P9-BHV-084

PRESENTED TO

BY

ON

THY WORD IS A LAMP UNTO MY FEET, AND A LIGHT UNTO MY PATH. PSALM 119:105

Old Testament Chronology

Creation

Fall

Flood

Babel

?

?

?

?

New Testament Chronology

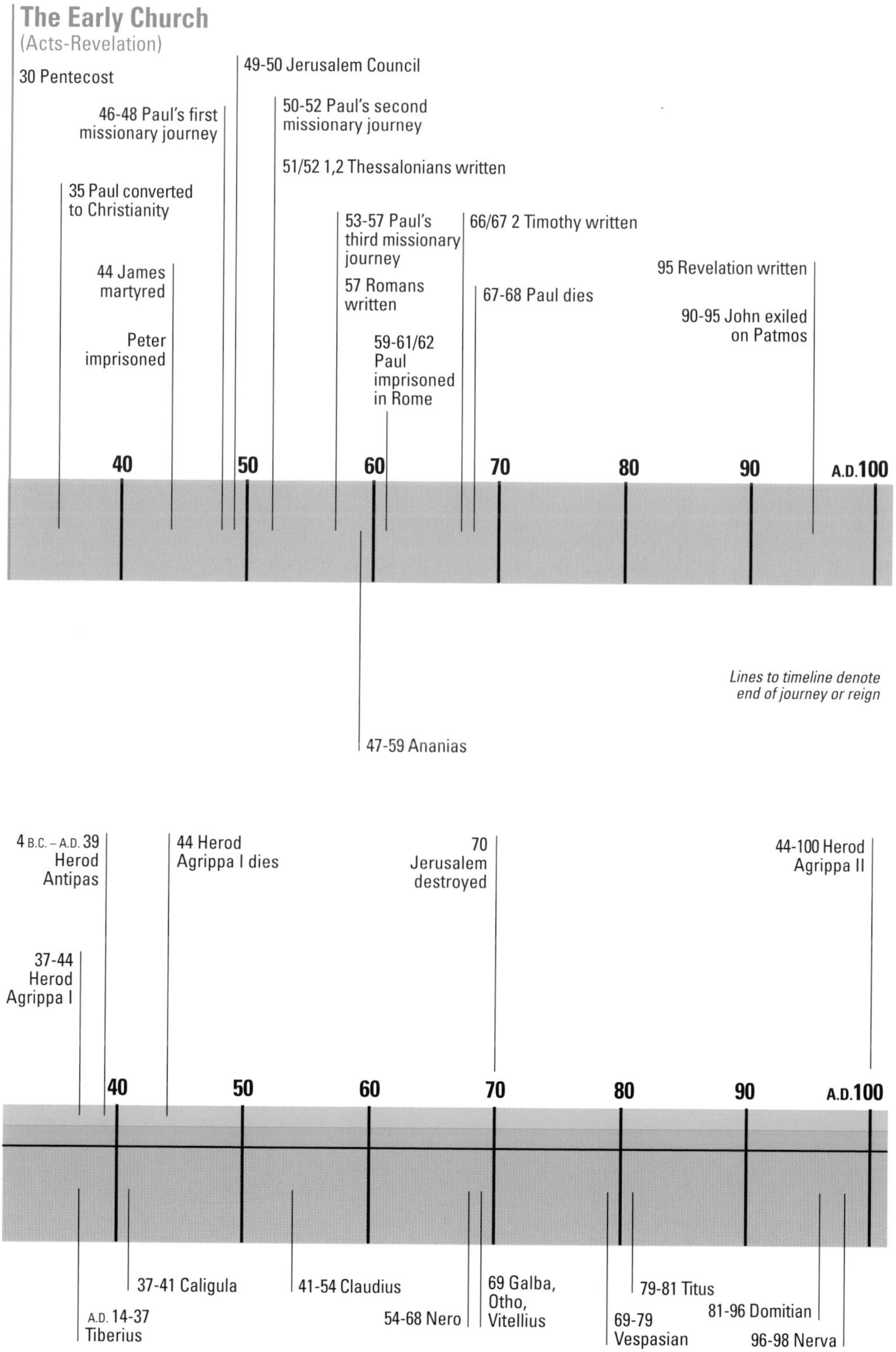

The Early Church
(Acts-Revelation)
30 Pentecost
35 Paul converted to Christianity
44 James martyred
Peter imprisoned
46-48 Paul's first missionary journey
49-50 Jerusalem Council
50-52 Paul's second missionary journey
51/52 1,2 Thessalonians written
53-57 Paul's third missionary journey
57 Romans written
59-61/62 Paul imprisoned in Rome
66/67 2 Timothy written
67-68 Paul dies
95 Revelation written
90-95 John exiled on Patmos
40
50
60
70
80
90
A.D.100
47-59 Ananias
Lines to timeline denote end of journey or reign
4 B.C. – A.D. 39 Herod Antipas
37-44 Herod Agrippa I
44 Herod Agrippa I dies
70 Jerusalem destroyed
44-100 Herod Agrippa II
40
50
60
70
80
90
A.D.100
A.D. 14-37 Tiberius
37-41 Caligula
41-54 Claudius
54-68 Nero
69 Galba, Otho, Vitellius
69-79 Vespasian
79-81 Titus
81-96 Domitian
96-98 Nerva

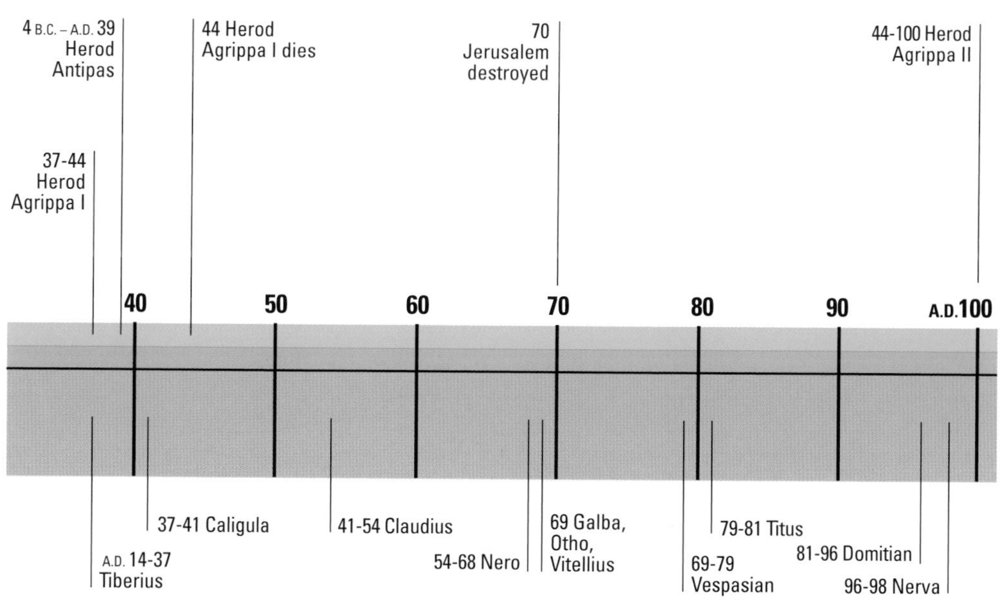

New Testament Chronology

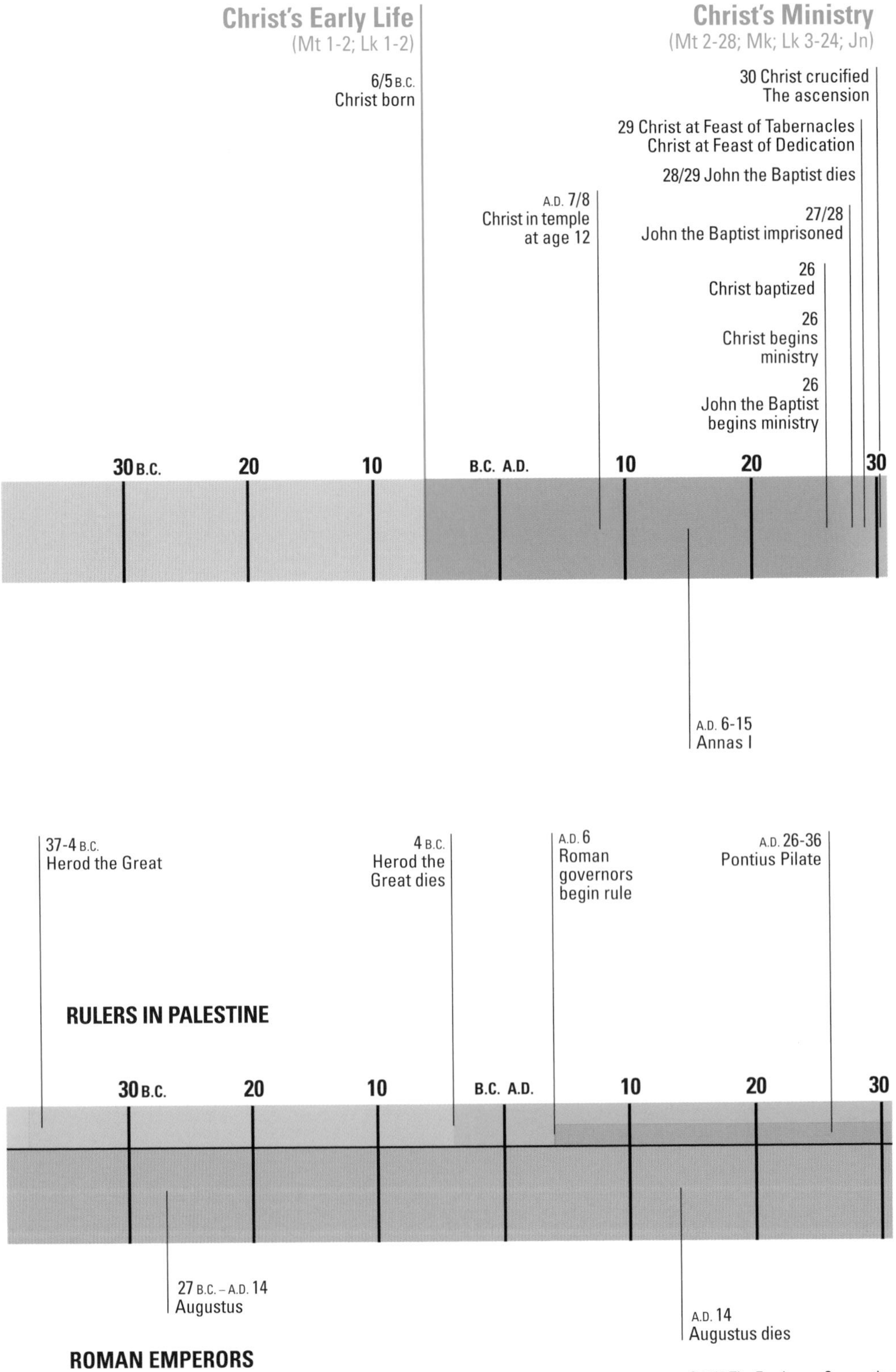

Christ's Early Life
(Mt 1-2; Lk 1-2)

6/5 B.C.
Christ born

A.D. 7/8
Christ in temple
at age 12

Christ's Ministry
(Mt 2-28; Mk; Lk 3-24; Jn)

30 Christ crucified
The ascension

29 Christ at Feast of Tabernacles
Christ at Feast of Dedication

28/29 John the Baptist dies

27/28
John the Baptist imprisoned

26
Christ baptized

26
Christ begins
ministry

26
John the Baptist
begins ministry

30 B.C. | 20 | 10 | B.C. A.D. | 10 | 20 | 30

A.D. 6-15
Annas I

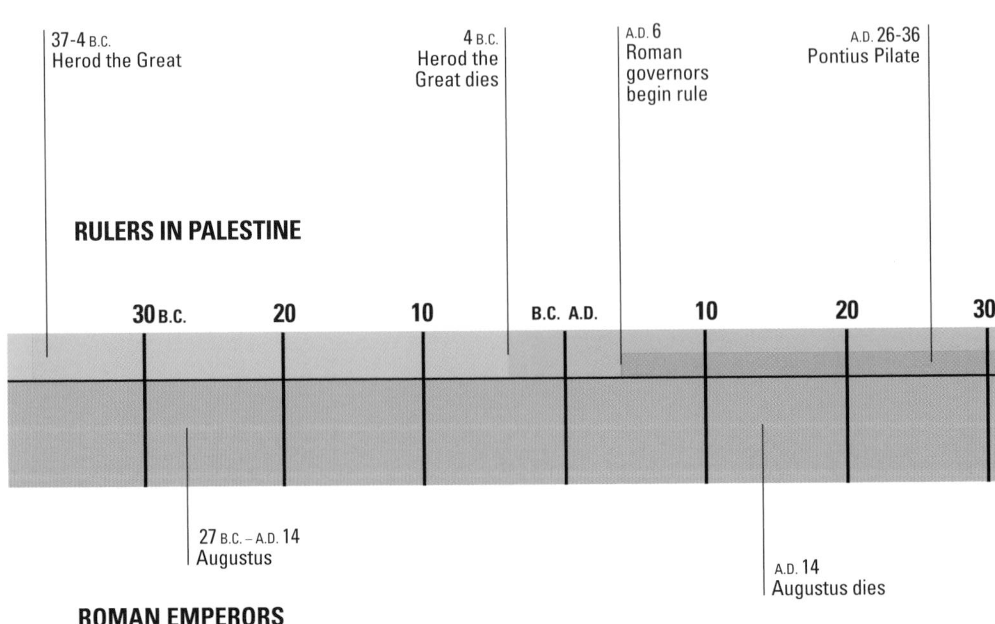

Old Testament Chronology

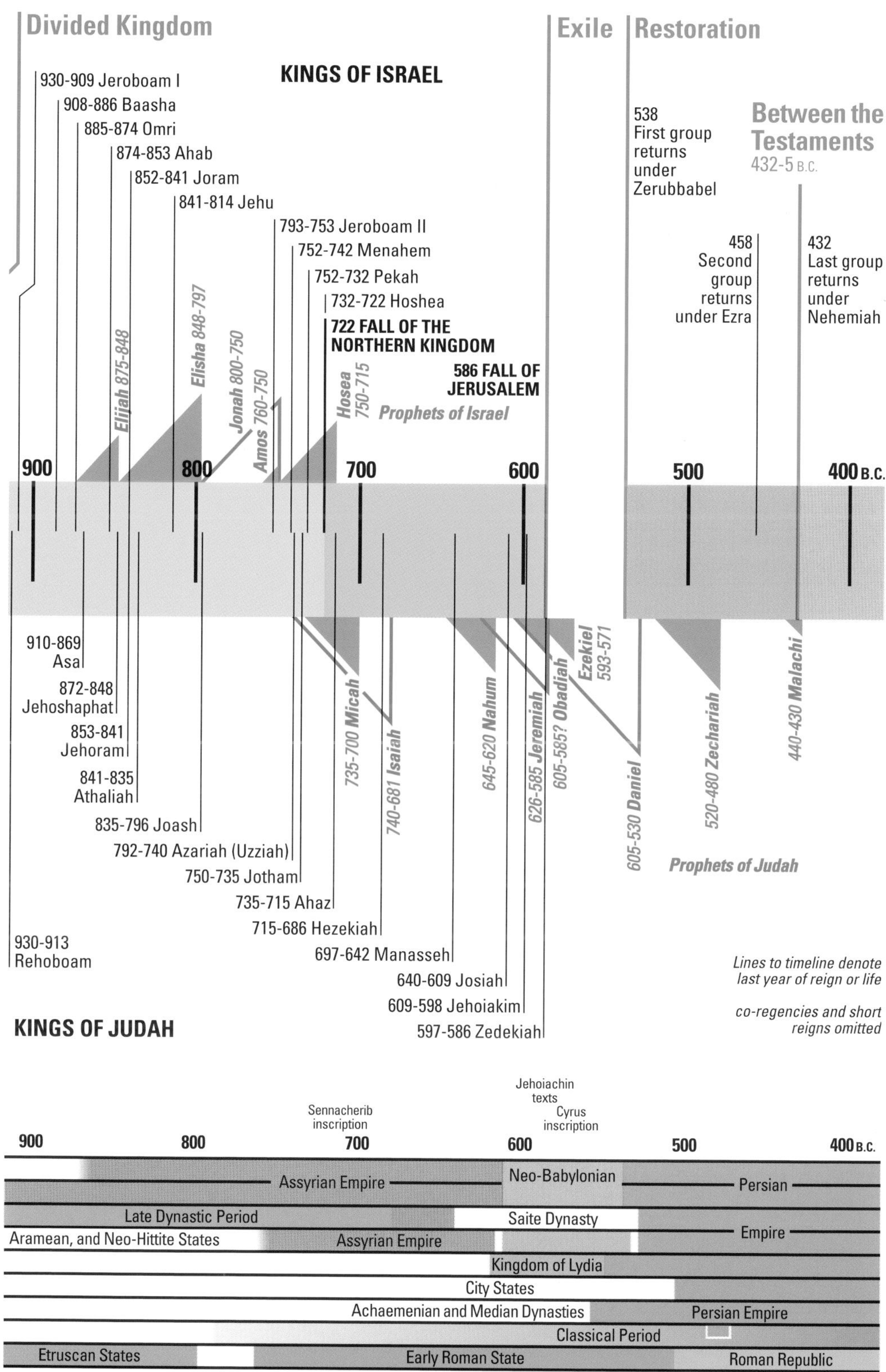

Divided Kingdom
Exile
Restoration
KINGS OF ISRAEL
930-909 Jeroboam I
908-886 Baasha
885-874 Omri
874-853 Ahab
852-841 Joram
841-814 Jehu
793-753 Jeroboam II
752-742 Menahem
752-732 Pekah
732-722 Hoshea
722 FALL OF THE NORTHERN KINGDOM
586 FALL OF JERUSALEM
538 First group returns under Zerubbabel
Between the Testaments
432-5 B.C.
458 Second group returns under Ezra
432 Last group returns under Nehemiah
Elijah 875-848
Elisha 848-797
Jonah 800-750
Amos 760-750
Hosea 750-715
Prophets of Israel
900
800
700
600
500
400 B.C.
910-869 Asa
872-848 Jehoshaphat
853-841 Jehoram
841-835 Athaliah
835-796 Joash
792-740 Azariah (Uzziah)
750-735 Jotham
735-715 Ahaz
715-686 Hezekiah
697-642 Manasseh
640-609 Josiah
609-598 Jehoiakim
597-586 Zedekiah
930-913 Rehoboam
KINGS OF JUDAH
735-700 Micah
740-681 Isaiah
645-620 Nahum
626-585 Jeremiah
605-585? Obadiah
Ezekiel 593-571
605-530 Daniel
520-480 Zechariah
440-430 Malachi
Prophets of Judah
Lines to timeline denote last year of reign or life
co-regencies and short reigns omitted
Jehoiachin texts
Sennacherib inscription
Cyrus inscription
900
800
700
600
500
400 B.C.
Assyrian Empire
Neo-Babylonian
Persian
Late Dynastic Period
Saite Dynasty
Aramean, and Neo-Hittite States
Assyrian Empire
Empire
Kingdom of Lydia
City States
Achaemenian and Median Dynasties
Persian Empire
Classical Period
Etruscan States
Early Roman State
Roman Republic

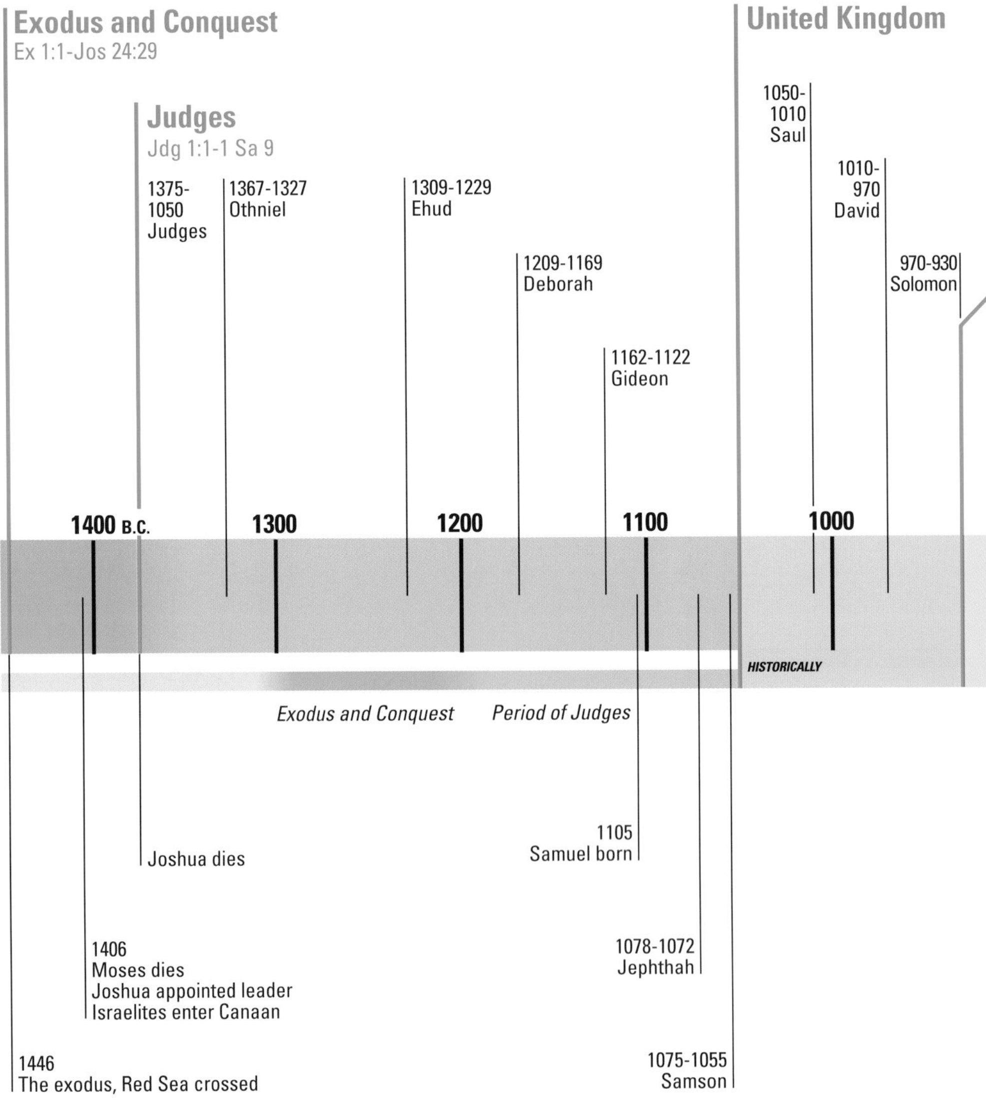

Nuzi texts · Ugaritic texts · Amarna texts (c. 1400–1350) · Merneptah inscription (c. 1210) · Medinet Habu inscriptions (c. 1180) · Shishak inscription (c. 925)

	1400 B.C.	1300	1200	1100	1000
S. MESOPOTAMIA	Kassite Period				
N. MESOPOTAMIA	←Mitannian Kingdom		Middle Assyrian Period		
EGYPT	New Kingdom				
SYRIA-PALESTINE	Late Canaanite Period		Sea Peoples		Phoenician,
ANATOLIA	Hittite Empire		Phrygian Period		
CRETE	Late Minoan Period				Dorian States
PERSIA					
GREECE	Late Helladic (Mycenean) Period			Dorian States	
ITALY					

Old Testament Chronology

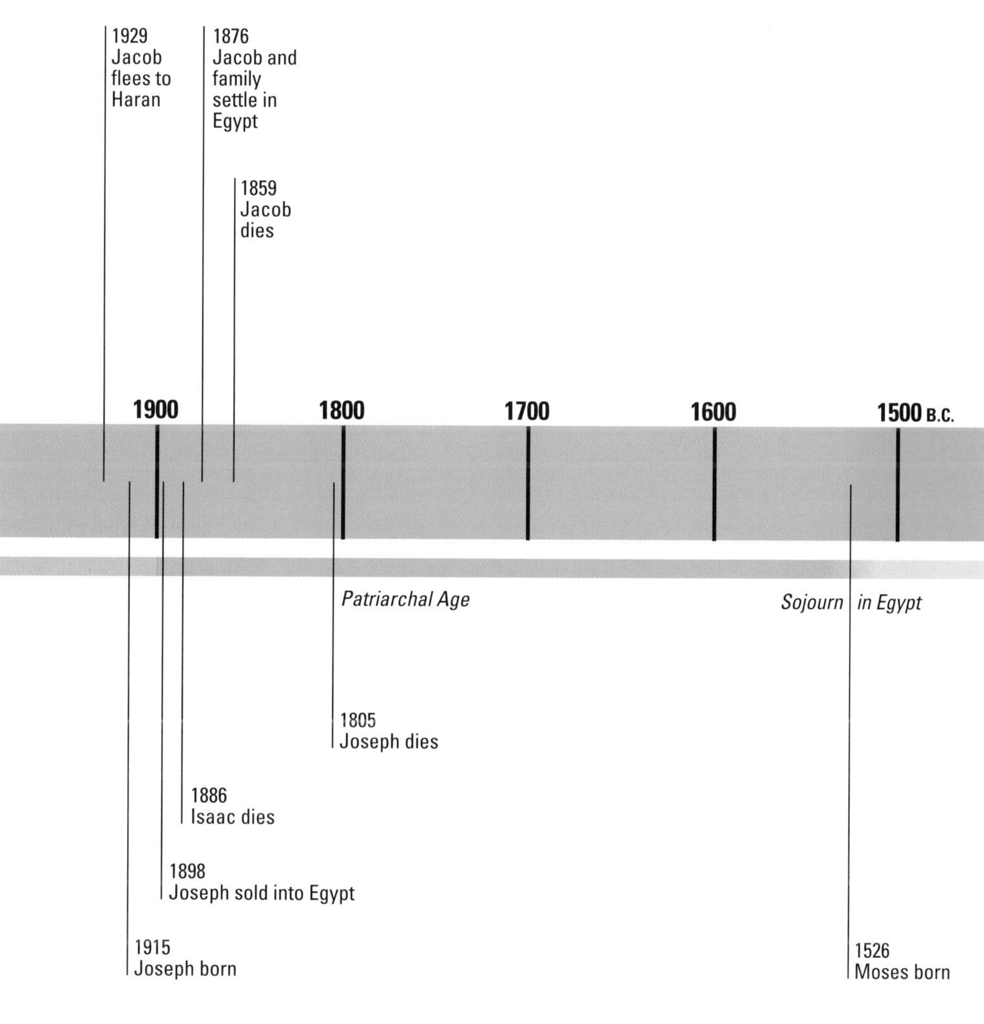

Cappadocian texts 1900	1800	Mari texts	Hammurapi texts 1700	1600	1500 B.C.
Isin-Larsa Period					
		Old Babylonian Period			
Middle Kingdom		2nd Intermediate (Hyksos) Period			New Kingdom
Amorite Period			Hyksos Period		Late Canaanite Period
				Hittite Old Kingdom	
Middle Minoan Period					
Middle Helladic Period					

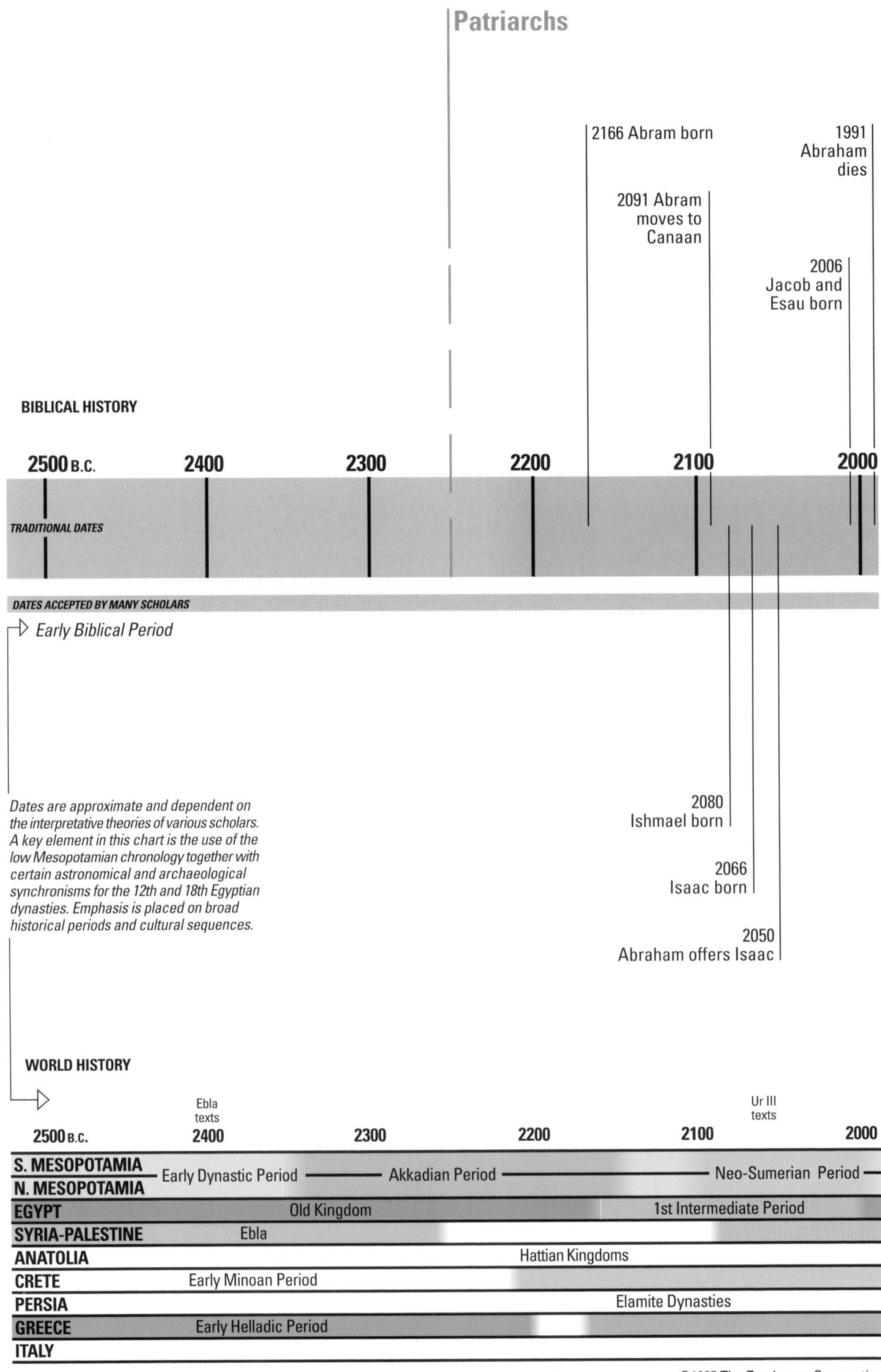
Patriarchs
2166 Abram born
1991 Abraham dies
2091 Abram moves to Canaan
2006 Jacob and Esau born
BIBLICAL HISTORY
2500 B.C.
2400
2300
2200
2100
2000
TRADITIONAL DATES
DATES ACCEPTED BY MANY SCHOLARS
Early Biblical Period
2080 Ishmael born
2066 Isaac born
2050 Abraham offers Isaac
Dates are approximate and dependent on the interpretative theories of various scholars. A key element in this chart is the use of the low Mesopotamian chronology together with certain astronomical and archaeological synchronisms for the 12th and 18th Egyptian dynasties. Emphasis is placed on broad historical periods and cultural sequences.
WORLD HISTORY
Ebla texts
Ur III texts
2500 B.C.
2400
2300
2200
2100
2000
S. MESOPOTAMIA
N. MESOPOTAMIA
Early Dynastic Period
Akkadian Period
Neo-Sumerian Period
EGYPT
Old Kingdom
1st Intermediate Period
SYRIA-PALESTINE
Ebla
ANATOLIA
Hattian Kingdoms
CRETE
Early Minoan Period
PERSIA
Elamite Dynasties
GREECE
Early Helladic Period
ITALY

ZONDERVAN

KJV
STUDY BIBLE

KING JAMES VERSION

GENERAL EDITOR

KENNETH BARKER

ASSOCIATE EDITORS

DONALD BURDICK JOHN STEK

WALTER WESSEL RONALD YOUNGBLOOD

CONSULTING EDITORS

EDWARD HINDSON DANIEL MITCHELL

GRAND RAPIDS, MICHIGAN 49530

WWW.ZONDERVAN.COM

ZONDERVAN™

The Zondervan KJV Study Bible

Library of Congress Catalog Card Number: 2001098540

Published by ZONDERVAN™
Grand Rapids, Michigan 49530, USA
http://www.zondervan.com

Printed in the United States of America

3 4 5 6 7 8 9 / 08 07

RRD-C

TABLE OF CONTENTS

THE OLD TESTAMENT

THE NEW TESTAMENT

STUDY HELPS

MAPS

CHARTS

PREFACE TO THE KING JAMES VERSION

1873 EDITION

The most time-honored and widely used edition of the English Bible is the translation of 1611, commonly known as the Authorized Version or King James Version (KJV). But though it has served as the standard translation for millions of users through nearly four centuries, there has never been a standard edition to which all printings are conformed.

No two early printings of the KJV were identical—not even the two printings of 1611—and no two modern settings are identical, either. These differences are due to accidental human error as well as to intentional changes by printers and editors, who sought to eliminate what they judged to be the errors of others and to conform the text to their standards of English usage. This said, most differences involve only spelling, punctuation, and italics, and few variations materially affect the meaning of the text.

As early as 1616 there were systematic attempts to revise and standardize the KJV. Other important early editions were issued by Cambridge in 1629 and 1638. In the eighteenth century, the two great English universities (who were also officially chartered printers) commissioned thorough and systematic revisions. The edition of Dr. F. S. Paris was published by Cambridge in 1762 and that of Dr. Benjamin Blayney by Oxford in 1769. Though far from perfect, these remained the standard editions until *The Cambridge Paragraph Bible* of 1873.

The Cambridge Paragraph Bible began with the simple plan of arranging the text of the KJV according to the sense of the literature: arranging the prose sections into paragraphs and the poetic sections into parallel lines. This simple plan, however, was enhanced by the editor's desire to create the most thorough standardization of the text ever attempted. To this task Dr. F. H. A. Scrivener devoted seven laborious years: 1866 to 1873.

Because the translators' original manuscript no longer exists, the KJV text must be established by consulting the earliest settings. Dr. Scrivener compared at least 15 early settings and important revisions, including both settings of 1611; Bibles of 1612, 1613, 1616, 1617, 1629, 1630, 1634, 1638, 1640; and the significant editions of Drs. Paris (1762) and Blayney (1769).

In his 120-page introduction, Dr. Scrivener addressed the various features of the KJV he worked to standardize:

Marginal notes. The KJV does not contain explanatory or doctrinal comments but does include annotations "for the explanation of the Hebrew and Greek words." In the Old Testament of 1611, there are 6,637 such notes. The more literal meaning of the original Hebrew or Aramaic ("Chaldee") is expressed in 4,111 notes, indicated by the abbreviation "Heb." or "Chald."; 2,156 give alternate renderings, indicated by the word "Or"; 63 give the meaning of proper names; 240 harmonize parallel passages; and 67 refer to various readings in the Hebrew manuscripts used by the translators.

In the New Testament of 1611, there are 765 marginal notes. Alternate translations are given in 583 notes, indicated by the word "Or"; 112 provide a more literal rendering of the Greek, indicated by the abbreviation "Gr."; 35 are explanatory notes or brief expositions; and 35 relate to alternate readings in the Greek manuscripts used by the translators.

Significant notes from later editions have also been included in square brackets [ ]. There are 368 additional notes in the Old Testament (for example, Gen. 1:20) and 105 in the New (for example, Mat. 1:20,21).

The KJV Study Bible includes a significant system of cross references in addition to the translators' notes. Cross references are indicated by letters (*a, b, c,* etc.), while translators' notes are indicates by numbers (1, 2, 3, etc.).

Italic type. Italic type was used in the KJV, as in the Geneva Bible, to indicate words in the English translation that have no exact representative in the original language. Dr. Scrivener, following many earlier scholars, noted that the KJV translators were noticeably inconsistent in their use of italics, sometimes even in the same paragraph and verse. To cite one small pattern from the 1611 edi-

tion, Leviticus 11:20 has "upon all foure," while for the same Hebrew 11:21 and 42 have "upon *all* foure," and 11:27 has "on *all* foure."

Dr. Scrivener carefully analyzed why italic type was used throughout the KJV, reduced this analysis to 14 major principles, and then applied these principles with meticulous consistency throughout the entire Bible. A substantial portion of the editor's "seven laborious years" was devoted to this significant improvement.

Punctuation. Later printings of the KJV added a great deal of punctuation to the editions of 1611. Dr. Scrivener restored the major punctuation (periods, colons, parentheses, question marks) of 1611, and used commas and semicolons to help divide longer sentences into more manageable units for reading.

Spelling and capital letters. Spelling of proper names and common words was very fluid in the sixteenth and seventeenth centuries: "Inquire" and "enquire" were interchangeable, as were "ceiling," "cieling," and "sieling." Most differences between modern settings of the KJV and early settings involve standardization of spelling. Dr. Scrivener's general rule was that whenever a word was spelled more than one way, he conformed all occurrences to the standard spelling of the late nineteenth century. Proper names, on the other hand, vary according to their spelling in the original languages, so "Elijah" throughout 1 and 2 Kings and in Malachi 4:5 becomes "Elias" throughout the New Testament, as in Matthew 11:14 and 17:3.

Paragraphs and poetry. According to Dr. Scrivener and other scholars, the paragraph marks (¶) were unequally and inconsistently distributed, and they disappear altogether after Acts 20:26. So, while consulted, the original marks were not always followed in *The Cambridge Paragraph Bible*. Hebrew poetry is characterized by rhyming of thoughts rather than rhyming of words. In *The Cambridge Paragraph Bible*, as well as in most modern translations, lines of similar or contrasting content are set in parallel lines to show this parallelism of thought. In Psalm 1, verse 5 has two lines of similar parallelism, while verse 6 has two lines of contrasting parallelism:

5 Therefore the ungodly shall not stand in the judgment,
Nor sinners in the congregation of the righteous.
6 For the LORD knoweth the way of the righteous:
But the way of the ungodly shall perish.

The KJV Study Bible is a verse setting, that is, each verse begins a new line. Paragraphs are indicated with the traditional paragraph mark (¶). However, poetry is set as poetry.

With *The KJV Study Bible,* Zondervan conforms its setting of the King James or Authorized Version to its most highly regarded edition: *The Cambridge Paragraph Bible* of 1873, edited by F. H. A. Scrivener. As in the case of the first edition of the version of 1611, this is done out of "zeal to promote the common good, whether it be by devising any thing ourselves, or revising that which hath been laboured by others" ("The Translators to the Reader," the preface to the version of 1611). With the original translators, we hope our efforts will be "welcomed," not "with suspicion" but with "love," and that the reissue of this edition will contribute to improvement of this great treasure of the English-speaking church.

JOHN R. KOHLENBERGER III

EPISTLE DEDICATORY

TO THE MOST HIGH AND MIGHTY PRINCE
JAMES
BY THE GRACE OF GOD
KING OF GREAT BRITAIN, FRANCE, AND IRELAND
DEFENDER OF THE FAITH, &c.

The Translators of the Bible wish Grace, Mercy, and Peace
through JESUS CHRIST our Lord

Great and manifold were the blessings, most dread Sovereign, which Almighty God, the Father of all mercies, bestowed upon us the people of *England,* when first he sent Your Majesty's Royal Person to rule and reign over us. For whereas it was the expectation of many, who wished not well unto our *Sion,* that upon the setting of that bright *Occidental Star,* Queen *Elizabeth* of most happy memory, some thick and palpable clouds of darkness would so have overshadowed this Land, that men should have been in doubt which way they were to walk; and that it should hardly be known, who was to direct the unsettled State; the appearance of Your Majesty, as of the *Sun* in his strength, instantly dispelled those supposed and surmised mists, and gave unto all that were well affected exceeding cause of comfort; especially when we beheld the Government established in Your Highness, and Your hopeful Seed, by an undoubted Title, and this also accompanied with peace and tranquility at home and abroad.

But among all our joys, there was no one that more filled our hearts, than the blessed continuance of the preaching of God's sacred Word among us; which is that inestimable treasure, which excelleth all the riches of the earth; because the fruit thereof extendeth itself, not only to the time spent in this transitory world, but directeth and disposeth men unto that eternal happiness which is above in heaven.

Then not to suffer this to fall to the ground, but rather to take it up, and to continue it in that state, wherein the famous Predecessor of Your Highness did leave it: nay, to go forward with the confidence and resolution of a Man in maintaining the truth of Christ, and propagating it far and near, is that which hath so bound and firmly knit the hearts of all Your Majesty's loyal and religious people unto You, that Your very name is precious among them: their eye doth behold You with comfort, and they bless You in their hearts, as that sanctified Person who, under God, is the immediate Author of their true happiness. And this their contentment doth not diminish or decay, but every day increaseth and taketh strength, when they observe, that the zeal of Your Majesty toward the house of God doth not slack or go backward, but is more and more kindled, manifesting itself abroad in the farthest parts of *Christendom,* by writing in defence of the Truth, (which hath given such a blow unto that man of sin, as will not be healed,) and every day at home, by religious and learned discourse, by frequenting the house of God, by hearing the Word preached, by cherishing the Teachers thereof, by caring for the Church, as a most tender and loving nursing Father.

There are infinite arguments of this right Christian and religious affection in Your Majesty; but none is more forcible to declare it to others than the vehement and perpetuated desire of accomplishing and publishing of this work, which now with all humility we present unto Your Majesty. For when Your Highness had once out of deep judgment apprehended how convenient it was, that out of the Original Sacred Tongues, together with comparing of the labours, both in our own, and other foreign Languages, of many worthy men who went before us, there should be one more exact Transla-

tion of the holy Scriptures into the *English Tongue;* Your Majesty did never desist to urge and to excite those to whom it was commended, that the work might be hastened, and that the business might be expedited in so decent a manner, as a matter of such importance might justly require.

And now at last, by the mercy of God, and the continuance of our labours, it being brought unto such a conclusion, as that we have great hopes that the Church of *England* shall reap good fruit thereby; we hold it our duty to offer it to Your Majesty, not only as to our King and Sovereign, but as to the principal Mover and Author of the work: humbly craving of Your most Sacred Majesty, that since things of this quality have ever been subject to the censures of illmeaning and discontented persons, it may receive approbation and patronage from so learned and judicious a Prince as Your Highness is, whose allowance and acceptance of our labours shall more honour and encourage us, than all the calumniations and hard interpretations of other men shall dismay us. So that if, on the one side, we shall be traduced by Popish Persons at home or abroad, who therefore will malign us, because we are poor instruments to make God's holy Truth to be yet more and more known unto the people, whom they desire still to keep in ignorance and darkness; or if, on the other side, we shall be maligned by self-conceited Brethren, who run their own ways, and give liking unto nothing, but what is framed by themselves, and hammered on their anvil; we may rest secure, supported within by the truth and innocency of a good conscience, having walked the ways of simplicity and integrity, as before the Lord; and sustained without by the powerful protection of Your Majesty's grace and favour, which will ever give countenance to honest and Christian endeavours against bitter censures and uncharitable imputations.

The Lord of heaven and earth bless Your Majesty with many and happy days, that, as his heavenly hand hath enriched Your Highness with many singular and extraordinary graces, so You may be the wonder of the world in this latter age for happiness and true felicity, to the honour of that great GOD, and the good of his Church, through Jesus Christ our Lord and only Saviour.

INTRODUCTION

ABOUT THE ZONDERVAN KJV STUDY BIBLE

The Zondervan KJV Study Bible is an adaptation of the *Zondervan NASB Study Bible*. Both titles use the basic note structure that appears in the *NIV Study Bible, 10th Anniversary Edition*. The special symbol (‡) that appears next to many of the notes in this volume indicates that these notes were altered in some way by the editorial team that completed this adaptation (see p. xvi).

The Zondervan KJV Study Bible is the work of a transdenominational team of conservative Biblical scholars. All confess the authority of the Bible as God's infallible word to humanity. They have sought to clarify understanding of, develop appreciation for, and provide insight into that word.

But why a study Bible when the text itself is clearly written? Surely there is no substitute for the reading of the text itself; nothing people write about God's word can be on a level with the word itself. Further, it is the Holy Spirit alone—not fallible human beings—who can open the human mind to the divine message.

However, the Spirit also uses people to explain God's word to others. It was the Spirit who led Philip to the Ethiopian eunuch's chariot, where he asked, "Understandest thou what thou readest?" (Ac 8:30). "How can I," the Ethiopian replied, "except some man should guide me?" Philip then showed him how an Old Testament passage in Isaiah related to the good news of Jesus.

This interrelationship of the Scriptures—so essential to understanding the complete Biblical message—is a major theme of the notes in *The Zondervan KJV Study Bible*.

Doctrinally, *The Zondervan KJV Study Bible* reflects traditional evangelical theology. Where editors were aware of significant differences of opinion on key passages or doctrines, they tried to follow an evenhanded approach by indicating those differences (e.g., see note on Rev 20:2). In finding solutions to problems mentioned in the book introductions, they went only as far as evidence (Biblical and non-Biblical) could carry them.

The result is a study Bible that can be used profitably by all Christians who want to be serious Bible students.

FEATURES OF THE ZONDERVAN KJV STUDY BIBLE

The Zondervan KJV Study Bible features the text of the King James Version, study notes keyed to and listed with Bible verses, introductions and outlines to books of the Bible, text notes, a cross-reference system (tens of thousands of entries), parallel passages, a concordance (nearly 20,000 references), charts, maps, essays and comprehensive indexes.

The text of the King James Version, which is presented in verse-by-verse format, is organized into sections with headings.

Study Notes

The outstanding feature of this study Bible is that it contains nearly 20,000 study notes located on the same pages as the verses and passages they explain.

The study notes provide new information to supplement that found in the KJV text notes. Among other things, they

1. explain important words and concepts (see note on Lev 11:44 about "holiness");
2. interpret "difficult verses" (see notes on Mal 1:3 and Luke 14:26 for the concept of "hating" your parents);

3. draw parallels between specific people and events (see note on Ex 32:30 for the parallels between Moses and Christ as mediators);
4. describe historical and textual contexts of passages (see note on 1 Cor 8:1 for the practice of touching or eating meat sacrificed to idols); and
5. demonstrate how one passage sheds light on another (see note on Ps 26:8 for how the presence of God's glory marked his presence in the tabernacle, in the temple, and finally in Jesus Christ himself).

Some elements of style should be noted:

1. Study notes on a passage precede notes on individual verses within that passage.
2. When a book of the Bible is referred to within a note on that book, the book name is not repeated. For example, a reference to 2 Timothy 2:18 within the notes on 2 Timothy is written 2:18, not 2 Tim 2:18.
3. In lists of references within a note, references from the book under discussion are placed first. The rest appear in Biblical order.

Introductions to Books of the Bible

Each introduction to each book of the Bible is different. Introductions vary in length and reflect both the nature of the material itself and the strengths and interests of contributing editors.

An introduction frequently reports on a book's title, author, and date of writing. It details the book's background and purpose, explores themes and theological significance, and points out special problems and distinctive literary features. Where appropriate, such as in Paul's letters to the churches, it describes the original recipients of a book and the city in which they lived.

A complete outline of the book's content is provided in each introduction (except for the introduction to Psalms). For Genesis, two outlines—a literary and a thematic—are given. Pairs of books that were originally one literary work, such as 1 and 2 Samuel, 1 and 2 Kings, and 1 and 2 Chronicles, are outlined together.

Marginal Notes

The KJV translation's extensive text notes appear within the center-column reference system. They examine such things as alternate translations, meanings of Hebrew and Greek terms, Old Testament quotations and variant readings in ancient Biblical manuscripts.

Cross-Reference System

Marginal notes and cross references appear in the center column on each page of Scripture. They are listed under the verse numbers to which they refer. Superior numbers refer to literal renderings, alternate translations, or explanations. Superior letters refer to cross-references.

Genesis 1:1-2 provides a good example of the resources of this cross-reference system.

The two lists of references in 1:1 relate to creation, but each takes a different perspective. Note *a* takes up the time of creation: "in the beginning," and directs the reader to two other instances where this time is discussed. Note *b* addresses God's activity in creation, as well as His preexistence and His wondrous power.

The creation

1 In the [a]beginning [b]God created the
heaven and the earth.
2 And the earth was [a]without form, and
void; and darkness *was* upon the face of the
deep. [b]And the Spirit of God moved upon the
face of the waters.
3 ¶ [a]And God said, [b]Let there be light: and
there was light.
4 And God saw the light, that *it was* good:
and God divided [1]the light from the darkness.
5 And God called the light [a]Day, and the
darkness he called Night. [1]And the evening
and the morning were the first day.
6 ¶ And God said, [a]Let there be a [1]firmament in the midst of the waters, and let it di-

1:1 [a]John 1:1,2; Heb. 1:10 [b]Ps. 8:3; Is. 44:24; Acts 17:24; Rev. 4:11
1:2 [a]Jer. 4:23 [b]Ps. 33:6; Is. 40:13,14
1:3 [a]Ps. 33:9 [b]2 Cor. 4:6
1:4 [1]Heb. *between the light and between the darkness*
1:5 [1]Heb. *And the evening was, and the morning was, etc.* [a]Ps. 74:16
1:6 [1]Heb. *expansion* [a]Job 37:18; Jer. 10:12
1:7 [a]Prov. 8:28 [b]Ps. 148:4

Genesis 1:5 provides an example of how the KJV marginal notes work in tandem with the cross references. Note that the superscript numbers refer to notes that can be found in the center column. These literal renderings, alternate translations or explanations always come first under the verse heading in the center column, despite their relative position in the note. The note's cross-references appear after the notes indicated by the superscript numbers.

Concordance

The concordance is designed as a quick-reference tool to enhance Bible study. By looking up key words, you can find verses for which you remember a word or two but not their location. For example, to find the verse that says, "Thy word is a lamp unto my feet, And a light unto my path," you could look in the concordance under either "word," "lamp," "light" or "path."

Maps

The Zondervan KJV Study Bible includes 59 maps: 13 full-color and 46 black-and-white. The 13 full-color maps at the end of this Bible cover nearly 4,000 years of history, from the patriarchs to Christianity in the world today.

Strategically placed throughout the text are almost four dozen black-and-white maps. The Contents: Maps page contains a complete list of the topics covered.

The cities of Jerusalem, Damascus, Rome, Corinth, Ephesus and Philippi have been reconstructed as they might have been in ancient times. These recreations allow Bible students to visualize David's city and, in the New Testament, the places through which Paul traveled on his missionary journeys.

Charts

Complementing the study notes are 46 charts, diagrams and drawings. Two full-color time lines, located in the front of this Bible, pinpoint significant dates in the Old and New Testaments. Other charts, carefully placed within the text, give detailed information about ancient, non-Biblical texts; about Old Testament covenants, sacrifices, and feast days; about Jewish sects; and about major archaeological finds relating to the New Testament.

Essays

Five brief essays provide additional information on specific sections of the Bible: Wisdom Literature, the Minor Prophets, the Synoptic Gospels, the Pastoral Letters, and the General Letters.

A sixth essay confronts the ethical question of war, and a seventh details the history, literature and social developments of the 400 years between the Old and New Testaments.

Subject, Notes and Map Indexes

The subject index contains references to key Biblical information and important topics. The notes index pinpoints other references to persons, places, events and topics mentioned in *The Zondervan KJV Study Bible* notes.

Two map indexes help in locating place-names on a map.

Harmony of the Gospels

As an additional study tool for the Gospels and the life of Christ, this Bible contains a portion of *The NIV Harmony of the Gospels* by Robert L. Thomas and Stanley N. Gundry.

ACKNOWLEDGMENTS

The *Zondervan KJV Study Bible* is an adaptation of *The Zondervan NASB Study Bible*. Both of these titles are adaptations of *The NIV Study Bible: 10th Anniversary Edition.* The following acknowledgments recognize the contributions of those individuals involved in the development of *The NIV Study Bible*.

My greatest debt of gratitude is owed to God for giving me the privilege of serving as General Editor of *The NIV Study Bible.* Special thanks go to the four Associate Editors: Donald W. Burdick, John H. Stek, Walter W. Wessel, and Ronald Youngblood. Without their help, it would have been impossible to complete this project in a little over seven years.

In addition, grateful acknowledgment is given to all those listed on the Contributors page. Obviously the editors and contributors have profited immensely from the labors of others. We feel deeply indebted to all the commentaries and other sources we have used in our work.

I should also thank the following individuals for rendering help in various ways (though I fear that I have inadvertently omitted a few names): Caroline Blauwkamp, David R. Douglass, Stanley N. Gundry, N. David Hill, Betty Hockenberry, Charles E. Hummel, Alan F. Johnson, Janet Johnston, Donald H. Madvig, Frances Steenwyk, and Edward Viening.

Nehemiah 8:7–8, 12 says:

The Levites . . . instructed the people in the Law while the people were standing there. They read from the Book of the Law of God, making it clear and giving the meaning so that the people could understand what was being read. . . . Then all the people went away . . . to celebrate with great joy, because they now understood the words that had been made known to them. *(NIV)*

My associates and I will feel amply rewarded if those who use this study Bible have an experience similar to that of God's people in Nehemiah's time.

Kenneth L. Barker
General Editor
The NIV Study Bible

Tribute to Edwin H. Palmer

Edwin H. Palmer, who had served so capably as Executive Secretary of the NIV Committee on Bible Translation and as coordinator of all translation work on the NIV, was appointed general editor of *The NIV Study Bible* by Zondervan Bible Publishers in 1979. On September 16, 1980, he departed this life to "be with Christ, which is better by far" (Philippians 1:23, NIV). Before his death, however, he had laid most of the plans for *The NIV Study Bible,* had recruited the majority of the contributors, and had done some editorial work on the first manuscripts submitted. We gratefully acknowledge his significant contributions to the earliest stages of this project.

CONTRIBUTORS

General Editor:	Kenneth L. Barker	
Associate Editors:	Donald W. Burdick	Walter W. Wessel
	John H. Stek	Ronald Youngblood
Consulting Editors:	Edward Hindson	Daniel Mitchell
KJV Notes Adaptation Team:	James Borland	Donald Fowler
	James Freerkson	Harvey Hartman
	Gary Yates	

The *Zondervan KJV Study Bible* is an adaptation of *The Zondervan NASB Study Bible*. Both of these titles are adaptations of *The NIV Study Bible: 10th Anniversary Edition.*

The individuals named below contributed and/or reviewed material for *The NIV Study Bible.* However, since the General Editor and the Associate Editors extensively edited the notes on most books, they alone are responsible for their final form and content.

The chief contributors of original material to *The NIV Study Bible* are listed first. Where the Associate Editors and General Editor contributed an unusually large number of notes on certain books, their names are also listed.

Genesis	Ronald Youngblood
Exodus	Ronald Youngblood
	Walter C. Kaiser, Jr.
Leviticus	R. Laird Harris
	Ronald Youngblood
Numbers	Ronald B. Allen
	Kenneth L. Barker
Deuteronomy	Earl S. Kalland
	Kenneth L. Barker
Joshua	Arthur Lewis
Judges	John J. Davis
	Herbert Wolf
Ruth	Marvin R. Wilson
	John H. Stek
1,2 Samuel	J. Robert Vannoy
1,2 Kings	J. Robert Vannoy
1,2 Chronicles	Raymond Dillard
Ezra	Edwin Yamauchi
	Ronald Youngblood
Nehemiah	Edwin Yamauchi
	Ronald Youngblood
Esther	Raymond Dillard
	Edwin Yamauchi
Job	Elmer B. Smick
	Ronald Youngblood
Psalms	John H. Stek
Proverbs	Herbert Wolf
Ecclesiastes	Derek Kidner
Song of Solomon	John H. Stek
Isaiah	Herbert Wolf
	John H. Stek
Jeremiah	Ronald Youngblood
Lamentations	Ronald Youngblood
Ezekiel	Mark Hillmer
Daniel	Gleason L. Archer, Jr.
	Ronald Youngblood
Hosea	Jack P. Lewis
Joel	Jack P. Lewis
Amos	Alan R. Millard
	John H. Stek
Obadiah	John M. Zinkand
Jonah	Marvin R. Wilson
	John H. Stek
Micah	Allan A. MacRae
	Thomas E. McComiskey
Nahum	G. Herbert Livingston
	Kenneth L. Barker
Habakkuk	Roland K. Harrison
	William C. Williams
Zephaniah	Roland K. Harrison
Haggai	Herbert Wolf
Zechariah	Kenneth L. Barker
	Larry L. Walker
Malachi	Herbert Wolf
	John H. Stek
Matthew	Ralph Earle
	Walter W. Wessel
Mark	Walter W. Wessel
	William L. Lane
Luke	Lewis Foster
John	Leon Morris
Acts	Lewis Foster
Romans	Walter W. Wessel
1 Corinthians	W. Harold Mare
2 Corinthians	Philip E. Hughes
Galatians	Robert Mounce
Ephesians	Walter L. Liefeld
Philippians	Richard B. Gaffin, Jr.
Colossians	Gerald F. Hawthorne
	Wilber B. Wallis
1,2 Thessalonians	Leon Morris
1,2 Timothy	Walter W. Wessel
	George W. Knight, III
Titus	D. Edmond Hiebert
Philemon	John Werner
Hebrews	Philip E. Hughes
	Donald W. Burdick
James	Donald W. Burdick
1,2 Peter	Donald W. Burdick
	John H. Skilton
1,2,3 John	Donald W. Burdick
Jude	Donald W. Burdick
	John H. Skilton
Revelation	Robert Mounce
"The Time between the Testaments" (essay)	David O'Brien

ABBREVIATIONS AND SPECIAL MARKINGS

GENERAL

Aram	*Aramaic*
Chald	*Chaldean [Aramaic]*
DSS	*Dead Sea Scrolls*
Gr	*Greek translation of O.T. (Septuagint or LXX) or Greek text of N.T.*
Heb	*Hebrew text, usually Masoretic*
Lat	*Latin*
M.T.	*Masoretic text*
Syr	*Syriac*
Lit	*A literal translation*
Or	*An alternate translation justified by the Hebrew, Aramaic, or Greek*
[ ]	*In margin, brackets indicate notes from editions later than the 1611 edition of the King James Version*
cf	*compare*
f, ff	*following verse or verses*
marg	*Refers to a marginal reading on another verse*
ms, mss	*manuscript, manuscripts*
v, vv	*verse, verses*

BOOKS OF THE BIBLE

The Old Testament

Genesis	Gen
Exodus	Ex
Leviticus	Lev
Numbers	Num
Deuteronomy	Deut
Joshua	Josh
Judges	Judg
Ruth	Ruth
First Samuel	1 Sam
Second Samuel	2 Sam
First Kings	1 Ki
Second Kings	2 Ki
First Chronicles	1 Chr
Second Chronicles	2 Chr
Ezra	Ezra
Nehemiah	Neh
Esther	Esth
Job	Job
Psalms	Ps
Proverbs	Prov
Ecclesiastes	Eccl
Song of Solomon	Sol
Isaiah	Is
Jeremiah	Jer
Lamentations	Lam
Ezekiel	Ezek
Daniel	Dan
Hosea	Hos
Joel	Joel
Amos	Amos
Obadiah	Obad
Jonah	Jonah
Micah	Mic
Nahum	Nah
Habakkuk	Hab
Zephaniah	Zeph
Haggai	Hag
Zechariah	Zech
Malachi	Mal

The New Testament

Matthew	Mat
Mark	Mark
Luke	Luke
John	John
Acts	Acts
Romans	Rom
First Corinthians	1 Cor
Second Corinthians	2 Cor
Galatians	Gal
Ephesians	Eph
Philippians	Phil
Colossians	Col
First Thessalonians	1 Thes
Second Thessalonians	2 Thes
First Timothy	1 Tim
Second Timothy	2 Tim
Titus	Tit
Philemon	Philem
Hebrews	Heb
James	Jas
First Peter	1 Pet
Second Peter	2 Pet
First John	1 John
Second John	2 John
Third John	3 John
Jude	Jude
Revelation	Rev

TRANSLITERATIONS

A simplified system has been used for transliterating words from ancient Biblical languages into English. The only transliterations calling for comment are these:

Transliteration	Pronunciation
'	Glottal stop
ḥ	Similar to the "ch" in the German word *Buch*
ṭ	Similar to the "t" in the verb "tear"
'	Similar to the glottal stop
ṣ	Similar to the "ts" in "hits"
ś	Similar to the "s" in "sing"

Ancient Texts Relating to the Old Testament

Major representative examples of ancient Near Eastern non-Biblical documents that provide parallels to or shed light on various OT passages.

AMARNA LETTERS **Canaanite Akkadian** *14th century B.C.*	Hundreds of letters, written primarily by Canaanite scribes, illuminate social, political and religious relationships between Canaan and Egypt during the reigns of Amunhotep III and Akhenaten.
AMENEMOPE'S WISDOM **Egyptian** *Early 1st millennium B.C.*	Thirty chapters of wisdom instruction are similar to Prov 22:17-24:22 and provide the closest external parallels to OT wisdom literature.
ATRAHASIS EPIC **Akkadian** *Early 2nd millennium B.C.*	A cosmological epic depicts creation and early human history, including the flood (cf. Gen 1-9).
BABYLONIAN THEODICY **Akkadian** *Early 1st millennium B.C.*	A sufferer and his friend dialogue with each other (cf. Job).
CYRUS CYLINDER **Akkadian** *6th century B.C.*	King Cyrus of Persia records the conquest of Babylon (cf. Dan 5:30; 6:28) and boasts of his generous policies toward his new subjects and their gods.
DEAD SEA SCROLLS **Hebrew, Aramaic, Greek** *3rd century B.C. to 1st century A.D.*	Several hundred scrolls and fragments include the oldest copies of OT books and passages.
EBLA TABLETS **Sumerian, Eblaite** *Mid-3rd millennium B.C.*	Thousands of commercial, legal, literary and epistolary texts describe the cultural vitality and political power of a pre-patriarchal civilization in northern Syria.
ELEPHANTINE PAPYRI **Aramaic** *Late 5th century B.C.*	Contracts and letters document life among Jews who fled to southern Egypt after Jerusalem was destroyed in 586 B.C.
ENUMA ELISH **Akkadian** *Early 2nd millennium B.C.*	Marduk, the Babylonian god of cosmic order, is elevated to the supreme position in the pantheon. The 7-tablet epic contains an account of creation (cf. Gen 1–2).
GEZER CALENDAR **Hebrew** *10th century B.C.*	A schoolboy from west-central Israel describes the seasons, crops and farming activity of the agricultural year.
GILGAMESH EPIC **Akkadian** *Early 2nd millennium B.C.*	Gilgamesh, ruler of Uruk, experiences numerous adventures, including a meeting with Utnapishtim, the only survivor of a great deluge (cf. Gen 6–9).
HAMMURAPI'S CODE **Akkadian** *18th century B.C.*	Together with similar law codes that preceded and followed it, the Code of Hammurapi exhibits close parallels to numerous passages in the Mosaic legislation of the OT.
HYMN TO THE ATEN **Egyptian** *14th century B.C.*	The poem praises the beneficence and universality of the sun in language somewhat similar to that used in Ps 104.
ISHTAR'S DESCENT **Akkadian** *1st millennium B.C.*	The goddess Ishtar temporarily descends to the nether world, which is pictured in terms reminiscent of OT descriptions of Sheol.
JEHOIACHIN'S RATION DOCKETS **Akkadian** *Early 6th century B.C.*	Brief texts from the reign of Nebuchadnezzar II refer to rations allotted to Judah's exiled king Jehoiachin and his sons (cf. 2 Ki 25:27-30).
KING LISTS **Sumerian** *Late 3rd millennium B.C.*	The reigns of Sumerian kings before the flood are described as lasting for thousands of years, reminding us of the longevity of the preflood patriarchs in Gen 5.
LACHISH LETTERS **Hebrew** *Early 6th century B.C.*	Inscriptions on pottery fragments vividly portray the desperate days preceding the Babylonian siege of Jerusalem in 588-586 B.C. (cf. Jer 34:7).
LAMENTATION OVER THE DESTRUCTION OF UR **Sumerian** *Early 2nd millennium B.C.*	The poem mourns the destruction of the city of Ur at the hands of the Elamites (cf. the OT book of Lamentations).
LUDLUL BEL NEMEQI **Akkadian** *Late 2nd millennium B.C.*	A suffering Babylonian nobleman describes his distress in terms faintly reminiscent of the experiences of Job.

MARI TABLETS **Akkadian** *18th century B.C.*	Letters and administrative texts provide detailed information regarding customs, language and personal names that reflect the culture of the OT patriarchs.
MERNEPTAH STELE **Egyptian** *13th century B.C.*	Pharaoh Merneptah figuratively describes his victory over various peoples in western Asia, including "Israel."
MESHA STELE (MOABITE STONE) **Moabite** *9th century B.C.*	Mesha, king of Moab (see 2 Ki 3:4), rebels against a successor of Israel's king Omri.
MURASHU TABLETS **Akkadian** *5th century B.C.*	Commercial documents describe financial transactions engaged in by Murashu and Sons, a Babylonian firm that did business with Jews and other exiles.
MURSILIS'S TREATY WITH DUPPI-TESSUB **Hittite** *Mid-2nd millennium B.C.*	King Mursilis imposes a suzerainty treaty on King Duppi-tessub. The literary outline of this and other Hittite treaties is strikingly paralleled in OT covenants established by God with his people.
NABONIDUS CHRONICLE **Akkadian** *Mid-6th century B.C.*	The account describes the absence of King Nabonidus from Babylon. His son Belshazzar is therefore the regent in charge of the kingdom (cf. Dan 5:29-30).
NEBUCHADNEZZAR CHRONICLE **Akkadian** *Early 6th century B.C.*	A chronicle from the reign of Nebuchadnezzar II includes the Babylonian account of the siege of Jerusalem in 597 B.C. (see 2 Ki 24:10-17).
NUZI TABLETS **Akkadian** *Mid-2nd millennium B.C.*	Adoption, birthright-sale and other legal documents graphically illustrate OT patriarchal customs current centuries earlier.
PESSIMISTIC DIALOGUE **Akkadian** *Early 1st millennium B.C.*	A master and his servant discuss the pros and cons of various activities (cf. Eccl 1-2).
RAS SHAMRA TABLETS **Ugaritic** *15th century B.C.*	Canaanite deities and rulers experience adventures in epics that enrich our understanding of Canaanite mythology and religion and of OT poetry.
SARGON LEGEND **Akkadian** *1st millennium B.C.*	Sargon I (the Great), ruler of Akkad in the late 3rd millennium B.C., claims to have been rescued as an infant from a reed basket found floating in a river (cf. Ex 2).
SARGON'S DISPLAY INSCRIPTION **Akkadian** *8th century B.C.*	Sargon II takes credit for the conquest of Samaria in 722/721 B.C. and states that he captured and exiled 27,290 Israelites.
SENNACHERIB'S PRISM **Akkadian** *Early 7th century B.C.*	Sennacherib vividly describes his siege of Jerusalem in 701 B.C., making Hezekiah a prisoner in his own royal city (but cf. 2 Ki 19:35-37).
SEVEN LEAN YEARS TRADITION **Egyptian** *2nd century B.C.*	Egypt experiences 7 years of low Niles and famine, which, by a contractual agreement between Pharaoh Djoser (28th century B.C.) and a god, will be followed by prosperity (cf. Gen 41).
SHALMANESER'S BLACK OBELISK **Akkadian** *9th century B.C.*	Israel's king Jehu (or his servant) presents tribute to Assyria's king Shalmaneser III. Additional Assyrian and Babylonian texts refer to other kings of Israel and Judah.
SHISHAK'S GEOGRAPHICAL LIST **Egyptian** *10th century B.C.*	Pharaoh Shishak lists the cities that he captured or made tributary during his campaign in Judah and Israel (cf. 1 Ki 14:25-26).
SILOAM INSCRIPTION **Hebrew** *Late 8th century B.C.*	A Judahite workman describes the construction of an underground conduit to guarantee Jerusalem's water supply during Hezekiah's reign (cf. 2 Ki 20:20; 2 Chr 32:30).
SINUHE'S STORY **Egyptian** *20th-19th centuries B.C.*	An Egyptian official of the 12th dynasty goes into voluntary exile in Syria and Canaan during the OT patriarchal period.
TALE OF TWO BROTHERS **Egyptian** *13th century B.C.*	A young man rejects the amorous advances of his older brother's wife (cf. Gen 39).
WENAMUN'S JOURNEY **Egyptian** *11th century B.C.*	An official of the Temple of Amun at Thebes in Egypt is sent to Byblos in Canaan to buy lumber for the ceremonial barge of his god.

THE OLD TESTAMENT

The First Book of Moses, Called
Genesis

INTRODUCTION

Title

The first phrase in the Hebrew text of 1:1 is *bereshith* ("in [the] beginning"), which is also the Hebrew title of the book (books in ancient times customarily were named after their first word or two). The English title, Genesis, is Greek in origin and comes from the word *geneseos,* which appears in the Greek translation (Septuagint) of 2:4; 5:1. Depending on its context, the word can mean "birth," "genealogy," or "history of origin." In both its Hebrew and Greek forms, then, the title of Genesis appropriately describes its contents, since it is primarily a book of beginnings.

Background

Chs. 1—38 reflect a great deal of what we know from other sources about ancient Mesopotamian life and culture. Creation, genealogies, destructive floods, geography and mapmaking, construction techniques, migrations of peoples, sale and purchase of land, legal customs and procedures, sheepherding and cattle-raising—all these subjects and many others were matters of vital concern to the peoples of Mesopotamia during this time. They were also of interest to the individuals, families and tribes of whom we read in the first 38 chapters of Genesis. The author appears to locate Eden, man's first home, in or near Mesopotamia; the tower of Babel was built there; Abram was born there; Isaac took a wife from there; and Jacob lived there for 20 years. Although these patriarchs settled in Canaan, their original homeland was Mesopotamia.

The closest ancient literary parallels to Gen 1—38 also come from Mesopotamia. *Enuma elish,* the story of the god Marduk's rise to supremacy in the Babylonian pantheon, is similar in some respects (though thoroughly mythical and polytheistic) to the Gen 1 creation account. Some of the features of certain king lists from Sumer bear striking resemblance to the genealogy in Gen 5. The 11th tablet of the *Gilgamesh* epic is quite similar in outline to the flood narrative in Gen 6—8. Several of the major events of Gen 1—8 are narrated in the same order as similar events in the *Atrahasis* epic. In fact, the latter features the same basic motif of creation-rebellion-flood as the Biblical account. Clay tablets found recently at the ancient (c. 2500–2300 B.C.) site of Ebla (modern Tell Mardikh) in northern Syria may also contain some intriguing parallels (see chart, p. xix).

Two other important sets of documents demonstrate the reflection of Mesopotamia in the first 38 chapters of Genesis. From the Mari letters (see chart, p. xix), dating from the patriarchal period, we learn that the names of the patriarchs (including especially Abram, Jacob and Job) were typical of that time. The letters also clearly illustrate the freedom of travel that was possible between various parts of the Amorite world in which the patriarchs lived. The Nuzi tablets (see chart, p. xix), though a few centuries later than the patriarchal period, shed light on patriarchal customs, which tended to survive virtually intact for many centuries. The inheritance right of an adopted household member or slave (see 15:1–4), the obligation of a barren wife to furnish her husband with sons through a servant girl (see 16:2–4), strictures against expelling such a servant girl and her son (see 21:10–11), the authority of oral statements in ancient Near Eastern law, such as the deathbed bequest (see 27:1–4,22–23,33)—these and other legal customs, social contracts and provisions are graphically illustrated in Mesopotamian documents.

As Gen 1—38 is Mesopotamian in character and background, so chs. 39—50 reflect Egyptian influence—though in not quite so direct a way. Examples of such influence are: Egyptian grape cultivation (40:9–11), the riverside scene (ch. 41), Egypt as Canaan's breadbasket (ch. 42), Canaan as the source of numerous products for Egyptian consumption (ch. 43), Egyptian religious and social customs (the end of chs. 43; 46), Egyptian administrative procedures (ch. 47), Egyptian funerary practices (ch. 50) and several Egyptian words and names used throughout these chapters. The closest specific literary parallel from Egypt is the *Tale of Two Brothers,* which bears some resemblance to the story of Joseph and Potiphar's wife (ch. 39). Egyptian autobiographical narratives (such as the *Story*

of Sinuhe and the *Report of Wenamun*) and certain historical legends offer more general literary parallels.

Author and Date of Writing

Historically, Jews and Christians alike have held that Moses was the author/compiler of the first five books of the OT. These books, known also as the Pentateuch (meaning "five-volumed book"), were referred to in Jewish tradition as the five fifths of the law (of Moses). The Bible itself suggests Mosaic authorship of Genesis, since Acts 15:1 refers to circumcision as "the manner of Moses," an allusion to Gen 17. However, a certain amount of later editorial updating does appear to be indicated (see, e.g., notes on 14:14; 36:31; 47:11).

The historical period during which Moses lived seems to be fixed with a fair degree of accuracy by 1 Kings. We are told that "the fourth year of Solomon's reign over Israel" was the same as "the four hundred and eightieth year after the children of Israel were come out of the land of Egypt" (1 Ki 6:1). Since the former was c. 966 B.C., the latter—and thus the date of the exodus—was c. 1446 (assuming that the 480 in 1 Ki 6:1 is to be taken literally; see Introduction to Judges: Background). The 40-year period of Israel's wanderings in the wilderness, which lasted from c. 1446 to c. 1406, would have been the most likely time for Moses to write the bulk of what is today known as the Pentateuch.

During the last three centuries many scholars have claimed to find in the Pentateuch four underlying sources. The presumed documents, allegedly dating from the tenth to the fifth centuries B.C., are called J (for Jahweh/Yahweh, the personal OT name for God), E (for Elohim, a generic name for God), D (for Deuteronomic) and P (for Priestly). Each of these documents is claimed to have its own characteristics and its own theology, which often contradicts that of the other documents. The Pentateuch is thus depicted as a patchwork of stories, poems and laws. However, this view is not supported by conclusive evidence, and intensive archaeological and literary research has tended to undercut many of the arguments used to challenge Mosaic authorship.

Theme and Message

Genesis speaks of beginnings—of the heavens and the earth, of light and darkness, of seas and skies, of land and vegetation, of sun and moon and stars, of sea and air and land animals, of human beings (made in God's own image, the climax of His creative activity), of sin and redemption, of blessing and cursing, of society and civilization, of marriage and family, of art and craft and industry. The list could go on and on. A key word in Genesis is the Hebrew word for "generations," which also serves to divide the book into its ten major parts (see Literary Features and Literary Outline) and which includes such concepts as birth, genealogy and history.

The book of Genesis is foundational to the understanding of the rest of the Bible. Its message is rich and complex, and listing its main elements gives a succinct outline of the Biblical message as a whole. It is supremely a book of relationships, highlighting those between God and nature, God and man, and man and man. It is thoroughly monotheistic, taking for granted that there is only one God worthy of the name and opposing the ideas that there are many gods (polytheism), that there is no god at all (atheism) and that everything is divine (pantheism). It clearly teaches that the one true God is sovereign over all that exists (i.e., His entire creation), and that by divine election He often exercises His unlimited freedom to overturn human customs, traditions and plans. It introduces us to the way in which God initiates and makes covenants with His chosen people, pledging His love and faithfulness to them and calling them to promise theirs to Him. It establishes sacrifice as the substitution of life for life (ch. 22). It gives us the first hint of God's provision for redemption from the forces of evil (compare 3:15 with Rom 16:17–20) and contains the oldest and most profound definition of faith (15:6). More than half of Heb 11—the NT roll of the faithful—refers to characters in Genesis.

Literary Features

The message of a book is often enhanced by its literary structure and characteristics. Genesis is divided into ten main sections, which begin with the Hebrew word translated "generation[s]" (see 2:4; 5:1; 6:9; 10:1; 11:10; 11:27; 25:12; 25:19; 36:1—repeated for emphasis at 36:9—and 37:2). The first five sections can be grouped together and, along with the introduction to the book as a whole (1:1—2:3), can be appropriately called "primeval history" (1:1—11:26), sketching the period from Adam to Abraham. The last five sections constitute a much longer (but equally unified) account, and relate the story of God's dealings with Abraham, Isaac, Jacob and Joseph and their families—a section often called "patriarchal history" (11:27—50:26). This section is in turn composed of three narrative

cycles (Abraham-Isaac, 11:27—25:11; Isaac-Jacob, 25:19—35:29; 37:1; Jacob-Joseph, 37:2—50:26), interspersed by the genealogies of Ishmael (25:12–18) and Esau (ch. 36).

The narrative frequently concentrates on the life of a later son in preference to the firstborn: Seth over Cain, Isaac over Ishmael, Jacob over Esau, Judah and Joseph over their brothers, and Ephraim over Manasseh. Such emphasis on divinely chosen men and their families is perhaps the most obvious literary and theological characteristic of the book of Genesis as a whole. It strikingly underscores the fact that the people of God are not the product of natural human developments, but are the result of God's sovereign and gracious intrusion in human history. He brings out of the fallen human race a new humanity consecrated to Himself, called and destined to be the people of His kingdom and the channel of His blessing to the whole earth.

Numbers with symbolic significance figure prominently in Genesis. The number ten, in addition to being the number of sections into which Genesis is divided, is also the number of names appearing in the genealogies of chs. 5 and 11 (see note on 5:5). The number seven also occurs frequently. The Hebrew text of 1:1 consists of exactly seven words and that of 1:2 of exactly 14 (twice seven). There are seven days of creation, seven names in the genealogy of ch. 4 (see note on 4:17–18; see also 4:15,24; 5:31), various sevens in the flood story, 70 descendants of Noah's sons (ch. 10), a sevenfold promise to Abram (12:2–3), seven years of abundance and then seven of famine in Egypt (ch. 41), and 70 descendants of Jacob (ch. 46). Other significant numbers, such as 12 and 40, are used with similar frequency.

The book of Genesis is basically prose narrative, punctuated here and there by brief poems (the longest is the so-called Blessing of Jacob in 49:2–27). Much of the prose has a lyrical quality and uses the full range of figures of speech and other devices that characterize the world's finest epic literature. Vertical and horizontal parallelism between the two sets of three days in the creation account (see note on 1:11); the ebb and flow of sin and judgment in ch. 3 (the serpent and woman and man sin successively; then God questions them in reverse order; then He judges them in the original order); the powerful monotony of "and he died" in the genealogies in ch. 5; the climactic hinge effect of the phrase "And God remembered Noah" (8:1) at the midpoint of the flood story; the hourglass structure of the account of the tower of Babel in 11:1–9 (narrative in vv. 1–2,8–9; discourse in vv. 3–4,6–7; v. 5 acting as transition); the macabre pun in 40:19 (see 40:13); the alternation between brief accounts about firstborn sons and lengthy accounts about younger sons—these and numerous other literary devices add interest to the narrative and provide interpretive signals to which the reader should pay close attention.

It is no coincidence that many of the subjects and themes of the first three chapters of Genesis are reflected in the last three chapters of Revelation. We can only marvel at the superintending influence of the Lord Himself, who assures us that "all scripture is given by inspiration of God" (2 Tim 3:16) and that "holy men of God spake as they were moved by the Holy Ghost" (2 Pet 1:21).

Outlines

Literary Outline:

I. Introduction (1:1—2:3)
II. Body (2:4—50:26)
   A. "The generations of the heavens and of the earth" (2:4—4:26)
   B. "The book of the generations of Adam" (5:1—6:8)
   C. "The generations of Noah" (6:9—9:29)
   D. "The generations of the sons of Noah, Shem, Ham, and Japheth" (10:1—11:9)
   E. "The generations of Shem" (11:10–26)
   F. "The generations of Terah" (11:27—25:11)
   G. "The generations of Ishmael, Abraham's son" (25:12–18)
   H. "The generations of Isaac, Abraham's son" (25:19—35:29)
   I. "The generations of Esau" (36:1—37:1)
   J. "The generations of Jacob" (37:2—50:26)

Thematic Outline:

I. Primeval History (1:1—11:26)
   A. Creation (1:1—2:3)
      1. Introduction (1:1–2)
      2. Body (1:3–31)

3. Conclusion (2:1–3)
- B. Adam and Eve in Eden (2:4–25)
- C. The Fall and Its Consequences (ch. 3)
- D. The Rapid "Progress" of Sin (4:1–16)
- E. Two Genealogies (4:17—5:32)
  1. The genealogy of pride (4:17–24)
  2. The genealogy of death (4:25—5:32)
- F. The Extent of Sin before the Flood (6:1–8)
- G. The Great Flood (6:9—9:29)
  1. Preparing for the flood (6:9—7:10)
  2. Judgment and redemption (7:11—8:19)
     - a. The rising of the waters (7:11–24)
     - b. The receding of the waters (8:1–19)
  3. The flood's aftermath (8:20—9:29)
     - a. A new promise (8:20–22)
     - b. New ordinances (9:1–7)
     - c. A new relationship (9:8–17)
     - d. A new temptation (9:18–23)
     - e. A final word (9:24–29)
- H. The Spread of the Nations (10:1—11:26)
  1. The diffusion of nations (ch. 10)
  2. The confusion of tongues (11:1–9)
  3. The first Semitic genealogy (11:10–26)

II. Patriarchal History (11:27—50:26)
- A. The Life of Abraham (11:27—25:11)
  1. Abraham's background (11:27–32)
  2. Abraham's land (chs. 12—14)
  3. Abraham's people (chs. 15—24)
  4. Abraham's last days (25:1–11)
- B. The Descendants of Ishmael (25:12–18)
- C. The Life of Jacob (25:19—35:29)
  1. Jacob at home (25:19—27:46)
  2. Jacob abroad (chs. 28—30)
  3. Jacob at home again (chs. 31—35)
- D. The Descendants of Esau (36:1—37:1)
- E. The Life of Joseph (37:2—50:26)
  1. Joseph's career (37:2—41:57)
  2. Jacob's migration (chs. 42—47)
  3. Jacob's last days (48:1—50:14)
  4. Joseph's last days (50:15–26)

The creation

1 In the [a]beginning [b]God created the
heaven and the earth.
2 And the earth was [a]without form, and
void; and darkness *was* upon the face of the
deep. [b]And the Spirit of God moved upon the
face of the waters.
3 ¶ [a]And God said, [b]Let there be light: and
there was light.
4 And God saw the light, that *it was* good:
and God divided [1]the light from the darkness.
5 And God called the light [a]Day, and the
darkness he called Night. [1]And the evening
and the morning were the first day.
6 ¶ And God said, [a]Let there be a [1]firma-
ment in the midst of the waters, and let it divide the waters from the waters.
7 And God made the firmament, [a]and di-

1:1 [a]John 1:1,2; Heb. 1:10 [b]Ps. 8:3; Is. 44:24; Acts 17:24; Rev. 4:11
1:2 [a]Jer. 4:23 [b]Ps. 33:6; Is. 40:13,14
1:3 [a]Ps. 33:9 [b]2 Cor. 4:6
1:4 [1]Heb. *between the light and between the darkness*
1:5 [1]Heb. *And the evening was, and the morning was, etc.* [a]Ps. 74:16
1:6 [1]Heb. *expansion* [a]Job 37:18; Jer. 10:12
1:7 [a]Prov. 8:28 [b]Ps. 148:4
1:9 [a]Job 26:10; Prov. 8:29; Jer. 5:22; 2 Pet. 3:5

vided the waters which *were* under the firmament from the waters which *were* [b]above the
firmament: and it was so.
8 And God called the firmament Heaven.
And the evening and the morning were the
second day.
9 ¶ And God said, [a]Let the waters under the
heaven be gathered together unto one place,
and let the dry *land* appear: and it was so.
10 And God called the dry *land* Earth; and
the gathering together of the waters called he
Seas: and God saw that *it was* good.
11 And God said, Let the earth [a]bring forth
[1]grass, the herb yielding seed, *and* the fruit
tree yielding [b]fruit after his kind, whose seed
is in itself, upon the earth: and it was so.

1:11 [1]Heb. *tender grass* [a]Heb. 6:7 [b]Luke 6:44

‡1:1 The Bible begins with an affirmation of God's existence and His creative activity. The opening verse is a summary statement introducing the six days of creation. The truth of this majestic verse was joyfully affirmed by poet (Ps 102:25) and prophet (Is 40:21). *In the beginning God.* The Bible always assumes, and never argues, God's existence. Although everything else had a beginning, God has always been (Ps 90:2). *In the beginning.* John 1:1–10, which stresses the work of Christ in creation, opens with the same phrase. *God created.* The Hebrew noun *Elohim* is plural but the verb is singular, a normal usage in the OT when reference is to the one true God. This use of the plural expresses intensification rather than number and has been called the plural of majesty, or of potentiality. In the OT the Hebrew verb for "create" is used only of divine, never of human, activity. *the heaven and the earth.* "All things" (Is 44:24). That God created everything is also taught in Eccl 11:5; Jer 10:16; John 1:3; Col 1:16; Heb 1:2. The positive, life-oriented teaching of v. 1 is beautifully summarized in Is 45:18.

1:2 *earth.* The focus of this account. *without form, and void.* The phrase, which appears elsewhere only in Jer 4:23, gives structure to the rest of the chapter (see note on v. 11). God's "dividing" and "gathering" on days 1–3 gave form, and His "making" and "filling" on days 4–6 removed the void. *darkness . . . the waters.* Completes the picture of a world awaiting God's light-giving, order-making and life-creating word. *And.* Or "but." The awesome (and, for ancient man, fearful) picture of the original state of the visible creation is relieved by the majestic announcement that the mighty Spirit of God hovers over creation. The announcement anticipates God's creative words that follow. *Spirit of God.* He was active in creation, and His creative power continues today (see Job 33:4; Ps 104:30). *moved upon.* Like a bird that provides for and protects its young (see Deut 32:11; Is 31:5).

1:3 *God said.* Merely by speaking, God brought all things into being (Ps 33:6,9; 148:5; Heb 11:3). *Let there be light.* God's first recorded creative word called forth light in the midst of the primeval darkness. Light is necessary for making God's creative works visible and life possible. In the OT it is also symbolic of life and blessing (see 2 Sam 22:29; Job 3:20; 30:26; 33:30; Ps 49:19; 56:13; 97:11; 112:4; Is 53:11; 58:8,10; 59:9; 60:1,3). Paul uses this word to illustrate God's re-creating work in sin-darkened hearts (2 Cor 4:6).

1:4 Everything God created is good (see vv. 10,12,18,21,25); in fact, the conclusion declares it to be "very good" (v. 31). The creation, as fashioned and ordered by God, had no lingering traces of disorder and no dark and threatening forces arrayed against God or man. Even darkness and the deep were given benevolent functions in a world fashioned to bless and sustain life (see Ps 104:19–26; 127:2).

‡1:5 *called.* See vv. 8,10. In ancient times, to name something or someone implied having dominion or ownership (see 17:5,15; 41:45; 2 Ki 23:34; 24:17; Dan 1:7). Both day and night belong to the Lord (Ps 74:16). *the first day.* Some say that the creation days were literal 24-hour days, others that they were indefinite periods. Several factors, however, support the first interpretation: 1. Though the Hebrew word for "Day" (*yom*) has multiple possible meanings, one might expect a primary (i.e. literal) meaning in its first reference to time in the OT, i.e. a literal day rather than a secondary (i.e. non-literal or metaphorical) meaning; 2. The normal and usual interpretation of *yom* accompanied by a numerical adjective (e.g. "first," "second," etc.) in the OT is a literal day; 3. The qualifying phrase "and the evening and the morning were the . . . day" suggests a 24-hour day-night cycle; and 4. A creative week of seven indefinite periods of time would hardly serve as a meaningful pattern for man's cycle of work and rest (Ex 20:11). Moreover, Moses had at his disposal words in the Hebrew language that represented long periods of time, thus he was capable of providing necessary clarification if something other than a 24-hour day had been intended.

1:6 *firmament.* The atmosphere, or "Heaven" (v. 8), as seen from the earth. "Strong, and as a molten looking glass" (Job 37:18) and "as a curtain" (Is 40:22) are among the many pictorial phrases used to describe it.

1:7 *and it was so.* The only possible outcome, whether stated (vv. 9,11,15,24,30) or implied, to God's "Let there be."

1:9 *one place.* A picturesque way of referring to the "Seas" (v. 10) that surround the dry ground on all sides and into which the waters of the lakes and rivers flow. The earth was "standing out of the water" (2 Pet 3:5) and "founded . . . upon the seas" (Ps 24:2), and the waters are not to cross the boundaries set for them (Ps 104:7–9; Jer 5:22).

1:11 *God said.* This phrase is used twice on the third day (vv. 9,11) and three times (vv. 24,26,29) on the sixth day. These two days are climactic, as the following structure of ch. 1 reveals (see note on v. 2 regarding "without form, and void"):

Days of forming	*Days of filling*
1. "light" (v. 3)	4. "lights" (v. 14)
2. "waters . . . under the firmament. . . waters . . . above the firmament" (v. 7)	5. "every living creature that moveth, which the waters brought forth abundantly. . . every winged fowl" (v. 21)
3a. "dry land" (v. 9)	$6a_1$. "cattle, and creeping thing, and beast of the earth" (v. 24)
	$6a_2$. "man" (v. 26)
b. "grass" (v. 11)	b. "every green herb for meat" (v. 30)

12 And the earth brought forth grass, *and* herb yielding seed after his kind, and the tree yielding fruit, whose seed *was* in itself, after his kind: and God saw that *it was* good.

13 And the evening and the morning were the third day.

14 ¶ And God said, Let there be lights in the firmament of the heaven to divide [1]the day from the night; and let them be for signs, and for seasons, and for days, and years:

15 And let them be for lights in the firmament of the heaven to give light upon the earth: and it was so.

16 And God made two great lights; the [a]greater light [1]to rule the day, and the [b]lesser light to rule the night: *he made* [c]the stars also.

17 And God set them in the firmament of the heaven to give light upon the earth,

18 And to [a]rule over the day and over the night, and to divide the light from the darkness: and God saw that *it was* good.

19 And the evening and the morning were the fourth day.

20 ¶ And God said, Let the waters bring forth abundantly the [1]moving [2]creature that hath life, and [3]fowl *that* may fly above the earth in the [4]open firmament of heaven.

21 And [a]God created great whales, and every living creature that moveth, which the waters brought forth abundantly, after their kind, and every winged fowl after his kind: and God saw that *it was* good.

22 And God blessed them, saying, [a]Be fruitful, and multiply, and fill the waters in the seas, and let fowl multiply in the earth.

23 And the evening and the morning were the fifth day.

24 ¶ And God said, Let the earth bring forth the living creature after his kind, cattle, and creeping thing, and beast of the earth after his kind: and it was so.

25 And God made the beast of the earth after his kind, and cattle after their kind, and every thing that creepeth upon the earth after his kind: and God saw that *it was* good.

26 ¶ And God said, [a]Let us make man in our image, after our likeness: and [b]let them have dominion over the fish of the sea, and over the fowl of the air, and over the cattle, and over all the earth, and over every creeping thing that creepeth upon the earth.

27 So God created man in his own image, [a]in the image of God created he him; [b]male and female created he them.

28 And God blessed them, and God said unto them, [a]Be fruitful, and multiply, and replenish the earth, and subdue it: and have dominion over the fish of the sea, and over the fowl of the air, and over every living thing that [1]moveth upon the earth.

29 ¶ And God said, Behold, I have given

1:14 [1]Heb. *between the day and between the night*
1:16 [1]Heb. *for the rule of the day, etc.* [a]Ps. 136:8 [b]Ps. 8:3 [c]Job 38:7
1:18 [a]Jer. 31:35
1:20 [1]Or, *creeping* [2]Heb. *soul* [3][Heb. *let fowl fly*] [4]Heb. *face of the firmament of heaven*
1:21 [a]Ps. 104:26
1:22 [a]ch. 8:17
1:26 [a]Ps. 100:3; Eccl. 7:29; Eph. 4:24; Jas. 3:9 [b]ch. 9:2; Ps. 8:6
1:27 [a]1 Cor. 11:7 [b]ch. 5:2; Mat. 19:4
1:28 [1]Heb. *creepeth* [a]ch. 9:1,7; Lev. 26:9

Both the horizontal and vertical relationships between the days demonstrate the literary beauty of the chapter and stress the orderliness and symmetry of God's creative activity. *kind.* See vv. 12,21,24–25. Both creation and reproduction are orderly.

1:14 *be for signs.* In the ways mentioned here, not in any astrological or other such sense.

1:16 *two great lights.* The words "sun" and "moon" seem to be avoided deliberately here, since both were used as proper names for the pagan deities associated with these heavenly bodies. They are light-givers to be appreciated, not powers to be feared, because the one true God made them (see Is 40:26). Perhaps because of the emphasis on the greater light and lesser light, the stars seem to be mentioned almost as an afterthought. But Ps 136:9 indicates that the stars help the moon "rule by night." *to rule.* The great Creator-King assigns subordinate regulating roles to certain of His creatures (see vv. 26,28).

1:17–18 The three main functions of the heavenly bodies.

1:21 *great whales.* Lit. "sea monsters." The Hebrew word underlying this phrase was used in Canaanite mythology to name a dreaded sea monster. He is often referred to figuratively in OT poetry as one of God's most powerful opponents. He is pictured as national (Babylon, Jer 51:34; Egypt, Is 51:9; Ezek 29:3; 32:2) or cosmic (Job 7:12; Ps 74:13; Is 27:1, though some take the latter as a reference to Egypt). In Genesis, however, the creatures of the sea are portrayed not as enemies to be feared but as part of God's good creation to be appreciated. *winged fowl.* The term denotes anything that flies, including insects (see Deut 14:19–20).

1:22 *Be fruitful, and multiply.* God's benediction on living things that inhabit the water and that fly in the air. By His blessing they flourish and fill both realms with life (see note on v. 28). God's rule over His created realm promotes and blesses life.

1:26 *us . . . our . . . our.* God speaks as the Creator-King, announcing His crowning work to the members of His heavenly court (see 3:22; 11:7; Is 6:8; see also 1 Ki 22:19–23; Job 15:8; Jer 23:18). *image . . . likeness.* No distinction should be made between "image" and "likeness," which are synonyms in both the OT (5:1; 9:6) and the NT (1 Cor 11:7; Col 3:10; Jas 3:9). Since man is made in God's image, every human being is worthy of honor and respect; he is neither to be murdered (9:6) nor cursed (Jas 3:9). "Image" includes such characteristics as "righteousness and true holiness" (Eph 4:24) and "knowledge" (Col 3:10). Believers are to be "conformed to the image" of Christ (Rom 8:29) and will someday be "like him" (1 John 3:2). *have dominion..* Man is the climax of God's creative activity, and God has crowned him "with glory and honour" and made him "to have dominion" over the rest of His creation (Ps 8:5–8). Since man was created in the image of the divine King, delegated sovereignty (kingship) was bestowed on him. (For redeemed man's ultimate kingship see notes on Heb 2:5–9.)

1:27 This highly significant verse is the first occurrence of poetry in the OT (which is about 40 percent poetry). *created.* The word is used here three times to describe the central divine act of the sixth day (see note on v. 1). *male and female.* Alike they bear the image of God, and together they share in the divine benediction that follows.

1:28 *God blessed them . . . replenish. . . subdue . . . have dominion.* Man goes forth under this divine benediction—flourishing, filling the earth with his kind, and exercising dominion over the other earthly creatures (see v. 26; 2:15; Ps 8:6–8). Human culture, accordingly, is not anti-God (though fallen man often has turned his efforts into proud rebellion against God). Rather, it is the expression of man's bearing the image of his Creator and sharing, as God's servant, in God's kingly rule. As God's representative in the creaturely realm, he is steward of God's creatures. He is not to exploit, waste or despoil them, but to care for them and use them in the service of God and man.

1:29–30 People and animals seem to be portrayed as originally vegetarian (see 9:3).

you every herb [1]bearing seed, which *is* upon
the face of all the earth, and every tree, in the
which *is* the fruit of a tree [1]yielding seed; [a]to
you it shall be for meat.
30 And to [a]every beast of the earth, and to
every [b]fowl of the air, and to every *thing* that
creepeth upon the earth, wherein *there is*
[1]life, *I have given* every green herb for meat:
and it was so.
31 And [a]God saw every thing that he had
made, and behold, *it was* very good. And the
evening and the morning were the sixth day.

2 Thus the heavens and the earth were finished, and [a]all the host of them.
2 [a]And on the seventh day God ended his
work which he had made; and he rested on
the seventh day from all his work which he
had made.
3 And God [a]blessed the seventh day, and
sanctified it: because that in it he had rested
from all his work which God [1]created and
made.

Adam and Eve

4 ¶ [a]These *are* the generations of the heavens and of the earth when they were created,
in the day that the LORD God made the earth
and the heavens,
5 And every [a]plant of the field before it
was in the earth, and every herb of the field
before it grew: for the LORD God had not
[b]caused it to rain upon the earth, and *there*
was not a man [c]to till the ground.
6 But [1]there went up a mist from the
earth, and watered the whole face of the
ground.
7 And the LORD God formed man [1]*of* the
[a]dust of the ground, and [b]breathed into his
[c]nostrils the breath of life; and [d]man became a
living soul.
8 ¶ And the LORD God planted [a]a garden
[b]eastward in [c]Eden; and there he put the man
whom he had formed.
9 And out of the ground made the LORD
God to grow [a]every tree that is pleasant to the
sight, and good for food; [b]the tree of life also in
the midst of the garden, and the tree of knowledge of good and evil.
10 And a river went out of Eden to water
the garden; and from thence it was parted, and
became into four heads.
11 The name of the first *is* Pison: that *is it*
which compasseth [a]the whole land of Havilah,
where *there is* gold;

1:29 [1]Heb. *seeding seed* [a]ch. 9:3; Ps. 104:14,15
1:30 [1]Heb. *a living soul* [a]Ps. 145:15 [b]Job 38:41
1:31 [a]Ps. 104:24
2:1 [a]Ps. 33:6
2:2 [a]Ex. 20:11; Heb. 4:4
2:3 [1]Heb. *created to make* [a]Is. 58:13
2:4 [a]ch. 1:1
2:5 [a]ch. 1:12 [b]Job 38:26-28 [c]ch. 3:23
2:6 [1]Or, *a mist which went up from, etc.*
2:7 [1]Heb. *dust of the ground* [a]ch. 3:19,23; Ps. 103:14 [b]Job 33:4 [c]ch. 7:22 [d]1 Cor. 15:45
2:8 [a]Is. 51:3 [b]ch. 3:24 [c]ch. 4:16
2:9 [a]Ezek. 31:8 [b]ch. 3:22; Rev. 2:7
2:11 [a]ch. 25:18

1:31 *very good.* See note on v. 4. *the sixth day.* Perhaps to stress the finality and importance of this day, in the Hebrew text the definite article is first used here in regard to the creation days.
2:2 *ended . . . rested.* God ceased on the seventh day, not because He was weary, but because nothing formless or empty remained. His creative work was completed—and it was totally effective, absolutely perfect, "very good" (1:31). It did not have to be repeated, repaired or revised, and the Creator rested to commemorate it.
2:3 *God blessed the seventh day, and sanctified it . . . rested.* Although the word "sabbath" is not used here, the Hebrew verb translated "rested" (see v. 2) is the origin of the noun "sabbath." Ex 20:11 quotes the first half of v. 3, but substitutes "sabbath" for "seventh," clearly equating the two. The first record of obligatory sabbath observance is of Israel on her way from Egypt to Sinai (Ex 16), and according to Neh 9:13–14 the sabbath was not an official covenant obligation until the giving of the law at mount Sinai.
2:4 *generations.* The Hebrew word for "generations" occurs ten times in Genesis—at the beginning of each main section (see Introduction: Literary Features). *the heavens and of the earth.* See note on 1:1. The phrase "the generations [i.e., "account"] of the heavens and of the earth" introduces the record of what happened to God's creation. The blight of sin and rebellion brought a threefold curse that darkens the story of Adam and Eve in God's good and beautiful garden: (1) on Satan (3:14); (2) on the ground, because of man (3:17); and (3) on Cain (4:11). 1:1–2:3 is a general account of creation, while 2:4–4:26 focuses on the beginning of human history. *LORD God.* "LORD" (Hebrew *YHWH,* "Yahweh") is the personal and covenant name of God (see note on Ex 3:15), emphasizing His role as Israel's Redeemer and covenant Lord (see note on Ex 6:6), while "God" (Hebrew *Elohim*) is a general term. Both names occur thousands of times in the OT, and often, as here, they appear together—clearly indicating that they refer to the same one and only God.
2:7 *formed.* The Hebrew for this verb commonly referred to the work of a potter (see Is 45:9; Jer 18:6), who fashions vessels from clay (see Job 33:6). "Make" (1:26), "created" (1:27) and "form" are used to describe God's creation of both man and animals (v. 19; 1:21,25). *man.* The Hebrew for "man" (*adam*) sounds like and may be related to the Hebrew for "ground" (*adamah*); it is also the name Adam (see 2:20). *breath of life.* Humans and animals alike have the breath of life in them (see 1:30; Job 33:4). *man became a living soul.* The Hebrew phrase here translated "living soul" is translated "creature that hath life" in 1:20 and "living creature" in 1:24. The words of 2:7 therefore imply that people, at least physically, have affinity with the animals. The great difference is that man is made "in the image of God" (1:27) and has an absolutely unique relation both to God as His servant and to the other creatures as their divinely appointed steward (Ps 8:5–8).
2:8 *eastward.* From the standpoint of the author of Genesis. The garden was perhaps near where the Tigris and Euphrates rivers (see v. 14) meet, in what is today southern Iraq. *Eden.* A name synonymous with "paradise" and related to either (1) a Hebrew word meaning "bliss" or "delight" or (2) a Mesopotamian word meaning "a plain." Perhaps the author subtly suggests both.
2:9 *tree of life.* Signifying and giving life, without death, to those who eat its fruit (see 3:22; Rev 2:7; 22:2,14). *tree of knowledge of good and evil.* Signifying and giving knowledge of good and evil, leading ultimately to death, to those who eat its fruit (v. 17; 3:3). "Knowledge of good and evil" refers to moral knowledge or ethical discernment (see Deut 1:39; Is 7:15–16). Adam and Eve possessed both life and moral discernment as they came from the hand of God. Their access to the fruit of the tree of life showed that God's will and intention for them was life. Ancient pagans believed that the gods intended for man always to be mortal. In eating the fruit of the tree of the knowledge of good and evil, Adam and Eve sought a creaturely source of discernment in order to be morally independent of God.
2:11 *Pison.* Location unknown. The Hebrew word may be a common noun meaning "gusher." *Havilah.* Location unknown; perhaps mentioned again in 10:29. It is probably to be distinguished from the Havilah of 10:7, which was in Egypt.

12 And the gold of that land *is* good: [a]there *is* bdellium and the onyx stone.

13 And the name of the second river *is* Gihon: the same *is it* that compasseth the whole land of [1]Ethiopia.

14 And the name of the third river *is* [a]Hiddekel: that *is it* which goeth [1]toward the east of Assyria. And the fourth river *is* Euphrates.

15 And the LORD God took [1]the man, and put him into the garden of Eden to dress it and to keep it.

16 And the LORD God commanded the man, saying, Of every tree of the garden [1]thou mayest freely eat:

17 But of the tree of the knowledge of good and evil, [a]thou shalt not eat of it: for in the day that thou eatest thereof [b][1]thou shalt surely die.

18 ¶ And the LORD God said, *It is* not good that the man should be alone; [a]I will make him a help [1]meet for him.

19 [a]And out of the ground the LORD God formed every beast of the field, and every fowl of the air; and [b]brought *them* unto [1]Adam to see what he would call them: and whatsoever Adam called every living creature, that *was* the name thereof.

20 And Adam [1]gave names to all cattle, and to the fowl of the air, and to every beast of the field; but for Adam there was not found a help meet for him.

21 And the LORD God caused a [a]deep sleep to fall upon Adam, and he slept: and he took one of his ribs, and closed up the flesh instead thereof;

22 And the rib, which the LORD God had taken from man, [1]made he a woman, and [a]brought her unto the man.

23 And Adam said, This *is* now [a]bone of my bones, and flesh of my flesh: she shall be called [1]Woman, because she was [b]taken out of [2]Man.

24 [a]Therefore shall a man leave his father and his mother, and shall cleave unto his wife: and they shall be one flesh.

25 [a]And they were both naked, the man and his wife, and were not [b]ashamed.

The fall of man

3 Now [a]the serpent was [b]more subtil than any beast of the field which the LORD God had made. And he said unto the woman, [1]Yea, hath God said, Ye shall not eat of every tree of the garden?

2 And the woman said unto the serpent, We may eat of the fruit of the trees of the garden:

3 But of the fruit of the tree which *is* in the midst of the garden, God hath said, Ye shall not eat of it, neither shall ye touch it, lest ye die.

4 [a]And the serpent said unto the woman, Ye shall not surely die:

5 For God doth know that in the day ye eat thereof, then your eyes shall be opened, and ye shall be as gods, knowing good and evil.

6 And when the woman saw that the tree *was* good for food, and that it *was* [1]pleasant to the eyes, and a tree to be desired to make *one* wise, she took of the fruit thereof, [a]and did eat, and gave also unto her husband with her; and he did eat.

7 And the eyes of them both were opened,

2:12 [a]Num. 11:7
2:13 [1]Heb. *Cush*
2:14 [1]Or, *eastward* to *Assyria* [a]Dan. 10:4
2:15 [1]Or, *Adam*
2:16 [1]Heb. *eating thou shalt eat*
2:17 [1]Heb. *dying thou shalt die* [a]ch. 3:1,3,11,17 [b]ch. 3:3,19; Rom. 6:23
2:18 [1]Heb. *as before him* [a]1 Cor. 11:9; 1 Tim. 2:13
2:19 [1]Or, *the man* [a]ch. 1:20,24 [b]Ps. 8:6
2:20 [1]Heb. *called*
2:21 [a]1 Sam. 26:12
2:22 [1]Heb. *builded* [a]Heb. 13:4
2:23 [1][Heb. *Isha*] [2][Heb. *Ish*] [a]ch. 29:14; Eph. 5:30 [b]1 Cor. 11:8
2:24 [a]Mat. 19:5; Eph. 5:31
2:25 [a]ch. 3:7,10 [b]Is. 47:3
3:1 [1]Heb. *Yea, because, etc.* [a]Rev. 12:9 [b]2 Cor. 11:3
3:4 [a]2 Cor. 11:3
3:6 [1]Heb. *a desire* [a]1 Tim. 2:14

2:13 *Gihon.* Location unknown. The Hebrew word may be a common noun meaning "spurter." Both the Pison and the Gihon may have been streams in Lower Mesopotamia near the Persian Gulf. The names were those current when Moses wrote.
‡2:14 *Hiddekel.* The Tigris river. *Assyria.* Lit. "Asshur," an ancient capital city of Assyria ("Assyria" and "Asshur" are related words). *Euphrates.* Often called simply "the river" (1 Ki 4:21,24) because of its size and importance.
2:15 *dress . . . keep.* See note on 1:28. Man is now charged to govern the earth responsibly under God's sovereignty.
2:16 *every tree.* Including the tree of life (v. 9).
2:17 *surely die.* Despite the serpent's denial (3:4), disobeying God ultimately results in death.
2:18–25 The only full account of the creation of woman in ancient Near Eastern literature.
2:18 *not good . . . should be alone.* Without female companionship and a partner in reproduction, the man could not fully realize his humanity.
2:19 *call them.* His first act of dominion over the creatures around him (see note on 1:5).
2:24 *leave his father and his mother.* Instead of remaining under the protective custody of his parents a man leaves them and, with his wife, establishes a new family unit. *cleave . . . one flesh.* The divine intention for husband and wife was monogamy. Together they were to form an inseparable union, of which "one flesh" is both a sign and an expression.
2:25 *naked . . . not ashamed.* Freedom from shame, signifying moral innocence, would soon be lost as a result of sin (see 3:7).
3:1 *serpent.* The great deceiver clothed himself as a serpent, one of God's good creatures. He insinuated a falsehood and portrayed rebellion as clever, but essentially innocent, self-interest. Therefore "the devil, or Satan," is later referred to as "that old serpent" (Rev 12:9; 20:2). *subtil.* The Hebrew words for "subtil" and "naked" are almost identical. Though naked, the man and his wife felt no shame (2:25). The craftiness of the serpent led them to sin, and they then became ashamed of their nakedness (see v. 7). *Yea, hath God said . . . ?* The question and the response changed the course of human history. By causing the woman to doubt God's word, Satan brought evil into the world. Here the deceiver undertook to alienate man from God. In Job 1–2 he, as the accuser, acted to alienate God from man (see also Zech 3:1).
3:3 *Ye shall not . . . touch it.* The woman adds to God's word, distorting His directive and demonstrating that the serpent's subtle challenge was working its poison.
3:4 *Ye shall not surely die.* The blatant denial of a specific divine pronouncement (see 2:17).
‡3:5 *God doth know.* Satan accuses God of having unworthy motives. In Job 1:9–11; 2:4–5 he accuses the righteous man of the same. *your eyes shall be opened, and ye shall be as gods.* [the Hebrew word *Elohim* would be better rendered "God" here]. The statement is only half true. Their eyes were opened, to be sure (see v. 7), but the result was quite different from what the serpent had promised. *knowing good and evil.* See note on 2:9.
3:6 *good for food . . . pleasant to the eyes . . . to be desired to make one wise.* Three aspects of temptation. Cf. 1 John 2:16; Luke 4:3,5,9.

[a]and they knew that they *were* naked; and they sewed fig leaves together, and made themselves [1]aprons.

8 And they heard [a]the voice of the LORD God walking in the garden in the [1]cool of the day: and Adam and his wife [b]hid themselves from the presence of the LORD God amongst the trees of the garden.

9 And the LORD God called unto Adam, and said unto him, Where *art* thou?

10 And he said, I heard thy voice in the garden, [a]and I was afraid, because I *was* naked; and I hid myself.

11 And he said, Who told thee that thou *wast* naked? Hast thou eaten of the tree, whereof I commanded thee that thou shouldest not eat?

12 And the man said, [a]The woman whom thou gavest *to be* with me, she gave me of the tree, and I did eat.

13 And the LORD God said unto the woman, What *is* this *that* thou hast done? And the woman said, [a]The serpent beguiled me, and I did eat.

14 And the LORD God said unto the serpent, Because thou hast done this, thou *art* cursed above all cattle, and above every beast of the field; upon thy belly shalt thou go, and [a]dust shalt thou eat all the days of thy life:

15 And I will put enmity between thee and the woman, and between [a]thy seed and [b]her seed; [c]it shall bruise thy head, and thou shalt bruise his heel.

16 Unto the woman he said, I will greatly multiply thy sorrow and thy conception; [a]in sorrow thou shalt bring forth children; [b]and thy desire *shall be* [1]to thy husband, and he shall [c]rule over thee.

17 And unto Adam he said, [a]Because thou hast hearkened unto the voice of thy wife, and hast eaten of the tree, [b]of which I commanded thee, saying, Thou shalt not eat of it: [c]cursed *is* the ground for thy sake; [d]in sorrow shalt thou eat *of* it all the days of thy life;

18 Thorns also and thistles shall it [1]bring forth to thee; and [a]thou shalt eat the herb of the field;

19 [a]In the sweat of thy face shalt thou eat bread, till thou return unto the ground; for out of it wast thou taken: [b]for dust thou *art,* and [c]unto dust shalt thou return.

20 And Adam called his wife's name [1]Eve; because she was the mother of all living.

21 Unto Adam also and to his wife did the LORD God make coats of skins, and clothed them.

22 And the LORD God said, Behold, the man is become as one of us, to know good and evil: and now, lest he put forth his hand, and take also of the tree of life, and eat, and live for ever:

23 Therefore the LORD God sent him forth from the garden of Eden, [a]to till the ground from whence he was taken.

24 So he drove out the man; and he placed [a]at the east of the garden of Eden [b]Cherubims, and a flaming sword which turned every way, to keep the way of the tree of life.

3:7 [1]Or, *things to gird about* [a]ch. 2:25
3:8 [1]Heb. *wind* [a]Job 38:1 [b]Job 31:33; Jer. 23:24
3:10 [a]ch. 2:25; 1 John 3:20
3:12 [a]Prov. 28:13
3:13 [a]ver. 4; 2 Cor. 11:3; 1 Tim. 2:14
3:14 [a]Is. 65:25
3:15 [a]John 8:44; Acts 13:10; 1 John 3:8 [b]Is. 7:14; Luke 1:31,34,35 [c]Rom. 16:20; Rev. 12:7
3:16 [1]Or, *subject to thy husband* [a]Is. 13:8; John 16:21 [b]ch. 4:7 [c]1 Cor. 11:3; Eph. 5:22
3:17 [a]1 Sam. 15:23 [b]ch. 2:17 [c]Rom. 8:20 [d]Eccl. 2:23
3:18 [1]Heb. *cause to bud* [a]Ps. 104:14
3:19 [a]2 Thes. 3:10 [b]ch. 2:7 [c]Job 21:26; Eccl. 3:20
3:20 [1]Heb. *Chavah.* [That is, *Living*]
3:23 [a]ch. 4:2; 9:20
3:24 [a]ch. 2:8 [b]Ps. 104:4; Heb. 1:7

3:7 *they knew that they were naked.* No longer innocent like children, they had a new awareness of themselves and of each other in their nakedness and shame. *they . . . made . . . aprons.* Their own feeble and futile attempt to hide their shame, which only God could cover (see note on v. 21).

3:8 *the garden.* Once a place of joy and fellowship with God, it became a place of fear and of hiding from God.

3:9 *Where art thou?* A rhetorical question (see 4:9).

3:12 *The woman whom thou gavest . . . gave me.* The man blames God and the woman—anyone but himself—for his sin.

3:13 *The serpent beguiled me.* The woman blames the serpent rather than herself.

3:14 *cursed.* The serpent, the woman and the man were all judged, but only the serpent and the ground were cursed—the latter because of Adam (v. 17). *dust.* The symbol of death itself (v. 19) would be the serpent's food.

3:15 *it shall bruise thy head, and thou shalt bruise his heel.* The antagonism between people and snakes is used to symbolize the outcome of the titanic struggle between God and the evil one, a struggle played out in the hearts and history of mankind. The offspring of the woman would eventually crush the serpent's head, a promise fulfilled in Christ's victory over Satan—a victory in which all believers will share (see Rom 16:20).

3:16 *thy sorrow and thy conception.* Her judgment fell on what was most uniquely hers as a woman and as a "help meet" (2:20) for her husband. Similarly, the man's "sorrow" (v. 17) was a judgment on him as worker of the soil. Some believe that the Hebrew root underlying "sorrow" should here be understood in the sense of burdensome labor (see Prov 5:10, "labours"; 14:23, "labour"). *bring forth children.* As a sign of grace in the midst of judgment, the human race would continue. *desire . . . rule.* Her sexual attraction for the man, and his headship over her, will become intimate aspects of her life in which she experiences trouble and anguish rather than unalloyed joy and blessing.

3:17–19 *shalt thou eat.* Though he would have to work hard and long (judgment), the man would be able to produce food that would sustain life (grace).

3:19 *return unto the ground . . . unto dust shalt thou return.* Man's labor would not be able to stave off death. The origin of his body (see 2:7) and the source of his food (see v. 17) became a symbol of his eventual death.

‡3:21 *clothed them.* God graciously provided Adam and Eve with more effective clothing (cf. v. 7) to cover their shame (cf. v. 10). God's act of clothing them with skins, thus requiring the death of innocent animals, is symbolic of the merits of Christ's future sacrifice for sins upon the cross whereby the unrighteous sinner can be clothed in Christ's righteousness (2 Cor 5:21). It is possible that it is here that God instructed Adam and Eve concerning the need of animal sacrifice as a part of worship.

3:22 *us.* See note on 1:26. *to know good and evil.* In a terribly perverted way, Satan's prediction (v. 5) came true. *live for ever.* Sin, which always results in death (Rom 6:23; Jas 1:14–15), cuts the sinner off from God's gift of eternal life.

3:23 *sent him forth from the garden of Eden, to till the ground.* Before he sinned, man had worked in a beautiful and pleasant garden (2:15). Now he would have to work hard ground cursed with thorns and thistles (v. 18).

3:24 *Cherubims.* Similar to the statues of winged figures that stood guard at the entrances to palaces and temples in ancient Mesopotamia (see note on Ex 25:18). *to keep.* The sword of God's judgment stood between fallen man and God's garden. The reason is given in v. 22. Only through God's redemption in Christ does man have access again to the tree of life (see Rev 2:7; 22:2,14,19).

Cain and Abel

4 And Adam knew Eve his wife; and she
conceived, and bare [1]Cain, and said, I
have gotten a man from the LORD.
2 And she again bare his brother [1]Abel.
And Abel was [2]a keeper of sheep, but Cain
was a tiller of the ground.
3 And [1]in process of time it came to pass,
that Cain brought [a]of the fruit of the ground
an offering unto the LORD.
4 And Abel, he also brought of [a]the
firstlings of his [1]flock and of [b]the fat thereof.
And the LORD had [c]respect unto Abel and to
his offering:
5 But unto Cain and to his offering he had
not respect. And Cain was very wroth, [a]and
his countenance fell.
6 And the LORD said unto Cain, Why art
thou wroth? and why is thy countenance fallen?
7 If thou doest well, *shalt thou* not [1]be accepted? and if thou doest not well, sin lieth at
the door. And [a2]unto thee *shall be* his desire,
and thou shalt rule over him.
8 And Cain talked with Abel his brother:
and it came to pass, when they were in the
field, that Cain rose up against Abel his brother, and [a]slew him.
9 And the LORD said unto Cain, Where *is*
Abel thy brother? And he said, [a]I know not:
Am I my brother's keeper?
10 And he said, What hast thou done? the
voice of thy brother's [1]blood [a]crieth unto me
from the ground.
11 And now *art* thou cursed from the
earth, which hath opened her mouth to receive thy brother's blood from thy hand.
12 When thou tillest the ground, it shall
not henceforth yield unto thee her strength; a
fugitive and a vagabond shalt thou be in the
earth.
13 And Cain said unto the LORD, [1]My punishment *is* greater than *I* can bear.
14 Behold, thou hast driven me out *this*
day from the face of the earth; and [a]from thy
face shall I be hid; and I shall be a fugitive and
a vagabond in the earth; and it shall come to
pass, [b]*that* every one that findeth me shall slay
me.
15 And the LORD said unto him, Therefore
whosoever slayeth Cain, vengeance shall be
taken on him [a]sevenfold. And the LORD set a
mark upon Cain, lest any finding him should
kill him.
16 And Cain [a]went out from the presence
of the LORD, and dwelt in the land of Nod, on
the east of Eden.
17 And Cain knew his wife; and she conceived, and bare [1]Enoch: and he builded a
city, [a]and called the name of the city, after the
name of his son, Enoch.
18 And unto Enoch was born Irad: and Irad

4:1 [1][That is, *Gotten*, or, *Acquired*]
4:2 [1]Heb. *Hebel* [2]Heb. *a feeder*
4:3 [1]Heb. *at the end of days* [a]Num. 18:12
4:4 [1]Heb. *sheep*, or, *goats* [a]Num. 18:17 [b]Lev. 3:16 [c]Heb. 11:4
4:5 [a]ch. 31:2
4:7 [1]Or, *have the excellency* [2]Or, *subject unto thee* [a]ch. 3:16
4:8 [a]Mat. 23:35
4:9 [a]John 8:44
4:10 [1]Heb. *bloods* [a]Heb. 12:24; Rev. 6:10
4:13 [1]Or, *Mine iniquity is greater than that it may be forgiven*
4:14 [a]Ps. 51:11 [b]ch. 9:6; Num. 35:19,21,27
4:15 [a]Ps. 79:12
4:16 [a]2 Ki. 13:23; 24:20; Jer. 23:39; 52:3
4:17 [1]Heb. *Chanoch* [a]Ps. 49:11

4:1 *from the LORD.* Eve acknowledged that God is the ultimate source of life (see Acts 17:25).

4:2 *Abel.* The name means "breath" or "temporary" or "meaningless" (the translation of the same basic Hebrew word that is in Eccl 1:2; 12:8) and hints at the shortness of Abel's life.

4:3–4 *Cain brought . . . fruit . . . Abel . . . brought of the firstlings of his flock and of the fat thereof.* The contrast is not between an offering of plant life and an offering of animal life, but between a careless, thoughtless offering and a choice, generous offering (cf. Lev 3:16). Motivation and heart attitude are all-important, and God looked with favor on Abel and his offering because of Abel's faith (Heb 11:4). *firstlings.* Indicative of the recognition that all the productivity of the flock is from the Lord and all of it belongs to Him.

4:5 *wroth.* God did not look with favor on Cain and his offering, and Cain (whose motivation and attitude were bad from the outset) reacted predictably.

4:7 *sin lieth at the door.* The Hebrew word for "lieth" is the same as an ancient Babylonian word referring to an evil demon crouching at the door of a building to threaten the people inside. Sin may thus be pictured here as just such a demon, waiting to pounce on Cain—it desires to have him. He may already have been plotting his brother's murder. *unto thee shall be his desire.* In Hebrew, the same expression as that for "thy desire shall be to [thy husband]" in 3:16 (see also Sol 7:10).

4:8 *rose up against . . . his brother, and slew him.* The first murder was especially monstrous because it was committed against a brother (see vv. 9–11; 1 John 3:12) and against a good man (Mat 23:35; Heb 11:4)—a striking illustration of the awful consequences of the fall.

4:9 *Where . . . ?* A rhetorical question (see 3:9). *I know not.* An outright lie. *Am I my brother's keeper?* A statement of callous indifference—all too common through the whole course of human history.

4:10 *thy brother's blood crieth unto me.* Abel, in one sense a prophet (Luke 11:50–51), still speaks, though dead (Heb 11:4), for his spilled blood continues to cry out to God against all those who do violence to their human brothers. But the blood of Christ "speaketh better things than that of Abel" (Heb 12:24).

4:11 *cursed.* The ground had been cursed because of human sin (3:17), and now Cain himself is cursed. Formerly he had worked the ground, and it had produced life for him (vv. 2–3). Now the ground, soaked with his brother's blood, would symbolize death and would no longer yield for him its produce (v. 12).

4:12 *vagabond.* Estranged from his fellowman and finding even the ground inhospitable, he became a wanderer in the land of wandering (see note on v. 16).

4:13 *My punishment is greater than I can bear.* Confronted with his crime and its resulting curse, Cain responded not with remorse but with self-pity. His sin was virtually uninterrupted: impiety (v. 3), anger (v. 5), jealousy, deception and murder (v. 8), falsehood (v. 9) and self-seeking (v. 13). The final result was alienation from God Himself (vv. 14,16).

4:14–15 *every one . . . whosoever . . . any.* These words seem to imply the presence of substantial numbers of people outside Cain's immediate family, but perhaps they only anticipate the future rapid growth of the race.

4:15 *mark.* A warning sign to protect him from an avenger. For the time being, the life of the murderer is spared (but see 6:7; 9:6). For a possible parallel see Ezek 9:4.

4:16 *Nod.* Location unknown. The name "Nod" is from the same Hebrew word as "vagabond" in verses 12, 14.

4:17–18 *Cain . . . Enoch . . . Irad . . . Mehujael . . . Methusael . . . Lamech.* Together with that of Adam, these names add up to a total of seven, a number often signifying completeness (see v. 15). Each of the six names listed here is paralleled by a similar or identical name in the genealogy of Seth in ch. 5 as follows: Cainan (5:12), Enoch (5:21), Jared (5:18), Mahalaleel (5:15), Methuselah (5:25), Lamech (5:28). The similarity between the

begat Mehujael: and Mehujael begat Methusael: and Methusael begat [1]Lamech.
19 And Lamech took unto him two wives:
the name of the one *was* Adah, and the name
of the other Zillah.
20 And Adah bare Jabal: he was the father
of such as dwell in tents, and *of such as have*
cattle.
21 And his brother's name *was* Jubal: he
was the father of all such as handle the harp
and organ.
22 And Zillah, she also bare Tubal-cain, an
[1]instructor of every artificer in brass and iron:
and the sister of Tubal-cain *was* Naamah.
23 And Lamech said unto his wives,
Adah and Zillah, Hear my voice;
Ye wives of Lamech, hearken unto my
speech:
For [1]I have slain a man to my
wounding,
And a young man [2]to my hurt.
24 [a]If Cain shall be avenged sevenfold,
Truly Lamech seventy and sevenfold.
25 And Adam knew his wife again; and she
bare a son, and [a]called his name [1]Seth: For
God, *said she,* hath appointed me another
seed instead of Abel, whom Cain slew.
26 And to Seth, [a]*to* him also there was
born a son; and he called his name [1]Enos;
then began *men* [b2]to call upon the name of
the LORD.

4:18 [1]Heb. *Lemech*
4:22 [1]Heb. *whetter*
4:23 [1]Or, *I would slay a man in my wound, etc.* [2]Or, *in my hurt*
4:24 [a]ver. 15
4:25 [1]Heb. *Sheth.* [That is, *Appointed,* or, *Put*] [a]ch. 5:3
4:26 [1]Heb. *Enosh* [2]Or, *to call* themselves *by the name of the LORD* [a]ch. 5:6 [b]1 Ki. 18:24; Ps. 116:17; 1 Cor. 1:2
5:1 [a]ch. 1:26; Eph. 4:24; Col. 3:10
5:2 [a]ch. 1:27
5:3 [a]ch. 4:25
5:4 [a]1 Chr. 1:1 [b]ch. 1:28
5:5 [a]ch. 3:19; Heb. 9:27
5:6 [1]Heb. *Enosh* [a]ch. 4:26
5:9 [1]Heb. *Kenan*
5:12 [1]Gr. *Maleleel*

The descendants of Adam

5 This *is* the book of the generations of
Adam. In the day that God created man,
in [a]the likeness of God made he him;
2 [a]Male and female created he them; and
blessed them, and called their name Adam, in
the day when they were created.
3 And Adam lived an hundred and thirty
years, and begat *a son* in his own likeness, after his image; and [a]called his name Seth:
4 [a]And the days of Adam after he had begotten Seth were eight hundred years: [b]and he
begat sons and daughters:
5 And all the days that Adam lived were
nine hundred and thirty years: [a]and he died.
6 And Seth lived an hundred and five
years, and [a]begat [1]Enos:
7 And Seth lived after he begat Enos eight
hundred and seven years, and begat sons and
daughters:
8 And all the days of Seth were nine hundred and twelve years: and he died.
9 And Enos lived ninety years, and begat
[1]Cainan:
10 And Enos lived after he begat Cainan
eight hundred and fifteen years, and begat
sons and daughters:
11 And all the days of Enos were nine hundred and five years: and he died.
12 And Cainan lived seventy years, and begat [1]Mahalaleel:
13 And Cainan lived after he begat Maha-

two sets of names is striking and may suggest the selective nature of such genealogies (see note on 5:5). See also Introduction to 1 Chronicles: Genealogies.

4:17 *city.* The Hebrew for this word can refer to any permanent settlement, however small. Cain tried to redeem himself from his wandering state by the activity of his own hands—in the land of wandering he builds a city.

4:19 *took unto him two wives.* Polygamy entered history. Haughty Lamech, the seventh from Adam in the line of Cain, perhaps sought to attain the benefits of God's primeval blessing (see 1:28 and note) by his own device—multiplying his wives. Monogamy, however, was the original divine intention (see 2:23–24).

4:20–22 *Jabal . . . Jubal . . . Tubal-cain.* Lamech's three sons had similar names, each derived from a Hebrew verb meaning "to bring, carry, lead," and emphasizing activity. Tubal-cain's name was especially appropriate, since "Cain" means "metalsmith."

‡4:22 *instructor . . . brass and iron.* He made implements for agriculture and construction, but they were also weapons.

4:23 *slain a man to my wounding.* Violent and wanton destruction of human life by one who proclaimed his complete independence from God by taking vengeance with his own hands (see Deut 32:35). Lamech proudly claimed to be master of his own destiny, thinking that he and his sons, by their own achievements, would redeem themselves from the curse on the line of Cain. This titanic claim climaxes the catalog of sins that began with Cain's prideful selfishness at the beginning of the chapter.

4:24 *seventy and sevenfold.* Lamech's vicious announcement of personal revenge found its counterpoint in Jesus' response to Peter's question about forgiveness in Mat 18:21–22.

4:25 *again . . . another seed.* Abel was dead, and Cain was alienated; so Adam and Eve were granted a third son to carry on the family line.

4:26 *Enos.* The name, like "Adam" (see note on 2:7), means "man." *began . . . to call upon the name of the LORD.* Lamech's proud self-reliance, so characteristic of the line of Cain, is contrasted with dependence on God found in the line of Seth.

5:1 *generations.* See note on 2:4. *likeness.* See note on 1:26.

5:2 *Male and female.* See note on 1:27. *blessed them.* See 1:28 and note. *called their name.* See note on 1:5. *Adam.* The Hebrew word for "man," which often refers to both sexes (mankind) in the early chapters of Genesis (see, e.g., 3:22–24).

5:3 *his own likeness . . . his image.* See note on 1:26. As God created man in His own perfect image, so now sinful Adam has a son in his own imperfect image.

5:5 *nine hundred and thirty years.* See notes on v. 27; 6:3. Whether the large numbers describing human longevity in the early chapters of Genesis are literal or have a conventional literary function—or both—is uncertain. Some believe that several of the numbers have symbolic significance, such as Enoch's 365 (v. 23) years (365 being the number of days in a year, thus a full life) and Lamech's 777 (v. 31) years (777 being an expansion and multiple of seven, the number of completeness; cf. the "seventy and sevenfold" of Lamech's namesake in 4:24). The fact that there are exactly ten names in the Gen 5 list (as in the genealogy of 11:10–26) makes it likely that it includes gaps, the lengths of which may be summarized in the large numbers. Other ancient genealogies outside the Bible exhibit similarly large figures. For example, three kings in a Sumerian list (which also contains exactly ten names) are said to have reigned 72,000 years each—obviously exaggerated time spans. *and he died.* Repeated as a sad refrain throughout the chapter, the only exception being Enoch (see note on v. 24). The phrase is a stark reminder of God's judgment on sin resulting from Adam's fall.

laleel eight hundred and forty years, and begat sons and daughters:

14 And all the days of Cainan were nine hundred and ten years: and he died.

15 And Mahalaleel lived sixty and five years, and begat [1]Jared:

16 And Mahalaleel lived after he begat Jared eight hundred and thirty years, and begat sons and daughters:

17 And all the days of Mahalaleel were eight hundred ninety and five years: and he died.

18 And Jared lived an hundred sixty and two years, and he begat [a]Enoch:

19 And Jared lived after he begat Enoch eight hundred years, and begat sons and daughters:

20 And all the days of Jared were nine hundred sixty and two years: and he died.

21 And Enoch lived sixty and five years, and begat [1]Methuselah:

22 And Enoch [a]walked with God after he begat Methuselah three hundred years, and begat sons and daughters:

23 And all the days of Enoch were three hundred sixty and five years:

24 And [a]Enoch walked with God: and he *was* not; for God took him.

25 And Methuselah lived an hundred eighty and seven years, and begat Lamech:

26 And Methuselah lived after he begat [1]Lamech seven hundred eighty and two years, and begat sons and daughters:

27 And all the days of Methuselah were nine hundred sixty and nine years: and he died.

28 And Lamech lived an hundred eighty and two years, and begat a son:

29 And he called his name [1]Noah, saying, This *same* shall comfort us concerning our work and toil of our hands, because of the ground [a]which the LORD hath cursed.

30 And Lamech lived after he begat Noah five hundred ninety and five years, and begat sons and daughters:

31 And all the days of Lamech were seven hundred seventy and seven years: and he died.

32 And Noah was five hundred years old: and Noah begat [a]Shem, Ham, [b]and Japheth.

The flood

6 And it came to pass, [a]when men began to multiply on the face of the earth, and daughters were born unto them,

2 That the sons of God saw the daughters of men that they *were* fair; and they [a]took them wives of all which they chose.

3 And the LORD said, [a]My spirit shall not always strive with man, [b]for that he also *is* flesh: yet his days shall be an hundred and twenty years.

4 There were giants in the earth in those days; and also after that, when the sons of God came in unto the daughters of men, and they bare *children* to them, the same *became* mighty *men* which *were* of old, men of renown.

5 And GOD saw that the wickedness of man *was* great in the earth, and *that* [1]every [a]imagination of the thoughts of his heart *was* only evil [2]continually.

6 And [a]it repented the LORD that he had

5:15 [1]Heb. *Jered*
5:18 [a]Jude 14,15
5:21 [1]Gr. *Mathusala*
5:22 [a]ch. 6:9; 17:1; 2 Ki. 20:3; Ps. 16:8; Mic. 6:8; Mal. 2:6
5:24 [a]2 Ki. 2:11; Heb. 11:5
5:26 [1]Heb. *Lemech*
5:29 [1]Gr. *Noe.* [That is, *Rest,* or, *Comfort*] [a]ch. 3:17
5:32 [a]ch. 6:10 [b]ch. 10:21
6:1 [a]ch. 1:28
6:2 [a]Deut. 7:3
6:3 [a]Gal. 5:16; 1 Pet. 3:19 [b]Ps. 78:39
6:5 [1]Or, *the whole imagination:* The Hebrew word signifieth not only *the imagination,* but also *the purposes and desires* [2]Heb. *every day* [a]ch. 8:21
6:6 [a]1 Sam. 15:11,29; 2 Sam. 24:16; Mal. 3:6; Jas. 1:17

5:22 *walked with God.* The phrase replaces the word "lived" in the other genealogies of the chapter and reminds us that there is a difference between walking with God and merely living.

5:24 *and he was not; for God took him.* The phrase replaces "and he died" in the other genealogies of the chapter. Like Elijah, who was "taken" (2 Ki 2:10) to heaven, Enoch was taken away (cf. Ps 49:15; 73:24) to the presence of God without experiencing death (Heb 11:5). Lamech, the seventh from Adam in the genealogy of Cain, was evil personified. But "Enoch also, the seventh from Adam" (Jude 14) in the genealogy of Seth, "had this testimony, that he pleased God" (Heb 11:5).

5:27 *nine hundred sixty and nine years.* Only Noah and his family survived the flood. If the figures concerning life spans are literal, Methuselah died in the year of the flood (the figures in vv. 25,28 and 7:6 add up to exactly 969).

6:1 *multiply.* See note on 1:22.

6:2 *sons of God saw . . . daughters of men . . . and they took them wives.* See v. 4. The phrase "sons of God" here has been interpreted to refer either to angels or to human beings. In such places as Job 1:6; 2:1 it refers to angels, and perhaps also in Ps 29:1 fn (where it is translated "sons of the mighty"). Some interpreters also appeal to Jude 6–7 (as well as to Jewish literature) in referring the phrase here to angels.

Others, however, maintain that intermarriage and cohabitation between angels and human beings, though commonly mentioned in ancient mythologies, are surely excluded by the very nature of the created order (ch. 1; Mark 12:25). Elsewhere, expressions equivalent to "sons of God" often refer to human beings, though in contexts quite different from the present one (see Deut 14:1; 32:5; Ps 73:15; Is 43:6; Hos 1:10; 11:1; Luke 3:38; 1 John 3:1–2,10). "Sons of God" (vv. 2,4) possibly refers to godly men, and "daughters of men" to sinful women (significantly, they are not called "daughters of God"), probably from the wicked line of Cain. If so, the context suggests that vv. 1–2 describe the intermarriage of the Sethites ("sons of God") of ch. 5 with the Cainites ("daughters of men") of ch. 4, indicating a breakdown in the separation of the two groups.

Another plausible suggestion is that the "sons of God" refers to royal figures (kings were closely associated with gods in the ancient Near East) who proudly perpetuated and aggravated the corrupt life-style of Lamech son of Cain (virtually a royal figure) and established for themselves royal harems.

6:3 Two key phrases in the Hebrew of this verse are obscure: the one rendered "strive with" (which could be translated "remain in") and the one rendered "is flesh" (which could be translated "is corrupt"). The verse seems to announce that the period of grace between God's declaration of judgment and its arrival would be 120 years (cf. 1 Pet 3:20). But if "remain in" is accepted, the verse announces that man's life span would henceforth be limited to 120 years (but see 11:10–26).

6:4 *giants.* People of great size and strength (see Num 13:31–33). The Hebrew word is *nephilim,* which means "fallen ones." In men's eyes they were "the mighty men . . . of old, men of renown," but in God's eyes they were sinners ("fallen ones") ripe for judgment.

6:5 One of the Bible's most vivid descriptions of total depravity. And because man's nature remained unchanged, things were no better after the flood (8:21).

6:6 *it repented the LORD . . . it grieved him at his heart.* Man's sin is God's sorrow (see Eph 4:30).

made man on the earth, and it [b]grieved him at
his heart.
7 And the LORD said, I will destroy man
whom I have created from the face of the
earth; [1]both man, and beast, and the creeping
thing, and the fowls of the air; for it repenteth
me that I have made them.
8 But Noah [a]found grace in the eyes of the
LORD.
9 ¶ These *are* the generations of Noah:
[a]Noah was a just man *and* [1]perfect in his generations, *and* Noah [b]walked with God.
10 And Noah begat three sons, [a]Shem,
Ham, and Japheth.
11 The earth also was corrupt [a]before God,
and the earth was [b]filled *with* violence.
12 And God [a]looked upon the earth, and
behold, it was corrupt; for all flesh had corrupted his way upon the earth.
13 And God said unto Noah, [a]The end of
all flesh is come before me; for the earth is
filled *with* violence through them; [b]and behold, I will destroy them [1]with the earth.
14 Make thee an ark of gopher wood;
[1]rooms shalt thou make *in* the ark, and shalt
pitch it within and without with pitch.
15 And this *is the fashion* which thou shalt
make it *of:* the length of the ark *shall be* three
hundred cubits, the breadth of it fifty cubits,
and the height of it thirty cubits.
16 A window shalt thou make to the ark,
and in a cubit shalt thou finish it above; and

6:6 [b]Is. 63:10
6:7 [1]Heb. *from man unto beast*
6:8 [a]ch. 19:19; Ex. 33:12; Luke 1:30; Acts 7:46
6:9 [1]Or, *upright* [a]ch. 7:1; Ezek. 14:14,20; Heb. 11:7; 2 Pet. 2:5 [b]ch. 5:22
6:10 [a]ch. 5:32
6:11 [a]Rom. 2:13 [b]Ezek. 8:17
6:12 [a]Ps. 14:2; 53:2,3
6:13 [1]Or, *from the earth* [a]Jer. 51:13; 1 Pet. 4:7 [b]ver. 17
6:14 [1]Heb. *nests*
6:17 [a]ch. 7:4,21-23; 2 Pet. 2:5
6:18 [a]ch. 7:1,7,13; 1 Pet. 3:20; 2 Pet. 2:5
6:19 [a]ch. 7:8,9,15,16
6:20 [a]ch. 7:9,15
6:22 [a]Heb. 11:7; See Ex. 40:16 [b]ch. 7:5,9,16
7:1 [a]Mat. 24:38; Luke 17:26; Heb. 11:7; 1 Pet. 3:20; 2 Pet. 2:5 [b]ch. 6:9; Ps. 33:18; Prov. 10:9; 2 Pet. 2:9
7:2 [1]Heb. *seven seven* [a]Lev. ch. 11 [b]Lev. 10:10; Ezek. 44:23

the door of the ark shalt thou set in the side
thereof; *with* lower, second, and third *stories*
shalt thou make it.
17 [a]And behold, I, even I, do bring a flood of
waters upon the earth, to destroy all flesh,
wherein *is* the breath of life, from under heav-
en; *and* every *thing* that *is* in the earth shall die.
18 But with thee will I establish my cov-
enant; and [a]thou shalt come into the ark,
thou, and thy sons, and thy wife, and thy sons'
wives with thee.
19 And of every living *thing* of all flesh,
[a]two of every *sort* shalt thou bring into the
ark, to keep *them* alive with thee; they shall be
male and female.
20 Of fowls after their kind, and of cattle
after their kind, of every creeping thing of the
earth after his kind, two of every *sort* [a]shall
come unto thee, to keep *them* alive.
21 And take thou unto thee of all food that
is eaten, and thou shalt gather *it* to thee; and it
shall be for food for thee, and for them.
22 [a]Thus did Noah; [b]according to all that
God commanded him, so did he.
7 And the LORD said unto Noah, [a]Come
thou and all thy house into the ark; for
[b]thee have I seen righteous before me in this
generation.
2 Of every [a]clean beast thou shalt take to
thee [1]by sevens, the male and his female:
[b]and of beasts that *are* not clean by two, the
male and his female.

6:7 *I will destroy man . . . from the face of the earth.* The period of grace (see v. 3 and note) was coming to an end. *beast . . . creeping thing . . . fowls.* Though morally innocent, the animal world, as creatures under man's corrupted rule, shared in his judgment.

6:8–9 *found grace . . . just . . . perfect . . . walked with God.* See note on 5:22. Noah's godly life was a powerful contrast to the wicked lives of his contemporaries (see v. 5 and note; see also v. 12). This description of Noah does not imply sinless perfection.

6:9 *generations.* See note on 2:4. *just.* See note on Ps 1:5.

6:14 *ark.* The Hebrew for this word is used elsewhere only in reference to the basket that saved the baby Moses (Ex 2:3,5). *pitch it . . . with pitch.* Moses' mother made his basket watertight in the same way (see Ex 2:3).

‡6:17 *flood of waters upon the earth, to destroy all flesh . . . under heaven.* The Bible describes the deluge as worldwide, because of the universal terms of the text—both here and elsewhere (vv. 7,12–13; 7:4,19, 21–23; 8:21; 9:11,15). Others argue that nothing in the narrative of chs. 6–9 prevents the flood from being understood as regional—destroying everything in its wake, but of relatively limited scope and universal only from the standpoint of Moses' geographic knowledge. (See the universal language used to describe the drought and famine in the time of Joseph—41:54,57; see also note on 41:57.) The purpose of the flood was to destroy all land-living, air-breathing creatures (including sinful mankind). Our present knowledge of the spread of the ancient human population would seem to necessitate a worldwide flood in order to accomplish this. Other factors supporting a global deluge include the size of the ark, the extent of the flood and the duration of the flood (over one year). The promise of God not to send such a flood in the future was signified by the rainbow as a divine commitment to future generations (9:8-17). The apostle Peter, likewise, seems to assume that the flood and its devastation were universal and total, except for Noah and his family (2 Pet 3:6)

6:18 *covenant.* See note on 9:9. Noah would understand the full implications of God's covenant with him only after the floodwaters had dried up (see 9:8–17). *come into the ark.* The story of Noah's salvation from the flood illustrates God's redemption of His children (see Heb 11:7; 2 Pet 2:5) and typifies baptism (see 1 Pet 3:20–21). *thy sons, and thy wife, and thy sons' wives with thee.* God extends His loving concern to the whole family of righteous Noah—a consistent pattern in God's dealings with His people, underscoring the moral and responsible relationship of parents to their children (see 17:7–27; 18:19; Deut 30:19; Ps 78:1–7; 102:28; 103:17–18; 112:1–2; Acts 2:38–39; 16:31; 1 Cor 7:14).

6:19 *two of every sort. . . to keep them alive.* Most animals were doomed to die in the flood (see note on v. 7), but at least one pair of each kind was preserved to restock the earth after the waters subsided.

6:20 *kind.* See note on 1:11.

6:22 *according to all that God commanded him, so did he.* The account stresses Noah's obedience (see 7:5,9,16).

7:1 *Come . . . into the ark.* The beginning of God's final word to Noah before the flood. God's first word to Noah after the flood begins similarly:"Go forth of the ark" (8:16). *righteous.* See note on 6:8–9. As a "preacher of righteousness" (2 Pet 2:5), Noah warned his contemporaries of coming judgment and testified to the vitality of his own faith (see Heb 11:7).

7:2 *every clean beast . . . by sevens . . . and of beasts . . . not clean by two.* The ceremonially unclean animals would only have to reproduce themselves after the flood, but ceremonially clean animals would be needed also for the burnt offerings that Noah would sacrifice (see 8:20) and for food (see 9:3).

3 Of fowls also of the air [1]by sevens, the male and the female; to keep seed alive upon the face of all the earth.

4 For yet seven days, *and* I will cause it to rain upon the earth [a]forty days and forty nights; and every living substance that I have made will I [1]destroy from off the face of the earth.

5 [a]And Noah did according unto all that the LORD commanded him.

6 And Noah *was* six hundred years old when the flood of waters was upon the earth.

7 [a]And Noah went in, and his sons, and his wife, and his sons' wives with him, into the ark, because of the waters of the flood.

8 Of clean beasts, and of beasts that *are* not clean, and of fowls, and of every *thing* that creepeth upon the earth,

9 There went in two and two unto Noah into the ark, the male and the female, as God had commanded Noah.

10 ¶ And it came to pass [1]after seven days, that the waters of the flood were upon the earth.

11 In the six hundredth year of Noah's life, in the second month, the seventeenth day of the month, the same day were all [a]the fountains of the great deep broken up, and the [b1]windows of heaven were opened.

12 [a]And the rain was upon the earth forty days and forty nights.

13 In the selfsame day entered Noah, and Shem, and Ham, and Japheth, the sons of Noah, and Noah's wife, and the three wives of his sons with them, into the ark;

14 [a]They, and every beast after his kind, and all the cattle after their kind, and every creeping thing that creepeth upon the earth after his kind, and every fowl after his kind, every bird of every [1]sort.

15 And they [a]went in unto Noah into the ark, two and two of all flesh, wherein *is* the breath of life.

16 And they that went in, went in male and female of all flesh, [a]as God had commanded him: and the LORD shut him in.

17 [a]And the flood was forty days upon the earth; and the waters increased, and bare up the ark, and it was lift up above the earth.

18 And the waters prevailed, and were increased greatly upon the earth; [a]and the ark went upon the face of the waters.

19 And the waters prevailed exceedingly upon the earth; and all the high hills, that *were* under the whole heaven, were covered.

20 Fifteen cubits upward did the waters prevail; and the mountains were covered.

21 [a]And all flesh died that moved upon the earth, *both* of fowl, and of cattle, and of beast, and of every creeping thing that creepeth upon the earth, and every man:

22 All in [a]whose nostrils *was* [1]the breath of life, of all that *was* in the dry *land,* died.

23 And every living substance was destroyed which *was* upon the face of the ground, both man, and cattle, and the creeping things, and the fowl of the heaven; and they were destroyed from the earth: and [a]Noah only remained *alive,* and *they* that *were* with him in the ark.

24 [a]And the waters prevailed upon the earth an hundred and fifty days.

8 And God [a]remembered Noah, and every living thing, and all the cattle that *was* with him in the ark: [b]and God made a wind to pass over the earth, and the waters asswaged;

2 [a]The fountains also of the deep and the windows of heaven were stopped, and [b]the rain from heaven was restrained;

3 And the waters returned from off the earth [1]continually: and after the end [a]of the hundred and fifty days the waters were abated.

4 And the ark rested in the seventh month, on the seventeenth day of the month, upon the mountains of Ararat.

5 And the waters [1]decreased continually

7:3 [1]Heb. *seven seven*
7:4 [1]Heb. *blot out* [a]ver. 12,17
7:5 [a]ch. 6:22
7:7 [a]ver. 1
7:10 [1]Or, *on the seventh day*
7:11 [1]Or, *floodgates* [a]ch. 8:2; Prov. 8:28; Ezek. 26:19 [b]ch. 8:2; Ps. 78:23
7:12 [a]ver. 4,17
7:14 [1]Heb. *wing* [a]ch. 6:19
7:15 [a]ch. 6:20
7:16 [a]ver. 2,3
7:17 [a]ver. 4,12
7:18 [a]Ps. 104:26
7:21 [a]ch. 6:13,17
7:22 [1]Heb. *the breath of the spirit of life* [a]ch. 2:7
7:23 [a]1 Pet. 3:20; 2 Pet. 2:5
7:24 [a]ch. 8:3; 8:4; compared with ver. 11 of this chapter
8:1 [a]ch. 19:29; Ex. 2:24; 1 Sam. 1:19; Ps. 106:4 [b]Ex. 14:21
8:2 [a]ch. 7:11 [b]Job 38:37
8:3 [1]Heb. *in going and returning* [a]ch. 7:24
8:5 [1]Heb. *were in going and decreasing*

7:4 *forty days and forty nights.* A length of time often characterizing a critical period in redemptive history (see v. 12; Deut 9:11; Mat 4:1–11).

7:7 *went in . . into the ark, because of the waters.* Noah and his family were saved, but life as usual continued for everyone else until it was too late (see Mat 24:37–39).

7:13 *Noah, and . . . the sons of Noah, and Noah's wife, and the three wives of his sons.* "A few, that is, eight souls" (1 Pet 3:20; see 2 Pet 2:5), survived the flood.

7:14 *every beast . . . all the cattle . . . every creeping thing that creepeth upon the earth . . . every fowl.* Four of the five categories of animate life mentioned in 1:21–25. The fifth category—sea creatures—could remain alive outside the ark.

7:16 *God had commanded him . . . the LORD shut him in.* "God" gave the command, but in His role as redeeming "LORD" (see notes on 2:4; Ex 6:6) He closed the door of the ark behind Noah and his family. Neither divine name is mentioned in the rest of ch. 7, as the full fury of the flood was unleashed on sinful mankind.

7:20 *Fifteen cubits upward . . . and the mountains were covered.* The ark was 30 cubits high (6:15), so the water was deep enough to keep it from running aground.

7:22 *breath of life.* God's gift at creation (see 1:30; 2:7) was taken away because of sin.

8:1 So far the flood narrative has been an account of judgment; from this point on it is a story of redemption. *God remembered Noah.* Though He had not been mentioned since 7:16 or heard from for 150 days (see 7:24), God had not forgotten Noah and his family. To "remember" in the Bible is not merely to recall to mind; it is to express concern for someone, to act with loving care for him. When God remembers His people, He does so "for good" (Neh 5:19; 13:31). *wind.* The Hebrew word translated "Spirit" in 1:2 is here rendered "wind," and introduces a series of parallels between the events of chs. 8–9 and those of ch. 1 in their literary order: Compare 8:2 with 1:7; 8:5 with 1:9; 8:7 with 1:20; 8:17 with 1:25; 9:1 with 1:28a; 9:2 with 1:28b; 9:3 with 1:30. Ch. 1 describes the original beginning, while chs. 8–9 describe a new beginning after the flood.

8:4 *mountains.* The word is plural and refers to a range of mountains. *Ararat.* The name is related to Assyrian Urartu, which became an extensive and mountainous kingdom (see Jer 51:27; see also Is 37:38), including much of the territory north of Mesopotamia and east of modern Turkey. The ark's landfall was probably in southern Urartu.

until the tenth month: in the tenth *month,* on
the first *day* of the month, were the tops of the
mountains seen.
6 And it came to pass at the end of forty
days, that Noah opened [a]the window of the
ark which he had made:
7 And he sent forth a raven, which went
forth [1]to and fro, until the waters were dried
up from off the earth.
8 Also he sent forth a dove from him, to
see if the waters were abated from off the face
of the ground;
9 But the dove found no rest for the sole of
her foot, and she returned unto him into the
ark, for the waters *were* on the face of the
whole earth: then he put forth his hand, and
took her, and [1]pulled her in unto him into the
ark.
10 And he stayed yet other seven days; and
again he sent forth the dove out of the ark;
11 And the dove came in to him in the
evening; and lo, in her mouth *was* an olive leaf
pluckt off: so Noah knew that the waters were
abated from off the earth.
12 And he stayed yet other seven days; and
sent forth the dove; which returned not again
unto him any more.
13 ¶ And it came to pass in the six hundredth and first year, in the first *month,* the
first *day* of the month, the waters were dried
up from off the earth: and Noah removed the
covering of the ark, and looked, and behold,
the face of the ground was dry.
14 And in the second month, on the seven
and twentieth day of the month, was the earth
dried.
15 And God spake unto Noah, saying,
16 Go forth of the ark, [a]thou, and thy wife,
and thy sons, and thy sons' wives with thee.

8:6 [a]ch. 6:16
8:7 [1]Heb. *in going forth and returning*
8:9 [1]Heb. *caused her to come*
8:16 [a]ch. 7:13
8:17 [a]ch. 1:22
8:19 [1]Heb. *families*
8:20 [a]Lev. ch. 11
8:21 [1]Heb. *a savour of rest* [2][Or, *though*] [a]Lev. 1:9; Ezek. 20:41; 2 Cor. 2:15; Eph. 5:2 [b]ch. 3:17; 6:17 [c]ch. 6:5; Job 14:4; Jer. 17:9 [d]ch. 9:11,15
8:22 [1]Heb. *As yet all the days of the earth* [a]Is. 54:9 [b]Jer. 33:20,25
9:1 [a]ver. 7,19; ch. 1:28; 10:32
9:2 [a]ch. 1:28; Hos. 2:18
9:3 [a]Deut. 12:15; 14:3,9,11; Acts 10:12,13 [b]ch. 1:29 [c]Rom. 14:14,20; 1 Cor. 10:23,26; Col. 2:16; 1 Tim. 4:3,4
9:4 [a]Lev. 17:10,11,14; Deut. 12:23; 1 Sam. 14:33

17 Bring forth with thee every living thing
that *is* with thee, of all flesh, *both* of fowl, and
of cattle, and of every creeping thing that
creepeth upon the earth; that they may breed
abundantly in the earth, and [a]be fruitful, and
multiply upon the earth.
18 And Noah went forth, and his sons, and
his wife, and his sons' wives with him:
19 Every beast, every creeping thing, and
every fowl, *and* whatsoever creepeth upon the
earth, after their [1]kinds, went forth out of the
ark.
20 ¶ And Noah builded an altar unto the
LORD; and took of [a]every clean beast, and of
every clean fowl, and offered burnt offerings
on the altar.
21 And the LORD smelled [a][1]a sweet savour;
and the LORD said in his heart, I will not again
[b]curse the ground any more for man's sake;
[2]for the [c]imagination of man's heart *is* evil
from his youth; [d]neither will I again smite any
more every *thing* living, as I have done.
22 [a][1]While the earth remaineth, seedtime
and harvest, and cold and heat, and summer
and winter, and [b]day and night shall not cease.

The covenant with Noah

9 And God blessed Noah and his sons, and
said unto them, [a]Be fruitful, and multiply, and replenish the earth.
2 [a]And the fear of you and the dread of you
shall be upon every beast of the earth, and
upon every fowl of the air, upon all that moveth
upon the earth, and upon all the fishes of the
sea; into your hand are they delivered.
3 [a]Every moving thing that liveth shall be
meat for you; *even* as the [b]green herb have I
given you [c]all *things.*
4 [a]But flesh with the life thereof, *which is*
the blood thereof, shall you not eat.

8:11 *the dove came in to him . . . in her mouth was an olive leaf pluckt off.* Olives do not grow at high elevations, and the fresh leaf was a sign to Noah that the water had receded from the earth. The modern symbol of peace represented by a dove carrying an olive branch in its beak has its origin in this story.

8:13 *in the six hundredth and first year, in the first month, the first day of the month.* The date formula signals mankind's new beginning after the flood.

8:14 *in the second month, on the seven and twentieth day of the month.* More than a year after the flood began (see 7:11).

8:16 *Go forth of the ark.* See note on 7:1.

8:17 *breed abundantly . . . be fruitful . . . multiply.* See 1:22 and note. The animals and birds could now repopulate their former habitats.

8:20 *LORD.* Since worship is a very personal matter, it is to God as "the LORD" (see note on 2:4) that Noah brought his sacrifice (see 4:4). *burnt offerings.* See Lev 1:3–4 and notes.

8:21 *smelled a sweet savour.* A figurative way of saying that the Lord takes delight in His children's worship of Him (see Eph 5:2; Phil 4:18). *curse the ground.* Although the Hebrew here has a different word for "curse," the reference appears to be to the curse of 3:17. It may be that the Lord here pledged never to add curse upon curse as He had in regard to Cain (4:12). *for the imagination of man's heart is evil.* For almost identical phraseology see 6:5. Because of man's extreme wickedness, God had destroyed him (6:7) by means of a flood (6:17). Although righteous Noah and his family had been saved, he and his offspring were descendants of Adam and carried in their hearts the inheritance of sin. God graciously promises never again to deal with sin by sending such a devastating deluge (see 9:11,15). Human history is held open for God's dealing with sin in a new and redemptive way—the way that was prepared for by God's action at Babel (see notes on 11:6,8) and that begins to unfold with the call of Abram (12:1). *from his youth.* The phrase replaces "continually" in 6:5 and emphasizes the truth that sin infects a person's life from his conception and birth (Ps 51:5; 58:3).

8:22 Times and seasons, created by God in the beginning (see 1:14), will never cease till the end of history.

9:1–7 At this new beginning, God renewed His original benediction (1:28) and His provision for man's food (cf. v. 3; 1:29–30). But because sin had brought violence into man's world and because God now appointed meat as a part of man's food (v. 3), further divine provisions and stipulations are added (vv. 4–6). Yet God's benediction dominates and encloses the whole (see v. 7).

9:2 *into your hand are they delivered.* God reaffirmed that mankind would rule over all creation, including the animals (see note on 1:26).

9:3 *Every moving thing that liveth shall be meat.* Meat would now supplement mankind's diet.

9:4 *flesh with the life thereof, which is the blood thereof, shall you not eat.* Lev 17:14 stresses the intimate relationship between

Major Covenants in the Old Testament

COVENANTS	REFERENCE	TYPE	PARTICIPANT	DESCRIPTION
NOAHIC	Gen 9:8-17	Royal Grant	Made with "righteous" (6:9) Noah (and his descendants and every living thing on earth—all life that is subject to man's jurisdiction)	An unconditional divine promise never to destroy all earthly life with some natural catastrophe; the covenant "token" being the rainbow in the storm cloud
ABRAHAMIC A	Gen 15:9-21	Royal (land) Grant	Made with "righteous" (his faith was "counted to him as righteousness," v. 6) Abram (and his descendants, v. 16)	An unconditional divine promise to fulfill the grant of the land; a self-maledictory oath symbolically enacted it (v. 17)
ABRAHAMIC B	Gen 17	Suzerain-vassal	Made with Abraham as patriarchal head of his household	A conditional divine pledge to be Abraham's God and the God of his descendants (cf. "As for me," v. 4; "Thou shalt keep," v. 9); the condition: total consecration to the Lord as symbolized by circumcision
SINAITIC	Ex 19-24	Suzerain-vassal	Made with Israel as the descendants of Abraham, Isaac and Jacob and as the people the Lord has redeemed from bondage to an earthly power	A conditional divine pledge to be Israel's God (as her Protector and the Guarantor of her blessed destiny); the condition: Israel's total consecration to the Lord as His people (His kingdom) who live by His rule and serve His purposes in history
PHINEHAS	Num 25:10-13	Royal Grant	Made with the zealous priest Phinehas	An unconditional divine promise to maintain the family of Phinehas in an "everlasting priesthood" (implicitly a pledge to Israel to provide her forever with a faithful priesthood)
DAVIDIC	2 Sam 7:5-16	Royal Grant	Made with faithful King David after his devotion to God as Israel's king and the Lord's anointed vassal had come to special expression (v. 2)	An unconditional divine promise to establish and maintain the Davidic dynasty on the throne of Israel (implicitly a pledge to Israel) to provide her forever with a godly king like David and through that dynasty to do for her what He had done through David—bring her into rest in the promised land (1 Ki 4:20-21; 5:3-4)
NEW	Jer 31:31-34	Royal Grant	Promised to rebellious Israel as she is about to be expelled from the promised land in actualization of the most severe covenant curse (Lev 26:27-39; Deut 28:36-37, 45-68)	An unconditional divine promise to unfaithful Israel to forgive her sins and establish His relationship with her on a new basis by writing His law "in their hearts"—a covenant of pure grace

Major Types of Royal Covenants/Treaties in the Ancient Near East

ROYAL GRANT (UNCONDITIONAL)
A king's grant (of land or some other benefit) to a loyal servant for faithful or exceptional service. The grant was normally perpetual and unconditional, but the servant's heirs benefited from it only as they continued their father's loyalty and service. (Cf. 1 Sam 8:14; 22:7; 27:6; Esth 8:1.)

PARITY
A covenant between equals, binding them to mutual friendship or at least to mutual respect for each other's spheres and interests. Participants called each other "brethren." (Cf. Gen 21:27; 26:31; 31:44-54; 1 Ki 5:12; 15:19; 20:32-34; Amos 1:9.)

SUZERAIN-VASSAL (CONDITIONAL)
A covenant regulating the relationship between a great king and one of his subject kings. The great king claimed absolute right of sovereignty, demanded total loyalty and service (the vassal must "love" his suzerain) and pledged protection of the subject's realm and dynasty, conditional on the vassal's faithfulness and loyalty to him. The vassal pledged absolute loyalty to his suzerain—whatever service his suzerain demanded—and exclusive reliance on the suzerain's protection. Participants called each other "lord" and "servant" or "father" and "son." (Cf. Josh 9:6,8; Ezek 17:13-18; Hos 12:1.)

Commitments made in these covenants were accompanied by self-maledictory oaths (made orally, ceremonially or both). The gods were called upon to witness the covenants and implement the curses of the oaths if the covenants were violated.

5 And surely your blood of your lives will I
require; [a]at the hand of every beast will I require it, and [b]at the hand of man; at the hand
of every [c]man's brother will I require the life
of man.
6 [a]Whoso sheddeth man's blood, by man
shall his blood be shed: [b]for in the image of
God made he man.
7 And you, [a]be ye fruitful, and multiply;
bring forth abundantly in the earth, and multiply therein.
8 ¶ And God spake unto Noah, and to his
sons with him, saying,
9 And I, [a]behold I establish [b]my covenant
with you and with your seed after you;
10 [a]And with every living creature that *is*
with you, of the fowl, of the cattle, and of
every beast of the earth with you; from all that
go out of the ark, to every beast of the earth.
11 And [a]I will establish my covenant with
you; neither shall all flesh be cut off any more
by the waters of a flood; neither shall there
any more be a flood to destroy the earth.
12 And God said, [a]This *is* the token of the
covenant which I make between me and you
and every living creature that *is* with you, for
perpetual generations:
13 I do set [a]my bow in the cloud, and it
shall be for a token of a covenant between me
and the earth.
14 And it shall come to pass, when I bring
a cloud over the earth, that the bow shall be
seen in the cloud:
15 And [a]I will remember my covenant,
which *is* between me and you and every living
creature of all flesh; and the waters shall no
more become a flood to destroy all flesh.
16 And the bow shall be in the cloud; and
I will look upon it, that I may remember [a]the
everlasting covenant between God and every
living creature of all flesh that *is* upon the
earth.
17 And God said unto Noah, This *is* the token of the covenant, which I have established
between me and all flesh that *is* upon the
earth.

Canaan cursed; Shem blessed

18 ¶ And the sons of Noah, that went forth
of the ark, were Shem, and Ham, and Japheth:
[a]and Ham *is* the father of [1]Canaan.
19 [a]These *are* the three sons of Noah: [b]and
of them was the whole earth overspread.
20 And Noah began *to be* [a]a husbandman,
and he planted a vineyard:
21 And he drank of the wine, [a]and was
drunken; and he was uncovered within his
tent.
22 And Ham, the father of Canaan, saw the
nakedness of his father, and told his two
brethren without.
23 [a]And Shem and Japheth took a garment,
and laid *it* upon both their shoulders, and
went backward, and covered the nakedness of
their father; and their faces *were* backward,
and they saw not their father's nakedness.
24 And Noah awoke from his wine, and
knew what his younger son had done unto him.
25 And he said,
[a]Cursed *be* Canaan;

9:5 [a]Ex. 21:28 [b]ch. 4:9,10; Ps. 9:12 [c]Acts 17:26
9:6 [a]Ex. 21:12,14; Lev. 24:17; Mat. 26:52 [b]ch. 1:27
9:7 [a]ver. 1,19
9:9 [a]ch. 6:18 [b]Is. 54:9
9:10 [a]Ps. 145:9
9:11 [a]Is. 54:9
9:12 [a]ch. 17:11
9:13 [a]Rev. 4:3
9:15 [a]Lev. 26:42,45
9:16 [a]ch. 17:13,19; Is. 55:3; Jer. 32:40; Heb. 13:20
9:18 [1]Heb. *Chenaan* [a]ch. 10:6
9:19 [a]ch. 5:32 [b]ch. 10:32; 1 Chr. 1:4
9:20 [a]ch. 3:19,23; 4:2; Prov. 12:11
9:21 [a]Prov. 20:1; 1 Cor. 10:12
9:23 [a]Ex. 20:12; Gal. 6:1
9:25 [a]Deut. 27:16; Josh. 9:23,27

blood and life by twice declaring that "the life of all flesh is the blood thereof." Life is the precious and mysterious gift of God, and man is not to seek to preserve it or increase the life-force within him by eating "life" that is "in the blood" (Lev 17:11)—as many pagan peoples throughout history have thought they could do.

9:5 *your blood of your lives will I require; at the hand of every beast will I require it.* God Himself is the great defender of human life (see 4:9–12), which is precious to Him because man was created in His image (v. 6) and because man is the earthly representative and focal point of God's kingdom. In the theocracy (kingdom of God) established at Sinai, a domestic animal that had taken human life was to be stoned to death (Ex 21:28–32).

9:6 *Whoso sheddeth man's blood, by man shall his blood be shed.* In the later theocracy, those guilty of premeditated murder were to be executed (see Ex 21:12–14; Num 35:16–32; see also Rom 13:3–4; 1 Pet 2:13–14). *for in the image of God made he man.* See 1:26 and note. In killing a human being, a murderer demonstrates his contempt for God as well as for his fellowman.

9:9 *I establish my covenant.* God sovereignly promised in this covenant to Noah, to Noah's descendants and to all other living things (as a kind of gracious reward to righteous Noah, the new father of the human race—see 6:18) never again to destroy man and the earth until His purposes for His creation are fully realized ("while the earth remaineth," 8:22). For similar commitments by God see His covenants with Abram (15:18–20), Phinehas (Num 25:10–13) and David (2 Sam 7). See chart, p. 16.

9:11 *neither shall all flesh be cut off any more by the waters of a flood.* A summary of the provisions of the Lord's covenant with Noah—an eternal covenant, as seen in such words and phrases as "any more" (vv. 11,15), "for perpetual generations" (v. 12) and "everlasting" (v. 16).

9:12 *token.* A covenant token or sign was a visible seal and reminder of covenant commitments. Circumcision would become the sign of the covenant with Abraham (see 17:11), and the sabbath would be the sign of the covenant with Israel at Sinai (see Ex 31:16–17).

9:13 *bow.* Rain and the rainbow doubtless existed long before the time of Noah's flood, but after the flood the rainbow took on new meaning as the sign of the Noahic covenant.

9:19 *overspread.* Thus anticipating the table of nations (see note on 11:8).

9:20 *a husbandman.* Noah, like his father Lamech (see 5:29), was a farmer.

9:21 *he drank of the wine, and was drunken.* The first reference to wine connects it with drunkenness. *he was uncovered within his tent.* Excessive use of wine led, among other things, to immodest behavior (see 19:30–35).

9:22 *father of Canaan.* Mentioned here because Ham, in acting as he did, showed himself to be the true father of Canaan (i.e., of the Canaanites; see note on 15:16). *told his two brethren.* He broadcast, rather than covered, his father's immodesty.

9:23 *faces were backward, and they saw not their father's nakedness.* They wanted to avoid further disgrace to their father.

9:24 *from his wine.* From the drunkenness caused by the wine.

9:25 *Cursed be Canaan.* Some maintain that Ham's son (see vv. 18,22) was to be punished because of his father's sin (see Ex 20:5), but Ex 20 restricts such punishment to "them that hate me." It is probably better to hold that Canaan and his descendants were to be punished because they were going to be even

[b]A servant of servants shall he be unto
his brethren.
26 And he said,
[a]Blessed *be* the LORD God of Shem;
And Canaan shall be [1]his servant.
27 God shall [1]enlarge Japheth,
[a]And he shall dwell in the tents of
Shem;
And Canaan shall be his servant.
28 And Noah lived after the flood three
hundred and fifty years.
29 And all the days of Noah were nine
hundred and fifty years: and he died.

Descendants of Noah's sons

10 Now these *are* the generations of the
sons of Noah, Shem, Ham, and Japheth: [a]and unto them were sons born after
the flood.
2 [a]The sons of Japheth; Gomer, and Magog,
and Madai, and Javan, and Tubal, and Meshech, and Tiras.
3 And the sons of Gomer; Ashkenaz, and
Riphath, and Togarmah.

9:25 [b]Josh. 9:23; 1 Ki. 9:20,21
9:26 [1]Or, *servant to them* [a]Ps. 144:15; Heb. 11:16
9:27 [1]Or, *persuade* [a]Eph. 2:13,14; 3:6
10:1 [a]ch. 9:1,7,19
10:2 [a]1 Chr. 1:5
10:4 [1][Or, as some read it, *Rodanim*]
10:5 [a]Ps. 72:10; Jer. 2:10; 25:22
10:6 [a]1 Chr. 1:8
10:9 [a]Jer. 16:16; Mic. 7:2 [b]ch. 6:11
10:10 [1]Gr. *Babylon* [a]Mic. 5:6
10:11 [1]Or, *he went out* into *Assyria* [2]Or, *the streets of the city*

4 And the sons of Javan; Elishah, and Tarshish, Kittim, and [1]Dodanim.
5 By these were [a]the isles of the Gentiles
divided in their lands; every one after his
tongue, after their families, in their nations.
6 ¶ [a]And the sons of Ham; Cush, and Mizraim, and Phut, and Canaan.
7 And the sons of Cush; Seba, and Havilah,
and Sabtah, and Raamah, and Sabtecha: and
the sons of Raamah; Sheba, and Dedan.
8 And Cush begat Nimrod: he began to be
a mighty *one* in the earth.
9 He was a mighty [a]hunter [b]before the
LORD: wherefore it is said, *Even* as Nimrod the
mighty hunter before the LORD.
10 [a]And the beginning of his kingdom was
[1]Babel, and Erech, and Accad, and Calneh, in
the land of Shinar.
11 Out of that land [1]went forth Asshur,
and builded Nineveh, and [2]the city Rehoboth,
and Calah,
12 And Resen between Nineveh and Calah: the same *is* a great city.
13 And Mizraim begat Ludim, and
Anamim, and Lehabim, and Naphtuhim,

worse than Ham (Lev 18:2–3,6–30). *servant of servants.* Joshua's subjection of the Gibeonites (Josh 9:27) is one of the fulfillments (see also Josh 16:10; Judg 1:28,30,33,35; 1 Ki 9:20–21). Noah's prophecy cannot be used to justify the enslavement of blacks, since those cursed here were Canaanites, who were Caucasian.

9:26 *Blessed be the LORD.* The Lord (instead of Shem) is blessed (praised) because He is the source of Shem's blessing. He is also the "God of Shem" (and his descendants, the Semites—which included the Israelites) in a special sense.

9:27 *dwell in the tents of Shem.* Share in the blessings bestowed on Shem.

9:29 *and he died.* See note on 5:5. As the tenth and last member of the genealogy of Seth (5:3–32), Noah had an obituary that ends like those of his worthy ancestors.

10:1 *generations.* See note on 2:4. The links affirmed here may not all be based on strictly physical descent, but may include geographical, historical and linguistic associations (see note on v. 5.) For example, the Hebrew for "sons" can mean "descendants" or "successors" or "nations," and the Hebrew for "father" can mean "ancestor" or "predecessor" or "founder." See also Introduction to 1 Chronicles: Genealogies.

10:2 *Japheth.* As the least involved in the Biblical narrative and perhaps also as the oldest of Noah's sons (see note on v. 21), his descendants or successors are listed first. The genealogy of Shem, the chosen line, appears last in the chapter (see vv. 21–31; see also 11:10–26). The 14 nations that came from Japheth plus the 30 from Ham and the 26 from Shem add up to 70 (the multiple of 10 and 7, both numbers signifying completeness; see note on 5:5), perhaps in anticipation of the 70 members of Jacob's family in Egypt (see 46:27; Ex 1:5; also Deut 32:8). The Japhethites lived generally north and west of Canaan in Eurasia. *Gomer.* The people of Gomer (the later Cimmerians) and related nations (see v. 3) lived near the Black Sea. *Magog.* Possibly the father of a Scythian people who inhabited the Caucasus and adjacent regions southeast of the Black Sea. *Madai.* The later Medes. *Javan.* Ionia (southern Greece) and perhaps western Asia Minor. *Tubal, and Meshech.* Not related to Tobolsk and Moscow in modern Russia. Together with Magog they are mentioned in later Assyrian inscriptions. See also Ezek 38:2. Probably Tubal was in Pontus, and Meshech was in the Moschian Mountains. Their movement was from eastern Asia Minor north to the Black Sea. *Tiras.* Possibly the Thrace of later times.

10:3 *Ashkenaz.* The later Scythians. All three names in this verse refer to peoples located in the upper Euphrates region.

‡**10:4** *Elishah.* Either Alashia (an ancient name for Cyprus) or a reference to Sicily and southern Italy. *Tarshish.* Probably southern Spain. *Kittim.* A people living on Cyprus. *Dodanim.* Some manuscripts have "Rodanim," a people whose name is perhaps reflected in Rhodes (a Greek isle). The Hebrew letters for *d* and *r* were easily confused by scribes (copyists) because of their similarity in form.

10:5 See vv. 20,31. *lands . . . tongue . . . families . . . nations.* Geographic, ethnic, political and linguistic terms, respectively. These several criteria were used to differentiate the various groups of people.

10:6 *Ham.* The Hamites were located in southwestern Asia and northeast Africa. *Cush.* The upper Nile region, south of Egypt. *Mizraim.* Means "two Egypts," a reference to Upper and Lower Egypt. *Phut.* Either Libya (see note on v. 13) or the land the ancient Egyptians called Punt (modern Somalia). *Canaan.* The name means "land of purple" (as does Phoenicia, the Greek name for the same general region)—so called because Canaan was a major producer and exporter of purple dye, highly prized by royalty. The territory was much later called Palestine after the Philistim (see v. 14).

10:7 *sons of Cush.* The seven Cushite nations here mentioned were all in Arabia. Sheba and Dedan (or their namesakes) reappear as two of Abraham's grandsons (see 25:3). Together with Raamah they are mentioned in Ezek 27:20–22.

10:8 *Cush.* Probably not the same as that in vv. 6–7. Located in Mesopotamia, its name may be related to that of the later Kassites. *Nimrod.* Possibly the Hebrew name of Sargon I, an early ruler of Accad (see v. 10).

10:10 *Erech.* The Hebrew name for Uruk (modern Warka), one of the important cities in ancient Mesopotamia.

10:12 *great city.* Possibly a reference to Calah (or even Resen), but most likely to Nineveh (see Jonah 1:2; 3:2; 4:11), either alone or including the surrounding urban areas.

10:13 *Ludim.* Perhaps the Lydians in Asia Minor (see note on v. 22). *Anamim.* Located in north Africa, west of Egypt, near Cy-

14 And Pathrusim, and Casluhim, ([a]out of whom came Philistim) and Caphtorim.
15 And Canaan begat [1]Sidon his firstborn, and Heth,
16 And the Jebusite, and the Amorite, and the Girgashite,
17 And the Hivite, and the Arkite, and the Sinite,
18 And the Arvadite, and the Zemarite, and the Hamathite: and afterward were the families of the Canaanites spread abroad.
19 [a]And the border of the Canaanites was from Sidon, as thou comest to Gerar, unto [1]Gaza; as thou goest unto Sodom, and Gomorrah, and Admah, and Zeboim, even unto Lasha.

10:14 [a]1 Chr. 1:12
10:15 [1]Heb. *Tzidon*
10:19 [1]Heb. *Azzah* [a]ch. 13:12, 14,15,17; 15:18-21
10:22 [1]Heb. *Arpachshad* [a]1 Chr. 1:17
10:24 [1]Heb. *Shelah* [a]ch. 11:12
10:25 [1][That is, *Division*] [a]1 Chr. 1:19

20 These *are* the sons of Ham, after their families, after their tongues, in their countries, *and* in their nations.
21 ¶ Unto Shem also, the father of all the children of Eber, the brother of Japheth the elder, even to him were *children* born.
22 The [a]children of Shem; Elam, and Asshur, and [1]Arphaxad, and Lud, and Aram.
23 And the children of Aram; Uz, and Hul, and Gether, and Mash.
24 And Arphaxad begat [a][1]Salah; and Salah begat Eber.
25 [a]And unto Eber were born two sons: the name of one *was* [1]Peleg; for in his days was the earth divided; and his brother's name *was* Joktan.

rene. *Lehabim.* Perhaps the Libyan desert tribes (see note on v. 6). *Naphtuhim.* People of Lower Egypt.
10:14 *Pathrusim.* The inhabitants of Upper Egypt (see note on v. 6). *Caphtorim.* Crete, known as Caphtor in ancient times, was for a while the homeland of various Philistine groups (see Jer 47:4; Amos 9:7). The Philistines themselves were a vigorous Indo-European maritime people who invaded Egypt early in the 12th century B.C. After being driven out, they migrated in large numbers to southwest Canaan, later extending their influence over most of the land. The Philistines of the patriarchal period (see 21:32,34; 26:1,8,14–15,18) no doubt had earlier settled in Canaan more peacefully and in smaller numbers.
10:15 *Sidon.* An important commercial city on the northwest coast of Canaan. *Heth.* The progenitor of the Hittites, a powerful people, centered in Asia Minor, who dominated much of Canaan from c. 1800 to c. 1200 B.C.
10:16 *Jebusite.* Inhabited Jerusalem at the time of Israel's conquest of Canaan. Jerusalem was also known as Jebus during part of its history (see Judg 19:10–11; 1 Chr 11:4). *Amorite.* The name comes from an Akkadian word meaning "westerner" (west from the Babylonian perspective). Amorites lived in the hill country of Canaan at the time of the Israelite conquest.
10:17–18 Together with the Girgashites (v. 16), these groups inhabited small city-states for the most part.
10:19 *Sodom, and Gomorrah, and Admah, and Zeboim.* See 14:2,8 (see also note on 13:10); probably located east and/or southeast of the Dead Sea.
10:21 *Unto Shem also . . . were children born.* The descendants of Shem were called Shemites (later modified to Semites). *Eber.* Though a distant descendant of Shem (see vv. 24–25; 11:14–17), Eber's importance as the ancestor of the Hebrews ("Eber" is the origin of the Hebrew word for "Hebrew") is already hinted at here. The Ebla tablets (see Introduction: Background) frequently refer to a king named Ebrium, who ruled Ebla for 28 years. It is possible that Ebrium and Eber were the same person.
10:22 *Elam.* The Elamites lived east of Mesopotamia. *Asshur.* An early name for Assyria (see note on 2:14) in northern Mesopotamia. *Arphaxad.* See also 11:10–13; perhaps a compound form of the Hebrew word for Chaldea, in southern Mesopotamia. *Lud.* Probably the Lydians of Asia Minor (see note on v. 13). *Aram.* Located northeast of Canaan, the area known today as Syria.
10:24 *Salah.* See 11:12–15.
10:25 *Peleg.* Peleg means "division" (see 11:16–19).

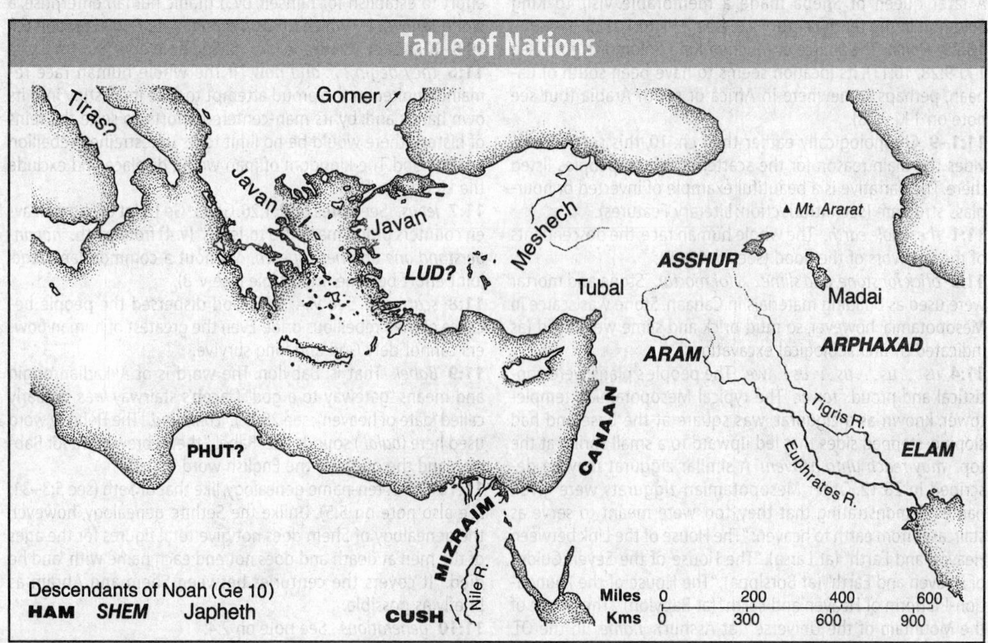

26 And Joktan begat Almodad, and Sheleph, and Hazarmaveth, and Jerah,

27 And Hadoram, and Uzal, and Diklah,

28 And Obal, and Abimael, and Sheba,

29 And Ophir, and Havilah, and Jobab: all these *were* the sons of Joktan.

30 And their dwelling was from Mesha, as thou goest unto Sephar, a mount of the east.

31 These *are* the sons of Shem, after their families, after their tongues, in their lands, after their nations.

32 [a]These *are* the families of the sons of Noah, after their generations, in their nations: [b]and by these were the nations divided in the earth after the flood.

The tower of Babel

11 And the whole earth was *of* one [1]language, and *of* one [2]speech.

2 And it came to pass, as they journeyed [1]from the east, that they found a plain in the land of Shinar; and they dwelt there.

3 And [1]they said one to another, Go to, let us make brick, and [2]burn *them* thoroughly. And they had brick for stone, and slime had they for morter.

4 And they said, Go to, let us build us a city and a tower, [a]whose top *may reach* unto heaven; and let us make us a name, lest we be scattered abroad upon the face of the whole earth.

5 [a]And the LORD came down to see the city and the tower, which the children of men builded.

6 And the LORD said, Behold, [a]the people *is* one, and they have all [b]one language; and this they begin to do: and now nothing will be restrained from them, which they have [c]imagined to do.

7 Go to, [a]let us go down, and there confound their language, that they may [b]not understand one another's speech.

8 So [a]the LORD scattered them abroad from thence [b]upon the face of all the earth: and they left off to build the city.

9 Therefore is the name of it called [1]Babel; [a]because the LORD did there confound the language of all the earth: and from thence did the LORD scatter them abroad upon the face of all the earth.

The descendants of Shem

10 ¶ [a]These *are* the generations of Shem: Shem *was* an hundred years old, and begat Arphaxad two years after the flood:

11 And Shem lived after he begat Arphaxad five hundred years, and begat sons and daughters.

12 And Arphaxad lived five and thirty years, [a]and begat Salah:

13 And Arphaxad lived after he begat Salah four hundred and three years, and begat sons and daughters.

14 And Salah lived thirty years, and begat Eber:

15 And Salah lived after he begat Eber four hundred and three years, and begat sons and daughters.

10:32 [a]ver. 1 [b]ch. 9:19
11:1 [1]Heb. *lip* [2]Heb. *words*
11:2 [1][Or, *eastward*, as ch. 13:11; 2 Sam. 6:2; with 1 Chr. 13:6]
11:3 [1]Heb. *a man said to his neighbour* [2]Heb. *burn* them *to a burning*
11:4 [a]Deut. 1:28
11:5 [a]ch. 18:21
11:6 [a]ch. 9:19; Acts 17:26
11:6 [b]ver. 1 [c]Ps. 2:1
11:7 [a]ch. 1:26 [b]ch. 42:23; 1 Cor. 14:2,11
11:8 [a]Luke 1:51 [b]ch. 10:25,32
11:9 [1]That is, *Confusion* [a]1 Cor. 14:23
11:10 [a]ch. 10:22; 1 Chr. 1:17
11:12 [a]See Luke 3:36

10:26 *Joktan.* The predecessor of numerous south Arabian kingdoms.

10:28 *Sheba.* In southwest Arabia (roughly the area of Yemen). A later queen of Sheba made a memorable visit to King Solomon in the tenth century B.C. (see 1 Ki 10:1–13).

10:29 *Ophir.* The source of much of King Solomon's gold (see 1 Ki 9:28; 10:11). Its location seems to have been south of Canaan, perhaps somewhere in Africa or south Arabia (but see note on 1 Ki 9:28).

11:1–9 Chronologically earlier than ch. 10, this section provides the main reason for the scattering of the peoples listed there. The narrative is a beautiful example of inverted or hourglass structure (see Introduction: Literary Features).

11:1 *the whole earth.* The whole human race, the descendants of the survivors of the flood (see vv. 4,8–9).

11:3 *brick for stone, and slime . . . for mortar.* Stone and mortar were used as building materials in Canaan. Stone was scarce in Mesopotamia, however, so mud brick and slime were used (as indicated by archaeological excavations).

11:4 *us . . . us . . . us . . . us . . . we.* The people's plans were egotistical and proud. *tower.* The typical Mesopotamian temple-tower, known as a ziggurat, was square at the base and had sloping, stepped sides that led upward to a small shrine at the top. *may reach unto heaven.* A similar ziggurat may be described in 28:12. Other Mesopotamian ziggurats were given names demonstrating that they, too, were meant to serve as staircases from earth to heaven: "The House of the Link between Heaven and Earth" (at Larsa), "The House of the Seven Guides of Heaven and Earth" (at Borsippa), "The House of the Foundation-Platform of Heaven and Earth" (at Babylon), "The House of the Mountain of the Universe" (at Asshur). *name.* In the OT, "name" also refers to reputation, fame or renown. (The giants [*nephilim*] were "men of renown [lit. 'name']," 6:4.) At Babel (see note on v. 9) rebellious man undertook a united and godless effort to establish for himself, by a titanic human enterprise, a world renown by which he would dominate God's creation (cf. 10:8–12; 2 Sam 18:18). *scattered.* See note on v. 8.

11:6 *they begin . . . and now.* If the whole human race remained united in the proud attempt to take its destiny into its own hands and, by its man-centered efforts, to seize the reins of history, there would be no limit to its unrestrained rebellion against God. The kingdom of man would displace and exclude the kingdom of God.

11:7 *let us.* See notes on 1:1,26. God's "Go to, let us" from heaven counters proud man's "Go to, let us" (v. 4) from earth. *not understand one another's speech.* Without a common language, joint effort became impossible (see v. 8).

11:8 *scattered.* See v. 4; 9:19. God dispersed the people because of their rebellious pride. Even the greatest of human powers cannot defy God and long survive.

11:9 *Babel.* That is, Babylon. The word is of Akkadian origin and means "gateway to a god" (Jacob's stairway was similarly called "gate of heaven"; see 28:17). *confound.* The Hebrew word used here (*balal*) sounds like "Babel," the Hebrew word for Babylon and the origin of the English word "babel."

11:10–26 A ten-name genealogy, like that of Seth (see 5:3–31; see also note on 5:5). Unlike the Sethite genealogy, however, the genealogy of Shem does not give total figures for the ages of the men at death and does not end each name with "and he died." It covers the centuries between Shem and Abram as briefly as possible.

11:10 *generations.* See note on 2:4.

16 [a]And Eber lived four and thirty years,
and begat [1]Peleg:
17 And Eber lived after he begat Peleg four
hundred and thirty years, and begat sons and
daughters.
18 And Peleg lived thirty years, and begat
Reu:
19 And Peleg lived after he begat Reu two
hundred and nine years, and begat sons and
daughters.
20 And Reu lived two and thirty years, and
begat [1]Serug:
21 And Reu lived after he begat Serug two
hundred and seven years, and begat sons and
daughters.
22 And Serug lived thirty years, and begat
Nahor:
23 And Serug lived after he begat Nahor two
hundred years, and begat sons and daughters.
24 And Nahor lived nine and twenty years,
and begat [1]Terah:
25 And Nahor lived after he begat Terah an
hundred and nineteen years, and begat sons
and daughters.
26 And Terah lived seventy years, and [a]be-
gat Abram, Nahor, and Haran.
27 ¶ Now these *are* the generations of Terah: Terah begat Abram, Nahor, and Haran;
and Haran begat Lot.
28 And Haran died before his father Terah
in the land of his nativity, in Ur of the Chaldees.
29 And Abram and Nahor took them

11:16 [1]Called, Luke 3:35, *Phalec* [a]1 Chr. 1:19
11:20 [1]Luke 3:35, *Saruch*
11:24 [1]Luke 3:34, *Thara*
11:26 [a]Josh. 24:2; 1 Chr. 1:26
11:29 [a]ch. 17:15; 20:12 [b]ch. 22:20
11:30 [a]ch. 16:1,2; Luke 1:36
11:31 [a]ch. 12:1 [b]Neh. 9:7; Acts 7:4 [c]ch. 10:19
12:1 [a]Acts 7:3; Heb. 11:8
12:2 [a]ch. 17:6; 18:18; Deut. 26:5; 1 Ki. 3:8 [b]ch. 24:35 [c]ch:28:4; Gal. 3:14
12:3 [a]ch. 27:29; Ex. 23:22; Num. 24:9 [b]ch. 18:18; 22:18; 26:4; Ps. 72:17; Acts 3:25; Gal. 3:8
12:5 [a]ch. 14:14 [b]ch. 11:31

wives: the name of Abram's wife *was* [a]Sarai;
and the name of Nahor's wife, [b]Milcah, the
daughter of Haran, the father of Milcah, and
the father of Iscah.
30 But [a]Sarai was barren; she had no child.
31 And Terah [a]took Abram his son, and Lot
the son of Haran his son's son, and Sarai his
daughter in law, his son Abram's wife; and
they went forth with them from [b]Ur of the
Chaldees, to go into [c]the land of Canaan; and
they came unto Haran, and dwelt there.
32 And the days of Terah were two hundred and five years: and Terah died in Haran.

The call of Abram

12 Now the [a]LORD had said unto Abram,
Get thee out of thy country, and from
thy kindred, and from thy father's house, unto
a land that I will shew thee:
2 [a]And I will make of thee a great nation,
[b]and I will bless thee, and make thy name
great; [c]and thou shalt be a blessing:
3 [a]And I will bless them that bless thee,
and curse him that curseth thee: [b]and in thee
shall all families of the earth be blessed.
4 So Abram departed, as the LORD had spoken unto him; and Lot went with him: and
Abram *was* seventy and five years old when he
departed out of Haran.
5 And Abram took Sarai his wife, and Lot
his brother's son, and all their substance that
they had gathered, and [a]the souls that they
had gotten [b]in Haran; and they went forth to

11:26 *Terah . . . begat Abram, Nahor, and Haran.* As in the case of Shem, Ham and Japheth, the names of the three sons may not be in chronological order by age (see 9:24; see also 10:21). Haran died while his father was still alive (see v. 28).

11:27 *generations.* See note on 2:4.

‡11:28 *Ur of the Chaldees.* Possibly the site on the Euphrates in southern Iraq excavated by Leonard Woolley between 1922 and 1934. Ruins and artifacts from Ur reveal a civilization and culture that reached high levels before Abram's time. King Ur-Nammu, who may have been Abram's contemporary, is famous for his law code. It is argued that since the moon-god was worshiped at both Ur and Haran (v. 31), and since Terah was an idolater (see Josh 24:2) he probably felt at home in either place. Another possible site is located in northern Mesopotamia and north of Haran. Haran seems to be too far north to be on the travel route from southern Ur to Canaan. Though etymology of names is not an exact science, it is worth noting that in addition to Haran (v.26), the names of Serug (v. 21), Nahor (v. 22), and Terah (v. 24), all in the family line of Abraham, are represented in names of ancient sites in the vicinity of what has been identified as ancient Haran. Furthermore, Genesis 24:4-7,10 defines northern Mesopotamia (Heb. is *Aram-nahariam,* i.e."Aram of the two rivers") as the land of Abraham's kindred.

11:30 *Sarai was barren.* The sterility of Abram's wife (see 15:2–3; 17:17) emphasized the fact that God's people would not come by natural generation from the post-Babel peoples. God was bringing a new humanity into being, of whom Abram was father (17:5), just as Adam and Noah were fathers of the fallen human race.

11:31 *they came unto Haran.* In Hebrew the name of the town is spelled differently from that of Abram's brother (v. 26). Haran was a flourishing caravan city in the 19th century B.C. In the 18th century it was ruled by Amorites (see note on 10:16).

12:1 *had said.* God had spoken to Abram "when he was in Mesopotamia, before he dwelt in Charran [Haran]" (Acts 7:2). *Get thee out . . . shew thee.* Abram must leave the settled world of the post-Babel nations and begin a pilgrimage with God to a better world of God's making (see 24:7).

12:2–3 God's promise to Abram has a sevenfold structure: (1) "I will make of thee a great nation," (2) "I will bless thee," (3) "and make thy name great," (4) "thou shalt be a blessing," (5) "I will bless them that bless thee," (6) "curse him that curseth thee," and (7) "in thee shall all families of the earth be blessed." God's original blessing on all mankind (1:28) would be restored and fulfilled through Abram and his offspring. In various ways and degrees, these promises were reaffirmed to Abram (v. 7; 15:5–21; 17:4–8; 18:18–19; 22:17–18), to Isaac (26:2–4), to Jacob (28:13–15; 35:11–12; 46:3) and to Moses (Ex 3:6–8; 6:2–8). The seventh promise is quoted in Acts 3:25 with reference to Peter's Jewish listeners (see Acts 3:12)—Abram's physical descendants—and in Gal 3:8 with reference to Paul's Gentile listeners—Abram's spiritual descendants.

12:4 *Abram departed, as the LORD had spoken unto him.* See Heb 11:8. Prompt obedience grounded in faith characterized this patriarch throughout his life (see 17:23; 21:14; 22:3). *Lot went with him.* See 13:1,5. Lot at first was little more than Abram's ward. *seventy and five years old.* Although advanced in age at the time of his call, Abram would live for another full century (see 25:7; see also note on 5:5).

12:5 *souls that they had gotten.* Wealthy people in that ancient world always had servants to help them with their flocks and herds (see 15:3; 24:2). Not all servants were slaves; many were voluntarily employed.

go into the land of Canaan; and into the land of Canaan they came.

6 And Abram [a]passed through the land unto the place of Sichem, [b]unto the plain of Moreh. [c]And the Canaanite *was* then in the land.

7 [a]And the LORD appeared unto Abram, and said, [b]Unto thy seed will I give this land: and there builded he an [c]altar unto the LORD, who appeared unto him.

8 And he removed from thence unto a mountain on the east of Beth-el, and pitched his tent, *having* Beth-el on the west, and Hai on the east: and there he builded an altar unto the LORD, and [a]called upon the name of the LORD.

9 And Abram journeyed, [a][1]going on still toward the south.

Abram goes to Egypt

10 ¶ And there was [a]a famine in the land: and Abram [b]went down into Egypt to sojourn there; for the famine *was* [c]grievous in the land.

11 And it came to pass, when he was come near to enter into Egypt, that he said unto Sarai his wife, Behold now, I know that thou *art* [a]a fair woman to look upon:

12 Therefore it shall come to pass, when the Egyptians shall see thee, that they shall say, This *is* his wife: and they [a]will kill me, but they will save thee alive.

13 [a]Say, I pray thee, thou *art* my sister: that it may be well with me for thy sake; and my soul shall live because of thee.

14 And it came to pass, that, when Abram was come into Egypt, the Egyptians beheld the woman that she *was* very fair.

15 The princes also of Pharaoh saw her, and commended her before Pharaoh: and the woman was taken into Pharaoh's house.

16 And he [a]entreated Abram well for her sake: and he had sheep, and oxen, and he asses, and menservants, and maidservants, and she asses, and camels.

17 And the LORD [a]plagued Pharaoh and his house with great plagues because of Sarai Abram's wife.

18 And Pharaoh called Abram, and said, [a]What *is* this *that* thou hast done unto me? why didst thou not tell me that she *was* thy wife?

19 Why saidst thou, She *is* my sister? so I might have taken her to me to wife: now therefore behold thy wife, take *her,* and go thy way.

20 [a]And Pharaoh commanded *his* men concerning him: and they sent him away, and his wife, and all that he had.

Abram and Lot part

13 And Abram went up out of Egypt, he, and his wife, and all that he had, and Lot with him, [a]into the south.

2 [a]And Abram *was* very rich in cattle, in silver, and in gold.

3 And he went on his journeys [a]from the south even to Beth-el, unto the place where his tent had been at the beginning, between Beth-el and Hai;

4 Unto the [a]place of the altar, which he had made there at the first: and there Abram [b]called on the name of the LORD.

5 And Lot also, which went with Abram, had flocks, and herds, and tents.

6 And [a]the land was not able to bear them, that they might dwell together: for their substance was great, so that they could not dwell together.

7 And there was [a]a strife between the herdmen of Abram's cattle and the herdmen of

12:6 [a]Heb. 11:9 [b]Deut. 11:30; Judg. 7:1 [c]ch. 10:18,19
12:7 [a]ch. 17:1 [b]ch. 13:15; 17:8; Ps. 105:9,11 [c]ch. 13:4
12:8 [a]ch. 13:4
12:9 [1]Heb. *in going and journeying* [a]ch. 13:3
12:10 [a]ch. 26:1 [b]Ps. 105:13 [c]ch. 43:1
12:11 [a]ver. 14; ch. 26:7
12:12 [a]ch. 20:11; 26:7
12:13 [a]ch. 20:5,13
12:16 [a]ch. 20:14
12:17 [a]ch. 20:18; 1 Chr. 16:21; Ps. 105:14
12:18 [a]ch. 20:9; 26:10
12:20 [a]Prov. 21:1
13:1 [a]ch. 12:9
13:2 [a]ch. 24:35; Ps. 112:3; Prov. 10:22
13:3 [a]ch. 12:8,9
13:4 [a]ch. 12:7,8 [b]Ps. 116:17
13:6 [a]ch. 36:7
13:7 [a]ch. 26:20

‡**12:6** *place of Sichem, unto the plain of Moreh.* See perhaps 35:4; Judg 9:6,37. A famous sanctuary was located at Sichem [i.e. Shechem] in central Canaan. "Plain" is better rendered "oak" or "terebinth." A large tree was often a conspicuous feature at such holy places. But Abram worshiped the Lord there, not the local deity.
12:7 *the LORD appeared.* The Lord frequently appeared visibly to Abram and to others, but not in all His glory (see Ex 33:18–20; John 1:18). *an altar.* The first of several that Abram built at places where he had memorable spiritual experiences (see v. 8; 13:18; 22:9). He acknowledged that the land of Canaan belonged to the Lord in a special way (see Ex 20:24; Josh 22:19).
12:8 *Beth-el.* Just north of Jerusalem, it was an important town in the religious history of God's ancient people (see, e.g., 28:10–22; 35:1–8; 1 Ki 12:26–29). Only Jerusalem is mentioned more often in the OT.
12:9 *south.* The dry wasteland stretching southward from Beer-sheba. The same Hebrew word *negev* is translated "southward" in 13:14.
12:10 *went down into Egypt . . . for the famine was grievous.* Egypt's food supply was usually plentiful because the Nile's water supply was normally dependable.
12:11 *fair.* See v. 14. She was 65 at the time (see v. 4; 17:17). The Genesis Apocryphon (one of the Dead Sea Scrolls) praises Sarai's beauty. Abram's experience in this episode foreshadows Israel's later experience in Egypt, as the author of Genesis, writing after the exodus, was very much aware. Abram was truly the "father" of Israel.
12:13 *Say, I pray thee, thou art my sister.* If Pharaoh were to add Sarai to his harem while knowing that she was Abram's wife, he would have to kill Abram first.
12:15 *Pharaoh.* See note on Ex 1:11.
12:16 Livestock was an important measure of wealth in ancient times (see 13:2). *menservants, and maidservants.* See note on v. 5. *camels.* Although camels were not widely used until much later (see, e.g., Judg 6:5), archaeology has confirmed their occasional domestication as early as the patriarchal period.
12:19 *Why saidst thou, She is my sister?* Egyptian ethics emphasized the importance of absolute truthfulness, and Abram was put in the uncomfortable position of being exposed as a liar.
12:20 *Pharaoh commanded his men.* See Ex 12:31–32.
13:2 *very rich.* Abram left Egypt with greater wealth than he had before—even as Israel would later leave Egypt laden with wealth from the Egyptians (Ex 3:22; 12:36).
13:4 *Abram called on the name of the LORD.* As he had done earlier at the same place (see 12:8).
13:6 *the land was not able to bear them.* Livestock made up the greater part of their possessions, and the region around Beth-el and Ai did not have enough water or pasture for such large flocks and herds (see v. 10; 26:17–22,32; 36:7).

Lot's cattle: [b]and the Canaanite and the Perizzite dwelled then in the land.
8 And Abram said unto Lot, [a]Let there be
no strife, I pray thee, between me and thee,
and between my herdmen and thy herdmen;
for we *be* [b][1]brethren.
9 [a]*Is* not the whole land before thee? separate thyself, I pray thee, from me: [b]if *thou wilt*
take the left hand, then I will go to the right;
or if *thou depart to* the right hand, then I will
go to the left.
10 And Lot lifted up his eyes, and beheld
all [a]the plain of Jordan, that it *was* well watered every where, before the LORD [b]destroyed
Sodom and Gomorrah, [c]*even* as the garden of
the LORD, like the land of Egypt, as thou
comest unto [d]Zoar.
11 Then Lot chose him all the plain of Jordan; and Lot journeyed east: and they separated themselves the one from the other.
12 Abram dwelled in the land of Canaan,
and Lot [a]dwelled in the cities of the plain, and
[b]pitched his tent toward Sodom.
13 But the men of Sodom [a]*were* wicked
and [b]sinners before the LORD exceedingly.
14 ¶ And the LORD said unto Abram, after
that Lot [a]was separated from him, Lift up now
thine eyes, and look from the place where
thou *art* [b]northward, and southward, and eastward, and westward:
15 For all the land which thou seest, [a]to
thee will I give it, and [b]to thy seed for ever.
16 And [a]I will make thy seed as the dust of
the earth: so that if a man can number the dust
of the earth, *then* shall thy seed also be numbered.
17 Arise, walk through the land in the

13:7 [b]ch. 12:6
13:8 [1]Heb. *men brethren:* So Ex. 2:14 (Heb.)
[a]1 Cor. 6:7 [b]See ch. 11:27,31
13:9 [a]ch. 20:15; 34:10 [b]Rom. 12:18
13:10 [a]ch. 19:17 [b]ch. 19:24 [c]ch. 2:10; Is. 51:3 [d]ch. 14:2,8; 19:22
13:12 [a]ch. 19:29 [b]ch. 14:12; 19:1
13:13 [a]ch. 18:20; 2 Pet. 2:7 [b]ch. 6:11
13:14 [a]ver. 11 [b]ch. 28:14
13:15 [a]ch. 12:7; 15:18; Deut. 34:4; Acts 7:5 [b]2 Chr. 20:7; Ps. 37:22
13:16 [a]ch. 22:17; Ex. 32:13
13:18 [1]Heb. *plains* [a]ch. 14:13 [b]ch. 35:27
14:1 [a]ch. 10:10; 11:2 [b]Is. 11:11
14:2 [a]Deut. 29:23 [b]ch. 19:22
14:3 [a]Num. 34:12; Deut. 3:17; Josh. 3:16
14:4 [a]ch. 9:26
14:5 [1]Or, *The plain of Kiriathaim* [a]ch. 15:20 [b]Deut. 2:20 [c]Deut. 2:10
14:6 [1]Or, *The plain of Paran* [a]Deut. 2:12,22
14:7 [a]2 Chr. 20:2

length of it and in the breadth of it; for I will
give it unto thee.
18 Then Abram removed his tent, and
came and [a]dwelt in the [1]plain of Mamre,
[b]which *is* in Hebron, and built there an altar
unto the LORD.

The wars of the kings

14 And it came to pass in the days of
Amraphel king [a]of Shinar, Arioch
king of Ellasar, Chedorlaomer king of [b]Elam,
and Tidal king of nations;
2 *That these* made war with Bera king of
Sodom, and with Birsha king of Gomorrah,
Shinab king of [a]Admah, and Shemeber king of
Zeboiim, and the king of Bela, which *is* [b]Zoar.
3 All these were joined together in the vale
of Siddim, [a]which *is* the salt sea.
4 Twelve years [a]they served Chedorlaomer, and *in* the thirteenth year they rebelled.
5 And in the fourteenth year came Chedorlaomer, and the kings that *were* with him,
and smote [a]the Rephaims in Ashteroth Karnaim, and [b]the Zuzims in Ham, [c]and the Emims
in [1]Shaveh Kiriathaim,
6 [a]And the Horites in their mount Seir,
unto [1]El-paran, which *is* by the wilderness.
7 And they returned, and came to En-mishpat, which *is* Kadesh, and smote all the country of the Amalekites, and also the Amorites,
that dwelt [a]in Hazezon-tamar.
8 And there went out the king of Sodom,
and the king of Gomorrah, and the king of Admah, and the king of Zeboiim, and the king of
Bela (the same *is* Zoar); and they joined battle
with them in the vale of Siddim;
9 With Chedorlaomer the king of Elam,
and *with* Tidal king of nations, and Amraphel

13:7 *the Perizzite.* May refer to rural inhabitants in contrast to city dwellers.
13:8 *brethren.* Relatives (as often in the Bible).
13:9 Abram, always generous, gave his young nephew the opportunity to choose the land he wanted. He himself would not obtain wealth except by the Lord's blessing (see 14:22–24).
13:10 *plain.* The Hebrew for this word picturesquely describes this section of the Jordan Valley as oval in shape. *like the land of Egypt.* Because of its abundant and dependable water supply (see note on 12:10), Egypt came the closest to matching Eden's ideal conditions (see 2:10). *the LORD destroyed Sodom and Gomorrah.* See especially 18:16–19:29. The names of Sodom and Gomorrah became proverbial for vile wickedness and for divine judgment on sin. Archaeology has confirmed that, prior to this catastrophe, the now dry area east and southeast of the Dead Sea (see note on 10:19) had ample water and was well populated.
13:12 *Lot . . . pitched his tent toward Sodom.* Since the men of Sodom were known to be wicked (see v. 13), Lot was flirting with temptation by choosing to live near them. Contrast the actions of Abram (v. 18).
13:14 *Lift up now thine eyes, and look.* See Deut 34:1–4. Lot and Abram are a study in contrasts. The former looked selfishly and coveted (v. 10); the latter looked as God commanded and was blessed.
13:16 *as the dust of the earth.* A simile (common in the ancient Near East) for the large number of Abram's offspring (see 28:14; 2 Chr 1:9; see also Num 23:10). Similar phrases are: "as the stars of the heaven" and "as the sand which is upon the sea shore" (22:17).
13:17 *walk through the land in the length of it and in the breadth of it.* Either to inspect it or to exercise authority over it, demonstrating the promised ownership.
13:18 *plain.* See note on 12:6. *Mamre.* A town named after one of Abram's allies (see 14:13). *Hebron.* Kirjath-arba (see note on 23:2). *altar.* See note on 12:7.
14:1 *Amraphel king of Shinar.* Not the great Babylonian king Hammurapi, as once thought. *Elam.* See note on 10:22. *nations.* The Hebrew word *goiim* means "Gentile nations" and may be a common noun here (as in Is 9:1).
14:3 *salt sea.* The Dead Sea, whose water contains a 25 percent concentration of chloride and bromide salts, making it the densest large body of water on earth.
14:6 *Horites.* Formerly thought to be cave dwellers (the Hebrew word *ḥor* means "cave"), they are now known to have been the Hurrians, a non-Semitic people widely dispersed throughout the ancient Near East.
14:7 *En-mishpat.* Another name for Kadesh, it means "spring of judgment/justice." It is called Meribah-Kadesh, "quarreling/litigation at Kadesh," in Deut 32:51 (see Num 27:14). *Kadesh.* Located in the southwest Negev (see note on 12:9), it was later called Kadesh-barnea (see Num 32:8). *Amalekites.* A tribal people living in the Negev and in the Sinai peninsula. *Amorites.* See note on 10:16.

king of Shinar, and Arioch king of Ellasar; four kings with five.

10 And the vale of Siddim *was* full of [a]slimepits; and the kings of Sodom and Gomorrah fled, and fell there; and they that remained fled [b]to the mountain.

11 And they took [a]all the goods of Sodom and Gomorrah, and all their victuals, and went their way.

12 And they took Lot, Abram's [a]brother's son, [b]who dwelt in Sodom, and his goods, and departed.

13 And there came one that had escaped, and told Abram the Hebrew; for [a]he dwelt in the plain of Mamre the Amorite, brother of Eshcol, and brother of Aner: [b]and these *were* confederate with Abram.

14 And when Abram heard that [a]his brother was taken captive, he [1]armed his [2]trained *servants,* [b]born in his own house, three hundred and eighteen, and pursued *them* [c]unto Dan.

15 And he divided himself against them, he and his servants, by night, and [a]smote them, and pursued them unto Hobah, which *is* on the left hand of Damascus.

16 And he brought back all the goods, and also brought again his brother Lot, and his goods, and the women also, and the people.

Melchizedek blesses Abram

17 ¶ And the king of Sodom [a]went out to meet him [b]after his return from the slaughter of Chedorlaomer, and of the kings that *were* with him, at the valley of Shaveh, which *is* the [c]king's dale.

18 And [a]Melchizedek king of Salem brought forth bread and wine: and he *was* [b]the priest of [c]the most high God.

19 And he blessed him, and said, [a]Blessed *be* Abram of the most high God, [b]possessor of heaven and earth:

20 And [a]blessed *be* the most high God, which hath delivered thine enemies into thy hand. And he gave him tithes [b]of all.

21 And the king of Sodom said unto Abram, Give me the [1]persons, and take the goods to thyself.

22 And Abram said to the king of Sodom, I [a]have lift up mine hand unto the LORD, the most high God, [b]the possessor of heaven and earth,

23 That [a]I will not *take* from a thread even to a shoelatchet, and that I will not take any thing that *is* thine, lest thou shouldest say, I have made Abram rich:

24 Save only that which the young men have eaten, and the portion of the men which went with me, Aner, Eshcol, and Mamre; let them take their portion.

The covenant with Abram

15 After these things the word of the LORD came unto Abram [a]in a vision,

14:10 [a]ch. 11:3 [b]ch. 19:17,30
14:11 [a]ver. 16,21
14:12 [a]ch. 12:5 [b]ch. 13:12
14:13 [a]ch. 13:18 [b]ver. 24
14:14 [1]Or, *led forth* [2]Or, *instructed* [a]ch. 13:8 [b]ch. 15:3 [c]Deut. 34:1
14:15 [a]Is. 41:2,3
14:17 [a]1 Sam. 18:6
14:17 [b]Heb. 7:1 [c]2 Sam. 18:18
14:18 [a]Heb. 7:1 [b]Ps. 110:4; Heb. 5:6 [c]Acts 16:17
14:19 [a]Ruth 3:10 [b]ver. 22
14:20 [a]ch. 24:27 [b]Heb. 7:4
14:21 [1]Heb. *souls*
14:22 [a]Dan. 12:7 [b]ver. 19
14:23 [a]See Esth. 9:15,16
15:1 [a]Dan. 10:1

14:10 *slimepits.* Lumps of asphalt are often seen even today floating in the southern end of the Dead Sea. *mountain.* The Dead Sea, the lowest body of water on earth (about 1,300 feet below sea level), is flanked by hills on both sides.

‡14:12 *Lot . . . who dwelt in Sodom.* He had moved into the town and was living among its wicked people (see 2 Pet 2:8). Though Lot was "righteous," he was now in danger of imitating the sensual conduct of wicked men (2 Pet 2:7).

14:13 *Hebrew.* Abram, the father of the Hebrew people, is the first Biblical character to be called a Hebrew (see "Eber" in note on 10:21). Usually an ethnic term in the Bible, it was normally used by non-Israelites in a disparaging sense (see, e.g., 39:17). Outside the Bible, people known as the Habiru/Apiru (a word probably related to Hebrew) are referred to as a propertyless, dependent, immigrant (foreign) social class rather than as a specific ethnic group. Negative descriptions of them are given in the Amarna letters (clay tablets found in Egypt). *Mamre.* A town was named after him (see 13:18 and note).

14:14 *his trained servants, born in his own house, three hundred and eighteen.* A clear indication of Abram's great wealth. The Hebrew for "trained servants" is found only here in the Bible. A related word used elsewhere in very ancient texts means "armed retainers." *Dan.* This well-known city in the north was not given the name "Dan" until the days of the judges (see Judg 18:29). The designation here is thus an editorial updating subsequent to Moses' time.

14:17 *king's dale.* Near Jerusalem, probably to the east (see 2 Sam 18:18).

14:18 *Melchizedek king of Salem . . . priest.* See Heb 7:1. In ancient times, particularly in non-Israelite circles, kingly and priestly duties were often performed by the same individual. "Melchizedek" means "My king is righteousness" or "King of righteousness" (see Heb 7:2). "Salem" is a shortened form of "Jerusalem" (see Ps 76:2) and is related to the Hebrew word for "peace" (see Heb 7:2). The name of Adoni-zedek, another king of Jerusalem (see Josh 10:1), is very similar to that of Melchizedek and means "My lord is righteousness" or "lord of righteousness." *bread and wine.* An ordinary meal (see Judg 19:19), in no way related to the NT ordinance of communion. Melchizedek offered the food and drink as a show of friendship and hospitality.

14:19 *most high God, possessor of heaven and earth.* The titles "most high," "lord of heaven" and "creator of earth" were frequently applied to the chief Canaanite deity in ancient times. Terminology and location (Jerusalem was in central Canaan) thus indicate that Melchizedek was probably a Canaanite king-priest. But Abram, by identifying Melchizedek's "most high God" with "the LORD" (see v. 22), bore testimony to the one true God, whom Melchizedek had come to know.

14:20 *he gave him tithes of all.* Although Melchizedek's view of God was no doubt deficient, Abram's response to his blessing seems to indicate that he recognized that Melchizedek served the same God as he (see v. 18). So Abram took the occasion to offer him a tithe of his spoils for the most high God. A tenth was the king's share (see 1 Sam 8:15,17). Melchizedek is later spoken of as a type or prefiguration of Jesus, our "great high priest" (Heb 4:14), whose priesthood is therefore in "the order of Melchisedec," not "after the order of Aaron" (Heb 7:11; see Ps 110:4).

14:22 *I have lift up mine hand.* The raising of the hand when making an oath was common practice in ancient times (see Deut 32:40; Rev 10:5–6).

14:23 *I will not take any thing that is thine.* Cf. 2 Ki 5:16. Abram refused to let himself become obligated to anyone but the Lord. Had he done so, this Canaanite king might later have claimed the right of kingship over Abram.

saying, [b]Fear not, Abram: I *am* thy [c]shield, *and* thy exceeding [d]great reward.

2 And Abram said, Lord GOD, what wilt thou give me, [a]seeing I go childless, and the steward of my house *is* this Eliezer of Damascus?

3 And Abram said, Behold, to me thou hast given no seed: and lo, [a]one born in my house is mine heir.

4 And behold, the word of the LORD *came* unto him, saying, This shall not be thine heir; but he that [a]shall come forth out of thine own bowels shall be thine heir.

5 And he brought him forth abroad, and said, Look now towards heaven, and [a]tell the [b]stars, if thou be able to number them: and he said unto him, [c]So shall thy seed be.

6 And he [a]believed in the LORD; and he [b]counted it to him *for* righteousness.

7 And he said unto him, I *am* the LORD that [a]brought thee out of [b]Ur of the Chaldees, [c]to give thee this land to inherit it.

8 And he said, Lord GOD, [a]whereby shall I know that I shall inherit it?

9 And he said unto him, Take me a heifer of three years old, and a she goat of three years old, and a ram of three years old, and a turtledove, and a young pigeon.

10 And he took unto him all these, and [a]divided them in the midst, and laid each piece one against another: but [b]the birds divided he not.

11 And when the fowls came down upon the carcases, Abram drove them away.

12 And when the sun was going down, [a]a deep sleep fell upon Abram; and, lo, a horror of great darkness fell upon him.

13 And he said unto Abram, Know of a surety [a]that thy seed shall be a stranger in a land *that is* not theirs, and shall serve them; and [b]they shall afflict them four hundred years;

14 And also that nation, whom they shall serve, [a]will I judge: and afterward [b]shall they come out with great substance.

15 And [a]thou shalt go [b]to thy fathers in peace; [c]thou shalt be buried in a good old age.

16 But [a]*in* the fourth generation they shall come hither again: for the iniquity [b]of the Amorites [c]*is* not yet full.

17 And it came to pass, that, when the sun went down, and it was dark, behold a smoking furnace, and [1]a burning lamp that passed between those pieces.

18 In the same day the LORD [a]made a covenant with Abram, saying, [b]Unto thy seed have I given this land, from the river of Egypt unto the great river, the river Euphrates:

19 The Kenites, and the Kenizzites, and the Kadmonites,

15:1 [b]ch. 26:24; Dan. 10:12 [c]Ps. 3:3; 84:11; 91:4 [d]Prov. 11:18
15:2 [a]Acts 7:5
15:3 [a]ch. 14:14
15:4 [a]2 Sam. 7:12
15:5 [a]Ps. 147:4 [b]Jer. 33:22 [c]Ex. 32:13; Heb. 11:12
15:6 [a]Rom. 4:3,9,22; Gal. 3:6 [b]Ps. 106:31
15:7 [a]ch. 12:1 [b]ch. 11:28,31 [c]Ps. 105:42,44
15:8 [a]See ch. 24:13,14; 1 Sam. 14:9,10
15:10 [a]Jer. 34:18
15:10 [b]Lev. 1:17
15:12 [a]ch. 2:21
15:13 [a]Ex. 1:11; Acts 7:6 [b]Ex. 12:40
15:14 [a]Ex. 6:6 [b]Ex. 12:36
15:15 [a]Job 5:26 [b]Acts 13:36 [c]ch. 25:8
15:16 [a]Ex. 12:41 [b]1 Ki. 21:26 [c]Mat. 23:32
15:17 [1]Heb. *a lamp of fire*
15:18 [a]ch. 24:7 [b]ch. 12:7; Ex. 23:31; Num. 34:3; Deut. 11:24; Josh. 1:4

15:1 *I am thy shield.* Whether "shield" or "sovereign" is meant (it can be translated either way), the reference is to the Lord as Abram's King. As elsewhere, "shield" stands for king (e.g., Deut 33:29; 2 Sam 22:3; Ps 7:10; 84:9). *thy exceeding great reward.* Though Abram was quite rich (13:2), God Himself was Abram's greatest treasure (cf. Deut 10:9).

15:2 *Eliezer of Damascus.* A servant probably acquired by Abram on his journey southward from Haran (see 12:5). He may also be the unnamed "servant" of 24:2.

15:3–4 Ancient documents uncovered at Nuzi (see chart, p. xix) near Kirkuk on a branch of the Tigris River, as well as at other places, demonstrate that a childless man could adopt one of his own male servants to be heir and guardian of his estate. Abram apparently contemplated doing this with Eliezer, or perhaps had already done so.

15:5 *tell the stars, if thou be able to number them.* See 22:17. More than 8,000 stars are clearly visible in the darkness of a Near Eastern night. *So shall thy seed be.* The promise was initially fulfilled in Egypt (see Ex 1; see also Deut 1:10; Heb 11:12). Ultimately, all who belong to Christ are Abram's offspring (see Gal 3:29).

15:6 Abram is the "father of all them that believe" (Rom 4:11), and this verse is the first specific reference to faith in God's promises. It also teaches that God graciously responds to a man's faith by crediting righteousness to him (see Heb 11:7).

15:7 *I am the LORD that brought thee out.* Ancient royal covenants often began with (1) the self-identification of the king and (2) a brief historical prologue, as here (see Ex 20:2).

15:8 *whereby shall I know . . . ?* Cf. Luke 1:18. Abram believed God's promise of a son, but he asked for a guarantee of the promise of the land.

15:9 *three years old.* The prime age for most sacrificial animals (see 1 Sam 1:24).

15:10 *the birds divided he not.* Perhaps because they were too small (see Lev 1:17).

15:13 *land that is not theirs.* Egypt (see 46:3–4). *four hundred years.* A round number. According to Ex 12:40 Israel spent 430 years in Egypt.

15:15 The fulfillment is recorded in 25:8.

15:16 *in the fourth generation.* That is, after 400 years (see v. 13). A "generation" was the age of a man when his first son (from the legal standpoint) was born—in Abram's case, 100 years (see 21:5). *the iniquity of the Amorites is not yet full.* Just how sinful many Canaanite religious practices were is now known from archaeological artifacts and from their own epic literature, discovered at Ras Shamra (ancient Ugarit) on the north Syrian coast beginning in 1929 (see chart, p. xix). Their "worship" was polytheistic and included child sacrifice, idolatry, religious prostitution and divination (cf. Deut 18:9–12). God was patient in judgment, even with the wicked Canaanites.

15:17 *smoking furnace, and a burning lamp.* Symbolizing the presence of God (see Ex 3:2; 14:24; 19:18; 1 Ki 18:38; Acts 2:3–4). *passed between those pieces.* Of the slaughtered animals (v. 10). In ancient times the parties solemnized a covenant by walking down an aisle flanked by the pieces of slaughtered animals (see Jer 34:18–19). The practice signified a self-maledictory oath: "May it be so done to me if I do not keep my oath and pledge." Having credited Abram's faith as righteousness, God now graciously ministered to his need for assurance concerning the land. He granted Abram a promissory covenant, as He had to Noah (see 9:9 and note; see also chart, p. 16).

15:18 *made a covenant.* Lit. "cut a covenant," referring to the slaughtering of the animals (the same Hebrew verb is translated "made" and "cut" in Jer 34:18). *have I given this land.* The Lord initially fulfilled this covenant through Joshua (see Josh 1:2–9; 21:43; see also 1 Ki 4:20–21). *river of Egypt.* Probably the modern Wadi el-Arish in northeastern Sinai.

15:19–21 A similar list of ten peoples is found in 10:15–18 (see notes there). The number ten signifies completeness.

20 And the Hittites, and the Perizzites, and the Rephaims,

21 And the Amorites, and the Canaanites, and the Girgashites, and the Jebusites.

Hagar and Ishmael

16 Now Sarai Abram's wife [a]bare him no *children:* and she had a handmaid, [b]an Egyptian, whose name *was* [c]Hagar.

2 [a]And Sarai said unto Abram, Behold now, the LORD [b]hath restrained me from bearing: I pray thee, [c]go in unto my maid; it may be that I may [1]obtain children by her. And Abram [d]hearkened to the voice of Sarai.

3 And Sarai Abram's wife took Hagar her maid the Egyptian, after Abram [a]had dwelt ten years in the land of Canaan, and gave her to her husband Abram to be his wife.

4 And he went in unto Hagar, and she conceived: and when she saw that she had conceived, her mistress was [a]despised in her eyes.

5 And Sarai said unto Abram, My wrong *be* upon thee: I have given my maid into thy bosom; and when she saw that she had conceived, I was despised in her eyes: [a]the LORD judge between me and thee.

6 [a]But Abram said unto Sarai, Behold, thy maid *is* in thy hand; do to her [1]as it pleaseth thee. And when Sarai [2]dealt hardly with her, [b]she fled from her face.

7 And the angel of the LORD found her by a fountain of water in the wilderness, [a]by the fountain in the way to [b]Shur.

8 And he said, Hagar, Sarai's maid, whence camest thou? and whither wilt thou go? And she said, I flee from the face of my mistress Sarai.

9 And the angel of the LORD said unto her, Return to thy mistress, and [a]submit thyself under her hands.

10 And the angel of the LORD said unto her, [a]I will multiply thy seed exceedingly, that it shall not be numbered for multitude.

11 And the angel of the LORD said unto her, Behold, thou *art* with child, and shalt bear a son, [a]and shalt call his name [1]Ishmael; because the LORD hath heard thy affliction.

12 [a]And he will be a wild man; his hand *will be* against every man, and every man's hand against him; [b]and he shall dwell in the presence of all his brethren.

13 And she called the name of the LORD that spake unto her, Thou God seest me: for she said, Have I also here looked after him [a]that seeth me?

14 Wherefore the well was called [a][1]Beer-lahai-roi; behold, *it is* [b]between Kadesh and Bered.

15 And [a]Hagar bare Abram a son: and Abram called his son's name, which Hagar bare, Ishmael.

16 And Abram *was* fourscore and six years old, when Hagar bare Ishmael to Abram.

The covenant of circumcision

17 And when Abram was ninety years old and nine, the LORD appeared to Abram, and said unto him, [a]I *am* the Almighty God; [b]walk before me, and be thou [c][1]perfect.

16:1 [a]ch. 15:2,3 [b]ch. 21:9 [c]Gal. 4:24
16:2 [1]Heb. *be builded by her* [a]ch. 30:3 [b]ch. 20:18 [c]ch. 30:3,9 [d]ch. 3:17
16:3 [a]ch. 12:5
16:4 [a]Prov. 30:21,23
16:5 [a]ch. 31:53
16:6 [1]Heb. *that which is good in thine eyes* [2]Heb. *afflicted her* [a]1 Pet. 3:7 [b]Ex. 2:15
16:7 [a]ch. 25:18 [b]Ex. 15:22
16:9 [a]Tit. 2:9
16:10 [a]ch. 17:20
16:11 [1]That is, *God shall hear* [a]Luke 1:13,31
16:12 [a]ch. 21:20 [b]ch. 25:18
16:13 [a]ch. 31:42
16:14 [1]That is, *The well of him that liveth* and *seeth me* [a]ch. 24:62 [b]Num. 13:26
16:15 [a]Gal. 4:22
17:1 [1]Or, *upright,* or, *sincere* [a]ch. 28:3; Ex. 6:3 [b]2 Ki. 20:3 [c]Deut. 18:13

16:1 *no children.* See note on 11:30. *Egyptian.* Perhaps Hagar was acquired while Abram and Sarai were in Egypt (see 12:10–20).
16:2 *the LORD hath restrained me from bearing.* Some time had passed since the revelation of 15:4 (see 16:3), and Sarai impatiently implied that God was not keeping His promise. *go in unto my maid.* An ancient custom, illustrated in Old Assyrian marriage contracts, the Code of Hammurapi and the Nuzi tablets (see note on 15:3–4), to ensure the birth of a male heir. Sarai would herself solve the problem of her barrenness.
16:3 *ten years.* Abram was now 85 years old (see 12:4; 16:16).
16:4 *mistress was despised.* Peninnah acted similarly toward Hannah (see 1 Sam 1:6).
16:5 *the LORD judge between me and thee.* An expression of hostility or suspicion (see 31:53; see also 31:49).
16:7 *the angel of the LORD.* Since the angel of the Lord speaks for God in the first person (v. 10) and Hagar is said to name "the LORD that spake unto her, Thou God seest me" (v. 13), the angel appears to be both distinguished from the Lord (in that he is called "messenger"—the Hebrew for "angel" means "messenger") and identified with Him. Similar distinction and identification can be found in 19:1,21; 31:11,13; Ex 3:2,4; Judg 2:1–5; 6:11–12,14; 13:3,6,8–11,13,15–17,20–23; Zech 3:1–6; 12:8. Traditional Christian interpretation has held that this "angel" was a preincarnate manifestation of Christ as God's Messenger-Servant. It may be, however, that, as the Lord's personal messenger who represented Him and bore His credentials, the angel could speak on behalf of (and so be identified with) the One who sent him (see especially 19:21; cf. 18:2,22; 19:2). Whether this "angel" was the second person of the Trinity remains therefore uncertain. *Shur.* Located east of Egypt (see 25:18; 1 Sam 15:7).
16:8 *I flee from the face of my mistress.* Not yet knowing exactly where she was going, Hagar answered only the first of the angel's questions.
16:10 A promise reaffirmed in 17:20 and fulfilled in 25:13–16.
16:11 *Ishmael.* See 17:20.
‡16:12 *wild man.* Lit. "wild donkey of a man." Away from human settlements, Ishmael would roam the desert like a wild donkey (see Job 24:5; Hos 8:9). *in the presence of.* Lit. "to the face of," possibly suggesting "in defiance of." The hostility would be that between Sarai and Hagar (see vv. 4–6), which was passed on to their descendants (see 25:18).
‡16:13 *Have I also here looked after him that seeth me?* She marvels that she is living, having just seen God. Cf. Ex 33:23; to see God's face was believed to bring death (see 32:30; Ex 33:20).
‡16:14 *Beer-lahai-roi.* The name means "the well of the living one who sees me." Another possible translation that fits the context equally well is: "well of the one who sees me and who lives." *Kadesh.* See note on 14:7
‡17:1 *ninety years old and nine.* Thirteen years had passed since Ishmael's birth (see 16:16; 17:24–25). *appeared.* See note on 12:7. *I am.* See note on 15:7. *the Almighty God.* The Hebrew (*El-Shaddai*) perhaps means "God, the Mountain One," either highlighting the invincible power of God or referring to the mountains as God's symbolic home (see Ps 121:1). It was the special name by which God revealed Himself to the patriarchs (see Ex 6:3). Another possible meaning finds the root of *Shaddai* in the verb *shadad,* "to destroy," or "to overpower." Thus God is the "one who overpowers." Such meaning fits the context well. God introduces Himself to Abraham by this name before declaring that Sarai, who is barren and beyond the years of childbearing, will have her natural condition overpowered by

2 And I will make my covenant between me
and thee, and [a]will multiply thee exceedingly.
3 And Abram fell on his face: and God
talked with him, saying,
4 *As for* me, behold, my covenant *is* with
thee, and thou shalt be [a]a father of [1]many nations.
5 Neither shall thy name any more be
called Abram, but [a]thy name shall be [1]Abra-
ham; [b]for a father of many nations have I
made thee.
6 And I will make thee exceeding fruitful,
and I will make [a]nations of thee, and [b]kings
shall come out of thee.
7 And I will [a]establish my covenant between me and thee and thy seed after thee in
their generations for an everlasting covenant,
[b]to be a God unto thee, and to [c]thy seed after
thee.
8 And [a]I will give unto thee, and to thy
seed after thee, the land [b1]wherein thou art a
stranger, all the land of Canaan, for an everlasting possession; and [c]I will be their God.
9 And God said unto Abraham, Thou shalt
keep my covenant therefore, thou, and thy
seed after thee in their generations.
10 This *is* my covenant, which ye shall
keep, between me and you and thy seed after
thee; [a]Every man *child* among you shall be
circumcised.

17:2 [a]ch. 12:2
17:4 [1]Heb. *multitude of nations* [a]Rom. 4:11,12,16
17:5 [1][That is, *Father of a great multitude*] [a]Neh. 9:7 [b]Rom. 4:17
17:6 [a]ch. 35:11 [b]Mat. 1:6
17:7 [a]Gal. 3:17
17:7 [b]ch. 26:24; 28:13 [c]Rom. 9:8
17:8 [1]Heb. *of thy sojournings* [a]ch. 12:7 [b]ch. 23:4; 28:4 [c]Ex. 6:7; Lev. 26:12
17:10 [a]Acts 7:8

God and she will bear a son. *Shaddai* occurs 31 times in the book of Job and 17 times in the rest of the Bible. *walk before me, and be thou perfect.* Perhaps equivalent to "Walk with Me, and be blameless" (see notes on 5:22; 6:8–9). After Abram's and Sarai's attempt to obtain the promised offspring by using a surrogate mother, God appeared to Abram. The Lord made it clear that, if Abram was to receive God's promised and covenanted benefits, he must be God's faithful and obedient servant. His faith must be accompanied by the "obedience to the faith" (Rom 1:5; see ch. 22).

17:2 *my covenant.* See 12:2–3; 13:14–16; 15:4–5. The covenant is God's. God calls it "my covenant" nine times in vv. 2–21, and He initiates (see 15:18), confirms (v. 2) and establishes (v. 7) it. *multiply thee.* See 13:16 and note. Earlier God had covenanted to keep His promise concerning the land (ch. 15); here He broadens His covenant to include the promised offspring. See chart, p. 16.

17:5 *Abram . . . Abraham.* The first name means "Exalted Father," probably in reference to God (i.e., "[God is] Exalted Father"); the second means "father of many," in reference to Abraham. *thy name shall be.* By giving Abram a new name (see Neh 9:7) God marked him in a special way as His servant (see notes on 1:5; 2:19).

17:6 *nations . . . kings.* This promise came also to Sarah (v. 16) and was renewed to Jacob (35:11; see 48:19). It referred to the proliferation of Abraham's offspring, who, like the descendants of Noah (see ch. 10), would someday become many nations and spread over the earth. Ultimately it finds fulfillment in such passages as Rom 4:16–18; 15:8–12; Gal 3:29; Rev 7:9; 21:24.

17:7 *everlasting.* From God's standpoint (see vv. 13,19), but capable of being broken from man's standpoint (see v. 14; cf. Is 24:5; Jer 31:32). *to be a God unto thee.* The heart of God's covenant promise, repeated over and over in the OT (see, e.g., v. 8; Jer 24:7; 31:33; Ezek 34:30–31; Hos 2:23; Zech 8:8). This is God's pledge to be the protector of His people and the One who provides for their well-being and guarantees their future blessing (see 15:1).

17:8 *land.* See 12:7; 15:18; Acts 7:5. *everlasting possession.* The land, though an everlasting possession given by God, could be temporarily lost because of disobedience (see Deut 28:62–63; 30:1–10).

17:9 *Thou* [i.e. "as for you"]. Balances the "As for me" of v. 4. Having reviewed His covenanted commitment to Abraham (see 15:8–21), and having broadened it to include the promise of offspring, God now called upon Abraham to make a covenanted commitment to Him—to "walk before me, and be thou perfect" (v. 1). *keep my covenant.* Participation in the blessings of the Abrahamic covenant was conditioned on obedience (see 18:19; 22:18; 26:4–5).

17:10 *circumcised.* Circumcision was God's appointed "token of the covenant" (v. 11), which signified Abraham's covenanted commitment to the Lord—that the Lord alone would be his

Angel of the LORD

When the "angel of the LORD" appears in the Bible, he is identified with God and yet distinguished from Him. He is also referred to as "the angel of His presence" (Isaiah 63:9). The same statements that are made about the nature, character, mission and activities of the angel of the LORD are stated of Jesus. The "angel of the LORD" is thought by many to be God the Son, appearing in human history before Jesus came to earth as a man.

ANGEL OF THE LORD	ACTIVITY OR ATTRIBUTE	JESUS
Genesis 16:7,13	Called "LORD"	John 20:28
Genesis 48:15–16	Called "God"	Hebrews 1:8
Exodus 3:2–14	"I AM"	John 8:58
Exodus 23:20–23	Sent from God	John 5:30; 6:38
Joshua 5:13–15	Captain of the LORD'S host	Revelation 19:1–14
Judges 13:15–18	Name is "Wonderful"	Isaiah 9:6
Isaiah 63:9	Redeemed his own	Ephesians 5:25

11 And ye shall circumcise the flesh of your foreskin; and it shall be [a]a token of the covenant betwixt me and you.

12 And [1]he that is eight days old [a]shall be circumcised among you, every man *child* in your generations, he that is born in the house, or bought with money of any stranger, which *is* not of thy seed.

13 He that is born in thy house, and he that is bought with thy money, must needs be circumcised: and my covenant shall be in your flesh for an everlasting covenant.

14 And the uncircumcised man *child* whose flesh of his foreskin is not circumcised, that soul [a]shall be cut off from his people; he hath broken my covenant.

15 And God said unto Abraham, *As for* Sarai thy wife, thou shalt not call her name Sarai, but [1]Sarah *shall* her name *be.*

16 And I will bless her, [a]and give thee a son also of her: yea, I will bless her, and [1]she shall be *a mother* [b]of nations; kings of people shall be of her.

17 Then Abraham fell upon his face, [a]and laughed, and said in his heart, Shall *a child* be born unto him that is an hundred years old? and shall Sarah, that is ninety years old, bear?

18 And Abraham said unto God, O that Ishmael might live before thee!

19 And God said, [a]Sarah thy wife shall bear thee a son indeed; and thou shalt call his name Isaac: and I will establish my covenant with him for an everlasting covenant, *and* with his seed after him.

20 And as for Ishmael, I have heard thee: Behold, I have blessed him, and will make him fruitful, and [a]will multiply him exceedingly; [b]twelve princes shall he beget, [c]and I will make him a great nation.

21 But my covenant will I establish with Isaac, [a]which Sarah shall bear unto thee at this set time in the next year.

22 And he left off talking with him, and God went up from Abraham.

23 ¶ And Abraham took Ishmael his son, and all that were born in his house, and all that were bought with his money, every male among the men of Abraham's house; and circumcised the flesh of their foreskin in the selfsame day, as God had said unto him.

24 And Abraham *was* ninety years old and nine, when he was circumcised *in* the flesh of his foreskin.

25 And Ishmael his son *was* thirteen years old, when he was circumcised in the flesh of his foreskin.

26 In the selfsame day was Abraham circumcised, and Ishmael his son.

27 And [a]all the men of his house, born in the house, and bought with money of the stranger, were circumcised with him.

The three visitors

18 And the LORD appeared unto him in the [a]plains of Mamre: and he sat *in* the tent door in the heat of the day;

2 [a]And he lift up his eyes and looked, and lo, three men stood by him: [b]and when he saw *them,* he ran to meet them from the tent door, and bowed himself toward the ground,

17:11 [a]Rom. 4:11
17:12 [1]Heb. *a son of eight days* [a]Lev. 12:3; Luke 2:21
17:14 [a]Ex. 4:24
17:15 [1][That is, *Princess*]
17:16 [1]Heb. *she shall become nations* [a]ch. 18:10 [b]ch. 35:11; Gal. 4:31; 1 Pet. 3:6
17:17 [a]ch. 18:12; 21:6
17:19 [a]ch. 18:10; 21:2; Gal. 4:28
17:20 [a]ch. 16:10 [b]ch. 25:12,16 [c]ch. 21:18
17:21 [a]ch. 21:2
17:27 [a]ch. 18:19
18:1 [a]ch. 13:18; 14:13
18:2 [a]Heb. 13:2 [b]ch. 19:1; 1 Pet. 4:9

God, whom he would trust and serve. It symbolized a self-maledictory oath (analogous to the oath to which God had submitted Himself; see note on 15:17): "If I am not loyal in faith and obedience to the Lord, may the sword of the Lord cut off me and my offspring (see v. 14) as I have cut off my foreskin." Thus Abraham was to place himself under the rule of the Lord as his King, consecrating himself, his offspring and all he possessed to the service of the Lord. For circumcision as signifying consecration to the Lord see Ex 6:12; Lev 19:23; 26:41; Deut 10:16; 30:6; Jer 4:4; 6:10; 9:25–26; Ezek 44:7,9. Other nations also practiced circumcision (see Jer 9:25–26; Ezek 32:18–19), but not for the covenant reasons that Israel did.

17:11 *token of the covenant.* See notes on 9:12; 15:17. As the covenant sign, circumcision also (see note on v. 10) marked Abraham as the one to whom God had made covenant commitment (15:7–21) in response to Abraham's faith, which He "counted ... to him for righteousness" (15:6). Paul comments on this aspect of the covenant sign in Rom 4:11.

17:12 *eight days old.* See 21:4 and Acts 7:8 (Isaac); Luke 1:59 (John the Baptist); 2:21 (Jesus); Phil 3:5 (Paul). Abraham was 99 years old when the newly initiated rite of circumcision was performed on him (see v. 24). The Arabs, who consider themselves descendants of Ishmael, are circumcised at the age of 13 (see v. 25). For them, as for other peoples, it serves as a rite of transition from childhood to manhood, thus into full participation in the community.

17:14 *cut off from his people.* Removed from the covenant people by divine judgment (see note on v. 10).

17:15 *Sarai ... Sarah.* Both names evidently mean "princess." The renaming stressed that she was to be the mother of nations and kings (see v. 16) and thus to serve the Lord's purpose (see note on v. 5).

17:16 *son.* Fulfilled in Isaac (see 21:2–3).

17:17 *laughed.* In temporary disbelief (see 18:12; cf. Rom 4:19–21). The verb is a pun on the name "Isaac," which means "he laughs" (see v. 19; 18:12–15; 21:3,6).

17:20 *multiply him.* See note on 13:16. *twelve princes shall he beget.* Fulfilled in 25:16.

17:21 Paul cites the choice of Isaac (and not Ishmael) as one proof of God's sovereign right to choose to save by grace alone (see Rom 9:6–13). *at this set time in the next year.* See 21:2.

17:22 *God went up from Abraham.* A solemn conclusion to the conversation.

17:23 *in the selfsame day.* Abraham was characterized by prompt obedience (see note on 12:4).

18:1 *appeared.* See note on 12:7. *plains.* See note on 12:6. *Mamre.* See note on 13:18. *the heat of the day.* Early afternoon.

18:2 *three men.* At least two of the "men" were angels (see 19:1; see also note on 16:7). The third may have been the Lord Himself (see vv. 1,13,17,20,26,33; see especially v. 22). *ran.* The story in vv. 2–8 illustrates Near Eastern hospitality in several ways: 1. Abraham gave prompt attention to the needs of his guests (vv. 2,6–7). 2. He bowed low to the ground (v. 2). 3. He politely addressed one of his guests as "my Lord" and called himself "your servant" (vv. 3,5), a common way of speaking when addressing a superior (see, e.g., 19:2,18–19). 4. He acted as if it would be a favor to him if they allowed him to serve them (vv. 3–5). 5. He asked that water be brought to wash their feet (see v. 4), an act of courtesy to refresh a traveler in a hot, dusty climate (see 19:2; 24:32; 43:24). 6. He prepared a lavish meal for them (vv. 5–8; a

3 And said, My Lord, if now I have found favour in thy sight, pass not away, I pray thee, from thy servant:

4 Let [a]a little water, I pray you, be fetched, and wash your feet, and rest yourselves under the tree:

5 And [a]I will fetch a morsel of bread, and [b][1]comfort ye your hearts; after *that* you shall pass on: [c]for therefore [2]are you come to your servant. And they said, So do, as thou hast said.

6 And Abraham hastened into the tent unto Sarah, and said, [1]Make ready quickly three measures of fine meal, knead *it,* and make cakes upon the hearth.

7 And Abraham ran unto the herd, and fetcht a calf tender and good, and gave *it* unto a young man; and he hasted to dress it.

8 And [a]he took butter, and milk, and the calf which he had dressed, and set *it* before them; and he stood by them under the tree, and they did eat.

9 And they said unto him, Where *is* Sarah thy wife? And he said, Behold, [a]in the tent.

10 And he said, I [a]will certainly return unto thee [b]according to the time of life; and lo, [c]Sarah thy wife shall have a son. And Sarah heard *it in* the tent door, which *was* behind him.

11 Now [a]Abraham and Sarah *were* old *and* well stricken in age; *and* it ceased to be with Sarah [b]after the manner of women.

12 Therefore Sarah [a]laughed within herself, saying, [b]After I am waxed old shall I have pleasure, my [c]lord being old also?

13 And the LORD said unto Abraham, Wherefore did Sarah laugh, saying, Shall I of a surety bear *a child,* which am old?

14 [a]Is any thing too hard for the LORD? [b]At the time appointed I will return unto thee, according to the time of life, and Sarah shall have a son.

15 Then Sarah denied, saying, I laughed not; for she was afraid. And he said, Nay; but thou didst laugh.

Abraham pleads for Sodom

16 ¶ And the men rose up from thence, and looked toward Sodom: and Abraham went with them [a]to bring them on the way.

17 And the LORD said, [a]Shall I hide from Abraham *that thing* which I do;

18 Seeing that Abraham shall surely become a great and mighty nation, and all the nations of the earth shall be [a]blessed in him?

19 For I know him, [a]that he will command his children and his household after him, and they shall keep the way of the LORD, to do justice and judgment; that the LORD may bring upon Abraham that which he hath spoken of him.

20 And the LORD said, Because [a]the cry of Sodom and Gomorrah is great, and because their sin is very grievous;

21 [a]I will go down now, and see whether they have done altogether according to the cry of it, which is come unto me; and if not, [b]I will know.

22 And the men turned their faces from thence, [a]and went toward Sodom: but Abraham [b]stood yet before the LORD.

23 ¶ And Abraham [a]drew near, and said, [b]Wilt thou also destroy the righteous with the wicked?

24 [a]Peradventure there be fifty righteous within the city: wilt thou also destroy and not spare the place for the fifty righteous that *are* therein?

25 That be far from thee to do after this manner, to slay the righteous with the wicked: and [a]that the righteous should be as the wicked, that be far from thee: [b]Shall not the Judge of all the earth do right?

18:4 [a]ch. 19:2; 43:24
18:5 [1]Heb. *stay* [2]Heb. *you have passed* [a]Judg. 6:18; 13:15 [b]Judg. 19:5; Ps. 104:15 [c]ch. 19:8; 33:10
18:6 [1]Heb. *Hasten*
18:8 [a]ch. 19:3
18:9 [a]ch. 24:67
18:10 [a]ver. 14 [b]2 Ki. 4:16 [c]ch. 17:19,21; 21:2; Rom. 9:9
18:11 [a]ch. 17:17; Rom. 4:19; Heb. 11:11,12,19 [b]ch. 31:35
18:12 [a]ch. 17:17 [b]Luke 1:18 [c]1 Pet. 3:6
18:14 [a]Num. 11:23; Jer. 32:17; Zech. 8:6; Mat. 3:9; Luke 1:37 [b]ver. 10; ch. 17:21; 2 Ki. 4:16
18:16 [a]Acts 15:3; Rom. 15:24; 3 John 6
18:17 [a]Ps. 25:14; Amos 3:7; John 15:15
18:18 [a]ch. 12:3; 22:18; Acts 3:25; Gal. 3:8
18:19 [a]Deut. 4:9,10; 6:7; Josh. 24:15; Eph. 6:4
18:20 [a]ch. 4:10
18:21 [a]ch. 11:5 [b]Deut. 8:2; 13:3; Josh. 22:22; Luke 16:15; 2 Cor. 11:11
18:22 [a]ch. 19:1 [b]ver. 1
18:23 [a]Heb. 10:22 [b]Num. 16:22
18:24 [a]Jer. 5:1
18:25 [a]Job 8:20; Is. 3:10,11 [b]Job 8:3; 34:17; Ps. 58:11; 94:2; Rom. 3:6

similar lavish offering was presented to a divine messenger in Judg 6:18–19; 13:15–16). 7. He stood nearby (v. 8), assuming the posture of a servant (see v. 22), to meet their every wish. Heb 13:2 is probably a reference to vv. 2–8 and 19:1–3.

18:6 *cakes.* Probably round, thin loaves.

18:10 See 17:21. Paul quotes this promise of Isaac's birth (see v. 14) in Rom 9:9 and relates it to Abraham's spiritual offspring (see Rom 9:7–8).

18:12 *laughed.* In disbelief, as also Abraham had at first (see note on 17:17).

18:14 *Is any thing too hard for the LORD?* The answer is no, for Sarah as well as for her descendants Mary and Elisabeth (see Luke 1:34–37). Nothing within God's will, including creation (see Jer 32:17) and redemption (see Mat 19:25–26), is impossible for Him.

18:16 *Sodom.* See notes on 10:19; 13:10.

18:17 Abraham was God's friend (see v. 19; 2 Chr 20:7; Jas 2:23; see also Is 41:8, but see note there). And because he was now God's covenant friend (see Job 29:4), God convened His heavenly council (see note on 1:26) at Abraham's tent. There He announced His purpose for Abraham (v. 10) and for the wicked of the plain (vv. 20–21)—redemption and judgment. He thus even gave Abraham opportunity to speak in His court and to intercede for the righteous in Sodom and Gomorrah. Abraham was later called a prophet (20:7). Here, in Abraham, is exemplified the great privilege of God's covenant people throughout the ages: God has revealed His purposes to them and allows their voice to be heard (in intercession) in the court of heaven.

18:18 *a great and mighty nation . . . shall be blessed.* See note on 12:2–3.

18:19 *know.* In Hebrew usage, "to know" sometimes connotes "to choose" (see, e.g., Amos 3:2).

18:20 *cry.* A cry of righteous indignation (cf. the blood of Abel, 4:10) that became one of the reasons for the destruction of the cities (see 19:13). *Gomorrah.* See notes on 10:19; 13:10. *sin is very grievous.* The sin of Sodom (and probably of Gomorrah as well) was already proverbial (see 13:13) and remained so for centuries (see Ezek 16:49–50).

18:21 *I will go down.* The result would be judgment (as in 11:5–9), but God also comes down to redeem (as in Ex 3:8). *see.* Not a denial of God's infinite knowledge but a figurative way of stating that He does not act out of ignorance or on the basis of mere complaints.

18:22 *Abraham stood yet before the LORD.* Illustrates the mutual accessibility that existed between God and His servant.

18:23 The second time Abraham intervened for his relatives and for Sodom (see 14:14–16).

18:25 *Judge of all the earth.* Abraham based his plea on the justice and authority ("Judge" could be translated "Ruler") of God, confident that God would do what was right (see Deut 32:4).

26 And the LORD said, [a]If I find in Sodom fifty righteous within the city, then I will spare all the place for their sakes.

27 And Abraham answered and said, [a]Behold now, I have taken upon me to speak unto the Lord, which *am* [b]*but* dust and ashes:

28 Peradventure there shall lack five of the fifty righteous: wilt thou destroy all the city for *lack of* five? And he said, If I find there forty and five, I will not destroy *it.*

29 And he spake unto him yet again, and said, Peradventure there shall be forty found there. And he said, I will not do *it* for forty's sake.

30 And he said *unto him,* Oh let not the Lord be angry, and I will speak: Peradventure there shall thirty be found there. And he said, I will not do *it,* if I find thirty there.

31 And he said, Behold now, I have taken upon me to speak unto the Lord: Peradventure there shall be twenty found there. And he said, I will not destroy *it* for twenty's sake.

32 And he said, [a]Oh let not the Lord be angry, and I will speak yet but *this* once: Peradventure ten shall be found there. [b]And he said, I will not destroy *it* for ten's sake.

33 And the LORD went his way, as soon as he had left communing with Abraham: and Abraham returned unto his place.

Sodom and Gomorrah destroyed

19 And there [a]came two angels to Sodom at even; and Lot sat in the gate of Sodom: and [b]Lot seeing *them* rose up to meet them; and he bowed himself with his face toward the ground;

2 And he said, Behold now, my lords, [a]turn in, I pray you, into your servant's house, and tarry all night, and [b]wash your feet, and ye shall rise up early, and go on your ways. And they said, [c]Nay; but we will abide in the street all night.

3 And he pressed upon them greatly; and they turned in unto him, and entered into his house; [a]and he made them a feast, and did bake unleavened bread, and they did eat.

4 But before they lay down, the men of the city, *even* the men of Sodom, compassed the house round, both old and young, all the people from every quarter:

5 [a]And they called unto Lot, and said unto him, Where *are* the men which came in to thee this night? [b]bring them out unto us, that we [c]may know them.

6 And [a]Lot went out at the door unto them, and shut the door after him,

7 And said, I pray you, brethren, do not *so* wickedly.

8 [a]Behold now, I have two daughters which have not known man; let me, I pray you, bring them out unto you, and do ye to them as *is* good in your eyes: only unto these men do nothing; [b]for therefore came they under the shadow of my roof.

9 And they said, Stand back. And they said *again, This* one *fellow* [a]came in to sojourn, [b]and he will needs be a judge: now will we deal worse with thee, than with them. And they pressed sore upon the man, *even* Lot, and came near to break the door.

10 But the men put forth their hand, and pulled Lot into the house to them, and shut to the door.

11 And they smote the men that *were at* the door of the house with blindness, both small and great; so that they wearied themselves to find the door.

12 And the men said unto Lot, Hast thou here any besides? son in law, and thy sons, and thy daughters, and whatsoever thou hast in the city, [a]bring *them* out of *this* place:

13 For we will destroy this place, because the [a]cry of them is waxen great before the face of the LORD; and [b]the LORD hath sent us to destroy it.

14 And Lot went out, and spake unto his sons in law, [a]which married his daughters, and said, [b]Up, get ye out of this place; for the

18:26 [a]Jer. 5:1; Ezek. 22:30
18:27 [a]Luke 18:1 [b]ch. 3:19; Job 4:19; Eccl. 12:7; 1 Cor. 15:47,48; 2 Cor. 5:1
18:32 [a]Judg. 6:39 [b]Jas. 5:16
19:1 [a]ch. 18:22 [b]ch. 18:1
19:2 [a]Heb. 13:2 [b]ch. 18:4 [c]See Luke 24:28
19:3 [a]ch. 18:8
19:5 [a]Is. 3:9 [b]Judg. 19:22 [c]ch. 4:1; Rom. 1:24,27; Jude 7
19:6 [a]Judg. 19:23
19:8 [a]See Judg. 19:24 [b]See ch. 18:5
19:9 [a]2 Pet. 2:7,8 [b]Ex. 2:14
19:12 [a]ch. 7:1; 2 Pet. 2:7,9
19:13 [a]ch. 18:20 [b]1 Chr. 21:15
19:14 [a]Mat. 1:18 [b]Num. 16:21,45

18:27 *Lord.* Abraham used the title "Lord," not the intimate name "LORD," throughout his prayer. He was appealing to God as "Judge of all the earth." *dust and ashes.* In contrast to God's exalted position, Abraham described himself as insignificant (see Job 30:19; 42:6).

18:32 *but this once.* Abraham's questioning in vv. 23–32 did not arise from a spirit of haggling but of compassion for his relatives and of wanting to know God's ways. *ten.* Perhaps Abraham stopped at ten because he had been counting while praying: Lot, his wife, possibly two sons (see 19:12), at least two married daughters and their husbands (see 19:14), and two unmarried daughters (see 19:8).

18:33 *his place.* Mamre (see v. 1). The next morning Abraham went back to see what God had done (see 19:27).

19:1–3 See note on 18:2.

19:1 *two angels.* See notes on 16:7; 18:2. *Lot sat in the gate of Sodom.* Lot had probably become a member of Sodom's ruling council, since a city gateway served as the administrative and judicial center where legal matters were discussed and prosecuted (see Ruth 4:1–12).

19:2 *street.* A large open space near the main city gateway (see 2 Chr 32:6) where public gatherings were held. Important cities like Jerusalem could have two or more such places (see Neh 8:16).

19:3 *unleavened bread.* So that it could be baked quickly (see 18:6; Ex 12:39).

19:4–9 See Judg 19:22–25.

19:5 *we may know them.* Euphemistic for sexual relations (see 4:1). Homosexuality was so characteristic of the men of Sodom (see Jude 7) that it is still often called sodomy.

19:8 *under the shadow of my roof.* Ancient hospitality obliged a host to protect his guests in every situation.

19:9 *This one fellow came in to sojourn, and he will needs be a judge.* Centuries later, Moses was also considered an outsider and accused of setting himself up as a judge (see Ex 2:14; Acts 7:27).

19:13 *we will destroy this place.* Sodom's wickedness had made it ripe for destruction (see Is 3:9; Jer 23:14; Lam 4:6; Zeph 2:8–9; 2 Pet 2:6; Jude 7).

19:14 *he seemed as one that mocked unto his sons in law.* Lot apparently had lost his power of moral persuasion even among his family members.

LORD will destroy this city. [c]But he seemed as one that mocked unto his sons in law.

15 And when the morning arose, then the angels hastened Lot, saying, [a]Arise, take thy wife, and thy two daughters, which [1]are here; lest thou be consumed in the [2]iniquity of the city.

16 And while he lingered, the men laid hold upon his hand, and upon the hand of his wife, and upon the hand of his two daughters; [a]the LORD being merciful unto him: [b]and they brought him forth, and set him without the city.

17 And it came to pass, when they had brought them forth abroad, that he said, [a]Escape for thy life; [b]look not behind thee, neither stay thou in all the plain; escape to the mountain, lest thou be consumed.

18 And Lot said unto them, Oh, [a]not so, my Lord:

19 Behold now, thy servant hath found grace in thy sight, and thou hast magnified thy mercy, which thou hast shewed unto me in saving my life; and I cannot escape to the mountain, lest *some* evil take me, and I die:

20 Behold now, this city *is* near to flee unto, and it *is* a little one: Oh, let me escape thither, (*is* it not a little one?) and my soul shall live.

21 And he said unto him, See, [a]I have accepted [1]thee concerning this thing, that I will not overthrow *this* city, for the which thou hast spoken.

22 Haste thee, escape thither; for [a]I cannot do any thing till thou be come thither. Therefore [b]the name of the city was called [1]Zoar.

23 The sun was [1]risen upon the earth when Lot entered into Zoar.

24 Then [a]the LORD rained upon Sodom and upon Gomorrah brimstone and fire from the LORD out of heaven;

25 And he overthrew those cities, and all the plain, and all the inhabitants of the cities, and [a]that which grew upon the ground.

26 But his wife looked back from behind him, and she became [a]a pillar of salt.

27 And Abraham gat up early in the morning to the place where [a]he stood before the LORD:

28 And he looked toward Sodom and Gomorrah, and toward all the land of the plain, and beheld, and lo, [a]the smoke of the country went up as the smoke of a furnace.

29 And it came to pass, when God destroyed the cities of the plain, that God [a]remembered Abraham, and sent Lot out of the midst of the overthrow, when he overthrew the cities in the which Lot dwelt.

The sin of Lot's daughters

30 ¶ And Lot went up out of Zoar, and [a]dwelt in the mountain, and his two daughters with him; for he feared to dwell in Zoar: and he dwelt in a cave, he and his two daughters.

31 And the firstborn said unto the younger, Our father *is* old, and *there is* not a man in the earth [a]to come in unto us after the manner of all the earth:

32 Come, let us make our father drink wine, and we will lie with him, that we [a]may preserve seed of our father.

33 And they made their father drink wine that night: and the firstborn went in, and lay with her father; and he perceived not when she lay down, nor when she arose.

34 And it came to pass on the morrow, that the firstborn said unto the younger, Behold, I lay yesternight with my father: let us make him drink wine this night also; and go thou in, *and* lie with him, that we may preserve seed of our father.

35 And they made their father drink wine that night also: and the younger arose, and lay with him; and he perceived not when she lay down, nor when she arose.

36 Thus were both the daughters of Lot with child by their father.

37 And the firstborn bare a son, and called his name Moab: [a]the same *is* the father of the Moabites unto *this* day.

38 And the younger, she also bare a son, and called his name Ben-ammi: [a]the same *is* the father of the children of Ammon unto *this* day.

Abraham and Abimelech

20 And Abraham journeyed from [a]thence toward the south country, and dwelled between [b]Kadesh and Shur, and [c]sojourned in Gerar.

2 And Abraham said of Sarah his wife, [a]She

19:14 [c]Ex. 9:21; Luke 17:28; 24:11
19:15 [1]Heb. *are found* [2]Or, *punishment* [a]Num. 16:24,26; Rev. 18:4
19:16 [a]Luke 18:13 [b]Ps. 34:22
19:17 [a]1 Ki. 19:3 [b]ver. 26; Mat. 24:16-18; Luke 9:62; Phil. 3:13,14
19:18 [a]Acts 10:14
19:21 [1]Heb. *thy face* [a]Job 42:8,9; Ps. 145:19
19:22 [1][That is, *Little,* ver. 20] [a]See ch. 32:25,26; Ex. 32:10; Deut. 9:14; Mark 6:5 [b]ch. 13:10; 14:2
19:23 [1]Heb. *gone forth*
19:24 [a]Deut. 29:23; Is. 13:19; Jer. 20:16; Ezek. 16:49,50; Hos. 11:8; Luke 17:29; 2 Pet. 2:6; Jude 7
19:25 [a]ch. 14:3; Ps. 107:34
19:26 [a]Luke 17:32
19:27 [a]ch. 18:22
19:28 [a]Rev. 18:9
19:29 [a]ch. 8:1; 18:23
19:30 [a]ver. 17,19
19:31 [a]ch. 16:2,4; 38:8,9; Deut. 25:5
19:32 [a]Mark 12:19
19:37 [a]Deut. 2:9
19:38 [a]Deut. 2:19
20:1 [a]ch. 18:1 [b]ch. 16:7,14 [c]ch. 26:6
20:2 [a]ch. 12:13; 26:7

19:16 *lingered.* Perhaps because of reluctance to leave his material possessions. *his hand, and upon the hand of his wife, and upon the hand of his two daughters.* The ten righteous people required to save Sodom (see 18:32) had now been reduced to four. *the LORD being merciful unto him.* Deliverance is due to divine mercy, not to human righteousness (cf. Tit 3:5).

19:24 *rained ... brimstone and fire.* Perhaps from a violent earthquake spewing up asphalt, such as is still found in this region.

19:26 *his wife looked back ... and she became a pillar of salt.* Her disobedient hesitation (see v. 17) became proverbial in later generations (see Luke 17:32). Even today, grotesque salt formations near the southern end of the Dead Sea are reminders of her folly.

19:29 *God remembered Abraham.* See note on 8:1. *God ... sent Lot out of the midst of the overthrow.* Lot's deliverance was the main concern of Abraham's prayer (18:23–32), which God now answered.

19:33 *they made their father drink wine ... and the firstborn went in, and lay with her father.* Though Lot's role was somewhat passive, he bore the basic responsibility for the drunkenness and incest that eventually resulted in his two daughters' becoming pregnant by him (see v. 36).

19:36–38 The sons born to Lot's daughters were the ancestors of the Moabites and Ammonites (see Deut 2:9,19), two nations that were to become bitter enemies of Abraham's descendants (see, e.g., 1 Sam 14:47; 2 Chr 20:1).

20:1 *between Kadesh and Shur.* See notes on 14:7; 16:7. *Gerar.*

is my sister: and Abimelech king of Gerar sent, and [b]took Sarah.

3 But [a]God came to Abimelech [b]in a dream by night, and said to him, [c]Behold, thou *art but* a dead man, for the woman which thou hast taken; for she *is* [1]a man's wife.

4 But Abimelech had not come near her: and he said, Lord, [a]wilt thou slay also a righteous nation?

5 Said he not unto me, She *is* my sister? and she, even she herself said, He *is* my brother: [a]in the [1]integrity of my heart and innocency of my hands have I done this.

6 And God said unto him in a dream, Yea, I know that thou didst this in the integrity of thy heart; for [a]I also withheld thee from sinning [b]against me: therefore suffered I thee not to touch her.

7 Now therefore restore the man *his* wife; [a]for he *is* a prophet, and he shall pray for thee, and thou shalt live: and if thou restore *her* not, [b]know thou that thou shalt surely die, thou, [c]and all that *are* thine.

8 Therefore Abimelech rose early in the morning, and called all his servants, and told all these things in their ears: and the men were sore afraid.

9 Then Abimelech called Abraham, and said unto him, What hast thou done unto us? and what have I offended thee, [a]that thou hast brought on me and on my kingdom a great sin? thou hast done deeds unto me [b]that ought not to be done.

10 And Abimelech said unto Abraham, What sawest thou, that thou hast done this thing?

11 And Abraham said, Because I thought, Surely [a]the fear of God *is* not in this place; and [b]they will slay me for my wife's sake.

12 And yet indeed [a]*she is* my sister; she *is* the daughter of my father, but not the daughter of my mother; and she became my wife.

13 And it came to pass, when [a]God caused me to wander from my father's house, that I said unto her, This *is* thy kindness which thou shalt shew unto me; at every place whither we shall come, [b]say of me, He *is* my brother.

14 And Abimelech [a]took sheep, and oxen, and menservants, and womenservants, and gave *them* unto Abraham, and restored him Sarah his wife.

15 And Abimelech said, Behold, [a]my land *is* before thee: dwell [1]where it pleaseth thee.

16 And unto Sarah he said, Behold, I have given thy brother a thousand *pieces* of silver: [a]behold, he *is* to thee [b]a covering of the eyes, unto all that *are* with thee, and with all *other:* thus she was reproved.

17 So Abraham [a]prayed unto God: and God healed Abimelech, and his wife, and his maidservants; and they bare *children.*

18 For the LORD [a]had fast closed up all the wombs of the house of Abimelech, because of Sarah Abraham's wife.

The birth of Isaac; Hagar and Ishmael cast out

21 And the LORD [a]visited Sarah as he had said, and the LORD did unto Sarah [b]as he had spoken.

2 For Sarah [a]conceived, and bare Abraham a son in his old age, [b]at the set time of which God had spoken to him.

3 And Abraham called the name of his son that was born unto him, whom Sarah bare to him, [a]Isaac.

4 And Abraham [a]circumcised his son Isaac being eight days old, [b]as God had commanded him.

5 And [a]Abraham *was* an hundred years old, when his son Isaac was born unto him.

6 And Sarah said, [a]God hath made me to laugh, *so that* all that hear [b]will laugh with me.

7 And she said, Who would have said unto Abraham, that Sarah should have given children suck? [a]for I have born *him* a son in his old age.

8 And the child grew, and was weaned: and Abraham made a great feast the *same* day that Isaac was weaned.

9 And Sarah saw the son of Hagar [a]the Egyptian, [b]which she had born unto Abraham, [c]mocking.

20:2 [b]ch. 12:15
20:3 [1]Heb. *married to a husband* [a]Ps. 105:14 [b]Job 33:15 [c]ver. 7
20:4 [a]ch. 18:23
20:5 [1]Or, *simplicity,* or, *sincerity* [a]2 Ki. 20:3
20:6 [a]ch. 31:7; 35:5; Ex. 34:24; 1 Sam. 25:26,34 [b]ch. 39:9; Lev. 6:2; Ps. 51:4
20:7 [a]1 Sam. 7:5; 2 Ki. 5:11; Job 42:8; Jas. 5:14,15 [b]ch. 2:17 [c]Num. 16:32,33
20:9 [a]ch. 26:10; Ex. 32:21; Josh. 7:25 [b]ch. 34:7
20:11 [a]ch. 42:18; Ps. 36:1; Prov. 16:6 [b]ch. 12:12; 26:7
20:12 [a]See ch. 11:29
20:13 [a]ch. 12:1,9,11; Heb. 11:8 [b]ch. 12:13
20:14 [a]ch. 12:16
20:15 [1]Heb. *as is good in thine eyes* [a]ch. 13:9
20:16 [a]ch. 26:11 [b]ch. 24:65
20:17 [a]Job 42:9
20:18 [a]ch. 12:17
21:1 [a]1 Sam. 2:21 [b]ch. 17:19; Gal. 4:23,28
21:2 [a]Acts 7:8; Gal. 4:22; Heb. 11:11 [b]ch. 17:21
21:3 [a]ch. 17:19
21:4 [a]Acts 7:8 [b]ch. 17:10,12
21:5 [a]ch. 17:1,17
21:6 [a]Ps. 126:2; Is. 54:1 [b]Luke 1:58
21:7 [a]ch. 18:11,12
21:9 [a]ch. 16:1 [b]ch. 16:15 [c]Gal. 4:29

Located at the edge of Philistine territory, about halfway between Gaza on the Mediterranean coast and Beer-sheba in the northern Negev.

20:2 *Abimelech.* Probably the father or grandfather of the later king who bore the same name (see 26:1).

20:3 *dream.* Once again God intervened to spare the mother of the promised offspring. Dreams were a frequent mode of revelation in the OT (see 28:12; 31:10–11; 37:5–9; 40:5; 41:1; Num 12:6; Judg 7:13; 1 Ki 3:5; Dan 2:3; 4:5; 7:1).

20:7 *prophet.* See note on 18:17. Abraham was the first man to bear this title (see Ps 105:15).

20:11 *fear of God.* A conventional phrase equivalent to "true religion." "Fear" in this phrase has the sense of reverential trust in God that includes commitment to His revealed will (word).

20:12 *she is my sister; she is the daughter of my father, but not the daughter of my mother.* Abraham's half-truth was a sinful deception, not a legitimate explanation.

20:14–16 Abimelech's generosity was a strong contrast to Abraham's fearfulness and deception.

20:16 *pieces.* That is, shekels. Originally the shekel was only a weight, not a coin, since coinage was not invented till the seventh century B.C.

21:1 *visited Sarah as he had said.* See 17:16. *did unto Sarah as he had spoken.* See Gal 4:22–23,28.

21:3 *Isaac.* See note on 17:17.

21:4 See notes on 17:10,12.

21:5 Abraham, in fulfillment of the promise made to him (see 17:16), miraculously became a father at the age of 100 years (see 17:17).

21:6 *made me to laugh . . . laugh.* See note on 17:17.

21:8 *weaned.* At age two or three, as was customary in the ancient Near East.

21:9 *the son of Hagar the Egyptian, which she had born.* Ishmael, who was in his late teens at this time (see 16:15–16). *mocking.* Or "at play." In either case, Sarah saw Ishmael as a potential threat to Isaac's inheritance (v. 10).

10 Wherefore she said unto Abraham, [a]Cast out this bondwoman and her son: for the son of this bondwoman shall not be heir with my son, *even* with Isaac.

11 And the thing was very grievous in Abraham's sight [a]because of his son.

12 And God said unto Abraham, Let it not be grievous in thy sight because of the lad, and because of thy bondwoman; in all that Sarah hath said unto thee, hearken unto her voice; for [a]in Isaac shall thy seed be called.

13 And also of the son of the bondwoman will I make [a]a nation, because he *is* thy seed.

14 And Abraham rose up early in the morning, and took bread, and a bottle of water, and gave *it* unto Hagar, putting *it* on her shoulder, and the child, and [a]sent her away: and she departed, and wandered in the wilderness of Beer-sheba.

15 And the water was spent in the bottle, and she cast the child under one of the shrubs.

16 And she went, and sat her down over against *him* a good way off, as it were a bowshot: for she said, Let me not see the death of the child. And she sat over against *him,* and lift up her voice, and wept.

17 And [a]God heard the voice of the lad; and the angel of God called to Hagar out of heaven, and said unto her, What aileth thee, Hagar? fear not; for God hath heard the voice of the lad where he *is.*

18 Arise, lift up the lad, and hold him in thine hand; for [a]I will make him a great nation.

19 And [a]God opened her eyes, and she saw a well of water; and she went, and filled the bottle *with* water, and gave the lad drink.

20 And God [a]was with the lad; and he grew, and dwelt in the wilderness, [b]and became an archer.

21 And he dwelt in the wilderness of Paran: and his mother [a]took him a wife out of the land of Egypt.

Covenant with Abimelech

22 ¶ And it came to pass at that time, that [a]Abimelech and Phichol the chief captain of his host spake unto Abraham, saying, [b]God *is* with thee in all that thou doest:

23 Now therefore [a]swear unto me here by God [1]that thou wilt not deal falsely with me, nor with my son, nor with my son's son: *but* according to the kindness that I have done unto thee, thou shalt do unto me, and to the land wherein thou hast sojourned.

24 And Abraham said, I will swear.

25 And Abraham reproved Abimelech because of a well of water, which Abimelech's servants [a]had violently taken away.

26 And Abimelech said, I wot not who hath done this thing: neither didst thou tell me, neither yet heard I *of it,* but to day.

27 And Abraham took sheep and oxen, and gave *them* unto Abimelech; and both of them [a]made a covenant.

28 And Abraham set seven ewe lambs of the flock by themselves.

29 And Abimelech said unto Abraham, [a]What *mean* these seven ewe lambs which thou hast set by themselves?

30 And he said, For *these* seven ewe lambs shalt thou take of my hand, that [a]they may be a witness unto me, that I have digged this well.

31 Wherefore he [a]called that place [1]Beer-sheba; because there they sware both of them.

32 Thus they made a covenant at Beer-sheba: then Abimelech rose up, and Phichol the chief captain of his host, and they returned into the land of the Philistines.

33 And *Abraham* planted a [1]grove in Beer-sheba, and [a]called there on the name of the LORD, [b]the everlasting God.

21:10 [a]Gal. 4:30; See ch. 25:6; 36:6,7
21:11 [a]ch. 17:18
21:12 [a]Rom. 9:7,8; Heb. 11:18
21:13 [a]ver. 18; ch. 16:10; 17:20
21:14 [a]John 8:35
21:17 [a]Ex. 3:7
21:18 [a]ver. 13
21:19 [a]Num. 22:31
21:20 [a]ch. 28:15; 39:2,3,21 [b]ch. 16:12
21:21 [a]ch. 24:4
21:22 [a]ch. 20:2; 26:26 [b]ch:26:28
21:23 [1]Heb. *if thou shalt lie unto me* [a]Josh. 2:12; 1 Sam. 24:21
21:25 [a]See ch. 26:15,18,20-22
21:27 [a]ch. 26:31; 31:44; 1 Sam. 18:3
21:29 [a]ch. 33:8
21:30 [a]ch. 31:48,52
21:31 [1]That is, *The well of the oath* [a]ch. 26:33
21:33 [1]Or, *tree* [a]ch. 4:26 [b]Deut. 33:27

21:10 *Cast out this bondwoman and her son.* See Gal 4:21–31. Driving them out would have had the effect of disinheriting Ishmael.

21:11 *the thing was very grievous in Abraham's sight.* Both love and legal custom played a part in Abraham's anguish. He knew that the customs of his day, illustrated later in the Nuzi tablets (see chart, p. xix), prohibited the arbitrary expulsion of a servant girl's son (whose legal status was relatively weak in any case).

21:12 *in all that Sarah hath said unto thee, hearken unto her voice.* God overruled in this matter (as He had done earlier; see 15:4), promising Abraham that both Isaac and Ishmael would have numerous descendants. *in Isaac shall thy seed be called.* See Rom 9:6–8 and Heb 11:17–19 for broader spiritual applications of this statement.

21:14 *early in the morning.* Though Abraham would now be separated from Ishmael for the first time, he responded to God's command with prompt obedience (see note on 12:4). *Beer-sheba.* See note on v. 31.

21:15 *one of the shrubs.* See note on v. 33.

21:17 *God heard . . . God hath heard.* A pun on the name "Ishmael," which means "God hears"(see 16:11; 17:20).

21:21 *wilderness of Paran.* Located in north central Sinai. *his mother took him a wife out of the land of Egypt.* Parents often arranged their children's marriages (see ch. 24).

21:22 *Abimelech.* See 20:2 and note. *Phichol.* Either a family name or an official title, since it reappears over 60 years later (25:26) in a similar context (26:26).

21:23 *swear unto me . . . by God . . . the kindness that I have done . . . thou shalt do unto me.* Phrases commonly used when making covenants or treaties (see vv. 27,32). "Kindness" as used here refers to acts of friendship (cf. v. 27; 20:14). Such covenants always involved oaths.

21:27 *sheep and oxen.* Probably to be used in the treaty ceremony (see 15:10).

21:31 *Beer-sheba; because there they sware both of them.* Beer-sheba can mean "well of seven" or "well of the oath." For a similar pun on the name see 26:33. Beer-sheba, an important town in the northern Negev, marked the southernmost boundary of the Israelite monarchy in later times (see, e.g., 2 Sam 17:11). An ancient well there is still pointed out as "Abraham's well" (see v. 25), but its authenticity is not certain.

21:32 *Philistines.* See note on 10:14.

21:33 *grove* [i.e. a tamarisk]. A shrub or small tree that thrives in arid regions. Its leafy branches provide welcome shade, and it is probably the unidentified bush under which Hagar put Ishmael in v. 15. *everlasting God.* Hebrew *El Olam,* a phrase unique to this passage. It is one of a series of names that include *El,* "God," as an element (see 14:19 and note; 17:1 and note; 33:20; 35:7).

34 And Abraham sojourned in the Philistines' land many days.

God tests Abraham

22 And it came to pass after these things, that [a]God did tempt Abraham, and said unto him, Abraham: and he said, [1]Behold, *here* I *am.*

2 And he said, Take now thy son, [a]thine only *son* Isaac, whom thou lovest, and get thee [b]into the land of Moriah; and offer him there for a burnt offering upon one of the mountains which I will tell thee of.

3 And Abraham rose up early in the morning, and saddled his ass, and took two of his young men with him, and Isaac his son, and clave the wood for the burnt offering, and rose up, and went unto the place of which God had told him.

4 Then on the third day Abraham lift up his eyes, and saw the place afar off.

5 And Abraham said unto his young men, Abide you here with the ass; and I and the lad will go yonder and worship, and come again to you.

6 And Abraham took the wood of the burnt offering, and [a]laid *it* upon Isaac his son; and he took the fire in his hand, and a knife; and they went both of them together.

7 And Isaac spake unto Abraham his father, and said, My father: and he said, [1]Here *am* I, my son. And he said, Behold the fire and the wood: but where *is* the [2]lamb for a burnt offering?

8 And Abraham said, My son, God will provide himself a lamb for a burnt offering: so they went both of them together.

9 And they came to the place which God had told him of; and Abraham built an altar there, and laid the wood in order, and bound Isaac his son, and [a]laid him on the altar upon the wood.

10 And Abraham stretched forth his hand, and took the knife to slay his son.

11 And the angel of the LORD called unto him out of heaven, and said, Abraham, Abraham: and he said, Here *am* I.

12 And he said, [a]Lay not thine hand upon the lad, neither do thou any thing unto him: for [b]now I know that thou fearest God, seeing thou hast not withheld thy son, thine only *son* from me.

13 And Abraham lifted up his eyes, and looked, and behold behind *him* a ram caught in a thicket by his horns: and Abraham went and took the ram, and offered him up for a burnt offering in the stead of his son.

14 And Abraham called the name of that place [1]Jehovah-jireh: as it is said *to this* day, In the mount of the LORD it shall be seen.

15 And the angel of the LORD called unto Abraham out of heaven the second time,

16 And said, [a]By myself have I sworn, saith the LORD, for because thou hast done this thing, and hast not withheld thy son, thine only *son:*

17 That in blessing I will bless thee, and in multiplying I will multiply thy seed [a]as the

22:1 [1]Heb. *Behold me* [a]1 Cor. 10:13; Heb. 11:17; Jas. 1:12; 1 Pet. 1:7
22:2 [a]Heb. 11:17 [b]2 Chr. 3:1
22:6 [a]John 19:17
22:7 [1]Heb. *Behold me* [2]Or, *kid*
22:9 [a]Heb. 11:17; Jas. 2:21
22:12 [a]1 Sam. 15:22 [b]ch. 26:5; Jas. 2:22
22:14 [1]That is, *The LORD will see,* or, *provide*
22:16 [a]Ps. 105:9; Luke 1:73; Heb. 6:13,14
22:17 [a]ch. 15:5; Jer. 33:22

22:1 *after these things.* Isaac had grown into adolescence or young manhood, as implied also by 21:34 ("many days"). *did tempt* [i.e."tested"]. God does not tempt (Jas 1:13). Satan tempts us (see 1 Cor 7:5) in order to make us fall; God tests us in order to confirm our faith (Ex 20:20) or prove our commitment (Deut 8:2). See note on Mat 4:1. *here I am.* Abraham answered with the response of a servant, as did Moses and Samuel when God called them by name (see Ex 3:4; 1 Sam 3:4,6,8).

‡22:2 *thy son, thine only son Isaac, whom thou lovest.* In the Hebrew text, Isaac's name is placed last in this sequence in order to heighten the effect. He was the "only son" of the promise (21:12). *land of Moriah.* The author of Chronicles identifies the area as the temple mount in Jerusalem (2 Chr 3:1). Today "Mount Moriah" is occupied by the Dome of the Rock, an impressive Muslim structure erected in A.D. 691. A large outcropping of rock inside the building is still pointed to as the traditional site of the intended sacrifice of Isaac. *offer him there for a burnt offering.* Abraham had committed himself by covenant to be obedient to the Lord and had consecrated his son Isaac to the Lord by circumcision. The Lord put His servant's faith and loyalty to the supreme test, thereby instructing Abraham, Isaac and their descendants as to the kind of total consecration the Lord's covenant requires. The test also foreshadowed the perfect consecration in sacrifice that another offspring of Abraham would undergo (see note on v. 16) in order to wholly consecrate Abraham and his spiritual descendants to God and to fulfill the covenant promises.

22:3 *early in the morning.* Prompt obedience, even under such trying circumstances, characterized Abraham's response to God (see note on 12:4).

22:4 *third day.* Three days would be necessary for the journey from Beer-sheba (see v. 19) to Jerusalem.

22:5 *lad.* See v. 12. The Hebrew for this word has a wide range of meaning, from an infant (see Ex 2:6) to a young man of military age (see 1 Chr 12:28). *I and the lad . . . come again to you.* Abraham, the man of faith and "the father of all them that believe" (Rom 4:11), considered "that God was able to raise him up, even from the dead" (Heb 11:19) if that were necessary to fulfill His promise.

22:8 *God will provide himself a lamb.* The immediate fulfillment of Abraham's trusting response was the ram of v. 13, but its ultimate fulfillment is the Lamb of God (John 1:29,36).

22:9 *laid him on the altar upon the wood.* Isaac is here a type (prefiguration) of Christ (see note on v. 16).

22:11 *angel of the LORD.* See note on 16:7. *Abraham, Abraham.* The repetition of the name indicates urgency (see 46:2; Ex 3:4; 1 Sam 3:10; Acts 9:4). *Here am I.* See note on v. 1.

22:12 *fearest God.* See note on 20:11. *thou hast not withheld thy son, thine only son from me*. See v. 16. Abraham's faith was "made perfect" by what he did (Jas 2:21–22).

22:13 *in the stead of.* Substitutionary sacrifice of one life for another is here mentioned for the first time. As the ram died in Isaac's place, so also Jesus gave His life as a ransom "for" (lit. "instead of") many (Mark 10:45).

22:14 *mount of the LORD.* During the Israelite monarchy the phrase referred to the temple mount in Jerusalem (see Ps 24:3; Is 2:3; 30:29; Zech 8:3).

22:16 *By myself have I sworn.* There is no greater name in which the Lord can take an oath (see Heb 6:13). *thou . . . hast not withheld thy son, thine only son.* Abraham's devotion is paralleled by God's love to us in Christ as reflected in John 3:16 and Rom 8:32, which may allude to this verse.

stars of the heaven, [b]and as the sand which *is*
upon the sea [1]shore; and [c]thy seed shall possess [d]the gate of his enemies;
18 [a]And in thy seed shall all the nations of
the earth be blessed; [b]because thou hast
obeyed my voice.
19 So Abraham returned unto his young
men, and they rose up and went together to
[a]Beer-sheba; and Abraham dwelt at Beer-sheba.
20 ¶ And it came to pass after these things,
that it was told Abraham, saying, Behold,
[a]Milcah, she hath also born children unto thy
brother Nahor;
21 [a]Huz his firstborn, and Buz his brother,
and Kemuel the father [b]of Aram,
22 And Chesed, and Hazo, and Pildash,
and Jidlaph, and Bethuel.
23 And [a]Bethuel begat [b]Rebekah: these
eight Milcah did bear to Nahor, Abraham's
brother.
24 And his concubine, whose name *was*
Reumah, she bare also Tebah, and Gaham, and
Thahash, and Maachah.

The death of Sarah

23 And Sarah was an hundred and sev-
en and twenty years old: *these were*
the years of the life of Sarah.
2 And Sarah died in [a]Kirjath-arba; the same
is [b]Hebron in the land of Canaan: and Abraham came to mourn for Sarah, and to weep for
her.
3 And Abraham stood up from before his
dead, and spake unto the sons of Heth, saying,
4 [a]I *am* a stranger and a sojourner with
you: [b]give me a possession of a buryingplace
with you, that I may bury my dead out of my
sight.

22:17 [1]Heb. *lip* [b]ch. 13:16 [c]ch. 24:60 [d]Mic. 1:9
22:18 [a]ch. 12:3; 18:18; 26:4; Acts 3:25; Gal. 3:8,9,16,18 [b]ver. 3,10; ch. 26:5
22:19 [a]ch. 21:31
22:20 [a]ch. 11:29
22:21 [a]Job 1:1 [b]Job 32:2
22:23 [a]ch. 24:15 [b]Called, Rom. 9:10, *Rebecca*
23:2 [a]Josh. 14:15 [b]ver. 19; ch. 13:18
23:4 [a]ch. 17:8; 1 Chr. 29:15; Ps. 105:12; Heb. 11:9,13 [b]Acts 7:5

23:6 [1]Heb. *a prince of God* [a]ch. 13:2; 14:14; 24:35
23:9 [1]Heb. *full money*
23:10 [1]Heb. *ears* [a]ch. 34:20,24; Ruth 4:4
23:11 [a]See 2 Sam. 24:21-24
23:15 [a]Ex. 30:13; Ezek. 45:12

5 And the children of Heth answered Abraham, saying unto him,
6 Hear us, my lord: thou *art* [a][1]a mighty
prince among us: in the choice of our sepulchres bury thy dead; none of us shall withhold
from thee his sepulchre, but that thou mayest
bury thy dead.
7 And Abraham stood up, and bowed himself to the people of the land, *even* to the children of Heth.
8 And he communed with them, saying, If
it be your mind that I should bury my dead out
of my sight; hear me, and intreat for me to
Ephron the son of Zohar,
9 That he may give me the cave of Machpelah, which he hath, which *is* in the end of
his field; for [1]as much money as it is worth he
shall give it me for a possession of a buryingplace amongst you.
10 And Ephron dwelt amongst the children
of Heth: and Ephron the Hittite answered
Abraham in the [1]audience of the children of
Heth, *even* of all that [a]went in *at* the gate of
his city, saying,
11 [a]Nay, my lord, hear me: the field give I
thee, and the cave that *is* therein, I give it
thee; in the presence of the sons of my people
give I it thee: bury thy dead.
12 And Abraham bowed down himself before the people of the land.
13 And he spake unto Ephron in the audience of the people of the land, saying, But if
thou *wilt give it,* I pray thee, hear me: I will
give *thee* money for the field; take *it* of me,
and I will bury my dead there.
14 And Ephron answered Abraham, saying
unto him,
15 My lord, hearken unto me: the land *is*
worth four hundred [a]shekels of silver; what *is*

22:17 *multiply thy seed as the stars of the heaven.* See 13:16; 15:5 and notes. *sand which is upon the sea shore.* Fulfilled, at least in part, during Solomon's reign (see 1 Ki 4:20). *gate.* Taking possession of the gate of a city was tantamount to occupying the city itself (see 24:60).

22:18 *shall all the nations of the earth be blessed.* See note on 12:2–3. *because thou hast obeyed my voice.* See note on 17:9.

22:23–24 Abraham's brother Nahor (see 11:26) became the father of eight sons by his wife and four by his concubine (see note on 25:6). They would later become the ancestors of 12 Aramean (see v. 21) tribes, just as Abraham's grandson Jacob would become the ancestor of the 12 tribes of Israel (see 49:28).

23:2 *Kirjath-arba.* Means "the town of Arba" (Arba was the most prominent member of a tribe living in the Hebron area [see Josh 14:15]). It can also mean "the town of four," referring to the place where Anak (see Josh 15:13–14; 21:11) and his three sons lived (see Judg 1:10,20). *came.* Either from Beer-sheba to Hebron or into where Sarah's body was lying.

23:3 *sons of Heth.* See note on 10:15. They were apparently in control of the Hebron area at this time.

23:4 *a stranger and a sojourner.* This and similar phrases were used often by the patriarchs and their descendants in reference to themselves (see 1 Chr 29:15; Ps 39:12; see also Heb 11:13). On this earth Abraham was dwelling in tents (Heb 11:9), the most temporary of dwellings. But he looked forward to the more permanent home promised him, which the author of Hebrews calls "a city which hath foundations, whose builder and maker is God" (Heb 11:10).

23:6 *thou art a mighty prince.* Probably intended as words of flattery.

23:9 *cave of Machpelah.* Though inaccessible today, the tombs of several patriarchs and their wives—Abraham and Sarah, Isaac and Rebekah, Jacob and Leah (see v. 19; 25:8–10; 49:30–31; 50:12–13)—are, according to tradition, located in a large cave deep beneath the Mosque of Abraham, a Muslim shrine in Hebron. *end of his field.* Because buying the entire field would have made Abraham responsible for certain additional financial and social obligations, he wanted to buy only a small part of it. Hittite laws stipulated that when a landowner sold only part of his property to someone else, the original and principal landowner had to continue paying all dues on the land. But if the landowner disposed of an entire tract, the new owner had to pay the dues.

23:10 *in the audience of the children of Heth . . . all that went in at the gate.* The main gateway of a city was usually the place where legal matters were transacted and attested (see v. 18; see also note on 19:1).

23:11 *my lord.* Perhaps intended to flatter Abraham (see v. 15). *give.* Or "sell."

23:15 *four hundred shekels of silver; what is that betwixt me and thee?* See note on 20:16. Despite Ephron's pretense of generosity, 400 shekels of silver was an exorbitant price for a field

that betwixt me and thee? bury therefore thy
dead.
16 And Abraham hearkened unto Ephron;
and Abraham [a]weighed to Ephron the silver,
which he had named in the audience of the
sons of Heth, four hundred shekels of silver,
current *money* with the merchant.
17 And [a]the field of Ephron, which *was* in
Machpelah, which *was* before Mamre, the
field, and the cave which *was* therein, and all
the trees that *were* in the field, that *were* in all
the borders round about, were made sure
18 Unto Abraham for a possession in the
presence of the children of Heth, before all
that went in *at* the gate of his city.
19 And after this, Abraham buried Sarah
his wife in the cave of the field of Machpelah
before Mamre: the same *is* Hebron in the land
of Canaan.
20 And the field, and the cave that *is* therein, [a]were made sure unto Abraham for a possession of a buryingplace by the sons of Heth.

Isaac and Rebekah

24 And Abraham [a]was old, *and* [1]well
stricken in age: and the LORD [b]had
blessed Abraham in all things.
2 And Abraham said [a]unto his eldest servant
of his house that [b]ruled over all that he had,
[c]Put, I pray thee, thy hand under my thigh:
3 And I will make thee [a]swear by the LORD,
the God of heaven, and the God of the earth,
that [b]thou shalt not take a wife unto my son of
the daughters of the Canaanites, amongst
whom I dwell:
4 [a]But thou shalt go [b]unto my country, and
to my kindred, and take a wife unto my son
Isaac.
5 And the servant said unto him, Peradventure the woman will not be willing to follow me unto this land: must I needs bring thy
son again unto the land from whence thou
camest?
6 And Abraham said unto him, Beware
thou that thou bring not my son thither again.
7 The LORD God of heaven, which [a]took
me from my father's house, and from the land
of my kindred, and which spake unto me, and
that sware unto me, saying, [b]Unto thy seed
will I give this land; [c]he shall send his angel
before thee, and thou shalt take a wife unto
my son from thence.
8 And if the woman will not be willing to
follow thee, then [a]thou shalt be clear from this
my oath: only bring not my son thither again.
9 And the servant put his hand under the
thigh of Abraham his master, and sware to him
concerning that matter.
10 ¶ And the servant took ten camels of the
camels of his master, and departed; [a][1]for all
the goods of his master *were* in his hand: and
he arose, and went to Mesopotamia, unto [b]the
city of Nahor.
11 And he made *his* camels to kneel down
without the city by a well of water at the time
of the evening, *even* the time [a][1]that *women*
go out to draw *water*.
12 And he said, [a]O LORD God of my master
Abraham, I pray thee, [b]send me good speed
this day, and shew kindness unto my master
Abraham.
13 Behold, [a]I stand *here* by the well of water; and [b]the daughters of the men of the city
come out to draw water:
14 And let it come to pass, *that* the damsel
to whom I shall say, Let down thy pitcher, I pray
thee, that I may drink; and she shall say, Drink,
and I will give thy camels drink also: *let the
same be* she *that* thou hast appointed for thy
servant Isaac; and [a]thereby shall I know that
thou hast shewed kindness unto my master.
15 And it came to pass, before he had done

23:16 [a]Jer.32:9 **23:17** [a]ch. 25:9; 49:30-32; 50:13; Acts 7:16 **23:20** [a]Jer. 32:10,11
24:1 [1]Heb. *gone into days* [a]ch. 21:5 [b]ver. 35; ch. 13:2; Ps. 112:3; Prov. 10:22 **24:2** [a]ch. 15:2 [b]ver. 10; ch. 39:4-6 [c]ch. 47:29; 1 Chr. 29:24 **24:3** [a]ch. 14:22; Deut. 6:13; Josh. 2:12 [b]ch. 26:35; 28:2; Ex. 34:16; Deut. 7:3 **24:4** [a]ch. 28:2 [b]ch. 12:1
24:7 [a]ch. 12:1 [b]ch. 12:7; 13:15; 17:8; Ex. 32:13; Deut. 1:8; 34:4; Acts 7:5 [c]Ex. 23:20,23; 33:2; Heb. 1:14 **24:8** [a]Josh. 2:17,20 **24:10** [1]Or, *and* [a]ver. 2 [b]ch. 27:43 **24:11** [1]Heb. *that* women *which draw* water *go forth* [a]Ex. 2:16; 1 Sam. 9:11 **24:12** [a]ver. 27; ch. 26:24; 32:9; Ex. 3:6,15 [b]Neh. 1:11; Ps. 37:5 **24:13** [a]ver. 43 [b]Ex. 2:16 **24:14** [a]See Judg. 6:17,37; 1 Sam. 6:7; 14:10; 20:7

(see, e.g., Jer 32:9). Ephron was taking advantage of Abraham during a time of grief and bereavement. He knew that Abraham had to deal quickly in order to have a place to bury Sarah, so he insisted that Abraham buy the entire lot and assume responsibility for the dues as well.

23:16 *current money with the merchant* [i.e. commercial standard]. Subject to more variation and therefore greater dishonesty than the later royal standard (see 2 Sam 14:26), which was carefully regulated and more precise.

23:17 *the field, and the cave which was therein, and all the trees.* In order to be free of all obligations relating to the field in which the cave of Machpelah was located, Ephron had held out for the sale of the entire field and its contents (see note on v. 9).

23:19 *buried Sarah his wife . . . in the land of Canaan.* In that culture, people had a strong desire to be buried "with their fathers" (see note on 25:8) in their native land. By purchasing a burial place in Canaan, Abraham indicated his unswerving commitment to the Lord's promise. Canaan was his new homeland.

24:2 *his eldest servant of his house.* Probably Eliezer of Damascus (see note on 15:2). *Put . . . thy hand under my thigh.* Near the organ of procreation, probably because this oath was related to the continuation of Abraham's line through Isaac (see 47:29).

24:3 *the LORD, the God of heaven, and the God of the earth.* See v. 7. For a similar majestic title used by Abraham in an oath see 14:22.

24:4 *my country.* Mesopotamia (see note on v. 10). *take a wife unto my son.* See note on 21:21.

24:7 *Unto thy seed will I give this land.* Repeats the promise of 12:7. *his angel.* See note on 16:7.

24:10 *camels.* See note on 12:16. *Mesopotamia.* Hebrew *Aram-naharaim,* meaning "Aram of the two rivers"—the Euphrates and the Tigris. Aram (see note on 10:22) Naharaim was the northern part of the area called later by the Greeks "Mesopotamia," meaning "between the rivers." *city of Nahor.* Perhaps named after Abraham's brother (see v. 15; 11:26). It is mentioned in clay tablets excavated by the French beginning in 1933 at the ancient city of Mari on the Euphrates (see chart, p. xix). Nahor was located in the Haran (see note on 11:31) district and was ruled by an Amorite prince in the 18th century B.C.

24:11 *at the time of the evening, even the time that women go out to draw water.* The coolest time of day.

24:14 *thereby shall I know.* Like his master Abraham, the servant asked God for a sign to validate his errand (see note on 15:8). *kindness.* See v. 27; probably a reference to God's covenant with Abraham, which had promised numerous descendants through Isaac (see 17:19; 21:12).

24:15 *before he had done speaking.* God had already begun to

speaking, that behold, Rebekah came out, who
was born to Bethuel, son of [a]Milcah, the wife
of Nahor, Abraham's brother, with her pitcher
upon her shoulder.
16 And the damsel [a]*was* very [1]fair to look
upon, a virgin, neither had any man known
her: and she went down to the well, and filled
her pitcher, and came up.
17 And the servant ran to meet her, and
said, Let me, I pray thee, drink a little water of
thy pitcher.
18 [a]And she said, Drink, my lord: and she
hasted, and let down her pitcher upon her
hand, and gave him drink.
19 And when she had done giving him
drink, she said, I will draw *water* for thy
camels also, until they have done drinking.
20 And she hasted, and emptied her pitcher into the trough, and ran again unto the well
to draw *water,* and drew for all his camels.
21 And the man wondering at her held his
peace, to wit whether [a]the LORD had made his
journey prosperous or not.
22 And it came to pass, as the camels had
done drinking, that the man took a golden
[a][1]earring of half a shekel weight, and two
bracelets for her hands of ten *shekels* weight
of gold;
23 And said, Whose daughter *art* thou? tell
me, I pray thee: is there room *in* thy father's
house for us to lodge in?
24 And she said unto him, [a]I *am* the
daughter of Bethuel the son of Milcah, which
she bare unto Nahor.
25 She said moreover unto him, We have
both straw and provender enough, and room
to lodge in.
26 And the man [a]bowed down his head,
and worshipped the LORD.
27 And he said, [a]Blessed *be* the LORD God
of my master Abraham, who hath not left destitute my master of [b]his mercy and his truth: I
being in the way, the LORD [c]led me to the
house of my master's brethren.
28 And the damsel ran, and told *them of*
her mother's house these things.
29 And Rebekah had a brother, and his
name *was* [a]Laban: and Laban ran out unto the
man, unto the well.
30 And it came to pass, when he saw the
earring and bracelets upon his sister's hands,
and when he heard the words of Rebekah his
sister, saying, Thus spake the man unto me;
that he came unto the man; and behold, he
stood by the camels at the well.
31 And he said, Come in, [a]thou blessed of
the LORD; wherefore standest thou without?

24:15 [a]ch. 11:29; 22:23
24:16 [1]Heb. *good of countenance* [a]ch. 26:7
24:18 [a]1 Pet. 3:8
24:21 [a]ver. 12,56
24:22 [1]Or, *jewel for the forehead* [a]Ex. 32:2,3; Is. 3:19-21
24:24 [a]ch. 22:23
24:26 [a]ver. 52; Ex. 4:31
24:27 [a]Ex. 18:10; Ruth 4:14; 1 Sam. 25:32,39 [b]ch. 32:10; Ps. 98:3 [c]ver. 48
24:29 [a]ch. 29:5
24:31 [a]ch. 26:29; Judg. 17:2; Ruth 3:10; Ps. 115:15
24:32 [a]ch. 43:24; Judg. 19:21
24:33 [a]Job 23:12; John 4:34; Eph. 6:5-7
24:35 [a]ver. 1; ch. 13:2
24:36 [a]ch. 21:2 [b]ch. 21:10; 25:5
24:37 [a]ver. 3
24:38 [a]ver. 4
24:39 [a]ver. 5
24:40 [a]ver. 7 [b]ch. 17:1
24:41 [a]ver. 8
24:42 [a]ver. 12
24:43 [a]ver. 13
24:45 [a]ver. 15 [b]1 Sam. 1:13

for I have prepared the house, and room for
the camels.
32 And the man came into the house: and
he ungirded *his* camels, and [a]gave straw and
provender for the camels, and water to wash
his feet, and the men's feet that *were* with
him.
33 And there was set *meat* before him to
eat: but he said, [a]I will not eat, until I have
told mine errand. And he said, Speak on.
34 And he said, I *am* Abraham's servant.
35 And the LORD [a]hath blessed my master
greatly; and he is become great: and he hath
given him flocks, and herds, and silver, and
gold, and menservants, and maidservants, and
camels, and asses.
36 And Sarah my master's wife [a]bare a son
to my master when she was old: and [b]unto
him hath he given all that he hath.
37 And my master [a]made me swear, saying, Thou shalt not take a wife to my son of the
daughters of the Canaanites, in whose land I
dwell:
38 [a]But thou shalt go unto my father's
house, and to my kindred, and take a wife
unto my son.
39 [a]And I said unto my master, Peradventure the woman will not follow me.
40 [a]And he said unto me, The LORD, [b]be-
fore whom I walk, will send his angel with
thee, and prosper thy way; and thou shalt take
a wife for my son of my kindred, and of my father's house:
41 [a]Then shalt thou be clear from *this* my
oath, when thou comest to my kindred; and if
they give not thee *one,* thou shalt be clear
from my oath.
42 And I came this day unto the well, and
said, [a]O LORD God of my master Abraham, if
now thou do prosper my way which I go:
43 [a]Behold, I stand by the well of water;
and it shall come to pass, *that when* the virgin
cometh forth to draw *water,* and I say to her,
Give me, I pray thee, a little water of thy pitcher to drink;
44 And she say to me, Both drink thou, and
I will also draw for thy camels: *let* the same *be*
the woman whom the LORD hath appointed
out for my master's son.
45 [a]And before I had done [b]speaking in
mine heart, behold, Rebekah came forth with
her pitcher on her shoulder; and she went
down unto the well, and drew *water:* and I
said unto her, Let me drink, I pray thee.
46 And she made haste, and let down her
pitcher from her *shoulder,* and said, Drink,
and I will give thy camels drink also: so I
drank, and she made the camels drink also.

answer. *Rebekah . . . was born to Bethuel, son of . . . the wife of Nahor, Abraham's brother.* Isaac would thus be marrying his father's grandniece (see v. 48).

24:22 *half a shekel.* See note on 20:16; see also Ex 38:26.

24:32–33 See note on 18:2.

24:34–49 The servant explained his mission to Rebekah's family. His speech, which summarizes the narrative of the earlier part of the chapter, is an excellent example of the ancient storyteller's art, which was designed to fix the details of a story in the hearer's memory.

24:40 *before whom I walk.* See notes on 5:22; 6:8–9; 17:1.

47 And I asked her, and said, Whose daughter *art* thou? And she said, The daughter of Bethuel, Nahor's son, whom Milcah bare unto him: and I [a]put the earring upon her face, and the bracelets upon her hands.

48 [a]And I bowed down my head, and worshipped the LORD, and blessed the LORD God of my master Abraham, which had led me in the right way to take [b]my master's brother's daughter unto his son.

49 And now if ye will [a]deal kindly and truly with my master, tell me: and if not, tell me; that I may turn to the right hand, or to the left.

50 Then Laban and Bethuel answered and said, [a]The thing proceedeth from the LORD: we cannot [b]speak unto thee bad or good.

51 Behold, Rebekah [a]*is* before thee, take *her,* and go, and let her be thy master's son's wife, as the LORD hath spoken.

52 And it came to pass, that, when Abraham's servant heard their words, he [a]worshipped the LORD, *bowing himself* to the earth.

53 And the servant brought forth [a][1]jewels of silver, and jewels of gold, and raiment, and gave *them* to Rebekah: he gave also to her brother and to her mother [b]precious things.

54 And they did eat and drink, he and the men that *were* with him, and tarried all night; and they rose up in the morning, and he said, [a]Send me away unto my master.

55 And her brother and her mother said, Let the damsel abide with us [1]*a few* days, at the least ten; after *that* she shall go.

56 And he said unto them, Hinder me not, seeing the LORD hath prospered my way; send me away that I may go to my master.

57 And they said, We will call the damsel, and inquire at her mouth.

58 And they called Rebekah, and said unto her, Wilt thou go with this man? And she said, I will go.

59 And they sent away Rebekah their sister, and [a]her nurse, and Abraham's servant, and his men.

60 And they blessed Rebekah, and said unto her, Thou *art* our sister, be thou [a]*the mother* of thousands of millions, and [b]let thy seed possess the gate of those which hate them.

61 ¶ And Rebekah arose, and her damsels, and they rode upon the camels, and followed the man: and the servant took Rebekah, and went his way.

62 And Isaac came from the way of the [a]well Lahai-roi; for he dwelt in the south country.

63 And Isaac went out [a][1]to meditate in the field at the eventide: and he lift up his eyes, and saw, and behold, the camels *were* coming.

64 And Rebekah lift up her eyes, and when she saw Isaac, [a]she lighted off the camel.

65 For she had said unto the servant, What man *is* this that walketh in the field to meet us? And the servant had said, It *is* my master: therefore she took a vail, and covered herself.

66 And the servant told Isaac all things that he had done.

67 And Isaac brought her into his mother Sarah's tent, and took Rebekah, and she became his wife; and he loved her: and Isaac [a]was comforted after his mother's *death.*

The death of Abraham

25 Then again Abraham took a wife, and her name *was* Keturah.

2 And [a]she bare him Zimran, and Jokshan, and Medan, and Midian, and Ishbak, and Shuah.

3 And Jokshan begat Sheba, and Dedan. And the sons of Dedan were Asshurim, and Letushim, and Leummim.

4 And the sons of Midian; Ephah, and Epher, and Hanoch, and Abidah, and Eldaah. All these *were* the children of Keturah.

5 And [a]Abraham gave all that he had unto Isaac.

6 But unto the sons of the concubines, which Abraham had, Abraham gave gifts, and [a]sent them away from Isaac his son, while he yet lived, eastward, unto [b]the east country.

7 And these *are* the days of the years of Abraham's life which he lived, an hundred threescore and fifteen years.

8 Then Abraham gave up the ghost, and [a]died in a good old age, an old man, and full *of years;* and [b]was gathered to his people.

9 And [a]his sons Isaac and Ishmael buried him in the cave of Machpelah, in the field of

24:47 [a]Ezek. 16:11,12
24:48 [a]ver. 26 [b]ch. 22:23
24:49 [a]ch. 47:29; Josh. 2:14
24:50 [a]Ps. 118:23; Mat. 21:42 [b]ch. 31:24
24:51 [a]ch. 20:15
24:52 [a]ver. 26
24:53 [1]Heb. *vessels* [a]Ex. 3:22; 11:2; 12:35 [b]2 Chr. 21:3; Ezra 1:6
24:54 [a]ver. 56,59
24:55 [1]Or, *a full year, or ten* months
24:59 [a]ch. 35:8
24:60 [a]ch. 17:16 [b]ch. 22:17
24:62 [a]ch. 25:11
24:63 [1]Or, *to pray* [a]Josh. 1:8; Ps. 1:2; 77:12; 119:15; 143:5
24:64 [a]Josh. 15:18
24:67 [a]ch. 38:12
25:2 [a]1 Chr. 1:32
25:5 [a]ch. 24:36
25:6 [a]ch. 21:14 [b]Judg. 6:3
25:8 [a]ch. 15:15 [b]ch. 35:29; 49:33
25:9 [a]ch. 35:29; 50:13

24:53 The rich gifts bestowed on Rebekah and her family indicated the wealth of the household into which she was being asked to marry—far from her loved ones and homeland.
24:60 See 22:17 and note.
24:62 *the well Lahai-roi.* See note on 16:14.
24:65 *she took a vail, and covered herself.* Apparently a sign that she was unmarried (cf. 38:14,19).
24:67 *tent.* Often used as a bridal chamber (see Ps 19:4–5).
25:1 *again Abraham took a wife.* Or "married another woman"—his "concubine" (1 Chr 1:32). *took.* Or "had taken", since Abraham would have been 140 years old at this time if the order is chronological.
25:5 *gave all that he had unto Isaac.* The law of primogeniture provided that at least a double share of the father's property be given to the firstborn son when the father died (Deut 21:15–17). Parallels to this practice come from Nuzi, from Larsa in the Old Babylonian period and from Assyria in the Middle Assyrian period. Isaac was Abraham's firstborn son according to law.
25:6 *concubines.* Secondary wives; polygamy was practiced even by godly men in ancient times, though it was not the original divine intention (see note on 4:19). *gifts.* These doubtless represented the inheritance left to Abraham's other sons.
25:7 *an hundred threescore and fifteen years.* Abraham lived for a full century after "he departed out of Haran" (12:4).
25:8 *died in a good old age.* As God had promised (see 15:15). *an old man, and full of years.* A phrase used also of the patriarch Job (see Job 42:17). *was gathered to his people.* Joined his ancestors and/or deceased relatives in death (see 2 Ki 22:20; 2 Chr 34:28).
25:9 *Isaac and Ishmael.* Isaac, legally the firstborn (see note on v. 5), is listed first.

Ephron the son of Zohar the Hittite, which *is* before Mamre;

10 [a]The field which Abraham purchased of the sons of Heth: [b]there was Abraham buried, and Sarah his wife.

11 And it came to pass after the death of Abraham, that God blessed his son Isaac; and Isaac dwelt by the [a]well Lahai-roi.

The descendants of Ishmael

12 ¶ Now these *are* the generations of Ishmael, Abraham's son, [a]whom Hagar the Egyptian, Sarah's handmaid, bare unto Abraham:

13 And [a]these *are* the names of the sons of Ishmael, by their names, according to their generations: the firstborn of Ishmael, Nebajoth; and Kedar, and Adbeel, and Mibsam,

14 And Mishma, and Dumah, and Massa,

15 [1]Hadar, and Tema, Jetur, Naphish, and Kedemah:

16 These *are* the sons of Ishmael, and these *are* their names, by their towns, and by their castles; [a]twelve princes according to their nations.

17 And these *are* the years of the life of Ishmael, an hundred and thirty and seven years: and [a]he gave up the ghost and died; and was gathered unto his people.

18 [a]And they dwelt from Havilah unto Shur, that *is* before Egypt, as thou goest towards Assyria: *and* he [1]died [b]in the presence of all his brethren.

Jacob and Esau

19 ¶ And these *are* the generations of Isaac, Abraham's son: [a]Abraham begat Isaac:

20 And Isaac was forty years old when he took Rebekah to wife, [a]the daughter of Bethuel the Syrian of Padan-aram, [b]the sister to Laban the Syrian.

21 And Isaac intreated the LORD for his wife, because she *was* barren: [a]and the LORD was intreated of him, and [b]Rebekah his wife conceived.

22 And the children struggled together within her; and she said, If *it be* so, why *am* I thus? [a]And she went to inquire of the LORD.

23 And the LORD said unto her,

[a]Two nations *are* in thy womb,
And two manner of people shall be separated from thy bowels;
And [b]*the one* people shall be stronger than *the other* people;
And [c]the elder shall serve the younger.

24 ¶ And when her days to be delivered were fulfilled, behold, *there were* twins in her womb.

25 And the first came out red, [a]all over like a hairy garment; and they called his name Esau.

26 And after that came his brother out, and [a]his hand took hold on Esau's heel; and [b]his name was called Jacob: and Isaac *was* threescore years old when she bare them.

27 And the boys grew: and Esau was [a]a cunning hunter, a man of the field; and Jacob *was* [b]a plain man, [c]dwelling in tents.

28 And Isaac loved Esau, because [1]he did [a]eat of *his* venison: [b]but Rebekah loved Jacob.

29 ¶ And Jacob sod pottage: and Esau came from the field, and he *was* faint:

30 And Esau said to Jacob, Feed me, I pray thee, [1]with that same red *pottage;* for I *am* faint: therefore was his name called [2]Edom.

31 And Jacob said, Sell me *this* day thy birthright.

32 And Esau said, Behold, I *am* [1]at the point to die: and what profit shall this birthright do to me?

33 And Jacob said, Swear to me *this* day; and he sware to him: and [a]he sold his birthright unto Jacob.

34 Then Jacob gave Esau bread and pottage of lentiles; and [a]he did eat and drink, and rose

25:10 [a]ch. 23:16 [b]ch. 49:31
25:11 [a]ch. 16:14
25:12 [a]ch. 16:15
25:13 [a]1 Chr. 1:29
25:15 [1][Or, *Hadad,* 1 Chr. 1:30]
25:16 [a]ch. 17:20
25:17 [a]ver. 8
25:18 [1]Heb. *fell* [a]1 Sam. 15:7 [b]ch. 16:12
25:19 [a]Mat. 1:2
25:20 [a]ch. 22:23 [b]ch. 24:29
25:21 [a]1 Chr. 5:20; 2 Chr. 33:13; Ezra 8:23
25:21 [b]Rom. 9:10
25:22 [a]1 Sam. 9:9; 10:22
25:23 [a]ch. 17:16; 24:60 [b]2 Sam. 8:14 [c]ch. 27:29; Mal. 1:3; Rom. 9:12
25:25 [a]ch. 27:11,16,23
25:26 [a]Hos. 12:3 [b]ch. 27:36
25:27 [a]ch. 27:3,5 [b]Job 1:1,8 [c]Heb. 11:9
25:28 [1]Heb. *venison was in his mouth* [a]ch. 27:19,25,31 [b]ch. 27:6
25:30 [1]Heb. *with that red, with that red pottage* [2][That is, *Red*]
25:32 [1]Heb. *going to die*
25:33 [a]Heb. 12:16
25:34 [a]Eccl. 8:15; Is. 22:13; 1 Cor. 15:32

25:11 *well Lahai-roi.* See note on 16:14.

25:12 *generations.* See note on 2:4.

25:13 *names of the sons of Ishmael.* Many are Arab names, giving credence to the Arab tradition that Ishmael is their ancestor.

25:16 *twelve princes.* Twelve major tribes descended from Abraham's son Ishmael (as predicted in 17:20)—as was also true of Abraham's brother Nahor (see note on 22:23–24).

‡25:18 *died.* Lit. "he fell." May have the meaning "he settled" or "he dwelt." *in the presence.* Perhaps "in defiance of." See note on 16:12; or possibly "to the east of" (see also 25:6).

25:19 *generations.* See note on 2:4.

25:20 *Padan-aram.* Means "plain of Aram," another name for Aram-naharaim (Northwest Mesopotamia; see note on 24:10).

25:22 *struggled together.* The struggle between Jacob and Esau began in the womb (see also v. 26). *went.* Perhaps to a nearby place of worship.

25:23 *the elder shall serve the younger.* The ancient law of primogeniture (see note on v. 5) provided that, under ordinary circumstances, the younger of two sons would be subservient to the older. God's election of the younger son highlights the fact that God's people are the product not of natural or worldly development but of His sovereign intervention in the affairs of men (see note on 11:30). Part of this verse is quoted in Rom 9:10–12 as an example of God's sovereign right to do whatever He pleases (Ps 115:3)—not in an arbitrary way (see Rom 9:14), but according to His own perfect will.

25:24–26 For another unusual birth of twin boys see 38:27–30.

25:25 *red.* A pun on Edom, one of Esau's other names (Esau may mean "hairy").

25:26 *his hand took hold on Esau's heel.* Hostility between the Israelites (Jacob's descendants) and Edomites (Esau's descendants) became the rule rather than the exception (see, e.g., Num 20:14–21; Obad 9–10). *Jacob.* The name became proverbial for the unsavory quality of deceptiveness (see Jer 9:4).

25:31 *Sell me . . . thy birthright.* In ancient times the birthright included the inheritance rights of the firstborn (see Heb 12:16; see also note on v. 5). Jacob was ever the schemer, seeking by any means to gain advantage over others. But it was by God's appointment and care, not Jacob's wits, that he came into the blessing.

25:33 *Swear to me.* A verbal oath was all that was required to make the transaction legal.

25:34 *lentiles.* A small pea-like annual plant, the pods of which turn reddish-brown when boiled. It grows well even in bad soil

up, and went his way: thus Esau despised *his* birthright.

Isaac and Abimelech

26 And there was a famine in the land, besides the [a]first famine that was in the days of Abraham. And Isaac went unto [b]Abimelech king of the Philistims unto Gerar.

2 And the LORD appeared unto him, and said, Go not down into Egypt; dwell in [a]the land which I shall tell thee of:

3 [a]Sojourn in this land, and [b]I will be with thee, and [c]will bless thee; for unto thee, and unto thy seed, [d]I will give all these countries, and I will perform [e]the oath which I sware unto Abraham thy father;

4 And [a]I will make thy seed to multiply as the stars of heaven, and will give unto thy seed all these countries; [b]and in thy seed shall all the nations of the earth be blessed;

5 [a]Because that Abraham obeyed my voice, and kept my charge, my commandments, my statutes, and my laws.

6 And Isaac dwelt in Gerar:

7 And the men of the place asked *him* of his wife; and [a]he said, She *is* my sister: for [b]he feared to say, *She is* my wife; lest, *said he,* the men of the place should kill me for Rebekah; because she [c]*was* fair to look upon.

8 And it came to pass, when he had been there a long time, that Abimelech king of the Philistims looked out at a window, and saw, and behold, Isaac *was* sporting with Rebekah his wife.

9 And Abimelech called Isaac, and said, Behold, of a surety she *is* thy wife: and how saidst thou, She *is* my sister? And Isaac said unto him, Because I said, Lest I die for her.

10 And Abimelech said, What *is* this thou hast done unto us? one of the people might lightly have lien with thy wife, and [a]thou shouldest have brought guiltiness upon us.

11 And Abimelech charged all *his* people, saying, He that [a]toucheth this man or his wife shall surely be put to death.

12 Then Isaac sowed in that land, and [1]received in the same year [a]an hundredfold: and the LORD [b]blessed him.

13 And the man [a]waxed great, and [1]went forward, and grew until he became very great:

14 For he had possession of flocks, and possession of herds, and great store of [1]servants: and the Philistims [a]envied him.

15 For all the wells [a]which his father's servants had digged in the days of Abraham his father, the Philistims had stopped them, and filled them *with* earth.

16 And Abimelech said unto Isaac, Go from us; for [a]thou art much mightier than we.

17 ¶ And Isaac departed thence, and pitched his tent in the valley of Gerar, and dwelt there.

18 And Isaac digged again the wells of water, which they had digged in the days of Abraham his father; for the Philistims had stopped them after the death of Abraham: [a]and he called their names after the names by which his father had called them.

19 And Isaac's servants digged in the valley, and found there a well of [1]springing water.

20 And the herdmen of Gerar [a]did strive with Isaac's herdmen, saying, The water *is* ours: and he called the name of the well [1]Esek; because they strove with him.

21 And they digged another well, and strove for that also: and he called the name of it [1]Sitnah.

22 And he removed from thence, and digged another well; and for that they strove not: and he called the name of it [1]Rehoboth; and he said, For now the LORD hath made

26:1 [a]ch. 12:10 [b]ch. 20:2
26:2 [a]ch. 12:1
26:3 [a]ch. 20:1; Ps. 39:12; Heb. 11:9 [b]ch. 28:15 [c]ch. 12:2 [d]ch. 13:15 [e]ch. 22:16; Ps. 105:9
26:4 [a]ch. 15:5; 22:17 [b]ch. 12:3; 22:18
26:5 [a]ch. 22:16,18
26:7 [a]ch. 12:13; 20:2,13 [b]Prov. 29:25 [c]ch. 24:16
26:10 [a]ch. 20:9
26:11 [a]Ps. 105:15
26:12 [1]Heb. *found* [a]Mat. 13:8; Mark 4:8 [b]ver. 3; Job 42:12
26:13 [1]Heb. *went going* [a]ch. 24:35; Prov. 10:22
26:14 [1]Or, *husbandry* [a]ch. 37:11; Eccl. 4:4
26:15 [a]ch. 21:30
26:16 [a]Ex. 1:9
26:18 [a]ch. 21:31
26:19 [1]Heb. *living*
26:20 [1]That is, *Contention* [a]ch. 21:25
26:21 [1]That is, *Hatred*
26:22 [1]That is, *Room*

and has provided an important source of nourishment in the Near East since ancient times (see 2 Sam 17:28; 23:11; Ezek 4:9). *Esau despised his birthright.* In so doing, he proved himself to be "profane" (Heb 12:16), since at the heart of the birthright were the covenant promises that Isaac had inherited from Abraham.

26:1–33 The events of some of these verses (e.g., vv. 1–11) occurred before the birth of Esau and Jacob. Verses 1–11 are placed here to highlight the fact that the birthright and blessing Jacob struggled to obtain from his father (see 25:22,31–33; 27:5–29) involved the covenant inheritance of Abraham that Isaac had received.

26:1 *the first famine . . . in the days of Abraham.* See 12:10. *Abimelech.* Probably the son or grandson of the earlier king who bore the same name (see 20:2). *Philistims.* See note on 10:14. *Gerar.* See note on 20:1.

26:2 *appeared.* See note on 12:7.

26:3 *I will be with thee.* God's promise to be a sustainer and protector of His people is repeated often (see, e.g., v. 24; 28:15; 31:3; Josh 1:5; Is 41:10; Jer 1:8,19; Mat 28:20; Acts 18:10; see also Gen 17:7 and note). *the oath which I sware unto Abraham thy father.* See 22:16–18.

26:4 *seed . . . as the stars of heaven.* See 13:16; 15:5 and notes. *in thy seed shall all the nations of the earth be blessed.* See note on 12:2–3.

26:5 *Because that Abraham obeyed my voice.* See note on 17:9. *charge . . . commandments . . . statutes . . . laws.* Legal language describing various aspects of the divine regulations that God's people were expected to keep (see Lev 26:14–15,46; Deut 11:1). Addressing Israel after the covenant at Sinai, the author of Genesis used language that strictly applied only to that covenant. But he emphasized to Israel that their father Abraham had been obedient to God's will in his time and that they must follow his example if they were to receive the covenant promises.

26:7 *because she was fair to look upon.* See 12:11,14.

26:8 *sporting* [i.e.,"caressing"]. The word in Hebrew (a form of the verb translated "laugh" in 17:17; 18:12–13,15; 21:6 and "mock" in 21:9) is yet another pun on Isaac's name.

26:16 *thou art much mightier than we.* An indication that the covenant promises were being fulfilled. Already in the days of the patriarchs, the presence of God's people in the land was seen as a threat by the peoples of the world. As the world's people pursued their own godless living, God's people aroused their hostility. A similar complaint was voiced by an Egyptian pharaoh hundreds of years later (Ex 1:9).

26:20 *The water is ours:* In those arid regions, disputes over water rights and pasturelands were common (see 13:6–11; 21:25; 36:7).

room for us, and we shall [a]be fruitful in the land.

23 And he went up from thence to Beer-sheba.

24 And the LORD appeared unto him the same night, and said, [a]I *am* the God of Abraham thy father: [b]fear not, for [c]I *am* with thee, and will bless thee, and multiply thy seed for my servant Abraham's sake.

25 And he [a]builded an altar there, and [b]called upon the name of the LORD, and pitched his tent there: and there Isaac's servants digged a well.

26 Then Abimelech went to him from Gerar, and Ahuzzath *one* of his friends, [a]and Phichol the chief captain of his army.

27 And Isaac said unto them, Wherefore come ye to me, seeing [a]ye hate me, and have [b]sent me away from you?

28 And they said, [1]We saw certainly that the LORD [a]was with thee: and we said, Let there be now an oath betwixt us, *even* betwixt us and thee, and let us make a covenant with thee;

29 [1]That thou wilt do us no hurt, as we have not touched thee, and as we have done unto thee nothing but good, and have sent thee away in peace: [a]thou *art* now the blessed of the LORD.

30 [a]And he made them a feast, and they did eat and drink.

31 And they rose up betimes in the morning, and [a]sware one to another: and Isaac sent them away, and they departed from him in peace.

32 And it came to pass the same day, that Isaac's servants came, and told him concerning the well which they had digged, and said unto him, We have found water.

33 And he called it [1]Shebah: [a]therefore the name of the city *is* [2]Beer-sheba unto this day.

34 [a]And Esau was forty years old when he took to wife Judith the daughter of Beeri the Hittite, and Bashemath the daughter of Elon the Hittite:

35 Which [a]were [1]a grief of mind unto Isaac and to Rebekah.

Jacob's stolen blessing

27 And it came to pass, that when Isaac was old, and [a]his eyes were dim, so that he could not see, he called Esau his eldest son, and said unto him, My son: and he said unto him, Behold, *here am* I.

2 And he said, Behold now, I am old, I [a]know not the day of my death:

3 [a]Now therefore take, I pray thee, thy weapons, thy quiver and thy bow, and go out to the field, and [1]take me *some* venison;

4 And make me savoury meat, such as I love, and bring *it* to me, that I may eat; that my soul [a]may bless thee before I die.

5 And Rebekah heard when Isaac spake to Esau his son. And Esau went to the field to hunt for venison, *and* to bring *it*.

6 And Rebekah spake unto Jacob her son, saying, Behold, I heard thy father speak unto Esau thy brother, saying,

7 Bring me venison, and make me savoury meat, that I may eat, and bless thee before the LORD before my death.

8 Now therefore, my son, [a]obey my voice according to *that* which I command thee.

9 Go now to the flock, and fetch me from thence two good kids of the goats; and I will make them [a]savoury meat for thy father, such as he loveth:

10 And thou shalt bring *it* to thy father, that he may eat, and that he [a]may bless thee before his death.

11 And Jacob said to Rebekah his mother, Behold, [a]Esau my brother *is* a hairy man, and I *am* a smooth man:

12 My father peradventure will [a]feel me, and I shall seem to him as a deceiver; and I shall bring [b]a curse upon me, and not a blessing.

13 And his mother said unto him, [a]Upon

26:22 [a]ch. 17:6; 28:3; 41:52; Ex. 1:7
26:24 [a]ch. 17:7; 24:12 [b]ch. 15:1 [c]ver. 3,4
26:25 [a]ch. 12:7; 13:18 [b]Ps. 116:17
26:26 [a]ch. 21:22
26:27 [a]Judg. 11:7 [b]ver. 16
26:28 [1]Heb. *Seeing we saw* [a]ch. 21:22,23
26:29 [1]Heb. *If thou shalt, etc.* [a]ch. 24:31; Ps. 115:15
26:30 [a]ch. 19:3
26:31 [a]ch. 21:31
26:33 [1]That is, *An oath* [2]That is, *The well of the oath* [a]ch. 21:31
26:34 [a]ch. 36:2
26:35 [1]Heb. *bitterness of spirit* [a]ch. 27:46; 28:1,8
27:1 [a]ch. 48:10; 1 Sam. 3:2
27:2 [a]Prov. 27:1; Jas. 4:14
27:3 [1]Heb. *hunt* [a]ch. 25:27,28
27:4 [a]ver. 27; ch. 48:9,15; 49:28; Deut. 33:1
27:8 [a]ver. 13
27:9 [a]ver. 4
27:10 [a]ver. 4
27:11 [a]ch. 25:25
27:12 [a]ver. 22 [b]ch. 9:25; Deut. 27:18
27:13 [a]ch. 43:9; 1 Sam. 25:24; 2 Sam. 14:9; Mat. 27:25

26:25 *builded an altar.* See note on 12:7. *called upon the name of the LORD.* See 4:26 and note.
26:26 *Phichol.* See note on 21:22.
26:30 *made them a feast.* Covenants were often concluded with a shared meal, signifying the bond of friendship (see 31:54; Ex 24:11).
26:33 *the name of the city is Beer-sheba.* See note on 21:31.
26:34 *Esau was forty years old when he took to wife.* As had his father Isaac (see 25:20). Forty years was roughly equivalent to a generation in later times (see Num 32:13). *Judith . . . Bashemath.* In addition to these two wives, Esau also married Mahalath, who was the sister of Nebajoth and daughter of Ishmael (28:9). The Esau genealogy of ch. 36 also mentions three wives, but they are identified as "Adah the daughter of Elon the Hittite," "Aholibamah the daughter of Anah . . . the Hivite" and "Bashemath, Ishmael's daughter, sister of Nebajoth" (36:2–3). Possibly the lists have suffered in transmission, or perhaps alternate names or nicknames are used. It may also be that Esau married more than three wives.
26:35 *were a grief of mind.* Isaac and Rebekah were determined not to allow Jacob to make the same mistake of marrying Hittite or Canaanite women (see 27:46–28:2).
27:1 *his eyes were dim, so that he could not see.* In ancient times, blindness and near blindness were common among elderly people (see 48:10; 1 Sam 4:15). *here am I.* See note on 22:1.
27:4 *savoury meat, such as I love.* Rebekah and Jacob took advantage of Isaac's love for a certain kind of food (see vv. 9,14). *my soul may bless thee before I die.* Oral statements, including deathbed bequests (see 49:28–33), had legal force in ancient Near Eastern law. *bless.* See note on v. 36.
‡27:5 *heard.* She was eavesdropping.
27:6 *Rebekah.* Throughout the Jacob story the author develops a wordplay on "birthright" (*bekorah*) and "blessing" (*berakah*), both of which Jacob seeks to obtain; and Rebekah (*ribqah*) does her best to further the cause of her favorite son. *spake unto Jacob her son.* The parental favoritism mentioned in 25:28 is about to bear its poisonous fruit.
27:8 *my son, obey my voice according to that which I command thee.* Rebekah proves to be just as deceitful as Jacob, whose very name signifies deceit (see v. 36; 25:26 and note).

me *be* thy curse, my son: only obey my voice, and go fetch me *them.*

14 And he went, and fetched, and brought *them* to his mother: and his mother [a]made savoury meat, such as his father loved.

15 And Rebekah took [a][1]goodly raiment of her eldest son Esau, which *were* with her in the house, and put them upon Jacob her younger son:

16 And she put the skins of the kids of the goats upon his hands, and upon the smooth of his neck:

17 And she gave the savoury meat and the bread, which she had prepared, into the hand of her son Jacob.

18 And he came unto his father, and said, My father: and he said, Here *am* I; who *art* thou, my son?

19 And Jacob said unto his father, I *am* Esau thy firstborn; I have done according as thou badest me: arise, I pray thee, sit and eat of my venison, [a]that thy soul may bless me.

20 And Isaac said unto his son, How *is* it *that* thou hast found *it so* quickly, my son? And he said, Because the LORD thy God brought *it* [1]to me.

21 And Isaac said unto Jacob, Come near, I pray thee, that I [a]may feel thee, my son, whether thou *be* my very son Esau or not.

22 And Jacob went near unto Isaac his father; and he felt him, and said, The voice *is* Jacob's voice, but the hands *are* the hands of Esau.

23 And he discerned him not, because [a]his hands were hairy, as his brother Esau's hands: so he blessed him.

24 And he said, *Art* thou my very son Esau? And he said, I *am.*

25 And he said, Bring *it* near to me, and I will eat of my son's venison, [a]that my soul may bless thee. And he brought *it* near to him, and he did eat: and he brought him wine, and he drank.

26 And his father Isaac said unto him, Come near now, and kiss me, my son.

27 And he came near, and kissed him: and he smelled the smell of his raiment, and blessed him, and said,

See, [a]the smell of my son *is* as the
smell of a field which the LORD hath
blessed:

27:14 [a]Prov. 23:3; Luke 21:34
27:15 [1]Heb. *desirable* [a]ver. 27
27:19 [a]ver. 4
27:20 [1]Heb. *before me*
27:21 [a]ver. 12
27:23 [a]ver. 16
27:25 [a]ver. 4,10,19,31
27:27 [a]Sol. 4:11; Hos. 14:6
27:28 [a]Heb. 11:20 [b]Deut. 33:13,28; 2 Sam. 1:21; Ps. 133:3; Mic. 5:7 [c]ch. 45:18 [d]Deut. 33:28
27:29 [a]ch. 9:25; 25:23 [b]ch. 49:8 [c]ch. 12:3; Num. 24:9; Zeph. 2:8
27:31 [a]ver. 4
27:33 [1]Heb. *trembled with a great trembling greatly* [2]Heb. *hunted* [a]ch. 28:3,4; Rom. 11:29
27:34 [a]Heb. 12:17
27:36 [1]That is, *A supplanter* [a]ch. 25:26 [b]ch. 25:33
27:37 [1]Or, *supported* [a]Fulfilled, 2 Sam. 8:14 [b]ver. 28
27:38 [a]Heb. 12:17

28 Therefore [a]God give thee of [b]the dew
of heaven,
And [c]the fatness of the earth,
And [d]plenty of corn and wine:
29 [a]Let people serve thee,
And nations bow down to thee:
Be lord over thy brethren,
And [b]let thy mother's sons bow down
to thee:
[c]Cursed *be* every one that curseth
thee,
And blessed *be* he that blesseth thee.

30 And it came to pass, as soon as Isaac had made an end of blessing Jacob, and Jacob was yet scarce gone out from the presence of Isaac his father, that Esau his brother came in from his hunting.

31 And he also had made savoury meat, and brought *it* unto his father, and said unto his father, Let my father arise, and [a]eat of his son's venison, that thy soul may bless me.

32 And Isaac his father said unto him, Who *art* thou? And he said, I *am* thy son, thy firstborn Esau.

33 And Isaac [1]trembled very exceedingly, and said, Who? where *is* he that hath [2]taken venison, and brought *it* me, and I have eaten of all before thou camest, and have blessed him? yea, [a]*and* he shall be blessed.

34 And when Esau heard the words of his father, [a]he cried with a great and exceeding bitter cry, and said unto his father, Bless me, *even* me also, O my father.

35 And he said, Thy brother came with subtilty, and hath taken away thy blessing.

36 And he said, [a]Is not he rightly named [1]Jacob? for he hath supplanted me these two times: [b]he took away my birthright; and behold, now he hath taken away my blessing. And he said, Hast thou not reserved a blessing for me?

37 And Isaac answered and said unto Esau, [a]Behold, I have made him thy lord, and all his brethren have I given to him for servants; and [b]with corn and wine have I [1]sustained him: and what shall I do now unto thee, my son?

38 And Esau said unto his father, Hast thou but one blessing, my father? bless me, *even* me also, O my father. And Esau lift up his voice, [a]and wept.

27:13 *Upon me be thy curse.* Cf. the similar self-imprecation in Mat 27:25.

27:20 *thy God.* Consistent with Jacob's language elsewhere (31:5,42; 32:9). Not until his safe return from Haran did he speak of the Lord as his own God (cf. 28:20–22; 33:18–20).

27:24 *Art thou my very son Esau?* To the very end of the charade, Isaac remained suspicious.

27:27 *kissed him.* In his attempt to obtain the covenant blessing, Jacob the father of Israel betrayed with a kiss. Jesus the great Son of Israel, who ultimately obtained the blessing for Israel, was betrayed with a kiss (Mat 26:48–49; Luke 22:48).

27:29 *Be lord over thy brethren.* Isaac was unwittingly blessing Jacob and thus fulfilling God's promise to Rebekah in 25:23.

27:33 *yea, and he shall be blessed.* The ancient world believed that blessings and curses had a kind of magical power to accomplish what they pronounced. But Isaac, as heir and steward of God's covenant blessing, acknowledged that he had solemnly transmitted that heritage to Jacob by way of a legally binding bequest (see note on v. 4).

27:34 *great and exceeding bitter cry.* Esau's tears provided "no place for repentance" (Heb 12:17).

27:36 *Is not he rightly named Jacob?* Jacob means "he grasps the heel" (figuratively, "he deceives"); see 25:26 and note. *he took away my birthright . . . now he hath taken away my blessing.* The Hebrew for "birthright" is *bekorah,* and for "blessing" it is *berakah* (see note on v. 6). Though Esau tried to separate birthright from blessing, the former led inevitably to the latter, since both involved the inheritance of the firstborn (see Heb 12:16–17).

39 And Isaac his father answered and said unto him,
Behold, [a]thy dwelling shall be [1]the
fatness of the earth,
And of the dew of heaven from above;
40 And by thy sword shalt thou live,
And [a]shalt serve thy brother;
And [b]it shall come to pass when thou
shalt have the dominion,
That thou shalt break his yoke from off
thy neck.

Isaac sends Jacob to Laban

41 ¶ And Esau [a]hated Jacob because of the blessing wherewith his father blessed him: and Esau said in his heart, [b]The days of mourning for my father are at hand; [c]then will I slay my brother Jacob.

42 And these words of Esau her elder son were told to Rebekah: and she sent and called Jacob her younger son, and said unto him, Behold, thy brother Esau, as touching thee, doth [a]comfort himself, *purposing* to kill thee.

43 Now therefore, my son, obey my voice; and arise, flee thou to Laban my brother [a]to Haran;

44 And tarry with him a few days, until thy brother's fury turn away;

45 Until thy brother's anger turn away from thee, and he forget *that* which thou hast done to him: then I will send, and fetch thee from thence: why should I be deprived also of you both *in* one day?

46 And Rebekah said to Isaac, [a]I am weary of my life because of the daughters of Heth: [b]if Jacob take a wife of the daughters of Heth, such as these *which are* of the daughters of the land, what good shall my life do me?

28 And Isaac called Jacob, and [a]blessed him, and charged him, and said unto him, [b]Thou shalt not take a wife of the daughters of Canaan.

2 [a]Arise, go to [b]Padan-aram, to the house of [c]Bethuel thy mother's father; and take thee a wife from thence of the daughters of [d]Laban thy mother's brother.

3 [a]And God Almighty bless thee, and make thee fruitful, and multiply thee, that thou mayest be [1]a multitude of people;

4 And give thee [a]the blessing of Abraham, to thee, and to thy seed with thee; that thou mayest inherit the land [b][1]wherein thou art a stranger, which God gave unto Abraham.

5 And Isaac sent away Jacob: and he went to Padan-aram unto Laban, son of Bethuel the Syrian, the brother of Rebekah, Jacob's and Esau's mother.

6 When Esau saw that Isaac had blessed Jacob, and sent him away to Padan-aram, to take him a wife from thence; and that as he blessed him he gave him a charge, saying, Thou shalt not take a wife of the daughters of Canaan;

7 And that Jacob obeyed his father and his mother, and was gone to Padan-aram;

8 And Esau seeing [a]that the daughters of Canaan [1]pleased not Isaac his father;

9 Then went Esau unto Ishmael, and took unto the wives which he had [a]Mahalath the daughter of Ishmael Abraham's son, [b]the sister of Nebajoth, to be his wife.

Jacob's dream at Beth-el

10 ¶ And Jacob [a]went out from Beer-sheba, and went toward [b]Haran.

11 And he lighted upon a *certain* place, and tarried there all night, because the sun was set; and he took of the stones of *that* place, and put *them for* his pillows, and lay down in that place to sleep.

12 And he [a]dreamed, and behold a ladder set up on the earth, and the top of it reached to heaven: and behold [b]the angels of God ascending and descending on it.

13 [a]And behold, the LORD stood above it, and said, [b]I *am* the LORD God of Abraham thy father, and the God of Isaac: [c]the land whereon thou liest, to thee will I give it, and to thy seed;

14 And [a]thy seed shall be as the dust of the earth, and thou shalt [1]spread abroad [b]to the west, and to the east, and to the north, and to

27:39 [1]Or, *of the fatness* [a]ver. 28; Heb. 11:20
27:40 [a]ch. 25:23; 2 Sam. 8:14; Obad. 18-20 [b]2 Ki. 8:20
27:41 [a]ch. 37:4,8 [b]ch. 50:3,4,10 [c]Obad. 10
27:42 [a]Ps. 64:5
27:43 [a]ch. 11:31
27:46 [a]ch. 26:35; 28:8 [b]ch. 24:3
28:1 [a]ch. 27:33 [b]ch. 24:3
28:2 [a]Hos. 12:12 [b]ch. 25:20 [c]ch. 22:23 [d]ch. 24:29
28:3 [1]Heb. *an assembly of people* [a]ch. 17:1,6
28:4 [1]Heb. *of thy sojournings* [a]ch. 12:2 [b]ch. 17:8
28:8 [1]Heb. were *evil in the eyes, etc.* [a]ch. 24:3; 26:35
28:9 [a]ch. 36:3, she is called *Bashemath* [b]ch. 25:13
28:10 [a]Hos. 12:12 [b]Called, Acts 7:2; *Charran*
28:12 [a]ch. 41:1 [b]John 1:51; Heb. 1:14
28:13 [a]ch. 35:1; 48:3 [b]ch. 26:24 [c]ch. 13:15; 35:12
28:14 [1]Heb. *break forth* [a]ch. 13:16 [b]ch. 13:14; Deut. 12:20

‡27:39 *shall be the fatness of the earth . . . of the dew of heaven.* The Hebrew suggests Esau would live *away from* the fatness of the earth, *away from* the dew of heaven; i.e. outside Canaan. Cf. v. 28. Isaac's secondary blessing of Esau could be only a parody of his primary blessing of Jacob.
27:40 See 25:23 and notes on 25:22,26.
27:43 *obey my voice.* Bad advice earlier (see vv. 8,13), but sensible counsel this time.
27:44 *a few days.* Twenty years, as it turned out (see 31:38,41).
27:45 *you both.* Either Jacob and Isaac or Jacob and Esau, who would become a target for blood revenge if he killed Jacob (cf. 2 Sam 14:6–7).
27:46 See note on 26:35.
28:2 *Padan-aram.* Means "plain of Aram," another name for Aram-naharaim (see note on 24:10). *take thee a wife from thence.* See 24:3–4.
28:3 *God Almighty.* See note on 17:1.
28:4 *the blessing of Abraham.* For Paul's application of this phrase to Christian believers see Gal 3:14.
28:5 See map, p. 48.
28:9 *unto the wives which he had.* See 26:34 and note.
28:11 *of the stones . . . for his pillows.* In ancient times headrests (e.g., in Egypt) were often quite hard, sometimes being made of metal. People were used to sleeping on the ground.
28:12 *ladder.* Not a ladder with rungs, it was more likely a stairway such as mounted the sloping side of a ziggurat (see note on 11:4). *angels of God ascending and descending on it.* A sign that the Lord offered to be Jacob's God. Jesus told a disciple that he would "see heaven open, and the angels of God ascending and descending upon the Son of man" (John 1:51). Jesus Himself is the bridge between heaven and earth (see John 14:6), the only "mediator between God and men" (1 Tim 2:5).
28:13 *the LORD stood above it.* Mesopotamian ziggurats were topped with a small shrine where worshipers prayed to their gods.
28:14 *as the dust of the earth.* See note on 13:16. *in thee. . . shall all the families of the earth be blessed.* Repeats the blessing of 12:3.

the south: and in thee and [c]in thy seed shall all the families of the earth be blessed.

15 And behold, [a]I *am* with thee, and will [b]keep thee in all *places* whither thou goest, and will [c]bring thee again into this land; for [d]I will not leave thee, [e]until I have done *that* which I have spoken to thee of.

16 And Jacob awaked out of his sleep, and he said, Surely the LORD is in [a]this place; and I knew *it* not.

17 And he was afraid, and said, How dreadful *is* this place! this *is* none other but the house of God, and this *is* the gate of heaven.

18 And Jacob rose up early in the morning, and took the stone that he had put *for* his pillows, and [a]set it up *for* a pillar, [b]and poured oil upon the top of it.

19 And he called the name of [a]that place [1]Beth-el: but the name of *that* city *was called* Luz at the first.

20 [a]And Jacob vowed a vow, saying, If [b]God will be with me, and will keep me in this way that I go, and will give me [c]bread to eat, and raiment to put on,

21 So that [a]I come again to my father's house in peace; [b]then shall the LORD be my God:

22 And this stone, which I have set *for* a pillar, [a]shall be God's house: [b]and of all that thou shalt give me I will surely give the tenth unto thee.

Jacob meets Rachel

29 Then Jacob [1]went on his journey, [a]and came into the land of the [2]people of the east.

2 And he looked, and behold a well in the field, and lo, there *were* three flocks of sheep lying by it; for out of that well they watered the flocks: and a great stone *was* upon the well's mouth.

3 And thither were all the flocks gathered: and they rolled the stone from the well's mouth, and watered the sheep, and put the stone again upon the well's mouth in his place.

4 And Jacob said unto them, My brethren, whence *be* ye? And they said, Of Haran *are* we.

5 And he said unto them, Know ye Laban the son of Nahor? And they said, We know *him.*

6 And he said unto them, [a1]*Is* he well? And they said, *He is* well: and behold, Rachel his daughter cometh with the sheep.

7 And he said, Lo, [1]*it is* yet high day, neither *is it* time that the cattle should be gathered together: water ye the sheep, and go *and* feed *them.*

8 And they said, We cannot, until all the flocks be gathered together, and *till* they roll the stone from the well's mouth; then we water the sheep.

9 And while he yet spake with them, [a]Rachel came with her father's sheep: for she kept them.

10 And it came to pass, when Jacob saw Rachel the daughter of Laban his mother's brother, and the sheep of Laban his mother's brother, that Jacob went near, and [a]rolled the stone from the well's mouth, and watered the flock of Laban his mother's brother.

11 And Jacob [a]kissed Rachel, and lifted up his voice, and wept.

12 And Jacob told Rachel that he *was* [a]her father's brother, and that he *was* Rebekah's son: [b]and she ran and told her father.

13 And it came to pass, when Laban heard the [1]tidings of Jacob his sister's son, that [a]he ran to meet him, and embraced him, and kissed him, and brought him to his house. And he told Laban all these things.

14 And Laban said to him, [a]Surely thou *art* my bone and my flesh. And he abode with him [1]the space of a month.

15 And Laban said unto Jacob, Because thou *art* my brother, shouldest thou therefore serve me for nought? tell me, what *shall* thy wages *be?*

16 And Laban had two daughters: the name of the elder *was* Leah, and the name of the younger *was* Rachel.

17 Leah was tender eyed; but Rachel was beautiful and well favoured.

18 And Jacob loved Rachel; and said, [a]I will serve thee seven years for Rachel thy younger daughter.

19 And Laban said, *It is* better that I give her to thee, than that I should give her to another man: abide with me.

20 And Jacob [a]served seven years for Ra-

28:14 [c]ch. 12:3; 18:18; 22:18; 26:4
28:15 [a]See ver. 20,21 [b]ch. 48:16 [c]ch. 35:6 [d]Deut. 31:6,8; Josh. 1:5; 1 Ki. 8:57; Heb. 13:5 [e]Num. 23:19
28:16 [a]Ex. 3:5; Josh. 5:15
28:18 [a]ch. 31:13,45 [b]Lev. 8:10-12
28:19 [1]That is, *The house of God* [a]Judg. 1:23,26; Hos. 4:15
28:20 [a]ch. 31:13; Judg. 11:30; 2 Sam. 15:8 [b]ver. 15 [c]1 Tim. 6:8
28:21 [a]Judg. 11:31; 2 Sam. 19:24,30 [b]Deut. 26:17; 2 Sam. 15:8
28:22 [a]ch. 35:7,14 [b]Lev. 27:30
29:1 [1]Heb. *lift up his feet* [2]Heb. *children* [a]Num. 23:7; Hos. 12:12
29:6 [1]Heb. Is there *peace to him?* [a]ch. 43:27
29:7 [1]Heb. *yet the day is great*
29:9 [a]Ex. 2:16
29:10 [a]Ex. 2:17
29:11 [a]ch. 33:4; 45:14,15
29:12 [a]ch. 13:8; 14:14,16 [b]ch. 24:28
29:13 [1]Heb. *hearing* [a]ch. 24:29
29:14 [1]Heb. *a month of days* [a]ch. 2:23; Judg. 9:2; 2 Sam. 5:1; 19:12,13
29:18 [a]ch. 31:41; 2 Sam. 3:14
29:20 [a]ch. 30:26; Hos. 12:12

28:15 *I am with thee.* See note on 26:3. *I will not leave thee.* Unlike the gods of pagan religions, in which the gods were merely local deities who gave protection only within their own territories, the one true God assured Jacob that He would always be with him wherever he went.

28:17 *house of God . . . gate of heaven.* Phrases that related Jacob's stairway to the Mesopotamian ziggurats (see notes on 11:4,9).

28:18 *pillar.* A memorial of worship or of communion between man and God, common in ancient times. *poured oil upon the top of it.* To consecrate it (see Ex 30:25–29).

28:21 *come again . . . in peace.* Partially fulfilled in 33:18. *shall the LORD be my God.* For the first time Jacob considered (conditionally: "If . . .") acknowledging the God of Abraham and Isaac (see v. 13; 27:20) as his own. His full acknowledgment came only after his safe return from Haran (see 33:20 and note).

28:22 *this stone . . . shall be God's house.* In the sense that it would memorialize Jacob's meeting with God at Beth-el (Beth-el means "house of God"). *of all that thou shalt give me I will surely give the tenth to thee.* A way of acknowledging the Lord as his God and King (see note on 14:20).

29:5 *son.* Or "grandson" (see note on 10:1; see also 24:15,29).

29:9 *father's sheep: for she kept them.* The task of caring for sheep and goats in the Middle East was shared by men and women.

29:10 *rolled the stone.* A feat of unusual strength for one man, because the stone was large (see v. 2).

29:11 *wept.* For joy.

29:14 *my bone and my flesh.* A Hebrew phrase that stresses blood kinship (see, e.g., 2:23).

29:16 *Leah . . . Rachel.* The names mean "cow" and "ewe" respectively, appropriate in a herdsman's family.

chel; and they seemed unto him *but* a few days, for the love he had to her.

Jacob marries Leah and Rachel

21 ¶ And Jacob said unto Laban, Give *me* my wife, for my days are fulfilled, that I may [a]go in unto her.

22 And Laban gathered together all the men of the place, and [a]made a feast.

23 And it came to pass in the evening, that he took Leah his daughter, and brought her to him; and he went in unto her.

24 And Laban gave unto his daughter Leah Zilpah his maid *for* a handmaid.

25 And it came to pass, that in the morning, behold, it *was* Leah: and he said to Laban, What *is* this thou hast done unto me? did not I serve with thee for Rachel? wherefore then hast thou beguiled me?

26 And Laban said, It must not be so done in our [1]country, to give the younger before the firstborn.

27 [a]Fulfil her week, and we will give thee this also for the service which thou shalt serve with me yet seven other years.

28 And Jacob did so, and fulfilled her week: and he gave him Rachel his daughter to wife *also.*

29 And Laban gave to Rachel his daughter Bilhah his handmaid to be her maid.

30 And he went in also unto Rachel, and he [a]loved also Rachel more than Leah, and served with him [b]yet seven other years.

The sons of Jacob

31 ¶ And when the LORD [a]saw that Leah *was* hated, he [b]opened her womb: but Rachel *was* barren.

32 And Leah conceived, and bare a son, and she called his name [1]Reuben: for she said, Surely the LORD hath [a]looked upon my affliction; now therefore my husband will love me.

33 And she conceived again, and bare a son; and said, Because the LORD hath heard that I *was* hated, he hath therefore given me this *son* also: and she called his name [1]Simeon.

34 And she conceived again, and bare a son; and said, Now *this* time will my husband be joined unto me, because I have born him three sons: therefore was his name called [1]Levi.

35 And she conceived again, and bare a son: and she said, Now will I praise the LORD: therefore she called his name [a][1]Judah; and [2]left bearing.

30 And when Rachel saw that [a]she bare Jacob no *children,* Rachel [b]envied her sister; and said unto Jacob, Give me children, [c]or else I die.

2 And Jacob's anger was kindled against Rachel: and he said, [a]*Am* I in God's stead, who hath withheld from thee the fruit of the womb?

3 And she said, Behold [a]my maid Bilhah, go in unto her; [b]and she shall bear upon my knees, [c]that I may also [1]have children by her.

4 And she gave him Bilhah her handmaid [a]to wife: and Jacob went in unto her.

5 And Bilhah conceived, and bare Jacob a son.

6 And Rachel said, God hath [a]judged me, and hath also heard my voice, and hath given me a son: therefore called she his name [1]Dan.

7 And Bilhah Rachel's maid conceived again, and bare Jacob a second son.

8 And Rachel said, With [1]great wrestlings have I wrestled with my sister, and I have prevailed: and she called his name [2][3]Naphtali.

9 When Leah saw that she had left bearing, she took Zilpah her maid, and [a]gave her Jacob to wife.

10 And Zilpah Leah's maid bare Jacob a son.

11 And Leah said, A troop cometh: and she called his name [1]Gad.

12 And Zilpah Leah's maid bare Jacob a second son.

13 And Leah said, [1]Happy am I, for the

29:21 [a]Judg. 15:1
29:22 [a]Judg. 14:10; John 2:1,2
29:26 [1]Heb. *place*
29:27 [a]Judg. 14:12
29:30 [a]Deut. 21:15 [b]ch. 30:26; 31:41; Hos. 12:12
29:31 [a]Ps. 127:3 [b]ch. 30:1
29:32 [1]That is, *See a son* [a]Ex. 4:31; Deut. 26:7; Ps. 25:18
29:33 [1]That is, *Hearing*
29:34 [1]That is, *Joined*
29:35 [1]That is, *Praise* [2]Heb. *stood from bearing* [a]Mat. 1:2
30:1 [a]ch. 29:31 [b]ch. 37:11 [c]Job 5:2
30:2 [a]ch. 16:2; 1 Sam. 1:5
30:3 [1]Heb. *be built by her* [a]ch. 16:2 [b]ch. 50:23; Job 3:12 [c]ch. 16:2
30:4 [a]ch. 16:3
30:6 [1]That is, *Judging* [a]Lam. 3:59
30:8 [1]Heb. *wrestlings of God* [2]That is, *My wrestling* [3]Called, Mat. 4:13, *Nephthalim*
30:9 [a]ver. 4
30:11 [1]That is, *A troop,* or, *company*
30:13 [1]Heb. *In my happiness*

29:21 *my wife.* If Jacob had said "Rachel," Laban would have had no excuse for giving him Leah.
29:22 *feast.* A wedding feast was usually seven days long (see vv. 27–28; Judg 14:10,12).
29:23 *in the evening . . . he went in unto her.* The darkness, or perhaps a veil (see 24:65), may have concealed Leah's identity.
29:24 See v. 29; a wedding custom documented in Old Babylonian marriage contracts.
29:25 *hast thou beguiled me?* Jacob, the deceiver in name (see note on 25:26) as well as in behavior (see 27:36), had himself been deceived. The one who had tried everything to obtain the benefits of the firstborn had now, against his will, received the firstborn (vv. 16,26).
29:28 *he gave him Rachel his daughter.* Before Jacob worked another seven years (see v. 30).
29:30 *he loved also Rachel more than Leah.* Not only because Rachel had been his choice from the beginning but also, no doubt, because Laban had tricked Jacob into marrying Leah.
29:31–35 Leah, though unloved, nevertheless became the mother of Jacob's first four sons, including Levi (ancestor of the Aaronic priestly line) and Judah (ancestor of David and his royal line, and ultimately of Jesus).
29:32 *called his name Reuben . . . Surely the LORD hath looked upon my affliction.* Ishmael had received his name in similar circumstances (see 16:11).
30:1 *Rachel envied her sister.* As Jacob did of his older brother. *Give me children, or else I die.* Tragically prophetic words (see 35:16–19).
30:2 *Am I in God's stead . . . ?* Jacob was forever trying to secure the blessing by his own efforts. Here he has to acknowledge that the blessing of offspring could come only from God (see 31:7–13 for the blessing of flocks). Joseph later echoed these words (see 50:19).
30:3 *go in unto her.* See v. 9; see also 16:2 and note. *upon my knees.* Apparently an expression symbolic of adoption (see 48:10–16) and meaning "as though my own" (see note on 50:23).
30:4 *to wife.* As a concubine (see 35:22).
30:5–12 Jacob's fifth, sixth, seventh and eighth sons were born to him through his maidservant concubines.

daughters [a]will call me blessed: and she called
his name [2]Asher.
14 And Reuben went in the days of wheat
harvest, and found mandrakes in the field, and
brought them unto his mother Leah. Then Rachel said to Leah, [a]Give me, I pray thee, of thy
son's mandrakes.
15 And she said unto her, [a]*Is it* a small
matter that thou hast taken my husband? and
wouldest thou take away my son's mandrakes
also? And Rachel said, Therefore he shall lie
with thee to night for thy son's mandrakes.
16 And Jacob came out of the field in the
evening, and Leah went out to meet him, and
said, Thou must come in unto me; for surely I
have hired thee with my son's mandrakes.
And he lay with her that night.
17 And God hearkened unto Leah, and she
conceived, and bare Jacob the fifth son.
18 And Leah said, God hath given *me* my
hire, because I have given my maiden to my
husband: and she called his name [1]Issachar.
19 And Leah conceived again, and bare Jacob the sixth son.
20 And Leah said, God hath endued me
with a good dowry; now will my husband
dwell with me, because I have born him six
sons: and she called his name [1][2]Zebulun.
21 And afterwards she bare a daughter, and
called her name [1]Dinah.
22 And God [a]remembered Rachel, and
God hearkened to her, and [b]opened her
womb.
23 And she conceived, and bare a son; and
said, God hath taken away [a]my reproach:
24 And she called his name [1]Joseph; and
said, [a]The LORD shall add to me another son.

Jacob's bargain with Laban

25 ¶ And it came to pass, when Rachel had
born Joseph, that Jacob said unto Laban, [a]Send
me away, that I may go unto [b]mine own place,
and to my country.
26 Give *me* my wives and my children,
[a]for whom I have served thee, and let me go:
for thou knowest my service which I have
done thee.
27 And Laban said unto him, I pray thee, if
I have found favour in thine eyes, *tarry: for* [a]I
have learned by experience that the LORD hath
blessed me [b]for thy sake.
28 And he said, [a]Appoint me thy wages,
and I will give *it.*
29 And he said unto him, [a]Thou knowest
how I have served thee, and how thy cattle
was with me.
30 For *it was* little which thou hadst before
I *came,* and it is *now* [1]increased unto a multitude; and the LORD hath blessed thee [2]since
my coming: and now when shall I [a]provide for
mine own house also?
31 And he said, What shall I give thee?
And Jacob said, Thou shalt not give me any
thing: if thou wilt do this thing for me, I will
again feed *and* keep thy flock:
32 I will pass through all thy flock to day,
removing from thence all the speckled and
spotted cattle, and all the brown cattle among
the sheep, and the spotted and speckled
among the goats: and [a]*of such* shall be my
hire.
33 So shall my [a]righteousness answer for
me [1]in time to come, when it shall come for
my hire before thy face: every one that *is* not
speckled and spotted amongst the goats, and
brown amongst the sheep, that *shall be counted* stolen with me.
34 And Laban said, Behold, I would it
might be according to thy word.
35 And he removed that day the he goats
that were ringstraked and spotted, and all the
she goats that were speckled and spotted, *and*
every one that had *some* white in it, and all
the brown amongst the sheep, and gave *them*
into the hand of his sons.
36 And he set three days' journey betwixt
himself and Jacob: and Jacob fed the rest of Laban's flocks.
37 ¶ And [a]Jacob took him rods of green
poplar, and of the hazel and chesnut tree; and
pilled white strakes in them, and made the
white appear which *was* in the rods.
38 And he set the rods which he had pilled
before the flocks in the gutters in the watering

30:13 [2]That is, *Happy* [a]Prov. 31:28; Luke 1:48
30:14 [a]ch. 25:30
30:15 [a]Num. 16:9,13
30:18 [1]That is, *A hire*
30:20 [1]That is, *Dwelling* [2]Called, Mat. 4:13, *Zabulon*
30:21 [1]That is, *Judgment*
30:22 [a]1 Sam. 1:19 [b]ch. 29:31
30:23 [a]1 Sam. 1:6; Is. 4:1; Luke 1:25
30:24 [1]That is, *Adding* [a]ch. 35:17
30:25 [a]ch. 24:54,56 [b]ch. 18:33
30:26 [a]ch. 29:20,30
30:27 [a]ch. 39:3,5 [b]See ch. 26:24
30:28 [a]ch. 29:15
30:29 [a]ch. 31:6,38-40; Mat. 24:45; Tit. 2:10
30:30 [1]Heb. *broken forth* [2]Heb. *at my foot* [a]1 Tim. 5:8
30:32 [a]ch. 31:8
30:33 [1]Heb. *to morrow* [a]Ps. 37:6
30:37 [a]See ch. 31:9-12

30:14 *Give me . . . of thy son's mandrakes.* The mandrake has fleshy, forked roots that resemble the lower part of a human body and were therefore superstitiously thought to induce pregnancy when eaten (see Sol 7:13). Rachel, like Jacob (vv. 37–43), tried to obtain what she wanted by magical means.
30:16 *hired.* The Hebrew for this word is a pun on the name Issachar. (Issachar sounds like the Hebrew for "reward.")
30:17–20 Jacob's ninth and tenth sons were born through Leah, who was thus the mother of half of Jacob's 12 sons (see note on 29:31–35).
30:20 *endued. . .dowry.* The Hebrew terms for these words are puns on the name Zebulun. (Zebulun probably means "honor.")
30:21 *Dinah.* See ch. 34.
30:22 *God remembered Rachel.* See note on 8:1.
30:23 *reproach.* Barrenness was considered to be shameful, a mark of divine disfavor (see 16:2; 30:2).
30:24 *The LORD shall add to me another son.* The fulfillment of Rachel's wish would bring about her death (see 35:16–19).

‡30:27 *learned by experience* [i.e. divined]. The attempt to discover hidden knowledge through mechanical means (see 44:5), the interpretation of omens (see Ezek 21:21) or the aid of supernatural powers (see Acts 16:16). It was strictly forbidden to Israel (Lev 19:26; Deut 18:10,14) because it reflected a pagan concept of the world controlled by evil forces, and therefore obviously not under the sovereign rule of the Lord. *the LORD hath blessed me for thy sake.* Cf. 21:22; 26:28–29. The offspring of Abraham were a source of blessing (see 12:2).

30:35 *he removed.* Secretly and without telling Jacob.

30:37 *poplar . . . white.* The Hebrew terms for these words are puns on the name Laban. As Jacob had gotten the best of Esau (whose other name, Edom, means "red"; see note on 25:25) by means of red stew (25:30), so he now tries to get the best of Laban (whose name means "white") by means of white branches. In effect, Jacob was using Laban's own tactic (deception) against him.

troughs when the flocks came to drink, that they should conceive when they came to drink.

39 And the flocks conceived before the rods, and brought forth cattle ringstraked, speckled, and spotted.

40 And Jacob did separate the lambs, and set the faces of the flocks toward the ringstraked, and all the brown in the flock of Laban; and he put his own flocks by themselves, and put them not unto Laban's cattle.

41 And it came to pass, whensoever the stronger cattle did conceive, that Jacob laid the rods before the eyes of the cattle in the gutters, that they might conceive among the rods.

42 But when the cattle were feeble, he put *them* not in: so the feebler were Laban's, and the stronger Jacob's.

43 And the man [a]increased exceedingly, and [b]had much cattle, and maidservants, and menservants, and camels, and asses.

Jacob flees from Laban

31 And he heard the words of Laban's sons, saying, Jacob hath taken away all that *was* our father's; and of *that* which *was* of our father's hath he gotten all this [a]glory.

2 And Jacob beheld [a]the countenance of Laban, and behold, it *was* not [b]toward him [1]as before.

3 And the LORD said unto Jacob, [a]Return unto the land of thy fathers, and to thy kindred; and I will be with thee.

4 And Jacob sent and called Rachel and Leah to the field unto his flock,

5 And said unto them, [a]I see your father's countenance, that it *is* not toward me as before; but the God of my father [b]hath been with me.

6 And [a]ye know that with all my power I have served your father.

7 And your father hath deceived me, and [a]changed my wages [b]ten times; but God [c]suffered him not to hurt me.

8 If he said thus, [a]The speckled shall be thy wages; then all the cattle bare speckled: and if he said thus, The ringstraked shall be thy hire; then bare all the cattle ringstraked.

9 Thus God hath [a]taken away the cattle of your father, and given *them* to me.

10 And it came to pass at the time that the cattle conceived, that I lifted up mine eyes, and saw in a dream, and behold, the [1]rams which leaped upon the cattle *were* ringstraked, speckled, and grisled.

11 And [a]the angel of God spake unto me in a dream, *saying,* Jacob: And I said, Here *am* I.

12 And he said, Lift up now thine eyes, and see, all the rams which leap upon the cattle *are* ringstraked, speckled, and grisled: for [a]I have seen all that Laban doeth unto thee.

13 I *am* the God of Beth-el, [a]where thou anointedst the pillar, *and* where thou vowedst a vow unto me: now [b]arise, get thee out from this land, and return unto the land of thy kindred.

14 And Rachel and Leah answered and said unto him, [a]*Is there* yet any portion or inheritance for us in our father's house?

15 Are we not counted of him strangers? for [a]he hath sold us, and hath quite devoured also our money.

16 For all the riches which God hath taken from our father, that *is* ours, and our children's: now then, whatsoever God hath said unto thee, do.

17 ¶ Then Jacob rose up, and set his sons and his wives upon camels;

18 And he carried away all his cattle, and all his goods which he had gotten, the cattle of his getting, which he had gotten in Padan-aram, for to go to Isaac his father in the land of Canaan.

19 And Laban went to shear his sheep: and Rachel had stolen the [a][1]images [b]that *were* her father's.

20 And Jacob stale away [1]unawares to Laban the Syrian, in that he told him not that he fled.

21 So he fled with all that he had; and he rose up, and passed over the river, and [a]set his face *toward* the mount Gilead.

30:43 [a]ver. 30 [b]ch. 13:2; 24:35; 26:13,14
31:1 [a]Ps. 49:16
31:2 [1]Heb. *as yesterday* and *the day before* [a]ch. 4:5 [b]Deut. 28:54
31:3 [a]ch. 28:15,20,21; 32:9
31:5 [a]ver. 2 [b]ver. 3
31:6 [a]ver. 38-41; ch. 30:29
31:7 [a]ver. 41 [b]Num. 14:22; Neh. 4:12; Job 19:3; Zech. 8:23 [c]ch. 20:6; Job 1:10; Ps. 37:28; 105:14
31:8 [a]ch. 30:32
31:9 [a]ver. 1,16
31:10 [1]Or, *he goats*
31:11 [a]ch. 48:16
31:12 [a]Ex. 3:7; Ps. 139:3; Eccl. 5:8
31:13 [a]ch. 28:18-20 [b]ver. 3; ch. 32:9
31:14 [a]ch. 2:24
31:15 [a]ch. 29:15,27; Neh. 5:8
31:19 [1]Heb. *teraphim* [a]ch. 35:2 [b]Judg. 17:5; 1 Sam. 19:13; Hos. 3:4
31:20 [1]Heb. *the heart of Laban*
31:21 [a]ch. 46:28; 2 Ki. 12:17; Luke 9:51,53

30:39 The scheme worked—but only because of God's intervention (see Jacob's own admission in 31:9), not because of Jacob's superstition.

30:43 *the man increased exceedingly.* Over a period of six years (see 31:41). While in Haran Jacob obtained both family and wealth.

31:3 *Return unto the land of thy fathers.* Every sign Jacob was getting—from his wives (see vv. 14–16), from Laban (see v. 2), from Laban's sons (see v. 1) and now from God Himself—told him that it was time to return to Canaan. *I will be with thee.* See note on 26:3.

31:4 *Rachel and Leah.* At long last (see v. 14) Rachel, the younger, has been given precedence over Leah—but she will soon become a deceiver like her husband Jacob (see vv. 31,35).

31:7 *ten times.* See v. 41. "Ten" here probably signifies completeness. In effect, Jacob accused Laban of cheating him at every turn.

31:9 See note on 30:39.

31:11 *angel of God.* See note on 16:7. *Here am I.* See note on 22:1.

31:13 *Beth-el, where thou anointedst the pillar.* See note on 28:18.

31:18 *Padan-aram.* Means "plain of Aram," another name for Aram-naharaim (see note on 24:10). See map below.

‡31:19 *images.* Hebrew *teraphim.* Small portable idols, which Rachel probably stole because she thought they would bring her protection and blessing. Or perhaps she wanted to have something tangible to worship on the long journey ahead, a practice referred to much later in the writings of Josephus, a first-century Jewish historian. In any case, Rachel was not yet free of her pagan background (see 35:2; Josh 24:2).

31:21 *So he fled.* As he had fled earlier from Esau (27:42–43). Jacob's devious dealings produced only hostility from which he had to flee. *Gilead.* A fertile region southeast of the Sea of Galilee.

22 And it was told Laban on the third day
that Jacob was fled.
23 And he took [a]his brethren with him,
and pursued after him seven days' journey;
and they overtook him in the mount Gilead.
24 And God [a]came to Laban the Syrian in a
dream by night, and said unto him, Take heed
that thou [b]speak not to Jacob [1]either good or
bad.
25 Then Laban overtook Jacob. Now Jacob
had pitched his tent in the mount: and Laban
with his brethren pitched in the mount of Gilead.
26 And Laban said to Jacob, What hast
thou done, that thou hast stolen away unawares
to me, and [a]carried away my daughters,
as captives taken with the sword?
27 Wherefore didst thou flee away secretly,
and [1]steal away from me; and didst not tell
me, that I might have sent thee away with
mirth, and with songs, with tabret, and with
harp?

31:23 [a]ch. 13:8
31:24 [1]Heb. *from good to bad* [a]ch. 20:3; Job 33:15; Mat. 1:20 [b]ch. 24:50
31:26 [a]1 Sam. 30:2
31:27 [1]Heb. *hast stolen me*
31:28 [a]ver. 55; Ruth 1:9,14; 1 Ki. 19:20; Acts 20:37 [b]1 Sam. 13:13; 2 Chr. 16:9
31:29 [a]ver. 53; ch. 28:13 [b]ver. 24
31:30 [a]ver. 19; Judg. 18:24
31:32 [a]See ch. 44:9

28 And hast not suffered me [a]to kiss my
sons and my daughters? [b]thou hast now done
foolishly in *so* doing.
29 It is in the power of my hand to do you
hurt: but the [a]God of your father spake unto
me [b]yesternight, saying, Take thou heed that
thou speak not to Jacob either good or bad.
30 And now, *though* thou wouldest needs
be gone, because thou sore longedst after thy
father's house, *yet* wherefore hast thou [a]stolen
my gods?
31 And Jacob answered and said to Laban,
Because I was afraid: for I said, Peradventure
thou wouldest take by force thy daughters
from me.
32 With whomsoever thou findest thy
gods, [a]let him not live: before our brethren
discern thou what *is* thine with me, and take
it to thee. For Jacob knew not that Rachel had
stolen them.
33 And Laban went into Jacob's tent, and
into Leah's tent, and into the two maidser-

31:26 *thou hast stolen away unawares to me.* Lit. "you have stolen my heart"; i.e., "you have deceived me." Jacob's character, reflected in his name (see note on 25:26; see also 27:36), is emphasized in the narrative again and again.

‡31:27 *harp.* Probably the lyre which is much smaller, and with fewer strings (usually 6 to 12), than a modern harp.

31:32 *With whomsoever thou findest thy gods, let him not live.* Cf. 44:7–12. Though he made the offer in all innocence, Jacob

Jacob's Journeys

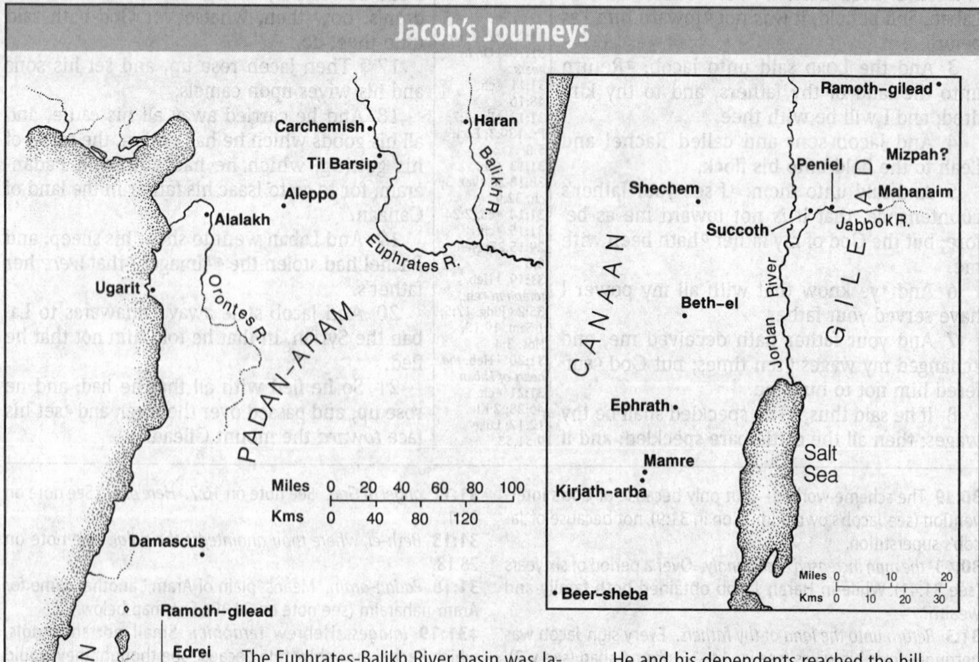

The Euphrates-Balikh River basin was Jacob's destination as he fled from Esau, ultimately reaching the home of his maternal uncle (Laban) near Haran.

His lengthy sojourn ended in a dispute with Laban and another flight—this time back to Canaan. His route likely took him toward Aleppo, then to Damascus and Edrei before reaching Peniel on the Jabbok River.

He and his dependents reached the hill country of Gilead before their caravan was overtaken by Laban. The covenant at Mizpah was celebrated on one of the hills later used as a border station between Aramean and Israelite territories.

Jacob tarried at Succoth, entered Canaan and proceeded to Shechem, where he erected an altar to the Lord.

vants' tents; but he found *them* not. Then went he out of Leah's tent, and entered into Rachel's tent.

34 Now Rachel had taken the images, and put them in the camel's furniture, and sat upon them. And Laban [1]searched all the tent, but found *them* not.

35 And she said to her father, Let it not displease my lord that I cannot [a]rise up before thee; for the custom of women *is* upon me. And he searched, but found not the images.

36 And Jacob was wroth, and chode with Laban: and Jacob answered and said to Laban, What *is* my trespass? what *is* my sin, that thou hast *so* hotly pursued after me?

37 Whereas thou hast [1]searched all my stuff, what hast thou found of all thy household stuff? set *it* here before my brethren and thy brethren, that they may judge betwixt us both.

38 This twenty years *have* I *been* with thee; thy ewes and thy she goats have not cast their young, and the rams of thy flock have I not eaten.

39 [a]That which was torn *of beasts* I brought not unto thee; I bare the loss of it; of [b]my hand didst thou require it, *whether* stolen by day, or stolen by night.

40 *Thus* I was in the day, the drought consumed me, and the frost by night; and my sleep departed from mine eyes.

41 Thus have I been twenty years in thy house; I [a]served thee fourteen years for thy two daughters, and six years for thy cattle: and [b]thou hast changed my wages ten times.

42 [a]Except the God of my father, the God of Abraham, and [b]the fear of Isaac, had been with me, surely thou hadst sent me away now empty. [c]God hath seen mine affliction and the labour of my hands, and [d]rebuked *thee* yesternight.

43 And Laban answered and said unto Jacob, *These* daughters *are* my daughters, and *these* children *are* my children, and *these* cattle *are* my cattle, and all that thou seest *is* mine: and what can I do *this* day unto these

31:34 [1] Heb. *felt*
31:35 [a] Ex. 20:12; Lev. 19:32
31:37 [1] Heb. *felt*
31:39 [a] Ex. 22:10 [b] Ex. 22:12
31:41 [a] ch. 29:27,28 [b] ver. 7
31:42 [a] Ps. 124:1,2 [b] ver. 53; Is. 8:13 [c] ch. 29:32; Ex. 3:7 [d] 1 Chr. 12:17
31:44 [a] ch. 26:28 [b] Josh. 24:27
31:45 [a] ch. 28:18
31:47 [1] That is, *The heap of witness.* [Chald.] [2] That is, *The heap of witness.* [Heb.]
31:48 [a] Josh. 24:27
31:49 [1] That is, *A beacon,* or, *watchtower* [a] Judg. 11:29; 1 Sam. 7:5
31:53 [a] ch. 16:5 [b] ch. 21:23 [c] ver. 42
31:54 [1] Or, *killed beasts*
31:55 [a] ch. 28:1 [b] ch. 18:33; 30:25; Num. 24:25
32:1 [a] Ps. 91:11; Heb. 1:14

my daughters, or unto their children which they have born?

44 Now therefore come thou, [a]let us make a covenant, I and thou; [b]and let it be for a witness between me and thee.

45 And Jacob [a]took a stone, and set it up *for* a pillar.

46 And Jacob said unto his brethren, Gather stones; and they took stones, and made a heap: and they did eat there upon the heap.

47 And Laban called it [1]Jegar-sahadutha: but Jacob called it [2]Galeed.

48 And Laban said, [a]This heap *is* a witness between me and thee *this* day. Therefore was the name of it called Galeed;

49 And [a][1]Mizpah; for he said, The LORD watch between me and thee, when we are absent one from another.

50 If thou shalt afflict my daughters, or if thou shalt take *other* wives beside my daughters, no man *is* with us; see, God *is* witness betwixt me and thee.

51 And Laban said to Jacob, Behold this heap, and behold *this* pillar, which I have cast betwixt me and thee;

52 This heap *be* witness, and *this* pillar *be* witness, that I will not pass over this heap to thee, and that thou shalt not pass over this heap and this pillar unto me, for harm.

53 The God of Abraham, and the God of Nahor, the God of their father, [a]judge betwixt us. And Jacob [b]sware by [c]the fear of his father Isaac.

54 Then Jacob [1]offered sacrifice upon the mount, and called his brethren to eat bread: and they did eat bread, and tarried all night in the mount.

55 And early in the morning Laban rose up, and kissed his sons and his daughters, and [a]blessed them: and Laban departed, and [b]returned unto his place.

Jacob prepares to meet Esau

32 And Jacob went on his way, and [a]the angels of God met him.

2 And when Jacob saw them, he said, This

---

almost lost his beloved Rachel. He had now been deceived even by his wife.

31:34 *in the camel's furniture* [i.e. saddle] *. . . sat upon them.* Indicating the small size and powerlessness of the household gods.

31:35 *I cannot rise up before thee; for the custom of women is upon me.* In later times, anything a menstruating woman sat on was considered ritually unclean (Lev 15:20). Rachel, too, had become a deceiver.

31:42 *fear.* Here a surrogate for God. Or perhaps the Hebrew for this word means "Kinsman," stressing the intimacy of God's relationship to the patriarch.

31:46 *did eat.* See note on 26:30.

31:48 For the naming of an altar under similar circumstances see Josh 22:10–12,34.

31:49 *The LORD . . . another.* The so-called Mizpah benediction, which in context is in fact a denunciation or curse.

31:51 *heap . . . pillar . . . betwixt me and thee.* Boundary markers between Laban's territory and Jacob's territory. Galeed, Jacob's name for the heap, is a pun on Gilead (see v. 47, where Aramaic *Jegar-sahadutha* means "witness heap"; *Galeed* also means "witness heap").

31:53 *God of their father.* Or possibly "gods of their father [i.e., Terah]," reflecting Laban's polytheistic background (see Josh 24:2). *fear of his father Isaac.* See note on v. 42. Jacob had met the "God of Isaac" (28:13) at Beth-el 20 years earlier.

31:54 *sacrifice . . . to eat bread.* Two important aspects of the covenant-making (see v. 44) process (see Ex 24:5–8,11). *brethren.* Those with whom he had now entered into a covenant. The common meal indicated mutual acceptance (see note on 26:30).

31:55 *blessed.* Or "said farewell to"; also in 47:10).

32:1 *angels of God met him.* Jacob had just left the region of the hostile Laban and is about to enter the region of the hostile Esau. He was met by the angels of God, whom he had seen at Beth-el when he was fleeing from Esau to go to Laban (28:12). Thus God was with Jacob, as He had promised (see 28:15; 31:3; see also note on 26:3).

is God's [a]host: and he called the name of that
place [1]Mahanaim.
3 And Jacob sent messengers before him to
Esau his brother [a]unto the land of Seir, [b]the
[1]country of Edom.
4 And he commanded them, saying, [a]Thus
shall ye speak unto my lord Esau; Thy servant
Jacob saith thus, I have sojourned with Laban,
and stayed *there* until now:
5 And [a]I have oxen, and asses, flocks, and
menservants, and womenservants: and I have
sent to tell my lord, that [b]I may find grace in
thy sight.
6 And the messengers returned to Jacob,
saying, We came to thy brother Esau, and also
[a]he cometh to meet thee, and four hundred
men with him.
7 Then Jacob was greatly afraid and [a]dis-
tressed: and he divided the people that *was*
with him, and the flocks, and herds, and the
camels, into two bands;
8 And said, If Esau come to the one company, and smite it, then the *other* company
which is left shall escape.
9 [a]And Jacob said, [b]O God of my father
Abraham, and God of my father Isaac, the
LORD [c]which saidst unto me, Return unto thy
country, and to thy kindred, and I will deal
well with thee:
10 [1]I am not worthy of the least of all the
[a]mercies, and of all the truth, which thou hast
shewed unto thy servant; for with [b]my staff I
passed over this Jordan; and now I am become
two bands.
11 [a]Deliver me, I pray thee, from the hand
of my brother, from the hand of Esau: for I fear
him, lest he will come and smite me, *and* [b]the
mother [1]with the children.
12 And [a]thou saidst, I will surely do thee
good, and make thy seed as the sand of the
sea, which cannot be numbered for multitude.
13 And he lodged there that *same* night;
and took of that which came to his hand [a]a
present for Esau his brother;

32:2 [1]That is, *Two hosts,* or, *camps* [a]Josh. 5:14; Ps. 103:21; 148:2; Luke 2:13
32:3 [1]Heb. *field* [a]ch. 33:14,16 [b]ch. 36:6-8; Deut. 2:5; Josh. 24:4
32:4 [a]Prov. 15:1
32:5 [a]ch. 30:43 [b]ch. 33:8,15
32:6 [a]ch. 33:1
32:7 [a]ch. 35:3
32:9 [a]Ps. 50:15 [b]ch. 28:13 [c]ch. 31:3,13
32:10 [1]Heb. *I am less than all, etc.* [a]ch. 24:27 [b]Job 8:7
32:11 [1]Heb. *upon* [a]Ps. 59:1,2 [b]Hos. 10:14
32:12 [a]ch. 28:13-15
32:13 [a]ch. 43:11; Prov. 18:16
32:20 [1]Heb. *my face* [a]Prov. 21:14
32:22 [a]Deut. 3:16
32:23 [1]Heb. *caused to pass*
32:24 [1]Heb. *ascending of the morning* [a]Hos. 12:3,4
32:25 [a]See Mat. 26:41; 2 Cor. 12:7
32:26 [a]See Luke 24:28 [b]Hos. 12:4

14 Two hundred she goats, and twenty he
goats, two hundred ewes, and twenty rams,
15 Thirty milch camels with their colts,
forty kine, and ten bulls, twenty she asses, and
ten foals.
16 And he delivered *them* into the hand of
his servants, every drove by themselves; and
said unto his servants, Pass over before me,
and put a space betwixt drove and drove.
17 And he commanded the foremost, saying, When Esau my brother meeteth thee, and
asketh thee, saying, Whose *art* thou? and whither goest thou? and whose *are* these before thee?
18 Then thou shalt say, *They be* thy servant
Jacob's; it *is* a present sent unto my lord Esau:
and behold, also he *is* behind us.
19 And so commanded he the second, and
the third, and all that followed the droves, saying, On this manner shall you speak unto
Esau, when you find him.
20 And say ye moreover, Behold, thy servant Jacob *is* behind us. For he said, I will [a]ap-
pease him with the present that goeth before
me, and afterward I will see his face; peradventure he will accept [1]of me.
21 So went the present over before him:
and himself lodged that night in the company.
22 And he rose up that night, and took his
two wives, and his two womenservants, and his
eleven sons, [a]and passed over the ford Jabbok.
23 And he took them, and [1]sent them over
the brook, and sent over that he had.

Jacob's wrestling at Peniel

24 ¶ And Jacob was left alone; and there
[a]wrestled a man with him until the [1]breaking
of the day.
25 And when he saw that he prevailed not
against him, he touched the hollow of his
thigh; and [a]the hollow of Jacob's thigh was out
of joint, as he wrestled with him.
26 And [a]he said, Let me go, for the day
breaketh. And he said, [b]I will not let thee go,
except thou bless me.

32:2 *Mahanaim.* Means "two camps" and is located in Gilead (see note on 31:21) east of the Jordan and north of the Jabbok (see note on v. 22). Two camps had just met in hostility and separated in peace. Two camps were again about to meet (in hostility, Jacob thought) and separate in peace. But Jacob called this crucial place "two camps" after seeing the angelic encampment, suggesting that he saw God's encampment as a divine assurance. God's host had come to escort him safely to Canaan (see 33:12,15). Yet he also feared meeting with Esau, so he divided his household into two camps (see vv. 7,10), still trying to protect himself by his own devices.

32:3 *Seir . . . Edom.* Far to the south of Jacob's ultimate destination, but he assumed that Esau would come seeking revenge as soon as he heard that Jacob was on his way back.

32:4 *Thy servant.* A phrase suggesting both courtesy and humility.

32:6 *four hundred.* A round number for a sizable unit of fighting men (see 1 Sam 22:2; 25:13; 30:10).

32:9 *Jacob said.* His first recorded prayer since leaving Beth-el.

32:11 *mother with the children.* Jacob was afraid that Esau's wrath would extend to Jacob's family as well.

32:12 *thy seed as the sand of the sea.* A reference to God's promise in 28:14 (see 22:17 and note).

32:13 *present.* Probably a wordplay: Out of his "two companies" (Hebrew *maḥanayim,* v. 2; see vv. 7–8,10) Jacob selects a "present" (*minḥah*) for his brother.

32:22 *Jabbok.* Today called the Wadi Zerqa, flowing westward into the Jordan about 20 miles north of the Dead Sea.

32:24 *left alone.* As he had been at Beth-el (28:10–22). *wrestled.* God wrestled (*ye'abeq*) with Jacob (*ya'aqob*) by the Jabbok (*yabboq*)—the author delighted in wordplay. Jacob had struggled all his life to prevail, first with Esau, then with Laban. Now, as he was about to reenter Canaan, he was shown that it was with God that he must "wrestle." It was God who held his destiny in His hands. *a man.* God Himself (as Jacob eventually realized; see v. 30) in the form of an angel (see Hos 12:3–4 and note on Gen 16:7).

32:25 *prevailed not against him . . . touched the hollow of his thigh.* God came to him in such a form that Jacob could wrestle with Him successfully, yet He showed Jacob that He could disable him at will.

32:26 *I will not let thee go.* Jacob's persistence was soon re-

27 And he said unto him, What *is* thy
name? And he said, Jacob.
28 And he said, [a]Thy name shall be called
no more Jacob, but [1]Israel: for as a prince hast
thou [b]power with God and [c]with men, and
hast prevailed.
29 And Jacob asked *him,* and said, Tell *me,*
I pray thee, thy name. And he said, [a]Where-
fore *is* it *that* thou dost ask after my name?
And he blessed him there.
30 And Jacob called the name of the place
[1]Peniel: for [a]I have seen God face to face, and
my life is preserved.
31 And as he passed over Penuel the sun
rose upon him, and he halted upon his thigh.
32 Therefore the children of Israel eat not
of the sinew which shrank, which *is* upon the
hollow of the thigh, unto this day: because he
touched the hollow of Jacob's thigh in the
sinew that shrank.

Jacob and Esau meet

33 And Jacob lifted up his eyes, and
looked, and behold, [a]Esau came, and
with him four hundred men. And he divided
the children unto Leah, and unto Rachel, and
unto the two handmaids.
2 And he put the handmaids and their children foremost, and Leah and her children after, and Rachel and Joseph hindermost.
3 And he passed over before them, and
[a]bowed himself to the ground seven times, until he came near to his brother.
4 [a]And Esau ran to meet him, and embraced him, [b]and fell on his neck, and kissed
him: and they wept.
5 And he lift up his eyes, and saw the
women and the children; and said, Who *are*
those [1]with thee? And he said, The children
[a]which God hath graciously given thy servant.
6 Then the handmaidens came near, they
and their children, and they bowed themselves.
7 And Leah also with her children came

32:28 [1][That is, *A prince of God*] [a]ch. 35:10; 2 Ki. 17:34 [b]Hos. 12:3,4 [c]ch. 25:31; 27:33
32:29 [a]Judg. 13:18
32:30 [1]That is, *The face of God* [a]ch. 16:13; Ex. 24:11; Deut. 5:24; Judg. 6:22; Is. 6:5
33:1 [a]ch. 32:6
33:3 [a]ch. 18:2; 42:6
33:4 [a]ch. 32:28 [b]ch. 45:14,15
33:5 [1]Heb. *to thee?* [a]ch. 48:9; Ps. 127:3; Is. 8:18
33:8 [1]Heb. *What is all this band to thee?* [a]ch. 32:16 [b]ch. 32:5
33:9 [1]Heb. *be that to thee that is thine*
33:10 [a]ch. 43:3; 2 Sam. 3:13; 14:24,28,32
33:11 [1][Heb. *all* things] [a]Judg. 1:15; 1 Sam. 25:27; 30:26 [b]2 Ki. 5:23
33:14 [1]Heb. *according to the foot of the work, etc. and according to the foot of the children* [a]ch. 32:3
33:15 [1]Heb. *set,* or, *place* [2]Heb. *Wherefore is this?* [a]ch. 34:11; 47:25; Ruth 2:13
33:17 [1]That is, *Booths* [a]Josh. 13:27; Judg. 8:5; Ps. 60:6
33:18 [1]Called, Acts 7:16, *Sychem* [a]John 3:23 [b]Josh. 24:1; Judg. 9:1

near, and bowed themselves: and after came
Joseph near and Rachel, and they bowed themselves.
8 And he said, [1]What meanest thou by [a]all
this drove which I met? And he said, *These*
are [b]to find grace in the sight of my lord.
9 And Esau said, I have enough, my brother; [1]keep that thou hast unto thyself.
10 And Jacob said, Nay, I pray thee, if now
I have found grace in thy sight, then receive
my present at my hand: for therefore I [a]have
seen thy face, as though I had seen the face of
God, and thou wast pleased with me.
11 Take, I pray thee, [a]my blessing that is
brought to thee; because God hath dealt graciously with me, and because I have [1]enough.
[b]And he urged him, and he took *it.*
12 And he said, Let us take our journey,
and let us go, and I will go before thee.
13 And he said unto him, My lord knoweth
that the children *are* tender, and the flocks and
herds with young *are* with me: and if *men*
should overdrive them one day, all the flock
will die.
14 Let my lord, I pray thee, pass over before his servant: and I will lead on softly, [1]ac-
cording as the cattle that goeth before me and
the children be able to endure, until I come
unto my lord [a]unto Seir.
15 And Esau said, Let me now [1]leave with
thee *some* of the folk that *are* with me. And he
said, [2]What needeth it? [a]let me find grace in
the sight of my lord.
16 So Esau returned that day on his way
unto Seir.
17 And Jacob journeyed to [a]Succoth, and
built him a house, and made booths for his cattle: therefore the name of the place is called
[1]Succoth.
18 And Jacob came to [a]Shalem, a city of
[b][1]Shechem, which *is* in the land of Canaan,
when he came from Padan-aram; and pitched
his tent before the city.

warded (v. 29). *except thou bless me.* Jacob finally acknowledged that the blessing must come from God.

32:28 *Thy name shall be called no more Jacob.* Now that Jacob had acknowledged God as the source of blessing and was about to reenter the promised land, the Lord acknowledged Jacob as His servant by changing his name (see 17:5 and note). *Israel.* Means "he struggles with God." Here in Father Jacob/Israel, the nation of Israel got her name and her characterization: the people who struggle with God (memorialized in the name Israel) and with men (memorialized in the name Jacob) and overcome. God later confirmed Jacob's new name (35:10).

32:29 *Wherefore is it that thou dost ask after my name?* Such a request of God is both unworthy and impossible to fulfill (see Judg 13:17–18).

32:30 *I have seen God face to face, and my life is preserved.* See note on 16:13; see also Judg 6:22–23; 13:22. Only God's "back parts" (see Ex 33:23) or "feet" (see Ex 24:10) or "similitude" (see Num 12:8), in a symbolic sense, may be seen.

32:32 *eat not of the sinew.* Probably the sciatic muscle. Mentioned nowhere else in the Bible, this dietary prohibition is found in the later writings of Judaism. Jacob retained in his body, and Israel retained in her dietary practice, a perpetual reminder of this fateful encounter with God.

33:2 *Rachel and Joseph hindermost.* Jacob wanted to keep his favorite wife and child farthest away from potential harm.

33:3 *bowed himself to the ground seven times.* A sign of total submission, documented also in texts found at Tell el-Amarna in Egypt and dating to the 14th century B.C. (see chart, p. xix).

33:4 All Jacob's fears proved unfounded. God had been at work and had so blessed Esau (v. 9) that he no longer held a grudge against Jacob.

33:9 *my brother.* Esau's generous and loving response was in contrast to Jacob's cautious and fearful "my lord" (v. 8).

‡33:11 *blessing.* Though a reference to the present in v. 10, the Hebrew word is the same as that used for "blessing" in 27:35. The author of Genesis was conscious of the irony that Jacob now acknowledged that the blessing he had struggled for was from God. In his last attempt to express reconciliation with Esau, Jacob in a sense gave back the "blessing" he had stolen from his brother, doing so from the blessings the Lord had given him.

33:14 *until I come unto my lord unto Seir.* But Jacob, still the deceiver, had no intention of following Esau all the way to Seir.

‡33:18 *came to Shalem.* The Hebrew can be rendered adver-

19 And [a]he bought a parcel of a field,
where he had spread his tent, at the hand of
the children of [1]Hamor, Shechem's father, for
an hundred [2]pieces of money.
20 And he erected there an altar, and
[a]called it [1]El-Elohe-Israel.

The defiling of Dinah

34 And [a]Dinah the daughter of Leah,
which she bare unto Jacob, [b]went
out to see the daughters of the land.
2 And when Shechem the son of Hamor
the Hivite, prince of the country, [a]saw her, he
[b]took her, and lay with her, and [1]defiled her.
3 And his soul clave unto Dinah the daughter of Jacob, and he loved the damsel, and
spake [1]kindly unto the damsel.
4 And Shechem [a]spake unto his father Hamor, saying, Get me this damsel to wife.
5 And Jacob heard that he had defiled Dinah his daughter: now his sons were with his
cattle in the field: and Jacob [a]held his peace
until they were come.
6 And Hamor the father of Shechem went
out unto Jacob to commune with him.
7 And the sons of Jacob came out of the
field when they heard *it:* and the men were
grieved, and they [a]were very wroth, because
he [b]had wrought folly in Israel in lying with Jacob's daughter; [c]which thing ought not to be
done.
8 And Hamor communed with them, saying, The soul of my son Shechem longeth for
your daughter: I pray you give her him to wife.
9 And make ye marriages with us, *and* give
your daughters unto us, and take our daughters unto you.
10 And ye shall dwell with us: and [a]the
land shall be before you; dwell and [b]trade you
therein, and [c]get you possessions therein.
11 And Shechem said unto her father and
unto her brethren, Let me find grace in your
eyes, and what ye shall say unto me I will give.
12 Ask me never so much [a]dowry and gift,
and I will give according as ye shall say unto
me: but give me the damsel to wife.
13 And the sons of Jacob answered Shechem and Hamor his father [a]deceitfully, and
said, because he had defiled Dinah their sister:
14 And they said unto them, We cannot do
this thing, to give our sister to one that is uncircumcised; for [a]that *were* a reproach unto us:
15 But in this will we consent unto you: If
ye will be as we *be,* that every male of you be
circumcised;
16 Then will we give our daughters unto
you, and we will take your daughters to us,
and we will dwell with you, and we will become one people.
17 But if ye will not hearken unto us, to be
circumcised; then will we take our daughter,
and we will be gone.
18 And their words pleased Hamor, and
Shechem Hamor's son.
19 And the young man deferred not to do
the thing, because he had delight in Jacob's
daughter: and he *was* [a]more honourable than
all the house of his father.
20 And Hamor and Shechem his son came
unto the gate of their city, and communed
with the men of their city, saying,
21 These men *are* peaceable with us;
therefore let them dwell in the land, and trade
therein; for the land, behold, *it is* large enough
for them; let us take their daughters to us for
wives, and let us give them our daughters.
22 Only herein will the men consent unto
us for to dwell with us, to be one people, if
every male among us be circumcised, as they
are circumcised.
23 *Shall* not their cattle and their substance and every beast of theirs *be* ours? only
let us consent unto them, and they will dwell
with us.
24 And unto Hamor and unto Shechem his
son hearkened all that [a]went out of the gate of
his city; and every male was circumcised, all
that went out of the gate of his city.

33:19 [1]Called, Acts 7:16, *Emor* [2]Or, *lambs* [a]Josh. 24:32; John 4:5
33:20 [1]That is, *God the God of Israel* [a]ch. 35:7
34:1 [a]ch. 30:21 [b]Tit. 2:5
34:2 [1]Heb. *humbled her* [a]ch. 6:2; Judg. 14:1 [b]ch. 20:2
34:3 [1]Heb. *to her heart.* [*to the heart of the damsel*] more exactly
34:4 [a]Judg. 14:2
34:5 [a]1 Sam. 10:27; 2 Sam. 13:22
34:7 [a]ch. 49:7; 2 Sam. 13:21 [b]Josh. 7:15; Judg. 20:6 [c]Deut. 23:17; 2 Sam. 13:12
34:10 [a]ch. 13:9; 20:15 [b]ch. 42:34 [c]ch. 47:27
34:12 [a]Ex. 22:16,17; Deut. 22:29; 1 Sam. 18:25
34:13 [a]See 2 Sam. 13:24
34:14 [a]Josh. 5:9
34:19 [a]1 Chr. 4:9
34:24 [a]ch. 23:10,18

bially, not as a noun; i.e."came safely to Shechem," thus the answer to Jacob's prayer of 20 years earlier (see 28:21). *Shechem.* An important city in central Canaan, first built and inhabited during the patriarchal period. Jacob followed in the footsteps of Father Abraham (see 12:6). Jacob dug a well there (see John 4:5–6) that can still be seen today. *Padan-aram.* Means "plain of Aram," another name for Aram-naharaim (see note on 24:10).

33:19 *pieces of money.* The Hebrew word translated by this phrase (*qesitah,* a unit of money of unknown weight and value) is always found in patriarchal contexts (see Josh 24:32; Job 42:11).

‡33:20 *erected there an altar.* See note on 12:7. *called it El-Elohe-Israel* [i.e."God, the God of Israel]. Jacob formally acknowledged the God of his fathers as his God also (see 28:21). But he lingered at Shechem and did not return to Beth-el (see 35:1), and that meant trouble (see ch. 34).

34:1–31 The name of God ends ch. 33 and begins ch. 35, but it is completely absent from this sordid chapter (see note on 7:16).

34:2 *Shechem.* See 33:19. He was probably named after the city.

34:4 *Get me this damsel to wife.* See note on 21:21.

34:7 *Israel.* The clan of Israel. *which thing ought not to be done.* Cf. Tamar's plea to Amnon in a similar situation (2 Sam 13:12).

34:9 *make ye marriages with us.* The Canaanites wanted to absorb Israel (see v. 16) in order to benefit from the blessings Jacob had received from the Lord (both his offspring and his possessions—vv. 21–23). This was a danger Israel constantly faced from other peoples and nations—either absorption or hostility, both of which are perpetual threats to the people of God.

34:12 *dowry and gift.* For a specific example of this marriage custom see 24:53.

34:13 *sons of Jacob answered . . . deceitfully.* Like father, like son (see 27:24; see also note on 25:26).

34:15 Using a sacred ceremony for a sinful purpose (see vv. 24–25).

34:20 *gate of their city.* See notes on 19:1; 23:10.

34:23 The greed of the men of Shechem led to their destruction.

34:24 The Canaanites were even willing to submit to Israel's covenant rite in order to attain their purposes.

25 And it came to pass on the third day,
when they were sore, that two of the sons of
Jacob, [a]Simeon and Levi, Dinah's brethren,
took each man his sword, and came upon the
city boldly, and slew all the males.
26 And they slew Hamor and Shechem his
son with the [1]edge of the sword, and took Dinah out of Shechem's house, and went out.
27 The sons of Jacob came upon the slain,
and spoiled the city, because they had defiled
their sister.
28 They took their sheep, and their oxen,
and their asses, and that which *was* in the city,
and that which *was* in the field,
29 And all their wealth, and all their little
ones, and their wives took they captive, and
spoiled even all that *was* in the house.
30 And Jacob said to Simeon and Levi, [a]Ye
have [b]troubled me [c]to make me to stink
among the inhabitants of the land, amongst
the Canaanites and the Perizzites: [d]and I *be-*
ing few in number, they shall gather themselves together against me, and slay me; and I
shall be destroyed, I and my house.
31 And they said, Should he deal with our
sister as with a harlot?

Jacob returns to Beth-el

35 And God said unto Jacob, Arise, go
up to [a]Beth-el, and dwell there: and
make there an altar unto God, [b]that appeared
unto thee [c]when thou fleddest from the face of
Esau thy brother.
2 Then Jacob said unto his [a]household, and
to all that *were* with him, Put away [b]the
strange gods that *are* among you, and [c]be
clean, and change your garments:
3 And let us arise, and go up to Beth-el; and
I will make there an altar unto God, [a]who answered me in the day of my distress, [b]and was
with me in the way which I went.
4 And they gave unto Jacob all the strange
gods which *were* in their hand, and *all their*
[a]earrings which *were* in their ears; and Jacob
hid them under [b]the oak which *was* by Shechem.
5 And they journeyed: and [a]the terror of
God was upon the cities that *were* round about
them, and they did not pursue after the sons of
Jacob.
6 So Jacob came to [a]Luz, which *is* in the
land of Canaan, that *is,* Beth-el, he and all the
people that *were* with him.
7 And he [a]built there an altar, and called
the place [1]El-beth-el: because [b]there God appeared unto him, when he fled from the face
of his brother.
8 But [a]Deborah Rebekah's nurse died, and
she was buried beneath Beth-el under an oak:
and the name of it was called [1]Allon-bachuth.
9 And [a]God appeared unto Jacob again,
when he came out of Padan-aram, and blessed
him.
10 And God said unto him, Thy name *is* Jacob: [a]thy name shall not be called any more Jacob, [b]but Israel shall be thy name: and he
called his name Israel.
11 And God said unto him, [a]I *am* God
Almighty: be fruitful and multiply; [b]a nation
and a company of nations shall be of thee, and
kings shall come out of thy loins;
12 And the land [a]which I gave Abraham
and Isaac, to thee I will give it, and to thy seed
after thee will I give the land.
13 And God [a]went up from him in the
place where he talked with him.
14 And Jacob [a]set up a pillar in the place
where he talked with him, *even* a pillar of
stone: and he poured a drink offering thereon,
and he poured oil thereon.
15 And Jacob called the name of the place
where God spake with him, [a]Beth-el.

The deaths of Rachel and Isaac

16 ¶ And they journeyed from Beth-el; and
there was but [1]a little way to come to Ephrath:
and Rachel travailed, and she had hard labour.
17 And it came to pass, when she was in

34:25 [a]ch. 49:5-7
34:26 [1]Heb. *mouth*
34:30 [a]ch. 49:6 [b]Josh. 7:25 [c]Ex. 5:21; 1 Sam. 13:4 [d]Deut. 4:27; Ps. 105:12
35:1 [a]ch. 28:19 [b]ch. 28:13 [c]ch. 27:43
35:2 [a]ch. 18:19; Josh. 24:15 [b]ch. 31:19,34; Josh. 24:2,23; 1 Sam. 7:3 [c]Ex. 19:10
35:3 [a]ch. 32:7,24 [b]ch. 28:20; 31:3,42
35:4 [a]Hos. 2:13
35:4 [b]Josh. 24:26; Judg. 9:6
35:5 [a]Ex. 15:16; Deut. 11:25; Josh. 2:9; 1 Sam. 14:15
35:6 [a]ch. 28:19,22
35:7 [1]That is, *The God of Beth-el* [a]Eccl. 5:4 [b]ch. 28:13
35:8 [1]That is, *The oak of weeping* [a]ch. 24:59
35:9 [a]Hos. 12:4
35:10 [a]ch. 17:5 [b]ch. 32:28
35:11 [a]ch. 17:1; 48:3,4; Ex. 6:3 [b]ch. 17:5,6,16; 28:3; 48:4
35:12 [a]ch. 12:7; 13:15; 26:3,4; 28:13
35:13 [a]ch. 17:22
35:14 [a]ch. 28:18
35:15 [a]ch. 28:19
35:16 [1]Heb. *a little piece of ground*

34:25 *Simeon and Levi.* Because they slaughtered the men of Shechem, their own descendants would be scattered far and wide (see note on 49:7). *Dinah's brethren.* All three were children of Leah (29:33–34; 30:21). *slew all the males.* Shechem's crime, serious as it was, hardly warranted such brutal and extensive retaliation (see vv. 27–29).
34:30 *Perizzites.* See note on 13:7.
35:1 *God . . . appeared unto thee when thou fleddest.* See v. 7; 28:13.
35:2 *strange gods that are among you.* See note on 31:19 (see also Josh 24:23).
35:3 *God . . . was with me.* See 28:15; see also note on 26:3.
35:4 *earrings.* Worn as amulets or charms; a pagan religious custom (cf. Hos 2:13). *the oak . . . by Shechem.* Obviously a well-known tree, perhaps the "oak" mentioned in 12:6 (see Josh 24:26).
35:5 *the terror of God.* God protected His servant.
35:7 *built there an altar.* See note on 12:7.
35:8 *Deborah Rebekah's nurse died.* After long years of faithful service (see 24:59). *beneath.* Either "lower than" or "to the south of." *an oak.* Again probably a well-known tree (see note on v. 4), perhaps the "oak" mentioned in 1 Sam 10:3.
35:9 *Jacob . . . when he came.* See map, p. 48. *Padan-aram.* Means "plain of Aram," another name for Aram-naharaim (see note on 24:10).
35:10 *Jacob . . . Israel.* The previous assignment of an additional name (see 32:28) is here confirmed. For similar examples compare 21:31 with 26:33, and 28:19 with 35:15.
35:11–12 This event climaxes the Isaac-Jacob cycle (see Introduction: Literary Features). Now that Jacob was at last back at Beth-el, where God had begun His direct relationship with him, God confirmed to this chosen son of Isaac the covenant promises made to Abraham (17:1–8; see 28:3). His words echo His original benediction pronounced on man in the beginning (1:28) and renewed after the flood (9:1,7). God's blessing on mankind would be fulfilled in and through Jacob and his offspring. See also 47:27; Ex 1:7.
35:13 See note on 17:22.
35:14 See 28:18 and note. *drink offering.* A liquid poured out as a sacrifice to a deity.
35:15 See 28:19; see also note on v. 10.
35:16 *Ephrath.* The older name for Beth-lehem (see v. 19) in Judah (see Ruth 1:2; Mic 5:2).

hard labour, that the midwife said unto her, Fear not; [a]thou shalt have this son also.

18 And it came to pass, as her soul was in departing (for she died) that she called his name [1]Ben-oni: but his father called him [2]Benjamin.

19 And [a]Rachel died, and was buried in the way to [b]Ephrath, which *is* Beth-lehem.

20 And Jacob set a pillar upon her grave: that *is* the pillar of Rachel's grave [a]unto *this* day.

21 And Israel journeyed, and spread his tent beyond [a]the tower of Edar.

22 And it came to pass, when Israel dwelt in that land, that Reuben went and [a]lay with Bilhah his father's concubine: and Israel heard *it.* Now the sons of Jacob were twelve:

23 The sons of Leah; [a]Reuben, Jacob's firstborn, and Simeon, and Levi, and Judah, and Issachar, and Zebulun:

24 The sons of Rachel; Joseph, and Benjamin:

25 And the sons of Bilhah, Rachel's handmaid; Dan, and Naphtali:

26 And the sons of Zilpah, Leah's handmaid; Gad, and Asher: these *are* the sons of Jacob, which were born to him in Padan-aram.

27 And Jacob came unto Isaac his father unto [a]Mamre, unto the [b]city of Arbah, which *is* Hebron, where Abraham and Isaac sojourned.

28 And the days of Isaac were an hundred and fourscore years.

29 And Isaac gave up the ghost, and died, and [a]was gathered unto his people, *being* old and full of days: and [b]his sons Esau and Jacob buried him.

The descendants of Esau

36 Now these *are* the generations of Esau, [a]who *is* Edom.

2 [a]Esau took his wives of the daughters of Canaan; Adah the daughter of Elon the Hittite,

35:17 [a]ch. 30:24; 1 Sam. 4:20
35:18 [1]That is, *The son of my sorrow* [2]That is, *The son of the right hand*
35:19 [a]ch. 48:7 [b]Ruth 1:2; Mic. 5:2; Mat. 2:6
35:20 [a]1 Sam. 10:2
35:21 [a]Mic. 4:8
35:22 [a]ch. 49:4; 1 Chr. 5:1
35:23 [a]ch. 46:8; Ex. 1:2
35:27 [a]ch. 13:18 [b]Josh. 14:15
35:29 [a]ch. 15:15; 25:8 [b]See ch. 25:9; 49:31
36:1 [a]ch. 25:30
36:2 [a]ch. 26:34
36:2 [b]ver. 25
36:3 [a]ch. 28:9
36:4 [a]1 Chr. 1:35
36:6 [1]Heb. *souls*
36:7 [a]ch. 13:6,11 [b]ch. 17:8; 28:4
36:8 [a]ch. 32:3; Deut. 2:5; Josh. 24:4 [b]ver. 1
36:9 [1]Heb. *Edom*
36:10 [a]1 Chr. 1:35
36:11 [1][Or, *Zephi,* 1 Chr. 1:36]
36:12 [a]Ex. 17:8,14; Num. 24:20; 1 Sam. 15:2,3

and [b]Aholibamah the daughter of Anah the daughter of Zibeon the Hivite;

3 And [a]Bashemath Ishmael's daughter, sister of Nebajoth.

4 And [a]Adah bare to Esau Eliphaz; and Bashemath bare Reuel;

5 And Aholibamah bare Jeush, and Jaalam, and Korah: these *are* the sons of Esau, which were born unto him in the land of Canaan.

6 And Esau took his wives, and his sons, and his daughters, and all the [1]persons of his house, and his cattle, and all his beasts, and all his substance, which he had got in the land of Canaan; and went into the country from the face of his brother Jacob.

7 [a]For their riches were more than that they might dwell together; and [b]the land wherein they were strangers could not bear them because of their cattle.

8 Thus dwelt Esau in [a]mount Seir: [b]Esau *is* Edom.

9 ¶ And these *are* the generations of Esau the father of [1]the Edomites in mount Seir:

10 These *are* the names of Esau's sons; [a]Eliphaz the son of Adah the wife of Esau, Reuel the son of Bashemath the wife of Esau.

11 And the sons of Eliphaz were Teman, Omar, [1]Zepho, and Gatam, and Kenaz.

12 And Timna was concubine to Eliphaz Esau's son; and she bare to Eliphaz [a]Amalek: these *were* the sons of Adah Esau's wife.

13 And these *are* the sons of Reuel; Nahath, and Zerah, Shammah, and Mizzah: these were the sons of Bashemath Esau's wife.

14 And these were the sons of Aholibamah, the daughter of Anah, daughter of Zibeon, Esau's wife: and she bare to Esau Jeush, and Jaalam, and Korah.

15 These *were* dukes of the sons of Esau: the sons of Eliphaz the firstborn *son* of Esau; duke Teman, duke Omar, duke Zepho, duke Kenaz,

35:17 *thou shalt have this son also.* An echo of Rachel's own plea at the time of Joseph's birth (see 30:24).
35:18 *Benjamin.* The name can mean "son of the right hand" or "son of the south"—in distinction from the other sons, who were born in the north. One set of Hebrew terms for indicating direction was based on facing east, so south was on the right.
35:19 *Rachel died.* In childbirth (see note on 30:1).
35:20 *Rachel's grave.* See 1 Sam 10:2. The traditional, though not authentic, site is near Beth-lehem.
35:21 *tower of Edar.* Means "tower of the flock," doubtless referring to a watchtower built to discourage thieves from stealing sheep and other animals (see, e.g., 2 Chr 26:10). The same Hebrew phrase is used figuratively in Mic 4:8, where "flock" refers to the people of Judah (see Mic 4:6–7).
35:22 Reuben's act was an arrogant and premature claim to the rights of the firstborn—here the right to inherit his father's concubine. For this he would lose his legal status as firstborn (see 49:3–4; 1 Chr 5:1; see also note on 37:21).
35:26 *sons of Jacob . . . born to him in Padan-aram.* Obviously a summary statement since Benjamin was born in Canaan (see vv. 16–18).
35:27 *Mamre, unto the city of Arba, which is, Hebron.* See notes on 13:18; 23:2.
35:29 See note on 25:8. *buried him.* In the family tomb, the cave of Machpelah (49:30–31).
36:1 *generations.* See note on 2:4. Though repeated in v. 9, the word does not mark the start of a new main section there since the information in vv. 9–43 is merely an expansion of that in vv. 1–8. *Esau, who is, Edom.* See note on 25:25. Reddish rock formations, primarily sandstone, are conspicuous in the territory of the Edomites, located south and southeast of the Dead Sea.
36:2–3 See note on 26:34.
36:7 See 13:6; see also 26:20 and note.
36:8 *Seir.* Another name for Edom. The word itself is related to the Hebrew word meaning "hair," a possible meaning also for the name "Esau" (see note on 25:25). Esau's clan must have driven away the original Horite (see v. 20) inhabitants of Seir (see 14:6 and note). The descendants of Seir are listed in vv. 20–28.
36:10–14 The same list of Esau's descendants (see 1 Chr 1:35–37) is repeated in vv. 15–19 as a list of tribal chieftains.
36:11 *Eliphaz . . . Teman.* One of Job's friends was named Eliphaz the Temanite (Job 2:11), and Job himself was from the land of Uz (Job 1:1). Thus Job probably lived in Edom (see vv. 28,34).
36:12 *Amalek.* See note on 14:7.

16 Duke Korah, duke Gatam, *and* duke Amalek: these *are* the dukes *that came* of Eliphaz in the land of Edom; these *were* the sons of Adah.

17 And these *are* the sons of Reuel Esau's son; duke Nahath, duke Zerah, duke Shammah, duke Mizzah: these *are* the dukes *that came* of Reuel in the land of Edom; these *are* the sons of Bashemath Esau's wife.

18 And these *are* the sons of Aholibamah Esau's wife; duke Jeush, duke Jaalam, duke Korah: these *were* the dukes *that came* of Aholibamah the daughter of Anah, Esau's wife.

19 These *are* the sons of Esau, who *is* Edom, and these *are* their dukes.

20 ¶ [a]These *are* the sons of Seir [b]the Horite, who inhabited the land; Lotan, and Shobal, and Zibeon, and Anah,

21 And Dishon, and Ezer, and Dishan: these *are* the dukes of the Horites, the children of Seir in the land of Edom.

22 And the children of Lotan were Hori and [1]Hemam; and Lotan's sister *was* Timna.

23 And the children of Shobal *were* these; [1]Alvan, and Manahath, and Ebal, [2]Shepho, and Onam.

24 And these *are* the children of Zibeon; both Aiah, and Anah: this *was that* Anah that found [a]the mules in the wilderness, as he fed the asses of Zibeon his father.

25 And the children of Anah *were* these; Dishon, and Aholibamah the daughter of Anah.

26 And these *are* the children of Dishon; [1]Hemdan, and Eshban, and Ithran, and Cheran.

27 The children of Ezer *are* these; Bilhan, and Zaavan, and [1]Akan.

28 The children of Dishan *are* these; Uz, and Aran.

29 These *are* the dukes *that came* of the Horites; duke Lotan, duke Shobal, duke Zibeon, duke Anah,

30 Duke Dishon, duke Ezer, duke Dishan: these *are* the dukes *that came* of Hori, among their dukes in the land of Seir.

The kings of Edom

31 ¶ And [a]these *are* the kings that reigned in the land of Edom, before there reigned *any* king over the children of Israel.

32 And Bela the son of Beor reigned in Edom: and the name of his city *was* Dinhabah.

33 And Bela died, and Jobab the son of Zerah of Bozrah reigned in his stead.

34 And Jobab died, and Husham of the land of Temani reigned in his stead.

35 And Husham died, and Hadad the son of Bedad, who smote Midian in the field of Moab, reigned in his stead: and the name of his city *was* Avith.

36 And Hadad died, and Samlah of Masrekah reigned in his stead.

37 And Samlah died, and Saul of [a]Rehoboth *by* the river reigned in his stead.

38 And Saul died, and Baal-hanan the son of Achbor reigned in his stead.

39 And Baal-hanan the son of Achbor died, and [a]Hadar reigned in his stead: and the name of his city *was* Pau; and his wife's name *was* Mehetabel, the daughter of Matred, the daughter of Mezahab.

40 And these *are* the names of [a]the dukes *that came* of Esau, according to their families, after their places, by their names; duke Timnah, duke [1]Alvah, duke Jetheth,

41 Duke Aholibamah, duke Elah, duke Pinon,

42 Duke Kenaz, duke Teman, duke Mibzar,

43 Duke Magdiel, duke Iram: these *be* the dukes of Edom, according to their habitations in the land of their possession: he *is* Esau the father of [1]the Edomites.

Joseph's dream

37 And Jacob dwelt in the land [a1]wherein his father was a stranger, in the land of Canaan.

2 These *are* the generations of Jacob. Joseph, *being* seventeen years old, was feeding the flock with his brethren; and the lad *was* with the sons of Bilhah, and with the sons of Zilpah, his father's wives: and Joseph brought unto his father [a]their evil report.

3 Now Israel loved Joseph more than all his children, because he *was* [a]the son of his old age: and he made him a coat of many [b1]colours.

36:20 [a]1 Chr. 1:38 [b]ch. 14:6; Deut. 2:12,22
36:22 [1][Or, *Homam,* 1 Chr. 1:39]
36:23 [1][Or, *Alian,* 1 Chr. 1:40] [2][Or, *Shephi,* 1 Chr. 1:40]
36:24 [a]See Lev. 19:19
36:26 [1][Or, *Amram,* 1 Chr. 1:41]
36:27 [1][Or, *Jakan,* 1 Chr. 1:42]
36:31 [a]1 Chr. 1:43
36:37 [a]ch. 10:11
36:39 [a]1 Chr. 1:50, *Hadad Pai*
36:40 [1][Or, *Aliah*] [a]1 Chr. 1:51
36:43 [1]Heb. *Edom*
37:1 [1]Heb. *of his father's sojournings* [a]ch. 17:8; 23:4; 28:4; 36:7; Heb. 11:9
37:2 [a]1 Sam. 2:22-24
37:3 [1]Or, *pieces* [a]ch. 44:20 [b]Judg. 5:30; 2 Sam. 13:18

36:20–28 See note on v. 8. The same list of Seir's descendants (see 1 Chr 1:38–42) is repeated in abbreviated form in vv. 29–30 as a list of tribal chieftains.
36:31 *before there reigned any king over the children of Israel.* Presupposes the later Israelite monarchy and is therefore an editorial updating subsequent to Moses' time (see note on 14:14).
36:43 *these . . . possession.* A summary statement for the whole chapter (just as v. 1 is a title for the whole chapter).
37:1 *Canaan.* Jacob made the promised land his homeland and was later buried there (49:29–30; 50:13). His son Joseph also insisted on being buried in Canaan, which he recognized as the land the Lord had promised to Israel (50:24–25). The Jacob-Joseph cycle (see Introduction: Literary Features) begins and ends with references to the land of promise.
37:2 *generations.* See note on 2:4. The word here introduces the tenth and final main section of Genesis. *Joseph.* The author immediately introduces Joseph, on whom the last cycle of the patriarchal narrative centers. In his generation, he, more than any other, represented Israel—as a people who struggled with God and with men and overcame (see note on 32:28) and as a source of blessing to the nations (see 12:2–3). It is, moreover, through the life of Joseph that the covenant family in Canaan becomes an emerging nation in Egypt, thus setting the stage for the exodus. The story of God's dealings with the patriarchs foreshadows the subsequent Biblical account of God's purpose with Israel. It begins with the election and calling out of Abram from the post-Babel nations and ends with Israel in Egypt (in the person of Joseph) preserving the life of the nations (see 41:57; 50:20). So God would deliver Israel out of the nations (the exodus), eventually to send them on a mission of life to the nations (cf. Mat 28:18–20; Acts 1:8). *their evil report.* Doubtless about all his brothers (as the later context indicates), not just the sons of his father's concubines.
37:3 *coat of many colours.* A mark of Jacob's favoritism, "for

4 And when his brethren saw that their father loved him more than all his brethren, they [a]hated him, and could not speak peaceably unto him.

5 And Joseph dreamed a dream, and he told *it* his brethren: and they hated him yet the more.

6 And he said unto them, Hear, I pray you, this dream which I have dreamed:

7 For, [a]behold, we *were* binding sheaves in the field, and lo, my sheaf arose, and also stood upright; and behold, your sheaves stood round about, and made obeisance to my sheaf.

8 And his brethren said to him, Shalt thou indeed reign over us? or shalt thou indeed have dominion over us? And they hated him yet the more for his dreams, and for his words.

9 And he dreamed yet another dream, and told it his brethren, and said, Behold, I have dreamed a dream more; and behold, [a]the sun and the moon and the eleven stars made obeisance to me.

10 And he told *it* to his father, and to his brethren: and his father rebuked him, and said unto him, What *is* this dream that thou hast dreamed? Shall I and thy mother and [a]thy brethren indeed come to bow down ourselves to thee to the earth?

11 And [a]his brethren envied him; but his father [b]observed the saying.

Joseph sold to merchants

12 ¶ And his brethren went to feed their father's flock in [a]Shechem.

13 And Israel said unto Joseph, Do not thy brethren feed *the flock* in Shechem? come, and I will send thee unto them. And he said to him, Here *am* I.

14 And he said to him, Go, I pray thee, [1]see whether it be well with thy brethren, and well with the flocks; and bring me word again. So he sent him out of the vale of [a]Hebron, and he came to Shechem.

15 And a *certain* man found him, and behold, *he was* wandering in the field: and the man asked him, saying, What seekest thou?

16 And he said, I seek my brethren: [a]tell me, I pray thee, where they feed *their flocks.*

17 And the man said, They are departed hence; for I heard *them* say, Let us go to Dothan. And Joseph went after his brethren, and found them in [a]Dothan.

18 And when they saw him afar off, even before he came near unto them, [a]they conspired against him to slay him.

19 And they said one to another, Behold, this [1]dreamer cometh.

20 [a]Come now therefore, and let us slay him, and cast him into some pit, and we will say, *Some* evil beast hath devoured him: and we shall see what will become of his dreams.

21 And [a]Reuben heard *it,* and he delivered him out of their hands; and said, Let us not kill him.

22 And Reuben said unto them, Shed no blood, *but* cast him into this pit that *is* in the wilderness, and lay no hand upon him, that he might rid him out of their hands, to deliver him to his father again.

23 And it came to pass, when Joseph was come unto his brethren, that they stript Joseph out of his coat, *his* coat of many [1]colours that *was* on him;

24 And they took him, and cast him into a pit: and the pit *was* empty, *there was* no water in it.

25 [a]And they sat down to eat bread: and they lift up their eyes and looked, and behold, a company of [b]Ishmeelites came from Gilead with their camels bearing spicery and [c]balm and myrrh, going to carry *it* down to Egypt.

26 And Judah said unto his brethren, What

37:4 [a]ch. 27:41; 49:23
37:7 [a]ch. 42:6,9; 43:26; 44:14
37:9 [a]ch. 46:29
37:10 [a]ch. 27:29
37:11 [a]Acts 7:9 [b]Dan. 7:28; Luke 2:19,51
37:12 [a]ch. 33:18
37:14 [1]Heb. *see the peace of thy brethren, etc.*
37:14 [a]ch. 13:18; 35:27
37:16 [a]Sol. 1:7
37:17 [a]2 Ki. 6:13
37:18 [a]1 Sam. 19:1; Mat. 27:1; Mark 14:1; Acts 23:12
37:19 [1]Heb. *master of dreams*
37:20 [a]Prov. 1:11
37:21 [a]ch. 42:22
37:23 [1]Or, *pieces*
37:25 [a]Prov. 30:20 [b]See ver. 28,36 [c]Jer. 8:22

with such robes were the king's daughters that were virgins apparelled" (2 Sam 13:18).

37:5 *dream.* See note on 20:3.

37:7 *made obeisance.* Joseph's dream would later come true (42:6; 43:26; 44:14).

‡37:8 *Shalt thou indeed reign over us?* Joseph would later become the one "that was separated from his brethren" (Deut 33:16) and receive "the birthright"(1 Chr 5:2), at least the double portion of the inheritance (see note on 25:5), since his father adopted his two sons (48:5).

37:10 *thy mother.* Jacob possibly refers to Leah, since Rachel has already died (see 35:19). *bow down ourselves to thee.* An unsettling echo of a hope expressed earlier to Jacob by his father Isaac (see 27:29).

37:11 *observed the saying.* A hint that Jacob later recalled Joseph's dreams when events brought about their fulfillment. Cf. Mary's equally sensitive response to events during Jesus' boyhood days (Luke 2:19,51).

37:12 *Shechem.* See note on 33:18.

37:17 *Dothan.* Located about 13 miles north of Shechem, Dothan was already an ancient city by this time.

37:19 *dreamer.* The Hebrew for this word means "master of dreams" or "dream expert" and is here used with obvious sarcasm.

37:21 *Reuben . . . delivered him.* As Jacob's firstborn, he felt responsible for Joseph. He would later remind his brothers of this day (42:22). Initially Reuben's attempts to influence events seemed successful (30:14–17). But after his arrogant incest with Bilhah (see 35:22 and note) his efforts were always ineffective (see 42:37–38)—demonstrating his loss of the status of firstborn (see 49:3–4). Effective leadership passed to Judah (see vv. 26–27; 43:3–5,8–10; 44:14–34; 46:28; 49:8–12).

37:23–24 Similarly, in Egypt Joseph (though innocent of any wrongdoing) would be stripped of his position of privilege and thrown into prison—also as a result of domestic intrigue (ch. 39). His cloak also would be torn from him and shown to Potiphar, but he would be rescued (41:14).

37:25 *Ishmeelites.* Also called Midianites (v. 28; see Judg 8:22,24,26) and Medanites (the literal Hebrew for "Midianites" in v. 36). These various tribal groups were interrelated, since Midian and Medan, like Ishmael, were also sons of Abraham (25:2). *Gilead.* See note on 31:21. *balm.* An oil or gum, with healing properties (see Jer 51:8), exuded by the fruit or stems of one or more kinds of small trees. The balm of Gilead was especially effective (see Jer 8:22; 46:11). *myrrh.* Probably to be identified with labdanum, an aromatic gum (see Ps 45:8; Prov 7:17; Sol 3:6; 5:13) exuded from the leaves of the cistus rose. Its oil was used in beauty treatments (see Esth 2:12), and it was sometimes

profit *is it* if we slay our brother, and [a]conceal his blood?

27 Come, and let us sell him to the Ishmeelites, and [a]let not our hand be upon him; for he *is* [b]our brother *and* [c]our flesh. And his brethren [1]were content.

28 Then there passed by [a]Midianites merchantmen; and they drew and lift up Joseph out of the pit, [b]and sold Joseph to the Ishmeelites for [c]twenty *pieces* of silver: and they brought Joseph into Egypt.

29 And Reuben returned unto the pit; and behold, Joseph *was* not in the pit; and he [a]rent his clothes.

30 And he returned unto his brethren, and said, The child [a]*is* not; and I, whither shall I go?

31 And they took [a]Joseph's coat, and killed a kid of the goats, and dipped the coat in the blood;

32 And they sent the coat of many colours, and they brought *it* to their father; and said, This have we found: know now whether it *be* thy son's coat or no.

33 And he knew it, and said, *It is* my son's coat; an [a]evil beast hath devoured him; Joseph is without doubt rent in pieces.

34 And Jacob [a]rent his clothes, and put sackcloth upon his loins, and mourned for his son many days.

35 And all his sons and all his daughters [a]rose up to comfort him; but he refused to be comforted; and he said, For [b]I will go down into the grave unto my son mourning. Thus his father wept for him.

36 And [a]the Medanites sold him into Egypt unto Potiphar, an [1]officer of Pharaoh's, *and* [2][3]captain of the guard.

37:26 [a]ver. 20 37:27 [1]Heb. *hearkened* [a]1 Sam. 18:17 [b]ch. 42:21 [c]ch. 29:14 37:28 [a]Judg. 6:3 [b]Ps. 105:17; Acts 7:9 [c]See Mat. 27:9 37:29 [a]Job 1:20 37:30 [a]ch. 42:13,36 37:31 [a]ver. 23 37:33 [a]ver. 20 37:34 [a]2 Sam. 3:31 37:35 [a]2 Sam. 12:17 [b]ch. 42:38 37:36 [1]Heb. *eunuch:* But the word doth signify not only *eunuchs,* but also *chamberlains, courtiers,* and *officers* [2]Heb. *chief of the slaughtermen,* or, *executioners* [3]Or, *chief marshal* [a]ch. 39:1 38:1 [a]2 Ki. 4:8 38:2 [a]ch. 34:2 [b]1 Chr. 2:3 38:4 [a]Num. 26:19 38:5 [a]Num. 26:20 38:6 [a]ch. 21:21 38:7 [a]Num. 26:19 [b]1 Chr. 2:3 38:8 [a]Deut. 25:5 38:9 [a]Deut. 25:6 38:10 [1]Heb. *was evil in the eyes of the LORD* [a]ch. 46:12 38:11 [a]Ruth 1:13

Judah and Tamar

38 And it came to pass at that time, that Judah went down from his brethren, and [a]turned in to a certain Adullamite, whose name *was* Hirah.

2 And Judah [a]saw there a daughter of a certain Canaanite, whose name *was* [b]Shuah; and he took her, and went in unto her.

3 And she conceived, and bare a son; and he called his name Er.

4 And she conceived again, and bare a son; and she called his name [a]Onan.

5 And she yet again conceived, and bare a son; and called his name [a]Shelah: and he was at Chezib, when she bare him.

6 And Judah [a]took a wife for Er his firstborn, whose name *was* Tamar.

7 And [a]Er, Judah's firstborn, was wicked in the sight of the LORD; [b]and the LORD slew him.

8 And Judah said unto Onan, Go in unto [a]thy brother's wife, and marry her, and raise up seed to thy brother.

9 And Onan knew that the seed should not be [a]his; and it came to pass, when he went in unto his brother's wife, that he spilled *it* on the ground, lest that he should give seed to his brother.

10 And *the thing* which he did [1]displeased the LORD: wherefore he slew [a]him also.

11 Then said Judah to Tamar his daughter in law, [a]Remain a widow *at* thy father's house, till Shelah my son be grown: for he said, Lest

---

mixed with wine and drunk to relieve pain (see Mark 15:23). As a gift fit for a king, myrrh was brought to Jesus after His birth (Mat 2:11) and applied to His body after His death (John 19:39–40).

37:28 *twenty pieces of silver.* In later times, this amount was the value of a male of Joseph's age who had been dedicated to the Lord (see Lev 27:5).

37:31–33 Again a slaughtered goat figures prominently in an act of deception (see 27:5–13).

37:34 *rent his clothes.* See v. 29. *put sackcloth upon his loins.* Wearing coarse and uncomfortable sackcloth instead of ordinary clothes was a sign of mourning.

37:35 *daughters.* The term can include daughters-in-law (e.g., a daughter-in-law of Jacob is mentioned in 38:2). *the grave.* According to some, the Hebrew word *Sheol* can also refer in a more general way to the realm of the dead, the netherworld, where, it was thought, departed spirits live (for a description of *Sheol* see, e.g., Job 3:13–19).

37:36 *sold.* "For a servant" (Ps 105:17). The peoples of the Arabian Desert were long involved in international slave trade (cf. Amos 1:6,9). *guard.* The Hebrew for this word can mean "executioners" (the captain of whom was in charge of the royal prisoners; see 40:4), or it can mean "butchers" (the captain of whom was the chief cook in the royal court; cf. 1 Sam 9:23–24).

38:1–30 The unsavory events of this chapter illustrate the danger that Israel as God's separated people faced if they remained among the Canaanites (see 15:16 and note). In Egypt the Israelites were kept separate because the Egyptians despised them (43:32; 46:34). While there, God's people were able to develop into a nation without losing their identity. Judah's actions contrasted with those of Joseph (ch. 39)—demonstrating the moral superiority of Joseph, to whom leadership in Israel fell in his generation (see 37:5–9).

38:1 *went down from his brethren.* Joseph was separated from his brothers by force, but Judah voluntarily separated himself to seek his fortune among the Canaanites. *Adullamite.* Adullam was a town southwest of Jerusalem (see 2 Chr 11:5,7).

38:3–4 *Er . . . Onan.* The names also appear as designations of tribes in Mesopotamian documents of this time.

38:5 *Chezib.* Probably the same as Achzib (Josh 15:44), three miles west of Adullam. The "men of Chozeba" (another form of the same word) were descendants of Shelah son of Judah (see 1 Chr 4:21–22). The Hebrew root of the name means "deception" (see Mic 1:14 and note), a theme running throughout the story of Jacob and his sons.

38:6 *Judah took a wife for Er.* See note on 21:21.

38:8 A concise description of the custom known as "levirate marriage" (Latin *levir* means "brother-in-law"). Details of the practice are given in Deut 25:5–6, where it is laid down as a legal obligation within Israel (cf. Mat 22:24). The custom is illustrated in Ruth 4:5, though there it is extended to the nearest living relative (see Ruth 3:12 and note on Ruth 2:20), since neither Boaz nor the nearer kinsman was a brother-in-law.

38:9 *knew that the seed should not be his.* Similarly, Ruth's nearest kinsman was fearful that if he married Ruth he would endanger his own estate (Ruth 4:5–6). *spilled it on the ground.* A means of birth control sometimes called "onanism" (after Onan).

38:10 *the thing which he did.* His refusal to perform his levirate duty.

peradventure he die also, as his brethren *did.*
And Tamar went and dwelt [b]*in* her father's
house.
12 And [1]in process of time the daughter of
Shuah Judah's wife died; and Judah [a]was comforted, and went up unto his sheepshearers to
Timnath, he and his friend Hirah the Adullamite.
13 And it was told Tamar, saying, Behold
thy father in law goeth up [a]to Timnath to
shear his sheep.
14 And she put her widow's garments off
from her, and covered her with a vail, and
wrapped herself, and [a]sat in [1]an open place,
which *is* by the way to Timnath; for she saw
[b]that Shelah was grown, and she was not giv-
en unto him to wife.
15 When Judah saw her, he thought her to
be a harlot; because she had covered her face.
16 And he turned unto her by the way, and
said, Go to, I pray thee, let me come in unto
thee; (for he knew not that she *was* his daughter in law:) and she said, What wilt thou give
me, that thou mayest come in unto me?
17 And he said, [a]I will send *thee* [1]a kid
from the flock. And she said, [b]Wilt thou give
me a pledge, till thou send *it?*
18 And he said, What pledge shall I give
thee? And she said, [a]Thy signet, and thy
bracelets, and thy staff that *is* in thine hand.
And he gave *it* her, and came in unto her, and
she conceived by him.
19 And she arose, and went away, and
[a]laid by her vail from her, and put on the garments of her widowhood.
20 And Judah sent the kid by the hand of
his friend the Adullamite, to receive *his* pledge
from the woman's hand: but he found her not.
21 Then he asked the men of that place,
saying, Where *is* the harlot, that *was* [1]openly
by the way side? And they said, There was no
harlot in this *place.*

38:11 [b]Lev. 22:13
38:12 [1]Heb. *the days were multiplied* [a]2 Sam. 13:39
38:13 [a]Josh. 15:10,57
38:14 [1]Heb. *the door of eyes,* or, *of Enajim* [a]Prov. 7:12 [b]ver. 11,26
38:17 [1]Heb. *a kid of the goats* [a]Ezek. 16:33 [b]ver. 20
38:18 [a]ver. 25
38:19 [a]ver. 14
38:21 [1]Or, *in Enajim*
38:23 [1]Heb. *become a contempt*
38:24 [a]Judg. 19:2 [b]Lev. 21:9; Deut. 22:21
38:25 [a]ch. 37:32 [b]ver. 18
38:26 [a]ch. 37:33 [b]1 Sam. 24:17 [c]ver. 14 [d]Job 34:31,32
38:29 [1]Or, *Wherefore hast thou made* this *breach against thee?* [2]That is, *A breach* [a]ch. 46:12; Num. 26:20; 1 Chr. 2:4; Mat. 1:3
39:1 [a]ch. 37:36; Ps:105:17 [b]ch. 37:28

22 And he returned to Judah, and said, I
cannot find her; and also the men of the place
said, *that* there was no harlot in this *place.*
23 And Judah said, Let her take *it* to her,
lest we [1]be shamed: behold, I sent this kid,
and thou hast not found her.
24 And it came to pass about three months
after, that it was told Judah, saying, Tamar thy
daughter in law hath [a]played the harlot; and
also, behold, she *is* with child by whoredom.
And Judah said, Bring her forth, [b]and let her
be burnt.
25 When she *was* brought forth, she sent
to her father in law, saying, By the man, whose
these *are, am* I with child: and she said, [a]Dis-
cern, I pray thee, whose *are* these, [b]the signet,
and bracelets, and staff.
26 And Judah [a]acknowledged *them,* and
said, [b]She hath been more righteous than I;
because that [c]I gave her not to Shelah my son.
And he knew her again [d]no more.
27 And it came to pass in the time of her
travail, that, behold, twins *were* in her womb.
28 And it came to pass, when she travailed, that *the one* put out *his* hand: and the
midwife took and bound upon his hand a scarlet thread, saying, This came out first.
29 And it came to pass, as he drew back his
hand, that, behold, his brother came out: and
she said, [1]How hast thou broken forth? *this*
breach *be* upon thee: therefore his name was
called [a][2]Pharez.
30 And afterward came out his brother,
that had the scarlet thread upon his hand: and
his name was called Zarah.

Joseph and Potiphar's wife

39 And Joseph was brought down to
Egypt; and [a]Potiphar, an officer of
Pharaoh, captain of the guard, an Egyptian,
[b]bought him of the hand of the Ishmeelites,
which had brought him down thither.

38:11 *he said, Lest peradventure he die also, as his brethren did.* Thus Judah had no intention of giving Shelah to Tamar (see v. 14).

38:12 *Timnath.* Exact location unknown, but somewhere in the hill country of Judah (see Josh 15:48,57).

‡38:14 *sat . . . by the way.* Prostitutes (see v. 15) customarily stationed themselves by the roadside (Jer 3:2). *an open place* [lit. "the gate of Enaim"]. Enaim means "two springs"; probably the same as Enam in the western foothills of Judah (see Josh 15:33–34).

38:18 *signet, and thy bracelets.* Probably a small cylinder seal of the type used to sign clay documents by rolling them over the clay. The owner wore it around his neck on a cord threaded through a hole drilled lengthwise through it.

‡38:21 *harlot.* The Hebrew here differs from that used for "harlot" in v. 15 and means "temple prostitute". Judah's friend perhaps deliberately used the more acceptable term, since ritual prostitutes enjoyed a higher social status in Canaan than did ordinary prostitutes.

38:24 *let her be burnt.* In later times, burning was the legal penalty for prostitution (see Lev 21:9).

38:27–30 For a similarly unusual birth of twin boys see 25:24–26.

38:29 *Pharez.* Became the head of the leading clan in Judah and the ancestor of David (see Ruth 4:18–22) and ultimately of Christ (see Mat 1:1–6).

39:1 See 37:36. *brought down to Egypt.* Joseph's experiences in Egypt, as well as those of his youth in Canaan (see note on 37:23–24), are similar to Israel's national experiences in Egypt. Initially, because of God's blessing, Joseph attains a position of honor (in Potiphar's house); he is then unjustly thrown into prison, his only crime being his attractiveness and moral integrity; and finally he is raised up among the Egyptians as the one who, because God is with him, holds their lives in his hands. Similarly Israel was first received with honor in Egypt (because of Joseph); then she was subjected to cruel bondage, her only crime being God's evident blessings upon her; and finally God raised her up in the eyes of the Egyptians (through the ministry of Moses) as they came fearfully to recognize that these people and their God did indeed hold their lives in their hands. The author of Genesis knew the events of the exodus and shows how the history of God and the patriarchs moved forward to and foreshadowed that event (see also 15:13–16; 48:21–22; 50:24–25). *Ishmeelites.* See note on 37:25.

39:2–6 See vv. 20–23. Though Joseph's situation changed drastically, God's relationship to him remained the same.

2 And [a]the LORD was with Joseph, and he was a prosperous man; and he was in the house of his master the Egyptian.

3 And his master saw that the LORD *was* with him, and *that* the LORD [a]made all that he did to prosper in his hand.

4 And Joseph [a]found grace in his sight, and he served him: and he made him [b]overseer over his house, and all *that* he had he put into his hand.

5 And it came to pass from the time *that* he had made him overseer in his house, and over all that he had, that [a]the LORD blessed the Egyptian's house for Joseph's sake; and the blessing of the LORD was upon all that he had in the house, and in the field.

6 And he left all that he had in Joseph's hand; and he knew not ought he had, save the bread which he did eat. And Joseph [a]was *a* goodly *person,* and well favoured.

7 And it came to pass after these things, that his master's wife cast her eyes upon Joseph; and she said, [a]Lie with me.

8 But he refused, and said unto his master's wife, Behold, my master wotteth not what *is* with me in the house, and he hath committed all that he hath to my hand;

9 *There is* none greater in this house than I; neither hath he kept back any thing from me but thee, because thou *art* his wife: [a]how then can I do this great wickedness, and [b]sin against God?

10 And it came to pass, as she spake to Joseph day by day, that he hearkened not unto her, to lie by her, *or* to be with her.

11 And it came to pass about this time, that *Joseph* went into the house to do his business; and *there was* none of the men of the house there within.

12 And [a]she caught him by his garment, saying, Lie with me: and he left his garment in her hand, and fled, and got him out.

13 And it came to pass, when she saw that he had left his garment in her hand, and was fled forth,

14 That she called unto the men of her house, and spake unto them, saying, See, he hath brought in a Hebrew unto us to mock us; he came in unto me to lie with me, and I cried with a [1]loud voice:

15 And it came to pass, when he heard that I lifted up my voice and cried, that he left his garment with me, and fled, and got him out.

16 And she laid up his garment by her, until his lord came home.

17 And she [a]spake unto him according to these words, saying, The Hebrew servant, which thou hast brought unto us, came in unto me to mock me:

18 And it came to pass, as I lift up my voice and cried, that he left his garment with me, and fled out.

19 And it came to pass, when his master heard the words of his wife, which she spake unto him, saying, After this manner did thy servant to me; that his [a]wrath was kindled.

20 And Joseph's master took him, and [a]put him into the [b]prison, a place where the king's prisoners *were* bound: and he was there in the prison.

21 But the LORD was with Joseph, and [1]shewed him mercy, and [a]gave him favour in the sight of the keeper of the prison.

22 And the keeper of the prison [a]committed to Joseph's hand all the prisoners that *were* in the prison; and whatsoever they did there, he was the doer *of it.*

23 The keeper of the prison looked not to any thing *that was* under his hand; because [a]the LORD *was* with him, and *that* which he did, the LORD made *it* to prosper.

Joseph interprets dreams

40 And it came to pass after these things, *that* the [a]butler of the king of Egypt and *his* baker had offended their lord the king of Egypt.

2 And Pharaoh was [a]wroth against two *of* his officers, against the chief of the butlers, and against the chief of the bakers.

3 [a]And he put them in ward *in* the house of the captain of the guard, into the prison, the place where Joseph *was* bound.

4 And the captain of the guard charged Joseph with them, and he served them: and they continued a season in ward.

5 And they dreamed a dream both of them, each man his dream in one night, each man according to the interpretation of his dream,

39:2 [a]ver. 21; ch. 21:22; 26:24,28; 28:15; 1 Sam. 16:18; 18:14,28; Acts 7:9
39:3 [a]Ps. 1:3
39:4 [a]ver. 21 [b]ch. 24:2
39:5 [a]ch. 30:27
39:6 [a]1 Sam. 16:12
39:7 [a]2 Sam. 13:11
39:9 [a]Prov. 6:29,32 [b]ch. 20:6
39:12 [a]Prov. 7:13
39:14 [1]Heb. *great*
39:17 [a]Ex. 23:1; Ps. 120:3
39:19 [a]Prov. 6:34,35
39:20 [a]Ps. 105:18; 1 Pet. 2:19 [b]See ch. 40:3,15; 41:14
39:21 [1]Heb. *extended kindness unto him* [a]Ex. 3:21; Prov. 16:7; Dan. 1:9; Acts 7:9,10
39:22 [a]ch. 40:3,4
39:23 [a]ver. 2,3
40:1 [a]Neh. 1:11
40:2 [a]Prov. 16:14
40:3 [a]ch. 39:20,23

39:2 *the LORD was with Joseph.* See note on 26:3. This fact, mentioned several times here (vv. 3,21,23), is stressed also by Stephen (Acts 7:9).

39:5 *the LORD blessed the Egyptian's house for Joseph's sake.* The offspring of Abraham are becoming a blessing to the nations (see 12:2–3; 30:27).

39:6 *left all that he had in Joseph's hand.* Joseph had full responsibility for the welfare of Potiphar's house, as later he would have full responsibility in prison (vv. 22–23) and later still in all Egypt (41:41). Always this Israelite came to hold the welfare of his "world" in his hands—but always by the blessing and overruling of God, never by his own wits, as his father Jacob had so long attempted. In the role that he played in Israel's history and in the manner in which he lived it, Joseph was a true representative of Israel.

39:7 *cast her eyes upon*. The phrase is used in the same sense in Akkadian in Section 25 of the Code of Hammurapi.

39:9 *sin against God.* All sin is against God, first and foremost (see Ps 51:4).

39:10 *as she spake to Joseph day by day, that he hearkened not.* Samson twice succumbed under similar pressure (Judg 14:17; 16:16–17).

39:14 *a Hebrew.* See v. 17; see also note on 14:13.

39:20–23 See note on vv. 2–6.

39:20 *a place where the king's prisoners were bound.* Though understandably angry (see v. 19), Potiphar put Joseph in the "house of the captain of the guard" (40:3)—certainly not the worst prison available.

40:2 *chief of the butlers.* Would be the divinely appointed agent for introducing Joseph to Pharaoh (see 41:9–14).

40:5 *each man according to the interpretation of his dream.* Throughout the ancient Near East it was believed that dreams

the butler and the baker of the king of Egypt, which *were* bound in the prison.

6 And Joseph came in unto them in the morning, and looked upon them, and behold, they *were* sad.

7 And he asked Pharaoh's officers that *were* with him in the ward of his lord's house, saying, Wherefore [1]look ye *so* sadly to day?

8 And they said unto him, [a]We have dreamed a dream, and *there is* no interpreter of it. And Joseph said unto them, [b]*Do* not interpretations *belong* to God? tell me *them,* I pray you.

9 And the chief butler told his dream to Joseph, and said to him, In my dream, behold, a vine *was* before me;

10 And in the vine *were* three branches: and it *was* as though it budded, *and* her blossoms shot forth; *and* the clusters thereof brought forth ripe grapes:

11 And Pharaoh's cup *was* in my hand: and I took the grapes, and pressed them into Pharaoh's cup, and I gave the cup into Pharaoh's hand.

12 And Joseph said unto him, [a]This *is* the interpretation of it: The three branches [b]*are* three days:

13 Yet within three days shall Pharaoh [a1]lift up thine head, and restore thee unto thy place: and thou shalt deliver Pharaoh's cup into his hand, after the former manner when thou wast his butler.

14 But [a1]think on me when it shall be well with thee, and [b]shew kindness, I pray thee, unto me, and make mention of me unto Pharaoh, and bring me out of this house:

15 For indeed I was stolen away out of the land of the Hebrews: [a]and here also have I done nothing that they should put me into the dungeon.

16 When the chief baker saw that the interpretation was good, he said unto Joseph, I also *was* in my dream, and behold, *I had* three [1]white baskets on my head:

17 And in the uppermost basket *there was* of all *manner of* [1]bakemeats for Pharaoh; and the birds did eat them out of the basket upon my head.

40:7 [1]Heb. are *your faces evil?* 40:8 [a]ch. 41:15 [b]See ch. 41:16; Dan. 2:11,28,47 40:12 [a]ver. 18; ch. 41:12,25; Judg. 7:14; Dan. 2:36; 4:19 [b]ch. 41:26 40:13 [1]Or, *reckon* [a]2 Ki. 25:27; Ps. 3:3; Jer. 52:31 40:14 [1]Heb. *remember me with thee* [a]Luke 23:42 [b]Josh. 2:12; 1 Sam. 20:14,15; 2 Sam. 9:1; 1 Ki. 2:7 40:15 [a]ch. 39:20 40:16 [1]Or, *full of holes* 40:17 [1]Heb. *meat of Pharaoh, the work of a baker,* or, *cook*

40:18 [a]ver. 12 40:19 [1]Or, *reckon thee,* and take thy office *from thee* [a]ver. 13 40:20 [1]Or, *reckoned* [a]Mat. 14:6 [b]Mark 6:21 [c]ver. 13,19; Mat. 25:19 40:21 [a]ver. 13 [b]Neh. 2:1 40:22 [a]ver. 19 40:23 [a]Job 19:14; Eccl. 9:15,16; Amos 6:6 41:5 [1]Heb. *fat* 41:8 [a]Dan. 2:1; 4:5,19 [b]Ex. 7:11,22; Is. 29:14; Dan. 1:20; 2:2; 4:7 [c]Mat. 2:1

18 And Joseph answered and said, [a]This *is* the interpretation thereof: The three baskets *are* three days:

19 [a]Yet within three days shall Pharaoh [1]lift up thy head from off thee, and shall hang thee on a tree; and the birds shall eat thy flesh from off thee.

20 And it came to pass the third day, *which was* Pharaoh's [a]birthday, that he [b]made a feast unto all his servants: and he [c1]lifted up the head of the chief butler and of the chief baker among his servants.

21 And he [a]restored the chief butler unto his butlership again; and [b]he gave the cup into Pharaoh's hand:

22 But he [a]hanged the chief baker: as Joseph had interpreted to them.

23 Yet did not the chief butler remember Joseph, but [a]forgat him.

Pharaoh's dreams

41 And it came to pass at the end of two full years, that Pharaoh dreamed: and behold, he stood by the river.

2 And behold, there came up out of the river seven well favoured kine and fatfleshed; and they fed in a meadow.

3 And behold, seven other kine came up after them out of the river, ill favoured and leanfleshed; and stood by the *other* kine upon the brink of the river.

4 And the ill favoured and leanfleshed kine did eat up the seven well favoured and fat kine. So Pharaoh awoke.

5 And he slept and dreamed the second time: and behold, seven ears of corn came up upon one stalk, [1]rank and good.

6 And behold, seven thin ears and blasted with the east wind sprang up after them.

7 And the seven thin ears devoured the seven rank and full ears. And Pharaoh awoke, and behold, *it was* a dream.

8 And it came to pass in the morning [a]that his spirit was troubled; and he sent and called for all [b]the magicians of Egypt, and all the [c]wise men thereof: and Pharaoh told them his

had specific meanings and that proper interpretation of them could help the dreamer predict his future (see note on 20:3). God was beginning to prepare the way for Joseph's rise in Egypt.

40:8 *interpretations belong to God.* Only God can interpret dreams properly and accurately (see 41:16,25,28; Dan 2:28). *tell me them.* Joseph presents himself as God's agent through whom God will make known the revelation contained in their dreams—Israel is God's prophetic people through whom God's revelation comes to the nations (see 18:17 and note; 41:16,28, 32).

40:13 *lift up thine head, and restore thee unto thy place.* See Ps 3:3; 27:6. For this meaning of the idiom "lift up one's head" see 2 Ki 25:27 and Jer 52:31, where the Hebrew for "released" in the context of freeing a prisoner means lit. "lifted up the head of."

40:14 *think on me when it shall be well with thee.* Unfortunately, the cupbearer did not remember Joseph (v. 23) until two full years later (see 41:1,9–13).

40:15 *dungeon.* Probably hyperbole to reflect Joseph's despair (see note on 39:20). Since the same Hebrew word is translated "pit" in 37:24, the author of Genesis has established a link with Joseph's earlier experience at the hands of his brothers.

40:19 *lift up thy head.* A grisly pun based on the same idiom used in v. 13.

40:20 *Pharaoh's birthday.* Centuries later, the birthday of Herod the tetrarch would become the occasion for another beheading (see Mat 14:6–10).

41:2 *up out of the river seven well favoured kine.* Cattle often submerged themselves up to their necks in the Nile to escape sun and insects.

41:6 *blasted with the east wind.* The Palestinian sirocco (in Egypt the khamsin), which blows in from the desert (see Hos 13:15) in late spring and early fall, often withers vegetation (see Is 40:7; Ezek 17:10).

41:8 *his spirit was troubled.* See 40:6–7. *magicians.* Probably priests who claimed to possess occult knowledge. *none that could interpret them unto Pharaoh.* See Dan 2:10–11.

dream; but *there was* none that could interpret them unto Pharaoh.
9 Then spake the chief butler unto Pharaoh, saying, I do remember my faults *this* day:
10 Pharaoh was [a]wroth with his servants,
[b]and put me in ward *in* the captain of the
guard's house, *both* me and the chief baker:
11 And [a]we dreamed a dream in one night,
I and he; we dreamed each man according to
the interpretation of his dream.
12 And *there was* there with us a young
man, a Hebrew, [a]servant to the captain of the
guard; and we told him, and he [b]interpreted to
us our dreams; to each man according to his
dream he did interpret.
13 And it came to pass, [a]as he interpreted
to us, so it was; me he restored unto mine office, and him he hanged.
14 ¶ [a]Then Pharaoh sent and called Joseph,
and they [b][1]brought him hastily [c]out of the
dungeon: and he shaved *himself,* and changed
his raiment, and came in unto Pharaoh.
15 And Pharaoh said unto Joseph, I have
dreamed a dream, and *there is* none that can
interpret it: [a]and I have heard say of thee, *that*
[1]thou canst understand a dream to interpret it.
16 And Joseph answered Pharaoh, saying,
[a]*It is* not in me: [b]God shall give Pharaoh an
answer of peace.
17 And Pharaoh said unto Joseph, [a]In my
dream, behold, I stood upon the bank of the
river:
18 And behold, there came up out of the
river seven kine, fatfleshed and well favoured;
and they fed in a meadow:
19 And behold, seven other kine came up
after them, poor and very ill favoured and
leanfleshed, such as I never saw in all the land
of Egypt for badness:
20 And the lean and the ill favoured kine
did eat up the first seven fat kine:
21 And when they had [1]eaten them up, it
could not be known that they had [1]eaten
them; but they *were still* ill favoured, as at the
beginning. So I awoke.
22 And I saw in my dream, and behold,
seven ears came up in one stalk, full and good:
23 And behold, seven ears, [1]withered,
thin, *and* blasted with the east wind, sprung
up after them:
24 And the thin ears devoured the seven
good ears: and [a]I told *this* unto the magicians;
but *there was* none that could declare *it* to me.

41:10 [a]ch. 40:2,3 [b]ch. 39:20
41:11 [a]ch. 40:5
41:12 [a]ch. 37:36 [b]ch. 40:12
41:13 [a]ch. 40:22
41:14 [1]Heb. *made him run* [a]Ps. 105:20 [b]Dan. 2:25 [c]1 Sam. 2:8; Ps. 113:7,8
41:15 [1]Or, when *thou hearest a dream thou canst interpret it* [a]ver. 12; Dan. 5:16
41:16 [a]Dan. 2:30; Acts 3:12; 2 Cor. 3:5 [b]ch. 40:8; Dan. 2:22,28,47; 4:2
41:17 [a]ver. 1
41:21 [1]Heb. *come to the inward parts of them*
41:23 [1]Or, *small*
41:24 [a]ver. 8; Dan. 4:7
41:25 [a]Dan. 2:28,29,45; Rev. 4:1
41:27 [a]2 Ki. 8:1
41:28 [a]ver. 25
41:29 [a]ver. 47
41:30 [a]ver. 54 [b]ch. 47:13
41:31 [1]Heb. *heavy*
41:32 [1]Or, *prepared of God* [a]Num. 23:19; Is. 46:10,11
41:34 [1]Or, *overseers* [a]Prov. 6:6-8
41:35 [a]ver. 48
41:36 [1]Heb. *be not cut off* [a]ch. 47:15,19
41:37 [a]Ps. 105:19; Acts 7:10
41:38 [a]Num. 27:18; Job 32:8; Prov. 2:6; Dan. 4:8,18; 5:11,14; 6:3
41:40 [a]Ps. 105:21; Acts 7:10

25 And Joseph said unto Pharaoh, The
dream of Pharaoh *is* one: [a]God hath shewed
Pharaoh what he *is* about to do.
26 The seven good kine *are* seven years;
and the seven good ears *are* seven years: the
dream *is* one.
27 And the seven thin and ill favoured kine
that came up after them *are* seven years; and
the seven empty ears blasted with the east
wind shall be [a]seven years of famine.
28 [a]This *is* the thing which I have spoken
unto Pharaoh: What God *is* about to do he
sheweth unto Pharaoh.
29 Behold, there come [a]seven years of
great plenty throughout all the land of Egypt:
30 And there shall [a]arise after them seven
years of famine; and all the plenty shall be forgotten in the land of Egypt; and the famine
[b]shall consume the land;
31 And the plenty shall not be known in
the land by reason of that famine following; for
it *shall be* very [1]grievous.
32 And for that the dream was doubled
unto Pharaoh twice; *it is* because the [a]thing *is*
[1]established by God, and God will shortly
bring it to pass.
33 Now therefore let Pharaoh look out a
man discreet and wise, and set him over the
land of Egypt.
34 Let Pharaoh do *this,* and let him appoint
[1]officers over the land, and [a]take up the fifth
part of the land of Egypt in the seven plenteous years.
35 And [a]let them gather all the food of
those good years that come, and lay up corn
under the hand of Pharaoh, and let them keep
food in the cities.
36 And *that* food shall be for store to the
land against the seven years of famine, which
shall be in the land of Egypt; that the land
[a][1]perish not through the famine.

Pharaoh makes Joseph a ruler

37 ¶ And [a]the thing was good in the eyes of
Pharaoh, and in the eyes of all his servants.
38 And Pharaoh said unto his servants,
Can we find *such a one* as this *is,* a man [a]in
whom the spirit of God *is?*
39 And Pharaoh said unto Joseph, Forasmuch as God hath shewed thee all this, *there*
is none so discreet and wise as thou *art:*
40 [a]Thou shalt be over my house, and according unto thy word shall all my people be

41:13 *as he interpreted.* Because his words were from the Lord (see Ps 105:19).

41:14 *Pharaoh sent and called Joseph.* Effecting his permanent release from prison (see Ps 105:20). *shaved.* Egyptians were normally smooth-shaven, while Palestinians wore beards (see 2 Sam 10:5; Jer 41:5).

41:16 *It is not in me: God shall give Pharaoh an answer of peace.* See 40:8; Dan 2:27–28,30; 2 Cor 3:5.

41:27 *seven years of famine.* See Acts 7:11. Long famines were rare in Egypt because of the regularity of the annual overflow of the Nile, but not uncommon elsewhere (see 2 Ki 8:1). According to the NT, the great famine in the time of Elijah lasted three and a half years (Jas 5:17), thus half of seven years; it had been cut short by Elijah's intercession (1 Ki 18:42; Jas 5:18).

41:32 Repetition of a divine revelation was often used for emphasis (see 37:5–9; Amos 7:1–6,7–9; 8:1–3).

‡41:38 *spirit of God.* Perhaps "spirit of the gods," since spoken by Pharaoh. The word "spirit" should probably not be capitalized in such passages, since reference to the Holy Spirit would be out of character in statements by pagan rulers.

41:40 *Thou shalt be over my house.* Pharaoh took Joseph's advice (see v. 33) and decided that Joseph himself should be "governor over Egypt" (Acts 7:10; see also Ps 105:21). *according unto*

[1]ruled: only *in* the throne will I be greater
than thou.
41 And Pharaoh said unto Joseph, See, I
have [a]set thee over all the land of Egypt.
42 And Pharaoh [a]took off his ring from his
hand, and put it upon Joseph's hand, and [b]ar-
rayed him in vestures of [1]fine linen, [c]and put
a gold chain about his neck;
43 And he made him to ride in the second
chariot which he had; [a]and they cried before
him, [1][2]Bow the knee: and he made him *ruler*
[b]over all the land of Egypt.
44 And Pharaoh said unto Joseph, I *am*
Pharaoh, and without thee shall no man lift up
his hand or foot in all the land of Egypt.
45 And Pharaoh called Joseph's name
[1]Zaphnath-paaneah; and he gave him to wife
Asenath the daughter of Poti-pherah [2]priest of
On. And Joseph went out over *all* the land of
Egypt.
46 ¶ And Joseph *was* thirty years old when
he [a]stood before Pharaoh king of Egypt. And Joseph went out from the presence of Pharaoh,
and went throughout all the land of Egypt.
47 And in the seven plenteous years the
earth brought forth by handfuls.
48 And he gathered up all the food of the
seven years, which were in the land of Egypt,
and laid up the food in the cities: the food of
the field, which *was* round about every city,
laid he up in the same.
49 And Joseph gathered corn [a]as the sand
of the sea, very much, until he left numbering;
for *it was* without number.
50 [a]And unto Joseph were born two sons
before the years of famine came, which Asenath the daughter of Poti-pherah [1]priest of On
bare unto him.
51 And Joseph called the name of the first-

41:40 [1]Heb. *[be] armed,* or, *kiss*
41:41 [a]Dan. 6:3
41:42 [1]Or, *silk* [a]Esth. 3:10 [b]Esth. 8:15 [c]Dan. 5:7,29
41:43 [1]Or, *tender father* [2]Heb. *Abrech* [a]Esth. 6:9 [b]ch. 42:6; Acts 7:10
41:45 [1][Which in the Coptic signifies, *A revealer of secrets,* or, *The man to whom secrets are revealed*] [2]Or, *prince*
41:46 [a]1 Sam. 16:21; 1 Ki. 12:6,8; Dan. 1:19
41:49 [a]ch. 22:17; Judg. 7:12; 1 Sam. 13:5
41:50 [1]Or, *prince* [a]ch. 46:20; 48:5
41:51 [1]That is, *Forgetting*
41:52 [1]That is, *Fruitful* [a]ch. 49:22
41:54 [a]Ps. 105:16; Acts 7:11 [b]ver. 30
41:56 [1]Heb. *all wherein* was [a]ch. 42:6
41:57 [a]Deut. 9:28
42:1 [a]Acts 7:12
42:2 [a]ch. 43:8; Is. 38:1
42:4 [a]ver. 38
42:5 [a]Acts 7:11

born [1]Manasseh: For God, *said he,* hath made
me forget all my toil, and all my father's house.
52 And the name of the second called he
[1]Ephraim: For God hath caused me to be
[a]fruitful in the land of my affliction.
53 ¶ And the seven years of plenteousness,
that was in the land of Egypt, were ended.
54 [a]And the seven years of dearth began to
come, [b]according as Joseph had said: and the
dearth was in all lands; but in all the land of
Egypt there was bread.
55 And when all the land of Egypt was famished, the people cried to Pharaoh for bread:
and Pharaoh said unto all the Egyptians, Go
unto Joseph; what he saith to you, do.
56 And the famine was over all the face of
the earth: And Joseph opened [1]all the storehouses, and [a]sold unto the Egyptians; and the
famine waxed sore in the land of Egypt.
57 [a]And all countries came into Egypt to
Joseph for to buy *corn;* because that the
famine was *so* sore in all lands.

Joseph's brethren visit Egypt

42 Now when [a]Jacob saw that there was
corn in Egypt, Jacob said unto his
sons, Why do ye look one upon another?
2 And he said, Behold, I have heard that
there is corn in Egypt: get you down thither,
and buy for us from thence; that we may [a]live,
and not die.
3 And Joseph's ten brethren went down to
buy corn in Egypt.
4 But Benjamin, Joseph's brother, Jacob
sent not with his brethren; for he said, [a]Lest
peradventure mischief befall him.
5 And the sons of Israel came to buy *corn*
among those that came: for the famine was [a]in
the land of Canaan.

thy word shall all my people be ruled. More lit. "at your command all my people are to kiss (you)"—i.e., kiss your hands or feet in an act of homage and submission (see Ps 2:12 and note).

41:42 Three symbols of transfer and/or sharing of royal authority, referred to also in Esth 3:10 (ring); Esth 6:11 (apparel); and Dan 5:7,16,29 (chain of gold).

41:43 *he made him to ride in the second chariot.* The position was probably that of vizier, the highest executive office below that of the king himself. *Bow the knee.* The Hebrew here may be an Egyptian imperative of a Semitic loanword.

41:45 *called Joseph's name Zaphnath-paaneah.* As a part of assigning Joseph an official position within his royal administration (see note on 1:5). Pharaoh presumed to use this marvelously endowed servant of the Lord for his own royal purposes—as a later Pharaoh would attempt to use divinely blessed Israel for the enrichment of Egypt (Ex 1). He did not recognize that Joseph served a Higher Power, whose kingdom and redemptive purposes are being advanced. (The meaning of Joseph's Egyptian name is uncertain.) *Asenath.* The name is Egyptian and probably means "She belongs to (the goddess) Neith." *Poti-phera.* Not the same person as "Potiphar" (37:36; 39:1); the name (also Egyptian) means "he whom (the sun-god) Ra has given." *On.* Located ten miles northeast of modern Cairo, it was called Heliopolis ("city of the sun") by the Greeks and was an important center for the worship of Ra, who had a temple there. Poti-phera therefore bore an appropriate name.

41:46 *thirty years old.* In just 13 years (see 37:2), Joseph had become second-in-command (v. 43) in Egypt.

41:49 *as the sand of the sea.* A simile also for the large number of offspring promised to Abraham and Jacob (see 22:17; 32:12).

41:52 *Ephraim.* The wordplay on the name (Ephraim sounds like the Hebrew for "twice fruitful") reflects the fact that God gave Joseph "two" (see v. 50) sons.

41:57 *all countries.* The known world from the writer's perspective (the Middle East). This description of the famine in the time of Joseph echoes the author's description of the flood in the time of Noah. God saved only Noah and his family from the flood, so that Noah became the new (after Adam) father of the race. With the call of Abram out of the post-flood and post-Babel nations, God once more singled out one man, now to be the father of His special people. God promised that, through this man and his descendants, "shall all families of the earth be blessed" (12:3). The author highlights the fact that in this new crisis hope rested with one of these descendants.

42:2–3 Stephen refers to this incident (Acts 7:12).

42:4 *Benjamin, Joseph's brother, Jacob sent not.* Their mother Rachel had died (35:19), and Jacob thought Joseph also was dead (37:33). Jacob did not want to lose Benjamin, the remaining son of his beloved Rachel.

42:5 *famine was in the land of Canaan.* As in the time of Abram (see 12:10 and note).

6 And Joseph *was* the governor [a]over the land, *and* he *it was* that sold to all the people of the land: and Joseph's brethren came, and [b]bowed down themselves before him *with* their faces to the earth.

7 And Joseph saw his brethren, and he knew them, but made himself strange unto them, and spake [1]roughly unto them; and he said unto them, Whence come ye? And they said, From the land of Canaan to buy food.

8 And Joseph knew his brethren, but they knew not him.

9 And Joseph [a]remembered the dreams which he dreamed of them, and said unto them, Ye *are* spies; to see the nakedness of the land you are come.

10 And they said unto him, Nay, my lord, but to buy food are thy servants come.

11 We *are* all one man's sons; we *are* true *men*, thy servants are no spies.

12 And he said unto them, Nay, but to see the nakedness of the land you are come.

13 And they said, Thy servants *are* twelve brethren, the sons of one man in the land of Canaan; and behold, the youngest *is this* day with our father, and one [a]*is* not.

14 And Joseph said unto them, That *is it* that I spake unto you, saying, Ye *are* spies:

15 Hereby ye shall be proved: [a]By the life of Pharaoh ye shall not go forth hence, except your youngest brother come hither.

16 Send one of you, and let him fetch your brother, and ye shall be [1]kept in prison, that your words may be proved, whether *there be any* truth in you: or else by the life of Pharaoh surely ye *are* spies.

17 And he [1]put them all together into ward three days.

18 And Joseph said unto them the third day, This do, and live; [a]*for* I fear God:

19 If ye *be* true *men*, let one of your brethren be bound in the house of your prison: go ye, carry corn *for* the famine of your houses:

20 But [a]bring your youngest brother unto me; so shall your words be verified, and ye shall not die. And they did so.

21 And they said one to another, [a]We *are* verily guilty concerning our brother, in that we saw the anguish of his soul, when he besought us, and we would not hear; [b]therefore is this distress come upon us.

22 And Reuben answered them, saying, [a]Spake I not unto you, saying, Do not sin against the child; and ye would not hear? therefore, behold, also his blood is [b]required.

23 And they knew not that Joseph understood *them;* for [1]he spake unto them by an interpreter.

24 And he turned himself about from them, and wept; and returned to them *again*, and communed with them, and took from them Simeon, and bound him before their eyes.

25 Then Joseph commanded to fill their sacks *with* corn, and to restore every man's money into his sack, and to give them provision for the way: and [a]thus did he unto them.

26 ¶ And they laded their asses with the corn, and departed thence.

27 And as [a]one *of them* opened his sack to give his ass provender in the inn, he espied his money; for behold, it *was* in his sack's mouth.

28 And he said unto his brethren, My money is restored; and lo, *it is* even in my sack: and their heart [1]failed *them*, and they were afraid, saying one to another, What *is* this *that* God hath done unto us?

29 And they came unto Jacob their father unto the land of Canaan, and told him all that befell unto them; saying,

30 The man, *who is* the lord of the land, [a]spake [1]roughly to us, and took us for spies of the country.

31 And we said unto him, We *are* true *men;* we are no spies:

32 We *be* twelve brethren, sons of our father; one *is* not, and the youngest *is this* day with our father in the land of Canaan.

33 And the man, the lord of the country, said unto us, [a]Hereby shall I know that ye *are* true *men;* leave one of your brethren *here* with me, and take *food for* the famine of your households, and be gone:

34 And bring your youngest brother unto me: then shall I know that ye *are* no spies, but *that* ye *are* true *men: so* will I deliver you your brother, and ye shall [a]traffick in the land.

35 And it came to pass as they emptied their sacks, that behold, [a]every man's bundle of money *was* in his sack: and when *both* they and their father saw the bundles of money, they were afraid.

36 And Jacob their father said unto them, Me have ye [a]bereaved of my children: Joseph *is* not, and Simeon *is* not, and ye will take Benjamin *away:* all these things are against me.

42:6 [a]ch. 41:41 [b]ch. 37:7
42:7 [1]Heb. *hard* things *with them*
42:9 [a]ch. 37:5,9
42:13 [a]ch. 37:30; Lam. 5:7; See ch. 44:20
42:15 [a]See 1 Sam. 1:26; 17:55
42:16 [1]Heb. *bound*
42:17 [1]Heb. *gathered*
42:18 [a]Lev. 25:43; Neh. 5:15
42:20 [a]ver. 34; ch. 43:5; 44:23
42:21 [a]Job 36:8,9; Hos. 5:15 [b]Prov. 21:13; Mat. 7:2
42:22 [a]ch. 37:21 [b]ch. 9:5; 1 Ki. 2:32; 2 Chr. 24:22; Ps. 9:12; Luke 11:50,51
42:23 [1]Heb. *an interpreter* was *between them*
42:25 [a]Mat. 5:44; Rom. 12:17,20,21
42:27 [a]See ch. 43:21
42:28 [1]Heb. *went forth*
42:30 [1]Heb. *with us hard* things [a]ver. 7
42:33 [a]ver. 15,19,20
42:34 [a]ch. 34:10
42:35 [a]See ch. 43:21
42:36 [a]ch. 43:14

42:6 *bowed down themselves before him.* In fulfillment of Joseph's dreams (see 37:7,9).

42:8 *Joseph knew his brethren.* Although at least 20 years had passed since he had last seen them (see 37:2; 41:46,53–54), they had been adults at the time and their appearance had not changed much. *they knew not him.* Joseph, a teenager at the time of his enslavement, was now an adult in an unexpected position of authority, wearing Egyptian clothes and speaking to his brothers through an interpreter (see v. 23). He was, moreover, shaven in the Egyptian manner (see note on 41:14).

42:10 *my lord . . . thy servants.* Unwittingly, Joseph's brothers again fulfilled his dreams and their own scornful fears (see 37:8).

42:15 *By the life of Pharaoh.* The most solemn oaths were pronounced in the name of the reigning monarch (as here) or of the speaker's deities (Ps 16:4; Amos 8:14) or of the Lord Himself (Judg 8:19; 1 Sam 14:39,45; 19:6).

42:21 *anguish of his soul . . . is this distress come upon us.* The brothers realized they were beginning to reap what they had sown (see Gal 6:7).

42:22 See 37:21–22 and note on 37:21.

42:24 *took from them Simeon.* Jacob's second son (see 29:32–33) is imprisoned instead of the firstborn Reuben, perhaps because the latter had saved Joseph's life years earlier (37:21–22).

37 And Reuben spake unto his father, saying, Slay my two sons, if I bring him not to
thee: deliver him into my hand, and I will
bring him to thee again.
38 And he said, My son shall not go down
with you; for [a]his brother is dead, and he is
left alone: [b]if mischief befall him by the way in
the which ye go, then shall ye [c]bring down my
gray hairs with sorrow to the grave.

The second trip to Egypt

43 And the famine *was* [a]sore in the
land.
2 And it came to pass, when they had eat-
en up the corn which they had brought out of
Egypt, their father said unto them, Go again,
buy us a little food.
3 And Judah spake unto him, saying, The
man [1]did solemnly protest unto us, saying, Ye
shall not see my face, except your [a]brother *be*
with you.
4 If thou wilt send our brother with us, we
will go down and buy thee food:
5 But if thou wilt not send *him*, we will not
go down: for the man said unto us, Ye shall not
see my face, except your brother *be* with you.
6 And Israel said, Wherefore dealt ye *so* ill
with me, *as* to tell the man whether ye had yet
a brother?
7 And they said, The man [1]asked us straitly of our state, and of our kindred, saying, *Is*
your father yet alive? have ye *another* brother?
and we told him according to the [2]tenor of
these words: [3]could we certainly know that he
would say, Bring your brother down?
8 And Judah said unto Israel his father,
Send the lad with me, and we will arise and
go; that we may live, and not die, both we, and
thou, *and* also our little ones.
9 I will be surety for him; of my hand shalt
thou require him: [a]if I bring him not unto
thee, and set him before thee, then let me
bear the blame for ever:
10 For except we had lingered, surely now
we had returned [1]this second time.
11 And their father Israel said unto them,
If *it must be* so now, do this; take of the best
fruits in the land in your vessels, and [a]carry
down the man a present, a little [b]balm, and a
little honey, spices, and myrrh, nuts, and almonds:
12 And take double money in your hand;
and the money [a]that was brought again in the
mouth of your sacks, carry *it* again in your
hand; peradventure it *was* an oversight:
13 Take also your brother, and arise, go
again unto the man:
14 And God Almighty give you mercy before the man, that he may send away your other brother, and Benjamin. [a 1]If I be bereaved of
my children, I am bereaved.
15 ¶ And the men took that present, and
they took double money in their hand, and
Benjamin; and rose up, and went down *to*
Egypt, and stood before Joseph.
16 And when Joseph saw Benjamin with
them, he said to the [a]ruler of his house, Bring
these men home, and [1]slay, and make ready;
for *these* men shall [2]dine with me at noon.
17 And the man did as Joseph bade; and
the man brought the men into Joseph's house.
18 And the men were afraid, because they
were brought into Joseph's house; and they
said, Because of the money that was returned
in our sacks at the first time *are* we brought in;
that he may [1]seek occasion against us, and fall
upon us, and take us for bondmen, and our
asses.
19 And they came near to the steward of
Joseph's house, and they communed with him
at the door of the house,
20 And said, O sir, [a 1]we came indeed
down at the first time to buy food:
21 And [a]it came to pass, when we came to
the inn, that we opened our sacks, and behold,
every man's money *was* in the mouth of his
sack, our money in full weight: and we have
brought it again in our hand.
22 And other money have we brought
down in our hands to buy food: we cannot tell
who put our money in our sacks.
23 And he said, Peace *be* to you, fear not:
your God, and the God of your father, hath giv-
en you treasure in your sacks: [1]I had your
money. And he brought Simeon out unto
them.
24 And the man brought the men into Joseph's house, and [a]gave *them* water, and they
washed their feet; and he gave their asses
provender.
25 And they made ready the present
against Joseph came at noon: for they heard
that they should eat bread there.
26 And when Joseph came home, they

42:38 [a]ver. 13; ch. 37:33; 44:28 [b]ver. 4; ch. 44:29 [c]ch. 37:35; 44:31
43:1 [a]ch. 41:54,57
43:3 [1]Heb. *protesting he protested* [a]ch. 42:20; 44:23
43:7 [1]Heb. *asking he asked us* [2]Heb. *mouth* [3]Heb. *knowing could we know*
43:9 [a]ch. 44:32; Philem. 18,19
43:10 [1]Or, *twice by this*
43:11 [a]ch. 32:20; Prov. 18:16 [b]ch. 37:25; Jer. 8:22
43:12 [a]ch. 42:25,35
43:14 [1]Or, *And I, as I have been, etc.* [a]Esth. 4:16
43:16 [1]Heb. *kill a killing* [2]Heb. *eat* [a]ch. 24:2; 39:4; 44:1
43:18 [1]Heb. *roll himself upon us*
43:20 [1]Heb. *coming down we came down* [a]ch. 42:3,10
43:21 [a]ch. 42:27,35
43:23 [1]Heb. *your money came to me*
43:24 [a]ch. 18:4; 24:32

42:37 *my two sons.* Reuben's generous offer as security for Benjamin's safety (see note on 37:21).

43:3 *Judah spake unto him.* From this point on, Judah became the spokesman for his brothers (see vv. 8–10; 44:14–34; 46:28). His tribe would become preeminent among the 12 (see 49:8–10), and he would be an ancestor of Jesus (see Mat 1:2,17; Luke 3:23,33).

43:9 Judah offered himself as security for Benjamin's safety—an even more generous gesture than that of Reuben (see 42:37 and note).

‡43:11 *carry . . . a present.* A customary practice when approaching one's superior, whether political (see 1 Sam 16:20), military (see 1 Sam 17:18) or religious (see 2 Ki 5:15). *balm . . . myrrh.* See 37:25 and note. *honey.* Either that produced by bees, or an inferior substitute made by boiling grape or date juice down to a thick syrup. *nuts.* Pistachio nuts, mentioned only here in the Bible; the fruit of a small, broad-crowned tree that is native to Asia Minor, Syria and Canaan but not to Egypt.

43:14 *God Almighty.* See note on 17:1. *If I be bereaved . . . I am bereaved.* Cf. Esther's similar phrase of resignation in Esth 4:16.

43:21 The brothers' statement to Joseph's steward compressed the details (see 42:27,35).

43:23 *your God . . . hath given you treasure.* The steward spoke better than he knew.

43:24 See note on 18:2.

brought him the present which *was* in their hand into the house, and [a]bowed themselves to him to the earth.

27 And he asked them of *their* [a 1]welfare, and said, [2]*Is* your father well, the old man [b]of whom ye spake? *Is* he yet alive?

28 And they answered, Thy servant our father *is* in good health, he *is* yet alive. [a]And they bowed down their heads, and made obeisance.

29 And he lift up his eyes, and saw his brother Benjamin, [a]his mother's son, and said, *Is* this your younger brother, [b]of whom ye spake unto me? And he said, God be gracious unto thee, my son.

30 And Joseph made haste; for [a]his bowels did yern upon his brother: and he sought *where* to weep; and he entered into *his* chamber, and [b]wept there.

31 And he washed his face, and went out, and refrained himself, and said, Set on [a]bread.

32 And they set on for him by himself, and for them by themselves, and for the Egyptians, which did eat with him, by themselves: because the Egyptians might not eat bread with the Hebrews; for that *is* [a]an abomination unto the Egyptians.

33 And they sat before him, the firstborn according to his birthright, and the youngest according to his youth: and the men marvelled one at another.

34 And he took *and sent* messes unto them from before him: but Benjamin's mess was [a]five times so much as any of theirs. And they drunk, and [1]were merry with him.

The missing silver cup

44 And he commanded [1]the steward of his house, saying, Fill the men's sacks *with* food, as much as they can carry, and put every man's money in his sack's mouth.

2 And put my cup, the silver cup, in the sack's mouth of the youngest, and his corn money. And he did according to the word that Joseph had spoken.

3 As soon as the morning was light, the men were sent away, they and their asses.

4 *And* when they were gone out of the city, *and* not *yet* far off, Joseph said unto his steward, Up, follow after the men; and when thou dost overtake them, say unto them, Wherefore have ye rewarded evil for good?

5 *Is* not this *it* in which my lord drinketh, and whereby indeed he [1]divineth? ye have done evil in *so* doing.

6 And he overtook them, and he spake unto them these *same* words.

7 And they said unto him, Wherefore saith my lord these words? God forbid that thy servants should do according to this thing:

8 Behold, [a]the money, which we found in our sacks' mouths, we brought again unto thee out of the land of Canaan: how then should we steal out of thy lord's house silver or gold?

9 With whom*soever* of thy servants it be found, [a]both let him die, and we also will be my lord's bondmen.

10 And he said, Now also *let* it *be* according unto your words: he with whom it is found shall be my servant; and ye shall be blameless.

11 Then they speedily took down every man his sack to the ground, and opened every man his sack.

12 And he searched, *and* began at the eldest, and left at the youngest: and the cup was found in Benjamin's sack.

13 Then they [a]rent their clothes, and laded every man his ass, and returned to the city.

14 ¶ And Judah and his brethren came to Joseph's house; for he *was* yet there: and they [a]fell before him on the ground.

15 And Joseph said unto them, What deed *is* this that ye have done? wot ye not that such a man as I can certainly [1]divine?

16 And Judah said, What shall we say unto my lord? what shall we speak? or how shall we clear ourselves? God hath found out the iniquity of thy servants: behold, [a]we *are* my lord's servants, both we, and *he* also with whom the cup is found.

17 And he said, [a]God forbid that I should do so: *but* the man in whose hand the cup is found, he shall be my servant; and as for you, get you up in peace unto your father.

18 Then Judah came near unto him, and said, O my lord, let thy servant, I pray thee, speak a word in my lord's ears, and [a]let not

43:26 [a]ch. 37:7,10
43:27 [1]Heb. *peace* [2]Heb. Is there *peace to your father* [a]ch. 37:14 [b]ch. 42:11,13
43:28 [a]ch. 37:7,10
43:29 [a]ch. 35:17,18 [b]ch. 42:13
43:30 [a]1 Ki. 3:26 [b]ch. 42:24
43:31 [a]ver. 25
43:32 [a]ch. 46:34; Ex. 8:26
43:34 [1]Heb. *they drank largely* [a]ch. 45:22
44:1 [1]Heb. him *that* was *over his house*
44:5 [1]Or, *maketh trial?*
44:8 [a]ch. 43:21
44:9 [a]ch. 31:32
44:13 [a]ch. 37:29,34; Num. 14:6; 2 Sam. 1:11
44:14 [a]ch. 37:7
44:15 [1]Or, *make trial?*
44:16 [a]ver. 9
44:17 [a]Prov. 17:15
44:18 [a]ch. 18:30,32; Ex. 32:22

43:26 *bowed themselves to him to the earth.* Additional fulfillment of Joseph's dreams (37:7,9; see also 42:6; 43:28).
43:29 *Benjamin, his mother's son.* Joseph's special relationship to Benjamin is clear. *God be gracious unto thee.* Later blessings and benedictions would echo these words (see Num 6:25; Ps 67:1).
43:30 *Joseph . . . wept.* Both emotional and sensitive, he wept often (see 42:24; 45:2,14–15; 46:29).
43:32 *Egyptians might not eat bread with the Hebrews.* The taboo was probably based on ritual or religious reasons (see Ex 8:26), unlike the Egyptian refusal to associate with shepherds (see 46:34), which was probably based on social custom.
43:34 *Benjamin's mess was five times so much.* Again reflecting his special status with Joseph (see note on v. 29; see also 45:22).
44:4 *the city.* Identity unknown, though Memphis (about 13 miles south of modern Cairo) and Zoan (in the eastern delta region) have been suggested.
44:5 *he divineth.* See v. 15; see also note on 30:27.
44:9 *With whomsoever of thy servants it be found, both let him die.* Years earlier, Jacob had given Laban a similar rash response (see 31:32 and note).
44:10 The steward softened the penalty contained in the brothers' proposal.
44:12 *began at the eldest, and left at the youngest.* For a similar building up of suspense see 31:33.
44:13 *rent their clothes.* A sign of distress and grief (see 37:29).
44:14 *fell before him on the ground.* Further fulfillment of Joseph's dreams in 37:7,9 (see 42:6; 43:26,28).
44:16 *God hath found out the iniquity of thy servants.* Like Joseph's steward (see note on 43:23), Judah spoke better than he knew—or perhaps his words had a double meaning (see 42:21).
44:18 *Judah . . . said.* See note on 43:3. *lord . . . servant.* See note on 42:10. *thou art even as Pharaoh.* Words more flattering than true (see 41:40,43).

thine anger burn against thy servant: for thou *art* even as Pharaoh.

19 My lord asked his servants, saying, Have ye a father, or a brother?

20 And we said unto my lord, We have a father, an old man, and [a]a child of *his* old age, a little one; and his brother is dead, and he alone is left of his mother, and his father loveth him.

21 And thou saidst unto thy servants, [a]Bring him down unto me, that I may set mine eyes upon him.

22 And we said unto my lord, The lad cannot leave his father: for *if* he should leave his father, *his father* would die.

23 And thou saidst unto thy servants, [a]Except your youngest brother come down with you, ye shall see my face no more.

24 And it came to pass when we came up unto thy servant my father, we told him the words of my lord.

25 And [a]our father said, Go again, *and* buy us a little food.

26 And we said, We cannot go down: if our youngest brother be with us, then will we go down: for we may not see the man's face, except our youngest brother *be* with us.

27 And thy servant my father said unto us, Ye know that [a]my wife bare me two *sons:*

28 And the one went out from me, and I said, [a]Surely he is torn in pieces; and I saw him not since:

29 And if ye [a]take this also from me, and mischief befall him, ye shall bring down my gray hairs with sorrow to the grave.

30 Now therefore when I come to thy servant my father, and the lad *be* not with us; seeing that [a]his life *is* bound up in *the lad's* life;

31 It shall come to pass, when he seeth that the lad *is* not *with us,* that he will die: and thy servants shall bring down the gray hairs of thy servant our father with sorrow to the grave.

32 For thy servant became surety for the lad unto my father, saying, [a]If I bring him not unto thee, then I shall bear the blame to my father for ever.

33 Now therefore, I pray thee, [a]let thy servant abide instead of the lad a bondman to my lord; and let the lad go up with his brethren.

34 For how shall I go up to my father, and the lad *be* not with me? lest peradventure I see the evil that shall [1]come on my father.

Joseph reveals his identity

45 Then Joseph could not refrain himself before all them that stood by him; and he cried, Cause every man to go out from me. And there stood no man with him, while Joseph made himself known unto his brethren.

2 And he [1]wept aloud: and the Egyptians and the house of Pharaoh heard.

3 And Joseph said unto his brethren, [a]I *am* Joseph; doth my father yet live? And his brethren could not answer him; for they were [b1]troubled at his presence.

4 And Joseph said unto his brethren, Come near to me, I pray you. And they came near. And he said, I *am* Joseph your brother, [a]whom ye sold into Egypt.

5 Now therefore be not grieved, [1]nor angry with yourselves, that ye sold me hither: [a]for God did send me before you to preserve life.

6 For these two years *hath* the famine *been* in the land: and yet *there are* five years, *in* the which *there shall* neither *be* earing nor harvest.

7 And God sent me before you [1]to preserve you a posterity in the earth, and to save your lives by a great deliverance.

8 So now *it was* not you *that* sent me hither, but God: and he hath made me [a]a father to Pharaoh, and lord of all his house, and a ruler throughout all the land of Egypt.

9 Haste you, and go up to my father, and say unto him, Thus saith thy son Joseph, God hath made me lord of all Egypt: come down unto me, tarry not:

10 And [a]thou shalt dwell in the land of Goshen, and thou shalt be near unto me, thou, and thy children, and thy children's children, and thy flocks, and thy herds, and all that thou hast:

11 And there will I nourish thee; for yet *there are* five years of famine; lest thou, and thy household, and all that thou hast, come to poverty.

44:20 [a]ch. 37:3
44:21 [a]ch. 42:15,20
44:23 [a]ch. 43:3,5
44:25 [a]ch. 43:2
44:27 [a]ch. 46:19
44:28 [a]ch. 37:33
44:29 [a]ch. 42:36,38
44:30 [a]1 Sam. 18:1
44:32 [a]ch. 43:9
44:33 [a]Ex. 32:32

44:34 [1]Heb. *find my father*
45:2 [1]Heb. *gave forth his voice in weeping*
45:3 [1]Or, *terrified* [a]Acts 7:13 [b]Job 4:5; 23:15; Mat. 14:26; Mark 6:50
45:4 [a]ch. 37:28
45:5 [1]Heb. *neither let there be anger in your eyes* [a]ch. 50:20; Ps. 105:16,17
45:7 [1]Heb. *to put for you a remnant*
45:8 [a]ch. 41:43; Judg. 17:10
45:10 [a]ch. 47:1

44:30 *his life is bound up in the lad's life.* The Hebrew underlying this clause is later used for "the soul of Jonathan" being "knit with the soul of David" (1 Sam 18:1).

44:33 *instead of the lad.* Judah's willingness to be a substitute for Benjamin helped make amends for his role in selling Joseph (see 37:26–27).

44:34 *lest peradventure I see the evil.* Judah remembers an earlier scene (37:34–35).

45:2 *wept.* See vv. 14–15; see also 43:30 and note.

45:3 *brethren . . . were troubled.* Either because they thought they were seeing a ghost or because they were afraid of what Joseph would do to them.

45:4 *I am Joseph your brother.* See v. 3; Acts 7:13. This time Joseph emphasized his relationship to them. *ye sold.* See note on 37:28.

45:5 *God did send me.* See vv. 7–9; Acts 7:9. God had a purpose to work through the brothers' thoughtless and cruel act (see Acts 2:23; 4:28).

45:6 Joseph was now 39 years old (see 41:46,53).

45:7 *a posterity* [i.e. remnant]. Although none had been lost, they had escaped a great threat to them all; so Joseph called them a remnant in the confidence that they would live to produce a great people.

45:8 *father.* A title of honor given to viziers (see note on 41:43) and other high officials (in the Apocrypha see 1 Maccabees 11:32). All three titles of Joseph in this verse were originally Egyptian.

45:9 *Haste you . . . tarry not.* Joseph is anxious to see Jacob as soon as possible (see v. 13).

45:10 *Goshen.* A region in the eastern part of the Nile delta, it was very fertile (see v. 18) and remains so today.

12 And behold, your eyes see, and the eyes
of my brother Benjamin, that *it is* [a]my mouth
that speaketh unto you.
13 And you shall tell my father of all my
glory in Egypt, and of all that you have seen;
and ye shall haste and [a]bring down my father
hither.
14 And he fell upon his brother Benjamin's
neck, and wept; and Benjamin wept upon his
neck.
15 Moreover he kissed all his brethren,
and wept upon them: and after that his
brethren talked with him.
16 ¶ And the fame *thereof* was heard *in*
Pharaoh's house, saying, Joseph's brethren are
come: and it [1]pleased Pharaoh well, and his
servants.
17 And Pharaoh said unto Joseph, Say unto
thy brethren, This do ye; lade your beasts, and
go, get you unto the land of Canaan;
18 And take your father and your households, and come unto me: and I will give you
the good of the land of Egypt, and ye shall eat
[a]the fat of the land.
19 Now thou art commanded, this do ye;
take you wagons out of the land of Egypt for
your little ones, and for your wives, and bring
your father, and come.
20 Also [1]regard not your stuff; for the good
of all the land of Egypt *is* yours.
21 And the children of Israel did so: and Joseph gave them wagons, according to the
[1]commandment of Pharaoh, and gave them
provision for the way.
22 To all of them he gave each man
changes of raiment; but to Benjamin he gave
three hundred *pieces* of silver, and [a]five
changes of raiment.
23 And to his father he sent after this manner; ten asses [1]laden with the good things of
Egypt, and ten she asses [1]laden with corn and
bread and meat for his father by the way.
24 So he sent his brethren away, and they
departed: and he said unto them, See that ye
fall not out by the way.
25 And they went up out of Egypt, and
came *into* the land of Canaan unto Jacob their
father,

45:12 [a]ch. 42:23
45:13 [a]Acts 7:14
45:16 [1]Heb. *was good in the eyes of Pharaoh*
45:18 [a]ch. 27:28; Num. 18:12,29
45:20 [1]Heb. *let not your eye spare, etc.*
45:21 [1]Heb. *mouth*
45:22 [a]ch. 43:34
45:23 [1]Heb. *carrying*
45:26 [1]Heb. *his* [a]Job 29:24; Ps. 126:1; Luke 24:11,41
46:1 [a]ch. 21:31,33; 28:10 [b]ch. 26:24,25; 28:13; 31:42
46:2 [a]ch. 15:1; Job 33:14,15
46:3 [a]ch. 28:13 [b]ch. 12:2; Deut. 26:5
46:4 [a]ch. 28:15; 48:21 [b]ch. 15:16; 50:13,24,25; Ex. 3:8 [c]ch. 50:1
46:5 [a]Acts 7:15 [b]ch. 45:19,21
46:6 [a]Deut. 26:5; Josh. 24:4; Ps. 105:23; Is. 52:4
46:8 [a]Ex. 1:1 [b]Num. 26:5
46:10 [1][Or, *Nemuel*] [2][Or, *Jarib*] [3][Or, *Zerah*] [a]Ex. 6:15
46:11 [1][Or, *Gershom*] [a]1 Chr. 6:1,16

26 And told him, saying, Joseph *is* yet
alive, and he *is* governor over all the land of
Egypt. [a]And [1]*Jacob's* heart fainted, for he believed them not.
27 And they told him all the words of Joseph, which he had said unto them: and when
he saw the wagons which Joseph had sent to
carry him, the spirit of Jacob their father revived:
28 And Israel said, *It is* enough; Joseph my
son *is* yet alive: I will go and see him before I
die.

Jacob goes to Egypt

46 And Israel took his journey with all
that he had, and came to [a]Beer-she-
ba, and offered sacrifices [b]unto the God of his
father Isaac.
2 And God spake unto Israel [a]in the visions
of the night, and said, Jacob, Jacob. And he
said, Here *am* I.
3 And he said, I *am* God, [a]the God of thy
father: fear not to go down into Egypt; for I
will there [b]make of thee a great nation.
4 [a]I will go down with thee into Egypt; and
I will also surely [b]bring thee up *again:* and [c]Jo-
seph shall put his hand upon thine eyes.
5 And [a]Jacob rose up from Beer-sheba: and
the sons of Israel carried Jacob their father,
and their little ones, and their wives, in the
wagons [b]which Pharaoh had sent to carry him.
6 And they took their cattle, and their
goods, which they had gotten in the land of
Canaan, and came into Egypt, [a]Jacob, and all
his seed with him:
7 His sons, and his sons' sons with him, his
daughters, and his sons' daughters, and all his
seed brought he with him into Egypt.
8 ¶ And [a]these *are* the names of the children of Israel, which came into Egypt, Jacob
and his sons: [b]Reuben, Jacob's firstborn.
9 And the sons of Reuben; Hanoch, and
Phallu, and Hezron, and Carmi.
10 And [a]the sons of Simeon; [1]Jemuel, and
Jamin, and Ohad, and [2]Jachin, and [3]Zohar,
and Shaul the son of a Canaanitish woman.
11 And the sons of [a]Levi; [1]Gershon, Kohath, and Merari.

45:12 *my mouth that speaketh.* Not through an interpreter as before (see 42:23).
45:14 *wept.* See 43:30 and note.
45:15 *his brethren talked with him.* In intimate fellowship and friendship, rather than hostility or fear, for the first time in over 20 years (see 37:2 and note on 45:6).
45:18 *ye shall eat the fat of the land.* An echo of Isaac's blessing on Jacob (see 27:28).
45:22 *to Benjamin he gave . . . five changes of raiment.* See note on 43:34. *pieces.* See note on 20:16.
45:24 *fall not out by the way.* Joseph wanted nothing to delay their return (see note on v. 9), and he wanted them to avoid mutual accusation and recrimination concerning the past.
46:1 *took his journey.* Probably from the family estate at Hebron (see 35:27). *came to Beer-sheba, and offered sacrifices.* Abraham and Isaac had also worshiped the Lord there (see 21:33; 26:23–25).
46:2 *God spake unto Israel in the visions of the night.* See 26:24. *Jacob, Jacob.* See note on 22:11. *Here am I.* See note on 22:1.
46:3–4 As Israel and his family were about to leave Canaan, God reaffirmed His covenant promises.
46:3 *I am . . . the God of thy father: fear not.* A verbatim repetition of God's statement to Isaac in 26:24. *I will there make of thee a great nation.* The Lord reaffirmed one aspect of His promise to Abraham (see 12:2). *there.* See Ex 1:7.
46:4 *I will go down with thee into Egypt.* God would be with Jacob as he went south to Egypt just as He was with him when he went north to Haran, and would again bring him back as He had done before (see 28:15; see also 15:16; 48:21).
46:8 *these are the names of the children of Israel which came into Egypt.* The Hebrew here is repeated verbatim in Ex 1:1 (see note there), where it introduces the background for the story of the exodus (predicted here in v. 4).

12 And the sons of [a]Judah; Er, and Onan, and Shelah, and Pharez, and Zerah: but [b]Er and Onan died in the land of Canaan. And [c]the sons of Pharez were Hezron and Hamul.

13 [a]And the sons of Issachar; Tola, and [1]Phuvah, and Job, and Shimron.

14 And the sons of Zebulun; Sered, and Elon, and Jahleel.

15 These *be* the sons of Leah, which she bare unto Jacob in Padan-aram, with his daughter Dinah: all the souls of his sons and his daughters *were* thirty and three.

16 And the sons of Gad; [a]Ziphion, and Haggi, Shuni, and [1]Ezbon, Eri, and [2]Arodi, and Areli.

17 [a]And the sons of Asher; Jimnah, and Ishuah, and Ishui, and Beriah, and Serah their sister: and the sons of Beriah; Heber, and Malchiel.

18 [a]These *are* the sons of Zilpah, [b]whom Laban gave to Leah his daughter, and these she bare unto Jacob, *even* sixteen souls.

19 The sons of Rachel [a]Jacob's wife; Joseph, and Benjamin.

20 [a]And unto Joseph in the land of Egypt were born Manasseh and Ephraim, which Asenath the daughter of Poti-pherah [1]priest of On bare unto him.

21 [a]And the sons of Benjamin *were* Belah, and Becher, and Ashbel, Gera, and Naaman, [1]Ehi, and Rosh, [2]Muppim, and [3]Huppim, and Ard.

22 These *are* the sons of Rachel, which were born to Jacob: all the souls *were* fourteen.

23 [a]And the sons of Dan; [1]Hushim.

24 [a]And the sons of Naphtali; Jahzeel, and Guni, and Jezer, and Shillem.

25 [a]These *are* the sons of Bilhah, [b]which Laban gave unto Rachel his daughter, and she bare these unto Jacob: all the souls *were* seven.

26 [a]All the souls that came with Jacob into Egypt, which came out of his [1]loins, besides Jacob's sons' wives, all the souls *were* threescore and six;

27 And the sons of Joseph, which were born him in Egypt, *were* two souls: [a]all the souls of the house of Jacob, which came into Egypt, *were* threescore and ten.

28 ¶ And he sent Judah before him unto Joseph, [a]to direct his face unto Goshen; and they came [b]into the land of Goshen.

29 And Joseph made ready his chariot, and went up to meet Israel his father, to Goshen, and presented himself unto him; and he [a]fell on his neck, and wept on his neck a good while.

30 And Israel said unto Joseph, [a]Now let me die, since I have seen thy face, because thou *art* yet alive.

31 And Joseph said unto his brethren, and unto his father's house, [a]I will go up, and shew Pharaoh, and say unto him, My brethren, and my father's house, which *were* in the land of Canaan, are come unto me;

32 And the men *are* shepherds, for [1]their trade hath been to feed cattle; and they have brought their flocks, and their herds, and all that they have.

33 And it shall come to pass, when Pharaoh shall call you, and shall say, [a]What *is* your occupation?

34 That ye shall say, Thy servants' [a]trade hath been about cattle [b]from our youth even until now, both we, *and* also our fathers: that ye may dwell in the land of Goshen; for every shepherd *is* [c]an abomination unto the Egyptians.

47 Then Joseph [a]came and told Pharaoh, and said, My father and my brethren, and their flocks, and their herds, and all that they have, are come out of the land of Canaan; and behold, they *are* in [b]the land of Goshen.

2 And he took some of his brethren, *even* five men, and [a]presented them unto Pharaoh.

3 And Pharaoh said unto his brethren, [a]What *is* your occupation? And they said unto Pharaoh, [b]Thy servants *are* shepherds, both we, *and* also our fathers.

4 They said moreover unto Pharaoh, [a]For to sojourn in the land are we come; for thy servants have no pasture for their flocks; [b]for the famine *is* sore in the land of Canaan: now therefore, we pray thee, let thy servants [c]dwell in the land of Goshen.

5 And Pharaoh spake unto Joseph, saying, Thy father and thy brethren are come unto thee:

6 [a]The land of Egypt *is* before thee; in the best of the land make thy father and brethren to dwell; [b]in the land of Goshen let them dwell: and if thou knowest *any* man of activity amongst them, then make them rulers over my cattle.

7 And Joseph brought in Jacob his father, and set him before Pharaoh: and Jacob blessed Pharaoh.

46:12 [a]1 Chr. 2:3; 4:21 [b]ch. 38:3,7,10 [c]ch. 38:29
46:13 [1][Or, *Puah, and Jashub*] [a]1 Chr. 7:1
46:16 [1][Or, *Ozni*] [2][Or, *Arod*] [a]Num. 26:15, *Zephon*
46:17 [a]1 Chr. 7:30
46:18 [a]ch. 30:10 [b]ch. 29:24
46:19 [a]ch. 44:27
46:20 [1]Or, *prince* [a]ch. 41:50
46:21 [1][Num. 26:38, *Ahiram*] [2][Num. 26:39, *Shupham.* 1 Chr. 7:12, *Shuppim*] [3][*Hupham,* Num. 26:39] [a]1 Chr. 7:6; 8:1
46:23 [1][Or, *Shuham,* Num. 26:42] [a]1 Chr. 7:12
46:24 [a]1 Chr. 7:13
46:25 [a]ch. 30:5,7 [b]ch. 29:29
46:26 [1]Heb. *thigh* [a]Ex. 1:5
46:27 [a]Deut. 10:22; See Acts 7:14
46:28 [a]ch. 31:21 [b]ch. 47:1
46:29 [a]ch. 45:14
46:30 [a]Luke 2:29,30
46:31 [a]ch. 47:1
46:32 [1]Heb. *they are men of cattle*
46:33 [a]ch. 47:2,3
46:34 [a]ver. 32 [b]ch. 30:35; 34:5; 37:12 [c]ch. 43:32; Ex. 8:26
47:1 [a]ch. 46:31 [b]ch. 45:10; 46:28
47:2 [a]Acts 7:13
47:3 [a]ch. 46:33 [b]ch. 46:34
47:4 [a]ch. 15:13; Deut. 26:5 [b]ch. 43:1; Acts 7:11 [c]ch. 46:34
47:6 [a]ch. 20:15 [b]ver. 4

46:15 *Padan-aram.* See note on 25:20. *were thirty and three.* There are 34 names in vv. 8–15. To bring the number to 33 the name Ohad in v. 10 should probably be removed, since it does not appear in the parallel lists in Num 26:12–13; 1 Chr 4:24. The Hebrew form of "Ohad" looks very much like that of the nearby "Zohar" (see Ex 6:15), and a later scribe probably added Ohad to the text accidentally.

46:20 See note on 41:45.

46:26 *All the souls that came with Jacob into Egypt . . . were threescore and six.* The total of 33 (see v. 15 and note), 16 (v. 18), 14 (v. 22) and 7 (see v. 25) is 70 (v. 27). To arrive at 66 we must subtract Er and Onan, who "died in the land of Canaan" (v. 12), and Manasseh and Ephraim (v. 20), who "were born . . . in Egypt" (v. 27).

46:27 *threescore and ten.* See Deut 10:22. Seventy is the ideal and complete number (see Introduction: Literary Features; see also notes on 5:5; 10:2) of Jacob's descendants who would have been in Egypt if Er and Onan had not died earlier (see 38:7–10). For the number 75 in Acts 7:14 see note there.

46:28 *he sent Judah before him.* See note on 43:3.

46:29 *wept.* See 43:30 and note.

46:34 *every shepherd is an abomination unto the Egyptians.* See note on 43:32.

8 And Pharaoh said unto Jacob, [1]How old *art* thou?

9 And Jacob said unto Pharaoh, [a]The days of the years of my pilgrimage *are* an hundred and thirty years: [b]few and evil have the days of the years of my life been, and [c]have not attained unto the days of the years of the life of my fathers in the days of their pilgrimage.

10 And Jacob [a]blessed Pharaoh, and went out from before Pharaoh.

11 And Joseph placed his father and his brethren, and gave them a possession in the land of Egypt, in the best of the land, in the land of [a]Rameses, [b]as Pharaoh had commanded.

12 And Joseph nourished his father, and his brethren, and all his father's household, *with* bread, [1][2]according to *their* families.

Joseph and the famine

13 ¶ And *there was* no bread in all the land; for the famine *was* very sore, [a]so that the land of Egypt and *all* the land of Canaan fainted by reason of the famine.

14 [a]And Joseph gathered up all the money that was found in the land of Egypt, and in the land of Canaan, for the corn which they bought: and Joseph brought the money into Pharaoh's house.

15 And when money failed in the land of Egypt, and in the land of Canaan, all the Egyptians came unto Joseph, and said, Give us bread: for [a]why should we die in thy presence? for the money faileth.

16 And Joseph said, Give your cattle; and I will give you for your cattle, if money fail.

17 And they brought their cattle unto Joseph: and Joseph gave them bread *in exchange* for horses, and for the flocks, and for the cattle of the herds, and for the asses: and he [1]fed them with bread for all their cattle for that year.

18 When that year was ended, they came unto him the second year, and said unto him, We will not hide *it* from my lord, how that our money is spent; my lord also had our herds of cattle; there is not ought left in the sight of my lord, but our bodies, and our lands:

19 Wherefore shall we die before thine eyes, both we and our land? buy us and our land for bread, and we and our land will be servants unto Pharaoh: and give *us* seed, that we may live, and not die, that the land be not desolate.

20 And Joseph bought all the land of Egypt for Pharaoh; for the Egyptians sold every man his field, because the famine prevailed over them: so the land became Pharaoh's.

21 And as for the people, he removed them to cities from *one* end of the borders of Egypt even to the *other* end thereof.

22 [a]Only the land of the [1]priests bought he not; for the priests had a portion assigned them of Pharaoh, and did eat their portion which Pharaoh gave them: wherefore they sold not their lands.

23 Then Joseph said unto the people, Behold, I have bought you *this* day and your land for Pharaoh: lo, *here is* seed for you, and ye shall sow the land.

24 And it shall come to pass in the increase, that you shall give the fifth *part* unto Pharaoh, and four parts shall be your own, for seed of the field, and for your food, and for them of your households, and for food for your little ones.

25 And they said, Thou hast saved our lives: [a]let us find grace in the sight of my lord, and we will be Pharaoh's servants.

26 And Joseph made it a law over the land of Egypt unto this day, *that* Pharaoh should have the fifth *part;* [a]except the land of the [1]priests only, *which* became not Pharaoh's.

27 ¶ And Israel [a]dwelt in the land of Egypt, in the country of Goshen; and they had possession therein, and [b]grew, and multiplied exceedingly.

28 And Jacob lived in the land of Egypt seventeen years: so [1]the whole age of Jacob was an hundred forty and seven years.

29 And the time [a]drew nigh that Israel must die: and he called his son Joseph, and said unto him, If now I have found grace in thy sight, [b]put, I pray thee, thy hand under my thigh, and [c]deal kindly and truly with me; [d]bury me not, I pray thee, in Egypt:

30 But [a]I will lie with my fathers, and thou shalt carry me out of Egypt, and [b]bury me in their buryingplace. And he said, I will do as thou hast said.

31 And he said, Swear unto me. And he sware unto him. And [a]Israel bowed himself upon the bed's head.

47:8 [1]Heb. *How many are the days of the years of thy life?*
47:9 [a]Ps. 39:12; Heb. 11:9,13 [b]Job 14:1 [c]ch. 25:7; 35:28
47:10 [a]ver. 7
47:11 [a]Ex. 1:11; 12:37 [b]ver. 6
47:12 [1]Or, *as a little child is nourished* [2]Heb. *according to the little ones*
47:13 [a]ch. 41:30; Acts 7:11
47:14 [a]ch. 41:56
47:15 [a]ver. 19
47:17 [1]Heb. *led them*
47:22 [1]Or, *princes* [a]Ezra 7:24
47:25 [a]ch. 33:15
47:26 [1]Or, *princes* [a]ver. 22
47:27 [a]ver. 11 [b]ch. 46:3
47:28 [1]Heb. *the days of the years of his life*
47:29 [a]See Deut. 31:14; 1 Ki. 2:1 [b]ch. 24:2 [c]ch. 24:49 [d]See ch. 50:25
47:30 [a]2 Sam. 19:37 [b]ch. 49:29; 50:5,13
47:31 [a]ch. 48:2; 1 Ki. 1:47; Heb. 11:21

47:9 *pilgrimage.* Jacob referred to the itinerant nature of patriarchal life in general and of his own in particular as he hopefully awaited the fulfillment of the promise of a land (see also Deut 26:5). *have not attained unto the days of the years of the life of my fathers.* Abraham lived to the age of 175 (25:7), Isaac to 180 (35:28).
47:11 *best of the land.* See note on 45:10. *land of Rameses.* The city of Rameses is mentioned in Ex 1:11; 12:37; Num 33:3,5. The name doubtless refers to the great Egyptian pharaoh Rameses II, who reigned centuries later (the designation here involves an editorial updating). In addition to being known as Goshen (see v. 27), the "land of Rameses" was called the "field of Zoan" in Ps 78:12,43 (see note on Gen 44:4).
47:13 *the famine was very sore.* After the people used up all their money to buy corn (see vv. 14–15), they traded their cattle (vv. 16–17), then their land (v. 20), then themselves (v. 21).
47:21 The Egyptians were to move temporarily into the cities until seed could be distributed to them for planting (see v. 23).
47:26 *Pharaoh should have the fifth part.* The same was true "in the seven plenteous years" (41:34)—but now all the land on which the produce grew belonged to Pharaoh as well.
47:27 *Israel . . . grew, and multiplied exceedingly.* See 35:11–12; 46:3 and notes.
47:29 *put . . . thy hand under my thigh.* See 24:2 and note. In both cases, ties of family kinship are being stressed.
47:30 *lie with my fathers.* See note on 25:8. *bury me in their buryingplace.* In the cave of Machpelah (see 50:12–13).
47:31 *bowed himself upon the bed's head.* Cf. 48:2.

Jacob blesses Joseph's sons

48 And it came to pass after these
things, that *one* told Joseph, Behold,
thy father *is* sick: and he took with him his
two sons, Manasseh and Ephraim.
2 And *one* told Jacob, and said, Behold, thy
son Joseph cometh unto thee: and Israel
strengthened himself, and sat upon the bed.
3 And Jacob said unto Joseph, God
Almighty appeared unto me at [a]Luz in the land
of Canaan, and blessed me,
4 And said unto me, Behold, I will make
thee fruitful, and multiply thee, and I will
make of thee a multitude of people; and will
give this land to thy seed after thee [a]*for* an
everlasting possession.
5 And now thy [a]two sons, Ephraim and
Manasseh, which were born unto thee in the
land of Egypt before I came unto thee into
Egypt, *are* mine; as Reuben and Simeon, they
shall be mine.
6 And thy issue, which thou begettest after
them, shall be thine, *and* shall be called after
the name of their brethren in their inheritance.
7 And as for me, when I came from Padan,
[a]Rachel died by me in the land of Canaan in
the way, when yet *there was* but a little way to
come unto Ephrath: and I buried her there in
the way of Ephrath; the same *is* Beth-lehem.
8 And Israel beheld Joseph's sons, and said,
Who *are* these?
9 And Joseph said unto his father, [a]They
are my sons, whom God hath given me in this
place. And he said, Bring them, I pray thee,
unto me, and [b]I will bless them.
10 Now [a]the eyes of Israel were [1]dim for
age, *so that* he could not see. And he brought
them near unto him; and [b]he kissed them, and
embraced them.
11 And Israel said unto Joseph, [a]I had not
thought to see thy face: and lo, God hath
shewed me also thy seed.
12 And Joseph brought them out from between his knees, and he bowed himself with
his face to the earth.
13 And Joseph took them both, Ephraim in
his right hand toward Israel's left hand, and
Manasseh in his left hand towards Israel's
right hand, and brought *them* near unto him.
14 And Israel stretched out his right hand,
and laid *it* upon Ephraim's head, who *was* the
younger, and his left hand upon Manasseh's
head, [a]guiding his hands wittingly; for Manasseh *was* the firstborn.
15 And [a]he blessed Joseph, and said, God,
[b]before whom my fathers Abraham and Isaac
did walk, the God which fed me all my life
long unto this day,
16 The Angel [a]which redeemed me from
all evil, bless the lads; and let [b]my name be
named on them, and the name of my fathers
Abraham and Isaac; and let them [1]grow into a
multitude in the midst of the earth.
17 And when Joseph saw that his father
[a]laid his right hand upon the head of Ephraim,
it [1]displeased him: and he held up his father's
hand, to remove it from Ephraim's head unto
Manasseh's head.
18 And Joseph said unto his father, Not so,
my father: for this *is* the firstborn; put thy
right hand upon his head.
19 And his father refused, and said, [a]I
know *it,* my son, I know *it:* he also shall become a people, and he also shall be great: but
truly [b]his younger brother shall be greater

48:3 [a]ch. 28:13,19; 35:6,9
48:4 [a]ch. 17:8
48:5 [a]ch. 41:50; 46:20; Josh. 13:7; 14:4
48:7 [a]ch. 35:9,16,19
48:9 [a]See ch. 33:5 [b]ch. 27:4
48:10 [1]Heb. *heavy* [a]ch. 27:1
48:10 [b]ch. 27:27
48:11 [a]ch. 45:26
48:14 [a]ver. 19
48:15 [a]Heb. 11:21 [b]ch. 17:1
48:16 [1]Heb. *as fishes do increase* [a]ch. 28:15; Ps. 34:22; 121:7 [b]Amos 9:12; Acts 15:17
48:17 [1][*was evil in his eyes*] [a]ver. 14
48:19 [a]ver. 14 [b]Num. 1:33,35; Deut. 33:17

48:3 *God Almighty.* See note on 17:1. *Luz.* The older name for Beth-el (see 28:19).

48:5 *thy two sons . . . are mine.* Jacob would adopt them as his own. *Ephraim and Manasseh.* See v. 1 for the expected order, since Manasseh was Joseph's firstborn (see 41:51). Jacob mentions Ephraim first because he intends to give him the primary blessing and thus "set Ephraim before Manasseh" (v. 20). *mine; as Reuben and Simeon.* Joseph's first two sons would enjoy equal status with Jacob's first two sons (35:23) and in fact would eventually supersede them. Because of an earlier sinful act (see 35:22 and note), Reuben would lose his birthright to Jacob's favorite son, Joseph (see 49:3–4; 1 Chr 5:2), and thus to Joseph's sons (see 1 Chr 5:1).

48:6 *thy issue, which thou begettest after them, shall be thine.* They would take the place of Ephraim and Manasseh, whom Jacob had adopted. *shall be called after the name of their brethren in their inheritance.* They would perpetuate the names of Ephraim and Manasseh for purposes of inheritance (for a similar provision see 38:8 and note; Deut 25:5–6). Joseph's territory would thus be divided between Ephraim and Manasseh, but Levi (Jacob's third son; see 35:23) would not receive a share of the land (Josh 14:4). The total number of tribal allotments would therefore remain the same.

48:7 *Padan.* That is, Padan-aram, meaning "plain of Aram," another name for Aram-naharaim (see note on 24:10). *Rachel died.* See 35:16–19. Adopted by Joseph's father, Ephraim and Manasseh in effect took the place of other sons whom Joseph's mother, Rachel, might have borne had she not died. *Ephrath.* See note on 35:16.

48:8 *Israel . . . said, Who are these?* Either because he had never met them or because, being old, he could not see them clearly.

48:10 *eyes . . . dim for age, so that he could not see.* See note on 27:1. *kissed them, and embraced them.* While they were on Jacob's knees (see v. 12), probably symbolizing adoption (see note on 30:3).

48:13–20 See note on Acts 6:6.

48:13 *Manasseh . . . towards Israel's right hand.* Joseph wanted Jacob to bless Manasseh, Joseph's firstborn, by placing his right hand on Manasseh's head.

48:15 *blessed.* As his father Isaac had blessed him (27:27–29). *Joseph.* Used here collectively for Ephraim and Manasseh (the Hebrew for "you" and "your" in v. 21 is plural). *before whom . . . Abraham and Isaac did walk.* See notes on 5:22; 17:1. *which fed me* [lit. "shepherded me"]. An intimate royal metaphor for God (see Ps 23:1), used in Genesis only here and in Jacob's later blessing of Joseph (49:24).

48:16 *Angel.* See note on 16:7. The angel—God Himself—had earlier blessed Jacob (see 32:29; see also note on 32:24).

48:19 *his younger brother shall be greater than he.* See note on 25:23. During the divided monarchy (930–722 B.C.), Ephraim's descendants were the most powerful tribe in the north. "Ephraim" was often used to refer to the northern kingdom as a whole (see, e.g., Is 7:2,5,8–9; Hos 9:13; 12:1,8).

48:20 *he set Ephraim before Manasseh.* Jacob, the younger son

than he, and his seed shall become a [1]multi-
tude of nations.
20 And he blessed them that day, saying,
[a]In thee shall Israel bless, saying, God make
thee as Ephraim and as Manasseh: and he set
Ephraim before Manasseh.
21 And Israel said unto Joseph, Behold, I
die: but [a]God shall be with you, and bring you
again unto the land of your fathers.
22 Moreover [a]I have given to thee one portion above thy brethren, which I took out of
the hand [b]of the Amorite with my sword and
with my bow.

Jacob blesses his sons

49 And Jacob called unto his sons, and
said, Gather yourselves together, that
I may [a]tell you *that* which shall befall you [b]in
the last days.

2 Gather yourselves together, and hear,
ye sons of Jacob;
And hearken unto Israel your father.
3 Reuben, thou *art* [a]my firstborn,
My might, and the beginning of my
strength,
The excellency of dignity, and the
excellency of power:
4 Unstable as water, [1]thou shalt not
excel;
Because thou [a]wentest up to thy
father's bed;
Then defiledst thou *it:* [2]he went up to
my couch.
5 [a]Simeon and Levi *are* brethren;
[1]Instruments of cruelty *are in* their
habitations.
6 O my soul, [a]come not thou into their
secret;
[b]Unto their assembly, mine honour, be
not thou united:
For [c]in their anger they slew a man,
And in their selfwill they [1]digged
down a wall.
7 Cursed *be* their anger, for *it was* fierce;
And their wrath, for it was cruel:
I will divide them in Jacob,
And scatter them in Israel.

48:19 [1]Heb. *fulness*
48:20 [a]See Ruth 4:11,12
48:21 [a]ch. 46:4
48:22 [a]Josh. 24:32; John 4:5 [b]ch. 34:28
49:1 [a]Deut. 33:1; Amos 3:7 [b]Deut. 4:30; Is. 39:6; Jer. 23:20; Heb. 1:2
49:3 [a]ch. 29:32
49:4 [1]Heb. *do not thou excel* [2]Or, *my couch is gone* [a]ch. 35:22; Deut. 27:20
49:5 [1]Or, *Their swords are weapons of violence* [a]ch. 29:33,34
49:6 [1]Or, *houghed oxen* [a]Prov. 1:15,16 [b]Ps. 26:9; Eph. 5:11 [c]ch. 34:26

who struggled with Esau for the birthright and blessing and who preferred the younger sister (Rachel) above the older (Leah), now advanced Joseph's younger son ahead of the older.
48:21 *Joseph.* See note on v. 15. *I die.* Years later, Joseph spoke these words to his brothers (50:24).
48:22 *one portion above.* The Hebrew for this phrase is identical with the place-name Shechem, where Joseph was later buried in a plot of ground inherited by his descendants (see Josh 24:32; see also 33:19; John 4:5). *I took out of the hand of the Amorite.* Possibly referring to the event of 34:25–29.
49:2–27 Often called the "Blessing of Jacob," this is the longest poem in Genesis. Its various blessings were intended not only for Jacob's 12 sons but also for the tribes that descended from them (see v. 28). For other poetic blessings in Genesis see 9:26–27; 14:19–20; 27:27–29; 27:39–40; 48:15–16; 48:20.
49:4 *Unstable.* Reuben's descendants were characterized by indecision (see Judg 5:15–16). *thou shalt not excel; Because thou wentest up to thy father's bed.* See 35:22 and note; see also notes on 37:21; 48:5.
49:5 *Simeon and Levi are brethren.* They shared the traits of violence, anger and cruelty (see vv. 6–7).
49:7 *I will divide them.* Fulfilled when Simeon's descendants were absorbed into the territory of Judah (see Josh 19:1,9) and when Levi's descendants were dispersed throughout the land, living in 48 towns and the surrounding pasturelands (see note on 48:6; see also Num 35:2,7; Josh 14:4; 21:41).

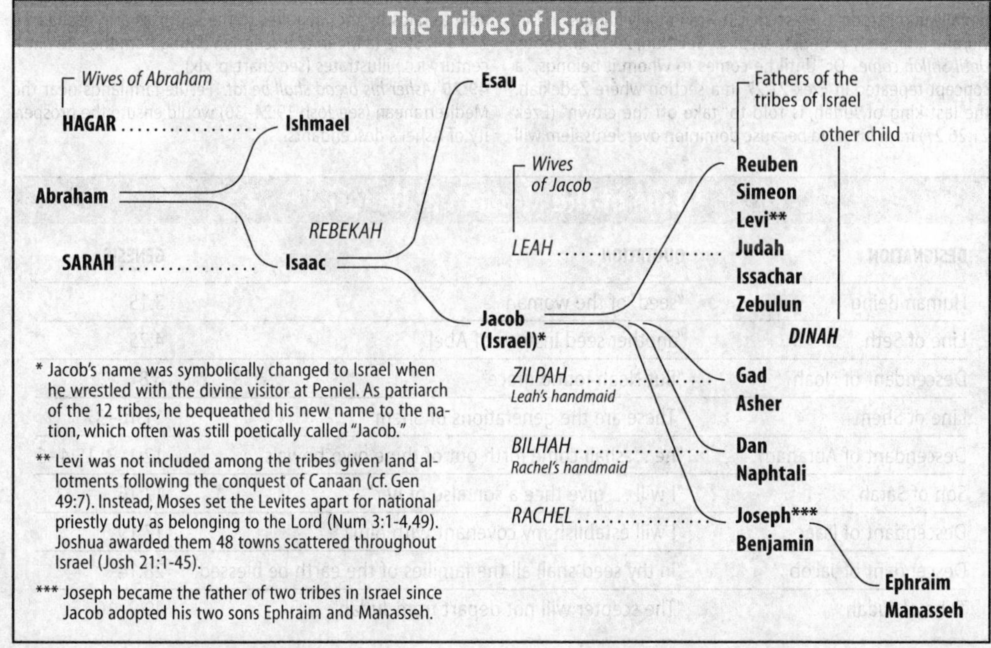
The Tribes of Israel
Wives of Abraham
HAGAR
Ishmael
Abraham
SARAH
Isaac
REBEKAH
Esau
Jacob
(Israel)*
Wives of Jacob
LEAH
ZILPAH
Leah's handmaid
BILHAH
Rachel's handmaid
RACHEL
Fathers of the tribes of Israel
other child
Reuben
Simeon
Levi**
Judah
Issachar
Zebulun
DINAH
Gad
Asher
Dan
Naphtali
Joseph***
Benjamin
Ephraim
Manasseh
* Jacob's name was symbolically changed to Israel when he wrestled with the divine visitor at Peniel. As patriarch of the 12 tribes, he bequeathed his new name to the nation, which often was still poetically called "Jacob."
** Levi was not included among the tribes given land allotments following the conquest of Canaan (cf. Gen 49:7). Instead, Moses set the Levites apart for national priestly duty as belonging to the Lord (Num 3:1-4,49). Joshua awarded them 48 towns scattered throughout Israel (Josh 21:1-45).
*** Joseph became the father of two tribes in Israel since Jacob adopted his two sons Ephraim and Manasseh.

8 [a]Judah, thou *art he* whom thy brethren
shall praise:
[b]Thy hand *shall be* in the neck of thine
enemies;
[c]Thy father's children shall bow down
before thee.
9 Judah *is* [a]a lion's whelp:
From the prey, my son, thou art gone
up:
[b]He stooped down, he couched as a
lion,
And as an old lion; who shall rouse
him up?
10 [a]The sceptre shall not depart from
Judah,
Nor [b]a lawgiver from between his feet,
[c]Until Shiloh come;
[d]And unto him *shall* the gathering of
the people *be*.
11 Binding his foal unto the vine,
And his ass's colt unto the choice vine;
He washed his garments in wine,
And his clothes in the blood of grapes:

49:8 [a]Deut. 33:7 [b]Ps. 18:40 [c]1 Chr. 5:2
49:9 [a]Rev. 5:5 [b]Num. 23:24; 24:9
49:10 [a]Num. 24:17; Jer. 30:21 [b]Ps. 60:7 [c]Is. 11:1; Mat. 21:9 [d]Is. 60:1-5; Luke 2:30-32
49:13 [a]Deut. 33:18,19; Josh. 19:10,11
49:15 [a]1 Sam. 10:9
49:16 [a]Deut. 33:22
49:17 [1]Heb. *An arrow-snake* [a]Judg. 18:27
49:18 [a]Ps. 25:5; Is. 25:9
49:19 [a]Deut. 33:20; 1 Chr. 5:18
49:20 [a]Deut. 33:24; Josh. 19:24

12 *His* eyes *shall be* red with wine,
And *his* teeth white with milk.
13 [a]Zebulun shall dwell at the haven of
the sea;
And he *shall be* for a haven of ships;
And his border *shall be* unto Zidon.
14 Issachar *is* a strong ass
Couching down between two burdens:
15 And he saw that rest *was* good,
And the land that *it was* pleasant;
And bowed [a]his shoulder to bear,
And became a servant unto tribute.
16 [a]Dan shall judge his people,
As one of the tribes of Israel.
17 [a]Dan shall be a serpent by the way,
[1]An adder in the path,
That biteth the horse heels,
So that his rider shall fall backward.
18 [a]I have waited for thy salvation,
O LORD.
19 [a]Gad, a troop shall overcome him:
But he shall overcome at the last.
20 [a]Out of Asher his bread *shall be* fat,

49:8 Cf. 27:29,40; 37:7,9. *Judah . . . thy brethren . . . shall bow down before thee.* See note on 43:3. As those who would become the leading tribes of southern and northern Israel respectively, Judah and Joseph were given the longest (vv. 8–12 and vv. 22–26) of Jacob's blessings. Judah was the fourth of Leah's sons and also the fourth son born to Jacob (29:35), but Reuben, Simeon and Levi had forfeited their right of leadership. So Jacob assigns leadership to Judah (a son of Leah) but a double portion to Joseph (a son of Rachel). See also 1 Chr 5:2.
49:9 *Judah is a lion's whelp.* A symbol of sovereignty, strength and courage. Judah (or Israel) is often pictured as a lion in later times (see Ezek 19:1–7; Mic 5:8; and especially Num 24:9). Judah's greatest descendant, Jesus Christ (see note on 43:3), is Himself called "the Lion of the tribe of Juda" (Rev 5:5).
49:10 Though difficult to translate, the verse has been traditionally understood as Messianic. It was initially fulfilled in David, and ultimately in Christ. *sceptre.* See Num 24:17 and note. *Until Shiloh come.* Or "Until he comes to whom it belongs," a concept repeated in Ezek 21:27 in a section where Zedekiah, the last king of Judah, is told to "take off the crown" (Ezek 21:26,27) from his head because dominion over Jerusalem will ultimately be given to the one "whose right it is."
49:11 Judah's descendants would someday enjoy a settled and prosperous life.
49:13 Though landlocked by the tribes of Asher and Manasseh, the descendants of Zebulun were close enough to the Mediterranean (within ten miles) to "suck of the abundance of the seas" (Deut 33:19).
49:17 *Dan shall be a serpent.* The treachery of a group of Danites in later times is described in Judg 18:27. *That biteth the horse heels.* Samson, from the tribe of Dan, would single-handedly hold the Philistines at bay (Judg 14–16).
49:18 Jacob pauses midway through his series of blessings to utter a brief prayer for God's help.
49:19 *Gad, a troop shall overcome him.* Located east of the Jordan (see Josh 13:24–27), the descendants of Gad were vulnerable to raids by the Moabites to the south, as the Mesha (see 2 Ki 3:4) Stele (a Moabite inscription dating from the late ninth century B.C.) illustrates (see chart, p. xix).
49:20 *Asher his bread shall be fat.* Fertile farmlands near the Mediterranean (see Josh 19:24–30) would ensure the prosperity of Asher's descendants.

Line of the Messiah in Genesis

DESIGNATION	QUOTATION	GENESIS
Human Being	"seed" of the woman	3:15
Line of Seth	"another seed instead of Abel"	4:25
Descendant of Noah	"But Noah found grace"	6:8
Line of Shem	"These are the generations of Shem"	11:10–32
Descendant of Abraham	"he . . . shall come forth out of thine own bowels"	12:1–3; 15:4–6
Son of Sarah	"I will . . . give thee a son also of her"	17:16
Descendant of Isaac	"I will establish my covenant with him"	17:19
Descendant of Jacob	"in thy seed shall all the families of the earth be blessed"	28:14
Tribe of Judah	"The scepter will not depart from Judah"	49:9–10

And he shall yield royal dainties.
21 [a]Naphtali *is* a hind let loose:
He giveth goodly words.
22 Joseph *is* a fruitful bough,
Even a fruitful bough by a well;
Whose [1]branches run over the wall.
23 The archers have [a]sorely grieved him,
And shot *at him,* and hated him:
24 But his [a]bow abode in strength,
And the arms of his hands were made strong
By the hands of [b]the mighty *God* of Jacob;
([c]From thence [d]*is* the shepherd, [e]the stone of Israel:)
25 [a]*Even* by the God of thy father, who shall help thee;
[b]And *by* the Almighty, [c]who shall bless thee
With blessings of heaven above,
Blessings of the deep that lieth under,
Blessings of the breasts, and of the womb:
26 The blessings of thy father have prevailed above the blessings of my progenitors
[a]Unto the utmost bound of the everlasting hills:
[b]They shall be on the head of Joseph,
And on the crown of the head of him *that was* separate from his brethren.
27 Benjamin shall [a]ravin *as* a wolf:
In the morning he shall devour the prey,
[b]And at night he shall divide the spoil.

The death of Jacob

28 ¶ All these *are* the twelve tribes of Israel: and this *is it* that their father spake unto
them, and blessed them; every one according
to his blessing he blessed them.
29 And he charged them, and said unto
them, I [a]*am to be* gathered unto my people:
[b]bury me with my fathers [c]in the cave that *is*
in the field of Ephron the Hittite,
30 In the cave that *is* in the field of Machpelah, which *is* before Mamre, in the land of
Canaan, [a]which Abraham bought with the
field of Ephron the Hittite for a possession of a
buryingplace.
31 [a]There they buried Abraham and Sarah
his wife; [b]there they buried Isaac and Rebekah
his wife; and there I buried Leah.
32 The purchase of the field and of the
cave that *is* therein *was* from the children of
Heth.
33 And when Jacob had made an end of
commanding his sons, he gathered up his feet
into the bed, and yielded up the ghost, and
[a]was gathered unto his people.
50 And Joseph [a]fell upon his father's
face, and [b]wept upon him, and
kissed him.
2 And Joseph commanded his servants the
physicians to [a]embalm his father: and the
physicians embalmed Israel.
3 And forty days were fulfilled for him; for
so are fulfilled the days of those which are embalmed: and the Egyptians [a][1]mourned for him
threescore and ten days.
4 And when the days of his mourning were
past, Joseph spake unto [a]the house of Pharaoh,
saying, If now I have found grace in your eyes,
speak, I pray you, in the ears of Pharaoh, saying,
5 [a]My father made me swear, saying, Lo, I
die: in my grave [b]which I have digged for me
in the land of Canaan, there shalt thou bury
me. Now therefore let me go up, I pray thee,
and bury my father, and I will come again.
6 And Pharaoh said, Go up, and bury thy
father, according as he made thee swear.
7 And Joseph went up to bury his father:
and with him went up all the servants of Pharaoh, the elders of his house, and all the elders
of the land of Egypt,

49:21 [a]Deut. 33:23
49:22 [1]Heb. *daughters*
49:23 [a]ch. 37:4,24; Ps. 118:13
49:24 [a]Job 29:20; Ps. 37:15 [b]Ps. 132:2,5 [c]ch. 45:11; 47:12 [d]Ps. 80:1 [e]Is. 28:16
49:25 [a]ch. 28:13; 35:3; 43:23 [b]ch. 17:1; 35:11 [c]Deut. 33:13
49:26 [a]Deut. 33:15; Hab. 3:6 [b]Deut. 33:16
49:27 [a]Judg. 20:21,25 [b]Num. 23:24; Esth. 8:11; Ezek. 39:10; Zech. 14:1
49:29 [a]ch. 15:15; 25:8 [b]ch. 47:30; 2 Sam. 19:37 [c]ch. 50:13
49:30 [a]ch. 23:16
49:31 [a]ch. 23:19; 25:9 [b]ch. 35:29
49:33 [a]ver. 29
50:1 [a]ch. 46:4 [b]2 Ki. 13:14
50:2 [a]ver. 26; 2 Chr. 16:14; Luke 24:1; John 19:39,40
50:3 [1]Heb. *wept* [a]Num. 20:29; Deut. 34:8
50:4 [a]Esth. 4:2
50:5 [a]ch. 47:29 [b]2 Chr. 16:14; Is. 22:16

49:21 *Naphtali is a hind let loose.* Perhaps a reference to an independent spirit fostered in the descendants of Naphtali by their somewhat isolated location in the hill country north of the Sea of Galilee (see Josh 19:32–38).

49:22 *fruitful . . . fruitful.* A pun on the name Ephraim (see note on 41:52), who Jacob predicted would be greater than Joseph's firstborn son Manasseh (48:19–20). *branches run over the wall.* Ephraim's descendants tended to expand their territory (see Josh 17:14–18).

49:24 *his bow abode in strength.* The warlike Ephraimites (see Judg 8:1; 12:1) would often prove victorious in battle (see Josh 17:18). *mighty God of Jacob.* Stresses the activity of God in saving and redeeming His people (see Is 49:26). *shepherd.* See note on 48:15. *stone of Israel.* Israel's sure defense (see Deut 32:4,15,18, 30–31)—a figure often used also in Psalms and Isaiah.

49:25 *Almighty.* See note on 17:1. *blessings of heaven . . . of the deep.* The fertility of the soil watered by rains from above and springs and streams from below. *of the breasts, and of the womb.* The fertility of man and animals. For the later prosperity of Ephraim's descendants see Hos 12:8.

49:26 *Joseph . . . him that was separate from his brethren.* See note on v. 8. Ephraim would gain supremacy, especially over the northern tribes (see Josh 16:9; Is 7:1–2; Hos 13:1).

49:27 *Benjamin shall ravin as a wolf.* See the exploits of Ehud (Judg 3:12–30) and Saul and Jonathan (1 Sam 11–15). See Judg 19–21 for examples of the savagery that characterized one group of Benjamin's descendants.

49:28 *twelve tribes of Israel.* See note on vv. 2–27.

49:29 *bury me with my fathers.* See note on 25:8. Jacob does not forget that the land of his fathers is his God-appointed homeland (see note on 23:19).

49:33 *was gathered unto his people.* See note on 25:8.

50:1 *wept.* See note on 43:30.

50:2 *physicians embalmed Israel.* Professional embalmers could have been hired for the purpose, but Joseph perhaps wanted to avoid involvement with the pagan religious ceremonies accompanying their services.

50:3 *forty days . . . threescore and ten days.* The two periods probably overlapped.

50:5 *My father made me swear.* See 47:29–31. *digged.* Or "bought," as the Hebrew for this verb is translated in Hos 3:2 (see also Deut 2:6). *go up.* To Hebron, which has a higher elevation than Goshen.

8 And all the house of Joseph, and his brethren, and his father's house: only their little ones, and their flocks, and their herds, they left in the land of Goshen.

9 And there went up with him both chariots and horsemen: and it was a very great company.

10 And they came to the threshingfloor of Atad, which *is* beyond Jordan, and there they [a]mourned with a great and very sore lamentation: [b]and he made a mourning for his father seven days.

11 And when the inhabitants of the land, the Canaanites, saw the mourning in the floor of Atad, they said, This *is* a grievous mourning to the Egyptians: wherefore the name of it was called [1]Abel-mizraim, which *is* beyond Jordan.

12 And his sons did unto him according as he commanded them:

13 For [a]his sons carried him into the land of Canaan, and buried him in the cave of the field of Machpelah, which Abraham [b]bought with the field for a possession of a buryingplace of Ephron the Hittite, before Mamre.

14 And Joseph returned into Egypt, he, and his brethren, and all that went up with him to bury his father, after he had buried his father.

15 ¶ And when Joseph's brethren saw that their father was dead, [a]they said, Joseph will peradventure hate us, and will certainly requite us all the evil which we did unto him.

16 And they [1]sent a messenger unto Joseph, saying, Thy father did command before he died, saying,

17 So shall ye say unto Joseph, Forgive, I pray thee now, the trespass of thy brethren, and their sin; [a]for they did unto thee evil: and now, we pray thee, forgive the trespass of the servants of [b]the God of thy father. And Joseph wept when they spake unto him.

18 And his brethren also went and [a]fell down before his face; and they said, Behold, we *be* thy servants.

19 And Joseph said unto them, [a]Fear not: [b]for *am* I in the place of God?

20 [a]But as for you, ye thought evil against me; *but* [b]God meant it unto good, to bring to pass, as *it is* this day, to save much people alive.

21 Now therefore fear ye not: [a]I will nourish you and your little ones. And he comforted them, and spake [1]kindly unto them.

The death of Joseph

22 ¶ And Joseph dwelt in Egypt, he, and his father's house: and Joseph lived an hundred and ten years.

23 And Joseph saw Ephraim's children [a]of the third *generation:* [b]the children also of Machir the son of Manasseh [c]were [1]brought up upon Joseph's knees.

24 And Joseph said unto his brethren, I die: and [a]God will surely visit you, and bring you out of this land unto the land [b]which he sware to Abraham, to Isaac, and to Jacob.

25 And [a]Joseph took an oath of the children of Israel, saying, God will surely visit you, and ye shall carry up my bones from hence.

26 So Joseph died, *being* an hundred and ten years old: and they embalmed him, and he was put in a coffin in Egypt.

50:10 [a]Acts 8:2 [b]1 Sam. 31:13; Job 2:13
50:11 [1]That is, *The mourning of the Egyptians*
50:13 [a]ch. 49:29; Acts 7:16 [b]ch. 23:16
50:15 [a]Job 15:21
50:16 [1]Heb. *charged*
50:17 [a]Prov. 28:13 [b]ch. 49:25
50:18 [a]ch. 37:7,10
50:19 [a]ch. 45:5 [b]2 Ki. 5:7
50:20 [a]Ps. 56:5 [b]Acts 3:13-15
50:21 [1]Heb. *to their hearts* [a]Mat. 5:44
50:23 [1]Heb. *born* [a]Job 42:16 [b]Num. 32:39 [c]ch. 30:3
50:24 [a]ch. 15:14; 46:4; 48:21; Ex. 3:16,17; Heb. 11:22 [b]ch. 26:3; 35:12; 46:4
50:25 [a]Ex. 13:19; Josh. 24:32; Acts 7:16

50:10 *threshingfloor.* Grain was threshed on a flat circular area, either of rock or of pounded earth. Threshing floors were located on an elevated open place exposed to the wind, usually at the edge of town or near the main gate (see 1 Ki 22:10). See note on Ruth 1:22.

50:15 *hate us, and . . . requite us.* Similarly, Esau had once planned to kill Jacob as soon as Isaac died (see 27:41).

50:17 *Joseph wept.* See note on 43:30. Joseph may have been saddened by the thought that his brothers might be falsely implicating their father in their story. Or he may have regretted his failure to reassure them sooner that he had already forgiven them.

50:18 *fell down before his face.* A final fulfillment of Joseph's earlier dreams (see note on 37:7; see also 37:9) *we be thy servants.* They had earlier expressed a similar willingness, but under quite different circumstances (see 44:9,33).

50:19 *am I in the place of God?* See note on 30:2.

50:20 *God meant it unto good.* Their act, out of personal animosity toward a brother, had been used by God to save life—the life of the Israelites, the Egyptians and all the nations that came to Egypt to buy food in the face of a famine that threatened the known world. At the same time, God showed by these events that His purpose for the nations is life and that this purpose would be effected through the descendants of Abraham.

50:23 *saw . . . the third generation.* Cf. Job's experience (Job 42:16). *Machir.* Manasseh's firstborn son and the ancestor of the powerful Gileadites (Josh 17:1). The name of Machir later became almost interchangeable with that of Manasseh himself (see Judg 5:14). *brought up upon Joseph's knees.* Joseph probably adopted Machir's children (see note on 30:3).

50:24 *brethren.* Perhaps used here in a broader sense than siblings. *I die.* See note on 48:21. *God will . . . bring you out of this land.* Joseph did not forget God's promises (cf. 15:16; 46:4; 48:21) concerning "the departing" (Heb 11:22).

‡50:25 See 47:29–31 for a similar request by Jacob. *carry up my bones from hence.* Centuries later Moses did so to fulfill his ancestor's oath (see Ex 13:19). Joseph's bones were eventually "buried . . . in Shechem, in a parcel of ground which Jacob bought of the sons of Hamor" (Josh 24:32; see Gen 33:19).

50:26 *Joseph died, being an hundred and ten years old.* See v. 22. Ancient Egyptian records indicate that 110 years was considered to be the ideal life span; to the Egyptians this would have signified divine blessing upon Joseph.

The Second Book of Moses, Called
Exodus

INTRODUCTION

Title

"Exodus" is a Latin word derived from Greek *Exodos,* the name given to the book by those who translated it into Greek. The word means "exit," "departure" (see Luke 9:31; Heb 11:22). The name was retained by the Latin Vulgate, by the Jewish author Philo (a contemporary of Christ) and by the Syriac version. In Hebrew the book is named after its first two words, *we'elleh shemoth* ("these are the names of"). The same phrase occurs in Gen 46:8, where it likewise introduces a list of the names of those Israelites "which came into Egypt" (1:1). Thus Exodus was not intended to exist separately, but was thought of as a continuation of a narrative that began in Genesis and was completed in Leviticus, Numbers and Deuteronomy. The first five books of the Bible are together known as the Pentateuch (see Introduction to Genesis: Author and Date of Writing).

Author and Date of Writing

Several statements in Exodus indicate that Moses wrote certain sections of the book (see 17:14; 24:4; 34:27). In addition, Josh 8:31 refers to the command of Ex 20:25 as having been "written in the book of the law of Moses." The NT also claims Mosaic authorship for various passages in Exodus (see, e.g., Mark 7:10; 12:26 and text notes; see also Luke 2:22–23). Taken together, these references strongly suggest that Moses was largely responsible for writing the book of Exodus—a traditional view not convincingly challenged by the commonly held notion that the Pentateuch as a whole contains four underlying sources (see Introduction to Genesis: Author and Date of Writing).

Chronology

According to 1 Ki 6:1, the exodus took place 480 years before "the fourth year of Solomon's reign over Israel." Since that year was c. 966 B.C., it has been traditionally held that the exodus occurred c. 1446. The "three hundred years" of Judg 11:26 fits comfortably within this time span (see Introduction to Judges: Background). In addition, although Egyptian chronology relating to the 18th dynasty remains somewhat uncertain, recent research tends to support the traditional view that two of this dynasty's pharaohs, Thutmose III and his son Amunhotep II, were the pharaohs of the oppression and the exodus respectively (see notes on 2:15,23; 3:10).

On the other hand, the appearance of the name Raamses in 1:11 has led many to the conclusion that the 19th-dynasty pharaoh Seti I and his son Rameses II were the pharaohs of the oppression and the exodus respectively. Furthermore, archaeological evidence of the destruction of numerous Canaanite cities in the 13th century B.C. has been interpreted as proof that Joshua's troops invaded the promised land in that century. These and similar lines of argument lead to a date for the exodus of c. 1290 (see Introduction to Joshua: Historical Setting).

The identity of the cities' attackers, however, cannot be positively ascertained. The raids may have been initiated by later Israelite armies, or by Philistines or other outsiders. In addition, the archaeological evidence itself has become increasingly ambiguous, and recent evaluations have tended to redate some of it to the 18th dynasty. Also, the name Raamses in 1:11 could very well be the result of an editorial updating by someone who lived centuries after Moses—a procedure that probably accounts for the appearance of the same word in Gen 47:11 (see note there).

In short, there are no compelling reasons to modify in any substantial way the traditional 1446 B.C. date for the exodus of the Israelites from Egyptian bondage.

The Route of the Exodus

At least three routes of escape from Pithom and Raamses (1:11) have been proposed: (1) a northern route through the land of the Philistines (but see 13:17); (2) a middle route leading eastward across Sinai to Beersheba; and (3) a southern route along the west coast of Sinai to the southeastern

extremities of the peninsula. The southern route seems most likely, since several of the sites in Israel's wilderness itinerary have been tentatively identified along it. See map No. 3 at the end of the study Bible. The exact place where Israel crossed the "Red sea" is uncertain, however (see notes on 13:18; 14:2).

Themes and Theology

Exodus lays a foundational theology in which God reveals His name, His attributes, His redemption, His law and how He is to be worshiped. It also reports the appointment and work of the first covenant mediator (Moses), describes the beginnings of the priesthood, defines the role of the prophet and relates how the ancient covenant relationship between God and His people came under a new administration (the Sinai covenant).

Profound insights into the nature of God are found in chs. 3; 6; 33—34. The focus of these texts is on the fact and importance of His presence (as signified by His name Yahweh and by His glory). But emphasis is also placed on His attributes of justice, truthfulness, mercy, faithfulness and holiness. Thus to know God's "name" is to know Him and His character (see 3:13–15; 6:3).

God is also the Lord of history, for there is no one like Him: "glorious in holiness, Fearful in praises, doing wonders" (15:11). Neither the affliction of Israel nor the plagues in Egypt were outside His control. Pharaoh, the Egyptians and all Israel saw the power of God.

It is reassuring to know that God remembers and is concerned about His people (see 2:24). What He had promised centuries earlier to Abraham, Isaac and Jacob He now begins to bring to fruition as Israel is freed from Egyptian bondage and sets out for the land of promise. The covenant at Sinai is but another step in God's fulfillment of His promise to the patriarchs (3:15–17; 6:2–8; 19:3–8).

The theology of salvation is likewise one of the strong emphases of the book. The verb "redeem" is used, e.g., in 6:6; 15:13. But the heart of redemption theology is best seen in the passover narrative of ch. 12 and the sealing of the covenant in ch. 24. The apostle Paul viewed the death of the passover lamb as fulfilled in Christ (1 Cor 5:7). Indeed, John the Baptist called Jesus the "Lamb of God, which taketh away the sin of the world" (John 1:29).

The foundation of Biblical ethics and morality is laid out first in the gracious character of God as revealed in the exodus itself and then in the ten commandments (20:1–17) and the ordinances of the book of the covenant (20:22—23:33), which taught Israel how to apply in a practical way the principles of the commandments.

The book concludes with an elaborate discussion of the theology of worship. Though costly in time, effort and monetary value, the tabernacle, in meaning and function, points to the chief end of man: "to glorify God and to enjoy him forever" (Westminster Shorter Catechism). By means of the tabernacle, the omnipotent, unchanging and transcendent God of the universe came to "dwell" or "tabernacle" with His people, thereby revealing His gracious nearness as well. God is not only mighty in Israel's behalf; He is also present in her midst.

However, these theological elements do not merely sit side by side in the Exodus narrative. They receive their fullest and richest significance from the fact that they are embedded in the account of God's raising up His servant Moses (1) to liberate His people from Egyptian bondage, (2) to inaugurate His earthly kingdom among them by bringing them into a special national covenant with Him, and (3) to erect within Israel God's royal tent. And this account of redemption from bondage leading to consecration in covenant and the pitching of God's royal tent in the earth, all through the ministry of a chosen mediator, discloses God's purpose in history—the purpose He would fulfill through Israel, and ultimately through Jesus Christ the supreme Mediator.

Outline

- I. Divine Redemption (chs. 1—18)
  - A. Fulfilled Multiplication (ch. 1)
    1. The promised increase (1:1–7)
    2. The first pogrom (1:8–14)
    3. The second pogrom (1:15–21)
    4. The third pogrom (1:22)
  - B. Preparations for Deliverance (2:1—4:26)
    1. Preparing a leader (2:1–10)
    2. Extending the time of preparation (2:11–22)
    3. Preparing the people (2:23–25)

   4. Calling a deliverer (3:1–10)
   5. Answering inadequate objections (3:11—4:17)
   6. Preparing a leader's family (4:18–26)
 C. First Steps in Leadership (4:27—7:5)
   1. Reinforced by brothers (4:27–31)
   2. Rebuffed by the enemy (5:1–14)
   3. Rebuffed by the enslaved (5:15–21)
   4. Revisited by old objections (5:22–23)
   5. Reinforced by the name of God (6:1–8)
   6. Reminded of one's lowly origins (6:9—7:5)
 D. Judgment and Salvation through the Plagues (7:6—11:10)
   1. Presenting the signs of divine authority (7:6–13)
   2. First plague: water turned to blood (7:14–24)
   3. Second plague: frogs (7:25—8:15)
   4. Third plague: lice (8:16–19)
   5. Fourth plague: flies (8:20–32)
   6. Fifth plague: against livestock (9:1–7)
   7. Sixth plague: boils (9:8–12)
   8. Seventh plague: hail (9:13–35)
   9. Eighth plague: locusts (10:1–20)
   10. Ninth plague: darkness (10:21–29)
   11. Tenth plague announced: death of the firstborn (ch. 11)
 E. The Passover (12:1–28)
   1. Preparations for the passover (12:1–13)
   2. Preparations for unleavened bread (12:14–20)
   3. Celebration of the passover (12:21–28)
 F. The Exodus from Egypt (12:29–51)
   1. Death at midnight (12:29–32)
   2. Expulsion from Egypt (12:33–42)
   3. Regulations for the passover (12:43–51)
 G. The Consecration of the Firstborn (13:1–16)
 H. Crossing the "Red Sea" (13:17—15:21)
   1. Into the wilderness (13:17–22)
   2. At the "Red sea" (14:1–14)
   3. Across the "Red sea" (14:15–31)
   4. Song at the sea (15:1–21)
 I. Journey to Sinai (15:22—18:27)
   1. The waters of Marah (15:22–27)
   2. The manna and the quails (ch. 16)
   3. The waters of Meribah (17:1–7)
   4. The war with Amalek (17:8–16)
   5. The wisdom of Jethro (ch. 18)
II. Covenant at Sinai (chs. 19—24)
 A. The Covenant Proposed (ch. 19)
 B. The Decalogue (20:1–17)
 C. The Reaction of the People to God's Fiery Presence (20:18–21)
 D. The Book of the Covenant (20:22—23:33)
   1. Prologue (20:22–26)
   2. Laws on slaves (21:1–11)
   3. Laws on homicide (21:12–17)
   4. Laws on bodily injuries (21:18–32)
   5. Laws on property damage (21:33—22:15)
   6. Laws on society (22:16–31)
   7. Laws on justice and neighborliness (23:1–9)
   8. Laws on sacred seasons (23:10–19)
   9. Epilogue (23:20–33)
 E. Ratification of the Covenant (ch. 24)

- III. Divine Worship (chs. 25—40)
  - A. Instructions concerning the Tabernacle (chs. 25—31)
    1. Collection of the materials (25:1–9)
    2. Ark and mercy seat (25:10–22)
    3. Table of the shewbread (25:23–30)
    4. Golden candlestick (25:31–40)
    5. Curtains and boards (ch. 26)
    6. Brasen altar (27:1–8)
    7. Court of the tabernacle (27:9–19)
    8. Priesthood (27:20—28:5)
    9. Garments of the priests (28:6–43)
    10. Ordination of the priests (ch. 29)
    11. Altar of incense (30:1–10)
    12. Census tax (30:11–16)
    13. Laver of brass (30:17–21)
    14. Anointing oil and incense (30:22–38)
    15. Appointment of craftsmen (31:1–11)
    16. Sabbath rest (31:12–18)
  - B. False Worship (chs. 32—34)
    1. The golden calf (32:1–29)
    2. Moses' mediation (32:30–35)
    3. Threatened separation and Moses' prayer (ch. 33)
    4. Renewal of the covenant (ch. 34)
  - C. The Building of the Tabernacle (chs. 35—40)
    1. Summons to build (35:1–19)
    2. Voluntary gifts (35:20–29)
    3. Bezaleel and his craftsmen (35:30—36:7)
    4. Progress of the work (36:8—39:31)
    5. Moses' blessing (39:32–43)
    6. Erection of the tabernacle (40:1–33)
    7. Dedication of the tabernacle (40:34–38)

Israel's growth and bondage

1 Now [a]these *are* the names of the children of Israel, which came into Egypt;
every man and his household came with Jacob.
2 Reuben, Simeon, Levi, and Judah,
3 Issachar, Zebulun, and Benjamin,
4 Dan, and Naphtali, Gad, and Asher.
5 And all the souls that came *out of* the
[1]loins of Jacob were [a]seventy souls: for Joseph
was in Egypt *already.*
6 And [a]Joseph died, and all his brethren,
and all that generation.
7 ¶ [a]And the children of Israel were fruitful, and increased abundantly, and multiplied,
and waxed exceeding mighty; and the land
was filled with them.
8 Now there arose up a new king over
Egypt, which knew not Joseph.
9 And he said unto his people, Behold,
[a]the people of the children of Israel *are* moe
and mightier than we:
10 [a]Come on, let us [b]deal wisely with
them; lest they multiply, and it come to pass,
that, when there falleth out any war, they join
also unto our enemies, and fight against us,
and *so* get them up out of the land.
11 Therefore they did set over them
taskmasters [a]to afflict them with their [b]bur-
dens. And they built for Pharaoh treasure cities, Pithom [c]and Raamses.
12 [1]But the more they afflicted them, the
more they multiplied and grew. And they were
grieved because of the children of Israel.
13 And the Egyptians made the children of
Israel to serve with rigour:
14 And they [a]made their lives bitter with
hard bondage, [b]in morter, and in brick, and in
all manner of service in the field: all their service, wherein they made them serve, *was* with
rigour.
15 ¶ And the king of Egypt spake to the Hebrew midwives, of which the name of the one
was Shiphrah, and the name of the other Puah:
16 And he said, When ye do the office of a
midwife to the Hebrew women, and see *them*
upon the stools; if it *be* a son, then ye shall kill
him: but if it *be* a daughter, then she shall live.
17 But the midwives [a]feared God, and did
not [b]as the king of Egypt commanded them,
but saved the men children alive.
18 And the king of Egypt called for the
midwives, and said unto them, Why have ye
done this thing, and have saved the men children alive?
19 And [a]the midwives said unto Pharaoh,
Because the Hebrew women *are* not as the
Egyptian women; for they *are* lively, and are
delivered ere the midwives come in unto
them.
20 [a]Therefore God dealt well with the midwives: and the people multiplied, and waxed
very mighty.
21 And it came to pass, because the midwives feared God, [a]that he made them houses.
22 And Pharaoh charged all his people,
saying, [a]Every son that is born ye shall cast
into the river, and every daughter ye shall save
alive.

Moses' birth

2 And there went [a]a man of the house of
Levi, and took *to wife* a daughter of Levi.
2 And the woman conceived, and bare a
son: and [a]when she saw him that he *was a*
goodly *child,* she hid him three months.

1:1 [a]Gen. 46:8
1:5 [1]Heb. *thigh* [a]Gen. 46:26,27
1:6 [a]Gen. 50:26; Acts 7:15
1:7 [a]Gen. 46:3; Deut. 26:5; Ps. 105:24; Acts 7:17
1:9 [a]Ps. 105:24
1:10 [a]Ps. 83:3,4 [b]Prov. 16:25; Acts 7:19
1:11 [a]Gen. 15:13; ch. 3:7; Deut. 26:6 [b]ch. 5:4,5 [c]Gen. 47:11
1:12 [1]Heb. *And as they afflicted them, so they multiplied, etc.*
1:14 [a]ch. 2:23; 6:9; Num. 20:15; Acts 7:19,34 [b]Ps. 81:6
1:17 [a]Prov. 16:6 [b]Dan. 3:16,18; Acts 5:29
1:19 [a]See Josh. 2:4; 2 Sam. 17:19,20
1:20 [a]Prov. 11:18; Eccl. 8:12; Is. 3:10; Heb. 6:10
1:21 [a]See 1 Sam. 2:35; 2 Sam. 7:11,13,27,29; 1 Ki. 11:38; Ps. 127:1
1:22 [a]Acts 7:19
2:1 [a]ch. 6:20; Num. 26:59; 1 Chr. 23:14
2:2 [a]Acts 7:20; Heb. 11:23

‡1:1–5 These verses clearly indicate that Exodus was written as a continuation of Genesis. The Israelites lived in Egypt 430 years (see 12:40). Exodus is the story of Israel's exit from bondage in Egypt.

1:1 *these are the names of.* The same expression appears in Gen 46:8 at the head of a list of Jacob's descendants. *Israel . . . Jacob.* Jacob had earlier been given the additional name Israel (see Gen 32:28; 35:10 and notes).

1:2–4 The sons of Leah (Reuben through Zebulun) and Rachel (Benjamin; Joseph is not mentioned because the list includes only those "which came into Egypt . . . with Jacob," v. 1) are listed in the order of their seniority and before the sons of Rachel's and Leah's handmaids: Bilhah had Dan and Naphtali, Zilpah had Gad and Asher (see Gen 35:23–26).

1:5 *seventy.* See note on Gen 46:27.

1:6–7 From the death of Joseph to the rise of a new king (v. 8) was more than 200 years.

1:7 See Acts 7:17. God's promised blessing of fruitfulness and increase had been given to Adam (Gen 1:28), Noah (Gen 8:17; 9:1,7), Abraham (Gen 17:2,6; 22:17), Isaac (Gen 26:4) and Jacob (Gen 28:14; 35:11; 48:4). God continued to fulfill His promise during the 430-year sojourn in Egypt. *the land was filled with them.* The Hebrew used here echoes the blessing of Adam (Gen 1:28)—God's initial blessing of mankind was being fulfilled in Israel. The Israelites who left Egypt are said to number about 600,000 men, "beside" (12:37). *land.* Goshen (see note on Gen 45:10).

1:8 See Acts 7:18. *new king.* Probably Ahmose, the founder of the 18th dynasty, who expelled the Hyksos (foreign—predominantly Semitic—rulers of Egypt).

1:11 *taskmasters.* The same official Egyptian designation appears on a wall painting in the Theban tomb of Rekhmire during the reign of the 18th-dynasty pharaoh Thutmose III (see Introduction: Chronology). *Raamses.* See note on Gen 47:11. *Pharaoh.* The word, which is Egyptian in origin and means "great house," is a royal title rather than a personal name.

1:14 *made their lives bitter.* A fact commemorated in the passover meal, which was eaten with "bitter herbs" (12:8). *all manner of service in the field.* Including pumping the waters of the Nile into the fields to irrigate them (see Deut 11:10).

1:15 *Hebrew.* See note on Gen 14:13. *Shiphrah, and . . . Puah.* Semitic, not Egyptian, names. Since the Israelites were so numerous, there were probably other midwives under Shiphrah and Puah.

1:16 *stools.* The Hebrew term means lit. "two stones"; a woman sat on them while giving birth.

1:17 See Acts 5:29 for a parallel in the early church. *feared God.* See note on Gen 20:11.

2:1 *a man . . . a daughter of Levi.* Perhaps Amram and Jochebed (but see note on 6:20).

2:2 *he was a goodly child.* Moses was "exceeding fair" (Acts 7:20; cf. Heb 11:23). The account of Moses' remarkable deliverance in infancy foreshadows the deliverance from Egypt that God would later effect through him.

3 And when she could not longer hide
him, she took for him an ark of bulrushes, and
daubed it with slime and with pitch, and put
the child therein; and she laid *it* in the flags by
the river's brink.
4 [a]And his sister stood afar off, to wit what
would be done to him.
5 And the [a]daughter of Pharaoh came
down to wash *herself* at the river; and her
maidens walked along by the river's side; and
when she saw the ark among the flags, she
sent her maid to fetch it.
6 And when she had opened *it*, she saw
the child: and behold, the babe wept. And she
had compassion on him, and said, This *is one*
of the Hebrews' children.
7 Then said his sister to Pharaoh's daughter, Shall I go and call to thee a nurse of the
Hebrew women, that she may nurse the child
for thee?
8 And Pharaoh's daughter said to her, Go.
And the maid went and called the child's
mother.
9 And Pharaoh's daughter said unto her,
Take this child away, and nurse it for me, and
I will give *thee* thy wages. And the woman
took the child, and nursed it.
10 And the child grew, and she brought
him unto Pharaoh's daughter, and he became
[a]her son. And she called his name [1]Moses:
and she said, Because I drew him out of the
water.

Moses flees to Midian

11 ¶ And it came to pass in those days,
[a]when Moses was grown, that he went out
unto his brethren, and looked on their [b]bur-
dens: and he spied an Egyptian smiting a Hebrew, *one* of his brethren.
12 And he looked this way and that way,
and when he saw that *there was* no man, he
[a]slew the Egyptian, and hid him in the sand.
13 And [a]when he went out the second day,
behold, two men of the Hebrews strove together: and he said to him that did the wrong,
Wherefore smitest thou thy fellow?
14 And he said, [a]Who made thee [1]a prince
and a judge over us? intendest thou to kill me,
as thou killedst the Egyptian? And Moses
feared, and said, Surely *this* thing is known.
15 Now when Pharaoh heard this thing, he
sought to slay Moses. But [a]Moses fled from the
face of Pharaoh, and dwelt in the land of Midian: and he sat down by [b]a well.
16 [a]Now the [1]priest of Midian had seven
daughters: [b]and they came and drew water, and
filled the troughs to water their father's flock.
17 And the shepherds came and drove
them away: but Moses stood up and helped
them, and [a]watered their flock.
18 And when they came to [a]Reuel their father, he said, How *is it that* you are come so
soon to day?
19 And they said, An Egyptian delivered us
out of the hand of the shepherds, and also drew
water enough for us, and watered the flock.
20 And he said unto his daughters, And
where *is* he? why *is* it *that* ye have left the
man? call him, that he may [a]eat bread.
21 And Moses was content to dwell with
the man: and he gave Moses [a]Zipporah his
daughter.
22 And she bare *him* a son, and he called
his name [a][1]Gershom: for he said, I have been
[b]a stranger in a strange land.
23 ¶ And it came to pass [a]in process of
time, that the king of Egypt died: and the children of Israel [b]sighed by reason of the
bondage, and they cried, and [c]their cry came
up unto God by reason of the bondage.

2:4 [a]ch. 15:20; Num. 26:59 **2:5** [a]Acts 7:21 **2:10** [1]That is, *Drawn out* [a]Acts 7:21 **2:11** [a]Acts 7:23,24; Heb. 11:24-26 [b]ch. 1:11

2:12 [a]Acts 7:24 **2:13** [a]Acts 7:26 **2:14** [1]Heb. *a man a prince* [a]Acts 7:27,28 **2:15** [a]Acts 7:29; Heb. 11:27 [b]Gen. 24:11; 29:2 **2:16** [1]Or, *prince* [a]ch. 3:1 [b]Gen. 24:11; 1 Sam. 9:11 **2:17** [a]Gen. 29:10 **2:18** [a]Num. 10:29; Called also *Jethro*, or, *Jether*; ch. 3:1; 4:18 **2:20** [a]Gen. 31:54 **2:21** [a]ch. 18:2 **2:22** [1][That is, *A stranger here*] [a]ch. 18:3 [b]Acts 7:29 **2:23** [a]Acts 7:30 [b]Deut. 26:7 [c]ch. 3:9; Jas. 5:4

‡2:3 *ark of bulrushes.* Each of the two Hebrew words lying behind this phrase is of Egyptian origin. The word for "ark" is used only here and of Noah's ark (see note on Gen 6:14). Moses' ark was a miniature version of the large, seaworthy "vessels of bulrushes" mentioned in Is 18:2. *flags* [i.e., reeds]. A word of Egyptian derivation, reflected in the proper name "Red sea" (Hebrew *Yam Suph*, "Sea of Reeds").

2:4 *his sister.* Miriam (see 15:20).

2:5 *the daughter of Pharaoh.* Perhaps the famous 18th-dynasty princess who later became Queen Hatshepsut. *maidens.* They stayed on the river bank to bathe the princess.

2:10 See Acts 7:21–22. *he became her son.* Throughout this early part of Exodus, all the pharaoh's efforts to suppress Israel were thwarted by women: the midwives (1:17), the Israelite mothers (1:19), Moses' mother and sister (vv. 3–4,7–9), the pharaoh's daughter (here). The pharaoh's impotence to destroy the people of God is thus ironically exposed. *Moses.* The name, of Egyptian origin, means "is born" and forms the second element in such pharaonic names as Ahmose (see note on 1:8), Thutmose and Raamses (see note on 1:11). *drew him out.* A Hebrew wordplay on the name Moses (which sounds like the Hebrew for "draw out"), emphasizing his providential rescue from the Nile. Thus Moses' name may also have served as a reminder of the great act of deliverance God worked through him at the "Red sea" (see 13:17–14:31).

2:11–15 See Acts 7:23–29; Heb 11:24–27.

2:11 *Moses was grown.* He was now 40 years old (see Acts 7:23).

2:14 *Who made thee a prince and a judge . . . ?* Unwittingly, the speaker made a prediction that would be fulfilled 40 years later (see Acts 7:27,30,35). The Hebrew word for "judge" could also refer to a deliverer, as in the book of Judges (see Acts 7:35); it was often a synonym for "ruler" in the OT (see Gen 18:25 and note) as well as in ancient Canaanite usage. *Moses feared.* See note on Heb 11:27.

2:15 *Pharaoh.* Probably Thutmose III (see Introduction: Chronology). *Midian.* Named after one of Abraham's younger sons (see Gen 25:2; see also note on Gen 37:25). Midian was located in southeastern Sinai and west central Arabia, flanking the eastern arm of the Red sea (Gulf of Aqaba) on both sides. Dry and desolate, it formed a stark contrast to Moses' former home in the royal court. He lived in Midian 40 years (see Acts 7:29–30).

2:16 *priest of Midian.* Reuel (see v. 18), which means "friend of God." His other name, Jethro (see 3:1), may be a title meaning "his excellency."

2:23 *in process of time.* Thutmose III (see note on v. 15) enjoyed a long reign.

2:24 *covenant with Abraham.* See Gen 15:17–18; 17:7 and notes. *Isaac.* See Gen 17:19; 26:24. *Jacob.* See Gen 35:11–12.

24 And God [a]heard their groaning, and
God [b]remembered his [c]covenant with Abraham, with Isaac, and with Jacob.
25 And God [a]looked upon the children of
Israel, and God [b][1]had respect unto *them.*

Moses and the burning bush

3 Now Moses kept the flock of Jethro his father in law, [a]the priest of Midian: and he
led the flock to the backside of the desert, and
came to [b]the mountain of God, *even* to Horeb.
2 And [a]the angel of the LORD appeared unto
him in a flame of fire out of the midst of a bush:
and he looked, and behold, the bush burned
with fire, and the bush was not consumed.
3 And Moses said, I will now turn aside,
and see this [a]great sight, why the bush is not
burnt.
4 And when the LORD saw that he turned
aside to see, God called [a]unto him out of the
midst of the bush, and said, Moses, Moses.
And he said, Here *am* I.
5 And he said, Draw not nigh hither: [a]put
off thy shoes from off thy feet, for the place
whereon thou standest *is* holy ground.
6 Moreover he said, [a]I *am* the God of thy
father, the God of Abraham, the God of Isaac,
and the God of Jacob. And Moses hid his face;
for [b]he was afraid to look upon God.
7 And the LORD said, [a]I have surely seen
the affliction of my people which *are* in Egypt,
and have heard their cry [b]by reason of their
taskmasters; for [c]I know their sorrows;
8 And [a]I am come down to [b]deliver them
out of the hand of the Egyptians, and to bring
them up out of that land [c]unto a good land and
a large, unto a land [d]flowing with milk and
honey; unto the place of [e]the Canaanites, and
the Hittites, and the Amorites, and the Perizzites, and the Hivites, and the Jebusites.
9 Now therefore, behold, [a]the cry of the
children of Israel is come unto me: and I have
also seen the [b]oppression wherewith the
Egyptians oppress them.
10 [a]Come now therefore, and I will send
thee unto Pharaoh, that thou mayest bring forth
my people the children of Israel out of Egypt.
11 And Moses said unto God, [a]Who *am* I,
that I should go unto Pharaoh, and that I should
bring forth the children of Israel out of Egypt?
12 And he said, [a]Certainly I will be with
thee; and this *shall be* a token unto thee, that
I have sent thee: When thou hast brought
forth the people out of Egypt, ye shall serve
God upon this mountain.
13 And Moses said unto God, Behold, *when*
I come unto the children of Israel, and shall say
unto them, The God of your fathers hath sent
me unto you; and they shall say to me, What *is*
his name? what shall I say unto them?
14 And God said unto Moses, I AM THAT I
AM: and he said, Thus shalt thou say unto the
children of Israel, [a]I AM hath sent me unto you.
15 And God said moreover unto Moses,
Thus shalt thou say unto the children of Israel,
The LORD God of your fathers, the God of
Abraham, the God of Isaac, and the God of Jacob, hath sent me unto you: this *is* [a]my name
for ever, and this *is* my memorial unto all generations.

2:24 [a]ch. 6:5 [b]ch. 6:5; Ps. 105:8,42 [c]Gen. 15:14
2:25 [1]Heb. *knew* [a]ch. 4:31; Luke 1:25 [b]ch. 3:7
3:1 [a]ch. 2:16 [b]ch. 18:5; 1 Ki. 19:8
3:2 [a]Deut. 33:16; Acts 7:30
3:3 [a]Acts 7:31
3:4 [a]Deut. 33:16
3:5 [a]Josh. 5:15
3:6 [a]Gen. 28:13; ch. 4:5; Mat. 22:32; Acts 7:32 [b]See 1 Ki. 19:13
3:7 [a]ch. 2:23-25; Ps. 106:44 [b]ch. 1:11 [c]Gen. 18:21; ch. 2:25
3:8 [a]Gen. 50:24 [b]ch. 6:6,8
3:8 [c]Deut. 1:25; 8:7-9 [d]ver. 17; ch. 13:5; Jer. 11:5; Ezek. 20:6 [e]Gen. 15:21
3:9 [a]ch. 2:23 [b]ch. 1:11,13,14
3:10 [a]Mic. 6:4
3:11 [a]See ch. 6:12; 1 Sam. 18:18
3:12 [a]Gen. 31:3; Josh. 1:5; Rom. 8:31
3:14 [a]ch. 6:3; John 8:58; Heb. 13:8
3:15 [a]Ps. 135:13

3:1 Like David (2 Sam 7:8), Moses was called from tending the flock to be the shepherd of God's people. *Jethro.* See note on 2:16. *Horeb.* Means "desert," "desolation"; either (1) an alternate name for mount Sinai or (2) another high mountain in the same vicinity in the southeast region of the Sinai peninsula. Tradition identifies mount Horeb with Ras es-Safsaf ("willow peak"), 6,500 feet high, and mount Sinai with Jebel Musa ("mountain of Moses"), 7,400 feet high, but both identifications are uncertain.

3:2 *angel of the LORD.* Used interchangeably with "the LORD" and "God" in v. 4 (see note on Gen 16:7). *appeared unto him in a flame of fire.* God's revelation of Himself and His will was often accompanied by fire (see 13:21; 19:18; 1 Ki 18:24,38).

3:4 Every true prophet was called by God (see, e.g., 1 Sam 3:4; Is 6:8; Jer 1:4–5; Ezek 2:1–8; Hos 1:2; Amos 7:15; Jonah 1:1–2; see also note on 7:1–2). *Moses, Moses . . . Here am I.* See notes on Gen 22:1,11.

3:5 *put off thy shoes.* A practice still followed by Muslims before entering a mosque. *holy.* The ground was not holy by nature but was made so by the divine presence (see, e.g., Gen 2:3). Holiness involves being consecrated to the Lord's service and thus being separated from the commonplace.

3:6 See 2:24 and note. *afraid to look upon God.* See notes on Gen 16:13; 32:30. Later, as the Lord's servant, Moses would meet with God on mount Sinai (19:3) and even ask to see God's glory (33:18).

3:8 *I am come down to deliver.* God may also come down to judge (see Gen 11:5–9; 18:21). *land flowing with milk and honey.* The traditional and proverbial description of the hill country of Canaan—in its original pastoral state (see note on Is 7:15). *Canaanites . . . Jebusites.* See notes on Gen 10:6,15–16; 13:7. The list of the Canaanite nations ranges from two names (see Gen 13:7) to five (see Num 13:29) to six (as here; see also Judg 3:5) to ten (see Gen 15:19–21) to twelve (see Gen 10:15–18). The classic description includes seven names (see, e.g., Deut 7:1), seven being the number of completeness (see note on Gen 4:17–18).

3:10 *Pharaoh.* Probably Amunhotep II (see Introduction: Chronology).

3:11 Moses' first expression of reluctance (see v. 13; 4:1,10,13).

3:12 *I will be with thee.* See note on Gen 26:3. The Hebrew word translated "I will be" is the same as the one translated "I AM" in v. 14. *token.* A visible proof or guarantee that what God had promised He would surely fulfill (see notes on 4:8; Gen 15:8).

3:13 Moses' second expression of reluctance. *What is his name?* God had not yet identified Himself to Moses by name (see v. 6; cf. Gen 17:1).

3:14 *I AM THAT I AM.* The name by which God wished to be known and worshiped in Israel—the name that expressed His character as the dependable and faithful God who desires the full trust of His people (see v. 12, where "I will be" is completed by "with you"; see also 34:5–7). *I AM.* Jesus applied the phrase to Himself; in so doing He claimed to be God and risked being stoned for blasphemy (see John 8:58–59).

3:15 *The LORD.* The Hebrew for this name is *Yahweh* (often incorrectly spelled "Jehovah"; see note on Deut 28:58). It means "He is" or "He will be" and is the third-person form of the verb translated "I will be" in v. 12 and "I AM" in v. 14. When God speaks of Himself He says, "I AM," and when we speak of Him we say, "He is."

16 Go, and [a]gather the elders of Israel together, and say unto them, The LORD God of your fathers, the God of Abraham, of Isaac, and of Jacob, appeared unto me, saying, [b]I have surely visited you, and *seen* that which is done to you in Egypt:

17 And I have said, [a]I will bring you up out of the affliction of Egypt unto the land of the Canaanites, and the Hittites, and the Amorites, and the Perizzites, and the Hivites, and the Jebusites, unto a land flowing with milk and honey.

18 And [a]they shall hearken to thy voice: and [b]thou shalt come, thou and the elders of Israel, unto the king of Egypt, and you shall say unto him, The LORD God of the Hebrews hath [c]met with us: and now let us go, we beseech thee, three days' journey into the wilderness, that we may sacrifice to the LORD our God.

19 And I am sure that the king of Egypt [a]will not let you go, [1]no, not by a mighty hand.

20 And I will [a]stretch out my hand, and smite Egypt with [b]all my wonders which I will do in the midst thereof: and [c]after that he will let you go.

21 And [a]I will give this people favour in the sight of the Egyptians: and it shall come to pass, that, when ye go, ye shall not go empty:

22 [a]But every woman shall borrow of her neighbour, and of her that sojourneth in her house, jewels of silver, and jewels of gold, and raiment: and ye shall put *them* upon your sons, and upon your daughters; and [b]ye shall spoil [1]the Egyptians.

God equips Moses

4 And Moses answered and said, But behold, they will not believe me, nor hearken unto my voice: for they will say, The LORD hath not appeared unto thee.

2 And the LORD said unto him, What *is* that in thine hand? And he said, [a]A rod.

3 And he said, Cast it on the ground. And he cast it on the ground, and it became a serpent; and Moses fled from before it.

4 And the LORD said unto Moses, Put forth thine hand, and take it by the tail. And he put forth his hand, and caught it, and it became a rod in his hand:

5 That they may [a]believe that [b]the LORD God of their fathers, the God of Abraham, the God of Isaac, and the God of Jacob, hath appeared unto thee.

6 And the LORD said furthermore unto him, Put now thine hand into thy bosom. And he put his hand into his bosom: and when he took it out, behold, his hand *was* leprous [a]as snow.

7 And he said, Put thine hand into thy bosom again. And he put his hand into his bosom again; and plucked it out of his bosom, and behold, [a]it was turned again as his *other* flesh.

8 And it shall come to pass, if they will not believe thee, neither hearken to the voice of the first sign, that they will believe the voice of the latter sign.

9 And it shall come to pass, if they will not believe also these two signs, neither hearken unto thy voice, that thou shalt take of the water of the river, and pour *it upon* the dry *land:* and [a]the water which thou takest out of the river [1]shall become blood upon the dry *land.*

10 And Moses said unto the LORD, O my Lord, I *am* not [1]eloquent, neither [2]heretofore, nor since thou hast spoken unto thy servant: but [a]I *am* slow of speech, and of a slow tongue.

11 And the LORD said unto him, [a]Who hath made man's mouth? or who maketh the dumb, or deaf, or the seeing, or the blind? have not I the LORD?

12 Now therefore go, and I will be [a]with thy mouth, and teach thee what thou shalt say.

13 And he said, O my Lord, [a]send, I pray thee, by the hand *of him whom* thou [1]wilt send.

14 And the anger of the LORD was kindled against Moses, and he said, Is not Aaron the

3:16 [a]ch. 4:29 [b]ch. 2:25; Luke 1:68
3:17 [a]Gen. 15:14,16
3:18 [a]ch. 4:31 [b]ch. 5:1,3 [c]Num. 23:3,4,15,16
3:19 [1]Or, *but by strong hand* [a]ch. 5:2
3:20 [a]ch. 6:6; 9:15 [b]Deut. 6:22; Neh. 9:10; Acts 7:36 [c]ch. 12:31
3:21 [a]ch. 11:3; 12:36; Prov. 16:7
3:22 [1]Or, *Egypt* [a]ch. 11:2 [b]Job 27:17; Prov. 13:22; Ezek. 39:10
4:2 [a]ver. 17,20
4:5 [a]ch. 19:9 [b]ch. 3:15
4:6 [a]Num. 12:10; 2 Ki. 5:27
4:7 [a]Num. 12:13,14; Deut. 32:39
4:9 [1]Heb. *shall be and shall be* [a]ch. 7:19
4:10 [1]Heb. *a man of words* [2]Heb. *since yesterday, nor since the third day* [a]ch. 6:12; Jer. 1:6
4:11 [a]Ps. 94:9
4:12 [a]Is. 50:4; Jer. 1:9; Mat. 10:19; Mark 13:11; Luke 12:11,12; 21:14,15
4:13 [1]Or, *shouldest* [a]See Jonah 1:3

3:16 *elders.* The Hebrew for this word means lit. "bearded ones," perhaps reflecting the age, wisdom, experience and influence necessary for a man expected to function as an elder. As heads of local families and tribes, "elders" had a recognized position also among the Babylonians, Hittites, Egyptians (see Gen 50:7), Moabites and Midianites (see Num 22:7). Their duties included judicial arbitration and sentencing (see Deut 22:13–19) as well as military leadership (see Josh 8:10) and counsel (see 1 Sam 4:3).

3:18 *Hebrews.* See note on Gen 14:13. *three days' journey.* Probably a conventional expression for a short trip rather than a journey of exactly three days. *wilderness.* God had met with Moses there (see vv. 1–2) and would meet with him there again (see v. 12).

3:20 *wonders.* A prediction of the plagues that God would send against Egypt (see 7:14–12:30).

3:21–22 See 11:2–3; 12:35–36.

3:21 *when ye go, ye shall not go empty.* God had promised Abraham that after Israel had served for 400 years they would "come out with great substance" (Gen 15:14; see Ps 105:37). Israel herself was to live by the same principle of providing gifts to a released slave (see Deut 15:12–15).

4:1 Moses' third expression of reluctance (in spite of God's assurance in 3:18).

4:2 *rod.* Probably a shepherd's crook.

4:3 *serpent.* See 7:9–10 and note. Throughout much of Egypt's history the pharaoh wore a cobra made of metal on the front of his headdress as a symbol of his sovereignty.

4:8 *sign.* A supernatural event or phenomenon designed to demonstrate authority, provide assurance (see Josh 2:12–13), bear testimony (see Is 19:19–20), give warning (see Num 17:10) or encourage faith. See note on 3:12.

4:10 Moses' fourth expression of reluctance. *I am slow of speech, and of a slow tongue.* Not in the sense of a speech impediment (see Acts 7:22). He complained, instead, of not being eloquent or quick-witted enough to respond to the pharaoh (see 6:12). Cf. the description of Paul in 2 Cor 10:10.

4:13 Moses' fifth and final expression of reluctance.

4:14 *the anger of the LORD was kindled against Moses.* Although the Lord is "longsuffering" (34:6), He does not withhold His

Levite thy brother? I know that he can speak well. And also, behold, [a]he cometh forth to meet thee: and when he seeth thee, he will be glad in his heart.

15 And [a]thou shalt speak unto him, and [b]put words in his mouth: and I will be with thy mouth, and with his mouth, and [c]will teach you what ye shall do.

16 And he shall be thy spokesman unto the people: and he shall be, *even* he shall be to thee instead of a mouth, and [a]thou shalt be to him instead of God.

17 And thou shalt take [a]this rod in thine hand, wherewith thou shalt do signs.

18 And Moses went and returned to [1]Jethro his father in law, and said unto him, Let me go, I pray thee, and return unto my brethren which *are* in Egypt, and see whether they be yet alive. And Jethro said to Moses, Go in peace.

19 And the LORD said unto Moses in Midian, Go, return *into* Egypt: for [a]all the men are dead which sought thy life.

20 And Moses took his wife and his sons, and set them upon an ass, and he returned to the land of Egypt: and Moses took [a]the rod of God in his hand.

21 And the LORD said unto Moses, When thou goest to return into Egypt, see that thou do all *those* [a]wonders before Pharaoh, which I have put in thine hand: but [b]I will harden his heart, that he shall not let the people go.

22 And thou shalt say unto Pharaoh, Thus saith the LORD, [a]Israel *is* my son, [b]*even* my firstborn:

23 And I say unto thee, Let my son go, that he may serve me: and *if* thou refuse to let him go, behold, [a]I will slay thy son, *even* thy firstborn.

Moses returns to Egypt

24 ¶ And it came to pass by the way in the inn, that the LORD [a]met him, and sought to [b]kill him.

25 Then Zipporah took [a][1]a sharp stone, and cut off the foreskin of her son, and [2]cast *it* at his feet, and said, Surely a bloody husband *art* thou to me.

26 So he let him go: then she said, A bloody husband *thou art,* because of the circumcision.

27 And the LORD said to Aaron, Go into the wilderness [a]to meet Moses. And he went, and met him in [b]the mount of God, and kissed him.

28 And Moses told [a]Aaron all the words of the LORD who had sent him, and all the [b]signs which he had commanded him.

29 And Moses and Aaron [a]went and gathered together all the elders of the children of Israel:

30 [a]And Aaron spake all the words which the LORD had spoken unto Moses, and did the signs in the sight of the people.

31 And the people [a]believed: and when they heard that the LORD had [b]visited the children of Israel, and that he [c]had looked upon their affliction, then [d]they bowed their heads and worshipped.

Pharaoh oppresses Israel

5 And afterward Moses and Aaron went in, and told Pharaoh, Thus saith the LORD God of Israel, Let my people go, that they may hold [a]a feast unto me in the wilderness.

2 And Pharaoh said, [a]Who *is* the LORD, that I should obey his voice to let Israel go? I know not the LORD, [b]neither will I let Israel go.

3 And they said, [a]The God of the Hebrews hath met with us: let us go, we pray thee, three days' journey into the desert, and sacrifice unto the LORD our God; lest he fall upon us with pestilence, or with the sword.

4 And the king of Egypt said unto them, Wherefore do ye, Moses and Aaron, let the people from their works? get you unto your [a]burdens.

5 And Pharaoh said, Behold, the people of the land now *are* [a]many, and you make them rest from their burdens.

4:14 [a]ver. 27; 1 Sam. 10:2,3,5
4:15 [a]ch. 7:1,2 [b]Num. 23:5,12,16 [c]Deut. 5:31
4:16 [a]ch. 7:1
4:17 [a]ver. 2
4:18 [1][Heb. *Jether*]
4:19 [a]ch. 2:15,23; Mat. 2:20
4:20 [a]Num. 20:8,9
4:21 [a]ch. 3:20 [b]ch. 7:3,13; 9:12,35; Deut. 2:30; Josh. 11:20; Is. 63:17; John 12:40
4:22 [a]Hos. 11:1; Rom. 9:4; 2 Cor. 6:18 [b]Jer. 31:9; Jas. 1:18
4:23 [a]ch. 11:5; 12:29
4:24 [a]Num. 22:22 [b]Gen. 17:14
4:25 [1]Or, *knife* [a]Josh. 5:2,3
4:25 [2]Heb. *made* it *touch*
4:27 [a]ver. 14 [b]ch. 3:1
4:28 [a]ver. 15,16 [b]ver. 8,9
4:29 [a]ch. 3:16
4:30 [a]ver. 16
4:31 [a]ver. 8,9; ch. 3:18 [b]ch. 3:16 [c]ch. 2:25; 3:7 [d]Gen. 24:26; 1 Chr. 29:20
5:1 [a]ch. 10:9
5:2 [a]2 Ki. 18:35; Job 21:15 [b]ch. 3:19
5:3 [a]ch. 3:18
5:4 [a]ch. 1:11
5:5 [a]ch. 1:7,9

anger or punishment from His disobedient children forever (see 34:7). *Levite.* Under Aaron's leadership Israel's priesthood would come from the tribe of Levi.

4:15–16 See note on 7:1–2.

4:19 *all the men are dead.* Including Thutmose III (see 2:15,23; see also Introduction: Chronology).

4:20 *sons.* Gershom (see 2:22) and Eliezer. The latter, though unmentioned by name until 18:4, had already been born.

4:21 *wonders.* See note on 3:20. *I will harden his heart.* Nine times in Exodus the hardening of the pharaoh's heart is ascribed to God (here; 7:3; 9:12; 10:1,20,27; 11:10; 14:4,8; see Rom 9:17–18 and notes); another nine times the pharaoh is said to have hardened his own heart (7:13–14,22; 8:15,19,32; 9:7,34–35). The pharaoh alone was the agent of the hardening in each of the first five plagues. Not until the sixth plague did God confirm the pharaoh's willful action (see 9:12), as he had told Moses he would do (see similarly Rom 1:24–28).

4:22 *son.* Used collectively of the Israelites also in Hos 11:1. *my firstborn.* A figure of speech indicating Israel's special relationship with God (see Jer 31:9; Hos 11:1).

4:23 *slay . . . thy firstborn.* Anticipates the tenth plague (see 11:5; 12:12).

4:24 *inn.* Perhaps near water, where travelers could spend the night. *the LORD . . . sought to kill him.* Evidently because Moses had failed to circumcise his son (see Gen 17:9–14).

4:25 *Zipporah . . . cut off the foreskin of her son.* Sensing that divine displeasure had threatened Moses' life, she quickly performed the circumcision on their young son. *sharp stone* [i.e., flint]. Continued to be used for circumcision long after metal was introduced, probably because flint knives were sharper than the metal instruments available and thus more efficient for the surgical procedure (see Josh 5:2 and note). *feet.* Probably a euphemism for "genitals," as in Deut 28:57 ("between her feet").

4:26 *bloody husband.* Circumcision may have been repulsive to Zipporah—though it was practiced for various reasons among many peoples of the ancient Near East.

4:30 *Aaron spake all the words which the LORD had spoken unto Moses.* See note on 7:1–2.

5:1 *Pharaoh.* See note on 3:10.

5:3 See 3:18 and note. The reason for sacrificing where the

6 And Pharaoh commanded the same day the [a]taskmasters of the people, and their officers, saying,

7 Ye shall no more give the people straw to make brick, as heretofore: let them go and gather straw for themselves.

8 And the tale of the bricks, which they did make heretofore, you shall lay upon them; you shall not diminish *ought* thereof: for they *be* idle; therefore they cry, saying, Let us go *and* sacrifice to our God.

9 [1]Let there more work be laid upon the men, that they may labour therein; and let them not regard vain words.

10 And the taskmasters of the people went out, and their officers, and they spake to the people, saying, Thus saith Pharaoh, I will not give you straw.

11 Go ye, get you straw where you can find *it:* yet not ought of your work *shall be* diminished.

12 So the people were scattered abroad throughout all the land of Egypt to gather stubble instead of straw.

13 And the taskmasters hasted *them,* saying, Fulfil your works, [1]*your* daily tasks, as when there was straw.

14 And the officers of the children of Israel, which Pharaoh's taskmasters had set over them, were beaten, *and* demanded, Wherefore have ye not fulfilled your task in making brick both yesterday and to day, as heretofore?

15 Then the officers of the children of Israel came and cried unto Pharaoh, saying, Wherefore dealest thou thus with thy servants?

16 *There is* no straw given unto thy servants, and they say to us, Make brick: and behold, thy servants *are* beaten; but the fault *is* in thine own people.

17 But he said, Ye *are* idle, *ye are* idle: therefore ye say, Let us go *and* do sacrifice to the LORD.

18 Go therefore now, *and* work; for there shall no straw be given you, yet shall ye deliver the tale of bricks.

19 And the officers of the children of Israel did see *that* they *were* in evil *case,* after it was said, Ye shall not minish *ought* from your bricks of *your* daily task.

20 And they met Moses and Aaron, who stood in the way, as they came forth from Pharaoh:

21 [a]And they said unto them, The LORD look upon you, and judge; because you have made our savour [1]to be abhorred in the eyes of Pharaoh, and in the eyes of his servants, to put a sword in their hand to slay us.

God's promise of deliverance

22 ¶ And Moses returned unto the LORD, and said, Lord, wherefore hast thou *so* evil entreated this people? why *is* it *that* thou hast sent me?

23 For since I came to Pharaoh to speak in thy name, he hath done evil to this people; [1]neither hast thou delivered thy people at all.

6 Then the LORD said unto Moses, Now shalt thou see what I will do to Pharaoh: for [a]with a strong hand shall he let them go, and with a strong hand [b]shall he drive them out of his land.

2 And God spake unto Moses, and said unto him, I *am* [1]the LORD:

3 And I appeared unto Abraham, unto Isaac, and unto Jacob, by *the name of* [a]God Almighty, but *by* my name [b]JEHOVAH was I not known to them.

4 [a]And I have also established my covenant with them, [b]to give them the land of Canaan, the land of their pilgrimage, wherein they were strangers.

5 And [a]I have also heard the groaning of the children of Israel, whom the Egyptians keep in bondage; and I have remembered my covenant.

6 Wherefore say unto the children of Israel, I *am* the LORD, and [a]I will bring you out from under the burdens of the Egyptians, and I will rid you out of their bondage, and I will [b]redeem you with a stretched out arm, and with great judgments:

7 And I will [a]take you to me for a people,

5:6 [a]ch. 1:11
5:9 [1]Heb. *Let the work be heavy upon the men*
5:13 [1]Heb. *a matter of a day in his day*
5:21 [1]Heb. *to stink* [a]ch. 6:9
5:23 [1]Heb. *delivering thou hast not delivered*
6:1 [a]ch. 3:19 [b]ch. 12:31,33,39
6:2 [1][Or, *JEHOVAH*]
6:3 [a]Gen. 17:1; 35:11; 48:3 [b]ch. 3:14; Ps. 83:18; John 8:58
6:4 [a]Gen. 15:18 [b]Gen. 28:4
6:5 [a]ch. 2:24
6:6 [a]ch. 3:17; Deut. 26:8 [b]Deut. 7:8; 1 Chr. 17:21
6:7 [a]Deut. 4:20; 2 Sam. 7:24

Egyptians could not see them is given in 8:26 (see note on Gen 43:32).

5:6 *taskmasters.* See note on 1:11. *officers.* Israelite supervisors whose method of appointment and whose functions are indicated in vv. 14–16.

5:7 *straw.* Chopped and mixed with the clay as binder to make the bricks stronger.

5:9 *vain words.* The pharaoh labels all hopes of a quick release for Israel as presumptuous and false.

5:21 *The LORD look upon you, and judge.* See Gen 16:5; 31:49 and notes.

6:1 *Now.* Without further delay, God will act.

6:2 *I am the LORD.* Appears four times in this passage: (1) to introduce the message; (2) to confirm God's promise of redemption (v. 6) based on the evidence of vv. 2–5; (3) to underscore God's intention to adopt Israel (v. 7); (4) to confirm His promise of the land and to conclude the message (v. 8).

6:3 *God Almighty.* See note on Gen 17:1. *by my name JEHOVAH was I not known to them.* See notes on 3:14–15. This does not necessarily mean that the patriarchs were totally ignorant of the name Yahweh ("the LORD"), but it indicates that they did not understand its full implications as the name of the One who would redeem His people (see notes on v. 6; Gen 2:4). That fact could be comprehended only by the Israelites who were to experience the exodus, and by their descendants. *was I not known.* This experiential sense of the verb "to know" is intended also in its repeated use throughout the account of the plagues (see v. 7; 7:17; 8:10,22; 9:14,29; 10:2; 11:7) and in connection with the exodus itself (see 14:4,18; 16:6,8,12; 18:11).

6:5 *remembered.* See note on Gen 8:1.

6:6 *I will bring you out . . . will rid you . . . will redeem you.* The verbs stress the true significance of the name Yahweh—"the LORD"—who is the Redeemer of His people (see note on v. 3). *great judgments.* See 7:4. The Lord's acts include redemption (for Israel) and judgment (against Egypt).

6:7–8 *bringeth you out from . . . will bring you in unto the land.* Redemption means not only release from slavery and suffering but also deliverance to freedom and joy.

and [b]I will be to you a God: and ye shall know that I *am* the LORD your God, which bringeth you out [c]from under the burdens of the Egyptians.

8 And I will bring you in unto the land, *concerning* the which I did [a][1]swear to give it to Abraham, to Isaac, and to Jacob; and I will give it you *for* an heritage: I *am* the LORD.

9 And Moses spake so unto the children of Israel: [a]but they hearkened not unto Moses for [1]anguish of spirit, and for cruel bondage.

10 ¶ And the LORD spake unto Moses, saying,

11 Go in, speak unto Pharaoh king of Egypt, that he let the children of Israel go out of his land.

12 And Moses spake before the LORD, saying, Behold, the children of Israel have not hearkened unto me; how then shall Pharaoh hear me, [a]who *am* of uncircumcised lips?

13 And the LORD spake unto Moses and unto Aaron, and gave them a charge unto the children of Israel, and unto Pharaoh king of Egypt, to bring the children of Israel out of the land of Egypt.

The descendants of Israel

14 ¶ These *be* the heads of their fathers' houses: [a]The sons of Reuben the firstborn of Israel; Hanoch, and Pallu, Hezron, and Carmi: these *be* the families of Reuben.

15 [a]And the sons of Simeon; Jemuel, and Jamin, and Ohad, and Jachin, and Zohar, and Shaul the son of a Canaanitish woman: these *are* the families of Simeon.

16 And these *are* the names of [a]the sons of Levi according to their generations; Gershon, and Kohath, and Merari: and the years of the life of Levi *were* an hundred thirty and seven years.

17 [a]The sons of Gershon; Libni, and Shimi, according to their families.

18 And [a]the sons of Kohath; Amram, and Izhar, and Hebron, and Uzziel: and the years of the life of Kohath *were* an hundred thirty and three years.

6:7 [b]ch. 29:45,46; Rev. 21:7 [c]ch. 5:4,5
6:8 [1]Heb. *lift up my hand* [a]Gen. 15:18; 26:3
6:9 [1]Heb. *shortness, or, straitness* [a]ch. 5:21
6:12 [a]ver. 30; ch. 4:10; Jer. 1:6
6:14 [a]Gen. 46:9; 1 Chr. 5:3
6:15 [a]Gen. 46:10; 1 Chr. 4:24
6:16 [a]Gen. 46:11; Num. 3:17
6:17 [a]1 Chr. 6:17
6:18 [a]1 Chr. 6:2,18
6:19 [a]1 Chr. 6:19; 23:21
6:20 [a]ch. 2:1,2
6:21 [a]1 Chr. 6:37,38
6:22 [a]Lev. 10:4
6:23 [a]Ruth 4:19,20; Mat. 1:4 [b]Lev. 10:1; Num. 3:2; 26:60
6:24 [a]Num. 26:11
6:25 [a]Num. 25:7,11; Josh. 24:33
6:26 [a]ch. 7:4; 12:17,51; Num. 33:1
6:27 [a]ver. 13; ch. 32:7; 33:1; Ps. 77:20
6:29 [a]ver. 11; ch. 7:2
6:30 [a]ver. 12; ch. 4:10
7:1 [a]ch. 4:16; Jer. 1:10 [b]ch. 4:16
7:2 [a]ch. 4:15

19 And [a]the sons of Merari; Mahali and Mushi: these *are* the families of Levi according to their generations.

20 And [a]Amram took him Jochebed his father's sister to wife; and she bare him Aaron and Moses: and the years of the life of Amram *were* an hundred and thirty and seven years.

21 And [a]the sons of Izhar; Korah, and Nepheg, and Zichri.

22 And [a]the sons of Uzziel; Mishael, and Elzaphan, and Zithri.

23 And Aaron took him Elisheba, daughter of [a]Amminadab, sister of Naashon, to wife; and she bare him [b]Nadab, and Abihu, Eleazar, and Ithamar.

24 And the [a]sons of Korah; Assir, and Elkanah, and Abiasaph: these *are* the families of the Korhites.

25 And Eleazar Aaron's son took him *one* of the daughters of Putiel to wife; and [a]she bare him Phinehas: these *are* the heads of the fathers of the Levites according to their families.

26 *These are* that Aaron and Moses, to whom the LORD said, Bring out the children of Israel from the land of Egypt according to their [a]armies.

27 *These are* they which spake to Pharaoh king of Egypt, [a]to bring out the children of Israel from Egypt: *these are* that Moses and Aaron.

Aaron to speak for Moses

28 ¶ And it came to pass on the day *when* the LORD spake unto Moses in the land of Egypt,

29 That the LORD spake unto Moses, saying, I *am* the LORD: [a]speak thou unto Pharaoh king of Egypt all that I say unto thee.

30 And Moses said before the LORD, Behold, [a]I *am* of uncircumcised lips, and how shall Pharaoh hearken unto me?

7 And the LORD said unto Moses, See, I have made thee [a]a god to Pharaoh: and Aaron thy brother shall be [b]thy prophet.

2 Thou [a]shalt speak all that I command thee: and Aaron thy brother shall speak unto

6:7 *I will take you to me for a people, and I will be to you a God.* Words that anticipate the covenant at mount Sinai (see 19:5–6; see also Jer 31:33).

6:8 See Gen 22:15–17. *did swear.* See note on Gen 14:22.

6:12 *am of uncircumcised lips.* See note on 4:10.

6:13 *unto Moses and unto Aaron.* The genealogy contained in vv. 14–25 gives details concerning the background of Moses and Aaron. Only the first three of Jacob's 12 sons (Reuben, Simeon and Levi) are listed since Moses and Aaron were from the third tribe.

6:16 *Merari.* The name is of Egyptian origin, as are those of Putiel and Phinehas (see v. 25) and of Moses himself (see note on 2:10). *the years of the life of Levi were an hundred thirty and seven years.* See vv. 18,20. In the OT, attention is usually called to a person's life span only when it exceeds 100 years.

6:20 *Amram . . . Aaron and Moses.* There is some reason to believe that Amram and Jochebed were not the immediate parents but the ancestors of Aaron and Moses. Kohath, Amram's father (see v. 18), was born before Jacob's (Israel's) descent into Egypt (see Gen 46:11), where the Israelites then stayed 430 years (see 12:40–41). Since Moses was 80 years old at the time of the exodus (see 7:7), he must have been born at least 350 years after Kohath, who consequently could not have been Moses' grandfather (see v. 18). Therefore Amram must not have been Moses' father, and the Hebrew verb for "bare" must have the same meaning it sometimes has in Gen 10 (see Gen 10:8, where it is translated "begat," which can indicate an ancestor or predecessor or founder; see also note on Gen 10:1). *Jochebed.* The name appears to mean "The LORD is glory." If so, it shows that the name Yahweh (here abbreviated as *Jo-*) was known before Moses was born (see note on v. 3). *Aaron and Moses.* Aaron, as the firstborn (see 7:7), is listed first in the official genealogy.

6:30 *of uncircumcised lips.* See v. 12 and note on 4:10.

7:1–2 As God transmits His word through His prophets to His people, so Moses will transmit God's message through Aaron to the pharaoh. The prophet's task was to speak God's word on God's behalf. He was God's "mouth" (4:15–16).

Pharaoh, that he send the children of Israel out of his land.

3 And [a]I will harden Pharaoh's heart, and [b]multiply my [c]signs and my wonders in the land of Egypt.

4 But Pharaoh shall not hearken unto you, [a]that I may lay my hand upon Egypt, and bring forth mine armies, *and* my people the children of Israel, out of the land of Egypt [b]by great judgments.

5 And the Egyptians [a]shall know that I *am* the LORD, when I [b]stretch forth mine hand upon Egypt, and bring out the children of Israel from among them.

6 And Moses and Aaron [a]did as the LORD commanded them, so did they.

7 And Moses *was* [a]fourscore years old, and Aaron fourscore and three years old, when they spake unto Pharaoh.

The rod becomes a serpent

8 ¶ And the LORD spake unto Moses and unto Aaron, saying,

9 When Pharaoh shall speak unto you, saying, [a]Shew a miracle for you: then thou shalt say unto Aaron, [b]Take thy rod, and cast *it* before Pharaoh, *and* it shall become a serpent.

10 And Moses and Aaron went in unto Pharaoh, and they did so [a]as the LORD had commanded: and Aaron cast down his rod before Pharaoh, and before his servants, and it [b]became a serpent.

11 Then Pharaoh also [a]called the wise men and [b]the sorcerers: now the magicians of Egypt, they also [c]did in like manner with their enchantments.

12 For they cast down every man his rod, and they became serpents: but Aaron's rod swallowed up their rods.

13 And he hardened Pharaoh's heart, that he hearkened not unto them; as the LORD had said.

7:3 [a]ch. 4:21 [b]ch. 11:9 [c]ch. 4:7
7:4 [a]ch. 10:1; 11:9 [b]ch. 6:6
7:5 [a]ver. 17; ch. 8:22; 14:4,18; Ps. 9:16 [b]ch. 3:20
7:6 [a]ver. 2
7:7 [a]Deut. 29:5; 31:2; 34:7; Acts 7:23,30
7:9 [a]Is. 7:11; John 2:18; 6:30 [b]ch. 4:2,17
7:10 [a]ver. 9 [b]ch. 4:3
7:11 [a]Gen. 41:8 [b]2 Tim. 3:8 [c]ver. 22; ch. 8:7,18
7:14 [a]ch. 8:15; 10:1,20,27
7:15 [a]ver. 10; ch. 4:2,3
7:16 [a]ch. 3:18 [b]ch. 3:12,18; 5:1,3
7:17 [a]ver. 5; ch. 5:2 [b]ch. 4:9 [c]Rev. 16:4,6
7:18 [a]ver. 24
7:19 [1]Heb. *gathering of their waters* [a]ch. 8:5,6,16; 9:22; 10:12,21; 14:21,26
7:20 [a]ch. 17:5 [b]Ps. 78:44; 105:29
7:21 [a]ver. 18

The water becomes blood

14 ¶ And the LORD said unto Moses, [a]Pharaoh's heart *is* hardened, he refuseth to let the people go.

15 Get thee unto Pharaoh in the morning; lo, he goeth out unto the water; and thou shalt stand by the river's brink against he come; and [a]the rod which was turned to a serpent shalt thou take in thine hand.

16 And thou shalt say unto him, [a]The LORD God of the Hebrews hath sent me unto thee, saying, Let my people go, [b]that they may serve me in the wilderness: and behold, hitherto thou wouldest not hear.

17 Thus saith the LORD, In this [a]thou shalt know that I *am* the LORD: behold, I will smite with the rod that *is* in mine hand upon the waters which *are* in the river, and [b]they shall be turned [c]to blood.

18 And the fish that *is* in the river shall die, and the river shall stink; and the Egyptians shall [a]lothe to drink of the water of the river.

19 And the LORD spake unto Moses, Say unto Aaron, Take thy rod, and [a]stretch out thine hand upon the waters of Egypt, upon their streams, upon their rivers, and upon their ponds, and upon all their [1]pools of water, that they may become blood; and *that* there may be blood throughout all the land of Egypt, both in *vessels of* wood, and in *vessels of* stone.

20 And Moses and Aaron did so, as the LORD commanded; and he [a]lift up the rod, and smote the waters that *were* in the river, in the sight of Pharaoh, and in the sight of his servants; and all the [b]waters that *were* in the river were turned to blood.

21 And the fish that *was* in the river died; and the river stunk, and the Egyptians [a]could not drink of the water of the river; and there was blood throughout all the land of Egypt.

7:3 *harden.* See note on 4:21. *signs.* See notes on 3:12; 4:8.
7:4 *great judgments.* See note on 6:6.
7:7 *Moses was fourscore years old.* See notes on 2:11,15.
7:9–10 *serpent.* The Hebrew for this word is different from that used in 4:3 (see Ps 74:13, "dragon"). A related word (also translated "dragon") is used in Ezek 29:3 as a designation for Egypt and her king.
7:11 *wise men and . . . magicians.* See note on Gen 41:8. According to tradition, two of the magicians who opposed Moses were named Jannes and Jambres (see 2 Tim 3:8; the first is also mentioned in the pre-Christian Dead Sea Scrolls). *the magicians of Egypt, they also did in like manner with their enchantments.* Either through sleight of hand or by means of demonic power.
7:12 *Aaron's rod swallowed up their rods.* Demonstrating God's mastery over the pharaoh and the gods of Egypt.
7:13 *he hardened Pharaoh's heart.* See note on 4:21.
7:14–10:29 The first nine plagues can be divided into three groups of three plagues each—7:14–8:19; 8:20–9:12; 9:13–10:29—with the first plague in each group (the first, the fourth and the seventh) introduced by a warning delivered to the pharaoh in the morning as he went out to the Nile (see v. 15; 8:20; 9:13).
‡7:17 *waters . . . in the river. . . shall be turned to blood.* See Ps 78:44; 105:29. Some scholars believe that the first nine plagues may have been a series of miraculous intensifications of natural events taking place in less than a year, and coming at God's bidding and timing. If so, the first plague resulted from the flooding of the Nile in late summer and early fall as large quantities of red sediment were washed down from Ethiopia, causing the water to become as red as blood (see the similar incident in 2 Ki 3:22). However, the details of the account of the plagues cannot be easily reconciled with the intensification theory. For example, this explanation does not account for the description of water stored in pools and in vessels (see v. 19). A natural event, though intensified, would not necessarily affect all available water in Egypt. Nor would it explain its occurrence at Moses' signal. See further problems with this view below.
7:19 *thy rod.* Aaron was acting on Moses' behalf (see v. 17). *in vessels of wood, and in vessels of stone.* Lit. "in/on the wooden things and in/on the stone things." Some think that, since the Egyptians believed that their gods inhabited idols and images made of wood, clay and stone (see Deut 29:16–17), the plague may have been intended as a rebuke to their religion (see 12:12).
7:20 *river.* Egypt's dependence on the life-sustaining waters of the Nile led to its deification as the god Hapi, for whom hymns of adoration were composed. See note on v. 19.

22 [a]And the magicians of Egypt did so with their enchantments: and Pharaoh's heart was hardened, neither did he hearken unto them; [b]as the LORD had said.

23 And Pharaoh turned and went into his house, neither did he set his heart to this also.

24 And all the Egyptians digged round about the river *for* water to drink; for they could not drink of the water of the river.

25 And seven days were fulfilled, after *that* the LORD had smitten the river.

The plague of frogs

8 And the LORD spake unto Moses, Go unto Pharaoh, and say unto him, Thus saith the LORD, Let my people go, [a]that they may serve me.

2 And if thou [a]refuse to let *them* go, behold, I will smite all thy borders with [b]frogs:

3 And the river shall bring forth frogs abundantly, which shall go up and come into thine house, and into [a]thy bedchamber, and upon thy bed, and into the house of thy servants, and upon thy people, and into thine ovens, and into thy [1]kneadingtroughs:

4 And the frogs shall come up *both* on thee, and upon thy people, and upon all thy servants.

5 And the LORD spake unto Moses, Say unto Aaron, [a]Stretch forth thine hand with thy rod over the streams, over the rivers, and over the ponds, and cause frogs to come up upon the land of Egypt.

6 And Aaron stretched out his hand over the waters of Egypt; and [a]the frogs came up, and covered the land of Egypt.

7 [a]And the magicians did so with their enchantments, and brought up frogs upon the land of Egypt.

8 Then Pharaoh called for Moses and Aaron, and said, [a]Intreat the LORD, that he may take away the frogs from me, and from my people; and I will let the people go, that they may do sacrifice unto the LORD.

9 And Moses said unto Pharaoh, [1]Glory over me: [2]when shall I intreat for thee, and for thy servants, and for thy people, [3]to destroy the frogs from thee and thy houses, *that* they may remain in the river only?

7:22 [a]ver. 11 [b]ver. 3
8:1 [a]ch. 3:12,18
8:2 [a]ch. 7:14; 9:2 [b]Rev. 16:13
8:3 [1]Or, *dough* [a]Ps. 105:30
8:5 [a]ch. 7:19
8:6 [a]Ps. 78:45; 105:30
8:7 [a]ch. 7:11
8:8 [a]ch. 9:28; 10:17
8:9 [1]Or, *Have this honour over me, etc.* [2]Or, *against when* [3]Heb. *to cut off*

8:10 [1]Or, *Against to morrow* [a]ch. 9:14; Deut. 33:26; 2 Sam. 7:22; 1 Chr. 17:20; Is. 46:9; Jer. 10:6,7
8:12 [a]ver. 30; ch. 9:33; 10:18; 32:11; Jas. 5:16-18
8:15 [a]Eccl. 8:11 [b]ch. 7:14
8:17 [a]Ps. 105:31
8:18 [a]ch. 7:11 [b]Dan. 5:8; 2 Tim. 3:8,9
8:19 [a]1 Sam. 6:3,9; Ps. 8:3; Mat. 12:28; Luke 11:20 [b]ver. 15
8:20 [a]ch. 7:15 [b]ver. 1
8:21 [1]Or, *a mixture of noisome beasts, etc.*

10 And he said, [1]To morrow. And he said, *Be it* according to thy word: that thou mayest know that [a]*there is* none like unto the LORD our God.

11 And the frogs shall depart from thee, and from thy houses, and from thy servants, and from thy people; they shall remain in the river only.

12 And Moses and Aaron went out from Pharaoh: and Moses [a]cried unto the LORD because of the frogs which he had brought against Pharaoh.

13 And the LORD did according to the word of Moses; and the frogs died out of the houses, out of the villages, and out of the fields.

14 And they gathered them together upon heaps: and the land stank.

15 But when Pharaoh saw that there was [a]respite, [b]he hardened his heart, and hearkened not unto them; as the LORD had said.

The plague of lice

16 ¶ And the LORD said unto Moses, Say unto Aaron, Stretch out thy rod, and smite the dust of the land, that it may become lice throughout all the land of Egypt.

17 And they did so; for Aaron stretched out his hand with his rod, and smote the dust of the earth, and [a]it became lice in man, and in beast; all the dust of the land became lice throughout all the land of Egypt.

18 And [a]the magicians did so with their enchantments to bring forth lice, but they [b]could not: so there were lice upon man, and upon beast.

19 Then the magicians said unto Pharaoh, This *is* [a]the finger of God: and Pharaoh's [b]heart was hardened, and he hearkened not unto them; as the LORD had said.

The swarms of flies

20 ¶ And the LORD said unto Moses, [a]Rise up early in the morning, and stand before Pharaoh; lo, he cometh forth to the water; and say unto him, Thus saith the LORD, [b]Let my people go, that they may serve me.

21 Else, if thou wilt not let my people go, behold, I will send [1]swarms *of flies* upon thee,

---

‡7:24 *digged round about the river for water to drink.* The Egyptians supposed that if the water of the Nile were filtered through sandy soil near the river bank, the polluted water would become safe for drinking. However, it is not stated that the Egyptians were able to find pure water in their efforts.

7:25 *seven days were fulfilled.* The plagues did not follow each other in rapid succession.

8:2 *I will smite all thy borders with frogs.* The frog (or toad) was deified in the goddess Heqt, who assisted women in childbirth.

‡8:3 *go up.* Some suggest (see note on 7:17) that the frogs abandoned the Nile and swarmed over the land, perhaps because the unusually high concentration of bacteria-laden algae had by now proved fatal to most of the fish, thus polluting the river. The evidence, however, supports a supernatural multiplication of frogs that came out of the river at Moses' signal to invade the land.

‡8:13 *the LORD did according to the word of Moses.* For similar occurrences see v. 31; 1 Sam 12:18; 1 Ki 18:42–45; Amos 7:1–6. *the frogs died.* Some (see note on 7:17) say the frogs died probably because they had been infected by the bacteria (*Bacillus anthracis*) in the Nile algae (see note on v. 3). However, in answer to Moses' prayer, all the frogs on land died, but apparently those still in the Nile lived (v. 11).

‡8:16 *dust . . . may become lice* [better rendered "gnats"]. Some have proposed (see note on 7:17) that the word "dust" is perhaps a reference to the enormous number (see, e.g., Gen 13:16) of the gnats, bred in the flooded fields of Egypt in late autumn. However, this plague did not occur until Aaron actually struck "the dust of the earth" with his rod (v. 17).

8:19 *finger of God.* A concise and colorful figure of speech referring to God's miraculous power (see 31:18; Ps 8:3). Jesus drove out demons "with the finger of God" (Luke 11:20). Cf. the similar use of the phrase "hand of the LORD" in 9:3.

8:21 *I will send swarms of flies.* Probably *Stomoxys calcitrans,*

and upon thy servants, and upon thy people,
and into thy houses: and the houses of the
Egyptians shall be full of swarms *of flies,* and
also the ground whereon they *are.*
22 And [a]I will sever in that day the land of
Goshen, in which my people dwell, that no
swarms *of flies* shall be there; to the end thou
mayest know that I *am* the LORD in the midst
of the earth.
23 And I will put [1]a division between my
people and thy people: [2]to morrow shall this
sign be.
24 And the LORD did so; and [a]there came a
grievous swarm *of flies* into the house of Pharaoh, and *into* his servants' houses, and into all
the land of Egypt: the land was [1]corrupted by
reason of the swarm *of flies.*
25 And Pharaoh called for Moses and for
Aaron, and said, Go ye, sacrifice to your God
in the land.
26 And Moses said, It is not meet so to do;
for we shall sacrifice [a]the abomination of the
Egyptians to the LORD our God: lo, shall we
sacrifice the abomination of the Egyptians before their eyes, and will they not stone us?
27 We will go [a]three days' journey into the
wilderness, and sacrifice to the LORD our God,
as [b]he shall command us.
28 And Pharaoh said, I will let you go, that
ye may sacrifice to the LORD your God in the
wilderness; only you shall not go very far
away: [a]intreat for me.
29 And Moses said, Behold, I go out from
thee, and I will intreat the LORD that the swarms
of flies may depart from Pharaoh, from his servants, and from his people, to morrow: but let
not Pharaoh [a]deal deceitfully any more in not
letting the people go to sacrifice to the LORD.
30 And Moses went out from Pharaoh, and
[a]intreated the LORD.
31 And the LORD did according to the word
of Moses; and he removed the swarms *of flies*
from Pharaoh, from his servants, and from his
people; there remained not one.

8:22 [a]ch. 9:4,6,26; 10:23; 11:6,7; 12:13
8:23 [1]Heb. *a redemption* [2]Or, *by to morrow*
8:24 [1]Or, *destroyed* [a]Ps. 78:45; 105:31
8:26 [a]Gen. 43:32; 46:34; Deut. 7:25,26; 12:31
8:27 [a]ch. 3:18 [b]ch. 3:12
8:28 [a]ver. 8; ch. 9:28; 1 Ki. 13:6
8:29 [a]ver. 15
8:30 [a]ver. 12
8:32 [a]ver. 15; ch. 4:21
9:1 [a]ch. 8:1
9:2 [a]ch. 8:2
9:3 [a]ch. 7:4
9:4 [a]ch. 8:22
9:6 [a]Ps. 78:50
9:7 [a]ch. 7:14; 8:32
9:9 [a]Rev. 16:2
9:10 [a]Deut. 28:27

32 And Pharaoh [a]hardened his heart at this
time also, neither would he let the people go.

The death of Egyptian cattle

9 Then the LORD said unto Moses, [a]Go in
unto Pharaoh, and tell him, Thus saith
the LORD God of the Hebrews, Let my people
go, that they may serve me.
2 For if thou [a]refuse to let *them* go, and
wilt hold them still,
3 Behold, the [a]hand of the LORD is upon
thy cattle which *is* in the field, upon the
horses, upon the asses, upon the camels, upon
the oxen, and upon the sheep: *there shall be* a
very grievous murrain.
4 And [a]the LORD shall sever between the
cattle of Israel and the cattle of Egypt: and
there shall nothing die of all *that is* the children's of Israel.
5 And the LORD appointed a set time, saying, To morrow the LORD shall do this thing in
the land.
6 And the LORD did that thing on the morrow, and [a]all the cattle of Egypt died: but of the
cattle of the children of Israel died not one.
7 And Pharaoh sent, and behold, there was
not one of the cattle of the Israelites dead. And
[a]the heart of Pharaoh was hardened, and he
did not let the people go.

The plague of boils and blains

8 ¶ And the LORD said unto Moses and unto
Aaron, Take to you handfuls of ashes of the furnace, and let Moses sprinkle it towards the
heaven in the sight of Pharaoh.
9 And it shall become small dust in all the
land of Egypt, and shall be [a]a boil breaking
forth *with* blains upon man, and upon beast,
throughout all the land of Egypt.
10 And they took ashes of the furnace, and
stood before Pharaoh; and Moses sprinkled it
up toward heaven; and it became [a]a boil
breaking forth *with* blains upon man, and
upon beast.

which would have multiplied rapidly as the receding Nile left breeding places in its wake. Full-grown, such insects infest houses and stables and bite men and animals.

8:22 *I will sever.* See 33:16. God makes a "division" (v. 23) between Moses' people and the pharaoh's people in this plague as well as in the fifth (see 9:4,6), the seventh (see 9:26), the ninth (see 10:23) and the tenth (see 11:7)—and probably also the sixth and eighth (see 9:11; 10:6)—demonstrating that the Lord can preserve His own people while judging Egypt. *Goshen.* See note on Gen 45:10.

8:26 *the abomination of the Egyptians.* See Gen 46:34; see also Gen 43:32 and note.

8:31 *the LORD did according to the word of Moses.* See note on v. 13.

‡9:3 *hand of the LORD.* See note on 8:19. *very grievous murrain.* Some propose that the flies of the fourth plague (see note on 8:21) probably carried the anthrax bacteria (see note on 8:13) that would now infect the animals, which had been brought into the fields again as the floodwaters subsided. Nevertheless, this plague struck the Egyptians' animals at the appointed time as predicted (v. 5). The Egyptians worshiped many animals and animal-headed deities, including the bull-gods Apis and Mnevis, the cow-god Hathor and the ram-god Khnum. Thus Egyptian religion is again rebuked and ridiculed (see note on 7:19).

9:4 *shall sever between.* See note on 8:22.

9:5 *To morrow.* To give those Egyptians who feared God time to bring their livestock in from the fields and out of danger (see also v. 20).

9:6 *all the cattle of Egypt died.* That is, all that were left out in the fields. Protected livestock remained alive (see vv. 19–21).

‡9:8 *Take . . . ashes. . . sprinkle it toward the heaven.* Perhaps symbolizing either the widespread extent of the plague of boils or their black coloration. *furnace.* Used for firing bricks, the symbol of Israel's bondage (see 1:14; 5:7–19). The same Hebrew word appears in Gen 19:28 and is used as a simile for the destruction of Sodom and Gomorrah.

9:9 *boil.* Probably skin anthrax (a variety of the plague that struck the livestock in vv. 1–7), a black, burning abscess that develops into a pustule. *upon man, and upon beast.* The plague on the livestock now extended to other animals as well as to the people of Egypt.

11 And the [a]magicians could not stand before Moses because of the boils; for the boil was upon the magicians, and upon all the Egyptians.

12 And the LORD hardened the heart of Pharaoh, and he hearkened not unto them; [a]as the LORD had spoken unto Moses.

The plague of hail and fire

13 ¶ And the LORD said unto Moses, [a]Rise up early in the morning, and stand before Pharaoh, and say unto him, Thus saith the LORD God of the Hebrews, Let my people go, that they may serve me.

14 For I will at this time send all my plagues upon thine heart, and upon thy servants, and upon thy people; [a]that thou mayest know that *there is* none like me in all the earth.

15 For now I will [a]stretch out my hand, that I may smite thee and thy people with pestilence; and thou shalt be cut off from the earth.

16 And in very deed for [a]this cause have I [1]raised thee up, for to shew *in* thee my power; and that my name may be declared throughout all the earth.

17 As yet exaltest thou thyself against my people, that *thou* wilt not let them go?

18 Behold, to morrow about *this* time I will cause it to rain a very grievous hail, such as hath not been in Egypt since the foundation thereof even until now.

19 Send therefore now, *and* gather thy cattle, and all that thou hast in the field; *for upon* every man and beast which shall be found in the field, and shall not be brought home, the hail shall come down upon them, and they shall die.

20 He that feared the word of the LORD amongst the servants of Pharaoh made his servants and his cattle flee into the houses:

21 And he that [1]regarded not the word of the LORD left his servants and his cattle in the field.

22 And the LORD said unto Moses, Stretch forth thine hand toward heaven, that there may be [a]hail in all the land of Egypt, upon man, and upon beast, and upon every herb of the field, throughout the land of Egypt.

23 And Moses stretched forth his rod toward heaven: and [a]the LORD sent thunder and hail, and the fire ran along upon the ground; and the LORD rained hail upon the land of Egypt.

24 So there was hail, and fire mingled with the hail, very grievous, such as there was none like it in all the land of Egypt since it became a nation.

25 And the hail smote throughout all the land of Egypt all that *was* in the field, both man and beast; and the hail [a]smote every herb of the field, and brake every tree of the field.

26 [a]Only in the land of Goshen, where the children of Israel *were*, was there no hail.

27 And Pharaoh sent, and called for Moses and Aaron, and said unto them, [a]I have sinned *this* time: [b]the LORD *is* righteous, and I and my people *are* wicked.

28 [a]Intreat the LORD (for *it is* enough) that there be no *more* [1]mighty thunderings and hail; and I will let you go, and ye shall stay no longer.

29 And Moses said unto him, As soon as I am gone out of the city, I will [a]spread abroad my hands unto the LORD; *and* the thunder shall cease, neither shall there be any more hail; that thou mayest know how that the [b]earth *is* the LORD's.

30 But as for thee and thy servants, [a]I know that ye will not yet fear the LORD God.

31 And the flax and the barley was smitten: [a]for the barley *was* in the ear, and the flax *was* bolled.

32 But the wheat and the rye were not smitten: for they *were* [1]not grown up.

33 And Moses went out of the city from Pharaoh, and [a]spread abroad his hands unto the LORD: and the thunders and hail ceased, and the rain was not poured upon the earth.

34 And when Pharaoh saw that the rain and the hail and the thunders were ceased, he sinned yet more, and hardened his heart, he and his servants.

35 And [a]the heart of Pharaoh was hardened, neither would he let the children of Israel go; as the LORD had spoken [1]by Moses.

The plague of locusts

10 And the LORD said unto Moses, Go in unto Pharaoh: [a]for I have hardened his heart, and the heart of his servants, [b]that I might shew these my signs before him:

2 And that [a]thou mayest tell in the ears of thy son, and of thy son's son, what things I

9:11 [a]ch. 8:18,19; 2 Tim. 3:9
9:12 [a]ch. 4:21
9:13 [a]ch. 8:20
9:14 [a]ch. 8:10
9:15 [a]ch. 3:20
9:16 [1]Heb. *made thee stand* [a]See ch. 14:17; Prov. 16:4; Rom. 9:17; 1 Pet. 2:9
9:21 [1]Heb. *set not his heart unto*
9:22 [a]Rev. 16:21
9:23 [a]Josh. 10:11; Ps. 18:13; 78:47; 105:32; 148:8; Is. 30:30; Ezek. 38:22; Rev. 8:7
9:25 [a]Ps. 105:33
9:26 [a]ch. 8:22; 9:4,6; 10:23; 11:7; 12:13; Is. 32:18,19
9:27 [a]ch. 10:16 [b]2 Chr. 12:6; Lam. 1:18
9:28 [1]Heb. *voices of God* [a]ch. 8:8,28; 10:17; Acts 8:24
9:29 [a]1 Ki. 8:22,38; Ps. 143:6; Is. 1:15 [b]Ps. 24:1; 1 Cor. 10:26,28
9:30 [a]Is. 26:10
9:31 [a]Ruth 1:22; 2:23
9:32 [1]Heb. *hidden*, or, *dark*
9:33 [a]ver. 29; ch. 8:12
9:35 [1]Heb. *by the hand of Moses* [a]ch. 4:21
10:1 [a]ch. 4:21; 7:14 [b]ch. 7:4
10:2 [a]Deut. 4:9; Ps. 44:1; 71:18; 78:5; Joel 1:3

9:11 *magicians could not stand.* The "botch [i.e. "boils"] of Egypt" (Deut 28:27) affected the knees and legs (see Deut 28:35).

9:12 *the LORD hardened the heart of Pharaoh.* See note on 4:21.

9:16 Paul quotes this verse as an outstanding illustration of the sovereignty of God (see Rom 9:17).

‡9:18 *I will cause it to rain a very grievous hail.* If the first six plagues occurred during the autumn flooding season, the hailstorm is in the proper chronological position, taking place in January or February when the flax and barley were in flower but the wheat and rye had not yet germinated (see vv. 31–32).

9:19–21 See note on v. 6.

9:27 *I have sinned this time.* For the first time the pharaoh acknowledges his sinfulness and perceives its devastating results.

9:29 *spread abroad my hands.* See 1 Ki 8:22,38,54; 2 Chr 6:12–13,29; Ezra 9:5; Ps 44:20; 88:9; 143:6; Is 1:15; 1 Tim 2:8. Statues of men praying with hands upraised have been found by archaeologists at several ancient sites in the Middle East.

9:30 *LORD God.* See note on Gen 2:4.

9:31–32 See note on v. 18.

‡9:32 *rye* [i.e., spelt]. Grains of spelt, a member of the grass family allied to wheat, have been found in ancient Egyptian tombs. Although inferior to wheat, it grows well in poorer and drier soil.

10:2 *tell . . . thy son.* The memory of God's redemptive acts is to be kept alive by reciting them to our descendants (see

have wrought in Egypt, and my signs which I have done amongst them; that ye may know how that I *am* the LORD.

3 And Moses and Aaron came in unto Pharaoh, and said unto him, Thus saith the LORD God of the Hebrews, How long wilt thou refuse to [a]humble thyself before me? let my people go, that they may serve me.

4 Else, if thou refuse to let my people go, behold, to morrow will I bring the [a]locusts into thy coast:

5 And they shall cover the [a1]face of the earth, that *one* cannot be able to see the earth: and [b]they shall eat the residue of that which is escaped which remaineth unto you from the hail, and shall eat every tree which groweth for you out of the field:

6 And they shall fill thy houses, and the houses of all thy servants, and the houses of all the Egyptians; which neither thy fathers, nor thy fathers' fathers have seen, since the day that they were upon the earth unto this day. And he turned himself, and went out from Pharaoh.

7 And Pharaoh's servants said unto him, How long shall this *man* be [a]a snare unto us? let the men go, that they may serve the LORD their God: knowest thou not yet that Egypt is destroyed?

8 And Moses and Aaron were brought again unto Pharaoh: and he said unto them, Go, serve the LORD your God: *but* [1]who *are* they that shall go?

9 And Moses said, We will go with our young and with our old, with our sons and with our daughters, with our flocks and with our herds will we go; for [a]we *must hold* a feast unto the LORD.

10 And he said unto them, Let the LORD be so with you, as I will let you go, and your little ones: look *to it;* for evil *is* before you.

11 Not so: go now ye *that are* men, and serve the LORD; for that you did desire. And they were driven out from Pharaoh's presence.

12 And the LORD said unto Moses, [a]Stretch out thine hand over the land of Egypt for the locusts, that they may come up upon the land of Egypt, and [b]eat every herb of the land, *even* all that the hail hath left.

13 And Moses stretched forth his rod over the land of Egypt, and the LORD brought an east wind upon the land all that day, and all *that* night; *and* when it was morning, the east wind brought the locusts.

14 And [a]the locusts went up over all the land of Egypt, and rested in all the coasts of Egypt: very grievous *were they;* [b]before them there were no such locusts as they, neither after them shall be such.

15 For they [a]covered the face of the whole earth, so that the land was darkened; and they [b]did eat every herb of the land, and all the fruit of the trees which the hail had left: and there remained not any green thing in the trees, or in the herbs of the field, through all the land of Egypt.

16 Then Pharaoh [1]called for Moses and Aaron in haste; and he said, [a]I have sinned against the LORD your God, and against you.

17 Now therefore forgive, I pray thee, my sin only *this* once, and [a]intreat the LORD your God, that he may take away from me this death only.

18 And he [a]went out from Pharaoh, and intreated the LORD.

19 And the LORD turned a mighty strong west wind, which took away the locusts, and [1]cast them [a]into the Red sea; there remained not one locust in all the coasts of Egypt.

20 But the LORD [a]hardened Pharaoh's heart, so that he would not let the children of Israel go.

The plague of darkness

21 ¶ And the LORD said unto Moses, [a]Stretch out thine hand toward heaven, that there may be darkness over the land of Egypt, [1]even darkness *which* may be felt.

22 And Moses stretched forth his hand toward heaven; and there was a [a]thick darkness in all the land of Egypt three days:

23 They saw not one another, neither rose any from his place for three days: [a]but all the children of Israel had light in their dwellings.

24 And Pharaoh called unto Moses, and [a]said, Go ye, serve the LORD; only let your flocks and your herds be stayed: let your [b]little ones also go with you.

25 And Moses said, Thou must give [1]us also sacrifices and burnt offerings, that we may sacrifice unto the LORD our God.

26 Our cattle also shall go with us; there shall not a hoof be left behind; for thereof must we take to serve the LORD our God; and

10:3 [a]1 Ki. 21:29; Job 42:6; Jas. 4:10
10:4 [a]Prov. 30:27; Rev. 9:3
10:5 [1]Heb. *eye* [a]ver. 15 [b]ch. 9:32; Joel 1:4; 2:25
10:7 [a]ch. 23:33; Josh. 23:13; 1 Sam. 18:21; Eccl. 7:26; 1 Cor. 7:35
10:8 [1]Heb. *who and who, etc.*
10:9 [a]ch. 5:1
10:12 [a]ch. 7:19 [b]ver. 4,5
10:14 [a]Ps. 78:46; 105:34 [b]Joel 2:2
10:15 [a]ver. 5 [b]Ps. 105:35
10:16 [1]Heb. *hastened to call* [a]ch. 9:27
10:17 [a]ch. 9:28; 1 Ki. 13:6
10:18 [a]ch. 8:30
10:19 [1]Heb. *fastened* [a]Joel 2:20
10:20 [a]ch. 4:21; 11:10
10:21 [1]Heb. *that one may feel darkness* [a]ch. 9:22
10:22 [a]Ps. 105:28
10:23 [a]ch. 8:22
10:24 [a]ver. 8 [b]ver. 10
10:25 [1]Heb. *into our hands*

12:26–27; 13:8,14–15; Deut 4:9; Ps 77:11–20; 78:4–6,43–53; 105:26–38; 106:7–12; 114:1–3; 135:8–9; 136:10–15).

10:4 *will I bring the locusts.* In March or April the prevailing east winds (see v. 13) would bring in hordes of migratory locusts at their immature and most voracious stage. As also today, locust plagues were greatly feared in ancient times and became a powerful symbol of divine judgment (see Joel 1:4–7; 2:1–11; Amos 7:1–3).

10:7 *How long . . . ?* The pharaoh's officials ironically echo the phrase used by Moses in v. 3. *Egypt is destroyed.* Human rebellion and disobedience always bring death and destruction in their wake.

10:11 *go now ye that are men.* From the pharaoh's standpoint, (1) the women and children should remain behind as hostages, and (2) it was typically only the men who participated fully in worship.

10:13 *east wind.* See note on v. 4.

10:19 *the LORD turned a mighty strong west wind.* The forces of nature are compelled to obey His sovereign will (see 14:21; Mat 8:23–27). *Red sea.* See note on 2:3.

‡10:21 *there may be darkness over . . . Egypt.* Like the third and sixth plagues, this ninth plague was unannounced to Pharaoh. Some suggest that the darkeness was caused by the arrival of an unusually severe khamsin, the blinding sandstorm that blows in from the desert each year in the early spring. However, like the other plagues, the darkness came at Moses'

we know not with what we must serve the LORD, until we come thither.

27 But the LORD [a]hardened Pharaoh's heart, and he would not let them go.

28 And Pharaoh said unto him, Get thee from me, take heed to thyself, see my face no more; for in *that* day thou seest my face thou shalt die.

29 And Moses said, Thou hast spoken well, [a]I will see thy face again no more.

The last plague

11 (And the LORD said unto Moses, Yet will I bring one plague *more* upon Pharaoh, and upon Egypt; afterwards he will let you go hence: [a]when he shall let *you* go, he shall surely thrust you out hence altogether.

2 Speak now in the ears of the people, and let every man borrow of his neighbour, and every woman of her neighbour, [a]jewels of silver, and jewels of gold.

3 [a]And the LORD gave the people favour in the sight of the Egyptians. Moreover the man [b]Moses *was* very great in the land of Egypt, in the sight of Pharaoh's servants, and in the sight of the people.)

4 And Moses said, Thus saith the LORD, [a]About midnight will I go out into the midst of Egypt:

5 And [a]all the firstborn in the land of Egypt shall die, from the firstborn of Pharaoh that sitteth upon his throne, *even* unto the firstborn of the maidservant that *is* behind the mill; and all the firstborn of beasts.

6 [a]And there shall be a great cry throughout all the land of Egypt, such as there was none like it, nor shall be like it any more.

7 [a]But against any of the children of Israel [b]shall not a dog move his tongue, against man or beast: that ye may know how that the LORD doth put a difference between the Egyptians and Israel.

8 And [a]all these thy servants shall come down unto me, and bow down themselves unto me, saying, Get thee out, and all the people [1]that follow thee: and after that I will go out. And he went out from Pharaoh in [2]a great anger.

9 And the LORD said unto Moses, [a]Pharaoh shall not hearken unto you; that [b]my wonders may be multiplied in the land of Egypt.

10 And Moses and Aaron did all these wonders before Pharaoh: [a]and the LORD hardened Pharaoh's heart, so that he would not let the children of Israel go out of his land.

The passover

12 And the LORD spake unto Moses and Aaron in the land of Egypt, saying,

2 [a]This month *shall be* unto you the beginning of months: it *shall be* the first month of the year to you.

3 Speak ye unto all the congregation of Israel, saying, In the tenth *day* of this month they shall take to them every man a [1]lamb, according to the house of *their* fathers, a [1]lamb for a house:

4 And if the household be too little for the lamb, let him and his neighbour next unto his house take *it* according to the number of the souls; every man according to his eating shall make your count for the lamb.

5 Your lamb shall be [a]without blemish, a male [1]of the first year: ye shall take *it* out from the sheep, or from the goats:

6 And ye shall keep it *up* until the [a]fourteenth day of the same month: and the whole assembly of the congregation of Israel shall kill it [1]in the evening.

7 And they shall take of the blood, and strike *it* on the two side posts and on the upper door post of the houses, wherein they shall eat it.

8 And they shall eat the flesh in that night,

10:27 [a]ver. 20; ch. 4:21; 14:4,8
10:29 [a]Heb. 11:27
11:1 [a]ch. 12:31,33,39
11:2 [a]ch. 3:22; 12:35
11:3 [a]ch. 3:21; 12:36; Ps. 106:46 [b]2 Sam. 7:9; Esth. 9:4
11:4 [a]ch. 12:12,23,29
11:5 [a]ch. 12:12,29; Amos 4:10
11:6 [a]ch. 12:30; Amos 5:17
11:7 [a]ch. 8:22 [b]Josh. 10:21

11:8 [1]Heb. *that is at thy feet* [2]Heb. *heat of anger* [a]ch. 12:33
11:9 [a]ch. 3:19; 7:4; 10:1 [b]ch. 7:3
11:10 [a]ch. 10:20,27; Rom. 2:5; 9:22
12:2 [a]ch. 13:4; Deut. 16:1
12:3 [1]Or, *kid*
12:5 [1]Heb. *son of a year* [a]Lev. 22:19-21; Mal. 1:8,14; Heb. 9:14
12:6 [1]Heb. *between the two evenings* [a]Lev. 23:5; Num. 9:3; Deut. 16:1,6

---

signal and, supernaturally, a distinction was made for the Israelites, who enjoyed light. The darkness was an insult to the sun-god Ra (or Re), one of the chief deities of Egypt.

10:28 Pharaoh declares that he will never again grant Moses an audience. *in that day thou seest my face.* During a plague of darkness, these words are somewhat ironic.

11:1 *when he shall let you go.* The Hebrew for this phrase can also be read "as one sends away [a bride]"—i.e., laden with gifts (see Gen 24:53).

11:2–3 See 12:35–36.

11:4 *Moses said.* Continuing the speech of 10:29.

11:5 *all the firstborn in . . . Egypt shall die.* See Ps 78:51; 105:36; 135:8; 136:10. This is the ultimate disaster, since all the plans and dreams of a father were bound up in his firstborn son, who received a double share of the family estate when the father died (see Deut 21:17 and note). Moreover, judgment on the firstborn represented judgment on the entire community. *maidservant that is behind the mill.* The lowliest of occupations (see Is 47:2).

11:7 *difference.* See note on 8:22.

12:2 *This month shall be . . . the beginning of months.* The inauguration of the religious calendar in Israel (see chart, p. 92). In the ancient Near East, new year festivals normally coincided with the new season of life in nature. The designation of this month as Israel's religious New Year reminded Israel that her life as the people of God was grounded in God's redemptive act in the exodus. The Canaanite name for this month was Abib (see 13:4; 23:15; 34:18; Deut 16:1), which means "young head of grain." Later the Babylonian name Nisan was used (see Neh 2:1; Esth 3:7). Israel's agricultural calendar began in the fall (see note on 23:16), and during the monarchy it dominated the nation's civil calendar. Both calendars (civil and religious) existed side by side until after the exile. Judaism today uses only the calendar that begins in the fall.

12:3 *congregation of Israel.* The Israelites gathered in assembly.

12:5 *lamb . . . without blemish.* See Lev 22:18–25. Similarly, Jesus was like "a lamb without blemish and without spot" (1 Pet 1:19).

12:6 *in the evening.* Lit. "between the two evenings," an idiom meaning either (1) between the decline of the sun and sunset, or (2) between sunset and nightfall—which has given rise to disputes about when the sabbath and other holy days begin.

12:7 *blood.* Symbolizes a sacrifice offered as a substitute, one life laid down for another (see Lev 17:11). Thus Israel escapes the judgment about to fall on Egypt only through the mediation of a sacrifice (see Heb 9:22; 1 John 1:7).

Hebrew Calendar and Selected Events

NUMBER OF MONTH		HEBREW NAME	MODERN EQUIVALENT	BIBLICAL REFERENCES	AGRICULTURE	FEASTS
1 Sacred sequence begins	7	**Abib; Nisan**	March–April	Ex 12:2; 13:4; 23:15; 34:18; Deut 16:1; Neh 2:1; Esth 3:7	Spring (later) rains; barley and flax harvest begins	Passover; Unleavened Bread; Firstfruits
2	8	**Ziv (Iyyar)***	April–May	1 Ki 6:1,37	Barley harvest; dry season begins	
3	9	**Sivan**	May–June	Esth 8:9	Wheat harvest	Pentecost (Weeks)
4	10	**(Tammuz)***	June–July		Tending vines	
5	11	**(Ab)***	July–August		Ripening of grapes, figs and olives	
6	12	**Elul**	August–September	Neh 6:15	Processing grapes, figs and olives	
7	1 Civil sequence	**Ethanim (Tishri)***	September–October	1 Ki 8:2	Autumn (early) rains begin; plowing	Trumpets; Atonement; Tabernacles
8	2	**Bul (Marcheshvan)***	October–November	1 Ki 6:38	Sowing of wheat and barley	
9	3	**Kislev**	November–December	Neh 1:1; Zech 7:1	Winter rains begin (snow in some areas)	Hanukkah ("Dedication")
10	4	**Tebeth**	December–January	Esth 2:16		
11	5	**Shebat**	January–February	Zech 1:7		
12	6	**Adar**	February–March	Ezra 6:15; Esth 3:7,13; 8:12; 9:1,15,17,19,21	Almond trees bloom; citrus fruit harvest	Purim
		(Adar Sheni)* — Second Adar	This intercalary month was added about every three years so the lunar calendar would correspond to the solar year.			

*Names in parentheses are not in the Bible

roast with fire, and [a]unleavened bread; *and*
with bitter *herbs* they shall eat it.
9 Eat not of it raw, nor sodden at all with
water, but [a]roast with fire; his head with his
legs, and with the purtenance thereof.
10 [a]And ye shall let nothing of it remain
until the morning; and that which remaineth
of it until the morning ye shall burn with fire.
11 And thus shall ye eat it; *with* your loins
girded, your shoes on your feet, and your staff
in your hand; and ye shall eat it in haste: [a]it *is*
the LORD's passover.
12 For I [a]will pass through the land of
Egypt this night, and will smite all the firstborn in the land of Egypt, both man and beast;
and [b]against all the [1]gods of Egypt I will execute judgment: [c]I *am* the LORD.
13 And the blood shall be to you for a token upon the houses where you *are:* and when
I see the blood, I will pass over you, and the
plague shall not be upon you [1]to destroy *you,*
when I smite the land of Egypt.
14 And this day shall be unto you [a]for a
memorial; and you shall keep it a [b]feast to the
LORD throughout your generations; you shall
keep it a feast [c]by an ordinance for ever.
15 [a]Seven days shall ye eat unleavened
bread; even the first day ye shall put away
leaven out of your houses: for whosoever
eateth leavened bread from the first day until
the seventh day, [b]that soul shall be cut off
from Israel.
16 And in the first day *there shall be* [a]a
holy convocation, and in the seventh day there
shall be a holy convocation to you; no *manner
of* work shall be done in them, save *that* which
every [1]man must eat, that only may be done of
you.
17 And ye shall observe the *feast of* un-

12:8 [a]ch. 34:25; Deut. 16:3; 1 Cor. 5:8
12:9 [a]Deut. 16:7
12:10 [a]ch. 23:18; 34:25
12:11 [a]Deut. 16:5
12:12 [1]Or, *princes* [a]ch. 11:4,5; Amos 5:17 [b]Num. 33:4 [c]ch. 6:2
12:13 [1]Heb. *for a destruction*
12:14 [a]ch. 13:9 [b]Lev. 23:4,5; 2 Ki. 23:21 [c]ver. 24,43; ch. 13:10
12:15 [a]ch. 13:6,7; 23:15; Lev. 23:5,6; Deut. 16:3,8; 1 Cor. 5:7 [b]Gen. 17:14; Num. 9:13
12:16 [1]Heb. *soul* [a]Lev. 23:7,8; Num. 28:18,25
12:17 [a]ch. 13:3
12:18 [a]Lev. 23:5; Num. 28:16
12:19 [a]ch. 23:15; 34:18
12:21 [1]Or, *kid* [a]ver. 3; Num. 9:4; Josh. 5:10; 2 Ki. 23:21; Ezra 6:20; Mark 14:12-16
12:22 [a]Heb. 11:28 [b]ver. 7
12:23 [a]ver. 12,13 [b]Ezek. 9:6; Rev. 7:3 [c]2 Sam. 24:16; 1 Cor. 10:10; Heb. 11:28
12:25 [a]ch. 3:8,17
12:26 [a]ch. 13:8,14; Deut. 32:7; Josh. 4:6

leavened bread; for [a]in this selfsame day have
I brought your armies out of the land of Egypt:
therefore shall ye observe this day in your generations by an ordinance for ever.
18 [a]In the first *month,* on the fourteenth
day of the month at even, ye shall eat unleavened bread, until the one and twentieth day of
the month at even.
19 [a]Seven days shall there be no leaven
found in your houses: for whosoever eateth
that which is leavened, even that soul shall be
cut off from the congregation of Israel,
whether he be a stranger, or born in the land.
20 Ye shall eat nothing leavened; in all
your habitations shall ye eat unleavened
bread.
21 ¶ Then Moses called for all the elders of
Israel, and said unto them, [a]Draw out and take
you a [1]lamb according to your families, and
kill the passover.
22 [a]And ye shall take a bunch of hyssop,
and dip *it* in the blood that *is* in the bason, and
[b]strike the lintel and the two side posts with
the blood that *is* in the bason; and none of you
shall go out at the door of his house until the
morning.
23 [a]For the LORD will pass through to smite
the Egyptians; and when he seeth the blood
upon the lintel, and on the two side posts, the
LORD will pass over the door, and [b]will not suffer [c]the destroyer to come in unto your houses
to smite *you.*
24 And ye shall observe this thing for an
ordinance to thee and to thy sons for ever.
25 And it shall come to pass, when ye be
come to the land which the LORD will give you,
[a]according as he hath promised, that ye shall
keep this service.
26 [a]And it shall come to pass, when your

12:8 *unleavened bread.* Reflecting the haste with which the people left Egypt (see vv. 11,39; Deut 16:3). *bitter herbs.* Endive, chicory and other bitter-tasting plants are indigenous to Egypt. Eating them would recall the bitter years of servitude there (see 1:14).

12:9 *roast . . . head . . . legs . . . purtenance thereof.* The method wandering shepherds used to cook meat.

12:11 *passover.* Explained in vv. 13,23,27 to mean that the Lord would "pass over" and not destroy the occupants of houses that were under the sign of the blood.

12:12 *against all the gods of Egypt . . . judgment.* Some had already been judged (see notes on 7:19; 8:2; 9:3; 10:21), and now all would be: (1) They would be shown to be powerless to deliver from the impending slaughter, and (2) many animals sacred to the gods would be killed.

12:13 *token* [i.e. "sign"]. Just as the plagues were miraculous signs of judgment on Pharaoh and his people (see 8:23), so the Lord's "passing over" the Israelites who placed themselves under the sign of blood was a pledge of God's mercy.

12:14 *keep it a feast . . . by an ordinance.* Frequent references to passover observance occur in the rest of Scripture (see Num 9:1–5; Josh 5:10; 2 Ki 23:21–23; 2 Chr 30:1–27; 35:1–19; Ezra 6:19–22; Luke 2:41–43; John 2:13,23; 6:4; 11:55—12:1). The ordinance is still kept by practicing Jews today.

12:15 *put away leaven out of your houses.* Yeast later was often used as a symbol of sin, such as "hypocrisy" (Luke 12:1) or "malice and wickedness" (1 Cor 5:8). Before celebrating passover, the observant Jew today conducts a systematic (often symbolic) search of his house to remove every crumb of leavened bread that might be there (see v. 19). *cut off from Israel.* Removed from the covenant people by execution (see, e.g., 31:14; Lev 20:2–3) or banishment. See also Gen 17:14 and note.

12:17 *feast of unleavened bread.* Began with the passover meal and continued for seven days (see vv. 18–19; see also Mark 14:12).

12:21 *passover.* Jesus is "our passover" (1 Cor 5:7), sacrificed "once" (Heb 7:27) for us.

12:22 *hyssop.* Here probably refers to an aromatic plant (*Origanum maru*) of the mint family with a straight stalk (see John 19:29) and white flowers. The hairy surface of its leaves and branches held liquids well and made it suitable as a sprinkling device for use in purification rituals (see Lev 14:4,6,49,51–52; Num 19:6,18; Heb 9:19; see also Ps 51:7). *dip it in the blood.* Today at passover meals a sprig of parsley or other plant is dipped in salt water to symbolize the lowly diet and tears of the Israelites during their time of slavery.

‡12:23 *pass over.* See note on v. 11. *the destroyer.* In Ps 78:49 the agent of God's wrath against the Egyptians is described as "evil angels" [lit. "angels of evil ones," i.e. "adversities"]. God often used angels to bring destructive plagues (see 2 Sam 24:15–16; 2 Ki 19:35; see also 1 Cor 10:10, a reference to Num 16:41–49).

children shall say unto you, What mean you by this service?

27 That ye shall say, [a]It *is* the sacrifice of the LORD'S passover, who passed over the houses of the children of Israel in Egypt, when he smote the Egyptians, and delivered our houses. And the people [b]bowed the head and worshipped.

28 And the children of Israel went away, and [a]did as the LORD had commanded Moses and Aaron, so did they.

The exodus begins

29 ¶ [a]And it came to pass, that at midnight [b]the LORD smote all the firstborn in the land of Egypt, [c]from the firstborn of Pharaoh that sat on his throne unto the firstborn of the captive that *was* in the [1]dungeon; and all the firstborn of cattle.

30 And Pharaoh rose up in the night, he, and all his servants, and all the Egyptians; and there was a [a]great cry in Egypt; for *there was* not a house where *there was* not one dead.

31 And [a]he called for Moses and Aaron by night, and said, Rise up, *and* get you forth from amongst my people, [b]both you and the children of Israel; and go, serve the LORD, as ye have said.

32 [a]Also take your flocks and your herds, as ye have said, and be gone; and [b]bless me also.

33 [a]And the Egyptians were urgent upon the people, that they might send them out of the land in haste; for they said, [b]We *be* all dead *men.*

34 And the people took their dough before it was leavened, their [1]kneadingtroughs being bound up in their clothes upon their shoulders.

35 And the children of Israel did according to the word of Moses; and they borrowed of the Egyptians [a]jewels of silver, and jewels of gold, and raiment:

36 [a]And the LORD gave the people favour in the sight of the Egyptians, so that they lent unto them *such things as they required.* And [b]they spoiled the Egyptians.

37 ¶ And [a]the children of Israel journeyed from [b]Rameses to Succoth, about [c]six hundred thousand on foot *that were* men, beside children.

38 And [1]a mixed multitude went up also with them; and flocks, and herds, *even* very much cattle.

39 And they baked unleavened cakes of the dough which they brought forth out of Egypt, for it was not leavened; because [a]they were thrust out of Egypt, and could not tarry, neither had they prepared for themselves *any* victual.

40 Now the sojourning of the children of Israel, who dwelt in Egypt, *was* [a]four hundred and thirty years.

41 And it came to pass at the end of the four hundred and thirty years, even the selfsame day it came to pass, *that* all [a]the hosts of the LORD went out from the land of Egypt.

42 It *is* [a] [1]a night to be much observed unto the LORD for bringing them out from the land of Egypt: this *is* that night of the LORD [1]to be observed of all the children of Israel in their generations.

The law of the passover

43 ¶ And the LORD said unto Moses and Aaron, This *is* [a]the ordinance of the passover: There shall no stranger eat thereof:

44 But every man's servant that is bought for money, when thou hast [a]circumcised him, then shall he eat thereof.

45 [a]A foreigner and a hired servant shall not eat thereof.

46 In one house shall it be eaten; thou shalt not carry forth *ought* of the flesh abroad out of the house; [a]neither shall ye break a bone thereof.

47 [a]All the congregation of Israel shall [1]keep it.

48 And [a]when a stranger shall sojourn with thee, and will keep the passover to the LORD, let all his males be circumcised, and then let him come near and keep it; and he shall be as one that is born in the land: for no uncircumcised person shall eat thereof.

49 [a]One law shall be to him that is homeborn, and unto the stranger that sojourneth among you.

50 Thus did all the children of Israel; as the LORD commanded Moses and Aaron, so did they.

51 [a]And it came to pass the selfsame day, *that* the LORD did bring the children of Israel out of the land of Egypt [b]by their armies.

12:27 [a]ver. 11 [b]ch. 4:31
12:28 [a]Heb. 11:28
12:29 [1]Heb. *house of the pit* [a]ch. 11:4 [b]Num. 8:17; 33:4; Ps. 78:51; 105:36 [c]ch. 4:23; 11:5
12:30 [a]ch. 11:6; Prov. 21:13; Amos 5:17
12:31 [a]ch. 11:1; Ps. 105:38 [b]ch. 10:9
12:32 [a]ch. 10:26 [b]Gen. 27:34
12:33 [a]ch. 11:8; Ps. 105:38 [b]Gen. 20:3
12:34 [1]Or, *dough*
12:35 [a]ch. 3:22
12:36 [a]ch. 3:21 [b]Gen. 15:14; ch. 3:22; Ps. 105:37
12:37 [a]Num. 33:3,5 [b]Gen. 47:11 [c]Gen. 12:2; Num. 11:21
12:38 [1]Heb. *a great mixture*
12:39 [a]ver. 33; ch. 6:1
12:40 [a]Gen. 15:13; Acts 7:6; Gal. 3:17
12:41 [a]ch. 7:4
12:42 [1]Heb. *a night of observations* [a]See Deut. 16:6
12:43 [a]Num. 9:14
12:44 [a]Gen. 17:12,13
12:45 [a]Lev. 22:10
12:46 [a]Num. 9:12; John 19:33,36
12:47 [1]Heb. *do it* [a]ver. 6; Num. 9:13
12:48 [a]Num. 9:14
12:49 [a]Num. 9:14; 15:15,16; Gal. 3:28
12:51 [a]ver. 41 [b]ch. 6:26

12:26 *your children shall say unto you, What mean you by this service?* See 13:14. The passover was to be observed as a memorial feast commemorating Israel's redemption and appropriating it anew. As observed today, it includes the asking of similar questions by the youngest child present.

12:27 *sacrifice . . . passover.* See note on v. 21. *passed over.* See note on v. 11.

12:29 *captive that was in the dungeon.* The lowliest of situations (see note on 11:5).

12:31 *he called for Moses.* Though he had sworn never again to grant Moses an audience (see 10:28 and note), Pharaoh now summons Moses (and Aaron) into his presence.

12:35–36 See 3:21–22; 11:2–3.

12:37 *journeyed from Rameses.* See 1:11; see also note on Gen 47:11. The Israelite departure took place "on the morrow after the passover" (Num 33:3). *Succoth.* Probably modern Tell el-Maskhutah in the Wadi Tumeilat, west of the Bitter Lakes. *about six hundred thousand . . . men.* A round number for 603,550 (see note on 38:26).

12:38 *a mixed multitude.* Possibly including such Egyptians as those mentioned in 9:20.

12:41 *four hundred and thirty years, even the selfsame day.* See notes on Gen 15:13; Acts 7:6.

12:46 *neither . . . break a bone thereof.* See Num 9:12; Ps 34:20; quoted in John 19:36 in reference to Jesus.

12:48 *no uncircumcised person shall eat thereof.* Only those consecrated to the Lord in covenant commitment could partake of passover; only for them could it have its full meaning (see Gen 17:9–14). Concerning participants in the Lord's supper see 1 Cor 11:28.

The firstborn set apart

13 And the LORD spake unto Moses, saying,

2 [a]Sanctify unto me all the firstborn, whatsoever openeth the womb among the children of Israel, *both* of man and of beast: it *is* mine.

3 And Moses said unto the people, [a]Remember this day, *in* which ye came out from Egypt, out of the house of [1]bondage; for [b]by strength of hand the LORD brought you out from this *place:* [c]there shall no leavened bread be eaten.

4 [a]*This* day came ye out in the month Abib.

5 And it shall be when the LORD shall [a]bring thee into the land of the Canaanites, and the Hittites, and the Amorites, and the Hivites, and the Jebusites, which he [b]sware unto thy fathers to give thee, a land flowing with milk and honey, [c]that thou shalt keep this service in this month.

6 [a]Seven days thou shalt eat unleavened bread, and in the seventh day *shall be* a feast to the LORD.

7 Unleavened bread shall be eaten seven days; and there shall [a]no leavened bread be seen with thee, neither shall there be leaven seen with thee in all thy quarters.

8 And thou shalt [a]shew thy son in that day, saying, *This is done* because of that *which* the LORD did unto me when I came forth out of Egypt.

9 And it shall be for [a]a sign unto thee upon thine hand, and for a memorial between thine eyes, that the LORD's law may be in thy mouth: for with a strong hand hath the LORD brought thee out of Egypt.

10 [a]Thou shalt therefore keep this ordinance in his season from year to year.

11 And it shall be when the LORD shall bring thee into the land of the Canaanites, as he sware unto thee and to thy fathers, and shall give it thee,

12 [a]That thou shalt [1]set apart unto the LORD all that openeth the matrix, and every firstling that cometh of a beast which thou hast; the males *shall be* the LORD's.

13 And [a]every firstling of an ass thou shalt redeem with a [1]lamb; and if thou wilt not redeem *it,* then thou shalt break his neck: and all the firstborn of man amongst thy children [b]shalt thou redeem.

14 [a]And it shall be when thy son asketh thee [1]in time to come, saying, What *is* this? that thou shalt say unto him, [b]By strength of hand the LORD brought us out from Egypt, from the house of [2]bondage:

15 And it came to pass, when Pharaoh would hardly let us go, that [a]the LORD slew all the firstborn in the land of Egypt, both the firstborn of man, and the firstborn of beast: therefore I sacrifice to the LORD all that openeth the matrix, being males; but all the firstborn of my children I redeem.

16 And it shall be for [a]a token upon thine hand, and for frontlets between thine eyes: for by strength of hand the LORD brought us forth out of Egypt.

Crossing the Red sea

17 ¶ And it came to pass, when Pharaoh had let the people go, that God led them not *through* the way of the land of the Philistines, although that *was* near; for God said, Lest peradventure the people [a]repent when they see war, and [b]they return to Egypt:

18 But God [a]led the people about, *through* the way of the wilderness of the Red sea: and the children of Israel went up [1]harnessed out of the land of Egypt.

19 And Moses took the bones of Joseph with him: for he had straitly sworn the children of Israel, saying, [a]God will surely visit you; and ye shall carry up my bones away hence with you.

20 And [a]they took their journey from Succoth, and encamped in Etham, in the edge of the wilderness.

21 And [a]the LORD went before them by day in a pillar of a cloud, to lead them the way; and

13:2 [a]ver. 12,13,15; ch. 22:29,30; Num. 3:13; Deut. 15:19; Luke 2:23
13:3 [1]Heb. *servants* [a]ch. 12:42; Deut. 16:3 [b]ch. 6:1 [c]ch. 12:8
13:4 [a]ch. 23:15; 34:18; Deut. 16:1
13:5 [a]ch. 3:8 [b]ch. 6:8 [c]ch. 12:25,26
13:6 [a]ch. 12:15,16
13:7 [a]ch. 12:19
13:8 [a]ver. 14; ch. 12:26
13:9 [a]See ver. 16; Deut. 6:8; Mat. 23:5
13:10 [a]ch. 12:14,24
13:12 [1]Heb. *cause to pass over* [a]ver. 2; Lev. 27:26
13:13 [1]Or, *kid* [a]ch. 34:20; Num. 18:15 [b]Num. 3:46,47; 18:15,16
13:14 [1]Heb. *to morrow* [2]Heb. *servants* [a]ch. 12:26; Deut. 6:20; Josh. 4:6,21 [b]ver. 3
13:15 [a]ch. 12:29
13:16 [a]ver. 9
13:17 [a]ch. 14:11; Num. 14:1-4 [b]Deut. 17:16
13:18 [1]Or, *by five in a rank* [a]ch. 14:2; Num. 33:6
13:19 [a]Gen. 50:25; Josh. 24:32
13:20 [a]Num. 33:6
13:21 [a]ch. 14:19,24; Num. 9:15; 14:14; Deut. 1:33; Neh. 9:12; Ps. 78:14; 99:7; Is. 4:5; 1 Cor. 10:1

13:2 *Sanctify unto me all the firstborn . . . among the children.* God had adopted Israel as His firstborn (see 4:22) and had delivered every firstborn among the Israelites, whether man or animal, from the tenth plague (see 12:12–13). All the firstborn in Israel were therefore His. Jesus, Mary's firstborn son (see Luke 2:7), was presented to the Lord in accordance with this law (see Luke 2:22–23).

13:5 See note on 3:8.

13:9 *sign . . . upon thine hand, and for a memorial between thine eyes.* A figure of speech (see v. 16; Deut 6:8; 11:18; see also Prov 3:3; 6:21; 7:3; Sol 8:6). A literal reading of this verse has led to the practice of writing the texts of vv. 1–10, vv. 11–16, Deut 6:4–9 and Deut 11:13–21 on separate strips of parchment and placing them in two small leather boxes, which the observant Jew straps on his forehead and left arm before his morning prayers. The boxes are called "phylacteries" (Mat 23:5). This practice seems to have originated after the exile to Babylon.

13:13 *every firstling of an ass.* The economic importance of pack animals allowed for their redemption through sacrificing a lamb. *redeem.* See 6:6. The verb means "obtain release by means of payment." *all the firstborn . . . amongst thy children.* Humans were to be consecrated to the Lord by their life, not by their death (see Gen 22:12; Num 3:39–51; cf. Rom 12:1).

13:14 See note on 12:26.

13:16 See note on v. 9.

13:17 *way of the land of the Philistines.* Although the most direct route from Goshen to Canaan, it was heavily guarded by a string of Egyptian fortresses.

‡13:18 *way of the wilderness.* Leading south along the west coast of the Sinai peninsula. *Red sea.* See note on 2:3. Various locations of the crossing have been proposed along the line of the modern Suez Canal and including the northern end of the Gulf of Suez (see map No. 3 at the end of the study Bible; but see also note on 14:2). *harnessed* [i.e., in martial array]. Probably armed only with spears, bows and slings.

13:19 See notes on Gen 50:24–25.

13:20 *Succoth.* See note on 12:37. *Etham.* Location unknown.

13:21 *pillar of a cloud . . . pillar of fire.* The visible symbol of God's presence among His people (see 14:24; see also note on

by night in a pillar of fire, to give them light; to go by day and night:

22 He took not away the pillar of the cloud by day, nor the pillar of fire by night, *from* before the people.

14 And the LORD spake unto Moses, saying,

2 Speak unto the children of Israel, [a]that they turn and encamp before [b]Pi-hahiroth, between [c]Migdol and the sea, over against Baal-zephon: before it shall ye encamp by the sea.

3 For Pharaoh will say of the children of Israel, [a]They *are* entangled in the land, the wilderness hath shut them in.

4 And [a]I will harden Pharaoh's heart, that he shall follow after them; and I [b]will be honoured upon Pharaoh, and upon all his host; [c]that the Egyptians may know that I *am* the LORD. And they did so.

5 And it was told the king of Egypt that the people fled: and [a]the heart of Pharaoh and of his servants was turned against the people, and they said, Why have we done this, that we have let Israel go from serving us?

6 And he made ready his chariot, and took his people with him:

7 And he took [a]six hundred chosen chariots, and all the chariots of Egypt, and captains over every one of them.

8 And the LORD [a]hardened the heart of Pharaoh king of Egypt, and he pursued after the children of Israel: and [b]the children of Israel went out with a high hand.

9 But the [a]Egyptians pursued after them (all the horses *and* chariots of Pharaoh, and his horsemen, and his army) and overtook them encamping by the sea, beside Pi-hahiroth, before Baal-zephon.

10 ¶ And when Pharaoh drew nigh, the children of Israel lift up their eyes, and behold, the Egyptians marched after them; and they were sore afraid: and the children of Israel [a]cried out unto the LORD.

11 [a]And they said unto Moses, Because *there were* no graves in Egypt, hast thou taken us away to die in the wilderness? wherefore hast thou dealt thus with us, to carry us forth out of Egypt?

12 [a]*Is* not this the word that we did tell thee in Egypt, saying, Let us alone, that we may serve the Egyptians? For *it had been* better for us to serve the Egyptians, than that we should die in the wilderness.

13 And Moses said unto the people, [a]Fear ye not, stand still, and see the salvation of the LORD, which he will shew to you to day: [1]for the Egyptians whom ye have seen to day, ye shall see them again no more for ever.

14 [a]The LORD shall fight for you, and ye shall [b]hold your peace.

15 And the LORD said unto Moses, Wherefore criest thou unto me? speak unto the children of Israel, that they go forward:

16 But [a]lift thou up thy rod, and stretch out thine hand over the sea, and divide it: and the children of Israel shall go on dry *ground* through the midst of the sea.

17 And I, behold, I will [a]harden the hearts of the Egyptians, and they shall follow them: and I will [b]get me honour upon Pharaoh, and upon all his host, upon his chariots, and upon his horsemen.

18 And the Egyptians [a]shall know that I *am* the LORD, when I have gotten me honour upon Pharaoh, upon his chariots, and upon his horsemen.

19 And the angel of God, [a]which went before the camp of Israel, removed and went behind them; and the pillar of the cloud went from before their face, and stood behind them:

20 And it came between the camp of the Egyptians and the camp of Israel; and [a]it was a cloud and darkness *to them,* but it gave light by night *to these:* so that the one came not near the other all the night.

21 ¶ And Moses stretched out his hand over the sea; and the LORD caused the sea to go *back* by a strong east wind all *that* night, and [a]made the sea dry *land,* and the waters were [b]divided.

22 And [a]the children of Israel went into the midst of the sea upon the dry *ground:* and the waters *were* [b]a wall unto them on their right hand, and on their left.

14:2 [a]ch. 13:18 [b]Num. 33:7 [c]Jer. 44:1
14:3 [a]Ps. 71:11
14:4 [a]ch. 4:21; 7:3 [b]ver. 17,18; ch. 9:16; Rom. 9:17,22,23 [c]ch. 7:5
14:5 [a]Ps. 105:25
14:7 [a]ch. 15:4
14:8 [a]ver. 4 [b]ch. 6:1; 13:9; Num. 33:3
14:9 [a]ch. 15:9; Josh. 24:6
14:10 [a]Josh. 24:7; Neh. 9:9; Ps. 34:17
14:11 [a]Ps. 106:7,8
14:12 [a]ch. 5:21
14:13 [1]Or, *for whereas you have seen the Egyptians to day, etc.* [a]2 Chr. 20:15,17; Is. 41:10
14:14 [a]ver. 25; Deut. 1:30; Josh. 10:14,42; 2 Chr. 20:29; Is. 31:4 [b]Is. 30:15
14:16 [a]ver. 21,26
14:17 [a]ver. 8 [b]ver. 4
14:18 [a]ver. 4
14:19 [a]ch. 13:21; Is. 63:9
14:20 [a]See Is. 8:14; 2 Cor. 4:3
14:21 [a]Ps. 66:6 [b]ch. 15:8; Josh. 3:16; Neh. 9:11; Ps. 74:13; Is. 63:12
14:22 [a]ch. 15:19; Ps. 66:6; Is. 63:13; 1 Cor. 10:1; Heb. 11:29 [b]Hab. 3:10

3:2). The Lord often spoke to them from the pillar (see Num 12:5–6; Deut 31:15–16; Ps 99:6–7).

14:2 *turn.* Northward, in the general direction from which they had come. *Pi-hahiroth.* Lies "before Baal-zephon" (Num 33:7). *Migdol.* Location unknown. The name means "watchtower." *sea.* The sea that established tradition calls the Red sea—in Hebrew *Yam Suph,* i.e., Sea of Reeds (see notes on 2:3; 13:18). Reference can hardly be to the northern end of the Gulf of Suez since reeds do not grow in salt water. Moreover, an Egyptian papyrus locates Baal-zephon in the vicinity of Tahpanhes (see note on Jer 2:16), a site near Lake Menzaleh about 20 miles east of Rameses. The crossing of the "Red sea" thus probably occurred at the southern end of Lake Menzaleh (see map, p. 97; but see note on 13:18). *Baal-zephon.* Means "Baal of the north" or "Baal of North (Mountain)"—also the name of a Canaanite god.

14:4 *know that I am the LORD.* See note on 6:3.

14:7 *captains.* The Hebrew for the singular of this word means "third man," perhaps referring to his place in a chariot crew.

14:14 *The LORD shall fight for you.* A necessary reminder that although Israel was armed for battle (13:18), and "went out with a high hand [i.e. boldly]" (v. 8), the victory would be won by God alone.

14:19 *angel of God.* See note on Gen 16:7; here associated with the cloud (see 13:21).

14:20 *came between the camp of the Egyptians and . . . Israel.* The pillar of cloud (signifying the Lord's presence) protected Israel (see Ps 105:39).

14:21 *strong east wind.* See 10:13. In 15:8 the poet praises the Lord and calls the wind the "blast of thy nostrils," affirming (as here) that the miracle occurred in accordance with God's timing and under His direction (see 15:10).

14:22 *into . . . the sea upon the dry ground.* In later times, psalmists and prophets reminded Israel of what God had done for them (see Ps 66:6; 106:9; 136:13–14; Is 51:10; 63:11–13). *waters were a wall.* See v. 29. The waters were "gathered together" (15:8) on both sides.

The Exodus

The exodus and conquest narratives form the classic historical and spiritual drama of OT times. Subsequent ages looked back to this period as one of obedient and victorious living under divine guidance. Close examination of the environment and circumstances also reveals the strenuous exertions, human sin and bloody conflicts of the era.

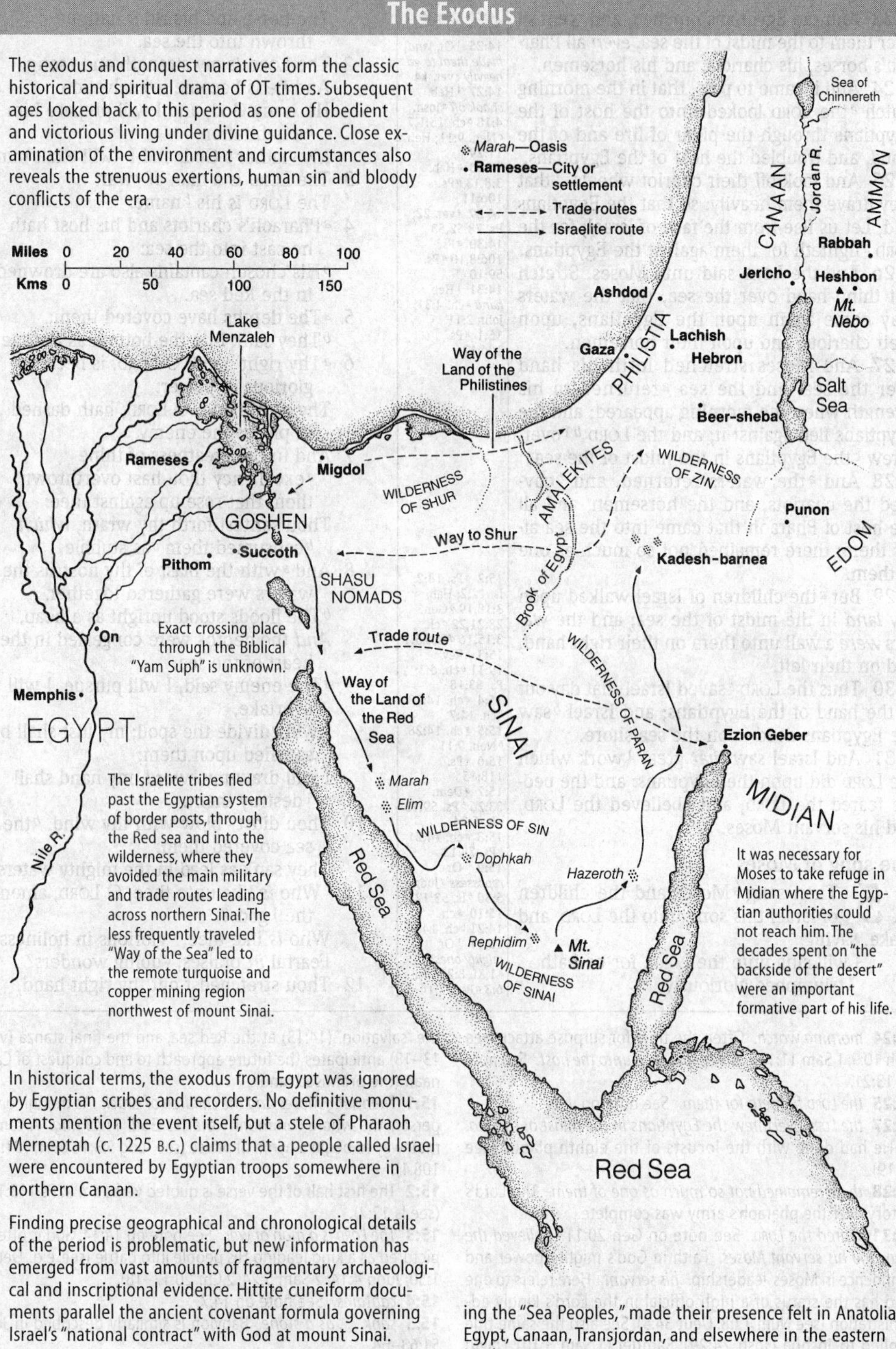

In historical terms, the exodus from Egypt was ignored by Egyptian scribes and recorders. No definitive monuments mention the event itself, but a stele of Pharaoh Merneptah (c. 1225 B.C.) claims that a people called Israel were encountered by Egyptian troops somewhere in northern Canaan.

Finding precise geographical and chronological details of the period is problematic, but new information has emerged from vast amounts of fragmentary archaeological and inscriptional evidence. Hittite cuneiform documents parallel the ancient covenant formula governing Israel's "national contract" with God at mount Sinai.

The Late Bronze Age (c. 1550-1200 B.C.) was a time of major social migrations. Egyptian control over the Semites in the eastern Nile delta was harsh, with a system of brickmaking quotas imposed on the labor force, often the landless, low-class "Apiru." Numerous Canaanite towns were violently destroyed. New populations, including the "Sea Peoples," made their presence felt in Anatolia, Egypt, Canaan, Transjordan, and elsewhere in the eastern Mediterranean.

Correspondence from Canaanite town rulers to the Egyptian court in the time of Akhenaten (c. 1375 B.C.) reveals a weak structure of alliances, with an intermittent Egyptian military presence and an ominous fear of people called "Habiru" ("Apiru").

23 And the Egyptians pursued, and went in
after them to the midst of the sea, *even* all Pharaoh's horses, his chariots, and his horsemen.
24 And it came to pass, that in the morning
watch [a]the LORD looked unto the host of the
Egyptians through the pillar of fire and of the
cloud, and troubled the host of the Egyptians,
25 And took off their chariot wheels, [1]that
they drave them heavily: so that the Egyptians
said, Let us flee from the face of Israel; for the
LORD [a]fighteth for them against the Egyptians.
26 And the LORD said unto Moses, Stretch
out thine hand over the sea, that the waters
may come again upon the Egyptians, upon
their chariots, and upon their horsemen.
27 And Moses stretched forth his hand
over the sea, and the sea [a]returned to his
strength when the morning appeared; and the
Egyptians fled against it; and the LORD [b][1]over-
threw [c]the Egyptians in the midst of the sea.
28 And [a]the waters returned, and [b]cov-
ered the chariots, and the horsemen, and all
the host of Pharaoh that came into the sea after them; there remained not so much as one
of them.
29 But [a]the children of Israel walked upon
dry *land* in the midst of the sea; and the waters *were* a wall unto them on their right hand,
and on their left.
30 Thus the LORD [a]saved Israel that day out
of the hand of the Egyptians; and Israel [b]saw
the Egyptians dead upon the sea shore.
31 And Israel saw *that* great [1]work which
the LORD did upon the Egyptians: and the people feared the LORD, and [a]believed the LORD,
and his servant Moses.

The song of Moses

15 Then sang [a]Moses and the children
of Israel this song unto the LORD, and
spake, saying,

I will sing unto the LORD, for he hath
triumphed gloriously:
The horse and his rider hath he
thrown into the sea.
2 The LORD *is* my strength and [a]song,
And he is become my salvation:
He *is* my God, and I will prepare him
[b]a habitation;
My [c]father's God, and I [d]will exalt him.
3 The LORD *is* a man of [a]war:
The LORD *is* his [b]name.
4 [a]Pharaoh's chariots and his host hath
he cast into the sea:
[b]His chosen captains also are drowned
in the Red sea.
5 [a]The depths have covered them:
[b]They sank into the bottom as a stone.
6 [a]Thy right hand, O LORD, is become
glorious in power:
Thy right hand, O LORD, hath dashed
in pieces the enemy.
7 And in the greatness of thine
[a]excellency thou hast overthrown
them that rose up against thee:
Thou sentest forth thy wrath, *which*
[b]consumed them [c]as stubble.
8 And [a]with the blast of thy nostrils the
waters were gathered together,
[b]The floods stood upright as a heap,
And the depths were congealed in the
heart of the sea.
9 [a]The enemy said, I will pursue, I will
overtake,
I will [b]divide the spoil; my lust shall be
satisfied upon them;
I will draw my sword, my hand shall
[1]destroy them.
10 Thou didst [a]blow with thy wind, [b]the
sea covered them:
They sank as lead in the mighty waters.
11 [a]Who *is* like unto thee, O LORD, among
the [1]gods?
Who *is* like thee, [b]glorious in holiness,
Fearful *in* praises, [c]doing wonders?
12 Thou stretchedst out thy right hand,

14:24 [a]See Ps. 77:17 **14:25** [1]Or, [*and*] *made them to go heavily* [a]ver. 14 **14:27** [1]Heb. *shook off* [a]Josh. 4:18 [b]ch. 15:1,7 [c]Neh. 9:11; Heb. 11:29 **14:28** [a]Hab. 3:8,13 [b]Ps. 106:11 **14:29** [a]ver. 22; Ps. 78:52,53 **14:30** [a]Ps. 106:8,10 [b]Ps. 59:10 **14:31** [1]Heb. *hand* [a]ch. 4:31; John 2:11 **15:1** [a]Ps. 106:12

15:2 [a]Ps. 18:2; Is. 12:2; Hab. 3:18,19 [b]Gen. 28:21,22 [c]ch. 3:15,16 [d]Is. 25:1 **15:3** [a]Rev. 19:11 [b]ch. 6:3; Ps. 83:18 **15:4** [a]ch. 14:28 [b]ch. 14:7 **15:5** [a]ch. 14:28 [b]Neh. 9:11 **15:6** [a]Ps. 118:15 **15:7** [a]Deut. 33:26 [b]Ps. 59:13 [c]Is. 5:24 **15:8** [a]ch. 14:21 [b]Ps. 78:13 **15:9** [1]Or, *repossess* [a]Judg. 5:30 [b]Is. 53:12 **15:10** [a]ch. 14:21 [b]ch. 14:28 **15:11** [1]Or, *mighty ones?* [a]1 Ki. 8:23 [b]Is. 6:3 [c]Ps. 77:14

14:24 *morning watch.* Often the time for surprise attack (see Josh 10:9; 1 Sam 11:11). *the LORD looked unto the host.* See note on 13:21.
14:25 *the LORD fighteth for them.* See note on v. 14.
14:27 *the LORD overthrew the Egyptians in the midst of the sea.* As He had done with the locusts of the eighth plague (see 10:19).
14:28 *there remained not so much as one of them.* The Lord's victory over the pharaoh's army was complete.
14:31 *feared the LORD.* See note on Gen 20:11. *believed the LORD, and his servant Moses.* Faith in God's mighty power and confidence in Moses' leadership. *his servant.* Here refers to one who has the status of a high official in the Lord's kingly administration (see Num 12:8; Deut 34:5). See also the same title applied to Joshua (Josh 24:29), Samuel (1 Sam 3:10), David (2 Sam 3:18) and Elijah (2 Ki 9:36).
15:1–18 A hymn celebrating God's spectacular victory over the pharaoh and his army. The focus of the song is God Himself (see v. 11); the divine name Yahweh ("the LORD") appears ten times. Similes—"as a stone" (v. 5), "as a heap" (v. 8) and "as lead" (v. 10)—mark the conclusion of three of the five stanzas. The first four stanzas (vv. 1–5, 6–8, 9–10, 11–12) retell the story of the "salvation" (14:13) at the Red sea, and the final stanza (vv. 13–18) anticipates the future approach to and conquest of Canaan (the promised land).
15:1 *Then sang Moses and the children of Israel.* As though one person, the whole community praises God. *I will sing.* A common way to begin a hymn of praise (see Judg 5:3; Ps 89:1; 101:1; 108:1).
15:2 The first half of the verse is quoted verbatim in Ps 118:14 (see Is 12:2).
15:3 *The LORD is a man of war.* See note on 14:14. God is often pictured as a king leading His people into battle (see, e.g., Deut 1:30; Judg 4:14; 2 Sam 5:24; 2 Chr 20:17–18).
15:4 *captains.* See note on 14:7.
15:5 *sank . . . as a stone.* Babylon is similarly described in Jer 51:63–64.
15:8 See note on 14:22. *blast of thy nostrils.* See note on 14:21; see also Ps 18:15.
15:10 *Thou didst blow with thy wind.* See note on 14:21.
15:11 *Who is like unto thee. . . ?* See Ps 35:10; 71:19; 89:6; 113:5; Mic 7:18. The Lord, who tolerates no rivals, has defeated all the gods of Egypt and their worshipers.
15:12 *earth.* Perhaps refers to Sheol or the grave (see Deut

The earth swallowed them.
13 Thou in thy mercy hast [a]led forth the
people *which* thou hast redeemed:
Thou hast guided *them* in thy strength
unto [b]thy holy habitation.
14 [a]The people shall hear, *and* be afraid:
[b]Sorrow shall take hold on the
inhabitants of Palestina.
15 [a]Then [b]the dukes of Edom shall be
amazed;
[c]The mighty men of Moab, trembling
shall take hold upon them;
[d]All the inhabitants of Canaan shall
melt away.
16 [a]Fear and dread shall fall upon them;
By the greatness of thine arm they
shall be *as* still [b]as a stone;
Till thy people pass over, O LORD,
Till the people pass over, [c]*which* thou
hast purchased.
17 Thou shalt bring them in, and [a]plant
them in the mountain of thine
inheritance,
In the place, O LORD, *which* thou hast
made for thee to dwell in,
In the [b]Sanctuary, O Lord, *which* thy
hands have established.
18 [a]The LORD shall reign for ever and ever.
19 ¶ For the [a]horse of Pharaoh went in
with his chariots and with his horsemen into
the sea, and [b]the LORD brought again the waters
of the sea upon them; but the children of
Israel went on dry *land* in the midst of the sea.
20 And Miriam [a]the prophetess, [b]the sister
of Aaron, [c]took a timbrel in her hand; and
all the women went out after her [d]with timbrels
and with dances.
21 And Miriam [a]answered them,
[b]Sing ye to the LORD, for he hath
triumphed gloriously;
The horse and his rider hath he
thrown into the sea.

Bitter waters made sweet

22 ¶ So Moses brought Israel from the Red
sea, and they went out into the wilderness of
[a]Shur; and they went three days in the wilderness,
and found no water.
23 And when they came to [a]Marah, they
could not drink of the waters of Marah, for
they *were* bitter: therefore the name of it was
called [1]Marah.
24 And the people [a]murmured against Moses,
saying, What shall we drink?
25 And he cried unto the LORD; and the
LORD shewed him a tree, [a]*which* when he had
cast into the waters, the waters were made
sweet: there he [b]made for them a statute and
an ordinance, and there [c]he proved them,
26 And said, [a]If thou wilt diligently hearken
to the voice of the LORD thy God, and wilt
do that which is right in his sight, and wilt give
ear to his commandments, and keep all his statutes,
I will put none of *these* [b]diseases upon
thee, which I have brought upon the Egyptians:
for I *am* the LORD [c]that healeth thee.
27 [a]And they came to Elim, where *were*
twelve wells of water, and threescore and ten
palm trees: and they encamped there by the
waters.

Quails and manna provided

16 And they [a]took their journey from
Elim, and all the congregation of the
children of Israel came unto the wilderness of
[b]Sin, which *is* between Elim and Sinai, on the

15:13 [a]Ps. 77:15,20 [b]Ps. 78:54
15:14 [a]Josh. 2:9 [b]Ps. 48:6
15:15 [a]Gen. 36:40 [b]Deut. 2:4 [c]Num. 22:3 [d]Josh. 5:1
15:16 [a]Josh. 2:9 [b]1 Sam. 25:37 [c]Ps. 74:2; Jer. 31:11; 1 Pet. 2:9
15:17 [a]Ps. 44:2 [b]Ps. 78:54
15:18 [a]Is. 57:15
15:19 [a]ch. 14:23 [b]ch. 14:28
15:20 [a]Judg. 4:4 [b]Num. 26:59 [c]1 Sam. 18:6 [d]Judg. 11:34; 2 Sam. 6:16; Ps. 150:4
15:21 [a]1 Sam. 18:7
15:21 [b]ver. 1
15:22 [a]Gen. 25:18
15:23 [1]That is, *Bitterness* [a]Num. 33:8
15:24 [a]ch. 16:2
15:25 [a]See 2 Ki. 2:21 [b]See Josh. 24:25 [c]Deut. 8:2,16; Judg. 3:1,4; Ps. 66:10
15:26 [a]Deut. 7:12,15 [b]Deut. 28:27,60 [c]ch. 23:25; Ps. 103:3
15:27 [a]Num. 33:9
16:1 [a]Num. 33:10,11 [b]Ezek. 30:15

32:22; Ps 63:9; 71:20), the realm of death below, since it was the sea that swallowed the Egyptians.

15:13 *people which thou hast redeemed.* See note on 6:6. *thy holy habitation.* Perhaps a reference to the house of worship at Shiloh (see Jer 7:12), and ultimately the temple on mount Zion (see Ps 76:2), the "place" God "shall choose" (Deut 12:14,18,26; 14:25; 16:7,15–16; 17:8,10; 18:6; 31:11) to put "his name" (Deut 12:5,11,21; 14:23–24; 16:2,6,11; 26:2). But the phrase may refer to the promised land, which is called "the place . . . for thee to dwell in" and "the Sanctuary . . . thy hands have established" in v. 17.

15:14–15 *Palestina . . . Edom . . . Moab . . . Canaan.* The order is roughly that along the route Israel would follow from mount Sinai to the promised land.

15:15 *dukes.* The term used earlier of the Edomite rulers (see Gen 36:15–19,21,29–30,40,43).

15:16 *dread shall fall upon them.* See note on 1 Chr 14:17. *purchased.* Or "created" (the same alternative translation is possible in Deut 32:6). In Ps 74:2 the meaning "bought" or "purchased" is found in context with "redeemed" (see note on 13:13).

15:17 *inheritance.* The promised land (see 1 Sam 26:19; Ps 79:1).

15:20 *prophetess.* See Num 12:1–2 for a statement by Miriam concerning her prophetic gift (see note on 7:1–2). Other prophetesses in the Bible were Deborah (Judg 4:4), Isaiah's wife (Is 8:3, but see note there), Huldah (2 Ki 22:14), Noadiah (Neh 6:14), Anna (Luke 2:36) and Philip's daughters (Acts 21:9). *women went out after her with timbrels and with dances.* Such celebration was common after victory in battle (see 1 Sam 18:6; 2 Sam 1:20).

15:21 Miriam repeats the first four lines of the victory hymn (see v. 1), changing only the form of the first verb.

15:22 *wilderness of Shur.* Located east of Egypt (see Gen 25:18; 1 Sam 15:7) in the northwestern part of the Sinai peninsula. In Num 33:8 it is called the "wilderness of Etham." Shur and Etham both mean "fortress wall" (Shur in Hebrew, Etham in Egyptian).

15:23 *Marah.* Probably modern Ain Hawarah, inland from the Gulf of Suez and 50 miles south of its northern end.

15:24 *murmured.* During their wilderness wanderings, the Israelites grumbled against Moses and Aaron whenever they faced a crisis (see 16:2; 17:3; Num 14:2; 16:11,41). In reality, however, they were grumbling "against the LORD" (16:8). Paul warns us not to follow their example (see 1 Cor 10:10).

15:25 *which when he had cast into the waters, the waters were made sweet.* For a similar occurrence see 2 Ki 2:19–22. *a statute and an ordinance.* Technical terms presumably referring to what follows in v. 26. *proved.* See note on Gen 22:1. God tested Israel also in connection with His provision of manna (see 16:4; Deut 8:2–3) and the giving of the ten commandments (see 20:20).

15:27 *Elim.* Seven miles south of Ain Hawarah (see note on v. 23) in the well-watered valley of Gharandel. *palm trees.* Elim means "large trees."

16:1 *from Elim . . . unto the wilderness of Sin.* See Num 33:10–11. The wilderness of Sin was in southwestern Sinai ("Sin"

fifteenth day of the second month after their
departing out of the land of Egypt.
2 And the whole congregation of the children of Israel [a]murmured against Moses and
Aaron in the wilderness:
3 And the children of Israel said unto
them, [a]Would to God we had died by the hand
of the LORD in the land of Egypt, [b]when we sat
by the flesh pots, *and* when we did eat bread
to the full; for ye have brought us forth into
this wilderness, to kill this whole assembly
with hunger.
4 Then said the LORD unto Moses, Behold,
I will rain [a]bread from heaven for you; and the
people shall go out and gather [1]a certain rate
every day, that I may [b]prove them, whether
they will walk in my law, or no.
5 And it shall come to pass, that on the
sixth day they shall prepare *that* which they
bring in; and [a]it shall be twice as much as they
gather daily.
6 And Moses and Aaron said unto all the
children of Israel, [a]At even, then ye shall
know that the LORD hath brought you out from
the land of Egypt:
7 And in the morning, then ye shall see
[a]the glory of the LORD; for that he heareth your
murmurings against the LORD: and [b]what *are*
we, that ye murmur against us?
8 And Moses said, *This shall be,* when the
LORD shall give you in the evening flesh to eat,
and in the morning bread to the full; for that
the LORD heareth your murmurings which ye
murmur against him: and what *are* we? your
murmurings *are* not against us, but [a]against
the LORD.
9 And Moses spake unto Aaron, Say unto
all the congregation of the children of Israel,
[a]Come near before the LORD: for he hath
heard your murmurings.
10 And it came to pass, as Aaron spake
unto the whole congregation of the children of
Israel, that they looked toward the wilderness,
and behold, the glory of the LORD [a]appeared in
the cloud.
11 And the LORD spake unto Moses, saying,
12 [a]I have heard the murmurings of the
children of Israel: speak unto them, saying,
[b]At even ye shall eat flesh, and [c]in the morning ye shall be filled *with* bread; and ye shall
know that I *am* the LORD your God.
13 And it came to pass, that at even [a]the
quails came up, and covered the camp: and in
the morning [b]the dew lay round about the host.
14 And when the dew that lay was gone
up, behold, upon the face of the wilderness
there lay [a]a small round thing, *as* small as the
hoar frost on the ground.
15 And when the children of Israel saw *it,*
they said one to another, [1]It *is* manna: for they
wist not what it *was.* And Moses said unto
them, [a]This *is* the bread which the LORD hath
given you to eat.
16 This *is* the thing which the LORD hath
commanded, Gather of it every man according
to his eating, [a]an omer [1]for every man, *according to* the number of your [2]persons; take
ye every man for *them* which *are* in his tents.
17 And the children of Israel did so, and
gathered, some more, some less.
18 And when they did mete *it* with an omer,
[a]he that gathered much had nothing over, and
he that gathered little had no lack; they gathered every man according to his eating.
19 And Moses said, Let no man leave of it
till the morning.
20 Notwithstanding they hearkened not
unto Moses; but some of them left of it until
the morning, and it bred worms, and stank:
and Moses was wroth with them.
21 And they gathered it every morning,
every man according to his eating: and when
the sun waxed hot, it melted.
22 And it came to pass, *that* on the sixth
day they gathered twice as much bread, two
omers for one *man:* and all the rulers of the
congregation came and told Moses.
23 And he said unto them, This *is that*
which the LORD hath said, To morrow *is* [a]the
rest of the holy sabbath unto the LORD: bake
that which you will bake *to day,* and seethe that
ye will seethe; and that which remaineth over
lay up for you to be kept until the morning.
24 And they laid it up till the morning, as

16:2 [a]1 Cor. 10:10
16:3 [a]Lam. 4:9 [b]Num. 11:4
16:4 [1]Heb. *the portion of a day in his day* [a]John 6:31 [b]Deut. 8:2,16
16:5 [a]See ver. 22; Lev. 25:21
16:6 [a]See ver. 12,13; ch. 6:7; Num. 16:28-30
16:7 [a]See ver. 10; Is. 35:2; 40:5; John 11:4,40 [b]Num. 16:11
16:8 [a]See 1 Sam. 8:7; Luke 10:16; Rom. 13:2
16:9 [a]Num. 16:16
16:10 [a]ver. 7; ch. 13:21; Num. 16:19; 1 Ki. 8:10,11
16:12 [a]ver. 8 [b]ver. 6 [c]ver. 7
16:13 [a]Num. 11:31; Ps. 78:27,28; 105:40 [b]Num. 11:9
16:14 [a]Num. 11:7; Deut. 8:3; Neh. 9:15; Ps. 78:24; 105:40
16:15 [1]Or, *What is this?* or, *It is a portion* [a]John 6:31,49,58; 1 Cor. 10:3
16:16 [1]Heb. *by the poll,* or, *head* [2]Heb. *souls* [a]ver. 36
16:18 [a]2 Cor. 8:15
16:23 [a]Gen. 2:3; ch. 20:8; 31:15; 35:3; Lev. 23:3

is probably derived from "Sinai") in the region today called Debbet er-Ramleh. *fifteenth day of the second month.* Exactly one month had passed since Israel's exodus from Egypt (see 12:2,6,29,31).

16:2 *murmured.* See note on 15:24.

16:3 *flesh pots.* Num 11:5 lists additional items of food from Egypt that the Israelites craved.

16:4 *bread from heaven.* Jesus called Himself "the true bread from heaven" (John 6:32), "the bread of God" (John 6:33), "the bread of life" (John 6:35,48), "the living bread which came down from heaven" (John 6:51)—all in the spiritual sense (John 6:63). For a similar application see Deut 8:3 and Jesus' quotation of it in Mat 4:4. *go out and gather a certain rate every day.* Probably the background for Jesus' model petition in Mat 6:11; Luke 11:3. *prove.* See notes on 15:25; Gen 22:1.

16:5 *sixth day . . . twice as much as they gather daily.* To provide for "the seventh day, which is the sabbath" (v. 26), "the rest of the holy sabbath" (v. 23). See v. 29.

16:6 *know.* See note on 6:3.

16:8 *in the evening flesh . . . in the morning bread.* See vv. 13–14.

16:10 *glory of the LORD appeared in the cloud.* See 24:15–17; see also note on 13:21.

16:12 *At even.* See note on 12:6.

16:13 *quails came up.* For a similar incident see Num 11:31–33.

16:14 *a small round thing.* See note on Num 11:7.

‡16:15 *It is manna.* Lit., "What is it?" Thus the name "Manna" (see v. 31).

16:18 See 2 Cor 8:15, where Paul quotes the heart of the verse as an illustration of Christians who share with each other what they possess.

16:23 *sabbath.* The first occurrence of the word itself, though the principle of the seventh day as a day of rest and holiness is set forth in the account of creation (see note on Gen 2:3).

Moses bade: and it did not [a]stink, neither was
there any worm therein.
25 And Moses said, Eat that to day; for to
day *is* a sabbath unto the LORD: to day ye shall
not find it in the field.
26 [a]Six days ye shall gather it; but on the
seventh day, *which is* the sabbath, in it there
shall be none.
27 And it came to pass, *that* there went out
some of the people on the seventh day for to
gather, and they found none.
28 And the LORD said unto Moses, How
long [a]refuse ye to keep my commandments
and my laws?
29 See, for that the LORD hath given you
the sabbath, therefore he giveth you on the
sixth day the bread of two days; abide ye every
man in his place, let no man go out of his place
on the seventh day.
30 So the people rested on the seventh day.
31 And the house of Israel called the name
thereof Manna: and [a]it *was* like coriander
seed, white; and the taste of it *was* like wafers
made with honey.
32 And Moses said, This *is* the thing which
the LORD commandeth, Fill an omer of it to be
kept for your generations; that they may see
the bread wherewith I have fed you in the
wilderness, when I brought you forth from the
land of Egypt.
33 And Moses said unto Aaron, [a]Take a
pot, and put an omer full of manna therein,
and lay it up before the LORD, to be kept for
your generations.
34 As the LORD commanded Moses, so Aaron laid it up [a]before the Testimony, to be kept.
35 And the children of Israel did eat manna [a]forty years, [b]until they came to a land inhabited; they did eat manna, until they came
unto the borders of the land of Canaan.
36 Now an omer *is* the tenth *part* of an
ephah.

16:24 [a]ver. 20
16:26 [a]ch. 20:9,10
16:28 [a]2 Ki. 17:14; Ps. 78:10,22
16:31 [a]Num. 11:7,8
16:33 [a]Heb. 9:4
16:34 [a]ch. 25:16,21; 40:20; Num. 17:10; Deut. 10:5
16:35 [a]Num. 33:38; John 6:31,49 [b]Josh. 5:12

17:1 [a]Num. 33:12,14
17:2 [a]Num. 20:3 [b]Deut. 6:16; Ps. 78:18,41
17:3 [a]ch. 16:2
17:4 [a]ch. 14:15 [b]John 8:59; 10:31
17:5 [a]Ezek. 2:6 [b]Num. 20:8
17:6 [a]Num. 20:10,11
17:7 [1]That is, *Tentation* [2]That is, *Chiding*, or, *Strife* [a]Num. 20:13
17:8 [a]Gen. 36:12; Deut. 25:17
17:9 [a]Called *Jesus*, Acts 7:45 [b]ch. 4:20

The water from the rock

17 And [a]all the congregation of the children of Israel journeyed from the
wilderness of Sin, after their journeys, according to the commandment of the LORD, and
pitched in Rephidim: and *there was* no water
for the people to drink.
2 [a]Wherefore the people did chide with
Moses, and said, Give us water that we may
drink. And Moses said unto them, Why chide
you with me? wherefore do ye [b]tempt the
LORD?
3 And the people thirsted there for water;
and the people [a]murmured against Moses, and
said, Wherefore *is* this *that* thou hast brought
us up out of Egypt, to kill us and our children
and our cattle with thirst?
4 And Moses [a]cried unto the LORD, saying,
What shall I do unto this people? they be almost ready to [b]stone me.
5 And the LORD said unto Moses, [a]Go on
before the people, and take with thee of the
elders of Israel; and thy rod, wherewith [b]thou
smotest the river, take in thine hand, and go.
6 [a]Behold, I will stand before thee there
upon the rock in Horeb; and thou shalt smite
the rock, and there shall come water out of it,
that the people may drink. And Moses did so
in the sight of the elders of Israel.
7 And he called the name of the place
[a][1]Massah, and [2]Meribah, because of the chiding of the children of Israel, and because they
tempted the LORD, saying, Is the LORD amongst
us, or not?

The defeat of Amalek

8 ¶ [a]Then came Amalek, and fought with
Israel in Rephidim.
9 And Moses said unto [a]Joshua, Choose us
out men, and go out, fight with Amalek: to
morrow I will stand on the top of the hill with
[b]the rod of God in mine hand.

16:29 See note on v. 5.
16:31 *Manna.* See note on Num 11:7.
16:33 *pot.* Said in Heb 9:4 to be made of gold.
16:34 *Testimony.* Anticipates the later description of the tablets containing the ten commandments as the "two tables of Testimony" (31:18; 32:15; 34:29), which gave their name to the "ark of the Testimony" (25:22; 26:33) in which they were placed (see 25:16,21) along with the pot of manna (see Heb 9:4; see also Rev 2:17 and note).
16:35 *did eat manna forty years until they came to . . . Canaan.* The manna stopped at the time the Israelites celebrated their first passover in Canaan (see Josh 5:10–12).
17:1 *journeyed . . . after their journeys.* For the places to which they journeyed see Num 33:12–14. *Rephidim.* Probably either the Wadi Refayid or the Wadi Feiran, both near Jebel Musa (see note on 3:1) in southern Sinai.
17:2 *tempt the LORD.* Israel fails the Lord's testing of her (see 16:4) by putting the Lord to the test.
17:3 *murmured.* See note on 15:24.
17:4 *this people.* The same note of distance and alienation ("this people" instead of "my people") in such situations (see also the interplay in 32:7, 9–11; 33:13) is found often in the prophets (see, e.g., Is 6:9; Hag 1:2).
17:6 *I will stand . . . there upon the rock.* Paul may have had this incident in mind when he spoke of Christ as "that spiritual Rock that followed" Israel (see 1 Cor 10:4; see also Heb 11:24–26). *Horeb.* See note on 3:1. *smite the rock, and there shall come water out.* The event was later celebrated by Israel's hymn writers and prophets (see Ps 78:15–16,20; 105:41; 114:8; Is 48:21).
17:7 *Massah, and Meribah.* Heb 3:7–8,15 (quoting Ps 95:7–8) gives the meaning "day of temptation" for Massah and "provocation" for Meribah. Another Meribah, where a similar incident occurred near Kadesh-barnea (see note on Gen 14:7), is referred to in Num 20:13,24; 27:14; Deut 32:51; 33:8; Ps 81:7; 106:32; Ezek 47:19; 48:28.
17:8 *Amalek.* See note on Gen 14:7.
‡17:9 *Joshua.* The name given by Moses to Hoshea son of Nun (see Num 13:16). "Oshea" means "salvation," while "Joshua [or Jehoshua]" means "The LORD saves." The Greek form of the name Joshua is the same as that of the name Jesus. Joshua was from the tribe of Ephraim (Num 13:8), one of the most powerful of the 12 tribes (see notes on Gen 48:6,19). *fight with Amalek.* Joshua's military prowess uniquely suited him to be the conqueror of Canaan 40 years later, while his faith in God and loyalty to Moses suited him to be Moses' aide, or "minister" (24:13; 33:11), and successor (see Deut 1:38; 3:28; 31:14; 34:9; Josh 1:5).

10 So Joshua did as Moses had said to him,
and fought with Amalek: and Moses, Aaron,
and Hur went up *to* the top of the hill.
11 And it came to pass, when Moses [a]held
up his hand, that Israel prevailed: and when
he let down his hand, Amalek prevailed.
12 But Moses' hands *were* heavy; and they
took a stone, and put *it* under him, and he sat
thereon; and Aaron and Hur stayed up his
hands, the one on the one side, and the other
on the other side; and his hands were steady
until the going down of the sun.
13 And Joshua discomfited Amalek and his
people with the edge of the sword.
14 And the LORD said unto Moses, [a]Write
this *for* a memorial in a book, and rehearse *it* in
the ears of Joshua: for [b]I will utterly put out the
remembrance of Amalek from under heaven.
15 And Moses built an altar, and called the
name of it [1]Jehovah-nissi:
16 For he said, [1]Because [2]the LORD hath
sworn *that* the LORD *will have* war with Amalek from generation *to* generation.

The coming of Jethro

18 When [a]Jethro, the priest of Midian,
Moses' father in law, heard of all that
[b]God had done for Moses, and for Israel his
people, *and* that the LORD had brought Israel
out of Egypt;
2 Then Jethro, Moses' father in law, took
Zipporah, Moses' wife, [a]after he had sent her
back,
3 And her [a]two sons; of which the [b]name
of the one *was* [1]Gershom; for he said, I have
been an alien in a strange land:
4 And the name of the other *was* [1]Eliezer;
for the God of my father, *said he, was* mine
help, and delivered me from the sword of
Pharaoh:
5 And Jethro, Moses' father in law, came
with his sons and his wife unto Moses into the
wilderness, where he encamped *at* [a]the
mount of God:
6 And he said unto Moses, I thy father in
law Jethro am come unto thee, and thy wife,
and her two sons with her.
7 And Moses [a]went out to meet his father
in law, and did obeisance, and [b]kissed him;
and they asked each other of *their* [1]welfare;
and they came into the tent.
8 And Moses told his father in law all that
the LORD had done unto Pharaoh and to the
Egyptians for Israel's sake, *and* all the travail
that had [1]come upon them by the way, and
how the LORD [a]delivered them.
9 And Jethro rejoiced for all the goodness
which the LORD had done to Israel, whom he
had delivered out of the hand of the Egyptians.
10 And Jethro said, [a]Blessed *be* the LORD,
who hath delivered you out of the hand of the
Egyptians, and out of the hand of Pharaoh,
who hath delivered the people from under the
hand of the Egyptians.
11 Now I know that the LORD *is* [a]greater
than all gods: [b]for in the thing wherein they
dealt [c]proudly *he was* above them.
12 And Jethro, Moses' father in law, took a
burnt offering and sacrifices for God: and Aaron came, and all the elders of Israel, to eat
bread with Moses' father in law [a]before God.
13 ¶ And it came to pass on the morrow,
that Moses sat to judge the people: and the
people stood by Moses from the morning unto
the evening.
14 And when Moses' father in law saw all
that he did to the people, he said, What *is* this
thing that thou doest to the people? why
sittest thou thyself alone, and all the people
stand by thee from morning unto even?
15 And Moses said unto his father in law,
Because [a]the people come unto me to inquire
of God:
16 When they have [a]a matter, they come
unto me; and I judge between [1]one and another, and I do [b]make *them* know the statutes
of God, and his laws.

17:11 [a]Jas. 5:16
17:14 [a]ch. 34:27 [b]1 Sam. 15:3,7; 30:1,17
17:15 [1]That is, *The LORD my banner:* [See Judg. 6:24]
17:16 [1]Or, *Because the hand* of Amalek is *against the throne of the LORD,* therefore, etc. [2]Heb. *the hand upon the throne of the LORD*
18:1 [a]ch. 2:16 [b]Ps. 106:2,8
18:2 [a]ch. 4:26
18:3 [1]That is, *A stranger there* [a]Acts 7:29 [b]ch. 2:22
18:4 [1]That is, *My God is a help*
18:5 [a]ch. 3:1,12
18:7 [1]Heb. *peace* [a]Gen. 18:2 [b]Gen. 29:13
18:8 [1]Heb. *found them* [a]Ps. 81:7
18:10 [a]Gen. 14:20; 2 Sam. 18:28
18:11 [a]2 Chr. 2:5 [b]ch. 1:10,16,22 [c]Luke 1:51
18:12 [a]Deut. 12:7
18:15 [a]Lev. 24:12
18:16 [1]Heb. *a man and his fellow* [a]ch. 24:14 [b]Lev. 24:15

17:10 *Hur.* Perhaps the same Hur who was the son of Caleb and the grandfather of Bezaleel (see 1 Chr 2:19–20), one of the builders of the tabernacle (see 31:2–5).
17:11 *held up his hand.* A symbol of appeal to God for help and enablement (see note on 9:29; see also 9:22; 10:12; 14:16).
17:14 *Write.* See 24:4; 34:27–28; Num 33:2; Deut 28:58; 29:20,21,27; 30:10; 31:9,19,22,24; see also Introduction: Author and Date of Writing. *book.* Or "scroll," a long strip of leather or papyrus on which scribes wrote in columns (see Jer 36:23) with pen (see Is 8:1) and ink (see Jer 36:18), sometimes on both sides (see Ezek 2:10; Rev 5:1). After being rolled into a scroll, the "book" was often sealed (see Is 29:11; Dan 12:4; Rev 5:1–2,5,9) to protect its contents. Scrolls were of various sizes (see Is 8:1; Rev 10:2,9–10). Certain Egyptian examples reached lengths of over 100 feet; Biblical scrolls, however, rarely exceeded 30 feet in length, as in the case of a book like Isaiah (see Luke 4:17). Reading the contents of a scroll involved the awkward procedure of unrolling it with one hand while rolling it up with the other (see Is 34:4; Ezek 2:10; Luke 4:17,20; Rev 6:14). Shortly after the time of Christ the scroll gave way to the book form still used today.
17:15 *Jehovah-nissi* [i.e. "the LORD is my banner"]. Recalling Moses' petition with upraised hands (see vv. 11–12,16) and testifying to the power of God displayed in defense of His people.
18:1 *Jethro, the priest of Midian.* See note on 2:16.
18:2 *sent her back.* Apparently Moses sent Zipporah to her father with the news that the Lord had blessed his mission (see v. 1) and that he was in the vicinity of mount Sinai with Israel.
18:5 *mount of God.* See 3:1 and note.
18:11 *Now I know that the LORD is greater than all gods.* See the similar confession of Naaman in 2 Ki 5:15.
18:12 *took.* The verb means "provided" an animal for sacrifice (see, e.g., 25:2; Lev 12:8), not "officiated at" a sacrifice. *eat bread with.* A token of friendship (contrast the battle with the Amalekites, 17:8–16). Such a meal often climaxed the establishment of a treaty (see Gen 31:54; Ex 24:11).
18:15 *to inquire of God.* Usually by going to a place of worship (see Gen 25:22 and note; Num 27:21) or to a prophet (see 1 Sam 9:9; 1 Ki 22:8).
18:16 *statutes of God, and his laws.* The process of compiling and systematizing the body of divine law that would govern the newly formed nation of Israel may have already begun (see 15:25–26 and note on Gen 26:5).

17 And Moses' father in law said unto him,
The thing that thou doest *is* not good.
18 [1]Thou wilt surely wear away, both
thou, and this people that *is* with thee: for *this*
thing *is* too heavy for thee; [a]thou art not able
to perform it thyself alone.
19 Hearken now unto my voice, I will give
thee counsel, and [a]God shall be with thee: be
thou [b]for the people to God-ward, that thou
mayest [c]bring the causes unto God:
20 And thou shalt [a]teach them ordinances
and laws, and shalt shew them [b]the way
wherein they must walk, and [c]the work that
they must do.
21 Moreover thou shalt provide out of all
the people [a]able men, such as [b]fear God,
[c]men of truth, [d]hating covetousness; and
place *such* over them, *to be* rulers of thousands, *and* rulers of hundreds, rulers of fifties,
and rulers of tens:
22 And let them judge the people [a]at all
seasons: [b]and it shall be, *that* every great matter they shall bring unto thee, but every small
matter they shall judge: so shall it be easier for
thyself, and [c]they shall bear *the burden* with
thee.
23 If thou shalt do this thing, and God
command thee *so,* then thou shalt be [a]able to
endure, and all this people shall also go to
[b]their place in peace.
24 So Moses hearkened to the voice of his
father in law, and did all that he had said.
25 And [a]Moses chose able men out of all
Israel, and made them heads over the people,
rulers of thousands, rulers of hundreds, rulers
of fifties, and rulers of tens.
26 And they [a]judged the people at all seasons: the [b]hard causes they brought unto Moses, but every small matter they judged themselves.
27 And Moses let his father in law depart;
and [a]he went his way into his own land.

At mount Sinai

19 In the third month, when the children of Israel were gone forth out of
the land of Egypt, the same day [a]came they
into the wilderness of Sinai.
2 For they were departed from [a]Rephidim,
and were come *to* the desert of Sinai, and had
pitched in the wilderness; and there Israel
camped before [b]the mount.
3 And [a]Moses went up unto God, and the
LORD [b]called unto him out of the mountain,
saying, Thus shalt thou say to the house of Jacob, and tell the children of Israel;
4 [a]Ye have seen what I did unto the Egyptians, and *how* [b]I bare you on eagles' wings,
and brought you unto myself.
5 Now [a]therefore, if ye will obey my voice
indeed, and keep my covenant, then [b]ye shall
be a peculiar treasure unto me above all people: for [c]all the earth *is* mine:
6 And ye shall be unto me a [a]kingdom of
priests, and a [b]holy nation. These *are* the
words which thou shalt speak unto the children of Israel.
7 And Moses came and called for the elders
of the people, and laid before their faces all
these words which the LORD commanded him.
8 And [a]all the people answered together,
and said, All that the LORD hath spoken we
will do. And Moses returned the words of the
people unto the LORD.
9 And the LORD said unto Moses, Lo, I
come unto thee [a]in a thick cloud, [b]that the
people may hear when I speak with thee, and
[c]believe thee for ever. And Moses told the
words of the people unto the LORD.
10 ¶ And the LORD said unto Moses, Go
unto the people, and [a]sanctify them to day and
to morrow, and let them [b]wash their clothes,
11 And be ready against the third day: for
the third day the LORD [a]will come down in the
sight of all the people upon mount Sinai.
12 And thou shalt set bounds unto the people round about, saying, Take heed to yourselves, *that ye* go *not* up into the mount, or
touch the border of it: [a]whosoever toucheth
the mount shall be surely put to death:
13 There shall not a hand touch it, but he
shall surely be stoned, or shot through;

18:18 [1]Heb. *Fading thou wilt fade* [a]Num. 11:14,17
18:19 [a]ch. 3:12 [b]ch. 4:16 [c]Num. 27:5
18:20 [a]Deut. 5:1 [b]Ps. 143:8 [c]Deut. 1:18
18:21 [a]ver. 25; 2 Chr. 19:5-10; Acts 6:3 [b]2 Sam. 23:3 [c]Ezek. 18:8 [d]Deut. 16:19
18:22 [a]ver. 26 [b]Lev. 24:11; Deut. 1:17 [c]Num. 11:17
18:23 [a]ver. 18 [b]ch. 16:29; 2 Sam. 19:39
18:25 [a]Deut. 1:15
18:26 [a]ver. 22 [b]Job 29:16
18:27 [a]Num. 10:29,30
19:1 [a]Num. 33:15
19:2 [a]ch. 17:1,8 [b]ch. 3:1,12
19:3 [a]Acts 7:38 [b]ch. 3:4
19:4 [a]Deut. 29:2 [b]Is. 63:9
19:5 [a]Deut. 5:2 [b]Deut. 7:6; 14:2,21; 1 Ki. 8:53; Ps. 135:4 [c]ch. 9:29; Deut. 10:14; Job 41:11; Ps. 24:1
19:6 [a]Deut. 33:2-4; 1 Pet. 2:5,9 [b]Deut. 7:6; Is. 62:12; 1 Cor. 3:17
19:8 [a]Deut. 5:27
19:9 [a]Mat. 17:5 [b]Deut. 4:12,36; John 12:29,30 [c]ch. 14:31
19:10 [a]Lev. 11:44,45; Heb. 10:22 [b]ver. 14
19:11 [a]ver. 16,18; ch. 34:5
19:12 [a]Heb. 12:20

18:21 *men, such as fear God.* See note on Gen 20:11.
19:2 *desert of Sinai.* Located in the southeast region of the peninsula (see note on 3:1). The narrator locates there the events recorded in the rest of Exodus, all of Leviticus, and Num 1:1–10:10.
19:3 *Jacob . . . Israel.* See note on 1:1.
19:4 *I bare you on eagles' wings.* The description best fits the female golden eagle.
19:5 *if . . . then.* The covenant between God and Israel at mount Sinai is the outgrowth and extension of the Lord's covenant with Abraham and his descendants 600 years earlier (see chart, p. 16). Participation in the divine blessings is conditioned on obedience added to faith (see note on Gen 17:9). *my covenant.* See note on Gen 9:9. *a peculiar treasure unto me above all people.* The equivalent phrases used of Christians in 1 Pet 2:9 are "chosen generation" and "a peculiar people" (see Deut 7:6; 14:2; 26:18; Ps 135:4; Mal 3:17). *all the earth is mine.* God is the Creator and Possessor of the earth and everything in it (see Gen 14:19,22; Ps 24:1–2).
19:6 *kingdom of priests.* Israel was to constitute the Lord's kingdom (the people who acknowledged Him as their King) and, like priests, was to be wholly consecrated to His service (see Is 61:6; cf. 1 Pet 2:5; Rev 1:6; 5:10; 20:6). *holy nation.* See 1 Pet 2:9. God's people, both individually and collectively, are to be set apart (see note on 3:5) to do His will (see Deut 7:6; 14:2,21; 26:19; Is 62:12).
19:8 *All that the LORD hath spoken we will do.* The people promised to obey the terms of the covenant (see 24:3,7; Deut 5:27).
19:9 *thick cloud.* See 13:21 and note. *the people may hear when I speak.* See Deut 4:33. *believe thee for ever.* See 14:31 and note.
19:10–11 Outward preparation to meet God symbolizes the inward consecration God requires of His people.
19:12–13 The whole mountain becomes holy because of God's presence (see 3:5 and note). Israel must keep herself from the mountain even as she is to keep herself from the tabernacle (see Num 3:10).

whether *it be* beast or man, it shall not live:
when the [a][1]trumpet soundeth long, they shall
come up to the mount.
14 And Moses went down from the mount
unto the people, and sanctified the people;
and they washed their clothes.
15 And he said unto the people, Be ready
against the third day: [a]come not at *your* wives.
16 And it came to pass on the third day in
the morning, that there were [a]thunders and
lightnings, and a [b]thick cloud upon the mount,
and the [c]voice of the trumpet exceeding loud;
so that all the people that *was* in the camp
[d]trembled.
17 And [a]Moses brought forth the people
out of the camp to meet with God; and they
stood at the nether part of the mount.
18 And [a]mount Sinai was altogether on a
smoke, because the LORD descended upon it
[b]in fire: [c]and the smoke thereof ascended as
the smoke of a furnace, and [d]the whole mount
quaked greatly.
19 And when the voice of the trumpet
sounded long, and waxed louder and louder,
[a]Moses spake, and [b]God answered him by a
voice.
20 And the LORD came down upon mount
Sinai, on the top of the mount: and the LORD
called Moses *up* to the top of the mount; and
Moses went up.
21 And the LORD said unto Moses, Go
down, [1]charge the people, lest they break
through unto the LORD [a]to gaze, and many of
them perish.
22 And let the priests also, which come
near to the LORD, [a]sanctify themselves, lest the
LORD [b]break forth upon them.
23 And Moses said unto the LORD, The
people cannot come up to mount Sinai: for
thou [1]chargedst us, saying, [a]Set bounds about
the mount, and sanctify it.
24 And the LORD said unto him, Away, get
thee down, and thou shalt come up, thou, and
Aaron with thee: but let not the priests and
the people break through to come up unto the
LORD, lest he break forth upon them.
25 So Moses went down unto the people,
and spake unto them.

The ten commandments

20 And God spake [a]all these words, saying,
2 [a]I *am* the LORD thy God, which have
brought thee out of the land of Egypt, [b]out of
the house of [1]bondage.
3 [a]Thou shalt have no other gods before
me.
4 [a]Thou shalt not make unto thee *any*
graven image, or any likeness *of any thing* that
is in heaven above, or that *is* in the earth beneath, or that *is* in the water under the earth:
5 [a]Thou shalt not bow down thyself to
them, nor serve them: for I the LORD thy God
am [b]a jealous God, [c]visiting the iniquity of the

19:13 [1]Or, *cornet* [a]ver. 16,19
19:15 [a]1 Cor. 7:5
19:16 [a]Heb. 12:18,19; Rev. 8:5 [b]ch. 40:34; 2 Chr. 5:14 [c]Rev. 4:1 [d]Heb. 12:21
19:17 [a]Deut. 4:10
19:18 [a]Deut. 4:11; 33:2; Judg. 5:5; Hab. 3:3 [b]ch. 3:2; 24:17; 2 Chr. 7:1-3 [c]Gen. 15:17; Ps. 144:5; Rev. 15:8 [d]Ps. 68:8; Jer. 4:24; Heb. 12:26
19:19 [a]Heb. 12:21 [b]Neh. 9:13; Ps. 81:7
19:21 [1]Heb. *contest*
19:21 [a]See ch. 3:5; 1 Sam. 6:19
19:22 [a]Lev. 10:3 [b]2 Sam. 6:7,8
19:23 [1]Heb. *contest* [a]ver. 12
20:1 [a]Deut. 5:22
20:2 [1]Heb. *servants* [a]Hos. 13:4 [b]ch. 13:3
20:3 [a]Jer. 35:15
20:4 [a]Deut. 27:15
20:5 [a]Is. 44:15,19 [b]Deut. 4:24 [c]Num. 14:18,33; 1 Ki. 21:29; Ps. 79:8; Jer. 32:18

19:15 *come not at your wives.* Not because sex is sinful but because it may leave the participants ceremonially unclean (see Lev 15:18; see also 1 Sam 21:4–5).

19:16 *thunders . . . lightnings . . . voice of the trumpet exceeding loud.* God's appearance is often accompanied by an impressive display of meteorological sights and sounds (see, e.g., 1 Sam 7:10; 12:18; Job 38:1; 40:6; Ps 18:13–14). *thick cloud.* See 13:21 and note.

19:18 *fire . . . smoke of a furnace.* See Gen 15:17 and note.

19:22 *priests.* See also v. 24. Before the Aaronic priesthood was established (see 28:1), priestly functions were performed either by the elders (see note on 3:16; see also 3:18; 12:21; 18:12) or by designated younger men (see 24:5). But perhaps the verse anticipates the regulations for the Aaronic priests who will be appointed. *which come near to the LORD.* To officiate at sacrifices (see 40:32; Lev 21:23).

20:1–17 See Deut 5:6–21; see also Mat 5:21,27; 19:17–19; Mark 10:19; Luke 18:20; Rom 13:9; Eph 6:2–3.

20:1 *words.* A technical term for "(covenant) stipulations" in the ancient Near East (e.g., among the Hittites; see also 24:3,8; 34:28). The basic code in Israel's divine law is found in vv. 2–17, elsewhere called the "ten commandments" (34:28; Deut 4:13; 10:4), the Hebrew words for which mean lit. "ten words." "Decalogue," a term of Greek origin often used as a synonym for the ten commandments, also means lit. "ten words."

20:2 *I am the LORD thy God, which have brought thee out.* The Decalogue reflects the structure of the contemporary royal treaties (see note on Gen 15:7). On the basis of (1) a preamble, in which the great king identified himself ("I am the LORD thy God"), and (2) a historical prologue, in which he sketched his previous gracious acts toward the subject king or people ("which have brought thee out . . ."), the Lord then set forth (3) the treaty (covenant) stipulations (see Deut 5:1–3,7–21) to be obeyed (in this case, ten in number: vv. 3–17). Use of this ancient royal treaty pattern shows that the Lord is here formally acknowledged as Israel's King and that Israel is His subject people. As His subjects, His covenant people are to render complete submission, allegiance and obedience to Him out of gratitude for His mercies, reverence for His sovereignty, and trust in His continuing care. See chart, p. 16.

‡20:3 *before.* Lit. "to the face of." The Hebrew for this word may have the meaning of "in defiance of" in Gen 16:12; 25:18; (see notes). Something of that sense may be intended here. In any event, no deity, real or imagined, is to rival the one true God in Israel's heart and life.

20:4 *graven image, or any likeness.* Because God has no visible form, any idol intended to resemble Him would be a sinful misrepresentation of Him (see Deut 4:12,15–18). Since other gods are not to be worshiped (see v. 5), making idols of them would be equally sinful (see Deut 4:19,23–28).

20:5 *jealous God.* God will not put up with rivalry or unfaithfulness. Usually His "jealousy" concerns Israel and assumes the covenant relationship (analogous to marriage) and the Lord's exclusive right to possess Israel and to claim her love and allegiance. Actually, jealousy is part of the vocabulary of love. The "jealousy" of God (1) demands exclusive devotion to Himself (see 34:14; Deut 4:24; 32:16,21; Josh 24:19; Ps 78:58; 1 Cor 10:22; Jas 4:5), (2) delivers to judgment all who oppose Him (see Deut 29:20; 1 Ki 14:22; Ps 79:5; Is 42:13; 59:17; Ezek 5:13; 16:38; 23:25; 36:5; Nah 1:2; Zeph 1:18; 3:8) and (3) vindicates His people (see 2 Ki 19:31; Is 9:7; 26:11; Ezek 39:25; Joel 2:18; Zech 1:14; 8:2). In some of these passages the meaning is closer to "zeal" (the same Hebrew word may be translated either way, depending on context). *unto the third and fourth generation of them that hate me.* Those Israelites who blatantly violate God's covenant and thus show that they reject the Lord as their King will bring down

fathers upon the children unto the third and fourth *generation* of them that hate me;

6 And [a]shewing mercy unto thousands of them that love me, and keep my commandments.

7 [a]Thou shalt not take the name of the LORD thy God in vain; for the LORD [b]will not hold him guiltless that taketh his name in vain.

8 [a]Remember the sabbath day, to keep it holy.

9 [a]Six days shalt thou labour, and do all thy work:

10 But the [a]seventh day *is* the sabbath of the LORD thy God: *in it* thou shalt not do any work, thou, nor thy son, nor thy daughter, thy manservant, nor thy maidservant, nor thy cattle, [b]nor thy stranger that *is* within thy gates:

11 For [a]*in* six days the LORD made heaven and earth, the sea, and all that in them *is,* and rested the seventh day: wherefore the LORD blessed the sabbath day, and hallowed it.

12 [a]Honour thy father and thy mother: that thy days may be long upon the land which the LORD thy God giveth thee.

13 [a]Thou shalt not kill.

14 [a]Thou shalt not commit adultery.

15 [a]Thou shalt not steal.

16 [a]Thou shalt not bear false witness against thy neighbour.

17 [a]Thou shalt not covet thy neighbour's house, [b]thou shalt not covet thy neighbour's wife, nor his manservant, nor his maidservant, nor his ox, nor his ass, nor any thing that *is* thy neighbour's.

Making an altar of earth

18 ¶ And [a]all the people [b]saw the thunderings, and the lightnings, and the noise of the trumpet, and the mountain [c]smoking: and when the people saw *it,* they removed, and stood afar off.

19 And they said unto Moses, [a]Speak thou with us, and we will hear: but [b]let not God speak with us, lest we die.

20 And Moses said unto the people, [a]Fear not: [b]for God is come to prove you, and [c]that his fear may be before your faces, that ye sin not.

21 And the people stood afar off, and Moses drew near unto [a]the thick darkness where God *was.*

22 And the LORD said unto Moses, Thus thou shalt say unto the children of Israel, Ye have seen that I have talked with you [a]from heaven.

23 Ye shall not make [a]with me gods of silver, neither shall ye make unto you gods of gold.

24 An altar of earth thou shalt make unto

20:6 [a]Deut:7:9; Rom. 11:28
20:7 [a]Mat. 5:33 [b]Mic. 6:11
20:8 [a]Lev. 26:2
20:9 [a]Ezek. 20:12; Luke 13:14
20:10 [a]Gen. 2:2,3 [b]Neh. 13:16-19
20:11 [a]Gen. 2:2
20:12 [a]Lev. 19:3; Deut. 5:16; Eph. 6:2
20:13 [a]Rom. 13:9
20:14 [a]Deut. 5:18
20:15 [a]Lev. 19:11
20:16 [a]ch. 23:1; Deut. 5:20
20:17 [a]Luke 12:15; Eph. 5:3,5; Heb. 13:5 [b]Mat. 5:28
20:18 [a]Heb. 12:18 [b]Rev. 1:10,12 [c]ch. 19:18
20:19 [a]Gal. 3:19 [b]Deut. 5:25
20:20 [a]Is. 41:10,13 [b]Deut. 13:3 [c]Prov. 16:6; Is. 8:13
20:21 [a]ch. 19:16
20:22 [a]Deut. 4:36
20:23 [a]ch. 32:1,2,4

judgment on themselves and their households (see, e.g., Num 16:31–34; Josh 7:24 and note)—households were usually extended to "three or four" generations. See note on Ps 109:12. *hate.* In covenant contexts the terms "hate" and "love" (v. 6) were conventionally used to indicate rejection of or loyalty to the covenant Lord.

20:6 *unto thousands of them.* See 1 Chr 16:15; Ps 105:8. *love me, and keep my commandments.* See John 14:15; 1 John 5:3. In the treaty language of the ancient Near East the "love" owed to the great king was a conventional term for total allegiance and implicit trust expressing itself in obedient service.

20:7 *take the name of the LORD . . . in vain.* By profaning God's name—e.g., by swearing falsely by it (see Lev 19:12; see also Jer 7:9), as on the witness stand in court. Jesus elaborates on oath-taking in Mat 5:33–37.

20:8 See Gen 2:3. *sabbath.* See note on 16:23. *holy.* See note on 3:5.

20:9 *Six days.* The question of a shorter "work week" in a modern industrialized culture is not in view.

20:10 *in it thou shalt not do any work.* Two reasons (one here and one in Deuteronomy) are given: (1) Having completed His work of creation God "rested on the seventh day" (v. 11), and the Israelites are to observe the same pattern in their service of God in the creation; (2) the Israelites must cease all labor so that their servants can also participate in the sabbath-rest—just as God had delivered His people from the burden of slavery in Egypt (see Deut 5:14–15). The sabbath thus became a "sign" of the covenant between God and Israel at mount Sinai (see 31:12–17; see also note on Gen 9:12).

20:12 *Honour.* (1) Prize highly (see Prov 4:8), (2) care for (see Ps 91:15), (3) show respect for (see Lev 19:3; 20:9), and (4) obey (see Deut 21:18–21; cf. Eph 6:1). *that thy days may be long.* "The first commandment with a promise" (Eph 6:2). See also note on Deut 6:2.

20:13 See Mat 5:21–26. *kill.* The Hebrew for this verb usually refers to a premeditated and deliberate act.

20:14 See Mat 5:27–30. *adultery.* A sin "against God" (Gen 39:9) as well as against the marriage partner.

20:17 *covet.* Desire something with evil motivation (see Mat 15:19). To break God's commandments inwardly is equivalent to breaking them outwardly (see Mat 5:21–30).

20:18–21 Concludes the account of the giving of the Decalogue. The order of the narrative appears to be different from the order of events, since v. 18 is most likely a continuation of 19:25. On this reading, the proclamation of the Decalogue took place after Moses approached God (v. 21). Biblical writers often did not follow chronological sequence in their narratives for various literary reasons. The purpose of chronological displacement here may have been either (1) to keep the Decalogue distinct from the "book of the covenant" (24:7) that follows (20:22–23:19), or (2) to conclude the account with the formal institution of Moses' office as covenant mediator—or both.

20:19 See Heb 12:19–20. Israel requests a mediator to stand between them and God, a role fulfilled by Moses and subsequently by priests, prophets and kings—and ultimately by Jesus Christ (see 1 Tim 2:5).

20:20 *Fear not.* Do not think that God's display of His majesty is intended simply to fill you with abject fear. He has come to enter into covenant with you as your heavenly King. *prove.* See note on Gen 22:1. *his fear.* See note on Gen 20:11.

20:22–23:19 The stipulations of the "book of the covenant" (24:7), consisting largely of expansions on and expositions of the ten commandments. See chart, p. 256.

20:22–26 Initial stipulations governing Israel's basic relationship with God (cf. v. 3).

20:22 *heaven.* God's dwelling place. Even on "the top of the mount" (19:20) God spoke from heaven.

20:23 See vv. 3–4. The contrast between the one true God "in the heavens," who "hath done whatsoever he pleased" (Ps 115:3), and idols of silver or gold, who can do nothing at all (see Ps 115:4–7; see also Ps 135:5–6,15–17), is striking indeed.

20:24 *altar of earth.* Such an altar, with dimensions the same

me, and shalt sacrifice thereon thy burnt offerings, and thy peace offerings, [a]thy sheep, and thine oxen: in all [b]places where I record my name I will come unto thee, and I will [c]bless thee.

25 And [a]if thou wilt make me an altar of stone, thou shalt not [1]build it *of* hewn stone: for if thou lift up thy tool upon it, thou hast polluted it.

26 Neither shalt thou go up by steps unto mine altar, that thy nakedness be not discovered thereon.

Laws about servants

21 Now these *are* the judgments which thou shalt [a]set before them.

2 [a]If thou buy a Hebrew servant, six years he shall serve: and in the seventh he shall go out free for nothing.

3 If he came in [1]by himself, he shall go out by himself: if he *were* married, then his wife shall go out with him.

4 If his master have given him a wife, and she have born him sons or daughters; the wife and her children shall be her master's, and he shall go out by himself.

5 [a]And if the servant [1]shall plainly say, I love my master, my wife, and my children; I will not go out free:

6 Then his master shall bring him unto the [a]judges; he shall also bring him to the door, or unto the door post; and his master shall [b]bore his ear through with an aul; and he shall serve him for ever.

7 And if a man [a]sell his daughter to be a maidservant, she shall not go out as the menservants do.

8 If she [1]please not her master, who hath betrothed her to himself, then shall he let her be redeemed: to sell her unto a strange nation he shall have no power, seeing he hath dealt deceitfully with her.

9 And if he have betrothed her unto his son, he shall deal with her after the manner of daughters.

10 If he take him another *wife;* her food, her raiment, [a]and her duty of marriage, shall he not diminish.

11 And if he do not these three unto her, then shall she go out free without money.

Laws about murder and strife

12 ¶ [a]He that smiteth a man, so that he die, shall be surely put to death.

13 And [a]if a man lie not in wait, but God [b]deliver *him* into his hand; then [c]I will appoint thee a place whither he shall flee.

14 But if a man come [a]presumptuously upon his neighbour, to slay him with guile; [b]thou shalt take him from mine altar, that he may die.

20:24 [a]Lev. 1:2 [b]Deut. 16:6,11; 1 Ki. 9:3; 2 Chr. 6:6 [c]Gen. 12:2
20:25 [1]Heb. *build them with hewing* [a]Deut. 27:5
21:1 [a]Deut. 4:14
21:2 [a]Jer. 34:14
21:3 [1]Heb. *with his body*
21:5 [1]Heb. *saying shall say* [a]Deut. 15:16,17
21:6 [a]ch. 12:12
21:6 [b]Ps. 40:6
21:7 [a]Neh. 5:5
21:8 [1]Heb. *be evil in the eyes of, etc.*
21:10 [a]1 Cor. 7:5
21:12 [a]Gen. 9:6; Mat. 26:52
21:13 [a]Deut. 19:4,5 [b]1 Sam. 24:4,10,18 [c]Num. 35:11; Deut. 19:3; Josh. 20:2
21:14 [a]Deut. 19:11,12; Heb. 10:26 [b]1 Ki. 2:28-34

as those of the altar in the tabernacle (see 27:1), has been found in the excavated ruins of a small Iron Age (10th, or possibly 11th, century B.C.) Israelite temple at Arad in southern Israel. *burnt offerings.* See note on Lev 1:3. *peace offerings.* See note on Lev 3:1. *all places.* The numerous temporary places of worship (see, e.g., Josh 8:30–31; Judg 6:24; 21:4; 1 Sam 7:17; 14:35; 2 Sam 24:25; 1 Ki 18:30).

20:25 *thou shalt not build it of hewn stone.* Many ancient altars of undressed stones (from various periods) have been found in Israel. *if thou lift up thy tool upon it, thou hast polluted it.* For reasons not now clear, but perhaps related to pagan practices.

20:26 *steps.* The oldest stepped altar known in Israel is at Megiddo and dates between 3000 and 2500 B.C. *nakedness be not discovered.* Men who ascended to such altars would expose their nakedness in the presence of God. Although Aaron and his descendants served at stepped altars (see Lev 9:22; Ezek 43:17), they were instructed to wear linen undergarments (see 28:42–43; Lev 6:10; 16:3–4; Ezek 44:17–18).

21:2–11 See Jer 34:8–22.

21:2 *Hebrew.* See note on Gen 14:13. *in the seventh he shall go out free for nothing.* The Lord's servants are not to be anyone's perpetual slaves (see 20:10 and note).

21:6 *judges.* See 22:8–9,28. *bore his ear through with an aul.* See Deut 15:17. Submission to this rite symbolized willing service (see Ps 40:6–8 and note on Ps 40:6).

21:12–15 See 20:13 and note; see also Num 35:16–34; Deut 19:1–13; 21:1–9; 24:7; 27:24–25; Josh 20:1–9.

21:12 See Gen 9:6 and note.

21:13 *lie not in wait.* Related terms and expressions are "at unawares" (Num 35:11), "without enmity" (Num 35:22), "was not his enemy" (Num 35:23), "neither sought his harm" (Num 35:23) and "hated not in time past" (Deut 19:4). Premeditated murder is thus distinguished from accidental manslaughter. *God deliver him into his hand.* The event is beyond human control—in modern legal terminology, an "act of God." *place.* A city of refuge (see Num 35:6–32; Deut 19:1–13; Josh 20:1–9; 21:13,21, 27,32,38).

21:14 *from mine altar.* The horns of the altar were a final refuge for those subject to judicial action (see 1 Ki 1:50–51; 2:28; Amos 3:14 and notes).

The Purpose of the Law of God

EXODUS 20:3–12	**EXODUS 20:13–17**
Spirituality	Morality
Our Relation to God	Our Relation to Others
Love Your God (Matthew 22:37–38)	Love Your Neighbor (Matthew 22:39–40)
Sanctity of character	Slander
Sanctity of contentment	Covetousness

15 And he that smiteth his father, or his mother, shall be surely put to death.

16 And [a]he that stealeth a man, and [b]selleth him, or if he be [c]found in his hand, he shall surely be put to death.

17 And [a]he that [1]curseth his father, or his mother, shall surely be put to death.

18 And if men strive together, and one smite [1]another with a stone, or with *his* fist, and he die not, but keepeth *his* bed:

19 If he rise again, and walk abroad [a]upon his staff, then shall he that smote *him* be quit: only he shall pay *for* [1]the loss of his time, and shall cause *him* to be thoroughly healed.

20 And if a man smite his servant, or his maid, with a rod, and he die under his hand; he shall be surely [1]punished.

21 Notwithstanding, if he continue a day or two, he shall not be punished: for he *is* his money.

22 If men strive, and hurt a woman with child, so that her fruit depart *from her,* and yet no mischief follow: he shall be surely punished, according as the woman's husband will lay upon him; and he shall [a]pay as the judges determine.

23 And if *any* mischief follow, then thou shalt give life for life,

24 [a]Eye for eye, tooth for tooth, hand for hand, foot for foot,

25 Burning for burning, wound for wound, stripe for stripe.

26 And if a man smite the eye of his servant, or the eye of his maid, that it perish; he shall let him go free for his eye's sake.

27 And if he smite out his manservant's tooth, or his maidservant's tooth; he shall let him go free for his tooth's sake.

28 ¶ If an ox gore a man or a woman, that they die: then [a]the ox shall be surely stoned, and his flesh shall not be eaten; but the owner of the ox *shall be* quit.

29 But if the ox *were* wont to push with his horn in time past, and it hath been testified to his owner, and he hath not kept him in, but that he hath killed a man or a woman; the ox shall be stoned, and his owner also shall be put to death.

21:16 [a]Deut. 24:7 [b]Gen. 37:28 [c]ch. 22:4
21:17 [1]Or, *revileth* [a]Mark 7:10
21:18 [1]Or, *his neighbour*
21:19 [1]Heb. [*his*] *ceasing* [a]2 Sam. 3:29
21:20 [1]Heb. *avenged*
21:22 [a]ver. 30; Deut. 22:18,19
21:24 [a]Lev. 24:20; Deut. 19:21; Mat. 5:38
21:28 [a]Gen. 9:5

21:30 [a]ver. 22; Num. 35:31
21:32 [a]See Zech. 11:12,13; Mat. 26:15; 27:3,9 [b]ver. 28
22:1 [1]Or, *goat* [a]2 Sam. 12:6; See Prov. 6:31; Luke 19:8
22:2 [a]Mat. 24:43 [b]Num. 35:27
22:3 [a]ch. 21:2
22:4 [a]ch. 21:16 [b]See ver. 1,7; Prov. 6:31

30 If there be laid on him a sum of money, then he shall give *for* [a]the ransom of his life whatsoever is laid upon him.

31 Whether he have gored a son, or have gored a daughter, according to this judgment shall it be done unto him.

32 If the ox shall push a manservant or a maidservant; he shall give unto their master [a]thirty shekels *of* silver, and the [b]ox shall be stoned.

33 And if a man shall open a pit, or if a man shall dig a pit, and not cover it, and an ox or an ass fall therein;

34 The owner of the pit shall make *it* good, *and* give money unto the owner of them; and the dead *beast* shall be his.

35 And if one man's ox hurt another's, that he die; then they shall sell the live ox, and divide the money of it; and the dead *ox* also they shall divide.

36 Or *if* it be known that the ox *hath* used to push in time past, and his owner hath not kept him in; he shall surely pay ox for ox; and the dead shall be his own.

Laws about property

22 If a man shall steal an ox, or a [1]sheep, and kill it, or sell it; he shall restore five oxen for an ox, and [a]four sheep for a sheep.

2 If a thief be found [a]breaking up, and be smitten that he die, *there shall* [b]no blood *be shed* for him.

3 If the sun be risen upon him, *there shall be* blood *shed* for him; *for* he should make full restitution; if he have nothing, then he shall be [a]sold for his theft.

4 If the theft be certainly [a]found in his hand alive, whether it be ox, or ass, or sheep; he shall [b]restore double.

5 ¶ If a man shall cause a field or vineyard to be eaten, and shall put in his beast, and shall feed in another man's field; of the best of his own field, and of the best of his own vineyard, shall he make restitution.

6 If fire break out, and catch in thorns, so that the stacks of corn, or the standing corn, or

21:15 See 20:12.
21:16 See 20:15.
21:19 *walk abroad upon his staff.* Is convalescing in a satisfactory way. *loss of his time.* Lit. "his sitting," i.e., his enforced idleness.
21:20–21 Benefit of doubt was granted to the slaveholder where no homicidal intentions could be proved.
21:23–25 See Deut 19:21. The so-called law of retaliation, as its contexts show, was meant to limit the punishment to fit the crime. By invoking the law of love, Jesus corrected the popular misunderstanding of the law of retaliation (see Mat 5:38–42). See note on Lev 24:20.
21:23 *any mischief follow.* Any further injury either to mother or to child.
21:26–27 Humane applications of the law of retaliation.
21:28–32 The law of the goring ox.
21:28 *the ox shall be surely stoned.* By killing someone, the ox becomes accountable for that person's life (see Gen 9:5).
21:30 *If there be laid on him a sum of money.* If the victim's family is willing to accept a ransom payment instead of demanding the death penalty. *he shall give for the ransom of his life.* The ransom is not to compensate the victim's family but to save the negligent man's life.
21:32 *thirty shekels of silver.* Apparently the standard price for a slave. It was also the amount Judas was willing to accept as his price for betraying Jesus (see Mat 26:14–15; see also Zech 11:12–13). *shekels.* See note on Gen 20:16.
21:33–36 Laws concerning injuries to animals.
22:1–15 Laws concerning property rights (see 20:15).
22:2 An act of self-defense in darkness does not produce bloodguilt.
22:3 Killing an intruder in broad daylight is not justifiable.
22:5 *of the best.* Restitution should always err on the side of quality and generosity.
22:6 *thorns.* Often used as hedges (see Mic 7:4) bordering cultivated areas.

the field, be consumed *therewith;* he that kindled the fire shall surely make restitution.
7 If a man shall deliver unto his neighbour
money or stuff to keep, and it be stolen out of
the man's house; [a]if the thief be found, let him
pay double.
8 If the thief be not found, then the master
of the house shall be brought unto the [a]judges,
to see whether he have put his hand unto his
neighbour's goods.
9 For all manner of trespass, *whether it be*
for ox, for ass, for sheep, for raiment, *or* for
any manner of lost *thing,* which *another* chal-
lengeth to be his, the [a]cause of both parties
shall come before the judges; *and* whom the
judges shall condemn, he shall pay double
unto his neighbour.
10 If a man deliver unto his neighbour an
ass, or an ox, or a sheep, or any beast, to keep;
and it die, or be hurt, or driven away, no man
seeing *it:*
11 *Then* shall an [a]oath of the LORD be between them both, that he hath not put his
hand unto his neighbour's goods; and the owner of it shall accept *thereof,* and he shall not
make *it* good.
12 And [a]if it be stolen from him, he shall
make restitution unto the owner thereof.
13 If it be torn in pieces, *then* let him bring
it *for* witness, *and* he shall not make good that
which was torn.
14 And if a man borrow *ought* of his neighbour, and it be hurt, or die, the owner thereof
being not with it, he shall surely make *it* good.
15 *But* if the owner thereof *be* with it, he
shall not make *it* good: if it *be* a hired *thing,* it
came for his hire.

Laws about personal actions

16 ¶ And [a]if a man entice a maid that is not
betrothed, and lie with her, he shall surely endow her to be his wife.
17 If her father utterly refuse to give her
unto him, he shall [1]pay money according to
the [a]dowry of virgins.
18 [a]Thou shalt not suffer a witch to live.
19 [a]Whosoever lieth with a beast shall
surely be put to death.
20 [a]He that sacrificeth unto *any* god, save
unto the LORD only, he shall be utterly destroyed.
21 ¶ [a]Thou shalt neither vex a stranger, nor
oppress him: for ye were strangers in the land
of Egypt.
22 [a]Ye shall not afflict any widow, or fatherless child.
23 If thou afflict them in any wise, and they
[a]cry at all unto me, I will surely [b]hear their cry;
24 And my [a]wrath shall wax hot, and I will
kill you with the sword; and [b]your wives shall
be widows, and your children fatherless.
25 ¶ [a]If thou lend money to *any of* my people *that is* poor by thee, thou shalt not be to
him as an usurer, neither shalt thou lay upon
him usury.
26 [a]If thou at all take thy neighbour's raiment to pledge, thou shalt deliver it unto him
by that the sun goeth down:
27 For that *is* his covering only, it *is* his raiment for his skin: wherein shall he sleep? and
it shall come to pass, when he crieth unto me,
that I will hear; for I *am* [a]gracious.
28 ¶ [a]Thou shalt not revile the [b][1]gods, nor
curse the ruler of thy people.
29 Thou shalt not delay *to offer* [a]*the first of*
[1]thy ripe fruits, and *of* thy [2]liquors: [b]the firstborn of thy sons shalt thou give unto me.
30 [a]Likewise shalt thou do with thine
oxen, *and* with thy sheep: [b]seven days it shall
be with his dam; on the eighth day thou shalt
give it me.
31 And ye shall be [a]holy men unto me:
[b]neither shall ye eat *any* flesh *that is* torn *of*
beasts in the field; ye shall cast it to the dogs.

22:7 [a]ver. 4
22:8 [a]ch. 21:6; ver. 28
22:9 [a]Deut. 25:1; 2 Chr. 19:10
22:11 [a]Heb. 6:16
22:12 [a]Gen. 31:39
22:16 [a]Deut. 22:28,29
22:17 [1]Heb. *weigh* [a]Gen. 34:12
22:18 [a]1 Sam. 28:3
22:19 [a]Lev. 18:23
22:20 [a]Deut. 17:2,3,5
22:21 [a]Deut. 10:19
22:22 [a]Jas. 1:27
22:23 [a]Luke 18:7 [b]Ps. 18:6
22:24 [a]Ps. 69:24 [b]Ps. 109:9
22:25 [a]Ps. 15:5
22:26 [a]Deut. 24:6
22:27 [a]ch. 34:6
22:28 [1]Or, *judges* [a]Eccl. 10:20 [b]Ps. 82:6
22:29 [1]Heb. *thy fulness* [2]Heb. *tear* [a]ch. 23:16 [b]ch. 13:2,12
22:30 [a]Deut. 15:19 [b]Lev. 22:27
22:31 [a]Lev. 19:2 [b]Ezek. 4:14

22:11 See 20:7 and note. *an oath of the LORD.* The judges were God's representatives in court cases (see 21:6; 22:8–9,28).

22:12–13 Similar laws apparently existed as early as the patriarchal period (see Gen 31:39).

22:16–31 General laws related to social obligations.

22:16 *shall surely endow her.* A gift, usually substantial, was given by the prospective groom to the bride's family as payment for her (see Gen 24:53). The custom is still followed today in parts of the Middle East.

22:18 See Deut 18:10,14; 1 Sam 28:9; Is 47:12–14.

22:19 Ancient myths and epics describe acts of bestiality performed by pagan gods and demigods in Babylon and Canaan.

22:20 See 20:3–5. The total destruction of the idolatrous Canaanites was later commanded by the Lord (see Num 21:2; Deut 2:34; 3:6; 7:2; 13:15; 20:17; Josh 2:10; 6:17,21; 8:25; 10:1,28,35,37,39–40; 11:11–12,20–21; Judg 1:17).

22:21–27 That the poor, the widow, the orphan, the alien—in fact, all defenseless people—are objects of God's special concern and providential care is clear from the writings of Moses (see 21:26–27; 23:6–12; Lev 19:9–10; Deut 14:29; 16:11,14; 24:19–21; 26:12–13), the psalmists (see Ps 10:14,17–18; 68:5; 82:3; 146:9) and the prophets (see Is 1:23; 10:2; Jer 7:6; 22:3; Zech 7:10; Mal 3:5) as well as from the teachings of Jesus (see, e.g., Mat 25:34–45).

22:25–27 Laws dealing with interest on loans (see Lev 25:35–37; Deut 15:7–11; 23:19–20; see also Neh 5:7–12; Job 24:9; Prov 28:8; Ezek 18:13; 22:12). Interest for profit was not to be charged at the expense of the poor. Generosity in such matters was extended even further by Jesus (see Luke 6:34–35).

22:26–27 If all that a man had to offer as his pledge for a loan was his cloak, he was among the poorest of the poor (see Amos 2:8 and note).

22:28 *not revile the gods.* Or "not revile the judges." *nor curse the ruler of thy people.* A ruler was God's representative; quoted by a penitent Paul after he had unwittingly insulted the high priest (see Acts 23:4–5).

22:29 *firstborn . . . give unto me.* See notes on 4:22; 13:2,13; see also 13:15.

22:30 *Likewise shalt thou do with thine oxen, and with thy sheep.* See notes on 13:2; 13:13; see also 13:12,15. *on the eighth day thou shalt give it me.* The same principle applied in a different way to firstborn sons as well (see note on Gen 17:12).

22:31 Since God's people were "a kingdom of priests" (see 19:6 and note), they were to obey a law later specified for members of the Aronic priesthood (see Lev 22:8) as well.

23 Thou [a]shall not [1]raise a false report:
put not thine hand with the wicked
to be an [b]unrighteous witness.
2 [a]Thou shalt not follow a multitude to *do*
evil; [b]neither shalt thou [1]speak in a cause to
decline after many to wrest *judgment:*
3 Neither shalt thou countenance a poor
man in his cause.
4 [a]If thou meet thine enemy's ox or his ass
going astray, thou shalt surely bring it back to
him again.
5 [a]If thou see the ass of him that hateth
thee lying under his burden, [1]and wouldest
forbear to help him, thou shalt surely help
with him.
6 [a]Thou shalt not wrest the judgment of
thy poor in his cause.
7 [a]Keep thee far from a false matter; [b]and
the innocent and righteous slay thou not: for
[c]I will not justify the wicked.
8 And [a]thou shalt take no gift: for the gift
blindeth [1]the wise, and perverteth the words
of the righteous.
9 Also [a]thou shalt not oppress a stranger:
for ye know the [1]heart of a stranger, seeing ye
were strangers in the land of Egypt.

The law about the Sabbath

10 ¶ And [a]six years thou shalt sow thy
land, and shalt gather in the fruits thereof:
11 But the seventh *year* thou shalt let it
rest and lie still; that the poor of thy people
may eat: and what they leave the beasts of the
field shall eat. In like manner thou shalt deal
with thy vineyard, *and* with thy [1]oliveyard.
12 [a]Six days thou shalt do thy work, and
on the seventh day thou shalt rest: that thine
ox and thine ass may rest, and the son of thy
handmaid, and the stranger, may be refreshed.
13 And in all *things* that I have said unto

23:1 [1]Or, *receive* [a]Ps. 101:5 [b]Acts 6:11
23:2 [1]Heb. *answer* [a]Gen. 7:1 [b]Lev. 19:15
23:4 [a]Rom. 12:20
23:5 [1]Or, *wilt thou cease to help him? or, and wouldest cease to leave* thy business *for him: thou shalt surely leave* it to join *with him* [a]Deut. 22:4
23:6 [a]Eccl. 5:8
23:7 [a]Eph. 4:25 [b]Mat. 27:4 [c]Rom. 1:18
23:8 [1]Heb. *the seeing* [a]Prov. 15:27
23:9 [1]Heb. *soul* [a]ch. 22:21
23:10 [a]Lev. 25:3,4
23:11 [1]Or, *olive trees*
23:12 [a]Luke 13:14
23:13 [a]1 Tim. 4:16 [b]Num. 32:38
23:14 [a]ch. 34:23
23:15 [a]ch. 12:15 [b]ch. 34:20
23:16 [a]ch. 34:22 [b]Deut. 16:13
23:17 [a]Deut. 16:16
23:18 [1]Or, *feast* [a]Deut. 16:4
23:19 [a]Deut. 26:10 [b]Deut. 14:21
23:20 [a]ch. 14:19
23:21 [a]Num. 14:11; Ps. 78:40, 56 [b]Deut. 18:19; 1 John 5:16 [c]Is. 9:6; Jer. 23:6
23:22 [1]Or, *I will afflict them that afflict thee* [a]Deut. 30:7; Jer. 30:20
23:23 [a]ver. 20

you [a]be circumspect: and [b]make no mention
of the name of other gods, neither let it be
heard out of thy mouth.

Laws about appointed feasts

14 ¶ [a]Three times thou shalt keep a feast
unto me in the year.
15 [a]Thou shalt keep the feast of unleavened bread: thou shalt eat unleavened bread
seven days, as I commanded thee, in the time
appointed of the month Abib; for in it thou
camest out from Egypt: [b]and none shall appear
before me empty:
16 [a]And the feast of harvest, the firstfruits
of thy labours, which thou hast sown in the
field: and [b]the feast of ingathering, *which is* in
the end of the year, when thou hast gathered
in thy labours out of the field.
17 [a]Three times in the year all thy males
shall appear before the Lord GOD.
18 [a]Thou shalt not offer the blood of my
sacrifice with leavened bread; neither shall the
fat of my [1]sacrifice remain until the morning.
19 [a]The first of the firstfruits of thy land
thou shalt bring *into* the house of the LORD thy
God. [b]Thou shalt not seethe a kid in his mother's milk.

Promise of God's protection

20 ¶ [a]Behold, I send an Angel before thee,
to keep thee in the way, and to bring thee into
the place which I have prepared.
21 Beware of him, and obey his voice,
[a]provoke him not; for he will [b]not pardon
your transgressions: for [c]my name *is* in him.
22 But if thou shalt indeed obey his voice,
and do all that I speak; then [a]I will be an enemy unto thine enemies, and [1]an adversary
unto thine adversaries.
23 [a]For mine Angel shall go before thee,

23:1–9 Most of the regulations in this section pertain to 20:16.
23:1 See Lev 19:16; Deut 22:13–19; 1 Ki 21:10–13.
23:4–5 Those hostile to you are to be shown the same consideration as others (see Deut 22:1–4; Prov 25:21). Jesus teaches that this means "love your enemies" (Mat 5:44).
23:7 1 Ki 21:10–13 is a vivid illustration of violation of this law.
23:8 See Deut 16:19. Samuel exemplifies faithful stewardship in this regard (see 1 Sam 12:3), while his sons do not (see 1 Sam 8:3).
23:10–13 Extensions of the principles taught in 20:8–11; Deut 5:12–15.
23:14–19 See 34:18–26; Lev 23:4–44; Num 28:16–29:40; Deut 16:1–17.
23:15 *feast of unleavened bread.* Celebrated from the 15th through the 21st days of the first month (usually about mid-March to mid-April; see note on 12:2) at the beginning of the barley harvest; it commemorated the exodus.
23:16 *feast of harvest.* Also called the "feast of weeks" (34:22) because it was held seven weeks after the feast of unleavened bread. It was celebrated on the sixth day of the third month (usually about mid-May to mid-June) during the wheat harvest. In later Judaism it came to commemorate the giving of the law on mount Sinai, though there is no evidence of this significance in the OT. In NT times it was called "(the day of) Pentecost" (Acts 2:1; 20:16; 1 Cor 16:8), which means "50" (see Lev 23:16). *feast of ingathering.* Also called the "feast of tabernacles" (Lev 23:34) because the Israelites lived in temporary shelters when God brought them out of Egypt (see Lev 23:43). It was celebrated from the 15th through the 22nd days of the seventh month (usually about mid-September to mid-October) when the produce of the orchards and vines had been harvested; it commemorated the wilderness wanderings after the exodus. *end of the year.* End of the agricultural year, which began in the fall (see note on 12:2).
23:17 *all thy males.* Normally accompanied by their families (see, e.g., 1 Sam 1).
23:18 *not . . . with leavened bread.* See note on 12:15. *neither. . . remain until the morning.* See 12:9–10.
23:19 *firstfruits.* Representative of the whole harvest. The offering of firstfruits was an acknowledgment that the harvest was from the Lord and belonged wholly to Him. *Thou shalt not seethe a kid in his mother's milk.* Perhaps a protest against a Canaanite pagan ritual (see v. 33; 34:15).
23:20 *Angel.* See 14:19; see also note on Gen 16:7. *place . . . I have prepared.* Canaan (cf. the similar statement of Jesus in John 14:2–3).
23:21 *name.* Representing God's presence.
23:22 *if.* See note on 19:5.
23:23 See 3:8 and note.

and [b]bring thee in unto the Amorites, and the Hittites, and the Perizzites, and the Canaanites, the Hivites, and the Jebusites: and I will cut them off.

24 Thou shalt not [a]bow down to their gods, nor serve them, [b]nor do after their works: [c]but thou shalt utterly overthrow them, and quite break down their images.

25 And ye shall [a]serve the LORD your God, and [b]he shall bless thy bread, and thy water; and [c]I will take sickness away from the midst of thee.

26 [a]There shall nothing cast their young, nor be barren, in thy land: the number of thy days I will [b]fulfil.

27 I will send [a]my fear before thee, and will [b]destroy all the people to whom thou shalt come, and I will make all thine enemies turn their [1]backs unto thee.

28 And [a]I will send hornets before thee, which shall drive out the Hivite, the Canaanite, and the Hittite, from before thee.

29 [a]I will not drive them out from before thee in one year; lest the land become desolate, and the beast of the field multiply against thee.

30 By little and little I will drive them out from before thee, until thou be increased, and inherit the land.

31 And [a]I will set thy bounds from the Red sea even unto the sea of the Philistines, and from the desert unto the river: for I will [b]deliver the inhabitants of the land into your hand; and thou shalt drive them out before thee.

32 [a]Thou shalt make no covenant with them, nor with their gods.

33 They shall not dwell in thy land, lest they make thee sin against me: for if thou serve their gods, [a]it will surely be a snare unto thee.

23:23 [b]Josh. 24:8
23:24 [a]ch. 20:5 [b]Deut. 12:30,31 [c]Num. 33:52
23:25 [a]Deut. 6:13; Mat. 4:10 [b]Deut. 28:5 [c]ch. 15:26; Deut. 7:15
23:26 [a]Deut. 7:14; 28:4; Mal. 3:11 [b]1 Chr. 23:1
23:27 [1]Heb. *neck* [a]Deut. 2:25 [b]Deut. 7:23
23:28 [a]Josh. 24:12
23:29 [a]Deut. 7:22
23:31 [a]Gen. 15:18; Deut. 11:24; 1 Ki. 4:21,24 [b]Josh. 21:44
23:32 [a]ch. 34:12,15
23:33 [a]1 Sam. 18:21; Ps. 106:36
24:1 [a]Lev. 10:1,2 [b]ch. 1:5; Num. 11:16
24:3 [a]ver. 7; ch. 19:8; Deut. 5:27; Gal. 3:19
24:4 [a]Deut. 31:9 [b]Gen. 28:18
24:6 [a]Heb. 9:18
24:7 [a]Heb. 9:19
24:8 [a]1 Pet. 1:2
24:10 [a]John 1:18; 1 John 4:12

The covenant affirmed

24 And he said unto Moses, Come up unto the LORD, thou, and Aaron, [a]Nadab, and Abihu, [b]and seventy of the elders of Israel; and worship ye afar off.

2 And Moses alone shall come near the LORD: but they shall not come nigh; neither shall the people go up with him.

3 And Moses came and told the people all the words of the LORD, and all the judgments: and all the people answered *with* one voice, and said, [a]All the words which the LORD hath said will we do.

4 And Moses [a]wrote all the words of the LORD, and rose up early in the morning, and builded an altar under the hill, and twelve [b]pillars, according to the twelve tribes of Israel.

5 And he sent young men of the children of Israel, which offered burnt offerings, and sacrificed peace offerings *of* oxen unto the LORD.

6 And Moses [a]took half of the blood, and put *it* in basons; and half of the blood he sprinkled on the altar.

7 And he [a]took the book of the covenant, and read in the audience of the people: and they said, All that the LORD hath said will we do, and be obedient.

8 And Moses took the blood, and sprinkled *it* on the people, and said, Behold [a]the blood of the covenant, which the LORD hath made with you concerning all these words.

9 Then went up Moses, and Aaron, Nadab, and Abihu, and seventy of the elders of Israel:

10 And they [a]saw the God of Israel: and *there was* under his feet as it were a paved

23:28 *hornets.* The meaning of the Hebrew for this word is uncertain. The Septuagint (the Greek translation of the OT) renders it "wasp," but the translators may have been guessing. In any event, the Lord promises to send some agent to disable or frighten the peoples of Canaan so that they will not be able to resist Israel's invasion. But probably the word involves concrete imagery and the focus of the statement is on the effects—therefore we are not to look for some historical agent to which the word metaphorically refers (cf. Is 7:18).

23:30 *By little and little.* See Judg 1.

23:31 See Gen 15:18; 1 Ki 4:21. *Red sea.* The (south)eastern border (here the modern Gulf of Aqaba; see note on 1 Ki 9:26). *sea of the Philistines.* The western border (the Mediterranean). *the desert.* The southern border (northeastern Sinai; see note on Gen 15:18). *the river.* The northern border (the Euphrates River).

23:33 *snare.* A symbol of destruction (see 10:7; Job 18:9; Ps 18:5; Prov 13:14; 21:6; Is 24:17–18).

24:1 *Come up.* The action, temporarily interrupted for the book of the covenant (20:22–23:33), is resumed from 20:21. Moses and his associates would ascend the mountain after the events of vv. 3–8. *Nadab, and Abihu.* Aaron's two oldest sons. Nadab would have succeeded Aaron as high priest, but he and his brother died because they offered unauthorized fire before the Lord (see Lev 10:1–2; Num 3:4). *seventy ... elders.* Cf. Num 11:16; perhaps representing Jacob's 70 descendants (see 1:5; Gen 46:27 and note). *elders.* See note on 3:16. *afar off.* See 20:21.

24:2 *Moses alone.* The mediator between God and the people of Israel. Jesus, who is greater than Moses (see Heb 3:1–6), is the "mediator of the new covenant" (Heb 12:24).

24:3 *words.* Probably refers to the ten commandments (see 20:1 and note). *judgments.* Probably refers to the stipulations of the book of the covenant (21:1–23:19). *will we do.* See v. 7; see also 19:8 and note.

24:4 *Moses wrote.* See note on 17:14; see also Introduction: Author and Date of Writing. *twelve pillars.* See Josh 4:5,20; 1 Ki 18:31.

24:5 *young men ... offered.* See note on 19:22.

24:6 *half of the blood ... and half.* The division of the blood points to the twofold aspect of the "blood of the covenant" (v. 8): The blood on the altar symbolizes God's forgiveness and His acceptance of the offering; the blood on the people points to an oath that binds them in obedience (see vv. 3,7).

24:7 *book of the covenant.* Strictly speaking, 20:22–23:19 (see note there)—but here implying also the stipulations of 20:2–17; 23:20–33. *will we do, and be obedient.* See v. 3; see also 19:8 and note.

24:8 Only after the people agreed to obey the Lord could they participate in His covenant with them. *blood of the covenant.* See Mark 14:24 and note.

24:9 *went up.* See v. 1 and note.

24:10 *saw ... God.* But not in the fullness of His glory (see 33:20; see also notes on 3:6; Gen 16:13; Num 12:8; Ezek 1:28).

work of a [b]sapphire stone, and as it were the [c]body of heaven in *his* clearness.

11 And upon the nobles of the children of Israel he [a]laid not his hand: also [b]they saw God, and did [c]eat and drink.

12 ¶ And the LORD said unto Moses, [a]Come up to me into the mount, and be there: and I will give thee [b]tables of stone, and a law, and commandments which I have written; that thou mayest teach them.

13 And Moses rose up, and [a]his minister Joshua: and Moses went up into the mount of God.

14 And he said unto the elders, Tarry ye here for us, until we come again unto you: and behold, Aaron and Hur *are* with you: if any man have any matters to do, let him come unto them.

15 And Moses went up into the mount, and [a]a cloud covered the mount.

16 And [a]the glory of the LORD abode upon mount Sinai, and the cloud covered it six days: and the seventh day he called unto Moses out of the midst of the cloud.

17 And the sight of the glory of the LORD *was* like [a]devouring fire on the top of the mount in the eyes of the children of Israel.

18 And Moses went into the midst of the cloud, and gat him up into the mount: and [a]Moses was in the mount forty days and forty nights.

24:10 [b]Ezek. 1:26; Rev. 4:3 [c]Mat. 17:2
24:11 [a]ch. 19:21 [b]Gen. 32:30; Judg. 13:22 [c]1 Cor. 10:18
24:12 [a]ver. 2,15 [b]ch. 32:15
24:13 [a]ch. 32:17
24:15 [a]ch. 19:9; Mat. 17:5
24:16 [a]ch. 16:10
24:17 [a]ch. 3:2; Deut. 4:36; Heb. 12:18,29
24:18 [a]ch. 34:28; Deut. 9:9

25:2 [1]Heb. *take for me* [2]Or, *heave offering* [a]ch. 35:5,21; 1 Chr. 29:3,5,9,14; Ezra 2:68; Neh. 11:2; 2 Cor. 8:12; 9:7
25:3 [1]Or, *heave offering*
25:4 [1]Or, *silk* [a]Gen. 41:42
25:6 [a]ch. 27:20 [b]ch. 30:23 [c]ch. 30:34
25:7 [a]ch. 28:4,6 [b]ch. 28:15
25:8 [a]ch. 36:1,3,4; Lev. 4:6; 10:4; 21:12; Heb. 9:1,2 [b]ch. 29:45; 1 Ki. 6:13; 2 Cor. 6:16; Heb. 3:6; Rev. 21:3

Offerings for the tabernacle

25 And the LORD spake unto Moses, saying,

2 Speak unto the children of Israel, that they [1]bring me an [2]offering: [a]of every man that giveth it willingly with his heart ye shall take my [2]offering.

3 And this *is* the [1]offering which ye shall take of them; gold, and silver, and brass,

4 And blue, and purple, and scarlet, and [a][1]fine linen, and goats' *hair,*

5 And rams' skins dyed red, and badgers' skins, and shittim wood,

6 [a]Oil for the light, [b]spices for anointing oil, and for [c]sweet incense,

7 Onyx stones, and stones to be set in the [a]ephod, and in the [b]breastplate.

8 And let them make me a [a]sanctuary; that [b]I may dwell amongst them.

9 [a]According to all that I shew thee, *after* the pattern of the tabernacle, and the pattern of all the instruments thereof, even so shall ye make *it.*

The ark

10 ¶ [a]And they shall make an ark of shittim wood: two cubits and a half *shall be* the length thereof, and a cubit and a half the breadth thereof, and a cubit and a half the height thereof.

25:9 [a]ver. 40 **25:10** [a]ch. 37:1; Deut. 10:3; Heb. 9:4

---

sapphire. Or "lapis lazuli." *heaven.* Symbolized by the blue color of the "lapis lazuli" (see Ezek 1:26).

24:11 *nobles.* Lit. "corners," "corner supports"; used in the sense of "nobles" only here. Cf. Gal 2:9. *laid not his hand.* See 9:15. *did eat and drink.* A covenant meal (cf. Gen 26:30; 31:54), celebrating the sealing of the covenant described in vv. 3–8. It foreshadows the Lord's supper, which celebrates the new covenant sealed by Christ's death (see 1 Cor 11:25–26).

24:12 *Come up.* See note on v. 1. *tables of stone.* See note on 31:18. *that thou mayest teach them.* As instruction from the covenant Lord, the laws were divine directives.

24:13 *his minister Joshua.* See note on 17:9.

24:14 *Hur.* See note on 17:10.

24:17 *glory of the LORD.* See 16:10.

24:18 *was in the mount.* Moses did not come down until he had received instructions concerning the tabernacle and its furnishings (see 32:15). *forty days and forty nights.* Jesus, the new Moses (see note on v. 2), fasted for the same length of time (see Mat 4:2).

25:2 *offering.* Here refers to a voluntary contribution.

25:4 *blue, and purple, and scarlet.* Royal colors. *blue, and purple.* Dyes derived from various shellfish (primarily the *murex*) that swarm in the waters of the northeast Mediterranean. So important for the local economy was the dyeing industry that the promised land was known as Canaan (which means "land of purple"), later called Phoenicia (also meaning "land of purple") by the Greeks. *scarlet.* Derived from the eggs and carcasses of the worm *Coccus ilicis,* which attaches itself to the leaves of the holly plant. *fine linen.* A very high quality cloth (often used by Egyptian royalty) made from thread spun from the fibers of flax straw. The Hebrew for this term derives ultimately from Egyptian. Excellent examples of unusually white, tightly woven linen have been found in ancient Egyptian tombs. Some are so finely woven that they cannot be distinguished from silk without the use of a magnifying glass. *goats' hair.* From long-haired goats. A coarse, black (cf. Sol 1:5; 6:5) material, it was often used to weave cloth for tents.

‡25:5 *rams' skins dyed red.* After all the wool had been removed from the skins. The final product was similar to present-day morocco leather. *badgers'.* Now understood to be "porpoises" which were native to the Red sea. *shittim.* [i.e., acacia]. The wood is darker and harder than oak and is avoided by wood-eating insects. It is common in the Sinai peninsula.

25:6 *spices.* Those used in the anointing oil are identified in 30:23–24 as myrrh (balsam sap), cinnamon (bark of the cinnamon tree, a species of laurel), cane (pith from the root of a reed plant) and cassia (made from dried flowers of the cinnamon tree). Those used in the fragrant incense are identified in 30:34 as stacte (a powder taken from the middle of hardened drops of myrrh—rare and very valuable), onycha (made from mollusk shells) and galbanum (a rubbery resin taken from the roots of a flowering plant that thrives in Syria and Persia).

25:7 *stones to be set.* See 28:17–20.

25:8 *sanctuary.* Lit. "holy place," "place set apart." See note on 3:5.

25:9 *tabernacle.* Lit. "dwelling place." The word is rarely used of human dwellings; it almost always signifies the place where God dwells among His people (see v. 8; 29:45–46; Lev 26:11; Ezek 37:27; cf. John 1:14; Rev 21:3). *pattern.* See note on v. 40.

25:10 *ark.* That is, "chest" (such was its form and function). The Hebrew for this word is translated by the more traditional term "ark" throughout the rest of Exodus (see also Deut 10:1–3); it is different from that used to refer to Noah's ark and to the reed basket in which the infant Moses was placed (see note on 2:3). Of all the tabernacle furnishings, the ark is mentioned first probably because it symbolized the throne of the Lord (see 1 Sam 4:4; 2 Sam 6:2), the great King, who chose to dwell among His people (see note on v. 9).

11 And thou shalt overlay it with pure gold,
within and without shalt thou overlay it, and
shalt make upon it a crown *of* gold round about.
12 And thou shalt cast four rings of gold for
it, and put *them* in the four corners thereof;
and two rings *shall be* in the one side of it, and
two rings in the other side of it.
13 And thou shalt make staves of shittim
wood, and overlay them with gold.
14 And thou shalt put the staves into the
rings by the sides of the ark, that the ark may
be borne with them.
15 [a]The staves shall be in the rings of the
ark: they shall not be taken from it.
16 And thou shalt put into the ark [a]the Testimony which I shall give thee.
17 And [a]thou shalt make a mercy seat *of*
pure gold: two cubits and a half *shall be* the
length thereof, and a cubit and a half the
breadth thereof.

25:15 [a]1 Ki. 8:8
25:16 [a]ch. 16:34; 31:18; Deut. 31:26; 1 Ki. 8:9; 2 Ki. 11:12; Heb. 9:4
25:17 [a]ch. 37:6; Rom. 3:25; Heb. 9:5
25:19 [1]Or, *of the matter of the mercy seat*
25:20 [a]1 Ki. 8:7; 1 Chr. 28:18; Heb. 9:5
25:21 [a]ch. 26:34 [b]ver. 16
25:22 [a]ch. 29:42,43 [b]Num. 7:89; 1 Sam. 4:4; 2 Sam. 6:2; 2 Ki. 19:15; Ps. 80:1; Is. 37:16

18 And thou shalt make two cherubims *of*
gold, *of* beaten work shalt thou make them, in
the two ends of the mercy seat.
19 And make one cherub on the one end,
and the other cherub on the other end: *even*
[1]of the mercy seat shall ye make the cherubims on the two ends thereof.
20 And [a]the cherubims shall stretch forth
their wings on high, covering the mercy seat
with their wings, and their faces *shall look* one
to another; toward the mercy seat shall the
faces of the cherubims be.
21 [a]And thou shalt put the mercy seat
above upon the ark; and [b]in the ark thou shalt
put the Testimony that I shall give thee.
22 And [a]there I will meet with thee, and I
will commune with thee from above the mercy seat, from [b]between the two cherubims
which *are* upon the ark of the Testimony, of all

25:11 *pure gold.* Uncontaminated by silver or other impurities.
25:12 *rings.* Lit. "houses," "housings," into which poles were inserted to carry the ark (see v. 14).
25:16 *Testimony.* The two tables on which were inscribed the ten commandments as the basic stipulations of the Sinai covenant (see 20:1–17; 31:18). The Hebrew word for "testimony" is related to a Babylonian word meaning "covenant stipulations." See also notes on v. 22; 16:34.
25:17 *mercy.* Or "atonement." It speaks of reconciliation, the divine act of grace whereby God draws to Himself and makes "at one" with Him those who were once alienated from Him. In the OT, the shed blood of sacrificial offerings effected atonement (see Lev 17:11 and note); in the NT, the blood of Jesus, shed once for all time, does the same (see Rom 3:25; 1 John 2:2). *mercy seat.* Or "atonement cover" (see note on Lev 16:2). That God's symbolic throne was capped with an atonement cover signified His great mercy toward His people—only such a God can be revered (see Ps 130:3–4).
25:18 *cherubims.* Probably similar to the carvings of winged sphinxes that adorned the armrests of royal thrones (see note on v. 10) in many parts of the ancient Near East (see also note on Gen 3:24). In the OT the cherubim were symbolic attendants that marked the place of the Lord's "enthronement" in His earthly kingdom (see 1 Sam 4:4; 2 Sam 6:2; 2 Ki 19:15; Ps 99:1). From the cover of the ark (God's symbolic throne) the Lord gave directions to Moses (see v. 22; Num 7:89). Later the ark's presence in the temple at Jerusalem would designate it as God's earthly royal city (see Ps 9:11; 18:10 and notes).
25:22 *I will meet with thee.* See note on 27:21. *ark of the Testimony.* Called this because it contained the Testimony (see note

Tabernacle Design: Only a Shadow

The tabernacle, which literally means "dwelling place" or "tent of meeting," was a symbol of God's presence with his people. God himself furnished the details of its pattern (Exodus 25—27), because it was "a copy and shadow of what is in heaven" (Hebrews 8:5). The book of Hebrews goes on to tell us that even God's law is only a shadow of the good things that God has in store for us (Hebrews 7; 10; see also Exodus 10:1). Jesus is the ultimate fulfillment of what God designed the tabernacle to be. The priests offered sacrifices continually, but Jesus' sacrifice is far superior because he offered the sacrifice in "heaven itself" (Hebrews 9:23–28).

TABERNACLE TYPES	DESCRIPTIONS OF JESUS	REFERENCE
One Entry	"I am the door"	John 10:9
Brasen Altar	"Behold the Lamb of God"	John 1:29
Laver for washing	"If I wash thee not"	John 13:8–10
Candlestick	"I am the light"	John 8:12
Shewbread	"I am that bread of life"	John 6:48
Incense	"I pray for them"	John 17:9
Vail	"Through the vail, that is to say, his flesh"	Hebrews 10:20
Mercy Seat	"Enter into the holiest by the blood of Jesus"	Hebrews 10:19
Glory of God	"We beheld his glory"	John 1:14

things which I will give thee in commandment unto the children of Israel.

The table

23 ¶ [a]Thou shalt also make a table *of* shittim wood: two cubits *shall be* the length thereof, and a cubit the breadth thereof, and a cubit and a half the height thereof.

24 And thou shalt overlay it with pure gold, and make thereto a crown *of* gold round about.

25 And thou shalt make unto it a border of a handbreadth round about, and thou shalt make a golden crown to the border thereof round about.

26 And thou shalt make for it four rings of gold, and put the rings in the four corners that *are* on the four feet thereof.

27 Over against the border shall the rings be for places of the staves to bear the table.

28 And thou shalt make the staves *of* shittim wood, and overlay them with gold, that the table may be borne with them.

29 And thou shalt make [a]the dishes thereof, and spoons thereof, and covers thereof, and bowls thereof, [1]to cover withal: *of* pure gold shalt thou make them.

30 And thou shalt set upon the table [a]shewbread before me alway.

The candlestick

31 ¶ [a]And thou shalt make a candlestick of pure gold: *of* beaten work shall the candlestick be made: his shaft, and his branches, his bowls, his knops, and his flowers, shall be of the same.

32 And six branches shall come out of the sides of it; three branches of the candlestick out of the one side, and three branches of the candlestick out of the other side:

33 [a]Three bowls made like unto almonds, *with* a knop and a flower in one branch; and three bowls made like almonds in the other branch, *with* a knop and a flower: so in the six branches that come out of the candlestick.

34 And [a]in the candlestick *shall be* four bowls made like unto almonds, *with* their knops and their flowers.

35 And *there shall be* a knop under two branches of the same, and a knop under two branches of the same, and a knop under two branches of the same, according to the six branches that proceed out of the candlestick.

36 Their knops and their branches shall be of the same: all it *shall be* one beaten work *of* pure gold.

37 And thou shalt make the seven lamps thereof: and [a]they shall [1]light the lamps thereof, that they may [b]give light over against [2]it.

38 And the tongs thereof, and the snuffdishes thereof, *shall be of* pure gold.

39 *Of* a talent of pure gold shall he make it, with all these vessels.

40 And [a]look that thou make *them* after their pattern, [1]which was shewed thee in the mount.

The tabernacle

26 Moreover [a]thou shalt make the tabernacle *with* ten curtains *of* fine twined linen, and blue, and purple, and scarlet: *with* cherubims [1]*of* cunning work shalt thou make them.

2 The length of one curtain *shall be* eight and twenty cubits, and the breadth of one curtain four cubits: *and* every one of the curtains shall have one measure.

3 The five curtains shall be coupled together one to another; and *other* five curtains *shall be* coupled one to another.

4 And thou shalt make loops of blue upon the edge of the one curtain from the selvedge in the coupling; and likewise shalt thou make

25:23 [a]ch. 37:10; 1 Ki. 7:48; 2 Chr. 4:8; Heb. 9:2
25:29 [1]Or, *to pour out withal* [a]ch. 37:16; Num. 4:7
25:30 [a]Lev. 24:5,6
25:31 [a]ch. 37:17; 1 Ki. 7:49; Zech. 4:2; Heb. 9:2; Rev. 1:12
25:33 [a]ch. 37:19
25:34 [a]ch. 37:20-22
25:37 [1]Or, *cause to ascend* [2]Heb. *the face of it* [a]ch. 27:21; 30:8; Lev. 24:3,4; 2 Chr. 13:11 [b]Num. 8:2
25:40 [1]Heb. *which thou* wast *caused to see* [a]ch. 26:30; Num. 8:4; 1 Chr. 28:11,19; Acts 7:44; Heb. 8:5
26:1 [1]Heb. *the work of a cunning workman,* or, *embroiderer* [a]ch. 36:8

on v. 16). The phrase "ark of the Testimony" is a synonym of the more familiar phrase "ark of the covenant" (see, e.g., Num 10:33).

25:23 *table.* The table taken from the second (Zerubbabel's) temple by Antiochus Epiphanes is depicted on the Arch of Titus among the items the Romans took back to Rome after conquering Jerusalem in A.D. 70.

25:26 *rings.* See note on v. 12.

25:30 *shewbread.* Lit. "bread of the presence." In this phrase, "presence" refers to the presence of God Himself (as in 33:14–15; Is 63:9). The bread (twelve loaves, one for each tribe) represented a perpetual bread offering to the Lord by which Israel declared that she consecrated to God the fruits of her labors, and by which she at the same time acknowledged that all such fruit had been hers only by God's blessing. See Lev 24:5–9.

25:31 *his bowls, his knops, and his flowers.* The design is patterned after an almond tree (see v. 33), the first of the trees in the Near East to blossom in spring. The cups of the candlestick resemble either the calyx (outer covering of the flower) or the almond nut.

25:37 *seven.* Signifying completeness. *lamps.* The ancient lamp was a small clay saucer with part of its rim pinched together to form a spout from which protruded the top of a wick fed by oil contained in the saucer. (Examples of seven-spouted lamps come from the time of Moses.) The ruins of Beth Shan and Megiddo have yielded examples of a metal pedestal topped by a ledge designed to carry a lamp. The classic representation of the shape of the tabernacle candlestick comes from the time of Herod the Great and may be seen on the Arch of Titus in Rome. The lamps were to burn all night in the tabernacle, tended by the priests. Oil for the lamps was to be supplied by the people; the light from the lamps represented the glory of the Lord reflected in the consecrated lives of the Israelites—Israel's glory answering to God's glory in the tabernacle (29:43). See 27:20–21.

25:40 Quoted in Heb 8:5 in order to contrast the "shadow" (the trappings of the old covenant) with the reality (the Christ of the new covenant). See also Heb 10:1.

26:1 *tabernacle.* See note on 25:9. Its basic structure was to be 15 feet wide by 45 feet long by 15 feet high. Over an inner lining of embroidered linen (vv. 1–6), it was to have a covering woven of goat hair (vv. 7–13) and two additional coverings of leather, one made from ram skins dyed red and one from the hides of porpoises ("badgers' skins," v. 14). Internally, the ceiling was probably flat, but whether the leather coverings had a ridge line with sloping sides (like a tent) is not known. Symbolically the tabernacle represented God's royal tent. *fine twined linen, and blue, and purple, and scarlet.* See note on 25:4. *cherubims.* Signifying a royal chamber (see 25:18 and note).

in the uttermost edge of *another* curtain, in the coupling of the second.

5 Fifty loops shalt thou make in the one curtain, and fifty loops shalt thou make in the edge of the curtain that *is* in the coupling of the second; that the loops may take hold one of another.

6 And thou shalt make fifty taches of gold, and couple the curtains together with the taches: and it shall be one tabernacle.

7 ¶ And [a]thou shalt make curtains *of* goats' *hair* to be a covering upon the tabernacle: eleven curtains shalt thou make.

8 The length of one curtain *shall be* thirty cubits, and the breadth of one curtain four cubits: *and* the eleven curtains *shall be all* of one measure.

9 And thou shalt couple five curtains by themselves, and six curtains by themselves, and shalt double the sixth curtain in the forefront of the tabernacle.

10 And thou shalt make fifty loops on the edge of the one curtain *that is* outmost in the coupling, and fifty loops in the edge of the curtain which coupleth the second.

26:7 [a]ch. 36:14
26:11 [1]Or, *covering*
26:13 [1]Heb. *in the remainder*, or, *surplusage*
26:14 [a]ch. 36:19
26:17 [1]Heb. *hands*

11 And thou shalt make fifty taches of brass, and put the taches into the loops, and couple the [1]tent together, that it may be one.

12 And the remnant that remaineth of the curtains of the tent, the half curtain that remaineth, shall hang over the backside of the tabernacle.

13 And a cubit on the one side, and a cubit on the other side [1]of that which remaineth in the length of the curtains of the tent, it shall hang over the sides of the tabernacle on this side and on that side, to cover it.

14 And [a]thou shalt make a covering for the tent *of* rams' skins dyed red, and a covering above of badgers' skins.

15 ¶ And thou shalt make boards for the tabernacle *of* shittim wood standing up.

16 Ten cubits *shall be* the length of a board, and a cubit and a half *shall be* the breadth of one board.

17 Two [1]tenons *shall there be* in one board, set in order one against another: thus shalt thou make for all the boards of the tabernacle.

18 And thou shalt make the boards for the

26:7 *goats' hair.* See note on 25:4.
26:14 *rams' skins dyed red . . . badgers' skins.* See note on 25:5.
26:17 *tenons.* Lit. "hands"; probably the two at the bottom of each frame that were inserted into its two bases (see v. 19).

The Tabernacle

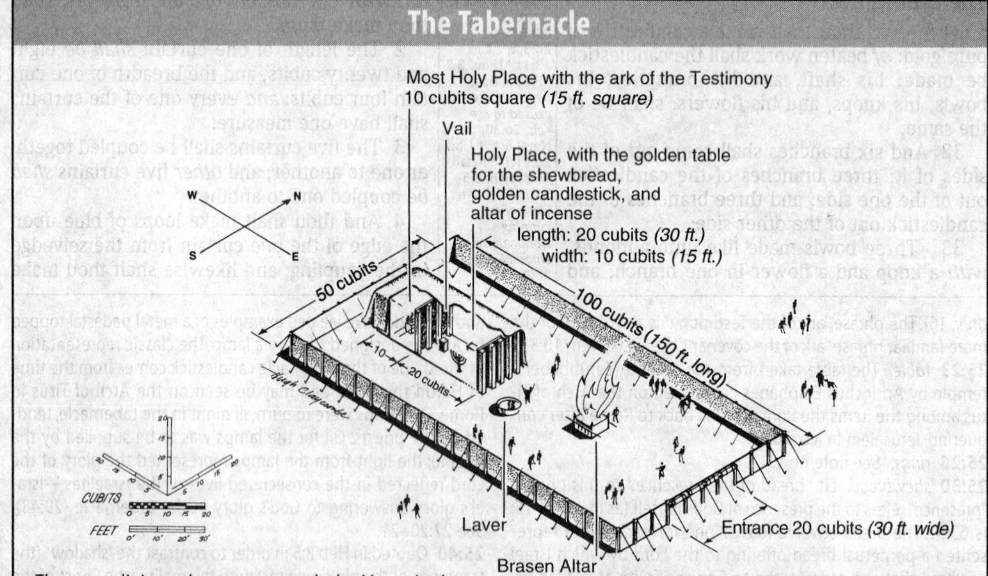

The new religious observances taught by Moses in the wilderness centered on rituals connected with the tabernacle, and amplified Israel's sense of separateness, purity and oneness under the Lordship of Yahweh.

A few wilderness shrines have been found in Sinai, notably at Serabit el-Khadem and at Timnah in the Negev, and show marked Egyptian influence.

Specific cultural antecedents to portable shrines carried on poles and covered with thin sheets of gold can be found in ancient Egypt as early as the Old Kingdom (2800-2250 B.C.), but were especially prominent in the 18th and 19th dynasties (1570-1180). The best examples come from the fabulous tomb of Tutankhamun, c. 1350.

Comparisons of construction details in the text of Ex 25-40 with the frames, shrines, poles, sheathing, draped fabric covers, gilt rosettes, and winged protective figures from the shrine of Tutankhamun are instructive. The period, the Late Bronze Age, is equivalent in all dating systems to the era of Moses and the exodus.

tabernacle, twenty boards on the south side southward.

19 And thou shalt make forty sockets of silver under the twenty boards; two sockets under one board for his two tenons, and two sockets under another board for his two tenons.

20 And for the second side of the tabernacle on the north side *there shall be* twenty boards:

21 And their forty sockets *of* silver; two sockets under one board, and two sockets under another board.

22 And for the sides of the tabernacle westward thou shalt make six boards.

23 And two boards shalt thou make for the corners of the tabernacle in the two sides.

24 And they shall be [1]coupled together beneath, and they shall be [1]coupled together above the head of it unto one ring: thus shall it be for them both; they shall be for the two corners.

25 And they shall be eight boards, and their sockets *of* silver, sixteen sockets; two sockets under one board, and two sockets under another board.

26 And thou shalt make bars *of* shittim wood; five for the boards of the one side of the tabernacle,

27 And five bars for the boards of the other side of the tabernacle, and five bars for the boards of the side of the tabernacle, for the two sides westward.

28 And the middle bar in the midst of the boards shall reach from end to end.

29 And thou shalt overlay the boards with gold, and make their rings *of* gold *for* places for the bars: and thou shalt overlay the bars with gold.

30 And thou shalt rear up the tabernacle [a]according to the fashion thereof which was shewed thee in the mount.

31 ¶ And [a]thou shalt make a vail *of* blue, and purple, and scarlet, and fine twined linen *of* cunning work: *with* cherubims shall it be made:

26:24 [1]Heb. *twinned*

26:30 [a]ch. 25:9,40; 27:8; Acts 7:44; Heb. 8:5

26:31 [a]ch. 36:35; Lev. 16:2; 2 Chr. 3:14; Mat. 27:51; Heb. 9:3

26:19 *forty sockets of silver.* These plus the 40 in v. 21, the 16 in v. 25 and the 4 in v. 32 make up a grand total of 100, the number of talents of silver obtained from the Israelite community to be used to cast the bases ("sockets"). See 38:27.

26:23 *corners.* Or "angles," perhaps referring to mitered joints at the corners.

26:26 *bars.* To strengthen the frames on the north, south and west sides.

26:29 *rings.* Lit. "houses," "housings" (see note on 25:12).

26:30 *fashion* [i.e., plan]. See note on 25:40.

26:31–35 A vail was to divide the tabernacle into two rooms, the holy place and the most holy place, with the former twice

Tabernacle Furnishings

The symbolism of God's redemptive covenant was preserved in the tabernacle, making each element an object lesson for the worshiper. The Levitical priests, including some with Egyptian names and perhaps Egyptian training, gave meticulous attention to facts about the shrine. Reconstruction of the furnishings is possible because of extremely detailed descriptions and precise measurements recorded in Exodus 25–40.

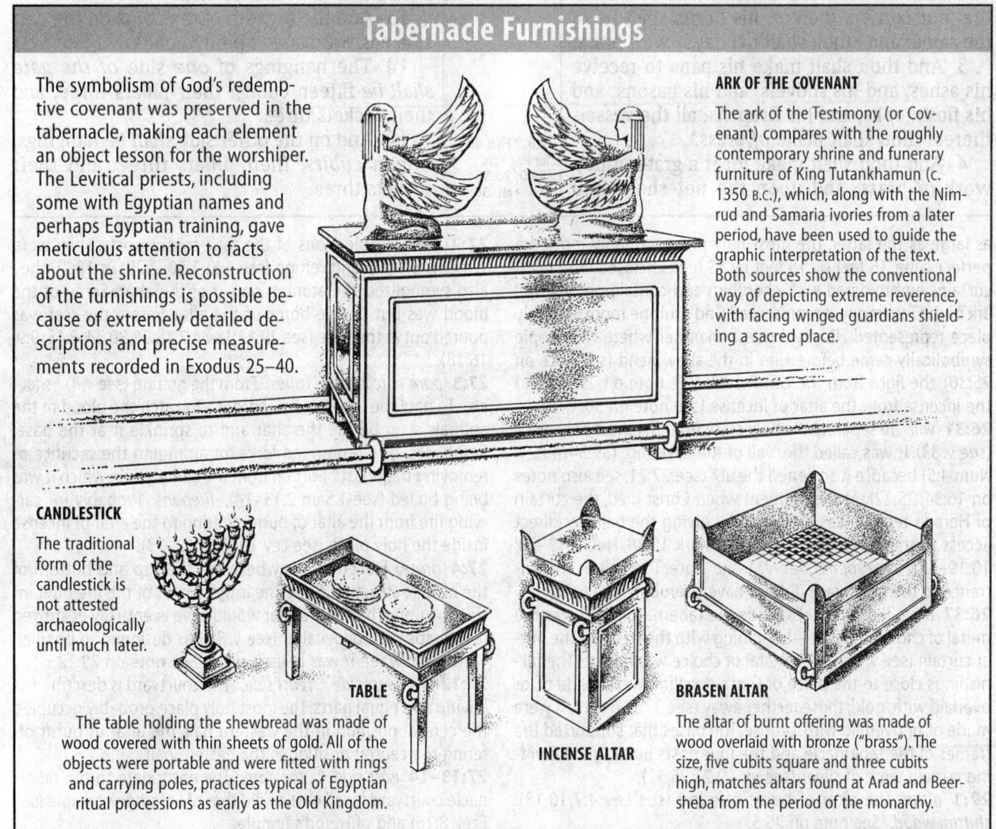

ARK OF THE COVENANT

The ark of the Testimony (or Covenant) compares with the roughly contemporary shrine and funerary furniture of King Tutankhamun (c. 1350 B.C.), which, along with the Nimrud and Samaria ivories from a later period, have been used to guide the graphic interpretation of the text. Both sources show the conventional way of depicting extreme reverence, with facing winged guardians shielding a sacred place.

CANDLESTICK

The traditional form of the candlestick is not attested archaeologically until much later.

TABLE

The table holding the shewbread was made of wood covered with thin sheets of gold. All of the objects were portable and were fitted with rings and carrying poles, practices typical of Egyptian ritual processions as early as the Old Kingdom.

INCENSE ALTAR

BRASEN ALTAR

The altar of burnt offering was made of wood overlaid with bronze ("brass"). The size, five cubits square and three cubits high, matches altars found at Arad and Beersheba from the period of the monarchy.

32 And thou shalt hang it upon four pillars
of shittim *wood* overlaid with gold: their
hooks *shall be of* gold, upon the four sockets of
silver.
33 And thou shalt hang up the vail under
the taches, that thou mayest bring in thither
within the vail [a]the ark of the Testimony: and
the vail shall divide unto you between [b]the
holy *place* and the most holy.
34 And [a]thou shalt put the mercy seat upon
the ark of the Testimony in the most holy *place.*
35 And [a]thou shalt set the table without
the vail, and [b]the candlestick over against the
table on the side of the tabernacle toward the
south: and thou shalt put the table on the
north side.
36 And [a]thou shalt make a hanging for the
door of the tent, *of* blue, and purple, and scarlet, and fine twined linen, wrought with
needlework.
37 And thou shalt make for the hanging
[a]five pillars of shittim *wood,* and overlay them
with gold, *and* their hooks *shall be of* gold: and
thou shalt cast five sockets of brass for them.

The altar

27 And thou shalt make [a]an altar *of*
shittim wood, five cubits long, and
five cubits broad; the altar shall be foursquare:
and the height thereof *shall be* three cubits.
2 And thou shalt make the horns of it upon
the four corners thereof: his horns shall be of
the same: and [a]thou shalt overlay it with brass.
3 And thou shalt make his pans to receive
his ashes, and his shovels, and his basons, and
his fleshhooks, and his firepans: all the vessels
thereof thou shalt make *of* brass.
4 And thou shalt make for it a grate of network *of* brass; and upon the net shalt thou
make four brasen rings in the four corners
thereof.
5 And thou shalt put it under the compass
of the altar beneath, that the net may be even
to the midst of the altar.
6 And thou shalt make staves for the altar,
staves of shittim wood, and overlay them with
brass.
7 And the staves shall be put into the rings,
and the staves shall be upon the two sides of
the altar, to bear it.
8 Hollow with boards shalt thou make it:
[a]as [1]it was shewed thee in the mount, so shall
they make *it.*

The court of the tabernacle

9 ¶ And [a]thou shalt make the court of the
tabernacle: for the south side southward *there
shall be* hangings for the court *of* fine twined
linen of an hundred cubits long for one side:
10 And the twenty pillars thereof and their
twenty sockets *shall be of* brass; the hooks of
the pillars and their fillets *shall be of* silver.
11 And likewise for the north side in
length *there shall be* hangings of an hundred
cubits long, and his twenty pillars and their
twenty sockets *of* brass; the hooks of the pillars and their fillets *of* silver.
12 And *for* the breadth of the court on the
west side *shall be* hangings of fifty cubits: their
pillars ten, and their sockets ten.
13 And the breadth of the court on the east
side eastward *shall be* fifty cubits.
14 The hangings of *one* side *of the gate
shall be* fifteen cubits: their pillars three, and
their sockets three.
15 And on the other side *shall be* hangings,
fifteen *cubits:* their pillars three, and their
sockets three.

26:33 [a]ch. 25:16; 40:21 [b]Lev. 16:2; Heb. 9:2,3
26:34 [a]ch. 25:21; 40:20; Heb. 9:5
26:35 [a]ch. 40:22; Heb. 9:2 [b]ch. 40:24
26:36 [a]ch. 36:37
26:37 [a]ch. 36:38
27:1 [a]ch. 38:1; Ezek. 43:13
27:2 [a]See Num. 16:38
27:8 [1]Heb. *he shewed* [a]ch. 25:40; 26:30
27:9 [a]ch. 38:9

as large as the latter. The most holy place probably formed a perfect cube, 15 feet by 15 feet by 15 feet. Enclosed with linen curtains embroidered with cherubim and containing only the ark of the Testimony, it represented God's throne room. The holy place represented His royal guest chamber where His people symbolically came before Him in the shewbread (see note on 25:30), the light from the candlestick (see note on 25:37) and the incense from the altar of incense (see note on 30:1).

26:31 *vail.* To separate the holy place from the most holy place (see v. 33). It was called the "vail of the covering" (39:34; 40:21; Num 4:5) because it screened the ark (see 27:21; see also notes on 16:34; 25:22). At the moment when Christ died, the curtain of Herod's temple was torn, thereby giving the believer direct access to the presence of God (see Mark 15:38; Heb 6:19–20; 10:19–22). *cherubims.* See v. 1 and note. The vail at the entrance to the holy place did not have cherubim (see v. 36).

26:37 *brass* [i.e., bronze]. Inside the tabernacle, gold was the metal of choice; outside—beginning with the bases of the outer curtain (see v. 36)—the metal of choice was bronze. The furnishings close to the place of God's dwelling were made of, or overlaid with, gold; those farther away (see 27:2–6; 30:18) were made of, or overlaid with, bronze. The bases that supported the frames of the tabernacle and the four posts holding the dividing curtain were of silver (see vv. 19,21,25,32).

27:1 *altar.* The altar of burnt offering (see Lev 4:7,10,18). *shittim wood.* See note on 25:5.

27:2 *horns.* Projections of the four corner posts. They were symbols of help and refuge (see 1 Ki 1:50; 2:28; Ps 18:2). They also symbolized the atoning power of the altar: Some of the blood was put on the horns of the altar before the rest was poured out at the base (see 29:12; Lev 4:7,18,25,30,34; 8:15; 9:9; 16:18).

27:3 *pans to receive his ashes.* From the grating (see v. 4). *shovels.* To haul the ashes away. *basons.* To catch the blood of the animals slain beside the altar and to sprinkle it at the base. *fleshhooks.* Three-pronged forks for arranging the sacrifice or removing the priests' portion from the container in which it was being boiled (see 1 Sam 2:13–14). *firepans.* Probably for carrying fire from the altar of burnt offering to the altar of incense inside the holy place (see Lev 10:1; 16:12–13).

27:4 *grate.* Placed midway between the top and bottom of the boxlike structure. Since the intense heat of the fire built inside the upper half of the altar would have eventually destroyed it, perhaps the hollow altar (see v. 8) was designed to be filled with earth when it was in use. *rings.* See note on 25:12.

27:12–13 *west side . . . east side.* The courtyard is described as having two equal parts. The most holy place probably occupied the central position in the western half, the altar of burnt offering the central position in the eastern half.

27:13–14 *east side . . . the gate.* The entry gate to the tabernacle courtyard faced east, as did that of Solomon's temple (see Ezek 8:16) and of Herod's temple.

16 And for the gate of the court *shall be* a hanging of twenty cubits, *of* blue, and purple, and scarlet, and fine twined linen, wrought with needlework: *and* their pillars *shall be* four, and their sockets four.

17 All the pillars round about the court *shall be* filleted *with* silver; their hooks *shall be of* silver, and their sockets *of* brass.

18 The length of the court *shall be* an hundred cubits, and the breadth [1]fifty every where, and the height five cubits *of* fine twined linen, and their sockets *of* brass.

19 All the vessels of the tabernacle in all the service thereof, and all the pins thereof, and all the pins of the court, *shall be of* brass.

Oil for the lamp

20 ¶ And [a]thou shalt command the children of Israel, that they bring thee pure oil olive beaten for the light, to cause the lamp [1]to burn always.

21 In the tabernacle of the congregation [a]without the vail, which *is* before the Testimony, [b]Aaron and his sons shall order it from evening to morning before the LORD: [c]*it shall be* a statute for ever unto their generations on the behalf of the children of Israel.

The priest's garments

28 And take thou unto thee [a]Aaron thy brother, and his sons with him, from among the children of Israel, that he may minister unto me in the priest's office, *even* Aaron, Nadab and Abihu, Eleazar and Ithamar, Aaron's sons.

2 And [a]thou shalt make holy garments for Aaron thy brother, for glory and for beauty.

3 And [a]thou shalt speak unto all *that are* wise hearted, [b]whom I have filled with the spirit of wisdom, that they may make Aaron's garments to consecrate him, that he may minister unto me in the priest's office.

4 And these *are* the garments which they shall make; [a]a breastplate, and [b]an ephod, and [c]a robe, and [d]a broidered coat, a mitre, and a girdle: and they shall make holy garments for Aaron thy brother, and his sons, that he may minister unto me in the priest's office.

5 And they shall take gold, and blue, and purple, and scarlet, and fine linen.

6 ¶ [a]And they shall make the ephod *of* gold, *of* blue, and *of* purple, *of* scarlet, and fine twined linen, *with* cunning work.

7 It shall have the two shoulderpieces *thereof* joined at the two edges thereof; and *so* it shall be joined together.

8 And the [1]curious girdle of the ephod, which *is* upon it, shall be of the same, according to the work thereof; *even of* gold, *of* blue, and purple, and scarlet, and fine twined linen.

9 And thou shalt take two onyx stones, and grave on them the names of the children of Israel:

10 Six of their names on one stone, and the *other* six names of the rest on the other stone, according to their birth.

11 *With* the work of an engraver in stone, *like* the engravings of a signet, shalt thou engrave the two stones with the names of the children of Israel: thou shalt make them to be set *in* ouches *of* gold.

12 And thou shalt put the two stones upon the shoulders of the ephod *for* stones of memorial unto the children of Israel: and [a]Aaron shall bear their names before the LORD upon his two shoulders [b]for a memorial.

13 And thou shalt make ouches *of* gold;

14 And two chains *of* pure gold at the ends; *of* wreathen work shalt thou make them, and fasten the wreathen chains to the ouches.

The priest's breastplate

15 ¶ And [a]thou shalt make the breastplate of judgment *with* cunning work; after the work of the ephod thou shalt make it; *of* gold, *of* blue, and *of* purple, and *of* scarlet, and *of* fine twined linen, shalt thou make it.

16 Foursquare it shall be *being* doubled; a span *shall be* the length thereof, and a span *shall be* the breadth thereof.

17 [a]And thou shalt [1]set in it settings of stones, *even* four rows of stones: *the first* row

27:18 [1]Heb. *fifty by fifty* 27:20 [1]Heb. *to ascend up* [a]Lev. 24:2 27:21 [a]ch. 26:31,33 [b]ch. 30:8; 1 Sam. 3:3; 2 Chr. 13:11 [c]ch. 28:43; 29:9,28; Lev. 3:17; 16:34; Num. 18:23; 19:21 28:1 [a]Num. 18:7; Heb. 5:1,4 28:2 [a]ch. 29:5,29; 31:10; 39:1,2; Lev. 8:7,30; Num. 20:26,28 28:3 [a]ch. 31:6; 36:1 [b]ch. 31:3; 35:30,31 28:4 [a]ver. 15 [b]ver. 6 [c]ver. 31 [d]ver. 39

28:6 [a]ch. 39:2 28:8 [1]Or, *embroidered* 28:12 [a]ver. 29; ch. 39:7 [b]See Josh. 4:7; Zech. 6:14 28:15 [a]ch. 39:8 28:17 [1]Heb. *fill in it fillings of stone* [a]ch. 39:10

27:18 *five cubits.* Five cubits equaled about seven and a half feet, high enough to block the view of people standing outside the courtyard, thus protecting the sanctity and privacy of the worship taking place inside.

27:20 *pure oil olive beaten.* Unripe olives were crushed in a mortar. The pulpy mass was then placed in a cloth basket through the bottom of which the oil dripped, producing a clear fuel that burned with little or no smoke.

27:21 *tabernacle of the congregation.* The tabernacle was not a place where God's people met for collective worship but one where God Himself met—by appointment, not by accident—with His people (see 29:42–43). *vail, which is before the Testimony.* See note on 26:31. *order it from evening to morning.* The lamps were lit in the evening (see 30:8) and apparently extinguished in the morning (1 Sam 3:3).

28:1 *his sons . . . Nadab and Abihu.* See note on 24:1. *minister unto me in the priest's office.* In order to "offer both gifts and sacrifices for sins" and to "have compassion on the ignorant, and on them that are out of the way" (Heb 5:1–2). Another important function of the priests was to read the law of Moses to the people and remind them of their covenant obligations (see Deut 31:9–13; Neh 8:2–3).

28:2 *for glory and for beauty.* The garments were to exalt the office and functions of lesser priests (see v. 40) as well as of the high priest.

28:6 *ephod.* A sleeveless vestment worn by the high priest. Sometimes the word refers to an otherwise unidentified object of worship (see, e.g., Judg 8:27; 18:17; Hos 3:4).

28:8 *girdle.* Apparently to hold the front and the back of the ephod to the priest's body.

28:12 *Aaron shall bear their names . . . upon his two shoulders.* To symbolize the fact that the high priest represents all Israel when he ministers in the tabernacle.

28:15 *of judgment.* By means of the Urim and Thummim (see note on v. 30).

shall be a [2]sardius, a topaz, and a carbuncle: this *shall be* the first row.

18 And the second row *shall be* an emerald, a sapphire, and a diamond.

19 And the third row a ligure, an agate, and an amethyst.

20 And the fourth row a beryl, and an onyx, and a jasper: they shall be set in gold in their [1]inclosings.

21 And the stones shall be with the names of the children of Israel, twelve, according to their names, *like* the engravings of a signet; every one with his name shall they be according to the twelve tribes.

22 And thou shalt make upon the breastplate chains at the ends *of* wreathen work *of* pure gold.

23 And thou shalt make upon the breastplate two rings of gold, and shalt put the two rings on the two ends of the breastplate.

24 And thou shalt put the two wreathen *chains of* gold in the two rings *which are* on the ends of the breastplate.

25 And *the other* two ends of the two wreathen *chains* thou shalt fasten in the two ouches, and put *them* on the shoulderpieces of the ephod before it.

26 And thou shalt make two rings of gold, and thou shalt put them upon the two ends of the breastplate in the border thereof, which *is* in the side of the ephod inward.

27 And two *other* rings of gold thou shalt make, and shalt put them on the two sides of the ephod underneath, towards the forepart thereof, over against *the other* coupling thereof, above the curious girdle of the ephod.

28 And they shall bind the breastplate by the rings thereof unto the rings of the ephod with a lace of blue, that *it* may be above the curious girdle of the ephod, and that the breastplate be not loosed from the ephod.

29 And Aaron shall bear the names of the children of Israel in the breastplate of judgment upon his heart, when he goeth in unto the holy *place,* [a]for a memorial before the LORD continually.

30 And [a]thou shalt put in the breastplate of judgment the Urim and the Thummim; and they shall be upon Aaron's heart, when he goeth in before the LORD: and Aaron shall bear the judgment of the children of Israel upon his heart before the LORD continually.

28:17 [2]Or, *ruby*
28:20 [1]Heb. *fillings*
28:29 [a]ver. 12
28:30 [a]Lev. 8:8; Num. 27:21; Deut. 33:8; 1 Sam. 28:6; Ezra 2:63; Neh. 7:65

The priest's robe

31 ¶ And [a]thou shalt make the robe of the ephod all of blue.

32 And there shall be a hole in the top of it, in the midst thereof: it shall have a binding of woven work round about the hole of it, as it were the hole of an habergeon, *that* it be not rent.

33 And *beneath* upon the [1]hem of it thou shalt make pomegranates of blue, and of purple, and of scarlet, round about the hem thereof; and bells of gold between them round about:

34 A golden bell and a pomegranate, a golden bell and a pomegranate, upon the hem of the robe round about.

35 And it shall be upon Aaron to minister: and his sound shall be heard when he goeth in unto the holy *place* before the LORD, and when he cometh out, that he die not.

36 And [a]thou shalt make a plate *of* pure gold, and grave upon it, *like* the engravings of a signet, HOLINESS TO THE LORD.

37 And thou shalt put it on a blue lace, that it may be upon the mitre; upon the forefront of the mitre it shall be.

38 And it shall be upon Aaron's forehead, that Aaron may [a]bear the iniquity of the holy *things,* which the children of Israel shall hallow in all their holy gifts; and it shall be always upon his forehead, that they may be [b]accepted before the LORD.

39 ¶ And thou shalt embroider the coat of fine linen, and thou shalt make the mitre *of* fine linen, and thou shalt make the girdle *of* needlework.

40 [a]And for Aaron's sons thou shalt make coats, and thou shalt make for them girdles, and bonnets shalt thou make for them, for glory and for beauty.

41 And thou shalt put them upon Aaron thy brother, and his sons with him; and shalt [a]anoint them, and [b][1]consecrate them, and sanctify them, that they may minister unto me in the priest's office.

42 And thou shalt make them [a]linen breeches to cover [1]*their* nakedness; from the loins even unto the thighs they shall [2]reach:

43 And they shall be upon Aaron, and upon his sons, when they come in unto the tabernacle of the congregation, or when they come near [a]unto the altar to minister in the

28:31 [a]ch. 39:22
28:33 [1]Or, *skirts*
28:36 [a]ch. 39:30; Zech. 14:20
28:38 [a]ver. 43; Lev. 10:17; 22:9; Num. 18:1; Is. 53:11; Ezek. 4:4-6; John 1:29; Heb. 9:28; 1 Pet. 2:24 [b]Lev. 1:4; 22:27; Is. 56:7
28:40 [a]ver. 4; ch. 39:27-29,41; Ezek. 44:17,18
28:41 [1]Heb. *fill their hand* [a]ch. 29:7; 30:30; 40:15; Lev. 10:7 [b]ch. 29:9; Lev. 8; Heb. 7:28
28:42 [1]Heb. *flesh of* their *nakedness* [2]Heb. *be* [a]ch. 39:28; Lev. 6:10; 16:4; Ezek. 44:18
28:43 [a]ch. 20:26

28:29 *Aaron shall bear the names . . . upon his heart.* Thus the nation was doubly represented before the Lord (see v. 12 and note).

28:30 *the Urim and the Thummim.* The Hebrew for this phrase probably means "the lights [or possibly 'curses'] and the perfections." The Hebrew word *Urim* begins with the first letter of the Hebrew alphabet (*aleph*) and *Thummim* begins with the last letter (*taw*). They were sacred lots and were often used in times of crisis to determine the will of God (see Num 27:21). It has been suggested that if Urim (or "lights") dominated when the lots were cast the answer was "no," but if Thummim (or "perfections") dominated it was "yes." In any event, "the whole disposing" was "of the LORD" (Prov 16:33).

28:31 *robe.* Worn under the ephod.

28:35 According to Jewish tradition, one end of a length of rope was tied to the high priest's ankle and the other end remained outside the tabernacle. If the bells on his robe stopped tinkling while he was in the holy place, the assumption that he had died could be tested by pulling gently on the rope.

28:38 *bear the iniquity.* Symbolically.

28:39 *coat.* Worn under the robe.

28:40 *for glory and for beauty.* See note on v. 2.

28:42–43 See note on 20:26.

28:43 *tabernacle of the congregation.* See note on 27:21.

holy *place;* that they [b]bear not iniquity, and die: [c]*it shall be* a statute for ever unto him and his seed after him.

Consecrating the priests

29 And this *is* the thing that thou shalt do unto them to hallow them, to minister unto me in the priest's office: [a]Take one young bullock, and two rams without blemish,

2 And [a]unleavened bread, and cakes unleavened tempered with oil, and wafers unleavened anointed with oil: *of* wheaten flour shalt thou make them.

3 And thou shalt put them into one basket, and bring them in the basket, with the bullock and the two rams.

4 And Aaron and his sons thou shalt bring unto the door of the tabernacle of the congregation, [a]and shalt wash them with water.

5 [a]And thou shalt take the garments, and put upon Aaron the coat, and the robe of the ephod, and the ephod, and the breastplate, and gird him with [b]the curious girdle of the ephod:

6 [a]And thou shalt put the mitre upon his head, and put the holy crown upon the mitre.

7 Then shalt thou take the anointing [a]oil, and pour *it* upon his head, and anoint him.

8 And [a]thou shalt bring his sons, and put coats upon them.

9 And thou shalt gird them *with* girdles, Aaron and his sons, and [1]put the bonnets on them: and [a]the priest's office shall be theirs for a perpetual statute: and thou shalt [b][2]consecrate Aaron and his sons.

10 And thou shalt cause a bullock to be brought before the tabernacle of the congregation: and [a]Aaron and his sons shall put their hands upon the head of the bullock.

11 And thou shalt kill the bullock before the LORD, *by* the door of the tabernacle of the congregation.

12 And thou [a]shalt take of the blood of the bullock, and put *it* upon [b]the horns of the altar with thy finger, and pour all the blood beside the bottom of the altar.

13 And [a]thou shalt take all the fat that covereth the inwards, and [1]the caul *that is* above the liver, and the two kidneys, and the fat that *is* upon them, and burn *them* upon the altar.

14 But [a]the flesh of the bullock, and his

28:43 [b]Lev. 5:1,17; 20:19,20; 22:9; Num. 9:13; 18:22 [c]ch. 27:21; Lev. 17:7
29:1 [a]Lev. 8:2
29:2 [a]Lev. 2:4; 6:20-22
29:4 [a]ch. 40:12; Lev. 8:6; Heb. 10:22
29:5 [a]ch. 28:2; Lev. 8:7 [b]ch. 28:8
29:6 [a]Lev. 8:9
29:7 [a]ch. 30:25; Lev. 8:12; 10:7; 21:10; Num. 35:25
29:8 [a]Lev. 8:13
29:9 [1]Heb. *bind* [2]Heb. *fill the hand of* [a]Num. 18:7 [b]ch. 28:41; Lev. 8:22; Heb. 7:28
29:10 [a]Lev. 1:4; 8:14
29:12 [a]Lev. 8:15 [b]ch. 27:2
29:13 [1]It seemeth by Anatomy, and the Hebrew Doctors, to be *the midriff* [a]Lev. 3:3
29:14 [a]Lev. 4:11,12,21; Heb. 13:11

29:1 *hallow them.* See note on 19:10–11. *without blemish.* See note on 12:5.
29:4 *tabernacle of the congregation.* See note on 27:21. *wash them with water.* Symbolizing the removal of ceremonial uncleanness (cf. Heb 10:22) and thus signifying the purity that must characterize them.
29:7 *anoint him.* Symbolizing spiritual enduement for serving God (see Is 61:1).
29:10 *cause a bullock to be brought.* As a sin offering (see v. 14) to atone for the past sins of Aaron and his sons (see Lev 4:3). *put their hands upon the head of the bullock.* As a symbol of (1) the animal's becoming their substitute and (2) transferring their sins to the sin-bearer (see Lev 16:20–22 and note).
29:12 *horns of the altar.* See note on 27:2.
29:13 *fat.* The most select parts of the bull (see Lev 3:3–5,16) were burned on the altar as a sacrifice to the Lord.

The Messiah: Our Priest For Ever

The system of animal sacrifices and the functions of the Old Testament priesthood were intended to be in effect for only a period of time (Exodus 29). The sacrificial system was never intended to remove the people's sins but only to cover sin until God's promised Messiah would come to accomplish once and for all what the Old Testament system could not. The priests were ordinary men with human flaws, men who, like ourselves, needed to be rescued from the effects of sin. At best they could only represent what Jesus would later do perfectly. Jesus is called "a high priest for ever, after the order of Melchisedec" (Hebrews 6:20). Melchisedec was introduced as the "priest of the most high God" before Levi's family line had been chosen for the priesthood (Genesis 14:18–20). In the same way, Jesus is our priest—even though he is from the family of Judah—because God specifically chose him. The book of Hebrews explains how Jesus' priesthood takes the place of the Levitical priesthood (Hebrews 7:17–19).

LEVI'S PRIESTHOOD	JESUS AS OUR PRIEST	HEBREWS
Temporary	Eternal	7:21–23
Fallible	Sinless	7:26
Changeable	Unchanging	7:24
Continual	Permanent	9:12,26
Imperfect	Perfect	2:14–18
Incomplete	Complete	7:25
Insufficient	All-sufficient	10:11–12

skin, and his dung, shalt thou burn with fire without the camp: it *is* a sin offering.

15 [a]Thou shalt also take one ram; and Aaron and his sons shall [b]put their hands upon the head of the ram.

16 And thou shalt slay the ram, and thou shalt take his blood, and sprinkle *it* round about upon the altar.

17 And thou shalt cut the ram in pieces, and wash the inwards of him, and his legs, and put *them* [1]unto his pieces, and [1]unto his head.

18 And thou shalt burn the whole ram upon the altar: it *is* a burnt offering unto the LORD: it *is* a [a]sweet savour, an offering made by fire unto the LORD.

19 [a]And thou shalt take the other ram; and Aaron and his sons shall put their hands upon the head of the ram.

20 Then shalt thou kill the ram, and take of his blood, and put *it* upon the tip of the *right* ear of Aaron, and upon the tip of the right ear of his sons, and upon the thumb of their right hand, and upon the great toe of their right foot, and sprinkle the blood upon the altar round about.

21 And thou shalt take of the blood that *is* upon the altar, and of [a]the anointing oil, and sprinkle *it* upon Aaron, and upon his garments, and upon his sons, and upon the garments of his sons with him: and [b]he shall be hallowed, and his garments, and his sons, and his sons' garments with him.

22 Also thou shalt take of the ram the fat and the rump, and the fat that covereth the inwards, and the caul *above* the liver, and the two kidneys, and the fat that *is* upon them, and the right shoulder; for it *is* a ram of consecration:

23 [a]And one loaf of bread, and one cake of oiled bread, and one wafer out of the basket of the unleavened bread that *is* before the LORD:

24 And thou shalt put all in the hands of Aaron, and in the hands of his sons; and shalt [a][1]wave them *for* a wave offering before the LORD.

25 [a]And thou shalt receive them of their hands, and burn *them* upon the altar for a burnt offering, for a sweet savour before the LORD: it *is* an offering made by fire unto the LORD.

26 And thou shalt take [a]the breast of the ram of Aaron's consecrations, and wave it *for* a wave offering before the LORD: and [b]it shall be thy part.

27 And thou shalt sanctify [a]the breast of the wave offering, and the shoulder of the heave offering, which is waved, and which is heaved up, of the ram of the consecration, *even* of *that* which *is* for Aaron, and of *that* which *is* for his sons:

28 And it shall be Aaron's and his sons' [a]by a statute for ever from the children of Israel: for it *is* a heave offering: and [b]it shall be a heave offering from the children of Israel of the sacrifice of their peace offerings, *even* their heave offering unto the LORD.

29 And the holy garments of Aaron [a]shall be his sons' after him, [b]to be anointed therein, and to be consecrated in them.

30 *And* [a][1]that son that is priest in his stead shall put them on [b]seven days, when he cometh into the tabernacle of the congregation to minister in the holy *place.*

31 And thou shalt take the ram of the consecration, and [a]seethe his flesh in the holy place.

32 And Aaron and his sons shall eat the flesh of the ram, and the [a]bread that *is* in the basket, *by* the door of the tabernacle of the congregation.

33 And [a]they shall eat those *things* wherewith the atonement was made, to consecrate *and* to sanctify them: [b]but a stranger shall not eat *thereof,* because they *are* holy.

34 And if *ought* of the flesh of the consecrations, or of the bread, remain unto the morning, then [a]thou shalt burn the remainder with fire: it shall not be eaten, because it *is* holy.

35 And thus shalt thou do unto Aaron, and to his sons, according to all *things* which I have commanded thee: [a]seven days shalt thou consecrate them.

36 ¶ And thou shalt [a]offer every day a bullock *for* a sin offering for atonement: and thou shalt cleanse the altar, when thou hast made an atonement for it, [b]and thou shalt anoint it, to sanctify it.

37 Seven days thou shalt make an atonement for the altar, and sanctify it; [a]and it shall be an altar most holy: [b]whatsoever toucheth the altar shall be holy.

38 ¶ Now this *is that* which thou shalt offer upon the altar; [a]two lambs of the first year [b]day by day continually.

39 The one lamb thou shalt offer [a]in the morning; and the other lamb thou shalt offer at even:

40 And with the one lamb a tenth deal of flour mingled with the fourth part of a hin of beaten oil; and the fourth *part* of a hin of wine *for* a drink offering.

41 And the other lamb thou shalt [a]offer at

29:15 [a]Lev. 8:18 [b]Lev. 1:4-9
29:17 [1]Or, *upon*
29:18 [a]Gen. 8:21
29:19 [a]ver. 3; Lev. 8:22
29:21 [a]ch. 30:25,31 [b]ver. 1; Heb. 9:22
29:23 [a]Lev. 8:26
29:24 [1]Or, *shake to and fro* [a]Lev. 7:30
29:25 [a]Lev. 8:28
29:26 [a]Lev. 8:29 [b]Lev. 7:33
29:27 [a]Lev. 7:31,34; Num. 18:11,18; Deut. 18:3
29:28 [a]Lev. 10:15 [b]Lev. 7:34
29:29 [a]Num. 20:26,28 [b]Num. 18:8
29:30 [1]Heb. he *of his sons* [a]Num. 20:28 [b]Lev. 8:35; 9:1,8
29:31 [a]Lev. 8:31
29:32 [a]Mat. 12:4
29:33 [a]Lev. 10:14,15,17 [b]Lev. 22:10
29:34 [a]Lev. 7:18; 8:32
29:35 [a]Lev. 8:33-35
29:36 [a]Heb. 10:11 [b]ch. 40:10
29:37 [a]ch. 40:10 [b]Mat. 23:19
29:38 [a]Num. 28:3; 1 Chr. 16:40; Ezra 3:3 [b]See Dan. 12:11
29:39 [a]Ezek. 46:13-15
29:41 [a]1 Ki. 18:29,36; 2 Ki. 16:15; Ezra 9:4,5; Ps. 141:2

29:14 *flesh . . . skin. . . dung.* Thought of as bearing sin, and thus burned outside the camp (see Heb 13:11–13).
29:18 *burn the whole ram.* Symbolizing total dedication.
29:20 *right ear.* Symbolizing sensitivity to God and His word. *right hand . . . right foot.* Symbolizing a life of service to others on God's behalf.
29:24 *wave offering.* See note on Lev 7:30–32.
29:28 *Aaron's and his sons' by a statute for ever.* Parts of certain sacrificial animals were set aside as food for the priests and their families (see Lev 10:14).
29:31 *the holy place.* Probably the tabernacle courtyard.
29:38–39 Institution of the daily morning and evening offerings—sometimes observed even during days of apostasy (see 2 Ki 16:15).

even, *and* shalt do thereto according to the meat offering of the morning, and according to the drink offering thereof, for a sweet savour, an offering made by fire unto the LORD.

42 *This shall be* [a]a continual burnt offering throughout your generations *at* the door of the tabernacle of the congregation before the LORD: [b]where I will meet you, to speak there unto thee.

43 And there I will meet with the children of Israel, and [1]*the tabernacle* [a]shall be sanctified by my glory.

44 And I will sanctify the tabernacle of the congregation, and the altar: I will [a]sanctify also both Aaron and his sons, to minister to me in the priest's office.

45 And [a]I will dwell amongst the children of Israel, and will be their God.

46 And they shall know that [a]I *am* the LORD their God, that brought them forth out of the land of Egypt, that I may dwell amongst them: I *am* the LORD their God.

The altar of incense

30 And thou shalt make [a]an altar [b]to burn incense upon: *of* shittim wood shalt thou make it.

2 A cubit *shall be* the length thereof, and a cubit the breadth thereof; foursquare shall it be: and two cubits *shall be* the height thereof: the horns thereof *shall be* of the same.

3 And thou shalt overlay it with pure gold, the [1]top thereof, and the [2]sides thereof round about, and the horns thereof; and thou shalt make unto it a crown *of* gold round about.

4 And two golden rings shalt thou make to it under the crown of it, by the two [1]corners thereof, upon the two sides of it shalt thou make *it;* and they shall be for places for the staves to bear it withal.

5 And thou shalt make the staves *of* shittim wood, and overlay them with gold.

6 And thou shalt put it before the vail that *is* by the ark of the Testimony, before the [a]mercy seat that *is* over the Testimony, where I will meet with thee.

7 And Aaron shall burn thereon [a][1]sweet incense every morning: when [b]he dresseth the lamps, he shall burn incense upon it.

8 And when Aaron [1]lighteth the lamps [2]at even, he shall burn incense upon it, a perpetual incense before the LORD throughout your generations.

9 Ye shall offer no [a]strange incense thereon, nor burnt sacrifice, nor meat offering; neither shall ye pour drink offering thereon.

10 And [a]Aaron shall make an atonement upon the horns of it once in a year with the blood of the sin offering of atonements: once in the year shall he make atonement upon it throughout your generations: it *is* most holy unto the LORD.

The offerings for the tabernacle

11 ¶ And the LORD spake unto Moses, saying,

12 [a]When thou takest the sum of the children of Israel after [1]their number, then shall they give every man [b]a ransom for his soul unto the LORD, when *thou* numberest them; that there be no [c]plague amongst them, when *thou* numberest them.

13 [a]This they shall give, every one that passeth among them that are numbered, half a shekel after the shekel of the sanctuary: ([b]a shekel *is* twenty gerahs:) [c]a half shekel *shall be* the offering of the LORD.

14 Every one that passeth among them that are numbered, from twenty years old and above, shall give an offering unto the LORD.

15 The [a]rich shall not [1]give more, and the poor shall not [2]give less than half a shekel, when *they* give an offering unto the LORD, to make an atonement for your souls.

16 And thou shalt take the atonement money of the children of Israel, and [a]shalt appoint it for the service of the tabernacle of the congregation; that it may be [b]a memorial unto the children of Israel before the LORD, to make an atonement for your souls.

The laver, oil and perfume

17 ¶ And the LORD spake unto Moses, saying,

18 [a]Thou shalt also make a laver *of* brass, and his foot *also of* brass, to wash *withal:* and thou shalt [b]put it between the tabernacle of the congregation and the altar, and thou shalt put water therein.

19 For Aaron and his sons [a]shall wash their hands and their feet thereat:

20 When they go into the tabernacle of the

29:42 [a]ch. 30:8 [b]ch. 25:22
29:43 [1]Or, Israel [a]1 Ki. 8:11; 2 Chr. 5:14; Ezek. 43:5; Hag. 2:7,9
29:44 [a]Lev. 21:15
29:45 [a]Ex. 25:8; Lev. 26:12; Zech. 2:10; John 14:17,23; Rev. 21:3
29:46 [a]ch. 20:2
30:1 [a]ch. 37:25 [b]See ver. 7,8,10; Rev. 8:3
30:3 [1]Heb. *roof* [2]Heb. *walls*
30:4 [1]Heb. *ribs*
30:6 [a]ch. 25:21,22
30:7 [1]Heb. *incense of spices* [a]ver. 34; 1 Sam. 2:28; 1 Chr. 23:13; Luke 1:9 [b]ch. 27:21
30:8 [1]Or, *setteth up.* Heb. *causeth to ascend* [2]Heb. *between the two evens*
30:9 [a]Lev. 10:1
30:10 [a]Lev. 16:18
30:12 [1]Heb. *them that are to be numbered* [a]2 Sam. 24:2 [b]See Num. 31:50; Mat. 20:28; 1 Pet. 1:18,19 [c]2 Sam. 24:15
30:13 [a]Mat. 17:24 [b]Num. 3:47 [c]ch. 38:26
30:15 [1]Heb. *multiply* [2]Heb. *diminish* [a]Prov. 22:2; Eph. 6:9
30:16 [a]ch. 38:25 [b]Num. 16:40
30:18 [a]ch. 38:8; 1 Ki. 7:38 [b]ch. 40:30
30:19 [a]ch. 40:31,32; Ps. 26:6; Is. 52:11; John 13:10; Heb. 10:22

29:42–43 *I will meet.* See note on 27:21.

29:43 *my glory.* Symbolic of God's presence over the ark of the Testimony (see note on 25:10; see also 40:34–35; 1 Ki 8:10–13).

29:45–46 *dwell amongst.* See note on 25:9.

29:45 *I will . . . be their God.* Commonly denotes the essence of the divine promise pledged in His covenant with His people (see note on 6:7).

29:46 *I am the LORD . . . that brought them forth.* See note on 20:2.

30:1 *incense.* Its fragrant smoke symbolized the prayers of God's people (see Ps 141:2; Luke 1:10; Rev 5:8; 8:3–4).

30:3 *gold.* See note on 26:37.

30:4 *rings.* See note on 25:12.

30:6 *vail that is by the ark of the Testimony.* See notes on 25:16,22; 26:31.

30:10 *atonement . . . once in a year.* See Lev 16:34.

30:12 *takest the sum of the children of Israel.* Perhaps such censuses were taken on various occasions (and at stated intervals) to enter the Israelites into an official roll for public duties in the Lord's service (see Num 1:2; 26:2). *give every man a ransom for his soul.* An extension of the principle stated in 13:13,15 (see note on 13:13).

30:14 *twenty years old and above.* Of military age (see Num 1:3).

30:16 *taberncle of the congregation.* See note on 27:21.

30:18 *laver.* Made from bronze ("brass") mirrors contributed by Israelite women (see 38:8). *to wash.* See note on 29:4.

congregation, they shall wash *with* water, that they die not; or when they come near to the altar to minister, to burn offering made by fire unto the LORD:

21 So they shall wash their hands and their feet, that they die not: and [a]it shall be a statute for ever to them, *even* to him and to his seed throughout their generations.

22 ¶ Moreover the LORD spake unto Moses, saying,

23 Take thou also unto thee [a]principal spices, of pure [b]myrrh five hundred *shekels,* and of sweet cinnamon half so much, *even* two hundred and fifty *shekels,* and of sweet [c]calamus two hundred and fifty *shekels,*

24 And of [a]cassia five hundred *shekels,* after the shekel of the sanctuary, and of oil olive a [b]hin:

25 And thou shalt make it an oil of holy ointment, an ointment compound *after* the art of the [1]apothecary: it shall be [a]a holy anointing oil.

26 [a]And thou shalt anoint the tabernacle of the congregation therewith, and the ark of the Testimony,

27 And the table and all his vessels, and the candlestick and his vessels, and the altar of incense,

28 And the altar of burnt offering with all his vessels, and the laver and his foot.

29 And thou shalt sanctify them, that they may be most holy: [a]whatsoever toucheth them shall be holy.

30 [a]And thou shalt anoint Aaron and his sons, and consecrate them, that *they* may minister unto me in the priest's office.

31 And thou shalt speak unto the children of Israel, saying, This shall be a holy anointing oil unto me throughout your generations.

32 Upon man's flesh shall it not be poured, neither shall ye make *any other* like it, after the composition of it: [a]it *is* holy, *and* it shall be holy unto you.

33 [a]Whosoever compoundeth *any* like it, or whosoever putteth *any* of it upon a stranger, [b]shall even be cut off from his people.

34 ¶ And the LORD said unto Moses, [a]Take unto thee sweet spices, stacte, and onycha, and galbanum; *these* sweet spices with pure frankincense: of each shall there be a like *weight:*

35 And thou shalt make it a perfume, a confection [a]*after* the art of the apothecary, [1]tempered together, pure *and* holy:

30:21 [a]ch. 28:43
30:23 [a]Sol. 4:14; Ezek. 27:22 [b]Ps. 45:8; Prov. 7:17 [c]Sol. 4:14; Jer. 6:20
30:24 [a]Ps. 45:8 [b]ch. 29:40
30:25 [1]Or, *perfumer* [a]ch. 37:29; Num. 35:25; Ps. 89:20; 133:2
30:26 [a]ch. 40:9; Lev. 8:10; Num. 7:1
30:29 [a]ch. 29:37
30:30 [a]ch. 29:7; Lev. 8:12,30
30:32 [a]ver. 25,37
30:33 [a]ver. 38 [b]Gen. 17:14; ch. 12:15; Lev. 7:20,21
30:34 [a]ch. 25:6; 37:29
30:35 [1]Heb. *salted* [a]ver. 25
30:36 [a]ch. 29:42; Lev. 16:2 [b]ver. 32; ch. 29:37; Lev. 2:3
30:37 [a]ver. 32
30:38 [a]ver. 33
31:2 [a]ch. 35:30; 36:1 [b]1 Chr. 2:20
31:3 [a]ch. 35:31; 1 Ki. 7:14
31:6 [a]ch. 35:34 [b]ch. 28:3; 35:10,35; 36:1
31:7 [1]Heb. *vessels* [a]ch. 36:8 [b]ch. 37:1 [c]ch. 37:6
31:8 [1]Heb. *vessels* [a]ch. 37:10 [b]ch. 37:17
31:9 [1]Heb. *vessels* [a]ch. 38:1 [b]ch. 38:8
31:10 [a]ch. 39:1,41; Num. 4:5,6
31:11 [a]ch. 30:25,31 [b]ch. 30:34
31:13 [a]Lev. 19:3,30; 26:2; Ezek. 20:12,20

36 And thou shalt beat *some* of it very small, and put of it before the Testimony in the tabernacle of the congregation, [a]where I will meet with thee: [b]it shall be unto you most holy.

37 And *as for* the perfume which thou shalt make, [a]you shall not make to yourselves according to the composition thereof: it shall be unto thee holy for the LORD.

38 [a]Whosoever shall make like unto that, to smell thereto, shall even be cut off from his people.

The appointment of the workmen

31 And the LORD spake unto Moses, saying,

2 [a]See, I have called by name Bezaleel the [b]son of Uri, the son of Hur, of the tribe of Judah:

3 And I have [a]filled him *with* the spirit of God, in wisdom, and in understanding, and in knowledge, and in all *manner of* workmanship,

4 To devise cunning works, to work in gold, and in silver, and in brass,

5 And in cutting of stones, to set *them,* and in carving of timber, to work in all *manner of* workmanship.

6 And I, behold, I have given with him [a]Aholiab, the son of Ahisamach, of the tribe of Dan: and in the hearts of all that are [b]wise hearted I have put wisdom, that they may make all that I have commanded thee;

7 [a]The tabernacle of the congregation, and [b]the ark of the Testimony, and [c]the mercy seat that *is* thereupon, and all the [1]furniture of the tabernacle,

8 And [a]the table and his [1]furniture, and [b]the pure candlestick with all his [1]furniture, and the altar of incense,

9 And [a]the altar of burnt offering with all his [1]furniture, and [b]the laver and his foot,

10 And [a]the clothes of service, and the holy garments for Aaron the priest, and the garments of his sons, to minister in the priest's office,

11 [a]And the anointing oil, and [b]sweet incense for the holy *place:* according to all that I have commanded thee shall they do.

The sabbath

12 ¶ And the LORD spake unto Moses, saying,

13 Speak thou also unto the children of Israel, saying, [a]Verily my sabbaths ye shall keep: for it *is* a sign between me and you throughout

30:23–24 *myrrh . . . cinnamon . . . calamus . . . cassia.* See note on 25:6.
30:33 *cut off from his people.* See note on 12:15.
30:34 *stacte, and onycha, and galbanum.* See note on 25:6. *frankincense.* A resin from the bark of *Boswellia carteri,* which grows in southern Arabia.
31:2 *Bezaleel.* Means "in the shadow/protection of God." *Hur.* See note on 17:10.
31:3 *filled him with the spirit of God.* Ability to work as a skilled craftsman was a spiritual gift, equipping a person for special service to God.
31:6 *Aholiab.* Means "The (divine) father is my tent/tabernacle." The names of Bezaleel (see note on v. 2) and Aholiab were appropriate for the chief craftsmen working on the tabernacle.
31:7 *tabernacle of the congregation.* See note on 27:21.
31:13 *my sabbaths ye shall keep.* Instructions for building the tabernacle and making the priestly garments are concluded by impressing on the Israelites the importance and necessity of keeping the sabbath even while carrying out this special task.

your generations; that *ye* may know that I *am*
the LORD that doth sanctify you.
14 [a]Ye shall keep the sabbath therefore; for
it *is* holy unto you: *every* one that defileth it
shall surely be put to death: for [b]whosoever
doeth *any* work therein, that soul shall be cut
off from amongst his people.
15 [a]Six days may work be done; but in the
[b]seventh *is* the sabbath of rest, [1]holy to the
LORD: whosoever doeth *any* work in the sabbath day, he shall surely be put to death.
16 Wherefore the children of Israel shall
keep the sabbath, to observe the sabbath
throughout their generations, *for* a perpetual
covenant.
17 It *is* [a]a sign between me and the children of Israel for ever: for [b]*in* six days the
LORD made heaven and earth, and on the seventh day he rested, and was refreshed.
18 And he gave unto Moses, when he had
made an end of communing with him upon
mount Sinai, [a]two tables of Testimony, tables
of stone, written with the finger of God.

The golden calf

32 And when the people saw that Moses [a]delayed to come down out of the
mount, the people gathered themselves together unto Aaron, and said unto him, [b]Up,
make us gods, which shall [c]go before us; for *as*
for this Moses, the man that brought us up out
of the land of Egypt, we wot not what is become of him.
2 And Aaron said unto them, Break off the
[a]golden earrings, which *are* in the ears of your
wives, of your sons, and of your daughters,
and bring *them* unto me.

31:14 [a]ch. 20:8; Deut. 5:12 [b]Num. 15:35
31:15 [1]Heb. *holiness* [a]ch. 20:9 [b]Gen. 2:2
31:17 [a]ver. 13 [b]Gen. 2:2
31:18 [a]ch. 32:15; Deut. 4:13; 5:22; 2 Cor. 3:3
32:1 [a]ch. 24:18; Deut. 9:9 [b]Acts 7:40 [c]ch. 13:21
32:2 [a]Judg. 8:24-27
32:4 [a]ch. 20:23; Deut. 9:16; Judg. 17:3,4; 1 Ki. 12:28; Neh. 9:18; Ps. 106:19; Acts 7:41
32:5 [a]Lev. 23:2,4,21,37; 2 Ki. 10:20; 2 Chr. 30:5
32:6 [a]1 Cor. 10:7
32:7 [a]Deut. 9:12; Dan. 9:24 [b]Gen. 6:11,12
32:8 [a]ch. 20:3,4,23 [b]1 Ki. 12:28
32:9 [a]2 Chr. 30:8; Is. 48:4; Acts 7:51
32:10 [a]Deut. 9:14,19 [b]ch. 22:24 [c]Num. 14:12
32:11 [1]Heb. *the face of the LORD* [a]Deut. 9:18,26-29

3 And all the people brake off the golden
earrings which *were* in their ears, and brought
them unto Aaron.
4 [a]And he received *them* at their hand, and
fashioned it with a graving tool, after he had
made it a molten calf: and they said, These *be*
thy gods, O Israel, which brought thee up out
of the land of Egypt.
5 And when Aaron saw *it,* he built an altar
before it; and Aaron made [a]proclamation, and
said, To morrow *is* a feast to the LORD.
6 And they rose up early on the morrow,
and offered burnt offerings, and brought peace
offerings; and the [a]people sat down to eat and
to drink, and rose up to play.
7 ¶ And the LORD said unto Moses, [a]Go, get
thee down; for thy people, which thou
broughtest out of the land of Egypt, [b]have corrupted *themselves:*
8 They have turned aside quickly out of the
way which [a]I commanded them: they have
made them a molten calf, and have worshipped it, and have sacrificed thereunto, and
said, [b]These *be* thy gods, O Israel, which have
brought thee up out of the land of Egypt.
9 And the LORD said unto Moses, [a]I have
seen this people, and behold, it *is* a stiffnecked
people:
10 Now therefore [a]let me alone, that [b]my
wrath may wax hot against them, and that I
may consume them: and [c]I will make of thee a
great nation.
11 [a]And Moses besought [1]the LORD his
God, and said, LORD, why doth thy wrath wax
hot against thy people, which thou hast
brought forth out of the land of Egypt with
great power, and with a mighty hand?

31:14 *cut off from amongst his people.* See note on 12:15.
31:16–17 *covenant . . . sign.* In her rhythm of work and rest in the service of God, Israel is to emulate God's pattern in creation as an ever-renewed sign of her covenant with God (see note on Gen 9:12).
31:18 *two tables.* In keeping with ancient Near Eastern practice, these were duplicates of the covenant document, not two sections of the ten commandments. One copy belonged to each party of the covenant. Since Israel's copy was to be laid up in the presence of her God (according to custom), both covenant tables (God's and Israel's) were placed in the ark (see 25:21). *Testimony.* See notes on 16:34; 25:16. *written with the finger of God.* Because it was God's covenant (see 19:5–6), and the stipulations of the covenant (20:1–17) were His.
32:1 *delayed.* Forty days and forty nights (see 24:18 and note). *the people.* Probably the tribe and clan leaders. *Moses . . . that brought us up out of . . . Egypt.* A rebellious contrast to the gracious statement of Israel's covenant Lord (see 20:2 and note; 29:46).
32:2 *golden earrings.* Probably part of the plunder brought from Egypt (see 3:21–22; 11:2–3; 12:35–36).
32:4 *made it a molten calf.* Either gold plating over a carved wooden calf (it was later burned, v. 20) or crudely cast in solid gold and then further shaped with a tool, later to be melted down in the fire. The calf was probably similar to representations of the Egyptian bull-god Apis (see note on Jer 46:15). Its manufacture was a flagrant violation of the second commandment (20:4–5). *they.* The leaders among the people (see note on v. 1). *These be thy gods . . . up out of the land of Egypt.* A parody of 20:2 (see note on v. 1). Centuries later, King Jeroboam would quote these words when he set up two golden calves in the northern kingdom of Israel (see 1 Ki 12:28–29).
32:5 *altar before it . . . feast to the LORD.* Apparently Aaron recognized the idolatrous consequences of his deed and acted quickly to keep the people from turning completely away from the Lord.
32:6 *the people sat down . . . rose up to play.* A pagan symbol evoked pagan religious practices. Paul quotes this sentence as a vivid example of Israel's tendency toward idolatry (see 1 Cor 10:7). The Hebrew verb translated "rose up to play" often has sexual connotations (see, e.g., "caressing," Gen 26:8). Immoral orgies frequently accompanied pagan worship in ancient times.
32:7,9 *thy people . . . this people.* By not calling Israel "my people" (as, e.g., in 3:10), God indicates that He is disowning them for breaking His covenant with them.
32:7 *corrupted.* And, therefore, ripe for destruction (see v. 10; Gen 6:11–13).
‡32:9 *stiffnecked* [i.e. obstinate]. Like unresponsive oxen or horses (see Jer 27:11–12; see also note on Neh 3:5).
32:10 *I will make of thee a great nation.* After Israel—Abraham's descendants—has been destroyed, God will transfer to Moses the pledge originally given to Abraham (see Gen 12:2).
32:11 *thy people.* Using God's own words (see v. 7 and note), Moses appeals to God's special relationship to Israel, then to God's need to vindicate His name in the eyes of the Egyptians (see v. 12), and finally to the great patriarchal promises (see v. 13).

12 [a]Wherefore should the Egyptians speak,
and say, For mischief did he bring them out, to
slay them in the mountains, and to consume
them from the face of the earth? Turn from thy
fierce wrath, and [b]repent of *this* evil against
thy people.
13 Remember Abraham, Isaac, and Israel,
thy servants, to whom thou [a]swarest by thine
own self, and saidst unto them, [b]I will multiply your seed as the stars of heaven, and all
this land that I have spoken of will I give unto
your seed, and they shall inherit *it* for ever.
14 And the LORD [a]repented of the evil
which he thought to do unto his people.
15 ¶ And [a]Moses turned, and went down
from the mount, and the two tables of the Testimony *were* in his hand: the tables *were* written on both their sides; on the one side and on
the other *were* they written.
16 And the [a]tables *were* the work of God,
and the writing *was* the writing of God, graven
upon the tables.
17 And when Joshua heard the noise of the
people as they shouted, he said unto Moses,
There is a noise of war in the camp.
18 And he said, *It is* not the voice of *them*
that shout for mastery, neither *is it* the voice of
them that cry for [1]being overcome: *but* the
noise of *them that* sing do I hear.
19 And it came to pass, as soon as he came
nigh unto the camp, that [a]he saw the calf, and
the dancing: and Moses' anger waxed hot, and
he cast the tables out of his hands, and brake
them beneath the mount.
20 [a]And he took the calf which they had
made, and burnt *it* in the fire, and ground *it* to
powder, and strawed *it* upon the water, and
made the children of Israel drink *of it*.
21 And Moses said unto Aaron, [a]What did
this people unto thee, that thou hast brought
so great a sin upon them?

32:12 [a]Num. 14:13 [b]ver. 14
32:13 [a]Gen. 22:16; Heb. 6:13 [b]Gen. 12:7; 13:15; 15:7,18; 26:4; 35:11,12
32:14 [a]2 Sam. 24:16
32:15 [a]Deut. 9:15
32:16 [a]ch. 31:18
32:18 [1]Heb. *weakness*
32:19 [a]Deut. 9:16,17
32:20 [a]Deut. 9:21
32:21 [a]Gen. 26:10
32:22 [a]ch. 14:11
32:25 [1]Heb. *those that rose up against them* [a]ch. 33:4,5 [b]2 Chr. 28:19
32:27 [a]Num. 25:5
32:29 [1]Or, *And Moses said, Consecrate yourselves to day to the LORD, because every man* hath been *against his son, and against his brother, etc.* [2]Heb. *Fill your hands* [a]1 Sam. 15:18,22; Prov. 21:3; Zech. 13:3
32:30 [a]1 Sam. 12:20,23 [b]2 Sam. 16:12 [c]Num. 25:13
32:31 [a]Deut. 9:18 [b]ch. 20:23

22 And Aaron said, Let not the anger of my
lord wax hot: [a]thou knowest the people, that
they *are set* on mischief.
23 For they said unto me, Make us gods,
which shall go before us: for *as for* this Moses,
the man that brought us up out of the land of
Egypt, we wot not what is become of him.
24 And I said unto them, Whosoever hath
any gold, let them break *it* off. So they gave *it*
me: then I cast it into the fire, and there came
out this calf.
25 And when Moses saw that the people
were [a]naked; (for Aaron [b]had made them
naked unto *their* shame amongst [1]their enemies:)
26 Then Moses stood in the gate of the
camp, and said, Who *is* on the LORD's side? *let*
him come unto me. And all the sons of Levi
gathered themselves together unto him.
27 And he said unto them, Thus saith the
LORD God of Israel, Put every man his sword
by his side, *and* go in and out from gate to gate
throughout the camp, and [a]slay every man his
brother, and every man his companion, and
every man his neighbour.
28 And the children of Levi did according
to the word of Moses: and there fell of the people that day about three thousand men.
29 [a][1]For Moses had said, [2]Consecrate
yourselves to day to the LORD, even every man
upon his son, and upon his brother; that he
may bestow upon you a blessing *this* day.
30 ¶ And it came to pass on the morrow,
that Moses said unto the people, [a]Ye have
sinned a great sin: and now I will go up unto
the LORD; [b]peradventure I shall [c]make an
atonement for your sin.
31 And Moses [a]returned unto the LORD,
and said, Oh, this people have sinned a great
sin, and have [b]made them gods of gold.
32 Yet now, if thou wilt forgive their sin;

32:13 *Israel.* Jacob (see 33:1; see also Gen 32:28).

32:14 *the LORD repented.* See note on Jer 18:7–10; see also 2 Sam 24:16; Ps 106:45; Amos 7:1–6; Jas 5:16.

32:15 *went down from the mount.* See note on 24:18. *two tables.* See note on 31:18. *Testimony.* See notes on 16:34; 25:16. *written on both their sides.* Tablets were often thus inscribed in ancient times.

32:16 *work of God . . . writing of God.* See 31:18.

32:17 *Joshua.* Perhaps he had accompanied Moses part of the way up the mountain (see 24:13).

32:19 *brake them.* Thus testifying against Israel that they had broken the covenant.

32:20 *burnt it . . . ground it to powder.* King Jeroboam's altar (see note on v. 4) at Beth-el received the same treatment (see 2 Ki 23:15).

32:22–24 In his desperation, Aaron blamed the people (see notes on Gen 3:12–13).

32:24 *there came out this calf.* Aaron could hardly have thought that Moses would believe such an incredible story.

32:25 *were naked . . . made them naked.* The Hebrew root can also be translated "without restraint" or "out of control." Anarchy reigns among people who refuse to obey and worship the Lord.

32:26 *Who is on the LORD's side? let him come unto me.* See Josh 24:15; 1 Ki 18:21; Mat 6:24. *all.* A generalization since Deut 33:9 implies that some of the Levites were also slain. *sons of Levi.* The descendants of Levi (Gen 29:34) may have originally been regarded as priests (Deut 18:6–8). But at some stage they became subordinate to the priests who were descendants of Aaron, the brother of Moses (38:21; Num 3:9–10; 1 Chr 16:4–6, 37–42).

32:27 *slay every man his brother . . . his companion . . . his neighbour.* See Mat 10:37; Luke 14:26.

32:28 *the children of Levi did according to the word of Moses.* Their zeal for the Lord is later matched by Aaron's grandson Phinehas, resulting in a perpetual covenant of the priesthood (see Num 25:7–13).

32:29 *Consecrate yourselves to day to the LORD.* Because of their zeal for the Lord the Levites were set apart to be caretakers of the tabernacle and aides to the priests (see Num 1:47–53; 3:5–9, 12,41,45; 4:2–3).

32:30 *make an atonement for your sin.* By making urgent intercession before God, as the mediator God had appointed between Himself and Israel. No sacrifice that Israel or Moses might bring could atone for this sin. But Moses so identified himself with Israel that he made his own death the condition for God's destruction of the nation (see v. 32). Jesus Christ, the great Mediator, offered Himself on the cross to make atonement for His people.

and if not, [a]blot me, I pray thee, [b]out of thy book which thou hast written.

33 And the LORD said unto Moses, [a]Whosoever hath sinned against me, him will I blot out of my book.

34 Therefore now go, lead the people unto *the place* of which I have spoken unto thee: [a]behold, mine Angel shall go before thee: nevertheless [b]in the day when I visit, I will visit their sin upon them.

35 And the LORD plagued the people, because [a]they made the calf, which Aaron made.

The renewal of the covenant

33 And the LORD said unto Moses, Depart, *and* go up hence, thou [a]and the people which thou hast brought up out of the land of Egypt, unto the land which I sware unto Abraham, to Isaac, and to Jacob, saying, [b]Unto thy seed will I give it:

2 [a]And I will send an angel before thee; [b]and I will drive out the Canaanite, the Amorite, and the Hittite, and the Perizzite, the Hivite, and the Jebusite:

3 [a]Unto a land flowing with milk and honey: for I will not go up in the midst of thee; for thou *art* a [b]stiffnecked people: lest [c]I consume thee in the way.

4 And when the people heard these evil tidings, [a]they mourned: [b]and no man did put on him his ornaments.

5 For the LORD had said unto Moses, Say unto the children of Israel, Ye *are* a stiffnecked people: I will come up [a]into the midst of thee in a moment, and consume thee: therefore now put off thy ornaments from thee, that I may [b]know what to do unto thee.

6 And the children of Israel stript themselves of their ornaments by the mount Horeb.

7 ¶ And Moses took the tabernacle, and pitched it without the camp, afar off from the camp, [a]and called it the Tabernacle of the Congregation. And it came to pass, *that* every one which [b]sought the LORD went out unto the Tabernacle of the Congregation, which *was* without the camp.

8 And it came to pass, when Moses went out unto the tabernacle, *that* all the people rose up, and stood every man [a]*at* his tent door, and looked after Moses, until he was gone into the tabernacle.

9 And it came to pass, as Moses entered into the tabernacle, the cloudy pillar descended, and stood *at* the door of the tabernacle, and *the LORD* [a]talked with Moses.

10 And all the people saw the cloudy pillar stand *at* the tabernacle door: and all the people rose up and [a]worshipped, every man *in* his tent door.

11 And [a]the LORD spake unto Moses face to face, as a man speaketh unto his friend. And he turned again into the camp: but [b]his servant Joshua, the son of Nun, a young man, departed not out of the tabernacle.

12 And Moses said unto the LORD, See, [a]thou sayest unto me, Bring up this people: and thou hast not let me know whom thou wilt send with me. Yet thou hast said, [b]I know thee by name, and thou hast also found grace in my sight.

13 Now therefore, I pray thee, [a]if I have found grace in thy sight, [b]shew me now thy way, that I may know thee, that I may find grace in thy sight: and consider that this nation *is* [c]thy people.

14 And he said, [a]My presence shall go *with thee,* and I will give thee [b]rest.

15 And he said unto him, [a]If thy presence go not *with me,* carry us not up hence.

16 For wherein shall it be known here that I and thy people have found grace in thy sight? [a]*is it* not in that thou goest with us? so [b]shall we be separated, I and thy people, from all the people that *are* upon the face of the earth.

Moses beholds God's glory

17 And the LORD said unto Moses, [a]I will do this thing also that thou hast spoken: for [b]thou hast found grace in my sight, and I know thee by name.

32:32 [a]Ps. 69:28; Rom. 9:3 [b]Dan. 12:1; Phil. 4:3; Rev. 3:5; 21:27
32:33 [a]Lev. 23:30; Ezek. 18:4
32:34 [a]ch. 33:2,14 [b]Deut. 32:35; Rom. 2:5,6
32:35 [a]2 Sam. 12:9
33:1 [a]ch. 32:7 [b]Gen. 12:7
33:2 [a]ch. 32:34 [b]Josh. 24:11
33:3 [a]ch. 3:8 [b]ch. 32:9 [c]Num. 16:21,45
33:4 [a]Num. 14:1,39 [b]Ezra 9:3; Esth. 4:1,4; Ezek. 24:17,23
33:5 [a]See Num. 16:45,46 [b]Ps. 139:23
33:7 [a]ch. 29:42,43 [b]Deut. 4:29
33:8 [a]Num. 16:27
33:9 [a]ch. 25:22; 31:18; Ps. 99:7
33:10 [a]ch. 4:31
33:11 [a]Num. 12:8; Deut. 34:10 [b]ch. 24:13
33:12 [a]ch. 32:34 [b]ver. 17; John 10:14,15; 2 Tim. 2:19
33:13 [a]ch. 34:9 [b]Ps. 25:4; 27:11; 86:11; 119:33 [c]Deut. 9:26,29
33:14 [a]Is. 63:9 [b]Josh. 21:44
33:15 [a]ver. 3
33:16 [a]Num. 14:14 [b]ch. 34:10; Deut. 4:7,34
33:17 [a]Jas. 5:16 [b]ver. 12

32:32 *book which thou hast written.* See notes on Ps 9:5; 51:1; 69:28.
32:33 *Whosoever hath sinned . . . him will I blot out.* Moses' gracious offer is refused, because the person who sins is responsible for his own sin (see Deut 24:16; Ezek 18:4 and note).
32:34 *now go, lead the people.* Thus Moses received assurance that the Lord will continue His covenant with wayward Israel and fulfill His promise concerning the land. *the place of which I have spoken unto thee.* Canaan (see 33:1).
33:2 *Canaanite . . . Jebusite.* See note on 3:8.
33:3 *land flowing with milk and honey.* See note on 3:8. *I will not go up in the midst of thee.* The Lord's presence, earlier assured to His people (see 23:21 and note), is now temporarily withdrawn because of sin. *stiffnecked.* See note on 32:9.
33:6 *stript themselves of their ornaments.* As a sign of mourning (see Ezek 26:16–17).
33:7 *Tabernacle of the Congregation, which was without the camp.* Not the tabernacle (contrast 27:21), which occupied a central location within the Israelite camp, but a temporary structure where the people could inquire of the Lord until the more durable tabernacle was completed.
33:9 *cloudy pillar descended.* Symbolizing God's communication with Moses "as a man speaketh unto his friend" (v. 11). Later, a similar descent crowned the completion of the tabernacle (see 40:33–34; see also note on 13:21).
33:11 *the LORD spake unto Moses face to face.* As the OT mediator, Moses was unique among the prophets. *Joshua . . . departed not out of the tabernacle.* Probably his task was to guard the tent against intrusion by others.
33:12 *thou hast not let me know whom thou wilt send with me.* See note on v. 3. Moses objects that a mere angel is no substitute for God's own presence. *I know thee by name.* I have chosen you for my special purpose.
33:13 *shew me now thy way.* A prayer that is answered in 34:6–7.
33:14 *My presence shall go with thee.* The Lord's gracious response to Moses' concern (see note on v. 12).
33:17 *for thou hast found grace in my sight.* How much more does God hear the prayers of His Son Jesus Christ (see Mat 17:5; Heb 3:1–6)!

18 And he said, I beseech thee, shew me [a]thy glory.

19 And he said, I will make all my goodness pass before thee, and I will proclaim the name of the LORD before thee; [a]and will be [b]gracious to whom I will be gracious, and will shew mercy on whom I will shew mercy.

20 And he said, Thou canst not see my face: for [a]there shall no man see me, and live.

21 And the LORD said, Behold, *there is* a place by me, and thou shalt stand upon a rock:

22 And it shall come to pass, while my glory passeth by, that I will put thee [a]in a clift of the rock, and will [b]cover thee with my hand while I pass by:

23 And I will take away mine hand, and thou shalt see my back parts: but my face shall [a]not be seen.

The second tables of stone

34 And the LORD said unto Moses, [a]Hew thee two tables of stone like unto the first: [b]and I will write upon *these* tables the words that were in the first tables, which thou brakest.

2 And be ready in the morning, and come up in the morning unto mount Sinai, and present thyself there to me [a]in the top of the mount.

3 And no man shall [a]come up with thee, neither let any man be seen throughout all the mount; neither let the flocks nor herds feed before that mount.

4 And he hewed two tables of stone like unto the first; and Moses rose up early in the morning, and went up unto mount Sinai, as the LORD had commanded him, and took in his hand the two tables of stone.

5 And the LORD descended in the cloud, and stood with him there, and [a]proclaimed the name of the LORD.

6 And the LORD passed by before him, and proclaimed, The LORD, The LORD [a]God, merciful and gracious, longsuffering, and abundant in [b]goodness and [c]truth,

7 [a]Keeping mercy for thousands, [b]forgiving iniquity and transgression and sin, and [c]*that* will by no means clear *the guilty;* visiting the iniquity of the fathers upon the children, and upon the children's children, unto the third and to the fourth *generation.*

8 And Moses made haste, and [a]bowed his head toward the earth, and worshipped.

9 And he said, If now I have found grace in thy sight, O Lord, [a]let my Lord, I pray thee, go amongst us; for [b]it *is* a stiffnecked people; and pardon our iniquity and our sin, and take us for [c]thine inheritance.

10 And he said, Behold, [a]I make a covenant: before all thy people I will [b]do marvels, such as have not been done in all the earth, nor in any nation: and all the people among which thou *art* shall see the work of the LORD: for it *is* [c]a terrible thing that I will do with thee.

11 [a]Observe thou that which I command thee *this* day: behold, [b]I drive out before thee the Amorite, and the Canaanite, and the Hittite, and the Perizzite, and the Hivite, and the Jebusite.

12 [a]Take heed to thyself, lest thou make a covenant with the inhabitants of the land whither thou goest, lest it be for [b]a snare in the midst of thee:

13 But ye shall [a]destroy their altars, break their [1]images, and [b]cut down their groves:

14 For thou shalt worship [a]no other god: for the LORD, whose [b]name *is* Jealous, *is* a [c]jealous God:

15 [a]Lest thou make a covenant with the inhabitants of the land, and they [b]go a whoring after their gods, and do sacrifice unto their gods, and *one* [c]call thee, and thou [d]eat of his sacrifice;

16 And thou take of [a]their daughters unto thy sons, and their daughters [b]go a whoring after their gods, and make thy sons go a whoring after their gods.

17 [a]Thou shalt make thee no molten gods.

33:18 [a]1 Tim. 6:16
33:19 [a]Rom. 9:15,16,18 [b]Rom. 4:4,16
33:20 [a]Gen. 32:30
33:22 [a]Is. 2:21 [b]Ps. 91:1,4
33:23 [a]John 1:18
34:1 [a]ch. 32:16,19 [b]ver. 28; Deut. 10:2,4
34:2 [a]ch. 19:20
34:3 [a]ch. 19:12,13,21
34:5 [a]ch. 33:19
34:6 [a]Neh. 9:17; Joel 2:13 [b]Rom. 2:4 [c]Ps. 108:4
34:7 [a]ch. 20:6 [b]Ps. 103:3; 130:4; Dan. 9:9; Eph. 4:32; 1 John 1:9 [c]Josh. 24:19; Job 10:14; Mic. 6:11; Nah. 1:3
34:8 [a]ch. 4:31
34:9 [a]ch. 33:15,16 [b]ch. 33:3 [c]Ps. 33:12; 94:14
34:10 [a]Deut. 5:2 [b]Deut. 4:32; Ps. 77:14 [c]Ps. 145:6
34:11 [a]Deut. 6:25 [b]ch. 33:2
34:12 [a]ch. 23:32 [b]ch. 23:33
34:13 [1]Heb. *statues* [a]Deut. 12:3 [b]2 Ki. 18:4; 2 Chr. 34:3,4
34:14 [a]ch. 20:3,5 [b]See Is. 9:6; 57:15 [c]ch. 20:5
34:15 [a]ver. 12 [b]Judg. 2:17 [c]Num. 25:2 [d]1 Cor. 8:4,7,10
34:16 [a]Deut. 7:3; 1 Ki. 11:2; Ezra 9:2; Neh. 13:25 [b]Num. 25:1,2; 1 Ki. 11:4
34:17 [a]ch. 32:8

33:18 See v. 22. In a sense, Moses' prayer was finally answered on the mount of Transfiguration (Luke 9:30–32), where he shared a vision—however brief—of the Lord's glory with Elijah and three of Jesus' disciples.

33:19 *goodness.* God's nature and character. *name.* A further symbol of God's nature, character and person (see Ps 20:1; John 1:12; 17:6). Here His name implies His mercy (grace) and His compassion (as it does also in 34:6).

33:20 See note on Gen 16:13; see also John 1:18; 6:46; 1 Tim 1:17; 1 John 4:12.

33:21–23 God speaks of Himself in human language. See 34:5–7 for the fulfillment of His promise.

34:1 *two tables of stone . . . I will write upon these tables.* See note on 31:18. *words.* See note on 20:1.

34:5 *name.* See note on 33:19.

34:6–7 See 33:19 and note. The Lord's proclamation of the meaning and implications of His name in these verses became a classic exposition that was frequently recalled elsewhere in the OT (see Num 14:18; Neh 9:17; Ps 86:15; 103:8; 145:8; Joel 2:13; Jonah 4:2). See also notes on 3:14–15; 6:2–3.

34:7 *for thousands.* Or "to thousands" (see 20:6). *iniquity and transgression and sin.* See Is 59:12 and note.

34:10 *make a covenant.* Renewing the covenant he had earlier made (chs. 19–24). Verses 10–26, many of which are quoted almost verbatim from previous sections of Exodus (compare especially vv. 18–26 with 23:14–19), are sometimes referred to as the "Ritual Decalogue."

34:12 *lest thou make a covenant with the inhabitants of the land.* Israel is not to make a treaty of peace with any of the people of Canaan to let them live in the land.

34:13 *groves.* Hebrew *Asherim.* Symbols of Asherah, the name of the consort (wife) of El, the chief Canaanite god. Wooden poles, perhaps carved in her image, were often set up in her honor and placed near other pagan objects of worship (see, e.g., Judg 6:25).

34:14 *whose name is Jealous.* See note on 20:5.

34:15 *go a whoring.* See Judg 2:17 and note. *eat of his sacrifice.* Partaking of food sacrificed to a pagan deity invites compromise (cf. 1 Cor 8; 10:18–21).

34:17 *make . . . no molten gods.* As Aaron had done when he made the golden calf (see 32:4).

18 The feast of [a]unleavened bread shalt thou keep: seven days thou shalt eat unleavened bread, as I commanded thee, in the time of the month Abib: for in the [b]month Abib thou camest out from Egypt.

19 [a]All that openeth the matrix *is* mine; and every firstling amongst thy cattle, *whether* ox or [1]sheep, *that* is male.

20 But [a]the firstling of an ass thou shalt redeem with a [1]lamb: and if thou redeem *him* not, then shalt thou break his neck. All the firstborn of thy sons thou shalt redeem: and none shall appear before me [b]empty.

21 [a]Six days thou shalt work, but on the seventh day thou shalt rest: in earing time and in harvest thou shalt rest.

22 [a]And thou shalt observe the feast of weeks, of the firstfruits of wheat harvest, and the feast of ingathering *at* the [1]year's end.

23 [a]Thrice in the year shall all your men children appear before the Lord GOD, the God of Israel.

24 For I will [a]cast out the nations before thee, and [b]enlarge thy borders: [c]neither shall any man desire thy land, when thou shalt go up to appear before the LORD thy God thrice in the year.

25 [a]Thou shalt not offer the blood of my sacrifice with leaven; [b]neither shall the sacrifice of the feast of the passover be left unto the morning.

26 [a]The first of the firstfruits of thy land thou shalt bring *unto* the house of the LORD thy God. [b]Thou shalt not seethe a kid in his mother's milk.

27 And the LORD said unto Moses, Write thou [a]these words: for after the tenor of these words I have made a covenant with thee and with Israel.

28 [a]And he was there with the LORD forty days and forty nights; he did neither eat bread, nor drink water. And [b]he wrote upon the tables the words of the covenant, the ten [1]commandments.

Moses' shining face

29 ¶ And it came to pass, when Moses came down from mount Sinai with the [a]two tables of Testimony in Moses' hand, when he came down from the mount, that Moses wist not that [b]the skin of his face shone while he talked with him.

30 And when Aaron and all the children of Israel saw Moses, behold, the skin of his face shone; and they were afraid to come nigh him.

31 And Moses called unto them; and Aaron and all the rulers of the congregation returned unto him: and Moses talked with them.

32 And afterward all the children of Israel came nigh: [a]and he gave them in commandment all that the LORD had spoken with him in mount Sinai.

33 And *till* Moses had done speaking with them, he put [a]a vail on his face.

34 But [a]when Moses went in before the LORD to speak with him, he took the vail off, until he came out. And he came out, and spake unto the children of Israel *that* which he was commanded.

35 And the children of Israel saw the face of Moses, that the skin of Moses' face shone: and Moses put the vail upon his face again, until he went in to speak with him.

Sabbath regulations

35 And Moses gathered all the congregation of the children of Israel together, and said unto them, [a]These *are* the words which the LORD hath commanded, that *ye* should do them.

2 [a]Six days shall work be done, but on the seventh day there shall be to you [1]a holy *day*, a sabbath of rest to the LORD: whosoever doeth work therein shall be put to death.

3 [a]Ye shall kindle no fire throughout your habitations upon the sabbath day.

4 And Moses spake unto all the congregation of the children of Israel, saying, [a]This *is* the thing which the LORD commanded, saying,

5 Take ye from amongst you an offering unto the LORD: [a]whosoever *is* of a willing heart, let him bring it, an offering of the LORD; gold, and silver, and brass,

6 And blue, and purple, and scarlet, and fine linen, and goats' *hair*,

7 And rams' skins dyed red, and badgers' skins, and shittim wood,

8 And oil for the light, [a]and spices for anointing oil, and for the sweet incense,

34:18 [a]ch. 12:15 [b]ch. 13:4 **34:19** [1]Or, *kid* [a]ch. 22:29 **34:20** [1]Or, *kid* [a]ch. 13:13 [b]ch. 23:15; Deut. 16:16; 1 Sam. 9:7,8; 2 Sam. 24:24 **34:21** [a]ch. 20:9; Luke 13:14 **34:22** [1]Heb. *revolution of the year* [a]ch. 23:16 **34:23** [a]ch. 23:14,17 **34:24** [a]ch. 33:2; Ps. 78:55 [b]Deut. 12:20; 19:8 [c]See Gen. 35:5; Acts 18:10 **34:25** [a]ch. 23:18 [b]ch. 12:10 **34:26** [a]ch. 23:19 [b]ch. 23:19 **34:27** [a]Deut. 31:9 **34:28** [1]Heb. *words* [a]ch. 24:18 [b]ver. 1; ch. 31:18; Deut. 4:13; 10:2,4 **34:29** [a]ch. 32:15

34:29 [b]Mat. 17:2; 2 Cor. 3:7,13 **34:32** [a]ch. 24:3 **34:33** [a]2 Cor. 3:13 **34:34** [a]2 Cor. 3:16 **35:1** [a]ch. 34:32 **35:2** [1]Heb. *holiness* [a]ch. 20:9; Lev. 23:3 **35:3** [a]ch. 16:23 **35:4** [a]ch. 25:1,2 **35:5** [a]ch. 25:2 **35:8** [a]ch. 25:6

34:18–26 See notes on 23:14–19.

34:21 *in earing time and in harvest thou shalt rest.* Just as they were also to rest while building the tabernacle (see notes on 31:13,16–17).

34:27 *Write thou these words.* As he had earlier written down similar words (see 24:4).

34:28 *he wrote.* Here the Lord, rather than Moses, is probably the subject (see v. 1). *the words of the covenant, the ten commandments.* The two phrases are synonymous (see note on 20:1).

34:29 *Testimony.* See notes on 16:34; 25:16. *shone.* He who had asked to see God's glory (33:18) now, quite unawares, reflects the divine glory. The Hebrew for "shone" is related to the Hebrew noun for "horn." The meaning of the phrase was therefore misunderstood by the Vulgate (the Latin translation), and thus European medieval art often showed horns sprouting from Moses' head.

34:33 *he put a vail on his face.* So that the Israelites would not see the fading away of the radiance but would continue to honor Moses as the one who represented God. For a NT reflection on Moses' action see 2 Cor 3:7–18 and notes.

35:1–3 Just as the Israelites had been reminded of the importance of sabbath observance immediately after the instructions for building the tabernacle and making the priestly garments (see note on 31:13), so now—just before the fulfilling of those instructions—the people are given the same reminder.

35:4–39:43 For the most part repeated from chs. 25–28; 30:1–5; 31:1–11 (see notes on those passages), sometimes verbatim, but with the verbs primarily in the past rather than the future tense and with the topics arranged in a different order.

9 And onyx stones, and stones to be set for the ephod, and for the breastplate.

10 And [a]every wise hearted among you shall come, and make all that the LORD hath commanded;

11 [a]The tabernacle, his tent, and his covering, his taches, and his boards, his bars, his pillars, and his sockets,

12 [a]The ark, and the staves thereof, *with* the mercy seat, and the vail of the covering,

13 The [a]table, and his staves, and all his vessels, [b]and the shewbread,

14 [a]The candlestick also for the light, and his furniture, and his lamps, with the oil for the light,

15 [a]And the incense altar and his staves, [b]and the anointing oil, and [c]the sweet incense, and the hanging for the door at the entering in of the tabernacle,

16 [a]The altar of burnt offering with his brasen grate, his staves, and all his vessels, the laver and his foot,

17 [a]The hangings of the court, his pillars, and their sockets, and the hanging for the door of the court,

18 The pins of the tabernacle, and the pins of the court, and their cords,

19 [a]The clothes of service, to do service in the holy *place,* the holy garments for Aaron the priest, and the garments of his sons, to minister in the priest's office.

Offerings for the tabernacle

20 ¶ And all the congregation of the children of Israel departed from the presence of Moses.

21 And they came, every one [a]whose heart stirred him up, and every one whom his spirit made willing, *and* they brought the LORD's offering to the work of the tabernacle of the congregation, and for all his service, and for the holy garments.

22 And they came, both men and women, as many as were willing hearted, *and* brought bracelets, and earrings, and rings, and tablets, all jewels of gold: and every man that offered *offered* an offering of gold unto the LORD.

23 And [a]every man, with whom was found blue, and purple, and scarlet, and fine linen, and goats' *hair,* and red skins of rams, and badgers' skins, brought *them.*

24 Every one that did offer an offering of silver and brass brought the LORD's offering: and every man, with whom was found shittim wood for any work of the service, brought *it.*

25 And all the women that were [a]wise hearted did spin with their hands, and brought that which they had spun, *both* of blue, and of purple, *and* of scarlet, and of fine linen.

26 And all the women whose heart stirred them up in wisdom spun goats' *hair.*

35:10 [a]ch. 31:6
35:11 [a]ch. 26:1,2
35:12 [a]ch. 25:10
35:13 [a]ch. 25:23 [b]ch. 25:30; Lev. 24:5,6
35:14 [a]ch. 25:31
35:15 [a]ch. 30:1 [b]ch. 30:25 [c]ch. 30:34
35:16 [a]ch. 27:1
35:17 [a]ch. 27:9
35:19 [a]ch. 31:10; 39:1,41; Num. 4:5,6
35:21 [a]ver. 5,22,26,29; ch. 36:2
35:23 [a]1 Chr. 29:8
35:25 [a]ch. 28:3; 31:6; 36:1
35:27 [a]1 Chr. 29:6; Ezra 2:68
35:28 [a]ch. 30:23
35:29 [a]ver. 21; 1 Chr. 29:9
35:30 [a]ch. 31:2
35:34 [a]ch. 31:6
35:35 [a]ver. 31; ch. 31:3,6; 1 Ki. 7:14; 2 Chr. 2:14; Is. 28:26
36:1 [a]ch. 28:3; 31:6; 35:10,35 [b]ch. 25:8
36:2 [a]ch. 35:21,26; 1 Chr. 29:5
36:3 [a]ch. 35:27
36:5 [a]2 Cor. 8:2,3

27 And [a]the rulers brought onyx stones, and stones to be set, for the ephod, and for the breastplate;

28 And [a]spice, and oil for the light, and for the anointing oil, and for the sweet incense.

29 The children of Israel brought a [a]willing offering unto the LORD, every man and woman, whose heart made them willing to bring for all *manner of* work, which the LORD had commanded to be made by the hand of Moses.

The workmen gathered

30 ¶ And Moses said unto the children of Israel, See, [a]the LORD hath called by name Bezaleel the son of Uri, the son of Hur, of the tribe of Judah;

31 And he hath filled him *with* the spirit of God, in wisdom, in understanding, and in knowledge, and in all *manner of* workmanship;

32 And to devise curious works, to work in gold, and in silver, and in brass,

33 And in the cutting of stones, to set *them,* and in carving of wood, to make any *manner of* cunning work.

34 And he hath put in his heart that *he* may teach, *both* he, and [a]Aholiab, the son of Ahisamach, of the tribe of Dan.

35 Them hath he [a]filled *with* wisdom of heart, to work all *manner of* work, of the engraver, and of the cunning workman, and of the embroiderer, in blue, and in purple, in scarlet, and in fine linen, and of the weaver, *even* of them that do any work, and of those that devise cunning work.

36 Then wrought Bezaleel and Aholiab, and every [a]wise hearted man, in whom the LORD put wisdom and understanding to know how to work all *manner of* work for the service of the [b]sanctuary, according to all that the LORD had commanded.

2 And Moses called Bezaleel and Aholiab, and every wise hearted man, in whose heart the LORD had put wisdom, *even* every one [a]whose heart stirred him up to come unto the work to do it:

3 And they received of Moses all the offering, which the children of Israel [a]had brought for the work of the service of the sanctuary, to make it *withal.* And they brought yet unto him free offerings every morning.

4 And all the wise *men,* that wrought all the work of the sanctuary, came every man from his work which they made;

5 And they spake unto Moses, saying, [a]The people bring much more than enough for the service of the work, which the LORD commanded to make.

6 And Moses gave commandment, and

Such repetition was a common feature of ancient Near Eastern literature and was intended to fix the details of a narrative in the reader's mind (see note on Gen 24:34–49).

35:5 *whosoever is of a willing heart.* The voluntary motivation behind the offering of materials and services for the tabernacle is stressed (see vv. 21–22,26,29; 36:2–3).

35:21 *tabernacle of the congregation.* See note on 27:21.

36:1–38 See note on 35:4–39:43.

they caused it to be proclaimed throughout the camp, saying, Let neither man nor woman make any more work for the offering of the sanctuary. So the people were restrained from bringing.

7 For the stuff *they had* was sufficient for all the work to make it, and too much.

The work for the tabernacle

8 ¶ [a]And every wise hearted *man* among them that wrought the work *of* the tabernacle made ten curtains *of* fine twined linen, and blue, and purple, and scarlet: *with* cherubims *of* cunning work made he them.

9 The length of one curtain *was* twenty and eight cubits, and the breadth of one curtain four cubits: the curtains *were* all of one size.

10 And he coupled the five curtains one unto another: and *the other* five curtains he coupled one unto another.

11 And he made loops of blue on the edge of one curtain from the selvedge in the coupling: likewise he made in the uttermost side of *another* curtain, in the coupling of the second.

12 [a]Fifty loops made he in one curtain, and fifty loops made he in the edge of the curtain which *was* in the coupling of the second: the loops held one *curtain* to another.

13 And he made fifty taches of gold, and coupled the curtains one unto another with the taches: so it became one tabernacle.

14 [a]And he made curtains *of* goats' *hair* for the tent over the tabernacle: eleven curtains he made them.

15 The length of one curtain *was* thirty cubits, and four cubits *was* the breadth of one curtain: the eleven curtains *were* of one size.

16 And he coupled five curtains by themselves, and six curtains by themselves.

17 And he made fifty loops upon the uttermost edge of the curtain in the coupling, and fifty loops made he upon the edge of the curtain which coupleth the second.

18 And he made fifty taches of brass to couple the tent together, that *it* might be one.

19 [a]And he made a covering for the tent *of* rams' skins dyed red, and a covering of badgers' skins above *that*.

20 [a]And he made boards for the tabernacle *of* [b]shittim wood, standing up.

21 The length of a board *was* ten cubits, and the breadth of a board one cubit and a half.

22 One board had two tenons, equally distant one from another: thus did he make for all the boards of the tabernacle.

23 And he made boards for the tabernacle; twenty boards for the south side southward:

24 And forty sockets of silver he made under the twenty boards; two sockets under one board for his two tenons, and two sockets under another board for his two tenons.

25 And for the other side of the tabernacle, *which is* toward the north corner, he made twenty boards,

26 And their forty sockets *of* silver; two sockets under one board, and two sockets under another board.

27 And for the sides of the tabernacle westward he made six boards.

28 And two boards made he for the corners of the tabernacle in the two sides.

29 And they were [1]coupled beneath, and [1]coupled together at the head thereof, to one ring: thus he did to both of them in both the corners.

30 And there were eight boards; and their sockets *were* sixteen sockets *of* silver, [1]under every board two sockets.

31 And he made [a]bars of shittim wood; five for the boards of the one side of the tabernacle,

32 And five bars for the boards of the other side of the tabernacle, and five bars for the boards of the tabernacle for the sides westward.

33 And he made the middle bar to shoot through the boards from the one end to the other.

34 And he overlaid the boards with gold, and made their rings *of* gold *to be* places for the bars, and overlaid the bars with gold.

35 ¶ And he made [a]a vail *of* blue, and purple, and scarlet, and fine twined linen: *with* cherubims made he it *of* cunning work.

36 And he made thereunto four pillars of shittim *wood*, and overlaid them with gold: their hooks *were of* gold; and he cast for them four sockets of silver.

37 And he made a [a]hanging for the tabernacle door *of* blue, and purple, and scarlet, and fine twined linen, [1]*of* needlework;

38 And the five pillars of it with their hooks: and he overlaid their chapiters and their fillets with gold: but their five sockets *were of* brass.

The construction of the ark

37 And Bezaleel made [a]the ark *of* shittim wood: two cubits and a half *was* the length of it, and a cubit and a half the breadth of it, and a cubit and a half the height of it:

2 And he overlaid it with pure gold within and without, and made a crown *of* gold to it round about.

3 And he cast for it four rings of gold, *to be set* by the four corners of it; even two rings upon the one side of it, and two rings upon the other side of it.

4 And he made staves of shittim wood, and overlaid them with gold.

36:8 [a]ch. 26:1
36:12 [a]ch. 26:5
36:14 [a]ch. 26:7
36:19 [a]ch. 26:14
36:20 [a]ch. 26:15 [b]ch. 25:5,10; Num. 15:1; Deut. 10:3; Josh. 2:1
36:29 [1]Heb. *twinned*
36:30 [1]Heb. *two sockets, two sockets under one board*
36:31 [a]ch. 26:26
36:35 [a]ch. 26:31
36:37 [1]Heb. *the work of a needleworker,* or, *embroiderer* [a]ch. 26:36
37:1 [a]ch. 25:10

37:1–29 See note on 35:4–39:43.
37:1 *Bezaleel made the ark.* The chief craftsman (see 31:2–3) was given the honor of making the most sacred object (see 25:10 and note) among the furnishings for the tabernacle.

5 And he put the staves into the rings by
the sides of the ark, to bear the ark.
6 And he made the [a]mercy seat *of* pure
gold: two cubits and a half *was* the length
thereof, and one cubit and a half the breadth
thereof.
7 And he made two cherubims *of* gold,
beaten out of one piece made he them, [1]on
the two ends of the mercy seat;
8 One cherub [1]on the end on this side, and
another cherub [1]on the *other* end on that side:
out of the mercy seat made he the cherubims
on the two ends thereof.
9 And the cherubims spread out *their*
wings on high, *and* covered with their wings
over the mercy seat, with their faces one to another; *even* to the mercy seatward were the
faces of the cherubims.

The table and the candlestick

10 ¶ And he made [a]the table *of* shittim
wood: two cubits *was* the length thereof, and
a cubit the breadth thereof, and a cubit and a
half the height thereof:
11 And he overlaid it with pure gold, and
made thereunto a crown *of* gold round about.
12 Also he made thereunto a border of a
handbreadth round about; and made a crown
of gold for the border thereof round about.
13 And he cast for it four rings of gold, and
put the rings upon the four corners that *were*
in the four feet thereof.
14 Over against the border were the rings,
the places for the staves to bear the table.
15 And he made the staves *of* shittim
wood, and overlaid them with gold, to bear
the table.
16 And he made the vessels which *were*
upon the table, his [a]dishes, and his spoons,
and his bowls, and *his* covers [1]to cover withal,
of pure gold.
17 ¶ And he made the [a]candlestick *of* pure
gold: *of* beaten work made he the candlestick;
his shaft, and his branch, his bowls, his knops,
and his flowers, were of the same:
18 And six branches going out of the sides
thereof; three branches of the candlestick out
of the one side thereof, and three branches of
the candlestick out of the other side thereof:
19 Three bowls made after the fashion of
almonds in one branch, a knop and a flower;
and three bowls made like almonds in another
branch, a knop and a flower: so throughout
the six branches going out of the candlestick.
20 And in the candlestick *were* four bowls
made like almonds, his knops, and his flowers:
21 And a knop under two branches of the
same, and a knop under two branches of the
same, and a knop under two branches of the
same, according to the six branches going
out of it.
22 Their knops and their branches were of
the same: all of it *was* one beaten work *of* pure
gold.
23 And he made his seven lamps, and his
snuffers, and his snuffdishes, *of* pure gold.
24 *Of* a talent *of* pure gold made he it, and
all the vessels thereof.

The altar of incense

25 ¶ [a]And he made the incense altar *of*
shittim wood: the length of it *was* a cubit, and
the breadth of it a cubit; *it was* foursquare; and
two cubits *was* the height of it; the horns
thereof were of the same.
26 And he overlaid it with pure gold, *both*
the top of it, and the sides thereof round
about, and the horns of it: also he made unto it
a crown *of* gold round about.
27 And he made two rings of gold for it under the crown thereof, by the two corners of
it, upon the two sides thereof, to be places for
the staves to bear it withal.
28 And he made the staves *of* shittim
wood, and overlaid them with gold.
29 ¶ And he made [a]the holy anointing oil,
and the pure incense of sweet spices, *accord-*
ing to the work of the apothecary.

The altar of burnt offering

38 And [a]he made the altar of burnt offering *of* shittim wood: five cubits
was the length thereof, and five cubits the
breadth thereof; *it was* foursquare; and three
cubits the height thereof.
2 And he made the horns thereof on the
four corners of it; the horns thereof were of
the same: and he overlaid it with brass.
3 And he made all the vessels of the altar,
the pots, and the shovels, and the basons, *and*
the fleshhooks, and the firepans: all the vessels
thereof made he *of* brass.
4 And he made for the altar a brasen grate
of network under the compass thereof beneath
unto the midst of it.
5 And he cast four rings for the four ends of
the grate of brass, *to be* places for the staves.
6 And he made the staves *of* shittim wood,
and overlaid them with brass.
7 And he put the staves into the rings on
the sides of the altar, to bear it withal; he made
the altar hollow with boards.
8 And he made [a]the laver *of* brass, and the
foot of it *of* brass, of the [1]looking-glasses of *the*
women [2]assembling, which [2]assembled *at* the
door of the tabernacle of the congregation.

The court of the tabernacle

9 ¶ And he made [a]the court: on the south
side southward the hangings of the court *were*
of fine twined linen, an hundred cubits:
10 Their pillars *were* twenty, and their
brasen sockets twenty; the hooks of the pillars
and their fillets *were of* silver.
11 And for the north side *the hangings*

37:6 [a]ch. 25:17
37:7 [1]Or, *out of, etc.*
37:8 [1]Or, *out of, etc.*
37:10 [a]ch. 25:23
37:16 [1]Or, *to pour out withal* [a]ch. 25:29
37:17 [a]ch. 25:31
37:25 [a]ch. 30:1; 40:26; 1 Ki. 9:25; 2 Chr. 29:6,7; Is. 60:6; Heb. 7:25
37:29 [a]ch. 30:23,34; Ps. 133:2; Is. 11:2; 61:1; 1 John 2:20
38:1 [a]ch. 27:1
38:8 [1]Or, *brasen glasses* [2]Heb. *assembling by troops,* as 1 Sam. 2:22 [a]ch. 30:18
38:9 [a]ch. 27:9

38:1–31 See note on 35:4–39:43.
38:8 *brass . . . looking-glasses.* Mirrored glass was unknown in ancient times, but highly polished bronze ("brass") gave adequate reflection. *tabernacle of the congregation.* See note on 27:21.

were an hundred cubits, their pillars *were* twenty, and their sockets *of* brass twenty; the hooks of the pillars and their fillets *of* silver.

12 And for the west side *were* hangings of fifty cubits, their pillars ten, and their sockets ten; the hooks of the pillars and their fillets *of* silver.

13 And for the east side eastward fifty cubits.

14 The hangings of the *one* side *of the gate were* fifteen cubits; their pillars three, and their sockets three.

15 And for the other side of the court gate, on this hand and that hand, *were* hangings of fifteen cubits; their pillars three, and their sockets three.

16 All the hangings of the court round about *were of* fine twined linen.

17 And the sockets for the pillars *were of* brass; the hooks of the pillars and their fillets *of* silver; and the overlaying of their chapiters *of* silver; and all the pillars of the court *were* filleted *with* silver.

18 And the hanging for the gate of the court *was* needlework, *of* blue, and purple, and scarlet, and fine twined linen: and twenty cubits *was* the length, and the height in the breadth *was* five cubits, answerable to the hangings of the court.

19 And their pillars *were* four, and their sockets *of* brass four; their hooks *of* silver, and the overlaying of their chapiters and their fillets *of* silver.

20 And all the [a]pins of the tabernacle, and of the court round about, *were of* brass.

The valuable metals used

21 ¶ This is the sum of the tabernacle, *even* of [a]the tabernacle of Testimony, as it was counted, according to the commandment of Moses, *for* the service of the Levites, [b]by the hand of Ithamar, son to Aaron the priest.

22 And [a]Bezaleel the son of Uri, the son of Hur, of the tribe of Judah, made all that the LORD commanded Moses.

23 And with him *was* Aholiab, son of Ahisamach, of the tribe of Dan, an engraver, and a cunning workman, and an embroiderer in blue, and in purple, and in scarlet, and fine linen.

24 All the gold that was occupied for the work in all the work of the holy *place*, even the gold of the offering, was twenty and nine talents, and seven hundred and thirty shekels, after [a]the shekel of the sanctuary.

25 And the silver of them that were numbered of the congregation *was* an hundred talents, and a thousand seven hundred and threescore and fifteen shekels, after the shekel of the sanctuary:

38:20 [a]ch. 27:19
38:21 [a]Num. 1:50,53; 9:15; 10:11; 17:7,8; 2 Chr. 24:6; Acts 7:44 [b]Num. 4:28,33
38:22 [a]ch. 31:2,6
38:24 [a]ch. 30:13,24; Lev. 5:15; 27:3,25; Num. 3:47; 18:16
38:26 [1]Heb. *a poll* [a]ch. 30:13,15 [b]Num. 1:46
38:27 [a]ch. 26:19,21,25,32
38:28 [a]ch. 27:17
39:1 [a]ch. 35:23 [b]ch. 31:10; 35:19 [c]ch. 28:4
39:2 [a]ch. 28:6
39:6 [a]ch. 28:9
39:7 [a]ch. 28:12
39:8 [a]ch. 28:15

26 [a]A bekah for [1]every man, *that is,* half a shekel, after the shekel of the sanctuary, for every one that went to be numbered, from twenty years old and upward, for [b]six hundred thousand and three thousand and five hundred and fifty *men.*

27 And of the hundred talents of silver were cast [a]the sockets of the sanctuary, and the sockets of the vail; an hundred sockets of the hundred talents, a talent for a socket.

28 And of the thousand seven hundred seventy and five *shekels* he made hooks for the pillars, and overlaid their chapiters, and [a]filleted them.

29 And the brass of the offering *was* seventy talents, and two thousand and four hundred shekels.

30 And therewith he made the sockets to the door of the tabernacle of the congregation, and the brasen altar, and the brasen grate for it, and all the vessels of the altar,

31 And the sockets of the court round about, and the sockets of the court gate, and all the pins of the tabernacle, and all the pins of the court round about.

The garments of the priesthood

39 And of [a]the blue, and purple, and scarlet, they made [b]clothes of service, to do service in the holy *place,* and made the holy garments for Aaron; [c]as the LORD commanded Moses.

2 [a]And he made the ephod *of* gold, blue, and purple, and scarlet, and fine twined linen.

3 And they did beat the gold into thin plates, and cut *it into* wires, to work *it* in the blue, and in the purple, and in the scarlet, and in the fine linen, *with* cunning work.

4 They made shoulderpieces for it, to couple *it* together: by the two edges was it coupled together.

5 And the curious girdle of his ephod, that *was* upon it, *was* of the same, according to the work thereof; *of* gold, blue, and purple, and scarlet, and fine twined linen; as the LORD commanded Moses.

6 [a]And they wrought onyx stones inclosed *in* ouches *of* gold, graven *as* signets are graven, with the names of the children of Israel.

7 And he put them on the shoulders of the ephod, *that they should be* stones for a [a]memorial to the children of Israel; as the LORD commanded Moses.

The priest's breastplate

8 [a]And he made the breastplate *of* cunning work, like the work of the ephod; *of* gold, blue, and purple, and scarlet, and fine twined linen.

38:25 *an hundred talents, and a thousand seven hundred and threescore and fifteen shekels.* Since there are 3,000 shekels in a talent, 100 talents equals 300,000 shekels, which, when added to the 1,775 shekels, gives a grand total of 301,775—half a shekel for each of the 603,550 men of military age (v. 26).

38:26 *six hundred thousand and three thousand and five hundred and fifty men.* The number is doubtless to be understood literally, since the figures in the tribal census (see Num 1:21–43; 2:4–31) total 603,550 (see Num 1:46 and note). See Introduction to Numbers: Special Problem.

38:27 *a talent for a socket.* See note on 26:19.

39:1–43 See note on 35:4–39:43.

9 It was foursquare; they made the breastplate double: a span *was* the length thereof,
and a span the breadth thereof, *being* doubled.
10 [a]And they set in it four rows of stones:
the first row *was* a [1]sardius, a topaz, and a carbuncle: *this was* the first row.
11 And the second row, an emerald, a sapphire, and a diamond.
12 And the third row, a ligure, an agate,
and an amethyst.
13 And the fourth row, a beryl, an onyx,
and a jasper: *they were* inclosed *in* ouches *of*
gold in their inclosings.
14 And the stones *were* according to the
names of the children of Israel, [a]twelve, according to their names, *like* the engravings of
a signet, every one with his name, according
to the twelve tribes.
15 And they made upon the breastplate
chains at the ends, *of* wreathen work *of* pure
gold.
16 And they made two ouches *of* gold, and
two gold rings; and put the two rings in the
two ends of the breastplate.
17 And they put the [a]two wreathen *chains*
of gold in the two rings on the ends of the
breastplate.
18 And the two ends of the two wreathen
chains they fastened in the two ouches, and
put them on the shoulderpieces of the ephod,
before it.
19 And they made two rings of gold, and
put *them* on the two ends of the breastplate,
upon the border of it, which *was* on the side of
the ephod inward.
20 And they made two *other* golden rings,
and put them on the two sides of the ephod
underneath, toward the forepart of it, over
against the *other* coupling thereof, above the
curious girdle of the ephod.
21 And they did bind the breastplate by his
rings unto the rings of the ephod with a lace of
blue, that *it* might be above the curious girdle
of the ephod, and that the breastplate might
not be loosed from the ephod; as the LORD
commanded Moses.

The robe of the ephod

22 [a]And he made the robe of the ephod *of*
woven work, all of blue.
23 And *there was* a hole in the midst of the
robe, as the hole of an habergeon, *with* a band
round about the hole, *that* it should not rend.
24 And they made upon the hems of the
robe pomegranates of blue, and purple, and
scarlet, *and* twined *linen.*
25 And they made [a]bells of pure gold, and
put the bells between the pomegranates upon
the hem of the robe, round about between the
pomegranates;

39:10 [1]Or, *ruby* [a]ch. 28:17
39:14 [a]Rev. 21:12
39:17 [a]Ex. 28:40
39:22 [a]ch. 28:31
39:25 [a]ch. 28:33
39:27 [a]ch. 28:39,40
39:28 [a]ch. 28:4,39; Ezek. 44:18 [b]ch. 28:42
39:29 [a]ch. 28:39
39:30 [a]ch. 28:36,37
39:32 [a]ver. 42,43; ch. 25:40
39:38 [1]Heb. *the incense of sweet spices*
39:42 [a]ch. 35:10
39:43 [a]Lev. 9:22,23; Num. 6:23; Josh. 22:6; 2 Sam. 6:18; 1 Ki. 8:14; 2 Chr. 30:27

26 A bell and a pomegranate, a bell and a
pomegranate, round about the hem of the robe
to minister *in;* as the LORD commanded Moses.
27 [a]And they made coats *of* fine linen *of*
woven work for Aaron, and for his sons,
28 [a]And a mitre *of* fine linen, and goodly
bonnets *of* fine linen, and [b]linen breeches *of*
fine twined linen,
29 [a]And a girdle *of* fine twined linen, and
blue, and purple, and scarlet, *of* needlework;
as the LORD commanded Moses.
30 [a]And they made the plate of the holy
crown *of* pure gold, and wrote upon it a writing, *like to* the engravings of a signet, HOLI-
NESS TO THE LORD.
31 And they tied unto it a lace of blue, to
fasten *it* on high upon the mitre; as the LORD
commanded Moses.

The tabernacle finished

32 ¶ Thus was all the work of the tabernacle of the tent of the congregation finished:
and the children of Israel did [a]according to all
that the LORD commanded Moses, so did they.
33 And they brought the tabernacle unto
Moses, the tent, and all his furniture, his taches, his boards, his bars, and his pillars, and his
sockets,
34 And the covering of rams' skins dyed
red, and the covering of badgers' skins, and
the vail of the covering,
35 The ark of the Testimony, and the staves
thereof, and the mercy seat,
36 The table, *and* all the vessels thereof,
and the shewbread,
37 The pure candlestick, *with* the lamps
thereof, *even with* the lamps to be set in order,
and all the vessels thereof, and the oil for light,
38 And the golden altar, and the anointing
oil, and [1]the sweet incense, and the hanging
for the tabernacle door,
39 The brasen altar, and his grate of brass,
his staves, and all his vessels, the laver and his
foot,
40 The hangings of the court, his pillars,
and his sockets, and the hanging for the court
gate, his cords, and his pins, and all the vessels
of the service of the tabernacle, for the tent of
the congregation,
41 The clothes of service to do service in
the holy *place,* and the holy garments for Aaron the priest, and his sons' garments, to minister in the priest's office.
42 According to all that the LORD commanded Moses, so the children of Israel
[a]made all the work.
43 And Moses did look upon all the work,
and behold, they had done it as the LORD had
commanded, *even* so had they done it: and
Moses [a]blessed them.

39:30 *holy crown.* An official designation (not found in 28:36–37) for the plate of the turban ("mitre").

39:32 *all the work of the tabernacle . . . finished.* Reminiscent of the concluding words of the creation narrative (see Gen 2:1–3).

39:43 *Moses blessed them.* For the faithfulness with which the Israelites had donated their gifts, time and talents in building the tabernacle and all its furnishings—faithfulness in service brings divine benediction.

40:2 *first day of the first month.* The tabernacle was set up al-

Assembling the tabernacle

40 And the LORD spake unto Moses, saying,

2 On the first day of the [a]first month shalt thou set up [b]the tabernacle of the tent of the congregation.

3 And [a]thou shalt put therein the ark of the Testimony, and cover the ark with the vail.

4 And [a]thou shalt bring in the table, and [b]set in order [1]the things that are to be set in order upon it; [c]and thou shalt bring in the candlestick, and light the lamps thereof.

5 [a]And thou shalt set the altar of gold for the incense before the ark of the Testimony, and put the hanging of the door to the tabernacle.

6 And thou shalt set the altar of the burnt offering before the door of the tabernacle of the tent of the congregation.

7 And [a]thou shalt set the laver between the tent of the congregation and the altar, and shalt put water therein.

8 And thou shalt set up the court round about, and hang up the hanging at the court gate.

9 And thou shalt take the anointing oil, and [a]anoint the tabernacle, and all that *is* therein, and shalt hallow it, and all the vessels thereof: and it shall be holy.

10 And thou shalt anoint the altar of the burnt offering, and all his vessels, and sanctify the altar: and [a]it shall be an altar [1]most holy.

11 And thou shalt anoint the laver and his foot, and sanctify it.

12 [a]And thou shalt bring Aaron and his sons unto the door of the tabernacle of the congregation, and wash them with water.

13 And thou shalt put upon Aaron the holy garments, [a]and anoint him, and sanctify him; that he may minister unto me in the priest's office.

14 And thou shalt bring his sons, and clothe them with coats:

15 And thou shalt anoint them, as thou didst anoint their father, that they may minister unto me in the priest's office: for their anointing shall surely be [a]an everlasting priesthood throughout their generations.

16 Thus did Moses: according to all that the LORD commanded him, so did he.

17 ¶ And it came to pass in the first month in the second year, on the first *day* of the month, *that* the [a]tabernacle was reared up.

18 And Moses reared up the tabernacle, and fastened his sockets, and set up the boards thereof, and put in the bars thereof, and reared up his pillars.

19 And he spread abroad the tent over the tabernacle, and put the covering of the tent above upon it; as the LORD commanded Moses.

20 And he took and put [a]the Testimony into the ark, and set the staves on the ark, and put the mercy seat above upon the ark:

21 And he brought the ark into the tabernacle, and [a]set up the vail of the covering, and covered the ark of the Testimony; as the LORD commanded Moses.

22 [a]And he put the table in the tent of the congregation, upon the side of the tabernacle northward, without the vail.

23 [a]And he set the bread in order upon it before the LORD; as the LORD had commanded Moses.

24 [a]And he put the candlestick in the tent of the congregation, over against the table, on the side of the tabernacle southward.

25 And [a]he lighted the lamps before the LORD; as the LORD commanded Moses.

26 [a]And he put the golden altar in the tent of the congregation before the vail:

27 [a]And he burnt sweet incense thereon; as the LORD commanded Moses.

28 [a]And he set up the hanging at the door of the tabernacle.

29 [a]And he put the altar of burnt offering *by* the door of the tabernacle of the tent of the congregation, and [b]offered upon it the burnt offering and the meat offering; as the LORD commanded Moses.

30 [a]And he set the laver between the tent of the congregation and the altar, and put water there, to wash *withal.*

31 And Moses and Aaron and his sons washed their hands and their feet thereat:

32 When they went into the tent of the congregation, and when they came near unto the altar, they washed; [a]as the LORD commanded Moses.

33 [a]And he reared up the court round about the tabernacle and the altar, and set up the hanging of the court gate. So Moses finished the work.

The glory of the LORD

34 ¶ [a]Then a cloud covered the tent of the congregation, and the glory of the LORD filled the tabernacle.

35 And Moses [a]was not able to enter into the tent of the congregation, because the cloud abode thereon, and the glory of the LORD filled the tabernacle.

40:2 [a]ch. 12:2; 13:4 [b]ver. 17; ch. 26:1,30
40:3 [a]ver. 21; ch. 26:33; Num. 4:5
40:4 [1]Heb. *the order thereof* [a]ver. 22; ch. 26:35 [b]ver. 23; ch. 25:30 [c]ver. 24,25
40:5 [a]ver. 26
40:7 [a]ver. 30; ch. 30:18
40:9 [a]ch. 30:26
40:10 [1]Heb. *holiness of holinesses* [a]ch. 29:36,37
40:12 [a]Lev. 8:1-13
40:13 [a]ch. 28:41
40:15 [a]Num. 25:13
40:17 [a]ver. 2; Num. 7:1
40:20 [a]ch. 25:16
40:21 [a]ch. 26:33
40:22 [a]ch. 26:35
40:23 [a]ver. 4
40:24 [a]ch. 26:35
40:25 [a]ver. 4; ch. 25:37
40:26 [a]ver. 5; ch. 30:6
40:27 [a]ch. 30:7
40:28 [a]ver. 5; ch. 26:36
40:29 [a]ver. 6 [b]ch. 29:38
40:30 [a]ver. 7; ch. 30:18
40:32 [a]ch. 30:19,20
40:33 [a]ver. 8; ch. 27:9,16
40:34 [a]ch. 29:43; Lev. 16:2; Num. 9:15; 1 Ki. 8:10,11; 2 Chr. 5:13; 7:2; Is. 6:4; Hag. 2:7,9; Rev. 15:8
40:35 [a]Lev. 16:2; 1 Ki. 8:11; 2 Chr. 5:14

---

most a year after the institution of the passover (see v. 17; 12:2,6).

40:16 *according to all that the LORD commanded him, so did he.* Moses' obedience to God's command is a key theme of the final chapter of Exodus (see vv. 19,21,23,25,27,29,32). It was the people who provided all the resources and made all the components, but it was the Lord's servant Moses who was authorized to erect the tabernacle and prepare it for the Lord's entry.

40:33 *Moses finished the work.* See note on 39:32.

40:34 With the glory of the Lord entering the tabernacle, the great series of events that began with the birth of Moses and his rescue from the Nile, foreshadowing the deliverance of Israel from Egypt, comes to a grand climax. From now on, the Israelites march through the wilderness, and through history, with the Lord tenting among them and leading them to the land of fulfilled promises.

36 [a]And when the cloud was taken up
from over the tabernacle, the children of Israel [1]went onward in all their journeys:
37 But [a]if the cloud were not taken up,
then they journeyed not till the day that it was
taken up.
38 For [a]the cloud of the LORD *was* upon the
tabernacle by day, and fire was on it by night,
in the sight of all the house of Israel, throughout all their journeys.

40:36 [1]Heb. *journeyed* [a]Num. 9:17; 10:11; Neh. 9:19
40:37 [a]Num. 9:19-22
40:38 [a]ch. 13:21; Num. 9:15

40:38 See note on 13:21. *house of Israel.* The nation, viewed as an extended family household.

The Third Book of Moses, Called Leviticus

INTRODUCTION

Author and Date

See note on 1:1 and Introduction to Genesis: Author and Date of Writing.

Title

Leviticus receives its name from the Septuagint (the Greek translation of the OT) and means "relating to the Levites." Its Hebrew title, *wayyiqra',* is the first word in the Hebrew text of the book and means "And He [i.e., the Lord] called." Although Leviticus does not deal only with the special duties of the Levites, it is so named because it concerns mainly the service of worship at the tabernacle, which was conducted by the priests who were the sons of Aaron, assisted by many from the rest of the tribe of Levi. Exodus gave the directions for building the tabernacle, and now Leviticus gives the laws and regulations for worship there, including instructions on ceremonial cleanness, moral laws, holy days, the sabbath year and the year of jubile. These laws were given, at least for the most part, during the year that Israel camped at mount Sinai, when God directed Moses in organizing Israel's worship, government and military forces. The book of Numbers continues the history with preparations for moving on from Sinai to Canaan.

Themes

The key thought of Leviticus is holiness (see note on 11:44)—the holiness of God and man (man must revere God in "holiness"). In Leviticus spiritual holiness is symbolized by physical perfection. Therefore the book demands perfect animals for its many sacrifices (chs. 1—7) and requires priests without deformity (chs. 8—10). A woman's hemorrhaging after giving birth (ch. 12); sores, burns or baldness (chs. 13—14); a man's bodily discharge (15:1–18); specific activities during a woman's monthly period (15:19–33)—all may be signs of blemish (a lack of perfection) and may symbolize man's spiritual defects, which break his spiritual wholeness. The person with visible skin disease must be banished from the camp, the place of God's special presence, just as Adam and Eve were banished from the Garden of Eden. Such a person can return to the camp (and therefore to God's presence) when he is pronounced whole again by the examining priests. Before he can reenter the camp, however, he has to offer the prescribed, perfect sacrifices (symbolizing the perfect, whole sacrifice of Christ).

After the covenant at Sinai, Israel was the earthly representation of God's kingdom (the theocracy), and, as her King, the Lord established His administration over all of Israel's life. Her religious, communal and personal life was so regulated as to establish her as God's holy people and to instruct her in holiness. Special attention was given to Israel's religious ritual. The sacrifices were to be offered at an approved sanctuary, which would symbolize both God's holiness and His compassion. They were to be controlled by the priests, who by care and instruction would preserve them in purity and carefully teach their meaning to the people. Each particular sacrifice was to have meaning for the people of Israel but would also have spiritual and symbolic import.

For more information on the meaning of sacrifice in general see the solemn ritual of the day of atonement (ch. 16). For the meaning of the blood of the offering see 17:11; Gen 9:4. For the emphasis on substitution see 16:21.

Some suppose that the OT sacrifices were remains of old agricultural offerings—a human desire to offer part of one's possessions as a love gift to the deity. But the OT sacrifices were specifically prescribed by God and received their meaning from the Lord's covenant relationship with Israel—whatever their superficial resemblances to pagan sacrifices. They indeed include the idea of a gift, but this is accompanied by such other values as dedication, communion, propitiation (appeasing God's judicial wrath against sin) and restitution. The various offerings have differing functions, the primary ones being atonement (see note on Ex 25:17) and worship.

Outline

The subjects treated in Leviticus, as in any book of laws and regulations, cover several categories:

I. The Five Main Offerings (chs. 1—7)
  A. Their Content, Purpose and Manner of Offering (1:1—6:7)
  B. Additional Regulations (6:8—7:38)
II. The Ordination, Installation and Work of Aaron and His Sons (chs. 8—10)
III. Laws of Cleanness—Food, Childbirth, Diseases, etc. (chs. 11—15)
IV. The Day of Atonement and the Centrality of Worship at the Tabernacle (chs. 16—17)
V. Moral Laws Covering Incest, Honesty, Thievery, Idolatry, etc. (chs. 18—20)
VI. Regulations for the Priests, the Offerings and the Annual Feasts (21:1—24:9)
VII. Punishment for Blasphemy, Murder, etc. (24:10–23)
VIII. The Sabbath Year, Jubile, Land Tenure and Reform of Slavery (ch. 25)
IX. Blessings and Curses for Covenant Obedience and Disobedience (ch. 26)
X. Regulations for Offerings Vowed to the Lord (ch. 27)

The law of burnt offerings

1 And the LORD [a]called unto Moses, and
spake unto him [b]out of the tabernacle of
the congregation, saying,
2 Speak unto the children of Israel, and say
unto them, [a]If *any* man of you bring an offering unto the LORD, ye shall bring your offering
of the cattle, *even* of the herd, and of the flock.
3 If his offering *be* a burnt sacrifice of the
herd, let him offer a male [a]without blemish:
he shall offer it of his own voluntary will at the
door of the tabernacle of the congregation before the LORD.
4 [a]And he shall put his hand upon the head
of the burnt offering; and it shall be [b]accepted
for him [c]to make atonement for him.
5 And he shall kill the [a]bullock before the
LORD: [b]and the priests, Aaron's sons, shall
bring the blood, [c]and sprinkle the blood round
about upon the altar that *is by* the door of the
tabernacle of the congregation.
6 And he shall flay the burnt offering, and
cut it into his pieces.
7 And the sons of Aaron the priest shall put
fire upon the altar, and [a]lay the wood in order
upon the fire:
8 And the priests, Aaron's sons, shall lay the
parts, the head, and the fat, in order upon the
wood that *is* on the fire which *is* upon the altar:
9 But his inwards and his legs shall he
wash in water: and the priest shall burn all on
the altar, *to be* a burnt sacrifice, an offering
made by fire, of a [a]sweet savour unto the
LORD.
10 And if his offering *be* of the flocks,
namely, of the sheep, or of the goats, for a
burnt sacrifice; he shall bring it a male [a]with-
out blemish.
11 [a]And he shall kill it on the side of the altar northward before the LORD: and the
priests, Aaron's sons, shall sprinkle his blood
round about upon the altar.
12 And he shall cut it into his pieces, with
his head and his fat: and the priest shall lay
them in order on the wood that *is* on the fire
which *is* upon the altar.
13 But he shall wash the inwards and the
legs with water: and the priest shall bring *it*
all, and burn *it* upon the altar: it *is* a burnt sacrifice, an offering made by fire, of a sweet
savour unto the LORD.
14 And if the burnt sacrifice for his offering
to the LORD *be* of fowls, then he shall bring his
offering of [a]turtledoves, or of young pigeons.
15 And the priest shall bring it unto the altar, and [1]wring off his head, and burn *it* on the
altar; and the blood thereof shall be wrung out
at the side of the altar:

1:1 [a]Ex. 19:3 [b]Ex. 40:34
1:2 [a]ch. 22:18,19
1:3 [a]Deut. 15:21; Eph. 5:27; Heb. 9:14; 1 Pet. 1:19
1:4 [a]ch. 3:2,8,13; 4:15 [b]Rom. 12:1; Phil. 4:18 [c]2 Chr. 29:23,24
1:5 [a]Mic. 6:6 [b]2 Chr. 35:11 [c]Heb. 12:24
1:7 [a]Gen. 22:9
1:9 [a]Gen. 8:21; Ezek. 20:28,41; 2 Cor. 2:15
1:10 [a]ver. 3
1:11 [a]ver. 5; Ex. 40:22; Ezek. 8:5
1:14 [a]ch. 5:7
1:15 [1]Or, *pinch off the head with the nail*

‡1:1 Leviticus contains the Biblical regulations for the priestly worship and Israel's sacrificial system. Verse one emphasizes that the contents of Leviticus were given to Moses by God at mount Sinai. Cf. also the concluding verse (27:34). In more than 50 places it is said that the Lord spoke to Moses. Modern criticism has attributed practically the whole book to priestly legislation written during or after the exile. But this is without objective evidence, is against the repeated claim of the book to be Mosaic, is against the traditional Jewish view, and runs counter to other OT and NT witness (Rom 10:5). Many items in Leviticus are now seen to be best explained in terms of a second-millennium B.C. date, which is also the most likely time for Moses to have written the Pentateuch (see Introduction to Genesis: Author and Date of Writing). There is no convincing reason not to take at face value the many references to Moses and his work. *tabernacle of the congregation.* The tabernacle, where God met with Israel (see note on Ex 27:21).

1:2 *bring an offering.* The Hebrew word for "offering" used here *(qorban)* comes from the word translated "brings." An "offering" is something that someone "brings" to God as a gift (most offerings were voluntary, such as the burnt offering). This word for "offering" is also used in Mark 7:11 ("Corban"), where Mark translates it as a "gift" (see note there).

‡1:3 *burnt sacrifice.* See further priestly regulations in 6:8–13 (see also chart, p. 141). A burnt offering was offered every morning and evening for all Israel (Ex 29:39–42). Double burnt offerings were brought on the sabbath (Num 28:9–10) and extra ones on feast days (Num 28–29). In addition, anyone could offer special burnt offerings to express devotion to the Lord. *male.* The burnt offering had to be a male animal because of its greater value, and also perhaps because it was thought to better represent vigor and fertility. It was usually a young sheep or goat (for the average individual), but bulls (for the wealthy) and doves or pigeons (for the poor) were also specified. *without blemish.* The animal had to be unblemished (cf. Mal 1:8). As in all offerings, the offerer was to lay his hand on the head of the animal to express identification between himself and the animal (16:21), whose death would then be accepted in "atonement" (v. 4). The blood was sprinkled on the sides of the great altar (located outside the tabernacle—later the temple—in the eastern half of the courtyard), where the fire of sacrifice was never to go out (6:13). The whole sacrifice was to be burned up (v. 9), including the head, legs, fat and inner organs. It is therefore sometimes called a holocaust offering (*holo* means "whole," and *caust* means "burnt"). When a bull was offered, however, the officiating priest could keep its hide (7:8). The burnt offering may have been the usual sacrifice offered by the patriarchs. It was the most comprehensive in its meaning. Its Hebrew name means "going up," perhaps symbolizing worship and prayer as its aroma ascended to the Lord (v. 17). The completeness of its burning also speaks of dedication on the part of the worshiper. *door of the tabernacle of the congregation.* Where the altar of burnt offering was (see Ex 40:29). *before the* LORD. Lit. "for acceptance for him before the Lord." See Rom 12:1; Phil 4:18.

1:4 *put his hand upon.* See notes on v. 3; Ex 29:10. *atonement.* See notes on 16:20–22; 17:11.

1:5 Only after the offerer killed the animal (symbolizing substitution of a perfect animal sacrifice for a sinful human life) did the priestly work begin. *blood.* See notes on 17:11; Heb 9:18. *sprinkle . . . round about upon the altar.* See Ex 24:6; Heb 9:19–21.

1:6 *flay.* The whole animal was burned except the hide, which was given to the priest (7:8).

1:9,13,17 *sweet savour unto the* LORD. The OT sacrifices foreshadowed Christ, who was an "offering . . . a sweetsmelling savour" (Eph 5:2; cf. Phil 4:18).

1:11 *northward.* See diagram, p. 114.

1:14 *fowls.* Three categories of sacrifices are mentioned: (1) herds (vv. 3–9), (2) flocks (vv. 10–13) and (3) fowls (vv. 14–17). Sacrifices of birds were allowed for the poor (see 5:7; 12:8; Luke 2:24).

16 And he shall pluck away his crop with
[1]his feathers, and cast it [a]beside the altar on
the east part, by the place of the ashes:
17 And he shall cleave it with the wings
thereof, *but* [a]shall not divide *it* asunder: and
the priest shall burn it upon the altar, upon the
wood that *is* upon the fire: [b]it *is* a burnt sacrifice, an offering made by fire, of a sweet
savour unto the LORD.

The law of meat offerings

2 And when any will offer [a]a meat offering
unto the LORD, his offering shall be *of*
fine flour; and he shall pour oil upon it, and
put frankincense thereon:
2 And he shall bring it to Aaron's sons the
priests: and he shall take thereout his handful
of the flour thereof, and of the oil thereof, with
all the frankincense thereof; and the priest
shall burn [a]the memorial of it upon the altar,
to be an offering made by fire, of a sweet
savour unto the LORD:
3 And [a]the remnant of the meat offering
shall be Aaron's and his sons': [b]*it is a thing*
most holy of the offerings of the LORD made by
fire.
4 And if thou bring an oblation of a meat
offering baken in the oven, *it shall be* unleavened cakes of fine flour mingled with oil, or
unleavened wafers [a]anointed with oil.
5 And if thy oblation *be* a meat offering
baken [1]in a pan, it shall be *of* fine flour unleavened, mingled with oil.
6 Thou shalt part it in pieces, and pour oil
thereon: it *is* a meat offering.
7 And if thy oblation *be* a meat offering
baken in the fryingpan, it shall be made *of* fine
flour with oil.
8 And thou shalt bring the meat offering
that is made of these *things* unto the LORD: and
when it is presented unto the priest, he shall
bring it unto the altar.
9 And the priest shall take from the meat
offering [a]a memorial thereof, and shall burn *it*
upon the altar: *it is* an [b]offering made by fire,
of a sweet savour unto the LORD.
10 And [a]that which is left of the meat offering *shall be* Aaron's and his sons': *it is* a
thing most holy of the offerings of the LORD
made by fire.
11 No meat offering, which ye shall bring
unto the LORD, shall be made *with* [a]leaven: for
ye shall burn no leaven, nor any honey, *in* any
offering of the LORD made by fire.
12 [a]*As for* the oblation of the firstfruits, ye
shall offer them unto the LORD: but they shall
not [1]be burnt on the altar for a sweet savour.
13 And every oblation of thy meat offering
[a]shalt thou season with salt; neither shalt thou
suffer [b]the salt of the covenant of thy God to
be lacking from thy meat offering: [c]with all
thine offerings thou shalt offer salt.
14 And if thou offer a meat offering of *thy*
firstfruits unto the LORD, [a]thou shalt offer for
the meat offering of thy firstfruits green ears of
corn dried by the fire, *even* corn beaten out of
[b]full ears.
15 And [a]thou shalt put oil upon it, and lay
frankincense thereon: it *is* a meat offering.
16 And the priest shall burn [a]the memorial
of it, *part* of the beaten corn thereof, and *part*
of the oil thereof, with all the frankincense
thereof: *it is* an offering made by fire unto the
LORD.

The law of peace offerings

3 And if his oblation *be* a [a]sacrifice of
peace offering, if he offer *it* of the herd;
whether *it be* a male or female, he shall offer it
[b]without blemish before the LORD.

1:16 [1]Or, *the filth thereof* [a]ch. 6:10
1:17 [a]Gen. 15:10 [b]ver. 9,13
2:1 [a]ch. 6:14; 9:17; Num. 15:4
2:2 [a]ver. 9; ch. 5:12; 6:15; 24:7; Is. 66:3; Acts 10:4
2:3 [a]ch. 7:9; 10:12,13 [b]Ex. 29:37; Num. 18:9
2:4 [a]Ex. 29:2
2:5 [1]Or, *on a flat plate,* or, *slice*
2:9 [a]ver. 2; ch. 6:15 [b]Ex. 29:18
2:10 [a]ver. 3
2:11 [a]ch. 6:17; See Mat. 16:12; Mark 8:15; Luke 12:1; 1 Cor. 5:8; Gal. 5:9
2:12 [1]Heb. *ascend* [a]Ex. 22:29; ch. 23:10,11
2:13 [a]Mark 9:49; Col. 4:6 [b]Num. 18:19 [c]Ezek. 43:24
2:14 [a]ch. 23:10,14 [b]2 Ki. 4:42
2:15 [a]ver. 1
2:16 [a]ver. 2
3:1 [a]ch. 7:11,29; 22:21 [b]ch. 1:3

1:17 *not divide it.* See note on Gen 15:10.

‡2:1 *meat offering.* What is rendered "meat offering" is seen from the context to refer to a "meal" or "grain" offering. See further priestly regulations in 6:14–23; 7:9–10. It was made of grain or fine flour. If baked or cooked, it consisted of cakes or wafers made in a pan or oven or on a griddle. It was the only bloodless offering, but it was to accompany the burnt offering (see Num 28:3–6), sin offering (see Num 6:14–15) and peace offering (see 9:4; Num 6:17). The amounts of grain offering ingredients specified to accompany a bull, ram or lamb sacrificed as a burnt offering are given in Num 28:12–13. A representative handful of flour was to be burned on the altar with the accompanying offerings, and the balance was to be baked without yeast and eaten by the priests in their holy meals (6:14–17). The flour that was burned on the altar was mixed with olive oil for shortening, salted for taste and accompanied by incense, but it was to have no yeast or honey—neither of which was allowed on the altar (vv. 11–13). The cooked product was similar to pie crust. The worshiper was not to eat any of the grain offering, and the priests were not to eat any of their own grain offerings, which were to be totally burned (6:22–23). The Hebrew word for grain offering can mean "present" or "gift" and is often used in that way (see Gen 43:11). The sacred gifts expressed devotion to God (see v. 2). *fine flour.* Grain that was milled and sifted. *oil.* Olive oil is often mentioned in connection with grain and new wine as fresh products of the harvest (see Deut 7:13). Used extensively in cooking, it was a suitable part of the worshiper's gift. *frankincense.* The chief ingredient in incense (see Ex 30:34–35).

2:3 *thing most holy.* For this reason, the priests were to eat it in the sanctuary area proper and not feed their families with it (6:16–18).

2:4 *unleavened.* See notes on Ex 12:8,15.

2:5 *pan.* A clay pan that rested on a stone heated by a fire. Later, iron pans were sometimes used.

2:11 *honey.* It was forbidden on the altar perhaps because of its use in brewing beer (as an aid to fermentation), though some suggest that it was because of its use in Canaanite cultic practice.

2:12 *firstfruits.* See 23:10–11; Ex 23:16,19; Num 15:18–20; Deut 18:4–5; 26:1–11.

2:13 *salt of the covenant.* In ancient times salt was often costly and a valuable part of the diet. Perhaps this is why it was used as a covenant sign and was required for sacrifices.

3:1 *peace offering.* See further priestly regulations in 7:11–21, 28–34. Two basic ideas are included in this offering: peace and fellowship. The traditional translation is "peace offering," a name that comes from the Hebrew word for the offering, which in turn is related to the Hebrew word *shalom,* meaning "peace" or "wholeness." Thus the offering perhaps symbolized peace be-

2 And [a]he shall lay his hand upon the head of his offering, and kill it *at* the door of the tabernacle of the congregation: and Aaron's sons the priests shall sprinkle the blood upon the altar round about.

3 And he shall offer of the sacrifice of the peace offering an offering made by fire unto the LORD; [a]the [1]fat that covereth the inwards, and all the [1]fat that *is* upon the inwards,

4 And the two kidneys, and the fat that *is* on them, which *is* by the flanks, and the [1]caul above the liver, with the kidneys, it shall he take away.

5 And Aaron's sons [a]shall burn it on the altar upon the burnt sacrifice, which *is* upon the wood that *is* on the fire: *it is* an offering made by fire, of a sweet savour unto the LORD.

6 And if his offering for a sacrifice of peace offering unto the LORD *be* of the flock, male or female, [a]he shall offer it without blemish.

7 If he offer a lamb for his offering, then shall he offer it before the LORD.

8 And he shall lay his hand upon the head of his offering, and kill it before the tabernacle of the congregation: and Aaron's sons shall sprinkle the blood thereof round about upon the altar.

9 And he shall offer of the sacrifice of the peace offering an offering made by fire unto the LORD; the fat thereof, *and* the whole rump, it shall he take off hard by the back bone; and the fat that covereth the inwards, and all the fat that *is* upon the inwards,

10 And the two kidneys, and the fat that *is* upon them, which *is* by the flanks, and the caul above the liver, with the kidneys, it shall he take away.

11 And the priest shall burn it upon the altar: *it is* [a]the food of the offering made by fire unto the LORD.

12 And if his offering *be* a goat, then [a]he shall offer it before the LORD.

13 And he shall lay his hand upon the head of it, and kill it before the tabernacle of the congregation: and the sons of Aaron shall sprinkle the blood thereof upon the altar round about.

14 And he shall offer thereof his offering, *even* an offering made by fire unto the LORD; the fat that covereth the inwards, and all the fat that *is* upon the inwards,

15 And the two kidneys, and the fat that *is* upon them, which *is* by the flanks, and the caul above the liver, with the kidneys, it shall he take away.

16 And the priest shall burn them upon the altar: *it is* the food of the offering made by fire for a sweet savour: [a]all the fat *is* the LORD's.

17 *It shall be* a [a]perpetual statute for your generations throughout all your dwellings, *that* ye eat neither [b]fat nor [c]blood.

The sin offering

4 And the LORD spake unto Moses, saying,

2 Speak unto the children of Israel, saying, [a]If a soul shall sin through ignorance against any of the commandments of the LORD (*concerning things* which ought not to be done), and shall do against any of them:

3 [a]If the priest that is anointed do sin according to the sin of the people; then let him bring for his sin, which he hath sinned, [b]a young bullock without blemish unto the LORD for a sin offering.

4 And he shall bring the bullock [a]unto the door of the tabernacle of the congregation before the LORD; and shall lay his hand upon the bullock's head, and kill the bullock before the LORD.

3:2 [a]Ex. 29:10; ch. 1:4,5
3:3 [1]Or, *suet* [a]Ex. 29:13,22; ch. 4:8,9
3:4 [1]Or, *midriff over the liver,* and *over the kidneys*
3:5 [a]Ex. 29:13; ch. 6:12
3:6 [a]ver. 1
3:11 [a]See ch. 21:6,8,17, 21,22; 22:25; Ezek. 44:7; Mal. 1:7,12
3:12 [a]ver. 1,7
3:16 [a]ch. 7:23,25; 1 Sam. 2:15; 2 Chr. 7:7
3:17 [a]ch. 6:18; 7:36; 17:7; 23:14 [b]ver. 16; compare with Deut. 32:14; Neh. 8:10 [c]Gen. 9:4; ch. 7:23,26; 17:10,14; Deut. 12:16; 1 Sam. 14:33; Ezek. 44:7,15
4:2 [a]ch. 5:15,17; Num. 15:22; 1 Sam. 14:27; Ps. 19:12
4:3 [a]ch. 8:12 [b]ch. 9:2
4:4 [a]ch. 1:3,4

tween God and man as well as the inward peace that resulted. The peace offering was the only sacrifice of which the offerer might eat a part. Fellowship was involved because the offerer, on the basis of the sacrifice, had fellowship with God and with the priest, who also ate part of the offering (7:14–15, 31–34). This sacrifice—along with others—was offered by the thousands during the three annual festivals in Israel (see Ex 23:14–17; Num 29:39) because multitudes of people came to the temple to worship and share in a communal meal. During the monarchy, the animals offered by the people were usually supplemented by large numbers given by the king. At the dedication of the temple, Solomon offered 20,000 cattle and 120,000 sheep and goats as peace offerings over a period of 14 days (1 Ki 8:63–65).

3:2 *lay his hand upon.* See notes on 1:3; Ex 29:10.

3:5 *upon the burnt sacrifice.* The burnt offerings for the nation as a whole were offered every morning and evening, and the peace offerings were offered on top of them.

3:9 *whole rump* [i.e. fat tail]. A breed of sheep still much used in the Middle East has a tail heavy with fat.

3:11,16 *upon the altar: it is the food.* Israelite sacrifices were not "food for the gods" (as in other ancient cultures; see Ezek 16:20; cf. Ps 50:9–13) but were sometimes called "food" metaphorically (21:6,8,17,21; 22:25) in the sense that they were gifts to God and that He received them with delight.

3:17 *eat neither fat nor blood.* See note on 17:11.

4:2 *through ignorance.* See 5:15; contrast Num 15:30–31. Four classes of people involved in committing unintentional sins are listed: (1) "the priest that is anointed" (vv. 3–12), (2) the "whole congregation of Israel" (vv. 13–21), (3) a "ruler" (vv. 22–26) and (4) "any one of the common people" (vv. 27–35). Heb 9:7 speaks of "the errors of the people" in referring to the day of atonement.

4:3 *the priest that is anointed.* The high priest (see 6:20,22). *do sin.* All high priests sinned except the high priest Jesus Christ (Heb 5:1–3; 7:26–28). *according to the sin of the people.* The relationship of the priests to the people was so intimate in Israel (as a nation consecrated to God) that the people became guilty when the priest sinned. *let him.* Although the burnt, meat and peace offerings (chs. 1–3) were voluntary, the sin offering was compulsory (see vv. 14,23,28). *without blemish.* A defective sacrifice could not be a substitute for a defective people. The final perfect sacrifice for the sins of God's people was the crucified Christ, who was without any moral defect (Heb 9:13–14; 1 Pet 1:19). *sin offering.* See further priestly regulations in 6:24–30; Num 15:22–29. As soon as an "anointed priest" (or a person from one of the other classes of people) became aware of unintentional sin, he was to bring his sin offering to the Lord. On the other hand, should the priest (or others) remain unaware of unintentional sin, this lack was atoned for on the day of atonement.

4:4 Three principles of atonement are found in this verse:

5 And the priest that is anointed [a]shall take of the bullock's blood, and bring it to the tabernacle of the congregation:

6 And the priest shall dip his finger in the blood, and sprinkle of the blood seven times before the LORD, before the vail of the sanctuary.

7 And the priest shall [a]put *some* of the blood upon the horns of the altar of sweet incense before the LORD, which *is* in the tabernacle of the congregation; and shall pour [b]all the blood of the bullock at the bottom of the altar of the burnt offering, which *is at* the door of the tabernacle of the congregation.

8 And he shall take off from it all the fat of the bullock *for* the sin offering; the fat that covereth the inwards, and all the fat that *is* upon the inwards,

9 And the two kidneys, and the fat that *is* upon them, which *is* by the flanks, and the caul above the liver, with the kidneys, it shall he take away,

10 [a]As it was taken off from the bullock of the sacrifice of peace offerings: and the priest shall burn them upon the altar of the burnt offering.

11 [a]And the skin of the bullock, and all his flesh, with his head, and with his legs, and his inwards, and his dung,

12 Even the whole bullock shall he carry forth [1]without the camp unto a clean place, [a][2]where the ashes are poured out, and [b]burn him on the wood with fire: [2]where the ashes are poured out shall he be burnt.

13 ¶ And [a]if the whole congregation of Israel sin through ignorance, [b]and the thing be hid from the eyes of the assembly, and they have done somewhat against any of the commandments of the LORD *concerning things* which should not be done, and are guilty;

14 When the sin, which they have sinned against it, is known, then the congregation shall offer a young bullock for the sin, and bring him before the tabernacle of the congregation.

15 And the elders of the congregation [a]shall lay their hands upon the head of the bullock before the LORD: and the bullock shall be killed before the LORD.

16 [a]And the priest that is anointed shall bring of the bullock's blood to the tabernacle of the congregation:

17 And the priest shall dip his finger *in some* of the blood, and sprinkle *it* seven times before the LORD, *even* before the vail.

18 And he shall put *some* of the blood upon the horns of the altar which *is* before the LORD, that *is* in the tabernacle of the congregation, and shall pour out all the blood at the bottom of the altar of the burnt offering, which *is at* the door of the tabernacle of the congregation.

19 And he shall take all his fat from him, and burn *it* upon the altar.

20 And he shall do with the bullock as he did [a]with the bullock for a sin offering, so shall he do with this: [b]and the priest shall make an atonement for them, and it shall be forgiven them.

21 And he shall carry forth the bullock without the camp, and burn him as he burned the first bullock: it *is* a sin offering for the congregation.

22 ¶ When a ruler hath sinned, and [a]done somewhat through ignorance against any of the commandments of the LORD his God *concerning things* which should not be done, and is guilty;

4:5 [a]ch. 16:14; Num. 19:4
4:7 [a]ch. 8:15; 9:9; 16:18 [b]ch. 5:9
4:10 [a]ch. 3:3-5
4:11 [a]Ex. 29:14; Num. 19:5
4:12 [1]Heb. *to without the camp* [2]Heb. *at the pouring out of the ashes* [a]ch. 6:11 [b]Heb. 13:11
4:13 [a]Num. 15:24; Josh. 7:11 [b]ch. 5:2-4,17
4:15 [a]ch. 1:4
4:16 [a]ver. 5; Heb. 9:12-14
4:20 [a]ver. 3 [b]Num. 15:25
4:22 [a]ver. 2,13

(1) substitution ("bring the bullock"), (2) identification ("lay his hand upon the bullock's head") and (3) the death of the substitute ("kill the bullock").

4:5 *blood.* See note on 17:11. There were two types of sin offerings. The first (vv. 3–21) and more important involved sprinkling the blood in the tabernacle in front of the inner curtain or, in the case of the solemn day of atonement (ch. 16), on and in front of the mercy seat itself. This type of sin offering was not eaten. The fat, kidneys and covering of the liver were burned on the great altar, but all the rest was burned outside the camp (v. 12). Heb 13:11–13 clearly draws the parallel to our sin offering, Jesus, who suffered outside the city gate. This type of sin offering was offered by and for a priest or by the elders for the whole community. In general, the animal to be sacrificed was a young bull, but on the day of atonement the sin offering was to be a goat (16:9).

The second type of sin offering (4:22–5:13) was for a leader of the nation or a private individual. Some of the blood was applied to the horns of the great altar, the rest poured out at its base. The fat, etc., was burned on the altar, but the rest of the offering was given to the priest and his male relatives as food to be eaten in a holy place (6:29–30; see 10:16–20). The sin offering brought by a private person was to be a female goat or lamb. If the person was poor, he could bring two turtledoves or young pigeons (5:7–8; 12:6,8; cf. Luke 2:24), or even about two quarts of flour (5:11). The offering included confession (5:5) and the symbolic transfer of guilt by laying hands on the sacrifice (v. 29; 16:21). Then the priest who offered the sacrifice made atonement for the sin, and the Lord promised forgiveness (5:13). By bringing such a sin offering, a faithful Israelite under conviction of sin sought restoration of fellowship with God.

4:6 *finger.* The right forefinger (see 14:16). *seven.* The number was symbolic of perfection and completeness (see note on Gen 5:5). *vail.* The great curtain that separated the holy place from the most holy place (Ex 26:33).

4:7 *horns.* The four horns of the altar (see Ex 30:1–3) were symbols of the atoning power of the sin offering (Ex 30:10).

4:8–10 See 3:3–5.

4:12 *without the camp.* See note on 13:45–46. So also Jesus was crucified outside Jerusalem (Heb 13:11–13; see 9:11; 16:26–28; Num 19:3; Ezek 43:21). *clean.* The distinction between clean and unclean was a matter of ritual or religious purity, not a concern for physical cleanliness (see chs. 11–15 for examples; see also Mark 7:1–4). *burn.* Since the sins of the offerer were symbolically transferred to the sacrificial bull, the bull had to be entirely destroyed and not thrown on the ash pile of 1:16.

4:15 *elders.* See note on Ex 3:16.

4:18 *altar.* Of incense (see v. 7).

4:20 *sin offering.* The offering of the priest who had sinned (v. 3). *shall be forgiven.* In 4:20–6:7 this is a key phrase, occurring nine times and referring to forgiveness by God.

Old Testament Sacrifices

SACRIFICE	OT REFERENCES	ELEMENTS	PURPOSE
Burnt Offering	Lev 1; 6:8-13; 8:18-21; 16:24	Bullock, ram or male bird (turtledove or young pigeon for the poor); wholly consumed; no defect	Voluntary act of worship; atonement for unintentional sin in general; expression of devotion, commitment and complete surrender to God
Meat [Grain] Offering	Lev 2; 6:14-23	Grain, fine flour, oil, frankincense, baked bread (cakes or wafers), salt; no yeast or honey; accompanied burnt offering and peace offering (along with drink offering)	Voluntary act of worship; recognition of God's goodness and provisions; devotion to God
Peace Offering	Lev 3; 7:11-34	Any animal without defect from herd or flock; variety of breads	Voluntary act of worship; thanksgiving and fellowship (it included a communal meal)
Sin Offering	Lev 4:1–5:13; 6:24-30; 8:14-17; 16:3-22	1. Young bullock: for high priest and congregation 2. Male goat: for ruler 3. Female goat or lamb: for common person 4. Two turtledoves or pigeons: for the poor 5. Tenth of an ephah of fine flour: for the very poor	Mandatory atonement for specific unintentional sin; confession of sin; forgiveness of sin; cleansing from defilement
Trespass Offering	Lev 5:14–6:7; 7:1-6	Ram	Mandatory atonement for unintentional sin requiring restitution; cleansing from defilement; make restitution; pay 20% fine

When more than one kind of offering was presented (as in Num 7:16,17), the procedure was usually as follows: (1) sin offering or trespass offering, (2) burnt offering, (3) peace offering and meat offering (along with a drink offering). This sequence furnishes part of the spiritual significance of the sacrificial system. First, sin had to be dealt with (sin offering or trespass offering). Second, the worshiper committed himself completely to God (burnt offering and meat offering). Third, fellowship or communion between the Lord, the priest and the worshiper (peace offering) was established. To state it another way, there were sacrifices of expiation (sin offerings and trespass offerings), consecration (burnt offerings and meat offerings) and communion (peace offerings—these included vow offerings, thank offerings and voluntary offerings).

23 Or [a]if his sin, wherein he hath sinned, come to his knowledge, he shall bring his offering, a kid of the goats, a male without blemish;

24 And [a]he shall lay his hand upon the head of the goat, and kill it in the place where they kill the burnt offering before the LORD: it *is* a sin offering.

25 [a]And the priest shall take of the blood of the sin offering with his finger, and put *it* upon the horns of the altar of burnt offering, and shall pour out his blood at the bottom of the altar of burnt offering.

26 And he shall burn all his fat upon the altar, as [a]the fat of the sacrifice of peace offerings: [b]and the priest shall make an atonement for him as concerning his sin, and it shall be forgiven him.

27 ¶ And [a]if [1]any one of the [2]common people sin through ignorance, while he doeth somewhat against *any of* the commandments of the LORD *concerning things* which ought not to be done, and be guilty;

28 Or [a]if his sin, which he hath sinned, come to his knowledge, then he shall bring his offering, a kid of the goats, a female without blemish, for his sin which he hath sinned.

29 [a]And he shall lay his hand upon the head of the sin offering, and slay the sin offering in the place of the burnt offering.

30 And the priest shall take of the blood thereof with his finger, and put *it* upon the horns of the altar of burnt offering, and shall pour out all the blood thereof at the bottom of the altar.

31 And [a]he shall take away all the fat thereof, [b]as the fat is taken away from off the sacrifice of peace offerings; and the priest shall burn *it* upon the altar for a [c]sweet savour unto the LORD; [d]and the priest shall make an atonement for him, and it shall be forgiven him.

32 And if he bring a lamb for a sin offering, [a]he shall bring it a female without blemish.

33 And he shall lay his hand upon the head of the sin offering, and slay it for a sin offering in the place where they kill the burnt offering.

34 And the priest shall take of the blood of the sin offering with his finger, and put *it* upon the horns of the altar of burnt offering, and shall pour out all the blood thereof at the bottom of the altar;

35 And he shall take away all the fat thereof, as the fat of the lamb is taken away from the sacrifice of the peace offerings; and the priest shall burn them upon the altar, [a]according to the offerings made by fire unto the LORD; [b]and the priest shall make an atonement for his sin that he hath committed, and it shall be forgiven him.

4:23 [a]ver. 14; ch. 5:4
4:24 [a]ver. 4; Is. 53:6
4:25 [a]ver. 30
4:26 [a]ch. 3:5 [b]ver. 20; Num. 15:28
4:27 [1]Heb. *any soul* [2]Heb. *people of the land* [a]ver. 2; Num. 15:27
4:28 [a]ver. 23
4:29 [a]ver. 4,24
4:31 [a]ch. 3:14 [b]ch. 3:3 [c]Gen. 8:21; Ex. 29:18; ch. 1:9; Ezra 6:10 [d]ver. 26
4:32 [a]ver. 28
4:35 [a]ch. 3:5 [b]ver. 26,31
5:1 [a]1 Ki. 8:31; Prov. 29:24; Mat. 26:63 [b]ver. 17; ch. 7:18; 17:16; 19:8; 20:17; Num. 9:13
5:2 [a]ch. 11:24, 28,31,39; Num. 19:11,13,16 [b]ver. 17
5:3 [a]ch. 12; 13; 15
5:4 [a]See 1 Sam. 25:22; Acts 23:12 [b]See Mark 6:23
5:5 [a]ch. 16:21; 26:40; Num. 5:7; Ezra 10:11,12
5:7 [1]Heb. *his hand cannot reach to the sufficiency of a lamb* [a]ch. 12:8; 14:21 [b]ch. 1:14
5:8 [a]ch. 1:15
5:9 [a]ch. 4:7,18,30,34
5:10 [1]Or, *ordinance* [a]ch. 1:14 [b]ch. 4:26

5 And if a soul sin, [a]and hear the voice of swearing, and *is* a witness, whether he hath seen or known *of it;* if he do not utter *it,* then he shall [b]bear his iniquity.

2 Or [a]if a soul touch any unclean thing, whether *it be* a carcase of an unclean beast, or a carcase of unclean cattle, or the carcase of unclean creeping things, and *if* it be hidden from him; he also shall be unclean, and [b]guilty.

3 Or if he touch [a]the uncleanness of man, whatsoever uncleanness *it be* that a man shall be defiled withal, and it be hid from him; when he knoweth *of it,* then he shall be guilty.

4 Or if a soul swear, pronouncing with *his* lips [a]to do evil, or [b]to do good, whatsoever *it be* that a man shall pronounce with an oath, and it be hid from him; when he knoweth *of it,* then he shall be guilty in one of these.

5 And it shall be, when he shall be guilty in one of these *things,* that he shall [a]confess that he hath sinned in that *thing:*

6 And he shall bring his trespass offering unto the LORD for his sin which he hath sinned, a female from the flock, a lamb or a kid of the goats, for a sin offering; and the priest shall make an atonement for him concerning his sin.

7 And [a]if [1]he be not able to bring a lamb, then he shall bring for his trespass, which he hath committed, two [b]turtledoves, or two young pigeons, unto the LORD; one for a sin offering, and the other for a burnt offering.

8 And he shall bring them unto the priest, who shall offer *that* which *is* for the sin offering first, and [a]wring off his head from his neck, but shall not divide *it* asunder:

9 And he shall sprinkle of the blood of the sin offering upon the side of the altar; and [a]the rest of the blood shall be wrung out at the bottom of the altar: it *is* a sin offering.

10 And he shall offer the second *for* a burnt offering, according to the [a] [1]manner: [b]and the priest shall make an atonement for him for his sin which he had sinned, and it shall be forgiven him.

11 But if he be not able to bring two turtledoves, or two young pigeons, then he that sinned shall bring for his offering the tenth

4:23 *kid of the goats, a male.* Less valuable animals were sacrificed for those with lesser standing in the community or of lesser economic means. Thus a bullock was required for the high priest (v. 3) and the whole community (v. 14), but a male goat for a civic leader (v. 23) and a female goat (v. 28) or lamb (v. 32) for an ordinary Israelite. If an offerer was too poor, then turtledoves and pigeons were sufficient (5:7) or even a handful of fine flour (5:11–12).

4:25 *priest.* The priest who officiated for the civil authority or the lay person (see vv. 30,34).

4:28 *kid of the goats, a female.* See note on v. 23.

4:29 *lay his hand upon.* See notes on 1:3; Ex 29:10.

4:30 *horns.* See note on v. 7.

4:32 *lamb . . . female.* See note on v. 23.

4:35 *fat . . . of the peace offerings.* See 3:3–5.

5:1–4 Four examples of the unintentional sins (see 4:2–3,13, 22,27) the sin offering covers.

5:2 *unclean.* See note on 4:12.

5:3 *uncleanness of man.* See chs. 11–15.

5:5 *confess.* The offerer had to acknowledge his sin to God in order to receive forgiveness.

5:7 *two turtledoves . . . pigeons.* See note on 4:23.

part of an ephah of fine flour for a sin offering;
[a]he shall put no oil upon it, neither shall he
put *any* frankincense thereon: for it *is* a sin offering.
12 Then shall he bring it to the priest, and
the priest shall take his handful of it, [a]*even* a
memorial thereof, and burn *it* on the altar, [b]ac-
cording to the offerings made by fire unto the
LORD: it *is* a sin offering.
13 [a]And the priest shall make an atonement for him as touching his sin that he hath
sinned in one of these, and it shall be forgiven
him: and [b]*the remnant* shall be the priest's, as
a meat offering.
14 ¶ And the LORD spake unto Moses, saying,
15 [a]If a soul commit a trespass, and sin
through ignorance, in the holy *things* of the
LORD; then [b]he shall bring for his trespass unto
the LORD a ram without blemish out of the
flocks, with thy estimation *by* shekels of silver,
after [c]the shekel of the sanctuary, for a trespass offering:
16 And he shall make amends for the harm
that he hath done in the holy *thing,* and [a]shall
add the fifth *part* thereto, and give it unto the
priest: [b]and the priest shall make an atonement for him with the ram of the trespass offering, and it shall be forgiven him.
17 And if a soul sin, and commit any *of
these things* which are forbidden to be done
by the commandments of the LORD; [a]though
he wist *it* not, yet is he [b]guilty, and shall bear
his iniquity.
18 [a]And he shall bring a ram without
blemish out of the flock, with thy estimation,
for a trespass offering, unto the priest: [b]and
the priest shall make an atonement for him
concerning his ignorance wherein he erred
and wist *it* not, and it shall be forgiven him.
19 It *is* a trespass offering: [a]he hath certainly trespassed against the LORD.
6 And the LORD spake unto Moses, saying,
2 If a soul sin, and [a]commit a trespass
against the LORD, and [b]lie unto his neighbour
in that [c]which was delivered him to keep, or
[1]in [2]fellowship, or in a thing taken away by violence, or hath [d]deceived his neighbour;
3 Or [a]have found that which was lost, and
lieth concerning it, and [b]sweareth falsely; in
any of all *these* that a man doeth, sinning
therein:

5:11 [a]Num. 5:15
5:12 [a]ch. 2:2 [b]ch. 4:35
5:13 [a]ch. 4:26 [b]ch. 2:3
5:15 [a]ch. 22:14 [b]Ezra 10:19 [c]Ex. 30:13; ch. 27:25
5:16 [a]ch. 6:5; 22:14; 27:13,15, 27,31; Num. 5:7 [b]ch. 4:26
5:17 [a]ver. 15; ch. 4:2,13,22,27 [b]ver. 1,2
5:18 [a]ver. 15 [b]ver. 16
5:19 [a]Ezra 10:2
6:2 [1]Or, *in dealing* [2]Heb. *putting of the hand* [a]Num. 5:6 [b]ch. 19:11; Acts 5:4; Col. 3:9 [c]Ex. 22:7,10 [d]Prov. 24:28; 26:19
6:3 [a]Deut. 22:1-3 [b]Ex. 22:11; ch. 19:12; Jer. 7:9; Zech. 5:4
6:5 [1]Or, *in the day of his being found guilty* [2]Heb. *in the day of his trespass* [a]ch. 5:16; Num. 5:7; 2 Sam. 12:6
6:6 [a]ch. 5:15
6:7 [a]ch. 4:26
6:9 [1]Or, *for the burning*
6:10 [a]Ex. 28:39-41,43; ch. 16:4; Ezek. 44:17,18 [b]ch. 1:16
6:11 [a]Ezek. 44:19 [b]ch. 4:12
6:12 [a]ch. 3:3,9,14
6:14 [a]ch. 2:1; Num. 15:4

4 Then it shall be, because he hath sinned,
and is guilty, that he shall restore that which he
took violently away, or the thing which he hath
deceitfully gotten, or that which was delivered
him to keep, or the lost *thing* which he found,
5 Or all *that* about which he hath sworn
falsely; he shall even [a]restore it in the principal, and shall add the fifth *part* more thereto,
and give it unto him to whom it appertaineth,
[1][2]in the day of his trespass offering.
6 And he shall bring his trespass offering
unto the LORD, [a]a ram without blemish out of
the flock, with thy estimation, for a trespass offering, unto the priest:
7 [a]And the priest shall make an atonement
for him before the LORD: and it shall be forgiv-
en him for any *thing* of all that he hath done in
trespassing therein.

The burnt offering

8 ¶ And the LORD spake unto Moses, saying,
9 Command Aaron and his sons, saying,
This *is* the law of the burnt offering: It *is* the
burnt offering, [1]because of the burning upon
the altar all night unto the morning, and the
fire of the altar shall be burning in it.
10 [a]And the priest shall put on his linen
garment, and *his* linen breeches shall he put
upon his flesh, and take up the ashes which
the fire hath consumed with the burnt offering
on the altar, and he shall put them [b]besides
the altar.
11 And [a]he shall put off his garments, and
put on other garments, and carry forth the
ashes without the camp [b]unto a clean place.
12 And the fire upon the altar shall be
burning in it; it shall not be put out: and the
priest shall burn wood on it every morning,
and lay the burnt offering in order upon it; and
he shall burn thereon [a]the fat of the peace offerings.
13 The fire shall ever be burning upon the
altar; it shall never go out.

The meat offering

14 ¶ [a]And this *is* the law of the meat offering: the sons of Aaron shall offer it before the
LORD, before the altar.
15 And he shall take of it his handful, of
the flour of the meat offering, and of the oil
thereof, and all the frankincense which *is*
upon the meat offering, and shall burn *it upon*

5:11 *fine flour.* See note on 4:23. Although no blood was used with a flour offering, it was offered "according to the offerings made by fire unto the LORD" (v. 12). Heb 9:22 may refer to such a situation.

5:15 *trespass offering* [i.e., guilt offering]. See further priestly regulations in 7:1–6 (see also Is 53:10). Traditionally called the "trespass offering," it was very similar to the sin offering (cf. 7:7), and the Hebrew words for the two were apparently sometimes interchanged. The major difference between the trespass and sin offerings was that the trespass offering was brought in cases where restitution for the sin was possible and therefore required (v. 16). Thus in cases of theft and cheating (6:2–5) the stolen property had to be returned along with 20 percent indemnity. By contrast, the sin offering was prescribed in cases of sin where no restitution was possible. The animal sacrificed as a trespass offering was always a ram.

6:3 *that which was lost.* See Deut 22:1–3.

6:6 *unto the LORD . . . unto the priest.* Sacrifices were brought to the Lord, but priests were His authorized representatives.

6:8–7:36 Further regulations concerning the sacrifices, dealing mainly with the portions to be eaten by the priests or, in the case of the peace offering, by the one offering the sacrifice.

6:9 *burnt offering.* See ch. 1; Num 15:1–16 and notes.

6:13 The perpetual fire on the altar represented uninterrupted offering to and appeal to God on behalf of Israel.

6:14 *meat offering* [i.e., grain offering]. See ch. 2 and notes.

the altar *for* a sweet savour, *even* the [a]memorial of it, unto the LORD.

16 And [a]the remainder thereof shall Aaron and his sons eat: [b]*with* unleavened bread shall it be eaten in the holy place; in the court of the tabernacle of the congregation they shall eat it.

17 [a]It shall not be baken *with* leaven. [b]I have given it *unto them for* their portion of my offerings made by fire; [c]it *is* most holy, as *is* the sin offering, and as the trespass offering.

18 [a]All the males among the children of Aaron shall eat of it. [b]*It shall be* a statute for ever in your generations concerning the offerings of the LORD made by fire: [c]every one that toucheth them shall be holy.

19 ¶ And the LORD spake unto Moses, saying,

20 [a]This *is* the offering of Aaron and of his sons, which they shall offer unto the LORD in the day when he is anointed; the tenth *part* of an [b]ephah of fine flour *for* a meat offering perpetual, half of it in the morning, and half thereof at night.

21 In a pan it shall be made with oil; *and when it is* baken, thou shalt bring it in: *and* the baken pieces of the meat offering shalt thou offer *for* a sweet savour unto the LORD.

22 And the priest of his sons [a]that is anointed in his stead shall offer it: *it is* a statute for ever unto the LORD; [b]it shall be wholly burnt.

23 For every meat offering for the priest shall be wholly *burnt:* it shall not be eaten.

The sin offering

24 ¶ And the LORD spake unto Moses, saying,

25 Speak unto Aaron and to his sons, saying, [a]This *is* the law of the sin offering: [b]In the place where the burnt offering is killed shall the sin offering be killed before the LORD: [c]it *is* most holy.

26 [a]The priest that offereth it for sin shall eat it: [b]in the holy place shall it be eaten, in the court of the tabernacle of the congregation.

27 [a]Whatsoever shall touch the flesh thereof shall be holy: and when there is sprinkled of the blood thereof upon *any* garment, thou shalt wash that whereon it was sprinkled in the holy place.

28 But the earthen vessel wherein it is sodden [a]shall be broken: and if it be sodden in a brasen pot, it shall be both scoured, and rinsed in water.

6:15 [a]ch. 2:2,9
6:16 [a]ch. 2:3; Ezek. 44:29 [b]ver. 26; ch. 10:12,13; Num. 18:10
6:17 [a]ch. 2:11 [b]Num. 18:9,10 [c]ver. 25; Ex. 29:37; ch. 2:3; 7:1
6:18 [a]ver. 29; Num. 18:10 [b]ch. 3:17 [c]Ex. 29:37; ch. 22:3-7
6:20 [a]Ex. 29:2 [b]Ex. 16:36
6:22 [a]ch. 4:3 [b]Ex. 29:25
6:25 [a]ch. 4:2 [b]ch. 1:3,5,11 [c]ver. 17
6:26 [a]ch. 10:17,18; Num. 18:9,10; Ezek. 44:28,29 [b]ver. 16
6:27 [a]Ex. 29:37; 30:29
6:28 [a]ch. 11:33; 15:12
6:29 [a]ver. 18; Num. 18:10 [b]ver. 25
6:30 [a]ch. 4:7,11, 12,18,21; 10:18; 16:27; Heb. 13:11
7:1 [a]ch. 5; 6:1-7 [b]ch. 6:17,25; 21:22
7:2 [a]ch. 1:3,5,11; 4:24,29,33
7:3 [a]Ex. 29:13; ch. 3:4,9,10,14-16; 4:8,9
7:6 [a]ch. 6:16-18; Num. 18:9,10 [b]ch. 2:3
7:7 [a]ch. 6:25,26; 14:13
7:9 [1]Or, *on the flat plate*, or, *slice* [a]ch. 2:3,10; Num. 18:9; Ezek. 44:29
7:11 [a]ch. 3:1; 22:18,21; Ezek. 45:15
7:12 [a]ch. 2:4; Num. 6:15
7:13 [a]Amos 4:5

29 [a]All the males among the priests shall eat thereof: [b]it *is* most holy.

30 [a]And no sin offering, whereof *any* of the blood is brought into the tabernacle of the congregation to reconcile *withal* in the holy *place,* shall be eaten: it shall be burnt in the fire.

The trespass offering

7 Likewise [a]this *is* the law of the trespass offering: [b]it *is* most holy.

2 [a]In the place where they kill the burnt offering shall they kill the trespass offering: and the blood thereof shall he sprinkle round about upon the altar.

3 And he shall offer of it [a]all the fat thereof; the rump, and the fat that covereth the inwards,

4 And the two kidneys, and the fat that *is* on them, which *is* by the flanks, and the caul *that is* above the liver, with the kidneys, it shall he take away:

5 And the priest shall burn them upon the altar *for* an offering made by fire unto the LORD: it *is* a trespass offering.

6 [a]Every male among the priests shall eat thereof: it shall be eaten in the holy place: [b]it *is* most holy.

7 As the sin offering *is,* so *is* [a]the trespass offering: *there is* one law for them: the priest that maketh atonement therewith shall have *it.*

8 And the priest that offereth *any* man's burnt offering, *even* the priest shall have to himself the skin of the burnt offering which he hath offered.

9 And [a]all the meat offering that is baken in the oven, and all *that* is dressed in the fryingpan, and [1]in the pan, shall be the priest's that offereth it.

10 And every meat offering, mingled with oil, and dry, shall all the sons of Aaron have, one *as much* as another.

The peace offering

11 ¶ And [a]this *is* the law of the sacrifice of peace offerings, which he shall offer unto the LORD.

12 If he offer it for a thanksgiving, then he shall offer with the sacrifice of thanksgiving unleavened cakes mingled with oil, and unleavened wafers [a]anointed with oil, and cakes mingled with oil, of fine flour, fried.

13 Besides the cakes, he shall offer *for* his offering [a]leavened bread with the sacrifice of thanksgiving of his peace offerings.

14 And of it he shall offer one out of the

6:25 *sin offering.* See 4:1–5:13 and notes.

6:28 *earthen vessel.* Ordinary kitchen utensils and domestic ware were made of clay, usually fired in a kiln and often painted or burnished.

7:2 *place.* On the north side of the altar of burnt offering in front of the tabernacle (1:11). *trespass offering.* See 5:14–6:7 and notes.

7:3 *rump.* See note on 3:9.

7:7–10 See Num 18:8–20; 1 Cor 9:13.

7:11–36 This section supplements ch. 3, adding regulations about (1) three types of peace offerings (thanksgiving, vv. 12–15; vow, v. 16; voluntary, v. 16), (2) prohibition of eating fat and blood (vv. 22–27) and (3) the priests' share (vv. 28–36).

7:12–15 Thanksgiving offerings were given in gratitude for deliverance from sickness (Ps 116:17), trouble (Ps 107:22) or death (Ps 56:12), or for a blessing received.

7:13 *leavened.* This regulation was not against the prohibition of 2:11 or Ex 23:18 since the offering here was not burned on the altar.

whole oblation *for* a heave offering unto the
LORD, [a]*and* it shall be the priest's that sprinkleth the blood of the peace offerings.
15 [a]And the flesh of the sacrifice of his
peace offerings for thanksgiving shall be eaten
the same day that it is offered; he shall not
leave *any* of it until the morning.
16 But [a]if the sacrifice of his offering *be* a
vow, or a voluntary offering, it shall be eaten
the *same* day that he offereth his sacrifice: and
on the morrow also the remainder of it shall
be eaten:
17 But the remainder of the flesh of the
sacrifice on the third day shall be burnt with
fire.
18 And if *any* of the flesh of the sacrifice of
his peace offerings be eaten at all on the third
day, it shall not be accepted, neither shall it be
[a]imputed unto him that offereth it: it shall be
an [b]abomination, and the soul that eateth of it
shall bear his iniquity.
19 And the flesh that toucheth any unclean
thing shall not be eaten; it shall be burnt with
fire: and *as for* the flesh, all that be clean shall
eat thereof.
20 But the soul that eateth *of* the flesh of the
sacrifice of peace offerings, that *pertain* unto
the LORD, [a]having his uncleanness upon him,
even that soul [b]shall be cut off from his people.
21 Moreover the soul that shall touch any
unclean *thing, as* [a]the uncleanness of man, or
any [b]unclean beast, or any [c]abominable unclean *thing,* and eat of the flesh of the sacrifice
of peace offerings, which *pertain* unto the
LORD, even that soul [d]shall be cut off from his
people.

Forbidden portions

22 ¶ And the LORD spake unto Moses, saying,
23 Speak unto the children of Israel, saying, [a]Ye shall eat no *manner* fat, of ox, or of
sheep, or of goat.
24 And the fat of the [a][1]beast that dieth of
itself, and the fat of that which is torn *with*
beasts, may be used in any *other* use: but ye
shall in no wise eat of it.

7:14 [a]Num. 18:8,11,19
7:15 [a]ch. 22:30
7:16 [a]ch. 19:6-8
7:18 [a]Num. 18:27 [b]ch. 11:10,11,41; 19:7
7:20 [a]ch. 15:3; 1 Cor. 11:28 [b]Gen. 17:14
7:21 [a]ch. 12; 13; 15 [b]ch. 11:24,28 [c]Ezek. 4:14 [d]ver. 20
7:23 [a]ch. 3:17
7:24 [1]Heb. *carcase* [a]ch. 17:15; Deut. 14:21; Ezek. 4:14; 44:31
7:26 [a]Gen. 9:4; ch. 3:17; 17:10-14; Ezek. 33:25; John 6:53; Acts 15:20,29
7:29 [a]ch. 3:1; 22:21; Ezek. 45:15
7:30 [a]ch. 3:3,4,9,14 [b]Ex. 29:24,27; ch. 8:27; 9:21; Num. 6:20
7:31 [a]ch. 3:5,11,16 [b]ver. 34
7:32 [a]ver. 34; ch. 9:21; Num. 6:20
7:34 [a]Ex. 29:28; ch. 10:14,15; Num. 18:18,19; Deut. 18:3
7:36 [a]Ex. 40:13,15; ch. 8:12,30

25 For whosoever eateth the fat of the
beast, of which *men* offer an offering made by
fire unto the LORD, even the soul that eateth *it*
shall be cut off from his people.
26 [a]Moreover ye shall eat no *manner of*
blood, *whether it be* of fowl or of beast, in any
of your dwellings.
27 Whatsoever soul *it be* that eateth any
manner of blood, even that soul shall be cut off
from his people.

The portion for priests

28 ¶ And the LORD spake unto Moses, saying,
29 Speak unto the children of Israel, saying, [a]He that offereth the sacrifice of his peace
offerings unto the LORD shall bring his oblation
unto the LORD of the sacrifice of his peace offerings.
30 [a]His own hands shall bring the offerings
of the LORD made by fire, the fat with the
breast, it shall he bring, that [b]the breast may
be waved *for* a wave offering before the LORD.
31 [a]And the priest shall burn the fat upon
the altar: [b]but the breast shall be Aaron's and
his sons'.
32 And [a]the right shoulder shall ye give
unto the priest *for* a heave offering of the sacrifices of your peace offerings.
33 He among the sons of Aaron, that offereth the blood of the peace offerings, and the
fat, shall have the right shoulder for *his* part.
34 For [a]the wave breast and the heave
shoulder have I taken of the children of Israel
from off the sacrifices of their peace offerings,
and have given them unto Aaron the priest
and unto his sons by a statute for ever from
among the children of Israel.
35 ¶ This *is the portion* of the anointing of
Aaron, and of the anointing of his sons, out of
the offerings of the LORD made by fire, in the
day *when* he presented them to minister unto
the LORD in the priest's office;
36 Which the LORD commanded to be giv-
en them of the children of Israel, [a]in the day
that he anointed them, *by* a statute for ever
throughout their generations.

7:15–18 See 19:5–8. All meat had to be eaten promptly (in the case of the thanksgiving offering on the same day, and in the case of the vow and voluntary offerings within two days). One reason may have been that in Canaan meat spoiled quickly and thus became ceremonially impure (v. 18) because it was not then perfect (1:3; see 21:16–23). The prohibition applied also to the passover (Ex 12:10).
7:16 *vow.* See 22:18–23. A vow was a solemn promise to offer a gift to God in response to a divine deliverance or blessing. Such vows often accompanied prayers for deliverance or blessing (see note on Ps 7:17). *voluntary offering.* See 22:18–23.
7:19 *unclean.* See note on 4:12.
7:20 *cut off from his people.* Removed from the covenant people through direct divine judgment (Gen 17:14), or (as here and in vv. 21,25,27; 17:4,9–10,14; 18:29; 19:8; 20:3,5–6,17–18; 23:29) through execution (see, e.g., 20:2–3; Ex 31:14), or possibly sometimes through banishment.
7:21 *abominable.* The penalty for doing things that were abominable in the Lord's eyes was severe (see note on v. 20; see also 18:29; 20:13).
7:22–27 See note on 17:11.
7:23 *fat.* The prohibition of fat for food was as strict as that of blood, but the reason was different. The fat of the peace offerings was the Lord's and was to be burned on the altar. There was no explicit prohibition of eating the fat of hunted animals like the gazelle or deer, but probably that was included (see 3:17; Deut 12:15–22).
7:26 *eat no manner of blood.* See note on 17:11; see also 3:17; 19:26; Gen 9:4–6; Deut 12:16,23–25; 15:23; 1 Sam 14:32–34; Ezek 33:25.
7:28–36 See 10:12–15; Num 18:8–20; Deut 18:1–5.
7:30–32 *breast . . . right shoulder* [i.e., thigh]. The breast and right thigh given to the priest were first presented to the Lord with gestures described as waving the breast and presenting the thigh (v. 34). See 8:25–29; 9:21; 10:14–15; Ex 29:26–27; Num 6:20; 18:11,18.

37 This *is* the law [a]of the burnt offering, [b]of the meat offering, [c]and of the sin offering, [d]and of the trespass offering, [e]and of the consecrations, and [f]of the sacrifice of the peace offerings;

38 Which the LORD commanded Moses in mount Sinai, in the day that he commanded the children of Israel [a]to offer their oblations unto the LORD, in the wilderness of Sinai.

The anointing of priests

8 And the LORD spake unto Moses, saying,

2 [a]Take Aaron and his sons with him, and [b]the garments, and [c]the anointing oil, and a bullock *for* the sin offering, and two rams, and a basket of unleavened bread;

3 And gather thou all the congregation together unto the door of the tabernacle of the congregation.

4 And Moses did as the LORD commanded him; and the assembly was gathered together unto the door of the tabernacle of the congregation.

5 And Moses said unto the congregation, [a]This *is* the thing which the LORD commanded to be done.

6 And Moses brought Aaron and his sons, [a]and washed them with water.

7 [a]And he put upon him the [b]coat, and girded him with the girdle, and clothed him with the robe, and put the ephod upon him, and he girded him with the curious girdle of the ephod, and bound *it* unto him therewith.

8 And he put the breastplate upon him: also he [a]put in the breastplate the Urim and the Thummim.

9 [a]And he put the mitre upon his head; also upon the mitre, *even* upon his forefront, did he put the golden plate, the holy crown; as the LORD [b]commanded Moses.

10 [a]And Moses took the anointing oil, and anointed the tabernacle and all that *was* therein, and sanctified them.

11 And he sprinkled thereof upon the altar seven times, and anointed the altar and all his vessels, both the laver and his foot, to sanctify them.

12 And he [a]poured of the anointing oil upon Aaron's head, and anointed him, to sanctify him.

13 [a]And Moses brought Aaron's sons, and put coats upon them, and girded them *with* girdles, and [1]put bonnets upon them; as the LORD commanded Moses.

14 [a]And he brought the bullock *for* the sin offering: and Aaron and his sons [b]laid their hands upon the head of the bullock *for* the sin offering.

15 And he slew *it;* [a]and Moses took the blood, and put *it* upon the horns of the altar round about with his finger, and purified the altar, and poured the blood at the bottom of the altar, and sanctified it, to make reconciliation upon it.

16 [a]And he took all the fat that *was* upon the inwards, and the caul *above* the liver, and the two kidneys, and their fat, and Moses burned *it* upon the altar.

17 But the bullock, and his hide, his flesh, and his dung, he burnt with fire without the camp; as the LORD [a]commanded Moses.

18 [a]And he brought the ram for the burnt offering: and Aaron and his sons laid their hands upon the head of the ram.

19 And he killed *it;* and Moses sprinkled the blood upon the altar round about.

20 And he cut the ram into pieces; and Moses burnt the head, and the pieces, and the fat.

21 And he washed the inwards and the legs in water; and Moses burnt the whole ram upon the altar: it *was* a burnt sacrifice for a sweet savour, *and* an offering made by fire unto the LORD; [a]as the LORD commanded Moses.

22 And [a]he brought the other ram, the ram of consecration: and Aaron and his sons laid their hands upon the head of the ram.

23 And he slew *it;* and Moses took of the blood of it, and put *it* upon the tip of Aaron's right ear, and upon the thumb of his right hand, and upon the great toe of his right foot.

24 And he brought Aaron's sons, and Moses put of the blood upon the tip of their right ear, and upon the thumbs of their right hands, and upon the great toes of their right feet: and Moses sprinkled the blood upon the altar round about.

25 [a]And he took the fat, and the rump, and all the fat that *was* upon the inwards, and the caul *above* the liver, and the two kidneys, and their fat, and the right shoulder:

26 [a]And out of the basket of unleavened bread, that *was* before the LORD, he took one unleavened cake, and a cake of oiled bread, and one wafer, and put *them* on the fat, and upon the right shoulder:

7:37 [a]ch. 6:9 [b]ch. 6:14 [c]ch. 6:25 [d]ver. 1 [e]Ex. 29:1; ch. 6:20 [f]ver. 11
7:38 [a]ch. 1:2
8:2 [a]Ex. 29:1-3 [b]Ex. 28:2,4 [c]Ex. 30:24,25
8:5 [a]Ex. 29:4
8:6 [a]Ex. 29:4
8:7 [a]Ex. 29:5 [b]Ex. 28:4
8:8 [a]Ex. 28:30
8:9 [a]Ex. 29:6 [b]Ex. 28:37
8:10 [a]Ex. 30:26-29
8:12 [a]Ex. 29:7; 30:30; ch. 21:10,12; Ps. 133:2
8:13 [1]Heb. *bound* [a]Ex. 29:8,9
8:14 [a]Ex. 29:10; Ezek. 43:19 [b]ch. 4:4
8:15 [a]Ex. 29:12,36; ch. 4:7; Ezek. 43:20,26; Heb. 9:22
8:16 [a]Ex. 29:13; ch. 4:8
8:17 [a]Ex. 29:14; ch. 4:11,12
8:18 [a]Ex. 29:15
8:21 [a]Ex. 29:18
8:22 [a]Ex. 29:19,31
8:25 [a]Ex. 29:22
8:26 [a]Ex. 29:23

7:37–38 A summary of chs. 1–7.
7:37 *consecrations.* See 8:14–36; Ex 29:1–35.
8:2 *the garments.* See Ex 39:1–31; 40:12–16. The garments that the high priest was to wear when he ministered are detailed in Ex 28:4–43 (see notes there). *anointing oil.* See note on Ex 25:6. The oil was used to anoint the tabernacle, sacred objects and consecrated priests (vv. 10–12,30). It was later used to anoint leaders and kings (1 Sam 10:1; 16:13). See also note on Ex 29:7.
8:6 *washed them with water.* In the bronze basin ("laver," see v. 11) in the courtyard of the tabernacle (see Ex 30:17–21).
8:7 *ephod.* See note on Ex 28:6.
8:8 *Urim and the Thummim.* See notes on Ex 28:30; 1 Sam 2:28.
8:9 *holy crown.* See note on Ex 39:30.
8:11 *seven times.* See note on 4:6.
8:12 *oil upon Aaron's head.* See Ps 133.
8:14 *sin offering.* See 4:3–11 and notes. The consecration service included a sin offering for atonement, a burnt offering for worship (v. 18) and a "ram of consecration" (v. 22), whose blood was applied to the high priest on his right ear, thumb and toe (v. 23). After this was done, Aaron offered sacrifices for the people (9:15–21). Then he blessed the people in his capacity as priest, and the Lord accepted his ministry with the sign of miraculous fire (9:23–24). *laid their hands upon.* See notes on 1:3; Ex 29:10.

27 And he put all [a]upon Aaron's hands, and upon his sons' hands, and waved them *for* a wave offering before the LORD.

28 [a]And Moses took them from off their hands, and burnt *them* on the altar upon the burnt offering: they *were* consecrations for a sweet savour: it *is* an offering made by fire unto the LORD.

29 And Moses took the breast, and waved it *for* a wave offering before the LORD: *for* of the ram of consecration it was Moses' [a]part; as the LORD commanded Moses.

30 And [a]Moses took of the anointing oil, and of the blood which *was* upon the altar, and sprinkled *it* upon Aaron, *and* upon his garments, and upon his sons, and upon his sons' garments with him; and sanctified Aaron, *and* his garments, and his sons, and his sons' garments with him.

31 ¶ And Moses said unto Aaron and to his sons, [a]Boil the flesh *at* the door of the tabernacle of the congregation: and there eat it with the bread that *is* in the basket of consecrations, as I commanded, saying, Aaron and his sons shall eat it.

32 [a]And that which remaineth of the flesh and of the bread shall ye burn with fire.

33 And ye shall not go out of the door of the tabernacle of the congregation *in* seven days, until the days of your consecration be at an end: for [a]seven days shall he consecrate you.

34 [a]As he hath done this day, *so* the LORD hath commanded to do, to make an atonement for you.

35 Therefore shall ye abide *at* the door of the tabernacle of the congregation day and night seven days, and [a]keep the charge of the LORD, that ye die not: for so I am commanded.

36 So Aaron and his sons did all things which the LORD commanded by the hand of Moses.

The offerings of Aaron

9 And [a]it came to pass on the eighth day, *that* Moses called Aaron and his sons, and the elders of Israel;

2 And he said unto Aaron, [a]Take thee a young calf for a sin offering, [b]and a ram for a burnt offering, without blemish, and offer *them* before the LORD.

3 And unto the children of Israel thou shalt speak, saying, [a]Take ye a kid of the goats for a sin offering; and a calf and a lamb, both of the first year, without blemish, for a burnt offering;

4 Also a bullock and a ram for peace offerings, to sacrifice before the LORD; and [a]a meat offering mingled with oil: for [b]to day the LORD will appear unto you.

5 And they brought *that* which Moses commanded before the tabernacle of the congregation: and all the congregation drew near and stood before the LORD.

6 And Moses said, This *is* the thing which the LORD commanded *that* ye should do: and [a]the glory of the LORD shall appear unto you.

7 And Moses said unto Aaron, Go unto the altar, and [a]offer thy sin offering, and thy burnt offering, and make an atonement for thyself, and for the people: and [b]offer the offering of the people, and make an atonement for them; as the LORD commanded.

8 ¶ Aaron therefore went unto the altar, and slew the calf of the sin offering, which *was* for himself.

9 [a]And the sons of Aaron brought the blood unto him: and he dipt his finger in the blood, and [b]put *it* upon the horns of the altar, and poured out the blood at the bottom of the altar:

10 [a]But the fat, and the kidneys, and the caul above the liver of the sin offering, he burnt upon the altar; [b]as the LORD commanded Moses.

11 [a]And the flesh and the hide he burnt with fire without the camp.

12 And he slew the burnt offering; and Aaron's sons presented unto him the blood, [a]which he sprinkled round about upon the altar.

13 [a]And they presented the burnt offering unto him, with the pieces thereof, and the head: and he burnt *them* upon the altar.

14 [a]And he did wash the inwards and the legs, and burnt *them* upon the burnt offering on the altar.

15 ¶ [a]And he brought the people's offering, and took the goat, which *was* the sin offering for the people, and slew it, and offered it for sin, as the first.

16 And he brought the burnt offering, and offered it [a]according to the [1]manner.

17 And he brought [a]the meat offering, and [1]took a handful thereof, and burnt *it* upon the altar, [b]beside the burnt sacrifice of the morning.

18 He slew also the bullock and the ram *for* [a]a sacrifice of peace offerings, which *was* for the people: and Aaron's sons presented unto him the blood, which he sprinkled upon the altar round about,

19 And the fat of the bullock and of the ram, the rump, and that which covereth *the inwards*, and the kidneys, and the caul *above* the liver:

20 And they put the fat upon the breasts, [a]and he burnt the fat upon the altar:

21 And the breasts and the right shoulder Aaron waved [a]*for* a wave offering before the LORD; as Moses commanded.

8:27 [a]Ex. 29:24
8:28 [a]Ex. 29:25
8:29 [a]Ex. 29:26
8:30 [a]Ex. 29:21; 30:30; Num. 3:3
8:31 [a]Ex. 29:31,32; 1 Sam. 2:13-17
8:32 [a]Ex. 29:34
8:33 [a]Ex. 29:30,35; Ezek. 43:25,26
8:34 [a]Heb. 7:16
8:35 [a]Num. 3:7; 9:19; Deut. 11:1; 1 Ki. 2:3
9:1 [a]Ezek. 43:27
9:2 [a]Ex. 29:1; ch. 4:3; 8:14 [b]ch. 8:18
9:3 [a]ch. 4:23; Ezra 6:17; 10:19
9:4 [a]ch. 2:4 [b]ver. 6,23; Ex. 29:43
9:6 [a]ver. 23; Ex. 24:16; 2 Chr. 5:13,14
9:7 [a]ch. 4:3; 1 Sam. 3:14; Heb. 5:3; 7:27; 9:7 [b]ch. 4:16,20; Heb. 5:1
9:9 [a]ch. 8:15 [b]See ch. 4:7; Heb. 9:22,23
9:10 [a]ch. 8:16 [b]ch. 4:8
9:11 [a]ch. 4:11; 8:17
9:12 [a]ch. 1:5; 8:19
9:13 [a]ch. 8:20
9:14 [a]ch. 8:21
9:15 [a]ver. 3; Is. 53:10; Heb. 2:17; 5:3
9:16 [1]Or, *ordinance* [a]ch. 1:3,10
9:17 [1]Heb. *filled his hand out of it* [a]ver. 4; ch. 2:1,2 [b]Ex. 29:38
9:18 [a]ch. 3:1
9:20 [a]ch. 3:5,16
9:21 [a]Ex. 29:24; ch. 7:30-34

8:28 *upon the burnt offering.* See note on 3:5.
8:31 *saying, Aaron and his sons shall eat it.* Quoted from Ex 29:32.
9:1 *eighth day.* After the seven days of consecration (8:33).
9:2 *sin offering.* See notes on 4:3,5. *burnt offering.* See note on 1:3.
9:4 *peace offerings.* See note on 3:1. *meat offering.* See note on 2:1. *LORD will appear.* See vv. 6,23; see also note on Gen 12:7.
9:17 *burnt sacrifice of the morning.* See Ex 29:38–42.
9:21 *wave offering.* See note on 7:30–32.

22 ¶ And Aaron lift up his hand towards the people, and [a]blessed them, and came down from offering of the sin offering, and the burnt offering, and peace offerings.

23 And Moses and Aaron went into the tabernacle of the congregation, and came out, and blessed the people: [a]and the glory of the LORD appeared unto all the people.

24 And [a]there came a fire out from before the LORD, and consumed upon the altar the burnt offering and the fat: *which* when all the people saw, [b]they shouted, and fell on their faces.

The death of Nadab and Abihu

10 And [a]Nadab and Abihu, the sons of Aaron, [b]took either of them his censer, and put fire therein, and put incense thereon, and offered [c]strange fire before the LORD, which he commanded them not.

2 And there [a]went out fire from the LORD, and devoured them, and they died before the LORD.

3 Then Moses said unto Aaron, This *is it* that the LORD spake, saying, I will be sanctified in them [a]that come nigh me, and before all the people I will be [b]glorified. [c]And Aaron held his peace.

4 And Moses called Mishael and Elzaphan, the sons of [a]Uzziel the uncle of Aaron, and said unto them, Come near, carry your brethren from before the sanctuary out of the camp.

5 So they went near, and carried them in their coats out of the camp; as Moses had said.

6 And Moses said unto Aaron, and unto Eleazar and unto Ithamar his sons, [a]Uncover not your heads, neither rend your clothes; lest you die, and lest [b]wrath come upon all the people: but let your brethren, the whole house of Israel, bewail the burning which the LORD hath kindled.

7 [a]And ye shall not go out from the door of the tabernacle of the congregation, lest you die: [b]for the anointing oil of the LORD *is* upon you. And they did according to the word of Moses.

8 ¶ And the LORD spake unto Aaron, saying,

9 [a]Do not drink wine nor strong drink, thou, nor thy sons with thee, when ye go into the tabernacle of the congregation, lest ye die: *it shall be* a statute for ever throughout your generations:

10 And that *ye* may [a]put difference between holy and unholy, and between unclean and clean;

11 [a]And that *ye* may teach the children of Israel all the statutes which the LORD hath spoken unto them by the hand of Moses.

12 ¶ And Moses spake unto Aaron, and unto Eleazar and unto Ithamar his sons that were left, Take [a]the meat offering that remaineth of the offerings of the LORD made by fire, and eat it without leaven beside the altar: for [b]it *is* most holy:

13 And ye shall eat it in the holy place, because it *is* thy due, and thy sons' due, of the sacrifices of the LORD made by fire: for [a]so I am commanded.

14 And [a]the wave breast and heave shoulder shall ye eat in a clean place; thou, and thy sons, and thy daughters with thee: for *they be* thy due, and thy sons' due, *which* are given out of the sacrifices of peace offerings of the children of Israel.

15 [a]The heave shoulder and the wave breast shall they bring with the offerings made by fire of the fat, to wave *it for* a wave offering before the LORD; and it shall be thine, and thy sons' with thee, by a statute for ever; as the LORD hath commanded.

16 ¶ And Moses diligently sought [a]the goat of the sin offering, and behold, it was burnt: and he was angry with Eleazar and Ithamar the sons of Aaron which were left *alive,* saying,

17 [a]Wherefore have ye not eaten the sin offering in the holy place, seeing it *is* most holy, and *God* hath given it you to bear the iniquity of the congregation, to make atonement for them before the LORD?

18 Behold, [a]the blood of it was not brought in within the holy *place:* ye should indeed have eaten it in the holy *place,* [b]as I commanded.

9:22 [a]Num. 6:23; Deut. 21:5; Luke 24:50
9:23 [a]ver. 6; Num. 14:10
9:24 [a]Gen. 4:4; Judg. 6:21; 1 Ki. 18:38; 2 Chr. 7:1; Ps. 20:3 [b]1 Ki. 18:39; 2 Chr. 7:3; Ezra 3:11
10:1 [a]Num. 3:3,4; 1 Chr. 24:2 [b]ch. 16:12 [c]Ex. 30:9
10:2 [a]Num. 16:35
10:3 [a]Ex. 19:22; Is. 52:11; Ezek. 20:41 [b]Ezek. 28:22 [c]Ps. 39:9
10:4 [a]Ex. 6:18,22; Num. 3:19,30
10:6 [a]ch. 21:10; Num. 6:6,7 [b]Num. 16:22,46; Josh. 7:1; 2 Sam. 24:1
10:7 [a]ch. 21:12 [b]ch. 8:30
10:9 [a]Luke 1:15; 1 Tim. 3:3; Tit. 1:7
10:10 [a]Ezek. 44:23
10:11 [a]Deut. 24:8; Neh. 8:2,8; Jer. 18:18; Mal. 2:7
10:12 [a]Num. 18:9 [b]ch. 21:22
10:13 [a]ch. 2:3; 6:16
10:14 [a]Ex. 29:24,26,27; ch. 7:31,34; Num. 18:11
10:15 [a]ch. 7:29,30
10:16 [a]ch. 9:3,15
10:17 [a]ch. 6:26,29
10:18 [a]ch. 6:30 [b]ch. 6:26,30

9:22 *blessed.* The Aaronic benediction, a threefold blessing, is given in Num 6:23–26. Cf. the threefold apostolic benediction in 2 Cor 13:14.

9:23 *glory of the LORD.* See v. 6; cf. the display of the Lord's glory at the erection of the tabernacle (Ex 40:34–35); cf. also God's acceptance of sacrifices at the dedication of Solomon's temple (2 Chr 7:1).

9:24 *came a fire out from before the LORD.* See 10:2; 1 Ki 18:38.

10:1 *censer.* Ceremonial vessels containing hot coals and used for burning incense (see 16:12–13; 2 Chr 26:19; Rev 8:3–4).

10:2 *died before the LORD.* Aaron's older sons are mentioned also in Ex 6:23; 24:1,9; 28:1; Num 3:2–4; 26:60–61; 1 Chr 6:3; 24:1–2. They are regularly remembered as having died before the Lord and as having had no sons. Their death was tragic and at first seems harsh, but no more so than that of Ananias and Sapphira (Acts 5:1–11). In both cases a new era was being inaugurated (cf. also the judgment on Achan, Josh 7, and on Uzzah, 2 Sam 6:1–7). The new community had to be made aware that it existed for God, not vice versa.

10:6 *rend your clothes.* See 21:10; see also note on Gen 44:13.

10:7 *not go out.* To join the mourners (see 21:11–12).

10:10 *between holy and unholy.* The distinction between what was holy (sacred) and what was profane (common) was carefully maintained (see Ezek 22:26; 42:20; 44:23; 48:14–15).

10:12–15 See 7:28–36; Num 18:8–20; Deut 18:1–5.

10:18 *the blood of it was not brought in . . . ye should . . . have eaten.* There were two types of sin offerings: (1) those in which the blood was sprinkled within the tabernacle, and (2) those in which it was sprinkled only on the great altar. Portions of the second type normally should have been eaten (see note on 4:5). But Moses was satisfied when he learned that Aaron had acted sincerely and not in negligence or rebellion (vv. 19–20).

10:19 *such things have befallen me.* Perhaps referring to the death of his two oldest sons (v. 2), for which he mourned by fasting. Or possibly something had occurred that made him ceremonially unclean.

19 And Aaron said unto Moses, Behold,
[a]*this* day have they offered their sin offering
and their burnt offering before the LORD; and
such things have befallen me: and *if* I had eat-
en the sin offering to day, [b]should it have been
accepted in the sight of the LORD?
20 And when Moses heard *that,* he was
content.

Clean and unclean animals

11 And the LORD spake unto Moses and
to Aaron, saying unto them,
2 Speak unto the children of Israel, saying,
[a]These *are* the beasts which ye shall eat
among all the beasts that *are* on the earth.
3 Whatsoever parteth the hoof, and *is*
clovenfooted, *and* cheweth cud, among the
beasts, that shall ye eat.
4 Nevertheless these shall ye not eat of
them that chew the cud, or of them that divide
the hoof: *as* the camel, because he cheweth
the cud, but divideth not the hoof; he *is* unclean unto you.
5 And the cony, because he cheweth the
cud, but divideth not the hoof; he *is* unclean
unto you.
6 And the hare, because he cheweth the
cud, but divideth not the hoof; he *is* unclean
unto you.
7 And the swine, though he divide the
hoof, and *be* clovenfooted, yet he cheweth not
the cud; [a]he *is* unclean to you.
8 Of their flesh shall ye not eat, and their
carcase shall ye not touch; [a]they *are* unclean
to you.
9 ¶ [a]These shall ye eat of all that *are* in the
waters: whatsoever hath fins and scales in the
waters, in the seas, and in the rivers, them
shall ye eat.
10 And all that have not fins nor scales in
the seas, and in the rivers, of all that move in
the waters, and of any living thing which *is* in
the waters, they *shall be* an [a]abomination unto
you:
11 They shall be even an abomination unto
you: ye shall not eat of their flesh, but you
shall have their carcases in abomination.
12 Whatsoever hath no fins nor scales in the
waters, that *shall be* an abomination unto you.
13 ¶ [a]And these *are they which* ye shall
have in abomination among the fowls; they
shall not be eaten, they *are* an abomination:
the eagle, and the ossifrage, and the ospray,
14 And the vulture, and the kite after his
kind;

10:19 [a]ch. 9:8,12 [b]Is. 1:11-15
11:2 [a]Deut. 14:4; Ezek. 4:14; Dan. 1:8; Mat. 15:11; Acts 10:12,14; Rom. 14:14; Heb. 9:10; 13:9
11:7 [a]Is. 65:4; 66:3,17
11:8 [a]Is. 52:11; Mark 7:2,15,18; Acts 10:14,15; 15:29; 1 Cor. 8:8; Heb. 9:10
11:9 [a]Deut. 14:9
11:10 [a]ch. 7:18; Deut. 14:3
11:13 [a]Deut. 14:12
11:22 [a]Mat. 3:4; Mark 1:6
11:25 [a]ch. 14:8; 15:5; Num. 19:10,22; 31:24; Rev. 7:14
11:29 [a]Is. 66:17
11:32 [a]ch. 15:12

15 Every raven after his kind;
16 And the owl, and the night hawk, and
the cuckow, and the hawk after his kind,
17 And the little owl, and the cormorant,
and the great owl,
18 And the swan, and the pelican, and the
gier eagle,
19 And the stork, the heron after her kind,
and the lapwing, and the bat.
20 ¶ All fowls that creep, going upon *all*
four, *shall be* an abomination unto you.
21 Yet these may ye eat of every flying
creeping thing that goeth upon *all* four, which
have legs above their feet, to leap withal upon
the earth;
22 *Even* these of them ye may eat; [a]the locust after his kind, and the bald locust after his
kind, and the beetle after his kind, and the
grasshopper after his kind.
23 But all *other* flying creeping things,
which have four feet, *shall be* an abomination
unto you.
24 And for these ye shall be unclean:
whosoever toucheth the carcase of them shall
be unclean until the even.
25 And whosoever beareth *ought* of the
carcase of them [a]shall wash his clothes, and be
unclean until the even.
26 *The carcases* of every beast which divideth the hoof, and *is* not clovenfooted, nor
cheweth the cud, *are* unclean unto you: every
one that toucheth them shall be unclean.
27 And whatsoever goeth upon his paws,
among all *manner of* beasts that go on *all* four,
those *are* unclean unto you: whoso toucheth
their carcase shall be unclean until the even.
28 And he that beareth the carcase of them
shall wash his clothes, and be unclean until
the even: they *are* unclean unto you.
29 ¶ These also *shall be* unclean unto you
among the creeping things that creep upon the
earth; the weasel, and [a]the mouse, and the
tortoise after his kind,
30 And the ferret, and the chameleon, and
the lizard, and the snail, and the mole.
31 These *are* unclean to you among all that
creep: whosoever doth touch them, when
they be dead, shall be unclean until the even.
32 And upon whatsoever *any* of them,
when they are dead, doth fall, it shall be unclean; whether *it be* any vessel of wood, or raiment, or skin, or sack, whatsoever vessel *it be,*
wherein *any* work is done, [a]it must be put into
water, and it shall be unclean until the even;
so it shall be cleansed.

11:2 *These . . . ye shall eat.* Ch. 11 is closely paralleled in Deut 14:3–21 but is more extensive. The animals acceptable for human consumption were those that chewed the cud and had a split hoof (v. 3). Of marine life, only creatures with fins and scales were permissible (v. 9). Birds and insects are also covered in the instructions (vv. 13–23). The distinction between clean and unclean food was as old as the time of Noah (Gen 7:2). The main reason for the laws concerning clean and unclean food is the same as for other laws concerning the clean and unclean—to preserve the sanctity of Israel as God's holy people (see v. 44). Some hold that certain animal life was considered unclean for health considerations, but it is difficult to substantiate this idea. Uncleanness typified sin and defilement. For the uncleanness of disease and bodily discharges see chs. 13–15.

11:6 *hare.* Does not technically chew the cud with regurgitation. The apparent chewing movements of the rabbit caused it to be classified popularly with cud chewers.

11:20 *all four.* Although insects have six legs, perhaps people in ancient times did not count as ordinary legs the two large hind legs used for jumping.

33 And every earthen vessel, whereinto
any of them falleth, whatsoever *is* in it shall be
unclean; and [a]ye shall break it.
34 Of all meat which may be eaten, *that* on
which *such* water cometh shall be unclean:
and all drink that may be drunk in every *such*
vessel shall be unclean.
35 And every *thing* whereupon *any part* of
their carcase falleth shall be unclean; *whether
it be* oven, or ranges for pots, they shall be
broken down: *for* they *are* unclean, and shall
be unclean unto you.
36 Nevertheless a fountain or pit, [1]*wherein there is* plenty of water, shall be clean: but
that which toucheth their carcase shall be unclean.
37 And if *any part* of their carcase fall upon
any sowing seed which is to be sown, it *shall
be* clean.
38 But if *any* water be put upon the seed,
and *any part* of their carcase fall thereon, it
shall be unclean unto you.
39 And if any beast, of which ye may eat,
die; he that toucheth the carcase thereof shall
be unclean until the even.
40 And [a]he that eateth of the carcase of it
shall wash his clothes, and be unclean until
the even: he also that beareth the carcase of it
shall wash his clothes, and be unclean until
the even.
41 And every creeping thing that creepeth
upon the earth *shall be* an abomination; it
shall not be eaten.
42 Whatsoever goeth upon the belly, and
whatsoever goeth upon *all* four, or whatsoever
[1]hath more feet among all creeping things that
creep upon the earth, them ye shall not eat;
for they *are* an abomination.
43 [a]Ye shall not make your[1]selves abominable with any creeping thing that creepeth,
neither shall ye make yourselves unclean with
them, that ye should be defiled thereby.
44 For I *am* the LORD your God: ye shall
therefore sanctify yourselves, and [a]ye shall be
holy; for I *am* holy: neither shall ye defile yourselves with any *manner of* creeping thing that
creepeth upon the earth.
45 [a]For I *am* the LORD that bringeth you up
out of the land of Egypt, to be your God: [b]ye
shall therefore be holy, for I *am* holy.

11:33 [a]ch. 6:28; 15:12; Ps. 2:9; Jer. 48:38; 2 Tim. 2:21; Rev. 2:27
11:36 [1]Heb. *a gathering together of waters*
11:40 [a]ch. 17:15; 22:8; Deut. 14:21; Ezek. 4:14; 44:31
11:42 [1]Heb. *doth multiply feet*
11:43 [1]Heb. *souls* [a]ch. 20:25
11:44 [a]Ex. 19:6; ch. 19:2; 20:7,26; Amos 3:3; Mat. 5:48; 1 Thes. 4:7; 1 Pet. 1:15,16; Rev. 22:11,14
11:45 [a]Ex. 6:7; 20:2; Ps. 105:43-45; Hos. 11:1 [b]ver. 44
11:47 [a]ch. 10:10; Ezek. 44:23; Mal. 3:18
12:2 [a]ch. 15:19; Job 14:4; Ps. 51:5 [b]Luke 2:22 [c]ch. 15:19
12:3 [a]Gen. 17:12; Luke 1:59; 2:21; John 7:22,23; Rom. 3:19; Gal. 5:3
12:6 [1]Heb. *son of his year* [a]Luke 2:22
12:8 [1]Heb. *her hand find not sufficiency of* [a]ch. 5:7; Luke 2:24 [b]ch. 4:26

46 This *is* the law of the beasts, and of the
fowl, and of every living creature that moveth
in the waters, and of every creature that creepeth upon the earth:
47 [a]To make a difference between the unclean and the clean, and between the beast
that may be eaten and the beast that may not
be eaten.

Purification after childbirth

12 And the LORD spake unto Moses, saying,
2 Speak unto the children of Israel, saying,
If a [a]woman have conceived seed, and born a
man child: then [b]she shall be unclean seven
days; [c]according to the days of the separation
for her infirmity shall she be unclean.
3 And in the [a]eighth day the flesh of his
foreskin shall be circumcised.
4 And she shall *then* continue in the blood
of her purifying three and thirty days; she shall
touch no hallowed *thing,* nor come into the
sanctuary, until the days of her purifying be
fulfilled.
5 But if she bear a maid child, then she
shall be unclean two weeks, as *in* her separation: and she shall continue in the blood of her
purifying threescore and six days.
6 And [a]when the days of her purifying are
fulfilled, for a son, or for a daughter, she shall
bring a lamb [1]of the first year for a burnt offering, and a young pigeon, or a turtledove, for
a sin offering, unto the door of the tabernacle
of the congregation, unto the priest:
7 Who shall offer it before the LORD, and
make an atonement for her; and she shall be
cleansed from the issue of her blood. This *is*
the law for her that hath born a male or a female.
8 [a]And if [1]she be not able to bring a lamb,
then she shall bring two turtles, or two young
pigeons; the one for the burnt offering, and
the other for a sin offering: [b]and the priest
shall make an atonement for her, and she shall
be clean.

Laws about skin plagues

13 And the LORD spake unto Moses and
Aaron, saying,
2 When a man shall have in the skin of his

11:36 *pit, wherein there is . . . water.* The use of waterproof plaster for lining cisterns dug in the ground was an important factor in helping the Israelites to settle the dry areas of Canaan after the conquest (cf. 2 Chr 26:10).

11:41 *earth.* Verses 29–30 identify the animals that move about (or swarm) on the ground.

11:44 *be holy; for I am holy.* Holiness is the key theme of Leviticus, ringing like a refrain in various forms throughout the book (e.g., v. 45; 19:2; 20:7,26; 21:8,15; 22:9,16,32). The word "holy" appears more often in Leviticus than in any other book of the Bible. Israel was to be totally consecrated to God. Her holiness was to be expressed in every aspect of her life, to the extent that all of life had a certain ceremonial quality. Because of who God is and what He has done (v. 45), His people must dedicate themselves fully to Him (cf. Mat 5:48). See Rom 12:1.

11:45 *bringeth . . . out of the land of Egypt.* A refrain found 8 more times in Leviticus (19:36; 22:33; 23:43; 25:38,42,55; 26:13,45) and nearly 60 times in 18 other books of the OT.

11:46–47 A summary of ch. 11.

12:2 *unclean.* The uncleanness came from the bleeding (vv. 4–5,7), not from the birth. It is not clear why the period of uncleanness after the birth of a baby boy (40 days) was half the period for a girl (80 days). *separation for her infirmity* [i.e., her menstruation]. See 15:19–24.

12:3 See notes on Gen 17:10,12.

12:6 *burnt offering.* See note on 1:3. *sin offering.* See notes on 4:3,5.

12:8 See 1:14–17 and note on 1:14; see also 5:7–10; 14:21–22; and especially Luke 2:24 (Mary's offering for Jesus).

13:1–46 This section deals with preliminary symptoms of skin

flesh a [1]rising, [a]a scab, or bright spot, and it be
in the skin of his flesh like the plague of leprosy; [b]then he shall be brought unto Aaron the
priest, or unto one of his sons the priests:
3 And the priest shall look on the plague in
the skin of the flesh: and *when* the hair in the
plague is turned white, and the plague in sight
be deeper than the skin of his flesh, it *is* a
plague of leprosy: and the priest shall look on
him, and pronounce him unclean.
4 If the bright spot *be* white in the skin of
his flesh, and in sight *be* not deeper than the
skin, and the hair thereof be not turned white;
then the priest shall shut up *him that hath* the
plague seven days:
5 And the priest shall look on him the seventh day: and behold, *if* the plague in his sight
be at a stay, *and* the plague spread not in the
skin; then the priest shall shut him up seven
days more:
6 And the priest shall look on him again
the seventh day: and behold, *if* the plague *be*
somewhat dark, and the plague spread not in
the skin, the priest shall pronounce him clean:
it *is but* a scab: and he [a]shall wash his clothes,
and be clean.
7 But if the scab spread much abroad in the
skin, after that he hath been seen of the priest
for his cleansing, he shall be seen of the priest
again:
8 And *if* the priest see that behold, the scab
spreadeth in the skin, then the priest shall pronounce him unclean: it *is* a leprosy.
9 ¶ When the plague of leprosy is in a man,
then he shall be brought unto the priest;
10 [a]And the priest shall see *him:* and behold, *if* the rising *be* white in the skin, and it
have turned the hair white, and *there be*
[1]quick raw flesh in the rising;
11 It *is* an old leprosy in the skin of his
flesh, and the priest shall pronounce him unclean, *and* shall not shut him up: for he *is* unclean.
12 And if a leprosy break out abroad in the
skin, and the leprosy cover all the skin of *him*
that hath the plague from his head even to his
foot, wheresoever the priest looketh;
13 Then the priest shall consider: and behold, *if* the leprosy have covered all his flesh,
he shall pronounce *him* clean *that hath* the
plague: it is all turned white: he *is* clean.
14 But when raw flesh appeareth in him,
he shall be unclean.
15 And the priest shall see the raw flesh,
and pronounce him to be unclean: *for* the raw
flesh *is* unclean: it *is* a leprosy.
16 Or if the raw flesh turn again, and be
changed unto white, he shall come unto the
priest;
17 And the priest shall see him: and behold, *if* the plague be turned into white; then
the priest shall pronounce *him* clean *that hath*
the plague: he *is* clean.
18 ¶ The flesh also, in which, *even* in the
skin thereof, was a [a]boil, and is healed,
19 And in the place of the boil there be a
white rising, or a bright spot, white, *and* somewhat reddish, and it be shewed to the priest;
20 And if, when the priest seeth it, behold,
it *be* in sight lower than the skin, and the hair
thereof be turned white; the priest shall pronounce him unclean: it *is* a plague of leprosy
broken out of the boil.
21 But if the priest look on it, and behold,
there be no white hairs therein, and *if* it *be* not
lower than the skin, but *be* somewhat dark;
then the priest shall shut him up seven days:
22 And if it spread much abroad in the
skin, then the priest shall pronounce him unclean: it *is* a plague.
23 But if the bright spot stay in his place,
and spread not, it *is* a burning boil; and the
priest shall pronounce him clean.
24 ¶ Or if there be *any* flesh, in the skin
whereof *there is* [1]a hot burning, and the quick
flesh that burneth have a white bright spot,
somewhat reddish, or white;
25 Then the priest shall look upon it: and
behold, *if* the hair in the bright spot be turned
white, and it *be* in sight deeper than the skin;
it *is* a leprosy broken out of the burning:
wherefore the priest shall pronounce him unclean: it *is* the [a]plague of leprosy.
26 But if the priest look on it, and behold,
there be no white hair in the bright spot, and
it *be* no lower than the *other* skin, but *be*
somewhat dark; then the priest shall shut him
up seven days:
27 And the priest shall look upon him the
seventh day: *and* if it be spread much abroad
in the skin, then the priest shall pronounce
him unclean: it *is* the plague of leprosy.
28 And if the bright spot stay in his place,
and spread not in the skin, but it *be* somewhat
dark; it *is* a rising of the burning, and the
priest shall pronounce him clean: for it *is* an
inflammation of the burning.
29 ¶ If a man or woman hath a plague upon
the head or the beard;
30 Then the [a]priest shall see the plague: and
behold, *if* it *be* in sight deeper than the skin;
and *there be* in it a yellow thin hair; then the
priest shall pronounce him unclean: it *is* a dry
[b]scall, *even* a leprosy upon the head or beard.

13:2 [1]Or, *swelling* [a]Deut. 28:27; Is. 3:17 [b]Deut. 17:8,9; 24:8; Mal. 2:7; Luke 17:14
13:6 [a]ch. 11:25; 14:8
13:10 [1]Heb. *the quickening of living flesh* [a]Num. 12:10,12; 2 Ki. 5:27; 2 Chr. 26:20
13:18 [a]Ex. 9:9; 15:26
13:24 [1]Heb. *a burning of fire*
13:25 [a]Ex. 4:6,7; Num. 12:10; 2 Sam. 3:29; 2 Ki. 5:27; Luke 5:12-14
13:30 [a]Deut. 24:8; Mal. 2:7; 1 Cor. 12:9 [b]Deut. 28:27; Is. 3:17

diseases (vv. 1–8) and then with the symptoms of (1) raw flesh (vv. 9–17), (2) boils (vv. 18–23), (3) burns (vv. 24–28), (4) sores on the head or chin (vv. 29–37), (5) white spots (vv. 38–39) and (6) skin diseases on the head that cause baldness (vv. 40–44).
‡13:2 *in the skin of his flesh like the plague.* The Hebrew probably refers simply to "skin disease." Such diseases show visible defects that could function aptly as a symbol for defilement—as could mildew (cf. vv. 47–59). *leprosy.* The Hebrew word was used for various diseases affecting the skin—not necessarily leprosy; see also 22:4–8; Num 5:2–4; Deut 24:8–9. The symptoms described, and the fact that they may rapidly change (vv. 6,26–27,32–37), show that the disease was not true leprosy (Hansen's disease). They apply also to a number of other diseases, as well as to rather harmless skin eruptions. The Hebrew word translated "plague of leprosy" apparently can also mean "mildew" (see leprosy of a garment and of a house, v. 47; 14:34).

31 And if the priest look on the plague of the scall, and behold, it *be* not in sight deeper than the skin, and *that there is* no black hair in it; then the priest shall shut up *him that hath* the plague of the scall seven days:

32 And in the seventh day the priest shall look on the plague: and behold, *if* the scall spread not, and there be in it no yellow hair, and the scall *be* not in sight deeper than the skin;

33 He shall be [a]shaven, but the scall shall he not shave; and the priest shall shut up *him that hath* the scall seven days more:

34 And in the seventh day the priest shall look on the scall: and behold, *if* the scall be not spread in the skin, nor *be* in sight deeper than the skin; then the priest shall pronounce him clean: and he shall wash his clothes, and be clean.

35 But if the scall spread much in the skin after his cleansing;

36 Then the priest shall look on him: and behold, *if* the scall be spread in the skin, the priest shall not seek for yellow hair: he *is* unclean.

37 But if the scall be in his sight at a stay, and *that* there is black hair grown up therein; the scall is healed, he *is* clean: and the [a]priest shall pronounce him clean.

38 ¶ If a man also or a woman have in the skin of their flesh bright spots, *even* white bright spots;

39 Then the priest shall look: and behold, *if* the bright spots in the skin of their flesh *be* darkish white; it *is* a freckled spot *that* groweth in the skin: he *is* clean.

40 And the man whose [1]hair is fallen off his head, he *is* [a]bald: *yet is* he clean.

41 And he that hath his hair fallen off from the part of *his head toward* his face, he *is* forehead bald: *yet is* he clean.

42 And if there be in the bald head, or bald forehead, a white reddish sore; it *is* a leprosy sprung up in his bald head, or his bald forehead.

43 Then the priest shall look upon it: and behold, *if* the rising of the sore *be* white reddish in his bald head, or in his bald forehead, as the leprosy appeareth in the skin of the flesh;

44 He *is* a leprous man, he *is* unclean: the priest shall pronounce him utterly unclean, his plague *is* in his head.

45 And the leper in whom the plague *is*, his clothes shall be rent, and his head bare, and he shall [a]put a covering upon *his* upper lip, and shall cry, [b]Unclean, unclean.

13:33 [a]Job 1:20; Rom. 8:13
13:37 [a]ch. 10:10; Jer. 15:19; Ezek. 22:26; 44:23
13:40 [1]Heb. *head is pilled* [a]Is. 15:2; Amos 8:10
13:45 [a]Ezek. 24:17,22; Mic. 3:7 [b]Lam. 4:15

13:46 [a]Num. 5:2; 12:14; 2 Ki. 7:3; 15:5; 2 Chr. 26:21; Luke 17:12
13:48 [1]Heb. *work of*
13:49 [1]Heb. *vessel*, or, *instrument*
13:51 [a]ch. 14:44
13:55 [1]Heb. whether *it* be *bald in the head thereof, or in the forehead thereof*

46 All the days wherein the plague *shall be* in him he shall be defiled; he *is* unclean: he shall dwell alone; [a]without the camp *shall* his habitation *be*.

Leprosy in garments

47 ¶ The garment also that the plague of leprosy is in, *whether it be* a woollen garment, or a linen garment;

48 Whether *it be* in the warp, or woof; of linen, or of woollen; whether in a skin, or in any [1]thing made of skin;

49 And *if* the plague be greenish or reddish in the garment, or in the skin, either in the warp, or in the woof, or in any [1]thing of skin; it *is* a plague of leprosy, and shall be shewed unto the priest:

50 And the priest shall look upon the plague, and shut up *it that hath* the plague seven days:

51 And he shall look on the plague on the seventh day: if the plague be spread in the garment, either in the warp, or in the woof, or in a skin, *or* in any work that is made of skin; the plague *is* [a]a fretting leprosy; it *is* unclean.

52 He shall therefore burn *that* garment, whether warp or woof, in woollen or in linen, or any thing of skin, wherein the plague is: for it *is* a fretting leprosy; it shall be burnt in the fire.

53 And if the priest shall look, and behold, the plague be not spread in the garment, either in the warp, or in the woof, or in any thing of skin;

54 Then the priest shall command that they wash *the thing* wherein the plague *is*, and he shall shut it up seven days more:

55 And the priest shall look on the plague, after *that* it is washed: and behold, *if* the plague have not changed his colour, and the plague be not spread; it *is* unclean; thou shalt burn it in the fire; it *is* fret inward, [1]*whether* it *be* bare within or without.

56 And if the priest look, and behold, the plague *be* somewhat dark after the washing of it; then he shall rend it out of the garment, or out of the skin, or out of the warp, or out of the woof:

57 And if it appear still in the garment, either in the warp, or in the woof, or in any thing of skin; it *is* a spreading *plague:* thou shalt burn that wherein the plague *is* with fire.

58 And the garment, either warp, or woof, or whatsoever thing of skin *it be*, which thou shalt wash, if the plague be departed from them, then it shall be washed the second time, and shall be clean.

13:45–46 The ceremonially unclean were excluded from the camp (the area around the tabernacle and courtyard), where the Israelites lived in tents. Later, no unclean person was allowed in the temple area, where he could mingle with others. Not only was God present in the tabernacle in a special way, but also in the camp (Num 5:3; Deut 23:14). Therefore unclean people were not to be in the camp (see Num 5:1–4; 12:14–15, Miriam; 31:19–24; see also Lev 10:4–5; Num 15:35–36; 2 Ki 7:3–4; 2 Chr 26:21, Uzziah). As a result of their separation from God, the unclean were to exhibit their grief by tearing their clothes, by having unkempt hair and by partially covering their faces (v. 45).

13:47 *leprosy.* Or "mildew." During Israel's rainy season (October through March), mildew is a problem along the coast and by the sea of Galilee, where it is very humid.

13:54 *wash.* See vv. 34,55–56,58. The treatment of disorders commonly included washing.

59 This *is* the law of the plague of leprosy
in a garment of woollen or linen, either *in* the
warp, or woof, or any thing of skins, to pronounce it clean, or to pronounce it unclean.

The cleansing of lepers

14 And the LORD spake unto Moses, saying,
2 This shall be the law of the leper in the
day of his cleansing: He [a]shall be brought unto
the priest:
3 And the priest shall go forth out of the
camp; and the priest shall look, and behold, *if*
the plague of leprosy be healed in the leper;
4 Then shall the priest command to take
for him that is to be cleansed two [1]birds alive
and clean, and [a]cedar wood, and [b]scarlet, and
[c]hyssop:
5 And the priest shall command that one of
the birds be killed in an earthen vessel over
running water:
6 As for the living bird, he shall take it, and
the cedar wood, and the scarlet, and the hyssop, and shall dip them and the living bird in
the blood of the bird *that was* killed over the
running water:
7 And he shall [a]sprinkle upon him that is
to be cleansed from the leprosy [b]seven times,
and shall pronounce him clean, and shall let
the living bird loose [1]into the open field.
8 And he that is to be cleansed [a]shall wash
his clothes, and shave off all his hair, [b]and
wash *himself* in water, that he may be clean:
and after *that* he shall come into the camp, and
[c]shall tarry abroad out of his tent seven days.
9 But it shall be on the seventh day, *that* he
shall shave all his hair off his head and his
beard and his eyebrows, even all his hair he
shall shave off: and he shall wash his clothes,
also he shall wash his flesh in water, and he
shall be clean.
10 And on the eighth day [a]he shall take
two he lambs without blemish, and one ewe
lamb [1]of the first year without blemish, and
three tenth deals of fine flour *for* [b]a meat offering, mingled with oil, and one log of oil.
11 And the priest that maketh *him* clean
shall present the man that is to be made clean,
and those *things,* before the LORD, *at* the door
of the tabernacle of the congregation:
12 And the priest shall take one he lamb,
and [a]offer him for a trespass offering, and the
log of oil, and [b]wave them *for* a wave offering
before the LORD:
13 And he shall slay the lamb [a]in the place
where he shall kill the sin offering and the
burnt offering, in the holy place: for [b]as the sin
offering *is* the priest's, *so is* the trespass offering: [c]it *is* most holy:
14 And the priest shall take *some* of the
blood of the trespass offering, and the priest
shall put *it* [a]upon the tip of the right ear of him
that is to be cleansed, and upon the thumb of
his right hand, and upon the great toe of his
right foot:
15 And the priest shall take *some* of the log
of oil, and pour *it* into the palm of his own left
hand:
16 And the priest shall dip his right finger
in the oil that *is* in his left hand, and shall
sprinkle of the oil with his finger seven times
before the LORD:
17 And of the rest of the oil that *is* in his
hand shall the priest put upon the tip of the
right ear of him that is to be cleansed, and
upon the thumb of his right hand, and upon
the great toe of his right foot, upon the blood
of the trespass offering:
18 And the remnant of the oil that *is* in the
priest's hand he shall pour upon the head of
him that is to be cleansed: [a]and the priest shall
make an atonement for him before the LORD.
19 And the priest shall offer [a]the sin offering, and make an atonement for him that is to
be cleansed from his uncleanness; and afterward he shall kill the burnt offering:
20 And the priest shall offer the burnt offering and the meat offering upon the altar:
and the priest shall make an atonement for
him, and he shall be clean.
21 ¶ And [a]if he *be* poor, and [1]cannot get *so
much;* then he shall take one lamb *for* a trespass offering [2]to be waved, to make an atonement for him, and one tenth deal of fine flour
mingled with oil for a meat offering, and a log
of oil;
22 [a]And two turtledoves, or two young pigeons, such as he is able to get; and the one
shall be a sin offering, and the other a burnt offering.
23 [a]And he shall bring them on the eighth
day for his cleansing unto the priest, unto the
door of the tabernacle of the congregation, before the LORD.

14:2 [a]Mat. 8:2,4; Mark 1:40,44; Luke 5:12,14; 17:14
14:4 [1]Or, *sparrows* [a]Num. 19:6 [b]Heb. 9:19 [c]Ps. 51:7
14:7 [1]Heb. *upon the face of the field* [a]Num. 19:18,19; Is. 52:15; Heb. 9:13,21; 12:24 [b]2 Ki. 5:10,14; Ps. 51:2
14:8 [a]ch. 13:6 [b]ch. 11:25; Eph. 5:26; Heb. 10:22; Rev. 1:5,6 [c]Num. 12:15
14:10 [1]Heb. *the daughter of her year* [a]Mat. 8:4; Mark 1:44; Luke 5:14 [b]ch. 2:1; Num. 15:4
14:12 [a]ch. 5:2,18; 6:6,7
14:12 [b]Ex. 29:24
14:13 [a]Ex. 29:11; ch. 1:5; 4:4 [b]ch. 7:7 [c]ch. 2:3; 7:6; 21:22
14:14 [a]Ex. 29:20; ch. 8:23
14:18 [a]ch. 4:26; 5:6
14:19 [a]ch. 5:1,6; 12:7
14:21 [1]Heb. *his hand reach not* [2]Heb. *for a waving* [a]ch. 5:7; 12:8
14:22 [a]ch. 12:8; 15:14,15
14:23 [a]ver. 10,11

13:59 A summary of ch. 13.

14:1–32 The ritual after the skin disease had been cured had three parts: (1) ritual for the first week (outside the camp, vv. 1–7), (2) ritual for the second week (inside the camp, vv. 8–20) and (3) special permission for the poor (vv. 21–32).

14:4 *hyssop.* A plant used in ceremonial cleansing (see note on Ex 12:22).

14:5 *be killed.* Diseases and disorders were a symbol of sin and rendered a person or object ceremonially unclean. The prescribed cleansing included sacrifice as well as washing (see note on 13:54).

14:6 *cedar . . . scarlet . . . hyssop.* Also used for cleansing in vv. 51–52; Num 19:6.

14:7,16,51 *seven times.* See note on 4:6.

14:7 *clean.* Perhaps the string and cedar stick were used as well as the hyssop plant to sprinkle the blood for cleansing (see Ps 51:7). Further sacrifices are specified in vv. 10–31. *let the living bird loose.* Cf. 16:22; see note on 16:5.

14:8 The Levites were similarly cleansed (see Num 8:7).

14:10 *meat offering.* See note on 2:1.

14:12 *trespass offering.* See 5:14–6:7 and note on 5:15. *wave offering.* See note on 7:30–32.

14:14 See note on 8:14.

14:19 *sin offering.* See 4:1–5:13 and notes on 4:3,5. *burnt offering.* See note on 1:3.

14:20 *meat offering.* See note on 2:1.

24 [a]And the priest shall take the lamb of the trespass offering, and the log of oil, and the priest shall wave them *for* a wave offering before the LORD:

25 And he shall kill the lamb of the trespass offering, [a]and the priest shall take *some* of the blood of the trespass offering, and put *it* upon the tip of the right ear of him that is to be cleansed, and upon the thumb of his right hand, and upon the great toe of his right foot:

26 And the priest shall pour of the oil into the palm of his own left hand:

27 And the priest shall sprinkle with his right finger *some* of the oil that *is* in his left hand seven times before the LORD:

28 And the priest shall put of the oil that *is* in his hand upon the tip of the right ear of him that is to be cleansed, and upon the thumb of his right hand, and upon the great toe of his right foot, upon the place of the blood of the trespass offering:

29 And the rest of the oil that *is* in the priest's hand he shall put upon the head of him that is to be cleansed, to make an atonement for him before the LORD.

30 And he shall offer the one of [a]the turtledoves, or of the young pigeons, such as he can get;

31 *Even* such as he is able to get, the one *for* a sin offering, and the other *for* a burnt offering, with the meat offering: and the priest shall make an atonement for him that is to be cleansed before the LORD.

32 This *is* the law *of him* in whom *is* the plague of leprosy, whose hand is not able to get [a]*that which pertaineth* to his cleansing.

Leprosy in houses

33 ¶ And the LORD spake unto Moses and unto Aaron, saying,

34 [a]When ye be come into the land of Canaan, which I give to you for a possession, and I put the plague of leprosy in a house of the land of your possession;

35 And he that owneth the house shall come and tell the priest, saying, It seemeth to me *there is* as it were [a]a plague in the house:

36 Then the priest shall command that they [1]empty the house, before the priest go *into it* to see the plague, that all that *is* in the house be not *made* unclean: and afterward the priest shall go in to see the house:

37 And he shall look on the plague, and behold, *if* the plague *be* in the walls of the house with hollow strakes, greenish or reddish, which in sight *are* lower than the wall;

38 Then the priest shall go out of the house to the door of the house, and shut up the house seven days:

39 And the priest shall come again the seventh day, and shall look: and behold, *if* the plague be spread in the walls of the house;

40 Then the priest shall command that they take away the stones in which the plague *is,* and they shall cast them into an unclean place without the city:

41 And he shall cause the house to be scraped within round about, and they shall pour out the dust that they scrape off without the city into an unclean place:

42 And they shall take other stones, and put *them* in the place of *those* stones; and he shall take other morter, and shall plaister the house.

43 And if the plague come again, and break out in the house, after *that* he hath taken away the stones, and after he hath scraped the house, and after it is plaistered;

44 Then the priest shall come and look, and behold, *if* the plague be spread in the house, it *is* [a]a fretting leprosy in the house: it *is* unclean.

45 And he shall break down the house, the stones of it, and the timber thereof, and all the morter of the house; and he shall carry *them* forth out of the city into an unclean place.

46 Moreover he that goeth into the house all the while that it is shut up shall be unclean until the even.

47 And he that lieth in the house shall wash his clothes; and he that eateth in the house shall wash his clothes.

48 And if the priest [1]shall come in, and look *upon it,* and behold, the plague hath not spread in the house, after the house was plaistered: then the priest shall pronounce the house clean, because the plague is healed.

49 And [a]he shall take to cleanse the house two birds, and cedar wood, and scarlet, and hyssop:

50 And he shall kill the one of the birds in an earthen vessel over running water:

51 And he shall take the cedar wood, and the hyssop, and the scarlet, and the living bird, and dip them in the blood of the slain bird, and in the running water, and sprinkle the house seven times:

52 And he shall cleanse the house with the blood of the bird, and with the running water, and with the living bird, and with the cedar wood, and with the hyssop, and with the scarlet:

53 But he shall let go the living bird out of the city into the open fields, and [a]make an atonement for the house: and it shall be clean.

54 ¶ This *is* the law for all *manner of* plague of leprosy, and [a]scall,

55 And for the [a]leprosy of a garment, [b]and of a house,

56 And [a]for a rising, and for a scab, and for a bright spot:

57 To [a]teach [1]when *it is* unclean, and when *it is* clean: this *is* the law of leprosy.

14:24 [a]ver. 12
14:25 [a]ver. 14,17
14:30 [a]ver. 22; ch. 15:14,15
14:32 [a]ver. 10
14:34 [a]Gen. 17:8; Num. 32:22; Deut. 7:1; 32:49
14:35 [a]Ps. 91:10; Prov. 3:33; Zech. 5:4
14:36 [1]Or, *prepare*
14:44 [a]ch. 13:51; Zech. 5:4
14:48 [1]Heb. *in coming in shall come in, etc.*
14:49 [a]ver. 4
14:53 [a]ver. 20
14:54 [a]ch. 13:30
14:55 [a]ch. 13:47 [b]ver. 34
14:56 [a]ch. 13:2
14:57 [1]Heb. *in the day of the unclean, and in the day of the clean* [a]Deut. 24:8; Ezek. 44:23

14:33–53 There are many similarities between this section and the previous one, particularly in the manner of restoration.

14:45 *break down.* A house desecrated by mildew (see note on 13:47), mold or fungus would be a defiled place to live in, so drastic measures had to be taken.

Laws about uncleanness

15 And the LORD spake unto Moses and to Aaron, saying,

2 Speak unto the children of Israel, and say unto them, [a]When any man hath a [1]running issue out of his flesh, *because of* his issue he *is* unclean.

3 And this shall be his uncleanness in his issue: *whether* his flesh run with his issue, or his flesh be stopped from his issue, it *is* his uncleanness.

4 Every bed, whereon he lieth that hath the issue, is unclean: and every [1]thing, whereon he sitteth, shall be unclean.

5 And whosoever toucheth his bed shall wash his clothes, [a]and bathe *himself* in water, and be unclean until the even.

6 And he that sitteth on *any* thing whereon he sat that hath the issue shall wash his clothes, and bathe *himself* in water, and be unclean until the even.

7 And he that toucheth the flesh of him that hath the issue shall wash his clothes, and bathe *himself* in water, and be unclean until the even.

8 And if he that hath the issue spit upon him that is clean; then he shall wash his clothes, and bathe *himself* in water, and be unclean until the even.

9 And what saddle soever he rideth upon that hath the issue shall be unclean.

10 And whosoever toucheth any *thing* that was under him shall be unclean until the even: and he that beareth *any of* those *things* shall wash his clothes, and bathe *himself* in water, and be unclean until the even.

11 And whomsoever he toucheth that hath the issue, and hath not rinsed his hands in water, he shall wash his clothes, and bathe *himself* in water, and be unclean until the even.

12 And the [a]vessel of earth, that he toucheth which hath the issue, shall be broken: and every vessel of wood shall be rinsed in water.

13 And when he that hath an issue is cleansed of his issue; then [a]he shall number to himself seven days for his cleansing, and wash his clothes, and bathe his flesh in running water, and shall be clean.

14 And on the eighth day he shall take to him [a]two turtledoves, or two young pigeons, and come before the LORD unto the door of the tabernacle of the congregation, and give them unto the priest:

15 And the priest shall offer them, [a]the one *for* a sin offering, and the other *for* a burnt offering; [b]and the priest shall make an atonement for him before the LORD for his issue.

16 And [a]if any man's seed of copulation go out from him, then he shall wash all his flesh in water, and be unclean until the even.

17 And every garment, and every skin, whereon is the seed of copulation, shall be washed with water, and be unclean until the even.

18 The woman also with whom man shall lie *with* seed of copulation, they shall *both* bathe *themselves* in water, and [a]be unclean until the even.

19 ¶ And [a]if a woman have an issue, *and* her issue in her flesh be blood, she shall be [1]put apart seven days: and whosoever toucheth her shall be unclean until the even.

20 And every *thing* that she lieth upon in her separation shall be unclean: every *thing* also that she sitteth upon shall be unclean.

21 And whosoever toucheth her bed shall wash his clothes, and bathe *himself* in water, and be unclean until the even.

22 And whosoever toucheth any thing that she sat upon shall wash his clothes, and bathe *himself* in water, and be unclean until the even.

23 And if it *be* on *her* bed, or on *any* thing whereon she sitteth, when he toucheth it, he shall be unclean until the even.

24 And [a]if any man lie with her at all, and her flowers be upon him, he shall be unclean seven days; and all the bed whereon he lieth shall be unclean.

25 And if [a]a woman have an issue of her blood many days out of the time of her separation, or if it run beyond the time of her separation; all the days of the issue of her uncleanness shall be as the days of her separation: she *shall be* unclean.

26 Every bed whereon she lieth all the days of her issue shall be unto her as the bed of her separation: and whatsoever she sitteth upon shall be unclean, as the uncleanness of her separation.

15:2 [1]Or, *running of the reins* [a]ch. 22:4; Num. 5:2; 2 Sam. 3:29
15:4 [1]Heb. *vessel*
15:5 [a]ch. 11:25; 17:15
15:12 [a]ch. 6:28; 11:32,33
15:13 [a]ver. 28; ch. 14:8; Num. 19:11,12
15:14 [a]ch. 14:22,23
15:15 [a]ch. 14:30,31 [b]ch. 14:19,31
15:16 [a]ch. 22:4; Deut. 23:10
15:18 [a]Ex. 19:15; 1 Sam. 21:4; 1 Cor. 6:18
15:19 [1]Heb. *in her separation* [a]ch. 12:2
15:24 [a]See ch. 20:18
15:25 [a]Mat. 9:20; Mark 5:25; Luke 8:43

15:1–33 The chapter deals with (1) male uncleanness caused by bodily discharge (vv. 2–15) or emission of semen (vv. 16–18); (2) female uncleanness caused by her monthly period (vv. 19–24) or lengthy hemorrhaging (vv. 25–30); (3) summary (vv. 31–33).
15:2 *running issue out of his flesh.* Probably either diarrhea or urethral discharge (various kinds of infections). The contamination of anything under the man (v. 10), whether he sat (vv. 4,6,9) or lay (v. 4) on it, indicates that the bodily discharge had to do with the buttocks or genitals.
15:4 *bed.* Something like a mat (cf. 2 Sam 11:13).
15:13 *cleansed.* God brought about the healing; the priest could only ascertain that a person was already healed.
15:16 *seed of copulation.* Normal sexual activity and a woman's menstruation required no sacrifices but only washing and a minimal period of uncleanness.
15:19 *seven days.* See 12:2. This regulation is the background of 2 Sam 11:4 (Bath-sheba).
15:20 See note on Gen 31:35.
15:24 A case of the woman's period beginning during intercourse. This is different from 18:19 and 20:18. *flowers.* Or menstrual impurity. During her period a woman was protected from sexual activity. No offering was required for uncleanness contracted by a man in this way, but the uncleanness lasted seven days.
15:25 *issue of her blood many days.* As, e.g., the woman in Mat 9:20. *beyond the time of her separation.* An unnatural discharge, possibly caused by disease, was treated like a sickness and required an offering upon recovery (vv. 28–30; see vv. 14–15).

27 And whosoever toucheth those *things*
shall be unclean, and shall wash his clothes,
and bathe *himself* in water, and be unclean until the even.
28 But [a]if she be cleansed of her issue,
then she shall number to herself seven days,
and after *that* she shall be clean.
29 And on the eighth day she shall take
unto her two turtles, or two young pigeons,
and bring them unto the priest, to the door of
the tabernacle of the congregation.
30 And the priest shall offer the one *for* a sin
offering, and the other *for* a burnt offering; and
the priest shall make an atonement for her before the LORD for the issue of her uncleanness.
31 ¶ Thus shall ye [a]separate the children of
Israel from their uncleanness; that they die not
in their uncleanness, when they [b]defile my
tabernacle that *is* among them.
32 [a]This *is* the law of him that hath an issue, [b]and *of him* whose seed goeth from him,
and is defiled therewith;
33 [a]And of her that is sick of her flowers,
and of him that hath an issue, of the man,
[b]and of the woman, [c]and of him that lieth
with her which is unclean.

The day of atonement

16 And the LORD spake unto Moses after
[a]the death of the two sons of Aaron,
when they offered before the LORD, and died;
2 And the LORD said unto Moses, Speak
unto Aaron thy brother, that he [a]come not at
all times into the holy *place* within the vail before the mercy seat, which *is* upon the ark;
that he die not: for [b]I will appear in the cloud
upon the mercy seat.
3 Thus shall Aaron [a]come into the holy
place: [b]with a young bullock for a sin offering,
and a ram for a burnt offering.
4 He shall put on [a]the holy linen coat, and
he shall have the linen breeches upon his
flesh, and shall be girded with a linen girdle,
and with the linen mitre shall he be attired:
these *are* holy garments; therefore [b]shall he
wash his flesh in water, and *so* put them on.
5 And he shall take of [a]the congregation of
the children of Israel two kids of the goats for
a sin offering, and one ram for a burnt offering.
6 And Aaron shall offer *his* bullock of the
sin offering, which *is* for himself, and [a]make
an atonement for himself, and for his house.
7 And he shall take the two goats, and present them before the LORD *at* the door of the
tabernacle of the congregation.
8 And Aaron shall cast lots upon the two
goats; one lot for the LORD, and the other lot
for the [1]scapegoat.
9 And Aaron shall bring the goat upon
which the LORD's lot [1]fell, and offer him *for* a
sin offering.
10 But the goat, on which the lot fell to be
the scapegoat, shall be presented alive before
the LORD, to make [a]an atonement with him,
and to let him go for a scapegoat into the
wilderness.

15:28 [a]ver. 13-15
15:31 [a]ch. 11:47; Deut. 24:8; Ezek. 44:23; Heb. 12:15 [b]Num. 5:3; 19:13,20; Ezek. 5:11; 23:38
15:32 [a]ver. 2 [b]ver. 16
15:33 [a]ver. 19 [b]ver. 25 [c]ver. 24
16:1 [a]ch. 10:1,2
16:2 [a]Ex. 30:10; ch. 23:27; Heb. 9:7; 10:19
16:2 [b]Ex. 25:22; 40:34; 1 Ki. 8:10-12
16:3 [a]Ex. 25:21 [b]ch. 4:3
16:4 [a]Ex. 28:39,42,43; ch. 6:10; Ezek. 44:17,18 [b]Ex. 30:20; ch. 8:6,7
16:5 [a]See ch. 4:14; Num. 29:11; 2 Chr. 29:21; Ezra 6:17; Ezek. 45:22,23
16:6 [a]ch. 9:7; Heb. 5:2; 7:27,28; 9:7
16:8 [1]Heb. *Azazel*
16:9 [1]Heb. *went up*
16:10 [a]1 John 2:2

15:31 Addressed to the priests, thus emphasizing the importance of the regulations. Since God dwelt in the tabernacle, any unholiness, symbolized by the discharges of ch. 15, could result in death if the people came into His presence. Sin separates all people from a holy God and results in their death, unless atonement is made (see the next chapter).

16:1–34 See 23:26–32; 25:9; Ex 30:10; Num 29:7–11; Heb 9:7. The order of ritual for the day of atonement was as follows: 1. The high priest went to the basin in the courtyard, removed his regular garments, washed himself (v. 4) and went into the holy place to put on the special garments for the day of atonement (v. 4). 2. He went out to sacrifice a bull at the altar of burnt offering as a sin offering for himself and the other priests (v. 11). 3. He went into the most holy place with some of the bull's blood, with incense and with coals from the altar of burnt offering (vv. 12–13). The incense was placed on the burning coals, and the smoke of the incense hid the ark from view. 4. He sprinkled some of the bull's blood on and in front of the mercy seat (v. 14). 5. He went outside the tabernacle and cast lots for two goats to see which was to be sacrificed and which was to be the scapegoat (vv. 7–8). 6. At the altar of burnt offering the high priest killed the goat for the sin offering for the people, and for a second time he went into the most holy place, this time to sprinkle the goat's blood in front of and on the mercy seat (vv. 5,9,15–16a). 7. He returned to the holy place (called "tabernacle of the congregation" in v. 16) and sprinkled the goat's blood there (v. 16b). 8. He went outside to the altar of burnt offering and sprinkled it (v. 18) with the blood of the bull (for himself, v. 11) and of the goat (for the people, v. 15). 9. While in the courtyard, he laid both hands on the second goat, thus symbolizing the transfer of Israel's sin, and sent it out into the wilderness (vv. 20–22). 10. The man who took the goat away, after he accomplished his task, washed himself and his clothes outside the camp (v. 26) before rejoining the people. 11. The high priest entered the holy place to remove his special garments (v. 23). 12. He went out to the laver to wash and put on his regular priestly clothes (v. 24). 13. As a final sacrifice he went out to the great altar and offered a ram (v. 3) as a burnt offering for himself, and another ram (v. 5) for the people (v. 24). 14. The conclusion of the entire day was the removal of the sacrifices for the sin offerings to a place outside the camp, where they were burned, and there the man who performed this ritual bathed and washed his clothes (vv. 27–28) before rejoining the people.

16:1 *death of the two sons of Aaron.* See 10:1–3.

16:2 *mercy seat.* See Ex 25:17 and note. Blood sprinkled on the lid of the ark made atonement for Israel on the day of atonement (vv. 15–17). In the Septuagint (the Greek translation of the OT) the word for "mercy seat" is the same one used of Christ and translated "propitiation" in Rom 3:25 (see note there).

16:3 *bullock.* For Aaron's cleansing (vv. 6,11). Before Aaron could minister in the holy place for the nation, he himself had to be cleansed (Heb 5:1–3); not so Christ, who is our high priest and Aaron's antitype (Heb 7:26–28).

16:5 *two kids of the goats for a sin offering.* One was the usual sin offering (see notes on 4:3,5) and the other a scapegoat. No single offering could fully typify the atonement of Christ. The one goat was killed, its blood sprinkled in the holy place and its body burned outside the camp (vv. 15,27), symbolizing the payment of the price of Christ's atonement. The other goat, sent away alive and bearing the sins of the nation (v. 21), symbolized the removal of sin and its guilt. *ram.* For the sins of the people; the one in v. 3 was for the sins of the high priest. Both were sacrificed at the end of the ceremony (v. 24).

16:6–10 An outline of vv. 11–22.

11 And Aaron shall bring the bullock of the
sin offering, which *is* for himself, and shall
make an atonement for himself, and for his
house, and shall kill the bullock of the sin offering which *is* for himself:
12 And he shall take [a]a censer full of burning coals of fire from off the altar before the
LORD, and his hands full of [b]sweet incense
beaten small, and bring *it* within the vail:
13 [a]And he shall put the incense upon the
fire before the LORD, that the cloud of the incense may cover the [b]mercy seat that *is* upon
the Testimony, that he die not:
14 And [a]he shall take of the blood of the
bullock, and [b]sprinkle *it* with his finger upon
the mercy seat eastward; and before the mercy
seat shall he sprinkle of the blood with his finger seven times.
15 [a]Then shall he kill the goat of the sin offering, that *is* for the people, and bring his
blood [b]within the vail, and do with that blood
as he did with the blood of the bullock, and
sprinkle it upon the mercy seat, and before the
mercy seat:
16 And he shall [a]make an atonement for
the holy *place,* because of the uncleanness of
the children of Israel, and because of their
transgressions in all their sins: and so shall he
do for the tabernacle of the congregation, that
[1]remaineth among them in the midst of their
uncleanness.
17 [a]And there shall be no man in the tabernacle of the congregation when he goeth in
to make an atonement in the holy *place,* until
he come out, and have made an atonement for
himself, and for his household, and for all the
congregation of Israel.
18 And he shall go out unto the altar that *is*
before the LORD, and [a]make an atonement for
it; and shall take of the blood of the bullock,
and of the blood of the goat, and put *it* upon
the horns of the altar round about.
19 And he shall sprinkle of the blood upon
it with his finger seven times, and cleanse it,
and [a]hallow it from the uncleanness of the
children of Israel.
20 And when he hath made an end of [a]rec-
onciling the holy *place,* and the tabernacle of
the congregation, and the altar, he shall bring
the live goat:
21 And Aaron shall lay both his hands

16:12 [a]ch. 10:1; Num. 16:18,46; Rev. 8:5 [b]Ex. 30:34
16:13 [a]Ex. 30:7,8; Num. 16:7,18,46 [b]Ex. 25:21
16:14 [a]ch. 4:5; Heb. 9:25; 10:4 [b]ch. 4:6
16:15 [a]Heb. 2:17; 5:2; 9:7,28 [b]ver. 2; Heb. 6:19; 9:3,7,12
16:16 [1]Heb. *dwelleth* [a]See Ex. 29:36; Ezek. 45:18; Heb. 9:22,23
16:17 [a]See Ex. 34:3; Luke 1:10
16:18 [a]Ex. 30:10; ch. 4:7,18; Heb. 9:22,23
16:19 [a]Ezek. 43:20
16:20 [a]ver. 16; Ezek. 45:20
16:21 [1]Heb. *a man of opportunity* [a]Is. 53:6
16:22 [1]Heb. *of separation* [a]Is. 53:11,12; John 1:29; Heb. 9:28; 1 Pet. 2:24
16:23 [a]Ezek. 42:14; 44:19
16:24 [a]ver. 3,5
16:25 [a]ch. 4:10
16:26 [a]ch. 15:5
16:27 [a]ch. 4:12,21; 6:30; Heb. 13:11
16:29 [a]Ex. 30:10; ch. 23:27; Num. 29:7
16:30 [a]Jer. 33:8; Eph. 5:26; Heb. 9:13,14; 10:1,2; 1 John 1:7,9
16:31 [a]ch. 23:32
16:32 [1]Heb. *fill his hand* [a]ch. 4:3,5,16 [b]Ex. 29:29,30; Num. 20:26,28 [c]ver. 4

upon the head of the live goat, and confess
over him all the iniquities of the children of Israel, and all their transgressions in all their
sins, [a]putting them upon the head of the goat,
and shall send *him* away by the hand of [1]a fit
man into the wilderness:
22 And the goat shall [a]bear upon him all
their iniquities unto a land [1]not inhabited: and
he shall let go the goat in the wilderness.
23 And Aaron shall come into the tabernacle of the congregation, [a]and shall put off the
linen garments, which he put on when he
went into the holy *place,* and shall leave them
there:
24 And he shall wash his flesh with water
in the holy place, and put on his garments, and
come forth, [a]and offer his burnt offering, and
the burnt offering of the people, and make an
atonement for himself, and for the people.
25 And [a]the fat of the sin offering shall he
burn upon the altar.
26 And he that let go the goat for the
scapegoat shall wash his clothes, [a]and bathe
his flesh in water, and afterward come into the
camp.
27 [a]And the bullock for the sin offering,
and the goat for the sin offering, whose blood
was brought in to make atonement in the holy
place, shall *one* carry forth without the camp;
and they shall burn in the fire their skins, and
their flesh, and their dung.
28 And he that burneth them shall wash
his clothes, and bathe his flesh in water, and
afterward he shall come into the camp.
29 ¶ And *this* shall be a statute for ever
unto you: *that* [a]in the seventh month, on the
tenth *day* of the month, ye shall afflict your
souls, and do no work *at all, whether it be* one
of your own country, or a stranger that sojourneth among you:
30 For on that day shall *the priest* make an
atonement for you, to [a]cleanse you, *that* ye may
be clean from all your sins before the LORD.
31 [a]It *shall be* a sabbath of rest unto you,
and ye shall afflict your souls, *by* a statute for
ever.
32 [a]And the priest, whom he shall anoint,
and whom he shall [b][1]consecrate to minister in
the priest's office in his father's stead, shall
make the atonement, and [c]shall put on the
linen clothes, *even* the holy garments:

16:11 *make an atonement for himself.* See note on v. 3.

16:13 The smoke of the incense covered the ark so that the high priest would not see the glorious presence of God (v. 2) and thus die.

16:14 See Rom 3:25. *seven times.* See note on 4:6.

16:16 *tabernacle of the congregation.* Here and in vv. 17,20,33 the term means the holy place.

16:20–22 A summary description of substitutionary atonement. The sin of the worshipers was confessed and symbolically transferred to the sacrificial animal, on which hands were laid (see notes on 1:3; Ex 29:10; see also Lev 1:4; 3:8; 4:4).

16:24 *holy place.* Cf. 6:26. *burnt offering . . . burnt offering.* The two rams mentioned in vv. 3,5.

16:25 *fat of the sin offering.* See 4:8–10.

16:27 *without the camp.* See note on 4:12.

16:29 *seventh month.* Tishri, the seventh month, begins with the blowing of trumpets (see note on 23:24). The day of atonement follows on the 10th day, and on the 15th day the feast of tabernacles begins (see 23:23–36).

‡16:29,31 *afflict your souls.* Or humble your souls. The expression came to be used of fasting (Ps 35:13). The day of atonement was the only regular fast day stipulated in the OT (see 23:27,29,32, where humbling oneself probably implies fasting), though tradition later added other fast days to the Jewish calendar (see Zech 7:5; 8:19).

16:30 *clean from all your sins.* On the day of atonement the repentant Israelite was assured of sins forgiven.

33 And [a]he shall make an atonement for the holy sanctuary, and he shall make an atonement for the tabernacle of the congregation, and for the altar, and he shall make an atonement for the priests, and for all the people of the congregation.

34 [a]And this shall be an everlasting statute unto you, to make an atonement for the children of Israel for all their sins [b]once a year. And he did as the LORD commanded Moses.

Laws about special sacrifices

17 And the LORD spake unto Moses, saying,

2 Speak unto Aaron, and unto his sons, and unto all the children of Israel, and say unto them; This *is* the thing which the LORD hath commanded, saying,

3 What man soever *there be* of the house of Israel, [a]that killeth an ox, or lamb, or goat, in the camp, or that killeth *it* out of the camp,

4 [a]And bringeth it not unto the door of the tabernacle of the congregation, to offer an offering unto the LORD before the tabernacle of the LORD; blood shall be [b]imputed unto that man; he hath shed blood; and that man [c]shall be cut off from among his people:

5 To the end that the children of Israel may bring their sacrifices, [a]which they offer in the open field, even that they may bring them unto the LORD, unto the door of the tabernacle of the congregation, unto the priest, and offer them *for* peace offerings unto the LORD.

6 And the priest [a]shall sprinkle the blood upon the altar of the LORD *at* the door of the tabernacle of the congregation, and [b]burn the fat for a sweet savour unto the LORD.

7 And they shall no more offer their sacrifices [a]unto devils, after whom they [b]have gone a whoring. This shall be a statute for ever unto them throughout their generations.

8 And thou shalt say unto them, Whatsoever man *there be* of the house of Israel, or of the strangers which sojourn among you, [a]that offereth a burnt offering or sacrifice,

9 And bringeth it not unto the door of the tabernacle of the congregation, to offer it unto the LORD; even that man shall be cut off from among his people.

10 ¶ [a]And whatsoever man *there be* of the house of Israel, or of the strangers that sojourn among you, that eateth any *manner of* blood; [b]I will even set my face against *that* soul that eateth blood, and will cut him off from among his people.

11 For the life of the flesh *is* in the blood: and I have given it to you upon the altar [a]to make an atonement for your souls: for [b]it *is* the blood *that* maketh an atonement for the soul.

12 Therefore I said unto the children of Israel, No soul of you shall eat blood, neither shall any stranger that sojourneth among you eat blood.

13 And whatsoever man *there be* of the children of Israel, or of the strangers that sojourn among you, [1]which [a]hunteth and catcheth *any* beast or fowl that may be eaten; he shall even [b]pour out the blood thereof, and [c]cover it with dust.

14 [a]For *it is* the life of all flesh; the blood of it *is* for the life thereof: therefore I said unto the children of Israel, Ye shall eat the blood of no *manner of* flesh: for the life of all flesh *is* the blood thereof: whosoever eateth it shall be cut off.

15 [a]And every soul that eateth [1]that which died of itself, or that which was torn *with beasts, whether it be* one of your own country, or a stranger, [b]he shall both wash his clothes, [c]and bathe *himself* in water, and be unclean until the even: then shall he be clean.

16 But if he wash *them* not, nor bathe his flesh; then [a]he shall bear his iniquity.

Unlawful sexual relations

18 And the LORD spake unto Moses, saying,

2 Speak unto the children of Israel, and say unto them, [a]I *am* the LORD your God.

3 [a]After the doings of the land of Egypt,

16:33 [a]ver. 6,16-18,24
16:34 [a]ch. 23:31; Num. 29:7 [b]Ex. 30:10; Heb. 9:7,25
17:3 [a]See Deut. 12:5,15,21
17:4 [a]Deut. 12:5,6,13,14 [b]Rom. 5:13 [c]Gen. 17:14
17:5 [a]Gen. 21:33; 22:2; 31:54; Deut. 12:2
17:6 [a]ch. 3:2 [b]Ex. 29:18; Num. 18:17
17:7 [a]Deut. 32:17; 2 Chr. 11:15; 1 Cor. 10:20 [b]Ex. 34:15; Deut. 31:16; Ezek. 23:8
17:8 [a]ch. 1:2,3
17:10 [a]Gen. 9:4; Deut. 12:16,23; 15:23; 1 Sam. 14:33 [b]ch. 20:3,5,6
17:11 [a]Mat. 26:28; Rom. 3:25; Eph. 1:7; Col. 1:14,20; 1 Pet. 1:2; 1 John 1:7 [b]Heb. 9:22
17:13 [1]Heb. *that hunteth* any *hunting* [a]ch. 7:26 [b]Deut. 12:16,24 [c]Ezek. 24:7
17:14 [a]ver. 11,12; Gen. 9:4; Deut. 12:23
17:15 [1]Heb. *a carcase* [a]Ex. 22:31; Ezek. 4:14; 44:31 [b]ch. 11:25 [c]ch. 15:5
17:16 [a]ch. 5:1
18:2 [a]Ex. 6:7; Ezek. 20:5,7,19,20
18:3 [a]Ezek. 20:7

16:34 *once a year.* Heb 9:11–10:14 repeatedly points out this contrast with Christ's "once for all" sacrifice.

17:4 *tabernacle of the LORD.* The people, with few exceptions (e.g., Deut 12:15,20–21), were directed to sacrifice only at the central sanctuary (Deut 12:5–6). Sennacherib's representative referred to Hezekiah's requiring worship only in Jerusalem (2 Ki 18:22). One reason for such a regulation was to keep the Israelites from becoming corrupted by the Canaanites' pagan worship. *cut off from among his people.* See note on 7:20.

17:5 *unto the priest . . . unto the LORD.* See note on 6:6.

17:7 *have gone a whoring.* See 20:5–6; see also Judg 2:17 and note.

17:11 *the life of the flesh is in the blood.* See note on Gen 9:4. The blood shed in the sacrifices was sacred. It epitomized the life of the sacrificial victim. Since life was sacred, blood (a symbol of life) had to be treated with respect (Gen 9:5–6). Eating blood was therefore strictly forbidden (see 7:26–27; Deut 12:16,23–25; 15:23; 1 Sam 14:32–34). *blood that maketh an atonement.* Practically every sacrifice included the sprinkling or smearing of blood on the altar or within the tabernacle (v. 6; 1:5; 3:2; 4:6,25; 7:2), thus teaching that atonement involves the substitution of life for life. The blood of the OT sacrifice pointed forward to the blood of the Lamb of God, who obtained for His people "eternal redemption" (Heb 9:12). "Without shedding of blood there is no remission" (Heb 9:22).

17:15 *died . . . torn.* Such animals would not have had the blood drained from them and therefore would be forbidden.

18:1–20:27 Here God's people are given instructions concerning interpersonal relations and a morality reflecting God's holiness. Israel was thereby prepared for a life different from the Canaanites, whose life-style was deplorably immoral. Ch. 18 contains prohibitions in the moral sphere, ch. 19 expands the ten commandments to detail correct morality, and ch. 20 assesses the penalties for violating God's standard of morality. See chart, p. 256.

18:2 In chs. 18–26 the phrase "I am the LORD" occurs 47 times. The Lord's name (i.e., His revealed character as Yahweh, "the LORD") is the authority that stands behind His instructions. See note on Ex 3:15.

18:3 Six times in this chapter Israel is warned not to follow the example of pagans (here, two times; see also vv. 24,26–27,30).

wherein ye dwelt, shall ye not do: and [b]after
the doings of the land of Canaan, whither I
bring you, shall ye not do: neither shall ye
walk in their ordinances.
4 [a]Ye shall do my judgments, and keep
mine ordinances, to walk therein: I *am* the
LORD your God.
5 Ye shall therefore keep my statutes, and
my judgments: [a]which if a man do, he shall
live in them: [b]I *am* the LORD.
6 ¶ None of you shall approach to any that
is [1]near of kin to him, to uncover *their* nakedness: I *am* the LORD.
7 [a]The nakedness of thy father, or the
nakedness of thy mother, shalt thou not uncover: she *is* thy mother; thou shalt not uncover her nakedness.
8 [a]The nakedness of thy father's wife shalt
thou not uncover: it *is* thy father's nakedness.
9 [a]The nakedness of thy sister, the daughter of thy father, or daughter of thy mother,
whether she be born at home, or born abroad,
even their nakedness thou shalt not uncover.
10 The nakedness of thy son's daughter, or
of thy daughter's daughter, *even* their nakedness thou shalt not uncover: for theirs *is* thine
own nakedness.
11 The nakedness of thy father's wife's
daughter, begotten of thy father, she *is* thy sister, thou shalt not uncover her nakedness.
12 [a]Thou shalt not uncover the nakedness
of thy father's sister: she *is* thy father's near
kinswoman.
13 Thou shalt not uncover the nakedness
of thy mother's sister: for she *is* thy mother's
near kinswoman.
14 [a]Thou shalt not uncover the nakedness
of thy father's brother, thou shalt not approach
to his wife: she *is* thine aunt.
15 [a]Thou shalt not uncover the nakedness
of thy daughter in law: she *is* thy son's wife;
thou shalt not uncover her nakedness.
16 [a]Thou shalt not uncover the nakedness
of thy brother's wife: it *is* thy brother's nakedness.

18:3 [b]Ex. 23:24
18:4 [a]Ezek. 20:19
18:5 [a]Ezek. 20:11,13,21; Rom. 10:5; Gal. 3:12 [b]Ex. 6:2,6
18:6 [1]Heb. *remainder of his flesh*
18:7 [a]ch. 20:11
18:8 [a]Gen. 49:4; ch. 20:11; 1 Cor. 5:1
18:9 [a]ch. 20:17
18:12 [a]ch. 20:19
18:14 [a]ch. 20:20
18:15 [a]Gen. 38:18,26
18:16 [a]See Deut. 25:5
18:17 [a]ch. 20:14
18:18 [1]Or, one *wife to another* [a]1 Sam. 1:6,8
18:19 [a]ch. 20:18; Ezek. 18:6; 22:10
18:20 [a]Ex. 20:14; ch. 20:10; Deut. 5:18; 22:22; Mat. 5:27; Rom. 2:22; 1 Cor. 6:9; Heb. 13:4
18:21 [a]ch. 20:2; 2 Ki. 16:3 [b]1 Ki. 11:7,33; Called, Acts 7:43, *Moloch* [c]ch. 19:12; 20:3; Ezek. 36:20
18:22 [a]ch. 20:13; 1 Cor. 6:9; 1 Tim. 1:10
18:23 [a]Ex. 22:19 [b]ch. 20:12
18:24 [a]Mat. 15:18-20; 1 Cor. 3:17 [b]Deut. 18:12
18:25 [a]Num. 35:34; Ezek. 36:17 [b]Is. 26:21; Jer. 5:9
18:26 [a]ver. 5,30
18:28 [a]Jer. 9:19

17 [a]Thou shalt not uncover the nakedness
of a woman and her daughter, neither shalt
thou take her son's daughter, or her daughter's
daughter, to uncover her nakedness; *for* they
are her near kinswomen: it *is* wickedness.
18 Neither shalt thou take [1]a wife to her
sister, [a]to vex *her*, to uncover her nakedness,
besides the other in her life *time*.
19 [a]Also thou shalt not approach unto a
woman to uncover her nakedness, as long as
she is put apart for her uncleanness.
20 Moreover [a]thou shalt not lie carnally
with thy neighbour's wife, to defile *thyself*
with her.
21 And thou shalt not let *any* of thy seed
[a]pass through *the fire* to [b]Molech, neither
shalt thou [c]profane the name of thy God: I *am*
the LORD.
22 [a]Thou shalt not lie with mankind, as
with womankind: it *is* abomination.
23 [a]Neither shalt thou lie with any beast to
defile *thyself* therewith: neither shall any
woman stand before a beast to lie down thereto: it *is* [b]confusion.
24 [a]Defile not you yourselves in any of
these *things*: [b]for in all these the nations are
defiled which I cast out before you:
25 And [a]the land is defiled: therefore I do
[b]visit the iniquity thereof upon it, and the land
itself vomiteth out her inhabitants.
26 [a]Ye shall therefore keep my statutes and
my judgments, and shall not commit any of
these abominations; *neither* any of your own
nation, nor any stranger that sojourneth
among you:
27 (For all these abominations have the
men of the land done, which *were* before you,
and the land is defiled;)
28 That [a]the land spue not you out also,
when ye defile it, as it spued out the nations
that *were* before you.
29 For whosoever shall commit any of
these abominations, even the souls that commit *them* shall be cut off from among their
people.

18:5 *live.* With God's full blessing. The law was the way of life for the redeemed (see Ezek 20:11,13,21), not a way of salvation for the lost (see Rom 10:5; Gal 3:12).

18:6 A summary of the laws against incest (vv. 7–18). Penalties for incestuous relations are given in ch. 20.

18:7 This prohibition applied also after the father's death. If the father was still living, the act was adulterous and therefore forbidden.

18:8 *thy father's wife.* Other than your mother—assuming there is more than one wife.

18:11 *sister.* There would be many half-sisters in a polygamous society. Tamar claimed that an exception to this prohibition could be made (2 Sam 13:12–13; but see note there).

18:14 *thine aunt.* See 20:20. If the father's brother was alive, the act would be adulterous. If he was dead, one could rationalize such a marriage because the aunt was not a blood relative—but it was forbidden.

18:15 Cf. the account of Judah and Tamar (Gen 38:18).

18:16 *thy brother's wife.* The law also applied to a time after divorce or the brother's death. To marry one's brother's widow was not immoral but might damage the brother's inheritance. The levirate law of Deut 25:5–6 offered an exception that preserved the dead brother's inheritance and continued his line.

18:17 *daughter.* Stepdaughter (granddaughter-in-law is also covered in the verse). The law applied even after the mother's death.

18:18 Cf. the account of Jacob with Leah and Rachel (Gen 29:23–30).

18:19 See Ezek 18:6; 22:10.

18:21 *Molech.* The god of the Ammonites (see 20:2–5; 1 Ki 11:5 and note). The detestable practice of sacrificing children to Molech was common in Phoenicia and other surrounding countries. Cf. 2 Ki 3:26–27. King Manasseh evidently sacrificed his sons to Molech (2 Chr 33:6; see 2 Ki 23:10). Jer 32:35 protests the practice.

18:22 *lie with mankind.* See 20:13, where the penalty for homosexual acts is death.

18:29 *abominations.* See note on 7:21. *cut off from among their people.* See note on 7:20.

30 Therefore ye shall keep mine ordinance, [a]that *ye* commit not *any one* of *these* abominable customs, which were committed before you, and that ye defile not yourselves therein: I *am* the LORD your God.

Personal conduct

19 And the LORD spake unto Moses, saying,

2 Speak unto all the congregation of the children of Israel, and say unto them, [a]Ye shall be holy: for I the LORD your God *am* holy.

3 [a]Ye shall fear every man his mother, and his father, and [b]keep my sabbaths: I *am* the LORD your God.

4 [a]Turn ye not unto idols, [b]nor make to yourselves molten gods: I *am* the LORD your God.

5 ¶ And [a]if ye offer a sacrifice of peace offerings unto the LORD, ye shall offer it at your own will.

6 It shall be eaten the *same* day ye offer it, and on the morrow: and if ought remain until the third day, it shall be burnt in the fire.

7 And if it be eaten at all on the third day, it *is* abominable; it shall not be accepted.

8 Therefore *every one* that eateth it shall bear his iniquity, because he hath profaned the hallowed *thing* of the LORD: and that soul shall be cut off from among his people.

9 ¶ And [a]when ye reap the harvest of your land, thou shalt not wholly reap the corners of thy field, neither shalt thou gather the gleanings of thy harvest.

10 And thou shalt not glean thy vineyard, neither shalt thou gather *every* grape of thy vineyard; thou shalt leave them for the poor and stranger: I *am* the LORD your God.

11 [a]Ye shall not steal, neither deal falsely, [b]neither lie one to another.

12 And ye shall not [a]swear by my name falsely, [b]neither shalt thou profane the name of thy God: I *am* the LORD.

13 [a]Thou shalt not defraud thy neighbour, neither rob *him:* [b]the wages of him that is hired shall not abide with thee all night until the morning.

14 Thou shalt not curse the deaf, [a]nor put a stumblingblock before the blind, but shalt fear thy God: I *am* the LORD.

18:30 [a]ver. 3
19:2 [a]ch. 11:44
19:3 [a]Ex. 20:12 [b]Ex. 20:8
19:4 [a]Ex. 20:4 [b]Ex. 34:17
19:5 [a]ch. 7:16
19:9 [a]Deut. 24:19
19:11 [a]Ex. 20:15 [b]Eph. 4:25
19:12 [a]Ex. 20:7; Deut. 5:11; Mat. 5:33; Jas. 5:12 [b]ch. 18:21
19:13 [a]Mark 10:19 [b]Mal. 3:5
19:14 [a]Deut 27:18
19:16 [a]Ex. 23:1 [b]Ex. 23:1,7; 1 Ki. 21:13
19:17 [1]Or, *that thou bear not sin for him* [a]1 John 2:9,11; 3:15 [b]Mat. 18:15; Eph. 5:11; 1 Tim. 5:20
19:18 [a]Rom. 12:17,19 [b]Mat. 5:43
19:19 [a]Deut. 22:9,10 [b]Deut. 22:11
19:20 [1]Or, *abused by any* [2]Heb. *reproached by,* (or, *for*) *man* [3]Or, *they* [4]Heb. *there shall be a scourging*
19:21 [a]ch. 5:15
19:24 [1]Heb. *holiness of praises to the LORD* [a]Deut. 12:17,18; Prov. 3:9
19:26 [a]ch. 17:10 [b]Deut. 18:10,11,14; 1 Sam. 15:23; 2 Chr. 33:6; Mal. 3:5
19:27 [a]ch. 21:5; Is. 15:2; Jer. 9:26

15 Ye shall do no unrighteousness in judgment: thou shalt not respect the person of the poor, nor honour the person of the mighty: *but* in righteousness shalt thou judge thy neighbour.

16 [a]Thou shalt not go up and down *as* a talebearer among thy people: neither shalt thou [b]stand against the blood of thy neighbour: I *am* the LORD.

17 [a]Thou shalt not hate thy brother in thine heart: [b]thou shalt in any wise rebuke thy neighbour, [1]and not suffer sin upon him.

18 [a]Thou shalt not avenge, nor bear any grudge against the children of thy people, [b]but thou shalt love thy neighbour as thyself: I *am* the LORD.

19 ¶ Ye shall keep my statutes. Thou shalt not let thy cattle gender with a diverse kind: [a]thou shalt not sow thy field with mingled seed: [b]neither shall a garment mingled of linen and woollen come upon thee.

20 And whosoever lieth carnally with a woman that *is* a bondmaid, [1][2]betrothed to a husband, and not at all redeemed, nor freedom given her; [3][4]she shall be scourged, they shall not be put to death, because she was not free.

21 And [a]he shall bring his trespass offering unto the LORD, unto the door of the tabernacle of the congregation, *even* a ram for a trespass offering.

22 And the priest shall make an atonement for him with the ram of the trespass offering before the LORD for his sin which he hath done: and the sin which he hath done shall be forgiven him.

23 And when ye shall come into the land, and shall have planted all *manner of* trees for food, then ye shall count the fruit thereof as uncircumcised: three years shall it be as uncircumcised unto you: it shall not be eaten of.

24 But in the fourth year all the fruit thereof shall be [1]holy [a]to praise the LORD *withal.*

25 And in the fifth year shall ye eat of the fruit thereof, that *it* may yield unto you the increase thereof: I *am* the LORD your God.

26 ¶ [a]Ye shall not eat *any thing* with the blood: [b]neither shall ye use enchantment, nor observe times.

27 [a]Ye shall not round the corners of your heads, neither shalt thou mar the corners of thy beard.

19:1 See note on 18:1–20:27.
19:2 *be holy.* See note on 11:44.
19:3–4 See v. 30; Ex 20:4–6,8–11. See also chart, p. 256.
19:5 *peace offerings.* See note on 3:1.
19:6 *third day.* See note on 7:15–18.
19:8 *cut off from among his people.* See note on 7:20.
19:9–10 See 23:22; see also Deut 24:19–21. Ruth 2 gives an example of the application of the law of gleaning.
19:11–12 See Ex 20:7,15–16.
19:13 *wages of him that is hired.* See Deut 24:14–15; Mat 20:8.
19:17 *not hate thy brother.* See 1 John 2:9,11; 3:15; 4:20.
19:18 *love thy neighbour as thyself.* Quoted by Christ (Mat 22:39; Mark 12:31; Luke 10:27), Paul (Rom 13:9; Gal 5:14) and James (2:8). The stricter Pharisees (school of Shammai) added to this command what they thought it implied: "Hate thine enemy" (Mat 5:43). Jesus' reaction, "Love your enemies," was in line with true OT teaching (see vv. 17,34) and was more in agreement with the middle-of-the-road Pharisees. Rabbi Nahmanides caught their sentiments: "One should place no limitations upon the love for the neighbor, but instead a person should love to do an abundance of good for his fellow being as he does for himself." "Neighbor" does not merely mean one who lives nearby, but anyone with whom one comes in contact.
19:21–22 *trespass offering.* See 5:14–6:7 and note on 5:15.
‡19:26 *any thing with the blood.* See note on 17:11. *observe times.* Lit. "practice soothsaying." See v. 31; Ex 22:18; Deut 18:14; 1 Sam 28:9; Is 47:12–14.
19:27 *not round the corners of your heads.* A prohibition still followed by orthodox Jews.

28 Ye shall not [a]make any cuttings in your
flesh for the dead, nor print any marks upon
you: I *am* the LORD.
29 [a]Do not [1]prostitute thy daughter, to
cause her to be a whore; lest the land fall to
whoredom, and the land become full of
wickedness.
30 [a]Ye shall keep my sabbaths, and [b]rever-
ence my sanctuary: I *am* the LORD.
31 [a]Regard not them that have familiar
spirits, neither seek after wizards, to be defiled by them: I *am* the LORD your God.
32 [a]Thou shalt rise up before the hoary
head, and honour the face of the old man, and
[b]fear thy God: I *am* the LORD.
33 And [a]if a stranger sojourn with thee in
your land, ye shall not [1]vex him.
34 [a]*But* the stranger that dwelleth with
you shall be unto you as one born amongst
you, and [b]thou shalt love him as thyself; for ye
were strangers in the land of Egypt: I *am* the
LORD your God.
35 [a]Ye shall do no unrighteousness in judgment, in meteyard, in weight, or in measure.
36 [a]Just balances, just [1]weights, a just
ephah, and a just hin, shall ye have: I *am* the
LORD your God, which brought you out of the
land of Egypt.
37 [a]Therefore shall ye observe all my statutes, and all my judgments, and do them: I *am*
the LORD.

Punishments for sin

20 And the LORD spake unto Moses, saying,
2 [a]Again, thou shalt say to the children of
Israel, [b]Whosoever *he be* of the children of Israel, or of the strangers that sojourn in Israel,
that giveth *any* of his seed unto Molech; he
shall surely be put to death: the people of the
land shall stone him with stones.
3 And [a]I will set my face against that man,
and will cut him off from among his people;
because he hath given of his seed unto Molech, to [b]defile my sanctuary, and [c]to profane
my holy name.
4 And if the people of the land do any ways
hide their eyes from the man, when he giveth
of his seed unto Molech, and [a]kill him not:
5 Then [a]I will set my face against that man,
and [b]against his family, and will cut him off,
and all that [c]go a whoring after him, to commit whoredom with Molech, from among
their people.
6 And [a]the soul that turneth after such as
have familiar spirits, and after wizards, to go a
whoring after them, I will even set my face
against that soul, and will cut him off from
among his people.
7 [a]Sanctify yourselves therefore, and be ye
holy: for I *am* the LORD your God.
8 [a]And ye shall keep my statutes, and do
them: [b]I *am* the LORD which sanctify you.
9 [a]For every one that curseth his father or
his mother shall be surely put to death: he
hath cursed his father or his mother; [b]his
blood *shall be* upon him.
10 ¶ And [a]the man that committeth adultery with *another* man's wife, *even he* that
committeth adultery with his neighbour's
wife, the adulterer and the adulteress shall
surely be put to death.
11 [a]And the man that lieth with his father's wife hath uncovered his father's nakedness: both of them shall surely be put to death;
their blood *shall be* upon them.
12 [a]And if a man lie with his daughter in
law, both of them shall surely be put to death:
[b]they have wrought confusion; their blood
shall be upon them.
13 [a]If a man also lie with mankind, as he lieth with a woman, both of them have committed an abomination: they shall surely be
put to death; their blood *shall be* upon them.
14 [a]And if a man take a wife and her mother, it *is* wickedness: they shall be burnt with
fire, both he and they; that there be no
wickedness among you.
15 [a]And if a man lie with a beast, he shall
surely be put to death: and ye shall slay the
beast.
16 And if a woman approach unto any
beast, and lie down thereto, thou shalt kill the
woman and the beast: they shall surely be put
to death; their blood *shall be* upon them.
17 [a]And if a man shall take his sister, his
father's daughter, or his mother's daughter,
and see her nakedness, and she see his nakedness; it *is* a wicked thing; and they shall be
cut off in the sight of their people: he hath uncovered his sister's nakedness; he shall bear
his iniquity.

19:28 [a]Jer. 16:6
19:29 [1]Heb. *profane* [a]Deut. 23:17
19:30 [a]ver. 3; ch. 26:2 [b]Eccl. 5:1
19:31 [a]Ex. 22:18; Is. 8:19; Acts 16:16
19:32 [a]1 Tim. 5:1 [b]ver. 14
19:33 [1]Or, *oppress* [a]Ex. 22:21
19:34 [a]Ex. 12:48 [b]Deut. 10:19
19:35 [a]ver. 15
19:36 [1]Heb. *stones* [a]Deut. 25:13,15
19:37 [a]ch. 18:4,5; Deut. 4:5,6; 5:1; 6:25
20:2 [a]ch. 18:2 [b]ch. 18:21; 2 Ki. 23:10; 2 Chr. 33:6; Jer. 7:31
20:3 [a]ch. 17:10 [b]Ezek. 5:11; 23:38,39 [c]ch. 18:21
20:4 [a]Deut. 17:2,3,5
20:5 [a]ch. 17:10 [b]Ex. 20:5
20:5 [c]ch. 17:7
20:6 [a]ch. 19:31
20:7 [a]ch. 19:2
20:8 [a]ch. 19:37 [b]Ex. 31:13
20:9 [a]Ex. 21:17; Deut. 27:16; Prov. 20:20; Mat. 15:4 [b]ver. 11,12, 13,16,27; 2 Sam. 1:16
20:10 [a]ch. 18:20; Deut. 22:22
20:11 [a]ch. 18:8; Deut. 27:23
20:12 [a]ch. 18:15 [b]ch. 18:23
20:13 [a]ch. 18:22; Deut. 23:17; Gen. 19:5; Judg. 19:22
20:14 [a]ch. 18:17; Deut. 27:23
20:15 [a]ch. 18:23; Deut. 27:21
20:17 [a]ch. 18:9; Deut. 27:22; Gen. 20:12

19:28 There was to be no disfiguring of the body, after the manner of the pagans (see note on 21:5).
19:34 *ye were strangers in . . . Egypt.* See Deut 5:15.
19:35 *do no unrighteousness in judgment.* In a culture with no bureau of weights and measures, cheating in business transactions by falsification of standards was common (see Deut 25:13–16; Prov 11:1; 16:11; 20:10,23). The prophets also condemned such sin (Amos 8:5; Mic 6:10–11).
20:1–27 In ch. 20 many of the same sins listed in ch. 18 are mentioned again, but this time usually with the death penalty specified. Israel's God is a jealous God and tolerates no rivals (see note on Ex 20:5). He requires exclusive allegiance (see Ex 20:3). See note on 18:1–20:27.
20:2–5 *Molech.* See note on 18:21.
20:3 *cut him off from among his people.* See note on 7:20.
20:5 *go a whoring.* See v. 6; 17:7; see also note on Ex 34:15.
20:6 *after such as have familiar spirits, and after wizards.* Consulting a medium was no less a sin than being one (v. 27). See Deut 18:10–11. Only God was to be consulted—through either the priest or a prophet.
20:7 *be ye holy.* See note on 11:44.
20:8 *which sanctify.* This phrase and the expression, "I am the LORD (your God)," are characteristic of chs. 18–26.
20:9 Cf. the penalty of a profligate son in Deut 21:20–21.
20:10 See 18:20.
20:12 See 18:15.
20:13 *abomination.* See note on 7:21.
20:15–16 See 18:23.

18 [a]And if a man shall lie with a woman having her sickness, and shall uncover her nakedness; he hath [1]discovered her fountain, and she hath uncovered the fountain of her blood: and both of them shall be cut off from among their people.

19 [a]And thou shalt not uncover the nakedness of thy mother's sister, nor of thy father's sister: [b]for he [1]uncovereth his near kin: they shall bear their iniquity.

20 [a]And if a man shall lie with his uncle's wife, he hath uncovered his uncle's nakedness: they shall bear their sin; they shall die childless.

21 [a]And if a man shall take his brother's wife, it *is* [1]an unclean thing: he hath uncovered his brother's nakedness; they shall be childless.

22 ¶ Ye shall therefore keep all my [a]statutes, and all my judgments, and do them: that the land, whither I bring you to dwell therein, [b]spue you not out.

23 [a]And ye shall not walk in the manners of the nation, which I cast out before you: for they committed all these *things,* and [b]therefore I abhorred them.

24 But [a]I have said unto you, Ye shall inherit their land, and I will give it unto you to possess it, a land that floweth with milk and honey: I *am* the LORD your God, [b]which have separated you from *other* people.

25 [a]Ye shall therefore put difference between clean beasts and unclean, and between unclean fowls and clean: [b]and ye shall not make your souls abominable by beast, or by fowl, or by any *manner of living thing* that [1]creepeth *on* the ground, which I have separated from you as unclean.

26 And ye shall be holy unto me: [a]for I the LORD *am* holy, and have severed you from *other* people, that *ye* should be mine.

27 [a]A man also or woman that hath a familiar spirit, or that is a wizard, shall surely be put to death: they shall stone them with stones: [b]their blood *shall be* upon them.

The sanctity of the priesthood

21 And the LORD said unto Moses, Speak unto the priests the sons of Aaron, and say unto them, [a]There shall none be defiled for the dead among his people:

2 But for his kin, that is near unto him, *that is,* for his mother, and for his father, and for his son, and for his daughter, and for his brother,

3 And for his sister a virgin, that is nigh unto him, which hath had no husband; for her may he be defiled.

4 *But* [1]he shall not defile himself, *being* a chief man among his people, to profane himself.

5 [a]They shall not make baldness upon their head, neither shall they shave off the corner of their beard, nor make any cuttings in their flesh.

6 They shall be holy unto their God, and [a]not profane the name of their God: for the offerings of the LORD made by fire, *and* the bread of their God, they do offer: therefore they shall be holy.

7 [a]They shall not take a wife *that is* a whore, or profane; neither shall they take a woman [b]put away from her husband: for he *is* holy unto his God.

8 Thou shalt sanctify him therefore; for he offereth the bread of thy God: he shall be holy unto thee: for I the LORD, which sanctify you, *am* holy.

9 [a]And the daughter of any priest, if she profane herself by playing the whore, she profaneth her father: she shall be burnt with fire.

10 ¶ [a]And *he that is* the high priest among his brethren, upon whose head the anointing oil was poured, and [b]that is consecrated to put on the garments, [c]shall not uncover his head, nor rend his clothes;

11 Neither shall he [a]go in to any dead body, nor defile himself for his father, or for his mother;

12 [a]Neither shall he go out of the sanctuary, nor profane the sanctuary of his God; for [b]the crown of the anointing oil of his God *is* upon him: I *am* the LORD.

13 And [a]he shall take a wife in her virginity.

14 A widow, or a divorced *woman,* or profane, *or* a harlot, these shall he not take: but he shall take a virgin of his own people to wife.

15 Neither shall he profane his seed among his people: for [a]I the LORD do sanctify him.

16 ¶ And the LORD spake unto Moses, saying,

17 Speak unto Aaron, saying, Whosoever *he be* of thy seed in their generations that hath *any* blemish, let him not [a]approach to offer the [1]bread of his God.

20:18 [1]Heb. *made naked* [a]ch. 15:24
20:19 [1]Heb. *made naked* [a]ch. 18:12 [b]ch. 18:6
20:20 [a]ch. 18:14
20:21 [1]Heb. *a separation* [a]ch. 18:16
20:22 [a]ch. 18:26; 19:37 [b]ch. 18:25
20:23 [a]ch. 18:3,24 [b]ch. 18:27; Deut. 9:5
20:24 [a]Ex. 3:17; 6:8 [b]ver. 26; Ex. 19:5; 33:16; Deut. 7:6; 14:2; 1 Ki. 8:53
20:25 [1]Or, *moveth* [a]ch. 11:47; Deut. 14:4 [b]ch. 11:43
20:26 [a]ver. 7; ch. 19:2; 1 Pet. 1:16
20:27 [a]ch. 19:31 [b]ver. 9
21:1 [a]Ezek. 44:25
21:4 [1]Or, *being a husband among his people, he shall not defile himself* for his wife, etc.
21:5 [a]ch. 19:27
21:6 [a]ch. 18:21; 19:12
21:7 [a]Ezek. 44:22 [b]See Deut. 24:1,2
21:9 [a]Gen. 38:24
21:10 [a]Ex. 29:29; ch. 8:12 [b]Ex. 28:2; ch. 16:32 [c]ch. 10:6
21:11 [a]Num. 19:14
21:12 [a]ch. 10:7 [b]Ex. 28:36; ch. 8:9,12,30
21:13 [a]ver. 7; Ezek. 44:22
21:15 [a]ver. 8
21:17 [1]Or, *food* [a]ch. 10:3; Num. 16:5

20:18 See 18:19.
20:20 See 18:14.
20:21 See 18:16 and note.
20:24 *land that floweth with milk and honey.* A common phrase in Exodus, Numbers and Deuteronomy (see Ex 3:8 and note; see also Josh 5:6; Jer 11:5; 32:22; Ezek 20:6,15).
20:25 See ch. 11 and notes.
20:27 See note on v. 6.
21:1–22:33 Directions for the priests' conduct, especially about separation from ceremonial uncleanness.
21:1 *for the dead.* Touching a corpse (Num 19:11) or entering the home of a person who had died (Num 19:14) made one unclean. A priest was only to contract such uncleanness at the death of a close relative (vv. 2–3), and the regulations for the high priest denied him even this (vv. 11–12).
21:5 *cuttings in their flesh.* See 19:27–28. Such lacerations and disfigurement were common among pagans as signs of mourning and to secure the attention of their deity (see 1 Ki 18:28). Israelite faith had a much less grotesque view of death (see, e.g., vv. 1–4; Gen 5:24; 2 Sam 12:23; Heb 11:19).
21:8 *I . . . am holy.* See note on 11:44.
21:9 See Gen 38:24 and note.
21:11–12 See note on v. 1.
21:17 *blemish.* Like the sacrifices that had to be without defect, the priests were to typify Christ's perfection (Heb 9:13–14).

18 For whatsoever man *he be* that hath a blemish, he shall not approach: a blind man, or a lame, or he that hath a flat nose, or any thing [a]superfluous,

19 Or a man that is brokenfooted, or brokenhanded,

20 Or crookbackt, or [1]a dwarf, or that hath a blemish in his eye, or be scurvy, or scabbed, or [a]hath his stones broken;

21 No man that hath a blemish, of the seed of Aaron the priest, shall come nigh to [a]offer the offerings of the LORD made by fire: he hath a blemish; he shall not come nigh to offer the bread of his God.

22 He shall eat the bread of his God, *both* of the [a]most holy, and of the [b]holy.

23 Only he shall not go in unto the vail, nor come nigh unto the altar, because he hath a blemish; that [a]he profane not my sanctuaries: for I the LORD do sanctify them.

24 And Moses told *it* unto Aaron, and to his sons, and unto all the children of Israel.

22 And the LORD spake unto Moses, saying,

2 Speak unto Aaron and to his sons, that they [a]separate themselves from the holy *things* of the children of Israel, and that they [b]profane not my holy name *in those things* which they [c]hallow unto me: I *am* the LORD.

3 Say unto them, Whosoever *he be* of all your seed among your generations, that goeth unto the holy *things* which the children of Israel hallow unto the LORD, [a]having his uncleanness upon him, that soul shall be cut off from my presence: I *am* the LORD.

4 What man soever of the seed of Aaron *is* a leper, or hath [a]a [1]running issue; he shall not eat of the holy *things*, [b]until he be clean. And [c]whoso toucheth any *thing that is* unclean *by* the dead, or [d]a man whose seed goeth from him;

5 Or [a]whosoever toucheth any creeping thing, whereby he may be made unclean, or [b]a man of whom he may take uncleanness, whatsoever uncleanness he hath;

6 The soul which hath touched *any* such shall be unclean until even, and shall not eat of the holy *things*, unless he [a]wash his flesh with water.

7 And when the sun is down, he shall be clean, and shall afterward eat of the holy *things;* because [a]it *is* his food.

8 [a]That which dieth of itself, or is torn *with beasts,* he shall not eat to defile *himself* therewith: I *am* the LORD.

21:18 [a]ch. 22:23
21:20 [1]Or, *too slender* [a]Deut. 23:1
21:21 [a]ver. 6
21:22 [a]ch. 2:3,10; 6:17,29; 7:1; 24:9; Num. 18:9 [b]ch. 22:10-12; Num. 18:19
21:23 [a]ver. 12
22:2 [a]Num. 6:3 [b]ch. 18:21 [c]Ex. 28:38; Num. 18:32; Deut. 15:19
22:3 [a]ch. 7:20
22:4 [1]Heb. *running of the reins* [a]ch. 15:2 [b]ch. 14:2; 15:13 [c]Num. 19:11 [d]ch. 15:16
22:5 [a]ch. 11:24 [b]ch. 15:7,19
22:6 [a]ch. 15:5
22:7 [a]ch. 21:22; Num. 18:11,13
22:8 [a]Ex. 22:31; ch. 17:15; Ezek. 44:31
22:9 [a]Ex. 28:43
22:10 [a]See 1 Sam. 21:6
22:11 [1]Heb. with *the purchase of his money* [a]Num. 8:11,13
22:12 [1]Heb. *a man a stranger*
22:13 [a]Gen. 38:11 [b]ch. 10:14
22:14 [a]ch. 5:15,16; Num. 18:11,19
22:15 [a]Num. 18:32
22:16 [1]Or, *lade themselves* with *the iniquity of trespass in their eating* [a]ver. 9
22:18 [a]ch. 1:2,3,10
22:19 [a]ch. 1:3
22:20 [a]Deut. 15:21; Mal. 1:8,14; Eph. 5:27; Heb. 9:14; 1 Pet. 1:19
22:21 [1]Or, *goats* [a]ch. 3:1,6 [b]Num. 15:3,8; Ps. 61:8; 65:1; Eccl. 5:4,5
22:22 [a]ver. 20; Mal. 1:8 [b]ch. 1:9,13; 3:3,5
22:23 [1]Or, *kid* [a]ch. 21:18

9 They shall therefore keep mine ordinance, [a]lest they bear sin for it, and die therefore, if they profane it: I the LORD do sanctify them.

10 ¶ [a]There shall no stranger eat *of* the holy *thing:* a sojourner of the priest's, or a hired servant, shall not eat *of* the holy *thing.*

11 But if the priest buy *any* soul [1]with his money, he shall eat of it, and he that is born in his house: [a]they shall eat of his meat.

12 If the priest's daughter also be *married* unto [1]a stranger, she may not eat of an offering of the holy *things.*

13 But if the priest's daughter be a widow, or divorced, and have no child, and is [a]returned unto her father's house, [b]as *in* her youth, she shall eat of her father's meat: but there shall no stranger eat thereof.

14 [a]And if a man eat *of* the holy *thing* unwittingly, then he shall put the fifth *part* thereof unto it, and shall give *it* unto the priest with the holy *thing.*

15 And [a]they shall not profane the holy *things* of the children of Israel, which they offer unto the LORD;

16 Or [1]suffer them [a]to bear the iniquity of trespass, when they eat their holy *things:* for I the LORD do sanctify them.

Sacrifices of blemished animals

17 ¶ And the LORD spake unto Moses, saying,

18 Speak unto Aaron, and to his sons, and unto all the children of Israel, and say unto them, [a]Whatsoever *he be* of the house of Israel, or of the strangers in Israel, that will offer his oblation for all his vows, and for all his freewill offerings, which they will offer unto the LORD for a burnt offering;

19 [a]*Ye shall offer* at your own will a male without blemish, of the beeves, of the sheep, or of the goats.

20 [a]*But* whatsoever hath a blemish, *that* shall ye not offer: for it shall not be acceptable for you.

21 And [a]whosoever offereth a sacrifice of peace offerings unto the LORD [b]to accomplish *his* vow, or a freewill offering in beeves or [1]sheep, it shall be perfect to be accepted; there shall be no blemish therein.

22 [a]Blind, or broken, or maimed, or having a wen, or scurvy, or scabbed, ye shall not offer these unto the LORD, nor make [b]an offering by fire of them upon the altar unto the LORD.

23 Either a bullock or a [1]lamb that hath any thing [a]superfluous or lacking in his parts,

21:23 *vail.* Between the holy place and the most holy place (see Ex 26:33).
22:3 *cut off from my presence.* Excluded from the worshiping community.
22:4 See 13:1–46 and note on 13:45–46; 15:1–18 and notes; 21:11.
22:5 See 11:29–31.
22:8 See 17:15 and note.
22:9 *die . . . if they profane it.* The laws of cleanness were the same for priests and people, but the penalties were far more severe for the priests, who had greater responsibility. Cf. Nadab and Abihu (10:1–3) and the faithless priests of Malachi's day (Mal 1:6–2:9). *sanctify.* See note on 11:44.
22:14 *the fifth part . . . unto the priest.* Cf. 5:16.
22:16 *holy.* See note on 11:44.
22:18 *burnt offering.* See note on 1:3.
22:20–22 See Mal 1:8.
22:21 *peace offerings.* See note on 3:1.

that mayest thou offer *for* a freewill offering; but for a vow it shall not be accepted.

24 Ye shall not offer unto the LORD that which is bruised, or crushed, or broken, or cut; neither shall you make *any* offering *thereof* in your land.

25 Neither [a]from a stranger's hand shall ye offer [b]the bread of your God of any of these; because their [c]corruption *is* in them, *and* blemishes *be* in them: they shall not be accepted for you.

26 ¶ And the LORD spake unto Moses, saying,

27 [a]When a bullock, or a sheep, or a goat, is brought forth, then it shall be seven days under the dam; and from the eighth day and thenceforth it shall be accepted for an offering made by fire unto the LORD.

28 And *whether it be* cow or [1]ewe, ye shall not kill it [a]and her young both in one day.

29 And when ye will [a]offer a sacrifice of thanksgiving unto the LORD, offer *it* at your own will.

30 On the same day it shall be eaten up; ye shall leave [a]none of it until the morrow: I *am* the LORD.

31 ¶ [a]Therefore shall ye keep my commandments, and do them: I *am* the LORD.

32 [a]Neither shall ye profane my holy name; but [b]I will be hallowed among the children of Israel: I *am* the LORD which [c]hallow you,

33 [a]That brought you out of the land of Egypt, to be your God: I *am* the LORD.

Feasts of the LORD

23 And the LORD spake unto Moses, saying,

2 Speak unto the children of Israel, and say unto them, *Concerning* [a]the feasts of the LORD, which ye shall [b]proclaim *to be* holy convocations, *even* these *are* my feasts.

3 ¶ [a]Six days shall work be done: but the seventh day *is* the sabbath of rest, a holy convocation; ye shall do no work *therein:* it *is* the sabbath of the LORD in all your dwellings.

4 ¶ [a]These *are* the feasts of the LORD, *even* holy convocations, which ye shall proclaim in their seasons.

5 [a]In the fourteenth *day* of the first month at even *is* the LORD's passover.

6 And on the fifteenth day of the same month *is* the feast of unleavened bread unto the LORD: seven days ye must eat unleavened bread.

7 [a]In the first day ye shall have a holy convocation: ye shall do no servile work *therein.*

8 But ye shall offer an offering made by fire unto the LORD seven days: in the seventh day *is* a holy convocation: ye shall do no servile work *therein.*

9 ¶ And the LORD spake unto Moses, saying,

10 Speak unto the children of Israel, and say unto them, [a]When ye be come into the land which I give unto you, and shall reap the harvest thereof, then ye shall bring a [1 2]sheaf of [b]the firstfruits of your harvest unto the priest:

11 And he shall [a]wave the sheaf before the LORD, to be accepted for you: on the morrow after the sabbath the priest shall wave it.

12 And ye shall offer that day when ye wave the sheaf a he lamb without blemish of the first year for a burnt offering unto the LORD.

13 [a]And the meat offering thereof *shall be* two tenth deals *of* fine flour mingled with oil, an offering made by fire unto the LORD *for* a sweet savour: and the drink offering thereof *shall be of* wine, the fourth *part* of a hin.

14 And ye shall eat neither bread, nor parched *corn,* nor green ears, until the selfsame day that ye have brought an offering unto your God: *it shall be* a statute for ever throughout your generations in all your dwellings.

15 ¶ And [a]ye shall count unto you from the morrow after the sabbath, from the day that ye brought the sheaf of the wave offering; seven sabbaths shall be complete:

16 Even unto the morrow after the seventh sabbath shall ye number [a]fifty days; and ye shall offer [b]a new meat offering unto the LORD.

17 Ye shall bring out of your habitations two wave loaves of two tenth deals: they shall be *of* fine flour; they shall be baken *with* leaven; *they are* [a]the firstfruits unto the LORD.

18 And ye shall offer with the bread seven lambs without blemish of the first year, and one young bullock, and two rams: they shall

22:25 [a]Num. 15:15,16 [b]ch. 21:6,17 [c]Mal. 1:14
22:27 [a]Ex. 22:30
22:28 [1]Or, *she goat* [a]Deut. 22:6
22:29 [a]ch. 7:12; Ps. 107:22; 116:17; Amos 4:5
22:30 [a]ch. 7:15
22:31 [a]ch. 19:37; Num. 15:40; Deut. 4:40
22:32 [a]ch. 18:21 [b]ch. 10:3; Mat. 6:9; Luke 11:2 [c]ch. 20:8
22:33 [a]ch. 19:36; Num. 15:41
23:2 [a]ver. 4,37 [b]Ex. 32:5; 2 Ki. 10:20; Ps. 81:3
23:3 [a]Ex. 20:9; 23:12; 31:15; ch. 19:3; Deut. 5:13; Luke 13:14
23:4 [a]ver. 37; Ex. 23:14
23:5 [a]Ex. 12:6,14,18; 13:3,10; Deut. 16:1-8
23:7 [a]Ex. 12:16; Num. 28:18,25
23:10 [1]Or, *handful* [2]Heb. *omer* [a]Ex. 34:26; Deut. 16:9; Josh. 3:15 [b]Rom. 11:16; Jas. 1:18; Rev. 14:4
23:11 [a]Ex. 29:24
23:13 [a]ch. 2:14-16
23:15 [a]Ex. 34:22; ch. 25:8; Deut. 16:9
23:16 [a]Acts 2:1 [b]Num. 28:26
23:17 [a]Ex. 23:16,19; Num. 15:17-21

22:24 *bruised, or crushed, or broken, or cut.* Castrated animals were not acceptable offerings.

22:28 Perhaps the prohibition was humanitarian (see v. 27), or possibly it was practical: The mother was to be saved to build up the flock (see Deut 22:6–7). Or it may have been a law to avoid an otherwise unknown pagan custom (see note on Ex 23:19).

22:30 *the same day.* The rule applied also to the passover (Ex 34:25); however, the peace offering could be saved and eaten on the following day (7:16).

23:2 *feasts.* See Ex 23:14–17 and notes; 34:18–25; Num 28–29; Deut 16:1–17. The parallel in Numbers (the fullest and closest to Leviticus) specifies in great detail the offerings to be made at each feast. See chart, pp. 166.

23:3 *sabbath.* See notes on Ex 16:23; 20:9–10. The sabbath is associated with the annual feasts also in Ex 23:12. Two additional lambs were to be sacrificed as a burnt offering every weekly sabbath (Num 28:9–10).

23:5 *first month.* See note on Ex 12:2. The Israelites had three systems of referring to months. In one, the months were simply numbered (as here and in v. 24). In another, the Canaanite names were used (Abib, Bul, etc.), of which only four are known. In the third system, the Babylonian names (Nisan, Adar, Tishri, Kislev, etc.) were used—in the exilic and postexilic books only—and are still used today. See chart, p. 92. *passover.* See notes on Ex 12:11,14,21.

23:6 *feast of unleavened bread.* See note on Ex 23:15. During the feast the first sheaf of the barley harvest was brought (see vv. 10–11).

23:15 *seven sabbaths shall be complete.* Or seven full weeks. See note on Ex 23:16.

23:16 *fifty days.* The NT name for the feast of weeks was Pentecost (see Acts 2:1; 20:16; 1 Cor 16:8), meaning "fifty."

be *for* a burnt offering unto the LORD, with their meat offering, and their drink offerings, *even* an offering made by fire, of sweet savour unto the LORD.

19 Then ye shall sacrifice [a]one kid of the goats for a sin offering, and two lambs of the first year for a sacrifice of [b]peace offerings.

20 And the priest shall wave them with the bread of the firstfruits *for* a wave offering before the LORD, with the two lambs: [a]they shall be holy to the LORD for the priest.

21 And ye shall proclaim on the selfsame day, *that* it may be a holy convocation unto you: ye shall do no servile work *therein: it shall be* a statute for ever in all your dwellings throughout your generations.

22 And [a]when ye reap the harvest of your land, thou shalt not make clean riddance of the corners of thy field when thou reapest, neither shalt thou gather *any* gleaning of thy harvest: thou shalt leave them unto the poor, and to the stranger: I *am* the LORD your God.

23 ¶ And the LORD spake unto Moses, saying,

24 Speak unto the children of Israel, saying, In the [a]seventh month, in the first *day* of the month, shall ye have a sabbath, [b]a memorial of blowing of trumpets, a holy convocation.

25 Ye shall do no servile work *therein:* but ye shall offer an offering made by fire unto the LORD.

26 ¶ And the LORD spake unto Moses, saying,

27 [a]Also on the tenth *day* of this seventh month *there shall be* a day of atonement: it shall be a holy convocation unto you; and ye shall afflict your souls, and offer an offering made by fire unto the LORD.

28 And ye shall do no work in that same day: for it *is* a day of atonement, to make an atonement for you before the LORD your God.

29 For whatsoever soul *it be* that shall not be afflicted in that same day, [a]he shall be cut off from among his people.

30 And whatsoever soul *it be* that doeth any work in that same day, [a]the same soul will I destroy from among his people.

31 Ye shall do no *manner of* work: *it shall be* a statute for ever throughout your generations in all your dwellings.

32 It *shall be* unto you a sabbath of rest, and ye shall afflict your souls: in the ninth *day* of the month at even, from even unto even, shall ye [1]celebrate your sabbath.

33 ¶ And the LORD spake unto Moses, saying,

34 Speak unto the children of Israel, saying, [a]The fifteenth day of this seventh month *shall be* the feast of tabernacles *for* seven days unto the LORD.

35 On the first day *shall be* a holy convocation: ye shall do no servile work *therein.*

36 Seven days ye shall offer an offering made by fire unto the LORD: [a]on the eighth day shall be a holy convocation unto you; and ye shall offer an offering made by fire unto the LORD: it *is* a [b][1]solemn assembly; *and* ye shall do no servile work *therein.*

37 [a]These *are* the feasts of the LORD, which ye shall proclaim *to be* holy convocations, to offer an offering made by fire unto the LORD, a burnt offering, and a meat offering, a sacrifice, and drink offerings, every thing upon his day:

38 [a]Beside the sabbaths of the LORD, and beside your gifts, and beside all your vows, and beside all your freewill offerings, which ye give unto the LORD.

39 Also in the fifteenth day of the seventh month, when ye have [a]gathered in the fruit of the land, ye shall keep a feast unto the LORD seven days: on the first day *shall be* a sabbath, and on the eighth day *shall be* a sabbath.

40 And [a]ye shall take you on the first day the [1]boughs of goodly trees, branches of palm trees, and the boughs of thick trees, and willows of the brook; [b]and ye shall rejoice before the LORD your God seven days.

41 [a]And ye shall keep it a feast unto the LORD seven days in the year. *It shall be* a statute for ever in your generations: ye shall celebrate it in the seventh month.

42 [a]Ye shall dwell in booths seven days; all that are Israelites born shall dwell in booths:

43 [a]That your generations may know that I made the children of Israel to dwell in booths, when I brought them out of the land of Egypt: I *am* the LORD your God.

44 And Moses [a]declared unto the children of Israel the feasts of the LORD.

23:19 [a]ch. 4:23,28; Num. 28:30 [b]ch. 3:1
23:20 [a]Num. 18:12; Deut. 18:4
23:22 [a]ch. 19:9
23:24 [a]Num. 29:1 [b]ch. 25:9
23:27 [a]ch. 16:30; Num. 29:7
23:29 [a]Gen. 17:14
23:30 [a]ch. 20:3,5,6
23:32 [1]Heb. *rest*
23:34 [a]Ex. 23:16; Num. 29:12; Deut. 16:13; Ezra 3:4; Neh. 8:14; Zech. 14:16; John 7:2
23:36 [1]Heb. day of *restraint* [a]Num. 29:35; Neh. 8:18; John 7:37 [b]Deut. 16:8; 2 Chr. 7:9
23:37 [a]ver. 2,4
23:38 [a]Num. 29:39
23:39 [a]Ex. 23:16; Deut. 16:13
23:40 [1]Heb. *fruit* [a]Neh. 8:15 [b]Deut. 16:14,15
23:41 [a]Num. 29:12; Neh. 8:18
23:42 [a]Neh. 8:14-16
23:43 [a]Deut. 31:13
23:44 [a]ver. 2

23:22 See note on 19:9–10.

23:24 *seventh month, in the first day of the month.* Today known as the Jewish New Year (*Rosh Hashanah,* "the beginning of the year"), but not so called in the Bible (the Hebrew expression is only used in Ezek 40:1 in a date formula). *blowing of trumpets.* Trumpets were blown on the first of every month (Ps 81:3). With no calendars available, the trumpets sounding across the land were an important signal of the beginning of the new season, the end of the agricultural year. See note on 16:29; see also chart, p. 92.

23:27 *day of atonement.* For details see notes on 16:1–34. Aaron was to enter the most holy place only once a year (16:29–34) on the day called by modern Jews *Yom Kippur.* The Biblical name, however, is the plural *Yom Hakkippurim* (as in this verse), derived from the Hebrew words *yom* ("day") and *kipper* ("to atone"). The day was typological, foreshadowing the work of Christ, our high priest (see Heb 9:7; 13:11–12). *afflict your souls.* See note on 16:29,31.

23:29 *cut off from among his people.* See note on 7:20.

23:34 *feast of tabernacles.* See notes on Ex 23:16; John 7:37–39. This was the last of the three annual pilgrimage festivals (Ex 23:14–17; Deut 16:16).

23:42 *booths.* The Hebrew for this word is *Sukkot* and can also be translated "tabernacles." Even today, orthodox Jews construct small booths (see Neh 8:13–17) to remind them of the booths they lived in when God brought them out of Egypt at the time of the exodus (v. 43).

The oil and the shewbread

24 And the LORD spake unto Moses, saying,
2 [a]Command the children of Israel, that they bring unto thee pure oil olive beaten for the light, [1]to cause the lamps to burn continually.
3 Without the vail of the Testimony, in the tabernacle of the congregation, shall Aaron order it from the evening unto the morning before the LORD continually: *it shall be* a statute for ever in your generations.
4 He shall order the lamps upon [a]the pure candlestick before the LORD continually.
5 ¶ And thou shalt take fine flour, and bake twelve [a]cakes thereof: two tenth deals shall be *in* one cake.
6 And thou shalt set them *in* two rows, six on a row, [a]upon the pure table before the LORD.
7 And thou shalt put pure frankincense upon *each* row, that it may be on the bread for a memorial, *even* an offering made by fire unto the LORD.
8 [a]Every sabbath he shall set it in order before the LORD continually, *being taken* from the children of Israel *by* an everlasting covenant.
9 And [a]it shall be Aaron's and his sons'; [b]and they shall eat it in the holy place: for it *is* most holy unto him of the offerings of the LORD made by fire, *by* a perpetual statute.

24:2 [1]Heb. *to cause to ascend* [a]Ex. 27:20
24:4 [a]Ex. 31:8; 39:37
24:5 [a]Ex. 25:30
24:6 [a]1 Ki. 7:48; 2 Chr. 4:19; 13:11; Heb. 9:2
24:8 [a]Num. 4:7; 1 Chr. 9:32; 2 Chr. 2:4
24:9 [a]1 Sam. 21:6; Mat. 12:4; Mark 2:26; Luke 6:4 [b]Ex. 29:33; ch. 8:31

24:2–4 See Ex 27:20–21.
24:3 *Testimony.* See note on Ex 16:34. *order it.* Keep the lamps burning (see vv. 2,4). *continually.* Every night without interruption, but not throughout the day. See 1 Sam 3:3 and note.
24:5 *two tenth deals.* Supposedly the unit of measurement is an ephah; i.e., about four quarts per cake (the Hebrew word *ephah* is not expressed). Either the loaves were quite large or a smaller unit of measurement is intended.
24:7 *pure frankincense.* Not used as a condiment for the bread, but burned either in piles on the table or in small receptacles alongside the rows of bread.
24:8 *it.* The shewbread, often called the "bread of the Presence" (see Ex 25:30 and note). It represented a gift from the 12 tribes and signified the fact that God sustained His people. It was eaten by the priests (24:9).
24:9 See 1 Sam 21:4–6.

Old Testament Feasts and Other Sacred Days

NAME	OLD TESTAMENT REFERENCES	OT TIME	MODERN EQUIVALENT
Sabbath	Ex 20:8-11; 31:12-17; Lev 23:3; Deut 5:12-15	7th day	Same
Sabbath Year	Ex 23:10-11; Lev 25:1-7	7th year	Same
Year of Jubilee	Lev 25:8-55; 27:17-24; Num 36:4	50th year	Same
Passover	Ex 12:1-14; Lev 23:5; Num 9:1-14; 28:16; Deut 16:1-3a,4b-7	1st month (Abib) 14	Mar.–Apr.
Unleavened Bread	Ex 12:15-20; 13:3-10; 23:15; 34:18; Lev 23:6-8; Num 28:17-25; Deut 16:3b,4a,8	1st month (Abib) 15-21	Mar.–Apr.
First fruits	Lev 23:9-14	1st month (Abib) 16	Mar.–Apr.
Weeks (Pentecost)(Harvest)	Ex 23:16a; 34:22a; Lev 23:15-21; Num 28:26-31; Deut 16:9-12	3rd month (Sivan) 6	May–June
Trumpets (Later: Rosh Hashanah–New Year's Day)	Lev 23:23-25; Num 29:1-6	7th month (Tishri) 1	Sept.–Oct.
Day of Atonement (Yom Kippur)	Lev 16; 23:26-32; Num 29:7-11	7th month (Tishri) 10	Sept.–Oct.
Booths (Tabernacles)(Ingathering)	Ex 23:16b; 34:22b; Lev 23:33-36a,39-43; Num 29:12-34; Deut 16:13-15; Zech 14:16-19	7th month (Tishri) 15-21	Sept.–Oct.
Holy Convocation	Lev 23:36b; Num 29:35-38	7th month (Tishri) 22	Sept.–Oct.
Purim	Esth 9:18-32	12th month (Adar) 14,15	Feb.–Mar.

On Kislev 25 (mid-December) Hanukkah, the feast of dedication or festival of lights, commemorated the purification of the temple and altar in the Maccabean period (165/4 B.C.). This feast is mentioned in John 10:22.

Death for blasphemy

10 ¶ And the son of an Israelitish woman, whose father *was* an Egyptian, went out among the children of Israel: and *this* son of the Israelitish *woman* and a man of Israel strove together in the camp;

11 And the Israelitish woman's son blasphemed the name *of the LORD,* and [a]cursed. And they [b]brought him unto Moses: (and his mother's name *was* Shelomith, the daughter of Dibri, of the tribe of Dan:)

12 And they [a]put him in ward, [b][1]that the mind of the LORD might be shewed them.

13 And the LORD spake unto Moses, saying,

14 Bring forth him that hath cursed without the camp; and let all that heard *him* [a]lay their hands upon his head, and let all the congregation stone him.

24:11 [a]Job 1:5,11,22; Is. 8:21 [b]Ex. 18:22,26
24:12 [1]Heb. *to expound unto them according to the mouth of the LORD* [a]Num. 15:34 [b]Ex. 18:15; Num. 27:5
24:14 [a]Deut. 13:9; 17:7
24:15 [a]ch. 20:17; Num. 9:13
24:16 [a]1 Ki. 21:10,13; Mat. 12:31; Mark 3:28
24:17 [1]Heb. *smiteth the life of a man* [a]Ex. 21:12; Num. 35:31; Deut. 19:11,12

15 And thou shalt speak unto the children of Israel, saying, Whosoever curseth his God [a]shall bear his sin.

16 And he that [a]blasphemeth the name of the LORD, he shall surely be put to death, *and* all the congregation shall certainly stone him: as well the stranger, as he that is born in the land, when he blasphemeth the name *of the LORD,* shall be put to death.

17 [a]And he that [1]killeth any man shall surely be put to death.

18 [a]And he that [1]killeth a beast shall make it good; [2]beast for beast.

19 And if a man cause a blemish in his neighbour; as [a]he hath done, so shall it be done to him;

20 Breach for breach, eye for eye, tooth for

24:18 [1]Heb. *smiteth the life of a man* [2]Heb. *life for life* [a]ver. 21
24:19 [a]Ex. 21:24; Deut. 19:21; Mat. 5:38; 7:2

24:10 *father was an Egyptian.* An alien. The laws, at least in the judicial sphere, applied equally to both the alien and the native-born Israelite (v. 22; see Ex 12:49).
24:11 *blasphemed.* See Ex 20:7 and note.
24:17,21 See Gen 9:6 and note.

24:20 *eye for eye, tooth for tooth.* See note on Ex 21:23–25. This represents a statement of principle: The penalty is to fit the crime, not exceed it. An actual eye or tooth was not to be required, nor is there evidence that such a penalty was ever exacted. A similar law of retaliation is found in the Code of Ham-

DESCRIPTION	PURPOSE	NEW TESTAMENT REFERENCES
Day of rest; no work	Rest for people and animals	Mat 12:1-14; 28:1; Luke 4:16; John 5:9; Acts 13:42; Col 2:16; Heb 4:1-11
Year of rest; fallow fields	Rest for land	
Canceled debts; liberation of slaves and indentured servants; land returned to original family owners	Help for poor; stabilize society	
Slaying and eating a lamb, together with bitter herbs and bread made without yeast, in every household	Remember Israel's deliverance from Egypt	Mat 26:17; Mark 14:12-26; John 2:13; 11:55; 1 Cor 5:7; Heb 11:28
Eating bread made without yeast; holding several assemblies; making designated offerings	Remember how the Lord brought the Israelites out of Egypt in haste	Mark 14:1; Acts 12:3; 1 Cor 5:6-8
Presenting a sheaf of the first of the barley harvest as a wave offering; making a burnt offering and a grain offering	Recognize the Lord's bounty in the land	Rom 8:23; 1 Cor 15:20-23
A festival of joy; mandatory and voluntary offerings, including the first fruits of the wheat harvest	Show joy and thankfulness for the Lord's blessing of harvest	Acts 2:1-4; 20:16; 1 Cor 16:8
An assembly on a day of rest commemorated with trumpet blasts and sacrifices	Present Israel before the Lord for his favor	
A day of rest, fasting and sacrifices of atonement for priests and people and atonement for the tabernacle and altar	Cleanse priests and people from their sins and purify the holy place	Rom 3:24-26; Heb 9:7; 10:3,19-22
A week of celebration for the harvest; living in booths and offering sacrifices	Memorialize the journey from Egypt to Canaan; give thanks for the productivity of Canaan	John 7:2,37
A day of convocation, rest and offering sacrifices	Commemorate the closing of the cycle of feasts	
A day of joy and feasting and giving presents	Remind the Israelites of their national deliverance in the time of Esther	

In addition, new moons were often special feast days (Num 10:10; 1 Chr 23:31; Ezra 3:5; Neh 10:33; Ps 81:3; Is 1:13-14; 66:23; Hos 5:7; Amos 8:5; Col 2:16).

tooth: as he hath caused a blemish in a man,
so shall it be done to him *again.*
21 [a]And he that killeth a beast, he shall restore it: [b]and he that killeth a man, he shall be
put to death.
22 Ye shall have [a]one manner of law, as
well for the stranger, as for one of your own
country: for I *am* the LORD your God.
23 And Moses spake to the children of Israel, [a]that they should bring forth him that
had cursed out of the camp, and stone him
with stones. And the children of Israel did as
the LORD commanded Moses.

Sabbath and jubile years

25 And the LORD spake unto Moses in
mount Sinai, saying,
2 Speak unto the children of Israel, and say
unto them, When ye come into the land which
I give you, then shall the land [1]keep [a]a sabbath unto the LORD.
3 Six years thou shalt sow thy field, and six
years thou shalt prune thy vineyard, and gather in the fruit thereof;
4 But in the seventh year shall be a sabbath
of rest unto the land, a sabbath for the LORD:
thou shalt neither sow thy field, nor prune thy
vineyard.
5 [a]That which groweth of it own accord of
thy harvest thou shalt not reap, neither gather
the grapes [1]of thy vine undressed: *for* it is a
year of rest unto the land.
6 And the sabbath of the land shall be meat
for you; for thee, and for thy servant, and for
thy maid, and for thy hired servant, and for thy
stranger that sojourneth with thee,
7 And for thy cattle, and for the beast that
are in thy land, shall all the increase thereof be
meat.
8 ¶ And thou shalt number seven sabbaths
of years unto thee, seven times seven years;
and the space of the seven sabbaths of years
shall be unto thee forty and nine years.
9 Then shalt thou cause the trumpet [1]of the
jubile to sound on the tenth *day* of the seventh
month, [a]in the day of atonement shall ye make
the trumpet sound throughout all your land.
10 And ye shall hallow the fiftieth year, and
[a]proclaim liberty throughout *all* the land unto
all the inhabitants thereof: it shall be a jubile
unto you; [b]and ye shall return every man unto
his possession, and ye shall return every man
unto his family.
11 A jubile shall that fiftieth year be unto
you: [a]ye shall not sow, neither reap that which
groweth of itself in it, nor gather *the grapes* in
it of thy vine undressed.
12 For it *is* the jubile; it shall be holy unto
you: [a]ye shall eat the increase thereof out of
the field.
13 [a]In the year of this jubile ye shall return
every man unto his possession.
14 And if thou sell ought unto thy neighbour, or buyest *ought* of thy neighbour's hand,
ye shall not oppress one another:
15 [a]According to the number of years after
the jubile thou shalt buy of thy neighbour, *and*
according unto the number of years of the
fruits he shall sell unto thee:
16 According to the multitude of years
thou shalt increase the price thereof, and according to the fewness of years thou shalt diminish the price of it: for *according to* the
number *of the years* of the fruits doth he sell
unto thee.
17 [a]Ye shall not therefore oppress one another; [b]but thou shalt fear thy God: for I *am*
the LORD your God.
18 ¶ [a]Wherefore ye shall do my statutes,
and keep my judgments, and do them; [b]and ye
shall dwell in the land in safety.
19 And the land shall yield her fruit, and
[a]ye shall eat *your* fill, and dwell therein in
safety.
20 And if ye shall say, [a]What shall we eat
the seventh year? behold, [b]we shall not sow,
nor gather in our increase:
21 Then I will [a]command my blessing
upon you in the sixth year, and it shall bring
forth fruit for three years.
22 [a]And ye shall sow the eighth year, and
eat *yet* of [b]old fruit until the ninth year; until
her fruits come in ye shall eat *of* the old *store.*
23 ¶ The land shall not be sold [1]for ever:

24:21 [a]Ex. 21:33 [b]ver. 17
24:22 [a]Ex. 12:49; ch. 19:34; Num. 15:16
24:23 [a]ver. 14
25:2 [1]Heb. *rest* [a]Ex. 23:10; See ch. 26:34,35
25:5 [1]Heb. *of thy separation* [a]2 Ki. 19:29
25:9 [1]Heb. *loud of sound* [a]ch. 23:24,27
25:10 [a]Is. 61:2; 63:4; Jer. 34:8,15,17; Luke 4:19 [b]ver. 13; Num. 36:4
25:11 [a]ver. 5
25:12 [a]ver. 6,7
25:13 [a]ver. 10; ch. 27:24; Num. 36:4
25:15 [a]ch. 27:18
25:17 [a]ver. 14 [b]ver. 43; ch. 19:14,32
25:18 [a]ch. 19:37 [b]ch. 26:5; Deut. 12:10; Ps. 4:8
25:19 [a]ch. 26:5; Ezek. 34:25
25:20 [a]Mat. 6:25 [b]ver. 4,5
25:21 [a]See Ex. 16:29
25:22 [a]2 Ki. 19:29 [b]Josh. 5:11
25:23 [1]Or, *to be quite cut off.* Heb. *for cutting off*

murapi, which also seems not to have been literally applied. Christ, like the middle-of-the-road Pharisees (school of Hillel), objected to an extremist use of this judicial principle to excuse private vengeance, such as by the strict Pharisees (school of Shammai); see Mat 5:38–42.

24:22 See note on v. 10.

25:4 *a sabbath of rest unto the land.* See Ex 23:10–11. The Israelites did not practice crop rotation, but the fallow year (when the crops were not planted) served somewhat the same purpose. And just as the land was to have a sabbath year, so the servitude of a Hebrew slave was limited to six years, apparently whether or not the year he was freed was a sabbath year (see Ex 21:2 and note). Deut 15:1–11 specifies that debts were also to be canceled in the sabbath year. The care for the poor in the laws of Israel (see Ex 23:11) is noteworthy. See 23:7,35; Deut 31:10; Neh 10:31.

25:9 *day of atonement.* See notes on 16:1–34; see also 23:27.

25:10 *fiftieth year.* Possibly a fallow year in addition to the seventh sabbath year, or perhaps the same as the 49th year (counting the first and last years). Jewish sources from the period between the Testaments favor the latter interpretation. *proclaim liberty . . . inhabitants.* See vv. 39–43,47–55. The Liberty Bell in Philadelphia is so named because this statement was written on it. Cf. Is 61:1–2; Luke 4:16–21. *jubile.* The Hebrew for this word is the same as and may be related to one of the Hebrew words for "[ram's] horn," "trumpet" (see, e.g., Ex 19:13), though in v. 9 a different Hebrew word for "trumpet" is used. Trumpets were blown at the close of the day of atonement to inaugurate the year of jubile. Cf. 23:24.

25:13 *return . . . his possession.* See v. 10. The Lord prohibited the accumulation of property to the detriment of the poor. "The land is mine," said the Lord (v. 23). God's people are only tenants (see 1 Chr 29:15; Heb 11:13).

25:15 *number of years of the fruits.* The number of years left for harvesting. In a way, the sale of land in Israel was a lease until the year of jubile (see 27:18,23).

for [a]the land *is* mine; for ye *were* [b]strangers and sojourners with me.

24 And in all the land of your possession ye shall grant a redemption for the land.

25 [a]If thy brother be waxen poor, and hath sold away *some* of his possession, and *if* [b]*any of* his kin come to redeem it, then shall he redeem that which his brother sold.

26 And if the man have none to redeem *it*, and [1]himself be able to redeem it;

27 Then [a]let him count the years of the sale thereof, and restore the overplus unto the man to whom he sold it; that he may return unto his possession.

28 But if he be not able to restore *it* to him, then that which is sold shall remain in the hand of him that hath bought it until the year of jubile: [a]and in the jubile it shall go out, and he shall return unto his possession.

29 And if a man sell a dwelling house in a walled city, then he may redeem it within a whole year after it is sold; *within* a full year may he redeem it.

30 And if it be not redeemed within the space of a full year, then the house that *is* in the walled city shall be stablished for ever to him that bought it throughout his generations: it shall not go out in the jubile.

31 But the houses of the villages which have no wall round about them shall be counted as the fields of the country: [1]they may be redeemed, and they shall go out in the jubile.

32 Notwithstanding [a]the cities of the Levites, *and* the houses of the cities of their possession, may the Levites redeem at any time.

33 And if [1]a man purchase of the Levites, then the house that was sold, and the city of his possession, shall go out in the *year of* jubile: for the houses of the cities of the Levites *are* their possession among the children of Israel.

34 But [a]the field of the suburbs of their cities may not be sold; for it *is* their perpetual possession.

35 ¶ And if thy brother be waxen poor, and [1]fallen in decay with thee; then thou shalt [a2]relieve him: *yea, though he be* a stranger, or a sojourner; that he may live with thee.

36 [a]Take thou no usury of him, or increase: but [b]fear thy God; that thy brother may live with thee.

37 Thou shalt not give him thy money upon usury, nor lend him thy victuals for increase.

38 [a]I *am* the LORD your God, which brought you forth out of the land of Egypt, to give you the land of Canaan, *and* to be your God.

39 ¶ And [a]if thy brother *that dwelleth* by thee be waxen poor, and be sold unto thee; thou shalt not [1]compel him to serve as a bondservant:

40 *But* as a hired servant, *and* as a sojourner, he shall be with thee, *and* shall serve thee unto the year of jubile:

41 And *then* shall he depart from thee, *both* he and his children [a]with him, and shall return unto his own family, and [b]unto the possession of his fathers shall he return.

42 For they *are* [a]my servants, which I brought forth out of the land of Egypt: they shall not be sold [1]as bondmen.

43 [a]Thou shalt not rule over him [b]with rigour; but [c]shalt fear thy God.

44 Both thy bondmen, and thy bondmaids, which thou shalt have, *shall be* of the heathen that *are* round about you; of them shall ye buy bondmen and bondmaids.

45 Moreover of [a]the children of the strangers that do sojourn among you, of them shall ye buy, and of their families that *are* with you, which they begat in your land: and they shall be your possession.

46 And [a]ye shall take them as an inheritance for your children after you, to inherit *them for* a possession; [1]they shall be your bondmen for ever: but over your brethren the children of Israel, ye shall not rule one over another with rigour.

47 ¶ And if a sojourner or stranger [1]wax rich by thee, and [a]thy brother *that dwelleth* by him wax poor, and sell himself unto the stranger *or* sojourner by thee, or to the stock of the stranger's family:

48 After *that* he is sold he may be redeemed again; one of his brethren may [a]redeem him:

49 Either his uncle, or his uncle's son, may redeem him, or *any* that is nigh of kin unto him of his family may redeem him; or if [a]he be able, he may redeem himself.

50 And he shall reckon with him that bought him from the year that he was sold to him unto the year of jubile: and the price of his sale shall be according unto the number of years, [a]according to the time of a hired servant shall it be with him.

51 If *there be* yet many years *behind*, according unto them he shall give again the price of his redemption out of the money that he was bought for.

52 And if there remain but few years unto the year of jubile, then he shall count with him, *and* according unto his years shall he give *him* again the price of his redemption.

53 *And* as a yearly hired servant shall he be with him: *and the other* shall not rule with rigour over him in thy sight.

25:23 [a]Deut. 32:43 [b]Ps. 39:12
25:25 [a]Ruth 2:20 [b]See Ruth 3:2,9,12
25:26 [1]Heb. *his hand hath attained and found sufficiency*
25:27 [a]ver. 50-52
25:28 [a]ver. 13
25:31 [1]Heb. *redemption belongeth unto it*
25:32 [a]See Num. 35:2
25:33 [1]Or, one *of the Levites redeem* them
25:34 [a]See Acts 4:36,37
25:35 [1]Heb. *his hand faileth* [2]Heb. *strengthen* [a]Deut. 15:7; Luke 6:35; 1 John 3:17
25:36 [a]Ex. 22:25; Deut. 23:19 [b]Neh. 5:9
25:38 [a]ch. 22:32,33
25:39 [a]Ex. 21:2; Deut. 15:12; 1 Ki. 9:22
25:39 [1]Heb. *serve* thyself *with him* with *the service, etc.*
25:41 [a]Ex. 21:3 [b]ver. 28
25:42 [1]Heb. with *the sale of a bondman* [a]ver. 55; Rom. 6:22; 1 Cor. 7:23
25:43 [a]Eph. 6:9 [b]Ex. 1:13 [c]Ex. 1:17; Deut. 25:18; Mal. 3:5
25:45 [a]Is. 56:3,6
25:46 [1]Heb. *ye shall serve* yourselves *with them* [a]Is. 14:2
25:47 [1]Heb. *his hand obtain, etc.* [a]ver. 25,35
25:48 [a]Neh. 5:5
25:49 [a]ver. 26
25:50 [a]Job 7:1; Is. 16:14

25:24 *redemption for the land.* That is, the right to repurchase the land by (or for) the original family.

25:25 *his kin come to redeem it.* See Jer 32:6–15. This is apparently what the nearest relative was to do for Naomi and Ruth (Ruth 4:1–4), but he was also obligated to marry the widow and support the family (see Deut 25:5–10). Only Boaz was willing to do both (Ruth 4:9–10).

25:33 *cities of the Levites.* See Num 35:1–8; Josh 21:1–42.

25:36 *usury* [i.e., interest]. The main idea was not necessarily to forbid all interest, but to assist the poor. The law did not forbid lending so much as it encouraged giving.

54 And if he be not redeemed [1]in these *years,* then he shall go out in the year of jubile, *both* he, and his children with him.

55 For unto me the children of Israel *are* servants; they *are* my servants whom I brought forth out of the land of Egypt: I *am* the LORD your God.

The blessings for obedience

26 Ye shall make you [a]no idols nor graven image, neither rear you up a [1]standing image, neither shall ye set up *any* [2]image of stone in your land, to bow down unto it: for I *am* the LORD your God.

2 [a]Ye shall keep my sabbaths, and reverence my sanctuary: I *am* the LORD.

3 ¶ [a]If ye walk in my statutes, and keep my commandments, and do them;

4 [a]Then I will give you rain in due season, [b]and the land shall yield her increase, and the trees of the field shall yield their fruit.

5 And [a]your threshing shall reach unto the vintage, and the vintage shall reach unto the sowing time: and [b]ye shall eat your bread to the full, and [c]dwell in your land safely.

6 And [a]I will give peace in the land, and [b]ye shall lie down, and none shall make *you* afraid: and I will [1]rid [c]evil beasts out of the land, neither shall [d]the sword go through your land.

7 And ye shall chase your enemies, and they shall fall before you by the sword.

8 And [a]five of you shall chase an hundred, and an hundred of you shall put ten thousand to flight: and your enemies shall fall before you by the sword.

9 For I will [a]have respect unto you, and [b]make you fruitful, and multiply you, and establish my covenant with you.

10 And ye shall eat [a]old store, and bring forth the old because of the new.

11 [a]And I will set my tabernacle amongst you: and my soul shall not abhor you.

12 [a]And I will walk among you, and will be your God, and ye shall be my people.

13 I *am* the LORD your God, which brought you forth out of the land of Egypt, that *ye* should not be their bondmen; and I have broken the bands of your yoke, and made you go upright.

The punishments for disobedience

14 ¶ [a]But if ye will not hearken unto me, and will not do all these commandments;

15 And if ye shall despise my statutes, or if your soul abhor my judgments, so that *ye* will not do all my commandments, *but* that ye break my covenant:

16 I also will do this unto you; I will even appoint [1]over you terror, [a]consumption, and the burning ague, that shall [b]consume the eyes, and cause sorrow of heart: and [c]ye shall sow your seed in vain, for your enemies shall eat it.

17 And [a]I will set my face against you, and [b]ye shall be slain before your enemies; [c]they that hate you shall reign over you; and [d]ye shall flee when none pursueth you.

18 And if ye will not yet for *all* this hearken unto me, then I will punish you [a]seven *times* more for your sins.

19 And I will [a]break the pride of your power; and I [b]will make your heaven as iron, and your earth as brass:

20 And your [a]strength shall be spent in vain: for [b]your land shall not yield her increase, neither shall the trees of the land yield their fruits.

21 And if ye walk [1]contrary unto me, and will not hearken unto me; I will bring seven *times* moe plagues upon you according to your sins.

22 [a]I will also send wild beasts among you, which shall rob you of your children, and destroy your cattle, and make you few in number; and [b]your *high* ways shall be desolate.

23 And if ye [a]will not be reformed by me by these *things,* but will walk contrary unto me;

24 [a]Then will I also walk contrary unto you, and will punish you yet seven *times* for your sins.

25 And [a]I will bring a sword upon you, that shall avenge the quarrel of *my* covenant: and when ye are gathered together within your cities, [b]I will send the pestilence among you; and ye shall be delivered into the hand of the enemy.

26 [a]*And* when I have broken the staff of your bread, ten women shall bake your bread in one oven, and they shall deliver *you* your bread again by weight: and [b]ye shall eat, and not be satisfied.

27 And if ye will not for *all* this hearken unto me, but walk contrary unto me;

28 Then I will walk contrary unto you also [a]in fury; and I, even I, will chastise you seven *times* for your sins.

29 [a]And ye shall eat the flesh of your sons, and the flesh of your daughters shall ye eat.

25:54 [1]Or, *by these* means
26:1 [1]Or, *pillar* [2]Or, *figured stone.* Heb. *a stone of picture* [a]Ex. 20:4,5; Deut. 5:8
26:2 [a]ch. 19:30
26:3 [a]Deut. 28:1-14
26:4 [a]Is. 30:23 [b]Ps. 67:6; Zech. 8:12
26:5 [a]Amos 9:13 [b]ch. 25:19 [c]ch. 25:18
26:6 [1]Heb. *cause to cease* [a]Is. 45:7 [b]Ps. 4:8; Hos. 2:18; Zeph. 3:13 [c]2 Ki. 17:25 [d]Ezek. 14:17
26:8 [a]Deut. 32:30
26:9 [a]Ex. 2:25 [b]Gen. 17:6,7; Ps. 107:38
26:10 [a]ch. 25:22
26:11 [a]Ex. 25:8; Josh. 22:19; Ps. 76:2; Rev. 21:3
26:12 [a]2 Cor. 6:16
26:14 [a]Deut. 28:15; Lam. 2:17; Mal. 2:2
26:16 [1]Heb. *upon you* [a]Deut. 28:22 [b]1 Sam. 2:33 [c]Deut. 28:33,51; Job 31:8; Mic. 6:15
26:17 [a]ch. 17:10 [b]Deut. 28:25 [c]Ps. 106:41 [d]ver. 36; Ps. 53:5
26:18 [a]1 Sam. 2:5
26:19 [a]Is. 25:11 [b]Deut. 28:23
26:20 [a]Ps. 127:1 [b]Deut. 11:17
26:21 [1]Or, *at all adventures with me,* and so ver. 24
26:22 [a]Deut. 32:24 [b]2 Chr. 15:5; Zech. 7:14
26:23 [a]Jer. 2:30; Amos 4:6-12
26:24 [a]Ps. 18:26
26:25 [a]Ezek. 5:17 [b]Deut. 28:21
26:26 [a]Ps. 105:16 [b]Mic. 6:14
26:28 [a]Jer. 21:5; Ezek. 5:13,15; 8:18
26:29 [a]Deut. 28:53

25:55 *servants.* Covenant terminology, similar to "vassals." Slavery, however demeaning, is not brutal where the masters truly recognize themselves as God's servants. Cf. Paul's exhortation to both slaves and masters (Eph 6:5–9; Col 3:22–4:1).

26:1 *Ye shall make you no idols.* This verse probably does not forbid making statues, but it does forbid worshiping God in any material form (see Ex 20:4 and note)."God is a Spirit" (John 4:24; see Deut 4:15–19).

26:3 *keep my commandments.* Obedience is the key to blessing (see Gal 6:7–10; Jas 1:22–25). Compare the blessings promised in vv. 3–13 with those in Deut 28:1–14.

26:9 *fruitful, and multiply.* See note on Gen 1:22; cf. Lev 26:22.

26:12 *your God . . . my people.* Covenantal terms later made famous by Hosea (1:9–10; 2:23). See Jer 31:33; Ezek 36:28; Heb 8:10.

26:14 *if ye will not hearken unto me.* The list of curses for covenant disobedience (see vv. 14–39) is usually much longer than that of blessings for obedience (as in vv. 3–13; see Deut 28:15–29:28; cf. Deut 28:1–14).

26:17 See v. 36 and the allusion to this statement in Prov 28:1.

30 And [a]I will destroy your high places, and cut down your images, and cast your carcases upon the carcases of your idols, and my soul shall abhor you.

31 And I will make your cities waste, and [a]bring your sanctuaries unto desolation, and I will not smell the savour of your sweet odours.

32 [a]And I will bring the land into desolation: and your enemies which dwell therein shall be astonished at it.

33 And [a]I will scatter you among the heathen, and will draw out a sword after you: and your land shall be desolate, and your cities waste.

34 [a]Then shall the land enjoy her sabbaths, as long as it lieth desolate, and ye *be* in your enemies' land; *even* then shall the land rest, and enjoy her sabbaths.

35 As long as it lieth desolate it shall rest; because it did not rest in your [a]sabbaths, when ye dwelt upon it.

36 And *upon* them that are left *alive* of you [a]I will send a faintness into their hearts in the lands of their enemies; and [b]the sound of a [1]shaken leaf shall chase them; and they shall flee, as fleeing from a sword; and they shall fall when none pursueth.

37 And [a]they shall fall one upon another, as it were before a sword, when none pursueth: and [b]ye shall have no power to stand before your enemies.

38 And ye shall perish among the heathen, and the land of your enemies shall eat you up.

39 And they that are left of you [a]shall pine away in their iniquity in your enemies' lands; and also in the iniquities of their fathers shall they pine away with them.

40 [a]If they shall confess their iniquity, and the iniquity of their fathers, with their trespass which they trespassed against me, and that also they have walked contrary unto me;

41 *And that* I also have walked contrary unto them, and have brought them into the land of their enemies; if then their [a]uncircumcised hearts be [b]humbled, and they then accept of the punishment of their iniquity:

42 Then will I [a]remember my covenant with Jacob, and also my covenant with Isaac, and also my covenant with Abraham will I remember; and I will [b]remember the land.

43 [a]The land also shall be left of them, and shall enjoy her sabbaths, while she lieth desolate without them: and they shall accept of the punishment of their iniquity: because, even because they [b]despised my judgments, and because their soul abhorred my statutes.

44 And yet for all that, when they be in the land of their enemies, [a]I will not cast them away, neither will I abhor them, to destroy them utterly, and to break my covenant with them: for I *am* the LORD their God.

45 But I will [a]for their sakes remember the covenant of their ancestors, [b]whom I brought forth out of the land of Egypt [c]in the sight of the heathen, that *I* might be their God: I *am* the LORD.

46 [a]These *are* the statutes and judgments and laws, which the LORD made between him and the children of Israel [b]in mount Sinai by the hand of Moses.

26:30 [a]2 Chr. 34:3; Ezek. 6:3-6,13
26:31 [a]Ps. 74:7
26:32 [a]Jer. 9:11
26:33 [a]Deut. 4:27; Ezek. 12:15; 20:23; 22:15; Zech. 7:14
26:34 [a]2 Chr. 36:21
26:35 [a]ch. 25:2
26:36 [1]Heb. *driven* [a]Ezek. 21:7,12,15 [b]ver. 17; Prov. 28:1
26:37 [a]See Judg. 7:22; 1 Sam. 14:15,16; Is. 10:4 [b]Josh. 7:12,13; Judg. 2:14
26:39 [a]Deut. 28:65; Zech. 10:9
26:40 [a]Num. 5:7; Neh. 9:2; Luke 15:18; 1 John 1:9
26:41 [a]Acts 7:51; Rom. 2:29 [b]2 Chr. 12:6,7
26:42 [a]Ex. 2:24; 6:5; Ezek. 16:60 [b]Ps. 136:23
26:43 [a]ver. 34,35
26:43 [b]ver. 15
26:44 [a]Deut. 4:31; 2 Ki. 13:23; Rom. 11:2
26:45 [a]Rom. 11:28 [b]ch. 22:33; 25:38 [c]Ps. 98:2; Ezek. 20:9,14,22
26:46 [a]ch. 27:34; Deut. 6:1; 12:1; John 1:17 [b]ch. 25:1
27:2 [a]Num. 6:2; See Judg. 11:30,31,39; 1 Sam. 1:11,28
27:3 [a]Ex. 30:13

Vows and tithes to the LORD

27 And the LORD spake unto Moses, saying,

2 Speak unto the children of Israel, and say unto them, [a]When a man shall make a singular vow, the persons *shall be* for the LORD by thy estimation.

3 And thy estimation shall be, of the male from twenty years old even unto sixty years old, even thy estimation shall be fifty shekels of silver, [a]after the shekel of the sanctuary.

4 And if it *be* a female, then thy estimation shall be thirty shekels.

5 And if *it be* from five years old even unto twenty years old, then thy estimation shall be of the male twenty shekels, and for the female ten shekels.

6 And if *it be* from a month old even unto five years old, then thy estimation shall be of the male five shekels of silver, and for the female thy estimation *shall be* three shekels of silver.

7 And if *it be* from sixty years old and above; if *it be* a male, then thy estimation shall be fifteen shekels, and for the female ten shekels.

8 But if he be poorer than thy estimation, then he shall present himself before the priest, and the priest shall value him; according to his ability that vowed shall the priest value him.

9 ¶ And if *it be* a beast, whereof *men* bring an offering unto the LORD, all that *any man* giveth of such unto the LORD shall be holy.

10 He shall not alter it, nor change it, a good for a bad, or a bad for a good: and if he shall at all change beast for beast, then it and the exchange thereof shall be holy.

11 And if *it be* any unclean beast, of which

26:41 *uncircumcised hearts.* See note on Gen 17:10.

26:44 *not cast them away.* See Jer 31:37; 33:25–26; Rom 11:1–29.

26:46 A summary statement concerning chs. 1–26.

27:1–34 This final chapter concerns things promised to the Lord in kind—servants, animals, houses or lands. But provisions were made to give money instead of the item, in which case usually the adding of a fifth of its value was required. Such vows were expressions of special thanksgiving (cf. Hannah, 1 Sam 1:28) and were given over and above the expected sacrifices.

27:2 *a singular vow.* Possibly to give slaves to the service of the temple, but more likely to offer oneself or a member of one's family. Since only Levites were acceptable for most work of this kind, other people gave the monetary equivalent—but see 1 Sam 1:11.

27:9 *shall be holy.* An animal given for a sacrifice could not be exchanged for another (v. 10). The people of Malachi's day chose the poorest animals after having vowed to offer good ones (Mal 1:13–14). If an unclean animal was given, it could be redeemed with the 20 percent penalty (vv. 11–13).

they do not offer a sacrifice unto the LORD, then he shall present the beast before the priest:

12 And the priest shall value it, whether it be good or bad: [1]as thou valuest it, *who art* the priest, so shall it be.

13 [a]But if he will at all redeem it, then he shall add a fifth *part* thereof unto thy estimation.

14 ¶ And when a man shall sanctify his house *to be* holy unto the LORD, then the priest shall estimate it, whether it be good or bad: as the priest shall estimate it, so shall it stand.

15 [a]And if he that sanctified *it* will redeem his house, then he shall add the fifth *part* of the money of thy estimation unto it, and it shall be his.

16 And if a man shall sanctify unto the LORD *some part* of a field of his possession, then thy estimation shall be according to the seed thereof: [1]a homer of barley seed *shall be valued* at fifty shekels of silver.

17 If he sanctify his field from the year of jubile, according to thy estimation it shall stand.

18 But if he sanctify his field after the jubile, then the priest shall [a]reckon unto him the money according to the years that remain, *even* unto the year of the jubile, and it shall be abated from thy estimation.

19 [a]And if he that sanctified the field will in any wise redeem it, then he shall add the fifth *part* of the money of thy estimation unto it, and it shall be assured to him.

20 And if he will not redeem the field, or if he have sold the field to another man, it shall not be redeemed any more.

21 But the field, [a]when it goeth out in the jubile, shall be holy unto the LORD, as a field [b]devoted; [c]the possession thereof shall be the priest's.

22 And if *a man* sanctify unto the LORD a field which he hath bought, which *is* not of the fields of [a]his possession;

23 [a]Then the priest shall reckon unto him the worth of thy estimation, *even* unto the year of the jubile: and he shall give thine estimation in that day, *as* a holy *thing* unto the LORD.

24 [a]In the year of the jubile the field shall return unto him of whom it was bought, *even* to him to whom the possession of the land *did belong.*

25 And all thy estimations shall be according to the shekel of the sanctuary: [a]twenty gerahs shall be the shekel.

26 ¶ Only the [a 1]firstling of the beasts, which should be the LORD's firstling, no man shall sanctify it; whether *it be* ox, or sheep: it *is* the LORD's.

27 And if *it be* of an unclean beast, then he shall redeem *it* according to thine estimation, [a]and shall add a fifth *part* of it thereto: or if it be not redeemed, then it shall be sold according to thy estimation.

28 [a]Notwithstanding no devoted thing, that a man shall devote unto the LORD of all that he hath, *both* of man and beast, and of the field of his possession, shall be sold or redeemed: every devoted thing *is* most holy unto the LORD.

29 [a]None devoted, which shall be devoted of men, shall be redeemed; *but* shall surely be put to death.

30 ¶ And [a]all the tithe of the land, *whether* of the seed of the land, *or* of the fruit of the tree, *is* the LORD's: *it is* holy unto the LORD.

31 [a]And if a man will at all redeem *ought* of his tithes, he shall add thereto the fifth *part* thereof.

32 And *concerning* the tithe of the herd, or of the flock, *even of* whatsoever [a]passeth under the rod, the tenth shall be holy unto the LORD.

33 He shall not search whether it be good or bad, [a]neither shall he change it: and if he change it at all, then both it and the change thereof shall be holy; it shall not be redeemed.

34 [a]These *are* the commandments, which the LORD commanded Moses for the children of Israel in mount Sinai.

27:12 [1]Heb. *according to thy estimation, O priest, etc.*
27:13 [a]ver. 15,19
27:15 [a]ver. 13
27:16 [1]Or, the land of *a homer, etc.*
27:18 [a]ch. 25:15,16
27:19 [a]ver. 13
27:21 [a]ch. 25:10,28,31 [b]ver. 28 [c]Num. 18:14; Ezek. 44:29
27:22 [a]ch. 25:10,25
27:23 [a]ver. 18
27:24 [a]ch. 25:28
27:25 [a]Ex. 30:13; Num. 3:47; 18:16; Ezek. 45:12
27:26 [1]Heb. *firstborn, etc.* [a]Ex. 13:2,12; 22:30
27:27 [a]ver. 11,12
27:28 [a]ver. 21; Josh. 6:17-19
27:29 [a]Num. 21:2
27:30 [a]Gen. 28:22; Num. 18:21,24; 2 Chr. 31:5,6,12; Neh. 13:12; Mal. 3:8
27:31 [a]ver. 13
27:32 [a]Jer. 33:13; Ezek. 20:37; Mic. 7:14
27:33 [a]ver. 10
27:34 [a]ch. 26:46

27:28 *shall devote unto the LORD.* Devoting something was far more serious than dedicating it to sacred use. The devoted thing became totally the Lord's. Achan's sin was the greater because he stole what had been devoted to the Lord (Josh 7:11). Persons devoted to destruction were usually the captives in the wars of Canaan (cf. 1 Sam 15:3,18).

27:29 Saul sinned in this regard when he did not totally destroy the Amalekites (1 Sam 15).

27:30 *tithe.* A tenth (see Num 18:21–29; Deut 12:6–18; 14:22–29; 26:12). From these passages it appears that Israel actually had three tithes: (1) the general tithe (here), paid to the Levites (Num 18:21), who in turn had to give a tenth of that to the priests (Num 18:26); (2) the tithe associated with the sacred meal involving offerer and Levite (Deut 14:22–27); (3) the tithe paid every three years to the poor (Deut 14:28–29).

27:34 *These are the commandments, which the LORD commanded Moses.* See 1:1; 7:37–38; 25:1; 26:46. This is strong testimony for the Mosaic authorship and divine origin of the book.

The Fourth Book of Moses, Called Numbers

INTRODUCTION

Title

The English name of the book comes from the Septuagint (the Greek translation of the OT) and is based on the census lists found in chs. 1 and 26. The Hebrew title of the book (*bemidbar,* "in the wilderness") is more descriptive of its contents. Numbers presents an account of the 38-year period of Israel's wandering in the wilderness following the establishment of the covenant of Sinai (compare 1:1 with Deut 1:1).

Author and Date

The book has traditionally been ascribed to Moses. This conclusion is based on (1) statements concerning Moses' writing activity (e.g., 33:1–2; Ex 17:14; 24:4; 34:27) and (2) the assumption that the first five books of the Bible, the Pentateuch, are a unit and come from one author. See Introduction to Genesis: Author and Date of Writing.

It is not necessary, however, to claim that Numbers came from Moses' hand complete and in final form. Portions of the book were probably added by scribes or editors from later periods of Israel's history. For example, the protestation of the humility of Moses (12:3) would hardly be convincing if it came from his own mouth. But it seems reasonable to assume that Moses wrote the essential content of the book.

Contents

Numbers relates the story of Israel's journey from mount Sinai to the plains of Moab on the border of Canaan. Much of its legislation for people and priests is similar to that in Exodus, Leviticus and Deuteronomy. The book tells of the murmuring and rebellion of God's people and of their subsequent judgment. Those whom God had redeemed from slavery in Egypt and with whom He had made a covenant at mount Sinai responded not with faith, gratitude and obedience but with unbelief, ingratitude and repeated acts of rebellion, which came to extreme expression in their refusal to undertake the conquest of Canaan (ch. 14). The community of the redeemed forfeited their part in the promised land. They were condemned to live out their lives in the wilderness; only their children would enjoy the fulfillment of the promise that had originally been theirs (cf. Heb 3:7—4:11).

Theological Teaching

In telling the story of Israel's wilderness wanderings, Numbers offers much that is theologically significant. During the first year after Israel's deliverance from Egypt, she entered into covenant with the Lord at Sinai to be the people of His kingdom, among whom He pitched His royal tent (the tabernacle)—this is the story of Exodus. As the account of Numbers begins, the Lord organizes Israel into a military camp. Leaving Sinai, she marches forth as His conquering army, with the Lord at her head, to establish His kingdom in the promised land in the midst of the nations. The book graphically portrays Israel's identity as the Lord's redeemed covenant people and her vocation as the servant people of God, charged with establishing His kingdom on earth. God's purpose in history is implicitly disclosed: to invade the arena of fallen humanity and effect the redemption of His creation—the mission in which His people are also to be totally engaged.

Numbers also presents the chastening wrath of God against His disobedient people. Because of her rebellion (and especially her refusal to undertake the conquest of Canaan), Israel was in breach of covenant. The fourth book of the Pentateuch presents a sobering reality: The God who had entered into covenant with Abraham (Gen 15; 17), who had delivered His people from bondage in the exodus (Ex 14—15), who had brought Israel into covenant with Himself as His "peculiar treasure" (Ex 19:5) and who had revealed His holiness and the gracious means of approaching Him (Lev 1—7) was

also a God of wrath. His wrath extended to His errant children as well as to the enemy nations of Egypt and Canaan.

Even Moses, the great prophet and servant of the Lord, was not exempt from God's wrath when he disobeyed God. Ch. 20, which records his error, begins with the notice of Miriam's death (20:1) and concludes with the record of Aaron's death (20:22–29). Here is the passing of the old guard. Those whom God has used to establish the nation are dying before the nation has come into its own.

The questions arise: Is God finished with the nation as a whole (cf. Rom 11:1)? Are His promises a thing of the past? In one of the most remarkable sections of the Bible—the account of Balaam, the pagan diviner (chs. 22—24)—the reply is given. The Lord, working in a providential and direct way, proclaims His continued faithfulness to His purpose for His people despite their unfaithfulness to Him.

Balaam is Moab's answer to Moses, the man of God. He is an internationally known prophet who shares the pagan belief that the God of Israel is like any other deity who might be manipulated by acts of magic or sorcery. But from the early part of the narrative, when Balaam first encounters the one true God in visions, and in the narrative of the journey on the donkey (ch. 22), he begins to learn that dealing with the true God is fundamentally different from anything he has ever known. When he attempts to curse Israel at the instigation of Balak king of Moab, Balaam finds his mouth unable to express the curse he desires to pronounce. Instead, from his lips come blessings on Israel and curses on her enemies (chs. 23—24).

In his seven prophetic oracles, Balaam proclaims God's great blessing for His people (see 23:20). Though the immediate enjoyment of this blessing will always depend on the faithfulness of His people, the ultimate realization of God's blessing is sure—because of the character of God (see 23:19). Thus Numbers reaffirms the ongoing purposes of God. Despite His judgment on His rebellious people, God is still determined to bring Israel into the land of promise. His blessing to her rests in His sovereign will.

The teaching of the book has lasting significance for Israel and for the church (cf. Rom 15:4; 1 Cor 10:6,11). God does display His wrath even against His errant people, but His grace is renewed as surely as is the dawn and His redemptive purpose will not be thwarted.

Special Problem

The large numbers of men conscripted into Israel's army puzzle modern scholars (see, e.g., the figures in 1:46; 26:51). These numbers of men mustered for warfare demand a total population in excess of 2,000,000. Such numbers seem to be exceedingly large for the times, for the locale, for the wilderness wanderings, and in comparison with the inhabitants of Canaan. See note on 3:43.

Various possibilities have been suggested to solve this problem. Some have thought that the numbers may have been corrupted in transmission. The present text, however, does not betray textual difficulties with the numbers.

Others have felt that the Hebrew word for "thousand" might have a different meaning here from its usual numerical connotation. In some passages, for example, it has been proposed that the word is a technical term for a company of men (i.e., "family division" or "clan") that may or may not equal 1,000 (e.g., Josh 22:14; 1 Sam 23:23). Further, some have postulated that this Hebrew word means "chief" (or "duke" as in Gen 36:15). In this way the figure 53,400 (26:47) would mean "53 chiefs plus 400 men." Such a procedure would yield a greatly reduced total, but it would be at variance with the fact that the Hebrew text adds the "thousands" in the same way it adds the "hundreds" for a large total. Also, this would make the proportion of chiefs to fighting men top-heavy (59 chiefs for 300 men in Simeon).

Another option is to read the Hebrew word for "thousand" with a dual meaning of "chief" and "1,000," with the chiefs numbering one less than the stated figure. For example, the 46,500 of Reuben (1:21) is read as 45 chiefs and 1,500 fighting men, the 59,300 of Simeon (1:23) is read as 58 chiefs and 1,300 fighting men, etc. But in this case, as in the former, the totals of 1:46 and 2:32 must then be regarded as errors of understanding (perhaps by later scribes).

Still another approach is to regard the numbers as symbolic figures rather than as strictly mathematical. The numerical value of the Hebrew letters in the expression *bene yisra'el* ("all the congregation of the children of Israel," 1:2) equals 603 (the number of the thousands of the fighting men, 1:46); the remaining 550 (plus 1 for Moses) might come from the numerical equivalent of the Hebrew letters in the expression "all that are able to go forth to war in Israel" (1:3). This symbolic use

of numbers (called "gematria") is not unknown in the Bible (see Rev 13:18), but it is not likely in Numbers, where there are no literary clues pointing in that direction.

While the problem of the large numbers has not been satisfactorily solved, the Bible does point to a remarkable increase of Jacob's descendants during the four centuries of their sojourn in Egypt (see Ex 1:7–12). With all their difficulties, these numbers also point to the great role of providence and miracles in God's dealings with his people during their life in the wilderness (see note on 1:46).

Structure and Outline

The book has three major divisions, based on Israel's geographical locations. Each of the three divisions has two parts, as the following breakdown demonstrates: (1) Israel at Sinai, preparing to depart for the land of promise (1:1—10:10), followed by the journey from Sinai to Kadesh (10:11—12:16); (2) Israel at Kadesh, delayed as a result of rebellion (13:1—20:13), followed by the journey from Kadesh to the plains of Moab (20:14—22:1); (3) Israel on the plains of Moab, anticipating the conquest of the land of promise (22:2—32:42), followed by appendixes dealing with various matters (chs. 33—36).

- I. Israel at Sinai, Preparing to Depart for the Promised Land (1:1—10:10)
  - A. The Commands for the Census of the People (chs. 1—4)
    1. The numbers of men from each tribe mustered for war (ch. 1)
    2. The placement of the tribes around the tabernacle and their order for march (ch. 2)
    3. The placement of the Levites around the tabernacle, and the numbers of the Levites and the firstborn of Israel (ch. 3)
    4. The numbers of the Levites in their tabernacle service for the Lord (ch. 4)
  - B. The Commands for Purity of the People (5:1—10:10)
    1. The test for purity in the law of jealousy (ch. 5)
    2. The Nazarite vow and the Aaronic benediction (ch. 6)
    3. The offerings of the 12 leaders at the dedication of the tabernacle (ch. 7)
    4. The setting up of the lamps and the separation of the Levites (ch. 8)
    5. The observance of the passover (9:1–14)
    6. The covering cloud and the silver trumpets (9:15—10:10)
- II. The Journey from Sinai to Kadesh (10:11—12:16)
  - A. The Beginning of the Journey (10:11–36)
  - B. The Beginning of the Sorrows: Fire and Quails (ch. 11)
  - C. The Opposition of Miriam and Aaron (ch. 12)
- III. Israel at Kadesh, the Delay Resulting from Rebellion (13:1—20:13)
  - A. The 12 Spies and Their Mixed Report of the Good Land (ch. 13)
  - B. The People's Rebellion against God's Commission, and Their Defeat (ch. 14)
  - C. A Collection of Laws on Offerings, the Sabbath and Tassels on Garments (ch. 15)
  - D. The Rebellion of Korah and His Allies (ch. 16)
  - E. The Budding of Aaron's Rod: A Sign for Rebels (ch. 17)
  - F. Concerning Priests, Their Duties and Their Support (ch. 18)
  - G. The Red Heifer and the Cleansing Water (ch. 19)
  - H. The Sin of Moses (20:1–13)
- IV. The Journey from Kadesh to the Plains of Moab (20:14—22:1)
  - A. The Resistance of Edom (20:14–21)
  - B. The Death of Aaron (20:22–29)
  - C. The Destruction of Arad (21:1–3)
  - D. The Serpent of Brass (21:4–9)
  - E. The Song of the Well and the Journey to Moab (21:10–20)
  - F. The Defeat of Sihon and Og (21:21–35)
  - G. Israel Returns to Moab (22:1)
- V. Israel on the Plains of Moab, in Anticipation of Taking the Promised Land (22:2—32:42)
  - A. Balak of Moab Hires Balaam to Curse Israel (22:2–41)
  - B. Balaam Blesses Israel in Seven Oracles (chs. 23—24)
  - C. The Baal of Peor and Israel's Apostasy (ch. 25)
  - D. The Second Census (ch. 26)
  - E. Instructions for the New Generation (chs. 27—30)
    1. The inheritance for women (27:1–11)

2. The successor to Moses (27:12–23)
3. Commands regarding offerings (28:1–15)
4. Commands regarding festivals (28:16—29:40)
5. Commands regarding vows (ch. 30)

F. The War against Midian (ch. 31)
G. The Settlement of the Tribes East of the Jordan (ch. 32)

VI. Appendixes Dealing with Various Matters (chs. 33—36)

A. The Stages of the Journey (ch. 33)
B. The Land of Inheritance (chs. 34—35)
C. The Inheritance for Women (ch. 36)

The census of the people

1 And the LORD spake unto Moses [a]in the wilderness of Sinai, [b]in the tabernacle of the congregation, on the first *day* of the second month, in the second year after they were come out of the land of Egypt, saying,

2 [a]Take ye the sum of all the congregation of the children of Israel, after their families, by the house of their fathers, with the number of *their* names, every male by their polls;

3 From twenty years old and upward, all that *are able to* go forth *to* war in Israel: thou and Aaron shall number them by their armies.

4 And with you there shall be a man of every tribe; every one head of the house of his fathers.

5 ¶ And these *are* the names of the men that shall stand with you: of *the tribe of* Reuben; Elizur the son of Shedeur.

6 Of Simeon; Shelumiel the son of Zurishaddai.

7 Of Judah; Nahshon the son of Amminadab.

8 Of Issachar; Nethaneel the son of Zuar.

9 Of Zebulun; Eliab the son of Helon.

10 Of the children of Joseph: of Ephraim; Elishama the son of Ammihud: of Manasseh; Gamaliel the son of Pedahzur.

11 Of Benjamin; Abidan the son of Gideoni.

12 Of Dan; Ahiezer the son of Ammishaddai.

13 Of Asher; Pagiel the son of Ocran.

14 Of Gad; Eliasaph the son of [1]Deuel.

15 Of Naphtali; Ahira the son of Enan.

16 [a]These *were* the renowned of the congregation, princes of the tribes of their fathers, [b]heads of thousands in Israel.

17 And Moses and Aaron took these men which are expressed [a]by *their* names:

18 And they assembled all the congregation together on the first *day* of the second month, and they declared their [a]pedigrees after their families, by the house of their fathers, according to the number of the names, from twenty years old and upward, by their polls.

19 As the LORD commanded Moses, so he numbered them in the wilderness of Sinai.

20 ¶ And the [a]children of Reuben, Israel's eldest son, *by* their generations, after their families, by the house of their fathers, according to the number of the names, by their polls, every male from twenty years old and upward, all that *were able to* go forth *to* war;

21 Those that were numbered of them, *even* of the tribe of Reuben, *were* forty and six thousand and five hundred.

22 Of the [a]children of Simeon, *by* their generations, after their families, by the house of their fathers, those that were numbered of them, according to the number of the names, by their polls, every male from twenty years old and upward, all that *were able to* go forth *to* war;

23 Those that were numbered of them, *even* of the tribe of Simeon, *were* fifty and nine thousand and three hundred.

24 Of the [a]children of Gad, *by* their generations, after their families, by the house of their fathers, according to the number of the names, from twenty years old and upward, all that *were able to* go forth *to* war;

25 Those that were numbered of them, *even* of the tribe of Gad, *were* forty and five thousand six hundred and fifty.

26 Of the [a]children of Judah, *by* their generations, after their families, by the house of their fathers, according to the number of the names, from twenty years old and upward, all that *were able to* go forth *to* war;

27 Those that were numbered of them,

1:1 [a]Ex. 19:1; ch. 10:11,12 [b]Ex. 25:22
1:2 [a]Ex. 30:12; 38:26; ch. 26:2,63,64; 2 Sam. 24:2; 1 Chr. 21:2
1:14 [1][ch. 2:14, he is called *Reuel*]
1:16 [a]ch. 7:2; 1 Chr. 27:16 [b]Ex. 18:21,25
1:17 [a]Is. 43:1
1:18 [a]Ezra 2:59
1:20 [a]ch. 2:10,11; 32:6,15,21,29
1:22 [a]ch. 2:12,13; 26:12-14
1:24 [a]ch. 2:14,15; 26:15-18; 32:2,29; 34:14
1:26 [a]ch. 2:3,4; 26:19-22; 2 Sam. 24:9

1:1 *the LORD spake unto Moses.* One of the most pervasive emphases in Numbers is the fact that the Lord spoke to Moses and through Moses to Israel. From the opening words to the closing words (36:13), this is stated over 150 times and in more than 20 ways. The Lord's use of Moses as His prophet is described in 12:6–8. One of the Hebrew names for the book is *wayedabber* ("And He [the LORD] spoke"), from the first word in the Hebrew text. *wilderness of Sinai.* The more common Hebrew name for Numbers is *bemidbar* ("in the wilderness"), the fifth word in the Hebrew text. The events of Numbers cover a period of 38 years and nine or ten months, i.e., the period of Israel's wilderness wanderings. *first day of the second month . . . second year.* Thirteen months after the exodus, Numbers begins. Israel had spent the previous year in the region of mount Sinai receiving the law and erecting the tabernacle. Now she was to be mustered as a military force for an orderly march. Dating events from the exodus (for another example see 1 Ki 6:1) is similar to the Christian practice of dating years in reference to the incarnation of Christ (B.C. and A.D.). The exodus was God's great act of deliverance of His people from bondage.

1:2 *Take.* The Hebrew for this word is plural, indicating that Moses and Aaron were to complete this task together (see v. 3, "thou and Aaron"), but the primary responsibility lay with Moses. *sum.* Its main purpose was to form a military roster, not a social, political or taxing document.

1:3 *able to go forth to war.* Refers to the principal military purpose of the census. The phrase occurs 14 times in ch. 1 and again in 26:2.

1:4 *a man of every tribe.* By having a representative from each tribe assist Moses and Aaron, the count would be regarded as legitimate by all.

1:5–16 The names of these men occur again in chs. 2; 7; 10. Most contain within them a reference to the name of God. Levi is not represented in the list (see vv. 47–53).

1:19 *so he numbered them in the wilderness of Sinai.* A summary statement; vv. 20–43 provide the details.

1:20–43 For each tribe there are two verses in repetitive formulaic structure, giving: (1) the name of the tribe, (2) the specifics of those numbered, (3) the name of the tribe again and (4) the total count for that tribe. The numbers for each tribe are rounded off to the hundred (but Gad to the 50, v. 25). The same numbers are given for each tribe in ch. 2, where there are four triads of tribes. A peculiarity in the numbers that leads some to believe that they are symbolic is that the hundreds are grouped between 200 and 700. Also, various speculations have arisen regarding the meaning of the Hebrew word for "thousand" (see Introduction: Special Problem). In this chapter, the word has been used to mean 1,000 in order for the totals to be achieved.

even of the tribe of Judah, *were* [a]threescore and fourteen thousand and six hundred.

28 Of the [a]children of Issachar, *by* their generations, after their families, by the house of their fathers, according to the number of the names, from twenty years old and upward, all that *were able to* go forth *to* war;

29 Those that were numbered of them, *even* of the tribe of Issachar, *were* fifty and four thousand and four hundred.

30 Of the [a]children of Zebulun, *by* their generations, after their families, by the house of their fathers, according to the number of the names, from twenty years old and upward, all that *were able to* go forth *to* war;

31 Those that were numbered of them, *even* of the tribe of Zebulun, *were* fifty and seven thousand and four hundred.

32 Of the children of Joseph, *namely,* of the [a]children of Ephraim, *by* their generations, after their families, by the house of their fathers, according to the number of the names, from twenty years old and upward, all that *were able to* go forth *to* war;

33 Those that were numbered of them, *even* of the tribe of Ephraim, *were* forty thousand and five hundred.

34 Of the [a]children of Manasseh, *by* their generations, after their families, by the house of their fathers, according to the number of the names, from twenty years old and upward, all that *were able to* go forth *to* war;

35 Those that were numbered of them, *even* of the tribe of Manasseh, *were* thirty and two thousand and two hundred.

36 Of the [a]children of Benjamin, *by* their generations, after their families, by the house of their fathers, according to the number of the names, from twenty years old and upward, all that *were able to* go forth *to* war;

37 Those that were numbered of them, *even* of the tribe of Benjamin, *were* thirty and five thousand and four hundred.

38 Of the [a]children of Dan, *by* their generations, after their families, by the house of their fathers, according to the number of the names, from twenty years old and upward, all that *were able to* go forth *to* war;

39 Those that were numbered of them, *even* of the tribe of Dan, *were* threescore and two thousand and seven hundred.

40 Of the [a]children of Asher, *by* their generations, after their families, by the house of their fathers, according to the number of the names, from twenty years old and upward, all that *were able to* go forth *to* war;

41 Those that were numbered of them, *even* of the tribe of Asher, *were* forty and one thousand and five hundred.

42 *Of* the children of Naphtali, *throughout* their generations, after their families, by the house of their fathers, according to the number of the names, from twenty years old and upward, all that *were able to* go forth *to* war;

43 Those that were numbered of them, *even* of the tribe of Naphtali, *were* fifty and three thousand and four hundred.

44 [a]These *are* those that were numbered, which Moses and Aaron numbered, and the princes of Israel, *being* twelve men: each one was for the house of his fathers.

45 So were all those that were numbered of the children of Israel, by the house of their fathers, from twenty years old and upward, all that *were able to* go forth *to* war in Israel;

46 Even all they that were numbered were [a]six hundred thousand and three thousand and five hundred and fifty.

47 ¶ But [a]the Levites after the tribe of their fathers were not numbered among them.

48 For the LORD had spoken unto Moses, saying,

49 [a]Only thou shalt not number the tribe of Levi, neither take the sum of them among the children of Israel:

50 [a]But thou shalt appoint the Levites over the tabernacle of Testimony, and over all the vessels thereof, and over all *things* that *belong* to it: they shall bear the tabernacle, and all the vessels thereof; and they shall minister unto it, [b]and shall encamp round about the tabernacle.

51 [a]And when the tabernacle setteth forward, the Levites shall take it down: and when

1:27 [a]2 Chr. 17:14
1:28 [a]ch. 2:5,6
1:30 [a]ch. 2:7,8; 26:26,27
1:32 [a]ch. 2:18,19; 26:35-37
1:34 [a]ch. 2:20,21; 26:28-34
1:36 [a]ch. 2:22,23; 26:38-41
1:38 [a]ch. 2:25,26; 26:42,43
1:40 [a]ch. 2:27,28; 26:44-47
1:44 [a]ch. 26:64
1:46 [a]Ex. 38:26; See Ex. 12:37; ch. 2:32; 26:51
1:47 [a]ch. 2:33; See ch. 3; 4; 26:57; 1 Chr. 6; 21:6
1:49 [a]ch. 2:33; 26:62
1:50 [a]Ex. 38:21; ch. 3:7,8; 4:15,25-27,33 [b]ch. 3:23,29,35,38
1:51 [a]ch. 10:17,21

1:32–35 Because the descendants of Levi were excluded from the census (see note on v. 47), the descendants of Joseph are listed according to the families of his two sons, Ephraim (vv. 32–33) and Manasseh (vv. 34–35). In this way the traditional tribal number of 12 is maintained, and Joseph is given the "double portion" of the ranking heir (cf. Gen 49:22–26; Deut 33:13–17; 2 Ki 2:9).

1:46 *six hundred thousand and three thousand and five hundred and fifty.* Except for Joshua and Caleb, all these died in the wilderness. The mathematics of these numbers is accurate and complex. It is complex in that the totals are reached in two ways: (1) a linear listing of 12 units (vv. 20–43), with the total given (v. 46); (2) four sets of triads, each with a subtotal, and then the grand total (2:3–32). These figures are also consistent with those in Ex 12:37; 38:26. This large number of men conscripted for the army suggests a population for the entire community in excess of 2,000,000 (see Introduction: Special Problem). Ex 1:7 describes the remarkable growth of the Hebrew people in Egypt during the 400-year sojourn. They had become so numerous that they were regarded as a grave threat to the security of Egypt (Ex 1:9–10,20). Israel's amazing growth from the 70 who entered Egypt (Ex 1:5) was an evidence of God's great blessing and His faithfulness to His covenant with Abraham (Gen 12:2; 15:5; 17:4–6; 22:17).

1:47 Because of their special tasks, the Levites were excluded from this military count. They too had to perform service to the Lord, but they were to be engaged in the ceremonies and maintenance of the tabernacle (see note on vv. 32–35).

1:50 *Testimony.* The ten commandments written on stone tablets (see Ex 31:18; 32:15; 34:29), which were placed in the ark (Ex 25:16,21; 40:20), leading to the phrase the "ark of the Testimony" (Ex 25:22; 26:33,34).

1:51 *stranger.* The Hebrew word is often translated "stranger," "alien" or "foreigner" (e.g., Is 1:7; Hos 7:9). Thus a non-Levite Israelite was considered an alien to the religious duties of the tabernacle (see Ex 29:33; 30:33; Lev 22:12). *death.* See 3:10,38; 18:7; cf. 16:31–33; 1 Sam 6:19.

the tabernacle is to be pitched, the Levites shall set it up: [b]and the stranger that cometh nigh shall be put to death.

52 And the children of Israel shall pitch their tents, [a]every man by his own camp, and every man by his own standard, throughout their hosts.

53 [a]But the Levites shall pitch round about the tabernacle of Testimony, that there be no [b]wrath upon the congregation of the children of Israel: and the Levites shall keep the charge of the tabernacle of Testimony.

54 And the children of Israel did according to all that the LORD commanded Moses, so did they.

The camps and tribal captains

2 And the LORD spake unto Moses and unto Aaron, saying,

2 [a]Every man of the children of Israel shall pitch by his own standard, with the ensign of their father's house: [b][1]far off about the tabernacle of the congregation shall they pitch.

3 ¶ And on the east side toward the rising of the sun *shall* they of the standard of the camp of Judah pitch throughout their armies: and [a]Nahshon the son of Amminadab *shall be* captain of the children of Judah.

4 And his host, and those that were numbered of them, *were* threescore and fourteen thousand and six hundred.

5 And those that do pitch next unto him *shall be* the tribe of Issachar: and Nethaneel the son of Zuar *shall be* captain of the children of Issachar.

6 And his host, and those that were numbered thereof, *were* fifty and four thousand and four hundred.

1:51 [b]ch. 3:10,38; 18:22
1:52 [a]ch. 2:2,34
1:53 [a]ver. 50 [b]Lev. 10:6; ch. 8:19; 16:46; 18:5; 1 Sam. 6:19

2:2 [1]Heb. *over against* [a]ch. 1:52 [b]Josh. 3:4
2:3 [a]ch. 10:14; Ruth 4:20; 1 Chr. 2:10; Mat. 1:4

1:53 *pitch round about the tabernacle.* See 3:21–38. *wrath.* The Levites formed a protective hedge against trespassing by the non-Levites to keep them from experiencing divine wrath.
1:54 *the LORD commanded Moses, so did they.* In view of Israel's great disobedience in the later chapters of Numbers, these words of initial compliance have a special poignancy.
2:1–34 This chapter is symmetrically structured:

Summary command (vv. 1–2)
Details of execution (vv. 3–33)
Eastern camp (vv. 3–9)
Southern camp (vv. 10–16)
Tent and Levites (v. 17)
Western camp (vv. 18–24)
Northern camp (vv. 25–31)
Summary totals (vv. 32–33)
Summary conclusion (v. 34)

In ch. 1 the nation is mustered, and the genealogical relationships are clarified. In ch. 2 the nation is put in structural order, and the line of march and place of encampment are established. The numbers of ch. 1 are given in a new pattern, and the same leaders are named here again.
2:2 *Every man.* Each was to know his exact position within the camp. *standard . . . ensign.* Each tribe had its banner, and each triad of tribes had its standard. Jewish tradition suggests that the tribal banners corresponded in color to the 12 stones in the breastplate of the high priest (Ex 28:15–21). Tradition also holds that the standard of the triad led by Judah had the figure of a lion, that of Reuben the figure of a man, that of Ephraim the figure of an ox and that of Dan the figure of an eagle (see the four living creatures described by Ezek 1:10; cf. Rev 4:7). But these traditions are not otherwise substantiated. See diagram below. *far off.* See 1:52–53.
2:3–7 *Judah . . . Issachar . . . Zebulun.* The fourth, fifth and sixth sons of Jacob and Leah. It is somewhat surprising to have these three tribes first in the order of march, since Reuben is regularly noted as Jacob's firstborn son (1:20). However, because of the failure of the older brothers (Reuben, Simeon and Levi; see Gen 49:3–7), Judah is granted pride of place among his brothers (Gen 49:8). Judah produced the royal line from which the Messiah came (Gen 49:10; Ruth 4:18–21; Mat 1:1–16).

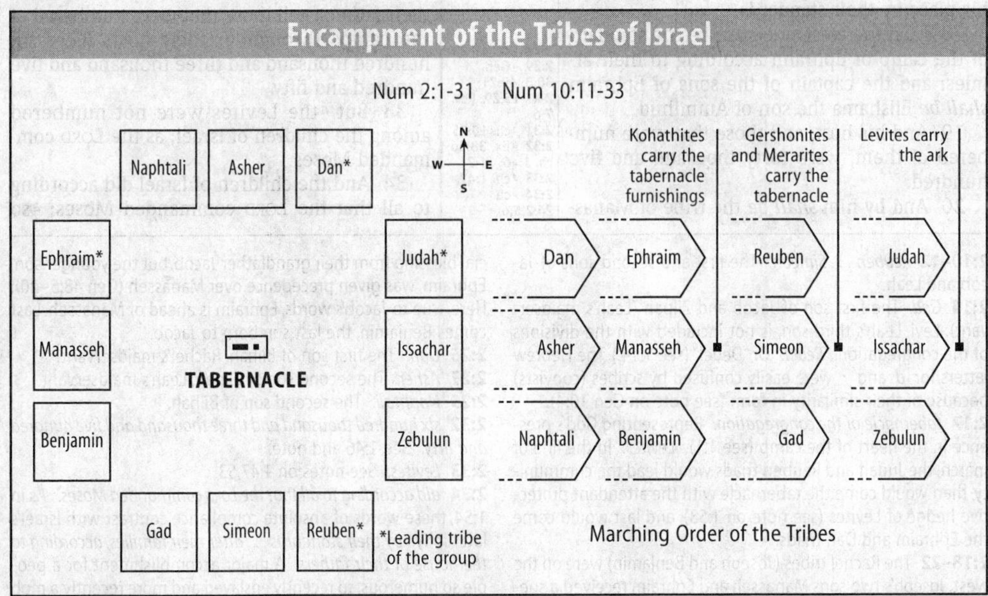

7 *Then* the tribe of Zebulun: and Eliab the son of Helon *shall be* captain of the children of Zebulun.

8 And his host, and those that were numbered thereof, *were* fifty and seven thousand and four hundred.

9 All that were numbered in the camp of Judah *were* an hundred thousand and fourscore thousand and six thousand and four hundred, throughout their armies. [a]*These* shall first set forth.

10 ¶ On the south side *shall be* the standard of the camp of Reuben according to their armies: and the captain of the children of Reuben *shall be* Elizur the son of Shedeur.

11 And his host, and those that were numbered thereof, *were* forty and six thousand and five hundred.

12 And those which pitch by him *shall be* the tribe of Simeon: and the captain of the children of Simeon *shall be* Shelumiel the son of Zurishaddai.

13 And his host, and those that were numbered of them, *were* fifty and nine thousand and three hundred.

14 Then the tribe of Gad: and the captain of the sons of Gad *shall be* Eliasaph the son of [1]Reuel.

15 And his host, and those that were numbered of them, *were* forty and five thousand and six hundred and fifty.

16 All that were numbered in the camp of Reuben *were* an hundred thousand and fifty and one thousand and four hundred and fifty, throughout their armies. [a]And they shall set forth in the second rank.

17 ¶ [a]Then the tabernacle of the congregation shall set forward *with* the camp of the Levites in the midst of the camp: as they encamp, so shall they set forward, every man in his place by their standards.

18 ¶ On the west side *shall be* the standard of the camp of Ephraim according to their armies: and the captain of the sons of Ephraim *shall be* Elishama the son of Ammihud.

19 And his host, and those that were numbered of them, *were* forty thousand and five hundred.

20 And by him *shall be* the tribe of Manasseh: and the captain of the children of Manasseh *shall be* Gamaliel the son of Pedahzur.

21 And his host, and those that were numbered of them, *were* thirty and two thousand and two hundred.

22 Then the tribe of Benjamin: and the captain of the sons of Benjamin *shall be* Abidan the son of Gideoni.

23 And his host, and those that were numbered of them, *were* thirty and five thousand and four hundred.

24 All that were numbered of the camp of Ephraim *were* an hundred thousand and eight thousand and an hundred, throughout their armies. [a]And they shall go forward in the third rank.

25 ¶ The standard of the camp of Dan *shall be* on the north side by their armies: and the captain of the children of Dan *shall be* Ahiezer the son of Ammishaddai.

26 And his host, and those that were numbered of them, *were* threescore and two thousand and seven hundred.

27 And those that encamp by him *shall be* the tribe of Asher: and the captain of the children of Asher *shall be* Pagiel the son of Ocran.

28 And his host, and those that were numbered of them, *were* forty and one thousand and five hundred.

29 Then the tribe of [a]Naphtali: and the captain of the children of Naphtali *shall be* Ahira the son of Enan.

30 And his host, and those that were numbered of them, *were* fifty and three thousand and four hundred.

31 All they that were numbered in the camp of Dan *were* an hundred thousand and fifty and seven thousand and six hundred. [a]They shall go hindmost with their standards.

32 ¶ These *are* those which were numbered of the children of Israel by the house of their fathers: [a]all those that were numbered of the camps throughout their hosts *were* six hundred thousand and three thousand and five hundred and fifty.

33 But [a]the Levites were not numbered among the children of Israel; as the LORD commanded Moses.

34 And the children of Israel did according to all that the LORD commanded Moses: [a]so

2:9 [a]ch. 10:14
2:14 [1][*Deuel*, ch. 1:14; 7:42,47; 10:20]
2:16 [a]ch. 10:18
2:17 [a]ch. 10:17,21
2:24 [a]ch. 10:22
2:29 [a]Gen. 30:8; 49:21; 2 Ki. 15:29; Rev. 7:6
2:31 [a]ch. 10:25
2:32 [a]Ex. 38:26; ch. 1:46; 11:21
2:33 [a]ch. 1:47
2:34 [a]ch. 24:2,5,6

2:10–12 *Reuben . . . Simeon.* The first and second sons of Jacob and Leah.
2:14 *Gad.* The first son of Jacob and Zilpah (Leah's maidservant). Levi, Leah's third son, is not included with the divisions of the congregation. *Reuel.* Or "Deuel" (see 1:14.). The Hebrew letters for *d* and *r* were easily confused by scribes (copyists) because of their similarity in form (see note on Gen 10:4).
2:17 *tabernacle of the congregation.* Representing God's presence in the heart of the camp (see 1:1). *Levites.* In the line of march, the Judah and Reuben triads would lead the community, then would come the tabernacle with the attendant protective hedge of Levites (see note on 1:53), and last would come the Ephraim and Dan triads.
2:18–22 The Rachel tribes (Joseph and Benjamin) were on the west. Joseph's two sons Manasseh and Ephraim received a special blessing from their grandfather Jacob, but the younger son, Ephraim, was given precedence over Manasseh (Gen 48:5–20). Here, true to Jacob's words, Ephraim is ahead of Manasseh. Last comes Benjamin, the last son born to Jacob.
2:25 *Dan.* The first son of Bilhah, Rachel's maidservant.
2:27 *Asher.* The second son of Zilpah, Leah's maidservant.
2:29 *Naphtali.* The second son of Bilhah.
2:32 *six hundred thousand and three thousand and five hundred and fifty.* See 1:46 and note.
2:33 *Levites.* See notes on 1:47,53.
2:34 *did according to all that the LORD commanded Moses.* As in 1:54, these words of absolute compliance contrast with Israel's later folly. *by their standards . . . after their families, according to the house of their fathers.* A major accomplishment for a people so numerous, so recently enslaved and more recently a mob

they pitched by their standards, and so they
set forward, every one after their families, according to the house of their fathers.

The Levites

3 These also *are* the generations of Aaron
and Moses in the day that the LORD spake
with Moses in mount Sinai.
2 And these *are* the names of the sons of
Aaron; Nadab the [a]firstborn, and Abihu, Eleazar, and Ithamar.
3 These *are* the names of the sons of Aaron,
[a]the priests which were anointed, [1]whom he
consecrated to minister in the priest's office.
4 [a]And Nadab and Abihu died before the
LORD, when they offered strange fire before
the LORD, in the wilderness of Sinai, and they
had no children: and Eleazar and Ithamar ministered in the priest's office in the sight of Aaron their father.
5 ¶ And the LORD spake unto Moses, saying,
6 [a]Bring the tribe of Levi near, and present
them before Aaron the priest, that they may
minister unto him.
7 And they shall keep his charge, and the
charge of the whole congregation before the
tabernacle of the congregation, to do [a]the service of the tabernacle.
8 And they shall keep all the instruments
of the tabernacle of the congregation, and the
charge of the children of Israel, to do the service of the tabernacle.
9 And [a]thou shalt give the Levites unto
Aaron and to his sons: they *are* wholly given
unto him out of the children of Israel.
10 And thou shalt appoint Aaron and his

3:2 [a]Ex. 6:23
3:3 [1]Heb. *whose hand he filled* [a]Ex. 28:41; Lev. 8
3:4 [a]Lev. 10:1; ch. 26:61; 1 Chr. 24:2
3:6 [a]ch. 8:6; 18:2
3:7 [a]See ch. 1:50; 8:11,15,24,26
3:9 [a]ch. 8:19; 18:6
3:10 [a]ch. 18:7 [b]ver. 38; ch. 1:51; 16:40
3:12 [a]ver. 41; ch. 8:16; 18:6
3:13 [a]Ex. 13:2; Lev. 27:26; ch. 8:17; Luke 2:23 [b]Ex. 13:12,15; ch. 8:17
3:15 [a]ver. 39; ch. 26:62
3:16 [1]Heb. *mouth*
3:17 [a]Gen. 46:11; Ex. 6:16; ch. 26:57; 1 Chr. 6:1,16; 23:6
3:18 [a]Ex. 6:17
3:19 [a]Ex. 6:18
3:20 [a]Ex. 6:19

sons, [a]and they shall wait on their priest's office: [b]and the stranger that cometh nigh shall
be put to death.
11 And the LORD spake unto Moses, saying,
12 And I, behold, [a]I have taken the Levites
from among the children of Israel instead of all
the firstborn that openeth the matrix among
the children of Israel: therefore the Levites
shall be mine;
13 Because [a]all the firstborn *are* mine; [b]*for*
on the day that I smote all the firstborn in the
land of Egypt I hallowed unto me all the firstborn in Israel, both man and beast: mine they
shall be: I *am* the LORD.
14 ¶ And the LORD spake unto Moses in the
wilderness of Sinai, saying,
15 Number the children of Levi after the
house of their fathers, by their families: [a]every
male from a month old and upward shalt thou
number them.
16 And Moses numbered them according
to the [1]word of the LORD, as he was commanded.
17 [a]And these were the sons of Levi by
their names; Gershon, and Kohath, and Merari.
18 And these *are* the names of the sons of
Gershon by their families; [a]Libni, and Shimei.
19 And the sons of Kohath by their families; [a]Amram, and Izehar, Hebron, and Uzziel.
20 [a]And the sons of Merari by their families; Mahli, and Mushi. These *are* the families
of the Levites according to the house of their
fathers.
21 ¶ Of Gershon *was* the family of the Libnites, and the family of the Shimites: these *are*
the families of the Gershonites.

in disarray. It may have been the orderliness of this encampment that led Balaam to say: "How goodly are thy tents, O Jacob, And thy tabernacles, O Israel!" (24:5).

3:1 *Aaron and Moses.* At first glance, the names seem out of order, but the emphasis is correct: It is the family of Aaron that is about to be described (see v. 2).

3:3 *the priests which were anointed.* Ex 28:41 records God's command to Moses to anoint his brother Aaron and his sons as priests of the Lord (see Ex 30:30; Lev 8:30). By this solemn act they were consecrated in a special way to the Lord. Kings (1 Sam 16:13) were also anointed with oil for special service to God. Physical objects could be anointed as well (see Gen 28:18; Ex 29:36). The Hebrew term for "anointed" (*mashiah*) later became the specific term for the Messiah. "The Christ" (Greek) and "the Messiah" (Hebrew) both mean "the Anointed One." *consecrated.* The Hebrew for this word means lit. "fill your hand." By this act there was an investing of authority, a consecration and a setting apart.

3:4 *Nadab and Abihu.* See Lev 10:1–3 and notes. *strange fire.* This seems to be a deliberately obscure expression, as though the narrator finds the very concept distasteful. They were using fire that the Lord had not commanded (see Lev 10:1). Proximity to God's holiness requires righteousness and obedience from His priests. For all time, the deaths of Aaron's newly consecrated sons serve to warn God's ministers of the awesome seriousness of their tasks (cf. 1 Sam 2:12–17, 22–25,27–36; 3:11–14; 4:1–11). For similar divine judgments at the beginning of new stages in salvation history see Josh 7; 2 Sam 6:7; Acts 5:1–11.

3:5–10 These commands are not followed by a report of obedience as were the commands in chs. 1–2, but further details are given in ch. 8. Clear distinctions are made here between the priestly house (the sons of Aaron) and the Levites. The latter were to be aides to the priests, and they served not only Aaron but the whole nation in the process (see vv. 7–8).

3:9 *unto him.* It appears that the issue here is service to Aaron (and through him to the Lord); in 8:16 the service is to the Lord.

3:10 *stranger.* Anyone lacking authorization. Service at the tabernacle may be performed only at the express appointment of the Lord. The words of v. 10 follow the paragraph telling of the death of Aaron's sons. They were authorized persons, but used unauthorized means. If the sons of Aaron were put to death at the commencement of their duties, how dare an unauthorized person even think to trespass? See v. 38; 18:7.

3:12 *instead of.* An example of the practice of substitution (see Gen 22:13 and note; Mat 20:28).

3:13 See note on Ex 13:2. *mine.* Repeated for emphasis.

3:15 *a month old and upward.* The counting of the Levites corresponds to that of the other tribes in chs. 1–2, except that all males from the age of one month, rather than from 20 years, were to be counted. The Levites were not being mustered for war, but for special service in the sacred precincts of the Lord.

3:16 *as he was commanded.* The obedience of Moses to the Lord's command is explicit and total.

3:21–38 The words of 1:53, "pitch round about the tabernacle of Testimony," are detailed by the four paragraphs in this section: (1) Gershon to the west (vv. 21–26); (2) Kohath to the south (vv. 27–32); (3) Merari to the north (vv. 33–37); (4) Moses and Aaron and sons to the east (v. 38). The other tribes began with

22 Those that were numbered of them, according to the number of all the males, from a month old and upward, *even* those that were numbered of them *were* seven thousand and five hundred.

23 [a]The families of the Gershonites shall pitch behind the tabernacle westward.

24 And the chief of the house of the father of the Gershonites *shall be* Eliasaph the son of Lael.

25 And [a]the charge of the sons of Gershon in the tabernacle of the congregation *shall be* [b]the tabernacle, and [c]the tent, [d]the covering thereof, and [e]the hanging for the door of the tabernacle of the congregation,

26 And [a]the hangings of the court, and [b]the curtain for the door of the court, which *is* by the tabernacle, and by the altar round about, and [c]the cords of it for all the service thereof.

27 ¶ [a]And of Kohath *was* the family of the Amramites, and the family of the Izeharites, and the family of the Hebronites, and the family of the Uzzielites: these *are* the families of the Kohathites.

28 In the number of all the males, from a month old and upward, *were* eight thousand and six hundred, keeping the charge of the sanctuary.

29 [a]The families of the sons of Kohath shall pitch on the side of the tabernacle southward.

30 And the chief of the house of the father of the families of the Kohathites *shall be* Elizaphan the son of Uzziel.

31 And [a]their charge *shall be* [b]the ark, and [c]the table, and [d]the candlestick, and [e]the altars, and the vessels of the sanctuary wherewith they minister, and [f]the hanging, and all the service thereof.

32 And Eleazar the son of Aaron the priest *shall be* chief over the chief of the Levites, *and have* the oversight of them that keep the charge of the sanctuary.

33 ¶ Of Merari *was* the family of the Mahlites, and the family of the Mushites: these *are* the families of Merari.

3:23 [a]ch. 1:53
3:25 [a]ch. 4:24-26 [b]Ex. 25:9 [c]Ex. 26:1 [d]Ex. 26:7,14 [e]Ex. 26:36
3:26 [a]Ex. 27:9 [b]Ex. 27:16 [c]Ex. 35:18
3:27 [a]1 Chr. 26:23
3:29 [a]ch. 1:53
3:31 [a]ch. 4:15 [b]Ex. 25:10 [c]Ex. 25:23 [d]Ex. 25:31 [e]Ex. 27:1; 30:1 [f]Ex. 26:32

34 And those that were numbered of them, according to the number of all the males, from a month old and upward, *were* six thousand and two hundred.

35 And the chief of the house of the father of the families of Merari *was* Zuriel the son of Abihail: [a]*these* shall pitch on the side of the tabernacle northwards.

36 And [a][1]under the custody and charge of the sons of Merari *shall be* the boards of the tabernacle, and the bars thereof, and the pillars thereof, and the sockets thereof, and all the vessels thereof, and all that serveth thereto,

37 And the pillars of the court round about, and their sockets, and their pins, and their cords.

38 ¶ [a]But those that encamp before the tabernacle toward the east, *even* before the tabernacle of the congregation eastward, *shall be* Moses, and Aaron and his sons, [b]keeping the charge of the sanctuary [c]for the charge of the children of Israel; and [d]the stranger that cometh nigh shall be put to death.

39 [a]All that were numbered of the Levites, which Moses and Aaron numbered at the commandment of the LORD, throughout their families, all the males from a month old and upward, *were* twenty and two thousand.

40 ¶ And the LORD said unto Moses, [a]Number all the firstborn of the males of the children of Israel from a month old and upward, and take the number of their names.

41 [a]And thou shalt take the Levites for me (I *am* the LORD) instead of all the firstborn among the children of Israel; and the cattle of the Levites instead of all the firstlings among the cattle of the children of Israel.

42 And Moses numbered, as the LORD commanded him, all the firstborn among the children of Israel.

43 And all the firstborn males by the number of names, from a month old and upward, of those that were numbered of them, were twenty and two thousand two hundred and threescore and thirteen.

3:35 [a]ch. 1:53
3:36 [1]Heb. *the office of the charge* [a]ch. 4:31,32
3:38 [a]ch. 1:53 [b]ch. 18:5 [c]ver. 7,8 [d]ver. 10
3:39 [a]See ch. 26:62
3:40 [a]ver. 15
3:41 [a]ver. 12,45

the most favored: (1) Judah on the east (2:3); (2) Reuben on the south (2:10); (3) Ephraim on the west (2:18); (4) Dan on the north (2:25). The Levitical clans lead up to the most favored. The leaders of the Levitical houses correspond to the leaders of the other tribes (see note on 1:5–16). As the names of the other tribal leaders include a form of God's name, so do these names.

3:24 *Eliasaph.* Means "(My) God has added." *Lael.* Means "belonging to God."

3:25–26 There were three curtains or covering screens for the tabernacle: (1) for the door at the gate of the courtyard (v. 26; 4:26); (2) at the entrance to the tabernacle (vv. 25,31; 4:25); (3) between the most holy place and the holy place (4:5).

3:27 *Amramites.* Aaron was an Amramite (see Ex 6:20); thus he and Moses were from the family of Kohath. To the Kohathites was given the care of the most holy things (see 4:4–18).

3:28 *eight thousand and six hundred.* The total number of Levites given in v. 39 is 22,000—300 less than the totals of 7,500 Gershonites (v. 22), 8,600 Kohathites (here) and 6,200 Merarites (v. 34). Many believe that a copyist may have made a mistake here, and that the correct number is 8,300.

3:30 *Elizaphan.* Means "(My) God has protected." *Uzziel.* Means "My strength is God."

3:35 *Zuriel.* Means "My Rock is God." *Abihail.* Means "My (divine) Father is power."

‡3:38 *toward the east.* The direction of the sunrise was the most honored location, but Moses and Aaron were placed there for a representative ministry (on behalf of the Israelites). *the stranger . . . shall be put to death.* Service in the tabernacle was an act of mercy, a means for the people to come before God. Yet it was marked by strict discipline—it had to be done in God's way. The sovereignty of God was evident in His limitations on the means to approach Him (see v. 10; 1:51; 18:7).

3:41 *I am the LORD.* What is being commanded conforms to God's character as Yahweh ("the LORD"; see note on Ex 3:14).

3:43 *twenty and two thousand two hundred and threescore and thirteen.* Seems too small for a population in excess of 2,000,000, and is used as an argument for attempting to find a means of reducing the total number of the people (calculations based on this number suggest a total population of about 250,000). Some suggest that the 22,273 firstborn of Israel were

44 And the LORD spake unto Moses, saying,

45 [a]Take the Levites instead of all the firstborn among the children of Israel, and the cattle of the Levites instead of their cattle; and the Levites shall be mine: I *am* the LORD.

46 And for those that are *to be* [a]redeemed of the two hundred and threescore and thirteen of the firstborn of the children of Israel, [b]which are more than the Levites;

47 Thou shalt even take [a]five shekels apiece by the poll, after the shekel of the sanctuary shalt thou take *them:* ([b]the shekel *is* twenty gerahs:)

48 And thou shalt give the money, wherewith the odd number of them is *to be* redeemed, unto Aaron and to his sons.

49 And Moses took the redemption money of them that were over and above them that were redeemed by the Levites:

50 Of the firstborn of the children of Israel took he the money; [a]a thousand three hundred and threescore and five *shekels,* after the shekel of the sanctuary:

51 And Moses [a]gave the money of them that were redeemed unto Aaron and to his sons, according to the word of the LORD, as the LORD commanded Moses.

The descendants of Kohath

4 And the LORD spake unto Moses and unto Aaron, saying,

2 Take the sum of the sons of Kohath from among the sons of Levi, after their families, by the house of their fathers,

3 [a]From thirty years old and upward even until fifty years old, all that enter into the host, to do the work in the tabernacle of the congregation.

4 [a]This *shall be* the service of the sons of Kohath in the tabernacle of the congregation, *about* [b]the most holy *things:*

5 And when the camp setteth forward, Aaron shall come, and his sons, and they shall take down [a]the covering vail, and cover the [b]ark of Testimony with it:

6 And shall put thereon the covering of badgers' skins, and shall spread over *it* a cloth wholly of blue, and shall put in [a]the staves thereof.

7 And upon the [a]table of shewbread they shall spread a cloth of blue, and put thereon the dishes, and the spoons, and the bowls, and covers to [1]cover withal: and the continual bread shall be thereon:

8 And they shall spread upon them a cloth of scarlet, and cover the same with a covering of badgers' skins, and shall put in the staves thereof.

9 And they shall take a cloth of blue, and cover the [a]candlestick of the light, [b]and his lamps, and his tongs, and his snuffdishes, and all the oil vessels thereof, wherewith they minister unto it:

10 And they shall put it and all the vessels thereof within a covering of badgers' skins, and shall put *it* upon a bar.

11 And upon [a]the golden altar they shall spread a cloth of blue, and cover it with a covering of badgers' skins, and shall put to the staves thereof:

12 And they shall take all the instruments of ministry, wherewith they minister in the sanctuary, and put *them* in a cloth of blue, and cover them with a covering of badgers' skins, and shall put *them* on a bar:

13 And they shall take away the ashes from the altar, and spread a purple cloth thereon:

14 And they shall put upon it all the vessels thereof, wherewith they minister about it, *even* the censers, the fleshhooks, and the shovels, and the [1]basons, all the vessels of the altar; and they shall spread upon it a covering of badgers' skins, and put to the staves of it.

15 And when Aaron and his sons have made an end of covering the sanctuary, and all the vessels of the sanctuary, as the camp is to set forward; after that, [a]the sons of Kohath shall come to bear *it:* [b]but they shall not touch *any* holy *thing,* lest they die. [c]These *things are* the burden of the sons of Kohath in the tabernacle of the congregation.

16 And *to* the office of Eleazar the son of Aaron the priest *pertaineth* [a]the oil for the light, and the [b]sweet incense, and [c]the daily meat offering, and the [d]anointing oil, *and* the oversight of all the tabernacle, and of all that therein *is,* in the sanctuary, and in the vessels thereof.

17 And the LORD spake unto Moses and unto Aaron, saying,

18 Cut ye not off the tribe of the families of the Kohathites from among the Levites:

19 But thus do unto them, that they may live, and not die, when they approach unto [a]the most holy *things:* Aaron and his sons shall go in, and appoint them every one to his service and to his burden:

20 [a]But they shall not go in to see when the holy *things* are covered, lest they die.

3:45 [a]ver. 12,41 **3:46** [a]Ex. 13:13; ch. 18:15 [b]ver. 39,43 **3:47** [a]Lev. 27:6; ch. 18:16 [b]Ex. 30:13 **3:50** [a]ver. 46,47 **3:51** [a]ver. 48 **4:3** [a]See ch. 8:24; 1 Chr. 23:3,24,27 **4:4** [a]ver. 15 [b]ver. 19 **4:5** [a]Ex. 26:31 [b]Ex. 25:10,16 **4:6** [a]Ex. 25:13 **4:7** [1]Or, *pour out withal* [a]Ex. 25:23,29,30 **4:9** [a]Ex. 25:31 [b]Ex. 25:37,38 **4:11** [a]Ex. 30:1,3 **4:14** [1]Or, *bowls* **4:15** [a]ch. 7:9; 10:21; Deut. 31:9; 2 Sam. 6:13; 1 Chr. 15:2,15 [b]2 Sam. 6:6,7; 1 Chr. 13:9,10 [c]ch. 3:31 **4:16** [a]Ex. 25:6; Lev. 24:2 [b]Ex. 30:34 [c]Ex. 29:38 [d]Ex. 30:25 **4:19** [a]ver. 4 **4:20** [a]See Ex. 19:21; 1 Sam. 6:19

those born since the exodus, all the firstborn at the time of the exodus having already been set apart for the Lord at the first passover (see Ex 12:22–23). This, however, creates a new problem since nowhere is that allegedly distinct group assigned any special service of the Lord. See Introduction: Special Problem.

4:3 *thirty . . . until fifty years.* Ch. 3 listed all males over the age of one month (3:15). Ch. 4 lists those Levites who were of age to serve in the tabernacle. Of the 22,000 Levite males (3:39), 8,580 were of age for service (v. 48). From 8:24 we learn that the beginning age for service was 25; perhaps the first 5 years were something of an apprenticeship.

4:4 *most holy things.* Despite the fact that the primary care of these holy things was given to the Kohathites, they were forbidden to touch them (v. 15) or even to look at them (v. 20), on pain of death. All the work of the Kohathites was to be strictly supervised by Aaron and his sons, and only the priests were able to touch and look at the unveiled holy things.

4:16 *the office of Eleazar . . . the priest.* The high priest could draw near to the most holy things on behalf of the people. If he had not been able to do so, there could have been no worship by the community.

The descendants of Gershon

21 ¶ And the LORD spake unto Moses, saying,

22 Take also the sum of the sons of Gershon, throughout the houses of their fathers, by their families;

23 [a]From thirty years old and upward until fifty years old shalt thou number them; all that enter in [1]to perform the service, to do the work in the tabernacle of the congregation.

24 This *is* the service of the families of the Gershonites, to serve, and for [1]burdens:

25 And [a]they shall bear the curtains of the tabernacle, and the tabernacle of the congregation, his covering, and the covering of the badgers' skins that *is* above upon it, and the hanging for the door of the tabernacle of the congregation,

26 And the hangings of the court, and the hanging for the door of the gate of the court, which *is* by the tabernacle and by the altar round about, and their cords, and all the instruments of their service, and all that is made for them: so shall they serve.

27 At the [1]appointment of Aaron and his sons shall be all the service of the sons of the Gershonites, in all their burdens, and in all their service: and ye shall appoint unto them in charge all their burdens.

28 This *is* the service of the families of the sons of Gershon in the tabernacle of the congregation: and their charge *shall be* [a]under the hand of Ithamar the son of Aaron the priest.

The descendants of Merari

29 ¶ *As for* the sons of Merari, thou shalt number them after their families, by the house of their fathers;

30 [a]From thirty years old and upward even unto fifty years old shalt thou number them, every one that entereth into the [1]service, to do the work of the tabernacle of the congregation.

31 And [a]this *is* the charge of their burden, according to all their service in the tabernacle of the congregation; [b]the boards of the tabernacle, and the bars thereof, and the pillars thereof, and sockets thereof,

32 And the pillars of the court round about, and their sockets, and their pins, and their cords, with all their instruments, and with all their service: and by name ye shall [a]reckon the instruments of the charge of their burden.

33 This *is* the service of the families of the sons of Merari, according to all their service, in the tabernacle of the congregation, under the hand of Ithamar the son of Aaron the priest.

The results of the census

34 ¶ [a]And Moses and Aaron and the chief of the congregation numbered the sons of the Kohathites after their families, and after the house of their fathers,

35 From thirty [a]years old and upward even unto fifty years old, every one that entereth into the service, for the work in the tabernacle of the congregation:

36 And those that were numbered of them by their families were two thousand seven hundred and fifty.

37 These *were* they that were numbered of the families of the Kohathites, all that *might* do service in the tabernacle of the congregation, which Moses and Aaron did number according to the commandment of the LORD by the hand of Moses.

38 And those that were numbered of the sons of Gershon, throughout their families, and by the house of their fathers,

39 From thirty years old and upward even unto fifty years old, every one that entereth into the service, for the work in the tabernacle of the congregation,

40 Even those that were numbered of them, throughout their families, by the house of their fathers, were two thousand and six hundred and thirty.

41 [a]These *are* they that were numbered of the families of the sons of Gershon, of all that *might* do service in the tabernacle of the congregation, whom Moses and Aaron did number according to the commandment of the LORD.

42 And those that were numbered of the families of the sons of Merari, throughout their families, by the house of their fathers,

43 From thirty years old and upward even unto fifty years old, every one that entereth into the service, for the work in the tabernacle of the congregation,

44 Even those that were numbered of them after their families, were three thousand and two hundred.

45 These *be* those that were numbered of the families of the sons of Merari, whom Moses and Aaron numbered [a]according to the word of the LORD by the hand of Moses.

46 All those that were numbered of the Levites, whom Moses and Aaron and the chief of Israel numbered, after their families, and after the house of their fathers,

47 [a]From thirty years old and upward even unto fifty years old, every one that came to do the service of the ministry, and the service of the burden in the tabernacle of the congregation,

48 Even those that were numbered of them, were eight thousand and five hundred and fourscore.

49 According to the commandment of the LORD they were numbered by the hand of Moses, [a]every one according to his service, and according to his burden: thus *were they* numbered of him, [b]as the LORD commanded Moses.

Concerning the unclean

5 And the LORD spake unto Moses, saying,
2 Command the children of Israel, that they put out of the camp every [a]leper, and

4:23 [1]Heb. *to war the warfare* [a]ver. 3
4:24 [1]Or, *carriage*
4:25 [a]ch. 3:25,26
4:27 [1]Heb. *mouth*
4:28 [a]ver. 33
4:30 [1]Heb. *warfare* [a]ver. 3
4:31 [a]ch. 3:36,37 [b]Ex. 26:15
4:32 [a]Ex. 38:21
4:34 [a]ver. 2
4:35 [a]ver. 47; ch. 8:24,26; 1 Chr. 23:24; Luke 3:23; 1 Tim. 3:6

4:41 [a]ver. 22
4:45 [a]ver. 29
4:47 [a]ver. 3,23,30
4:49 [a]ver. 15,24,31 [b]ver. 1,21
5:2 [a]Lev. 13:3,46

5:2 *leper.* See note on Lev 13:2; cf. Luke 5:12–16; 17:11–19. *issue.* See note on Lev 15:2. Such discharges were primarily from the sexual organs and were chronic in nature (cf. Luke 8:43–48). The people who suffered from them became living object les-

every one that hath an [b]issue, and whosoever is defiled by the [c]dead:

3 Both male and female shall ye put out, without the camp shall ye put them; that they defile not their camps, [a]in the midst whereof I dwell.

4 And the children of Israel did so, and put them out without the camp: as the LORD spake unto Moses, so did the children of Israel.

Suspected adultery

5 ¶ And the LORD spake unto Moses, saying,

6 Speak unto the children of Israel, [a]When a man or woman shall commit any sin that men commit, to do a trespass against the LORD, and that person be guilty;

7 [a]Then they shall confess their sin which they have done: and he shall recompense his trespass [b]with the principal thereof, and add unto it the fifth *part* thereof, and give *it* unto *him* against whom he hath trespassed.

8 But if the man have no kinsman to recompense the trespass unto, *let* the trespass *be* recompensed unto the LORD, *even* to the priest; beside [a]the ram of the atonement, whereby an atonement shall be made for him.

9 And every [a][1]offering of all the holy *things* of the children of Israel, which they bring unto the priest, shall be his.

10 And every man's hallowed *things* shall be his: whatsoever any man giveth the priest, it shall be [a]his.

11 ¶ And the LORD spake unto Moses, saying,

12 Speak unto the children of Israel, and say unto them, If any man's wife go aside, and commit a trespass against him,

13 And a man [a]lie with her carnally, and it be hid from the eyes of her husband, and be kept close, and she be defiled, and *there be* no witness against her, neither she be taken *with the manner;*

14 And the spirit of jealousy come upon him, and he be jealous of his wife, and she be defiled: or if the spirit of jealousy come upon him, and he be jealous of his wife, and she be not defiled:

15 Then shall the man bring his wife unto the priest, and he shall [a]bring her offering for her, the tenth *part* of an ephah of barley meal; he shall pour no oil upon it, nor put frankincense thereon; for it *is* an offering of jealousy, an offering of memorial, [b]bringing iniquity to remembrance.

16 And the priest shall bring her near, and set her before the LORD:

17 And the priest shall take holy water in an earthen vessel; and of the dust that is in the floor of the tabernacle the priest shall take, and put *it* into the water:

18 And the priest shall set the woman before the LORD, and uncover the woman's head,

5:2 [b]Lev. 15:2 [c]Lev. 21:1; ch. 9:6,10; 19:11,13; 31:19
5:3 [a]Lev. 26:11,12; 2 Cor. 6:16
5:6 [a]Lev. 6:2,3
5:7 [a]Lev. 5:5; 26:40; Josh. 7:19 [b]Lev. 6:5
5:8 [a]Lev. 6:6,7; 7:7
5:9 [1]Or, *heave offering* [a]Ex. 29:28; Lev. 6:17,18,26; 7:6,7,9,10,14
5:10 [a]Lev. 10:13
5:13 [a]Lev. 18:20
5:15 [a]Lev. 5:11 [b]1 Ki. 17:18; Ezek. 29:16

sons to the whole camp on the necessity for all people to be "clean" in their approach to God. *defiled.* Ceremonially unfit to be with the community, and a possible contaminant to the tabernacle and the pure worship of the Lord. Aspects of uncleanness were not left in the abstract or theoretical; the focus was on tangible issues, such as clearly evident skin diseases and discharges. *the dead.* The ultimate tangible sign of uncleanness. Processes of decay and disease in dead flesh were evident to all. Physical contact with a corpse was a sure mark of uncleanness; normal contacts with the living would have to be curtailed until proper cleansing had been made. See note on 6:6 for application to the Nazarite vow. Jesus reached out to the dead as well as to the living; His raising of Jairus's daughter began with holding her limp hand (Luke 8:54).

5:3 *male and female.* The concept of clean versus unclean cuts across sexual lines. The essential issue was the presence of the Lord in the camp; there can be no uncleanness where He dwells. In the new Jerusalem (Rev 21:2–3) the dwelling of God with man will be uncompromised by any form of uncleanness (Rev 21:27).

5:5–10 The connection of these verses (on personal wrongs) with the first paragraph (on ritual uncleanness) may be that of moving from the outward, visible defects to the inward, more secret faults that mar the purity of the community. Those with evident marks of uncleanness are to be expelled for the duration of their malady. But more insidious are those people who have overtly sinned against others in the community, and who think that they may continue to function as though they had done nothing wrong.

5:11–31 Again, the connection with the preceding two paragraphs seems to be a movement from the more open, obvious sins to the more personal, hidden ones. Issues of purity begin with physical marks (vv. 1–4), are expanded to interpersonal relationships (vv. 5–10), and then intrude into the most intimate of relationships—the purity of a man and woman in their marriage bed. A test for marital fidelity is far more difficult to prove than a test for a skin disorder; hence, the larger part of the chapter is given to this most sensitive of issues.

5:14 *spirit of jealousy.* This may have been provoked on the basis of good cause, and the issue must be faced. The concern is not just for the bruised feelings of the husband but is ultimately based on the reality of God's dwelling among His people (v. 3). Yet the chapter is designed to prevent unfounded charges of unfaithfulness. This text was not to be used by a capricious, petty or malevolent husband to badger an innocent woman. *defiled.* The subject of the chapter is consistent; the purity of the camp where God dwells (v. 3) is the burden of the passage.

5:15–28 The actions presented here seem severe and harsh. But the consequences would have been worse for a woman charged with adultery by an angry husband if there was no provision for her guilt or innocence to be demonstrated. That she was taken to the priest (v. 15) is finally an act of mercy. The gravity of the ritual for a suspected unfaithful wife shows that the law regards marital infidelity most seriously. This was not just a concern of a jealous husband. The entire community was affected by this breach of faith; hence, the judgment was in the context of the community.

5:18 *uncover the woman's head.* A sign of openness; for the guilty, an expectation of judgment and mourning. *bitter water that causeth the curse.* Or "curse-bringing water of bitterness." It is not just that the water was bitter tasting but that the water had the potential of bringing with it a bitter curse. The Lord's role in the proceedings (vv. 16,21,25) is emphasized repeatedly to show that this potion was neither simply a tool of magic nor merely a psychological device to determine stress. The verdict with respect to the woman was precipitated by her physiological and psychological responses to the bitter water, but the judgment was from the Lord.

and put the offering of memorial in her hands, which *is* the jealousy offering: and the priest shall have in his hand the bitter water that causeth the curse:

19 And the priest shall charge her by an oath, and say unto the woman, If no man have lain with thee, and if thou hast not gone aside *to* uncleanness [1]*with another* instead of thy husband, be thou free from this bitter water that causeth the curse:

20 But if thou hast gone aside *to another* instead of thy husband, and if thou be defiled, and *some* man hath lain with thee beside thine husband:

21 Then the priest shall [a]charge the woman with an oath of cursing, and the priest shall say unto the woman, [b]The LORD make thee a curse and an oath among thy people, when the LORD doth make thy thigh to [1]rot, and thy belly to swell;

22 And this water that causeth the curse [a]shall go into thy bowels, to make *thy* belly to swell, and *thy* thigh to rot: [b]And the woman shall say, Amen, amen.

23 And the priest shall write these curses in a book, and he shall blot *them* out with the bitter water:

24 And he shall cause the woman to drink the bitter water that causeth the curse: and the water that causeth the curse shall enter into her, and become bitter.

25 Then the priest shall take the jealousy offering out of the woman's hand, and shall [a]wave the offering before the LORD, and offer it upon the altar:

26 [a]And the priest shall take a handful of the offering, *even* the memorial thereof, and burn *it* upon the altar, and afterward shall cause the woman to drink the water.

27 And when he hath made her to drink the water, then it shall come to pass, *that,* if she be defiled, and have done trespass against her husband, that the water that causeth the curse shall enter into her, and become bitter, and her belly shall swell, and her thigh shall rot: and the woman [a]shall be a curse among her people.

5:19 [1]Or, being *in the power of thy husband.* Heb. *under thy husband*
5:21 [1]Heb. *fall* [a]Josh. 6:26; 1 Sam. 14:24; Neh. 10:29 [b]Jer. 29:22
5:22 [a]Ps. 109:18 [b]Deut. 27:15
5:25 [a]Lev. 8:27
5:26 [a]Lev. 2:2,9
5:27 [a]ver. 21
5:29 [a]ver. 19
5:31 [a]Lev. 20:17,19,20
6:2 [1]Or, *make* themselves *Nazarites* [a]Lev. 27:2; Judg. 13:5; Acts 21:23; Rom. 1:1
6:3 [a]Amos 2:12; Luke 1:15
6:4 [1]Or, *Nazariteship* [2]Heb. *vine of the wine*
6:5 [a]Judg. 13:5; 16:17; 1 Sam. 1:11
6:6 [a]Lev. 21:11; ch. 19:11,16
6:7 [1]Heb. *separation* [a]Lev. 21:1,2,11; ch. 9:6
6:8 [a]2 Cor. 6:17,18
6:9 [a]Acts 18:18; 21:24

28 And if the woman be not defiled, but *be* clean; then she shall be free, and shall conceive seed.

29 This *is* the law of jealousies, when a wife goeth aside *to another* [a]instead of her husband, and is defiled;

30 Or when the spirit of jealousy cometh upon him, and he be jealous over his wife, and shall set the woman before the LORD, and the priest shall execute upon her all this law.

31 Then shall the man be guiltless from iniquity, and this woman [a]shall bear her iniquity.

The law of a Nazarite

6 And the LORD spake unto Moses, saying,
2 Speak unto the children of Israel, and say unto them, When either man or woman shall [a]separate *themselves* to vow a vow of a Nazarite, [1]to separate *themselves* unto the LORD:

3 [a]He shall separate *himself* from wine and strong drink, *and* shall drink no vinegar of wine, or vinegar of strong drink, neither shall he drink any liquor of grapes, nor eat moist grapes, or dried.

4 All the days of his [1]separation shall he eat nothing that is made of the [2]vine tree, from the kernels even to the husk.

5 All the days of the vow of his separation there shall no [a]rasor come upon his head: until the days be fulfilled, *in* the which he separateth *himself* unto the LORD, he shall be holy, *and* shall let the locks of the hair of his head grow.

6 All the days that he separateth *himself* unto the LORD [a]he shall come at no dead body.

7 [a]He shall not make himself unclean for his father, or for his mother, for his brother, or for his sister, when they die: because the [1]consecration of his God *is* upon his head.

8 [a]All the days of his separation he *is* holy unto the LORD.

9 And if any man die very suddenly by him, and he hath defiled the head of his consecration; then he shall [a]shave his head in the day of his cleansing, on the seventh day shall he shave it.

5:21 *thy thigh to rot, and thy belly to swell.* The figurative language here (and in vv. 22,27) speaks of the loss of the capacity for childbearing (and, if pregnant, the miscarriage of the child). This is demonstrated by the determination of the fate of a woman wrongly charged (v. 28). For a woman in the ancient Near East to be denied the ability to bear children was a personal loss of inestimable proportions. Since it was in the bearing of children that a woman's worth was realized in the ancient world, this was a grievous punishment indeed.

6:2 *man or woman.* See ch. 30 for the differences between the vows of men and women. *vow . . . Nazarite.* Involved separation or consecration for a specific period of special devotion to God—on occasion even for life. Attention is usually given to the prohibitions for the Nazarite; more important to the Lord is the positive separation (see v. 8). This was not just a vow of personal self-discipline; it was an act of total devotion to the Lord.

6:4 *nothing that is made of the vine tree.* Not only was the fermented beverage forbidden, but even the seed and skin of the grape. During the period of a Nazarite's vow, three areas of his (or her) life were governed: (1) diet, (2) appearance and (3) associations. Every Israelite was regulated in these areas, but for the Nazarite each regulation was heightened. An analogy may be the practice of some Christians to forgo certain (good) foods during the period of Lent to enhance spiritual devotion to Christ in the special period of remembering His sufferings.

6:5 *no rasor.* See Judg 13:5. The unusually long hair of a Nazarite would become a physical mark of his (or her) vow of special devotion to the Lord. Cf. Lev 21:5.

6:6 *dead body.* See note on 5:2. For the Nazarite, the prohibition of contact with dead bodies extended even to the deceased within his (or her) own family (v. 7; contrast Lev 21:1–3).

6:9–12 The provisions of the Nazarite vow concerned areas where he (or she) was able to make conscious decisions. This section deals with the unexpected and the unplanned events of daily living.

10 And [a]on the eighth day he shall bring two turtles, or two young pigeons, to the priest, to the door of the tabernacle of the congregation:

11 And the priest shall offer the one for a sin offering, and the other for a burnt offering, and make an atonement for him, for that he sinned by the dead, and shall hallow his head that *same* day.

12 And he shall consecrate unto the LORD the days of his separation, and shall bring a lamb of the first year [a]for a trespass offering: but the days that were before shall [1]be lost, because his separation was defiled.

13 And this *is* the law of the Nazarite, [a]when the days of his separation are fulfilled: he shall be brought unto the door of the tabernacle of the congregation:

14 And he shall offer his offering unto the LORD, one he lamb of the first year without blemish for a burnt offering, and one ewe lamb of the first year without blemish [a]for a sin offering, and one ram without blemish [b]for peace offerings,

15 And a basket of unleavened bread, [a]cakes *of* fine flour mingled with oil, and wafers of unleavened bread [b]anointed with oil, and their meat offering, and their [c]drink offerings.

16 And the priest shall bring *them* before the LORD, and shall offer his sin offering, and his burnt offering:

17 And he shall offer the ram *for* a sacrifice of peace offerings unto the LORD, with the basket of unleavened bread: the priest shall offer also his meat offering, and his drink offering.

18 [a]And the Nazarite shall shave the head of his separation *at* the door of the tabernacle of the congregation, and shall take the hair of the head of his separation, and put *it* in the fire which *is* under the sacrifice of the peace offerings.

19 And the priest shall take the [a]sodden shoulder of the ram, and one unleavened cake out of the basket, and one unleavened wafer, and [b]shall put *them* upon the hands of the Nazarite, after *the hair of* his separation is shaven:

20 And the priest shall wave them *for* a wave offering before the LORD: [a]this *is* holy for the priest, with the wave breast and heave shoulder: and after *that* the Nazarite may drink wine.

21 This *is* the law of the Nazarite who hath vowed, *and of* his offering unto the LORD for his separation, besides *that* that his hand shall get: according to the vow which he vowed, so he must do after the law of his separation.

6:10 [a]Lev. 5:7; 14:22; 15:14,29
6:12 [1]Heb. *fall* [a]Lev. 5:6
6:13 [a]Acts 21:26
6:14 [a]Lev. 4:2,27,32 [b]Lev. 3:6
6:15 [a]Lev. 2:4 [b]Ex. 29:2 [c]ch. 15:5,7,10
6:18 [a]Acts 21:24
6:19 [a]1 Sam. 2:15 [b]Ex. 29:23,24
6:20 [a]Ex. 29:27,28

The Aaronic benediction

22 ¶ And the LORD spake unto Moses, saying,

23 Speak unto Aaron and unto his sons, saying, On this wise [a]ye shall bless the children of Israel, saying unto them,

24 ¶ The LORD bless thee, and [a]keep thee:

25 ¶ The LORD [a]make his face shine upon thee, and [b]be gracious unto thee:

26 ¶ [a]The LORD lift up his countenance upon thee, and [b]give thee peace.

27 ¶ [a]And they shall put my name upon the children of Israel; and [b]I will bless them.

The dedication offerings

7 And it came to pass on the day that Moses had fully [a]set up the tabernacle, and had anointed it, and sanctified it, and all the instruments thereof, both the altar and all the vessels thereof, and had anointed them, and sanctified them;

2 That [a]the princes of Israel, heads of the house of their fathers, who *were* the princes of the tribes, [1]and were over them that were numbered, offered:

3 And they brought their offering before the LORD, six covered wagons, and twelve oxen; a wagon for two of the princes, and for *each* one an ox: and they brought them before the tabernacle.

4 And the LORD spake unto Moses, saying,

5 Take *it* of them, that they may be to do the service of the tabernacle of the congregation; and thou shalt give them unto the Levites, to every man according to his service.

6 And Moses took the wagons and the oxen, and gave them unto the Levites.

7 Two wagons and four oxen [a]he gave unto the sons of Gershon, according to their service:

8 [a]And four wagons and eight oxen he gave unto the sons of Merari, according unto

6:23 [a]Lev. 9:22; Deut. 10:8; 21:5; Josh. 8:33; 1 Chr. 23:13
6:24 [a]Ps. 121:7; John 17:11
6:25 [a]Ps. 31:16; 67:1; 80:3,7,19; 119:135; Dan. 9:17 [b]Gen. 43:29; Ex. 33:19; Mal. 1:9
6:26 [a]Ps. 4:6 [b]John 14:27; Phil. 4:7; 2 Thes. 3:16
6:27 [a]Deut. 28:10; 2 Chr. 7:14; Is. 43:7; Dan. 9:18,19 [b]ch. 23:20; Ps. 5:12; 67:7; 115:12,13; Eph. 1:3
7:1 [a]Ex. 40:18; Lev. 8:10,11
7:2 [1]Heb. *who stood* [a]ch. 1:4
7:7 [a]ch. 4:23
7:8 [a]ch. 4:33

6:13–20 The offerings of the Nazarite at the completion of the period of the vow were extensive, expensive and expressive of the spirit of total commitment to the Lord during this time of special devotion. In addition to these several offerings the Nazarite burned his (or her) hair (the sign of the vow).

6:21 *This is the law of the Nazarite.* Summary statements such as this not only end a section, but also solemnize its contents.

6:24–26 The Aaronic benediction. The threefold repetition of the divine name Yahweh ("the LORD") is for emphasis and gives force to the expression in v. 27: "And they shall put my name upon the children of Israel." Each verse conveys two elements of benediction, and the verses are progressively longer (in the Hebrew text, the first verse has three words, the second has five and the third has seven).

6:25 *make his face shine upon thee.* In acceptance and favor.

6:26 *peace.* The Hebrew for this word is *shalom,* here seen in its most expressive fullness—not the absence of war, but a positive state of rightness and well-being. Such peace comes only from the Lord.

7:1–89 See Ex 40, which describes the setting up of the tabernacle and ends with the report of the cloud covering and the presence of the Lord filling the tabernacle. With much repetition of language, this chapter (the longest in the Pentateuch) records the magnificent (and identical) gifts to the Lord for tabernacle service from the leaders of the 12 tribes. The fact that the record of these gifts follows the text of the Aaronic benediction (6:24–26) seems fitting: In response to God's promise to bless His people, they bring gifts to Him in 12 sequential days of celebrative pageantry.

their service, [b]under the hand of Ithamar the son of Aaron the priest.

9 But unto the sons of Kohath he gave none: because [a]the service of the sanctuary belonging unto them [b]*was that* they should bear upon *their* shoulders.

10 And the princes offered *for* [a]dedicating of the altar in the day that it was anointed, even the princes offered their offering before the altar.

11 And the LORD said unto Moses, They shall offer their offering, each prince on *his* day, for the dedicating of the altar.

12 ¶ And he that offered his offering the first day was [a]Nahshon the son of Amminadab, of the tribe of Judah:

13 And his offering *was* one silver charger, the weight thereof *was* an hundred and thirty *shekels,* one silver bowl of seventy shekels, after [a]the shekel of the sanctuary; both of them *were* full *of* fine flour mingled with oil for a [b]meat offering:

14 One spoon of ten *shekels* of gold, full *of* [a]incense:

15 [a]One young bullock, one ram, one lamb [b]of the first year, for a burnt offering:

16 One kid of the goats for a [a]sin offering:

17 And for [a]a sacrifice of peace offerings, two oxen, five rams, five he goats, five lambs of the first year: this *was* the offering of Nahshon the son of Amminadab.

18 ¶ On the second day Nethaneel the son of Zuar, prince of Issachar, did offer:

19 He offered *for* his offering one silver charger, the weight whereof *was* an hundred and thirty *shekels,* one silver bowl of seventy shekels, after the shekel of the sanctuary; both of them full *of* fine flour mingled with oil for a meat offering:

20 One spoon of gold of ten *shekels,* full *of* incense:

21 One young bullock, one ram, one lamb of the first year, for a burnt offering:

22 One kid of the goats for a sin offering:

23 And for a sacrifice of peace offerings, two oxen, five rams, five he goats, five lambs of the first year: this *was* the offering of Nethaneel the son of Zuar.

24 ¶ On the third day Eliab the son of Helon, prince of the children of Zebulun, *did offer:*

25 His offering *was* one silver charger, the weight whereof *was* an hundred and thirty *shekels,* one silver bowl of seventy shekels, after the shekel of the sanctuary; both of them full *of* fine flour mingled with oil for a meat offering:

26 One golden spoon of ten *shekels,* full *of* incense:

27 One young bullock, one ram, one lamb of the first year, for a burnt offering:

7:8 [b]ch. 4:28,33
7:9 [a]ch. 4:15 [b]ch. 4:6,8,10,12,14; 2 Sam. 6:13
7:10 [a]See Deut. 20:5; 1 Ki. 8:63; 2 Chr. 7:5,9; Ezra 6:16; Neh. 12:27
7:12 [a]ch. 2:3
7:13 [a]Ex. 30:13 [b]Lev. 2:1
7:14 [a]Ex. 30:34
7:15 [a]Lev. 1:2 [b]Ex. 12:5
7:16 [a]Lev. 4:23
7:17 [a]Lev. 3:1

7:30 [a]ch. 1:5; 2:10
7:36 [a]ver. 41; ch. 1:6; 2:12
7:42 [a]ch. 1:14; 2:14
7:45 [a]Ps. 40:6
7:48 [a]ch. 1:10; 2:18

28 One kid of the goats for a sin offering:

29 And for a sacrifice of peace offerings, two oxen, five rams, five he goats, five lambs of the first year: this *was* the offering of Eliab the son of Helon.

30 ¶ On the fourth day [a]Elizur the son of Shedeur, prince of the children of Reuben, *did offer:*

31 His offering *was* one silver charger of the weight of an hundred and thirty *shekels,* one silver bowl of seventy shekels, after the shekel of the sanctuary; both of them full *of* fine flour mingled with oil for a meat offering:

32 One golden spoon *of* ten *shekels,* full *of* incense:

33 One young bullock, one ram, one lamb of the first year, for a burnt offering:

34 One kid of the goats for a sin offering:

35 And for a sacrifice of peace offerings, two oxen, five rams, five he goats, five lambs of the first year: this *was* the offering of Elizur the son of Shedeur.

36 ¶ On the fifth day [a]Shelumiel the son of Zurishaddai, prince of the children of Simeon, *did offer:*

37 His offering *was* one silver charger, the weight whereof *was* an hundred and thirty *shekels,* one silver bowl of seventy shekels, after the shekel of the sanctuary; both of them full *of* fine flour mingled with oil for a meat offering:

38 One golden spoon of ten *shekels,* full *of* incense:

39 One young bullock, one ram, one lamb of the first year, for a burnt offering:

40 One kid of the goats for a sin offering:

41 And for a sacrifice of peace offerings, two oxen, five rams, five he goats, five lambs of the first year: this *was* the offering of Shelumiel the son of Zurishaddai.

42 ¶ On the sixth day [a]Eliasaph the son of Deuel, prince of the children of Gad, *offered:*

43 His offering *was* one silver charger of the weight of an hundred and thirty *shekels,* a silver bowl of seventy shekels, after the shekel of the sanctuary; both of them full *of* fine flour mingled with oil for a meat offering:

44 One golden spoon of ten *shekels,* full *of* incense:

45 One young bullock, one ram, one lamb of the first year, for [a]a burnt offering:

46 One kid of the goats for a sin offering:

47 And for a sacrifice of peace offerings, two oxen, five rams, five he goats, five lambs of the first year: this *was* the offering of Eliasaph the son of Deuel.

48 ¶ On the seventh day [a]Elishama the son of Ammihud, prince of the children of Ephraim, *offered:*

7:12–78 The leaders of the 12 tribes have already been named in 1:5–15; 2:3–32. The order of the presentation of their offerings to the Lord is the same as the order of march: first, the triad of tribes camped east of the tabernacle (Judah, Issachar and Zebulun: 2:3–9; 7:12,18,24); second, the triad camped to the south (Reuben, Simeon and Gad: 2:10–16; 7:30,36,42); third, the triad to the west (Ephraim, Manasseh and Benjamin: 2:18–24; 7:48,54,60); finally, those to the north (Dan, Asher and Naphtali: 2:25–31; 7:66,72,78). See diagram, p. 179.

49 His offering *was* one silver charger, the weight whereof *was* an hundred and thirty *shekels,* one silver bowl of seventy shekels, after the shekel of the sanctuary; both of them full *of* fine flour mingled with oil for a meat offering:

50 One golden spoon of ten *shekels,* full *of* [a]incense:

51 One young bullock, one ram, one lamb of the first year, for a burnt offering:

52 One kid of the goats for a sin offering:

53 And for a sacrifice of peace offerings, two oxen, five rams, five he goats, five lambs of the first year: this *was* the offering of Elishama the son of Ammihud.

54 ¶ On the eighth day *offered* [a]Gamaliel the son of Pedahzur, prince of the children of Manasseh:

55 His offering *was* one silver charger of the weight of an hundred and thirty *shekels,* one silver bowl of seventy shekels, after the shekel of the sanctuary; both of them full *of* fine flour mingled with oil for a meat offering:

56 One golden spoon of ten *shekels,* full *of* incense:

57 One young bullock, one ram, one lamb of the first year, for a burnt offering:

58 One kid of the goats for a sin offering:

59 And for a sacrifice of peace offerings, two oxen, five rams, five he goats, five lambs of the first year: this *was* the offering of Gamaliel the son of Pedahzur.

60 ¶ On the ninth day [a]Abidan the son of Gideoni, prince of the children of Benjamin, *offered:*

61 His offering *was* one silver charger, the weight whereof *was* an hundred and thirty *shekels,* one silver bowl of seventy shekels, after the shekel of the sanctuary; both of them full *of* fine flour mingled with oil for a meat offering:

62 One golden spoon of ten *shekels,* full *of* incense:

63 One young bullock, one ram, one lamb of the first year, for a burnt offering:

64 One kid of the goats for a sin offering:

65 And for a sacrifice of peace offerings, two oxen, five rams, five he goats, five lambs of the first year: this *was* the offering of Abidan the son of Gideoni.

66 ¶ On the tenth day [a]Ahiezer the son of Ammishaddai, prince of the children of Dan, *offered:*

67 His offering *was* one silver charger, the weight whereof *was* an hundred and thirty *shekels,* one silver bowl of seventy shekels, after the shekel of the sanctuary; both of them full *of* fine flour mingled with oil for a meat offering:

68 One golden spoon of ten *shekels,* full *of* incense:

69 One young bullock, one ram, one lamb of the first year, for a burnt offering:

7:50 [a]Deut. 33:10; Ps. 66:15; 141:2; Ezek. 8:11; Mal. 1:11; Luke 1:10; Rev. 5:8; 8:3
7:54 [a]ch. 1:10; 2:20
7:60 [a]ch. 1:11; 2:22
7:66 [a]ch. 1:12; 2:25
7:72 [a]ch. 1:13; 2:27
7:78 [a]ch. 1:15; 2:29
7:84 [a]2 Chr. 7:9 [b]Judg. 5:9
7:85 [a]Ex. 30:13,24; 38:24-26; Lev. 5:15; 27:3,25; ch. 3:47
7:88 [a]ver. 1

70 One kid of the goats for a sin offering:

71 And for a sacrifice of peace offerings, two oxen, five rams, five he goats, five lambs of the first year: this *was* the offering of Ahiezer the son of Ammishaddai.

72 ¶ On the eleventh day [a]Pagiel the son of Ocran, prince of the children of Asher, *offered:*

73 His offering *was* one silver charger, the weight whereof *was* an hundred and thirty *shekels,* one silver bowl of seventy shekels, after the shekel of the sanctuary; both of them full *of* fine flour mingled with oil for a meat offering:

74 One golden spoon of ten *shekels,* full *of* incense:

75 One young bullock, one ram, one lamb of the first year, for a burnt offering:

76 One kid of the goats for a sin offering:

77 And for a sacrifice of peace offerings, two oxen, five rams, five he goats, five lambs of the first year: this *was* the offering of Pagiel the son of Ocran.

78 ¶ On the twelfth day [a]Ahira the son of Enan, prince of the children of Naphtali, *offered:*

79 His offering *was* one silver charger, the weight whereof *was* an hundred and thirty *shekels,* one silver bowl of seventy shekels, after the shekel of the sanctuary; both of them full *of* fine flour mingled with oil for a meat offering:

80 One golden spoon of ten *shekels,* full *of* incense:

81 One young bullock, one ram, one lamb of the first year, for a burnt offering:

82 One kid of the goats for a sin offering:

83 And for a sacrifice of peace offerings, two oxen, five rams, five he goats, five lambs of the first year: this *was* the offering of Ahira the son of Enan.

84 ¶ This *was* [a]the dedication of the altar, in the day when it was anointed, by [b]the princes of Israel: twelve chargers of silver, twelve silver bowls, twelve spoons of gold:

85 Each charger of silver *weighing* an hundred and thirty *shekels,* each bowl seventy: all the silver vessels *weighed* two thousand and four hundred *shekels,* after the [a]shekel of the sanctuary:

86 The golden spoons *were* twelve, full *of* incense, *weighing* ten *shekels* apiece, after the shekel of the sanctuary: all the gold of the spoons *was* an hundred and twenty *shekels.*

87 All the oxen for the burnt offering *were* twelve bullocks, the rams twelve, the lambs of the first year twelve, with their meat offering: and the kids of the goats for sin offering twelve.

88 And all the oxen for the sacrifice of the peace offerings *were* twenty and four bullocks, the rams sixty, the he goats sixty, the lambs of the first year sixty. This *was* the dedication of the altar, after *that* it was [a]anointed.

7:84–88 The totals of the 12 sets of gifts.

The candlestick

89 ¶ And when Moses was gone into the tabernacle of the congregation [a]to speak with [1]him, then he heard [b]the voice of one speaking unto him from off the mercy seat that *was* upon the ark of Testimony, from between the two cherubims: and he spake unto him.

8 And the LORD spake unto Moses, saying,
2 Speak unto Aaron, and say unto him, When thou [a]lightest the lamps, the seven lamps shall give light over against the candlestick.

3 And Aaron did so; he lighted the lamps thereof over against the candlestick, as the LORD commanded Moses.

4 [a]And this work of the candlestick *was of* beaten gold, unto the shaft thereof, unto the flowers thereof, *was* [b]beaten work: [c]according unto the pattern which the LORD had shewed Moses, so he made the candlestick.

Purification of the Levites

5 ¶ And the LORD spake unto Moses, saying,

6 Take the Levites from among the children of Israel, and cleanse them.

7 And thus shalt thou do unto them, to cleanse them: Sprinkle [a]water of purifying upon them, and [b][1]let them shave all their flesh, and let them wash their clothes, and *so* make themselves clean.

8 Then let them take a young bullock with [a]his meat offering, *even* fine flour mingled with oil, and another young bullock shalt thou take for a sin offering.

9 [a]And thou shalt bring the Levites before the tabernacle of the congregation: [b]and thou shalt gather the whole assembly of the children of Israel together:

10 And thou shalt bring the Levites before the LORD: and the children of Israel [a]shall put their hands upon the Levites:

11 And Aaron shall [1]offer the Levites before the LORD *for* an [2]offering of the children of Israel, that [3]they may execute the service of the LORD.

12 [a]And the Levites shall lay their hands upon the heads of the bullocks: and thou shalt offer the one *for* a sin offering, and the other *for* a burnt offering, unto the LORD, to make an atonement for the Levites.

13 And thou shalt set the Levites before Aaron, and before his sons, and offer them *for* an offering unto the LORD.

14 Thus shalt thou separate the Levites from among the children of Israel: and the Levites shall be [a]mine.

15 And after that shall the Levites go in to do the service of the tabernacle of the congregation: and thou shalt cleanse them, and [a]offer them *for* an offering.

16 For they *are* wholly given unto me from among the children of Israel; [a]instead of such as open every womb, *even instead of* the firstborn of all the children of Israel, have I taken them unto me.

17 [a]For all the firstborn of the children of Israel *are* mine, *both* man and beast: on the day that I smote every firstborn in the land of Egypt, I sanctified them for myself.

18 And I have taken the Levites for all the firstborn of the children of Israel.

19 And [a]I have given the Levites *as* [1]a gift to Aaron and to his sons from among the children of Israel, to do the service of the children of Israel in the tabernacle of the congregation, and to make an atonement for the children of Israel: [b]that there be no plague among the children of Israel, when the children of Israel come nigh unto the sanctuary.

20 And Moses, and Aaron, and all the congregation of the children of Israel, did to the Levites according unto all that the LORD commanded Moses concerning the Levites, so did the children of Israel unto them.

21 [a]And the Levites were purified, and they washed their clothes; and Aaron offered them *as* an offering before the LORD; and Aaron made an atonement for them to cleanse them.

22 [a]And after that went the Levites in to do their service in the tabernacle of the congregation before Aaron, and before his sons: [b]as the LORD had commanded Moses concerning the Levites, so did they unto them.

23 ¶ And the LORD spake unto Moses, saying,

7:89 [1]That is, *God* [a]Ex. 33:9,11 [b]Ex. 25:22
8:2 [a]Ex. 25:37; 40:25
8:4 [a]Ex. 25:31 [b]Ex. 25:18 [c]Ex. 25:40
8:7 [1]Heb. *let them cause a rasor to pass over, etc.* [a]ch. 19:9,17,18 [b]Lev. 14:8,9
8:8 [a]Lev. 2:1
8:9 [a]See Ex. 29:4; 40:12 [b]Lev. 8:3
8:10 [a]Lev. 1:4
8:11 [1]Heb. *wave* [2]Heb. *wave offering* [3]Heb. *they may be to execute, etc.*
8:12 [a]Ex. 29:10
8:14 [a]ch. 3:45; 16:9
8:15 [a]ver. 11,13
8:16 [a]ch. 3:12,45
8:17 [a]Ex. 13:2,12,13,15; ch. 3:13; Luke 2:23
8:19 [1]Heb. *given* [a]ch. 3:9 [b]ch. 1:53; 16:46; 18:5; 2 Chr. 26:16
8:21 [a]ver. 7
8:22 [a]ver. 15 [b]ver. 5

7:89 The climax: Communion is established between the Lord and His prophet. The people have an advocate with God.
8:2 *over against the candlestick.* The area of the holy place in the tabernacle (see Ex 25:37; 26:33; 27:21).
8:5–26 Describes the cleansing of the Levites and may be compared with the account of the ordination of Aaron and his sons to the priesthood (Lev 8). The Levites are helpers to the priests, and the language describing their consecration is somewhat different from that of the priests. The priests were made holy, the Levites clean; the priests were anointed and washed, the Levites sprinkled; the priests were given new garments, the Levites washed theirs; blood was applied to the priests, it was waved over the Levites.
8:7 *shave all their flesh.* Symbolic of the completeness of their cleansing, as in the case of the ritual cleansing of one cured of skin disease (Lev 14:8).
8:10 *children of Israel shall put their hands upon the Levites.* The Levites were substitutes for the nation; by laying hands on them, the other people of the nation were acknowledging this substitutionary act (see vv. 16–18).
8:16 *unto me.* See note on 3:9.
8:19 *I have given the Levites as a gift to Aaron and to his sons.* The Levites were given to the Lord for His exclusive use (see v. 14). Now the Lord gives His Levites to the priests as their aides for the work of ministry in the tabernacle worship. *that there be no plague among the children of Israel.* The Levites were a protective hedge for the community against trespassing in the sacred precincts of the tabernacle (see note on 1:53).
8:20 *according unto all that the LORD commanded Moses.* See vv. 4,22; 1:54; 2:34; 3:16,51; 4:49; 5:4; 9:5,23. The implicit obedience of Moses and the Israelites to God's commands in the areas of ritual and regimen stands in sharp contrast to the people's complaints against the Lord's loving character and to their breaches of faith that begin in ch. 11.

24 This *is it* that *belongeth* unto the Levites: [a]from twenty and five years old and upward they shall go in [1]to wait upon the service
of the tabernacle of the congregation:
25 And from the age of fifty years they shall
[1]cease waiting upon the service *thereof,* and
shall serve no more:
26 But shall minister with their brethren
in the tabernacle of the congregation, [a]to keep
the charge, and shall do no service. Thus shalt
thou do unto the Levites touching their
charge.

The passover command

9 And the LORD spake unto Moses in the
wilderness of Sinai, in the first month of
the second year after they were come out of
the land of Egypt, saying,
2 Let the children of Israel also keep [a]the
passover at his appointed season.
3 In the fourteenth day of this month, [1]at
even, ye shall keep it in his appointed season:
according to all the rites of it, and according to
all the ceremonies thereof, shall ye keep it.
4 And Moses spake unto the children of Israel, that they should keep the passover.
5 And [a]they kept the passover on the fourteenth day of the first month at even in the
wilderness of Sinai: according to all that the
LORD commanded Moses, so did the children
of Israel.
6 ¶ And there were *certain* men, who were
[a]defiled by the dead body of a man, that they
could not keep the passover on that day: [b]and
they came before Moses and before Aaron on
that day:
7 And those men said unto him, We *are* defiled by the dead body of a man: wherefore are
we kept back, that *we* may not offer an offering of the LORD in his appointed season among
the children of Israel?
8 And Moses said unto them, Stand still,
and [a]I will hear what the LORD will command
concerning you.
9 ¶ And the LORD spake unto Moses, saying,
10 Speak unto the children of Israel, saying, If any man of you or of your posterity shall
be unclean by reason of a dead body, or *be* in a
journey afar off, yet he shall keep the passover
unto the LORD.
11 [a]The fourteenth day of the second
month at even they shall keep it, *and* [b]eat it
with unleavened bread and bitter *herbs.*
12 [a]They shall leave none of it unto the
morning, [b]nor break any bone of it: [c]according
to all the ordinances of the passover they shall
keep it.
13 But the man that *is* clean, and is not in
a journey, and forbeareth to keep the passover,
even the same soul [a]shall be cut off from
among his people: because he [b]brought not
the offering of the LORD in his appointed season, that man shall [c]bear his sin.
14 And if a stranger shall sojourn among
you, and will keep the passover unto the LORD;
according to the ordinance of the passover, and
according to the manner thereof, so shall he
do: [a]ye shall have one ordinance, both for the
stranger, and for him that was born in the land.

The cloud of guidance

15 ¶ And [a]on the day that the tabernacle
was reared up, the cloud covered the tabernacle, *namely,* the tent of the Testimony: and [b]at
even there was upon the tabernacle as it were
the appearance of fire, until the morning.
16 So it was alway: the cloud covered it *by
day,* and the appearance of fire by night.

8:24 [1]Heb. *to war the warfare of, etc.* [a]See ch. 4:3; 1 Chr. 23:3,24,27
8:25 [1]Heb. *return from the warfare of the service*
8:26 [a]ch. 1:53
9:2 [a]Ex. 12:1; Lev. 23:5; ch. 28:16; Deut. 16:1,2
9:3 [1]Heb. *between the two evenings*
9:5 [a]Josh. 5:10
9:6 [a]ch. 5:2; 19:11,16; See John 18:28 [b]Ex. 18:15,19,26; ch. 27:2
9:8 [a]ch. 27:5
9:11 [a]2 Chr. 30:2,15 [b]Ex. 12:8
9:12 [a]Ex. 12:10 [b]Ex. 12:46; John 19:36 [c]Ex. 12:43
9:13 [a]Gen. 17:14; Ex. 12:15 [b]ver. 7 [c]ch. 5:31
9:14 [a]Ex. 12:49
9:15 [a]Ex. 40:34; Neh. 9:12,19; Ps. 78:14 [b]Ex. 13:21; 40:38

8:24 *twenty and five years old.* See note on 4:3. The age at which the Levites entered service was reduced to 20 by David (see 1 Chr 23:24,27), as the circumstances of their work had greatly changed by the time of the monarchy (see 1 Chr 23:26). It is difficult to imagine a change in circumstances between 4:3 and this verse, however. Therefore the rabbinical suggestion that these two verses indicate a five-year period of apprenticeship seems reasonable.

8:26 *but shall minister.* After a Levite had reached the mandatory retirement age of 50 (see v. 25), he was still free to assist his younger co-workers (perhaps at festivals), but he was no longer to do the difficult work he had done in his prime.

9:1–14 This unit is in four parts: (1) the command to keep the passover (vv. 1–5); (2) the question concerning those ceremonially unclean (vv. 6–8); (3) the response of the Lord—giving permission for legitimate delay, but judgment for willful neglect (vv. 9–13); (4) the rights of the alien at passover (v. 14). The first passover was held in Egypt (see Ex 12). The second is here at Sinai a year later. Because of Israel's rebellion and God's judgment on her (ch. 14), Israel would not celebrate the passover again until she entered the promised land (see Josh 5:10).

9:1 *first month of the second year.* The events of this chapter preceded the beginning of the census in ch. 1 (see 1:1).

9:3 *at even.* Traditional Jewish practice regards this period as the end of one day and the beginning of the next.

9:7 *wherefore are we kept back, that we may not offer an offering of the LORD* Those with ceremonial uncleanness had a keen desire to worship the Lord "in spirit and in truth" (John 4:24).

9:10 *he shall keep.* God's gracious provision for these people was an alternative day one month later (v. 11) so that they would not be excluded totally from the passover celebration. The Lord thus demonstrates the reality of the distance that uncleanness brings between a believer and his (or her) participation in the worship of the community, but He also provides a merciful alternative.

9:12 *nor break any bone of it.* When Jesus ("our passover," 1 Cor 5:7; cf. John 1:29) was crucified, it was reported that none of His bones was broken, in fulfillment of Scripture (John 19:36). See also Ex 12:46; Ps 34:20.

9:13 *forbeareth to keep . . . cut off.* The NT also issues grave warnings concerning the abuse or misuse of the celebration of the Lord's supper (1 Cor 11:28–30). See note on Ex 12:15.

9:14 *stranger.* Must first be circumcised before participating in the passover celebration (Ex 12:48).

9:15 *cloud covered the tabernacle.* See notes on Ex 13:21; 40:34. The cloud was the visible symbol of the Lord's presence hovering above the tabernacle. That this was no ordinary cloud is attested not only by its spontaneous appearance at the completion of the setting up of the tabernacle, but also by the fact that at night it had the appearance of fire. The Lord also directed the movements of His people by means of the cloud (vv. 17–18).

17 And when the cloud [a]was taken up
from the tabernacle, then after that the children of Israel journeyed: and in the place
where the cloud abode, there the children of
Israel pitched their tents.
18 At the commandment of the LORD the
children of Israel journeyed, and at the commandment of the LORD they pitched: [a]as long
as the cloud abode upon the tabernacle they
rested in the tents.
19 And when the cloud [1]tarried long upon
the tabernacle many days, then the children of
Israel [a]kept the charge of the LORD, and journeyed not.
20 And *so* it was, when the cloud was a
few days upon the tabernacle; according to the
commandment of the LORD they abode in their
tents, and according to the commandment of
the LORD they journeyed.
21 And *so* it was, when the cloud [1]abode
from even unto the morning, and *that* the
cloud was taken up in the morning, then they
journeyed: whether *it was* by day or by night
that the cloud was taken up, they journeyed.
22 Or *whether it were* two days, or a
month, or a year, that the cloud tarried upon
the tabernacle, remaining thereon, the children of Israel [a]abode in their tents, and journeyed not: but when it was taken up, they
journeyed.
23 At the commandment of the LORD they
rested in the tents, and at the commandment
of the LORD they journeyed: they [a]kept the
charge of the LORD, at the commandment of
the LORD by the hand of Moses.

The two silver trumpets

10 And the LORD spake unto Moses, saying,
2 Make thee two trumpets of silver; of a
whole piece thou shalt make them: that thou
mayest use them for the [a]calling of the assembly, and for the journeying of the camps.
3 And when [a]they shall blow with them,
all the assembly shall assemble themselves to
thee at the door of the tabernacle of the congregation.
4 And if they blow *but* with one *trumpet,*
then the princes, *which are* [a]heads of the
thousands of Israel, shall gather themselves
unto thee.
5 When ye blow an alarm, then [a]the camps
that lie on the east parts shall go forward.
6 When you blow an alarm the second
time, then the camps that lie [a]on the south
side shall take their journey: they shall blow
an alarm for their journeys.
7 But when the congregation is to be gathered together, [a]you shall blow, but you shall
not [b]sound an alarm.
8 [a]And the sons of Aaron, the priests, shall
blow with the trumpets; and they shall be to
you for an ordinance for ever throughout your
generations.
9 And [a]if ye go *to* war in your land against
the enemy that [b]oppresseth you, then ye shall
blow an alarm with the trumpets; and ye shall
be [c]remembered before the LORD your God,
and ye shall be saved from your enemies.
10 Also [a]in the day of your gladness, and in
your solemn days, and in the beginnings of
your months, ye shall blow with the trumpets
over your burnt offerings, and over the sacrifices of your peace offerings; that they may be
to you [b]for a memorial before your God: I *am*
the LORD your God.

The departure from Sinai

11 ¶ And it came to pass on the twentieth
day of the second month, in the second year,
that the cloud [a]was taken up from off the tabernacle of the Testimony.
12 And the children of Israel took [a]their
journeys out of the [b]wilderness of Sinai; and
the cloud rested in the [c]wilderness of Paran.
13 And they first took their journey [a]ac-
cording to the commandment of the LORD by
the hand of Moses.
14 [a]In the first *place* went the standard of
the camp of the children of Judah according to

9:17 [a]Ex. 40:36; ch. 10:11,33,34; Ps. 80:1
9:18 [a]1 Cor. 10:1
9:19 [1]Heb. *prolonged* [a]ch. 1:53; 3:8
9:21 [1]Heb. *was*
9:22 [a]Ex. 40:36,37
9:23 [a]ver. 19
10:2 [a]Is. 1:13
10:3 [a]Jer. 4:5; Joel 2:15
10:4 [a]Ex. 18:21; ch. 1:16; 7:2
10:5 [a]ch. 2:3
10:6 [a]ch. 2:10
10:7 [a]ver. 3 [b]Joel 2:1
10:8 [a]ch. 31:6; Josh. 6:4; 1 Chr. 15:24; 2 Chr. 13:12
10:9 [a]ch. 31:6; Josh. 6:5; 2 Chr. 13:14 [b]Judg. 2:18; 4:3; 6:9; 10:8,12 [c]Gen. 8:1; Ps. 106:4
10:10 [a]ch. 29:1; Lev. 23:24; 1 Chr. 15:24 [b]ver. 9
10:11 [a]ch. 9:17
10:12 [a]Ex. 40:36; ch. 2:9,16 [b]Ex. 19:1; ch. 1:1; 9:5 [c]Gen. 21:21; ch. 12:16; 13:3,26
10:13 [a]ver. 5,6
10:14 [a]ch. 2:3,9

9:18 *At the commandment of the LORD.* The lifting and settling of the cloud are identified with the Lord's command.

9:23 *kept the charge of the LORD.* The repetitious nature of vv. 15–23 enhances the expectation of continued complete obedience to the Lord's direction of Israel's movements through the wilderness. The role of Moses is mentioned for balance: Moses was the Lord's agent, who interpreted the movement of the cloud as signaling the movement of the people. The tragedy of their subsequent disobedience (ch. 11) is heightened by this paragraph on their obedience.

10:2 *trumpets.* Long, straight, slender metal tubes with flared ends. They were blown for order and discipline.

10:3 *when they shall blow.* Not only for assembling but also for marching (vv. 5–6), battle (v. 9) and festivals (v. 10). Since different signals were used (v. 7), a guild of priestly musicians was developed (v. 8). See Josh 6:4 for the use of seven trumpets of rams' horns (Hebrew *shophar*) in the battle of Jericho.

10:10 *in your solemn days . . . blow with the trumpets.* As an introit to prepare the people for communion with God. Later, David expanded the instruments to include the full orchestra in the worship of the Lord (see, e.g., 1 Chr 25), but he maintained the playing of the silver trumpets regularly before the ark of the covenant (1 Chr 16:6).

10:11–28 The structure of this section is: (1) v. 11, time frame; (2) vv. 12–13, introductory summary of setting out; (3) vv. 14–17, setting out of the tribes led by Judah (see 2:3–9); (4) vv. 18–21, setting out of the tribes led by Reuben (see 2:10–16); (5) vv. 22–24, setting out of the tribes led by Ephraim (see 2:18–24); (6) vv. 25–27, setting out of the tribes led by Dan (see 2:25–31); (7) v. 28, concluding summary of the line of march.

10:11 *twentieth day of the second month.* After 11 months in the region of mount Sinai, the people set out for the promised land, led by the cloud. This verse begins the second great section of the book of Numbers (10:11–22:1). Israel leaves on a journey that in a few months should have led to the conquest of Canaan.

10:14–27 The names of the leaders of the 12 tribes are given for the fourth time in the book (see 1:5–15; 2:3–31; 7:12–83). The order of the line of march is essentially the same as that in ch. 2. The new details are that the Gershonites and Merarites, who carry the tabernacle, follow the triad of the Judah tribes

their armies: and over his host *was* [b]Nahshon
the son of Amminadab.
15 And over the host of the tribe of the
children of Issachar *was* Nethaneel the son of
Zuar.
16 And over the host of the tribe of the
children of Zebulun *was* Eliab the son of Helon.
17 And [a]the tabernacle was taken down;
and the sons of Gershon and the sons of Merari set forward, [b]bearing the tabernacle.
18 ¶ And [a]the standard of the camp of Reuben set forward according to their armies: and
over his host *was* Elizur the son of Shedeur.
19 And over the host of the tribe of the
children of Simeon *was* Shelumiel the son of
Zurishaddai.
20 And over the host of the tribe of the
children of Gad *was* Eliasaph the son of Deuel.
21 And the Kohathites set forward, bearing
the [a]sanctuary: and [1]*the other* did set up the
tabernacle against they came.
22 ¶ And [a]the standard of the camp of the
children of Ephraim set forward according to
their armies: and over his host *was* Elishama
the son of Ammihud.
23 And over the host of the tribe of the
children of Manasseh *was* Gamaliel the son of
Pedahzur.
24 And over the host of the tribe of the
children of Benjamin *was* Abidan the son of
Gideoni.
25 ¶ And [a]the standard of the camp of the
children of Dan set forward, *which was* the
rereward of all the camps throughout their
hosts: and over his host *was* Ahiezer the son of
Ammishaddai.
26 And over the host of the tribe of the
children of Asher *was* Pagiel the son of Ocran.
27 And over the host of the tribe of the children of Naphtali *was* Ahira the son of Enan.
28 [a][1]Thus *were* the journeyings of the children of Israel according to their armies, when
they set forward.
29 ¶ And Moses said unto Hobab, the son
of [a]Raguel the Midianite, Moses' father in law,
We *are* journeying unto the place of which the
LORD said, [b]I will give it you: come thou with
us, and [c]we will do thee good: for [d]the LORD
hath spoken good concerning Israel.
30 And he said unto him, I will not go; but
I will depart to mine own land, and to my kindred.
31 And he said, Leave us not, I pray thee;
forasmuch as thou knowest how we are to encamp in the wilderness, and thou mayest be to
us [a]instead of eyes.
32 And it shall be, if thou go with us, yea,
it shall be, *that* [a]what goodness the LORD shall
do unto us, the same will we do unto thee.
33 ¶ And they departed from [a]the mount of
the LORD three days' journey: and the ark of
the covenant of the LORD [b]went before them
in the three days' journey, to search out a resting place for them.
34 And [a]the cloud of the LORD *was* upon
them by day, when they went out of the camp.
35 And it came to pass, when the ark set
forward, that Moses said,

[a]Rise up, LORD, and let thine enemies
be scattered;
And let them that hate thee flee before
thee.

36 ¶ And when it rested, he said,

Return, O LORD, *unto* the [1]many
thousands of Israel.

The people complain

11 And [a]*when* the people [1]complained,
[2]it displeased the LORD: and the LORD
heard *it;* [b]and his anger was kindled; and the
[c]fire of the LORD burnt among them, and consumed *them that were* in the uttermost parts
of the camp.
2 And the people cried unto Moses; and
when Moses [a]prayed unto the LORD, the fire
[1]was quenched.
3 And he called the name of the place
[1]Taberah: because the fire of the LORD burnt
among them.

God sends quails

4 ¶ And the [a]mixt multitude that *was*
among them [1]fell a lusting: and the children of

10:14 [a]ch. 2:3,9 [b]ch. 1:7
10:17 [a]ch. 1:51 [b]ch. 4:24,31
10:18 [a]ch. 2:16
10:21 [1]That is, *the Gershonites and the Merarites* [a]ch. 4:4,15; 7:9
10:22 [a]ch. 2:24
10:25 [a]ch. 2:31; Josh. 6:9
10:28 [1]Heb. *These* [a]ch. 2:34
10:29 [a]Ex. 2:18
10:29 [b]Gen. 12:7 [c]Judg. 1:16 [d]Gen. 32:12; Ex. 3:8
10:31 [a]Job 29:15
10:32 [a]Judg. 1:16
10:33 [a]See Ex. 3:1 [b]Deut. 1:33; Josh. 3:3,4,6; Ezek. 20:6
10:34 [a]Ex. 13:21; Neh. 9:12,19
10:35 [a]Ps. 68:1,2; 132:8
10:36 [1]Heb. *ten thousand thousands*
11:1 [1]Or, *were as it were complainers* [2]Heb. it was *evil in the ears of, etc.* [a]Deut. 9:22 [b]Ps. 78:21 [c]Lev. 10:2; 2 Ki. 1:12
11:2 [1]Heb. *sunk* [a]Jas. 5:16
11:3 [1]That is, *A burning*
11:4 [1]Heb. *lusted a lust* [a]As Ex. 12:38

(v. 17), and the Kohathites, who carry the holy things, follow the triad of the Reuben tribes (v. 21) (see diagram, p. 179).

10:14 *standard.* As in 2:3,10,18,25, each of the four triads of tribes had a standard or banner for rallying and organization.

‡10:29 *Hobab, the son of Raguel.* Thus Hobab was Moses' brother-in-law. *Raguel* [Greek Septuagint has Raguel, Hebrew has Reuel]. Jethro (see Ex 2:18; 3:1).

10:31 *be to us instead of eyes.* Judg 1:16 indicates that Hobab acceded to Moses' request.

10:33 *three days' journey.* Because of the huge numbers of people in the tribes of Israel, and because this was their first organized march, it is not likely that this first journey covered much territory.

10:35–36 Reinforces the portrayal of Israel as the Lord's army on the march, with the Lord in the vanguard.

10:35 Later used in the opening words of a psalm celebrating God's triumphal march from Sinai to Jerusalem (see Ps 68:1).

11:1 *the people complained.* The first ten chapters of Numbers repeatedly emphasize the complete obedience of Moses and the people to the dictates of the Lord. But only three days into their march, the people reverted to disloyal complaints. They had expressed the same complaints a year earlier only three days after their deliverance at the waters of the "Red sea" (Ex 15:22–27) and subsequently had complained about manna (Ex 16) and a lack of water (Ex 17:1–7). *fire of the LORD.* By God's mercy, this purging fire was limited to the outskirts of the camp. The phrase sometimes refers to fire ignited by lightning (as probably in 1 Ki 18:38).

11:3 *Taberah.* Means "burning."

11:4 *mixt multitude.* I.e. rabble. A term for the non-Israelite mixed group of people who followed the Israelites out of Egypt, pointing to a recurring source of complaints and trouble in the camp. Those who did not know the Lord and His mercies incited those who did know Him to rebel against Him. *Who shall give us flesh to eat?* As in Ex 16, the people began to complain about their diet, forgetting what God had done for them (see

Israel also [2]wept again, and said, [b]Who shall
give us flesh to eat?
5 [a]We remember the fish, which we did
eat in Egypt freely; the cucumbers, and the
melons, and the leeks, and the onions, and the
garlick:
6 But now [a]our soul *is* dried away: *there is*
nothing at all, beside *this* manna, *before* our
eyes.
7 And [a]the manna *was* as coriander seed,
and the [1]colour thereof as the colour of bdellium.
8 *And* the people went about, and gathered
it, and ground *it* in mills, or beat *it* in a mortar,
and baked *it* in pans, and made cakes *of* it: and
[a]the taste of it was as the taste of fresh oil.
9 And [a]when the dew fell upon the camp
in the night, the manna fell upon it.
10 Then Moses heard the people weep
throughout their families, every man in the
door of his tent: and [a]the anger of the LORD was
kindled greatly; Moses also was displeased.
11 [a]And Moses said unto the LORD, Wherefore hast thou afflicted thy servant? and
wherefore have I not found favour in thy sight,
that *thou* layest the burden of all this people
upon me?
12 Have I conceived all this people? have I
begotten them, that thou shouldest say unto
me, [a]Carry them in thy bosom, as a [b]nursing
father beareth the sucking child, unto the land
which thou [c]swarest unto their fathers?
13 [a]Whence should I have flesh to give

11:4 [2]Heb. *returned and wept* [b]Ps. 78:18; 1 Cor. 10:6
11:5 [a]Ex. 16:3
11:6 [a]ch. 21:5
11:7 [1]Heb. *eye of it as the eye of* [a]Ex. 16:14,31
11:8 [a]Ex. 16:31
11:9 [a]Ex. 16:13,14
11:10 [a]Ps. 78:21
11:11 [a]Deut. 1:12
11:12 [a]Is. 40:11 [b]Is. 49:23; 1 Thes. 2:7 [c]Gen. 26:3; 50:24; Ex. 13:5
11:13 [a]Mat. 15:33; Mark 8:4
11:14 [a]Ex. 18:18
11:15 [a]See 1 Ki. 19:4; Jonah 4:3 [b]Rev. 3:17
11:16 [a]See Ex. 24:1,9 [b]Deut. 16:18
11:17 [a]ver. 25; Ex. 19:20 [b]1 Sam. 10:6; 2 Ki. 2:15
11:18 [a]Ex. 19:10 [b]Ex. 16:7 [c]ver. 5; Acts 7:39
11:20 [1]Heb. *month of days* [a]Ps. 78:29; 106:15 [b]ch. 21:5
11:21 [a]Gen. 12:2; Ex. 12:37; ch. 1:46

unto all this people? for they weep unto me,
saying, Give us flesh, that we may eat.
14 [a]I am not able to bear all this people
alone, because *it is* too heavy for me.
15 And if thou deal thus with me, [a]kill me, I
pray thee, out of hand, if I have found favour in
thy sight; and let me not [b]see my wretchedness.
16 ¶ And the LORD said unto Moses, Gather
unto me [a]seventy men of the elders of Israel,
whom thou knowest to be the elders of the
people, and [b]officers over them; and bring
them unto the tabernacle of the congregation,
that they may stand there with thee.
17 And I will [a]come down and talk with
thee there: and [b]I will take of the spirit which
is upon thee, and will put *it* upon them; and
they shall bear the burden of the people with
thee, that thou bear *it* not thyself alone.
18 And say thou unto the people, [a]Sanctify
yourselves against to morrow, and ye shall eat
flesh: for you have wept [b]in the ears of the
LORD, saying, Who shall give us flesh to eat?
[c]for *it was* well with us in Egypt: therefore the
LORD will give you flesh, and ye shall eat.
19 Ye shall not eat one day, nor two days,
nor five days, neither ten days, nor twenty days;
20 [a]*But* even a [1]whole month, until it come
out at your nostrils, and it be loathsome unto
you: because that ye have despised the LORD
which *is* among you, and have wept before him,
saying, [b]Why came we forth out of Egypt?
21 And Moses said, [a]The people, amongst
whom I *am, are* six hundred thousand foot-

Ps 106:14). Certainly meat was not their common fare when they were slaves in Egypt. Now that they were in a new type of distress, the people romanticized the past and minimized its discomforts.

11:5 *fish . . . cucumbers . . . garlick.* Suggestive of the varieties of foods available in Egypt, in contrast to the diet of manna in the wilderness.

11:7 *manna.* Several naturalistic explanations for the manna have been given. For example, some equate it with the sticky and often granular honeydew that is excreted in Sinai in early June by various scale insects and that solidifies rapidly through evaporation. But no naturally occurring substance fits all the data of the text, and several factors suggest that manna was in fact the Lord's unique provision for His people in the wilderness: 1. The meaning of the Hebrew word for "manna" suggests that it was something unknown by the people at the time (see note on Ex 16:15). 2. The appearance and taste of the manna (see Ex 16:31) suggest that it is not something experienced by other peoples in other times. 3. The daily abundance of the manna and its regular periodic surge and slump (double amounts on the sixth day but none on the seventh day, Ex 16:22,27) hardly fit a natural phenomenon. 4. Its availability in ample supply for the entire wilderness experience, no matter where the people were (Ex 16:35), argues against a natural substance. 5. The keeping of a sample of the manna in the ark for future generations (Ex 16:33–34) suggests that it was a unique food.

11:10 *the anger of the LORD was kindled greatly.* The rejection of His gracious gift of heavenly food (called "bread from heaven" in Ex 16:4) angered the Lord. God had said that the reception of the manna by the people would be a significant test of their obedience (Ex 16:4). In view of the good things He was to give them (10:32), the people were expected to receive each day's supply of manna as a gracious gift of a merciful God, and a promise of abundance to come. In spurning the manna, the people had spurned the Lord. They had failed the test of faith. *Moses also was displeased.* The people's reaction to God's provision of manna was troubling to Moses as well. Instead of asking the Lord to understand the substance of their complaint, Moses asked Him why he was given such an ungrateful people to lead.

11:11–15 A prayer of distress and complaint, filled with urgency, irony and passion.

11:12 *Have I conceived all this people?* The implication is that the Lord conceived the people of Israel, that He was their nurse and that their promises were His. Moses asks that he be relieved of his mediatorial office, for "it is too heavy for me" (v. 14; cf. Elijah, 1 Ki 19). Even death, Moses asserts (v. 15), would be preferable to facing the continuing complaints of the people.

11:16–34 The Lord's response to the great distress of His prophet was twofold—mercy and curse: 1. There was mercy to Moses in that his responsibility was now to be shared by 70 leaders (vv. 16–17). 2. There was a curse on the people that was analogous to their complaint: They asked for meat and would now become sick with meat (vv. 18–34).

11:18 *ye shall eat flesh.* Their distress at the lack of variety in the daily manna had led the people to challenge the Lord's goodness. They had wailed for meat. Now they were going to get their fill of meat, so much that it would make them physically ill (v. 20).

11:20 *ye have despised the LORD.* The principal issue was not meat at all, but a failure to demonstrate proper gratitude to the Lord, who was in their midst and who was their constant source of good.

11:21 *people . . . are six hundred thousand footmen.* The num-

men; and thou hast said, I will give them flesh, that they may eat a whole month.

22 [a]Shall the flocks and the herds be slain for them, to suffice them? or shall all the fish of the sea be gathered together for them, to suffice them?

23 And the LORD said unto Moses, [a]Is the LORD's hand waxed short? thou shalt see now whether [b]my word shall come to pass unto thee or not.

24 And Moses went out, and told the people the words of the LORD, and [a]gathered the seventy men of the elders of the people, and set them round about the tabernacle.

25 And the LORD [a]came down in a cloud, and spake unto him, and took of the spirit that *was* upon him, and gave *it* unto the seventy elders: and it came to pass, that [b]when the spirit rested upon them, [c]they prophesied, and did not cease.

26 But there remained two *of the* men in the camp, the name of the one *was* Eldad, and the name of the other Medad: and the spirit rested upon them; and they *were* of them that were written, but [a]went not out unto the tabernacle: and they prophesied in the camp.

27 And there ran a young man, and told Moses, and said, Eldad and Medad do prophesy in the camp.

28 And Joshua the son of Nun, the servant of Moses, *one* of his young men, answered and said, My lord Moses, [a]forbid them.

29 And Moses said unto him, Enviest thou for my sake? [a]would God that all the LORD's people were prophets, *and* that the LORD would put his spirit upon them!

30 And Moses gat him into the camp, he and the elders of Israel.

31 ¶ And there went forth a [a]wind from the LORD, and brought quails from the sea, and let *them* fall by the camp, [1]as it were a day's journey on this side, and [2]as it were a day's journey on the other side, round about the camp, and as it were two cubits *high* upon the face of the earth.

32 And the people stood up all that day, and all *that* night, and all the next day, and they gathered the quails: he that gathered least gathered ten [a]homers: and they spread *them* all abroad for themselves round about the camp.

33 And while the [a]flesh *was* yet between their teeth, ere it was chewed, the wrath of the LORD was kindled against the people, and the LORD smote the people *with* a very great plague.

34 And he called the name of that place [1]Kibroth-hattaavah: because there they buried the people that lusted.

35 [a]*And* the people journeyed from Kibroth-hattaavah *unto* Hazeroth; and [1]abode at Hazeroth.

Miriam and Aaron

12 And Miriam and Aaron spake against Moses because of the [1]Ethiopian woman whom he had [2]married: for [a]he had [2]married an [1]Ethiopian woman.

2 And they said, Hath the LORD indeed spoken only by Moses? [a]hath he not spoken also by us? And the LORD [b]heard *it*.

3 (Now the man Moses *was* very meek, above all the men which *were* upon the face of the earth.)

4 [a]And the LORD spake suddenly unto Moses, and unto Aaron, and unto Miriam, Come out ye three unto the tabernacle of the congregation. And they three came out.

5 [a]And the LORD came down in the pillar of the cloud, and stood *in* the door of the tabernacle, and called Aaron and Miriam: and they both came forth.

11:22 [a]See 2 Ki. 7:2
11:23 [a]Is. 50:2; 59:1 [b]ch. 23:19; Ezek. 12:25
11:24 [a]ver. 16
11:25 [a]ver. 17; ch. 12:5 [b]See 2 Ki. 2:15 [c]See 1 Sam. 10:5,6,10; Joel 2:28; Acts 2:17,18; 1 Cor. 14:1
11:26 [a]See 1 Sam. 20:26; Jer. 36:5
11:28 [a]See Mark 9:38; Luke 9:49
11:29 [a]1 Cor. 14:5
11:31 [1]Heb. *as it were the way of, a day* [a]Ex. 16:13; Ps. 78:26-28
11:31 [2]Heb. *as it were the way of, a day*
11:32 [a]Ex. 16:36; Ezek. 45:11
11:33 [a]Ps. 78:30,31
11:34 [1]That is, *The graves of lust*
11:35 [1]Heb. *they were in, etc.* [a]ch. 33:17
12:1 [1]Or, *Cushite* [2]Heb. *taken* [a]Ex. 2:21
12:2 [a]Ex. 15:20; Mic. 6:4 [b]Gen. 29:33; ch. 11:1; 2 Ki. 19:4; Is. 37:4; Ezek. 35:12,13
12:4 [a]Ps. 76:9
12:5 [a]ch. 11:25; 16:19

bers are consistent: A marching force of this size suggests a total population of over 2,000,000 (see note on 1:46). Moses' distress at providing meat for this immense number of people (v. 22) is nearly comical—the task is impossible.

11:23 *Is the LORD's hand waxed short?* The human impossibility is an occasion for demonstrating the Lord's power.

‡11:25 *they prophesied.* Probably means that they gave ecstatic expression to an intense religious experience (see 1 Sam 10:5–6; 18:10; 19:20–24; 1 Ki 18:29). *and did not cease.* A literal rendering is "and they added not," seemingly meaning that they did not do it again. It seems that the temporary gift of prophecy to the elders was primarily to establish their credentials as Spirit-empowered leaders.

11:29 *Enviest thou for my sake?* Here the true spirit of Moses is demonstrated. Rather than being threatened by the public demonstration of the gifts of the Spirit by Eldad and Medad, Moses desired that all God's people might have the full gifts of the Spirit (cf. Phil 1:15–18). This verse is a fitting introduction to the inexcusable challenge to Moses' leadership in ch. 12.

11:31–32 Cf. the great provision of Jesus in the feeding of the 5,000 (John 6:5–13) and the 4,000 (Mat 15:29–39). In those cases the feeding was a demonstration of God's grace; in this instance it was of God's wrath.

11:34 *Kibroth-hattaavah.* See KJV marg. These graves marked the death camp of those who had turned against the food of the Lord's mercy.

‡12:1 *Ethiopian woman.* See KJV marg. Cush was the first son of Ham, the father of the southernmost peoples known to the Hebrews (Gen 10:6–7), living in the southern Nile valley. Moses' wife Zipporah may be referred to here (see Ex 2:15–22); if so, the term "Cushite" is used in contempt of her Midianite ancestry. It is more likely, however, that the reference is to a new wife taken by Moses, perhaps after the death of his first wife. The attack on the woman was a pretext; its focus was the prophetic gift of Moses and his special relationship with the Lord (v. 2).

12:2 *hath he not spoken also by us?* Of course He had. Mic 6:4 speaks of Moses, Aaron and Miriam as God's gracious provision for Israel. The prophetic gifting of the 70 elders (11:24–30) seems to have been the immediate provocation for the attack of Miriam and Aaron on their brother.

12:3 Perhaps a later addition to the text, alerting the reader to the great unfairness of the charge of arrogance against Moses.

12:4 *suddenly.* The abruptness of the Lord's response instilled terror (see Job 22:10; Is 47:11; Jer 4:20).

12:5 *came down.* Often used of divine manifestations. In 11:25 the Lord came down in grace; here and in Gen 11:5 He came down in judgment. In a sense every theophany (appearance of

6 And he said, Hear now my words: If
there be a prophet among you, *I* the LORD will
make myself known unto him [a]in a vision, *and*
will speak unto him [b]in a dream.
7 [a]My servant Moses *is* not so, [b]who *is*
faithful in all [c]mine house.
8 With him will I speak [a]mouth to mouth,
even [b]apparently, and not in dark speeches;
and [c]the similitude of the LORD shall he behold: wherefore then [d]were ye not afraid to
speak against my servant Moses?
9 And the anger of the LORD was kindled
against them; and he departed.
10 And the cloud departed from off the tabernacle; and [a]behold, Miriam *became* [b]lep-
rous, *white* as snow: and Aaron looked upon
Miriam, and behold, *she was* leprous.
11 And Aaron said unto Moses, Alas, my
lord, I beseech thee, [a]lay not the sin upon us,
wherein we have done foolishly, and wherein
we have sinned.
12 Let her not be [a]as one dead, of whom
the flesh is half consumed when he cometh
out of his mother's womb.
13 And Moses cried unto the LORD, saying,
Heal her now, O God, I beseech thee.
14 And the LORD said unto Moses, If her father had but spit in her face, should she not be
ashamed seven days? let her be [a]shut out from
the camp seven days, and after *that* let her be
received in *again.*
15 [a]And Miriam was shut out from the
camp seven days: and the people journeyed
not till Miriam was brought in *again.*
16 And afterward the people removed
from [a]Hazeroth, and pitched in the wilderness
of Paran.

Twelve spies sent to Canaan

13 And the LORD spake unto Moses, saying,
2 [a]Send thou men, that they may search
the land of Canaan, which I give unto the children of Israel: of every tribe of their fathers
shall ye send a man, every one a ruler among
them.
3 And Moses by the commandment of the
LORD sent them [a]from the wilderness of Paran:
all those men *were* heads of the children of Israel.
4 And these *were* their names: of the tribe
of Reuben, Shammua the son of Zaccur.
5 Of the tribe of Simeon, Shaphat the son
of Hori.
6 [a]Of the tribe of Judah, [b]Caleb the son of
Jephunneh.
7 Of the tribe of Issachar, Igal the son of Joseph.
8 Of the tribe of Ephraim, [a]Oshea the son
of Nun.
9 Of the tribe of Benjamin, Palti the son of
Raphu.
10 Of the tribe of Zebulun, Gaddiel the son
of Sodi.
11 Of the tribe of Joseph, *namely,* of the
tribe of Manasseh, Gaddi the son of Susi.
12 Of the tribe of Dan, Ammiel the son of
Gemalli.
13 Of the tribe of Asher, Sethur the son of
Michael.
14 Of the tribe of Naphtali, Nahbi the son
of Vophsi.
15 Of the tribe of Gad, Geuel the son of
Machi.
16 These *are* the names of the men which
Moses sent to spy out the land. And Moses
called [a]Oshea the son of Nun, Jehoshua.
17 And Moses sent them to spy out the
land of Canaan, and said unto them, Get you
up this *way* [a]southward, and go up into [b]the
mountain:
18 And see the land, what it *is;* and the
people that dwelleth therein, whether they *be*
strong or weak, few or many;
19 And what the land *is* that they dwell in,
whether it *be* good or bad; and what cities

12:6 [a]Gen. 46:2; Job 33:15; Ezek. 1:1; Dan. 8:2; 10:8,16; Luke 1:11; Acts 10:11,17; 22:17,18 [b]Gen. 31:10; 1 Ki. 3:5; Mat. 1:20
12:7 [a]Ps. 105:26 [b]Heb. 3:2,5 [c]1 Tim. 3:11
12:8 [a]Ex. 33:11; Deut. 34:10 [b]1 Cor. 13:12 [c]Ex. 33:19 [d]2 Pet. 2:10; Jude 8
12:10 [a]Deut. 24:9 [b]2 Ki. 5:27; 15:5; 2 Chr. 26:19,20
12:11 [a]2 Sam. 24:10; Prov. 30:32
12:12 [a]Ps. 88:4
12:14 [a]Lev. 13:46; ch. 5:2,3
12:15 [a]Deut. 24:9; 2 Chr. 26:20,21
12:16 [a]ch. 11:35; 33:18
13:2 [a]ch. 32:8; Deut. 1:22
13:3 [a]ch. 12:16; 32:8; Deut. 1:19; 9:23
13:6 [a]ch. 34:19; 1 Chr. 4:15 [b]ver. 30; ch. 14:6,30; Josh. 14:6,7,13,14; Judg. 1:12
13:8 [a]ver. 16
13:16 [a]ver. 8; Ex. 17:9; ch. 14:6
13:17 [a]ver. 21 [b]Judg. 1:9

God) is a picture and promise of the grand theophany, the incarnation of Jesus, both in grace and in judgment.

12:6–8 The poetic cast of these words adds a sense of solemnity to them. The point of the poem is clear: All true prophetic vision is from the Lord, but in the case of Moses his position and faithfulness enhance his special relationship with the Lord.

12:7 *My servant.* See notes on Ex 14:31; Ps 18 title; Is 41:8–9; 42:1. *mine house.* The household of God's people Israel.

12:8 *apparently, and not in dark speeches.* God's revelation does not come with equal clarity to His servants. There may be oracles of the Lord that a prophet might not fully understand at the time; to him they may be riddles and mysteries (cf. 1 Pet 1:10–11). But to Moses, God spoke with special clarity, as though face to face (see also Deut 34:10).

12:10 *leprous.* See note on Lev 13:2. Miriam, the principal offender against her brother Moses, has become an outcast, as she now suffers from a skin disease that would exclude her from the community of Israel (see 5:1–4).

12:11 *my lord, I beseech thee.* Aaron's repentance for the sin of presumption is touching, both in its intensity and in his concern for his (and Moses') sister.

12:14 *be ashamed seven days.* An act of public rebuke (see Deut 25:9) demands a period of public shame. A period of seven days was a standard time for uncleanness occasioned by being in contact with a dead body (see 19:11,14,16).

12:16 *wilderness of Paran.* The southernmost region of the promised land. The people's opportunity to conquer the land was soon to come.

13:2 *search the land of Canaan.* The use of spies was a common practice in the ancient Near East (see note on Josh 2:1–24). From Deut 1:22–23 it appears that this directive of the Lord was in response to the people's request. Thus the very sending of the spies was an expression of God's grace.

13:4–15 The names listed here are different from those in chs. 1–2; 7; 10. Presumably the tribal leaders in the four earlier lists were older men. The task for the spies called for men who were younger and more robust, but no less respected by their peers.

13:16 *Moses called Oshea* [Hoshea] *the son of Nun, Jehoshua* [Joshua]. A parenthetical statement anticipating the later prominence of Joshua. The reader is alerted to the significance of this name in the list of the spies; here is a man of destiny. Hoshea means "salvation"; Joshua means "The LORD saves" ("Jesus" is the Greek form of Hebrew "Joshua").

13:17–20 Moses' instruction to the 12 spies was comprehensive;

they be that they dwell in, whether in tents, or
in strong holds;
20 And what the land *is,* whether it *be* [a]fat
or lean, whether there be wood therein, or
not. And [b]be ye of good courage, and bring of
the fruit of the land. Now the time *was* the
time of the first ripe grapes.
21 So they went up, and searched the land
[a]from the wilderness of Zin unto [b]Rehob, as
men come to Hamath.
22 And they ascended by the south, and
came unto Hebron; where [a]Ahiman, Sheshai,
and Talmai, [b]the children of Anak, *were.* (Now
[c]Hebron was built seven years before [d]Zoan in
Egypt.)
23 [a]And they came unto the [1]brook of Eshcol, and cut down from thence a branch with
one cluster of grapes, and they bare it between
two upon a staff; and *they brought* of the
pomegranates, and of the figs.
24 The place was called the [1]brook [2]Esh-
col, because of the cluster of grapes which the
children of Israel cut down from thence.
25 And they returned from searching of
the land after forty days.

The spies return

26 ¶ And they went and came to Moses,
and to Aaron, and to all the congregation of
the children of Israel, [a]unto the wilderness of
Paran, to [b]Kadesh; and brought back word
unto them, and unto all the congregation, and
shewed them the fruit of the land.
27 And they told him, and said, We came
unto the land whither thou sentest us, and
surely it floweth with [a]milk and honey; [b]and
this *is* the fruit of it.
28 Nevertheless [a]the people *be* strong that
dwell in the land, and the cities *are* walled,
and very great: and moreover we saw [b]the
children of Anak there.

13:20 [a]Neh. 9:25,35; Ezek. 34:14 [b]Deut. 31:6,7,23
13:21 [a]ch. 34:3; Josh. 15:1 [b]Josh. 19:28
13:22 [a]Josh. 15:13,14 [b]ver. 33 [c]Josh. 21:11 [d]Ps. 78:12; Is. 19:11
13:23 [1]Or, *valley* [a]Deut. 1:24,25
13:24 [1]Or, *valley* [2]That is, *A cluster of grapes*
13:26 [a]ver. 3 [b]ch. 20:1; Deut. 1:19; Josh. 14:6
13:27 [a]Ex. 3:8 [b]Deut. 1:25
13:28 [a]Deut. 1:28 [b]ver. 33
13:29 [a]Ex. 17:8; Judg. 6:3
13:30 [a]See ch. 14:6,24
13:31 [a]ch. 32:9; Deut. 1:28; Josh. 14:8
13:32 [1]Heb. *men of statures* [a]ch. 14:36,37 [b]Amos 2:9
13:33 [a]Deut. 9:2 [b]Is. 40:22 [c]1 Sam. 17:42
14:1 [a]ch. 11:4
14:2 [a]Ex. 16:2 [b]See ver. 28,29
14:4 [a]Neh. 9:17 [b]See Deut. 17:16; Acts 7:39
14:5 [a]ch. 16:4,22

29 [a]The Amalekites dwell in the land of
the south: and the Hittites, and the Jebusites,
and the Amorites, dwell in the mountains: and
the Canaanites dwell by the sea, and by the
coast of Jordan.
30 And [a]Caleb stilled the people before
Moses, and said, Let us go up at once, and possess it; for we are well able to overcome it.
31 [a]But the men that went up with him
said, We be not able to go up against the people; for they *are* stronger than we.
32 And they [a]brought up an evil report of
the land which they had searched unto the
children of Israel, saying, The land, through
which we have gone to search it, *is* a land that
eateth up the inhabitants thereof; and [b]all the
people that we saw in it *are* [1]men of a great
stature.
33 And there we saw the giants, [a]the sons
of Anak, *which come* of the giants: and we
were in our own sight [b]as grasshoppers, and
so we were [c]in their sight.

The rebellion of Israel

14 And all the congregation lifted up
their voice, and cried; and [a]the people wept that night.
2 [a]And all the children of Israel murmured
against Moses and against Aaron: and the
whole congregation said unto them, Would
God that we had died in the land of Egypt! or
[b]would God we had died in this wilderness!
3 And wherefore *hath* the LORD brought us
unto this land, to fall by the sword, *that* our
wives and our children should be a prey? were
it not better for us to return into Egypt?
4 And they said one to another, [a]Let us
make a captain, and [b]let us return into Egypt.
5 Then [a]Moses and Aaron fell on their
faces before all the assembly of the congregation of the children of Israel.

a thorough report of the land and its produce and the peoples and their towns was required in their reconnaissance mission.

13:21 *searched the land.* The journey of the spies began in the southernmost extremity of the land (the wilderness of Zin) and took them to the northernmost point (Rehob, near Lebo Hamath; see 34:8). This journey of about 250 miles each way took them 40 days (v. 25), perhaps a round number.

13:22 *Hebron.* The first city the spies came to in Canaan. The parenthetical comment about the city's being built seven years before Zoan in Egypt may have been prompted by their amazement at the size and fortifications of the city that was so closely associated with the lives of their ancestors four centuries before this time (see Gen 13:14–18; 14:13; 23:2; 25:9; 35:27–29; 50:13). In the stories of the ancestors of their people, Hebron had not been a great city, but a dwelling and trading place for shepherds and herdsmen. *children of Anak.* Three notable Anak descendants are mentioned as living at Hebron. The Anakim were men of great stature; their physical size brought fear to the people (see vv. 32–33). In a later day of faith, Caleb was to drive them from their city (Josh 15:14; Judg 1:10).

‡13:23 *brook of Eshcol.* "Eshcol" means "cluster." This "brook," or valley is near Hebron; presumably the spies cut the cluster of grapes on their return journey. The size of the grape cluster should have indicated the goodness of the land God was giving them.

13:26–29 The first part of the spies' report was truthful, but the goodness of the land was offset in their fearful eyes by the powerful peoples who lived there.

13:30 *Caleb stilled the people.* Only Caleb and Hoshea (Joshua) gave a report prompted by faith in God.

13:32 *evil report of the land.* The promised land was a good land, a gracious gift from God. By speaking bad things about it, the faithless spies were speaking evil of the Lord (cf. 10:29).

‡13:33 Their words became exaggerations and distortions. The Anakim were now said to be Nephilim (see note on Gen 6:4). The reference to the Nephilim seems deliberately intended to evoke fear. The term "Nephalim" also had come to be used of "giants" in general, and does not refer to the same people as Gen 6:4. The exaggeration of the faithless led to their final folly: "we were in our own sight as grasshoppers."

14:1 *all . . . the people wept.* The frightening words of the faithless spies led to mourning by the entire community and to their great rebellion against the Lord. They forgot all the miracles the Lord had done for them, they despised His mercies, and they spurned His might. In their ingratitude they preferred death (v. 2).

14:3 *children.* The most reprehensible charge against God's grace was that concerning their children. Only their children would survive (see vv. 31–33).

6 [a]And Joshua the son of Nun, and Caleb
the son of Jephunneh, *which were* of them
that searched the land, rent their clothes:
7 And they spake unto all the company of
the children of Israel, saying, [a]The land,
which we passed through to search it, *is* an exceeding good land.
8 If the LORD [a]delight in us, then he will
bring us into this land, and give it us; [b]a land
which floweth with milk and honey.
9 Only [a]rebel not ye against the LORD, [b]nei-
ther fear ye the people of the land; for [c]they *are*
bread for us: their [1]defence is departed from
them, [d]and the LORD *is* with us: fear them not.
10 [a]But all the congregation bade stone
them with stones. And [b]the glory of the LORD
appeared in the tabernacle of the congregation
before all the children of Israel.
11 And the LORD said unto Moses, How
long will this people [a]provoke me? and how
long will it be ere they [b]believe me, for all the
signs which I have shewed among them?
12 I will smite them with the pestilence,
and disinherit them, and [a]will make of thee a
greater nation and mightier than they.
13 And [a]Moses said unto the LORD, Then
the Egyptians shall hear *it,* (for thou broughtest
up this people in thy might from among them;)
14 And they will tell *it* to the inhabitants of
this land: [a]*for* they have heard that thou LORD
art among this people, that thou LORD *art* seen
face to face, and *that* [b]thy cloud standeth over
them, and *that* thou goest before them, by day
time in a pillar of a cloud, and in a pillar of fire
by night.
15 Now *if* thou shalt kill *all* this people as
one man, then the nations which have heard
the fame of thee will speak, saying,
16 Because the LORD was not [a]able to bring
this people into the land which he sware unto
them, therefore he hath slain them in the
wilderness.
17 And now, I beseech thee, let the power
of my Lord be great, according as thou hast
spoken, saying,
18 The LORD *is* [a]longsuffering, and of great

14:6 [a]ch. 13:6,8
14:7 [a]ch. 13:27
14:8 [a]Deut. 10:15; 2 Sam. 15:25,26; 1 Ki. 10:9; Ps. 147:11 [b]ch. 13:27
14:9 [1]Heb. *shadow* [a]Deut. 9:7,23,24 [b]Deut. 7:18 [c]ch. 24:8 [d]Gen. 48:21; Deut. 20:1,3,4; 31:6,8
14:10 [a]Ex. 17:4 [b]Ex. 16:10; Lev. 9:23
14:11 [a]ver. 23; Ps. 95:8; Heb. 3:8 [b]Deut. 9:23; Ps. 78:22,32,42; John 12:37
14:12 [a]Ex. 32:10
14:13 [a]Ex. 32:12; Ezek. 20:9,14
14:14 [a]Ex. 15:14 [b]Ex. 13:21; Neh. 9:12
14:16 [a]Deut. 9:28
14:18 [a]Ex. 34:6,7
14:18 [a]Ex. 34:6,7 [b]Ex. 20:5
14:19 [1]Or, *hitherto* [a]Ex. 34:9 [b]Ps. 106:45 [c]Ps. 78:38
14:20 [a]1 John 5:14-16
14:21 [a]Ps. 72:19
14:22 [a]Deut. 1:35; Heb. 3:17 [b]Gen. 31:7
14:23 [1]Heb. *If they see the land* [a]ch. 32:11; Ezek. 20:15
14:24 [a]Josh. 14:6,8,9,14 [b]ch. 32:12
14:25 [a]Deut. 1:40
14:27 [a]Ex. 16:28 [b]Ex. 16:12
14:28 [a]ver. 21; Deut. 1:35; Heb. 3:17 [b]See ver. 2
14:29 [a]ch. 1:45; 26:64
14:30 [1]Heb. *lifted up my hand* [a]ver. 38; Deut. 1:36,38

mercy, forgiving iniquity and transgression,
and by no means clearing *the guilty,* [b]visiting
the iniquity of the fathers upon the children
unto the third and fourth *generation.*
19 [a]Pardon, I beseech thee, the iniquity of
this people [b]according unto the greatness of
thy mercy, and [c]as thou hast forgiven this people, from Egypt even [1]until now.
20 And the LORD said, I have pardoned [a]ac-
cording to thy word:
21 But *as* truly *as* I live, [a]all the earth shall
be filled *with* the glory of the LORD.
22 [a]Because all *those* men which have
seen my glory, and my miracles, which I did in
Egypt and in the wilderness, and have tempted me *now* [b]these ten times, and have not
hearkened to my voice;
23 [a][1]Surely they shall not see the land
which I sware unto their fathers, neither shall
any of them that provoked me see it:
24 But my servant [a]Caleb, because he had
another spirit with him, and [b]hath followed
me fully, him will I bring into the land whereinto he went; and his seed shall possess it.
25 (Now the Amalekites and the Canaanites dwelt in the valley.) To morrow turn you,
[a]and get you *into* the wilderness *by* the way of
the Red sea.
26 ¶ And the LORD spake unto Moses and
unto Aaron, saying,
27 [a]How long *shall I bear* with this evil
congregation, which murmur against me? [b]I
have heard the murmurings of the children of
Israel, which they murmur against me.
28 Say unto them, [a]*As truly as* I live, saith
the LORD, [b]as ye have spoken in mine ears, so
will I do to you:
29 Your carcases shall fall in this wilderness; and [a]all that were numbered of you, according to your whole number, from twenty
years old and upward, which have murmured
against me,
30 Doubtless ye shall not come into the
land, *concerning* which I [1]sware to make you
dwell therein, [a]save Caleb the son of Jephunneh, and Joshua the son of Nun.

14:9 *the LORD is with us.* There are no walls, no fortifications, no factors of size or bearing, and certainly no gods that can withstand the onslaught of God's people when the Lord is with them.

14:10 *the glory of the LORD appeared.* The theophany (manifestation of God) must have been staggering in its sudden and intense display of His majesty and wrath.

14:11 *provoke me.* By refusing to believe in the Lord's power, especially in view of all the wonders they had experienced, the people of Israel were spurning Him.

14:12 *will make of thee a greater nation.* For the second time since the exodus, God speaks of starting over with Moses in creating a people faithful to Himself (see Ex 32:10).

14:13 *the Egyptians shall hear it.* Moses desires to protect the Lord's reputation. The enemies of God's people will charge the Lord with inability to complete His deliverance and will be contemptuous of His power.

14:17–19 Moses now moves from the Lord's reputation to His character, presenting a composite quotation of His own words of loyal love for and faithful discipline of His people (see Ex 20:6; 34:6–7).

14:22 *ten times.* Perhaps to be enumerated as follows: (1) Ex 14:10–12; (2) Ex 15:22–24; (3) Ex 16:1–3; (4) Ex 16:19–20; (5) Ex 16:27–30; (6) Ex 17:1–4; (7) Ex 32:1–35; (8) Num 11:1–3; (9) 11:4–34; (10) 14:3. But "ten times" may also be a way of saying "many times."

14:24 *my servant Caleb . . . had another spirit.* Caleb seems to be singled out; perhaps the words of vv. 7–9 were his, and he was joined in them by Joshua. Caleb's ultimate vindication came 45 years later (see note on 13:22; see also Josh 14:10).

14:28 *as ye have spoken . . . so will I do to you.* The people of Israel brought upon themselves their punishment. They had said that they would rather die in the wilderness (v. 2) than be led into Canaan to die by the sword. All those 20 years old or more, who were counted in the census, were to die in the wilderness (v. 29). The only exceptions would be Joshua and Caleb (v. 30). Only their children would survive (v. 31)—the children that the people said God would allow to die in the wilderness (v. 3).

31 [a]But your little ones, which ye said
should be a prey, them will I bring in, and they
shall know the land which [b]ye have despised.
32 But *as for* you, [a]your carcases, they
shall fall in this wilderness.
33 And your children shall [a][1]wander in
the wilderness [b]forty years, and [c]bear your
whoredoms, until your carcases be wasted in
the wilderness.
34 [a]After the number of the days *in* which
ye searched the land, *even* [b]forty days, each
day for a year, shall ye bear your iniquities,
even forty years, [c]and ye shall know my
[1]breach of promise.
35 [a]I the LORD have said, I will surely do it
unto all [b]this evil congregation, that are gathered together against me: in this wilderness
they shall be consumed, and there they shall
die.
36 [a]And the men, which Moses sent to
search the land, who returned, and made all
the congregation to murmur against him, by
bringing up a slander upon the land,
37 Even *those* men that did bring up the
evil report upon the land, [a]died by the plague
before the LORD.
38 [a]But Joshua the son of Nun, and Caleb
the son of Jephunneh, *which were* of the men
that went to search the land, lived *still.*
39 And Moses told these sayings unto all
the children of Israel: [a]and the people
mourned greatly.
40 ¶ And they rose up early in the morning,
and gat them up into the top of the mountain,
saying, Lo, [a]we *be here,* and will go up unto
the place which the LORD hath promised: for
we have sinned.
41 And Moses said, Wherefore now do ye
transgress [a]the commandment of the LORD?
but it shall not prosper.
42 [a]Go not up, for the LORD *is* not among
you; that ye be not smitten before your enemies.
43 For the Amalekites and the Canaanites
are there before you, and ye shall fall by the
sword: [a]because ye are turned away from the
LORD, therefore the LORD will not be with you.

14:31 [a]Deut. 1:39 [b]Ps. 106:24
14:32 [a]1 Cor. 10:5
14:33 [1]Or, *feed* [a]ch. 32:13; Ps. 107:40 [b]See Deut. 2:14 [c]Ezek. 23:35
14:34 [1]Or, *altering of my purpose* [a]ch. 13:25 [b]Ps. 95:10; Ezek. 4:6 [c]See 1 Ki. 8:56; Heb. 4:1
14:35 [a]ch. 23:19 [b]ver. 27,29; 1 Cor. 10:5
14:36 [a]ch. 13:31,32
14:37 [a]1 Cor. 10:10
14:38 [a]Josh. 14:6,10
14:39 [a]Ex. 33:4
14:40 [a]Deut. 1:41
14:41 [a]ver. 25; 2 Chr. 24:20
14:42 [a]Deut. 1:42
14:43 [a]2 Chr. 15:2
14:44 [a]Deut. 1:43
14:45 [a]ver. 43; Deut. 1:44 [b]ch. 21:3; Judg. 1:17
15:2 [a]ver. 18; Lev. 23:10; Deut. 7:1
15:3 [1]Heb. *separating* [a]Lev. 1:2,3 [b]Lev. 7:16; 22:18,21 [c]Lev. 23:8,12,36; ch. 28:19,27; Deut. 16:10 [d]Gen. 8:21; Ex. 29:18
15:4 [a]Lev. 2:1; 6:14 [b]Ex. 29:40; Lev. 23:13 [c]Lev. 14:10; ch. 28:5
15:5 [a]ch. 28:7,14
15:6 [a]ch. 28:12,14
15:8 [a]Lev. 7:11
15:9 [a]ch. 28:12,14
15:11 [a]ch. 28

44 [a]But they presumed to go up unto the
hill top: nevertheless the ark of the covenant
of the LORD, and Moses, departed not out of
the camp.
45 [a]Then the Amalekites came down, and
the Canaanites which dwelt in that hill, and
smote them, and discomfited them, *even* unto
[b]Hormah.

Offerings required of Israel

15 And the LORD spake unto Moses, saying,
2 [a]Speak unto the children of Israel, and
say unto them, When ye be come into the land
of your habitations, which I give unto you,
3 And [a]will make an offering by fire unto
the LORD, a burnt offering, or a sacrifice [b]in
[1]performing a vow, or in a freewill offering, or
[c]in your solemn feasts, to make a [d]sweet savour
unto the LORD, of the herd, or of the flock:
4 Then [a]shall he that offereth his offering
unto the LORD bring [b]a meat offering of a tenth
deal *of* flour mingled [c]with the fourth *part* of a
hin of oil.
5 [a]And the fourth *part* of a hin *of* wine for
a drink offering shalt thou prepare with the
burnt offering or sacrifice, for one lamb.
6 [a]Or for a ram, thou shalt prepare *for* a
meat offering two tenth deals *of* flour mingled
with the third *part* of a hin of oil.
7 And for a drink offering thou shalt offer
the third *part* of a hin *of* wine, *for* a sweet
savour unto the LORD.
8 And when thou preparest a bullock *for* a
burnt offering, or *for* a sacrifice in performing
a vow, or [a]peace offerings unto the LORD:
9 Then shall he bring [a]with a bullock a
meat offering of three tenth deals *of* flour mingled with half a hin of oil.
10 And thou shalt bring for a drink offering
half a hin *of* wine, *for* an offering made by fire,
of a sweet savour unto the LORD.
11 [a]Thus shall it be done for one bullock,
or for one ram, or for a lamb, or a kid.
12 According to the number that ye shall
prepare, so shall ye do to *every* one according
to their number.

14:34 The 40 days of the travels of the spies became the numerical pattern for their suffering: one year for one day—for 40 years they would recount their misjudgment, and for 40 years the people 20 years old or more would be dying, so that only the young generation might enter the land. Significantly, Israel's refusal to carry out the Lord's commission to conquer His land is the climactic act of rebellion for which God condemns Israel to die in the wilderness.

14:37 *those men that did bring up the evil report upon the land, died.* The judgment on the ten evil spies was immediate; the generation that they influenced would live out their lives in the wilderness.

14:40 *we . . . will go up.* Now, too late, the people determine to go up to the land they had refused. Such a course of action was doomed to failure. Not only was the Lord not with them; He was against them (v. 41). Their subsequent defeat (v. 45) was another judgment the rebellious people brought down upon their own heads.

15:1–41 This chapter is divided into three units, each introduced by the phrase, "The LORD spake unto Moses" (vv. 1,17,37). The people were under terrible judgment because they had disobeyed the specific commands of the Lord and had despised His character.

15:2 *When ye be come into the land.* The juxtaposition of this clause with the sad ending of ch. 14 is dramatic. The sins of the people were manifold; they would be judged. The grace and mercy of the Lord are magnified as He points to the ultimate realization of His ancient promise to Abraham (Gen 12:7), as well as to His continuing promise to the nation that they would indeed enter the land.

15:3–12 Grain and wine offerings were to accompany the offerings by fire; the grain was to be mixed with oil. The offerings increased in amounts with the increase of size of the sacrificial animal (vv. 6–12). These passages are the first to indicate that wine offerings must accompany all burnt and fellowship offerings.

13 All that are born of the country shall do these *things* after this manner, in offering an offering made by fire, of a sweet savour unto the LORD.

14 And if a stranger sojourn with you, or whosoever *be* among you in your generations, and will offer an offering made by fire, of a sweet savour unto the LORD; as ye do, so he shall do.

15 [a]One ordinance *shall be both* for you *of* the congregation, and also for the stranger that sojourneth *with you,* an ordinance for ever in your generations: as ye *are,* so shall the stranger be before the LORD.

16 One law and one manner shall be for you, and for the stranger that sojourneth with you.

17 ¶ And the LORD spake unto Moses, saying,

18 [a]Speak unto the children of Israel, and say unto them, When ye come into the land whither I bring you,

19 Then it shall be, *that* when ye eat of [a]the bread of the land, ye shall offer up a heave offering unto the LORD.

20 [a]Ye shall offer up a cake *of* the first of your dough *for* a heave offering: as *ye do* [b]the heave offering of the threshingfloor, so shall ye heave it.

21 Of the first of your dough ye shall give unto the LORD a heave offering in your generations.

Offering for unintentional sins

22 And [a]if ye have erred, and not observed all these commandments, which the LORD hath spoken unto Moses,

23 *Even* all that the LORD hath commanded you by the hand of Moses, from the day that the LORD commanded *Moses,* and henceforward among your generations;

24 Then it shall be, [a]if *ought* be committed by ignorance [1]without the knowledge of the congregation, that all the congregation shall offer one young bullock for a burnt offering, for a sweet savour unto the LORD, [b]with his meat offering, and his drink offering, according to the [2]manner, and [c]one kid of the goats for a sin offering.

25 [a]And the priest shall make an atonement for all the congregation of the children of Israel, and it shall be forgiven them; for it *is* ignorance: and they shall bring their offering, a sacrifice made by fire unto the LORD, and their sin offering before the LORD, for their ignorance:

26 And it shall be forgiven all the congregation of the children of Israel, and the stranger that sojourneth among them; seeing all the people were in ignorance.

27 And [a]if any soul sin through ignorance, then he shall bring a she goat of the first year for a sin offering.

28 [a]And the priest shall make an atonement for the soul that sinneth ignorantly, when he sinneth by ignorance before the LORD, to make an atonement for him; and it shall be forgiven him.

29 [a]You shall have one law for him that [1]sinneth through ignorance, *both for* him that is born amongst the children of Israel, and for the stranger that sojourneth among them.

30 [a]But the soul that doeth *ought* [1]presumptuously, *whether he be* born in the land, or a stranger, the same reproacheth the LORD; and that soul shall be cut off from among his people.

31 Because he hath [a]despised the word of the LORD, and hath broken his commandment, that soul shall utterly be cut off; [b]his iniquity *shall be* upon him.

Stoning the sabbath breaker

32 ¶ And while the children of Israel were in the wilderness, [a]they found a man that gathered sticks upon the sabbath day.

33 And they that found him gathering sticks brought him unto Moses and Aaron, and unto all the congregation.

34 And they put him [a]in ward, because it was not declared what should be done to him.

35 And the LORD said unto Moses, [a]The man shall be surely put to death: all the congregation shall [b]stone him with stones without the camp.

36 And all the congregation brought him without the camp, and stoned him with stones, and he died; as the LORD commanded Moses.

15:15 [a]ver. 29; Ex. 12:49; ch. 9:14
15:18 [a]ver. 2; Deut. 26:1
15:19 [a]Josh. 5:11,12
15:20 [a]Deut. 26:2,10; Prov. 3:9,10 [b]Lev. 2:14; 23:10,16
15:22 [a]Lev. 4:2
15:24 [1]Heb. *from the eyes* [2]Or, *ordinance* [a]Lev. 4:13 [b]ver. 8-10 [c]See Lev. 4:23
15:25 [a]Lev. 4:20
15:27 [a]Lev. 4:27,28
15:28 [a]Lev. 4:35
15:29 [1]Heb. *doth* [a]ver. 15
15:30 [1]Heb. *with a high hand* [a]Deut. 17:12; Ps. 19:13; Heb. 10:26
15:31 [a]2 Sam. 12:9; Prov. 13:13 [b]Lev. 5:1; Ezek. 18:20
15:32 [a]Ex. 31:14,15; 35:2,3
15:34 [a]Lev. 24:12
15:35 [a]Ex. 31:14,15 [b]Lev. 24:14; 1 Ki. 21:13; Acts 7:58

15:14 *stranger.* As in the case of the celebration of the passover (see note on 9:14), the alien had the same regulations as the native-born Israelite. The commonwealth of Israel would always be open to proselytes. Indeed, the charter of Israel's faith embraces all peoples of the earth (Gen 12:3).

15:20 *of the first of your dough.* This law also looks forward to the time when the Israelites would be in the land. The first of the threshed grain was to be made into a cake and presented to the Lord. This concept of the firstfruits is a symbol that all blessing is from the Lord and all produce belongs to Him.

15:22 *if ye have erred.* Sins may be unintentional, but they still need to be dealt with (see note on Lev 4:2). Such unintentional sins may be committed by the people as a whole (vv. 22–26) or by an individual (vv. 27–29).

15:30 *presumptuously.* Lit. "with a high hand." Unlike unintentional sins, for which there are provisions of God's mercy, one who sets his hand defiantly to despise the word of God and to blaspheme His name must be punished. This was the experience of the nation in ch. 14, and it is described in the case of an individual here in vv. 32–36. *cut off from among his people.* See note on Ex 12:15.

15:32 *gathered sticks upon the sabbath day.* The penalty for breaking the sabbath was death (v. 36; Ex 31:15; 35:2). As in the case of the willful blasphemer (Lev 24:10–16), the sabbath breaker was guilty of high-handed rebellion (see note on v. 30) and was judged with death. By the time of Christ, sabbath-keeping had become distorted to the point that its regulations were regarded as more important than the needs of people. Jesus confronted the Pharisees on this issue on several occasions (see, e.g., Mat 12:1–14). From their point of view, these regulations (vv. 32–36) gave them reasons to seek His death (Mat 12:14).

The fringes of remembrance

37 ¶ And the LORD spake unto Moses, saying,
38 Speak unto the children of Israel, and
bid [a]them that they make them fringes in the
borders of their garments throughout their
generations, and that they put upon the fringe
of the borders a ribband of blue:
39 And it shall be unto you for a fringe, that
ye may look upon it, and remember all the
commandments of the LORD, and do them; and
that ye [a]seek not after your own heart and your
own eyes, after which ye use [b]to go a whoring:
40 That ye may remember, and do all my
commandments, and be [a]holy unto your God.
41 I *am* the LORD your God, which brought
you out of the land of Egypt, to be your God: I
am the LORD your God.

The rebellion of Korah

16 Now [a]Korah, the son of Izhar, the
son of Kohath, the son of Levi, and
Dathan and Abiram, the sons of Eliab, and On,
the son of Peleth, sons of Reuben, took *men:*
2 And they rose up before Moses, with certain of the children of Israel, two hundred and
fifty princes of the assembly, [a]famous in the
congregation, men of renown:
3 And [a]they gathered themselves together
against Moses and against Aaron, and said
unto them, [1]*Ye take* too much upon you, seeing [b]all the congregation *are* holy, every one of
them, [c]and the LORD *is* among them: wherefore then lift you up yourselves above the congregation of the LORD?
4 And when Moses heard *it,* [a]he fell upon
his face:
5 And he spake unto Korah and unto all his
company, saying, Even to morrow the LORD
will shew who *are* his, and *who is* [a]holy; and
will cause *him* to come near unto him: even
him whom he hath [b]chosen will he cause to
[c]come near unto him.
6 This do; Take you censers, Korah, and all
his company;
7 And put fire therein, and put incense in

15:38 [a]Deut. 22:12; Mat. 23:5
15:39 [a]See Deut. 29:19 [b]Ps. 73:27; 106:39; Jas. 4:4
15:40 [a]Lev. 11:44,45; Rom. 12:1; Col. 1:22; 1 Pet. 1:15,16
16:1 [a]Ex. 6:21; ch. 26:9; 27:3; Jude 11
16:2 [a]ch. 26:9
16:3 [1]Heb. It is *much for you* [a]Ps. 106:16 [b]Ex. 19:6 [c]Ex. 29:45; ch. 14:14; 35:34
16:4 [a]ch. 14:5; 20:6
16:5 [a]ver. 3; Lev. 21:6-8,12,15 [b]Ex. 28:1; ch. 17:5; 1 Sam. 2:28 [c]Ezek. 40:46; 44:15,16
16:9 [a]1 Sam. 18:23; Is. 7:13 [b]ch. 3:41,45; 8:14; Deut. 10:8
16:11 [a]Ex. 16:8
16:13 [a]Ex. 2:14; Acts 7:27,35
16:14 [1]Heb. *bore out* [a]Ex. 3:8; Lev. 20:24
16:15 [a]Gen. 4:4,5 [b]1 Sam. 12:3; Acts 20:33
16:16 [a]ver. 6,7 [b]1 Sam. 12:3,7

them before the LORD to morrow: and it shall
be *that* the man whom the LORD doth choose,
he *shall be* holy: *ye take* too much upon you,
ye sons of Levi.
8 And Moses said unto Korah, Hear, I pray
you, ye sons of Levi:
9 *Seemeth it but* [a]a small thing unto you,
that the God of Israel hath [b]separated you
from the congregation of Israel, to bring you
near to himself to do the service of the tabernacle of the LORD, and to stand before the congregation to minister unto them?
10 And he hath brought thee near *to him,*
and all thy brethren the sons of Levi with thee:
and seek ye the priesthood also?
11 For which cause *both* thou and all thy
company *are* gathered together against the
LORD: [a]and what *is* Aaron, that ye murmur
against him?
12 And Moses sent to call Dathan and Abiram, the sons of Eliab: which said, We will not
come up:
13 *Is it* a small thing that thou hast brought
us up out of a land that floweth with milk and
honey, to kill us in the wilderness, except thou
[a]make thyself altogether a prince over us?
14 Moreover thou hast not brought us into
[a]a land that floweth with milk and honey, or
given us inheritance of fields and vineyards:
wilt thou [1]put out the eyes of these men? we
will not come up.
15 And Moses was very wroth, and said
unto the LORD, [a]Respect not thou their offering: [b]I have not taken one ass from them, neither have I hurt one of them.
16 And Moses said unto Korah, [a]Be thou
and all thy company [b]before the LORD, thou,
and they, and Aaron, to morrow:
17 And take every man his censer, and put
incense in them, and bring ye before the LORD
every man his censer, two hundred and fifty
censers; thou also, and Aaron, each *of you* his
censer.
18 And they took every man his censer,
and put fire in them, and laid incense thereon,

15:38 *fringes in the borders of their garments.* As one would walk along, the fringes [tassels] would swirl about at the edge of his garment (cf. v. 39), serving as excellent memory prods to obey God's commands (cf. Deut 6:4–9).

15:41 *I am the LORD your God, which brought you out.* The demands that God made upon His people were grounded in His act of redemption (see Ex 20:2 and note).

‡16:1–7 Earlier, Miriam and Aaron had led a rebellion against the leadership of Moses (ch. 12). Now Korah and his allies attack the leadership of Moses and Aaron. Korah was descended from Levi through Kohath. As a Kohathite, he had high duties in the service of the Lord at the tabernacle (see 4:1–20), but he desired more. His passion was to assume the role of priest, and he used deception to advance his claim. Korah was joined by the Reubenites, Dathan, Abiram and On, and about 250 other leaders of Israel who had their own complaints. Their charge against Moses and Aaron was "Ye take too much upon you" (v. 3) in taking the role of spiritual leadership of the people; "all the congregation are holy" (v. 3). To this abusive charge Moses retorts, "ye take too much upon you, ye sons of Levi" (v. 7), and sets up a trial by fire.

16:12 *Dathan and Abiram.* Their charge against Moses was that he had not led them into the land of promise. They claimed that Moses had in fact led the people "out of a land that floweth with milk and honey" (v. 13). By this strange alchemy, in their minds the land of Egypt has been transformed from prison to paradise.

16:15 *neither have I hurt one of them.* Moses' humanity is seen in his plea of innocence.

16:18–21 The trial was to be by fire: Which men would the Lord accept as His priests in the holy tabernacle? The 250 men allied with Korah came with arrogance to withstand Moses and Aaron at the entrance to the tabernacle. The revelation of the Lord's glory was sure and sudden (v. 19), with words of impending doom for the rebellious people (v. 21). The punishment was fittingly ironic. Those 250 men who dared to present themselves as priests before the Lord with fire in their censers were themselves put to death by fire (perhaps lightning) from the Lord (see v. 35).

and stood *in* the door of the tabernacle of the
congregation with Moses and Aaron.
19 And Korah gathered all the congregation against them unto the door of the tabernacle of the congregation: and [a]the glory of
the LORD appeared unto all the congregation.
20 And the LORD spake unto Moses and
unto Aaron, saying,
21 [a]Separate yourselves from among this
congregation, that I may [b]consume them in a
moment.
22 And they [a]fell upon their faces, and
said, O God, [b]the God of the spirits of all flesh,
shall one man sin, and wilt thou be wroth with
all the congregation?
23 And the LORD spake unto Moses, saying,
24 Speak unto the congregation, saying,
Get you up from about the tabernacle of Korah, Dathan, and Abiram.
25 And Moses rose up and went unto Dathan and Abiram; and the elders of Israel followed him.
26 And he spake unto the congregation,
saying, [a]Depart, I pray you, from the tents of
these wicked men, and touch nothing of
theirs, lest ye be consumed in all their sins.
27 So they gat up from the tabernacle of
Korah, Dathan, and Abiram, on every side:
and Dathan and Abiram came out, and stood
in the door of their tents, and their wives, and
their sons, and their little children.
28 And Moses said, [a]Hereby ye shall know
that the LORD hath sent me to do all these
works; for *I have* not *done them* [b]of mine own
mind.
29 If these *men* die [1]the common death of
all men, or if they be [a]visited after the visitation of all men; *then* the LORD hath not sent
me.
30 But if the LORD [1]make [a]a new thing,
and the earth open her mouth, and swallow
them up, with all that *appertain* unto them,
and they [b]go down quick into the pit; then ye
shall understand that these men have provoked the LORD.
31 [a]And it came to pass, as he had made an
end of speaking all these words, that the
ground clave asunder that *was* under them:
32 And the earth opened her mouth, and
swallowed them up, and their houses, and [a]all
the men that *appertained* unto Korah, and all
their goods.
33 They, and all that *appertained* to them,

16:19 [a]ver. 42; Ex. 16:7,10; Lev. 9:6,23; ch. 14:10
16:21 [a]ver. 45; See Gen. 19:17,22; Jer. 51:6 [b]ver. 45; Ex. 32:10; 33:5
16:22 [a]ver. 45; ch. 14:5 [b]ch. 27:16; Job 12:10; Eccl. 12:7; Heb. 12:9
16:26 [a]Gen. 19:12,14
16:28 [a]Ex. 3:12; John 5:36 [b]ch. 24:13; Ezek. 13:17; John 5:30; 6:38
16:29 [1]Heb. *as every man dieth* [a]Ex. 20:5; 32:34; Job 35:15
16:30 [1]Heb. *create a creature* [a]Job 31:3; Is. 28:21 [b]ver. 33; Ps. 55:15
16:31 [a]ch. 26:10; 27:3; Deut. 11:6; Ps. 106:17
16:32 [a]See ver. 17; ch. 26:11; 1 Chr. 6:22,37
16:35 [a]Lev. 10:2; ch. 11:1; Ps. 106:18 [b]ver. 17
16:37 [a]See Lev. 27:28
16:38 [a]Prov. 20:2; Hab. 2:10 [b]ch. 17:10; 26:10; Ezek. 14:8
16:40 [a]ch. 3:10; 2 Chr. 26:18
16:41 [a]ch. 14:2; Ps. 106:25
16:42 [a]Ex. 40:34 [b]ver. 19; ch. 20:6
16:45 [a]ver. 21,24 [b]ver. 22; ch. 20:6
16:46 [a]Lev. 10:6; ch. 8:19; 11:33; 1 Chr. 27:24

went down alive into the pit, and the earth
closed upon them: and they perished from
among the congregation.
34 And all Israel that *were* round about
them fled at the cry of them: for they said, Lest
the earth swallow us up *also.*
35 And there [a]came out a fire from the
LORD, and consumed [b]the two hundred and
fifty men that offered incense.
36 ¶ And the LORD spake unto Moses, saying,
37 Speak unto Eleazar the son of Aaron the
priest, that he take up the censers out of the
burning, and scatter thou the fire yonder; for
[a]they are hallowed.
38 The censers of these [a]sinners against
their own souls, let them make them broad
plates *for* a covering of the altar: for they offered them before the LORD, therefore they are
hallowed: [b]and they shall be a sign unto the
children of Israel.
39 And Eleazar the priest took the brasen
censers, wherewith they that were burnt had
offered; and they were made broad *plates for* a
covering of the altar:
40 *To be* a memorial unto the children of
Israel, [a]that no stranger, which *is* not of the
seed of Aaron, come near to offer incense before the LORD; that he be not as Korah, and as
his company: as the LORD said to him by the
hand of Moses.
41 ¶ But on the morrow [a]all the congregation of the children of Israel murmured against
Moses and against Aaron, saying, Ye have
killed the people of the LORD.
42 And it came to pass, when the congregation was gathered against Moses and against
Aaron, that they looked toward the tabernacle
of the congregation: and behold, [a]the cloud
covered it, and [b]the glory of the LORD appeared.
43 And Moses and Aaron came before the
tabernacle of the congregation.
44 And the LORD spake unto Moses, saying,
45 [a]Get you up from among this congregation, that I may consume them as in a moment. And [b]they fell upon their faces.
46 And Moses said unto Aaron, Take a
censer, and put fire therein from off the altar,
and put on incense, and go quickly unto the
congregation, and make an atonement for
them: [a]for there is wrath gone out from the
LORD; the plague is begun.

16:22 Here the magnanimity of Moses and Aaron is seen.

16:24 *Get you up from.* God's judgment was going to be severe, but He did not want to lash out against bystanders. It appears that Korah himself had left the 250 false priests and was standing with Dathan and Abiram to continue their opposition to Moses.

16:30 *new thing.* Moses wished to assure the people that the imminent judgment was the direct work of the Lord and not a chance event that might be interpreted differently. The opening of the earth to swallow the rebels was a sure sign of the wrath of God and the vindication of Moses and Aaron.

16:32 *swallowed them up, and their houses.* The sons of Korah did not die (26:11); apparently they did not join their father in his rash plan. The households of the other rebels died with them.

16:37 *take up the censers.* The true priests took the censers of the 250 deceased impostors from their charred remains and hammered them into bronze sheets for the altar as a memorial of the folly of a self-proclaimed priest (v. 40).

16:41 *all the congregation . . . murmured.* Again the community attacked Moses, unfairly charging him with the death of the Lord's people. Except for the intervention of Moses and Aaron (see vv. 4,22), the entire nation might have been destroyed because of their continued rebellion (see v. 45).

47 And Aaron took as Moses commanded, and ran into the midst of the congregation; and behold, the plague was begun among the people: and he put on incense, and made an atonement for the people.

48 And he stood between the dead and the living; and [a]the plague was stayed.

49 Now they that died in the plague were fourteen thousand and seven hundred, beside them that died about the matter of Korah.

50 And Aaron returned unto Moses unto the door of the tabernacle of the congregation: and the plague was stayed.

The budding of Aaron's rod

17 And the LORD spake unto Moses, saying,

2 Speak unto the children of Israel, and take of every one of them a rod according to the house of *their* fathers, of all their princes according to the house of their fathers twelve rods: write thou every man's name upon his rod.

3 And thou shalt write Aaron's name upon the rod of Levi: for one rod *shall be* for the head of the house of their fathers.

4 And thou shalt lay them up in the tabernacle of the congregation before the Testimony, [a]where I will meet with you.

5 And it shall come to pass, *that* the man's rod, [a]whom I shall choose, shall blossom: and I will make to cease from me the murmurings of the children of Israel, [b]whereby they murmur against you.

6 And Moses spake unto the children of Israel, and every one of their princes gave him [1]a rod apiece, for each prince one, according to their fathers' houses, *even* twelve rods: and the rod of Aaron *was* among their rods.

7 And Moses laid up the rods before the LORD in [a]the tabernacle of Witness.

16:48 [a]ch. 25:8; Ps. 106:30
17:4 [a]Ex. 25:22; 29:42,43; 30:36
17:5 [a]ch. 16:5 [b]ch. 16:11
17:6 [1]Heb. *a rod for one prince, a rod for one prince*
17:7 [a]Ex. 38:21; ch. 18:2; Acts 7:44

17:10 [1]Heb. *children of rebellion* [a]Heb. 9:4 [b]ch. 16:38 [c]ver. 5
17:13 [a]ch. 1:51,53; 18:4,7
18:1 [a]ch. 17:13 [b]Ex. 28:38
18:2 [a]See Gen. 29:34 [b]ch. 3:6,7 [c]ch. 3:10
18:3 [a]ch. 3:25,31,36 [b]ch. 16:40 [c]ch. 4:15
18:4 [a]ch. 3:10

8 And it came to pass, that on the morrow Moses went into the tabernacle of Witness; and behold, the rod of Aaron for the house of Levi was budded, and brought forth buds, and bloomed blossoms, and yielded almonds.

9 And Moses brought out all the rods from before the LORD unto all the children of Israel: and they looked, and took every man his rod.

10 And the LORD said unto Moses, Bring [a]Aaron's rod again before the Testimony, to be kept [b]for a token against the [1]rebels; [c]and thou shalt quite take away their murmurings from me, that they die not.

11 And Moses did *so:* as the LORD commanded him, so did he.

12 And the children of Israel spake unto Moses, saying, Behold, we die, we perish, we all perish.

13 [a]Whosoever cometh any thing near unto the tabernacle of the LORD shall die: shall we be consumed with dying?

Duties of priests and Levites

18 And the LORD said unto Aaron, [a]Thou and thy sons and thy father's house with thee shall [b]bear the iniquity of the sanctuary: and thou and thy sons with thee shall bear the iniquity of your priesthood.

2 And thy brethren also *of* the tribe of Levi, the tribe of thy father, bring thou with thee, that they may be [a]joined unto thee, and [b]minister unto thee: but [c]thou and thy sons with thee *shall minister* before the tabernacle of Witness.

3 And they shall keep thy charge, and [a]the charge of all the tabernacle: [b]only they shall not come nigh the vessels of the sanctuary and the altar, [c]that neither they, nor you also, die.

4 And they shall be joined unto thee, and keep the charge of the tabernacle of the congregation, for all the service of the tabernacle: [a]and a stranger shall not come nigh unto you.

16:49 *they that died . . . were fourteen thousand and seven hundred.* The number makes sense only if the community is as large as the census lists of ch. 2 suggest.

17:1–13 This story follows the account of the divine judgment of Korah (16:1–35) and the narrative of the symbolic use given to the censers of the rebels and its aftermath (16:36–50). Ch. 17 is thus the third in a series of accounts vindicating the Aaronic priesthood against all opposition. The selection of 12 rods, one from each tribe, was a symbolic act whereby the divine choice of Aaron would be indicated again.

17:3 *write Aaron's name upon the rod of Levi.* The test needed to be unequivocal because of the wide support given to Korah's rebellion. The 250 who had joined with Korah were from many, perhaps all, of the tribes.

17:4 *before the Testimony.* In front of the ark, with the ten commandments, thus probably in the holy place, near the altar of incense.

17:8 *was budded, and brought forth buds . . . blossoms . . . almonds.* God exceeded the demands of the test so that there might be no uncertainty as to who had acted or what He intended by His action.

17:10 *before the Testimony.* Aaron's rod joined the stone tables of the law of Moses (see note on Ex 25:16) and the jar of manna (Ex 16:33–34) within or near the ark of the covenant (see Heb 9:4). These holy symbols were ever before the Lord as memorials of His special deeds in behalf of His people. Moreover, should anyone of a later age dare to question the unique and holy place of the Aaronic priests in the Lord's service, this symbolic memorial of God's choice of Aaron would stand in opposition to his audacity. It is difficult to overestimate the importance of the role of Aaron and his sons in the worship of Israel (see note on 18:1–7).

17:12 *we die.* At last the people realized the sin of their arrogance in challenging Aaron's role. The appropriate ways of approaching the Lord are detailed in chs. 18–19.

18:1–7 Aaron and his family, chosen by the Lord to be the true priests of holy worship, faced a burdensome task. The lament of the people in 17:12–13 was real; grievous sins against the holy meeting place of the Lord and His people would be judged by death. The Lord's mercy in providing a legitimate priesthood was actually an aspect of His grace (cf. Ps 99:6–8), because it was the people's only hope for deliverance from judgment.

18:2 *thy brethren also of the tribe of Levi . . . bring.* The Aaronic priests were to be assisted by the others in the tribe of Levi, but the assistants were not to go beyond their serving role. If they did so, not only would they die, but so would the priests who were responsible (v. 3).

5 And ye shall keep [a]the charge of the sanctuary, and the charge of the altar: [b]that there be no wrath any more upon the children of Israel.

6 And I, behold, I have [a]taken your brethren the Levites from among the children of Israel: [b]to you *they are* given *as* a gift for the LORD, to do the service of the tabernacle of the congregation.

7 Therefore [a]thou and thy sons with thee shall keep your priest's office for every thing of the altar, and [b]within the vail; and ye shall serve: I have given your priest's office *unto you as* a service of gift: and the stranger that cometh nigh shall be put to death.

Tithes and offerings

8 And the LORD spake unto Aaron, Behold, [a]I also have given thee the charge of mine heave offerings of all the hallowed *things* of the children of Israel; unto thee have I given them [b]by reason of the anointing, and to thy sons, by an ordinance for ever.

9 This shall be thine of the most holy *things, reserved* from the fire: every oblation of theirs, every [a]meat offering of theirs, and every [b]sin offering of theirs, and every [c]trespass offering of theirs, which they shall render unto me, *shall be* most holy for thee and for thy sons.

10 [a]In the most holy *place* shalt thou eat it; every male shall eat it: it shall be holy unto thee.

11 And this *is* thine; [a]the heave offering of their gift, with all the wave offerings of the children of Israel: I have given them unto thee, and to thy sons and to thy daughters with thee, by a statute for ever: [b]every one *that is* clean in thy house shall eat of it.

12 [a]All the [1]best of the oil, and all the [1]best of the wine, and of the wheat, [b]the firstfruits of them which they shall offer unto the LORD, them have I given thee.

13 *And* whatsoever is first ripe in the land, [a]which they shall bring unto the LORD, shall be thine; every one *that is* clean in thine house shall eat *of* it.

14 [a]Every thing devoted in Israel shall be thine.

15 Every thing that openeth [a]the matrix in all flesh, which they bring unto the LORD, *whether it be* of men or beasts, shall be thine: nevertheless [b]the firstborn of man shalt thou surely redeem, and the firstling of unclean beasts shalt thou redeem.

16 And those that are *to be* redeemed from a month old shalt thou redeem, [a]according to thine estimation, *for* the money of five shekels, after the shekel of the sanctuary, [b]which *is* twenty gerahs.

17 [a]But the firstling of a cow, or the firstling of a sheep, or the firstling of a goat, thou shalt not redeem; they *are* holy: [b]thou shalt sprinkle their blood upon the altar, and shalt burn their fat *for* an offering made by fire, for a sweet savour unto the LORD.

18 And the flesh of them shall be thine, as the [a]wave breast and as the right shoulder are thine.

19 All the heave offerings of the holy *things,* which the children of Israel offer unto the LORD, have I given thee, and thy sons and thy daughters with thee, by a statute for ever: [a]it *is* a covenant of salt for ever before the LORD unto thee and to thy seed with thee.

20 ¶ And the LORD spake unto Aaron, Thou shalt have no inheritance in their land, neither shalt thou have any part among them: [a]I *am* thy part and thine inheritance among the children of Israel.

21 And behold, [a]I have given the children of Levi all the tenth in Israel for an inheritance, for their service which they serve, *even* [b]the service of the tabernacle of the congregation.

22 [a]Neither must the children of Israel henceforth come nigh the tabernacle of the congregation, [b]lest they bear sin, [1]and die.

23 [a]But the Levites shall do the service of the tabernacle of the congregation, and they shall bear their iniquity: *it shall be* a statute for ever throughout your generations, that among the children of Israel they have no inheritance.

24 But the tithes of the children of Israel, which they offer *as* a heave offering unto the LORD, I have given to the Levites to inherit: therefore I have said unto them, Among the children of Israel they shall have no inheritance.

18:5 [a]Ex. 27:21; 30:7; Lev. 24:3; ch. 8:2 [b]ch. 16:46
18:6 [a]ch. 3:12,45 [b]ch. 3:9; 8:19
18:7 [a]ver. 5; ch. 3:10 [b]Heb. 9:3,6
18:8 [a]Lev. 6:16,18; 7:6,32; ch. 5:9 [b]Ex. 29:29; 40:13,15
18:9 [a]Lev. 2:2,3; 10:12,13 [b]Lev. 6:25,26 [c]Lev. 7:7
18:10 [a]Lev. 6:16,26
18:11 [a]Ex. 29:27,28 [b]Lev. 22:2,3
18:12 [1]Heb. *fat* [a]Ex. 23:19; Neh. 10:35,36 [b]Ex. 22:29
18:13 [a]Ex. 23:19; Lev. 2:14; Deut. 26:2
18:14 [a]Lev. 27:28
18:15 [a]Ex. 13:2; Lev. 27:26; ch. 3:13 [b]Ex. 13:13
18:16 [a]Lev. 27:6 [b]Ex. 30:13
18:17 [a]Deut. 15:19 [b]Lev. 3:2,5
18:18 [a]Ex. 29:26,28
18:19 [a]Lev. 2:13; 2 Chr. 13:5
18:20 [a]Deut. 10:9; 12:12; 14:27,29; 18:1,2; Josh. 13:14,33; 14:3; 18:7; Ezek. 44:28
18:21 [a]ver. 24,26; Lev. 27:30,32; Neh. 10:37; 12:44; Heb. 7:5,8,9 [b]ch. 3:7,8
18:22 [1]Heb. *to die* [a]ch. 1:51 [b]Lev. 22:9
18:23 [a]ch. 3:7

18:7 *given your priest's office unto you as a service of gift.* Of all men, the priests were privileged to approach the holy place and minister before the Lord. The priesthood was a gift of God's grace to both priests and people.

18:8 *by reason of the anointing . . . an ordinance for ever.* The priests were to be supported in their work of ministry (see Lev 6:14–7:36). Since the Levites as a whole and the priests in particular had no part in the land that God was going to give them, it was necessary that the means for their provision be spelled out fully. They were not to have a part in the land; their share was the Lord Himself (v. 20).

18:11 *to thy sons and to thy daughters.* Provision was made not only for the priests, but for their families as well. Only family members who were ceremonially unclean were forbidden to eat the gifts and offerings of the people (see v. 13). Provisions for cleansing were stated in Lev 22:4–8.

18:12 *best of the oil . . . wine . . . wheat.* Since the best items of produce were to be given to the Lord, these became the special foods of the priests and their families. The NT writers similarly argue that those who minister the word of God in the present period should also be paid suitably for their work (see, e.g., 1 Cor 9:3–10 and notes).

18:19 *covenant of salt for ever.* A permanent provision for the priests. The phrase "covenant of salt" (see 2 Chr 13:5) remains obscure. In Lev 2:13 the salt that must accompany grain offerings is called the "salt of the covenant." According to Ezek 43:24, salt is also to be sprinkled on burnt offerings, and Ex 30:35 specifies salt as one of the ingredients in the special incense compounded for the sanctuary. A "covenant of salt" is perhaps an allusion to the salt used in the sacrificial meal that commonly accompanied the making of a covenant (see Gen 31:54; Ex 24:5–11; Ps 50:5).

25 ¶ And the LORD spake unto Moses, saying,

26 Thus speak unto the Levites, and say unto them, When ye take of the children of Israel the tithes which I have given you from them for your inheritance, then ye shall offer up a heave offering of it for the LORD, *even* [a]a tenth *part* of the tithe.

27 And *this* your heave offering shall be reckoned unto you, as though it were the corn of the threshingfloor, and as the fulness of the winepress.

28 Thus you also shall offer a heave offering unto the LORD of all your tithes, which ye receive of the children of Israel; and ye shall give thereof the LORD'S heave offering to Aaron the priest.

29 Out of all your gifts ye shall offer every heave offering of the LORD, of all the [1]best thereof, *even* the hallowed *part* thereof out of it.

30 Therefore thou shalt say unto them, When ye have heaved the [1]best thereof from it, [a]then it shall be counted unto the Levites as the increase of the threshingfloor, and as the increase of the winepress.

31 And ye shall eat it in every place, ye and your households: for it *is* [a]your reward for your service in the tabernacle of the congregation.

32 And ye shall [a]bear no sin by reason of it, when ye have heaved from it the best of it: neither shall ye [b]pollute the holy *things* of the children of Israel, lest ye die.

Purification of the unclean

19 And the LORD spake unto Moses and unto Aaron, saying,

2 This *is* the ordinance of the law which the LORD hath commanded, saying, Speak unto the children of Israel, that they bring thee a red heifer without spot, wherein *is* no blemish, [a]*and* upon which never came yoke:

3 And ye shall give her unto Eleazar the priest, that he may bring her [a]forth without the camp, and *one* shall slay her before his face:

4 And Eleazar the priest shall take of her blood with his finger, and [a]sprinkle of her blood directly before the tabernacle of the congregation seven times:

5 And *one* shall burn the heifer in his sight; [a]her skin, and her flesh, and her blood, with her dung, shall he burn:

6 And the priest shall take [a]cedar wood, and hyssop, and scarlet, and cast *it* into the midst of the burning of the heifer.

7 [a]Then the priest shall wash his clothes, and he shall bathe his flesh in water, and afterward he shall come into the camp, and the priest shall be unclean until the even.

8 And he that burneth her shall wash his clothes in water, and bathe his flesh in water, and shall be unclean until the even.

9 And a man *that is* clean shall gather up [a]the ashes of the heifer, and lay *them* up without the camp in a clean place, and it shall be kept for the congregation of the children of Israel [b]for a water of separation: it *is* a purification for sin.

10 And he that gathereth the ashes of the heifer shall wash his clothes, and be unclean until the even: and it shall be unto the children of Israel, and unto the stranger that sojourneth among them, for a statute for ever.

11 ¶ [a]He that toucheth the dead *body* of any [1]man shall be unclean seven days.

12 [a]He shall purify himself with it on the third day, and on the seventh day he shall be clean: but if he purify not himself the third day, then the seventh day he shall not be clean.

13 Whosoever toucheth the dead *body* of *any* man that is dead, and purifieth not himself, [a]defileth the tabernacle of the LORD; and that soul shall be cut off from Israel: because [b]the water of separation was not sprinkled upon him, he shall be unclean; [c]his uncleanness *is* yet upon him.

14 This *is* the law, when a man dieth in a tent: all that come into the tent, and all that *is* in the tent, shall be unclean seven days.

15 And every [a]open vessel, which hath no covering bound upon it, *is* unclean.

18:26 [a]Neh. 10:38
18:29 [1]Heb. *fat*
18:30 [1]Heb. *fat* [a]ver. 27
18:31 [a]Mat. 10:10; Luke 10:7; 1 Cor. 9:13; 1 Tim. 5:18
18:32 [a]Lev. 19:8; 22:16 [b]Lev. 22:2,15
19:2 [a]Deut. 21:3; 1 Sam. 6:7
19:3 [a]Lev. 4:12,21; 16:27; Heb. 13:11
19:4 [a]Lev. 4:6; 16:14,19; Heb. 9:13
19:5 [a]Ex. 29:14; Lev. 4:11,12
19:6 [a]Lev. 14:4,6,49
19:7 [a]Lev. 11:25; 15:5
19:9 [a]Heb. 9:13 [b]ver. 13,20,21
19:11 [1]Heb. *soul* [*of man*] [a]ver. 16; Lev. 21:1; ch. 5:2; 9:6,10; 31:19; Lam. 4:14; Hag. 2:13
19:12 [a]ch. 31:19
19:13 [a]Lev. 15:31 [b]ver. 9; ch. 8:7 [c]Lev. 7:20; 22:3
19:15 [a]Lev. 11:32; ch. 31:20

18:26–32 Although the Levites were the recipients of the tithe given to the Lord, they were not themselves exempt from worshiping God by tithing. They in turn were to give a tenth of their income to Aaron (v. 28) and were to be sure that the best part was given as the Lord's portion (v. 29). By obedient compliance the Levites would escape judicial death (v. 32).

19:2 *red heifer.* The qualifying words, "without spot . . . no blemish," are familiar in contexts of sacrificial worship in the OT. But this is not a sacrificial animal. It is a cow, not an ox; it is to be slaughtered, not sacrificed; and it is to be killed outside the camp, not at the holy altar. The ashes of the red heifer (v. 9) are the primary focus of this act, for they will be used in the ritual of the water of cleansing. The burning of the animal with its blood and dung (v. 5) is unprecedented in the OT. The normal pattern for the sacrifice of the burnt offering is given in Lev 1:3–9. In every respect the killing of the red heifer is distinct: A female animal was taken outside the camp to be killed; the priest had to be present, but he did not identify himself with it; and a bit of the heifer's blood was sprinkled from the priest's finger toward the tabernacle seven times, but the rest of the animal was to be burned in its entirety, without the draining of its blood or the cleansing of its dung.

19:6 *cedar wood, and hyssop, and scarlet.* Associated with the cleansing properties of the ashes of the red heifer.

19:12 *purify himself with it.* The ashes from the red heifer were kept outside the camp and would be mixed as needed with water to provide a means of cleansing after contact with dead bodies.

19:13 *defileth the tabernacle of the LORD.* Willful neglect of the provision for cleansing brought not only judgment on the person, but also a pollution of the tabernacle itself. *cut off from Israel.* See note on Ex 12:15.

19:14 *all that is in the tent.* There would be many occasions in which a person would become unclean, not because of deliberate contact with a dead body, but just by being in the proximity of one who died.

16 And [a]whosoever toucheth one that is slain with a sword in the open fields, or a dead *body,* or a bone of a man, or a grave, shall be unclean seven days.

17 And for an unclean *person* they shall take of the [a][1]ashes of the burnt *heifer* of purification for sin, and [2]running water shall be put thereto in a vessel:

18 And a clean person shall take [a]hyssop, and dip *it* in the water, and sprinkle *it* upon the tent, and upon all the vessels, and upon the persons that were there, and upon him that touched a bone, or one slain, or one dead, or a grave:

19 And the clean *person* shall sprinkle upon the unclean on the third day, and on the seventh day: [a]and on the seventh day he shall purify him*self,* and wash his clothes, and bathe *himself* in water, and shall be clean at even.

20 But the man that shall be unclean, and shall not purify himself, that soul shall be cut off from among the congregation, because he hath [a]defiled the sanctuary of the LORD: the water of separation hath not been sprinkled upon him; he *is* unclean.

21 And it shall be a perpetual statute unto them, that he that sprinkleth the water of separation shall wash his clothes; and he that toucheth the water of separation shall be unclean until even.

22 And [a]whatsoever the unclean *person* toucheth shall be unclean; and [b]the soul that toucheth *it* shall be unclean until even.

Water from the rock

20 Then [a]came the children of Israel, *even* the whole congregation, *into* the desert of Zin in the first month: and the people abode in Kadesh; and [b]Miriam died there, and was buried there.

2 [a]And there was no water for the congregation: [b]and they gathered themselves together against Moses and against Aaron.

3 And the people [a]chode with Moses, and spake, saying, Would God that we had died [b]when our brethren died before the LORD!

4 And [a]why have ye brought up the congregation of the LORD into this wilderness, that we and our cattle should die there?

5 And wherefore have ye made us to come up out of Egypt, to bring us in unto this evil place? it *is* no place of seed, or of figs, or vines, or of pomegranates; neither *is there any* water to drink.

6 And Moses and Aaron went from the presence of the assembly unto the door of the tabernacle of the congregation, and [a]they fell upon their faces: and [b]the glory of the LORD appeared unto them.

7 And the LORD spake unto Moses, saying,

8 [a]Take the rod, and gather thou the assembly together, thou, and Aaron thy brother, and speak ye unto the rock before their eyes; and it shall give forth his water, and [b]thou shalt bring forth to them water out of the rock: so thou shalt give the congregation and their beasts drink.

9 And Moses took the rod [a]from before the LORD, as he commanded him.

10 And Moses and Aaron gathered the congregation together before the rock, and he said unto them, [a]Hear now, ye rebels; must we fetch you water out of this rock?

11 And Moses lift up his hand, and with his rod he smote the rock twice: and [a]the water came out abundantly, and the congregation drank, and their beasts *also.*

12 And the LORD spake unto Moses and

19:16 [a]ver. 11
19:17 [1]Heb. *dust* [2]Heb. *living waters shall be given* [a]ver. 9
19:18 [a]Ps. 51:7
19:19 [a]Lev. 14:9
19:20 [a]ver. 13
19:22 [a]Hag. 2:13 [b]Lev. 15:5
20:1 [a]ch. 33:36
20:1 [b]Ex. 15:20; ch. 26:59
20:2 [a]Ex. 17:1 [b]ch. 16:19,42
20:3 [a]Ex. 17:2; ch. 14:2 [b]ch. 11:1,33; 14:37; 16:32,35,49
20:4 [a]Ex. 17:3
20:6 [a]ch. 14:5; 16:4,22,45 [b]ch. 14:10
20:8 [a]Ex. 17:5 [b]Neh. 9:15; Is. 43:20; 48:21
20:9 [a]ch. 17:10
20:10 [a]Ps. 106:33
20:11 [a]Ex. 17:6; Deut. 8:15; 1 Cor. 10:4

19:18 *hyssop, and dip it in the water, and sprinkle.* Here the method of the cleansing ritual is explained. A ceremonially clean person had to sprinkle the ceremonially unclean person or thing. The cleansing power of the blood of Christ is specifically contrasted ("much more"; Heb 9:13–14) with the cleansing effectiveness of the water of the ashes of the red heifer.

20:1–29 This chapter begins with the death of Miriam (v. 1), concludes with the death of Aaron (v. 28), includes the record of the conflict with Edom (vv. 14–21) and centers on the tragic sin of Moses (vv. 11–12). Such was the sad beginning of Israel's last year in the wilderness.

20:1 *first month.* The year is not given, but a comparison of vv. 22–29 with 33:38 leads to the conclusion that this chapter begins in the 40th year after the exodus (see notes on 1:1; 9:1). Most of the people 20 years old or more at the time of the rebellion at Kadesh (chs. 13–14) would already have died. *in Kadesh.* The larger part of the wilderness wandering is left without record. The people may have gone through a cycle of roving travels, seeking the water sources and the sparse vegetation, supported primarily by manna. But their circuits would bring them back to the central camp at Kadesh, the scene of their great rebellion (chs. 13–14). They have now come full circle; the land of promise lies before them again.

20:2 *no water.* Forty years earlier, the Lord had instructed Moses to take the rod he had used to strike the Nile (Ex 7:17) and to strike the rock at Horeb to initiate a flow of water (Ex 17:1–7). Now, 40 years later, at the place of Israel's worst acts of rebellion, the scene was recurring. The children of the rebellious nation now desire to die with their parents; the complaints about the bread from heaven are repeated by the sons.

20:8 *speak ye unto the rock.* Moses was told to take his rod, through which God had performed wonders in Egypt and in the wilderness all these years, but this time he was merely to speak to the rock and it would pour out its water for the people. Cf. Ps 114:8.

20:10 *Hear now, ye rebels.* At once the accumulated anger, exasperation and frustration of 40 years came to expression (see Ps 106:33).

20:11 *with his rod he smote the rock twice.* In his rage Moses disobeyed the Lord's instruction to speak to the rock (v. 8). Moses' rash action brought a stern rebuke from the Lord (v. 12). The nature of Moses' offense is not clearly stated in this text, but these factors appear to be involved: 1. Moses' action was a lack of trust in God (v. 12), as though he believed that a word alone would not suffice. 2. God's holiness was offended by Moses' rash action (v. 12), for he had not shown proper deference to God's presence.

20:12 *ye shall not bring this congregation into the land.* The end result of Moses' action is sure: Neither Aaron nor Moses would enter the land of promise. Of their contemporaries only Joshua

Aaron, Because [a]ye believed me not, to [b]sanctify me in the eyes of the children of Israel, therefore ye shall not bring this congregation into the land which I have given them.

13 [a]This *is* the water of [b][1]Meribah; because the children of Israel strove with the LORD, and he was sanctified in them.

Edom refuses Israel passage

14 ¶ [a]And Moses sent messengers from Kadesh unto the king of Edom, [b]Thus saith thy brother Israel, Thou knowest all the travail that hath [1]befallen us:

15 [a]How our fathers went down into Egypt, [b]and we have dwelt in Egypt a long time; [c]and the Egyptians vexed us, and our fathers:

16 And [a]when we cried unto the LORD, he heard our voice, and [b]sent an angel, and hath brought us forth out of Egypt: and behold, we *are* in Kadesh, a city in the uttermost of thy border:

17 [a]Let us pass, I pray thee, through thy country: we will not pass through the fields, or through the vineyards, neither will we drink *of* the water of the wells: we will go *by* the king's *high* way, we will not turn *to* the right hand nor *to* the left, until we have passed thy borders.

18 And Edom said unto him, Thou shalt not pass by me, lest I come out against thee with the sword.

19 And the children of Israel said unto him, We will go by the high way: and if I and my cattle drink *of* thy water, [a]then I will pay for it: I will only, without *doing any* thing *else,* go through on my feet.

20 And he said, [a]Thou shalt not go through. And Edom came out against him with much people, and with a strong hand.

21 Thus Edom [a]refused to give Israel passage through his border: wherefore Israel [b]turned away from him.

The death of Aaron

22 ¶ And the children of Israel, *even* the whole congregation, journeyed from [a]Kadesh, [b]and came *unto* mount Hor.

23 And the LORD spake unto Moses and Aaron in mount Hor, by the coast of the land of Edom, saying,

24 Aaron shall be [a]gathered unto his people: for he shall not enter into the land which I have given unto the children of Israel, because [b]ye rebelled against my [1]word at the water of Meribah.

25 [a]Take Aaron and Eleazar his son, and bring them up *unto* mount Hor:

26 And strip Aaron of his garments, and put them upon Eleazar his son: and Aaron shall be gathered *unto his people,* and shall die there.

27 And Moses did as the LORD commanded: and they went up into mount Hor in the sight of all the congregation.

28 [a]And Moses stripped Aaron of his garments, and put them upon Eleazar his son; and [b]Aaron died there in the top of the mount: and Moses and Eleazar came down from the mount.

29 And when all the congregation saw that Aaron was dead, they mourned for Aaron [a]thirty days, *even* all the house of Israel.

21 And *when* [a]king Arad the Canaanite, which dwelt *in* the south, heard *tell* that Israel came [b]*by* the way of the spies; then he fought against Israel, and took *some* of them prisoners.

2 [a]And Israel vowed a vow unto the LORD, and said, If thou wilt indeed deliver this people into my hand, then [b]I will utterly destroy their cities.

3 And the LORD hearkened to the voice of Israel, and delivered up the Canaanites; and they utterly destroyed them and their cities: and he called the name of the place [1]Hormah.

20:12 [a]Deut. 1:37 [b]Lev. 10:3; Ezek. 20:41; 36:23; 1 Pet. 3:15
20:13 [1]That is, *Strife* [a]Deut. 33:8; Ps. 106:32 [b]Ex. 17:7
20:14 [1]Heb. *found us* [a]Judg. 11:16,17 [b]Deut. 2:4; Obad. 10,12
20:15 [a]Gen. 46:6; Acts 7:15 [b]Ex. 12:40 [c]Ex. 1:11; Deut. 26:6; Acts 7:19
20:16 [a]Ex. 2:23; 3:7 [b]Ex. 3:2; 14:19
20:17 [a]See ch. 21:22
20:19 [a]Deut. 2:6
20:20 [a]Judg. 11:17
20:21 [a]See Deut. 2:27,29 [b]Deut. 2:8; Judg. 11:18
20:22 [a]ch. 33:37 [b]ch. 21:4
20:24 [1]Heb. *mouth* [a]Gen. 25:8; Deut. 32:50 [b]ver. 12
20:25 [a]ch. 33:38; Deut. 32:50
20:28 [a]Ex. 29:29,30 [b]ch. 33:38; Deut. 10:6
20:29 [a]Deut. 34:8
21:1 [a]ch. 33:40; Judg. 1:16 [b]ch. 13:21
21:2 [a]Gen. 28:20; Judg. 11:30 [b]Lev. 26:25
21:3 [1]That is, *Utter destruction*

and Caleb would survive to enter the land. The inclusion of Aaron demonstrates his partnership with his brother in the breach against God's holiness.

20:13 *Meribah.* Means "contention." The same name was used 40 years earlier at the first occasion of bringing water from the rock (Ex 17:7, where it is also called Massah, "testing"). Ps 95:8 laments the rebellion at Meribah and Massah.

20:14–21 Moses' attempt to pass through the territory of Edom by peaceful negotiation and payment for services rendered is met by arrogant rebuff.

20:14 *thy brother Israel.* The people of Edom were descended from Esau, the brother of Jacob (see Gen 36:1).

20:17 *king's high way.* The major north-south trade route in the region east of the Jordan, extending from Arabia to Damascus.

20:20 *with much people, and . . . strong hand.* The show of force by Edom caused Israel to turn away so as not to risk conflict with this brother nation. Israel was forbidden by the Lord to take even a foothold in Edom (see Deut 2:4–6).

20:22 *mount Hor.* Other than its proximity to the border of Edom (v. 23), nothing is known for certain about its location.

20:24 *gathered unto his people.* A euphemism for death (see, e.g., Gen 25:8,17; 35:29). *ye.* The Hebrew is plural. Aaron had joined Moses in rebellion against God (v. 12); his impending death was a precursor of Moses' death as well (see Deut 34).

20:25 *Aaron and Eleazar his son.* There was no doubt about Aaron's successor, just as there was no doubt about Moses' successor (see Deut 34).

20:26–28 While Aaron was still alive, his garments were to be placed on his son; only then did he die.

20:29 *mourned for Aaron.* His death (and that of Moses) marked the passing of a generation. The old generation was now nearly gone; in 40 years there had been almost a complete turnover of the people 20 years old or more.

21:1–3 The first battle of the new community against the Canaanites was provoked by the king of Arad, perhaps as he was raiding them. The result was a complete victory for the Israelites—a new day for them, since they had been defeated by the Amalekites and Canaanites a generation before (14:41–45).

21:2 *utterly destroy.* The Hebrew term refers to the irrevocable giving over of things or persons to the Lord, often by totally destroying them.

21:3 *Hormah.* See KJV marg.; the association with Israel's earlier defeat is made certain by the use of this place-name (see 14:45).

The serpent of brass

4 ¶ And [a]they journeyed from mount Hor
by the way of the Red sea, to [b]compass the
land of Edom: and the soul of the people was
much [1]discouraged because of the way.
5 And the people [a]spake against God, and
against Moses, [b]Wherefore have ye brought us
up out of Egypt to die in the wilderness? for
there is no bread, neither *is there any* water;
and [c]our soul loatheth *this* light bread.
6 And [a]the LORD sent [b]fiery serpents
among the people, and they bit the people;
and much people of Israel died.
7 [a]Therefore the people came to Moses,
and said, We have sinned, for [b]we have spoken against the LORD, and against thee; [c]pray
unto the LORD, that he take away the serpents
from us. And Moses prayed for the people.
8 And the LORD said unto Moses, Make
thee a fiery *serpent,* and set it upon a pole: and
it shall come to pass, that every one that is bitten, when he looketh upon it, shall live.
9 And [a]Moses made a serpent of brass, and
put it upon a pole, and it came to pass, that if
a serpent had bitten *any* man, when he beheld
the serpent of brass, he lived.

Israel moves on

10 And the children of Israel set forward,
and [a]pitched in Oboth.
11 And they journeyed from Oboth, and
[a]pitched at [1]Ije-abarim, in the wilderness
which *is* before Moab, toward the sunrising.
12 [a]From thence they removed, and
pitched in the valley of Zared.
13 From thence they removed, and pitched
on the *other* side of Arnon, which *is* in the
wilderness that cometh out of the coasts of the
Amorites: for [a]Arnon *is* the border of Moab,
between Moab and the Amorites.
14 Wherefore it is said in the book of the
wars of the LORD,
[1]What he did in the Red sea,
And *in* the brooks of Arnon,
15 And *at* the stream of the brooks that
goeth down to the dwelling of Ar,
[a]And [1]lieth upon the border of Moab.
16 And from thence *they went* [a]to Beer:
that *is* the well whereof the LORD spake unto
Moses, Gather the people together, and I will
give them water.
17 [a]Then Israel sang this song,
[1]Spring up, O well;
[2]Sing ye unto it:
18 The princes digged the well,
The nobles of the people digged it,
By the direction of [a]the lawgiver, with
their staves.
And from the wilderness *they went to* Mattanah:
19 And from Mattanah *to* Nahaliel: and
from Nahaliel *to* Bamoth:
20 And from Bamoth *in* the valley, that *is*
in the [1]country of Moab, *to* the top of [2]Pisgah,
which looketh [a]toward [3]Jeshimon.

Defeat of Sihon and Og

21 ¶ And [a]Israel sent messengers unto Sihon king of the Amorites, saying,
22 [a]Let me pass through thy land: we will
not turn into the fields, or into the vineyards;
we will not drink *of* the waters of the well: *but*
we will go along by the king's *high* way, until
we be past thy borders.
23 [a]And Sihon would not suffer Israel to
pass through his border: but Sihon gathered all
his people together, and went out against Israel into the wilderness: [b]and he came *to* Jahaz,
and fought against Israel.
24 And [a]Israel smote him with the edge of
the sword, and possessed his land from Arnon
unto Jabbok, *even* unto the children of Ammon: for the border of the children of Ammon
was strong.
25 And Israel took all these cities: and Israel dwelt in all the cities of the Amorites, in
Heshbon, and in all the [1]villages thereof.
26 For Heshbon *was* the city of Sihon the
king of the Amorites, who had fought against

21:4 [1]Or, *grieved.* Heb. *shortened* [a]ch. 20:22; 33:41 [b]Judg. 11:18
21:5 [a]Ps. 78:19 [b]Ex. 17:3 [c]ch. 11:6
21:6 [a]1 Cor. 10:9 [b]Deut. 8:15
21:7 [a]Ps. 78:34 [b]ver. 5 [c]Ex. 8:8; 1 Sam. 12:19; 1 Ki. 13:6; Acts 8:24
21:9 [a]2 Ki. 18:4; John 3:14,15
21:10 [a]ch. 33:43
21:11 [1]Or, *heaps of Abarim* [a]ch. 33:44
21:12 [a]Deut. 2:13
21:13 [a]ch. 22:36; Judg. 11:18
21:14 [1]Or, *Vaheb in Suphah*
21:15 [1]Heb. *leaneth* [a]Deut. 2:18,29
21:16 [a]Judg. 9:21
21:17 [1]Heb. *Ascend* [2]Or, *Answer* [a]Ex. 15:1; Ps. 105:2; 106:12
21:18 [a]Is. 33:22
21:20 [1]Heb. *field* [2]Or, *[the] hill* [3]Or, *the wilderness* [a]ch. 23:28
21:21 [a]Deut. 2:26,27; Judg. 11:19
21:22 [a]ch. 20:17
21:23 [a]Deut. 29:7 [b]Deut. 2:32; Judg. 11:20
21:24 [a]Deut. 2:33; Josh. 12:1; Neh. 9:22; Ps. 135:10; 136:19; Amos 2:9
21:25 [1]Heb. *daughters*

21:4 With Moses' determination not to engage Edom in battle (see note on 20:20), the people became impatient with him and with the direction the Lord was taking them. Flushed with victory, they were confident in themselves. They forgot that their victory over Arad was granted by the Lord in response to their solemn pledge (v. 2); now they were ready to rebel again.

21:5 *our soul loatheth this light bread.* The people's impatience (v. 4) led them to blaspheme God, to reject His servant Moses and to despise the bread from heaven. This is the most bitter of their several attacks on the manna (see note on 11:7). Just as Moses' attack on the rock was more than it appeared to be (see note on 20:11), so the people's contempt for the heavenly bread was more serious than one might think. Rejecting the heavenly manna was tantamount to spurning God's grace (cf. John 6:32–35,48–51,58).

21:8–9 In response to the people's confession of sin (v. 7), God directed Moses to make an image of a serpent and put it on a pole, so that anyone who had been bitten could look at it and live. See the typological use of this incident in John 3:14–15.

21:10–13 The people skirt Edom and make their way to the Arnon, the wadi that serves as the border between Moab and the region of the Amorites and that flows west into the midpoint of the Dead Sea.

21:14 *book of the wars of the LORD.* Mentioned only here in the OT. This is not in existence today; it was presumably an ancient collection of songs of war in praise of God (see note on 10:3 for music in war). Cf. the "book of Jasher" (Josh 10:13; 2 Sam 1:18).

21:16 *I will give them water.* The quest for water had been a constant problem during the wilderness experience (see ch. 20; Ex 17).

21:17–18 The "song of the well" may also come from the book of the wars of the LORD (v. 14).

21:21–26 As with Edom (20:14–19), Israel requested freedom to pass through the land of the Amorites. When Sihon, their king, tried to meet Israel with a show of force, he suffered an overwhelming defeat. The land of the Amorites was east of the Jordan, extending from the Arnon River (at the midpoint of the Dead Sea) to the Jabbok River (v. 24), which flows into the Jordan some 24 miles north of the Dead Sea.

the former king of Moab, and taken all his land
out of his hand, *even* unto Arnon.
27 Wherefore they that speak in proverbs
say,

Come *into* Heshbon,
Let the city of Sihon be built and
prepared:
28 For there is [a]a fire gone out of
Heshbon,
A flame from the city of Sihon:
It hath consumed [b]Ar of Moab,
And the lords of the high places of
Arnon.
29 Woe to thee, Moab!
Thou art undone, O people of
[a]Chemosh:
He hath given his sons that escaped,
And his daughters into captivity
Unto Sihon king of the Amorites.
30 We have shot at them;
Heshbon is perished even [a]unto
Dibon,
And we have laid *them* waste even
unto Nophah,
Which *reacheth* unto [b]Medeba.

31 Thus Israel dwelt in the land of the Amorites.
32 And Moses sent to spy out [a]Jaazer, and
they took the villages thereof, and drove out
the Amorites that *were* there.
33 [a]And they turned and went up *by* the
way of Bashan: and Og the king of Bashan
went out against them, he, and all his people,
to the battle [b]*at* Edrei.
34 And the LORD said unto Moses, [a]Fear
him not: for I have delivered him into thy
hand, and all his people, and his land; and
[b]thou shalt do to him as thou didst unto Sihon
king of the Amorites, which dwelt at Heshbon.
35 [a]So they smote him, and his sons, and
all his people, until there was none left him
alive: and they possessed his land.

21:28 [a]Jer. 48:45,46 [b]Deut. 2:9,18; Is. 15:1
21:29 [a]Judg. 11:24; 1 Ki. 11:7,33; 2 Ki. 23:13; Jer. 48:7,13
21:30 [a]Jer. 48:18,22 [b]Is. 15:2
21:32 [a]ch. 32:1; Jer. 48:32
21:33 [a]Deut. 3:1; 29:7 [b]Josh. 13:12
21:34 [a]Deut. 3:2 [b]ver. 24; Ps. 135:10; 136:20
21:35 [a]Deut. 3:3; 29:7; Josh. 13:12; Ps. 135:10

22:1 [a]ch. 33:48
22:2 [a]Judg. 11:25
22:3 [a]Ex. 15:15
22:4 [a]ch. 31:8; Josh. 13:21
22:5 [1]Heb. *eye* [a]Deut. 23:4; Josh. 13:22; 24:9; Neh. 13:1,2; Mic. 6:5; 2 Pet. 2:15; Jude 11; Rev. 2:14 [b]See ch. 23:7; Deut. 23:4
22:6 [a]ch. 23:7
22:7 [a]1 Sam. 9:7,8
22:8 [a]ver. 19
22:9 [a]ver. 20; Gen. 20:3

Balak sends for Balaam

22 And [a]the children of Israel set forward, and pitched in the plains of
Moab on *this* side Jordan *by* Jericho.
2 And [a]Balak the son of Zippor saw all that
Israel had done to the Amorites.
3 And [a]Moab was sore afraid of the people,
because they *were* many: and Moab was distressed because of the children of Israel.
4 And Moab said unto [a]the elders of Midian, Now shall *this* company lick up all *that are*
round about us, as the ox licketh up the grass
of the field. And Balak the son of Zippor *was*
king of the Moabites at that time.
5 [a]He sent messengers therefore unto Balaam the son of Beor to [b]Pethor, which *is* by
the river *of* the land of the children of his people, to call him, saying, Behold, there is a people come out from Egypt: behold, they cover
the [1]face of the earth, and they abide over
against me:
6 Come now therefore, I pray thee, [a]curse
me this people; for they *are* too mighty for me:
peradventure I shall prevail, *that* we may smite
them, and *that* I may drive them out of the
land: for I wot that *he* whom thou blessest *is*
blessed, and *he* whom thou cursest is cursed.
7 And the elders of Moab and the elders of
Midian departed with [a]the rewards of divination in their hand; and they came unto Balaam, and spake unto him the words of Balak.
8 And he said unto them, [a]Lodge here *this*
night, and I will bring you word again, as the
LORD shall speak unto me: and the princes of
Moab abode with Balaam.
9 [a]And God came unto Balaam, and said,
What men *are* these with thee?
10 And Balaam said unto God, Balak the
son of Zippor, king of Moab, hath sent unto
me, *saying,*
11 Behold, *there is* a people come out of
Egypt, which covereth the face of the earth:

21:27–30 This third ancient poem in ch. 21 was an Amorite taunt song about their earlier victory over Moab (v. 29). Perhaps the "song of Heshbon" was also preserved in the book of the wars of the LORD (v. 14).
21:33 *Bashan.* The region northeast of the sea of Galilee.
21:35 *smote him.* By defeating Og, Israel now controlled the area east of the Jordan, from Moab to the heights of Bashan in the vicinity of mount Hermon. The victory over Sihon and Og became a subject of song (Ps 135:11; 136:19–20), and is a regular part of the commemoration of the works of the Lord in the passover celebration.
22:1 *plains of Moab.* Israel now marched back to their staging area east of the Jordan and just north of the Dead Sea. From this point they would launch their attack on Canaan, beginning with the ancient city of Jericho. Moab did not trust Israel's intentions, however. Moab's fear leads to a remarkable interval in the story of Israel: the account of Balak and Balaam (chs. 22–24).
22:3 *Moab was sore afraid.* Balak king of Moab did not know that Israel had no plans against him.
22:4 *said unto the elders of Midian.* Balak made an alliance with the Midianites to oppose Israel (see v. 7). *as the ox licketh up the grass of the field.* A proverbial simile particularly fitting for a pastoral people.
22:5 *sent messengers therefore unto Balaam.* Since Balak believed that there was no military way to withstand Israel, he sought to oppose them through pagan divination (vv. 6–7), sending for a diviner with an international reputation. (One of Balaam's non-Biblical prophecies is preserved in an Aramaic text from Deir Alla in the Jordan Valley dating to c. 700 B.C.)
22:8 *bring you word . . . as the LORD shall speak.* The language here and in v. 18 ("the LORD my God") has led some to believe that Balaam was a believer in Yahweh ("the LORD"), God of Israel. Based on the subsequent narrative, however, it seems best to take Balaam's words as claiming to be the spokesman for any god. Balaam is universally condemned in Scripture for moral, ethical and religious faults (see 31:7–8,15–16; Deut 23:3–6; Josh 13:22; 24:9–10; Neh 13:1–3; Mic 6:5; 2 Pet 2:15–16; Jude 11; Rev 2:14).
22:9 *God came unto Balaam.* The author shows his aversion to the pagan prophet Balaam by using "God" instead of "the LORD" (Yahweh), as Balaam does (e.g., in v. 8). By this subtle device, the narrator distances himself from Balaam's outrageous claims. That God spoke to Balaam is not to be denied, but Balaam did not yet realize that the God of Israel was unlike the supposed deities that he usually schemed against.

come now, curse me them; peradventure [1]I shall be able to overcome them, and drive them out.

12 And God said unto Balaam, Thou shalt not go with them; thou shalt not curse the people: for [a]they *are* blessed.

13 And Balaam rose up in the morning, and said unto the princes of Balak, Get you into your land: for the LORD refuseth to give me leave to go with you.

14 And the princes of Moab rose up, and they went unto Balak, and said, Balaam refuseth to come with us.

15 And Balak sent yet again princes, more, and more honourable than they.

16 And they came to Balaam, and said to him, Thus saith Balak the son of Zippor, [1]Let nothing, I pray thee, hinder thee from coming unto me:

17 For I will promote thee unto very great honour, and I will do whatsoever thou sayest unto me: [a]come therefore, I pray thee, curse me this people.

18 And Balaam answered and said unto the servants of Balak, [a]If Balak would give me his house full *of* silver and gold, [b]I cannot go beyond the word of the LORD my God, to do less or more.

19 Now therefore, I pray you, [a]tarry ye also here *this* night, that I may know what the LORD will say unto me more.

20 [a]And God came unto Balaam at night, and said unto him, If the men come to call thee, rise up, *and* go with them; but [b]yet the word which I shall say unto thee, that shalt thou do.

Balaam's ass speaks

21 And Balaam rose up in the morning, and saddled his ass, and went with the princes of Moab.

22 And God's anger was kindled because he went: [a]and the angel of the LORD stood in the way for an adversary against him. Now he was riding upon his ass, and his two servants *were* with him.

23 And [a]the ass saw the angel of the LORD standing in the way, and his sword drawn in his hand: and the ass turned aside out of the way, and went into the field: and Balaam smote the ass, to turn her *into* the way.

22:11 [1]Heb. *I shall prevail in fighting against him*
22:12 [a]ch. 23:20; Rom. 11:28
22:16 [1]Heb. *Be not thou letted from, etc.*
22:17 [a]ver. 6
22:18 [a]ch. 24:13 [b]1 Ki. 22:14; 2 Chr. 18:13
22:19 [a]ver. 8
22:20 [a]ver. 9 [b]ver. 35; ch. 23:12,26; 24:13
22:22 [a]Ex. 4:24
22:23 [a]See 2 Ki. 6:17; Dan. 10:7; Acts 22:9; 2 Pet. 2:16; Jude 11
22:28 [a]2 Pet. 2:16
22:29 [a]Prov. 12:10
22:30 [1]Heb. *who hast ridden upon me* [2]Or, *ever since thou* wast, etc. [a]2 Pet. 2:16
22:31 [1][Or,] *bowed himself* [a]See Gen. 21:19; 2 Ki. 6:17; Luke 24:16,31 [b]Ex. 34:8
22:32 [1]Heb. *to be an adversary* unto thee [a]2 Pet. 2:14,15
22:34 [1]Heb. be *evil in thine eyes* [a]1 Sam. 15:24,30; 26:21; 2 Sam. 12:13; Job 34:31,32
22:35 [a]ver. 20
22:36 [a]Gen. 14:17 [b]ch. 21:13

24 But the angel of the LORD stood in a path of the vineyards, a wall *being* on this side, and a wall on that side.

25 And when the ass saw the angel of the LORD, she thrust herself unto the wall, and crusht Balaam's foot against the wall: and he smote her again.

26 And the angel of the LORD went further, and stood in a narrow place, where *was* no way to turn *either to* the right hand or *to* the left.

27 And when the ass saw the angel of the LORD, she fell down under Balaam: and Balaam's anger was kindled, and he smote the ass with a staff.

28 And the LORD [a]opened the mouth of the ass, and she said unto Balaam, What have I done unto thee, that thou hast smitten me these three times?

29 And Balaam said unto the ass, Because thou hast mocked me: I would there were a sword in mine hand, [a]for now would I kill thee.

30 [a]And the ass said unto Balaam, *Am* not I thine ass, [1]upon which thou hast ridden [2]ever since *I was* thine unto this day? was I ever wont to do so unto thee? And he said, Nay.

31 Then the LORD [a]opened the eyes of Balaam, and he saw the angel of the LORD standing in the way, and his sword drawn in his hand: and he [b]bowed down his head, and [1]fell flat on his face.

32 And the angel of the LORD said unto him, Wherefore hast thou smitten thine ass these three times? behold, I went out [1]to withstand thee, because *thy* way is [a]perverse before me:

33 And the ass saw me, and turned from me these three times: unless she had turned from me, surely now also I had slain thee, and saved her alive.

34 And Balaam said unto the angel of the LORD, [a]I have sinned; for I knew not that thou stoodest in the way against me: now therefore, if it [1]displease thee, I will get me back again.

35 And the angel of the LORD said unto Balaam, Go with the men: [a]but only the word that I shall speak unto thee, that thou shalt speak. So Balaam went with the princes of Balak.

36 And when Balak heard that Balaam was come, [a]he went out to meet him unto a city of Moab, [b]which *is* in the border of Arnon, which *is* in the utmost coast.

22:12 *they are blessed.* Israel was under the Lord's blessing promised to Abraham (see note on Gen 12:2–3).

22:20 *go with them.* There appears to be a contradiction between the permission God grants Balaam here and the prohibition He had given earlier (v. 12), and then the anger the Lord displayed against Balaam on his journey (v. 22). The difficulty is best understood as lying in the contrary character of Balaam. God had forbidden him to go to curse Israel. He then allowed Balaam to go, but only if he would follow the Lord's direction. But Balaam's real intentions were known to the Lord, and so with severe displeasure He confronted the pagan prophet.

22:23 *the ass saw the angel of the LORD.* The internationally known seer is blind to spiritual reality, but his proverbially dumb beast is able to see the angel of the Lord on the path. As a pagan prophet, Balaam was a specialist in animal divination, but his animal saw what he was blind to observe.

22:29 *I would there were a sword in mine hand.* A ridiculous picture of the hapless Balaam. A sword was nearby (see vv. 23,31–33), but its victim was not going to be the donkey.

22:31 *Then the LORD opened the eyes of Balaam.* The language follows the same structure as the opening words of v. 28. In some ways, the opening of the eyes of the pagan prophet to see the reality of the angel was the greater miracle.

22:35 *only the word that I shall speak unto thee, that thou shalt speak.* The one great gain was that Balaam was now more aware of the seriousness of the task before him; he would not be able to change the word the Lord would give him (see 23:12,20,26).

37 And Balak said unto Balaam, Did I not
earnestly send unto thee to call thee? wherefore camest thou not unto me? am I not able
indeed [a]to promote thee to honour?
38 And Balaam said unto Balak, Lo, I am
come unto thee: have I now any power at all to
say any thing? [a]the word that God putteth in
my mouth, that shall I speak.
39 And Balaam went with Balak, and they
came *unto* [1]Kirjath-huzoth.
40 And Balak offered oxen and sheep, and
sent to Balaam, and to the princes that *were*
with him.
41 And it came to pass on the morrow, that
Balak took Balaam, and brought him up *into*
the [a]high places of Baal, that thence he might
see the utmost part of the people.

Balaam's parables

23 And Balaam said unto Balak, [a]Build
me here seven altars, and prepare
me here seven oxen and seven rams.
2 And Balak did as Balaam had spoken; and
Balak and Balaam [a]offered on *every* altar a bullock and a ram.
3 And Balaam said unto Balak, [a]Stand by
thy burnt offering, and I will go: peradventure
the LORD will come [b]to meet me: and whatsoever he sheweth me I will tell thee. And [1]he
went to a high place.
4 [a]And God met Balaam: and he said unto
him, I have prepared seven altars, and I have
offered upon *every* altar a bullock and a ram.
5 And the LORD [a]put a word in Balaam's
mouth, and said, Return unto Balak, and thus
thou shalt speak.
6 And he returned unto him, and lo, *he*
stood by his burnt sacrifice, he, and all the
princes of Moab.
7 And he [a]took up his parable, and said,
Balak the king of Moab hath brought
me from Aram,
Out of the mountains of the east,
saying,
[b]Come, curse me Jacob,
And come, [c]defy Israel.
8 [a]How shall I curse, whom God hath
not cursed?
Or how shall I defy, *whom* the LORD
hath not defied?
9 For from the top of the rocks I see him,
And from the hills I behold him:
Lo, [a]the people shall dwell alone,
And [b]shall not be reckoned among the
nations.
10 [a]Who can count the dust of Jacob,
And the number *of* the fourth part of
Israel?
Let [1]me die [b]the death of the righteous,
And let my last end be like his!
11 And Balak said unto Balaam, What hast
thou done unto me? [a]I took thee to curse mine
enemies, and behold, thou hast blessed *them*
altogether.
12 And he answered and said, [a]Must I not
take heed to speak that which the LORD hath
put in my mouth?
13 And Balak said unto him, Come, I pray
thee, with me unto another place, from
whence thou mayest see them: thou shalt see
but the utmost part of them, and shalt not see
them all: and curse me them from thence.
14 And he brought him *into* the field of Zo-
phim, to the top of [1]Pisgah, [a]and built seven
altars, and offered a bullock and a ram on *every*
altar.
15 And he said unto Balak, Stand here by
thy burnt offering, while I meet *the LORD* yonder.
16 And the LORD met Balaam, and [a]put a
word in his mouth, and said, Go again unto Balak, and say thus.
17 And when he came to him, behold, he
stood by his burnt offering, and the princes of
Moab with him. And Balak said unto him,
What hath the LORD spoken?
18 And he took up his parable, and said,
[a]Rise up, Balak, and hear;
Hearken unto me, thou son of Zippor:
19 [a]God *is* not a man, that he should lie;
Neither the son of man, that he should
repent:

22:37 [a]ver. 17; ch. 24:11
22:38 [a]ch. 23:26; 24:13; 1 Ki. 22:14; 2 Chr. 18:13
22:39 [1]Or, *a city of streets*
22:41 [a]Deut. 12:2
23:1 [a]ver. 29
23:2 [a]ver. 14,30
23:3 [1]Or, *he went solitary* [a]ver. 15 [b]ch. 24:1
23:4 [a]ver. 16
23:5 [a]ver. 16; ch. 22:35; Deut. 18:18; Jer. 1:9
23:7 [a]ver. 18; ch. 24:3,15,23; Job 27:1; 29:1; Ps. 78:2 [b]ch. 22:6,11,17 [c]1 Sam. 17:10
23:8 [a]Is. 47:12
23:9 [a]Deut. 33:28 [b]Ex. 33:16; Ezra 9:2; Eph. 2:14
23:10 [1]Heb. *my soul,* or, *my life* [a]Gen. 13:16; 22:17 [b]Ps. 116:15
23:11 [a]ch. 22:11
23:12 [a]ch. 22:38
23:14 [1]Or, *the hill* [a]ver. 1,2
23:16 [a]ver. 5; ch. 22:35
23:18 [a]Judg. 3:20
23:19 [a]1 Sam. 15:29; Mal. 3:6; Jas. 1:17

22:37 *Did I not earnestly send unto thee to call thee?* The comic element of the story is seen not only in the hapless Balaam but also in the frustrated Balak (see 23:11,25; 24:10).

22:40 *Balak offered oxen and sheep.* Not sacrifices to the Lord. The pieces given to Balaam would have included the livers, for, as a pagan diviner, Balaam was a specialist in liver divination. Balaam subsequently gave up his acts of sorcery as the power of the Lord's word came upon him (24:1).

23:1 *seven altars . . . seven oxen and seven rams.* These sacrifices were prepared as a part of Balaam's pagan actions. The number seven (signifying completeness) was held in high regard among Semitic peoples in general; the many animals would provide abundant liver and organ materials for the diviner from the east.

23:2 *Balak did as Balaam had spoken.* Balaam is in charge; Balak is now his subordinate.

23:7–24:24 There are seven poetic oracles here: The first four are longer, have introductory narrative bridges and are written in exquisite poetry (23:7–10; 23:18–24; 24:3–9; 24:15–19). The last three are brief, are much more difficult to understand, and follow one another in a staccato pattern (24:20,21–22, 23–24).

23:7 *parable.* Hebrew *mashal,* usually translated "proverb" or "oracle." By this word the distinctive nature of Balaam's prophecies is established; none of the prophecies of Israel's true prophets is described by this term.

23:8 *How shall I curse, whom God hath not cursed?* That which Balaam had been hired to do he was unable to do. God kept him from pronouncing a curse on His people, who were unlike the nations of the world (v. 9).

23:10 *Let me die the death of the righteous.* A wish not granted (see 31:8,16). *let my last end be like his!* He who had come to curse desired to share in Israel's blessing.

23:13 *shalt not see them all.* Balak attempted to reduce Israel's power by selecting a point where their immense numbers would be obscured. Unfortunately for Balak, the oracle that followed (vv. 18–24) exceeded the first in its blessing on Israel.

23:19 *God is not a man, that he should lie.* These sublime words describe the immutability of the Lord and the integrity of His

Hath he said, and shall he not do *it?*
Or hath he spoken, and shall he not
make it good?
20 Behold, I have received *commandment*
to bless: and [a]he hath blessed;
And I cannot reverse it.
21 [a]He hath not beheld iniquity in Jacob,
Neither hath he seen perverseness in
Israel:
The LORD his God *is* with him,
[b]And the shout of a king *is* among
them.
22 [a]God brought them out of Egypt;
He hath as it were [b]the strength of an
unicorn.
23 Surely *there is* no enchantment
[1]against Jacob,
Neither *is there* any divination [1]against
Israel:
According to *this* time it shall be said
of Jacob and of Israel,
[a]What hath God wrought!
24 Behold, the people shall rise up [a]as a
great lion,
And lift up himself as a young lion:
[b]He shall not lie down until he eat *of*
the prey,
And drink the blood of the slain.
25 And Balak said unto Balaam, Neither
curse them at all, nor bless them at all.
26 But Balaam answered and said unto Balak, Told not I thee, saying, [a]All that the LORD
speaketh, that I must do?
27 And Balak said unto Balaam, [a]Come, I
pray thee, I will bring thee unto another place;
peradventure it will please God that thou
mayest curse me them from thence.
28 And Balak brought Balaam *unto* the top
of Peor, that looketh [a]toward Jeshimon.
29 And Balaam said unto Balak, [a]Build me
here seven altars, and prepare me here seven
bullocks and seven rams.

23:20 [a]Gen. 12:2; 22:17; ch. 22:12
23:21 [a]Rom. 4:7,8 [b]Ps. 89:15
23:22 [a]ch. 24:8 [b]Deut. 33:17; Job 39:10
23:23 [1]Or, *in* [a]Ps. 31:19; 44:1
23:24 [a]Gen. 49:9 [b]Gen. 49:27
23:26 [a]ver. 12; ch. 22:38
23:27 [a]ver. 13
23:28 [a]ch. 21:10
23:29 [a]ver. 1

24:1 [1]Heb. *to the meeting of enchantments* [a]ch. 23:3,15
24:2 [a]ch. 2:2 [b]ch. 11:25; 1 Sam. 10:10; 19:20,23; 2 Chr. 15:1
24:3 [1]Heb. *who had his eyes shut,* but now open[ed] [a]ch. 23:7,18
24:4 [a]See 1 Sam. 19:24; Ezek. 1:28
24:6 [a]Ps. 1:3; Jer. 17:8 [b]Ps. 104:16
24:7 [a]Jer. 51:13; Rev. 17:1,15 [b]1 Sam. 15:9 [c]2 Sam. 5:12; 1 Chr. 14:2
24:8 [a]ch. 23:22 [b]ch. 14:9; 23:24 [c]Ps. 2:9; Jer. 50:17 [d]Ps. 45:5
24:9 [a]Gen. 49:9 [b]Gen. 12:3

30 And Balak did as Balaam had said, and
offered a bullock and a ram on *every* altar.

24 And when Balaam saw that it pleased
the LORD to bless Israel, he went not,
as at [a]other times, [1]to seek for enchantments,
but he set his face toward the wilderness.
2 And Balaam lift up his eyes, and he saw
Israel [a]abiding *in his tents* according to their
tribes; and [b]the spirit of God came upon him.
3 [a]And he took up his parable, and said,
Balaam the son of Beor hath said,
And the man [1]whose eyes are open
hath said:
4 He hath said, which heard the words
of God,
Which saw the vision of the Almighty,
[a]Falling *into a trance,* but having his
eyes open:
5 How goodly are thy tents, O Jacob,
And thy tabernacles, O Israel!
6 As the valleys are they spread forth,
As gardens by the river side,
[a]As the trees of lign aloes [b]*which* the
LORD hath planted,
And as cedar trees beside the waters.
7 He shall pour the water out of his
buckets,
And his seed *shall be* [a]in many waters,
And his king shall be higher than [b]Agag,
And his [c]kingdom shall be exalted.
8 [a]God brought him forth out of Egypt;
He hath as it were the strength of an
unicorn:
He shall [b]eat up the nations his enemies,
And shall [c]break their bones,
And [d]pierce *them* through *with* his
arrows.
9 [a]He couched, he lay down as a lion,
And as a great lion: who shall stir
him up?
[b]Blessed *is* he that blesseth thee,
And cursed *is* he that curseth thee.

---

word. Balaam is a foil for God—constantly shifting, prevaricating, equivocating, changing—a prime example of the distinction between God and man.

23:21 *the shout of a king is among them.* That the first explicit declaration of the Lord's kingship in the Pentateuch was made by Balaam is a suitable improbability. Because God is King (Sovereign), He was able to use Balaam for his own ends—to bless his people in a new and wonderful manner.

23:22 *unicorn.* Or "aurochs" or "oryx," a traditional image of power in the ancient Near East (see also 24:8).

23:23 *no enchantment against Jacob.* Balaam speaks from his frightful experience. He had no means in his bag of tricks to withstand God's blessing of Israel.

23:24 *as a great lion.* Israel was about to arise and devour its foes, like a lioness on the hunt (see 24:9; Gen 49:9).

24:1 *went not . . . to seek for enchantments.* Balaam's magic and sorcery are identified here (see notes on 22:40; 23:1).

24:2 *the spirit of God came upon him.* Not to be confused with the filling of the Spirit (Acts 2:1–4), or with the anointing of the Spirit (Is 61:1). This unexpected language prepares the reader for the heightened revelation that is about to come from the unwitting messenger.

24:3–4 The extensive introduction of this oracle describes Balaam's experience in the Lord's presence. Now Balaam's eyes were opened (see note on 22:31).

24:6–7 Balaam speaks here in general, but luxuriant, terms of the blessings that will come to the Israelites as they settle in their new land. The lushness of their blessing from the Lord is reminiscent of Eden.

24:7 *higher than Agag.* Possibly a specific future prophecy concerning the opponent of King Saul (1 Sam 15:32–33)—setting the stage for the even more remarkable words of the fourth oracle (vv. 15–19). But it may be that Agag was a common name among Amalekite kings and that the allusion here is to the Amalekites who attacked Israel when she came out of Egypt (see Ex 17:8–13) and again when she first approached Canaan (see 14:45).

24:8 *God brought him forth out of Egypt.* These central words about Israel's salvation are recited by one who was a hostile outsider (see notes on 23:21; 25:1–18).

24:9 *Blessed is he that blesseth thee . . . curseth thee.* The theology of blessing and cursing in the promises made to Abraham (Gen 12:2–3) is now a part of this oracle of blessing. Perhaps here Balaam was reasserting his desire to be a part of Israel's blessing (see note on 23:10).

10 And Balak's anger was kindled against
Balaam, and he [a]smote his hands together:
and Balak said unto Balaam, [b]I called thee to
curse mine enemies, and behold, thou hast altogether blessed *them* these three times.
11 Therefore now flee thou to thy place: [a]I
thought to promote thee unto great honour; but
lo, the LORD hath kept thee back from honour.
12 And Balaam said unto Balak, Spake I not
also to thy messengers which thou sentest
unto me, saying,
13 [a]If Balak would give me his house full *of*
silver and gold, I cannot go beyond the commandment of the LORD, to do *either* good or
bad of mine own mind; *but* what the LORD
saith, that will I speak?
14 And now behold, I go unto my people:
come *therefore, and* [a]I will advertise thee
what this people shall do to thy people [b]in the
latter days.
15 And he took up his parable, and said,
Balaam the son of Beor hath said,
And the man whose eyes are open
hath said:
16 He hath said, which heard the words
of God,
And knew the knowledge of the most
High,
Which saw the vision of the Almighty,
Falling *into a trance,* but having his
eyes open:
17 [a]I shall see him, but not now:
I shall behold him, but not nigh:
There shall come [b]a Star out of Jacob,
And [c]a Sceptre shall rise out of Israel,
And shall [d][1]smite the corners of Moab,
And destroy all the children of Sheth.
18 And [a]Edom shall be a possession,
Seir also shall be a possession for his
enemies;
And Israel shall do valiantly.
19 [a]Out of Jacob shall come *he* that shall
have dominion,
And shall destroy him that remaineth
of the city.
20 ¶ And when he looked on Amalek, he
took up his parable, and said,
Amalek *was* [a][1]the first of the nations;
But his latter end [b][2]*shall be* that he
perish for ever.
21 ¶ And he looked on the Kenites, and
took up his parable, and said,
Strong *is* thy dwelling place,
And thou puttest thy nest in a rock.
22 Nevertheless [1]the Kenite shall be
wasted,
[2]Until Asshur shall carry thee away
captive.
23 ¶ And he took up his parable, and said,
Alas, who shall live when God doeth
this!
24 And ships *shall come* from the coast of
[a]Chittim,
And shall afflict Asshur, and shall afflict
[b]Eber,
And he also shall perish for ever.
25 And Balaam rose up, and went and [a]re-
turned to his place: and Balak also went his
way.

Israel's idolatry in Shittim

25 And Israel abode in [a]Shittim, and
[b]the people begun to commit whoredom with the daughters of Moab.
2 And [a]they called the people unto [b]the
sacrifices of their gods: and the people did eat,
and [c]bowed down to their gods.
3 And Israel joined himself unto Baal-peor:
and [a]the anger of the LORD was kindled against
Israel.
4 And the LORD said unto Moses, [a]Take all
the heads of the people, and hang them up before the LORD against the sun, [b]that the fierce
anger of the LORD may be turned away from
Israel.
5 And Moses said unto [a]the judges of Israel,

24:10 [a]Ezek. 21:14,17 [b]ch. 23:11; Neh. 13:2
24:11 [a]ch. 22:17,37
24:13 [a]ch. 22:18
24:14 [a]Mic. 6:5; Rev. 2:14 [b]Gen. 49:1; Dan. 2:28
24:17 [1]Or, *smite through the princes of Moab* [a]Rev. 1:7 [b]Mat. 2:2 [c]Gen. 49:10 [d]2 Sam. 8:2
24:18 [a]2 Sam. 8:14
24:19 [a]Gen. 49:10
24:20 [1]*The first of the nations that warred against Israel* [2]Or, shall be *even to destruction* [a]Ex. 17:8 [b]Ex. 17:14
24:22 [1]Heb. *Kain* [2]Or, *How long* shall it be ere *Asshur carry thee away captive?*
24:24 [a]Gen. 10:4 [b]Gen. 10:21,25
24:25 [a]See ch. 31:8
25:1 [a]ch. 33:49; Josh. 2:1 [b]1 Cor. 10:8
25:2 [a]Josh. 22:17; Hos. 9:10 [b]Ex. 34:15 [c]Ex. 20:5
25:3 [a]Ps. 106:29
25:4 [a]Deut. 4:3 [b]ver. 11; Deut. 13:17
25:5 [a]Ex. 18:21

24:11 *the LORD hath kept thee back from honour.* In his disgust with Balaam's failure to curse Israel, Balak now dismisses him without pay—the ultimate insult to his greed (see 2 Pet 2:15).
24:14 *in the latter days.* The distant (Messianic) future is usually indicated by this expression (see, e.g., Jer 48:47 and note).
24:15–16 As in the third oracle (see vv. 3–4), the introduction to the fourth oracle is lengthy, helping to prepare the reader for the startling words of the prophecy.
24:17 *Star . . . Sceptre.* Perhaps fulfilled initially in David, but ultimately in the coming Messianic ruler. Israel's future Deliverer will be like a star (cf. Rev 22:16) and scepter in his royalty and will bring victory over the enemies of his people (see v. 19). *Sheth.* Possibly the early inhabitants of Moab known as the Shutu people in ancient Egyptian documents.
24:20 *Amalek was the first.* The first to attack Israel and oppose the Lord's purpose with his people (see Ex 17:8–13).
24:21 *Kenites.* The name suggests a tribe of metal workers. In other passages the Kenites are allied with Israel (see, e.g., Judg 1:16; 4:11; 1 Sam 15:6). Since Moses' father-in-law was a Kenite but also associated with Midian (see Ex 2:16), it may be that Balaam's reference is to Midianites (see 22:4,7). *nest.* Hebrew *qen,* a wordplay on the word for Kenites (Hebrew *qeni*).
24:22 *Asshur.* Assyria.
24:24 *Chittim.* Probably ancient Kition in Cyprus. *And shall afflict Asshur, and shall afflict Eber, And . . . perish.* One nation will rise and supplant another, only to face its own doom. By contrast, there is the implied ongoing blessing on Israel, and their sure promise of a future deliverer who will have the final victory (vv. 17–19).
25:1–18 It is not until 31:8,16 that we learn that the principal instigator of Israel's apostasy was Balaam (see notes on 22:5,8). Failing to destroy Israel by means of the mantic curse, Balaam seduced Israel by the Canaanite fertility rites of Baal.
25:1 *Shittim.* Another name for the region of Israel's staging for the conquest of Canaan; it was across the Jordan River opposite the ancient city of Jericho (see Josh 2:1). *commit whoredom.* Israel's engagement in the fertility rites of Baal involved not only the evil of sexual immorality. It was also a breach of covenant with the Lord, a worship of the gods of the land (vv. 2–3) and a foretaste of the people's ruin in the unfolding of their history.
25:4 *hang them up . . . against the sun.* The special display of the corpses would warn survivors of the consequences of sin.

[b]Slay ye every one his men that were joined
unto Baal-peor.
6 And behold, one of the children of Israel
came and brought unto his brethren a Midianitish *woman* in the sight of Moses, and in
the sight of all the congregation of the children
of Israel, [a]who *were* weeping *before* the door
of the tabernacle of the congregation.
7 And [a]when Phinehas, [b]the son of Eleazar, the son of Aaron the priest, saw *it,* he rose
up from amongst the congregation, and took a
javelin in his hand;
8 And he went after the man of Israel into
the tent, and thrust both of them through, the
man of Israel, and the woman through her belly. So [a]the plague was stayed from the children
of Israel.
9 And [a]those that died in the plague were
twenty and four thousand.
10 ¶ And the LORD spake unto Moses, saying,
11 [a]Phinehas, the son of Eleazar, the son of
Aaron the priest, hath turned my wrath away
from the children of Israel, while he was zealous [1]for my sake among them, that I consumed
not the children of Israel in [b]my jealousy.
12 Wherefore say, [a]Behold, I give unto him
my covenant of peace:
13 And he shall have it, and [a]his seed after
him, *even* the covenant of [b]an everlasting
priesthood; because he was [c]zealous for his
God, and [d]made an atonement for the children of Israel.
14 Now the name of the Israelite that was
slain, *even* that was slain with the Midianitish
woman, *was* Zimri, the son of Salu, a prince of
a [1]chief house among the Simeonites.
15 And the name of the Midianitish
woman that was slain *was* Cozbi, the daughter
of [a]Zur; he *was* head over a people, *and* of a
chief house in Midian.

25:5 [b]Deut. 13:6,9
25:6 [a]Joel 2:17
25:7 [a]Ps. 106:30 [b]Ex. 6:25
25:8 [a]Ps. 106:30
25:9 [a]Deut. 4:3; 1 Cor. 10:8
25:11 [1][Heb. *with my zeal:* See 2 Cor. 11:2] [a]Ps. 106:30 [b]Ex. 20:5; Ps. 78:58; Ezek. 16:38
25:12 [a]Mal. 2:4,5
25:13 [a]See 1 Chr. 6:4 [b]Ex. 40:15 [c]Acts 22:3; Rom. 10:2 [d]Heb. 2:17
25:14 [1]Heb. *house of a father*
25:15 [a]ch. 31:8; Josh. 13:21
25:17 [a]ch. 31:2
25:18 [a]ch. 31:16; Rev. 2:14
26:2 [a]Ex. 30:12; 38:25,26; ch. 1:2 [b]ch. 1:3
26:3 [a]ver. 63; ch. 22:1; 31:12; 33:48; 35:1
26:4 [a]ch. 1:1
26:5 [a]Gen. 46:8; Ex. 6:14; 1 Chr. 5:1
26:9 [a]ch. 16:1,2

16 ¶ And the LORD spake unto Moses, saying,
17 [a]Vex the Midianites, and smite them:
18 For they vex you with their [a]wiles,
wherewith they have beguiled you in the matter of Peor, and in the matter of Cozbi, the
daughter of a prince of Midian, their sister,
which was slain in the day of the plague for
Peor's sake.

Israel's second census

26 And it came to pass after the plague,
that the LORD spake unto Moses and
unto Eleazar the son of Aaron the priest, saying,
2 [a]Take the sum of all the congregation of
the children of Israel, [b]from twenty years old
and upward, throughout their fathers' house,
all that *are able to* go *to* war in Israel.
3 And Moses and Eleazar the priest spake
with them [a]in the plains of Moab by Jordan
near Jericho, saying,
4 *Take the sum of the people,* from twenty
years old and upward; as the LORD [a]command-
ed Moses and the children of Israel, which
went forth out of the land of Egypt.
5 ¶ [a]Reuben, the eldest son of Israel: the
children of Reuben; Hanoch, *of whom cometh*
the family of the Hanochites: of Pallu, the family of the Palluites:
6 Of Hezron, the family of the Hezronites:
of Carmi, the family of the Carmites.
7 These *are* the families of the Reubenites:
and they that were numbered of them were
forty and three thousand and seven hundred
and thirty.
8 And the sons of Pallu; Eliab.
9 And the sons of Eliab; Nemuel, and Dathan, and Abiram. This *is that* Dathan and Abiram, *which were* [a]famous in the congregation,
who strove against Moses and against Aaron in

25:6 *brought unto his brethren a Midianitish woman.* The contempt for the holy things and the word of the Lord shown by Zimri (v. 14) and his lover Cozbi (v. 15) is unimaginable.

25:9 *twenty and four thousand.* The number of those who died because of the flagrant actions of the people in their worship of Baal exceeded even those who died in the rebellion of Korah and his allies (14,700; see 16:49). Again, the large number of those who died fits well with the immense number of the people stated in the first census (1:46) and the second (26:51).

25:11 *he was zealous for my sake.* Cf. Ex 20:4–6. The zeal of Phinehas for the Lord's honor became the occasion for the Lord's covenanting with him and his descendants as God's true priests (see note on Gen 9:9). This son of Eleazar contrasts with the casual wickedness of his uncles, Nadab and Abihu (see Lev 10:1–3 and notes).

25:17 *Vex the Midianites.* Because of their active participation in the seduction of the Israelites. Midianites had been in league with Balak from the beginning of the confrontation (see 22:4,7) and became the objects of a holy war (31:1–24).

26:1–51 The first census of those who were mustered for the war of conquest had been taken over 38 years earlier. That first generation of men 20 years old or more had nearly all died. It was now time for the new generation to be numbered and mustered for the campaign that awaited them. The aged Moses was joined in the task this time by his nephew Eleazar; Aaron was dead (see 20:28). In this second census the prominent clans of each tribe are listed. The numbers of most of the tribes increase. Reuben is one of the tribes that shows a decline. It is possible that the slight reduction of the families of Reuben was brought about by the judgment on their members during the rebellion of Korah and his Reubenite allies (see note on v. 9). In the intervening years the family of Reuben had nearly caught up with its former numbers (see note on v. 14). Note the comparison of the numbers of each tribe from the first census to the second:

Tribe	*First Census*	*Second Census*
Reuben	46,500	43,730
Simeon	59,300	22,200
Gad	45,650	40,500
Judah	74,600	76,500
Issachar	54,400	64,300
Zebulun	57,400	60,500
Ephraim	40,500	32,500
Manasseh	32,200	52,700
Benjamin	35,400	45,600
Dan	62,700	64,400
Asher	41,500	53,400
Naphtali	53,400	45,400
Total	603,550	601,730

26:9 *Dathan and Abiram.* The listing of Reuben's families becomes an occasion to remind the reader of the part that certain

the company of Korah, when they strove against the LORD:

10 [a]And the earth opened her mouth, and swallowed them up together with Korah, when that company died, what time the fire devoured two hundred and fifty men: [b]and they became a sign.

11 Notwithstanding [a]the children of Korah died not.

12 ¶ The sons of Simeon after their families: of [1]Nemuel, the family of the Nemuelites: of Jamin, the family of the Jaminites: of [2]Jachin, the family of the Jachinites:

13 Of [1]Zerah, the family of the Zarhites: of Shaul, the family of the Shaulites.

14 These *are* the families of the Simeonites, twenty and two thousand and two hundred.

15 ¶ The children of Gad after their families: of [1]Zephon, the family of the Zephonites: of Haggi, the family of the Haggites: of Shuni, the family of the Shunites:

16 Of [1]Ozni, the family of the Oznites: of Eri, the family of the Erites:

17 Of [1]Arod, the family of the Arodites: of Areli, the family of the Arelites.

18 These *are* the families of the children of Gad according to those that were numbered of them, forty thousand and five hundred.

19 ¶ [a]The sons of Judah *were* Er and Onan: and Er and Onan died in the land of Canaan.

20 And [a]the sons of Judah after their families were, of Shelah, the family of the Shelanites: of Pharez, the family of the Pharzites: of Zerah, the family of the Zarhites.

21 And the sons of Pharez were; of Hezron, the family of the Hezronites: of Hamul, the family of the Hamulites.

22 These *are* the families of Judah according to those that were numbered of them, threescore and sixteen thousand and five hundred.

23 ¶ [a]*Of* the sons of Issachar after their families: *of* Tola, the family of the Tolaites: of [1]Pua, the family of the Punites:

24 Of [1]Jashub, the family of the Jashubites: of Shimron, the family of the Shimronites.

25 These *are* the families of Issachar according to those that were numbered of them, threescore and four thousand and three hundred.

26 ¶ [a]*Of* the sons of Zebulun after their families: of Sered, the family of the Sardites: of Elon, the family of the Elonites: of Jahleel, the family of the Jahleelites.

27 These *are* the families of the Zebulunites according to those that were numbered of them, threescore thousand and five hundred.

28 ¶ [a]The sons of Joseph after their families *were* Manasseh and Ephraim.

29 *Of* the sons of Manasseh: of [a]Machir, the family of the Machirites: and Machir begat Gilead: of Gilead *come* the family of the Gileadites.

30 These *are* the sons of Gilead: *of* [1]Jeezer, the family of the Jeezerites: of Helek, the family of the Helekites:

31 And *of* Asriel, the family of the Asrielites: and *of* Shechem, the family of the Shechemites:

32 And *of* Shemida, the family of the Shemidaites: and *of* Hepher, the family of the Hepherites.

33 And [a]Zelophehad the son of Hepher had no sons, but daughters: and the names of the daughters of Zelophehad *were* Mahlah, and Noah, Hoglah, Milcah, and Tirzah.

34 These *are* the families of Manasseh, and those that were numbered of them, fifty and two thousand and seven hundred.

35 These *are* the sons of Ephraim after their families: of Shuthelah, the family of the Shuthalhites: of [1]Becher, the family of the Bachrites: of Tahan, the family of the Tahanites.

36 And these *are* the sons of Shuthelah: of Eran, the family of the Eranites.

37 These *are* the families of the sons of Ephraim according to those that were numbered of them, thirty and two thousand and five hundred. These *are* the sons of Joseph after their families.

38 ¶ [a]The sons of Benjamin after their families: of Bela, the family of the Belaites: of Ashbel, the family of the Ashbelites: of [1]Ahiram, the family of the Ahiramites:

39 Of [1]Shupham, the family of the Shuphamites: of Hupham, the family of the Huphamites.

40 And the sons of Bela were [1]Ard and Naaman: *of Ard,* the family of the Ardites: *and* of Naaman, the family of the Naamites.

41 These *are* the sons of Benjamin after their families: and they that were numbered of them *were* forty and five thousand and six hundred.

42 ¶ [a]These *are* the sons of Dan after their families: of [1]Shuham, the family of the Shuhamites. These *are* the families of Dan after their families.

26:10 [a]ch. 16:32,35 [b]ch. 16:38; See 1 Cor. 10:6; 2 Pet. 2:6
26:11 [a]Ex. 6:24; 1 Chr. 6:22
26:12 [1][Gen. 46:10, *Jemuel*] [2][1 Chr. 4:24, *Jarib*]
26:13 [1][Gen. 46:10, *Zohar*]
26:15 [1][Gen. 46:16, *Ziphion*]
26:16 [1][Or, *Ezbon,* Gen. 46:16]
26:17 [1][Gen. 46:16, *Arodi*]
26:19 [a]Gen. 38:2; 46:12
26:20 [a]1 Chr. 2:3
26:23 [1][Or, *Phuvah,* Gen. 46:13, and here, but *Puah* in 1 Chr. 7:1] [a]Gen. 46:13; 1 Chr. 7:1
26:24 [1][Or, *Job*]
26:26 [a]Gen. 46:14
26:28 [a]Gen. 46:20
26:29 [a]Josh. 17:1; 1 Chr. 7:14,15
26:30 [1][Called *Abiezer,* Josh. 17:2; Judg. 6:11,24,34]
26:33 [a]ch. 27:1; 36:11
26:35 [1][1 Chr. 7:20, *Bered*]
26:38 [1][Gen. 46:21, *Ehi;* 1 Chr. 8:1, *Aharah*] [a]Gen. 46:21; 1 Chr. 7:6
26:39 [1][Gen. 46:21, *Muppim and Huppim*]
26:40 [1][1 Chr. 8:3, *Addar*]
26:42 [1][Or, *Hushim*] [a]Gen. 46:23

of their number had in Korah's rebellion (see 16:1; cf. Jude 11).

26:14 *twenty and two thousand and two hundred.* The greatest loss was in the tribe of Simeon (down from 59,300). Zimri was from the house of Simeon (25:14). Perhaps most of the 24,000 who died in the plague of that time were from Simeon. The judgment was so recent that the tribe had not had time to recover, as had the tribe of Reuben (see note on vv. 1–51).

26:19 *Er and Onan.* The names of the evil sons of Judah had not been forgotten, but they had no heritage (see Gen 38:1–10).

26:20 *Pharez.* The line of David and Jesus would be traced through him (Ruth 4:18–22; Mat 1:1–3).

26:29,35 *Manasseh . . . Ephraim.* The order of the tribes is the same as in ch. 1, except for the inversion of Ephraim and Manasseh.

26:33 *Zelophehad . . . daughters.* See 27:1–11; 36.

26:34 *fifty and two thousand and seven hundred.* The greatest gain was in the tribe of Manasseh (up from 32,200). The reason for this increase is not known.

43 All the families of the Shuhamites, according to those that were numbered of them,
were threescore and four thousand and four
hundred.
44 ¶ [a]*Of* the children of Asher after their
families: of Jimna, the family of the Jimnites: of
Jesui, the family of the Jesuites: of Beriah, the
family of the Beriites.
45 Of the sons of Beriah: of Heber, the family of the Heberites: of Malchiel, the family of
the Malchielites.
46 And the name of the daughter of Asher
was Sarah.
47 These *are* the families of the sons of
Asher according to those that were numbered
of them; *who were* fifty and three thousand
and four hundred.
48 ¶ [a]*Of* the sons of Naphtali after their
families: of Jahzeel, the family of the Jahzeel-
ites: of Guni, the family of the Gunites:
49 Of Jezer, the family of the Jezerites: of
[1]Shillem, the family of the Shillemites.
50 These *are* the families of Naphtali according to their families: and they that were
numbered of them *were* forty and five thousand and four hundred.
51 [a]These *were* the numbered of the children of Israel, six hundred thousand and a
thousand seven hundred and thirty.
52 ¶ And the LORD spake unto Moses, saying,
53 [a]Unto these the land shall be divided
for an inheritance according to the number of
names.
54 [a]To many thou shalt [1]give the more inheritance, and to few thou shalt [2]give the less
inheritance: *to* every one shall his inheritance
be given according to those that were numbered of him.
55 Notwithstanding the land shall be [a]di-
vided by lot: according to the names of the
tribes of their fathers they shall inherit.
56 According to the lot shall the possession
thereof be divided between many and few.
57 ¶ [a]And these *are* they that were numbered of the Levites after their families: of Gershon, the family of the Gershonites: of Kohath,
the family of the Kohathites: of Merari, the
family of the Merarites.
58 These *are* the families of the Levites:
the family of the Libnites, the family of the Hebronites, the family of the Mahlites, the family
of the Mushites, the family of the Korahites.
And Kohath begat Amram.
59 And the name of Amram's wife *was*
[a]Jochebed, the daughter of Levi, whom *her
mother* bare to Levi in Egypt: and she bare
unto Amram Aaron and Moses, and Miriam
their sister.
60 [a]And unto Aaron was born Nadab, and
Abihu, Eleazar, and Ithamar.
61 And [a]Nadab and Abihu died, when they
offered strange fire before the LORD.
62 [a]And those that were numbered of
them were twenty and three thousand, all
males from a month old and upward: [b]for they
were not numbered among the children of Israel, because there was [c]no inheritance given
them among the children of Israel.
63 These *are* they that were numbered by
Moses and Eleazar the priest, who numbered
the children of Israel [a]in the plains of Moab by
Jordan *near* Jericho.
64 [a]But among these there was not a man
of them whom Moses and Aaron the priest
numbered, when they numbered the children
of Israel in the wilderness of Sinai.
65 For the LORD had said of them, They
[a]shall surely die in the wilderness. And there
was not left a man of them, [b]save Caleb the
son of Jephunneh, and Joshua the son of Nun.

The daughters of Zelophehad

27 Then came the daughters of
[a]Zelophehad, the son of Hepher, the
son of Gilead, the son of Machir, the son of
Manasseh, of the families of Manasseh the son
of Joseph: and these *are* the names of his
daughters; Mahlah, Noah, and Hoglah, and
Milcah, and Tirzah.
2 And they stood before Moses, and before
Eleazar the priest, and before the princes and
all the congregation, *by* the door of the tabernacle of the congregation, saying,
3 Our father [a]died in the wilderness, and
he was not in the company of them that gathered themselves together against the LORD [b]in
the company of Korah; but died in his own sin,
and had no sons.
4 Why should the name of our father be
[1]done away from among his family, because
he hath no son? [a]Give unto us *therefore* a possession among the brethren of our father.

26:44 [a]Gen. 46:17; 1 Chr. 7:30
26:48 [a]Gen. 46:24; 1 Chr. 7:13
26:49 [1][1 Chr. 7:13, *Shallum*]
26:51 [a]See ch. 1:46
26:53 [a]Josh. 11:23; 14:1
26:54 [1]Heb. *multiply his inheritance* [2]Heb. *diminish his inheritance* [a]ch. 33:54
26:55 [a]ch. 33:54; 34:13; Josh. 11:23; 14:2
26:57 [a]Gen. 46:11; Ex. 6:16-19; 1 Chr. 6:1,16
26:59 [a]Ex. 2:1,2; 6:20
26:60 [a]ch. 3:2
26:61 [a]Lev. 10:1,2; ch. 3:4; 1 Chr. 24:2
26:62 [a]See ch. 3:39 [b]ch. 1:49 [c]ch. 18:20,23,24; Deut. 10:9; Josh. 13:14,33
26:63 [a]ver. 3
26:64 [a]ch. 1; Deut. 2:14,15
26:65 [a]ch. 14:28,29; 1 Cor. 10:5,6 [b]ch. 14:30
27:1 [a]ch. 26:33; 36:1,11; Josh. 17:3
27:3 [a]ch. 14:35; 26:64,65 [b]ch. 16:1,2
27:4 [1]Heb. *diminished* [a]Josh. 17:4

26:46 *daughter . . . was Sarah.* The listing of this solitary daughter is striking.

26:51 *six hundred thousand and a thousand seven hundred and thirty.* Despite all that the people had been through during the years of wilderness experience, their total number was nearly the same as that of those who were first numbered. This remarkable fact is to be regarded as the blessing of the Lord, in fulfillment of His many promises to give numerical strength to the people descended from Abraham through Jacob (see note on Gen 12:2–3). This grand total and its parts are in accord with the general pattern of the numbers in the book (see note on 1:46).

26:53 *divided . . . according to the number.* Larger tribes would receive larger shares, but decisions of place would be made by lot (see 33:54).

26:57 *Levites.* As in the first census (ch. 3), the Levites were counted separately.

27:1–11 The daughters of a man who had no son (see 26:33) were concerned about their rights of inheritance and the preservation of their father's name in the land (v. 4). Their action in approaching Moses, Eleazar and the leaders of the nation was unprecedented, an act of courage and conviction.

27:3 *died in his own sin.* A particular case from among those who died in the wilderness (see 26:64–65). These pious women had a sound understanding of the nature of the wilderness experience and a just claim for their family.

5 And Moses [a]brought their cause before the LORD.

6 And the LORD spake unto Moses, saying,

7 The daughters of Zelophehad speak right: [a]thou shalt surely give them a possession of an inheritance among their father's brethren; and thou shalt cause the inheritance of their father to pass unto them.

8 And thou shalt speak unto the children of Israel, saying, If a man die, and have no son, then ye shall cause his inheritance to pass unto his daughter.

9 And if he have no daughter, then ye shall give his inheritance unto his brethren.

10 And if he have no brethren, then ye shall give his inheritance unto his father's brethren.

11 And if his father have no brethren, then ye shall give his inheritance unto his kinsman that is next to him of his family, and he shall possess it: and it shall be unto the children of Israel [a]a statute of judgment, as the LORD commanded Moses.

Joshua to succeed Moses

12 ¶ And the LORD said unto Moses, [a]Get thee up into this mount Abarim, and see the land which I have given unto the children of Israel.

13 And when thou hast seen it, thou also [a]shalt be gathered unto thy people, as Aaron thy brother was gathered.

14 For ye [a]rebelled against my commandment in the desert of Zin, in the strife of the congregation, to sanctify me at the water before their eyes: that *is* the [b]water of Meribah in Kadesh *in* the wilderness of Zin.

15 And Moses spake unto the LORD, saying,

16 Let the LORD, [a]the God of the spirits of all flesh, set a man over the congregation,

17 [a]Which may go out before them, and which may go in before them, and which may lead them out, and which may bring them in; that the congregation of the LORD be not [b]as sheep which have no shepherd.

18 And the LORD said unto Moses, Take thee Joshua the son of Nun, a man [a]in whom *is* the spirit, and [b]lay thine hand upon him;

19 And set him before Eleazar the priest, and before all the congregation; and [a]give him a charge in their sight.

20 And [a]thou shalt put *some* of thine honour upon him, that all the congregation of the children of Israel [b]may be obedient.

21 [a]And he shall stand before Eleazar the priest, who shall ask *counsel* for him [b]after the judgment of Urim before the LORD: [c]at his word shall they go out, and at his word they shall come in, *both* he, and all the children of Israel with him, even all the congregation.

22 And Moses did as the LORD commanded him: and he took Joshua, and set him before Eleazar the priest, and before all the congregation:

23 And he laid his hands upon him, [a]and gave him a charge, as the LORD commanded by the hand of Moses.

The daily burnt offering

28 And the LORD spake unto Moses, saying,

2 Command the children of Israel, and say unto them, My offering, *and* [a]my bread for my sacrifices made by fire, *for* [1]a sweet savour unto me, shall ye observe to offer unto me in their due season.

3 And thou shalt say unto them, [a]This *is* the offering made by fire which ye shall offer unto the LORD; two lambs of the first year without spot [1]day by day, *for* a continual burnt offering.

4 The one lamb shalt thou offer in the morning, and the other lamb shalt thou offer [1]at even;

5 And [a]a tenth *part* of an ephah *of* flour for a [b]meat offering, mingled with the fourth *part* of a [c]hin of beaten oil.

6 *It is* [a]a continual burnt offering, which was ordained in mount Sinai for a sweet savour, a sacrifice made by fire unto the LORD.

7 And the drink offering thereof *shall be* the fourth *part* of a hin for the one lamb: [a]in the holy *place* shalt thou cause the strong wine to be poured unto the LORD *for* a drink offering.

8 And the other lamb shalt thou offer at even: as the meat offering of the morning, and as the drink offering thereof, thou shalt offer *it*, a sacrifice made by fire, *of* a sweet savour unto the LORD.

27:5 [a]Ex. 18:15,19 **27:7** [a]ch. 36:2 **27:11** [a]ch. 35:29 **27:12** [a]ch. 33:47; Deut. 3:27; 32:49 **27:13** [a]ch. 20:24,28; 31:2; Deut. 10:6 **27:14** [a]ch. 20:12,24; Deut. 1:37; 32:51; Ps. 106:32 [b]Ex. 17:7 **27:16** [a]ch. 16:22; Heb. 12:9 **27:17** [a]Deut. 31:2; 1 Sam. 8:20; 18:13; 2 Chr. 1:10 [b]1 Ki. 22:17; Zech. 10:2; Mat. 9:36; Mark 6:34 **27:18** [a]Gen. 41:38; Judg. 3:10; 1 Sam. 16:13,18 [b]Deut. 34:9

27:19 [a]Deut. 31:7 **27:20** [a]See ch. 11:17,28 [b]Josh. 1:16,17 **27:21** [a]Judg. 20:18,23,26; 1 Sam. 23:9; 30:7 [b]Ex. 28:30 [c]Josh. 9:14; 1 Sam. 22:10,13,15 **27:23** [a]Deut. 3:28; 31:7 **28:2** [1]Heb. *a savour of my rest* [a]Lev. 3:11; 21:6,8; Mal. 1:7,12 **28:3** [1]Heb. *in a day* [a]Ex. 29:38 **28:4** [1]Heb. *between the two evenings* **28:5** [a]Ex. 16:36; ch. 15:4 [b]Lev. 2:1 [c]Ex. 29:40 **28:6** [a]Ex. 29:42; See Amos 5:25 **28:7** [a]Ex. 29:42

27:5 *Moses brought their cause before the LORD.* This verse indicates how case law might have operated in Israel. The general laws would be proclaimed. Then legitimate exceptions or special considerations would come to the elders, and perhaps to Moses himself. He then would await a decision from the Lord. In this case, the Lord gave a favorable decision for these women. Ch. 36 provides an appendix to this account.

27:12–23 The juxtaposition of the story of Zelophehad's daughters' request for an inheritance in the land (vv. 1–11) and the Lord's words to Moses about his own exclusion from the land (vv. 12–14) is touching. Provisions are made for exceptions and irregularities in the inheritance laws, but there is no provision for Moses. His sin at the waters of Meribah at Kadesh (20:1–13) was always before him.

27:16 *set a man.* Moses' reaction to this reassertion of his restriction is a prayer for his successor.

27:18 *Take thee Joshua.* As Moses and Aaron needed to determine the true successor of Aaron before his death (20:22–29), so the true successor of Moses also needed to be established. Joshua and Caleb were the two heroes in the darkest hour of Israel's apostasy (chs. 13–14). It was fitting that the Lord selected one of them (cf. Ex 17:9–14; 24:13; 32:17; 33:11).

27:20 *put some of thine honour upon him.* The transition from Moses' leadership to that of any successor would be difficult. The change would be smoother by a gradual shift of power while Moses was still alive.

28:1–29:40 These chapters attest to the all-pervasiveness of sacrifice in the life of the people and to the enormity of the work of the priests. Perhaps the reason for these passages at this time is to give continuity to the impending transition from the leadership of Moses to that of Joshua (27:12–23).

28:1–8 See Ex 29:38–41; Lev 1–7 and notes.

The offering on the sabbath

9 ¶ And on the sabbath day two lambs of
the first year without spot, and two tenth deals
of flour *for* a meat offering, mingled with oil,
and the drink offering thereof:
10 *This is* [a]the burnt offering of every sabbath, beside the continual burnt offering, and
his drink offering.

The offering at the new moon

11 ¶ And [a]in the beginnings of your
months ye shall offer a burnt offering unto the
LORD; two young bullocks, and one ram, seven
lambs of the first year without spot;
12 And [a]three tenth deals *of* flour *for* a
meat offering, mingled with oil, for one bullock; and two tenth deals *of* flour *for* a meat offering, mingled with oil, for one ram;
13 And a several tenth deal of flour mingled with oil *for* a meat offering unto one
lamb; *for* a burnt offering *of* a sweet savour, a
sacrifice made by fire unto the LORD.
14 And their drink offerings shall be half a
hin of wine unto a bullock, and the third *part*
of a hin unto a ram, and a fourth *part* of a hin
unto a lamb: this *is* the burnt offering of every
month throughout the months of the year.
15 And [a]one kid of the goats for a sin offering unto the LORD shall be offered, besides the
continual burnt offering, and his drink offering.

The feast of unleavened bread

16 ¶ [a]And in the fourteenth day of the first
month *is* the passover of the LORD.
17 [a]And in the fifteenth day of this month
is the feast: seven days shall unleavened bread
be eaten.
18 In the [a]first day *shall be* a holy convocation; ye shall do no *manner of* servile work
therein:
19 But ye shall offer a sacrifice made by fire
for a burnt offering unto the LORD; two young
bullocks, and one ram, and seven lambs of the
first year: [a]they shall be unto you without
blemish:
20 And their meat offering *shall be of* flour
mingled with oil: three tenth deals shall ye offer for a bullock, and two tenth deals for a ram;
21 A several tenth deal shalt thou offer for
every lamb, throughout the seven lambs;
22 And [a]one goat for a sin offering, to
make an atonement for you.
23 Ye shall offer these beside the burnt offering in the morning, which *is* for a continual
burnt offering.
24 After this manner ye shall offer daily,
throughout the seven days, the meat of the
sacrifice made by fire, *of* a sweet savour unto
the LORD: it shall be offered beside the continual burnt offering, and his drink offering.
25 And [a]on the seventh day ye shall have a
holy convocation; ye shall do no servile work.
26 ¶ Also [a]in the day of the firstfruits,
when ye bring a new meat offering unto the
LORD, after your weeks *be out,* ye shall have a
holy convocation; ye shall do no servile work:
27 But ye shall offer the burnt offering for a
sweet savour unto the LORD; [a]two young bullocks, one ram, seven lambs of the first year;
28 And their meat offering *of* flour mingled
with oil, three tenth deals unto one bullock,
two tenth deals unto one ram,
29 A several tenth deal unto one lamb,
throughout the seven lambs;
30 *And* one kid of the goats, to make an
atonement for you.
31 Ye shall offer *them* besides the continual burnt offering, and his meat offering, ([a]they
shall be unto you without blemish) and their
drink offerings.

Feast of the trumpets offerings

29 And in the seventh month, on the
first *day* of the month, ye shall have a
holy convocation; ye shall do no servile work:
[a]it is a day of blowing the trumpets unto you.
2 And ye shall offer a burnt offering for a
sweet savour unto the LORD; one young bullock, one ram, *and* seven lambs of the first year
without blemish:
3 And their meat offering *shall be of* flour
mingled with oil, three tenth deals for a bullock, *and* two tenth deals for a ram,
4 And one tenth deal for one lamb,
throughout the seven lambs:
5 And one kid of the goats for a sin offering, to make an atonement for you:
6 Beside [a]the burnt offering of the month,
and his meat offering, and [b]the daily burnt offering, and his meat offering, and their drink
offerings, [c]according unto their manner, for a
sweet savour, a sacrifice made by fire unto the
LORD.

Day of atonement offerings

7 ¶ And [a]ye shall have on the tenth *day* of
this seventh month a holy convocation; and ye

28:10 [a]Ezek. 46:4
28:11 [a]ch. 10:10; 1 Sam. 20:5; 1 Chr. 23:31; 2 Chr. 2:4; Ezra 3:5; Neh. 10:33; Is. 1:13,14; Ezek. 45:17; 46:6; Hos. 2:11; Col. 2:16
28:12 [a]ch. 15:4-12
28:15 [a]ver. 22; ch. 15:24
28:16 [a]Ex. 12:6,18; Lev. 23:5; ch. 9:3; Deut. 16:1; Ezek. 45:21
28:17 [a]Lev. 23:6
28:18 [a]Ex. 12:16; Lev. 23:7
28:19 [a]ver. 31; Lev. 22:20; ch. 29:8; Deut. 15:21
28:22 [a]ver. 15
28:25 [a]Ex. 13:6; Lev. 23:8
28:26 [a]Ex. 23:16; 34:22; Lev. 23:10,15; Deut. 16:10; Acts 2:1
28:27 [a]See Lev. 23:18,19
28:31 [a]ver. 19
29:1 [a]Lev. 23:24
29:6 [a]ch. 28:11 [b]ch. 28:3 [c]ch. 15:11,12
29:7 [a]Lev. 16:29; 23:27

28:9–10 The sabbath offerings were in addition to the daily offerings.

28:11–15 The sacrifices at the beginning of the month were of great significance. These were times for celebration and blowing of trumpets in worship (see 10:10).

28:16–25 The priests are instructed as to the proper preparation for the passover in the first month of the year. Passover is also associated with the feast of unleavened bread (see Ex 12:15; Lev 23:4–8). The number 7 (and 14, its multiple) reappears frequently in the paragraph.

28:26–31 The feast of weeks came 50 days after the feast of unleavened bread (see Lev 23:9–22); from this number the term "Pentecost" (meaning "fifty") was used in the NT (Acts 2:1).

29:1–6 The feast of the trumpets came at the beginning of the seventh month, a busy month for the worship of the Lord in holy festivals (see Lev 23:23–25; see also chart, pp. 166–167). Later in Jewish tradition this feast commemorated the New Year, *Rosh Hashanah.* The trumpet used was the *shophar,* the ram's horn.

29:7–11 The feast of the trumpets leads into the day of atonement, a time of confession, contrition and celebration (see Lev 16; 23:26–32).

shall [b]afflict your souls: ye shall not do any work *therein:*

8 But ye shall offer a burnt offering unto the LORD *for* a sweet savour; one young bullock, one ram, *and* seven lambs of the first year; [a]they shall be unto you without blemish:

9 And their meat offering *shall be of* flour mingled with oil, three tenth deals to a bullock, *and* two tenth deals to one ram,

10 A several tenth deal for one lamb, throughout the seven lambs:

11 One kid of the goats *for* a sin offering; beside [a]the sin offering of atonement, and the continual burnt offering, and the meat offering of it, and their drink offerings.

Feast of tabernacles offerings

12 ¶ And [a]on the fifteenth day of the seventh month ye shall have a holy convocation; ye shall do no servile work, and ye shall keep a feast unto the LORD seven days:

13 And [a]ye shall offer a burnt offering, a sacrifice made by fire, *of* a sweet savour unto the LORD; thirteen young bullocks, two rams, *and* fourteen lambs of the first year; they shall be without blemish:

14 And their meat offering *shall be of* flour mingled with oil, three tenth deals unto every bullock of the thirteen bullocks, two tenth deals to each ram of the two rams,

15 And a several tenth deal to each lamb of the fourteen lambs:

16 And one kid of the goats *for* a sin offering; beside the continual burnt offering, his meat offering, and his drink offering.

17 And on the second day *ye shall offer* twelve young bullocks, two rams, fourteen lambs of the first year without spot:

18 And their meat offering and their drink offerings for the bullocks, for the rams, and for the lambs, *shall be* according to their number, [a]after the manner:

19 And one kid of the goats *for* a sin offering; beside the continual burnt offering, and the meat offering thereof, and their drink offerings.

20 And on the third day eleven bullocks, two rams, fourteen lambs of the first year without blemish;

21 And their meat offering and their drink offerings for the bullocks, for the rams, and for the lambs, *shall be* according to their number, [a]after the manner:

22 And one goat for a sin offering; beside the continual burnt offering, and his meat offering, and his drink offering.

23 And on the fourth day ten bullocks, two rams, *and* fourteen lambs of the first year without blemish:

24 Their meat offering and their drink offerings for the bullocks, for the rams, and for the lambs, *shall be* according to their number, after the manner:

25 And one kid of the goats *for* a sin offering; beside the continual burnt offering, his meat offering, and his drink offering.

26 And on the fifth day nine bullocks, two rams, *and* fourteen lambs of the first year [a]without spot:

27 And their meat offering and their drink offerings for the bullocks, for the rams, and for the lambs, *shall be* according to their number, after the manner:

28 And one goat for a sin offering; beside the continual burnt offering, and his meat offering, and his drink offering.

29 And on the sixth day eight bullocks, two rams, *and* fourteen lambs of the first year without blemish:

30 And their meat offering and their drink offerings for the bullocks, for the rams, and for the lambs, *shall be* according to their number, after the manner:

31 And one goat for a sin offering; beside the continual burnt offering, his meat offering, and his drink offering.

32 And on the seventh day seven bullocks, two rams, *and* fourteen lambs of the first year without blemish:

33 And their meat offering and their drink offerings for the bullocks, for the rams, and for the lambs, *shall be* according to their number, after the manner:

34 And one goat for a sin offering; beside the continual burnt offering, his meat offering, and his drink offering.

35 On the eighth day ye shall have a [a]solemn assembly; ye shall do no servile work *therein:*

36 But ye shall offer a burnt offering, a sacrifice made by fire, *of* a sweet savour unto the LORD: one bullock, one ram, seven lambs of the first year without blemish:

37 Their meat offering and their drink offerings for the bullock, for the ram, and for the lambs, *shall be* according to their number, after the manner:

38 And one goat for a sin offering; beside the continual burnt offering, and his meat offering, and his drink offering.

39 These *things* ye shall [1]do unto the LORD in your [a]set feasts, besides your [b]vows, and your freewill offerings, for your burnt offerings, and for your meat offerings, and for your drink offerings, and for your peace offerings.

40 And Moses told the children of Israel according to all that the LORD commanded Moses.

The laws about vows

30 And Moses spake unto [a]the heads of the tribes concerning the children of

29:7 [b]Ps. 35:13; Is. 58:5
29:8 [a]ch. 28:19
29:11 [a]Lev. 16:3,5
29:12 [a]Lev. 23:34; Deut. 16:13; Ezek. 45:25
29:13 [a]Ezra 3:4; Dan. 9:24; Heb. 7:18,19; 8:13; 10:1-18
29:18 [a]ver. 3,4,9,10; ch. 15:12; 28:7,14
29:21 [a]ver. 18
29:26 [a]Heb. 7:26; 1 Pet. 1:19; Rev. 5:6-14
29:35 [a]Lev. 23:36
29:39 [1]Or, *offer* [a]Lev. 23:2; 1 Chr. 23:31; 2 Chr. 31:3; Ezra 3:5; Neh. 10:33; Is. 1:14 [b]Lev. 7:11,16; 22:21,23
30:1 [a]ch. 1:4,16; 7:2

29:12–34 In the seventh month the feast of the trumpets took place on the first day, the day of atonement occurred on the tenth day, and the feast of tabernacles began on the 15th day and lasted for seven days (see Lev 23:33–44). Each day of the feast of tabernacles had its own order for sacrifice.

29:40 *Moses told the children of Israel.* The recapitulation of these festivals was a necessary part of the transfer of power from Moses to Joshua.

30:1–16 The principal OT passage on vows (see Deut

Israel, saying, This *is* the thing which the LORD hath commanded.

2 [a]If a man vow a vow unto the LORD, or [b]swear an oath to bind his soul with a bond; he shall not [1]break his word, he shall [c]do according to all that proceedeth out of his mouth.

3 If a woman also vow a vow unto the LORD, and bind *herself by* a bond, *being* in her father's house in her youth;

4 And her father hear her vow, and her bond wherewith she hath bound her soul, and her father shall hold his peace at her: then all her vows shall stand, and every bond wherewith she hath bound her soul shall stand.

5 But if her father disallow her in the day that he heareth; not any of her vows, or of her bonds wherewith she hath bound her soul, shall stand: and the LORD shall forgive her, because her father disallowed her.

6 And if she had at all a husband, when [a][1]she vowed, or uttered ought out of her lips, wherewith she bound her soul;

7 And her husband heard *it,* and held his peace at her in the day that he heard *it:* then her vows shall stand, and her bonds wherewith she bound her soul shall stand.

8 But if her husband [a]disallow her on the day that he heard *it;* then he shall make her vow which she vowed, and that which she uttered with her lips, wherewith she bound her soul, of none effect: and the LORD shall forgive her.

9 But every vow of a widow, and of her that is divorced, wherewith they have bound their souls, shall stand against her.

10 And if she vowed *in* her husband's house, or bound her soul by a bond with an oath;

11 And her husband heard *it,* and held his peace at her, *and* disallowed her not: then all her vows shall stand, and every bond wherewith she bound her soul shall stand.

12 But if her husband hath utterly made them void on the day he heard *them; then* whatsoever proceeded out of her lips concerning her vows, or concerning the bond of her soul, shall not stand: her husband hath made them void; and the LORD shall forgive her.

13 Every vow, and every binding oath to afflict the soul, her husband may establish it, or her husband may make it void.

14 But if her husband altogether hold his peace at her from day to day; then he establisheth all her vows, or all her bonds, which *are* upon her: he confirmeth them, because he held his peace at her in the day that he heard *them.*

15 But if he shall any ways make them void after *that* he hath heard *them;* then he shall bear her iniquity.

16 These *are* the statutes, which the LORD commanded Moses, between a man and his wife, between the father and his daughter, *being yet* in her youth *in* her father's house.

The killing of the Midianites

31 And the LORD spake unto Moses, saying,

2 [a]Avenge the children of Israel of the Midianites: afterward shalt thou [b]be gathered unto thy people.

3 And Moses spake unto the people, saying, Arm some of yourselves unto the war, and let them go against the Midianites, and avenge the LORD of Midian.

4 [1]Of every tribe a thousand, throughout all the tribes of Israel, shall ye send to the war.

5 So there were delivered out of the thousands of Israel, a thousand of *every* tribe, twelve thousand armed for war.

6 And Moses sent them to the war, a thousand of *every* tribe, them and Phinehas the son of Eleazar the priest, to the war, with the holy instruments, and [a]the trumpets to blow in his hand.

7 And they warred against the Midianites, as the LORD commanded Moses; and [a]they slew all the [b]males.

8 And they slew the kings of Midian, beside *the rest of* them that were slain; *namely,* [a]Evi, and Rekem, and Zur, and Hur, and Reba,

30:2 [1]Heb. *profane* [a]Lev. 27:2; Deut. 23:21; Judg. 11:30,35; Eccl. 5:4 [b]Lev. 5:4; Mat. 14:9; Acts 23:14 [c]Job 22:27; Ps. 22:25; 50:14; 66:13,14; 116:14,18; Nah. 1:15
30:6 [1]Heb. *her vows* were *upon her* [a]Ps. 56:12
30:8 [a]Gen. 3:16

31:2 [a]ch. 25:17 [b]ch. 27:13
31:4 [1]Heb. *A thousand of a tribe, a thousand of a tribe*
31:6 [a]ch. 10:9
31:7 [a]Deut. 20:13; Judg. 21:11; 1 Sam. 27:9; 1 Ki. 11:15,16 [b]See Judg. 6:1,2,33
31:8 [a]Josh. 13:21

23:21–23). A vow is not to be made rashly (cf. Eccl 5:1–7), and a vow to the Lord must be kept.

30:3–5 The vow of an unmarried woman still under her father's protection might be nullified by her father. This and the following law were probably designed for the protection of the woman, who in ancient Near Eastern society was subject to strong societal pressures, some of which would leave her without defense.

30:6–8 The vow of a married woman might be nullified by her husband.

30:9 *widow, and . . . her that is divorced.* She is her own agent in the taking of vows.

30:10–15 Further examples of the complications that come in the taking of vows within the husband-wife relationship. Such complications may have come up much as in the case of Zelophehad's daughters (27:1–11). One case after another presented itself, resulting in this final codification. Presumably, in the centuries leading up to the NT, the legal decisions on vows became even more complex. The words of Jesus that one is to avoid complications connected with oaths (Mat 5:33–37) are liberating.

31:1–24 The Lord declares a holy war (see essay, p. 272) against the Midianites as one of Moses' last actions before the end of his life. Moses was not motivated by petty jealousy; rather, the war was the LORD'S vengeance (v. 3) for the Midianites' part in seducing the Israelites to engage in sexual immorality and to worship the Baal of Peor. (See 25:16–18, where the specific mention of Cozbi, a Midianite woman, heightens the anger expressed in ch. 31.)

31:2 *gathered unto thy people.* A euphemism for death (see, e.g., Gen 25:8,17; 35:29).

31:4 *Of every tribe a thousand . . . Israel.* The burden of the holy war had to be shared equally among the tribes.

31:6 *Phinehas.* His zeal for the Lord's honor led him to execute Zimri and Cozbi (25:8). Now he leads in the sacred aspects of the battle to demonstrate that this is a holy war. *trumpets.* See note on 10:3.

31:7 *as the LORD commanded Moses.* The battle was the Lord's.

five kings of Midian: [b]Balaam also the son of Beor they slew with the sword.

9 And the children of Israel took *all* the women of Midian captives, and their little ones, and took the spoil of all their cattle, and all their flocks, and all their goods.

10 And they burnt all their cities wherein they dwelt, and all their goodly castles, with fire.

11 And [a]they took all the spoil, and all the prey, *both* of men and of beasts.

12 And they brought the captives, and the prey, and the spoil, unto Moses, and Eleazar the priest, and unto the congregation of the children of Israel, unto the camp at the plains of Moab, which *are* by Jordan *near* Jericho.

Purification of those who killed

13 ¶ And Moses, and Eleazar the priest, and all the princes of the congregation, went forth to meet them without the camp.

14 And Moses was wroth with the officers of the host, *with* the captains over thousands, and captains over hundreds, which came from the [1]battle.

15 And Moses said unto them, Have ye saved [a]all the women alive?

16 Behold, [a]these caused the children of Israel, through the [b]counsel of Balaam, to commit trespass against the LORD in the matter of Peor, and [c]there was a plague among the congregation of the LORD.

17 Now therefore [a]kill every male among the little ones, and kill every woman that hath known man by lying with [1]him.

18 But all the women children, that have not known a man by lying with him, keep alive for yourselves.

19 And [a]do ye abide without the camp seven days: whosoever hath killed *any* person, and [b]whosoever hath touched *any* slain, purify *both* yourselves and your captives on the third day, and on the seventh day.

20 And purify all *your* raiment, and all [1]that is made of skins, and all work of goats' *hair,* and all things made of wood.

21 And Eleazar the priest said unto the men of war which went to the battle, This *is* the ordinance of the law which the LORD commanded Moses;

22 Only the gold, and the silver, the brass, the iron, the tin, and the lead,

23 Every thing that may abide the fire, ye shall make *it* go through the fire, and it shall be clean: nevertheless it shall be purified [a]with the water of separation: and all that abideth not the fire ye shall make go through the water.

24 [a]And ye shall wash your clothes on the seventh day, and ye shall be clean, and afterward ye shall come into the camp.

The division of the prey

25 ¶ And the LORD spake unto Moses, saying,

26 Take the sum of the prey [1]that was taken, *both* of man and of beast, thou, and Eleazar the priest, and the chief fathers of the congregation:

27 And [a]divide the prey into two parts; between them that took the war upon them, who went out to battle, and between all the congregation:

28 And levy a tribute unto the LORD of the men of war which went out to battle: [a]one soul of five hundred, *both* of the persons, and of the beeves, and of the asses, and of the sheep:

29 Take *it* of their half, and give *it* unto Eleazar the priest, *for* a heave offering of the LORD.

30 And of the children of Israel's half, thou shalt take [a]one portion of fifty, of the persons, of the beeves, of the asses, and of the [1]flocks, of all *manner of* beasts, and give them unto the Levites, [b]which keep the charge of the tabernacle of the LORD.

31 And Moses and Eleazar the priest did as the LORD commanded Moses.

32 And the booty, *being* the rest of the prey which the men of war had caught, was six hundred thousand and seventy thousand and five thousand sheep,

33 And threescore and twelve thousand beeves,

34 And threescore and one thousand asses,

35 And thirty and two thousand persons in all, of women that had not known man by lying with him.

36 And the half, *which was* the portion of them that went out to war, was *in* number three hundred thousand and seven and thirty thousand and five hundred sheep:

37 And the LORD'S [a]tribute of the sheep was six hundred *and* threescore and fifteen.

38 And the beeves *were* thirty and six thousand; of which the LORD'S tribute *was* threescore and twelve.

39 And the asses *were* thirty thousand and five hundred; of which the LORD'S tribute *was* threescore and one.

40 And the persons *were* sixteen thousand; of which the LORD'S tribute *was* thirty and two persons.

31:8 [b]Josh. 13:22
31:11 [a]Deut. 20:14
31:14 [1]Heb. *host of war*
31:15 [a]See Deut. 20:14; 1 Sam. 15:3
31:16 [a]ch. 25:2 [b]ch. 24:14; 2 Pet. 2:15; Rev. 2:14 [c]ch. 25:9
31:17 [1]Heb. *a male* [a]Judg. 21:11
31:19 [a]ch. 5:2 [b]ch. 19:11
31:20 [1]Heb. *instrument,* or, *vessel of skins*
31:23 [a]ch. 19:9,17
31:24 [a]Lev. 11:25
31:26 [1]Heb. *of the captivity*
31:27 [a]Josh. 22:8; 1 Sam. 30:24
31:28 [a]See ver. 30,47; ch. 18:26
31:30 [1]Or, *goats* [a]See ver. 42-47 [b]ch. 3:7,8,25,31,36; 18:3,4
31:37 [a]Lev. 25:23; Deut. 10:14; Job 41:11; Ps. 24:1; 50:12; Prov. 3:9; Luke 20:25; 1 Cor. 10:26,28

31:8 *Balaam . . . they slew with the sword.* Ch. 25 lacks the name of the principal instigator of the seduction of the Israelite men to the depraved worship of Baal. But here he is found among the dead. What Balaam had been unable to accomplish through acts of magic or sorcery (chs. 22–24) he was almost able to achieve by his advice to the Midianites (v. 16).

31:9–18 While the troops killed the men of Midian, they spared the women and children as plunder. Moses commanded that only the virgin women (who were thus innocent of the indecencies at Peor) could be spared; the guilty women and the boys (who might endanger the inheritance rights of Israelite men) were to be put to death (vv. 15–17).

31:19–24 Since this was holy war, both people (vv. 19–20) and things (vv. 21–24) had to be cleansed (cf. 19:11–13).

31:26–35 Another aspect of holy war was the fair distribution of the spoils of war, both among those who fought in the battle and among those who stayed with the community, with appropriate shares to be given to the Lord, whose battle it was (v. 28).

41 And Moses gave the tribute, *which was* the LORD'S heave offering, unto Eleazar the priest, [a]as the LORD commanded Moses.

42 And of the children of Israel's half, which Moses divided from the men that warred,

43 (Now the half that pertained unto the congregation was three hundred thousand and thirty thousand *and* seven thousand and five hundred sheep,

44 And thirty and six thousand beeves,

45 And thirty thousand asses and five hundred,

46 And sixteen thousand persons;)

47 Even [a]of the children of Israel's half, Moses took one portion of fifty, *both* of man and of beast, and gave them unto the Levites, which kept the charge of the tabernacle of the LORD; as the LORD commanded Moses.

48 ¶ And the officers which *were* over thousands of the host, the captains of thousands, and captains of hundreds, came near unto Moses:

49 And they said unto Moses, Thy servants have taken the sum of the men of war which *are* under our [1]charge, and there lacketh not one man of us.

50 We have therefore brought an oblation for the LORD, what every man hath [1]gotten, *of* jewels of gold, chains, and bracelets, rings, earrings, and tablets, [a]to make an atonement for our souls before the LORD.

51 And Moses and Eleazar the priest took the gold of them, *even* all wrought jewels.

52 And all the gold of the [1]offering that they offered up to the LORD, of the captains of thousands, and of the captains of hundreds, was sixteen thousand seven hundred and fifty shekels.

53 (*For* [a]the men of war had taken spoil, every man for himself.)

54 And Moses and Eleazar the priest took the gold of the captains of thousands and of hundreds, and brought it into the tabernacle of the congregation, [a]*for* a memorial for the children of Israel before the LORD.

Tribes to possess Gilead

32 Now the children of Reuben and the children of Gad had a very great multitude of cattle: and when they saw the land of [a]Jazer, and the land of Gilead, that behold, the place *was* a place for cattle;

2 The children of Gad and the children of Reuben came and spake unto Moses, and to Eleazar the priest, and unto the princes of the congregation, saying,

3 Ataroth, and Dibon, and Jazer, and [1]Nimrah, and Heshbon, and Elealeh, and [2]Shebam, and Nebo, and [3]Beon,

4 *Even* the country [a]which the LORD smote before the congregation of Israel, *is* a land for cattle, and thy servants have cattle:

5 Wherefore, said they, if we have found grace in thy sight, let this land be given unto thy servants for a possession, *and* bring us not over Jordan.

6 And Moses said unto the children of Gad and to the children of Reuben, Shall your brethren go to war, and shall ye sit here?

7 And wherefore [1]discourage ye the heart of the children of Israel from going over into the land which the LORD hath given them?

8 Thus did your fathers, [a]when I sent them from Kadesh-barnea [b]to see the land.

9 For [a]when they went up unto the valley of Eshcol, and saw the land, they discouraged the heart of the children of Israel, that *they* should not go into the land which the LORD had given them.

10 [a]And the LORD'S anger was kindled the same time, and he sware, saying,

11 Surely none of the men that came up out of Egypt, [a]from twenty years old and upward, shall see the land which I sware unto Abraham, unto Isaac, and unto Jacob; because [b]they have not [1]wholly followed me:

12 Save Caleb the son of Jephunneh the Kenezite, and Joshua the son of Nun: [a]for they have wholly followed the LORD.

13 And the LORD'S anger was kindled against Israel, and he made them [a]wander in the wilderness forty years, until [b]all the generation, that had done evil in the sight of the LORD, was consumed.

14 And behold, ye are risen up in your fathers' stead, an increase of sinful men, to augment yet the [a]fierce anger of the LORD toward Israel.

15 For if ye [a]turn away from after him, he will yet again leave them in the wilderness; and ye shall destroy all this people.

16 And they came near unto him, and said, We will build sheepfolds here for our cattle, and cities for our little ones:

17 But [a]we ourselves will go ready armed before the children of Israel, until we have brought them unto their place: and our little ones shall dwell in the fenced cities because of the inhabitants of the land.

18 [a]We will not return unto our houses, until the children of Israel have inherited every man his inheritance.

19 For we will not inherit with them on *yonder* side Jordan, or forward; [a]because our

31:41 [a]See ch. 18:8,19
31:47 [a]ver. 30
31:49 [1]Heb. *hand*
31:50 [1]Heb. *found* [a]Ex. 30:12,16
31:52 [1]Heb. *heave offering*
31:53 [a]Deut. 20:14
31:54 [a]Ex. 30:16
32:1 [a]ch. 21:32; Josh. 13:25; 2 Sam. 24:5
32:3 [1][ver. 36, *Beth-nimrah*] [2][ver. 38, *Shibmah*] [3][ver. 38, *Baal-meon*]
32:4 [a]ch. 21:24,34
32:7 [1]Heb. *break*
32:8 [a]ch. 13:3,26 [b]Deut. 1:22
32:9 [a]ch. 13:24,31; Deut. 1:24,28
32:10 [a]ch. 14:11,21; Deut. 1:34
32:11 [1]Heb. *fulfilled after me* [a]ch. 14:28,29; Deut. 1:35 [b]ch. 14:24,30
32:12 [a]ch. 14:24; Deut. 1:36; Josh. 14:8,9
32:13 [a]ch. 14:33-35 [b]ch. 26:64,65
32:14 [a]Deut. 1:34
32:15 [a]Deut. 30:17; Josh. 22:16,18; 2 Chr. 7:19
32:17 [a]Josh. 4:12,13
32:18 [a]Josh. 22:4
32:19 [a]ver. 33; Josh. 12:1; 13:8

32:1 *children of Reuben and the children of Gad.* The abundance of fertile grazing land east of the Jordan prompted the leaders of these two tribes to request that they be allowed to settle there and not cross the Jordan. This area too was a gift of God won by conquest.

32:8 *Thus did your fathers.* Moses' fear was that the failure of these two tribes to stay with the whole community in conquering Canaan would be the beginning of a general revolt against entering the land. It would be the failure of Kadesh (chs. 13–14) all over again. Moreover, the conquest of Canaan was a commission to all Israel.

32:17 *we ourselves will go ready armed.* The leaders of Reuben and Gad sought to assure Moses that they did not wish to shirk their duty in helping to conquer the land. They would join their brothers in battle but wished to leave their families and livestock behind in the territory of their choosing.

inheritance is fallen to us on *this* side Jordan
eastward.
20 And [a]Moses said unto them, If ye will
do this thing, if ye will go armed before the
LORD to war,
21 And will go all of you armed over Jordan
before the LORD, until he hath driven out his
enemies from before him,
22 And [a]the land be subdued before the
LORD: then afterward [b]ye shall return, and be
guiltless before the LORD, and before Israel;
and [c]this land shall be your possession before
the LORD.
23 But if ye will not do so, behold, ye have
sinned against the LORD: and be sure [a]your sin
will find you out.
24 [a]Build ye cities for your little ones, and
folds for your sheep; and do that which hath
proceeded out of your mouth.
25 And the children of Gad and the children of Reuben spake unto Moses, saying, Thy
servants will do as my lord commandeth.
26 [a]Our little ones, our wives, our flocks,
and all our cattle, shall be there in the cities of
Gilead:
27 [a]But thy servants will pass over, every
man armed for war, before the LORD to battle,
as my lord saith.
28 So [a]concerning them Moses commanded Eleazar the priest, and Joshua the son of
Nun, and the chief fathers of the tribes of the
children of Israel:
29 And Moses said unto them, If the children of Gad and the children of Reuben will
pass with you over Jordan, every man armed
to battle, before the LORD, and the land shall
be subdued before you; then ye shall give
them the land of Gilead for a possession:
30 But if they will not pass over with you
armed, they shall have possessions among you
in the land of Canaan.
31 And the children of Gad and the children of Reuben answered, saying, As the LORD
hath said unto thy servants, so will we do.
32 We will pass over armed before the
LORD *into* the land of Canaan, that the possession of our inheritance on *this* side Jordan *may
be* ours.
33 And [a]Moses gave unto them, *even* to
the children of Gad, and to the children of
Reuben, and unto half the tribe of Manasseh
the son of Joseph, [b]the kingdom of Sihon king
of the Amorites, and the kingdom of Og king
of Bashan, the land, with the cities thereof in
the coasts, *even* the cities of the country round
about.
34 ¶ And the children of Gad built [a]Dibon,
and Ataroth, and [b]Aroer,
35 And Atroth, Shophan, and [1]Jaazer, and
Jogbehah,
36 And [1]Beth-nimrah, and Beth-haran,
[a]fenced cities: and folds for sheep.
37 And the children of Reuben [a]built
Heshbon, and Elealeh, and Kirjathaim,
38 And [a]Nebo, and [b]Baal-meon, ([c]*their
names being changed,*) and Shibmah: and
[1]gave other names unto the cities which they
builded.
39 And the children of [a]Machir the son of
Manasseh went to Gilead, and took it, and dispossessed the Amorite which *was* in it.
40 And Moses [a]gave Gilead unto Machir
the son of Manasseh; and he dwelt therein.
41 And [a]Jair the son of Manasseh went and
took the small towns thereof, and called them
[b]Havoth-jair.
42 And Nobah went and took Kenath, and
the villages thereof, and called it Nobah, after
his own name.

Journey from Egypt to Canaan

33 These *are* the journeys of the children of Israel, which went forth out
of the land of Egypt with their armies under
the hand of Moses and Aaron.
2 And Moses wrote their goings out according to their journeys by the commandment of the LORD: and these *are* their journeys
according to their goings out.
3 And they [a]departed from Rameses in
[b]the first month, on the fifteenth day of the
first month; on the morrow after the passover
the children of Israel went out [c]with a high
hand in the sight of all the Egyptians.
4 For the Egyptians buried all *their* firstborn, [a]which the LORD had smitten among
them: [b]upon their gods also the LORD executed
judgments.
5 [a]And the children of Israel removed from
Rameses, and pitched in Succoth.

32:20 [a]Deut. 3:18; Josh. 1:14; 4:12,13 **32:22** [a]Deut. 3:20; Josh. 11:23; 18:1 [b]Josh. 22:4 [c]Deut. 3:12,15,16,18; Josh. 1:15; 13:8,32; 22:4,9 **32:23** [a]Gen. 4:7; 44:16; Is. 59:12 **32:24** [a]ver. 16,34 **32:26** [a]Josh. 1:14 **32:27** [a]Josh. 4:12 **32:28** [a]Josh. 1:13 **32:33** [a]Deut. 3:12-17; 29:8; Josh. 12:6; 13:8; 22:4 [b]ch. 21:24,33,35 **32:34** [a]ch. 33:45,46 [b]Deut. 2:36 **32:35** [1][ver. 1,3, *Jazer*] **32:36** [1][ver. 3, *Nimrah*] [a]ver. 24 **32:37** [a]ch. 21:27 **32:38** [1]Heb. *they called by names the names of the cities* [a]Is. 46:1 [b]ch. 22:41 [c]See ver. 3; Ex. 23:13; Josh. 23:7 **32:39** [a]Gen. 50:23 **32:40** [a]Deut. 3:12,13,15; Josh. 13:31; 17:1 **32:41** [a]Deut. 3:14; Josh. 13:30; 1 Chr. 2:21 [b]Judg. 10:4; 1 Ki. 4:13 **33:3** [a]Ex. 12:37 [b]Ex. 12:2; 13:4 [c]Ex. 14:8 **33:4** [a]Ex. 12:29 [b]Ex. 12:12; 18:11; Is. 19:1; Rev. 12:8 **33:5** [a]Ex. 12:37

32:23 *be sure your sin will find you out.* The bargain was struck, but not without strong warnings if they failed to live up to their word.

32:33 *half the tribe of Manasseh.* It appears that after the requirements for settlement east of the Jordan were established with the tribes of Reuben and Gad, half the tribe of Manasseh joined with them.

33:1–49 The numerous places (significantly 40 in number between Rameses and the plains of Moab) in Israel's wilderness experience are listed. Unfortunately, most of the sites were wilderness encampments, not cities with lasting archaeological records; so they are difficult to locate. Many of the places (e.g., in vv. 19–29) are not recorded elsewhere in Exodus and Numbers. Some of the places mentioned elsewhere (e.g., Taberah, 11:3; see 21:19) are missing here. The data warrant these conclusions: 1. Moses recorded the list at the Lord's command (v. 2). 2. The list should be taken seriously, as an accurate recapitulation of the stages of the journey, despite difficulty in locating many of the sites. 3. The numerical factor of 40 sites between Rameses and the plains of Moab suggests some styling of the list, which helps to account for the sites not included. 4. As in the case of genealogies in the Pentateuch, some factors of ancient significance may not be clear to us today. 5. Ultimately the record is a recital of the Lord's blessing on His people for the extended period of their wilderness experience. Although certainly not without geographical importance, the listing of the stages of Israel's experience in the wilderness is fundamentally a religious document, a litany of the Lord's deliverance of His people.

6 And they departed from [a]Succoth, and pitched in Etham, which *is* in the edge of the wilderness.

7 And [a]they removed from Etham, and turned again unto Pi-hahiroth, which *is* before Baal-zephon: and they pitched before Migdol.

8 And they departed from before *Pi*-hahiroth, and [a]passed through the midst of the sea into the wilderness, and went three days' journey in the wilderness of Etham, and pitched in Marah.

9 And they removed from Marah, and [a]came unto Elim: and in Elim *were* twelve fountains of water, and threescore and ten palm trees; and they pitched there.

10 And they removed from Elim, and encamped by the Red sea.

11 And they removed from the Red sea, and encamped in the [a]wilderness of Sin.

12 And they took their journey out of the wilderness of Sin, and encamped in Dophkah.

13 And they departed from Dophkah, and encamped in Alush.

14 And they removed from Alush, and encamped at [a]Rephidim, where was no water for the people to drink.

15 And they departed from Rephidim, and pitched in the [a]wilderness of Sinai.

16 And they removed from the desert of Sinai, and pitched [a]at [1]Kibroth-hattaavah.

17 And they departed from Kibroth-hattaavah, and [a]encamped at Hazeroth.

18 And they departed from Hazeroth, and pitched in [a]Rithmah.

19 And they departed from Rithmah, and pitched at Rimmon-parez.

20 And they departed from Rimmon-parez, and pitched in Libnah.

21 And they removed from Libnah, and pitched at Rissah.

22 And they journeyed from Rissah, and pitched in Kehelathah.

23 And they went from Kehelathah, and pitched in mount Shapher.

24 And they removed from mount Shapher, and encamped in Haradah.

25 And they removed from Haradah, and pitched in Makheloth.

26 And they removed from Makheloth, and encamped at Tahath.

27 And they departed from Tahath, and pitched at Tarah.

28 And they removed from Tarah, and pitched in Mithcah.

29 And they went from Mithcah, and pitched in Hashmonah.

30 And they departed from Hashmonah, and [a]encamped at Moseroth.

31 And they departed from Moseroth, and pitched in Bene-jaakan.

32 And they removed from [a]Bene-jaakan, and [b]encamped at Hor-hagidgad.

33 And they went from Hor-hagidgad, and pitched in Jotbathah.

34 And they removed from Jotbathah, and encamped at Ebronah.

35 And they departed from Ebronah, [a]and encamped at Ezion-gaber.

36 And they removed from Ezion-gaber, and pitched in the [a]wilderness of Zin, which *is* Kadesh.

37 And they removed from [a]Kadesh, and pitched in mount Hor, in the edge of the land of Edom.

38 And [a]Aaron the priest went up into mount Hor at the commandment of the LORD, and died there, in the fortieth year after the children of Israel were come out of the land of Egypt, in the first *day* of the fifth month.

39 And Aaron *was* an hundred and twenty and three years old when he died in mount Hor.

40 And [a]king Arad the Canaanite, which dwelt in the south in the land of Canaan, heard of the coming of the children of Israel.

41 And they departed from mount [a]Hor, and pitched in Zalmonah.

42 And they departed from Zalmonah, and pitched in Punon.

43 And they departed from Punon, and [a]pitched in Oboth.

44 And [a]they departed from Oboth, and pitched in [b1]Ije-abarim, in the border of Moab.

45 And they departed from Iim, and pitched [a]in Dibon-gad.

46 And they removed from Dibon-gad, and encamped in Almon-[a]diblathaim.

47 And they removed from Almon-diblathaim, [a]and pitched in the mountains of Abarim, before Nebo.

48 And they departed from the mountains of Abarim, and [a]pitched in the plains of Moab by Jordan *near* Jericho.

49 And they pitched by Jordan, from Beth-jesimoth *even* unto [a1]Abel-shittim in the plains of Moab.

50 ¶ And the LORD spake unto Moses in the plains of Moab by Jordan *near* Jericho, saying,

51 Speak unto the children of Israel, and say unto them, [a]When ye are passed over Jordan into the land of Canaan;

52 [a]Then ye shall drive out all the inhabitants of the land from before you, and destroy all their pictures, and destroy all their molten images, and quite pluck down all their high places:

53 And ye shall dispossess *the inhabitants of* the land, and dwell therein: for I have given you the land to possess it.

54 And [a]ye shall divide the land by lot for an inheritance among your families: *and* to the

33:6 [a]Ex. 13:20
33:7 [a]Ex. 14:2,9
33:8 [a]Ex. 14:22; 15:22,23
33:9 [a]Ex. 15:27
33:11 [a]Ex. 16:1
33:14 [a]Ex. 17:1; 19:2
33:15 [a]Ex. 16:1; 19:1,2
33:16 [1]That is, *the graves of lust* [a]ch. 11:34
33:17 [a]ch. 11:35
33:18 [a]ch. 12:16
33:30 [a]Deut. 10:6
33:32 [a]See Gen. 36:27; Deut. 10:6; 1 Chr. 1:42 [b]Deut. 10:7
33:35 [a]Deut. 2:8; 1 Ki. 9:26; 22:48
33:36 [a]ch. 20:1; 27:14
33:37 [a]ch. 20:22,23; 21:4
33:38 [a]ch. 20:25,28; Deut. 10:6; 32:50
33:40 [a]ch. 21:1
33:41 [a]ch. 21:4
33:43 [a]ch. 21:10
33:44 [1]Or, *heaps of Abarim* [a]ch. 21:11 [b]ch. 21:11
33:45 [a]ch. 32:34
33:46 [a]Jer. 48:22; Ezek. 6:14
33:47 [a]ch. 21:20; Deut. 32:49
33:48 [a]ch. 22:1
33:49 [1]Or, *the plains of Shittim* [a]ch. 25:1; Josh. 2:1
33:51 [a]Deut. 7:1,2; 9:1; Josh. 3:17
33:52 [a]Ex. 23:24,33; 34:13; Deut. 7:2,5; 12:3; Josh. 11:12; Judg. 2:2
33:54 [a]ch. 26:53-55

33:52 *drive out all the inhabitants of the land . . . destroy all their molten images.* What Israel had accomplished in the war against the Midianites (ch. 31) was now to be extended to all the inhabitants of Canaan. Particularly important was the command to destroy all symbols of the pagan religious system of the Canaanites.

moe ye shall [1]give the more inheritance, and
to the fewer ye shall [2]give the less inheritance: every man's *inheritance* shall be in the
place where his lot falleth; according to the
tribes of your fathers ye shall inherit.
55 But if ye will not drive out the inhabitants of the land from before you; then it shall
come to pass, *that those* which ye let remain
of them *shall be* [a]pricks in your eyes, and
thorns in your sides, and shall vex you in the
land wherein ye dwell.
56 Moreover it shall come to pass, *that* I
shall do unto you, as I thought to do unto
them.

The borders of Canaan

34 And the LORD spake unto Moses, saying,
2 Command the children of Israel, and say
unto them, When ye come into [a]the land of
Canaan; (this *is* the land that shall fall unto
you for an inheritance, *even* the land of Canaan with the coasts thereof:)
3 Then [a]your south quarter shall be from
the wilderness of Zin along by the coast of
Edom, and your south border shall be the outmost coast of [b]the salt sea eastward:
4 And your border shall turn from the
south [a]to the ascent of Akrabbim, and pass on
to Zin: and the going forth thereof shall be
from the south [b]to Kadesh-barnea, and shall go
on *to* [c]Hazar-addar, and pass on to Azmon:
5 And the border shall fetch a compass
from Azmon [a]unto the river of Egypt, and the
goings out of it shall be at the sea.
6 And *as for* the western border, you shall
even have the great sea for a border: this shall
be your west border.
7 And this shall be your north border: from
the great sea you shall point out for you
[a]mount Hor:
8 From mount Hor ye shall point out *your
border* [a]unto the entrance of Hamath; and the
goings forth of the border shall be to [b]Zedad:
9 And the border shall go on to Ziphron,
and the goings out of it shall be at [a]Hazar-
enan: this shall be your north border.
10 And ye shall point out your east border
from Hazar-enan to Shepham:
11 And the coast shall go down from Shepham [a]*to* Riblah, on the east side of Ain; and
the border shall descend, and shall reach unto
the [1]side of the sea [b]of Chinnereth eastward:
12 And the border shall go down to Jordan,
and the goings out of it shall be *at* [a]the salt sea:
this shall be your land with the coasts thereof
round about.

33:54 [1]Heb. *multiply his inheritance* [2]Heb. *diminish his inheritance* 33:55 [a]Josh. 23:13; Judg. 2:3; Ps. 106:34,36 34:2 [a]Gen. 17:8; Deut. 1:7; Ps. 78:55; Ezek. 47:14 34:3 [a]Josh. 15:1; See Ezek. 47:13 [b]Gen. 14:3; Josh. 15:2 34:4 [a]Josh. 15:3 [b]ch. 13:26; 32:8 [c]See Josh. 15:3,4 34:5 [a]Gen. 15:18; Josh. 15:4,47; 1 Ki. 8:65; Is. 27:12 34:7 [a]ch. 33:37 34:8 [a]ch. 13:21; 2 Ki. 14:25 [b]Ezek. 47:15 34:9 [a]Ezek. 47:17 34:11 [1]Heb. *shoulder* [a]2 Ki. 23:33; Jer. 39:5,6 [b]Deut. 3:17; Josh. 11:2; 19:35; Mat. 14:34; Luke 5:1 34:12 [a]ver. 3

34:13 [a]ver. 2; Josh. 14:1,2 34:14 [a]ch. 32:33; Josh. 14:2 34:17 [a]Josh. 14:1; 19:51 34:18 [a]ch. 1:4,16 35:1 [a]See ch. 33:50 35:2 [a]Josh. 14:3,4; 21:2; See Ezek. 45:1; 48:8 [b]See Lev. 25:34

13 And Moses commanded the children of
Israel, saying, [a]This *is* the land which ye shall
inherit by lot, which the LORD commanded to
give unto the nine tribes, and *to* the half tribe:
14 [a]For the tribe of the children of Reuben
according to the house of their fathers, and the
tribe of the children of Gad according to the
house of their fathers, have received *their inheritance;* and half the tribe of Manasseh have
received their inheritance:
15 The two tribes and the half tribe have
received their inheritance on *this* side Jordan
near Jericho eastward, toward the sunrising.
16 ¶ And the LORD spake unto Moses, saying,
17 These *are* the names of the men which
shall divide the land unto you: [a]Eleazar the
priest, and Joshua the son of Nun.
18 And ye shall take one [a]prince of every
tribe, to divide the land by inheritance.
19 And the names of the men *are* these: Of
the tribe of Judah, Caleb the son of Jephunneh.
20 And of the tribe of the children of Simeon, Shemuel the son of Ammihud.
21 Of the tribe of Benjamin, Elidad the son
of Chislon.
22 And the prince of the tribe of the children of Dan, Bukki the son of Jogli.
23 The prince of the children of Joseph, for
the tribe of the children of Manasseh, Hanniel
the son of Ephod.
24 And the prince of the tribe of the children of Ephraim, Kemuel the son of Shiphtan.
25 And the prince of the tribe of the children of Zebulun, Elizaphan the son of Parnach.
26 And the prince of the tribe of the children of Issachar, Paltiel the son of Azzan.
27 And the prince of the tribe of the children of Asher, Ahihud the son of Shelomi.
28 And the prince of the tribe of the children of Naphtali, Pedahel the son of Ammihud.
29 These *are they* whom the LORD commanded to divide the inheritance unto the
children of Israel in the land of Canaan.

Cities for the Levites

35 And the LORD spake unto Moses in
[a]the plains of Moab by Jordan *near*
Jericho, saying,
2 [a]Command the children of Israel, that
they give unto the Levites of the inheritance of
their possession cities to dwell in; and ye shall
give *also* unto the Levites [b]suburbs for the cities round about them.
3 And the cities shall they have to dwell in;

34:3–12 The listing of the four boundaries is not only for information, but also to display again the dimensions of God's great gift to His people.

34:13–15 The new realities that the settlement of Reuben, Gad and the half tribe of Manasseh east of the Jordan brought about (see ch. 32).

34:16–29 The listing of the new tribal leaders recalls the listing of the leaders of the first generation (1:5–16). This time the promise will be realized; these new leaders will assist Eleazar and Joshua in actually allotting the land.

35:1–5 Since the Levites would not receive an allotment with the other tribes in the land (1:47–53), they would need towns in which to live and to raise their families and care for their livestock. The Levites were to be spread throughout the land, not in an isolated encampment. Josh 21 presents the fulfillment of this command.

and the suburbs of them shall be for their cattle, and for their goods, and for all their beasts.
4 And the suburbs of the cities, which ye
shall give unto the Levites, *shall reach* from
the wall of the city and outward a thousand cubits round about.
5 And ye shall measure from without the
city *on* the east side two thousand cubits, and
on the south side two thousand cubits, and *on*
the west side two thousand cubits, and *on* the
north side two thousand cubits; and the city
shall be in the midst: this shall be to them the
suburbs of the cities.
6 And *among* the cities which ye shall give
unto the Levites *there shall be* [a]six cities for
refuge, which ye shall appoint for the manslayer, that he may flee thither: and [1]to them ye
shall add forty and two cities.
7 *So* all the cities which ye shall give to the
Levites *shall be* [a]forty and eight cities: them
shall ye give with their suburbs.
8 And the cities which ye shall give *shall
be* [a]of the possession of the children of Israel:
[b]from *them that have* many ye shall give
many; but from *them that have* few ye shall
give few: every one shall give of his cities unto
the Levites according to his inheritance which
[1]he inheriteth.

The cities of refuge

9 ¶ And the LORD spake unto Moses, saying,
10 Speak unto the children of Israel, and
say unto them, [a]When ye be come over Jordan
into the land of Canaan;

35:6 [1]Heb. *above them ye shall give* [a]ver. 13; Deut. 4:41; Josh. 20:2,7,8; 21:3,13
35:7 [a]Josh. 21:41
35:8 [1]Heb. *they inherit* [a]Josh. 21:3 [b]ch. 26:54
35:10 [a]Deut. 19:2; Josh. 20:2
35:11 [1]Heb. *by error* [a]Ex. 21:13
35:12 [a]Deut. 19:6; Josh. 20:3,5,6
35:13 [a]ver. 6
35:14 [a]Deut. 4:41; Josh. 20:8
35:15 [a]ch. 15:16
35:16 [a]Ex. 21:12,14; Lev. 24:17; Deut. 19:11,12
35:17 [1]Heb. *with a stone of the hand*
35:19 [a]ver. 21,24,27; Deut. 19:6,12; Josh. 20:3,5
35:20 [a]Gen. 4:8; 2 Sam. 3:27; 20:10; 1 Ki. 2:31,32 [b]Ex. 21:14; Deut. 19:11

11 Then [a]ye shall appoint you cities to be
cities of refuge for you; that the slayer may flee
thither, which killeth *any* person [1]at unawares.
12 [a]And they shall be unto you cities for
refuge from the avenger; that the manslayer
die not, until he stand before the congregation
in judgment.
13 And *of these* cities which ye shall give
[a]six cities shall ye have for refuge.
14 [a]Ye shall give three cities on *this* side
Jordan, and three cities shall ye give in the
land of Canaan, *which* shall be cities of refuge.
15 These six cities shall be a refuge, *both*
for the children of Israel, and [a]for the stranger,
and for the sojourner among them: that every
one that killeth *any* person unawares may flee
thither.
16 [a]And if he smite him with an instrument of iron, so that he die, he *is* a murderer:
the murderer shall surely be put to death.
17 And if he smite him [1]with throwing a
stone, wherewith he may die, and he die, he
is a murderer: the murderer shall surely be put
to death.
18 Or *if* he smite him with a hand weapon
of wood, wherewith he may die, and he die,
he *is* a murderer: the murderer shall surely be
put to death.
19 [a]The revenger of blood himself shall
slay the murderer: when he meeteth him, he
shall slay him.
20 But [a]if he thrust him of hatred, or hurl
at him [b]by laying of wait, that he die;

35:6–15 Six Levitical cities were to be stationed strategically in the land—three east of the Jordan and three in Canaan proper—as cities of refuge, where a person guilty of unintentional manslaughter might escape blood revenge. Josh 20 describes the sites that were chosen.

35:16–21 Various descriptions of the taking of life are pre-

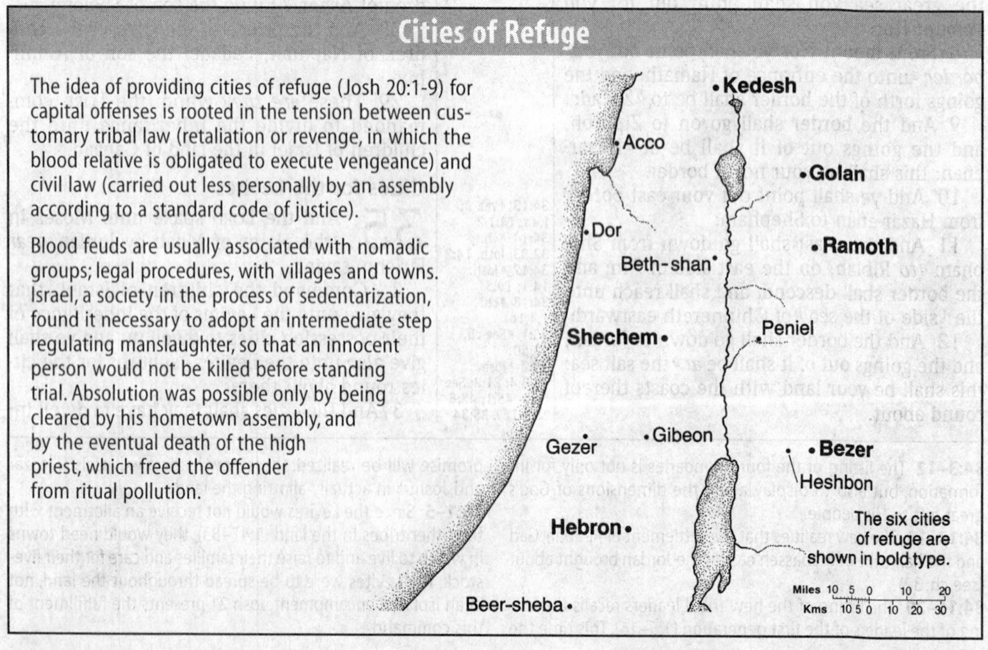

Cities of Refuge

The idea of providing cities of refuge (Josh 20:1-9) for capital offenses is rooted in the tension between customary tribal law (retaliation or revenge, in which the blood relative is obligated to execute vengeance) and civil law (carried out less personally by an assembly according to a standard code of justice).

Blood feuds are usually associated with nomadic groups; legal procedures, with villages and towns. Israel, a society in the process of sedentarization, found it necessary to adopt an intermediate step regulating manslaughter, so that an innocent person would not be killed before standing trial. Absolution was possible only by being cleared by his hometown assembly, and by the eventual death of the high priest, which freed the offender from ritual pollution.

21 Or in enmity smite him with his hand, that he die: he that smote *him* shall surely be put to death; *for* he *is* a murderer: the revenger of blood shall slay the murderer, when he meeteth him.

22 But if he thrust him suddenly [a]without enmity, or have cast upon him any thing without laying of wait,

23 Or with any stone, wherewith *a man* may die, seeing *him* not, and cast *it* upon him, that he die, and *was* not his enemy, neither sought his harm:

24 Then [a]the congregation shall judge between the slayer and the revenger of blood according to these judgments:

25 And the congregation shall deliver the slayer out of the hand of the revenger of blood, and the congregation shall restore him to the city of his refuge, whither he was fled: and [a]he shall abide in it unto the death of the high priest, [b]which was anointed with the holy oil.

26 But if the slayer shall at any time come *without* the border of the city of his refuge, whither he was fled;

27 And the revenger of blood find him without the borders of the city of his refuge, and the revenger of blood kill the slayer; [a][1]he shall not be guilty of blood:

28 Because he should have remained in the city of his refuge until the death of the high priest: but after the death of the high priest the slayer shall return into the land of his possession.

29 So these *things* shall be for [a]a statute of judgment unto you throughout your generations in all your dwellings.

30 Whoso killeth *any* person, the murderer shall be put to death by the [a]mouth of witnesses: but one witness shall not testify against *any* person *to cause him* to die.

31 Moreover ye shall take no satisfaction for the life of a murderer, which *is* [1]guilty of death: but he shall be surely put to death.

32 And ye shall take no satisfaction for him that is fled to the city of his refuge, that he should come again to dwell in the land, until the death of the priest.

33 So ye shall not pollute the land wherein ye *are:* for blood [a]it defileth the land: and [1]the land cannot be cleansed of the blood that is shed therein, but [b]by the blood of him that shed it.

34 [a]Defile not therefore the land which ye shall inhabit, wherein I dwell: for [b]I the LORD dwell among the children of Israel.

The marriage of heiresses

36 And the chief fathers of the families of the [a]children of Gilead, the son of Machir, the son of Manasseh, of the families of the sons of Joseph, came near, and spake before Moses, and before the princes, the chief fathers of the children of Israel:

2 And they said, [a]The LORD commanded my lord to give the land for an inheritance by lot to the children of Israel: and [b]my lord was commanded by the LORD to give the inheritance of Zelophehad our brother unto his daughters.

3 And *if* they be married to any of the sons of the *other* tribes of the children of Israel, then shall their inheritance be [a]taken from the inheritance of our fathers, and shall be put to the inheritance of the tribe [1]whereinto they are received: so shall it be taken from the lot of our inheritance.

4 And when [a]the jubile of the children of Israel shall be, then shall their inheritance be put unto the inheritance of the tribe [1]whereunto they are received: so shall their inheritance be taken away from the inheritance of the tribe of our fathers.

5 And Moses commanded the children of Israel according to the word of the LORD, saying, The tribe of the sons of Joseph [a]hath said well.

6 This *is* the thing which the LORD doth command concerning the daughters of Zelophehad, saying, Let them [1]marry to whom they think best; [a]only to the family of the tribe of their father shall they [2]marry.

7 So shall not the inheritance of the children of Israel remove from tribe to tribe: for every one of the children of Israel shall [a]keep himself to the inheritance of the tribe of his fathers.

8 And [a]every daughter, that possesseth an inheritance in any tribe of the children of Israel, shall be wife unto one of the family of the tribe of her father, that the children of Israel may enjoy every man the inheritance of his fathers.

9 Neither shall the inheritance remove

35:22 [a]Ex. 21:13
35:24 [a]ver. 12; Josh. 20:6
35:25 [a]Josh. 20:6 [b]Ex. 29:7; Lev. 4:3; 21:10
35:27 [1]Heb. *no blood* shall be *to him* [a]Ex. 22:2
35:29 [a]ch. 27:11
35:30 [a]Deut. 17:6; 19:15; Mat. 18:16; 2 Cor. 13:1; Heb. 10:28
35:31 [1]Heb. *faulty to die*
35:33 [1]Heb. *there can be no expiation for the land* [a]Ps. 106:38; Mic. 4:11 [b]Gen. 9:6
35:34 [a]Lev. 18:25; Deut. 21:23 [b]Ex. 29:45,46
36:1 [a]ch. 26:29
36:2 [a]ch. 26:55; 33:54; Josh. 17:4 [b]ch. 27:1,7; Josh. 17:3,4
36:3 [1]Heb. *unto whom they shall be* [a]ch. 27:4 marg.
36:4 [1]Heb. *unto whom they shall be* [a]Lev. 25:10
36:5 [a]ch. 27:7
36:6 [1]Heb. *be wives* [2]Heb. *cleave to the, etc.* [a]ver. 11,12
36:7 [a]1 Ki. 21:3
36:8 [a]1 Chr. 23:22

sented that would indicate willful murder.

35:22 *without enmity.* The cities of refuge were to be established for the person who had committed an act of involuntary manslaughter.

35:24 *according to these judgments.* Any gracious provision is subject to abuse. For this reason the case of the involuntary slayer had to be determined by the judges. Further, the accused man had to stay in the city of refuge until the death of the high priest (when there would be a general amnesty). If the accused left the city of refuge, he would become fair game again for the avenger of blood.

35:25–28 See note on Josh 20:6.

35:30 *witnesses.* To avoid the possibility of an innocent party being accused and sentenced to death on insufficient evidence.

35:32 Not even an involuntary slayer could leave the city of refuge on the payment of a ransom.

35:33 *blood it defileth the land.* The crime of murder is not only an offense against the sanctity of life; it is in fact a pollutant to the Lord's sacred land.

36:1–13 Presents an interesting further development of the account of Zelophehad's daughters (see 27:1–11). Since the Lord had instructed Moses that the women might inherit their father's land, new questions arose: What will happen to the family lands if these daughters marry among other tribes? Will not the original intention of the first provision be frustrated? Such questions led to the decision that marriage is to be kept within one's own tribe, so that the family allotments will not pass "from one tribe to another tribe" (v. 9).

from *one* tribe to another tribe; but every one
of the tribes of the children of Israel shall keep
himself to his own inheritance.
10 Even as the LORD commanded Moses,
so did the daughters of Zelophehad:
11 [a]For Mahlah, Tirzah, and Hoglah, and
Milcah, and Noah, the daughters of Zelophehad,
were married unto their father's brothers' sons:
12 *And* they were married [1]into the families
of the sons of Manasseh the son of Joseph,
and their inheritance remained in the tribe of
the family of their father.
13 These *are* the commandments and the
judgments, [a]which the LORD commanded by
the hand of Moses unto the children of Israel
[b]in the plains of Moab by Jordan *near* Jericho.

36:11 [a]ch. 27:1
36:12 [1]Heb. to some that were *of the families*
36:13 [a]Deut. 33:4 [b]ch. 26:3; 33:50

36:10 *Even as the LORD commanded Moses, so did the daughters of Zelophehad.* The book of Numbers, which so often presents the rebellion of God's people against His grace and in defiance of His will, ends on a happy note. These noble women, who were concerned for their father's name and their own place in the land, obeyed the Lord.

The Fifth Book of Moses, Called
Deuteronomy

INTRODUCTION

Title

The word "Deuteronomy" (meaning "repetition of the law"), the name of the last book of the Pentateuch, arose from a mistranslation in the Greek Septuagint and the Latin Vulgate of a phrase in Deut 17:18, which in Hebrew means "copy of this law." The error is not serious, however, since Deuteronomy is, in a certain sense, a "repetition of the law" (see Structure and Outline). The Hebrew name of the book is *'elleh haddebarim* ("These are the words") or, more simply, *debarim* ("words"; see 1:1).

Author

The book itself testifies that, for the most part, Moses wrote it (1:5; 31:9,22,24), and other OT books agree (1 Ki 2:3; 8:53; 2 Ki 14:6; 18:12)—though the preamble (1:1–5) may have been written by someone else, and the report of Moses' death (ch. 34) was almost certainly written by someone else. Jesus also bears testimony to Mosaic authorship (Mat 19:7–8; Mark 10:3–5; John 5:46–47), and so do other NT writers (Acts 3:22–23; 7:37–38; Rom 10:19). Moreover, Jesus quotes Deuteronomy as authoritative (Mat 4:4,7,10). In the NT there are almost 100 quotations of and allusions to Deuteronomy. Tradition uniformly testifies to the Mosaic authorship of the book (see, e.g., Mark 12:19). See Introduction to Genesis: Author and Date of Writing.

Date

The book is probably to be dated c. 1406 B.C. (see Introduction to Genesis: Author and Date of Writing).

Historical Setting

Deuteronomy locates Moses and the Israelites in the territory of Moab in the area where the Jordan flows into the Dead Sea (1:5). As his final act at this important time of transferring leadership to Joshua, Moses delivered his farewell addresses to prepare the people for their entrance into Canaan. These addresses were actually a covenant renewal (see Structure and Outline). In them, Moses emphasized the laws that were especially needed at such a time, and he presented them in a way appropriate to the situation. In contrast to the matter-of-fact narratives of Leviticus and Numbers, the book of Deuteronomy comes to us from Moses' heart in a warm, personal, sermonic form of expression.

Theological Teaching

The love relationship of the Lord to His people and that of the people to the Lord as their sovereign God pervade the whole book. Deuteronomy's spiritual emphasis and its call to total commitment to the Lord in worship and obedience inspired references to its message throughout the rest of Scripture.

Structure and Outline

Deuteronomy's literary structure supports its historical setting. By its interpretive, repetitious, reminiscent and somewhat irregular style it shows that it is a series of more or less extemporaneous addresses, sometimes describing events in nonchronological order (see, e.g., 10:3). But it also bears in its structure clear reflections of the suzerain-vassal treaties (see chart, p. 16) of the preceding and then-current Near Eastern states, a structure that lends itself to the Biblical emphasis on the covenant between the Lord and His people. In this sense Deuteronomy is a covenant renewal document, as the following outline shows:

I. The Preamble (1:1–5)
II. The Historical Prologue (1:6—4:43)
III. The Stipulations of the Covenant (4:44—26:19)
    A. The Great Commandment: The Demand for Absolute Allegiance (4:44—11:32)
    B. Supplementary Requirements (chs. 12—26)
        1. Ceremonial consecration (12:1—16:17)
        2. Governmental leaders and a righteous nation (16:18—21:21)
        3. Sanctity of God's kingdom (21:22—25:19)
        4. Confession of God as Redeemer-King (ch. 26)
IV. Ratification; Curses and Blessings (chs. 27—30)
V. Leadership Succession under the Covenant (chs. 31—34)
    A. Change of Leadership (31:1–29)
    B. Song of Moses (31:30—32:47)
    C. Moses' Testamental Blessing on the Tribes (32:48—33:29)
    D. Death of Moses and Succession of Joshua (ch. 34)

The book is sometimes divided into three addresses:

I. First Address (1:1—4:43)
II. Second Address (4:44—28:68)
III. Third Address (chs. 29—33)
IV. Moses' Death (ch. 34)

Moses tells of God's guidance

1 These *be* the words which Moses spake
unto all Israel [a]on *this* side Jordan in the
wilderness, in the plain over against [1]the Red
sea, between Paran, and Tophel, and Laban,
and Hazeroth, and Dizahab.
2 (*There are* eleven days' *journey* from Horeb *by* the way of mount Seir [a]unto Kadesh-
barnea.)
3 And it came to pass [a]in the fortieth year,
in the eleventh month, on the first *day* of the
month, *that* Moses spake unto the children of
Israel, according unto all that the LORD had giv-
en him in commandment unto them;
4 [a]After he had slain Sihon the king of the
Amorites, which dwelt in Heshbon, and Og
the king of Bashan, which dwelt at Astaroth
[b]in Edrei:
5 On *this* side Jordan, in the land of Moab,
began Moses to declare this law, saying,
6 ¶ The LORD our God spake unto us [a]in
Horeb, saying, Ye have dwelt long [b]enough in
this mount:
7 Turn you, and take your journey, and go
to the mount of the Amorites, and unto [1]all
the places nigh thereunto, in the plain, in the
hills, and in the vale, and in the south, and by
the sea side, *to* the land of the Canaanites, and
unto Lebanon, unto the great river, the river
Euphrates.
8 Behold, I have [1]set the land before you: go
in and possess the land which the LORD sware
unto your fathers, [a]Abraham, Isaac, and Jacob,
to give unto them and to their seed after them.

The choice of leaders

9 ¶ And [a]I spake unto you at that time, saying, I am not able to bear you myself alone:
10 The LORD your God hath multiplied you,
and behold, [a]you *are this* day as the stars of
heaven for multitude.

1:1 [1]Or, *Zuph* [a]Josh. 9:1,10
1:2 [a]Num. 13:26; ch. 9:23
1:3 [a]Num. 33:38
1:4 [a]Num. 21:24,33 [b]Num. 21:33; Josh. 13:12
1:6 [a]Ex. 3:1 [b]See Ex. 19:1; Num. 10:11
1:7 [1]Heb. *all his neighbours*
1:8 [1]Heb. *given* [a]Gen. 12:7; 15:18; 17:7,8; 26:4; 28:13
1:9 [a]Ex. 18:18; Num. 11:14
1:10 [a]Gen. 15:5; ch. 10:22; 28:62
1:11 [a]2 Sam. 24:3 [b]Gen. 15:5; 22:17; 26:4; Ex. 32:13
1:12 [a]1 Ki. 3:8,9
1:13 [1]Heb. *Give*
1:15 [1]Heb. *gave* [a]Ex. 18:25 [b]Ex. 18:25
1:16 [a]ch. 16:18; John 7:24 [b]Lev. 24:22
1:17 [1]Heb. *acknowledge faces* [a]Lev. 19:15; ch. 16:19; 1 Sam. 16:7; Prov. 24:23; Jas. 2:1 [b]2 Chr. 19:6 [c]Ex. 18:22,26
1:19 [a]Num. 10:12; ch. 8:15; Jer. 2:6 [b]Num. 13:26

11 ([a]The LORD God of your fathers make
you a thousand times so many moe as ye *are,*
and bless you, [b]as he hath promised you!)
12 [a]How can I myself alone bear your
cumbrance, and your burden, and your strife?
13 [1]Take ye wise men, and understanding,
and known among your tribes, and I will make
them rulers over you.
14 And ye answered me, and said, The
thing which thou hast spoken *is* good *for us* to
do.
15 So I took [a]the chief of your tribes, wise
men, and known, [b]and [1]made them heads
over you, captains over thousands, and captains over hundreds, and captains over fifties,
and captains over tens, and officers among
your tribes.
16 And I charged your judges at that time,
saying, Hear *the causes* between your brethren, and [a]judge righteously between every
man and his [b]brother, and the stranger *that is*
with him.
17 [a]Ye shall not [1]respect persons in judgment; *but* you shall hear the small as well as
the great; you shall not be afraid of the face of
man; for [b]the judgment *is* God's: and the cause
that is too hard for you, [c]bring *it* unto me, and
I will hear it.
18 And I commanded you at that time all
the things which ye should do.

The report of the spies

19 ¶ And when we departed from Horeb,
[a]we went *through* all that great and terrible
wilderness, which you saw *by* the way of the
mountain of the Amorites, as the LORD our
God commanded us; and [b]we came to Kadesh-
barnea.
20 And I said unto you, Ye are come unto
the mountain of the Amorites, which the LORD
our God doth give unto us.

---

‡1:1–5 The preamble gives the historical setting for the entire book. It involves a second giving of the law to the generation that was born after the exodus.

‡1:1 *Moses spake.* Almost all of Deuteronomy is made up of speeches by Moses during the final months of his life, just before the Israelites crossed the Jordan to enter Canaan. *in the plain* [*Arabah* in Hebrew]. Includes the valley of the Jordan (from the sea of Galilee to the southern end of the Dead Sea) and the valley extending down to the Gulf of Aqaba. *the Red sea* [*Suph* in Hebrew] . . . *Paran, and Tophel, and Laban, and Hazeroth, and Dizahab.* Places along the route from Sinai to the territory of Moab.

1:2 *Horeb.* The usual name for mount Sinai in Deuteronomy (the only exception is in 33:2). *Seir.* See note on Gen 36:8. *Kadesh-barnea.* See note on Gen 14:7.

1:3 *fortieth year.* After leaving Egypt. The Lord had condemned Israel to 40 years of wandering in Sinai as punishment for not entering Canaan as He had commanded them to do at Kadesh (Num 14:33–34). The 40 years included the time spent at Sinai and on the journey to Kadesh as well as the next 38 years (see 2:14). See 8:2–5; 29:5–6; Num 14:29–35; 32:13; Heb 3:7–19. *eleventh month.* January-February.

1:5 *this law.* The ten commandments and other laws given at mount Sinai and recorded in Ex 20–24, Leviticus and Numbers. In Deuteronomy the laws are summarized and interpreted, and adjusted to the new, specific situation Israel would face in Canaan. Thus Deuteronomy is, in essence, a covenant renewal (and updating) document.

‡1:7 See Josh 1:4. The land is described by its various geographical areas (see map No. 2 at the end of the study Bible). *the plain.* See note on v. 1; here the Jordan Valley and the Dead Sea area. *hills.* The midsection running north and south. *vale.* Sloping toward the Mediterranean. *south. Negev* in Hebrew. See note on Gen 12:9. *sea side.* The Mediterranean coastal strip. The "land of the Canaanites" and "Lebanon, unto . . . Euphrates" make up the northern sector. The "mount of the Amorites" is, in general, the central and southern mountains. This description of the land agrees with that in the promise (see v. 8) to Abraham in Gen 15:18–21, a promise later limited to Isaac's descendants (Gen 26:2–4) and still later to the descendants of Jacob (Gen 35:11–12).

1:9–18 Cf. 16:18–20; Ex 18:13–26.

1:10 *The LORD your God.* This title occurs almost 300 times in Deuteronomy in addition to the many times that "LORD" is used alone or in other combinations. *as the stars of heaven.* See 10:22; 28:62; Gen 13:16 and note; 15:5 and note; 22:17; 26:4; Ex 32:13.

1:19–46 See Num 13–14.

21 Behold, the LORD thy God hath set the land before thee: go up *and* possess *it,* as the LORD God of thy fathers hath said unto thee; [a]fear not, neither be discouraged.

22 And ye came near unto me every one of you, and said, We will send men before us, and they shall search us out the land, and bring us word again by what way we must go up, and into what cities we shall come.

23 And the saying pleased me well: and [a]I took twelve men of you, one of a tribe:

24 And [a]they turned and went up into the mountain, and came unto the valley of Eshcol, and searched it out.

25 And they took of the fruit of the land in their hands, and brought *it* down unto us, and brought us word again, and said, [a]*It is* a good land which the LORD our God doth give us.

The murmuring of Israel

26 [a]Notwithstanding ye would not go up, but rebelled against the commandment of the LORD your God:

27 And ye murmured in your tents, and said, Because the LORD [a]hated us, he hath brought us forth out of the land of Egypt, to deliver us into the hand of the Amorites, to destroy us.

28 Whither shall we go up? our brethren have [a][1]discouraged our heart, saying, [b]The people *is* greater and taller than we; the cities *are* great and walled up to heaven; and moreover we have seen the sons of the [c]Anakims there.

29 Then I said unto you, Dread not, neither be afraid of them.

30 [a]The LORD your God which goeth before you, he shall fight for you, according to all that he did for you in Egypt before your eyes;

31 And in the wilderness, where thou hast seen how that the LORD thy God [a]bare thee, as a man doth bear his son, in all the way that ye went, until ye came into this place.

32 Yet in this thing [a]ye did not believe the LORD your God,

33 [a]Who went in the way before you, [b]to search you out a place to pitch your tents *in,* in fire by night, to shew you by what way ye should go, and in a cloud by day.

34 And the LORD heard the voice of your words, and was wroth, [a]and sware, saying,

35 [a]Surely there shall not one of these men of this evil generation see that good land, which I sware to give unto your fathers,

36 [a]Save Caleb the son of Jephunneh, he shall see it, and to him will I give the land that he hath trodden upon, and to his children, because [b]he hath [1]wholly followed the LORD.

37 [a]Also the LORD was angry with me for your sakes, saying, Thou also shalt not go in thither.

38 [a]*But* Joshua the son of Nun, [b]which standeth before thee, he shall go in thither: [c]encourage him: for he shall cause Israel to inherit it.

39 [a]Moreover your little ones, which [b]ye said should be a prey, and your children, which *in that* day [c]had no knowledge between good and evil, they shall go in thither, and unto them will I give it, and they shall possess it.

40 [a]But *as for* you, turn ye, and take your journey into the wilderness *by* the way of the Red sea.

41 Then ye answered and said unto me, [a]We have sinned against the LORD, we will go up and fight, according to all that the LORD our God commanded us. And when ye had girded on every man his weapons of war, ye were ready to go up into the hill.

42 And the LORD said unto me, Say unto them, [a]Go not up, neither fight; for I *am* not among you; lest ye be smitten before your enemies.

43 So I spake unto you; and you would not hear, but rebelled against the commandment of the LORD, and [a][1]went presumptuously up into the hill.

44 And the Amorites, which dwelt in that mountain, came out against you, and chased you, [a]as bees do, and destroyed you in Seir, *even* unto Hormah.

1:21 [a]Josh. 1:9
1:23 [a]Num. 13:3
1:24 [a]Num. 13:22-24
1:25 [a]Num. 13:27
1:26 [a]Num. 14:1-4; Ps. 106:24
1:27 [a]ch. 9:28
1:28 [1]Heb. *melted* [a]Josh. 2:11 [b]Num. 13:28,31-33; ch. 9:1,2 [c]Num. 13:28
1:30 [a]Ex. 14:14; Neh. 4:20
1:31 [a]Ex. 19:4; ch. 32:11,12; Is. 46:3,4; 63:9; Hos. 11:3; See Acts 13:18
1:32 [a]Ps. 106:24; Jude 5
1:33 [a]Ex. 13:21; Ps. 78:14 [b]Num. 10:33; Ezek. 20:6
1:34 [a]ch. 2:14,15
1:35 [a]Num. 14:22; Ps. 95:11
1:36 [1]Heb. *fulfilled* to go *after* [a]Num. 14:24; Josh. 14:9 [b]Num. 14:24
1:37 [a]Num. 20:12; 27:14; ch. 3:26; 4:21; 34:4; Ps. 106:32
1:38 [a]Num. 14:30 [b]Ex. 24:13; 33:11; See 1 Sam. 16:22 [c]Num. 27:18,19; ch. 31:7,23
1:39 [a]Num. 14:31 [b]Num. 14:3 [c]Is. 7:15,16; Rom. 9:11
1:40 [a]Num. 14:25
1:41 [a]Num. 14:40
1:42 [a]Num. 14:42
1:43 [1]Heb. *you were presumptuous, and went up* [a]Num. 14:44
1:44 [a]Ps. 118:12

1:21 *as the LORD . . . hath said unto thee.* The promise of the land (see note on v. 7) was reaffirmed to Moses at the burning bush (v. 8; Ex 3:8,17). Now the Israelites are told to enter the land and conquer it. *fear not, neither be discouraged.* See 31:8; Josh 1:9; 8:1; 10:25.

1:23 *twelve.* They are named in Num 13:4–15.

1:24 *Eshcol.* See Num 13:23 and note.

1:26 *ye . . . rebelled.* Although they themselves had not rebelled, the people were being addressed as a nation united with the earlier rebellious generation (see 5:2; cf. 29:1).

1:27 *murmured.* See note on Ex 15:24. *the LORD hated us.* The people's statement is ironic indeed in the light of Deuteronomy's major theme (see Introduction: Theological Teaching).

1:28 *Anakims.* Earlier inhabitants of Canaan, described as giants (see 2:10,21; 9:2; Num 13:32).

1:30 *all that he did for you in Egypt.* See Ex 14:1–15:19.

1:31 *God bare thee.* See notes on Is 41:10,13; 43:1–2; cf. Is 40:11; Jer 31:10; Ezek 34:11–16.

1:33 *in fire by night . . . a cloud by day.* The presence of the Lord was in the cloud over the tabernacle to guide the Israelites through their wilderness journeys (see Ex 13:21 and note; 40:34–38).

1:36 *Caleb.* See Num 13:30–14:38; Josh 14:6–15.

1:37 *for your sakes.* See 3:26; 4:21. God was angry with Moses when in a wrong spirit he struck the rock at Meribah to get water (Num 20:9–13; 27:12–14). And since it was the Israelites who had incited him to sin, God was angry with them too. This event (v. 37) occurred almost 40 years after that of the preceding verses (vv. 34–36), but Moses, interested in telling of the Israelites' sin and his own, brings the two events together.

1:39 *had no knowledge between good and evil.* See notes on Gen 2:9; Is 7:15.

1:41 *ye.* See note on v. 26.

1:43 *you . . . rebelled against the commandment of the LORD.* The same charge as in v. 26. First the people rebelled against the Lord's command to go into the land, then against His command not to enter the land. After their first rebellion the Lord would not go with them. His presence was essential, and Israel needed to learn that lesson.

1:44 *bees.* See note on Ex 23:28.

45 And ye returned and wept before the
LORD; but the LORD would not hearken to your
voice, nor give ear unto you.
46 [a]So ye abode in Kadesh many days, according unto the days that ye abode *there.*

The years in the wilderness

2 Then we turned, and took our journey
into the wilderness *by* the way of the Red
sea, [a]as the LORD spake unto me: and we compassed mount Seir many days.
2 And the LORD spake unto me, saying,
3 Ye have compassed this mountain [a]long
enough: turn you northward.
4 And command thou the people, saying,
[a]Ye are to pass through the coast of your brethren the children of Esau, which dwell in Seir;
and they shall be afraid of you: take ye good
heed unto yourselves therefore:
5 Meddle not with them; for I will not give
you of their land, [1]no, not so much as a foot
breadth; [a]because I have given mount Seir
unto Esau *for* a possession.
6 Ye shall buy meat of them for money, that
ye may eat; and ye shall also buy water of them
for money, that ye may drink.
7 For the LORD thy God hath blessed thee
in all the works of thy hand: he knoweth thy
walking *through* this great wilderness: [a]these
forty years the LORD thy God *hath been* with
thee; thou hast lacked nothing.
8 [a]And when we passed by from our brethren the children of Esau, which dwelt in Seir,
through the way of the plain from [b]Elath, and
from Ezion-gaber, we turned and passed *by* the
way of the wilderness of Moab.
9 And the LORD said unto me, [1]Distress not
the Moabites, neither contend with them *in*
battle: for I will not give thee of their land *for*
a possession; because I have given [a]Ar unto
[b]the children of Lot *for* a possession.
10 ([a]The Emims dwelt therein in times
past, a people great, and many, and tall, as [b]the
Anakims;
11 Which also were accounted giants, as the
Anakims; but the Moabites call them Emims.
12 [a]The Horims also dwelt in Seir beforetime; but the children of Esau [1]succeeded
them, when they had destroyed them from before them, and dwelt in their [2]stead; as Israel
did unto the land of his possession, which the
LORD gave unto them.)
13 Now rise up, *said I,* and get you over
[a]the [1]brook Zered. And we went over the
[1]brook Zered.
14 And the space in which we came [a]from
Kadesh-barnea, until we were come over the
[1]brook Zered, *was* thirty and eight years; [b]un-
til all the generation of the men of war were
wasted out from among the host, [c]as the LORD
sware unto them.
15 For indeed the [a]hand of the LORD was
against them, to destroy them from among the
host, until they were consumed.
16 ¶ So it came to pass, when all the men
of war were consumed and dead from among
the people,
17 That the LORD spake unto me, saying,
18 Thou art to pass over *through* Ar, the
coast of Moab, *this* day:
19 And *when* thou comest nigh over
against the children of Ammon, distress them
not, nor meddle with them: for I will not give
thee of the land of the children of Ammon *any*
possession; because I have given it unto [a]the
children of Lot *for* a possession.
20 (That also was accounted a land of giants: giants dwelt therein in old time; and the
Ammonites call them [1]Zamzummims;
21 [a]A people great, and many, and tall, as
the Anakims; but the LORD destroyed them before them; and they succeeded them, and
dwelt in their stead:
22 As he did to the children of Esau, [a]which
dwelt in Seir, when he destroyed [b]the Horims
from before them; and they succeeded them,
and dwelt in their stead *even* unto this day:
23 And [a]the Avims which dwelt in Hazer-
im, *even* unto Azzah, [b]the Caphtorims, which
came forth out of Caphtor, destroyed them,
and dwelt in their stead.)
24 Rise ye up, take your journey, and [a]pass
over the river Arnon: behold, I have given into
thy hand Sihon the Amorite, king of Heshbon,
and his land: [1]begin to possess *it,* and contend
with him *in* battle.

1:46 [a]Num. 13:25; 20:1,22; Judg. 11:17
2:1 [a]Num. 14:25; ch. 1:40
2:3 [a]See ver. 7,14
2:4 [a]Num. 20:14
2:5 [1]Heb. *even to the treading of the sole of the foot* [a]Gen. 36:8; Josh. 24:4
2:7 [a]ch. 8:2-4
2:8 [a]Judg. 11:18 [b]1 Ki. 9:26
2:9 [1]Or, *Use no hostility against Moab* [a]Num. 21:28 [b]Gen. 19:36,37
2:10 [a]Gen. 14:5 [b]Num. 13:22,33; ch. 9:2
2:12 [1]Heb. *inherited them* [a]ver. 22; Gen. 14:6; 36:20
2:12 [2]Or, *room*
2:13 [1]Or, *valley* [a]Num. 21:12
2:14 [1]Or, *valley* [a]Num. 13:26 [b]Num. 14:33; 26:64 [c]Num. 14:35; ch. 1:34,35; Ezek. 20:15
2:15 [a]Ps. 78:33; 106:26
2:19 [a]Gen. 19:38
2:20 [1][Gen. 14:5, *Zuzims*]
2:21 [a]See ver. 10
2:22 [a]Gen. 36:8 [b]Gen. 14:6; 36:20-30
2:23 [a]Josh. 13:3 [b]Gen. 10:14; Amos 9:7
2:24 [1]Heb. *begin, possess* [a]Num. 21:13; Judg. 11:18

1:45 *before the LORD.* At the tabernacle.
2:1–3:11 See Num 20:14–21:35.
2:1 *Red sea.* Here probably the Gulf of Aqaba (see note on 1 Ki 9:26). *mount Seir.* The mountainous area south of the Dead Sea.
2:5 *I will not give you of their land.* See vv. 9,19. The Lord told Moses to bypass Edom, Moab and Ammon because of their blood relationship to Israel. The Israelites were to take over only those lands east of the Jordan that were in the hands of the Amorites (see v. 24; 3:2). *I have given.* See vv. 9,19. The Lord had given the descendants of Esau (Edomites) and Lot (Moabites and Ammonites) their lands, just as He was giving the Israelites the territories "beyond Jordan" and Canaan.
2:8 *Elath, and . . . Ezion-gaber.* At the head of the Gulf of Aqaba. The "Arabah road" ran from the head of the gulf northward and to the east of Moab.
2:9 *Ar.* Location unknown.
2:10 *Emims.* Possibly meaning "terrors." *Anakims.* See note on 1:28.
‡2:11 *giants.* Hebrew *Rephaim.* Ancient people of large stature.
2:12 *Horims.* See note on Gen 14:6. *the land . . . the LORD gave unto them.* Either (1) the region beyond the Jordan (see 2:24–3:20), (2) Canaan itself or (3) both. If either (2) or (3) is intended, editorial updating is involved (see note on Gen 14:14).
2:13 *Zered.* The main stream (intermittent) that flows into the southern end of the Dead Sea from the east (see map No. 4 at the end of the study Bible).
2:14 *thirty and eight years.* See note on 1:3.
2:20 *Zamzummims.* Possibly meaning "murmurers," and perhaps to be identified with the Zuzites of Gen 14:5.
2:23 *Avims.* Pre-Philistine people otherwise unknown (Josh 13:3). *Caphtorims.* See note on Gen 10:14.
2:24 *Arnon.* See note on Num 21:10–13.

25 [a]This day will I begin to put the dread of thee and the fear of thee upon the nations *that are* under the whole heaven, who shall hear report of thee, and shall tremble, and be in anguish because of thee.

The victory over Sihon

26 ¶ And I sent messengers out of the wilderness of Kedemoth unto Sihon king of Heshbon [a]*with* words of peace, saying,

27 [a]Let me pass through thy land: I will go along by the high way, I will neither turn *unto* the right hand nor *to* the left.

28 Thou shalt sell me meat for money, that I may eat; and give me water for money, that I may drink: [a]only I will pass through on my feet;

29 ([a]As the children of Esau which dwell in Seir, and the Moabites which dwell in Ar, did unto me;) until I shall pass over Jordan into the land which the LORD our God giveth us.

30 [a]But Sihon king of Heshbon would not let us pass by him: for [b]the LORD thy God [c]hardened his spirit, and made his heart obstinate, that he might deliver him into thy hand, as *appeareth* this day.

31 And the LORD said unto me, Behold, I have begun to [a]give Sihon and his land before thee: begin to possess, that *thou* mayest inherit his land.

32 [a]Then Sihon came out against us, he and all his people, to fight *at* Jahaz.

33 And [a]the LORD our God delivered him before us; and [b]we smote him, and his sons, and all his people.

34 And we took all his cities at that time, and [a]utterly destroyed [1]the men, and the women, and the little ones, of every city, we left none to remain:

35 Only the cattle we took for a prey unto ourselves, and the spoil of the cities which we took.

36 [a]From Aroer, which *is* by the brink of the river of Arnon, and *from* the city that *is* by the river, even unto Gilead, there was not one city too strong for us: [b]the LORD our God delivered all unto us:

2:25 [a]Ex. 15:14,15
2:26 [a]ch. 20:10
2:27 [a]Num. 21:21,22; Judg. 11:19
2:28 [a]Num. 20:19
2:29 [a]See Num. 20:18; ch. 23:3,4; Judg. 11:17
2:30 [a]Num. 21:23 [b]Josh. 11:20 [c]Ex. 4:21
2:31 [a]ch. 1:8
2:32 [a]Num. 21:23
2:33 [a]ch. 7:2; 20:16 [b]Num. 21:24; ch. 29:7
2:34 [1]Heb. *every city of men, and women, and little ones* [a]Lev. 27:28; ch. 7:2,26
2:36 [a]ch. 3:12; 4:48; Josh. 13:9 [b]Ps. 44:3
2:37 [a]Gen. 32:22; Num. 21:24; ch. 3:16 [b]ver. 5,9,19
3:1 [a]Num. 21:33; ch. 29:7 [b]ch. 1:4
3:2 [a]Num. 21:34
3:3 [a]Num. 21:35
3:4 [a]1 Ki. 4:13
3:6 [a]ch. 2:24; Ps. 135:10-12
3:9 [a]ch. 4:48 [b]1 Chr. 5:23
3:10 [a]ch. 4:49 [b]Josh. 12:5; 13:11
3:11 [a]Amos 2:9 [b]Gen. 14:5 [c]2 Sam. 12:26; Jer. 49:2; Ezek. 21:20

37 Only unto the land of the children of Ammon thou camest not, *nor unto* any place of the river [a]Jabbok, nor *unto* the cities in the mountains, nor *unto* [b]whatsoever the LORD our God forbad *us.*

The victory over Og

3 Then we turned, and went up the way to Bashan: and [a]Og the king of Bashan came out against us, he and all his people, to battle [b]*at* Edrei.

2 And the LORD said unto me, Fear him not: for I will deliver him, and all his people, and his land, into thy hand; and thou shalt do unto him as thou didst unto [a]Sihon king of the Amorites, which dwelt at Heshbon.

3 So the LORD our God delivered into our hands Og also, the king of Bashan, and all his people: [a]and we smote him until none was left to him remaining.

4 And we took all his cities at that time, there was not a city which we took not from them, threescore cities, [a]all the region of Argob, the kingdom of Og in Bashan.

5 All these cities *were* fenced *with* high walls, gates, and bars; beside unwalled towns a great many.

6 And we utterly destroyed them, as we did unto Sihon king [a]of Heshbon, utterly destroying the men, women, and children, of every city.

7 But all the cattle, and the spoil of the cities, we took for a prey to ourselves.

8 And we took at that time out of the hand of the two kings of the Amorites the land that *was* on *this* side Jordan, from the river of Arnon unto mount Hermon;

9 (*Which* [a]Hermon the Sidonians call Sirion; and the Amorites call it [b]Shenir;)

10 [a]All the cities of the plain, and all Gilead, and [b]all Bashan, unto Salchah and Edrei, cities of the kingdom of Og in Bashan.

11 [a]For only Og king of Bashan remained of the remnant of [b]giants; behold, his bedstead *was* a bedstead of iron; *is* it not in [c]Rabbath of the children of Ammon? nine cubits *was* the

2:26 *Kedemoth.* Means "eastern regions."

2:30 *hardened his spirit, and made his heart obstinate.* In the OT, actions are often attributed to God without the mention of mediate or contributing situations or persons. Sihon by his own conscious will refused Israel passage, but it was God who would give Sihon's land to Israel (see note on Ex 4:21).

2:32 *Jahaz.* See note on Is 15:4.

2:34 *utterly destroyed.* The Hebrew for this expression usually denotes the destruction of everyone and everything that could be destroyed. Objects like gold, silver and bronze, not subject to destruction, were put in a secure place as God's possession. Destruction of people and things made them useless to the conquerors but put them in the hands of God. So the word is sometimes translated "destroyed" and sometimes "accursed" (see, e.g., Josh 6:17). The practice was sometimes limited, as when God assigned captured livestock and other plunder to His people as recompense for service in His army (see v. 35; 3:7; Jos 8:2).

2:36 *Aroer.* See note on Is 17:2. *Gilead.* See note on Gen 31:21.

2:37 *Jabbok.* See note on Gen 32:22.

3:3 *delivered into our hands Og.* As in 2:26–37.

3:4 *threescore cities.* The cities were large and walled (1 Ki 4:13), implying a heavily populated territory (see v. 5). *region of Argob.* An otherwise unidentified area in Bashan (see vv. 13–14; 1 Ki 4:13).

3:6–7 See note on 2:34.

3:8 *mount Hermon.* Snowcapped throughout the year and rising to a height of over 9,200 feet, it is one of the most prominent and beautiful mountains in Lebanon.

3:9 *Sirion.* This name for mount Hermon is found also in a Canaanite document contemporary with Moses. *Shenir.* This name for mount Hermon is also found in Assyrian sources.

3:10 *Salchah.* A city marking the eastern boundary of Bashan (see Josh 13:11).

3:11 *bedstead of iron.* Sarcophagi (stone coffins) of basalt have been found in Bashan, and the Hebrew for "bedstead" (which can be translated "sarcophagus") and "iron" may reflect this. If an actual bed, it was probably made of wood but with certain

length thereof, and four cubits the breadth of it, after the cubit of a man.

The distribution of the land

12 And this land, *which* we possessed at that time, [a]from Aroer, which *is* by the river Arnon, and half mount Gilead, and [b]the cities thereof, gave I unto the Reubenites and to the Gadites.

13 [a]And the rest of Gilead, and all Bashan, *being* the kingdom of Og, gave I unto the half tribe of Manasseh; all the region of Argob, with all Bashan, which was called the land of giants.

14 [a]Jair the son of Manasseh took all the country of Argob [b]unto the coasts of Geshuri and Maachathi; and [c]called them after his own name, Bashan-havoth-jair, unto this day.

15 [a]And I gave Gilead unto Machir.

16 And unto the Reubenites [a]and unto the Gadites I gave from Gilead even unto the river Arnon, half the valley, and the border, even unto the river Jabbok, [b]*which is* the border of the children of Ammon;

17 The plain also, and Jordan, and the coast *thereof,* from [a]Chinnereth [b]even unto the sea of the plain, [c]*even* the salt sea, [1]under Ashdoth-pisgah eastward.

Moses forbidden to cross Jordan

18 ¶ And I commanded you at that time, saying, The LORD your God hath given you this land to possess it: [a]ye shall pass over armed before your brethren the children of Israel, all *that are* [1]meet for the war.

19 But your wives, and your little ones, and your cattle, (*for* I know that ye have much cattle,) shall abide in your cities which I have given you;

20 Until the LORD have given rest unto your brethren, as well as *unto* you, and *until* they also possess the land which the LORD your God hath given them beyond Jordan: and *then* shall ye [a]return every man unto his possession, which I have given you.

3:12 [a]ch. 2:36; Josh. 12:2 [b]Num. 32:33; Josh. 12:6; 13:8
3:13 [a]Josh. 13:29
3:14 [a]1 Chr. 2:22 [b]Josh. 13:13; 2 Sam. 3:3; 10:6 [c]Num. 32:41
3:15 [a]Num. 32:39
3:16 [a]2 Sam. 24:5 [b]Num. 21:24; Josh. 12:2
3:17 [1]Or, *under the springs of Pisgah,* or, *the hill* [a]Num. 34:11 [b]Num. 34:12; ch. 4:49; Josh. 12:3 [c]Gen. 14:3
3:18 [1]Heb. *sons of power* [a]Num. 32:20
3:20 [a]Josh. 22:4
3:21 [a]Num. 27:23
3:22 [a]Ex. 14:14; ch. 1:30; 20:4
3:23 [a]See 2 Cor. 12:8,9
3:24 [a]ch. 11:2 [b]Ex. 15:11; 2 Sam. 7:22; Ps. 71:19; 86:8; 89:6,8
3:25 [a]Ex. 3:8; ch. 4:22
3:26 [a]ch. 1:37; 31:2
3:27 [1]Or, *the hill* [a]Num. 27:12
3:28 [a]Num. 27:18,23; ch. 31:3,7
3:29 [a]ch. 34:6
4:1 [a]Lev. 19:37; ch. 5:1; Ezek. 20:11; Rom. 10:5
4:2 [a]Josh. 1:7

21 And [a]I commanded Joshua at that time, saying, Thine eyes have seen all that the LORD your God hath done unto these two kings: so shall the LORD do unto all the kingdoms whither thou passest.

22 Ye shall not fear them: for [a]the LORD your God he shall fight for you.

23 And [a]I besought the LORD at that time, saying,

24 O Lord GOD, thou hast begun to shew thy servant [a]thy greatness, and thy mighty hand: for [b]what God *is there* in heaven or in earth, that can do according to thy works, and according to thy might?

25 I pray thee, let me go over, and see [a]the good land that *is* beyond Jordan, that goodly mountain, and Lebanon.

26 But the LORD [a]was wroth with me for your sakes, and would not hear me: and the LORD said unto me, Let it suffice thee; speak no more unto me of this matter.

27 [a]Get thee up *into* the top of [1]Pisgah, and lift up thine eyes westward, and northward, and southward, and eastward, and behold *it* with thine eyes: for thou shalt not go over this Jordan.

28 But [a]charge Joshua, and encourage him, and strengthen him: for he shall go over before this people, and he shall cause them to inherit the land which thou shalt see.

29 So we abode in [a]the valley over against Beth-peor.

Moses commands obedience

4 Now therefore hearken, O Israel, unto [a]the statutes and unto the judgments, which I teach you, for to do *them,* that ye may live, and go in and possess the land which the LORD God of your fathers giveth you.

2 [a]Ye shall not add unto the word which I command you, neither shall you diminish ought from it, that *ye* may keep the commandments of the LORD your God which I command you.

---

iron fixtures, as were the "chariots of iron" (see note on Josh 17:16). *Rabbath of the children of Ammon.* Called Philadelphia in NT times, Rabbah was the capital of ancient Ammon (Amos 1:13–14). Today its name is Amman, the capital of the kingdom of Jordan.

3:12–20 See Num 32; 34:13–15.

3:14 *Jair . . . Bashan-havoth-jair.* See note on Judg 10:3. *Geshuri and Maachathi.* Two comparatively small kingdoms, Geshur was east of the sea of Galilee and Maacah was east of the waters of Merom (see note on Josh 11:5) and north of Geshur.

3:15 *Machir.* See note on Gen 50:23.

‡3:17 *Chinnereth.* See note on Mark 1:16. *Ashdoth-pisgah* [i.e. "the slopes of Pisgah"]. On the edge of the high plateau overlooking the Dead Sea from the east.

3:20 *rest.* A peaceful situation—free from external threat and oppression, and untroubled within by conflict, famine or plague (see 12:9–10; 25:19; see also notes on Josh 1:13; 1 Ki 5:4; Heb 4:1–11).

3:22 *God he shall fight.* The conquest narratives emphasize the truth that without the Lord's help Israel's victory would be impossible. The Lord's power, not Israel's unaided strength, achieved victory. Moses bolstered Israel's resolve and faith by this assurance (see 1:30; 2:21–22,31; 20:4).

3:23–25 Moses' final plea to be allowed to enter the land (see 1:37 and note; 31:2).

3:26 *for your sakes.* See note on 1:37.

3:27 *Get thee up into the top of Pisgah.* Moses did so after he had expounded the law to the Israelites to prepare them for life in the promised land (see 32:48–52; 34:1–6). *Pisgah.* See note on v. 17. *lift up thine eyes westward, and northward, and southward, and eastward.* Like Abraham (see Gen 13:14), Moses would inherit the promised land only through his descendants (see 34:1–4).

3:28 *charge Joshua.* See 31:7–8.

3:29 *Beth-peor.* Means "house/sanctuary of Peor." Very likely, reference is to the cult place where the Baal of Peor was worshiped (see Num 23:28; 25:3,5).

4:1 *hearken, O Israel.* God's call to His people to hear and obey is a frequent theme in Deuteronomy (see, e.g., 5:1; 6:3–4; 9:1; 20:3) and elsewhere in the OT. See also note on 6:4–9.

4:2 *Ye shall not add . . . neither shall you diminish.* The revelation the Lord gives is sufficient. All of it must be obeyed, and

3 Your eyes have seen what the LORD did because of [a]Baal-peor: for all the men that followed Baal-peor, the LORD thy God hath destroyed them from among you.

4 But ye that did cleave unto the LORD your God *are* alive every one of you *this* day.

5 Behold, I have taught you statutes and judgments, even as the LORD my God commanded me, that *ye* should do so in the land whither ye go to possess it.

6 Keep therefore and do *them;* for this *is* [a]your wisdom and your understanding in the sight of the nations, which shall hear all these statutes, and say, Surely this great nation *is* a wise and understanding people.

7 For [a]what nation *is there so* great, who hath [b]God *so* nigh unto them, as the LORD our God *is* in all *things that* we call upon him *for?*

8 And what nation *is there so* great, that hath statutes and judgments *so* righteous as all this law, which I set before you *this* day?

9 Only take heed to thyself, and [a]keep thy soul diligently, lest thou forget the things which thine eyes have seen, and lest they depart from thy heart all the days of thy life: but [b]teach them thy sons, and thy sons' sons;

10 *Specially* [a]the day that thou stoodest before the LORD thy God in Horeb, when the LORD said unto me, Gather me the people together, and I will make them hear my words, that they may learn to fear me all the days that they shall live upon the earth, and *that* they may teach their children.

11 And ye came near and stood under the mountain; and the [a]mountain burnt with fire unto the [1]midst of heaven, *with* darkness, clouds, and thick darkness.

12 [a]And the LORD spake unto you out of the midst of the fire: ye heard the voice of the words, but saw no similitude; [b] [1]only *ye heard* a voice.

13 [a]And he declared unto you his covenant, which he commanded you to perform, *even* [b]ten commandments; and [c]he wrote them upon two tables of stone.

14 And [a]the LORD commanded me at that time to teach you statutes and judgments, that ye might do them in the land whither ye go over to possess it.

4:3 [a]Josh. 22:17; Ps. 106:28
4:6 [a]Job 28:28; Ps. 19:7; Prov. 1:7
4:7 [a]2 Sam. 7:23 [b]Ps. 46:1; Is. 55:6
4:9 [a]Prov. 4:23 [b]Gen. 18:19; ch. 6:7; 11:19; Ps. 78:5,6; Eph. 6:4
4:10 [a]Ex. 19:9,16
4:11 [1]Heb. *heart* [a]Ex. 19:18
4:12 [1]Heb. *save a voice* [a]ch. 5:4,22 [b]Ex. 20:22; 1 Ki. 19:12
4:13 [a]ch. 9:9,11 [b]Ex. 34:28 [c]Ex. 24:12; 31:18
4:14 [a]Ex. 21:1; ch. 22; ch. 23
4:15 [a]Josh. 23:11 [b]Is. 40:18
4:16 [a]Ex. 32:7 [b]ver. 23; Ex. 20:4,5; ch. 5:8 [c]Rom. 1:23
4:19 [1]Or, *imparted* [a]ch. 17:3; Job 31:26 [b]2 Ki. 21:3 [c]Rom. 1:25
4:20 [a]1 Ki. 8:51; Jer. 11:4 [b]Ex. 19:5; ch. 9:29
4:21 [a]Num. 20:12; ch. 1:37; 3:26
4:22 [a]See 2 Pet. 1:13-15 [b]ch. 3:27 [c]ch. 3:25
4:23 [a]ver. 9 [b]ver. 16; Ex. 20:4,5
4:24 [a]Ex. 24:17; ch. 9:3; Is. 33:14; Heb. 12:29 [b]Ex. 20:5; ch. 6:15
4:25 [a]2 Ki. 17:17
4:26 [a]ch. 30:18,19; Is. 1:2; Mic. 6:2

Idolatry forbidden

15 [a]Take ye therefore good heed unto yourselves; for ye saw no *manner of* [b]similitude on the day *that* the LORD spake unto you in Horeb out of the midst of the fire:

16 Lest ye [a]corrupt *yourselves,* and [b]make you a graven image, the similitude of any figure, [c]the likeness of male or female,

17 The likeness of any beast that *is* on the earth, the likeness of any winged fowl that flieth in the air,

18 The likeness of any *thing* that creepeth on the ground, the likeness of any fish that *is* in the waters beneath the earth:

19 And lest thou [a]lift up thine eyes unto heaven, and when thou seest the sun, and the moon, and the stars, *even* [b]all the host of heaven, shouldest be driven to [c]worship them, and serve them, which the LORD thy God hath [1]divided unto all nations under the whole heaven.

20 But the LORD hath taken you, and [a]brought you forth out of the iron furnace, *even* out of Egypt, [b]to be unto him a people of inheritance, as *ye are* this day.

21 Furthermore [a]the LORD was angry with me for your sakes, and sware that I should not go over Jordan, and that *I* should not go in unto *that* good land, which the LORD thy God giveth thee *for* an inheritance:

22 But [a]I *must* die in this land, [b]I *must* not go over Jordan: but ye *shall* go over, and possess [c]that good land.

23 Take heed unto yourselves, [a]lest ye forget the covenant of the LORD your God, which he made with you, [b]and make you a graven image, *or* the likeness of any *thing,* which the LORD thy God hath forbidden thee.

24 For [a]the LORD thy God *is* a consuming fire, *even* [b]a jealous God.

25 When thou shalt beget children, and children's children, and ye shall have remained long in the land, and shall corrupt *yourselves,* and make a graven image, *or* the likeness of any *thing,* and [a]shall do evil in the sight of the LORD thy God, to provoke him to anger:

26 [a]I call heaven and earth to witness

anything that adulterates or contradicts it cannot be tolerated (see 12:32; Prov 30:6; Gal 3:15; Rev 22:18–19).

4:4 *did cleave.* See note on 10:20.

4:7 *nigh . . . that we call upon him for.* The Israelites always had access to the Lord in prayer. His presence was symbolized by the tabernacle in the center of the camp, and by the pillar of cloud over the tabernacle (see Ex 40:34–38; Num 23:21).

4:9 *teach them thy sons.* See v. 10; 11:19; cf. Ex 12:26–27.

4:10–14 See Ex 19–24.

‡4:10 The divine call to Israel to remember the Lord's past redemptive acts—especially how He delivered them from slavery in Egypt—is a common theme in Deuteronomy (5:15; 7:18; 8:2,18; 9:7,27; 11:2; 15:15; 16:3,12; 24:9,18,22; 25:17) and is summarized in 32:7: "Remember the days of old."

4:12 *no similitude* [i.e. form]. See v. 15; see also note on Ex 20:4. "God is a Spirit" (John 4:24; cf. Is 31:3).

4:13 *his covenant . . . even ten commandments.* See notes on Ex 20:1; 34:28. *two tables of stone.* See note on Ex 31:18.

4:15–18 See note on Ex 20:4.

4:19 *lest . . . be driven to worship.* As kings of Judah would be later (2 Ki 23:5).

4:20 *iron furnace.* Suggests that the period in Egypt was a time of affliction, testing and refinement for the Israelites (see 1 Ki 8:51; Jer 11:4; see also Is 48:10).

4:21 *for your sakes.* See note on 1:37.

4:24 *consuming fire.* See 9:3; see also note on Ex 24:17. *jealous God.* See 5:9; 6:15; see also note on Ex 20:5.

4:25 *When thou . . . have remained long in the land.* The pattern of Israel's rebellion, resulting in expulsion from the land, and then their repentance, leading to restoration to the land, is prominent in Deuteronomy (see, e.g., the blessing and curse formulas in chs. 27–28).

against you *this* day, that ye shall soon utterly perish from off the land whereunto you go over Jordan to possess it; ye shall not prolong *your* days upon it, but shall utterly be destroyed.

27 And the LORD [a]shall scatter you among the nations, and ye shall be left few in number among the heathen, whither the LORD shall lead you.

28 And [a]there ye shall serve gods, the work of men's hands, wood and stone, [b]which neither see, nor hear, nor eat, nor smell.

29 [a]But if from thence thou shalt seek the LORD thy God, thou shalt find *him,* if thou seek him with all thy heart and with all thy soul.

30 When thou art in tribulation, and all these things [1]are come upon thee, [a]*even* in the latter days, if thou [b]turn to the LORD thy God, and shalt be obedient unto his voice;

31 (For the LORD thy God *is* [a]a merciful God;) he will not forsake thee, neither destroy thee, nor forget the covenant of thy fathers which he sware unto them.

Israel as a chosen nation

32 For [a]ask now of the days that are past, which were before thee, since the day that God created man upon the earth, and *ask* [b]from the one side of heaven unto the other, whether there hath been *any such thing* as this great thing *is,* or hath been heard like it?

33 [a]Did *ever* people hear the voice of God speaking out of the midst of the fire, as thou hast heard, and live?

34 Or hath God assayed to go *and* take him a nation from the midst of *another* nation, [a]by temptations, [b]by signs, and by wonders, and by war, and [c]by a mighty hand, and [d]by a stretched out arm, [e]and by great terrors, according to all that the LORD your God did for you in Egypt before your eyes?

35 Unto thee it was shewed, that thou mightest know that the LORD he *is* God; [a]*there is* none else besides him.

36 [a]Out of heaven he made thee to hear his voice, that he might instruct thee: and upon earth he shewed thee his great fire; and thou heardest his words out of the midst of the fire.

37 And because [a]he loved thy fathers, therefore he chose their seed after them, and [b]brought thee out in his sight with his mighty power out of Egypt;

38 [a]To drive out nations from before thee greater and mightier than thou *art,* to bring thee in, to give thee their land *for* an inheritance, as *it is* this day.

39 Know therefore *this* day, and consider *it* in thine heart, that [a]the LORD he *is* God in heaven above, and upon the earth beneath: *there is* none else.

40 [a]Thou shalt keep therefore his statutes, and his commandments, which I command thee *this* day, [b]that it may go well with thee, and with thy children after thee, and that thou mayest prolong *thy* days upon the earth, which the LORD thy God giveth thee, for ever.

41 ¶ Then Moses [a]severed three cities on *this* side Jordan toward the sunrising;

42 [a]That the slayer might flee thither, which should kill his neighbour unawares, and hated him not in times past; and that fleeing unto one of these cities he might live:

43 *Namely,* [a]Bezer in the wilderness, in the plain country, of the Reubenites; and Ramoth in Gilead, of the Gadites; and Golan in Bashan, of the Manassites.

44 And this *is* the law which Moses set before the children of Israel:

45 These *are* the testimonies, and the statutes, and the judgments, which Moses spake unto the children of Israel, after they came forth out of Egypt,

46 On *this* side Jordan, [a]in the valley over against Beth-peor, in the land of Sihon king of the Amorites, who dwelt at Heshbon, whom Moses and the children of Israel [b]smote, after they were come forth out of Egypt:

47 And they possessed his land, and the land [a]of Og king of Bashan, two kings of the Amorites, which *were* on *this* side Jordan *toward* the sunrising;

48 [a]From Aroer, which *is* by the bank of the river Arnon, even unto mount Sion, which *is* [b]Hermon,

49 And all the plain on *this* side Jordan eastward, even unto the sea of the plain, under the [a]springs of Pisgah.

The ten commandments

5 And Moses called all Israel, and said unto them, Hear, O Israel, the statutes and judgments which I speak in your ears *this* day, that ye may learn them, and [1]keep, and do them.

2 [a]The LORD our God made a covenant with us in Horeb.

4:27 [a]Lev. 26:33; Neh. 1:8 **4:28** [a]ch. 28:64; 1 Sam. 26:19; Jer. 16:13 [b]Ps. 115:4,5; 135:15,16; Is. 44:9; 46:7 **4:29** [a]Lev. 26:39; ch. 30:1-3; 2 Chr. 15:4; Neh. 1:9; Is. 55:6,7 **4:30** [1]Heb. *have found thee* [a]Gen. 49:1; ch. 31:29; Jer. 23:20; Hos. 3:5 [b]Joel 2:12 **4:31** [a]2 Chr. 30:9; Neh. 9:31; Ps. 116:5; Jonah 4:2 **4:32** [a]Job 8:8 [b]Mat. 24:31 **4:33** [a]Ex. 24:11; 33:20; ch. 5:24,26 **4:34** [a]ch. 7:19 [b]Ex. 7:3 [c]Ex. 13:3 [d]Ex. 6:6 [e]ch. 26:8; 34:12 **4:35** [a]ch. 32:39; 1 Sam. 2:2; Is. 45:5,18; Mark 12:29 **4:36** [a]Ex. 19:9,19; 20:18,22; 24:16; Heb. 12:18 **4:37** [a]ch. 10:15 [b]Ex. 13:3,9,14 **4:38** [a]ch. 7:1; 9:1,4,5 **4:39** [a]Josh. 2:11 **4:40** [a]Lev. 22:31 [b]ch. 5:16; 6:3,18; 12:25,28; 22:7; Eph. 6:3 **4:41** [a]Num. 35:6 **4:42** [a]ch. 19:4 **4:43** [a]Josh. 20:8 **4:46** [a]ch. 3:29 [b]Num. 21:24; ch. 1:4 **4:47** [a]Num. 21:35; ch. 3:3,4 **4:48** [a]ch. 2:36; 3:12 [b]ch. 3:9; Ps. 133:3 **4:49** [a]ch. 3:17 **5:1** [1]Heb. *keep to do them* **5:2** [a]Ex. 19:5; ch. 4:23

4:26 *heaven and earth to witness.* See notes on 30:19; Ps 50:1; Isa 1:2.

4:27 *shall scatter you.* See note on 28:64.

4:29 *with all thy heart and . . . soul.* Indicates total involvement and commitment. The phrase is applied not only to how the Lord's people should seek Him, but also to how they should fear (revere) Him, live in obedience to Him, love and serve Him (6:5; 10:12; 11:13; 13:3; 30:6), and, after forsaking Him, renew their allegiance and commitment (26:16; 30:2,10).

4:31 *covenant . . . he sware unto them.* See notes on Gen 21:23; 22:16; Heb 6:13,18. In ancient times, parties to a covenant were expected to confirm their intentions by means of a self-maledictory oath (see note on Gen 15:17).

4:35 *that thou mightest know.* See v. 10. *there is none else besides him.* See v. 39; 5:7; 6:4 and note; 32:39. Moses' belief in one God was total and uncompromising (see note on Gen 1:1).

4:37 *he loved.* The first reference in Deuteronomy to God's love for His people (see Introduction: Theological Teaching). See note on 7:8; see also 5:10; 7:9,13; 10:15; 23:5. The corollary truth is that His people should love Him (see note on 6:5).

4:39 See v. 35 and note.

4:41–43 See 19:1–13; Num 35:9–28; Josh 20.

4:43 *Bezer.* About 20 miles east of the northeast corner of the Dead Sea.

5:1 *Hear, O Israel.* See note on 4:1.

5:2 *covenant with us in Horeb.* See note on Ex 19:5. God's cov-

3 The LORD [a]made not this covenant with our fathers, but with us, *even* us, who *are* all of us here alive *this* day.

4 [a]The LORD talked with you face to face in the mount out of the midst of the fire,

5 ([a]I stood between the LORD and you at that time, to shew you the word of the LORD: for [b]ye were afraid by reason of the fire, and went not up into the mount;) saying,

6 ¶ [a]I *am* the LORD thy God, which brought thee out of the land of Egypt, from the house of [1]bondage.

7 [a]Thou shalt have none other gods before me.

8 [a]Thou shalt not make thee *any* graven image, *or* any likeness *of any thing* that *is* in heaven above, or that *is* in the earth beneath, or that *is* in the waters beneath the earth:

9 Thou shalt not bow down thyself unto them, nor serve them: for I the LORD thy God *am* a jealous God, [a]visiting the iniquity of the fathers upon the children unto the third and fourth *generation* of them that hate me,

10 [a]And shewing mercy unto thousands of them that love me and keep my commandments.

11 [a]Thou shalt not take the name of the LORD thy God in vain: for the LORD will not hold *him* guiltless that taketh his name in vain.

12 [a]Keep the sabbath day to sanctify it, as the LORD thy God hath commanded thee.

13 [a]Six days thou shalt labour, and do all thy work:

14 But the seventh day *is* the [a]sabbath of the LORD thy God: *in it* thou shalt not do any work, thou, nor thy son, nor thy daughter, nor thy manservant, nor thy maidservant, nor thine ox, nor thine ass, nor any of thy cattle, nor thy stranger that *is* within thy gates; that thy manservant and thy maidservant may rest as well as thou.

15 [a]And remember that thou wast a servant in the land of Egypt, and *that* the LORD thy God brought thee out thence [b]through a mighty hand and by a stretched out arm: therefore the LORD thy God commanded thee to keep the sabbath day.

16 [a]Honour thy father and thy mother, as the LORD thy God hath commanded thee; [b]that thy days may be prolonged, and that it may go well with thee, in the land which the LORD thy God giveth thee.

17 [a]Thou shalt not kill.

18 [a]Neither shalt thou commit adultery.

19 [a]Neither shalt thou steal.

20 [a]Neither shalt thou bear false witness against thy neighbour.

21 [a]Neither shalt thou desire thy neighbour's wife, neither shalt thou covet thy neighbour's house, his field, or his manservant, or his maidservant, his ox, or his ass, or any *thing* that *is* thy neighbour's.

22 ¶ These words the LORD spake unto all your assembly in the mount out of the midst of the fire, of the cloud, and of the thick darkness, *with* a great voice: and he added no more. And [a]he wrote them in two tables of stone, and delivered them unto me.

23 [a]And it came to pass, when ye heard the voice out of the midst of the darkness, (for the mountain did burn with fire,) that ye came near unto me, *even* all the heads of your tribes, and your elders;

24 And ye said, Behold, the LORD our God hath shewed us his glory and his greatness, and [a]we have heard his voice out of the midst of the fire: we have seen this day that God doth talk with man, and he [b]liveth.

25 Now therefore why should we die? for this great fire will consume us: [a]if we [1]hear the voice of the LORD our God any more, then we shall die.

26 [a]For who *is there of* all flesh, that hath heard the voice of the living God speaking out of the midst of the fire, as we *have,* and lived?

27 Go thou near, and hear all that the LORD our God shall say: and [a]speak thou unto us all that the LORD our God shall speak unto thee; and we will hear *it,* and do *it.*

28 And the LORD heard the voice of your words, when ye spake unto me; and the LORD said unto me, I have heard the voice of the words of this people, which they have spoken

5:3 [a]See Mat. 13:17; Heb. 8:9
5:4 [a]Ex. 19:9,19; 20:22; ch. 4:33,36; 34:10
5:5 [a]Ex. 20:21; Gal. 3:19 [b]Ex. 19:16; 20:18; 24:2
5:6 [1]Heb. *servants* [a]Ex. 20:2
5:7 [a]Ex. 20:3
5:8 [a]Ex. 20:4
5:9 [a]Ex. 34:7
5:10 [a]Jer. 32:18; Dan. 9:4
5:11 [a]Ex. 20:7; Lev. 19:12; Mat. 5:33
5:12 [a]Ex. 20:8
5:13 [a]Ex. 23:12; 35:2; Ezek. 20:12
5:14 [a]Gen. 2:2; Ex. 16:29; Heb. 4:4
5:15 [a]ch. 15:15; 16:12; 24:18,22 [b]ch. 4:34,37
5:16 [a]Ex. 20:12; Lev. 19:3; ch. 27:16; Eph. 6:2,3; Col. 3:20 [b]ch. 4:40
5:17 [a]Ex. 20:13; Mat. 5:21
5:18 [a]Ex. 20:14; Luke 18:20; Jas. 2:11
5:19 [a]Ex. 20:15; Rom. 13:9
5:20 [a]Ex. 20:16
5:21 [a]Ex. 20:17; Mic. 2:2; Hab. 2:9; Luke 12:15; Rom. 7:7
5:22 [a]Ex. 24:12; 31:18; ch. 4:13
5:23 [a]Ex. 20:18,19
5:24 [a]Ex. 19:19 [b]ch. 4:33; Judg. 13:22
5:25 [1]Heb. *add to hear* [a]ch. 18:16
5:26 [a]ch. 4:33
5:27 [a]Ex. 20:19; Heb. 12:19

enant with Israel, given at mount Horeb (Sinai) and now being confirmed, bound Israel to the Lord as their absolute Sovereign, and to His laws and regulations as their way of life. Adherence to the covenant would bring to Israel the blessings of the Lord, while breaking the covenant would bring against them the punishments described as "curses" (see, e.g., 28:15–20). Jer 31:31–34 predicted the establishing of a new covenant, which made the Sinaitic covenant obsolete (see Heb 7:22; see also Heb 8:6–13; 10:15–18 and notes). See chart, p. 16.

5:3 *not . . . with our fathers, but with us.* The covenant was made with those who were present at Sinai, but since they were representatives of the nation, it was made with all succeeding generations as well.

5:5 See vv. 23–26; Ex 20:18–21.

5:6–21 The ten commandments are both the basis and the heart of Israel's relationship with the Lord. It is almost impossible to exaggerate their effect on subsequent history. They constitute the basis of moral principles throughout the Western world, and they summarize what the one true God expects of His people in terms of faith, worship and conduct (see notes on Ex 20:3–17).

5:12 *as the LORD thy God hath commanded thee.* Missing from the parallel verse in Exodus (20:8), this clause reminds the people of the divine origin of the ten commandments 40 years earlier (see vv. 15–16).

5:14 *that thy manservant and thy maidservant may rest.* See note on Ex 20:10; see also v. 15.

5:15 *remember.* See note on 4:10.

5:16–21 The NT quotes often from this section of the ten commandments (see cross references).

5:20 See 19:18–19.

5:22 *words.* See note on Ex 20:1. *two tables of stone.* See note on Ex 31:18.

5:25 *we shall die.* See notes on Gen 16:13; 32:30.

5:27 *we will hear it, and do it.* See note on Ex 19:8.

unto thee: [a]they have well *said* all that they
have spoken.
29 [a]O that there were such a heart in
them, that they would fear me, and [b]keep all
my commandments always, [c]that it might be
well with them, and with their children for
ever!
30 Go say to them, Get you into your tents
again.
31 But *as for* thee, stand thou here by me,
[a]and I will speak unto thee all the commandments, and the statutes, and the judgments,
which thou shalt teach them, that they may
do *them* in the land which I give them to possess it.
32 Ye shall observe to do therefore as the
LORD your God hath commanded you: [a]ye shall
not turn aside *to* the right hand or *to* the left.
33 You shall walk in [a]all the ways which
the LORD your God hath commanded you, that
ye may live, [b]and *that it may be* well with you,
and *that* ye may prolong *your* days in the land
which ye shall possess.

Love the LORD thy God

6 Now these *are* [a]the commandments, the
statutes, and the judgments, which the
LORD your God commanded to teach you, that
ye might do *them* in the land whither ye [1]go
to possess it:
2 [a]That thou mightest fear the LORD thy
God, to keep all his statutes and his commandments, which I command thee, thou, and thy
son, and thy son's son, all the days of thy life;
[b]and that thy days may be prolonged.
3 Hear therefore, O Israel, and observe to
do *it;* that it may be well with thee, and that ye
may increase mightily, [a]as the LORD God of thy
fathers hath promised thee, *in* [b]the land that
floweth with milk and honey.
4 [a]Hear, O Israel: The LORD our God *is* one
LORD:
5 And [a]thou shalt love the LORD thy God
[b]with all thine heart, and with all thy soul, and
with all thy might.

6 And [a]these words, which I command
thee *this* day, shall be in thine heart:
7 And [a]thou shalt [1]teach them diligently
unto thy children, and shalt talk of them when
thou sittest in thine house, and when thou
walkest by the way, and when thou liest down,
and when thou risest up.
8 [a]And thou shalt bind them for a sign
upon thine hand, and they shall be as frontlets
between thine eyes.
9 [a]And thou shalt write them upon the
posts of thy house, and on thy gates.
10 And it shall be, when the LORD thy God
shall have brought thee into the land which he
sware unto thy fathers, to Abraham, to Isaac,
and to Jacob, to give thee great and goodly cities, [a]which thou buildedst not,
11 And houses full *of* all good *things,*
which thou filledst not, and wells digged,
which thou diggedst not, vineyards and olive
trees, which thou plantedst not; [a]when thou
shalt have eaten and be full;
12 *Then* beware lest thou forget the LORD,
which brought thee forth out of the land of
Egypt, from the house of [1]bondage.
13 Thou shalt [a]fear the LORD thy God, and
serve him, and [b]shalt swear by his name.
14 Ye shall not go after other gods, [a]of the
gods of the people which *are* round about you;
15 (For [a]the LORD thy God *is* a jealous God
among you) [b]lest the anger of the LORD thy
God be kindled against thee, and destroy thee
from off the face of the earth.
16 [a]Ye shall not tempt the LORD your God,
[b]as ye tempted *him* in Massah.
17 You shall [a]diligently keep the commandments of the LORD your God, and his testimonies, and his statutes, which he hath commanded thee.
18 And thou [a]shalt do *that which is* right
and good in the sight of the LORD: that it may
be well with thee, and *that* thou mayest go in
and possess the good land which the LORD
sware unto thy fathers,

5:28 [a]ch. 18:17
5:29 [a]ch. 32:29; Ps. 81:13; Is. 48:18; Mat. 23:37; Luke 19:42 [b]ch. 11:1 [c]ch. 4:40
5:31 [a]Gal. 3:19
5:32 [a]ch. 17:20; 28:14; Josh. 1:7; Prov. 4:27
5:33 [a]ch. 10:12; Jer. 7:23 [b]ch. 4:40
6:1 [1]Heb. *pass over* [a]ch. 12:1
6:2 [a]ch. 10:12,13; Eccl. 12:13 [b]ch. 4:40; Prov. 3:1,2
6:3 [a]Gen. 22:17 [b]Ex. 3:8
6:4 [a]John 17:3; 1 Cor. 8:4,6
6:5 [a]Mat. 22:37; Mark 12:30 [b]2 Ki. 23:25
6:6 [a]ch. 11:18; Ps. 119:11,98
6:7 [1]Heb. *whet,* or, *sharpen* [a]ch. 11:19; Ps. 78:4-6
6:8 [a]Prov. 6:21; 7:3
6:9 [a]ch. 11:20; Is. 57:8
6:10 [a]Josh. 24:13; Ps. 105:44
6:11 [a]ch. 8:10
6:12 [1]Heb. *bondmen,* or, *servants*
6:13 [a]Mat. 4:10; Luke 4:8 [b]Is. 45:23; 65:16; Jer. 4:2
6:14 [a]ch. 13:7
6:15 [a]Ex. 20:5; ch. 4:24 [b]ch. 7:4; 11:17
6:16 [a]Mat. 4:7; Luke 4:12 [b]1 Cor. 10:9
6:17 [a]Ps. 119:4
6:18 [a]Ex. 15:26; ch. 12:28; 13:18

6:2 *fear the LORD.* See note on Gen 20:11. *days may be prolonged.* See 4:40; 5:16,33. By obeying the Lord and keeping His decrees, individual Israelites would enjoy long life in the land, and the people as a whole would enjoy a long national existence in the land.

6:3 *land that floweth with milk and honey.* See note on Ex 3:8. The phrase is used 14 times from Exodus through Deuteronomy and 5 times elsewhere in the OT (see especially 32:13–14).

6:4–9 Known as the *Shema,* Hebrew for "Hear." It has become the Jewish confession of faith, recited daily by the pious (see Mat 22:37–38; Mark 12:29–30; Luke 10:27).

6:4 *Hear, O Israel.* See note on 4:1. *The LORD . . . is one LORD.* A divinely revealed insight, especially important in view of the multiplicity of Baals and other gods of Canaan and elsewhere (see, e.g., Judg 2:11–13).

6:5 *thou shalt love the LORD.* Love for God and neighbor (see Lev 19:18) is built on the love that the Lord has for His people (1 John 4:19–21) and on His identification with them. Such love is to be total, involving one's whole being (see notes on 4:29; Josh 22:5).

6:6 *words . . . shall be in thine heart.* A feature that would especially characterize the "new covenant" (Jer 31:31; see Jer 31:33).

6:8–9 Many Jews take these verses literally and tie phylacteries (see note on Mat 23:5) to their foreheads and left arms. They also attach mezuzot (small wooden or metal containers in which passages of Scripture are placed) to the doorframes of their houses. But a figurative interpretation is supported by 11:18–20; Ex 13:9,16. See note on Ex 13:9.

6:10–12 Because the emphasis in Scripture is always on what God does and not on what His people achieve, they are never to forget what He has done for them.

6:13 Quoted in part by Jesus in response to Satan's temptation (Mat 4:10; Luke 4:8). Jesus quoted from Deuteronomy in response to the devil's other two temptations as well (see notes on v. 16; 8:3).

6:15 *jealous God.* See note on Ex 20:5.

6:16 Quoted in part by Jesus in Mat 4:7; Luke 4:12 (see also note on v. 13). *as ye tempted him in Massah.* See 9:22; 33:8; see also note on Ex 17:7.

19 [a]To cast out all thine enemies from before thee, as the LORD hath spoken.
20 *And* [a]when thy son asketh thee [1]in time
to come, saying, What *mean* the testimonies,
and the statutes, and the judgments, which the
LORD our God hath commanded you?
21 Then thou shalt say unto thy son, We
were Pharaoh's bondmen in Egypt; and the
LORD brought us out of Egypt [a]with a mighty
hand:
22 [a]And the LORD shewed signs and wonders, great and [1]sore, upon Egypt, upon Pharaoh, and upon all his household, before our
eyes:
23 And he brought us out from thence,
that he might bring us in, to give us the land
which he sware unto our fathers.
24 And the LORD commanded us to do all
these statutes, [a]to fear the LORD our God, [b]for
our good always, that [c]he might preserve us
alive, as *it is at* this day.
25 And [a]it shall be our righteousness, if we
observe to do all these commandments before
the LORD our God, as he hath commanded us.

God will defeat the nations

7 When the [a]LORD thy God shall bring thee
into the land whither thou goest to possess it, and hath cast out many nations before
thee, [b]the Hittites, and the Girgashites, and
the Amorites, and the Canaanites, and the Perizzites, and the Hivites, and the Jebusites, sev-
en nations [c]greater and mightier than thou;
2 And when the LORD thy God shall [a]deliver
them before thee; thou shalt smite them, *and*
[b]utterly destroy them; [c]thou shalt make no covenant with them, nor shew mercy unto them:
3 [a]Neither shalt thou make marriages with
them; thy daughter thou shalt not give unto
his son, nor his daughter shalt thou take unto
thy son.
4 For they will turn away thy son from following me, that they may serve other gods:
[a]so will the anger of the LORD be kindled
against you, and destroy thee suddenly.
5 But thus shall ye deal with them; ye shall
[a]destroy their altars, and break down their
[1]images, and cut down their groves, and burn
their graven images with fire.
6 [a]For thou *art* a holy people unto the LORD
thy God: [b]the LORD thy God hath chosen thee
to be a special people unto himself, above all
people that *are* upon the face of the earth.
7 The LORD did not set his love upon you,
nor choose you, because ye were moe in number than any people; for ye *were* [a]the fewest of
all people:
8 But [a]because the LORD loved you, and because he would keep [b]the oath which he had
sworn unto your fathers, [c]hath the LORD
brought you out with a mighty hand, and redeemed you out of the house of bondmen,
from the hand of Pharaoh king of Egypt.
9 Know therefore that the LORD thy God,
he *is* God, [a]the faithful God, [b]which keepeth
covenant and mercy with them that love him
and keep his commandments to a thousand
generations;
10 And [a]repayeth them that hate him to
their face, to destroy them: [b]he will not be
slack to him that hateth him, he will repay
him to his face.
11 Thou shalt therefore keep the commandments, and the statutes, and the judgments,
which I command thee *this* day, to do them.
12 [a]Wherefore it shall come to pass, [1]if ye
hearken to these judgments, and keep, and do
them, that the LORD thy God shall keep unto
thee [b]the covenant and the mercy which he
sware unto thy fathers:
13 And he will [a]love thee, and bless thee,
and multiply thee: [b]he will also bless the fruit of
thy womb, and the fruit of thy land, thy corn,
and thy wine, and thine oil, the increase of thy
kine, and the flocks of thy sheep, in the land
which he sware unto thy fathers to give thee.
14 Thou shalt be blessed above all people:
[a]there shall not be male or female barren
among you, or among your cattle.
15 And the LORD will take away from thee
all sickness, and will put none of the [a]evil diseases of Egypt, which thou knowest, upon
thee; but will lay them upon all *them* that hate
thee.

6:19 [a]Num. 33:52,53
6:20 [1]Heb. *to morrow* [a]Ex. 13:14
6:21 [a]Ex. 13:3
6:22 [1]Heb. *evil* [a]Ex. 7; 8; 9; 10
6:24 [a]ver. 2 [b]Job 35:7,8; Jer. 32:39 [c]ch. 4:1; Ps. 41:2
6:25 [a]Lev. 18:5; Rom. 10:3,5
7:1 [a]ch. 31:3 [b]Ex. 33:2 [c]ch. 4:38
7:2 [a]ch. 23:14 [b]Josh. 6:17; 8:24; 9:24 [c]Josh. 2:14; Judg. 1:24; 2:2
7:3 [a]1 Ki. 11:2; Ezra 9:2
7:4 [a]ch. 6:15
7:5 [a]Ex. 23:24; 34:13; ch. 12:2,3
7:5 [1]Heb. *statues,* or, *pillars*
7:6 [a]Ps. 50:5; Jer. 2:3 [b]Ex. 19:5; Amos 3:2; 1 Pet. 2:9
7:7 [a]ch. 10:22
7:8 [a]ch. 10:15 [b]Luke 1:55,72, 73 [c]Ex. 13:3,14
7:9 [a]1 Cor. 1:9; 2 Cor. 1:18; 2 Thes. 3:3; 2 Tim. 2:13; Heb. 11:11 [b]Neh. 1:5; Dan. 9:4
7:10 [a]Is. 59:18 [b]ch. 32:35
7:12 [1]Heb. *because* [a]ch. 28:1 [b]Ps. 105:8,9
7:13 [a]John 14:21 [b]ch. 28:4
7:14 [a]Ex. 23:26
7:15 [a]Ex. 15:26; ch. 28:27,60

6:20 See Ex 12:26 and note.
6:23 *brought us out . . . bring us in.* See note on Ex 6:7–8.
6:25 *righteousness.* Probably here refers to a true, personal relationship with the covenant Lord that manifests itself in the daily lives of God's people (see 24:13).
7:1 *Hittites . . . Jebusites.* See 20:17; see also notes on Gen 10:6,15–18; 13:7. *seven nations.* See note on Ex 3:8.
7:2 *utterly destroy them.* See note on 2:34.
7:2–5 *thou shalt make no covenant . . . make marriages . . . destroy their altars.* Israel was to have no association—political, social or religious—with the idol worshipers of Canaan (see v. 16; see also note on 2:34).
7:4 *turn away thy son . . . may serve other gods.* The Lord's command against intermarriage with foreigners was not racially motivated but was intended to prevent spiritual contamination and apostasy (see, e.g., 1 Ki 11:1–11; Neh 13:25–27).
‡7:5 *altars . . . images . . . groves* [*Asherim* in Hebrew]. Cult objects of Canaanite idolatrous worship (see 12:3; 16:21–22). Asherim were wooden symbols of the goddess Asherah (see Ex 34:13 and note.)
7:6 *holy.* Separated from all corrupting people or things and consecrated totally to the Lord (see note on Ex 3:5). *a special people unto himself.* See note on Ex 19:5.
7:8 *because the LORD loved you.* His "covenant and mercy" (vv. 9,12) stem from God's love for His people, based on His character and embodied in His covenant; they do not stem from the numerical greatness of the people or any virtue of theirs. His love must be reciprocated by His people (see vv. 9–10; 9:4–6; see also note on 6:5).
7:9 *Know . . . that the LORD . . . is God.* See Ps 100:3. *to a thousand generations.* See note on Ex 20:6.
7:12–15 The blessings are elaborated in 28:1–14; 30:1–10.
‡7:13 *corn* [i.e. grain] *. . . wine . . . oil.* A common OT summary of the produce of field, vineyard and olive grove (see, e.g., 11:14; 14:23; 18:4; 28:51).
7:15 *put none . . . diseases . . . upon thee.* See note on 28:60.

16 And [a]thou shalt consume all the people which the LORD thy God shall deliver thee; [b]thine eye shall have no pity upon them: neither shalt thou serve their gods; for that *will be* [c]a snare unto thee.

17 If thou shalt say in thine heart, These nations *are* moe than I; how can I [a]dispossess them?

18 [a]Thou shalt not be afraid of them: *but* shalt well [b]remember what the LORD thy God did unto Pharaoh, and unto all Egypt;

19 [a]The great temptations which thine eyes saw, and the signs, and the wonders, and the mighty hand, and the stretched out arm, where*by* the LORD thy God brought thee out: so shall the LORD thy God do unto all the people of whom thou *art* afraid.

20 [a]Moreover the LORD thy God will send the hornet among them, until they that are left, and hide themselves from thee, be destroyed.

21 Thou shalt not be affrighted at them: for the LORD thy God *is* [a]among you, [b]a mighty God and terrible.

22 [a]And the LORD thy God will [1]put out those nations before thee by little and little: thou mayest not consume them at once, lest the beasts of the field increase upon thee.

23 But the LORD thy God shall deliver them [1]unto thee, and shall destroy them *with* a mighty destruction, until they be destroyed.

24 And [a]he shall deliver their kings into thine hand, and thou shalt destroy their name [b]from under heaven: [c]there shall no man *be able to* stand before thee, until thou have destroyed them.

25 The graven images of their gods [a]shall ye burn with fire: thou [b]shalt not desire the silver or gold *that is* on them, nor take *it* unto thee, lest thou be [c]snared therein: for it *is* [d]an abomination to the LORD thy God.

26 Neither shalt thou bring an abomination into thine house, lest thou be a cursed thing like it: *but* thou shalt utterly detest it, and thou shalt utterly abhor it; [a]for it *is* a cursed thing.

God's mercies in the wilderness

8 All the commandments which I command thee *this* day [a]shall ye observe to do, that ye may live, and multiply, and go in and possess the land which the LORD sware unto your fathers.

2 And thou shalt remember all the way which the LORD thy God [a]led thee these forty years in the wilderness, to humble thee, *and* [b]to prove thee, [c]to know what *was* in thine heart, whether thou wouldest keep his commandments, or no.

3 And he humbled thee, and [a]suffered thee to hunger, and [b]fed thee with manna, which thou knewest not, neither did thy fathers know; that he might make thee know that man doth [c]not live by bread only, but by every *word* that proceedeth out of the mouth of the LORD doth man live.

4 [a]Thy raiment waxed not old upon thee, neither did thy foot swell, these forty years.

5 [a]Thou shalt also consider in thine heart, that, as a man chasteneth his son, *so* the LORD thy God chasteneth thee.

6 Therefore thou shalt keep the commandments of the LORD thy God, [a]to walk in his ways, and to fear him.

7 For the LORD thy God bringeth thee into a good land, [a]a land of brooks of water, of fountains and depths that spring out of the valleys and hills;

8 A land of wheat, and barley, and vines, and fig trees, and pomegranates; a land [1]of oil olive, and honey;

9 A land wherein thou shalt eat bread without scarceness, thou shalt not lack any *thing* in it; a land [a]whose stones *are* iron, and out of whose hills thou mayest dig brass.

10 [a]When thou hast eaten and art full, then thou shalt bless the LORD thy God for the good land which he hath given thee.

Warning against pride

11 Beware that thou forget not the LORD thy God, in not keeping his commandments, and his judgments, and his statutes, which I command thee *this* day:

12 [a]Lest *when* thou hast eaten and art full, and hast built goodly houses, and dwelt *therein;*

13 And *when* thy herds and thy flocks multiply, and thy silver and thy gold is multiplied, and all that thou hast is multiplied;

7:16 [a]ver. 2 [b]ch. 19:13,21 [c]Judg. 8:27
7:17 [a]Num. 33:53
7:18 [a]ch. 31:6 [b]Ps. 105:5
7:19 [a]ch. 4:34; 29:3
7:20 [a]Josh. 24:12
7:21 [a]Num. 16:3; Josh. 3:10 [b]Neh. 9:32
7:22 [1]Heb. *pluck off* [a]Ex. 23:29,30
7:23 [1]Heb. *before thy face*
7:24 [a]Josh. 10:24,25,42 [b]Ex. 17:14 [c]Josh. 23:9
7:25 [a]Ex. 32:20; 1 Chr. 14:12 [b]Josh. 7:1,21 [c]Judg. 8:27; Zeph. 1:3 [d]ch. 17:1
7:26 [a]Lev. 27:28; Josh. 6:17; 7:1
8:1 [a]ch. 4:1; 5:32,33; 6:1-3
8:2 [a]ch. 1:3; 2:7; Amos 2:10 [b]Ex. 16:4; ch. 13:3 [c]John 2:25
8:3 [a]Ex. 16:2,3 [b]Ex. 16:12,14,35 [c]Mat. 4:4; Luke 4:4
8:4 [a]ch. 29:5; Neh. 9:21
8:5 [a]2 Sam. 7:14; Ps. 89:32; Prov. 3:12; Heb. 12:5,6; Rev. 3:19
8:6 [a]ch. 5:33
8:7 [a]ch. 11:10-12
8:8 [1]Heb. *of olive tree of oil*
8:9 [a]ch. 33:25
8:10 [a]ch. 6:11,12
8:12 [a]ch. 28:47; 32:15; Hos. 13:6

7:16 See essay, p. 272.
7:18 *remember.* See note on 4:10.
7:20 *hornet.* See note on Ex 23:28.
7:22 *God will put out.* See note on 3:22.
7:25–26 Cf. the story of Achan (Josh 6:17–19; 7:1,20–25).
‡7:26 *be a cursed thing.* See note on 2:34.
‡8:2 *remember.* See note on 4:10. *to prove* [i.e. test]. See v. 16; see also note on Gen 22:1.
8:3 *manna.* See v. 16; see also note on Num 11:7. *man doth not live by bread only.* See note on 6:13; quoted by Jesus in response to the devil's temptation (see Mat 4:4; Luke 4:4). Bread sustains but does not guarantee life, which is God's gift to those who trust in and live by His word: His commands and promises (see vv. 1,18). God's chastening (v. 5) of His people by bringing them through the wilderness taught them this fundamental truth. There they were humbled (cf. v. 14) by being cast in total dependence on the Lord.
8:7–9 A concise description of the rich and fertile land of promise that the Israelites were about to enter and possess (see 11:8–12). See map No. 2 at the end of the study Bible.
‡8:9 *iron . . . brass* [i.e. copper]. The mountains of southern Lebanon and the regions east of the sea of Galilee and south of the Dead Sea contain iron. Both copper and iron were plentiful in the part of the Arabah south of the Dead Sea. Some of the copper mines date to the time of Solomon and earlier. Zarthan was a center for bronze works in Solomon's time (1 Ki 7:45–46). Some bronze objects from this site precede the Solomonic period, and today there are copper works at Timnah in the Negev.
8:11,14,19 *forget.* See note on 4:10.

14 [a]Then thine heart be lifted up, and thou [b]forget the LORD thy God, which brought thee forth out of the land of Egypt, from the house of bondage;

15 Who [a]led thee through *that* great and terrible wilderness, [b]*wherein were* fiery serpents, and scorpions, and drought, where *there was* no water; [c]who brought thee forth water out of the rock of flint;

16 Who fed thee in the wilderness with [a]manna, which thy fathers knew not, that he might humble thee, and that he might prove thee, [b]to do thee good at thy latter end;

17 [a]And thou say in thine heart, My power and the might of mine hand hath gotten me this wealth.

18 But thou shalt remember the LORD thy God: [a]for *it is* he that giveth thee power to get wealth, [b]that he may establish his covenant which he sware unto thy fathers, as *it is* this day.

19 And it shall be, if thou do at all forget the LORD thy God, and walk after other gods, and serve them, and worship them, [a]I testify against you *this* day that ye shall surely perish.

20 As the nations which the LORD destroyeth before your face, [a]so shall ye perish; because ye would not be obedient unto the voice of the LORD your God.

The golden calf

9 Hear, O Israel: Thou art to [a]pass over Jordan *this* day, to go in to possess nations [b]greater and mightier than thyself, cities great and [c]fenced up to heaven,

2 A people great and tall, [a]the children of the Anakims, whom thou knowest, and *of whom* thou hast heard *say,* Who can stand before the children of Anak!

3 Understand therefore *this* day, that the LORD thy God *is* he which [a]goeth over before thee; *as* a [b]consuming fire [c]he shall destroy them, and he shall bring them down before thy face: [d]so shalt thou drive them out, and destroy them quickly, as the LORD hath said unto thee.

4 [a]Speak not thou in thine heart, after that the LORD thy God hath cast them out from before thee, saying, For my righteousness the LORD hath brought me in to possess this land: but [b]for the wickedness of these nations the LORD doth drive them out from before thee.

5 [a]Not for thy righteousness, or for the uprightness of thine heart, dost thou go to possess their land: but for the wickedness of these nations the LORD thy God doth drive them out from before thee, and that he may perform [b]the word which the LORD sware unto thy fathers, Abraham, Isaac, and Jacob.

6 Understand therefore, that the LORD thy God giveth thee not this good land to possess it for thy righteousness; for thou *art* [a]a stiffnecked people.

7 Remember, *and* forget not, how thou provokedst the LORD thy God to wrath in the wilderness: [a]from the day that thou didst depart out of the land of Egypt, until ye came unto this place, ye have been rebellious against the LORD.

8 Also [a]in Horeb ye provoked the LORD to wrath, so that the LORD was angry with you to have destroyed you.

9 [a]When I was gone up into the mount to receive the tables of stone, *even* the tables of the covenant which the LORD made with you, then [b]I abode in the mount forty days and forty nights, I neither did eat bread nor drink water:

10 [a]And the LORD delivered unto me two tables of stone written with the finger of God; and on them *was written* according to all the words, which the LORD spake with you in the mount out of the midst of the fire [b]in the day of the assembly.

11 And it came to pass at the end of forty days and forty nights, *that* the LORD gave me the two tables of stone, *even* the tables of the covenant.

12 And the LORD said unto me, [a]Arise, get thee down quickly from hence; for thy people which thou hast brought forth out of Egypt have corrupted *themselves;* they are [b]quickly turned aside out of the way which I commanded them; they have made them a molten image.

13 Furthermore [a]the LORD spake unto me, saying, I have seen this people, and behold, [b]it *is* a stiffnecked people:

14 [a]Let me alone, that I may destroy them, and [b]blot out their name from under heaven: [c]and I will make of thee a nation mightier and greater than they.

15 [a]So I turned and came down from the mount, and [b]the mount burned with fire: and the two tables of the covenant *were* in my two hands.

8:14 [a]1 Cor. 4:7 [b]Ps. 106:21
8:15 [a]Is. 63:12-14; Jer. 2:6 [b]Num. 21:6; Hos. 13:5 [c]Num. 20:11
8:16 [a]Ex. 16:15 [b]Jer. 24:5,6; Heb. 12:11
8:17 [a]ch. 9:4
8:18 [a]Prov. 10:22; Hos. 2:8 [b]ch. 7:8,12
8:19 [a]ch. 4:26; 30:18
8:20 [a]Dan. 9:11,12
9:1 [a]ch. 11:31; Josh. 3:16; 4:19 [b]ch. 4:38; 11:23 [c]ch. 1:28
9:2 [a]Num. 13:22, 28,32,33
9:3 [a]ch. 31:3; Josh. 3:11 [b]ch. 4:24; Heb. 12:29 [c]ch. 7:23 [d]Ex. 23:31; ch. 7:24
9:4 [a]ch. 8:17; Rom. 11:6,20; 1 Cor. 4:4,7 [b]Gen. 15:16; Lev. 18:24; ch. 18:12
9:5 [a]Tit. 3:5 [b]Gen. 12:7; 13:15; 15:7; 17:8; 26:4
9:6 [a]ver. 13; Ex. 32:9; 33:3; 34:9
9:7 [a]Ex. 14:11; 16:2; 17:2; Num. 11:4; 20:2; 25:2; ch. 31:27
9:8 [a]Ex. 32:4; Ps. 106:19
9:9 [a]Ex. 24:12,15 [b]Ex. 24:18; 34:28
9:10 [a]Ex. 31:18 [b]Ex. 19:17; 20:1; ch. 4:10; 10:4
9:12 [a]Ex. 32:7 [b]ch. 31:29; Judg. 2:17
9:13 [a]Ex. 32:9 [b]ver. 6; ch. 10:16; 31:27; 2 Ki. 17:14
9:14 [a]Ex. 32:10 [b]ch. 29:20 [c]Num. 14:12
9:15 [a]Ex. 32:15 [b]Ex. 19:18; ch. 4:11; 5:23

8:15 *water out of the rock.* See Ex 17:6 and note.

8:16 *prove.* See v. 2; see also note on Gen 22:1.

8:17–18 See Zech 4:6 and note.

8:18 *remember.* See note on 4:10.

9:1 *Hear, O Israel:* See note on 4:1.

9:2 *Anakims.* See note on 1:28.

9:3 *consuming fire.* See 4:24; see also note on Ex 24:17. *he shall bring them down before thy face: so shalt thou drive them out.* The Lord not only went ahead of the Israelites, but He also exerted His power alongside them and through them to assure victory. The Lord's involvement, together with that of the Israelite armies, continues throughout Deuteronomy and the conquest narratives.

9:4 *For my righteousness.* See note on 7:8. *wickedness of these nations.* See note on Gen 15:16.

‡9:6,13 *stiffnecked* [i.e. stubborn]. See 10:16; 31:27; see also note on Ex 32:9.

9:7,27 *Remember.* See note on 4:10.

9:9 *tables of stone . . . of the covenant.* See notes on Ex 20:1; 34:28.

9:10 *two tables of stone.* See note on Ex 31:18. *finger of God.* See note on Ex 8:19.

9:11–21 See Ex 31:18–32:20.

16 And [a]I looked, and behold, ye had
sinned against the LORD your God, *and* had
made you a molten calf: ye had turned aside
quickly out of the way which the LORD had
commanded you.
17 And I took the two tables, and cast
them out of my two hands, and brake them before your eyes.
18 And I [a]fell down before the LORD, as at
the first, forty days and forty nights: I did neither eat bread, nor drink water, because of all
your sins which ye sinned, in doing wickedly
in the sight of the LORD, to provoke him to
anger.
19 [a]For I was afraid of the anger and hot
displeasure, where*with* the LORD was wroth
against you to destroy you. [b]But the LORD hearkened unto me at that time also.
20 And the LORD was very angry with Aaron to have destroyed him: and I prayed for
Aaron also the same time.
21 And [a]I took your sin, the calf which ye
had made, and burnt it with fire, and stamped
it, *and* ground *it* very small, *even* until *it was*
as small as dust: and I cast the dust thereof
into the brook that descended out of the
mount.
22 And at [a]Taberah, and at [b]Massah, and at
[c]Kibroth-hattaavah, ye provoked the LORD to
wrath.
23 Likewise [a]when the LORD sent you from
Kadesh-barnea, saying, Go up and possess the
land which I have given you; then you rebelled against the commandment of the LORD
your God, and [b]ye believed him not, nor hearkened to his voice.
24 [a]You have been rebellious against the
LORD from the day that I knew you.
25 [a]Thus I fell down before the LORD forty
days and forty nights, as I fell down *at the first;*
because the LORD had said he would destroy
you.
26 [a]I prayed therefore unto the LORD, and
said, O Lord GOD, destroy not thy people and
thine inheritance, which thou hast redeemed
through thy greatness, which thou hast
brought forth out of Egypt with a mighty hand.
27 Remember thy servants, Abraham,
Isaac, and Jacob; look not unto the stubbornness of this people, nor to their wickedness,
nor to their sin:
28 Lest [a]the land whence thou broughtest
us out say, [b]Because the LORD was not able to
bring them into the land which he promised
them, and because he hated them, he hath
brought them out to slay them in the wilderness.
29 [a]Yet they *are* thy people and thine inheritance, which thou broughtest out by thy
mighty power and by thy stretched out arm.

The second tables of stone

10 At that time the LORD said unto me,
[a]Hew thee two tables of stone like
unto the first, and come up unto me into the
mount, and [b]make thee an ark of wood.
2 And I will write on the tables the words
that were in the first tables which thou brakest, and [a]thou shalt put them in the ark.
3 And I made an ark of [a]shittim wood, and
[b]hewed two tables of stone like unto the first,
and went up into the mount, having the two
tables in mine hand.
4 And he wrote on the tables, according to
the first writing, the ten [1]commandments,
[a]which the LORD spake unto you in the mount
out of the midst of the fire in the day of the assembly: and the LORD gave them unto me.
5 And I turned myself and [a]came down
from the mount, and [b]put the tables in the ark
which I had made; [c]and there they be, as the
LORD commanded me.
6 And the children of Israel took their journey from Beeroth [a]of the children of Jaakan *to*
[b]Mosera: [c]there Aaron died, and there he was
buried; and Eleazar his son ministered in the
priest's office in his stead.
7 [a]From thence they journeyed *unto* Gudgodah; and from Gudgodah to Jotbath, a land
of rivers of waters.
8 At that time [a]the LORD separated the
tribe of Levi, [b]to bear the ark of the covenant
of the LORD, [c]to stand before the LORD to minister unto him, and [d]to bless in his name, unto
this day.
9 [a]Wherefore Levi hath no part nor inheritance with his brethren; the LORD *is* his inheritance, according as the LORD thy God promised him.
10 And [a]I stayed in the mount, according
to the [1]first time, forty days and forty nights;
and [b]the LORD hearkened unto me at that time
also, *and* the LORD would not destroy thee.
11 [a]And the LORD said unto me, Arise,
[1]take thy journey before the people, that they
may go in and possess the land, which I sware
unto their fathers to give unto them.

God's great requirement

12 ¶ And now, Israel, [a]what doth the LORD

9:16 [a]Ex. 32:19
9:18 [a]Ex. 34:28
9:19 [a]Ex. 32:10,11 [b]Ex. 32:14; 33:17; ch. 10:10; Ps. 106:23
9:21 [a]Ex. 32:20; Is. 31:7
9:22 [a]Num. 11:1,3,5 [b]Ex. 17:7 [c]Num. 11:4,34
9:23 [a]Num. 13:3; 14:1 [b]Ps. 106:24,25
9:24 [a]ch. 31:27
9:25 [a]ver. 18
9:26 [a]Ex. 32:11
9:28 [a]Ex. 6:6-8; 1 Sam. 14:25 [b]Ex. 32:12; Num. 14:16
9:29 [a]ch. 4:20; 1 Ki. 8:51; Neh. 1:10
10:1 [a]Ex. 34:1,2 [b]Ex. 25:10
10:2 [a]Ex. 25:16,21
10:3 [a]Ex. 25:5,10 [b]Ex. 34:4
10:4 [1]Heb. *words* [a]Ex. 20:1
10:5 [a]Ex. 34:29 [b]Ex. 40:20 [c]1 Ki. 8:9
10:6 [a]Num. 33:31 [b]Num. 33:30 [c]Num. 20:28; 33:38
10:7 [a]Num. 33:32,33
10:8 [a]Num. 3:6 [b]Num. 4:15 [c]ch. 18:5 [d]Num. 6:23; ch. 21:5
10:9 [a]ch. 18:1,2; Ezek. 44:28
10:10 [1]Or, *former days* [a]Ex. 34:28; ch. 9:18,25 [b]Ex. 32:14,33,34; 33:17; ch. 9:19
10:11 [1]Heb. *go in journey* [a]Ex. 33:1
10:12 [a]Mic. 6:8

9:19 *the LORD hearkened unto me at that time also.* Moses' intercessory prayer on this occasion (vv. 26–29) ranks among the great prayers for Israel's national survival (see 1 Sam 7:5,8–9; Jer 15:1).

9:22 *Taberah.* Means "burning"; see Num 11:3. *Massah.* See 6:16; 33:8; see also note on Ex 17:7. *Kibroth-hattaavah.* Means "graves of craving"; see Num 11:34.

9:23 *Kadesh-barnea.* See note on Gen 14:7.

9:27 *look not unto.* See note on Acts 17:30.

10:1–3 *ark.* See note on Ex 25:10.

10:1 *two tables of stone.* See note on Ex 31:18.

10:2 *put them in the ark.* See notes on Ex 16:34; 25:16.

10:3 Ex 34–37 show that the order of events here is different from that in Exodus (see Introduction: Structure and Outline).

10:6–9 A historical parenthesis, apparently stemming from Moses' prayer for Aaron and the Israelites (9:26–29) and the reference to the ark (vv. 1–5).

10:8 *bear the ark.* See note on Num 1:50. *to minister.* See note on 21:5.

10:9 See Num 18:20,24.

thy God require of thee, but [b]to fear the LORD
thy God, [c]to walk in all his ways, and [d]to love
him, and to serve the LORD thy God with all
thy heart and with all thy soul,
13 To keep the commandments of the
LORD, and his statutes, which I command thee
this day [a]for thy good?
14 Behold, [a]the heaven and the heaven of
heavens *is* the LORD's thy God, [b]the earth *also,*
with all that therein *is.*
15 [a]Only the LORD had a delight in thy fathers to love them, and he chose their seed after
them, *even* you above all people, as *it is* this day.
16 Circumcise therefore [a]the foreskin of
your heart, and be no more [b]stiffnecked.
17 For the LORD your God *is* [a]God of gods,
and [b]Lord of lords, a great God, [c]a mighty, and
a terrible, which [d]regardeth not persons, nor
taketh reward:
18 [a]He doth execute the judgment of the
fatherless and widow, and loveth the stranger,
in giving him food and raiment.
19 [a]Love ye therefore the stranger: for ye
were strangers in the land of Egypt.
20 [a]Thou shalt fear the LORD thy God; him
shalt thou serve, and to him shalt thou
[b]cleave, [c]and swear by his name.
21 [a]He *is* thy praise, and he *is* thy God,
[b]that hath done for thee these great and terrible *things,* which thine eyes have seen.
22 Thy fathers went down into Egypt
[a]with threescore and ten persons; and now
the LORD thy God hath made thee [b]as the stars
of heaven for multitude.

Love and obey God

11 Therefore thou shalt [a]love the LORD
thy God, and [b]keep his charge, and
his statutes, and his judgments, and his commandments alway.
2 And know you *this* day: for *I speak* not
with your children which have not known,
and which have not seen [a]the chastisement of
the LORD your God, [b]his greatness, his mighty
hand, and his stretched out arm,
3 [a]And his miracles, and his acts, which he
did in the midst of Egypt unto Pharaoh the
king of Egypt, and unto all his land;
4 And what he did unto the army of Egypt,
unto their horses, and to their chariots; [a]how
he made the water of the Red sea to overflow
them as they pursued after you, and *how* the
LORD hath destroyed them unto this day;
5 And what he did unto you in the wilderness, until ye came into this place;
6 And [a]what he did unto Dathan and Abiram, the sons of Eliab, the son of Reuben: how
the earth opened her mouth, and swallowed
them up, and their households, and their
tents, and all the [1]substance that [2]*was* in their
possession, in the midst of all Israel:
7 But [a]your eyes have seen all the great
acts of the LORD which he did.
8 Therefore shall ye keep all the commandments which I command you *this* day, that ye
may [a]be strong, and go in and possess the
land, whither ye go to possess it;
9 And [a]that ye may prolong *your* days in
the land, [b]which the LORD sware unto your fathers to give unto them and to their seed, [c]a
land that floweth with milk and honey.
10 For the land, whither thou goest in to
possess it, *is* not as the land of Egypt, from
whence ye came out, where thou sowedst thy
seed, and wateredst *it* with thy foot, as a garden of herbs:
11 [a]But the land, whither ye go to possess
it, *is* a land of hills and valleys, *and* drinketh
water of the rain of heaven:
12 A land which the LORD thy God [1]careth
for: [a]the eyes of the LORD thy God *are* always
upon it, from the beginning of the year even
unto the end of the year.
13 And it shall come to pass, if you shall
hearken [a]diligently unto my commandments
which I command you *this* day, [b]to love the
LORD your God, and to serve him with all your
heart and with all your soul,
14 That [a]I will give *you* the rain of your
land in his due season, [b]the first rain and the
latter rain, that thou mayest gather in thy
corn, and thy wine, and thine oil.
15 [a]And I will [1]send grass in thy fields for
thy cattle, that thou mayest [b]eat and be full.
16 Take heed to yourselves, [a]that your
heart be not deceived, and ye turn aside, and
[b]serve other gods, and worship them;
17 And *then* [a]the LORD's wrath be kindled
against you, and he [b]shut up the heaven, that
there be no rain, and *that* the land yield not
her fruit; and *lest* [c]ye perish quickly from off
the good land which the LORD giveth you.

10:12 [b]ch. 6:13 [c]ch. 5:33 [d]ch. 6:5; Mat. 22:37
10:13 [a]ch. 6:24
10:14 [a]1 Ki. 8:27 [b]Ex. 19:5
10:15 [a]ch. 4:37
10:16 [a]ch. 30:6; Jer. 4:4; Rom. 2:28,29; Col. 2:11 [b]ch. 9:6,13
10:17 [a]Dan. 2:47 [b]Rev. 19:16 [c]ch. 7:21 [d]Acts 10:34; Rom. 2:11; Eph. 6:9; 1 Pet. 1:17
10:18 [a]Ps. 68:5
10:19 [a]Lev. 19:33,34
10:20 [a]Mat. 4:10 [b]ch. 11:22 [c]Ps. 63:11
10:21 [a]Ex. 15:2; Jer. 17:14 [b]Ps. 106:21,22
10:22 [a]Gen. 46:27; Acts 7:14 [b]Gen. 15:5
11:1 [a]ch. 10:12 [b]Zech. 3:7
11:2 [a]ch. 8:5 [b]ch. 5:24
11:3 [a]Ps. 78:12; 135:9
11:4 [a]Ps. 106:11
11:6 [1]Or, *living substance which followed them* [2]Heb. was *at their feet* [a]Num. 16:1,31
11:7 [a]ch. 5:3; 7:19
11:8 [a]Josh. 1:6,7
11:9 [a]ch. 4:40; Prov. 10:27 [b]ch. 9:5 [c]Ex. 3:8
11:11 [a]ch. 8:7
11:12 [1]Heb. *seeketh* [a]1 Ki. 9:3
11:13 [a]ver. 22; ch. 6:17 [b]ch. 10:12
11:14 [a]Lev. 26:4; ch. 28:12 [b]Joel 2:23; Jas. 5:7
11:15 [1]Heb. *give* [a]Ps. 104:14 [b]ch. 6:11; Joel 2:19
11:16 [a]ch. 29:18; Job 31:27 [b]ch. 8:19
11:17 [a]ch. 6:15 [b]1 Ki. 8:35; 2 Chr. 6:26 [c]ch. 4:26; 8:19,20; Josh. 23:13,15,16

10:12 *fear the LORD.* See note on Gen 20:11. *love him.* See notes on 4:29,37; 6:5.
10:13 *for thy good.* See 6:24; see also note on 6:2.
10:16 *Circumcise . . . your heart.* See note on Gen 17:10. *be no more stiffnecked.* See 9:6,13; 31:27; see also note on Ex 32:9.
10:20 *cleave.* As a man "cleaves" to his wife (Gen 2:24), and as Ruth "clave" to Naomi (Ruth 1:14). See 4:4; 11:22; 13:4; 30:20.
10:22 *threescore and ten.* See notes on Gen 46:26–27; see also Ex 1:5. *as the stars of heaven.* See note on 1:10.
11:2–7 Moses continually emphasizes the involvement of his listeners in the Lord's works of providence and deliverance. In 5:3 it was not the fathers but they themselves with whom the covenant was made. Here it is not their children but they themselves who saw God's great deeds.
11:2 *know.* See note on 4:10.
11:8–12 See note on 8:7–9.
11:9 *prolong your days.* See note on 6:2.
11:10 *wateredst it with thy foot.* Irrigation channels dug by foot and/or fed by devices powered by foot brought the water of the Nile to the gardens in Egypt, in contrast to the rains that watered Canaan (v. 11).
11:13 See note on 4:29.
11:14 *first rain and the latter rain.* The rainy season in the Holy Land begins in October and ends in April.
11:17 *shut up the heaven.* The all-important seasonal rains (see v. 14) were controlled by the Lord—not by Baal, as the inhabitants of Canaan thought (cf. Hos 2:8,17).

18 Therefore [a]shall ye lay up these my
words in your heart and in your soul, and
[b]bind them for a sign upon your hand, that
they may be as frontlets between your eyes.
19 [a]And ye shall teach them your children,
speaking of them when thou sittest in thine
house, and when thou walkest by the way,
when thou liest down, and when thou risest
up.
20 [a]And thou shalt write them upon the
door posts of thine house, and upon thy gates:
21 That [a]your days may be multiplied, and
the days of your children, in the land which
the LORD sware unto your fathers to give them,
[b]as the days of heaven upon the earth.
22 For if [a]ye shall diligently keep all these
commandments which I command you, to do
them, to love the LORD your God, to walk in all
his ways, and [b]to cleave unto him;
23 Then will the LORD [a]drive out all these
nations from before you, and ye shall [b]possess
greater nations and mightier than yourselves.
24 [a]Every place whereon the soles of your
feet shall tread shall be yours: [b]from the
wilderness and Lebanon, from the river, the
river Euphrates, even unto the uttermost sea
shall your coast be.
25 [a]There shall no man *be able to* stand before you: *for* the LORD your God shall [b]lay the
fear of you and the dread of you upon all the
land that ye shall tread upon, [c]as he hath said
unto you.
26 ¶ [a]Behold, I set before you *this* day a
blessing and a curse;
27 [a]A blessing, if ye obey the commandments of the LORD your God, which I command you *this* day:
28 And a [a]curse, if ye will not obey the
commandments of the LORD your God, but
turn aside out of the way which I command
you *this* day, to go after other gods, which ye
have not known.
29 And it shall come to pass, when the
LORD thy God hath brought thee in unto the
land whither thou goest to possess it, that thou
shalt put [a]the blessing upon mount Gerizim,
and the curse upon mount Ebal.
30 *Are* they not on the *other* side Jordan,
by the way where the sun goeth down, in the
land of the Canaanites, which dwell in the
champaign over against Gilgal, [a]beside the
plains of Moreh?
31 [a]For ye shall pass over Jordan to go in to
possess the land which the LORD your God
giveth you, and ye shall possess it, and dwell
therein.
32 And ye shall observe [a]to do all the statutes and judgments which I set before you *this*
day.

Sacrifice at one altar only

12 These [a]*are* the statutes and judgments, which ye shall observe to do
in the land, which the LORD God of thy fathers
giveth thee to possess it, [b]all the days that ye
live upon the earth.
2 [a]Ye shall utterly destroy all the places,
wherein the nations which ye shall [1]possess
served their gods, [b]upon the high mountains,
and upon the hills, and under every green tree:
3 And [a]you shall [1]overthrow their altars,
and break their pillars, and burn their groves
with fire; and you shall hew down the graven
images of their gods, and destroy the names of
them out of that place.
4 [a]Ye shall not do so unto the LORD your
God.
5 But unto the place which the LORD your
God shall [a]choose out of all your tribes to put
his name there, *even* unto his habitation shall
ye seek, and thither thou shalt come:
6 And [a]thither ye shall bring your burnt offerings, and your sacrifices, and your [b]tithes,
and heave offerings of your hand, and your
vows, and your freewill offerings, and the
firstlings of your herds and of your flocks:
7 And [a]there ye shall eat before the LORD
your God, and [b]ye shall rejoice in all that you
put your hand unto, ye and your households,
where*in* the LORD thy God hath blessed thee.
8 Ye shall not do after all *the things* that we
do here *this* day, [a]every man whatsoever *is*
right in his own eyes.
9 For ye are not as yet come to the rest and
to the inheritance, which the LORD your God
giveth you.
10 But *when* [a]ye go over Jordan and dwell
in the land which the LORD your God giveth

11:18 [a]ch. 6:6; 32:46 [b]ch. 6:8
11:19 [a]ch. 4:9,10; 6:7
11:20 [a]ch. 6:9
11:21 [a]ch. 4:40; Prov. 3:2; 4:10 [b]Ps. 72:5; 89:29
11:22 [a]ver. 13; ch. 6:17 [b]ch. 10:20; 30:20
11:23 [a]ch. 4:38 [b]ch. 9:1
11:24 [a]Josh. 1:3; 14:9 [b]Gen. 15:18; Ex. 23:31; Num. 34:3
11:25 [a]ch. 7:24 [b]ch. 2:25 [c]Ex. 23:27
11:26 [a]ch. 30:1,15,19
11:27 [a]ch. 28:2
11:28 [a]ch. 28:15
11:29 [a]ch. 27:12,13; Josh. 8:33
11:30 [a]Gen. 12:6; Judg. 7:1
11:31 [a]ch. 9:1; Josh. 1:11
11:32 [a]ch. 5:32; 12:32
12:1 [a]ch. 6:1 [b]ch. 4:10; 1 Ki. 8:40
12:2 [1]Or, *inherit* [a]Ex. 34:13; ch. 7:5 [b]2 Ki. 16:4; 17:10,11; Jer. 3:6
12:3 [1]Heb. *break down* [a]Num. 33:52; Judg. 2:2
12:4 [a]ver. 31
12:5 [a]ver. 11; ch. 26:2; Josh. 9:27; 1 Ki. 8:29; 2 Chr. 7:12
12:6 [a]Lev. 17:3,4 [b]ver. 17; ch. 14:22,23; 15:19,20
12:7 [a]ch. 14:26 [b]ver. 12,18; Lev. 23:40; ch. 16:11,14,15
12:8 [a]Judg. 17:6; 21:25
12:10 [a]ch. 11:31

11:18–20 See note on 6:8–9.
11:22 *cleave.* See note on 10:20.
11:24 *Every place whereon the soles of your feet shall tread.* See note on 1:7.
11:26–30 The blessings and curses proclaimed on mount Gerizim and mount Ebal are detailed in chs. 27–28.
11:28 *known.* Experienced or acknowledged (see 13:2,6,13; 28:64; 29:26; 32:17; see also note on Ex 6:3).
‡11:30 *way.* Probably the north-south road that ran parallel to the Jordan between the sea of Galilee and the Dead Sea. *the champaign* [*Arabah* in Hebrew]. See note on 1:1. The Canaanites who lived there controlled the territory around Gerizim and Ebal. *plains of Moreh.* See note on Gen 12:6.
12:3 *altars . . . pillars . . . groves.* See note on 7:5.
12:4 *not do so.* The rituals and accessories of idolatrous worship were not to be used to worship the Lord, the one true God (cf. vv. 29–31).
12:5 *the place which the LORD . . . shall choose . . . to put his name.* The tabernacle, the Lord's dwelling place during the wilderness journey, will be located in the city in Canaan where the Lord would choose to dwell. Moses stresses the importance of centralizing the place of worship as he prepares the people for settlement in the promised land, where the Canaanites had established many places of worship. See vv. 11,14,18,21,26; 14:23–24; 16:2,6,11; 26:2.
12:6 See v. 11 and chart, p. 141.
12:8 *that we do here this day.* Israel was not able to follow all the procedures of the sacrificial system during the wilderness wandering and conquest periods. Moses was giving directives for their worship and way of life when settled in the land (vv. 10–14). *whatsoever is right in his own eyes.* See note on Judg 17:6.
12:9 *the rest.* See note on 3:20.

you to inherit, and *when* he giveth you rest from all your enemies round about, so that ye dwell in safety;

11 Then there shall be [a]a place which the LORD your God shall choose to cause his name to dwell there; thither shall ye bring all that I command you; your burnt offerings, and your sacrifices, your tithes, and the heave offering of your hand, and all [1]your choice vows which ye vow unto the LORD:

12 And [a]ye shall rejoice before the LORD your God, ye, and your sons, and your daughters, and your menservants, and your maidservants, and the Levite that *is* within your gates; forasmuch as [b]he hath no part nor inheritance with you.

13 [a]Take heed to thyself that thou offer not thy burnt offerings in every place that thou seest:

14 [a]But in the place which the LORD shall choose in one of thy tribes, there thou shalt offer thy burnt offerings, and there thou shalt do all that I command thee.

15 Notwithstanding [a]thou mayest kill and eat flesh in all thy gates, whatsoever thy soul lusteth after, according to the blessing of the LORD thy God which he hath given thee: [b]the unclean and the clean may eat thereof, [c]as of the roebuck, and as of the hart.

16 [a]Only ye shall not eat the blood; ye shall pour it upon the earth as water.

17 Thou mayest not eat within thy gates the tithe of thy corn, or of thy wine, or of thy oil, or the firstlings of thy herds or of thy flock, nor any of thy vows which thou vowest, nor thy freewill offerings, or heave offering of thine hand:

18 [a]But thou must eat them before the LORD thy God in the place which the LORD thy God shall choose, thou, and thy son, and thy daughter, and thy manservant, and thy maidservant, and the Levite that *is* within thy gates: and thou shalt rejoice before the LORD thy God in all that thou puttest thine hands unto.

19 [a]Take heed to thyself that thou forsake not the Levite [1]as long as thou livest upon the earth.

20 When the LORD thy God shall enlarge thy border, [a]as he hath promised thee, and thou shalt say, I will eat flesh, because thy soul longeth to eat flesh; thou mayest eat flesh, whatsoever thy soul lusteth after.

21 If the place which the LORD thy God hath chosen to put his name there be too far from thee, then thou shalt kill of thy herd and of thy flock, which the LORD hath given thee, as I have commanded thee, and thou shalt eat in thy gates whatsoever thy soul lusteth after.

22 [a]Even as the roebuck and the hart is eaten, so thou shalt eat them: the unclean and the clean shall eat of them alike.

23 [a]Only [1]be sure that thou eat not the blood: [b]for the blood *is* the life; and thou mayest not eat the life with the flesh.

24 Thou shalt not eat it; thou shalt pour it upon the earth as water.

25 Thou shalt not eat it; [a]that it may go well with thee, and with thy children after thee, [b]when thou shalt do *that which is* right in the sight of the LORD.

26 Only thy [a]holy *things* which thou hast, and [b]thy vows, thou shalt take, and go unto the place which the LORD shall choose:

27 And [a]thou shalt offer thy burnt offerings, the flesh and the blood, upon the altar of the LORD thy God: and the blood of thy sacrifices shall be poured out upon the altar of the LORD thy God, and thou shalt eat the flesh.

28 Observe and hear all these words which I command thee, [a]that it may go well with thee, and with thy children after thee for ever, when thou doest *that which is* good and right in the sight of the LORD thy God.

29 When [a]the LORD thy God shall cut off the nations from before thee, whither thou goest to possess them, and thou [1]succeedest them, and dwellest in their land;

30 Take heed to thyself that thou be not snared [1]by following them, after that they be destroyed from before thee; and that thou inquire not after their gods, saying, How did these nations serve their gods? even so will I do likewise.

31 [a]Thou shalt not do so unto the LORD thy God: for every [1]abomination to the LORD, which he hateth, have they done unto their gods; for [b]even their sons and their daughters they have burnt in the fire to their gods.

32 What thing soever I command you, observe to do it: [a]thou shalt not add thereto, nor diminish from it.

Warning against idolatry

13 If there arise among you a prophet, or a [a]dreamer of dreams, [b]and giveth thee a sign or a wonder,

2 And [a]the sign or the wonder come to pass, whereof he spake unto thee, saying, Let

12:11 [1]Heb. *the choice of your vows* [a]ver. 5,14,18,21,26; ch. 14:23; 15:20; 16:2; Josh. 18:1; 1 Ki. 8:29
12:12 [a]ver. 7 [b]ch. 10:9; 14:29
12:13 [a]Lev. 17:4
12:14 [a]ver. 11
12:15 [a]ver. 21 [b]ver. 22 [c]ch. 14:5; 15:22
12:16 [a]Gen. 9:4; Lev. 7:26; 17:10; ch. 15:23; ver. 23
12:18 [a]ver. 11,12; ch. 14:23
12:19 [1]Heb. *all thy days* [a]ch. 14:27
12:20 [a]Gen. 15:18; 28:14; Ex. 34:24; ch. 11:24; 19:8
12:22 [a]ver. 15
12:23 [1]Heb. *be strong* [a]ver. 16 [b]Gen. 9:4; Lev. 17:11,14
12:25 [a]ch. 4:40; Is. 3:10 [b]Ex. 15:26; ch. 13:18; 1 Ki. 11:38
12:26 [a]Num. 5:9,10 [b]1 Sam. 1:21,22,24
12:27 [a]Lev. 1:5,9,13; 17:11
12:28 [a]ver. 25
12:29 [1]Heb. *inheritest,* or, *possessest them* [a]Ex. 23:23; ch. 19:1; Josh. 23:4
12:30 [1]Heb. *after them*
12:31 [1]Heb. *abomination of the* [a]Lev. 18:3,26,30 [b]ch. 18:10; Jer. 32:35; Ezek. 23:37
12:32 [a]ch. 4:2; Josh. 1:7; Rev. 22:18
13:1 [a]Zech. 10:2 [b]Mat. 24:24; 2 Thes. 2:9
13:2 [a]See ch. 18:22; Mat. 7:22

12:11 *cause his name to dwell.* Equivalent to "a dwelling for Himself." See notes on Ex 3:13–15.

12:12 *rejoice before the LORD.* Joy, based on the Lord's blessings, was to be a major feature of Hebrew life and worship in the promised land (vv. 7,18). *Levite . . . hath no . . . inheritance.* See 10:9; Num 18:20,24.

12:13 *not . . . in every place that thou seest.* Sacrifices and offerings to the Lord were to be brought only to the central sanctuary, not to the various Canaanite worship sites.

12:16 *ye shall not eat the blood.* See v. 24; see also notes on Gen 9:4; Lev 17:11.

12:31 *sons and their daughters . . . burnt in the fire.* See 18:10; see also note on Lev 18:21.

12:32 *shalt not add thereto, nor diminish from it.* See note on 4:2.

13:1–5 Eventual fulfillment is one test of true prophecy (18:21–22), but the more stringent rule given here guards against intelligent foresight masquerading as prophecy and against coincidental fulfillment of the predictions of false prophets.

us go after other gods, which thou hast not
known, and let us serve them;
3 Thou shalt not hearken unto the words of
that prophet, or that dreamer of dreams: for
the LORD your God [a]proveth you, to know
whether you love the LORD your God with all
your heart and with all your soul.
4 Ye shall [a]walk after the LORD your God,
and fear him, and keep his commandments,
and obey his voice, and you shall serve him,
and [b]cleave unto him.
5 And [a]that prophet, or that dreamer of
dreams, shall be put to death; because he hath
[1]spoken to turn *you* away from the LORD your
God, which brought you out of the land of
Egypt, and redeemed you out of the house of
bondage, to thrust thee out of the way which
the LORD thy God commanded thee to walk in.
[b]So shalt thou put the evil away from the
midst of thee.
6 [a]If thy brother, the son of thy mother, or
thy son, or thy daughter, or [b]the wife of thy
bosom, or thy friend, [c]which *is* as thine own
soul, entice thee secretly, saying, Let us go and
serve other gods, which thou hast not known,
thou, nor thy fathers;
7 *Namely,* of the gods of the people which
are round about you, nigh unto thee, or far off
from thee, from the *one* end of the earth even
unto the *other* end of the earth;
8 Thou shalt [a]not consent unto him, nor
hearken unto him; neither shall thine eye pity
him, neither shalt thou spare, neither shalt
thou conceal him:
9 But [a]thou shalt surely kill him; [b]thine
hand shall be first upon him to put him to death,
and afterwards the hand of all the people.
10 And thou shalt stone him with stones,
that he die; because he hath sought to thrust
thee away from the LORD thy God, which
brought thee out of the land of Egypt, from the
house of [1]bondage.
11 And [a]all Israel shall hear, and fear, and
shall do no more any such wickedness as this
is among you.
12 [a]If thou shalt hear *say* in one of thy cities, which the LORD thy God hath given thee
to dwell there, saying,
13 *Certain* men, [1]the children of Belial,
[a]are gone out from among you, and have
[b]withdrawn the inhabitants of their city, saying, [c]Let us go and serve other gods, which ye
have not known;

13:3 [a]ch. 8:2; See Mat. 24:24; 2 Thes. 2:11
13:4 [a]2 Ki. 23:3; 2 Chr. 34:31 [b]ch. 30:20
13:5 [1]Heb. *spoken revolt against the LORD* [a]Jer. 14:15; Zech. 13:3 [b]ch. 17:7; 1 Cor. 5:13
13:6 [a]ch. 17:2 [b]See Gen. 16:5; ch. 28:54; Prov. 5:20 [c]1 Sam. 18:1,3; 20:17
13:8 [a]Prov. 1:10
13:9 [a]ch. 17:5 [b]ch. 17:7; Acts 7:58
13:10 [1]Heb. *bondmen*
13:11 [a]ch. 19:20
13:12 [a]Judg. 20:1,2
13:13 [1]Or, *naughty men* [a]1 John 2:19; Jude 19 [b]2 Ki. 17:21 [c]ver. 2,6
13:15 [a]Lev. 27:28; Josh. 6:17,21
13:16 [a]Josh. 6:24 [b]Josh. 8:28; Jer. 49:2
13:17 [1]Or, *devoted* [a]Josh. 6:18 [b]Josh. 7:26 [c]Gen. 22:17; 26:4,24; 28:14
13:18 [a]ch. 12:25,28,32
14:1 [a]Rom. 8:16; 9:8,26; Gal. 3:26 [b]Lev. 19:28; 21:5; Jer. 16:6; 41:5; 47:5; 1 Thes. 4:13
14:2 [a]Lev. 20:26; ch. 7:6; 26:18,19
14:3 [a]Ezek. 4:14; Acts 10:13,14
14:4 [a]Lev. 11:2
14:5 [1]Or, *bison.* Heb. *dishon*

14 Then shalt thou inquire, and make
search, and ask diligently; and behold, *if it be*
truth, *and* the thing certain, *that* such abomination is wrought among you;
15 Thou shalt surely smite the inhabitants
of that city with the edge of the sword, [a]de-
stroying it utterly, and all that *is* therein, and
the cattle thereof, with the edge of the sword.
16 And thou shalt gather all the spoil of it
into the midst of the street thereof, and shalt
[a]burn with fire the city, and all the spoil thereof every whit, for the LORD thy God: and it shall
be [b]a heap for ever; it shall not be built again.
17 And [a]there shall cleave nought of the
[1]cursed thing to thine hand: that the LORD
may [b]turn from the fierceness of his anger, and
shew thee mercy, and have compassion upon
thee, and multiply thee, [c]as he hath sworn
unto thy fathers;
18 When thou shalt hearken to the voice of
the LORD thy God, [a]to keep all his commandments which I command thee *this* day, to do
that which is right in the eyes of the LORD thy
God.

14 Ye *are* [a]the children of the LORD your
God: [b]ye shall not cut yourselves,
nor make *any* baldness between your eyes for
the dead.
2 [a]For thou *art* a holy people unto the LORD
thy God, and the LORD hath chosen thee to be
a peculiar people unto himself, above all the
nations that *are* upon the earth.

Clean and unclean animals

3 ¶ [a]Thou shalt not eat any abominable
thing.
4 [a]These *are* the beasts which ye shall eat:
the ox, the sheep, and the goat,
5 The hart, and the roebuck, and the fallow
deer, and the wild goat, and the [1]pygarg, and
the wild ox, and the chamois.
6 And every beast that parteth the hoof,
and cleaveth the cleft *into* two claws, *and*
cheweth the cud amongst the beasts: that ye
shall eat.
7 Nevertheless these ye shall not eat of
them that chew the cud, or of them that divide
the cloven hoof; *as* the camel, and the hare,
and the coney: for they chew the cud, but divide not the hoof; *therefore* they *are* unclean
unto you.
8 And the swine, because it divideth the
hoof, yet *cheweth* not the cud, it *is* unclean

13:3 *proveth.* See note on Gen 22:1. *all your heart.* See note on 4:29.

13:4 *cleave.* See note on 10:20.

13:5 *prophet . . . shall be put to death.* See 18:20; Jer 28:15–17. *shalt thou put the evil away from the midst of thee.* Repeated in 17:7; 19:19; 21:21; 22:21,24; 24:7, and quoted in 1 Cor 5:13. The purpose was to eliminate the evildoers as well as the evil itself.

‡13:13 *children of Belial* [i.e. worthless men]. See 1 Sam 1:16; 2:12; 25:17. The same Hebrew word is also used, e.g., in 1 Sam 10:27; 30:22; 1 Ki 21:10,13; Prov 6:12. Later, *Belial* was used as a name for Satan (2 Cor 6:15), who is the personification of wickedness, lawlessness and worthlessness.

13:15 *destroying it utterly.* See note on 2:34.

‡14:1 *cut yourselves.* A pagan religious custom (see 1 Ki 18:28). *make any baldness* [i.e. shave]. Shaving the forehead was a practice of mourners in Canaan.

14:2,21 *holy people unto the LORD.* See note on Lev 11:44. The regulations regarding clean and unclean foods were intended to separate Israel from things the Lord had identified as detestable and ceremonially unclean.

14:2 *a peculiar people unto himself.* See note on Ex 19:5.

14:3–21 The subject of clean and unclean food is discussed in greater detail in Lev 11 (see notes there).

unto you: ye shall not eat of their flesh, [a]nor
touch their dead carcase.
9 ¶ [a]These ye shall eat of all that *are* in the
waters: all that have fins and scales shall ye
eat:
10 And whatsoever hath not fins and scales
ye may not eat; it *is* unclean unto you.
11 ¶ *Of* all clean birds ye shall eat.
12 [a]But these *are they* of which ye shall
not eat: the eagle, and the ossifrage, and the
ospray,
13 And the glede, and the kite, and the vulture after his kind,
14 And every raven after his kind,
15 And the owl, and the night hawk, and
the cuckow, and the hawk after his kind,
16 The little owl, and the great owl, and
the swan,
17 And the pelican, and the gier eagle, and
the cormorant,
18 And the stork, and the heron after her
kind, and the lapwing, and the bat.
19 And [a]every creeping thing that flieth *is*
unclean unto you: [b]they shall not be eaten.
20 *But* of all clean fowls ye may eat.

Laws about tithes

21 ¶ [a]Ye shall not eat of any thing that dieth
of itself: thou shalt give it unto the stranger
that *is* in thy gates, that he may eat it; or thou
mayest sell *it* unto an alien: [b]for thou *art* a holy
people unto the LORD thy God. [c]Thou shalt not
seethe a kid in his mother's milk.
22 [a]Thou shalt truly tithe all the increase
of thy seed, that the field bringeth forth year
by year.
23 [a]And thou shalt eat before the LORD thy
God, in the place which he shall choose to
place his name there, the tithe of thy corn, of
thy wine, and of thine oil, and [b]the firstlings of
thy herds and of thy flocks; that thou mayest
learn to fear the LORD thy God always.
24 And if the way be too long for thee, so
that thou art not able to carry it; *or* [a]if the
place be too far from thee, which the LORD thy
God shall choose to set his name there, when
the LORD thy God hath blessed thee:
25 Then shalt thou turn *it* into money, and
bind up the money in thine hand, and shalt go
unto the place which the LORD thy God shall
choose:
26 And thou shalt bestow *that* money for
whatsoever thy soul lusteth after, for oxen, or
for sheep, or for wine, or for strong drink, or
for whatsoever thy soul [1]desireth: [a]and thou
shalt eat there before the LORD thy God, and
thou shalt rejoice, thou and thine household,
27 And [a]the Levite that *is* within thy gates;
thou shalt not forsake him; for [b]he hath no
part nor inheritance with thee.
28 [a]At the end of three years thou shalt
bring forth all the tithe of thine increase the
same year, and shalt lay *it* up within thy gates:
29 [a]And the Levite, (because [b]he hath no
part nor inheritance with thee,) and the
stranger, and the fatherless, and the widow,
which *are* within thy gates, shall come, and
shall eat and be satisfied; that [c]the LORD thy
God may bless thee in all the work of thine
hand which thou doest.

The sabbath years of release

15 At the end of [a]*every* seven years thou
shalt make a release.
2 And this *is* the manner of the release:
Every [1]creditor that lendeth *ought* unto his
neighbour shall release *it;* he shall not exact *it*
of his neighbour, or of his brother; because it
is called the LORD'S release.
3 [a]Of a foreigner thou mayest exact *it*
again: but *that* which is thine with thy brother thine hand shall release;
4 [1]Save when there shall be no poor
among you; [a]for the LORD shall greatly bless
thee in the land which the LORD thy God
giveth thee *for* an inheritance to possess it:
5 Only [a]if thou carefully hearken unto the
voice of the LORD thy God, to observe to do all
these commandments which I command thee
this day.
6 For the LORD thy God blesseth thee, as he
promised thee: and [a]thou shalt lend unto
many nations, but thou shalt not borrow; and
[b]thou shalt reign over many nations, but they
shall not reign over thee.
7 If there be among you a poor man of one

14:8 [a]Lev. 11:26,27
14:9 [a]Lev. 11:9
14:12 [a]Lev. 11:13
14:19 [a]Lev. 11:20 [b]See Lev. 11:21
14:21 [a]Lev. 17:15; 22:8; Ezek. 4:14 [b]ver. 2 [c]Ex. 23:19; 34:26
14:22 [a]Lev. 27:30; ch. 12:6,17; Neh. 10:37
14:23 [a]ch. 12:5-7,17,18 [b]ch. 15:19,20
14:24 [a]ch. 12:21
14:26 [1]Heb. *asketh of thee* [a]ch. 12:7,18; 26:11
14:27 [a]ch. 12:12,18,19 [b]Num. 18:20; ch. 18:1,2
14:28 [a]ch. 26:12; Amos 4:4
14:29 [a]ch. 26:12 [b]ver. 27; ch. 12:12 [c]ch. 15:10; See Mal. 3:10
15:1 [a]Ex. 21:2; 23:10,11; Lev. 25:2,4; ch. 31:10; Jer. 34:14
15:2 [1]Heb. *master of the lending of his hand*
15:3 [a]See ch. 23:20
15:4 [1]Or, *To the end that there be no poor among you* [a]ch. 28:8
15:5 [a]ch. 28:1
15:6 [a]ch. 28:12,44 [b]ch. 28:13; Prov. 22:7

14:21 *shall not eat . . . dieth of itself.* Because of the prohibition against eating blood, since the dead animal's blood would not be properly drained (see 12:16,24; see also notes on Gen 9:4; Lev 17:11). *shalt not seethe a kid in his mother's milk.* See note on Ex 23:19.

14:22–29 See Num 18:21–29. Taken together, the two passages suggest the following: 1. Annually, a tenth of all Israelite produce was to be taken to the city of the central sanctuary for distribution to the Levites. 2. At that time, at an initial festival, all Israelites ate part of the tithe. 3. The rest, which would be by far the major part of it, belonged to the Levites. 4. Every third year the tithe was gathered in the towns and stored for distribution to the Levites and the less fortunate: aliens, fatherless and widows (see 26:12). 5. The Levites were to present to the Lord a tenth of their tithe. See note on Lev 27:30.

14:22 *tithe.* See notes on Gen 14:20; 28:22.

14:23 *choose to place his name.* See note on 12:5.

14:25 *money.* Pieces of silver of various weights were a common medium of exchange, but not in the form of coins (see note on Gen 20:16).

15:1 *every seven years.* See Ex 23:10–11; Lev 25:1–7.

15:3 *Of a foreigner thou mayest exact it.* Since he was not subject to the command to allow his fields to lie fallow during the seventh year, a foreigner would probably be financially able to pay his debts if asked to do so.

15:4 *there shall be no poor among you.* Because of the Lord's reward for obedience (vv. 4–6), and because of the sabbath-year arrangement (vv. 7–11). This "year of release" (v. 9) gave Israelites who had experienced economic reverses a way to gain release from indebtedness and so, in a measure, a way to equalize wealth. Cf. the provisions of the year of jubile (Lev 25:8–38).

15:6 *thou shalt lend.* If Israel failed to follow the Lord's commands, the reverse would be true (see 28:43–44).

of thy brethren within any of thy gates in thy
land which the LORD thy God giveth thee,
[a]thou shalt not harden thy heart, nor shut
thine hand from thy poor brother:
8 [a]But thou shalt open thine hand wide
unto him, and shalt surely lend him sufficient
for his need, *in that* which he wanteth.
9 Beware that there be not a [1]thought in
thy [2]wicked heart, saying, The seventh year,
the year of release, is at hand; and thine [a]eye
be evil against thy poor brother, and thou
givest him nought; and [b]he cry unto the LORD
against thee, and [c]it be sin unto thee.
10 Thou shalt surely give him, and [a]thine
heart shall not be grieved when thou givest
unto him: because that [b]for this thing the
LORD thy God shall bless thee in all thy works,
and in all that thou puttest thine hand unto.
11 For [a]the poor shall never cease out of
the land: therefore I command thee, saying,
Thou shalt open thine hand wide unto thy
brother, to thy poor, and to thy needy, in thy
land.

Hebrew slaves to be freed

12 ¶ *And* [a]if thy brother, a Hebrew man, or
a Hebrew woman, be sold unto thee, and
serve thee six years; then in the seventh year
thou shalt let him go free from thee.
13 And when thou sendest him out free
from thee, thou shalt not let him go away
empty:
14 Thou shalt furnish him liberally out of
thy flock, and out of thy floor, and out of thy
winepress: *of that* where*with* the LORD thy
God hath [a]blessed thee thou shalt give unto
him.
15 And [a]thou shalt remember that thou
wast a bondman in the land of Egypt, and the
LORD thy God redeemed thee: therefore I command thee this thing to day.
16 And it shall be, [a]if he say unto thee, I
will not go away from thee; because he loveth
thee and thine house, because he is well with
thee;
17 Then thou shalt take an aul, and thrust
it through his ear unto the door, and he shall
be thy servant for ever. And also unto thy
maidservant thou shalt do likewise.
18 It shall not seem hard unto thee, when
thou sendest him away free from thee; for he
hath been worth [a]a double hired servant *to
thee,* in serving thee six years: and the LORD
thy God shall bless thee in all that thou doest.

Offering the firstlings

19 ¶ [a]All the firstling males that come of
thy herd and of thy flock thou shalt sanctify
unto the LORD thy God: thou shalt do no work
with the firstling of thy bullock, nor shear the
firstling of thy sheep.
20 [a]Thou shalt eat it before the LORD thy
God year by year in the place which the LORD
shall choose, thou and thy household.
21 [a]And if there be *any* blemish therein, *as
if it be* lame, or blind, *or have* any ill blemish,
thou shalt not sacrifice it unto the LORD thy
God.
22 Thou shalt eat it within thy gates: [a]the
unclean and the clean *person shall eat it* alike,
as the roebuck, and as the hart.
23 [a]Only thou shalt not eat the blood
thereof; thou shalt pour it upon the ground as
water.

The passover

16 Observe the [a]month of Abib, and
keep the passover unto the LORD thy
God: for [b]in the month of Abib the LORD thy
God brought thee forth out of Egypt [c]by night.
2 Thou shalt therefore sacrifice the
passover unto the LORD thy God, *of* the flock
and [a]the herd, in the [b]place which the LORD
shall choose to place his name there.
3 [a]Thou shalt eat no leavened bread with
it; seven days shalt thou eat unleavened bread
therewith, *even* the bread of affliction; for
thou camest forth out of the land of Egypt in
haste: that thou mayest remember the day
when thou camest forth out of the land of
Egypt all the days of thy life.
4 [a]And there shall be no leavened bread
seen with thee in all thy coast seven days;
[b]neither shall there *any thing* of the flesh,
which thou sacrificedst the first day at even,
remain all night until the morning.
5 Thou mayest not [1]sacrifice the passover
within any of thy gates, which the LORD thy
God giveth thee:
6 But at the place which the LORD thy God
shall choose to place his name *in,* there thou
shalt sacrifice the passover [a]at even, at the go-

15:7 [a]1 John 3:17
15:8 [a]Lev. 25:35; Mat. 5:42; Luke 6:34,35
15:9 [1]Heb. *word* [2]Heb. *Belial* [a]ch. 28:54,56; Mat. 20:15 [b]ch. 24:15 [c]Mat. 25:41,42
15:10 [a]2 Cor. 9:5,7 [b]ch. 14:29; 24:19
15:11 [a]Mat. 26:11; Mark 14:7; John 12:8
15:12 [a]Ex. 21:2; Lev. 25:39; Jer. 34:14
15:14 [a]Prov. 10:22
15:15 [a]ch. 5:15; 16:12
15:16 [a]Ex. 21:5,6
15:18 [a]See Is. 16:14; 21:16
15:19 [a]Ex. 13:2; 34:19; Lev. 27:26; Num. 3:13
15:20 [a]ch. 12:5-7,17; 14:23; 16:11,14
15:21 [a]Lev. 22:20
15:22 [a]ch. 12:15,22
15:23 [a]ch. 12:16,23
16:1 [a]Ex. 12:2 [b]Ex. 13:4 [c]Ex. 12:29,42
16:2 [a]Num. 28:19 [b]ch. 12:5,26
16:3 [a]Ex. 12:15,19,39; 13:3,6,7; 34:18
16:4 [a]Ex. 13:7 [b]Ex. 12:10; 34:25
16:5 [1]Or, *kill*
16:6 [a]Ex. 12:6

15:11 *the poor shall never cease out of the land.* See also Jesus' statement in Mat 26:11. Even in the best of societies under the most enlightened laws, the uncertainties of life and the variations among citizens result in some people becoming poor. In such cases the Lord commands that generosity and kindness be extended to them.

15:15 *remember.* See note on 4:10.

15:16 *because he loveth thee* In Ex 21:5–6 an additional reason is given: The servant may want to stay with his family.

15:17 *take an aul, and thrust it through his ear.* See note on Ex 21:6.

15:18 *double hired servant.* A Hebrew servant worked twice as many years as the Code of Hammurapi, e.g., required for release from debt (see chart, p. xix). Other ancient legal texts, however, support "equivalent to" as a possible translation of the phrase.

15:19 *the firstling males . . . sanctify.* Because the Lord saved His people from the plague of death on the firstborn in Egypt (see Ex 12:12,29; 13:2 and note; 13:15).

15:21 *if there be any blemish . . . thou shalt not sacrifice it.* See note on Lev 1:3.

15:23 See 12:16,24; see also notes on Gen 9:4; Lev 17:11.

16:1–17 See chart, pp. 116–117; see also Ex 23:14–19 and notes; 34:18–26; Lev 23:4–44 and notes; Num 28:16–29:40.

16:1–8 See Ex 12:1–28; 13:1–16 and notes.

16:1 *Abib.* See chart, p. 92.

16:3,12 *remember.* See note on 4:10.

ing down of the sun, *at* the season that thou
camest forth out of Egypt.
7 And thou shalt [a]roast and eat *it* [b]in the
place which the LORD thy God shall choose:
and thou shalt turn in the morning, and go
unto thy tents.
8 Six days thou shalt eat unleavened bread:
and [a]on the seventh day *shall be* a [1]solemn assembly to the LORD thy God: thou shalt do no
work *therein.*

Feasts of weeks and tabernacles

9 ¶ [a]Seven weeks shalt thou number unto
thee: begin to number the seven weeks from
such time as thou beginnest *to put* the sickle
to the corn.
10 And thou shalt keep the feast of weeks
unto the LORD thy God *with* [1]a tribute of a
freewill offering of thine hand, which thou
shalt give *unto the LORD thy God,* [a]according
as the LORD thy God hath blessed thee:
11 And [a]thou shalt rejoice before the LORD
thy God, thou, and thy son, and thy daughter,
and thy manservant, and thy maidservant, and
the Levite that *is* within thy gates, and the
stranger, and the fatherless, and the widow,
that *are* among you, in the place which the
LORD thy God hath chosen to place his name
there.
12 [a]And thou shalt remember that thou
wast a bondman in Egypt: and thou shalt observe and do these statutes.
13 ¶ [a]Thou shalt observe the feast of tabernacles seven days, after that thou hast gathered in thy [1]corn and thy wine:
14 And [a]thou shalt rejoice in thy feast,
thou, and thy son, and thy daughter, and thy
manservant, and thy maidservant, and the Levite, the stranger, and the fatherless, and the
widow, that *are* within thy gates.
15 [a]Seven days shalt thou keep a solemn
feast unto the LORD thy God in the place which
the LORD shall choose: because the LORD thy
God shall bless thee in all thy increase, and in
all the works of thine hands, therefore thou
shalt surely rejoice.
16 [a]Three times in a year shall all thy
males appear before the LORD thy God in the
place which he shall choose; in the feast of unleavened bread, and in the feast of weeks, and
in the feast of tabernacles: and [b]they shall not
appear before the LORD empty:

16:7 [a]Ex. 12:8,9; 2 Chr. 35:13 [b]2 Ki. 23:23; John 2:13; 11:55
16:8 [1]Heb. *restraint* [a]Ex. 12:16; 13:6; Lev. 23:8
16:9 [a]Ex. 23:16; 34:22; Lev. 23:15; Acts 2:1
16:10 [1]Or, *sufficiency* [a]1 Cor. 16:2
16:11 [a]ver. 14; ch. 12:7,12
16:12 [a]ch. 15:15
16:13 [1]Heb. *floor, and thy winepress* [a]Ex. 23:16; Lev. 23:34; Num. 29:12
16:14 [a]Neh. 8:9
16:15 [a]Lev. 23:39
16:16 [a]Ex. 23:14; 34:23 [b]Ex. 23:15; 34:20
16:17 [1]Heb. *according to the gift of his hand* [a]ver. 10
16:18 [a]ch. 1:16; 1 Chr. 23:4; 2 Chr. 19:5
16:19 [1]Or, *matters* [a]Ex. 23:2,6; Lev. 19:15 [b]ch. 1:17 [c]Ex. 23:8; Eccl. 7:7
16:20 [1]Heb. *Justice, justice* [a]Ezek. 18:5
16:21 [a]Ex. 34:13; 1 Ki. 14:15; 16:33; 2 Ki. 17:16; 21:3; 2 Chr. 33:3
16:22 [1]Or, *statue,* or, *pillar* [a]Lev. 26:1
17:1 [1]Or, *goat* [a]ch. 15:21; Mal. 1:8,13
17:2 [a]ch. 13:6 [b]Josh. 7:11; 23:16; Judg. 2:20; 2 Ki. 18:12; Hos. 8:1
17:3 [a]ch. 4:19; Job 31:26 [b]Jer. 7:22,23; 19:5; 32:35
17:4 [a]ch. 13:12,14
17:5 [a]Lev. 24:14; ch. 13:10; Josh. 7:25
17:6 [a]Num. 35:30; ch. 19:15; Mat. 18:16; John 8:17; 2 Cor. 13:1; 1 Tim. 5:19; Heb. 10:28

17 Every man *shall give* [1]as he is able, [a]ac-
cording to the blessing of the LORD thy God
which he hath given thee.

Appointment of judges and officers

18 ¶ [a]Judges and officers shalt thou make
thee in all thy gates, which the LORD thy God
giveth thee, throughout thy tribes: and they
shall judge the people *with* just judgment.
19 [a]Thou shalt not wrest judgment; [b]thou
shalt not respect persons, [c]neither take a gift:
for a gift doth blind the eyes of the wise, and
pervert the [1]words of the righteous.
20 [1]That which is altogether just shalt
thou follow, that thou mayest [a]live, and inherit the land which the LORD thy God giveth
thee.
21 ¶ [a]Thou shalt not plant thee a grove *of*
any trees near unto the altar of the LORD thy
God, which thou shalt make thee.
22 [a]Neither shalt thou set thee up *any* [1]im-
age; which the LORD thy God hateth.
17 Thou [a]shalt not sacrifice unto the
LORD thy God *any* bullock, or [1]sheep,
wherein is blemish, *or* any evil favouredness:
for that *is* an abomination unto the LORD thy
God.

The administration of justice

2 ¶ [a]If there be found among you, within
any of thy gates which the LORD thy God
giveth thee, man or woman, that hath
wrought wickedness in the sight of the LORD
thy God, [b]in transgressing his covenant,
3 And hath gone and served other gods,
and worshipped them, either [a]the sun, or
moon, or any of the host of heaven, [b]which I
have not commanded;
4 [a]And it be told thee, and thou hast heard
of it, and inquired diligently, and behold, *it is*
true, *and* the thing certain, *that* such abomination is wrought in Israel:
5 Then shalt thou bring forth that man or
that woman, which have committed that
wicked thing, unto thy gates, *even that* man or
that woman, and [a]shalt stone them with
stones, till they die.
6 [a]At the mouth of two witnesses, or three
witnesses, shall he that is *worthy* of death be
put to death; *but* at the mouth of one witness
he shall not be put to death.

---

‡16:6 *at the season that thou camest forth out of.* Or "on the anniversary of your departure from." The Hebrew for "season" is "appointed time," referring either to the time of day or to the anniversary of the day it first occurred.

16:7 *unto thy tents.* To wherever they were staying while at the festival, whether in permanent or temporary quarters.

16:8 *assembly.* Probably refers to closing assembly (cf. Lev 23:36).

16:9 *time as thou beginnest to put the sickle to the corn.* Abib 16, the second day of the passover feast.

16:15 *thou shalt surely rejoice.* As a result of God's blessing (cf. John 3:29; 15:11; 16:24; Phil 2:2; 1 John 1:4; 2 John 12).

16:16 *Three times in a year.* The three annual pilgrimage festivals (see Ex 23:14,17; 34:23).

16:17 *give . . . according to the blessing of the LORD.* See v. 10; cf. 2 Cor 8:12.

16:18–20 Cf. 1:9–18; Ex 18:13–26.

16:19 See Ex 23:8 and note.

16:21–22 *grove . . . image.* See note on 7:5.

17:1 *blemish, or any evil favouredness.* See note on Lev 1:3.

17:3 *worshipped them, either the sun . . . moon . . . host of heaven.* See 2 Ki 17:16; 21:3,5; 23:4–5.

17:6 *two witnesses, or three.* A further specification of the law set forth in Num 35:30. See 19:15; cf. Mat 18:16; 2 Cor 13:1; 1 Tim 5:19; Heb 10:28.

7 [a]The hands of the witnesses shall be first upon him to put him to death, and afterward the hands of all the people. So [b]thou shalt put the evil away from among you.

8 ¶ [a]If there arise a matter too hard for thee in judgment, [b]between blood and blood, between plea and plea, and between stroke and stroke, *being* matters of controversy within thy gates: then shalt thou arise, [c]and get thee up into the place which the LORD thy God shall choose;

9 And [a]thou shalt come unto the priests the Levites, and [b]unto the judge that shall be in those days, and inquire; [c]and they shall shew thee the sentence of judgment:

10 And thou shalt do according to the sentence, which *they* of that place which the LORD shall choose shall shew thee; and thou shalt observe to do according to all that they inform thee:

11 According to the sentence of the law which they shall teach thee, and according to the judgment which they shall tell thee, thou shalt do: thou shalt not decline from the sentence which they shall shew thee, *to* the right hand, nor *to* the left.

12 And [a]the man that will do presumptuously, [1]and will not hearken unto the priest [b]that standeth to minister there before the LORD thy God, or unto the judge, even that man shall die: and [c]thou shalt put away the evil from Israel.

13 [a]And all the people shall hear, and fear, and do no more presumptuously.

The choice of a king

14 ¶ When thou art come unto the land which the LORD thy God giveth thee, and shalt possess it, and shalt dwell therein, and shalt say, [a]I will set a king over me, like as all the nations that *are* about me;

15 Thou shalt in any wise set *him* king over thee, [a]whom the LORD thy God shall choose: *one* [b]from among thy brethren shalt thou set king over thee: thou mayest not set a stranger over thee, which *is* not thy brother.

16 But he shall not multiply [a]horses to himself, nor cause the people [b]to return to Egypt, to the end that he should multiply horses: forasmuch as [c]the LORD hath said unto you, [d]Ye shall henceforth return no more that way.

17 Neither shall he multiply wives to himself, that [a]his heart turn not away: neither shall he greatly multiply to himself silver and gold.

18 [a]And it shall be, when he sitteth upon the throne of his kingdom, that he shall write him a copy of this law in a book out of [b]*that which is* before the priests the Levites:

19 And [a]it shall be with him, and he shall read therein all the days of his life: that he may learn to fear the LORD his God, to keep all the words of this law and these statutes, to do them:

20 That his heart be not lifted up above his brethren, and that *he* [a]turn not aside from the commandment, *to* the right hand, or *to* the left: to the end that he may prolong *his* days in his kingdom, he, and his children, in the midst of Israel.

The portion for the priests

18 The priests the Levites, *and* all the tribe of Levi, [a]shall have no part nor inheritance with Israel: they [b]shall eat the offerings of the LORD made by fire, and his inheritance.

2 Therefore shall they have no inheritance among their brethren: the LORD *is* their inheritance, as he hath said unto them.

3 And this shall be the priest's due from the people, from them that offer a sacrifice, whether *it be* ox or sheep; and [a]they shall give unto the priest the shoulder, and the two cheeks, and the maw.

4 [a]The firstfruit *also* of thy corn, of thy wine, and of thy oil, and the first of the fleece of thy sheep, shalt thou give him.

5 For [a]the LORD thy God hath chosen him out of all thy tribes, [b]to stand to minister in the name of the LORD, him and his sons for ever.

6 And if a Levite come from any of thy gates out of all Israel, where he [a]sojourned, and come with all the desire of his mind [b]unto the place which the LORD shall choose;

7 Then he shall minister in the name of the LORD his God, [a]as all his brethren the Levites *do*, which stand there before the LORD.

17:7 [a]ch. 13:9; Acts 7:58 [b]ch. 13:5; 19:19
17:8 [a]2 Chr. 19:10; Hag. 2:11; Mal. 2:7 [b]Ex. 21:13, 20,22,28 [c]ch. 12:5; 19:17
17:9 [a]Jer. 18:18 [b]ch. 19:17 [c]Ezek. 44:24
17:12 [1]Heb. *not to hearken* [a]Num. 15:30 [b]ch. 18:5,7 [c]ch. 13:5
17:13 [a]ch. 13:11; 19:20
17:14 [a]1 Sam. 8:5,19,20
17:15 [a]1 Sam. 10:24; 1 Chr. 22:10 [b]Jer. 30:21
17:16 [a]1 Ki. 4:26; 10:26,28 [b]Is. 31:1; Ezek. 17:15 [c]Ex. 13:17; Num. 14:3
17:16 [d]ch. 28:68; Jer. 42:15; Hos. 11:5
17:17 [a]See 1 Ki. 11:3,4
17:18 [a]2 Ki. 11:12 [b]ch. 31:9; 2 Ki. 22:8
17:19 [a]Ps. 119:97,98
17:20 [a]ch. 5:32; 1 Ki. 15:5
18:1 [a]Num. 18:20; 26:62; ch. 10:9 [b]Num. 18:8; 1 Cor. 9:13
18:3 [a]Lev. 7:30-34
18:4 [a]Ex. 22:29; Num. 18:12
18:5 [a]Ex. 28:1; Num. 3:10 [b]ch. 10:8
18:6 [a]Num. 35:2 [b]ch. 12:5
18:7 [a]2 Chr. 31:2

17:7 *thou shalt put the evil away from among you.* See v. 12; see also note on 13:5.

17:14 *a king . . . like as all the nations . . . about me.* Moses, Joshua and a succession of judges were chosen directly by the Lord to govern Israel on His behalf. As Gideon later said, "The LORD shall rule over you" (Judg 8:23; see note there). Moses here, however, anticipates a time when the people would ask for a king (see 1 Sam 8:4–9) contrary to the Lord's ideal for them (see notes on 7:2–5; 1 Sam 8:1–12:25; see also Lev 20:23). So Moses gives guidance concerning the eventual selection of a king.

17:16–17 The very things that later kings were guilty of, beginning especially with Solomon (1 Ki 4:26; 11:1–4)—except that they did not make Israel return to Egypt (but see Jer 42:13–43:7).

17:18 *write him a copy of this law.* As a sign of submission to the Lord as his King, and as a guide for his rule in obedience to his heavenly Suzerain. This was required procedure for vassal kings under the suzeraintly treaties among the Hittites and others before and during this period (see note on 31:9). See chart, p. 16.

17:20 *his heart be not lifted up.* The king was not above God's law, any more than were the humblest of his subjects.

18:1 *no part nor inheritance.* No private ownership of land. Towns and surrounding pasturelands were set aside for the use of the Levites (Josh 21:41–42), as were the tithes and parts of sacrifices (see 14:22–29 and note; Lev 27:30 and note; Num 18:21–29).

18:4 *firstfruit.* See Ex 23:19 and note; 34:26; Lev 23:10–11; Num 15:18–20; 18:12–13.

18:5 See note on 21:5.

8 They shall have like [a]portions to eat, beside [1]that which cometh of the sale of his pat-
rimony.

Forbidden pagan practices

9 ¶ When thou art come into the land
which the LORD thy God giveth thee, [a]thou
shalt not learn to do after the abominations of
those nations.
10 There shall not be found among you *any*
one that maketh his son or his daughter [a]to
pass through the fire, [b]*or* that useth divination, *or* an observer of times, or an enchanter,
or a witch,
11 [a]Or a charmer, or a consulter with familiar spirits, or a wizard, or a [b]necromancer.
12 For all that do these *things are* an abomination unto the LORD: and [a]because of these
abominations the LORD thy God doth drive
them out from before thee.
13 Thou shalt be [a][1]perfect with the LORD
thy God.
14 For these nations, which thou shalt
[1]possess, hearkened unto observers of times,
and unto diviners: but *as for* thee, the LORD
thy God hath not suffered thee so *to do*.

The promise of a prophet

15 ¶ [a]The LORD thy God will raise up unto
thee a Prophet from the midst of thee, of thy
brethren, like unto me; unto him ye shall
hearken;
16 According to all that thou desiredst of
the LORD thy God in Horeb [a]in the day of the
assembly, saying, [b]Let me not hear again the
voice of the LORD my God, neither let me see
this great fire any more, that I die not.
17 And the LORD said unto me, [a]They have
well *spoken that* which they have spoken.
18 [a]I will raise them up a Prophet from
among their brethren, like unto thee, and
[b]will put my words in his mouth; [c]and he shall
speak unto them all that I shall command him.
19 [a]And it shall come to pass, *that* whosoever will not hearken unto my words which he
shall speak in my name, I will require *it* of him.
20 But [a]the prophet, which shall presume
to speak a word in my name, which I have not
commanded him to speak, or [b]that shall speak
in the name of other gods, even that prophet
shall die.
21 And if thou say in thine heart, How
shall we know the word which the LORD hath
not spoken?
22 [a]When a prophet speaketh in the name
of the LORD, [b]if the thing follow not, nor come
to pass, that *is* the thing which the LORD hath
not spoken, *but* the prophet hath spoken it
[c]presumptuously: thou shalt not be afraid of
him.

Cities of refuge for murderers

19 When the LORD thy God [a]hath cut off
the nations, whose land the LORD thy
God giveth thee, and thou [1]succeedest them,
and dwellest in their cities, and in their
houses;
2 [a]Thou shalt separate three cities for thee
in the midst of thy land, which the LORD thy
God giveth thee to possess it.
3 Thou shalt prepare thee a way, and divide the coasts of thy land, which the LORD thy
God giveth thee to inherit, into three parts,
that every slayer may flee thither.
4 And [a]this *is* the case of the slayer, which
shall flee thither, that he may live: Whoso killeth his neighbour ignorantly, whom he hated
not [1]in time past;
5 As when *a man* goeth into the wood with
his neighbour to hew wood, and his hand
fetcheth a stroke with the axe to cut down the
tree, and the [1]head slippeth from the [2]helve,
and [3]lighteth upon his neighbour, that he die;
he shall flee unto one of those cities, and live:
6 [a]Lest the avenger of the blood pursue the
slayer, while his heart is hot, and overtake
him, because the way is long, and [1]slay him;
whereas he *was* not worthy of death, inasmuch as he hated him not [2]in time past.
7 Wherefore I command thee, saying,
Thou shalt separate three cities for thee.
8 And if the LORD thy God [a]enlarge thy
coast, as he hath sworn unto thy fathers, and
give thee all the land which he promised to
give unto thy fathers;
9 If thou shalt keep all these command-

18:8 [1]Heb. *his sales by the fathers* [a]2 Chr. 31:4; Neh. 12:44
18:9 [a]Lev. 18:26,27,30; ch. 12:29
18:10 [a]Lev. 18:21; ch. 12:31 [b]Lev. 20:27; Is. 8:19
18:11 [a]Lev. 20:27 [b]1 Sam. 28:7
18:12 [a]Lev. 18:24; ch. 9:4
18:13 [1]Or, *upright*, or, *sincere* [a]Gen. 17:1
18:14 [1]Or, *inherit*
18:15 [a]John 1:45; Acts 3:22
18:16 [a]ch. 9:10 [b]Ex. 20:19; Heb. 12:19
18:17 [a]ch. 5:28
18:18 [a]John 1:45; Acts 3:22 [b]Is. 51:16; John 17:8 [c]John 4:25; 8:28; 12:49,50
18:19 [a]Acts 3:23
18:20 [a]Jer. 14:14,15
18:20 [b]ch. 13:1,2; Jer. 2:8
18:22 [a]Jer. 28:9 [b]See ch. 13:2 [c]ver. 20
19:1 [1]Heb. *inheritest*, or, *possessest* [a]ch. 12:29
19:2 [a]Ex. 21:13; Num. 35:10,14; Josh. 20:2
19:4 [1]Heb. *from yesterday the third day* [a]Num. 35:15; ch. 4:42
19:5 [1]Heb. *iron* [2]Heb. *wood* [3]Heb. *findeth*
19:6 [1]Heb. *smite him* in *life* [2]Heb. *from yesterday [the] third day* [a]Num. 35:12
19:8 [a]Gen. 15:18; ch. 12:20

18:9 *abominations of those nations.* What follows is the most complete list of magical or spiritistic arts in the OT. All were practiced in Canaan, and all are condemned and prohibited. The people are not to resort to such sources for their information, guidance or revelation. Rather, they are to listen to the Lord's true prophets (see vv. 14–22; Is 8:19–20).

‡18:10 *maketh his son or his daughter to pass through the fire.* See 12:31; see also note on Lev 18:21. *observer of times.* One practicing sorcery. *enchanter.* One who interprets omens.

‡18:11 *charmer.* One who casts spells. *consulter with familiar spirits.* A medium. *wizard.* A spiritist. *necromancer.* One who consults the dead.

18:15 *Prophet . . . like unto me.* Verse 16, as well as the general context (see especially vv. 20–22), indicates that a series of prophets is meant. At mount Horeb the people requested that Moses take the message from God and deliver it to them (see Ex 20:19 and note). But now that Moses is to leave them, he says that another spokesman will take his place, and then another will be necessary for the next generation. This is therefore a collective reference to the prophets who will follow. As such, it is also the basis for Messianic expectation and receives a unique fulfillment in Jesus who is the ultimate Prophet of God. (see John 1:21,25,45; 5:46; 6:14; 7:40; Acts 3:22–26; 7:37).

18:16 See Ex 20:18–19; Heb 12:18–21.

18:18 *my words in his mouth.* See Ex 4:15–16; Jer 1:9; see also note on Ex 7:1–2.

18:20 *prophet, which shall presume to speak.* See note on 13:1–5. *shall die.* See 13:5; Jer 28:15–17.

‡18:21–22 This negative form of statement is always true. But see also note on 13:1–5. These verses serve as a warning against false prophets and the deceptive nature of their messages. By contrast, true prophets of God speak in God's name and their predictions of the future come true.

19:1–13 See 4:41–43; Num 35:9–28; Josh 20.

ments to do them, which I command thee *this*
day, to love the LORD thy God, and to walk ever
in his ways; [a]then shalt thou add three cities
moe for thee, beside these three:
10 That innocent blood be not shed in thy
land, which the LORD thy God giveth thee *for*
an inheritance, and *so* blood be upon thee.
11 But [a]if any man hate his neighbour, and
lie in wait for him, and rise up against him,
and smite him [1]mortally that he die, and
fleeth into one of these cities:
12 Then the elders of his city shall send
and fetch him thence, and deliver him into the
hand of the avenger of blood, that he may die.
13 [a]Thine eye shall not pity him, [b]but thou
shalt put away *the guilt of* innocent blood from
Israel, that *it may go* well with thee.

Laws about witnesses

14 ¶ [a]Thou shalt not remove thy neighbour's landmark, which they of old time have
set in thine inheritance, which thou shalt inherit in the land that the LORD thy God giveth
thee to possess it.
15 [a]One witness shall not rise up against a
man for any iniquity, or for any sin, in any sin
that he sinneth: at the mouth of two witnesses, or at the mouth of three witnesses,
shall the matter be stablished.
16 If a false witness [a]rise up against any man
to testify against him [1]*that which is* wrong;
17 Then both the men, between whom the
controversy *is,* shall stand before the LORD,
[a]before the priests and the judges, which shall
be in those days;
18 And the judges shall make diligent inquisition: and behold, *if* the witness *be* a false
witness, *and* hath testified falsely against his
brother;
19 [a]Then shall ye do unto him, as he had
thought to have done unto his brother: so
[b]shalt thou put the evil away from among you.
20 [a]And those which remain shall hear,
and fear, and shall henceforth commit no more
any such evil among you.
21 [a]And thine eye shall not pity; *but* [b]life
shall go for life, eye for eye, tooth for tooth,
hand for hand, foot for foot.

Laws about military service

20 When thou goest out to battle against
thine enemies, and seest [a]horses,
and chariots, *and* a people more than thou, be
not afraid of them: for the LORD thy God *is*
[b]with thee, which brought thee up out of the
land of Egypt.
2 And it shall be, when ye are come nigh
unto the battle, that the priest shall approach
and speak unto the people,
3 And shall say unto them, Hear, O Israel,
you approach *this* day unto battle against your
enemies: let not your hearts [1]faint, fear not,
and do not [2]tremble, neither be ye terrified
because of them;
4 For the LORD your God *is* he that goeth
with you, [a]to fight for you against your enemies, to save you.
5 ¶ And the officers shall speak unto the
people, saying, What man *is there* that hath
built a new house, and hath not [a]dedicated it?
let him go and return to his house, lest he die
in the battle, and another man dedicate it.
6 And what man *is he* that hath planted a
vineyard, and hath not *yet* [a][1]eaten of it? let
him *also* go and return unto his house, lest he
die in the battle, and another man eat of it.
7 [a]And what man *is there* that hath betrothed a wife, and hath not taken her? let him
go and return unto his house, lest he die in the
battle, and another man take her.
8 And the officers shall speak further unto
the people, and they shall say, [a]What man *is
there that is* fearful and fainthearted? let him
go and return unto his house, lest his brethren's heart [1]faint as well as his heart.
9 And it shall be, when the officers have
made an end of speaking unto the people, that
they shall make captains of the armies [1]to lead
the people.
10 ¶ When thou comest nigh unto a city to
fight against it, [a]then proclaim peace unto it.
11 And it shall be, if it make thee answer of
peace, and open unto thee, then it shall be,
that all the people that is found therein shall be
tributaries unto thee, and they shall serve thee.
12 And if it will make no peace with thee,
but will make war against thee, then thou
shalt besiege it:
13 And when the LORD thy God hath delivered it into thine hands, [a]thou shalt smite
every male thereof with the edge of the sword:
14 But the women, and the little ones, and
[a]the cattle, and all that is in the city, *even* all
the spoil thereof, shalt thou [1]take unto thyself;
and [b]thou shalt eat the spoil of thine enemies,
which the LORD thy God hath given thee.

19:9 [a]Josh. 20:7
19:11 [1]Heb. in *life* [a]Num. 35:16,24; ch. 27:24; Prov. 28:17
19:13 [a]ch. 13:8 [b]Num. 35:33,34; 1 Ki. 2:31
19:14 [a]ch. 27:17; Prov. 22:28; Hos. 5:10
19:15 [a]Num. 35:30; ch. 17:6; Mat. 18:16; John 8:17; 2 Cor. 13:1; 1 Tim. 5:19; Heb. 10:28
19:16 [1]Or, *falling away* [a]Ps. 27:12; 35:11
19:17 [a]ch. 17:9; 21:5
19:19 [a]Prov. 19:5; Dan. 6:24 [b]ch. 13:5; 17:7; 21:21; 22:21
19:20 [a]ch. 17:13; 21:21
19:21 [a]ver. 13 [b]Ex. 21:23,24; Lev. 24:20; Mat. 5:38
20:1 [a]See Ps. 20:7; Is. 31:1
20:1 [b]Num. 23:21; ch. 31:6,8; 2 Chr. 13:12; 32:7,8
20:3 [1]Heb. *be tender* [2]Heb. *make haste*
20:4 [a]ch. 1:30; 3:22; Josh. 23:10
20:5 [a]See Neh. 12:27
20:6 [1]Heb. *made it common?* [a]See Lev. 19:23,24; ch. 28:30
20:7 [a]ch. 24:5
20:8 [1]Heb. *melt* [a]Judg. 7:3
20:9 [1]Heb. to be *in the head of the people*
20:10 [a]2 Sam. 20:18,20
20:13 [a]Num. 31:7
20:14 [1]Heb. *spoil* [a]Josh. 8:2 [b]Josh. 22:8

19:14 *landmark.* Such stones were set up to indicate the perimeters of fields and landed estates. Moving them illegally to increase one's own holdings was considered a serious crime.

19:15 See note on 17:6.

19:18 *false witness.* See 5:20; Lev 19:11–13; 1 Ki 21:10,13.

19:19 *shalt thou put the evil away from among you.* See note on 13:5.

19:21 *life shall go for life.* See notes on Ex 21:23–25; Lev 24:20; see also Mat 5:38–42.

20:2 *priest shall . . . speak.* Not merely a recitation of ritual. Priests sometimes accompanied the army when it went into battle (see, e.g., Josh 6:4–21; 2 Chr 20:14–22).

20:3 *Hear, O Israel.* See note on 4:1.

20:4 See note on 3:22.

20:5–8 *let him . . . return to his house.* See the curses in 28:30. Israel was not to trust in the size of its army but in the Lord. Exemptions from military duty were sometimes extensive (see, e.g., Judg 7:2–8).

20:10–15 Rules regarding warfare against nations outside the promised land.

‡20:11 *shall be tributaries unto thee* [i.e. forced labor to serve you]. A fulfillment of Noah's curse on Canaan (see Gen 9:25 and note).

15 Thus shalt thou do unto all the cities
which are very far off from thee, which *are* not
of the cities of these nations.
16 But [a]of the cities of these people, which
the LORD thy God doth give thee *for* an inheritance, thou shalt save alive nothing that
breatheth:
17 But thou shalt utterly destroy them;
namely, the Hittites, and the Amorites, the
Canaanites, and the Perizzites, the Hivites,
and the Jebusites; as the LORD thy God hath
commanded thee:
18 That [a]they teach you not to do after all
their abominations, which they have done
unto their gods; so should ye [b]sin against the
LORD your God.
19 ¶ When thou shalt besiege a city a long
time, in making war against it to take it, thou
shalt not destroy the trees thereof by forcing
an axe against them: for thou mayest eat of
them, and thou shalt not cut them down ([1]for
the tree of the field *is* man's *life*) [2]to employ
them in the siege:
20 Only the trees which thou knowest that
they *be* not trees for meat, thou shalt destroy
and cut them down; and thou shalt build bulwarks against the city that maketh war with
thee, until [1]it be subdued.

Laws about unsolved murders

21 If *one* be found slain in the land
which the LORD thy God giveth thee
to possess it, lying in the field, *and* it be not
known who hath slain him:
2 Then thy elders and thy judges shall
come forth, and they shall measure unto the
cities which *are* round about him that is slain:
3 And it shall be, *that* the city *which is*
next unto the slain *man,* even the elders of
that city shall take a heifer, which hath not
been wrought with, *and* which hath not
drawn in the yoke;
4 And the elders of that city shall bring
down the heifer unto a rough valley, which is
neither eared nor sown, and shall strike off the
heifer's neck there in the valley:
5 And the priests the sons of Levi shall
come near; for [a]them the LORD thy God hath
chosen to minister unto him, and to bless in the
name of the LORD; and [b]by their [1]word shall
every controversy and every stroke be *tried:*

20:16 [a]Num. 21:2,3,35; 33:52; ch. 7:1,2; Josh. 11:14
20:18 [a]ch. 7:4; 12:30,31; 18:9 [b]Ex. 23:33
20:19 [1]Or, *for, O man, the tree of the field is to be employed in the siege* [2]Heb. *to go from before thee*
20:20 [1]Heb. *it come down*
21:5 [1]Heb. *mouth* [a]ch. 10:8; 1 Chr. 23:13 [b]ch. 17:8,9
21:6 [a]See Ps. 19:12; 26:6; Mat. 27:24
21:8 [1]Heb. *in the midst* [a]Jonah 1:14
21:9 [a]ch. 19:13
21:12 [1]Or, *suffer to grow.* Heb. *make,* or, *dress*
21:13 [a]See Ps. 45:10
21:14 [a]Gen. 34:2; ch. 22:29; Judg. 19:24
21:15 [a]Gen. 29:33
21:16 [a]1 Chr. 5:2; 26:10; 2 Chr. 11:19,22
21:17 [1]Heb. *that is found with him* [a]See 1 Chr. 5:1 [b]Gen. 49:3

6 And all the elders of that city, *that are*
next unto the slain *man,* [a]shall wash their
hands over the heifer that is beheaded in the
valley:
7 And they shall answer and say, Our
hands have not shed this blood, neither have
our eyes seen *it.*
8 Be merciful, O LORD, unto thy people Israel, whom thou hast redeemed, [a]and lay not
innocent blood [1]unto thy people of Israel's
charge. And the blood shall be forgiven them.
9 So [a]shalt thou put away the *guilt of* innocent blood from among you, when thou shalt
do *that which is* right in the sight of the LORD.

Laws about captive wives

10 ¶ When thou goest forth to war against
thine enemies, and the LORD thy God hath delivered them into thine hands, and thou hast
taken them captive,
11 And seest among the captives a beautiful woman, and hast a desire unto her, that
thou wouldest have *her* to thy wife;
12 Then thou shalt bring her home to
thine house; and she shall shave her head, and
[1]pare her nails;
13 And she shall put the raiment of her
captivity from off her, and shall remain in
thine house, and [a]bewail her father and her
mother a full month: and after that thou shalt
go in unto her, and be her husband, and she
shall be thy wife.
14 And it shall be, if thou have no delight
in her, then thou shalt let her go whither she
will; but thou shalt not sell her at all for money, thou shalt not make merchandise of her,
because thou hast [a]humbled her.

Laws concerning sons

15 ¶ If a man have two wives, one beloved,
[a]and another hated, and they have born him
children, *both* the beloved and the hated; and
if the firstborn son be hers that was hated:
16 Then it shall be, [a]when he maketh his
sons to inherit *that* which he hath, *that* he
may not make the son of the beloved firstborn
before the son of the hated, *which is indeed*
the firstborn:
17 But he shall acknowledge the son of the
hated *for* the firstborn, [a]by giving him a double portion of all [1]that he hath: for he *is* [b]the

20:17 *Hittites . . . Jebusites.* See 7:1; see also notes on Gen 10:6,15–18; 13:7.

20:19 *thou shalt not destroy the trees thereof.* The failure of later armies to follow this wise rule stripped bare much of the Holy Land (though the absence of woodlands there today is of relatively recent origin).

21:5 *to minister.* To officiate at the place of worship before the Lord on behalf of the people (see 10:8; 18:5). *to bless.* See Num 6:22–27.

21:6 *wash their hands.* Symbolic of a declaration of innocence (v. 7; see Mat 27:24).

21:10 *against thine enemies.* The enemies here are those outside Canaan (see 20:14–15); so the woman (v. 11) could be taken captive and would not be subject to total destruction.

21:12 *shave her head.* Indicative of leaving her former life and beginning a new life, or perhaps symbolic of mourning (v. 13; see, e.g., Jer 47:5; Mic 1:16) or of humiliation (see note on Is 7:20). For cleansing rites see Lev 14:8; Num 8:7; cf. 2 Sam 19:24.

21:14 *humbled.* Twelve other times the Hebrew for this word is used of men forcing women to have sexual intercourse with them (22:24,29; Gen 34:2; Judg 19:24; 20:5; 2 Sam 13:12,14,22, 32; Lam 5:11; Ezek 22:10–11).

21:15 *two wives.* See notes on Gen 4:19; 25:6.

21:16 *before.* The order of birth rather than parental favoritism governed succession, though the rule was sometimes set aside with divine approval (cf., e.g., Jacob or Solomon).

21:17 *double portion.* In Israel the oldest son enjoyed a double share of the inheritance. Parallels to this practice come from

beginning of his strength; [c]the right of the firstborn *is* his.

18 ¶ If a man have a stubborn and rebellious son, which will not obey the voice of his father, or the voice of his mother, and *that,* when they have chastened him, will not hearken unto them:

19 Then shall his father and his mother lay hold on him, and bring him out unto the elders of his city, and unto the gate of his place;

20 And they shall say unto the elders of his city, This our son *is* stubborn and rebellious, he will not obey our voice; *he is* a glutton, and a drunkard.

21 And all the men of his city shall stone him with stones, that he die: [a]so shalt thou put evil away from among you; [b]and all Israel shall hear, and fear.

Miscellaneous laws

22 ¶ And if a man have committed a sin [a]worthy of death, and he be *to be* put to death, and thou hang him on a tree:

23 [a]His body shall not remain all night upon the tree, but thou shalt in any wise bury him that day; (for [b]he that is hanged *is* [c][1]accursed of God;) that [d]thy land be not defiled, which the LORD thy God giveth thee *for* an inheritance.

22 Thou [a]shalt not see thy brother's ox or his sheep go astray, and hide thyself from them: thou shalt in any case bring them again unto thy brother.

2 And if thy brother *be* not nigh unto thee, or *if* thou know him not, then thou shalt bring it unto thine own house, and it shall be with thee until thy brother seek after it, and thou shalt restore it to him again.

3 In like manner shalt thou do with his ass; and so shalt thou do with his raiment; and with all lost *thing* of thy brother's, which he hath lost, and thou hast found, shalt thou do likewise: thou mayest not hide thyself.

4 [a]Thou shalt not see thy brother's ass or his ox fall down by the way, and hide thyself from them: thou shalt surely help him to lift *them* up again.

5 ¶ The woman shall not wear that which pertaineth unto a man, neither shall a man put on a woman's garment: for all that do so *are* abomination unto the LORD thy God.

6 If a bird's nest chance to be before thee in the way in any tree, or on the ground, *whether they be* young ones, or eggs, and the dam sitting upon the young, or upon the eggs, [a]thou shalt not take the dam with the young:

7 *But* thou shalt in any wise let the dam go, and take the young to thee; [a]that it may be well with thee, and *that* thou mayest prolong *thy* days.

8 When thou buildest a new house, then thou shalt make a battlement for thy roof, that thou bring not blood upon thine house, if any man fall from thence.

9 [a]Thou shalt not sow thy vineyard with divers seeds: lest the [1]fruit of *thy* seed which thou hast sown, and the fruit of thy vineyard, be defiled.

10 [a]Thou shalt not plow with an ox and an ass together.

11 [a]Thou shalt not wear a garment of divers sorts, *as* of woollen and linen together.

12 Thou shalt make thee [a]fringes upon the four [1]quarters of thy vesture, wherewith thou coverest *thyself.*

Laws about sexual conduct

13 ¶ If any man take a wife, and go in unto her, and hate her,

14 And give occasions of speech against her, and bring up an evil name upon her, and say, I took this woman, and when I came to her, I found her not a maid:

15 Then shall the father of the damsel, and her mother, take and bring forth *the tokens of* the damsel's virginity unto the elders of the city in the gate:

16 And the damsel's father shall say unto the elders, I gave my daughter unto this man to wife, and he hateth her;

17 And lo, he hath given occasions of speech *against her,* saying, I found not thy daughter a maid; and *yet* these *are the tokens of* my daughter's virginity. And they shall spread the cloth before the elders of the city.

18 And the elders of that city shall take *that* man and chastise him;

19 And they shall amerce him in an hundred *shekels* of silver, and give *them* unto the

21:17 [c]Gen. 25:31,33 **21:21** [a]ch. 13:5; 19:19,20; 22:21,24 [b]ch. 13:11 **21:22** [a]ch. 19:6; 22:26; Acts 23:29; 25:11,25; 26:31 **21:23** [1]Heb. *the curse of God* [a]Josh. 8:29; 10:26,27; John 19:31 [b]Gal. 3:13 [c]Num. 25:4; 2 Sam. 21:6 [d]Lev. 18:25; Num. 35:34 **22:1** [a]Ex. 23:4 **22:4** [a]Ex. 23:5

22:6 [a]Lev. 22:28 **22:7** [a]ch. 4:40 **22:9** [1]Heb. *fulness of the seed* [a]Lev. 19:19 **22:10** [a]See 2 Cor. 6:14-16 **22:11** [a]Lev. 19:19 **22:12** [1]Heb. *wings* [a]Num. 15:38

Nuzi, Larsa in the Old Babylonian period, and Assyria in the Middle Assyrian period (see chart, p. xix). Receiving a double portion of an estate was also tantamount to succession. Thus Elisha succeeded Elijah (2 Ki 2:9). *beginning of his strength.* The first result of a man's procreative ability.

21:18 *stubborn and rebellious . . . will not obey.* In wicked defiance of the fifth commandment (see 5:16; Ex 20:12 and note).

21:21 *stone him with stones.* See 5:16; 27:16; Ex 21:15,17. *so shalt thou put evil away from among you.* See note on 13:5.

21:22 *put to death . . . on a tree.* The offender was first executed, then "hung on a tree" (see Gen 40:19), or, as the Hebrew for this phrase doubtless intends, "impaled on a pole" (see note on Esth 2:23).

21:23 *not remain all night upon the tree.* Prolonged exposure gives undue attention to the crime and the criminal. *accursed of God.* God had condemned murder, and hanging on a tree symbolized divine judgment and rejection. Christ accepted the full punishment of our sins, thus becoming "a curse for us" (Gal 3:13).

22:1 *not see . . . and hide thyself from them.* See vv. 3–4. The Biblical legislation was intended not only to punish criminal behavior but also to express concern for people and their possessions. See chart, p. 256.

22:5 Probably intended to prohibit such perversions as transvestism and homosexuality, especially under religious auspices. The God-created differences between men and women are not to be disregarded (see Lev 18:22; 20:13).

‡22:14 *found her not a maid.* I.e., virgin. Find a blood-stained cloth or garment (see vv. 15,17,20).

22:15 *elders . . . in the gate.* See 25:7; see also notes on Gen 19:1; Ruth 4:1.

22:19 *hundred shekels of silver.* A heavy fine—several times

father of the damsel, because he hath brought
up an evil name upon a virgin of Israel: and
she shall be his wife; he may not put her away
all his days.
20 But if this thing be true, *and the tokens
of* virginity be not found for the damsel:
21 Then they shall bring out the damsel to
the door of her father's house, and the men of
her city shall stone her with stones that she
die: because she hath [a]wrought folly in Israel,
to play the whore *in* her father's house: [b]so
shalt thou put evil away from among you.
22 ¶ [a]If a man be found lying with a
woman married to a husband, then they shall
both of them die, *both* the man that lay with
the woman, and the woman: so shalt thou put
away evil from Israel.
23 If a damsel *that is* a virgin be [a]betrothed
unto a husband, and a man find her in the city,
and lie with her;
24 Then ye shall bring them both out unto
the gate of that city, and ye shall stone them
with stones that they die; the damsel, because
she cried not, *being* in the city; and the man,
because he hath [a]humbled his neighbour's wife:
[b]so thou shalt put away evil from among you.
25 But if a man find a betrothed damsel in
the field, and the man [a][1]force her, and lie with
her: then the man only that lay with her shall
die:
26 But unto the damsel thou shalt do nothing; *there is* in the damsel no sin *worthy* of
death: for as when a man riseth against his
neighbour, and slayeth him, even so *is* this
matter:
27 For he found her in the field, *and* the
betrothed damsel cried, and *there was* none to
save her.
28 [a]If a man find a damsel *that is* a virgin,
which is not betrothed, and lay hold on her,
and lie with her, and they be found;
29 Then the man that lay with her shall

22:21 [a]Gen. 34:7; Judg. 20:6,10; 2 Sam. 13:12,13 [b]ch. 13:5
22:22 [a]Lev. 20:10; John 8:5; Num. 5:22-27
22:23 [a]Mat. 1:18,19
22:24 [a]ch. 21:14 [b]ver. 21,22; 1 Cor. 5:2,13
22:25 [1]Or, *take strong hold of her* [a]2 Sam. 13:14
22:28 [a]Ex. 22:16,17

what Hosea paid to buy Gomer back (Hos 3:2) or what Jeremiah paid for the field at Anathoth (Jer 32:9). It may have been about twice the average bride-price (see note on v. 29). The high fine, in addition to the no-divorce rule, was intended to restrain not only a husband's charges against his wife but also easy divorce.

22:21,24 *so shalt thou put evil away from among you.* See v. 22; see also note on 13:5.
22:22 See Lev 20:10.
22:29 *fifty shekels of silver.* Probably equaled the average bride-price, which must have varied with the economic status of the participants (see note on Ex 22:16).

Major Social Concerns in the Covenant

1. Personhood
Everyone's person is to be secure (Ex 20:13; Deut 5:17; Ex 21:16-21,26-31; Lev 19:14; Deut 24:7; 27:18).

2. False Accusation
Everyone is to be secure against slander and false accusation (Ex 20:16; Deut 5:20; Ex 23:1-3; Lev 19:16; Deut 19:15-21).

3. Woman
No woman is to be taken advantage of within her subordinate status in society (Ex 21:7-11,20,26-32; 22:16-17; Deut 21:10-14; 22:13-30; 24:1-5).

4. Punishment
Punishment for wrongdoing shall not be excessive so that the culprit is dehumanized (Deut 25:1-5).

5. Dignity
Every Israelite's dignity and right to be God's freedman and servant are to be honored and safeguarded (Ex 21:2,5-6; Lev 25; Deut 15:12-18).

6. Inheritance
Every Israelite's inheritance in the promised land is to be secure (Lev 25; Num 27:5-7; 36:1-9; Deut 25:5-10).

7. Property
Everyone's property is to be secure (Ex 20:15; Deut 5:19; Ex 21:33-36; 22:1-15; 23:4-5; Lev 19:35-36; Deut 22:1-4; 25:13-15).

8. Fruit of Labor
Everyone is to receive the fruit of his labors (Lev 19:13; Deut 24:14; 25:4).

9. Fruit of the Ground
Everyone is to share the fruit of the ground (Ex 23:10-11; Lev 19:9-10; 23:22; 25:3-55; Deut 14:28-29; 24:19-21).

10. Rest on Sabbath
Everyone, down to the humblest servant and the resident alien, is to share in the weekly rest of God's sabbath (Ex 20:8-11; Deut 5:12-15; Ex 23:12).

11. Marriage
The marriage relationship is to be kept inviolate (Ex 20:14; Deut 5:18; see also Lev 18:6-23; 20:10-21; Deut 22:13-30).

12. Exploitation
No one, however disabled, impoverished or powerless, is to be oppressed or exploited (Ex 22:21-27; Lev 19:14,33-34; 25:35-36; Deut 23:19; 24:6,12-15,17; 27:18).

13. Fair Trial
Everyone is to have free access to the courts and is to be afforded a fair trial (Ex 23:6,8; Lev 19:15; Deut 1:17; 10:17-18; 16:18-20; 17:8-13; 19:15-21).

14. Social Order
Every person's God-given place in the social order is to be honored (Ex 20:12; Deut 5:16; Ex 21:15,17; 22:28; Lev 19:3,32; 20:9; Deut 17:8-13; 21:15-21; 27:16).

15. Law
No one shall be above the law, not even the king (Deut 17:18-20).

16. Animals
Concern for the welfare of other creatures is to be extended to the animal world (Ex 23:5,11; Lev 25:7; Deut 22:4,6-7; 25:4).

give unto the damsel's father fifty *shekels* of silver, and she shall be his wife; [a]because he hath humbled her, he may not put her away all his days.

30 ¶ [a]A man shall not take his father's wife, nor [b]discover his father's skirt.

Persons to be excluded

23 He that is wounded in the stones, or hath *his* privy member cut off, shall not enter into the congregation of the LORD.

2 A bastard shall not enter into the congregation of the LORD; even *to* his tenth generation shall he not enter into the congregation of the LORD.

3 [a]An Ammonite or Moabite shall not enter into the congregation of the LORD; even *to* their tenth generation shall they not enter into the congregation of the LORD for ever:

4 [a]Because they met you not with bread and with water in the way, when ye came forth out of Egypt; and [b]because they hired against thee Balaam the son of Beor of Pethor of Mesopotamia, to curse thee.

5 Nevertheless the LORD thy God would not hearken unto Balaam; but the LORD thy God turned the curse into a blessing unto thee, because the LORD thy God loved thee.

6 [a]Thou shalt not seek their peace nor their [1]prosperity all thy days for ever.

7 Thou shalt not abhor an Edomite; [a]for he *is* thy brother: thou shalt not abhor an Egyptian; because [b]thou wast a stranger in his land.

8 The children that are begotten of them shall enter into the congregation of the LORD *in* their third generation.

Camp sanitation in wartime

9 ¶ When the host goeth forth against thine enemies, then keep thee from every wicked thing.

10 [a]If there be among you any man, that is not clean by reason of *uncleanness* that chanceth him by night, then shall he go abroad out of the camp, he shall not come within the camp:

11 But it shall be, when evening [1]cometh on, [a]he shall wash *himself* with water: and when the sun is down, he shall come into the camp *again.*

22:29 [a]ver. 24
22:30 [a]Lev. 18:8; 20:11; ch. 27:20; 1 Cor. 5:1 [b]See Ruth 3:9; Ezek. 16:8
23:3 [a]Neh. 13:1,2
23:4 [a]See ch. 2:29 [b]Num. 22:5,6
23:6 [1]Heb. *good* [a]Ezra 9:12
23:7 [a]Gen. 25:24-26; Obad. 10,12 [b]Ex. 22:21; 23:9; Lev. 19:34; ch. 10:19
23:10 [a]Lev. 15:16
23:11 [1]Heb. *turneth toward* [a]Lev. 15:5
23:13 [1]Heb. *sittest down*
23:14 [1]Heb. *nakedness of* any *thing* [a]Lev. 26:12
23:15 [a]1 Sam. 30:15
23:16 [1]Heb. is *good for him* [a]Ex. 22:21
23:17 [1]Or, *sodomitess* [a]Lev. 19:29; See Prov. 2:16 [b]Gen. 19:5; 2 Ki. 23:7
23:19 [a]Ex. 22:25; Lev. 25:36,37
23:20 [a]See Lev. 19:34; ch. 15:3 [b]ch. 15:10
23:21 [a]Num. 30:2; Eccl. 5:4,5
23:23 [a]Num. 30:2; Ps. 66:13,14

12 Thou shalt have a place also without the camp, whither thou shalt go forth abroad:

13 And thou shalt have a paddle upon thy weapon; and it shall be, when thou [1]wilt ease thyself abroad, thou shalt dig therewith, and shalt turn back and cover that which cometh from thee:

14 For the LORD thy God [a]walketh in the midst of thy camp, to deliver thee, and to give up thine enemies before thee; therefore shall thy camp be holy: that he see no [1]unclean thing in thee, and turn away from thee.

Various laws

15 ¶ [a]Thou shalt not deliver unto his master the servant which is escaped from his master unto thee:

16 He shall dwell with thee, *even* among you, in *that* place which he shall choose in one of thy gates, where it [1]liketh him best: [a]thou shalt not oppress him.

17 There shall be no [1]whore [a]of the daughters of Israel, nor [b]a sodomite of the sons of Israel.

18 Thou shalt not bring the hire of a whore, or the price of a dog, *into* the house of the LORD thy God for any vow: for even both these *are* abomination unto the LORD thy God.

19 [a]Thou shalt not lend upon usury to thy brother; usury of money, usury of victuals, usury of any thing that is lent upon usury:

20 [a]Unto a stranger thou mayest lend upon usury; but unto thy brother thou shalt not lend upon usury: [b]that the LORD thy God may bless thee in all that thou settest thine hand to in the land whither thou goest to possess it.

21 [a]When thou shalt vow a vow unto the LORD thy God, thou shalt not slack to pay it: for the LORD thy God will surely require it of thee; and it would be sin in thee.

22 But if thou shalt forbear to vow, it shall be no sin in thee.

23 [a]That which is gone out of thy lips thou shalt keep and perform; *even* a freewill offering, according as thou hast vowed unto the LORD thy God, which thou hast promised with thy mouth.

24 When thou comest into thy neighbour's vineyard, then thou mayest eat grapes thy fill

22:30 *his father's wife.* Refers to a wife other than his mother (see 27:20). *discover his father's skirt.* See notes on Ruth 3:9; Ezek 16:8.

23:1 For blessings on eunuchs in later times see Is 56:4–5; Acts 8:26–39.

23:2–3 *even to his tenth generation.* Perhaps forever, since ten is symbolic of completeness or finality. In v. 6 the equivalent expression is "all thy days for ever."

23:3 Ruth is an outstanding exception to Moabite exclusion from Israel (see Introduction to Ruth: Theme and Theology).

23:4 *Balaam the son of Beor.* See Num 22:4–24:25.

23:6 *shalt not seek their peace nor ... prosperity.* See the prophets' denunciation of Moab, Ammon and Edom (Is 15–16; Jer 48:1–49:6; Ezek 25:1–11; Amos 1:13–2:3; Zeph 2:8–11).

23:7 *Edomite ... thy brother.* Edom (Esau) is often condemned for his hostility against his brother Jacob (Israel; see Amos 1:11; Obad 10; see also notes on Gen 25:22,26).

23:9–14 Sanitary rules for Israel's military camps. For similar rules for the people in general see Lev 15.

23:15 *the servant which is escaped ... unto thee.* A foreign slave seeking freedom in Israel (see v. 16). Cf. 24:7.

23:17–18 See notes on Ex 34:15; Judg 2:17.

23:18 *dog.* A word often associated with moral or spiritual impurity (cf. Mat 7:6; 15:26; Phil 3:2). Here it probably refers to a male prostitute.

‡23:19 *usury* [i.e. interest]. See notes on Ex 22:25–27; Lev 25:36.

‡23:20 *a stranger ... lend* [i.e. charge]. A foreign businessman would come into Israel for financial advantage and so would be subject to paying interest.

23:21–23 See notes on Num 30; see also Eccl 5:4–6.

at thine own pleasure; but thou shalt not put *any* in thy vessel.

25 When thou comest into the standing corn of thy neighbour's, [a]then thou mayest pluck the ears with thine hand; but thou shalt not move a sickle unto thy neighbour's standing corn.

24 When a [a]man hath taken a wife, and married her, and it come to pass that she find no favour in his eyes, because he hath found [1]some uncleanness in her: then let him write her a bill of [2]divorcement, and give *it* in her hand, and send her out of his house.

2 And when she is departed out of his house, she may go and be another man's *wife.*

3 And *if* the latter husband hate her, and write her a bill of divorcement, and giveth *it* in her hand, and sendeth her out of his house; or if the latter husband die, which took her *to be* his wife;

4 [a]Her former husband, which sent her away, may not take her again to be his wife, after that she is defiled; for that *is* abomination before the LORD: and thou shalt not cause the land to sin, which the LORD thy God giveth thee *for* an inheritance.

5 [a]When a man hath taken a new wife, he shall not go out to war, [1]neither shall he be charged with any business: *but* he shall be free at home one year, and shall [b]cheer up his wife which he hath taken.

6 ¶ No *man* shall take the nether or the upper millstone to pledge: for he taketh *a man's* life to pledge.

7 [a]If a man be found stealing any of his brethren of the children of Israel, and maketh merchandise of him, or selleth him; then that thief shall die; [b]and thou shalt put evil away from among you.

8 Take heed in [a]the plague of leprosy, that *thou* observe diligently, and do according to all that the priests the Levites shall teach you: as I commanded them, *so* ye shall observe to do.

9 [a]Remember what the LORD thy God did [b]unto Miriam by the way, after that ye were come forth out of Egypt.

10 When thou dost [1]lend thy brother any thing, thou shalt not go into his house to fetch his pledge.

11 Thou shalt stand abroad, and the man to whom thou dost lend shall bring out the pledge abroad unto thee.

12 And if the man *be* poor, thou shalt not sleep with his pledge:

13 [a]In any case thou shalt deliver him the pledge again when the sun goeth down, that he may sleep in his own raiment, and [b]bless thee: and [c]it shall be righteousness unto thee before the LORD thy God.

14 Thou shalt not [a]oppress a hired servant *that is* poor and needy, *whether he be* of thy brethren, or of thy strangers that *are* in thy land within thy gates:

15 At his day [a]thou shalt give *him* his hire, neither shall the sun go down upon it; for he *is* poor, and [1]setteth his heart upon it: [b]lest he cry against thee unto the LORD, and it be sin unto thee.

16 [a]The fathers shall not be put to death for the children, neither shall the children be put to death for the fathers: every man shall be put to death for his own sin.

17 [a]Thou shalt not pervert the judgment of the stranger, *nor* of the fatherless; [b]nor take a widow's raiment to pledge:

18 But [a]thou shalt remember that thou wast a bondman in Egypt, and the LORD thy God redeemed thee thence: therefore I command thee to do this thing.

19 [a]When thou cuttest down thine harvest in thy field, and hast forgot a sheaf in the field, thou shalt not go again to fetch it: it shall be for the stranger, for the fatherless, and for the widow: that the LORD thy God may [b]bless thee in all the work of thine hands.

20 When thou beatest thine olive tree, [1]thou shalt not go over the boughs again: it shall be for the stranger, for the fatherless, and for the widow.

21 When thou gatherest the grapes of thy vineyard, thou shalt not glean *it* [1]afterward: it shall be for the stranger, for the fatherless, and for the widow.

22 And [a]thou shalt remember that thou wast a bondman in the land of Egypt: therefore I command thee to do this thing.

25 If there be a [a]controversy between men, and they come unto judgment, that *the judges* may judge them; then they [b]shall justify the righteous, and condemn the wicked.

2 And it shall be, if the wicked *man be* [a]worthy to be beaten, that the judge shall cause him to lie down, [b]and to be beaten before his face, according to his fault, by a *certain* number.

3 [a]Forty stripes he may give him, *and* not exceed: lest, *if* he should exceed, and beat him above these *with* many stripes, then thy brother should [b]seem vile unto thee.

23:25 [a]Mat. 12:1; Mark 2:23; Luke 6:1
24:1 [1]Heb. *matter of nakedness* [2]Heb. *cutting off* [a]Mat. 5:31; 19:7; Mark 10:4
24:4 [a]Jer. 3:1
24:5 [1]Heb. *not any thing shall pass upon him* [a]ch. 20:7 [b]Prov. 5:18
24:7 [a]Ex. 21:16 [b]ch. 19:19
24:8 [a]Lev. 13:2; 14:2
24:9 [a]See Luke 17:32; 1 Cor. 10:6 [b]Num. 12:10
24:10 [1]Heb. *lend the loan of any thing to, etc.*
24:13 [a]Ex. 22:26

24:13 [b]Job 29:11; 2 Cor. 9:13; 2 Tim. 1:18 [c]Dan. 4:27
24:14 [a]Mal. 3:5
24:15 [1]Heb. *he lifteth his soul unto it* [a]Lev. 19:13; Jer. 22:13; Jas. 5:4 [b]Jas. 5:4
24:16 [a]Jer. 31:29; Ezek. 18:20
24:17 [a]Prov. 22:22; Jer. 5:28; Ezek. 22:29; Zech. 7:10 [b]Ex. 22:26
24:18 [a]ver. 22; ch. 16:12
24:19 [a]Lev. 19:9; 23:22 [b]Ps. 41:1; Prov. 19:17
24:20 [1]Heb. *thou shalt not bough it after thee*
24:21 [1]Heb. *after thee*
24:22 [a]ver. 18
25:1 [a]ch. 19:17; Ezek. 44:24 [b]See Prov. 17:15
25:2 [a]Luke 12:48 [b]Mat. 10:17
25:3 [a]2 Cor. 11:24 [b]Job 18:3

24:1–4 In the books of Moses divorce was permitted and regulated (see Lev 21:7,14; 22:13; Num 30:9). Jesus conditioned the law of 24:1 in the Sermon on the Mount (Mat 5:31–32) and cited the higher law of creation (Mat 19:3–9).

24:5 *cheer up.* Marital bliss was held in high regard.

24:6 *millstone.* Used for grinding grain for flour and daily food (see note on Judg 9:53).

24:7 *thou shalt put evil away from among you.* See note on 13:5.

24:8 *leprosy.* See note on Lev 13:2.

24:9 *Remember.* See vv. 18, 22; see also note on 4:10.

24:10–13 See note on Ex 22:26–27.

24:16 *every man shall be put to death for his own sin.* See Ezek 18:4 and note.

24:17–18 When the Israelites were in trouble, the Lord helped them. Therefore they were not to take advantage of others in difficulty.

24:19–21 See note on Lev 19:9–10.

25:3 *Forty stripes . . . and not exceed.* Beating could subject the culprit to abuse, so the law kept the punishment from becoming inhumane. Cf. Paul's experience (2 Cor 11:24).

4 [a]Thou shalt not muzzle the ox when he [1]treadeth out *the corn.*

5 [a]If brethren dwell together, and one of them die, and have no child, the wife of the dead shall not marry without unto a stranger: her [b][1]husband's brother shall go in unto her, and take her to him to wife, and [2]perform the duty of a husband's brother unto her.

6 And it shall be, *that* the firstborn which she beareth [a]shall succeed in the name of his brother which is dead, that [b]his name be not put out of Israel.

7 And if the man like not to take his [1]brother's wife, then let his [2]brother's wife go up to the [a]gate unto the elders, and say, My husband's brother refuseth to raise up unto his brother a name in Israel, he will not perform the duty of my husband's brother.

8 Then the elders of his city shall call him, and speak unto him: and *if* he stand *to it,* and say, [a]I like not to take her;

9 Then shall his brother's wife come unto him in the presence of the elders, and [a]loose his shoe from off his foot, and spit in his face, and shall answer and say, So shall it be done unto *that* man that will not [b]build up his brother's house.

10 And his name shall be called in Israel, The house of him that hath his shoe loosed.

11 ¶ When men strive together one with another, and the wife of the one draweth near for to deliver her husband out of the hand of him that smiteth him, and putteth forth her hand, and taketh him by the secrets:

12 Then thou shalt cut off her hand, [a]thine eye shall not pity *her.*

13 [a]Thou shalt not have in thy bag [1]divers weights, a great and a small.

14 Thou shalt not have in thine house [1]divers measures, a great and a small.

15 *But* thou shalt have a perfect and just weight, a perfect and just measure shalt thou have: [a]that thy days may be lengthened in the land which the LORD thy God giveth thee.

16 For [a]all that do such *things, and* all that do unrighteously, *are* an abomination unto the LORD thy God.

17 ¶ [a]Remember what Amalek did unto thee by the way, when ye were come forth out of Egypt;

18 How he met thee by the way, and smote the hindmost of thee, *even* all that were feeble

25:4 [1]Heb. *thresheth* [a]Prov. 12:10; 1 Tim. 5:18
25:5 [1]Or, *next kinsman* [2]Or, *next kinsman* [a]Mat. 22:24; Luke 20:28 [b]Gen. 38:8; Ruth 1:12,13; 3:9
25:6 [a]Gen. 38:9 [b]Ruth 4:10
25:7 [1]Or, *next kinsman's wife* [2]Or, *next kinsman's wife* [a]Ruth 4:1,2
25:8 [a]Ruth 4:6
25:9 [a]Ruth 4:7 [b]Ruth 4:11
25:12 [a]ch. 19:13
25:13 [1]Heb. *a stone and a stone* [a]Lev. 19:35,36; Prov. 11:1; Ezek. 45:10; Mic. 6:11
25:14 [1]Heb. *an ephah and an ephah*
25:15 [a]Ex. 20:12
25:16 [a]Prov. 11:1; 1 Thes. 4:6
25:17 [a]Ex. 17:8
25:18 [a]Ps. 36:1; Prov. 16:6; Rom. 3:18
25:19 [a]1 Sam. 15:3 [b]Ex. 17:14
26:2 [a]Ex. 23:19; 34:26; Num. 18:13; ch. 16:10; Prov. 3:9 [b]ch. 12:5
26:5 [a]Hos. 12:12 [b]Gen. 43:1,2; 45:7,11 [c]Gen. 46:1,6; Acts 7:15 [d]Gen. 46:27; ch. 10:22
26:6 [a]Ex. 1:11,14
26:7 [a]Ex. 2:23-25; 3:9; 4:31
26:8 [a]Ex. 12:37,51; 13:3,14,16; ch. 5:15 [b]ch. 4:34
26:9 [a]Ex. 3:8

behind thee, when thou *wast* faint and weary; and he [a]feared not God.

19 Therefore it shall be, [a]when the LORD thy God hath given thee rest from all thine enemies round about, in the land which the LORD thy God giveth thee *for* an inheritance to possess it, *that* thou shalt [b]blot out the remembrance of Amalek from under heaven; thou shalt not forget *it.*

Firstfruits and tithes

26 And it shall be, when thou art come in unto the land which the LORD thy God giveth thee *for* an inheritance, and possessest it, and dwellest therein;

2 [a]That thou shalt take of the first of all the fruit of the earth, which thou shalt bring of thy land that the LORD thy God giveth thee, and shalt put *it* in a basket, and shalt [b]go unto the place which the LORD thy God shall choose to place his name there.

3 And thou shalt go unto the priest that shall be in those days, and say unto him, I profess *this* day unto the LORD thy God, that I am come unto the country which the LORD sware unto our fathers for to give us.

4 And the priest shall take the basket out of thine hand, and set it down before the altar of the LORD thy God.

5 And thou shalt speak and say before the LORD thy God, [a]A Syrian [b]ready to perish *was* my father, and [c]he went down into Egypt, and sojourned there with a [d]few, and became there a nation, great, mighty, and populous:

6 And [a]the Egyptians evil entreated us, and afflicted us, and laid upon us hard bondage:

7 And [a]when we cried unto the LORD God of our fathers, the LORD heard our voice, and looked on our affliction, and our labour, and our oppression:

8 And [a]the LORD brought us forth out of Egypt with a mighty hand, and with an outstretched arm, and [b]with great terribleness, and with signs, and with wonders:

9 And he hath brought us into this place, and hath given us this land, *even* [a]a land that floweth with milk and honey.

10 And now, behold, I have brought the firstfruits of the land, which thou, O LORD, hast given me. And thou shalt set it before the LORD thy God, and worship before the LORD thy God:

---

‡25:4 Applied to ministers of Christ in 1 Cor 9:9–10; 1 Tim 5:17–18. *treadeth out the corn* [i.e. threshing]. See notes on Gen 50:10; Ruth 1:22.

25:5–6 The continuity of each family and the decentralized control of land through family ownership were basic to the Mosaic economy (see note on Gen 38:8).

25:7 *if the man like not to take his brother's wife.* See vv. 8–10; note the experiences, with some variations, described in Gen 38:8–10; Ruth 4:1–12. *to the gate unto the elders.* See 22:15; see also notes on Gen 19:1; Ruth 4:1.

25:11–12 Cf. Ex 21:22–25.

25:13–16 See note on Lev 19:35.

25:14 *measures.* Of quantity.

25:17 *Remember.* See note on 4:10. *Amalek.* See Ex 17:8–16; Num 14:45.

25:18 *feared not God.* See note on Gen 20:11.

25:19 *rest.* See note on 3:20.

26:1 *inheritance.* See note on Ex 32:13.

26:2 *first of all the fruit of the earth.* The offering described here occurred only once and must not be confused with the annual offerings of firstfruits (see 18:4 and note). *the place which the LORD . . . choose to place his name.* See note on 12:5.

‡26:5 *Syrian ready to perish* [i.e."wandering Aramean"]. A reference to Jacob, who had wandered from southern Canaan to Haran and back (Gen 27–35) and who later migrated to Egypt (see Gen 46:3–7). He also married two Aramean women (see

11 And [a]thou shalt rejoice in every good
thing which the LORD thy God hath given unto
thee, and unto thine house, thou, and the Levite, and the stranger that *is* among you.
12 ¶ When thou hast made an end of
tithing all the [a]tithes of thine increase the
third year, *which is* [b]the year of tithing, and
hast given *it* unto the Levite, the stranger, the
fatherless, and the widow, that they may eat
within thy gates, and be filled;
13 Then thou shalt say before the LORD thy
God, I have brought away the hallowed *things*
out of *mine* house, and also have given them
unto the Levite, and unto the stranger, to the
fatherless, and to the widow, according to all
thy commandments which thou hast commanded me: I have not transgressed thy commandments, [a]neither have I forgotten *them:*
14 [a]I have not eaten thereof in my mourning, neither have I taken away *ought* thereof
for *any* unclean *use,* nor given *ought* thereof
for the dead: *but* I have hearkened to the voice
of the LORD my God, *and* have done according
to all that thou hast commanded me.
15 [a]Look down from thy holy habitation,
from heaven, and bless thy people Israel, and
the land which thou hast given us, as thou
swarest unto our fathers, a land that floweth
with milk and honey.
16 This day the LORD thy God hath commanded thee to do these statutes and judgments: thou shalt therefore keep and do them
with all thine heart, and with all thy soul.
17 Thou hast [a]avouched the LORD *this* day
to be thy God, and to walk in his ways, and to
keep his statutes, and his commandments, and
his judgments, and to hearken unto his voice:
18 And [a]the LORD hath avouched thee *this*
day to be his peculiar people, as he hath promised thee, and that *thou* shouldest keep all his
commandments;
19 And to make thee [a]high above all nations which he hath made, in praise, and in
name, and in honour; and that thou mayest be
[b]a holy people unto the LORD thy God, as he
hath spoken.

The altar at mount Ebal

27 And Moses with the elders of Israel
commanded the people, saying, Keep
all the commandments which I command you
this day.
2 And it shall be on the day [a]when you
shall pass over Jordan unto the land which the
LORD thy God giveth thee, that [b]thou shalt set
thee up great stones, and plaister them with
plaister:
3 And thou shalt write upon them all the
words of this law, when thou art passed over,
that thou mayest go in unto the land which
the LORD thy God giveth thee, a land that
floweth with milk and honey; as the LORD God
of thy fathers hath promised thee.
4 Therefore it shall be when ye be gone
over Jordan, *that* ye shall set up these stones,
which I command you *this* day, [a]in mount
Ebal, and thou shalt plaister them with plaister.
5 And there shalt thou build an altar unto
the LORD thy God, an altar of stones: [a]thou
shalt not lift up *any* iron *tool* upon them.
6 Thou shalt build the altar of the LORD thy
God *of* whole stones: and thou shalt offer burnt
offerings thereon unto the LORD thy God:
7 And thou shalt offer peace offerings, and
shalt eat there, and rejoice before the LORD thy
God.
8 And thou shalt write upon the stones all
the words of this law very plainly.
9 ¶ And Moses and the priests the Levites
spake unto all Israel, saying, Take heed, and
hearken, O Israel; [a]this day thou art become
the people of the LORD thy God.
10 Thou shalt therefore obey the voice of
the LORD thy God, and do his commandments
and his statutes, which I command thee *this*
day.
11 ¶ And Moses charged the people the
same day, saying,
12 These shall stand [a]upon mount Gerizzim to bless the people, when ye are come
over Jordan; Simeon, and Levi, and Judah, and
Issachar, and Joseph, and Benjamin:
13 And [a]these shall stand upon mount Ebal
[1]to curse; Reuben, Gad, and Asher, and Zebulun, Dan, and Naphtali.
14 And [a]the Levites shall speak, and say
unto all the men of Israel *with* a loud voice,
15 [a]Cursed *be* the man that maketh *any*
graven or molten image, an abomination unto
the LORD, the work of the hands of the crafts-

26:11 [a]ch. 12:7,12,18; 16:11
26:12 [a]Lev. 27:30; Num. 18:24 [b]ch. 14:28,29
26:13 [a]Ps. 119:141, 153,176
26:14 [a]Lev. 7:20; 21:1,11; Hos. 9:4
26:15 [a]Is. 63:15; Zech. 2:13
26:17 [a]Ex. 20:19
26:18 [a]Ex. 6:7; 19:5; ch. 7:6; 14:2; 28:9
26:19 [a]ch. 4:7,8; 28:1 [b]Ex. 19:6; ch. 7:6; 28:9; 1 Pet. 2:9
27:2 [a]Josh. 4:1 [b]Josh. 8:32
27:4 [a]ch. 11:29; Josh. 8:30,31
27:5 [a]Ex. 20:25; Josh. 8:31
27:9 [a]ch. 26:18
27:12 [a]ch. 11:29; Josh. 8:33; Judg. 9:7
27:13 [1]Heb. *for a cursing* [a]ch. 11:29; Josh. 8:33
27:14 [a]ch. 33:10; Josh. 8:33; Dan. 9:11
27:15 [a]Ex. 20:4,23; 34:17; Lev. 19:4; 26:1; ch. 4:16,23; 5:8; Is. 44:9; Hos. 13:2

Gen 28:5; 29:16,28). *few . . . a. nation . . . populous.* See Ex 1:5; 1:7 and note.
26:11 *rejoice.* See note on 12:12.
26:12 See note on 14:22–29.
26:16 *with all thine heart . . . soul.* See note on 4:29.
26:17 The terminology is that of a covenant or treaty, involving a renewal of Israel's vow that the Lord was God and that they would obey Him (see note on Ex 19:8).
26:18 *peculiar people.* See note on Ex 19:5.
27:2–8 Setting up stones inscribed with messages to be remembered was a common practice in the ancient Near East.
‡27:2,4 *plaister them with plaister.* Probably a whitewashing with lime so that the writing inscribed on them would stand out clearly (see v. 8).
27:3,8 *all the words of this law.* The stipulations (see note on Ex 20:1) of the covenant that Moses' reaffirmation contained.
27:5 *build . . . an altar of stones.* Different from the altars of the tabernacle, both in form and in use (see note on Ex 20:25).
27:9 *thou art become the people of the LORD.* The language of covenant renewal.
27:12 *These shall stand upon mount Gerizzim.* All six were descendants of Jacob by Leah and Rachel (see Gen 35:23–24). See 11:30 and note. *to bless.* No blessings appear in vv. 15–26, which consist entirely of 12 curses (see 28:15–68). Blessings, however, are listed and described in 28:1–14.
27:13 *these shall stand upon mount Ebal.* Reuben and Zebulun were descendants of Jacob by Leah; the rest were his descendants by the handmaids Zilpah and Bilhah (see Gen 35:23, 25–26).
27:15 *maketh any graven or molten image.* In violation of the

man, and putteth *it* in *a* secret *place.* [b]And all
the people shall answer and say, Amen.
16 [a]Cursed *be* he that setteth light by his
father or his mother. And all the people shall
say, Amen.
17 [a]Cursed *be* he that removeth his neighbour's landmark. And all the people shall say,
Amen.
18 [a]Cursed *be* he that maketh the blind to
wander out of the way. And all the people shall
say, Amen.
19 [a]Cursed *be* he that perverteth the judgment of the stranger, fatherless, and widow.
And all the people shall say, Amen.
20 [a]Cursed *be* he that lieth with his father's wife; because he uncovereth his father's
skirt. And all the people shall say, Amen.
21 [a]Cursed *be* he that lieth with any *manner of* beast. And all the people shall say,
Amen.
22 [a]Cursed *be* he that lieth with his sister,
the daughter of his father, or the daughter of
his mother. And all the people shall say, Amen.
23 [a]Cursed *be* he that lieth with his mother in law. And all the people shall say, Amen.
24 [a]Cursed *be* he that smiteth his neighbour secretly. And all the people shall say,
Amen.
25 [a]Cursed *be* he that taketh reward to
slay an innocent person. And all the people
shall say, Amen.
26 [a]Cursed *be* he that confirmeth not *all*
the words of this law to do them. And all the
people shall say, Amen.

The blessings of obedience

28 And it shall come to pass, [a]if thou
shalt hearken diligently unto the
voice of the LORD thy God, to observe *and* to
do all his commandments which I command
thee *this* day, that the LORD thy God [b]will set
thee on high above all nations of the earth:
2 And all these blessings shall come on
thee, and [a]overtake thee, if thou shalt hearken
unto the voice of the LORD thy God.
3 [a]Blessed *shalt* thou *be* in the city, and
blessed *shalt* thou *be* [b]in the field.
4 Blessed *shall be* [a]the fruit of thy body,
and the fruit of thy ground, and the fruit of thy
cattle, the increase of thy kine, and the flocks
of thy sheep.
5 Blessed *shall be* thy basket and thy
[1]store.
6 [a]Blessed *shalt* thou *be* when thou comest
in, and blessed *shalt* thou *be* when thou goest
out.
7 The LORD [a]shall cause thine enemies that
rise up against thee *to be* smitten before thy
face: they shall come out against thee one way,
and flee before thee seven ways.
8 The LORD shall [a]command the blessing
upon thee in thy [1]storehouses, and in all that
thou [b]settest thine hand unto; and he shall
bless thee in the land which the LORD thy God
giveth thee.
9 [a]The LORD shall establish thee a holy people unto himself, as he hath sworn unto thee,
if thou shalt keep the commandments of the
LORD thy God, and walk in his ways.
10 And all people of the earth shall see that
thou art [a]called by the name of the LORD; and
they shall be [b]afraid of thee.
11 And [a]the LORD shall make thee plenteous [1]in goods, in the fruit of thy [2]body, and
in the fruit of thy cattle, and in the fruit of thy
ground, in the land which the LORD sware
unto thy fathers to give thee.
12 The LORD shall open unto thee his good
treasure, the heaven [a]to give the rain unto thy
land in his season, and [b]to bless all the work of
thine hand: and [c]thou shalt lend unto many
nations, and thou shalt not borrow.
13 And the LORD shall make thee [a]the
head, and not the tail; and thou shalt be above
only, and thou shalt not be beneath; if that
thou hearken unto the commandments of the
LORD thy God, which I command thee *this* day,
to observe and to do *them:*
14 [a]And thou shalt not go aside from any of
the words which I command thee *this* day, *to*
the right hand, or *to* the left, to go after other
gods to serve them.

The curses of disobedience

15 ¶ But it shall come to pass, [a]if thou wilt
not hearken unto the voice of the LORD thy
God, to observe to do all his commandments
and his statutes which I command thee *this*
day; that all these curses shall come upon
thee, and overtake thee:
16 Cursed *shalt* thou *be* in the city, and
cursed *shalt* thou *be* in the field.

27:15 [b]See Num. 5:22; Jer. 11:5; 1 Cor. 14:16
27:16 [a]Ex. 20:12; 21:17; Lev. 19:3; ch. 21:18
27:17 [a]ch. 19:14; Prov. 22:28
27:18 [a]Lev. 19:14
27:19 [a]Ex. 22:21,22; ch. 10:18; 24:17; Mal. 3:5
27:20 [a]Lev. 18:8; ch. 22:30
27:21 [a]Lev. 18:23
27:22 [a]Lev. 18:9
27:23 [a]Lev. 18:17
27:24 [a]Ex. 20:13; Lev. 24:17; Num. 35:31
27:25 [a]Ex. 23:7,8; ch. 10:17; Ezek. 22:12
27:26 [a]Jer. 11:3; Gal. 3:10
28:1 [a]Ex. 15:26; Lev. 26:3; Is. 55:2 [b]ch. 26:19
28:2 [a]Zech. 1:6
28:3 [a]Ps. 128:1,4 [b]Gen. 39:5
28:4 [a]Gen. 22:17; 49:25; ch. 7:13; Prov. 10:22
28:5 [1]Or, *dough,* or, *kneading-trough*
28:6 [a]Ps. 121:8
28:7 [a]Lev. 26:7,8; 2 Sam. 22:38,39,41
28:8 [1]Or, *barns* [a]Lev. 25:21 [b]ch. 15:10
28:9 [a]Ex. 19:5,6; ch. 7:6; 26:18,19
28:10 [a]Num. 6:27; 2 Chr. 7:14; Is. 63:19; Dan. 9:18,19 [b]ch. 11:25
28:11 [1]Or, *for good* [2]Heb. *belly* [a]ch. 30:9; Prov. 10:22
28:12 [a]Lev. 26:4; ch. 11:14 [b]ch. 14:29 [c]ch. 15:6
28:13 [a]Is. 9:14,15
28:14 [a]ch. 5:32
28:15 [a]Lev. 26:14; Lam. 2:17; Dan. 9:11; Mal. 2:2

first and second commandments of the Decalogue (see note on Ex 20:1). See 4:28; 5:6–10; 31:29; Is 40:19–20; 41:7; 44:9–20; 45:16; Jer 10:3–9; Hos 8:4–6; 13:2. *Amen.* Not simply approval but a solemn, formal assertion that the people accept and agree to the covenant and its curses and blessings (see vv. 16–26).

27:16 See 5:16; Ex 20:12 and note.

27:17 See note on 19:14.

27:19 See 24:17–18 and note.

27:20 Cf. 22:30; see Lev 18:8.

27:21 See Ex 22:19 and note; Lev 18:23; 20:15–16.

27:22 See Lev 18:9.

27:23 See Lev 18:8.

27:24–25 See 5:17; Ex 20:13; 21:12; Lev 24:17,21.

27:26 Quoted in Gal 3:10 to prove that mankind is under a curse because no one follows the law of God fully. *to do them.* It is not enough to assert allegiance to the law; one must live according to its stipulations.

28:1–14 These blessings are the opposites of the curses in vv. 15–44 (compare especially vv. 3–6 with vv. 16–19).

‡28:5,17 *basket . . . store* [i.e. kneading bowl]. Used at home for storage and for the preparation of foods, particularly bread.

28:7 For the reverse see v. 25.

‡28:12 *treasure, the heaven.* For the heavens as the treasure or storehouse of rain, snow, hail and wind see Job 38:22; Ps 135:7; Jer 10:13; 51:16. *thou shalt lend.* For the opposite see v. 44; see also note on 15:6.

28:13 *the head, and not the tail.* For the reverse see v. 44.

17 Cursed *shall be* thy basket and thy store.

18 Cursed *shall be* the fruit of thy body, and the fruit of thy land, the increase of thy kine, and the flocks of thy sheep.

19 Cursed *shalt* thou *be* when thou comest in, and cursed *shalt* thou *be* when thou goest out.

20 The LORD shall send upon thee [a]cursing, [b]vexation, and [c]rebuke, in all that thou settest thine hand unto [1]for to do, until thou be destroyed, and until thou perish quickly; because of the wickedness of thy doings, where*by* thou hast forsaken me.

21 The LORD shall make [a]the pestilence cleave unto thee, until he have consumed thee from off the land, whither thou goest to possess it.

22 [a]The LORD shall smite thee with a consumption, and with a fever, and with an inflammation, and with an extreme burning, and with the [1]sword, and with [b]blasting, and with mildew; and they shall pursue thee until thou perish.

23 And [a]thy heaven that *is* over thy head shall be brass, and the earth that *is* under thee *shall be* iron.

24 The LORD shall make the rain of thy land powder and dust: from heaven shall it come down upon thee, until thou be destroyed.

25 [a]The LORD shall cause thee *to be* smitten before thine enemies: thou shalt go out one way against them, and flee seven ways before them: and [b]shalt be [1]removed into all the kingdoms of the earth.

26 And [a]thy carcase shall be meat unto all fowls of the air, and unto the beasts of the earth, and no man shall fray *them* away.

27 The LORD will smite thee with [a]the botch of Egypt, and with [b]the emerods, and with the scab, and with the itch, where*of* thou canst not be healed.

28 The LORD shall smite thee with madness, and blindness, and [a]astonishment of heart:

29 And thou shalt [a]grope at noondays, as the blind gropeth in darkness, and thou shalt not prosper in thy ways: and thou shalt be only oppressed and spoiled evermore, and no man shall save *thee.*

30 [a]Thou shalt betroth a wife, and another man shall lie with her: [b]thou shalt build a house, and thou shalt not dwell therein: [c]thou shalt plant a vineyard, and shalt not [1]gather the grapes thereof.

31 Thine ox *shall be* slain before thine eyes, and thou shalt not eat thereof: thine ass *shall be* violently taken away from before thy face, and [1]shall not be restored to thee: thy sheep *shall be* given unto thine enemies, and thou shalt have none to rescue *them.*

32 Thy sons and thy daughters *shall be* given unto another people, and thine eyes shall look, and [a]fail *with longing* for them all the day long: and *there shall be* no might in thine hand.

33 [a]The fruit of thy land, and all thy labours, shall a nation which thou knowest not eat up; and thou shalt be only oppressed and crushed alway:

34 So that thou shalt be mad for the sight of thine eyes which thou shalt see.

35 The LORD shall smite thee in the knees, and in the legs, with a sore botch that cannot be healed, from the sole of thy foot unto the top of thy head.

36 The LORD shall [a]bring thee, and thy king which thou shalt set over thee, unto a nation which neither thou nor thy fathers have known; and [b]there shalt thou serve other gods, wood and stone.

37 And thou shalt become [a]an astonishment, a proverb, [b]and a byword, among all nations whither the LORD shall lead thee.

38 [a]Thou shalt carry much seed out *into* the field, and shalt gather *but* little in; for [b]the locust shall consume it.

39 Thou shalt plant vineyards, and dress *them,* but shalt neither drink *of* the wine, nor gather *the grapes;* for the worms shall eat them.

40 Thou shalt have olive trees throughout all thy coasts, but thou shalt not anoint *thyself with* the oil; for thine olive shall cast *his fruit.*

41 Thou shalt beget sons and daughters, but [1]thou shalt not enjoy them; for [a]they shall go into captivity.

42 All thy trees and fruit of thy land shall the locust [1]consume.

43 The stranger that *is* within thee shall get up above thee very high; and thou shalt come down very low.

44 [a]He shall lend to thee, and thou shalt not lend to him: [b]he shall be the head, and thou shalt be the tail.

45 Moreover [a]all these curses shall come upon thee, and shall pursue thee, and overtake thee, till thou be destroyed; because thou hearkenedst not unto the voice of the LORD thy God, to keep his commandments and his statutes which he commanded thee:

46 And they shall be upon thee [a]for a sign and for a wonder, and upon thy seed for ever.

47 [a]Because thou servedst not the LORD thy God with joyfulness, and with gladness of heart, [b]for the abundance of all *things;*

48 Therefore shalt thou serve thine enemies which the LORD shall send against thee, in hunger, and in thirst, and in nakedness, and in want of all *things:* and he [a]shall put a yoke of iron upon thy neck, until he have destroyed thee.

49 [a]The LORD shall bring a nation against thee from far, from the end of the earth, [b]*as*

28:20 [1]Heb. *which thou wouldest do* [a]Mal. 2:2 [b]1 Sam. 14:20; Zech. 14:13 [c]Is. 30:17; 51:20; 66:15
28:21 [a]Lev. 26:25
28:22 [1]Or, *drought* [a]Lev. 26:16 [b]Amos 4:9
28:23 [a]Lev. 26:19
28:25 [1]Heb. *for a removing* [a]ch. 32:30; Is. 30:17 [b]Jer. 15:4; 24:9; Ezek. 23:46
28:26 [a]1 Sam. 17:44,46; Jer. 7:33; 16:4
28:27 [a]Ex. 15:26 [b]1 Sam. 5:6
28:28 [a]Jer. 4:9
28:29 [a]Job 5:14; Is. 59:10
28:30 [1]Heb. *profane, or, use it as common meat* [a]Job 31:10; Jer. 8:10 [b]Job 31:8; Jer. 12:13; Amos 5:11; Mic. 6:15; Zeph. 1:13 [c]ch. 20:6
28:31 [1]Heb. *shall not return to thee*
28:32 [a]Ps. 119:82
28:33 [a]Lev. 26:16; Jer. 5:17
28:36 [a]2 Ki. 17:4,6; 24:12,14; 2 Chr. 33:11 [b]ch. 4:28; Jer. 16:13
28:37 [a]Jer. 24:9; Zech. 8:13 [b]Ps. 44:14
28:38 [a]Mic. 6:15; Hag. 1:6 [b]Joel 1:4
28:41 [1]Heb. *they shall not be thine* [a]Lam. 1:5
28:42 [1]Or, *possess*
28:44 [a]ver. 12 [b]ver. 13
28:45 [a]ver. 15
28:46 [a]Is. 8:18; Ezek. 14:8
28:47 [a]Neh. 9:35-37 [b]ch. 32:15
28:48 [a]Jer. 28:14
28:49 [a]Jer. 5:15; 6:22,23; Luke 19:43 [b]Jer. 48:40; 49:22; Lam. 4:19; Hos. 8:1

28:23 *heaven . . . brass . . . earth . . . iron.* No rain would pierce the sky or penetrate the ground (see v. 22).
28:25 For the reverse see v. 7.
‡28:27 *botch of Egypt.* The boils of Egypt. See note on Ex 9:9.
28:30 See 20:5–7.
28:35 See note on Ex 9:11.
28:44 See notes on vv. 12–13.
28:49 *end of the earth.* An indefinite figurative expression

swift as the eagle flieth; a nation whose tongue
thou shalt not [1] understand;
50 A nation [a] [1] of fierce countenance,
[b] which shall not regard the person of the old,
nor shew favour to the young:
51 And he shall [a] eat the fruit of thy cattle,
and the fruit of thy land, until thou be destroyed: which *also* shall not leave thee *either*
corn, wine, or oil, *or* the increase of thy kine,
or flocks of thy sheep, until he have destroyed
thee.
52 And he shall [a] besiege thee in all thy
gates, until thy high and fenced walls come
down, wherein thou trustedst, throughout all
thy land: and he shall besiege thee in all thy
gates throughout all thy land, which the LORD
thy God hath given thee.
53 And [a] thou shalt eat the fruit of thine
own [1] body, the flesh of thy sons and of thy
daughters, which the LORD thy God hath given
thee, in the siege, and in the straitness,
wherewith thine enemies shall distress thee:
54 *So that* the man *that is* tender among
you, and very delicate, [a] his eye shall be evil toward his brother, and toward [b] the wife of his
bosom, and towards the remnant of his children which he shall leave:
55 So that *he* will not give to any of them
of the flesh of his children whom he shall eat:
because he hath nothing left him in the siege,
and in the straitness, wherewith thine enemies shall distress thee in all thy gates.
56 The tender and delicate *woman* among
you, which would not adventure to set the
sole of her foot upon the ground for delicate-
ness and tenderness, [a] her eye shall be evil towards the husband of her bosom, and towards
her son, and towards her daughter,
57 And towards her [1] young one that
cometh out [a] from between her feet, and towards her children which she shall bear: for
she shall eat them for want of all *things* secretly in the siege and straitness, wherewith
thine enemy shall distress thee in thy gates.
58 ¶ If thou wilt not observe to do all the
words of this law that are written in this book,

28:49 [1] Heb. *hear*
28:50 [1] Heb. *strong of face* [a] Prov. 7:13; Eccl. 8:1; Dan. 8:23 [b] 2 Chr. 36:17; Is. 47:6
28:51 [a] ver. 33; Is. 1:7
28:52 [a] 2 Ki. 25:1,2,4
28:53 [1] Heb. *belly* [a] Lev. 26:29; 2 Ki. 6:28,29; Jer. 19:9; Lam. 2:20; 4:10
28:54 [a] ch. 15:9 [b] ch. 13:6
28:56 [a] ver. 54
28:57 [1] Heb. *afterbirth* [a] Gen. 49:10
28:58 [a] Ex. 6:3
28:59 [a] Dan. 9:12
28:60 [a] ch. 7:15
28:61 [1] Heb. *cause to ascend*
28:62 [a] ch. 4:27 [b] ch. 10:22; Neh. 9:23
28:63 [a] ch. 30:9; Jer. 32:41 [b] Prov. 1:26; Is. 1:24
28:64 [a] Lev. 26:33; ch. 4:27,28; Neh. 1:8; Jer. 16:13 [b] ver. 36
28:65 [a] Amos 9:4 [b] Lev. 26:36 [c] Lev. 26:16
28:67 [a] Job 7:4 [b] ver. 34
28:68 [a] Jer. 43:7; Hos. 8:13; 9:3 [b] ch. 17:16

that *thou* mayest fear [a] this glorious and fearful
name, THE LORD THY GOD;
59 Then the LORD will make thy plagues
[a] wonderful, and the plagues of thy seed, *even*
great plagues, and of long continuance, and
sore sicknesses, and of long continuance.
60 Moreover he will bring upon thee all
[a] the diseases of Egypt, which thou wast afraid
of; and they shall cleave unto thee.
61 Also every sickness, and every plague,
which *is* not written in the book of this law,
them will the LORD [1] bring upon thee, until
thou be destroyed.
62 And ye [a] shall be left few in number,
whereas ye were [b] as the stars of heaven for
multitude; because thou wouldest not obey
the voice of the LORD thy God.
63 And it shall come to pass, *that* as the
LORD [a] rejoiced over you to do you good, and to
multiply you; so the LORD [b] will rejoice over
you to destroy you, and to bring you to nought;
and ye shall be plucked from off the land
whither thou goest to possess it.
64 And the LORD [a] shall scatter thee among
all people, from the *one* end of the earth even
unto the other; and [b] there thou shalt serve
other gods, which neither thou nor thy fathers
have known, *even* wood and stone.
65 And [a] among these nations shalt thou
find no ease, neither shall the sole of thy foot
have rest: [b] but the LORD shall give thee there
a trembling heart, and failing of eyes, and [c] sorrow of mind:
66 And thy life shall hang in doubt before
thee; and thou shalt fear day and night, and
shalt have none assurance of thy life:
67 [a] In the morning thou shalt say, Would
God it were even! and at even thou shalt say,
Would God it were morning! for the fear of
thine heart where*with* thou shalt fear, and [b] for
the sight of thine eyes which thou shalt see.
68 And the LORD [a] shall bring thee *into*
Egypt again with ships, by the way where*of* I
spake unto thee, [b] Thou shalt see it no more
again: and there ye shall be sold unto your enemies for bondmen and bondwomen, and no
man shall buy *you.*

---

meaning "far away"—anywhere from the horizon to the perimeter of the then-known world. *eagle flieth.* Symbolic of the speed and power of the Assyrians (see Hos 8:1) and Babylonians (see Jer 48:40; 49:22). *whose tongue thou shalt not understand.* Though related to Hebrew, the languages of Assyria and Babylonia were not understood by the average Israelite (see Is 28:11; 33:19 and note; 1 Cor 14:21).

‡28:53 *thou shalt eat . . . sons and . . . daughters.* For the actualizing of this curse see 2 Ki 6:24–29; Lam 2:20; 4:10. *the straitness* [i.e., distress], *wherewith thine enemies shall distress thee.* See vv. 55, 57. The repetition of the clause emphasizes the distress that the Israelites would suffer if they refused to obey the Lord.

28:58 *words of this law.* See note on 31:24. *this glorious and fearful name, THE LORD.* See note on Ex 3:15. One of the oddities of history and revelation is the loss of the proper pronunciation of the Hebrew word *YHWH,* the most intimate and personal name of God in the OT (see note on Gen 2:4). "Jehovah" is a spelling that developed from combining the consonants of the name with the vowels of a word for "Lord" (*Adonai*). "Yahweh" is probably the original pronunciation. The name eventually ceased to be pronounced because later Jews thought it too holy to be uttered and feared violating Ex 20:7 and Lev 24:16. It is translated "LORD" in this version.

28:60 *diseases of Egypt.* Those brought on the Egyptians during the plagues (see 7:15; Ex 15:26).

28:61 *book of this law.* See note on 31:24.

28:62 *as the stars of heaven.* See 1:10; see also notes on Gen 13:16; 15:5.

28:64 *shall scatter thee.* Experienced by Israel in the Assyrian (722–721 B.C.) and Babylonian (586 B.C.) exiles (see 2 Ki 17:6; 25:21).

28:68 *the way whereof I spake . . . Thou shalt see it no more again.* See 17:16; Ex 13:17; Num 14:3–4.

Keep the covenant

29 These *are* the words of the covenant,
which the LORD commanded Moses
to make with the children of Israel in the land
of Moab, beside [a]the covenant which he made
with them in Horeb.
2 ¶ And Moses called unto all Israel, and
said unto them, [a]Ye have seen all that the
LORD did before your eyes in the land of Egypt
unto Pharaoh, and unto all his servants, and
unto all his land;
3 [a]The great temptations which thine eyes
have seen, the signs, and those great miracles:
4 Yet [a]the LORD hath not given you a heart
to perceive, and eyes to see, and ears to hear,
unto this day.
5 [a]And I have led you forty years in the
wilderness: [b]your clothes are not waxen old
upon you, and thy shoe is not waxen old upon
thy foot.
6 [a]Ye have not eaten bread, neither have
you drunk wine or strong drink: that ye might
know that I *am* the LORD your God.
7 And when ye came unto this place, [a]Si-
hon the king of Heshbon, and Og the king of
Bashan, came out against us unto battle, and
we smote them:
8 And we took their land, and [a]gave it for
an inheritance unto the Reubenites, and to the
Gadites, and to the half tribe of Manasseh.
9 [a]Keep therefore the words of this covenant, and do them, that ye may [b]prosper *in*
all that ye do.
10 ¶ Ye stand *this* day all of you before the
LORD your God; your captains of your tribes,
your elders, and your officers, *with* all the men
of Israel,
11 Your little ones, your wives, and thy
stranger that *is* in thy camp, from [a]the hewer
of thy wood unto the drawer of thy water:
12 That thou shouldest [1]enter into covenant with the LORD thy God, and [a]into his
oath, which the LORD thy God maketh with
thee *this* day:
13 That he may [a]establish thee to day for a
people unto himself, and *that* he may be unto
thee a God, [b]as he hath said unto thee, and [c]as
he hath sworn unto thy fathers, to Abraham,
to Isaac, and to Jacob.
14 Neither with you only [a]do I make this
covenant and this oath;
15 But with *him* that standeth here with us
this day before the LORD our God, [a]and also
with *him* that *is* not here with us *this* day:
16 (For ye know how we have dwelt in the
land of Egypt; and how we came through the
nations which ye passed by;
17 And ye have seen their abominations,
and their [1]idols, wood and stone, silver and
gold, which *were* among them:)
18 Lest there should be among you man, or
woman, or family, or tribe, [a]whose heart turneth away *this* day from the LORD our God, to go
and serve the gods of these nations; [b]lest there
should be among you a root that beareth [1]gall
and wormwood;
19 And it come to pass, when he heareth
the words of this curse, that he bless himself
in his heart, saying, I shall have peace, though
I walk [a]in the [b 1]imagination of mine heart, [c]to
add [2]drunkenness *to* thirst:
20 [a]The LORD will not spare him, but then
[b]the anger of the LORD and [c]his jealousy shall
smoke against that man, and all the curses that
are written in this book shall lie upon him,
and the LORD [d]shall blot out his name from under heaven.
21 And the LORD [a]shall separate him unto
evil out of all the tribes of Israel, according to
all the curses of the covenant that [1]are written
in this book of the law:
22 So that the generation to come of your
children that shall rise up after you, and the
stranger that shall come from a far land, shall
say, when they see the plagues of that land,
and the sicknesses [1]which the LORD hath laid
upon it;
23 *And that* the whole land thereof *is* brimstone, [a]and salt, *and* burning, *that* it is not
sown, nor beareth, nor any grass groweth
therein, [b]like the overthrow of Sodom, and
Gomorrah, Admah, and Zeboim, which the
LORD overthrew in his anger, and in his wrath:
24 Even all nations shall say, [a]Wherefore
hath the LORD done thus unto this land? what
meaneth the heat of this great anger?
25 Then *men* shall say, Because they have
forsaken the covenant of the LORD God of their
fathers, which he made with them when he
brought them forth out of the land of Egypt:
26 For they went and served other gods,
and worshipped them, gods whom they knew
not, and [1]*whom* he had not [2]given unto them:
27 And the anger of the LORD was kindled

29:1 [a]ch. 5:2,3
29:2 [a]Ex. 19:4
29:3 [a]ch. 4:34; 7:19
29:4 [a]See Is. 6:9,10; 63:17; John 8:43; Acts 28:26,27; Eph. 4:18
29:5 [a]ch. 1:3; 8:2 [b]ch. 8:4
29:6 [a]Ex. 16:12; ch. 8:3
29:7 [a]Num. 21:23,24,33; ch. 2:32
29:8 [a]Num. 32:33; ch. 3:12,13
29:9 [a]ch. 4:6; 1 Ki. 2:3 [b]Josh. 1:7
29:11 [a]See Josh. 9:21,23,27
29:12 [1]Heb. *pass* [a]Neh. 10:29
29:13 [a]ch. 28:9 [b]Ex. 6:7 [c]Gen. 17:7
29:14 [a]Jer. 31:31
29:15 [a]Acts 2:39; 1 Cor. 7:14
29:17 [1]Heb. *dungy gods*
29:18 [1]Or, *a poisonful herb.* Heb. *rosh* [a]ch. 11:16 [b]Acts 8:23; Heb. 12:15
29:19 [1]Or, *stubbornness* [2]Heb. *the drunken* to *the thirsty* [a]Num. 15:39; Eccl. 11:9 [b]Jer. 3:17; 7:24 [c]Is. 30:1
29:20 [a]Ezek. 14:7 [b]Ps. 74:1 [c]Ps. 79:5; Ezek. 23:25 [d]ch. 9:14
29:21 [1]Heb. *is written* [a]Mat. 24:51
29:22 [1]Heb. *wherewith the* LORD *hath made it sick*
29:23 [a]Jer. 17:6; Zeph. 2:9 [b]Gen. 19:24; Jer. 20:16
29:24 [a]1 Ki. 9:8,9; Jer. 22:8,9
29:26 [1]Or, *who had not given to them* any portion [2]Heb. *divided*

29:1 See notes on 5:2–3.
29:2 *Ye have seen.* Only those who were less than 20 years old (Num 14:29) when Israel followed the majority spy report at Kadesh-barnea and refused to enter Canaan would have actually experienced life in Egypt before the exodus. But Moses is speaking to the people as a nation and referring to the national experience (see note on 5:3).
29:4 Quoted in Rom 11:8 and applied to hardened Israel.
29:8 *gave it for an inheritance.* See 3:12–17.
29:9–15 A clear summary of the nature of covenant reaffirmation.
29:18 *root that beareth gall and wormwood.* The poison of idolatry, involving the rejection of the Lord.
29:20 *The LORD will not spare him.* Lit. "The LORD will not be willing to forgive (or pardon) him." Not to be taken as contradictory to 2 Pet 3:9 ("not willing that any should perish"). Peter, too, says that those who deny the Lord bring "upon themselves swift destruction" (2 Pet 2:1). *this book.* See note on 31:24. *blot out his name.* See 9:14; Ex 32:32–33; Rev 3:5.
29:21 *book of the law.* See note on 31:24.
29:23 *overthrow of Sodom.* See Gen 19:24–25; see also notes on Gen 10:19; 13:10.

against this land, [a]to bring upon it all the curses that are written in this book:

28 And the LORD [a]rooted them out of their land in anger, and in wrath, and in great indignation, and cast them into another land, as *it is* this day.

29 The secret *things belong* unto the LORD our God: but *those things* which are revealed *belong* unto us and to our children for ever, that *we* may do all the words of this law.

The rewards of repentance

30 And [a]it shall come to pass, when [b]all these things are come upon thee, the blessing and the curse, which I have set before thee, and [c]thou shalt call *them* to mind among all the nations, whither the LORD thy God hath driven thee,

2 And shalt [a]return unto the LORD thy God, and shalt obey his voice according to all that I command thee *this* day, thou and thy children, with all thine heart, and with all thy soul;

3 [a]That then the LORD thy God will turn thy captivity, and have compassion upon thee, and will return and [b]gather thee from all the nations, whither the LORD thy God hath scattered thee.

4 [a]If *any* of thine be driven out unto the outmost parts of heaven, from thence will the LORD thy God gather thee, and from thence will he fetch thee:

5 And the LORD thy God will bring thee into the land which thy fathers possessed, and thou shalt possess it; and he will do thee good, and multiply thee above thy fathers.

6 And [a]the LORD thy God will circumcise thine heart, and the heart of thy seed, to love the LORD thy God with all thine heart, and with all thy soul, that thou mayest live.

7 And the LORD thy God will put all these curses upon thine enemies, and on them that hate thee, which persecuted thee.

8 And thou shalt return and obey the voice of the LORD, and do all his commandments which I command thee *this* day.

9 [a]And the LORD thy God will make thee plenteous in every work of thine hand, in the fruit of thy body, and in the fruit of thy cattle, and in the fruit of thy land, for good: for the LORD will again [b]rejoice over thee for good, as he rejoiced over thy fathers:

10 If thou shalt hearken unto the voice of the LORD thy God, to keep his commandments and his statutes which are written in this book of the law, *and* if thou turn unto the LORD thy God with all thine heart, and with all thy soul.

11 For this commandment which I command thee *this* day, [a]it *is* not hidden from thee, neither *is* it far off.

12 [a]It *is* not in heaven, that *thou* shouldest say, Who shall go up for us to heaven, and bring it unto us, that we may hear it, and do it?

13 Neither *is* it beyond the sea, that *thou* shouldest say, Who shall go over the sea for us, and bring it unto us, that we may hear it, and do it?

14 But the word *is* very nigh unto thee, in thy mouth, and in thy heart, that *thou* mayest do it.

Closing advice

15 ¶ See, [a]I have set before thee *this* day life and good, and death and evil;

16 In that I command thee *this* day to love the LORD thy God, to walk in his ways, and to keep his commandments and his statutes and his judgments, that thou mayest live and multiply: and the LORD thy God shall bless thee in the land whither thou goest to possess it.

17 But if thine heart turn away, so that thou wilt not hear, but shalt be drawn away, and worship other gods, and serve them;

18 [a]I denounce unto you *this* day, that ye shall surely perish, *and that* ye shall not prolong *your* days upon the land, whither thou passest over Jordan to go to possess it.

19 [a]I call heaven and earth to record *this* day against you, *that* [b]I have set before you life and death, blessing and cursing: therefore choose life, that *both* thou and thy seed may live:

20 That thou mayest love the LORD thy God, *and* that thou mayest obey his voice, and that thou mayest cleave unto him: for he *is* thy [a]life, and the length of thy days: that thou mayest dwell in the land which the LORD sware unto thy fathers, to Abraham, to Isaac, and to Jacob, to give them.

The appointment of Joshua

31 And Moses went and spake these words unto all Israel.

2 And he said unto them, I [a]*am* an hundred and twenty years old *this* day; I can no more

29:27 [a]Dan. 9:11,13,14
29:28 [a]1 Ki. 14:15; Ps. 52:5; Prov. 2:22
30:1 [a]Lev. 26:40 [b]ch. 28 [c]ch. 4:29,30; 1 Ki. 8:47
30:2 [a]Neh. 1:9; Is. 55:7; Lam. 3:40; Joel 2:12
30:3 [a]Ps. 106:45; 126:1,4; Jer. 29:14; Lam. 3:22,32 [b]Ps. 147:2; Jer. 32:37; Ezek. 34:13; 36:24
30:4 [a]ch. 28:64; Neh. 1:9
30:6 [a]ch. 10:16; Jer. 32:39; Ezek. 11:19; 36:26
30:9 [a]ch. 28:11 [b]ch. 28:63; Jer. 32:41
30:11 [a]Is. 45:19
30:12 [a]Rom. 10:6
30:15 [a]ver. 1,19; ch. 11:26
30:18 [a]ch. 4:26; 8:19
30:19 [a]ch. 4:26; 31:28 [b]ver. 15
30:20 [a]Ps. 27:1; 66:9; John 11:25
31:2 [a]Ex. 7:7; ch. 34:7

29:27 *this book.* See note on 31:24.
29:28 *as it is this day.* This would be said when Israel was in exile (see v. 25).
29:29 *secret things.* The hidden events of Israel's future relative to the blessings and curses; but the phrase can also have wider application. *things which are revealed.* Primarily the "words of this law."
30:2,6,10 *with all thine heart . . . soul.* See note on 4:29.
30:6 *circumcise thine heart.* See note on Gen 17:10.
30:7 *curses upon thine enemies.* Fulfilling Gen 12:3.
30:9 *thy fathers.* The patriarchs (see v. 20).
30:10 *book of the law.* See note on 31:24.
30:12,14 *It is not in heaven . . . the word is very nigh unto thee.* Moses declares that understanding, believing and obeying the covenant were not beyond them. Paul applies this passage to the availability of the "word of faith" (Rom 10:6–10).
30:19 *I call heaven and earth to record.* The typical ancient covenant outside the OT contained a list of gods who served as "witnesses" to its provisions. The covenant in Deuteronomy was "witnessed" by heaven and earth (see 31:28; 32:1; see also notes on Ps 50:1; Is 1:2).
30:20 *cleave.* See note on 10:20. *he is thy life.* When they chose the Lord, they chose life (v. 19). In 32:46–47 "all the words of this law" are said to be their life. The law, the Lord and life are bound together. "Life" in this context refers to all that makes life rich, full and productive—as God created it to be.

[b]go out and come in: also the LORD hath said
unto me, [c]Thou shalt not go over this Jordan.
3 The LORD thy God, [a]he will go over before thee, *and* he will destroy these nations
from before thee, and thou shalt possess them:
and Joshua, he shall go over before thee, [b]as
the LORD hath said.
4 [a]And the LORD shall do unto them [b]as he
did to Sihon and to Og, kings of the Amorites,
and unto the land of them, whom he destroyed.
5 And [a]the LORD shall give them up before
your face, that ye may do unto them according
unto all the commandments which I have
commanded you.
6 [a]Be strong and of a good courage, [b]fear
not, nor be afraid of them: for the LORD thy
God, [c]he *it is* that doth go with thee; [d]he will
not fail thee, nor forsake thee.
7 ¶ And Moses called unto Joshua, and said
unto him in the sight of all Israel, [a]Be strong
and of a good courage: for thou must go with
this people unto the land which the LORD hath
sworn unto their fathers to give them; and
thou shalt cause them to inherit it.
8 And the LORD, [a]he *it is* that doth go before thee; [b]he will be with thee, he will not
fail thee, neither forsake thee: fear not, neither be dismayed.

Provision for teaching the law

9 ¶ And Moses wrote this law, [a]and delivered it unto the priests the sons of Levi,
[b]which bare the ark of the covenant of the
LORD, and unto all the elders of Israel.
10 And Moses commanded them, saying,
At the end of *every* seven years, in the solemnity of the [a]year of release, [b]in the feast of
tabernacles,
11 When all Israel is come to [a]appear before the LORD thy God in the place which he
shall choose, [b]thou shalt read this law before
all Israel in their hearing.
12 [a]Gather the people together, men, and
women, and children, and thy stranger that *is*
within thy gates, that they may hear, and that
they may learn, and fear the LORD your God,
and observe to do all the words of this law:
13 And *that* their children, [a]which have
not known *any thing,* [b]may hear, and learn to
fear the LORD your God, as long as ye live in the
land whither ye go over Jordan to possess it.

31:2 [b]Num. 27:17; 1 Ki. 3:7 [c]Num. 20:12; 27:13; ch. 3:27
31:3 [a]ch. 9:3 [b]Num. 27:21; ch. 3:28
31:4 [a]ch. 3:21 [b]Num. 21:24,33
31:5 [a]ch. 7:2
31:6 [a]Josh. 10:25; 1 Chr. 22:13 [b]ch. 1:29; 7:18 [c]ch. 20:4 [d]Josh. 1:5; Heb. 13:5
31:7 [a]ver. 23; ch. 1:38; 3:28; Josh. 1:6
31:8 [a]Ex. 13:21; 33:14; ch. 9:3 [b]Josh. 1:5,9; 1 Chr. 28:20
31:9 [a]ver. 25; ch. 17:18 [b]Num. 4:15; Josh. 3:3; 1 Chr. 15:12,15
31:10 [a]ch. 15:1 [b]Lev. 23:34
31:11 [a]ch. 16:16 [b]Josh. 8:34,35; 2 Ki. 23:2; Neh. 8:1-3
31:12 [a]ch. 4:10
31:13 [a]ch. 11:2 [b]Ps. 78:6,7

The LORD appears to Moses

14 ¶ And the LORD said unto Moses, [a]Be-
hold, thy days approach that *thou* must die:
call Joshua, and present yourselves in the tabernacle of the congregation, that [b]I may give
him a charge. And Moses and Joshua went,
and presented themselves in the tabernacle of
the congregation.
15 And [a]the LORD appeared in the tabernacle in a pillar of a cloud: and the pillar of the
cloud stood over the door of the tabernacle.
16 And the LORD said unto Moses, Behold,
thou shalt [1]sleep with thy fathers; and this
people will [a]rise up, and [b]go a whoring after
the gods of the strangers of the land, whither
they go *to be* amongst them, and will [c]forsake
me, and [d]break my covenant which I have
made with them.
17 Then my anger shall be kindled against
them in that day, and [a]I will forsake them, and
I will [b]hide my face from them, and they shall
be devoured, and many evils and troubles shall
[1]befall them; so that they will say in that day,
[c]Are not these evils come upon us, because
our God *is* [d]not amongst us?
18 And [a]I will surely hide my face in that
day for all the evils which they shall have
wrought, in that they are turned unto other
gods.
19 Now therefore write ye this song for
you, and teach it the children of Israel: put it
in their mouths, that this song may be [a]a witness for me against the children of Israel.
20 *For* when I shall have brought them
into the land which I sware unto their fathers,
that floweth with milk and honey; and they
shall have eaten and filled *themselves,* [a]and
waxen fat; [b]then will they turn unto other
gods, and serve them, and provoke me, and
break my covenant.
21 And it shall come to pass, [a]when many
evils and troubles are befallen them, that this
song shall testify [1]against them as a witness;
for it shall not be forgotten out of the mouths
of their seed: for [b]I know their imagination
[c]which they [2]go about, *even* now, before I
have brought them into the land which I
sware.
22 Moses therefore wrote this song the
same day, and taught it the children of Israel.
23 [a]And he gave Joshua the son of Nun a

31:14 [a]Num. 27:13; ch. 34:5 [b]Num. 27:19
31:15 [a]Ex. 33:9
31:16 [1]Heb. *lie down* [a]Ex. 32:6 [b]Ex:34:15; Judg. 2:17 [c]ch. 32:15; Judg. 2:12; 10:6,13 [d]Judg. 2:20
31:17 [1]Heb. *find them* [a]2 Chr. 15:2 [b]ch. 32:20; Is. 8:17; 64:7; Ezek. 39:23 [c]Judg. 6:13 [d]Num. 14:42
31:18 [a]ver. 17
31:19 [a]ver. 26
31:20 [a]ch. 32:15; Neh. 9:25; Hos. 13:6 [b]ver. 16
31:21 [1]Heb. *before* [2]Heb. *do* [a]ver. 17 [b]Hos. 5:3; 13:5,6 [c]Amos 5:25,26
31:23 [a]ver. 14

31:2 *can no more go out and come in.* Not a reference to physical disability (see 34:7). The Lord did not allow Moses to lead the people into Canaan because of his sin (see 1:37; 3:23–27; 4:21–22; 32:48–52; Num 20:2–13).

31:4 *as he did to Sihon and to Og.* See 2:26–3:11.

31:6 *Be strong and of a good courage.* The Lord's exhortation, often through His servants, to the people of Israel (Josh 10:25), to Joshua (vv. 7,23; Josh 1:6–7,9,18), to Solomon (1 Chr 22:13; 28:20) and to Hezekiah's military officers (2 Chr 32:7). By trusting in the Lord and obeying Him, His followers would be victorious in spite of great obstacles. *he will not fail thee, nor forsake thee.* See v. 8; Josh 1:5; 1 Ki 8:57; see also note on Gen 28:15.

31:9 *wrote this law, and delivered it unto the priests.* Ancient treaties specified that a copy of the treaty was to be placed before the gods at the religious centers of the nations involved. For Israel, that meant to place it in or near the ark of the Testimony (cf. notes on Ex 16:34; 31:18).

31:10 *every seven years.* See 15:4 and note; Ex 23:10–11; Lev 25:1–7; see also chart, pp. 166–167.

31:11 *place which he shall choose.* See note on 12:5. *read this law before all Israel.* Reading the law to the Israelites (and teaching it to them) was one of the main duties of the priests (see 33:10; Mal 2:4–9).

31:14 *I may give him a charge.* See v. 23; cf. Num 27:18–23.

31:19 *write ye this song . . . and teach it.* See v. 22; 31:30–32:43.

charge, and said, [b]Be strong and of a good courage: for thou shalt bring the children of Israel into the land which I sware unto them: and I will be with thee.

24 ¶ And it came to pass, when Moses had made an end of writing the words of this law in a book, until they were finished,

25 That Moses commanded the Levites, which bare the ark of the covenant of the LORD, saying,

26 Take this book of the law, [a]and put it in the side of the ark of the covenant of the LORD your God, that it may be there [b]for a witness against thee.

27 [a]For I know thy rebellion, and thy [b]stiff neck: behold, while I am yet alive with you *this* day, ye have been rebellious against the LORD; and how much more after my death?

28 Gather unto me all the elders of your tribes, and your officers, that I may speak these words in their ears, [a]and call heaven and earth to record against them.

29 For I know that after my death ye will utterly [a]corrupt *yourselves,* and turn aside from the way which I have commanded you; and [b]evil will befall you [c]in the latter days; because ye will do evil in the sight of the LORD, to provoke him to anger through the work of your hands.

30 And Moses spake in the ears of all the congregation of Israel the words of this song, until they were ended.

The song of Moses

32 Give [a]ear, O ye heavens, and I will speak;
And hear, O earth, the words of my mouth.
2 [a]My doctrine shall drop as the rain,
My speech shall distil as the dew,
[b]As the small rain upon the tender herb,
And as the showers upon the grass:
3 Because I will publish the name of the LORD:
[a]Ascribe ye greatness unto our God.
4 *He is* [a]the Rock, [b]his work *is* perfect:
For all his ways *are* judgment:
[c]A God of truth and [d]without iniquity,
Just and right *is* he.
5 [a][1]They have corrupted themselves,
[2]their spot *is* not *the spot* of his children:
They are a [b]perverse and crooked generation.
6 Do ye thus [a]requite the LORD,
O foolish people and unwise?
Is not he [b]thy father *that* hath [c]bought thee?
Hath he *not* [d]made thee, and established thee?
7 Remember the days of old,
Consider the years of [1]many generations:
[a]Ask thy father, and he will shew thee;
Thy elders, and they will tell thee.
8 When the most High [a]divided to the nations their inheritance,
When he [b]separated the sons of Adam,
He set the bounds of the people
According to the number of the children of Israel.
9 For [a]the LORD'S portion *is* his people;
Jacob *is* the [1]lot of his inheritance.
10 He found him [a]in a desert land,
And in the waste howling wilderness;
He [1]led him about, he instructed him,
He [b]kept him as the apple of his eye.
11 [a]As an eagle stirreth up her nest,
Fluttereth over her young,
Spreadeth abroad her wings, taketh them,
Beareth them on her wings:
12 *So* the LORD alone did lead him,
And *there was* no strange god with him.
13 [a]He made him ride on the high places of the earth,
That he might eat the increase of the fields;
And he made him to suck honey out of the rock,
And oil out of the flinty rock;
14 Butter of kine, and milk of sheep,

31:23 [b]ver. 7; Josh. 1:6 **31:26** [a]See 2 Ki. 22:8 [b]ver. 19 **31:27** [a]ch. 9:24; 32:20 [b]Ex. 32:9; ch. 9:6 **31:28** [a]ch. 30:19; 32:1 **31:29** [a]ch. 32:5; Judg. 2:19; Hos. 9:9 [b]ch. 28:15 [c]Gen. 49:1; ch. 4:30 **32:1** [a]Is. 1:2 **32:2** [a]1 Cor. 3:6 [b]Ps. 72:6 **32:3** [a]1 Chr. 29:11 **32:4** [a]Ps. 18:2 [b]2 Sam. 22:31 **32:4** [c]Jer. 10:10 [d]Job 34:10 **32:5** [1]Heb. *He hath corrupted to himself* [2]Or, that they are *not his children,* that is *their blot* [a]ch. 31:29 [b]Phil. 2:15 **32:6** [a]Ps. 116:12 [b]Is. 63:16 [c]Ps. 74:2 [d]ver. 15 **32:7** [1]Heb. *generation and generation* [a]Ex. 13:14 **32:8** [a]Zech. 9:2 [b]Gen. 11:8 **32:9** [1]Heb. *cord* [a]Ex. 19:5 **32:10** [1]Or, *compassed him about* [a]Jer. 2:6 [b]Ps. 17:8 **32:11** [a]Is. 31:5 **32:13** [a]Is. 58:14

31:23 *Be strong and of a good courage.* See note on v. 6.
31:24 *words of this law . . . finished.* The book of Deuteronomy up to this place (see note on v. 9).
31:26 *put it in the side of the ark.* See note on v. 9.
‡31:27 *thy stiff neck* [i.e. stubbornness]. See 9:6,13; 10:16; see also note on Ex 32:9.
31:28 *heaven and earth to record.* See note on 30:19.
31:29 *the work of your hands.* A reference to idols (see 4:28; 27:15 and note).
31:30–32:43 The song of Moses (see notes on Ex 15:1–18; Rev 15:3).
32:1 *Give ear, O ye heavens.* For similar introductions see Is 1:2 and note; 34:1; Mic 1:2; 6:1–2.
32:4 *the Rock.* A major theme of the song of Moses (see vv. 15,18,30–31; see also note on Gen 49:24).
32:5 *perverse and crooked generation.* See Phil 2:15.
32:6 *father.* See Is 63:16; 64:8.
32:7 *Remember the days of old.* See note on 4:10.
32:8 *most High.* The only occurrence in Deuteronomy of this name for God (see note on Gen 14:19). It emphasizes the Lord's sovereignty over all creation. *divided to the nations their inheritance.* See Gen 10. *According to the number of the children of Israel.* Perhaps referring to the Lord's grant of Canaan to Israel as sufficient to sustain their expected population (see note on Gen 10:2).
32:10 *apple of his eye.* Lit. "little man of his eye," referring to the pupil, a delicate part of the eye that is essential for vision and that therefore must be protected at all costs.
32:13 *honey out of the rock.* See Ps 81:16. In Canaan, bees sometimes built their hives in clefts of rocks (cf. Is 7:18–19). *oil out of the flinty rock.* Olive trees often grew on rocky hillsides, as on the mount of Olives east of Jerusalem.
32:14 *Bashan.* See note on Ezek 39:18. *blood of the grape.* Wine (see Gen 49:11).

With fat of lambs, and rams of the
breed of Bashan,
And goats, [a]with the fat of kidneys of
wheat;
And thou didst drink the pure [b]blood
of the grape.
15 But Jeshurun waxed fat, and kicked:
[a]Thou art waxed fat, thou art grown
thick, thou art covered *with fatness;*
Then he [b]forsook God *which* [c]made
him,
And lightly esteemed the [d]Rock of his
salvation.
16 [a]They provoked him to jealousy with
strange *gods,*
With abominations provoked they him
to anger.
17 [a]They sacrificed unto devils, [1]not *to*
God;
To gods whom they knew not,
To new *gods that* came newly up,
Whom your fathers feared not.
18 [a]Of the Rock *that* begat thee thou art
unmindful,
And hast [b]forgotten God that formed
thee.
19 And when the LORD saw *it,* he
[1]abhorred *them,*
Because of the provoking of his sons,
and of his daughters.
20 And he said, I will hide my face from
them,
I will see what their end *shall be:*
For they *are* a very froward generation,
[a]Children in whom *is* no faith.
21 [a]They have moved me to jealousy with
that which is not God;
They have provoked me to anger [b]with
their vanities:
And [c]I will move them to jealousy with
those which are not a people;
I will provoke them to anger with a
foolish nation.
22 For [a]a fire is kindled in my anger,
And [1]shall burn unto the lowest hell,
And [2]shall consume the earth with her
increase,
And set on fire the foundations of the
mountains.
23 I will [a]heap mischiefs upon them;
[b]I will spend mine arrows upon them.
24 *They shall be* burnt with hunger, and
devoured with [1]burning heat,
And with bitter destruction:
I will also send the teeth of beasts
upon them,
With the poison of serpents of the
dust.
25 The sword without,
And terror [1]within, shall [2]destroy
Both the young man and the virgin,
The suckling *also* with the man of gray
hairs.
26 I said, I would scatter them into
corners,
I would make the remembrance of
them to cease from among men:
27 Were it not that I feared the wrath of
the enemy,
Lest their adversaries should behave
themselves strangely,
And lest they should say, [1]Our hand is
high,
And the LORD hath not done all this.
28 For they *are* a nation void of counsel,
Neither *is there any* understanding in
them.
29 [a]O that they were wise, *that* they
understood this,
That they would consider their latter
end!
30 How should one chase a thousand,
And two put ten thousand to flight,
Except their Rock [a]had sold them,
And the LORD had shut them up?
31 For their rock *is* not as our Rock,
[a]Even our enemies themselves *being*
judges.
32 For [a]their vine [1]*is* of the vine of
Sodom,
And of the fields of Gomorrah:
Their grapes *are* grapes of gall,
Their clusters *are* bitter:
33 Their wine *is* [a]the poison of dragons,
And the cruel [b]venom of asps.
34 *Is* not this [a]laid up in store with me,
And sealed up among my treasures?
35 [a]To me *belongeth* vengeance, and
recompence;
Their foot shall slide in *due* time:
For [b]the day of their calamity *is* at
hand,
And the things that shall come upon
them make haste.
36 [a]For the LORD shall judge his people,
[b]And repent himself for his servants,
When he seeth that *their* [1]power is
gone,
And [c]*there is* none shut up, or left.
37 And he shall say, [a]Where *are* their
gods,
Their rock in whom they trusted,
38 Which did eat the fat of their sacrifices,
And drank the wine of their drink
offerings?
Let them rise up and help you,

32:14 [a]Ps. 81:16 [b]Gen. 49:11
32:15 [a]ch. 31:20 [b]Is. 1:4 [c]Is. 51:13 [d]Ps. 95:1
32:16 [a]1 Cor. 10:22
32:17 [1]Or, which were *not God* [a]Rev. 9:20
32:18 [a]Is. 17:10 [b]Jer. 2:32
32:19 [1]Or, *despised*
32:20 [a]Mat. 17:17
32:21 [a]Ps. 78:58 [b]Ps. 31:6 [c]Rom. 10:19
32:22 [1]Or, *hath burned* [2]Or, *hath consumed* [a]Lam. 4:11
32:23 [a]Is. 26:15 [b]Ps. 7:12,13
32:24 [1]Heb. *burning coals*
32:25 [1]Heb. *from the chambers* [2]Heb. *bereave*
32:27 [1]Or, *Our high hand, and not the LORD, hath done all this*
32:29 [a]Luke 19:42
32:30 [a]Ps. 44:12
32:31 [a]1 Sam. 4:8; Jer. 40:3
32:32 [1]Or, is worse *than the vine of Sodom, etc.* [a]Is. 1:10
32:33 [a]Ps. 58:4 [b]Rom. 3:13
32:34 [a]Jer. 2:22; Rom. 2:5
32:35 [a]Heb. 10:30 [b]2 Pet. 2:3
32:36 [1]Heb. *hand* [a]Ps. 135:14 [b]Jer. 31:20; Joel 2:14 [c]2 Ki. 14:26
32:37 [a]Judg. 10:14; Jer. 2:28

32:15 *Jeshurun.* Means "the upright one," i.e., Israel; see also Is 44:2 and note. *Rock.* See v. 18 and note on v. 4.

32:21 Quoted in part in Rom 10:19 to illustrate Israel's failure to understand the good news about Christ.

‡32:22 *lowest hell* [*sheol* in Hebrew]. See note on Gen 37:35.

32:30 *their Rock.* Israel's God.

32:31 *their rock.* The god of Israel's enemy.

32:34 *sealed up among my treasures.* The Lord's plans for the future are fixed and certain. Sin will be punished in due time.

32:35–36 Quoted in part in Heb 10:30 as a warning against rejecting the Son of God.

32:35 *To me belongeth vengeance, and recompence.* Quoted in Rom 12:19 to affirm that avenging is God's prerogative.

And be [1]your protection.
39 See now that [a]I, *even* I, *am* he,
And [b]*there is* no god with me:
[c]I kill, and I make alive;
I wound, and I heal:
Neither *is there any* that can deliver
out of my hand.
40 For I lift up my hand to heaven,
And say, I live for ever.
41 [a]If I whet my glittering sword,
And mine hand take hold on judgment;
I will render vengeance to mine
enemies,
And will reward them that hate me.
42 I will make mine arrows [a]drunk with
blood,
And my sword shall devour flesh;
And that with the blood of the slain
and of the captives,
From the beginning of [b]revenges upon
the enemy.
43 [a][1]Rejoice, O ye nations, *with* his
people:
For he will [b]avenge the blood of his
servants,
And will render vengeance to his
adversaries,
And [c]will be merciful *unto* his land,
and to his people.

44 ¶ And Moses came and spake all the words of this song in the ears of the people, he and [1]Hoshea the son of Nun.

45 And Moses made an end of speaking all these words to all Israel:

46 And he said unto them, [a]Set your hearts unto all the words which I testify among you *this* day, which ye shall command your children to observe to do, all the words of this law.

47 For it *is* not a vain thing for you; [a]because it *is* your life: and through this thing ye shall prolong *your* days in the land, whither ye go over Jordan to possess it.

Moses to die on mount Nebo

48 ¶ [a]And the LORD spake unto Moses that selfsame day, saying,

49 Get thee up into this [a]mountain Abarim, *unto* mount Nebo, which *is* in the land of Moab, that *is* over against Jericho; and behold the land of Canaan, which I give unto the children of Israel for a possession:

50 And die in the mount whither thou goest up, and be gathered unto thy people; as [a]Aaron thy brother died in mount Hor, and was gathered unto his people:

51 Because [a]ye trespassed against me among the children of Israel at the waters of [1]Meribah-Kadesh, *in* the wilderness of Zin; because ye [b]sanctified me not in the midst of the children of Israel.

52 [a]Yet thou shalt see the land before *thee;* but thou shalt not go thither unto the land which I give the children of Israel.

Moses blesses the tribes

33 And this *is* [a]the blessing, wherewith Moses [b]the man of God blessed the children of Israel before his death.

2 And he said,
[a]The LORD came from Sinai,
And rose up from Seir unto them;
He shined forth from mount Paran,
And he came with [b]ten thousands of
saints:
From his right hand *went* [1]a fiery law
for them.
3 Yea, [a]he loved the people;
[b]All his saints *are* in thy hand:
And they [c]sat down at thy feet;
Every one shall [d]receive of thy words.
4 [a]Moses commanded us a law,
[b]*Even* the inheritance of the
congregation of Jacob.
5 And he was [a]king in [b]Jeshurun,
When the heads of the people
And the tribes of Israel were gathered
together.
6 Let Reuben live, and not die;
And let *not* his men be few.
7 And this *is the blessing* of Judah: and
he said,
Hear, LORD, the voice of Judah,
And bring him unto his people:
[a]Let his hands *be* sufficient for him;
And be thou [b]a help *to him* from his
enemies.
8 And of Levi he said,
[a]*Let* thy Thummim and thy Urim *be*
with thy holy one,
[b]Whom thou didst prove at Massah,
And with whom thou didst strive at the
waters of Meribah;
9 Who said unto his father and to his
mother, I have not [a]seen him;

32:38 [1]Heb. *a hiding for you* **32:39** [a]Ps. 102:27 [b]Is. 45:5,18,22 [c]1 Sam. 2:6; Hos. 6:1 **32:41** [a]Is. 66:16 **32:42** [a]Jer. 46:10 [b]Jer. 30:14; Lam. 2:5 **32:43** [1]Or, *Praise his people, ye nations:* or, *Sing ye* [a]Rom. 15:10 [b]Rev. 19:2 [c]Ps. 85:1 **32:44** [1]Or, *Joshua* **32:46** [a]Ezek. 40:4 **32:47** [a]Prov. 3:2; Rom. 10:5 **32:48** [a]Num. 27:12,13 **32:49** [a]ch. 34:1 **32:50** [a]Num. 20:25,28 **32:51** [1]Or, *strife at Kadesh* [a]Num. 20:11-13 [b]See Lev. 10:3 **32:52** [a]Num. 27:12 **33:1** [a]Gen. 49:28 [b]Ps. 90, title **33:2** [1]Heb. *a fire of law* [a]Hab. 3:3 [b]Dan. 7:10; Rev. 5:11 **33:3** [a]Ps. 47:4; Hos. 11:1 [b]1 Sam. 2:9 [c]Luke 10:39 [d]Prov. 2:1 **33:4** [a]John 1:17 [b]Ps. 119:111 **33:5** [a]See Gen. 36:31 [b]ch. 32:15 **33:7** [a]Gen. 49:8 [b]Ps. 146:5 **33:8** [a]Ex. 28:30 [b]ch. 8:2,3,16; Ps. 81:7 **33:9** [a]Gen. 29:32

32:39 *no god with me.* See note on 4:35. *I kill, and I make alive.* See Is 45:7 and note.
32:47 *it is your life.* See note on 30:20.
32:50 *gathered unto thy people.* See note on Gen 25:8. *Aaron . . . died in mount Hor.* See 10:6; Num 20:22–29.
32:51 *ye trespassed against me.* See 1:37; 3:23–26; 4:21–22; 31:2; Num 20:12. *Meribah-Kadesh, in the wilderness of Zin.* See 33:8; see also notes on Ex 17:7; Num 20:13.
33:1 *blessing.* See Gen 12:1–3; 22:15–18; 27:27–29; 28:10–15; 49:1–28. Moses' blessings on the tribes (vv. 6–25) should be compared particularly with Jacob's blessings on his sons in Gen 49. *man of God.* The first occurrence of this title. It appears next in Josh 14:6 (also of Moses; see Ps 90 title). Later it designates other messengers of God (see note on 1 Sam 2:27).
33:2 *Sinai . . . Seir . . . Paran.* Mountains associated with the giving of the law (see Gen 21:21 and note; Judg 5:4–5; Hab 3:3). *ten thousands of saints* ["myriads of holy ones" in Hebrew]. A reference to angels.
33:3 *saints* ["holy ones" in Hebrew]. Israelites (see 7:6; 14:2; 26:19; 28:9).
33:5 *king.* The Lord, not an earthly monarch, was to be king over Israel (see Judg 8:23 and note). *Jeshurun.* Means "the upright one," i.e. Israel; also in v. 26 (see Is 44:2 and note).
33:8 *Thummim . . . Urim.* See note on Ex 28:30. *Massah.* See 6:16; 9:22; see also note on Ex 17:7. *Meribah.* See 32:51; see also note on Ex 17:7.

[b]Neither did he acknowledge his
brethren,
Nor knew his own children:
For [c]they have observed thy word,
And kept thy covenant.
10 [a] [1]They shall teach Jacob thy
judgments,
And Israel thy law:
[2]They shall put incense [3]before thee,
[b]And whole *burnt sacrifice* upon thine
altar.
11 Bless, LORD, his substance,
And [a]accept the work of his hands:
Smite through the loins of them that
rise against him,
And of them that hate him, that they
rise not again.
12 *And* of Benjamin he said,
The beloved of the LORD shall dwell in
safety by him;
And the LORD shall cover him all the
day long,
And he shall dwell between his
shoulders.
13 And of Joseph he said,
[a]Blessed of the LORD *be* his land,
For the precious things of heaven, for
[b]the dew,
And for the deep that coucheth
beneath,
14 And for the precious fruits brought
forth by the sun,
And for the precious things [1]put forth
by the [2]moon,
15 And for the chief things of [a]the ancient
mountains,
And for the precious things [b]of the
lasting hills,
16 And for the precious things of the
earth and fulness thereof,
And *for* the good will of [a]him that
dwelt in the bush:
Let *the blessing* [b]come upon the head
of Joseph,
And upon the top of the head of him
that was separated from his brethren.
17 His glory *is like* the [a]firstling of his
bullock,
And his horns *are like* [b]the horns of
[1]unicorns:
With them [c]he shall push the people
together *to* the ends of the earth:
And [d]they *are* the ten thousands of
Ephraim,
And they *are* the thousands of
Manasseh.
18 And of Zebulun he said,
[a]Rejoice, Zebulun, in thy going out;
And, Issachar, in thy tents.
19 They shall [a]call the people *unto* the
mountain;
There [b]they shall offer sacrifices of
righteousness:
For they shall suck *of* the abundance of
the seas,
And *of* treasures hid in the sand.
20 And of Gad he said,
Blessed *be* he that [a]enlargeth Gad:
He dwelleth as a lion,
And teareth the arm with the crown of
the head.
21 And [a]he provided the first *part* for
himself,
Because there, *in* a portion of the
lawgiver, *was he* [1]seated;
And [b]he came *with* the heads of the
people,
He executed the justice of the LORD,
And his judgments with Israel.
22 And of Dan he said,
Dan *is* a lion's whelp:
[a]He shall leap from Bashan.
23 And of Naphtali he said,
O Naphtali, [a]satisfied with favour,
And full *with* the blessing of the LORD:
[b]Possess thou the west and the south.
24 And of Asher he said,
[a]*Let* Asher *be* blessed with children;
Let him be acceptable to his brethren,
And let him [b]dip his foot in oil.
25 [1]Thy shoes *shall be* [a]iron and brass;
And as thy days, *so shall* thy strength
be.
26 *There is* [a]none like unto the God of
[b]Jeshurun,
[c]*Who* rideth *upon* the heaven in thy
help,
And in his excellency *on* the sky.
27 The eternal God *is thy* [a]refuge,
And underneath *are* the everlasting
arms:
And [b]he shall thrust out the enemy
from before thee;
And shall say, Destroy *them.*
28 [a]Israel then shall dwell *in* safety alone:

33:9 [b]Ex. 32:26,27,28 [c]Mal. 2:5,6
33:10 [1]Or, *Let them teach, etc.* [2]Or, *Let them put incense* [3]Heb. *at thy nose* [a]Lev. 10:11; Mal. 2:7 [b]Lev. 1:9; Ps. 51:19
33:11 [a]2 Sam. 24:23; Ezek. 20:40
33:13 [a]Gen. 49:25 [b]Gen. 27:28
33:14 [1]Heb. *thrust forth* [2]Heb. *moons*
33:15 [a]Gen. 49:26 [b]Hab. 3:6
33:16 [a]Ex. 3:2,4 [b]Gen. 49:26
33:17 [1][Heb. *an unicorn*] [a]1 Chr. 5:1 [b]Num. 23:22 [c]Ps. 44:5
33:17 [d]Gen. 48:19
33:18 [a]Gen. 49:13
33:19 [a]Is. 2:3 [b]Ps. 4:5
33:20 [a]1 Chr. 12:8
33:21 [1]Heb. *cieled* [a]Num. 32:16,17 [b]Josh. 4:12
33:22 [a]Josh. 19:47
33:23 [a]Gen. 49:21 [b]See Josh. 19:32
33:24 [a]Gen. 49:20 [b]Job 29:6
33:25 [1]Or, Under *thy shoes* shall be *iron* [a]ch. 8:9
33:26 [a]Ex. 15:11 [b]ch. 32:15 [c]Ps. 68:4
33:27 [a]Ps. 90:1 [b]ch. 9:3-5
33:28 [a]Jer. 23:6

33:9 *they have observed thy word.* The Levites had charge of the tabernacle with its ark, in which the book of the law was placed (see note on 31:9).
33:10 *teach Jacob thy judgments.* See note on 31:11.
33:13 *of Joseph.* Moses included the blessing on the two tribes of Ephraim and Manasseh (v. 17), Joseph's sons, with that of Joseph himself. *the dew . . . the deep.* See note on Gen 49:25.
33:15–16 See Gen 49:26 and note.
33:16 *precious things of the earth.* Under the Lord's blessing, Joseph's land in the central part of Canaan was to be unusually fertile and productive. *him that dwelt in the bush.* See Ex 3:1–6.
33:19 *abundance of the seas . . . treasures hid in the sand.* References to maritime wealth (see note on Gen 49:13).
33:21 *he provided the first part.* For his livestock (see 3:12–20).
33:22 *leap from Bashan.* The lion's cub, not Dan, is the subject. Another possible translation is "keeps away from the viper." Although someday he would be like a viper himself (see Gen 49:17), the early history of Dan pictured him as being somewhat more timid.
33:23 *west* [*yam* in Hebrew, i.e. "sea"]. The sea of Galilee. Naphtali's area extended from north of the waters of Merom to south of the sea of Galilee.
33:26 *Jeshurun.* See note on 32:15. *rideth . . . the sky.* See note on Ps 68:4.

[b]The fountain of Jacob *shall be* upon a
land of corn and wine;
Also his [c]heavens shall drop down dew.
29 [a]Happy *art* thou, O Israel:
[b]Who *is* like unto thee, O people saved
by the LORD,
[c]The shield of thy help, and who *is* the
sword of thy excellency!
And thine enemies [d][1]shall be found
liars unto thee;
And [e]thou shalt tread upon their high
places.

The death of Moses

34 And Moses went up from the plains
of Moab [a]unto the mountain of
Nebo, *to* the top of [1]Pisgah, that *is* over
against Jericho. And the LORD [b]shewed him all
the land of Gilead, [c]unto Dan,
2 And all Naphtali, and the land of Ephraim, and Manasseh, and all the land of Judah,
[a]unto the utmost sea,
3 And the south, and the plain of the valley
of Jericho, [a]the city of palm trees, unto Zoar.
4 And the LORD said unto him, [a]This *is* the
land which I sware unto Abraham, unto Isaac,
and unto Jacob, saying, I will give it unto thy
seed: [b]I have caused thee to see *it* with thine
eyes, but thou shalt not go over thither.
5 [a]So Moses the servant of the LORD died
there in the land of Moab, according to the
word of the LORD.
6 And he buried him in a valley in the land
of Moab, over against Beth-peor: but [a]no man
knoweth of his sepulchre unto this day.
7 [a]And Moses *was* an hundred and twenty
years old when he died: [b]his eye was not dim,
nor his [1]natural force [2]abated.
8 And the children of Israel wept for Moses in the plains of Moab [a]thirty days: so the
days of weeping *and* mourning for Moses
were ended.
9 And Joshua the son of Nun was full *of* the
[a]spirit of wisdom; for [b]Moses had laid his
hands upon him: and the children of Israel
hearkened unto him, and did as the LORD commanded Moses.
10 And there [a]arose not a prophet since in
Israel like unto Moses, [b]whom the LORD knew
face to face,
11 In all [a]the signs and the wonders,
which the LORD sent him to do in the land of
Egypt to Pharaoh, and to all his servants, and
to all his land,
12 And in all *that* mighty hand, and in all
the great terror which Moses shewed in the
sight of all Israel.

33:28 [b]ch. 8:7,8 [c]Gen. 27:28
33:29 [1]Or, *shall be subdued* [a]Ps. 144:15 [b]2 Sam. 7:23 [c]Ps. 115:9 [d]Ps. 18:44 [e]ch. 32:13
34:1 [1]Or, *the hill* [a]Num. 27:12 [b]ch. 3:27 [c]Gen. 14:14
34:2 [a]ch. 11:24
34:3 [a]2 Chr. 28:15
34:4 [a]Gen. 12:7 [b]ch. 3:27
34:5 [a]ch. 32:50
34:6 [a]See Jude 9
34:7 [1]Heb. *moisture* [2]Heb. *fled* [a]ch. 31:2 [b]Gen 27:1
34:8 [a]See Gen. 50:3,10; Num. 20:29
34:9 [a]Is. 11:2; Dan. 6:3 [b]Num. 27:18,23
34:10 [a]ch. 18:15 [b]Ex. 33:11; ch. 5:4
34:11 [a]ch. 7:19

33:29 *shield.* See note on Gen 15:1. *high places.* See note on 1 Ki 3:2.

34:1 *Moses went up . . . unto the mountain of Nebo.* In obedience to the Lord's command in 32:48–52.

34:4 *land which I sware.* See 1:8; Gen 12:1; 15:18 and note; Ex 33:1.

34:5 *servant of the LORD.* A special title used to refer to those whom the Lord, as the Great King, has taken into His service; they serve as members of God's royal administration. For example, it was used especially of Abraham (Gen 26:24), Moses (Ex 14:31), Joshua (Josh 24:29), David (2 Sam 7:5), the prophets (2 Ki 9:7), Israel collectively (Is 41:8), and even a foreign king the Lord used to carry out His purposes (Jer 25:9). See notes on Ex 14:31; Is 42:1–4.

34:6 *Beth-peor.* See note on 3:29.

34:7 *an hundred and twenty years old.* See 31:2; perhaps a round number, indicating three generations of about 40 years each.

34:8 *wept . . . thirty days.* See Gen 50:3 and note.

34:10 *arose not a prophet since in Israel like unto Moses.* See note on 18:15. Until Jesus came, no one was superior to Moses. See Heb 3:1–6, where Moses the "servant" (Heb 3:5) is contrasted with Christ the "Son" (Heb 3:6). *face to face.* See Num 12:8 and note.

The Conquest and the Ethical Question of War

Many readers of Joshua (and other OT books) are deeply troubled by the role that warfare plays in this account of God's dealings with His people. Not a few relieve their ethical scruples by ascribing the author's perspective to a pre-Christian (and sub-Christian) stage of moral development that the Christian, in the light of Christ's teaching, must repudiate and transcend. Hence the main thread of the narrative line of Joshua is an offense to them.

It must be remembered, however, that the book of Joshua does not address itself to the abstract ethical question of war as a means for gaining human ends. It can only be understood in the context of the history of redemption unfolding in the Pentateuch, with its interplay of divine grace and judgment. Of that story it is the direct continuation.

Joshua is not an epic account of Israel's heroic generation or the story of Israel's conquest of Canaan with the aid of her national deity. It is rather the story of how God, to whom the whole world belongs, at one stage in the history of redemption reconquered a portion of the earth from the powers of this world that had claimed it for themselves, defending their claims by force of arms and reliance on their false gods. It tells how God commissioned His people, under His servant Joshua, to take Canaan in His name out of the hands of the idolatrous and dissolute Canaanites (whose measure of sin was now full; see Gen 15:16). It tells how He aided them in that enterprise and gave them conditional tenancy in His land in fulfillment of the ancient pledge.

Joshua is the story of the kingdom of God breaking into the world of nations at a time when national and political entities were viewed as the creation of the gods and living proofs of their power. Thus the Lord's triumph over the Canaanites testified to the world that the God of Israel is the one true and living God, whose claim on the world is absolute. It was also a warning to the nations that the irresistible advance of the kingdom of God would ultimately disinherit all those who opposed it, giving place in the earth only to those who acknowledge and serve the Lord. At once an act of redemption and of judgment, it gave notice of the outcome of history and anticipated the eschatological destiny of mankind and the creation.

The battles for Canaan were therefore the Lord's war, undertaken at a particular time in the program of redemption. God gave His people under Joshua no commission or license to conquer the world with the sword but a particular, limited mission. The conquered land itself would not become Israel's national possession by right of conquest, but it belonged to the Lord. So the land had to be cleansed of all remnants of paganism. Its people and their wealth were not for Israel to seize as the booty of war from which to enrich themselves (as Achan tried to do, ch. 7) but were placed under God's ban (were to be devoted to God to dispense with as He pleased). On that land Israel was to establish a commonwealth faithful to the righteous rule of God and thus be a witness (and a blessing) to the nations. If she herself became unfaithful and conformed to Canaanite culture and practice, she would in turn lose her place in the Lord's land—as she almost did in the days of the judges, and as she did eventually in the exile.

War is a terrible curse that the human race brings on itself as it seeks to possess the earth by its own unrighteous ways. But it pales before the curse that awaits all those who do not heed God's testimony to Himself or His warnings—those who oppose the rule of God and reject His offer of grace. The God of the second Joshua (Jesus) is the God of the first Joshua also. Although now for a time He reaches out to the whole world with the gospel (and commissions His people urgently to carry His offer of peace to all nations), the sword of His judgment waits in the wings—and His second Joshua will wield it (Rev 19:11–16).

The Book of Joshua

INTRODUCTION

Title and Theme

Joshua is a story of conquest and fulfillment for the people of God. After many years of slavery in Egypt and 40 years in the wilderness, the Israelites were finally allowed to enter the land promised to their fathers. Abraham, always a migrant, never possessed the country to which he was sent, but he left to his children the legacy of God's covenant that made them the eventual heirs of all of Canaan (see Gen 15:13,16,18; 17:8). Joshua was destined to turn that promise into reality.

Where Deuteronomy ends, the book of Joshua begins: The tribes of Israel are still camped on the east side of the Jordan River. The narrative opens with God's command to move forward and pass through the river on dry land. Then it relates the series of victories in central, southern and northern Canaan that gave the Israelites control of all the hill country and the Negev. It continues with a description of the tribal allotments and ends with Joshua's final addresses to the people. The theme of the book, therefore, is the establishment of Israel in the promised land.

Earlier in his life Joshua was called simply Yeshua [Oshea] (Num 13:8,16), meaning "salvation." But later Moses changed his name to Jehoshua [Joshua], meaning "The LORD saves" (or "The LORD gives victory"). When this same name (the Greek form of which is Jesus) was given to Mary's firstborn son, it became the most loved of names.

In the Hebrew Bible the book of Joshua initiates a division called the Former Prophets, including also Judges, Samuel and Kings—all historical in content but written from a prophetic standpoint. They do more than merely record the nation's development from Moses to the fall of Judah in 586 B.C. They prophetically interpret God's covenant ways with Israel in history—how He fulfills and remains true to His promises (especially through His servants such as Joshua, the judges, Samuel and David) and how He deals with the waywardness of the Israelites. In Joshua it was the Lord who won the victories and "gave unto Israel all the land which he sware to give unto their fathers" (21:43).

Author and Date

In the judgment of many scholars Joshua was not written until the end of the period of the kings, some 800 years after the actual events. But there are significant reasons to question this conclusion and to place the time of composition much earlier. The earliest Jewish traditions (Talmud) claim that Joshua wrote his own book except for the final section about his funeral, which is attributed to Eleazar son of Aaron (the last verse must have been added by a later editor).

On at least two occasions the text reports writing at Joshua's command or by Joshua himself. When the tribes received their territories, Joshua instructed his men, "Go and walk through the land, and describe it" (18:8). Then in the last scene of the book, when Joshua led Israel in a renewal of the covenant with the Lord, he "set them a statute and an ordinance" (24:25). On yet another occasion the one telling the story appears also to have been a participant in the event; he uses the pronoun "us" (5:6).

Moreover, the author's observations are accurate and precise. He is thoroughly at ease with the antiquated names of cities, such as "the Jebusite" city (15:8; 18:16,28) for Jerusalem, Kirjath-arba (14:15; 15:54; 20:7; 21:11) for Hebron, and great Zidon (11:8; 19:28) for what later became simply Sidon. Tyre is mentioned (19:29), but in the days of Joshua it had not yet developed into a port of major importance.

But if some features suggest Joshua's own lifetime, others point to a time somewhat later. The account of the long day when the sun stood still at Ajalon is substantiated by a quotation from another source, the book of Jasher (10:13). This would hardly be natural for an eyewitness of the miracle, writing shortly after it happened. Also, there are 12 instances where the phrase "unto this day" is employed by the author.

It seems safe to conclude that the book, at least in its early form, dates from the beginning of the

monarchy. Some think that Samuel may have had a hand in shaping or compiling the materials of the book, but in fact we are unsure who the final author or editor was.

The Life of Joshua

Joshua's remarkable life was filled with excitement, variety, success and honor. He was known for his deep trust in God and as "a man in whom is the spirit" (Num 27:18). As a youth he lived through the bitter realities of slavery in Egypt, but he also witnessed the supernatural plagues and the miracle of Israel's escape from the army of the Egyptians when the waters of the sea opened before them. In the Sinai peninsula it was Joshua who led the troops of Israel to victory over the Amalekites (Ex 17:8–13). He alone was allowed to accompany Moses up the holy mountain where the tables of the Testimony were received (Ex 24:13–14). And it was he who stood watch at the temporary tabernacle of the congragation Moses set up before the tabernacle was erected (Ex 33:11).

Joshua was elected to represent his own tribe of Ephraim when the 12 spies were sent into Canaan to look over the land. Only Joshua and his friend Caleb were ready to follow God's will and take immediate possession of the land (see Num 14:26–34). The rest were condemned to die in the wilderness. Even Moses died short of the goal and was told to turn everything over to Joshua. God promised to guide and strengthen Joshua, just as He had Moses (Deut 31:23).

Joshua proved to be not only a military strategist in the battles that followed, but also a statesman in the way he governed the tribes. Above all, he was God's chosen servant (see 24:29 and note on Deut 34:5) to bring Moses' work to completion and establish Israel in the promised land. In that role he was a striking OT type (foreshadowing) of Christ (see notes on Heb 4:1,6–8).

Historical Setting

At the time of the Israelite migration into Canaan the superpowers of the ancient Near East were relatively weak. The Hittites had faded from the scene. Neither Babylon nor Egypt could maintain a military presence in Canaan, and the Assyrians would not send in their armies until centuries later.

As the tribes circled east of the Dead Sea, only the stronghold of Edom offered any resistance. Moab was forced to let Israel pass through her territory and camp in her plains. When Og and Sihon, two regional Amorite kings east of the Jordan, tried to stop the Israelites, they were easily defeated and their lands occupied.

Biblical archaeologists call this period the Late Bronze Age (1550–1200 B.C.). Today thousands of artifacts give testimony to the richness of the Canaanite material culture, which was in many ways superior to that of the Israelites. When the ruins of the ancient kingdom of Ugarit were discovered at modern Ras Shamra on the northern coast of Syria (see chart on "Ancient Texts Relating to the OT," p. xix), a wealth of new information came to light concerning the domestic, commercial and religious life of the Canaanites. From a language close to Hebrew came stories of ancient kings and gods that revealed their immoral behavior and cruelty. In addition, pagan temples, altars, tombs and ritual vessels have been uncovered, throwing more light on the culture and customs of the peoples surrounding Israel.

Excavations at the ancient sites of Megiddo, Beth Shan and Gezer show how powerfully fortified these cities were and why they were not captured and occupied by Israel in Joshua's day. Many other fortified towns were taken, however, so that Israel became firmly established in the land as the dominant power. Apart from Jericho and Ai, Joshua is reported to have burned only Hazor (11:13), so attempts to date these events by destruction levels in the mounds of Canaan's ancient cities are questionable undertakings. It must also be remembered that other groups were involved in campaigns in the region about this time, among whom were Egyptian rulers and the Sea Peoples (including the Philistines). There had also been much intercity warfare among the Canaanites, and afterward the period of the judges was marked by general turbulence.

Much of the data from archaeology appears to support a date for Joshua's invasion c. 1250 B.C. This fits well with an exodus that would then have taken place 40 years earlier under the famous Rameses II, who ruled from the Nile delta at a city with the same name (Ex 1:11). It also places Joseph in Egypt in a favorable situation. Four hundred years before Rameses II the pharaohs were the Semitic Hyksos, who also ruled from the delta near the land of Goshen.

On the other hand, a good case can be made for the traditional viewpoint that the invasion occurred c. 1406 B.C. The oppression would have taken place under Amunhotep II after the death of his father Thutmose III, who is known to have used slave labor in his building projects. The earlier date also fits better with the two numbers found in Judg 11:26 and 1 Ki 6:1, since it allows for an addi-

tional 150 years between Moses and the monarchy. See also the Introductions to Genesis: Author and Date of Writing; Exodus: Chronology; and Judges: Background.

Outline

- I. The Entrance into the Land (1:1—5:12)
  - A. The Exhortations to Conquer (ch. 1)
  - B. The Reconnaissance of Jericho (ch. 2)
  - C. The Crossing of the Jordan (chs. 3—4)
  - D. The Consecration at Gilgal (5:1–12)
- II. The Conquest of the Land (5:13—12:24)
  - A. The Initial Battles (5:13—8:35)
    1. The victory at Jericho (5:13—6:27)
    2. The failure at Ai because of Achan's sin (ch. 7)
    3. The victory at Ai (8:1–29)
    4. The covenant renewed at Shechem (8:30–35)
  - B. The Campaign in the South (chs. 9—10)
    1. The treaty with the Gibeonites (ch. 9)
    2. The long day of Joshua (10:1–15)
    3. The southern cities conquered (10:16–43)
  - C. The Campaign in the North (ch. 11)
  - D. The Defeated Kings of Canaan (ch. 12)
- III. The Distribution of the Land (chs. 13—21)
  - A. Areas Yet to Be Conquered (13:1–7)
  - B. The Land East of the Jordan for Reuben, Gad and Half of Manasseh (13:8–33)
  - C. The Lands Given to Judah and "Joseph" at Gilgal (chs. 14—17)
  - D. The Lands Given to the Remaining Tribes at Shiloh (chs. 18—19)
    1. The tabernacle at Shiloh (18:1–10)
    2. The allotments for Benjamin, Simeon, Zebulun, Issachar, Asher, Naphtali and Dan (18:11—19:48)
    3. The town given to Joshua (19:49–51)
  - E. The Cities Assigned to the Levites (chs. 20—21)
    1. The 6 cities of refuge (ch. 20)
    2. The 48 cities of the priests (ch. 21)
- IV. Epilogue: Tribal Unity and Loyalty to the Lord (chs. 22—24)
  - A. The Altar of Witness by the Jordan (ch. 22)
  - B. Joshua's Farewell Exhortation (ch. 23)
  - C. The Renewal of the Covenant at Shechem (24:1–28)
  - D. The Death and Burial of Joshua and Eleazar (24:29–33)

The LORD instructs Joshua

1 Now after the death of Moses the servant of the LORD it came to pass, that the LORD spake unto Joshua the son of Nun, Moses' [a]minister, saying,

2 [a]Moses my servant is dead; now therefore arise, go over this Jordan, thou, and all this people, unto the land which I do give to them, *even* to the children of Israel.

3 [a]Every place that the sole of your foot shall tread upon, that have I given unto you, as I said unto Moses.

4 [a]From the wilderness and this Lebanon even unto the great river, the river Euphrates, all the land of the Hittites, and unto the great sea *toward* the going down of the sun, shall be your coast.

5 [a]There shall not any man *be able to* stand before thee all the days of thy life: [b]as I was with Moses, *so* [c]I will be with thee: [d]I will not fail thee, nor forsake thee.

6 [a]Be strong and of a good courage: for [1]unto this people shalt thou divide for an inheritance the land, which I sware unto their fathers to give them.

7 Only be thou strong and very courageous, that *thou* mayest observe to do according to all the law, [a]which Moses my servant commanded thee: [b]turn not from it *to* the right hand or *to* the left, that thou mayest [1]prosper whithersoever thou goest.

1:1 [a]Ex. 24:13; Deut. 1:38
1:2 [a]Deut. 34:5
1:3 [a]Deut. 11:24
1:4 [a]Gen. 15:18; Ex. 23:31; Num. 34:3-12
1:5 [a]Deut. 7:24 [b]Ex. 3:12 [c]Deut. 31:8,23; ch. 3:7; 6:27; Is. 43:2,5 [d]Deut. 31:6,8
1:6 [1]Or, *thou shalt cause this people to inherit the land, etc.* [a]Deut. 31:7,23
1:7 [1]Or, *do wisely* [a]Num. 27:23; Deut. 31:7; ch. 11:15 [b]Deut. 5:32; 28:14
1:8 [1]Or, *do wisely* [a]Deut. 17:18,19 [b]Ps. 1:2
1:9 [a]Deut. 31:7,8,23 [b]Ps. 27:1; Jer. 1:8
1:11 [a]Deut. 9:1; 11:31
1:13 [a]Num. 32:20-28; ch. 22:2-4
1:14 [1]Heb. *marshalled by five*

8 [a]This book of the law shall not depart out of thy mouth; but [b]thou shalt meditate therein day and night, that thou mayest observe to do according to all that is written therein: for then thou shalt make thy way prosperous, and then thou shalt [1]have good success.

9 [a]Have not I commanded thee? Be strong and of a good courage; [b]be not afraid, neither be thou dismayed: for the LORD thy God *is* with thee whithersoever thou goest.

10 ¶ Then Joshua commanded the officers of the people, saying,

11 Pass through the host, and command the people, saying, Prepare you victuals; for [a]within three days ye shall pass over this Jordan, to go in to possess the land, which the LORD your God giveth you to possess it.

12 And to the Reubenites, and to the Gadites, and to half the tribe of Manasseh, spake Joshua, saying,

13 Remember [a]the word which Moses the servant of the LORD commanded you, saying, The LORD your God hath given you rest, and hath given you this land.

14 Your wives, your little ones, and your cattle, shall remain in the land which Moses gave you on *this* side Jordan; but ye shall pass before your brethren [1]armed, all the mighty *men* of valour, and help them;

15 Until the LORD have given your brethren rest, as *he hath given* you, and they also

---

1:1–18 The Lord initiates the action by charging Joshua, His chosen replacement for Moses (see Deut 31:1–8), to lead Israel across the Jordan and take possession of the promised land. He urges courage and promises success—but only if Israel obeys the law of God that Moses has given them. The chapter consists of speeches significant in their content and order: The Lord commands Joshua as His appointed leader over His people (vv. 1–9); Joshua, as the Lord's representative, addresses Israel (vv. 10–15); Israel responds to Joshua as the Lord's representative and successor to Moses (vv. 16–18). Thus the events of the book are set in motion and the roles of the main actors indicated.

1:1 *after the death of Moses.* Immediately the time and occasion of the action are set forth, showing that the story will continue where Deuteronomy ended, with the death of Moses. Cf. "after the death of Joshua" (Judg 1:1). *servant of the LORD.* See notes on Ex 14:31; Deut 34:5; Ps 18 title; Is 41:8–9; 42:1. *Moses' minister.* The title by which Joshua served for many years as second in command (see Num 11:28; see also Ex 24:13; 33:11; Deut 1:38).

1:2 *Jordan.* The flow of the Jordan near Jericho was not large during most of the year (only 80–100 feet wide), but at flood stage in the spring it filled its wider bed, which at places was a mile wide and far more treacherous to cross. *land which I do give to them.* A central theme of the Pentateuch (see Gen 12:1; 50:24; Ex 3:8; 23:31; Deut 1:8). Joshua records the fulfillment of this promise of God.

1:3–5 See Deut 11:24–25.

1:4 The dimensions of the land promised to Israel vary (compare this text and Gen 15:18 with Deut 34:1–4), but these are the farthest limits—conquered and held only by David and Solomon. Canaan was still called "Hatti-land" centuries after the Hittites had withdrawn to the north. But Joshua was to take all he set out to conquer; wherever he set his foot was his. His victories gave to the 12 tribes most of the central hill country and much of the Negev.

1:5 *I will be with thee.* To direct, sustain and assure success.

1:6 *land, which I sware unto their fathers.* The long-awaited inheritance pledged to the descendants of Abraham (Gen 15:7,8–21) and of Jacob (Gen 28:13).

1:7 *observe to do.* Success was not guaranteed unconditionally (see Deut 8:1; 11:8,22–25).

1:8 *book of the law.* A documentary form of the laws from Sinai was already extant. *mouth.* See Deut 4:9–10; 6:6–7; 11:19. The law was usually read orally (cf. Deut 30:9–14; Acts 8:30). *meditate.* See Ps 1:2.

1:9 *Have not I commanded thee?* A rhetorical question that emphasizes the authority of the speaker.

1:10 *Joshua commanded.* At this point Joshua assumes full command. *officers.* May refer to those whom Moses had appointed over the divisions within the tribes (Ex 18:21; Deut 1:15).

1:11 *victuals.* Foodstuffs needed for the next several days of march.

1:12–15 The threat from the two kings "on this side Jordan" was overcome by military victory and the occupation of the lands north of Moab and east of the Jordan River. The two and a half tribes who asked to remain had been charged by Moses to send their fighting men across with the rest to conquer Canaan (Num 21:21–35; 32:1–27). The conquest of the promised land must be an undertaking by all Israel.

1:13 *rest.* An important OT concept (see notes on Deut 3:20; 2 Sam 7:1,11), implying secure borders, peace with neighboring countries and absence of threat to life and well-being within the land (see note on 1 Ki 5:4).

1:14 *armed, all the mighty men of valour.* Those over 20 (see, e.g., Ex 38:26), known for their valor and able to equip themselves with the weapons of war.

have possessed the land which the LORD your God giveth them: [a]then ye shall return unto the land of your possession, and enjoy it, which Moses the LORD's servant gave you on *this* side Jordan *toward* the sunrising.

16 And they answered Joshua, saying, All that thou commandest us we will do, and whithersoever thou sendest us, we will go.

17 According as we hearkened unto Moses in all *things,* so will we hearken unto thee: only the LORD thy God [a]be with thee, as he was with Moses.

18 Whosoever *he be* that doth rebel against thy commandment, and will not hearken unto thy words in all that thou commandest him, he shall be put to death: only be strong and of a good courage.

Two spies sent to Jericho

2 And Joshua the son of Nun [1]sent [a]out of Shittim two men to spy secretly, saying, Go view the land, even Jericho. And they went, and [b]came *into* a harlot's house, named [c]Rahab, and [2]lodged there.

2 And [a]it was told the king of Jericho, saying, Behold, there came men in hither to night of the children of Israel to search out the country.

3 And the king of Jericho sent unto Rahab, saying, Bring forth the men that are come to thee, which are entered into thine house: for they be come to search out all the country.

4 [a]And the woman took the two men, and hid them, and said thus, There came men unto me, but I wist not whence they *were:*

5 And it came to pass *about the time* of shutting of the gate, when it was dark, that the men went out: whither the men went I wot not: pursue after them quickly; for ye shall overtake them.

6 But [a]she had brought them up to the roof of the house, and hid them with the stalks of flax, which she had laid in order upon the roof.

7 And the men pursued after them the way to Jordan unto the fords: and as soon as they which pursued after them were gone out, they shut the gate.

8 And before they were laid down, she came up unto them upon the roof;

9 And she said unto the men, I know that the LORD hath given you the land, and that [a]your terror is fallen upon us, and that all the inhabitants of the land [1]faint because of you.

10 For we have heard how the LORD [a]dried up the water of the Red sea for you, when you came out of Egypt; and [b]what you did unto the two kings of the Amorites, that *were* on the *other* side Jordan, Sihon and Og, whom ye utterly destroyed.

11 And as soon as we had [a]heard *these things,* [b]our hearts did melt, neither [1]did there remain any more courage in any man, because of you: for [c]the LORD your God, he *is* God in heaven above, and in earth beneath.

12 Now therefore, I pray you, [a]swear unto me by the LORD, since I have shewed you kindness, that ye will also shew kindness unto [b]my father's house, and [c]give me a true token:

13 And *that* ye will save alive my father, and my mother, and my brethren, and my sisters, and all that they have, and deliver our lives from death.

14 And the men answered her, Our life [1]for yours, if ye utter not this our business. And it

1:15 [a]ch. 22:4
1:17 [a]1 Sam. 20:13; 1 Ki. 1:37
2:1 [1][Or, *had sent*] [2]Heb. *lay* [a]Num. 25:1 [b]Heb. 11:31; Jas. 2:25 [c]Mat. 1:5
2:2 [a]ver. 22
2:4 [a]See 2 Sam. 17:19,20
2:6 [a]See Ex. 1:17; 2 Sam. 17:19
2:9 [1]Heb. *melt* [a]Gen. 35:5; Ex. 23:27; Deut. 2:25; 11:25
2:10 [a]Ex. 14:21; ch. 4:23 [b]Num. 21:24,34,35
2:11 [1]Heb. *rose up* [a]Ex. 15:14,15 [b]ch. 5:1; 7:5; Is. 13:7 [c]Deut. 4:39
2:12 [a]See 1 Sam. 20:14,15, 17 [b]See 1 Tim. 5:8 [c]ver. 18
2:14 [1]Heb. *instead of you to die*

1:18 *Whosoever he be that doth rebel.* Having just taken the oath of allegiance to Joshua, they now agree to the death penalty for any act of treason (e.g., the sin of Achan, 7:15). *be strong and of a good courage.* The people's words of encouragement to Joshua echo and reinforce those from the Lord (vv. 6–7,9).

2:1–24 The mission of the two spies and the account of Rahab. The practice of reconnaissance and espionage is as old as war itself (cf. Judg 7:10–11; 1 Sam 26:6–12). Rahab became a convert to the God of Israel and a famous woman among the Hebrews. She is honored in the NT for her faith (Heb 11:31) and for her good works (Jas 2:25).

2:1 *sent out of Shittim.* The invasion point was in the plains of Moab facing toward the Jordan and Jericho (Num 33:48–49). The Hebrew word *Shittim* means "acacia trees," which grow in the semi-arid conditions of the wilderness. *even Jericho.* The primary focus of the spies. It was a fortified city, was well supplied by strong springs, which helped to make it an oasis, and was located just five miles west of the Jordan. Its name probably means "moon city," and archaeological excavations there reveal continuous occupation back to at least 7000 B.C. *harlot's house.* Josephus and other early sources refer to Rahab as an "innkeeper," but see Heb 11:31; Jas 2:25.

2:2 *king of Jericho.* The major cities of Canaan were in reality small kingdoms, each ruled by a local king (attested also in the Amarna letters of the 14th century B.C.; see chart, p. xix).

2:6 *hid . . . with the stalks of flax.* Rooftops in the Near East are still used for drying grain or stalks. Rahab's cunning saved the lives of the two Israelites but put her own life in jeopardy.

2:7 *Jordan . . . fords.* Shallow crossings of the Jordan, where the depth of normal flow averages only three feet.

2:8–11 Rahab's confession has a significant concentric structure:

a. "I know";

b. "terror is fallen upon us . . . the inhabitants of the land";

c. "we have heard";

bb. "our hearts did melt, neither did there remain any more courage in any man";

aa. "the LORD your God, he is God."

Rahab's personal confession forms the outer frame (a.-aa.); the inner frame (b.-bb.) offers the military intelligence that the spies report back to Joshua; the center (c., v. 10) sums up the news about the Lord that occasioned both the Canaanite fear and Rahab's abandonment of Canaan and its gods for the Lord and Israel. Her confession of faith in the Lord and her accurate information about the Lord's triumphs over powerful enemies are astounding. That the hearts of the Canaanites were "faint" (v. 9) was vital information to the spies.

2:10 *utterly destroyed.* See note on Num 21:2.

2:12 *shew kindness unto my father's house.* The Hebrew for "kindness" or "kindly" is frequently translated "love" or "unfailing love" and often summarizes God's covenant favor toward His people or the love that people are to show to others. Rahab had acted toward the spies as though she was an Israelite, and now she asks that Israel treat her similarly. *true token.* Their oath to spare the whole family (v. 14).

shall be, when the LORD hath given us the land,
that [a]we will deal kindly and truly with thee.
15 Then she [a]let them down by a cord
through the window: for her house *was* upon
the town wall, and she dwelt upon the wall.
16 And she said unto them, Get you to the
mountain, lest the pursuers meet you; and hide
yourselves there three days, until the pursuers
be returned: and afterward may ye go your way.
17 And the men said unto her, We *will be*
[a]blameless of this thine oath which thou hast
made us swear.
18 [a]Behold, *when* we come into the land,
thou shalt bind this line of scarlet thread in the
window which thou didst let us down by:
[b]and thou shalt [1]bring thy father, and thy
mother, and thy brethren, and all thy father's
household, home unto thee.
19 And it shall be, *that* whosoever shall go
out of the doors of thy house into the street,
his blood *shall be* upon his head, and we *will*
be guiltless: and whosoever shall be with thee
in the house, [a]his blood *shall be* on our head,
if *any* hand be upon him.
20 And if thou utter this our business, then
we will be quit of thine oath which thou hast
made us to swear.
21 And she said, According unto your
words, so *be* it. And she sent them away, and
they departed: and she bound the scarlet line
in the window.
22 And they went, and came unto the
mountain, and abode there three days, until
the pursuers were returned: and the pursuers
sought *them* throughout all the way, but found
them not.

2:14 [a]Judg. 1:24; Mat. 5:7
2:15 [a]Acts 9:25
2:17 [a]Ex. 20:7
2:18 [1]Heb. *gather* [a]ver. 12 [b]ch. 6:23
2:19 [a]1 Ki. 2:32; Mat. 27:25
2:24 [1]Heb. *melt* [a]Ex. 23:31; ch. 6:2; 21:44
3:1 [a]ch. 2:1
3:2 [a]ch. 1:10,11
3:3 [a]See Num. 10:33 [b]Deut. 31:9,25
3:4 [1]Heb. *since yesterday, and the third day* [a]Ex. 19:12
3:5 [a]Ex. 19:10,14,15; Lev. 20:7; Num. 11:18; ch. 7:13; 1 Sam. 16:5; Joel 2:16
3:6 [a]Num. 4:15
3:7 [a]ch. 4:14; 1 Chr. 29:25; 2 Chr. 1:1

23 So the two men returned, and descended from the mountain, and passed over, and
came to Joshua the son of Nun, and told him
all *things* that befell them:
24 And they said unto Joshua, Truly [a]the
LORD hath delivered into our hands all the
land; for even all the inhabitants of the country do [1]faint because of us.

Israel crosses the Jordan

3 And Joshua rose early in the morning;
and they removed [a]from Shittim, and
came to Jordan, he and all the children of Israel, and lodged there before they passed over.
2 And it came to pass [a]after three days,
that the officers went through the host;
3 And they commanded the people, saying,
[a]When ye see the ark of the covenant of the
LORD your God, [b]and the priests the Levites
bearing it, then ye shall remove from your
place, and go after it.
4 [a]Yet there shall be a space between you
and it, about two thousand cubits by measure:
come not near unto it, that ye may know the
way by which ye must go: for ye have not
passed *this* way [1]heretofore.
5 And Joshua said unto the people, [a]Sancti-
fy yourselves: for to morrow the LORD will do
wonders among you.
6 And Joshua spake unto the priests, saying, [a]Take up the ark of the covenant, and
pass over before the people. And they took up
the ark of the covenant, and went before the
people.
7 ¶ And the LORD said unto Joshua, This day
will I begin to [a]magnify thee in the sight of all

2:14 *when the LORD hath given us the land.* All were convinced of the inevitable victory of the Israelites over the city of Jericho. *kindly and truly.* The terms of the pledge made by the spies echo Rahab's request (v. 12).

2:15 *her house was upon the town wall.* There is archaeological evidence that the people of Jericho would occasionally build their houses onto the city wall. Although this evidence predates the time of Joshua, it may still serve to illumine this verse. Alternatively, the Late Bronze fortifications at Jericho may have included a casemate wall (a hollow wall with partitions), and Rahab may have occupied one or more rooms inside it.

2:18 *line of scarlet thread in the window.* The function of the red marker was similar to that of the blood of the passover lamb when the Lord struck down the firstborn of Egypt (see Ex 12:13,22–23). The early church viewed the blood-colored cord as a type (symbol) of Christ's atonement.

2:19 *his blood shall be on our head.* A vow that accepted responsibility for the death of another, with its related guilt and the retribution meted out by either relatives or the state.

2:22 *the mountain.* Directly west of ancient Jericho were the high, rugged hills of the central mountain ridge in Canaan. They are honeycombed with caves, making the concealment and escape of the two spies relatively easy.

3:1–4:24 Details of the river crossing and the memorial of 12 stones set up in the camp at Gilgal. The great significance of this account can hardly be overemphasized, since it marks the crossing of the boundary into the promised land and parallels the miracle of the "Red sea" crossing in the exodus (Ex 14–15). The Israelites' faith in the God of their fathers was renewed and strengthened when it was about to be most severely challenged, while at the same time the Canaanites' fear was greatly increased (5:1). In this account the author uses an "overlay" technique in which, having narrated the crossing to its conclusion (ch. 3), he returns to various points in the event to enlarge on several details: the stones for a memorial (4:1–9); the successful crossing by all Israel (4:10–14); the renewed flow of the river after the crossing was completed (4:15–18). The final paragraph of ch. 4 (vv. 19–24) picks up the story again from 3:17 and completes the account by noting Israel's encampment at Gilgal and the erecting of the stone memorial.

3:3 *ark of the covenant.* The most sacred of the tabernacle furnishings (see Ex 25:10–22). Since it signified the Lord's throne, the Lord Himself went into the Jordan ahead of His people as He led them into the land of rest (see Num 10:33–36).

3:4 *space . . . about two thousand cubits.* There was evidently a line of march, with the priests and ark leading the way. Respect for the sacred symbol of the Lord's holy presence accounts for this gap of about 1,000 yards between the people and the priests bearing the ark.

3:5 *Sanctify yourselves.* Before their meeting with God at Sinai this had involved washing all their garments as well as their bodies, and also abstinence from sexual intercourse (see Ex 19:10,14–15).

3:7 *will I begin to magnify thee.* A prime objective for the divine intervention at the Jordan was to validate the leadership of Joshua. With a miraculous event so much like that of the "Red sea" crossing, Joshua's position as the Lord's servant would be shown to be comparable to that of Moses.

Israel, that they may know that, [b]as I was with
Moses, *so* I will be with thee.
8 And thou shalt command [a]the priests
that bear the ark of the covenant, saying,
When ye are come to the brink of the water of
Jordan, [b]ye shall stand still in Jordan.
9 And Joshua said unto the children of Israel, Come hither, and hear the words of the
LORD your God.
10 And Joshua said, Hereby ye shall know
that [a]the living God *is* among you, and *that* he
will without fail [b]drive out from before you
the Canaanites, and the Hittites, and the Hivites, and the Perizzites, and the Girgashites,
and the Amorites, and the Jebusites.
11 Behold, the ark of the covenant, *even*
[a]the Lord of all the earth passeth over before
you into Jordan.
12 Now therefore [a]take ye twelve men out
of the tribes of Israel, out of every tribe a man.
13 And it shall come to pass, [a]as soon as
the soles of the feet of the priests that bear the
ark of the LORD, [b]the Lord of all the earth, shall
rest in the waters of Jordan, *that* the waters of
Jordan shall be cut off *from* the waters that
come down from above; and they [c]shall stand
upon a heap.
14 ¶ And it came to pass, when the people
removed from their tents, to pass over Jordan,
and the priests bearing the [a]ark *of* the covenant before the people;
15 And as they that bare the ark were
come unto Jordan, and [a]the feet of the priests
that bare the ark were dipped in the brim of
the water, (for [b]Jordan overfloweth all his
banks [c]all the time of harvest,)
16 That the waters which came down from
above stood *and* rose up *upon* a heap very far,
from the city Adam, that *is* beside [a]Zaretan:
and those that came down [b]toward the sea of
the plain, *even* [c]the salt sea, failed, *and* were
cut off: and the people passed over right
against Jericho.
17 And the priests that bare the ark *of* the
covenant of the LORD stood firm on dry *ground*
in the midst of Jordan, [a]and all the Israelites
passed over on dry *ground,* until all the people
were passed clean over Jordan.
4 And it came to pass, when all the people
were clean passed [a]over Jordan, that the
LORD spake unto Joshua, saying,
2 [a]Take you twelve men out of the people,
out of every tribe a man,
3 And command you them, saying, Take
you hence out of the midst of Jordan, out of
the place where [a]the priests' feet stood firm,
twelve stones, and ye shall carry them over
with you, and leave them in [b]the lodging
place, where you shall lodge *this* night.
4 Then Joshua called the twelve men,
whom he had prepared of the children of Israel, out of every tribe a man:
5 And Joshua said unto them, Pass over before the ark of the LORD your God into the
midst of Jordan, and take ye up every man of
you a stone upon his shoulder, according unto
the number of the tribes of the children of Israel:
6 That this may be a sign among you, *that*
[a]when your children ask *their fathers* [1]in time
to come, saying, What mean you by these
stones?
7 Then ye shall answer them, That [a]the
waters of Jordan were cut off before the ark of

3:7 [b]ch. 1:5
3:8 [a]ver. 3 [b]ver. 17
3:10 [a]Deut. 5:26; 1 Sam. 17:26; 2 Ki. 19:4; Hos. 1:10; Mat. 16:16; 1 Thes. 1:9 [b]Ex. 33:2; Deut. 7:1; Ps. 44:2
3:11 [a]ver. 13; Mic. 4:13; Zech. 4:14; 6:5
3:12 [a]ch. 4:2
3:13 [a]ver. 15,16 [b]ver. 11 [c]Ps. 78:13; 114:3
3:14 [a]Acts 7:45
3:15 [a]ver. 13 [b]1 Chr. 12:15; Jer. 12:5; 49:19 [c]ch. 4:18; 5:10,12
3:16 [a]1 Ki. 4:12; 7:46 [b]Deut. 3:17 [c]Gen. 14:3; Num. 34:3
3:17 [a]See Ex. 14:29
4:1 [a]Deut. 27:2; ch. 3:17
4:2 [a]ch. 3:12
4:3 [a]ch. 3:13 [b]ver. 19,20
4:6 [1]Heb. *to morrow* [a]Ex. 12:26; 13:14; Deut. 6:20
4:7 [a]ch. 3:13,16

3:10 *Hereby ye shall know.* The manner by which God is about to bring Israel across the Jordan River, the watery boundary of the promised land, will bring assurance that the one true God is with them and that He will surely dislodge the present inhabitants of Canaan. Two fundamental issues are at stake: 1. Who is the true and mighty God—the God of Israel or the god on whom the Canaanites depend (Baal, who was believed to reign as king among the gods because he had triumphed over the sea-god)? By opening the way through the flooded Jordan the Lord would show both Israel and the Canaanites that He is Lord over the waters (as He was at the "Red sea," at the flood and at creation) and that He is able to establish His own order in the world. See 1 Ki 20:23; 2 Ki 18:32–35. 2. Who has the rightful claim to the land—the Lord or the Canaanites? (For the juridical aspect of such wars see Judg 11:27.) By passing safely through the Jordan at the head of His army the Lord showed the rightness of His claim on the land. In the ancient Near East a common way for obtaining the judicial verdict of the gods was by compelling the accused to submit to trial by water ordeal. Usually this involved casting him into a river (if the accused drowned, the gods had found him guilty; if not, the gods had declared him innocent). In Israel, however, another form of water ordeal was practiced (see Num 5:16–28). Significantly, the Lord would enter the Jordan first and then remain there until His whole army had crossed safely over. Thus His claim to the land was vindicated before the eyes of all who heard about it. And it was His claim, not Israel's; she came through the Jordan only with Him and as His army, "baptized" to His service. *Canaanites . . . Jebusites.* See notes on Gen 9:25; 10:6,15–16; 13:7; 15:16; 23:3; Ex 3:8; Judg 3:3; 6:10.

3:12 *take ye twelve men.* Joshua seems to anticipate the Lord's instructions concerning a stone monument of the event (see 4:2–3).

3:13 *cut off.* Blocked, stopped in its flow. *stand upon a heap.* The Hebrew for "heap" is found here, in v. 16 and also in the poetic accounts of the "Red sea" crossing (Ex 15:8; Ps 78:13). It is possible that God used a physical means (such as a landslide) to dam up the Jordan at the place called Adam (v. 16), near the entrance of the Jabbok. (As recently as 1927 a blockage of the water in this area was recorded that lasted over 20 hours.) But if so, the miraculous element is not diminished (see Ex 14:21).

3:15 *as.* The stoppage nearly 20 miles upstream (v. 16) would have happened several hours earlier to make the events coincide. *overfloweth all his banks.* Because of the spring rains and the melting of snow on mount Hermon. *harvest.* Grain harvest took place in April and May.

3:17 *the priests that bare the ark . . . stood firm on dry ground in the midst of Jordan.* Signifying that the Lord Himself remained in the place of danger until all Israel had crossed the Jordan.

4:3 *in the lodging place, where you shall lodge this night.* Indicating that the entire nation made the crossing in one day.

4:6 *What mean you by these stones?* A stone monument was commonly used as a memorial to remind future generations of what had happened at that place (24:26; 1 Sam 7:12).

the covenant of the LORD; when it passed over
Jordan, the waters of Jordan were cut off: and
these stones shall be for [b]a memorial unto the
children of Israel for ever.
8 And the children of Israel did so as Joshua commanded, and took up twelve stones out
of the midst of Jordan, as the LORD spake unto
Joshua, according to the number of the tribes
of the children of Israel, and carried them over
with them unto the place where they lodged,
and laid them down there.
9 And Joshua set up twelve stones in the
midst of Jordan, in the place where the feet of
the priests which bare the ark of the covenant
stood: and they are there unto this day.
10 For the priests which bare the ark stood
in the midst of Jordan, until every thing was
finished that the LORD commanded Joshua to
speak unto the people, according to all that
Moses commanded Joshua: and the people
hasted and passed over.
11 And it came to pass, when all the people were clean passed over, that the ark of the
LORD passed over, and the priests, in the presence of the people.
12 And [a]the children of Reuben, and the
children of Gad, and half the tribe of Manasseh, passed over armed before the children of
Israel, as Moses spake unto them:
13 About forty thousand [1]prepared for war
passed over before the LORD unto battle, to the
plains of Jericho.
14 On that day the LORD [a]magnified Joshua
in the sight of all Israel; and they feared him,
as they feared Moses, all the days of his life.
15 ¶ And the LORD spake unto Joshua, saying,
16 Command the priests that bear [a]the ark
of the Testimony, that they come up out of Jordan.
17 Joshua therefore commanded the
priests, saying, Come ye up out of Jordan.
18 And it came to pass, when the priests
that bare the ark of the covenant of the LORD
were come up out of the midst of Jordan, *and*
the soles of the priests' feet were [1]lift up unto
the dry *land,* that the waters of Jordan returned unto their place, [a]and [2]flowed over all
his banks, as *they did* before.
19 And the people came up out of Jordan on
the tenth *day* of the first month, and encamped
[a]in Gilgal, in the east border of Jericho.
20 And [a]those twelve stones, which they
took out of Jordan, did Joshua pitch in Gilgal.
21 And he spake unto the children of Israel, saying, [a]When your children shall ask their
fathers [1]in time to come, saying, What *mean*
these stones?
22 Then ye shall let your children know,
saying, [a]Israel came over this Jordan on dry
land.
23 For the LORD your God dried up the waters of Jordan from before you, until ye were
passed over, as the LORD your God did to the
Red sea, [a]which he dried up from before us,
until we were gone over:
24 [a]That all the people of the earth might
know the hand of the LORD, that it *is* [b]mighty:
that ye might [c]fear the LORD your God [1]for
ever.

5 And it came to pass, when all the kings
of the Amorites, which *were* on the side
of Jordan westward, and all the kings of the
Canaanites, [a]which *were* by the sea, [b]heard
that the LORD had dried up the waters of Jordan from before the children of Israel, until we
were passed over, that their heart melted,
[c]neither was there spirit in them any more,
because of the children of Israel.

Circumcising of the nation

2 ¶ At that time the LORD said unto Joshua,
Make thee [a][1]sharp knives, and circumcise
again the children of Israel the second time.
3 And Joshua made him [1]sharp knives, and
circumcised the children of Israel at [2]the hill
of the foreskins.

4:7 [b]Ex. 12:14; Num. 16:40
4:12 [a]Num. 32:20,27,28
4:13 [1]Or, *ready armed*
4:14 [a]ch. 3:7
4:16 [a]Ex. 25:16,22
4:18 [1]Heb. *plucked up* [2]Heb. *went* [a]ch. 3:15
4:19 [a]ch. 5:9
4:20 [a]ver. 3
4:21 [1]Heb. *to morrow* [a]ver. 6
4:22 [a]ch. 3:17
4:23 [a]Ex. 14:21
4:24 [1]Heb. *all days* [a]1 Ki. 8:42,43; 2 Ki. 19:19 [b]Ex. 15:16; 1 Chr. 29:12 [c]Ex. 14:31; Deut. 6:2; Jer. 10:7
5:1 [a]Num. 13:29 [b]Ex. 15:14,15 [c]1 Ki. 10:5
5:2 [1]Or, *knives of flints* [a]Ex. 4:25
5:3 [1]Or, *knives of flints* [2]Or, *Gibeah-haaraloth*

4:9 *Joshua set up twelve stones in.* Suggesting that Joshua set up a second pile in the middle of the river. An alternative translation ("Joshua set up the twelve stones that had been in") suggests that each tribe brought a stone for the monument from the riverbed to the new campsite at Gilgal, and Joshua constructed the monument there (see v. 20).

4:13 *About forty thousand.* Seems too few for the number of men listed in Num 26 for Reuben, Gad and half of Manasseh; the contingents were very likely representative since it would have been imprudent to leave the people undefended who settled east of the Jordan (cf. 22:8, "brethren"; Num 32:17).

4:19 *tenth day of the first month.* The day the passover lamb was to be selected (Ex 12:3). *Gilgal.* Usually identified with the ruins at Khirbet el-Mafjer, two miles northeast of Jericho.

4:23 *God dried up the . . . Jordan.* Still another descriptive phrase for the miracle, along with "the waters . . . stood," "rose up upon a heap" and "were cut off" (3:16).

4:24 *That all . . . might know.* The Lord's revelation of His power to the Israelites was a public event that all the Canaanites heard about (see 5:1), just as they had heard of the crossing of the "Red sea" and defeat of Sihon and Og (2:10). *ye.* The Hebrew can also be read as "they." *fear the LORD.* Worship and serve Him according to His commandments.

5:1–12 Two covenantal ceremonies were resumed at Gilgal in accordance with the laws from Sinai: the rite of circumcision and the feast of the passover. Both were significant preparations for the conquest of the promised land.

5:1 *Amorites . . . Canaanites.* Usually interchangeable, these general names included the many smaller nations in the land. Amorite meant "westerner," and Canaanite referred to the people living along the Mediterranean coast. This verse perhaps concludes the account of the crossing since it notes the effect of that event on the peoples of Canaan (see note on 3:10).

‡5:2 *sharp knives.* Lit. "flint knives." Metal knives were available, but flint made a more efficient surgical tool, as modern demonstrations have shown. Israel had to be consecrated to the Lord's service before she could undertake the Lord's warfare and take possession of the land (cf. Ex 4:24–26). *circumcise.* Circumcision marked every male as a son of Abraham (Gen 17:10–11) bound to the service of the Lord, and it was a prerequisite for the passover (Ex 12:48).

‡5:3 *the hill of the foreskins.* See KJV marg.

4 And this *is* the cause why Joshua did circumcise: [a]All the people that came out of Egypt, *that were* males, *even* all the men of war, died in the wilderness by the way, after they came out of Egypt.

5 Now all the people that came out were circumcised: but all the people *that were* born in the wilderness by the way as they came forth out of Egypt, *them* they had not circumcised.

6 For the children of Israel walked [a]forty years in the wilderness, till all the people *that were* men of war, which came out of Egypt, were consumed, because they obeyed not the voice of the LORD: unto whom the LORD sware that [b]*he* would not shew them the land, which the LORD sware unto their fathers that he would give us, [c]a land that floweth with milk and honey.

7 And [a]their children, *whom* he raised up in their stead, them Joshua circumcised: for they were uncircumcised, because they had not circumcised them by the way.

8 And it came to pass, [1]when they had done circumcising all the people, that they abode in their places in the camp, [a]till they were whole.

9 And the LORD said unto Joshua, *This* day have I rolled away [a]the reproach of Egypt from off you. Wherefore the name of the place is called [b][1]Gilgal unto this day.

10 ¶ And the children of Israel encamped in Gilgal, and kept the passover [a]on the fourteenth day of the month at even in the plains of Jericho.

5:4 [a]Num. 14:29; 26:64,65; Deut. 2:16
5:6 [a]Num. 14:33; Deut. 1:3 [b]Num. 14:23; Heb. 3:11 [c]Ex. 3:8
5:7 [a]Num. 14:31; Deut. 1:39
5:8 [1]Heb. *when the people had made an end to be circumcised* [a]See Gen. 34:25
5:9 [1]That is, *Rolling* [a]Gen. 34:14 [b]ch. 4:19
5:10 [a]Ex. 12:6; Num. 9:5
5:12 [a]Ex. 16:35
5:13 [a]Gen. 18:2; 32:24; Ex. 23:23; Zech. 1:8; Acts 1:10 [b]Num. 22:23
5:14 [1]Or, *prince* [a]Gen. 17:3
5:15 [a]Ex. 3:5; Acts 7:33
6:1 [1]Heb. *did shut up, and was shut up*
6:2 [a]ch. 2:9,24; 8:1 [b]Deut. 7:24

11 And they did eat of the old corn of the land on the morrow after the passover, unleavened *cakes,* and parched *corn* in the selfsame day.

12 And [a]the manna ceased on the morrow after they had eaten of the old corn of the land; neither had the children of Israel manna any more; but they did eat of the fruit of the land of Canaan that year.

The fall of Jericho

13 ¶ And it came to pass, when Joshua was by Jericho, that he lift up his eyes and looked, and behold, there stood [a]a man over against him [b]with his sword drawn in his hand: and Joshua went unto him, and said unto him, *Art* thou for us, or for our adversaries?

14 And he said, Nay; but *as* [1]captain of the host of the LORD am I now come. And Joshua [a]fell on his face to the earth, and did worship, and said unto him, What saith my lord unto his servant?

15 And the captain of the LORD's host said unto Joshua, [a]Loose thy shoe from off thy foot; for the place whereon thou standest *is* holy. And Joshua did so.

6 Now Jericho [1]was straitly shut up because of the children of Israel: none went out, and none came in.

2 And the LORD said unto Joshua, See, [a]I have given into thine hand Jericho, and the [b]king thereof, *and* the mighty *men* of valour.

3 And ye shall compass the city, all *ye* men

5:6 *forty years.* The time between their departure from Egypt and the crossing of the Jordan. Only 38 years had passed since they turned back at Kadesh-barnea (Num 14:20–22; Deut 2:14).
5:9 *reproach of Egypt.* Although the reference may be to Egypt's enslavement of Israel, it is much more likely that the author had in mind the reproach the Egyptians would have cast upon her and her God if Israel had perished in the wilderness (see Ex 32:12; Num 14:13; Deut 9:28). Now that the wilderness journey is over and Israel is safely in the promised land as His special people consecrated to Him by circumcision, the reproach of Egypt is rolled away.
5:10 *passover.* The ceremonies took place in the month of Abib, the first month of the year (Ex 12:2). At twilight on the 14th day of the month the passover lamb was to be slaughtered, then roasted and eaten that same night (Ex 12:5–8). Israel had not celebrated passover since Sinai, one year after her release from Egypt (Num 9:1–5). Before the next season she had rebelled at the border of Canaan, and the generation of the exodus had been condemned to die in the wilderness (Num 14:21–23, 29–35). For that generation the celebration of passover (deliverance from judgment) could have had little meaning.
5:11 *unleavened cakes.* Bread baked without yeast. It was to be eaten during the seven feast days that followed (Ex 12:15; Lev 23:6).
5:12 *manna ceased.* This transition from eating manna to eating the "old corn of the land" (v. 11) ended 40 years of dependence on God's special provision. Manna was God's gift for the wilderness journey; from now on He provided Israel with food from the promised land.
5:13–6:5 The narration of the conquest is introduced by the sudden appearance of a heavenly figure who calls himself the "captain of the host of the LORD" (5:14).
5:13 *Joshua was by Jericho.* The leader of God's army went to scout the nearest Canaanite stronghold, but another warrior was already on the scene. *stood a man.* The experience is taken by many to be an encounter with God in human form (theophany), or with Christ (Christophany). But angels also were sent on missions of this kind (Judg 6:11; 13:3), and some were identified as captains over the heavenly armies (Dan 10:5,20; 12:1).
5:14 *Nay; but.* Joshua and Israel must know their place—it is not that God is on their side; rather, they must fight God's battles. *captain of the host of the LORD.* God has sent the commander of His heavenly armies to take charge of the battle on earth. Joshua must take orders from him (6:2–5), and he can also know that the armies of heaven are committed to this war—as later events confirm. *my lord.* A term of respect for a superior.
5:15 Joshua is commissioned to undertake the Lord's battles for Canaan, just as Moses had been commissioned to confront Pharaoh (Ex 3:5).
‡6:1 *Jericho.* Modern Tell es-Sultan, site of more than two dozen ancient cities, built and destroyed, one above the other. Many had powerful, double walls. While none of the levels has been positively identified as the one that fell under Joshua, there is ample archaeological evidence of such a destruction. The tell (mound) is roughly 400 by 200 yards in size. Since Jericho may have been a center for the worship of the moon-god (Jericho probably means "moon city"), God was destroying not only Canaanite cities, but also Canaanite religion. See map No. 3 at the end of the study Bible.
6:2 *the LORD.* The Lord's command no doubt comes to Joshua through the "captain of the host of the LORD" (5:14), who orders the first conquest of a Canaanite city.
6:3 *compass the city.* A ritual act, signifying a siege of the city, that was to be repeated for six days.

of war, *and* go round about the city once. Thus
shalt thou do six days.
4 And seven priests shall bear before the
ark seven [a]trumpets of rams' horns: and the
seventh day ye shall compass the city seven
times, and [b]the priests shall blow with the
trumpets.
5 And it shall come to pass, *that* when *they*
make a long blast with the ram's horn, *and*
when ye hear the sound of the trumpet, all the
people shall shout *with* a great shout; and the
wall of the city shall fall down [1]flat, and the
people shall ascend up every man straight before him.
6 ¶ And Joshua the son of Nun called the
priests, and said unto them, Take up the ark of
the covenant, and let seven priests bear seven
trumpets of rams' horns before the ark of the
LORD.
7 And he said unto the people, Pass on,
and compass the city, and let him that is armed
pass on before the ark of the LORD.
8 And it came to pass, when Joshua had
spoken unto the people, that the seven priests
bearing the seven trumpets of rams' horns
passed on before the LORD, and blew with the
trumpets: and the ark of the covenant of the
LORD followed them.
9 And the armed men went before the
priests that blew *with* the trumpets, [a]and the
[1]rereward came after the ark, *the priests* going on, and blowing with the trumpets.
10 And Joshua had commanded the peo-
ple, saying, Ye shall not shout, nor [1]make any
noise with your voice, neither shall *any* word
proceed out of your mouth, until the day I bid
you shout; then shall ye shout.
11 So the ark of the LORD compassed the
city, going about *it* once: and they came *into*
the camp, and lodged in the camp.

6:4 [a]See Judg. 7:16,22 [b]Num. 10:8
6:5 [1]Heb. *under it*
6:9 [1]Heb. *gathering* host [a]Num. 10:25
6:10 [1]Heb. *make your voice to be heard*
6:12 [a]Deut. 31:25
6:17 [1]Or, *devoted* [a]ch. 2:4
6:18 [1]Or, *devoted* [a]Deut. 7:26; 13:17; ch. 7:1,11,12 [b]ch. 7:25; 1 Ki. 18:17,18; Jonah 1:12
6:19 [1]Heb. *holiness*
6:20 [1]Heb. *under it* [a]ver. 5; Heb. 11:30

12 And Joshua rose early in the morning,
[a]and the priests took up the ark of the LORD.
13 And seven priests bearing seven trumpets of rams' horns before the ark of the LORD
went on continually, and blew with the trumpets: and the armed men went before them;
but the rereward came after the ark of the
LORD, *the priests* going on, and blowing with
the trumpets.
14 And the second day they compassed the
city once, and returned *into* the camp: so they
did six days.
15 And it came to pass on the seventh day,
that they rose early about the dawning of the
day, and compassed the city after the same
manner seven times: only on that day they
compassed the city seven times.
16 And it came to pass at the seventh time,
when the priests blew with the trumpets,
Joshua said unto the people, Shout; for the
LORD hath given you the city.
17 And the city shall be [1]accursed, *even* it,
and all that *are* therein, to the LORD: only Rahab the harlot shall live, she and all that *are*
with her in the house, because [a]she hid the
messengers that we sent.
18 And you, [a]in any wise keep *yourselves*
from the [1]accursed thing, lest ye make *yourselves* accursed, when ye take of the [1]accursed
thing, and make the camp of Israel [1]a curse,
[b]and trouble it.
19 But all the silver, and gold, and vessels
of brass and iron, *are* [1]consecrated unto the
LORD: they shall come *into* the treasury of the
LORD.
20 So the people shouted when *the priests*
blew with the trumpets: and it came to pass,
when the people heard the sound of the trumpet, and the people shouted *with* a great
shout, that [a]the wall fell down [1]flat, so that

6:4 *ark.* Signified that the Lord was laying siege to the city. *trumpets of rams' horns.* Instruments not of music but of signaling, in both religious and military contexts (which appear to come together here). The trumpets were to be sounded (v. 8), as on the seventh day, announcing the presence of the Lord (see 2 Sam 6:15; 1 Chr 15:28; Zech 9:14). *seventh day.* No note is taken of the sabbath during this seven-day siege, but perhaps that was the day the Lord gave the city to Israel as the first pledge of the land of rest. To arrive at the goal of a long march on the seventh day is a motif found also in other ancient Near Eastern literature. In any event, the remarkable constellation of sevens (seven priests with trumpets, seven days, seven encirclements on the seventh day) underscores the sacred significance of the event (see Introduction to Revelation: Distinctive Feature) and is, perhaps, a deliberate evoking of the seven days of creation to signal the beginning of God's new order in the world.

6:5 *long blast . . . great shout.* Signaling the onset of the attack—psychological warfare, intended to create panic and confusion (see Judg 7). In the Dead Sea Scroll of "The War of the Sons of Light against the Sons of Darkness," the Levites are instructed to blow in unison a great battle fanfare to melt the heart of the enemy (see essay, p. 1344.) *every man straight before him.* Not a breach here and there but a general collapse of the walls, giving access to the city from all sides.

6:7 *him that is armed.* The Hebrew for this term differs from that in v. 3 but may be synonymous with it. It is to be expected that the ark led the procession. If so, the present reference may be to a kind of royal guard (but see v. 9 and note).

6:8–14 Throughout these verses the ark of the Lord is made the center of focus, highlighting the fact that it was the Lord Himself who besieged the city.

6:9 *rereward.* If the rear guard was made up of the final contingents of the army (see Num 10:25), the armed guard of vv. 7,9 constituted the main body of troops.

6:12–14 Literary repetition reflects repetition in action, a common feature in ancient Near Eastern literature.

6:17 *be accursed..* See vv. 18, 21; 2:10; see also note on Num 21:2. This placed all of Jericho's inhabitants under the curse of death and all of the city's treasures that could not be destroyed under consignment to the Lord's house (v. 19). According to the law of Moses this curse could be applied to animals for sacrifice, to property given to God, or to any person found worthy of death (Lev 27:28–29). It was Moses himself who ruled that all the inhabitants of Canaan be "devoted" (see KJV marg.) by execution for their idolatry and all its accompanying moral corruption (Deut 20:16–18). See note on Deut 2:34. *Rahab . . . shall live, she and all that are with her in the house.* Honoring the pledge made by the two spies (2:14).

6:18 *make the camp of Israel a curse.* See note on v. 17. If Isra-

the people went up into the city, every man
straight before him, and they took the city.
21 And they [a]utterly destroyed all that *was*
in the city, both man and woman, young and
old, and ox, and sheep, and ass, with the edge
of the sword.
22 But Joshua had said unto the two men
that had spied out the country, Go *into* the
harlot's house, and bring out thence the
woman, and all that she hath, [a]as ye sware
unto her.
23 And the young men that were spies
went in, and brought out Rahab, [a]and her father, and her mother, and her brethren, and all
that she had; and they brought out all her
[1]kindred, and left them without the camp of
Israel.
24 And they burnt the city with fire, and
all that *was* therein: [a]only the silver, and the
gold, and the vessels of brass and of iron, they
put *into* the treasury of the house of the LORD.
25 And Joshua saved Rahab the harlot
alive, and her father's household, and all that
she had; and [a]she dwelleth in Israel *even* unto
this day; because she hid the messengers,
which Joshua sent to spy out Jericho.
26 And Joshua adjured *them* at that time,
saying, [a]Cursed *be* the man before the LORD,
that riseth up and buildeth this city Jericho: he
shall lay the foundation thereof in his firstborn, and in his youngest *son* shall he set up
the gates of it.
27 [a]So the LORD was with Joshua; and [b]his
fame was *noised* throughout all the country.

Achan's sin

7 But the children of Israel committed a
trespass in the accursed thing: for
[a][1]Achan, the son of Carmi, the son of [2]Zabdi,
the son of Zerah, of the tribe of Judah, took of
the accursed thing: and the anger of the LORD
was kindled against the children of Israel.
2 And Joshua sent men from Jericho *to* Ai,
which *is* beside Beth-aven, on the east side of
Beth-el, and spake unto them, saying, Go up
and view the country. And the men went up
and viewed Ai.
3 And they returned to Joshua, and said
unto him, Let not all the people go up; *but* let
[1]about two or three thousand men go up and
smite Ai; *and* make not all the people to labour
thither; for they *are but* few.
4 So there went up thither of the people
about three thousand men: [a]and they fled before the men of Ai.
5 And the men of Ai smote of them about
thirty and six men: for they chased them *from*
before the gate *even* unto Shebarim, and
smote them [1]in the going down: wherefore
[a]the hearts of the people melted, and became
as water.
6 ¶ And Joshua [a]rent his clothes, and fell to
the earth upon his face before the ark of the
LORD until the eventide, he and the elders of
Israel, and [b]put dust upon their heads.
7 And Joshua said, Alas, O Lord GOD,
[a]wherefore hast thou at all brought this people
over Jordan, to deliver us into the hand of the
Amorites, to destroy us? would to God we had
been content, and dwelt on the *other* side Jordan!
8 O Lord, what shall I say, when Israel
turneth *their* [1]backs before their enemies!
9 For the Canaanites and all the inhabitants
of the land shall hear *of it,* and shall environ us
round, and [a]cut off our name from the earth:
and [b]what wilt thou do unto thy great name?
10 And the LORD said unto Joshua, Get
thee up; wherefore [1]liest thou thus upon thy
face?

6:21 [a]Deut. 7:2
6:22 [a]ch. 2:14; Heb. 11:31
6:23 [1]Heb. *families* [a]ch. 2:13
6:24 [a]ver. 19
6:25 [a]See Mat. 1:5
6:26 [a]1 Ki. 16:34
6:27 [a]ch. 1:5 [b]ch. 9:1,3
7:1 [1][1 Chr. 2:7, *Achar*] [2][Or, *Zimri,* 1 Chr. 2:6] [a]ch. 22:20
7:3 [1]Heb. *about* 2000 *men, or about* 3000 *men*
7:4 [a]Lev. 26:17; Deut. 28:25
7:5 [1]Or, *in Morad* [a]ch. 2:9,11; Lev. 26:36
7:6 [a]Gen. 37:29,34 [b]1 Sam. 4:12; 2 Sam. 1:2; 13:19; Neh. 9:1; Job 2:12
7:7 [a]Ex. 17:3; Num. 21:5
7:8 [1]Heb. *necks*
7:9 [a]Deut. 32:26 [b]See Ex. 32:12; Num. 14:13
7:10 [1]Heb. *fallest*

el took for herself anything that was under God's curse, she herself would fall under the curse.

6:25 *she dwelleth in Israel.* The faith of Rahab is noted twice in the NT (Heb 11:31; Jas 2:25).

6:26 *Cursed be the man.* Jericho itself was to be devoted to the Lord as a perpetual sign of God's judgment on the wicked Canaanites and as a firstfruits offering of the land. This was a way of signifying that the conquered land belonged to the Lord. The curse was fulfilled in the rebellious days of King Ahab (1 Ki 16:34).

7:1–26 The tragic story of Achan, which stands in sharp contrast to the story of Rahab. In the earlier event a Canaanite prostitute, because of her courageous allegiance to Israel and her acknowledgment of the Lord, was spared and received into Israel. She abandoned Canaan and its gods on account of the Lord and Israel, and so received Canaan back. In the present event an Israelite (of the tribe of Judah, no less), because of his disloyalty to the Lord and Israel, is executed as the Canaanites were. He stole the riches of Canaan from the Lord, and so lost his inheritance in the promised land. This is also a story of how one man's sin adversely affected the entire nation. Throughout this account (as often in the OT) Israel is considered a corporate unity in covenant with and in the service of the Lord. Thus even in the acts of one (Achan) or a few (the 3,000 defeated at Ai) all Israel is involved (see vv. 1,11; 22:20).

7:2 *from Jericho to Ai.* An uphill march of some 15 miles through a ravine to the top of the central Palestinian ridge. Strategically, an advance from Gilgal to Ai would bring Israel beyond the Jordan Valley and provide them a foothold in the central highlands. Ai in Hebrew means "the ruin." It is usually identified with et-Tell (meaning "the ruin" in Arabic), just two miles east of Beth-el, but some dispute this precise identification. *Beth-aven.* Means "house of wickedness," a derogatory designation of either Beth-el itself or a pagan shrine nearby (see 1 Sam 13:5; Hos 4:15; Amos 5:5). *view the country.* See note on 2:1–24.

7:5 *Shebarim.* Means "breaks," a fitting term for the rocky bluffs overlooking the Jordan Valley.

7:6 *Joshua rent his clothes.* A sign of great distress (see Gen 37:29,34; 44:13; Judg 11:35). Joshua's dismay (and that of the people), as indicated by his prayer, arose from his recognition that the Lord had not been with Israel's troops in the battle. And without the Lord the whole venture for which Israel had crossed the Jordan would be impossible. Moreover, the Canaanites would now judge that neither Israel nor her God was invincible. They would pour out of their fortified cities, combine forces and descend on Israel in the Jordan Valley, from which Israel could not escape across the flooding Jordan.

7:9 *thy great name.* Joshua pleads, as Moses had (Num 14:13–16; Deut 9:28–29), that God's honor in the eyes of all the world was at stake in the fortunes of His people.

11 [a]Israel hath sinned, and they have also transgressed my covenant which I commanded them: [b]for they have even taken of the accursed thing, and have also stolen, and [c]dissembled also, and they have put *it* even amongst their own stuff.

12 [a]Therefore the children of Israel could not stand before their enemies, *but* turned *their* backs before their enemies, because [b]they were accursed: neither will I be with you any more, except ye destroy the accursed from amongst you.

13 Up, [a]sanctify the people, and say, [b]Sanctify yourselves against to morrow: for thus saith the LORD God of Israel, *There is* an accursed thing in the midst of thee, O Israel: thou canst not stand before thine enemies, until ye take away the accursed thing from among you.

14 In the morning therefore ye shall be brought according to your tribes: and it shall be, *that* the tribe which [a]the LORD taketh shall come according to the families *thereof;* and the family which the LORD shall take shall come by households; and the household which the LORD shall take shall come man by man.

15 [a]And it shall be, *that* he that is taken with the accursed thing shall be burnt with fire, he and all that he hath: because he hath [b]transgressed the covenant of the LORD, and because he [c]hath wrought [1]folly in Israel.

16 ¶ So Joshua rose up early in the morning, and brought Israel by their tribes; and the tribe of Judah was taken:

17 And he brought the family of Judah; and he took the family of the Zarhites: and he brought the family of the Zarhites man by man; and Zabdi was taken:

18 And he brought his household man by man; and Achan, the son of Carmi, the son of Zabdi, the son of Zerah, of the tribe of Judah, [a]was taken.

19 And Joshua said unto Achan, My son, [a]give, I pray thee, glory to the LORD God of Israel, [b]and make confession unto him; and [c]tell me now what thou hast done; hide *it* not from me.

20 And Achan answered Joshua, and said, Indeed I have sinned against the LORD God of Israel, and thus and thus have I done:

21 When I saw among the spoils a goodly Babylonish garment, and two hundred shekels *of* silver, and a [1]wedge of gold of fifty shekels weight, then I coveted them, and took them; and behold, they *are* hid in the earth in the midst of my tent, and the silver under it.

22 So Joshua sent messengers, and they ran unto the tent; and behold, *it was* hid in his tent, and the silver under it.

23 And they took them out of the midst of the tent, and brought them unto Joshua, and unto all the children of Israel, and [1]laid them out before the LORD.

24 And Joshua, and all Israel with him, took Achan the son of Zerah, and the silver, and the garment, and the wedge of gold, and his sons, and his daughters, and his oxen, and his asses, and his sheep, and his tent, and all that he had: and they brought them *unto* [a]the valley of Achor.

25 And Joshua said, [a]Why hast thou troubled us? the LORD shall trouble thee this day. [b]And all Israel stoned him *with* stones, and burned them with fire, after they had stoned them with stones.

26 And they [a]raised over him a great heap of stones unto this day. So [b]the LORD turned from the fierceness of his anger. Wherefore the name of that place was called, [c]The valley of [1]Achor, unto this day.

The destruction of Ai

8 And the LORD said unto Joshua, [a]Fear not, neither be thou dismayed: take all the people of war with thee, and arise, go up *to* Ai: see, [b]I have given into thy hand the king of Ai, and his people, and his city, and his land:

7:11 [a]ver. 1 [b]ch. 6:17,18 [c]See Acts 5:1,2
7:12 [a]See Num. 14:45; Judg. 2:14 [b]Deut. 7:26; ch. 6:18; Hag. 2:13,14
7:13 [a]Ex. 19:10 [b]ch. 3:5
7:14 [a]Prov. 16:33
7:15 [1]Or, *wickedness* [a]See 1 Sam. 14:38,39 [b]ver. 11 [c]Gen. 34:7; Judg. 20:6
7:18 [a]1 Sam. 14:42
7:19 [a]See 1 Sam. 6:5; Jer. 13:16; John 9:24 [b]Num. 5:6,7; 2 Chr. 30:22; Ezra 10:10,11; Dan. 9:4 [c]1 Sam. 14:43
7:21 [1]Heb. *tongue*
7:23 [1]Heb. *poured*
7:24 [a]ver. 26; ch. 15:7
7:25 [a]ch. 6:18; 1 Chr. 2:7; Gal. 5:12 [b]Deut. 17:5
7:26 [1]That is, *Trouble* [a]ch. 8:29; 2 Sam. 18:17; Lam. 3:53 [b]Deut. 13:17; 2 Sam. 21:14 [c]ver. 24
8:1 [a]Deut. 1:21; 7:18; 31:8; ch. 1:9 [b]ch. 6:2

7:11 *Israel hath sinned.* One soldier's theft of the devoted goods brought collective guilt on the entire nation (see 22:20). *transgressed my covenant.* See v. 15. This is the main indictment; what follows is further specification.

7:12 *were accursed.* See note on 6:18.

7:13 *Sanctify yourselves.* A series of purifications to be undertaken by every Israelite in preparation for meeting with God, as before a solemn religious feast or a special assembly called by the Lord (see note on 3:5). Here God summons His people before Him for His judgment.

7:14 *tribe which the LORD taketh.* When the lots are cast, one of the tribes is taken by the LORD so that the search is narrowed until the Lord exposes the guilty persons. The lots may have been the Urim and Thummim from the ephod of the high priest (see notes on Ex 28:30; 1 Sam 2:28; see also 1 Sam 14:41).

7:15 *folly in Israel.* An act that within Israel, as the covenant people of the Lord, is an outrage of utter folly (see Deut 22:21; Judg 19:23–24; 20:6,10; 2 Sam 13:12).

7:19 *My son.* Joshua took a fatherly attitude toward Achan. *give . . . glory to the LORD.* A solemn charge to tell the truth. *make confession unto him.* Lit. "give praise to him."

7:21 *Babylonish garment.* A valuable import. *two hundred shekels . . . fifty shekels.* The silver would have weighed about five pounds, the gold about one and one-fourth pounds.

7:23 *before the LORD.* Who is here the Judge.

7:24 *Joshua . . . all Israel.* Joshua and all Israel were God's agents for executing His judgment on both the Canaanites and this violator of the covenant. *all that he had.* As the head of (and example for) his family, Achan involved his whole household in his guilt and punishment. This is in accordance with the principle of corporate solidarity—the whole community is represented in one member (especially the head of that community).

7:25 *stoned them.* Because Achan had been found guilty of violating the covenant of the holy Lord (see Ex 19:13; Lev 24:23; Num 15:36). Afterward the bodies were burned to purge the land of the evil.

7:26 *great heap of stones.* A second monument in the land to the events of the conquest—alongside the memorial at Gilgal (4:20). *Achor.* Means "trouble." Achor was also another form of Achan's name (see 1 Chr 2:7, where Achan is called "Achar").

8:1–29 Renewal of the conquest and the taking of Ai.

8:1 *Fear not.* Now that Israel is purged, the Lord reassures Joshua once more (see 1:3–5; 3:11–13; 6:2–5).

2 And thou shalt do to Ai and her king as
thou didst unto [a]Jericho and her king: only
[b]the spoil thereof, and the cattle thereof, shall
ye take for a prey unto yourselves: lay thee an
ambush for the city behind it.
3 So Joshua arose, and all the people of
war, to go up *against* Ai: and Joshua chose out
thirty thousand mighty *men* of valour, and sent
them away by night.
4 And he commanded them, saying, Be-
hold, [a]ye shall lie in wait against the city, *even*
behind the city: go not very far from the city,
but be ye all ready:
5 And I, and all the people that *are* with
me, will approach unto the city: and it shall
come to pass, when they come out against us,
as at the first, that [a]we will flee before them,
6 (For they will come out after us) till we
have [1]drawn them from the city; for they will
say, *They* flee before us, as at the first: therefore we will flee before them.
7 Then ye shall rise up from the ambush,
and seize upon the city: for the LORD your God
will deliver it into your hand.
8 And it shall be, when ye have taken the
city, *that* ye shall set the city on fire: according
to the commandment of the LORD shall ye do.
[a]See, I have commanded you.
9 Joshua therefore sent them forth: and
they went to lie in ambush, and abode between Beth-el and Ai, on the west side of Ai:
but Joshua lodged that night among the people.
10 And Joshua rose up early in the morning, and numbered the people, and went up,
he and the elders of Israel, before the people
to Ai.
11 [a]And all the people, *even the people* of
war that *were* with him, went up, and drew
nigh, and came before the city, and pitched on
the north side of Ai: now *there was* a valley between them and Ai.
12 And he took about five thousand men,
and set them to lie in ambush between Beth-el
and Ai, on the west side [1]of the city.
13 And when they had set the people, *even*
all the host that *was* on the north of the city,
and [1]their liers in wait on the west of the city,
Joshua went that night into the midst of the
valley.
14 And it came to pass, when the king of
Ai saw *it,* that they hasted and rose up early,
and the men of the city went out against Israel to battle, he and all his people, at a time appointed, before the plain; but he [a]wist not that
there were liers in ambush against him behind
the city.
15 And Joshua and all Israel [a]*made as if*
they were beaten before them, and fled *by* the
way of the wilderness.
16 And all the people that *were* in Ai were
called *together* to pursue after them: and they
pursued after Joshua, and were drawn away
from the city.
17 And there was not a man left in Ai or
Beth-el, that went not out after Israel: and they
left the city open, and pursued after Israel.
18 And the LORD said unto Joshua, Stretch
out the spear that *is* in thy hand toward Ai; for
I will give it into thine hand. And Joshua
stretched out the spear that *he had* in his hand
toward the city.
19 And the ambush arose quickly out of
their place, and they ran as soon as *he* had
stretched out his hand: and they entered *into*
the city, and took it, and hasted and set the
city on fire.
20 And when the men of Ai looked behind
them, they saw, and behold, the smoke of the
city ascended up to heaven, and they had no
[1]power to flee this way or that way: and the
people that fled *to* the wilderness turned back
upon the pursuers.
21 And when Joshua and all Israel saw that
the ambush had taken the city, and that the
smoke of the city ascended, then they turned
again, and slew the men of Ai.
22 And the other issued out of the city
against them; so they were in the midst of Israel, some on this side, and some on that side:
and they smote them, so that *they* [a]let none of
them remain or escape.
23 And the king of Ai they took alive, and
brought him to Joshua.
24 And it came to pass, when Israel had
made an end of slaying all the inhabitants of Ai
in the field, in the wilderness wherein they
chased them, and *when* they were all fallen on
the edge of the sword, until they were consumed, that all the Israelites returned *unto* Ai,
and smote it with the edge of the sword.
25 And *so* it was, *that* all that fell that day,
both of men and women, *were* twelve thousand, *even* all the men of Ai.
26 For Joshua drew not his hand back,
wherewith he stretched out the spear, until *he*
had utterly destroyed all the inhabitants of Ai.
27 [a]Only the cattle and the spoil of that
city Israel took for a prey unto themselves, according unto the word of the LORD which he
[b]commanded Joshua.

8:2 [a]ch. 6:21 [b]Deut. 20:14
8:4 [a]Judg. 20:29
8:5 [a]Judg. 20:32
8:6 [1]Heb. *pulled*
8:8 [a]2 Sam. 13:28
8:11 [a]ver. 5
8:12 [1]Or, *of Ai*
8:13 [1]Heb. *their lying in wait*
8:14 [a]Judg. 20:34; Eccl. 9:12
8:15 [a]Judg. 20:36
8:20 [1]Heb. *hand*
8:22 [a]Lev. 7:29; Deut. 7:2; Job 20:5; Luke 17:26-30; 1 Thes. 5:3
8:27 [a]Num. 31:22,26 [b]ver. 2

8:2 *spoil . . . prey unto yourselves.* The Lord now assigns the wealth of Canaan to His troops who fight His battles. *lay thee an ambush.* Still in command, the Lord directs the attack.

8:12 *five thousand.* Verse 3 speaks of a contingent of 30,000 assigned to the ambush. Perhaps Joshua assigned two different units to the task to assure success. Or from the original 30,000 a unit of 5,000 may have been designated to attack Ai itself while the remaining 25,000 served as a covering force to block the threat from Beth-el (see v. 17).

8:13 *host . . . on the north.* In full visibility Joshua's main force moved north of the city, then pretended to flee to the east, drawing out the entire army of defenders.

8:17 *Ai or Beth-el.* Their joint action indicates that the two cities were closely allied, though each is said to have had a king (12:9,16).

8:26 *he had utterly destroyed.* For the second time Joshua ordered the holy curse on the inhabitants of a Canaanite city (see notes on Num 21:2; Deut 2:34).

28 And Joshua burnt Ai, and made it [a]a heap for ever, *even* a desolation unto this day.

29 [a]And the king of Ai he hanged on a tree until eventide: [b]and as soon as the sun was down, Joshua commanded that they should take his carcase down from the tree, and cast it at the entering of the gate of the city, and [c]raise thereon a great heap of stones, *that remaineth* unto this day.

An altar built in mount Ebal

30 ¶ Then Joshua built an altar unto the LORD God of Israel [a]in mount Ebal,

31 As Moses the servant of the LORD commanded the children of Israel, as it is written in the [a]book of the law of Moses, an altar of whole stones, over which no *man* hath lift up *any* iron: and [b]they offered thereon burnt offerings unto the LORD, and sacrificed peace offerings.

32 And [a]he wrote there upon the stones a copy of the law of Moses, which he wrote in the presence of the children of Israel.

33 And all Israel, and their elders, and officers, and their judges, stood on this side the ark and on that side before the priests the Levites, [a]which bare the ark of the covenant of the LORD, as well [b]the stranger, as he that was born among them; half of them over against mount Gerizim, and half of them over against mount Ebal; [c]as Moses the servant of the LORD had commanded before, that they should bless the people of Israel.

34 And afterward [a]he read all the words of the law, [b]the blessings and cursings, according to all that is written in the book of the law.

35 There was not a word of all that Moses commanded, which Joshua read not before all the congregation of Israel, [a]with the women, and the little ones, and [b]the strangers that [1]were conversant among them.

The trickery of the Gibeonites

9 And it came to pass, when all the kings which *were* on *this* side Jordan, in the hills, and in the valleys, and in all the coasts of [a]the great sea over against Lebanon, [b]the Hittite, and the Amorite, the Canaanite, the Perizzite, the Hivite, and the Jebusite, heard *thereof;*

2 That they [a]gathered themselves together, to fight with Joshua and with Israel, *with* one [1]accord.

3 And when the inhabitants of [a]Gibeon [b]heard what Joshua had done unto Jericho and to Ai,

4 They did work wilily, and went and made as if they had been ambassadors, and took old sacks upon their asses, and wine bottles, old, and rent, and bound up;

8:28 [a]Deut. 13:16
8:29 [a]ch. 10:26 [b]Deut. 21:22,23; ch. 10:27 [c]ch. 7:26; 10:27
8:30 [a]Deut. 27:4,5
8:31 [a]Ex. 20:25; Deut. 27:5,6 [b]Ex. 20:24
8:32 [a]Deut. 27:2,8
8:33 [a]Deut. 31:9,25 [b]Deut. 31:12
8:33 [c]Deut. 11:29; 27:12
8:34 [a]Deut. 31:11; Neh. 8:3 [b]Deut. 28:2,15, 45; 29:20,21; 30:19
8:35 [1]Heb. *walked* [a]Deut. 31:12 [b]ver. 33
9:1 [a]Num. 34:6 [b]Ex. 3:17; 23:23
9:2 [1]Heb. *mouth* [a]Ps. 83:3,5
9:3 [a]ch. 10:2; 2 Sam. 21:1,2 [b]ch. 6:27

8:28 *burnt Ai.* As he had Jericho (6:24) and would later do to Hazor (11:11). *a desolation unto this day.* If the ruins of Ai have been correctly identified (see note on 7:2), the site shows signs of later occupation only from c. 1200 to 1100 B.C.

8:29 *the king of Ai he hanged on a tree.* The Israelites did not execute by hanging. "Tree" may refer to a pole on which the king's body was impaled after execution (see note on Deut 21:22). *until eventide.* According to Mosaic instructions (see Deut 21:22–23). *great heap of stones.* A third monument in the land (see note on 7:26).

8:30–35 The renewal of the covenant with the Lord as Moses had ordered (Deut 11:26–30; 27:1–8) concludes the account of the initial battles (see Introduction: Outline). The conquest of Canaan has already been put into rich theological perspective. This final event (see also Joshua's final official act, ch. 24) underscores Israel's servant relationship to the Lord. In conquest and occupation she must faithfully acknowledge her one identity as the people of the kingdom of God, subject to His commission and rule (see note on 5:14).

How Israel could assemble peacefully between mount Ebal and mount Gerizim without further conquest is a worrisome question—and has led to some radical reconstructions of Israel's history. It must be noted, however, that Biblical narrators at times followed a thematic rather than a strictly chronological order of events. That may be the case here, since it is clear that the story of the Gibeonite deception and submission (ch. 9) is included in the thematic development of how Israel came into possession of the rest of Canaan (see the author's introduction in 9:1–2). The Shechemites (Shechem was a major city lying between the two mountains mentioned) were Hivites (or were under Hivite domination; see Gen 34:2) and thus were related to the people of the Gibeonite cities (9:7; 11:19). Also, there was no important town between Gibeon and Shechem (Beth-el and Ai had been subdued). Perhaps the treaty of submission established between Israel and the Gibeonites (ch. 9) applied also to the Hivites of Shechem, and the covenant renewal ceremony that concludes ch. 8 (and the previous narrative section) actually took place chronologically after the events narrated in ch. 9. If this suggestion is correct, the Gibeonites or their representatives would have been among the "strangers" who participated with Israel in the covenant event (vv. 33,35).

8:30 *mount Ebal.* At the foot of this peak was the fortress city of Shechem, where Abraham had built an altar (Gen 12:6–7).

8:31 *burnt offerings.* See Lev 1:1–17. *peace offerings.* See Lev 3:1–17; 7:11–18.

8:32 *wrote . . . upon the stones.* Moses had ordered the people first to plaster the stones, then to inscribe on them the words of the law (Deut 27:2–4). These stones are the fourth monument in the land (see note on v. 29).

8:33 *stranger, as he that was born among them.* Israel now included those who were part of the "mixed multitude" (Ex 12:38) who had come out of Egypt, plus others who had associated with them during the wilderness wanderings (see note on vv. 30–35).

8:34 *the blessings and cursings.* See Deut 27–28 and notes.

9:1–27 The account of how the Gibeonites deceived the leaders of the tribes and obtained a treaty of submission to Israel. It is the first of three sections telling how Israel came into possession of the bulk of the land. Verses 1–2 introduce the three units.

9:1 *kings which were on this side Jordan.* Small, independent city-kingdoms were scattered over Canaan, inhabited by a variety of peoples who had come earlier from outside the land (compare vv. 1–2 with Gen 15:19).

9:3 *Gibeon.* A site just north of Jerusalem called el-Jib, showing the remains of a Late Bronze Age city with an excellent water supply. The Gibeonites were in league with a number of neighboring towns (v. 17) but seem to have been dominant in the confederation.

9:4 *They did work wilily.* Motivated by their fear of Israel's God,

5 And old shoes and clouted upon their
feet, and old garments upon them; and all the
bread of their provision was dry *and* mouldy.
6 And they went to Joshua [a]unto the camp
at Gilgal, and said unto him, and to the men of
Israel, We be come from a far country: now
therefore make ye a league with us.
7 And the men of Israel said unto the [a]Hi-
vites, Peradventure ye dwell among us; and
[b]how shall we make a league with you?
8 And they said unto Joshua, [a]We *are* thy
servants. And Joshua said unto them, Who *are*
ye? and from whence come ye?
9 And they said unto him, [a]From a very far
country thy servants are come because of the
name of the LORD thy God: for we have [b]heard
the fame of him, and all that he did in Egypt,
10 And [a]all that he did to the two kings of
the Amorites, that *were* beyond Jordan, to Sihon king of Heshbon, and to Og king of Bashan, which *was* at Ashtaroth.
11 Wherefore our elders and all the inhabitants of our country spake to us, saying, Take
victuals [1]with you for the journey, and go to
meet them, and say unto them, We *are* your servants: therefore now make ye a league with us.
12 This our bread we took hot for our provision out of our houses on the day we came
forth to go unto you; but now, behold, it is dry,
and it is mouldy:
13 And these bottles of wine, which we
filled, *were* new; and behold, they be rent: and
these our garments and our shoes are become
old by reason of the very long journey.
14 And [1]the men took of their victuals, [a]and
asked not *counsel* at the mouth of the LORD.
15 And Joshua [a]made peace with them,
and made a league with them, to let them live:
and the princes of the congregation sware
unto them.
16 ¶ And it came to pass at the end of three
days after they had made a league with them,
that they heard that they *were* their neighbours, and *that* they dwelt among them.
17 And the children of Israel journeyed,

9:6 [a]ch. 5:10
9:7 [a]ch. 11:19 [b]Ex. 23:32; Deut. 7:2; Judg. 2:2
9:8 [a]Deut. 20:11
9:9 [a]Deut. 20:15 [b]Ex. 15:14; Josh. 2:10
9:10 [a]Num. 21:24,33
9:11 [1]Heb. *in your hand*
9:14 [1]Or, *they received the men by reason of their victuals* [a]Num. 27:21
9:15 [a]ch. 11:19; 2 Sam. 21:2

9:17 [a]ch. 18:25, 26,28; Ezra 2:25
9:18 [a]Ps. 15:4; Eccl. 5:2
9:20 [a]See 2 Sam. 21:1,2,6; Ezek. 17:13, 15,18,19; Zech. 5:3,4; Mal. 3:5
9:21 [a]Deut. 29:11 [b]ver. 15
9:22 [a]ver. 6,9 [b]ver. 16
9:23 [1]Heb. *not be cut off from you* [a]Gen. 9:25
9:24 [a]Ex. 23:32; Deut. 7:1,2 [b]Ex. 15:14
9:25 [a]Gen. 16:6
9:27 [1][Heb. *gave,* or, *delivered* to be; 1 Chr. 9:2; Ezra 8:20] [a]ver. 21,23 [b]Deut. 12:5

and came unto their cities on the third day.
Now their cities *were* [a]Gibeon, and Chephirah, and Beeroth, and Kirjath-jearim.
18 And the children of Israel smote them
not, [a]because the princes of the congregation
had sworn unto them by the LORD God of Israel. And all the congregation murmured against
the princes.
19 But all the princes said unto all the congregation, We have sworn unto them by the
LORD God of Israel: now therefore we may not
touch them.
20 This we will do to them; we will even
let them live, lest [a]wrath be upon us, because
of the oath which we sware unto them.
21 And the princes said unto them, Let
them live; but let them be [a]hewers of wood
and drawers of water unto all the congregation; as the princes had [b]promised them.
22 And Joshua called for them, and he
spake unto them, saying, Wherefore have ye
beguiled us, saying, [a]We *are* very far from you;
when [b]ye dwell among us?
23 Now therefore ye *are* [a]cursed, and
there shall [1]none of you be freed from being
bondmen, and hewers of wood and drawers of
water for the house of my God.
24 And they answered Joshua, and said,
Because it was certainly told thy servants, how
that the LORD thy God [a]commanded his servant Moses to give you all the land, and to destroy all the inhabitants of the land from before you, therefore [b]we were sore afraid of our
lives because of you, and have done this thing.
25 And now, behold, we *are* [a]in thine
hand: as it seemeth good and right unto thee
to do unto us, do.
26 And so did he unto them, and delivered
them out of the hand of the children of Israel,
that they slew them not.
27 And Joshua [1]made them that day [a]hew-
ers of wood and drawers of water for the congregation, and for the altar of the LORD, *even*
unto this day, [b]in the place which he should
choose.

the Gibeonites used pretense to trick Joshua into a treaty that would allow them to live.

9:6 *make ye a league with us.* In this request they were offering to submit themselves by treaty to be subjects of the Israelites (see v. 11, where they call themselves "your servants"—unmistakable language in the international diplomacy of that day). They chose submission rather than certain death (v. 24).

9:7 *Hivites.* Possibly Horites, an ethnic group living in Canaan related to the Hurrians of northern Mesopotamia (11:19; Gen 10:17; Ex 23:23; Judg 3:3).

9:9 *heard the fame of him.* The same reports that had been heard in Jericho (see 2:10).

9:14 *asked not . . . the LORD.* Did not consult their King, whose mission they were on.

9:15 *made peace . . . a league.* A covenant to let them live was sworn by the heads of the tribes—i.e., an oath was taken in the holy name of God. All such oaths were binding in Israel (see Ex 20:7; Lev 19:12; 1 Sam 14:24).

9:18 *all the congregation murmured.* Perhaps the people feared the consequences of not following through on the earlier divine order to destroy all the Canaanites, but more likely they grumbled because they could not take over the Gibeonite cities and possessions.

9:21 *hewers of wood and drawers of water.* A conventional phrase for household servants.

9:23 *cursed.* Noah's prediction that Canaan would someday be the servant of Shem (Gen 9:25–26) has part of its fulfillment in this event. *for the house of my God.* Probably specifies how the Gibeonites were to serve "all the congregation" (v. 21). Worship at the tabernacle (and later at the temple) required much wood and water (for sacrifices and washing) and consequently a great deal of menial labor. From now on, that labor was to be supplied by the Gibeonites, perhaps on a rotating basis. In this way they entered the Lord's service. When Solomon became king, the tabernacle and altar were at Gibeon (2 Chr 1:3,5).

9:27 *the place which he should choose.* Joshua moved the tabernacle (and its altar) to Shiloh, and there it would reside at least until the days of Samuel (1 Sam 4:3). Later, the Lord chose Jerusalem (1 Ki 9:3).

The sun stands still

10 Now it came to pass, when Adoni-zedek king of Jerusalem had heard how
Joshua had taken Ai, and had utterly destroyed
it; [a]as he had done to Jericho and her king, so
he had done to [b]Ai and her king; and [c]how the
inhabitants of Gibeon had made peace with Israel, and were among them;
2 That they [a]feared greatly, because Gibeon *was* a great city, as one of the [1]royal cities,
and because it *was* greater than Ai, and all the
men thereof *were* mighty.
3 Wherefore Adoni-zedek king of Jerusalem sent unto Hoham king of Hebron, and
unto Piram king of Jarmuth, and unto Japhia
king of Lachish, and unto Debir king of Eglon,
saying,
4 Come up unto me, and help me, that we
may smite Gibeon: [a]for it hath made peace
with Joshua and with the children of Israel.
5 Therefore the five kings of the Amorites,
the king of Jerusalem, the king of Hebron, the
king of Jarmuth, the king of Lachish, the king of
Eglon, [a]gathered themselves together, and went
up, they and all their hosts, and encamped before Gibeon, and made war against it.
6 And the men of Gibeon sent unto Joshua
[a]to the camp to Gilgal, saying, Slack not thy
hand from thy servants; come up to us quickly,
and save us, and help us: for all the kings of
the Amorites that dwell in the mountains are
gathered together against us.
7 So Joshua ascended from Gilgal, he, and
[a]all the people of war with him, and all the
mighty *men* of valour.
8 And the LORD said unto Joshua, [a]Fear
them not: for I have delivered them into thine
hand; [b]there shall not a man of them stand before thee.
9 Joshua therefore came unto them suddenly, *and* went up from Gilgal all night.

10:1 [a]ch. 6:21 [b]ch. 8:22,26,28 [c]ch. 9:15
10:2 [1]Heb. *cities of the kingdom* [a]Ex. 15:14-16; Deut. 11:25
10:4 [a]ver. 1; ch. 9:15
10:5 [a]ch. 9:2
10:6 [a]ch. 5:10; 9:6
10:7 [a]ch. 8:1
10:8 [a]ch. 11:6; Judg. 4:14 [b]ch. 1:5

10 And the LORD [a]discomfited them before
Israel, and slew them *with* a great slaughter at
Gibeon, and chased them *along* the way that
goeth up [b]to Beth-horon, and smote them to
[c]Azekah, and unto Makkedah.
11 And it came to pass, as they fled from
before Israel, *and* were in the going down to
Beth-horon, [a]that the LORD cast down great
stones from heaven upon them unto Azekah,
and they died: *they were* moe which died with
hailstones than *they* whom the children of Israel slew with the sword.
12 ¶ Then spake Joshua to the LORD in the
day when the LORD delivered up the Amorites
before the children of Israel, and he said in the
sight of Israel,
[a]Sun, [1]stand thou still upon Gibeon;
And thou, Moon, in the valley of
[b]Ajalon.
13 And the sun stood still, and the moon
stayed,
Until the people had avenged
themselves upon their enemies.
[a]*Is* not this written in the book of
[1]Jasher?
So the sun stood still in the midst of
heaven,
And hasted not to go down about a
whole day.
14 And there was [a]no day like that before
it or after it, that the LORD hearkened unto the
voice of a man: for [b]the LORD fought for Israel.
15 ¶ [a]And Joshua returned, and all Israel
with him, unto the camp to Gilgal.
16 But these five kings fled, and hid themselves in a cave at Makkedah.
17 And it was told Joshua, saying, The five
kings are found hid in a cave at Makkedah.
18 And Joshua said, Roll great stones upon
the mouth of the cave, and set men by it for to
keep them:

10:10 [a]Judg. 4:15; 1 Sam. 7:10,12; Is. 28:21 [b]ch. 16:3,5 [c]ch. 15:35
10:11 [a]Is. 30:30; Rev. 16:21
10:12 [1]Heb. *be silent* [a]Is. 28:21; Hab. 3:11 [b]Judg. 12:12
10:13 [1]Or, *the upright?* [a]2 Sam. 1:18
10:14 [a]See Is. 38:8 [b]ver. 42; Deut. 1:30; ch. 23:3
10:15 [a]ver. 43

10:1–43 The army under Joshua comes to the defense of Gibeon and defeats the coalition of southern kings at Ajalon, then subdues all the southern cities of Judah and the Negev.

10:1 *Adoni-zedek.* Means "lord of righteousness" or "My (divine) lord is righteous." An earlier king of Jerusalem had a similar name (Melchizedek; see Gen 14:18 and note). *Jerusalem.* City of the Jebusites.

10:2 *great city.* Gibeon was not only larger in size than Beth-el or Ai, but also closer to Jerusalem. With Beth-el and Ai conquered and the Gibeonite league in submission, the Israelites were well established in the central highlands, virtually cutting the land in two. Naturally the king of Jerusalem felt threatened, and he wanted to reunite all the Canaanites against Israel. Perhaps he also held (or claimed) some political dominion over the Gibeonite cities and viewed their submission to Israel as rebellion. *mighty.* Men famous for their courage in battle, yet wise enough to have made peace with the Israelites.

10:5 *five kings of the Amorites.* Rulers over five of the major cities in the southern mountains. The Amorites of the hills are here distinguished from the Canaanites along the coast.

10:6 *come . . . and save us.* An urgent appeal for deliverance to a man whose name means "The LORD saves." A treaty such as Joshua had made with the Gibeonites usually obliged the ruling nation to come to the aid of the subject peoples if they were attacked.

10:9 *suddenly.* Joshua attacked early in the morning, perhaps while the moon was still up (v. 12). *went up . . . all night.* Gilgal was about 20 miles east of Gibeon, a steep uphill climb for Joshua's men.

10:10 *discomfited.* The Hebrew for this word implies terror or panic.

10:11 *the going down to Beth-horon.* A long descent to the plain of Aijalon below, following the main east-west crossroad just north of Jerusalem. *great stones from heaven.* For the Lord's use of the elements of nature as His armaments see Judg 5:20; 1 Sam 7:10; Job 38:22.

10:13 *book of Jasher.* An early account of Israel's wars (perhaps all in poetic form; see 2 Sam 1:18; see also note on Judg 5:1–31), but never a part of canonical Scripture. *hasted not to go down.* Some believe that God extended the hours of daylight for the Israelites to defeat their enemies. Others suggest that the sun remained cool (perhaps as the result of an overcast sky) for an entire day, allowing the fighting to continue through the afternoon. The fact is we do not know what happened, except that it involved divine intervention.

10:16 *Makkedah.* A town near Azekah (v. 10) in the western foothills where Joshua's troops made their camp.

19 And stay you not, *but* pursue after your enemies, and [1]smite the hindmost of them; suffer them not to enter into their cities: for the LORD your God hath delivered them into your hand.

20 And it came to pass, when Joshua and the children of Israel had made an end of slaying them *with* a very great slaughter, till they were consumed, that the rest *which* remained of them entered into fenced cities.

21 And all the people returned to the camp to Joshua *at* Makkedah in peace: [a]none moved his tongue against any of the children of Israel.

22 Then said Joshua, Open the mouth of the cave, and bring out those five kings unto me out of the cave.

23 And they did so, and brought forth those five kings unto him out of the cave, the king of Jerusalem, the king of Hebron, the king of Jarmuth, the king of Lachish, *and* the king of Eglon.

24 And it came to pass, when they brought out those kings unto Joshua, that Joshua called for all the men of Israel, and said unto the captains of the men of war which went with him, Come near, [a]put your feet upon the necks of these kings. And they came near, and put their feet upon the necks of them.

25 And Joshua said unto them, [a]Fear not, nor be dismayed, be strong and of good courage: for [b]thus shall the LORD do to all your enemies against whom ye fight.

26 And afterward Joshua smote them, and slew them, and hanged them on five trees: and they [a]were hanging upon the trees until the evening.

27 And it came to pass at the time of the going down of the sun, *that* Joshua commanded, and they [a]took them down off the trees, and cast them into the cave wherein they had been hid, and laid great stones in the cave's mouth, *which remain* until this very day.

Conquest of the south

28 ¶ And that day Joshua took Makkedah, and smote it with the edge of the sword, and the king thereof he utterly destroyed, them, and all the souls that *were* therein; he let none remain: and he did to the king of Makkedah [a]as he did unto the king of Jericho.

29 Then Joshua passed from Makkedah, and all Israel with him, *unto* Libnah, and fought against Libnah:

30 And the LORD delivered it also, and the king thereof, into the hand of Israel; and he smote it with the edge of the sword, and all the souls that *were* therein; he let none remain in it; but did unto the king thereof as he did unto the king of Jericho.

31 And Joshua passed from Libnah, and all Israel with him, unto Lachish, and encamped against it, and fought against it:

32 And the LORD delivered Lachish into the hand of Israel, which took it on the second day, and smote it with the edge of the sword, and all the souls that *were* therein, according to all that he had done to Libnah.

33 Then Horam king of [a]Gezer came up to help Lachish; and Joshua smote him and his people, until *he* had left him none remaining.

34 And from Lachish Joshua passed unto Eglon, and all Israel with him; and they encamped against it, and fought against it:

35 And they took it on that day, and smote it with the edge of the sword, and all the souls that *were* therein he utterly destroyed that day, according to all that he had done to Lachish.

36 And Joshua went up from Eglon, and all Israel with him, unto [a]Hebron; and they fought against it:

37 And they took it, and smote it with the edge of the sword, and the king thereof, and all the cities thereof, and all the souls that *were* therein; he left none remaining, according to all that he had done to Eglon; but destroyed it utterly, and all the souls that *were* therein.

38 And Joshua returned, and all Israel with him, to [a]Debir; and fought against it:

39 And he took it, and the king thereof, and all the cities thereof; and they smote them with the edge of the sword, and utterly destroyed all the souls that *were* therein; he left none remaining: as he had done to Hebron, so he did to Debir, and to the king thereof; as he had done also to Libnah, and to her king.

40 ¶ So Joshua smote all the country of the hills, and of the south, and of the vale, and of the springs, and all their kings: he left none remaining, but utterly destroyed all that breathed, as the LORD God of Israel [a]commanded.

41 And Joshua smote them from Kadesh-

10:19 [1]Heb. *cut off the tail*
10:21 [a]Ex. 11:7
10:24 [a]Ps. 107:40; Is. 26:5,6; Mal. 4:3
10:25 [a]Deut. 31:6,8; ch. 1:9 [b]Deut. 3:21; 7:19
10:26 [a]ch. 8:29
10:27 [a]Deut. 21:23; ch. 8:29
10:28 [a]ch. 6:21
10:33 [a]ch. 16:3,10; 1 Ki. 9:16,17; 1 Chr. 20:4
10:36 [a]See ch. 14:13; 15:13; Judg. 1:10
10:38 [a]See ch. 15:15; Judg. 1:11
10:40 [a]Deut. 20:16,17

10:19 *pursue after your enemies.* Most of the fighting men defending the southern cities were caught and killed before they could reach the safety of their fortresses.

10:21 *none moved his tongue.* The thought here appears to be that no one dared even to raise his voice against the Israelites anymore.

10:24 *put your feet upon the necks.* Public humiliation of defeated enemy chieftains was the usual climax of warfare in the ancient Near East.

10:26 *hanged them on five trees.* See note on Deut 21:22.

10:27 *laid great stones.* A fifth monument in the land to the events of the conquest (see note on 8:32).

10:28 *destroyed . . . all the souls.* The holy curse was placed on the people of Makkedah, meaning they were "devoted" to death for their wicked deeds (see notes on Num 21:2; Deut 2:34). The same fate came to the other major cities of the south (vv. 29–42).

10:33 *Horam king of Gezer.* An important detail: the defeat of the king of the most powerful city in the area. Gezer was eventually taken over by the Egyptians and given to King Solomon as a wedding gift (see 1 Ki 9:16).

10:38 *Debir.* In the past, Debir (also known as Kirjath-sepher, 15:15) was identified with Tell Beit Mirsim. More recently, however, it has been equated with Khirbet Rabud, about five miles southwest of Hebron.

10:41 *Kadesh-barnea . . . Gaza.* The south-to-north limits in

barnea even unto [a]Gaza, [b]and all the country
of Goshen, even unto Gibeon.
42 And all these kings and their land did
Joshua take *at* one time, [a]because the LORD
God of Israel fought for Israel.
43 And Joshua returned, and all Israel with
him, unto the camp to Gilgal.

Conquest of the north

11 And it came to pass, when Jabin king
of Hazor had heard *those things,* that
he [a]sent to Jobab king of Madon, and to the
king [b]of Shimron, and to the king of Achshaph,
2 And to the kings that *were* on the north
of the mountains, and of the plains south of
[a]Cinneroth, and in the valley, and in the borders [b]of Dor on the west,
3 *And to* the Canaanite on the east and on
the west, and *to* the Amorite, and the Hittite,
and the Perizzite, and the Jebusite in the
mountains, [a]and *to* the Hivite under [b]Hermon
[c]in the land of Mizpeh.
4 And they went out, they and all their
hosts with them, much people, [a]*even* as the
sand that *is* upon the sea shore in multitude,
with horses and chariots very many.
5 And when all these kings were [1]met together, they came and pitched together at the
waters of Merom, to fight against Israel.
6 ¶ And the LORD said unto Joshua, [a]Be not
afraid because of them: for to morrow about
this time will I deliver them up all slain before
Israel: thou shalt [b]hough their horses, and
burn their chariots with fire.
7 So Joshua came, and all the people of war
with him, against them by the waters of Merom suddenly; and they fell upon them.
8 And the LORD delivered them into the

10:41 [a]Gen. 10:19 [b]ch. 11:16
10:42 [a]ver. 14
11:1 [a]ch. 10:3 [b]ch. 19:15
11:2 [a]Num. 34:11 [b]ch. 17:11; Judg. 1:27; 1 Ki. 4:11
11:3 [a]Judg. 3:3 [b]ch. 13:11 [c]Gen. 31:49
11:4 [a]Gen. 22:17; 32:12; Judg. 7:12; 1 Sam. 13:5
11:5 [1]Heb. *assembled by appointment*
11:6 [a]ch. 10:8 [b]2 Sam. 8:4
11:8 [1]Or, *Zidon-rabbah* [2]Or, *Salt pits.* Heb. *Burning[s] of waters* [a]ch. 13:6
11:11 [1]Heb. *any breath*
11:12 [a]Num. 33:52
11:13 [1]Heb. *on their heap*
11:15 [1]Heb. *he removed nothing* [a]Ex. 34:11,12 [b]Deut. 31:7,8 [c]ch. 1:7
11:16 [a]ch. 12:8 [b]ch. 10:41
11:17 [1]Or, *the smooth mountain* [a]ch. 12:7

hand of Israel, who smote them, and chased
them unto [1]great Zidon, and unto [a2]Misre-
photh-maim, and unto the valley of Mizpeh
eastward; and they smote them, until *they* left
them none remaining.
9 And Joshua did unto them as the LORD
bade him: he houghed their horses, and burnt
their chariots with fire.
10 And Joshua at that time turned back,
and took Hazor, and smote the king thereof
with the sword: for Hazor beforetime *was* the
head of all those kingdoms.
11 And they smote all the souls that *were*
therein with the edge of the sword, utterly destroying *them:* there was not [1]any left to
breathe: and he burnt Hazor with fire.
12 And all the cities of those kings, and all
the kings of them, did Joshua take, and smote
them with the edge of the sword, *and* he utterly destroyed them, [a]as Moses the servant of
the LORD commanded.
13 But *as for* the cities that stood still [1]in
their strength, Israel burned none of them,
save Hazor only; *that* did Joshua burn.
14 And all the spoil of these cities, and the
cattle, the children of Israel took for a prey
unto themselves; but every man they smote
with the edge of the sword, until they had destroyed them, neither left they any to breathe.
15 [a]As the LORD commanded Moses his
servant, so [b]did Moses command Joshua, and
[c]so did Joshua; [1]he left nothing undone of all
that the LORD commanded Moses.
16 So Joshua took all that land, [a]the hills,
and all the south *country,* [b]and all the land of
Goshen, and the valley, and the plain, and the
mountain of Israel, and the valley of the same;
17 [a]*Even* from [1]the mount Halak, that

the western part of the region. *Goshen.* A seldom-used name for the eastern Negev, not to be confused with the Goshen in the delta of Egypt; it is also the name of a town (15:51). Goshen and Gibeon mark the south-to-north limits in the eastern part of the region.

11:1–23 Only the northern cities remained to be conquered. The major battle for the hills of Galilee is fought and won against Hazor and the coalition of other northern city-states. A summary follows of all Joshua's victories in the southern and central regions as well.

11:1 *Jabin king of Hazor.* Jabin is perhaps a dynastic name, used again in the days of Deborah (Judg 4:2). The archaeological excavation of Hazor shows that it was the largest and best fortified of all the Canaanite cities. Its lower city measured 175 acres.

‡11:2 *Cinneroth.* Means "harp"; the sea of Galilee (which is shaped like a harp).

11:4 *much people . . . as the sand . . . upon the sea shore.* A widely used figure of speech for indicating large numbers (see note on Gen 22:17).

11:5 *all these kings.* Jabin's muster extended as far as the Arabah (v. 2) in the Jordan Valley and as far as Dor on the Mediterranean, south of mount Carmel. *Merom.* Probably modern Meirun, just northwest of Safed near the source of the Wadi Ammud (Marun)—some eight miles northwest of the sea of Galilee.

‡11:6 *hough* [i.e. hamstring] *their horses.* Done by cutting the tendon above the hock or ankle, crippling the horse so that it cannot walk again. *burn their chariots.* These advanced implements of war were not used by the armies of Israel until the time of Solomon (see 1 Ki 9:22; 10:26–29).

11:10 *Joshua . . . took Hazor.* Perhaps his greatest victory. Hazor's armed forces, however, had been defeated earlier at Merom. The archaeological site reveals extensive damage and the burning of the Canaanite city c. 1400 B.C., c. 1300 and again c. 1230. Since the destruction level at c. 1300 probably indicates the burning of the city by Pharaoh Seti I, this leaves the destruction levels at c. 1400 and c. 1230 for Joshua's conquest. Those who hold to the late date of the conquest opt for the 1230 level; those who hold to the early date opt for 1400 (see Introduction: Historical Setting). Once again the curse of total destruction was applied (v. 11).

11:13 *strength.* The Hebrew word is *tel* (Arabic *tell*), a hill formed by the accumulated debris of many ancient settlements one above the other (see note on 7:2).

11:15 *he left nothing undone.* Joshua's success should be measured in the light of the specific orders given by God, which he carried out fully, rather than by the total area that eventually would have to be occupied by Israel.

11:16 *all that land.* A lesson in the geography of Canaan follows. See map No. 2 at the end of the study Bible.

11:17 *mount Halak.* A wilderness peak to the east of Kadesh-barnea marking Israel's southern extremity. *Baal-gad.* The first valley west of mount Hermon.

goeth up *to* Seir, even unto Baal-gad in the valley of Lebanon under mount Hermon: and [b]all their kings he took, and smote them, and slew them.

18 Joshua made war a long time with all those kings.

19 There was not a city that made peace with the children of Israel, save [a]the Hivites the inhabitants of Gibeon: all *other* they took in battle.

20 For [a]it was of the LORD to harden their hearts, that *they* should come against Israel *in* battle, that *he* might destroy them utterly, *and* that they might have no favour, but that *he* might destroy them, [b]as the LORD commanded Moses.

21 And at that time came Joshua, and cut off [a]the Anakims from the mountains, from Hebron, from Debir, from Anab, and from all the mountains of Judah, and from all the mountains of Israel: Joshua destroyed them utterly with their cities.

22 There was none of the Anakims left in the land of the children of Israel: only in Gaza, in [a]Gath, [b]and in Ashdod, there remained.

23 So Joshua took the whole land, [a]according to all that the LORD said unto Moses; and Joshua gave it for an inheritance unto Israel [b]according to their divisions by their tribes. [c]And the land rested from war.

Defeated kings

12 Now these *are* the kings of the land, which the children of Israel smote, and possessed their land on the *other* side Jordan toward the rising of the sun, [a]from the river Arnon [b]unto mount Hermon, and all the plain on the east:

2 [a]Sihon king of the Amorites, who dwelt in Heshbon, *and* ruled from Aroer, which *is* upon the bank of the river of Arnon, and *from* the middle of the river, and *from* half Gilead, even unto the river Jabbok, *which is* the border of the children of Ammon;

3 And [a]*from* the plain to the sea of Cinneroth on the east, and unto the sea of the plain, *even* the salt sea on the east, [b]the way to Beth-jeshimoth; and from [1]the south, under [c][2]Ashdoth-pisgah:

4 And [a]the coast of Og king of Bashan, *which was* of [b]the remnant of the giants, [c]that dwelt at Ashtaroth and at Edrei,

5 And reigned in [a]mount Hermon, [b]and in Salcah, and in all Bashan, [c]unto the border of the Geshurites and the Maachathites, and half Gilead, the border of Sihon king of Heshbon.

6 [a]Them did Moses the servant of the LORD and the children of Israel smite: and [b]Moses the servant of the LORD gave it *for* a possession unto the Reubenites, and the Gadites, and the half tribe of Manasseh.

7 ¶ And these *are* the kings of the country [a]which Joshua and the children of Israel smote on *this* side Jordan on the west, from Baal-gad in the valley of Lebanon even unto the mount Halak, that goeth up to [b]Seir; which Joshua [c]gave unto the tribes of Israel *for* a possession according to their divisions;

8 [a]In the mountains, and in the valleys, and in the plains, and in the springs, and in the wilderness, and in the south *country;* [b]the Hittites, the Amorites, and the Canaanites, the Perizzites, the Hivites, and the Jebusites:

9 [a]The king of Jericho, one; [b]the king of Ai, which *is* beside Beth-el, one;

10 [a]The king of Jerusalem, one; the king of Hebron, one;

11 The king of Jarmuth, one; the king of Lachish, one;

12 The king of Eglon, one; [a]the king of Gezer, one;

13 [a]The king of Debir, one; the king of Geder, one;

14 The king of Hormah, one; the king of Arad, one;

15 [a]The king of Libnah, one; the king of Adullam, one;

16 [a]The king of Makkedah, one; [b]the king of Beth-el, one;

17 The king of Tappuah, one; [a]the king of Hepher, one;

18 The king of Aphek, one; the king of [1]Lasharon, one;

19 The king of Madon, one; [a]the king of Hazor, one;

20 The king of [a]Shimron-meron, one; the king of Achshaph, one;

21 The king of Taanach, one; the king of Megiddo, one;

11:17 [b]Deut. 7:24; ch. 12:7
11:19 [a]ch. 9:3,7
11:20 [a]Deut. 2:30; Judg. 14:4; 1 Sam. 2:25 [b]Deut. 20:16,17
11:21 [a]Num. 13:22,33; Deut. 1:28; ch. 15:13,14
11:22 [a]1 Sam. 17:4 [b]ch. 15:46
11:23 [a]Num. 34:2 [b]Num. 26:53; ch. 14; 15 [c]ver. 18; ch. 14:15; 21:44; 22:4; 23:1
12:1 [a]Num. 21:24 [b]Deut. 3:8,9
12:2 [a]Num. 21:24
12:3 [1]Or, *Teman* [2]Or, *the springs of Pisgah,* or, *the hill* [a]Deut. 3:17 [b]ch. 13:20 [c]Deut. 3:17; 4:49
12:4 [a]Num. 21:33; Deut. 3:4,10
12:4 [b]Deut. 3:11; ch. 13:12 [c]Deut. 1:4
12:5 [a]Deut. 3:8 [b]Deut. 3:10; ch. 13:11 [c]Deut. 3:14
12:6 [a]Num. 21:24,35 [b]Num. 32:29,33; ch. 13:8
12:7 [a]ch. 11:17 [b]Gen. 14:6; 32:3; Deut. 2:1,4 [c]ch. 11:23
12:8 [a]ch. 10:40; 11:16 [b]Ex. 3:8; 23:23; ch. 9:1
12:9 [a]ch. 6:2 [b]ch. 8:29
12:10 [a]ch. 10:23
12:12 [a]ch. 10:33
12:13 [a]ch. 10:38,39
12:15 [a]ch. 10:29,30
12:16 [a]ch. 10:28 [b]ch. 8:17; Judg. 1:22
12:17 [a]1 Ki. 4:10
12:18 [1]Or, *Sharon*
12:19 [a]ch. 11:10
12:20 [a]ch. 11:1; 19:15

11:18 *a long time.* An estimation of the duration of Joshua's conquests can be made from the life-span of Caleb: Seven years had elapsed from the beginning of the conquest (age 78; compare 14:7 with Deut 2:14) until he took Hebron (age 85; see 14:10).

11:20 *the LORD . . . their hearts.* God has sovereign control of history, yet His will never denies our personal and moral freedom (cf. the case of Pharaoh, Ex 8:32; 9:12).

11:21 *Anakims.* Had been reported by the 12 spies to be people "of a great stature" (Num 13:32), whom the Israelites had feared so much that they had refused to undertake the conquest. They were related to the Nephilim (see note on Gen 6:4) and were named after their forefather, Anak. Joshua shared with Caleb his victory over the Anakites (14:12–15).

12:1–24 A conclusion to the first section of Joshua, and a summary of the victories of the Israelites and the cities whose kings had been defeated (see map No. 3 at the end of the study Bible).

12:1 *land . . . other side Jordan.* The unity of the nation is reaffirmed by the inclusion of these lands east of the Jordan. *river Arnon.* Marked the border with Moab to the south. *mount Hermon.* The upper limits of Israel's land to the north.

12:4 *Og king of Bashan.* Og and Sihon (v. 2) met defeat under the command of Moses, a long-remembered tribute to God's mighty power (see Neh 9:22; Ps 135:11).

12:7 *the country . . . on the west.* Canaan proper (9:1; 11:16–17; 24:11; Gen 15:18–19).

12:12 *king of Gezer.* Had been defeated in the siege of Lachish (10:33), but the city itself was not captured by Joshua, nor were the cities of Aphek, Taanach, Megiddo or Dor (vv. 18–23; see Judg 1:27–31).

22 [a]The king of Kedesh, one; the king of
Jokneam of Carmel, one;
23 The king of Dor in the [a]coast of Dor,
one; the king of [b]the nations of Gilgal, one;
24 The king of Tirzah, one: all the kings
thirty and one.

Land yet to be conquered

13 Now Joshua [a]was old *and* stricken in
years; and the LORD said unto him,
Thou art old *and* stricken in years, and there
remaineth *yet* very much land [b][1]to be possessed.
2 [a]This is the land that *yet* remaineth: [b]all
the borders of the Philistines, and all
[c]Geshuri,
3 [a]From Sihor, which *is* before Egypt, even
unto the borders of Ekron northward, *which* is
counted to the Canaanite: [b]five lords of the
Philistines; the Gazathites, and the Ashdothites, the Eshkalonites, the Gittites, and the
Ekronites; also [c]the Avites:
4 From the south, all the land of the
Canaanites, and [1]Mearah that *is* beside the
Sidonians, [a]unto Aphek, to the borders of [b]the
Amorites:
5 And the land of [a]the Giblites, and [1]all
Lebanon, *toward* the sunrising, [b]from Baal-gad
under mount Hermon unto the entering into
Hamath.
6 All the inhabitants of the hill country
from Lebanon unto [a]Misrephoth-maim, *and* all
the Sidonians, them [b]will I drive out from before the children of Israel: only [c]divide thou it

12:22 [a]ch. 19:37
12:23 [a]ch. 11:2 [b]Gen. 14:1,2; Is. 9:1
13:1 [1]Heb. *to possess it* [a]See ch. 14:10 [b]Deut. 31:3
13:2 [a]Judg. 3:1 [b]Joel 3:4 [c]ver. 13; 2 Sam. 3:3
13:3 [a]Jer. 2:18 [b]Judg. 3:3 [c]Deut. 2:23
13:4 [1]Or, *the cave* [a]ch. 19:30 [b]See Judg. 1:34
13:5 [1]Or, *the cave* [a]1 Ki. 5:18; Ezek. 27:9 [b]ch. 12:7
13:6 [a]ch. 11:8 [b]ch. 23:13; Judg. 2:21,23 [c]ch. 14:1,2

13:1–32 The heavenly King, who has conquered the land, begins the administration of His realm by assigning specific territories to the several tribes. Much of chs. 13–21 reads like administrative documents. The account begins by noting the land still to be subdued (but to be allotted) and by recalling the assignments already made by Moses to the two and a half tribes east of the Jordan (see map No. 4 at the end of the study Bible).
13:1 *Joshua was old.* Between 90 and 100 years of age; Caleb was 85 (14:10).

13:3 *Sihor.* Another name for the Wadi el-Arish below Gaza at the eastern entrance to the Sinai. *lords.* The Hebrew for this word is probably derived from a Greek term for "tyrant," indicating the Aegean background of the Philistines. See map, p. 313.

13:5 *Giblites.* Inhabitants of the ancient city of Byblos just north of modern Beirut. The Phoenicians and the Philistines held most of the territory still to be occupied by Israel.

Conquest of Canaan

Damascus
Great Sea
Mt. Hermon
NORTHERN CAMPAIGN
BASHAN
Hazor
Acco
Chinnereth
Sea of Chinnereth
Edrei
Dor
Megiddo
Beth-shan
Taanach
Ibleam
Dothan
Jordan R.
Mt. Ebal
Mt. Gerizim
CENTRAL CAMPAIGN
See right-hand page
Beth-el
Gibeon
Jericho
Heshbon
Mt. Nebo
Gath
Salt Sea
Jahaz
Hebron
Dibon
SOUTHERN CAMPAIGN
See right-hand page
Beer-sheba
Miles 10 5 0 10 20
Kms 10 5 0 10 20 30

4. THE NORTHERN CAMPAIGN

Late Bronze Age Hazor was burned by Joshua (Josh 11:13). Excavations have revealed three clearly datable destruction layers, one of which may provide the strongest evidence yet for a historically verifiable date for the conquest.

The excavator thought Joshua burned the latest level (c. 1230 B.C.), but others argue that it must actually have been the earliest of the three levels, c. 1400 B.C.

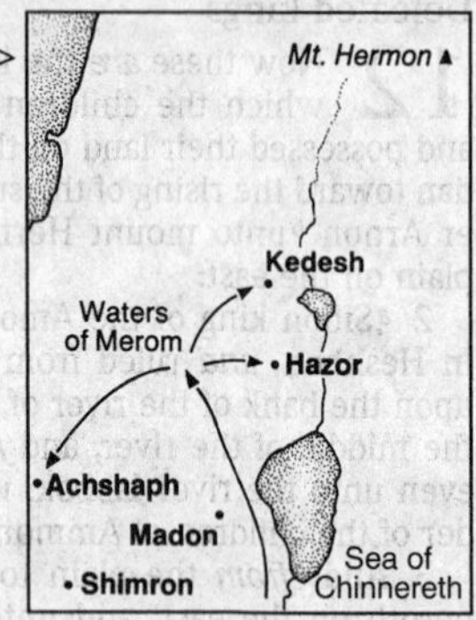

1. ENTRY INTO CANAAN

When the Israelite tribes approached Canaan after four decades of desert existence, they had to overcome the two Amorite kingdoms on the plain of Medeba and in Bashan. Under Moses' leadership, they also subdued the Midianites in order to consolidate their control over the region east of the Jordan.

The conquest of Canaan followed a course that in retrospect appears as though it had been planned by a brilliant strategist. Taking Jericho gave Israel control of its strategic plains, fords and roads as a base of operations. When Israel next gained control of the Beth-el, Gibeon and Upper Beth-horon region, she dominated the center of the north-south Palestinian ridge. Subsequently, she was able to break the power of the allied urban centers in separate campaigns south and north.

by lot unto the Israelites for an inheritance, as I have commanded thee.

7 Now therefore divide this land for an inheritance unto the nine tribes, and the half tribe of Manasseh,

Land east of the Jordan

8 With whom the Reubenites and the Gadites have received their inheritance, [a]which Moses gave them, beyond Jordan eastward, *even* as Moses the servant of the LORD gave them;

9 From Aroer, that *is* upon the bank of the river Arnon, and the city that *is* in the midst of the river, [a]and all the plain of Medeba unto Dibon;

10 And [a]all the cities of Sihon king of the Amorites, which reigned in Heshbon, unto the border of the children of Ammon;

11 [a]And Gilead, and the border of the Geshurites and Maachathites, and all mount Hermon, and all Bashan unto Salcah;

13:8 [a]Num. 32:33; Deut. 3:12,13; ch. 22:4
13:9 [a]ver. 16; Num. 21:30
13:10 [a]Num. 21:24,25
13:11 [a]ch. 12:5
13:12 [a]Deut. 3:11; ch. 12:4 [b]Num. 21:24,35
13:13 [a]ver. 11
13:14 [a]Num. 18:20,23,24; ch. 14:3,4 [b]ver. 33
13:16 [a]ch. 12:2 [b]Num. 21:28 [c]ver. 9; Num. 21:30

12 All the kingdom of Og in Bashan, which reigned in Ashtaroth and in Edrei, who remained of [a]the remnant of the giants: [b]for these did Moses smite, and cast them out.

13 (Nevertheless the children of Israel expelled [a]not the Geshurites, nor the Maachathites: but the Geshurites and the Maachathites dwell among the Israelites until this day.)

14 [a]Only unto the tribe of Levi he gave none inheritance; the sacrifices of the LORD God of Israel made by fire *are* their inheritance, [b]as he said unto them.

15 ¶ And Moses gave unto the tribe of the children of Reuben *inheritance* according to their families.

16 And their coast was [a]from Aroer, that *is* on the bank of the river Arnon, [b]and the city that *is* in the midst of the river, [c]and all the plain by Medeba;

17 Heshbon, and all her cities that *are* in

13:9 *Aroer.* This town on the Arnon River marked the southern boundary of Israel. From here the land extended through Gilead and Bashan to the slopes of mount Hermon in the north, the territory once dominated by the two kings of the Amorites, Sihon and Og.

13:14 *the sacrifices . . . are their inheritance.* See Deut 18:1–8 and note on Deut 18:1.

13:15 *Moses gave unto . . . Reuben.* The land east of the Jordan between the Arnon River (boundary of Moab) and Heshbon (the old royal city of Sihon).

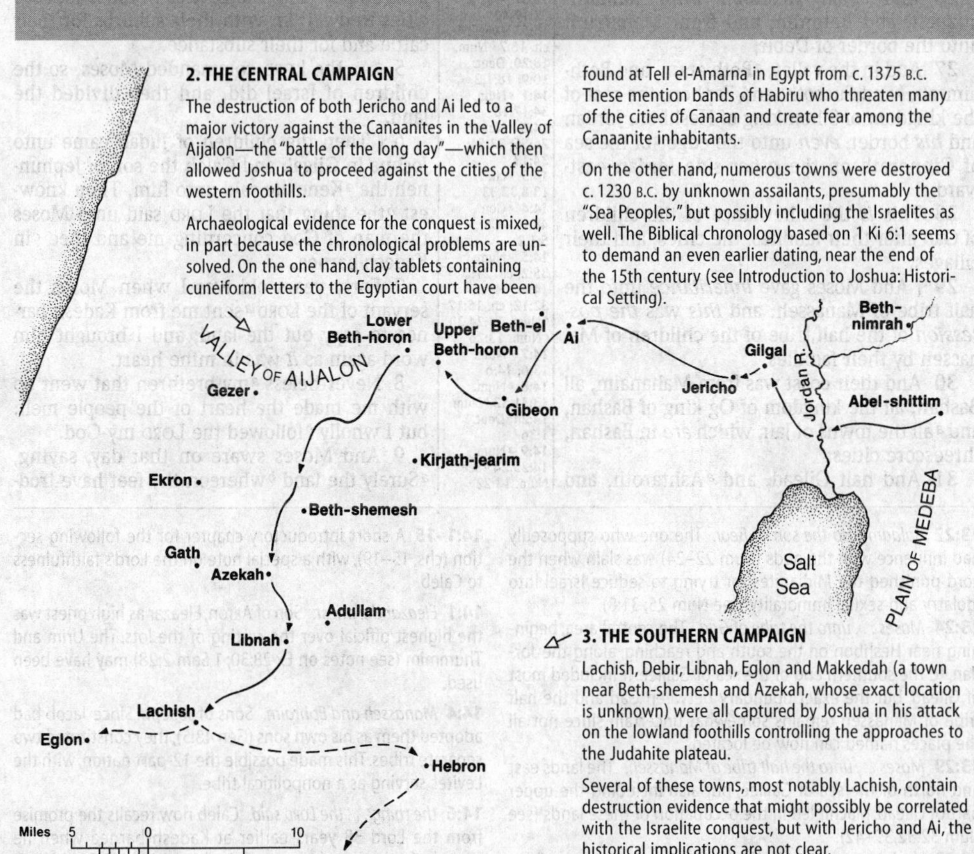

2. THE CENTRAL CAMPAIGN

The destruction of both Jericho and Ai led to a major victory against the Canaanites in the Valley of Aijalon—the "battle of the long day"—which then allowed Joshua to proceed against the cities of the western foothills.

Archaeological evidence for the conquest is mixed, in part because the chronological problems are unsolved. On the one hand, clay tablets containing cuneiform letters to the Egyptian court have been found at Tell el-Amarna in Egypt from c. 1375 B.C. These mention bands of Habiru who threaten many of the cities of Canaan and create fear among the Canaanite inhabitants.

On the other hand, numerous towns were destroyed c. 1230 B.C. by unknown assailants, presumably the "Sea Peoples," but possibly including the Israelites as well. The Biblical chronology based on 1 Ki 6:1 seems to demand an even earlier dating, near the end of the 15th century (see Introduction to Joshua: Historical Setting).

3. THE SOUTHERN CAMPAIGN

Lachish, Debir, Libnah, Eglon and Makkedah (a town near Beth-shemesh and Azekah, whose exact location is unknown) were all captured by Joshua in his attack on the lowland foothills controlling the approaches to the Judahite plateau.

Several of these towns, most notably Lachish, contain destruction evidence that might possibly be correlated with the Israelite conquest, but with Jericho and Ai, the historical implications are not clear.

the plain; Dibon, and [a][1]Bamoth-baal, and
Beth-baal-meon,
18 [a]And Jahazah, and Kedemoth, and
Mephaath,
19 [a]And Kirjathaim, and [b]Sibmah, and
Zareth-shahar in the mount of the valley,
20 And Beth-peor, and [a][1]Ashdoth-pisgah,
and Beth-jeshimoth,
21 [a]And all the cities of the plain, and all
the kingdom of Sihon king of the Amorites,
which reigned in Heshbon, [b]whom Moses
smote [c]with the princes of Midian, Evi, and
Rekem, and Zur, and Hur, and Reba, *which
were* dukes of Sihon, dwelling in the country.
22 [a]Balaam also the son of Beor, the [1]sooth-
sayer, did the children of Israel slay with the
sword among them that were slain by them.
23 And the border of the children of Reuben
was Jordan, and the border *thereof.* This *was*
the inheritance of the children of Reuben after
their families, the cities and villages thereof.
24 ¶ And Moses gave *inheritance* unto the
tribe of Gad, *even* unto the children of Gad according to their families.
25 [a]And their coast was Jazer, and all the
cities of Gilead, [b]and half the land of the children of Ammon, unto Aroer that *is* before
[c]Rabbah;
26 And from Heshbon unto Ramath-
mizpeh, and Betonim; and from Mahanaim
unto the border of Debir;
27 And in the valley, [a]Beth-aram, and Beth-
nimrah, [b]and Succoth, and Zaphon, the rest of
the kingdom of Sihon king of Heshbon, Jordan
and *his* border, *even* unto the edge [c]of the sea
of Cinnereth on the *other* side Jordan eastward.
28 This *is* the inheritance of the children
of Gad after their families, the cities, and their
villages.
29 ¶ And Moses gave *inheritance* unto the
half tribe of Manasseh: and *this* was *the possession* of the half tribe of the children of Manasseh by their families.
30 And their coast was from Mahanaim, all
Bashan, all the kingdom of Og king of Bashan,
and [a]all the towns of Jair, which *are* in Bashan,
threescore cities:
31 And half Gilead, and [a]Ashtaroth, and
Edrei, cities of the kingdom of Og in Bashan,
were pertaining unto the children of Machir
the son of Manasseh, *even* to the one half of
the [b]children of Machir by their families.
32 These *are the countries* which Moses
did distribute for inheritance in the plains of
Moab, on the *other* side Jordan, *by* Jericho,
eastward.
33 [a]But unto the tribe of Levi Moses gave
not *any* inheritance: the LORD God of Israel
was their inheritance, [b]as he said unto them.

Land west of the Jordan

14 And these *are the countries* which
the children of Israel inherited in the
land of Canaan, [a]which Eleazar the priest, and
Joshua the son of Nun, and the heads of the fathers of the tribes of the children of Israel, distributed for inheritance to them.
2 [a]By lot *was* their inheritance, as the LORD
commanded by the hand of Moses, for the
nine tribes, and *for* the half tribe.
3 [a]For Moses had given the inheritance of
two tribes and a half tribe on the *other* side
Jordan: but unto the Levites he gave none inheritance among them.
4 For [a]the children of Joseph were two
tribes, Manasseh and Ephraim: therefore they
gave no part unto the Levites in the land, save
cities to dwell *in,* with their suburbs for their
cattle and for their substance.
5 [a]As the LORD commanded Moses, so the
children of Israel did, and they divided the
land.
6 ¶ Then the children of Judah came unto
Joshua in Gilgal: and Caleb the son of Jephunneh the [a]Kenezite said unto him, Thou knowest [b]the thing that the LORD said unto Moses
the man of God concerning me and thee [c]in
Kadesh-barnea.
7 Forty years old *was* I when Moses the
servant of the LORD [a]sent me from Kadesh-barnea to espy out the land; and I brought him
word again as *it was* in mine heart.
8 Nevertheless [a]my brethren that went up
with me made the heart of the people melt:
but I wholly [b]followed the LORD my God.
9 And Moses sware on that day, saying,
[a]Surely the land [b]whereon thy feet have trod-

13:17 [1]Or, *the high places of Baal, and house of Baal-meon* [a]Num. 32:38
13:18 [a]Num. 21:23
13:19 [a]Num. 32:37 [b]Num. 32:38
13:20 [1]Or, *springs of Pisgah,* or, *the hill* [a]Deut. 3:17; ch. 12:3
13:21 [a]Deut. 3:10 [b]Num. 21:24 [c]Num. 31:8
13:22 [1]Or, *diviner* [a]Num. 22:5; 31:8
13:25 [a]Num. 32:35 [b]Compare Num. 21:26,28, 29 with Deut. 2:19; Judg. 11:13,15 [c]2 Sam. 11:1; 12:26
13:27 [a]Num. 32:36 [b]Gen. 33:17; 1 Ki. 7:46 [c]Num. 34:11
13:30 [a]Num. 32:41; 1 Chr. 2:23
13:31 [a]ch. 12:4
13:31 [b]Num. 32:39,40
13:33 [a]ver. 14; ch. 18:7 [b]Num. 18:20; Deut. 10:9; 18:1,2
14:1 [a]Num. 34:17,18
14:2 [a]Num. 26:55; 33:54; 34:13
14:3 [a]ch. 13:8,32,33
14:4 [a]Gen. 48:5; 1 Chr. 5:1,2
14:5 [a]Num. 35:2; ch. 21:2
14:6 [a]Num. 32:12; ch. 15:17 [b]Num. 14:24,30 [c]Num. 13:26
14:7 [a]Num. 13:6; 14:6
14:8 [a]Num. 13:31,32 [b]Num. 14:24; Deut. 1:36
14:9 [a]Num. 14:23,24 [b]See Num. 13:22

13:22 *Balaam also the son of Beor.* The one who supposedly had influence with the gods (Num 22–24) was slain when the Lord punished the Midianites for trying to seduce Israel into idolatry and sexual immorality (see Num 25; 31:8).

13:24 *Moses . . . unto the tribe of Gad.* The central area, beginning near Heshbon on the south and reaching, along the Jordan, to the southern end of the sea of Galilee. It included most of Gilead, but the exact boundary between Gad and the half tribe of Manasseh remains somewhat uncertain since not all the places named can now be located.

13:29 *Moses . . . unto the half tribe of Manasseh.* The lands east and north of the sea of Galilee, but also including the upper part of Gilead. Machir led in the occupation of these lands (see Num 32:32,39–42).

13:33 *the LORD . . . was their inheritance.* See v.14; see also Deut 18:1–8 and note on Deut 18:1.

14:1–15 A short introductory chapter for the following section (chs. 15–19), with a special note on the Lord's faithfulness to Caleb.

14:1 *Eleazar the priest.* Son of Aaron, Eleazar as high priest was the highest official over the casting of the lots. The Urim and Thummim (see notes on Ex 28:30; 1 Sam 2:28) may have been used.

14:4 *Manasseh and Ephraim.* Sons of Joseph. Since Jacob had adopted them as his own sons (Gen 48:5), they constituted two separate tribes. This made possible the 12-part nation, with the Levites serving as a nonpolitical tribe.

14:6 *the thing . . . the LORD said.* Caleb now recalls the promise from the Lord 38 years earlier at Kadesh-barnea when he brought back a good report of the land (Num 13:30; 14:6–9; Deut 1:34–36).

den shall be thine inheritance, and thy children's for ever, because thou hast wholly followed the LORD my God.

10 And now behold, the LORD hath kept me alive, [a]as he said, these forty and five years, *even* since the LORD spake this word unto Moses, while *the children of* Israel [1]wandered in the wilderness: and now lo, I *am this* day fourscore and five years old.

11 [a]As yet I *am as* strong *this* day as *I was* in the day that Moses sent me: as my strength *was* then, even so *is* my strength now, for war, both [b]to go out, and to come in.

12 Now therefore give me this mountain, whereof the LORD spake in that day; for thou heardest in that day how [a]the Anakims *were* there, and *that* the cities *were* great *and* fenced: [b]if so be the LORD *will be* with me, then [c]I shall *be able to* drive them out, as the LORD said.

13 And Joshua [a]blessed him, [b]and gave unto Caleb the son of Jephunneh Hebron for an inheritance.

14 [a]Hebron therefore became the inheritance of Caleb the son of Jephunneh the Kenezite unto this day, because that he [b]wholly followed the LORD God of Israel.

15 And [a]the name of Hebron before *was* Kirjath-arba; which *Arba was* a great man among the Anakims. [b]And the land had rest from war.

The borders of Judah

15 *This* then was the lot of the tribe of the children of Judah by their families; [a]*even* to the border of Edom, the [b]wilderness of Zin southward *was* the uttermost part of the south *coast.*

2 And their south border was from the shore of the salt sea, from the [1]bay that looketh southward:

3 And it went out to the south side [a]to [1]Maaleh-acrabbim, and passed along to Zin, and ascended up on the south side unto Kadesh-barnea, and passed along *to* Hezron, and went up to Adar, and fetched a compass to Karkaa:

4 *From thence* it passed [a]toward Azmon, and went out *unto* the river of Egypt; and the goings out of that coast were at the sea: this shall be your south coast.

5 And the east border *was* the salt sea,

14:10 [1]Heb. *walked* [a]Num. 14:30
14:11 [a]See Deut. 34:7 [b]Deut. 31:2
14:12 [a]Num. 13:28,33 [b]Rom. 8:31 [c]ch. 15:14; Judg. 1:20
14:13 [a]ch. 22:6 [b]ch. 10:37; 15:13
14:14 [a]ch. 21:12 [b]ver. 8,9
14:15 [a]Gen. 23:2; ch. 15:13 [b]ch. 11:23
15:1 [a]Num. 34:3 [b]Num. 33:36
15:2 [1]Heb. *tongue*
15:3 [1]Or, *the going up to Acrabbim* [a]Num. 34:4
15:4 [a]Num. 34:5
15:6 [a]ch. 18:19 [b]ch. 18:17
15:7 [a]ch. 7:26 [b]2 Sam. 17:17; 1 Ki. 1:9
15:8 [a]ch. 18:16; 2 Ki. 23:10; Jer. 19:2,6 [b]ch. 18:28; Judg. 1:21; 19:10 [c]ch. 18:16
15:9 [a]ch. 18:15 [b]1 Chr. 13:6 [c]Judg. 18:12
15:10 [a]Gen. 38:13; Judg. 14:1
15:11 [a]ch. 19:43
15:12 [a]ver. 47; Num. 34:6,7
15:13 [1]Or, *Kirjath-arba* [a]ch. 14:13 [b]ch. 14:15
15:14 [a]Judg. 1:11,20 [b]Num. 13:22
15:15 [a]ch. 10:38; Judg. 1:11

even unto the end of Jordan. And *their* border in the north quarter *was* from the bay of the sea at the uttermost part of Jordan:

6 And the border went up *to* [a]Beth-hogla, and passed along by the north of Beth-arabah; and the border went up [b]*to* the stone of Bohan the son of Reuben:

7 And the border went up toward Debir from [a]the valley of Achor, and *so* northward, looking toward Gilgal, that *is* before the going up to Adummim, which *is* on the south side of the river: and the border passed towards the waters of En-shemesh, and the goings out thereof were at [b]En-rogel:

8 And the border went up [a]*by* the valley of the son of Hinnom unto the south side of the [b]Jebusite; the same *is* Jerusalem: and the border went up to the top of the mountain that *lieth* before the valley of Hinnom westward, which *is* at the end [c]of the valley of the giants northward:

9 And the border was drawn from the top of the hill unto [a]the fountain of the water of Nephtoah, and went out to the cities of mount Ephron; and the border was drawn [b]*to* Baalah, which *is* [c]Kirjath-jearim:

10 And the border compassed from Baalah westward unto mount Seir, and passed along unto the side of mount Jearim, which *is* Chesalon, on the north side, and went down *to* Beth-shemesh, and passed on *to* [a]Timnah:

11 And the border went out unto the side of [a]Ekron northward: and the border was drawn to Shicron, and passed along *to* mount Baalah, and went out *unto* Jabneel; and the goings out of the border were at the sea.

12 And the west border *was* [a]to the great sea, and the coast *thereof.* This *is* the coast of the children of Judah round about according to their families.

13 ¶ [a]And unto Caleb the son of Jephunneh he gave a part among the children of Judah, according to the commandment of the LORD to Joshua, *even* [b][1]the city of Arba the father of Anak, which *city is* Hebron.

14 And Caleb drove thence [a]the three sons of Anak, [b]Sheshai, and Ahiman, and Talmai, the children of Anak.

15 And [a]he went up thence to the inhabitants of Debir: and the name of Debir before *was* Kirjath-sepher.

14:12 *this mountain.* Hebron is situated high in the Judahite hill country, about 25 miles south of Jerusalem. *Anakims.* See note on 11:21.

14:15 *Kirjath-arba.* Means "the town of Arba" and was named for Arba, the father of the Anakites (15:13; 21:11). It can also mean "the town of four." Hebron means "union." *And the land had rest from war.* Since the Judahites and Caleb approached Joshua concerning their territory while he was still headquartered at Gilgal, it may be that they did so shortly before the wars fought under Joshua were ended (see 11:23).

15:1–63 Judah is the first of the west bank tribes to have its territory delineated. First the outer limits are listed, then the area apportioned to Caleb and Othniel; finally the Canaanite cities allotted to the clans of Judah are named region by region.

15:1 *tribe of . . . Judah.* Judah's priority is anchored in the oracle of Jacob (Gen 49:8–12) and upheld in the history of the nation (2 Ki 17:18).

15:4 *south coast.* The points listed formed a curved line beginning at the lower tip of the Dead Sea and moving under Kadesh-barnea to join the Mediterranean coast at the mouth of the Wadi el-Arish (see note on 13:3).

15:5 *border in the north.* Judah's border with Benjamin ran in a westerly line from the mouth of the Jordan through the Hinnom Valley, just south of Jerusalem, over to Timnah, then northwest to the coastal city of Jabneel (later called Jamnia), about ten miles south of Joppa.

15:15 *he went up . . . to . . . Debir.* See note on 10:38.

16 [a]And Caleb said, He that smiteth Kirjath-sepher, and taketh it, to him will I give Achsah my daughter to wife.

17 And [a]Othniel the [b]son of Kenaz, the brother of Caleb, took it: and he gave him Achsah his daughter to wife.

18 [a]And it came to pass, as she came *unto him,* that she moved him to ask of her father a field: and [b]she lighted off *her* ass; and Caleb said unto her, What wouldest thou?

19 Who answered, Give me a [a]blessing; for thou hast given me a south land; give me also springs of water. And he gave her the upper springs, and the nether springs.

20 ¶ This *is* the inheritance of the tribe of the children of Judah according to their families.

21 And the uttermost cities of the tribe of the children of Judah toward the coast of Edom southward were Kabzeel, and Eder, and Jagur,

22 And Kinah, and Dimonah, and Adadah,

23 And Kedesh, and Hazor, and Ithnan,

24 Ziph, and Telem, and Bealoth,

25 And Hazor, Hadattah, and Kerioth, *and* Hezron, which *is* Hazor,

26 Amam, and Shema, and Moladah,

27 And Hazar-gaddah, and Heshmon, and Beth-palet,

28 And Hazar-shual, and Beer-sheba, and Bizjothjah,

29 Baalah, and Iim, and Azem,

30 And Eltolad, and Chesil, and Hormah,

31 And [a]Ziklag, and Madmannah, and Sansannah,

32 And Lebaoth, and Shilhim, and Ain, and Rimmon: all the cities *are* twenty and nine, with their villages.

33 ¶ *And* in the valley, [a]Eshtaol, and Zoreah, and Ashnah,

34 And Zanoah, and En-gannim, Tappuah, and Enam,

35 Jarmuth, and Adullam, Socoh, and Azekah,

36 And Sharaim, and Adithaim, and Gederah, [1]and Gederothaim; fourteen cities with their villages.

37 Zenan, and Hadashah, and Migdal-gad,

38 And Dilean, and Mizpeh, [a]and Joktheel,

39 Lachish, and Bozkath, and Eglon,

40 And Cabbon, and Lahmam, and Kithlish,

15:16 [a]Judg. 1:12
15:17 [a]Judg. 1:13; 3:9 [b]Num. 32:12; ch. 14:6
15:18 [a]Judg. 1:14 [b]See Gen. 24:64; 1 Sam. 25:23
15:19 [a]Gen. 33:11
15:31 [a]1 Sam. 27:6
15:33 [a]Num. 13:23
15:36 [1]Or, *or*
15:38 [a]2 Ki. 14:7

15:46 [1]Heb. *by the place of*
15:47 [a]ver. 4 [b]Num. 34:6
15:51 [a]ch. 10:41; 11:16
15:53 [1]Or, *Janus*
15:54 [a]ver. 13; ch. 14:15
15:60 [a]ch. 18:14
15:63 [a]See Judg. 1:8,21; 2 Sam. 5:6 [b]Judg. 1:21
16:1 [1]Heb. *went forth*

41 And Gederoth, Beth-dagon, and Naamah, and Makkedah; sixteen cities with their villages.

42 Libnah, and Ether, and Ashan,

43 And Jiphtah, and Ashnah, and Nezib,

44 And Keilah, and Achzib, and Mareshah; nine cities with their villages.

45 Ekron, with her towns and her villages:

46 From Ekron even unto the sea, all that *lay* [1]near Ashdod, with their villages:

47 Ashdod *with* her towns and her villages, Gaza *with* her towns and her villages, unto [a]the river of Egypt, and [b]the great sea, and the border *thereof.*

48 ¶ And in the mountains, Shamir, and Jattir, and Socoh,

49 And Dannah, and Kirjath-sannah, which *is* Debir,

50 And Anab, and Eshtemoh, and Anim,

51 [a]And Goshen, and Holon, and Giloh; eleven cities with their villages.

52 Arab, and Dumah, and Eshean,

53 And [1]Janum, and Beth-tappuah, and Aphekah,

54 And Humtah, and [a]Kirjath-arba, which *is* Hebron, and Zior; nine cities with their villages.

55 Maon, Carmel, and Ziph, and Juttah,

56 And Jezreel, and Jokdeam, and Zanoah,

57 Cain, Gibeah, and Timnah; ten cities with their villages.

58 Halhul, Beth-zur, and Gedor,

59 And Maarath, and Beth-anoth, and Eltekon; six cities with their villages.

60 [a]Kirjath-baal, which *is* Kirjath-jearim, and Rabbah; two cities with their villages.

61 ¶ In the wilderness, Beth-arabah, Middin, and Secacah,

62 And Nibshan, and the city of salt, and En-gedi; six cities with their villages.

63 As for the Jebusites the inhabitants of Jerusalem, [a]the children of Judah could not drive them out: [b]but the Jebusites dwell with the children of Judah at Jerusalem unto this day.

Ephraim and Manasseh

16 And the lot of the children of Joseph [1]fell from Jordan *by* Jericho, unto the water of Jericho on the east, *to* the wilderness that goeth up from Jericho throughout mount Beth-el,

15:17 *Othniel.* See Judg 3:7–11 for his service as judge in Israel.
15:19 *upper . . . nether* [i.e. lower] *springs.* They still water the local farms in Hebron.
15:21 *uttermost cities. . . of Judah . . . southward.* Most of the first 29 villages were assigned to the tribe of Simeon (cf. 19:1–9).
15:33 *valley.* The Hebrew for this term is *Shephelah.* This area between the highlands of central Judah and the Philistine coast was for the most part not occupied by Israel until the victories of King David. Some of the places on this list were reassigned to the tribe of Dan (cf. 19:41–43).
15:48 *mountains.* The high region south of Jerusalem. The Septuagint adds 11 names, including Tekoa and Beth-lehem, to this list.
15:61 *wilderness.* The chalky, dry region east and south of Jerusalem that borders the Dead Sea.
15:62 Only Engedi can be positively located, though the "city of salt" is believed by many to be Qumran, where, centuries later, the scribes who produced the Dead Sea Scrolls lived.
15:63 *Jebusites.* A victory over the city of the Jebusites by the men of Judah is recorded in Judg 1:8, but evidently this did not result in its permanent occupation. Both Benjamin and Judah failed to take the Jebusite fortress of Jerusalem (Judg 1:21).
16:1–17:18 Two chapters are devoted to the lands given to the "children of Joseph" (Ephraim and the half tribe of Manasseh that settled west of the Jordan). Following Judah, the Joseph tribes were given priority.
16:1 *lot of . . . Joseph.* Ephraim's southern border moved west

2 And goeth out from Beth-el to [a]Luz, and passeth along unto the borders of Archi *to* Ataroth,

3 And goeth down westward to the coast of Japhleti, [a]unto the coast of Beth-horon the nether, and to [b]Gezer: and the goings out thereof are at the sea.

4 [a]So the children of Joseph, Manasseh and Ephraim, took their inheritance.

5 ¶ And the border of the children of Ephraim according to their families was *thus:* even the border of their inheritance on the east side was [a]Ataroth-addar, [b]unto Beth-horon the upper;

6 And the border went out toward the sea *to* [a]Michmethah on the north side; and the border went about eastward *unto* Taanath-shiloh, and passed by it on the east *to* Janohah;

7 And it went down from Janohah *to* Ataroth, [a]and to Naarath, and came to Jericho, and went out *at* Jordan.

8 The border went *out* from Tappuah westward *unto* the [a]river Kanah; and the goings out thereof were at the sea. This *is* the inheritance of the tribe of the children of Ephraim by their families.

9 And [a]the separate cities for the children of Ephraim *were* among the inheritance of the children of Manasseh, all the cities with their villages.

10 [a]And they drave not out the Canaanites that dwelt in Gezer: but the Canaanites dwell among the Ephraimites unto this day, and serve under tribute.

17 There was also a lot for the tribe of Manasseh; for he *was* the [a]firstborn of Joseph; *to wit,* for [b]Machir the firstborn of Manasseh, the father of Gilead: because he was a man of war, therefore he had [c]Gilead and Bashan.

2 There was also *a lot* for [a]the rest of the children of Manasseh by their families; [b]for the children of [1]Abiezer, and for the children of Helek, [c]and for the children of Asriel, and for the children of Shechem, [d]and for the children of Hepher, and for the children of Shemida: these *were* the male children of Manasseh the son of Joseph by their families.

3 But [a]Zelophehad, the son of Hepher, the son of Gilead, the son of Machir, the son of Manasseh, had no sons, but daughters: and these *are* the names of his daughters, Mahlah, and Noah, Hoglah, Milcah, and Tirzah.

4 And they came near before [a]Eleazar the priest, and before Joshua the son of Nun, and before the princes, saying, [b]The LORD commanded Moses to give us an inheritance among our brethren. Therefore according to the commandment of the LORD he gave them an inheritance among the brethren of their father.

5 And there fell ten portions to Manasseh, beside the land of Gilead and Bashan, which *were* on the *other* side Jordan;

6 Because the daughters of Manasseh had an inheritance among his sons: and the rest of Manasseh's sons had the land of Gilead.

7 ¶ And the coast of Manasseh was from Asher *to* [a]Michmethah, that *lieth* before Shechem; and the border went *along* on the right hand unto the inhabitants of En-tappuah.

8 *Now* Manasseh had the land of Tappuah: but [a]Tappuah on the border of Manasseh *belonged* to the children of Ephraim;

9 And the coast descended *unto* the [1]river Kanah, southward of the river: [a]these cities of Ephraim *are* among the cities of Manasseh: the coast of Manasseh also *was* on the north side of the river, and the outgoings of it were at the sea:

10 Southward *it was* Ephraim's, and northward *it was* Manasseh's, and the sea is his border; and they met together in Asher on the north, and in Issachar on the east.

11 [a]And Manasseh had in Issachar and in Asher [b]Beth-shean and her towns, and Ibleam and her towns, and the inhabitants of Dor and her towns, and the inhabitants of Endor and her towns, and the inhabitants of Taanach and her towns, and the inhabitants of Megiddo and her towns, *even* three countries.

12 Yet [a]the children of Manasseh could not drive out *the inhabitants of* those cities; but the Canaanites would dwell in that land.

13 Yet it came to pass, when the children of Israel were waxen strong, that they put the Canaanites to [a]tribute; but did not utterly drive them out.

14 ¶ [a]And the children of Joseph spake unto Joshua, saying, Why hast thou given me

16:2 [a]ch. 18:13; Judg. 1:26
16:3 [a]ch. 18:13; 2 Chr. 8:5 [b]1 Ki. 9:15; 1 Chr. 7:28
16:4 [a]ch. 17:14
16:5 [a]ch. 18:13 [b]2 Chr. 8:5
16:6 [a]ch. 17:7
16:7 [a]1 Chr. 7:28
16:8 [a]ch. 17:9
16:9 [a]ch. 17:9
16:10 [a]Judg. 1:29; See 1 Ki. 9:16
17:1 [a]Gen. 41:51; 46:20; 48:18 [b]Gen. 50:23 [c]Deut. 3:15
17:2 [1][Num. 26:30, *Jeezer*] [a]Num. 26:29-32 [b]1 Chr. 7:18 [c]Num. 26:31 [d]Num. 26:32
17:3 [a]Num. 26:33; 27:1; 36:2
17:4 [a]ch. 14:1 [b]Num. 27:6,7
17:7 [a]ch. 16:6
17:8 [a]ch. 16:8
17:9 [1]Or, *brook of reeds* [a]ch. 16:9
17:11 [a]1 Chr. 7:29 [b]1 Sam. 31:10; 1 Ki. 4:12
17:12 [a]Judg. 1:27,28
17:13 [a]ch. 16:10
17:14 [a]ch. 16:4

from Jericho past Beth-el and down to Gezer and the Mediterranean coast.

16:5 *border.* Ephraim's northern border began down by the Jordan and ran west near Shiloh, but south of Shechem, then followed the Wadi Kanah down to the Mediterranean Sea.

16:10 *Gezer.* See note on 10:33. *serve under tribute.* I.e., became forced laborers. Since Gezer does not appear to have come under Israelite control until the days of Solomon (1 Ki 9:15–16), this may be a note added after that event (but see 2 Sam 5:25).

17:1 *Manasseh . . . the firstborn of Joseph.* A reminder to the proud Ephraimites that Manasseh had been the firstborn, though Jacob gave priority to Ephraim when he adopted Joseph's two sons (Gen 48:14,19).

17:3 *Zelophehad . . . had . . . but daughters.* Before Moses died, he promised the daughters an allotment along with their relatives (see Num 26:33; 27:1–7).

17:5 *ten portions.* Manasseh's territory was second only to Judah's in size. The ten portions went to the five brothers (minus Hepher) and to the five granddaughters of Hepher. For the law protecting the inheritance rights of a daughter without brothers see Num 27:8–11.

17:11 *Beth-shean . . . Megiddo.* These powerfully fortified cities, and others along Manasseh's common border with Issachar and Asher, were not conquered until later. When King Saul died in battle, the victorious Philistines fastened his body to the wall of Beth-shean (see 1 Sam 31:10), which suggests that that city was in league with the Philistines.

17:13 *when the children of Israel were waxen strong.* Possibly referring to the days of David and Solomon (see note on 16:10).

but [b]one lot and one portion to inherit, seeing
I *am* [c]a great people, forasmuch as the LORD
hath blessed me hitherto?
15 And Joshua answered them, If thou *be* a
great people, *then* get thee up to the wood
country, and cut down for thyself there in the
land of the Perizzites and of the [1]giants, if
mount Ephraim be too narrow for thee.
16 And the children of Joseph said, The hill
is not enough for us: and all the Canaanites
that dwell in the land of the valley have [a]char-
iots of iron, *both they* who *are* of Beth-shean
and her towns, and *they* who *are* [b]of the valley
of Jezreel.
17 And Joshua spake unto the house of Joseph, *even* to Ephraim and to Manasseh, saying, Thou *art* a great people, and hast great
power: thou shalt not have one lot *only:*
18 But the mountain shall be thine; for it *is*
a wood, and thou shalt cut it down: and the
outgoings of it shall be thine: for thou shalt
drive out the Canaanites, [a]though they have
iron chariots, *and* though they *be* strong.

Assigning the inherited land

18 And the whole congregation of the
children of Israel assembled together
[a]*at* Shiloh, and [b]set up the tabernacle of the
congregation there. And the land was subdued
before them.
2 And there remained among the children
of Israel seven tribes, which had not *yet* received their inheritance.
3 And Joshua said unto the children of Israel, [a]How long *are* you slack to go to possess
the land, which the LORD God of your fathers
hath given you?
4 Give out from among you three men for
each tribe: and I will send them, and they shall
rise, and go through the land, and describe it
according to the inheritance of them; and they
shall come *again* to me.
5 And they shall divide it into seven parts:
[a]Judah shall abide in their coast on the south,
and [b]the house of Joseph shall abide in their
coasts on the north.
6 Ye shall therefore describe the land *into*
seven parts, and bring *the description* hither
to me, [a]that I may cast lots for you here before
the LORD our God.
7 [a]But the Levites have no part among you;
for the priesthood of the LORD *is* their inheritance: [b]and Gad, and Reuben, and half the
tribe of Manasseh, have received their inheritance beyond Jordan on the east, which Moses
the servant of the LORD gave them.
8 And the men arose, and went away: and
Joshua charged them that went to describe the
land, saying, Go and walk through the land, and
describe it, and come again to me, that I may
here cast lots for you before the LORD in Shiloh.
9 And the men went and passed through
the land, and described it by cities into seven
parts in a book, and came *again* to Joshua to
the host *at* Shiloh.
10 And Joshua cast lots for them in Shiloh
before the LORD: and there Joshua divided the
land unto the children of Israel according to
their divisions.

The land of Benjamin

11 ¶ And the lot of the tribe of the children
of Benjamin came up according to their families:
and the coast of their lot came forth between
the children of Judah and the children of Joseph.
12 [a]And their border on the north side was
from Jordan; and the border went up to the
side of Jericho on the north side, and went up
through the mountains westward; and the goings out thereof were at the wilderness of
Beth-aven.

17:14 [b]Gen. 48:22 [c]Gen. 48:19; Num. 26:34,37
17:15 [1]Or, *Rephaims*
17:16 [a]Judg. 1:19; 4:3 [b]ch. 19:18; 1 Ki. 4:12
17:18 [a]Deut. 20:1
18:1 [a]ch. 19:51; 21:2; 22:9; Jer. 7:12 [b]Judg. 18:31; 1 Sam. 1:3,24; 4:3,4
18:3 [a]Judg. 18:9
18:5 [a]ch. 15:1 [b]ch. 16:1,4
18:6 [a]ver. 10; ch. 14:2
18:7 [a]ch. 13:33 [b]ch. 13:8
18:12 [a]See ch. 16:1

‡17:14 *children of Joseph . . . great people* [i.e."numerous"]. The reference is to both Ephraim and Manasseh (see v. 17). The allotment to the Joseph tribes is here handled as one (see 16:1,4)—though the two subdivisions are then described separately (16:5–17:11).

‡17:15 *cut down for thyself.* This region of Canaan was still heavily forested. It seems that the Israelites viewed their assigned territories primarily in terms of the number of cities that had their land cleared for farming and pasturage, not in terms of the size of the region in which these cities were located. The region assigned to the Joseph tribes was at the time not as heavily populated as others. *Perizzites and . . . giants* [*Rephaim* in Hebrew]. Here listed as neighboring peoples, though elsewhere the Perizzites are said to have lived on the west bank in Canaan (3:10; 12:8) and the Rephaites in the kingdom of Og east of the Jordan (12:4; 13:12). See notes on Gen 13:7; Deut 2:11. *mount Ephraim.* The territory of the Joseph tribes—under the name of the legal firstborn (see note on v. 1).

17:16 *in the land of the valley.* Only in the plains were chariots effective. *chariots of iron.* Chariots with certain parts made of iron (see note on 2 Sam 8:7), perhaps the axles—the use of iron was a new development (see note on 11:6).

18:1–19:51 Seven tribes remained to be assigned land: Benjamin, Simeon, Zebulun, Issachar, Asher, Naphtali and Dan. Their lots were cast at Shiloh, after which a special portion was awarded to Joshua.

18:1 *Shiloh.* About ten miles northeast of Beth-el, a little east of the main road from Beth-el to Shechem. *tabernacle of the congregation.* The tabernacle (see note on Ex 27:21) with its sacred ark of the Testimony. It would remain at Shiloh until the time of Samuel (1 Sam 4:3).

18:3 *possess.* Conquest had to be followed by settlement, which required a survey, then a fair distribution, and then a full occupation of the land. A distinction must therefore be made between the national wars of conquest (Joshua) and the tribal wars of occupation (Judg 1–2).

18:5 *north.* Relative to the territory of Judah.

18:6 *I may cast lots for you.* See note on 14:1.

18:7 *priesthood of the LORD is their inheritance.* See 13:14; see also Deut 18:1–8 and note on Deut 18:1.

18:9 *book.* The actual form of the document was probably that of a scroll.

18:11 *lot . . . Benjamin.* A buffer zone between Judah and Ephraim, the two dominant tribes. Its northern line was the same as Ephraim's southern border (see note on 16:1), and its southern line the same as Judah's northernmost boundary (see note on 15:5).

13 And the border went over from thence
toward Luz, to the side of Luz, [a]which *is* Beth-
el, southward; and the border descended *to*
Ataroth-adar, near the hill that *lieth* on the
south side [b]of the nether Beth-horon.
14 And the border was drawn *thence,* and
compassed the corner of the sea southward,
from the hill that *lieth* before Beth-horon southward; and the goings out thereof were at [a]Kir-
jath-baal, which *is* Kirjath-jearim, a city of the
children of Judah: this *was* the west quarter.
15 And the south quarter *was* from the end
of Kirjath-jearim, and the border went out on
the west, and went out to [a]the well of waters
of Nephtoah:
16 And the border came down to the end
of the mountain that *lieth* before [a]the valley of
the son of Hinnom, *and* which *is* in the valley
of the giants on the north, and descended *to*
the valley of Hinnom, to the side of Jebusi on
the south, and descended *to* [b]En-rogel,
17 And was drawn from the north, and
went forth *to* En-shemesh, and went forth toward Geliloth, which *is* over against the going
up of Adummim, and descended *to* [a]the stone
of Bohan the son of Reuben,
18 And passed along toward the side over
against [a][1]Arabah northward, and went down
unto Arabah:
19 And the border passed along to the side
of Beth-hoglah northward: and the outgoings
of the border were at the north [1]bay of the salt
sea at the south end of Jordan: this *was* the
south coast.
20 And Jordan was the border of it on the
east side. This *was* the inheritance of the children of Benjamin, by the coasts thereof round
about, according to their families.
21 ¶ Now the cities of the tribe of the children of Benjamin according to their families
were Jericho, and Beth-hoglah, and the valley
of Keziz,
22 And Beth-arabah, and Zemaraim, and
Beth-el,
23 And Avim, and Parah, and Ophrah,
24 And Chephar-haammonai, and Ophni,
and Gaba; twelve cities with their villages.
25 Gibeon, and Ramah, and Beeroth,
26 And Mizpeh, and Chephirah, and Mozah,
27 And Rekem, and Irpeel, and Taralah,
28 And Zelah, Eleph, and [a]Jebusi, which *is*
Jerusalem, Gibeath, *and* Kirjath; fourteen cities with their villages. This *is* the inheritance
of the children of Benjamin according to their
families.

The land of Simeon

19 And the second lot came forth to
Simeon, *even* for the tribe of the children of Simeon according to their families:
[a]and their inheritance was within the inheritance of the children of Judah.
2 And [a]they had in their inheritance Beer-
sheba, or Sheba, and Moladah,
3 And Hazar-shual, and Balah, and Azem,
4 And Eltolad, and Bethul, and Hormah,
5 And Ziklag, and Beth-marcaboth, and Hazar-susah,
6 And Beth-lebaoth, and Sharuhen; thirteen cities and their villages:
7 Ain, Remmon, and Ether, and Ashan;
four cities and their villages:
8 And all the villages that *were* round
about these cities to Baalath-beer, Ramath of
the south. This *is* the inheritance of the tribe
of the children of Simeon according to their
families.
9 Out of the portion of the children of Judah *was* the inheritance of the children of
Simeon: for the part of the children of Judah
was too much for them: [a]therefore the children of Simeon had their inheritance within
the inheritance of them.

The land of Zebulun

10 ¶ And the third lot came up for the children of Zebulun according to their families: and
the border of their inheritance was unto Sarid:
11 [a]And their border went up toward the
sea, and Maralah, and reached to Dabbasheth,
and reached to the river that *is* [b]before Jokneam;
12 And turned from Sarid eastward *toward*
the sunrising unto the border of Chisloth-ta-
bor, and *then* goeth out to Daberath, and goeth
up *to* Japhia,
13 And from thence passeth on along on
the east to Gittah-hepher, to Ittah-kazin, and
goeth out *to* Remmon-[1]methoar *to* Neah;
14 And the border compasseth it on the
north side *to* Hannathon: and the outgoings
thereof are *in* the valley of Jiphthah-el:
15 And Kattath, and Nahallal, and Shimron, and Idalah, and Beth-lehem: twelve cities
with their villages.
16 This *is* the inheritance of the children
of Zebulun according to their families, these
cities with their villages.

The land of Issachar

17 ¶ *And* the fourth lot came out to Issachar, for the children of Issachar according to
their families.
18 And their border was toward Jezreel,
and Chesulloth, and Shunem,
19 And Hapharaim, and Shion, and Ana-
harath,
20 And Rabbith, and Kishion, and Abez,
21 And Remeth, and En-gannim, and En-
haddah, and Beth-pazzez;

18:13 [a]Gen. 28:19; Judg. 1:23 [b]ch. 16:3
18:14 [a]See ch. 15:9
18:15 [a]ch. 15:9
18:16 [a]ch. 15:8 [b]ch. 15:7
18:17 [a]ch. 15:6
18:18 [1]Or, *the plain* [a]ch. 15:6
18:19 [1]Heb. *tongue*
18:28 [a]ch. 15:8
19:1 [a]ver. 9
19:2 [a]1 Chr. 4:28
19:9 [a]ver. 1
19:11 [a]Gen. 49:13 [b]ch. 12:22
19:13 [1]Or, *which is drawn*

18:23 *Avim.* The people of Ai.

19:1 *second lot . . . Simeon.* Cities within the borders of Judah (15:21) in the Negev along Judah's southern border (1 Chr 4:24–42).

19:10 *third lot came up for the children of Zebulun.* To this tribe went a portion of lower Galilee west of the sea of Galilee and in the vicinity of NT Nazareth.

19:17 *fourth lot . . . to Issachar.* Southwest of the sea of Galilee reaching down to Beth-shean and west to the Jezreel Valley. mount Tabor marked its northern border.

22 And the coast reacheth to Tabor, and Shahazimah, and Beth-shemesh; and the outgoings of their border were *at* Jordan: sixteen cities with their villages.

23 This *is* the inheritance of the tribe of the children of Issachar according to their families, the cities and their villages.

The land of Asher

24 ¶ And the fifth lot came out for the tribe of the children of Asher according to their families.

25 And their border was Helkath, and Hali, and Beten, and Achshaph,

26 And Alammelech, and Amad, and Misheal; and reacheth to Carmel westward, and to Shihor-libnath;

27 And turneth *toward* the sunrising *to* Beth-dagon, and reacheth to Zebulun, and to the valley of Jiphthah-el toward the north side *of* Beth-emek, and Neiel, and goeth out to Cabul on the left hand,

28 And Hebron, and Rehob, and Hammon, and Kanah, [a]*even* unto great Zidon;

29 And *then* the coast turneth *to* Ramah, and to the strong city [a][1]Tyre; and the coast turneth *to* Hosah; and the outgoings thereof are at the sea from the coast to [b]Achzib:

30 Ummah also, and Aphek, and Rehob: twenty and two cities with their villages.

31 This *is* the inheritance of the tribe of the children of Asher according to their families, these cities with their villages.

The land of Naphtali

32 ¶ The sixth lot came out to the children of Naphtali, *even* for the children of Naphtali according to their families.

33 And their coast was from Heleph, from Allon to Zaanannim, and Adami, Nekeb, and Jabneel, unto Lakum; and the outgoings thereof were *at* Jordan:

34 And *then* [a]the coast turneth westward *to* Aznoth-tabor, and goeth out from thence to Hukkok, and reacheth to Zebulun on the south side, and reacheth to Asher on the west side, and to Judah upon Jordan *toward* the sunrising.

35 And the fenced cities *are* Ziddim, Zer, and Hammath, Rakkath, and [a]Chinnereth,

36 And Adamah, and Ramah, and Hazor,

37 And Kedesh, and Edrei, and En-hazor,

38 And Iron, and Migdal-el, Horem, and Beth-anath, and Beth-shemesh; nineteen cities with their villages.

39 This *is* the inheritance of the tribe of the children of Naphtali according to their families, the cities and their villages.

The land of Dan

40 ¶ *And* the seventh lot came out for the tribe of the children of Dan according to their families.

41 And the coast of their inheritance was Zorah, and Eshtaol, and Ir-shemesh,

42 And [a]Shaalabbin, and Aijalon, and Jethlah,

43 And Elon, and Thimnathah, and Ekron,

44 And Eltekeh, and Gibbethon, and Baalath,

45 And Jehud, and Bene-berak, and Gath-rimmon,

46 And Me-jarkon, and Rakkon, with the border [1]before [2]Japho.

47 And [a]the coast of the children of Dan went out *too little* for them: therefore the children of Dan went up to fight against Leshem, and took it, and smote it with the edge of the sword, and possessed it, and dwelt therein, and called Leshem, [b]Dan, after the name of Dan their father.

48 This *is* the inheritance of the tribe of the children of Dan according to their families, these cities with their villages.

49 ¶ When they had made an end of dividing the land for inheritance by their coasts, the children of Israel gave an inheritance to Joshua the son of Nun among them:

50 According to the word of the LORD they gave him the city which he asked, *even* [a]Timnath-[b]serah in mount Ephraim: and he built the city, and dwelt therein.

51 [a]These *are* the inheritances, which Eleazar the priest, and Joshua the son of Nun, and the heads of the fathers of the tribes of the children of Israel, divided for an inheritance by lot [b]in Shiloh before the LORD, *at* the door of the tabernacle of the congregation. So they made an end of dividing the country.

19:28 [a]ch. 11:8; Judg. 1:31
19:29 [1]Heb. *Tzor* [a]2 Sam. 5:11 [b]Judg. 1:31
19:34 [a]Deut. 33:23
19:35 [a]Deut. 3:17; ch. 11:2; 12:3; Mark 6:53; Luke 5:1
19:42 [a]Judg. 1:35
19:46 [1]Or, *over against* [2]Or, *Joppa*
19:47 [a]See Judg. 18 [b]Judg. 18:29
19:50 [a]ch. 24:30 [b]1 Chr. 7:24
19:51 [a]Num. 34:17; ch. 14:1 [b]ch. 18:1,10

19:24 *fifth lot . . . for . . . Asher.* Asher was given the coastal area as far north as Sidon in Phoenicia and as far south as mount Carmel.

19:32 *sixth lot . . . to . . . Naphtali.* An area mostly to the north of the sea of Galilee, taking in the modern Huleh Valley and the mountains bordering on Asher to the west. Its southernmost point was at the lower edge of the sea of Galilee.

19:40 *seventh lot . . . for . . . Dan.* An elbow of land squeezed between Ephraim and Judah and west of Benjamin. The port of Joppa marked the northwestern corner of Dan.

19:47 *coast of . . . Dan went out too little for them.* Lit. "went out from them," probably indicating they were not able to maintain control over it. The Amorites of this area "forced the children of Dan into the mountain" (Judg 1:34), so most of the tribe migrated to the upper Jordan Valley, where they seized the town of Leshem (or Laish, Judg 18:2–10,27–29) and renamed it Dan.

19:49 *gave an inheritance to Joshua.* In the account of the distribution of the promised land (the territory west of the Jordan), the assignment to Caleb is treated first (14:6–15), the assignment to Joshua last. Thus the allotting of inheritance to these two dauntless servants of the Lord from the wilderness generation (see Num 13:30; 14:6,24,30) frames the whole account—and both received the territory they asked for. Appropriately, Joshua's allotment came last; he was not a king or a warlord but the servant of God commissioned to bring the Lord's people into the promised land.

19:50 *Timnath-serah.* Located in the southwestern corner of Ephraim, facing out to the sea. Here Joshua was also buried (24:30).

The six cities of refuge

20 The LORD also spake unto Joshua, saying,

2 Speak to the children of Israel, saying, [a]Appoint out for you cities of refuge, whereof I spake unto you by the hand of Moses:

3 That the slayer that killeth *any* person unawares *and* unwittingly may flee thither: and they shall be your refuge from the avenger of blood.

4 And when he that doth flee unto one of those cities shall stand *at* the entering of the gate of the city, and shall declare his cause in the ears of the elders of that city, they shall take him into the city unto them, and give him a place, that he may dwell among them.

5 [a]And if the avenger of blood pursue after him, then they shall not deliver the slayer up into his hand; because he smote his neighbour unwittingly, and hated him not beforetime.

6 And he shall dwell in that city, [a]until he stand before the congregation for judgment, *and* until the death of the high priest that shall be in those days: then shall the slayer return, and come unto his own city, and unto his own house, unto the city from whence he fled.

7 And they [1]appointed [a]Kedesh in Galilee in mount Naphtali, and [b]Shechem in mount Ephraim, and [c]Kirjath-arba, which *is* Hebron, in [d]the mountain of Judah.

8 And on the *other* side Jordan *by* Jericho eastward, they assigned [a]Bezer in the wilderness upon the plain out of the tribe of Reuben, and [b]Ramoth in Gilead out of the tribe of Gad, and [c]Golan in Bashan out of the tribe of Manasseh.

9 [a]These were the cities appointed for all the children of Israel, and for the stranger that sojourneth among them, that whosoever killeth *any* person at unawares might flee thither, and not die by the hand of the avenger of blood, [b]until he stood before the congregation.

20:2 [a]Ex. 21:13; Num. 35:6,11, 14; Deut. 19:2,9
20:5 [a]Num. 35:12
20:6 [a]Num. 35:12,25
20:7 [1]Heb. *sanctified* [a]ch. 21:32; 1 Chr. 6:76 [b]ch. 21:21; 2 Chr. 10:1 [c]ch. 14:15; 21:11,13 [d]Luke 1:39
20:8 [a]Deut. 4:43; ch. 21:36; 1 Chr. 6:78 [b]ch. 21:38; 1 Ki. 22:3 [c]ch. 21:27
20:9 [a]Num. 35:15 [b]ver. 6

21:1 [a]ch. 14:1; 17:4
21:2 [a]ch. 18:1 [b]Num. 35:2
21:4 [a]ver. 8,19 [b]See ch. 24:33
21:5 [a]ver. 20
21:6 [a]ver. 27
21:7 [a]ver. 34
21:8 [a]ver. 3 [b]Num. 35:2
21:9 [1]Heb. *called*

Cities for the Levites

21 Then came near the heads of the fathers of the Levites unto [a]Eleazar the priest, and unto Joshua the son of Nun, and unto the heads of the fathers of the tribes of the children of Israel;

2 And they spake unto them at [a]Shiloh in the land of Canaan, saying, [b]The LORD commanded by the hand of Moses to give us cities to dwell in, with the suburbs thereof for our cattle.

3 And the children of Israel gave unto the Levites out of their inheritance, at the commandment of the LORD, these cities and their suburbs.

4 And the lot came out for the families of the Kohathites: and [a]the children of Aaron the priest, *which were* of the Levites, [b]had by lot out of the tribe of Judah, and out of the tribe of Simeon, and out of the tribe of Benjamin, thirteen cities.

5 And [a]the rest of the children of Kohath had by lot out of the families of the tribe of Ephraim, and out of the tribe of Dan, and out of the half tribe of Manasseh, ten cities.

6 And [a]the children of Gershon *had* by lot out of the families of the tribe of Issachar, and out of the tribe of Asher, and out of the tribe of Naphtali, and out of the half tribe of Manasseh in Bashan, thirteen cities.

7 [a]The children of Merari by their families *had* out of the tribe of Reuben, and out of the tribe of Gad, and out of the tribe of Zebulun, twelve cities.

8 [a]And the children of Israel gave by lot unto the Levites these cities with their suburbs, [b]as the LORD commanded by the hand of Moses.

9 ¶ And they gave out of the tribe of the children of Judah, and out of the tribe of the children of Simeon, these cities which are *here* [1]mentioned by name,

10 Which the children of Aaron, *being* of

20:1–9 Having distributed the land to the tribes, the Lord's next administrative regulation (see note on 13:1–32) provided an elementary system of government, specifically a system of regional courts to deal with capital offenses having to do with manslaughter. Thus this most inflammatory of cases was removed from local jurisdiction, and a safeguard was created against the easy miscarriage of justice (with its potential for endless blood feuds) when retribution for manslaughter was left in the hands of family members. The cities chosen were among those also assigned to the Levites, where ideally the law of Moses would especially be known and honored.

20:2 *whereof I spake unto you by the hand of Moses.* See Num 35:6–34.

20:3 *avenger of blood.* Also translated "near kinsman" (Ruth 3:9), or "redeemer" (Ps 19:14). The avenger was a near relative with the obligation of exacting retribution (see Lev 24:17; Num 35:16–28).

20:4 *gate of the city.* Traditional place for trials, where the elders sat to hold court (see Ruth 4:1 and note; see also Job 29:7).

20:6 *congregation.* Made up of the adult males of the city. Their function in the trial before the elders (v. 4) is not clear, but perhaps they witnessed the trial to see that it was fair (closed courts are notoriously corruptible). *death of the high priest.* See Num 35:25–28. Either an atoning effect or a kind of amnesty was achieved by the high priest's death.

20:7 *they appointed Kedesh.* A wordplay in the Hebrew: "they consecrated (the town of) consecration." The other two cities west of the Jordan already had sacred associations: For Shechem see 8:30–35 and note; Gen 12:6–7; for Hebron see Gen 23:2; 49:29–32. The geographical distribution of the cities was important: one in the north, one in the midlands and one in the south. (See v. 8, where the order of the three cities of refuge east of the Jordan is reversed: Bezer in the south, Ramoth in the midlands and Golan in the north.) See map, p. 226.

20:9 *the stranger.* Evidence of the equal protection granted to the foreigners living in Israel (cf. Lev 19:33–34; Deut 10:18–19).

21:1–45 Finally the Levites are allotted their towns and adjoining pasturelands—with the priestly families being given precedence (see v. 10).

21:4 *Kohathites.* The three sons of Levi were Kohath, Gershon and Merari (Ex 6:16; Num 3:17). *Judah . . . Simeon . . . Benjamin.* Tribal areas close to Jerusalem, which would later be the site of the temple. The remaining Kohathites received cities in adjoining tribes.

the families of the Kohathites, *who were* of the children of Levi, had: for theirs was the first lot.

11 [a]And they gave them [1]the city of Arbah the father of [b]Anak, which *city is* Hebron, [c]in the hill *country* of Judah, with the suburbs thereof round about it.

12 But [a]the fields of the city, and the villages thereof, gave they to Caleb the son of Jephunneh for his possession.

13 Thus [a]they gave to the children of Aaron the priest [b]Hebron with her suburbs, *to be* a city of refuge for the slayer; [c]and Libnah with her suburbs,

14 And [a]Jattir with her suburbs, [b]and Eshtemoa with her suburbs,

15 And [1]Holon with her suburbs, [a]and Debir with her suburbs,

16 And [a][1]Ain with her suburbs, [b]and Juttah with her suburbs, *and* [c]Beth-shemesh with her suburbs; nine cities out of those two tribes.

17 And out of the tribe of Benjamin, [a]Gibeon with her suburbs, [1]Geba with her suburbs,

18 Anathoth with her suburbs, and [1]Almon with her suburbs; four cities.

19 All the cities of the children of Aaron, the priests, *were* thirteen cities with their suburbs.

20 ¶ [a]And the families of the children of Kohath, the Levites which remained of the children of Kohath, even they had the cities of their lot out of the tribe of Ephraim.

21 For they gave them [a]Shechem with her suburbs in mount Ephraim, *to be* a city of refuge for the slayer; and Gezer with her suburbs,

22 And Kibzaim with her suburbs, and Beth-horon with her suburbs; four cities.

23 And out of the tribe of Dan, Eltekeh with her suburbs, Gibbethon with her suburbs,

24 Aijalon with her suburbs, Gath-rimmon with her suburbs; four cities.

25 And out of the half tribe of Manasseh, Tanach with her suburbs, and Gath-rimmon with her suburbs; two cities.

26 All the cities *were* ten with their suburbs for the families of the children of Kohath that remained.

27 ¶ [a]And unto the children of Gershon, of the families of the Levites, out of the *other* half tribe of Manasseh *they gave* [b]Golan in Bashan with her suburbs, *to be* a city of refuge for the slayer; and Beeshterah with her suburbs; two cities.

28 And out of the tribe of Issachar, Kishon with her suburbs, Dabareh with her suburbs,

21:11 [1]Or, *Kirjath-arbah* [a]1 Chr. 6:55 [b]ch. 15:13,14 [c]ch. 20:7; Luke 1:39
21:12 [a]ch. 14:14; 1 Chr. 6:56
21:13 [a]1 Chr. 6:57 [b]ch. 15:54; 20:7 [c]ch. 15:42
21:14 [a]ch. 15:48 [b]ch. 15:50
21:15 [1][1 Chr. 6:58, *Hilen;* ch. 15:51] [a]ch. 15:49
21:16 [1][1 Chr. 6:59, *Ashan*] [a]ch. 15:42 [b]ch. 15:55 [c]ch. 15:10
21:17 [1][ch. 18:24, *Gaba*] [a]ch. 18:25
21:18 [1][1 Chr. 6:60, *Alemeth*]
21:20 [a]ver. 5; 1 Chr. 6:66
21:21 [a]ch. 20:7
21:27 [a]ver. 6; 1 Chr. 6:71 [b]ch. 20:8

29 Jarmuth with her suburbs, En-gannim with her suburbs; four cities.

30 And out of the tribe of Asher, Mishal with her suburbs, Abdon with her suburbs,

31 Helkath with her suburbs, and Rehob with her suburbs; four cities.

32 And out of the tribe of Naphtali, [a]Kedesh in Galilee with her suburbs, *to be* a city of refuge for the slayer; and Hammoth-dor with her suburbs, and Kartan with her suburbs; three cities.

33 All the cities of the Gershonites according to their families *were* thirteen cities with their suburbs.

34 ¶ [a]And unto the families of the children of Merari, the rest of the Levites, out of the tribe of Zebulun, Jokneam with her suburbs, and Kartah with her suburbs,

35 Dimnah with her suburbs, Nahalal with her suburbs; four cities.

36 And out of the tribe of Reuben, [a]Bezer with her suburbs, and Jahazah with her suburbs,

37 Kedemoth with her suburbs, and Mephaath with her suburbs; four cities.

38 And out of the tribe of Gad, [a]Ramoth in Gilead with her suburbs, *to be* a city of refuge for the slayer; and Mahanaim with her suburbs,

39 Heshbon with her suburbs, Jazer with her suburbs; four cities in all.

40 So all the cities for the children of Merari by their families, which were remaining of the families of the Levites, were *by* their lot twelve cities.

41 [a]All the cities of the Levites within the possession of the children of Israel *were* forty and eight cities with their suburbs.

42 These cities were every one with their suburbs round about them: thus *were* all these cities.

43 ¶ And the LORD gave unto Israel [a]all the land which he sware to give unto their fathers; and they possessed it, and dwelt therein.

44 [a]And the LORD gave them rest round about, according to all that he sware unto their fathers: and [b]there stood not a man of all their enemies before them; the LORD delivered all their enemies into their hand.

45 [a]There failed not ought of any good thing which the LORD had spoken unto the house of Israel; all came to pass.

21:32 [a]ch. 20:7
21:34 [a]ver. 7; See 1 Chr. 6:77
21:36 [a]ch. 20:8
21:38 [a]ch. 20:8
21:41 [a]Num. 35:7
21:43 [a]Gen. 13:15; 15:18; 26:3; 28:4,13
21:44 [a]ch. 11:23; 22:4 [b]Deut. 7:24
21:45 [a]ch. 23:14

Eastern tribes return home

22 Then Joshua called the Reubenites, and the Gadites, and the half tribe of Manasseh,

21:11 *Hebron.* Caleb's city (14:13–15). The priests and Levites were to be given space in their assigned cities along with the other inhabitants.

21:27 *children of Gershon.* Received cities in the northern tribes of Asher, Naphtali and Issachar.

21:34 *families of the children of Merari.* Their 12 cities were scattered over Reuben, Gad and Zebulun.

21:43–45 A concluding summary statement of how the Lord had fulfilled His sworn promise to give Israel this land (see Gen 15:18–21). The occupation of the land was not yet complete (see 23:4–5; Judg 1–2), but the national campaign was over and Israel was finally established in the promised land. No power was left in Canaan that could threaten to dislodge her.

21:44 *rest round about.* See note on 1:13.

22:1–34 The two and a half tribes from east of the Jordan, faithful in battle, are now commended by Joshua and sent to

2 And said unto them, Ye have kept [a]all that Moses the servant of the LORD commanded you, [b]and have obeyed my voice in all that I commanded you:

3 Ye have not left your brethren these many days unto this day, but have kept the charge of the commandment of the LORD your God.

4 And now the LORD your God hath given rest unto your brethren, as he promised them: therefore now return ye, and get ye unto your tents, *and* unto the land of your possession, [a]which Moses the servant of the LORD gave you on the *other* side Jordan.

5 But [a]take diligent heed to do the commandment and the law, which Moses the servant of the LORD charged you, [b]to love the LORD your God, and to walk in all his ways, and to keep his commandments, and to cleave unto him, and to serve him with all your heart and with all your soul.

6 So Joshua [a]blessed them, and sent them away: and they went unto their tents.

7 Now to the *one* half of the tribe of Manasseh Moses had given *possession* in Bashan: [a]but unto the *other* half thereof gave Joshua among their brethren on *this* side Jordan westward. And when Joshua sent them away also unto their tents, then he blessed them,

8 And he spake unto them, saying, Return with much riches unto your tents, and with very much cattle, with silver, and with gold, and with brass, and with iron, and with very much raiment: [a]divide the spoil of your enemies with your brethren.

9 And the children of Reuben and the children of Gad and the half tribe of Manasseh returned, and departed from the children of Israel out of Shiloh, which *is* in the land of Canaan, to go unto [a]the country of Gilead, to the land of their possession, whereof they were possessed, according to the word of the LORD by the hand of Moses.

10 And when they came unto the borders of Jordan, that *are* in the land of Canaan, the children of Reuben and the children of Gad and the half tribe of Manasseh built there an altar by Jordan, a great altar to see to.

22:2 [a]Num. 32:20; Deut. 3:18 [b]ch. 1:16,17
22:4 [a]Num. 32:33
22:5 [a]Deut. 6:6,17; 11:22; Jer. 12:16 [b]Deut. 10:12
22:6 [a]Gen. 47:7; Ex. 39:43; ch. 14:13; 2 Sam. 6:18; Luke 24:50
22:7 [a]ch. 17:5
22:8 [a]Num. 31:27; 1 Sam. 30:24
22:9 [a]Num. 32:1,26,29
22:11 [a]Deut. 13:12; Judg. 20:12
22:12 [a]Judg. 20:1
22:13 [a]Deut. 13:14; Judg. 20:12 [b]Ex. 6:25; Num. 25:7,11-13
22:14 [1]Heb. *house of the father* [a]Num. 1:4
22:16 [a]See Lev. 17:8,9; Deut. 12:13,14
22:17 [a]Num. 25:3,4; Deut. 4:3
22:18 [a]Num. 16:22
22:19 [a]ch. 18:1
22:20 [a]ch. 7:1,5

11 ¶ And the children of Israel [a]heard say, Behold, the children of Reuben and the children of Gad and the half tribe of Manasseh have built an altar over against the land of Canaan, in the borders of Jordan, at the passage of the children of Israel.

12 And when the children of Israel heard *of it,* [a]the whole congregation of the children of Israel gathered themselves together *at* Shiloh, to go up to war against them.

13 And the children of Israel [a]sent unto the children of Reuben, and to the children of Gad, and to the half tribe of Manasseh, into the land of Gilead, [b]Phinehas the son of Eleazar the priest,

14 And with him ten princes, of each [1]chief house a prince throughout all the tribes of Israel; and [a]each one *was* a head of the house of their fathers among the thousands of Israel.

15 And they came unto the children of Reuben, and to the children of Gad, and to the half tribe of Manasseh, unto the land of Gilead, and they spake with them, saying,

16 Thus saith the whole congregation of the LORD, What trespass *is* this that ye have committed against the God of Israel, to turn away *this* day from following the LORD, in that ye have builded you an altar, [a]that ye might rebel *this* day against the LORD?

17 *Is* the iniquity [a]of Peor *too* little for us, from which we are not cleansed until this day, although there was a plague in the congregation of the LORD,

18 But that ye must turn away *this* day from following the LORD? and it will be, *seeing* ye rebel to day against the LORD, that to morrow [a]he will be wroth with the whole congregation of Israel.

19 Notwithstanding, if the land of your possession *be* unclean, *then* pass ye over unto the land of the possession of the LORD, [a]wherein the LORD's tabernacle dwelleth, and take possession among us: but rebel not against the LORD, nor rebel against us, in building you an altar beside the altar of the LORD our God.

20 [a]Did not Achan the son of Zerah commit a trespass in the accursed thing, and wrath

---

their homes. But their "altar of witness" (see vv. 26–27,34) was misunderstood, and disciplinary action against them was narrowly averted.

22:2 *all that Moses . . . commanded.* Moses had ordered them to join the other tribes in the conquest of Canaan (Num 32:16–27; Deut 3:18).

22:5 *love the LORD . . . serve him with all your heart.* Both Moses and Joshua saw that obedience to the laws of God would require love and service from the heart. In the ancient Near East, "love" was also a political term, indicating truehearted loyalty to one's king.

22:8 *divide . . . with your brethren.* Moses also had seen the need for a fair sharing of the spoils of war (Num 31:25–27).

22:10 *borders of Jordan.* Understood in the Septuagint to be Gilgal, next to Jericho; more likely it was a site east of Shiloh along the Jordan River (18:17).

22:11 *And the children of Israel heard.* Anxiety about apostasy led to hasty conclusions. They thought the altar had been set up as a rival to the true altar at Shiloh.

22:12 *gathered . . . at Shiloh.* In the presence of God at the tabernacle. *to go up to war against them.* To take disciplinary action (cf. Deut 13:12–18; Judg 20).

22:13–14 A prestigious delegation is sent to try to turn the tribes east of the Jordan from their (supposed) act of rebellion against the Lord.

22:16 *What trespass is this . . . ?* The accusations were very grave: You have committed apostasy and rebellion.

22:17 *Peor.* Where some of the Israelites became involved in the Moabite worship of Baal-Peor (Num 25:1–5).

22:19 *be unclean.* By pagan worship, corrupting its inhabitants. *the land of the . . . LORD.* The promised land proper had never included territory east of the Jordan. Canaan was the land the Lord especially claimed as His own and promised to the descendants of Abraham, Isaac and Jacob.

22:20 *Achan . . . all the congregation of Israel.* See note on 7:1–26.

fell on all the congregation of Israel? and that man perished not alone in his iniquity.

21 ¶ Then the children of Reuben and the children of Gad and the half tribe of Manasseh answered, and said unto the heads of the thousands of Israel,

22 The LORD [a]God of gods, the LORD God of gods, he [b]knoweth, and Israel he shall know; if *it be* in rebellion, or if in transgression against the LORD, (save us not this day,)

23 That we have built us an altar to turn from following the LORD; or if to offer thereon burnt offering or meat offering, or if to offer peace offerings thereon, let the LORD himself [a]require *it;*

24 And if we have not *rather* done it for fear of *this* thing, saying, [1]In time to come your children might speak unto our children, saying, What have you to do with the LORD God of Israel?

25 For the LORD hath made Jordan a border between us and you, ye children of Reuben and children of Gad; ye have no part in the LORD: so shall your children make our children cease from fearing the LORD:

26 Therefore we said, Let us now prepare to build us an altar, not for burnt offering, nor for sacrifice:

27 But *that* it *may be* [a]a witness between us, and you, and our generations after us, that *we* might [b]do the service of the LORD before him with our burnt offerings, and with our sacrifices, and with our peace offerings; that your children may not say to our children in time to come, Ye have no part in the LORD.

28 Therefore said we, that it shall be, when they should *so* say to us or to our generations in time to come, that we may say *again,* Behold the pattern of the altar of the LORD, which our fathers made, not for burnt offerings, nor for sacrifices; but it *is* a witness between us and you.

29 God forbid that we should rebel against the LORD, and turn *this* day from following the LORD, [a]to build an altar for burnt offerings, for meat offerings, or for sacrifices, besides the altar of the LORD our God that *is* before his tabernacle.

30 ¶ And when Phinehas the priest, and the princes of the congregation and heads of the thousands of Israel which *were* with him, heard the words that the children of Reuben and the children of Gad and the children of Manasseh spake, [1]it pleased them.

31 And Phinehas the son of Eleazar the priest said unto the children of Reuben, and to the children of Gad, and to the children of Manasseh, *This* day we perceive that the LORD *is* [a]among us, because ye have not committed this trespass against the LORD: [1]now ye have delivered the children of Israel out of the hand of the LORD.

32 And Phinehas the son of Eleazar the priest, and the princes, returned from the children of Reuben, and from the children of Gad, out of the land of Gilead, unto the land of Canaan, to the children of Israel, and brought them word again.

33 And the thing pleased the children of Israel; and the children of Israel [a]blessed God, and did not intend to go up against them in battle, to destroy the land wherein the children of Reuben and Gad dwelt.

34 And the children of Reuben and the children of Gad called the altar [a 1]*Ed:* for it *shall be* a witness between us that the LORD *is* God.

Joshua's address to Israel

23 And it came to pass a long time after that the LORD [a]had given rest unto Israel from all their enemies round about, that Joshua [b]waxed old *and* [1]stricken in age.

2 And Joshua [a]called for all Israel, *and* for their elders, and for their heads, and for their judges, and for their officers, and said unto them, I am old *and* stricken in age:

3 And ye have seen all that the LORD your God hath done unto all these nations because of you; for the [a]LORD your God *is* he that hath fought for you.

4 Behold, [a]I have divided unto you *by lot* these nations that remain, to be an inheritance for your tribes, from Jordan, with all the nations that I have cut off, even *unto* the great sea [1]westward.

5 And the LORD your God, [a]he shall expel them from before you, and drive them from out of your sight; and ye shall possess their land, [b]as the LORD your God hath promised unto you.

6 [a]Be ye therefore very courageous to keep and to do all that is written in the book of the

22:22 [a]Deut. 10:17 [b]Job 10:7; 23:10; Jer. 12:3; 2 Cor. 11:11,31
22:23 [a]Deut. 18:19; 1 Sam. 20:16
22:24 [1]Heb. *To morrow*
22:27 [a]ver. 34; Gen. 31:48; ch. 24:27 [b]Deut. 12:5
22:29 [a]Deut. 12:13,14
22:30 [1]Heb. *it was good in their eyes*
22:31 [1]Heb. *then* [a]Lev. 26:11,12; 2 Chr. 15:2
22:33 [a]1 Chr. 29:20; Neh. 8:6; Dan. 2:19; Luke 2:28
22:34 [1]That is, A witness [a]ch. 24:27
23:1 [1]Heb. *come into days* [a]ch. 21:44; 22:4 [b]ch. 13:1
23:2 [a]Deut. 31:28; ch. 24:1; 1 Chr. 28:1
23:3 [a]Ex. 14:14; ch. 10:14,42
23:4 [1]Heb. at *the sunset* [a]ch. 13:2,6; 18:10
23:5 [a]Ex. 23:30; 33:2; 34:11; Deut. 11:23; ch. 13:6 [b]Num. 33:53
23:6 [a]ch. 1:7

22:22 *The LORD God of gods.* See note on Ps 50:1. The repetition of the sacred names gives an oath-like quality to this strong denial of any wrongdoing.

22:27 *witness.* The altar, presumably of uncut stone (see 8:31; Ex 20:25), was to serve as a testimony to the commitment of the tribes across the Jordan to remain loyal to the Lord, and to their continued right to worship the Lord at the tabernacle—even though they lived outside the land of promise. It constitutes the sixth memorial monument in the land noted by the author of Joshua (see note on 10:27).

22:31 *ye have delivered the children of Israel.* Their words prevented a terrible punishment that the other tribes were about to inflict as a divine act of judgment (consider the implications of v. 20).

23:1–16 Joshua, the Lord's servant, delivers a farewell address recalling the victories the Lord has given, but also reminding the people of areas yet to be possessed and of the need to be loyal to God's covenant laws. Their mission remains—to be the people of God's kingdom in the world.

23:1 *rest.* See note on 1:13. *striken in age.* Joshua was approaching the age of 110 (24:29).

23:6 *Be ye therefore very courageous to . . . do.* Echoing the Lord's instructions at the beginning (1:7–8; see 22:5). *book of the law.* A reference to canonical written materials from the time of Moses (cf. Deut 30:10,19; 31:9,24,26).

23:11 *love the LORD your God.* A concluding summation (see note on 22:5).

23:12 *if ye do in any wise go back.* Remaining in the promised

law of Moses, [b]that *ye* turn not aside therefrom *to* the right hand or *to* the left;

7 That *ye* [a]come not among these nations, these that remain amongst you; neither [b]make mention of the name of their gods, nor cause to swear *by them,* neither serve them, nor bow yourselves unto them.

8 [1]But [a]cleave unto the LORD your God, as ye have done unto this day.

9 [a] [1]For the LORD hath driven out from before you great nations and strong: but *as for* you, [b]no man hath *been able to* stand before you unto this day.

10 [a]One man of you shall chase a thousand: for the LORD your God, he *it is* that fighteth for you, [b]as he hath promised you.

11 [a]Take good heed therefore unto your[1] selves, that ye love the LORD your God.

12 Else if ye do in any wise [a]go back, and cleave unto the remnant of these nations, *even* these that remain among you, and shall [b]make marriages with them, and go in unto them, and they to you:

13 Know for a certainty that [a]the LORD your God will no more drive out *any of* these nations from before you; [b]but they shall be snares and traps unto you, and scourges in your sides, and thorns in your eyes, until ye perish from off this good land which the LORD your God hath given you.

14 And behold, *this* day [a]I am going the way of all the earth: and ye know in all your hearts and in all your souls, that [b]not one thing hath failed of all the good things which the LORD your God spake concerning you; all are come to pass unto you, *and* not one thing hath failed thereof.

15 [a]Therefore it shall come to pass, *that* as all good things are come upon you, which the LORD your God promised you; so shall the LORD bring upon you [b]all evil things, until he have destroyed you from off this good land which the LORD your God hath given you.

16 When ye have transgressed the covenant of the LORD your God, which he commanded you, and have gone and served other gods, and bowed yourselves to them; then shall the anger of the LORD be kindled against you, and ye shall perish quickly from off the good land which he hath given unto you.

23:6 [b]Deut. 5:32; 28:14
23:7 [a]Ex. 23:33; Deut. 7:2,3; Prov. 4:14; Eph. 5:11 [b]Ex. 23:13; Jer. 5:7; Zeph. 1:5; See Num. 32:38
23:8 [1]Or, *For if you will cleave, etc.* [a]Deut. 10:20; ch. 22:5
23:9 [1]Or, *Then the LORD will drive* [a]Deut. 11:23 [b]ch. 1:5
23:10 [a]Lev. 26:8; Deut. 32:30 [b]Ex. 14:14; Deut. 3:22
23:11 [1]Heb. *souls* [a]ch. 22:5
23:12 [a]2 Pet. 2:20,21 [b]Deut. 7:3
23:13 [a]Judg. 2:3 [b]Ex. 23:33; 1 Ki. 11:4
23:14 [a]1 Ki. 2:2 [b]Luke 21:33
23:15 [a]Deut. 28:63 [b]Deut. 28:15,16

24:1 [a]Gen. 35:4 [b]ch. 23:2 [c]1 Sam. 10:19
24:2 [a]Gen. 11:26,31 [b]ver. 14
24:3 [a]Gen. 12:1; Acts 7:2,3 [b]Ps. 127:3
24:4 [a]Gen. 25:24-26 [b]Gen. 36:8; Deut. 2:5 [c]Gen. 46:1,6
24:5 [a]Ex. 3:10 [b]Ex. 7; 8; 9; 10
24:6 [a]Ex. 12:37,51 [b]Ex. 14:2 [c]Ex. 14:9
24:7 [a]Ex. 14:20 [b]Ex. 14:27,28 [c]Deut. 4:34 [d]ch. 5:6
24:8 [a]Num. 21:21,33; Deut. 2:32
24:9 [a]Judg. 11:25 [b]Num. 22:5
24:10 [a]Deut. 23:5 [b]Num. 23:11,20
24:11 [a]ch. 3:14,17 [b]ch. 6:1; 10:1

Israel renews the covenant

24 And Joshua gathered all the tribes of Israel to [a]Shechem, and [b]called for the elders of Israel, and for their heads, and for their judges, and for their officers; and they [c]presented themselves before God.

2 And Joshua said unto all the people, Thus saith the LORD God of Israel, [a]Your fathers dwelt on the *other* side of the flood in old time, *even* Terah, the father of Abraham, and the father of Nachor: and [b]they served other gods.

3 And [a]I took your father Abraham from the *other* side of the flood, and led him throughout all the land of Canaan, and multiplied his seed, and [b]gave him Isaac.

4 And I gave unto Isaac [a]Jacob and Esau: and I gave unto [b]Esau mount Seir, to possess it; [c]but Jacob and his children went down *into* Egypt.

5 [a]I sent Moses also and Aaron, and [b]I plagued Egypt, according to *that* which I did amongst them: and afterward I brought you out.

6 And I [a]brought your fathers out of Egypt: and [b]you came unto the sea; [c]and the Egyptians pursued after your fathers with chariots and horsemen *unto* the Red sea.

7 And when they cried unto the LORD, [a]he put darkness between you and the Egyptians, [b]and brought the sea upon them, and covered them; and [c]your eyes have seen what I have done in Egypt: and ye dwelt in the wilderness [d]a long season.

8 And I brought you into the land of the Amorites, which dwelt on the *other* side Jordan; [a]and they fought with you: and I gave them into your hand, that ye might possess their land; and I destroyed them from before you.

9 Then [a]Balak the son of Zippor, king of Moab, arose and warred against Israel, and [b]sent and called Balaam the son of Beor to curse you:

10 [a]But I would not hearken unto Balaam; [b]therefore he blessed you still: so I delivered you out of his hand.

11 And [a]ye went over Jordan, and came unto Jericho: and [b]the men of Jericho fought against you, the Amorites, and the Perizzites,

land was conditioned on faithfulness to the Lord and separation from the idolaters still around them. Failure to meet these conditions would bring Israel's banishment from the land (cf. vv. 13,15–16; 2 Ki 17:7–8; 2 Chr 7:14–20). *cleave unto . . . make marriages with them.* The Lord prohibited alliances, either national or domestic, with the peoples of Canaan because such alliances would tend to compromise Israel's loyalty to the Lord (see Ex 34:15–16; Deut 7:2–4).

23:13 *snares and traps.* Joshua's warning echoes Ex 23:33; 34:12; Deut 7:16.

24:1–33 Once more Joshua assembled the tribes at Shechem to call Israel to a renewal of the covenant (see 8:30–35). It was his final official act as the Lord's servant, mediator of the Lord's rule over His people. In this he followed the example of Moses, whose final official act was also a call to covenant renewal—of which Deuteronomy is the preserved document.

‡24:2 *Thus saith the LORD.* Only a divinely appointed mediator would dare to speak for God with direct discourse, as in vv. 2–13. *the flood.* Lit. "the river," i.e. the Euphrates. *in old time.* In accordance with the common ancient Near Eastern practice of making treaties (covenants), a brief recital of the past history of the relationship precedes the making of covenant commitments. Joshua here focuses on the separation of Abraham from his polytheistic family, the deliverance of Israel from Egypt and the Lord's establishment of His people in Canaan.

‡24:6 *Red sea.* Lit. the "Sea of Reeds." See note on Ex. 14:2.

24:10 *I would not hearken unto Balaam.* Not only did the Lord reject Balaam's prayers; He also turned his curse into a blessing (see Num 23–24).

and the Canaanites, and the Hittites, and the Girgashites, the Hivites, and the Jebusites; and I delivered them into your hand.

12 And [a]I sent the hornet before you, which drave them out from before you, *even* the two kings of the Amorites; *but* [b]not with thy sword, nor with thy bow.

13 And I have given you a land for which ye did not labour, and [a]cities which ye built not, and ye dwell in them; of the vineyards and oliveyards which ye planted not do ye eat.

14 [a]Now therefore fear the LORD, and serve him in [b]sincerity and in truth: and [c]put away the gods which your fathers served on the *other* side of the flood, and [d]in Egypt; and serve ye the LORD.

15 And if it seem evil unto you to serve the LORD, [a]choose you *this* day whom you will serve; whether [b]the gods which your fathers served that *were* on the *other* side of the flood, or [c]the gods of the Amorites, in whose land ye dwell: [d]but as for me and my house, we will serve the LORD.

16 ¶ And the people answered and said, God forbid that we should forsake the LORD, to serve other gods;

17 For the LORD our God, he *it is* that brought us up and our fathers out of the land of Egypt, from the house of bondage, and which did those great signs in our sight, and preserved us in all the way wherein we went, and among all the people through whom we passed:

18 And the LORD drave out from before us all the people, even the Amorites which dwelt in the land: *therefore* will we also serve the LORD; for he *is* our God.

19 And Joshua said unto the people, [a]Ye cannot serve the LORD: for he *is* a [b]holy God; he *is* [c]a jealous God; [d]he will not forgive your transgressions nor your sins.

24:12 [a]Ex. 23:28; Deut. 7:20 [b]Ps. 44:3,6
24:13 [a]Deut. 6:10,11
24:14 [a]Deut. 10:12; 1 Sam. 12:24 [b]Gen. 17:1; 20:5; Deut. 18:13; 2 Cor. 1:12 [c]ver. 2,23; Ezek. 20:18 [d]Ezek. 20:7,8; 23:3
24:15 [a]Ruth 1:15; 1 Ki. 18:21 [b]ver. 2 [c]Ex. 23:24,32,33 [d]Gen. 18:19
24:19 [a]Mat. 6:24 [b]1 Sam. 6:20 [c]Ex. 20:5 [d]Ex. 23:21
24:20 [a]1 Chr. 28:9; Ezra 8:22; Is. 1:28; Jer. 17:13 [b]ch. 23:15; Is. 63:10; Acts 7:42
24:22 [a]Ps. 119:173
24:23 [a]ver. 14; Gen. 35:2
24:25 [a]Ex. 15:25; 2 Ki. 11:17 [b]ver. 1
24:26 [a]Deut. 31:24 [b]Judg. 9:6 [c]Gen. 28:18; ch. 4:3 [d]Gen. 35:4
24:27 [a]See Gen. 31:48,52 [b]Deut. 32:1
24:28 [a]Judg. 2:6
24:29 [a]Judg. 2:8
24:30 [a]ch. 19:50
24:31 [a]Judg. 2:7

20 [a]If ye forsake the LORD, and serve strange gods, [b]then he will turn and do you hurt, and consume you, after that he hath done you good.

21 And the people said unto Joshua, Nay; but we will serve the LORD.

22 And Joshua said unto the people, Ye *are* witnesses against yourselves that [a]ye have chosen you the LORD, to serve him. And they said, *We are* witnesses.

23 Now therefore [a]put away, *said he,* the strange gods which *are* among you, and incline your heart unto the LORD God of Israel.

24 And the people said unto Joshua, The LORD our God will we serve, and his voice will we obey.

25 So Joshua [a]made a covenant with the people that day, and set them a statute and an ordinance [b]in Shechem.

26 ¶ And Joshua [a]wrote these words in the book of the law of God, and took [b]a great stone, and [c]set it up there [d]under an oak, that *was* by the sanctuary of the LORD.

27 And Joshua said unto all the people, Behold, this stone shall be [a]a witness unto us; for [b]it hath heard all the words of the LORD which he spake unto us: it shall be therefore a witness unto you, lest ye deny your God.

The death of Joshua

28 ¶ So [a]Joshua let the people depart, every man unto his inheritance.

29 [a]And it came to pass after these things, that Joshua the son of Nun, the servant of the LORD, died, *being* an hundred and ten years old.

30 And they buried him in the border of his inheritance in [a]Timnath-serah, which *is* in mount Ephraim, on the north side of the hill of Gaash.

31 And [a]Israel served the LORD all the days of Joshua, and all the days of the elders that

24:12 *the hornet.* Lower (northern) Egypt had long used the hornet as a national symbol, so Egypt's military campaigns in Canaan may have been in mind. But "the hornet" may also refer to the reports about Israel that spread panic among the Canaanites (2:11; 5:1; 9:24). See note on Ex 23:28.

24:14 *fear the LORD.* Trust, serve and worship Him. *gods which your fathers served on the other side of the flood, and in Egypt.* See v. 2. Joshua appealed to the Israelites to put away the gods their forefathers had worshiped in Mesopotamia and Egypt. In Ur and Haran, Terah's family would have been exposed to the worship of the moon-god, Nanna(r) or Sin. The golden calf of Ex 32:4 may be an example of their worship of the gods of Egypt. It was probably patterned after Apis, the sacred bull of Egypt; see note on Ex 32:4. (Jeroboam's golden calves at Bethel and Dan, on the other hand, probably represented mounts or pedestals for a riding or standing deity; see 1 Ki 12:28–29.)

24:15 *as for me.* Joshua publicly makes his commitment, hoping to elicit the same from Israel.

24:17–18 A creedal statement based on the miraculous events of the exodus and ending with "he is our God."

24:19 *Ye cannot.* Strong words to emphasize the danger of overconfidence.

24:22 *witnesses.* See v. 27; a normal part of treaty/covenant-making (see Deut 30:19).

24:23 *strange gods.* The other gods were represented by idols of wood and metal, which could be thrown away and destroyed.

24:25 *covenant with the people.* Consisting of the pledges they had agreed to and the decrees and laws from God.

24:26 *great stone.* Set up as a witness to the covenant renewal that closed Joshua's ministry, this is the seventh memorial in the land reminding Israel of what the Lord had done for them through His servant (see note on 22:27). To these memorials were added the perpetual ruins of Jericho (6:26). Thus the promised land itself bore full testimony to Israel (seven being the number of completeness)—how she had come into possession of the land and how she would remain in the land only by fulfilling the covenant conditions. The land shouted its own story. *oak.* See note on Gen 12:6.

24:29–33 Three burials. Since it was a deep desire of the ancients to be buried in their homeland, these notices not only mark the conclusion of the story and the close of an era but also underscore the fact that Israel had indeed been established in the promised homeland—the Lord had kept His covenant.

24:29 *an hundred and ten.* For the significance of this number see note on Gen 50:26.

24:30 *buried him . . . in Timnath-serah.* See 19:50 and note.

[1] overlived Joshua, and which had [b] known all
the works of the LORD, that he had done for Israel.
32 ¶ And the [a] bones of Joseph, which the
children of Israel brought up out of Egypt,
buried they in Shechem, in a parcel of ground
[b] which Jacob bought of the sons of Hamor the
father of Shechem for an hundred [1] pieces of
silver: and it became the inheritance of the
children of Joseph.
33 And Eleazar the son of Aaron died; and
they buried him in a hill that pertained to
[a] Phinehas his son, which was given him in
mount Ephraim.

24:31 [1] Heb. *prolonged* their *days after Joshua* [b] Deut. 11:2
24:32 [1] Or, *lambs* [a] Gen. 50:25; Ex. 13:19 [b] Gen. 33:19
24:33 [a] Ex. 6:25; Judg. 20:28

24:31 The story told in Joshua is a testimony to Israel's faithfulness in that generation. The author anticipates the quite different story that would follow.

24:32 *bones of Joseph.* Returning his bones to Shechem was significant not only because of the ancient plot of land Jacob bought from Hamor (Gen 33:19), but also because Shechem was to be the center of the tribes of Ephraim and Manasseh, the two sons of Joseph. Also, the return fulfilled an oath sworn to Joseph on his deathbed (Gen 50:25; Ex 13:19).

‡24:33 *Eleazar.* The high priest who served Joshua, as Aaron had served Moses. *hill.* Hebrew is *Gibeah.* Not the Benjamite city, but a place in Ephraim near Shiloh.

The Book of Judges

INTRODUCTION

Title

The title describes the leaders Israel had from the time of the elders who outlived Joshua until the time of the monarchy. Their principal purpose is best expressed in 2:16: "Nevertheless the LORD raised up judges, which delivered them out of the hand of those that spoiled them." Since it was God who permitted the oppressions and raised up deliverers, He Himself was Israel's ultimate Judge and Deliverer (11:27; see 8:23, where Gideon, a judge, insists that the Lord is Israel's true ruler).

Author and Date

Although, according to tradition, Samuel wrote the book, authorship is actually uncertain. It is possible that Samuel assembled some of the accounts from the period of the judges and that such prophets as Nathan and Gad, both of whom were associated with David's court, had a hand in shaping and editing the material (see 1 Chr 29:29).

The date of composition is also unknown, but it was undoubtedly during the monarchy. The frequent expression "In those days there was no king in Israel" (17:6; 18:1; 19:1; 21:25) suggests a date after the establishment of the monarchy. The observation that the Jebusites still controlled Jerusalem (1:21) has been taken to indicate a time before David's capture of the city c. 1000 B.C. (see 2 Sam 5:6–10). But the new conditions in Israel alluded to in chs. 17—21 suggest a time after the Davidic dynasty had been effectively established (tenth century B.C.).

Theme and Theology

The book of Judges describes the life of Israel in the promised land from the death of Joshua to the rise of the monarchy. On the one hand, it is an account of frequent apostasy, provoking divine chastening. On the other hand, it tells of urgent appeals to God in times of crisis, moving the Lord to raise up leaders (judges) through whom He throws off foreign oppressors and restores the land to peace.

After Israel was established in the promised land through the ministry of Joshua, her pilgrimage ended. Many of the covenant promises God had given to the patriarchs in Canaan and to the fathers in the wilderness had now been fulfilled. The Lord's land, where Israel was to enter into rest, lay under her feet; it remained only for her to occupy it, to displace the Canaanites and to cleanse it of paganism. The time had come for Israel to be the kingdom of God in the form of an established commonwealth on earth.

But in Canaan Israel quickly forgot the acts of God that had given her birth and had established her in the land. Consequently she lost sight of her unique identity as God's people, chosen and called to be His army and the loyal citizens of His emerging kingdom. She settled down and attached herself to Canaan's peoples, morals, gods, and religious beliefs and practices as readily as to Canaan's agriculture and social life.

Throughout Judges the fundamental issue is the lordship of God in Israel—i.e., Israel's acknowledgment of and loyalty to His rule. His kingship over Israel had been uniquely established by the covenant at Sinai (Ex 19—24), which was later renewed by Moses on the plains of Moab (Deut 29) and by Joshua at Shechem (Josh 24). The author accuses Israel of having rejected the kingship of the Lord again and again. She stopped fighting the Lord's battles, turned to the gods of Canaan to secure the blessings of family, flocks and fields, and abandoned God's laws for daily living. In the very center of the cycle of the judges (see Outline), Gideon had to remind Israel that the Lord was her King (see note on 8:23). The recurring lament, and indictment, of chs. 17—21 (see Outline) is: "In those days there was no king in Israel, but every man did that which was right in his own eyes" (see note on 17:6). The primary reference here is doubtless to the earthly mediators of the Lord's rule (i.e., human kings), but the implicit charge is that Israel did not truly acknowledge or obey her heavenly King either.

Only by the Lord's sovereign use of foreign oppression to chasten His people—thereby implementing the covenant curses (see Lev 26:14–45; Deut 28:15–68)—and by His raising up deliverers when His people cried out to Him did He maintain His kingship in Israel and preserve the embryonic kingdom from extinction. Israel's flawed condition was graphically exposed; she continued to need new saving acts by God in order to enter into the promised rest (see note on Josh 1:13).

Out of the recurring cycles of disobedience, foreign oppression, cries of distress, and deliverance (see 2:11–19; Neh 9:26–31) emerges another important theme—the covenant faithfulness of the Lord. The amazing patience and long-suffering of God are no better demonstrated than during this unsettled period.

Remarkably, this age of Israel's failure, following directly on the redemptive events that came through Moses and Joshua, is in a special way the OT age of the Spirit. God's Spirit enabled men to accomplish feats of victory in the Lord's holy war against the powers that threatened His kingdom (see 3:10; 6:34; 11:29; 13:25; 14:6,19; 15:14; see also 1 Sam 10:6,10; 11:6; 16:13). This same Spirit, poured out on the church following the redemptive work of the second Joshua (Jesus), empowered the people of the Lord to begin the task of preaching the gospel to all nations and of advancing the kingdom of God (see notes on Acts 1:2,8).

Background

Fixing precise dates for the judges is difficult and complex. The dating system followed here is based primarily on 1 Ki 6:1, which speaks of an interval of 480 years between the exodus and the fourth year of Solomon's reign. This would place the exodus c. 1446 B.C. and the period of the judges between c. 1380 and the rise of Saul, c. 1050. Jephthah's statement that Israel had occupied Heshbon for 300 years (11:26) generally agrees with these dates.

Some maintain, however, that the number 480 in 1 Ki 6:1 is somewhat artificial, arrived at by multiplying 12 (perhaps in reference to the 12 judges) by 40 (a conventional number of years for a generation). They point out the frequent use of the round numbers 10, 20, 40 and 80 in the book of Judges itself. A later date for the exodus would of course require a much shorter period of time for the judges (see Introduction to Exodus: Chronology).

Literary Features

Even a quick reading of Judges discloses its basic threefold division: (1) a prologue (1:1—3:6), (2) a main body (3:7—16:31) and (3) an epilogue (chs. 17—21). Closer study brings to light a more complex structure, with interwoven themes that bind the whole into an intricately designed portrayal of the character of an age.

The prologue (1:1—3:6) has two parts, and each serves a different purpose. They are not chronologically related, nor does either offer a strict chronological scheme of the time as a whole. The first part (1:1—2:5) sets the stage historically for the narratives that follow. It describes Israel's occupation of the promised land—from her initial success to her large-scale failure and divine rebuke.

The second part (2:6—3:6) indicates a basic perspective on the period from the time of Joshua to the rise of the monarchy, a time characterized by recurring cycles of apostasy, oppression, cries of distress and gracious divine deliverance. The author summarizes and explains the Lord's dealings with his rebellious people and introduces some of the basic vocabulary and formulas he will use in the later narratives: "did evil in the sight of the LORD," 2:11 (see 3:7,12; 4:1; 6:1; 10:6); "delivered them into the hands of," 2:14 (see 6:1; 13:1); and "sold them," 2:14 (see 3:8; 4:2; 10:7).

The main body of the book (3:7—16:31), which gives the actual accounts of the recurring cycles (apostasy, oppression, distress, deliverance), has its own unique design. Each cycle has a similar beginning ("The children of Israel did evil in the sight of the LORD"; see note on 3:7) and a recognizable conclusion ("the land had rest . . . years" or "judged Israel . . . years"; see note on 3:11). The first of these cycles (Othniel; see 3:7–11 and note) provides the "report form" used for each successive story of oppression and deliverance.

The remaining five cycles form the following narrative units, built around the rest of the major judges:

1. Ehud (3:12–30), a lone hero from the tribe of Benjamin who delivers Israel from oppression from the east.

2. Deborah (chs. 4—5), a woman from one of the Joseph tribes (Ephraim, west of the Jordan) who judges at a time when Israel is being overrun by a coalition of Canaanites under Sisera.

3. Gideon and his son Abimelech (chs. 6—9), who form the central account. In many ways Gide-

on is the ideal judge, evoking memory of Moses, while his son is the very antithesis of a responsible and faithful judge.

4. Jephthah (10:6—12:7), a social outcast from the other Joseph tribe (Manasseh, east of the Jordan) who judges at a time when Israel is being threatened by a coalition of powers under the king of Ammon.

5. Samson (chs. 13—16), a lone hero from the tribe of Dan who delivers Israel from oppression from the west.

The arrangement of these narrative units is significant. The central accounts of Gideon (the Lord's ideal judge) and Abimelech (the anti-judge) are bracketed by the parallel narratives of the woman Deborah and the social outcast Jephthah—which in turn are framed by the stories of the lone heroes Ehud and Samson. In this way even the structure focuses attention on the crucial issue of the period of the judges: Israel's attraction to the Baals of Canaan (shown by Abimelech; see note on 9:1–57) versus the Lord's kingship over His people (encouraged by Gideon; see note on 8:23).

The epilogue (chs. 17—21) characterizes the era in yet another way, depicting religious and moral corruption on the part of individuals, cities and tribes. Like the introduction, it has two divisions that are neither chronologically related nor expressly dated to the careers of specific judges. The events must have taken place, however, rather early in the period of the judges (see notes on 18:30; 20:1,28).

By dating the events of the epilogue only in relationship to the monarchy (see the recurring refrain in 17:6; 18:1; 19:1; 21:25), the author contrasts the age of the judges with the better time that the monarchy inaugurated, undoubtedly having in view the rule of David and his dynasty (see note on 17:1—21:25). The book mentions two instances of the Lord's assigning leadership to the tribe of Judah: (1) in driving out the Canaanites (1:1–2), and (2) in disciplining a tribe in Israel (20:18). The author views the ruler from the tribe of Judah as the savior of the nation.

The first division of the epilogue (chs. 17—18) relates the story of Micah's development of a paganized place of worship and tells of the tribe of Dan abandoning their allotted territory while adopting Micah's corrupted religion. The second division (chs. 19—21) tells the story of a Levite's sad experience at Gibeah in Benjamin and records the disciplinary removal of the tribe of Benjamin because it had defended the degenerate town of Gibeah.

The two divisions have several interesting parallels:

1. Both involve a Levite's passing between Beth-lehem (in Judah) and Ephraim across the Benjamin-Dan corridor.

2. Both mention 600 warriors—those who led the tribe of Dan and those who survived from the tribe of Benjamin.

3. Both conclude with the emptying of a tribal area in that corridor (Dan and Benjamin).

Not only are these Benjamin-Dan parallels significant within the epilogue, but they also form a notable link to the main body of the book. The tribe of Benjamin, which in the epilogue undertook to defend gross immorality, setting ties of blood above loyalty to the Lord, was the tribe from which the Lord raised up the deliverer Ehud (3:15). The tribe of Dan, which in the epilogue retreated from its assigned inheritance and adopted pagan religious practices, was the tribe from which the Lord raised up the deliverer Samson (13:2,5). Thus the tribes that in the epilogue depict the religious and moral corruption of Israel are the very tribes from which the deliverers were chosen whose stories frame the central account of the book (Gideon-Abimelech).

The whole design of the book from prologue to epilogue, the unique manner in which each section deals with the age as a whole, and the way the three major divisions are interrelated clearly portray an age gone awry—an age when "there was no king in Israel" and "every man did that which was right in his own eyes" (see note on 17:6). Of no small significance is the fact that the story is in episodes and cycles. It is given as the story of all Israel, though usually only certain areas are directly involved. The book portrays the centuries after Joshua as a time of Israelite unfaithfulness to the Lord and of her surrender to the allurements of Canaan. Only by the mercies of God was Israel not overwhelmed and absorbed by the pagan nations around her. Meanwhile, however, the history of redemption virtually stood still—awaiting the forward thrust of the Lord's servant David and the establishment of his dynasty.

Outline

I. Prologue: Incomplete Conquest and Apostasy (1:1—3:6)
   A. First Episode: Israel's Failure to Purge the Land (1:1—2:5)
   B. Second Episode: God's Dealings with Israel's Rebellion (2:6—3:6)

II. Oppression and Deliverance (3:7—16:31)

Major Judges	*Minor Judges*
A. Othniel Defeats Mesopotamia (3:7–11)	
B. Ehud Defeats Moab (3:12–30)	
	1. Shamgar (3:31)
C. Deborah Defeats Canaan (chs. 4—5)	
D. Gideon Defeats Midian (chs. 6—8)	
(Abimelech, the anti-judge, ch. 9)	
	2. Tola (10:1–2)
	3. Jair (10:3–5)
E. Jephthah Defeats Ammon (10:6—12:7)	
	4. Ibzan (12:8–10)
	5. Elon (12:11–12)
	6. Abdon (12:13–15)
F. Samson Checks Philistia (chs. 13—16)	

III. Epilogue: Religious and Moral Disorder (chs. 17—21)
- A. First Episode (chs. 17—18; see 17:6; 18:1)
  1. Micah's corruption of religion (ch. 17)
  2. The Danites' departure from their tribal territory (ch. 18)
- B. Second Episode (chs. 19—21; see 19:1; 21:25)
  1. Gibeah's corruption of morals (ch. 19)
  2. The Benjamites' removal from their tribal territory (chs. 20—21)

Fighting the Canaanites

1 Now after the death of Joshua it came to pass, that the children of Israel [a]asked the LORD, saying, Who shall go up for us against the Canaanites first, to fight against them?

2 And the LORD said, [a]Judah shall go up: behold, I have delivered the land into his hand.

3 And Judah said unto Simeon his brother, Come up with me into my lot, that we may fight against the Canaanites; and [a]I likewise will go with thee into thy lot. So Simeon went with him.

4 And Judah went up; and the LORD delivered the Canaanites and the Perizzites into their hand: and they slew *of* them in [a]Bezek ten thousand men.

5 And they found Adoni-bezek in Bezek: and they fought against him, and they slew the Canaanites and the Perizzites.

6 But Adoni-bezek fled; and they pursued after him, and caught him, and cut off his thumbs and his great toes.

7 And Adoni-bezek said, Threescore and ten kings, having [1]their thumbs and their great toes cut off, [2]gathered *their meat* under my table: [a]as I have done, so God hath requited me. And they brought him *to* Jerusalem, and there he died.

8 Now [a]the children of Judah had fought against Jerusalem, and had taken it, and smitten it with the edge of the sword, and set the city on fire.

9 ¶ [a]And afterward the children of Judah went down to fight against the Canaanites, that dwelt in the mountain, and in the south, and in the [1]valley.

10 And Judah went against the Canaanites that dwelt in Hebron: (now the name of Hebron before *was* [a]Kirjath-arba:) and they slew Sheshai, and Ahiman, and Talmai.

11 [a]And from thence he went against the inhabitants of Debir: and the name of Debir before *was* Kirjath-sepher.

12 [a]And Caleb said, He that smiteth Kirjath-sepher, and taketh it, to him will I give Achsah my daughter to wife.

13 And Othniel the son of Kenaz, [a]Caleb's younger brother, took it: and he gave him Achsah his daughter to wife.

14 [a]And it came to pass, when she came *to him,* that she moved him to ask of her father a field: and she lighted from off *her* ass; and Caleb said unto her, What wilt thou?

15 And she said unto him, [a]Give me a blessing: for thou hast given me a south land; give me also springs of water. And Caleb gave her the upper springs and the nether springs.

16 ¶ [a]And the children of the Kenite, Moses' father in law, went up out [b]of the city of palm trees with the children of Judah *into* the wilderness of Judah, which *lieth* in the south of [c]Arad; [d]and they went and dwelt among the people.

17 [a]And Judah went with Simeon his brother, and they slew the Canaanites that inhabited Zephath, and utterly destroyed it: and the name of the city was called [b]Hormah.

1:1 [a]Num. 27:21; ch. 20:18
1:2 [a]Gen. 49:8
1:3 [a]ver. 17
1:4 [a]1 Sam. 11:8
1:7 [1]Heb. *the thumbs of their hands and of their feet* [2]Or, *gleaned* [a]Lev. 24:19; 1 Sam. 15:33; Jas. 2:13
1:8 [a]See Josh. 15:63
1:9 [a]Josh. 10:36; 11:21; 15:13
1:9 [1]Or, *low country*
1:10 [a]Josh. 14:15; 15:13,14
1:11 [a]Josh. 15:15
1:12 [a]Josh. 15:16,17
1:13 [a]ch. 3:9
1:14 [a]Josh. 15:18,19
1:15 [a]Gen. 33:11
1:16 [a]ch. 4:11,17; 1 Sam. 15:6; 1 Chr. 2:55 [b]Deut. 34:3 [c]Num. 21:1 [d]1 Sam. 15:6
1:17 [a]ver. 3 [b]Num. 21:3; Josh. 19:4

---

‡1:1–3:6 The book of Judges picks up the story of Israel's attempts to settle the promised land. The introduction is in two parts: (1) an account of Israel's failure to lay claim completely to the promised land as the Lord had directed (1:1–36) and of His rebuke for their disloyalty (2:1–5); (2) an overview of the main body of the book (3:7–16:31), portraying Israel's rebellious ways in the centuries after Joshua's death and showing how the Lord dealt with her in that period (2:6–3:6). See Introduction: Literary Features.

1:1–36 Judah is assigned leadership in occupying the land (v. 2; see 20:18). Her vigorous efforts (together with those of Simeon) highlight by contrast the sad story of failure that follows. Only Ephraim's success at Beth-el (vv. 22–26) breaks the monotony of that story.

1:1 *after the death of Joshua.* The book of Judges, like that of Joshua, tells of an era following the death of a leading figure in the history of redemption (see Josh 1:1). Joshua probably died c. 1390 B.C. The battles under his leadership broke the power of the Canaanites to drive the Israelites out of the land. The task that now confronted Israel was the actual occupation of Canaanite territory (see notes on Josh 18:3; 21:43–45). *asked the LORD.* Probably by the priestly use of Urim and Thummim (see notes on Ex 28:30; 1 Sam 2:28). *go up.* The main Israelite encampment was at Gilgal, near Jericho in the Jordan Valley (about 800 feet below sea level), while the Canaanite cities were mainly located in the central hill country (about 2,500–3,500 feet above sea level).

1:2 *Judah shall go up.* See 20:18. Judah was also the first to be assigned territory west of the Jordan (Josh 15). The leadership role of the tribe of Judah had been anticipated in the blessing of Jacob (Gen 49:8–12).

1:3 *Simeon.* Joshua assigned to Simeon cities within the territory of Judah (Josh 19:1,9; see Gen 49:5–7).

1:4 *Canaanites.* See note on Gen 10:6. *Perizzites.* See note on Gen 13:7. *Bezek.* Location unknown. Saul marshaled his army there before going to Jabesh-gilead (1 Sam 11:9).

1:5 *Adoni-bezek.* Means "lord of Bezek."

1:6 *cut off his thumbs and his great toes.* Physically mutilating prisoners of war was a common practice in the ancient Near East (see note on 16:21). It rendered them unfit for military service.

1:7 *Threescore and ten kings.* Canaan was made up of many small city-states, each of which was ruled by a king. "Seventy" may be a round number, or it may be symbolic of a large number. *under my table.* Humiliating treatment, like that given to a dog (see Mat 15:27; Luke 16:21). *God has requited me.* See note on Ex 21:23–25.

1:8 *fought against Jerusalem.* Although the city was defeated, it was not occupied by the Israelites at this time (see v. 21). Israel did not permanently control the city until David captured it c. 1000 B.C. (2 Sam 5:6–10).

1:10 *Kirjath-arba.* See note on Josh 14:15.

1:11 *Debir.* See note on Josh 10:38.

1:12 *Caleb.* He and Joshua had brought back an optimistic report about the prospects of conquering Canaan (Num 14:6–9). *daughter to wife.* Victory in battle was one way to pay the bride-price for a girl (see 1 Sam 18:25).

1:13 *Othniel.* First major judge (see 3:7–11).

‡1:15 *upper . . . nether* [i.e. lower] *springs.* They still water the local farms in Hebron.

1:16 *Moses' father in law.* See note on Ex 2:16.

1:17 *Judah . . . Simeon.* Judah was fulfilling her commitment (v. 3).

18 Also Judah took [a]Gaza with the coast thereof, and Askelon with the coast thereof, and Ekron with the coast thereof.
19 And [a]the LORD was with Judah; and [1]he drave out *the inhabitants of* the mountain; but could not drive out the inhabitants of the valley, because they had [b]chariots of iron.
20 [a]And they gave Hebron unto Caleb, as Moses said: and he expelled thence the three sons of Anak.
21 [a]And the children of Benjamin did not drive out the Jebusites that inhabited Jerusalem; but the Jebusites dwell with the children of Benjamin in Jerusalem unto this day.

1:18 [a]Josh. 11:22
1:19 [1]Or, *he possessed the mountain* [a]ver. 2; 2 Ki. 18:7 [b]Josh. 17:16,18
1:20 [a]Num. 14:24; Deut. 1:36; Josh. 14:9,13,14; 15:13,14
1:21 [a]See Josh. 15:63; 18:28
1:22 [a]ver. 19
1:23 [a]Josh. 2:1; 7:2; ch. 18:2 [b]Gen. 28:19
1:24 [a]Josh. 2:12,14

22 ¶ And the house of Joseph, they also went up *against* Beth-el: [a]and the LORD *was* with them.
23 And the house of Joseph [a]sent to descry Beth-el. (Now the name of the city before *was* [b]Luz.)
24 And the spies saw a man come forth out of the city, and they said unto him, Shew us, we pray thee, the entrance into the city, and [a]we will shew thee mercy.
25 And when he shewed them the entrance into the city, they smote the city with the edge of the sword; but they let go the man and all his family.

1:18 *Gaza . . . Askelon . . . Ekron.* Three of the five main cities inhabited by the Philistines (see map below).
1:19 *could not drive out the inhabitants.* Israel failed to comply with God's commands (Deut 7:1–5; 20:16–18) to drive the Canaanites out of the land. Five factors were involved in that failure: (1) The Canaanites possessed superior weapons (v. 19); (2) Israel disobeyed God by making treaties with the Canaanites (2:1–3); (3) Israel violated the covenant the Lord had made with their forefathers (2:20–21); (4) God was testing Israel's faithfulness to obey His commands (2:22–23; 3:4); (5) God was giving Israel, as His army, the opportunity to develop her skills in warfare (3:1–2). *chariots of iron.* Wooden vehicles with certain iron fittings, perhaps axles.
1:20 *as Moses said.* See Num 14:24; Deut 1:36; Josh 14:9–14. *Anak.* See note on Num 13:22.
1:21 *children of Benjamin did not drive out.* See note on v. 8. Jerusalem lay on the border between Benjamin and Judah but was allotted to Benjamin (Josh 18:28). *Jebusites.* See note on Gen 10:16.
1:22 *house of Joseph.* Ephraim and West Manasseh. *Beth-el.* See note on Gen 12:8. There is archaeological evidence of a destruction in the 13th century B.C. that may reflect the battle mentioned in this verse.
‡1:23 *to descry.* I.e. "to spy out." See note on Num 13:2.
1:25 *let go the man.* Cf. the treatment of Rahab (Josh 6:25).

Five Cities of the Philistines

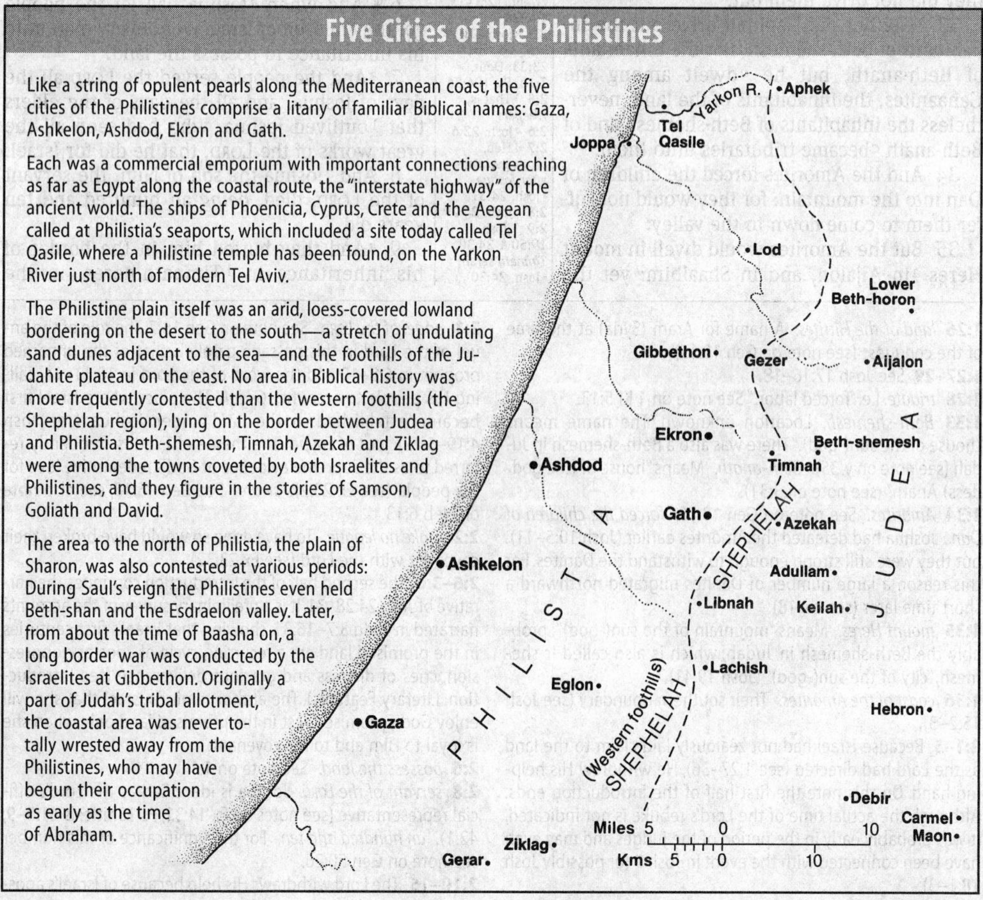

Like a string of opulent pearls along the Mediterranean coast, the five cities of the Philistines comprise a litany of familiar Biblical names: Gaza, Ashkelon, Ashdod, Ekron and Gath.

Each was a commercial emporium with important connections reaching as far as Egypt along the coastal route, the "interstate highway" of the ancient world. The ships of Phoenicia, Cyprus, Crete and the Aegean called at Philistia's seaports, which included a site today called Tel Qasile, where a Philistine temple has been found, on the Yarkon River just north of modern Tel Aviv.

The Philistine plain itself was an arid, loess-covered lowland bordering on the desert to the south—a stretch of undulating sand dunes adjacent to the sea—and the foothills of the Judahite plateau on the east. No area in Biblical history was more frequently contested than the western foothills (the Shephelah region), lying on the border between Judea and Philistia. Beth-shemesh, Timnah, Azekah and Ziklag were among the towns coveted by both Israelites and Philistines, and they figure in the stories of Samson, Goliath and David.

The area to the north of Philistia, the plain of Sharon, was also contested at various periods: During Saul's reign the Philistines even held Beth-shan and the Esdraelon valley. Later, from about the time of Baasha on, a long border war was conducted by the Israelites at Gibbethon. Originally a part of Judah's tribal allotment, the coastal area was never totally wrested away from the Philistines, who may have begun their occupation as early as the time of Abraham.

26 And the man went *into* the land of the Hittites, and built a city, and called the name thereof Luz: which *is* the name thereof unto this day.

27 ¶ [a]Neither did Manasseh drive out *the inhabitants of* Beth-shean and her towns, nor Taanach and her towns, nor the inhabitants of Dor and her towns, nor the inhabitants of Ibleam and her towns, nor the inhabitants of Megiddo and her towns: but the Canaanites would dwell in that land.

28 And it came to pass, when Israel was strong, that they put the Canaanites to tribute, and did not utterly drive them out.

29 ¶ [a]Neither did Ephraim drive out the Canaanites that dwelt in Gezer; but the Canaanites dwelt in Gezer among them.

30 Neither did Zebulun drive out the inhabitants of Kitron, nor the [a]inhabitants of Nahalol; but the Canaanites dwelt among them, and became tributaries.

31 [a]Neither did Asher drive out the inhabitants of Accho, nor the inhabitants of Zidon, nor of Ahlab, nor of Achzib, nor of Helbah, nor of Aphik, nor of Rehob:

32 But the Asherites [a]dwelt among the Canaanites, the inhabitants of the land: for they did not drive them out.

33 [a]Neither did Naphtali drive out the inhabitants of Beth-shemesh, nor the inhabitants of Beth-anath; but he [b]dwelt among the Canaanites, the inhabitants of the land: nevertheless the inhabitants of Beth-shemesh and of Beth-anath [c]became tributaries unto them.

34 And the Amorites forced the children of Dan into the mountain: for they would not suffer them to come down to the valley:

35 But the Amorites would dwell in mount Heres [a]in Aijalon, and in Shaalbim: yet the hand of the house of Joseph [1]prevailed, so that they became tributaries.

36 And the coast of the Amorites *was* [a]from [1]the going up to Akrabbim, from the rock, and upward.

Israel's disobedience

2 And an [1]angel of the LORD came up from Gilgal [a]to Bochim, and said, I made you to go up out of Egypt, and have brought you unto the land which I sware unto your fathers; and [b]I said, I will never break my covenant with you.

2 And [a]ye shall make no league with the inhabitants of this land; [b]you shall throw down their altars: [c]but ye have not obeyed my voice: why have ye done this?

3 Wherefore I also said, I will not drive them out from before you; but they shall be [a]*as thorns* in your sides, and [b]their gods shall be a [c]snare unto you.

4 And it came to pass, when the angel of the LORD spake these words unto all the children of Israel, that the people lift up their voice, and wept.

5 And they called the name of that place [1]Bochim: and they sacrificed there unto the LORD.

6 ¶ And when [a]Joshua had let the people go, the children of Israel went every man unto his inheritance to possess the land.

7 [a]And the people served the LORD all the days of Joshua, and all the days of the elders that [1]outlived Joshua, who had seen all the great works of the LORD, that he did for Israel.

8 And [a]Joshua the son of Nun, the servant of the LORD, died, *being* an hundred and ten years old.

9 [a]And they buried him in the border of his inheritance in [1]Timnath-heres, in the

1:27 [a]Josh. 17:11-13
1:29 [a]Josh. 16:10; 1 Ki. 9:16
1:30 [a]Josh. 19:15
1:31 [a]Josh. 19:24-30
1:32 [a]Ps. 106:34,35
1:33 [a]Josh. 19:38 [b]ver. 32 [c]ver. 30
1:35 [a]Josh. 19:42
1:35 [1]Heb. *was heavy*
1:36 [1]Or, *Maaleh-akrabbim* [a]Num. 34:4; Josh. 15:3
2:1 [1]Or, *messenger* [a]ver. 5 [b]Gen. 17:7
2:2 [a]Deut. 7:2 [b]Deut. 12:3 [c]Ps. 106:34
2:3 [a]Josh. 23:13 [b]ch. 3:6 [c]Ex. 23:33; Deut. 7:16; Ps. 106:36
2:5 [1]That is, *Weepers*
2:6 [a]Josh. 22:6
2:7 [1]Heb. *prolonged days after Joshua* [a]Josh. 24:31
2:8 [a]Josh. 24:29
2:9 [1][Josh. 19:50 & 24:30, *Timnath-serah*] [a]Josh. 24:30

1:26 *land of the Hittites.* A name for Aram (Syria) at the time of the conquest (see note on Gen 10:15).
1:27–29 See Josh 17:16–18.
1:28 *tribute.* I.e. "forced labor." See note on 1 Ki 5:13.
1:33 *Beth-shemesh.* Location unknown. The name means "house of the sun(-god)." There was also a Beth-shemesh in Judah (see note on v. 35). *Beth-anath.* Means "house of (the goddess) Anath" (see note on 3:31).
1:34 *Amorites.* See note on Gen 10:16. *forced the children of Dan.* Joshua had defeated the Amorites earlier (Josh 10:5–11), but they were still strong enough to withstand the Danites. For this reason a large number of Danites migrated northward a short time later (see ch. 18).
1:35 *mount Heres.* Means "mountain of the sun(-god)"; probably the Beth-shemesh in Judah, which is also called Ir-shemesh, "city of the sun(-god)" (Josh 19:41).
1:36 *coast of the Amorites.* Their southern boundary (see Josh 15:2–3).
2:1–5 Because Israel had not zealously laid claim to the land as the Lord had directed (see 1:27–36), He withdrew His helping hand. On this note the first half of the introduction ends. Although the actual time of the Lord's rebuke is not indicated, it was probably early in the period of the judges and may even have been connected with the event in Josh 9 (or possibly Josh 18:1–3).
2:1 *angel of the LORD.* See note on Gen 16:7. The role of the angel of the Lord in this passage parallels that of the unnamed prophet in 6:8–10 and the word of the Lord in 10:11–14, calling His people to account. *Gilgal.* The place where Israel first became established in the land under Joshua (see Josh 4:19–5:12). *out of Egypt.* The theme of Exodus, frequently referred to as the supreme evidence of God's redemptive love for His people (see Ex 20:2). *sware.* See Gen 15:18; see also note on Heb 6:13.
2:2 *make no league.* To have done so would have broken their covenant with the Lord (see Ex 23:32).
2:6–3:6 The second half of the introduction continues the narrative of Josh 24:28–31. It is a preliminary survey of the accounts narrated in Judg 3:7–16:31, showing that Israel's first centuries in the promised land are a recurring cycle of apostasy, oppression, cries of distress and gracious deliverance (see Introduction: Literary Features). The author reminds Israel that she will enjoy God's promised rest in the promised land only when she is loyal to Him and to His covenant.
2:6 *possess the land.* See note on 1:1.
2:8 *servant of the LORD.* Joshua is identified as the Lord's official representative (see notes on Ex 14:31; Ps 18 title; Is 41:8–9; 42:1). *an hundred and ten.* For the significance of this number see note on Gen 50:26.
2:10–15 The Lord withdraws His help because of Israel's apos-

mount of Ephraim, on the north side of the hill Gaash.

The LORD raises up judges

10 ¶ And also all that generation were gathered unto their fathers: and there arose another generation after them, which [a]knew not the LORD, nor yet the works which he had done for Israel.

11 And the children of Israel did evil in the sight of the LORD, and served Baalim:

12 And they [a]forsook the LORD God of their fathers, which brought them out of the land of Egypt, and followed [b]other gods, of the gods of the people that *were* round about them, and [c]bowed themselves unto them, and provoked the LORD to anger.

13 And they forsook the LORD, [a]and served Baal and Ashtaroth.

14 [a]And the anger of the LORD was hot against Israel, and he [b]delivered them into the hands of spoilers that spoiled them, and [c]he sold them into the hands of their enemies round about, so that they [d]could not any longer stand before their enemies.

15 Whithersoever they went out, the hand of the LORD was against them for evil, as the LORD had said, and [a]as the LORD had sworn unto them: and they were greatly distressed.

16 Nevertheless [a]the LORD raised up judges, which [1]delivered them out of the hand of those that spoiled them.

17 And yet they would not hearken unto their judges, but they [a]went a whoring after other gods, and bowed themselves unto them: they turned quickly out of the way which their fathers walked in, obeying the commandments of the LORD; *but* they did not so.

18 And when the LORD raised them up judges, then [a]the LORD was with the judge, and delivered them out of the hand of their enemies all the days of the judge: [b]for it repented the LORD because of their groanings by reason of them that oppressed them and vexed them.

19 And it came to pass, [a]when the judge was dead, *that* they returned, and [1]corrupted *themselves* more than their fathers, in following other gods to serve them, and to bow down unto them; [2]they ceased not from their own doings, nor from their stubborn way.

20 [a]And the anger of the LORD was hot against Israel; and he said, Because that this people hath [b]transgressed my covenant which I commanded their fathers, and have not hearkened unto my voice;

21 [a]I also will not henceforth drive out any from before them of the nations which Joshua left when he died:

22 [a]That through them I may [b]prove Israel, whether they will keep the way of the LORD to walk therein, as their fathers did keep *it*, or not.

23 Therefore the LORD [1]left those nations, without driving them out hastily; neither delivered he them into the hand of Joshua.

3 Now these *are* [a]the nations which the LORD left, to prove Israel by them, *even* as many *of Israel* as had not known all the wars of Canaan;

2 Only that the generations of the children of Israel might know, to teach them war, at the least such as before knew nothing thereof:

2:10 [a]Ex. 5:2; 1 Sam. 2:12; 1 Chr. 28:9; Gal. 4:8; Tit. 1:16
2:12 [a]Deut. 31:16 [b]Deut. 6:14 [c]Ex. 20:5
2:13 [a]ch. 10:6; Ps. 106:36
2:14 [a]ch. 3:8; Ps. 106:40-42 [b]2 Ki. 17:20 [c]ch. 3:8; Is. 50:1 [d]Lev. 26:37; Josh. 7:12,13
2:15 [a]Lev. 26; Deut. 28
2:16 [1]Heb. *saved* [a]ch. 3:9,10,15
2:17 [a]Ex. 34:15; Lev. 17:7
2:18 [a]Josh. 1:5 [b]Gen. 6:6; Ps. 106:44
2:19 [1]Or, *were corrupt* [2]Heb. *they let nothing fall of their* [a]ch. 3:12
2:20 [a]ver. 14 [b]Josh. 23:16
2:21 [a]Josh. 23:13
2:22 [a]ch. 3:1,4 [b]Deut. 8:2,16
2:23 [1]Or, *suffered*
3:1 [a]ch. 2:21,22

tasy. He "sells" the people He had "purchased" (Ex 15:16) and redeemed (Ex 15:13; cf. Ps 74:2).

2:10 *gathered unto their fathers.* See Gen 15:15; see also note on Gen 25:8. *which knew not the LORD . . . Israel.* They had no direct experience of the Lord's acts (see Ex 1:8).

2:11 *did evil in the sight of the LORD.* The same expression is used in 3:7,12; 4:1; 6:1; 10:6. *Baalim.* The many local forms of this Canaanite deity (see note on v. 13).

2:12 *provoked the LORD to anger.* See Deut 4:25; see also note on Zec 1:2.

2:13 *Baal.* Means "lord." Baal, the god worshiped by the Canaanites and Phoenicians, was variously known to them as the son of Dagon and the son of El. In Aram (Syria) he was called Hadad and in Babylonia Adad. Believed to give fertility to the womb and life-giving rain to the soil, he is pictured as standing on a bull, a popular symbol of fertility and strength (see 1 Ki 12:28). The storm cloud was his chariot, thunder his voice, and lightning his spear and arrows. The worship of Baal involved sacred prostitution and sometimes even child sacrifice (see Jer 19:5). The stories of Elijah and Elisha (1 Ki 17–2 Ki 13), as well as many other OT passages, directly or indirectly protest Baalism (e.g., Ps 29:3–9; 68:1–4,32–34; 93:1–5; 97:1–5; Jer 10:12–16; 14:22; Hos 2:8,16–17; Amos 5:8). *Ashtaroth.* Female deities such as Ashtoreth (consort of Baal) and Asherah (consort of El, the chief god of the Canaanite pantheon). Ashtoreth was associated with the evening star and was the beautiful goddess of war and fertility. She was worshiped as Ishtar in Babylonia and as Athtart in Aram. To the Greeks she was Astarte or Aphrodite, and to the Romans, Venus. Worship of the Ashtoreths involved extremely lascivious practices (1 Ki 14:24; 2 Ki 23:7).

2:14 *delivered them into the hands of.* The same expression is used in 6:1; 13:1. *sold them.* The same expression is used in 3:8; 4:2; 10:7.

2:16–19 The Lord was merciful to His people in times of distress, sending deliverers to save them from oppression. But Israel continually forgot these saving acts, just as she had those He had performed through Moses and Joshua.

2:16 *judges.* See Introduction: Title. There were six major judges (Othniel, Ehud, Deborah, Gideon, Jephthah and Samson) and six minor ones (Shamgar, Tola, Jair, Ibzan, Elon and Abdon).

2:17 *went a whoring.* Since the Hebrew for Baal (meaning "lord") was also used by women to refer to their husbands, it is understandable that the metaphor of adultery was commonly used in connection with Israelite worship of Baal (see Hos 2:2–3,16–17).

2:18 *groanings . . . oppressed.* The language of the Egyptian bondage (see Ex 2:24; 3:9; 6:5).

2:20–23 The Lord decided to leave the remaining nations to test Israel's loyalty.

3:1–6 The list of nations the Lord left roughly describes an arc along the western and northern boundaries of the area actually occupied by Israel at the death of Joshua (vv. 1–4). Within Israelite-occupied territory there were large groups of native peoples (v. 5; see 1:27–36) with whom the Israelites intermingled, often adopting their religions (v. 6).

3:2 *to teach them war.* As His covenant servant, Israel was the Lord's army for fighting against the powers of the world that were settled in His land. In view of the incomplete conquest,

3 *Namely,* [a]five lords of the Philistines, and
all the Canaanites, and the Sidonians, and the
Hivites that dwelt in mount Lebanon, from
mount Baal-hermon unto the entering in of
Hamath.
4 [a]And they were to prove Israel by them,
to know whether they would hearken unto the
commandments of the LORD, which he commanded their fathers by the hand of Moses.

Othniel

5 ¶ [a]And the children of Israel dwelt among
the Canaanites, Hittites, and Amorites, and
Perizzites, and Hivites, and Jebusites:
6 And [a]they took their daughters to be
their wives, and gave their daughters to their
sons, and served their gods.
7 [a]And the children of Israel did evil in the
sight of the LORD, and forgat the LORD their
God, [b]and served Baalim and [c]the groves.
8 Therefore the anger of the LORD was hot
against Israel, and he [a]sold them into the hand
of [b]Chushan-rishathaim king of [1]Mesopota-
mia: and the children of Israel served
Chushan-rishathaim eight years.
9 And when the children of Israel [a]cried
unto the LORD, the LORD [b]raised up a [1]deliver-
er to the children of Israel, who delivered
them, *even* [c]Othniel the son of Kenaz, Caleb's
younger brother.
10 And [a]the spirit of the LORD [1]came upon
him, and he judged Israel, and went out to
war: and the LORD delivered Chushan-rishathaim king of [2]Mesopotamia into his hand;
and his hand prevailed against Chushan-rishathaim.
11 And the land had rest forty years. And
Othniel the son of Kenaz died.

Ehud

12 ¶ [a]And the children of Israel did evil
again in the sight of the LORD: and the LORD
strengthened [b]Eglon the king of Moab against
Israel, because they had done evil in the sight
of the LORD.
13 And he gathered unto him the children
of Ammon and [a]Amalek, and went and smote
Israel, and possessed [b]the city of palm trees.
14 So the children of Israel [a]served Eglon
the king of Moab eighteen years.
15 But when the children of Israel [a]cried
unto the LORD, the LORD raised them up a deliverer, Ehud the son of Gera, [1]a Benjamite, a
man [b][2]lefthanded: and by him the children of
Israel sent a present unto Eglon the king of
Moab.
16 But Ehud made him a dagger which had
two edges, of a cubit length; and he did gird it
under his raiment upon his right thigh.
17 And he brought the present unto Eglon
king of Moab: and Eglon *was* a very fat man.
18 And when he had made an end to offer
the present, he sent away the people that bare
the present.
19 But he himself turned again [a]from the
[1]quarries that *were* by Gilgal, and said, I have

3:3 [a]Josh. 13:3
3:4 [a]ch. 2:22
3:5 [a]Ps. 106:35
3:6 [a]Ex. 34:16; Deut. 7:3
3:7 [a]ch. 2:11 [b]ch. 2:13 [c]Ex. 34:13; Deut. 16:21; ch. 6:25
3:8 [1]Heb. *Aram-naharaim* [a]ch. 2:14 [b]Hab. 3:7
3:9 [1]Heb. *saviour* [a]ver. 15; ch. 4:3; 6:7; 10:10; Ps. 22:5; 106:44 [b]ch. 2:16 [c]ch. 1:13
3:10 [1]Heb. *was* [a]Num. 27:18; ch. 6:34; 11:29; 13:25; 14:6,19; 1 Sam. 11:6; 2 Chr. 15:1
3:10 [2]Heb. *Aram*
3:12 [a]ch. 2:19 [b]1 Sam. 12:9
3:13 [a]ch. 5:14 [b]ch. 1:16
3:14 [a]Deut. 28:48
3:15 [1]Or, *the son of Jemini* [2]Heb. *shut of his right hand* [a]ver. 9; Ps. 78:34 [b]ch. 20:16
3:19 [1]Or, *graven images* [a]Josh. 4:20

succeeding generations in Israel needed to become capable warriors. "Only" probably here means "especially."

‡3:3 *five lords.* The Hebrew for "lords" is related to the word "tyrant" (see note on Josh 13:3) and is used only of Philistine rulers. These rulers had control of a five-city confederacy. At one point Judah defeated three of these cities (1:18) but was unable to hold them. The Philistines were also called "sea peoples" in non-biblical texts. They controlled the coast of Israel during the period of the Judges. *Sidonians.* Here used collectively of the Phoenicians. *Hivites.* Here identified with a region in northern Canaan reaching all the way to Hamath (see also Josh 11:3). *mount Baal-hermon.* Probably mount Hermon (see 1 Chr 5:23).

3:6 *took their daughters . . . and served their gods.* See note on Josh 23:12. The degenerating effect of such intermarriage is well illustrated in Solomon's experience (1 Ki 11:1–8).

3:7–11 In the account of Othniel's judgeship the author provides the basic literary form he uses in his accounts of the major judges (i.e., beginning statement; cycle of apostasy, oppression, distress, deliverance; recognizable conclusion), adding only the brief details necessary to complete the report (see Introduction: Literary Features).

‡3:7 *did evil in the sight of the LORD.* A recurring expression (see v. 12; 4:1; 6:1; 10:6; 13:1) used to introduce the cycles of the judges (see Introduction: Literary Features). *Baalim.* See note on 2:13. *groves.* Hebrew *Asheroth.* See notes on 2:13; Ex 34:13.

3:8 *Chushan-rishathaim.* Probably means "doubly wicked Cushan," perhaps a caricature of his actual name (see note on 10:6 regarding Baal-zebub). *Mesopotamia.* See note on Gen 24:10.

3:9 *Israel cried unto the LORD.* The Israelites' cries of distress occurred in each recurring cycle of the judges (see Introduction: Literary Features). *Othniel.* See 1:13.

3:10 *spirit of the LORD came upon him.* The Spirit empowered Othniel to deliver His people, as He did Gideon (6:34), Jephthah (11:29), Samson (14:6,19) and also David (1 Sam 16:13). Cf. Num 11:25–29.

3:11 *the land had rest . . . years.* A recognizable conclusion to the cycle of a judge (noted only here and in v. 30; 5:31; 8:28). After the judgeship of Gideon this formula is replaced by "judged Israel . . . years" (12:7; 15:20; 16:31). See Introduction: Literary Features. *forty years.* A conventional number of years for a generation (see Introduction: Background).

3:12–30 Ehud's triumph over Eglon king of Moab. The left-handed Benjamite was an authentic hero. All alone, and purely by his wits, he cut down the king of Moab, who had established himself in Canaan near Jericho. This account balances that of Samson in the five narrative units central to the book of Judges (see Introduction: Literary Features).

3:12 *Moab.* See note on Gen 19:36–38.

3:13 *children of Ammon.* See note on Gen 19:33. *children of . . . Amalek.* These descendants of Esau (Gen 36:12,16) lived in the Negev (Num 13:29). See note on Gen 14:7.

3:14 *children of Israel.* Here mainly Benjamin and Ephraim.

3:15 *man lefthanded.* Left-handedness was noteworthy among Benjamites (see 20:15–16)—which is ironic since Benjamin means "son of (my) right hand." Being left-handed, Ehud could conceal his dagger on the side where it was not expected (see v. 21). *present.* An annual payment, perhaps of agricultural products (cf. 2Ki 3:4).

3:16 *a dagger which had two edges.* During the period of the judges, Israelite weapons were often fashioned or improvised for the occasion: Shamgar's ox goad (v. 31), Jael's tent peg (4:22), Gideon's pitchers and lamps (7:20), the woman's millstone (9:53) and Samson's donkey jawbone (15:15). See 1 Sam 13:19.

3:19 *quarries.* Lit. "carved (stone) things," a frequent Hebrew

a secret errand unto thee, O king: who said, Keep silence. And all that stood by him went out from him.

20 And Ehud came unto him; and he was sitting in [a][1]a summer parlour, which he had for himself alone. And Ehud said, I have a message from God unto thee. And he arose out of *his* seat.

21 And Ehud put forth his left hand, and took the dagger from his right thigh, and thrust it into his belly:

22 And the haft also went in after the blade; and the fat closed upon the blade, so that he could not draw the dagger out of his belly; and [1]the dirt came out.

23 Then Ehud went forth through the porch, and shut the doors of the parlour upon him, and locked *them.*

24 When he was gone out, his servants came; and when they saw that behold, the doors of the parlour *were* locked, they said, Surely he [a][1]covereth his feet in *his* summer chamber.

25 And they tarried till *they* were ashamed: and behold, he opened not the doors of the parlour; therefore they took a key, and opened *them:* and behold, their lord *was* fallen down dead on the earth.

26 And Ehud escaped while they tarried, and passed beyond the quarries, and escaped unto Seirath.

27 And it came to pass, when he was come, that [a]he blew a trumpet in the [b]mountain of Ephraim, and the children of Israel went down with him from the mount, and he before them.

28 And he said unto them, Follow after me: for [a]the LORD hath delivered your enemies the Moabites into your hand. And they went down after him, and took [b]the fords of Jordan toward Moab, and suffered not a man to pass over.

29 And they slew *of* Moab at that time about ten thousand men, all [1]lusty, and all men of valour; and there escaped not a man.

30 So Moab was subdued that day under the hand of Israel. And [a]the land had rest fourscore years.

31 ¶ And after him was [1]Shamgar the son of Anath, which slew *of* the Philistines six hundred men [a]with an ox goad: [b]and he also delivered [2]Israel.

Deborah

4 And [a]the children of Israel again did evil in the sight of the LORD, when Ehud was dead.

2 And the LORD [a]sold them into the hand of Jabin king of Canaan, that reigned in [b]Hazor; the captain of whose host *was* [1]Sisera, which dwelt in [c]Harosheth of the Gentiles.

3 And the children of Israel cried unto the LORD: for he had nine hundred [a]chariots of iron; and twenty years [b]he mightily oppressed the children of Israel.

4 And Deborah, a prophetess, the wife of Lapidoth, she judged Israel at that time.

5 [a]And she dwelt under the palm tree of Deborah between Ramah and Beth-el in mount Ephraim: and the children of Israel came up to her for judgment.

6 And she sent and called [a]Barak the son of Abinoam out [b]of Kedesh-naphtali, and said unto him, Hath not the LORD God of Israel

3:20 [1]Heb. *a parlour of cooling* [a]Amos 3:15
3:22 [1]Or, *it came out at the fundament*
3:24 [1]Or, *doeth his easement* [a]1 Sam. 24:3
3:27 [a]ch. 5:14; 6:34; 1 Sam. 13:3 [b]Josh. 17:15
3:28 [a]ch. 7:9,15; 1 Sam. 17:47 [b]Josh. 2:7; ch. 12:5
3:29 [1]Heb. *fat*
3:30 [a]ver. 11
3:31 [1][ch. 5:6,8; 1 Sam. 13:19,22. It seems to concern only the country next to the Philistines] [2][So part is called Israel, ch. 4:1,3, etc.; 10:7,17; 11:4, etc.; 1 Sam. 4:1] [a]1 Sam. 17:47,50 [b]ch. 2:16
4:1 [a]ch. 2:19
4:2 [1][1 Sam. 12:9; Ps. 83:9. It seems to concern only North-Israel] [a]ch. 2:14 [b]Josh. 11:1,10; 19:36 [c]ver. 13,16
4:3 [a]ch. 1:19 [b]ch. 5:8; Ps. 106:42
4:5 [a]Gen. 35:8
4:6 [a]Heb. 11:32 [b]Josh. 19:37

word for stone idols. But here the reference may be to carved stone statues of Eglon, marking the boundary of the territory he now claims as part of his expanded realm—a common practice in the ancient Near East.

3:20 *summer parlour.* I.e. a roof chamber. Rooms were built on the flat roofs of houses (2 Ki 4:10–11) and palaces (Jer 22:13–14), and had latticed windows (2 Ki 1:2) that provided comfort in the heat of summer.

3:28 *took the fords.* This move prevented the Moabites from sending reinforcements and also enabled the Israelites to cut off the Moabites fleeing Jericho.

3:30 *fourscore years.* Round numbers are frequently used in Judges (see Introduction: Background).

3:31 *Shamgar.* The first of six minor judges and a contemporary of Deborah (see 5:6–7). His name is foreign, so he was probably not an Israelite. *son of Anath.* Indicates either that Shamgar came from the town of Beth-anath (see 1:33) or that his family worshiped the goddess Anath. Since Anath, Baal's sister, was a goddess of war who fought for Baal, the expression "son of Anath" may have been a military title, meaning "a warrior." *ox goad.* A long, wooden rod, sometimes having a metal tip, used for driving draft animals (see 1 Sam 13:21).

4:1–5:31 Deborah's triumph over Sisera (commander of a Canaanite army)—first narrated in prose (ch. 4), then celebrated in song (ch. 5). At the time of the Canaanite threat from the north, Israel remained incapable of united action until a woman (Deborah) summoned them to the Lord's battle. Because the warriors of Israel lacked the courage to rise up and face the enemy, the glory of victory went to a woman (Jael)—and she may not have been an Israelite.

4:1–2 Except for the Canaanites, Israel's enemies came from outside the territory she occupied. Nations like Mespotamia, Moab, Midian and Ammon were mainly interested in plunder, but the Canaanite uprising of chs. 4–5 was an attempt to restore Canaanite power in the north. The Philistines engaged in continual struggle with Israel for permanent control of the land in the southern and central regions.

4:2 *Jabin.* See Ps 83:9–10. The name was possibly royal rather than personal. Joshua is credited with having earlier slain a king by the same name (Josh 11:1,10). *Hazor.* The original royal city of the Jabin dynasty; it may still have been in ruins (see note on Josh 11:10). Sisera sought to recover the territory once ruled by the kings of Hazor. *Sisera.* His name suggests he was not a Canaanite.

4:3 *nine hundred.* The number probably represents a coalition rather than the chariot force of one city. In the 15th century B.C., Pharaoh Thutmose III boasted of having captured 924 chariots at the battle of Megiddo. *children of Israel.* Mainly Zebulun and Naphtali, but West Manasseh, Issachar and Asher were also affected.

4:4 *Deborah.* Means "bee"; cf. Deut 1:44. She is the only judge said to have been a prophet(ess). Other women spoken of as prophetesses are Miriam (Ex 15:20), Huldah (2 Ki 22:14), Noadiah (Neh 6:14) and Anna (Luke 2:36), but see also Acts 21:9.

4:6 *Barak.* Means "thunderbolt"—which suggests that he is summoned to be the Lord's "glittering sword" (Deut 32:41). He

commanded, *saying,* Go and draw toward mount Tabor, and take with thee ten thousand men of the children of Naphtali and of the children of Zebulun?

7 And [a]I will draw unto thee to the [b]river Kishon Sisera, the captain of Jabin's army, with his chariots and his multitude; and I will deliver him into thine hand.

8 And Barak said unto her, If thou wilt go with me, then I will go: but if thou wilt not go with me, *then* I will not go.

9 And she said, I will surely go with thee: notwithstanding the journey that thou takest shall not be for thine honour; for the LORD shall [a]sell Sisera into the hand of a woman. And Deborah arose, and went with Barak to Kedesh.

10 And Barak called [a]Zebulun and Naphtali to Kedesh; and he went up with ten thousand men [b]at his feet: and Deborah went up with him.

11 Now Heber [a]the Kenite, *which was* of the children of [b]Hobab the father in law of Moses, had severed himself from the Kenites, and pitched his tent unto the plain of Zaanaim, [c]which *is* by Kedesh.

12 And they shewed Sisera that Barak the son of Abinoam was gone up *to* mount Tabor.

13 And Sisera [1]gathered together all his chariots, *even* nine hundred chariots of iron, and all the people that *were* with him, from Harosheth of the Gentiles unto the river of Kishon.

14 And Deborah said unto Barak, Up; for this *is* the day in which the LORD hath delivered Sisera into thine hand: [a]is not the LORD gone out before thee? So Barak went down from mount Tabor, and ten thousand men after him.

15 And [a]the LORD discomfited Sisera, and all *his* chariots, and all *his* host, with the edge of the sword before Barak; so that Sisera lighted down off *his* chariot, and fled away on his feet.

16 But Barak pursued after the chariots, and after the host, unto Harosheth of the Gentiles: and all the host of Sisera fell upon the edge of the sword; *and* there was not [1]a man left.

17 Howbeit Sisera fled away on his feet to the tent of Jael the wife of Heber the Kenite: for *there was* peace between Jabin the king of Hazor and the house of Heber the Kenite.

18 And Jael went out to meet Sisera, and said unto him, Turn in, my lord, turn in to me; fear not. And when he had turned in unto her into the tent, she covered him with a [1]mantle.

19 And he said unto her, Give me, I pray thee, a little water to drink; for I am thirsty. And she opened [a]a bottle of milk, and gave him drink, and covered him.

20 Again he said unto her, Stand *in* the door of the tent, and it shall be, when any man doth come and inquire of thee, and say, Is there any man here? that thou shalt say, No.

21 Then Jael Heber's wife [a]took a nail of the tent, and [1]took a hammer in her hand, and went softly unto him, and smote the nail into his temples, and fastened *it* into the ground: for he was fast asleep and weary. So he died.

22 And behold, as Barak pursued Sisera, Jael came out to meet him, and said unto him, Come, and I will shew thee the man whom thou seekest. And when he came into her

4:7 [a]Ex. 14:4 [b]ch. 5:21; 1 Ki. 18:40; Ps. 83:9,10
4:9 [a]ch. 2:14
4:10 [a]ch. 5:18 [b]See Ex. 11:8; 1 Ki. 20:10
4:11 [a]ch. 1:16 [b]Num. 10:29 [c]ver. 6
4:13 [1]Heb. *gathered by cry,* or, *proclamation*
4:14 [a]Deut. 9:3; 2 Sam. 5:24; Ps. 68:7; Is. 52:12
4:15 [a]Ps. 83:9,10; See Josh. 10:10
4:16 [1]Heb. *unto one*
4:18 [1]Or, *rug,* or, *blanket*
4:19 [a]ch. 5:25
4:21 [1]Heb. *put*
[a]ch. 5:26

is named among the heroes of faith in Heb 11:32. *Kedesh-naphtali.* A town affected by the Canaanite oppression. *mount Tabor.* A mountain about 1,300 feet high, northeast of the battle site. *Naphtali and . . . Zebulun.* Issachar, a near neighbor of these tribes, is not mentioned here but is included in the poetic description of the battle in 5:15. In all, six tribes are mentioned as having participated in the battle.

4:7 With the Israelites encamped on the slopes of mount Tabor, safe from chariot attack, the Lord's strategy was to draw Sisera into a trap. For the battle site, Sisera cleverly chose the Valley of Jezreel along the Kishon River, where his chariot forces would have ample maneuvering space to range the battlefield and attack in numbers from any quarter. But that was his undoing, for he did not know the power of the Lord, who would fight from heaven for Israel with storm and flood (see 5:20–21), as He had done in the days of Joshua (Josh 10:11–14). Even in modern times storms have rendered the plain along the Kishon virtually impassable. In April of 1799 the flooded Kishon River aided Napoleon's victory over a Turkish army.

4:9 *a woman.* Barak's timidity (and that of Israel's other warriors, whom he exemplified) was due to lack of trust in the Lord and was thus rebuked (see note on 9:54).

4:11 *Heber the Kenite.* Since one meaning of Heber's name is "ally," and since "Kenite" identifies him as belonging to a clan of metalworkers, the author hints at the truth that this member of a people allied with Israel since the days of Moses has moved from south to north to ally himself (see v. 17) with the Canaanite king who is assembling a large force of chariots of iron. It is no doubt he who informs Sisera of Barak's military preparations. *the Kenites.* Settled in the south not far from Kadesh-barnea in the Negev (see 1:16). *Hobab.* See Num 10:29.

4:14 *gone out before thee.* As a king at the head of his army (see 1 Sam 8:20). See also Ex 15:3 ("The LORD is a man of war"); Josh 10:10–11; 2 Sam 5:24; 2 Chr 20:15–17,22–24. *Barak went down from mount Tabor.* The Lord's "thunderbolt" (see note on v. 6) descends the mountain to attack the Canaanite army.

4:15 *discomfited.* See note on v. 7. The Hebrew for this word is also used of the panic that overcame the Egyptians at the "Red sea" (Ex 14:24) and the Philistines at Mizpeh (1 Sam 7:10).

4:18 *he had turned in unto her . . . tent.* Since ancient Near Eastern custom prohibited any man other than a woman's husband or father from entering her tent, Jael seemed to offer Sisera an ideal hiding place.

4:19 *bottle.* Containers for liquids were normally made from the skins of goats or lambs. *milk.* See note on 5:25. Jael, whose name means "mountain goat," gave him milk to drink—and it was most likely goat's milk (see Ex 23:19; Prov 27:27).

‡4:21 *smote the nail* [i.e. tent peg] *into his temples.* The laws of hospitality normally meant that one tried to protect a guest from any harm (see 19:23; Gen 19:8). Jael remained true to her family's previous alliance with Israel (she may not have been an Israelite) and so undid her husband's deliberate breach of faith. Armed only with domestic implements, this dauntless woman destroyed the great warrior whom Barak had earlier feared.

4:22 *Sisera lay dead.* With Sisera dead the kingdom of Jabin was no longer a threat. The land "flowing with milk and honey" had been saved by the courage and faithfulness of "Bee" (see note on v. 4) and "Mountain Goat" (see note on v. 19).

tent, behold, Sisera lay dead, and the nail *was*
in his temples.
23 So God subdued on that day Jabin the
king of Canaan before the children of Israel.
24 And the hand of the children of Israel
[1]prospered, and prevailed against Jabin the
king of Canaan, until they had destroyed Jabin
king of Canaan.

The song of Deborah

5 Then [a]sang Deborah and Barak the son
of Abinoam on that day, saying,
2 Praise ye the LORD for the [a]avenging of
Israel,
[b]When the people willingly offered
themselves.
3 [a]Hear, O ye kings; give ear, O ye
princes;
I, *even* I, will sing unto the LORD;
I will sing *praise* to the LORD God of
Israel.
4 LORD, [a]when thou wentest out of Seir,
When thou marchedst out of the field
of Edom,
[b]The earth trembled, and the heavens
dropped,
The clouds also dropped water.
5 [a]The mountains [1]melted from before
the LORD,
Even [b]that Sinai from before the LORD
God of Israel.
6 In the days of Shamgar the son of Anath,
In the days of Jael, [a]the highways were
unoccupied,
And the [1]travellers walked *through*
[2]byways.

4:24 [1]Heb. *going, went and* was *hard*
5:1 [a]See Ex. 15:1
5:2 [a]Ps. 18:47 [b]2 Chr. 17:16
5:3 [a]Deut. 32:1,3
5:4 [a]Deut. 33:2 [b]Ps. 68:8
5:5 [1]Heb. *flowed* [a]Ps. 97:5 [b]Ex. 19:18
5:6 [1]Heb. *walkers of paths* [2]Heb. *crooked ways* [a]Is. 33:8
5:7 [a]Is. 49:23
5:8 [a]Deut. 32:16 [b]1 Sam. 13:19,22
5:10 [1]Or, *Meditate* [a]Ps. 145:5 [b]ch. 10:4 [c]Ps. 107:32
5:11 [1]Heb. *righteousnesses of the LORD* [a]Ps. 145:7
5:12 [a]Ps. 57:8 [b]Ps. 68:18
5:13 [a]Ps. 49:14

7 *The inhabitants of* the villages ceased,
they ceased in Israel,
Until that I Deborah arose,
That I arose [a]a mother in Israel.
8 They [a]chose new gods;
Then *was* war in the gates:
[b]Was there a shield or spear seen
Among forty thousand in Israel?
9 My heart *is* toward the governors of
Israel,
That offered themselves willingly
among the people.
Bless ye the LORD.
10 [a][1]Speak, ye [b]that ride on white asses,
[c]Ye that sit in judgment,
And walk by the way.
11 *They that are delivered* from the noise
of archers in the places of drawing
water,
There shall they rehearse the
[a][1]righteous acts of the LORD,
Even the [1]righteous acts *towards the*
inhabitants of his villages in Israel:
Then shall the people of the LORD go
down to the gates.
12 [a]Awake, awake, Deborah:
Awake, awake, utter a song:
Arise, Barak,
And [b]lead thy captivity captive, thou
son of Abinoam.
13 Then he made him that remaineth
[a]have dominion over the nobles
among the people:
The LORD made me have dominion
over the mighty.

5:1–31 To commemorate a national victory with songs was a common practice (see Ex 15:1–18; Num 21:27–30; Deut 32:1–43; 1 Sam 18:7). The "book of the wars of the LORD" (see note on Num 21:14) and the "book of Jasher" (see note on Josh 10:13) were probably collections of such songs.

The song was probably written by Deborah (see v. 7) and is thus one of the oldest poems in the Bible. It highlights some of the central themes of the narrative (cf. Ex 15:1–18; 1 Sam 2:1–10; 2 Sam 22; 23:1–7; Luke 1:46–55,68–79). In particular, it celebrates before the nations (v. 3) the righteous acts of the Lord and of His warriors (v. 11). The song may be divided into the following sections: (1) the purpose of the song (praise) and the occasion for the deeds it celebrates (vv. 2–9); (2) the exhortation to Israel to act in accordance with her heroic past (vv. 10–11a); (3) the people's appeal to Deborah (vv. 11b–12); (4) the gathering of warriors (vv. 13–18); (5) the battle (vv. 19–23); (6) the crafty triumph of Jael over Sisera (vv. 24–27); (7) the anxious waiting of Sisera's mother (vv. 28–30); and (8) the conclusion (v. 31).

5:4–5 Poetic recalling of the Lord's terrifying appearance in a storm cloud many years before, when he had brought Israel through the wilderness into Canaan (see Deut 33:2; Ps 68:7–8; Mic 1:3–4; see also Ps 18:7–15).

5:4 *Seir.* Mount Seir, in Edom. For a similar association of Seir (and mount Paran) with Sinai see Deut 33:2. *the heavens dropped.* See Ps 68:7–10.

5:5 *that Sinai.* See Ps 68:8. An earthquake and thunderstorm occurred when God appeared at mount Sinai (Ex 19:16–18).

5:6 *Shamgar.* See note on 3:31. *highways were unoccupied.* Because of enemy garrisons and marauding bands (see note on 4:1–2) the roads were unsafe.

5:7 *inhabitants of the villages ceased.* The inhabitants of villages fled to walled towns for protection.

5:8 A "shield or spear" was not seen in Israel, either because Israel had made peace with the native Canaanites (see 3:5–6) or because she had been disarmed (see 1 Sam 13:19–22).

5:10 *that ride on white asses.* An allusion to the nobles and the wealthy (see 10:4; 12:14).

5:11 *noise of archers.* Meaning of the Hebrew is uncertain. The leaders are encouraged by those at the watering places who rehearse the past heroic achievements of the Lord and His warriors.

5:12 *Awake.* A plea to take action (see Ps 44:23; Is 51:9). *lead thy captivity captive.* The same action is applied to God in Ps 68:18 and to Christ in Eph 4:8.

5:13–18 The warriors of the Lord who gathered for the battle. The tribes who came were Ephraim, Benjamin, Manasseh ("Machir" is possibly both East and West Manasseh; see Deut 3:15; Josh 13:29–31; 17:1), Zebulun (vv. 14,18), Issachar (v. 15) and Naphtali (v. 18). Especially involved were Zebulun and Naphtali (v. 18; see 4:10), the tribes most immediately affected by Sisera's tyranny. Reuben (vv. 15–16) and Gad (here referred to as Gilead, v. 17), from east of the Jordan, and Dan and Asher, from along the coast (v. 17), are rebuked for not responding. Judah and Simeon are not even mentioned, perhaps because they were already engaged with the Philistines. Levi is not mentioned because it did not have military responsibilities in the theocracy (kingdom of God).

14 Out of Ephraim *was there* a root of
them against Amalek;
After thee, Benjamin, among thy people;
Out of Machir came down governors,
And out of Zebulun they that [1]handle
the pen of the writer.
15 And the princes of Issachar *were* with
Deborah;
Even Issachar, *and* also Barak:
He was sent on [1]foot into the valley.
[2]For the divisions of Reuben *there*
were great [3]thoughts of heart.
16 Why abodest thou among the
sheepfolds,
To hear the bleatings of the flocks?
[1]For the divisions of Reuben *there*
were great searchings of heart.
17 [a]Gilead abode beyond Jordan:
And why did Dan remain *in* ships?
[b]Asher continued on the sea [1]shore,
And abode in his [2]breaches.
18 [a]Zebulun and Naphtali *were* a people
that [1]jeoparded their lives unto the
death
In the high places of the field.
19 The kings came *and* fought,
Then fought the kings of Canaan
In Taanach by the waters of Megiddo;
[a]They took no gain of money.
20 [a]They fought from heaven;
[b]The stars in their [1]courses fought
against Sisera.
21 [a]The river of Kishon swept them away,
That ancient river, the river Kishon.
O my soul, thou hast trodden down
strength.
22 Then were the horsehoofs broken by
the means of the [1]pransings,
The pransings of their mighty *ones.*
23 Curse ye Meroz, said the angel of the
LORD,
Curse ye bitterly the inhabitants thereof;
[a]Because they came not to the help [b]of
the LORD,
To the help of the LORD against the
mighty.
24 Blessed above women shall [a]Jael the
wife of Heber the Kenite be,
[b]Blessed shall she be above women in
the tent.
25 [a]He asked water, *and* she gave *him*
milk;
She brought forth butter in a lordly
dish.
26 She put her hand to the nail,
And her right hand to the workmen's
hammer;
And [1]with the hammer she smote
Sisera, she smote off his head,
When she had pierced and stricken
through his temples.
27 [1]At her feet he bowed, he fell, he lay
down:
[1]At her feet he bowed, he fell:
Where he bowed, there he fell down
[2]dead.
28 The mother of Sisera looked out at a
window,
And cried through the lattice,
Why is his chariot *so* long in coming?
Why tarry the wheels of his chariots?
29 Her wise ladies answered *her,*
Yea, she returned [1]answer to herself,
30 [a]Have they not sped? have they *not*
divided the prey;
[1]To every man a damsel *or* two;
To Sisera a prey of divers colours,
A prey of divers colours of needlework,
Of divers colours of needlework on
both sides,
Meet for the necks of *them that take*
the spoil?
31 [a]So let all thine enemies perish,
O LORD:

5:14 [1] Heb. *draw with the pen, etc.*
5:15 [1] Heb. *his feet* [2] Or, *In the divisions, etc.* [3] Heb. *impressions*
5:16 [1] Or, *In*
5:17 [1] Or, *port* [2] Or, *creeks* [a] See Josh. 13:25,31 [b] Josh. 19:29
5:18 [1] Heb. *exposed to reproach* [a] ch. 4:10
5:19 [a] Ps. 44:12
5:20 [1] Heb. *paths* [a] Ps. 77:17,18 [b] ch. 4:15
5:21 [a] ch. 4:7
5:22 [1] Or, *tramplings,* or, *plungings*
5:23 [a] Neh. 3:5 [b] 1 Sam. 18:17
5:24 [a] ch. 4:17 [b] Luke 1:28
5:25 [a] ch. 4:19
5:26 [1] Heb. [*she*] *hammered*
5:27 [1] Heb. *Between* [2] Heb. *destroyed*
5:29 [1] Heb. [*her*] *words*
5:30 [1] Heb. *To the head of a man* [a] Ex. 15:9
5:31 [a] Ps. 83:9,10

‡5:14 *root of them against* [lit."in"] *Amalek.* Some Amalekites apparently once lived in the hill country of Ephraim (see 12:15). *Machir.* The firstborn son of Manasseh (Josh 17:1). Although the descendants of Machir settled on both sides of the Jordan (see Deut 3:15; Josh 13:29–31; 17:1; 1 Chr 7:14–19), reference here is to those west of the Jordan (see v. 17; Josh 17:5).

5:18 *In the high places of the field.* Perhaps connected to Gen 49:21, where Naphtali is described as a "hind let loose."

5:19 *Megiddo.* Megiddo and Taanach dominated the main pass that runs northeast through the hill country from the plain of Sharon to the Valley of Jezreel. Because of its strategic location, the "valley of Megiddo" (2 Chr 35:22) has been a frequent battleground from the earliest times. There Pharaoh Thutmose III defeated a Canaanite coalition in 1468 B.C., and there in A.D. 1917 the British under General Allenby ended the rule of the Turks in Palestine by vanquishing them in the Valley of Jezreel opposite Megiddo. In Biblical history the forces of Israel under Deborah and Barak crushed the Canaanites "by the waters of Megiddo" (v. 19), and there Judah's good king Josiah died in battle against Pharaoh Neco II in 609 B.C. (2 Ki 23:29). See also the reference in Rev 16:16 to "a place called in the Hebrew tongue Armageddon" (i.e. "mount Megiddo") as the site of the "battle of that great day of God Almighty" (Rev 16:14).

5:20 *They fought . . . stars.* A poetic way of saying that the powers of heaven fought in Israel's behalf (see note on 4:7).

5:21 *swept them away.* See note on 4:7.

5:23 *Meroz.* Because of its refusal to help the army of the Lord, this Israelite town in Naphtali was cursed. Other cities were also punished severely for refusing to participate in the wars of the Lord (see 8:15–17; 21:5–10).

5:25 *butter.* Lit. "curds." Artificially soured milk was made by shaking milk in a skin-bottle and then allowing it to ferment (due to bacteria that remained in the skin from previous use).

5:28 This graphic picture of the anxious waiting of Sisera's mother heightens the triumph of Jael over the powerful Canaanite general and presents a contrast between this mother in Canaan and the triumphant Deborah, "a mother in Israel" (v. 7).

5:31 The song ends with a prayer that the present victory would be the pattern for all future battles against the Lord's enemies (see Num 10:35; Ps 68:1–2). *thine enemies . . . them that love him.* The two basic attitudes of people toward the Lord. As Lord of the covenant and royal Head of His people Israel, He demanded their love (see Ex 20:6), just as kings in the ancient Near East demanded the love of their subjects. *forty years.* A conventional number of years for a generation (see Introduction: Background).

But *let* them that love him *be* [b]as the
sun [c]when he goeth forth in his
might.

And the land had rest forty years.

Gideon

6 And [a]the children of Israel did evil in the sight of the LORD: and the LORD delivered them into the hand [b]of Midian seven years.

2 And the hand of Midian [1]prevailed against Israel: *and* because of the Midianites the children of Israel made them [a]the dens which *are* in the mountains, and caves, and strong holds.

3 And *so* it was, when Israel had sown, that the Midianites came up, and [a]the Amalekites, [b]and the children of the east, even they came up against them;

4 And they encamped against them, and [a]destroyed the increase of the earth, till thou come *unto* Gaza, and left no sustenance for Israel, neither [1]sheep, nor ox, nor ass.

5 For they came up with their cattle and their tents, and they came [a]as grasshoppers for multitude; *for* both they and their camels were without number: and they entered into the land to destroy it.

6 And Israel was greatly impoverished because of the Midianites; and the children of Israel [a]cried unto the LORD.

7 And it came to pass, when the children of Israel cried unto the LORD because of the Midianites,

8 That the LORD sent [1]a prophet unto the children of Israel, which said unto them, Thus saith the LORD God of Israel, I brought you up from Egypt, and brought you forth out of the house of bondage;

9 And I delivered you out of the hand of the Egyptians, and out of the hand of all that oppressed you, and [a]drave them out from before you, and gave you their land;

10 And I said unto you, I *am* the LORD your God; [a]fear not the gods of the Amorites, in whose land ye dwell: but ye have not obeyed my voice.

11 ¶ And there came an angel of the LORD, and sat under an oak which *was* in Ophrah, that *pertained* unto Joash [a]the Abi-ezrite: and his son [b]Gideon threshed wheat by the winepress, [1]to hide *it* from the Midianites.

12 And the [a]angel of the LORD appeared unto him, and said unto him, The LORD *is* [b]with thee, thou mighty *man* of valour.

13 And Gideon said unto him, O my lord, if the LORD be with us, why then is all this befallen us? and [a]where *be* all his miracles [b]which our fathers told us of, saying, Did not the LORD bring us up from Egypt? but now the LORD hath [c]forsaken us, and delivered us into the hands of the Midianites.

14 And the LORD looked upon him, and said, [a]Go in this thy might, and thou shalt save Israel from the hand of the Midianites: [b]have not I sent thee?

15 And he said unto him, O my Lord, wherewith shall I save Israel? behold, [a][1]my family *is* poor in Manasseh, and I *am* the least in my father's house.

16 And the LORD said unto him, [a]Surely I will be with thee, and thou shalt smite the Midianites as one man.

17 And he said unto him, If now I have found grace in thy sight, then [a]shew me a sign that thou talkest with me.

18 [a]Depart not hence, I pray thee, until I come unto thee, and bring forth my [1]present,

5:31 [b]2 Sam. 23:4 [c]Ps. 19:4,5
6:1 [a]ch. 2:19 [b]Hab. 3:7
6:2 [1]Heb. *was strong* [a]1 Sam. 13:6; Heb. 11:38
6:3 [a]ch. 3:13 [b]Gen. 29:1; ch. 7:12; 1 Ki. 4:30; Job 1:3
6:4 [1]Or, *goat* [a]Lev. 26:16; Deut. 28:30; Mic. 6:15
6:5 [a]ch. 7:12
6:6 [a]Hos. 5:15
6:8 [1]Heb. *a man a prophet*
6:9 [a]Ps. 44:2,3
6:10 [a]2 Ki. 17:35,37,38; Jer. 10:2
6:11 [1]Heb. *to cause* it *to flee* [a]Josh. 17:2 [b]Heb. 11:32, called *Gedeon*
6:12 [a]ch. 13:3; Luke 1:11,28 [b]Josh. 1:5
6:13 [a]Is. 59:1 [b]Ps. 44:1 [c]2 Chr. 15:2
6:14 [a]1 Sam. 12:11 [b]Josh. 1:9
6:15 [1]Or, *my thousand* is *the meanest* [a]See 1 Sam. 9:21
6:16 [a]Ex. 3:12
6:17 [a]ver. 36,37; 2 Ki. 20:8; Ps. 86:17; Is. 7:11
6:18 [1]Or, *meat offering* [a]Gen. 18:3,5

6:1–9:57 The Gideon and Abimelech narratives are a literary unit and constitute the center account of the judges. They are bracketed by the stories of Deborah (from Ephraim, a son of Joseph; west of the Jordan) and Jephthah (from Manasseh, the other son of Joseph; east of the Jordan)—which in turn are bracketed by the stories of the heroes Ehud (from Benjamin) and Samson (from Dan). In this center narrative, the crucial issues of the period of the judges are emphasized: the worship of Baal, and the Lord's kingship over His covenant people Israel (see note on 8:23).

6:1 *Midian.* See notes on Gen 37:25; Ex 2:15. Since they were apparently not numerous enough to wage war against the Israelites alone, they often formed coalitions with surrounding peoples—as with the Moabites (Num 22:4–6; 25:6–18), the Amalekites and other tribes from the east (v. 3). Their defeat was an event long remembered in Hebrew history (see Ps 83:9; Is 9:4; 10:26; Hab 3:7).

6:3 *Amalekites.* See note on Gen 14:7. Normally they were a people of the Negev, but they are in coalition here with the Midianites and other eastern peoples, who were nomads from the desert east of Moab and Ammon.

6:5 *as grasshoppers for multitude.* A vivid picture of the marauders who swarmed across the land, leaving it stripped bare (see 7:12; Ex 10:13–15; Joel 1:4). *camels.* The earliest OT reference to the use of mounted camels in warfare.

6:7 *cried unto the LORD.* The Israelites' cries of distress occurred in each recurring cycle of the judges (see Introduction: Literary Features).

6:8 *prophet.* See notes on 2:1; 10:11. The unnamed prophet rebuked Israel for forgetting that the Lord had saved them from Egyptian bondage and had given them the land (vv. 9–10).

6:10 *Amorites.* Probably here includes all the inhabitants of Canaan (see note on Gen 10:16).

6:11 *angel of the LORD.* See note on Gen 16:7. *Ophrah.* To be distinguished from the Benjamite Ophrah (Josh 18:23). *Abiezrite.* The Abi-ezrites (v. 24) were from the tribe of Manasseh (Josh 17:2). *threshed wheat by the winepress.* Rather than in the usual, exposed area (see note on Ruth 1:22). Gideon felt more secure threshing in this better protected but very confined space.

6:12 *mighty man of valour.* Apparently Gideon belonged to the upper class, perhaps a kind of aristocracy (see v. 27), in spite of his disclaimer in v. 15.

6:14 *LORD looked.* See vv. 22–23. Apparently this appearance of the "angel of the LORD" (v. 11) was a theophany (a manifestation of God). *Go . . . have not I sent thee?* Gideon was commissioned to deliver Israel as Moses had been (see Ex 3:7–10).

6:15 *wherewith shall I . . . ?* The Lord usually calls the lowly rather than the mighty to act for Him (see notes on Gen 25:23; 1 Sam 9:21).

6:17 *shew me a sign.* See vv. 36–40; cf. the signs the Lord gave Moses as assurance that He would be with him in his undertaking (see Ex 3:12; 4:1–17).

and set *it* before thee. And he said, I will tarry
until thou come again.
19 ¶ [a]And Gideon went in, and made ready
[1]a kid, and unleavened *cakes of* an ephah of
flour: the flesh he put in a basket, and he put
the broth in a pot, and brought *it* out unto him
under the oak, and presented *it.*
20 And the angel of God said unto him,
Take the flesh and the unleavened *cakes,* and
[a]lay *them* upon this rock, and [b]pour out the
broth. And he did so.
21 Then the angel of the LORD put forth the
end of the staff that *was* in his hand, and
touched the flesh and the unleavened *cakes;*
and [a]there rose up fire out of the rock, and
consumed the flesh and the unleavened *cakes.*
Then the angel of the LORD departed out of his
sight.
22 And when Gideon [a]perceived that he
was an angel of the LORD, Gideon said, Alas,
O Lord GOD! [b]for because I have seen an angel
of the LORD face to face.

6:19 [1]Heb. *a kid of the goats* [a]Gen. 18:6-8
6:20 [a]ch. 13:19 [b]See 1 Ki. 18:33,34
6:21 [a]Lev. 9:24
6:22 [a]ch. 13:21 [b]Gen. 16:13; Ex. 33:20; ch. 13:22
6:23 [a]Dan. 10:19
6:24 [1]That is, *The LORD send peace* [a]ch. 8:32
6:25 [1]Or, *and* [a]Ex. 34:13; Deut. 7:5
6:26 [1]Heb. *strong place* [2]Or, *in an orderly manner*

23 And the LORD said unto him, [a]Peace *be*
unto thee; fear not: thou shalt not die.
24 Then Gideon built an altar there unto
the LORD, and called it [1]Jehovah-shalom: unto
this day it *is* yet [a]in Ophrah of the Abi-ezrites.
25 ¶ And it came to pass the same night,
that the LORD said unto him, Take thy father's
young bullock, [1]even the second bullock of
seven years old, and throw down the altar of
Baal that thy father hath, and [a]cut down the
grove that *is* by it:
26 And build an altar unto the LORD thy
God upon the top of this [1]rock, [2]in the ordered place, and take the second bullock, and
offer a burnt sacrifice with the wood of the
grove which thou shalt cut down.
27 Then Gideon took ten men of his servants, and did as the LORD had said unto him:
and *so* it was, because he feared his father's
household, and the men of the city, that *he*
could not do *it* by day, that he did *it* by night.
28 And when the men of the city arose early in the morning, behold, the altar of Baal was

6:21 *consumed the flesh.* Indicating that Gideon's offering was accepted (see Lev 9:24).
6:23 *shalt not die.* See 13:22 and notes on Gen 16:13; 32:30.
6:25 *throw down the altar.* Gideon's first task as the Lord's warrior was to tear down an altar to Baal, as Israel had been commanded to do (see 2:2; Ex 34:13; Deut 7:5). *Baal.* See note on 2:13. *grove.* Hebrew *Asherah.* See notes on 2:13; Ex 34:13.
6:26 *altar . . . in the ordered place.* See Ex 20:25.

Gideon's Battles

The story of Gideon begins with a graphic portrayal of one of the most striking facts of life in the Fertile Crescent: the periodic migration of nomadic people from the Aramean desert into the settled areas of Canaan. Each spring the tents of the bedouin herdsmen appeared overnight almost as if by magic, scattered on the hills and fields of the farming districts. Conflict between these two ways of life (herdsmen and farmers) was inevitable.

In the Biblical period, the vast numbers and warlike practice of the herdsmen reduced the village people to near vassalage. Gideon's answer was twofold: (1) religious reform, starting with his own family; and (2) military action, based on a coalition of northern Israelite tribes. The location of Gideon's hometown, "Ophrah of the Abi-ezrites," is not known with certainty, but probably was ancient Aper (modern Afula) in the Valley of Jezreel.

The battle at the spring of Harod is justly celebrated for its strategic brilliance. Denied the use of the only local water source, the Midianites camped in the valley and fell victim to the small band of Israelites, who attacked them from the heights of the hill of Moreh.

The main battle took place north of the hill near the village of En-dor at the foot of mount Tabor. Fleeing by way of the Jordan Valley, the Midianites were trapped when the Ephraimites seized the fords of the Jordan from below Beth-shan to Beth-barah near Adam.

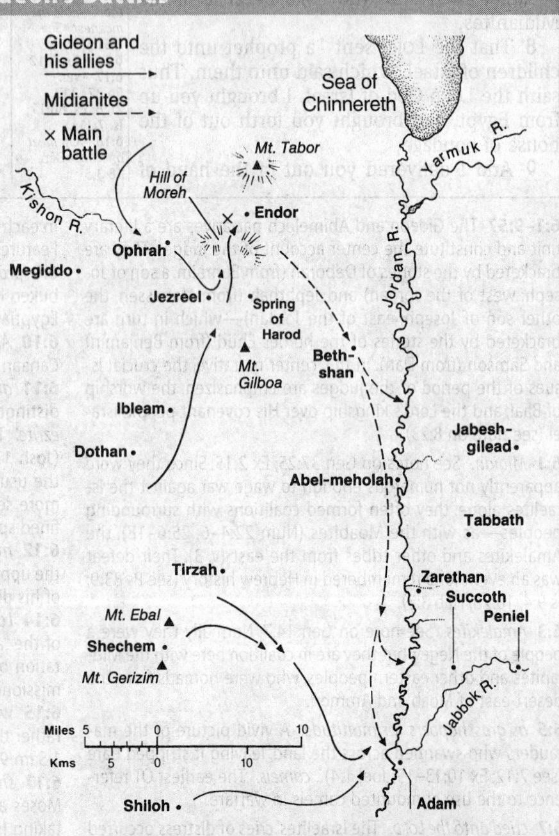

cast down, and the grove was cut down that *was* by it, and the second bullock was offered upon the altar that was built.

29 And they said one to another, Who hath done this thing? And when they inquired and asked, they said, Gideon the son of Joash hath done this thing.

30 Then the men of the city said unto Joash, Bring out thy son, that he may die: because he hath cast down the altar of Baal, and because he hath cut down the grove that *was* by it.

31 And Joash said unto all that stood against him, Will ye plead for Baal? will ye save him? he that will plead for him, let him be put to death whilst *it is yet* morning: if he *be* a god, let him plead for himself, because *one* hath cast down his altar.

32 Therefore on that day he called him [1]Jerubbaal, saying, Let Baal plead against him, because he hath thrown down his altar.

33 ¶ Then all [a]the Midianites and the Amalekites and the children of the east were gathered together, and went over, and pitched in [b]the valley of Jezreel.

34 But [a]the spirit of the LORD [1]came upon Gideon, and he [b]blew a trumpet; and Abi-ezer [2]was gathered after him.

35 And he sent messengers throughout all Manasseh; who also [1]was gathered after him: and he sent messengers unto Asher, and unto Zebulun, and unto Naphtali; and they came up to meet them.

36 ¶ And Gideon said unto God, If thou wilt save Israel by mine hand, as thou hast said,

37 [a]Behold, I will put a fleece of wool in the floor; *and* if the dew be on the fleece only, and *it be* dry upon all the earth *beside,* then shall I know that thou wilt save Israel by mine hand, as thou hast said.

38 And it was so: for he rose up early on the morrow, and thrust the fleece together, and wringed the dew out of the fleece, a bowl full *of* water.

39 And Gideon said unto God, [a]Let not thine anger be hot against me, and I will speak but *this* once: let me prove, I pray thee, but *this* once with the fleece; let it now be dry only upon the fleece, and upon all the ground let there be dew.

40 And God did so that night: for it was dry upon the fleece only, and there was dew on all the ground.

6:32 [1][That is, *Let Baal plead,* 1 Sam. 12:11. (2 Sam. 11:21, *Jerubbesheth*); that is, *Let the shameful* thing *plead,* see Jer. 11:13; Hos. 9:10]
6:33 [a]ver. 3 [b]Josh. 17:16
6:34 [1]Heb. *clothed* [2]Heb. *was called after him* [a]ch. 3:10; 1 Chr. 12:18; 2 Chr. 24:20 [b]Num. 10:3; ch. 3:27
6:35 [1]Heb. *was called after him*
6:37 [a]See Ex. 4:3-7
6:39 [a]Gen. 18:32

7:1 [a]ch. 6:32
7:2 [a]Deut. 8:17; 1 Cor. 1:29
7:3 [a]Deut. 20:8
7:7 [a]1 Sam. 14:6

The defeat of the Midianites

7 Then [a]Jerubbaal, who *is* Gideon, and all the people that *were* with him, rose up early, and pitched beside the well of Harod: so that the host of the Midianites were on the north side of them, by the hill of Moreh, in the valley.

2 And the LORD said unto Gideon, The people that *are* with thee *are* too many for me to give the Midianites into their hands, lest Israel [a]vaunt themselves against me, saying, Mine own hand hath saved me.

3 Now therefore go to, proclaim in the ears of the people, saying, [a]Whosoever *is* fearful and afraid, let him return and depart early from mount Gilead. And there returned of the people twenty and two thousand; and there remained ten thousand.

4 And the LORD said unto Gideon, The people *are* yet *too* many; bring them down unto the water, and I will try them for thee there: and it shall be, *that* of whom I say unto thee, This shall go with thee, the same shall go with thee; and of whomsoever I say unto thee, This shall not go with thee, the same shall not go.

5 So he brought down the people unto the water: and the LORD said unto Gideon, Every one that lappeth of the water with his tongue, as a dog lappeth, him shalt thou set by himself; likewise every one that boweth down upon his knees to drink.

6 And the number of them that lapped, putting their hand to their mouth, were three hundred men: but all the rest of the people bowed down upon their knees to drink water.

7 And the LORD said unto Gideon, [a]By the three hundred men that lapped will I save you, and deliver the Midianites into thine hand: and let all the *other* people go every man unto his place.

8 So the people took victuals in their hand, and their trumpets: and he sent all *the rest of*

6:30 *he may die.* The Israelites were so apostate that they were willing to kill one of their own people for the cause of Baal (contrast Deut 13:6–10, where God told Moses that idolaters must be stoned).
6:32 *Jerubbaal.* See KJV marg. This name later occurs as Jerubbesheth (2 Sam 11:21) by substituting a degrading term (Hebrew *bosheth,* "shameful thing") for the name of Baal, as in the change of the names Esh-baal and Merib-baal (1 Chr 8:33–34) to Ish-bosheth and Mephibosheth (see notes on 2 Sam 2:8; 4:4). *Let Baal plead against him.* Let Baal defend himself against Gideon.
6:33 *valley of Jezreel.* See note on 5:19.
6:34 *spirit . . . came upon.* Lit. "Spirit . . . clothed Himself with." This vivid figure, used only three times (here; 1 Chr 12:18; 2 Chr 24:20), emphasizes that the Spirit of the Lord empowered the human agent and acted through him (see note on 3:10).
6:35 *Manasseh.* West Manasseh. *Asher.* This tribe earlier had failed to answer the call to arms (5:17).
6:39 *speak but this once.* Cf. Abraham's words in Gen 18:32.
7:1–8 As supreme commander of Israel, the Lord reduced the army so that Israel would know that the victory was by His power, not theirs.
7:1 *Harod.* Means "trembling" and may refer to either the timidity of the Israelites (v. 3) or the great panic of the Midianites when Gideon attacked (v. 21). The Hebrew verb form is translated "discomfited" in 8:12. *hill of Moreh.* Located across the Valley of Jezreel, approximately four miles from the Israelite army.
7:3 *let him return.* Those who were afraid to fight the Lord's battle were not to go out with His army so that they would not demoralize the others (Deut 20:8). *mount Gilead.* Perhaps used here as another name for mount Gilboa.
‡7:6 *lapped.* The 300 lapped up the water from their hands.
7:8–14 The Lord provided Gideon with encouraging intelligence information for the battle.

Israel every man unto his tent, and retained *those* three hundred men: and the host of Midian was beneath him in the valley.

9 ¶ And it came to pass the same [a]night, that the LORD said unto him, Arise, get thee down unto the host; for I have delivered it into thine hand.

10 But if thou fear to go down, go thou with Phurah thy servant down to the host:

11 And thou shalt [a]hear what they say; and afterward shall thine hands be strengthened to go down unto the host. Then went he down with Phurah his servant unto the outside of the [1]armed *men* that *were* in the host.

12 And the Midianites and the Amalekites and [a]all the children of the east lay along in the valley like grasshoppers for multitude; and their camels *were* without number, as the sand by the sea side for multitude.

13 And when Gideon was come, behold, *there was* a man that told a dream unto his fellow, and said, Behold, I dreamed a dream, and lo, a cake of barley bread tumbled into the host of Midian, and came unto a tent, and smote it that it fell, and overturned it, that the tent lay along.

14 And his fellow answered and said, This *is* nothing else save the sword of Gideon the son of Joash, a man of Israel: *for* into his hand hath God delivered Midian, and all the host.

15 And it was *so,* when Gideon heard the telling of the dream, and [1]the interpretation thereof, that he worshipped, and returned into the host of Israel, and said, Arise; for the LORD hath delivered into your hand the host of Midian.

16 And he divided the three hundred men *into* three companies, and he put [1]a trumpet in every man's hand, with empty pitchers, and [2]lamps within the pitchers.

17 And he said unto them, Look on me, and do likewise: and behold, when I come to the outside of the camp, it shall be *that,* as I do, so shall ye do.

18 When I blow with a trumpet, I and all that *are* with me, then blow ye the trumpets also on every side of all the camp, and say, *The sword* of the LORD, and of Gideon.

19 So Gideon, and the hundred men that *were* with him, came unto the outside of the camp *in* the beginning of the middle watch; *and* they had but newly set the watch: and they blew the trumpets, and brake the pitchers that *were* in their hands.

20 And the three companies blew the trumpets, and brake the pitchers, and held the lamps in their left hands, and the trumpets in their right hands to blow *withal:* and they cried, The sword of the LORD, and of Gideon.

21 And they [a]stood every man in his place round about the camp: [b]and all the host ran, and cried, and fled.

22 And the three hundred [a]blew the trumpets, and [b]the LORD set [c]every man's sword against his fellow, even throughout all the host: and the host fled to Beth-shittah [1]in Zererath, *and* to the [2]border of Abel-meholah, unto Tabbath.

23 And the men of Israel gathered themselves together out of Naphtali, and out of Asher, and out of all Manasseh, and pursued after the Midianites.

24 ¶ And Gideon sent messengers throughout all [a]mount Ephraim, saying, Come down against the Midianites, and take before them the waters unto Beth-barah and Jordan. Then all the men of Ephraim gathered themselves together, and [b]took the waters unto [c]Beth-barah and Jordan.

25 And they took [a]two princes of the Midianites, Oreb and Zeeb; and they slew Oreb upon [b]the rock Oreb, and Zeeb they slew at the winepress of Zeeb, and pursued Midian, and brought the heads of Oreb and Zeeb to Gideon on the [c]*other* side Jordan.

8 And [a]the men of Ephraim said unto him, [1]Why hast thou served us thus, that *thou* calledst us not, when thou wentest to fight with the Midianites? And they did chide with him [2]sharply.

7:9 [a]Gen. 46:2,3
7:11 [1]Or, *ranks by five* [a]ver. 13-15; See Gen. 24:14; 1 Sam:14:9,10
7:12 [a]ch. 6:5,33; 8:10
7:15 [1]Heb. *the breaking thereof*
7:16 [1]Heb. *trumpets in the hand of all of them* [2]Or, *firebrands,* or, *torches*
7:21 [a]Ex. 14:13,14; 2 Chr. 20:17 [b]2 Ki. 7:7
7:22 [1]Or, *towards* [2]Heb. *lip* [a]Josh. 6:4,16,20; See 2 Cor. 4:7 [b]Ps. 83:9; Is. 9:4 [c]1 Sam. 14:20; 2 Chr. 20:23
7:24 [a]ch. 3:27 [b]ch. 3:28 [c]John 1:28
7:25 [a]ch. 8:3; Ps. 83:11 [b]Is. 10:26 [c]ch. 8:4
8:1 [1]Heb. *What thing* is *this thou hast done unto us?* [2]Heb. *strongly* [a]See ch. 12:1; 2 Sam. 19:41

7:13–14 Although revelations by dreams are frequently mentioned in the OT, here both dreamer and interpreter are non-Israelite. Contrast Joseph, who interpreted dreams in Egypt (Gen 40:1–22; 41:1–32), and Daniel, who interpreted dreams in Babylon (Dan 2:1–45; 4:4–27).

7:13 *cake of barley bread.* Since barley was considered an inferior grain and only one-half the value of wheat (see 2 Ki 7:1), it is a fitting symbol for Gideon and for Israel, which was inferior in numbers.

7:16 *three companies.* A strategy adopted by Israel on several occasions (9:43; 1 Sam 11:11; 2 Sam 18:2). *A trumpet.* Rams' horns (see Ex 19:13).

7:19 *middle watch.* The Hebrews divided the night into three watches (see note on Mat 14:25). The "beginning of the middle watch" would be after the enemy had gone to sleep.

‡7:22 *three hundred . . . trumpets.* Normally only a comparatively small number of men in an army carried trumpets. *every man's sword against his fellow.* God used Gideon and the trumpeters to scare the enemy. A similar panic occurred among the Ammonites, Moabites and Edomites (2 Chr 20:23) and, on a somewhat smaller scale, among the Philistines at Gibeah (1 Sam 14:20). See Ezek 38:21; Zech 14:13; see also note on Judg 4:15. *in Zererath.* Toward the southeast.

7:23 *gathered themselves together.* Encouraged by the turn of events, many of those who had departed now joined the battle.

7:24 *mount Ephraim.* Gideon needed the aid of the Ephraimites to cut off the retreat of the Midianites into the Jordan Valley. *waters . . . Jordan.* Probably the river crossings in the vicinity of Beth-shean. By controlling the river the Israelites could prevent the escape of the fleeing Midianites (see note on 3:28). *Beth-barah.* Exact location unknown, but it must have been some distance down the river. Gideon's pursuit of the enemy across the river took him to Succoth, a town near the Jabbok River (8:5).

7:25 *Oreb.* Means "raven." *Zeeb.* Means "wolf." *heads.* Frequently parts of the bodies of dead victims, such as heads, hands (8:6) and foreskins (1 Sam 18:25), were cut off and brought back as a kind of body count.

8:1 *men of Ephraim.* Contrast Gideon, who placates the wrath

2 And he said unto them, What have I done now in comparison of you? *Is* not the gleaning of the grapes of Ephraim better than the vintage of Abi-ezer?

3 [a]God hath delivered into your hands the princes of Midian, Oreb and Zeeb: and what was I able to do in comparison of you? Then their [b][1]anger was abated toward him, when he had said that.

4 ¶ And Gideon came to Jordan, *and* passed over, he, and the three hundred men that *were* with him, faint, yet pursuing *them.*

5 And he said unto the men of [a]Succoth, Give, I pray you, loaves of bread unto the people that follow me; for they *be* faint, and I am pursuing after Zebah and Zalmunna, kings of Midian.

6 And the princes of Succoth said, [a]*Are* the hands of Zebah and Zalmunna now in thine hand, that [b]we should give bread unto thine army?

7 And Gideon said, Therefore when the LORD hath delivered Zebah and Zalmunna into mine hand, [a]then I will [1]tear your flesh with the thorns of the wilderness and with briers.

8 And he went up thence [a]*to* Penuel, and spake unto them likewise: and the men of Penuel answered him as the men of Succoth had answered *him.*

9 And he spake also unto the men of Penuel, saying, When I [a]come again in peace, [b]I will break down this tower.

10 Now Zebah and Zalmunna *were* in Karkor, and their hosts with them, about fifteen thousand *men,* all that were left of [a]all the hosts of the children of the east: for there fell [b][1]an hundred and twenty thousand men that drew sword.

11 And Gideon went up *by* the way of them that dwelt in tents on the east of [a]Nobah and Jogbehah, and smote the host: for the host was [b]secure.

12 And when Zebah and Zalmunna fled, he pursued after them, and [a]took the two kings of Midian, Zebah and Zalmunna, and [1]discomfited all the host.

13 ¶ And Gideon the son of Joash returned from battle before the sun was up,

14 And caught a young man of the men of Succoth, and inquired of him: and he [1]described unto him the princes of Succoth, and the elders thereof, *even* threescore and seventeen men.

15 And he came unto the men of Succoth, and said, Behold Zebah and Zalmunna, with whom ye did [a]upbraid me, saying, *Are* the hands of Zebah and Zalmunna now in thine hand, that we should give bread unto thy men *that are* weary?

16 [a]And he took the elders of the city, and thorns of the wilderness and briers, and with them he [1]taught the men of Succoth.

17 [a]And he beat down the tower of [b]Penuel, and slew the men of the city.

18 Then said he unto Zebah and Zalmunna, What manner of men *were they* whom ye slew at [a]Tabor? And they answered, As thou *art,* so *were* they; *each* one [1]resembled the children of a king.

19 And he said, They *were* my brethren, *even* the sons of my mother: *as* the LORD liveth, if ye had saved them alive, I would not slay you.

20 And he said unto Jether his firstborn, Up, *and* slay them. But the youth drew not his sword: for he feared, because he *was* yet a youth.

21 Then Zebah and Zalmunna said, Rise thou, and fall upon us: for as the man *is, so is* his strength. And Gideon arose, and [a]slew Zebah and Zalmunna, and took away the [1]ornaments that *were* on their camels' necks.

Gideon refuses the kingship

22 ¶ Then the men of Israel said unto Gideon, Rule thou over us, both thou, and thy son, and thy son's son also: for thou hast delivered us from the hand of Midian.

23 And Gideon said unto them, I will not rule over you, neither shall my son rule over you: [a]the LORD shall rule over you.

24 And Gideon said unto them, I would desire a request of you, that you would give me every man the earrings of his prey. (For they had golden earrings, [a]because they *were* Ishmaelites.)

25 And they answered, We will willingly

8:3 [1]Heb. *spirit* [a]ch. 7:24,25; Phil. 2:3 [b]Prov. 15:1
8:5 [a]Gen. 33:17; Ps. 60:6
8:6 [a]See 1 Ki. 20:11 [b]See 1 Sam. 25:11
8:7 [1]Heb. *thresh* [a]ver. 16
8:8 [a]Gen. 32:30; 1 Ki. 12:25
8:9 [a]1 Ki. 22:27 [b]ver. 17
8:10 [1]Or, *an hundred and twenty thousand, every one drawing a sword* [a]ch. 7:12 [b]ch. 20:2,15,17,25; 2 Ki. 3:26
8:11 [a]Num. 32:35,42 [b]ch. 18:27; 1 Thes. 5:3
8:12 [1]Heb. *terrified* [a]Ps. 83:11
8:14 [1]Heb. *writ*
8:15 [a]ver. 6
8:16 [1]Heb. *made to know* [a]ver. 7
8:17 [a]ver. 9 [b]1 Ki. 12:25
8:18 [1]Heb. *according to the form, etc.* [a]ch. 4:6; Ps. 89:12
8:21 [1]Or, *ornaments like the moon* [a]Ps. 83:11
8:23 [a]1 Sam. 8:7; 10:19; 12:12
8:24 [a]Gen. 25:13; 37:25,28

of this tribe (vv. 2–3), with Jephthah, who brings humiliation and defeat to it (12:1–6).

8:2 *gleaning.* Leftover grain after the main gathering of the harvest (see note on Ruth 1:22). Here Gideon implies that Ephraim has accomplished more than he and all the other forces involved in the initial attack. *Abi-ezer.* Gideon's clan (see note on 6:11). The name means "My (divine) Father is helper" or "My (divine) Father is strong."

8:3 *their anger was abated.* "A soft answer turneth away wrath" (Prov 15:1).

8:5 *kings of Midian.* Zebah and Zalmunna may have belonged to different Midianite tribes (see Num 31:8).

8:6 *hands.* See note on 7:25. *that we should give bread . . . ?* The officials of Succoth doubted Gideon's ability to defeat the Midianite coalition and feared reprisal if they gave his army food.

8:8 *Penuel.* The place where Jacob had wrestled with God (Gen 32:30–31).

8:19 *sons of my mother.* In an age when men often had several wives it was necessary to distinguish between full brothers and half brothers.

8:21 *Rise thou.* Dying at the hands of a boy may have been considered a disgrace (see 1 Sam 17:42). *ornaments.* Probably crescent necklaces; see KJV marg. See also Is 3:18.

8:23 *I will not rule . . . the LORD shall rule.* Gideon, like Samuel (1 Sam 8:4–20), rejected the establishment of a monarchy because he regarded it as a replacement of the Lord's rule. God's rule over Israel (theocracy) is a central issue in Judges.

8:24 *earrings.* Or possibly "nose ring" (see Gen 24:47; Ezek 16:12). *Ishmaelites.* Related to the Midianites (Gen 25:1–2) and sometimes identified with them (vv. 22,24; Gen 37:25–28; 39:1). See note on Gen 37:25.

give *them.* And they spread a garment, and did
cast therein every man the earrings of his prey.
26 And the weight of the golden earrings
that he requested was a thousand and seven
hundred *shekels* of gold; beside ornaments,
and [1]collars, and purple raiment that *was* on
the kings of Midian, and beside the chains that
were about their camels' necks.
27 And Gideon [a]made an ephod thereof,
and put it in his city, *even* [b]in Ophrah: and all
Israel [c]went thither a whoring after it: which
thing became [d]a snare unto Gideon, and to his
house.
28 Thus was Midian subdued before the
children of Israel, so that they lifted up their
heads no more. [a]And the country was in quietness forty years in the days of Gideon.

Gideon's death

29 ¶ And Jerubbaal the son of Joash went
and dwelt in his own house.
30 And Gideon had [a]threescore and ten sons
[1]of his body begotten: for he had many wives.
31 [a]And his concubine that *was* in Shechem, she also bare him a son, whose name
he [1]called Abimelech.
32 And Gideon the son of Joash died [a]in a
good old age, and was buried in the sepulchre of
Joash his father, [b]in Ophrah of the Abi-ezrites.
33 And it came to pass, [a]as soon as Gideon
was dead, that the children of Israel turned
again, and [b]went a whoring after Baalim, [c]and
made Baal-berith their god.
34 And the children of Israel [a]remembered
not the LORD their God, who had delivered
them out of the hands of all their enemies on
every side:
35 [a]Neither shewed they kindness to the
house of Jerubbaal, *namely,* Gideon, according
to all the goodness which he had shewed unto
Israel.

Abimelech

9 And Abimelech the son of Jerubbaal
went to Shechem unto [a]his mother's
brethren, and communed with them, and with
all the family of the house of his mother's father, saying,
2 Speak, I pray you, in the ears of all the
men of Shechem, [1]Whether *is* better for you,
either that all the sons of Jerubbaal, *which are*
[a]threescore and ten persons, reign over you,
or that one reign over you? remember also
that I *am* [b]your bone and your flesh.
3 And his mother's brethren spake of him
in the ears of all the men of Shechem all these
words: and their hearts inclined [1]to follow
Abimelech; for they said, He *is* our [a]brother.
4 And they gave him threescore and ten
pieces of silver out of the house of [a]Baal-be-
rith, wherewith Abimelech hired [b]vain and
light persons, which followed him.
5 And he went unto his father's house [a]at
Ophrah, and [b]slew his brethren the sons of
Jerubbaal, *being* threescore and ten persons,
upon one stone: notwithstanding yet Jotham
the youngest son of Jerubbaal was left; for he
hid himself.

8:26 [1]Or, *sweet jewels*
8:27 [a]ch. 17:5 [b]ch. 6:24 [c]Ps. 106:39 [d]Deut. 7:16
8:28 [a]ch. 5:31
8:30 [1]Heb. *going out of his thigh* [a]ch. 9:2,5
8:31 [1]Heb. *set* [a]ch. 9:1
8:32 [a]Gen. 25:8; Job 5:26 [b]ver. 27; ch. 6:24
8:33 [a]ch. 2:19 [b]ch. 2:17 [c]ch. 9:4,46
8:34 [a]Ps. 78:11,42; 106:13,21
8:35 [a]ch. 9:16-18; Eccl. 9:14
9:1 [a]ch. 8:31
9:2 [1]Heb. *What is good? whether, etc.* [a]ch. 8:30 [b]Gen. 29:14
9:3 [1]Heb. *after* [a]Gen. 29:15
9:4 [a]ch. 8:33 [b]ch. 11:3; 2 Chr. 13:7; Acts 17:5
9:5 [a]ch. 6:24 [b]2 Ki. 11:1,2

8:27 *ephod.* Sometimes a holy garment associated with the priesthood (Ex 28:6–30; 39:2–26; Lev 8:7), at other times a pagan object associated with idols (17:5; 18:14,17).
8:28 *forty years.* A conventional number of years for a generation (see Introduction: Background).
8:29 *Jerubbaal.* See note on 6:32.
8:30 *threescore and ten sons.* A sign of power and prosperity (see 12:14; 2 Ki 10:1).
8:31 *concubine.* She was originally a slave in his household (9:18; see note on Gen 16:2). *Abimelech.* Appears elsewhere as a royal title (Gen 20:2; 26:1; Ps 34 title) and means "My (divine) Father is King." Gideon, in naming his son, acknowledges that the Lord (here called "Father") is King.
8:32 *a good old age.* A phrase used elsewhere only of Abraham (Gen 15:15; 25:8) and David (1 Chr 29:28).
8:33 *Baalim.* See notes on 2:11,13. *Baal-berith.* Means "lord of the covenant"; the same deity is called the god Berith ("god of the covenant") in 9:46. There was a temple dedicated to him (see 9:4) in Shechem. The word "covenant" in his name probably refers to a solemn treaty that bound together a league of Canaanite cities whose people worshiped him as their god. Ironically, Shechem (v. 31), near mount Ebal, was the site at which Joshua had twice renewed the Lord's covenant with Israel after they had entered Canaan (Josh 8:30–35; 24:25–27). See also note on 2:11.
9:1–57 The stories of Gideon and Abimelech form the literary center of Judges (see Introduction: Literary Features). Abimelech, who tried to set himself up like a Canaanite city king with the help of Baal (v. 4), stands in sharp contrast to his father Gideon (Jerubbaal), who had attacked Baal worship and insisted that the Lord ruled over Israel. Abimelech attempted this Canaanite revival in the very place where Joshua had earlier reaffirmed Israel's allegiance to the Lord (Josh 24:14–27). In every respect Abimelech was the antithesis of the Lord's appointed judges.
‡9:1 *Shechem.* See note on Gen 33:18. Ruins dating from the Canaanite era give evidence of a sacred area, probably to be associated with the temple of Baal-berith, or "the god Berith" (vv. 4,46). Archaeological evidence, which is compatible with the destruction of Shechem by Abimelech, indicates that its sacred area was never rebuilt after this time.
9:2 *men.* I.e., "leaders." The singular form of the Hebrew for this word is *ba'al.* It means "lord" or "owner" and probably refers here to the aristocracy or landowners of the city. *your bone and your flesh.* Being half-Canaanite, Abimelech intimated that it was in their best interest to make him king rather than be under the rule of Gideon's 70 sons. The following he gathered was based on this relationship and became a threat to the people of Israel.
9:4 *out of the house.* Ancient temples served as depositories for personal and civic funds. The payments of vows and penalties, as well as gifts, were also part of the temple treasury. The temple of Baal-berith is probably to be identified with a large building found at Shechem by archaeologists. *vain and light persons.* Use of mercenaries to accomplish political or military goals was common in ancient times. Others who used them are Jephthah (11:3), David (1 Sam 22:1–2), Absalom (2 Sam 15:1), Adonijah (1 Ki 1:5), Rezon (1 Ki 11:23–24) and Jeroboam (2 Chr 13:6–7).
9:5 *upon one stone.* Abimelech's 70 brothers were slaughtered like sacrificial animals (see 13:19–20; 1 Sam 14:33–34). In effect he inaugurated his kingship by using his Israelite half brothers as his coronation sacrifices (see 2 Sam 15:10,12; 1 Ki 1:5,9; 3:4).

6 And all the men of Shechem gathered together, and all the house of Millo, and went, and made Abimelech king, [1] by the plain of the pillar that *was* in Shechem.

7 ¶ And when they told *it* to Jotham, he went and stood in the top of [a] mount Gerizim, and lift up his voice, and cried, and said unto them, Hearken unto me, you men of Shechem, that God may hearken unto you.

8 [a] The trees went forth on a time to anoint a king over them; and they said unto the olive tree, [b] Reign thou over us.

9 But the olive tree said unto them, Should I leave my fatness, [a] wherewith by me they honour God and man, and [1] go to be promoted over the trees?

10 And the trees said to the fig tree, Come thou, *and* reign over us.

11 But the fig tree said unto them, Should I forsake my sweetness, and my good fruit, and go to be promoted over the trees?

12 Then said the trees unto the vine, Come thou, *and* reign over us.

13 And the vine said unto them, Should I leave my wine, [a] which cheereth God and man, and go to be promoted over the trees?

14 Then said all the trees unto the [1] bramble, Come thou, *and* reign over us.

15 And the bramble said unto the trees, If in truth ye anoint me king over you, *then* come *and* put your trust in my [a] shadow: and if not, [b] let fire come out of the bramble, and devour the [c] cedars of Lebanon.

16 Now therefore, if ye have done truly and sincerely, in that ye have made Abimelech king, and if ye have dealt well with Jerubbaal and his house, and have done unto him [a] according to the deserving of his hands;

17 (For my father fought for you, and [1] adventured his life far, and delivered you out of the hand of Midian:

18 [a] And ye are risen up against my father's house *this* day, and have slain his sons, threescore and ten persons, upon one stone, and have made Abimelech, the son of his maidservant, king over the men of Shechem, because he *is* your brother;)

19 If ye then have dealt truly and sincerely with Jerubbaal and with his house this day, *then* [a] rejoice ye in Abimelech, and let him also rejoice in you:

20 But if not, [a] let fire come out from Abimelech, and devour the men of Shechem, and the house of Millo; and let fire come out from the men of Shechem, and from the house of Millo, and devour Abimelech.

21 And Jotham ran away, and fled, and went to [a] Beer, and dwelt there, for fear of Abimelech his brother.

22 ¶ When Abimelech had reigned three years over Israel,

23 Then [a] God sent an evil spirit between Abimelech and the men of Shechem; and the men of Shechem [b] dealt treacherously with Abimelech:

24 [a] That the cruelty *done* to the threescore and ten sons of Jerubbaal might come, and their blood be laid upon Abimelech their brother, which slew them; and upon the men of Shechem, which [1] aided him in the killing of his brethren.

25 And the men of Shechem set liers in wait for him in the top of the mountains, and they robbed all that came along *that* way by them: and it was told Abimelech.

26 And Gaal the son of Ebed came with his brethren, and went over to Shechem: and the men of Shechem put their confidence in him.

27 And they went out *into* the fields, and gathered their vineyards, and trode *the grapes,* and made [1] merry, and went *into* [a] the house of their god, and did eat and drink, and cursed Abimelech.

28 And Gaal the son of Ebed said, [a] Who *is* Abimelech, and who *is* Shechem, that we should serve him? *is* not *he* the son of Jerubbaal? and Zebul his officer? serve the men of

9:6 [1] Or, *by the oak of the pillar*
9:7 [a] Deut. 11:29; 27:12; Josh. 8:33; John 4:20
9:8 [a] See 2 Ki. 14:9 [b] ch. 8:22,23
9:9 [1] Or, *go up and down for other trees* [a] Ps. 104:15
9:13 [a] Ps. 104:15
9:14 [1] Or, *thistle*
9:15 [a] Is. 30:2; Dan. 4:12; Hos. 14:7 [b] ver. 20; Num. 21:28; Ezek. 19:14 [c] 2 Ki. 14:9; Is. 2:13; 37:24; Ezek. 31:3
9:16 [a] ch. 8:35
9:17 [1] Heb. *cast his life*
9:18 [a] ver. 5,6
9:19 [a] Is. 8:6; Phil. 3:3
9:20 [a] ver. 15,56,57
9:21 [a] 2 Sam. 20:14
9:23 [a] 1 Sam. 16:14; 18:9,10; See 1 Ki. 22:22; 2 Chr. 18:22; Is. 19:14 [b] Is. 33:1
9:24 [1] Heb. *strengthened his hands to kill* [a] 1 Ki. 2:32; Esth. 9:25; Mat. 23:35,36
9:27 [1] Or, *songs* [a] ver. 4
9:28 [a] 1 Sam. 25:10; 1 Ki. 12:16

‡9:6 *house of Millo.* Hebrew *Beth-millo.* "Millo" is derived from a Hebrew verb meaning "to fill" and probably refers to the earthen fill used to erect a platform on which walls and other large structures were built. It may be identical to the "hold of the house" of v. 46. *plain.* Lit. "oak." See Josh 24:25–26; see also note on Gen 12:6.

9:7 *top.* Probably a ledge that overlooked the city.

9:8 *trees went forth.* Fables of this type, in which inanimate objects speak and act, were popular among Eastern peoples of that time (see 2 Ki 14:9).

9:9–13 The olive tree, the fig tree and the vine were all plants that produced fruit of great importance to the people of the Near East.

9:13 *cheereth God.* Cf. Ex 29:40.

9:14 *bramble.* Probably the well-known buckthorn, a scraggly bush common in the hills of Canaan and a constant menace to farming. It produced nothing of value and was an apt figure for Abimelech. See also KJV marg.

9:15 *shadow.* Ironically, in offering shade to the trees, the bramble symbolized the traditional role of kings as protectors of their subjects (see Is 30:2–3; 32:1–2; Lam 4:20; Dan 4:12). *cedars of Lebanon.* The most valuable of Near Eastern trees, here symbolic of the leading men of Shechem (see v. 20).

9:20 *fire come out . . . and devour.* A grim prediction that Abimelech and the people of Shechem would destroy each other. Fire spreads rapidly through bramble bushes and brings about swift destruction (see Ex 22:6; Is 9:18).

9:21 *Beer.* A very common name, meaning "a well."

9:22 *Israel.* Those Israelites who recognized Abimelech's authority, mainly in the vicinity of Shechem.

9:23 *evil spirit.* Perhaps a spirit of distrust and bitterness. The Hebrew for "spirit" is often used to describe an attitude or disposition. *dealt treacherously.* The one who founded his kingdom by treachery is himself undone by treachery.

9:26 *put their confidence in him.* Just as the fickle population had followed Abimelech, so they are now swayed by the deceptive proposals of Gaal.

9:27 *made merry.* The vintage harvest was one of the most joyous times of the year (see Is 16:9–10; Jer 25:30), but festivals and celebrations held at pagan temples often degenerated into debauched drinking affairs.

[b]Hamor the father of Shechem: for why should we serve him?

29 And [a]would to God this people were under my hand; then would I remove Abimelech. And he said to Abimelech, Increase thine army, and come out.

30 And when Zebul the ruler of the city heard the words of Gaal the son of Ebed, his anger was [1]kindled.

31 And he sent messengers unto Abimelech [1]privily, saying, Behold, Gaal the son of Ebed and his brethren be come to Shechem; and behold, they fortify the city against thee.

32 Now therefore up by night, thou and the people that *is* with thee, *and* lie in wait in the field:

33 And it shall be, *that* in the morning, as soon as the sun is up, thou shalt rise early, and set upon the city: and behold, *when* he and the people that *is* with him come out against thee, then mayest thou do to them [1]as thou shalt find occasion.

34 And Abimelech rose up, and all the people that *were* with him, by night, and they laid wait against Shechem *in* four companies.

35 And Gaal the son of Ebed went out, and stood *in* the entering of the gate of the city: and Abimelech rose up, and the people that *were* with him, from lying in wait.

36 And when Gaal saw the people, he said to Zebul, Behold, there come people down from the top of the mountains. And Zebul said unto him, Thou seest the shadow of the mountains as *if they were* men.

37 And Gaal spake again and said, See there come people down by the [1]middle of the land, and another company come along by the plain of [2]Meonenim.

38 Then said Zebul unto him, Where *is* now thy mouth, wherewith thou [a]saidst, Who *is* Abimelech, that we should serve him? *is* not this the people that thou hast despised? go out, I pray now, and fight with them.

39 And Gaal went out before the men of Shechem, and fought with Abimelech.

40 And Abimelech chased him, and he fled before him, and many were overthrown *and* wounded, *even* unto the entering of the gate.

41 And Abimelech dwelt at Arumah: and Zebul thrust out Gaal and his brethren, that *they* should not dwell in Shechem.

9:28 [b]Gen. 34:2,6
9:29 [a]2 Sam. 15:4
9:30 [1]Or, *hot*
9:31 [1]Heb. *craftily,* or, *to Tormah*
9:33 [1]Heb. *as thine hand shall find*
9:37 [1]Heb. *navel* [2]Or, *the regarders of times*
9:38 [a]ver. 28,29

9:45 [a]ver. 20 [b]Deut. 29:23; 1 Ki. 12:25; 2 Ki. 3:25
9:46 [a]ch. 8:33
9:48 [1]Heb. *I have done* [a]Ps. 68:14
9:53 [a]2 Sam. 11:21
9:54 [a]1 Sam. 31:4

42 And it came to pass on the morrow, that the people went out *into* the field; and they told Abimelech.

43 And he took the people, and divided them into three companies, and laid wait in the field, and looked, and behold, the people *were* come forth out of the city; and he rose up against them, and smote them.

44 And Abimelech, and the company that *was* with him, rushed forward, and stood *in* the entering of the gate of the city: and the two *other* companies ran upon all *the people* that *were* in the fields, and slew them.

45 And Abimelech fought against the city all that day; and [a]he took the city, and slew the people that *was* therein, and [b]beat down the city, and sowed it *with* salt.

46 And when all the men of the tower of Shechem heard *that,* they entered into a hold of the house [a]of the god Berith.

47 And it was told Abimelech, that all the men of the tower of Shechem were gathered together.

48 And Abimelech gat him up *to* mount [a]Zalmon, he and all the people that *were* with him; and Abimelech took an axe in his hand, and cut down a bough from the trees, and took it, and laid *it* on his shoulder, and said unto the people that *were* with him, What ye have seen [1]me do, make haste, *and* do as I *have done.*

49 And all the people likewise cut down every man his bough, and followed Abimelech, and put *them* to the hold, and set the hold on fire upon them; so that all the men of the tower of Shechem died also, about a thousand men and women.

50 ¶ Then went Abimelech to Thebez, and encamped against Thebez, and took it.

51 But there was a strong tower within the city, and thither fled all the men and women, and all they of the city, and shut *it* to them, and gat them up to the top of the tower.

52 And Abimelech came unto the tower, and fought against it, and went hard unto the door of the tower to burn it with fire.

53 And a certain woman [a]cast a piece of a millstone upon Abimelech's head, and all to brake his skull.

54 Then [a]he called hastily unto the young man his armourbearer, and said unto him, Draw thy sword, and slay me, that *men* say not

9:28 *Hamor.* The Hivite ruler who had founded the city of Shechem (Gen 33:19; 34:2; Josh 24:32).
9:32 *lie in wait.* Ambush succeeded against Gibeah in Benjamin (20:37) and against Ai (Josh 8:2).
9:34 *four companies.* Smaller segments meant less chance of detection. Also, attack from several directions was good strategy.
9:37 *middle of the land.* See note on Ezek 38:12. *plain of Meonenim.* Lit. "diviner's oak." Probably a sacred tree in some way related to the temple of Baal-berith (see note on Gen 12:6).
9:43 *three companies.* See note on 7:16.
9:45 *sowed it with salt.* To condemn it to perpetual barrenness and desolation (see Deut 29:23; Ps 107:33–34; Jer 17:6; Zeph 2:9).
9:46 *hold of the house.* Probably the house of Millo of v. 6. *god Berith.* Baal-berith (v. 4).
9:49 *set the hold on fire.* In fulfillment of Jotham's curse (v. 20).
9:53 *woman.* While the men used bows, arrows and spears, women helped to defend the tower by dropping heavy stones on those who came near it. *piece of a millstone.* See note on 3:16. The upper, revolving stone of a mill was circular, with a hole in the center. Grinding grain was women's work (see Ex 11:5), usually considered too lowly for men to perform (see 16:21). Abimelech was killed by a woman using a domestic implement (see also 4:21).
9:54 *armourbearer.* A military leader usually had a young man carry his shield and spear (see 1 Sam 14:6; 31:4). *A woman slew him.* It was considered a disgrace for a soldier to die at the hands of a woman. Abimelech's shameful death was long remembered (2 Sam 11:21).

of me, A woman slew him. And his young man
thrust him through, and he died.
55 And when the men of Israel saw that
Abimelech was dead, they departed every man
unto his place.
56 [a]Thus God rendered the wickedness of
Abimelech, which he did unto his father, in
slaying his seventy brethren:
57 And all the evil of the men of Shechem
did God render upon their heads: and upon
them came [a]the curse of Jotham the son of
Jerubbaal.

Israel cries for deliverance

10 And after Abimelech there [a]arose to
[1]defend Israel Tola the son of Puah,
the son of Dodo, a man of Issachar; and he
dwelt in Shamir in mount Ephraim.
2 And he judged Israel twenty and three
years, and died, and was buried in Shamir.
3 ¶ And after him arose Jair, a Gileadite,
and judged Israel twenty and two years.
4 And he had thirty sons that [a]rode on thirty ass colts, and they had thirty cities, [b]which
are called [c][1]Havoth-jair unto this day, which
are in the land of Gilead.
5 And Jair died, and was buried in Camon.
6 ¶ And [a]the children of Israel did evil
again in the sight of the LORD, and [b]served
Baalim, and Ashtaroth, and [c]the gods of Syria,
and the gods of [d]Zidon, and the gods of Moab,
and the gods of the children of Ammon, and
the gods of the Philistines, and forsook the
LORD, and served not him.
7 And the anger of the LORD was hot
against Israel, and he [a]sold them into the
hands of the Philistines, and into the hands of
the children of Ammon.
8 And that year they vexed and [1]oppressed
the children of Israel: eighteen years, all the
children of Israel that *were* on the *other* side
Jordan in the land of the Amorites, which *is* in
Gilead.
9 Moreover the children of Ammon passed
over Jordan to fight also against Judah, and
against Benjamin, and against the house of
Ephraim; so that Israel was sore distressed.
10 [a]And the children of Israel cried unto
the LORD, saying, We have sinned against thee,
both because we have forsaken our God, and
also served Baalim.
11 And the LORD said unto the children of
Israel, *Did* not *I deliver you* [a]from the Egyptians, and [b]from the Amorites, [c]from the children of Ammon, [d]and from the Philistines?
12 [a]The Zidonians also, [b]and the Amalekites, and the Maonites, [c]did oppress you; and
ye cried to me, and I delivered you out of their
hand.
13 [a]Yet ye have forsaken me, and served
other gods: wherefore I will deliver you no
more.
14 Go and [a]cry unto the gods which ye
have chosen; let them deliver you in the time
of your tribulation.
15 And the children of Israel said unto the
LORD, We have sinned: [a]do thou unto us whatsoever [1]seemeth good unto thee; deliver us
only, we pray thee, this day.
16 [a]And they put away the [1]strange gods
from among them, and served the LORD: and
[b]his soul [2]was grieved for the misery of Israel.
17 Then the children of Ammon were
[1]gathered together, and encamped in Gilead.
And the children of Israel assembled themselves together, and encamped in [a]Mizpeh.
18 And the people *and* princes of Gilead
said one to another, What man *is he* that will

9:56 [a]ver. 24; Job 31:3; Prov. 5:22
9:57 [a]ver. 20
10:1 [1]Or, *deliver.* Heb. *save* [a]ch. 2:16
10:4 [1]Or, *the villages of Jair* [a]ch. 5:10; 12:14 [b]Deut. 3:14 [c]Num. 32:41
10:6 [a]ch. 2:11; 3:7; 4:1; 6:1; 13:1 [b]ch. 2:13 [c]ch. 2:12 [d]1 Ki. 11:33; Ps. 106:36
10:7 [a]ch. 2:14; 1 Sam. 12:9
10:8 [1]Heb. *crushed*
10:10 [a]1 Sam. 12:10
10:11 [a]Ex. 14:30 [b]Num. 21:21,24,25 [c]ch. 3:12,13 [d]ch. 3:31
10:12 [a]ch. 5:19 [b]ch. 6:3 [c]Ps. 106:42,43
10:13 [a]Jer. 2:13
10:14 [a]Deut. 32:37,38
10:15 [1]Heb. is *good in thine eyes* [a]1 Sam. 3:18; 2 Sam. 15:26
10:16 [1]Heb. *gods of strangers* [2]Heb. *was shortened* [a]2 Chr. 7:14; 15:8; Jer. 18:7,8 [b]Ps. 106:44,45; Is. 63:9
10:17 [1]Heb. *cried together* [a]Gen. 31:49; ch. 11:11,29

9:56 *God rendered.* God was in control of the events. As Israel's true King, He brought Abimelech's wickedness to a quick and shameful end.

9:57 *curse of Jotham.* See v. 20.

10:1 *Tola the son of Puah . . . a man of Issachar.* Tola and Puah bear names of two of the sons of Issachar (Gen 46:13; Num 26:23; 1 Chr 7:1).

10:3 *Jair.* Since Jair came from Gilead (the territory assigned to Manasseh) and since a descendant of Manasseh bore the same name (Num 32:41; Deut 3:14; 1 Ki 4:13), it appears that Jair was a Manassite.

10:4 *thirty sons . . . thirty ass colts . . . thirty cities.* Evidence of wealth and position. *Havoth-jair.* I.e. "towns of Jair."

10:6–12:7 Israel now turned to Jephthah, a social outcast whom they had driven from the land and caused to become an outlaw without an inheritance in Israel. The author notes this to Israel's shame. The account of Jephthah's judgeship balances that of Deborah in the story of the judges (see note on 4:1–5:31; see also Introduction: Literary Features).

10:6 *gods of Syria.* The chief gods were Hadad (Baal), Mot, Anath and Rimmon. *gods of Zidon.* The Sidonians worshiped essentially the same gods as the Canaanites (see notes on 2:11,13). *gods of Moab.* The chief deity of Moab was Chemosh. *gods of the children of Ammon.* Molech was the chief Ammonite deity (see 1 Ki 11:7) and was sometimes worshiped by the offering of human sacrifice (Lev 18:21; 20:2–5; 2 Ki 23:10). This god is also called Milcom (see 1 Ki 11:5; 2 Ki 23:13; see also note on Lev 18:21). Both Molech and Milcom are forms of a Semitic word for "king." *gods of the Philistines.* While the Philistines worshiped most of the Canaanite gods, their most popular deities appear to have been Dagon and Baal-zebub. The name Dagon is the same as a Hebrew word for "grain," suggesting that he was a vegetation deity. He was worshiped in Babylonia as early as the second millennium B.C. Baal-zebub was worshiped in Ekron (2 Ki 1:2–3,6,16). The name means "lord of the flies," a deliberate change by followers of the Lord (Yahweh) to ridicule and protest the worship of Baal-zebul ("Baal the prince"), a name known from ancient Canaanite texts (see Mat 10:25; 12:24 and notes).

10:7 *Philistines.* The account of Philistine oppression is resumed in 13:1.

10:11 *the LORD said.* See note on 2:1. The Lord rebuked Israel for forgetting that He had delivered them from their oppressors in Canaan (see notes on 2:16–19; 6:8).

10:12 *Maonites.* Perhaps the same as the Mehunims, who along with the Philistines and Arabs opposed Israel (2 Chr 26:7).

10:17 *Mizpeh.* Means "watchtower." Several places bore this name. Jephthah's headquarters was a town or fortress in Gilead (11:11) called "Mizpeh of Gilead" (11:29). It may have been the same as Ramath-mizpeh (Josh 13:26), located about 30 miles east of Beth-shean.

10:18 The Gileadites wanted to resist the Ammonite incursion

begin to fight against the children of Ammon? he shall [a]be head over all the inhabitants of Gilead.

Jephthah

11 Now [1]Jephthah the Gileadite was [a]a mighty *man* of valour, and he *was* the son of [2]a harlot: and Gilead begat Jephthah.

2 And Gilead's wife bare him sons; and *his* wife's sons grew up, and they thrust out Jephthah, and said unto him, Thou shalt not inherit in our father's house; for thou *art* the son of a strange woman.

3 Then Jephthah fled [1]from his brethren, and dwelt in the land of Tob: and there were gathered [a]vain men to Jephthah, and went out with him.

4 And it came to pass [1]in process of time, that the children of Ammon made war against Israel.

5 And it was so, that when the children of Ammon made war against Israel, the elders of Gilead went to fetch Jephthah out of the land of Tob:

6 And they said unto Jephthah, Come, and be our captain, that we may fight with the children of Ammon.

7 And Jephthah said unto the elders of Gilead, [a]Did not ye hate me, and expel me out of my father's house? and why are ye come unto me now when ye are in distress?

8 [a]And the elders of Gilead said unto Jephthah, Therefore we [b]turn again to thee now, that thou mayest go with us, and fight against the children of Ammon, and be [c]our head over all the inhabitants of Gilead.

9 And Jephthah said unto the elders of Gilead, If ye bring me *home* again to fight against the children of Ammon, and the LORD deliver them before me, shall I be your head?

10 And the elders of Gilead said unto Jephthah, [a]The LORD [1]be witness between us, if we do not so according to thy words.

11 Then Jephthah went with the elders of Gilead, and the people made him [a]head and captain over them: and Jephthah uttered all his words [b]before the LORD in Mizpeh.

12 ¶ And Jephthah sent messengers unto the king of the children of Ammon, saying, What hast thou to do with me, that thou art come against me to fight in my land?

13 And the king of the children of Ammon answered unto the messengers of Jephthah, [a]Because Israel took away my land, when they came up out of Egypt, from Arnon even unto [b]Jabbok, and unto Jordan: now therefore restore those *lands* again peaceably.

14 And Jephthah sent messengers again unto the king of the children of Ammon:

15 And said unto him, Thus saith Jephthah, [a]Israel took not away the land of Moab, nor the land of the children of Ammon:

16 But when Israel came up from Egypt, and walked through the wilderness unto the Red sea, and [a]came to Kadesh;

17 Then [a]Israel sent messengers unto the king of Edom, saying, Let me, I pray thee, pass through thy land: [b]but the king of Edom would not hearken *thereto.* And in like manner they sent unto the king of Moab: but he would not consent: and Israel [c]abode in Kadesh.

18 Then they went along through the wilderness, and [a]compassed the land of Edom, and the land of Moab, and [b]came by the east side of the land of Moab, [c]and pitched on the *other* side of Arnon, but came not within the border of Moab: for Arnon *was* the border of Moab.

19 And [a]Israel sent messengers unto Sihon king of the Amorites, the king of Heshbon; and Israel said unto him, [b]Let us pass, we pray thee, through thy land into my place.

20 [a]But Sihon trusted not Israel to pass through his coast: but Sihon gathered all his people together, and pitched in Jahaz, and fought against Israel.

21 And the LORD God of Israel delivered Sihon and all his people into the hand of Israel, and they [a]smote them: so Israel possessed all the land of the Amorites, the inhabitants of that country.

22 And they possessed [a]all the coasts of the Amorites, from Arnon even unto Jabbok, and from the wilderness even unto Jordan.

23 So now the LORD God of Israel hath dispossessed the Amorites from before his people Israel, and shouldest thou possess it?

10:18 [a]ch. 11:8,11
11:1 [1]Heb. 11:32, called *Jephthae* [2]Heb. *a woman a harlot* [a]ch. 6:12; 2 Ki. 5:1
11:3 [1]Heb. *from the face* [a]ch. 9:4; 1 Sam. 22:2
11:4 [1]Heb. *after days*
11:7 [a]Gen. 26:27
11:8 [a]ch. 10:18 [b]Luke 17:4 [c]ch. 10:18
11:10 [1]Heb. *be the hearer between us* [a]Jer. 42:5
11:11 [a]ver. 8 [b]ch. 10:17; 20:1; 1 Sam. 10:17; 11:15
11:13 [a]Num. 21:24-26 [b]Gen. 32:22
11:15 [a]Deut. 2:9,19
11:16 [a]Num. 13:26; 20:1; Deut. 1:46
11:17 [a]Num. 20:14 [b]Num. 20:18,21 [c]Num. 20:1
11:18 [a]Num. 21:4; Deut. 2:1-8 [b]Num. 21:11 [c]Num. 21:13; 22:36
11:19 [a]Num. 21:21; Deut. 2:26 [b]Num. 21:22; Deut. 2:27
11:20 [a]Num. 21:23; Deut. 2:32
11:21 [a]Num. 21:24,25; Deut. 2:33,34
11:22 [a]Deut. 2:36

but lacked the courageous military leadership to press their cause. *people.* Fighting men.

11:1 *the son of a harlot.* Therefore Jephthah was a social outcast.

11:3 *Tob.* The men of Tob were later allied with the Ammonites against David (2 Sam 10:6–8). *vain men.* See note on 9:4.

11:8 *be our head.* In addition to their initial offer of military command during the war with Ammon (v. 6), the Gileadites now also offer to make Jephthah regional head after the fighting is over.

11:11 The proposal of the elders was ratified by the people, a process followed in the election of Saul (1 Sam 11:15), Rehoboam (1 Ki 12:1) and Jeroboam (1 Ki 12:20).

11:13 *my land.* When the Israelites had first approached Canaan, this area was ruled by the Amorite king Sihon, who had taken it from the Moabites (Num 21:29). The Ammonites had since become dominant over Moab and now claimed all previous Moabite territory.

11:14–27 Jephthah responded in accordance with international policies of the time; his letter is a classic example of contemporary international correspondence. It also reflects—and appeals to—the common recognition that the god(s) of a people established and protected their political boundaries and decided all boundary disputes. Jephthah's defense of Israel's claim to the land is threefold: (1) Israel took it from Sihon king of the Amorites, not from the Ammonites (vv. 15–22); (2) the Lord gave the land to Israel (vv. 23–25); (3) Israel had long possessed it (vv. 26–27).

11:16 *Kadesh.* Kadesh-barnea; see note on Num 20:1.

11:21 *LORD God of Israel.* War was viewed not only in military terms but also as a contest between deities (see v. 24; Ex 12:12; Num 33:4).

24 Wilt not thou possess that which [a]Chemosh thy god giveth thee to possess? So whomsoever [b]the LORD our God shall drive out from before us, them will we possess.

25 And now *art* thou any thing better than [a]Balak the son of Zippor, king of Moab? did he ever strive against Israel, or did he ever fight against them,

26 While Israel dwelt in [a]Heshbon and her towns, and in [b]Aroer and her towns, and in all the cities that *be* along by the coasts of Arnon, three hundred years? why therefore did ye not recover *them* within that time?

27 Wherefore I have not sinned against thee, but thou doest me wrong to war against me: the LORD [a]the Judge [b]be judge *this* day between the children of Israel and the children of Ammon.

28 Howbeit the king of the children of Ammon hearkened not unto the words of Jephthah which he sent him.

29 ¶ Then [a]the spirit of the LORD came upon [1]Jephthah, and he passed over Gilead and Manasseh, and passed over Mizpeh of Gilead, and from Mizpeh of Gilead he passed over *unto* the children of Ammon.

30 And Jephthah [a]vowed a vow unto the LORD, and said, If thou shalt without fail deliver the children of Ammon into mine hands,

31 Then it shall be, that [1]whatsoever cometh forth of the doors of my house to meet me, when I return in peace from the children of Ammon, [a]shall surely be the LORD'S, [b2]and I will offer it up *for* a burnt offering.

32 So Jephthah passed over unto the children of Ammon to fight against them; and the LORD delivered them into his hands.

33 And he smote them from Aroer, even till thou come *to* [a]Minnith, *even* twenty cities, and unto [1]the plain of the vineyards, *with* a very great slaughter. Thus the children of Ammon were subdued before the children of Israel.

34 ¶ And Jephthah came *to* [a]Mizpeh unto his house, and behold, [b]his daughter came out to meet him with timbrels and with dances: and she *was his* only child; [1]beside her he had neither son nor daughter.

35 And it came to pass, when he saw her, that he [a]rent his clothes, and said, Alas, my daughter, thou hast brought me very low, and thou art one of them that trouble me: for I [b]have opened my mouth unto the LORD, and [c]I cannot go back.

36 And she said unto him, My father, *if* thou hast opened thy mouth unto the LORD, [a]do to me according to that which hath proceeded out of thy mouth; forasmuch as [b]the LORD hath taken vengeance for thee of thine enemies, *even* of the children of Ammon.

37 And she said unto her father, Let this thing be done for me: let me alone two months, that I may [1]go up and down upon the mountains, and bewail my virginity, I and my fellows.

38 And he said, Go. And he sent her away *for* two months: and she went with her companions, and bewailed her virginity upon the mountains.

39 And it came to pass at the end of two months, that she returned unto her father, who [a]did with her *according to* his vow which he had vowed: and she knew no man. And it was a [1]custom in Israel,

40 *That* the daughters of Israel went [1]yearly [2]to lament the daughter of Jephthah the Gileadite four days in a year.

Jephthah and Ephraim

12 And [a]the men of Ephraim [1]gathered themselves together, and went northward, and said unto Jephthah, Wherefore passedst thou over to fight against the children of Ammon, and didst not call us to go with thee? we will burn thine house upon thee with fire.

2 And Jephthah said unto them, I and my people were at great strife with the children of Ammon; and when I called you, ye delivered me not out of their hands.

3 And when I saw that ye delivered *me* not, I [a]put my life in my hands, and passed over against the children of Ammon, and the LORD delivered them into my hand: wherefore then are ye come up unto me this day, to fight against me?

11:24 [a]Num. 21:29; 1 Ki. 11:7; Jer. 48:7 [b]Deut. 9:4,5; 18:12; Josh. 3:10
11:25 [a]Num. 22:2; See Josh. 24:9
11:26 [a]Num. 21:25 [b]Deut. 2:36
11:27 [a]Gen. 18:25 [b]Gen. 16:5; 31:53; 1 Sam. 24:12,15
11:29 [1][Jephthah seems to have been Judge only of North-east *Israel*] [a]ch. 3:10
11:30 [a]Gen. 28:20
11:31 [1]Heb. *that which cometh forth, [which] shall come forth* [2]Or, *[or] I will offer it, etc.* [a]See 1 Sam. 1:11,28 [b]Ps. 66:13
11:33 [1]Or, *Abel* [a]Ezek. 27:17
11:34 [1]Or, *he had not of his own* either *son or daughter.* Heb. *of himself* [a]ver. 11; ch. 10:17 [b]Ex. 15:20; Ps. 68:25; Jer. 31:4
11:35 [a]Gen. 37:29,34 [b]Eccl. 5:2 [c]Num. 30:2
11:36 [a]Num. 30:2 [b]2 Sam. 18:19,31
11:37 [1]Heb. *go and go down*
11:39 [1]Or, *ordinance* [a]ver. 31; 1 Sam. 1:22,24
11:40 [1]Heb. *from year to year* [2]Or, *to talk with*
12:1 [1]Heb. *were called* [a]See ch. 8:1
12:3 [a]1 Sam. 19:5; Ps. 119:109

11:24 *Chemosh.* The chief deity of the Moabites. At this time either the king of Ammon also ruled Moab or there was a military confederacy of the two peoples.

11:25 *Balak.* See Num 22–24.

11:26 *three hundred years.* For the relevance of this phrase in establishing the time span for Judges see Introduction: Background.

11:27 *Judge.* See 1 Sam 24:15. As the divine Judge, the Lord is the final court of appeal. It is significant that in the book of Judges the singular noun "judge" is found only here, where it is used of the Lord, Israel's true Judge.

11:29 *spirit of the LORD.* See note on 3:10. In the OT the unique empowering of the Spirit was given to an individual primarily to enable him to carry out the special responsibilities God had given him.

11:30 *vowed a vow.* A common practice among the Israelites (see Gen 28:20; 1 Sam 1:11; 2 Sam 15:8). The precise nature of this vow has been the subject of wide speculation, but v. 31 indicates the promise of a burnt offering and leads to the conclusion that Jephthah probably offered his daughter as a human sacrifice (v. 39). A vow was not to be broken (see Num 30:2; Deut 23:21–23; see also Eccl 5:4–5).

11:34 *dances.* It was customary for women to greet armies returning victoriously from battle in this way (see Ex 15:20; 1 Sam 18:6).

11:35 *rent his clothes.* A common practice for expressing extreme grief (see Gen 37:34 and note).

11:37 *my virginity.* To be kept from marrying and rearing children was a bitter prospect for an Israelite girl.

11:39 *custom in Israel.* Probably a local custom, since no other mention of it is found in the OT.

12:1 *burn thine house upon thee.* The Philistines issued a similar threat to Samson's wife (14:15). See also 20:48.

12:2 *said.* Again Jephthah tried diplomacy first (see 11:12,14; see also note on 8:1). *I called.* New information on the sequence of events.

4 Then Jephthah gathered together all the men of Gilead, and fought with Ephraim: and the men of Gilead smote Ephraim, because they said, Ye Gileadites [a]*are* fugitives of Ephraim among the Ephraimites, *and* among the Manassites.

5 And the Gileadites took the [a]passages of Jordan before the Ephraimites: and it was *so,* that when those Ephraimites which were escaped said, Let me go over; that the men of Gilead said unto him, *Art* thou an Ephraimite? If he said, Nay;

6 Then said they unto him, Say now [1]Shibboleth: and he said Sibboleth: for he could not frame to pronounce *it* right. Then they took him, and slew him at the passages of Jordan: and there fell at that time of the Ephraimites forty and two thousand.

7 And Jephthah judged Israel six years. Then died Jephthah the Gileadite, and was buried in *one of* the cities of Gilead.

Ibzan, Elon and Abdon

8 ¶ And after him [1]Ibzan of Beth-lehem judged Israel.

9 And he had thirty sons, and thirty daughters, *whom* he sent abroad, and took in thirty daughters from abroad for his sons. And he judged Israel seven years.

10 Then died Ibzan, and was buried at Beth-lehem.

11 ¶ And after him [1]Elon, a Zebulonite, judged Israel; and he judged Israel ten years.

12 And Elon the Zebulonite died, and was buried in Aijalon in the country of Zebulun.

13 ¶ And after him [1]Abdon the son of Hillel, a Pirathonite, judged Israel.

14 And he had forty sons and thirty [1]nephews, that [a]rode on threescore and ten ass colts: and he judged Israel eight years.

15 And Abdon the son of Hillel the Pirathonite died, and was buried in Pirathon in the land of Ephraim, [a]in the mount of the Amalekites.

The birth of Samson

13 And the children of Israel [a][1]did evil again in the sight of the LORD; [2]and the LORD delivered them [b]into the hand of the Philistines forty years.

2 And there was a certain man of [a]Zorah, of the family of the Danites, whose name *was* Manoah; and his wife *was* barren, and bare not.

3 And the [a]angel of the LORD appeared unto the woman, and said unto her, Behold now, thou *art* barren, and bearest not: but thou shalt conceive, and bear a son.

4 Now therefore beware, I pray thee, and [a]drink not wine nor strong drink, and eat not any unclean *thing:*

5 For lo, thou *shalt* conceive, and bear a son; and no [a]rasor shall come on his head: for the child shall be [b]a Nazarite unto God from the womb: and he shall [c]begin to deliver Israel out of the hand of the Philistines.

6 Then the woman came and told her husband, saying, [a]A man of God came unto me, and his [b]countenance *was* like the countenance of an angel of God, very terrible: but I [c]asked him not whence he *was,* neither told he me his name:

12:4 [a]See 1 Sam. 25:10
12:5 [a]Josh. 22:11; ch. 3:28
12:6 [1][Which signifieth *a stream,* or, *flood,* Ps. 69:2,15; Is. 27:12]
12:8 [1][He seems to have been only a civil Judge to do justice in North-east *Israel*]
12:11 [1][A civil Judge in North-east *Israel*]
12:13 [1][A civil Judge also in North-east *Israel*]
12:14 [1]Heb. *sons' sons* [a]ch. 5:10; 10:4
12:15 [a]ch. 3:13,27; 5:14
13:1 [1]Heb. *added to commit, etc.* [2][This seems a partial captivity] [a]ch. 2:11; 3:7; 4:1; 6:1; 10:6 [b]1 Sam. 12:9
13:2 [a]Josh. 19:41
13:3 [a]ch. 6:12; Luke 1:11,13, 28,31
13:4 [a]ver. 14; Num. 6:2,3; Luke 1:15
13:5 [a]Num. 6:5; 1 Sam. 1:11 [b]Num. 6:2 [c]See 1 Sam. 7:13; 2 Sam. 8:1; 1 Chr. 18:1
13:6 [a]Deut. 33:1; 1 Sam. 2:27; 9:6 [b]Mat. 28:3; Luke 9:29; Acts 6:15 [c]ver. 17,18

12:6 *Shibboleth.* Ironically, the word meant "floods" (see, e.g., Ps 69:2,15). Apparently the Israelites east of the Jordan pronounced its initial letter with a strong "sh" sound, while those in Canaan gave it a softer "s" sound. (Peter was similarly betrayed by his accent; see Mat 26:73.)

12:7 *judged Israel . . . years.* A new formula for closing out the account of a judge (see note on 3:11; see also Introduction: Literary Features).

12:8 *Beth-lehem.* Probably the Beth-lehem in western Zebulun.

12:9 *thirty sons, and thirty daughters.* See note on 10:4.

12:11 *Elon.* Also the name of a clan in the tribe of Zebulun (Gen 46:14; Num 26:26).

‡12:14 *forty sons and thirty nephews* [lit. "sons of sons," i.e. grandsons]. A total of 70 (see notes on 8:30; 10:4).

12:15 *mount of the Amalekites.* See note on 5:14. The background of this reference is unknown; the Amalekites are otherwise associated with the Negev (Num 13:29).

13:1–16:31 Samson (from the tribe of Dan), like Ehud (from the tribe of Benjamin), was a loner, whose heroic exploits involved single-handed triumphs over powerful enemies. His story therefore balances that of Ehud (3:12–30). He typifies the nation of Israel—born by special divine provision, consecrated to the Lord from birth and endowed with unique power among his fellowmen. The likeness is even more remarkable in light of his foolish chasing of foreign women, some of ill repute, until he was cleverly subdued by one of them. In this he exemplified Israel, who during the period of the judges constantly prostituted herself to Canaanite gods to her own destruction.

‡13:1 *did evil again in the sight of the LORD.* See note on 3:7. The story of the Philistine domination of the coastal farmlands of Israel is resumed here. It continues throughout the Biblical accounts of Samson, Samuel, Saul and David (see 1 Sam 4-7; 13-17; 27-31; 2 Sam 8:1; 23:8-17).

13:2 *Zorah.* A town first assigned to Judah (Josh 15:33), but later given to Dan (Josh 19:41). It became the point of departure for the Danite migration northward (18:2,8,11). *Danites.* See 1:34 and note. *barren, and bare not.* The same condition, before divine intervention, as that of Sarah, the mother of Isaac (Gen 11:30; 16:1); Rebekah, the mother of Jacob (Gen 25:21); Hannah, the mother of Samuel (1 Sam 1:2); and Elisabeth, the mother of John the Baptist (Luke 1:7).

13:3 *angel of the LORD.* See note on Gen 16:7. *thou shalt . . . bear a son.* Cf. the announcements of the births of Ishmael (Gen 16:11), Isaac (Gen 18:10), Immanuel (Is 7:14), John the Baptist (Luke 1:13) and Jesus (Luke 1:31).

13:5 *Nazarite.* From the Hebrew word meaning "separated" or "dedicated." For the stipulations of this vow see Num 6:1–21 and notes. Samson's vow was not voluntary, and it applied to his whole lifetime (v. 7). The same was true of Samuel (1 Sam 1:11) and John the Baptist (Luke 1:15). *begin to deliver Israel out of . . . Philistines.* The deliverance was continued in the time of Samuel (1 Sam 7:10–14) and completed under David (2 Sam 5:17–25; 8:1).

13:6 *man of God.* An expression often used of prophets (see Deut 33:1; 1 Sam 2:27; 9:6–10; 1 Ki 12:22), though it is clear from vv. 3,21 that this messenger was not a prophet but the angel of the Lord.

7 But he said unto me, Behold, thou *shalt* conceive, and bear a son; and now drink no wine nor strong drink, neither eat any unclean *thing:* for the child shall be a Nazarite to God from the womb to the day of his death.

8 ¶ Then Manoah intreated the LORD, and said, O my Lord, let the man of God which thou didst send come again unto us, and teach us what we shall do unto the child that shall be born.

9 And God hearkened to the voice of Manoah; and the angel of God came again unto the woman as she sat in the field: but Manoah her husband *was* not with her.

10 And the woman made haste, and ran, and shewed her husband, and said unto him, Behold, the man hath appeared unto me, that came unto me the *other* day.

11 And Manoah arose, and went after his wife, and came to the man, and said unto him, *Art* thou the man that spakest unto the woman? And he said, I *am.*

12 And Manoah said, Now let thy words come to pass. [1]How shall we order the child, and [2]*how* shall we do unto him?

13 And the angel of the LORD said unto Manoah, Of all that I said unto the woman let her beware.

14 She may not eat of any *thing* that cometh of the vine, [a]neither let her drink wine or strong drink, nor eat any unclean *thing:* all that I commanded her let her observe.

15 And Manoah said unto the angel of the LORD, I pray thee, [a]let us detain thee, until we shall have made ready a kid [1]for thee.

16 And the angel of the LORD said unto Manoah, Though thou detain me, I will not eat of thy bread: and if thou wilt offer a burnt offering, thou must offer it unto the LORD. For Manoah knew not that he *was* an angel of the LORD.

17 And Manoah said unto the angel of the LORD, What *is* thy name, that when thy sayings come to pass we may do thee honour?

18 And the angel of the LORD said unto him, [a]Why askest thou thus after my name, seeing it *is* [1]secret?

19 So Manoah took a kid with a meat offering, [a]and offered *it* upon a rock unto the LORD: and *the angel* did wondrously; and Manoah and his wife looked on.

20 For it came to pass, when the flame went up toward heaven from off the altar, that the angel of the LORD ascended in the flame of the altar. And Manoah and his wife looked on *it,* and [a]fell on their faces to the ground.

21 But the angel of the LORD did no more appear to Manoah and to his wife. [a]Then Manoah knew that he *was* an angel of the LORD.

22 And Manoah said unto his wife, [a]We shall surely die, because we have seen God.

23 But his wife said unto him, If the LORD were pleased to kill us, he would not have received a burnt offering and a meat offering at our hands, neither would he have shewed us all these *things,* nor would as *at this* time have told us *such things* as these.

24 ¶ And the woman bare a son, and called his name [a]Samson: and [b]the child grew, and the LORD blessed him.

25 [a]And the spirit of the LORD began to move him at times in [1]the camp of Dan, [b]between Zorah and Eshtaol.

The marriage of Samson

14 And Samson went down [a]*to* Timnath, and [b]saw a woman in Timnath of the daughters of the Philistines.

2 And he came up, and told his father and his mother, and said, I have seen a woman in Timnath of the daughters of the Philistines: now therefore [a]get her for me to wife.

3 Then his father and his mother said unto him, *Is there* never a woman among the daughters of [a]thy brethren, or among all my people, that thou goest to take a wife of the [b]uncircumcised Philistines? And Samson said unto his father, Get her for me; for [1]she pleaseth me well.

13:12 [1]Heb. *What shall be the manner of the, etc.* [2]Or, what *shall he do?* Heb. what shall be *his work?*
13:14 [a]ver. 4
13:15 [1]Heb. *before thee* [a]Gen. 18:5; ch. 6:18
13:18 [1]Or, *wonderful* [a]Gen. 32:29
13:19 [a]ch. 6:19,20
13:20 [a]Lev. 9:24; 1 Chr. 21:16; Ezek. 1:28; Mat. 17:6
13:21 [a]ch. 6:22
13:22 [a]Gen. 32:30; Ex. 33:20; Deut. 5:26; ch. 6:22
13:24 [a]Heb. 11:32 [b]1 Sam. 3:19; Luke 1:80; 2:52
13:25 [1][Heb. *Mahaneh-dan,* as ch. 18:12] [a]ch. 3:10; 1 Sam. 11:6; Mat. 4:1 [b]Josh. 15:33; ch. 18:11
14:1 [a]Gen. 38:13; Josh. 15:10 [b]Gen. 34:2
14:2 [a]Gen. 21:21; 34:4
14:3 [1]Heb. *she is right in mine eyes* [a]Gen. 24:3,4 [b]Gen. 34:14; Ex. 34:16; Deut. 7:3

13:8 *teach us.* Not the usual parental concern, but a special concern based on the boy's special calling.
13:12 *let thy words come to pass.* A declaration of faith. To Manoah it was not a matter of whether these events would occur, but of when (v. 17).
13:15 *detain thee . . . have made ready a kid.* Such food was considered a special delicacy. Hospitality of this kind was common in the ancient Near East (see 6:18–19; Gen 18:1–8).
13:17 *What is thy name . . . ?* A messenger's identity was considered very important. *when thy sayings come to pass.* Fulfilled prophecy was a sign of the authenticity of a prophet (Deut 18:21–22; 1 Sam 9:6).
‡13:18 *secret.* See KJV marg. In Is 9:6 the Hebrew for this phrase (translated "Wonderful") applies to One who would come as "The mighty God."
13:22 *surely die.* See 6:23 and notes on Gen 16:13; 32:30.
13:24 *Samson.* The name is derived from a Hebrew word meaning "sun" or "brightness," and is used here either as an expression of joy over the birth of the child or as a reference to the nearby town of Beth-shemesh, "house of the sun(-god)." *the child grew, and the LORD blessed him.* Cf. 1 Sam 2:26 (Samuel) and Luke 2:52 (Jesus).
‡13:25 *began to move him.* See notes on 3:10; 11:29. *camp of Dan.* Hebrew is *Mahaneh-dan.* See 18:12.
14:1 *Timnath.* Identified as Tell Batash in the Sorek Valley, west of Beth-shemesh. Archaeologists have uncovered the Philistine layer of the town. *one of the daughters of the Philistines.* The disappointment of Samson's parents (v. 3; cf. Esau, Gen 26:35; 27:46; 28:1) is understandable in light of the prohibition against marriage with the peoples of Canaan (Ex 34:11,16; Deut 7:1,3; see also Judg 3:5–6).
14:2 *get her for me.* See Gen 34:4. As the head of the family, the father exercised authority in all matters, often including the choice of wives for his sons (see 12:9; Gen 24:3–9; Neh 10:30).
14:3 *uncircumcised.* A term of scorn, referring to those not bound by covenant to the Lord, used especially of the Philistines (see note on 1 Sam 14:6). *she pleaseth me well.* The Hebrew for this expression is similar to that translated "did that which was right in his own eyes" in 17:6; 21:25. The author anticipates this theme, which recurs in chs. 17–21.

4 But his father and his mother knew not that it *was* [a]of the LORD, that he sought an occasion against the Philistines: for at that time [b]the Philistines had dominion over Israel.

5 Then went Samson down, and his father and his mother, *to* Timnath, and came to the vineyards of Timnath: and behold, a young lion roared [1]against him.

6 And [a]the spirit of the LORD came mightily upon him, and he rent him as *he* would have rent a kid, and *he had* nothing in his hand: but he told not his father or his mother what he had done.

7 And he went down, and talked with the woman; and she pleased Samson well.

8 ¶ And after a time he returned to take her, and he turned aside to see the carcase of the lion: and behold, *there was* a swarm of bees and honey in the carcase of the lion.

9 And he took thereof in his hands, and went on eating, and came to his father and mother, and he gave them, and they did eat: but he told not them that he had taken the honey out of the carcase of the lion.

10 So his father went down unto the woman: and Samson made there a feast; for so used the young men to do.

11 And it came to pass, when they saw him, that they brought thirty companions to be with him.

12 And Samson said unto them, I will now [a]put forth a riddle unto you: if you can certainly declare it me [b]*within* the seven days of the feast, and find *it* out, then I will give you thirty [1]sheets and thirty [c]change of garments:

13 But if ye cannot declare *it* me, then shall ye give me thirty [1]sheets and thirty change of garments. And they said unto him, Put forth thy riddle, that we may hear it.

14 And he said unto them,

Out of the eater came forth meat,
And out of the strong came forth
sweetness.

And they could not *in* three days expound the riddle.

15 And it came to pass on the seventh day, that they said unto Samson's wife, [a]Entice thy husband, that he may declare unto us the riddle, [b]lest we burn thee and thy father's house with fire: have ye called us [1]to take that we have? *is it* not *so?*

16 And Samson's wife wept before him, and said, [a]Thou dost but hate me, and lovest me not: thou hast put forth a riddle unto the children of my people, and hast not told *it* me. And he said unto her, Behold, I have not told *it* my father nor my mother, and shall I tell *it* thee?

17 And she wept before him [1]the seven days, while their feast lasted: and it came to pass on the seventh day, that he told her, because she lay sore upon him: and she told the riddle to the children of her people.

18 And the men of the city said unto him on the seventh day before the sun went down,

What *is* sweeter than honey?
And what *is* stronger than a lion?

And he said unto them,

If ye had not plowed with my heifer,
Ye had not found out my riddle.

19 And [a]the spirit of the LORD came upon him, and he went down *to* Ashkelon, and slew thirty men of them, and took their [1]spoil, and gave change *of garments* unto them which expounded the riddle. And his anger was kindled, and he went up *to* his father's house.

20 But Samson's wife [a]was *given* to his companion, whom he had used as [b]his friend.

The revenge of Samson

15 But it came to pass within a while after, in the time of wheat harvest, that Samson visited his wife with a kid; and he said, I will go in to my wife into the chamber. But her father would not suffer him to go in.

2 And her father said, I verily thought that thou hadst utterly [a]hated her; therefore I gave her to thy companion: *is* not her younger sister fairer than she? [1]take her, I pray thee, instead of her.

14:4 [a]Josh. 11:20; 1 Ki. 12:15; 2 Ki. 6:33; 2 Chr. 10:15; 22:7; 25:20 [b]ch. 13:1; Deut. 28:48
14:5 [1]Heb. *in meeting him*
14:6 [a]ch. 3:10; 13:25; 1 Sam. 11:6
14:12 [1]Or, *shirts* [a]1 Ki. 10:1; Ezek. 17:2; Luke 14:7 [b]Gen. 29:27 [c]Gen. 45:22; 2 Ki. 5:22
14:13 [1]Or, *shirts*
14:15 [1]Heb. *to possess us,* or, *to impoverish us?* [a]ch. 16:5 [b]ch. 15:6
14:16 [a]ch. 16:15
14:17 [1]Or, the rest of *the seven days, etc.*
14:19 [1]Or, *apparel* [a]ch. 3:10; 13:25
14:20 [a]ch. 15:2 [b]John 3:29
15:2 [1]Heb. *let her be thine* [a]ch. 14:20

14:4 *it was of the LORD.* See Josh 11:20; 1 Ki 12:15. The Lord uses even the sinful weaknesses of men to accomplish His purposes and bring praise to His name (see Gen 45:8; 50:20; 2 Chr 25:20; Acts 2:23; 4:28; Rom 8:28–29).
14:5 *vineyards of Timnath.* The Sorek Valley (in which Timnah was located) and its surrounding areas were noted for their luxurious vineyards. *young lion.* Lions were once common in southern Canaan (see 1 Sam 17:34; 2 Sam 23:20; 1 Ki 13:24; 20:36).
14:6 *spirit . . . came mightily upon him.* See 13:25; 14:19; 15:14; see also notes on 3:10; 11:29. *rent him.* David (1 Sam 17:34–37) and Benaiah (2 Sam 23:20) later performed similar feats.
14:10 *feast.* Such a special feast was common in the ancient Near East (see Gen 29:22) and here lasted seven days (v. 12; see Gen 29:27). Since it would have included drinking wine, Samson may have violated his Nazarite vow (see 13:4,7).
14:11 *companions.* These are the "attendants of the bridegroom" (cf. Mat 9:15). They were probably charged with protecting the wedding party against marauders.
14:12 *riddle.* The use of riddles at feasts and special occasions was popular in the ancient world. *change of garments.* Mentioned, together with silver, as gifts of great value in Gen 45:22; 2 Ki 5:22 (see also Zech 14:14).
14:16 *lovest me not.* Delilah used the same tactics (16:15).
14:18 *my heifer.* Samson's wife (see v. 15). Since heifers were not used for plowing, Samson is accusing them of unfairness.
14:19 *spirit . . . came upon him.* God's purposes for Samson included humbling the Philistines. *Ashkelon.* One of the five principal cities of the Philistines (see map, p. 313).
14:20 *companion.* See 15:2; probably the young man who had attended Samson (cf. John 3:29), in all likelihood one of his 30 companions (v. 11).
15:1 *time of wheat harvest.* Near the end of May or the beginning of June (see note on Ruth 1:22). *kid.* Such a gift was customary, as with Judah and Tamar (Gen 38:17).
15:2 *younger sister.* Samson's father-in-law felt he had to make a counterproposal because he had received the bride-price from Samson. Similar marital transactions were made by Laban and Jacob (Gen 29:16–28) and Saul and David (1 Sam 18:19–21).

3 And Samson said concerning them,
[1] Now shall I be more blameless than the Philistines, though I do them a displeasure.
4 And Samson went and caught three hundred foxes, and took [1] firebrands, and turned
tail to tail, and put a firebrand in the midst between two tails.
5 And when he had set the brands on fire,
he let *them* go into the standing corn of the
Philistines, and burnt up both the shocks, and
also the standing corn, with the vineyards *and*
olives.
6 Then the Philistines said, Who hath done
this? And they answered, Samson, the son in
law of the Timnite, because he had taken his
wife, and given her to his companion. [a] And
the Philistines came up, and burnt her and her
father with fire.
7 And Samson said unto them, Though ye
have done this, yet will I be avenged of you,
and after *that* I will cease.
8 And he smote them hip and thigh *with* a
great slaughter: and he went down and dwelt
in the top of the rock Etam.
9 ¶ Then the Philistines went up, and
pitched in Judah, and spread themselves [a] in
Lehi.
10 And the men of Judah said, Why are ye
come up against us? And they answered, To
bind Samson are we come up, to do to him as
he hath done to us.
11 Then three thousand men of Judah
[1] went to the top of the rock Etam, and said to
Samson, Knowest thou not that the Philistines
are [a] rulers over us? what *is* this *that* thou hast
done unto us? And he said unto them, As they
did unto me, so have I done unto them.
12 And they said unto him, We are come
down to bind thee, that we may deliver thee
into the hand of the Philistines. And Samson
said unto them, Swear unto me, that ye will
not fall upon me yourselves.
13 And they spake unto him, saying, No;
but we will bind thee fast, and deliver thee
into their hand: but surely we will not kill
thee. And they bound him with two new
cords, and brought him up from the rock.
14 *And* when he came unto Lehi, the Philistines shouted against him: and [a] the spirit of
the LORD came mightily upon him, and the
cords that *were* upon his arms became as flax
that was burnt with fire, and his bands [1] loosed
from off his hands.
15 And he found a [1] new jawbone of an ass,
and put forth his hand, and took it, and [a] slew
a thousand men therewith.
16 And Samson said,

With the jawbone of an ass, [1] heaps
upon heaps,
With the jaw of an ass have I slain a
thousand men.

17 And it came to pass, when he had made
an end of speaking, that he cast away the jawbone out of his hand, and called that place
[1] Ramath-lehi.
18 ¶ And he was sore athirst, and called on
the LORD, and said, [a] Thou hast given this great
deliverance into the hand of thy servant: and
now shall I die for thirst, and fall into the hand
of the uncircumcised?
19 But God clave a hollow place that *was*
in [1] the jaw, and there came water thereout;
and when he had drunk, [a] his spirit came
again, and he revived: wherefore he called the
name thereof [2] En-hakkore, which *is* in Lehi
unto this day.
20 [1] And he judged Israel [a] in the days of
the Philistines twenty years.

Samson and Delilah

16 Then went Samson to Gaza, and saw
there [1] a harlot, and went in unto her.
2 *And it was told* the Gazites, saying, Samson is come hither. And they [a] compassed *him*
in, and laid wait for him all night in the gate of
the city, and were [1] quiet all the night, saying,
In the morning, when it is day, we shall kill
him.
3 And Samson lay till midnight, and arose
at midnight, and took the doors of the gate of

15:3 [1] Or, *Now shall I be blameless from the Philistines, though, etc.* 15:4 [1] Or, *torches* 15:6 [a] ch. 14:15 15:9 [a] ver. 19 15:11 [1] Heb. *went down* [a] ch. 14:4

15:14 [1] Heb. *were melted* [a] ch. 3:10; 14:6 15:15 [1] Heb. *moist* [a] Lev. 26:8; Josh. 23:10; ch. 3:31 15:16 [1] Heb. *a heap, two heaps* 15:17 [1] That is, *the lifting up of the jawbone,* or, *casting away of the jawbone* 15:18 [a] Ps. 3:7 15:19 [1] Or, *Lehi* [2] That is, *the well of him that called,* or, *cried* [a] Gen. 45:27; Is. 40:29 15:20 [1] [He seems to have judged Southwest Israel during twenty years of their servitude of the Philistines] [a] ch. 13:1 16:1 [1] Heb. *a woman a harlot* 16:2 [1] Heb. *silent* [a] 1 Sam. 23:26; Acts 9:24

15:4 *foxes.* The Hebrew word may refer to foxes or jackals, both of which are still found in modern Israel.
15:5 *burnt up.* The wheat harvest (v. 1) comes at the end of a long dry season, thus making the fields extremely vulnerable to fire.
15:7 *be avenged.* A common feature of life in the ancient Near East. Six cities of refuge were designated by the Lord to prevent endless killings (Josh 20:1–9).
15:9 *Lehi.* Means "jawbone." This locality probably did not receive the name until after the events described here; the author uses the name in anticipation of those events—a common device in Hebrew narrative. The exact site of Lehi is not known.
15:11 *three thousand men of Judah.* The only time a force from Judah is explicitly mentioned in connection with any of the judges (but see note on 1:2). The men of Judah were well aware of Samson's capabilities, and even with a large force they did not attempt to tie him up without his consent (vv. 12–13). *Philistines are rulers over us.* Much of Judah was under Philistine rule, and the tribe was apparently content to accept it. They mustered a force, not to support Samson, but to capture him for the Philistines.
15:14 *shouted.* A battle cry (see 1 Sam 17:52). They came shouting against Samson as the lion had come roaring against him (14:5). *spirit of the LORD.* See notes on 3:10; 11:29; 14:19.
15:15 *slew a thousand men therewith.* Cf. the exploits of Shamgar, who struck down 600 Philistines with an ox goad (3:31).
15:18 *shall I die for thirst . . . ?* Mighty Samson was, after all, only a mortal man.
15:19 *came water thereout.* God provided for Samson as He had for Israel in the wilderness. See Ex 17:1–7 (Massah and Meribah); Num 20:2–13 (Meribah).
15:20 *judged Israel . . . years.* See note on 12:7. *twenty years.* Round numbers are frequently used in Judges (see Introduction: Background).
16:1 *Gaza.* An important Philistine seaport on the Mediterranean coast of the southwest portion of Canaan. *harlot.* While Samson certainly possessed physical strength, he lacked moral strength, which ultimately led to his ruin.
16:2 *morning, when it is day.* By that time they expected Samson to be exhausted and sleeping soundly.

the city, and the two posts, and went away
with them, [1]bar and all, and put *them* upon
his shoulders, and carried them up to the top
of a hill that *is* before Hebron.
4 ¶ And it came to pass afterward, that he
loved a woman [1]in the valley of Sorek, whose
name *was* Delilah.
5 And the lords of the Philistines came up
unto her, and said unto her, [a]Entice him, and
see wherein his great strength *lieth,* and by
what *means* we may prevail against him, that
we may bind him to [1]afflict him: and we will
give thee every one *of us* eleven hundred
pieces of silver.
6 And Delilah said to Samson, Tell me, I
pray thee, wherein thy great strength *lieth,*
and wherewith thou mightest be bound to afflict thee.
7 And Samson said unto her, If they bind me
with seven [1]green withs that were never dried,
then shall I be weak, and be as [2]another man.
8 Then the lords of the Philistines brought
up to her seven [1]green withs which had not
been dried, and she bound him with them.
9 Now *there were* men lying in wait, abiding with her in the chamber. And she said
unto him, The Philistines *be* upon thee, Samson. And he brake the withs, as a thread of
tow is broken when it [1]toucheth the fire. So
his strength was not known.
10 And Delilah said unto Samson, Behold,
thou hast mocked me, and told me lies: now
tell me, I pray thee, wherewith thou mightest
be bound.
11 And he said unto her, If they bind me fast
with new ropes [1]that never were occupied,
then shall I be weak, and be as another man.
12 Delilah therefore took new ropes, and
bound him therewith, and said unto him, The
Philistines *be* upon thee, Samson. And *there
were* liers in wait abiding in the chamber. And
he brake them from off his arms like a thread.
13 And Delilah said unto Samson, Hitherto
thou hast mocked me, and told me lies: tell me
wherewith thou mightest be bound. And he
said unto her, If thou weavest the seven locks
of my head with the web.
14 And she fastened *it* with the pin, and
said unto him, The Philistines *be* upon thee,
Samson. And he awaked out of his sleep, and
went away with the pin of the beam, and with
the web.
15 And she said unto him, [a]How canst
thou say, I love thee, when thine heart *is* not
with me? thou hast mocked me these three
times, and hast not told me wherein thy great
strength *lieth.*
16 And it came to pass, when she pressed
him daily with her words, and urged him, *so*
that his soul was [1]vexed unto death;
17 That he [a]told her all his heart, and said
unto her, [b]There hath not come a rasor upon
mine head; for I *have been* a Nazarite unto
God from my mother's womb: if I be shaven,
then my strength will go from me, and I shall
become weak, and be like any *other* man.
18 And when Delilah saw that he had told
her all his heart, she sent and called for the
lords of the Philistines, saying, Come up *this*
once, for he hath shewed me all his heart.
Then the lords of the Philistines came up unto
her, and brought money in their hand.
19 [a]And she made him sleep upon her
knees; and she called for a man, and she
caused *him* to shave off the seven locks of his
head; and she began to afflict him, and his
strength went from him.
20 And she said, The Philistines *be* upon
thee, Samson. And he awoke out of his sleep,
and said, I will go out as at other times *before,*
and shake myself. And he wist not that the
LORD [a]was departed from him.
21 But the Philistines took him, and [1]put
out his eyes, and brought him down to Gaza,
and bound him with fetters of brass; and he
did grind in the prison house.
22 Howbeit the hair of his head began to
grow *again* [1]after he was shaven.

16:3 [1]Heb. *with the bar*
16:4 [1]Or, *by the brook*
16:5 [1]Or, *humble* [a]ch. 14:15
16:7 [1]Or, *new cords.* Heb. *moist* [2]Heb. *one*
16:8 [1]Or, *new cords.* Heb. *moist*
16:9 [1]Heb. *smelleth*
16:11 [1]Heb. *wherewith work hath not been done*
16:15 [a]ch. 14:16
16:16 [1]Heb. *shortened*
16:17 [a]Mic. 7:5 [b]Num. 6:5; ch. 13:5
16:19 [a]Prov. 7:26,27
16:20 [a]Num. 14:9,42,43; Josh. 7:12; 1 Sam. 16:14; 18:12; 28:15,16; 2 Chr. 15:2
16:21 [1]Heb. *bored out*
16:22 [1]Or, *as when he was shaven*

16:3 *bar and all.* Probably made of bronze ("brasen bars," 1 Ki 4:13) or iron (Ps 107:16; Is 45:2). *before Hebron.* That is, in the direction of Hebron, which was 38 miles away in the hill country. Since Hebron was the chief city of Judah, this must be seen as Samson's response to what the men of Judah had done to him (see 15:11–13).

16:5 *lords of the Philistines.* See note on 3:3. *prevail against him.* The Philistines were not interested in killing him quickly; they sought revenge by a prolonged period of torture. *eleven hundred pieces of silver.* An extraordinarily generous payment in light of 17:10 (see note there). (The total amount paid by the five Philistines would have been equivalent to the price of 275 slaves, at the rate offered for Joseph centuries earlier; see Gen 37:28.) Micah stole a similar amount of silver from his mother (17:2).

‡16:7 *seven green withs.* Lit. "new cords." The number seven had special significance to the ancients, symbolizing completeness or fullness. Note that Samson's hair was divided into seven braids (v. 13).

16:11 *new ropes.* The Philistines apparently did not know that this method had already been tried and had failed (15:13–14).

16:13 In disdain, Samson played with his Philistine adversaries.

16:14 *she fastened it with the pin.* Probably from a weaver's shuttle. The details of the account suggest that the loom in question was the vertical type with a crossbeam from which warp threads were suspended. Samson's long hair was woven into the warp and beaten up into the web with the pin, thus forming a tight fabric.

16:19–20 *his strength went from him . . . the LORD was departed from him.* The source of Samson's strength was ultimately God Himself.

16:20 *he wist not.* One of the most tragic statements in the OT. Samson was unaware that he had betrayed his calling. He had permitted a Philistine woman to rob him of the sign of his special consecration to the Lord. The Lord's champion lay asleep and helpless in the arms of his paramour.

16:21 *put out his eyes.* Brutal treatment of prisoners of war to humiliate and incapacitate them was common (see 1 Sam 11:2; 2 Ki 25:7; see also note on Judg 1:6). *to Gaza.* In shame and weakness, Samson was led to Gaza, the place where he had displayed great strength (vv. 1–3). *he did grind in the prison.* See note on 9:53.

Samson's revenge and death

23 ¶ Then the lords of the Philistines gathered them together for to offer a great sacrifice
unto Dagon their god, and to rejoice: for they
said, Our god hath delivered Samson our enemy into our hand.
24 And when the people saw him, they
[a]praised their god: for they said, Our god hath
delivered into our hands our enemy, and the
destroyer of our country, [1]which slew many
of us.
25 And it came to pass, when their hearts
were [a]merry, that they said, Call for Samson,
that he may make us sport. And they called for
Samson out of the prison house; and he made
[1]them sport: and they set him between the
pillars.
26 And Samson said unto the lad that held
him by the hand, Suffer me that I may feel the
pillars whereupon the house standeth, that I
may lean upon them.
27 Now the house was full *of* men and
women; and all the lords of the Philistines
were there; and *there were* upon the [a]roof
about three thousand men and women, that
beheld while Samson made sport.
28 And Samson called unto the LORD, and
said, O Lord GOD, [a]remember me, I pray thee,
and strengthen me, I pray thee, only this once,
O God, that I may be at once avenged of the
Philistines for my two eyes.
29 And Samson took hold of the two middle pillars upon which the house stood, and
[1]on which it was borne up, of the one with his
right hand, and of the other with his left.
30 And Samson said, Let [1]me die with the
Philistines. And he bowed *himself* with *all his*
might; and the house fell upon the lords, and
upon all the people that *were* therein. So the
dead which he slew at his death were moe
than *they* which he slew in his life.
31 Then his brethren and all the house of
his father came down, and took him, and
brought *him* up, and [a]buried him between Zorah and Eshtaol in the buryingplace of Manoah
his father. And he judged Israel twenty years.

Micah's idols and priest

17 And there was a man of mount
Ephraim, whose name *was* Micah.
2 And he said unto his mother, The eleven
hundred *shekels* of silver that were taken from
thee, about which thou cursedst, and spakest
of also in mine ears, behold, the silver *is* with
me; I took it. And his mother said, [a]Blessed *be*
thou of the LORD, my son.
3 And when he had restored the eleven
hundred *shekels* of silver to his mother, his
mother said, I had wholly dedicated the silver
unto the LORD from my hand for my son, to
[a]make a graven image and a molten image:
now therefore I will restore it unto thee.
4 Yet he restored the money unto his mother; and his mother [a]took two hundred *shekels*
of silver, and gave them to the founder, who
made thereof a graven image and a molten image: and they were in the house of Micah.
5 And the man Micah had a house of gods,
and made an [a]ephod, and [b]teraphim, and
[c][1]consecrated one of his sons, who became
his priest.
6 [a]In those days *there was* no king in Israel, [b]*but* every man did *that* which *was* right in
his own eyes.

16:24 [1]Heb. *and who multiplied our slain* [a]Dan. 5:4
16:25 [1]Heb. *before them* [a]ch. 9:27
16:27 [a]Deut. 22:8
16:28 [a]Jer. 15:15
16:29 [1]Or, *he leaned on them*
16:30 [1]Heb. *my soul*
16:31 [a]ch. 13:25
17:2 [a]Gen. 14:19
17:3 [a]See Ex. 20:4,23; Lev. 19:4
17:4 [a]Is. 46:6
17:5 [1]Heb. *filled the hand* [a]ch. 8:27 [b]Gen. 31:19,30; Hos. 3:4 [c]Ex. 29:9
17:6 [a]ch. 18:1; 19:1; 21:25 [b]Deut. 12:8

16:23 *Dagon.* See note on 10:6. *Our god hath delivered.* It was common to attribute a victory to the national deities.
16:27 *upon the roof.* The temple complex probably surrounded an open court and had a flat roof where a large number of people had gathered to get a glimpse of the fallen champion.
16:30 *bowed himself.* Samson pushed the wooden pillars from their stone bases. Archaeologists have discovered a Philistine temple with a pair of closely spaced pillar bases. *slew . . . were moe* [i.e. more]. Samson previously had slain well over 1,000 people (see 15:15; see also 14:19; 15:8).
16:31 *came down, and took him.* The freedom of his family to secure his body and give it a burial indicates that the Philistines had no intention of further dishonoring him (contrast Saul's death, 1 Sam 31:9–10). *judged Israel . . . years.* See note on 12:7. *twenty years.* Round numbers are frequently used in Judges (see Introduction: Background).
17:1–21:25 Two episodes forming an epilogue to the story of the judges (see Introduction: Literary Features). The events narrated evidently took place fairly early in the period of the judges (see notes on 18:30; 20:1,28). They illustrate the religious and moral degeneracy that characterized the age—when "there was no king in Israel" and "every man did that which was right in his own eyes" (17:6; 21:25). Writing at a time when the monarchy under the Davidic dynasty had brought cohesion and order to the land and had reestablished a center for the worship of the Lord, the author portrays this earlier era of the judges as a dismal period of national decay, from which it was to be rescued by the house of David.
17:1–18:31 The first episode illustrates corruption in Israelite worship by telling of Micah's establishment of a local place of worship in Ephraim, aided by a Levite claiming descent from Moses. This paganized worship of the Lord is taken over by the tribe of Dan when that tribe abandons its appointed inheritance and migrates to Israel's northern frontier.
17:2 *eleven hundred shekels of silver.* See note on 16:5. *about which thou cursedst.* Fear of the curse seems to have motivated his returning the stolen money. *Blessed be thou . . . my son.* A blessing to counteract the curse.
17:3 *mother . . . son.* With their paganized view of the God of Israel, both were idolaters in disobedience to the law (Ex 20:4,23; Deut 4:16). *a graven image and a molten image.* The first was probably made of wood overlaid with silver; the second was made of solid silver or of cheaper metal overlaid with silver.
17:4 *founder.* A maker of idols, as in Acts 19:24 (cf. Is 40:19 and Jer 10:9, where the Hebrew for this word is translated "goldsmith").
17:5 *ephod.* See 8:27 and note on Ex 28:6. *teraphim.* Household gods, used in this case for divining (cf. Ezek 21:21; Zech 10:2). Some of them were in human form (1 Sam 19:13).
17:6 *was no king.* See 18:1; 19:1; 21:25; suggests that Judges was written after the establishment of the monarchy (see Introduction: Author and Date). *did that which was right in his own eyes.* The expression implies that Israel had departed from the covenant standards of conduct found in the law (see Deut 12:8).

7 ¶ And there was a young man out of [a]Beth-lehem-judah of the family of Judah, who *was* a Levite, and he sojourned there.

8 And the man departed out of the city from Beth-lehem-judah to sojourn where he could find *a place:* and he came *to* mount Ephraim to the house of Micah, [1]as he journeyed.

9 And Micah said unto him, Whence comest thou? And he said unto him, I *am* a Levite of Beth-lehem-judah, and I go to sojourn where I may find *a place.*

10 And Micah said unto him, Dwell with me, [a]and be unto me a [b]father and a priest, and I will give thee ten *shekels* of silver by the year, and [1]a suit of apparel, and thy victuals. So the Levite went *in.*

11 And the Levite was content to dwell with the man; and the young man was unto him as one of his sons.

12 And Micah [a]consecrated the Levite; and the young man [b]became his priest, and was in the house of Micah.

13 Then said Micah, Now know I that the LORD will do me good, seeing I have a Levite to *my* priest.

Danites overtake Laish

18 In [a]those days *there was* no king in Israel: and in those days [b]the tribe of the Danites sought them an inheritance to dwell *in;* for unto that day *all their* inheritance had not fallen unto them among the tribes of Israel.

2 And the children of Dan sent of their family five men from their coasts, [1]men of valour, from [a]Zorah and from Eshtaol, [b]to spy out the land, and to search it; and they said unto them, Go, search the land: who when they came *to* mount Ephraim, to the [c]house of Micah, they lodged there.

3 When they *were* by the house of Micah, they knew the voice of the young man the Levite: and they turned in thither, and said unto him, Who brought thee hither? and what makest thou in this *place?* and what hast thou here?

4 And he said unto them, Thus and thus dealeth Micah with me, and hath [a]hired me, and I am his priest.

5 And they said unto him, [a]Ask *counsel,* we pray thee, [b]of God, that we may know whether our way which we go shall be prosperous.

6 And the priest said unto them, [a]Go in peace: before the LORD *is* your way wherein ye go.

7 Then the five men departed, and came to [1]Laish, and saw the people that *were* therein, [a]how they dwelt careless, after the manner of the Zidonians, quiet and secure; and *there was* no [2]magistrate in the land, that might put *them* to shame in *any* thing; and they *were* far from the Zidonians, and had no business with *any* man.

8 And they came unto their brethren *to* [a]Zorah and Eshtaol: and their brethren said unto them, What *say* ye?

9 And they said, [a]Arise, that we may go up against them: for we have seen the land, and behold, it *is* very good: and *are* ye [b]still? be not slothful to go, *and* to enter to possess the land.

10 When ye go, ye shall come unto a people [a]secure, and to a large land: for God hath given it into your hands; [b]a place where *there is* no want of any thing that *is* in the earth.

11 ¶ And there went from thence of the family of the Danites, out of Zorah and out of Eshtaol, six hundred men [1]appointed *with* weapons of war.

12 And they went up, and pitched in [a]Kirjath-jearim, in Judah: wherefore they called

17:7 [a]See Josh. 19:15; ch. 19:1; Ruth 1:1,2; Mic. 5:2; Mat. 2:1,5,6
17:8 [1]Heb. *in making his way*
17:10 [1]Or, *a double suit, etc.* Heb. *an order of garments* [a]ch. 18:19 [b]Gen. 45:8; Job 29:16
17:12 [a]ver. 5 [b]ch. 18:30
18:1 [a]ch. 17:6; 21:25 [b]Josh. 19:47
18:2 [1]Heb. *sons* [a]ch. 13:25 [b]Num. 13:17; Josh. 2:1 [c]ch. 17:1
18:4 [a]ch. 17:10
18:5 [a]1 Ki. 22:5; Is. 30:1; Hos. 4:12 [b]See ch. 17:5; ver. 14
18:6 [a]1 Ki. 22:6
18:7 [1][Josh. 19:47, called, *Leshem*] [2]Heb. *possessor,* or, *heir of restraint* [a]ver. 27,28
18:8 [a]ver. 2
18:9 [a]Num. 13:30; Josh. 2:23,24 [b]1 Ki. 22:3
18:10 [a]ver. 7,27 [b]Deut. 8:9
18:11 [1]Heb. *girded*
18:12 [a]Josh. 15:60

17:7 *Beth-lehem-judah.* Not among the 48 designated Levitical cities (Josh 21).
17:8 *departed out of the city.* The failure of the Israelites to obey the law probably resulted in a lack of support for the Levites, which explains the man's wandering in search of his fortune.
17:10 *father.* A term of respect used also for Elijah (2 Ki 2:12) and Elisha (2 Ki 6:21; 13:14). See Gen 45:8; Mat 23:9. *ten shekels.* About four ounces. In the light of this remuneration for a year's service, the stated amounts in 16:5 and 17:2 take on special significance. The offer of wages, clothing and food was more than this Levite could resist (v. 11). Clearly material concerns were at the root of his decision, because later he accepts an even more attractive offer (18:19–20).
17:12 *consecrated the Levite.* An attempt to make his shrine legitimate and give it prestige. Micah probably removed his son (see v. 5).
18:1 *sought them an inheritance.* The Danite allotment was at the west end of the strip of land between Judah and Ephraim (Josh 19:41–46), but, due to the opposition of the Amorites (Judg 1:34) and the Philistines, the Danites were unable to occupy that territory (see note on 13:2).
18:2 *spy out.* See 1:23 and note on Num 13:2.
18:3 *knew the voice.* Perhaps they recognized him by his dialect or accent.
18:5 *Ask counsel . . . of God.* The request is for an oracle, probably by using the ephod and household gods (see note on 17:5). God had already revealed His will by the allotments given to the various tribes (Josh 14–20). They were searching for an oracle that would guarantee the success of their journey.
18:6 *Go in peace.* The Levite gave them the message they wanted to hear. He was even careful to use the name of the Lord to give the message credibility and authority.
18:7 *Laish.* The journey northward was about 100 miles from Zorah and Eshtaol (v. 2). This town is called Leshem in Josh 19:47. After its capture by the Danites, Laish was renamed Dan (v. 29), and it was Israel's northernmost settlement (see 20:1; 1 Sam 3:20; 2 Sam 3:10). Excavations there have disclosed that the earliest Israelite occupation of Dan was in the 12th century B.C. and that the first Israelite inhabitants apparently lived in tents or temporary huts. Occupation of the site continued into the Assyrian period, but the town was destroyed and rebuilt many times. A large high place attached to the city was often extensively rebuilt and refurbished and was in use into the Hellenistic period. *Zidonians.* A peaceful Phoenician people who engaged in commerce throughout the Mediterranean world. *had no business.* They did not feel threatened by other powers and therefore sought no treaties for mutual defense.
18:11 *six hundred men.* As leaders of the tribe of Dan, they represented the entire tribe's migration to its new location in

that place [b]Mahaneh-dan unto this day: behold, *it is* behind Kirjath-jearim.
13 And they passed thence *unto* mount
Ephraim, and came unto [a]the house of Micah.
14 [a]Then answered the five men that went
to spy out the country of Laish, and said unto
their brethren, Do ye know that [b]there is in
these houses an ephod, and teraphim, and a
graven image, and a molten image? now therefore consider what ye have to do.
15 And they turned thitherward, and came
to the house of the young man the Levite, *even*
unto the house of Micah, and [1]saluted him.
16 And the [a]six hundred men appointed
with their weapons of war, which *were* of the
children of Dan, stood *by* the entering of the
gate.
17 And [a]the five men that went to spy out
the land went up, *and* came in thither, *and*
took [b]the graven image, and the ephod, and
the teraphim, and the molten image: and the
priest stood *in* the entering of the gate with
the six hundred men that were appointed *with*
weapons of war.
18 And these went *into* Micah's house, and
fetched the carved image, the ephod, and the
teraphim, and the molten image. Then said
the priest unto them, What do ye?
19 And they said unto him, Hold thy
peace, [a]lay thine hand upon thy mouth, and go
with us, [b]and be to us a father and a priest: *is*
it better for thee to be a priest unto the house
of one man, or that thou be a priest unto a
tribe and a family in Israel?
20 And the priest's heart was glad, and he
took the ephod, and the teraphim, and the
graven image, and went in the midst of the
people.
21 So they turned and departed, and put
the little ones and the cattle and the carriage
before them.
22 ¶ *And* when they were a good way from
the house of Micah, the men that *were* in the
houses near to Micah's house were gathered
together, and overtook the children of Dan.
23 And they cried unto the children of
Dan. And they turned their faces, and said
unto Micah, What aileth thee, [1]that thou
comest with such a company?
24 And he said, Ye have taken away my
gods which I made, and the priest, and ye are
gone away: and what have I more? and what *is*
this *that* ye say unto me, What aileth thee?
25 And the children of Dan said unto him,
Let not thy voice be heard among us, lest [1]an-
gry fellows run upon thee, and thou lose thy
life, with the lives of thy household.
26 And the children of Dan went their
way: and when Micah saw that they *were* too
strong for him, he turned and went back unto
his house.
27 And they took *the things* which Micah
had made, and the priest which he had, and
came unto Laish, unto a people *that were* at quiet and secure: [a]and they smote them with the
edge of the sword, and burnt the city with fire.
28 And *there was* no deliverer, because it
was [a]far from Zidon, and they had no business
with *any* man; and it was in the valley that *li-*
eth [b]by Beth-rehob. And they built a city, and
dwelt therein,
29 And [a]they called the name of the city
[b]Dan, after the name of Dan their father, who
was born unto Israel: howbeit the name of the
city *was* Laish at the first.
30 And the children of Dan set up the
graven image: and Jonathan, the son of Gershom, the son of Manasseh, he and his sons
were priests to the tribe of Dan [a]until the day
of the captivity of the land.
31 And they set them up Micah's graven
image, which he made, [a]all the time that the
house of God was in Shiloh.

The Levite and his concubine

19 And it came to pass in those days,
[a]when *there was* no king in Israel,
that there was a certain Levite sojourning on
the side of mount Ephraim, who took to him
[1]a concubine out of [b]Beth-lehem-judah.

18:12 [b]ch. 13:25
18:13 [a]ver. 2
18:14 [a]1 Sam. 14:28 [b]ch. 17:5
18:15 [1]Heb. *asked him of peace*
18:16 [a]ver. 11
18:17 [a]ver. 2,14 [b]ch. 17:4,5
18:19 [a]Job 21:5; 29:9; 40:4; Mic. 7:16 [b]ch. 17:10
18:23 [1]Heb. *that thou art gathered together?*
18:25 [1]Heb. *bitter of soul*
18:27 [a]Josh. 19:47
18:28 [a]ver. 7 [b]Num. 13:21; 2 Sam. 10:6
18:29 [a]Josh. 19:47 [b]Gen. 14:14; ch. 20:1; 1 Ki. 12:29,30; 15:20
18:30 [a]ch. 13:1; 1 Sam. 4:2,3,10, 11
18:31 [a]Josh. 18:1; ch. 19:18; 21:12
19:1 [1]Heb. *a woman a concubine, or, a wife a concubine* [a]ch. 17:6; 18:1; 21:25 [b]ch. 17:7

the north. Cf. the 600 men who constituted the remnant of the tribe of Benjamin (20:47).

18:19 *father.* See note on 17:10. *a tribe and a family.* Only one clan from the tribe of Dan is ever mentioned—Shuham (Num 26:42; called Hushim in Gen 46:23). The Danites appealed to the Levite's vanity and materialism.

18:21 *before them.* For protection in case of attack; see Gen 33:2–3 (Jacob and Esau).

18:24 *Ye have taken away my gods.* Micah was concerned about the loss of gods that could not even protect themselves. *what have I more?* The agonizing cry of one whose faith is centered in helpless gods.

18:28 *Beth-rehob.* Probably the same as Rehob in Num 13:21.

18:30 *Manasseh.* The original reading appears to have been "Moses" (supported by an ancient Hebrew scribal tradition, some Greek Septuagint manuscripts and the Latin Vulgate). The Levite Jonathan would then be identified as the son of Gershom, the son of Moses (Ex 2:22; 18:3; 1 Chr 23:14–15). In an effort to prevent desecration of the name of Moses, later scribes modified the name slightly, making it read "Manasseh." If Jonathan was the grandson of Moses, the events in this chapter must have occurred early in the period of the judges (see notes on 20:1,28). *captivity of the land.* The date of this captivity has not been determined (see note on v. 7 regarding Laish).

18:31 *all the time that the house of God was in Shiloh.* See Josh 18:1. For Shiloh's destruction see Ps 78:60; Jer 7:12,14; 26:6. Archaeological work at Shiloh indicates that the site was destroyed c. 1050 B.C. and was left uninhabited for many centuries.

19:1–21:25 The second episode of the epilogue (see note on 17:1–18:31). It illustrates Israel's moral corruption by telling of the degenerate act of the men of Gibeah—an act remembered centuries later (Hos 9:9; 10:9). Although that town showed itself to be as wicked as any Canaanite town, it was defended by the rest of the tribe of Benjamin against the Lord's discipline through the Israelites, until nearly the whole tribe was destroyed.

19:1–30 An account of an Israelite town that revived the ways of Sodom (see Gen 19).

19:1 *Levite.* Unlike the Levite of chs. 17–18, this man is not named. *concubine.* See note on Gen 25:6.

2 And his concubine played the whore against him, and went away from him unto her father's house to Beth-lehem-judah, and was there [1]four whole months.

3 And her husband arose, and went after her, to speak [1]friendly unto her, *and* to bring her again, having his servant with him, and a couple of asses: and she brought him *into* her father's house: and when the father of the damsel saw him, he rejoiced to meet him.

4 And his father in law, the damsel's father, retained him; and he abode with him three days: so they did eat and drink, and lodged there.

5 And it came to pass on the fourth day, when they arose early in the morning, that he rose up to depart: and the damsel's father said unto his son in law, [a][1]Comfort thine heart *with* a morsel of bread, and afterward go your way.

6 And they sat down, and did eat and drink both of them together: for the damsel's father had said unto the man, Be content, I pray thee, and tarry all night, and let thine heart be merry.

7 And when the man rose up to depart, his father in law urged him: therefore he lodged there again.

8 And he arose early in the morning on the fifth day to depart: and the damsel's father said, Comfort thine heart, I pray thee. And they tarried [1]until afternoon, and they did eat both of them.

9 And when the man rose up to depart, he, and his concubine, and his servant, his father in law, the damsel's father, said unto him, Behold now, the day [1]draweth towards evening, I pray you tarry all night: behold, [2]the day groweth to an end, lodge here, that thine heart may be merry; and to morrow get you early on your way, that thou mayest go [3]home.

10 But the man would not tarry *that* night, but he rose up and departed, and came [1]over against [a]Jebus, which *is* Jerusalem; and *there were* with him two asses saddled, his concubine also *was* with him.

11 *And* when they *were* by Jebus, the day was far spent; and the servant said unto his master, Come, I pray thee, and let us turn in into this city [a]of the Jebusites, and lodge in it.

12 And his master said unto him, We will not turn aside hither into the city of a stranger, that *is* not of the children of Israel; we will pass over [a]to Gibeah.

13 And he said unto his servant, Come, and let us draw near to one of *these* places to lodge all night, in Gibeah, or in [a]Ramah.

14 And they passed on and went *their way;* and the sun went down upon them *when they were* by Gibeah, which *belongeth* to Benjamin.

15 And they turned aside thither, to go in *and* to lodge in Gibeah: and when he went in, he sat him down in a street of the city: for *there was* no man that [a]took them into *his* house to lodging.

16 ¶ And behold, there came an old man from [a]his work out of the field at even, which *was* also of mount Ephraim; and he sojourned in Gibeah: but the men of the place *were* Benjamites.

17 And when he had lift up his eyes, he saw a wayfaring man in the street of the city: and the old man said, Whither goest thou? and whence comest thou?

18 And he said unto him, We are passing from Beth-lehem-judah toward the side of mount Ephraim; from thence *am* I: and I went to Beth-lehem-judah, but I am *now* going *to* [a]the house of the LORD; and there *is* no man that [1]receiveth me to house.

19 Yet there is both straw and provender for our asses; and there is bread and wine also for me, and for thy handmaid, and for the young man *which is* with thy servants: *there is* no want of any thing.

20 And the old man said, [a]Peace *be* with thee; howsoever *let* all thy wants *lie* upon me; [b]only lodge not in the street.

21 [a]So he brought him into his house, and gave provender unto the asses: [b]and they washed their feet, and did eat and drink.

22 *Now* as they were making their hearts merry, behold, [a]the men of the city, certain [b]sons of Belial, beset the house round about, *and* beat at the door, and spake to the master of the house, the old man, saying, [c]Bring forth the man that came into thine house, that we may know him.

23 And [a]the man, the master of the house,

19:2 [1]Or, *a year and four months.* Heb. *days, four months*
19:3 [1]Heb. *to her heart*
19:5 [1]Heb. *Strengthen* [a]Gen. 18:5
19:8 [1]Heb. *till the day declined*
19:9 [1]Heb. *is weak* [2]Heb. it is *the pitching* time *of the day* [3]Heb. *to thy tent*
19:10 [1]Heb. *to over against Jebus* [a]Josh. 18:28
19:11 [a]Josh. 15:8,63
19:12 [a]Josh. 18:28
19:13 [a]Josh. 18:25
19:15 [a]Mat. 25:43
19:16 [a]Ps. 104:23
19:18 [1]Heb. *gathereth* [a]Josh. 18:1; ch. 18:31; 20:18; 1 Sam. 1:3,7
19:20 [a]Gen 43:23; ch. 6:23 [b]Gen. 19:2
19:21 [a]Gen. 24:32; 43:24 [b]Gen. 18:4; John 13:5
19:22 [a]Gen. 19:4; ch. 20:5; Hos. 9:9; 10:9 [b]Deut. 13:13 [c]Gen 19:5; Rom. 1:26,27
19:23 [a]Gen. 19:6,7

19:3 *rejoiced to meet him.* The separation of the concubine from the Levite was probably a matter of family disgrace, and so his father-in-law was glad for the prospect of the two being reunited.

19:10 *Jebus.* See 1:21; see also note on Gen 10:16.

19:12 *city of a stranger.* With the city under the control of the Jebusites, the Levite was afraid that he would receive no hospitality and might be in mortal danger.

19:14 *Gibeah . . . Benjamin.* Distinguished from the Gibeah in Judah (Josh 15:20,57) and the Gibeah in the hill country of Ephraim (Josh 24:33). As the political capital of Saul's kingdom, it is called Gibeah of Saul in 1 Sam 11:4; see also 1 Sam 13:15.

19:15 *took them into his house.* See notes on 13:15; Gen 18:2.

19:18 *the house of the LORD.* Apparently the Levite was planning to go to Shiloh (see 18:31; Josh 18:1) to present a thank offering to the Lord or a sin offering for himself and his concubine.

19:21 *washed their feet.* An evidence of hospitality in the ancient Near East, where travelers commonly wore sandals as they walked the dusty roads (see Gen 18:4; 24:32; 43:24; Luke 7:44; John 13:5–14).

19:22 *sons of Belial.* The Hebrew for this expression refers to the morally depraved (see note on Deut 13:13). Elsewhere the expression is associated with idolatry (Deut 13:13), drunkenness (1 Sam 1:16) and rebellion (1 Sam 2:12). Here the reference is to homosexuality. *Bring forth the man.* The sexual perversion of these wicked men is yet another example of the decadence of an age when "every man did that which was right in his own eyes" (17:6; 21:25). A similar request was made by the men of Sodom (Gen 19:5). Homosexuality was common among the Canaanites.

went out unto them, and said unto them, Nay,
my brethren, *nay,* I pray you, do not *so*
wickedly; seeing that this man is come into
mine house, [b]do not this folly.
24 [a]Behold, *here is* my daughter a maiden,
and his concubine; them I will bring out now,
and [b]humble ye them, and do with them what
seemeth good unto you: but unto this man do
not [1]so vile a thing.
25 But the men would not hearken to him:
so the man took his concubine, and brought
her forth unto them; and they [a]knew her, and
abused her all the night until the morning: and
when the day began to spring, they let her go.
26 Then came the woman in the dawning
of the day, and fell down *at* the door of the
man's house where her lord *was,* till it was
light.
27 And her lord rose up in the morning,
and opened the doors of the house, and went
out to go his way: and behold, the woman his
concubine *was* fallen down *at* the door of the
house, and her hands *were* upon the threshold.
28 And he said unto her, Up, and let us be
going. But [a]none answered. Then the man
took her *up* upon an ass, and the man rose up,
and gat him unto his place.
29 ¶ And when he was come into his
house, he took a knife, and laid hold on his
concubine, and [a]divided her, *together* with
her bones, into twelve pieces, and sent her
into all the coasts of Israel.
30 And it was so, that all that saw it said,
There was no such *deed* done nor seen from
the day that the children of Israel came up out
of the land of Egypt unto this day: consider of
it, [a]take advice, and speak *your minds.*

The rout of Benjamin

20 Then [a]all the children of Israel went
out, and the congregation was gathered together as one man, from [b]Dan even to
Beer-sheba, with the land of Gilead, unto the
LORD [c]*in* Mizpeh.
2 And the chief of all the people, *even* of all
the tribes of Israel, presented themselves in
the assembly of the people of God, four hundred thousand footmen [a]that drew sword.
3 (Now the children of Benjamin heard
that the children of Israel were gone up *to*
Mizpeh.) Then said the children of Israel, Tell
us, how was this wickedness?
4 And [1]the Levite, the husband of the
woman that was slain, answered and said, [a]I
came into Gibeah that *belongeth* to Benjamin,
I and my concubine, to lodge.
5 [a]And the men of Gibeah rose against me,
and beset the house round about upon me by
night, *and* thought to have slain me: [b]and my
concubine have they [1]forced, that she is dead.
6 And [a]I took my concubine, and cut her in
pieces, and sent her throughout all the country of the inheritance of Israel: for they [b]have
committed lewdness and folly in Israel.
7 Behold, ye *are* all children of Israel; [a]give
here your advice and counsel.
8 And all the people arose as one man, saying, We will not any *of us* go to his tent, neither will we any *of us* turn into his house.
9 But now this *shall be* the thing which we
will do to Gibeah; *we will go up* by lot against
it;
10 And we will take ten men of an hundred throughout all the tribes of Israel, and an
hundred of a thousand, and a thousand out of
ten thousand, to fetch victual for the people,
that *they* may do, when they come to Gibeah
of Benjamin, according to all the folly that they
have wrought in Israel.
11 So all the men of Israel were gathered
against the city, [1]knit together as one man.
12 ¶ [a]And the tribes of Israel sent men
through all the tribe of Benjamin, saying, What
wickedness *is* this that is done among you?
13 Now therefore deliver *us* the men, [a]the
children of Belial, which *are* in Gibeah, that
we may put them to death, and [b]put away evil
from Israel. But the children of Benjamin

19:23 [b]2 Sam. 13:12
19:24 [1]Heb. *the matter of this folly* [a]Gen. 19:8 [b]Gen. 34:2; Deut. 21:14
19:25 [a]Gen. 4:1
19:28 [a]ch. 20:5
19:29 [a]ch. 20:6; See 1 Sam. 11:7
19:30 [a]ch. 20:7
20:1 [a]ver. 11; Josh. 22:12; ch. 21:5; 1 Sam. 11:7 [b]ch. 18:29; 1 Sam. 3:20; 2 Sam. 3:10; 24:2 [c]Judg. 10:17; 11:11; 1 Sam. 7:5; 10:17
20:2 [a]ch. 8:10
20:4 [1]Heb. *the man the Levite* [a]ch. 19:15
20:5 [1]Heb. *humbled* [a]ch. 19:22 [b]ch. 19:25,26
20:6 [a]ch. 19:29 [b]Josh. 7:15
20:7 [a]ch. 19:30
20:11 [1]Heb. *fellows*
20:12 [a]Deut. 13:14; Josh. 22:13,16
20:13 [a]Deut. 13:13; ch. 19:22 [b]Deut. 17:12

19:23 *do not so wickedly.* An expression of outrage at the willful perversion of what is right and natural (see Gen 19:7; 2 Sam 13:12; see also Rom 1:27).

19:24 *my daughter a maiden, and his concubine.* The tragedy of this story lies not only in the decadence of Gibeah, but also in the callous selfishness of men who would betray defenseless women to be brutally violated for a whole night. Cf. Gen 19:8, where Lot offered his two daughters to the men of Sodom.

19:29 *divided her . . . into twelve pieces.* Dismembering the concubine's body and sending parts to each of the 12 tribes was intended to awaken Israel from its moral lethargy and to marshal the tribes to face up to their responsibility. It is ironic that the one who issued such a call was himself so selfish and insensitive. See also Saul's similar action in 1 Sam 11:7.

20:1–48 All Israel (except Jabesh-gilead; see 21:8–9) assembled before the Lord to deal with the moral outrage committed by the men of Gibeah. Having first inquired of God for divine direction, they marched against Gibeah and the Benjamites as the disciplinary arm of the Lord (see Josh 22:11–34), following Him as their King.

20:1 *gathered together . . . in Mizpeh.* A gathering place of the tribes during the days of Saul (1 Sam 7:5–17; 10:17). *as one man.* Cf. vv. 8,11; 1 Sam 11:7. *Dan even to Beer-sheba.* A conventional way of speaking of all Israel from north (Dan) to south (Beer-sheba); see 1 Sam 3:20; 2 Sam 3:10; 24:2; 1 Chr 21:2; 2 Chr 30:5. The use of this expression, however, does not mean that the events of this chapter occurred after Dan's move to the north (18:27–29); rather, it indicates the author's perspective at the time of writing (Judges was probably written after the Davidic dynasty was fully established; see Introduction: Author and Date). Here the expression refers to the disciplinary action of all Israel (except Jabesh-gilead; see 21:8–9) against Gibeah and the rest of the Benjamites. Such a united response must have occurred early in the time of the judges, before the period of foreign domination of various parts of the land.

20:9 *lot.* Casting lots was a common method of determining the will of God (see notes on Ex 28:30; Jonah 1:7; Acts 1:26).

20:10 *ten men.* Support for the large army had to be well organized and efficient. One man was responsible for providing food for nine men fighting at the front.

20:13 *deliver us . . . the children of Belial.* The demand of Israel was not unreasonable. They wanted to punish only those

would not hearken to the voice of their brethren the children of Israel:

14 But the children of Benjamin gathered themselves together out of the cities unto Gibeah, to go out to battle against the children of Israel.

15 And the children of Benjamin were numbered at that time out of the cities twenty and six thousand men that drew sword, beside the inhabitants of Gibeah, *which* were numbered seven hundred chosen men.

16 Among all this people *there were* seven hundred chosen men [a]lefthanded; every one could sling stones at a hair *breadth,* and not miss.

17 And the men of Israel, beside Benjamin, were numbered four hundred thousand men that drew sword: all these *were* men of war.

18 ¶ And the children of Israel arose, and [a]went up *to* the house of God, and [b]asked *counsel* of God, and said, Which of us shall go up first to the battle against the children of Benjamin? And the LORD said, Judah *shall go up* first.

19 And the children of Israel rose up in the morning, and encamped against Gibeah.

20 And the men of Israel went out to battle against Benjamin; and the men of Israel put *themselves* in array to fight against them at Gibeah.

21 And [a]the children of Benjamin came forth out of Gibeah, and destroyed *down* to the ground of the Israelites that day twenty and two thousand men.

22 And the people the men of Israel encouraged themselves, and set *their* battle again in array in the place where they put *themselves* in array the first day.

23 ([a]And the children of Israel went up and wept before the LORD until even, and asked *counsel* of the LORD, saying, Shall I go *up* again to battle against the children of Benjamin my brother? And the LORD said, Go up against him.)

24 And the children of Israel came near against the children of Benjamin the second day.

25 And [a]Benjamin went forth against them out of Gibeah the second day, and destroyed *down* to the ground of the children of Israel again eighteen thousand men; all these drew the sword.

26 Then all the children of Israel, and all the people, [a]went up, and came *unto* the house of God, and wept, and sat there before the LORD, and fasted that day until even, and offered burnt offerings and peace offerings before the LORD.

27 And the children of Israel inquired of the LORD, (for [a]the ark of the covenant of God *was* there in those days,

28 [a]And Phinehas, the son of Eleazar, the son of Aaron, [b]stood before it in those days,) saying, Shall I yet again go out to battle against the children of Benjamin my brother, or shall I cease? And the LORD said, Go up; for to morrow I will deliver them into thine hand.

29 And Israel [a]set liers in wait round about Gibeah.

30 And the children of Israel went up against the children of Benjamin on the third day, and put *themselves* in array against Gibeah, as at other times.

31 And the children of Benjamin went out against the people, *and* were drawn away from the city; and they began [1]to smite of the people, *and* kill, as at other times, in the highways, *of* which one goeth up *to* [2]the house of God, and the other to Gibeah in the field, about thirty men of Israel.

32 And the children of Benjamin said, They *are* smitten down before us, as at the first. But the children of Israel said, Let us flee, and draw them from the city unto the highways.

33 And all the men of Israel rose up out of their place, and put *themselves* in array at Baal-tamar: and the liers in wait of Israel came forth out of their places, *even* out of the meadows of Gibeah.

34 And there came against Gibeah ten thousand chosen men out of all Israel, and the battle was sore: [a]but they knew not that evil *was* near them.

35 And the LORD smote Benjamin before Israel: and the children of Israel destroyed of the Benjamites that day twenty and five thousand and an hundred men: all these drew the sword.

36 ¶ So the children of Benjamin saw that they were smitten: [a]for the men of Israel gave place to the Benjamites, because they trusted unto the liers in wait which they had set beside Gibeah.

20:16 [a]ch. 3:15; 1 Chr. 12:2
20:18 [a]ver. 23,26 [b]Num. 27:21; ch. 1:1
20:21 [a]Gen. 49:27
20:23 [a]ver. 26,27
20:25 [a]ver. 21
20:26 [a]ver. 18
20:27 [a]Josh. 18:1; 1 Sam. 4:3,4
20:28 [a]Josh. 24:33 [b]Deut. 10:8; 18:5
20:29 [a]See Josh. 8:4
20:31 [1]Heb. *to smite of the people wounded as at, etc.* [2]Or, *Beth-el*
20:34 [a]Josh. 8:14; Is. 47:11
20:36 [a]Josh. 8:15

directly involved in the crime. *children of Belial.* See note on Deut 13:13. *put them to death.* The sin of the men of Gibeah called for the death penalty, and Israel had to punish the sin if she was to avoid guilt herself (see Deut 13:5; 17:7; 19:19–20).

20:16 *lefthanded.* The Benjamite Ehud was also lefthanded (3:15). *sling stones.* Cf. Zech 9:15. The sling was a very effective weapon, as David later demonstrated in his encounter with Goliath (1 Sam 17:49). A slingstone, weighing one pound or more, could be hurled at 90–100 miles an hour. *miss.* In other contexts the Hebrew for this verb is translated "to sin."

‡20:18 *house of God.* Hebrew is *beth el.* At this time the ark of the covenant and the high priest Phinehas were at Beth-el (see vv. 26–28). *asked counsel of God.* Probably by priestly use of Urim and Thummim (see notes on Ex 28:30; 1 Sam 2:28). *Which of us shall go up first . . . ?* See 1:1–36. *Judah.* See note on 1:2.

20:21 *twenty and two thousand men.* A rousing victory for the Benjamites, who numbered 25,700 and therefore had slain nearly one man apiece.

20:27 *ark.* The only mention of the ark in Judges.

20:28 *Phinehas.* Phinehas was the priest in the tabernacle in the days of Joshua (Josh 22:13), and the fact that he was still serving is further evidence that these events took place early in the days of the judges (see notes on v. 1; 18:30).

20:29 *set liers in wait.* See 9:32; Josh 8:2.

20:33 *Baal-tamar.* Location unknown.

37 [a]And the liers in wait hasted, and rushed upon Gibeah; and the liers in wait [1]drew *themselves* along, and smote all the city with the edge of the sword.

38 Now there was an appointed [1]sign between the men of Israel [2]and the liers in wait, that they should make a great [3]flame with smoke rise up out of the city.

39 And when the men of Israel retired in the battle, Benjamin began [1]to smite *and* kill of the men of Israel about thirty persons: for they said, Surely they are smitten down before us, as *in* the first battle.

40 But when the flame began to arise up out of the city *with* a pillar of smoke, the Benjamites [a]looked behind them, and behold, [1]the flame of the city ascended up to heaven.

41 And when the men of Israel turned *again,* the men of Benjamin were amazed: for they saw that evil [1]was come upon them.

42 Therefore they turned *their backs* before the men of Israel unto the way of the wilderness; but the battle overtook them; and them which *came* out of the cities they destroyed in the midst of them.

43 *Thus* they inclosed the Benjamites round about, *and* chased them, *and* trode them down [1]with ease [2]over against Gibeah toward the sunrising.

44 And there fell of Benjamin eighteen thousand men; all these *were* men of valour.

45 And they turned and fled toward the wilderness unto the rock of [a]Rimmon: and they gleaned of them in the highways five thousand men; and pursued hard after them unto Gidom, and slew two thousand men of them.

46 So that all which fell that day of Benjamin were twenty and five thousand men that drew the sword; all these *were* men of valour.

47 [a]But six hundred men turned and fled to the wilderness unto the rock Rimmon, and abode in the rock Rimmon four months.

48 And the men of Israel turned again upon the children of Benjamin, and smote them with the edge of the sword, as well the men of *every* city, as the beast, and all that [1]came to hand: also they set on fire all the cities that [2]they came to.

Wives for the Benjamites

21 Now [a]the men of Israel had sworn in Mizpeh, saying, There shall not any of us give his daughter unto Benjamin to wife.

2 And the people came [a]*to* the house of God, and abode there till even before God, and lift up their voices, and wept sore;

3 And said, O LORD God of Israel, why is this come to pass in Israel, that there should be to day one tribe lacking in Israel?

4 And it came to pass on the morrow, that the people rose early, and [a]built there an altar, and offered burnt offerings and peace offerings.

5 And the children of Israel said, Who *is there* among all the tribes of Israel that came not up with the congregation unto the LORD? [a]For *they* had made a great oath concerning *him* that came not up to the LORD *to* Mizpeh, saying, He shall surely be put to death.

6 And the children of Israel repented them for Benjamin their brother, and said, There is one tribe cut off from Israel *this* day.

7 How shall we do for wives for them that remain, seeing we have sworn by the LORD that *we* will not give them of our daughters to wives?

8 And they said, What one *is there* of the tribes of Israel that came not up *to* Mizpeh to the LORD? And behold, there came none to the camp from [a]Jabesh-gilead to the assembly.

9 For the people were numbered, and behold, *there were* none of the inhabitants of Jabesh-gilead there.

10 And the congregation sent thither twelve thousand men of the valiantest, and commanded them, saying, [a]Go and smite the inhabitants of Jabesh-gilead with the edge of the sword, with the women and the children.

11 And this *is* the thing that ye shall do, [a]Ye shall utterly destroy every male, and every woman that [1]hath lien by man.

20:37 [1]Or, *made a long* sound with the trumpet [a]Josh. 8:19
20:38 [1]Or, *time* [2]Heb. *with* [3]Heb. *elevation*
20:39 [1]Heb. *to smite the wounded*
20:40 [1]Heb. *the whole* consumption [a]Josh. 8:20
20:41 [1]Heb. *touched them*
20:43 [1]Or, from *Menuchah, etc.* [2]Heb. *unto over against*
20:45 [a]Josh. 15:32
20:47 [a]ch. 21:13
20:48 [1]Heb. *was found* [2]Heb. *were found*
21:1 [a]ch. 20:1
21:2 [a]ch. 20:18,26
21:4 [a]2 Sam. 24:25
21:5 [a]ch. 5:23
21:8 [a]1 Sam 11:1; 31:11
21:10 [a]ver. 5; ch. 5:23; 1 Sam. 11:7
21:11 [1]Heb. *knoweth the lying with man* [a]Num. 31:17

20:36b–45 Details of the account in vv. 29–36a.
20:46 *twenty and five thousand.* A round number for 25,100 (v. 35).
20:47 *six hundred men.* If these had not escaped, the tribe of Benjamin would have been annihilated. The same number of Danites went to Laish (18:11).
21:1–25 Second thoughts about the slaughter of their Benjamite brothers caused the Israelites to grieve over the loss. Only 600 Benjamites were left alive, and the men of Israel decided to provide wives for them in order to keep the tribe from disappearing. After slaughtering most of the people of Jabesh-gilead, the Israelites took 400 girls from the survivors and gave them to 400 Benjamites. Shortly afterward, each of the remaining Benjamites seized a wife from the girls of Shiloh, and Benjamin began to be restored.
21:1 *sworn.* This vow, probably taken in the name of the Lord, was not an ordinary vow but invoked a curse on oneself if the vow was broken (v. 18; see also Acts 23:12–15).
21:2 *house of God.* See 20:18,26–27. *wept sore.* Earlier the Israelites wept because they were defeated by the Benjamites (20:23,26). Now they weep because the disciplinary action against the Benjamites has nearly annihilated one of the tribes (see v. 3).
21:5 *came not up with the congregation.* The tribes had a mutual responsibility in times of military action (see note on 5:13–18). Those who failed to participate were often singled out and sometimes punished (5:15–17,23). *great oath.* Complicating the situation for Israel was the fact that they had taken a second oath, calling for the death of those who did not participate in the battle.
21:10 *twelve thousand.* A thousand from each tribe (see Num 31:6), with 1,000 supplied to represent the tribe of Benjamin.
21:11 *destroy every male.* The punishment of Jabesh-gilead seems brutal, but the covenant bond between the tribes was extremely important. Even though delinquency on some occasions was not punished (5:15–17), the nature of the crime in this case, coupled with Benjamin's refusal to turn over the criminals, caused Israel to take this oath (v. 5).

12 And they found among the inhabitants
of Jabesh-gilead four hundred [1]young virgins,
that had known no man by lying with *any*
male: and they brought them unto the camp *to*
[a]Shiloh, which *is* in the land of Canaan.
13 And the whole congregation sent *some*
[1]to speak to the children of Benjamin [a]that
were in the rock Rimmon, and to [b][2]call peaceably unto them.
14 And Benjamin came again at that time;
and they gave them wives which they had
saved alive of the women of Jabesh-gilead: and
yet so they sufficed them not.
15 And the people [a]repented them for Benjamin, because that the LORD had made a
breach in the tribes of Israel.
16 ¶ Then the elders of the congregation
said, How shall we do for wives for them that
remain, seeing the women are destroyed out
of Benjamin?
17 And they said, *There must be* an inheritance for them that be escaped of Benjamin,
that a tribe be not destroyed out of Israel.
18 Howbeit we may not give them wives of
our daughters: [a]for the children of Israel have
sworn, saying, Cursed *be* he that giveth a wife
to Benjamin.
19 Then they said, Behold, *there is* a feast
of the LORD in Shiloh [1]yearly *in a place* which
is on the north side of Beth-el, [2]on the east
side [3]of the highway that goeth up from Beth-
el to Shechem, and on the south of Lebonah.
20 Therefore they commanded the children of Benjamin, saying, Go and lie in wait in
the vineyards;
21 And see, and behold, if the daughters of
Shiloh come out [a]to dance in dances, then
come ye out of the vineyards, and catch you
every man his wife of the daughters of Shiloh,
and go *to* the land of Benjamin.
22 And it shall be, when their fathers or
their brethren come unto us to complain, that
we will say unto them, [1]Be favourable unto
them for our sakes: because we reserved not
to each man his wife in the war: for ye did not
give unto them at *this* time, *that* you should be
guilty.
23 And the children of Benjamin did so,
and took *them* wives, according to their number, of them that danced, whom they caught:
and they went and returned unto their inheritance, and [a]repaired the cities, and dwelt in
them.
24 And the children of Israel departed
thence at that time, every man to his tribe and
to his family, and they went out from thence
every man to his inheritance.
25 [a]In those days *there was* no king in Israel: [b]every man did *that* which *was* right in
his own eyes.

21:12 [1]Heb. *young women virgins* [a]Josh. 18:1
21:13 [1]Heb. *and spake and called* [2]Or, *proclaim peace* [a]ch. 20:47 [b]Deut. 20:10
21:15 [a]ver. 6
21:18 [a]ver. 1; ch. 11:35
21:19 [1]Heb. *from year to year* [2]Or, *towards the sunrising*
21:19 [3]Or, *on*
21:21 [a]See Ex. 15:20; ch. 11:34; 1 Sam. 18:6
21:22 [1]Or, *Gratify us in them*
21:23 [a]See ch. 20:48
21:25 [a]ch. 17:6; 18:1; 19:1 [b]Deut. 12:8; ch. 17:6

21:12 *Canaan.* Emphasizes the fact that the women were brought across the Jordan from the east.
21:19 *feast of the LORD.* In light of the mention of vineyards (v. 20), it is likely that this reference is to the feast of tabernacles (see note on 1 Sam 1:3), though it may have been a local festival. *north side of Beth-el . . . south of Lebonah.* This detailed description of Shiloh's location may indicate that this material was written at a time when Shiloh was in ruins, perhaps after its destruction during the battle of Aphek (1 Sam 4:1–11).
21:21 *catch . . . his wife.* With the Benjamites securing wives in this manner, the other tribes were not actually "giving" their daughters to them (see note on v. 22).
21:22 *when their fathers or their brethren . . . complain.* It was customary for the brothers of a girl who had been abducted to demand satisfaction (see Gen 34:7–31; 2 Sam 13:20–38). It was therefore important that the elders anticipate this response and be prepared to get cooperation from the girls' families.
21:24 *went out from thence.* These soldiers had probably been away from home at least five months (see 20:47).
‡21:25 *there was no king in Israel.* See note on 17:6. The book of Judges ends with the reminder that Israel was still awaiting the arrival of its rightful King.

The Book of
Ruth

INTRODUCTION

Title

The book is named after one of its main characters, a young woman of Moab, the great-grandmother of David and an ancestress of Jesus (Mat 1:1,5). The only other Biblical book bearing the name of a woman is Esther.

Background

The story is set in the time of the judges, a time characterized in the book of Judges as a period of religious and moral degeneracy, national disunity and general foreign oppression. The book of Ruth reflects a temporary time of peace between Israel and Moab (contrast Judg 3:12–30). Like 1 Sam 1—2, it gives a series of intimate glimpses into the private lives of the members of an Israelite family. It also presents a delightful account of the remnant of true faith and piety in the period of the judges, relieving an otherwise wholly dark picture of that era.

Author and Date of Writing

The author is unknown. Jewish tradition points to Samuel, but it is unlikely that he is the author because the mention of David (4:17,22) implies a later date. Further, the literary style of Hebrew used in Ruth suggests that it was written during the period of the monarchy.

Theme and Theology

The author focuses on Ruth's unswerving and selfless devotion to desolate Naomi (1:16–17; 2:11–12; 3:10; 4:15) and on Boaz's kindness to these two widows (chs. 2—4). He presents striking examples of lives that embody in their daily affairs the self-giving love that fulfills God's law (Lev 19:18; cf. Rom 13:10). Such love also reflects God's love, in a marvelous joining of man's actions with God's (compare 2:12 with 3:9). In God's benevolence such lives are blessed and are made a blessing.

It may seem surprising that one who reflects God's love so clearly is a Moabitess (see map, p. 347). Yet her complete loyalty to the Israelite family into which she has been received by marriage and her total devotion to her desolate mother-in-law mark her as a true daughter of Israel and a worthy ancestress of David. She strikingly exemplifies the truth that participation in the coming kingdom of God is decided, not by blood and birth, but by the conformity of one's life to the will of God through the "obedience to the faith" (Rom 1:5). Her place in the ancestry of David signifies that all nations will be represented in the kingdom of David's greater Son.

As an episode in the ancestry of David, the book of Ruth sheds light on his role in the history of redemption. Redemption is a key concept throughout the account; the Hebrew word in its various forms occurs 23 times. The book is primarily a story of Naomi's transformation from despair to happiness through the selfless, God-blessed acts of Ruth and Boaz. She moves from emptiness to fullness (1:21; 3:17; see notes on 1:1,3,5–6,12,21–22; 3:17; 4:15), from destitution (1:1–5) to security and hope (4:13–17). Similarly, Israel was transformed from national desperation at the death of Eli (1 Sam 4:18) to peace and prosperity in the early days of Solomon (1 Ki 4:20–34; 5:4) through the selfless devotion of David, a true descendant of Ruth and Boaz. The author thus reminded Israel that the reign of the house of David, as the means of God's benevolent rule in Israel, held the prospect of God's promised peace and rest. But this rest would continue only so long as those who participated in the kingdom—prince and people alike—reflected in their daily lives the selfless love exemplified by Ruth and Boaz. In Jesus, the great "son of David" (Mat 1:1), and His redemptive work, the promised blessings of the kingdom of God find their fulfillment.

Literary Features

The book of Ruth is a Hebrew short story, told with consummate skill. Among historical narratives in Scripture it is unexcelled in its compactness, vividness, warmth, beauty and dramatic effectiveness—an exquisitely wrought jewel of Hebrew narrative art.

Marvelously symmetrical throughout (see Outline), the action moves from a briefly sketched account of distress (1:1–5; 71 words in Hebrew) through four episodes to a concluding account of relief and hope that is drawn with equal brevity (4:13–17; 71 words in Hebrew). The crucial turning point occurs exactly midway (see note on 2:20). The opening line of each of the four episodes signals its main development (1:6, the return; 2:1, the meeting with Boaz; 3:1, finding a home for Ruth; 4:1, the decisive event at the gate), while the closing line of each episode facilitates transition to what follows (see notes on 1:22; 2:23; 3:18; 4:12). Contrast is also used to good effect: pleasant (the meaning of "Naomi") and bitter (1:20), full and empty (1:21), and the living and the dead (2:20). Most striking is the contrast between two of the main characters, Ruth and Boaz: The one is a young, alien, destitute widow, while the other is a middle-aged, well-to-do Israelite securely established in his home community. For each there is a corresponding character whose actions highlight, by contrast, his or her selfless acts: Ruth—Orpah, Boaz—the unnamed kinsman.

When movements in space, time and circumstance all correspond in some way, a harmony results that both satisfies the reader's artistic sense and helps open doors to understanding. The author of Ruth keeps his readers from being distracted from the central story—Naomi's passage from emptiness to fullness through the selfless acts of Ruth and Boaz (see Theme and Theology). That passage, or restoration, first takes place in connection with her return from Moab to the promised land and to Beth-lehem ("house of bread"; see note on 1:1). It then progresses with the harvest season, when the fullness of the land is gathered in. All aspects of the story keep the reader's attention focused on the central issue. Consideration of these and other literary devices (mentioned throughout the notes) will aid understanding of the book of Ruth.

Outline

- I. Introduction: Naomi Emptied (1:1–5)
- II. Naomi Returns from Moab (1:6–22)
  - A. Ruth Clings to Naomi (1:6–18)
  - B. Ruth and Naomi Return to Beth-lehem (1:19–22)
- III. Ruth and Boaz Meet in the Harvest Fields (ch. 2)
  - A. Ruth Begins Work (2:1–7)
  - B. Boaz Shows Kindness to Ruth (2:8–16)
  - C. Ruth Returns to Naomi (2:17–23)
- IV. Ruth Goes to Boaz at the Threshingfloor (ch. 3)
  - A. Naomi Instructs Ruth (3:1–5)
  - B. Boaz Pledges to Secure Redemption (3:6–15)
  - C. Ruth Returns to Naomi (3:16–18)
- V. Boaz Arranges to Marry Ruth (4:1–12)
  - A. Boaz Confronts the Unnamed Kinsman (4:1–8)
  - B. Boaz Buys Naomi's Property and Announces His Marriage to Ruth (4:9–12)
- VI. Conclusion: Naomi Filled (4:13–17)
- VII. Epilogue: Genealogy of David (4:18–22)

Naomi and Ruth

1 Now it came to pass in the days when [a]the judges [1]ruled, that there was [b]a famine in the land. And a *certain* man of [c]Beth-lehem-judah went to sojourn in the country of Moab, he, and his wife, and his two sons.

2 And the name of the man *was* Elimelech, and the name of his wife Naomi, and the name of his two sons Mahlon and Chilion, [a]Ephrathites of Beth-lehem-judah. And they came [b]*into* the country of Moab, and [1]continued there.

3 And Elimelech Naomi's husband died; and she was left, and her two sons.

4 And they took them wives of the women of Moab; the name of the one *was* Orpah, and the name of the other Ruth: and they dwelled there about ten years.

5 And Mahlon and Chilion died also both of them; and the woman was left of her two sons and her husband.

6 ¶ Then she arose with her daughters in law, that she might return from the country of Moab: for she had heard in the country of Moab how that the LORD had [a]visited his people in [b]giving them bread.

7 Wherefore she went forth out of the place where she was, and her two daughters in law with her; and they went on the way to return unto the land of Judah.

8 And Naomi said unto her two daughters in law, [a]Go, return each to her mother's house: [b]the LORD deal kindly with you, as ye have dealt with [c]the dead, and with me.

9 The LORD grant you that you may find [a]rest, each *of you in* the house of her husband. Then she kissed them; and they lift up their voice, and wept.

1:1 [1]Heb. *judged* [a]Judg. 2:16 [b]Gen. 12:10; 26:1; 2 Ki. 8:1 [c]Judg. 17:8
1:2 [1]Heb. *were* [a]Gen. 35:19 [b]Judg. 3:30
1:6 [a]Ex. 4:31; Luke 1:68 [b]Mat. 6:11
1:8 [a]See Josh. 24:15 [b]2 Tim. 1:16-18 [c]ver. 5; ch. 2:20
1:9 [a]ch. 3:1

‡1:1 *when the judges ruled.* Probably from c. 1380 to c. 1050 B.C. (see Introduction to Judges: Background). By mentioning the judges, the author calls to mind that period of Israel's apostasy, moral degradation and oppression. By contrast the story of Ruth and Boaz adds a ray of light to the dark days of the judges. *Beth-lehem-judah.* David's hometown (1 Sam 16:18). Beth-lehem (the name suggests "house of bread") is empty.
1:2 *Elimelech.* Means "(My) God is King" (see note on Judg 8:23). *Naomi.* Means "pleasant." *Ephrathites.* Ephratah was a name for the area around Beth-lehem (see 4:11; Gen 35:19; 1 Sam 17:12; Mic 5:2).
1:3 *Elimelech Naomi's husband died.* Naomi's emptying begins (see v. 21).
‡1:4 *they took . . . women of Moab.* Prospect of continuing the family line remained. *women of Moab.* See Gen 19:36–37. Marriage with Moabite women was not forbidden, though no Moabite—or his sons to the tenth generation—was allowed to "enter into the congregation of the LORD" (Deut 23:3). *Ruth.* The name sounds like the Hebrew for "friendship." Ruth is one of four women in Matthew's genealogy of Jesus. The others are Tamar, Rahab and Bathsheba (Mat 1:3,5–6). Each one illustrates the magnitude of God's grace.
1:5 *Mahlon.* Ruth's husband (4:10), whose name probably means "weakling." *the woman was left of her . . . husband.* Naomi's emptiness is complete: She has neither husband nor sons. She has only two young daughters-in-law, both of them foreigners and childless.
1:6 *arose . . . that she might return.* Empty Naomi returns to the newly filled land of promise. *the LORD had visited his people.* At several points in the account, God's sovereign control of events is acknowledged (here; vv. 13,21; 2:20; 4:12–15). *bread.* I.e., "food." Beth-lehem ("house of bread") again has food.
1:8 *Go, return.* Desolate Naomi repeatedly urges her daughters-in-law to return to their original homes in Moab (here; vv. 11–12,15); she has nothing to offer them. *deal kindly.* See 2:20; 3:10.

The Book of Ruth

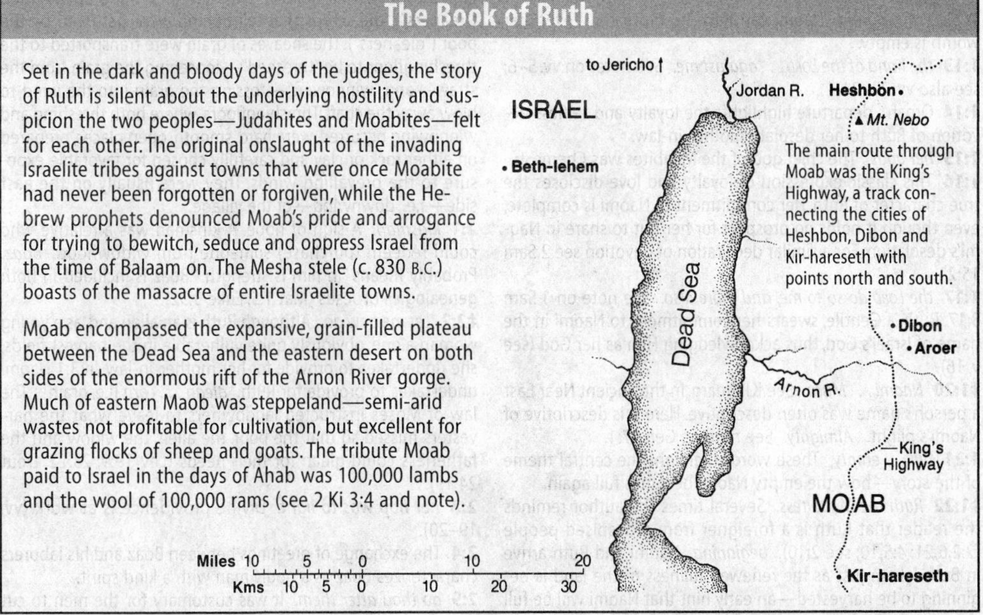

Set in the dark and bloody days of the judges, the story of Ruth is silent about the underlying hostility and suspicion the two peoples—Judahites and Moabites—felt for each other. The original onslaught of the invading Israelite tribes against towns that were once Moabite had never been forgotten or forgiven, while the Hebrew prophets denounced Moab's pride and arrogance for trying to bewitch, seduce and oppress Israel from the time of Balaam on. The Mesha stele (c. 830 B.C.) boasts of the massacre of entire Israelite towns.

Moab encompassed the expansive, grain-filled plateau between the Dead Sea and the eastern desert on both sides of the enormous rift of the Arnon River gorge. Much of eastern Maob was steppeland—semi-arid wastes not profitable for cultivation, but excellent for grazing flocks of sheep and goats. The tribute Moab paid to Israel in the days of Ahab was 100,000 lambs and the wool of 100,000 rams (see 2 Ki 3:4 and note).

10 And they said unto her, Surely we will
return with thee unto thy people.
11 And Naomi said, Turn again, my daughters: why will you go with me? *are there* yet
any moe sons in my womb, [a]that they may be
your husbands?
12 Turn again, my daughters, go *your way;*
for I am too old to have a husband. If I should
say, I have hope, [1]*if* I should have a husband
also to night, and should also bear sons;
13 Would ye [1]tarry for them till they were
grown? would ye stay for them from having
husbands? nay, my daughters; for [2]it grieveth
me much for your sakes that [a]the hand of the
LORD is gone out against me.
14 And they lift up their voice, and wept
again: and Orpah kissed her mother in law;
but Ruth [a]clave unto her.
15 And she said, Behold, thy sister in law
is gone back unto her people, and unto [a]her
gods: [b]return thou after thy sister in law.
16 And Ruth said, [a 1]Intreat me not to
leave thee, *or* to return from following after
thee: for whither thou goest, I will go; and
where thou lodgest, I will lodge: [b]thy people
shall be my people, and thy God my God:
17 Where thou diest, will I die, and there
will I be buried: [a]the LORD do so to me, and
more also, *if ought* but death part thee and me.
18 [a]When she saw that she [1]*was* stedfastly
minded to go with her, then she left speaking
unto her.
19 ¶ So they two went until they came *to*
Beth-lehem. And it came to pass, when they

1:11 [a]Gen. 38:11; Deut. 25:5
1:12 [1]Or, *if I were with a husband*
1:13 [1]Heb. *hope* [2]Heb. *I have much bitterness* [a]Judg. 2:15; Job 19:21
1:14 [a]Prov. 17:17; 18:24
1:15 [a]Judg. 11:24 [b]See Josh. 24:15,19; 2 Ki. 2:2; Luke 24:28
1:16 [1]Or, *Be not against me* [a]2 Ki. 2:2,4,6 [b]ch. 2:11,12
1:17 [a]1 Sam. 3:17; 25:22; 2 Sam. 19:13; 2 Ki. 6:31
1:18 [1]Heb. *strengthened herself* [a]Acts 21:14
1:19 [a]Mat. 21:10 [b]See Is. 23:7; Lam. 2:15
1:20 [1]That is, *Pleasant* [2]That is, *Bitter*
1:21 [a]Job 1:21
1:22 [a]Ex. 9:31,32; ch. 2:23; 2 Sam. 21:9
2:1 [1]Called, Mat. 1:5, *Booz* [a]ch. 3:2,12 [b]ch. 4:21
2:2 [a]Lev. 19:9; Deut. 24:19
2:3 [1]Heb. *hap happened*
2:4 [a]Luke 1:28; 2 Thes. 3:16

were come *to* Beth-lehem, that [a]all the city
was moved about them, and they said, [b]*Is* this
Naomi?
20 And she said unto them, Call me not
[1]Naomi, call me [2]Mara: for the Almighty hath
dealt very bitterly with me.
21 I went out full, [a]and the LORD hath
brought me *home* again empty: why *then* call
ye me Naomi, seeing the LORD hath testified
against me, and the Almighty hath afflicted me?
22 So Naomi returned, and Ruth the Moabitess, her daughter in law, with her, which returned out of the country of Moab: and they
came *to* Beth-lehem [a]in the beginning of barley harvest.

Boaz speaks with Ruth

2 And Naomi had a [a]kinsman of her husband's, a mighty man of wealth, of the
family of Elimelech; and his name *was* [b 1]Boaz.
2 And Ruth the Moabitess said unto Nao-
mi, Let me now go *to* the field, and [a]glean ears
of corn after *him* in whose sight I shall find
grace. And she said unto her, Go, my daughter.
3 And she went, and came, and gleaned in
the field after the reapers: and her [1]hap was to
light on a part of the field *belonging* unto
Boaz, who *was* of the kindred of Elimelech.
4 And behold, Boaz came from Beth-lehem, and said unto the reapers, [a]The LORD *be*
with you. And they answered him, The LORD
bless thee.
5 Then said Boaz unto his servant that was
set over the reapers, Whose damsel *is* this?

1:11 *sons . . . may be your husbands.* Naomi alludes to the Israelite law (Deut 25:5–6) regarding levirate marriage (see notes on Gen 38:8; Deut 25:5–10; see also Mark 12:18–23), which was given to protect the widow and guarantee continuance of the family line.

1:12 *I am too old.* Naomi can have no more sons; even her womb is empty.

1:13 *the hand of the LORD . . . against me.* See notes on vv. 5–6; see also vv. 20–21.

1:14 Orpah's departure highlights the loyalty and selfless devotion of Ruth to her desolate mother-in-law.

1:15 *her gods.* The chief god of the Moabites was Chemosh.

1:16 This classic expression of loyalty and love discloses the true character of Ruth. Her commitment to Naomi is complete, even though it holds no prospect for her but to share in Naomi's desolation. For a similar declaration of devotion see 2 Sam 15:21.

1:17 *the LORD do so to me, and more also.* See note on 1 Sam 3:17. Ruth, a Gentile, swears her commitment to Naomi in the name of Israel's God, thus acknowledging Him as her God (see v. 16).

‡1:20 *Naomi . . . Mara.* See KJV marg. In the ancient Near East a person's name was often descriptive. Here it is descriptive of Naomi's plight. *Almighty.* See note on Gen 17:1.

1:21 *full . . . empty.* These words highlight the central theme of the story—how the empty Naomi becomes full again.

‡1:22 *Ruth the Moabitess.* Several times the author reminds the reader that Ruth is a foreigner from a despised people (2:2,6,21; 4:5,10; see 2:10). *beginning.* Naomi and Ruth arrive in Beth-lehem just as the renewed fullness of the land is beginning to be harvested—an early hint that Naomi will be full again. Reference to the barley harvest also prepares the reader for the next major scene in the harvest fields (see Introduction: Literary Features). *harvest.* Harvesting grain in ancient Canaan took place in April and May (barley first, wheat a few weeks later; see 2:23). The harvest was cut and bundled by men ("reapers"), the scraps that fell behind were gathered by the poor ("gleaners"). The sheaves of grain were transported to the threshingfloor to be "threshed"—loosening the grain from the straw—and "winnowed"—tossing the grain into the wind to blow away the chaff. Threshingfloors, where both threshing and winnowing occurred, were hard, smooth, open places, prepared on either rock or clay and carefully chosen for favorable exposure to the prevailing winds. They were usually on the east side—i.e., downwind—of the village.

2:1 *kinsman.* A sign of hope. A kinsman was a relative who could redeem (purchase) someone from widowhood. *Boaz.* Probably means "In him is strength." Boaz is included in both genealogies of Jesus (Mat 1:5; Luke 3:32).

‡2:2 *Let me now go.* Although Ruth is an alien and, as a young woman alone, obviously quite vulnerable in the harvest fields, she undertakes to provide for her mother-in-law. In 3:1 Naomi undertakes to provide for Ruth. *glean . . . corn* [i.e, grain]. The law of Moses instructed landowners to leave what the harvesters missed so that the poor, the alien, the widow and the fatherless could glean for their needs (Lev 19:9; 23:22; Deut 24:19).

2:3 *her hap was to light.* Divine providence is at work (vv. 19–20).

2:4 The exchange of greetings between Boaz and his laborers characterizes Boaz as a godly man with a kind spirit.

2:9 *go thou after them.* It was customary for the men to cut

6 And the servant that was set over the reapers answered and said, It *is* the Moabitish damsel [a]that came back with Naomi out of the country of Moab:

7 And she said, I pray you, let me glean and gather after the reapers amongst the sheaves: so she came, and hath continued even from the morning until now, that she tarried a little in the house.

8 ¶ Then said Boaz unto Ruth, Hearest thou not, my daughter? Go not to glean in another field, neither go from hence, but abide here fast by my maidens:

9 *Let* thine eyes *be* on the field that they do reap, and go thou after them: have I not charged the young men that *they* shall not touch thee? and when thou art athirst, go unto the vessels, and drink of *that* which the young men have drawn.

10 Then she [a]fell on her face, and bowed herself to the ground, and said unto him, Why have I found grace in thine eyes, that *thou* shouldest take knowledge of me, seeing I *am* a stranger?

11 And Boaz answered and said unto her, It hath fully been shewed me, [a]all that thou hast done unto thy mother in law since the death of thine husband: and *how* thou hast left thy father and thy mother, and the land of thy nativity, and art come unto a people which thou knewest not heretofore.

12 [a]The LORD recompense thy work, and a full reward be given thee of the LORD God of Israel, [b]under whose wings thou art come to trust.

13 Then she said, [a][1]Let me find favour in thy sight, my lord; for that thou hast comforted me, and for that thou hast spoken [2]friendly unto thine handmaid, [b]though I be not like unto one of thy handmaidens.

14 And Boaz said unto her, At mealtime come thou hither, and eat of the bread, and dip thy morsel in the vinegar. And she sat beside the reapers: and he reached her parched *corn,* and she did eat, and [a]was sufficed, and left.

15 And when she was risen up to glean, Boaz commanded his young men, saying, Let her glean even among the sheaves, and [1]reproach her not:

16 And let fall also *some* of the handfuls of purpose for her, and leave *them,* that she may glean *them,* and rebuke her not.

17 So she gleaned in the field until even, and beat out that she had gleaned: and it was about an ephah of barley.

18 And she took *it* up, and went *into* the city: and her mother in law saw what she had gleaned: and she brought forth, and gave to her [a]that she had reserved after she was sufficed.

19 And her mother in law said unto her, Where hast thou gleaned to day? and where wroughtest thou? blessed be he that did [a]take knowledge of thee. And she shewed her mother in law with whom she had wrought, and said, The man's name with whom I wrought to day *is* Boaz.

20 And Naomi said unto her daughter in law, [a]Blessed *be* he of the LORD, who [b]hath not left off his kindness to the living and to the dead. And Naomi said unto her, The man *is* near of kin unto us, [c][1]one of our next kinsmen.

21 And Ruth the Moabitess said, He said unto me also, Thou shalt keep fast by my young men, until they have ended all my harvest.

22 And Naomi said unto Ruth her daughter in law, *It is* good, my daughter, that thou go out with his maidens, that they [1]meet thee not in *any* other field.

23 So she kept fast by the maidens of Boaz to glean unto the end of barley harvest and of wheat harvest; and dwelt with her mother in law.

Ruth visits Boaz

3 Then Naomi her mother in law said unto her, My daughter, [a]shall I not seek [b]rest for thee, that it may be well with thee?

2 And now *is* not Boaz of our kindred, [a]with whose maidens thou wast? Behold, he winnoweth barley to night in the threshingfloor.

2:6 [a]ch. 1:22
2:10 [a]1 Sam. 25:23
2:11 [a]ch. 1:14,16,17
2:12 [a]1 Sam. 24:19 [b]ch. 1:16; Ps. 17:8
2:13 [1]Or, *I find favour* [2]Heb. *to the heart* [a]Gen. 33:15; 1 Sam. 1:18 [b]1 Sam. 25:41
2:14 [a]ver. 18
2:15 [1]Heb. *shame her not*
2:18 [a]ver. 14
2:19 [a]ver. 10; Ps. 41:1
2:20 [1]Or, *one that hath right to redeem* [a]ch. 3:10; 2 Sam. 2:5; Job 29:13 [b]Prov. 17:17 [c]ch. 3:9; 4:6
2:22 [1]Or, *fall upon thee*
3:1 [a]1 Cor. 7:36; 1 Tim. 5:8 [b]ch. 1:9
3:2 [a]ch. 2:8

the grain and for the servant girls to go behind them to bind the grain into sheaves. Then Ruth could glean what they had left behind (see note on 1:22).

2:11 Ruth's commitment to care for her desolate mother-in-law remains the center of attention throughout the book.

2:12 *under whose wings.* A figure of a bird protecting her young under her wings (see Mat 23:37; see also note on 3:9).

2:13 *thine handmaid.* A polite reference to herself.

2:15 *commanded his young men.* Boaz goes beyond the requirement of the law in making sure that Ruth's labors are abundantly productive (see 3:15).

2:17 *beat out.* See note on 1:22. In Ruth's case, as in that of Gideon (Judg 6:11), the amount was small and could be threshed by hand simply by beating it with a club or stick. *ephah.* An ephah was probably about three-fifths of a bushel—an unusually large amount for one day's gleaning.

2:20 *the LORD, who hath not left off his kindness.* See 1:8. In 3:10 Boaz credits Ruth with demonstrating this same virtue. *next kinsmen.* Redemption is a key concept in Ruth (see Introduction: Theme and Theology). The "next kinsman," also known as a kinsman-redeemer, was responsible for protecting the interests of needy members of the extended family—e.g., to provide an heir for a brother who had died (Deut 25:5–10), to redeem land that a poor relative had sold outside the family (Lev 25:25–28), to redeem a relative who had been sold into slavery (Lev 25:47–49) and to avenge the killing of a relative (Num 35:19–21; Josh 20:6; avenger" and "kinsman-redeemer" are translations of the same Hebrew word). Naomi is encouraged when she hears that the Lord has led Ruth to the fields of a relative who might serve as their kinsman-redeemer. This moment of Naomi's awakened hope is the crucial turning point of the story.

2:23 *unto the end of . . . harvest.* This phrase rounds out the harvest episode and prepares for the next major scene on the threshingfloor (see Introduction: Literary Features).

3:1 Naomi's awakened hope (cf. 1:8–13) now moves her to undertake provision for Ruth's future (see note on 2:2).

3:2 *he winnoweth . . . to night.* See note on 1:22. In the threshing season it was customary for the landowner to spend the night near the threshing floor to protect his grain from theft.

3 Wash *thyself* therefore, [a]and anoint thee, and put thy raiment upon thee, and get thee down *to* the floor: *but* make not thyself known unto the man, until he shall have done eating and drinking.

4 And it shall be, when he lieth down, that thou shalt mark the place where he shall lie, and thou shalt go in, and [1]uncover his feet, and lay thee down; and he will tell thee what thou shalt do.

5 And she said unto her, All that thou sayest unto me I will do.

6 And she went down *unto* the floor, and did according to all that her mother in law bade her.

7 And when Boaz had eaten and drunk, and [a]his heart was merry, he went to lie down at the end of the heap *of corn:* and she came softly, and uncovered his feet, and laid her down.

8 And it came to pass at midnight, that the man was afraid, and [1]turned himself: and behold, a woman lay *at* his feet.

9 And he said, Who *art* thou? And she answered, I *am* Ruth thine handmaid: [a]spread therefore thy skirt over thine handmaid; for thou *art* [b1]a near kinsman.

10 And he said, [a]Blessed *be* thou of the LORD, my daughter: *for* thou hast shewed more kindness in the latter end than [b]at the beginning, inasmuch as *thou* followedst not young men, whether poor or rich.

11 And now, my daughter, fear not; I will do to thee all that thou requirest: for all the [1]city of my people doth know that thou *art* [a]a virtuous woman.

12 And now it is true that I *am thy* [a]near kinsman: howbeit [b]there is a kinsman nearer than I.

3:3 [a]2 Sam. 14:2
3:4 [1]Or, *lift up the clothes that are on his feet*
3:7 [a]Judg. 19:6,9,22; 2 Sam. 13:28; Esth. 1:10
3:8 [1]Or, *took hold on*
3:9 [1]Or, *one that hath right to redeem* [a]Ezek. 16:8 [b]ver. 12; ch. 2:20
3:10 [a]ch. 2:20 [b]ch. 1:8
3:11 [1]Heb. *gate* [a]Prov. 12:4
3:12 [a]ver. 9 [b]ch. 4:1

3:13 [a]Deut. 25:5; ch. 4:5; Mat. 22:24 [b]Judg. 8:19; Jer. 4:2
3:14 [a]Rom. 12:17; 14:16; 1 Cor. 10:32; 2 Cor. 8:21; 1 Thes. 5:22
3:15 [1]Or, *sheet, or, apron*
3:18 [a]Ps. 37:3,5
4:1 [a]ch. 3:12
4:2 [a]1 Ki. 21:8; Prov. 31:23

13 Tarry this night, and it shall be in the morning, *that* if he will [a]perform unto thee the part of a kinsman, well; let him do the kinsman's part: but if he will not do the part of a kinsman to thee, then will I do the part of a kinsman to thee, [b]*as* the LORD liveth: lie down until the morning.

14 And she lay *at* his feet until the morning: and she rose up before one could know another. And he said, [a]Let it not be known that a woman came *into* the floor.

15 Also he said, Bring the [1]vail that *thou hast* upon thee, and hold it. And when she held it, he measured six *measures* of barley, and laid *it* on her: and he went *into* the city.

16 And when she came to her mother in law, she said, Who *art* thou, my daughter? And she told her all that the man had done to her.

17 And she said, These six *measures* of barley gave he me; for he said to me, Go not empty unto thy mother in law.

18 Then said she, [a]Sit still, my daughter, until thou know how the matter will fall: for the man will not be in rest, until he have finished the thing *this* day.

Boaz and Ruth marry

4 Then went Boaz up *to* the gate, and sat him down there: and behold, [a]the kinsman of whom Boaz spake came by; unto whom he said, *Ho,* such a one, turn aside, sit down here. And he turned aside, and sat down.

2 And he took ten men of [a]the elders of the city, and said, Sit ye down here. And they sat down.

3 And he said unto the kinsman, Naomi, that is come again out of the country of Moab, selleth a parcel of land, which *was* our brother Elimelech's:

3:3 Ruth is instructed to prepare herself like a bride (see Ezek 16:9–12). *get thee down to the floor.* Women were not normally present at the evening revelries of the threshers (v. 14). *eating and drinking.* Harvest was a time of festivity (Is 9:3; 16:9–10; Jer 48:33).

3:4 *uncover his feet, and lay thee down.* Although Naomi's instructions may appear forward, the moral integrity of Naomi and Ruth is never in doubt (see v. 11). Naomi's advice to Ruth is clearly for the purpose of appealing to Boaz's kinsman obligation. Ruth's actions were a request for marriage. Tamar, the mother of Pharez (4:12), had also laid claim to the provision of the levirate (or kinsman-redeemer) law (Gen 38:13–30).

3:9 *spread therefore thy skirt over thine handmaid.* A request for marriage (see Ezek 16:8); a similar custom is still practiced in some parts of the Middle East today. There is a play on the words "wings" of the Lord (2:12) and "skirt" (lit. "wings") of the garment (here), both signifying protection. Boaz is vividly reminded that he must serve as the Lord's protective wing to watch over Ruth.

3:10 *shewed more kindness . . . than at the beginning.* See 2:11–12.

3:11 *virtuous woman.* See Prov 31:10. The Hebrew for this expression is similar to that used of Boaz in 2:1; thus the author maintains a balance between his descriptions of Ruth and Boaz.

3:12 *a kinsman nearer than I.* How Boaz was related to Ruth's former husband (Mahlon) is unknown, but the closest male relative had the primary responsibility to marry a widow. Naomi instructed Ruth to approach Boaz because he had already shown himself willing to be Ruth's protector. Boaz, however, would not bypass the directives of the law, which clearly gave priority to the nearest relative.

3:13 *as the LORD liveth.* Boaz commits himself by oath (cf. 1:17) to redeem the family property and to arrange Ruth's honorable marriage.

3:15 Boaz goes beyond the requirement of the law in supplying Ruth with grain from the threshingfloor (see 2:15).

3:17 *empty.* Again the empty-full motif (see note on 1:21).

3:18 *Sit still.* I.e. wait. The Hebrew underlying this word is translated "sat" in 4:1. Thus the author prepares the reader for the next major scene, in which Boaz sits at the town gate to see the matter through.

4:1 *gate.* The "town hall" of ancient Israel, the normal place for business and legal transactions, where witnesses were readily available (vv. 9–12; see note on Gen 19:1). *such a one.* The other kinsman remains unnamed.

4:2 *ten men of the elders.* A full court for legal proceedings.

4:3 *selleth a parcel of land.* See note on 2:20. Two interpretations are possible: 1. Naomi owns the land but is so destitute that she is forced to sell. It was the duty of the kinsman-redeemer to buy any land in danger of being sold outside the family. 2. Naomi does not own the land—it had been sold by

4 And [1]I thought to advertise thee, saying,
[a]Buy *it* [b]before the inhabitants, and before the
elders of my people. If thou wilt redeem *it,* redeem *it:* but if thou wilt not redeem *it, then*
tell me, that I may know: [c]for *there is* none to
redeem *it* besides thee; and I *am* after thee.
And he said, I will redeem *it.*
5 Then said Boaz, What day thou buyest
the field of the hand of Naomi, thou must buy
it also of Ruth the Moabitess, the wife of the
dead, [a]to raise up the name of the dead upon
his inheritance.
6 [a]And the kinsman said, I cannot redeem
it for myself, lest I mar mine own inheritance:
redeem thou my right to thyself; for I cannot
redeem *it.*
7 [a]Now this *was the manner* in former
time in Israel concerning redeeming and concerning changing, for to confirm all things; a
man plucked off his shoe, and gave *it* to his
neighbour: and this *was* a testimony in Israel.
8 Therefore the kinsman said unto Boaz,
Buy *it* for thee. So he drew off his shoe.
9 And Boaz said unto the elders, and *unto*
all the people, Ye *are* witnesses *this* day, that I
have bought all that *was* Elimelech's, and all
that *was* Chilion's and Mahlon's, of the hand
of Naomi.
10 Moreover Ruth the Moabitess, the wife
of Mahlon, have I purchased to be my wife, to
raise up the name of the dead upon his inheritance, [a]that the name of the dead be not cut
off from among his brethren, and from the
gate of his place: ye *are* witnesses *this* day.
11 And all the people that *were* in the gate,
and the elders, said, *We are* witnesses. [a]The
LORD make the woman that is come into thine
house like Rachel and like Leah, which two
did [b]build the house of Israel: and [1]do thou
worthily in [c]Ephratah, and [2]be famous in
Beth-lehem:
12 And let thy house be like the house of
Pharez, [a]whom Tamar bare unto Judah, of
[b]the seed which the LORD shall give thee of
this young woman.

Obed is born: the Davidic line

13 ¶ So Boaz [a]took Ruth, and she was his
wife: and when he went in unto her, [b]the
LORD gave her conception, and she bare a
son.
14 And [a]the women said unto Naomi,
Blessed *be* the LORD, which hath not [1]left thee
this day without a [2]kinsman, that his name
may be famous in Israel.
15 And he shall be unto thee a restorer of
thy life, and [1]a nourisher of [2]thine old age: for
thy daughter in law, which loveth thee, which
is [a]better to thee than seven sons, hath born
him.
16 And Naomi took the child, and laid it in
her bosom, and became nurse unto it.
17 [a]And the *women her* neighbours gave it
a name, saying, There is a son born to Naomi;

4:4 [1]Heb. *I said, I will reveal in thine ear* [a]Jer. 32:7,8 [b]Gen. 23:18 [c]Lev. 25:25
4:5 [a]Gen. 38:8; Deut. 25:5,6; ch. 3:13; Mat. 22:24
4:6 [a]ch. 3:12,13
4:7 [a]Deut. 25:7,9
4:10 [a]Deut. 25:6
4:11 [1]Or, *get thee riches*, or, *power* [2]Heb. *proclaim* thy *name* [a]Ps. 127:3; 128:3 [b]Deut. 25:9 [c]Gen. 35:16
4:12 [a]1 Chr. 2:4; Mat. 1:3 [b]1 Sam. 2:20
4:13 [a]ch. 3:11 [b]Gen. 29:31
4:14 [1]Heb. *caused to cease unto thee* [2]Or, *redeemer* [a]Luke 1:58
4:15 [1]Heb. *to nourish* [2]Heb. *thy gray hairs* [a]1 Sam. 1:8
4:17 [a]Luke 1:58

Elimelech before the family left for Moab—but by law she retains the right of redemption to buy the land back. Lacking funds to do so herself, she is dependent on a kinsman-redeemer to do it for her. It is the right of redemption that Naomi is "selling." *brother.* Used in the broader sense of "relative."

4:5 *buy it also . . . the wife of the dead.* Now Boaz reveals the other half of the obligation—the acquisition of Ruth. Levirate law (Deut 25:5–6) provided that Ruth's firstborn son would keep Mahlon's name alive and would possess the right of ownership of the family inheritance.

4:6 *I cannot redeem it.* Possibly he fears that, if he has a son by her and if that son is his only surviving heir, his own property will transfer to the family of Elimelech (see note on Gen 38:9). In that case his risk was no greater than that assumed by Boaz. This kinsman's refusal to assume the kinsman-redeemer's role highlights the kindness and generosity of Boaz toward the two widows—just as Orpah's return to her family highlights Ruth's selfless devotion and loyalty to Naomi.

‡4:7 *a man plucked off his shoe.* The process of renouncing one's property rights and passing them to another was publicly attested by taking off a sandal and transferring it to the new owner (cf. Amos 2:6; 8:6). The Nuzi documents (see chart, p. xix) refer to a similar custom. The symbolism of the act emphasizes the sincerity of one's "walk" in life.

4:9 *witnesses.* The role of public witnesses was to attest to all legal transactions and other binding agreements.

4:10 *name of the dead.* See Deut 25:6.

4:11 *Rachel and like Leah . . . build the house of Israel.* Cf. Deut 25:9. The Israelite readers of Ruth would have associated the house of Jacob (Israel), built up by Rachel and Leah, with the house of Israel, rebuilt by David, the descendant of Ruth and Boaz, after it had been threatened with extinction (1 Sam 4). They also knew that the Lord had covenanted to "build" the house of David as an enduring dynasty, through which Israel's blessed destiny would be assured (see 2 Sam 7:27–29). *Ephratah.* See note on 1:2.

‡4:12 *Pharez, whom Tamar bare unto Judah.* Pharez was Boaz's ancestor (vv. 18–21; Mat 1:3; Luke 3:33). His birth to Judah was from a union that involved challenges arising from the levirate practice (Gen 38:27–30; see note on 1:11). Despite these challenges, the descendants of Pharez had raised the tribe of Judah to a prominent place in Israel. So the blessing of the elders—that, through the offspring Ruth would bear to Boaz, his family would be like that of Pharez—was fully realized in David and his dynasty. Thus also v. 12 prepares the reader for the events briefly narrated in the conclusion.

4:13–17 The conclusion of the story balances the introduction (1:1–5): (1) In the Hebrew both have the same number of words; (2) both compress much into a short space; (3) both focus on Naomi; (4) the introduction emphasizes Naomi's emptiness, and the conclusion portrays her fullness.

4:13 *the LORD gave her conception.* See note on 1:6.

4:14 *kinsman.* The child Obed, as vv. 15–17 make clear. *his name may be famous.* This same wish is expressed concerning Boaz in v. 11.

4:15 *better to thee than seven sons.* See 1 Sam 1:8. Since seven was considered a number of completeness, to have seven sons was the epitome of all family blessings in Israel (see 1 Sam 2:5; Job 1:2; 42:13). Ruth's selfless devotion to Naomi receives its climactic acknowledgment.

4:16 *laid it in her bosom.* Possibly symbolizing adoption (see note on Gen 30:3).

4:17 *a son born to Naomi.* Through Ruth, aged Naomi, who can no longer bear children, obtains an heir in place of Mahlon. *Obed.* The name means "servant," in its full form possibly "servant of the LORD."

and they called his name Obed: he *is* the father of Jesse, the father of David.
18 ¶ Now these *are* the generations of Pharez: [a]Pharez begat Hezron,
19 And Hezron begat Ram, and Ram begat Amminadab,
20 And Amminadab begat [a]Nahshon, and Nahshon begat [b1]Salmon,
21 And Salmon begat Boaz, and Boaz begat Obed,
22 And Obed begat Jesse, and Jesse begat [a]David.

4:18 [a] 1 Chr. 2:4
4:20 [1] Or, *Salmah* [a] Num. 1:7 [b] Mat. 1:4
4:22 [a] 1 Chr. 2:15; Mat. 1:6

‡4:18–22 See 1 Chr 2:5–15; Mat 1:3–6; Luke 3:31–33. Like the genealogies of Gen 5:3–32; 11:10–26, this genealogy has ten names (see note on Gen 5:5). This may also reflect the author's response to Deut 23:2, in relation to the unusual nature of Pharez's birth. The ten names indicated David's right to rule as Israel's king. It brings to mind the reign of David, during which, in contrast to the turbulent period of the judges recalled in 1:1, Israel finally entered into rest in the promised land (see 1 Ki 5:4). It signifies that, just as Naomi was brought from emptiness to fullness through the selfless love of Ruth and Boaz, so the Lord brought Israel from unrest to rest through their descendant David, who selflessly gave himself to fight Israel's battles on the Lord's behalf. The ultimate end of this genealogy is Jesus Christ, the great "son of David" (Mat 1:1), who fulfills prophecy and will bring the Lord's people into final rest.

The First Book of Samuel

INTRODUCTION

Title

1 and 2 Samuel are named after the person God used to establish kingship in Israel. Samuel not only anointed both Saul and David, Israel's first two kings, but he also gave definition to the new order of God's rule over Israel that began with the incorporation of kingship into its structure. Samuel's importance as God's representative in this period of Israel's history is close to that of Moses (see Ps 99:6; Jer 15:1) since he, more than any other person, provided for covenant continuity in the transition from the rule of the judges to that of the monarchy.

1 and 2 Samuel were originally one book. It was divided into two parts by the translators of the Septuagint (the Greek translation of the OT)—a division subsequently followed by Jerome (the Latin Vulgate) and by modern versions. The title of the book has varied from time to time, having been designated "The First and Second Books of Kingdoms" (Septuagint), "First and Second Kings" (Vulgate) and "First and Second Samuel" (Hebrew tradition and most modern versions).

Literary Features, Authorship and Date

Many questions have arisen pertaining to the literary character, authorship and date of 1,2 Samuel. Certain literary characteristics of the book suggest that it was compiled with the use of a number of originally independent sources, which the author may have incorporated into his own composition as much as possible in their original, unedited form.

Who the author was cannot be known with certainty since the book itself gives no indication of his identity. Some have suggested Zabud, son of Nathan the prophet, who is referred to in 1 Ki 4:5 as King Solomon's "friend." He would have had access to information about David's reign from his father Nathan, as well as from court records. Whoever the author was, he must have lived shortly after Solomon's death (930 B.C.) and the division of the kingdom (see references to "Israel and Judah" in 11:8; 17:52; 18:16; 2 Sam 5:5; 24:1–9 and the expression "kings of Judah" in 1 Sam 27:6). Also, he doubtless had access to records of the life and times of Samuel, Saul and David. Explicit reference in the book itself is made to only one such source (the book of Jasher, 2 Sam 1:18), but the writer of Chronicles refers to four others that pertain to this period (the account of the book of King David, 1 Chr 27:24; the book of Samuel the seer; the book of Nathan the prophet; the chronicles of Gad the seer, 1 Chr 29:29).

Contents and Theme: Kingship and Covenant

1 Samuel portrays the establishment of kingship in Israel. Before the author describes this momentous change in the structure of the theocracy (God's rule), he effectively depicts the complexity of its context. The following events provide both historical and theological context for the birth of the monarchy:

1. *The birth, youth and calling of Samuel (chs. 1—3).* In a book dealing for the most part with the reigns of Israel's first two kings, Saul and David, it is significant that the author chose not to include a birth narrative of either of these men, but to describe the birth of their forerunner and anointer, the prophet Samuel. This in itself accentuates the importance the author attached to Samuel's role in the events that follow. He seems to be saying in a subtle way that flesh and blood are to be subordinated to word and Spirit in the process of the establishment of kingship. For this reason chs. 1—3 should be viewed as integrally related to what follows, not as a more likely component of the book of Judges or as a loosely attached prefix to the rest of 1,2 Samuel. Kingship is given its birth and then nurtured by the prophetic word and work of the prophet Samuel. Moreover, the events of Samuel's nativity thematically anticipate the story of God's working that is narrated in the rest of the book.

2. *The "ark narratives" (chs. 4—6).* This section describes how the ark of God was captured by the Philistines and then, after God wreaked havoc on several Philistine cities, how it was returned to

Israel. These narratives reveal the folly of Israel's notion that possession of the ark automatically guaranteed victory over her enemies. They also display the awesome power of the Lord (Yahweh, the God of Israel) and His superiority over the Philistine god Dagon. The Philistines were forced to confess openly their helplessness against God's power by their return of the ark to Israel. The entire ark episode performs a vital function in placing Israel's subsequent sinful desire for a human king in proper perspective.

3. *Samuel as a judge and deliverer (ch. 7)*. When Samuel called Israel to repentance and renewed dedication to the Lord, the Lord intervened mightily in Israel's behalf and gave victory over the Philistines. This narrative reaffirms the authority of Samuel as a divinely ordained leader; at the same time it provides evidence of divine protection and blessing for God's people when they place their confidence in the Lord and live in obedience to their covenant obligations.

All the material in chs. 1—7 serves as a necessary preface for the narratives of chs. 8—12, which describe the rise and establishment of kingship in Israel. The author has masterfully arranged the stories in chs. 8—12 in order to accentuate the serious theological conflict surrounding the historical events. In the study of these chapters, scholars have often noted the presence of a tension or ambivalence in the attitude toward the monarchy: On the one hand, Samuel is commanded by the Lord to give the people a king (8:7,9,22; 9:16–17; 10:24; 12:13); on the other hand, their request for a king is considered a sinful rejection of the Lord (8:7; 10:19; 12:12,17,19–20). These seemingly conflicting attitudes toward the monarchy must be understood in the context of Israel's covenant relationship with the Lord.

Moses had anticipated Israel's desire for a human king (Deut 17:18–20), but Israelite kingship was to be compatible with the continued rule of the Lord over His people as their Great King. Instead, when the elders asked Samuel to give them a king (8:5,19–20), they rejected the Lord's kingship over them (8:7; 10:19; 12:17,19). Their desire was for a king such as the nations around them had—to lead them in battle and give them a sense of national security and unity. The request for a king constituted a denial of their covenant relationship to the Lord, who was their King. Moreover, the Lord not only had promised to be their protector but had also repeatedly demonstrated His power in their behalf, most recently in the ark narratives (chs. 4—6), as well as in the great victory won over the Philistines under the leadership of Samuel (ch. 7).

Nevertheless the Lord instructed Samuel to give the people a king (8:7,9,22). By divine appointment Saul was brought into contact with Samuel, and Samuel was directed to anoint him privately as king (9:1—10:16). Subsequently, Samuel gathered the people at Mizpah, where, after again admonishing them concerning their sin in desiring a king (10:18–19), he presided over the selection of a king by lot. The lot fell on Saul and publicly designated him as the one whom God had chosen (10:24). Saul did not immediately assume his royal office, but returned home to work his fields (11:5,7). When the inhabitants of Jabesh-gilead were threatened by Nahash the Ammonite, Saul rose to the challenge, gathered an army and led Israel to victory in battle. His success placed a final seal of divine approval on Saul's selection to be king (cf. 10:24; 11:12–13) and occasioned the inauguration of his reign at Gilgal (11:14—12:25).

The question that still needed resolution, then, was not so much whether Israel should have a king (it was clearly the Lord's will to give them a king), but rather how they could maintain their covenant with God (i.e., preserve the theocracy) now that they had a human king. The problem was resolved when Samuel called the people to repentance and renewal of their allegiance to the Lord on the very occasion of the inauguration of Saul as king (11:14—12:25; see note on 10:25). By establishing kingship in the context of covenant renewal, Samuel placed the monarchy in Israel on a radically different footing from that in surrounding nations. The king in Israel was not to be autonomous in his authority and power; rather, he was to be subject to the law of the Lord and the word of the prophet (10:25; 12:23). This was to be true not only for Saul but also for all the kings who would occupy the throne in Israel in the future. The king was to be an instrument of the Lord's rule over His people, and the people as well as the king were to continue to recognize the Lord as their ultimate Sovereign (12:14–15).

Saul very quickly demonstrated that he was unwilling to submit to the requirements of his theocratic office (chs. 13—15). When he disobeyed the instructions of the prophet Samuel in preparation for battle against the Philistines (13:13), and when he refused to totally destroy the Amalekites as he had been commanded to do by the word of the Lord through Samuel (ch. 15), he ceased to be an instrument of the Lord's rule over His people. These abrogations of the requirements of his theocratic office led to his rejection as king (15:23).

The remainder of 1 Samuel (chs. 16—31) depicts the Lord's choice of David to be Saul's successor, and then describes the long road by which David is prepared for accession to the throne. Although Saul's rule became increasingly anti-theocratic in nature, David refused to usurp the throne by forceful means but left his accession to office in the Lord's hands. Eventually Saul was wounded in a battle with the Philistines and, fearing capture, took his own life. Three of Saul's sons, including David's loyal friend Jonathan, were killed in the same battle (ch. 31).

Chronology

Even though the narratives of 1,2 Samuel contain some statements of chronological import (see, e.g., 1 Sam 6:1; 7:2; 8:1,5; 13:1; 25:1; 2 Sam 2:10–11; 5:4–5; 14:28; 15:7), the data are insufficient to establish a precise chronology for the major events of this period of Israel's history. Except for the dates of David's birth and the duration of his reign, which are quite firm (see 2 Sam 5:4–5), most other dates can only be approximated. The textual problem with the chronological data on the age of Saul when he became king and the length of his reign (see note on 1 Sam 13:1) contributes to uncertainty concerning the precise time of his birth and the beginning of his reign. No information is given concerning the time of Samuel's birth (1 Sam 1:1) or death (25:1). His lifetime must have spanned, at least in part, that of Samson and that of Obed, son of Ruth and Boaz and grandfather of David. It is indicated that he was well along in years when the elders of Israel asked him to give them a king (see 8:1,5). One other factor contributing to chronological uncertainty is that the author has not always arranged his material in strict chronological sequence. It seems clear, for example, that 2 Sam 7 is to be placed chronologically after David's conquests described in 2 Sam 8:1–14 (see notes on 2 Sam 7:1; 8:1). The story of the famine sent by God on Israel during the reign of David because of Saul's violation of a treaty with the Gibeonites is found in 2 Sam 21:1–4, though chronologically it occurred prior to the time of Absalom's rebellion recorded in 2 Sam 15—18 (see further the notes on 2 Sam 21:1–2). The following dates, however, provide an approximate chronological framework for the times of Samuel, Saul and David.

1105 B.C.	Birth of Samuel (1 Sam 1:20)
1080	Birth of Saul
1050	Saul anointed to be king (1 Sam 10:1)
1040	Birth of David
1025	David anointed to be Saul's successor (1 Sam 16:1–13)
1010	Death of Saul and beginning of David's reign over Judah in Hebron (2 Sam 1:1; 2:1,4,11)
1003	Beginning of David's reign over all Israel and capture of Jerusalem (2 Sam 5)
997–992	David's wars (2 Sam 8:1–14)
991	Birth of Solomon (2 Sam 12:24; 1 Ki 3:7; 11:42)
980	David's census (2 Sam 24:1)
970	End of David's reign (2 Sam 5:4–5; 1 Ki 2:10–11)

Outline

- I. Historical Setting for the Establishment of Kingship in Israel (1 Sam 1—7)
  - A. Samuel's Birth, Youth and Calling to Be a Prophet; Judgment on the House of Eli (1 Sam 1—3)
  - B. Israel Defeated by the Philistines, the Ark of God Taken and the Ark Restored; Samuel's Role as Judge and Deliverer (1 Sam 4—7)
- II. The Establishment of Kingship in Israel under the Guidance of Samuel the Prophet (1 Sam 8—12)
  - A. The People's Sinful Request for a King and God's Intent to Give Them a King (1 Sam 8)
  - B. Samuel Anoints Saul Privately to Be King (1 Sam 9:1—10:16)
  - C. Saul Chosen to Be King Publicly by Lot at Mizpeh (1 Sam 10:17–27)
  - D. The Choice of Saul as King Confirmed by Victory over the Ammonites (1 Sam 11:1–13)
  - E. Saul's Reign Inaugurated at a Covenant Renewal Ceremony Convened by Samuel at Gilgal (1 Sam 11:14—12:25)
- III. Saul's Kingship a Failure (1 Sam 13—15)
- IV. David's Rise to the Throne; Progressive Deterioration and End of Saul's Reign (1 Sam 16:1—2 Sam 5:5)

- A. David Is Anointed Privately, Enters the Service of King Saul and Flees for His Life (1 Sam 16—26)
- B. David Seeks Refuge in Philistia, and Saul and His Sons Are Killed in Battle (1 Sam 27—31)
- C. David Becomes King over Judah (2 Sam 1—4)
- D. David Becomes King over All Israel (2 Sam 5:1–5)

V. David's Kingship in Its Accomplishments and Glory (2 Sam 5:6—9:12)

- A. David Conquers Jerusalem and Defeats the Philistines (2 Sam 5:6–25)
- B. David Brings the Ark to Jerusalem (2 Sam 6)
- C. God Promises David an Everlasting Dynasty (2 Sam 7)
- D. The Extension of David's Kingdom Externally and the Justice of His Rule Internally (2 Sam 8)
- E. David's Faithfulness to His Covenant with Jonathan (2 Sam 9)

VI. David's Kingship in Its Weaknesses and Failures (2 Sam 10—20)

- A. David Commits Adultery and Murder (2 Sam 10—12)
- B. David Loses His Sons Amnon and Absalom (2 Sam 13—20)

VII. Final Reflections on David's Reign (2 Sam 21—24)

Samuel's birth

1 Now there was a certain man of Ramathaim-zophim, of mount Ephraim, and his name *was* [a]Elkanah, the son of Jeroham, the son of Elihu, the son of Tohu, the son of Zuph, [b]an Ephrathite:

2 And he had two wives; the name of the one *was* Hannah, and the name of the other Peninnah: and Peninnah had children, but Hannah had no children.

3 And this man went up out of his city [a][1]yearly [b]to worship and to sacrifice unto the LORD of hosts in [c]Shiloh. And the two sons of Eli, Hophni and Phinehas, the priests of the LORD, *were* there.

4 And when the time was that Elkanah [a]offered, he gave to Peninnah his wife, and to all her sons and her daughters, portions:

5 But unto Hannah he gave [1]a worthy portion; for he loved Hannah: [a]but the LORD had shut up her womb.

6 And her adversary also [a][1]provoked her sore, for to make her fret, because the LORD had shut up her womb.

7 And *as* he did so year by year, [1]when she went up to the house of the LORD, so she provoked her; therefore she wept, and did not eat.

8 Then said Elkanah her husband to her, Hannah, why weepest thou? and why eatest thou not? and why is thy heart grieved? *am* not I [a]better to thee than ten sons?

9 ¶ So Hannah rose up after *they* had eaten in Shiloh, and after *they* had drunk. Now Eli the priest sat upon a seat by a post of [a]the temple of the LORD.

10 [a]And she *was* [1]in bitterness of soul, and prayed unto the LORD, and wept sore.

11 And she [a]vowed a vow, and said, O LORD of hosts, if thou wilt indeed [b]look on the affliction of thine handmaid, and [c]remember me, and not forget thine handmaid, but wilt give unto thine handmaid [1]a man child, then I will give him unto the LORD all the days of his life, and [d]there shall no rasor come upon his head.

12 And it came to pass, as she [1]continued praying before the LORD, that Eli marked her mouth.

13 Now Hannah, she spake in her heart; only her lips moved, but her voice was not heard: therefore Eli thought she had been drunken.

14 And Eli said unto her, How long wilt thou be drunken? put away thy wine from thee.

15 And Hannah answered and said, No, my lord, I *am* a woman [1]of a sorrowful spirit: I have drunk neither wine nor strong drink, but have [a]poured out my soul before the LORD.

1:1 [a]1 Chr. 6:27,34 [b]Ruth 1:2
1:3 [1]Heb. *from year to year* [a]Ex. 23:14; Luke 2:41 [b]Deut. 12:5 [c]Josh. 18:1
1:4 [a]Deut. 12:17
1:5 [1]Or, *a double portion* [a]Gen. 30:2
1:6 [1]Heb. *angered her* [a]Job 24:21
1:7 [1]Or, *from the time that she, etc.* Heb. *from her going up*
1:8 [a]Ruth 4:15
1:9 [a]ch. 3:3
1:10 [1]Heb. *bitter of soul* [a]Job 7:11
1:11 [1]Heb. *seed of men* [a]Gen. 28:20 [b]Ps. 25:18 [c]Gen. 8:1 [d]Num. 6:5
1:12 [1]Heb. *multiplied to pray*
1:15 [1]Heb. *hard of spirit* [a]Ps. 62:8

1:1 *Ramathaim-zophim.* The name occurs only here in the OT and appears to be another name for Ramah (see 1:19; 2:11; 7:17; 19:18; 25:1). It is perhaps to be identified with the Ramah of Benjamin (see Josh 18:25) located in the hill country about five miles north of Jerusalem near the border of Ephraim and Benjamin. *-zophim.* Or "a Zuphite." It is not entirely clear whether this word refers to the man or the place. If it refers to the man, it indicates his descent from Zuph (see 1 Chr 6:34–35). If it refers to the place, it designates the general area in which Ramathaim is located (see 9:5). *Ephrathite.* Although Elkanah is here called an Ephrathite, he was probably a Levite whose family belonged to the Kohathite clans that had been allotted towns in Ephraim (see Josh 21:20–21; 1 Chr 6:22–26).

1:2 *two wives.* See notes on Gen 4:19; 16:2; 25:6.

1:3 *this man went up . . . yearly.* Three times a year every Israelite male was required to appear before the Lord at the central sanctuary (Ex 23:14–19; 34:23; Deut 16:16–17). The festival referred to here was probably the feast of tabernacles, which not only commemorated God's care for His people during the wilderness journey to Canaan (see Lev 23:43) but more especially celebrated, with joy and feasting, God's blessing on the year's crops (see Deut 16:13–15). On such festive occasions Hannah's deep sorrow because of her own barrenness was the more poignant. *the LORD of hosts.* This is the first time in the Bible that God is designated by this title. The Hebrew for "host(s)" can refer to (1) human armies (Ex 7:4; Ps 44:9); (2) the celestial bodies such as the sun, moon and stars (Gen 2:1; Deut 4:19; Is 40:26); or (3) the heavenly creatures such as angels (Josh 5:14; 1 Ki 22:19; Ps 148:2). The title, "the LORD of hosts," is perhaps best understood as a general reference to the sovereignty of God over all powers in the universe. In the account of the establishment of kingship in Israel it became particularly appropriate as a reference to God as the God of armies—both of the heavenly army (Deut 33:2; Josh 5:14; Ps 68:17; Hab 3:8) and of the army of Israel (1 Sam 17:45). *Shiloh.* The town in Ephraim between Bethel and Shechem where the central sanctuary and the ark of the covenant were located (see Josh 18:1; Judg 21:19).

1:4 *offered.* Here refers to a sacrifice that was combined with a festive meal signifying fellowship and communion with the Lord and grateful acknowledgment of His mercies (see Lev 7:11–18; Deut 12:7,17–18).

1:5 *the LORD had shut up her womb.* The Lord gives and withholds children (see Gen 18:10; 29:31; 30:2,22).

1:6 *her adversary.* See note on Gen 16:4.

1:9 *temple.* Here and in 3:3 the central sanctuary, the tabernacle (the temple in Jerusalem had not yet been built), is referred to as "the temple of the LORD." It is also called "the house of the LORD" (v. 7; 3:15), "the tabernacle of the congregation" (2:22) and "my habitation" (2:32). The references to the tabernacle as a "house" and a "temple," as well as references to sleeping quarters and doors (3:2,15), give the impression that at this time the tabernacle was part of a larger, more permanent building complex to which the term "temple" could legitimately be applied (cf. Jer 7:12,14; 26:6).

1:11 *vow.* See Gen 28:20–22; Num 21:2; Ps 50:14; 76:11; 116:14,18; 132:2–5; Prov 20:25; 31:2. Regulations for the making of vows by women are found in Num 30. *remember.* To remember is more than simply to recall that Hannah existed. It is to go into action in her behalf (see v. 19; see also note on Gen 8:1). *all the days of his life.* In contrast to the normal period of service for Levites, which was from age 25 to 50 (see Num 8:23–26). *shall no rasor come.* Hannah voluntarily vows for her son that which God had required of Samson (Judg 13:5). Long hair was a symbol of dedication to the service of the Lord and was one of the characteristics of the Nazarite vow (see Num 6:1–21). The vow was normally taken for a limited time rather than for life.

1:13 *drunken.* Eli's mistake suggests that in those days it was not uncommon for drunken people to enter the sanctuary. Further evidence of the religious and moral deterioration of the time is found in the stories of Judg 17–21.

16 Count not thine handmaid for a daughter of [a]Belial: for out of the abundance of my
[1]complaint and grief have I spoken hitherto.
17 Then Eli answered and said, [a]Go in
peace: and [b]the God of Israel grant *thee* thy
petition that thou hast asked of him.
18 And she said, [a]Let thine handmaid find
grace in thy sight. So the woman [b]went her
way, and did eat, and her countenance was no
more *sad.*
19 And they rose up in the morning early,
and worshipped before the LORD, and returned, and came to their house to Ramah:
and Elkanah [a]knew Hannah his wife; and [b]the
LORD remembered her.
20 Wherefore it came to pass, [1]when the
time was come about after Hannah had conceived, that she bare a son, and called his
name [2]Samuel, *saying,* Because I have asked
him of the LORD.

Samuel dedicated

21 ¶ And the man Elkanah, and all his
house, [a]went up to offer unto the LORD the
yearly sacrifice, and his vow.
22 But Hannah went not up; for she said
unto her husband, *I will not go up* until the
child be weaned, and *then* I will [a]bring him,
that he may appear before the LORD, and there
[b]abide [c]for ever.
23 And [a]Elkanah her husband said unto
her, Do what seemeth thee good; tarry until
thou have weaned him; [b]only the LORD establish his word. So the woman abode, and gave
her son suck until she weaned him.
24 And when she had weaned him, she
[a]took him up with her, with three bullocks,
and one ephah of flour, and a bottle of wine,
and brought him *unto* [b]the house of the LORD
in Shiloh: and the child *was* young.
25 And they slew a bullock, and [a]brought
the child to Eli.
26 And she said, O my lord, [a]*as* thy soul
liveth, my lord, I *am* the woman that stood by
thee here, praying unto the LORD.
27 [a]For this child I prayed; and the LORD
hath given me my petition which I asked of
him:
28 Therefore also I have [1]lent him to the
LORD; as long as he liveth [2]he *shall be* lent to
the LORD. And he [a]worshipped the LORD there.

Hannah's song of praise

2 And Hannah [a]prayed, and said,
[b]My heart rejoiceth in the LORD,
[c]Mine horn is exalted in the LORD:
My mouth is enlarged over mine
enemies;
Because I [d]rejoice in thy salvation.
2 [a]*There is* none holy as the LORD:
For *there is* [b]none beside thee:
Neither *is there* any rock like our God.
3 Talk no more *so* exceeding proudly;
[a]Let *not* [1]arrogancy come out of your
mouth:
For the LORD *is* a God of knowledge,
And by him actions are weighed.
4 [a]The bows of the mighty *men are*
broken,
And they that stumbled are girt with
strength.
5 *They that were* full have hired out
themselves for bread;
And *they that were* hungry ceased:
So that [a]the barren hath born seven;
And [b]she that hath many children is
waxed feeble.

1:16 [1]Or, *meditation* [a]Deut. 13:13
1:17 [a]Judg. 18:6; Mark 5:34 [b]Ps. 20:4,5
1:18 [a]Ruth 2:13 [b]Eccl. 9:7
1:19 [a]Gen. 4:1 [b]Gen. 30:22
1:20 [1]Heb. [*in*] *revolution of days* [2]That is, *Asked of God*
1:21 [a]ver. 3
1:22 [a]Luke 2:22 [b]ver. 11:28 [c]Ex. 21:6
1:23 [a]Num. 30:7 [b]2 Sam. 7:25
1:24 [a]Deut. 12:5,6,11
1:24 [b]Josh. 18:1
1:25 [a]Luke 2:22
1:26 [a]2 Ki. 2:2,4,6
1:27 [a]Mat. 7:7
1:28 [1]Or, *returned him, whom I have obtained by petition, to the LORD* [2]Or, *he whom I have obtained by petition shall be returned* [a]Gen. 24:26,52
2:1 [a]Phil. 4:6 [b]See Luke 1:46 [c]Ps. 92:10 [d]Ps. 9:14
2:2 [a]Ex. 15:11 [b]Deut. 4:35
2:3 [1]Heb. *hard* [a]Ps. 94:4; Jude 15
2:4 [a]Ps. 37:15
2:5 [a]Ps. 113:9 [b]Is. 54:1

1:16 *Belial.* I.e. "worthless." See note on Deut 13:13.
1:20 *Samuel.* "Samuel" sounds like the Hebrew for "heard of God."
1:21 *yearly sacrifice.* See notes on vv. 3–4. *his vow.* Making vows to God was a common feature of OT piety, usually involving thank offerings and praise (see Lev 7:16; Ps 50:14; 56:12; 66:13–15; 116:17–18; Is 19:21). Elkanah no doubt annually made vows to the Lord as he prayed for God's blessing on his crops and flocks, and fulfilled those vows at the feast of tabernacles (see note on v. 3).
1:22 *weaned.* It was customary in the East to nurse children for three years or longer (in the Apocrypha see 2 Maccabees 7:27) since there was no way to keep milk sweet.
1:23 *his word.* No previous word from God is mentioned, unless this refers to the pronouncement of Eli in v. 17. The Dead Sea Scrolls, Septuagint (the Greek translation of the OT) and Syriac version resolve this problem by reading "your word."
1:26 *as thy soul liveth.* A customary way of emphasizing the truthfulness of one's words.
2:1 *prayed.* Hannah's prayer is a song of praise and thanksgiving to God (see Ps 72:20, where the psalms of David are designated "prayers"). This song has sometimes been termed the "Magnificat of the OT" because it is so similar to the Magnificat of the NT (Mary's song, Luke 1:46–55). It also has certain resemblances to the "Benedictus" (the song of Zacharias, Luke 1:67–79). Hannah's song of praise finds many echoes in David's song near the end of the book (2 Sam 22). These two songs frame the main narrative, and their themes highlight the ways of God that the narrative relates—they contain the theology of the book in the form of praise. Hannah speaks prophetically at a time when Israel is about to enter an important new period of her history with the establishment of kingship through her son, Samuel. *rejoiceth in the LORD.* The supreme source of Hannah's joy is not in the child, but in the God who has answered her prayer. *Mine horn is exalted in the LORD.* Cf. Deut 33:17; Ps 75:5,10; 92:10; 112:9; Luke 1:69. To have one's horn lifted up by God is to be delivered from disgrace to a position of honor and strength.
2:2 *none beside thee.* See 2 Sam 7:22; Deut 4:39; Is 45:6. *rock.* A metaphor to depict the strength and stability of the God of Israel as the unfailing source of security for His people (see 2 Sam 22:32; Deut 32:4,31; Ps 18:31; Is 30:29; 44:8).
2:3 *so exceeding proudly . . . arrogancy.* After the manner of Peninnah (and others in the narratives of 1,2 Samuel—Eli's sons, the Philistines, Saul, Nabal, Goliath, Absalom, Shimei and Sheba). *the LORD is a God of knowledge.* See 16:7; 1 Ki 8:39; Ps 139:1–6.
2:4–5 In a series of examples derived from everyday life Hannah shows that God often works contrary to natural expectations and brings about surprising reversals—seen frequently in the stories that follow.
2:5 *born seven.* See note on Ruth 4:15.

6 [a]The LORD killeth, and maketh alive:
He bringeth down *to* the grave, and
bringeth up.
7 The LORD [a]maketh poor, and maketh
rich:
[b]He bringeth low, and lifteth up.
8 [a]He raiseth up the poor out of the dust,
And lifteth up the beggar from the
dunghill,
[b]To set *them* among princes,
And to make them inherit the throne
of glory:
For [c]the pillars of the earth *are* the
LORD'S,
And he hath set the world upon them.
9 [a]He will keep the feet of his saints,
And the wicked shall be silent in
darkness;
For by strength shall no man prevail.
10 The adversaries of the LORD shall be
[a]broken to pieces;
[b]Out of heaven shall he thunder upon
them:
[c]The LORD shall judge the ends of the
earth;
And he shall give strength unto his
king,
And [d]exalt the horn of his anointed.
11 And Elkanah went to Ramah to his
house. [a]And the child did minister unto the
LORD before Eli the priest.

The sons of Eli

12 ¶ Now the sons of Eli *were* sons of Belial; [a]they knew not the LORD.
13 And the priests' custom with the people
was, that when any man offered sacrifice, the
priest's servant came, while the flesh was in
seething, with a fleshhook of three teeth in his
hand;
14 And he stroke *it* into the pan, or kettle,
or caldron, or pot; all that the fleshhook brought
up the priest took for himself. So they did in
Shiloh unto all the Israelites that came thither.
15 Also before they [a]burnt the fat, the
priest's servant came, and said to the man that
sacrificed, Give flesh to roast for the priest; for
he will not have sodden flesh of thee, but raw.
16 And *if any* man said unto him, Let them
not fail to burn the fat [1]presently, and *then*
take *as much* as thy soul desireth; then he
would answer him, *Nay;* but thou shalt give *it*
me now: and if not, I will take *it* by force.
17 Wherefore the sin of the young men
was very great [a]before the LORD: for men [b]ab-
horred the offering of the LORD.
18 ¶ [a]But Samuel ministered before the
LORD, *being* a child, [b]girded *with* a linen
ephod.

2:6 [a]Job 5:18; Hos. 6:1
2:7 [a]Job 1:21 [b]Ps. 75:7
2:8 [a]Luke 1:52 [b]Job 36:7 [c]Job 38:4-6
2:9 [a]Ps. 91:11
2:10 [a]Ps. 2:9 [b]Ps. 18:13 [c]Ps. 96:13 [d]Ps. 89:24
2:11 [a]ver. 18; ch. 3:1
2:12 [a]Judg. 2:10; Rom. 1:28
2:15 [a]Lev. 3:3,4,5,16
2:16 [1]Heb. *as on the day*
2:17 [a]Gen. 6:11 [b]Mal. 2:8
2:18 [a]ver. 11 [b]Ex. 28:4

2:6–8 Hannah declares that life and death, prosperity and adversity, are determined by the sovereign power of God—another theme richly illustrated in the following narrative (see Deut 32:39; 1 Ki 17:20–24; 2 Ki 4:32–35; John 5:21; 11:41–44).
‡2:6 *the grave.* Hebrew *Sheol;* i.e. the netherworld. See note on Gen 37:35.
2:8 *pillars of the earth.* A common figure in the OT for the solid base on which the earth (the dry land on which man lives, not planet earth; Gen 1:10) is founded. The phrase does not teach a particular theory of the structure of the universe (see Job 9:6; 38:6; Ps 75:3; 104:5; Zech 12:1).
2:9 *keep the feet.* Travel in ancient Israel was for the most part by foot over trails that were often rocky and dangerous (see Ps 91:11–12; 121:3). *saints.* People who are faithful to the Lord. The Hebrew root underlying this word is used of both God and His people in 2 Sam 22:26 (see also Ps 18:25) to characterize the nature of their mutual relationship. The word is also found in Ps 12:1; 32:6; Prov 2:8.
2:10 *judge.* Impose His righteous rule upon (see Ps 96:13; 98:9). *ends of the earth.* All nations and peoples (see Deut 33:17; Is 45:22). *his king.* Hannah's prayer is here prophetic, anticipating the establishment of kingship in Israel and the initial realization of the Messianic ideal in David (Luke 1:69). Ultimately her expectation finds fulfillment in Christ and His complete triumph over the enemies of God. *horn.* See note on v. 1. *anointed.* The first reference in the Bible to the Lord's anointed—i.e., His anointed king. (Priests were also anointed for God's service; see Ex 28:41; Lev 4:3.) The word is often synonymous with "king" (as here) and provides part of the vocabulary basis for the Messianic idea in the Bible. "Anointed" and "Messiah" are the translation and transliteration respectively of the same Hebrew word. The Greek translation of this Hebrew term is *Christos,* from which comes the English word "Christ" (see note on Mat 1:17). A king (coming from the tribe of Judah) is first prophesied by Jacob (Gen 49:10); kingship is further anticipated in the oracles of Balaam in Num 24:7,17. Also Deut 17:14–20 looks forward to the time when the Lord will place a king of His choice over His people after they enter the promised land. 1,2 Samuel shows how this expectation of the theocratic king is realized in the person of David. Hannah's prophetic anticipation of a king at the time of the dedication of her son Samuel, who was to be God's agent for establishing kingship in Israel, is entirely appropriate.
2:11 *minister.* Performed such services as a boy might render while assisting the high priest. *unto the LORD.* At the "house of the LORD" (1:24).
2:12 *sons of Belial.* See note on Deut 13:13. *knew not.* In OT usage, to "know" the Lord is not just intellectual or theoretical recognition. To know the Lord is to enter into fellowship with Him and acknowledge His claims on one's life. The term often has a covenantal connotation (see Jer 31:34; Hos 13:4).
2:13–16 Apparently vv. 13–14 describe the practice that had come to be accepted for determining the priests' portion of the peace offerings (Lev 7:31–36; 10:14–15; Deut 18:1–5)—a tradition presumably based on the assumption that a random thrust of the fork would providentially determine a fair portion. Verses 15–16 then describe how Eli's sons arrogantly violated that custom and the law.
2:15 *before they burnt the fat.* On the altar as the Lord's portion, which He was to receive first (see Lev 3:16; 4:10,26,31,35; 7:28,30–31; 17:6). *roast.* Boiling is the only form of cooking specified in the law for the priests' portion (Num 6:19–20). Roasting this portion is nowhere expressly forbidden in the law, but it is specified only for the passover lamb (Ex 12:8–9; Deut 16:7). The present passage seems to imply that for the priests to roast their portion of the sacrifices was unlawful.
2:16 *by force.* Presenting the priests' portion was to be a voluntary act on the part of the worshipers (see Lev 7:28–36; Deut 18:3).
2:18 *But Samuel.* Between 2:11 and 4:1 the author presents a series of sharp contrasts between Samuel and Eli's sons. *linen ephod.* A priestly garment worn by those who served before

19 Moreover his mother made him a little coat, and brought *it* to him from year to year, when she [a]came up with her husband to offer the yearly sacrifice.

20 And Eli [a]blessed Elkanah and his wife, and said, The LORD give thee seed of this woman for the [1]loan which is [b]lent to the LORD. And they went unto their own home.

21 And the LORD [a]visited Hannah, so that she conceived, and bare three sons and two daughters. And the child Samuel [b]grew before the LORD.

22 Now Eli was very old, and heard all that his sons did unto all Israel; and how they lay with [a]the women that [1]assembled *at* the door of the tabernacle of the congregation.

23 And he said unto them, Why do ye such things? for [1]I hear of your evil dealings by all this people.

24 Nay, my sons; for *it is* no good report that I hear: *ye* make the LORD'S people [1]to transgress.

25 If one man sin against another, the judge shall judge him: but if a man [a]sin against the LORD, who shall intreat for him? Notwithstanding they hearkened not unto the voice of their father, [b]because the LORD would slay them.

26 And the child Samuel [a]grew on, and was [b]in favour both with the LORD, and also with men.

The prophecy of doom to Eli

27 ¶ [a]And there came a man of God unto Eli, and said unto him, Thus saith the LORD, [b]Did I plainly appear unto the house of thy father, when they were in Egypt in Pharaoh's house?

28 And did I [a]choose him out of all the tribes of Israel to be my priest, to offer upon mine altar, to burn incense, to wear an ephod before me? and [b]did I give unto the house of thy father all the offerings made by fire of the children of Israel?

29 Wherefore [a]kick ye at my sacrifice and at mine offering, which I have commanded *in my* [b]habitation; and honourest thy sons above me, to make yourselves fat with the chiefest of all the offerings of Israel my people?

30 Wherefore the LORD God of Israel saith, [a]I said indeed *that* thy house, and the house of thy father, should walk before me for ever: but now the LORD saith, [b]Be it far from me; for them that honour me [c]I will honour, and [d]they that despise me shall be lightly esteemed.

31 Behold, [a]the days come, that I will cut off thine arm, and the arm of thy father's house, that there shall not be an old man in thine house.

32 And thou shalt see [1]an enemy *in my* habitation, in all *the wealth* which *God* shall give Israel: and there shall not be [a]an old man in thine house for ever.

33 And the man of thine, *whom* I shall not cut off from mine altar, *shall be* to consume thine eyes, and to grieve thine heart: and all

2:19 [a]ch. 1:3
2:20 [1]Or, *petition which he asked, etc.* [a]Gen. 14:19 [b]ch. 1:28
2:21 [a]Gen. 21:1 [b]ver. 26; Judg. 13:24
2:22 [1]Heb. *assembled by troops* [a]Ex. 38:8
2:23 [1]Or, *I hear evil words of you*
2:24 [1]Or, *to cry out*
2:25 [a]Num. 15:30 [b]Josh. 11:20
2:26 [a]ver. 21 [b]Prov. 3:4
2:27 [a]1 Ki. 13:1
2:27 [b]Ex. 4:14,27
2:28 [a]Ex. 28:1,4; Num. 16:5 [b]Lev. 2:3,10; 6:16; 7:7,8,34,35; Num. 5:9
2:29 [a]Deut. 32:15 [b]Deut. 12:5
2:30 [a]Ex. 29:9 [b]Jer. 18:9,10 [c]Ps. 91:14 [d]Mal. 2:9
2:31 [a]1 Ki. 2:27; See ch. 4:11,18,20; 14:3; 22:18
2:32 [1]Or, *the affliction of the tabernacle, for all* the wealth *which* God *would have given Israel* [a]Zech. 8:4

the Lord at His sanctuary (see 22:18; 2 Sam 6:14). It was a close-fitting, sleeveless pullover, usually of hip length, and is to be distinguished from the special ephod worn by the high priest (see note on v. 28; cf. Ex 39:1–26).

2:19 *little coat.* A sleeveless garment reaching to the knees, worn over the undergarment and under the ephod (see 15:27; 18:4). *yearly sacrifice.* See note on 1:3.

2:22 *lay with the women that assembled.* See Ex 38:8. There is no further reference to such women in the OT. Perhaps these women performed various menial tasks, but certainly their service is not to be confused with that of the Levites, which is prescribed in the Pentateuch (Num 1:50; 3:6–8; 8:15; 16:9; 18:2–3). The immoral acts of Eli's sons are reminiscent of the religious prostitution (fertility rites) at the Canaanite sanctuaries (see 1 Ki 14:24; 15:12; 22:46)—acts that were an abomination to the Lord and a desecration of His house (Deut 23:17–18).

2:23 *he said unto them.* Eli rebuked his sons but did not remove them from office. God would do that.

‡2:25 *the judge.* Hebrew *Elohim,* i.e. "God." Eli's argument is that when someone commits an offense against another man, there is recourse to a third party to decide the issue (whether this be understood as God or as God's representatives, the judges; see Ex 22:8–9 and note on Ex 22:11); but when the offense is against the Lord, there is no recourse, for God is both the one wronged and the judge. *the LORD would slay them.* This comment by the author of the narrative is not intended to excuse Eli's sons, but to indicate that Eli's warning was much too late. Eli's sons had persisted in their evil ways for so long that God's judgment on them was determined (v. 34; see Josh 11:20).

2:26 *grew on, and was in favour both with the LORD, and also with men.* Cf. Luke's description of Jesus (Luke 2:52).

2:27 *man of God.* Often a designation for a prophet (see 9:6,10; Deut 33:1; Josh 14:6; 1 Ki 13:1,6–8; 17:18,24; 2 Ki 4:7). *house of thy father.* The descendants of Aaron.

2:28 *to be my priest.* Three tasks of the priests are mentioned: 1. *to offer upon mine altar.* To perform the sacrificial rites at the altar of burnt offering in the courtyard of the tabernacle. 2. *to burn incense.* At the altar of incense in the holy place (Ex 30:1–10). 3. *to wear an ephod.* See note on v. 18. It would appear that the reference here is to the special ephod of the high priest (see Ex 28:4–13). The breastplate containing the Urim and Thummim was attached to the ephod of the high priest. The Urim and Thummim were a divinely ordained means of communication with God, placed in the custody of the high priest (see Ex 28:30 and note; see also 1 Sam 23:9–12; 30:7–8).

2:30 *I said indeed.* See Ex 29:9; Lev 8–9; Num 16–17; 25:13. *Be it far from me.* This is not to say that the promise of the priesthood to Aaron's house has been annulled, but that Eli and his house are to be excluded from participation in this privilege because of their sin. *them that honour me I will honour.* See v. 29. Spiritual privileges bring responsibilities and obligations; they are not to be treated as irrevocable rights (see 2 Sam 22:26–27).

2:31 *arm . . . arm.* Symbolic of strength. Eli's "arm" and that of his priestly family will be cut off (contrast David, 2 Sam 22:35). *not be an old man in thine house.* A prediction of the decimation of Eli's priestly family in the death of his sons (4:11), in the massacre of his descendants by Saul at Nob (22:18–19) and in the removal of Abiathar from his priestly office (1 Ki 2:26–27).

2:32 *enemy in my habitation.* Including the capture of the ark by the Philistines (4:1–10), the destruction of Shiloh (Jer 7:14) and the relocation of the tabernacle to Nob (21:1–6; see note on 21:1).

2:33 A reference apparently to Abiathar, who was expelled from office by Solomon (see 1 Ki 2:26–27) after an unsuccessful attempt to make Adonijah king as the successor to David.

the increase of thine house shall die [1]in the
flower of their age.
34 And this *shall be* [a]a sign unto thee, that
shall come upon thy two sons, on Hophni and
Phinehas; [b]in one day they shall die both of
them.
35 And [a]I will raise me up a faithful priest,
that shall do according to *that* which *is* in my
heart and in my mind: and [b]I will build him a
sure house; and he shall walk before [c]mine
anointed for ever.
36 [a]And it shall come to pass, *that* every
one that is left in thine house shall come and
crouch to him for a piece of silver and a morsel
of bread, and shall say, [1]Put me, I pray thee,
into [2]one of the priests' offices, that *I* may eat
a piece of bread.

The LORD calls Samuel

3 And [a]the child Samuel ministered unto
the LORD before Eli. And [b]the word of
the LORD was precious in those days; *there was*
no open vision.
2 And it came to pass at that time, when
Eli *was* laid down in his place, and his eyes
began *to wax* dim, *that* he could not see;
3 And ere [a]the lamp of God went out [b]in
the temple of the LORD, where the ark of God
was, and Samuel was laid down *to sleep;*
4 That the LORD called Samuel: and he answered, Here *am* I.
5 And he ran unto Eli, and said, Here *am* I;
for thou calledst me. And he said, I called not;
lie down again. And he went and lay down.
6 And the LORD called yet again, Samuel.
And Samuel arose and went to Eli, and said,
Here *am* I; for thou didst call me. And he answered, I called not, my son; lie down again.
7 [1]Now Samuel [a]did not yet know the
LORD, neither was the word of the LORD yet revealed unto him.
8 And the LORD called Samuel again the
third time. And he arose and went to Eli, and
said, Here *am* I; for thou didst call me. And Eli
perceived that the LORD had called the child.
9 Therefore Eli said unto Samuel, Go, lie
down: and it shall be, if he call thee, that thou
shalt say, Speak, LORD; for thy servant heareth.
So Samuel went and lay down in his place.
10 And the LORD came, and stood, and called
as at other times, Samuel, Samuel. Then Samuel
answered, Speak; for thy servant heareth.
11 And the LORD said to Samuel, Behold, I
will do a thing in Israel, [a]*at* which both the
ears of every one that heareth it shall tingle.
12 In that day I will perform against Eli [a]all
things which I have spoken concerning his
house: [1]when I begin, I will also make an end.
13 [a][1]For I have told him that I will [b]judge
his house for ever for the iniquity which he
knoweth; because [c]his sons made themselves
[2]vile, and he [d][3]restrained them not.
14 And therefore I have sworn unto the
house of Eli, that the iniquity of Eli's house
[a]shall not be purged with sacrifice nor offering
for ever.
15 And Samuel lay until the morning, and
opened the doors of the house of the LORD.
And Samuel feared to shew Eli the vision.
16 Then Eli called Samuel, and said, Samuel, my son. And he answered, Here *am* I.
17 And he said, What *is* the thing that *the*
LORD hath said unto thee? I pray thee hide *it*
not from me: [a]God do so to thee, and [1]more
also, if thou hide *any* [2]thing from me of all the
things that he said unto thee.

2:33 [1]Heb. *men* **2:34** [a]1 Ki. 13:3 [b]ch. 4:11 **2:35** [a]1 Ki. 2:35; Ezek. 44:15 [b]2 Sam. 7:11,27; 1 Ki. 11:38 [c]Ps. 18:50 **2:36** [1]Heb. *Join* [2]Or, *somewhat about the priesthood* [a]1 Ki. 2:27 **3:1** [a]ch. 2:11 [b]Ps. 74:9; Amos 8:11 **3:3** [a]Ex. 27:20 [b]ch. 1:9

3:7 [1]Or, *Thus* did *Samuel before he knew the LORD, and before the word of the LORD was revealed unto him* [a]See Acts 19:2 **3:11** [a]2 Ki. 21:12 **3:12** [1]Heb. *beginning and ending* [a]ch. 2:30-36 **3:13** [1]Or, *And I will tell him, etc.* [2]Or, *accursed* [3]Heb. *frowned not upon them* [a]ch. 2:29-31 [b]Ezek. 7:3; 18:30 [c]ch. 2:12,17,22 [d]ch. 2:23,25 **3:14** [a]Num. 15:30,31 **3:17** [1]Heb. *so add* [2]Or, *word* [a]Ruth 1:17

2:34 *a sign unto thee.* The death of Hophni and Phinehas (4:11) will confirm the longer-term predictions. Such confirmation of a prophetic word was not uncommon (see 10:7–9; 1 Ki 13:3; Jer 28:15–17; Luke 1:18–20).

2:35 *I will raise me up a faithful priest.* Initially fulfilled in the person of Zadok, who served as a priest during the time of David (see 2 Sam 8:17; 15:24,35; 20:25) and who eventually replaced Abiathar as high priest in the time of Solomon (see 1 Ki 2:35; 1 Chr 29:22). *build him a sure house.* Lit. "build for him a faithful house"; the faithful priest will be given a "faithful" (i.e., sure, enduring) priestly family. See the similar word spoken concerning David (25:28, "sure house"; see also 2 Sam 7:16; 1 Ki 11:38). The line of Zadok was continued by his son Azariah (see 1 Ki 4:1) and was still on the scene at the time of the return from the exile (see 1 Chr 6:14–15; Ezra 3:2). It continued in intertestamental times until Antiochus IV Epiphanes (175–164 B.C.) sold the priesthood to Menelaus (in the Apocrypha see 2 Maccabees 4:23–50), who was not of the priestly line. *mine anointed.* David and his successors (see note on v. 10).

3:1 *child Samuel.* See 2:11,18. Samuel is now no longer a little child (see 2:21,26). The Jewish historian Josephus places his age at 12 years; he may have been older. *word of the LORD was precious* [i.e. rare]. See Prov 29:18; Amos 8:11. During the entire period of the judges, apart from the prophet of 2:27–36, we are told of only two prophets (Judg 4:4; 6:8) and of five revelations (Judg 2:1–3; 6:11–23; 7:2–11; 10:11–14; 13:3–21). Possibly 2 Chr 15:3 also refers to this period. *vision.* Cf. Gen 15:1.

3:3 *ere the lamp of God went out.* The reference is to the golden candlestick, which stood opposite the table of shewbread (Ex 25:31–40) in the holy place. It was still night, but the early morning hours were approaching when the flame grew dim or went out (see Ex 27:20–21; 30:7–8; Lev 24:3–4; 2 Chr 13:11; Prov 31:18). For the lamp to be permitted to go out before morning was a violation of the Pentateuchal regulations. *temple.* See note on 1:9.

3:5 *he said.* Eli's failure to recognize at once that the Lord had called Samuel may be indicative of his own unfamiliarity with the Lord.

3:7 *did not yet know the LORD.* In the sense of having a direct experience of Him (see Ex 1:8), such as receiving a revelation from God (see the last half of the verse).

3:11–14 The Lord's first revelation to Samuel repeats the message Eli had already received from the "man of God" (2:27–36), thus confirming the fact that the youth had indeed received a revelation from God.

3:15 *doors of the house of the LORD.* See note on 1:9. The tabernacle itself did not have doors. This may refer to an enclosure in which it stood. *vision.* See note on vv. 11–14.

3:17 *God do so to thee, and more.* A curse formula (see 14:44; 20:13; 25:22; 2 Sam 3:9,35; 19:13; Ruth 1:17; 1 Ki 2:23; 2 Ki 6:31), usually directed against the speaker but here used by Eli against Samuel if he conceals anything the Lord said (see also note on 14:24).

18 And Samuel told him [1]every whit, and
hid nothing from him. And he said, [a]It *is* the
LORD: let him do what seemeth him good.
19 ¶ And Samuel [a]grew, and [b]the LORD was
with him, [c]and did let none of his words fall to
the ground.
20 And all Israel [a]from Dan even to Beer-
sheba knew that Samuel *was* [1]established to
be a prophet of the LORD.
21 And the LORD appeared again in Shiloh:
for the LORD revealed himself to Samuel in Shiloh by [a]the word of the LORD.

Israel defeated by the Philistines

4 And the word of Samuel [1]came to all Israel.
¶ Now Israel went out against the Philistines to battle, and pitched beside [a]Eben-ezer:
and the Philistines pitched in Aphek.
2 And the Philistines put *themselves* in array against Israel: and when [1]they joined battle, Israel was smitten before the Philistines:
and they slew of [2]the army in the field about
four thousand men.
3 And when the people were come into
the camp, the elders of Israel said, Wherefore
hath the LORD smitten us to day before the Philistines? Let us [1]fetch the ark of the covenant
of the LORD out of Shiloh unto us, that when it
cometh among us, it may save us out of the
hand of our enemies.
4 So the people sent *to* Shiloh, that they
might bring from thence the ark of the covenant of the LORD of hosts, [a]which dwelleth
between [b]the cherubims: and the two sons of
Eli, Hophni and Phinehas, *were* there with the
ark of the covenant of God.
5 And when the ark of the covenant of the
LORD came into the camp, all Israel shouted
with a great shout, so that the earth rang again.
6 And when the Philistines heard the noise
of the shout, they said, What *meaneth* the
noise of this great shout in the camp of the
Hebrews? And they understood that the ark of
the LORD was come into the camp.
7 And the Philistines were afraid, for they
said, God is come into the camp. And they
said, Woe unto us: for there hath not been
such *a thing* [1]heretofore.
8 Woe unto us: who shall deliver us out of
the hand of these mighty Gods? these *are* the
Gods that smote the Egyptians with all the
plagues in the wilderness.
9 [a]Be strong, and [1]quit yourselves like
men, O ye Philistines, that ye be not servants
unto the Hebrews, [b]as they have been to you:
[1]quit yourselves like men, and fight.
10 And the Philistines fought, and [a]Israel
was smitten, and they fled every man into his
tent: and there was a very great slaughter; for
there fell of Israel thirty thousand footmen.
11 And [a]the ark of God was taken; and
[b]the two sons of Eli, Hophni and Phinehas,
[1]were slain.

The death of Eli

12 ¶ And there ran a man of Benjamin out
of the army, and [a]came *to* Shiloh the same day

3:18 [1]Heb. *all the things,* or, *words* [a]Job 1:21; Is. 39:8
3:19 [a]ch. 2:21 [b]Gen. 39:2,21,23 [c]ch. 9:6
3:20 [1]Or, *faithful* [a]Judg. 20:1
3:21 [a]ver. 1,4
4:1 [1]Or, *came to pass.* Heb. *was* [a]ch. 7:12
4:2 [1]Heb. *the battle was spread* [2]Heb. *the array*
4:3 [1]Heb. *take unto us*
4:4 [a]2 Sam. 6:2
4:4 [b]Num. 7:89
4:7 [1]Heb. *yesterday,* or *the third day*
4:9 [1]Heb. *be men* [a]1 Cor. 16:13 [b]Judg. 13:1
4:10 [a]ver. 2; Lev. 26:17; Deut. 28:25
4:11 [1]Heb. *died* [a]ch. 2:32; Ps. 78:61 [b]ch. 2:34; Ps. 78:64
4:12 [a]2 Sam. 1:2

3:18 *let him do what seemeth him good.* Eli bows before God, accepting the judgment as righteous (see Ex 34:5–7).
3:19 *let none of his words fall to the ground.* Because none of Samuel's words proved unreliable, he was recognized as a prophet who spoke the word of the Lord (see vv. 20–21).
3:20 *Dan even to Beer-sheba.* A conventional expression often used in Samuel, Kings and Chronicles to denote the entire land (Dan was located in the far north and Beer-sheba in the far south).
3:21 *in Shiloh.* But not after the events narrated in chs. 4–6 (see Jer 7:12–14; 26:6).
4:1 *the word of Samuel came to all Israel.* Contrast 3:1. *Eben-ezer.* Means "stone of help." The precise location is unknown, but it was probably a short distance (see v. 6) to the east of Aphek—not to be confused with the location of the stone named Eben-ezer that was later erected by Samuel between Mizpeh and Shen (see 7:12) to commemorate a victory over the Philistines. *Aphek.* A town about 12 miles northeast of the coastal city of Joppa. Philistine presence this far north suggests an attempt to spread their control over the Israelite tribes of central Canaan (see v. 9; Judg 15:11).
4:3 *Wherefore hath the LORD smitten us . . . ?* The elders understood that their defeat was more an indication of God's displeasure than it was of Philistine military might. Israel's pagan neighbors also believed that the outcome of battle was decided by the gods. *that when it cometh among us, it may save us.* In an attempt to secure the Lord's presence with them in the struggle against the Philistines, the elders sent for the ark of the covenant. They were correct in thinking there was a connection between God's presence with His people and the ark (cf. v. 4), and no doubt they remembered the presence of the ark at notable victories in Israel's past history (see Num 10:33–36; Josh 3:3,11,14–17; 6:6,12–20). But they incorrectly believed that the Lord's presence with the ark was guaranteed, rather than being subject to His free decision. They reflect the pagan notion that the deity is identified with the symbol of His presence, and that God's favor could automatically be gained by manipulating the symbol.
4:4 *dwelleth between the cherubims.* On each end of the mercy seat of the ark of the covenant were golden cherubim with their wings spread upward over the ark (see Ex 25:17–22). In the space between these cherubim God's presence with His people was localized in a special way, so that the mercy seat of the ark came to be viewed as the throne of Israel's divine King (see 2 Sam 6:2; Ps 80:1; 99:1). *Hophni and Phinehas.* These wicked priests (see 2:12) did not restrain the army from its improper use of the ark but actually accompanied the ark to the battlefield.
4:6 *Hebrews.* See note on Gen 14:13.
4:7 *God is come into the camp.* The Philistines also identified the God of Israel with the symbol of His presence (see note on v. 3).
4:8 *mighty Gods.* The Philistines could think only in polytheistic terms. *Egyptians . . . plagues.* See note on 6:6.
4:11 *the ark of God was taken.* This phrase or a variation of it occurs five times in the chapter (here, vv. 17,19,21–22) and is the focal point of the narrative. In this disastrous event, God's word in 3:11 finds a swift fulfillment. *Hophni and Phinehas, were slain.* The fulfillment of 2:34; 3:12.
4:12 *his clothes rent, and with earth upon his head.* A sign of grief and sorrow, here marking the messenger as a bearer of bad news (see 2 Sam 1:2; 13:19; 15:32).

with his clothes rent, and [b]*with* earth upon his head.

13 And when he came, lo, Eli sat upon [a]a seat *by* the wayside watching: for his heart trembled for the ark of God. And when the man came into the city, and told *it,* all the city cried out.

14 And when Eli heard the noise of the crying, he said, What *meaneth* the noise of this tumult? And the man came in hastily, and told Eli.

15 Now Eli *was* ninety and eight years old; and [a]his eyes [1]were dim, that he could not see.

16 And the man said unto Eli, I *am* he that came out of the army, and I fled to day out of the army. And he said, [a]What [1]is there done, my son?

17 And the messenger answered and said, Israel is fled before the Philistines, and there hath been also a great slaughter among the people, and thy two sons also, Hophni and Phinehas, are dead, and the ark of God is taken.

18 And it came to pass, when he made mention of the ark of God, that he fell from off the seat backward by the side of the gate, and his neck brake, and he died: for he was an old man, and heavy. [1]And he had judged Israel forty years.

19 ¶ And his daughter in law, Phinehas' wife, was with child, *near* [1]to be delivered: and when she heard the tidings that the ark of God was taken, and that her father in law and her husband were dead, she bowed herself and travailed; for her pains [2]came upon her.

20 And about the time of her death [a]the *women* that stood by her said *unto her,* Fear not; for thou hast born a son. But she answered not, [1]neither did she regard *it.*

21 And she named the child [a1]Ichabod, saying, [b]The glory is departed from Israel: because the ark of God was taken, and because of her father in law and her husband.

22 And she said, The glory is departed from Israel: for the ark of God is taken.

The Philistines move the ark

5 And the Philistines took the ark of God, and brought it [a]from Eben-ezer unto Ashdod.

2 When the Philistines took the ark of God, they brought it *into* the house of [a]Dagon, and set it by Dagon.

3 And when they of Ashdod arose early on the morrow, behold, Dagon *was* [a]fallen upon his face to the earth before the ark of the LORD. And they took Dagon, and [b]set him in his place again.

4 And when they arose early on the morrow morning, behold, Dagon *was* fallen upon his face to the ground before the ark of the LORD; and [a]the head of Dagon and both the palms of his hands *were* cut off upon the threshold; only [1]*the stump of* Dagon was left to him.

5 Therefore neither the priests of Dagon, nor any that come *into* Dagon's house, [a]tread on the threshold of Dagon in Ashdod unto this day.

6 But [a]the hand of the LORD was heavy upon them of Ashdod, and he [b]destroyed them, and smote them with [c]emerods, *even* Ashdod and the coasts thereof.

4:12 [b]Josh. 7:6; 2 Sam. 13:19; 15:32; Neh. 9:1; Job 2:12
4:13 [a]ch. 1:9
4:15 [1]Heb. *stood* [a]ch. 3:2
4:16 [1]Heb. *is the thing* [a]2 Sam. 1:4
4:18 [1][He seems to have been a Judge to do justice only, and that in South-west *Israel*]
4:19 [1]Or, *to cry out* [2]Heb. *were turned*
4:20 [a]Gen. 35:17
4:20 [1]Heb. *set not her heart*
4:21 [1]That is, *Where* is *the glory?* or, There is *no glory* [a]ch. 14:3 [b]Ps. 26:8; 78:61
5:1 [a]ch. 4:1; 7:12
5:2 [a]Judg. 16:23
5:3 [a]Is. 19:1; 46:1,2 [b]Is. 46:7
5:4 [1]Or, *the fishy part* [a]Jer. 50:2; Ezek. 6:4,6; Mic. 1:7
5:5 [a]Zeph. 1:9
5:6 [a]ver. 7,11; Ex. 9:3; Ps. 32:4; Acts 13:11 [b]ch. 6:5 [c]Deut. 28:27; Ps. 78:66

4:13 *his heart trembled for the ark of God.* Eli had sufficient spiritual sensitivity to be aware of the danger inherent in the sinful and presumptuous act of taking the ark of God into the battle. And he seems to have been even more concerned for the ark than for his sons (see v. 18).

4:18 *he died.* The death of Eli marked the end of an era that had begun with the death of Joshua and the elders who served with him (see Josh 24:29,31). Incapable of restraining Israel or his sons from their wicked ways, and weakened and blinded by age, the old priest is an apt symbol of the flawed age now coming to its tragic close. He is also a striking contrast to the reign of David, which is the main focus of this narrative. *heavy.* A bit of information that not only helps explain why Eli's fall was fatal but also links his death with the judgment announced earlier: "Wherefore . . . honourest thy sons above me, to make yourselves fat . . .?" (2:29). *he had judged Israel forty years.* Eli is here included among the judges (see 2 Sam 7:11; Judg 2:16–19; Ruth 1:1), who served as leaders of Israel in the period between the deaths of Joshua and of the elders who outlived him and the establishment of kingship. It is likely that Eli's leadership of 40 years overlapped that of Jephthah, Ibzan, Elon and Abdon (Judg 12:7–14), as well as that of Samson (Judg 13–16).

4:21 *The glory is departed.* The glory of Israel was Israel's God, not the ark, and loss of the ark did not mean that God had abandoned His people—God was not inseparably bound to the ark (see Jer 3:16–17). Yet the removal of the ark from Israel did signal estrangement in the relationship between God and His people, and it demonstrated the gravity of their error in thinking that in spite of their wickedness they had the power to coerce God into doing their will simply because they possessed the ark.

5:1 *Ashdod.* One of the five major cities of the Philistines (Josh 13:3), it was located near the Mediterranean coast about 35 miles west of Jerusalem. See map, p.313.

5:2 *Dagon.* In Canaanite mythology the son (or brother) of El and the father of Baal. He was the principal god of the Philistines and was worshiped in temples at Gaza (Judg 16:21,23,26), Ashdod (here) and Beth-shan (31:10–12; 1 Chr 10:10). Veneration of this deity was widespread in the ancient world, extending from Mesopotamia to the Aramean and Canaanite area and attested in non-Biblical sources dating from the late third millennium B.C. until Maccabean times (second century B.C.; in the Apocrypha see 1 Maccabees 10:83–85). The precise nature of the worship of Dagon is obscure. Some have considered Dagon to be a fish god, but more recent evidence suggests either a storm or grain god. His name is related to a Hebrew word for "grain."

5:3 *Dagon was fallen upon his face.* The ark was placed next to the image of Dagon by the Philistines in order to demonstrate Dagon's superiority over the God of Israel, but the symbolism was reversed when Dagon was toppled to a position of homage before the ark of the Lord.

5:5 *tread on the threshold.* Apparently the threshold was considered to possess supernatural power because of its contact with parts of the fallen image of Dagon. Zeph 1:9 appears to be a reference to a more general and rather widespread pagan idea that the threshold was the dwelling place of spirits. *this day.* The time of the writing of 1,2 Samuel (see Introduction: Literary Features, Authorship and Date).

7 And when the men of Ashdod saw that *it was* so, they said, The ark of the God of Israel shall not abide with us: for his hand is sore upon us, and upon Dagon our god.

8 They sent therefore and gathered all the lords of the Philistines unto them, and said, What shall we do with the ark of the God of Israel? And they answered, Let the ark of the God of Israel be carried about *unto* Gath. And they carried the ark of the God of Israel about *thither.*

9 And it was *so,* that after they had carried it about, [a]the hand of the LORD was against the city [b]*with* a very great destruction: and [c]he smote the men of the city, both small and great, and they had emerods in their secret parts.

10 Therefore they sent the ark of God *to* Ekron. And it came to pass, as the ark of God came *to* Ekron, that the Ekronites cried out, saying, They have brought about the ark of the God of Israel to [1]us, to slay us and our people.

11 So they sent and gathered together all the lords of the Philistines, and said, Send away the ark of the God of Israel, and let it go again to his own place, that it slay [1]us not, and our people: for there was a deadly destruction throughout all the city; [a]the hand of God was very heavy there.

12 And the men that died not were smitten with the emerods: and the cry of the city went up *to* heaven.

The ark returned to Israel

6 And the ark of the LORD was in the country of the Philistines seven months.

2 And the Philistines [a]called for the priests and the diviners, saying, What shall we do to the ark of the LORD? tell us wherewith we shall send it to his place.

3 And they said, If ye send away the ark of the God of Israel, send it not [a]empty; but in any wise return him [b]a trespass offering: then ye shall be healed, and it shall [c]be known to you why his hand is not removed from you.

4 Then said they, What *shall be* the trespass offering which we shall return to him? They answered, Five golden emerods, and five golden mice, [a]*according to* the number of the lords of the Philistines: for one plague *was* on [1]you all, and on your lords.

5 Wherefore ye shall make images of your emerods, and images of your mice that [a]mar the land; and ye shall [b]give glory unto the God of Israel: peradventure he will [c]lighten his hand from off you, and from off [d]your gods, and from off your land.

6 Wherefore then do ye harden your hearts, [a]as the Egyptians and Pharaoh hardened their hearts? when he had wrought [1]wonderfully among them, [b]did they not let [2]the people go, and they departed?

7 Now therefore make [a]a new cart, and take two milch kine, [b]on which there hath come no yoke, and tie the kine to the cart, and bring their calves home from them:

8 And take the ark of the LORD, and lay it upon the cart; and put [a]the jewels of gold, which ye return him *for* a trespass offering, in a coffer by the side thereof; and send it away, that it may go.

9 And see, if it goeth up *by* the way of his own coast *to* [a]Beth-shemesh, *then* [1]he hath done us this great evil: but if not, then [b]we shall know that *it is* not his hand *that* smote us; it *was* a chance *that* happened to us.

10 ¶ And the men did so; and took two milch kine, and tied them to the cart, and shut up their calves at home:

11 And they laid the ark of the LORD upon

5:9 [a]Deut. 2:15; ch. 7:13; 12:15 [b]ver. 11 [c]ver. 6; Ps. 78:66
5:10 [1][Heb. *me, to slay me and my*]
5:11 [1][Heb. *me not, and my*] [a]ver. 6,9
6:2 [a]Gen. 41:8; Ex. 7:11; Dan. 2:2; 5:7; Mat. 2:4
6:3 [a]Ex. 23:15; Deut. 16:16 [b]Lev. 5:15,16 [c]ver. 9
6:4 [1]Heb. *them* [a]See ver. 17,18; Josh. 13:3; Judg. 3:3
6:5 [a]ch. 5:6 [b]Josh. 7:19; Is. 42:12; Mal. 2:2; John 9:24 [c]See ch. 5:6,11; Ps. 39:10 [d]ch. 5:3,4,7
6:6 [1]Or, *reproachfully* [2]Heb. *them* [a]Ex. 7:13; 8:15; 14:17 [b]Ex. 12:31
6:7 [a]2 Sam. 6:3 [b]Num. 19:2
6:8 [a]ver. 4,5
6:9 [1]Or, *it* [a]Josh. 15:10 [b]ver. 3

5:6 *the hand of the LORD was heavy.* Dagon's broken hand lay on the ground (v. 4), but the Lord shows the reality and strength of His own hand by bringing a plague (see note on 6:4) on the people of Ashdod and the surrounding area (see vv. 9,11). God would not be manipulated by His own people (see note on 4:3), nor would He permit the Philistines to think that their victory over the Israelites and the capture of the ark demonstrated the superiority of their god over the God of Israel.

5:8 *lords.* Of the five major cities of the Philistines (see 6:16; Josh 13:3; Judg 3:3). *Let the ark of the God of Israel be carried . . . unto Gath.* Evidently the leaders of the Philistines did not share the opinion of the Ashdodites that there was a direct connection between what had happened in Ashdod and the presence of the ark; they seem to have suspected that the sequence of events was merely coincidental (see 6:9). The removal of the ark to Gath put the matter to a test.

5:10 *Ekron.* The northernmost of the five major Philistine cities, located 11 miles northeast of Ashdod and close to Israelite territory (see map, p. 313).

5:11 *Send away the ark of the God of Israel.* After three successive towns had been struck by disease upon the arrival of the ark, there was little doubt in the people's minds that the power of the God of Israel was the cause of their distress.

6:2 *priests and . . . diviners.* The experts on religious matters (priests) and the discerners of hidden knowledge by interpretation of omens (diviners) were consulted (see Deut 18:10; Is 2:6; Ezek 21:21).

6:3 *trespass offering.* The priests and diviners suggest returning the ark with a gift, signifying recognition of guilt in taking the ark from Israel and compensation for this violation of the Lord's honor (see v. 5). For the trespass offering in Israel see Lev 5:14–6:7.

6:4 *Five golden emerods* [i.e. "tumors"]. Corresponding to the symptoms of the plague (see 5:6). *five golden mice.* The disease was accompanied by a plague of mice (v. 5). The Greek translation of the OT (the Septuagint) includes this information earlier in the narrative (at the end of 5:6). It is likely that the mice were carriers of the disease, which may have been a form of the plague.

6:5 *make images . . . and ye shall give glory unto the God of Israel.* The golden models were an acknowledgment that the disease and the mice were a judgment from the hand of the God of Israel (see note on v. 3).

6:6 *the Egyptians and Pharaoh.* The plagues that God inflicted on the Egyptians at the time of the exodus made a lasting impression on the surrounding nations (see 4:8; Josh 2:10).

6:7 *hath come no yoke.* Have not been trained to pull a cart. *bring their calves home.* Normally cows do not willingly leave their suckling calves.

6:9 *Beth-shemesh.* A town near the Philistine border, belonging to Judah (see Josh 15:10). Its name means "house (or sanctuary) of the sun (-god)."

the cart, and the coffer with the mice of gold
and the images of their emerods.
12 And the kine took the straight way to
the way of Beth-shemesh, *and* went along the
highway, lowing as they went, and turned not
aside *to* the right hand or *to* the left; and the
lords of the Philistines went after them unto
the border of Beth-shemesh.
13 And *they of* Beth-shemesh *were* reaping
their wheat harvest in the valley: and they lifted up their eyes, and saw the ark, and rejoiced
to see *it*.
14 And the cart came into the field of Joshua, a Beth-shemite, and stood there, where
there was a great stone: and they clave the
wood of the cart, and offered the kine a burnt
offering unto the LORD.
15 And the Levites took down the ark of
the LORD, and the coffer that *was* with it,
wherein the jewels of gold *were*, and put *them*
on the great stone: and the men of Beth-shemesh offered burnt offerings and sacrificed
sacrifices the same day unto the LORD.
16 And when [a]the five lords of the Philistines had seen *it*, they returned *to* Ekron the
same day.
17 [a]And these *are* the golden emerods which
the Philistines returned *for* a trespass offering
unto the LORD; for Ashdod one, for Gaza one, for
Askelon one, for Gath one, for Ekron one;
18 And the golden mice, *according to* the
number of all the cities of the Philistines *belonging* to the five lords, *both* of fenced cities,
and of country villages, even unto the [1]great
stone of Abel, whereon they set down the ark
of the LORD: *which stone remaineth* unto this
day in the field of Joshua, the Beth-shemite.

6:16 [a]Josh. 13:3
6:17 [a]ver. 4
6:18 [1]Or, *great stone*
6:19 [a]See Ex. 19:21; 2 Sam. 6:7
6:20 [a]2 Sam. 6:9; Mal. 3:2
6:21 [a]Josh. 18:14; 1 Chr. 13:5,6
7:1 [a]ch. 6:21; Ps. 132:6 [b]2 Sam. 6:4
7:3 [a]Deut. 30:2-10; Is. 55:7; Hos. 6:1; Joel 2:12 [b]Gen. 35:2; Josh. 24:14 [c]Judg. 2:13 [d]2 Chr. 30:19; Job 11:13 [e]Deut. 6:13; 10:20; Luke 4:8
7:4 [a]Judg. 2:11
7:5 [a]Judg. 20:1

19 ¶ And [a]he smote the men of Beth-shemesh, because they had looked into the ark of
the LORD, even he smote of the people fifty
thousand and threescore and ten men: and the
people lamented, because the LORD had smitten *many* of the people *with* a great slaughter.
20 And the men of Beth-shemesh said,
[a]Who is able to stand before this holy LORD
God? and to whom shall he go up from us?
21 And they sent messengers to the inhabitants of [a]Kirjath-jearim, saying, The Philistines have brought again the ark of the LORD;
come ye down, *and* fetch it up to you.
7 And the men of [a]Kirjath-jearim came,
and fetched up the ark of the LORD, and
brought it into the house of [b]Abinadab in the
hill, and sanctified Eleazar his son to keep the
ark of the LORD.

Philistines defeated at Mizpeh

2 ¶ And it came to pass, while the ark
abode in Kirjath-jearim, that the time was
long: for it was twenty years: and all the house
of Israel lamented after the LORD.
3 And Samuel spake unto all the house of
Israel, saying, If ye do [a]return unto the LORD
with all your hearts, *then* [b]put away the
strange gods and [c]Ashtaroth from among you,
and [d]prepare your hearts unto the LORD, and
[e]serve him only: and he will deliver you out of
the hand of the Philistines.
4 Then the children of Israel did put away
[a]Baalim and Ashtaroth, and served the LORD
only.
5 And Samuel said, [a]Gather all Israel to
Mizpeh, and I will pray for you unto the LORD.
6 And they gathered together to Mizpeh,

6:13 *reaping their wheat harvest.* The time of wheat harvest is from mid-April until mid-June.
6:14–15 The termination of the trip at Beth-shemesh is just as much a revelation of the hand of God as the journey itself, because it was one of the towns of Judah assigned to the priests at the time of the conquest (see Josh 21:13–16).
6:17 *trespass offering.* See note on v. 3.
6:18 *great stone of Abel.* A kind of monument to the event. *this day.* The time of the writing of 1,2 Samuel (see Introduction: Literary Features, Authorship and Date).
6:19 *looked into the ark.* The men of Beth-shemesh (Levites and priests among them) were judged by God for their irreverent curiosity. Because God had so closely linked the manifestation of His own presence among His people with the ark, it was to be treated with great honor and respect (see 2 Sam 6:7; Num 4:17–20). This attitude of respect, however, is quite different from the superstitious attitude that led the elders to take the ark into battle against the Philistines, thus treating it as an object with magical power (see note on 4:3). *fifty thousand and threescore and ten.* A few Hebrew manuscripts read "70." The additional 50,000 in most Hebrew manuscripts is apparently a copyist's mistake because it is added in an ungrammatical way (no conjunction). Furthermore, this small town could not have contained that many inhabitants.
6:20 *to whom shall he go up from us?* The inhabitants of Beth-shemesh respond to God's judgment in much the same way as the inhabitants of Ashdod, Gath and Ekron (see 5:8–10).
7:1 *house of Abinadab.* The ark remained in relative obscurity at Abinadab's house until David brought it to Jerusalem (2 Sam 6:2–3). Somehow the tabernacle of the congregation (and the altar of burnt offering) escaped the destruction of Shiloh (Jer 7:12,14; 26:6). It apparently was first moved to Nob (21:1–9). In David's and Solomon's days it was located at Gibeon (1 Chr 16:39; 21:29; 2 Chr 1:3,13), the city whose people had been condemned to be menial laborers at the Lord's sanctuary (Josh 9:23,27). Later, we are told, Solomon brought the tabernacle of the congregation to the completed temple (see notes on 1 Ki 3:4; 8:4).
7:2 *twenty years.* Probably the 20-year interval between the return of the ark to Israel and the assembly called by Samuel at Mizpeh (see v. 5).
7:3 *Ashtaroth.* The Hebrew plural of Ashtoreth, who was a goddess of love, fertility and war, worshiped in various forms by many peoples of the ancient Near East, including the Canaanites (see note on Judg 2:13). The worship of Ashtoreth is frequently combined with the worship of Baal (see v. 4; 12:10; Judg 2:13; 3:7; 10:6), in accordance with the common practice in fertility cults to associate male and female deities.
7:5 *Mizpeh.* A town in the territory of Benjamin (Josh 18:26), located about seven and a half miles north of Jerusalem. It was here that the Israelites had previously gathered to undertake disciplinary action against Benjamin (Judg 20:1; 21:1) after the abuse and murder of the concubine of a traveling Levite in Gibeah of Benjamin. Several other places bore the same name (see 22:3; Gen 31:49; Josh 11:3,8; 15:38). *I will pray.* See 7:8–9; 8:6; 12:17–19, 23; 15:11. Samuel, like Moses, was later remembered as a great intercessor (see Ps 99:6; Jer 15:1). Both were ap-

[a]and drew water, and poured *it* out before the LORD, and [b]fasted on that day, and said there, [c]We have sinned against the LORD. And Samuel judged the children of Israel in Mizpeh.

7 And when the Philistines heard that the children of Israel were gathered together to Mizpeh, the lords of the Philistines went up against Israel. And when the children of Israel heard *it,* they were afraid of the Philistines.

8 And the children of Israel said to Samuel, [a][1]Cease not to cry unto the LORD our God for us, that he will save us out of the hand of the Philistines.

9 And Samuel took a sucking lamb, and offered it *for* a burnt offering wholly unto the LORD: and [a]Samuel cried unto the LORD for Israel; and the LORD [1]heard him.

10 And as Samuel was offering up the burnt offering, the Philistines drew near to battle against Israel: [a]but the LORD thundered with a great thunder on that day upon the Philistines, and discomfited them; and they were smitten before Israel.

11 And the men of Israel went out of Mizpeh, and pursued the Philistines, and smote them, until *they came* under Beth-car.

12 Then Samuel [a]took a stone, and set *it* between Mizpeh and Shen, and called the name of it [b][1]Eben-ezer, saying, Hitherto hath the LORD helped us.

13 [a]So the Philistines were subdued, and they [b]came no more into the coast of Israel: and the hand of the LORD was against the Philistines all the days of Samuel.

14 And the cities which the Philistines had taken from Israel were restored to Israel, from Ekron even unto Gath; and the coasts thereof did Israel deliver out of the hands of the Philistines. And there was peace between Israel and the Amorites.

7:6 [a]2 Sam. 14:14 [b]Neh. 9:1,2; Dan. 9:3-5; Joel 2:12 [c]Judg. 10:10; Ps. 106:6
7:8 [1]Heb. *Be not silent from us from crying* [a]Is. 37:4
7:9 [1]Or, *answered* [a]Ps. 99:6; Jer. 15:1
7:10 [a]Josh. 10:10; Judg. 4:15; 5:20; ch. 2:10; 2 Sam. 22:14,15
7:12 [1]That is, *The stone of help* [a]Gen. 28:18; Josh. 4:9 [b]ch. 4:1
7:13 [a]Judg. 13:1 [b]ch. 13:5
7:15 [a]ch. 12:11; Judg. 2:16
7:16 [1]Heb. *and he circuited*
7:17 [a]ch. 8:4 [b]Judg. 21:4
8:1 [a]Deut. 16:18; 2 Chr. 19:5 [b]Judg. 10:4; 12:14, compared with Judg. 5:10
8:2 [1][*Vashni,* 1 Chr. 6:28]
8:3 [a]Jer. 22:15-17 [b]Ex. 18:21; 1 Tim. 3:3; 6:10 [c]Deut. 16:19; Ps. 15:5
8:5 [a]ver. 19,20; Deut. 17:14; Hos. 13:10; Acts 13:21
8:6 [1]Heb. *was evil in the eyes of Samuel*
8:7 [a]See Ex. 16:8 [b]ch. 10:19; 12:17,19; Hos. 13:10,11
8:9 [1]Or, *obey* [2]Or, *notwithstanding when thou hast solemnly protested against them, then thou shalt shew, etc.*

15 And Samuel [a]judged Israel all the days of his life.

16 And he went from year to year [1]in circuit *to* Beth-el, and Gilgal, and Mizpeh, and judged Israel in all those places.

17 And [a]his return *was* to Ramah; for there *was* his house; and there he judged Israel; and there he [b]built an altar unto the LORD.

Israel demands a king

8 And it came to pass, when Samuel was old, that he [a]made his [b]sons judges over Israel.

2 Now the name of his firstborn was [1]Joel; and the name of his second, Abiah: *they were* judges in Beer-sheba.

3 And his sons [a]walked not in his ways, but turned aside [b]after lucre, and [c]took bribes, and perverted judgment.

4 Then all the elders of Israel gathered themselves together, and came to Samuel unto Ramah,

5 And said unto him, Behold, thou art old, and thy sons walk not in thy ways: now [a]make us a king to judge us like all the nations.

6 But the thing [1]displeased Samuel, when they said, Give us a king to judge us. And Samuel prayed unto the LORD.

7 And the LORD said unto Samuel, Hearken unto the voice of the people in all that they say unto thee: for [a]they have not rejected thee, but [b]they have rejected me, that *I* should not reign over them.

8 According to all the works which they have done since the day that I brought them up out of Egypt even unto this day, wherewith they have forsaken me, and served other gods, so do they also unto thee.

9 Now therefore [1]hearken unto their voice: [2]howbeit yet protest solemnly unto

pointed by God to mediate His rule over His people, representing God to Israel and speaking on Israel's behalf to God.

7:6 *drew water, and poured it out before the LORD.* There is no other reference to this type of ceremony in the OT. It appears to symbolize the pouring out of one's heart in repentance and humility before the Lord. For related expressions see 1:15; Ps 62:8; Lam 2:19. *Samuel judged.* See v. 15; see also note on 4:18.

7:10 *the LORD thundered with a great thunder.* The Lord had promised to be the protector of His people when they were obedient to their covenant obligations (see Ex 23:22; Deut 20:1–4; see also 2 Sam 5:19–25; Josh 10:11–14; Judg 5:20–21; 2 Ki 7:6; 19:35; 2 Chr 20:17,22).

7:12 *Eben-ezer.* See note on 4:1.

7:13 *came no more into the coast of Israel.* Some interpreters see a contradiction between this statement and subsequent references to the Philistines in 9:16; 10:5; 13:3,5; 17:1; 23:27. This statement, however, only indicates that the Philistines did not immediately counterattack. See 2 Ki 6:23–24 for a similar situation.

7:15 A summary statement marking the end of the author's account of Samuel's ministry as Israel's leader (see v. 6).

7:16 *judged Israel.* See note on 4:18.

7:17 *Ramah.* See note on 1:1.

8:1–12:25 See Introduction: Contents and Theme.

8:1 *when Samuel was old.* Probably about 20 years after the victory at Mizpeh, when Samuel was approximately 65 years old (see Introduction: Chronology).

8:3 *took bribes.* Perversion of justice through bribery was explicitly forbidden in Pentateuchal law (see Ex 23:8; Deut 16:19).

8:5 *make us a king to judge us.* The elders cite Samuel's age and the misconduct of his sons as justifications for their request for a king. It soon becomes apparent, however, that the more basic reason for their request was a desire to be like the surrounding nations—to have a human king as a symbol of national power and unity who would lead them in battle and guarantee their security (see v. 20; 10:19; 12:12; see also Introduction: Contents and Theme).

8:7 *Hearken unto the voice of the people . . . that they say unto thee.* Anticipations of kingship in Israel are present already in the Pentateuch (Gen 49:10; Num 24:7,17; Deut 17:14–20); Samuel is therefore instructed to listen to the people's request (see vv. 9,22). *they have not rejected thee, but . . . me, that I should not reign over them.* Cf. Judg 8:23. The sin of Israel in requesting a king (see 10:19; 12:12,17,19–20) did not rest in any evil inherent in kingship itself, but in the kind of kingship the people envisioned and their reasons for requesting it (see Introduction: Contents and Theme). Their desire was for a form of kingship that denied their covenant relationship with the Lord, who Himself was pledged to be their savior and deliverer. In requesting a king "like all the nations" (v. 20) they broke the covenant, re-

them, and [a]shew them the manner of the king that shall reign over them.

10 ¶ And Samuel told all the words of the LORD unto the people that asked of him a king.

11 And he said, [a]This will be the manner of the king that shall reign over you: [b]He will take your sons, and appoint *them* for himself, for his chariots, and to be his horsemen; and *some* shall run before his chariots.

12 And he will appoint him captains over thousands, and captains over fifties; and *will set them* to ear his ground, and to reap his harvest, and to make his instruments of war, and instruments of his chariots.

13 And he will take your daughters to be confectionaries, and to be cooks, and to be bakers.

14 And [a]he will take your fields, and your vineyards, and your oliveyards, *even* the best *of them,* and give *them* to his servants.

15 And he will take the tenth of your seed, and of your vineyards, and give to his [1]officers, and to his servants.

16 And he will take your menservants, and your maidservants, and your goodliest young men, and your asses, and put *them* to his work.

17 He will take the tenth of your sheep: and ye shall be his servants.

18 And ye shall cry out in that day because of your king which ye shall have chosen you; and the LORD [a]will not hear you in that day.

19 ¶ Nevertheless the people [a]refused to obey the voice of Samuel; and they said, Nay, but we will have a king over us;

20 That we also may be [a]like all the nations; and that our king may judge us, and go out before us, and fight our battles.

21 And Samuel heard all the words of the people, and he rehearsed them in the ears of the LORD.

22 And the LORD said to Samuel, [a]Hearken unto their voice, and make them a king. And Samuel said unto the men of Israel, Go ye every man unto his city.

8:9 [a]ver. 11
8:11 [a]See Deut. 17:16; ch. 10:25 [b]ch. 14:52
8:14 [a]1 Ki. 21:7; See Ezek. 46:18
8:15 [1]Heb. *eunuchs*
8:18 [a]Is. 1:15; Mic. 3:4
8:19 [a]Jer. 44:16
8:20 [a]ver. 5
8:22 [a]ver. 7; Hos. 13:11

9:1 [1]Or, *the son of a man of Jemini* [2]Or, *substance* [a]ch. 14:51; 1 Chr. 8:33; 9:39
9:2 [a]ch. 10:23
9:4 [a]2 Ki. 4:42
9:6 [a]Deut. 33:1; 1 Ki. 13:1 [b]ch. 3:19
9:7 [1]Heb. *is gone out of, etc.* [2]Heb. is *with us* [a]See Judg. 6:18; 13:17; 1 Ki. 14:3; 2 Ki. 4:42; 8:8
9:8 [1]Heb. *there is found in my hand*
9:9 [a]Gen. 25:22 [b]2 Sam. 24:11; 2 Ki. 17:13; 1 Chr. 26:28; 29:29; 2 Chr. 16:7,10; Is. 30:10; Amos 7:12

Saul anointed by Samuel

9 Now there was a man of Benjamin, whose name *was* [a]Kish, the son of Abiel, the son of Zeror, the son of Bechorath, the son of Aphiah, [1]a Benjamite, a mighty *man* of [2]power.

2 And he had a son, whose name *was* Saul, a choice *young man,* and a goodly: and *there was* not among the children of Israel a goodlier person than he: [a]from his shoulders and upward *he was* higher than any of the people.

3 And the asses of Kish Saul's father were lost. And Kish said to Saul his son, Take now one of the servants with thee, and arise, go seek the asses.

4 And he passed through mount Ephraim, and passed through the land of [a]Shalisha, but they found *them* not: then they passed through the land of Shalim, and *there they were* not: and he passed through the land of the Benjamites, but they found *them* not.

5 *And* when they were come to the land of Zuph, Saul said to his servant that *was* with him, Come, and let us return; lest my father leave *caring* for the asses, and take thought for us.

6 And he said unto him, Behold now, *there is* in this city [a]a man of God, and *he is* an honourable man; [b]all that he saith cometh surely to pass: now let us go thither; peradventure he can shew us our way that we should go.

7 Then said Saul to his servant, But behold, *if* we go, [a]what shall we bring the man? for the bread [1]is spent in our vessels, and *there is* not a present to bring to the man of God: what [2]have we?

8 And the servant answered Saul again, and said, Behold, [1]I have here at hand the fourth part of a shekel of silver: *that* will I give to the man of God, to tell us our way.

9 (Beforetime in Israel, when a man [a]went to inquire of God, thus he spake, Come, and let us go to the seer: for *he that is* now *called* a Prophet was beforetime called [b]a Seer.)

jected the Lord who was their King (12:12; Num 23:21; Deut 33:5) and forgot His constant provision for their protection in the past (10:18; 12:8–11).

8:11 *the manner of the king.* Using a description of the policies of contemporary Canaanite kings (vv. 11–17), Samuel warns the people of the burdens associated with the type of kingship they long for.

8:15 *tenth.* This king's portion would be over and above the tenth Israel was to devote to the Lord (Lev 27:30–32; Num 18:26; Deut 14:22,28; 26:12). In fact, the demands of the king would parallel all that Israel was to consecrate to the Lord as her Great King (persons, lands, crops, livestock)—even the whole population (v. 17).

8:18 *cry out . . . because of your king.* See 1 Ki 12:4; Jer 22:13–17.

8:20 *like all the nations.* See notes on vv. 5,7.

9:2 *higher than any of the people.* Physically of kingly stature (see 10:23).

9:3 *asses . . . were lost.* Saul is introduced as a donkey wrangler sent in search of donkeys that had strayed from home—perhaps symbolizing Saul and the rebellious people who had asked for a king (cf. Is 1:3). David would be introduced as a shepherd caring for his father's flock and later pictured as the shepherd over the Lord's flock (2 Sam 5:2; 7:7–8; Ps 78:71–72).

9:6 *he said unto him.* Saul's ignorance of Samuel is indicative of his character. *this city.* Probably Ramah (see 7:17), the hometown of Samuel, to which he had just returned from a journey (see v. 12; 7:16). *man of God.* See note on 2:27; here a reference to Samuel. *all that he saith . . .* See 3:19 and note.

9:7 *what shall we bring the man?* Other examples of gifts offered to prophets are found in 1 Ki 14:3; 2 Ki 4:42; 5:15–16; 8:8–9. Whether Samuel accepted the gift and whether he was dependent on such gifts for a livelihood are not clear. Elisha refused the gift of Naaman (2 Ki 5:16). In later times false prophets adjusted their message to the desires of those who supported them (1 Ki 22:6,8,18; Mic 3:5,11).

9:8 *the fourth part of a shekel.* That is, about one-tenth of an ounce. Before the use of coins, gold or silver was weighed out for each monetary transaction (see 13:21; Job 28:15). The value of that amount of silver in Saul's time is not known.

9:9 *he that is now called a Prophet was beforetime called a Seer.* There was no essential difference between a seer and a prophet. The person popularly designated as a prophet at the time of

10 Then said Saul to his servant, [1]Well said; come, let us go. So they went unto the city where the man of God *was.*

11 *And* as they went up [1]the hill to the city, [a]they found young maidens going out to draw water, and said unto them, Is the seer here?

12 And they answered them, and said, He is; behold, *he is* before you: make haste now, for he came to day to the city; for [a]*there is* a [1]sacrifice of the people to day [b]in the high place:

13 As soon as ye be come *into* the city, ye shall straightway find him, before he go up to the high place to eat: for the people will not eat until he come, because he doth bless the sacrifice; *and* afterwards they eat that be bidden. Now therefore get you up; for about [1]*this* time ye shall find him.

14 And they went up *into* the city: *and* when they were come into the city, behold, Samuel came out against them, for to go up *to* the high place.

15 ¶ [a]Now the LORD had [1]told Samuel in his ear a day before Saul came, saying,

16 To morrow about *this* time I will send thee a man out of the land of Benjamin, [a]and thou shalt anoint him to be captain over my people Israel, that *he* may save my people out of the hand of the Philistines: for I have [b]looked upon my people, because their cry is come unto me.

17 And when Samuel saw Saul, the LORD said unto him, [a]Behold the man whom I spake to thee of: this *same* shall [1]reign over my people.

18 Then Saul drew near to Samuel in the gate, and said, Tell me, I pray thee, where the seer's house *is.*

19 And Samuel answered Saul, and said, I *am* the seer: go up before me *unto* the high place; for ye shall eat with me to day, and to morrow I will let thee go, and will tell thee all that *is* in thine heart.

20 And as for [a]thine asses that were lost [1]three days ago, set not thy mind on them; for they are found. And on whom [b]*is* all the desire of Israel? *Is it* not on thee, and on all thy father's house?

21 And Saul answered and said, [a]*Am* not I a Benjamite, of the [b]smallest of the tribes of Israel? and [c]my family the least of all the families of the tribe of Benjamin? wherefore then speakest thou [1]so to me?

22 And Samuel took Saul and his servant, and brought them into the parlour, and made them sit in the chiefest place among them that were bidden, which *were* about thirty persons.

23 And Samuel said unto the cook, Bring the portion which I gave thee, of which I said unto thee, Set it by thee.

24 And the cook took up [a]the shoulder, and *that* which *was* upon it, and set *it* before Saul. And *Samuel* said, Behold that which is [1]left; set *it* before thee, *and* eat: for unto *this* time *hath it* been kept for thee since *I* said, I have invited the people. So Saul did eat with Samuel that day.

25 ¶ And when they were come down from the high place *into* the city, *Samuel* communed with Saul upon [a]the top of the house.

26 And they arose early: and it came to pass about the spring of the day, that Samuel called Saul to the top of the house, saying, Up, that I may send thee away. And Saul arose, and they went out both of them, he and Samuel, abroad.

27 *And* as they were going down to the end of the city, Samuel said to Saul, Bid the servant pass on before us, (and he passed on,) but stand thou still [1]a while, that I may shew thee the word of God.

9:10 [1]Heb. *Thy word is good*
9:11 [1]Heb. *in the ascent of the city* [a]Gen. 24:11
9:12 [1]Or, *feast* [a]Gen. 31:54; ch. 16:2 [b]1 Ki. 3:2
9:13 [1]Heb. *to day*
9:15 [1]Heb. *revealed the ear of Samuel* [a]ch. 15:1; Acts 13:21
9:16 [a]ch. 10:1 [b]Ex. 2:25; 3:7,9
9:17 [1]Heb. *restrain in* [a]ch. 16:12; Hos. 13:11
9:20 [1]Heb. *to day three days* [a]ver. 3 [b]ch. 8:5,19; 12:13
9:21 [1]Heb. *according to this word?* [a]ch. 15:17 [b]Judg. 20:46-48 [c]See Judg. 6:15
9:24 [1]Or, *reserved* [a]Lev. 7:32,33; Ezek. 24:4
9:25 [a]Deut. 22:8; 2 Sam. 11:2; Acts 10:9
9:27 [1]Heb. *to day*

the writing of 1,2 Samuel was termed a seer in the time of Saul. This need not mean that the term "prophet" was unknown in the time of Saul or that the term "seer" was unknown in later times (see Is 30:10). The reference is to popular usage.

9:12 *high place.* See Lev 26:30. After entrance into the promised land, the Israelites often followed the custom of the Canaanites in building local altars on hills. (At this time the central sanctuary was not functioning because the ark of God was separated from the tabernacle; Shiloh had been destroyed, and the priestly family, after the death of Eli's sons, was apparently still inactive.) In later times, worship at these "high places" provided a means for the entrance of pagan practices into Israel's religious observances and, for this reason, it was condemned (see note on 1 Ki 3:2).

9:13 *he doth bless the sacrifice.* Samuel presided over the sacrificial meal (see 1:4; 2:13–16), at which he gave a prayer, probably similar to those referred to in the NT (see Mat 26:26–27; John 6:11, 23; 1 Tim 4:3–5).

9:16 *anoint him.* Priests were also anointed (see Ex 29:7; 40:12–15; Lev 4:3; 8:12), but from this point in the OT it is usually the king who is referred to as "the LORD's anointed" (see note on 2:10; cf. 12:3; 24:6; 26:9,11,16; 2 Sam 1:14,16; 19:21; 22:51; 23:1; Ps 2:2,6; but see also Zech 4:14). Anointing signifies separation to the Lord for a particular task and divine equipping for the task (see 10:1,6; 16:13; Is 61:1). *captain.* The Hebrew for this word indicates one designated (here by the Lord) to be the chief in rank. It served as a useful term to ease the transition between the time of the judges and that of the kings. *Philistines.* See note on 7:13.

9:20 *all the desire of Israel.* A reference to Israel's desire for a king.

9:21 *smallest of the tribes . . . least of all the families.* Saul's origins were among the humblest in Israel (Benjamin was the last of Jacob's sons, and the tribe had been greatly reduced in the time of the judges; see Judg 20:46–48). His elevation to king shows that God "raiseth up the poor" (2:8), which is one of the central themes running throughout Samuel. God's use of the powerless to promote His kingdom in the world is a common feature in the Biblical testimony and underscores the truth that His kingdom is not of this world.

9:24 *shoulder.* The Hebrew for this word specifies the thigh, which was normally reserved for the Lord's consecrated priest (see Ex 29:22,27; Lev 7:32–33,35; Num 6:20; 18:18). The presentation of this choice piece of the sacrificial animal to Saul was a distinct honor and anticipated his being designated the Lord's anointed.

10 Then [a]Samuel took a vial of oil, and poured *it* upon his head, [b]and kissed him, and said, *Is it* not because [c]the LORD hath anointed thee to be captain over [d]his inheritance?

2 When thou art departed from me to day, then thou shalt find two men by [a]Rachel's sepulchre in the border of Benjamin [b]at Zelzah; and they will say unto thee, The asses which thou wentest to seek are found: and lo, thy father hath left [1]the care of the asses, and sorroweth for you, saying, What shall I do for my son?

3 Then shalt thou go on forward from thence, and thou shalt come to the plain of Tabor, and there shall meet thee three men going up [a]to God *to* Beth-el, one carrying three kids, and another carrying three loaves of bread, and another carrying a bottle of wine:

4 And they will [1]salute thee, and give thee two *loaves* of bread; which thou shalt receive of their hands.

5 After that thou shalt come to the hill of God, [a]where *is* the garrison of the Philistines: and it shall come to pass, when thou art come thither *to* the city, that thou shalt meet a company of prophets coming down [b]from the high place with a psaltery, and a tabret, and a pipe, and a harp, before them; [c]and they shall prophesy:

6 And [a]the spirit of the LORD will come upon thee, and [b]thou shalt prophesy with them, and shalt be turned into another man.

7 [1]And let it be, when these [a]signs are come unto thee, [b][2]*that* thou do as occasion serve thee; for [c]God *is* with thee.

8 And thou shalt go down before me [a]*to* Gilgal; and behold, I will come down unto thee, to offer burnt offerings, *and* to sacrifice sacrifices of peace offerings: [b]seven days shalt thou tarry, till I come to thee, and shew thee what thou shalt do.

10:1 [a]ch. 9:16; 16:13; 2 Ki. 9:3,6 [b]Ps. 2:12 [c]Acts 13:21 [d]Deut. 32:9
10:2 [1]Heb. *the business* [a]Gen. 35:19,20 [b]Josh. 18:28
10:3 [a]Gen. 28:22; 35:1,3,7
10:4 [1]Heb. *ask thee of peace*
10:5 [a]ch. 13:3 [b]ch. 9:12 [c]Ex. 15:20,21; 2 Ki. 3:15; 1 Cor. 14:1
10:6 [a]Num. 11:25; ch. 16:13 [b]ver. 10; ch. 19:23,24
10:7 [1]Heb. *And it shall come to pass,* that *when these signs, etc.* [2]Heb. *do for thee as thine hand shall find* [a]Ex. 4:8; Luke 2:12 [b]Judg. 9:33 [c]Judg. 6:12
10:8 [a]ch. 11:14,15 [b]ch. 13:8
10:9 [1]Heb. *shoulder* [2]Heb. *turned*
10:10 [a]ver. 5 [b]ch. 19:20
10:11 [1]Heb. *a man to his neighbour* [a]Mat. 13:54,55; John 7:15; Acts 4:13
10:12 [1]Heb. *from thence* [a]Is. 54:13; John 6:45
10:17 [a]Judg. 11:11; 20:1 [b]ch. 7:5,6
10:18 [a]Judg. 6:8,9

Saul becomes king of Israel

9 ¶ And it was *so,* that when he had turned his [1]back to go from Samuel, God [2]gave him another heart: and all those signs came to pass that day.

10 And [a]when they came thither to the hill, behold, [b]a company of prophets met him; and the spirit of God came upon him, and he prophesied among them.

11 And it came to pass, when all that knew him beforetime saw that behold, he prophesied among the prophets, then the people said [1]one to another, What *is* this *that* is come unto the son of Kish? [a]*Is* Saul also among the prophets?

12 And one [1]of the same place answered and said, But [a]who *is* their father? Therefore it became a proverb, *Is* Saul also among the prophets?

13 And when he had made an end of prophesying, he came *to* the high place.

14 And Saul's uncle said unto him and to his servant, Whither went ye? And he said, To seek the asses: and when we saw that *they were* no where, we came to Samuel.

15 And Saul's uncle said, Tell me, I pray thee, what Samuel said unto you.

16 And Saul said unto his uncle, He told us plainly that the asses were found. But of the matter of the kingdom, whereof Samuel spake, he told him not.

17 ¶ And Samuel called the people together [a]unto the LORD [b]*to* Mizpeh;

18 And said unto the children of Israel, [a]Thus saith the LORD God of Israel, I brought up Israel out of Egypt, and delivered you out of the hand of the Egyptians, and out of the hand

10:1 *oil.* Perhaps spiced olive oil (see Ex 30:22–33). *Is it not because the LORD hath anointed thee . . . ?* See note on 9:16. *captain.* See 9:16. *his inheritance.* "My people Israel" (9:16). The Lord's inheritance includes both the people (see Ex 34:9) and the land (see Ex 15:17). After departing from Samuel, Saul is to receive three signs (see vv. 2–7) to authenticate Samuel's words and to assure him that the Lord has indeed chosen him to be king.

10:5 *the hill of God.* Or "Gibeah of God." Gibeah was Saul's hometown (see v. 26; 11:4), located in the tribal area of Benjamin (Josh 18:28; Judg 19:12–14). It was usually called "Gibeah" or "Gibeah of Benjamin" (as in 13:2,15), but twice "Gibeah of Saul" (15:34; 2 Sam 21:6). The present designation (used only here) may have been Samuel's way of reminding Saul that the land of Canaan belonged to God and not to the Philistines (see Deut 32:43; Is 14:2; Hos 9:3). *prophets.* The bands of prophets with which Samuel was associated (as also the "sons of the prophets" with whom Elijah and Elisha were associated; see note on 1 Ki 20:35) appear to have been small communities of men who banded together in spiritually decadent times for mutual cultivation of their religious zeal. *prophesy.* Here (and in vv. 6,10–11,13) appears to designate an enthusiastic praising of God inspired by the Holy Spirit (see Num 11:24–30 for similar use of the term).

10:7 *do as occasion serve thee.* Saul is to take whatever action is appropriate when the situation presents itself to manifest publicly his royal leadership (see 11:4–11).

10:8 *go down before me to Gilgal.* At some unspecified future time, perhaps previously discussed (see 9:25), Saul is to go to Gilgal and wait seven days for Samuel's arrival (see 13:7–14).

10:11 *Is Saul also among the prophets?* An expression of surprise at Saul's behavior (see note on v. 5) by those who had known him previously—another subtle indication of his character (see notes on 9:3,6).

10:12 *who is their father?* Some understand the question as an expression of contempt for prophets generally, others as implying the recognition that prophetic inspiration comes from God and therefore could be imparted to whomever God chose. However, since leading prophets were sometimes called "father" (2 Ki 2:12; 6:21; 13:14), the speaker may have intended a disdainful reference to Samuel or an ironical gibe at Saul.

10:17 *Samuel called the people.* After the private designation and anointing of Saul to be king (9:1–10:16), an assembly is called by Samuel to make the Lord's choice known to the people (v. 21) and to define the king's task (v. 25). *Mizpeh.* See note on 7:5.

10:18 *delivered you.* Speaking through Samuel, the Lord emphasizes to the people that He has been their deliverer throughout their history. He brought them out of Egypt and delivered them from all their enemies during the time of the judges. Al-

of all kingdoms, *and* of them that oppressed
you:
19 [a]And ye have *this* day rejected your
God, who himself saved you out of all your adversities and your tribulations; and ye have
said unto him, *Nay,* but set a king over us.
Now therefore present yourselves before the
LORD by your tribes, and by your thousands.
20 And when Samuel had [a]caused all the
tribes of Israel to come near, the tribe of Benjamin was taken.
21 When he had caused the tribe of Benjamin to come near by their families, the family
of Matri was taken, and Saul the son of Kish
was taken: and when they sought him, he
could not be found.
22 Therefore they [a]inquired of the LORD
further, if the man should yet come thither.
And the LORD answered, Behold, he hath hid
himself among the stuff.
23 And they ran and fetched him thence:
and when he stood among the people, [a]he was
higher than any of the people from his shoulders and upward.
24 And Samuel said to all the people, See
ye him [a]whom the LORD hath chosen, that
there is none like him among all the people?
And all the people shouted, and said, [b][1]God
save the king.
25 Then Samuel told the people [a]the manner of the kingdom, and wrote *it* in a book,
and laid *it* up before the LORD. And Samuel
sent all the people away, every man to his
house.
26 And Saul also went home [a]to Gibeah;
and there went with him a band of men,
whose hearts God had touched.
27 [a]But the [b]children of Belial said, How
shall this *man* save us? And they despised him,
[c]and brought him no presents. But [1]he held
his peace.

The Ammonites defeated

11 Then [a]Nahash the Ammonite came
up, and encamped against [b]Jabesh-
gilead: and all the men of Jabesh said unto Nahash, [c]Make a covenant with us, and we will
serve thee.
2 And Nahash the Ammonite answered
them, On this *condition* will I make *a covenant* with you, that *I* may thrust out all your
right eyes, and lay it *for* [a]a reproach upon all
Israel.
3 And the elders of Jabesh said unto him,
[1]Give us seven days' respite, that we may
send messengers unto all the coasts of Israel:
and then, if *there be* no man to save us, we
will come out to thee.
4 Then came the messengers [a]*to* Gibeah of
Saul, and told the tidings in the ears of the
people: and [b]all the people lift up their voices,
and wept.
5 And behold, Saul came after the herd out
of the field; and Saul said, What aileth the people that they weep? And they told him the tidings of the men of Jabesh.
6 [a]And the spirit of God came upon Saul
when he heard those tidings, and his anger
was kindled greatly.
7 And he took a yoke of oxen, and [a]hewed
them in pieces, and sent *them* throughout all
the coasts of Israel by the hands of messengers, saying, [b]Whosoever cometh not forth after Saul and after Samuel, so shall it be done

10:19 [a]ch. 8:7,19; 12:12
10:20 [a]Acts 1:24,26
10:22 [a]ch. 23:2,4,10,11
10:23 [a]ch. 9:2
10:24 [1]Heb. *Let the king live* [a]2 Sam. 21:6 [b]1 Ki. 1:25,39
10:25 [a]ch. 8:11
10:26 [a]Judg. 20:14; ch. 11:4
10:27 [1]Or, *he was as though he had been deaf* [a]ch. 11:12 [b]Deut. 13:13 [c]2 Sam. 8:2; 1 Ki. 4:21; Mat. 2:11
11:1 [a]ch. 12:12 [b]Judg. 21:8 [c]Gen. 26:28; 1 Ki. 20:34
11:2 [a]Gen. 34:14; ch. 17:26
11:3 [1]Heb. *Forbear us*
11:4 [a]ch. 10:26; 15:34; 2 Sam. 21:6 [b]Judg. 2:4
11:6 [a]Judg. 3:10; 6:34; ch. 10:10
11:7 [a]Judg. 19:29 [b]Judg. 21:5,8,10

though the judges themselves are sometimes referred to as Israel's deliverers (see Judg 3:9,15,31; 6:14; 10:1; 13:5), this was true only in a secondary sense, for they were instruments of the Lord's deliverance (see Judg 2:18). It was the Lord who sent them (see 12:11; Judg 6:14).

10:19 *rejected your God.* See note on 8:7.

10:20 *tribe of Benjamin was taken.* Probably by casting lots (see 14:41–42; Josh 7:15–18). The Urim and Thummim were used for this purpose (see notes on 2:28; Ex 28:30).

‡10:24 *God save the king.* See KJV marg.; 2 Sam 16:16.

10:25 *manner of the kingdom.* Samuel here takes the first step toward resolving the tension that existed between Israel's misdirected desire for a king (and their misconceived notion of what the king's role and function should be) and the Lord's intent to give them one (see Introduction: Contents and Theme). This description of the duties and prerogatives of the Israelite king was given for the benefit of both the people and the king-designate. It was intended to clearly distinguish Israelite kingship from that of the surrounding nations and to ensure that the king's role in Israel was compatible with the continued rule of the Lord over Israel as her Great King (see Deut 17:14–20). *laid it up before the LORD.* The written constitutional-legal document defining the role of the king in governing God's covenant people was preserved at the sanctuary (the tabernacle, later the temple). Other written documents defining Israel's covenant relationship with the Lord are referred to in Ex 24:7; Deut 31:26; Josh 24:26.

10:27 *children of Belial.* See note on Deut 13:13. *How shall this man save us?* Reflects the people's continued apostate idea that national security was to be sought in the person of the human king (see note on v. 18; cf. 8:20).

11:1 *Ammonite.* The Ammonites were descended from Lot (see Gen 19:38; Deut 2:19) and lived east of the tribal territory of Gad near the upper regions of the Jabbok River (see Deut 2:37; Josh 12:2). Previous attempts by the Ammonites to occupy Israelite territory are referred to in Judg 3:13; 11:4–32. The Philistine threat to Israel in the west presented the Ammonites with an opportunity to move against Israel from the east with supposed impunity. *Jabesh-gilead.* A town east of the Jordan in the tribal area of Manasseh.

11:2 *thrust out all your right eyes.* Besides causing humiliation (see note on Judg 16:21), the loss of the right eye would destroy the military capability of the archers.

11:4 *Gibeah of Saul.* See 10:26 and note on 10:5. Close family ties undoubtedly prompted the inhabitants of Jabesh to seek help from the tribe of Benjamin (see Judg 21:12–14).

11:5 *Saul came . . . out of the field.* After Saul's public selection as the king-designate at Mizpeh (10:17–27), he returned home (10:26) to resume his normal private activities and to wait for the Lord's leading for the next step in his elevation to the throne (see notes on v. 15; 10:7).

11:6 *the spirit of God came upon Saul.* For similar endowment of Israel's deliverers with extraordinary vigor by God's Spirit see 10:6,10; Judg 14:6,19; 15:14.

11:7 *sent them throughout . . . Israel.* For a similar case see Judg 19:29.

unto his oxen. And the fear of the LORD fell on the people, and they came out [1]with one consent.

8 And when he numbered them in [a]Bezek, the children [b]of Israel were three hundred thousand, and the men of Judah thirty thousand.

9 And they said unto the messengers that came, Thus shall ye say unto the men of Jabesh-gilead, To morrow, by *that time* the sun be hot, ye shall have [1]help. And the messengers came and shewed *it* to the men of Jabesh; and they were glad.

10 Therefore the men of Jabesh said, To morrow [a]we will come out unto you, and ye shall do with us all that seemeth good unto you.

11 And it was *so* on the morrow, that [a]Saul put the people [b]*in* three companies; and they came into the midst of the host in the morning watch, and slew the Ammonites until the heat of the day: and it came to pass, that they which remained were scattered, so that two of them were not left together.

12 ¶ And the people said unto Samuel, [a]Who *is* he that said, Shall Saul reign over us? [b]bring the men, that we may put them to death.

13 And Saul said, [a]There shall not a man be put to death this day: for to day [b]the LORD hath wrought salvation in Israel.

14 Then said Samuel to the people, Come, and let us go [a]*to* Gilgal, and renew the kingdom there.

15 And all the people went *to* Gilgal; and there they made Saul king [a]before the LORD in Gilgal; and [b]there they sacrificed sacrifices *of* peace offerings before the LORD; and there Saul and all the men of Israel rejoiced greatly.

11:7 [1]Heb. *as one man*
11:8 [a]Judg. 1:5 [b]2 Sam. 24:9
11:9 [1]Or, *deliverance*
11:10 [a]ver. 3
11:11 [a]See ch. 31:11 [b]Judg. 7:16
11:12 [a]ch. 10:27 [b]See Luke 19:27
11:13 [a]2 Sam. 19:22 [b]Ex. 14:13,30; ch. 19:5
11:14 [a]ch. 10:8
11:15 [a]ch. 10:17 [b]ch. 10:8
12:1 [a]ch. 8:5,19,20 [b]ch. 10:24
12:2 [a]Num. 27:17; ch. 8:20 [b]ch. 8:1,5
12:3 [1]Heb. *ransom* [2]Or, *that I should hide mine eyes at him* [a]ch. 24:6; 2 Sam. 1:14,16 [b]Num. 16:15; Acts 20:33; 1 Thes. 2:5 [c]Deut. 16:19
12:5 [a]John 18:38; Acts 23:9 [b]Ex. 22:4
12:6 [1]Or, *made* [a]Mic. 6:4
12:7 [1]Heb. *righteousnesses, or, benefits* [a]Is. 1:18; Mic. 6:2,3 [b]Judg. 5:11

Samuel addresses the people

12 And Samuel said unto all Israel, Behold, I have hearkened unto [a]your voice in all that ye said unto me, and [b]have made a king over you.

2 And now behold, the king [a]walketh before you: [b]and I am old and grayheaded; and behold, my sons *are* with you: and I have walked before you from my childhood unto this day.

3 Behold, here I *am:* witness against me before the LORD, and before [a]his anointed: [b]whose ox have I taken? or whose ass have I taken? or whom have I defrauded? whom have I oppressed? or of whose hand have I received *any* [1]bribe [2]to [c]blind mine eyes therewith? and I will restore *it* you.

4 And they said, Thou hast not defrauded us, nor oppressed us, neither hast thou taken ought of any man's hand.

5 And he said unto them, The LORD *is* witness against you, and his anointed *is* witness this day, [a]that ye have not found ought [b]in my hand. And they answered, *He is* witness.

6 And Samuel said unto the people, [a]*It is* the LORD that [1]advanced Moses and Aaron, and that brought your fathers up out of the land of Egypt.

7 Now therefore stand still, that I may [a]reason with you before the LORD of all the [b][1]righ-

11:8 *Bezek.* Located north of Shechem, west of the Jordan River but within striking distance of Jabesh-gilead.

11:11 *the morning watch.* The third watch, from about 2:00 A.M. until about 6:00 A.M. (see note on Mat 14:25).

11:13 *the LORD hath wrought salvation in Israel.* Saul recognizes Israel's true deliverer (see note on 10:18). The victory, in combination with Saul's confession, places yet another seal of divine approval on Saul as the man the Lord has chosen to be king.

11:14 *let us go to Gilgal, and renew the kingdom.* Samuel perceives that it is now the appropriate time for the people to renew their allegiance to the Lord. The kingship of which he speaks is the Lord's, not Saul's. Samuel calls for an assembly to restore the covenant relationship between the Lord and His people. He wants to inaugurate Saul's rule in a manner demonstrating that the continued rule of the Lord as Israel's Great King is in no way diminished or violated in the new era of the monarchy (see Introduction: Contents and Theme). Verses 14–15 are a brief synopsis of the Gilgal assembly and are prefaced to the more detailed account of the same assembly in ch. 12. *Gilgal.* Located east of Jericho near the Jordan River. It was a particularly appropriate place for Israel to renew her allegiance to the Lord (see Josh 4:19–5:11; 10:8–15).

11:15 *made Saul king before the LORD.* Saul had previously been anointed in private by Samuel at Ramah (10:1) and publicly selected as the king-designate at Mizpeh (10:17–27). In the subsequent Ammonite crisis (vv. 1–13) his leadership did not rest on public recognition of his royal authority, but on the military victory. Now at Gilgal Saul is inaugurated as God's chosen king and formally assumes the privileges and responsibilities of this office. *peace offerings.* This type of offering was an important element in the original ceremony of covenant ratification at Sinai (Ex 24:5,11). It represented the communion or peace between the Lord and His people when the people lived in conformity with their covenant obligations (see Lev 7:11–17; 22:21–23). *rejoiced greatly.* Rejoicing is the expression of people who have renewed their commitment to the Lord, confessed their sin (see 12:19) and been given a king.

12:3 *witness against me.* When Samuel presents the newly inaugurated king to the people, he seeks to establish publicly his own past faithfulness to the covenant as leader of the nation. His purpose is to exonerate himself and provide an example for Saul in his new responsibilities. *whose ox have I taken? or whose ass have I taken?* See Ex 20:17; 22:1,4,9. Samuel has not used his position for personal gain (see Num 16:15). *whom have I defrauded? whom have I oppressed?* See Lev 19:13; Deut 24:14. *of whose hand have I received any bribe . . . ?* See Ex 23:8; Deut 16:19.

12:6 *Samuel said unto the people.* Samuel turns from consideration of his previous leadership to the matter of the people's request for a king, which he views as a covenant-breaking act and a serious apostasy. *It is the LORD.* Samuel emphasizes that in the past the Lord had provided the necessary leadership for the nation.

12:7 *reason with you.* The terminology is that of a legal proceeding, as in vv. 2–5, but now the relationship of the parties is reversed. This time Samuel is the accuser, the people are the defendants, and the Lord is the Judge. *righteous acts of the LORD.* These righteous acts (see vv. 8–11) demonstrate the constancy of the Lord's covenant faithfulness toward His people in the past

teous acts of the LORD, which he did [2]to you
and [2]to your fathers.
8 [a]When Jacob was come *into* Egypt, and
your fathers [b]cried unto the LORD, then the
LORD [c]sent Moses and Aaron, which brought
forth your fathers out of Egypt, and made them
dwell in this place.
9 And when they [a]forgat the LORD their
God, [b]he sold them into the hand of Sisera,
captain of the host of Hazor, and into the hand
of [c]the Philistines, and into the hand of the
king [d]of Moab, and they fought against them.
10 And they cried unto the LORD, and said,
[a]We have sinned, because we have forsaken
the LORD, [b]and have served Baalim and Ashtaroth: but now [c]deliver us out of the hand of
our enemies, and we will serve thee.
11 And the LORD sent [a]Jerubbaal, and Be-
dan, and [b]Jephthah, and [c]Samuel, and delivered you out of the hand of your enemies on
every side, and ye dwelled safe.
12 And when ye saw that [a]Nahash the king
of the children of Ammon came against you,
[b]ye said unto me, Nay; but a king shall reign
over us: when [c]the LORD your God *was* your
king.
13 Now therefore [a]behold the king [b]whom
ye have chosen, *and* whom ye have desired:
and behold, [c]the LORD hath set a king over you.
14 If ye will [a]fear the LORD, and serve him,
and obey his voice, and not rebel against the
[1]commandment of the LORD, then shall both
ye and also the king that reigneth over you
[2]continue following the LORD your God:
15 But if ye will [a]not obey the voice of the
LORD, but rebel against the commandment of
the LORD, then shall the hand of the LORD be
against you, [b]as *it was* against your fathers.
16 Now therefore [a]stand and see this great
thing, which the LORD will do before your eyes.
17 *Is it* not [a]wheat harvest to day? [b]I will
call unto the LORD, and he shall send thunder
and rain; that ye may perceive and see that
[c]your wickedness *is* great, which ye have done
in the sight of the LORD, in asking you a king.
18 ¶ So Samuel called unto the LORD; and
the LORD sent thunder and rain that day: and
[a]all the people greatly feared the LORD and
Samuel.
19 And all the people said unto Samuel,
[a]Pray for thy servants unto the LORD thy God,
that we die not: for we have added unto all our
sins *this* evil, to ask us a king.
20 And Samuel said unto the people, Fear
not: ye have done all this wickedness: yet turn
not aside from following the LORD, but serve
the LORD with all your heart;
21 And [a]turn ye not aside: [b]for *then
should ye go* after vain *things,* which cannot
profit nor deliver; for they *are* vain.
22 For [a]the LORD will not forsake his people [b]for his great name's sake: because [c]it hath
pleased the LORD to make you his people.
23 Moreover as for me, God forbid that I
should sin against the LORD [a][1]in ceasing to
pray for you: but [b]I will teach you the [c]good
and the right way:
24 [a]Only fear the LORD, and serve him in

12:7 [2]Heb. *with* 12:8 [a]Gen. 46:5,6 [b]Ex. 2:23 [c]Ex. 3:10 12:9 [a]Judg. 3:7 [b]Judg. 4:2 [c]Judg. 10:7 [d]Judg. 3:12 12:10 [a]Judg. 10:10 [b]Judg. 2:13 [c]Judg. 10:15,16 12:11 [a]Judg. 6:14,32 [b]Judg. 11:1 [c]ch. 7:13 12:12 [a]ch. 11:1 [b]ch. 8:5,19 [c]Judg. 8:23; ch. 8:7 12:13 [a]ch. 10:24 [b]ch. 8:5 [c]Hos. 13:11 12:14 [1]Heb. *mouth* [2]Heb. *be after* [a]Josh. 24:14 12:15 [a]Lev. 26:14; Deut. 28:15; Josh. 24:20 12:15 [b]ver. 9 12:16 [a]Ex. 14:13 12:17 [a]Prov. 26:1 [b]Josh. 10:12; ch. 7:9,10; Jas. 5:16-18 [c]ch. 8:7 12:18 [a]Ex. 14:31; Ezra 10:9 12:19 [a]Ex. 9:28; 10:17; Jas. 5:15; 1 John 5:16 12:21 [a]Deut. 11:16 [b]Jer. 16:19; Hab. 2:18; 1 Cor. 8:4 12:22 [a]1 Ki. 6:13 [b]Josh. 7:9; Jer. 14:21 [c]Deut. 7:7,8 12:23 [1]Heb. *from ceasing* [a]Acts 12:5; Rom. 1:9; Col. 1:9; 2 Tim. 1:3 [b]Ps. 34:11; Prov. 4:11 [c]1 Ki. 8:36; 2 Chr. 6:27; Jer. 6:16 12:24 [a]Eccl. 12:13

and, by way of contrast, serve as an indictment of their present apostasy.

12:11 *LORD . . . delivered you.* The Lord repeatedly delivered Israel from her enemies right up to Samuel's own lifetime (see 7:3,8,10,12), demonstrating again the people's apostasy in desiring a king.

12:12 *when ye saw that Nahash . . . came against you.* In the face of the combined threat from the Philistines in the west (9:16) and the Ammonites in the east (11:1–13), the Israelites sought to find security in the person of a human king. *the LORD your God was your king.* The Israelite desire for and trust in a human leader constituted a rejection of the kingship of the Lord and betrayed a loss of confidence in His care, in spite of His faithfulness during the time of the exodus, conquest and judges (see note on 8:7).

12:13 *the LORD hath set a king over you.* In spite of the sinfulness of the people's request, the Lord had chosen to incorporate kingship into the structure of the theocracy (His kingdom). Kingship was given by the Lord to His people and was to function as an instrument of His rule over them (see Introduction: Contents and Theme).

12:14 *If ye will fear the LORD.* Samuel relates the old covenant condition (see Ex 19:5–6; Deut 8:19; 11:13–15,22–28; 28; 30:17–18; Josh 24:20) to the new era Israel is entering with the establishment of the monarchy. *ye and also the king . . . continue following the LORD your God.* Israel and her king are to demonstrate that although human kingship has been established, they will continue to recognize the Lord as their true King. In this new era where potential for divided loyalty between the Lord and the human king arises, Israel's loyalty to the Lord must remain inviolate. For similar use of the expression "to follow" see 2 Sam 2:10; 15:13; 1 Ki 12:20; 16:21.

12:15 *if ye will not obey.* Samuel confronts Israel with the same alternatives Moses had expressed centuries earlier (see Deut 28; 30:15–20). The introduction of kingship into Israel's socio-political structure has not changed the fundamental nature of Israel's relationship to the Lord.

12:16 *see this great thing.* Samuel calls the people to observe as the Lord Himself demonstrates His existence and power and authenticates the truthfulness and seriousness of Samuel's words.

12:17 *wheat harvest.* See note on 6:13.

12:19 *Pray . . . unto the LORD thy God.* Samuel's indictment (vv. 6–15) combined with the awesome sign of thunder and rain in the dry season (vv. 16–18) prompted the people to confess their sin and request Samuel's intercession for them.

12:20 *yet turn not aside from following the LORD.* Samuel again brings into focus the central issue in the controversy surrounding the establishment of kingship in Israel.

12:21 *vain things.* No rivals to the Lord can deliver or guarantee security.

12:23 *I will teach you the good and the right way.* Samuel is not retiring from his prophetic role when he presents the people with their king. He will continue to intercede for the people (see v. 19; 7:8–9) and will instruct them in their covenant obligations (see Deut 6:18; 12:28). Saul and all future kings are to be subject to instruction and correction by the Lord's prophets.

12:24 *fear the LORD.* Samuel summarizes Israel's obligation of loyalty to the Lord as an expression of gratitude for the great things He has done for them.

truth with all your heart: for [b]consider [1]how [c]great things he hath done for you.

25 But if ye shall still do wickedly, [a]ye shall be consumed, [b]both ye and your king.

Samuel rebukes Saul

13 Saul [1]reigned one year; and when he had reigned two years over Israel,

2 Saul chose him three thousand *men* of Israel; *whereof* two thousand were with Saul in Michmash and in mount Beth-el, and a thousand were with Jonathan in [a]Gibeah of Benjamin: and the rest of the people he sent every man to his tent.

3 And Jonathan smote [a]the garrison of the Philistines that *was* in [1]Geba, and the Philistines heard *of it.* And Saul blew the trumpet throughout all the land, saying, Let the Hebrews hear.

4 And all Israel heard say *that* Saul had smitten a garrison of the Philistines, and *that* Israel also [1]was had in abomination with the Philistines. And the people were called together after Saul *to* Gilgal.

5 And the Philistines gathered themselves together to fight with Israel, thirty thousand chariots, and six thousand horsemen, and people as the sand which *is* on the sea shore in multitude: and they came up, and pitched in Michmash, eastward from Beth-aven.

6 When the men of Israel saw that they were in a strait, (for the people were distressed,) then the people [a]did hide themselves in caves, and in thickets, and in rocks, and in high places, and in pits.

7 And *some of the* Hebrews went over Jordan *to* the land of Gad and Gilead. As for Saul, he *was* yet in Gilgal, and all the people [1]followed him trembling.

8 ¶ [a]And he tarried seven days, according to the set time that Samuel *had appointed:* but Samuel came not *to* Gilgal; and the people were scattered from him.

9 And Saul said, Bring hither a burnt offering to me, and peace offerings. And he offered the burnt offering.

10 And it came to pass, that as soon as he had made an end of offering the burnt offering, behold, Samuel came; and Saul went out to meet him, that he might [1]salute him.

11 And Samuel said, What hast thou done? And Saul said, Because I saw that the people were scattered from me, and *that* thou camest not within the days appointed, and *that* the Philistines gathered themselves together *at* Michmash;

12 Therefore said I, The Philistines will come down now upon me *to* Gilgal, and I have not [1]made supplication unto the LORD: I forced myself therefore, and offered a burnt offering.

13 And Samuel said to Saul, [a]Thou hast done foolishly: [b]thou hast not kept the commandment of the LORD thy God, which he commanded thee: for now would the LORD have established thy kingdom upon Israel for ever.

14 [a]But now thy kingdom shall not continue: [b]the LORD hath sought him a man after his own heart, and the LORD hath commanded him to be captain over his people, because thou hast not kept *that* which the LORD commanded thee.

Saul's small army

15 ¶ And Samuel arose, and gat him up from Gilgal *unto* Gibeah of Benjamin. And Saul numbered the people that were [1]present with him, [a]about six hundred men.

16 And Saul, and Jonathan his son, and the people that were [1]present with them, abode

12:24 [1]Or, *what a great thing, etc.* [b]Is. 5:12 [c]Deut. 10:21
12:25 [a]Josh. 24:20 [b]Deut. 28:36
13:1 [1]Heb. *the son of* one year *in his reigning*
13:2 [a]ch. 10:26
13:3 [1]Or, *the hill* [a]ch. 10:5
13:4 [1]Heb. *did stink*
13:6 [a]Judg. 6:2
13:7 [1]Heb. *trembled after him*
13:8 [a]ch. 10:8
13:10 [1]Heb. *bless him*
13:12 [1]Heb. *intreated the face*
13:13 [a]2 Chr. 16:9 [b]ch. 15:11
13:14 [a]ch. 15:28 [b]Ps. 89:20; Acts 13:22
13:15 [1]Heb. *found* [a]ch. 14:2
13:16 [1]Heb. *found*

12:25 *be consumed, both ye and your king.* Should the nation persist in covenant-breaking conduct, it will bring upon itself its own destruction.

‡13:1 *one year . . . two years.* The Hebrew gives evidence of a possible scribal omission, leaving the reading awkward and uncertain. If the wording of the verse follows the regularly used formula that introduces the reigns of later kings (see, e.g., 2 Sam 2:10; 5:4; 1 Ki 14:21; 2 Ki 8:26), then a conceivable reconstruction might be "When Saul was thirty years old he began to reign, and he reigned forty two years . . . ."

13:2 *Michmash.* Located southeast of Beth-el and northeast of Gibeah near a pass (see v. 23). *Jonathan.* Saul's oldest son (see 14:49), mentioned here for the first time.

13:3 *Geba.* Located across a ravine and south of Michmash.

13:4 *abomination.* A metaphor depicting an object of strong hostility, as in 2 Sam 10:6; 16:21; Gen 34:30; Ex 5:21. *Gilgal.* See note on 11:14. By prearrangement Saul had been instructed to wait for Samuel there (see notes on v. 8; 10:8).

13:5 *thirty thousand.* The Canaanites under Sisera (see Judg 4:13) had 900 chariots. The Israelites did not acquire chariots until the time of Solomon (see 1 Ki 4:26).

13:8 *set time that Samuel had appointed.* See note on 10:8. Saul is fully aware that Samuel's previous instructions had reference to this gathering at Gilgal. *the people were scattered.* The seven-day delay heightened the fear of the Israelite soldiers.

13:9 *Saul . . . offered the burnt offering.* Samuel had promised to make these offerings himself (see 10:8) before Israel went to battle (see 7:9), and he had directed Saul to await his arrival and instructions.

13:13 *Thou hast done foolishly.* The foolish and sinful aspect (see 26:21; 2 Sam 24:10; 1 Chr 21:8; 2 Chr 16:9) of Saul's act was that he thought he could strengthen Israel's chances against the Philistines while disregarding the instruction of the Lord's prophet Samuel. *thou hast not kept the commandment of the LORD thy God.* Saul was to recognize the word of the prophet Samuel as the word of the Lord (see 3:20; 15:1; Ex 20:18–19; see also note on Ex 7:1–2). In disobeying Samuel's instructions, Saul violated a fundamental requirement of his theocratic office. His kingship was not to function independently of the law and the prophets (see notes on 12:14,23; 15:11).

13:14 *thy kingdom shall not continue.* Saul will not be followed by his sons; there will be no dynasty bearing his name (contrast the Lord's word to David, 2 Sam 7:11–16). There is a striking parallel in the word of the Lord to Eli (see 2:30,35). *The LORD hath sought him a man after his own heart, and . . . commanded him.* Paul quotes from this passage at Antioch (Acts 13:22). *captain.* See 10:16.

13:15 *six hundred.* The seven-day delay had greatly depleted Saul's forces (see vv. 2,4,6–8).

in [2]Gibeah of Benjamin: but the Philistines encamped in Michmash.

17 And the spoilers came out of the camp of the Philistines *in* three companies: one company turned unto the way that leadeth to [a]Ophrah, unto the land of Shual:

18 And another company turned the way to [a]Beth-horon: and another company turned *to* the way of the border that looketh to the valley of [b]Zeboim toward the wilderness.

19 Now [a]there was no smith found throughout all the land of Israel: for the Philistines said, Lest the Hebrews make *them* swords or spears:

20 But all the Israelites went down *to* the Philistines, to sharpen every man his share, and his coulter, and his axe, and his mattock.

21 Yet they had [1]a file for the mattocks, and for the coulters, and for the forks, and for the axes, and [2]to sharpen the goads.

22 So it came to pass in the day of battle, that [a]there was neither sword nor spear found in the hand of any of the people that *were* with Saul and Jonathan: but with Saul and with Jonathan his son was there found.

23 [a]And the [1]garrison of the Philistines went out to the passage of Michmash.

Jonathan attacks the Philistines

14 Now [1]it came to pass upon a day, that Jonathan the son of Saul said unto the young man that bare his armour, Come, and let us go over to the Philistines' garrison, that *is* on the other side. But he told not his father.

2 And Saul tarried in the uttermost part of Gibeah under a pomegranate tree which *is* in Migron: and the people that *were* with him *were* [a]about six hundred men;

3 And [1]Ahiah, the son of Ahitub, [a]Ichabod's brother, the son of Phinehas, the son of Eli, the LORD's priest in Shiloh, [b]wearing an ephod. And the people knew not that Jonathan was gone.

4 And between the passages, *by* which Jonathan sought to go over [a]unto the Philistines' garrison, *there was* a sharp rock on the one side, and a sharp rock on the other side: and the name of the one *was* Bozez, and the name of the other Seneh.

5 The [1]forefront of the one *was* situate northward over against Michmash, and the other southward over against Gibeah.

6 And Jonathan said to the young man that bare his armour, Come, and let us go over unto the garrison of these uncircumcised: it may be that the LORD will work for us: for *there is* no restraint to the LORD [a]to save by many or by few.

7 And his armourbearer said unto him, Do all that *is* in thine heart: turn thee; behold, I *am* with thee according to thy heart.

8 Then said Jonathan, Behold, we will pass over unto *these* men, and we will discover ourselves unto them.

9 If they say thus unto us, [1]Tarry until we come to you; then we will stand still in our place, and will not go up unto them.

10 But if they say thus, Come up unto us; then we will go up: for the LORD hath delivered them into our hand: and [a]this *shall be* a sign unto us.

11 And both of them discovered themselves unto the garrison of the Philistines: and the Philistines said, Behold, the Hebrews come forth out of the holes where they had hid themselves.

12 And the men of the garrison answered Jonathan and his armourbearer, and said, Come up to us, and we will shew you a thing. And Jonathan said unto his armourbearer, Come up after me: for the LORD hath delivered them into the hand of Israel.

13 And Jonathan climbed up upon his hands and upon his feet, and his armourbearer after him: and they fell before Jonathan; and his armourbearer slew after him.

14 And *that* first slaughter, which Jonathan and his armourbearer made, was about twenty men, within as it were [1]a half acre of land, *which* a yoke *of oxen might plow.*

15 And [a]there was trembling in the host, in the field, and among all the people: the garrison, and [b]the spoilers, they also trembled, and the earth quaked: so it was [c1]a very great trembling.

13:16 [2][Heb. *Gebah*]
13:17 [a]Josh. 18:23
13:18 [a]Josh. 16:3; 18:13,14 [b]Neh. 11:34; Gen. 14:2
13:19 [a]See 2 Ki. 24:14; Jer. 24:1
13:21 [1]Heb. *a file with mouths* [2]Heb. *to set*
13:22 [a]See Judg. 5:8
13:23 [1]Or, *standing camp* [a]ch. 14:1,4
14:1 [1]Or, *there was a day*
14:2 [a]ch. 13:15
14:3 [1][ch. 22:9,11,20, called *Ahimelech*] [a]ch. 4:21 [b]ch. 2:28
14:4 [a]ch. 13:23
14:5 [1]Heb. *tooth*
14:6 [a]Judg. 7:4,7; 2 Chr. 14:11
14:9 [1]Heb. *Be still*
14:10 [a]See Gen. 24:14; Judg. 7:11
14:14 [1]Or, *half a furrow of an acre of land*
14:15 [1]Heb. *a trembling of God* [a]2 Ki. 7:7; Job 18:11 [b]ch. 13:17 [c]Gen. 35:5

13:17 *spoilers.* The purpose of these Philistine contingents was not to engage the Israelites in battle, but to plunder the land and demoralize its inhabitants.

13:18 *valley of Zeboim.* Located to the east toward the Jordan Valley.

13:19 *no smith.* A Philistine monopoly on the technology of iron production placed the Israelites at a great disadvantage in the fashioning and maintenance of agricultural implements and military weapons.

13:22 *neither sword nor spear.* The Israelites fought with bow and arrow and slingshot.

14:1 *on the other side.* The Philistines were encamped to the north of the pass and the Israelites to the south.

14:2 *Gibeah.* Saul had retreated farther south from Geba (13:3) to Gibeah. *under a pomegranate tree.* It appears to have been customary for leaders in early Israel to hold court under well-known trees (see 22:6; Judg 4:5).

14:3 *Ahiah.* Either the brother and predecessor of Ahimelech son of Ahitub (referred to in 21:1; 22:9,11) or an alternate name for Ahimelech. *Ichabod's brother.* See 4:21. *wearing an ephod.* See note on 2:28.

14:6 *uncircumcised.* A term of contempt (see 17:26,36; 31:4; 2 Sam 1:20; Judg 14:3; 15:18; 1 Chr 10:4), which draws attention to Israel's covenant relationship to the Lord (see note on Gen 17:10) and, by implication, to the illegitimacy of the Philistine presence in the land. *by many or by few.* See note on 17:47. Jonathan's bold plan is undertaken as an act of faith (cf. Heb 11:33–34) founded on God's promise (9:16).

14:10 *sign unto us.* See Judg 6:36–40; Is 7:11.

14:11 *Hebrews.* See 4:6; 13:3,7 and note on Gen 14:13.

14:15 *earth quaked.* See 7:10; Josh 10:11–14; Ps 77:18 for other instances of divine intervention in nature to bring deliverance to Israel.

The Philistines flee

16 ¶ And the watchmen of Saul in Gibeah
of Benjamin looked; and behold, the multitude
melted away, and they [a]went on beating down
one another.
17 Then said Saul unto the people that
were with him, Number now, and see who is
gone from us. And when they had numbered,
behold Jonathan and his armourbearer *were*
not *there.*
18 And Saul said unto Ahiah, Bring hither
the ark of God. For the ark of God was at that
time with the children of Israel.
19 And it came to pass, while Saul [a]talked
unto the priest, that the [1]noise that *was* in the
host of the Philistines went on and increased:
and Saul said unto the priest, Withdraw thine
hand.
20 And Saul and all the people that *were*
with him [1]assembled themselves, and they
came to the battle: and behold, [a]every man's
sword was against his fellow, *and there was* a
very great discomfiture.
21 Moreover the Hebrews *that* were with
the Philistines before that time, which went up
with them into the camp *from the country*
round about, even they also *turned* to be with
the Israelites that *were* with Saul and Jonathan.
22 Likewise all the men of Israel which
[a]had hid themselves in mount Ephraim, *when*
they heard that the Philistines fled, even they
also followed hard after them in the battle.
23 [a]So the LORD saved Israel that day: and
the battle passed over [b]*unto* Beth-aven.

Jonathan breaks Saul's oath

24 ¶ And the men of Israel were distressed
that day: for Saul had [a]adjured the people, saying, Cursed *be* the man that eateth *any* food
until evening, that I may be avenged on mine
enemies. So none of the people tasted *any* food.
25 [a]And all *they of* the land came to a
wood; and there was [b]honey upon the ground.
26 And when the people were come into
the wood, behold the honey dropped; but no
man put his hand to his mouth: for the people
feared the oath.
27 But Jonathan heard not when his father
charged the people with the oath: wherefore
he put forth the end of the rod that *was* in his
hand, and dipt it in a honeycomb, and put his
hand to his mouth; and his eyes were enlightened.
28 Then answered one of the people, and
said, Thy father straitly charged the people
with an oath, saying, Cursed *be* the man that
eateth *any* food *this* day. And the people were
[1]faint.
29 Then said Jonathan, My father hath
troubled the land: see, I pray you, how mine
eyes have been enlightened, because I tasted a
little of this honey.
30 How much more, if haply the people
had eaten freely to day of the spoil of their enemies which they found? for had there not
been now a much greater slaughter among the
Philistines?
31 And they smote the Philistines that day
from Michmash to Aijalon: and the people
were very faint.
32 And the people flew upon the spoil, and
took sheep, and oxen, and calves, and slew
them on the ground: and the people did eat
them [a]with the blood.
33 Then they told Saul, saying, Behold, the
people sin against the LORD, in that they eat
with the blood. And he said, Ye have [1]trans-
gressed: roll a great stone unto me *this* day.

14:16 [a]ver. 20 14:19 [1]Or, *tumult* [a]Num. 27:21 14:20 [1]Heb. *were cried together* [a]Judg. 7:22; 2 Chr. 20:23 14:22 [a]ch. 13:6 14:23 [a]Ex. 14:30; Hos. 1:7 [b]ch. 13:5 14:24 [a]Josh. 6:26

14:25 [a]Deut. 9:28; Mat. 3:5 [b]Ex. 3:8; Num. 13:27; Mat. 3:4 14:28 [1]Or, *weary* 14:32 [a]Lev. 3:17; 7:26; 17:10; 19:26; Deut. 12:16,23, 24 14:33 [1]Or, *dealt treacherously*

14:18 *Bring hither the ark of God.* Saul decides to seek God's will before entering into battle with the Philistines (see Num 27:21; Deut 20:2). Here the Septuagint (the Greek translation of the OT) may preserve the original text ("'Bring the ephod.' At that time he wore the ephod before the Israelites") for the following reasons: 1. In 7:1 the ark was located at Kirjath-jearim, where it remained until David brought it to Jerusalem (2 Sam 6), but the ephod was present in Saul's camp at Gibeah (see v. 3). 2. Nowhere else in the OT is the ark used to determine God's will, but the ephod (with the Urim and Thummim) was given for this purpose (see 23:9; 30:7 and notes on 2:18,28). 3. The command to the priest to withdraw his hand (v. 19) is more appropriate with the ephod than with the ark.
14:19 *Withdraw thine hand.* Due to the urgency of the moment, Saul decides that to wait for the word of the Lord might jeopardize his military advantage. As in 13:8–12, his decision rests on his own insight rather than on dependence upon the Lord and a commitment to obey Him.
14:23 *So the LORD saved Israel that day.* The writer attributes the victory to the Lord, not to either Saul or Jonathan (see vv. 6,10,15; 11:13).
14:24–46 Following the account of the great victory the Lord had given, the author relates Saul's actions that strikingly illustrated his lack of fitness to be king. This foolish curse before the battle (see note on v. 24) made the army "distressed" and, as Jonathan tellingly observed, "troubled the land" (v. 29) rather than contributing to the victory. And later, when hindered from taking advantage of the battle's outcome by the Lord's refusal to answer (v. 37), Saul was ready to execute Jonathan as the cause, though Jonathan had contributed most to the victory, as everyone else recognized (v. 45). Saul's growing egocentrism was turning into an all-consuming passion that threatened the very welfare of the nation. Rather than serving the cause of the Lord and His people, he was in fact becoming a king "like all the nations" (8:5).
14:24 *distressed.* Saul's rash action in requiring his troops to fast placed them at an unnecessary disadvantage in the battle (see vv. 29–30). *Cursed.* Thus Saul as king "charged the people with an oath" (v. 28), a most serious matter because an oath directly invoked God's involvement, whether it concerned giving testimony (Ex 20:7; Lev 19:12), making commitments (Gen 21:23–24; 24:3–4) or prohibiting action (here; Josh 6:24). It appealed to God as the supreme enforcement power and the all-knowing Judge of human actions. *I may be avenged on mine enemies.* Saul perceives the conflict with the Philistines more as a personal vendetta (see note on 15:12) than as a battle for the honor of the Lord and the security of the Lord's people (note the contrast between his attitude and that of Jonathan in vv. 6,10,12).
14:31 *Aijalon.* Located to the west near the Philistines' own territory (see Josh 10:12).
14:33 *eat with the blood.* The Israelites were not permitted to

34 And Saul said, Disperse yourselves
among the people, and say unto them, Bring
me hither every man his ox, and every man
his sheep, and slay *them* here, and eat; and sin
not against the LORD in eating with the blood.
And all the people brought every man his ox
[1]with him *that* night, and slew *them* there.
35 And Saul [a]built an altar unto the LORD:
[1]the same was the first altar that he built unto
the LORD.
36 ¶ And Saul said, Let us go down after
the Philistines by night, and spoil them until
the morning light, and let us not leave a man
of them. And they said, Do whatsoever
seemeth good unto thee. Then said the priest,
Let us draw near hither unto God.
37 And Saul asked *counsel* of God, Shall I
go down after the Philistines? wilt thou deliver them into the hand of Israel? But [a]he answered him not that day.
38 And Saul said, [a]Draw ye near hither, all
the [b1]chief of the people: and know and see
wherein this sin hath been *this* day.
39 For, [a]*as* the LORD liveth, which saveth
Israel, though it be in Jonathan my son, he
shall surely die. But *there was* not *a man*
among all the people *that* answered him.
40 Then said he unto all Israel, Be ye on
one side, and I and Jonathan my son will be on
the other side. And the people said unto Saul,
Do what seemeth good unto thee.
41 Therefore Saul said unto the LORD God
of Israel, [a1]Give a perfect *lot.* [b]And Saul and
Jonathan were taken: but the people [2]escaped.
42 And Saul said, Cast *lots* between me and
Jonathan my son. And Jonathan was taken.
43 Then Saul said to Jonathan, [a]Tell me
what thou hast done. And Jonathan told him,
and said, [b]I did but taste a little honey with
the end of the rod that *was* in mine hand, *and*
lo, I must die.
44 And Saul answered, [a]God do so and
more also: [b]for thou shalt surely die, Jonathan.
45 And the people said unto Saul, Shall
Jonathan die, who hath wrought this great salvation in Israel? God forbid: [a]*as* the LORD
liveth, there shall not one hair of his head fall
to the ground; for he hath wrought with God
this day. So the people rescued Jonathan, that
he died not.
46 Then Saul went up from following the
Philistines: and the Philistines went to their
own place.

Saul wars against other nations

47 ¶ So Saul took the kingdom over Israel,
and fought against all his enemies on every side,
against Moab, and against the children of [a]Am-
mon, and against Edom, and against the kings of
[b]Zobah, and against the Philistines: and whithersoever he turned himself, he vexed *them.*
48 And he [1]gathered a host, and [a]smote
the Amalekites, and delivered Israel out of the
hands of them that spoiled them.
49 Now [a]the sons of Saul were Jonathan,
and Ishui, and Melchishua: and the names of
his two daughters *were these;* the name of the
firstborn Merab, and the name of the younger
Michal:
50 And the name of Saul's wife *was* Ahinoam, the daughter of Ahimaaz: and the name of
the captain of his host *was* [1]Abner, the son of
Ner, Saul's uncle.
51 [a]And Kish *was* the father of Saul; and
Ner the father of Abner *was* the son of Abiel.
52 And there was sore war against the Philistines all the days of Saul: and when Saul saw
any strong man, or any valiant man, [a]he took
him unto him.

Saul rejected as king

15 Samuel also said unto Saul, [a]The
LORD sent me to anoint thee to be
king over his people, over Israel: now therefore hearken thou unto the voice of the words
of the LORD.
2 Thus saith the LORD of hosts, I remember
that which Amalek did to Israel, [a]how he laid

14:34 [1]Heb. *in his hand* **14:35** [1]Heb. *that altar he began to build unto the LORD* [a]ch. 7:17 **14:37** [a]ch. 28:6 **14:38** [1]Heb. *corners* [a]Josh. 7:14; ch. 10:19 [b]Judg. 20:2 **14:39** [a]2 Sam. 12:5 **14:41** [1]Or, *Shew the innocent* [2]Heb. *went forth* [a]Prov. 16:33; Acts 1:24 [b]Josh. 7:16; ch. 10:20,21 **14:43** [a]Josh. 7:19 [b]ver. 27 **14:44** [a]Ruth 1:17 [b]ver. 39 **14:45** [a]2 Sam. 14:11; 1 Ki. 1:52; Luke 21:18 **14:47** [a]ch. 11:11 [b]2 Sam. 10:6 **14:48** [1]Or, *wrought mightily* [a]ch. 15:3,7 **14:49** [a]ch. 31:2; 1 Chr. 8:33 **14:50** [1][Heb. *Abiner*] **14:51** [a]ch. 9:1 **14:52** [a]ch. 8:11 **15:1** [a]ch. 9:16 **15:2** [a]Ex. 17:8,14; Num. 24:20; Deut. 25:17-19

eat blood (see Gen 9:4; Lev 17:11; 19:26; Deut 12:16; Ezek 33:25; Acts 15:20 and notes). *transgressed.* See KJV marg. The same Hebrew term is translated "treacherous" in Jer 3:8–11.

14:35 *first altar that he built.* Another indication of Saul's personal lack of interest in religious matters (see notes on 9:6; 10:11).

‡14:36 *priest.* Ahiah (see v. 3).

14:37 *Saul asked counsel of God.* The means of ascertaining God's will appears to have been the ephod with its Urim and Thummim (see v. 3 and note on v. 18). *he answered him not.* Because an oath had been broken in the battle, God refused to answer Saul's inquiry concerning further military action.

14:39 *as the LORD liveth.* An oath formula (see note on v. 24; see also 19:6; Jer 4:2; Hos 4:15).

14:41 *taken.* See 10:20–21; Josh 7:14–18; Prov 16:33.

14:44 A curse formula (see note on v. 24; see also 3:17 and note).

14:45 *he hath wrought with God this day.* The men of Saul's army recognize the inappropriateness of taking the life of the one through whom God has delivered His people.

14:47–48 A summary of Saul's military victories to the east (Moab and the Ammonites), south (Edom), west (Philistines) and north (Zobah).

14:47 *children of Ammon.* See Deut 2:19–21,37.

14:48 *Amalekites.* See note on 15:2.

14:49 *sons of Saul.* See 2 Sam 2:8,10; 1 Chr 9:39; 10:2. *Merab . . . Michal.* See 18:17,20,27; 19:11–17; 25:44; 2 Sam 6:16–23.

14:50 *Ahinoam.* The only reference to a wife of Saul. His concubine Rizpah is mentioned in 2 Sam 3:7; 21:8–11.

14:52 *all the days of Saul.* Closes the main account of Saul's reign. *he took him unto him.* Saul developed a special cadre of professional soldiers bound to himself, much as David was to do later (see 22:2; 23:13; 25:13; 27:2–3; 29:2; 30:1,9; 2 Sam 2:3; 5:6; 8:18; 15:18; 23:8–39).

15:1–35 The event that occasioned Saul's rejection. Although no time designation is given, it evidently occurred after the conflicts of 14:47, in a time of relative peace and security. It is likely that David was anointed (16:1–13) shortly after the rejection of Saul (vv. 22,26,28), thus c. 1025 B.C.

15:2 *that which Amalek did to Israel.* See Ex 17:8–13; Num 14:43, 45; Deut 25:17–19; cf. Judg 3:13; 6:3–5,33; 7:12; 10:12. *Amalek.* A Bedouin people descended from Esau (see Gen

wait for him in the way, when he came up
from Egypt.
3 Now go and smite Amalek, and [a]utterly
destroy all that they have, and spare them not;
but slay both man and woman, infant and
suckling, ox and sheep, camel and ass.
4 And Saul gathered the people together,
and numbered them in Telaim, two hundred
thousand footmen, and ten thousand men of
Judah.
5 And Saul came to a city of Amalek, and
[1]laid wait in the valley.
6 And Saul said unto [a]the Kenites, [b]Go, depart, get you down from among the Amalekites, lest I destroy you with them: for [c]ye
shewed kindness to all the children of Israel,
when they came up out of Egypt. So the Kenites departed from among the Amalekites.
7 [a]And Saul smote the Amalekites from
[b]Havilah *until* thou comest *to* [c]Shur, that *is*
over against Egypt.
8 And [a]he took Agag the king of the
Amalekites alive, and [b]utterly destroyed all the
people with the edge of the sword.
9 But Saul and the people [a]spared Agag,
and the best of the sheep, and of the oxen, and
[1]of the fatlings, and the lambs, and all *that was*
good, and would not utterly destroy them: but
every thing *that was* vile and refuse, that they
destroyed utterly.
10 ¶ Then came the word of the LORD unto
Samuel, saying,
11 [a]It repenteth me that I have set up Saul
to be king: for he is [b]turned back from following me, [c]and hath not performed my commandments. And it [d]grieved Samuel; and he
cried unto the LORD all night.
12 And when Samuel rose early to meet

15:3 [a]Lev. 27:28,29; Josh. 6:17,21
15:5 [1]Or, *fought*
15:6 [a]Num. 24:21; Judg. 1:16; 4:11 [b]Gen. 18:25; 19:12,14; Rev. 18:4 [c]Ex. 18:10,19; Num. 10:29,32
15:7 [a]ch. 14:48 [b]Gen. 2:11; 25:18 [c]Gen. 16:7
15:8 [a]See 1 Ki. 20:34,35 [b]See ch. 30:1
15:9 [1]Or, *of the second sort* [a]ver. 3,15
15:11 [a]ver. 35; Gen. 6:6,7; 2 Sam. 24:16 [b]Josh. 22:16; 1 Ki. 9:6 [c]ver. 3,9; ch. 13:13 [d]ver. 35; ch. 16:1
15:12 [a]Josh. 15:55
15:13 [a]Gen. 14:19; Judg. 17:2; Ruth 3:10
15:15 [a]ver. 9,21; Gen. 3:12; Prov. 28:13
15:17 [a]ch. 9:21
15:18 [1]Heb. *they consume them*
15:20 [a]ver. 13
15:21 [a]ver. 15

Saul in the morning, it was told Samuel, saying, Saul came to [a]Carmel, and behold, he set
him up a place, and is gone about, and passed
on, and gone down *to* Gilgal.
13 And Samuel came to Saul: and Saul said
unto him, [a]Blessed *be* thou of the LORD: I have
performed the commandment of the LORD.
14 And Samuel said, What *meaneth* then
this bleating of the sheep in mine ears, and the
lowing of the oxen which I hear?
15 And Saul said, They have brought them
from the Amalekites: [a]for the people spared
the best of the sheep and of the oxen, to sacrifice unto the LORD thy God; and the rest we
have utterly destroyed.
16 Then Samuel said unto Saul, Stay, and I
will tell thee what the LORD hath said to me
this night. And he said unto him, Say on.
17 And Samuel said, [a]When thou *wast* little in thine own sight, *wast* thou not *made* the
head of the tribes of Israel, and the LORD
anointed thee king over Israel?
18 And the LORD sent thee on a journey,
and said, Go and utterly destroy the sinners
the Amalekites, and fight against them until
[1]they be consumed.
19 Wherefore then didst thou not obey the
voice of the LORD, but didst fly upon the spoil,
and didst evil in the sight of the LORD?
20 And Saul said unto Samuel, Yea, [a]I have
obeyed the voice of the LORD, and have gone
the way which the LORD sent me, and have
brought Agag the king of Amalek, and have utterly destroyed the Amalekites.
21 [a]But the people took of the spoil, sheep
and oxen, the chief of the things which should
have been utterly destroyed, to sacrifice unto
the LORD thy God in Gilgal.

36:12,16) usually located in the Negev and Sinai regions (see 27:8; 30:1; Gen 14:7; Ex 17:8; Num 13:29).

15:3 *utterly destroy.* See notes on Lev 27:28–29; Deut 2:34; Josh 6:17–18; see also Deut 13:12–18. Saul is given an opportunity as king to demonstrate his allegiance to the Lord by obedience in this assigned task.

15:4 *Telaim.* Probably the same as Telem in Josh 15:24, located in the southern part of Judah.

15:5 *city of Amalek.* A settlement of Amalekites, most likely located between Telaim and Kadesh-barnea, possibly the residence of their king.

15:6 *Kenites.* A Bedouin people of the Sinai, closely related to the Midianites. Moses had married a Kenite woman (see Ex 2:16,21–22; Num 10:29; Judg 1:16; 4:11), and some of the Kenites had accompanied the Israelites when they settled in the land of Canaan (see 27:10; Judg 1:16; 4:17–23; 5:24; 1 Chr 2:55).

15:7 *Havilah . . . to Shur.* The location of Havilah is uncertain. Shur was on the eastern frontier of Egypt (see 27:8; Gen 16:7; 20:1). Ishmael's descendants occupied this area (see Gen 25:18).

15:8 *all the people.* All the Amalekites they encountered. Some Amalekites survived (see 27:8; 30:1,18; 2 Sam 8:12; 1 Chr 4:43).

15:9 When Israel refused to obey the Lord's command (v. 3), their holy war against the Amalekites degenerated into personal aggrandizement, much like that of Achan at the time of the conquest of Canaan (see Josh 7:1). Giving to the Lord by destruction only what was despised and weak was a contemptible act (see Mal 1:7–12), not to be excused (see v. 19) by the protestation that the best had been preserved for sacrifice to the Lord (vv. 15,21).

15:11 *repenteth.* See note on v. 29. *he is turned back from following me.* A violation of the fundamental requirement of his office as king (see notes on 12:14–15).

‡15:12 *Carmel.* Located about seven miles south of Hebron (see 25:2; Josh 15:55). *set him up a place.* I.e. erected a monument to himself. Saul's self-glorification here contrasts sharply with his self-abasement after the victory over the Ammonites (see note on 11:13; cf. v. 17; 2 Sam 18:18). *Gilgal.* Saul returns to the place where he was inaugurated and instructed in the responsibilities of his office (see 11:14–12:25). This was also the place where he had been told that he would not have a continuing dynasty because of his disobedience (see 13:13–14).

15:13 *I have performed the commandment of the LORD.* Here and in v. 20 Saul is clearly less than honest in his statements to Samuel.

15:15 *the people spared the best . . . to sacrifice.* Saul attempts to shift responsibility from himself to the people and to excuse their action by claiming pious intentions. *the LORD thy God.* Saul's use of the pronoun "thy" instead of "my" here and in vv. 21,30 indicates an awareness of his own alienation from the Lord (see 12:19 for a similar case), even though he speaks of obedience and the intent to honor God by sacrifice.

15:17 *thou wast little in thine own sight.* See 9:21; 10:22.

22 And Samuel said,
[a]Hath the LORD *as great* delight in
burnt offerings and sacrifices,
As in obeying the voice of the LORD?
Behold, [b]to obey *is* better than
sacrifice,
And to hearken than the fat of rams.
23 For rebellion *is as* the sin of
[1]witchcraft,
And stubbornness *is as* iniquity and
idolatry.
Because thou hast rejected the word of
the LORD,
[a]He hath also rejected thee from *being*
king.
24 [a]And Saul said unto Samuel, I have
sinned: for I have transgressed the commandment of the LORD, and thy words: because I
[b]feared the people, and obeyed their voice.
25 Now therefore, I pray thee, pardon my
sin, and turn again with me, that I may worship the LORD.
26 And Samuel said unto Saul, I will not return with thee: [a]for thou hast rejected the
word of the LORD, and the LORD hath rejected
thee from being king over Israel.
27 And as Samuel turned about to go away,
[a]he laid hold upon the skirt of his mantle, and
it rent.
28 And Samuel said unto him, [a]The LORD
hath rent the kingdom of Israel from thee *this*
day, and hath given it to a neighbour of thine,
that is better than thou.

15:22 [a]Is. 1:11-13,16,17; Jer. 7:22,23; Mic. 6:6-8; Heb. 10:6-9 [b]Eccl. 5:1; Hos. 6:6; Mat. 5:24; 9:13; 12:7; Mark 12:33
15:23 [1]Heb. *divination* [a]ch. 13:14
15:24 [a]See 2 Sam. 12:13 [b]Ex. 23:2; Is. 51:12,13
15:26 [a]ch. 2:30
15:27 [a]See 1 Ki. 11:30
15:28 [a]ch. 28:17,18; 1 Ki. 11:31
15:29 [1]Or, *Eternity,* or, *Victory* [a]Num. 23:19; Ezek. 24:14; 2 Tim. 2:13; Tit. 1:2
15:30 [a]John 5:44; 12:43
15:33 [a]Ex. 17:11; Num. 14:45; See Judg. 1:7
15:34 [a]ch. 11:4
15:35 [a]See ch. 19:24 [b]ver. 11; ch. 16:1 [c]ver. 11
16:1 [a]ch. 15:35 [b]ch. 15:23 [c]ch. 9:16; 2 Ki. 9:1 [d]Ps. 78:70; Acts 13:22

29 And also the [1]Strength of Israel [a]will
not lie nor repent: for he *is* not a man, that *he*
should repent.
30 Then he said, I have sinned: *yet* [a]honour
me now, I pray thee, before the elders of my
people, and before Israel, and turn again with
me, that I may worship the LORD thy God.
31 So Samuel turned again after Saul; and
Saul worshipped the LORD.
32 ¶ Then said Samuel, Bring you hither to
me Agag the king of the Amalekites. And Agag
came unto him delicately. And Agag said, Surely the bitterness of death is past.
33 And Samuel said, [a]As thy sword hath
made women childless, so shall thy mother be
childless among women. And Samuel hewed
Agag in pieces before the LORD in Gilgal.
34 Then Samuel went to Ramah; and Saul
went up to his house *to* [a]Gibeah of Saul.
35 And [a]Samuel came no more to see Saul
until the day of his death: nevertheless Samuel
[b]mourned for Saul: and the LORD [c]repented
that he had made Saul king over Israel.

David chosen to be king

16 And the LORD said unto Samuel,
[a]How long wilt thou mourn for Saul,
seeing [b]I have rejected him from reigning over
Israel? [c]fill thine horn *with* oil, and go, I will
send thee to Jesse the Beth-lehemite: for [d]I
have provided me a king among his sons.
2 And Samuel said, How can I go? if Saul
hear *it,* he will kill me. And the LORD said,

15:22 Samuel does not suggest that sacrifice is unimportant but that it is acceptable only when brought with an attitude of obedience and devotion to the Lord (see Ps 15; Is 1:11–17; Hos 6:6; Amos 5:21–27; Mic 6:6–8). *fat of rams.* The fat of sacrificed animals belonged to the Lord (see 2:15; Ex 23:18; Lev 3:14–16; 7:30).

15:23 *rebellion.* Samuel charges Saul with violating the central requirement of the covenant condition given to him when he became king (see 12:14–15). *sin of witchcraft.* A serious offense against the Lord (see Lev 19:26; Deut 18:9–12), which Saul himself condemned (28:3,9). *thou hast rejected the word of the LORD.* A king who sets his own will above the command of the Lord ceases to be an instrument of the Lord's rule over His people, violating the very nature of his theocratic office. *He hath also rejected thee from being king.* The judgment here goes beyond the one given earlier (see note on 13:14). Now Saul himself is to be set aside as king. Although this did not happen immediately, as chs. 16–31 show, the process began that led to his death. It included in its relentless course the removal of God's Spirit and favor from him (16:14), the defection of his son Jonathan and daughter Michal to David, and the insubordination of his own officials (22:17).

15:24 Saul's confession retains an element of self-justification and a shift of blame (contrast David's confession, 2 Sam 12:13; Ps 51). Previously (vv. 15,21) he had attempted to justify the actions of those under him.

15:25 *turn again with me.* Saul's greatest concern was not to worship God but to avoid an open break with the prophet Samuel, a break that would undermine his authority as king (see v. 30).

15:28 *neighbour of thine.* David (see note on 13:14).

15:29 *Strength of Israel.* Lit. "Eminence of Israel," or "Glory." A title of God (see KJV marg.). Some translations read "the Glory of Israel"; see Mic 1:15; see also note on 4:21. Cf. Ps 89:17; 106:20; Is 13:19. *will not lie nor repent.* See Num 23:19; Ps 110:4; Jer 4:28; Mal 3:6 and notes. There is no conflict between this statement and vv. 11,35, where the Lord is said to "repent" that he had made Saul king. God has real emotions (one of the marks of personality).

15:31 *So Samuel turned again after Saul.* Samuel's purpose in agreeing to Saul's request is not to honor Saul, but to carry out the divine sentence on Agag and in so doing to reemphasize Saul's neglect of duty.

15:34 *Ramah.* Samuel's home (see 7:17). *Gibeah of Saul.* See note on 10:5.

15:35 *Samuel mourned.* Samuel regarded Saul as if dead (see the use of "lamented" in 6:19). Even though his love for him remained (see v. 11; 16:1), he sought no further contact with him because God had rejected him as king. Saul did come to Samuel on one other occasion (see 19:24).

16:1 *the LORD said unto Samuel.* Probably c. 1025 B.C. (see note on 15:1–35). *Jesse.* For Jesse's genealogy see Ruth 4:18–22; Mat 1:3–6. *Beth-lehemite.* Beth-lehem was a town five miles south of Jerusalem, formerly known as Ephrath (Gen 48:7). It was later to become renowned as the "city of David" (Luke 2:4) and the birthplace of Christ (Mic 5:2; Mat 2:1; Luke 2:4–7). *I have provided me a king among his sons.* See notes on 13:14; 15:28.

16:2 *Saul . . . will kill me.* The road from Ramah (where Samuel was, 15:34) to Beth-lehem passed through Gibeah of Saul. Saul already knew that the Lord had chosen someone to replace him as king (see 15:28). Samuel fears that jealousy will incite Saul to violence. Later incidents (18:10–11; 19:10; 20:33) demonstrate that Samuel's fears were well-founded. *say, I am*

Take a heifer [1]with thee, and say, [a]I am come to sacrifice to the LORD.

3 And call Jesse to the sacrifice, and [a]I will shew thee what thou shalt do: and [b]thou shalt anoint unto me *him* whom I name unto thee.

4 And Samuel did *that* which the LORD spake, and came *to* Beth-lehem. And the elders of the town [a]trembled at his [1]coming, and said, [b]Comest thou peaceably?

5 And he said, Peaceably: I am come to sacrifice unto the LORD: [a]sanctify yourselves, and come with me to the sacrifice. And he sanctified Jesse and his sons, and called them to the sacrifice.

6 And it came to pass, when they were come, that he looked on [1]Eliab, and [a]said, Surely the LORD's anointed *is* before him.

7 But the LORD said unto Samuel, Look not on [a]his countenance, or on the height of his stature; because I have refused him: [b]for *the LORD seeth* not as man seeth; for man [c]looketh on the [1]outward appearance, but the LORD looketh on the [d]heart.

8 Then Jesse called [a]Abinadab, and made him pass before Samuel. And he said, Neither hath the LORD chosen this.

9 Then Jesse made [a][1]Shammah to pass by. And he said, Neither hath the LORD chosen this.

10 Again, Jesse made seven of his sons to pass before Samuel. And Samuel said unto Jesse, The LORD hath not chosen these.

11 And Samuel said unto Jesse, Are here all *thy* children? And he said, [a]There remaineth yet the youngest, and behold, he keepeth the

16:2 [1]Heb. *in thine hand* [a]ch. 9:12; 20:29
16:3 [a]Ex. 4:15 [b]ch. 9:16
16:4 [1]Heb. *meeting* [a]ch. 21:1 [b]1 Ki. 2:13; 2 Ki. 9:22
16:5 [a]Ex. 19:10
16:6 [1][ch. 17:13; Called *Elihu*, 1 Chr. 27:18] [a]1 Ki. 12:26
16:7 [1]Heb. *eyes* [a]Ps. 147:10 [b]Is. 55:8 [c]2 Cor. 10:7 [d]1 Ki. 8:39
16:8 [a]ch. 17:13
16:9 [1][*Shimeah*, 2 Sam. 13:3; *Shimma*, 1 Chr. 2:13] [a]ch. 17:13
16:11 [a]ch. 17:12

come to sacrifice to the LORD. This response is true but incomplete, and it was intended to deceive Saul.
16:3 *anoint.* See note on 9:16.
16:5 *sanctify yourselves.* Involves preparing oneself spiritually as well as making oneself ceremonially clean by washing and putting on clean clothes (see Ex 19:10,14; Lev 15; Num 19:11–22).
16:6 *Eliab.* Jesse's oldest son (17:13).
16:7 *his countenance, or on the height.* Samuel is not to focus on these outward features, which had characterized Saul (see 9:2; 10:23–24). *heart.* The Lord is concerned with man's inner disposition and character (see 1 Ki 8:39; 1 Chr 28:9; Luke 16:15; John 2:25; Acts 1:24).
16:8 *Abinadab.* Jesse's second son.
16:9 *Shammah.* Jesse's third son.
16:11 *he keepeth the sheep.* The Lord's chosen one is a shepherd (see note on 9:3; see also 2 Sam 7:7–8; Ps 78:71–72).

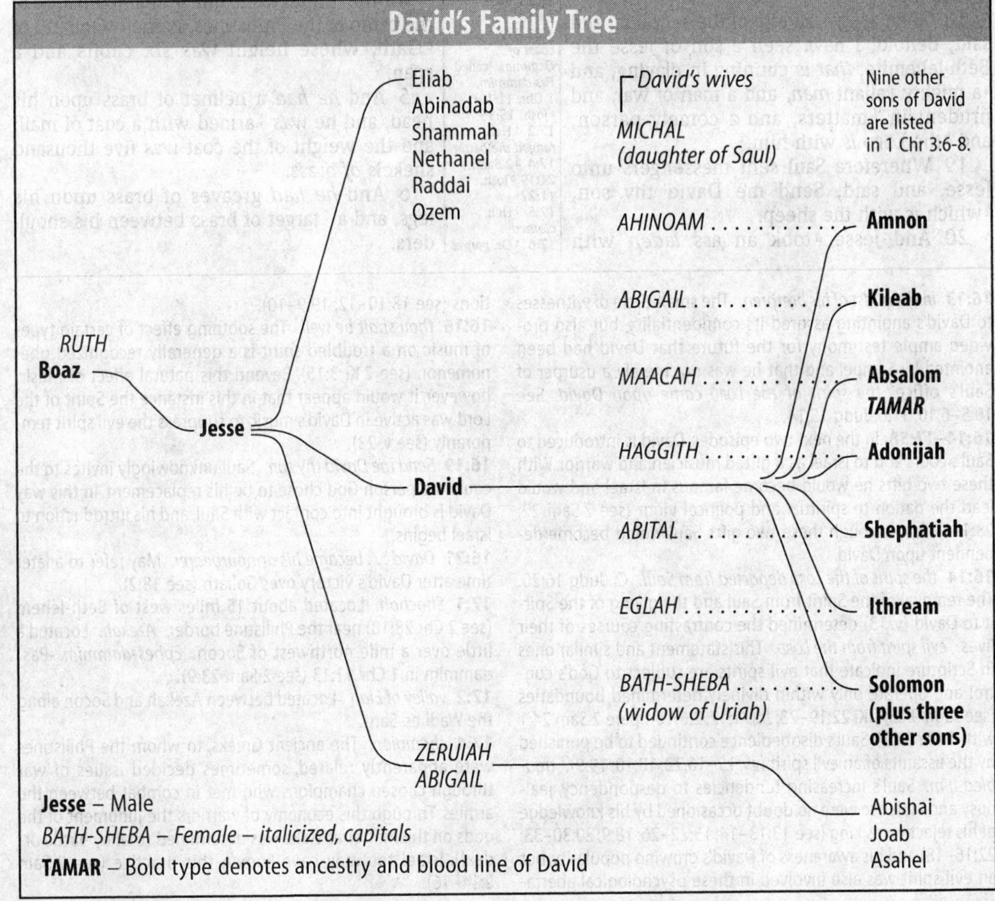

sheep. And Samuel said unto Jesse, [b]Send and
fetch him: for we will not sit [1]down till he
come hither.
12 And he sent, and brought him in. Now
he *was* [a]ruddy, *and* withal [1]of a beautiful
countenance, and goodly to look to. [b]And the
LORD said, Arise, anoint him: for this *is* he.
13 Then Samuel took the horn of oil, and
[a]anointed him in the midst of his brethren;
and [b]the spirit of the LORD came upon David
from that day forward. So Samuel rose up, and
went to Ramah.

David plays the harp

14 ¶ [a]But the spirit of the LORD departed
from Saul, and [b]an evil spirit from the LORD
[1]troubled him.
15 And Saul's servants said unto him, Behold now, an evil spirit from God troubleth
thee.
16 Let our lord now command thy servants
which are [a]before thee, to seek out a man,
who is a cunning player on a harp: and it shall
come to pass, when the evil spirit from God is
upon thee, that he shall [b]play with his hand,
and thou shalt be well.
17 And Saul said unto his servants, Provide
me now a man that can play well, and bring
him to me.
18 Then answered one of the servants, and
said, Behold, I have seen a son of Jesse the
Beth-lehemite, *that is* cunning in playing, and
[a]a mighty valiant *man*, and a man of war, and
prudent in [1]matters, and a comely person,
and [b]the LORD *is* with him.
19 Wherefore Saul sent messengers unto
Jesse, and said, Send me David thy son,
[a]which *is* with the sheep.
20 And Jesse [a]took an ass *laden* with
bread, and a bottle of wine, and a kid, and sent
them by David his son unto Saul.
21 And David came to Saul, and [a]stood before him: and he loved him greatly; and he became his armourbearer.
22 And Saul sent to Jesse, saying, Let David, I pray thee, stand before me; for he hath
found favour in my sight.
23 And it came to pass, when [a]the *evil*
spirit from God was upon Saul, that David took
a harp, and played with his hand: so Saul was
refreshed, and was well, and the evil spirit departed from him.

David and Goliath

17 Now the Philistines gathered together their armies to battle, and were
gathered together *at* [a]Shochoh, which *belongeth* to Judah, and pitched between
Shochoh and Azekah, in [1]Ephes-dammim.
2 And Saul and the men of Israel were
gathered together, and pitched by the valley of
Elah, and [1]set the battle in array against the
Philistines.
3 And the Philistines stood on a mountain
on the one side, and Israel stood on a mountain on the other side: and *there was* a valley
between them.
4 And there went out a champion out of
the camp of the Philistines, named [a]Goliath, of
[b]Gath, whose height *was* six cubits and a
span.
5 And *he had* a helmet of brass upon his
head, and he *was* [1]armed with a coat of mail;
and the weight of the coat *was* five thousand
shekels *of* brass.
6 And *he had* greaves of brass upon his
legs, and a [1]target of brass between his shoulders.

16:11 [1]Heb. *round* [b]2 Sam. 7:8
16:12 [1]Heb. *fair of eyes* [a]ch. 17:42 [b]See ch. 9:17
16:13 [a]ch. 10:1 [b]Num. 27:18; Judg. 11:29; 13:25; ch. 10:6,10
16:14 [1]Or, *terrified* [a]Judg. 16:20 [b]Judg. 9:23
16:16 [a]ver. 21,22; Gen. 41:46 [b]ver. 23; 2 Ki. 3:15
16:18 [1]Or, *speech* [a]ch. 17:32,34-36 [b]ch. 3:19; 18:12,14
16:19 [a]ver. 11; ch. 17:15
16:20 [a]ch. 10:27; 17:18
16:21 [a]Gen. 41:46
16:23 [a]ver. 14,16
17:1 [1]Or, *the coast of Dammim.* [called *Pas-dammim,* 1 Chr. 11:13] [a]Josh. 15:35
17:2 [1]Heb. *ranged the battle*
17:4 [a]2 Sam. 21:19 [b]Josh. 11:22
17:5 [1]Heb. *clothed*
17:6 [1]Or, *gorget*

16:13 *in the midst of his brethren.* The small circle of witnesses to David's anointing assured its confidentiality, but also provided ample testimony for the future that David had been anointed by Samuel and that he was not merely a usurper of Saul's office. *the spirit of the LORD came upon David.* See 10:5–6,10; 11:6; Judg 15:14.

16:14–17:58 In the next two episodes, David is introduced to Saul's court and to Israel as a gifted musician and warrior. With these two gifts he would become famous in Israel and would lead the nation to spiritual and political vigor (see 2 Sam 22; 23:1–7). Also through these two gifts Saul would become dependent upon David.

16:14 *the spirit of the LORD departed from Saul.* Cf. Judg 16:20. The removal of the Spirit from Saul and the giving of the Spirit to David (v. 13) determined the contrasting courses of their lives. *evil spirit from the LORD.* This statement and similar ones in Scripture indicate that evil spirits are subject to God's control and operate only within divinely determined boundaries (see Judg 9:23; 1 Ki 22:19–23; Job 1:12; 2:6; compare 2 Sam 24:1 with 1 Chr 21:1). Saul's disobedience continued to be punished by the assaults of an evil spirit (vv. 15–16,23; 18:10; 19:9). *troubled him.* Saul's increasing tendencies to despondency, jealousy and violence were no doubt occasioned by his knowledge of his rejection as king (see 13:13–14; 15:22–26; 18:9; 20:30–33; 22:16–18) and his awareness of David's growing popularity, but an evil spirit was also involved in these psychological aberrations (see 18:10–12; 19:9–10).

16:16 *thou shalt be well.* The soothing effect of certain types of music on a troubled spirit is a generally recognized phenomenon (see 2 Ki 3:15). Beyond this natural effect of music, however, it would appear that in this instance the Spirit of the Lord was active in David's music to suppress the evil spirit temporarily (see v. 23).

16:19 *Send me David thy son.* Saul unknowingly invites to the court the person God chose to be his replacement. In this way David is brought into contact with Saul, and his introduction to Israel begins.

16:21 *David . . . became his armourbearer.* May refer to a later time after David's victory over Goliath (see 18:2).

17:1 *Shochoh.* Located about 15 miles west of Beth-lehem (see 2 Chr 28:18) near the Philistine border. *Azekah.* Located a little over a mile northwest of Socoh. *Ephes-dammim.* Pas-dammim in 1 Chr 11:13 (see 2 Sam 23:9).

17:2 *valley of Elah.* Located between Azekah and Socoh along the Wadi es-Sant.

17:4 *champion.* The ancient Greeks, to whom the Philistines were apparently related, sometimes decided issues of war through chosen champions who met in combat between the armies. Through this economy of warriors the judgment of the gods on the matter at stake was determined (trial by battle ordeal). Israel too may have known this practice (see 2 Sam 2:14–16).

7 And the staff of his spear *was* like a weaver's beam; and his spear's head *weighed* six hundred shekels *of* iron: and one bearing a shield went before him.

8 And he stood and cried unto the armies of Israel, and said unto them, Why are ye come out to set *your* battle in array? *am* not I a Philistine, and you [a]servants to Saul? choose you a man for you, and let him come down to me.

9 If he be able to fight with me, and *to* kill me, then will we be your servants: but if I prevail against him, and kill him, then shall ye be our servants, and [a]serve us.

10 And the Philistine said, I [a]defy the armies of Israel this day; give me a man, that we may fight together.

11 When Saul and all Israel heard those words of the Philistine, they were dismayed, and greatly afraid.

12 ¶ Now David *was* [a]the son of that [b]Ephrathite of Beth-lehem-judah, whose name *was* Jesse; and he had [c]eight sons: and the man went among men *for* an old man in the days of Saul.

13 And the three eldest sons of Jesse went *and* followed Saul to the battle: and the [a]names of his three sons that went to the battle *were* Eliab the firstborn, and next unto him Abinadab, and the third Shammah.

14 And David *was* the youngest: and the three eldest followed Saul.

15 But David went and returned from Saul [a]to feed his father's sheep *at* Beth-lehem.

16 And the Philistine drew near morning and evening, and presented himself forty days.

17 And Jesse said unto David his son, Take now for thy brethren an ephah of this parched *corn,* and these ten loaves, and run *to* the camp to thy brethren;

18 And carry these ten [1]cheeses unto the [2]captain of *their* thousand, and [a]look how thy brethren fare, and take their pledge.

19 Now Saul, and they, and all the men of Israel, *were* in the valley of Elah, fighting with the Philistines.

20 And David rose up early in the morning, and left the sheep with a keeper, and took, and went, as Jesse had commanded him; and he came to the [a][1]trench, as the host was going forth to the [2]fight, and shouted for the battle.

17:8 [a]ch. 8:17
17:9 [a]ch. 11:1
17:10 [a]ver. 26; 2 Sam. 21:21
17:12 [a]ver. 58; Ruth 4:22; ch. 16:1,18 [b]Gen. 35:19 [c]ch. 16:10,11; See 1 Chr. 2:13-15
17:13 [a]ch. 16:6,8,9
17:15 [a]ch. 16:19
17:18 [1]Heb. *cheeses of milk* [2]Heb. *captain of a thousand* [a]Gen. 37:14
17:20 [1]Or, *place of the carriage* [2]Or, *battle ray,* or, *place of fight* [a]ch. 26:5
17:22 [1]Heb. *the vessels from upon him* [2]Heb. *asked his brethren of peace*
17:23 [a]ver. 8
17:24 [1]Heb. *from his face*
17:25 [a]Josh. 15:16
17:26 [a]ch. 11:2 [b]ch. 14:6 [c]ver. 10 [d]Deut. 5:26
17:27 [a]ver. 25
17:28 [a]Gen. 37:4,8,11; Mat. 10:36
17:29 [a]ver. 17
17:30 [1]Heb. *word* [a]ver. 26,27
17:31 [1]Heb. *took him*
17:32 [a]Deut. 20:1,3 [b]ch. 16:18
17:33 [a]See Num. 13:31; Deut. 9:2

21 For Israel and the Philistines had put *the battle* in array, army against army.

22 And David left [1]his carriage in the hand of the keeper of the carriage, and ran *into* the army, and came and [2]saluted his brethren.

23 And as he talked with them, behold, there came up the champion, the Philistine of Gath, Goliath by name, out of the armies of the Philistines, and spake [a]according to the same words: and David heard *them.*

24 And all the men of Israel, when they saw the man, fled [1]from him, and were sore afraid.

25 And the men of Israel said, Have ye seen this man that is come up? surely to defy Israel is he come up: and it shall be, *that* the man who killeth him, the king will enrich him *with* great riches, and [a]will give him his daughter, and make his father's house free in Israel.

26 And David spake to the men that stood by him, saying, What shall be done to the man that killeth this Philistine, and taketh away [a]the reproach from Israel? for who *is* this [b]uncircumcised Philistine, that he should [c]defy the armies of [d]the living God?

27 And the people answered him after this manner, saying, [a]So shall it be done to the man that killeth him.

28 And Eliab his eldest brother heard when he spake unto the men; and Eliab's [a]anger was kindled against David, and he said, Why camest thou down hither? and with whom hast thou left those few sheep in the wilderness? I know thy pride, and the naughtiness of thine heart; for thou art come down that *thou* mightest see the battle.

29 And David said, What have I now done? [a]*Is there* not a cause?

30 And he turned from him towards another, and [a]spake after the same [1]manner: and the people answered him again after the former [1]manner.

31 And when the words were heard which David spake, they rehearsed *them* before Saul: and he [1]sent for him.

32 ¶ And David said to Saul, [a]Let no man's heart fail because of him; [b]thy servant will go and fight with this Philistine.

33 And Saul said to David, [a]Thou art not

17:11 *Saul and all Israel . . . were . . . greatly afraid.* Israel's giant warrior (see 9:2; 10:23) quails before the Philistine champion. The fear of Saul and the Israelite army (see vv. 24,32) betrays a loss of faith in the covenant promises of the Lord (see Ex 23:22; Deut 3:22; 20:1–4). Their fear also demonstrates that the Israelite search for security in a human king (apart from trust in the Lord; see notes on 8:5,7) had failed. On the basis of God's covenant promises, Israel was never to fear her enemies but to trust in the Lord (see 2 Sam 10:12; Ex 14:13–14; Num 14:9; Josh 10:8; 2 Chr 20:17).

17:12 *Ephrathite.* See note on Ruth 1:2.

17:15 *David went and returned from Saul.* David's position at the court (see 16:21–23) was not permanent, but was performed on an intermittent basis. For the relationship between chs. 16 and 17 see note on v. 55.

17:24 *sore afraid.* See note on v. 11.

17:25 *the king will enrich . . . great riches.* See 8:14; 22:7. *give him his daughter.* See 18:17–26; cf. Josh 15:16.

17:26 *who is this . . .?* David sees the issues clearly—which sets him apart from Saul and all the other Israelites on that battlefield.

17:28 *Eliab's anger was kindled.* Eliab's anger may arise from jealousy toward his brother and a sense of guilt for the defeatist attitude of the Israelites. He recognizes, but does not comprehend, David's indomitable spirit (see 16:13).

17:32 *Let no man's heart fail because of him.* David's confidence does not rest in his own prowess (see vv. 37,47) but in the power of the living God, whose honor has been violated by the Philistines and whose covenant promises have been scorned by the Israelites.

able to go against this Philistine to fight with him: for thou *art but* a youth, and he a man of war from his youth.

34 And David said unto Saul, Thy servant kept his father's sheep, and there came a lion and a bear, and took a [1]lamb out of the flock:

35 And I went out after him, and smote him, and delivered *it* out of his mouth: and when he arose against me, I caught *him* by his beard, and smote him, and slew him.

36 Thy servant slew both the lion and the bear: and this uncircumcised Philistine shall be as one of them, seeing he hath defied the armies of the living God.

37 David said moreover, [a]The LORD that delivered me out of the paw of the lion, and out of the paw of the bear, he will deliver me out of the hand of this Philistine. And Saul said unto David, Go, and [b]the LORD be with thee.

38 And Saul [1]armed David with his armour, and he put a helmet of brass upon his head; also he armed him with a coat *of mail.*

39 And David girded his sword upon his armour, and he assayed to go; for he had not proved *it.* And David said unto Saul, I cannot go with these; for I have not proved *them.* And David put them off him.

40 And he took his staff in his hand, and chose him five smooth stones out of the [1]brook, and put them in a shepherd's [2]bag which he had, even in a scrip; and his sling *was* in his hand: and he drew near to the Philistine.

41 And the Philistine came on and drew near unto David; and the man that bare the shield *went* before him.

42 And when the Philistine looked about, and saw David, he [a]disdained him: for he was *but* a youth, and [b]ruddy, and of a fair countenance.

43 And the Philistine said unto David, [a]*Am* I a dog, that thou comest to me with staves? And the Philistine cursed David by his gods.

44 And the Philistine [a]said to David, Come to me, and I will give thy flesh unto the fowls of the air, and to the beasts of the field.

17:34 [1]Or, *kid*
17:37 [a]2 Cor. 1:10; 2 Tim. 4:17,18 [b]ch. 20:13; 1 Chr. 22:11,16
17:38 [1]Heb. *clothed David with his clothes*
17:40 [1]Or, *valley* [2]Heb. *vessel*
17:42 [a]1 Cor. 1:27,28 [b]ch. 16:12
17:43 [a]ch. 24:14; 2 Sam. 3:8; 9:8; 16:9; 2 Ki. 8:13
17:44 [a]1 Ki. 20:10,11

17:45 [a]2 Sam. 22:33,35; 2 Cor. 10:4; Heb. 11:33,34 [b]ver. 10
17:46 [1]Heb. *shut thee up* [a]Deut. 28:26 [b]Josh. 4:24; 1 Ki. 8:43; 18:36; 2 Ki. 19:19; Is. 52:10
17:47 [a]Hos. 1:7; Zech. 4:6 [b]2 Chr. 20:15
17:50 [a]ch. 21:9; See Judg. 3:31; 15:15; 2 Sam. 23:21
17:51 [a]Heb. 11:34
17:52 [a]Josh. 15:36

45 Then said David to the Philistine, Thou comest to me with a sword, and with a spear, and with a shield: [a]but I come to thee in the name of the LORD of hosts, the God of the armies of Israel, whom thou hast [b]defied.

46 This day will the LORD [1]deliver thee into mine hand; and I will smite thee, and take thine head from thee; and I will give [a]the carcases of the host of the Philistines this day unto the fowls of the air, and to the wild beasts of the earth; [b]that all the earth may know that there is a God in Israel.

47 And all this assembly shall know that the LORD [a]saveth not with sword and spear: for [b]the battle *is* the LORD's, and he will give you into our hands.

48 And it came to pass, when the Philistine arose, and came and drew nigh to meet David, that David hasted, and ran *toward* the army to meet the Philistine.

49 And David put his hand in *his* bag, and took thence a stone, and slang *it,* and smote the Philistine in his forehead, that the stone sunk into his forehead; and he fell upon his face to the earth.

50 So [a]David prevailed over the Philistine with a sling and with a stone, and smote the Philistine, and slew him; but *there was* no sword in the hand of David.

51 Therefore David ran, and stood upon the Philistine, and took his sword, and drew it out of the sheath thereof, and slew him, and cut off his head therewith. And when the Philistines saw their champion was dead, [a]they fled.

52 And the men of Israel and of Judah arose, and shouted, and pursued the Philistines, until thou come *to* the valley, and to the gates of Ekron. And the wounded of the Philistines fell down by the way to [a]Shaaraim, even unto Gath, and unto Ekron.

53 And the children of Israel returned from chasing after the Philistines, and they spoiled their tents.

54 And David took the head of the Philistine, and brought it *to* Jerusalem; but he put his armour in his tent.

17:33 *Thou art not able.* Saul does not take into account the power of God (see vv. 37,47).

17:34 *lion.* For the presence of lions in Canaan at that time see 2 Sam 23:20; Judg 14:5–18; 1 Ki 13:24–26; Amos 3:12. *bear.* See 2 Sam 17:8; 2 Ki 2:24; Amos 5:19.

17:36 *this uncircumcised Philistine.* See note on 14:6.

17:37 *The LORD . . . will deliver me.* Reliance on the Lord was essential for the true theocratic king (see notes on 10:18; 11:13). Here David's faith contrasts sharply with Saul's loss of faith (see 11:6–7 for Saul's earlier fearlessness). *Saul said unto David, Go.* Saul is now dependent on David not only for his sanity (see note on 16:16) but also for the security of his realm.

17:40 *his staff.* God's newly appointed shepherd of His people (see 2 Sam 5:2; 7:7; Ps 78:72) goes to defend the Lord's threatened and frightened flock. *stones.* Usually the stones chosen were round and smooth and somewhat larger than a baseball. When hurled by a master slinger, they probably traveled at close to 100 miles per hour. *his sling.* For the Benjamites' skill with a sling see Judg 20:16.

17:43 *Am I a dog . . . ?* See note on 2 Sam 9:8.

17:45 *in the name of the LORD of hosts.* David's strength was his reliance on the Lord (see Ps 9:10; Prov 18:10). For the expression "name of the LORD" see notes on Ex 3:13–14; Deut 12:11.

17:46 *all the earth may know.* The victory that David anticipates will demonstrate to all the world the existence and power of Israel's God (see Ex 7:17; 9:14,16,29; Deut 4:34–35; Josh 2:10–11; 4:23–24; 1 Ki 8:59–60; 18:36–39; 2 Ki 5:15; 19:19).

17:47 *the battle is the LORD's.* Both the Israelite and the Philistine armies will be shown the error of placing trust in human devices for personal or national security (see 2:10; 14:6; 2 Chr 14:11; 20:15; Ps 33:16–17; 44:6–7; Eccl 9:11; Hos 1:7; Zech 4:6).

17:51 *they fled.* Most likely the Philistines saw the fall of their champion as the judgment of the gods, but they did not honor Goliath's original proposal (see v. 9).

17:54 *brought it to Jerusalem.* Jerusalem had not at this time been conquered by the Israelites. David may have kept Goliath's head as a trophy of victory and brought the skull with him to Jerusalem when he took that city and made it his cap-

55 ¶ And when Saul saw David go forth against the Philistine, he said unto Abner, the captain of the host, Abner, [a]whose son *is* this youth? And Abner said, *As* thy soul liveth, O king, I cannot tell.

56 And the king said, Inquire thou whose son the stripling *is.*

57 And as David returned from the slaughter of the Philistine, Abner took him, and brought him before Saul [a]with the head of the Philistine in his hand.

58 And Saul said to him, Whose son *art* thou, *thou* young man? And David answered, [a]*I am* the son of thy servant Jesse the Bethlehemite.

Saul's hatred of David

18 And it came to pass, when he made an end of speaking unto Saul, that [a]the soul of Jonathan was knit with the soul of David, [b]and Jonathan loved him as his own soul.

2 And Saul took him that day, [a]and would let him go no more home *to* his father's house.

3 Then Jonathan and David made a covenant, because he loved him as his own soul.

4 And Jonathan stript himself of the robe that *was* upon him, and gave it to David, and his garments, even to his sword, and to his bow, and to his girdle.

5 And David went out whithersoever Saul sent him, *and* [1]behaved himself wisely: and Saul set him over the men of war, and he was accepted in the sight of all the people, and also in the sight of Saul's servants.

17:55 [a]See ch. 16:21,22
17:57 [a]ver. 54
17:58 [a]ver. 12
18:1 [a]Gen. 44:30 [b]ch. 19:2; 20:17; 2 Sam. 1:26; Deut. 13:6
18:2 [a]ch. 17:15
18:5 [1]Or, *prospered*
18:6 [1]Or, *Philistines* [2]Heb. *three-stringed instruments* [a]Ex. 15:20; Judg. 11:34
18:7 [a]Ex. 15:21 [b]ch. 21:11; 29:5
18:8 [1]Heb. *was evil in his eyes* [a]Eccl. 4:4 [b]ch. 15:28
18:10 [a]ch. 16:14 [b]ch. 19:24; 1 Ki. 18:29; Acts 16:16 [c]ch. 19:9
18:11 [a]ch. 19:10; 20:33
18:12 [a]ver. 15,29 [b]ch. 16:13,18 [c]ch. 16:14; 28:15
18:13 [a]ver. 16; Num. 27:17; 2 Sam. 5:2
18:14 [1]Or, *prospered* [a]Gen. 39:2,3,23; Josh. 6:27

6 And it came to pass as they came, when David was returned from the slaughter of the [1]Philistine, that [a]the women came out of all cities of Israel, singing and dancing, to meet king Saul, with tabrets, with joy, and with [2]instruments of musick.

7 And the women [a]answered *one another* as they played, and said,
[b]Saul hath slain his thousands,
And David his ten thousands.

8 And Saul was very wroth, and the saying [a][1]displeased him; and he said, They have ascribed unto David ten thousands, and to me they have ascribed *but* thousands: and *what* can he have more but [b]the kingdom?

9 And Saul eyed David from that day and forward.

10 ¶ And it came to pass on the morrow, that [a]the evil spirit from God came upon Saul, [b]and he prophesied in the midst of the house: and David played with his hand, as at other times: [c]and *there was* a javelin in Saul's hand.

11 And Saul [a]cast the javelin; for he said, I will smite David even to the wall *with it.* And David avoided out of his presence twice.

12 And Saul was [a]afraid of David, because [b]the LORD was with him, and was [c]departed from Saul.

13 Therefore Saul removed him from him, and made him his captain over a thousand; and [a]he went out and came in before the people.

14 And David [1]behaved himself wisely in all his ways; and [a]the LORD *was* with him.

15 Wherefore when Saul saw that he behaved himself very wisely, he was afraid of him.

ital (see 2 Sam 5:1–9). Or, having grown up almost under the shadow of the Jebusite city, he may have displayed Goliath's head to its defiant inhabitants as a warning of what the God of Israel was able to do and eventually would do. *put his armour in his tent.* As his personal spoils of the battle. Since Goliath's sword is later in the custody of the priest at Nob (see 21:9), he must have dedicated it to the Lord, the true victor in the fight (cf. 31:10).

17:55 *whose son is this youth?* The seeming contradiction between vv. 55–58 and 16:14–23 may be resolved by noting that prior to this time David was not a permanent resident at Saul's court (see v. 15; 18:2; see also note on 16:21), so that Saul's knowledge of David and his family may have been minimal. Further, Saul may have been so incredulous at David's courage that he was wondering if his family background and social standing might explain his extraordinary conduct.

18:1 It appears that David spoke with Saul at length, and he may have explained his actions as an expression of his faith in the Lord, thus attracting the love and loyalty of Jonathan (see v. 3; 14:6; 19:5). Their friendship endured even when it became clear that David was to replace him as the successor to his father's throne.

18:2 *Saul . . . would let him go no more home.* See note on 17:15.

‡18:3 *Jonathan and David made a covenant.* The Hebrew indicates the initiative comes from Jonathan. The terms of the agreement are not here specified (see further 19:1; 20:8,13–16, 41–42; 23:18) but would appear to involve a pledge of mutual loyalty and friendship. At the very least, Jonathan accepts David as his equal.

18:4 *stript himself of the robe . . . and gave it to David.* Jonathan ratifies the covenant in an act that symbolizes giving himself to David. His act may even signify his recognition that David was to assume his place as successor to Saul (see 20:14–15,31; 23:17)—a possibility that seems the more likely in that he also gave David "his sword, and . . . his bow, and . . . his girdle" (cf. 13:22).

18:5 *whithersoever Saul sent him.* During the rest of the campaign.

18:7 *David his ten thousands.* In accordance with the normal conventions of Hebrew poetry, this was the women's way of saying "Saul and David have slain thousands" (10,000 was normally used as the parallel of 1,000—see Deut 32:30; Ps 91:7; Mic 6:7; also in Canaanite poetry found at Ugarit). It is a measure of Saul's insecurity and jealousy that he read their intentions incorrectly and took offense. His resentment may have been initially triggered by the mention of David's name alongside his own. See note on 21:11 for how the Philistines interpreted the song.

18:10 *evil spirit from God.* See note on 16:14. *prophesied.* The Hebrew for this word is sometimes used to indicate uncontrolled ecstatic behavior (see note on 1 Ki 18:29) and is best understood in that sense in this context (see also note on 10:5). *as at other times.* See 16:14,23.

18:12 *the LORD was with him, and was departed from Saul.* See 16:14 and note.

18:13 *Saul removed him from him.* His apparent motive was the hope that David would be killed in battle (see vv. 17, 21, 25; 19:1), but the result was greater acclaim for David (see vv. 14,16,30).

16 But [a]all Israel and Judah loved David, because he went out and came in before them.

17 ¶ And Saul said to David, Behold my elder daughter Merab, [a]her will I give thee to wife: only be thou [1]valiant for me, and fight [b]the LORD'S battles. For Saul said, [c]Let not mine hand be upon him, but let the hand of the Philistines be upon him.

18 And David said unto Saul, [a]Who *am* I? and what *is* my life, *or* my father's family in Israel, that I should be son in law to the king?

19 But it came to pass at the time when Merab Saul's daughter should have been given to David, that she was given unto [a]Adriel the [b]Meholathite to wife.

20 [a]And Michal Saul's daughter loved David: and they told Saul, and the thing [1]pleased him.

21 And Saul said, I will give him her, that she may be a snare to him, and that [a]the hand of the Philistines may be against him. Wherefore Saul said to David, Thou shalt [b]*this* day be my son in law in *the one of* the twain.

22 And Saul commanded his servants, *saying,* Commune with David secretly, and say, Behold, the king hath delight in thee, and all his servants love thee: now therefore be the king's son in law.

23 And Saul's servants spake those words in the ears of David. And David said, Seemeth it to you a light *thing* to be a king's son in law, seeing that I *am* a poor man, and lightly esteemed?

24 And the servants of Saul told him, saying, [1]On this manner spake David.

25 And Saul said, Thus shall ye say to David, The king desireth not *any* [a]dowry, but an hundred foreskins of the Philistines, to be [b]avenged of the king's enemies. But Saul [c]thought to make David fall by the hand of the Philistines.

26 And when his servants told David these words, it pleased David well to be the king's son in law: and [a]the days were not [1]expired.

27 Wherefore David arose and went, he and [a]his men, and slew of the Philistines two hundred men; and [b]David brought their foreskins, and they gave them in full tale to the king, that he might be the king's son in law. And Saul gave him Michal his daughter to wife.

18:16 [a]ver. 5
18:17 [1]Heb. *a son of valour* [a]ch. 17:25 [b]Num. 32:20,27,29; ch. 25:28 [c]ver. 21,25; 2 Sam. 12:9
18:18 [a]See ver. 23; ch. 9:21; 2 Sam. 7:18
18:19 [a]2 Sam. 21:8 [b]Judg. 7:22
18:20 [1]Heb. *was right in his eyes* [a]ver. 28
18:21 [a]ver. 17 [b]See ver. 26
18:24 [1]Heb. *According to these words*
18:25 [a]Gen. 34:12; Ex. 22:17 [b]ch. 14:24 [c]ver. 17
18:26 [1]Heb. *fulfilled* [a]See ver. 21
18:27 [a]ver. 13 [b]2 Sam. 3:14
18:30 [1]Heb. *precious* [a]2 Sam. 11:1 [b]ver. 5
19:2 [a]ch. 18:1
19:4 [a]Prov. 31:8,9 [b]Gen. 42:22; Prov. 17:13
19:5 [a]Judg. 9:17 [b]ch. 17:49,50 [c]1 Sam. 11:13; 1 Chr. 11:14 [d]ch. 20:32 [e]Mat. 27:4
19:7 [1]Heb. *yesterday, third day* [a]ch. 16:21; 18:2,13
19:8 [1]Heb. *his face*
19:9 [a]ch. 16:14; 18:10,11

28 And Saul saw and knew that the LORD *was* with David, and *that* Michal Saul's daughter loved him.

29 And Saul was yet the more afraid of David; and Saul became David's enemy continually.

30 Then the princes of the Philistines [a]went forth: and it came to pass, after they went forth, *that* David [b]behaved himself more wisely than all the servants of Saul; so that his name was much [1]set by.

Saul tries to kill David

19 And Saul spake to Jonathan his son, and to all his servants, that they should kill David.

2 But Jonathan Saul's son [a]delighted much in David: and Jonathan told David, saying, Saul my father seeketh to kill thee: now therefore, I pray thee, take heed to thyself until the morning, and abide in a secret place, and hide thyself:

3 And I will go out and stand beside my father in the field where thou *art,* and I will commune with my father of thee; and what I see, that I will tell thee.

4 And Jonathan [a]spake good of David unto Saul his father, and said unto him, Let not the king [b]sin against his servant, against David; because he hath not sinned against thee, and because his works *have been* to thee-ward very good:

5 For he did put his [a]life in his hand, and [b]slew the Philistine, and [c]the LORD wrought a great salvation for all Israel: thou sawest *it,* and didst rejoice: [d]wherefore then wilt thou [e]sin against innocent blood, to slay David without a cause?

6 And Saul hearkened unto the voice of Jonathan: and Saul sware, *As* the LORD liveth, he shall not be slain.

7 And Jonathan called David, and Jonathan shewed him all those things. And Jonathan brought David to Saul, and he was in his presence, [a]as [1]in times past.

8 ¶ And there was war again: and David went out, and fought with the Philistines, and slew them *with* a great slaughter; and they fled from [1]him.

9 And [a]the evil spirit from the LORD was

18:17 *Behold my elder daughter.* David was entitled to have Saul's daughter as his wife because of his victory over Goliath (see 17:25). This promise had not been kept and is now made conditional on further military service, in which Saul hoped David would be killed. *the LORD's battles.* See 25:28.

18:25 *any dowry, but.* Normally a bride-price was paid by the bridegroom to the father of the bride (see Gen 34:12; Ex 22:16) as compensation for the loss of his daughter and insurance for her support if widowed. Saul requires David instead to pass a test appropriate for a great warrior, hoping that he will "fall" (see vv. 17,21).

18:28 *Michal . . . loved him.* God's favor on David is revealed not only in his military accomplishments, but also in Michal's love for him—now added to that of Jonathan. Everything Saul seeks to use against David turns to David's advantage.

18:29 *Saul was yet the more afraid of David.* Saul's perception that God's hand was on David did not lead him to repentance and acceptance of his own lot (see 15:26) but into greater fear and jealousy toward David.

19:1 *Saul spake to Jonathan . . . they should kill David.* Saul now abandons his indirect attempts on David's life (see 18:13,17,25) and adopts a more direct approach, leading to David's departure from the court and from service to Saul (see vv. 12,18; 20:42).

19:4 *Jonathan spake good of David.* Jonathan does not let his own personal ambition distort his perception of David's true theocratic spirit (see v. 5 and notes on 14:6; 17:11; 18:1).

19:6 *Saul hearkened . . . Saul sware.* See 14:24,44 for previous oaths that Saul did not keep (see note on 14:39).

19:9 *evil spirit from the LORD.* See note on 16:14; cf. 18:10–11.

upon Saul, as he sat in his house with his javelin in his hand: and David played with *his* hand.

10 And Saul sought to smite David even to the wall with the javelin; but he slipt away out of Saul's presence, and he smote the javelin into the wall: and David fled, and escaped that night.

11 [a]Saul also sent messengers unto David's house, to watch him, and to slay him in the morning: and Michal David's wife told him, saying, If thou save not thy life to night, to morrow thou *shalt be* slain.

12 ¶ So Michal [a]let David down through a window: and he went, and fled, and escaped.

13 And Michal took an [a][1]image, and laid *it* in the bed, and put a pillow of goats' *hair for* his bolster, and covered *it* with a cloth.

14 And when Saul sent messengers to take David, she said, He *is* sick.

15 And Saul sent the messengers *again* to see David, saying, Bring him up to me in the bed, that I may slay him.

16 And when the messengers were come in, behold *there was* an image in the bed, with a pillow of goats' *hair for* his bolster.

17 And Saul said unto Michal, Why hast thou deceived me so, and sent away mine enemy, that he is escaped? And Michal answered Saul, He said unto me, Let me go; [a]why should I kill thee?

18 ¶ So David fled, and escaped, and came to Samuel to Ramah, and told him all that Saul had done to him. And he and Samuel went and dwelt in Naioth.

19 And it was told Saul, saying, Behold, David *is* at Naioth in Ramah.

20 And [a]Saul sent messengers to take David: [b]and when they saw the company of the prophets prophesying, and Samuel standing *as* appointed over them, the spirit of God was upon the messengers of Saul, and they also [c]prophesied.

21 And when it was told Saul, he sent other messengers, and they prophesied likewise. And Saul sent messengers again the third time, and they prophesied also.

22 Then went he also to Ramah, and came to a great well that *is* in Sechu: and he asked and said, Where *are* Samuel and David? And *one* said, Behold, *they be* at Naioth in Ramah.

23 And he went thither to Naioth in Ramah: and [a]the spirit of God was upon him also, and he went on, and prophesied, until he came to Naioth in Ramah.

24 [a]And he stript off his clothes also, and prophesied before Samuel in like manner, and [1]lay down [b]naked all that day and all *that* night. Wherefore they say, [c]*Is* Saul also among the prophets?

David and Jonathan

20 And David fled from Naioth in Ramah, and came and said before Jonathan, What have I done? what *is* mine iniquity? and what *is* my sin before thy father, that he seeketh my life?

2 And he said unto him, God forbid; thou shalt not die: behold, my father will do nothing *either* great or small, but that he will [1]shew it me: and why should my father hide this thing from me? it *is* not *so.*

3 And David sware moreover, and said, Thy father certainly knoweth that I have found grace in thine eyes; and he saith, Let not Jonathan know this, lest he be grieved: but truly *as* the LORD liveth, and *as* thy soul liveth, *there is* but a step between me and death.

4 Then said Jonathan unto David, [1]Whatsoever thy soul [2]desireth, I will even do *it* for thee.

5 And David said unto Jonathan, Behold, to morrow *is* the [a]new moon, and I should not fail to sit with the king at meat: but let me go, that I may [b]hide myself in the fields unto the third *day* at even.

6 If thy father at all miss me, then say, David earnestly asked *leave* of me that *he* might run [a]*to* Beth-lehem his city: for *there is* a yearly [b][1]sacrifice there for all the family.

7 [a]If he say thus, *It is* well; thy servant shall have peace: but if he be very wroth, *then* be sure that [b]evil is determined by him.

8 Therefore thou shalt [a]deal kindly with thy servant; for [b]thou hast brought thy servant into a covenant of the LORD with thee:

19:11 [a]Ps. 59, title
19:12 [a]See Josh. 2:15; Acts 9:24,25
19:13 [1][Heb. *teraphim*] [a]Gen. 31:19
19:17 [a]2 Sam. 2:22
19:20 [a]See John 7:32,45 [b]ch. 10:5,6; 1 Cor. 14:3,24,25 [c]Num. 11:25; Joel 2:28

19:23 [a]ch. 10:10
19:24 [1]Heb. *fell* [a]Is. 20:2 [b]Mic. 1:8; See 2 Sam. 6:14,20 [c]ch. 10:11
20:2 [1]Heb. *uncover mine ear*
20:4 [1]Or, *Say what* is *thy mind, and I will do, etc.* [2]Heb. *speaketh,* or, *thinketh*
20:5 [a]Num. 10:10; 28:11 [b]ch. 19:2
20:6 [1]Or, *feast* [a]ch. 16:4 [b]ch. 9:12
20:7 [a]See Deut. 1:23; 2 Sam. 17:4 [b]ch. 25:17; Esth. 7:7
20:8 [a]Josh. 2:14 [b]ver. 16; ch. 18:3; 23:18

19:10 *with the javelin.* See 18:10–11; 20:33.
19:12 *through a window.* For similar escapes see Josh 2:15; Acts 9:25.
‡19:13 *image.* See KJV marg. See also note on Gen 31:19.
19:18 *Ramah.* Samuel's home (see 7:17 and note on 1:1). *Naioth.* Means "habitations" or "dwellings." The term appears to designate a complex of houses in a certain section of Ramah where a company of prophets resided (see vv. 19–20,22–23).
19:20 *company of the prophets.* See 10:5 and note. *prophesying.* See notes on 10:5; 18:10.
19:24 *he . . . lay down naked all that day and . . . night.* Saul was so overwhelmed by the power of the Spirit of God that he was prevented from carrying out his intention to take David's life. His frustrated attempts to kill David—his own inability to harm David and the thwarting of his plans by Jonathan's loyalty, by Michal's deception and by David's own cleverness—all reach their climax here. *Is Saul also among the prophets?* This second occasion reinforced the first (see 10:11 and note). Its repetition underscores how alien Saul's spirit was from that of these zealous servants of the Lord.
20:1 *Naioth in Ramah.* See note on 19:18.
20:3 *truly as the LORD liveth.* See note on 14:39.
20:5 *new moon.* Each month of the year was consecrated to the Lord by the bringing of special sacrifices (Num 28:11–15) and the blowing of trumpets (Num 10:10; Ps 81:3). This observance also involved cessation from normal work, especially at the beginning of the seventh month (Lev 23:24–25; Num 29:1–6; 2 Ki 4:23; Is 1:13; Am 8:5).
20:6 *yearly sacrifice.* David's statement indicates that it was customary for families to observe the new moon festival together once in the year. There is no other reference in the OT to this practice.
20:8 *covenant.* See note on 18:3.

notwithstanding, [c]if there be in me iniquity, slay me thyself; for why shouldest thou bring me to thy father?

9 And Jonathan said, Far be it from thee: for if I knew certainly that evil were determined by my father to come upon thee, then would not I tell it thee?

10 Then said David to Jonathan, Who shall tell me? or what *if* thy father answer thee roughly?

11 And Jonathan said unto David, Come, and let us go out *into* the field. And they went out both of them *into* the field.

12 And Jonathan said unto David, O LORD God of Israel, when I have [1]sounded my father about to morrow *any* time, *or* the third *day,* and behold, *if there be* good toward David, and I then send not unto thee, and [2]shew it thee;

13 [a]The LORD do so and much more to Jonathan: *but* if it please my father *to do* thee evil, then I will [1]shew it thee, and send thee away, that thou mayest go in peace: and [b]the LORD be with thee, as he hath been with my father.

14 And thou shalt not only while yet I live shew me the kindness of the LORD, that I die not:

15 But *also* [a]thou shalt not cut off thy kindness from my house for ever: no, not when the LORD hath cut off the enemies of David every one from the face of the earth.

16 So Jonathan [1]made *a covenant* with the house of David, *saying,* [a]Let the LORD even require *it* at the hand of David's enemies.

17 And Jonathan caused David to swear again, [1]because he loved him: [a]for he loved him as he loved his own soul.

18 Then Jonathan said to *David,* [a]To morrow *is* the new moon: and thou shalt be missed, because thy seat will be [1]empty.

19 And *when* thou hast stayed three days, *then* thou shalt go down [1]quickly, and come to [a]the place where thou didst hide thyself [2]when the business was *in hand,* and shalt remain by the stone [3]Ezel.

20 And I will shoot three arrows on the side *thereof,* as *though* I shot at a mark.

21 And behold, I will send a lad, *saying,* Go, find out the arrows. If I expressly say unto the lad, Behold, the arrows *are* on this side of thee, take them; then come thou: for *there is* peace to thee, and [1]no hurt; [a]*as* the LORD liveth.

22 But if I say thus unto the young man, Behold, the arrows *are* beyond thee; go *thy way:* for the LORD hath sent thee away.

20:8 [c]2 Sam. 14:32
20:12 [1]Heb. *searched* [2]Heb. *uncover thine ear*
20:13 [1]Heb. *uncover thine ear* [a]Ruth 1:17 [b]Josh. 1:5; ch. 17:37; 1 Chr. 22:11,16
20:15 [a]2 Sam. 9:1,3,7; 21:7
20:16 [1]Heb. *cut* [a]ch. 25:22; See ch. 31:2; 2 Sam. 4:7; 21:8
20:17 [1]Or, *by his love towards him* [a]ch. 18:1
20:18 [1]Heb. *missed* [a]ver. 5
20:19 [1]Or, *diligently.* Heb. *greatly* [2]Heb. *in the day of the business* [3]Or, *that sheweth the way* [a]ch. 19:2
20:21 [1]Heb. *not any thing* [a]Jer. 4:2

20:13 *the LORD do so and much more to Jonathan.* A common curse formula (see note on 3:17). *the LORD be with thee, as he hath been with my father.* A clear indication that Jonathan expects David to become king.

20:14 *that I die not.* It was quite common in the ancient world for the first ruler of a new dynasty to secure his position by murdering all potential claimants to the throne from the preceding dynasty (see 1 Ki 15:29; 16:11; 2 Ki 10:7; 11:1).

20:15 *thy kindness from my house.* This request was based on the covenant previously concluded between Jonathan and David (see note on 18:3) and was subsequently honored in David's dealings with Jonathan's son Mephibosheth (see 2 Sam 9:3,7; 21:7).

20:16 *Let the LORD even require it at the hand of David's enemies.* Jonathan aligns himself completely with David, calling for destruction of his enemies, even if that should include his father, Saul.

20:17 *swear again.* See vv. 14–15, 42; 18:3. *he loved him as he loved his own soul.* See 18:3; 2 Sam 1:26.

20:18 *new moon.* See note on v. 5.

20:19 *the place where thou didst hide.* Perhaps the place referred to in 19:2.

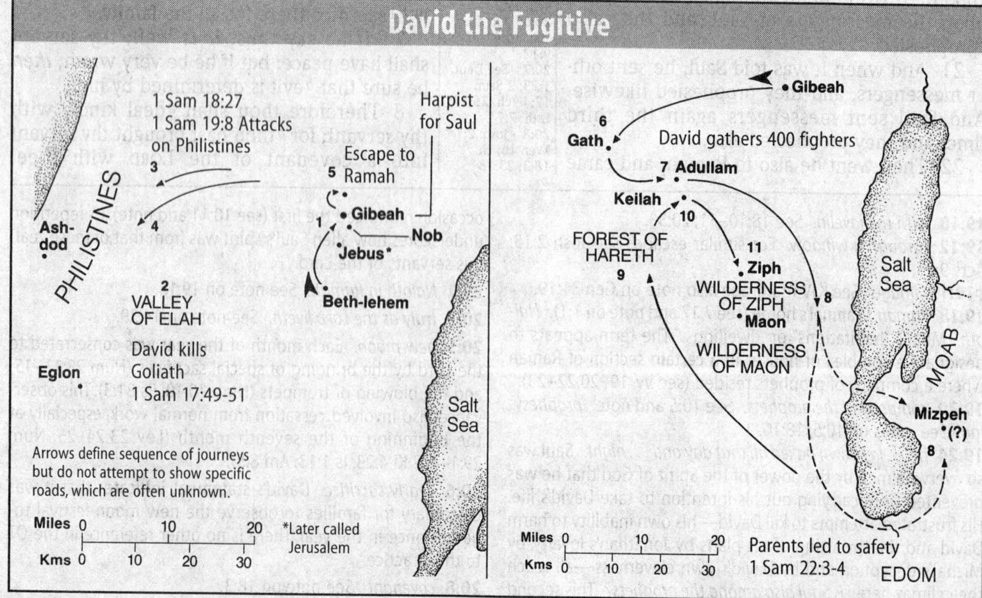

23 And *as touching* [a]the matter which thou and I have spoken of, behold, the LORD *be* between thee and me for ever.

24 ¶ So David hid himself in the field: and when the new moon was come, the king sat him down to eat meat.

25 And the king sat upon his seat, as at other times, *even* upon a seat by the wall: and Jonathan arose, and Abner sat by Saul's side, and David's place was empty.

26 Nevertheless Saul spake not any thing that day: for he thought, Something hath befallen him, he *is* [a]not clean; surely *he is* not clean.

27 And it came to pass on the morrow, *which was* the second *day* of the month, that David's place was empty: and Saul said unto Jonathan his son, Wherefore cometh not the son of Jesse to meat, neither yesterday, nor to day?

28 And Jonathan [a]answered Saul, David earnestly asked *leave* of me *to go* to Beth-lehem:

29 And he said, Let me go, I pray thee; for our family hath a sacrifice in the city; and my brother, he hath commanded me *to be there:* and now, if I have found favour in thine eyes, let me get away, I pray thee, and see my brethren. Therefore he cometh not unto the king's table.

30 Then Saul's anger was kindled against Jonathan, and he said unto him, [1]Thou son of the perverse rebellious *woman,* do not I know that thou hast chosen the son of Jesse to thine own confusion, and unto the confusion of thy mother's nakedness?

31 For as long as the son of Jesse liveth upon the ground, thou shalt not be stablished, nor thy kingdom. Wherefore now send and fetch him unto me, for he [1]shall surely die.

32 And Jonathan answered Saul his father, and said unto him, [a]Wherefore shall he be slain? what hath he done?

33 And Saul [a]cast a javelin at him to smite him: [b]whereby Jonathan knew that it was determined of his father to slay David.

34 So Jonathan arose from the table in fierce anger, and did eat no meat the second day of the month: for he was grieved for David, because his father had done him shame.

35 ¶ And it came to pass in the morning, that Jonathan went out *into* the field at the time appointed with David, and a little lad with him.

36 And he said unto his lad, Run, find out now the arrows which I shoot. *And* as the lad ran, he shot an arrow [1]beyond him.

37 And when the lad was come to the place of the arrow which Jonathan had shot, Jonathan cried after the lad, and said, *Is* not the arrow beyond thee?

38 And Jonathan cried after the lad, Make speed, haste, stay not. And Jonathan's lad gathered up the arrows, and came to his master.

39 But the lad knew not any thing: only Jonathan and David knew the matter.

40 And Jonathan gave his [1]artillery unto [2]his lad, and said unto him, Go, carry *them to* the city.

41 *And* as soon as the lad was gone, David arose out of *a place* toward the south, and fell on his face to the ground, and bowed himself three times: and they kissed one another, and wept one with another, until David exceeded.

42 And Jonathan said to David, [a]Go in peace, [1]forasmuch as we have sworn both of us in the name of the LORD, saying, The LORD be between me and thee, and between my seed and thy seed for ever. And he arose and departed: and Jonathan went *into* the city.

David visits Ahimelech

21 Then came David to Nob to [1]Ahimelech the priest: and Ahimelech was [a]afraid at the meeting of David, and said unto him, Why *art* thou alone, and no man with thee?

2 And David said unto Ahimelech the priest, The king hath commanded me a business, and hath said unto me, Let no man know any thing of the business whereabout I send thee, and what I have commanded thee: and I have appointed *my* servants to such and such a place.

3 Now therefore what is under thine hand? give *me* five *loaves of* bread in mine hand, or what there is [1]present.

20:23 [a]ver. 14,15; See ver. 42
20:26 [a]Lev. 7:21; 15:5
20:28 [a]ver. 6
20:30 [1]Or, *Thou perverse rebel.* Heb. *Son of perverse rebellion*
20:31 [1]Heb. is *the son of death*
20:32 [a]ch. 19:5; Mat. 27:23; Luke 23:22
20:33 [a]ch. 18:11 [b]ver. 7
20:36 [1]Heb. *to pass over him*
20:40 [1]Heb. *instruments* [2]Heb. *that* was *his*
20:42 [1]Or, the LORD be witness of that *which, etc.* [a]ch. 1:17
21:1 [1][ch. 14:3, called *Ahiah*]. [Called also *Abiathar,* Mark 2:26] [a]ch. 16:4
21:3 [1]Heb. *found*

20:23 *the matter which thou and I have spoken of.* See vv. 15–17. *the LORD be between.* The invoking of God to act as witness and judge between them ensures that their agreement will be kept.

20:25 *Abner.* Saul's cousin and the commander of his army (see 14:50).

20:26 *not clean.* See note on 16:5; cf. Lev 7:19–21; 15:16; Deut 23:10.

20:30 *son of the perverse rebellious woman.* The Hebrew idiom intends to characterize Jonathan, not his mother.

20:31 *thou shalt not be stablished, nor thy kingdom.* Saul is now convinced that David will succeed him if David is not killed (see notes on 18:13,17,29; 19:1), and he is incapable of understanding Jonathan's lack of concern for his own succession to the throne.

20:33 *cast a javelin.* See 18:11; 19:10.

20:41 *bowed himself three times.* A sign of submission and respect (see Gen 33:3; 42:6).

20:42 *sworn both of us.* See vv. 14–15,23; 18:3. *the city.* Gibeah (see 10:26).

21:1 *Nob.* A town northeast of Jerusalem and south of Gibeah where the tabernacle was relocated after the destruction of Shiloh (4:2–3; Jer 7:12). Although it appears that no attempt was made to bring the ark to this sanctuary (see note on 7:1), Ahimelech the high priest, 85 other priests (22:17–18), the ephod (v. 9) and the table of shewbread (v. 6) are mentioned in connection with it. *Ahimelech the priest.* See note on 14:3. It appears from 22:10,15 that David's purpose in coming to Nob was to seek the Lord's guidance by means of the Urim and Thummim (see notes on 2:28; Ex 28:30).

21:2 It is not clear why David resorts to deception in his response to Ahimelech. Perhaps it was an attempt to protect Ahimelech from the charge of involvement in David's escape from Saul. If so, his strategy was not successful (see 22:13–18).

4 And the priest answered David, and said, *There is* no common bread under mine hand, but there is [a]hallowed bread; [b]if the young men have kept themselves at least from women.

5 And David answered the priest, and said unto him, Of a truth women *have been* kept from us about these three days, since I came out, and the [a]vessels of the young men are holy, and *the bread is in* a manner common, [1]yea, though it were sanctified *this* day [b]in the vessel.

6 So the priest [a]gave him hallowed *bread:* for there was no bread there but the shewbread, [b]that was taken from before the LORD, to put hot bread in the day when it was taken away.

7 Now a *certain* man of the servants of Saul *was* there that day, detained before the LORD; and his name *was* [a]Doeg, an Edomite, the chiefest of the herdmen that *belonged* to Saul.

8 And David said unto Ahimelech, And is there not here under thine hand spear or sword? for I have neither brought my sword nor my weapons with me, because the king's business required haste.

9 And the priest said, The sword of Goliath the Philistine, whom thou slewest in [a]the valley of Elah, [b]behold, it *is here* wrapt in a cloth behind the ephod: if thou wilt take that, take *it:* for *there is* no other save that here. And David said, *There is* none like that; give it me.

David escapes to Gath

10 ¶ And David arose, and fled that day for fear of Saul, and went to [1]Achish the king of Gath.

11 And [a]the servants of Achish said unto him, *Is* not this David the king of the land? did they not sing one to another of him in dances, saying, [b]Saul hath slain his thousands, and David his ten thousands?

12 And David [a]laid up these words in his heart, and was sore afraid of Achish the king of Gath.

13 And [a]he changed his behaviour before them, and feigned himself mad in their hands, and [1]scrabled on the doors of the gate, and let his spittle fall down upon his beard.

14 Then said Achish unto his servants, Lo, you see the man [1]*is* mad: wherefore *then* have ye brought him to me?

15 *Have* I need of mad men, that ye have brought this *fellow* to play the mad man in my presence? shall this *fellow* come into my house?

David's flight continues

22 David therefore departed thence, and [a]escaped [b]to the cave Adullam: and when his brethren and all his father's house heard *it,* they went down thither to him.

2 [a]And every one *that was* in distress, and every one that [1]was in debt, and every one *that was* [2]discontented, gathered themselves unto him; and he became a captain over them: and there were with him about four hundred men.

3 And David went thence *to* Mizpeh of Moab: and he said unto the king of Moab, Let my father and my mother, I pray thee, come forth, *and be* with you, till I know what God will do for me.

4 And he brought them before the king of Moab: and they dwelt with him all the while that David was in the hold.

5 And the prophet [a]Gad said unto David, Abide not in the hold; depart, and get thee *into* the land of Judah. Then David departed, and came *into* the forest of Hareth.

Saul has Ahimelech killed

6 ¶ When Saul heard that David was discovered, and the men that *were* with him, (now Saul abode in Gibeah under a [1]tree in Ramah, having his spear in his hand, and all his servants *were* standing about him;)

21:4 [a]Ex. 25:30; Lev. 24:5; Mat. 12:4 [b]Ex. 19:15; Zech. 7:3
21:5 [1]Or, *especially when this day there is other sanctified in the vessel* [a]1 Thes. 4:4 [b]Lev. 8:26
21:6 [a]Mat. 12:3,4; Mark 2:25,26; Luke 6:3,4 [b]Lev. 24:8,9
21:7 [a]ch. 22:9; Ps. 52, title
21:9 [a]ch. 17:2,50 [b]See ch. 31:10
21:10 [1][Or, *Abimelech,* Ps. 34, title]
21:11 [a]Ps. 56, title [b]ch. 18:7; 29:5
21:12 [a]Luke 2:19
21:13 [1]Or, *made marks* [a]Ps. 34, title
21:14 [1]Or, *playeth the mad man*
22:1 [a]Ps. 57, title; 142, title [b]2 Sam. 23:13
22:2 [1]Heb. *had a creditor* [2]Heb. *bitter of soul* [a]Judg. 11:3
22:5 [a]2 Sam. 24:11; 1 Chr. 21:9; 2 Chr. 29:25
22:6 [1]Or, *grove in a high place*

‡21:4 *hallowed bread.* The "shewbread" (see v. 6; see note on Ex 25:30), which was placed in the holy place in the tabernacle and later in the temple as a thank offering to the Lord, symbolizing His provision of daily bread. *if the young men have kept themselves . . . from women.* Although the bread was to be eaten only by the priests (see Lev 24:9), Ahimelech agreed to give it to David and his men on the condition that they were ceremonially clean (see Ex 19:15; Lev 15:18). Jesus uses this incident to illustrate the principle that the ceremonial law was not to be viewed in a legalistic manner (see Mat 12:3–4). He also teaches that it is always lawful to do good and to save life (see Luke 6:9). Such compassionate acts are within the true spirit of the law.

21:9 *sword of Goliath.* See note on 17:54. *ephod.* See note on 2:28.

21:10 *Achish.* See note on Ps 34 title. *Gath.* One of the five major towns of the Philistines (Josh 13:3).

21:11 *king of the land.* The designation of David as "king" by the Philistines may be understood as a popular exaggeration expressing an awareness of the enormous success and popularity of David among the Israelite people.

22:1 *cave Adullam.* See 2 Sam 23:13; Gen 38:1; Josh 12:15; 15:35; 1 Chr 11:15 and note on Ps 142 title.

22:2 *with him about four hundred men.* David, officially an outlaw, was joined by others in similar circumstances, so that he began to develop the power base that would sustain him throughout his later years as king.

22:3 *Mizpeh of Moab.* Precise location unknown. *Let my father and my mother . . . come . . . and be with you.* The king of Moab was a natural ally for David because Saul had warred against him (see 14:47) and David's own great-grandmother was a Moabitess (see Ruth 4:13,22).

‡22:4 *hold* [i.e. "strong hold"]. Perhaps a specific fortress, but more likely a reference to a geographical area in which it was easy to hide (see 23:14; 2 Sam 5:17; 23:14).

22:5 *prophet Gad.* The king-designate is now served also by a prophet. Later a priest would come to him (v. 20) and complete the basic elements of a royal entourage—and they were all refugees from Saul's administration. This is the first appearance of the prophet who later assisted David in musical arrangements for the temple services (see 2 Chr 29:25), wrote a history of David's reign (see 1 Chr 29:29) and confronted David with the Lord's rebuke for his sin of numbering the Israelites (see 2 Sam 24:11–25). *forest of Hareth.* Located in the tribal area of Judah.

‡22:6 *Gibeah.* See note on 10:5. *tree.* Lit. "tamarisk tree." See note on 14:2.

7 Then Saul said unto his servants that stood about him, Hear now, ye Benjamites; will the son of Jesse [a]give every one of you fields and vineyards, *and* make you all captains of thousands, and captains of hundreds;

8 That all of you have conspired against me, and *there is* none that [1]sheweth me that [a]my son hath made *a league* with the son of Jesse, and *there is* none of you that is sorry for me, or sheweth unto me that my son hath stirred up my servant against me, to lie in wait, as at this day?

9 Then answered [a]Doeg the Edomite, which *was* set over the servants of Saul, and said, I saw the son of Jesse coming to Nob, to [b]Ahimelech the son of [c]Ahitub:

10 [a]And he inquired of the LORD for him, and [b]gave him victuals, and gave him the sword of Goliath the Philistine.

11 Then the king sent to call Ahimelech the priest, the son of Ahitub, and all his father's house, the priests that *were* in Nob: and they came all of them to the king.

12 And Saul said, Hear now, thou son of Ahitub. And he answered, [1]Here I *am,* my lord.

13 And Saul said unto him, Why have ye conspired against me, thou and the son of Jesse, in that thou hast given him bread and a sword, and hast inquired of God for him, that *he* should rise against me, to lie in wait, as at this day?

14 Then Ahimelech answered the king, and said, And who *is so* faithful among all thy servants as David, which *is* the king's son in law, and goeth at thy bidding, and *is* honourable in thine house?

15 Did I then begin to inquire of God for him? be it far from me: let not the king impute *any* thing unto his servant, *nor* to all the house of my father: for thy servant knew nothing of all this, [1]less or more.

16 And the king said, Thou shalt surely die, Ahimelech, thou, and all thy father's house.

17 And the king said unto the [1]footmen that stood about him, Turn, and slay the priests of the LORD; because their hand also *is* with David, and because they knew when he fled, and did not shew it to me. But the servants of the king [a]would not put forth their hand to fall upon the priests of the LORD.

18 And the king said to Doeg, Turn thou, and fall upon the priests. And Doeg the Edomite turned, and he fell upon the priests, and [a]slew on that day fourscore and five persons that did wear a linen ephod.

19 [a]And Nob, the city of the priests, smote he with the edge of the sword, both men and women, children and sucklings, and oxen, and asses, and sheep, with the edge of the sword.

20 ¶ [a]And one of the sons of Ahimelech the son of Ahitub, named Abiathar, [b]escaped, and fled after David.

21 And Abiathar shewed David that Saul had slain the LORD's priests.

22 And David said unto Abiathar, I knew *it* that day, when Doeg the Edomite *was* there, that he would surely tell Saul: I have occasioned *the death* of all the persons of thy father's house.

23 Abide thou with me, fear not: [a]for he that seeketh my life seeketh thy life: but with me thou *shalt be* in safeguard.

David at Keilah

23 Then they told David, saying, Behold, the Philistines fight against [a]Keilah, and they rob the threshingfloors.

2 Therefore David [a]inquired of the LORD, saying, Shall I go and smite these Philistines? And the LORD said unto David, Go, and smite the Philistines, and save Keilah.

3 And David's men said unto him, Behold, we *be* afraid here in Judah: how much more then if we come *to* Keilah against the armies of the Philistines?

4 Then David inquired of the LORD yet again. And the LORD answered him and said, Arise, go down *to* Keilah; for I will deliver the Philistines into thine hand.

5 So David and his men went *to* Keilah, and fought with the Philistines, and brought away their cattle, and smote them *with* a great slaughter. So David saved the inhabitants of Keilah.

6 And it came to pass, when Abiathar the son of Ahimelech [a]fled to David *to* Keilah, *that* he came down *with* an ephod in his hand.

7 ¶ And it was told Saul that David was come *to* Keilah. And Saul said, God hath delivered him into mine hand; for he is shut in, by entering into a town that hath gates and bars.

8 And Saul called all the people together to war, to go down *to* Keilah, to besiege David and his men.

22:7 [a]ch. 8:14
22:8 [1]Heb. *uncovereth mine ear* [a]ch. 18:3; 20:30
22:9 [a]ch. 21:7; Ps. 52, title; ver. 1-3 [b]ch. 21:1 [c]ch. 14:3
22:10 [a]Num. 27:21 [b]ch. 21:6,9
22:12 [1]Heb. *Behold me*
22:15 [1]Heb. *little or great*
22:17 [1]Or, *guard.* Heb. *runners* [a]See Ex. 1:17
22:18 [a]See ch. 2:31
22:19 [a]ver. 9,11
22:20 [a]ch. 23:6 [b]ch. 2:33
22:23 [a]1 Ki. 2:26
23:1 [a]Josh. 15:44
23:2 [a]ver. 4,6,9; ch. 30:8; 2 Sam. 5:19,23
23:6 [a]ch. 22:20

22:7 *Benjamites.* Saul, a Benjamite (9:1–2; 10:21), seeks to strengthen his position with his own officials by emphasizing tribal loyalty. David was from the tribe of Judah (see note on 16:1; 2 Sam 2:4). *give every one of you fields and vineyards.* Saul does exactly what Samuel had warned him that he would do—become like the kings of other nations (see 8:14). His actions are contrary to the covenantal ideal for kingship (see notes on 8:7; 10:25). *captains of thousands, and captains of hundreds.* See 8:12.

22:10 *he inquired of the LORD for him.* See note on 21:1.

22:17 *they knew when he fled.* How much the priests really knew is not clear. David himself had not told them (see 21:2–3,8).

22:18 *linen ephod.* See note on 2:18.

22:19 *Nob . . . smote he with the edge of the sword.* Thus the prophecy of judgment against the house of Eli is fulfilled (see 2:31).

22:20 *Abiathar, escaped, and fled after David.* See note on v. 5. Abiathar brought the high priestly ephod with him (see 23:6) and subsequently "inquired of the LORD" for David (see 23:2 and note; see also 23:4,9; 30:7–8; 2 Sam 2:1; 5:19,23). He served as high priest until removed from office by Solomon for participating in the rebellion of Adonijah (see 1 Ki 2:26–27).

23:2 *David inquired of the LORD.* By means of the Urim and Thummim through the high priest Abiathar (see vv. 6,9 and note on 2:28).

9 And David knew that Saul secretly prac-
tised mischief against him; and [a]he said to
Abiathar the priest, Bring hither the ephod.
10 Then said David, O LORD God of Israel,
thy servant hath certainly heard that Saul
seeketh to come to Keilah, [a]to destroy the city
for my sake.
11 Will the men of Keilah deliver me up
into his hand? Will Saul come down, as thy
servant hath heard? O LORD God of Israel, I beseech thee, tell thy servant. And the LORD said,
He will come down.
12 Then said David, Will the men of Keilah
[1]deliver me and my men into the hand of
Saul? And the LORD said, They will [1]deliver
thee up.
13 Then David and his men, [a]*which were*
about six hundred, arose and departed out of
Keilah, and went whithersoever they could go.
And it was told Saul that David was escaped
from Keilah; and he forbare to go forth.
14 And David abode in the wilderness in
strong holds, and remained in [a]a mountain in
the wilderness of [b]Ziph. And Saul [c]sought him
every day, but God delivered him not into his
hand.
15 And David saw that Saul was come out
to seek his life: and David *was* in the wilderness of Ziph in a wood.

Saul pursues David

16 ¶ And Jonathan Saul's son arose, and
went to David *into* the wood, and strengthened his hand in God.
17 And he said unto him, Fear not: for the
hand of Saul my father shall not find thee; and
thou shalt be king over Israel, and I shall be
next unto thee; and [a]that also Saul my father
knoweth.
18 And they two [a]made a covenant before
the LORD: and David abode in the wood, and
Jonathan went to his house.
19 ¶ Then [a]came up the Ziphites to Saul to
Gibeah, saying, Doth not David hide himself
with us in strong holds in the wood, in the hill
of Hachilah, which *is* [1]on the south of [2]Jeshi-
mon?
20 Now therefore, O king, come down according to all the desire of thy soul to come
down; and [a]our part *shall be* to deliver him
into the king's hand.

23:9 [a]Num. 27:21; ch. 30:7
23:10 [a]ch. 22:19
23:12 [1]Heb. *shut up*
23:13 [a]ch. 22:2; 25:13
23:14 [a]Ps. 11:1 [b]Josh. 15:55 [c]Ps. 54:3,4
23:17 [a]ch. 24:20
23:18 [a]ch. 18:3; 20:16,42; 2 Sam. 21:7
23:19 [1]Heb. *on the right hand* [2]Or, *the wilderness?* [a]See ch. 26:1; Ps. 54, title
23:20 [a]Ps. 54:3
23:22 [1]Heb. *foot shall be*
23:24 [a]Josh. 15:55; ch. 25:2
23:25 [1][Or, from *the rock*]
23:26 [a]Ps. 31:22 [b]Ps. 17:9
23:27 [1]Heb. *spread themselves upon, etc.* [a]See 2 Ki. 19:9
23:28 [1]That is, *the rock of divisions*
23:29 [a]2 Chr. 20:2
24:1 [1]Heb. *after* [a]ch. 23:28
24:2 [a]Ps. 38:12
24:3 [a]ver. 10 [b]Judg. 3:24 [c]Ps. 57, title; 142, title
24:4 [a]ch. 26:8

21 And Saul said, Blessed *be* ye of the
LORD; for ye have compassion on me.
22 Go, I pray you, prepare yet, and know
and see his place where his [1]haunt is, *and*
who hath seen him there: for it is told me *that*
he dealeth very subtilly.
23 See therefore, and take knowledge of all
the lurking places where he hideth himself,
and come ye again to me with the certainty,
and I will go with you: and it shall come to
pass, if he be in the land, that I will search him
out throughout all the thousands of Judah.
24 And they arose, and went to Ziph before Saul: but David and his men *were* in the
wilderness [a]of Maon, in the plain on the south
of Jeshimon.
25 Saul also and his men went to seek *him.*
And they told David: wherefore he came down
[1]*into* a rock, and abode in the wilderness of
Maon. And when Saul heard *that,* he pursued
after David *in* the wilderness of Maon.
26 And Saul went on this side of the mountain, and David and his men on that side of the
mountain: [a]and David made haste to get away
for fear of Saul; for Saul and his men [b]com-
passed David and his men round about to take
them.
27 [a]But there came a messenger unto Saul,
saying, Haste thee, and come; for the Philistines have [1]invaded the land.
28 Wherefore Saul returned from pursuing
after David, and went against the Philistines:
therefore they called that place [1]Sela-ham-
mahlekoth.

David spares Saul

29 ¶ And David went up from thence, and
dwelt in strong holds at [a]En-gedi.

24 And it came to pass, [a]when Saul was
returned from [1]following the Philistines, that it was told him, saying, Behold, David *is* in the wilderness of En-gedi.
2 Then Saul took three thousand chosen
men out of all Israel, and [a]went to seek David
and his men upon the rocks of the wild goats.
3 And he came to the sheepcotes by the
way, where *was* a cave; and [a]Saul went in to
[b]cover his feet: and [c]David and his men remained in the sides of the cave.
4 [a]And the men of David said unto him,
Behold the day of which the LORD said unto

23:9 *Bring hither the ephod.* See note on v. 2.

23:13 *about six hundred.* The number of David's men has grown significantly (cf. 22:2).

23:14 *wilderness in strong holds.* Inaccessible places (see note on 22:4). *wilderness of Ziph.* Located south of Hebron. *God delivered him not into his hand.* The reality of God's protection over David portrayed here contrasts sharply with the wishful thinking of Saul in v. 7.

23:17 *thou shalt be king over Israel.* See notes on 18:4; 20:13, 16,31. *I shall be next unto thee.* Jonathan's love and respect for David enable him to accept a role subordinate to David without any sign of resentment or jealousy (see notes on 18:3; 19:4). This is the last recorded meeting between Jonathan and David. *Saul . . . knoweth.* See 18:8 and note on 20:31.

23:18 *covenant.* See notes on 18:3; 20:14–15.

23:19 *strong holds.* Inaccessible places (see note on 22:4).

24:4 *Behold the day of which the LORD said.* There is no previous record of the divine revelation here alluded to by David's men. Perhaps this was their own interpretation of the anointing of David to replace Saul (see 16:13–14), or of assurances given to David that he would survive Saul's vendetta against him and ultimately become king (see 20:14–15; 23:17). This clause may also be rendered "today the LORD is saying." Then the reference would not be to a verbal communication from the Lord but to the providential nature of the incident itself, which David's men understood as a revelation from God that David should not ignore.

thee, Behold, I will deliver thine enemy into
thine hand, that thou mayest do to him as it
shall seem good unto thee. Then David arose,
and cut off the skirt of [1]Saul's robe privily.
5 And it came to pass afterward, that [a]Da-
vid's heart smote him, because he had cut off
Saul's skirt.
6 And he said unto his men, [a]The LORD forbid that I should do this thing unto my master,
the LORD's anointed, to stretch forth mine
hand against him, seeing he *is* the anointed of
the LORD.
7 So David [a][1]stayed his servants with
these words, and suffered them not to rise
against Saul. But Saul rose up out of the cave,
and went on *his* way.
8 David also rose afterward, and went out
of the cave, and cried after Saul, saying, My
lord the king. And when Saul looked behind
him, David stooped *with his* face to the earth,
and bowed himself.
9 ¶ And David said to Saul, [a]Wherefore
hearest thou men's words, saying, Behold, David seeketh thy hurt?
10 Behold, this day thine eyes have seen
how that the LORD had delivered thee to day
into mine hand in the cave: and *some* bade *me*
kill thee: but *mine eye* spared thee; and I said,
I will not put forth mine hand against my lord;
for he *is* the LORD's anointed.
11 Moreover, my father, see, yea see the
skirt of thy robe in my hand: for in that I cut
off the skirt of thy robe, and killed thee not,
know thou and see that *there is* [a]neither evil
nor transgression in mine hand, and I have not
sinned against thee; yet thou [b]huntest my soul
to take it.
12 [a]The LORD judge between me and thee,
and the LORD avenge me of thee: but mine
hand shall not be upon thee.
13 As saith the proverb of the ancients,
Wickedness proceedeth from the wicked: but
mine hand shall not be upon thee.
14 After whom is the king of Israel come
out? after whom dost thou pursue? [a]after a
dead dog, after [b]a flea.
15 [a]The LORD therefore be judge, and
judge between me and thee, and [b]see, and
[c]plead my cause, and [1]deliver me out of thine
hand.
16 ¶ And it came to pass, when David had
made an end of speaking these words unto
Saul, that Saul said, [a]*Is* this thy voice, my son
David? And Saul lift up his voice, and wept.
17 [a]And he said to David, Thou *art* [b]more
righteous than I: for [c]thou hast rewarded me
good, whereas I have rewarded thee evil.
18 And thou hast shewed *this* day how that
thou hast dealt well with me: forasmuch as
when [a]the LORD had [b][1]delivered me into thine
hand, thou killedst me not.
19 For if a man find his enemy, will he let
him go well away? wherefore the LORD reward
thee good for that thou hast done unto me this
day.
20 And now behold, [a]I know well that
thou shalt surely be king, and *that* the kingdom of Israel shall be established in thine
hand.
21 [a]Swear now therefore unto me by the
LORD, [b]that thou wilt not cut off my seed after
me, and that thou wilt not destroy my name
out of my father's house.
22 And David sware unto Saul. And Saul
went home; but David and his men gat them
up unto [a]the hold.

David, Nabal and Abigail

25 And [a]Samuel died; and all the Israelites were gathered together, and
[b]lamented him, and buried him in his house at
Ramah. And David arose, and went down [c]to
the wilderness of Paran.
2 And *there was* a man [a]in Maon, whose
[1]possessions *were* in [b]Carmel; and the man
was very great, and he had three thousand
sheep, and a thousand goats: and he was
shearing his sheep in Carmel.

24:4 [1]Heb. *the robe which was Saul's*
24:5 [a]2 Sam. 24:10
24:6 [a]ch. 26:11
24:7 [1]Heb. *cut off* [a]Ps. 7:4; Mat. 5:44; Rom. 12:17,19
24:9 [a]Ps. 141:6; Prov. 16:28; 17:9
24:11 [a]Ps. 7:3; 35:7 [b]ch. 26:20
24:12 [a]Gen. 16:5; Judg. 11:27; ch. 26:10; Job 5:8
24:14 [a]ch. 17:43; 2 Sam. 9:8 [b]ch. 26:20
24:15 [1]Heb. *judge* [a]ver. 12 [b]2 Chr. 24:22 [c]Ps. 35:1; 43:1; Mic. 7:9
24:16 [a]ch. 26:17
24:17 [a]ch. 26:21 [b]Gen. 38:26 [c]Mat. 5:44
24:18 [1]Heb. *shut up* [a]ch. 26:23 [b]ch. 23:12; 26:8
24:20 [a]ch. 23:17
24:21 [a]Gen. 21:23 [b]2 Sam. 21:6,8
24:22 [a]ch. 23:29
25:1 [a]ch. 28:3 [b]Num. 20:29; Deut. 34:8 [c]Gen. 21:21; Ps. 120:5
25:2 [1]Or, *business* [a]ch. 23:24 [b]Josh. 15:55

24:6 *he is the anointed of the LORD.* Because Saul's royal office carried divine sanction by virtue of his anointing (see note on 9:16), David is determined not to wrest the kingship from Saul but to leave its disposition to the Lord who gave it (see vv. 12,15; 26:10).

24:11 *my father.* Saul was David's father-in-law (see 18:27).

24:16 *lift up his voice, and wept.* Saul experiences temporary remorse (see 26:21) for his actions against David but quickly reverts to his former determination to kill him (see 26:2).

24:21 *not cut off my seed.* See notes on 20:14–15.

24:22 *hold.* An inaccessible place (see note on 22:4). From previous experience David did not place any confidence in Saul's words of repentance.

25:1 *all the Israelites . . . lamented him.* Samuel was recognized as a leader of national prominence who played a key role in the restructuring of the theocracy with the establishment of the monarchy (see chs. 8–12). The loss of his leadership was mourned much like that of other prominent figures in Israel's past history, including Jacob (Gen 50:10), Aaron (Num 20:29) and Moses (Deut 34:8). *Ramah.* See 7:17 and note on 1:1.

25:2–44 Nabal, the "fool" (see v. 25 and note), lived near Carmel, where Saul had erected a monument in his own honor (see 15:12) and had committed the act that led to his rejection (see 15:26). The account of Nabal effectively serves the author's purpose in a number of ways: 1. Nabal's general character, his disdainful attitude toward David though David had guarded his flocks, and his sudden death at the Lord's hand all parallel Saul (whose "flock" David had also protected). This allows the author indirectly to characterize Saul as a fool (see 13:13; 26:21) and to foreshadow his end. 2. David's vengeful attitude toward Nabal displays his natural tendency and highlights his restraint toward Saul, the Lord's anointed (this event is sandwiched between the two instances in which David spared Saul in spite of the urging of his men). 3. Abigail's prudent action prevents David from using his power as leader for personal vengeance (the very thing Saul was doing). In this way the Lord (who avenged His servant) keeps David's sword clean, teaching him a lesson he does not forget. 4. Abigail's confident acknowledgment of David's future accession to the throne foreshadows that event and even anticipates the Lord's commitment to establish David's house as a "sure house" (v. 28; cf. 2 Sam 7:11–16). 5. Abigail's marriage to David provides him with a wise and worthy wife, while Saul gives

3 Now the name of the man *was* Nabal; and the name of his wife Abigail: and *she was* a woman of good understanding, and of a beautiful countenance: but the man *was* churlish and evil *in* his doings; and he *was* of the house of Caleb.

4 And David heard in the wilderness that Nabal did [a]shear his sheep.

5 And David sent out ten young men, and David said unto the young men, Get you up to Carmel, and go to Nabal, and [1]greet him in my name:

6 And thus shall ye say to him that liveth *in prosperity,* [a]Peace *be* both *to* thee, and peace *be to* thine house, and peace *be unto* all that thou hast.

7 And now I have heard that thou hast shearers: now thy shepherds which were with us, we [1]hurt them not, [a]neither was there ought missing unto them, all the while they were in Carmel.

8 Ask thy young men, and they will shew thee. Wherefore let the young men find favour in thine eyes: for we come in [a]a good day: give, I pray thee, whatsoever cometh to thine hand unto thy servants, and to thy son David.

9 And when David's young men came, they spake to Nabal according to all those words in the name of David, and [1]ceased.

10 And Nabal answered David's servants, and said, [a]Who *is* David? and who *is* the son of Jesse? there be many servants now a days that break away every man from his master.

11 [a]Shall I then take my bread, and my water, and my [1]flesh that I have killed for my shearers, and give *it* unto men, whom I know not whence they *be?*

12 So David's young men turned their way, and went again, and came and told him all those sayings.

13 And David said unto his men, Gird you on every man his sword. And they girded on every man his sword; and David also girded on his sword: and there went up after David about four hundred men; and two hundred [a]abode by the stuff.

14 ¶ But one of the young men told Abigail, Nabal's wife, saying, Behold, David sent messengers out of the wilderness to salute our master; and he [1]railed on them.

15 But the men *were* very good unto us, and [a]we were not [1]hurt, neither missed we any thing, as long as we were conversant with them, when we were in the fields:

16 They were [a]a wall unto us both by night and day, all the while we were with them keeping the sheep.

17 Now therefore know and consider what thou wilt do; for [a]evil is determined against our master, and against all his household: for he *is such* a son of [b]Belial, that *a man* cannot speak to him.

18 Then Abigail made haste, and [a]took two hundred loaves, and two bottles of wine, and five sheep ready dressed, and five measures of parched *corn,* and an hundred [1]clusters of raisins, and two hundred cakes *of figs,* and laid *them* on asses.

19 And she said unto her servants, [a]Go on before me; behold, I come after you. But she told not her husband Nabal.

20 And it was *so, as* she rode on the ass, that she came down by the covert of the hill, and behold, David and his men came down against her; and she met them.

21 Now David had said, Surely in vain have I kept all that this *fellow* hath in the wilderness, so that nothing was missed of all that *pertained* unto him: and he hath [a]requited me evil for good.

22 [a]So and more also do God unto the enemies of David, if I [b]leave of all that *pertain* to him by the morning light [c]*any that* pisseth against the wall.

23 And when Abigail saw David, she hasted, and [a]lighted off the ass, and fell before David on her face, and bowed herself *to* the ground,

24 And fell at his feet, and said, Upon me, my lord, *upon* me *let this* iniquity *be:* and let thine handmaid, I pray thee, speak in thine [1]audience, and hear the words of thine handmaid.

25 Let not my lord, I pray thee, [1]regard this man of Belial, even Nabal: for as his name *is,* so *is* he; [2]Nabal *is* his name, and folly *is* with him: but I thine handmaid saw not the young men of my lord, whom thou didst send.

26 Now therefore, my lord, [a]*as* the LORD liveth, and *as* thy soul liveth, seeing the LORD

25:4 [a]Gen. 38:13; 2 Sam. 13:23
25:5 [1]Heb. *ask him in my name of peace*
25:6 [a]1 Chr. 12:18; Luke 10:5
25:7 [1]Heb. *shamed* [a]ver. 15,21
25:8 [a]Neh. 8:10; Esth. 9:19
25:9 [1]Heb. *rested*
25:10 [a]Judg. 9:28
25:11 [1]Heb. *slaughter* [a]Judg. 8:6
25:13 [a]ch. 30:24
25:14 [1]Heb. *flew upon them*
25:15 [1]Heb. *shamed* [a]ver. 7
25:16 [a]Ex. 14:22; Job 1:10
25:17 [a]ch. 20:7 [b]Deut. 13:13; Judg. 19:22
25:18 [1]Or, *lumps* [a]Gen. 32:13; Prov. 18:16; 21:14
25:19 [a]Gen. 32:16,20
25:21 [a]Ps. 109:5
25:22 [a]Ruth 1:17; ch. 3:17; 20:13,16 [b]ver. 34 [c]1 Ki. 14:10; 21:21; 2 Ki. 9:8
25:23 [a]Josh. 15:18; Judg. 1:14
25:24 [1]Heb. *ears*
25:25 [1]Heb. *lay it to his heart* [2][That is, *Fool*]
25:26 [a]2 Ki. 2:2

away David's wife Michal to another, illustrating how the Lord counters every move Saul makes against David.

25:3 *house of Caleb.* A descendant of Caleb (see Num 14:24), who settled at Hebron (see Josh 14:13) after the conquest of Canaan. Since Caleb's name can mean "dog," Nabal is subtly depicted as a dog as well as a fool. He would soon be a dead dog (see note on 2 Sam 9:8), when the Lord would avenge his acts of contempt toward David. The hint is strong that, when the Lord avenges Saul's sins against David (see 24:12,15), the king will no longer pursue a dead dog (see 24:14) but will himself become one—a case of biting irony.

25:4 *did shear his sheep.* A festive occasion (see v. 8; 2 Sam 13:23–24).

25:8 *whatsoever cometh to thine hand.* David and his men ask for some remuneration for their protection of Nabal's shepherds and flocks against pillage (see vv. 15–16,21).

25:17 *a son of Belial.* I.e. a worthless man. See note on Deut 13:13. *a man cannot speak to him.* In this way, too, Nabal is like Saul (cf., e.g., 20:27–33).

25:19 *told not her husband.* Cf. Michal's treatment of Saul (19:11–14).

25:22 *So and more also do God unto the enemies of David.* See note on 3:17. The sense may be: "As surely as God will punish my (David's) enemies, so surely will I kill every male in Nabal's household."

‡25:25 *man of Belial.* See v. 17 and note on Deut 13:13. *as his name is, so is he.* In ancient times a person's name was believed to reflect his nature and character. *Nabal is his name.* In Hebrew the name Nabal means "fool."

25:26 *as the LORD liveth.* See note on 14:39.

hath [b]withholden thee from coming to *shed* blood, and *from* [c][1]avenging thyself with thine own hand, now [d]let thine enemies, and they that seek evil to my lord, be as Nabal.

27 And now [a]this [1]blessing which thine handmaid hath brought unto my lord, let it even be given unto the young men that [2]follow my lord.

28 I pray thee, forgive the trespass of thine handmaid: for [a]the LORD will certainly make my lord a sure house; because my lord [b]fighteth the battles of the LORD, and [c]evil hath not been found in thee *all* thy days.

29 Yet a man is risen to pursue thee, and to seek thy soul: but the soul of my lord shall be bound in the bundle of life with the LORD thy God; and the souls of thine enemies, them shall he [a]sling out [1]*as out* of the middle of a sling.

30 And it shall come to pass, when the LORD shall have done to my lord according to all the good that he hath spoken concerning thee, and shall have appointed thee ruler over Israel;

31 That this shall be [1]no grief unto thee, nor offence of heart unto my lord, either that thou hast shed blood causeless, or that my lord hath avenged himself: but when the LORD shall have dealt well with my lord, then remember thine handmaid.

32 And David said to Abigail, [a]Blessed *be* the LORD God of Israel, which sent thee this day to meet me:

33 And blessed *be* thy advice, and blessed *be* thou, which hast [a]kept me this day from coming to *shed* blood, and *from* avenging myself with mine own hand.

34 For in very deed, *as* the LORD God of Israel liveth, which hath [a]kept me back from hurting thee, except thou hadst hasted and come to meet me, surely there had [b]not been left unto Nabal by the morning light *any that* pisseth against the wall.

35 So David received of her hand *that* which she had brought him, and said unto her, [a]Go up in peace to thine house; see, I have hearkened to thy voice, and have [b]accepted thy person.

36 ¶ And Abigail came to Nabal; and behold, [a]he held a feast in his house, like the feast of a king; and Nabal's heart *was* merry within him, for he *was* very drunken: wherefore she told him nothing, less or more, until the morning light.

37 But it came to pass in the morning, when the wine was gone out of Nabal, and his wife had told him these things, that his heart died within him, and he became *as* a stone.

38 And it came to pass about ten days *after,* that the LORD smote Nabal, that he died.

39 And when David heard that Nabal was dead, he said, [a]Blessed *be* the LORD, that hath [b]pleaded the cause of my reproach from the hand of Nabal, and hath [c]kept his servant from evil: for the LORD hath [d]returned the wickedness of Nabal upon his own head. And David sent and communed with Abigail, to take her to him to wife.

40 And when the servants of David were come to Abigail to Carmel, they spake unto her, saying, David sent us unto thee, to take thee to him to wife.

41 And she arose, and bowed herself *on her* face to the earth, and said, Behold, *let* thine handmaid *be* a servant to wash the feet of the servants of my lord.

42 And Abigail hasted, and rose, and rode upon an ass, with five damsels of hers that went [1]after her; and she went after the messengers of David, and became his wife.

43 David also took Ahinoam [a]of Jezreel; [b]and they were also both of them his wives.

44 But Saul had given [a]Michal his daughter, David's wife, to [1]Phalti the son of Laish, which *was* of [b]Gallim.

David spares Saul again

26 And the Ziphites came unto Saul to Gibeah, saying, [a]Doth not David hide himself in the hill of Hachilah, *which is* before Jeshimon?

2 Then Saul arose, and went down to the wilderness of Ziph, having three thousand chosen men of Israel with him, to seek David in the wilderness of Ziph.

25:26 [1]Heb. *saving thyself* [b]ver. 33; Gen. 20:6 [c]Rom. 12:19 [d]2 Sam. 18:32
25:27 [1]Or, *present* [2]Heb. *walk at the feet of, etc.* [a]Gen. 33:11; ch. 30:26; 2 Ki. 5:15
25:28 [a]2 Sam. 7:11,27; 1 Ki. 9:5; 1 Chr. 17:10,25 [b]ch. 18:17 [c]ch. 24:11
25:29 [1]Heb. *in the midst of the bought of a sling* [a]Jer. 10:18
25:31 [1]Heb. *no staggering,* or, *stumbling*
25:32 [a]Gen. 24:27; Ex. 18:10; Luke 1:68
25:33 [a]ver. 26
25:34 [a]ver. 26 [b]ver. 22
25:35 [a]ch. 20:42; 2 Sam. 15:9; 2 Ki. 5:19; Luke 7:50; 8:48 [b]Gen. 19:21
25:36 [a]2 Sam. 13:23
25:39 [a]ver. 32 [b]Prov. 22:23 [c]ver. 26,34 [d]1 Ki. 2:44
25:42 [1]Heb. *at her feet*
25:43 [a]Josh. 15:56 [b]ch. 27:3; 30:5
25:44 [1][*Phaltiel,* 2 Sam. 3:15] [a]2 Sam. 3:14 [b]Is. 10:30
26:1 [a]ch. 23:19; Ps. 54, title

25:28 *the LORD will certainly make . . . a sure house.* While the idea that David was destined to become king in place of Saul may have spread among the general populace, Abigail's assessment of David contrasts sharply with that of her husband (see v. 10). *fighteth the battles of the LORD.* Abigail is familiar with David's victories over the Philistines, in which he sought to glorify the Lord rather than advance his own honor (see 17:26,45–47; 18:16–17). *evil hath not been found in thee.* Abigail shows concern for the preservation of David's integrity in view of the office he was later to assume (see vv. 30–31,39).
25:29 *bound in the bundle of life.* Using the figure of placing a valuable possession in a carefully wrapped package for safekeeping, Abigail assures David that the Lord will preserve his life in the midst of danger.
25:30 *ruler.* See note on "captain" in 9:16 (same word in Hebrew).
25:31 *shed blood causeless.* See note on v. 28.
25:32 *which sent thee.* David recognizes the providential leading of the Lord in his encounter with Abigail (see v. 39).
25:36 *held a feast.* See Prov 30:21–22. *like the feast of a king.* Another clue that the author is using Nabal as a subtle portrayal of Saul.
25:37 *became as a stone.* Perhaps he suffered a stroke—he who was without moral sensitivity (was a *nabal;* see v. 25 and note) became as senseless as a stone.
25:43 *Ahinoam.* David's first wife (see 27:3; 30:5; 2 Sam 2:2) and mother of his first son, Amnon (see 2 Sam 3:2). *Jezreel.* Located near Carmel (see v. 2; Josh 15:55) and not to be confused with the northern town of the same name, where Israel camped against the Philistines (see 29:1,11) and where Ahab resided in later times (see 1 Ki 18:45–46).
25:44 *Michal . . . David's wife.* See 18:27.
26:1 *Ziphites.* See 23:19; see also note on 23:14. *Gibeah.* Saul's residence (see 10:26).
26:2 *three thousand.* Apparently Saul's standing army (see 24:2).

3 And Saul pitched in the hill of Hachilah,
which *is* before Jeshimon, by the way. But David abode in the wilderness, and he saw that
Saul came after him into the wilderness.
4 David therefore sent out spies, and understood that Saul was come in very deed.
5 And David arose, and came to the place
where Saul had pitched: and David beheld the
place where Saul lay, and [a]Abner the son of
Ner, the captain of his host: and Saul lay in the
[b1]trench, and the people pitched round about
him.
6 Then answered David and said to Ahimelech the Hittite, and to Abishai [a]the son of
Zeruiah, brother to Joab, saying, Who will [b]go
down with me to Saul to the camp? And
Abishai said, I will go down with thee.
7 So David and Abishai came to the people
by night: and behold, Saul lay sleeping within
the trench, and his spear stuck in the ground
at his bolster: but Abner and the people lay
round about him.
8 Then said Abishai to David, God hath
[a1]delivered thine enemy into thine hand *this*
day: now therefore let me smite him, I pray
thee, with the spear even to the earth at once,
and I will not *smite* him the second time.
9 And David said to Abishai, Destroy him
not: [a]for who can stretch forth his hand
against the LORD's anointed, and be guiltless?
10 David said furthermore, *As* the LORD
liveth, [a]the LORD shall smite him; or [b]his day
shall come to die; or he shall [c]descend into
battle, and perish.
11 [a]The LORD forbid that *I* should stretch
forth mine hand against the LORD's anointed:
but, I pray thee, take thou now the spear that
is at his bolster, and the cruse of water, and let
us go.
12 So David took the spear and the cruse of
water from Saul's bolster; and they gat them
away, and no man saw *it*, nor knew *it*, neither
awaked: for they *were* all asleep; because [a]a
deep sleep from the LORD was fallen upon them.
13 ¶ Then David went over *to* the *other*
side, and stood on the top of a hill afar off; a
great space *being* between them:

26:5 [1]Or, *midst of his carriages* [a]ch. 14:50; 17:55 [b]ch. 17:20
26:6 [a]1 Chr. 2:16 [b]Judg. 7:10,11
26:8 [1]Heb. *shut up* [a]ch. 24:18
26:9 [a]ch. 24:6,7; 2 Sam. 1:16
26:10 [a]ch. 25:38; Luke 18:7; Rom. 12:19 [b]See Gen. 47:29; Deut. 31:14; Job 7:1; 14:5 [c]ch. 31:6
26:11 [a]ch. 24:6,12
26:12 [a]Gen. 2:21; 15:12

26:16 [1]Heb. *the sons of death* [a]2 Sam. 12:5
26:17 [a]ch. 24:16
26:18 [a]ch. 24:9,11
26:19 [1]Heb. *smell* [2]Heb. *cleaving* [a]2 Sam. 16:11; 24:1 [b]Deut. 4:28 [c]2 Sam. 14:16; 20:19
26:20 [a]ch. 24:14
26:21 [a]ch. 15:24; 24:17 [b]ch. 18:30
26:23 [a]Ps. 7:8; 18:20

14 And David cried to the people, and to
Abner the son of Ner, saying, Answerest thou
not, Abner? Then Abner answered and said,
Who *art* thou *that* criest to the king?
15 And David said to Abner, *Art* not thou a
valiant man? and who *is* like to thee in Israel?
wherefore then hast thou not kept thy lord the
king? for there came one of the people in to
destroy the king thy lord.
16 This thing *is* not good that thou hast
done. *As* the LORD liveth, ye *are* [a1]worthy to
die, because ye have not kept your master, the
LORD's anointed. And now see where the
king's spear *is*, and the cruse of water that *was*
at his bolster.
17 And Saul knew David's voice, and said,
[a]*Is* this thy voice, my son David? And David
said, *It is* my voice, my lord, O king.
18 And he said, [a]Wherefore doth my lord
thus pursue after his servant? for what have I
done? or what evil *is* in mine hand?
19 Now therefore, I pray thee, let my lord
the king hear the words of his servant. If the
LORD have [a]stirred thee up against me, let him
[1]accept an offering: but if *they be* the children
of men, cursed *be* they before the LORD; [b]for
they have driven me out *this* day from [2]abid-
ing in the [c]inheritance of the LORD, saying,
Go, serve other gods.
20 Now therefore, let not my blood fall to
the earth before the face of the LORD: for the
king of Israel is come out to seek [a]a flea, as
when *one* doth hunt a partridge in the mountains.
21 Then said Saul, [a]I have sinned: return,
my son David: for I will no more do thee harm,
because my soul was [b]precious in thine eyes
this day: behold, I have played the fool, and
have erred exceedingly.
22 And David answered and said, Behold,
the king's spear; and let one of the young men
come over and fetch it.
23 [a]The LORD render to every man his righteousness and his faithfulness: for the LORD delivered thee into *my* hand to day, but I would
not stretch forth mine hand against the LORD's
anointed.

26:5 *lay.* David arrived at Saul's camp during the night when the men were sleeping. *Abner.* Saul's cousin (see 14:50).
26:6 *Ahimelech the Hittite.* Not referred to elsewhere. Hittites had long resided in Canaan (see note on Gen 10:15; see also Gen 15:20; 23:3–20; Deut 7:1; 20:17). Another Hittite in David's service was Uriah (see 2 Sam 11:3; 23:39). *Abishai the son of Zeruiah, brother to Joab.* Zeruiah was an older sister of David (1 Chr 2:16), so Abishai and Joab (and their brother Asahel, 2 Sam 2:18) were David's nephews as well as trusted military leaders. Joab would long serve as the commander of his army.
26:9 See note on 24:6.
26:10 *As the LORD liveth.* See note on 14:39.
26:12 *David took the spear and the cruse of water.* In this way he sought to prove again to Saul that he did not seek his life.
26:19 *let him accept an offering.* David knows no reason why God should be angry with him; but if for some reason God is behind Saul's determined effort to kill him, David appeals for God to accept an offering of appeasement (cf. 16:5)—in any event, to let the matter be settled between David and God, without Saul's involvement. *cursed be they before the LORD.* David commits any such men to the judgment of God. *the inheritance of the LORD.* See note on 10:1. David appeals to Saul's conscience by describing his present exclusion from the fellowship of God's people and from living at peace in the Lord's land. *Go, serve other gods.* In their view, to be expelled from the Lord's land was to be separated from the Lord's sanctuary (an OT form of excommunication) and left to serve the gods of whatever land one may settle in (see Josh 22:24–27).
26:20 *seek a flea.* See 24:14. David suggests that Saul is making a fool of himself in his fanatical pursuit of an innocent and undesigning man.
26:21 *I have sinned.* See 24:17. *I have played the fool.* Saul confesses that his behavior has been not only unwise but also ungodly (see notes on 13:13; 25:2–44).
26:23 *I would not stretch forth mine hand against the LORD's anointed.* See v. 9 and note on 24:6.

24 And behold, as thy life was much set by
this day in mine eyes, so let my life be much
set by in the eyes of the LORD, and let him deliver me out of all tribulation.
25 Then Saul said to David, Blessed *be*
thou, my son David: thou shalt both do great
things, and also shalt still [a]prevail. So David
went on his way, and Saul returned to his
place.

David lives with the Philistines

27 And David said in his heart, I shall
now [1]perish one day by the hand of
Saul: *there is* nothing better for me than that I
should speedily escape into the land of the Philistines; and Saul shall despair of me, to seek
me any more in any coast of Israel: so shall I
escape out of his hand.
2 And David arose, [a]and he passed over
with the six hundred men that *were* with
him [b]unto Achish, the son of Maoch, king of
Gath.
3 And David dwelt with Achish at Gath, he
and his men, every man with his household,
even David [a]with his two wives, Ahinoam the
Jezreelitess, and Abigail the Carmelitess, Nabal's wife.
4 And it was told Saul that David was fled
to Gath: and he sought no more again for him.
5 And David said unto Achish, If I have
now found grace in thine eyes, let them give
me a place in some town in the country, that I
may dwell there: for why should thy servant
dwell in the royal city with thee?
6 Then Achish gave him Ziklag that day:
wherefore [a]Ziklag pertaineth unto the kings of
Judah unto this day.
7 And [1]the time that David dwelt in the

26:25 [a]Gen. 32:28
27:1 [1]Heb. *be consumed*
27:2 [a]ch. 25:13
27:2 [b]ch. 21:10
27:3 [a]ch. 25:43
27:6 [a]See Josh. 15:31; 19:5
27:7 [1]Heb. *the number of days*

26:25 *thou shalt . . . prevail.* Saul makes a veiled reference to his own conviction that David will replace him as king (see 24:20).
27:1 *I shall now perish . . . by the hand of Saul.* David falters in his faith (see 23:14; 25:29) and under pressure of Saul's superior forces feels compelled to seek security outside Israel's borders. *land of the Philistines.* For the second time David seeks refuge in the land of the Philistines (see 21:10–15).
27:2 *Achish . . . king of Gath.* See 21:10. In contrast to David's previous excursion into Philistia, Achish is now ready to receive him because he has become known as a formidable adversary of Saul. Moreover, to offer sanctuary under the circumstances would obligate David and his men to serve at his call in any military venture (see 28:1).
27:3 *Ahinoam.* See note on 25:43. *Abigail.* See 25:39–42.
27:4 *he sought no more again for him.* Saul did not have sufficient military strength to make incursions into Philistine territory, and with David out of the country he no longer faced an internal threat to his throne.
27:5 *in some town in the country.* David desired more independence and freedom of movement than was possible while residing under the very eyes of the king of Gath. *why should thy servant dwell in the royal city with thee?* David implies that he is not worthy of this honor.
27:6 *Ziklag.* Location unknown, but it is included in a list of towns in southern Judah (see Josh 15:31). It was given to the tribe of Simeon (see Josh 19:1–5) and was presumably occupied by them (cf. Judg 1:17–18), only to be lost to the Philistines at a later, undisclosed time. *pertaineth unto the kings of Judah unto this day.* As royal property. This comment implies that the book of Samuel was written after the time of the division of Israel into the northern and southern kingdoms—an important consideration in determining the date of the writing of the book (see Introduction: Literary Features, Authorship and Date).
27:7 *David dwelt in the country of the Philistines . . . a full year and four months.* It was not until after the death of Saul that David moved his residence from Ziklag (see 2 Sam 1:1; 2:1–3) to Hebron.

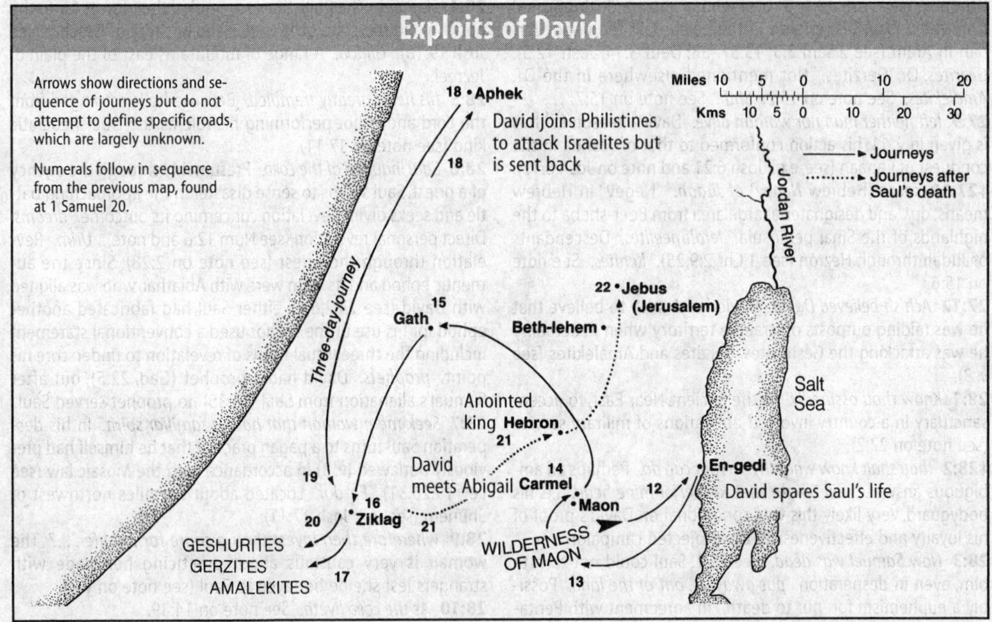

country of the Philistines was [a][2]a full year and
four months.

8 ¶ And David and his men went up, and
invaded [a]the Geshurites, [b]and the [1]Gezrites,
and the [c]Amalekites: for those *nations were* of
old the inhabitants of the land [d]as thou goest
to Shur, even unto the land of Egypt.

9 And David smote the land, and left neither man nor woman alive, and took away the
sheep, and the oxen, and the asses, and the
camels, and the apparel, and returned, and
came to Achish.

10 And Achish said, [1]Whither have ye
made a road to day? And David said, Against
the south of Judah, and against the south of
[a]the Jerahmeelites, and against the south of
[b]the Kenites.

11 And David saved neither man nor
woman alive, to bring *tidings to* Gath, saying,
Lest they should tell on us, saying, So did David, and so *will be* his manner all the while he
dwelleth in the country of the Philistines.

12 And Achish believed David, saying, He
hath made his people Israel [1]utterly to abhor
him; therefore he shall be my servant for
ever.

28 And [a]it came to pass in those days,
that the Philistines gathered their armies together for warfare, to fight with Israel.
And Achish said unto David, Know thou assuredly, that thou shalt go out with me to battle, thou and thy men.

2 And David said to Achish, Surely thou
shalt know what thy servant can do. And
Achish said to David, Therefore will I make
thee keeper of mine head for ever.

27:7 [2]Heb. a year of *days* [a]ch. 29:3
27:8 [1]Or, *Gerzites* [a]Josh. 13:2 [b]Josh. 16:10; Judg. 1:29 [c]Ex. 17:16; See ch. 15:7,8 [d]Gen. 25:18
27:10 [1]Or, *Did you not make a road, etc.* [a]See 1 Chr. 2:9,25 [b]Judg. 1:16
27:12 [1]Heb. *to stink*
28:1 [a]ch. 29:1

28:3 [a]ch. 5:1 [b]See ch 1:19 [c]ver. 9; Ex. 22:18; Lev. 19:31; 20:2; Deut. 18:10,11
28:4 [a]Josh. 19:18; 2 Ki. 4:8 [b]ch. 31:1
28:5 [a]Job 18:11
28:6 [a]ch. 14:37; Prov. 1:28; Lam. 2:9 [b]Num. 12:6 [c]Ex. 28:30; Num. 27:21; Deut. 33:8
28:8 [a]Deut. 18:11; 1 Chr. 10:13; Is. 8:19
28:9 [a]ver. 3

Saul and the woman at En-dor

3 ¶ Now [a]Samuel was dead, and all Israel
had lamented him, and buried him in [b]Ramah,
even in his own city. And Saul had put away
[c]those that had familiar spirits, and the wizards, out of the land.

4 And the Philistines gathered themselves
together, and came and pitched in [a]Shunem:
and Saul gathered all Israel together, and they
pitched in [b]Gilboa.

5 And when Saul saw the host of the Philistines, he was [a]afraid, and his heart greatly
trembled.

6 And when Saul inquired of the LORD,
[a]the LORD answered him not, neither by
[b]dreams, nor [c]by Urim, nor by prophets.

7 Then said Saul unto his servants, Seek
me a woman that hath a familiar spirit, that I
may go to her, and inquire of her. And his servants said to him, Behold, *there is* a woman
that hath a familiar spirit at En-dor.

8 And Saul disguised himself, and put on
other raiment, and he went, and two men
with him, and they came to the woman by
night: and [a]he said, I pray thee, divine unto
me by the familiar spirit, and bring me *him* up,
whom I shall name unto thee.

9 And the woman said unto him, Behold,
thou knowest what Saul hath done, how he
hath [a]cut off those that have familiar spirits,
and the wizards, out of the land: wherefore
then layest thou a snare for my life, to cause
me to die?

10 And Saul sware to her by the LORD, saying, *As* the LORD liveth, there shall no punishment happen to thee for this thing.

‡27:8 *Geshurites.* A people residing in the area south of Philistia who were not defeated by the Israelites at the time of the conquest (see Josh 13:1–3) and who are to be distinguished from the Geshurites residing in the north near the upper Jordan in Aram (see 2 Sam 3:3; 13:37–38; Deut 3:14; Josh 12:5). *Gezrites.* Or "Gerzites." Not mentioned elsewhere in the OT. *Amalekites.* See note on 15:2. *Shur.* See note on 15:7.

27:9 *left neither man nor woman alive.* David's reason for this is given in v. 11; his action conformed to that of Joshua in the conquest of Canaan (see, e.g., Josh 6:21 and note on Josh 6:17).

‡27:10 *south* [Hebrew *Negev*] *of Judah.* "Negev" in Hebrew means "dry" and designates a large area from Beer-sheba to the highlands of the Sinai peninsula. *Jerahmeelites.* Descendants of Judah through Hezron (see 1 Chr 2:9,25). *Kenites.* See note on 15:6.

27:12 *Achish believed David.* David led Achish to believe that he was raiding outposts of Israelite territory when in actuality he was attacking the Geshurites, Gerzites and Amalekites (see v. 8).

28:1 *Know thou assuredly.* In the ancient Near East, to accept sanctuary in a country involved obligations of military service (see note on 27:2).

‡28:2 *thou shalt know what thy servant can do.* Perhaps an ambiguous answer. *will I make thee keeper of mine head.* I.e. his bodyguard. Very likely this was conditional on David's proof of his loyalty and effectiveness in the projected campaign.

28:3 *Now Samuel was dead.* See 25:1. Saul could not turn to him, even in desperation. *put away . . . out of the land.* Possibly a euphemism for "put to death," in agreement with Pentateuchal law (see vv. 9,21). *those . . . familiar spirits . . . wizards.* See Lev 19:31; 20:6,27; Deut 18:11.

28:4 *Shunem.* The Philistines assembled their forces far to the north, along the plain of Jezreel in the territory of Issachar (see Josh 19:18). *Gilboa.* A range of mountains east of the plain of Jezreel.

28:5 *his heart greatly trembled.* Because he is estranged from the Lord and is not performing his role as the true theocratic king (see note on 17:11).

28:6 *Saul inquired of the LORD.* Presumably through the agency of a priest. Saul seems to sense disaster in the approaching battle and seeks divine revelation concerning its outcome. *dreams.* Direct personal revelation (see Num 12:6 and note). *Urim.* Revelation through the priest (see note on 2:28). Since the authentic ephod and its Urim were with Abiathar, who was aligned with David (see 23:2,6,9), either Saul had fabricated another ephod for his use or the author used a conventional statement including the three visual forms of revelation to underscore his point. *prophets.* David had a prophet (Gad, 22:5), but after Samuel's alienation from Saul (15:35) no prophet served Saul.

28:7 *Seek me a woman that hath a familiar spirit.* In his desperation Saul turns to a pagan practice that he himself had previously outlawed (v. 3) in accordance with the Mosaic law (see Lev 19:26,31). *En-dor.* Located about six miles northwest of Shunem (see v. 4; Josh 17:11).

28:9 *wherefore then layest thou a snare for my life . . .?* The woman is very cautious about practicing her trade with strangers lest she be betrayed to Saul (see note on v. 3).

28:10 *As the LORD liveth.* See note on 14:39.

11 Then said the woman, Whom shall I bring up unto thee? And he said, Bring me up Samuel.

12 And when the woman saw Samuel, she cried with a loud voice: and the woman spake to Saul, saying, Why hast thou deceived me? for thou *art* Saul.

13 And the king said unto her, Be not afraid: for what sawest thou? And the woman said unto Saul, I saw [a]gods ascending out of the earth.

14 And he said unto her, [1]What form is he of? And she said, An old man cometh up; and he *is* covered with [a]a mantle. And Saul perceived that it *was* Samuel, and he stooped *with his* face to the ground, and bowed himself.

15 ¶ And Samuel said to Saul, Why hast thou disquieted me, to bring me up? And Saul answered, [a]I am sore distressed; for the Philistines make war against me, and [b]God is departed from me, and [c]answereth me no more, neither [1]by prophets, nor by dreams: therefore I have called thee, that *thou* mayest make known unto me what I shall do.

16 Then said Samuel, Wherefore then dost thou ask of me, seeing the LORD is departed from thee, and is become thine enemy?

17 And the LORD hath done [1]to him, [a]as he spake by [2]me: for the LORD hath rent the kingdom out of thine hand, and given it to thy neighbour, *even* to David:

18 [a]Because thou obeyedst not the voice of the LORD, nor executedst his fierce wrath upon Amalek, therefore hath the LORD done this thing unto thee this day.

19 Moreover the LORD will also deliver Israel with thee into the hand of the Philistines: and to morrow *shalt* thou and thy sons *be* with me: the LORD also shall deliver the host of Israel into the hand of the Philistines.

20 ¶ Then Saul [1]fell straightway all along on the earth, and was sore afraid, because of the words of Samuel: and there was no strength in him; for he had eaten no bread all the day, nor all the night.

21 And the woman came unto Saul, and saw that he was sore troubled, and said unto him, Behold, thine handmaid hath obeyed thy voice, and I have [a]put my life in my hand, and have hearkened unto thy words which thou spakest unto me.

22 Now therefore, I pray thee, hearken thou also unto the voice of thine handmaid, and let me set a morsel of bread before thee; and eat, that thou mayest have strength, when thou goest on *thy* way.

23 But he refused, and said, I will not eat. But his servants, together with the woman, compelled him; and he hearkened unto their voice. So he arose from the earth, and sat upon the bed.

24 And the woman had a fat calf in the house; and she hasted, and killed it, and took flour, and kneaded *it*, and did bake unleavened bread thereof:

25 And she brought *it* before Saul, and before his servants; and they did eat. Then they arose up, and went away that night.

The Philistines dismiss David

29 Now [a]the Philistines gathered together all their armies [b]to Aphek: and the Israelites pitched by a fountain which *is* in Jezreel.

2 And the lords of the Philistines passed on by hundreds, and by thousands: but David and his men passed on in the rereward [a]with Achish.

3 Then said the princes of the Philistines, What *do* these Hebrews *here?* And Achish said unto the princes of the Philistines, *Is* not this David, the servant of Saul the king of Israel, which hath been with me [a]these days, or these years, and I have [b]found no *fault* in him since he fell *unto me* unto this day?

4 And the princes of the Philistines were wroth with him; and the princes of the Philistines said unto him, [a]Make *this* fellow return, that he may go again to his place, which thou hast appointed him, and let him not go down with us to battle, lest [b]in the battle he be an adversary to us: for wherewith should he reconcile himself unto his master? *should it* not *be* with the heads of these men?

5 *Is* not this David, of whom they sang one to another in dances, saying, [a]Saul slew his thousands, and David his ten thousands?

28:13 [a]Ex. 22:28
28:14 [1]Heb. *What is his form?* [a]ch. 15:27; 2 Ki. 2:8,13
28:15 [1]Heb. *by the hand of prophets* [a]Prov. 5:11-13; 14:14 [b]ch. 18:12 [c]ver. 6
28:17 [1]Or, *for himself* [2]Heb. *mine hand* [a]ch. 15:28
28:18 [a]ch. 15:9; 1 Ki. 20:42; 1 Chr. 10:13; Jer. 48:10
28:20 [1]Heb. *made haste and fell* with *the fulness of his stature*
28:21 [a]Judg. 12:3; ch. 19:5; Job 13:14
29:1 [a]ch. 28:1 [b]ch. 4:1
29:2 [a]ch. 28:1,2
29:3 [a]See ch. 27:7 [b]Dan. 6:5
29:4 [a]1 Chr. 12:19 [b]As ch. 14:21
29:5 [a]ch. 18:7; 21:11

28:12 *when the woman saw Samuel.* The episode has been understood in many different ways, among them the following: 1. God permitted the spirit of Samuel to appear to the woman. 2. The woman had contact with an evil or devilish spirit in the form of Samuel by whom she was deceived and controlled. 3. By using parapsychological powers such as telepathy or clairvoyance, the woman was able to discern Saul's thoughts and picture Samuel in her own mind. Whatever the explanation of this mysterious affair, the medium was used in some way to convey to Saul that the impending battle would bring death, would dash his hopes for a dynasty and would conclude his reign with a devastating defeat of Israel that would leave the nation at the mercy of the Philistines, the very people against whom he had struggled all his years as king. And this would come, as Samuel had previously announced (15:26,28), because of his unfaithfulness to the Lord. *she cried . . . thou art Saul.* By whatever means, the medium suddenly becomes aware that she is dealing with Saul.

28:14 *An old man . . . covered with a mantle.* Saul remembers Samuel as customarily dressed in this apparel (see 15:27).

28:21 *the woman came unto Saul.* This statement suggests that the woman removed herself from the direct view of Saul while she gave her oracles.

29:1 *the Philistines gathered . . . all their armies.* The narrative flow broken at 28:2 is resumed. *Aphek.* A place in the vicinity of Shunem (28:4), to be distinguished from another place of the same name referred to in 4:1 (see 1 Ki 20:26,30; 2 Ki 13:17).

29:2 *lords of the Philistines.* See note on 5:8.

29:3 *I have found no fault in him.* David's tactics described in 27:10–12 were highly successful.

29:4 *place, which thou hast appointed him.* See 27:6. *in the battle he be an adversary to us.* The Philistines had experienced just such a reversal on a previous occasion (see 14:21).

6 Then Achish called David, and said unto
him, Surely, *as* the LORD liveth, thou *hast been*
upright, and [a]thy going out and thy coming in
with me in the host *is* good in my sight: for [b]I
have not found evil in thee since the day of thy
coming unto me unto this day: nevertheless
[1]the lords favour thee not.
7 Wherefore now return, and go in peace,
that thou [1]displease not the lords of the Philistines.
8 And David said unto Achish, But what
have I done? and what hast thou found in thy
servant so long as I have been [1]with thee unto
this day, that I may not go fight against the enemies of my lord the king?
9 And Achish answered and said to David,
I know that thou *art* good in my sight, [a]as an
angel of God: notwithstanding [b]the princes of
the Philistines have said, He shall not go up
with us to the battle.
10 Wherefore now rise up early in the
morning with thy master's servants that are
come with thee: and as soon as ye be up early
in the morning, and have light, depart.
11 So David and his men rose up early to
depart in the morning, to return into the land
of the Philistines. [a]And the Philistines went
up *to* Jezreel.

David smites the Amalekites

30 And it came to pass, when David and
his men were come *to* Ziklag on the
third day, that the [a]Amalekites had invaded
the south, and Ziklag, and smitten Ziklag, and
burnt it with fire;
2 And had taken the women captives, that
were therein: they slew not any, either great
or small, but carried *them* away, and went on
their way.
3 So David and his men came to the city,
and behold, *it was* burnt with fire; and their
wives, and their sons, and their daughters,
were taken captives.
4 Then David and the people that *were*
with him lift up their voice and wept, until
they had no more power to weep.
5 And David's [a]two wives were taken captives, Ahinoam the Jezreelitess, and Abigail
the wife of Nabal the Carmelite.
6 And David was greatly distressed; [a]for
the people spake of stoning him, because the
soul of all the people was [1]grieved, every man
for his sons and for his daughters: but [b]David
encouraged himself in the LORD his God.
7 [a]And David said to Abiathar the priest,
Ahimelech's son, I pray thee, bring me hither
the ephod. And Abiathar brought thither the
ephod to David.
8 [a]And David inquired at the LORD, saying,
Shall I pursue after this troop? shall I overtake
them? And he answered him, Pursue: for thou
shalt surely overtake *them,* and without fail
recover *all.*
9 So David went, he and the six hundred
men that *were* with him, and came to the
brook Besor, where those that were left behind stayed.
10 But David pursued, he and four hundred men: [a]for two hundred abode *behind,*
which were so faint that they could not go
over the brook Besor.
11 ¶ And they found an Egyptian in the
field, and brought him to David, and gave him
bread, and he did eat; and they made him
drink water;
12 And they gave him a piece of [a]a cake *of
figs,* and two clusters of raisins: and [b]when he
had eaten, his spirit came again to him: for he
had eaten no bread, nor drunk *any* water,
three days and three nights.
13 And David said unto him, To whom *be-
longest* thou? and whence *art* thou? And he
said, I *am* a young man of Egypt, servant to an
Amalekite; and my master left me, because
three days agone I fell sick.
14 We made an invasion *upon* the south of
[a]the Cherethites, and upon *the coast* which
belongeth to Judah, and upon the south of
[b]Caleb; and we burnt Ziklag with fire.
15 And David said to him, Canst thou
bring me down to this company? And he said,
Swear unto me by God, that thou wilt neither
kill me, nor deliver me into the hands of my
master, and I will bring thee down to this company.
16 And when he had brought him down,
behold *they were* spread abroad upon all the
earth, [a]eating and drinking, and dancing, because of all the great spoil that they had taken
out of the land of the Philistines, and out of the
land of Judah.
17 And David smote them from the twi-

29:6 [1]Heb. *thou* art *not good in the eyes of the lords* [a]2 Sam. 3:25; 2 Ki. 19:27 [b]ver. 3
29:7 [1]Heb. *do not evil in the eyes of the lords*
29:8 [1]Heb. *before thee*
29:9 [a]2 Sam. 14:17,20; 19:27 [b]ver. 4
29:11 [a]2 Sam. 4:4
30:1 [a]See ch. 15:7; 27:8
30:5 [a]ch. 25:42,43; 2 Sam. 2:2
30:6 [a]Ex. 17:4

30:6 [1]Heb. *bitter* [b]Ps. 42:5; 56:3,4,11; Hab. 3:17,18
30:7 [a]ch. 23:6,9
30:8 [a]ch. 23:2,4
30:10 [a]ver. 21
30:12 [a]ch. 25:18; 2 Ki. 20:7 [b]Judg. 15:19; ch. 14:27
30:14 [a]ver. 16; 2 Sam. 8:18; 1 Ki. 1:38,44; Ezek. 25:16; Zeph. 2:5 [b]Josh. 14:13; 15:13
30:16 [a]1 Thes. 5:3

29:6 *as the LORD liveth.* See note on 14:39. Achish swears by the God of Israel apparently as a means of proving his sincerity to David.

29:8 *But what have I done?* David pretends disappointment in order to keep intact his strategy of deception. In reality this turn of events rescued David from a serious dilemma. *what hast thou found . . . that I may not go fight against the enemies of my lord the king?* David again uses an ambiguous statement (see 28:2). To whom was he referring as "my lord the king"—Achish or Saul or the Lord?

29:9 *as an angel of God.* A common simile.

29:11 *Jezreel.* The place of Israel's camp (see v. 1).

30:1–31:13 While Saul goes to his death at the hands of the Philistines, David is drawn into and pursues the Lord's continuing war with the Amalekites (see 15:2–3 and notes).

30:1 *Ziklag.* See note on 27:6. *Amalekites.* See 27:8 and note on 15:2. The absence of David and his warriors gave the Amalekites opportunity for revenge. *south.* See note on 27:10.

30:5 *Ahinoam.* See note on 25:43. *Abigail.* See 25:42.

30:7 *Abiathar the priest.* See note on 22:20. *ephod.* See note on 2:28.

30:14 *south.* See note on 27:10. *Cherethites.* Along with the Pelethites, they later contributed contingents of professional warriors to David's private army (see 2 Sam 15:18; 20:7; 1 Ki 1:38). The name may indicate that they originally came from the island of Crete (see note on "Caphtor" in Jer 47:4). *south of Caleb.* The area south of Hebron (see Josh 14:13).

light even unto the evening of [1]the next day: and there escaped not a man of them, save four hundred young men, which rode upon camels, and fled.

18 And David recovered all that the Amalekites had carried away: and David rescued his two wives.

19 And there was nothing lacking to them, neither small nor great, neither sons nor daughters, neither spoil, nor any *thing* that they had taken to them: [a]David recovered all.

20 And David took all the flocks and the herds, *which* they drave before those *other* cattle, and said, This *is* David's spoil.

21 ¶ And David came to the [a]two hundred men, which were so faint that they could not follow David, whom they had made also to abide at the brook Besor: and they went forth to meet David, and to meet the people that *were* with him: and when David came near to the people, he [1]saluted them.

22 Then answered all the wicked men and *men* [a]of Belial, of [1]those that went with David, and said, Because they went not with us, we will not give them *ought* of the spoil that we have recovered, save *to* every man his wife and his children, that they may lead *them* away, and depart.

23 Then said David, Ye shall not do so, my brethren, with *that* which the LORD hath given us, who hath preserved us, and delivered the company that came against us into our hand.

24 For who will hearken unto you in this matter? but [a]as his part *is* that goeth down to the battle, so *shall* his part *be* that tarrieth by the stuff: they shall part alike.

25 And it was *so* from that day [1]forward, that he made it a statute and an ordinance for Israel unto this day.

26 ¶ And when David came to Ziklag, he sent of the spoil unto the elders of Judah, *even* to his friends, saying, Behold a [1]present for you of the spoil of the enemies of the LORD;

27 To *them* which *were* in Beth-el, and to *them* which *were* in [a]south Ramoth, and to *them* which *were* in [b]Jattir,

28 And to *them* which *were* in [a]Aroer, and to *them* which *were* in Siphmoth, and to *them* which *were* in [b]Eshtemoa,

29 And to *them* which *were* in Rachal, and to *them* which *were* in the cities of [a]the Jerahmeelites, and to *them* which *were* in the cities of the [b]Kenites,

30 And to *them* which *were* in [a]Hormah, and to *them* which *were* in Chor-ashan, and to *them* which *were* in Athach,

31 And to *them* which *were* in [a]Hebron, and to all the places where David himself and his men were wont to haunt.

The death of Saul

31 Now [a]the Philistines fought against Israel: and the men of Israel fled from before the Philistines, and fell down [1]slain in mount [b]Gilboa.

2 And the Philistines followed hard upon Saul and upon his sons; and the Philistines slew [a]Jonathan, and Abinadab, and Malchishua, Saul's sons.

3 And [a]the battle went sore against Saul, and the [1]archers [2]hit him; and he was sore wounded of the archers.

4 [a]Then said Saul unto his armourbearer, Draw thy sword, and thrust me through therewith; lest [b]these uncircumcised come and thrust me through, and [1]abuse me. But his armourbearer would not; [c]for he was sore afraid: therefore Saul took a sword, and [d]fell upon it.

5 And when his armourbearer saw that Saul was dead, he fell likewise upon his sword, and died with him.

6 So Saul died, and his three sons, and his armourbearer, and all his men, that *same* day together.

7 ¶ And when the men of Israel that *were* on the *other* side of the valley, and *they* that *were* on the *other* side Jordan, saw that the men of Israel fled, and that Saul and his sons were dead, they forsook the cities, and fled; and the Philistines came and dwelt in them.

8 And it came to pass on the morrow, when the Philistines came to strip the slain, that they found Saul and his three sons fallen in mount Gilboa.

9 And they cut off his head, and stripped off his armour, and sent into the land of the Philistines round about, to [a]publish *it in* the house of their idols, and among the people.

30:17 [1]Heb. *their morrow* **30:19** [a]ver. 8 **30:21** [1]Or, *asked them how they did* [a]ver. 10 **30:22** [1]Heb. *men* [a]Deut. 13:13; Judg. 19:22 **30:24** [a]See Num. 31:27; Josh. 22:8 **30:25** [1]Heb. *and forward* **30:26** [1]Heb. *blessing* **30:27** [a]Josh. 19:8 [b]Josh. 15:48 **30:28** [a]Josh. 13:16 [b]Josh. 15:50

30:29 [a]ch. 27:10 [b]Judg. 1:16 **30:30** [a]Judg. 1:17 **30:31** [a]Josh. 14:13; 2 Sam. 2:1 **31:1** [1]Or, *wounded* [a]1 Chr. 10:1-12 [b]ch. 28:4 **31:2** [a]ch. 14:49 **31:3** [1]Heb. *shooters, men with bows* [2]Heb. *found him* [a]See 2 Sam. 1:6 **31:4** [1]Or, *mock me* [a]See Judg. 9:54 [b]ch. 14:6 [c]2 Sam. 1:14 [d]ch. 14:6 **31:9** [a]2 Sam. 1:20

‡**30:22** *men of Belial.* I.e. worthless men. See note on Deut 13:13.
30:23 *that which the LORD hath given us.* David gently but firmly rejects the idea that their victory is to be attributed to their own prowess. Because the Lord gave the victory, no segment of David's men could claim any greater right to the spoils than any other.
30:26 *elders of Judah . . . his friends.* David sent the plunder as an expression of gratitude to those who had assisted him during his flight from Saul (see v. 31), thus preparing the way for his later elevation to kingship in Judah (see 2 Sam 2:1–4).
30:29 *Jerahmeelites.* See note on 27:10. *Kenites.* See note on 15:6.
30:31 *Hebron.* The most important city in the southern part of Judah. The other locations mentioned are to the southwest and southeast of Hebron.
31:2 *Jonathan, and Abinadab, and Malchishua.* See note on 14:49. The surviving son, Ish-bosheth or Esh-baal (1 Chr 8:33; 9:39), was afterward promoted by Abner, who somehow survived the battle, to succeed his father as king (2 Sam 2:8–9).
31:4 *uncircumcised.* See 14:6 and note. *abuse me.* A practice that was not uncommon; previously the Philistines had mutilated and humiliated Samson after his capture (see Judg 16:23–25). *took a sword, and fell upon it.* The culmination of a long process of self-destruction.
31:6 *all his men.* Those who had served around him in his administration (but see note on v. 2).
31:9 *they cut off his head.* David had done the same to Goliath (see 17:51). *sent into the land.* Saul's head and armor served as proof and trophies of their victory.

10 [a]And they put his armour *in* the house
of [b]Ashtaroth: and [c]they fastened his body to
the wall of [d]Beth-shan.
11 [a]And when the inhabitants of Jabesh-
gilead heard [1]of that which the Philistines had
done to Saul,
12 [a]All the valiant men arose, and went all
night, and took the body of Saul and the bodies of his sons from the wall of Beth-shan, and
came to Jabesh, and [b]burnt them there.
13 And they took their bones, and [a]buried
them under a tree at Jabesh, [b]and fasted seven
days.

31:10 [a]ch. 21:9 [b]Judg. 2:13 [c]2 Sam. 21:12 [d]Josh. 17:11; Judg. 1:27
31:11 [1]Or, *concerning him* [a]ch. 11:3,9, 11
31:12 [a]See ch. 11:1-11; 2 Sam. 2:4-7
31:12 [b]2 Chr. 16:14; Jer. 34:5; Amos 6:10
31:13 [a]2 Sam. 21:12-14 [b]Gen. 50:10

31:10 *they put his armour in the house.* Symbolic of ascribing the victory to the Philistine gods.
31:11 *Jabesh-gilead.* See note on 11:1.
31:12 *took the body of Saul and . . . his sons.* The men of Jabesh-gilead had not forgotten how Saul had come to their defense when they were threatened by the Ammonites (see ch. 11). *burnt them.* Cremation was not customary in ancient Israel and here appears to have been done to prevent any further abuse of the bodies of Saul and his sons by the Philistines.
31:13 *took their bones, and buried them.* David later had their remains removed from Jabesh and placed in the family burial grounds of Zela in Benjamin (see 2 Sam 21:12–14). *fasted seven days.* As an indication of their mourning for Saul (cf. 2 Sam 1:12; 3:35; 12:16,21–23).

The Second Book of Samuel

INTRODUCTION

Title

1 and 2 Samuel were originally one book (see Introduction to 1 Samuel: Title).

Literary Features, Authorship and Date

See Introduction to 1 Samuel: Literary Features, Authorship and Date.

Contents and Theme: Kingship and Covenant

2 Samuel depicts David as a true (though imperfect) representative of the ideal theocratic king. David was initially acclaimed king at Hebron by the tribe of Judah (chs. 1—4), and subsequently was accepted by the remaining tribes after the murder of Ish-bosheth, one of Saul's surviving sons (5:1–5). David's leadership was decisive and effective. He captured Jerusalem from the Jebusites and made it his royal city and residence (5:6–14). Shortly afterward he brought the ark of the Lord from the house of Abinadab to Jerusalem, publicly acknowledging the Lord's kingship and rule over himself and the nation (ch. 6; Ps 132:3–5).

Under David's rule the Lord caused the nation to prosper, to defeat its enemies and, in fulfillment of His promise (see Gen 15:18), to extend its borders from Egypt to the Euphrates (ch. 8). David wanted to build a temple for the Lord—as His royal house, as a place for His throne (the ark) and as a place for Israel to worship Him. But the prophet Nathan told David that he was not to build the Lord a house (temple); rather, the Lord would build David a house (dynasty). Ch. 7 announces the Lord's promise that this Davidic dynasty would endure forever. This climactic chapter also describes the establishment of the Davidic covenant (see Ps 89:34–37), a covenant that promises ultimate victory over the evil one through the offspring of Eve (see Gen 3:15 and note). This promise—which had come to be focused on Shem and his descendants (see Gen 9:26–27 and notes), then on Abraham and his descendants (see Gen 12:2–3; 13:16; 15:5 and notes) and then on Judah and his (royal) descendants (see Gen 49:8–11 and notes)—is now focused specifically on the royal family of David. Later the prophets make clear that a descendant of David who sits on David's throne will perfectly fulfill the role of the theocratic king. He will complete the redemption of God's people (see Is 9:6–7; 11:1–16; Jer 23:5–6; 30:8–9; 33:14–16; Ezek 34:23–24; 37:24–25), thus enabling them to achieve the promised victory with Him (Rom 16:20).

After the description of David's rule in its glory and success, chs. 10—20 depict the darker side of his reign and describe David's weaknesses and failures. Even though David remained a king after God's own heart because he was willing to acknowledge his sin and repent (12:13), he nevertheless fell far short of the theocratic ideal and suffered the disciplinary results of his disobedience (12:10–12). His sin with Bath-sheba (chs. 11—12) and his leniency both with the wickedness of his sons (13:21; 14:1,33; 19:4–6) and with the insubordination of Joab (3:29,39; 20:10,23) led to intrigue, violence and bloodshed within his own family and the nation. It eventually drove him from Jerusalem at the time of Absalom's rebellion. Nonetheless the Lord was gracious to David, and his reign became a standard by which the reigns of later kings were measured (see 2 Ki 18:3; 22:2).

The book ends with David's own words of praise to God, who had delivered him from all his enemies (22:31–51), and with words of expectation for the fulfillment of God's promise that a king will come from the house of David and rule over men righteously (23:3–5). These songs echo many of the themes of Hannah's song (1 Sam 2:1–10), and together they frame (and interpret) the basic narrative.

Chronology

See Introduction to 1 Samuel: Chronology.

Outline

Below is an abbreviated outline for 2 Samuel. For the complete outline see Introduction to 1 Samuel: Outline.

IV. David's Rise to the Throne; Progressive Deterioration and End of Saul's Reign (1 Sam 16:1—2 Sam 5:5)
  - A. David Is Anointed Privately, Enters the Service of King Saul and Flees for His Life (1 Sam 16—26)
  - B. David Seeks Refuge in Philistia, and Saul and His Sons Are Killed in Battle (1 Sam 27—31)
  - C. David Becomes King over Judah (2 Sam 1—4)
  - D. David Becomes King over All Israel (2 Sam 5:1–5)

V. David's Kingship in Its Accomplishments and Glory (2 Sam 5:6—9:12)
  - A. David Conquers Jerusalem and Defeats the Philistines (2 Sam 5:6–25)
  - B. David Brings the Ark to Jerusalem (2 Sam 6)
  - C. God Promises David an Everlasting Dynasty (2 Sam 7)
  - D. The Extension of David's Kingdom Externally and the Justice of His Rule Internally (2 Sam 8)
  - E. David's Faithfulness to His Covenant with Jonathan (2 Sam 9)

VI. David's Kingship in Its Weaknesses and Failures (2 Sam 10—20)
  - A. David Commits Adultery and Murder (2 Sam 10—12)
  - B. David Loses His Sons Amnon and Absalom (2 Sam 13—20)

VII. Final Reflections on David's Reign (2 Sam 21—24)

The news of Saul's death

1 Now it came to pass after the death of Saul, when David was returned from [a]the slaughter of the Amalekites, and David had abode two days in Ziklag;

2 It came even to pass on the third day, that behold, [a]a man came out of the camp from Saul [b]with his clothes rent, and earth upon his head: and *so* it was, when he came to David, that he fell to the earth, and did obeisance.

3 And David said unto him, From whence comest thou? And he said unto him, Out of the camp of Israel am I escaped.

4 And David said unto him, [1]How went the matter? I pray thee, tell me. And he answered, That the people are fled from the battle, and many of the people also are fallen and dead; and Saul and Jonathan his son are dead also.

5 And David said unto the young man that told him, How knowest thou that Saul and Jonathan his son be dead?

6 And the young man that told him said, As I happened by chance upon [a]mount Gilboa, behold, [b]Saul leaned upon his spear; and lo, the chariots and horsemen followed hard after him.

7 And when he looked behind him, he saw me, and called unto me. And I answered, [1]Here *am* I.

8 And he said unto me, Who *art* thou? And I answered him, I *am* an Amalekite.

9 He said unto me again, Stand, I pray thee, upon me, and slay me: for [1]anguish is come upon me, because my life *is* yet whole in me.

10 So I stood upon him, and [a]slew him, because I was sure that he could not live after *that* he was fallen: and I took the crown that *was* upon his head, and the bracelet that *was* on his arm, and have brought them hither unto my lord.

11 Then David took hold on his clothes, and [a]rent them; and likewise all the men that *were* with him:

12 And they mourned, and wept, and fasted until even, for Saul, and for Jonathan his son, and for the people of the LORD, and for the house of Israel; because they were fallen by the sword.

13 And David said unto the young man that told him, Whence *art* thou? And he answered, I *am* the son of a stranger, an Amalekite.

14 And David said unto him, [a]How wast thou not [b]afraid to [c]stretch forth thine hand to destroy the LORD's anointed?

15 And [a]David called one of the young men, and said, Go near, *and* fall upon him. And he smote him that he died.

16 And David said unto him, [a]Thy blood *be* upon thy head; for [b]thy mouth hath testified against thee, saying, I have slain the LORD's anointed.

David's lament

17 ¶ And David lamented with this lamentation over Saul and over Jonathan his son:

18 ([a]Also he bade *them* teach the children of Judah the *use of the* bow: behold, *it is* written [b]in the book [1]of Jasher.)

19 The beauty of Israel *is* slain upon thy
high places:
[a]How are the mighty fallen!
20 [a]Tell *it* not in Gath,
Publish *it* not in the streets of Askelon;

1:1 [a]1 Sam. 30:17,26
1:2 [a]ch. 4:10 [b]1 Sam. 4:12
1:4 [1]Heb. *What was, etc.*
1:6 [a]1 Sam. 31:1 [b]See 1 Sam. 31:2-4
1:7 [1]Heb. *Behold me*
1:9 [1]Or, my *coat of mail, (*or, my *embroidered coat) hindereth me, that my, etc.*
1:10 [a]Judg. 9:54
1:11 [a]ch. 3:31; 13:31
1:14 [a]Num. 12:8 [b]1 Sam. 31:4 [c]1 Sam. 24:6; 26:9; Ps. 105:15
1:15 [a]ch. 4:10,12
1:16 [a]1 Sam. 26:9; 1 Ki. 2:32,33,37 [b]ver. 10; Luke 19:22
1:18 [1]Or, *of the upright* [a]1 Sam. 31:3 [b]Josh. 10:13
1:19 [a]ver. 27
1:20 [a]1 Sam. 31:9; Mic. 1:10; See Judg. 16:23

1:1 *after the death of.* See Josh 1:1; Judg 1:1. The narrative thread of 1 Samuel is continued. 1 and 2 Samuel were originally one book (see Introduction to 1 Samuel: Title). *David was returned from the slaughter of the Amalekites.* See 1 Sam 30:26. *Ziklag.* See note on 1 Sam 27:6.

1:2 *his clothes rent, and earth upon his head.* See note on 1 Sam 4:12; see also Josh 7:6; Acts 14:14.

1:8 *Amalekite.* It is not necessary to conclude from v. 3 that this Amalekite was a member of Saul's army. His statement that he "happened by chance upon mount Gilboa" (v. 6) is probably not as innocent as it appears. He may have been there as a scavenger to rob the fallen soldiers of their valuables and weapons. It is ironic that Saul's death is reported by an Amalekite (see 1 Sam 15).

1:10 *I stood upon him, and slew him.* The Amalekite's story conflicts with 1 Sam 31:3–6, where Saul is depicted as taking his own life. It appears that the Amalekite fabricated this version of Saul's death, expecting David to reward him (see 4:10). His miscalculation of David's response cost him his life (see v. 15). *I took the crown.* Apparently he got to Saul before the Philistines did (see 1 Sam 31:8–9).

1:11 *took hold on his clothes, and rent them.* See note on 1 Sam 4:12.

1:12 *mourned, and wept.* David and his men expressed their grief in typical Near Eastern fashion (see Gen 23:2; 1 Ki 13:30; Jer 22:18). *fasted.* See 3:35; 1 Sam 31:13.

1:13 *Amalekite.* The man was probably unaware of David's recent hostile encounters with the Amalekites (see v. 1; 1 Sam 30; see also note on 1 Sam 15:2).

1:14 The Amalekite understood nothing of the deep significance that David attached to the sanctity of the royal office in Israel (see note on 1 Sam 24:6). *the LORD's anointed.* See note on 1 Sam 9:16.

1:15 *fall upon him.* David displays no personal satisfaction over Saul's death and condemns to death the one he believes to be his murderer (see note on v. 10; see also 4:10).

1:16 *Thy blood be upon thy head.* The Amalekite's own testimony brought about his execution (see Josh 2:19; 1 Ki 2:37).

1:17 *lamentation.* It was a common practice in the ancient Near East to compose laments for fallen leaders and/or heroes.

1:18 *use of the bow.* Perhaps David taught his men to sing this lament while they practiced the bow (Israel's most common weapon; see, e.g., 22:35) as a motivation to master the weapon thoroughly so they would not experience a similar defeat (see note on Ezek 21:9). *book of Jasher.* See note on Josh 10:13.

1:19 *The beauty.* A reference to Saul and Jonathan as divinely designated leaders of God's covenant people, who had achieved many significant victories over Israel's enemies (see 1 Sam 14:47–48 and note). *high places.* Of Gilboa (see vv. 21,25; 1 Sam 31:1). *How are the mighty fallen!* The theme of David's lament (see v. 27). David's words contain no suggestion of bitterness toward Saul but rather recall the good qualities and accomplishments of Saul and Jonathan.

1:20 *Tell it not in Gath . . . Askelon.* As the major Philistine cit-

Lest [b]the daughters of the Philistines rejoice,
Lest the daughters of [c]the uncircumcised triumph.
21 Ye [a]mountains of Gilboa, [b]*let there be* no dew,
Neither *let there be* rain upon you, nor fields of offerings:
For there the shield of the mighty is vilely cast away,
The shield of Saul, *as though he had* not *been* [c]anointed with oil.
22 From the blood of the slain,
From the fat of the mighty,
[a]The bow of Jonathan turned not back,
And the sword of Saul returned not empty.
23 Saul and Jonathan *were* lovely and [1]pleasant in their lives,
And in their death they were not divided:
They were swifter than eagles,
They were [a]stronger than lions.
24 Ye daughters of Israel, weep over Saul,
Who clothed you in scarlet, with *other* delights,
Who put on ornaments of gold upon your apparel.
25 How are the mighty fallen in the midst of the battle!
O Jonathan, *thou wast* slain in thine high places.
26 I am distressed for thee, my brother Jonathan:
Very pleasant hast thou been unto me:
[a]Thy love to me was wonderful,
Passing the love of women.
27 [a]How are the mighty fallen,
And the weapons of war perished!

1:20 [b]See Ex. 15:20; Judg. 11:34; 1 Sam. 18:6 [c]1 Sam. 31:4
1:21 [a]1 Sam. 31:1 [b]Judg. 5:23; Job 3:3,4; Jer. 20:14 [c]1 Sam. 10:1
1:22 [a]1 Sam. 18:4
1:23 [1]Or, *sweet* [a]Judg. 14:18
1:26 [a]1 Sam. 18:1,3; 19:2; 20:17,41; 23:16
1:27 [a]ver. 19
2:1 [a]Judg. 1:1; 1 Sam. 23:2,4,9; 30:7,8 [b]ver. 11; 1 Sam. 30:31; ch. 5:1,3; 1 Ki. 2:11
2:2 [a]1 Sam. 30:5
2:3 [a]1 Sam. 27:2,3; 30:1; 1 Chr. 12:1
2:4 [a]ver. 11; ch. 5:5 [b]1 Sam. 31:11,13
2:5 [a]Ruth 2:20; 3:10
2:6 [a]2 Tim. 1:16,18
2:7 [1]Heb. *be ye the sons of valour*
2:8 [1]Heb. *the host which* was *Saul's* [2][Or, *Esh-baal*, 1 Chr. 8:33; 9:39] [a]1 Sam. 14:50

David anointed king of Judah

2 And it came to pass after this, that David
[a]inquired of the LORD, saying, Shall I go
up into any of the cities of Judah? And the LORD
said unto him, Go up. And David said, Whither
shall I go up? And he said, Unto [b]Hebron.
2 So David went up thither, and his [a]two
wives also, Ahinoam the Jezreelitess, and Abigail Nabal's wife the Carmelite.
3 And [a]his men that *were* with him did David bring up, every man with his household:
and they dwelt in the cities of Hebron.
4 [a]And the men of Judah came, and there
they anointed David king over the house of Judah. And they told David, saying, *That* [b]the
men of Jabesh-gilead *were they* that buried
Saul.
5 And David sent messengers unto the
men of Jabesh-gilead, and said unto them,
[a]Blessed *be* ye of the LORD, that ye have
shewed this kindness unto your lord, *even*
unto Saul, and have buried him.
6 And now [a]the LORD shew kindness and
truth unto you: and I also will requite you this
kindness, because ye have done this thing.
7 Therefore now let your hands be
strengthened, and [1]be ye valiant: for your
master Saul is dead, and also the house of Judah have anointed me king over them.
8 But [a]Abner the son of Ner, captain of
[1]Saul's host, took [2]Ish-bosheth the son of Saul,
and brought him over *to* Mahanaim;

ies located the closest and farthest from Israel's borders, Gath and Ashkelon represent the entire Philistine nation. David does not want the enemies of God's covenant people to take pleasure in Israel's defeat (as he knew they would; see 1 Sam 31:9–10) and thus bring reproach on the name of the Lord (see Ex 32:12; Num 14:13–19; Deut 9:28; Josh 7:9; Mic 1:10). *uncircumcised.* See note on 1 Sam 14:6.

1:21 *Ye mountains of Gilboa.* As an expression of profound grief, David rhetorically pronounces a curse on the place where Israel was defeated and Saul and Jonathan were killed (for other such rhetorical curses see Job 3:3–26; Jer 20:14–18). *not been anointed with oil.* Leather shields were rubbed with oil to preserve them (see Is 21:5).

1:23 *in their death they were not divided.* Even though Jonathan opposed his father's treatment of David, he gave his life beside his father in Israel's defense.

1:26 *was wonderful, Passing the love of women.* David is not suggesting that marital love is inferior to that of friendship, nor do his remarks have any sexual implications. He is simply calling attention to Jonathan's nearly inexplicable self-denying commitment to David, whom he had long recognized as the Lord's choice to succeed his father rather than himself (see notes on 1 Sam 20:13–16).

1:27 *weapons of war.* Probably a metaphor for Saul and Jonathan.

2:1 *David inquired of the LORD.* By means of the ephod through the priest Abiathar (see notes on Ex 28:30; 1 Sam 2:28; 23:2). *any of the cities of Judah.* Even though Saul was dead and David had many friends and contacts among the people of his own tribe (see 1 Sam 30:26–31), David did not presume to return from Philistine territory to assume the kingship promised to him without first seeking the Lord's guidance. *Hebron.* An old and important city (see Gen 13:18; 23:2; Josh 15:13–15; see also note on 1 Sam 30:31) centrally located in the tribe of Judah.

2:2 *Ahinoam the Jezreelitess.* See note on 1 Sam 25:43. *Abigail.* See 1 Sam 25.

2:3 *men that were with him.* See 1 Sam 22:2; 23:13; 30:3,9.

2:4 *anointed David king.* See notes on 1 Sam 2:10; 9:16. David had previously been anointed privately by Samuel in the presence of his own family (see note on 1 Sam 16:13). Here the anointing ceremony is repeated as a public recognition by his own tribe of his divine calling to be king. *over the house of Judah.* Very likely the tribe of Simeon was also involved (see Josh 19:1; Judg 1:3), but the Judahites in every way dominated the area. *men of Jabesh-gilead.* See notes on 1 Sam 11:1; 31:12. *buried Saul.* See note on 1 Sam 31:13.

2:7 *your master Saul is dead . . . the house of Judah have anointed me king over them.* David's concluding statement to the men of Jabesh-gilead is a veiled invitation to them to recognize him as their king just as the tribe of Judah had done. This appeal for their support, however, was ignored (see 1 Sam 2:8–9).

2:8 *Saul's host.* His small standing army of professionals loyal to him and his family (see 1 Sam 13:2,15; 14:2,52). *Ish-bosheth.* The name was originally Esh-baal (1 Chr 8:33) but was changed by the author of Samuel to Ish-bosheth, meaning "man of shame" (see note on 4:4). Evidently Baal (meaning "lord" or "master") was at this time still used to refer to the Lord. Later this was discontinued because of confusion with

9 And he made him king over Gilead, and over the Ashurites, and over Jezreel, and over Ephraim, and over Benjamin, and over all Israel.

10 Ish-bosheth Saul's son *was* forty years old when he *began* to reign over Israel, and reigned two years. But the house of Judah followed David.

11 And [a]the [1]time that David was king in Hebron over the house of Judah was seven years and six months.

War between Israel and Judah

12 ¶ And Abner the son of Ner, and the servants of Ish-bosheth the son of Saul, went out from Mahanaim to [a]Gibeon.

13 And Joab the son of Zeruiah, and the servants of David, went out, and met [1]together by [a]the pool of Gibeon: and they sat down, the one on the one side of the pool, and the other on the other side of the pool.

14 And Abner said to Joab, Let the young men now arise, and play before us. And Joab said, Let them arise.

15 Then there arose and went over by number twelve of Benjamin, which *pertained* to Ish-bosheth the son of Saul, and twelve of the servants of David.

16 And they caught every one his fellow by the head, and *thrust* his sword in his fellow's side; so they fell down together: wherefore that place was called [1]Helkath-hazzurim, which *is* in Gibeon.

17 And there was a very sore battle that day; and Abner was beaten, and the men of Israel, before the servants of David.

18 And there were [a]three sons of Zeruiah there, Joab, and Abishai, and Asahel: and Asahel *was* [b]as light [1]of foot [c2]as a wild roe.

19 And Asahel pursued after Abner; and in going he turned not to the right hand nor to the left [1]from following Abner.

20 Then Abner looked behind him, and said, *Art* thou Asahel? And he answered, I *am.*

21 And Abner said to him, Turn thee aside to thy right hand or to thy left, and lay thee hold on one of the young men, and take thee his [a1]armour. But Asahel would not turn aside from following of him.

22 And Abner said again to Asahel, Turn thee aside from following me: wherefore should I smite thee to the ground? how then should I hold up my face to Joab thy brother?

23 Howbeit he refused to turn aside: wherefore Abner with the hinder end of the spear smote him [a]under the fifth *rib,* that the spear came out behind him; and he fell down there, and died in the same place: and it came to pass, that as many as came to the place where Asahel fell down and died stood still.

24 Joab also and Abishai pursued after Abner: and the sun went down when they were come to the hill of Ammah, that *lieth* before Giah *by* the way of the wilderness of Gibeon.

25 And the children of Benjamin gathered themselves together after Abner, and became one troop, and stood on the top of a hill.

26 Then Abner called to Joab, and said, Shall the sword devour for ever? knowest thou not that it will be bitterness in the latter end? how long shall it be then, ere thou bid the people return from following their brethren?

27 And Joab said, *As* God liveth, unless [a]thou hadst spoken, surely then [1]in the morn-

2:11 [1]Heb. *number of days* [a]ch. 5:5; 1 Ki. 2:11
2:12 [a]Josh. 18:25
2:13 [1]Heb. *them together* [a]Jer. 41:12
2:16 [1]That is, *the field of strong men*
2:18 [a]1 Chr. 2:16
2:18 [1]Heb. *of his feet* [2]Heb. *as one of the roes that is in the field* [b]1 Chr. 12:8 [c]Ps. 18:33
2:19 [1]Heb. *from after Abner*
2:21 [1]Or, *spoil* [a]Judg. 14:19
2:23 [a]ch. 3:27; 4:6; 20:10
2:27 [1]Heb. *from the morning* [a]ver. 14; Prov. 17:14

the Canaanite god Baal, and the author of Samuel reflects the later sensitivity. *son of Saul.* See notes on 1 Sam 14:49; 31:2. *brought him.* Abner takes the initiative in the power vacuum created by Saul's death, using the unassertive Ish-bosheth as a pawn for his own ambitions (see 3:11; see also note on 4:1). There is no evidence that Ish-bosheth had strong support among the Israelites generally. *Mahanaim.* A Gileadite town east of the Jordan and thus beyond the sphere of Philistine domination—a kind of refugee capital.

2:9 *he made him king.* As a relative of Saul (see 1 Sam 14:50), Abner had both a family and a career interest in ensuring dynastic succession for Saul's house. *Gilead . . . all Israel.* This delineation of Ish-bosheth's realm suggests that his actual rule, while involving territory both east and west of the Jordan, was quite limited and that the last entry ("all Israel") was more claim than reality. David ruled over Judah and Simeon, and the Philistines controlled large sections of the northern tribal regions.

2:11 *seven years and six months.* Cf. Ish-bosheth's two-year reign in Mahanaim (v. 10). Because it appears that David was made king over all Israel shortly after Ish-bosheth's death (5:1–5) and moved his capital to Jerusalem not long afterward (5:6–12), reconciling the lengths of David's and Ish-bosheth's reigns is difficult. The difficulty is best resolved by assuming that it took Ish-bosheth a number of years to be recognized as his father's successor, and that the two years of his reign roughly correspond to the last two or three years of David's reign in Hebron.

2:12 Abner initiates an action to prevent David's sphere of influence from spreading northward out of Judah. Gibeon was located in the tribal area of Benjamin, to which Saul and his family belonged, and which the Philistines had not occupied.

2:13 *Joab the son of Zeruiah.* See note on 1 Sam 26:6. Joab became a figure of major importance during David's reign as a competent but ruthless military leader (see 10:7–14; 11:1; 12:26; 1 Ki 11:15–16). At times David was unable to control him (3:39; 18:5,14; 1 Ki 2:5–6), and he was eventually executed for his wanton assassinations and his part in the conspiracy to place Adonijah rather than Solomon on David's throne (1 Ki 2:28–34). *servants of David.* Some, at least, of David's small force of professionals that had gathered around him (see 1 Sam 22:1–2; 23:13; 27:2; 30:9).

2:15 *Benjamin.* At this time Ish-bosheth seems to have been supported mainly by his own tribesmen.

2:17 *there was a very sore battle that day.* Because the representative combat (see note on 1 Sam 17:4) by 12 men from each side was indecisive, a full-scale battle ensued in which David's forces were victorious. The attempt to use representative combat to avoid the decimation of civil war failed (see 3:1).

2:21 *Turn.* Abner tried unsuccessfully to avoid the necessity of killing Asahel.

2:22 *how then should I hold up my face to Joab thy brother?* Abner did not want the hostility between himself and Joab to be intensified by the practice of blood revenge (see note on 3:27).

2:26 *Shall the sword devour for ever?* Abner proposes an armistice as a means of avoiding the awful consequences of civil war.

2:27 *As God liveth.* An oath formula (see note on 1 Sam 14:39).

ing the people had [2]gone up every one from
following his brother.
28 So Joab blew a trumpet, and all the people stood still, and pursued after Israel no
more, neither fought they any more.
29 And Abner and his men walked all that
night through the plain, and passed over Jordan, and went *through* all Bithron, and they
came *to* Mahanaim.
30 And Joab returned from following Abner: and when he had gathered all the people
together, there lacked of David's servants nineteen men and Asahel.
31 But the servants of David had smitten of
Benjamin, and of Abner's men, *so that* three
hundred and threescore men died.
32 And they took up Asahel, and buried
him in the sepulchre of his father, which *was*
in Beth-lehem. And Joab and his men went all
night, and they came to Hebron at break of
day.
3 Now there was long war between the
house of Saul and the house of David:
but David waxed stronger and stronger, and
the house of Saul waxed weaker and weaker.
2 And [a]unto David were sons born in Hebron: and his firstborn was Amnon, [b]of Ahinoam the Jezreelitess;
3 And his second, [1]Chileab, of Abigail the
wife of Nabal the Carmelite; and the third, Absalom the son of Maacah the daughter of Talmai king [a]of Geshur;
4 And the fourth, [a]Adonijah the son of
Haggith; and the fifth, Shephatiah the son of
Abital;
5 And the sixth, Ithream, by Eglah David's
wife. These were born to David in Hebron.
6 ¶ And it came to pass, while there was
war between the house of Saul and the house
of David, that Abner made himself strong for
the house of Saul.
7 And Saul had a concubine, whose name
was [a]Rizpah, the daughter of Aiah: and *Ish-bo-*
sheth said to Abner, Wherefore hast thou
[b]gone in unto my father's concubine?
8 Then was Abner very wroth for the
words of Ish-bosheth, and said, *Am* I [a]a dog's
head, which against Judah do shew kindness
this day unto the house of Saul thy father, to
his brethren, and to his friends, and have not
delivered thee into the hand of David, that
thou chargest me to day with a fault concerning *this* woman?
9 [a]So do God to Abner, and more also, except, [b]as the LORD hath sworn to David, even
so I do to him;
10 To translate the kingdom from the
house of Saul, and to set up the throne of David over Israel and over Judah, [a]from Dan
even to Beer-sheba.
11 And he could not answer Abner a word
again, because he feared him.

Abner visits David

12 ¶ And Abner sent messengers to David
on his behalf, saying, Whose *is* the land? saying *also,* Make thy league with me, and behold, my hand *shall be* with thee, to bring
about all Israel unto thee.
13 And he said, Well; I will make a league
with thee: but one thing I require of thee,
[1]that is, [a]Thou shalt not see my face, except
thou first bring [b]Michal Saul's daughter, when
thou comest to see my face.
14 And David sent messengers to Ish-bosheth Saul's son, saying, Deliver *me* my wife

2:27 [2]Or, *gone away*
3:2 [a]1 Chr. 3:1-4 [b]1 Sam. 25:43
3:3 [1]Or, *Daniel,* 1 Chr. 3:1 [a]1 Sam. 27:8; ch. 13:37
3:4 [a]1 Ki. 1:5
3:7 [a]ch. 21:8,10 [b]ch. 16:21
3:8 [a]Deut. 23:18; 1 Sam. 24:14; ch. 9:8; 16:9
3:9 [a]Ruth 1:17; 1 Ki. 19:2 [b]1 Sam. 15:28; 16:1,12; 28:17; 1 Chr. 12:23
3:10 [a]Judg. 20:1; ch. 17:11; 1 Ki. 4:25
3:13 [1]Heb. *saying* [a]Gen. 43:3 [b]1 Sam. 18:20

2:28 *neither fought they anymore.* For the present the open conflict ceased, but the hostility remained (see 3:1).

‡2:29 *plain.* Hebrew *Arabah.* See note on Deut 1:1.

3:2–5 The list of six sons born to David in Hebron is given as an evidence of the strengthening of David's house in contrast to that of Saul (v. 1). That these six sons were each born of a different mother indirectly informs us that David married four additional wives (see 2:2) during his time in Hebron. The writer does not offer any direct criticism of this polygamous practice (see 5:13), which conflicts with Deut 17:17, but he lets the disastrous results in David's family life speak for themselves (see chs. 13–19; 1 Ki 1–2). *Amnon.* Later raped his sister Tamar and was killed by his brother Absalom (see ch. 13). *Ahinoam the Jezreelitess.* See note on 1 Sam 25:43.

3:3 *Chileab.* Called Daniel in 1 Chr 3:1. *Abigail.* See 1 Sam 25. *Absalom.* Later avenged the rape of Tamar by killing Amnon, and conspired against his father David in an attempt to make himself king (see chs. 13–18). *Maacah the daughter of Talmai.* David's marriage to Maacah undoubtedly had political implications. With Talmai as an ally on Ish-bosheth's northern border, David flanked the northern kingdom both south and north. *Geshur.* A small Aramean city kingdom (see 15:8) located northeast of the sea of Galilee (see Josh 12:5; 13:11–13).

3:4 *Adonijah.* Was put to death for attempting to take over the throne before Solomon could be crowned (see 1 Ki 1–2).

3:7 *Rizpah.* See 21:8–11. *Wherefore hast thou gone in unto my father's concubine?* Ish-bosheth suspects that Abner's act was part of a conspiracy to seize the kingship (cf. v. 6). Great significance was attached to taking the concubine of a former king (see note on 12:8; see also 16:21; 1 Ki 2:22).

3:9 *So do God to Abner, and more also.* A curse formula (see note on 1 Sam 3:17). *as the LORD hath sworn to David.* The knowledge of David's divine designation as successor to Saul had spread widely (see notes on 2:4; 1 Sam 16:13; 25:28).

3:10 *translate the kingdom.* Abner was the real power behind the throne. *Dan even to Beer-sheba.* See note on 1 Sam 3:20.

3:12 *Whose is the land?* Possibly a rhetorical question that presumed that the land belonged either to Abner or to David. The former seems more likely from the following sentence. *Make thy league with me.* Abner wants assurance that he will face no reprisals for his past loyalty to the house of Saul.

3:13 *Michal Saul's daughter.* Although Saul had given Michal to David (1 Sam 18:27), he later gave her to another man after David fled from his court (1 Sam 25:44). In the minds of the northern elders, the reunion of David and Michal would strengthen David's claim to the throne as a legitimate son-in-law of Saul.

3:14 *David sent messengers to Ish-bosheth.* David wanted Michal returned as an open and official act of Ish-bosheth himself, rather than as part of a subterfuge planned by Abner. David knew that Ish-bosheth would not dare to defy Abner's wishes (see v. 11). *an hundred foreskins of the Philistines.* See 1 Sam 18:25. Saul had required 100 Philistine foreskins; David presented him with 200 (1 Sam 18:27).

Michal, which I espoused to me [a]for an hundred foreskins of the Philistines.

15 And Ish-bosheth sent, and took her from *her* husband, *even* from [a]Phaltiel the son of Laish.

16 And her husband went with her [1]along weeping behind her to [a]Bahurim. Then said Abner unto him, Go, return. And he returned.

17 And Abner had communication with the elders of Israel, saying, Ye sought for David [1]in times past to be king over you:

18 Now then do *it:* [a]for the LORD hath spoken of David, saying, By the hand of my servant David I will save my people Israel out of the hand of the Philistines, and out of the hand of all their enemies.

19 And Abner also spake in the ears of [a]Benjamin: and Abner went also to speak in the ears of David in Hebron all that seemed good to Israel, and that seemed *good* to the whole house of Benjamin.

20 So Abner came to David *to* Hebron, and twenty men with him. And David made Abner and the men that *were* with him a feast.

21 And Abner said unto David, I will arise and go, and [a]will gather all Israel unto my lord the king, that they may make a league with thee, and that thou mayest [b]reign over all that thine heart desireth. And David sent Abner away; and he went in peace.

Joab kills Abner

22 ¶ And behold, the servants of David and Joab came from *pursuing* a troop, and brought in a great spoil with them: but Abner *was* not with David in Hebron; for he had sent him away, and he was gone in peace.

23 When Joab and all the host that *was* with him were come, they told Joab, saying, Abner the son of Ner came to the king, and he hath sent him away, and he is gone in peace.

24 Then Joab came to the king, and said, What hast thou done? behold, Abner came unto thee; why *is* it *that* thou hast sent him away, and he is quite gone?

25 Thou knowest Abner the son of Ner, that he came to deceive thee, and to know [a]thy going out and thy coming in, and to know all that thou doest.

26 And when Joab was come out from David, he sent messengers after Abner, which brought him again from the well of Sirah: but David knew *it* not.

27 And when Abner was returned *to* Hebron, Joab [a]took him aside in the gate to speak with him [1]quietly, and smote him there [b]*under* the fifth *rib,* that he died, for the blood of [c]Asahel his brother.

28 ¶ And afterward when David heard *it,* he said, I and my kingdom *are* guiltless before the LORD for ever from the [1]blood of Abner the son of Ner:

29 [a]Let it rest on the head of Joab, and on all his father's house; and let there not [1]fail from the house of Joab one [b]that hath an issue, or that is a leper, or that leaneth on a staff, or that falleth on the sword, or that lacketh bread.

30 So Joab and Abishai his brother slew Abner, because he had slain their brother [a]Asahel at Gibeon in the battle.

31 ¶ And David said to Joab, and to all the people that *were* with him, [a]Rent your clothes, and [b]gird you with sackcloth, and mourn before Abner. And king David *himself* followed the [1]bier.

32 And they buried Abner in Hebron: and the king lift up his voice, and wept at the grave of Abner; and all the people wept.

3:14 [a]1 Sam. 18:25,27
3:15 [a]1 Sam. 25:44; *Phalti*
3:16 [1]Heb. *going and weeping* [a]ch. 19:16
3:17 [1]Heb. *both yesterday and the third day*
3:18 [a]ver. 9
3:19 [a]1 Chr. 12:29
3:21 [a]ver. 10,12 [b]1 Ki. 11:37
3:25 [a]1 Sam. 29:6; Is. 37:28
3:27 [1]Or, *peaceably* [a]1 Ki. 2:5; ch. 20:9,10 [b]ch. 4:6 [c]ch. 2:23
3:28 [1]Heb. *bloods*
3:29 [1]Heb. *be cut off* [a]1 Ki. 2:32,33 [b]Lev. 15:2
3:30 [a]ch. 2:23
3:31 [1]Heb. *bed* [a]Josh. 7:6; ch. 1:2,11 [b]Gen. 37:34

3:16 *Bahurim.* The last Benjamite city on the way to Hebron (see 16:5; 17:18).

3:17 *elders of Israel.* The collective leadership of the various tribes comprised an informal national ruling body (see notes on Ex 3:16; Joel 1:2; Mat 15:2; Acts 24:1; see also 1 Sam 8:4; 2 Sam 5:3; 1 Ki 8:1,3; 20:7; 2 Ki 10:1; 23:1). *Ye sought for David ... to be king.* Apparently Ish-bosheth's support came mainly from the tribe of Benjamin (see 2:15 and note) and from Gilead across the Jordan (see 2:8; 1 Sam 11:9–11; 31:11–13).

3:18 *the LORD hath spoken of David.* By this time Samuel's anointing of David must have become common knowledge (see 5:2). Abner probably interpreted the anointing as a promise from the Lord, since Samuel was the Lord's much-revered prophet.

3:19 *Abner also spake in the ears of Benjamin.* Because Saul and his family were from the tribe of Benjamin, Abner was careful to consult the Benjamites concerning the transfer of kingship to the tribe of Judah. Apparently they consented, but Abner was not above representing matters in a way that was favorable to his purpose.

3:21 *make a league with thee.* See 5:3 and note.

3:25 *he came to deceive thee.* Joab despised Abner for killing his brother (2:18,23; 3:27) and sought to discredit him in David's eyes as a mere opportunist. Perhaps he also sensed that his own position of leadership would be threatened if Abner joined forces with David, since Abner was obviously a power among the northern tribes.

3:27 *Joab ... smote him there under the fifth rib, that he died.* Joab's murder of Abner is not to be excused either as an act of war or as justifiable blood revenge (cf. Num 35:12; Deut 19:11–13). Asahel had been killed by Abner in the course of battle (see 2:23; see also note on 2:21).

3:29 *Let it rest on the head of Joab, and on all his father's house.* After disclaiming any personal or official involvement in the plot to assassinate Abner (v. 28), David cursed Joab and thereby called on God to judge his wicked act. In this crucial hour when David's relationship to the northern tribes hung in the balance, he appears not to have felt sufficiently secure in his own position to bring Joab publicly to justice (see v. 39). The crime went unpunished until early in the reign of Solomon (1 Ki 2:5–6, 29–35).

3:31 *Joab.* He too was compelled to join the mourners. It may be that Joab's involvement was not widely known and that David hoped to keep the matter secret for the time being.

3:32 *Hebron.* David's royal city at the time. *the king lift up his voice, and wept at the grave of Abner.* Because Abner's murder had the potential of destroying the union of the nation under David's rule, David did everything possible to demonstrate his innocence to the people. In this he was successful (see vv. 36–37).

33 And the king lamented over Abner, and said,

Died Abner as a [a]fool dieth?

34 Thy hands *were* not bound,
Nor thy feet put into fetters:
As *a man* falleth before [1]wicked men,
So fellest thou.

¶ And all the people wept again over him.

35 And when all the people came [a]to cause David to eat meat while it was yet day, David sware, saying, [b]So do God to me, and more also, if I taste bread, or ought else, [c]till the sun be down.

36 And all the people took notice *of it,* and it [1]pleased them: as whatsoever the king did, [2]pleased all the people.

37 For all the people and all Israel understood that day that it was not of the king to slay Abner the son of Ner.

38 And the king said unto his servants, Know ye not that there is a prince and a great *man* fallen this day in Israel?

39 And I *am this* day [1]weak, though anointed king; and these men the sons of Zeruiah [a]*be* too hard for me: [b]the LORD shall reward the doer of evil according to his wickedness.

The murder of Ish-bosheth

4 And when Saul's son heard that Abner was dead in Hebron, [a]his hands were feeble, and all the Israelites were [b]troubled.

2 And Saul's son had two men *that were* captains of bands: the name of the one *was* Baanah, and the name of the [1]other Rechab, the sons of Rimmon a Beerothite, of the children of Benjamin: (for [a]Beeroth also was reckoned to Benjamin:

3 And the Beerothites fled to [a]Gittaim, and were sojourners there until this day.)

4 And [a]Jonathan, Saul's son, had a son *that was* lame of *his* feet, *and* was five years old when the tidings came of Saul and Jonathan [b]out of Jezreel, and his nurse took him up, and fled: and it came to pass, as she made haste to flee, that he fell, and became lame. And his name *was* [1]Mephibosheth.

5 And the sons of Rimmon the Beerothite, Rechab and Baanah, went, and came about the heat of the day to the house of Ish-bosheth, who lay on a bed at noon.

6 And they came thither into the midst of the house, *as though* they would have fetched wheat; and they smote him [a]under the fifth *rib:* and Rechab and Baanah his brother escaped.

7 For when they came *into* the house, he lay on his bed in his bedchamber, and they smote him, and slew him, and beheaded him, and took his head, and gat them away through the plain all night.

8 And they brought the head of Ish-bosheth unto David *to* Hebron, and said to the king, Behold the head of Ish-bosheth the son of Saul thine enemy, [a]which sought thy life; and the LORD hath avenged my lord the king this day of Saul, and of his seed.

9 And David answered Rechab and Baanah his brother, the sons of Rimmon the Beerothite, and said unto them, *As* the LORD liveth, [a]who hath redeemed my soul out of all adversity,

10 When [a]one told me, saying, Behold, Saul is dead, [1]thinking to have brought good tidings, I took hold of him, and slew him in Ziklag, [2]who *thought* that I would have given him a reward for *his* tidings:

11 How much more, when wicked men have slain a righteous person in his own house upon his bed? shall I not therefore now [a]require his blood of your hand, and take you away from the earth?

12 And David [a]commanded *his* young men, and they slew them, and cut off their hands and their feet, and hanged *them* up over the pool in Hebron. But they took the head of Ish-bosheth, and buried *it* in the [b]sepulchre of Abner in Hebron.

David made king of Israel

5 Then [a]came all the tribes of Israel to David unto Hebron, and spake, saying, Behold, [b]we *are* thy bone and thy flesh.

3:33 [a]ch. 13:12,13
3:34 [1]Heb. *children of iniquity*
3:35 [a]ch. 12:17; Jer. 16:7 [b]Ruth 1:17 [c]ch. 1:12
3:36 [1]Heb. *was good in their eyes* [2]Heb. *was good in their eyes*
3:39 [1]Heb. *tender* [a]ch. 19:7 [b]See ch. 19:13; 1 Ki. 2:5,6,33, 34; 2 Tim. 4:14
4:1 [a]Ezra 4:4; Is. 13:7 [b]Mat. 2:3
4:2 [1]Heb. *second* [a]Josh. 18:25
4:3 [a]Neh. 11:33
4:4 [1][Or, *Merib-baal,* 1 Chr. 8:34; 9:40] [a]ch. 9:3 [b]1 Sam. 29:1,11
4:6 [a]ch. 2:23
4:8 [a]1 Sam. 19:2,10,11
4:9 [a]Gen. 48:16; 1 Ki. 1:29
4:10 [1]Heb. *he was in his own eyes as a bringer, etc.* [2]Or, *which* was *the reward I gave him for his tidings* [a]ch. 1:2,4,15
4:11 [a]Gen. 9:5,6
4:12 [a]ch. 1:15 [b]ch. 3:32
5:1 [a]1 Chr. 11:1 [b]Gen. 29:14

3:35 *So do God to me, and more also.* A curse formula (see note on 1 Sam 3:17).
3:39 *the LORD shall reward the doer of evil.* See note on v. 29.
‡4:1 *his hands were feeble.* I.e. he lost courage. Ish-bosheth was very much aware of his dependence on Abner (see note on 2:8). *all the Israelites were troubled.* Civil strife threatened, and the northern tribes were now without a strong leader.
4:2 *Beeroth.* One of the Gibeonite cities (Josh 9:17) assigned to Benjamin (Josh 18:25).
4:3 *Gittaim.* Its location is not known (but see Neh 11:33).
4:4 *Jonathan, Saul's son, had a son that was lame of his feet.* The writer emphasizes that with the death of Ish-bosheth (see v. 6) there was no other viable claimant to the throne from the house of Saul. *tidings ... of Saul and Jonathan.* See 1:4; 1 Sam 31:2–4. *Mephibosheth.* See 9:1–13; 16:1–4; 19:24–30; 21:7–8. The name was originally Merib-baal (apparently meaning "opponent of Baal"; see 1 Chr 8:34), perhaps to be spelled "Meri-baal" (meaning "loved by Baal"), but was changed by the author of Samuel to Mephibosheth (meaning "from the mouth of the shameful thing"). See note on 2:8.
‡4:7 *plain.* See 2:29 and note on Deut 1:1.
4:8 *the LORD hath avenged my lord the king ... of Saul.* Rechab and Baanah depict their assassination of Ish-bosheth in pious terms, expecting David to commend them for their act—a serious miscalculation.
4:9 *As the LORD liveth.* An oath formula (see note on 1 Sam 14:39).
4:11 *require his blood of your hand.* An expression for the death penalty (see Gen 9:5–6). David here does what he was unable to do with Joab (see note on 3:29).
4:12 *their hands and their feet.* The hands that had assassinated Ish-bosheth and the feet that had run with the news.
5:1–24:25 Beginning with ch. 5 there are sections of 2 Samuel that have parallel passages in 1 Chronicles. In some instances these parallel accounts are nearly identical; in others there are variations.
5:1 *all the tribes of Israel.* Representatives of each tribe, including elders and armed soldiers (see 1 Chr 12:23–40). *thy*

2 Also in time past, when Saul was king
over us, [a]thou wast he that leddest out and
broughtest in Israel: and the LORD said to thee,
[b]Thou shalt feed my people Israel, and thou
shalt be a captain over Israel.
3 [a]So all the elders of Israel came to the
king to Hebron; [b]and king David made a
league with them in Hebron [c]before the LORD:
and they anointed David king over Israel.
4 David *was* thirty years old when he *began* to reign, [a]*and* he reigned forty years.
5 In Hebron he reigned over Judah [a]seven
years and six months: and in Jerusalem he
reigned thirty and three years over all Israel
and Judah.

The capture of Jerusalem

6 ¶ And the king and his men went [a]*to* Jerusalem unto [b]the Jebusites, the inhabitants of
the land: which spake unto David, saying, Except thou take away the blind and the lame,
thou shalt not come in hither: [1]thinking, David cannot come in hither.

5:2 [a]1 Sam. 18:13 [b]1 Sam. 16:1
5:3 [a]1 Chr. 11:3 [b]2 Ki. 11:17 [c]Judg. 11:11; 1 Sam. 23:18
5:4 [a]1 Chr. 26:31; 29:27
5:5 [a]ch. 2:11; 1 Chr. 3:4
5:6 [1]Or, *saying, David shall not, etc.* [a]Judg. 1:21 [b]Josh. 15:63; Judg. 1:8; 19:11,12

bone and thy flesh. The representatives of the various tribes cite three reasons for recognizing David as their king. The first of these is the acknowledgment that David is an Israelite. Even though national unity had been destroyed in the civil strife following Saul's death (2:8–3:1), this blood relationship had not been forgotten.

5:2 *he that leddest out and broughtest in Israel.* The second reason (see note on v. 1) for recognizing David as king (see 1 Sam 18:5, 13–14,16,30). *the LORD said to thee.* The third and most important reason (see 1 Sam 13:13–14; 16:1,13; 23:17; 25:26–31).

5:3 *king David made a league with them . . . before the LORD.* David and Israel entered into a covenant in which both the king and the people obligated themselves before the Lord to carry out their mutual responsibilities (see 2 Ki 11:17 and note). Thus, while David was king over Judah as the one elevated to that position by his tribe and later became king over Jerusalem by conquest (vv. 6–10), his rule over the northern tribes was by virtue of a treaty (covenant) of submission. That treaty was not renewed with David's grandson Rehoboam because he refused to negotiate its terms at the time of his accession to the throne (1 Ki 12:1–16). *they anointed David king over Israel.* The third time David was anointed (see note on 2:4).

5:5 *In Hebron he reigned . . . seven years and six months.* See 2:11. *Israel and Judah.* The specific relationship of David to these two segments of his realm appears to have remained distinct (see note on v. 3).

5:6 *Jerusalem.* One of the most significant accomplishments of David's reign was the establishment of Jerusalem as his royal city and the nation's capital (see Introduction: Contents and Theme). The site was first occupied in the third millennium B.C. and was a royal city in the time of Abraham (see note on Gen 14:18). It was located on the border between Judah and Benjamin but was controlled by neither tribe. At the time of the conquest both Judah and Benjamin had attacked the city (see notes on Judg 1:8,21), but it was quickly lost again to the Jebusites (Josh 15:63) and was sometimes referred to by the name Jebus (see Judg 19:10; 1 Chr 11:4). The city David conquered covered somewhat less than 11 acres and could have housed not many more than 3,500 inhabitants. By locating his royal city in a newly conquered town on the border between the two segments of his realm, David united the kingdom under his rule without seeming to subordinate one part to the other. *Jebusites.* A Canaanite people (Gen 10:15–16) inhabiting the area in (Josh 15:8; 18:16) and around (Num 13:29; Josh 11:3) Jerusalem. *the blind and the lame, thou shalt not come in hither.* Jerusalem was a natural fortress because of its location on a rise surrounded on three sides by deep valleys; so the Jebusites were confident that their walls could easily be defended.

The City of the Jebusites/David's Jerusalem

Substantial historical evidence, both Biblical and extra-Biblical, places the temple of Herod (and before it the temples of Zerubbabel and of Solomon) on the holy spot where King David built an altar to the Lord. David had purchased the land from Araunah the Jebusite, who was using the exposed bedrock as a threshingfloor (2 Sam 24:18–25). Tradition claims a much older sanctity for the site, associating it with the altar of Abraham on mount Moriah (Gen 22:1-19). The writer of Genesis equates Moriah with "the mount of the LORD," and other OT shrines originated in altars erected by Abraham.

c. 1000 B.C.

Barely 12 acres in size, Jebus, a Canaanite city, could well defend itself against attack, with walls atop steep canyons and shafts reaching an underground water source. David captured the stronghold c. 1000 B.C. and made it his capital.

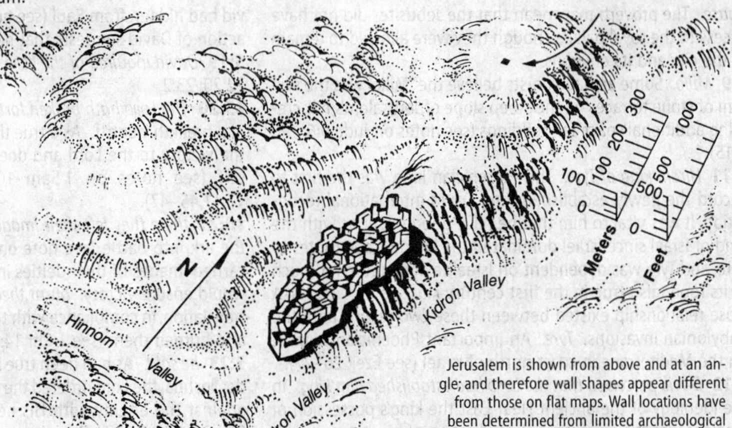

Jerusalem is shown from above and at an angle; and therefore wall shapes appear different from those on flat maps. Wall locations have been determined from limited archaeological evidence; houses are artist's concept.

7 Nevertheless David took the strong hold of Zion: [a]the same *is* the city of David.

8 And David said on that day, Whosoever getteth up to the gutter, and smiteth the Jebusites, and the lame and the blind, *that are* hated of David's soul, [a]*he shall be chief and captain.* [1]Wherefore they said, The blind and the lame shall not come into the house.

9 So David dwelt in the fort, and called it [a]the city of David. And David built round about from Millo and inward.

10 And David [1]went on, and grew great, and the LORD God of hosts *was* with him.

11 And [a]Hiram king of Tyre sent messengers to David, and cedar trees, and carpenters, and [1]masons: and they built David a house.

12 And David perceived that the LORD had established him king over Israel, and that he had exalted his kingdom for his people Israel's sake.

13 ¶ And [a]David took *him* mo concubines and wives out of Jerusalem, after he was come from Hebron: and there were yet sons and daughters born to David.

14 And [a]these *be* the names of those that were born unto him in Jerusalem; [1]Shammua, and Shobab, and Nathan, and Solomon,

15 Ibhar also, and [1]Elishua, and Nepheg, and Japhia,

5:7 [a]1 Ki. 2:10; 8:1
5:8 [1]Or, *Because they had said, even the blind and the lame, He shall not come into the house* [a]1 Chr. 11:6-9
5:9 [a]ver. 7
5:10 [1]Heb. *went, going and growing*
5:11 [1]Heb. *hewers of the stone of the wall* [a]1 Ki. 5:2
5:13 [a]Deut. 17:17; 1 Chr. 3:9
5:14 [1][Or, *Shimea*] [a]1 Chr. 3:5
5:15 [1][Or, *Elishama*]
5:16 [1][Or, *Beeliada*]
5:17 [a]1 Chr. 11:16 [b]ch. 23:14
5:18 [a]Josh. 15:8; Is. 17:5
5:19 [a]1 Sam. 23:2,4
5:20 [1]That is, *the plain of breaches* [a]Is. 28:21
5:21 [1]Or, *took them away* [a]Deut. 7:5,25
5:22 [a]1 Chr. 14:13
5:23 [a]ver. 19

16 And Elishama, and [1]Eliada, and Eliphalet.

The Philistines defeated

17 ¶ [a]But when the Philistines heard that they had anointed David king over Israel, all the Philistines came up to seek David; and David heard *of it,* [b]and went down to the hold.

18 The Philistines also came and spread themselves in [a]the valley of Rephaim.

19 And David [a]inquired of the LORD, saying, Shall I go up to the Philistines? wilt thou deliver them into mine hand? And the LORD said unto David, Go up: for I will doubtless deliver the Philistines into thine hand.

20 And David came to [a]Baal-perazim, and David smote them there, and said, The LORD hath broken forth upon mine enemies before me, as the breach of waters. Therefore he called the name of that place [1]Baal-perazim.

21 And there they left their images, and David and his men [a][1]burnt them.

22 [a]And the Philistines came up yet again, and spread themselves in the valley of Rephaim.

23 And when [a]David inquired of the LORD, he said, Thou shalt not go up; *but* fetch a compass behind them, and come upon them over against the mulberry trees.

5:7 *strong hold.* Probably the fortified city itself. *Zion.* The first occurrence of the name in the OT (its meaning is unknown). Originally the name appears to have been given to the southernmost hill of the city on which the Jebusite fortress was located. As the city expanded (from the days of Solomon onward), the name continued to be applied to the entire city (see Is 1:8; 2:3).

5:8 *David said on that day.* 1 Chr 11:6 may be combined with this verse for a more complete account. Joab's part in the conquest of the city demonstrated again his military prowess and reconfirmed him in the position of commander of David's armies. *gutter.* Although the Hebrew for this term is obscure, it appears that David knew of a secret tunnel—perhaps running from the Gihon spring outside the city into the fortress—that gave access to water when the city was under siege (see 2 Chr 32:30). *the lame and the blind.* An ironic reference to the Jebusites (cf. v. 6). *The blind and the lame shall not come into the house.* The proverb may mean that the Jebusites did not have access to the royal palace, though they were allowed to remain in the city and its environs.

5:9 *Millo.* Some archaeologists believe the "Millo" was the system of stone terraces on the steep slope of Jerusalem's hill, creating additional space for buildings (see notes on Judg 9:6; 1 Ki 9:15).

5:11 *Hiram king of Tyre.* This Phoenician king was the first to accord the newly established King David international recognition. It was vital to him that he have good relations with the king of Israel since Israel dominated the inland trade routes to Tyre, and Tyre was dependent on Israelite agriculture for much of its food (also true in the first century A.D.; see Acts 12:20). A close relationship existed between these two realms until the Babylonian invasions. *Tyre.* An important Phoenician seaport on the Mediterranean coast north of Israel (see Ezek 26–27).

5:12 *David perceived that the LORD had established him king.* In the ideology of the ancient Near East the king's possession of a palace was the chief symbolic indication of his status. *for his people Israel's sake.* David acknowledged that his elevation to kingship over all Israel was the Lord's doing and that it was an integral part of His continuing redemptive program for Israel—just as the ministries of Moses, Joshua, the judges and Samuel had been.

‡5:13 *David took him mo* [i.e. more] *concubines and wives.* See note on 3:2–5.

5:14 *Shammua, and Shobab, and Nathan, and Solomon.* 1 Chr 3:5 designates Bath-sheba as their mother.

5:17 *when the Philistines heard that they had anointed David king.* Chronologically it is likely that the Philistine attack followed immediately after the events of v. 3 and before the capture of Jerusalem (vv. 6–14). (The author arranged his narrative by topics; see note on 7:1.) The Philistines had not been disturbed by David's reign over Judah, but now they acted to protect their interests in the north, much of which they dominated after the defeat of Saul (1 Sam 31). *hold.* Probably a reference to the wilderness area in southern Judah where David had hidden from Saul (see notes on 1 Sam 22:4; 23:14). This action of David suggests that he had not yet taken Jerusalem.

5:19 *David inquired of the LORD.* See notes on 2:1; 1 Sam 2:28; 22:20; 23:2.

‡5:20 *The LORD hath broken forth . . . Baal-perazim* [i.e. "master of a breakthrough"]. As a true theocratic king, David attributes the victory to the Lord and does not claim the glory for himself (see notes on 1 Sam 10:18,27; 11:13; 12:11; 14:23; 17:11,45–47).

‡5:21 *there they left their images.* As the Israelites had taken the ark into battle (see note on 1 Sam 4:3), so the Philistines carried images of their deities into battle in the hope that this would ensure victory. *burnt them.* See KJV marg. for the literal translation. In compliance with the instruction of Deut 7:5, they also burned them (see 1 Chr 14:12).

5:23 *he said.* As had been true in the case of the conquest under Joshua, the Lord ordered the battle and He Himself marched against the enemy with His heavenly host (see Josh 6:2–5; 8:1–2; 10:8,14; 11:6). David's wars were a continuation and completion of the wars fought by Joshua.

24 And let it be, when thou [a]hearest the
sound of a going in the tops of the mulberry
trees, *that* then thou shalt bestir thyself: for
then [b]shall the LORD go out before thee, to
smite the host of the Philistines.
25 And David did so, as the LORD had commanded him; and smote the Philistines from
[1]Geba until thou come *to* [a]Gazer.

Bringing the ark to Jerusalem

6 Again, David gathered together all the
chosen *men* of Israel, thirty thousand.
2 And [a]David arose, and went with all the
people that *were* with him from [1]Baale of Judah, to bring up from thence the ark of God,
[2]whose name is called *by* the name of the
LORD of hosts [b]that dwelleth *between* the
cherubims.
3 And they [1]set the ark of God upon a new
cart, and brought it out of the house of Abinadab that *was* in [2]Gibeah: and Uzzah and Ahio,
the sons of Abinadab, drave the new cart.
4 And they brought it out of [a]the house of
Abinadab which *was* at Gibeah, [1]accompany-
ing the ark of God: and Ahio went before the
ark.
5 And David and all the house of Israel
played before the LORD on all *manner of instruments made of* fir wood, even on harps,
and on psalteries, and on timbrels, and on cornets, and on cymbals.
6 And when they came to [1]Nachon's
threshingfloor, Uzzah put forth *his hand* to the
ark of God, and took hold of it; for the oxen
[2]shook *it.*
7 And the anger of the LORD was kindled
against Uzzah; and [a]God smote him there for
his [1]error; and there he died by the ark of
God.
8 And David was displeased, because the
LORD had [1]made a breach upon Uzzah: and he
called *the name* of the place [2]Perez-uzzah to
this day.
9 And [a]David was afraid of the LORD that
day, and said, How shall the ark of the LORD
come to me?
10 So David would not remove the ark of
the LORD unto him into the city of David: but
David carried it aside *into* the house of Obed-
edom [a]the Gittite.
11 [a]And the ark of the LORD continued *in*
the house of Obed-edom the Gittite three
months: and the LORD [b]blessed Obed-edom,
and all his household.
12 ¶ And it was told king David, saying, The
LORD hath blessed the house of Obed-edom,
and all that *pertaineth* unto him, because of
the ark of God. [a]So David went and brought up
the ark of God from the house of Obed-edom
into the city of David with gladness.
13 And it was *so,* that when [a]they that
bare the ark of the LORD had gone six paces, he
sacrificed [b]oxen and fatlings.
14 And David [a]danced before the LORD
with all *his* might; and David *was* girded [b]*with*
a linen ephod.
15 [a]So David and all the house of Israel
brought up the ark of the LORD with shouting,
and with the sound of the trumpet.
16 And as the ark of the LORD came *into*
the city of David, Michal Saul's daughter
looked through a window, and saw king David
leaping and dancing before the LORD; and she
despised him in her heart.

5:24 [a]2 Ki. 7:6 [b]Judg. 4:14
5:25 [1][1 Chr. 14:16, *Gibeon*] [a]Josh. 16:10
6:2 [1][Or, *Baalah*, that is, *Kirjath-jearim*, Josh. 15:9,60] [2]Or, *at which the name, even the name of the LORD of hosts, was called upon* [a]1 Chr. 13:5,6 [b]1 Sam. 4:4; Ps. 80:1
6:3 [1]Heb. *made to ride* [2]Or, *the hill*
6:4 [1]Heb. *with* [a]1 Sam. 7:1
6:6 [1][1 Chr. 13:9, he is called, *Chidon*] [2]Or, *stumbled*
6:7 [a]1 Sam. 6:19
6:7 [1]Or, *rashness*
6:8 [1]Heb. *broken* [2]That is, *the breach of Uzzah*
6:9 [a]Ps. 119:120
6:10 [a]1 Chr. 13:13
6:11 [a]1 Chr. 13:14 [b]Gen. 39:5
6:12 [a]1 Chr. 15:25
6:13 [a]Num. 4:15; Josh. 3:3; 1 Chr. 15:2,15 [b]See 1 Ki. 8:5
6:14 [a]Ps. 30:11 [b]1 Sam. 2:18
6:15 [a]1 Chr. 15:28

5:24 *sound of a going.* The heavenly host of the Lord going into battle.

‡6:2 *Baale of Judah.* That is, Kirjath-jearim (see Josh 15:60; 18:14; 1 Sam 6:21; 7:1; see also note on 1 Ch 13:6). *ark of God.* See Ex 25:10–22; see also notes on 1 Sam 4:3–4,21. The ark had remained at Kirjath-jearim during the reign of Saul. *called by the name.* Used elsewhere to designate ownership (see 12:28; Deut 28:10; Is 4:1; 63:19). *LORD of hosts.* See note on 1 Sam 1:3. *dwelleth between the cherubims.* See note on 1 Sam 4:4; see also 1 Chr 28:2 ("footstool of our God"). David recognized the great significance of the ark as the earthly throne of Israel's God. As a true theocratic king, he wished to acknowledge the Lord's kingship and rule over both himself and the people by restoring the ark to a place of prominence in the nation.

6:3 *new cart.* David follows the example of the Philistines (see 1 Sam 6:7) rather than the instructions of Ex 25:12–14; Num 4:5–6,15, which require that the ark be carried on the shoulders of the Levites (see 1 Chr 15:13–15). *out of the house of Abinadab.* See 1 Sam 7:1. *Uzzah and Ahio, the sons of Abinadab.* 1 Sam 7:1 speaks of Eleazar as the son of Abinadab. The Hebrew word for "son" can have the broader meaning of "descendant."

6:7 *his error.* Although Uzzah's intent may have been good, he violated the clear instructions the Lord had given for handling the ark (see note on v. 3; cf. Ex 25:15; Num 4:5–6,15; 1 Chr 15:13–15; see also note on 1 Sam 6:19). At this important new beginning in Israel's life with the Lord, the Lord gives a shocking and vivid reminder to David and Israel that those who claim to serve Him must acknowledge His rule with absolute seriousness (see Lev 10:1–3; Josh 7:24–25; 24:19–20; Acts 5:1–11).

‡6:8 *David was displeased.* David's initial reaction was resentment that his attempt to honor the Lord had resulted in a display of God's wrath. *Perez-uzzah.* I.e. "the breakthrough of Uzzah." The place-name memorialized a divine warning that was not soon forgotten (see Josh 7:26 and note). *to this day.* Until the time of the writing of 2 Samuel.

6:9 *David was afraid of the LORD.* David's anger was accompanied by fear—not the wholesome fear of proper honor and respect for the Lord (1 Sam 12:24; Josh 24:14) but an anxiety arising from an acute sense of his own guilt (Gen 3:10; Deut 5:5).

6:10 *Obed-edom.* Perhaps means "servant of man." *Gittite.* He appears to have been a Levite (see note on 1 Chr 13:13; cf. 1 Chr 15:18,24; 16:5; 26:4–8,15; 2 Chr 25:24), though many think the term "Gittite" fixes his place of birth at the Philistine city of Gath (see 15:18). However, Gittite may be a reference to the Levitical city Gath-rimmon in Dan or Manasseh (Josh 21:20–25).

6:12 *David . . . brought up the ark.* God's blessing on the household of Obed-edom showed David that God's anger had been appeased.

6:13 *they that bare the ark.* David had become aware of his previous error (1 Chr 15:13–15). *six paces.* Sufficient to show that now God's blessing was on the Levites (see 1 Chr 15:26).

6:14 *linen ephod.* See note on 1 Sam 2:18.

6:16 *she despised him.* Michal had no appreciation for the significance of the event and deeply resented David's public display as unworthy of the dignity of a king (see vv. 20–23).

17 And [a]they brought in the ark of the LORD, and set it in [b]his place, in the midst of the tabernacle that David had [1]pitched for it: and David [c]offered burnt offerings and peace offerings before the LORD.

18 And as soon as David had made an end of offering burnt offerings and peace offerings, [a]he blessed the people in the name of the LORD of hosts.

19 [a]And he dealt among all the people, *even* among the whole multitude of Israel, as well to the women as men, to every one a cake of bread, and a good piece *of flesh,* and a flagon *of wine.* So all the people departed every one to his house.

20 [a]Then David returned to bless his household. And Michal the daughter of Saul came out to meet David, and said, How glorious was the king of Israel to day, who [b]uncovered himself to day in the eyes of the handmaids of his servants, as one of the [c]vain *fellows* [1]shamelessly uncovereth himself!

21 And David said unto Michal, *It was* before the LORD, [a]which chose me before thy father, and before all his house, to appoint me ruler over the people of the LORD, over Israel: therefore will I play before the LORD.

22 And I will yet be more vile than thus, and will be base in mine own sight: and [1]of the maidservants which thou hast spoken of, of them shall I be had in honour.

23 Therefore Michal the daughter of Saul had no child [a]unto the day of her death.

Nathan's prophecy

7 And it came to pass, [a]when the king sat in his house, and the LORD had given him rest round about from all his enemies;

2 That the king said unto Nathan the prophet, See now, I dwell in [a]a house of cedar, [b]but the ark of God dwelleth within [c]curtains.

3 And Nathan said to the king, Go, do all that *is* in thine heart; for the LORD *is* with thee.

4 And it came to pass that night, that the word of the LORD came unto Nathan, saying,

5 Go and tell [1]my servant David, Thus saith the LORD, [a]Shalt thou build me a house for me to dwell in?

6 Whereas I have not dwelt in *any* house [a]since the time that I brought up the children of Israel out of Egypt, even to this day, but have walked in [b]a tent and in a tabernacle.

7 In all *the places* wherein I have [a]walked with all the children of Israel spake I a word with [1]any of the tribes of Israel, whom I commanded [b]to feed my people Israel, saying, Why build ye not me a house of cedar?

8 Now therefore so shalt thou say unto my servant David, Thus saith the LORD of hosts, [a]I took thee from the sheepcote, [1]from following the sheep, to be ruler over my people, over Israel:

9 And [a]I was with thee whithersoever thou wentest, [b]and have cut off all thine enemies [1]out of thy sight, and have made thee a great name, like unto the name of the great *men* that *are* in the earth.

10 Moreover I will appoint a place for my people Israel, and will [a]plant them, that they may dwell in a place of their own, and move no more; [b]neither shall the children of wickedness afflict them any more, as beforetime,

11 And *as* [a]since the time that I commanded judges *to be* over my people Israel, and have caused thee to rest from all thine ene-

6:17 [1]Heb. *stretched* [a]1 Chr. 16:1 [b]1 Chr. 15:1; Ps. 132:8 [c]1 Ki. 8:5,62,63
6:18 [a]1 Ki. 8:55
6:19 [a]1 Chr. 16:3
6:20 [1]Or, *openly* [a]Ps. 30, title [b]ver. 14,16 [c]Judg. 9:4
6:21 [a]1 Sam. 13:14
6:22 [1]Or, *of the handmaids* of my servants
6:23 [a]See 1 Sam. 15:35; Is. 22:14
7:1 [a]1 Chr. 17:1
7:2 [a]ch. 5:11 [b]See Acts 7:46 [c]Ex. 26:1
7:5 [1]Heb. *to my servant, to David* [a]1 Ki. 5:3; 8:19; 1 Chr. 22:8
7:6 [a]1 Ki. 8:16 [b]Ex. 40:18,19,34
7:7 [1]In the 1 Chr. 17:6, *any of the judges* [a]Lev. 26:11; Deut. 23:14 [b]Mat. 2:6; Acts 20:28
7:8 [1]Heb. *from after* [a]1 Sam. 16:11,12
7:9 [1]Heb. *from thy face* [a]1 Sam. 18:14; ch. 5:10 [b]1 Sam. 31:6
7:10 [a]Ps. 44:2; 80:8; Jer. 24:6 [b]Ps. 89:22
7:11 [a]Judg. 2:14; 1 Sam. 12:9

6:17 *burnt offerings.* See Lev 1. *peace offerings.* See note on 1 Sam 11:15.

6:18 *he blessed the people.* As Solomon would later do at the dedication of the temple (1 Ki 8:55–61).

6:20 *uncovered himself.* An allusion to David's having worn only a linen ephod (v. 14) rather than his royal robe.

6:23 *Michal . . . had no child.* Probably a punishment for her pride and at the same time another manifestation of God's judgment on the house of Saul.

7:1–29 God's great promise to David (see Introduction: Contents and Theme). Although it is not expressly called a covenant here, it is elsewhere (23:5; Ps 89:3,28,34,39; cf. Ps 132:11), and David responds with language suggesting his recognition that a covenant had been made (see notes on vv. 20,28).

7:1 *when the king sat in his house.* See 5:11; see also note on 5:12. *and the LORD had given him rest . . . from all his enemies.* Chronologically the victories noted in 8:1–14 probably preceded the events of this chapter. The arrangement of material is topical (see also note on 5:17)—ch. 6 records the bringing of the ark to Jerusalem; ch. 7 tells of David's desire to build a temple in Jerusalem in which to house the ark.

‡7:2 *Nathan.* The first reference to this prophet (see 12:1–14; 1 Ki 1). *curtains.* I.e. tent curtains. See v. 6; 6:17. Now that he himself had a royal palace (symbolic of his established kingship), a tent did not seem to David to be an appropriate place for the throne of Israel's divine King (see note on 6:2; see also Ps 132:2–5; Acts 7:46). He wanted to build Israel's heavenly King a royal house in the capital city of his kingdom.

7:3 *Nathan said.* In consulting a prophet, David sought God's will, but Nathan boldly voiced approval of David's plans in the Lord's name before he had received a revelation from the Lord.

7:5 *Shalt thou build . . . ?* David's desire was commendable (1 Ki 8:18–19), but his gift and mission were to fight the Lord's battles until Israel was securely at rest in the promised land (see v. 10; 1 Ki 5:3).

‡7:7 *spake I a word . . . saying, Why build ye not me a house . . . ?* David misunderstood the Lord's priorities. He reflected the pagan notion that the gods were interested in human beings only as builders and maintainers of their temples and as practitioners of their cult. Instead, the Lord had raised up rulers in Israel only to shepherd His people (that is also why he had brought David "from the sheepcote [i.e. pasture]," v. 8).

7:9 *I . . . have cut off all thy enemies.* See note on v. 1.

7:10 *I will appoint a place for my people Israel.* It is for this purpose that the Lord has made David king, and through David He will do it. *as beforetime.* In Egypt.

7:11 *judges.* Leaders during the period of the judges (see Introduction to Judges: Title). *have caused thee to rest from all thine enemies.* See vv. 1,9. David's victories over threatening powers will be complete, so that the rest already enjoyed will be assured for the future. *The LORD . . . will make thee a house.* Compare this statement with the rhetorical question of v. 5. In a beautiful play on words God says that David is not to build Him a house (temple); rather, God will build David a house (roy-

mies. Also the LORD telleth thee [b]that he will make thee a house.

12 And [a]when thy days be fulfilled, and thou [b]shalt sleep with thy fathers, [c]I will set up thy seed after thee, which shall proceed out of thy bowels, and I will establish his kingdom.

13 [a]He shall build a house for my name, and I will [b]stablish the throne of his kingdom for ever.

14 [a]I will be his father, and he shall be my son. [b]If he commit iniquity, I will chasten him with the rod of men, and with the stripes of the children of men:

15 But my mercy shall not depart away from him, [a]as I took *it* from Saul, whom I put away before thee.

16 And [a]thine house and thy kingdom shall be stablished for ever before thee: thy throne shall be stablished for ever.

17 According to all these words, and according to all this vision, so did Nathan speak unto David.

David's prayer

18 ¶ Then went king David in, and sat before the LORD, and he said, [a]Who *am* I, O Lord GOD? and what *is* my house, that thou hast brought me hitherto?

19 And this was yet a small thing in thy sight, O Lord GOD; but thou hast spoken also of thy servant's house for a great while to come. [a]And *is* this the [1]manner of man, O Lord GOD?

20 And what can David say more unto thee? for thou, Lord GOD, [a]knowest thy servant.

21 For thy word's sake, and according to thine own heart, hast thou done all these great things, to make thy servant know *them*.

22 Wherefore [a]thou art great, O LORD God: for [b]*there is* none like thee, neither *is there any* God beside thee, according to all that we have heard with our ears.

23 And [a]what one nation in the earth *is* like thy people, *even* like Israel, whom God went to redeem for a people to himself, and to make him a name, and to do for you great things and terrible, for thy land, before [b]thy people, which thou redeemedst to thee from Egypt, *from* the nations and their gods?

24 For [a]thou hast confirmed to thyself thy people Israel to be a people unto thee for ever; [b]and thou, LORD, art become their God.

25 And now, O LORD God, the word that thou hast spoken concerning thy servant, and concerning his house, establish *it* for ever, and do as thou hast said.

26 And let thy name be magnified for ever, saying, The LORD of hosts *is* the God over Israel: and let the house of thy servant David be established before thee.

27 For thou, O LORD of hosts, God of Israel, hast [1]revealed to thy servant, saying, I will build thee a house: therefore hath thy servant found in his heart to pray this prayer unto thee.

7:11 [b]ver. 27; Ex. 1:21
7:12 [a]1 Ki. 2:1 [b]Deut. 31:16 [c]Ps. 132:11
7:13 [a]1 Ki. 5:5; 8:19 [b]ver. 16
7:14 [a]Heb. 1:5 [b]Ps. 89:30
7:15 [a]1 Sam. 15:23,28; 16:14
7:16 [a]ver. 13; John 12:34
7:18 [a]Gen. 32:10
7:19 [1]Heb. *law* [a]Is. 55:8
7:20 [a]Ps. 139:1
7:22 [a]1 Chr. 16:25; 2 Chr. 2:5; Jer. 10:6 [b]Deut. 3:24; 4:35; 32:39
7:23 [a]Ps. 147:20 [b]Deut. 9:26
7:24 [a]Deut. 26:18 [b]Ps. 48:14
7:27 [1]Heb. *opened the ear*

al dynasty) that will last forever (v. 16). God has been building Israel ever since the days of Abraham, and now He commits Himself to build David's royal house so that the promise to Israel may be fulfilled—rest in the promised land. It is God's building that effects His kingdom. This covenant with David is unconditional, like those with Noah, Abram and Phinehas (see note on Gen 9:9; see also chart, p. 16), grounded only in God's firm and gracious purpose. It finds its ultimate fulfillment in the kingship of Christ, who was born of the tribe of Judah and the house of David (see Ps 89:30–38; Is 9:1–7; Mat 1:1; Luke 1:32–33,69; Acts 2:30; 13:23; Rom 1:2–3; 2 Tim 2:8; Rev 3:7; 22:16).

7:12 *set up thy seed after thee.* The royal line of David, in contrast to that of Saul, would continue after David's death by dynastic succession.

7:13 *He shall build a house for my name.* God's priorities are that His own royal house, where His throne (the ark) can finally come to rest (1 Chr 6:31; 28:2), will wait until Israel is at rest and David's dynasty (in the person of his son) is secure. "Name" is equivalent to "me" in v. 5 (see note on 1 Sam 25:25).

7:14 *his father . . . my son.* This familial language expresses the special relationship God promises to maintain with the descendant(s) of David whom He will establish on David's throne. It marks him as the one God has chosen and enthroned to rule in His name as the official representative of God's rule over His people (see notes on Ps 2:7; 45:6; 89:27). In Jesus Christ this promise comes to ultimate fulfillment (see Mat 1:1; Mark 1:11; Heb 1:5).

7:15 *my mercy.* God's special and unfailing favor (see note on Ps 6:4).

7:16 *thy throne shall be stablished for ever.* See note on v. 11; see also Introduction: Contents and Theme. The promise of an everlasting kingdom for the house of David became the focal point for many later prophecies and powerfully influenced the development of the Messianic hope in Israel.

7:18–29 David's prayer expresses wonder that God would make such commitments to him and his descendants. But he also acknowledges that what God had pledged to him is for Israel's sake, that its purpose is the fulfillment of God's covenanted promises to His people—and that its ultimate effect will be the honor and praise of God throughout the world.

7:18 *went. . . in.* Presumably into the tent (6:17) in which the ark was kept. *sat before the LORD.* The ark was the symbol of God's presence with His people (see Ex 25:22; see also notes on 1 Sam 4:3–4,21).

7:19 *And is this the manner of man, O Lord GOD?* The meaning of this clause is uncertain (cf. 1 Chr 17:17). It has also been taken as an exclamation ("This is Your law for man, O Sovereign Lord!") and understood as a summation of the divine decree concerning David and his house.

7:20 *knowest.* Or "especially acknowledge" or "choose" (see Gen 18:19, "I know him"; Amos 3:2, "you only have I known"). David recognizes God's promise as a covenant (23:5).

7:21 *thy word's sake.* Probably God's covenant word of promise to His people.

7:22 *any God beside thee.* See 22:32; 1 Sam 2:2.

7:23 *one nation . . . God went to redeem for a people to himself.* Israel's uniqueness did not consist in her national achievements but in God's choice of her to be His own people (see Deut 7:6–8; 33:26–29). *to make him a name.* The basis for God's electing love, revealed in His dealings with Israel, did not lie in any meritorious characteristic of the Israelite people but in His own sovereign purposes (see Deut 7:6–8; 9:4–5; 1 Sam 12:22; Neh 9:10; Is 63:12; Jer 32:20–21; Ezek 36:22–38).

7:24 *thou, LORD, art become their God.* What God has pledged to David, He has pledged as the God of Israel.

7:27 *thy servant found in his heart to pray this prayer unto thee.* David's prayer lays claim on God's promise.

28 And now, O Lord GOD, thou *art* that God, and [a]thy words be true, and thou hast promised this goodness unto thy servant:

29 Therefore now [1]let it please thee to bless the house of thy servant, that *it* may continue for ever before thee: for thou, O Lord GOD, hast spoken *it:* and with thy blessing let the house of thy servant be blessed [a]for ever.

David's military victories

8 And after this it came to pass, that David smote the Philistines, and subdued them: and David took [1]Metheg-ammah out of the hand of the Philistines.

2 And [a]he smote Moab, and measured them with a line, casting them down to the ground; even *with* two lines measured he to put to death, and *with* one full line to keep alive. And *so* the Moabites became David's servants, and [b]brought gifts.

3 David smote also [1]Hadadezer, the son of Rehob, king of [a]Zobah, as he went to recover [b]his border at the river Euphrates.

4 And David took [1]from him a thousand [2]*chariots,* and seven hundred horsemen, and twenty thousand footmen: and David [a]houghed all the chariot *horses,* but reserved of them *for* an hundred chariots.

5 [a]And when the Syrians of Damascus came to succour Hadadezer king of Zobah, David slew of the Syrians two and twenty thousand men.

6 Then David put garrisons in Syria of Damascus: and the Syrians became servants to David, and brought gifts. [a]And the LORD preserved David whithersoever he went.

7 And David took [a]the shields of gold that were on the servants of Hadadezer, and brought them *to* Jerusalem.

8 And from [1]Betah, and from [2]Berothai, cities of Hadadezer, king David took exceeding much brass.

9 When [1]Toi king of Hamath heard that David had smitten all the host of Hadadezer,

10 Then Toi sent [a1]Joram his son unto king David, to [2]salute him, and to bless him, because he had fought against Hadadezer, and smitten him: for Hadadezer [3]had wars with Toi. And *Joram* [4]brought with him vessels of silver, and vessels of gold, and vessels of brass:

11 Which also king David [a]did dedicate unto the LORD, with the silver and gold that he had dedicated of all nations which he subdued;

12 Of Syria, and of Moab, and of the children of Ammon, and of the Philistines, and of Amalek, and of the spoil of Hadadezer, son of Rehob, king of Zobah.

13 And David gat *him* a name when he returned from [1]smiting of the Syrians in [a]the valley of salt, [b2]*being* eighteen thousand *men.*

14 And he put garrisons in Edom; throughout all Edom put he garrisons, and [a]all they of Edom became David's servants. And the LORD preserved David whithersoever he went.

15 ¶ And David reigned over all Israel; and David executed judgment and justice unto all his people.

16 [a]And Joab the son of Zeruiah *was* over the host; and [b]Jehoshaphat the son of Ahilud *was* [1]recorder;

17 And [a]Zadok the son of Ahitub, and Ahimelech the son of Abiathar, *were* the priests; and Seraiah *was* the [1]scribe;

7:28 [a]John 17:17
7:29 [1]Heb. *be thou pleased and bless* [a]ch. 22:51
8:1 [1]Or, *the bridle of Ammah*
8:2 [a]Num. 24:17 [b]See 1 Sam. 10:27
8:3 [1][Or, *Hadarezer,* 1 Chr. 18:3] [a]ch. 10:6; Ps. 60, title [b]See Gen. 15:18
8:4 [1]Or, *of his* [2]As 1 Chr. 18:4 [a]Josh. 11:6,9
8:5 [a]1 Ki. 11:23
8:6 [a]ver. 14; ch. 7:9
8:7 [a]See 1 Ki. 10:16
8:8 [1][Or, *Tibhath*] [2][Or, *Chun,* 1 Chr. 18:8]
8:9 [1][*Tou,* 1 Chr. 18:9]
8:10 [1][1 Chr. 18:10, *Hadoram*] [2]Heb. *ask him of peace* [3]Heb. *was a man of wars with* [4]Heb. *in his hand were* [a]1 Chr. 18:10; *Hadoram*
8:11 [a]1 Ki. 7:51
8:13 [1]Heb. *his smiting* [2][Or, slaying] [a]2 Ki. 14:7 [b]See 1 Chr. 18:12; Ps. 60, title
8:14 [a]Gen. 27:29,37,40; Num. 24:18
8:16 [1]Or, *remembrancer,* or, *writer of chronicles* [a]ch. 19:13; 20:23; 1 Chr. 11:6 [b]1 Ki. 4:3
8:17 [1]Or, *secretary* [a]1 Chr. 24:3

‡7:28 *goodness.* A common summary expression for covenant benefits from God (see also, e.g., Num 10:29; Josh 23:14, "good [words]"; Num 10:32; Isa 63:7, "goodness"; Deut 26:11; Josh 21:45, "good thing"; Jer 29:32; 32:40–41; 33:9, "good").

8:1 *after this it came to pass.* Chronologically the events of this chapter, or many of them, are probably to be placed between chs. 5 and 6 (see 7:1 and note). *Metheg-ammah.* An unknown site, perhaps near Gath (see 1 Chr 18:1).

8:2 *Moab.* Descendants of Lot (Gen 19:37), occupying territory east of the Dead Sea. Saul fought with the Moabites (1 Sam 14:47), and David sought refuge in Moab for his parents during his exile from Israel (1 Sam 22:3–4). See note on Ruth 1:22.

8:3 *Hadadezer.* Means "Hadad is (my) help." Hadad was an Aramean deity equivalent to the Canaanite Baal. *Zobah.* Saul had previously fought against the kings of Zobah (1 Sam 14:47), whose territory was apparently located in the Beqaa Valley between the Lebanon and Anti-Lebanon mountains, thus on Israel's northern border. *recover.* Saul's earlier victories over the kings of Zobah had extended Israelite control, if only briefly, as far as the fringes of the Euphrates Valley. *the river Euphrates.* The land promised to Abraham had included borders from Egypt to the Euphrates River (Gen 15:18–21; Deut 1:7; 11:24; Josh 1:4). Here is at least another provisional fulfillment of this promise (see 1 Ki 4:21–24; see also Gen 17:8; Josh 21:43–45). See map No. 5 at the end of the study Bible.

‡8:4 *houghed* [i.e. hamstrung] *all the chariot horses.* See Josh 11:6 and note. David may not have understood the value of the chariot as a military weapon.

8:5 *came to succour Hadadezer.* They feared Israelite expansion to the north.

8:7 *shields of gold.* Shields adorned with gold—the phrase is similar to "chariots of iron" (see Josh 17:16 and note).

8:8 *brass* [i.e. bronze]. Later used by Solomon in the construction of the temple (1 Chr 18:8).

8:9 *Hamath.* A kingdom centered on the Orontes River, north of Zobah (see v. 3 and note).

8:13 *valley of salt.* See 2 Ki 14:7; see also Ps 60 title.

8:15 *judgment and justice.* As a true theocratic king, David's reign was characterized by adherence to God's standards of right rule (see notes on 1 Sam 8:3; 12:3), as no doubt laid down in Samuel's "manner of the kingdom" (see 1 Sam 10:25 and note; 1 Ki 2:3–4).

8:16 *Joab the son of Zeruiah was over the host.* See notes on 2:13; 5:8. *recorder.* The precise duties of this official are not indicated, though the position was an important one in the court and was maintained throughout the period of the monarchy (see 2 Ki 18:18,37; 2 Chr 34:8; Is 36:3,11,22). He may have been a kind of chancellor or chief administrator of royal affairs, responsible among other things for the royal chronicles and annals.

8:17 *Zadok the son of Ahitub.* First mentioned here, Zadok was a descendant of Eleazar son of Aaron (see 1 Chr 6:4–8,50–52; 24:1–3). His father, Ahitub, is not to be identified with Ichabod's brother of the same name (1 Sam 14:3). Zadok remained loyal to David throughout his reign (15:24–29; 17:15–16; 19:11) and eventually anointed Solomon as David's successor (1 Ki 1:8,45;

18 [a]And Benaiah the son of Jehoiada *was*
over both the [b]Cherethites and the Pelethites;
and David's sons were [1]chief rulers.

David and Mephibosheth

9 And David said, Is there yet *any* that is
left of the house of Saul, that I may
[a]shew him kindness for Jonathan's sake?
2 And *there was* of the house of Saul a servant whose name *was* [a]Ziba. And when they
had called him unto David, the king said unto
him, *Art* thou Ziba? And he said, Thy servant
is he.
3 And the king said, *Is there* not yet any of
the house of Saul, that I may shew [a]the kindness of God unto him? And Ziba said unto the
king, Jonathan hath yet a son, *which is* [b]lame
on *his* feet.
4 And the king said unto him, Where *is*
he? And Ziba said unto the king, Behold, he *is*
in the house of [a]Machir, the son of Ammiel, in
Lo-debar.
5 Then king David sent, and fet him out of
the house of Machir, the son of Ammiel, from
Lo-debar.
6 Now when [1]Mephibosheth, the son of
Jonathan, the son of Saul, was come unto David, he fell on his face, and did reverence. And
David said, Mephibosheth. And he answered,
Behold thy servant.
7 And David said unto him, Fear not: for I

8:18 [1]Or, *princes*, ch. 20:26 [a]1 Chr. 18:17 [b]1 Sam. 30:14
9:1 [a]1 Sam. 18:3; Prov. 27:10
9:2 [a]ch. 16:1; 19:17,29
9:3 [a]1 Sam. 20:14 [b]ch. 4:4
9:4 [a]ch. 17:27
9:6 [1][Called *Merib-baal*, 1 Chr. 8:34; 9:40]
9:8 [a]ch. 16:9
9:9 [a]ch. 16:4; 19:29
9:10 [a]ver. 7,11,13; ch. 19:28 [b]ch. 19:17
9:12 [a]1 Chr. 8:34
9:13 [a]ver. 7,10; 2 Ki. 25:29 [b]ver. 3

will surely shew thee kindness for Jonathan
thy father's sake, and will restore thee all the
land of Saul thy father; and thou shalt eat
bread at my table continually.
8 And he bowed himself, and said, What *is*
thy servant, that thou shouldest look upon
such [a]a dead dog as I *am?*
9 Then the king called to Ziba, Saul's servant, and said unto him, [a]I have given unto
thy master's son all that pertained to Saul and
to all his house.
10 Thou therefore, and thy sons, and thy
servants, shall till the land for him, and thou
shalt bring in *the fruits,* that thy master's son
may have food to eat: but Mephibosheth thy
master's son [a]shall eat bread alway at my
table. Now Ziba had [b]fifteen sons and twenty
servants.
11 Then said Ziba unto the king, According
to all that my lord the king hath commanded
his servant, so shall thy servant do. As for Mephibosheth, *said the king,* he shall eat at my
table, as one of the king's sons.
12 And Mephibosheth had a young son,
[a]whose name *was* Micha. And all that dwelt in
the house of Ziba *were* servants unto Mephibosheth.
13 So Mephibosheth dwelt in Jerusalem:
[a]for he did eat continually at the king's table;
and [b]*was* lame on both his feet.

2:35; 4:4). *Ahimelech the son of Abiathar.* It appears that a copyist's error may have occurred here (repeated in 1 Chr 24:3,6,31) in which these two names have been transposed. Abiathar is referred to as son of Ahimelech in 1 Sam 22:20. While it is true that the Abiathar of 1 Sam 22:20 could have had a son named Ahimelech (after his grandfather), such a person does not appear elsewhere in the narratives of Samuel and Kings as a colleague of Zadok, but Abiathar consistently does (15:29,35; 17:15; 19:11; 20:25; 1 Ki 1:7–8,19; 2:27,35; 4:4). Abiathar was a descendant of Aaron through Ithamar (1 Chr 24:3) in the line of Eli (see notes on 1 Sam 2:31,33). *Seraiah.* Also called Sheva (20:25), Shisha (1 Ki 4:3) and Shavsha (1 Chr 18:16). *scribe.* His duties presumably included domestic and foreign correspondence, perhaps keeping records of important political events, and various administrative functions (2 Ki 12:10–12).

8:18 *Cherethites and the Pelethites.* See note on 1 Sam 30:14. Under the leadership of Benaiah, they formed a sort of special royal guard for David (23:22–23). "Pelethite" is probably an alternate form of "Philistine." *chief rulers.* The Hebrew has the common word for "priests" (see also 20:26), but the usage is obscure since that sense appears unlikely. Chronicles has "chief about the king" (see 1 Chr 18:17 and note), which supports the meaning "chief ministers."

9:1–20:26 These chapters, together with 1 Ki 1:1–2:46, are often referred to as the "Court History of David" and hailed as one of the finest examples of historical narrative to have been produced in the ancient world. Their intimate and precise detail marks them as the work of an eyewitness.

9:1–13 The events of this chapter cannot be dated precisely, but they occurred a number of years after David's capture of Jerusalem. Mephibosheth was five years old at the time of his father's death (4:4); now he has a son of his own (v. 12).

9:1 *I may shew him kindness for Jonathan's sake.* David has not forgotten his promise to Jonathan (see 1 Sam 20:15,42).

9:2 *Ziba.* The chief steward of Saul's estate, which had been inherited by Mephibosheth son of Jonathan, Saul's firstborn (see 16:1–4; 19:17).

9:3 *Jonathan hath yet a son.* Saul had other descendants (see 21:8), but Ziba mentions only the one in whom David would be chiefly interested.

9:4 *Machir.* Apparently a wealthy benefactor of Mephibosheth who later also came to David's aid (17:27). *Lo-debar.* A town deep in Gileadite territory east of the Jordan (Josh 13:26, "Debir"), far from the family estate and from David's court (see note on 2:8).

9:7 *restore thee.* The property Saul had acquired as king had either been taken over by David, or Ziba as steward had virtually taken possession of it and was profiting from its income (see 16:1–4; 19:26–30). *thou shalt eat bread at my table continually.* More a matter of high honor than economic assistance. Mephibosheth's general financial needs were to be cared for by the produce of Saul's estate (v. 10).

9:8 *dead dog as I.* An expression of deep self-abasement. The author has used the "dead dog" motif with great effect. First Goliath, scornfully disdaining the young warrior David, asks, "Am I a dog . . . ?" (1 Sam 17:43)—and unwittingly foreshadows his own end. Then David, in a self-deprecating manner, describes himself as a "dead dog" (1 Sam 24:14) to suggest to Saul that the king of Israel should not consider him worth so much attention. In the Nabal episode, that "dog" (a Calebite) and his sudden death characterize Saul and foreshadow his unhappy end (see note on 1 Sam 25:3). Here a grandson of Saul and in 16:9 a relative of the dead king who curses David are similarly described. For the author, "dead dog" fittingly characterizes those who foolishly scorn or oppose the Lord's anointed, while David's own self-deprecation (see 1 Sam 18:18; 2 Sam 7:18) is conducive to his exaltation.

9:12 *Micha.* See 1 Chr 8:35–39 for his descendants.

Victory over the children of Ammon

10 And it came to pass after this, that
the [a]king of the children of Ammon
died, and Hanun his son reigned in his stead.
2 Then said David, I will shew kindness
unto Hanun the son of Nahash, as his father
shewed kindness unto me. And David sent to
comfort him by the hand of his servants for his
father. And David's servants came *into* the
land of the children of Ammon.
3 And the princes of the children of Ammon said unto Hanun their lord, [1]Thinkest
thou that David doth honour thy father, that
he hath sent comforters unto thee? hath not
David *rather* sent his servants unto thee, to
search the city, and to spy it out, and to overthrow it?
4 Wherefore Hanun took David's servants,
and shaved off the *one* half of their beards, and
cut off their garments in the middle, [a]*even* to
their buttocks, and sent them away.
5 When they told *it* unto David, he sent to
meet them, because the men were greatly
ashamed: and the king said, Tarry at Jericho
until your beards be grown, and *then* return.
6 And when the children of Ammon saw
that they [a]stank before David, the children of
Ammon sent and hired [b]the Syrians of Beth-rehob, and the Syrians of Zoba, twenty thousand
footmen, and of king Maacah a thousand men,
and of [1]Ish-tob twelve thousand men.
7 And when David heard *of it,* he sent
Joab, and all the host *of* [a]the mighty *men.*
8 And the children of Ammon came out,
and put the battle in array *at* the entering in of
the gate: and [a]the Syrians of Zoba, and of Rehob, and Ish-tob, and Maacah, *were* by themselves in the field.
9 When Joab saw that the front of the battle was against him before and behind, he
chose of all the choice *men* of Israel, and put
them in array against the Syrians:
10 And the rest of the people he delivered
into the hand of Abishai his brother, that he
might put *them* in array against the children of
Ammon.
11 And he said, If the Syrians be too strong
for me, then thou shalt help me: but if the children of Ammon be too strong for thee, then I
will come and help thee.
12 [a]Be of good courage, and let us [b]play
the men for our people, and for the cities of
our God: and [c]the LORD do that which
seemeth him good.
13 And Joab drew nigh, and the people
that *were* with him, unto the battle against the
Syrians: and they fled before him.
14 And when the children of Ammon saw
that the Syrians were fled, *then* fled they *also*
before Abishai, and entered *into* the city. So
Joab returned from the children of Ammon,
and came *to* Jerusalem.
15 ¶ And when the Syrians saw that they
were smitten before Israel, they gathered
themselves together.
16 And Hadarezer sent, and brought out
the Syrians that *were* beyond [1]the river: and
they came *to* Helam; and [2]Shobach the captain
of the host of Hadarezer *went* before them.
17 And when it was told David, he gathered all Israel together, and passed over Jordan, and came to Helam. And the Syrians set
themselves in array against David, and fought
with him.
18 And the Syrians fled before Israel; and
David slew *the men of* seven hundred chariots
of the Syrians, and forty thousand [1]horsemen,
and smote Shobach the captain of their host,
who died there.
19 And when all the kings *that were* servants to Hadarezer saw that they were smitten
before Israel, they made peace with Israel, and
[a]served them. So the Syrians feared to help
the children of Ammon any more.

David's sin against Uriah

11 And it came to pass, [1]after the year
was expired, at the time when kings
go forth *to battle,* that [a]David sent Joab, and
his servants with him, and all Israel; and they
destroyed the children of Ammon, and besieged Rabbah. But David tarried *still* at Jerusalem.

10:1 [a]1 Chr. 19:1
10:3 [1]Heb. *In thine eyes doth David*
10:4 [a]Is. 20:4; 47:2
10:6 [1][Or, *the men of Tob.* See Judg. 11:3,5] [a]Gen. 34:30; Ex. 5:21; 1 Sam. 13:4 [b]ch. 8:3,5
10:7 [a]ch. 23:8
10:8 [a]ver. 6
10:12 [a]Deut. 31:6 [b]1 Sam. 4:9; 1 Cor. 16:13 [c]1 Sam. 3:18
10:16 [1][That is, *Euphrates*] [2][Or, *Shophach,* 1 Chr. 19:16]
10:18 [1][1 Chr. 19:18, *footmen*]
10:19 [a]ch. 8:6
11:1 [1]Heb. *at the return of the year* [a]1 Chr. 20:1

10:1 *king.* Nahash (see v. 2; 1 Sam 11). *children of Ammon.* See note on 1 Sam 11:1.

10:2 *shew kindness.* The Hebrew for this expression suggests that a formal treaty existed between the Israelites and the Ammonites. Perhaps this explains why there is no account of a war against the Ammonites in ch. 8, and why the Ammonites did not come to the assistance of the Moabites (8:2).

10:3 *city.* Rabbah, the capital (11:1; 12:26).

10:4 *shaved off the one half of their beards.* In the Eastern world of that time this was considered an insult of the most serious kind. A beard was shaved only as a sign of deep mourning (see Is 15:2; Jer 41:5; Ezek 5:1). *cut off their garments . . . even to their buttocks.* A customary way of degrading prisoners of war (see Is 20:4).

10:5 *Jericho.* See notes on Josh 6:1,26; 1 Ki 16:34. Jericho remained unrestored during the centuries between Joshua's conquest and the time of Ahab.

‡10:6 *Beth-rehob.* See Num 13:21; Judg 18:28. *Zoba.* See note on 8:3. *Maacah.* See Deut 3:14; Josh 12:5; 13:13. *Ish-tob.* See KJV marg.; also rendered "land of Tob."

10:10 *Abishai.* See note on 1 Sam 26:6.

‡10:16 *Hadarezer.* Hebrew *Hadadezer.* See note on 8:3. *Helam.* A town close to the northern border of Gilead.

10:18 *seven hundred.* Evidently a copyist's mistake; in 1 Chr 19:18 the figure is 7,000.

10:19 *they made peace with Israel.* There is no indication that Hadadezer himself made peace with Israel as his vassals did in the aftermath of this defeat. These events represent David's last major campaign against combined foreign powers.

‡11:1 *after the year was expired.* I.e. the spring of the year following the events reported in ch. 10. The time must have been about ten years after David became established in Jerusalem. *the time when kings go forth to battle.* Directly after the grain harvest in April and May. *Rabbah.* See note on 10:3. Though now alone (see 10:19), the Ammonites had not yet been subjugated.

2 And it came to pass in an eveningtide, that David arose from off his bed, [a]and walked upon the roof of the king's house: and from the roof he [b]saw a woman washing *herself;* and the woman *was* very beautiful to look upon.

3 And David sent and inquired after the woman. And *one* said, *Is* not this [1]Bath-sheba, the daughter of [2]Eliam, the wife [a]of Uriah the Hittite?

4 And David sent messengers, and took her; and she came in unto him, and [a]he lay with her; [1]for she was [b]purified from her uncleanness: and she returned unto her house.

5 And the woman conceived, and sent and told David, and said, I *am* with child.

6 And David sent to Joab, *saying,* Send me Uriah the Hittite. And Joab sent Uriah to David.

7 And when Uriah was come unto him, David demanded *of him* [1]how Joab did, and how the people did, and how the war prospered.

8 And David said to Uriah, Go down to thy house, and [a]wash thy feet. And Uriah departed out of the king's house, and there [1]followed him a mess *of meat* from the king.

9 But Uriah slept *at* the door of the king's house with all the servants of his lord, and went not down to his house.

10 And when they had told David, saying, Uriah went not down unto his house, David said unto Uriah, Camest thou not from *thy* journey? why *then* didst thou not go down unto thine house?

11 And Uriah said unto David, [a]The ark, and Israel, and Judah, abide in tents; and [b]my lord Joab, and the servants of my lord, are encamped in the open fields; shall I then go into mine house, to eat and to drink, and to lie with my wife? *as* thou livest, and *as* thy soul liveth, I will not do this thing.

12 And David said to Uriah, Tarry here to day also, and to morrow I will let thee depart. So Uriah abode in Jerusalem that day, and the morrow.

13 And when David had called him, he did eat and drink before him; and he made him [a]drunk: and at even he went out to lie on his bed [b]with the servants of his lord, but went not down to his house.

14 And it came to pass in the morning, that David [a]wrote a letter to Joab, and sent *it* by the hand of Uriah.

15 And he wrote in the letter, saying, Set ye Uriah in the forefront of the [1]hottest battle, and retire ye [2]from him, that he may [a]be smitten, and die.

16 And it came to pass, when Joab observed the city, that he assigned Uriah unto a place where he knew that valiant men *were.*

17 And the men of the city went out, and fought with Joab: and there fell *some* of the people of the servants of David; and Uriah the Hittite died also.

18 Then Joab sent and told David all the things concerning the war;

19 And charged the messenger, saying, When thou hast made an end of telling the matters of the war unto the king,

20 And if so be that the king's wrath arise, and he say unto thee, Wherefore approached ye *so* nigh unto the city when *ye* did fight? knew ye not that they would shoot from the wall?

21 Who smote [a]Abimelech the son of [1]Jerubbesheth? did not a woman cast a piece of a millstone upon him from the wall, that he died in Thebez? why went ye nigh the wall? then say thou, Thy servant Uriah the Hittite is dead also.

22 So the messenger went, and came and shewed David all that Joab had sent him for.

11:2 [a]Deut. 22:8 [b]Gen. 34:2; Job 31:1; Mat. 5:28
11:3 [1][Or, *Bath-shua,* 1 Chr. 3:5] [2][Or, *Ammiel*] [a]ch. 23:39
11:4 [1]Or, *and when she had purified herself, etc. she returned* [a]Ps. 51, title; Jas. 1:14 [b]Lev. 15:19,28; 18:19
11:7 [1]Heb. *of the peace of, etc.*
11:8 [1]Heb. *went out after him* [a]Gen. 18:4; 19:2
11:11 [a]ch. 7:2,6 [b]ch. 20:6
11:13 [a]Gen. 19:33,35 [b]ver. 9
11:14 [a]See 1 Ki. 21:8,9
11:15 [1]Heb. *strong* [2]Heb. *from after him* [a]ch. 12:9
11:21 [1][Judg. 6:32, *Jerubbaal*] [a]Judg. 9:53

11:2 *walked upon the roof.* The roofs were flat (see 1 Sam 9:25). David had probably gone there to enjoy the cool evening air.
11:3 *Eliam.* Perhaps the same Eliam who was a member of David's personal bodyguard (23:34) and a son of his counselor Ahithophel. *Uriah.* Also listed among those comprising David's royal guard (23:39). His name suggests that even though he was a Hittite, he had adopted the Israelite faith (Uriah means "My light is the LORD"). *Hittite.* See note on 1 Sam 26:6.
11:4 *David sent messengers, and took her.* Through this action David eventually becomes guilty of breaking the sixth, seventh, ninth and tenth commandments (Ex 20:13–17). *she came in unto him, and he lay with her.* Bath-sheba appears to have been an unprotesting partner in this adulterous relationship with David. *she was purified from her uncleanness.* Lev 15:18 required purification after sexual relations.
11:5 *I am with child.* Bath-sheba leaves the next step up to David. The law prescribed the death penalty for both David and Bath-sheba (Lev 20:10; Deut 22:22), as they well knew.
11:6 *Send me Uriah.* Under the pretense of seeking information about the course of the war, David brings Uriah back to Jerusalem.
‡11:8 *Go down to thy house, and wash thy feet.* In essence, David tells Uriah to go home and relax. What he does not say specifically is what is most important, and well understood by Uriah (v.11). *there followed him a mess of meat from the king.* The Hebrew word for "mess [i.e. portion]" has the meaning of "food" in Gen 43:34 ("mess" from the king's table). David wanted Uriah and Bath-sheba to enjoy their evening together.
11:11 *ark.* Uriah's statement suggests that the ark was in the field camp with the army rather than in the tent that David had set up for it in Jerusalem (6:17). If so, it was probably there for purposes of worship and to seek guidance for the war. But then the circumstances are even more damning for David—the Lord is in the field with His army while David stays at home in leisure. *shall I then go into mine house . . . ?* Uriah's devotion to duty exposes by sharp contrast David's dalliance at home while his men are in the field. *as thou livest, and as thy soul liveth.* See note on 1 Sam 1:26.
11:13 *he made him drunk.* In the hope that in this condition he would relent and go to Bath-sheba.
11:15 *that he may be smitten, and die.* Unsuccessful in making it appear that Uriah was the father of Bath-sheba's child, David plotted Uriah's death so he could marry Bath-sheba himself as quickly as possible.
11:21 *Jerubbesheth.* That is, Gideon. Another possible spelling is "Jerubbosheth." In Judges he is called Jerubbaal (see note on Judg 6:32). For similar name changes by the author of Samuel see notes on 2:8; 4:4. *millstone.* See Judg 9:52–53. *Uriah . . . is dead.* Joab knows that this news is of great importance to

23 And the messenger said unto David, Surely the men prevailed against us, and came out unto us *into* the field, and we were upon them *even* unto the entering of the gate.

24 And the shooters shot from off the wall upon thy servants; and *some* of the king's servants be dead, and thy servant Uriah the Hittite is dead also.

25 Then David said unto the messenger, Thus shalt thou say unto Joab, Let not this thing [1]displease thee, for the sword devoureth [2]one as well as another: make thy battle *more* strong against the city, and overthrow it: and encourage thou him.

26 And when the wife of Uriah heard that Uriah her husband was dead, she mourned for her husband.

27 And when the mourning was past, David sent and fet her to his house, and she [a]became his wife, and bare him a son. But the thing that David had done [1]displeased the LORD.

David repents

12 And the LORD sent Nathan unto David. And [a]he came unto him, and [b]said unto him, There were two men in one city; the one rich, and the other poor.

2 The rich *man* had exceeding many flocks and herds:

3 But the poor *man* had nothing, save one little ewe lamb, which he had bought and nourished up: and it grew up together with him, and with his children; it did eat of his own [1]meat, and drank of his own cup, and lay in his bosom, and was unto him as a daughter.

4 And there came a traveller unto the rich man, and he spared to take of his own flock and of his own herd, to dress for the wayfaring man that was come unto him; but took the poor man's lamb, and dressed it for the man that was come to him.

5 And David's anger was greatly kindled against the man; and he said to Nathan, *As* the LORD liveth, the man that hath done this *thing* [1]shall surely die:

6 And he shall restore the lamb [a]fourfold, because he did this thing, and because he had no pity.

7 And Nathan said to David, Thou *art* the man. Thus saith the LORD God of Israel, I [a]anointed thee king over Israel, and I delivered thee out of the hand of Saul;

8 And I gave thee thy master's house, and thy master's wives into thy bosom, and gave thee the house of Israel and of Judah; and if *that had been too* little, I would moreover have given unto thee such and such things.

9 [a]Wherefore hast thou [b]despised the commandment of the LORD, to do evil in his sight? [c]thou hast killed Uriah the Hittite with the sword, and hast taken his wife to be thy wife, and hast slain him with the sword of the children of Ammon.

10 Now therefore [a]the sword shall never depart from thine house, because thou hast despised me, and hast taken the wife of Uriah the Hittite to be thy wife.

11 Thus saith the LORD, Behold, I will raise up evil against thee out of thine own house, and I will [a]take thy wives before thine eyes, and give *them* unto thy neighbour, and he shall lie with thy wives in the sight of this sun.

12 For thou didst *it* secretly: [a]but I will do this thing before all Israel, and before the sun.

13 [a]And David said unto Nathan, [b]I have sinned against the LORD. And Nathan said unto David, The LORD also hath [c]put away thy sin; thou shalt not die.

14 Howbeit, because by this deed thou hast given great occasion to the enemies of the LORD [a]to blaspheme, the child also that is born unto thee shall surely die.

11:25 [1]Heb. *be evil in thine eyes* [2]Heb. *so and such*
11:27 [1]Heb. *was evil in the eyes of* [a]ch. 12:9
12:1 [a]Ps. 51, title [b]See ch. 14:5; 1 Ki. 20:35-41; Is. 5:3
12:3 [1]Heb. *morsel*
12:5 [1]Or, is *worthy to die,* [or, is *a son of death,* 1 Sam. 26:16]
12:6 [a]Ex. 22:1; Luke 19:8
12:7 [a]1 Sam. 16:13
12:9 [a]See 1 Sam. 15:19 [b]Num. 15:31 [c]ch. 11:15-17,27
12:10 [a]Amos 7:9
12:11 [a]Deut. 28:30; ch. 16:22
12:12 [a]ch. 16:22
12:13 [a]See 1 Sam. 15:24 [b]ch. 24:10; Job 7:20; Prov. 28:13 [c]ch. 24:10; Job 7:21; Mic. 7:18; Zech. 3:4
12:14 [a]Is. 52:5; Ezek. 36:20,23; Rom. 2:24

David, and he uses it to squelch any criticism David might otherwise have had of the battle tactics.

11:25 *David said unto the messenger.* David hid his satisfaction over the news with a hypocritical statement that war is war and the death of Uriah should not be a discouragement.

11:27 *when the mourning was past.* Presumably a period of seven days (Gen 50:10; 1 Sam 31:13). *she became his wife.* See notes on 3:2–5; 5:14. *the thing that David had done displeased the LORD.* Not only had David brazenly violated God's laws (see note on v. 4) but, even worse, he had shamelessly abused his royal power, which the Lord had entrusted to him to shepherd the Lord's people (5:2; 7:7–8).

12:1 *the LORD sent.* Prophets were messengers from the Lord. Here the Great King sends His emissary to rebuke and announce judgment on the king He had enthroned over His people. *Nathan.* See note on 7:2. *There were two men.* Nathan begins one of the most striking parables in the OT.

12:5 *As the LORD liveth.* See note on 1 Sam 14:39.

12:6 *fourfold.* In agreement with the requirements of Ex 22:1.

12:8 *thy master's wives.* Earlier narratives refer to only one wife of Saul (Ahinoam, 1 Sam 14:50) and one concubine (Rizpah, 2 Sam 3:7; 21:8). This statement suggests that there were others. But since it was customary for new kings to assume the harem of their predecessors (see note on 3:7), it may be that Nathan merely uses conventional language to emphasize that the Lord had placed David on Saul's throne. *I . . . gave thee the house of Israel and of Judah.* See 2:4; 5:2–3.

12:9 *despised the commandment of the LORD.* See notes on 11:4,27. *thou . . . hast slain him.* David is held directly responsible for Uriah's death even though he fell in battle (see 11:15).

12:10 *the sword shall never depart from thine house.* Three of David's sons came to violent deaths: Amnon (13:28–29), Absalom (18:14) and Adonijah (1 Ki 2:24,25).

12:11 *I will raise up evil against thee out of thine own house.* David was driven from Jerusalem by Absalom's conspiracy to seize the kingship from his own father (15:1–15). *he shall lie with thy wives in the sight of this sun.* Fulfilled at the time of Absalom's rebellion (see note on 16:22).

12:13 *I have sinned against the LORD.* David recognizes his guilt and confesses his sin in response to Nathan's rebuke (see Ps 51). There is a clear contrast between David's confession and Saul's (see note on 1 Sam 15:24). *The LORD also hath put away thy sin.* David experienced the joy of knowing his sin was forgiven (see Ps 32:1,5; cf. Ps 51:8,12). *thou shalt not die.* The Lord, in his grace, released David from the customary death penalty for adultery and murder (Lev 20:10; 24:17).

12:14 *thou hast given great occasion to the enemies of the LORD*

15 ¶ And Nathan departed unto his house.
And the LORD strake the child that Uriah's wife
bare unto David, and it was very sick.
16 David therefore besought God for the
child; and David [1]fasted, and went in, and [a]lay
all night upon the earth.
17 And the elders of his house arose, *and*
went to him, to raise him up from the earth:
but he would not, neither did he eat bread
with them.
18 And it came to pass on the seventh day,
that the child died. And the servants of David
feared to tell him that the child was dead: for
they said, Behold, while the child was *yet*
alive, we spake unto him, and he would not
hearken unto our voice: how will he then
[1]vex himself, if we tell him *that* the child is
dead?
19 But when David saw that his servants
whispered, David perceived that the child was
dead: therefore David said unto his servants, Is
the child dead? And they said, He is dead.
20 Then David arose from the earth, and
washed, and anointed *himself,* and changed
his apparel, and came *into* the house of the
LORD, and [a]worshipped: then he came to his
own house; and when he required, they set
bread before him, and he did eat.
21 Then said his servants unto him, What
thing *is* this that thou hast done? thou didst
fast and weep for the child, *while it was* alive;
but when the child was dead, thou didst rise
and eat bread.
22 And he said, While the child *was* yet
alive, I fasted and wept: [a]for I said, Who can
tell *whether* GOD will be gracious to me, that
the child may live?
23 But now he is dead, wherefore should I
fast? can I bring him back again? I shall go to
him, but [a]he shall not return to me.
24 And David comforted Bath-sheba his
wife, and went in unto her, and lay with her:
and [a]she bare a son, and [b]he called his name
Solomon: and the LORD loved him.
25 And he sent by the hand of Nathan the
prophet; and he called his name [1]Jedidiah, because of the LORD.

12:16 [1]Heb. *fasted a fast* [a]ch. 13:31
12:18 [1]Heb. *do hurt*
12:20 [a]Job 1:20
12:22 [a]See Is. 38:1,5; Jonah 3:9
12:23 [a]Job 7:8-10
12:24 [a]Mat. 1:6 [b]1 Chr. 22:9
12:25 [1]That is, *Beloved of the LORD*

12:26 [a]1 Chr. 20:1 [b]Deut. 3:11
12:28 [1]Heb. *my name be called upon it*
12:30 [1]Heb. *very great* [a]1 Chr. 20:2
13:1 [a]ch. 3:2,3 [b]1 Chr. 3:9
13:2 [1]Heb. *it was marvellous,* or, *hidden in the eyes of Amnon*
13:3 [a]See 1 Sam. 16:9
13:4 [1]Heb. *thin* [2]Heb. *morning by morning*

Victory over the children of Ammon

26 ¶ And [a]Joab fought against [b]Rabbah of
the children of Ammon, and took the royal
city.
27 And Joab sent messengers to David, and
said, I have fought against Rabbah, and have
taken the city of waters.
28 Now therefore gather the rest of the
people together, and encamp against the city,
and take it: lest I take the city, and [1]it be called
after my name.
29 And David gathered all the people together, and went to Rabbah, and fought against
it, and took it.
30 [a]And he took their king's crown from
off his head, the weight whereof *was* a talent
of gold with the precious stones: and it was *set*
on David's head. And he brought forth the
spoil of the city [1]in great abundance.
31 And he brought forth the people that
were therein, and put *them* under saws, and
under harrows of iron, and under axes of iron,
and made them pass through the brickkiln:
and thus did he unto all the cities of the children of Ammon. So David and all the people
returned *unto* Jerusalem.

Amnon defiles Tamar

13 And it came to pass after this, [a]that
Absalom the son of David had a fair
sister, whose name *was* [b]Tamar; and Amnon
the son of David loved her.
2 And Amnon was *so* vexed, that he fell
sick for his sister Tamar; for she *was* a virgin;
and [1]Amnon thought it hard for him to do any
thing to her.
3 But Amnon had a friend, whose name
was Jonadab, [a]the son of Shimeah David's
brother: and Jonadab *was* a very subtil man.
4 And he said unto him, Why *art* thou, *be-*
ing the king's son, [1]lean [2]from day to day? wilt
thou not tell me? And Amnon said unto him, I
love Tamar, my brother Absalom's sister.
5 And Jonadab said unto him, Lay *thee*
down on thy bed, and make thyself sick: and
when thy father cometh to see thee, say unto
him, I pray thee, let my sister Tamar come,

---

to blaspheme. David is required to suffer the disciplinary results of his sin in a manner open to public view.

12:20 *came into the house of the LORD, and worshipped.* In this way David clearly demonstrated his humble acceptance of the disciplinary results of his sin. Again (see note on v. 13) there is a contrast between David's attitude and Saul's (see note on 1 Sam 15:25).

12:23 *I shall go to him.* Like the child, David will die and join him in the grave (see note on Gen 37:35).

12:24 *Solomon.* See 1 Chr 22:9 and note.

12:25 *Jedidiah.* Means "beloved of the LORD." The giving of this name suggests that the Lord's special favor rested on Solomon from his birth. And since the name also contained an echo of David's name, it provided assurance to David that the Lord also loved him and would continue his dynasty.

12:26 *Joab fought against Rabbah.* The writer now returns to the outcome of the attack against the Ammonites (11:1,25), which provided the background for the story of David and Bath-sheba. Even while the Lord was displeased with David, He gave the Israelites victory over a people who had abused them.

12:30 *their king's crown . . . was set on David's head.* A crown of such weight (about 75 pounds) would have been worn only briefly and on very special occasions. Perhaps it was worn only once in a symbolic act of transferring to David sovereignty over Ammon.

12:31 *put them under saws . . . brickkiln.* Had them tortured and/or killed in keeping with their own cruel practices (see 1 Sam 11:2; Amos 1:13).

13:1–39 The trouble within David's family begins (see note on 12:10).

13:1 *Tamar.* David's daughter by Maacah of Geshur (3:3), and Absalom's full sister. *Amnon.* David's oldest son (3:2).

13:3 *Shimeah.* Called Shammah in 1 Sam 16:9.

David's Conquests

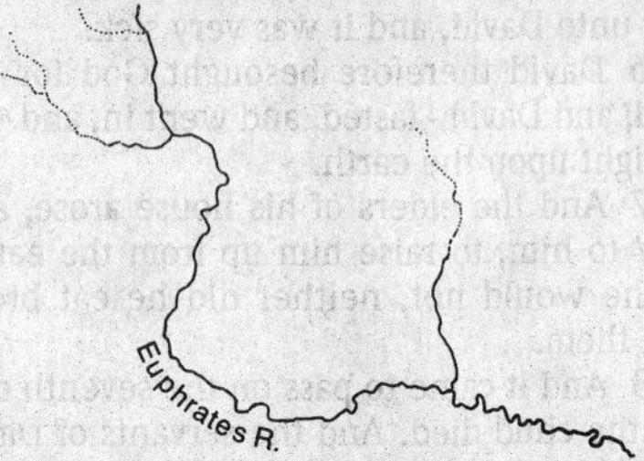

Once he had become king over all Israel (2 Sam 5:1-5), David:

1. Conquered the Jebusite citadel of Zion/Jerusalem and made it his royal city (2 Sam 5:6-10);
2. Received the recognition of and assurance of friendship from Hiram of Tyre, king of the Phoenicians (2 Sam 5:11-12);
3. Decisively defeated the Philistines so that their hold on Israelite territory was broken and their threat to Israel eliminated (2 Sam 5:17-25; 8:1);
4. Defeated the Moabites and imposed his authority over them (2 Sam 8:2);
5. Crushed the Aramean kingdoms of Hadadezer (king of Zobah), Damascus and Maacah and put them under tribute (2 Sam 8:3-8; 10:6-19). Talmai, the Aramean king of Geshur, apparently had made peace with David while he was still reigning in Hebron and sealed the alliance by giving his daughter in marriage to David (2 Sam 3:3; see 1 Chr 2:23);
6. Subdued Edom and incorporated it into his empire (2 Sam 8:13-14);
7. Defeated the Ammonites and brought them into subjection (2 Sam 12:19-31);
8. Subjugated the remaining Canaanite cities that had previously maintained their independence from and hostility toward Israel, such as Beth-shan, Megiddo, Taanach and Dor.

Since David had earlier crushed the Amalekites (1 Sam 30:17), his wars thus completed the conquest begun by Joshua and secured all the borders of Israel. His empire (united Israel plus the subjugated kingdoms) reached from Ezion-geber on the eastern arm of the Red sea to the Euphrates River.

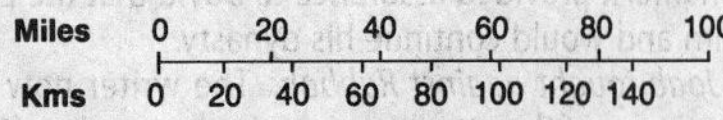

and give me meat, and dress the meat in my
sight, that I may see *it,* and eat *it* at her hand.
6 So Amnon lay down, and made himself
sick: and when the king was come to see him,
Amnon said unto the king, I pray thee, let Tamar my sister come, and [a]make *me* a couple of
cakes in my sight, that I may eat at her hand.
7 Then David sent home to Tamar, saying,
Go now *to* thy brother Amnon's house, and
dress him meat.
8 So Tamar went *to* her brother Amnon's
house; and he was laid down. And she took
[1]flour, and kneaded *it,* and made cakes in his
sight, and did bake the cakes.
9 And she took a pan, and poured *them* out
before him; but he refused to eat. And Amnon
said, [a]Have out all men from me. And they
went out every man from him.
10 And Amnon said unto Tamar, Bring the
meat *into* the chamber, that I may eat of thine
hand. And Tamar took the cakes which she
had made, and brought *them* into the chamber
to Amnon her brother.
11 And when she had brought *them* unto
him to eat, he [a]took hold of her, and said unto
her, Come lie with me, my sister.
12 And she answered him, Nay, my brother, do not [a][1]force me; for [b][2]no such thing
ought to be done in Israel: do not thou this
[c]folly.
13 And I, whither shall I cause my shame
to go? and *as for* thee, thou shalt be as one of
the fools in Israel. Now therefore, I pray thee,
speak unto the king; [a]for he will not withhold
me from thee.
14 Howbeit he would not hearken unto
her voice: but, being stronger than she,
[a]forced her, and lay with her.
15 Then Amnon hated her [1]exceedingly;
so that the hatred wherewith he hated her
was greater than the love wherewith he had
loved her. And Amnon said unto her, Arise, be
gone.
16 And she said unto him, *There is* no
cause: this evil in sending me away *is* greater
than the other that thou didst unto me. But he
would not hearken unto her.
17 Then he called his servant that ministered unto him, and said, Put now this *woman*
out from me, and bolt the door after her.
18 And *she had* [a]a garment of divers
colours upon her: for with such robes were
the king's daughters *that were* virgins apparelled. Then his servant brought her out, and
bolted the door after her.
19 And Tamar put [a]ashes on her head, and
rent her garment of divers colours that *was* on
her, and [b]laid her hand on her head, and went
on crying.
20 And Absalom her brother said unto her,
Hath [1]Amnon thy brother been with thee? but
hold now thy peace, my sister: he *is* thy brother; [2]regard not this thing. So Tamar remained
[3]desolate *in* her brother Absalom's house.
21 But when king David heard of all these
things, he was very wroth.
22 And Absalom spake unto his brother
Amnon [a]neither good nor bad: for Absalom
[b]hated Amnon, because he had forced his sister Tamar.

Absalom kills Amnon; Absalom flees to Geshur

23 ¶ And it came to pass after two full
years, that Absalom [a]had sheepshearers in
Baal-hazor, which *is* beside Ephraim: and Absalom invited all the king's sons.
24 And Absalom came to the king, and
said, Behold now, thy servant hath
sheepshearers; let the king, I beseech thee,
and his servants go with thy servant.
25 And the king said to Absalom, Nay, my
son, let us not all now go, lest we be chargeable unto thee. And he pressed him: howbeit
he would not go, but blessed him.
26 Then said Absalom, If not, I pray thee,
let my brother Amnon go with us. And the king
said unto him, Why should he go with thee?

13:6 [a]Gen. 18:6
13:8 [1]Or, *paste*
13:9 [a]Gen. 45:1
13:11 [a]Gen. 39:12
13:12 [1]Heb. *humble me* [2]Heb. *it ought not so to be done* [a]Gen. 34:2 [b]Lev. 18:9,11; 20:17 [c]Gen. 34:7; Judg. 19:23; 20:6
13:13 [a]See Lev. 18:9,11
13:14 [a]Deut. 22:25; See ch. 12:11
13:15 [1]Heb. with *great hatred greatly*
13:18 [a]Gen. 37:3; Judg. 5:30
13:19 [a]Josh. 7:6; ch. 1:2; Job 2:12 [b]Jer. 2:37
13:20 [1][Heb. *Aminon*] [2]Heb. *set not thine heart* [*upon*] [3]Heb. *and desolate*
13:22 [a]Gen. 24:50; 31:24 [b]Lev. 19:17,18
13:23 [a]See Gen. 38:12,13; 1 Sam. 25:4,36

13:13 *as for thee.* This act would jeopardize Amnon's position as crown prince and heir to the throne. *he will not withhold me from thee.* Possibly a futile attempt by Tamar to escape Amnon's immediate designs rather than a serious proposal, since such a marriage was prohibited in Israel (see Lev 18:9; 20:17; Deut 27:22).

13:15 *Amnon hated her.* The reversal in Amnon's feelings toward Tamar demonstrates that his former "love" (v. 1) was nothing but sensual desire.

13:16 *this evil in sending me away is greater.* No longer a virgin, she could not be offered by her father to any other potential husband (see v. 21 and note).

‡13:18 *garment of divers colours.* Hebrew is uncertain. Perhaps a long-sleeved or embroidered garment. See also Gen 37:3 and note.

13:19 *put ashes on her head.* A sign of great mourning. *rent her garment of divers colours.* Thus expressing her anguish and announcing that her virginity had been violated. *laid her hand on her head.* Also a sign of grief (see Jer 2:37).

13:20 *hold now thy peace, my sister . . . regard not this thing.* Absalom urges his sister not to make the matter a public scandal, and attempts to quiet her by minimizing its significance. Meanwhile, he formulates his own secret plans for revenge (see vv. 22,28,32).

13:21 *he was very wroth.* Although David was incensed by Amnon's rape of Tamar, there is no record that he took any punitive action against him. Perhaps the memory of his own sin with Bath-sheba adversely affected his judicious handling of the matter. Whatever the reason, David abdicated his responsibility both as king and as father. This disciplinary leniency toward his sons (see notes on 14:33; 1 Ki 1:6) eventually led to the death of Amnon and the revolts of Absalom and Adonijah.

13:22 *Absalom spake unto . . . Amnon neither good nor bad . . . Absalom hated Amnon.* He quietly bided his time.

13:23 *Absalom invited all the king's sons.* The time of sheepshearing was a festive occasion (see 1 Sam 25:4,8).

13:26 *let my brother Amnon go with us.* Upon David's refusal of the invitation, Absalom diplomatically requested that Amnon, the crown prince and oldest son, be his representative. *Why should he go with thee?* David's question suggests some misgivings because of the strained relationship between the two half brothers (see v. 22).

27 But Absalom pressed him, that he let Amnon and all the king's sons go with him.

28 Now Absalom had commanded his servants, saying, Mark ye now when Amnon's [a]heart is merry with wine, and when I say unto you, Smite Amnon; then kill him, fear not: [1]have not I commanded you? be courageous, and be [2]valiant.

29 And the servants of Absalom did unto Amnon as Absalom had commanded. Then all the king's sons arose, and every man [1]gat him up upon his mule, and fled.

30 And it came to pass, while they *were* in the way, that tidings came to David, saying, Absalom hath slain all the king's sons, and there is not one of them left.

31 Then the king arose, and [a]tare his garments, and [b]lay on the earth; and all his servants stood *by* with their clothes rent.

32 And [a]Jonadab, the son of Shimeah David's brother, answered and said, Let not my lord suppose *that* they have slain all the young men the king's sons; for Amnon only is dead: for by the [1]appointment of Absalom *this* hath been [2]determined from the day that he forced his sister Tamar.

33 Now therefore [a]let not my lord the king take the thing to his heart, to think *that* all the king's sons are dead: for Amnon only is dead.

34 [a]But Absalom fled. And the young man that kept the watch lift up his eyes, and looked, and behold, there came much people by the way of the hill side behind him.

35 And Jonadab said unto the king, Behold, the king's sons come: [1]as thy servant said, so it is.

36 And it came to pass, as soon as he had made an end of speaking, that behold, the king's sons came, and lift up their voice and wept: and the king also and all his servants wept [1]very sore.

37 But Absalom fled, and went to [a]Talmai, the son of [1]Ammihud, king of Geshur. And *David* mourned for his son every day.

38 So Absalom fled, and went to [a]Geshur, and was there three years.

39 And *the soul of* king David [1]longed to go forth unto Absalom: for he was [a]comforted concerning Amnon, seeing he was dead.

Absalom's return

14 Now Joab the son of Zeruiah perceived that the king's heart *was* [a]toward Absalom.

2 And Joab sent to [a]Tekoah, and fetcht thence a wise woman, and said unto her, I pray thee, feign thyself to be a mourner, [b]and put on now mourning apparel, and anoint not *thyself with* oil, but be as a woman *that had* a long time mourned for the dead:

3 And come to the king, and speak on this manner unto him. So Joab [a]put the words in her mouth.

4 And when the woman of Tekoah spake to the king, she [a]fell on her face to the ground, and did obeisance, and said, [b][1]Help, O king.

5 And the king said unto her, What aileth thee? And she answered, [a]I *am* indeed a widow woman, and mine husband is dead.

6 And thy handmaid had two sons, and they two strove together in the field, and *there was* [1]none to part them, but the one smote the other, and slew him.

7 And behold, the whole family is risen against thine handmaid, and they said, Deliver him that smote his brother, that we may kill him, for the life of his brother whom he slew; and we will destroy the heir also: and *so* they shall quench my coal which is left, and shall not leave to my husband *neither* name nor remainder [1]upon the earth.

8 And the king said unto the woman, Go to

13:28 [1]Or, will you *not, since I have commanded you?* [2]Heb. *sons of valour* [a]Judg. 19:6,9,22; Ruth 3:7; 1 Sam. 25:36; Esth. 1:10
13:29 [1]Heb. *rode*
13:31 [a]ch. 1:11 [b]ch. 12:16
13:32 [1]Heb. *mouth* [2]Or, *settled* [a]ver. 3
13:33 [a]ch. 19:19
13:34 [a]ver. 38
13:35 [1]Heb. *according to the word of thy servant*
13:36 [1]Heb. with *a great weeping greatly*
13:37 [1]Or, *Ammihur* [a]ch. 3:3
13:38 [a]ch. 14:23,32; 15:8
13:39 [1]Or, *was consumed* [a]Gen. 38:12
14:1 [a]ch. 13:39
14:2 [a]2 Chr. 11:6 [b]See Ruth 3:3
14:3 [a]ver. 19; Ex. 4:15
14:4 [1]Heb. *Save* [a]1 Sam. 20:41; ch. 1:2 [b]See 2 Ki. 6:26,28
14:5 [a]See ch. 12:1
14:6 [1]Heb. *no deliverer between them*
14:7 [1]Heb. *upon the face of the earth*

13:28 *kill him.* Absalom arranged for the murder of his half brother in violation of Eastern hospitality. In the wicked acts of Amnon and Absalom, David's oldest sons became guilty of sexual immorality and murder, as their father had before them. With the murder of Amnon, Absalom not only avenged the rape of his sister but also secured for himself the position of successor to the throne (see 3:3; 15:1–6). Chileab, David's second son (3:3), may have died in his youth since there is no reference to him beyond the announcement of his birth.

13:29 *mule.* Apparently the normal mount for royalty in David's kingdom (see 18:9; 1 Ki 1:33,38,44; see also note on 1 Ki 1:33).

13:31 *tare his garments, and lay on the earth.* Common ways of expressing grief (see Josh 7:6; 1 Ki 21:27; Esth 4:1,3; Job 1:20; 2:8).

13:37 *Talmai, the son of Ammihud, king of Geshur.* Absalom's grandfather (see 3:3).

13:39 *longed to go forth unto Absalom.* With Absalom a refugee, David had lost both of his oldest living sons.

14:1 *Joab the son of Zeruiah.* See note on 2:13. *the king's heart was toward Absalom.* Torn between anger and love (and perhaps remorse), David again leaves the initiative to others.

14:2 *And Joab sent.* Joab appears to have been motivated by a concern for the political implications of the unresolved dispute between David and the son in line for the throne. He attempts to move David to action by means of a story designed to elicit a response clearly applicable, by analogy, to David's own predicament. A similar technique was used by Nathan the prophet (12:1–7; see 1 Ki 20:38–43). *Tekoah.* A town a few miles south of Beth-lehem, from which the prophet Amos also came (Amos 1:1).

14:7 *the whole family is risen against thine handmaid.* It was customary in Israel for a murder victim's next of kin to avenge the blood of his relative by putting the murderer to death (see note on 3:27; see also Num 35:12; Deut 19:11–13). In the case presented, however, blood revenge would wipe out the family line, which was something Israelite law and custom tried to avoid if at all possible (see notes on Deut 25:5–6; Ruth 2:20). *destroy the heir also.* The woman suggests that the motivation for blood revenge was more a selfish desire to acquire the family inheritance than a desire for justice (see Num 27:11). *leave to my husband neither name nor remainder.* The implication is that it would be a more serious offense to terminate the woman's family line than to permit a murder to go unpunished by blood revenge. Apparently Joab hoped subtly to suggest to David that if he did not restore Absalom, a struggle for the throne would eventually ensue.

14:8 *I will give charge concerning thee.* David's judicial action

thine house, and I will give charge concerning thee.

9 And the woman of Tekoah said unto the king, My lord, O king, [a]the iniquity *be* on me, and on my father's house: [b]and the king and his throne *be* guiltless.

10 And the king said, Whosoever saith *ought* unto thee, bring him to me, and he shall not touch thee any more.

11 Then said she, I pray thee, let the king remember the LORD thy God, [1]that thou wouldest not suffer [a]the revengers of blood to destroy any more, lest they destroy my son. And he said, [b]*As* the LORD liveth, there shall not one hair of thy son fall to the earth.

12 Then the woman said, Let thine handmaid, I pray thee, speak *one* word unto my lord the king. And he said, Say on.

13 And the woman said, Wherefore then hast thou thought such a thing against [a]the people of God? for the king doth speak this thing as one which is faulty, in that the king doth not fetch *home* again [b]his banished.

14 For we [a]must needs die, and *are* as water spilt on the ground, which cannot be gathered up *again;* [1]neither doth God respect *any* person: yet doth he [b]devise means, that *his* banished be not expelled from him.

15 Now therefore that I am come to speak of this thing unto my lord the king, *it is* because the people have made me afraid: and thy handmaid said, I will now speak unto the king; it may be that the king will perform the request of his handmaid.

16 For the king will hear, to deliver his handmaid out of the hand of the man *that would* destroy me and my son together out of the inheritance of God.

17 Then thine handmaid said, The word of my lord the king shall now be [1]comfortable: for [a]as an angel of God, so *is* my lord the king [2]to discern good and bad: therefore the LORD thy God will be with thee.

18 Then the king answered and said unto the woman, Hide not from me, I pray thee, the thing that I shall ask thee. And the woman said, Let my lord the king now speak.

19 And the king said, *Is not* the hand of Joab with thee in all this? And the woman answered and said, *As* thy soul liveth, my lord the king, none can turn to the right hand or to the left from ought that my lord the king hath spoken: for thy servant Joab, he bade me, and [a]he put all these words in the mouth of thine handmaid:

20 To fetch about *this* form of speech hath thy servant Joab done this thing: and my lord *is* wise, [a]according to the wisdom of an angel of God, to know all *things* that *are* in the earth.

21 And the king said unto Joab, Behold now, I have done this thing: go therefore, bring the young man Absalom again.

22 And Joab fell to the ground on his face, and bowed himself, and [1]thanked the king: and Joab said, To day thy servant knoweth that I have found grace in thy sight, my lord, O king, in that the king hath fulfilled the request of [2]his servant.

23 So Joab arose [a]and went to Geshur, and brought Absalom *to* Jerusalem.

24 And the king said, Let him turn to his own house, and let him [a]not see my face. So Absalom returned to his own house, and saw not the king's face.

25 ¶ [1]But in all Israel there was none to be so much praised as Absalom for his beauty: [a]from the sole of his foot even to the crown of his head there was no blemish in him.

26 And when he polled his head, (for it was at every year's end that he polled *it:* because *the hair* was heavy on him, therefore he polled it:) he weighed the hair of his head *at* two hundred shekels after the king's weight.

14:9 [a]Gen. 27:13; 1 Sam. 25:24; Mat. 27:25 [b]ch. 3:28,29; 1 Ki. 2:33
14:11 [1]Heb. *that the revenger of blood do not multiply to destroy* [a]Num. 35:19 [b]1 Sam. 14:45; Acts 27:34
14:13 [a]Judg. 20:2 [b]ch. 13:37,38
14:14 [1]Or, *because God hath not taken away* his *life, he hath also devised means, etc.* [a]Job 34:15; Heb. 9:27 [b]Num. 35:15,25, 28
14:17 [1]Heb. *for rest* [a]ver. 20; ch. 19:27
14:17 [2]Heb. *to hear*
14:19 [a]ver. 3
14:20 [a]ver. 17; ch. 19:27
14:22 [1]Heb. *blessed* [2]Or, *thy*
14:23 [a]ch. 13:37
14:24 [a]Gen. 43:3; ch. 3:13
14:25 [1]Heb. *And as Absalom there was not a beautiful man in all Israel to praise greatly* [a]Is. 1:6

may have rested on the legal ground that the murder was not premeditated (see Deut 19:4–6).

14:9 *iniquity.* For the unpunished crime.

14:11 *let the king remember the LORD thy God.* The woman wants David to confirm his promise by an oath in the Lord's name. *As the LORD liveth.* An oath formula (see notes on Gen 42:15; 1 Sam 14:39) that solemnly binds David to his commitment.

14:13 *against the people of God.* The woman's suggestion is that David has done the same thing to Israel that her family members have done to her. The people of Israel want their crown prince returned safely to them. *the king . . . as one which is faulty.* The argument is that when David exempted the fictitious murderer from blood revenge, he in effect rendered himself guilty for not doing the same in the case of Absalom. The analogy places David in the position of the blood avenger.

14:14 *as water spilt on the ground.* Blood revenge will not return the victim of murder to life, just as water spilled on the ground cannot be recovered. *neither doth God respect any person.* Lit. "God does not take away life." In the suggestion that the avenging of blood is contrary to God's ways of dealing with people, the woman apparently distorts Biblical teaching of God's justice (see note on Gen 9:6). But she dwells on the mercy of God, who would rather preserve life than take it (see Ezek 18:23,32; 33:11). David's own guilt and subsequent experience of God's mercy appear to give added weight to the woman's argument (see notes on 12:13; 13:21).

14:15 *the people have made me afraid.* The woman reverts to her own fabricated story. "The people" are evidently those of her own family who are seeking blood revenge.

14:17 *as an angel of God . . . discern good and bad.* Possessing superhuman powers of discernment—as a king ideally should (see v. 20; 19:27).

14:21 *Joab.* He appears to have been present the whole time.

14:23 *Joab . . . went to Geshur.* See 13:37.

14:24 *let him not see my face.* David still vacillates (see note on v. 1); he does not offer forgiveness and restoration.

14:25 *none . . . so much praised.* Absalom's handsomeness brought him attention and popular favor—which he was soon to cultivate.

14:26 *hair of his head.* For the people of that time, hair was apparently a sign of vigor. Kings and heroic figures were usually portrayed with abundant locks, while baldness was a disgrace (see 2 Ki 2:23). In this, too, Absalom seemed destined for the throne. *king's weight.* The royal shekel was perhaps heavier than the sanctuary shekel (see Ex 30:13; Lev 5:15; Num 3:47).

27 And [a]unto Absalom there were born three sons, and one daughter, whose name *was* Tamar: she was a woman of a fair countenance.

28 So Absalom dwelt two full years in Jerusalem, [a]and saw not the king's face.

29 Therefore Absalom sent for Joab, to have sent him to the king; but he would not come to him: and when he sent again the second time, he would not come.

30 Therefore he said unto his servants, See, Joab's field is [1]near mine, and he hath barley there; go and set it on fire. And Absalom's servants set the field on fire.

31 Then Joab arose, and came to Absalom unto *his* house, and said unto him, Wherefore have thy servants set my field on fire?

32 And Absalom answered Joab, Behold, I sent unto thee, saying, Come hither, that I may send thee to the king, to say, Wherefore am I come from Geshur? *it had been* good for me *to have been* there still: now therefore let me see the king's face; and if there be *any* iniquity in me, let him kill me.

33 So Joab came to the king, and told him: and when he had called for Absalom, he came to the king, and bowed himself on his face to the ground before the king: and the king [a]kissed Absalom.

Absalom's revolt against David

15 And [a]it came to pass after this, that Absalom [b]prepared him chariots and horses, and fifty men to run before him.

2 And Absalom rose up early, and stood beside the way of the gate: and it was *so, that when* any man that had a controversy [1]came to the king for judgment, then Absalom called unto him, and said, Of what city *art* thou? And he said, Thy servant *is* of one of the tribes of Israel.

3 And Absalom said unto him, See, thy matters *are* good and right; but [1]*there is* no man *deputed* of the king to hear thee.

4 Absalom said moreover, [a]Oh that I were made judge in the land, that every man which hath *any* suit or cause might come unto me, and I would do him justice.

5 And it was *so,* that when any man came nigh *to him* to do him obeisance, he put forth his hand, and took him, and kissed him.

6 And on this manner did Absalom to all Israel that came to the king for judgment: [a]so Absalom stole the hearts of the men of Israel.

7 And it came to pass [a]after forty years, that Absalom said unto the king, I pray thee, let me go and pay my vow, which I have vowed unto the LORD, in Hebron.

8 [a]For thy servant [b]vowed a vow [c]while I abode at Geshur in Syria, saying, If the LORD shall bring me again indeed *to* Jerusalem, then I will serve the LORD.

9 And the king said unto him, Go in peace. So he arose, and went to Hebron.

10 But Absalom sent spies throughout all the tribes of Israel, saying, As soon as ye hear the sound of the trumpet, then ye shall say, Absalom reigneth in Hebron.

11 And with Absalom went two hundred men out of Jerusalem, *that were* [a]called; and they went [b]in their simplicity, and they knew not any thing.

12 And Absalom sent *for* Ahithophel the Gilonite, [a]David's counseller, from his city, *even* from [b]Giloh, while he offered sacrifices. And the conspiracy was strong; for the people [c]increased continually with Absalom.

David and his household flee

13 ¶ And there came a messenger to David, saying, [a]The hearts of the men of Israel are after Absalom.

14 And David said unto all his servants that *were* with him at Jerusalem, Arise, and let us

14:27 [a]See ch. 18:18
14:28 [a]ver. 24
14:30 [1]Heb. *near my place*
14:33 [a]Gen. 33:4; 45:15; Luke 15:20
15:1 [a]ch. 12:11 [b]1 Ki. 1:5
15:2 [1]Heb. *to come*
15:3 [1]Or, *none will hear thee from the king downward*
15:4 [a]Judg. 9:29
15:6 [a]Rom. 16:18
15:7 [a]1 Sam. 16:1
15:8 [a]1 Sam. 16:2 [b]Gen. 28:20,21 [c]ch. 13:38
15:11 [a]1 Sam. 9:13; 16:3,5 [b]Gen. 20:5
15:12 [a]Ps. 41:9; 55:12-14 [b]Josh. 15:51 [c]Ps. 3:1
15:13 [a]ver. 6; Judg. 9:3

14:27 *three sons.* Their names are unknown; 18:18 suggests that they died in their youth. *Tamar.* Absalom named his daughter after his sister (13:1). Maachah (1 Ki 15:2) was probably a daughter of Tamar, and Absalom's granddaughter (see note on 2 Chr 11:20).

14:32 *if there be any iniquity in me, let him kill me.* Absalom demands either full pardon and restoration or death, but he still gives no sign of repentance.

14:33 *the king kissed Absalom.* Signifying his forgiveness and Absalom's reconciliation with the royal family. David sidesteps repentance and justice, and in this way he probably contributes to the fulfillment of the prophecy of Nathan (12:10–12).

‡15:1 *chariots* [lit."a chariot"] *and horses.* As far as is known, Absalom was the first Israelite leader to acquire a chariot and horses (cf. Deut 17:16). *fifty men.* They probably functioned as bodyguards and provided a display of royal pomp that appealed to the masses. Adonijah later followed Absalom's example (1 Ki 1:5).

15:3 *thy matters are good.* Absalom seeks to ingratiate himself with the people by endorsing their grievances apart from any investigation into their legitimacy.

15:4 *Oh that I were made judge in the land.* Absalom presents himself as the solution to the people's legal grievances. In the case of Amnon, he had taken matters into his own hands because of his father's laxity. He has found, he believes, the weakness in his father's reign, and he capitalizes on it with political astuteness.

15:7 *forty years.* Some ancient manuscripts read "four years," i.e. four years after Absolom's return to the court (14:33). By this time he must have been about 30 years old, so his revolt must be dated early in the last decade of David's reign. *Hebron.* Where David was first proclaimed king (see notes on 2:1,4; 5:3,5) and where Absalom was born (3:2–3). Absalom may have had reason to believe that he could count on some local resentment over David's transfer of the capital to Jerusalem. Hebron was also the site of an important sanctuary.

15:8 *Geshur.* See 13:37.

15:12 *Ahithophel.* Bath-sheba's grandfather (see 11:3; 23:34) and a wise and respected counselor (16:23). He appears to have secretly aligned himself with Absalom's rebellion in its planning stage, perhaps in retaliation against David for his treatment of Bath-sheba and Uriah. This unsuspected betrayal by a trusted friend may have prompted David's statements in Ps 41:9; 55:12–14. *Gilonite.* Giloh was near Hebron (see Josh 15:51).

15:14 *we shall not else escape from Absalom.* Uncertain of the extent of Absalom's support (see v. 13), David fears being

[a]flee; for we shall not *else* escape from Absalom: make speed to depart, lest he overtake us suddenly, and [1]bring evil upon us, and smite the city with the edge of the sword.

15 And the king's servants said unto the king, Behold, thy servants *are ready to do* whatsoever my lord the king shall [1]appoint.

16 And [a]the king went forth, and all his household [1]after him. And the king left [b]ten women, *which were* concubines, to keep the house.

17 And the king went forth, and all the people after him, and tarried *in* a place that *was* far off.

18 And all his servants passed on beside him; [a]and all the Cherethites, and all the Pelethites, and all the Gittites, six hundred men which came after him from Gath, passed on before the king.

19 Then said the king to [a]Ittai the Gittite, Wherefore goest thou also with us? return to thy place, and abide with the king: for thou *art* a stranger, and also an exile.

20 *Whereas* thou camest *but* yesterday, should I *this* day [1]make thee go up and down with us? seeing I go [a]whither I may, return thou, and take back thy brethren: mercy and truth *be* with thee.

21 And Ittai answered the king, and said, [a]*As* the LORD liveth, and *as* my lord the king liveth, surely in what place my lord the king shall be, whether in death or life, even there *also* will thy servant be.

22 And David said to Ittai, Go and pass over. And Ittai the Gittite passed over, and all his men, and all the little ones that *were* with him.

23 And all the country wept *with* a loud voice, and all the people passed over: the king also *himself* passed over the brook [1]Kidron, and all the people passed over, toward the way of the [a]wilderness.

24 And lo Zadok also, and all the Levites *were* with him, bearing the ark of the covenant of God: and they set down the ark of God; and Abiathar went up, until all the people had done passing out of the city.

25 And the king said unto Zadok, Carry back the ark of God *into* the city: if I shall find favour in the eyes of the LORD, he [a]will bring me again, and shew me *both* it, and his habitation:

26 But if he thus say, I have no [a]delight in thee; behold, *here am* I, [b]let him do to me as seemeth good unto him.

27 The king said also unto Zadok the priest, *Art not* thou a [a]seer? return *into* the city in peace, and [b]your two sons with you, Ahimaaz thy son, and Jonathan the son of Abiathar.

28 See, [a]I will tarry in the plain of the wilderness, until there come word from you to certify me.

29 Zadok therefore and Abiathar carried the ark of God again *to* Jerusalem: and they tarried there.

30 ¶ And David went up by the ascent of *mount* Olivet, [1]and wept as he went up, and [a]had his head covered, and he went [b]barefoot: and all the people that *was* with him [c]covered every man his head, and they went up, [d]weeping as they went up.

31 And *one* told David, saying, [a]Ahithophel *is* among the conspirators with Absalom. And David said, O LORD, I pray thee, [b]turn the counsel of Ahithophel into foolishness.

32 And it came to pass, that *when* David was come to the top *of the mount,* where he worshipped God, behold, Hushai the [a]Archite *came* to meet him [b]with his coat rent, and earth upon his head:

33 Unto whom David said, If thou passest on with me, then thou shalt be [a]a burden unto me:

34 But if thou return *to* the city, and say unto Absalom, [a]I will be thy servant, O king; as I *have been* thy father's servant hitherto, so

15:14 [1]Heb. *thrust* [a]ch. 19:9; Ps. 3, title
15:15 [1]Heb. *choose*
15:16 [1]Heb. *at his feet* [a]Ps. 3, title [b]ch. 16:21,22
15:18 [a]ch. 8:18
15:19 [a]ch. 18:2
15:20 [1]Heb. *make thee wander in going* [a]1 Sam. 23:13
15:21 [a]Ruth 1:16,17
15:23 [1]Called, John 18:1, *Cedron* [a]ch. 16:2
15:25 [a]Ps. 43:3
15:26 [a]Num. 14:8; ch. 22:20; 1 Ki. 10:9; 2 Chr. 9:8; Is. 62:4 [b]1 Sam. 3:18
15:27 [a]1 Sam. 9:9 [b]See ch. 17:17
15:28 [a]ch. 17:16
15:30 [1]Heb. *going up and weeping* [a]ch. 19:4; Esth. 6:12 [b]Is. 20:2,4 [c]Jer. 14:3,4 [d]Ps. 126:6
15:31 [a]Ps. 3:1,2; 55:12 [b]ch. 16:23; 17:14,23
15:32 [a]Josh. 16:2 [b]ch. 1:2
15:33 [a]ch. 19:35
15:34 [a]ch. 16:19

trapped in Jerusalem, and he wants to spare the city a bloodbath.

15:16 *the king left ten women . . . concubines, to keep the house.* See 5:13; see also note on 3:2. David unknowingly arranges for the fulfillment of one of Nathan's prophecies (see note on 12:11; see also 20:3).

15:18 *Cherethites . . . Pelethites.* See note on 8:18. *Gittites, six hundred men.* Philistine soldiers from Gath under the command of Ittai who for some unknown reason had joined David's personal military force (see 18:2).

15:19 *return . . . and abide with the king.* David releases the Philistine contingent from further obligations to him.

15:21 *As the LORD liveth.* An oath of loyalty and devotion taken in the name of Israel's God (see note on 1 Sam 14:39). For a similar oath see Ruth 1:16–17.

15:24 *Zadok.* See note on 8:17. *Abiathar.* See note on 8:17; see also 1 Sam 22:20–23.

15:25 *Carry back the ark of God into the city.* David reveals a true understanding of the connection between the ark and God's presence with His people. He knows that possession of the ark does not guarantee God's blessing (see notes on 1 Sam 4:3,21). He also recognizes that the ark belongs in the capital city as a symbol of the Lord's rule over the nation (see note on 6:2), no matter who the king might be.

15:26 *let him do to me as seemeth good to him.* David confesses that he has no exclusive claim to the throne and that Israel's divine King is free to confer the kingship on whomever He chooses.

15:27 *Art not thou a seer?* Perhaps an allusion to the high priest's custody of the Urim and Thummim as a means of divine revelation (see notes on Ex 28:30; 1 Sam 2:28). See also note on 1 Sam 9:9.

‡15:28 *plain* [lit. "fjords"] *of the wilderness.* Fjords across the Jordan in the vicinity of Gilgal.

15:30 *had his head covered.* A sign of sorrow (see Esth 6:12; Jer 14:3–4). *he went barefoot.* Another sign of sorrow (see Is 20:2,4; Ezek 24:17; Mic 1:8).

15:31 *Ahithophel.* See note on v. 12.

15:32 *Hushai the Archite.* The Archites were a clan (some think non-Israelite) that inhabited an area southwest of Beth-el (Josh 16:2). Since Hushai was a trusted member of David's court (see note on v. 37), his appearance was the beginning of an answer to David's prayer (v. 31).

will I now also *be* thy servant: then mayest
thou for me defeat the counsel of Ahithophel.
35 And *hast thou* not there with thee Zadok and Abiathar the priests? therefore it shall
be, *that* what thing soever thou shalt hear out
of the king's house, [a]thou shalt tell *it* to Zadok
and Abiathar the priests.
36 Behold, *they have* there [a]with them
their two sons, Ahimaaz Zadok's *son,* and Jonathan Abiathar's *son;* and by them ye shall
send unto me every thing that ye can hear.
37 So Hushai [a]David's friend came *into* the
city, [b]and Absalom came *into* Jerusalem.

Ziba's lie

16 And [a]when David was a little past
the top *of the hill,* behold, [b]Ziba the
servant of Mephibosheth met him, with a couple of asses saddled, and upon them two hundred *loaves of* bread, and an hundred bunches
of raisins, and an hundred of summer fruits,
and a bottle of wine.
2 And the king said unto Ziba, What meanest thou by these? And Ziba said, The asses *be*
for the king's household to ride on; and the
bread and summer fruit for the young men to
eat; and the wine, [a]that such as be faint in the
wilderness may drink.
3 And the king said, And where *is* thy master's son? [a]And Ziba said unto the king, Behold, he abideth at Jerusalem: for he said, To
day shall the house of Israel restore me the
kingdom of my father.
4 Then said the king to Ziba, Behold, thine
are all that *pertained* unto Mephibosheth. And
Ziba said, [1]I humbly beseech thee *that* I may
find grace in thy sight, my lord, O king.

Shimei curses David

5 ¶ And when king David came to Bahurim,
behold, thence came out a man of the family of
the house of Saul, whose name *was* [a]Shimei,
the son of Gera: [1]he came forth, and cursed
still as he came.
6 And he cast stones at David, and at all the
servants of king David: and all the people and
all the mighty *men were* on his right hand and
on his left.
7 And thus said Shimei when he cursed,
Come out, come out, thou [1]bloody man, and
thou [a]man of Belial:
8 The LORD hath [a]returned upon thee all
[b]the blood of the house of Saul, in whose stead
thou hast reigned; and the LORD hath delivered
the kingdom into the hand of Absalom thy
son: and, [1]behold, thou *art taken* to thy mischief, because thou *art* a bloody man.
9 Then said Abishai the son of Zeruiah
unto the king, Why should this [a]dead dog
[b]curse my lord the king? let me go over, I pray
thee, and take off his head.
10 And the king said, [a]What have I to do
with you, ye sons of Zeruiah? so let him curse,
because [b]the LORD hath said unto him, Curse
David. [c]Who shall then say, Wherefore hast
thou done so?
11 And David said to Abishai, and to all his
servants, Behold, [a]my son, which [b]came forth
of my bowels, seeketh my life: how much
more now *may this* Benjamite *do it?* let him
alone, and let him curse; for the LORD hath bidden him.
12 It may be that the LORD will look on
mine [1]affliction, and that the LORD will [a]re-
quite me good for his cursing this day.
13 And as David and his men went by the
way, Shimei went along on the hill's side over
against him, and cursed as he went, and threw
stones at him, and [1]cast dust.
14 And the king, and all the people that
were with him, came weary, and refreshed
themselves there.

The advice of Ahithophel

15 ¶ And [a]Absalom, and all the people the
men of Israel, came *to* Jerusalem, and
Ahithophel with him.
16 And it came to pass, when Hushai the
Archite, [a]David's friend, was come unto Absalom, that Hushai said unto Absalom, [1]God
save the king, God save the king.
17 And Absalom said to Hushai, *Is* this thy
kindness to thy friend? [a]why wentest thou not
with thy friend?
18 And Hushai said unto Absalom, Nay;
but whom the LORD, and this people, and all
the men of Israel, choose, his will I be, and
with him will I abide.

15:35 [a]ch. 17:15,16
15:36 [a]ver. 27
15:37 [a]ch. 16:16; 1 Chr. 27:33 [b]ch. 16:15
16:1 [a]ch. 15:30,32 [b]ch. 9:2
16:2 [a]ch. 15:23; 17:29
16:3 [a]ch. 19:27
16:4 [1]Heb. *I do obeisance*
16:5 [1]Or, *he still came forth and cursed* [a]ch. 19:16; 1 Ki. 2:8,44
16:7 [1]Heb. *man of blood* [a]Deut. 13:13
16:8 [1]Heb. *behold thee in thy evil* [a]Judg. 9:24,56,57; 1 Ki. 2:32,33 [b]See ch. 1:16; 3:28,29; 4:11,12
16:9 [a]1 Sam. 24:14; ch. 9:8 [b]Ex. 22:28
16:10 [a]ch. 19:22; 1 Pet. 2:23 [b]See 2 Ki. 18:25; Lam. 3:38 [c]Rom. 9:20
16:11 [a]ch. 12:11 [b]Gen. 15:4
16:12 [1]Or, *tears.* Heb. *eye* [a]Rom. 8:28
16:13 [1]Heb. *dusted* him *with dust*
16:15 [a]ch. 15:37
16:16 [1]Heb. *Let the king live* [a]ch. 15:37
16:17 [a]ch. 19:25; Prov. 17:17

15:37 *Hushai David's friend.* 1 Chr 27:33 calls him the "king's companion," which seems to be an official title for the king's most trusted adviser (see 1 Ki 4:5).
16:1 *Ziba.* See ch. 9. *Mephibosheth.* See note on 4:4.
16:2 *Ziba said.* Since David assumed control of Saul's estate (9:7–10), Ziba, always the opportunist, seeks to profit from the political crisis.
16:3 *thy master's son.* "Son" here means "grandson," i.e. Mephibosheth (see 9:2–3,9).
16:4 *thine are all that pertained unto Mephibosheth.* Because the revolt was so widespread and loyalties so uncertain, David was quick to assume the worst.
16:5 *Bahurim.* On the eastern slope of the mount of Olives (see note on 3:16). *of the family of the house of Saul.* The clan of Matri (see 1 Sam 10:21). *Gera.* His exact relation to Saul is unknown (see note on 1 Kin 2:8).
16:6 *people and . . . mighty men.* The Cherethites, Pelethites and 600 Gittites (see 15:18).
‡16:7 *man of Belial.* I.e. worthless man. See note on Deut 13:13.
16:8 *blood of the house of Saul.* Shimei may be referring to the executions reported in 21:1–14, but the time of that event is uncertain (see note on 21:1).
16:9 *Abishai.* See note on 1 Sam 26:6. *this dead dog.* An expression of absolute contempt (see note on 9:8).
16:10 *because the LORD hath said unto him, Curse David.* David leaves open the possibility that God has seen fit to terminate his rule—the verdict is not yet in (see 15:26). For David's later actions regarding Shimei see 19:18–23; 1 Ki 2:8–9.
16:15 *Ahithophel.* See note on 15:12.
16:16 *Hushai the Archite, David's friend.* See notes on 15:32, 37.

19 And again, [a]whom should I serve?
should I not *serve* in the presence of his son?
as I have served in thy father's presence, so
will I be in thy presence.
20 ¶ Then said Absalom to Ahithophel,
Give counsel among you what we shall do.
21 And Ahithophel said unto Absalom, Go
in unto thy father's [a]concubines, which he
hath left to keep the house; and all Israel shall
hear that thou [b]art abhorred of thy father:
then shall [c]the hands of all that *are* with thee
be strong.
22 So they spread Absalom a tent upon the
top of the house; and Absalom went in unto
his father's concubines [a]in the sight of all Israel.
23 And the counsel of Ahithophel, which
he counselled in those days, *was* as if a man
had inquired at the [1]oracle of God: so *was* all
the counsel of Ahithophel [a]both with David
and with Absalom.

The advice of Hushai

17 Moreover Ahithophel said unto Absalom, Let me now choose out
twelve thousand men, and I will arise and pursue after David *this* night:
2 And I will come upon him while he *is*
[a]weary and weak handed, and will make him
afraid: and all the people that *are* with him
shall flee; and I will [b]smite the king only:
3 And I will bring back all the people unto
thee: the man whom thou seekest *is* as if all
returned: *so* all the people shall be *in* peace.
4 And the saying [a][1]pleased Absalom well,
and all the elders of Israel.
5 Then said Absalom, Call now Hushai the
Archite also, and let us hear likewise [1]what he
saith.
6 And when Hushai was come to Absalom,
Absalom spake unto him, saying, Ahithophel
hath spoken after this manner: shall we do *after* his [1]saying? if not; speak thou.
7 And Hushai said unto Absalom, The
counsel that Ahithophel hath [1]given *is* not
good at this time.
8 For, (said Hushai,) thou knowest thy father and his men, that they *be* mighty *men,*
and they *be* [1]chafed in their minds, as [a]a bear
robbed of her whelps in the field: and thy fa-

16:19 [a]ch. 15:34
16:21 [a]ch. 15:16; 20:3 [b]Gen. 34:30; 1 Sam. 13:4 [c]ch. 2:7; Zech. 8:13
16:22 [a]ch. 12:11,12
16:23 [1]Heb. *word* [a]ch. 15:12
17:2 [a]See Deut. 25:18; ch. 16:14 [b]Zech. 13:7
17:4 [1]Heb. *was right in the eyes of, etc.* [a]1 Sam. 18:20
17:5 [1]Heb. *what is in his mouth*
17:6 [1]Heb. *word?*
17:7 [1]Heb. *counselled*
17:8 [1]Heb. *bitter of soul* [a]Hos. 13:8

17:9 [1]Heb. *fallen*
17:10 [a]Josh. 2:11
17:11 [1]Heb. *that thy face,* or, *presence go, etc.* [a]Judg. 20:1 [b]Gen. 22:17
17:14 [1]Heb. *commanded* [a]ch. 15:31,34
17:15 [a]ch. 15:35
17:16 [a]ch. 15:28
17:17 [a]ch. 15:27,36 [b]Josh. 2:4 [c]Josh. 15:7; 18:16
17:18 [a]ch. 16:5

ther *is* a man of war, and will not lodge with
the people.
9 Behold, he is hid now in some pit, or in
some *other* place: and it will come to pass, when
some of them be [1]overthrown at the first, that
whosoever heareth *it* will say, There is a slaughter among the people that follow Absalom.
10 And he also *that is* valiant, whose heart
is as the heart of a lion, shall utterly [a]melt: for
all Israel knoweth that thy father *is* a mighty
man, and *they* which *be* with him *are* valiant
men.
11 Therefore I counsel *that* all Israel be
generally gathered unto thee, [a]from Dan even
to Beer-sheba, [b]as the sand that *is* by the sea
for multitude; and [1]*that* thou go to battle in
thine own person.
12 So shall we come upon him in some
place where he shall be found, and we *will light*
upon him as the dew falleth on the ground: and
of him and of all the men that *are* with him
there shall not be left so much as one.
13 Moreover, if he be gotten into a city,
then shall all Israel bring ropes to that city, and
we will draw it into the river, until there be
not one small stone found there.
14 And Absalom and all the men of Israel
said, The counsel of Hushai the Archite *is* better than the counsel of Ahithophel. For [a]the
LORD had [1]appointed to defeat the good counsel of Ahithophel, to the intent that the LORD
might bring evil upon Absalom.
15 ¶ [a]Then said Hushai unto Zadok and to
Abiathar the priests, Thus and thus did
Ahithophel counsel Absalom and the elders of
Israel; and thus and thus have I counselled.
16 Now therefore send quickly, and tell David, saying, Lodge not *this* night [a]in the plains
of the wilderness, but speedily pass over; lest
the king be swallowed up, and all the people
that *are* with him.
17 [a]Now Jonathan and Ahimaaz [b]stayed by
[c]En-rogel; for they might not be seen to come
into the city: and a wench went and told them;
and they went and told king David.
18 Nevertheless a lad saw them, and told
Absalom: but they went both of them away
quickly, and came to a man's house [a]in Bahurim, which had a well in his court; whither
they went down.

16:21 *Go in unto thy father's concubines.* This would signify Absalom's assumption of royal power; it would also be a definitive and irreversible declaration of the break between father and son (see notes on 3:7; 12:8; 1 Ki 2:22).

16:22 *Absalom went in unto his father's concubines.* A fulfillment of Nathan's prophecy (12:11–12). For additional significance see note on v. 21.

17:1–3 Ahithophel's advice to Absalom envisioned a cheap and easy victory that would not leave the nation weakened.

17:4 *all the elders of Israel.* See note on 3:17. Absalom's rebellion appears to have gained extensive backing from prominent tribal leaders.

17:5 *Hushai the Archite.* See 16:16–19; see also notes on 15:32,37.

17:7–13 Hushai's advice subtly capitalizes on Absalom's uncertainty, his fear and his egotism.

17:12 *we . . . we.* Hushai carefully links himself with the revolt.

17:14 *the LORD had appointed to defeat the good counsel of Ahithophel.* An answer to David's prayer (see 15:31; cf. Ps 33:10; Prov 21:30).

17:15 *Zadok and to Abiathar.* See 15:24–29,35–36.

17:16 *plains of the wilderness.* See 15:28 and note. *pass over.* Hushai advises David to cross the Jordan River, knowing that Absalom might change his mind and immediately set out after him.

17:17 *Jonathan and Ahimaaz.* See 15:36. *En-rogel.* A spring in the Kidron Valley just outside the walls of Jerusalem. *a wench.* I.e. a maidservant. A servant girl going to the spring for water would attract no attention.

17:18 *Bahurim.* See note on 16:5.

19 And [a]the woman took and spread a covering over the well's mouth, and spread
ground corn thereon; and the thing was not
known.
20 And when Absalom's servants came to
the woman to the house, they said, Where *is*
Ahimaaz and Jonathan? And [a]the woman said
unto them, They be gone over the brook of
water. And when they had sought and could
not find *them,* they returned *to* Jerusalem.
21 And it came to pass, after they were departed, that they came up out of the well, and
went and told king David, and said unto David, [a]Arise, and pass quickly over the water:
for thus hath Ahithophel counselled against
you.
22 Then David arose, and all the people
that *were* with him, and they passed over Jordan: by the morning light there lacked not one
of them that was not gone over Jordan.
23 ¶ And when Ahithophel saw that his
counsel was not [1]followed, he saddled *his* ass,
and arose, and gat him *home* to his house, to
[a]his city, and [b2]put his household in order,
and [c]hanged himself, and died, and was
buried in the sepulchre of his father.
24 Then David came to [a]Mahanaim. And
Absalom passed over Jordan, he and all the
men of Israel with him.
25 And Absalom made Amasa captain of
the host instead of Joab: which Amasa *was* a
man's son, whose name *was* [1]Ithra an Israelite, that went in to [a]Abigail the daughter of
[2]Nahash, sister to Zeruiah Joab's mother.
26 So Israel and Absalom pitched *in* the
land of Gilead.
27 And it came to pass, when David was
come to Mahanaim, that [a]Shobi the son of Nahash of Rabbah of the children of Ammon, and
[b]Machir the son of Ammiel of Lo-debar, and
[c]Barzillai the Gileadite of Rogelim,
28 Brought beds, and [1]basons, and earthen
vessels, and wheat, and barley, and flour, and
parched *corn,* and beans, and lentiles, and
parched *pulse,*
29 And honey, and butter, and sheep, and
cheese of kine, for David, and for the people
that *were* with him, to eat: for they said, The
people *is* hungry, and weary, and thirsty, [a]in
the wilderness.

Absalom killed by Joab

18 And David numbered the people that
were with him, and set captains of
thousands and captains of hundreds over
them.
2 And David sent forth a third part of the
people under the hand of Joab, and a third part
under the hand of Abishai the son of Zeruiah,
Joab's brother, [a]and a third part under the
hand of Ittai the Gittite. And the king said
unto the people, I will surely go forth with you
myself also.
3 [a]But the people answered, Thou shalt
not go forth: for if we flee away, they will not
[1]care for us; neither if half of us die, will they
[1]care for us: but now *thou art* [2]worth ten
thousand of us: therefore now *it is* better that
thou [3]succour us out of the city.
4 And the king said unto them, What
seemeth you best I will do. And the king stood
by the gate side, and all the people came out
by hundreds and by thousands.
5 And the king commanded Joab and
Abishai and Ittai, saying, *Deal* gently for my
sake with the young man, *even* with Absalom.
[a]And all the people heard when the king gave
all the captains charge concerning Absalom.
6 So the people went out *into* the field
against Israel: and the battle was in the [a]wood
of Ephraim;
7 Where the people of Israel were slain before the servants of David, and there was there
a great slaughter that day *of* twenty thousand
men.
8 For the battle was there scattered over
the face of all the country: and the wood [1]de-
voured more people that day than the sword
devoured.
9 And Absalom met the servants of David.
And Absalom rode upon a mule, and the mule
went under the thick boughs of a great oak,
and his head caught hold of the oak, and he
was taken up between the heaven and the
earth; and the mule that *was* under him went
away.

17:19 [a]See Josh. 2:6
17:20 [a]See Ex. 1:19; Josh. 2:4,5
17:21 [a]ver. 15,16
17:23 [1]Heb. *done* [2]Heb. *gave charge concerning his house* [a]ch. 15:12 [b]2 Ki. 20:1 [c]Mat. 27:5
17:24 [a]Gen. 32:2; Josh. 13:26; ch. 2:8
17:25 [1][Or, *Jether an Ishmaelite,* 1 Chr. 2:16,17] [2][Or, *Jesse.* See 1 Chr. 2:13-16] [a]1 Chr. 2:16,17
17:27 [a]See ch. 10:1; 12:29 [b]ch. 9:4 [c]ch. 19:31,32; 1 Ki. 2:7
17:28 [1]Or, *cups*
17:29 [a]ch. 16:2
18:2 [a]ch. 15:19
18:3 [1]Heb. *set their heart on us* [2]Heb. *as ten thousand of us* [3]Heb. *be to succour* [a]ch. 21:17
18:5 [a]ver. 12
18:6 [a]Josh. 17:15,18
18:8 [1]Heb. *multiplied to devour*

17:23 *his city.* Giloh (see note on 15:12). *hanged himself.* Ahithophel was convinced that the rebellion would fail and that he would be found guilty of treason as a co-conspirator.
17:24 *Mahanaim.* Ironically the same place where Ish-bosheth had sought refuge after Saul's death (2:8).
17:25 *Amasa.* Nephew of David and cousin of both Absalom and Joab son of Zeruiah. *Abigail the daughter of Nahash, sister to Zeruiah.* Zeruiah was David's sister (1 Chr 2:16). Since the father of Abigail and Zeruiah is Nahash rather than Jesse, it would appear that their unnamed mother married Jesse after the death of Nahash.
17:27 *Shobi the son of Nahash.* Apparently the brother of Hanun (see 10:2–4), whom David had defeated earlier in his reign (12:26–31). *Rabbah of the children of Ammon.* See note on 10:3. *Machir.* See note on 9:4. *Barzillai.* A wealthy benefactor of David during his flight to Mahanaim (see 19:32; 1 Ki 2:7). After the Babylonian exile, there were claimants to the priesthood among his descendants (Ezra 2:61–63; Neh 7:63).
18:2 *Ittai the Gittite.* See 15:18–22.
18:3 *Thou shalt not go forth.* In addition to the reason given, David was growing old and was no longer the warrior he had been (see note on 15:7). This is essentially the same idea that Ahithophel had expressed to Absalom (see 17:2).
18:5 *Deal gently for my sake with . . . Absalom.* David's love for his (now) oldest son was undying—and almost his undoing (see 19:5–7).
18:6 *Israel.* Absalom's army (see 15:13; 16:15; 17:4,11,24–26). *wood of Ephraim.* The battle was apparently fought in Gilead, east of the Jordan (see 17:24,26). Why this area is termed the "wood of Ephraim" is not clear (perhaps it comes from an Ephraimite claim on the area; see Judg 12:1–4).
18:8 *the battle was there scattered.* The armies apparently became dispersed, and many of the men got lost in the forest.
18:9 *a mule.* See note on 13:29. *his head caught hold of the*

10 And a certain man saw *it,* and told Joab, and said, Behold, I saw Absalom hanged in an oak.

11 And Joab said unto the man that told him, And behold, thou sawest *him,* and why didst thou not smite him there to the ground? and I would have given thee ten *shekels of* silver, and a girdle.

12 And the man said unto Joab, Though I should [1]receive a thousand *shekels of* silver in mine hand, *yet* would I not put forth mine hand against the king's son: [a]for in our hearing the king charged thee and Abishai and Ittai, saying, [2]Beware *that* none *touch* the young man Absalom.

13 Otherwise I should have wrought falsehood against mine own life: for there is no matter hid from the king, and thou thyself wouldest have set thyself against *me.*

14 Then said Joab, I may not tarry thus [1]with thee. And he took three darts in his hand, and thrust them through the heart of Absalom, while he *was* yet alive in the [2]midst of the oak.

15 And ten young men that bare Joab's armour compassed about and smote Absalom, and slew him.

16 And Joab blew the trumpet, and the people returned from pursuing after Israel: for Joab held back the people.

17 And they took Absalom, and cast him into a great pit in the wood, and [a]laid a very great heap of stones upon him: and all Israel fled every one to his tent.

18 Now Absalom in his lifetime had taken and reared up for himself a pillar, which *is* in [a]the king's dale: for he said, [b]I have no son to keep my name in remembrance: and he called the pillar after his own name: and it is called unto this day, Absalom's place.

David told of Absalom's death

19 ¶ Then said Ahimaaz the son of Zadok, Let me now run, and bear the king tidings, how that the LORD hath [1]avenged him of his enemies.

20 And Joab said unto him, Thou *shalt* not [1]bear tidings this day, but thou shalt bear tidings another day: but this day thou shalt bear no tidings, because the king's son is dead.

21 Then said Joab to Cushi, Go tell the king what thou hast seen. And Cushi bowed himself unto Joab, and ran.

22 Then said Ahimaaz the son of Zadok yet again to Joab, But [1]howsoever, let me, I pray thee, also run after Cushi. And Joab said, Wherefore wilt thou run, my son, seeing that thou hast no tidings [2]ready?

23 But howsoever, *said he,* let me run. And he said unto him, Run. Then Ahimaaz ran *by* the way of the plain, and overran Cushi.

24 And David sat between the two gates: and [a]the watchman went *up* to the roof over the gate unto the wall, and lift up his eyes, and looked, and behold a man running alone.

25 And the watchman cried, and told the king. And the king said, If he *be* alone, *there is* tidings in his mouth. And he came apace, and drew near.

26 And the watchman saw another man running: and the watchman called unto the porter, and said, Behold *another* man running alone. And the king said, He also bringeth tidings.

27 And the watchman said, [1]Me thinketh the running of the foremost *is* like the running of Ahimaaz the son of Zadok. And the king said, He *is* a good man, and cometh with good tidings.

28 And Ahimaaz called, and said unto the king, [1]All is well. And he fell down to the earth upon his face before the king, and said, Blessed *be* the LORD thy God, which hath [2]delivered up the men that lift up their hand against my lord the king.

29 And the king said, [1]*Is* the young man Absalom safe? And Ahimaaz answered, When Joab sent the king's servant, and *me* thy servant, I saw a great tumult, but I knew not what *it was.*

30 And the king said *unto him,* Turn aside, *and* stand here. And he turned aside, and stood still.

31 And behold, Cushi came; and Cushi said, [1]Tidings, my lord the king: for the LORD hath avenged thee *this* day of all them that rose up against thee.

32 And the king said unto Cushi, *Is* the young man Absalom safe? And Cushi answered, The enemies of my lord the king, and

18:12 [1]Heb. *weigh upon mine hand* [2]Heb. *Beware whosoever* ye be, *of, etc.* [a]ver. 5
18:14 [1]Heb. *before thee* [2]Heb. *heart*
18:17 [a]Josh. 7:26
18:18 [a]Gen. 14:17 [b]See ch. 14:27
18:19 [1]Heb. *judged him from the hand, etc.*
18:20 [1]Heb. be *a man of tidings*
18:22 [1]Heb. *be what* may [2]Or, *convenient*
18:24 [a]2 Ki. 9:17
18:27 [1]Heb. *I see the running*
18:28 [1]Or, *Peace* be to thee. Heb. *Peace* [2]Heb. *shut up*
18:29 [1]Heb. Is there *peace?*
18:31 [1]Heb. *Tidings is brought*

oak. Whether by the entanglement of his abundant hair (14:26) or by some other means is not stated, but his handsome head (see 14:25) was in the end—ironically—his undoing.

18:11 *I would have given thee.* Joab must be referring to an announced intent on his part to reward anyone killing Absalom. His actions and interests did not always coincide with David's wishes (see note on 2:13).

18:15 *slew him.* The easiest and most certain way of ending the rebellion—but the brutal overkill is indicative of the deep animosity felt by David's men against Absalom.

18:17 *great heap of stones.* A mound of rocks that mocked the monument Absalom himself had erected (v. 18). *all Israel.* See note on v. 6.

18:18 *reared up for himself a pillar.* As Saul had done (1 Sam 15:12). *king's dale.* Thought to be located near Jerusalem (see Gen 14:17; Josephus, *Antiquities,* 7.10.3). *I have no son.* See 14:27 and note. *Absalom's place.* Not to be confused with the much later monument of the same name that is still visible today in the valley east of Jerusalem.

18:19 *Ahimaaz the son of Zadok.* See 15:27; 17:17–21.

18:20 *Thou shalt not bear tidings this day.* The choice of a messenger depended on the content of the message (see v. 27 and note).

‡18:21 *Cushi.* Not a personal name, but the "Cushite," an unnamed alien from Cush (see notes on Gen 10:6–8; Amos 9:7).

18:27 *cometh with good tidings.* David presumed that Joab would not have sent someone like Ahimaaz to carry bad news (see v. 20 and note).

18:29 *I saw a great tumult.* Ahimaaz avoids a direct answer to David's question, though he knew Absalom was dead.

all that rise against thee to do *thee* hurt, be as
that young man *is.*
33 And the king was much moved, and
went up to the chamber over the gate, and
wept: and as he went, thus he said, [a]O my son
Absalom, my son, my son Absalom: would
God I had died for thee, O Absalom, my son,
my son.
19 And it was told Joab, Behold, the
king weepeth and mourneth for Absalom.
2 And the [1]victory that day was *turned*
into mourning unto all the people: for the people
heard say that day *how* the king was
grieved for his son.
3 And the people gat them by stealth that
day [a]*into* the city, as people being ashamed
steal away when they flee in battle.
4 But the king [a]covered his face, and the
king cried *with* a loud voice, [b]O my son Absalom,
O Absalom, my son, my son.
5 And Joab came *into* the house to the
king, and said, Thou hast shamed *this* day the
faces of all thy servants, which *this* day have
saved thy life, and the lives of thy sons and of
thy daughters, and the lives of thy wives, and
the lives of thy concubines;
6 [1]In that thou lovest thine enemies, and
hatest thy friends: for thou hast declared *this*
day, [2]that thou regardest neither princes nor
servants: for *this* day I perceive, that if Absalom
had lived, and all we had died *this* day,
then it had pleased thee well.
7 Now therefore arise, go forth, and speak
[1]comfortably unto thy servants: for I swear by
the LORD, if thou go not forth, there will not
tarry one with thee *this* night: and that *will be*
worse unto thee than all the evil that befell
thee from thy youth until now.
8 Then the king rose, and sat in the gate.
And they told unto all the people, saying, Behold,
the king doth sit in the gate. And all the
people came before the king: for Israel had
fled every man to his tent.

David's return to Jerusalem

9 ¶ And all the people were at strife
throughout all the tribes of Israel, saying, The
king saved us out of the hand of our enemies,
and he delivered us out of the hand of the Philistines;
and now he is [a]fled out of the land for
Absalom.
10 And Absalom, whom we anointed over
us, is dead in battle. Now therefore why
[1]speak ye not a word of bringing the king
back?
11 And king David sent to Zadok and to
Abiathar the priests, saying, Speak unto the
elders of Judah, saying, Why are ye the last to
bring the king back to his house? seeing the
speech of all Israel is come to the king, *even* to
his house.
12 Ye *are* my brethren, ye *are* [a]my bones
and my flesh: wherefore then are ye the last to
bring back the king?
13 [a]And say ye to Amasa, *Art* thou not *of*
my bone, and *of* my flesh? [b]God do so to me,
and more also, if thou be not captain of the
host before me continually in the room of
Joab.
14 And he bowed the heart of all the men
of Judah, [a]*even* as *the heart of* one man; so
that they sent *this word* unto the king, Return
thou, and all thy servants.
15 So the king returned, and came to Jordan.
And Judah came to [a]Gilgal, to go to meet
the king, to conduct the king over Jordan.
16 ¶ And [a]Shimei the son of Gera, a Benjamite,
which *was* of Bahurim, hasted and
came down with the men of Judah to meet
king David.
17 And *there were* a thousand men of Benjamin
with him, and [a]Ziba the servant of the
house of Saul, and his fifteen sons and his
twenty servants with him; and they went over
Jordan before the king.
18 And there went over a ferry boat to carry
over the king's household, and to do [1]what
he thought good. And Shimei the son of Gera
fell down before the king, as he was come over
Jordan;
19 And said unto the king, [a]Let not my
lord impute iniquity unto me, neither do thou
remember [b]*that* which thy servant did perversely
the day that my lord the king went out
of Jerusalem, that the king should [c]take *it* to
his heart.
20 For thy servant doth know that I have

18:33 [a]ch. 19:4
19:2 [1]Heb. *salvation, or, deliverance*
19:3 [a]ver. 32
19:4 [a]ch. 15:30 [b]ch. 18:33
19:6 [1]Heb. *By loving, etc.* [2]Heb. *that princes or servants are not to thee*
19:7 [1]Heb. *to the heart of thy servants*
19:9 [a]ch. 15:14
19:10 [1]Heb. *are ye silent?*
19:12 [a]ch. 5:1
19:13 [a]ch. 17:25 [b]Ruth 1:17
19:14 [a]Judg. 20:1
19:15 [a]Josh. 5:9
19:16 [a]ch. 16:5; 1 Ki. 2:8
19:17 [a]ch. 9:2,10; 16:1,2
19:18 [1]Heb. *the good in his eyes*
19:19 [a]1 Sam. 22:15 [b]ch. 16:5,6 [c]ch. 13:33

18:33 *O my son Absalom . . . my son.* One of the most moving expressions in all literature of a father's love for a son—in spite of all that Absalom had done.
19:5 *Joab came . . . to the king.* Apparently confident that the king was unaware of his part in Absalom's death. David never indicates that he learned of it (see 1 Ki 2:5). *Thou hast shamed . . . the faces of all thy servants.* Joab boldly rebukes David for allowing his personal grief to keep him from expressing his appreciation for the loyalty of those who risked their lives to preserve his throne. Joab warns David that his love for Absalom can still undo him.
19:9 *The king saved us.* With Absalom dead, the northern tribes remember what David had done for them (see 3:17–18; 5:2).
19:11 *Speak unto the elders of Judah.* Even though the rebellion had begun in Hebron in Judah (see 15:9–12), David appeals to the elders of his own tribe to take the initiative in restoring him to the throne in Jerusalem (see 2:4; 1 Sam 30:26). This appeal produced the desired result, but it also led to the arousal of tribal jealousies (see vv. 41–42).
19:13 *Amasa.* See 17:25 and note. Although Amasa deserved death for treason, David appointed him commander of his army in place of Joab, hoping to secure the allegiance of those who had followed Amasa, especially the Judahites (see 20:5). *God do so to me, and more also.* A curse formula (see note on 1 Sam 3:17).
19:15 *Gilgal.* See note on Josh 4:19.
19:17 *a thousand men of Benjamin.* No doubt fearing they would be suspected by the king of being implicated in Shimei's deed.
19:20 *thy servant doth know that I have sinned.* Shimei's guilt was common knowledge; he could only seize the most appropriate time to plead for mercy. *house of Joseph.* A common way

sinned: therefore, behold, I am come the first
this day of all [a]the house of Joseph to go down
to meet my lord the king.
21 But Abishai the son of Zeruiah answered and said, Shall not Shimei be put to
death for this, because he [a]cursed the LORD'S
anointed?
22 And David said, [a]What have I to do
with you, ye sons of Zeruiah, that ye should
this day be adversaries unto me? [b]shall there
any man be put to death *this* day in Israel? for
do not I know that I *am this* day king over Israel?
23 Therefore [a]the king said unto Shimei,
Thou shalt not die. And the king sware unto
him.
24 ¶ And [a]Mephibosheth the son of Saul
came down to meet the king, and had neither
dressed his feet, nor trimmed his beard, nor
washed his clothes, from the day the king departed until the day he came *again* in peace.
25 And it came to pass, when he was come
to Jerusalem to meet the king, that the king
said unto him, [a]Wherefore wentest not thou
with me, Mephibosheth?
26 And he answered, My lord, O king, my
servant deceived me: for thy servant said, I will
saddle me an ass, that I may ride thereon, and
go to the king; because thy servant *is* lame.
27 And [a]he hath slandered thy servant
unto my lord the king; [b]but my lord the king *is*
as an angel of God: do therefore what *is* good
in thine eyes.
28 For all *of* my father's house were but
[1]dead men before my lord the king: [a]yet didst
thou set thy servant among them that did eat
at thine own table. What right therefore have
I yet to cry any more unto the king?
29 And the king said unto him, Why speakest thou any more of thy matters? I have said,
Thou and Ziba divide the land.
30 And Mephibosheth said unto the king,
Yea, let him take all, forasmuch as my lord the
king is come *again* in peace unto his own
house.
31 ¶ And [a]Barzillai the Gileadite came
down from Rogelim, and went over Jordan
with the king, to conduct him *over* Jordan.
32 Now Barzillai was a very aged man,
even fourscore years old: and [a]he had provided the king of sustenance while he lay at Mahanaim; for he *was* a very great man.
33 And the king said unto Barzillai, Come
thou over with me, and I will feed thee with
me in Jerusalem.
34 And Barzillai said unto the king, [1]How
long have I to live, that I should go up with the
king *unto* Jerusalem?
35 I *am this* day [a]fourscore years old: *and*
can I discern between good and evil? can thy
servant taste what I eat or what I drink? can I
hear any more the voice of singing *men* and
singing *women?* wherefore then should thy
servant be yet a burden unto my lord the king?
36 Thy servant will go a little *way* over Jordan with the king: and why should the king
recompense *it* me *with* such a reward?
37 Let thy servant, I pray thee, turn back
again, that I may die in mine own city, *and be
buried* by the grave of my father and of my
mother. But behold thy servant [a]Chimham; let
him go over with my lord the king; and do to
him what shall seem good unto thee.
38 And the king answered, Chimham shall
go over with me, and I will do to him *that*
which shall seem good unto thee: and whatsoever thou shalt [1]require of me, *that* will I do
for thee.
39 And all the people went over Jordan.
And when the king was come over, the king
[a]kissed Barzillai, and blessed him; and he returned unto his own place.
40 Then the king went on to Gilgal, and
[1]Chimham went on with him: and all the people of Judah conducted the king, and also half
the people of Israel.
41 ¶ And behold, all the men of Israel came
to the king, and said unto the king, Why have
our brethren the men of Judah stolen thee
away, and [a]have brought the king, and his
household, and all David's men with him, over
Jordan?

19:20 [a]See ch. 16:5
19:21 [a]Ex. 22:28; 1 Sam. 26:9
19:22 [a]ch. 16:10 [b]1 Sam. 11:13
19:23 [a]1 Ki. 2:8,9,37,46
19:24 [a]ch. 9:6
19:25 [a]ch. 16:17
19:27 [a]ch. 16:3 [b]ch. 14:17,20
19:28 [1]Heb. *men of death* [a]ch. 9:7,10,13
19:31 [a]1 Ki. 2:7
19:32 [a]ch. 17:27
19:34 [1][Heb.] *How many days* are *the years of my life*
19:35 [a]Ps. 90:10
19:37 [a]1 Ki. 2:7; Jer. 41:17
19:38 [1]Heb. *choose*
19:39 [a]Gen. 31:55
19:40 [1][Heb. *Chimhan*]
19:41 [a]ver. 15

of referring to the northern tribes (see 1 Ki 11:28; Ezek 37:19; Amos 5:6; Zech 10:6)—of which Ephraim and Manasseh (sons of Joseph) were the most prominent (see Num 26:28; Josh 18:5; Judg 1:22).
19:21 *Abishai.* See 16:9; see also note on 1 Sam 26:6. *the LORD's anointed.* See note on 1 Sam 9:16; see also 1 Sam 24:6; 26:9–11; Ex 22:28; 1 Ki 21:10.
19:22 *shall there any man be put to death this day in Israel?* It was a day for general amnesty (see 1 Sam 11:13).
19:23 *Thou shalt not die.* David kept his pledge; he would not himself avenge the wrong committed against him (see note on 1 Sam 25:2–44). But on his deathbed he instructed Solomon to take Shimei's case in hand (see 1 Ki 2:8–9,36–46).
19:24 *Mephibosheth.* See 9:6–13.
19:25 *Wherefore wentest not thou with me . . . ?* David remembers Ziba's previous allegations (see 16:3).
19:26 *lame.* See 4:4; 9:3.
19:27 *he hath slandered thy servant.* See 16:3. *as an angel of God.* See 14:17 and note. *do therefore what is good in thine eyes.* Mephibosheth discreetly requests David to reconsider the grant of his property to Ziba (see 16:4).
19:29 *divide the land.* Faced with conflicting testimony that could not be corroborated, David withholds judgment and orders the division of Saul's estate.
19:31 *Barzillai.* See note on 17:27.
19:35 *discern between good and evil.* At his age, he would be indifferent to all the pleasures of the court.
19:37 *Chimham.* Likely a son of Barzillai (see 1 Kin 2:7).
19:41 *Why have . . . the men of Judah stolen thee away, and have brought the king . . . over Jordan?* It seems that the Jordan was a kind of psychological border to the land of Israel (see Josh 22:19,25; Judg 12:4)—which may also explain why Ish-bosheth (2:8), Mephibosheth (9:4) and even David himself (17:22) had sought refuge on the other side. That being the case, the protest of the Israelites may be that the Judahites had not waited for all Israel to assemble before bringing David across the Jordan, thus leaving the Israelites in a bad light—as though they were reluctant to receive the king back (see v. 43).

42 And all the men of Judah answered the
men of Israel, Because the king *is* [a]near of kin
to us: wherefore then be ye angry for this matter? have we eaten at all of the king's *cost?* or
hath he given us *any* gift?

43 And the men of Israel answered the
men of Judah, and said, We have ten parts in
the king, and we have also more *right* in David
than ye: why then did ye [1]despise us, that our
advice should not be first had in bringing back
our king? And [a]the words of the men of Judah
were fiercer than the words of the men of Israel.

Sheba leads Israel to revolt

20 And there happened to be there a
man of Belial, whose name *was* She-
ba, the son of Bichri, a Benjamite: and he blew
a trumpet, and said, [a]We have no part in David, neither have we inheritance in the son of
Jesse: [b]every man to his tents, O Israel.

2 So every man of Israel went up from after
David, *and* followed Sheba the son of Bichri:
but the men of Judah clave unto their king,
from Jordan even to Jerusalem.

3 And David came to his house *at* Jerusalem; and the king took the ten women *his*
[a]concubines, whom he had left to keep the
house, and put them *in* [1]ward, and fed them,
but went not in unto them. So they were
[2]shut up unto the day of their death, [3]living in
widowhood.

4 Then said the king to Amasa, [a][1]Assemble
me the men of Judah *within* three days, and be
thou here present.

5 So Amasa went to [1]assemble *the men of*
Judah: but he tarried longer than the set time
which he had appointed him.

6 And David said to Abishai, Now shall
Sheba the son of Bichri do us more harm than
did Absalom: take thou [a]thy lord's servants,
and pursue after him, lest he get him fenced
cities, and [1]escape us.

7 And there went out after him Joab's
men, and the [a]Cherethites, and the Pelethites, and all the mighty *men:* and they went
out of Jerusalem, to pursue after Sheba the
son of Bichri.

8 When they *were* at the great stone which
is in Gibeon, Amasa went before them. And
Joab's garment that he had put on *was* girded
unto him, and upon it a girdle with a sword
fastened upon his loins in the sheath thereof;
and as he went forth it fell out.

9 And Joab said to Amasa, *Art* thou in
health, my brother? [a]And Joab took Amasa by
the beard with the right hand to kiss him.

10 But Amasa took no heed to the sword
that *was* in Joab's hand: so [a]he smote him
therewith [b]in the fifth *rib,* and shed out his
bowels to the ground, and [1]strake him not
again; and he died. So Joab and Abishai his
brother pursued after Sheba the son of Bichri.

11 And one of Joab's men stood by him,
and said, He that favoureth Joab, and he that *is*
for David, *let him go* after Joab.

12 And Amasa wallowed in blood in the
midst of the highway. And when the man saw
that all the people stood still, he removed Amasa out of the highway *into* the field, and cast
a cloth upon him, when he saw that every one
that came by him stood still.

13 When he was removed out of the highway, all the people went on after Joab, to pursue after Sheba the son of Bichri.

14 ¶ And he went through all the tribes of
Israel unto [a]Abel, and *to* Beth-maachah, and
all the Berites: and they were gathered together, and went also after him.

15 And they came and besieged him in
Abel of Beth-maachah, and they [a]cast up a
bank against the city, and [1]it stood in the
trench: and all the people that *were* with Joab
[2]battered the wall, to throw *it* down.

16 Then cried a wise woman out of the
city, Hear, hear; say, I pray you, unto Joab,
Come near hither, that I may speak with thee.

17 And when he was come near unto her,
the woman said, *Art* thou Joab? And he answered, I *am he.* Then she said unto him, Hear

19:42 [a]ver. 12
19:43 [1]Heb. *set us at light* [a]See Judg. 8:1; 12:1
20:1 [a]ch. 19:43 [b]1 Ki. 12:16; 2 Chr. 10:16
20:3 [1]Heb. *a house of ward* [2]Heb. *bound* [3]Heb. in *widowhood of life* [a]ch. 15:16; 16:21,22
20:4 [1]Heb. *Call* [a]ch. 19:13
20:5 [1]Heb. *call*
20:6 [1]Heb. *deliver* himself from *our eyes* [a]ch. 11:11; 1 Ki. 1:33
20:7 [a]ch. 8:18; 1 Ki. 1:38
20:9 [a]Mat. 26:49; Luke 22:47
20:10 [1]Heb. *doubled not his* stroke [a]1 Ki. 2:5 [b]ch. 2:23
20:14 [a]2 Ki. 15:29; 2 Chr. 16:4
20:15 [1]Or, *it stood against the outmost wall* [2]Heb. *marred to throw down* [a]2 Ki. 19:32

19:43 *ten parts.* The ten tribes, excluding Judah and Simeon (see note on 2:4). *we have also more right in David.* The grounds for this assertion may be that the Lord had chosen David to reign in the place of Saul (see 3:17–18; 5:2).

‡20:1 *to be there.* In Gilgal (19:40–43). *man of Belial.* I.e. a worthless fellow. See note on Deut 13:13. *Bichri.* Benjamin's second son (Becher, Gen 46:21; 1 Chr 7:6–9). *Benjamite.* Tribal jealousy still simmered over the transfer of the royal house from Benjamin (Saul's tribe) to Judah. *We have no part in David.* Sheba appeals to the Israelite suspicion that David favored his own tribe Judah over the other tribes (see 1 Ki 12:16).

20:2 *every man of Israel.* Those referred to in 19:41–43.

20:3 *ten . . . concubines.* See notes on 15:16; 16:22.

20:4 *Amasa.* See notes on 17:25; 19:13. David bypasses Joab.

20:6 *Abishai.* David bypasses Joab a second time (see v. 7). *thy lord's servants.* "Joab's men" (v. 7).

20:7 *Joab's men.* See 18:2. It becomes clear that Joab also accompanied the soldiers and, though not in command (by the king's order), he was obviously the leader recognized by the soldiers (see vv. 7,11,15). *Cherethites and the Pelethites.* See note on 8:18. *mighty men.* See 23:8–39. Once more in a time of crisis David depended mainly on the small force of professionals (many of them non-Israelite) who made up his private army.

20:8 *Gibeon.* See note on 2:12. *Amasa went.* Apparently with some troops (see v. 11 and note).

20:10 *in the fifth rib.* See 2:23; 3:27. For the second time Joab commits murder to secure his position as commander of David's army (see 1 Ki 2:5–6). *Joab and Abishai his brother.* In defiance of David's order, Joab reassumes command on his own initiative (see v. 23).

20:11 *He that favoureth Joab, and he that is for David.* To dispel any idea that Joab was aligned with Sheba's conspiracy, an appeal is made to Amasa's troops to support Joab if they are truly loyal to David.

20:14 *Abel . . . Beth-maachah.* Located to the north of Dan (see 1 Ki 15:20; 2 Chr 16:4). Sheba's strategy was to gather as many volunteers for his revolt as possible, but he was obviously afraid to assemble his ragtag army anywhere within close reach of David's men. *Berites.* Otherwise unknown.

the words of thine handmaid. And he answered, I do hear.
18 Then she spake, saying, [1]They were
wont to speak in old time, saying, They shall
surely ask *counsel* at Abel: and so they ended
the matter.
19 I *am one of them that are* peaceable *and*
faithful in Israel: thou seekest to destroy a city
and a mother in Israel: why wilt thou swallow
up [a]the inheritance of the LORD?
20 And Joab answered and said, Far be it,
far be it from me, that I should swallow up or
destroy.
21 The matter *is* not so: but a man of
mount Ephraim, Sheba the son of Bichri [1]by
name, hath lift up his hand against the king,
even against David: deliver him only, and I will
depart from the city. And the woman said unto
Joab, Behold, his head *shall be* thrown to thee
over the wall.
22 Then the woman went unto all the people [a]in her wisdom. And they cut off the head
of Sheba the son of Bichri, and cast *it* out to
Joab. And he blew a trumpet, and they [1]re-
tired from the city, every man to his tent. And
Joab returned *to* Jerusalem unto the king.
23 ¶ Now [a]Joab *was* over all the host of Israel: and Benaiah the son of Jehoiada *was* over
the Cherethites and over the Pelethites:
24 And Adoram *was* [a]over the tribute: and
[b]Jehoshaphat the son of Ahilud *was* [1]recorder:
25 And Sheva *was* scribe: and [a]Zadok and
Abiathar *were* the priests:
26 [a]And Ira also the Jairite was [b][1]a chief
ruler about David.

David repays the Gibeonites

21 Then there was a famine in the days
of David three years, year after year;
and David [1]inquired of the LORD. And the
LORD answered, *It is* for Saul, and for *his*
bloody house, because he slew the Gibeonites.
2 And the king called the Gibeonites, and
said unto them; (now the Gibeonites *were* not
of the children of Israel, but [a]of the remnant of
the Amorites; and the children of Israel had
sworn unto them: and Saul sought to slay
them in his zeal to the children of Israel and
Judah.)
3 Wherefore David said unto the
Gibeonites, What shall I do for you? and
wherewith shall I make the atonement, that ye
may bless [a]the inheritance of the LORD?
4 And the Gibeonites said unto him, [1]We
will have no silver nor gold of Saul, nor of his
house; neither for us *shalt thou* kill any man in
Israel. And he said, What you shall say, *that*
will I do for you.

20:18 [1]Or, *They plainly spake in the beginning, saying, Surely they will ask of Abel, and so make an end*
20:19 [a]1 Sam. 26:19; ch. 21:3
20:21 [1]Heb. *by his name*
20:22 [1]Heb. *were scattered* [a]Eccl. 9:14,15
20:23 [a]ch. 8:16,18
20:24 [1]Or, *remembrancer* [a]1 Ki. 4:6 [b]ch. 8:16; 1 Ki. 4:3
20:25 [a]ch. 8:17; 1 Ki. 4:4
20:26 [1]Or, *a prince* [a]ch. 23:38 [b]Gen. 41:45; Ex. 2:16; ch. 8:18
21:1 [1]Heb. *sought the face, etc.*
21:2 [a]Josh. 9:3,15-17
21:3 [a]ch. 20:19
21:4 [1]Or, It is *not silver nor gold that we have to do with Saul or his house, neither* pertains it *to us to kill, etc.*

20:18 *ask counsel at Abel.* The city was famous for the wisdom of its inhabitants.

20:19 *a mother in Israel.* A town that produced faithful Israelites—cities were commonly personified as women (see Jer 50:12; Gal 4:26). *the inheritance of the LORD.* See note on 1 Sam 10:1.

20:21 *mount Ephraim.* Either Sheba, a Benjamite (see v. 1), lived in the tribal territory of Ephraim or this was the designation of a geographical, rather than a strictly tribal, region.

20:22 *Joab returned to Jerusalem unto the king.* See notes on vv. 7,10.

20:23–26 These royal officials apparently served David during most of his reign (see 8:15–18).

20:23 *Joab was over all the host of Israel.* Though in some disfavor, he held this position until he participated in Adonijah's conspiracy (1 Ki 1:7; 2:28–35). *Cherethites and . . . Pelethites.* See note on 8:18.

‡20:24 *Adoram was over the tribute.* A position not established in the early years of David's reign (see 8:15–16). Adoram (a variant of Adoniram) must have been a late appointee of David since he continued to serve under Solomon (1 Ki 4:6; 5:14) and was eventually killed in the early days of the reign of Rehoboam (1 Ki 12:18; 2 Chr 10:18). *tribute.* I.e. forced labor. Labor performed for the most part by prisoners of war from defeated nations (see Josh 9:21; 1 Ki 9:15,20–21). *recorder.* See note on 8:16.

20:25 *Sheva.* See note on 8:17 ("Seraiah"). *scribe.* See note on 8:17. *Zadok and Abiathar.* See note on 8:17.

20:26 *Jairite.* A reference either to Jair of the tribe of Manasseh (Num 32:41) or to a judge from Gilead (Judg 10:3,5). *chief ruler.* See note on 8:18.

21:1–24:25 This concluding section forms an appendix to 1,2 Samuel and contains additional materials (without concern for chronology) relating to David's reign. While its topical arrangement is striking, it also employs a literary pattern, *a-b-c/c-b-a,* frequently found elsewhere in OT literature. The first and last units (21:1–14; 24:1–25) are narratives of two events in which David had to deal with God's wrath against Israel (the first occasioned by an act of Saul, the second by his own). The second and fifth units (21:15–22; 23:8–39) are accounts of David's warriors (the second much longer than the first). At the center (22:1–23:7) are two songs of David (the first much longer than the second), one of which celebrates David's victories as warrior-king while the other recalls his role as psalmist (see note on 1 Sam 16:14–17:58). It is unknown if motivation for this arrangement went beyond aesthetic considerations. The triumph song of ch. 22 and the song of Hannah in 1 Sam 2:1–10 clearly form a literary frame enclosing the main composition (see note on 1 Sam 2:1).

21:1–14 This event appears to have occurred after David's kindness was extended to Mephibosheth (ch. 9) and before Absalom's rebellion (16:7–8; 18:28; see note on 16:8).

21:1 *he slew the Gibeonites.* Saul's action against the Gibeonites is not related elsewhere but appears to have been instituted early in his reign, motivated by an excessive nationalism (if not tribalism—the Gibeonites occupied territory partly assigned to Benjamin, and Saul's great-grandfather was known as the "father of Gibeon," 1 Chr 8:29; 9:35).

21:2 *Amorites.* A comprehensive name sometimes used to designate all the pre-Israelite inhabitants of Canaan (Gen 15:16; Josh 24:18; Judg 6:10; Amos 2:10). More precisely, the Gibeonites were called Hivites (Josh 9:7; 11:19). *the children of Israel had sworn unto them.* A pledge sworn in the name of the Lord (Josh 9:15,18–26). *sought to slay them.* The reason Saul was unsuccessful is not known.

21:3 *bless.* Since the oath sworn to them had been violated, they could rightly call down God's curse on the land. *the inheritance of the LORD.* See note on 1 Sam 10:1.

21:4 *neither for us shalt thou kill any man in Israel.* Bloodguilt could only be redressed by the shedding of blood, but as subject aliens the Gibeonites had no right to legal redress against an Israelite. This restriction must have been Saul's since it is contrary to the Mosaic law (see Ex 22:21; Lev 19:34; 24:22; Deut 1:16–17; 24:17; 27:19).

5 And they answered the king, The man that consumed us, and that [1]devised against us *that* we should be destroyed from remaining in any of the coasts of Israel,

6 Let seven men of his sons be delivered unto us, and we will hang them up unto the LORD [a]in Gibeah of Saul, [b][1]whom the LORD did choose. And the king said, I will give *them.*

7 But the king spared Mephibosheth, the son of Jonathan the son of Saul, because of [a]the LORD'S oath that *was* between them, between David and Jonathan the son of Saul.

8 But the king took the two sons of [a]Rizpah the daughter of Aiah, whom she bare unto Saul, Armoni and Mephibosheth; and the five sons of [1]Michal the daughter of Saul, whom she [2]brought up for Adriel the son of Barzillai the Meholathite:

9 And he delivered them into the hands of the Gibeonites, and they hanged them in the hill [a]before the LORD: and they fell *all* seven together, and were put to death in the days of harvest, in the first *days,* in the beginning of barley harvest.

10 And [a]Rizpah the daughter of Aiah took sackcloth, and spread it for her upon the rock, [b]from the beginning of harvest until water dropped upon them out of heaven, and suffered neither the birds of the air to rest on them by day, nor the beasts of the field by night.

11 And it was told David what Rizpah the daughter of Aiah, the concubine of Saul, had done.

12 And David went and took the bones of Saul and the bones of Jonathan his son from the men of [a]Jabesh-gilead, which had stolen them from the street of Beth-shan, where the Philistines had hanged them, when the Philistines had slain Saul in Gilboa:

13 And he brought up from thence the bones of Saul and the bones of Jonathan his son; and they gathered the bones of them that were hanged.

14 And the bones of Saul and Jonathan his son buried they in the country of Benjamin in [a]Zelah, in the sepulchre of Kish his father: and they performed all that the king commanded. And after that [b]God was intreated for the land.

Victories over the Philistines

15 ¶ Moreover the Philistines had yet war again with Israel; and David went down, and his servants with him, and fought against the Philistines: and David waxed faint.

16 And Ishbi-benob, which *was* of the sons of [1]the giant, the weight of whose [2]spear *weighed* three hundred *shekels* of brass *in* weight, he being girded *with* a new *sword,* thought to have slain David.

17 But Abishai the son of Zeruiah succoured him, and smote the Philistine, and killed him. Then the men of David sware unto him, saying, [a]Thou shalt go no more out with us to battle, that thou quench not the [b][1]light of Israel.

18 [a]And it came to pass after this, that there was again a battle with the Philistines at Gob: then [b]Sibbechai the Hushathite slew [1]Saph, which *was* of the sons of [2]the giant.

19 And there was again a battle in Gob with the Philistines, where Elhanan the son of [1]Jaare-oregim, a Beth-lehemite, slew [a]*the brother of* Goliath the Gittite, the staff of whose spear *was* like a weaver's beam.

20 And [a]there was yet a battle in Gath, where was a man of *great* stature, that had on every hand six fingers, and on every foot six toes, four and twenty *in* number; and he also was born to [1]the giant.

21:5 [1] Or, *cut us off*
21:6 [1] Or, *chosen of the LORD* [a] 1 Sam. 10:26 [b] 1 Sam. 10:24
21:7 [a] 1 Sam. 18:3; 20:8,15
21:8 [1] Or, *Michal's* sister [2] Heb. *bare to Adriel* [a] ch. 3:7
21:9 [a] ch. 6:17
21:10 [a] ver. 8; ch. 3:7 [b] See Deut. 21:23
21:12 [a] 1 Sam. 31:11-13
21:14 [a] Josh. 18:28 [b] See Josh. 7:26; ch. 24:25
21:16 [1] Or, *Rapha* [2] Heb. *the staff,* or, *the head*
21:17 [1] Heb. *candle,* or, *lamp* [a] ch. 18:3 [b] 1 Ki. 11:36
21:18 [1] [Or, *Sippai*] [2] Or, *Rapha* [a] 1 Chr. 20:4 [b] 1 Chr. 11:29
21:19 [1] [Or, *Jair*] [a] See 1 Chr. 20:5
21:20 [1] Or, *Rapha* [a] 1 Chr. 20:6

21:5 *The man.* Saul. *we should be destroyed . . . Israel.* Those who escaped Saul's attack had been driven from their towns and lands (see 4:2–3 and notes).

21:6 *seven.* Because it would represent a full number (seven symbolized completeness)—though many more Gibeonites had been slain. *Gibeah.* The place of Saul's residence (see 1 Sam 10:26).

21:7 *the LORD'S oath . . . between David and Jonathan.* See 4:4; 9:1–13; 1 Sam 18:3; 20:15.

‡21:8 *Rizpah.* See 3:7. *Michal.* See KJV marg.; see also 6:23. Two Hebrew manuscripts read "Merab." See 1 Sam 18:19. *Barzillai the Meholathite.* Not to be confused with Barzillai the Gileadite (17:27; 19:31).

21:9 *they fell all seven together.* This nearly extinguished the house of Saul, which God had rejected (see 1 Sam 13:13–14; 15:23–26). In 1 Chr 8:29–39; 9:35–44 no descendants of Saul are listed other than from the line of Jonathan. *the beginning of barley harvest.* About the middle of April (see note on Ruth 1:22).

21:10 *sackcloth.* See note on Gen 37:34. *water dropped . . . heaven.* An indication that the famine was caused by drought and evidence that the judgment on Israel for breaking the oath sworn to the Gibeonites (see v. 1) was now over.

21:12 *bones of Saul and . . . Jonathan his son.* See 1 Sam 31:11–13. David's final act toward Saul and Jonathan was a deed of deep respect for the king he had honored and the friend he had loved.

21:15–22 These four Philistine episodes (vv. 15–17, 18, 19, 20–21) cannot be chronologically located with any certainty (see note on 21:1–24:25). Each involves a heroic accomplishment by one of David's mighty men, resulting in the death of "sons of the giant" (see vv. 16,18,20,22).

21:16 *giant.* In saying the four formidable enemy warriors referred to in this series were "born to the giant in Gath" (v. 22), the writer may be linking them to Deut 2:10–11,20–21. In that case, they may have been related to the Anakim (see Josh 11:21–22). Cf. Gen 15:19–20, which in its list of ten peoples of Canaan mentions Rephaim but not Anakim, though the Anakim (but not Rephaim) figure significantly in the accounts of the conquest (Num 13:22,28,33; Deut 1:28; 9:2; Josh 14:12,15; Judg 1:20).

21:17 *Abishai.* See note on 1 Sam 26:6. *that thou quench not the light of Israel.* A striking metaphor depicting Israel's dependence on David for its security and continuing existence as a nation—its national hope (see 22:29; 23:3–4; 1 Ki 11:36).

21:18 *Gob.* Probably in the near vicinity of Gezer, where 1 Chr 20:4 locates this same battle. *Saph.* Called Sippai in 1 Chr 20:4.

‡21:19 *Elhanan . . . slew the brother of Goliath.* The Hebrew does not include "the brother of." Since it is clear from 1 Sam 17 that David killed Goliath, it is possible that an early copyist misread the Hebrew for "Lahmi the brother of" (see 1 Chr 20:5) as "a Beth-lehemite" (in Hebrew the word for "slew" stands first in the clause).

21 And when he [1]defied Israel, Jonathan
the son of [a]Shimea the brother of David slew
him.
22 [a]These four were born to the giant in
Gath, and fell by the hand of David, and by the
hand of his servants.

David's psalm of praise

22 And David [a]spake unto the LORD the
words of this song in the day *that* the
LORD had [b]delivered him out of the hand of all
his enemies, and out of the hand of Saul:
2 And he said,
[a]The LORD *is* my rock, and my fortress,
and my deliverer;
3 The God of my rock; [a]in him will I
trust:
He is my [b]shield, and the [c]horn of my
salvation, my high [d]tower, and my
[e]refuge,
My saviour; thou savest me from
violence.
4 I will call on the LORD, who is *worthy*
to be praised:
So shall I be saved from mine enemies.
5 When the [1]waves of death compassed
me,
The floods of [2]ungodly men made me
afraid;
6 The [a 1]sorrows of hell compassed me
about;
The snares of death prevented me:
7 In my distress [a]I called upon the LORD,
And cried to my God:
And he did [b]hear my voice out of his
temple,
And my cry *did enter* into his ears.
8 Then [a]the earth shook and trembled;
[b]The foundations of heaven moved
And shook, because he was wroth.
9 There went up a smoke [1]out of his
nostrils,
And [a]fire out of his mouth devoured:
Coals were kindled by it.
10 He [a]bowed the heavens also, and came
down;
And [b]darkness *was* under his feet.
11 And he rode upon a cherub, and did
fly:
And he was seen [a]upon the wings of
the wind.
12 And he made [a]darkness pavilions
round about him,
[1]Dark waters, *and* thick clouds of the
skies.
13 Through the brightness before him
Were [a]coals of fire kindled.
14 The LORD [a]thundered from heaven,
And the most High uttered his voice.
15 And he sent out [a]arrows, and scattered
them;
Lightning, and discomfited them.
16 And the channels of the sea appeared,
The foundations of the world were
discovered,
At the [a]rebuking of the LORD,
At the blast of the breath of his
[1]nostrils.
17 [a]He sent from above, he took me;
He drew me out of [1]many waters;
18 [a]He delivered me from my strong
enemy,
And from them that hated me: for they
were too strong for me.
19 They prevented me in the day of my
calamity:
But the LORD was my stay.
20 [a]He brought me forth also into a large
place:
He delivered me, because he
[b]delighted in me.
21 [a]The LORD rewarded me according to
my righteousness:

21:21 [1]Or, *reproached* [a]1 Sam. 16:9, *Shammah*
21:22 [a]1 Chr. 20:8
22:1 [a]Ex. 15:1; Judg. 5:1 [b]Ps. 18, title; 34:19
22:2 [a]Deut. 32:4
22:3 [a]Heb. 2:13 [b]Gen. 15:1 [c]Luke 1:69 [d]Prov. 18:10 [e]Ps. 9:9; Jer. 16:19
22:5 [1]Or, *pangs* [2]Heb. *Belial*
22:6 [1]Or, *cords* [a]Ps. 116:3
22:7 [a]Ps. 116:4 [b]Ex. 3:7
22:8 [a]Ps. 77:18 [b]Job 26:11
22:9 [1]Heb. *by*
22:9 [a]Ps. 97:3
22:10 [a]Is. 64:1 [b]Ex. 20:21
22:11 [a]Ps. 104:3
22:12 [1]Heb. *Binding of waters* [a]Ps. 97:2
22:13 [a]ver. 9
22:14 [a]1 Sam. 2:10
22:15 [a]Ps. 7:13
22:16 [1][Or, *anger*, Ps. 74:1] [a]Ex. 15:8
22:17 [1]Or, *great* [a]Ps. 144:7
22:18 [a]ver. 1
22:20 [a]Ps. 31:8 [b]ch. 15:26
22:21 [a]Ps. 7:8

21:21 *defied Israel.* As Goliath had done (see 1 Sam 17:10,25). *Shimea.* Also called Shammah (1 Sam 16:9; 17:13).
22:1 *this song.* Preserved also as Ps 18 (see notes on that psalm). Besides an introduction (vv. 2–4) and conclusion (vv. 47–51), the song consists of three major sections: The first describes David's deliverance from mortal danger at the hands of his enemies (vv. 5–20); the second sets forth the moral grounds for God's saving help (vv. 21–30); the third recounts the help that the Lord gave him (vv. 31–46). The song was probably composed shortly after David's victories over foreign enemies (8:1–14) and before his sin with Bath-sheba (compare vv. 21–25 with 1 Ki 15:5). *out of the hand of all his enemies.* See 8:1–14. *out of the hand of Saul.* See 1 Sam 18–31.
22:2 *my rock.* A figure particularly appropriate to David's experience (see vv. 32,47; 23:3; Deut 32:4,15,18,31; Ps 28:1; 31:2; 61:2; 78:35; 89:26; 94:22; 95:1). He had often taken refuge among the rocks of the wilderness (1 Sam 23:25; 24:2), but he realized that true security was found only in the Lord. *fortress.* The Hebrew for this word occurs in 5:17; 23:14; 1 Sam 22:4–5; 24:22, referring to places where David sought refuge.
22:3 *my shield.* See vv. 31,36; Gen 15:1; Deut 33:29. *horn.* Here symbolizes strength (see Deut 33:17; Jer 48:25; see also note on Luke 1:69).
22:5 *waves of death.* In vv. 5–6 David depicts his experiences in poetic figures of mortal danger.
‡22:6 *hell.* Hebrew *Sheol.* See note on Jonah 2:2.
22:7 *his temple.* Heaven, where the Lord is enthroned as King (see Ps 11:4; Is 6:1; Jonah 2:7).
22:8–16 See note on Ps 18:7–15.
22:9 *went up a smoke out of his nostrils.* God's power is portrayed in terms similar to those applied to the awesome beast, the Leviathan (Job 41:19–21).
22:11 *cherub.* See Ezek 1 and 10, where cherubim are said to be the bearers of the throne of God; see also notes on Gen 3:24; 1 Sam 4:4; Ezek 1:5.
22:14 *The LORD thundered.* The reference to thunder as the voice of God is common in the OT (see Ps 29; Job 37:2–5). Thunder is particularly suited to expressing God's power and majesty.
22:17 *He sent from above.* In vv. 17–20 David describes his deliverance, initially in figurative terms (v. 17; cf. v. 5) and subsequently in more literal language (vv. 18–20).
22:20 *delighted in.* The Hebrew underlying this expression is used in 15:26; Ps 22:8 (cf. Mat 3:17, "well-pleased") and expresses the idea of the sovereign good pleasure and favor of God toward His anointed one (v. 51).
22:21 *according to my righteousness.* In vv. 21–25 David refers

According to the [b]cleanness of my
hands hath he recompensed me.
22 For I have [a]kept the ways of the LORD,
And have not wickedly departed from
my God.
23 For all his [a]judgments *were* before me:
And *as for* his statutes, I did not depart
from them.
24 I was also [a]upright [1]before him,
And have kept myself from mine
iniquity.
25 Therefore [a]the LORD hath recompensed
me according to my righteousness;
According to my cleanness [1]in his eye
sight.
26 With [a]the merciful thou wilt shew
thyself merciful,
And with the upright man thou wilt
shew thyself upright.
27 With the pure thou wilt shew thyself
pure;
And [a]with the froward thou wilt
[1]shew thyself unsavoury.
28 And the [a]afflicted people thou wilt save:
But thine eyes *are* upon [b]the haughty,
that thou mayest bring *them* down.
29 For thou *art* my [1]lamp, O LORD:
And the LORD will lighten my darkness.
30 For by thee I have [1]run *through* a
troop:
By my God have I leaped over a wall.
31 *As for* God, [a]his way *is* perfect;
[b]The word of the LORD *is* [1]tried:
He *is* a buckler to all them that trust in
him.
32 For [a]who *is* God, save the LORD?
And who *is* a rock, save our God?
33 God *is* my [a]strength *and* power:
And he [b][1]maketh my way [c]perfect.
34 He [1]maketh my feet [a]like hinds' *feet:*
And [b]setteth me upon my high places.
35 [a]He teacheth my hands [1]to war;
So that a bow of steel is broken *by*
mine arms.
36 Thou hast also given me the shield of
thy salvation:
And thy gentleness hath [1]made me
great.
37 Thou hast [a]enlarged my steps under
me;
So that my [1]feet did not slip.
38 I have pursued mine enemies, and
destroyed them;

22:21 [b]Ps. 24:4
22:22 [a]Ps. 119:3
22:23 [a]Deut. 7:12
22:24 [1]Heb. *to him* [a]Job 1:1
22:25 [1]Heb. *before his eyes* [a]ver. 21
22:26 [a]Mat. 5:7
22:27 [1]Or, *wrestle* [a]Lev. 26:23
22:28 [a]Ps. 72:12 [b]Job 40:11
22:29 [1]Or, *candle*
22:30 [1]Or, *broken a troop*
22:31 [1]Or, *refined* [a]Dan. 4:37 [b]Ps. 12:6
22:32 [a]Is. 45:5,6
22:33 [1]Heb. *riddeth,* or, *looseth* [a]Ps. 27:1; Is. 12:2 [b]Heb. 13:21 [c]Ps. 101:2,6
22:34 [1]Heb. *equalleth* [a]ch. 2:18 [b]Is. 33:16
22:35 [1]Heb. *for the war* [a]Ps. 144:1
22:36 [1]Heb. *multiplied me*
22:37 [1]Heb. *ankles* [a]Prov. 4:12
22:39 [a]Mal. 4:3
22:40 [1]Heb. *caused to bow* [a]Ps. 18:32 [b]Ps. 44:5
22:41 [a]Gen. 49:8
22:42 [a]Prov. 1:28
22:43 [a]Ps. 18:42 [b]Is. 10:6
22:44 [a]ch. 3:1 [b]Deut. 28:13 [c]Is. 55:5
22:45 [1]Heb. *Sons of the stranger* [2]Or, *yield feigned obedience.* Heb. *lie*
22:46 [a]Mic. 7:17
22:47 [a]Ps. 89:26
22:48 [1]Heb. *giveth avengement for me* [a]1 Sam. 25:39 [b]Ps. 144:2
22:49 [a]Ps. 140:1
22:50 [a]Rom. 15:9
22:51 [a]Ps. 144:10

And turned not again until I had
consumed them.
39 And I have consumed them, and
wounded them, that they could not
arise:
Yea, they are fallen [a]under my feet.
40 For thou hast [a]girded me with strength
to battle:
[b]Them that rose up against me hast
thou [1]subdued under me.
41 Thou hast also given me the [a]necks of
mine enemies,
That I might destroy them that hate
me.
42 They looked, but *there was* none to
save;
Even [a]unto the LORD, but he answered
them not.
43 Then did I beat them *as* small [a]as the
dust of the earth,
I did stamp them [b]as the mire of the
street, *and* did spread them abroad.
44 [a]Thou also hast delivered me from the
strivings of my people,
Thou hast kept me to be [b]head of the
heathen:
[c]A people *which* I knew not shall serve
me.
45 [1]Strangers shall [2]submit themselves
unto me:
As soon as they hear, they shall be
obedient unto me.
46 Strangers shall fade away,
And they shall be afraid [a]out of their
close places.
47 The LORD liveth; and blessed *be* my
rock;
And exalted be the God of the [a]rock of
my salvation.
48 *It is* God that [a][1]avengeth me,
And that [b]bringeth down the people
under me,
49 And that bringeth me forth from mine
enemies:
Thou also hast lifted me up on high
above them that rose up against me:
Thou hast delivered me from the
[a]violent man.
50 Therefore I will give thanks unto thee,
O LORD, among [a]the heathen,
And I will sing praises unto thy name.
51 [a]*He is* the tower of salvation for his
king:

to the Lord's deliverances as a reward for his own righteousness. While these statements may give the impression of self-righteous boasting and a meritorious basis for divine favor, they should be understood in their context as: (1) David's desire to please the Lord in his service as the Lord's anointed (see note on v. 51); (2) his recognition that the Lord rewards those who faithfully seek to serve Him.

22:26–30 Because God responds to man in kind (see Job 34:11; Prov 3:34), David has experienced the Lord's favor.

22:28 *the haughty, that thou mayest bring them down.* The words of this verse fit well with David's experience in his conflict with Saul (see Hannah's song, 1 Sam 2:3–8).

22:29 *thou art my lamp.* The Lord causes David's life and undertakings to flourish (see Job 18:5–6; 21:17; see also note on Ps 27:1).

22:31 *his way is perfect.* The remainder of the song (vv. 31–51) accentuates David's praise to God for His deliverances.

22:32 *rock.* See note on v. 2.

22:47 *The LORD liveth.* God's interventions and blessings in David's behalf have shown Him to be the living God (see Deut 5:26).

22:50 *I will give thanks unto thee, O LORD, among the heathen.* For Paul's reference to this vow see Rom 15:9.

22:51 *his king . . . his anointed.* See notes on 1 Sam 10:25;

And sheweth mercy to his [b]anointed,
Unto David, and [c]to his seed for
evermore.

David's last words

23 Now these *be* the last words of David.
David the son of Jesse said,
[a]And the man *who* was raised up on
high,
[b]The anointed of the God of Jacob,
And the sweet psalmist of Israel, said,
2 [a]The Spirit of the LORD spake by me,
And his word *was* in my tongue.
3 The God of Israel said,
[a]The Rock of Israel spake to me,
[1]He that ruleth over men *must be* just,
Ruling [b]*in* the fear of God.
4 And *he shall be* as the light of the
morning, *when* the sun riseth,
Even a morning without clouds;
As the tender grass *springing* out of
the earth
By clear shining after rain.
5 Although my house *be* not so with God;
[a]Yet he hath made with me an
everlasting covenant,
Ordered in all *things,* and sure:
For *this is* all my salvation, and all *my*
desire,
Although he make *it* not to grow.
6 But *the sons of* Belial *shall be* all of
them as thorns thrust away,
Because they cannot be taken with
hands:
7 But the man *that* shall touch them
must be [1]fenced *with* iron and the
staff of a spear;
And they shall be utterly burnt with
fire in the same place.

22:51 [b]Ps. 89:20 [c]Ps. 89:29
23:1 [a]Ps. 78:70 [b]1 Sam. 16:12, 13; Ps. 89:20
23:2 [a]2 Pet. 1:21
23:3 [1]Or, Be thou *ruler, etc.* [a]Deut. 32:4 [b]Ex. 18:21
23:5 [a]Ps. 89:29
23:7 [1]Heb. *filled*
23:8 [1]Or, *Josheb-bassebet the Tachmonite, head of the three* [2]Supplied from 1 Chr. 11:11 [3]Heb. *slain*
23:9 [a]1 Chr. 11:12
23:11 [1]Or, *for foraging* [a]1 Chr. 11:27 [b]See 1 Chr. 11:13,14
23:13 [1]Or, *the three captains over the thirty* [a]1 Chr. 11:15 [b]1 Sam. 22:1 [c]ch. 5:18
23:14 [a]1 Sam. 22:4,5

David's mighty men

8 ¶ These *be* the names of the mighty *men*
whom David had: [1]The Tachmonite that sat in
the seat, chief among the captains; the same *was*
Adino the Eznite: [2]*he lift up his spear* against
eight hundred, [3]whom he slew at one time.
9 And after him *was* [a]Eleazar the son of
Dodo the Ahohite, *one* of the three mighty
men with David, when they defied the Philistines *that* were there gathered together to battle, and the men of Israel were gone away:
10 He arose, and smote the Philistines until his hand was weary, and his hand clave
unto the sword: and the LORD wrought a great
victory that day; and the people returned after
him only to spoil.
11 And after him *was* [a]Shammah the son
of Agee the Hararite. [b]And the Philistines
were gathered together [1]into a troop, where
was a piece of ground full *of* lentiles: and the
people fled from the Philistines.
12 But he stood in the midst of the ground,
and defended it, and slew the Philistines: and
the LORD wrought a great victory.
13 And [a][1]three of the thirty chief went
down, and came to David in the harvest time
unto [b]the cave of Adullam: and the troop of the
Philistines pitched in [c]the valley of Rephaim.
14 And David *was* then in [a]a hold, and the
garrison of the Philistines *was* then *in* Beth-
lehem.
15 And David longed, and said, Oh that
one would give me drink *of* the water of the
well of Beth-lehem, which *is* by the gate.
16 And the three mighty *men* brake
through the host of the Philistines, and drew
water out of the well of Beth-lehem, that *was*
by the gate, and took *it,* and brought *it* to David: nevertheless he would not drink thereof,
but poured it out unto the LORD.

12:14–15. David refers to himself in the third person in a way that acknowledges the covenantal character of his kingship. It is in the context of David's official capacity as the Lord's anointed that the entire song is to be read and understood (see note on v. 21). *his seed for evermore.* David speaks of God's promise through Nathan (see 7:12–16).

23:1 *last words of David.* Probably to be understood as David's last poetic testimony (in the manner of his psalms), perhaps composed at the time of his final instructions and warnings to his son Solomon (see 1 Ki 2:1–10).

23:2 *The Spirit of the LORD spake by me.* David was conscious of God's Spirit at work in him enabling him to speak under the Spirit's guidance (see notes on 2 Tim 3:16; 2 Pet 1:21).

23:3 *Rock.* See note on 22:2; see also 1 Sam 2:2; Deut 32:4,15,18,30–31. *He that ruleth over men must be just.* In brief and vivid strokes David portrays the ideal theocratic king—to be fully realized only in the rule of David's greater son, Jesus Christ. This prophetic utterance complements that of 7:12–16 and anticipates those of Is 9:7; 11:1–5; Jer 23:5–6; 33:15–16; Zec 9:9.

23:4 *as the light of the morning.* See notes on Ps 27:1; 36:9.

‡23:5 *my house be not so with God.* A statement recalling God's covenant with him and his dynasty (see 7:12–16). *everlasting covenant.* David expressly calls God's promise to him a covenant that will not be abrogated (see notes on 7:20,28; Is 55:3; see also Ps 89:3,28,34,39; 132:11). *make it not to grow.* Through David's promised descendants.

23:6 *sons of Belial . . . thrust away.* Godless people who have no interest in the righteous king will be destroyed (see Ps 2:9; 110:5–6).

23:8–39 See note on 21:1–24:25. This list of 37 (see v. 39) of David's most valiant warriors and the description of some of their exploits are paralleled in 1 Chr 11:11–41. There the list is expanded by 16 names (1 Chr 11:41–47).

23:8 *Tachmonite.* 1 Chr 11:11 reads "Hachmonite," derived from an unknown place-name. *captains.* Two groups of three warriors (vv. 8–12 and 13–23) and one group of 30 warriors (vv. 23–39) are mentioned (see note on v. 39 for the total number of warriors).

23:9 *Ahohite.* A descendant of Ahoah from the tribe of Benjamin (1 Chr 8:4).

23:13 *three.* Not the same as the three mighty men of v. 9. *thirty chief.* See vv. 23–24,39. *harvest time.* See 11:1 and note. The circumstances of this event suggest that it happened shortly after David had fled from Saul, when men first began to gather to his cause (see 1 Sam 22:1–4), or shortly after his conquest of Jerusalem (see 2 Sam 5:17–18). *cave of Adullam.* See 1 Sam 22:1. *Rephaim.* See 5:18.

23:14 *hold.* See note on 1 Sam 22:4.

23:15–16 See note on 1 Chr 11:15–19.

17 And he said, Be it far from me, O LORD, that I should do this: *is not this* [a]the blood of the men that went in *jeopardy of* their lives? therefore he would not drink it. These *things* did *these* three mighty *men.*

18 And [a]Abishai, the brother of Joab, the son of Zeruiah, *was* chief among three. And he lift up his spear against three hundred, [1]and slew them, and had the name among three.

19 Was he not most honourable of three? therefore he was their captain: howbeit he attained not unto the *first* three.

20 And Benaiah the son of Jehoiada, the son of a valiant man, of [a]Kabzeel, [1]who had done many acts, [b]he slew two [2]lion-like men of Moab: he went down also and slew a lion in the midst of a pit in time of snow:

21 And he slew an Egyptian, [1]a goodly man: and the Egyptian had a spear in his hand; but he went down to him with a staff, and plucked the spear out of the Egyptian's hand, and slew him with his own spear.

22 These *things* did Benaiah the son of Jehoiada, and had the name among three mighty *men.*

23 He was [1]more honourable than the thirty, but he attained not to the *first* three. And David set him [a]over his [2]guard.

24 ¶ [a]Asahel the brother of Joab *was* one of the thirty; Elhanan the son of Dodo *of* Beth-lehem,

25 [a]Shammah the Harodite, Elika the Harodite,

26 Helez the Paltite, Ira the son of Ikkesh the Tekoite,

27 Abiezer the Anethothite, Mebunnai the Hushathite,

28 Zalmon the Ahohite, Maharai the Netophathite,

29 Heleb the son of Baanah, a Netophathite, Ittai the son of Ribai out of Gibeah of the children of Benjamin,

30 Benaiah the Pirathonite, Hiddai of the [1]brooks of [a]Gaash,

31 Abialbon the Arbathite, Azmaveth the Barhumite,

32 Eliahba the Shaalbonite, *of* the sons of Jashen, Jonathan,

33 Shammah the Hararite, Ahiam the son of Sharar the Hararite,

34 Eliphelet the son of Ahasbai, the son of the Maachathite, Eliam the son of Ahithophel the Gilonite,

35 Hezrai the Carmelite, Paarai the Arbite,

36 Igal the son of Nathan of Zobah, Bani the Gadite,

37 Zelek the Ammonite, Naharai the Beerothite, armourbearer to Joab the son of Zeruiah,

38 [a]Ira an Ithrite, Gareb an Ithrite,

39 [a]Uriah the Hittite: thirty and seven *in* all.

The census of Israel and Judah

24 And [a]again the anger of the LORD was kindled against Israel, and [1]he moved David against them to say, [b]Go, number Israel and Judah.

2 For the king said to Joab the captain of the host, which *was* with him, [1]Go now through all the tribes of Israel, [a]from Dan even to Beer-sheba, and number ye the people, that [b]I may know the number of the people.

3 And Joab said unto the king, Now the

23:17 [a]Lev. 17:10
23:18 [1]Heb. *slain* [a]1 Chr. 11:20
23:20 [1]Heb. *great of acts* [2]Heb. *lion of God* [a]Josh. 15:21 [b]Ex. 15:15
23:21 [1]Heb. *a man of countenance,* or, *sight:* called, 1 Chr. 11:23, *a man of* great *stature*
23:23 [1]Or, *honourable among the thirty* [2]Or, *council.* Heb. *at his command* [a]ch. 8:18; 20:23
23:24 [a]ch. 2:18
23:25 [a]See 1 Chr. 11:27
23:30 [1]Or, *valleys* [a]Judg. 2:9
23:38 [a]ch. 20:26
23:39 [a]ch. 11:3,6
24:1 [1]*Satan* [a]ch. 20:1 [b]1 Chr. 27:23,24
24:2 [1]Or, *Compass* [a]Judg. 20:1 [b]Jer. 17:5

23:18 *Abishai.* See 10:10,14; 18:2; see also note on 1 Sam 26:6. *three.* Presumably those referred to in vv. 13–17.

23:20 *Benaiah the son of Jehoiada.* Commander of the Cherethites and Pelethites (8:18; 20:23; see v. 23 below) and of the division of troops for the third month of the year (1 Chr 27:5). He supported Solomon's succession to the throne (1 Ki 1–2) and eventually replaced Joab as commander of the army (1 Ki 2:35).

23:24 *Asahel.* See 2:18–23. *thirty.* Twenty-nine names are listed in vv. 24–39. Since the three of vv. 13–17 are also included in the thirty (see v. 13), the total number of warriors mentioned is 32. 1 Chr 11:26–47 lists 16 additional names for this group, so it appears that the list includes the names of replacements for vacancies when a warrior either dropped out or died.

23:34 *Eliam.* Father of Bath-sheba (see 11:3) and son of David's counselor Ahithophel, who joined in Absalom's conspiracy (see 15:12,31,34; 16:20–23; 17:1–23).

23:39 *Uriah.* Husband of Bath-sheba (see 11:3–27). *thirty and seven.* The total number of warriors referred to in vv. 8–39, including the three of vv. 8–12, the three of vv. 13–17, Abishai (vv. 18–19), Benaiah (vv. 20–23) and the 29 whose names are recorded in vv. 24–39 (see note on v. 24).

24:1 *again.* The previous occasion may have been the famine of 21:1. *the anger of the LORD was kindled against Israel.* The specific reason for the Lord's displeasure is not stated. Because the anger is said to be directed against Israel rather than David, some have concluded that it was occasioned by the widespread support among the people for the rebellions of Absalom and Sheba against David (see 15:12; 17:11,24–26; 18:7; 20:1–2), the divinely chosen and anointed theocratic king. This would mean that the events of this chapter are to be placed chronologically shortly after those of chs. 15–20 and so after 980 B.C. (see note on 15:7). *the LORD . . . moved David against them.* 1 Chr 21:1 says that Satan inspired David to take the census. Although Scripture is clear that God does not cause anyone to sin (Jas 1:13–15), it is also clear that man's—and Satan's—evil acts are under God's sovereign control (see Ex 4:21; 7:3; 9:12; 10:1,20,27; 11:10; 14:4; Josh 11:20; 1 Ki 22:22–23; Job 1:12; 2:10; Ezek 3:20; 14:9; Acts 4:28). *number Israel and Judah.* David's military census (see vv. 2–3) does not appear to have been prompted by any immediate external threat. Since he wanted to "know the number of the people" (v. 2), it is evident that his action was motivated either by pride in the size of the empire he had acquired or by reliance for his security on the size of the reserve of manpower he could muster in an emergency or, more likely, both. The mere taking of a census was hardly sinful (see Num 1:2–3; 26:2–4), but in this instance it represented an unwarranted glorying in and dependence on human power rather than the Lord (not much different from Israel's initial desire to have a king for their security; see 1 Sam 8–12). The act was uncharacteristic of David (see 1 Sam 17:26, 37,45–47; 2 Sam 22:2–4,47–51).

24:2 *Dan even to Beer-sheba.* See note on 1 Sam 3:20.

24:3 *but why . . . ?* David's directive does not go unchallenged. The fact that he does not answer suggests that he knew his rea-

LORD thy God add unto the people, how many soever they be, an hundredfold, and *that* the eyes of my lord the king may see *it:* but why doth my lord the king delight in this thing?

4 Notwithstanding the king's word prevailed against Joab, and against the captains of the host. And Joab and the captains of the host went out from the presence of the king, to number the people *of* Israel.

5 And they passed over Jordan, and pitched in [a]Aroer, *on* the right side of the city that *lieth* in the midst of the [1]river of Gad, and toward [b]Jazer:

6 Then they came to Gilead, and to the [1]land of Tahtim-hodshi; and they came to [a]Dan-jaan, and about to [b]Zidon,

7 And came *to* the strong hold of Tyre, and *to* all the cities of the Hivites, and of the Canaanites: and they went out to the south of Judah, *even to* Beer-sheba.

8 So when they had gone through all the land, they came *to* Jerusalem at the end of nine months and twenty days.

9 And Joab gave *up* the sum of the number of the people unto the king: [a]and there were in Israel eight hundred thousand valiant men that drew the sword; and the men of Judah *were* five hundred thousand men.

10 ¶ And [a]David's heart smote him after that he had numbered the people. And David said unto the LORD, [b]I have sinned greatly *in* that I have done: and now, I beseech thee, O LORD, take away the iniquity of thy servant; for I have [c]done very foolishly.

11 For when David was up in the morning, the word of the LORD came unto the prophet [a]Gad, David's [b]seer, saying,

12 Go and say unto David, Thus saith the LORD, I offer thee three *things;* choose thee one of them, that I may do *it* unto thee.

13 So Gad came to David, and told him, and said unto him, Shall [a]seven years of famine come unto thee in thy land? or wilt thou flee three months before thine enemies, while they pursue thee? or that there be three days' pestilence in thy land? now advise, and see what answer I shall return *to* him that sent me.

24:5 [1]Or, *valley* [a]Deut. 2:36; Josh. 13:9,16 [b]Num. 32:1,3
24:6 [1]Or, *nether land newly inhabited* [a]Josh. 19:47; Judg. 18:29 [b]Josh. 19:28; Judg. 18:28
24:9 [a]See 1 Chr. 21:5
24:10 [a]1 Sam. 24:5 [b]ch. 12:13 [c]1 Sam. 13:13
24:11 [a]1 Sam. 22:5 [b]1 Sam. 9:9; 1 Chr. 29:29
24:13 [a]See 1 Chr. 21:12
24:14 [1]Or, *many* [a]Ps. 103:8,13,14; 119:156 [b]See Is. 47:6; Zech. 1:15
24:15 [a]1 Chr. 21:14; 27:24
24:16 [1][1 Chr. 21:15, *Ornan:* See ver. 18] [a]Ex. 12:23 [b]Gen. 6:6; 1 Sam. 15:11; Joel 2:13,14 [c]2 Chr. 3:1
24:17 [a]1 Chr. 21:17
24:18 [1][Heb. *Araniah*] [a]1 Chr. 21:18
24:21 [a]See Gen. 23:8-16 [b]Num. 16:48,50
24:22 [a]1 Ki. 19:21
24:23 [a]Ezek. 20:40,41

14 And David said unto Gad, I am in a great strait: let us fall now into the hand of the LORD; [a]for his mercies *are* [1]great: and [b]let me not fall into the hand of man.

15 So [a]the LORD sent a pestilence upon Israel from the morning even to the time appointed: and there died of the people from Dan even to Beer-sheba seventy thousand men.

David builds an altar

16 ¶ [a]And when the angel stretched out his hand *upon* Jerusalem to destroy it, [b]the LORD repented him of the evil, and said to the angel that destroyed the people, *It is* enough: stay now thine hand. And the angel of the LORD was by the threshingplace of [c][1]Araunah the Jebusite.

17 And David spake unto the LORD when he saw the angel that smote the people, and said, Lo, [a]I have sinned, and I have done wickedly: but these sheep, what have they done? let thine hand, I pray thee, be against me, and against my father's house.

18 And Gad came that day to David, and said unto him, [a]Go up, rear an altar unto the LORD in the threshingfloor of [1]Araunah the Jebusite.

19 And David, according to the saying of Gad, went up as the LORD commanded.

20 And Araunah looked, and saw the king and his servants coming on toward him: and Araunah went out, and bowed himself before the king *on* his face upon the ground.

21 And Araunah said, Wherefore is my lord the king come to his servant? [a]And David said, To buy the threshingfloor of thee, to build an altar unto the LORD, that [b]the plague may be stayed from the people.

22 And Araunah said unto David, Let my lord the king take and offer up what seemeth good unto him: [a]behold, *here be* oxen for burnt sacrifice, and threshing instruments and *other* instruments of the oxen for wood.

23 All *these things* did Araunah, *as* a king, give unto the king. And Araunah said unto the king, The LORD thy God [a]accept thee.

24 And the king said unto Araunah, Nay; but I will surely buy *it* of thee at a price: nei-

---

sons were highly questionable. In any event, Joab's challenge renders David the more guilty.

24:5–8 The military census was begun east of the Jordan, first in the south, then it and moved northward, then back across the Jordan, moving from north to south.

24:9 *eight hundred thousand . . . five hundred thousand.* These figures differ from those of 1 Chr 21:5 (see notes on 1 Chr 21:5–6).

24:10 *I have sinned greatly.* See note on v. 1.

24:11 *the prophet Gad, David's seer.* See notes on 1 Sam 9:9; 22:5.

24:12 *Go and say unto David.* See 12:1 and note. *three things.* The three alternative judgments were all included in the curses that Moses said would come on God's people when they failed to adhere to their covenant obligations (see Deut 28:15–25).

24:14 *not fall into the hand of man.* David, who knew both God and war, knew that even in His anger God is more merciful than man let loose in the rampages of war (see Ps 30:5).

24:15 *Dan even to Beer-sheba.* See note on 1 Sam 3:20.

24:16 *angel.* Angels appear elsewhere in Scripture as instruments of God's judgment (see Ex 33:2; 2 Ki 19:35; Ps 35:5–6; 78:49; Mat 13:41; Acts 12:23). *the LORD repented.* See note on 1 Sam 15:29. *threshingplace of Araunah.* Located on mount Moriah, immediately north of David's city and overlooking it. Later it would become the site of the temple (see 1 Chr 22:1; 2 Chr 3:1). *Jebusite.* See note on 5:6.

24:17 *let thine hand . . . be against me, and against my father's house.* Although the people of Israel were not without guilt (see v. 1), David assumes full blame for his own act and acknowledges his responsibility as king for the well-being of the Lord's people (see 5:2; 7:7–8).

24:19 *as the LORD commanded.* The Lord Himself appointed the atoning sacrifice in answer to David's prayer.

24:21 *To buy the threshingfloor of thee.* David does not simply expropriate the property for his royal purposes (see 1 Sam 8:14).

ther will I offer burnt offerings unto the LORD
my God of that which doth cost me nothing.
So [a]David bought the threshingfloor and the
oxen for fifty shekels of silver.

24:24 [a]See 1 Chr. 21:24,25
24:25 [a]ch. 21:14 [b]ver. 21

25 And David built there an altar unto the
LORD, and offered burnt offerings and peace offerings. [a]So the LORD was intreated for the
land, and [b]the plague was stayed from Israel.

24:24 *burnt offerings.* See Lev 1:1–17. *David bought the threshingfloor.* Thus the later site of the temple (see note on v. 16) became the royal property of the house of David. *and the oxen.* David's haste could not wait for oxen to be brought some distance from his own herds. *fifty shekels.* See note on 1 Chr 21:25.
24:25 *peace offerings.* See note on 1 Sam 11:15. Reconciliation and restoration of covenant fellowship were obtained by the king's repentance, intercessory prayer and the offering of sacrifices.

The First Book of the Kings

INTRODUCTION

Title

1 and 2 Kings (like 1 and 2 Samuel and 1 and 2 Chronicles) are actually one literary work, called in Hebrew tradition simply "Kings." The division of this work into two books was introduced by the translators of the Septuagint (the Greek translation of the OT) and subsequently followed in the Latin Vulgate and most modern versions. In 1448 the division into two sections also appeared in a Hebrew manuscript and was perpetuated in later printed editions of the Hebrew text. Both the Septuagint and the Latin Vulgate further designated Samuel and Kings in a way that emphasized the relationship of these two works (Septuagint: First, Second, Third and Fourth Book of Kingdoms; Latin Vulgate: First, Second, Third and Fourth Kings). Together Samuel and Kings relate the whole history of the monarchy, from its rise under the ministry of Samuel to its fall at the hands of the Babylonians.

The division between 1 and 2 Kings has been made at an appropriate but somewhat arbitrary place, shortly after the deaths of Ahab of the northern kingdom (22:37) and Jehoshaphat of the southern kingdom (22:50). Placing the division at this point causes the account of the reign of Ahaziah of Israel to overlap the end of 1 Kings (22:51–53) and the beginning of 2 Kings (ch. 1). The same is true of the narration of the ministry of Elijah, which for the most part appears in 1 Kings (chs. 17—19). However, his final act of judgment and the passing of his cloak to Elisha at the moment of his ascension to heaven in a whirlwind are contained in 2 Kings (1:1—2:17).

Author, Sources and Date

There is little conclusive evidence as to the identity of the author of 1,2 Kings. Although Jewish tradition credits Jeremiah, few today accept this as likely. Whoever the author was, it is clear that he was familiar with the book of Deuteronomy—as were many of Israel's prophets. It is also clear that he used a variety of sources in compiling his history of the monarchy. Three such sources are named: "the book of the acts of Solomon" (11:41), "the book of the chronicles of the kings of Israel" (14:19), "the book of the chronicles of the kings of Judah" (14:29). It is likely that other written sources were also employed (such as those mentioned in Chronicles; see below).

Although some scholars have concluded that the three sources specifically cited in 1,2 Kings are to be viewed as official court annals from the royal archives in Jerusalem and Samaria, this is by no means certain. It seems at least questionable whether official court annals would have included details of conspiracies such as those referred to in 16:20; 2 Ki 15:15. It is also questionable whether official court annals would have been readily accessible for public scrutiny, as the author clearly implies in his references to them. Such considerations have led some scholars to conclude that these sources were probably records of the reigns of the kings of Israel and Judah compiled by the succession of Israel's prophets spanning the kingdom period. 1,2 Chronicles makes reference to a number of such writings: "in the book of Samuel the seer, and in the book of Nathan the prophet, and in the book of Gad the seer" (1 Chr 29:29), "the prophecy of Ahijah the Shilonite" and "the visions of Iddo the seer" (2 Chr 9:29), "the book of Shemaiah the prophet" (2 Chr 12:15), "the book of Jehu the son of Hanani" (2 Chr 20:34), "the story of the book of the kings" (2 Chr 24:27), the "acts of Uzziah . . . Isaiah the prophet, the son of Amoz [wrote]" (2 Chr 26:22; see also 2 Chr 32:32)—and there may have been others. It is most likely, for example, that for the ministries of Elijah and Elisha the author depended on a prophetic source (perhaps from the eighth century) that had drawn up an account of those two prophets in which they were already compared with Moses and Joshua.

Some scholars place the date of composition of 1,2 Kings in the time subsequent to Jehoiachin's release from prison (562 B.C.; 2 Ki 25:27–30) and prior to the end of the Babylonian exile in 538. This position is challenged by others on the basis of statements in 1,2 Kings that speak of certain things in the preexilic period that are said to have continued in existence "unto this day" (see, e.g., 8:8, the poles used to carry the ark; 9:20–21, conscripted labor; 12:19, Israel in rebellion against the

house of David; 2 Ki 8:22, Edom in rebellion against the kingdom of Judah). From such statements it is argued that the writer must have been a person living in Judah in the preexilic period rather than in Babylon in postexilic times. If this argument is accepted, one must conclude that the original book was composed about the time of the death of Josiah and that the material pertaining to the time subsequent to his reign was added during the exile c. 550. While this "two-edition" viewpoint is possible, it rests largely on the "unto this day" statements.

An alternative is to understand these statements as those of the original source used by the author rather than statements of the author himself. A comparison of 2 Chr 5:9 with 1 Ki 8:8 suggests that this is a legitimate conclusion. Chronicles is clearly a postexilic writing, yet the wording of the statement concerning the poles used to carry the ark ("there it is unto this day") is the same in Chronicles as it is in Kings. Probably the Chronicler was simply quoting his source, namely, 1 Ki 8:8. There is no reason that the author of 1,2 Kings could not have done the same thing in quoting from his earlier sources. This explanation allows for positing a single author living in exile and using the source materials at his disposal.

Theme: Kingship and Covenant

1,2 Kings contains no explicit statement of purpose or theme. Reflection on its content, however, reveals that the author has selected and arranged his material in a manner that provides a sequel to the history found in 1,2 Samuel—a history of kingship regulated by covenant. In general, 1,2 Kings describes the history of the kings of Israel and Judah in the light of God's covenants. The guiding thesis of the book is that the welfare of Israel and her kings depended on their obedience to their obligations as defined in the Mosaic covenant.

It is clearly not the author's intention to present a socio-politico-economic history of Israel's monarchy in accordance with the principles of modern historiography. The author repeatedly refers the reader to other sources for more detailed information about the reigns of the various kings (see, e.g., 11:41; 14:19,29; 15:7,31; 16:5,14,20,27), and he gives a covenantal rather than a social or political or economic assessment of their reigns. From the standpoint of a political historian, Omri would be considered one of the more important rulers in the northern kingdom. He established a powerful dynasty and made Samaria the capital city. According to the Moabite Stone (see chart, p. xix), Omri was the ruler who subjugated the Moabites to the northern kingdom. Long after Omri's death, Assyrian rulers referred to Jehu as the "son of Omri" (either mistakenly or merely in accordance with their literary conventions when speaking of a later king of a realm). Yet in spite of Omri's political importance, his reign is dismissed in six verses (16:23–28) with the statement that he "wrought evil in the eyes of the LORD, and did worse than all that were before him" (16:25). Similarly, the reign of Jeroboam II, who presided over the northern kingdom during the time of its greatest political and economic power, is treated only briefly (2 Ki 14:23–29).

Another example of the writer's covenantal rather than merely political or economic interest can be seen in the description of the reign of Josiah of Judah. Nothing is said about the early years of his reign, but a detailed description is given of the reformation and renewal of the covenant that he promoted in his 18th year as king (2 Ki 22:3—23:28). Nor is anything said of the motives leading Josiah to oppose Pharaoh Neco of Egypt at Megiddo, or of the major shift in geopolitical power from Assyria to Babylon that was connected with this incident (see notes on 2 Ki 23:29–30).

It becomes apparent, then, that the kings who receive the most attention in 1,2 Kings are those during whose reigns there was either notable deviation from or affirmation of the covenant (or significant interaction between a king and God's prophet; see below). Ahab son of Omri is an example of the former (17:1—22:39). His reign is given extensive treatment, not so much because of its extraordinary political importance, but because of the serious threat to covenant fidelity and continuity that arose in the northern kingdom during his reign. Ultimately the pagan influence of Ahab's wife Jezebel through Ahab's daughter Athaliah (whether she was Jezebel's daughter is unknown) nearly led to the extermination of the house of David in Judah (see 2 Ki 11:1–3).

Manasseh (2 Ki 21:1–18) is an example of a similar sort. Here again it is deviation from the covenant that is emphasized in the account of his reign rather than political features, such as involvement in the Assyrian-Egyptian conflict (mentioned in Assyrian records but not in 2 Kings). The extreme apostasy characterizing Manasseh's reign made exile for Judah inevitable (2 Ki 21:10–15; 23:26–27).

On the positive side, Hezekiah (2 Ki 18:1—20:21) and Josiah (2 Ki 22:1—23:29) are given extensive treatment because of their involvement in covenant renewal. These are the only two kings

given unqualified approval by the writer for their loyalty to the Lord (2 Ki 18:3; 22:2). It is noteworthy that all the kings of the northern kingdom are said to have done evil in the eyes of the Lord and walked in the ways of Jeroboam, who caused Israel to sin (see, e.g., 16:26,31; 22:52; 2 Ki 3:3; 10:29). It was Jeroboam who established the golden calf worship at Beth-el and Dan shortly after the division of the kingdom (see 12:26–33; 13:1–6).

While the writer depicts Israel's obedience or disobedience to the Sinai covenant as decisive for her historical destiny, he also recognizes the far-reaching historical significance of the Davidic covenant, which promised that David's dynasty would endure forever. This is particularly noticeable in references to the "lamp" that the Lord had promised David (see 11:36; 15:4; 2 Ki 8:19; see also note on 2 Sam 21:17). It also appears in more general references to the promise to David (8:20,25) and its consequences for specific historical developments in Judah's later history (11:12–13,32; 2 Ki 19:34; 20:6). In addition, the writer uses the life and reign of David as a standard by which the lives of later kings are measured (see, e.g., 9:4; 11:4,6,33,38; 14:8; 15:3,5,11; 2 Ki 16:2; 18:3; 22:2).

Another prominent feature of the narratives of 1,2 Kings is the emphasis on the relationship between prophecy and fulfillment in the historical developments of the monarchy. On at least 11 occasions a prophecy is recorded that is later said to have been fulfilled (see, e.g., 2 Sam 7:13 and 1 Ki 8:20; 1 Ki 11:29–39 and 1 Ki 12:15; 1 Ki 13 and 2 Ki 23:16–18). The result of this emphasis is that the history of the kingdom is not presented as a chain of chance occurrences or the mere interplay of human actions but as the unfolding of Israel's historical destiny under the guidance of an omniscient and omnipotent God—Israel's covenant Lord, who rules all history in accordance with His sovereign purposes (see 8:56; 2 Ki 10:10).

The author also stresses the importance of the prophets themselves in their role as official emissaries from the court of Israel's covenant Lord, the Great King to whom Israel and her king were bound in service through the covenant. The Lord sent a long succession of such prophets to call king and people back to covenant loyalty (2 Ki 17:13). For the most part their warnings and exhortations fell on deaf ears. Many of these prophets and prophetesses are mentioned in the narratives of 1,2 Kings (see, e.g., Ahijah, 11:29–40; 14:5–18; Shemaiah, 12:22–24; Micaiah, 22:8–28; Jonah, 2 Ki 14:25; Isaiah, 2 Ki 19:1–7,20–34; Huldah, 2 Ki 22:14–20), but particular attention is given to the ministries of Elijah and Elisha (1 Ki 17—19; 2 Ki 1—13).

Reflection on these features of 1,2 Kings suggests that it was written to explain to a people in exile that the reason for their condition of humiliation was their stubborn persistence in breaking the covenant. In bringing the exile upon His people, God, after much patience, imposed the curses of the covenant, which had stood as a warning to them from the beginning (see Lev 26:27–45; Deut 28:64–68). This is made explicit with respect to the captivity of the northern kingdom in 2 Ki 17:7–23; 18:10–12, and with respect to the southern kingdom in 2 Ki 21. The reformation under Josiah in the southern kingdom is viewed as too little, too late (see 2 Ki 23:26–27; 24:3).

The book, then, provides a retrospective analysis of Israel's history. It explains the reasons both for the destruction of Samaria and Jerusalem and their respective kingdoms and for the bitter experience of being forced into exile. This does not mean, however, that there is no hope for the future. The writer consistently keeps the promise to David in view as a basis on which Israel in exile may look to the future with hope rather than with despair. In this connection the final four verses of the book, reporting Jehoiachin's release from prison in Babylon and his elevation to a place of honor in the court there (2 Ki 25:27–30), take on added significance. The future remains open for a new work of the Lord in faithfulness to His promise to the house of David.

It is important to note that, although the author was undoubtedly a Judahite exile, and although the northern kingdom had been dispersed for well over a century and a half at the time of his writing, the scope of his concern was all Israel—the whole covenant people. Neither he nor the prophets viewed the division of the kingdom as an excommunication of the ten tribes, nor did they see the earlier exile of the northern kingdom as a final exclusion of the northern tribes from Israel's future.

Chronology

1,2 Kings presents the reader with abundant chronological data. Not only is the length of the reign of each king given, but during the period of the divided kingdom the beginning of the reign of each king is synchronized with the regnal year of the ruling king in the opposite kingdom. Often additional data, such as the age of the ruler at the time of his accession, are also provided.

By integrating Biblical data with those derived from Assyrian chronological records, the year 853

B.C. can be fixed as the year of Ahab's death, and the year 841 as the year Jehu began to reign. The years in which Ahab and Jehu had contacts with Shalmaneser III of Assyria can also be given definite dates (by means of astronomical calculations based on an Assyrian reference to a solar eclipse). With these fixed points, it is then possible to work both forward and backward in the lines of the kings of Israel and Judah to give dates for each king. By the same means it can be determined that the division of the kingdom occurred in 930, that Samaria fell to the Assyrians in 722–721 and that Jerusalem fell to the Babylonians in 586.

The synchronistic data correlating the reigns of the kings of Israel and Judah present some knotty problems, which have long been considered nearly insoluble. In more recent times, most of these problems have been resolved in a satisfactory way through recognizing such possibilities as overlapping reigns, co-regencies of sons with their fathers, differences in the time of the year in which the reign of a king officially began, and differences in the way a king's first year was reckoned (e.g., see notes on 15:33; 2 Ki 8:25; see also chart, pp. 478–479).

Content

1,2 Kings describes the history of Israel's monarchy from the closing days of the rule of David until the time of the Babylonian exile. After an extensive account of Solomon's reign, the narrative records the division of the kingdom and then, by means of its synchronistic accounts, presents an interrelated picture of developments within the two kingdoms.

Kingship in the northern kingdom was plagued with instability and violence. Twenty rulers represented nine different dynasties during the approximately 210 years from the division of the kingdom in 930 B.C. until the fall of Samaria in 722–721. In the southern kingdom there were also 20 rulers, but these were all descendants of David (except Athaliah, whose usurping of the throne interrupted the sequence for a few years) and spanned a period of about 345 years from the division of the kingdom until the fall of Jerusalem in 586.

Outline

1,2 Kings can be broadly outlined by relating its contents to the major historical periods it describes and to the ministries of Elijah and Elisha.

- I. The Solomonic Era (1:1—12:24)
  - A. Solomon's Succession to the Throne (1:1—2:12)
  - B. Solomon's Throne Consolidated (2:13–46)
  - C. Solomon's Wisdom (ch. 3)
  - D. Solomon's Reign Characterized (ch. 4)
  - E. Solomon's Building Projects (5:1—9:9)
    - 1. Preparation for building the temple (ch. 5)
    - 2. Building the temple (ch. 6)
    - 3. Building the palace (7:1–12)
    - 4. The temple furnishings (7:13–51)
    - 5. Dedication of the temple (ch. 8)
    - 6. The Lord's response and warning (9:1–9)
  - F. Solomon's Reign Characterized (9:10—10:29)
  - G. Solomon's Folly (11:1–13)
  - H. Solomon's Throne Threatened (11:14–43)
  - I. Rehoboam's Succession to the Throne (12:1–24)
- II. Israel and Judah from Jeroboam I/Rehoboam to Ahab/Asa (12:25—16:34)
  - A. Jeroboam I of Israel (12:25—14:20)
  - B. Rehoboam of Judah (14:21–31)
  - C. Abijam of Judah (15:1–8)
  - D. Asa of Judah (15:9–24)
  - E. Nadab of Israel (15:25–32)
  - F. Baasha of Israel (15:33—16:7)
  - G. Elah of Israel (16:8–14)
  - H. Zimri of Israel (16:15–20)
  - I. Omri of Israel (16:21–28)
  - J. Ahab of Israel (16:29–34)

III. The Ministries of Elijah and Elisha and Other Prophets from Ahab/Asa to Joram/Jehoshaphat (17:1—2 Ki 8:15)
  A. Elijah (and Other Prophets) in the Reign of Ahab (17:1—22:40)
    1. Elijah and the drought (ch. 17)
    2. Elijah on mount Carmel (ch. 18)
    3. Elijah's flight to Horeb (ch. 19)
    4. A prophet condemns Ahab for sparing Ben-hadad (ch. 20)
    5. Elijah condemns Ahab for seizing Naboth's vineyard (ch. 21)
    6. Micaiah prophesies Ahab's death; its fulfillment (22:1–40)
  B. Jehoshaphat of Judah (22:41–50)
  C. Ahaziah of Israel; Elijah's Last Prophecy (22:51—2 Ki 1:18)
  D. Elijah's Translation; Elisha's Inauguration (2 Ki 2:1–18)
  E. Elisha in the Reign of Jehoram (2:19—8:15)
    1. Elisha's initial miraculous signs (2:19–25)
    2. Elisha during the campaign against Moab (ch. 3)
    3. Elisha's ministry to needy ones in Israel (ch. 4)
    4. Elisha heals Naaman (ch. 5)
    5. Elisha's deliverance of one of the prophets (6:1–7)
    6. Elisha's deliverance of Joram from Aramean raiders (6:8–23)
    7. Aramean siege of Samaria lifted, as Elisha prophesied (6:24—7:20)
    8. The Shunammite's land restored (8:1–6)
    9. Elisha prophesies Hazael's oppression of Israel (8:7–15)
IV. Israel and Judah from Joram/Jehoram to the Exile of Israel (2 Ki 8:16—17:41)
  A. Jehoram of Judah (8:16–24)
  B. Ahaziah of Judah (8:25–29)
  C. Jehu's Revolt and Reign (chs. 9—10)
    1. Elisha orders Jehu's anointing (9:1–13)
    2. Jehu's assassination of Joram and Ahaziah (9:14–29)
    3. Jehu's execution of Jezebel (9:30–37)
    4. Jehu's slaughter of Ahab's family (10:1–17)
    5. Jehu's eradication of Baal worship (10:18–36)
  D. Athaliah and Joash of Judah; Repair of the Temple (chs. 11—12)
  E. Jehoahaz of Israel (13:1–9)
  F. Jehoash of Israel; Elisha's Last Prophecy (13:10–25)
  G. Amaziah of Judah (14:1–22)
  H. Jeroboam II of Israel (14:23–29)
  I. Azariah of Judah (15:1–7)
  J. Zechariah of Israel (15:8–12)
  K. Shallum of Israel (15:13–16)
  L. Menahem of Israel (15:17–22)
  M. Pekahiah of Israel (15:23–26)
  N. Pekah of Israel (15:27–31)
  O. Jotham of Judah (15:32–38)
  P. Ahaz of Judah (ch. 16)
  Q. Hoshea of Israel (17:1–6)
  R. Exile of Israel; Resettlement of the Land (17:7–41)
V. Judah from Hezekiah to the Babylonian Exile (2 Ki 18—25)
  A. Hezekiah (chs. 18—20)
    1. Hezekiah's good reign (18:1–8)
    2. The Assyrian threat and deliverance (18:9—19:37)
    3. Hezekiah's illness and alliance with Babylon (ch. 20)
  B. Manasseh (21:1–18)
  C. Amon (21:19–26)
  D. Josiah (22:1—23:30)
    1. Repair of the temple; discovery of the book of the law (ch. 22)
    2. Renewal of the covenant; end of Josiah's reign (23:1–30)
  E. Jehoahaz Exiled to Egypt (23:31–35)

F. Jehoiakim: First Babylonian Invasion (23:36—24:7)
G. Jehoiachin: Second Babylonian Invasion (24:8–17)
H. Zedekiah (24:18–20)
I. Babylonian Exile of Judah (25:1–21)
J. Removal of the Remnant to Egypt (25:22–26)
K. Elevation of Jehoiachin in Babylon (25:27–30)

Adonijah seeks to be king

1 Now king David was old *and* [1]stricken in
years; and they covered him with
clothes, but he gat no heat.
2 Wherefore his servants said unto him,
[1]Let there be sought for my lord the king [2]a
young virgin: and let her stand before the king,
and let her [3]cherish him, and let her lie in thy
bosom, that my lord the king may get heat.
3 So they sought for a fair damsel throughout all the coasts of Israel, and found Abishag
a [a]Shunammite, and brought her to the king.
4 And the damsel *was* very fair, and cherished the king, and ministered to him: but the
king knew her not.
5 ¶ Then [a]Adonijah the son of Haggith exalted himself, saying, I will [1]be king: and he
prepared him chariots and horsemen, and fifty
men to run before him.
6 And his father had not displeased him [1]at
any time in saying, Why hast thou done so?
and he also *was* a very goodly *man;* [a]and *his
mother* bare him after Absalom.
7 And [1]he conferred with Joab the son of
Zeruiah, and with [a]Abiathar the priest: and
[b]they [2]following Adonijah helped *him.*
8 But Zadok the priest, and Benaiah the
son of Jehoiada, and Nathan the prophet, and
[a]Shimei, and Rei, and [b]the mighty *men* which
belonged to David, were not with Adonijah.
9 And Adonijah slew sheep and oxen and
fat cattle by the stone of Zoheleth, which *is* by

1:1 [1]Heb. *entered into days* 1:2 [1]Heb. *Let them seek* [2]Heb. *a damsel, a virgin* [3]Heb. *be a cherisher unto him* 1:3 [a]Josh. 19:18 1:5 [1]Heb. *reign* [a]2 Sam. 3:4 1:6 [1]Heb. *from his days* [a]2 Sam. 3:3; 1 Chr. 3:2 1:7 [1]Heb. *his words were with Joab* [2]Heb. *helped after Adonijah* [a]2 Sam. 20:25 [b]ch. 2:22,28 1:8 [a]ch. 4:18 [b]2 Sam. 23:8

1:9 [1]Or, *The well Rogel* 1:11 [a]2 Sam. 3:4 1:13 [a]1 Chr. 22:9 1:14 [1]Heb. *fill up* 1:16 [1]Heb. *What to thee* 1:17 [a]ver. 13,30

[1]En-rogel, and called all his brethren the
king's sons, and all the men of Judah the king's
servants:
10 But Nathan the prophet, and Benaiah,
and the mighty *men,* and Solomon his brother,
he called not.
11 ¶ Wherefore Nathan spake unto Bath-
sheba the mother of Solomon, saying, Hast
thou not heard that Adonijah the son of [a]Hag-
gith doth reign, and David our lord knoweth *it*
not?
12 Now therefore come, let me, I pray
thee, give thee counsel, that thou mayest save
thine own life, and the life of thy son Solomon.
13 Go and get thee in unto king David, and
say unto him, Didst not thou, my lord O king,
swear unto thine handmaid, saying, [a]Assured-
ly Solomon thy son shall reign after me, and he
shall sit upon my throne? why then doth Adonijah reign?
14 Behold, while thou yet talkest there
with the king, I also will come in after thee,
and [1]confirm thy words.
15 And Bath-sheba went in unto the king
into the chamber: and the king was very old;
and Abishag the Shunammite ministered unto
the king.
16 And Bath-sheba bowed, and did obeisance unto the king. And the king said, [1]What
wouldest thou?
17 And she said unto him, My lord, [a]thou
swarest by the LORD thy God unto thine hand-

1:1–12:24 The narrative of the Solomonic era is an exquisite example of literary inversion, in this case consisting of nine sections. The first and last are parallel, as well as the second and eighth, etc.—and the fifth section, which occupies the central position in the structure, is the longest of the nine and describes Solomon's building projects (see Introduction: Outline).

1:1 *stricken in years.* 2 Sam 5:4 indicates that David died at about 70 years of age (cf. 1 Ki 2:11).

1:3 *Shunammite.* Abishag came from Shunem (2 Ki 4:8; Josh 19:18; 1 Sam 28:4), located near the plain of Jezreel in the tribal territory of Issachar.

‡1:4 *knew her not.* I.e. he had no intimate relations with her. Significant in connection with Adonijah's request to be given Abishag as his wife after the death of David (see notes on 2:17,22).

1:5 *Adonijah.* The fourth son of David (see 2 Sam 3:4), who was at this time approximately 35 years of age. It is likely that he was the oldest surviving son of David (see note on 2 Sam 13:28; see also 2 Sam 18:14). *exalted himself.* A unilateral attempt to usurp the throne, bypassing King David's right to designate his own successor (Adonijah must at least have known that his father favored Solomon; see v. 10). If successful, it would have thwarted God's and David's choice of Solomon (see vv. 13,17,30; 1 Chr 22:9–10; see also note on 2 Sam 12:25). *fifty men to run before him.* Adonijah here follows the example of Absalom before him (see note on 2 Sam 15:1).

1:6 *had not displeased him.* David appears to have been consistently negligent in disciplining his sons (see notes on 2 Sam 13:21; 14:33). *very goodly.* Attractive physical appearance was an important asset to an aspirant to the throne (see 1 Sam 9:2; 16:12; 2 Sam 14:25).

1:7 *Joab the son of Zeruiah.* See notes on 1 Sam 26:6; 2 Sam 2:13; 19:13; 20:10,23. Joab's alignment with Adonijah may have been motivated by a struggle for power with Benaiah (see v. 8; 2 Sam 8:18; 20:23; 23:20–23). Joab held his position more by his standing with the army than by the favor and confidence of David (see 2:5–6). *Abiathar the priest.* See note on 2 Sam 8:17.

1:8 *Zadok the priest.* See note on 2 Sam 8:17. *Benaiah the son of Jehoiada.* See note on 2 Sam 23:20. *Nathan the prophet.* See 2 Sam 12:1–25. *Shimei.* Not the Shimei of 2:8,46; 2 Sam 16:5–8; perhaps the same as Shimei son of Elah (4:18). *Rei.* Or "and his friends," i.e. friends of Shimei. If Rei is a proper name, this is its only occurrence in the OT. *mighty men which belonged to David.* See 2 Sam 23:8–39.

1:9 *Adonijah slew sheep . . . .* Here also (see note on v. 5) Adonijah followed the example of Absalom (see 2 Sam 15:7–12). *En-rogel.* Means "the spring of Rogel"; located just south of Jerusalem in the Kidron Valley. Apparently the site of a spring had some kind of symbolic significance for the business at hand (see v. 33 and note).

1:11 *Bath-sheba the mother of Solomon.* The queen mother held an important and influential position in the royal court (see 2:19; 15:13; 2 Ki 10:13; 2 Chr 15:16). *doth reign.* Although the preceding narrative does not relate the actual proclamation of Adonijah's kingship, it can be assumed (see v. 25; 2:15; cf. 2 Sam 15:10).

1:12 *save thine own life, and the life of thy son Solomon.* It was common in the ancient Near East for a usurper to liquidate all potential claimants to the throne in an attempt to secure his own position (see 15:29; 2 Ki 10:11; 11:1).

1:13 *Didst not thou . . . swear unto thine handmaid . . . ?* Although 2 Samuel does not record David's oath concerning the succession of Solomon, it does suggest that Solomon was the son through whom the Lord's promise to David for an eternal dynasty would be carried forward (see note on v. 5).

1:17 *thou swarest by the LORD thy God unto thine handmaid.* An

maid, *saying,* Assuredly Solomon thy son shall
reign after me, and he shall sit upon my
throne.
18 And now behold, Adonijah reigneth; and
now, my lord the king, thou knowest *it* not:
19 [a]And he hath slain oxen and fat cattle
and sheep in abundance, and hath called all
the sons of the king, and Abiathar the priest,
and Joab the captain of the host: but Solomon
thy servant hath he not called.
20 And thou, my lord O king, the eyes of
all Israel *are* upon thee, that *thou* shouldest
tell them who shall sit on the throne of my
lord the king after him.
21 Otherwise it shall come to pass, when
my lord the king shall [a]sleep with his fathers,
that I and my son Solomon shall be *counted*
[1]offenders.
22 And lo, while she yet talked with the
king, Nathan the prophet also came in.
23 And they told the king, saying, Behold
Nathan the prophet. And when he was come
in before the king, he bowed himself before
the king with his face to the ground.
24 And Nathan said, My lord O king, hast
thou said, Adonijah shall reign after me, and
he shall sit upon my throne?
25 [a]For he is gone down *this* day, and hath
slain oxen and fat cattle and sheep in abundance, and hath called all the king's sons, and
the captains of the host, and Abiathar the
priest; and behold, they eat and drink before
him, and say, [b][1]God save king Adonijah.
26 But me, *even* me thy servant, and Zadok
the priest, and Benaiah the son of Jehoiada,
and thy servant Solomon, hath he not called.
27 Is this thing done by my lord the king,
and thou hast not shewed *it* unto thy servant,
who should sit on the throne of my lord the
king after him?
28 Then king David answered and said,
Call me Bath-sheba. And she came [1]into the
king's presence, and stood before the king.

1:19 [a]ver. 7-9,25
1:21 [1]Heb. *sinners* [a]Deut. 31:16; ch. 2:10
1:25 [1]Heb. *Let king Adonijah live* [a]ver. 19 [b]1 Sam. 10:24
1:28 [1]Heb. *before the king*

1:29 [a]2 Sam. 4:9
1:30 [a]ver. 17
1:31 [a]Neh. 2:3; Dan 2:4
1:33 [1]Heb. *which* belongeth *to me* [a]2 Sam. 20:6 [b]2 Chr. 32:30
1:34 [a]1 Sam. 10:1; 16:3,12; 2 Sam. 2:4; 5:3; ch. 19:16; 2 Ki. 9:3; 11:12 [b]2 Sam. 15:10; 2 Ki 9:13; 11:14
1:37 [a]Josh. 1:5,17; 1 Sam. 20:13 [b]ver. 47
1:38 [a]2 Sam. 8:18; 23:20-23
1:39 [a]Ex. 30:23,25,32; Ps. 89:20 [b]1 Chr. 29:22

29 And the king sware, and said, [a]*As* the
LORD liveth, that hath redeemed my soul out of
all distress,
30 [a]Even as I sware unto thee by the LORD
God of Israel, saying, Assuredly Solomon thy
son shall reign after me, and he shall sit upon
my throne in my stead; even so will I certainly do this day.
31 Then Bath-sheba bowed *with her* face *to*
the earth, and did reverence to the king, and
said, [a]Let my lord king David live for ever.

Solomon anointed king

32 ¶ And king David said, Call me Zadok
the priest, and Nathan the prophet, and Benaiah the son of Jehoiada. And they came before
the king.
33 The king also said unto them, [a]Take
with you the servants of your lord, and cause
Solomon my son to ride upon [1]mine own
mule, and bring him down to [b]Gihon:
34 And let Zadok the priest and Nathan the
prophet [a]anoint him there king over Israel:
and [b]blow ye with the trumpet, and say, God
save king Solomon.
35 Then ye shall come up after him, that
he may come and sit upon my throne; for he
shall be king in my stead: and I have appointed him to be ruler over Israel and over Judah.
36 And Benaiah the son of Jehoiada answered the king, and said, Amen: the LORD
God of my lord the king say so *too.*
37 [a]As the LORD hath been with my lord
the king, even so be he with Solomon, and
[b]make his throne greater than the throne of
my lord king David.
38 So Zadok the priest, and Nathan the
prophet, [a]and Benaiah the son of Jehoiada,
and the Cherethites, and the Pelethites, went
down, and caused Solomon to ride upon king
David's mule, and brought him to Gihon.
39 And Zadok the priest took a horn of [a]oil
out of the tabernacle, and [b]anointed Solomon.

oath taken in the Lord's name was inviolable (see Ex 20:7; Lev 19:12; Josh 9:15,18,20; Judg 11:30,35; Eccl 5:4–7).

1:21 *sleep with his fathers.* A conventional expression for death (see Gen 47:30; Deut 31:16).

1:24 Nathan approached David diplomatically by raising a question that revealed the dilemma. Either David had secretly encouraged Adonijah to claim the throne and thereby had broken his oath to Bath-sheba and Solomon (see v. 27), or he had been betrayed by Adonijah.

‡1:25 *God save king Adonijah.* Lit. "may the king Adonijah live!" An expression of recognition and acclamation of the new king (see 1 Sam 10:24; 2 Sam 16:16; 2 Ki 11:12).

1:31 *Let my lord king David live for ever.* An expression of Bath-sheba's thanks in the stereotyped hyperbolic language of the court (see Neh 2:3; Dan 2:4; 3:9; 5:10; 6:21).

1:33 *the servants of your lord.* Presumably including the Cherethites and Pelethites (see v. 38). *mine own mule.* Although crossbreeding was forbidden in the Mosaic law (Lev 19:19), mules (perhaps imported; see Ezek 27:14) were used in the time of David, at least as mounts for royalty (see 2 Sam 13:29; 18:9). To ride on David's own mule was a public proclamation that Solomon's succession to the throne was sanctioned by David (see Gen 41:43; Esth 6:7–8). *Gihon.* The site of a spring on the eastern slope of mount Zion (see notes on v. 9; 2 Sam 5:8).

1:34 *anoint him.* See notes on 1 Sam 2:10; 9:16. *blow ye with the trumpet.* See 2 Ki 9:13; 2 Sam 15:10; 20:1. *God save king Solomon.* See note on v. 25.

1:35 *Israel and over Judah.* The distinction between Israel and Judah was rooted in the separate arrangements by which David became king over these two tribal units (see 2 Sam 2:4; 5:3).

1:36 *Amen: the LORD . . . say so too.* See Jer 28:6.

1:37 *greater.* Not a deprecation of David's accomplishments, but an expression of total loyalty to David and Solomon. Benaiah shared David's own desire for his chosen successor (see vv. 47–48).

1:38 *the Cherethites, and the Pelethites.* See note on 2 Sam 8:18.

1:39 *Zadok . . . anointed Solomon.* Kings chosen by God to rule over His people who were not in a line of dynastic succession were anointed by prophets (Saul, 1 Sam 9:16; David, 1 Sam 16:12; Jehu, 2 Ki 9). Kings who assumed office in the line of dynastic succession were anointed by priests (Solomon, here; Joash, 2 Ki 11:12). The distinction seems to be that the priest worked within the established order while the prophets intro-

And they blew the trumpet; [c]and all the people said, God save king Solomon.

40 And all the people came up after him, and the people piped with [1]pipes, and rejoiced *with* great joy, so that the earth rent with the sound of them.

41 ¶ And Adonijah and all the guests that *were* with him heard *it* as they had made an end of eating. And when Joab heard the sound of the trumpet, he said, Wherefore *is this* noise of the city being in an uproar?

42 And while he yet spake, behold, Jonathan the son of Abiathar the priest came: and Adonijah said *unto him,* Come in; for [a]thou *art* a valiant man, and bringest good tidings.

43 And Jonathan answered and said to Adonijah, Verily our lord king David hath made Solomon king.

44 And the king hath sent with him Zadok the priest, and Nathan the prophet, and Benaiah the son of Jehoiada, and the Cherethites, and the Pelethites, and they have caused him to ride upon the king's mule:

45 And Zadok the priest and Nathan the prophet have anointed him king in Gihon: and they are come up from thence rejoicing, so that the city rang again. This *is* the noise that ye have heard.

46 And also Solomon [a]sitteth on the throne of the kingdom.

47 And moreover the king's servants came to bless our lord king David, saying, [a]God make the name of Solomon better than thy name, and make his throne greater than thy throne. [b]And the king bowed himself upon the bed.

48 And also thus said the king, Blessed *be* the LORD God of Israel, which hath [a]given *one* to sit on my throne *this* day, mine eyes even seeing *it.*

1:39 [c]1 Sam. 10:24
1:40 [1]Or, *flutes*
1:42 [a]2 Sam. 18:27
1:46 [a]1 Chr. 29:23
1:47 [a]ver. 37 [b]Gen. 47:31
1:48 [a]ch. 3:6; Ps. 132:11,12
1:50 [a]ch. 2:28
1:52 [a]1 Sam. 14:45; 2 Sam. 14:11
2:1 [a]Gen. 47:29; Deut. 31:14
2:2 [a]Josh. 23:14 [b]Deut. 17:19,20
2:3 [1]Or, *do wisely* [a]Deut. 29:9; Josh. 1:7; 1 Chr. 22:12,13
2:4 [1]Heb. *be cut off from thee from the throne* [a]2 Sam. 7:25 [b]Ps. 132:12 [c]2 Ki. 20:3 [d]2 Sam. 7:12,13; ch. 8:25

49 And all the guests that *were* with Adonijah were afraid, and rose up, and went every man his way.

50 ¶ And Adonijah feared because of Solomon, and arose, and went, and [a]caught hold on the horns of the altar.

51 And it was told Solomon, saying, Behold, Adonijah feareth king Solomon: for lo, he hath caught hold on the horns of the altar, saying, Let king Solomon swear unto me to day that he will not slay his servant with the sword.

52 And Solomon said, If he will shew himself a worthy man, [a]there shall not a hair of him fall to the earth: but if wickedness shall be found in him, he shall die.

53 So king Solomon sent, and they brought him down from the altar. And he came and bowed himself to king Solomon: and Solomon said unto him, Go to thine house.

David's last words and death

2 Now [a]the days of David drew nigh that *he* should die; and he charged Solomon his son, saying,

2 [a]I go the way of all the earth: [b]be thou strong therefore, and shew thyself a man;

3 And keep the charge of the LORD thy God, to walk in his ways, to keep his statutes, *and* his commandments, and his judgments, and his testimonies, as *it is* written in the law of Moses, that thou mayest [a][1]prosper *in* all that thou doest, and whithersoever thou turnest thyself:

4 That the LORD may [a]continue his word which he spake concerning me, saying, [b]If thy children take heed to their way, to [c]walk before me in truth with all their heart and with all their soul, [d]there shall not [1]fail thee (said he) a man on the throne of Israel.

---

duced new divine initiatives. *horn of oil.* Perhaps containing the anointing oil described in Ex 30:22–33. *tabernacle.* The tent David had erected in Jerusalem to house the ark (see 2 Sam 6:17) rather than the tabernacle at Gibeon (see 3:4 and note; 2 Chr 1:3).

1:41 *heard it.* Although Gihon may not have been visible from En-rogel, the distance was not great and the sound would carry down the Kidron Valley.

1:42 *Jonathan the son of Abiathar.* See 2 Sam 17:17–21.

1:47 *better.* See note on v. 37.

1:48 *one to sit on my throne.* In Solomon's succession to the throne David sees a fulfillment of the promise in 2 Sam 7:12,16.

1:49 *went every man his way.* No one wanted to be identified with Adonijah's abortive coup now that it appeared certain to fail.

1:50 *caught hold on the horns of the altar.* The horns of the altar were vertical projections at each corner. The idea of seeking asylum at the altar was rooted in the Pentateuch (see Ex 21:13–14). The priest smeared the blood of the sacrifice on the horns of the altar (see Ex 29:12; Lev 4:7,18,25,30,34) during the sacrificial ritual. Adonijah thus seeks to place his own destiny under the protection of God.

1:52 *worthy man.* Who recognizes and submits to Solomon's office and authority. *if wickedness shall be found in him.* If he shows evidence of continuing opposition to Solomon's succession to the throne.

2:1 *he charged.* Moses (Deut 31:1–8), Joshua (Josh 23:1–16) and Samuel (1 Sam 12:1–25), as representatives of the Lord's rule, had all given final instructions and admonitions shortly before their deaths.

2:2 *the way of all the earth.* To the grave (see Josh 23:14). *be thou strong.* See Deut 31:7,23; Josh 1:6–7,9,18.

2:3 *keep the charge of the LORD thy God.* See Gen 26:5; Lev 18:30; Deut 11:1. *walk in his ways.* A characteristic expression of Deuteronomy for obedience to covenant obligations (Deut 5:33; 8:6; 10:12; 11:22; 19:9; 26:17; 28:9; 30:16). *his statutes, and his commandments, and his judgments, and his testimonies.* Four generally synonymous terms for covenant obligations (see 6:12; 8:58; 2 Ki 17:37; Deut 8:11; 11:1; 26:17; 28:15,45; 30:10,16). *that thou mayest prosper.* See Deut 29:9.

2:4 *That the LORD may continue his word . . . concerning me.* David here alludes to the covenanted promise of an everlasting dynasty given to him by God through Nathan the prophet (see notes on 2 Sam 7:11–16). Although the covenant promise to David was unconditional, individual participation in its blessing on the part of David's royal descendants was conditioned on obedience to the obligations of the Mosaic covenant (see 2 Chr 7:17–22). *with all their heart and . . . soul.* See Deut 4:29; 6:5; 10:12; 30:6. *there shall not fail thee . . . a man on the throne of Israel.* Both Solomon and his descendants fell short of their covenant obligations. This led to the division of the kingdom and eventually to the exile of both the northern and southern

5 Moreover thou knowest also what Joab the son of Zeruiah [a]did to me, *and* what he did to the two captains of the hosts of Israel, unto [b]Abner the son of Ner, and unto [c]Amasa the son of Jether, whom he slew, and [1]shed the blood of war in peace, and put the blood of war upon his girdle that *was* about his loins, and in his shoes that *were* on his feet.

6 Do therefore [a]according to thy wisdom, and let not his hoar head go down *to* the grave in peace.

7 But shew kindness unto the sons of [a]Barzillai the Gileadite, and let them be of *those* that [b]eat at thy table: for so [c]they came to me when I fled because of Absalom thy brother.

8 And behold, *thou hast* with thee [a]Shimei the son of Gera, a Benjamite of Bahurim, which cursed me *with* a [1]grievous curse in the day when I went *to* Mahanaim: but [b]he came down to meet me *at* Jordan, and [c]I sware to him by the LORD, saying, I will not put thee to death with the sword.

9 Now therefore [a]hold him not guiltless: for thou *art* a wise man, and knowest what thou oughtest to do unto him; but his hoar head [b]bring thou down *to* the grave with blood.

10 So [a]David slept with his fathers, and was buried in [b]the city of David.

11 And the days that David [a]reigned over Israel *were* forty years: seven years reigned he in Hebron, and thirty and three years reigned he in Jerusalem.

12 ¶ [a]Then sat Solomon upon the throne of David his father; and his kingdom was established greatly.

13 And Adonijah the son of Haggith came to Bath-sheba the mother of Solomon. And she said, [a]Comest thou peaceably? And he said, Peaceably.

14 He said moreover, I have somewhat to say unto thee. And she said, Say on.

2:5 [1]Heb. *put* [a]2 Sam. 3:39; 18:5,12,14 [b]2 Sam. 3:27 [c]2 Sam. 20:10
2:6 [a]ver. 9; Prov. 20:26
2:7 [a]2 Sam. 19:31,38 [b]2 Sam. 9:7,10; 19:28 [c]2 Sam. 17:27
2:8 [1]Heb. *strong* [a]2 Sam. 16:5 [b]2 Sam. 19:18 [c]2 Sam. 19:23
2:9 [a]Ex. 20:7; Job 9:28 [b]Gen. 42:38; 44:31
2:10 [a]ch. 1:21; Acts 2:29; 13:36 [b]2 Sam. 5:7
2:11 [a]2 Sam. 5:4; 1 Chr. 29:26,27
2:12 [a]1 Chr. 29:23; 2 Chr. 1:1
2:13 [a]1 Sam. 16:4,5

kingdoms. It was only in the coming of Christ that the fallen tent of David would be restored (see notes on Amos 9:11–15; Acts 15:16) and the promise of David's eternal dynasty ultimately fulfilled. When the nation and its king turned away from the requirements of the Sinai covenant, they experienced the covenant curses rather than blessings; but in all this God remained faithful to His covenant promises to Abraham and to David (see Lev 26:42–45; Is 9:6–7; 11:1–16; 16:5; 55:3; Jer 23:5–6; 30:9; 33:17,20–22,25–26; Ezek 34:23–24; 37:24–28).

2:5 *Joab the son of Zeruiah.* See note on 1:7. *Abner the son of Ner.* See notes on 2 Sam 3:25–32. *Amasa the son of Jether.* See 2 Sam 20:10. *shed the blood of war in peace.* Joab's actions were unlawful assassinations (see Deut 19:1–13; 21:1–9) and only served his own self-interest.

2:7 *sons of Barzillai.* See note on 2 Sam 17:27. *eat at thy table.* A position of honor that brought with it other benefits (see 18:19; 2 Ki 25:29; 2 Sam 9:7; 19:28; Neh 5:17).

2:8 See 2 Sam 16:5–13. *Shimei the son of Gera, a Benjamite.* Gera was probably the ancestor of Shimei's particular line of descent rather than his immediate father (see Gen 46:21; Judg 3:15). The Hebrew for "son" may mean "descendant," "successor," or "nation."

2:9 *hold him not guiltless.* The Mosaic law prohibited cursing a ruler (21:10; Ex 22:28).

2:10 *slept with his fathers.* See note on 1:21. *city of David.* See 2 Sam 5:7 and note. Peter implies that David's tomb is still known in his day (Acts 2:29).

2:11 *forty years.* See 2 Sam 5:4–5. David ruled c. 1010–970 B.C. (see Introduction to 1 Samuel: Chronology).

2:13 *Adonijah the son of Haggith.* See note on 1:5. *Comest thou peaceably?* The question (see 1 Sam 16:4; 2 Ki 9:22) reveals Bath-sheba's apprehension concerning Adonijah's intention (see 1:5).

Solomon's Jerusalem

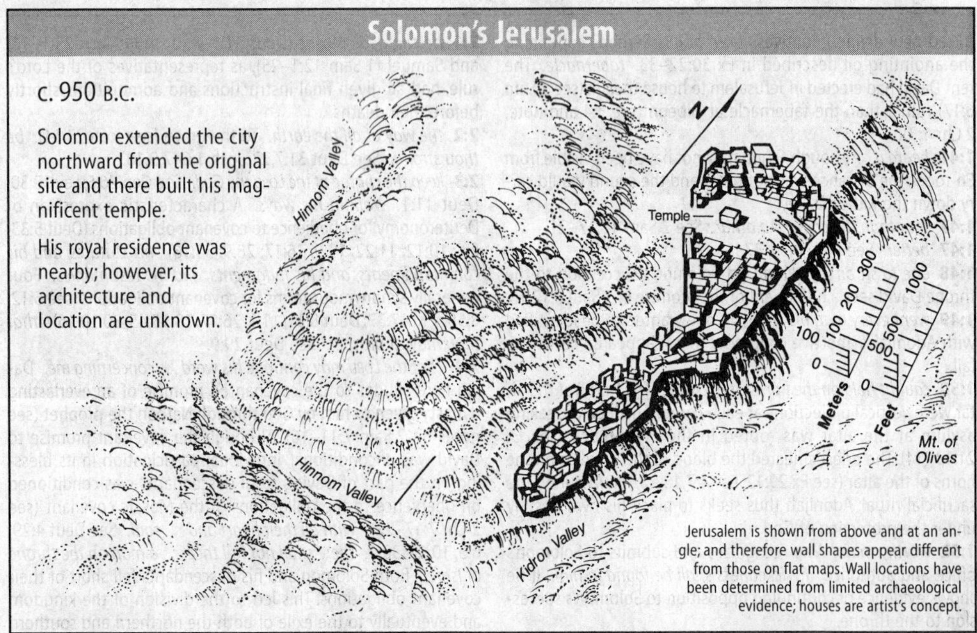

c. 950 B.C.
Solomon extended the city northward from the original site and there built his magnificent temple.
His royal residence was nearby; however, its architecture and location are unknown.
N
Hinnom Valley
Temple
Hinnom Valley
Kidron Valley
Mt. of Olives
Meters
0
100
200
300
Feet
0
500
1000

Jerusalem is shown from above and at an angle; and therefore wall shapes appear different from those on flat maps. Wall locations have been determined from limited archaeological evidence; houses are artist's concept.

15 And he said, Thou knowest that the kingdom was mine, and *that* all Israel set their faces on me, that *I* should reign: howbeit the kingdom is turned about, and is become my brother's: for [a]it was his from the LORD.

16 And now I ask one petition of thee, [1]deny me not. And she said unto him, Say on.

17 And he said, Speak, I pray thee, unto Solomon the king, (for he will not say thee nay,) that he give me [a]Abishag the Shunammite to wife.

18 And Bath-sheba said, Well; I will speak for thee unto the king.

19 Bath-sheba therefore went unto king Solomon, to speak unto him for Adonijah. And the king rose up to meet her, and [a]bowed himself unto her, and sat down on his throne, and caused a seat to be set for the king's mother; [b]and she sat on his right hand.

20 Then she said, I desire one small petition of thee; *I pray thee,* say me not nay. And the king said unto her, Ask on, my mother: for I will not say thee nay.

21 And she said, Let Abishag the Shunammite be given to Adonijah thy brother to wife.

22 And king Solomon answered and said unto his mother, And why dost thou ask Abishag the Shunammite for Adonijah? ask for him the kingdom also; for he *is* mine elder brother; even for him, and for [a]Abiathar the priest, and for Joab the son of Zeruiah.

23 Then king Solomon sware by the LORD, saying, [a]God do so to me, and more also, if Adonijah have not spoken this word against his own life.

24 Now therefore, *as* the LORD liveth, which hath established me, and set me on the throne of David my father, and who hath made me a house, as he [a]promised, Adonijah shall be put to death *this* day.

2:15 [a]1 Chr. 22:9,10; 28:5-7; Dan. 2:21
2:16 [1]Heb. *turn not away my face*
2:17 [a]ch. 1:3,4
2:19 [a]Ex. 20:12 [b]See Ps. 45:9
2:22 [a]ch. 1:7
2:23 [a]Ruth 1:17
2:24 [a]2 Sam. 7:11,13; 1 Chr. 22:10
2:26 [1]Heb. *a man of death* [a]Josh. 21:18 [b]1 Sam. 23:6; 2 Sam. 15:24,29 [c]1 Sam. 22:20,23; 2 Sam. 15:24
2:27 [a]1 Sam. 2:31-35
2:28 [a]ch. 1:7 [b]ch. 1:50
2:31 [a]Ex. 21:14 [b]Num. 35:33; Deut. 19:13; 21:8,9
2:32 [a]Judg. 9:24,57 [b]2 Chr. 21:13 [c]2 Sam. 3:27

25 And king Solomon sent by the hand of Benaiah the son of Jehoiada; and he fell upon him that he died.

26 ¶ And unto Abiathar the priest said the king, Get thee *to* [a]Anathoth, unto thine own fields; for thou *art* [1]worthy of death: but I will not at this time put thee to death, [b]because thou barest the ark of the Lord GOD before David my father, and because [c]thou hast been afflicted in all where*in* my father was afflicted.

27 So Solomon thrust out Abiathar from being priest unto the LORD; that *he* might [a]fulfil the word of the LORD, which he spake concerning the house of Eli in Shiloh.

28 ¶ Then tidings came to Joab: for Joab [a]had turned after Adonijah, though he turned not after Absalom. And Joab fled unto the tabernacle of the LORD, and [b]caught hold on the horns of the altar.

29 And it was told king Solomon that Joab was fled unto the tabernacle of the LORD; and behold, *he is* by the altar. Then Solomon sent Benaiah the son of Jehoiada, saying, Go, fall upon him.

30 And Benaiah came to the tabernacle of the LORD, and said unto him, Thus saith the king, Come forth. And he said, Nay; but I will die here. And Benaiah brought the king word again, saying, Thus said Joab, and thus he answered me.

31 And the king said unto him, [a]Do as he hath said, and fall upon him, and bury him; [b]that thou mayest take away the innocent blood, which Joab shed, from me, and from the house of my father.

32 And the LORD [a]shall return his blood upon his own head, who fell upon two men more righteous [b]and better than he, and slew them with the sword, my father David not knowing *thereof, to wit,* [c]Abner the son of

2:15 *the kingdom was mine.* See 1:11. *all Israel set their faces on me, that I should reign.* A gross exaggeration (see 1:7–8). *it was his from the LORD.* Adonijah professes to view Solomon's kingship as God's will and to have no further intentions of seeking the position for himself.

2:17 *give me Abishag the Shunammite to wife.* Adonijah's request has the appearance of being innocent (but see note on v. 22) since Abishag had remained a virgin throughout the period of her care for David (see 1:1–4; Deut 22:30).

2:19 *right hand.* The position of honor (see Ps 110:1; Mat 20:21).

2:20 *one small petition.* Bath-sheba does not seem to have attached any great significance to Adonijah's request.

2:22 *ask for him the kingdom also.* Solomon immediately understood Adonijah's request as another attempt to gain the throne. Possession of the royal harem was widely regarded as signifying the right of succession to the throne (see notes on 2 Sam 3:7; 12:8; 16:21). Although Abishag was a virgin, she would be regarded by the people as belonging to David's harem; so marriage to Abishag would greatly strengthen Adonijah's claim to the throne. *for Abiathar the priest, and for Joab the son of Zeruiah.* See note on 1:7. Solomon assumes that Abiathar and Joab continue to be involved in Adonijah's treacherous schemes.

2:23 *God do so to me, and more also.* A curse formula (see note on 1 Sam 3:17).

‡2:24 *hath established me.* Lit. "has made me a house." Solomon's son and successor, Rehoboam, was born shortly before Solomon became king (cf. 11:42; 14:21). *as he promised.* See 1 Chr 22:9–10.

2:25 *Benaiah the son of Jehoiada.* See notes on 1:7; 2 Sam 23:20.

2:26 *thou barest the ark.* See 2 Sam 15:24–25,29; 1 Chr 15:11–12. *hast been afflicted in all wherein my father was afflicted.* See 1 Sam 22:20–23; 23:6–9; 30:7; 2 Sam 17:15; 19:11.

2:27 *might fulfil the word of the LORD, which he spake concerning the house of Eli in Shiloh.* See notes on 1 Sam 2:30–35.

2:28 *tidings.* Of Adonijah's death and Abiathar's banishment. *turned after Adonijah.* See 1:7. *tabernacle of the LORD.* See note on 1:39. *caught hold on the horns of the altar.* See note on 1:50.

2:29 *fall upon him.* The right of asylum was extended only to those who accidentally caused someone's death (see Ex 21:14). Solomon was completely justified in denying this right to Joab, not only for his complicity in Adonijah's conspiracy, but also for his murder of Abner and Amasa (see vv. 31–33). In this incident Solomon finds a suitable occasion for carrying out his father's instruction (see vv. 5–6).

2:32 *fell upon two men . . . and slew them.* See 2 Sam 3:27; 20:9–10. *host of Israel.* See 2 Sam 2:8–9. *host of Judah.* See 2 Sam 20:4.

Ner, captain of the host of Israel, and [d]Amasa
the son of Jether, captain of the host of Judah.
33 Their blood shall therefore return upon
the head of Joab, and [a]upon the head of his
seed for ever: [b]but upon David, and upon his
seed, and upon his house, and upon his throne,
shall there be peace for ever from the LORD.
34 So Benaiah the son of Jehoiada went up,
and fell upon him, and slew him: and he was
buried in his own house in the wilderness.
35 And the king put Benaiah the son of Jehoiada in his room over the host: and [a]Zadok
the priest did the king put in the room of [b]Abi-
athar.
36 ¶ And the king sent and called for
[a]Shimei, and said unto him, Build thee a
house in Jerusalem, and dwell there, and go
not forth thence any whither.
37 For it shall be, *that* on the day thou
goest out, and passest over [a]the brook Kidron,
thou shalt know for certain that thou shalt
surely die: [b]thy blood shall be upon thine own
head.
38 And Shimei said unto the king, The saying *is* good: as my lord the king hath said, so
will thy servant do. And Shimei dwelt in Jerusalem many days.
39 And it came to pass at the end of three
years, that two of the servants of Shimei ran
away unto [a]Achish son of Maachah king of
Gath. And they told Shimei, saying, Behold,
thy servants *be* in Gath.
40 And Shimei arose, and saddled his ass,
and went to Gath to Achish to seek his servants: and Shimei went, and brought his servants from Gath.

2:32 [d]2 Sam. 20:10
2:33 [a]2 Sam. 3:29 [b]Prov. 25:5
2:35 [a]Num. 25:11-13; 1 Sam. 2:35; See 1 Chr. 6:53; 24:3 [b]ver. 27
2:36 [a]ver. 8; 2 Sam. 16:5
2:37 [a]2 Sam. 15:23 [b]Lev. 20:9; Josh. 2:19; 2 Sam. 1:16
2:39 [a]1 Sam. 27:2

41 And it was told Solomon that Shimei
had gone from Jerusalem *to* Gath, and was
come again.
42 And the king sent and called for Shimei,
and said unto him, Did I not make thee to
swear by the LORD, and protested unto thee,
saying, Know for a certain, on the day thou
goest out, and walkest *abroad* any whither,
that thou shalt surely die? and thou saidst unto
me, The word *that* I have heard *is* good.
43 Why then hast thou not kept the oath of
the LORD, and the commandment that I have
charged thee with?
44 The king said moreover to Shimei, Thou
knowest [a]all the wickedness which thine
heart is privy to, that thou didst to David my
father: therefore the LORD shall [b]return thy
wickedness upon thine own head;
45 And king Solomon *shall be* blessed, and
[a]the throne of David shall be established before the LORD for ever.
46 So the king commanded Benaiah the
son of Jehoiada; which went out, and fell upon
him, that he died. And the [a]kingdom was established in the hand of Solomon.

Prayer for wisdom granted

3 And [a]Solomon made affinity with Pharaoh king of Egypt, and took Pharaoh's
daughter, and brought her into the [b]city of David, until he had made an end of building his
[c]own house, and [d]the house of the LORD, and
[e]the wall of Jerusalem round about.
2 [a]Only the people sacrificed in high
places, because there was no house built unto
the name of the LORD, until those days.

2:44 [a]2 Sam. 16:5 [b]Ezek. 17:19
2:45 [a]Prov. 25:5
2:46 [a]ver. 12; 2 Chr. 1:1
3:1 [a]ch. 7:8; 9:24 [b]2 Sam. 5:7 [c]ch. 7:1 [d]ch. 6 [e]ch. 9:15,19
3:2 [a]Lev. 17:3-5; Deut. 12:2,4,5; ch. 22:43

2:34 *in his own house.* The tomb of Joab's father was located near Beth-lehem (see 2 Sam 2:32). *wilderness.* Of Judah, east of Beth-lehem.

2:35 *Benaiah the son of Jehoiada.* See note on 2 Sam 23:20. *Zadok the priest.* See notes on 1 Sam 2:35; 2 Sam 8:17.

2:36 *go not forth thence any whither.* Confinement to Jerusalem would greatly reduce the possibility of Shimei's (see v. 8) conspiring with any remaining followers of Saul against Solomon's rule.

2:39 *Achish son of Maachah king of Gath.* Gath was a major Philistine city (see Josh 13:3; 1 Sam 6:16–17). It is likely that Gath was ruled successively by Maoch, Achish the elder (1 Sam 27:2), Maachah and Achish the younger (here).

2:46 *fell upon him, that he died.* The third execution carried out by Benaiah (see vv. 25,34). It brought to completion the tasks assigned to Solomon by David just before his death (vv. 6,9).

‡3:1 *made affinity with Pharaoh.* I.e. he made a marriage alliance. It appears likely that Solomon established his marriage alliance with either Siamun or Psusennes II, the last kings of the 21st Egyptian dynasty (the first Egyptian pharaoh mentioned by name in the OT is Shishak—11:40; 14:25–26—who established the 22nd Egyptian dynasty c. 945 B.C.). Such an alliance attests Egyptian recognition of the growing importance and strength of the Israelite state. 1 Ki 9:16 indicates that the pharaoh gave his daughter the Canaanite town of Gezer as a dowry at the time of her marriage to Solomon. Gezer was located near the crossing of two important trade routes. One, to the west of Gezer, went from Egypt to the north and was very important for Egypt's commercial interests. The other, to the north of Gezer, went from Jerusalem to the Mediterranean Sea and the port of Joppa and was important to Solomon as a supply line for his building projects. The marriage alliance enabled both Solomon and the pharaoh to accomplish important economic and political objectives. No precise date is given for the conclusion of the marriage alliance, though it appears to have occurred in the third or fourth year of Solomon's reign (see 2:39). Solomon began construction of the temple in his fourth year (6:1), and control of the Gezer area was important to him for the beginning of this project. *city of David.* The Egyptian princess was given a temporary residence in the old fortress (see 2 Sam 5:7 and note) until a separate palace of her own could be constructed some 20 years later (7:8; 9:10; 2 Chr 8:11).

3:2 *high places.* Upon entering Canaan, the Israelites often followed the Canaanite custom of locating their altars on high hills, probably on the old Baal sites. The question of the legitimacy of Israelite worship at these high places has long been a matter of debate. It is clear that the Israelites were forbidden to take over pagan altars and high places and use them for the worship of the Lord (Num 33:52; Deut 7:5; 12:3). It is also clear that altars were to be built only at divinely sanctioned sites (see Ex 20:24; Deut 12:5,8,13–14). It is not so clear whether multiplicity of altars was totally forbidden provided the above conditions were met (see 19:10,14; Lev 26:30–31; Deut 12; 1 Sam 9:12). It seems, however, that these conditions were not followed even in the time of Solomon, and pagan high places were being used for the worship of the Lord. This would eventually lead to religious apostasy and syncretism and was strongly condemned (2 Ki 17:7–18; 21:2–9; 23:4–25). *because there was no*

3 And Solomon [a]loved the LORD, [b]walking
in the statutes of David his father: only he sacrificed and burnt incense in high places.
4 And [a]the king went to Gibeon to sacrifice
there; [b]for that *was* the great high place: a
thousand burnt offerings did Solomon offer up
on that altar.
5 ¶ [a]In Gibeon the LORD appeared to Solomon [b]in a dream by night: and God said, Ask
what I shall give thee.
6 [a]And Solomon said, Thou hast shewed
unto thy servant David my father great [1]mer-
cy, according as he [b]walked before thee in
truth, and in righteousness, and in uprightness
of heart with thee; and thou hast kept for him
this great kindness, that thou [c]hast given him
a son to sit on his throne, as *it is* this day.
7 And now, O LORD my God, thou hast
made thy servant king instead of David my father: and I *am but* a little child: I know not
how [a]to go out or come in.
8 And thy servant *is* in the midst of thy
people which thou [a]hast chosen, a great people, [b]that cannot be numbered nor counted for
multitude.
9 [a]Give therefore thy servant an [1]under-
standing heart [b]to judge thy people, that *I* may
[c]discern between good and bad: for who is
able to judge this thy *so* great a people?
10 And the speech pleased the Lord, that
Solomon had asked this thing.
11 And God said unto him, Because thou
hast asked this thing, and hast [a]not asked for
thyself [1]long life; neither hast asked riches for
thyself, nor hast asked the life of thine enemies; but hast asked for thyself understanding
[2]to discern judgment;
12 [a]Behold, I have done according to thy
word: [b]lo, I have given thee a wise and an understanding heart; so that there was none like
thee before thee, neither after thee shall any
arise like unto thee.
13 And I have also [a]given thee *that* which
thou hast not asked, both [b]riches, and honour:
so that there [1]shall not be any among the
kings like unto thee all thy days.
14 And if thou wilt walk in my ways, to
keep my statutes and my commandments, [a]as
thy father David did walk, then I will [b]length-
en thy days.
15 And Solomon [a]awoke; and behold, *it*
was a dream. And he came *to* Jerusalem, and
stood before the ark of the covenant of the
LORD, and offered up burnt offerings, and offered peace offerings, and [b]made a feast to all
his servants.

Solomon's wise decision

16 ¶ Then came there two women, *that*
were harlots, unto the king, and [a]stood before
him.
17 And the one woman said, O my lord, I
and this woman dwell in one house; and I was
delivered of a child with her in the house.
18 And it came to pass the third day after
that I was delivered, that this woman was delivered also: and we *were* together; *there was*
no stranger with us in the house, save we two
in the house.
19 And this woman's child died in the
night; because she overlaid it.
20 And she rose at midnight, and took my
son from beside me, while thine handmaid
slept, and laid it in her bosom, and laid her
dead child in my bosom.
21 And when I rose in the morning to give

3:3 [a]Deut. 6:5; 30:16,20; Rom. 8:28; 1 Cor. 8:3 [b]ver. 6,14
3:4 [a]2 Chr. 1:3 [b]1 Chr. 16:39; 2 Chr. 1:3
3:5 [a]ch. 9:2; 2 Chr. 1:7 [b]Num. 12:6; Mat. 1:20
3:6 [1]Or, *bounty* [a]2 Chr. 1:8 [b]ch. 2:4; 9:4; 2 Ki. 20:3 [c]ch. 1:48
3:7 [a]Num. 27:17
3:8 [a]Deut. 7:6 [b]Gen. 13:16; 15:5
3:9 [1]Heb. *hearing* [a]2 Chr. 1:10; Prov. 2:3-9; Jas. 1:5 [b]Ps. 72:1,2 [c]Heb. 5:14
3:11 [1]Heb. *many days* [2]Heb. *to hear* [a]Jas. 4:3
3:12 [a]1 John 5:14,15
3:12 [b]ch. 4:29-31; Eccl. 1:16
3:13 [1]Or, *hath not been* [a]Mat. 6:33; Eph. 3:20 [b]ch. 4:21,24
3:14 [a]ch. 15:5 [b]Ps. 91:16; Prov. 3:2
3:15 [a]Gen. 41:7 [b]Gen. 40:20; ch. 8:65; Esth. 1:3; Dan. 5:1; Mark 6:21
3:16 [a]Num. 27:2

house built. Worship at a variety of places was apparently considered normal prior to the building of the temple (see Judg 6:24; 13:19; 1 Sam 7:17; 9:12–13).

3:3 *only.* Solomon's one major fault early in his reign was inconsistency in meeting the Mosaic requirements concerning places of legitimate worship.

3:4 *Gibeon.* The Gibeonites tricked Joshua and Israel into a peace treaty at the time of the conquest of Canaan (see Josh 9:3–27). The city was subsequently given to the tribe of Benjamin and set apart for the Levites (Josh 18:25; 21:17). David avenged Saul's violation of the Gibeonite treaty by the execution of seven of Saul's descendants (see 2 Sam 21:1–9). *great high place.* The reason for Gibeon's importance was the presence there of the tabernacle and the ancient bronze altar (see 1 Chr 21:29; 2 Chr 1:2–6). These must have been salvaged after the destruction of Shiloh by the Philistines (see note on 1 Sam 7:1).

3:5 *dream.* Revelation through dreams is found elsewhere in the OT (see Gen 28:12; 31:11; 46:2; Num 12:6; Judg 7:13; Dan 2:4; 7:1), as well as in the NT (see, e.g., Mat 1:20; 2:12,22).

‡3:6 *mercy.* The Hebrew for this word, often translated "lovingkindness," refers to God's covenant favors (see note on 2 Sam 7:15). Solomon is praising the Lord for faithfulness to His promises to David (2 Sam 7:8–16). *according as.* See note on 2 Sam 22:21.

3:7 *I am but a little child.* The birth of Solomon is generally placed in approximately the middle of David's 40-year reign, meaning that Solomon was about 20 years old at the beginning of his own reign (see 2:11–12) and lacked experience in assuming the responsibilities of his office (cf. Jer 1:6).

3:8 *great people, that cannot be numbered . . . for multitude.* From the small beginnings of a single family living in Egypt (see Gen 46:26–27; Deut 7:7), the Israelites had increased to an extent approaching that anticipated in the promise given to Abraham (Gen 13:16; 22:17–18) and Jacob (Gen 32:12). See 4:20.

3:11 *long life . . . riches . . . life of thine enemies.* Typical desires of ancient Near Eastern monarchs.

3:12 *none like thee.* See 4:29–34; 10:1–13.

3:13 *I have also given thee that which thou hast not asked.* Cf. Jesus' promise in Luke 12:31.

3:14 *if thou wilt walk in my ways . . . I will lengthen thy days.* Echoes Deut 6:2; 17:20; 22:7. Unfortunately Solomon did not remain obedient to the covenant as his father David had (11:6), and he did not live to be much more than 60 years of age (see note on v. 7; cf. 11:42).

3:15 *ark of the covenant of the LORD.* See notes on 6:19; 2 Sam 6:2. *peace offerings.* See note on 1 Sam 11:15.

3:16 *came . . . unto the king.* It was possible for Israelites (and others within the realm) to bypass lower judicial officials (Deut 16:18) and appeal directly to the king (see 2 Ki 8:3; 2 Sam 15:2). *two . . . harlots.* It is not known if these two were Israelites or Jebusites—possibly the latter.

3:17 *dwell in one house.* Brothels were common in ancient Near Eastern cities.

my child suck, behold, it was dead: but when
I had considered it in the morning, behold, it
was not my son, which I did bear.
22 And the other woman said, Nay; but the
living *is* my son, and the dead *is* thy son. And
this said, No; but the dead *is* thy son, and the
living *is* my son. Thus they spake before the
king.
23 Then said the king, The one saith, This
is my son that liveth, and thy son *is* the dead:
and the other saith, Nay; but thy son *is* the
dead, and my son *is* the living.
24 And the king said, Bring me a sword.
And they brought a sword before the king.
25 And the king said, Divide the living
child in two, and give half to the one, and half
to the other.
26 Then spake the woman whose the living child *was* unto the king, for [a]her bowels
[1]yerned upon her son, and she said, O my
lord, give her the living child, and in no wise
slay it. But the other said, Let it be neither
mine nor thine, *but* divide *it*.
27 Then the king answered and said, Give
her the living child, and in no wise slay it: she
is the mother thereof.
28 And all Israel heard of the judgment
which the king had judged; and they feared
the king: for they saw that the [a]wisdom of God
was [1]in him, to do judgment.

Appointment of court officials

4 So king Solomon was king over all Israel.
2 And these *were* the princes which he
had; Azariah the son of Zadok [1]the priest,
3 Elihoreph and Ahiah, the sons of Shisha,
[1]scribes; [a]Jehoshaphat the son of Ahilud, the
[2]recorder.
4 And [a]Benaiah the son of Jehoiada *was*
over the host: and Zadok and [b]Abiathar *were*
the priests:

3:26 [1]Heb. *were hot* [a]Gen. 43:30; Is. 49:15; Jer. 31:20; Hos. 11:8
3:28 [1]Heb. *in the midst of him* [a]ver. 9,11,12
4:2 [1]Or, *the chief officer*
4:3 [1]Or, *secretaries* [2]Or, *remembrancer* [a]2 Sam. 8:16; 20:24
4:4 [a]ch. 2:35 [b]See ch. 2:27
4:5 [a]ver. 7 [b]2 Sam. 8:18; 20:26 [c]2 Sam. 15:37; 16:16; 1 Chr. 27:33
4:6 [1]Or, *levy* [a]ch. 5:14
4:8 [1]Or, *Ben-Hur*
4:9 [1]Or, *Ben-Dekar*
4:10 [1]Or, *Ben-Hesed*
4:11 [1]Or, *Ben-Abinadab*
4:13 [1]Or, *Ben-Geber* [a]Num. 32:41 [b]Deut. 3:4
4:14 [1]Or, *to Mahanaim*

5 And Azariah the son of Nathan *was* over
[a]the officers: and Zabud the son of Nathan *was*
[b]principal officer, *and* [c]the king's friend:
6 And Ahishar *was* over the household:
and [a]Adoniram the son of Abda *was* over the
[1]tribute.
7 And Solomon had twelve officers over all
Israel, which provided victuals for the king
and his household: each man *his* month in a
year made provision.
8 And these *are* their names: [1]The son of
Hur, in mount Ephraim:
9 [1]The son of Dekar, in Makaz, and in Shaalbim, and Beth-shemesh, and Elon-beth-
hanan:
10 [1]The son of Hesed, in Aruboth; to him
pertained Sochoh, and all the land of Hepher:
11 [1]The son of Abinadab, *in* all the region
of Dor; which had Taphath the daughter of Solomon to wife:
12 Baana the son of Ahilud; *to him pertained* Taanach and Megiddo, and all Beth-
shean, which *is* by Zartanah beneath Jezreel,
from Beth-shean to Abel-meholah, *even* unto
the place that is beyond Jokneam:
13 [1]The son of Geber, in Ramoth-gilead; to
him *pertained* [a]the towns of Jair the son of
Manasseh, which *are* in Gilead; to him *also
pertained* [b]the region of Argob, which *is* in Bashan, threescore great cities *with* walls and
brasen bars:
14 Ahinadab the son of Iddo *had* [1]Maha-
naim:
15 Ahimaaz *was* in Naphtali; he also took
Basmath the daughter of Solomon to wife:
16 Baanah the son of Hushai *was* in Asher
and in Aloth:
17 Jehoshaphat the son of Paruah, in Issachar:
18 Shimei the son of Elah, in Benjamin:
19 Geber the son of Uri *was* in the country

3:28 *they saw that the wisdom of God was in him.* This episode strikingly demonstrated that the Lord had answered Solomon's prayer for a discerning heart (vv. 9,12).

4:1 *king over all Israel.* Solomon ruled over an undivided kingdom, as his father had before him (see 2 Sam 8:15).

4:2 *son.* According to 2 Sam 15:27,36 and 1 Chr 6:8–9, Azariah was the son of Ahimaaz and the grandson of Zadok (see note on 2:8). Apparently Zadok's son Ahimaaz had died, so that Zadok was succeeded by his grandson Azariah. *Zadok.* See 2:27,35.

4:3 *Shisha.* See note on 2 Sam 8:17. *scribes.* See note on 2 Sam 8:17. *Jehoshaphat the son of Ahilud.* The same person who served in David's court (see 2 Sam 8:16). *recorder.* See note on 2 Sam 8:16.

4:4 *Benaiah.* Replaced Joab as commander of the army (see 2:35; 2 Sam 8:18). *Zadok and Abiathar.* Abiathar was banished at the beginning of Solomon's reign (2:27,35), and Zadok was succeeded by his grandson Azariah (v. 2).

4:5 *Nathan.* Either the prophet (1:11) or the son of David (2 Sam 5:14). *officers.* See vv. 7–19. *principal officer.* See note on 2 Sam 8:18 ("chief rulers"). *the king's friend.* See note on 2 Sam 15:37.

4:6 *over the household.* The first OT reference to an office mentioned frequently in 1,2 Kings (1 Ki 16:9; 18:3; 2 Ki 18:18,37; 19:2). It is likely that this official was administrator of the palace and steward of the king's properties. *Adoniram.* Served not only under Solomon, but also under David before him (2 Sam 20:24) and Rehoboam after him (1 Ki 12:18). *tribute.* I.e."forced labor." See notes on 9:15; 2 Sam 20:24.

‡4:7 *Solomon had twelve officers.* They administered 12 districts that were not identical to tribal territories, possibly because the tribes varied greatly in agricultural productivity. But Solomon's administrative decision violated traditional tribal boundaries and probably stirred up ancient tribal loyalties, eventually contributing to the disruption of the united kingdom.

4:8 *son of Hur.* Hebrew *Ben-hur.* The Hebrew *Ben* means "son of."

‡4:11 *son of Abinadab.* Hebrew *Ben-abinadab.* Most likely the "son of" David's brother Abinadab (see 1 Sam 16:8; 17:13), making him Solomon's first cousin (he was also his son-in-law).

4:12 *Baana the son of Ahilud.* Probably a brother of Jehoshaphat the recorder (v. 3).

4:16 *Baana the son of Hushai.* Perhaps the son of David's trusted adviser (see notes on 2 Sam 15:32,37).

4:18 *Shimei the son of Elah.* Perhaps the same Shimei mentioned in 1:8.

of Gilead, *in* [a]the country of Sihon king of the
Amorites, and of Og king of Bashan; and *he
was* the only officer which *was* in the land.
20 Judah and Israel *were* many, [a]as the
sand which *is* by the sea in multitude, [b]eating
and drinking, and making merry.

The household provisions

21 ¶ And [a]Solomon reigned over all kingdoms from [b]the river *unto* the land of the Philistines, and unto the border of Egypt: [c]they
brought presents, and served Solomon all the
days of his life.
22 And Solomon's [1]provision for one day
was thirty [2]measures of fine flour, and threescore [3]measures of meal,
23 Ten fat oxen, and twenty oxen out of
the pastures, and an hundred sheep, beside
harts, and roebucks, and fallowdeer, and fatted
fowl.
24 For he had dominion over all *the region*
on *this* side the river, from Tiphsah even to Azzah, over [a]all the kings on *this* side the river:
and [b]he had peace on all sides round about
him.
25 And Judah and Israel [a]dwelt [1]safely,
[b]every man under his vine and under his fig
tree, [c]from Dan even to Beer-sheba, all the
days of Solomon.
26 And [a]Solomon had forty thousand stalls
of [b]horses for his chariots, and twelve thousand horsemen.
27 And [a]those officers provided victual for
king Solomon, and for all that came unto king
Solomon's table, every man *in* his month: they
lacked nothing.
28 Barley also and straw for the horses and
[1]dromedaries brought they unto the place
where *the officers* were, every man according
to his charge.

Solomon's great wisdom

29 ¶ And [a]God gave Solomon wisdom and
understanding exceeding much, and largeness
of heart, *even* as the sand that *is* on the sea
shore.
30 And Solomon's wisdom excelled the
wisdom of all the children [a]of the east country,
and all [b]the wisdom of Egypt.
31 For he was [a]wiser than all men; [b]than
Ethan the Ezrahite, [c]and Heman, and Chalcol,
and Darda, the sons of Mahol: and his fame
was in all nations round about.
32 And [a]he spake three thousand proverbs: and his [b]songs were a thousand and five.
33 And he spake of trees, from the cedar
tree that *is* in Lebanon even unto the hyssop
that springeth out of the wall: he spake also of
beasts, and of fowl, and of creeping things, and
of fishes.
34 And [a]there came of all people to hear
the wisdom of Solomon, from all kings of the
earth, which had heard of his wisdom.

Preparing to build the temple

5 And [1]Hiram king of Tyre sent his servants unto Solomon; for he had heard
that they had anointed him king in the room
of his father: [a]for Hiram was ever a lover of
David.
2 And [a]Solomon sent to Hiram, saying,
3 Thou knowest how that David my father
could not build a house unto the name of the
LORD his God [a]for the wars which were about
him on every side, until the LORD put them under the soles of his feet.

4:19 [a]Deut. 3:8 **4:20** [a]Gen. 22:17; ch. 3:8; Prov. 14:28 [b]Ps. 72:3,7; Mic. 4:4 **4:21** [a]2 Chr. 9:26; Ps. 72:8 [b]Gen. 15:18; Josh. 1:4 [c]Ps. 68:29; 72:10,11 **4:22** [1]Heb. *bread* [2]Heb. *cors* [3]Heb. *cors* **4:24** [a]Ps. 72:11 [b]1 Chr. 22:9 **4:25** [1]Heb. *confidently* [a]See Jer. 23:6 [b]Mic. 4:4; Zech. 3:10 [c]Judg. 20:1 **4:26** [a]ch. 10:26; 2 Chr. 1:14 [b]See Deut. 17:16 **4:27** [a]ver. 7 **4:28** [1]Or, *mules,* or, *swift beasts*

4:29 [a]ch. 3:12 **4:30** [a]Gen. 25:6 [b]See Acts 7:22 **4:31** [a]ch. 3:12 [b]1 Chr. 15:19; Ps. 89, title [c]See 1 Chr. 2:6; 6:33; 15:19; Ps. 88, title **4:32** [a]Prov. 1:1; Eccl. 12:9 [b]Sol. 1:1 **4:34** [a]ch. 10:1; 2 Chr. 9:1,23 **5:1** [1][ver. 10, 18; 2 Chr. 2:3, *Huram*] [a]2 Sam. 5:11; 1 Chr. 14:1; Amos 1:9 **5:2** [a]2 Chr. 2:3 **5:3** [a]1 Chr. 22:8; 28:3

4:20 *many, as the sand which is by the sea.* See 3:8 and note; see also v. 29; Gen 22:17; 2 Sam 17:11; Is 10:22; Jer 33:22; Hos 1:10; cf. Gen 41:49; Josh 11:4; Judg 7:12; Ps 78:27. *eating and drinking, and making merry.* Judah and Israel prospered (see 5:4).

4:21 *from the river unto the land of the Philistines, and unto the border of Egypt.* The borders of Solomon's empire extended to the limits originally promised to Abraham (see note on 2 Sam 8:3). However, rebellion was brewing in Edom (11:14–21) and Damascus (11:23–25).

4:22 *Solomon's provision for one day.* For all his household, his palace servants and his court officials and their families.

‡4:24 *Tiphsah.* A city on the west bank of the Euphrates River. *Azzah.* I.e. *Gaza,* the southernmost city of the Philistines on the Mediterranean coast.

‡4:26 *forty thousand.* One manuscript reads four thousand, cf. 2 Chr. 9:25. 1 Ki 10:26 and 2 Chr 1:14 indicate that Solomon had 1,400 chariots, meaning he maintained stalls for two horses for each chariot, with places for about 1,200 reserve horses. By way of comparison, an Assyrian account of the battle of Qarqar in 853 B.C. (about a century after Solomon) speaks of 1,200 chariots from Damascus, 700 chariots from Hamath and 2,000 chariots from Israel (the northern kingdom).

4:29 *as the sand . . . on the sea shore.* See note on v. 20.

4:30 *children of the east country.* The phrase is general and appears to refer to the peoples of Mesopotamia (see Gen 29:1) and Arabia (see Jer 49:28; Ezek 25:4,10)—those associated with Israel's northeastern and eastern horizons, just as Egypt was the main region on her southwestern horizon. Many examples of Mesopotamian wisdom literature have been recovered. *wisdom of Egypt.* See Gen 41:8; Ex 7:11; Acts 7:22. Examples of Egyptian wisdom literature are to be found in the proverbs of Ptahhotep (c. 2450 B.C.) and Amenemope (see Introduction to Proverbs: Date).

4:31 *he was wiser than all men.* Until Jesus came (see Luke 11:31). *Ethan the Ezrahite.* See Ps 89 title. *Heman, and Chalcol, and Darda.* See note on 1 Chr 2:6.

4:32 *three thousand proverbs.* Only some of these are preserved in the book of Proverbs.

4:33 *beasts, and of fowl, and of creeping things, and of fishes.* Examples of Solomon's knowledge of these creatures are found in Prov 6:6–8; 26:2–3,11; 27:8; 28:1,15.

4:34 *all people . . . all kings of the earth.* A general statement referring to the Near Eastern world (cf. Gen 41:57).

5:1 *Hiram king of Tyre.* Hiram ruled over Tyre c. 978–944 B.C. He may have also served as co-regent with his father Abibaal as early as 993. Before Solomon was born, Hiram provided timber and workmen for the building of David's palace (see 2 Sam 5:11).

5:3 *could not build a house.* Although David was denied the privilege of building the temple, he did make plans and provisions for its construction (see 1 Chr 22:2–5; 28:2; cf. also Ps 30 title).

4 But now the LORD my God hath given me
[a]rest on every side, *so that there is* neither adversary nor evil occurrent.
5 [a]And behold, I [1]purpose to build a house
unto the name of the LORD my God, [b]as the
LORD spake unto David my father, saying, Thy
son, whom I will set upon thy throne in thy
room, he shall build a house unto my name.
6 Now therefore command thou that they
hew me [a]cedar trees out of Lebanon; and my
servants shall be with thy servants: and unto
thee will I give hire for thy servants according
to all that thou shalt [1]appoint: for thou knowest that *there is* not among us any *that* can skill
to hew timber like unto the Sidonians.
7 And it came to pass, when Hiram heard
the words of Solomon, that he rejoiced greatly,
and said, Blessed *be* the LORD *this* day, which
hath given unto David a wise son over this
great people.
8 And Hiram sent to Solomon, saying, I
have [1]considered *the things* which thou sentest to me *for: and* I will do all thy desire concerning timber of cedar, and concerning timber of fir.
9 My servants shall bring *them* down from
Lebanon unto the sea: and I will convey them
by sea *in* flotes unto the place that thou shalt
[1]appoint me, and will cause them to be dis-
charged there, and thou shalt receive *them:*
and thou shalt accomplish my desire, [a]in giving food for my household.
10 So Hiram gave Solomon cedar trees and
fir trees *according to* all his desire.
11 [a]And Solomon gave Hiram twenty thousand [1]measures of wheat *for* food to his house-

5:4 [a]ch. 4:24; 1 Chr. 22:9
5:5 [1]Heb. *say*
[a]2 Chr. 2:4
[b]2 Sam. 7:13; 1 Chr. 17:12
5:6 [1]Heb. *say*
[a]2 Chr. 2:8,10
5:8 [1]Heb. *heard*
5:9 [1]Heb. *send*
[a]See Ezra 3:7; Ezek. 27:17; Acts 12:20
5:11 [1]Heb. *cors*
[a]See 2 Chr. 2:10
5:11 [2]Heb. *cors*
5:12 [a]ch. 3:12
5:13 [1]Heb. *tribute* of men
5:14 [a]ch. 4:6
5:15 [a]ch. 9:21; 2 Chr. 2:18
5:17 [a]1 Chr. 22:2
5:18 [1]Or, *Giblites:* as Ezek. 27:9
6:1 [1]Heb. *built*
[a]2 Chr. 3:1,2
[b]Acts 7:47

hold, and twenty [2]measures of pure oil: thus
gave Solomon to Hiram year by year.
12 And the LORD gave Solomon wisdom,
[a]as he promised him: and there was peace between Hiram and Solomon; and they two
made a league *together.*
13 ¶ And king Solomon raised a [1]levy out
of all Israel; and the levy was thirty thousand
men.
14 And he sent them to Lebanon, ten thousand a month *by* courses: a month they were
in Lebanon, *and* two months at home: and
[a]Adoniram *was* over the levy.
15 [a]And Solomon had threescore and ten
thousand that bare burdens, and fourscore
thousand hewers in the mountains;
16 Besides the chief of Solomon's officers
which *were* over the work, three thousand
and three hundred, which ruled over the people that wrought in the work.
17 And the king commanded, and they
brought great stones, costly stones, *and*
[a]hewed stones, to lay the foundation of the
house.
18 And Solomon's builders and Hiram's
builders did hew *them,* and the [1]stonesquar-
ers: so they prepared timber and stones to
build the house.

The description of the temple

6 And [a]it came to pass in the four hundred
and eightieth year after the children of Israel were come out of the land of Egypt, in the
fourth year of Solomon's reign over Israel, in
the month Zif, which *is* the second month,
that [b]he [1]*began* to build the house of the LORD.

5:4 *rest.* Described here as "neither adversary nor evil occurrent." God's promises to His people (see Ex 33:14; Deut 25:19; Josh 1:13,15) and to David (2 Sam 7:11) have now been fulfilled (see 8:56), so that the Israelites are free to concentrate their strength and resources on building their Great King's royal house (see note on 2 Sam 7:11).

5:5 *name.* Signifies God's revealed character or self-revelation as a person (see, e.g., 8:16; Ex 20:24; Deut 12:5; 2 Sam 6:2; 7:13). *as the LORD spake unto David my father.* See 2 Sam 7:12–13; 1 Chr 22:8–10.

5:6 *command.* A more detailed account of Solomon's request is found in 2 Chr 2:3–10. *cedars trees out of Lebanon.* Widely used in the ancient Near East in the construction of royal houses and temples.

5:7 *Blessed be the LORD.* In polytheistic cultures it was common practice for the people of one nation to recognize the deities of another nation (see 10:9; 11:5) and even to ascribe certain powers to them (see 2 Ki 18:25; see also 2 Chr 2:12).

5:9 *place that thou shalt appoint me.* Joppa (2 Chr 2:16; see note on 1 Ki 3:1). *giving food for my household.* Provision of food for Hiram's court personnel appears to cover only the cost of the wood itself. In addition, Solomon would have to provide for the wages of the Phoenician laborers (v. 6). Comparison of v. 11 with 2 Chr 2:10 indicates that besides wheat and olive oil for Hiram's court, Solomon also sent barley and wine for labor costs. Hiram may have sold some of these provisions in order to pay the laborers.

‡5:11 *twenty thousand measures* [i.e."kors"] *of wheat.* About 125,000 bushels. By way of comparison, Solomon's court received 10,950 kors of flour and 21,900 kors of meal on an annual basis (see 4:22). Solomon's whole grain payment to Hiram of 20,000 kors of wheat and 20,000 kors of barley (2 Chr 2:10) would probably yield about 26,666 kors of refined flour and meal, or about 20 percent less than the requirements of Solomon's own court.

5:13 *levy.* I.e."forced laborers." See notes on 9:15; 2 Sam 20:24. Resentment among the people toward this sort of forced labor eventually led to a civil uprising and the division of Solomon's kingdom immediately after his death (12:1–18).

5:15 *threescore and ten thousand that bare burdens . . . fourscore thousand hewers.* Conscripted from the non-Israelite population that David had subdued and incorporated into his kingdom (see 2 Chr 2:17–18). *mountains.* The limestone hills of the Holy Land where the stone was quarried.

5:16 *three thousand and three hundred, which ruled . . . people.* 1 Ki 9:23 refers to 550 chief officers. If these are two different categories of supervisory personnel, the total is 3,850 men. 2 Chr 2:2 refers to 3,600 supervisors, and 2 Chr 8:10 speaks of 250 chief officers, which again yields a total of 3,850 men in a supervisory capacity.

5:17 *great stones, costly stones.* For the size of these stones see 7:10. Transportation of such stones to Jerusalem would require enormous manpower.

‡5:18 *stonesquarers.* Better rendered "Giblites" or "Gebalites." Gebal is also known as Byblos (see note on Ezek 27:9).

6:1–38 See drawing, p. 458.

6:1 *four hundred and eightieth year . . . fourth year.* Synchronizations between certain events in the reigns of later Israelite

2 And [a]the house which king Solomon built for the LORD, the length thereof *was* threescore cubits, and the breadth thereof twenty *cubits,* and the height thereof thirty cubits.

3 And the porch before the temple of the house, twenty cubits *was* the length thereof, according to the breadth of the house; *and* ten cubits *was* the breadth thereof before the house.

4 And for the house he made [a][1]windows of narrow lights.

5 And [1]against the wall of the house he built [a][2]chambers round about, *against* the walls of the house round about, *both* of the temple [b]and of the oracle: and he made [3]chambers round about:

6 The nethermost chamber *was* five cubits broad, and the middle *was* six cubits broad, and the third *was* seven cubits broad: for without *in the wall* of the house he made [1]narrowed rests round about, that *the beams* should not be fastened in the walls of the house.

7 And [a]the house, when it was in building, was built *of* stone made ready *before it was* brought *thither:* so that there was neither hammer nor axe *nor* any tool of iron heard in the house, while it was in building.

8 The door for the middle chamber *was* in the right [1]side of the house: and they went up with winding stairs into the middle *chamber,* and out of the middle into the third.

9 [a]So he built the house, and finished it; and covered the house [1]with beams and boards of cedar.

10 And *then* he built chambers against all the house, five cubits high: and they rested on the house with timber of cedar.

11 ¶ And the word of the LORD came to Solomon, saying,

12 *Concerning* this house which thou art in building, [a]if thou wilt walk in my statutes, and execute my judgments, and keep all my commandments to walk in them; then will I perform my word with thee, [b]which I spake unto David thy father:

13 And I [a]will dwell among the children of Israel, and will not [b]forsake my people Israel.

14 ¶ So Solomon built the house, and finished it.

15 And he built the walls of the house within with boards of cedar, [1]both the floor of the house, and the walls of the cieling: *and* he covered *them* on the inside with wood, and covered the floor of the house with planks of fir.

16 And he built twenty cubits on the sides of the house, both the floor and the walls with boards of cedar: he even built *them* for it within, *even* for the oracle, *even* for the [a]most holy *place.*

17 And the house, that *is,* the temple before it, was forty cubits *long.*

18 And the cedar of the house within *was* carved with [1]knops and [2]open flowers: all *was* cedar; there was no stone seen.

19 And the oracle he prepared in the house within, to set there the ark of the covenant of the LORD.

20 And the oracle in the forepart *was* twenty cubits in length, and twenty cubits in breadth, and twenty cubits in the height thereof: and he overlaid it with [1]pure gold; and *so* covered the altar *which was of* cedar.

6:2 [a]See Ezek. 41:1
6:4 [1]Or, *windows broad* within, and *narrow* without: or, *skewed* and *closed* [a]See Ezek. 40:16
6:5 [1]Or, *upon,* or, *joining to* [2]Heb. *floors* [3]Heb. *ribs* [a]See Ezek. 41:6 [b]ver. 16,19-21,31
6:6 [1]Heb. *narrowings,* or, *rebatements*
6:7 [a]See Deut. 27:5,6
6:8 [1]Heb. *shoulder*
6:9 [1]Or, *the vault-beams and the cielings with cedar* [a]ver. 14,38
6:12 [a]ch. 2:4; 9:4 [b]2 Sam. 7:13; 1 Chr. 22:10
6:13 [a]Ex. 25:8; 2 Cor. 6:16; Rev. 21:3 [b]Deut. 31:6
6:15 [1]Or, *from the floor of the house unto the walls, etc.* and so ver. 16
6:16 [a]Ex. 26:33; Lev. 16:2; ch. 8:6; 2 Chr. 3:8; Ezek. 45:3
6:18 [1]Or, *gourds* [2]Heb. *openings of flowers*
6:20 [1]Heb. *shut up*

kings and Assyrian chronological records fix the fourth year of Solomon's reign at c. 966 B.C. (see Introduction: Chronology). If Israel's exodus is placed 480 years prior to 966, it would have occurred c. 1446 (the chronology followed in this study Bible) during the rule of the 18th-dynasty Egyptian pharaoh, Amunhotep II. On the basis of Ex 1:11 and certain other historical considerations, however, some have concluded that the exodus could not have occurred prior to the rule of the 19th-dynasty pharaoh, Rameses II—thus not until c. 1290 (see note on Gen 47:11). This would mean that the 480 years of this verse would be understood as either a schematic (perhaps representative of 12 generations multiplied by the conventional, but not always actual, 40-year length of a generation) or aggregate figure (the combined total of a number of subsidiary time periods, which in reality were partly concurrent, examples of which are to be found in Egyptian and Mesopotamian records).

6:2 *house which king Solomon built.* The temple was patterned after the tabernacle (and, in general, other temples of the time) and was divided into three major areas: the most holy place, the holy place and the outer courtyard. The most holy place in the temple was cubical, as it probably was in the tabernacle. The dimensions of the temple in most instances seem to be double those of the tabernacle (see Ex 26:15–30; 36:20–34).

6:6 *narrowed rests.* To avoid making holes in the temple wall, it was built with a series of ledges on which the beams for the three floors of side chambers rested. This accounts for the different widths of the rooms on each floor.

6:11 *the word of the LORD came to Solomon.* As the temple neared completion the Lord spoke to Solomon, perhaps through an unnamed prophet (but see 3:5,11–14; 9:2–9).

6:12 *if thou wilt walk in my statutes . . . will I perform my word with thee.* In words similar to those spoken by David (see notes on 2:1–4), the Lord assures Solomon of a continuing dynasty (see 2 Sam 7:12–16) if he is faithful to the covenant.

6:13 *I will dwell among the children of Israel.* In the temple being built (see 9:3). To avoid any apprehension among the Israelites concerning His presence with them (cf. Ps 78:60; Jer 26:6,9; see note on 1 Sam 7:1), the Lord gives assurance that He will dwell in their midst (see 8:10–13; Lev 26:11).

6:16 *most holy place.* Similar terminology was used for the inner sanctuary housing the ark in the tabernacle (see Ex 26:33–34; Lev 16:2,16–17, 20, 23).

6:19 *ark of the covenant of the LORD.* The ten commandments are called the "words of the covenant" in Ex 34:28. The stone tablets on which the ten commandments were inscribed are called the "tables of the covenant" in Deut 9:9. The ark in which the tablets were kept (see Ex 25:16,21; 40:20; Deut 10:1–5) is thus sometimes called the "ark of the covenant of the LORD" (see Deut 10:8; 31:9,25; Josh 3:11). Elsewhere the ark is variously designated as the "ark of the LORD" (Josh 3:13; 4:11), the "ark of the Testimony" (Ex 30:6; 31:7) and the "ark of God" (1 Sam 3:3; 4:11,17,21; 5:1–2).

6:20 *pure gold.* The extensive use of gleaming gold probably symbolized the glory of God and His heavenly temple (cf. Rev 21:10–11,18,21).

21 So Solomon overlaid the house within
with pure gold: and he made a partition by the
chains of gold before the oracle; and he overlaid it with gold.
22 And the whole house he overlaid with
gold, until *he* had finished all the house: also
[a]the whole altar that *was* by the oracle he
overlaid with gold.
23 ¶ And within the oracle [a]he made two
cherubims *of* [1]olive tree, each ten cubits high.
24 And five cubits *was* the one wing of the
cherub, and five cubits the other wing of the
cherub: from the uttermost part of the one
wing unto the uttermost part of the other *were*
ten cubits.
25 And the other cherub *was* ten cubits:
both the cherubims *were* of one measure and
one size.
26 The height of the one cherub *was* ten
cubits, and so *was it* of the other cherub.
27 And he set the cherubims within the inner house: and [a][1]they stretched forth the wings
of the cherubims, so that the wing of the one
touched the *one* wall, and the wing of the other
cherub touched the other wall; and their wings
touched one another in the midst of the house.
28 And he overlaid the cherubims with
gold.
29 And he carved all the walls of the house
round about *with* carved figures of cherubims
and palm trees and [1]open flowers, within and
without.

6:22 [a]Ex. 30:1,3,6
6:23 [1]Or, *oily.* Heb. *trees of oil* [a]Ex. 37:7-9; 2 Chr. 3:10-12
6:27 [1]Or, *the cherubims stretched forth their wings* [a]Ex. 25:20; 37:9; 2 Chr. 5:8
6:29 [1]Heb. *openings of flowers*

6:21 *chains of gold.* The curtain covering the entrance to the most holy place was probably hung on these chains (see 2 Chr 3:14; Mat 27:51; Heb 6:19).
‡6:22 *altar that was by the oracle* [i.e. the inner sanctuary]. The incense altar (see 7:48; Ex 30:1,6; 37:25–28; Heb 9:3–4).
6:23 *cherubims.* See note on Ex 25:18. They were to stand as sentries on either side of the ark (8:6–7; 2 Chr 3:10–13). Two additional cherubim stood on the ark—one on each end of its atonement cover (Ex 25:17–22). *ten cubits high.* The most holy place, where the cherubim stood, was 20 cubits high (v. 16).
6:29 *he carved . . . cherubims.* Not a violation of the second commandment, which prohibited making anything to serve as a representation of God and worshiping it (see note on Ex 20:4). *palm trees and open flowers.* Early Jewish synagogues were adorned with similar motifs. The depiction of cherubim and beautiful trees and flowers is reminiscent of the Garden of Eden, from which man had been driven as a result of sin (Gen 3:24). In a symbolic sense, readmission to the paradise of God

Solomon's Temple

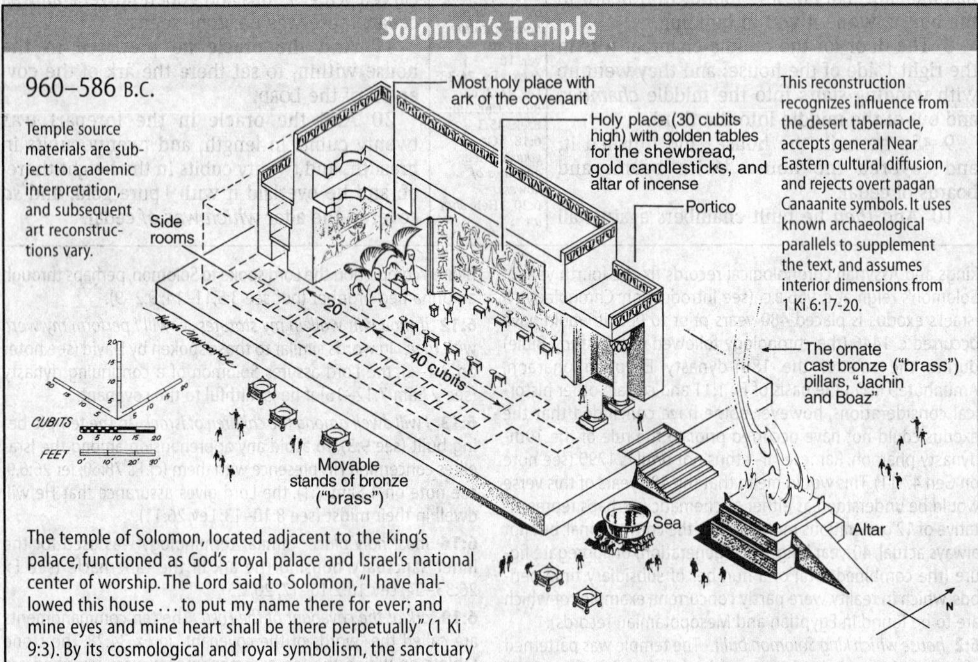

The temple of Solomon, located adjacent to the king's palace, functioned as God's royal palace and Israel's national center of worship. The Lord said to Solomon, "I have hallowed this house . . . to put my name there for ever; and mine eyes and mine heart shall be there perpetually" (1 Ki 9:3). By its cosmological and royal symbolism, the sanctuary taught the absolute sovereignty of the Lord over the whole creation and His special headship over Israel.

The floor plan is a type that has a long history in Semitic religion, particularly among the West Semites. An early example of the tripartite division into *'ulam*, *hekal*, and *debir* (portico, main hall, and inner sanctuary) has been found at Syrian Ebla (c. 2300 B.C.) and, much later but more contemporaneous with Solomon, at Tell Tainat in the Orontes basin (c. 900 B.C.). Like Solomon's, the later temple has three divisions, contains two columns supporting the entrance, and is located adjacent to the royal palace.

Many archaeological parallels can be drawn to the methods of construction used in the temple, e.g., the "stone and cedar beam" technique described in 1 Ki 6:36. Interestingly, evidence for the largest bronze-casting industry ever found in Palestine comes from the same locale and period as that indicated in Scripture: Zarethan in the Jordan Valley c. 1000 B.C.

30 And the floor of the house he overlaid
with gold, within and without.
31 ¶ And for the entering of the oracle he
made doors of olive tree: the lintel *and* side
posts *were* [1] a fifth *part of the wall.*
32 The [1] two doors also *were* of olive tree;
and he carved upon them carvings of cherubims and palm trees and [2] open flowers, and
overlaid *them* with gold, and spread gold upon
the cherubims, and upon the palm trees.
33 So also made he for the door of the temple posts of olive tree, [1] a fourth *part of the*
wall.
34 And the two doors *were* of fir tree: the
[a] two leaves of the one door *were* folding, and
the two leaves of the other door *were* folding.
35 And he carved *thereon* cherubims and
palm trees and open flowers: and covered
them with gold fitted upon the carved work.
36 And he built the inner court *with* three
rows of hewed stone, and a row of cedar
beams.
37 ¶ [a] In the fourth year was the foundation
of the house of the LORD laid, in the month Zif:
38 And in the eleventh year, in the month
Bul, which *is* the eighth month, was the house
finished [1] throughout all the parts thereof, and
according to all the fashion of it. So was he
[a] seven years in building it.

The palace buildings

7 But Solomon was building his own house
[a] thirteen years, and he finished all his
house.
2 He built also the house of the forest of
Lebanon; the length thereof *was* an hundred
cubits, and the breadth thereof fifty cubits,
and the height thereof thirty cubits, upon four
rows of cedar pillars, with cedar beams upon
the pillars.
3 And *it was* covered with cedar above
upon the [1] beams, that *lay* on forty five pillars,
fifteen *in* a row.

6:31 [1] Or, *fivesquare*
6:32 [1] Or, *leaves of the doors* [2] Heb. *openings of flowers*
6:33 [1] Or, *foursquare*
6:34 [a] Ezek. 41:23-25
6:37 [a] ver. 1
6:38 [1] Or, *with all the appurtenances thereof, and with all the ordinances thereof* [a] Compare; ver. 1
7:1 [a] ch. 9:10; 2 Chr. 8:1
7:3 [1] Heb. *ribs*
7:4 [1] Heb. *sight against sight*
7:5 [1] Or, *spaces and pillars* were *square in prospect*
7:6 [1] Or, *according to them*
7:7 [1] Heb. *from floor to floor*
7:8 [a] ch. 3:1; 2 Chr. 8:11
7:12 [a] John 10:23; Acts 3:11
7:13 [1] [2 Chr. 4:11, *Huram:* See ver. 40]
7:14 [1] Heb. *the son of a widow woman* [a] 2 Chr. 2:14 [b] 2 Chr. 4:16 [c] Ex. 31:3; 36:1

4 And *there were* windows *in* three rows,
and [1] light *was* against light *in* three ranks.
5 And all the [1] doors and posts *were*
square, *with the* windows: and light *was*
against light *in* three ranks.
6 And he made a porch of pillars; the
length thereof *was* fifty cubits, and the breadth
thereof thirty cubits: and the porch *was* [1] before them: and *the other* pillars and the thick
beam *were* [1] before them.
7 Then he made a porch for the throne
where he might judge, *even* the porch of judgment: and *it was* covered with cedar [1] from
one side of the floor to the other.
8 And his house where he dwelt *had* another court within the porch, *which* was of the
like work. Solomon made also a house for
Pharaoh's daughter, [a] whom he had taken *to*
wife, like unto this porch.
9 All these *were of* costly stones, according
to the measures of hewed stones, sawed with
saws, within and without, even from the foundation unto the coping, and *so* on the outside
toward the great court.
10 And the foundation *was of* costly
stones, *even* great stones, stones of ten cubits,
and stones of eight cubits.
11 And above *were* costly stones, after the
measures of hewed stones, and cedars.
12 And the great court round about *was with*
three rows *of* hewed stones, and a row of cedar
beams, both for the inner court of the house of
the LORD, [a] and for the porch of the house.

The temple furnishings

13 ¶ And king Solomon sent and fet [1] Hiram
out of Tyre.
14 [a] He *was* [1] a widow's son of the tribe of
Naphtali, and [b] his father *was* a man of Tyre, a
worker in brass: and [c] he was filled *with* wisdom, and understanding, and cunning to work
all works in brass. And he came to king Solomon, and wrought all his work.

is now to be found only by means of atonement for sin at the sanctuary.

6:36 *inner court.* Suggests that there was an outer courtyard (see 8:64). 2 Chr 4:9 refers to the "court of the priests" (inner) and the "great court" (outer). The inner court is also called the higher court (Jer 36:10) because of its higher position on the temple mount.

6:37 *fourth year.* Of Solomon's reign (see v. 1 and note).

6:38 *eleventh year.* Of Solomon's reign (959 B.C.).

7:1 *thirteen years.* Solomon spent almost twice as long building his own house as he did the Lord's house (see 6:38; see also Hag 1:2–4).

7:2 *house of the forest of Lebanon.* Four rows of cedar pillars in the palace created the impression of a great forest. *length . . . an hundred cubits, and the breadth . . . fifty cubits, and the height . . . thirty cubits.* About 150 feet long, 75 feet wide and 45 feet high. Compare these measurements with those of the temple in 6:2.

7:3 *forty five pillars, fifteen in a row.* Suggests that there were three floors in the building above the main hall on the ground level. The building included storage area for weaponry (see 10:16–17).

7:6 *porch.* Apparently an entrance hall to the palace of the forest of Lebanon. Its length (50 cubits) corresponds to the width of the palace.

7:7 *porch for the throne.* It is not clear whether the throne hall, the hall of judgment, Solomon's own living quarters (v. 8) and the palace for Pharaoh's daughter (v. 8) were separate buildings or locations within the palace of the forest of Lebanon.

7:9 *sawed with saws.* The pinkish white limestone of the Holy Land is easily cut when originally quarried, but gradually hardens with exposure.

7:12 *great court.* Constructed in the same way as the inner court of the temple (6:36).

7:13 *king Solomon sent.* Prior to the completion of the temple and the construction of Solomon's palace (see 2 Chr 2:7, 13–14). *Hiram.* His full name is Huram-abi (Huram is a variant of Hiram; 2 Chr 2:13).

7:14 *widow's son of the tribe of Naphtali.* 2 Chr 2:14 indicates that Huram-abi's mother was from Dan. Apparently she was born in the city of Dan in northern Israel close to the tribe of Naphtali, from which came her first husband. After he died, she married a man from Tyre. *all works in brass.* Huram-abi had a much wider range of skills as well (see 2 Chr 2:7,14).

15 For he [1]cast [a]two pillars *of* brass, of eighteen cubits high apiece: and a line of twelve cubits did compass either of them about.

16 And he made two chapiters *of* molten brass, to set upon the tops of the pillars: the height of the one chapiter *was* five cubits, and the height of the other chapiter *was* five cubits:

17 *And* nets of checker work, *and* wreaths of chain work, for the chapiters which *were* upon the top of the pillars; seven for the one chapiter, and seven for the other chapiter.

18 And he made the pillars, and two rows round about upon the one network, to cover the chapiters that *were* upon the top, *with* pomegranates: and so did he for the other chapiter.

19 (And the chapiters that *were* upon the top of the pillars *were* of lily work in the porch, four cubits).

20 And the chapiters upon the two pillars *had pomegranates* also above, over against the belly which *was* by the network: and the pomegranates *were* [a]two hundred *in* rows round about upon the other chapiter.

21 [a]And he set up the pillars in the porch of the temple: and he set up the right pillar, and called the name thereof [1]Jachin: and he set up the left pillar, and called the name thereof [2]Boaz.

22 And upon the top of the pillars *was* lily work: so was the work of the pillars finished.

23 ¶ And he made [a]a molten sea, ten cubits [1]from the one brim to the other: *it was* round all about, and his height *was* five cubits: and a line of thirty cubits did compass it round about.

24 And under the brim of it round about *there were* knops compassing it, ten in a cubit, [a]compassing the sea round about: the knops *were* cast *in* two rows, when it was cast.

7:15 [1]Heb. *fashioned* [a]2 Ki. 25:17; 2 Chr. 3:15; 4:12; Jer. 52:21
7:20 [a]See 2 Chr. 3:16; 4:13; Jer. 52:23
7:21 [1]That is, *He shall establish* [2]That is, *In it is strength* [a]2 Chr. 3:17
7:23 [1]Heb. *from his brim to his brim* [a]2 Ki. 25:13; 2 Chr. 4:2; Jer. 52:17
7:24 [a]2 Chr. 4:3

7:15 *two pillars of brass.* One was placed on each side of the main entrance to the temple (v. 21). Surely decorative, they may also have embodied a symbolism not known to us. It has been suggested that they were not freestanding but supported a roof (forming a portico to the temple) and an architrave.
7:21 *the right pillar.* The temple, like the tabernacle before it, faced east (see Ezek 8:16).
7:23 *molten sea.* This enormous reservoir of water corresponded to the bronze laver made for the tabernacle (see Ex 30:17–21; 38:8). Its water was used by the priests for ritual cleansing (2 Chr 4:6). *thirty cubits.* Technically speaking, this should be 31.416 cubits because of the ten-cubit diameter of the circular top. Thirty may be a round number here, or perhaps the measurement was taken a bit below the rim or on the inside circumference (see v. 26).
‡7:24 *knops* [i.e. "gourds"] . . . *ten in a cubit.* With ten gourds to a cubit it took 300 gourds to span the reservoir, or 600 gourds counting both rows.

Temple Furnishings

Glimpses of the rich ornamentation of Solomon's temple can be gained through recent discoveries that illumine the text of 1 Ki 6-7.

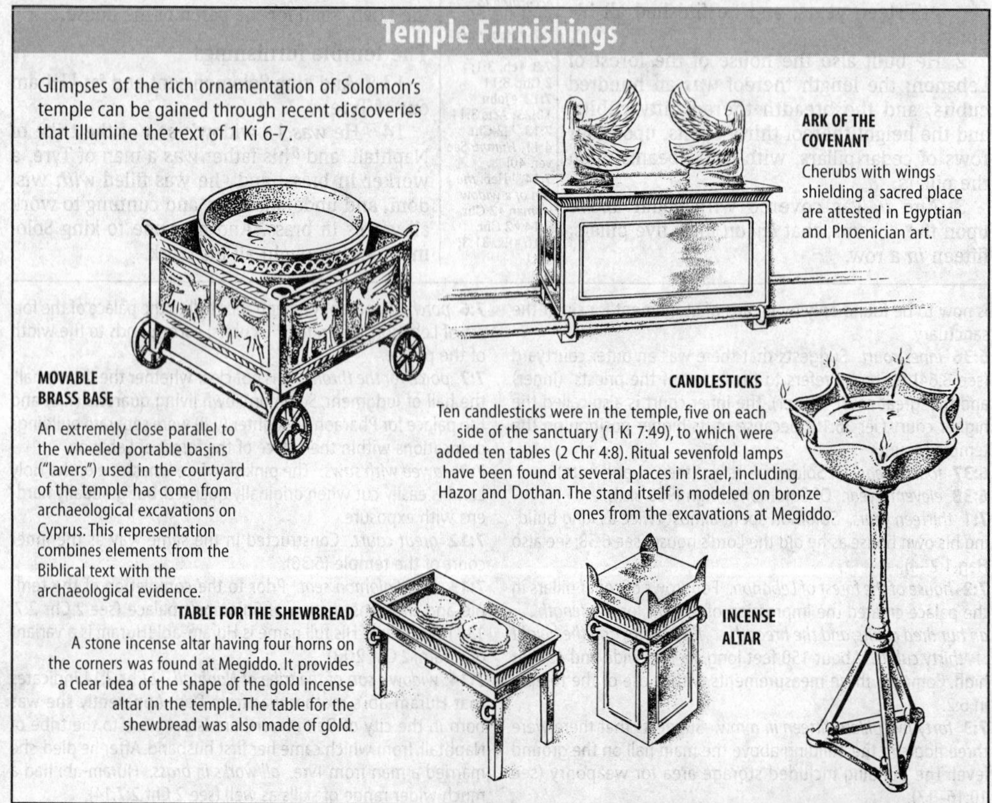

ARK OF THE COVENANT
Cherubs with wings shielding a sacred place are attested in Egyptian and Phoenician art.

MOVABLE BRASS BASE
An extremely close parallel to the wheeled portable basins ("lavers") used in the courtyard of the temple has come from archaeological excavations on Cyprus. This representation combines elements from the Biblical text with the archaeological evidence.

CANDLESTICKS
Ten candlesticks were in the temple, five on each side of the sanctuary (1 Ki 7:49), to which were added ten tables (2 Chr 4:8). Ritual sevenfold lamps have been found at several places in Israel, including Hazor and Dothan. The stand itself is modeled on bronze ones from the excavations at Megiddo.

TABLE FOR THE SHEWBREAD

INCENSE ALTAR
A stone incense altar having four horns on the corners was found at Megiddo. It provides a clear idea of the shape of the gold incense altar in the temple. The table for the shewbread was also made of gold.

25 It stood upon [a]twelve oxen, three looking toward the north, and three looking toward the west, and three looking toward the south, and three looking toward the east: and the sea *was set* above upon them, and all their hinder parts *were* inward.

26 And it *was* a handbreadth thick, and the brim thereof was wrought like the brim of a cup, *with* flowers of lilies: it contained [a]two thousand baths.

27 ¶ And he made ten bases of brass; four cubits *was* the length of one base, and four cubits the breadth thereof, and three cubits the height of it.

28 And the work of the bases *was on* this *manner:* they had borders, and the borders *were* between the ledges:

29 And on the borders that *were* between the ledges *were* [a]lions, oxen, and cherubims: and upon the ledges *there was* a base above: and beneath the lions and oxen *were certain* additions made of thin work.

30 And every base had four brasen wheels, and plates of brass: and the four corners thereof had undersetters: under the laver *were* undersetters molten, at the side of every addition.

31 And the mouth of it within the chapiter and above *was* a cubit: but the mouth thereof *was* round *after* the work of the base, a cubit and a half: and also upon the mouth of it *were* gravings with their borders, foursquare, not round.

32 And under the borders *were* four wheels; and the axletrees of the wheels *were* [1]joined to the base: and the height of a wheel *was* a cubit and half a cubit.

33 And the work of the wheels *was* like the work of a chariot wheel: their axletrees, and their naves, and their felloes, and their spokes, *were* all molten.

34 And *there were* four undersetters to the four corners of one base: *and* the undersetters *were* of the *very* base itself.

35 And in the top of the base *was there* a round compass of half a cubit high: and on the top of the base the ledges thereof and the borders thereof *were* of the same.

36 For on the plates of the ledges thereof, and on the borders thereof, he graved cherubims, lions, and palm trees, according to the [1]proportion of every one, and additions round about.

37 After this *manner* he made the ten bases: all of them had one casting, one measure, *and* one size.

38 Then [a]made he ten lavers of brass: one laver contained forty baths: *and* every laver was four cubits: *and* upon every one of the ten bases one laver.

39 And he put five bases on the right [1]side of the house, and five on the left side of the house: and he set the sea on the right side of the house eastward over against the south.

40 ¶ And [1]Hiram made the lavers, and the shovels, and the basons. So Hiram made an end of doing all the work that he made king Solomon *for* the house of the LORD:

41 The two pillars, and the two bowls of the chapiters that *were* on the top of the *two* pillars; and the two [a]networks, to cover the two bowls of the chapiters which *were* upon the top of the pillars;

42 And four hundred pomegranates for the two networks, *even* two rows *of* pomegranates for one network, to cover the two bowls of the chapiters that *were* [1]upon the pillars;

43 And the ten bases, and ten lavers on the bases;

44 And one sea, and twelve oxen under the sea;

45 [a]And the pots, and the shovels, and the basons: and all these vessels, which Hiram made to king Solomon *for* the house of the LORD, *were of* [1]bright brass.

46 [a]In the plain of Jordan did the king cast them, [1]in the clay ground between [b]Succoth and [c]Zarthan.

47 And Solomon left all the vessels *unweighed,* [1]because they were exceeding many: neither was the weight of the brass [a2]found out.

48 And Solomon made all the vessels that *pertained unto* the house of the LORD: [a]the altar of gold, and [b]the table *of* gold, whereupon [c]the shewbread *was,*

49 And the candlesticks *of* pure gold, five on the right side, and five on the left, before the oracle, with the flowers, and the lamps, and the tongs *of* gold,

7:25 [a]2 Chr. 4:4,5; Jer. 52:20
7:26 [a]See 2 Chr. 4:5
7:29 [a]Gen. 3:24; ch. 6:27; Ps. 18:10; Ezek. 1:10; 41:18,19; Rev. 4:6-8
7:32 [1]Heb. *in the base*
7:36 [1]Heb. *nakedness*
7:38 [a]2 Chr. 4:6
7:39 [1]Heb. *shoulder*
7:40 [1][Heb. *Hirom:* See ver. 13]
7:41 [a]ver. 17,18
7:42 [1]Heb. *upon the face [of the pillars]*
7:45 [1]Heb. *made bright,* or, *scoured* [a]Ex. 27:3; 2 Chr. 4:16
7:46 [1]Heb. *in the thickness of the ground* [a]2 Chr. 4:17 [b]Gen. 33:17 [c]Josh. 3:16
7:47 [1]Heb. *for the exceeding multitude* [2]Heb. *searched* [a]1 Chr. 22:14
7:48 [a]Ex. 37:25 [b]Ex. 37:10 [c]Lev. 24:5-8

‡7:27 *ten bases* [i.e."stands"]. These movable bronze ("brass") stands were designed to hold water basins ("lavers," v. 38) of much smaller dimensions than the molten sea. The water from the basins was used to wash certain prescribed parts of the animals that were slaughtered for burnt offerings (see Lev 1:9,13; 2 Chr 4:6).
7:36 *he graved cherubims, lions, and palm trees.* See note on 6:29.
7:40 *lavers.* Perhaps used for cooking meat to be eaten in connection with the peace offerings (see Lev 7:11–17; 22:21–23). *shovels.* Used for removing ashes from the altar. *basons.* For use by the priests in various rites involving the sprinkling of blood or water (see Ex 27:3).
7:41 *two networks.* See v. 17.
7:42 *four hundred pomegranates.* See vv. 18,20.
7:43 *ten bases, and ten lavers.* See vv. 27–37.
7:44 *one sea, and twelve oxen.* See vv. 23–26.
7:45 *pots, and the shovels, and the basons.* See v. 40.
7:46 *Succoth.* Located on the east side of the Jordan (Gen 33:17; Josh 13:27; Judg 8:4–5) just north of the Jabbok River. Excavations in this area have confirmed that Succoth was a center of metallurgy during the period of the monarchy. *Zarthan.* Located near Adam (see Josh 3:16) and Abel-meholah (4:12).
7:48 *altar of gold.* See 6:22. *table of gold.* The shewbread was placed on this table (see Ex 25:23–30; 1 Chr 9:32; 2 Chr 13:11; 29:18). Ten such golden tables are mentioned in 1 Chr 28:16 and 2 Chr 4:8,19, five on the right side and five on the left of the temple.
7:49 *candlesticks of pure gold.* Only one candlestick with seven arms had stood in the tabernacle, opposite the table for the shewbread (Ex 25:31–40; 26:35). The ten candlesticks in the temple, five on the right side and five on the left, created a lane of light in the holy place. *flowers . . . of gold.* See Ex 25:33. *lamps.* See Ex 25:37. *tongs.* See 2 Chr 4:21; Isa 6:6.

50 And the bowls, and the snuffers, and the basons, and the spoons, and the [1]censers *of* pure gold; and the hinges *of* gold, *both* for the doors of the inner house, the most holy *place, and* for the doors of the house, *to wit,* of the temple.

51 So was ended all the work that king Solomon made *for* the house of the LORD. And Solomon brought in the [1]*things* [a]which David his father had dedicated; *even* the silver, and the gold, and the vessels, did he put among the treasures of the house of the LORD.

The ark brought to the temple

8 Then [a]Solomon assembled the elders of Israel, and all the heads of the tribes, the [1]chief of the fathers of the children of Israel, unto king Solomon *in* Jerusalem, [b]that *they* might bring up the ark of the covenant of the LORD [c]out of the city of David, which *is* Zion.

2 And all the men of Israel assembled themselves unto king Solomon at the [a]feast in the month Ethanim, which *is* the seventh month.

3 And all the elders of Israel came, [a]and the priests took up the ark.

4 And they brought up the ark of the LORD, [a]and the tabernacle of the congregation, and all the holy vessels that *were* in the tabernacle, even those did the priests and the Levites bring up.

5 And king Solomon, and all the congregation of Israel, that were assembled unto him, *were* with him before the ark, [a]sacrificing sheep and oxen, that could not be told nor numbered for multitude.

6 And the priests [a]brought in the ark of the covenant of the LORD unto [b]his place, into the oracle of the house, to the most holy *place,* even [c]under the wings of the cherubims.

7 For the cherubims spread forth *their* two wings over the place of the ark, and the cherubims covered the ark and the staves thereof above.

8 And they [a]drew out the staves, that the [1]ends of the staves were seen out in the [2]holy *place* before the oracle, and they were not seen without: and there they are unto this day.

7:50 [1] Heb. *ash pans* 7:51 [1] Heb. [*holy*] things of *David* [a] 2 Sam. 8:11
8:1 [1] Heb. *princes* [a] 2 Chr. 5:2 [b] 2 Sam. 6:17 [c] 2 Sam. 5:7; 6:12,16
8:2 [a] Lev. 23:34; 2 Chr. 7:8
8:3 [a] Num. 4:15
8:4 [a] 2 Chr. 1:3
8:5 [a] 2 Sam. 6:13
8:6 [a] 2 Sam. 6:17 [b] Ex. 26:33,34; ch. 6:19 [c] ch. 6:27
8:8 [1] Heb. *heads* [2] Or, *ark:* as 2 Chr. 5:9 [a] Ex. 25:14
8:9 [1] Or, *where* [a] Ex. 25:21; Deut. 10:2 [b] Deut. 10:5; Heb. 9:4 [c] Ex. 40:20 [d] Ex. 34:27,28
8:10 [a] Ex. 40:34
8:12 [a] 2 Chr. 6:1 [b] Ps. 18:11
8:13 [a] 2 Sam. 7:13 [b] Ps. 132:14
8:14 [a] 2 Sam. 6:18
8:15 [a] Luke 1:68 [b] 2 Sam. 7:5,25
8:16 [a] ver. 29 [b] 1 Sam. 16:1; 2 Sam. 7:8; 1 Chr. 28:4
8:17 [a] 2 Sam. 7:2
8:18 [a] 2 Chr. 6:8,9
8:19 [a] 2 Sam. 7:5,12,13
8:20 [a] 1 Chr. 28:5,6
8:21 [a] ver. 9; Deut. 31:26

9 [a]*There was* nothing in the ark [b]save the two tables of stone, which Moses [c]put there at Horeb, [d][1]when the LORD made *a covenant* with the children of Israel, when they came out of the land of Egypt.

10 And it came to pass, when the priests were come out of the holy *place,* that the cloud [a]filled the house of the LORD,

11 So that the priests could not stand to minister because of the cloud: for the glory of the LORD had filled the house of the LORD.

12 ¶ [a]Then spake Solomon, The LORD said that *he* would dwell [b]in the thick darkness.

13 [a]I have surely built thee a house to dwell in, [b]a settled place for thee to abide in for ever.

14 And the king turned his face about, and [a]blessed all the congregation of Israel: (and all the congregation of Israel stood;)

15 And he said, [a]Blessed *be* the LORD God of Israel, which [b]spake with his mouth unto David my father, and hath with his hand fulfilled *it,* saying,

16 Since the day that I brought forth my people Israel out of Egypt, I chose no city out of all the tribes of Israel to build a house, that [a]my name might be therein; but I chose [b]David to be over my people Israel.

17 And [a]it was in the heart of David my father to build a house for the name of the LORD God of Israel.

18 [a]And the LORD said unto David my father, Whereas it was in thine heart to build a house unto my name, thou didst well that it was in thine heart.

19 Nevertheless [a]thou shalt not build the house; but thy son that shall come forth out of thy loins, he shall build the house unto my name.

20 And the LORD hath performed his word that he spake, and I am risen up in the room of David my father, and sit on the throne of Israel, [a]as the LORD promised, and have built a house for the name of the LORD God of Israel.

21 And I have set there a place for the ark, wherein *is* [a]the covenant of the LORD, which he made with our fathers, when he brought them out of the land of Egypt.

7:50 *censers.* See 2 Ki 25:15; 2 Chr 4:22; Jer 52:18–19.

7:51 *things which David his father had dedicated.* Valuable objects of silver and gold, either taken as booty in war or received as tribute from kings seeking David's favor (see 2 Sam 8:9–12; 1 Chr 18:7–11; 2 Chr 5:1). *treasures of the house of the LORD.* See 15:18; 2 Ki 12:18; 1 Chr 9:26; 26:20–26; 28:12.

8:1 *bring up the ark of the covenant.* David had previously brought the ark from the house of Obed-edom to Jerusalem (see 2 Sam 6). *the city of David, which is Zion.* See note on 2Sam 5:7.

‡8:2 *feast.* It is probable that Solomon waited 11 months (see 6:38) to dedicate the temple during the feast of tabernacles, which was observed in the seventh month of the year (Lev 23:34; Deut 16:13–15). *seventh month.* Presumably in the 12th year of Solomon's reign.

‡8:4 *tabernacle of the congregation.* The Mosaic tabernacle, which had been preserved at Gibeon (see notes on 3:4; 1 Sam 7:1; see also 2 Chr 5:4–5).

8:6 *under the wings of the cherubims.* See 6:23–28.

8:8 *the ends . . . were seen.* The staves [carrying poles] were always to remain in the gold rings of the ark (Ex 25:15). *there they are unto this day.* These words must be those of the original author of this description of the dedication of the temple rather than those of the final compiler of the books of Kings (see Introduction: Author, Sources and Date; see also 2 Chr 5:9).

8:9 *two tables of stone.* See Ex 25:16; 40:20. *the LORD made a covenant.* See Ex 24.

8:10 *the cloud filled the house of the LORD.* Just as a visible manifestation of the presence of the Lord had descended on the tabernacle at Sinai, so now the Lord came to take up His abode in the temple (see Ex 40:33–35; Ezek 10:3–5,18–19; 43:4–5).

8:12 *he would dwell in the thick darkness.* See Ex 19:9; 24:15,18; 33:9–10; 34:5; Lev 16:2; Deut 4:11; 5:22; Ps 18:10–11.

8:15 *fulfilled it.* See 2 Sam 7:5–16.

8:16 *my name.* Equivalent to the Lord Himself (see note on 5:5).

Solomon's prayer of dedication

22 ¶ And Solomon stood before [a]the altar
of the LORD in the presence of all the congregation of Israel, and [b]spread forth his hands
toward heaven:
23 And he said,
¶ LORD God of Israel, [a]*there is* no God like
thee, in heaven above, or on earth beneath,
[b]who keepest covenant and mercy with thy
servants that [c]walk before thee with all their
heart:
24 Who hast kept with thy servant David
my father that thou promisedst him: thou
spakest also with thy mouth, and hast fulfilled
it with thine hand, as *it is* this day.
25 Therefore now, LORD God of Israel, keep
with thy servant David my father that thou
promisedst him, saying, [a][1]There shall not fail
thee a man in my sight to sit on the throne of
Israel; [2]so that thy children take heed to their
way, that they walk before me as thou hast
walked before me.
26 [a]And now, O God of Israel, let thy
word, I pray thee, be verified, which thou
spakest unto thy servant David my father.
27 ¶ But [a]will God indeed dwell on the
earth? behold, the heaven and [b]heaven of
heavens cannot contain thee; how much less
this house that I have builded?
28 Yet have thou respect unto the prayer of
thy servant, and to his supplication, O LORD my
God, to hearken unto the cry and to the prayer,
which thy servant prayeth before thee to day:
29 That thine eyes may be open toward
this house night and day, *even* toward the
place of which thou hast said, [a]My name shall
be there: that *thou* mayest hearken unto the
prayer which thy servant shall make [b][1]to-
wards this place.
30 [a]And hearken thou to the supplication
of thy servant, and of thy people Israel, when
they shall pray [1]towards this place: and hear
thou in heaven thy dwelling place: and when
thou hearest, forgive.
31 ¶ If any man trespass against his neighbour, [a][1]and [b]an oath be laid upon him to
cause him to swear, and the oath come before
thine altar in this house:
32 Then hear thou *in* heaven, and do, and
judge thy servants, [a]condemning the wicked,
to bring his way upon his head; and justifying
the righteous, to give him according to his
righteousness.
33 ¶ [a]When thy people Israel be smitten
down before the enemy, because they have
sinned against thee, and [b]shall turn again to
thee, and confess thy name, and pray, and
make supplication unto thee [1]in this house:
34 Then hear thou *in* heaven, and forgive
the sin of thy people Israel, and bring them
again unto the land which thou gavest unto
their fathers.
35 ¶ [a]When heaven is shut up, and there is
no rain, because they have sinned against
thee; if they pray towards this place, and confess thy name, and turn from their sin, when
thou afflictest them:
36 Then hear thou *in* heaven, and forgive
the sin of thy servants, and of thy people Israel, that thou [a]teach them [b]the good way
wherein they should walk, and give rain upon
thy land, which thou hast given to thy people
for an inheritance.
37 ¶ [a]If there be in the land famine, if there
be pestilence, blasting, mildew, locust, *or* if
there be caterpillar; if their enemy besiege
them in the land of their [1]cities; whatsoever
plague, whatsoever sickness *there be;*

8:22 [a]2 Chr. 6:12 [b]Ex. 9:33; Ezra 9:5
8:23 [a]Ex. 15:11; 2 Sam. 7:22 [b]Deut. 7:9; Neh. 1:5; Dan. 9:4 [c]Gen. 17:1; ch. 3:6; 2 Ki. 20:3
8:25 [1]Heb. *There shall not be cut off unto thee a man from my sight* [2]Heb. *only if* [a]2 Sam. 7:12,16; ch. 2:4
8:26 [a]2 Sam. 7:25
8:27 [a]2 Chr. 2:6; Is. 66:1; Jer. 23:24; Acts 7:49; 17:24 [b]2 Cor. 12:2
8:29 [1]Or, *in this place* [a]Deut. 12:11 [b]Dan. 6:10
8:30 [1]Or, *in this place* [a]Neh. 1:6
8:31 [1]Heb. *and he require an oath of him* [a]Lev. 5:1 [b]Ex. 22:11
8:32 [a]Deut. 25:1
8:33 [1]Or, *towards* [a]Lev. 26:17; Deut. 28:25 [b]Lev. 26:39
8:35 [a]Lev. 26:19; Deut. 28:23
8:36 [a]Ps. 25:4; 27:11; 94:12 [b]1 Sam. 12:23
8:37 [1]Or, *jurisdiction* [a]Lev. 26:16,25,26

8:23 *no God like thee.* No other god has acted in history as has the God of Israel, performing great miracles and directing the course of events so that His long-range covenant promises are fulfilled (see Ex 15:11; Deut 4:39; 7:9; Ps 86:8–10).
8:24 *that thou promisedst.* See v. 15; 2 Sam 7:5–16.
8:25 *so that thy children . . . walk before me.* See 9:4–9; 2 Chr 7:17–22; see also note on 1 Ki 2:4.
8:27 *how much less this house that I have builded?* With the construction of the temple and the appearance of a visible manifestation of the presence of God within its courts, the erroneous notion that God was irreversibly and exclusively bound to the temple in a way that guaranteed His assistance to Israel no matter how the people lived could very easily arise (see Jer 7:4–14; Mic 3:11). Solomon confessed that even though God had chosen to dwell among His people in a special and localized way, He far transcended containment by anything in all creation.
8:29 *My name.* I the Lord (see note on 5:5).
8:30 *pray towards this place.* When an Israelite was unable to pray in the temple itself, he was to direct his prayers toward the place where God had pledged to be present among His people (see Dan 6:10). *heaven thy dwelling place.* See note on v. 27.
8:31 *an oath be laid upon him to cause him to swear.* In cases such as default in pledges (Ex 22:10–12) or alleged adultery (Num 5:11–31), when there was insufficient evidence to establish the legitimacy of the charge, the supposed offender was required to take an oath of innocence at the sanctuary. Such an oath, with its attendant blessings and curses, was considered a divinely given means of determining innocence or guilt since the consequences of the oath became apparent in the life of the individual either by his experiencing the blessing or the curse or by direct divine revelation through the Urim and Thummim (see Ex 28:29–30; Lev 8:8; Num 27:21).
8:32 *hear thou in heaven.* It is clear that Solomon viewed the oath as an appeal to God to act and not as an automatic power that worked in a magical way.
8:33 *smitten down before the enemy, because they have sinned against thee.* Defeat by enemies was listed in Deut 28:25 as one of the curses that would come on Israel if she disobeyed the covenant. Solomon's prayer reflects an awareness of the covenant obligations the Lord had placed on His people and a knowledge of the consequences that disobedience would entail.
8:34 *bring them again unto the land.* A reference to prisoners taken in battle.
8:35 *no rain.* Drought was another of the covenant curses listed in Deut 28:22–24.
8:36 *good way . . . they should walk.* In accordance with covenant obligations (see Deut 6:18; 12:25; 13:18; 1 Sam 12:23).
8:37 *famine.* See Deut 32:24. *pestilence.* See Deut 28:21–22; 32:24. *locust, or . . . caterpillar.* See Deut 28:38,42. *their enemy besiege them in the land of their cities.* See Deut 28:52. *plague.* See Deut 28:61; 31:29; 32:23–25. *sickness.* See Deut 28:22.

38 What prayer and supplication soever be *made* by any man, *or* by all thy people Israel, which shall know every man the plague of his own heart, and spread forth his hands towards this house:

39 Then hear thou *in* heaven thy dwelling place, and forgive, and do, and give to every man according to his ways, whose heart thou knowest; (for thou, *even* thou only, [a]knowest the hearts of all the children of men;)

40 [a]That they may fear thee all the days that they live in the land which thou gavest unto our fathers.

41 ¶ Moreover concerning a stranger, that *is* not of thy people Israel, but cometh out of a far country for thy name's sake;

42 (For they shall hear of thy great name, and of thy [a]strong hand, and of thy stretched out arm;) when he shall come and pray towards this house;

43 Hear thou *in* heaven thy dwelling place, and do according to all that the stranger calleth to thee for: [a]that all people of the earth may know thy name, to [b]fear thee, as *do* thy people Israel; and that *they* may know that [1]this house, which I have builded, is called by thy name.

44 ¶ If thy people go out to battle against their enemy, whithersoever thou shalt send them, and shall pray unto the LORD [1]toward the city which thou hast chosen, and *toward* the house that I have built for thy name:

45 Then hear thou *in* heaven their prayer and their supplication, and maintain their [1]cause.

46 If they sin against thee, ([a]for *there is* no man that sinneth not,) and thou be angry with them, and deliver them to the enemy, so that they carry them away captives [b]unto the land of the enemy, far or near;

47 [a]*Yet* if they shall [1]bethink themselves in the land whither they were carried captives, and repent, and make supplication unto thee in the land of them *that* carried them captives, [b]saying, We have sinned, and have done perversely, we have committed wickedness;

48 And *so* [a]return unto thee with all their heart, and with all their soul, in the land of their enemies, which led them away captive, and [b]pray unto thee toward their land, which thou gavest unto their fathers, the city which thou hast chosen, and the house which I have built for thy name:

49 Then hear thou their prayer and their supplication *in* heaven thy dwelling place, and maintain their [1]cause,

50 And forgive thy people that have sinned against thee, and all their transgressions wherein they have transgressed against thee, and [a]give them compassion before them who carried them captive, that they may have compassion on them:

51 For [a]they *be* thy people, and thine inheritance, which thou broughtest forth out of Egypt, [b]from the midst of the furnace of iron:

52 That thine eyes may be open unto the supplication of thy servant, and unto the supplication of thy people Israel, to hearken unto them in all that they call for unto thee.

53 For thou didst separate them from among all the people of the earth, to be thine inheritance, [a]as thou spakest by the hand of Moses thy servant, when thou broughtest our fathers out of Egypt, O Lord GOD.

54 ¶ And it was *so, that* when Solomon had made an end of praying all this prayer and supplication unto the LORD, he arose from before the altar of the LORD, from kneeling on his knees with his hands spread *up to* heaven.

55 And he stood, [a]and blessed all the congregation of Israel *with* a loud voice, saying,

56 Blessed *be* the LORD, that hath given rest unto his people Israel, according to all that he promised: [a]there hath not [1]failed one word of all his good promise, which he promised by the hand of Moses his servant.

8:39 [a]1 Sam. 16:7; 1 Chr. 28:9; Ps. 11:4; Jer. 17:10; Acts 1:24
8:40 [a]Ps. 130:4
8:42 [a]Deut. 3:24
8:43 [1]Heb. *thy name is called upon this house* [a]1 Sam. 17:46; 2 Ki. 19:19 [b]Ps. 102:15
8:44 [1]Heb. *the way of the city*
8:45 [1]Or, *right*
8:46 [a]2 Chr. 6:36; Eccl. 7:20; Jas. 3:2; 1 John 1:8,10 [b]Lev. 26:34,44; Deut. 28:36,64
8:47 [1]Heb. *bring back to their heart* [a]Lev. 26:40
8:47 [b]Neh. 1:6; Ps. 106:6; Dan. 9:5
8:48 [a]Jer. 29:12-14 [b]Dan. 6:10
8:49 [1]Or, *right*
8:50 [a]Ezra 7:6; Ps. 106:46
8:51 [a]Deut. 9:29; Neh. 1:10 [b]Deut. 4:20; Jer. 11:4
8:53 [a]Ex. 19:5; Deut. 9:26,29
8:55 [a]2 Sam. 6:18
8:56 [1]Heb. *fallen* [a]Deut. 12:10; Josh. 21:45; 23:14

8:38 *know every man the plague of his own heart.* Conscious of one's guilt before God, with an attitude of repentance and the desire for God's forgiveness and grace (see 2 Chr 6:29; Ps 38:17–18; Jer 17:9).

8:39 *give to every man according to his ways.* Not to be viewed as a request for retribution for the wrong committed (forgiveness and retribution are mutually exclusive), but as a desire for whatever discipline God in His wisdom may use to correct His people and to instruct them in the way of the covenant (see v. 40; Prov 3:11; Heb 12:5–15).

8:40 *fear thee.* Honor and obediently serve You (see Deut 5:29; 6:1–2; 8:6; 31:13; 2 Chr 6:31; Ps 130:4).

8:41 *stranger, that is not of thy people Israel.* One who comes from a foreign land to pray to Israel's God at the temple, as distinguished from a resident alien.

8:42 *they shall hear.* See 9:9 (foreign nations generally); 10:1 (queen of Sheba); Josh 2:9–11 (Rahab); 1 Sam 4:6–8 (Philistines). *thy great name, and of thy strong hand, and of thy stretched out arm.* God's great power, demonstrated by His interventions in the history of His people (see Deut 4:34; 5:15; 7:19; 11:2; 26:8).

8:44 *go out to battle . . . whithersoever thou shalt send them.* Military initiatives undertaken with divine sanction (see, e.g., Lev 26:7; Deut 20; 21:10; 1 Sam 15:3; 23:2,4; 30:8; 2 Sam 5:19,24). *toward the city which thou hast chosen.* See note on v. 30.

8:46 *the enemy, so that they carry them away captives.* On the basis of Lev 26:33–45; Deut 28:64–68; 30:1–5, Solomon knew that stubborn disobedience would lead to exile from the promised land.

8:51 *furnace of iron.* See Deut 4:20 and note.

8:53 *thou didst separate them . . . to be thine inheritance.* Solomon began his prayer with an appeal to the Davidic covenant (vv. 23–30), and he closes with an appeal to the Sinaitic covenant (see Ex 19:5; Lev 20:24,26; Deut 7:6; 32:9).

8:54 *kneeling on his knees.* Cf. v. 22; 2 Sam 7:18; 2 Chr 6:13; Luke 22:41; Eph 3:14.

8:56 *Blessed be the LORD.* Solomon understood this historic day to be a testimony to God's covenant faithfulness. *rest unto his people.* After the conquest of Canaan under the leadership of Joshua, the Lord gave the Israelites a period of rest from their enemies (Josh 11:23; 21:44; 22:4), even though there remained much land to be possessed (Josh 13:1; Judg 1). It was only with David's victories that the rest was made durable and complete (see 2 Sam 7:1; see also note on 1 Ki 5:4).

57 The LORD our God be with us, as he was with our fathers: [a]let him not leave us, nor forsake us:

58 That *he* may [a]incline our hearts unto him, to walk in all his ways, and to keep his commandments, and his statutes, and his judgments, which he commanded our fathers.

59 And let these my words, wherewith I have made supplication before the LORD, be nigh unto the LORD our God day and night, that *he* maintain the cause of his servant, and the cause of his people Israel [1]at all times, as the matter shall require:

60 [a]That all the people of the earth may know that [b]the LORD *is* God, *and that there is* none else.

61 Let your [a]heart therefore be perfect with the LORD our God, to walk in his statutes, and to keep his commandments, as at this day.

The offering and feast

62 ¶ And [a]the king, and all Israel with him, offered sacrifice before the LORD.

63 And Solomon offered a sacrifice of peace offerings, which he offered unto the LORD, two and twenty thousand oxen, and an hundred and twenty thousand sheep. So the king and all the children of Israel dedicated the house of the LORD.

64 [a]The same day did the king hallow the middle of the court that *was* before the house of the LORD: for there he offered burnt offerings, and meat offerings, and the fat of the peace offerings: because [b]the brasen altar that *was* before the LORD *was* too little to receive the burnt offerings, and meat offerings, and the fat of the peace offerings.

65 And at that time Solomon held [a]a feast, and all Israel with him, a great congregation, from [b]the entering in of Hamath unto [c]the river of Egypt, before the LORD our God, [d]seven days and seven days, *even* fourteen days.

66 [a]On the eighth day he sent the people away: and they [1]blessed the king, and went unto their tents joyful and glad of heart for all the goodness that the LORD had done for David his servant, and for Israel his people.

The covenant with Solomon

9 And [a]it came to pass, when Solomon had finished the building of the house of the LORD, [b]and the king's house, and [c]all Solomon's desire which he was pleased to do,

2 That the LORD appeared to Solomon the second time, [a]as he had appeared unto him at Gibeon.

3 And the LORD said unto him, [a]I have heard thy prayer and thy supplication, that thou hast made before me: I have hallowed this house, which thou hast built, [b]to put my name there for ever; [c]and mine eyes and mine heart shall be there perpetually.

4 And if thou wilt [a]walk before me, [b]as David thy father walked, in integrity of heart, and in uprightness, to do according to all that I have commanded thee, *and* wilt keep my statutes and my judgments:

5 Then I will establish the throne of thy kingdom upon Israel for ever, [a]as I promised to David thy father, saying, There shall not fail thee a man upon the throne of Israel.

6 [a]*But* if you shall at all turn from following me, you or your children, and will not keep my commandments *and* my statutes which I have set before you, but go and serve other gods, and worship them:

7 [a]Then will I cut off Israel out of the land which I have given them; and *this* house, which I have hallowed [b]for my name, will I cast out of my sight; [c]and Israel shall be a proverb and a byword among all people:

8 And [a]*at* this house, *which* is high, every one that passeth by it shall be astonished, and shall hiss; and they shall say, [b]Why hath the LORD done thus unto this land, and to this house?

9 And they shall answer, Because they forsook the LORD their God, who brought forth

8:57 [a]Deut. 31:6; Josh. 1:5
8:58 [a]Ps. 119:36
8:59 [1]Heb. *the thing of a day in his day*
8:60 [a]Josh. 4:24; 1 Sam. 17:46 [b]Deut. 4:35,39
8:61 [a]ch. 11:4; 15:3,14; 2 Ki. 20:3
8:62 [a]2 Chr. 7:4
8:64 [a]2 Chr. 7:7 [b]2 Chr. 4:1
8:65 [a]ver. 2; Lev. 23:34 [b]Num. 34:8; Josh. 13:5; Judg. 3:3; 2 Ki. 14:25 [c]Gen. 15:18; Num. 34:5 [d]2 Chr. 7:8
8:66 [1]Or, *thanked* [a]2 Chr. 7:9
9:1 [a]2 Chr. 7:11 [b]ch. 7:1 [c]2 Chr. 8:6
9:2 [a]ch. 3:5
9:3 [a]2 Ki. 20:5; Ps. 10:17 [b]ch. 8:29 [c]Deut. 11:12
9:4 [a]Gen. 17:1 [b]ch. 15:5
9:5 [a]2 Sam. 7:12,16; ch. 2:4; 1 Chr. 22:10
9:6 [a]2 Sam. 7:14; 2 Chr. 7:19,20
9:7 [a]2 Ki. 17:23; 25:21 [b]Jer. 7:14 [c]Deut. 28:37
9:8 [a]2 Chr. 7:21 [b]Deut. 29:24-26; Jer. 22:8,9

8:58 *incline our hearts unto him.* Solomon asks for a divine work of grace within his people that will enable them to be faithful to the covenant (see Deut 30:6; Ps 51:10; Phil 2:13).
8:59 *his servant.* The king, who, as the Lord's anointed, serves as the earthly representative of God's rule over His people (see notes on Ps 2:2,7).
8:60 *That all . . . may know.* See note on Ps 46:10.
8:63 *peace offerings.* Involved a communion meal (see note on 1 Sam 11:15). *two and twenty thousand oxen, and an hundred and twenty thousand sheep.* Although these numbers may seem large, there were vast numbers of people who participated in the dedication ceremony, which lasted 14 days (see vv. 1–2; see also v. 65).
8:65 *entering in of Hamath.* See note on Ezek 47:15. *river of Egypt.* Probably Wadi el-Arish (see note on Gen 15:18). People came to Jerusalem for the dedication of the temple from nearly the entire area of Solomon's dominion (see note on 4:21). *seven days and seven days, even fourteen days.* It appears that the seven-day celebration for the dedication of the temple was followed by the seven-day feast of tabernacles (see note on v. 2), which was observed from the 15th to the 21st of the seventh month. According to Chronicles, this was followed by a final assembly on the next day, in accordance with Lev 23:33–36; then on the 23rd of the month the people were sent to their homes (see 2 Chr 7:8–10).
9:1 *when Solomon had finished.* At the earliest this would be in the 24th year (4 + 7 + 13 = 24) of Solomon's reign—946 B.C. (see 6:1,37–38; 7:1; 9:10).
9:2 *he had appeared unto him at Gibeon.* See 3:4–15.
9:3 *to put my name there for ever.* See 8:10–13. *mine eyes and mine heart shall be there perpetually.* See 8:29.
9:4–5 *if thou wilt walk before me . . . in integrity of heart . . . I will establish the throne of thy kingdom upon Israel for ever.* See 8:25 and note on 2:4. The Lord reemphasizes to Solomon the importance of obedience to the covenant in order to experience its blessings rather than its curses. This was particularly necessary as Solomon's kingdom grew in influence and wealth, with all the potential for covenant-breaking that prosperity brought (see Deut 8:12–14,17; 31:20; 32:15).
9:6 *serve other gods, and worship them.* See 11:4–8.
9:7 *a proverb and a byword among all people.* See the covenant curse in Deut 28:37.

their fathers out of the land of Egypt, and have taken hold upon other gods, and have worshipped them, and served them: therefore hath the LORD brought upon them all this evil.

Solomon's accomplishments

10 ¶ And [a]it came to pass at the end of twenty years, when Solomon had built the two houses, the house of the LORD, and the king's house,

11 ([a]*Now* Hiram the king of Tyre had furnished Solomon with cedar trees and fir trees, and with gold, according to all his desire,) *that* then king Solomon gave Hiram twenty cities in the land of Galilee.

12 And Hiram came out from Tyre to see the cities which Solomon had given him; and they [1]pleased him not.

13 And he said, What cities *are* these which thou hast given me, my brother? [a]And he called them the land of [1]Cabul unto this day.

14 And Hiram sent to the king sixscore talents of gold.

15 ¶ And this *is* the reason of [a]the levy which king Solomon raised; for to build the house of the LORD, and his own house, and [b]Millo, and the wall of Jerusalem, and [c]Hazor, and [d]Megiddo, and [e]Gezer.

16 *For* Pharaoh king of Egypt had gone up, and taken Gezer, and burnt it with fire, [a]and slain the Canaanites that dwelt in the city, and given it *for* a present unto his daughter, Solomon's wife.

17 And Solomon built Gezer, and [a]Beth-horon the nether,

18 And [a]Baalath, and Tadmor in the wilderness, in the land,

19 And all the cities of store that Solomon had, and cities for [a]his chariots, and cities for his horsemen, and [1]that which Solomon [b]desired to build in Jerusalem, and in Lebanon, and in all the land of his dominion.

20 [a]*And* all the people that were left of the Amorites, Hittites, Perizzites, Hivites, and Jebusites, which *were* not of the children of Israel,

21 Their children [a]that were left after them in the land, [b]whom the children of Israel also were not able utterly to destroy, [c]upon those did Solomon levy a tribute of [d]bondservice unto this day.

22 But of the children of Israel did Solomon [a]make no bondman: but they *were* men of war, and his servants, and his princes, and his captains, and rulers of his chariots, and his horsemen.

23 These *were* the chief of the officers that *were* over Solomon's work, [a]five hundred and fifty, which bare rule over the people that wrought in the work.

24 But [a]Pharaoh's daughter came up out of the city of David unto [b]her house which *Solomon* had built for her: [c]then did he build Millo.

25 [a]And three times in a year did Solomon offer burnt offerings and peace offerings upon the altar which he built unto the LORD, and he burnt incense [1]upon the altar that *was* before the LORD. So he finished the house.

26 ¶ And [a]king Solomon made a navy *of ships* in [b]Ezion-geber, which *is* beside Eloth, on the [1]shore of the Red sea, in the land of Edom.

27 [a]And Hiram sent in the navy his servants, shipmen that had knowledge of the sea, with the servants of Solomon.

9:10 [a]ch. 6:37,38; 7:1; 2 Chr. 8:1
9:11 [a]2 Chr. 8:2
9:12 [1]Heb. *were not right in his eyes*
9:13 [1]That is, *displeasing,* or, *dirty* [a]Josh. 19:27
9:15 [a]ch. 5:13 [b]ver. 24; 2 Sam. 5:9 [c]Josh. 19:36 [d]Josh. 17:11 [e]Josh. 16:10
9:16 [a]Josh. 16:10
9:17 [a]Josh. 16:3; 2 Chr. 8:5
9:18 [a]Josh. 19:44; 2 Chr. 8:4,6
9:19 [1]Heb. *the desire of Solomon, which he desired* [a]ch. 4:26 [b]ver. 1
9:20 [a]2 Chr. 8:7
9:21 [a]Judg. 3:1 [b]Josh. 15:63; 17:12 [c]Judg. 1:28 [d]Ezra 2:55,58; Neh. 7:57
9:22 [a]Lev. 25:39
9:23 [a]See 2 Chr. 8:10
9:24 [a]ch. 3:1; 2 Chr. 8:11 [b]ch. 7:8 [c]2 Sam. 5:9; ch. 11:27; 2 Chr. 32:5
9:25 [1]Heb. *upon it* [a]2 Chr. 8:12,13,16
9:26 [1]Heb. *lip* [a]2 Chr. 8:17,18 [b]Num. 33:35; Deut. 2:8; ch. 22:48
9:27 [a]ch. 10:11

9:9 *therefore hath the LORD brought upon them all this evil.* See Deut 29:22–28; Jer 22:8–30.

9:10–28 See map No. 5 at the end of the study Bible.

9:11 *Solomon gave Hiram twenty cities in the land of Galilee.* Comparison of vv. 10–14 with 5:1–12 suggests that during Solomon's 20 years of building activity he became more indebted to Hiram than anticipated in their original agreement (see note on 5:9), which had provided for payment for labor (5:6) and wood (5:10–11). From vv. 11,14 it is evident that in addition to wood and labor Solomon had also acquired great quantities of gold from Hiram. It appears that Solomon gave Hiram the 20 towns in the Phoenician-Galilee border area as a surety for repayment of the gold. 2 Chr 8:1–2 indicates that at some later date when Solomon's gold reserves were increased, perhaps after the return of the expedition to Ophir (1 Ki 9:26–28; 10:11) or the visit of the queen of Sheba (10:1–13), he settled his debt with Hiram and recovered the 20 towns held as collateral.

‡9:15 *levy* [i.e. forced labor]. Non-Israelite slave labor of a permanent nature (in contrast to the temporary conscription of Israelite workmen described in 5:13–16). *Millo.* Probably for Solomon's expansion of Jerusalem on the ridge north from David's city (see note on 2 Sam 5:9). *Hazor.* Solomon's building activity at Hazor, Megiddo and Gezer was intended to strengthen the fortifications of these ancient, strategically located towns (Solomonic gates, probably built by the same masons, have been found at all three sites). Hazor was the most important fortress in the northern Galilee area, controlling the trade route running from the Euphrates River to Egypt. *Megiddo.* Another fortress along the great north-south trade route; it commanded the pass through the Carmel range from the plain of Jezreel to the coastal plain of Sharon. *Gezer.* See note on 3:1.

9:16 *slain the Canaanites . . . in the city.* Although Joshua had killed the king of Gezer at the time of the conquest (Josh 10:33; 12:12), the tribe of Ephraim had been unable to drive out its inhabitants (Josh 16:10; Judg 1:29).

‡9:17 *Beth-horon the nether* [i.e. lower Beth-horon]. Located about eight miles northwest of Jerusalem at a pass giving entrance to the Judahite highlands and Jerusalem from the coastal plain.

‡9:18 *Baalath.* To be identified with either the Bealoth of Josh 15:24 located to the south of Hebron in the tribe of Judah or the Baalath southwest of Beth-horon in the tribe of Dan (Josh 19:44). *Tadmor.* Hebrew *Tamor,* but see 2 Chr 8:4.

9:20 *Amorites . . . Jebusites.* See Deut 7:1; 20:17; see also notes on Gen 10:15–18; 13:7; 15:16; 23:9; Josh 5:1; Judg 3:3; 6:10; 2 Sam 21:2.

9:22 *of the children of Israel did Solomon make no bondman.* See note on v. 15.

9:23 *five hundred and fifty, which bare rule.* See note on 5:16.

9:25 *three times in a year.* On the occasion of the three important annual festivals: the feast of unleavened bread, the feast of weeks, and the feast of tabernacles (see Ex 23:14–17; 2 Chr 8:13).

9:26 *ships.* Used in a large trading business that brought great wealth to Solomon's court (see v. 28; 10:11). *Ezion-geber.* Located at the northern tip of the Gulf of Aqaba (see 22:48; Num

28 And they came to [a]Ophir, and fet from
thence gold, four hundred and twenty talents,
and brought *it* to king Solomon.

The visit of the queen of Sheba

10 And when the [a]queen of Sheba
heard of the fame of Solomon concerning the name of the LORD, she came [b]to
prove him with hard questions.
2 And she came to Jerusalem with a very
great train, *with* camels that bare spices, and
very much gold, and precious stones: and
when she was come to Solomon, she communed with him of all that was in her heart.
3 And Solomon told her all her [1]questions:
there was not *any* thing hid from the king,
which he told her not.
4 And when the queen of Sheba had seen
all Solomon's wisdom, and the house that he
had built,
5 And the meat of his table, and the sitting
of his servants, and the [1]attendance of his
ministers, and their apparel, and his [2]cupbear-
ers, [a]and his ascent *by* which he went up *unto*
the house of the LORD; there was no more spirit in her.
6 And she said to the king, It was a true
[1]report that I heard in mine own land of thy
[2]acts and of thy wisdom.
7 Howbeit I believed not the words, until I
came, and mine eyes had seen *it:* and behold,
the half was not told me: [1]thy wisdom and
prosperity exceedeth the fame which I heard.
8 [a]Happy *are* thy men, happy *are* these thy
servants, which stand continually before thee,
and that hear thy wisdom.

9:28 [a]Job 22:24
10:1 [a]2 Chr. 9:1; Mat. 12:42; Luke 11:31 [b]See Judg. 14:12; Prov. 1:6
10:3 [1]Heb. *words*
10:5 [1]Heb. *standing* [2]Or, *butlers* [a]1 Chr. 26:16
10:6 [1]Heb. *word* [2]Or, *sayings*
10:7 [1]Heb. *thou hast added wisdom and goodness to the fame*
10:8 [a]Prov. 8:34
10:9 [a]ch. 5:7 [b]2 Sam. 8:15; Ps. 72:2; Prov. 8:15
10:10 [a]Ps. 72:10,15
10:11 [1][2 Chr. 2:8; 9:10,11, *algum trees*] [a]ch. 9:27
10:12 [1]Or, *rails.* Heb. *a prop* [a]2 Chr. 9:11 [b]2 Chr. 9:10
10:13 [1]Heb. *according to the hand of king Solomon*
10:15 [1]Or, *captains* [a]2 Chr. 9:24; Ps. 72:10

9 [a]Blessed be the LORD thy God, which delighted in thee, to set thee on the throne of Israel: because the LORD loved Israel for ever,
therefore made he thee king, [b]to do judgment
and justice.
10 And she [a]gave the king an hundred and
twenty talents of gold, and of spices very great
store, and precious stones: there came no
more such abundance of spices as these which
the queen of Sheba gave to king Solomon.
11 [a]And the navy also of Hiram, that
brought gold from Ophir, brought in from
Ophir great plenty of [1]almug trees, and precious stones.
12 [a]And the king made *of* the almug trees
[1]pillars for the house of the LORD, and for the
king's house, harps also and psalteries for
singers: there came no such [b]almug trees, nor
were seen unto this day.
13 And king Solomon gave unto the queen
of Sheba all her desire, what*soever* she asked,
besides *that* which Solomon gave her [1]of his
royal bounty. So she turned and went to her
own country, she and her servants.

The splendor of Solomon

14 ¶ Now the weight of gold that came to
Solomon in one year was six hundred threescore and six talents of gold,
15 Besides *that he had* of the merchantmen, and *of* the traffick of the *spice* merchants, and [a]*of* all the kings of Arabia, and *of*
the [1]governors of the country.
16 And king Solomon made two hundred
targets *of* beaten gold: six hundred *shekels* of
gold went to one target.

33:35; Deut 2:8). *Red sea.* The Hebrew for this term, normally read as *Yam Suph* ("sea of reeds"), refers to the body of water through which the Israelites passed at the time of the exodus (see notes on Ex 13:18; 14:2). It can also be read, however, as *Yam Soph* ("sea of [land's] end"), a more likely reading when referring to the Red sea, and especially (as here) to its eastern arm (the Gulf of Aqaba).

9:28 *Ophir.* A source for gold (2 Chr 8:18; Job 28:16; Ps 45:9; Is 13:12), almug trees and precious stones (10:11), and silver, ivory, apes and baboons (10:22). Its location is disputed: Southeastern Arabia, southwestern Arabia, the northeastern African coast (in the area of Somalia), India and Zimbabwe have all been suggested. If Ophir was located in Arabia, it was probably a trading center for goods from farther east as well as from east Africa. But the three-year voyages of Solomon's merchant vessels (10:22) suggest a more distant location than the Arabian coast.

10:1 *Sheba.* Archaeological evidence suggests that Sheba is to be identified with a mercantile kingdom that flourished in southwest Arabia (see notes on Gen 10:28; Joel 3:8) c. 900–450 B.C. It profited from the sea trade of India and east Africa by transporting luxury commodities north to Damascus and Gaza on caravan routes through the Arabian Desert. It is possible that Solomon's fleet of ships threatened Sheba's continued dominance of this trading business. *concerning the name of the LORD.* The queen of Sheba recognized a connection between the wisdom of Solomon and the God he served. Jesus used her example to condemn the people of His own day who had not recognized that "a greater than Solomon" was in their midst (Mat 12:42; Luke 11:31).

10:9 *Blessed be the LORD thy God.* The queen of Sheba's confession is beautifully worded and reflects a profound understanding of Israel's covenant relationship with the Lord. However, it does not necessarily imply anything more than her recognition of the Lord as Israel's national God in conformity with the ideas of polytheistic paganism (see note on 5:7; see also 2 Chr 2:12; Dan 3:28–29). There is no confession that Solomon's God has become her God to the exclusion of all others.

10:10 *an hundred and twenty talents of gold.* See notes on 9:11,28.

10:11 *navy also of Hiram.* See 9:26–28. Hiram had supplied the wood, the sailors and the expertise in construction that Israel lacked. *almug trees.* Perhaps a variant of "algum trees" (2 Chr 9:10–11). Its identity is unknown, though some suggest it is juniper. It was apparently available from Lebanon as well as Ophir (2 Chr 2:8).

10:13 *all her desire, whatsoever she asked.* The exchange of gifts between Solomon and the queen may have signified the effecting of a trade agreement (see note on v. 1). There is no basis for the idea sometimes suggested that she desired offspring fathered by Solomon and left Jerusalem carrying his child.

10:15 *that he had of . . . the kings of Arabia.* Tribute from Bedouin sheiks for passage of their caravans into Israelite territory. *governors of the country.* See 4:7–19.

‡10:16 *targets* [i.e."large shields"]. Rectangular shields that afforded maximum protection (in distinction from the smaller round shields). These gold shields were probably not intended for battle but for ceremonial use, symbolizing Israel's wealth

17 And *he made* [a]three hundred shields *of* beaten gold; three pound *of* gold went to one shield: and the king put them *in* the [b]house of the forest of Lebanon.

18 [a]Moreover the king made a great throne of ivory, and overlaid it with the best gold.

19 The throne had six steps, and the top of the throne *was* round [1]behind: and *there were* [2]stays on either side on the place of the seat, and two lions stood beside the stays.

20 And twelve lions stood there on the one side and on the other upon the six steps: there was not [1]the like made in any kingdom.

21 [a]And all king Solomon's drinking vessels *were of* gold, and all the vessels of the house of the forest of Lebanon *were of* pure gold: [1]none *were of* silver: it was nothing accounted of in the days of Solomon.

22 For the king had at sea a navy of [a]Tharshish with the navy of Hiram: once in three years came the navy of Tharshish, bringing gold, and silver, [1]ivory, and apes, and peacocks.

23 So [a]king Solomon exceeded all the kings of the earth for riches and for wisdom.

24 And all the earth [1]sought to Solomon, to hear his wisdom, which God had put in his heart.

25 And they brought every man his present, vessels of silver, and vessels of gold, and garments, and armour, and spices, horses, and mules, a rate year by year.

26 [a]And Solomon [b]gathered together chariots and horsemen: and he had a thousand and four hundred chariots, and twelve thousand horsemen, whom he bestowed in the cities for chariots, and with the king at Jerusalem.

27 [a]And the king [1]made silver *to be* in Jerusalem as stones, and cedars made he *to be* as the sycomore trees that *are* in the vale, for abundance.

28 [a][1]And Solomon had horses brought out of Egypt, and linen yarn: the king's merchants received the linen yarn at a price.

29 And a chariot came up and went out of Egypt for six hundred *shekels* of silver, and a horse for an hundred and fifty: [a]and so for all the kings of the Hittites, and for the kings of Syria, did they bring *them* out [1]by their means.

Solomon takes foreign wives

11 But [a]king Solomon loved [b]many strange women, [1]together with the daughter of Pharaoh, *women of the* Moabites, Ammonites, Edomites, Zidonians, *and* Hittites;

2 Of the nations *concerning* which the LORD said unto the children of Israel, [a]Ye shall not go in to them, neither shall they come in unto you: *for* surely they will turn away your heart after their gods: Solomon clave unto these in love.

3 And he had seven hundred wives, princesses, and three hundred concubines: and his wives turned away his heart.

4 For it came to pass, when Solomon was old, [a]*that* his wives turned away his heart after other gods: and his [b]heart was not perfect with the LORD his God, [c]as *was* the heart of David his father.

5 For Solomon went after [a]Ashtoreth the goddess of the Zidonians, and after [1]Milcom the abomination of the Ammonites.

6 And Solomon did evil in the sight of the LORD, and [1]went not fully after the LORD, as *did* David his father.

7 [a]Then did Solomon build a high place for [b]Chemosh, the abomination of Moab, in [c]the hill that *is* before Jerusalem, and for Molech, the abomination of the children of Ammon.

8 And likewise did he for all his strange

10:17 [a]ch. 14:26 [b]ch. 7:2
10:18 [a]2 Chr. 9:17
10:19 [1]Heb. *on the hinder part thereof* [2]Heb. *hands*
10:20 [1]Heb. *so*
10:21 [1]Or, there was *no silver* in them [a]2 Chr. 9:20
10:22 [1]Or, *elephants' teeth* [a]Gen. 10:4; 2 Chr. 20:36
10:23 [a]ch. 3:12,13; 4:30
10:24 [1]Heb. *sought the face of*
10:26 [a]ch. 4:26; 2 Chr. 1:14; 9:25 [b]Deut. 17:16
10:27 [1]Heb. *gave* [a]2 Chr. 1:15-17
10:28 [1]Heb. *And the going forth of the horses which* was *Solomon's* [a]Deut. 17:16; 2 Chr. 1:16; 9:28
10:29 [1]Heb. *by their hand* [a]Josh. 1:4; 2 Ki. 7:6
11:1 [1]Or, *besides* [a]Neh. 13:26 [b]Deut. 17:17
11:2 [a]Ex. 34:16; Deut. 7:3,4
11:4 [a]Deut. 17:17; Neh. 13:26 [b]ch. 8:61 [c]ch. 9:4
11:5 [1][Called *Molech*, ver. 7] [a]ver. 33; Judg. 2:13; 2 Ki. 23:13
11:6 [1]Heb. *fulfilled not after*
11:7 [a]Num. 33:52 [b]Num. 21:29; Judg. 11:24 [c]2 Ki. 23:13

---

and glory. They were probably made of wood overlaid with gold. Shishak of Egypt carried them off as plunder in the fifth regnal year of Solomon's son Rehoboam (see 14:25–26).

‡10:22 *navy* [i.e. "ships"] *of Tharshish.* See 2 Chr 9:21. The same fleet is referred to in v. 11; 9:26–28. "Ships of Tharshish" are not necessarily ships that sail to Tarshish (see note on Jonah 1:3) but can designate large trading vessels.

10:26 *chariots and horsemen.* See note on 4:26. Accumulation of chariots and horses by the king was forbidden in the Mosaic law (Deut 17:16).

‡10:29 *Hittites.* See note on Gen 10:15. *Syria.* A people who occupied a large area north and east of the Sea of Galilee (cf. note on Aram in Gen 10:22). *did they bring them out.* I.e. they exported them. Through his agents Solomon was the middleman in a lucrative trading business.

‡11:1 *loved many strange* [i.e. "foreign"] *women.* Many of Solomon's marriages were no doubt for the purpose of sealing international relationships with various kingdoms, large and small—a common practice in the ancient Near East. But this violated not only Deut 17:17 with respect to the multiplicity of wives, but also the prohibition against taking wives from the pagan peoples among whom Israel settled (see Ex 34:16; Deut 7:1–3; Josh 23:12–13; Ezra 9:2; 10:2–3; Neh 13:23–27). *Moabites.* See note on Gen 19:36–38. *Ammonites.* See note on Gen 19:36–38; see also 14:21; Deut 23:3. *Edomites.* See notes on Gen 25:26; 36:1; Amos 1:11; 9:12; see also Deut 23:7–8. *Zidonians.* See 16:31.

11:2 *surely they will turn away your heart after their gods.* An example in Israel's earlier history is found in Num 25:1–15.

11:3 *seven hundred . . . three hundred.* Cf. Sol 6:8, but see note there.

11:4 *his heart was not perfect with the LORD his God.* See 8:61. The atmosphere of paganism and idolatry introduced into Solomon's court by his foreign wives gradually led Solomon into syncretistic religious practices.

11:5 *Ashtoreth.* See v. 33; 14:15; 2 Ki 23:13; see also note on Judg 2:13. *Milcom.* See 2 Ki 23:10,13. Molech and Milcom are alternate names for the same pagan deity. Worship of this god not only severely jeopardized the continued recognition of the absolute kingship of the Lord over His people, but also involved (on rare occasions) the abomination of child sacrifice (see 2 Ki 16:3; 17:17; 21:6; Lev 18:21; 20:2–5; see also note on Judg 10:6).

11:6 *as did David his father.* Although David committed grievous sins, he was repentant, and he was never involved in idolatrous worship.

11:7 *high place.* See note on 3:2. *Chemosh.* See note on 2 Ki 3:27.

wives, which burnt incense and sacrificed
unto their gods.
9 ¶ And the LORD was angry with Solomon,
because his heart was turned from the LORD
God of Israel, [a]which had appeared unto him
twice,
10 And [a]had commanded him concerning
this thing, that *he* should not go after other
gods: but he kept not *that* which the LORD
commanded.
11 Wherefore the LORD said unto Solomon,
Forasmuch as this [1]is done of thee, and thou
hast not kept my covenant and my statutes,
which I have commanded thee, [a]I will surely
rend the kingdom from thee, and will give it to
thy servant.
12 Notwithstanding in thy days I will not
do it for David thy father's sake: *but* I will rend
it out of the hand of thy son.
13 [a]Howbeit I will not rend away all the
kingdom; *but* will give [b]one tribe to thy son
for David my servant's sake, and for Jerusalem's sake, [c]which I have chosen.

Solomon's adversaries

14 ¶ And the LORD [a]stirred up an adversary
unto Solomon, Hadad the Edomite: he *was* of
the king's seed in Edom.
15 [a]For it came to pass, when David was in
Edom, and Joab the captain of the host was
gone up to bury the slain, [b]after he had smitten every male in Edom;
16 (For six months did Joab remain there
with all Israel, until he had cut off every male
in Edom:)
17 That Hadad fled, he and certain Edomites of his father's servants with him, to go *into*
Egypt; Hadad *being yet* a little child.
18 And they arose out of Midian, and came
to Paran: and they took men with them out of
Paran, and they came *to* Egypt, unto Pharaoh
king of Egypt; which gave him a house, and appointed him victuals, and gave him land.
19 And Hadad found great favour in the
sight of Pharaoh, so that he gave him *to* wife
the sister of his own wife, the sister of Tahpenes the queen.
20 And the sister of Tahpenes bare him Genubath his son, whom Tahpenes weaned in
Pharaoh's house: and Genubath was *in* Pharaoh's household among the sons of Pharaoh.
21 [a]And when Hadad heard in Egypt that
David slept with his fathers, and that Joab the
captain of the host was dead, Hadad said to
Pharaoh, [1]Let me depart, that I may go to
mine own country.
22 Then Pharaoh said unto him, But what
hast thou lacked with me, that behold, thou
seekest to go to thine own country? And he
answered, [1]Nothing: howbeit let me go in any
wise.
23 ¶ And God stirred him up *another* adversary, Rezon the son of Eliadah, which fled
from his lord [a]Hadadezer king of Zobah:
24 And he gathered men unto him, and became captain over a band, [a]when David slew
them *of Zobah:* and they went *to* Damascus,
and dwelt therein, and reigned in Damascus.
25 And he was an adversary to Israel all the
days of Solomon, beside the mischief that Hadad *did:* and he abhorred Israel, and reigned
over Syria.

Jeroboam's rebellion

26 ¶ And [a]Jeroboam the son of Nebat, an
Ephrathite of Zereda, Solomon's servant, whose
mother's name *was* Zeruah, a widow woman,
even he [b]lift up *his* hand against the king.
27 And this *was* the cause that he lift up *his*
hand against the king: [a]Solomon built Millo,

11:9 [a]ch. 3:5; 9:2
11:10 [a]ch. 6:12; 9:6
11:11 [1]Heb. *is with thee* [a]ver. 31; ch. 12:15,16
11:13 [a]2 Sam. 7:15 [b]ch. 12:20 [c]Deut. 12:11
11:14 [a]1 Chr. 5:26
11:15 [a]2 Sam. 8:14; 1 Chr. 18:12 [b]Num. 24:19; Deut. 20:13
11:21 [1]Heb. *Send me away* [a]ch. 2:10,34
11:22 [1]Heb. *Not*
11:23 [a]2 Sam. 8:3
11:24 [a]2 Sam. 8:3; 10:8,18
11:26 [a]ch. 12:2; 2 Chr. 13:6 [b]2 Sam. 20:21
11:27 [a]ch. 9:24

11:9 *appeared unto him twice.* See 3:4–5; 9:1–9.
11:11 *not kept my covenant.* Solomon had broken the most basic demands of the covenant (see Ex 20:2–5) and thereby severely undermined the entire covenant relationship between God and His people.
11:12 *for David thy father's sake.* Because of David's unwavering loyalty to the Lord and God's covenant with him (see 2 Sam 7:11–16).
11:13 *one tribe.* Judah (see note on vv. 31–32; see also 12:20). *for Jerusalem's sake, which I have chosen.* Now that Jerusalem contained the temple built by David's son in accordance with 2 Sam 7:13, the destiny of Jerusalem and the Davidic dynasty were closely linked (see 2 Ki 19:34; 21:7–8; Ps 132). The temple represented God's royal palace, where His earthly throne (the ark) was situated and where He had pledged to be present as Israel's Great King (9:3).
11:14 *Hadad.* A familiar name among Edomite kings (see Gen 36:35,39).
11:15 *David was in Edom.* See 2 Sam 8:13–14.
11:16 *all Israel . . . every male in Edom.* All those, on both sides, who took part in the campaign.
11:17 *a little child.* Probably in his early teens.
11:18 *Midian.* At this time Midianites inhabited a region on the eastern borders of Moab and Edom. *Paran.* A wilderness area southeast of Kadesh in the central area of the Sinai peninsula (see Num 10:12; 12:16; 13:3). *Pharaoh king of Egypt.* See note on 3:1. *gave him a house, and . . . victuals, and . . . land.* In a time of Israel's growing strength it was in Egypt's interest to befriend those who would harass Israel and keep her power in check.
11:21 *Let me depart.* It appears that Hadad returned to Edom during the early days of Solomon's reign.
11:22 *what hast thou lacked with me . . . ?* Because Egypt had by this time established relatively good relations with Israel (see note on 3:1), the pharaoh was reluctant to see Hadad return to Edom and provoke trouble with Solomon.
11:24 *captain over a band.* As David had been (1 Sam 22:1–2), and Jephthah before him (Judg 11:3). *they went to Damascus, and dwelt therein, and reigned.* Presumably this took place in the early part of Solomon's reign (see 2 Sam 8:6 for the situation in Damascus during the time of David). It is likely that Solomon's expedition (2 Chr 8:3) against Hamath-zobah (the kingdom formerly ruled by Hadadezer, 2 Sam 8:3–6) was provoked by opposition led by Rezon. Even though Solomon was able to retain control of the territory north of Damascus to the Euphrates (4:21,24), he was not able to drive Rezon from Damascus itself.
‡11:26 *lift up his hand* [i.e. "rebelled"] *against the king.* See note on v. 40.
11:27 *Millo.* See 9:15 and note.

and [1]repaired the breaches of the city of David
his father.
28 And the man Jeroboam *was* a mighty
man of valour: and Solomon seeing the young
man that he [1]was industrious, he made him
ruler over all the [2]charge of the house of Joseph.
29 And it came to pass at that time when
Jeroboam went out of Jerusalem, that the
prophet [a]Ahijah the Shilonite found him in
the way; and he had clad himself with a new
garment; and they two *were* alone in the field:
30 And Ahijah caught the new garment
that *was* on him, and [a]rent it *in* twelve pieces:
31 And he said to Jeroboam, Take thee ten
pieces: for [a]thus saith the LORD, the God of Israel, Behold, I will rent the kingdom out of the
hand of Solomon, and will give ten tribes to
thee:
32 (But he shall have one tribe for my servant David's sake, and for Jerusalem's sake, the
city which I have chosen out of all the tribes of
Israel:)
33 [a]Because that they have forsaken me,
and have worshipped Ashtoreth the goddess of
the Zidonians, Chemosh the god of the Moabites, and Milcom the god of the children of
Ammon, and have not walked in my ways, to
do *that* which *is* right in mine eyes, and *to*
keep my statutes and my judgments, as *did* David his father.
34 Howbeit I will not take the whole king-

11:27 [1]Heb. *closed*
11:28 [1]Heb. *did work* [2]Heb. *burden*
11:29 [a]ch. 14:2
11:30 [a]See 1 Sam. 15:27; 24:5
11:31 [a]ver. 11,13
11:33 [a]ver. 5-7
11:35 [a]ch. 12:16,17
11:36 [1]Heb. *lamp,* or, *candle* [a]ch. 15:4; 2 Ki. 8:19
11:38 [a]Josh. 1:5 [b]2 Sam. 7:11,27
11:41 [1]Or, *words,* or, *things* [2]Or, *words,* or, *things* [a]2 Chr. 9:29

dom out of his hand: but I will make him
prince all the days of his life for David my servant's sake, whom I chose, because he kept
my commandments and my statutes:
35 But [a]I will take the kingdom out of his
son's hand, and will give it unto thee, *even* ten
tribes.
36 And unto his son will I give one tribe,
that [a]David my servant may have a [1]light alway before me in Jerusalem, the city which I
have chosen me to put my name there.
37 And I will take thee, and thou shalt
reign according to all that thy soul desireth,
and shalt be king over Israel.
38 And it shall be, if thou wilt hearken
unto all that I command thee, and wilt walk in
my ways, and do that *is* right in my sight, to
keep my statutes and my commandments, as
David my servant did; that [a]I will be with
thee, and [b]build thee a sure house, as I built
for David, and will give Israel unto thee.
39 And I will for this afflict the seed of David, but not for ever.
40 Solomon sought therefore to kill Jeroboam. And Jeroboam arose, and fled *into* Egypt,
unto Shishak king of Egypt, and was in Egypt
until the death of Solomon.

The death of Solomon

41 ¶ And [a]the rest of the [1]acts of Solomon,
and all that he did, and his wisdom, *are* they not
written in the book of the [2]acts of Solomon?

11:28 *all the charge of the house of Joseph.* See 5:13–18. Jeroboam's supervision of the conscripted laborers from the tribes of Ephraim and Manasseh made him aware of the smoldering discontent among the people over Solomon's policies (see 12:4).
11:31–32 *ten tribes . . . one tribe.* The tradition of considering the ten northern tribes as a unit distinct from the southern tribes (Judah and Simeon—Levi received no territorial inheritance; see Josh 21) goes back to the period of the judges (see Judg 5:14–16). The reason, no doubt, was the continuing presence of a non-Israelite corridor (Jerusalem, Gibeonite league, Gezer) that separated the two Israelite regions (see map No. 4 at the end of the study Bible). Political division along the same line during the early years of David's reign and the different arrangements that brought the southern and northern segments under David's rule (see 2 Sam 2:4; 5:3) reinforced this sense of division. With the conquest of Jerusalem by David (2 Sam 5:6–7) and the pharaoh's gift of Gezer to Solomon's wife (9:16–17), all Israel was for the first time territorially united. (Now that Jerusalem and Gezer were under Israelite control, the Gibeonite league, which had submitted already to Joshua—see Josh 9—could be effectively absorbed politically.) In the division here announced, the "one tribe" refers to the area dominated by Judah (but including Simeon; see Josh 19:1–9), and the "ten tribes" refers to the region that came under David's rule at the later date (Ephraim and Manasseh, Joseph's sons, being counted as two tribes; see Gen 48:5; see also note on Josh 14:4). For further refinement of the new boundaries that came about see note on 12:21.
11:33 *forsaken me.* See vv. 5–7. *have not walked in my ways.* See vv. 1–2; 3:14.
11:34 *I will make him prince all the days of his life.* See vv. 12–13.
11:35 *out of his son's hand.* From Rehoboam (see 12:1–24).
11:36 *a light alway before me in Jerusalem.* Symbolizes the continuance of the Davidic dynasty in the city where God had chosen to cause His name to dwell (see v. 13 and note). In a number of passages, the burning or snuffing out of one's lamp signifies the flourishing or ceasing of one's life (Job 18:6; 21:17; Prov 13:9; 20:20; 24:20). Here (and in 15:4; 2 Ki 8:19; 2 Chr 21:7; Ps 132:17) the same figure is applied to David's dynasty (see especially Ps 132:17, where "ordained a lamp for mine anointed" is parallel to "make the horn of David to bud"). In David's royal sons his "lamp" continues to burn before the Lord in Jerusalem.
11:37 *Israel.* The northern ten tribes.
11:38 *if thou wilt hearken unto all that I command thee . . . I will be with thee.* Jeroboam was placed under the same covenant obligations as David and Solomon before him (see 2:3–4; 3:14; 6:12–13).
11:39 *afflict the seed of David.* The division of the kingdom considerably reduced the status and power of the house of David. *not for ever.* Anticipates a restoration (announced also in the Messianic prophecies of Jer 30:9; Ezek 34:23; 37:15–28; Hos 3:5; Amos 9:11–12) in which the nation is reunited under the rule of the house of David.
11:40 *Solomon sought therefore to kill Jeroboam.* Jeroboam, perhaps indifferent to the timing announced by Ahijah (vv. 34–35), may have made an abortive attempt to wrest the kingdom from Solomon (see v. 26). *Shishak king of Egypt.* See 14:25–26. This first Egyptian pharaoh to be mentioned by name in the OT was the Libyan founder of the 22nd dynasty (945–924 B.C.). Solomon's marriage ties were with the previous dynasty (see note on 3:1).
11:41 *acts of Solomon.* A written source concerning Solomon's life and administration, which was used by the writer of 1,2 Kings (see Introduction: Author, Sources and Date; see also 15:7,23).

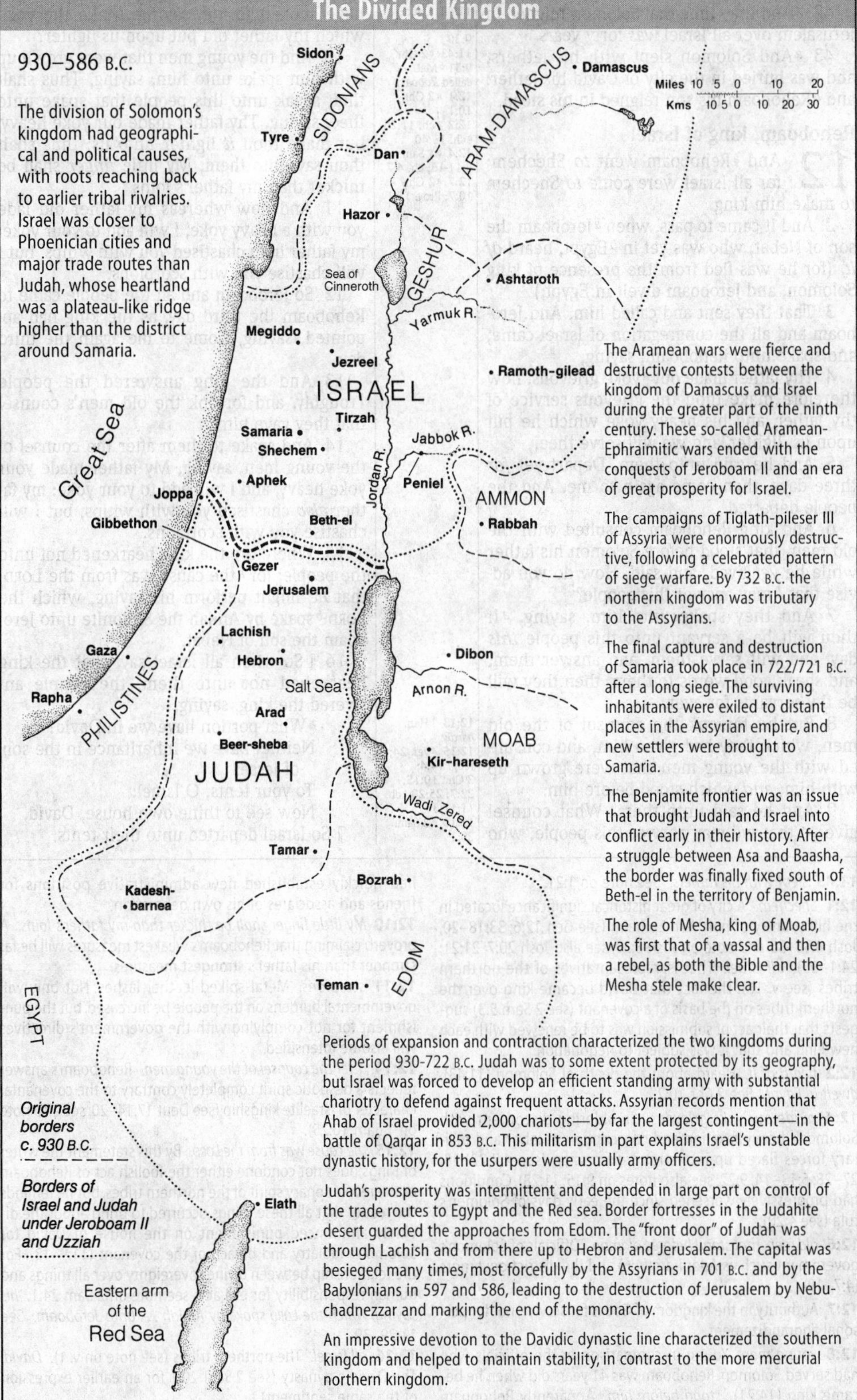
The Divided Kingdom
930–586 B.C.
The division of Solomon's kingdom had geographical and political causes, with roots reaching back to earlier tribal rivalries. Israel was closer to Phoenician cities and major trade routes than Judah, whose heartland was a plateau-like ridge higher than the district around Samaria.
Sidon
Tyre
SIDONIANS
Dan
ARAM-DAMASCUS
Damascus
Miles 10 5 0 10 20
Kms 10 5 0 10 20 30
Hazor
Sea of Cinneroth
GESHUR
Ashtaroth
Yarmuk R.
Megiddo
Jezreel
Ramoth-gilead
ISRAEL
Tirzah
Samaria
Shechem
Jabbok R.
Jordan R.
Peniel
Aphek
Joppa
Great Sea
AMMON
Gibbethon
Beth-el
Rabbah
Gezer
Jerusalem
Lachish
Gaza
Hebron
Dibon
Salt Sea
Arnon R.
Rapha
PHILISTINES
Arad
Beer-sheba
MOAB
JUDAH
Kir-hareseth
Wadi Zered
Tamar
Bozrah
Kadesh-barnea
Teman
EDOM
EGYPT
Elath
Eastern arm of the Red Sea
Original borders c. 930 B.C.
Borders of Israel and Judah under Jeroboam II and Uzziah
The Aramean wars were fierce and destructive contests between the kingdom of Damascus and Israel during the greater part of the ninth century. These so-called Aramean-Ephraimitic wars ended with the conquests of Jeroboam II and an era of great prosperity for Israel.
The campaigns of Tiglath-pileser III of Assyria were enormously destructive, following a celebrated pattern of siege warfare. By 732 B.C. the northern kingdom was tributary to the Assyrians.
The final capture and destruction of Samaria took place in 722/721 B.C. after a long siege. The surviving inhabitants were exiled to distant places in the Assyrian empire, and new settlers were brought to Samaria.
The Benjamite frontier was an issue that brought Judah and Israel into conflict early in their history. After a struggle between Asa and Baasha, the border was finally fixed south of Beth-el in the territory of Benjamin.
The role of Mesha, king of Moab, was first that of a vassal and then a rebel, as both the Bible and the Mesha stele make clear.
Periods of expansion and contraction characterized the two kingdoms during the period 930-722 B.C. Judah was to some extent protected by its geography, but Israel was forced to develop an efficient standing army with substantial chariotry to defend against frequent attacks. Assyrian records mention that Ahab of Israel provided 2,000 chariots—by far the largest contingent—in the battle of Qarqar in 853 B.C. This militarism in part explains Israel's unstable dynastic history, for the usurpers were usually army officers.
Judah's prosperity was intermittent and depended in large part on control of the trade routes to Egypt and the Red sea. Border fortresses in the Judahite desert guarded the approaches from Edom. The "front door" of Judah was through Lachish and from there up to Hebron and Jerusalem. The capital was besieged many times, most forcefully by the Assyrians in 701 B.C. and by the Babylonians in 597 and 586, leading to the destruction of Jerusalem by Nebuchadnezzar and marking the end of the monarchy.
An impressive devotion to the Davidic dynastic line characterized the southern kingdom and helped to maintain stability, in contrast to the more mercurial northern kingdom.

42 [a]And the [1]time that Solomon reigned in Jerusalem over all Israel *was* forty years.

43 [a]And Solomon slept with his fathers, and was buried in the city of David his father: and [b]Rehoboam his son reigned in his stead.

Rehoboam, king of Israel

12 And [a]Rehoboam went *to* Shechem: for all Israel were come *to* Shechem to make him king.

2 And it came to pass, when [a]Jeroboam the son of Nebat, who was yet in [b]Egypt, heard *of it,* (for he was fled from the presence of king Solomon, and Jeroboam dwelt in Egypt;)

3 That they sent and called him. And Jeroboam and all the congregation of Israel came, and spake unto Rehoboam, saying,

4 Thy father made our [a]yoke grievous: now therefore make thou the grievous service of thy father, and his heavy yoke which he put upon us, lighter, and we will serve thee.

5 And he said unto them, Depart yet *for* three days, then come again to me. And the people departed.

6 And king Rehoboam consulted with the old men, that stood before Solomon his father while he *yet* lived, and said, How do you advise that *I* may answer this people?

7 And they spake unto him, saying, [a]If thou wilt be a servant unto this people *this* day, and wilt serve them, and answer them, and speak good words to them, then they will be thy servants for ever.

8 But he forsook the counsel of the old men, which they had given him, and consulted with the young men that were grown up with him, *and* which stood before him:

9 And he said unto them, What counsel give ye that we may answer this people, who have spoken to me, saying, Make the yoke which thy father did put upon us lighter?

10 And the young men that were grown up with him spake unto him, saying, Thus shalt thou speak unto this people that spake unto thee, saying, Thy father made our yoke heavy, but make thou *it* lighter unto us; thus shalt thou say unto them, My little *finger* shall be thicker than my father's loins.

11 And now whereas my father did lade you with a heavy yoke, I will add to your yoke: my father hath chastised you with whips, but I will chastise you with scorpions.

12 So Jeroboam and all the people came to Rehoboam the third day, as the king had appointed, saying, Come to me again the third day.

13 And the king answered the people [1]roughly, and forsook the old men's counsel that they gave him;

14 And spake to them after the counsel of the young men, saying, My father made your yoke heavy, and I will add to your yoke: my father *also* chastised you with whips, but I will chastise you with scorpions.

15 Wherefore the king hearkened not unto the people; for [a]the cause was from the LORD, that *he* might perform his saying, which the LORD [b]spake by Ahijah the Shilonite unto Jeroboam the son of Nebat.

16 ¶ So when all Israel saw that the king hearkened not unto them, the people answered the king, saying,

[a]What portion have we in David?
Neither *have we* inheritance in the son
of Jesse:
To your tents, O Israel:
Now see to thine own house, David.
¶ So Israel departed unto their tents.

11:42 [1]Heb. *days* [a]2 Chr. 9:30
11:43 [a]2 Chr. 9:31 [b]Mat. 1:7, called *Roboam*
12:1 [a]2 Chr. 10:1
12:2 [a]ch. 11:26 [b]ch. 11:40
12:4 [a]1 Sam. 8:11-18; ch. 4:7
12:7 [a]2 Chr. 10:7; Prov. 15:1
12:13 [1]Heb. *hardly*
12:15 [a]ver. 24; Judg. 14:4; 2 Chr. 10:15; 22:7; 25:20 [b]ch. 11:11,31
12:16 [a]2 Sam. 20:1

11:43 *slept with his fathers.* See note on 1:21.

12:1 *Shechem.* A city of great historical significance located in the hill country of northern Ephraim (see Gen 12:6; 33:18–20; Josh 8:30–35 and note on Josh 8:30; see also Josh 20:7; 21:21; 24:1–33). *all Israel.* That is, representatives of the northern tribes (see v. 16). The fact that David became king over the northern tribes on the basis of a covenant (see 2 Sam 5:3) suggests that their act of submission was to be renewed with each new king and that it was subject to negotiation.

12:2 *heard of it.* Heard about the death of Solomon (11:43). *dwelt in Egypt.* See 2 Chr 10:2.

12:4 *made our yoke grievous.* Smoldering discontent with Solomon's heavy taxation and conscription of labor and military forces flared up into strong expression (see 4:7,22–23, 27–28; 5:13–14; 9:22; see also notes on 9:15; 11:28). Conditions had progressively worsened since the early days of Solomon's rule (see 4:20).

12:6 *old men, that stood before Solomon.* Officials of Solomon's government such as Adoniram (4:6) and the district governors (4:7–19).

12:7 Authority in the kingdom of God is for service, not for personal aggrandizement.

12:8 *young men.* Young in comparison to the officials who had served Solomon. Rehoboam was 41 years old when he became king (14:21). *stood before him.* Apparently Rehoboam had quickly established new administrative positions for friends and associates of his own generation.

12:10 *My little finger shall be thicker than my father's loins.* A proverb claiming that Rehoboam's weakest measures will be far stronger than his father's strongest measures.

12:11 *scorpions.* Metal-spiked leather lashes. Not only will governmental burdens on the people be increased, but the punishment for not complying with the government's directives will also be intensified.

12:14 *after the counsel of the young men.* Rehoboam's answer reflects a despotic spirit completely contrary to the covenantal character of Israelite kingship (see Deut 17:14–20; see also note on 1 Sam 10:25).

12:15 *the cause was from the LORD.* By this statement the writer of Kings does not condone either the foolish act of Rehoboam or the revolutionary spirit of the northern tribes, but he reminds the reader that all these things occurred to bring about the divinely announced punishment on the house of David for Solomon's idolatry and breach of the covenant (11:9–13). For the relationship between divine sovereignty over all things and human responsibility for evil acts see note on 2 Sam 24:1. *his saying, which the LORD spake by Ahijah . . . unto Jeroboam.* See 11:29–39.

12:16 *all Israel.* The northern tribes (see note on v. 1). *David.* The Davidic dynasty (see 2 Sam 20:1 for an earlier expression of the same sentiment).

17 But [a]*as for* the children of Israel which dwelt in the cities of Judah, Rehoboam reigned over them.

18 Then king Rehoboam [a]sent Adoram, who *was* over the tribute; and all Israel stoned him with stones, that he died. Therefore king Rehoboam [1]made speed to get *him* up to *his* chariot, to flee *to* Jerusalem.

19 So [a]Israel [1]rebelled against the house of David unto this day.

20 And it came to pass, when all Israel heard that Jeroboam was come again, that they sent and called him unto the congregation, and made him king over all Israel: there was none that followed the house of David, but the tribe of Judah [a]only.

21 ¶ And when [a]Rehoboam was come *to* Jerusalem, he assembled all the house of Judah, with the tribe of Benjamin, an hundred and fourscore thousand chosen *men*, which were warriors, to fight against the house of Israel, to bring the kingdom again to Rehoboam the son of Solomon.

22 But [a]the word of God came unto Shemaiah the man of God, saying,

23 Speak unto Rehoboam, the son of Solomon, king of Judah, and unto all the house of Judah and Benjamin, and *to* the remnant of the people, saying,

24 Thus saith the LORD, Ye shall not go up, nor fight against your brethren the children of Israel: return every man to his house; [a]for this thing is from me. They hearkened therefore to the word of the LORD, and returned to depart, according to the word of the LORD.

Two golden calves

25 ¶ Then Jeroboam [a]built Shechem in mount Ephraim, and dwelt therein; and went out from thence, and built [b]Penuel.

26 And Jeroboam said in his heart, Now shall the kingdom return to the house of David:

27 If this people [a]go up to do sacrifice in the house of the LORD at Jerusalem, then shall the heart of this people turn again unto their lord, *even* unto Rehoboam king of Judah, and they shall kill me, and go again to Rehoboam king of Judah.

28 Whereupon the king took counsel, and [a]made two calves of gold, and said unto them, *It is* too much for you to go up *to* Jerusalem: [b]behold thy gods, O Israel, which brought thee up out of the land of Egypt.

29 And he set the one in [a]Beth-el, and the other put he in [b]Dan.

30 And this thing became [a]a sin: for the people went *to worship* before the one, *even* unto Dan.

31 And he made a [a]house of high places, [b]and made priests of the lowest of the people, which were not of the sons of Levi.

12:17 [a]ch. 11:13,36
12:18 [1]Heb. *strengthened himself* [a]ch. 4:6; 5:14
12:19 [1]Or, *fell away* [a]2 Ki. 17:21
12:20 [a]ch. 11:13,32
12:21 [a]2 Chr. 11:1
12:22 [a]2 Chr. 11:2
12:24 [a]ver. 15
12:25 [a]See Judg. 9:45 [b]Judg. 8:17
12:27 [a]Deut. 12:5,6
12:28 [a]2 Ki. 10:29; 17:16 [b]Ex. 32:4,8
12:29 [a]Gen. 28:19; Hos. 4:15 [b]Judg. 18:29
12:30 [a]ch. 13:34; 2 Ki. 17:21
12:31 [a]ch. 13:32 [b]Num. 3:10; ch. 13:33; 2 Ki. 17:32; 2 Chr. 11:14,15

12:17 *children of Israel which dwelt in the cities of Judah.* People originally from the northern tribes who had settled in Judah. They were later to be joined by others from the north who desired to serve the Lord and worship at the temple (see 2 Chr 11:16–17).

‡12:18 *Adoram, who was over the tribute* [i.e. "forced labor"]. Adoram (a variant of Adoniram) had served in the same capacity under both David (2 Sam 20:24) and Solomon (1 Ki 4:6; 5:14).

12:19 *this day.* The time of the writing of the source from which the author of 1 Kings derived this account (see Introduction: Author, Sources and Date).

12:21 *tribe of Benjamin.* Although the bulk of Benjamin was aligned with the northern tribes (see note on 11:31–32), the area around Jerusalem remained under Rehoboam's control (as did the Gibeonite cities and Gezer). The northern boundary of Judah must have reached almost to Beth-el (12 miles north of Jerusalem)—which Abijah, Rehoboam's son, even held for a short while (see 2 Chr 13:19). *an hundred and fourscore thousand . . . warriors.* Probably includes all support personnel together with those who would actually be committed to battle.

12:22 *Shemaiah.* Wrote a history of Rehoboam's reign (2 Chr 12:15). Another of his prophecies is recorded in 2 Chr 12:5–8. *man of God.* A common way of referring to a prophet (see, e.g., 13:1; Deut 18:18; 33:1; 1 Sam 2:27; 9:9–10).

12:23 *remnant of the people.* See note on v. 17.

12:24 *returned to depart.* Although full-scale civil war was averted, intermittent skirmishes and battles between Israel and Judah continued throughout the reigns of Rehoboam, Abijah and Asa, until political instability in Israel after the death of Baasha finally brought the conflict to a halt. Asa's son Jehoshaphat entered into an alliance with Ahab and sealed the relationship by the marriage of his son Jehoram to Ahab's daughter Athaliah (see 14:30; 15:6,16; 22:2,44; 2 Ki 8:18).

12:25 *Penuel.* A town east of the Jordan (see Gen 32:31; Judg 8:9,17) of strategic importance for defense against the Arameans of Damascus (see 11:23–25) and the Ammonites.

12:26 *return to the house of David.* Jeroboam did not have confidence in the divine promise given to him through Ahijah (see 11:38) and thus took action that forfeited the theocratic basis for his kingship.

12:28 *two calves of gold.* Pagan gods of the Arameans and Canaanites were often represented as standing on calves or bulls as symbols of their strength and fertility (see note on Judg 2:13). *behold thy gods, O Israel, which brought thee up out of the land of Egypt.* Like Aaron (Ex 32:4–5), Jeroboam attempted to combine the pagan calf symbol with the worship of the Lord, though he attempted no physical representation of the Lord—no "god" stood on the backs of his bulls.

12:29 *Beth-el.* Located about 12 miles north of Jerusalem close to the border of Ephraim but within the territory of Benjamin (Josh 18:11–13,22). Beth-el held a prominent place in the history of Israel's worship of the Lord (see Gen 12:8; 28:11–19; 35:6–7; Judg 20:26–28; 1 Sam 7:16). *Dan.* Located in the far north of the land near mount Hermon. A similarly paganized worship was practiced here during the period of the judges (Judg 18:30–31).

12:30 *this thing became a sin.* Jeroboam's royal policy promoted violation of the second commandment (Ex 20:4–6). It inevitably led to Israel's violation of the first commandment also (Ex 20:3) and opened the door for the entrance of fully pagan practices into Israel's religious rites (especially in the time of Ahab). Jeroboam foolishly abandoned religious principle for political expediency and in so doing forfeited the promise given him by the prophet Ahijah (see 11:38).

12:31 *he made a house of high places.* See note on 3:2. *not of the sons of Levi.* Many of the priests and Levites of the northern kingdom migrated to Judah because Jeroboam bypassed them when appointing cult personnel in the north (see 2 Chr 11:13–14).

32 And Jeroboam ordained a feast in the
eighth month, on the fifteenth day of the
month, like unto [a]the feast that *is* in Judah,
and he [1]offered upon the altar (so did he in
Beth-el,) [2]sacrificing unto the calves that he
had made: [b]and he placed in Beth-el the
priests of the high places which he had made.
33 So he [1]offered upon the altar which he
had made in Beth-el the fifteenth day of the
eighth month, *even* in the month which he
had [a]devised of his own heart; and ordained a
feast unto the children of Israel: and he [1]of-
fered upon the altar, [2]and [b]burnt incense.

The man of God from Judah

13 And behold, there [a]came a man of
God out of Judah by the word of the
LORD unto Beth-el: [b]and Jeroboam stood by the
altar [1]to burn incense.
2 And he cried against the altar in the word
of the LORD, and said, O altar, altar, thus saith
the LORD; Behold, a child *shall be* born unto
the house of David, [a]Josiah by name; and upon
thee shall he offer the priests of the high
places that burn incense upon thee, and men's
bones shall be burnt upon thee.
3 And he gave [a]a sign the same day, saying,
This *is* the sign which the LORD hath spoken;
Behold, the altar *shall be* rent, and the ashes
that *are* upon it shall be poured out.
4 And it came to pass, when king Jeroboam
heard the saying of the man of God, which had
cried against the altar in Beth-el, that he put
forth his hand from the altar, saying, Lay hold
on him. And his hand, which he put forth
against him, dried up, so that he could not pull
it in again to him.
5 The altar also *was* rent, and the ashes
poured out from the altar, according to the
sign which the man of God had given by the
word of the LORD.
6 And the king answered and said unto the
man of God, [a]Intreat now the face of the LORD
thy God, and pray for me, that my hand may
be restored me again. And the man of God besought [1]the LORD, and the king's hand was restored him again, and became as *it was* before.
7 And the king said unto the man of God,
Come home with me, and refresh *thyself*, and
[a]I will give thee a reward.
8 And the man of God said unto the king,
[a]If thou wilt give me half thine house, I will
not go in with thee, neither will I eat bread
nor drink water in this place:
9 For so was it charged me by the word of
the LORD, saying, [a]Eat no bread, nor drink water, nor turn again by the *same* way that thou
camest.
10 So he went another way, and returned
not by the way that he came to Beth-el.
11 ¶ Now there dwelt an old prophet in
Beth-el; and his son came and told him all the
works that the man of God had done *that* day
in Beth-el: the words which he had spoken
unto the king, them they told also to their father.
12 And their father said unto them, What
way went he? For his sons had seen what way
the man of God went, which came from Judah.
13 And he said unto his sons, Saddle me
the ass. So they saddled him the ass: and he
rode thereon,
14 And went after the man of God, and
found him sitting under an oak: and he said
unto him, *Art* thou the man of God that
camest from Judah? And he said, I *am*.
15 Then he said unto him, Come home
with me, and eat bread.
16 And he said, [a]I may not return with
thee, nor go in with thee: neither will I eat
bread nor drink water with thee in this place:
17 For [1]it was said to me [a]by the word of
the LORD, Thou shalt eat no bread nor drink
water there, nor turn again to go by the way
that thou camest.
18 He said unto him, I *am* a prophet also as

12:32 [1]Or, *went up to the altar, etc.* [2]Or, *to sacrifice* [a]Lev. 23:33,34; Num. 29:12; ch. 8:2,5 [b]Amos 7:13
12:33 [1]Or, *went up to the altar, etc.* [2]Heb. *to burn incense* [a]Num. 15:39 [b]ch. 13:1
13:1 [1]Or, *to offer* [a]2 Ki. 23:17 [b]ch. 12:32,33
13:2 [a]2 Ki. 23:15,16
13:3 [a]Is. 7:14; John 2:18; 1 Cor. 1:22
13:6 [a]Ex. 8:8; 9:28; 10:17; Num. 21:7; Acts 8:24; Jas. 5:16
13:6 [1]Heb. *the face of the LORD*
13:7 [a]1 Sam. 9:7; 2 Ki. 5:15
13:8 [a]Num. 22:18; 24:13
13:9 [a]1 Cor. 5:11
13:16 [a]ver. 8:9
13:17 [1]Heb. *a word* was [a]ch. 20:35; 1 Thes. 4:15

12:32 *feast that is in Judah.* Apparently the feast of tabernacles, observed in Judah on the 15th to the 21st of the seventh month (see 8:2; Lev 23:34). *offered upon the altar.* Jeroboam overstepped the limits of his prerogatives as king and assumed the role of a priest (see 2 Chr 26:16–21).

13:1 *man of God.* See note on 12:22. *out of Judah . . . unto Beth-el.* God sent a prophet from the southern kingdom to Beth-el in the northern kingdom. Possibly He did this to emphasize that the divinely appointed political division (11:11,29–39; 12:15,24) was not intended to establish rival religious systems in the two kingdoms. Two centuries later the prophet Amos from Tekoa in Judah also went to Beth-el in the northern kingdom to pronounce God's judgment on Jeroboam II (Amos 7:10–17).

13:2 *Josiah.* A prophetic announcement of the rule of King Josiah, who came to the throne in Judah nearly 300 years after the division of the kingdom. *shall he offer the priests of the high places.* Fulfilled in 2 Ki 23:15–20.

13:3 *sign.* The immediate fulfillment of a short-term prediction would serve to authenticate the reliability of the longer-term prediction (see Deut 18:21–22).

13:5 *ashes poured out.* Visibly demonstrating God's power to fulfill the words of the prophet (see note on v. 3) and providing a clear sign that Jeroboam's offering was unacceptable to the Lord (see Lev 6:10–11).

13:6 *thy God.* Should not be taken as implying that Jeroboam no longer considered the Lord as his own God (cf. 2:3; Gen 27:20), but as suggesting that he recognized the prophet as his superior in the theocratic order. *king's hand was restored.* The Lord's gracious response to Jeroboam's request is to be seen as an additional sign (see v. 3) given to confirm the word of the prophet and to move Jeroboam to repentance.

13:7 *Come home with me.* Jeroboam attempted to renew his prestige in the eyes of the people by creating the impression that there was no fundamental break between himself and the prophetic order (see 1 Sam 15:30 for a similar situation).

13:9 *Eat no bread.* The prophet's refusal of Jeroboam's invitation rested on a previously given divine command. It underscored God's extreme displeasure with the apostate worship at Beth-el.

13:18 *I am a prophet also as thou art.* A half-truth. It is likely that the old prophet in Beth-el had faithfully proclaimed the word of the Lord in former days, but those days had long since passed.

thou *art;* and an angel spake unto me by the
word of the LORD, saying, Bring him back with
thee into thine house, that he may eat bread
and drink water. *But* he lied unto him.
19 So he went back with him, and did eat
bread in his house, and drank water.
20 And it came to pass, as they sat at the
table, that the word of the LORD came unto the
prophet that brought him back:
21 And he cried unto the man of God that
came from Judah, saying, Thus saith the LORD,
Forasmuch as thou hast disobeyed the mouth
of the LORD, and hast not kept the commandment which the LORD thy God commanded
thee,
22 But camest back, and hast eaten bread
and drunk water in the place, of the which *the*
LORD did say to thee, Eat no bread, and drink
no water; thy carcase shall not come unto the
sepulchre of thy fathers.
23 ¶ And it came to pass, after he had eaten
bread, and after he had drunk, that he saddled
for him the ass, *to wit,* for the prophet whom
he had brought back.
24 And when he was gone, [a]a lion met
him by the way, and slew him: and his carcase
was cast in the way, and the ass stood by it, the
lion also stood by the carcase.
25 And behold, men passed by, and saw
the carcase cast in the way, and the lion standing by the carcase: and they came and told *it* in
the city where the old prophet dwelt.
26 And when the prophet that brought
him back from the way heard *thereof,* he said,
It *is* the man of God, who was disobedient
unto the word of the LORD: therefore the LORD
hath delivered him unto the lion, which hath
[1]torn him, and slain him, according to the
word of the LORD, which he spake unto him.
27 And he spake to his sons, saying, Saddle
me the ass. And they saddled *him.*
28 And he went and found his carcase cast
in the way, and the ass and the lion standing
by the carcase: the lion had not eaten the carcase, nor [1]torn the ass.
29 And the prophet took up the carcase of
the man of God, and laid it upon the ass, and
brought it back: and the old prophet came to
the city, to mourn and to bury him.
30 And he laid his carcase in his own
grave; and they mourned over him, *saying,*
[a]Alas, my brother.
31 And it came to pass, after he had buried
him, that he spake to his sons, saying, When I
am dead, then bury me in the sepulchre
wherein the man of God *is* buried; [a]lay my
bones beside his bones:
32 [a]For the saying which he cried by the
word of the LORD against the altar in Beth-el,
and against all the houses of the high places
which *are* in the cities of [b]Samaria, shall surely come to pass.
33 ¶ [a]After this thing Jeroboam returned
not from his evil way, but [1]made again of the
lowest of the people priests of the high places:
whosoever would, he [b2]consecrated him, and
he became *one of* the priests of the high places.
34 [a]And this thing became sin unto the
house of Jeroboam, even [b]to cut *it* off, and to
destroy *it* from off the face of the earth.

The prophecy against Jeroboam

14 At that time Abijah the son of Jeroboam fell sick.
2 And Jeroboam said to his wife, Arise, I
pray thee, and disguise thyself, that thou be
not known to be the wife of Jeroboam; and get
thee *to* Shiloh: behold, there *is* Ahijah the

13:24 [a]ch. 20:36
13:26 [1]Heb. *broken*
13:28 [1]Heb. *broken*
13:30 [a]Jer. 22:18
13:31 [a]2 Ki. 23:17,18
13:32 [a]ver. 2; 2 Ki. 23:16,19 [b]See ch. 16:24
13:33 [1]Heb. *returned and made* [2]Heb. *filled his hand* [a]ch. 12:31,32; 2 Chr. 11:15; 13:9 [b]Judg. 17:12
13:34 [a]ch. 12:30 [b]ch. 14:10

13:19 *he went back with him.* Neither the old prophet's lie nor his own need justified disobedience to the direct and explicit command of the Lord. His public action in this matter undermined respect for the divine authority of all he had said at Beth-el.

13:20 *the word of the LORD came unto the prophet.* The fundamental distinction between a true and a false prophecy here becomes apparent. The false prophecy arises from one's own imagination (Jer 23:16; Ezek 13:2,7) while the true prophecy is from God (Ex 4:16; Deut 18:18; Jer 1:9; 2 Pet 1:21).

13:22 *thy carcase shall not come unto the sepulchre of thy fathers.* The man of God from Judah will die far from his own home and family burial plot.

13:24 *slew him.* A stern warning to Jeroboam that God takes His word very seriously. *the ass stood by it, the lion also.* The remarkable fact that the donkey did not run and the lion did not attack the donkey or disturb the man's body (v. 28) clearly stamped the incident as a divine judgment. This additional miracle was reported in Beth-el (v. 25) and provided yet another sign authenticating the message that the man of God from Judah had delivered at Jeroboam's altar. But Jeroboam was still not moved to repentance (v. 33).

13:30 *laid his carcase in his own grave.* See v. 22. The old prophet did the only thing left for him to do in order to make amends for his deliberate and fatal deception.

13:31 *sepulchre wherein the man of God is buried.* The old prophet chose in this way to identify himself with the message that the man of God from Judah had given at Beth-el.

13:32 *Samaria.* As the capital of the northern kingdom, Samaria is used to designate the entire territory of the northern ten tribes (see note on 16:24). However, Samaria was not established until about 50 years after this (16:23–24). The use of the name here reflects the perspective of the author of Kings (see note on Gen 14:14 for a similar instance of the use of a place-name—Dan—of later origin than the historical incident with which it is connected).

13:33 *made . . . of the lowest of the people priests.* See 12:31 and note.

13:34 *sin.* The sin in 12:30 was the establishment of a paganized worship; here it is persistence in this worship with all its attendant evils.

14:1 *At that time.* Probably indicating a time not far removed from the event narrated in ch. 13. *Abijah.* Means "My (divine) Father is the LORD," suggesting that Jeroboam, at least to some degree, desired to be regarded as a worshiper of the Lord.

14:2 *disguise thyself.* Jeroboam's attempt to mislead the prophet Ahijah into giving a favorable prophecy concerning the sick boy indicates (1) his consciousness of his own guilt, (2) his superstition that prophecy worked in a magical way and (3) his confused but real respect for the power of the Lord's prophet. *which told me that I should be king over this people.* See 11:29–39.

prophet, which told me that [a]I should be king
over this people.
3 [a]And take [1]with thee ten loaves, and
[2]cracknels, and a [3]cruse of honey, and go to him:
he shall tell thee what shall become of the child.
4 And Jeroboam's wife did so, and arose,
[a]and went *to* Shiloh, and came *to* the house of
Ahijah. But Ahijah could not see; for his eyes
[1]were set by reason of his age.
5 And the LORD said unto Ahijah, Behold,
the wife of Jeroboam cometh to ask a thing of
thee for her son; for he *is* sick: thus and thus
shalt thou say unto her: for it shall be, when
she cometh in, that she shall feign herself to
be another *woman.*
6 And it was *so,* when Ahijah heard the
sound of her feet, as she came in at the door,
that he said, Come in, thou wife of Jeroboam;
why feignest thou thyself to be another? for I
am sent to thee *with* [1]heavy *tidings.*
7 Go, tell Jeroboam, Thus saith the LORD
God of Israel, [a]Forasmuch as I exalted thee
from among the people, and made thee prince
over my people Israel,
8 And [a]rent the kingdom away from the
house of David, and gave it thee: and *yet* thou
hast not been as my servant David, [b]who kept
my commandments, and who followed me
with all his heart, to do *that* only which *was*
right in mine eyes;
9 But hast done evil above all that were before thee: [a]for thou hast gone and made thee
other gods, and molten images, to provoke me
to anger, and [b]hast cast me behind thy back:
10 Therefore, behold, [a]I will bring evil
upon the house of Jeroboam, and [b]will cut off

14:2 [a]ch. 11:31
14:3 [1]Heb. *in thine hand* [2]Or, *cakes* [3]Or, *bottle* [a]See 1 Sam. 9:7,8
14:4 [1]Heb. *stood for* [*his*] *hoariness* [a]ch. 11:29
14:6 [1]Heb. *hard*
14:7 [a]See 2 Sam. 12:7,8
14:8 [a]ch. 11:31 [b]ch. 11:33,38; 15:5
14:9 [a]ch. 12:28; 2 Chr. 11:15 [b]Neh. 9:26; Ps. 50:17
14:10 [a]ch. 15:29 [b]ch. 21:21; 2 Ki. 9:8
14:10 [c]Deut. 32:36; 2 Ki. 14:26
14:11 [a]ch. 16:4; 21:24
14:12 [a]ver. 17
14:13 [a]2 Chr. 12:12; 19:3
14:14 [a]ch. 15:27-29
14:15 [a]2 Ki. 17:6; Ps. 52:5 [b]Josh. 23:15,16 [c]2 Ki. 15:29 [d]Ex. 34:13; Deut. 12:3
14:16 [a]ch. 12:30; 13:34; 15:30,34; 16:2
14:17 [a]ch. 16:6,8 [b]ver. 12
14:18 [a]ver. 13

from Jeroboam *him that* pisseth against the
wall, [c]*and him that is* shut up and left in Israel, and will take away the remnant of the
house of Jeroboam, as *a man* taketh away
dung, till it be all gone.
11 [a]Him that dieth of Jeroboam in the city
shall the dogs eat; and him that dieth in the
field shall the fowls of the air eat: for the LORD
hath spoken *it.*
12 Arise thou therefore, get thee to thine
own house: *and* [a]when thy feet enter into the
city, the child shall die.
13 And all Israel shall mourn for him, and
bury him: for he only of Jeroboam shall come
to the grave, because in him [a]there is found
some good thing toward the LORD God of Israel in the house of Jeroboam.
14 [a]Moreover the LORD shall raise him up a
king over Israel, who shall cut off the house of
Jeroboam that day: but what? even now.
15 For the LORD shall smite Israel, as a reed
is shaken in the water, and he shall [a]root up Israel out of this [b]good land, which he gave to
their fathers, and shall scatter them [c]beyond
the river, [d]because they have made their
groves, provoking the LORD to anger.
16 And he shall give Israel up because of
the sins of Jeroboam, [a]who did sin, and who
made Israel to sin.
17 And Jeroboam's wife arose, and departed, and came to [a]Tirzah: *and* [b]when she came
to the threshold of the door, the child died;
18 And they buried him; and all Israel
mourned for him, [a]according to the word of
the LORD, which he spake by the hand of his
servant Ahijah the prophet.

14:3 *ten loaves.* The gift of an ordinary farmer (like Saul in 1 Sam 9:7–8) rather than that of a king (see 2 Ki 8:7–9).

14:5 *the LORD had said unto Ahijah.* See 1 Sam 9:15–17; 2 Ki 6:32 for other examples of divine revelation concerning an imminent visit.

14:6 *Come in, thou wife of Jeroboam.* Ahijah's recognition of the woman and his knowledge of the purpose of her visit served to authenticate his message as truly being the word of the Lord.

14:7–8 *exalted thee ... made thee prince ... rent the kingdom away.* Jeroboam is first reminded of the gracious acts of the Lord in his behalf (see 11:26,30–38).

14:8 *thou hast not been as my servant David.* Jeroboam had not responded to God's gracious acts and had ignored the requirements given when Ahijah told him he would become king (see 11:38).

14:9 *all that were before thee.* Jeroboam's wickedness surpassed that of Saul, David and Solomon in that he implemented a paganized system of worship for the entire populace of the northern kingdom. *other gods.* See notes on 12:28,30.

‡14:10 *him that is shut up and left.* I.e. the bond and the free without exception (see 21:21; 2 Ki 9:8; 14:26).

14:11 *him that dieth in the field shall the fowls of the air eat.* See note on 16:4. The covenant curse of Deut 28:26 is applied to Jeroboam's male descendants, none of whom will receive an honorable burial.

14:12 *child.* The Hebrew for this word allows for wide latitude in age (the same term is used for the young advisers of Rehoboam; see 12:8 and note). *shall die.* Although the death of Abijah was a severe disappointment to Jeroboam and his wife, it was an act of God's mercy to the prince, sparing him the disgrace and suffering that were to come on his father's house (see Is 57:1–2).

14:13 *all Israel shall mourn for him, and bury him.* Perhaps an indication that Abijah was the crown prince, and was well known and loved by the people. *grave.* He alone of Jeroboam's descendants would receive an honorable burial.

14:14 *a king ... who shall cut off the house of Jeroboam.* Ahijah looked beyond the brief reign of Nadab, Jeroboam's son (15:25–26), to the revolt of Baasha (15:27–16:7).

‡14:15 *as a reed is shaken in the water.* Descriptive of the instability of the royal house in the northern kingdom, which was to be characterized by assassinations and revolts (see 15:27–28; 16:16; 2 Ki 9:24; 15:10,14,25,30). *he shall root up Israel.* The list of curses for covenant breaking found in Deuteronomy climaxes in forced exile for God's people from the land of promise (Deut 28:63–64; 29:25–28). *groves.* Hebrew is *Asherim.* Ahijah perceived that Jeroboam's use of golden bulls in worship would inevitably lead to the adoption of other elements of Canaanite nature religion. The goddess Asherah was the consort of El (see notes on Ex 34:13; Judg 2:13), and the Asherim were probably wooden representations of the goddess (see note on Ex 34:13).

14:16 *sins of Jeroboam.* See 12:26–33; 13:33–34. *who made Israel to sin.* A phrase repeated often in 1,2 Kings (e.g., 15:26; 16:2,13,19,26).

14:17 *Tirzah.* Used by the kings of Israel as the royal city until Omri purchased and built up Samaria to serve that purpose (16:24). It is probably modern Tell el-Far'ah, about seven miles north of Shechem (see note on Sol 6:4).

19 And the rest of the acts of Jeroboam, how he [a]warred, and how he reigned, behold they *are* written in the book of the chronicles of the kings of Israel.

20 And the days which Jeroboam reigned *were* two and twenty years: and he [1]slept with his fathers, and Nadab his son reigned in his stead.

Rehoboam, king of Judah

21 ¶ And Rehoboam the son of Solomon reigned in Judah. [a]Rehoboam *was* forty and one years old when he *began* to reign, and he reigned seventeen years in Jerusalem, the city [b]which the LORD did choose out of all the tribes of Israel, to put his name there. [c]And his mother's name *was* Naamah an Ammonitess.

22 [a]And Judah did evil in the sight of the LORD, and they [b]provoked him to jealousy with their sins which they had committed, above all that their fathers had done.

23 For they also built them [a]high places, and [1]images, [b]and groves, on every high hill, and [c]under every green tree.

24 [a]And there were also sodomites in the land: *and* they did according to all the abominations of the nations which the LORD cast out before the children of Israel.

25 ¶ [a]And it came to pass in the fifth year of king Rehoboam, *that* Shishak king of Egypt came up against Jerusalem:

14:19 [a]2 Chr. 13:2
14:20 [1]Heb. *lay down*
14:21 [a]2 Chr. 12:13 [b]ch. 11:36 [c]ver. 31
14:22 [a]2 Chr. 12:1 [b]Deut. 32:21
14:23 [1]Or, *standing images,* or, *statues* [a]Deut. 12:2; Ezek. 16:24,25 [b]2 Ki. 17:9,10 [c]Is. 57:5
14:24 [a]Deut. 23:17; ch. 15:12; 2 Ki. 23:7
14:25 [a]ch. 11:40; 2 Chr. 12:2
14:26 [a]2 Chr. 12:9-11 [b]ch. 10:17
14:27 [1]Heb. *runners*
14:29 [a]2 Chr. 12:15
14:30 [a]ch. 12:24; 15:6; 2 Chr. 12:15
14:31 [1][2 Chr. 12:16, *Abijah*] [a]2 Chr. 12:16 [b]ver. 21 [c]Mat. 1:7, *Abia*
15:1 [a]2 Chr. 13:1
15:2 [1][2 Chr. 13:2, *Michaiah the daughter of Uriel*] [2][2 Chr. 11:21, *Absalom*] [a]2 Chr. 11:20-22

26 [a]And he took away the treasures of the house of the LORD, and the treasures of the king's house; he even took away all: and he took away all the shields of gold [b]which Solomon had made.

27 And king Rehoboam made in their stead brasen shields, and committed *them* unto the hands of the chief of the [1]guard, which kept the door of the king's house.

28 And it was *so,* when the king went *into* the house of the LORD, *that* the guard bare them, and brought them back into the guard chamber.

29 [a]Now the rest of the acts of Rehoboam, and all that he did, *are* they not written in the book of the chronicles of the kings of Judah?

30 And there was [a]war between Rehoboam and Jeroboam all *their* days.

31 [a]And Rehoboam slept with his fathers, and was buried with his fathers in the city of David. [b]And his mother's name *was* Naamah an Ammonitess. And [c][1]Abijam his son reigned in his stead.

Abijam, king of Judah

15 Now [a]in the eighteenth year of king Jeroboam the son of Nebat reigned Abijam over Judah.

2 Three years reigned he in Jerusalem. [a]And his mother's name *was* [1]Maachah, the daughter of [2]Abishalom.

3 And he walked in all the sins of his father,

14:19 *warred.* See v. 30; 15:6; 2 Chr 13:2–20. *chronicles of the kings of Israel.* A record of the reigns of the kings of the northern kingdom used by the author of 1,2 Kings and apparently accessible to those interested in further details of the history of the reigns of Israelite kings. It is not to be confused with the canonical book of 1,2 Chronicles, which was written later than 1,2 Kings and contains the history of the reigns of the kings of Judah only (see Introduction: Author, Sources and Date).

14:20 *two and twenty years.* 930–909 B.C. *slept with his fathers.* See note on 1:21. *Nadab.* See 15:25–32.

14:21 *forty and one years old.* Rehoboam was born shortly before David's death (see 11:42; see also note on 2:24). *seventeen years.* 930–913 B.C. *city which the LORD did choose . . . to put his name.* See 9:3; Ps 132:13.

14:22 *Judah did evil in the sight of the LORD.* The reign of Rehoboam is described in greater detail in 2 Chr 11–12. The priests and Levites who immigrated to Judah from the north led the country to follow the way of David and Solomon for the first three years of Rehoboam's reign (see 12:24; 2 Chr 11:17). In later years Rehoboam and the people of Judah turned away from the Lord (2 Chr 12:1).

‡14:23 *high places.* See note on 3:2. *images* [i.e. "sacred pillars"]. Stone pillars, bearing a religious significance, that were placed next to the altars. The use of such pillars was common among the Canaanites and was explicitly forbidden to the Israelites in the Mosaic law (Ex 23:24; Lev 26:1; Deut 16:21–22). It is likely that the pillars were intended to be representations of the deity (2 Ki 3:2). For legitimate uses of stone pillars see Gen 28:18; 31:45; Ex 24:4. *groves.* See note on v. 15.

‡14:24 *sodomites.* I.e. male cult prostitutes. Ritual prostitution was an important feature of Canaanite fertility religion. The Israelites had been warned by Moses not to engage in this abominable practice (see Deut 23:17–18; see also 1 Ki 15:12; 2 Ki 23:7; Hos 4:14).

14:25 *fifth year of king Rehoboam.* 926 B.C. *Shishak.* See notes on 3:1; 11:40. *came up against Jerusalem.* Shishak's invasion is described in more detail in 2 Chr 12:2–4 and is also attested in a victory inscription found on the walls of the temple of Amun in Thebes, where numerous cities that Shishak plundered in both Judah and the northern kingdom are listed. 2 Chr 12:5–8 indicates that fear of the impending invasion led to a temporary reformation in Judah.

14:26 *shields of gold which Solomon had made.* See 10:16–17.

14:27 *brasen shields.* The reduced realm could not match the great wealth Solomon had accumulated in Jerusalem (see 10:21,23,27).

14:29 *chronicles of the kings of Judah.* A record of the reigns of the kings of Judah similar to the one for the kings of the northern kingdom (see note on v. 19; see also Introduction: Author, Sources and Date).

14:30 *war . . . all their days.* See notes on v. 19; 12:24.

14:31 *slept with his fathers.* See note on 1:21.

15:1 *eighteenth year of king Jeroboam.* The first of numerous synchronisms in 1,2 Kings between the reigns of the kings in the north and those in Judah (see, e.g., vv. 9,25,33; 16:8,15,29; see also Introduction: Chronology). *Abijam.* A variant of Abijah; see note on 14:1. Both Rehoboam and Jeroboam had sons by this name.

‡15:2 *Three years.* 913–910 B.C. *Maachah, the daughter of Abishalom.* Absalom in 2 Chr 11:20. Abijah's mother is said to be a daughter of Uriel of Gibeah in 2 Chr 13:2. It is likely that Maachah was the granddaughter of Absalom and the daughter of a marriage between Tamar (Absalom's daughter; see 2 Sam 14:27) and Uriel. Absalom's mother was also named Maacah (2 Sam 3:3).

15:3 *sins of his father.* See 14:22–24. *not perfect with the LORD*

Rulers of the Divided Kingdom of Israel and Judah

DATA AND DATES IN ORDER OF SEQUENCE

SCRIPTURE	KINGS	SYNCHRONISM OR CORRELATION	LENGTH OF REIGN	HISTORICAL DATA	DATES
1. *1 Ki 12:1-24* *1 Ki 14:21-31*	***Rehoboam*** *(Judah)*		*17 years*		*930-913*
2. 1 Ki 12:25–14:20	**Jeroboam I** (Israel)		22 years		930-909
3. *1 Ki 15:1-8*	***Abijah (Abijam)*** *(Judah)*	*18th of Jeroboam*	*3 years*		*913-910*
4. *1 Ki 15:9-24*	***Asa*** *(Judah)*	*20th of Jeroboam*	*41 years*		*910-869*
5. 1 Ki 15:25-31	**Nadab** (Israel)	2nd of Asa	2 years		909-908
6. 1 Ki 15:32–16:7	**Baasha** (Israel)	3rd of Asa	24 years		908-886
7. 1 Ki 16:8-14	**Elah** (Israel)	26th of Asa	2 years		886-885
8. 1 Ki 16:15-20	**Zimri** (Israel)	27th of Asa	7days		885
9. 1 Ki 16:21-22	**Tibni** (Israel)			Overlap with Omri	885-880
10. 1 Ki 16:23-28	**Omri** (Israel)	27th of Asa 31st of Asa	 12 years	Made king by the people Overlap with Tibni Official reign = 11 actual years Beginning of sole reign	885 885-880 885-874 880
11. 1 Ki 16:29–22:40	**Ahab** (Israel)	38th of Asa	22 years	Official reign = 21 actual years	874-853
12. *1 Ki 22:41-50*	***Jehoshaphat*** *(Judah)*	 *4th of Ahab*	 *25 years*	*Co-regency with Asa* *Official reign* *Beginning of sole reign* *Has Jehoram as regent*	*872-869* *872-848* *869* *853-848*
13. 1 Ki 22:51– 2 Ki 1:18	**Ahaziah** (Israel)	17th of Jehoshaphat	2 years	Official reign = 1 yr. actual reign	853-852
14. 2 Ki 1:17 2 Ki 3:1–8:15	**Joram (Jehoram)** (Israel)	2nd of Jehoram 18th of Jehoshaphat	 12 years	 Official reign = 11 actual years	852 852-841
15. *2 Ki 8:16-24*	***Jehoram*** *(Judah)*	*5th of Joram*	 *8 years*	*Beginning of sole reign* *Official reign = 7 actual years*	*848* *848-841*
16. *2 Ki 8:25-29* *2 Ki 9:29*	***Ahaziah*** *(Judah)*	*12th of Joram* *11th of Joram*	*1 year*	*Nonaccession-year reckoning* *Accession-year reckoning*	*841* *841*
17. 2 Ki 9:30–10:36	**Jehu** (Israel)		28 years		841-814
18. *2 Ki 11*	***Athaliah*** *(Judah)*		*7 years*		*841-835*
19. *2 Ki 12*	***Joash (Jehoash)*** *(Judah)*	*7th of Jehu*	*40 years*		*835-796*
20. 2 Ki 13:1-9	**Jehoahaz** (Israel)	23rd of Joash	17 years		814-798
21. 2 Ki 13:10-25	**Jehoash (Joash)** (Israel)	37th of Joash	16 years		798-782

SCRIPTURE	KINGS	SYNCHRONISM OR CORRELATION	LENGTH OF REIGN	HISTORICAL DATA	DATES
22. *2 Ki 14:1-22*	***Amaziah*** *(Judah)*	*2nd of Jehoash*	*29 years*		*796-767*
				Overlap with Azariah	*792-767*
23. 2 Ki 14:23-29	**Jeroboam II** (Israel)			Co-regency with Jehoash	793-782
			41 years	Total reign	793-753
		15th of Amaziah		Beginning of sole reign	782
24. *2 Ki 15:1-7*	***Azariah (Uzziah)*** *(Judah)*			*Overlap with Amaziah*	*792-767*
			52 years	*Total reign*	*792-740*
		27th of Jeroboam		*Beginning of sole reign*	*767*
25. 2 Ki 15:8-12	**Zachariah** (Israel)	38th of Azariah	6 months		753
26. 2 Ki 15:13-15	**Shallum** (Israel)	39th of Azariah	1 month		752
27. 2 Ki 15:16-22	**Menahem** (Israel)	39th of Azariah	10 years	Ruled in Samaria	752-742
28. 2 Ki 15:23-26	**Pekahiah** (Israel)	50th of Azariah	2 years		742-740
29. 2 Ki 15:27-31	**Pekah** (Israel)			In Gilead; overlapping years	752-740
			20 years	Total reign	752-732
		52nd of Azariah		Beginning of sole reign	740
30. *2 Ki 15:32-38*	***Jotham*** *(Judah)*			*Co-regency with Azariah*	*750-740*
2 Ki 15:30			*16 years*	*Official reign*	*750-735*
				Reign to his 20th year	*750-732*
		2nd of Pekah		*Beginning of co-regency*	*750*
31. *2 Ki 16*	***Ahaz*** *(Judah)*			*Total reign*	*735-715*
		17th of Pekah			*735*
			16 years	*From 20th of Jotham*	*732-715*
32. 2 Ki 15:30	**Hoshea** (Israel)			20th of Jotham	732
2 Ki 17		12th of Ahaz*	9 years		732-722
33. *2 Ki 18:1–20:21*	***Hezekiah*** *(Judah)*	*3rd of Hoshea**	*29 years*		*715-686*
34. *2 Ki 21:1-18*	***Manasseh*** *(Judah)*			*Co-regency with Hezekiah*	*697-686*
			55 years	*Total reign*	*697-642*
35. *2 Ki 21:19-26*	***Amon*** *(Judah)*		*2 years*		*642-640*
36. *2 Ki 22:1–23:30*	***Josiah*** *(Judah)*		*31 years*		*640-609*
37. *2 Ki 23:31-33*	***Jehoahaz*** *(Judah)*		*3 months*		*609*
38. *2 Ki 23:34–24:7*	***Jehoiakim*** *(Judah)*		*11 years*		*609-598*
39. *2 Ki 24:8-17*	***Jehoiachin*** *(Judah)*		*3 months*		*598-597*
40. *2 Ki 24:18–25:26*	***Zedekiah*** *(Judah)*		*11 years*		*597-586*

*These data arise when the reign of Hoshea is thrown 12 years in advance of its historical position.

*Italics denote kings of **Judah**.*
Non-italic type denotes kings of **Israel**.

which he had done before him: and [a]his heart
was not perfect with the LORD his God, as the
heart of David his father.
4 Nevertheless [a]for David's sake did the
LORD his God give him a [b][1]lamp in Jerusalem,
to set up his son after him, and to establish Jerusalem:
5 Because David [a]did *that* which *was* right
in the eyes of the LORD, and turned not aside
from any *thing* that he commanded him all the
days of his life, [b]save only in the matter of Urijah the Hittite.
6 [a]And there was war between Rehoboam
and Jeroboam all the days of his life.
7 [a]Now the rest of the acts of Abijam, and
all that he did, *are* they not written in the book
of the chronicles of the kings of Judah? And
there was war between Abijam and Jeroboam.
8 [a]And Abijam slept with his fathers; and
they buried him in the city of David: and Asa
his son reigned in his stead.

Asa, king of Judah

9 ¶ And in the twentieth year of Jeroboam
king of Israel reigned Asa over Judah.
10 And forty and one years reigned he in
Jerusalem. And his [1]mother's name *was*
Maachah, the daughter of Abishalom.
11 [a]And Asa did *that* which *was* right in
the eyes of the LORD, as *did* David his father.
12 [a]And he took away the sodomites out of
the land, and removed all the idols that his fathers had made.
13 And also [a]Maachah his mother, even her
he removed from *being* queen, because she had
made an idol in a grove; and Asa [1]destroyed her
idol, and [b]burnt *it* by the brook Kidron.
14 [a]But the high places were not removed:
nevertheless Asa's [b]heart was perfect with the
LORD all his days.
15 And he brought in *the* [1]*things* which
his father had dedicated, and *the things* which
himself had dedicated, *into* the house of the
LORD, silver, and gold, and vessels.
16 ¶ And there was war between Asa and
Baasha king of Israel all their days.
17 And [a]Baasha king of Israel went up
against Judah, and built [b]Ramah, [c]that *he*
might not suffer *any* to go out or come in to
Asa king of Judah.
18 Then Asa took all the silver and the gold
that were left in the treasures of the house of
the LORD, and the treasures of the king's
house, and delivered them into the hand of his
servants: and king Asa sent them to [a]Ben-ha-
dad, the son of Tabrimon, the son of Hezion,
king of Syria, that dwelt at [b]Damascus, saying,
19 *There is* a league between me and thee,
and between my father and thy father: behold,
I have sent unto thee a present of silver and
gold; come *and* break thy league with Baasha
king of Israel, that he may [1]depart from me.

15:3 [a]ch. 11:4; Ps. 119:80
15:4 [1]Or, *candle* [a]ch. 11:32,36; 2 Chr. 21:7 [b]ch. 11:36
15:5 [a]ch. 14:8 [b]2 Sam. 11:4,15; 12:9
15:6 [a]ch. 14:30
15:7 [a]2 Chr. 13:2,3,22
15:8 [a]2 Chr. 14:1
15:10 [1]That is, *grandmother*['s]
15:11 [a]2 Chr. 14:2
15:12 [a]ch. 14:24; 22:46
15:13 [1]Heb. *cut off* [a]2 Chr. 15:16 [b]Ex. 32:20
15:14 [a]ch. 22:43; 2 Chr. 15:17,18 [b]See ver. 3
15:15 [1]Heb. *holy*
15:17 [a]2 Chr. 16:1 [b]Josh. 18:25 [c]See ch. 12:27
15:18 [a]2 Chr. 16:2 [b]ch. 11:23,24
15:19 [1]Heb. *go up*

his God, as . . . David his father. Although David fell into grievous sin, his heart was never divided between serving the Lord and serving the nature deities of the Canaanites.

15:4 *lamp in Jerusalem.* See note on 11:36.

15:5 *Urijah the Hittite.* See 2 Sam 11.

15:6 *Rehoboam.* See note on 12:24.

15:7 *rest of the acts of Abijam.* See 2 Chr 13. *chronicles of the kings of Judah.* See note on 14:29. *war between Abijam and Jeroboam.* Cf. v. 6; 14:30. From 2 Chr 13 it is clear that the chronic hostile relations of preceding years flared into serious combat in which Abijam defeated Jeroboam and took several towns from him, including Beth-el (2 Chr 13:19).

15:8 *slept with his fathers.* See note on 1:21.

15:9 *twentieth year of Jeroboam.* 910 B.C. (see note on 14:20).

15:10 *forty and one years.* 910–869 B.C. *Maachah, the daughter of Abishalom.* See note on v. 2.

15:12 *sodomites.* See note on 14:24. *removed all the idols that his fathers had made.* See 14:23.

‡15:13 *Maachah his mother . . . he removed.* 2 Chr 14:1–15:16 indicates a progression in Asa's reform over a period of years. Although Asa had destroyed pagan idols and altars early in his reign (2 Chr 14:2–3), it was not until after a victory over Zerah the Ethiopian (2 Chr 14:8–15) that Asa responded to the message of the prophet Azariah son of Oded by calling for a covenant renewal assembly in Jerusalem in the 15th year of his reign (2 Chr 15:10). After this assembly Asa deposed his grandmother (the Hebrew for "mother" here means "grandmother," a common usage) Maachah because of her idolatry (2 Chr 15:16). *made an idol in a grove.* See note on 14:15. It appears that Maachah's action was a deliberate attempt to counter Asa's reform.

15:14 *the high places were not removed.* The reference here and in 2 Chr 15:17 is to those high places where the Lord was worshiped (for the question of legitimacy of worship of the Lord at high places see note on 3:2). When 2 Chr 14:3 indicates that Asa removed the high places, it is to be taken as a reference to the high places that were centers of pagan Canaanite worship (see 2 Chr 17:6; 20:33 for the same distinction). This same statement of qualified approval that is made of Asa is made of five other kings of Judah prior to the time of Hezekiah (Jehoshaphat, 22:43; Joash, 2 Ki 12:3; Amaziah, 2 Ki 14:4; Azariah, 2 Ki 15:4; Jotham, 2 Ki 15:35). *perfect with the LORD.* See note on v. 3.

15:15 *things which himself had dedicated . . . silver, and gold.* Most likely consisting of war booty that Abijam had taken from Jeroboam (2 Chr 13) and that Asa acquired from Zerah the Ethiopian (2 Chr 14:8–15).

15:16 *war between Asa and Baasha . . . all their days.* A reference to the chronic hostile relations that had existed ever since the division of the kingdom, rather than to full-scale combat (see notes on v. 7; 12:24; see also 2 Chr 15:19).

‡15:17 *built* [i.e."fortified"] *Ramah.* Baasha had recaptured the territory previously taken from Jeroboam by Abijam (see note on v. 7; see also 2 Chr 13:19) since Ramah was located south of Beth-el and only about five miles north of Jerusalem. *might not suffer any to go out or come in to Asa.* See 2 Chr 15:9–10.

15:18 *silver and the gold that were left.* That which remained after the plundering of Jerusalem by Shishak of Egypt (see 14:25). *Hezion.* It is not clear whether Hezion is to be identified with Rezon of Damascus (see 11:23–25) or regarded as the founder of a new dynasty.

15:19 *league . . . between my father and thy father.* A reference to a previously unmentioned treaty between Abijam and Tabrimmon of Aram. When Tabrimmon died, Baasha succeeded in establishing a treaty with his successor Ben-hadad. Asa saw no hope for success against Baasha without the assistance provided by a renewal of the old treaty with Aram. Although his plan seemed to be successful, it was condemned by Hanani the prophet as a foolish act and a denial of reliance on the Lord (see 2 Chr 16:7–10). The true theocratic king was never to fear

20 So Ben-hadad hearkened unto king Asa,
and sent the captains of the hosts which he
had against the cities of Israel, and smote
[a]Ijon, and [b]Dan, and [c]Abel-beth-maachah, and
all Cinneroth, with all the land of Naphtali.
21 And it came to pass, when Baasha heard
thereof, that he left off building of Ramah, and
dwelt in Tirzah.
22 [a]Then king Asa made a proclamation
throughout all Judah; none *was* [1]exempted:
and they took away the stones of Ramah, and
the timber thereof, where*with* Baasha had
builded; and king Asa built with them [b]Geba
of Benjamin, and [c]Mizpah.
23 The rest of all the acts of Asa, and all his
might, and all that he did, and the cities which
he built, *are* they not written in the book of
the chronicles of the kings of Judah? Nevertheless [a]in the time of his old age he was diseased in his feet.
24 And Asa slept with his fathers, and was
buried with his fathers in the city of David his
father: [a]and [1]Jehoshaphat his son reigned in
his stead.

Nadab, king of Israel

25 ¶ And Nadab the son of Jeroboam [1]*began* to reign over Israel in the second year of
Asa king of Judah, and reigned over Israel two
years.
26 And he did evil in the sight of the LORD,
and walked in the way of his father, and in
[a]his sin wherewith he made Israel to sin.
27 [a]And Baasha the son of Ahijah, of the
house of Issachar, conspired against him; and
Baasha smote him at [b]Gibbethon, which *belongeth* to the Philistines; for Nadab and all Israel laid siege to Gibbethon.
28 Even in the third year of Asa king of Judah did Baasha slay him, and reigned in his
stead.
29 And it came to pass, when he reigned,
that he smote all the house of Jeroboam; he
left not to Jeroboam any that breathed, until
he had destroyed him, according unto [a]the
saying of the LORD, which he spake by his servant Ahijah the Shilonite:
30 [a]Because of the sins of Jeroboam which
he sinned, and which he made Israel sin, by
his provocation where*with* he provoked the
LORD God of Israel to anger.
31 Now the rest of the acts of Nadab, and
all that he did, *are* they not written in the book
of the chronicles of the kings of Israel?

Baasha, king of Israel

32 ¶ [a]And there was war between Asa and
Baasha king of Israel all their days.
33 In the third year of Asa king of Judah *began* Baasha the son of Ahijah to reign over all
Israel in Tirzah, twenty and four years.
34 And he did evil in the sight of the LORD,
and walked in [a]the way of Jeroboam and in his
sin wherewith he made Israel to sin.
16 Then the word of the LORD came to
[a]Jehu the son of Hanani against Baasha, saying,
2 [a]Forasmuch as I exalted thee out of the
dust, and made thee prince over my people Israel; and [b]thou hast walked in the way of Jero-

15:20 [a]2 Ki. 15:29 [b]Judg. 18:29 [c]2 Sam. 20:14
15:22 [1]Heb. *free* [a]2 Chr. 16:6 [b]Josh. 21:17 [c]Josh. 18:26
15:23 [a]2 Chr. 16:12
15:24 [1]Mat. 1:8, called *Josaphat* [a]2 Chr. 17:1
15:25 [1]Heb. *reigned*
15:26 [a]ch. 12:30; 14:16
15:27 [a]ch. 14:14
15:27 [b]Josh. 19:44
15:29 [a]ch. 14:10,14
15:30 [a]ch. 14:9,16
15:32 [a]ver. 16
15:34 [a]ch. 12:28,29; 13:33; 14:16
16:1 [a]ver. 7; 2 Chr. 19:2; 20:34
16:2 [a]ch. 14:7 [b]ch. 15:34

his enemies but to trust in the God of the covenant for security and protection (see note on 1 Sam 17:11). Ahaz was later to follow Asa's bad example and seek Assyria's help when he was attacked by Israel and Aram (see 2 Ki 16:5–9; Is 7).

15:20 *Naphtali.* The cities that Ben-hadad conquered in Naphtali were of particular importance because the major trade routes from Damascus going west to Tyre and southwest through the plain of Jezreel to the coastal plain and Egypt transversed this area. This same territory was later seized by the Assyrian ruler Tiglath-pileser III (2 Ki 15:29).

15:21 *Tirzah.* See note on 14:17.

15:22 *proclamation throughout all Judah.* Asa's action is reminiscent of the labor force conscripted by Solomon (5:13–14; 11:28). *Geba . . . Mizpah.* Asa established two border fortresses to check Baasha's desire to expand his territory southward. Geba was east of Ramah, and Mizpah was southwest of Ramah.

15:23 *rest of all the acts of Asa.* See 2 Chr 14:2–16:14. *chronicles of the kings of Judah.* See note on 14:29. *diseased in his feet.* See 2 Chr 16:12.

15:24 *slept with his fathers.* See note on 1:21. *Jehoshaphat his son reigned in his stead.* For the reign of Jehoshaphat see 22:41–50; 2 Chr 17:1–21:1.

15:25 *second year of Asa.* See note on v. 1. The second year of Asa of Judah corresponded to the 22nd and last year of Jeroboam of Israel (see v. 9; 14:20). *two years.* 909–908 B.C.

15:26 *his sin wherewith he made Israel to sin.* Jeroboam's sin (see note on 14:16). Although Abijam of Judah occupied Beth-el during the reign of Jeroboam (see note on v. 7), it is probable that the paganized worship Jeroboam initiated was continued elsewhere until control of Beth-el was regained by Baasha.

15:27 *Gibbethon.* A town located between Jerusalem and Joppa (probably a few miles west of Gezer) in the territory originally assigned to Dan (Josh 19:43–45). This Levitical city (Josh 21:23) probably fell into Philistine hands at the time of the Philistine expansion in the period of the judges.

15:28 *third year of Asa.* 908 B.C. (see note on v. 10). It is likely that Baasha was a commander in Nadab's army and was able to secure the support of the military for his revolt.

15:29 *the saying . . . he spake by . . . Ahijah.* See 14:10–11.

15:30 *sins of Jeroboam which he sinned, and which he made Israel sin.* See note on 14:16.

15:31 *chronicles of the kings of Israel.* See note on 14:19.

15:32 *war . . . all their days.* See note on v. 16. The demise of Jeroboam's dynasty did not improve relations between the two kingdoms.

15:33 *third year of Asa.* 908 B.C. (see note on v. 10). *Tirzah.* See note on 14:17. *twenty and four years.* 908–886 B.C. His official years were counted as 24, though his actual years were 23 (see 16:8; see also Introduction: Chronology).

15:34 *his sin wherewith he made Israel to sin.* See note on 14:16. The assessment of Baasha's reign indicates no improvement over the reign of Nadab, whom he replaced (see v. 26).

16:1 *Jehu.* Like his father before him (see 2 Chr 16:7–10), Jehu brought God's word of condemnation to a king. Much as the man of God from Judah (see note on 13:1) and later the prophet Amos, he was sent from the south to a northern king. His ministry continued for about 50 years until the reign of Jehoshaphat of Judah (2 Chr 19:2; 20:34).

16:2 *I exalted thee out of the dust.* Cf. 14:7. *walked in the way of Jeroboam.* See note on 14:16.

boam, and hast made my people Israel to sin,
to provoke me to anger with their sins;
3 Behold, I will [a]take away the posterity of
Baasha, and the posterity of his house; and will
make thy house like [b]the house of Jeroboam
the son of Nebat.
4 [a]Him that dieth of Baasha in the city shall
the dogs eat; and him that dieth of his in the
fields shall the fowls of the air eat.
5 Now the rest of the acts of Baasha, and
what he did, and his might, [a]*are* they not written in the book of the chronicles of the kings
of Israel?
6 So Baasha slept with his fathers, and was
buried in [a]Tirzah: and Elah his son reigned in
his stead.
7 And also by the hand of the prophet
[a]Jehu the son of Hanani came the word of the
LORD against Baasha, and against his house,
even for all the evil that he did in the sight of
the LORD, in provoking him to anger with the
work of his hands, in being like the house of
Jeroboam; and because [b]he killed him.

Elah, king of Israel

8 ¶ In the twenty and sixth year of Asa king
of Judah *began* Elah the son of Baasha to reign
over Israel in Tirzah, two years.
9 [a]And his servant Zimri, captain of half
his chariots, conspired against him, as he *was*
in Tirzah, drinking *himself* drunk *in* the house
of Arza [1]steward of *his* house in Tirzah.
10 And Zimri went in and smote him, and
killed him, in the twenty and seventh year of
Asa king of Judah, and reigned in his stead.
11 And it came to pass, when he *began* to
reign, as soon as he sat on his throne, *that* he
slew all the house of Baasha: he left him [a]not
one that pisseth against a wall, [1]neither *of* his
kinsfolks, nor *of* his friends.
12 Thus did Zimri destroy all the house of
Baasha, [a]according to the word of the LORD,
which he spake against Baasha [b1]by Jehu the
prophet,
13 For all the sins of Baasha, and the sins of
Elah his son, *by* which they sinned, and *by*
which they made Israel to sin, in provoking the
LORD God of Israel to anger [a]with their vanities.
14 Now the rest of the acts of Elah, and all
that he did, *are* they not written in the book of
the chronicles of the kings of Israel?

Zimri, king of Israel

15 ¶ In the twenty and seventh year of Asa
king of Judah did Zimri reign seven days in Tirzah. And the people *were* encamped [a]against
Gibbethon, which *belonged* to the Philistines.
16 And the people that *were* encamped
heard say, Zimri hath conspired, and hath also
slain the king: wherefore all Israel made Omri,
the captain of the host, king over Israel that
day in the camp.
17 And Omri went up from Gibbethon,
and all Israel with him, and they besieged Tirzah.
18 And it came to pass, when Zimri saw
that the city was taken, that he went into the
palace of the king's house, and burnt the king's
house over him with fire, and died,
19 For his sins which he sinned in doing
evil in the sight of the LORD, [a]in walking in the
way of Jeroboam, and in his sin which he did,
to make Israel sin.
20 Now the rest of the acts of Zimri, and
his treason that he wrought, *are* they not written in the book of the chronicles of the kings
of Israel?

Omri, king of Israel

21 ¶ Then were the people of Israel divided
into two parts: half of the people followed Tibni the son of Ginath, to make him king; and
half followed Omri.
22 But the people that followed Omri prevailed against the people that followed Tibni

16:3 [a]ver. 11 [b]ch. 14:10; 15:29
16:4 [a]ch. 14:11
16:5 [a]2 Chr. 16:1
16:6 [a]ch. 14:17; 15:21
16:7 [a]ver. 1 [b]ch. 15:27,29; See Hos. 1:4
16:9 [1]Heb. *which was over* [a]2 Ki. 9:31
16:11 [1]Or, *both his kinsmen and his friends* [a]1 Sam. 25:22
16:12 [a]ver. 3
16:12 [1]Heb. *by the hand of* [b]ver. 1
16:13 [a]Deut. 32:21; 1 Sam. 12:21; Is. 41:29; Jonah 2:8; 1 Cor. 8:4; 10:19
16:15 [a]ch. 15:27
16:19 [a]ch. 12:28; 15:26,34

16:3 *take away the posterity of Baasha, and . . . his house.* Cf. 14:10 (the house of Jeroboam); 21:21 (the house of Omri and Ahab).
16:4 Identical to the prophecy against Jeroboam's dynasty in 14:11.
16:5 *his might.* For the purposes of the writer of Kings (see Introduction: Theme), it was not necessary to list any of Baasha's achievements. He may have been a very successful ruler from a military-political point of view. *chronicles of the kings of Israel.* See note on 14:19.
16:6 *slept with his fathers.* See note on 1:21.
‡16:7 *evil that he did . . . like the house of Jeroboam.* See v. 2; 15:34. *he killed him.* Lit."he struck it" [i.e. he struck Jeroboam's house]. Although Baasha fulfilled God's purpose (14:10,14) in destroying the house of Jeroboam, he remained responsible for this violent and unlawful act (cf. Gen 50:20; Is 10:5–7,12).
16:8 *twenty and sixth year of Asa.* 886 B.C. (see note on 15:10; see also Introduction: Chronology). *two years.* 886–885 B.C.
16:9 *drinking himself drunk.* The fact that Elah was carousing at Tirzah while the army was laying siege to Gibbethon (v. 15) indicates he had little perception of his responsibilities as king.
16:10 *twenty and seventh year of Asa.* 885 B.C.
16:11 *slew all the house of Baasha.* See 15:29; 2 Ki 10:1–7; 11:1. *friends.* Probably including the chief adviser to the king (see note on 2 Sam 15:37).
16:12 *word of the LORD . . . by Jehu the prophet.* See vv. 1–4. Zimri did not consciously decide to fulfill Jehu's prophecy, but unwittingly he became the instrument by which Jehu's prediction was fulfilled (see note on v. 7) when he conspired against Elah and destroyed the dynasty of Baasha.
16:13 *sins of Baasha, and . . . Elah his son, by which they sinned.* See 15:34. *vanities.* A reference to all the paganism in Israel's religious observances, including the use of the golden calves in worship (see 12:28; 14:9).
16:14 *chronicles of the kings of Israel.* See note on 14:19.
16:15 *twenty and seventh year of Asa.* 885 B.C. (see notes on 15:1,10). *Gibbethon.* See notes on v. 9; 15:27.
16:16 *conspired, and . . . slain the king.* See vv. 9–12. *Omri, the captain of the host.* He held a higher rank than Zimri did under Elah (v. 9).
16:17 *Tirzah.* The royal residence (see vv. 8–10; see also note on 14:17).
16:19 *way of Jeroboam.* See note on 14:16.
16:20 *chronicles of the kings of Israel.* See note on 14:19.

the son of Ginath: so Tibni died, and Omri
reigned.
23 In the thirty and first year of Asa king of
Judah *began* Omri to reign over Israel, twelve
years: six years reigned he in Tirzah.
24 And he bought the hill Samaria of Shemer for two talents of silver, and built *on* the
hill, and called the name of the city which he
built, after the name of Shemer, owner of the
hill, [a][1]Samaria.
25 But [a]Omri wrought evil in the eyes of
the LORD, and did worse than all that *were* before him.
26 For he [a]walked in all the way of Jeroboam the son of Nebat, and in his sin wherewith
he made Israel to sin, to provoke the LORD God
of Israel to anger with their [b]vanities.
27 Now the rest of the acts of Omri which
he did, and his might that he shewed, *are* they
not written in the book of the chronicles of the
kings of Israel?
28 So Omri slept with his fathers, and was
buried in Samaria: and Ahab his son reigned in
his stead.

16:24 [1]Heb. *Shomeron* [a]See ch. 13:32; 2 Ki. 17:24; John 4:4
16:25 [a]Mic. 6:16
16:26 [a]ver. 19 [b]ver. 13

16:31 [1]Heb. *was it a light thing, etc.* [a]Deut. 7:3 [b]Judg. 18:7 [c]ch. 21:25,26; 2 Ki. 10:18; 17:16
16:32 [a]2 Ki. 10:21,26,27
16:33 [a]2 Ki. 13:6; 17:10; 21:3; Jer. 17:2 [b]ver. 30; ch. 21:25

Ahab, king of Israel

29 ¶ And in the thirty and eighth year of
Asa king of Judah *began* Ahab the son of Omri
to reign over Israel: and Ahab the son of Omri
reigned over Israel in Samaria twenty and two
years.
30 And Ahab the son of Omri did evil in
the sight of the LORD above all that *were* before
him.
31 And it came to pass, [1]as if it had been a
light thing for him to walk in the sins of Jeroboam the son of Nebat, [a]that he took *to* wife
Jezebel the daughter of Ethbaal king of the [b]Zi-
donians, [c]and went and served Baal, and worshipped him.
32 And he reared up an altar for Baal *in*
[a]the house of Baal, which he had built in
Samaria.
33 [a]And Ahab made a grove; and Ahab
[b]did more to provoke the LORD God of Israel to
anger than all the kings of Israel that were before him.
34 ¶ In his days did Hiel the Bethelite build
Jericho: he laid the foundation thereof in Abi-

16:22 *Tibni died.* It is not clear whether Tibni's death was due to natural causes or the result of the military struggle for control of the land.
16:23 *thirty and first year of Asa.* 880 B.C. (see note on 15:10; see also Introduction: Chronology). *began . . . to reign.* Became sole king. The struggle for control of the northern kingdom between Omri and Tibni lasted four years (compare this verse with v. 15). *twelve years.* 885–874. The 12 years of Omri's reign include the four years of struggle between Omri and Tibni (cf. vv. 15,29). *Tirzah.* See note on 14:17. Omri had been able to capture Tirzah in a matter of days (vv. 15–19).
16:24 *Samaria.* Seven miles northwest of Shechem, Samaria rose about 300 feet above the surrounding fertile valleys (referred to as a "crown" in Is 28:1). The original owner may have been persuaded to sell his property (see 21:3) on the condition that the city be named after him (cf. Ruth 4:5). The site provided an ideal location for a nearly impregnable capital city for the northern kingdom (see 20:1–21; 2 Ki 6:25; 18:9–10). With the establishment of this royal city, the kings of the north came to possess a royal citadel-city like that of the Davidic dynasty (see 2 Sam 5:6–12). Archaeologists have discovered that Omri and Ahab also adorned it with magnificent structures to rival those Solomon had erected in Jerusalem. From this time on, the northern kingdom could be designated by the name of the royal city, just as the southern kingdom could be designated by its capital, Jerusalem (see, e.g., 21:1; Is 10:10; Amos 6:1).
16:25 *did worse than all.* Omri's alliance with Ethbaal of Tyre and Sidon (Omri's son Ahab married Ethbaal's daughter Jezebel to seal the alliance) led to widespread Baal worship in the northern kingdom (vv. 31–33) and eventually to the near extinction of the Davidic line in the southern kingdom (see 2 Ki 11; see also note on 2 Ki 8:18). This marriage alliance must have been established in the early years of Omri's reign (see note on v. 23), perhaps to strengthen his hand against Tibni (see vv. 21–22).
16:26 *sin wherewith he made Israel to sin.* See 12:26–33; see also note on 14:16. *vanities.* See note on v. 13.
16:27 *his might that he shewed.* Omri's military and political accomplishments were not of importance for the purposes of the writer of Kings (see Introduction: Theme). Apart from establishing Samaria as the capital of the northern kingdom, about all that is known of him is that he organized a governmental structure in the northern kingdom that was in place during the rule of his son, Ahab (see 20:14–15). Omri's dynasty, however, endured for over 40 years. A century and a half later (732 B.C.) Tiglath-pileser III of Assyria referred to Israel as the "house of Omri" in his annals. *chronicles of the kings of Israel.* See note on 14:19.
16:28 *slept with his fathers.* See note on 1:21.
16:29 *thirty and eighth year of Asa.* 874 B.C. (see notes on 15:9–10). *twenty and two years.* 874–853 B.C.
16:30 *did evil . . . above all.* Omri sinned more than those before him (see v. 25), and Ahab sinned more than his father had. Evil became progressively worse in the royal house of the northern kingdom. Nearly a third of the narrative material in 1,2 Kings concerns the 34-year period of the reigns of Ahab and his two sons, Ahaziah and Joram. In this period the struggle between the kingdom of God (championed especially by Elijah and Elisha) and the kingdom of Satan was especially intense.
16:31 *took to wife Jezebel the daughter of Ethbaal.* The Jewish historian Josephus refers to Ethbaal as a king-priest who ruled over Tyre and Sidon for 32 years. Ahab had already married Jezebel during the reign of his father (see note on v. 25). *Baal.* Perhaps Melqart, the local manifestation of Baal in Tyre, whose worship was brought to Israel by Jezebel. It is probable that Ahab participated in the worship of this deity at the time of his marriage. The names of Ahab's sons (Ahaziah, "The LORD grasps"; Joram, "The LORD is exalted") suggest that Ahab did not intend to replace the worship of the Lord with the worship of Baal but to worship both deities in a syncretistic way.
16:32 *house of Baal, which he had built in Samaria.* Ahab imported the Phoenician Baal worship of his wife Jezebel into the northern kingdom by constructing a temple of Baal in Samaria, just as Solomon had erected the temple of the Lord in Jerusalem. This pagan temple and its sacred stone (see note on 14:23) were later destroyed by Jehu (2 Ki 10:21–27).
16:33 *grove.* See note on 14:15. *than all the kings of Israel.* See note on v. 30. Ahab elevated the worship of Baal to an official status in the northern kingdom at the beginning of his reign.
16:34 *build Jericho.* Does not mean that Jericho had remained uninhabited since its destruction by Joshua (see Josh 18:21;

ram his firstborn, and set up the gates thereof in his youngest *son* Segub, [a]according to the word of the LORD, which he spake by Joshua the son of Nun.

Elijah fed by ravens

17 And [1]Elijah the Tishbite, *who was* of the inhabitants of Gilead, said unto Ahab, [a]*As* the LORD God of Israel liveth, [b]before whom I stand, [c]there shall not be dew nor rain [d]these years, but according to my word.

2 And the word of the LORD came unto him, saying,

3 Get thee hence, and turn thee eastward, and hide thyself by the brook Cherith, that *is* before Jordan.

4 And it shall be, *that* thou shalt drink of the brook; and I have commanded the ravens to feed thee there.

5 So he went and did according unto the word of the LORD: for he went and dwelt by the brook Cherith, that *is* before Jordan.

6 And the ravens brought him bread and flesh in the morning, and bread and flesh in the evening; and he drank of the brook.

7 And it came to pass [1]after a while, that the brook dried up, because there had been no rain in the land.

16:34 [a]Josh. 6:26
17:1 [1]Heb. *Elijahu.* Luke 4:25, he is called *Elias* [a]2 Ki. 3:14 [b]Deut. 10:8 [c]Jas. 5:17 [d]Luke 4:25
17:7 [1]Heb. *at the end of days*

17:9 [1]Luke 4:26, called *Sarepta* [a]Obad. 20

Elijah raises the widow's son

8 ¶ And the word of the LORD came unto him, saying,

9 Arise, get thee to [a][1]Zarephath, which *belongeth* to Zidon, and dwell there: behold, I have commanded a widow woman there to sustain thee.

10 So he arose and went to Zarephath. And when he came to the gate of the city, behold, the widow woman *was* there gathering of sticks: and he called to her, and said, Fetch me, I pray thee, a little water in a vessel, that I may drink.

11 And as she was going to fetch *it,* he called to her, and said, Bring me, I pray thee, a morsel of bread in thine hand.

12 And she said, *As* the LORD thy God liveth, I have not a cake, but a handful of meal in a barrel, and a little oil in a cruse: and behold, I *am* gathering two sticks, that I may go in and dress it for me and my son, that we may eat it, and die.

13 And Elijah said unto her, Fear not; go *and* do as thou hast said: but make me thereof a little cake first, and bring *it* unto me, and after make for thee and for thy son.

14 For thus saith the LORD God of Israel, The barrel of meal shall not waste, neither

---

Judg 1:16; 3:13; 2 Sam 10:5), but that it had remained an unwalled town or village. During the rule of Ahab, Hiel fortified the city by reconstructing its walls and gates (see 9:17 for a similar use of "rebuilt"). This violated God's intention that the ruins of Jericho (Josh 6:26) be a perpetual reminder that Israel had received the land of Canaan from God's hand as a gift of grace. Accordingly, Hiel suffered the curse Joshua had pronounced.

‡17:1 *Elijah.* Elijah's name (meaning "The LORD is my God") was the essence of his message (18:21,39). He was sent to oppose vigorously, by word and action, both Baal worship and those who engaged in it. *of the inhabitants of Gilead.* Possibly rendered "from Tishbe of Gilead." Gilead was in the northern area across the Jordan. The precise location of Tishbe is unknown. *before whom I stand.* A technical expression indicating one who stands in the service of a king. Kings and priests in Israel were supposed to be anointed to serve as official representatives of the Lord, Israel's Great King, leading Israel in the way of faithfulness to the Lord and channeling His covenantal care and blessings to them. Since the days of Jeroboam the northern kingdom had not had such a priest (12:31), and its kings had all been unfaithful. Now, in the great crisis brought on by Ahab's promotion of Baal worship, the Lord sent Elijah (and after him Elisha) to serve as His representative (instead of king and priest), much as Moses had done long ago. The author of Kings highlights many parallels between the ministries of Elijah and Moses. *not be dew nor rain.* The drought was not only a divine judgment on a nation that had turned to idolatry, but also a demonstration that even though Baal was considered the god of fertility and lord of the rain clouds, he was powerless to give rain (cf. Lev 26:3–4; Hos 2:5,8).

‡17:3 *Get thee hence.* With this command God withdrew His prophet from His land and people to leave them isolated from His word and blessings. The absence of the prophet confirmed and intensified the judgment. *brook Cherith . . . before* [i.e. "east of"] *Jordan.* The location of Cherith is uncertain. Perhaps it was a gorge formed by one of the northern tributaries to the Yarmuk River.

17:4 *ravens to feed thee there.* The Lord's faithful servant Elijah was miraculously sustained beyond the Jordan (like Israel in the wilderness in the time of Moses) while Israel in the promised land was going hungry—a clear testimony against Israel's reliance on Baal. The fact that Elijah was sustained in a miraculous way apart from living among his own people demonstrated that the word of God was not dependent on the people, but the people were dependent on the word of God.

17:9 *Zarephath, which belongeth to Zidon.* A coastal town located between Tyre and Sidon in the territory ruled by Jezebel's father Ethbaal (16:31). Elijah is commanded to go and reside in the heart of the very land from which the Baal worship now being promoted in Israel had come. *I have commanded a widow woman there to sustain thee.* Elijah, as the bearer of God's word, was now to be sustained by human hands, but they were the hands of a poor widow facing starvation (v. 12). She was, moreover, from outside the circle of God's own people (cf. Luke 4:25–26)—in fact, she was from the pagan nation that at that time (much like Egypt earlier and Babylon later) represented the forces arrayed against God's kingdom.

‡17:10 *So he arose and went.* Elijah's reliance on the Lord demonstrated the faith in the Lord that Israel should have been living by.

17:12 *As the LORD thy God liveth.* Her oath in the name of the Lord was either an accommodation to Elijah, whom she recognized as an Israelite (see notes on 5:7; 10:9), or a genuine expression of previous knowledge of and commitment to the God of Israel.

17:13 *make me thereof a little cake first, and . . . after make for thee and for thy son.* As a prophet, Elijah's words are the command of the Lord. The widow is asked to give all she has to sustain the bearer of the word of God. The demand to give her all is in essence the demand of the covenant that Israel had broken.

17:14 *thus saith the LORD God of Israel.* Elijah can tell the widow "Fear not" (v. 13) because the demand of the covenant is not given without the promise of the covenant. The Lord does not ask more than He promises to give.

shall the cruse of oil fail, until the day *that* the
LORD [1] sendeth rain upon the earth.
15 And she went and did according to the
saying of Elijah: and she, and he, and her
house, did eat [1] *many* days.
16 *And* the barrel of meal wasted not, neither did the cruse of oil fail, according to the
word of the LORD, which he spake [1] by Elijah.
17 ¶ And it came to pass after these things,
that the son of the woman, the mistress of the
house, fell sick; and his sickness was so sore,
that there was no breath left in him.
18 And she said unto Elijah, [a] What have I
to do with thee, O thou man of God? art thou
come unto me to call my sin to remembrance,
and to slay my son?
19 And he said unto her, Give me thy son.
And he took him out of her bosom, and carried
him up into a loft, where he abode, and laid
him upon his own bed.
20 And he cried unto the LORD, and said,
O LORD my God, hast thou also brought evil
upon the widow with whom I sojourn, by slaying her son?
21 [a] And he [1] stretched himself upon the
child three times, and cried unto the LORD,
and said, O LORD my God, I pray thee, let this
child's soul come [2] into him again.
22 And the LORD heard the voice of Elijah;
and the soul of the child came into him again,
and he [a] revived.
23 And Elijah took the child, and brought
him down out of the chamber into the house,
and delivered him unto his mother: and Elijah
said, See, thy son liveth.

17:14 [1] Heb. *giveth*
17:15 [1] Or, *a full year*
17:16 [1] Heb. *by the hand of*
17:18 [a] See Luke 5:8
17:21 [1] Heb. *measured* [2] Heb. *into his inward parts* [a] 2 Ki. 4:34,35
17:22 [a] Heb. 11:35
17:24 [a] John 3:2; 16:30
18:1 [a] Luke 4:25; Jas. 5:17 [b] Deut. 28:12
18:3 [1] Heb. *Obadiahu* [2] Heb. *over his house*
18:4 [1] Heb. *Izebel*
18:5 [1] Heb. *that we cut not off ourselves from the beasts*

24 And the woman said to Elijah, Now *by*
this [a] I know that thou *art* a man of God, and
that the word of the LORD in thy mouth *is*
truth.

Elijah and Obadiah meet

18 And it came to pass *after* [a] many days,
that the word of the LORD came to
Elijah in the third year, saying, Go, shew thyself unto Ahab; and [b] I will send rain upon the
earth.
2 And Elijah went to shew himself unto
Ahab. And *there was* a sore famine in Samaria.
3 And Ahab called [1] Obadiah, which *was*
[2] the governor of *his* house. (Now Obadiah
feared the LORD greatly:
4 For it was *so,* when [1] Jezebel cut off the
prophets of the LORD, that Obadiah took an
hundred prophets, and hid them *by* fifty in a
cave, and fed them *with* bread and water.)
5 And Ahab said unto Obadiah, Go into the
land, unto all fountains of water, and unto all
brooks: peradventure we may find grass to
save the horses and mules alive, [1] that we
leese not all the beasts.
6 So they divided the land between them
to pass throughout it: Ahab went one way by
himself, and Obadiah went another way by
himself.
7 ¶ And as Obadiah was in the way, behold
Elijah met him: and he knew him, and fell on
his face, and said, *Art* thou that my lord Elijah?
8 And he answered him, I *am:* go, tell thy
lord, Behold, Elijah *is here.*
9 And he said, What have I sinned, that

17:15 *did according to the saying of Elijah.* By an act of faith the woman received the promised blessing. Israel had forsaken the covenant and followed Baal and Asherah in search of prosperity. Now in the midst of a pagan kingdom a widow realized that trustful obedience to the word of God is the way that leads to life.

17:16 *barrel of meal wasted not.* God miraculously provided for this non-Israelite who, in an act of faith in the Lord's word, had laid her life on the line. He gave her "manna" from heaven even while He was withholding food from His unfaithful people in the promised land. The warning of Deut 32:21 was being fulfilled (cf. Rom 10:19; 11:11,14).

17:18 *art thou come . . . to call my sin to remembrance, and to slay my son?* The widow concluded that Elijah's presence in her house had called God's attention to her sin, and that the death of her son was a divine punishment for this sin. Although her sense of guilt seems to have been influenced by pagan ideas, both she and Elijah are confronted with the question: Why did the God who promised life bring death instead?

17:21 *stretched himself upon the child three times.* The apparent intent of this physical contact was to transfer the bodily warmth and stimulation of the prophet to the child. Elijah's prayer, however, makes it clear that he expected the life of the child to return as an answer to prayer, not as a result of bodily contact. *let this child's soul come into him again.* Moved by a faith like that of Abraham (Rom 4:17; Heb 11:19), Elijah prayed for the child's return to life so that the veracity and trustworthiness of God's word might be demonstrated.

17:22 *the soul of the child came into him again.* The first instance of raising the dead recorded in Scripture. This non-Israelite widow was granted the supreme covenant blessing, the gift of life rescued from the power of death. This blessing came in the person of her son, the only hope for a widow in ancient society (see 2 Ki 4:14; Ruth 1:11–12; 4:15–17; Luke 7:12).

17:24 *thou art a man of God.* The widow had addressed Elijah as a man of God previously (v. 18), but now she knew in a much more experiential way that he truly was a prophet of the Lord (see note on 12:22). *the word of the LORD in thy mouth is truth.* God used this experience to convince the Phoenician widow that His word was completely reliable. Her confession was one that the Lord's own people in Israel had failed to make.

18:1 *third year.* Apparently of the drought. Later Jewish tradition indicates that the drought lasted three and a half years (cf. Luke 4:25; Jas 5:17), but that probably represents a symbolic number for a drought cut short (half of seven years; see Gen 41:27; 2 Ki 8:1). *shew thyself unto Ahab; and I will send rain upon the earth.* Elijah's return is not occasioned by repentance in Israel but by the command of the Lord, who in His sovereign grace determined to reveal Himself anew to His people.

18:3 *Obadiah.* A common OT name, meaning "servant of the LORD." *governor of his house.* See note on 4:6.

18:5 The famine did not move Ahab to repentance (contrast Ahab's response to the famine with that of David years earlier, 2 Sam 21:1). But when his military strength seemed to be jeopardized, he scoured the land for food and water (see 10:26; according to the annals of the Assyrian ruler Shalmaneser III, Ahab had a force of at least 2,000 chariots).

18:8 *tell thy lord, Behold, Elijah is here.* This action would publicly identify Obadiah with Elijah in contrast to his previous clandestine support of the prophets sought by Jezebel (see vv. 4,13).

thou wouldest deliver thy servant into the hand of Ahab, to slay me?

10 *As* the LORD thy God liveth, there is no nation or kingdom, whither my lord hath not sent to seek thee: and when they said, *He is* not *there;* he took an oath of the kingdom and nation, that they found thee not.

11 And now thou sayest, Go, tell thy lord, Behold, Elijah *is here.*

12 And it shall come to pass, *as soon as* I am gone from thee, that [a]the spirit of the LORD shall carry thee whither I know not; and *so* when I come and tell Ahab, and he cannot find thee, he shall slay me: but *I* thy servant fear the LORD from my youth.

13 Was it not told my lord what I did when Jezebel slew the prophets of the LORD, how I hid an hundred men of the LORD'S prophets by fifty in a cave, and fed them *with* bread and water?

14 And now thou sayest, Go, tell thy lord, Behold, Elijah *is here:* and he shall slay me.

15 And Elijah said, *As* the LORD of hosts liveth, before whom I stand, I will surely shew myself unto him to day.

16 So Obadiah went to meet Ahab, and told him: and Ahab went to meet Elijah.

Elijah on mount Carmel

17 ¶ And it came to pass, when Ahab saw Elijah, that Ahab said unto him, [a]*Art* thou he that [b]troubleth Israel?

18 And he answered, I have not troubled Israel; but thou, and thy father's house, [a]in that ye have forsaken the commandments of the LORD, and thou hast followed Baalim.

19 Now therefore send, *and* gather to me all Israel unto mount [a]Carmel, and the prophets of Baal four hundred and fifty, [b]and the prophets of the groves four hundred, which eat *at* Jezebel's table.

20 So Ahab sent unto all the children of Israel, and [a]gathered the prophets together unto mount Carmel.

21 And Elijah came unto all the people, and said, [a]How long halt ye between two [1]opinions? if the LORD *be* God, follow him: but if Baal, [b]*then* follow him. And the people answered him not a word.

22 Then said Elijah unto the people, [a]I, *even* I only, remain a prophet of the LORD; [b]but Baal's prophets *are* four hundred and fifty men.

23 Let them therefore give us two bullocks; and let them choose one bullock for themselves, and cut it in pieces, and lay *it* on wood, and put no fire *under:* and I will dress the other bullock, and lay *it* on wood, and put no fire *under:*

24 And call ye on the name of your gods, and I will call on the name of the LORD: and the God that [a]answereth by fire, let him be God. And all the people answered and said, [1]It is well spoken.

25 And Elijah said unto the prophets of Baal, Choose you one bullock for yourselves, and dress *it* first; for ye *are* many; and call on the name of your gods, but put no fire *under.*

26 And they took the bullock which was given them, and they dressed *it,* and called on the name of Baal from morning even until noon, saying, O Baal, [1]hear us. But *there was* [a]no voice, nor any that [2]answered. And they [3]leapt upon the altar which was made.

27 And it came to pass at noon, that Elijah mocked them, and said, Cry [1]aloud: for he *is* a god; either [2]he is talking, or he [3]is pursuing, or he is in a journey, *or* peradventure he sleepeth, and must be awaked.

28 And they cried loud, and [a]cut themselves after their manner with knives and lancets, till [1]the blood gushed out upon them.

29 And it came to pass, when midday was past, [a]and they prophesied until *the time* of

18:12 [a]2 Ki. 2:16; Ezek. 3:12,14; Mat. 4:1; Acts 8:39
18:17 [a]ch. 21:20 [b]Josh. 7:25; Acts 16:20
18:18 [a]2 Chr. 15:2
18:19 [a]Josh. 19:26 [b]ch. 16:33
18:20 [a]ch. 22:6
18:21 [1]Or, *thoughts?* [a]2 Ki. 17:41; Mat. 6:24 [b]See Josh. 24:15
18:22 [a]ch. 19:10,14 [b]ver. 19
18:24 [1]Heb. *The word is good* [a]ver. 38; 1 Chr. 21:26
18:26 [1]Or, *answer* [2]Or, *heard* [3]Or, *leaped up and down at the altar* [a]Ps. 115:5; Jer. 10:5; 1 Cor. 8:4
18:27 [1]Heb. *with a great voice* [2]Or, *he meditateth* [3]Heb. *hath a pursuit*
18:28 [1]Heb. *poured out blood upon them* [a]Lev. 19:28; Deut. 14:1
18:29 [a]1 Cor. 11:4,5

18:12 *the spirit of the LORD shall carry thee whither I know not.* Elijah's disappearance earlier and now his sudden reappearance suggested to Obadiah that God's Spirit was miraculously transporting the prophet about (see 2 Ki 2:16).

18:13 *Jezebel slew the prophets.* Possibly in an attempt to please Baal so he would send rain. *prophets of the LORD.* Probably members of the communities of "prophets" that had sprung up in Israel during this time of apostasy (see note on 20:35).

18:17 *he that troubleth Israel.* Ahab holds Elijah to account for the drought and charges him with a crime against the state worthy of death (he calls him a trouble bringer; see Josh 7:25).

18:18 *ye have forsaken the commandments of the LORD, and . . . followed Baalim.* The source of Israel's trouble was not Elijah or even the drought, but the breach of covenantal loyalty.

18:19 *mount Carmel.* A high ridge next to the Mediterranean Sea, where the effects of the drought would be least apparent (see Amos 1:2) and the power of Baal to nurture life would seem to be strongest. *prophets of Baal . . . prophets of the groves.* See v. 29 and note. *groves.* See note on 14:15. *eat at Jezebel's table.* See note on 2:7.

18:21 *halt.* The Hebrew for this word is the same as that used for "leapt" in v. 26 (see note there). Elijah speaks with biting irony: In her religious ambivalence Israel is but engaging in a wild and futile religious "dance." *if the LORD be God, follow him: but if Baal, then follow him.* Elijah placed a clear choice before the people. He drew a sharp contrast between the worship of the Lord and that of Baal, to eliminate the apostate idea that both deities could be worshiped in a syncretistic way.

18:22 *I, even I only, remain.* At least the only one to stand boldly and publicly against the king and the prophets of Baal (but see v. 4; 19:10,14; 20:13,28,35; 22:6,8; see also 19:18 and note).

18:24 *the God that answereth by fire, let him be God.* Both the Lord and Baal were said to ride the thunderstorm as their divine chariot (see Ps 104:3 and note); thunder was their voice (see Ps 29:3–9 and note) and lightning ("fire") their weapon (see Ps 18:14 and note). Elijah's challenge is direct. Cf. Lev 9:24.

18:26 *leapt upon the altar.* The ecstatic cultic dance was part of the pagan ritual intended to arouse the deity to perform some desired action.

18:27 *talking . . . sleepeth.* Elijah ridicules, but as he does he shows knowledge of the Baal myths.

18:28 *till the blood gushed out.* Self-inflicted wounds (causing blood to flow) were symbolic of self-sacrifice as an extreme method of arousing the deity to action. Such mutilation of the body was strictly forbidden in the Mosaic law (Lev 19:28; Deut 14:1).

the [1]offering of the *evening* sacrifice, that *there was* [b]neither voice, nor any to answer, nor any [2]that regarded.

30 And Elijah said unto all the people, Come near unto me. And all the people came near unto him. [a]And he repaired the altar of the LORD that was broken down.

31 And Elijah took twelve stones, according to the number of the tribes of the sons of Jacob, unto whom the word of the LORD came, saying, [a]Israel shall be thy name:

32 And *with* the stones he built an altar [a]in the name of the LORD: and he made a trench about the altar, as great as would contain two measures of seed.

33 And he [a]put the wood in order, and cut the bullock in pieces, and laid *him* on the wood, and said, Fill four barrels *with* water, and [b]pour *it* on the burnt sacrifice, and on the wood.

34 And he said, Do *it* the second time. And they did *it* the second time. And he said, Do *it* the third time. And they did *it* the third time.

35 And the water [1]ran round about the altar; and he filled [a]the trench also *with* water.

36 And it came to pass at *the time of* the offering of the *evening* sacrifice, that Elijah the prophet came near, and said, LORD [a]God of Abraham, Isaac, and of Israel, [b]let it be known *this* day that thou *art* God in Israel, and *that* I *am* thy servant, and *that* [c]I have done all these things at thy word.

37 Hear me, O LORD, hear me, that this people may know that thou *art* the LORD God, and *that* thou hast turned their heart back again.

38 Then [a]the fire of the LORD fell, and consumed the burnt sacrifice, and the wood, and the stones, and the dust, and licked up the water that *was* in the trench.

39 And when all the people saw *it,* they fell on their faces: and they said, [a]The LORD, he *is* the God; the LORD, he *is* the God.

40 And Elijah said unto them, [a][1]Take the prophets of Baal; let not one of them escape. And they [2]took them: and Elijah brought them down to the brook Kishon, and [b]slew them there.

41 ¶ And Elijah said unto Ahab, Get thee up, eat and drink; for *there is* [1]a sound of abundance of rain.

42 So Ahab went up to eat and to drink. And Elijah went up to the top of Carmel; [a]and he cast himself down upon the earth, and put his face between his knees,

43 And said to his servant, Go up now, look toward the sea. And he went up, and looked, and said, *There is* nothing. And he said, Go again seven times.

44 And it came to pass at the seventh *time,* that he said, Behold, there ariseth a little cloud out of the sea, like a man's hand. And he said, Go up, say unto Ahab, [1]Prepare *thy chariot,* and get thee down, that the rain stop thee not.

45 And it came to pass in the mean while, that the heaven was black *with* clouds and wind, and there was a great rain. And Ahab rode, and went to Jezreel.

46 And the hand of the LORD was on Elijah; and he [a]girded up his loins, and ran before Ahab [1]to the entrance of Jezreel.

Elijah flees from Jezebel

19 And Ahab told Jezebel all that Elijah had done, and withal how he had [a]slain all the prophets with the sword.

2 Then Jezebel sent a messenger unto Elijah, saying, [a]So let the gods do *to me,* and more also, if I make not thy life as the life of one of them *by* to morrow about *this* time.

3 And when he saw *that,* he arose, and

18:29 [1]Heb. *ascending* [2]Heb. *attention* [b]ver. 26
18:30 [a]ch. 19:10
18:31 [a]Gen. 32:28; 2 Ki. 17:34
18:32 [a]Col. 3:17
18:33 [a]Lev. 1:6-8 [b]See Judg. 6:20
18:35 [1]Heb. *went* [a]ver. 32,38
18:36 [a]Ex. 3:6 [b]ch. 8:43; 2 Ki. 19:19 [c]Num. 16:28
18:38 [a]Lev. 9:24; Judg. 6:21; 1 Chr. 21:26; 2 Chr. 7:1
18:39 [a]ver. 24
18:40 [1]Or, *Apprehend* [2]Or, *apprehended* [a]2 Ki. 10:25 [b]Deut. 13:5; 18:20
18:41 [1]Or, *a sound of a noise of rain*
18:42 [a]Jas. 5:17,18
18:44 [1]Heb. *Tie,* or, *Bind*
18:46 [1]Heb. *till thou come to Jezreel* [a]2 Ki. 4:29; 9:1
19:1 [a]ch. 18:40
19:2 [a]Ruth 1:17; ch. 20:10; 2 Ki. 6:31

18:29 *prophesied.* Indicative of ecstatic raving, in which the ritual reached its climax (see notes on 1 Sam 10:5; 18:10). *time of the . . . evening sacrifice.* See Ex 29:38–41; Num 28:3–8. *neither voice.* Dramatic demonstration of Baal's impotence (see Ps 115:5–8; 135:15–18; Jer 10:5).

18:30 *altar of the LORD that was broken down.* It is possible that the altar had been built by people of the northern ten tribes after the division of the kingdom (see note on 3:2) and that it had been destroyed by the agents of Jezebel (vv. 4,13; 19:10,14).

18:31 *twelve stones, according to the number of the tribes.* In this way Elijah called attention to the covenant unity of Israel as the people of God in spite of her political division. What was about to happen concerned the entire nation, not just the northern ten tribes.

18:33 *water.* By drenching the whole installation Elijah showed to all that he was using no tricks.

18:36 *said.* Elijah's simple but earnest prayer stands in sharp contrast to the frantic shouts and "dancing" and self-mutilation of the Baal prophets. *God of Abraham, Isaac, and of Israel.* An appeal to the Lord to remember His ancient covenant with the patriarchs, and to Israel to remember all that the Lord has done for her since the days of her forefathers.

18:38 *fire of the LORD fell.* See note on v. 24.

18:40 *slew them there.* Elijah, acting on the authority of the Lord, who sent him, carried out the sentence pronounced in the Mosaic law for prophets of pagan deities (Deut 13:13–18; 17:2–5).

18:41 *sound of abundance of rain.* Now that Baal worship has been struck a devastating blow, there is the promise of rain (see 17:1). Significantly, Ahab takes no action—either to carry out the Mosaic sentence or to halt Elijah.

18:42 *Elijah . . . cast himself down upon the earth, and put his face between his knees.* Now that the people had confessed that the Lord alone was God, Elijah prayed for the covenant curse to be lifted (see note on 17:1) by the coming of rain (see 8:35; 2 Chr 7:13–14).

18:43 *seven times.* The number symbolic of completeness.

18:44 *ariseth . . . out of the sea.* Appearing on the western horizon.

18:46 *ran before Ahab to the entrance of Jezreel.* Divinely energized by extraordinary strength, Elijah ran before Ahab's chariot to Jezreel. This dramatic scene, with the Lord's prophet running before the king and the Lord Himself racing behind him riding His mighty thundercloud chariot (see note on v. 24), served as a powerful appeal to Ahab to break once for all with Baal and henceforth to rule as the servant of the Lord.

19:2 *So let the gods do to me, and more also.* A curse formula (see note on 1 Sam 3:17). *one of them.* The dead prophets of Baal (v. 1).

19:3 *when he saw that, he arose, and went for his life.* In spite

went for his life, and came *to* Beer-sheba,
which *belongeth* to Judah, and left his servant
there.
4 But he himself went a day's journey into
the wilderness, and came and sat down under
a juniper tree: and he [a]requested [1]for himself
that he might die; and said, *It is* enough; now,
O LORD, take away my life; for I *am* not better
than my fathers.
5 And as he lay and slept under a juniper
tree, behold then, an angel touched him, and
said unto him, Arise *and* eat.
6 And he looked, and behold, *there was* a
cake baken on the coals, and a cruse of water
at his [1]head. And he did eat and drink, and
laid him down again.
7 And the angel of the LORD came again the
second time, and touched him, and said, Arise
and eat; because the journey *is* too great for
thee.
8 And he arose, and did eat and drink, and
went in the strength of that meat [a]forty days
and forty nights unto [b]Horeb the mount of
God.

Elijah in the mountain cave

9 ¶ And he came thither unto a cave, and
lodged there; and behold, the word of the
LORD *came* to him, and he said unto him,
What doest thou here, Elijah?
10 And he said, [a]I have been very [b]jealous
for the LORD God of hosts: for the children of
Israel have forsaken thy covenant, thrown
down thine altars, and [c]slain thy prophets
with the sword; and [d]I, *even* I only, am left;
and they seek my life, to take it away.
11 And he said, Go forth, and stand [a]upon
the mount before the LORD. And behold, the
LORD passed by, and [b]a great and strong wind
rent the mountains, and brake in pieces the
rocks before the LORD; *but* the LORD *was* not
in the wind: and after the wind an earthquake; *but* the LORD *was* not in the earthquake:
12 And after the earthquake a fire; *but* the
LORD *was* not in the fire: and after the fire a
still small voice.
13 And it was *so,* when Elijah heard *it,* that
[a]he wrapped his face in his mantle, and went
out, and stood *in* the entering in of the cave.
[b]And behold, *there came* a voice unto him,
and said, What doest thou here, Elijah?
14 [a]And he said, I have been very jealous
for the LORD God of hosts: because the children of Israel have forsaken thy covenant,
thrown down thine altars, and slain thy prophets with the sword; and I, *even* I only, am left;
and they seek my life, to take it away.
15 And the LORD said unto him, Go, return
on thy way to the wilderness of Damascus:
[a]and when thou comest, anoint Hazael to be
king over Syria:

19:4 [1]Heb. *for his life* [a]Num. 11:15; Jonah 4:3,8
19:6 [1]Heb. *bolster*
19:8 [a]Ex. 34:28; Deut. 9:9,18; Mat. 4:2 [b]Ex. 3:1
19:10 [a]Rom. 11:3 [b]Num. 25:11,13; Ps. 69:9
19:10 [c]ch. 18:4 [d]ch. 18:22; Rom. 11:3
19:11 [a]Ex. 24:12 [b]Ezek. 1:4; 37:7
19:13 [a]Ex. 3:6; Is. 6:2 [b]ver. 9
19:14 [a]ver. 10
19:15 [a]2 Ki. 8:12,13

of Elijah's great triumph in the trial on mount Carmel and the dramatic demonstration that Elijah's God is the Lord of heaven and earth and the source of Israel's blessings, Jezebel is undaunted. Hers is no empty threat, and Ahab has shown that he is either unwilling or unable to restrain her. So Elijah knows that one of the main sources of Israel's present apostasy is still spewing out its poison and that his own life is in danger. *Beer-sheba.* The southernmost city in Judah (see notes on Gen 21:31; Amos 5:5; see also Judg 20:1).

19:4 *juniper tree.* A wilderness shrub, sometimes large enough to offer some shade. *requested for himself that he might die.* Cf. Jonah 4:3,8. Elijah concluded that his work was fruitless and consequently that life was not worth living. He had lost his confidence in the triumph of the kingdom of God and was withdrawing from the arena of conflict.

19:7 *angel of the LORD.* See note on Gen 16:7. God in His mercy provided sustenance and rest for His discouraged servant. *the journey is too great for thee.* Evidently Elijah had already determined to go to mount Horeb, where God had established His covenant with His people. There is no indication that the Lord had instructed him to do this as He had previously directed him to go to Cherith (17:2–3) and to Zarephath (17:8–9) and to meet Ahab (18:1).

19:8 *forty days and forty nights.* Sustained by the Lord as Moses had been for the same length of time on mount Sinai (Ex 24:18; 34:28) and as Jesus would be in the wilderness (Mat 4:2,11). *Horeb the mount of God.* Probably an alternate name for mount Sinai (see Ex 3:1; 19:1–3), located in the wilderness apparently about 250 miles south of Beer-sheba.

19:9 *What doest thou here, Elijah?* The question implies that Elijah had come to Sinai for his own misguided reasons and not because the Lord had sent him.

19:10 Elijah did not give a direct answer to the Lord's question but implied that the work the Lord had begun centuries earlier with the establishment of the Sinai covenant had now come to nothing. Whereas Moses had interceded for Israel when they sinned with the golden calf (Ex 32:11–13), Elijah condemned the Israelites for breaking the covenant, and bitterly complained over the fruitlessness of his own work. *I, even I only, am left.* See note on 18:22.

19:12 *a still small voice.* In the symbolism of these occurrences (vv. 11–12) the Lord appears to be telling Elijah that although His servant's indictment of Israel was a call for God to judge His people with windstorm, earthquake and fire, it was not God's will to do so now. Elijah must return to continue God's mission to His people, and Elisha is to carry it on for another generation (v. 16).

19:13 *What doest thou here, Elijah?* After demonstrating His presence in the gentle whisper rather than in the wind, earthquake or fire, the Lord gave Elijah an opportunity to revise the answer he had previously given to the same question (vv. 9–10).

19:14 Elijah's unrevised answer demonstrated that he did not understand the significance of the divine revelation he had just witnessed.

19:15 *the LORD said unto him.* Giving instructions to Elijah that revealed His sovereign power over people and nations. Even though Israel would experience divine judgment through Hazael, Jehu and Elisha, God would continue to preserve a remnant faithful to Himself among the people. *return . . . to the wilderness of Damascus.* Apparently Elijah is to go back by way of the road east of the Dead Sea and the Jordan. As it turns out, all three anointings take place east of the Jordan, though it is Elisha who effects the anointing of the two kings. *anoint.* Appears to mean here no more than "designate as divinely appointed." This anointing was actually done by Elijah's successor Elisha (see 2 Ki 8:7–15). *Hazael.* Subsequently became a serious threat to Israel during the reigns of Joram, Jehu and Jehoahaz (see 2 Ki 8:28–29; 10:32–33; 12:17–18; 13:3,22).

16 And [a]Jehu the son of Nimshi shalt thou
anoint to be king over Israel: and [b]Elisha the
son of Shaphat of Abel-meholah shalt thou
anoint to be prophet in thy room.
17 And [a]it shall come to pass, *that* him that
escapeth the sword of Hazael shall Jehu slay:
and him that escapeth from the sword of Jehu
[b]shall Elisha slay.
18 [a]Yet [1]I have left *me* seven thousand in
Israel, all the knees which have not bowed
unto Baal, [b]and every mouth which hath not
kissed him.

19:16 [a]2 Ki. 9:1-3 [b]Luke 4:27, called *Eliseus*
19:17 [a]2 Ki. 8:12; 9:14; 10:6; 13:3 [b]See Hos. 6:5
19:18 [1]Or, *I will leave* [a]Rom. 11:4 [b]See Hos. 13:2
19:20 [1]Heb. *Go return* [a]Mat. 8:21,22; Luke 9:61,62

Elijah and Elisha

19 ¶ So he departed thence, and found Elisha the son of Shaphat, who *was* plowing *with*
twelve yoke *of oxen* before him, and he with
the twelfth: and Elijah passed by him, and cast
his mantle upon him.
20 And he left the oxen, and ran after Elijah, and said, [a]Let me, I pray thee, kiss my father and my mother, and *then* I will follow
thee. And he said unto him, [1]Go back again:
for what have I done to thee?
21 And he returned back from him, and

19:16 *Jehu ... shalt thou anoint.* Jehu was a military commander under Ahab and Joram, Ahab's son (2 Ki 9:5–6). He was anointed king over Israel by "one of the sons of the prophets" at the instruction of Elisha (2 Ki 9:1–16), with the mandate to destroy the house of Ahab. *Elisha.* As with Elijah (see note on 17:1), Elisha's name (meaning "God is salvation" or "God saves") was the essence of his ministry. His name evokes memory of Joshua ("The LORD saves"). Elijah is given someone to finish his work just as Moses was, and Elisha channels the covenant blessings to the faithful in Israel just as Joshua brought Israel into the promised land (see the account of Elisha's ministry in 2 Ki 2:19–8:15; 9:1–3; 13:14–20). In the NT John the Baptist ("Elijah," Mat 11:14; 17:12) was followed by Jesus ("Joshua"; see note on Mat 1:21) to complete God's saving work. *son of Shaphat.* Shaphat means "He judges," which is also in accordance with Elisha's ministry. *of Abel-meholah.* See map below.

19:17 *him that escapeth the sword of Hazael shall Jehu slay.* See 2 Ki 9:24. *him that escapeth from the sword of Jehu shall Elisha slay.* How this may have been fulfilled we are not told, but see 2 Ki 2:24; 8:1 (see also Hos 6:5).

19:18 *seven thousand.* A round number, no doubt symbolic of the fullness or completeness of the divinely preserved godly remnant (Rom 11:2–4). In any case Elijah had been mistaken in his conclusion that he alone had remained faithful (see vv. 10,14; 18:22 and note). *not kissed him.* See Hos 13:2.

19:19 *cast his mantle upon him.* Thus designating Elisha as his successor (see note on v. 16).

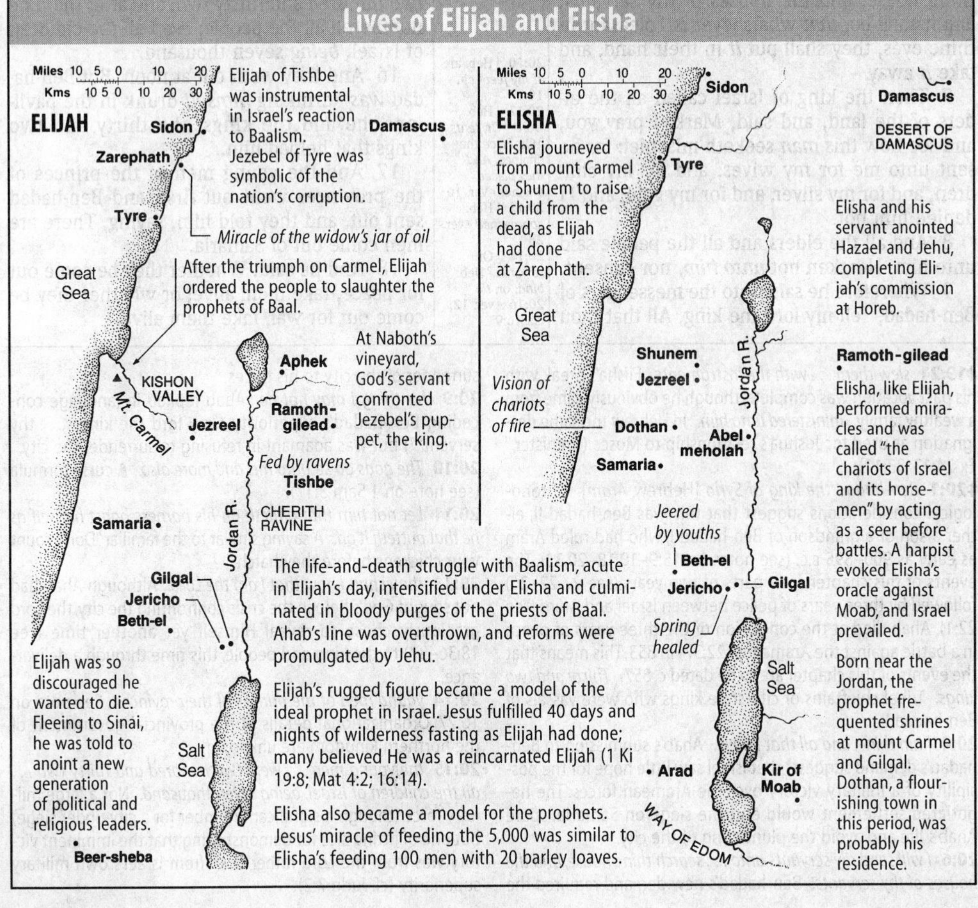
Lives of Elijah and Elisha
Miles 10 5 0 10 20
Kms 10 5 0 10 20 30
ELIJAH
Sidon
Damascus
Zarephath
Tyre
Great Sea
KISHON VALLEY
Mt. Carmel
Jezreel
Aphek
Ramoth-gilead
Tishbe
CHERITH RAVINE
Samaria
Jordan R.
Gilgal
Jericho
Beth-el
Salt Sea
Beer-sheba
Elijah of Tishbe was instrumental in Israel's reaction to Baalism. Jezebel of Tyre was symbolic of the nation's corruption.
Miracle of the widow's jar of oil
After the triumph on Carmel, Elijah ordered the people to slaughter the prophets of Baal.
At Naboth's vineyard, God's servant confronted Jezebel's puppet, the king.
Fed by ravens
Elijah was so discouraged he wanted to die. Fleeing to Sinai, he was told to anoint a new generation of political and religious leaders.
The life-and-death struggle with Baalism, acute in Elijah's day, intensified under Elisha and culminated in bloody purges of the priests of Baal. Ahab's line was overthrown, and reforms were promulgated by Jehu.
Elijah's rugged figure became a model of the ideal prophet in Israel. Jesus fulfilled 40 days and nights of wilderness fasting as Elijah had done; many believed He was a reincarnated Elijah (1 Ki 19:8; Mat 4:2; 16:14).
Elisha also became a model for the prophets. Jesus' miracle of feeding the 5,000 was similar to Elisha's feeding 100 men with 20 barley loaves.
Miles 10 5 0 10 20
Kms 10 5 0 10 20 30
ELISHA
Sidon
Damascus
DESERT OF DAMASCUS
Tyre
Great Sea
Elisha journeyed from mount Carmel to Shunem to raise a child from the dead, as Elijah had done at Zarephath.
Elisha and his servant anointed Hazael and Jehu, completing Elijah's commission at Horeb.
Shunem
Jezreel
Jordan R.
Ramoth-gilead
Vision of chariots of fire
Dothan
Abel-meholah
Samaria
Elisha, like Elijah, performed miracles and was called "the chariots of Israel and its horsemen" by acting as a seer before battles. A harpist evoked Elisha's oracle against Moab, and Israel prevailed.
Jeered by youths
Beth-el
Jericho
Gilgal
Spring healed
Salt Sea
Born near the Jordan, the prophet frequented shrines at mount Carmel and Gilgal. Dothan, a flourishing town in this period, was probably his residence.
Arad
Kir of Moab
WAY OF EDOM

took a yoke of oxen, and slew them, and
[a]boiled their flesh with the instruments of the
oxen, and gave unto the people, and they did
eat. Then he arose, and went after Elijah, and
ministered unto him.

Ahab defeats Ben-hadad

20 And Ben-hadad the king of Syria
gathered all his host together: and
there were thirty and two kings with him, and
horses, and chariots: and he went up and besieged Samaria, and warred against it.
2 And he sent messengers to Ahab king of
Israel into the city, and said unto him, Thus
saith Ben-hadad,
3 Thy silver and thy gold *is* mine; thy wives
also and thy children, *even* the goodliest, *are*
mine.
4 And the king of Israel answered and said,
My lord, O king, according to thy saying, I *am*
thine, and all that I have.
5 And the messengers came again, and
said, Thus speaketh Ben-hadad, saying, Although I have sent unto thee, saying, Thou
shalt deliver me thy silver, and thy gold, and
thy wives, and thy children;
6 Yet I will send my servants unto thee to
morrow about *this* time, and they shall search
thine house, and the houses of thy servants;
and it shall be, *that* whatsoever *is* [1]pleasant in
thine eyes, they shall put *it* in their hand, and
take *it* away.
7 Then the king of Israel called all the elders of the land, and said, Mark, I pray you,
and see how this *man* seeketh mischief: for he
sent unto me for my wives, and for my children, and for my silver, and for my gold; and [1]I
denied him not.
8 And all the elders and all the people said
unto him, Hearken not *unto him,* nor consent.
9 Wherefore he said unto the messengers of
Ben-hadad, Tell my lord the king, All that thou

19:21 [a]2 Sam. 24:22
20:6 [1]Heb. *desirable*
20:7 [1]Heb. *I kept not back from him*
20:10 [1]Heb. are *at my feet* [a]ch. 19:2
20:12 [1]Heb. *word* [2]Or, *tents* [3]Or, *Place* the engines. *And they placed* engines [a]ver. 16
20:13 [1]Heb. *approached* [a]ver. 28
20:14 [1]Or, *servants* [2]Heb. *bind,* or, *tie*
20:16 [a]ver. 12; ch. 16:9

didst send for to thy servant at the first I will
do: but this thing I may not do. And the messengers departed, and brought him word again.
10 And Ben-hadad sent unto him, and said,
[a]The gods do so unto me, and more also, if the
dust of Samaria shall suffice for handfuls for all
the people that [1]follow me.
11 And the king of Israel answered and
said, Tell *him,* Let not him that girdeth on *his*
harness boast himself as he that putteth *it* off.
12 And it came to pass, when *Ben-hadad*
heard this [1]message, as he *was* [a]drinking, he
and the kings in the [2]pavilions, that he said
unto his servants, [3]Set *yourselves in array.*
And they set *themselves in array* against the
city.
13 ¶ And behold, there [1]came a prophet
unto Ahab king of Israel, saying, Thus saith the
LORD, Hast thou seen all this great multitude?
behold, [a]I will deliver it into thine hand *this*
day; and thou shalt know that I *am* the LORD.
14 And Ahab said, By whom? And he said,
Thus saith the LORD, *Even* by the [1]young men
of the princes of the provinces. Then he said,
Who shall [2]order the battle? And he answered, Thou.
15 Then he numbered the young men of
the princes of the provinces, and they were
two hundred and thirty two: and after them he
numbered all the people, *even* all the children
of Israel, *being* seven thousand.
16 And they went out at noon. But Ben-hadad *was* [a]drinking *himself* drunk in the pavilions, he and the kings, the thirty and two
kings that helped him.
17 And the young men of the princes of
the provinces went out first; and Ben-hadad
sent out, and they told him, saying, There are
men come out of Samaria.
18 And he said, Whether they be come out
for peace, take them alive; or whether they be
come out for war, take them alive.

---

‡19:21 *slew them . . . with the instruments.* Elisha's break with his past vocation was complete, though he obviously came from a wealthy family. *ministered unto him.* In Hebrew the same designation as used for Joshua's relationship to Moses ("minister," Ex 24:13; 33:11).

‡20:1 *Ben-hadad the king of Syria* [Hebrew *Aram*]. Chronological considerations suggest that this was Ben-hadad II, either a son or a grandson of Ben-hadad I, who had ruled Aram as early as 900–895 B.C. (see notes on 15:9–10,18–20,33). The events of this chapter span parts of two years (see vv. 22–26) followed by three years of peace between Israel and Aram (see 22:1). Ahab died at the conclusion of the three years of peace in a battle against the Arameans (22:37) in 853. This means that the events of this chapter are to be dated c. 857. *Thirty and two kings.* Tribal chieftains or city-state kings who were vassals of Ben-hadad II.

20:4 *I am thine, and all that I have.* Ahab's submission to Ben-hadad's demand suggests that Israel saw little hope for the possibility of a military victory over the Aramean forces. The negotiated settlement would end the siege on Samaria, spare Ahab's life and avoid the plundering of the city.

20:6 *I will send my servants unto . . . search thine house, and the houses of thy servants.* Ben-hadad's new demand required the surrender of the city to his forces.

20:9 *this thing I may not do.* Ahab replied in language conceding Ben-hadad's superiority ("my lord the king," . . . thy servant' ") but was adamant in refusing to surrender the city.

20:10 *The gods do so unto me, and more also.* A curse formula (see note on 1 Sam 3:17).

20:11 *Let not him that girdeth on his harness boast himself as he that putteth it off.* A saying similar to the familiar "Don't count your chickens before they hatch."

20:13 *thou shalt know that I am the LORD.* Although Ahab had not sought God's help in the crisis confronting the city, the Lord graciously chose to reveal Himself yet another time (see 18:36–37) to the king and people, this time through a deliverance.

20:14 *young men of the princes of the provinces.* See note on 16:27. Organizational details of the provincial government of the northern kingdom are unknown.

20:15 *the young men . . . were two hundred and thirty two . . . all the children of Israel, being seven thousand.* Not a large military force (though a significant number for a city under siege) but one of fitting size for demonstrating that the imminent victory was from the Lord rather than from Israel's own military superiority (cf. Judg 7:2).

19 So these young men of the princes of
the provinces came out of the city, and the
army which followed them.
20 And they slew every one his man: and
the Syrians fled; and Israel pursued them: and
Ben-hadad the king of Syria escaped on a horse
with the horsemen.
21 And the king of Israel went out, and
smote the horses and chariots, and slew the
Syrians with a great slaughter.
22 ¶ And the prophet came to the king of
Israel, and said unto him, Go, strengthen thyself, and mark, and see what thou doest: [a]for
at the return of the year the king of Syria will
come up against thee.
23 And the servants of the king of Syria
said unto him, Their gods *are* gods of the hills;
therefore they were stronger than we; but let
us fight against them in the plain, and surely
we shall be stronger than they.
24 And do this thing, Take the kings away,
every man out of his place, and put captains in
their rooms:
25 And number thee an army, like the
army [1]that thou hast lost, horse for horse, and
chariot for chariot: and we will fight against
them in the plain, *and* surely we shall be
stronger than they. And he hearkened unto
their voice, and did so.
26 And it came to pass at the return of the
year, that Ben-hadad numbered the Syrians,
and went up to [a]Aphek, [1]to fight against Israel.
27 And the children of Israel were numbered, and [1]were all present, and went against
them: and the children of Israel pitched before
them like two little flocks of kids; but the Syrians filled the country.
28 And there came a man of God, and
spake unto the king of Israel, and said, Thus
saith the LORD, Because the Syrians have said,
The LORD *is* God of the hills, but he *is* not God
of the valleys, therefore [a]will I deliver all this
great multitude into thine hand, and ye shall
know that I *am* the LORD.
29 And they pitched one over against the
other seven days. And *so* it was, that in the
seventh day the battle was joined: and the
children of Israel slew *of* the Syrians an hundred thousand footmen in one day.
30 But the rest fled to Aphek, into the city;
and *there* a wall fell upon twenty and seven
thousand of the men that were left. And Ben-
hadad fled, and came into the city, [1]into an inner chamber.
31 And his servants said unto him, Behold
now, we have heard that the kings of the
house of Israel *are* merciful kings: let us, I pray
thee, [a]put sackcloth on our loins, and ropes
upon our heads, and go out to the king of Israel: peradventure he will save thy life.
32 So they girded sackcloth on their loins,
and *put* ropes on their heads, and came to the
king of Israel, and said, Thy servant Ben-hadad
saith, I pray thee, let me live. And he said, *Is*
he yet alive? he *is* my brother.
33 Now the men did diligently observe
whether *any thing would come* from him, and
did hastily catch *it:* and they said, Thy brother
Ben-hadad. Then he said, Go ye, bring him.
Then Ben-hadad came forth to him; and he
caused him to come up into the chariot.
34 And *Ben-hadad* said unto him, [a]The cities, which my father took from thy father, I
will restore; and thou shalt make streets for
thee in Damascus, as my father made in
Samaria. Then *said Ahab,* I will send thee

20:22 [a]2 Sam. 11:1
20:25 [1]Heb. *that was fallen*
20:26 [1]Heb. *to the war with Israel* [a]Josh. 13:4
20:27 [1]Or, *were victualled*
20:28 [a]ver. 13
20:30 [1]Or, *from chamber to chamber.* Heb. into *a chamber within a chamber*
20:31 [a]Gen. 37:34
20:34 [a]ch. 15:20

20:20 *they slew every one his man.* Apparently they were met by a small advance force like their own (see 2 Sam 2:15–16). *escaped on a horse with the horsemen.* Since fighting on horseback did not come until later, reference must be to chariot horses and charioteers. After their defeat, the Arameans seem to have withdrawn to Damascus.

20:22 *the king of Syria will come up against thee.* The anonymous prophet (see v. 13) warned Ahab against undue self-confidence. The prophet's announcement of an impending renewed attack by Ben-hadad should have driven Ahab to more complete reliance on the God who had revealed Himself on mount Carmel and in the recent military victory.

20:23 *gods of the hills.* An expression of the pagan idea that a deity's power extended only over the limited area of his particular jurisdiction. *therefore they were stronger than we.* The Arameans believed that the outcome of military conflicts depended on the relative strength of the gods of the opposing forces rather than on the inherent strength of the two armies. For this reason, their strategy was to fight the next battle in a way that advantageously maximized the supposed strengths and weaknesses of the deities involved.

20:26 *Aphek.* Presumably the Aphek located a few miles east of the sea of Galilee. The battle apparently took place in the Jordan Valley near the juncture of the Yarmuk and Jordan rivers.

20:28 *man of God.* Apparently the same prophet mentioned in vv. 13,22. *ye shall know that I am the LORD.* See note on v. 13. God will again demonstrate that He is the sovereign ruler over all nature and history and that the pagan nature deities are powerless before Him.

20:29 *slew . . . an hundred thousand footmen.* Probably includes all those who were driven from the field and the Aramean encampment, including support personnel.

20:30 *wall fell.* The God of Israel not only gave Israel's army a victory in battle but also caused an additional disaster to fall on the Aramean army. *twenty and seven thousand.* Aphek was certainly not so large a city that its wall could literally have collapsed on so many. Perhaps this is the number of troops that had taken refuge in Aphek and were left defenseless when the city walls gave way.

20:31 *kings of the house of Israel are merciful.* The Arameans recognized that Israel's kings were different from, e.g., the ruthless Assyrian kings. *sackcloth . . . ropes.* Perhaps here symbolic of humility and submission.

20:32 *Thy servant.* In the diplomatic language of the time, Ben-hadad acknowledged his inferiority and subordination to Ahab by designating himself Ahab's servant (see note on v. 9). *my brother.* Ahab disregarded Ben-hadad's concession and responded in terminology used by rulers who considered themselves equals (see 9:13). In doing this, Ahab gave much more than Ben-hadad had asked or expected.

20:33 *caused him to come up into the chariot.* Not the treatment normally accorded a defeated military opponent.

20:34 *cities, which my father took from thy father.* Perhaps Ramoth-gilead (see 22:3) along with some of the cities Ben-

away with *this* covenant. So he made a covenant with him, and sent him away.

Ahab judged

35 ¶ And a certain man of [a]the sons of the
prophets said unto his neighbour [b]in the word
of the LORD, Smite me, I pray thee. And the
man refused to smite him.
36 Then said he unto him, Because thou
hast not obeyed the voice of the LORD, behold,
as soon as thou art departed from me, a lion
shall slay thee. And as soon as he was departed from him, [a]a lion found him, and slew him.
37 Then he found another man, and said,
Smite me, I pray thee. And the man smote
him, [1]so that in smiting he wounded *him.*
38 So the prophet departed, and waited for
the king by the way, and disguised himself
with ashes upon his face.
39 And [a]as the king passed by, he cried
unto the king: and he said, Thy servant went
out into the midst of the battle; and behold, a
man turned aside, and brought a man unto
me, and said, Keep this man: if by any means
he be missing, then [b]shall thy life be for his
life, or else thou shalt [1]pay a talent of silver.
40 And as thy servant was busy here and
there, [1]he was gone. And the king of Israel
said unto him, So *shall* thy judgment *be;* thyself hast decided *it.*
41 And he hasted, and took the ashes away
from his face; and the king of Israel discerned
him that he *was* of the prophets.
42 And he said unto him, Thus saith the
LORD, [a]Because thou hast let go out of *thy* hand
a man whom I appointed to utter destruction,
therefore thy life shall go for his life, and thy
people for his people.
43 And the king of Israel [a]went to his
house heavy and displeased, and came to
Samaria.

Naboth's vineyard

21 And it came to pass after these
things, *that* Naboth the Jezreelite had
a vineyard, which *was* in Jezreel, hard by the
palace of Ahab king of Samaria.
2 And Ahab spake unto Naboth, saying,
Give me thy [a]vineyard, that I may have it for a
garden of herbs, because it *is* near unto my
house: and I will give thee for it a better vineyard than it; *or,* if it [1]seem good to thee, I will
give thee the worth of it *in* money.
3 And Naboth said to Ahab, The LORD forbid it me, [a]that I should give the inheritance
of my fathers unto thee.
4 And Ahab came into his house heavy and
displeased because of the word which Naboth
the Jezreelite had spoken to him: for he had
said, I will not give thee the inheritance of my
fathers. And he laid him down upon his bed,
and turned away his face, and would eat no
bread.
5 But Jezebel his wife came to him, and
said unto him, Why is thy spirit so sad, that
thou eatest no bread?
6 And he said unto her, Because I spake
unto Naboth the Jezreelite, and said unto him,

20:35 [a]2 Ki. 2:3,5,7,15 [b]ch. 13:17,18
20:36 [a]ch. 13:24
20:37 [1]Heb. *smiting and wounding*
20:39 [1]Heb. *weigh* [a]See 2 Sam. 12:1 [b]2 Ki. 10:24
20:40 [1]Heb. *he was not*
20:42 [a]ch. 22:31-37
20:43 [a]ch. 21:4
21:2 [1]Heb. *be good in thine eyes* [a]1 Sam. 8:14
21:3 [a]Lev. 25:23; Num. 36:7; Ezek. 46:18

hadad I had taken from Baasha (15:20) at an even earlier time. *make streets for thee.* Outlets for engaging in the lucrative international trade—a distinct economic advantage; usually such privileges were a jealously guarded local monopoly. *made a covenant with him, and sent him away.* A parity treaty (a peace treaty between equals) that included among its provisions the political and trade agreements proposed by Ben-hadad.

20:35 *sons of the prophets.* An expression designating members of prophetic companies (see 2 Ki 2:3,5,7,15; 4:1,38; 5:22; 6:1; 9:1). "Son" is not to be understood here as "male child" or "descendant" but as the member of a group. These companies of prophets were apparently religious communities that sprang up in the face of general indifference and apostasy for the purpose of mutual edification and the cultivation of the experience of God. It seems likely that they were known as prophets because their religious practices (sometimes ecstatic) were called prophesying (see 18:29; Num 11:25–27; 1 Sam 10:5–6,10–11; 18:10; 19:20–24)—to be distinguished from "prophet" in the sense of one bringing ("prophesying") a word from the Lord. The relationship of the Lord's great prophets (such as Samuel, Elijah and Elisha) to these communities was understandably a close one, the Lord's prophets probably being viewed as their spiritual mentors.

20:36 *as soon as thou art departed from me, a lion shall slay thee.* A penalty reminiscent of what happened to the man of God from Judah (13:23–24).

20:39 *talent.* About 75 pounds. Because few soldiers could have paid such a large sum, it would appear to Ahab that the man's life was at stake.

20:40 *So shall thy judgment be.* Ahab refused to grant clemency. Little did he know that he was pronouncing his own death sentence (cf. the similar technique used by Nathan the prophet, 2 Sam 12:1–12).

20:42 *a man whom I appointed to utter destruction.* The Hebrew refers to the irrevocable giving over of things or persons to the Lord, often by totally destroying them (see notes on Lev 27:28; Josh 6:17). It is not clear whether Ahab violated a previous revelation or erred by simply neglecting to inquire of the Lord before releasing Ben-hadad. In any case, the Lord had given Ben-hadad into Ahab's hand (see v. 28), and Ahab was responsible to the Lord for his custody. *thy life shall go for his life, and thy people for his people.* Because Ahab sinned in his official capacity as king, the sentence fell not only on Ahab personally but also on the people of the northern kingdom. Ahab died in battle against the Arameans (22:29–39), and Israel was severely humiliated by them during the reigns of Jehu and Jehoahaz (2 Ki 10:32; 13:3).

21:1 *hard by the palace of Ahab.* Ahab maintained a residence in Jezreel in addition to his official palace in Samaria (see 18:45; 2 Ki 9:30). *Samaria.* The entire northern kingdom is here represented by its capital city (see note on 16:24).

21:2 *Give me thy vineyard.* Because royal power in Israel was limited by covenantal law (see Deut 17:14–20; 1 Sam 10:25), Ahab was unable simply to confiscate privately held land, as was customary with Canaanite kings (see note on v. 7; see also 1 Sam 8:9–17).

21:3 Naboth's refusal to dispose of his land was based on the conviction that the land was the Lord's, that He had granted a perpetual lease to each Israelite family and that this lease was to be jealously preserved as the family's permanent inheritance in the promised land.

Give me thy vineyard for money; or *else,* if it
please thee, I will give thee *another* vineyard
for it: and he answered, I will not give thee my
vineyard.
7 And Jezebel his wife said unto him, Dost
thou now govern the kingdom of Israel? arise,
and eat bread, and let thine heart be merry: I
will give thee the vineyard of Naboth the Jezreelite.
8 So she wrote letters in Ahab's name, and
sealed *them* with his seal, and sent the letters
unto the elders and to the nobles that *were* in
his city, dwelling with Naboth.
9 And she wrote in the letters, saying, Proclaim a fast, and set Naboth [1]on high among
the people:
10 And set two men, sons of Belial, before
him, to bear witness against him, saying, Thou
didst [a]blaspheme God and the king. And *then*
carry him out, and [b]stone him, that he may
die.
11 And the men of his city, *even* the elders
and the nobles who *were* the inhabitants in
his city, did as Jezebel had sent unto them, *and*
as *it was* written in the letters which she had
sent unto them.
12 [a]They proclaimed a fast, and set Naboth
on high among the people.
13 And there came in two men, children of
Belial, and sat before him: and the men of Belial witnessed against him, *even* against Naboth, in the presence of the people, saying,
Naboth did blaspheme God and the king.
[a]Then they carried him forth out of the city,
and stoned him with stones, that he died.
14 Then they sent to Jezebel, saying, Naboth is stoned, and is dead.
15 And it came to pass, when Jezebel
heard that Naboth was stoned, and was dead,
that Jezebel said to Ahab, Arise, take possession of the vineyard of Naboth the Jezreelite,
which he refused to give thee for money: for
Naboth is not alive, but dead.
16 And it came to pass, when Ahab heard
that Naboth was dead, that Ahab rose up to go
down to the vineyard of Naboth the Jezreelite,
to take possession of it.
17 ¶ [a]And the word of the LORD came to
Elijah the Tishbite, saying,
18 Arise, go down to meet Ahab king of Israel, [a]which *is* in Samaria: behold, *he is* in the
vineyard of Naboth, whither he is gone down
to possess it.
19 And thou shalt speak unto him, saying,
Thus saith the LORD, Hast thou killed, and also
taken possession? And thou shalt speak unto
him, saying, Thus saith the LORD, [a]In the place
where dogs licked the blood of Naboth shall
dogs lick thy blood, even thine.
20 And Ahab said to Elijah, [a]Hast thou
found me, O mine enemy? And he answered,
I have found *thee:* because [b]thou hast sold thyself to work evil in the sight of the LORD,
21 Behold, [a]I will bring evil upon thee, and
will take away thy posterity, and will cut off
from Ahab [b]*him that* pisseth against the wall,
and [c]*him that is* shut up and left in Israel,
22 And will make thine house like the
house of [a]Jeroboam the son of Nebat, and like
the house of [b]Baasha the son of Ahijah, for the
provocation wherewith thou hast provoked
me to anger, and made Israel to sin.
23 And [a]of Jezebel also spake the LORD,
saying, The dogs shall eat Jezebel by the [1]wall
of Jezreel.
24 [a]Him that dieth of Ahab in the city the
dogs shall eat; and him that dieth in the field
shall the fowls of the air eat.
25 (But [a]there was none like unto Ahab,
which did sell himself to work wickedness in
the sight of the LORD, [b]whom Jezebel his wife
[1]stirred up.
26 And he did very abominably in following idols, according to all *things* [a]as did the
Amorites, whom the LORD cast out before the
children of Israel).
27 And it came to pass, when Ahab heard
those words, that he rent his clothes, and [a]put

21:9 [1]Heb. *in the top of the people* 21:10 [a]Ex. 22:28; Lev. 24:15,16; Acts 6:11 [b]Lev. 24:14 21:12 [a]Is. 58:4 21:13 [a]See 2 Ki. 9:26

21:17 [a]Ps. 9:12 21:18 [a]ch. 13:32; 2 Chr. 22:9 21:19 [a]ch. 22:38 21:20 [a]ch. 18:17 [b]2 Ki. 17:17; Rom. 7:14 21:21 [a]ch. 14:10; 2 Ki. 9:8 [b]1 Sam. 25:22 [c]ch. 14:10 21:22 [a]ch. 15:29 [b]ch. 16:3,11 21:23 [1]Or, *ditch* [a]2 Ki. 9:36 21:24 [a]ch. 14:11; 16:4 21:25 [1]Or, *incited* [a]ch. 16:30 [b]ch. 16:31 21:26 [a]Gen. 15:16; 2 Ki. 21:11 21:27 [a]Gen. 37:34

21:7 *Dost thou now govern the kingdom of Israel?* A sarcastic remark of incredulity spoken by one accustomed to the despotic practices of the Phoenician and Canaanite kings, who would not hesitate a moment to use their power to satisfy personal interests (contrast the attitude and practice of Samuel in the exercise of his civil power, 1 Sam 12:3–4).

21:9 *Proclaim a fast.* Jezebel attempted to create the impression that a disaster threatened the people that could be averted only if they would humble themselves before the Lord and remove any person whose sin had brought God's judgment on them (cf. Judg 20:26; 1 Sam 7:5–6; 2 Chr 20:2–4).

21:10 *two.* Mosaic law required two witnesses for capital offenses (Num 35:30; Deut 17:6; 19:15). *sons of Belial.* See note on Deut 13:13. *to bear witness.* The entire scenario was designed to give an appearance of legitimate judicial procedure (see Ex 20:16; 23:7; Lev 19:16). *Thou didst blaspheme God and the king.* For this the Mosaic law prescribed death by stoning (Lev 24:15–16).

21:13 *out of the city.* In accordance with Mosaic law (Lev 24:14; Num 15:35–36). Naboth was stoned on his own field (compare v. 19 with 2 Ki 9:21,26), and his sons were stoned with him (see 2 Ki 9:26; cf. the case of Achan, Josh 7:24–25), thus also eliminating his heirs.

21:19 *Hast thou killed, and also taken possession?* Ahab's willing compliance with Jezebel's scheme made him guilty of murder and theft. *In the place where dogs licked the blood of Naboth shall dogs lick thy blood.* Ahab's subsequent repentance (v. 29) occasioned the postponement of certain aspects of this prophecy until the time of his son Joram, whose body was thrown on the field of Naboth (2 Ki 9:25–26). Ahab himself was killed in battle at Ramoth-gilead (22:29–37) and his body brought to Samaria, where the dogs licked the blood being washed from his chariot (22:38).

21:21 *him that is shut up and left in Israel.* See note on 14:10.

21:22 *like the house of Jeroboam.* See 14:10; 15:28–30. *the house of Baasha.* See 16:3–4,11–13.

21:24 See notes on 14:11; 16:4.

21:25 *whom Jezebel his wife stirred up.* See 16:31; 18:4; 19:1–2; 21:7.

21:26 *Amorites.* Here a designation for the entire pre-Israelite population of Canaan (see Gen 15:16; Deut 1:7).

sackcloth upon his flesh, and fasted, and lay in
sackcloth, and went softly.
28 And the word of the LORD came to Elijah
the Tishbite, saying,
29 Seest thou how Ahab humbleth himself
before me? because he humbleth himself before me, I will not bring the evil in his days:
but [a]in his son's days will I bring the evil upon
his house.

Micaiah's prophecy

22 And they continued three years without war between Syria and Israel.
2 And it came to pass on the third year,
that [a]Jehoshaphat the king of Judah came
down to the king of Israel.
3 And the king of Israel said unto his servants, Know ye that [a]Ramoth in Gilead *is* ours,
and we *be* [1]still, and take it not out of the
hand of the king of Syria?
4 And he said unto Jehoshaphat, Wilt thou
go with me to battle *to* Ramoth-gilead? And Jehoshaphat said to the king of Israel, [a]I *am* as
thou *art*, my people as thy people, my horses
as thy horses.
5 And Jehoshaphat said unto the king of Israel, Inquire, I pray thee, at the word of the
LORD to day.
6 Then the king of Israel [a]gathered the
prophets together, about four hundred men,
and said unto them, Shall I go against Ramoth-
gilead to battle, or shall I forbear? And they
said, Go up; for the Lord shall deliver *it* into
the hand of the king.
7 And [a]Jehoshaphat said, *Is there* not here
a prophet of the LORD besides, that we might
inquire of him?
8 And the king of Israel said unto Jehoshaphat, *There is* yet one man, Micaiah the son of
Imlah, by whom *we* may inquire of the LORD:
but I hate him; for he doth not prophesy good
concerning me, but evil. And Jehoshaphat
said, Let not the king say so.
9 Then the king of Israel called an [1]officer,
and said, Hasten *hither* Micaiah the son of Imlah.
10 And the king of Israel and Jehoshaphat
the king of Judah sat each on his throne, having put on *their* robes, in a [1]void place *in* the
entrance of the gate of Samaria; and all the
prophets prophesied before them.
11 And Zedekiah the son of Chenaanah
made him horns of iron: and he said, Thus
saith the LORD, With these shalt thou push the
Syrians, until *thou* have consumed them.
12 And all the prophets prophesied so, saying, Go up *to* Ramoth-gilead, and prosper: for
the LORD shall deliver *it* into the king's hand.
13 ¶ And the messenger that was gone to
call Micaiah spake unto him, saying, Behold
now, the words of the prophets *declare* good
unto the king *with* one mouth: let thy word, I
pray thee, be like the word of one of them, and
speak *that which is* good.
14 And Micaiah said, *As* the LORD liveth,
[a]what the LORD saith unto me, that will I speak.
15 So he came to the king. And the king
said unto him, Micaiah, shall we go against Ramoth-gilead to battle, or shall we forbear? And
he answered him, Go, and prosper: for the
LORD shall deliver *it* into the hand of the king.

21:29 [a]2 Ki. 9:25
22:2 [a]2 Chr. 18:2
22:3 [1]Heb. *silent from taking it* [a]Deut. 4:43
22:4 [a]2 Ki. 3:7
22:6 [a]ch. 18:19
22:7 [a]2 Ki. 3:11
22:9 [1]Or, *eunuch*
22:10 [1]Heb. *floor*
22:14 [a]Num. 22:38

21:27 *sackcloth.* See note on Gen 37:34.

21:29 *in his son's days.* The judgment was postponed but not rescinded (see note on v. 19).

‡22:1 *three years.* See note on 20:1. *without war between Syria* [Hebrew *Aram*] *and Israel.* The annals of the Assyrian ruler Shalmaneser III (859–824 B.C.) record the participation of both "Ahab the Israelite" and Hadadezer (Ben-hadad) of Damascus in a coalition of 12 rulers that fought against Assyrian forces at Qarqar on the Orontes River in 853. According to the Assyrian records, Ahab contributed 2,000 chariots and 10,000 foot soldiers to the allied forces. Assyrian claims of victory appear exaggerated since they withdrew and did not venture westward again for four or five years.

22:2 *Jehoshaphat the king of Judah came down to the king of Israel.* Perhaps to congratulate him on the success of the western alliance against the Assyrian threat (see notes on v. 1; 2 Chr 18:2).

22:3 *Ramoth in Gilead.* Located near the Yarmuk River east of the Jordan; an Israelite city since the days of Moses (see 4:13; Deut 4:43; Josh 20:8). *is ours.* Israel could lay claim to Ramoth-gilead also by virtue of the treaty concluded with Ben-hadad a few years earlier (see 20:34), the provisions of which he had apparently failed to honor.

22:4 *Wilt thou go with me . . . ?* Even though Ahab had just been allied with the Arameans against the Assyrians, now that the Assyrian threat was over he did not hesitate to seize an opportunity to free Ramoth-gilead from Aramean control. *I am as thou art, my people as thy people, my horses as thy horses.* Jehoshaphat was later to be condemned by the prophet Jehu (2 Chr 19:2) for violating the Lord's will by joining forces with Ahab. In this alliance, Jehoshaphat completely reversed the policy of his father Asa, who had entered into an alliance with the Arameans against Baasha of the northern kingdom (see 15:17–23).

22:5 *Inquire . . . at the word of the LORD to day.* Jehoshaphat hesitated to proceed with the planned action without the assurance of the Lord's favor (see 1 Sam 23:1–4; 2 Sam 2:1).

22:6 *prophets.* No doubt associated with the paganized worship at Beth-el (see notes on 12:28–29), they exercised their "office" by proclaiming messages designed to please the king (see Amos 7:10–13).

22:7 *Is there not here a prophet of the LORD . . . ?* Jehoshaphat recognized that the 400 prophets were not to be relied on (see Ezek 13:2–3) and asked for consultation with a true prophet of the Lord.

22:8 *doth not prophesy good.* Ahab's assessment of a prophet depended on whether his message was favorable to him (see 18:17; 21:20).

22:11 *Zedekiah.* Evidently the spokesman for the 400 prophets. *horns of iron.* A symbol of power (see Deut 33:17).

22:13 *let thy word . . . be like the word of one of them.* A bit of advice reflecting the view that all prophets were merely self-serving.

22:15 *we.* A subtle shift (see v. 6) that seeks a favorable response by including Jehoshaphat as a co-sponsor of the enterprise. *Go . . . the LORD shall deliver it into the hand of the king.* Micaiah sarcastically mimics the 400 false prophets (see v. 12).

16 And the king said unto him, How many times shall I adjure thee that thou tell me nothing but *that which is* true in the name of the LORD?

17 And he said, I saw all Israel [a]scattered upon the hills, as sheep that have not a shepherd: and the LORD said, These have no master: let them return every man to his house in peace.

18 And the king of Israel said unto Jehoshaphat, Did I not tell thee that he would prophesy no good concerning me, but evil?

19 And he said, Hear thou therefore the word of the LORD: [a]I saw the LORD sitting on his throne, [b]and all the host of heaven standing by him on his right hand and on his left.

20 And the LORD said, Who shall [1]persuade Ahab, that he may go up and fall at Ramoth-gilead? And one said on this manner, and another said on that manner.

21 And there came forth a spirit, and stood before the LORD, and said, I will persuade him.

22 And the LORD said unto him, Wherewith? And he said, I will go forth, and I will be a lying spirit in the mouth of all his prophets. And he said, [a]Thou shalt persuade *him,* and prevail also: go forth, and do so.

23 [a]Now therefore behold, the LORD hath put a lying spirit in the mouth of all these thy prophets, and the LORD hath spoken evil concerning thee.

24 But Zedekiah the son of Chenaanah went near, and smote Micaiah on the cheek, and said, [a]Which way went the spirit of the LORD from me to speak unto thee?

25 And Micaiah said, Behold, thou shalt see in that day, when thou shalt go [1]into an inner chamber to hide thyself.

26 And the king of Israel said, Take Micaiah, and carry him back unto Amon the governor of the city, and to Joash the king's son;

27 And say, Thus saith the king, Put this *fellow in* the prison, and feed him with bread of affliction and with water of affliction, until I come in peace.

28 And Micaiah said, If thou return at all in peace, [a]the LORD hath not spoken by me. And he said, Hearken, O people, every one of you.

Ahab's defeat and death

29 ¶ So the king of Israel and Jehoshaphat the king of Judah went up *to* Ramoth-gilead.

30 And the king of Israel said unto Jehoshaphat, [1]I will disguise myself, and enter into the battle; but put thou on thy robes. And the king of Israel [a]disguised himself, and went into the battle.

31 But the king of Syria commanded his thirty and two captains that had rule over *his* chariots, saying, Fight neither with small nor great, save only with the king of Israel.

32 And it came to pass, when the captains of the chariots saw Jehoshaphat, that they said, Surely it *is* the king of Israel. And they turned aside to fight against him: and Jehoshaphat [a]cried out.

33 And it came to pass, when the captains of the chariots perceived that it *was* not the king of Israel, that they turned back from pursuing him.

34 And a *certain* man drew a bow [1]at a venture, and smote the king of Israel between the [2]joints of the harness: wherefore he said unto the driver of his chariot, Turn thine hand, and carry me out of the host; for I am [3]wounded.

35 And the battle [1]increased that day: and the king was stayed up in *his* chariot against the Syrians, and died at even: and the blood ran out of the wound into the [2]midst of the chariot.

36 And there went a proclamation throughout the host about the going down of the sun, saying, Every man to his city, and every man to his own country.

37 So the king died, and [1]was brought *to* Samaria; and they buried the king in Samaria.

38 And *one* washed the chariot in the pool of Samaria; and the dogs licked up his blood; and they washed his armour; according [a]unto the word of the LORD which he spake.

39 Now the rest of the acts of Ahab, and all

22:17 [a]Mat. 9:36
22:19 [a]Is. 6:1; Dan. 7:9 [b]Job 1:6; 2:1; Dan. 7:10; Zech. 1:10; Mat. 18:10; Heb. 1:7,14
22:20 [1]Or, *deceive*
22:22 [a]Judg. 9:23; Job 12:16; Ezek. 14:9; 2 Thes. 2:11
22:23 [a]Ezek. 14:9
22:24 [a]2 Chr. 18:23
22:25 [1]Or, from *chamber to chamber.* Heb. *chamber in a chamber*
22:28 [a]Num. 16:29; Deut. 18:20-22
22:30 [1]Or, *when he was to disguise himself, and enter into the battle* [a]2 Chr. 35:22
22:32 [a]2 Chr. 18:31; Prov. 13:20
22:34 [1]Heb. *in his simplicity* [2]Heb. *joints and the breastplate* [3]Heb. *made sick*
22:35 [1]Heb. *ascended* [2]Heb. *bosom*
22:37 [1]Heb. *came*
22:38 [a]ch. 21:19

22:16 *tell me nothing but that which is true.* Micaiah apparently betrayed his lack of seriousness, and Ahab immediately recognizes this.

22:17 *as sheep that have not a shepherd . . . These have no master.* Using the imagery of shepherd and sheep (see Num 27:16–17; Zech 13:7; Mat 9:36; 26:31), Micaiah depicts Ahab's death in the upcoming battle.

22:19 *I saw the LORD sitting on his throne.* A true prophet was one who had, as it were, been made privy to what had transpired in God's heavenly throne room and so could truthfully declare what God intended to do (see Is 6:1; Jer 23:16–22).

22:23 *the LORD hath put a lying spirit in the mouth of all these thy prophets.* Some view the lying spirit as Satan or one of his agents. Others have suggested a spirit of God who undertakes the task of a lying spirit (but see 1 Sam 15:29). Still others understand the lying spirit as a symbolic picture of the power of the lie. The Lord had given the 400 prophets over to the power of the lie because they did not love the truth and had chosen to speak out of their own hearts (see Jer 14:14; 23:16,26; Ezek 13:2–3,17; see also note on 2 Sam 24:1; cf. 2 Thes 2:9–12).

22:24 *Which way went the spirit of the LORD from me to speak unto thee?* By this sarcastic question Zedekiah suggests that one prophet can be a liar just as well as another.

22:25 *go into an inner chamber to hide.* Where Zedekiah will seek refuge (cf. 20:30). This will vindicate Micaiah's prophetic authority.

22:30 *disguise.* By this strategy he thought he could direct attention away from himself and so minimize any chance for fulfillment of Micaiah's prediction.

22:31 *only with the king of Israel.* If the leader was killed or captured, ancient armies usually fell apart (cf. vv. 35–36).

22:34 *driver of his chariot.* A war chariot normally carried two men—a fighter and a driver. Sometimes, it appears, there were three men, but the third seems to have been an officer who commanded a chariot unit (see 9:22; 2 Ki 9:25; Ex 14:7; 15:4).

22:35 *died at even.* Fulfilling Micaiah's prophecy (vv. 17,28).

22:38 *according unto the word of the LORD.* A partial fulfillment of Elijah's prophecy concerning Ahab's death (see note on 21:19).

that he did, and [a]the ivory house which he
made, and all the cities that he built, *are* they
not written in the book of the chronicles of the
kings of Israel?
40 So Ahab slept with his fathers; and Ahaziah his son reigned in his stead.

Jehoshaphat, king of Judah

41 ¶ And [a]Jehoshaphat the son of Asa *be-*
gan to reign over Judah in the fourth year of
Ahab king of Israel.
42 Jehoshaphat *was* thirty and five years
old when he *began* to reign; and he reigned
twenty and five years in Jerusalem. And his
mother's name *was* Azubah the daughter of
Shilhi.
43 And [a]he walked in all the ways of Asa
his father; he turned not aside from it, doing
that which *was* right in the eyes of the LORD:
nevertheless [b]the high places were not taken
away; *for* the people offered and burnt incense
yet in the high places.
44 And [a]Jehoshaphat made peace with the
king of Israel.
45 Now the rest of the acts of Jehoshaphat,
and his might that he shewed, and how he
warred, *are* they not written in the book of the
chronicles of the kings of Judah?
46 [a]And the remnant of the sodomites,
which remained in the days of his father Asa,
he took out of the land.
47 [a]*There was* then no king in Edom: a
deputy *was* king.
48 [a]Jehoshaphat [b][1]made ships of Tharshish to go to Ophir for gold: [c]but they went
not; for the ships were broken at [d]Ezion-geber.
49 Then said Ahaziah the son of Ahab unto
Jehoshaphat, Let my servants go with thy servants in the ships. But Jehoshaphat would not.
50 And [a]Jehoshaphat slept with his fathers, and was buried with his fathers in the
city of David his father: and Jehoram his son
reigned in his stead.

Ahaziah, king of Israel

51 ¶ [a]Ahaziah the son of Ahab *began* to
reign over Israel in Samaria the seventeenth
year of Jehoshaphat king of Judah, and reigned
two years over Israel.
52 And he did evil in the sight of the LORD,
and [a]walked in the way of his father, and in
the way of his mother, and in the way of Jeroboam the son of Nebat, who made Israel to
sin:
53 For [a]he served Baal, and worshipped
him, and provoked to anger the LORD God of
Israel, according unto all that his father had
done.

22:39 [a]Amos 3:15
22:41 [a]2 Chr. 20:31
22:43 [a]2 Chr. 17:3 [b]ch. 14:23; 15:14; 2 Ki. 12:3
22:44 [a]2 Chr. 19:2; 2 Cor. 6:14
22:46 [a]ch. 14:24; 15:12
22:47 [a]Gen. 25:23; 2 Sam. 8:14; 2 Ki. 3:9; 8:20
22:48 [1]Or, had *ten ships* [a]2 Chr. 20:35 [b]ch. 10:22 [c]2 Chr. 20:37 [d]ch. 9:26
22:50 [a]2 Chr. 21:1
22:51 [a]ver. 40
22:52 [a]ch. 15:26
22:53 [a]Judg. 2:11; ch. 16:31

22:39 *ivory house which he made.* Excavators of Samaria have found ivory inlays in some of the buildings dating from this period of Israel's history. Ahab's use of ivory in this way is indicative of the realm's economic prosperity during his reign. *cities that he built.* Excavators have found evidence that Ahab strengthened the fortifications of Megiddo and Hazor. *chronicles of the kings of Israel.* See note on 14:19.

22:40 *slept with his fathers.* See note on 1:21. *Ahaziah his son reigned in his stead.* For the reign of Ahaziah see vv. 51–53; 2 Ki 1.

22:41 *Jehoshaphat . . . began to reign over Judah in the fourth year of Ahab.* Appears to refer to the beginning of Jehoshaphat's reign as sole king in 869 B.C. (see notes on v. 42; 16:29; see also Introduction: Chronology).

22:42 *twenty and five years.* 872–848 B.C. The full span of Jehoshaphat's reign dates from the 39th year of King Asa, when he became co-regent with his father (see note on 15:10; see also 2 Chr 16:12).

22:43 *the high places were not taken away.* See notes on 3:2; 15:14.

22:44 *king.* Probably to be understood in the collective sense and as including Ahab, Ahaziah and Joram, all of whom ruled in the north during the reign of Jehoshaphat in the south (see note on v. 4).

22:45 *how he warred.* See 2 Ki 3; 2 Chr 17:11; 20. *chronicles of the kings of Judah.* See note on 14:29.

22:46 *sodomites.* See note on 14:24.

22:47 *no king in Edom.* Suggests that Edom was subject to Judah (see 2 Sam 8:14; 2 Ki 8:20).

22:48 *Ophir.* See note on 9:28. *broken at Ezion-geber.* The destruction of the trading ships was a judgment of God on Jehoshaphat for entering into an alliance with Ahaziah of the northern kingdom (see 2 Chr 20:35–37).

22:50 *slept with his fathers.* See note on 1:21. *Jehoram his son reigned in his stead.* For the reign of Jehoram see 2 Ki 8:16–24; 2 Chr 21.

22:51 *seventeenth year of Jehoshaphat.* 853 B.C. (see notes on vv. 41–42). *two years.* 853–852 (see note on 2 Ki 1:17).

22:52 *way of his father and . . . mother.* See 16:30–33. *way of Jeroboam.* See 12:28–33.

The Second Book of the
Kings

INTRODUCTION

See Introduction to 1 Kings.

Outline

Below is an abbreviated outline for 2 Kings. For the complete outline see Introduction to 1 Kings: Outline.

III. The Ministries of Elijah and Elisha and Other Prophets from Ahab/Asa to Joram/Jehoshaphat (1 Ki 17:1—2 Ki 8:15)
- A. Elijah (and Other Prophets) in the Reign of Ahab (1 Ki 17:1—22:40)
- B. Jehoshaphat of Judah (1 Ki 22:41–50)
- C. Ahaziah of Israel; Elijah's Last Prophecy (22:51—2 Ki 1:18)
- D. Elijah's Translation; Elisha's Inauguration (2 Ki 2:1–18)
- E. Elisha in the Reign of Jehoram (2:19—8:15)

IV. Israel and Judah from Joram/Jehoram to the Exile of Israel (2 Ki 8:16—17:41)
- A. Jehoram of Judah (8:16–24)
- B. Ahaziah of Judah (8:25–29)
- C. Jehu's Revolt and Reign (chs. 9—10)
- D. Athaliah and Joash of Judah; Repair of the Temple (chs. 11—12)
- E. Jehoahaz of Israel (13:1–9)
- F. Jehoash of Israel; Elisha's Last Prophecy (13:10–25)
- G. Amaziah of Judah (14:1–22)
- H. Jeroboam II of Israel (14:23–29)
- I. Azariah of Judah (15:1–7)
- J. Zechariah of Israel (15:8–12)
- K. Shallum of Israel (15:13–16)
- L. Menahem of Israel (15:17–22)
- M. Pekahiah of Israel (15:23–26)
- N. Pekah of Israel (15:27–31)
- O. Jotham of Judah (15:32–38)
- P. Ahaz of Judah (ch. 16)
- Q. Hoshea of Israel (17:1–6)
- R. Exile of Israel; Resettlement of the Land (17:7–41)

V. Judah from Hezekiah to the Babylonian Exile (2 Ki 18—25)
- A. Hezekiah (chs. 18—20)
- B. Manasseh (21:1–18)
- C. Amon (21:19–26)
- D. Josiah (22:1—23:30)
- E. Jehoahaz Exiled to Egypt (23:31–35)
- F. Jehoiakim: First Babylonian Invasion (23:36—24:7)
- G. Jehoiachin: Second Babylonian Invasion (24:8–17)
- H. Zedekiah (24:18–20)
- I. Babylonian Exile of Judah (25:1–21)
- J. Removal of the Remnant to Egypt (25:22–26)
- K. Elevation of Jehoiachin in Babylon (25:27–30)

Elijah's prophecy to Ahaziah

1 Then Moab [a]rebelled against Israel [b]after the death of Ahab.
2 And Ahaziah fell down through a lattice
in his upper chamber that *was* in Samaria, and
was sick: and he sent messengers, and said
unto them, Go, inquire of Baal-zebub the god
of [a]Ekron whether I shall recover of this disease.
3 But the angel of the LORD said to Elijah the
Tishbite, Arise, go up to meet the messengers
of the king of Samaria, and say unto them, *Is it*
not because *there is* not a God in Israel, *that* ye
go to inquire of Baal-zebub the god of Ekron?
4 Now therefore thus saith the LORD,
[1]Thou shalt not come down from *that* bed on
which thou art gone up, but shalt surely die.
And Elijah departed.
5 And when the messengers turned back
unto him, he said unto them, Why are ye now
turned back?
6 And they said unto him, There came a
man up to meet us, and said unto us, Go, turn
again unto the king that sent you, and say unto
him, Thus saith the LORD, *Is it* not because
there is not a God in Israel, *that* thou sendest
to inquire of Baal-zebub the god of Ekron?
therefore thou shalt not come down from *that*
bed on which thou art gone up, but shalt surely die.

1:1 [a]2 Sam. 8:2 [b]ch. 3:5
1:2 [a]1 Sam. 5:10
1:4 [1]Heb. *The bed whither thou art gone up, thou shalt not come down from it*
1:7 [1]Heb. *What was the manner of the man*
1:8 [a]See Zech. 13:4; Mat. 3:4
1:10 [a]Luke 9:54
1:13 [1]Heb. *bowed*

7 And he said unto them, [1]What manner of
man *was he* which came up to meet you, and
told you these words?
8 And they answered him, *He was* [a]a hairy
man, and girt *with* a girdle of leather about his
loins. And he said, It *is* Elijah the Tishbite.
9 Then the king sent unto him a captain of
fifty with his fifty. And he went up to him: and
behold, he sat on the top of a hill. And he
spake unto him, Thou man of God, the king
hath said, Come down.
10 And Elijah answered and said to the
captain of fifty, If I *be* a man of God, then [a]let
fire come down from heaven, and consume
thee and thy fifty. And there came down fire
from heaven, and consumed him and his fifty.
11 Again also he sent unto him another
captain of fifty with his fifty. And he answered
and said unto him, O man of God, thus hath
the king said, Come down quickly.
12 And Elijah answered and said unto
them, If I *be* a man of God, let fire come down
from heaven, and consume thee and thy fifty.
And the fire of God came down from heaven,
and consumed him and his fifty.
13 And he sent again a captain of the third
fifty with his fifty. And the third captain of fifty
went up, and came and [1]fell on his knees before Elijah, and besought him, and said unto
him, O man of God, I pray thee, let my life,

1:1 *Moab rebelled.* Moab had been brought into subjection by David (see 2 Sam 8:2), but when the northern tribes and those east of the Jordan rebelled and made Jeroboam their king, political domination of Moab probably also shifted to the northern kingdom. An inscription of Mesha king of Moab (see chart, p. xix) indicates that during the reign of Omri's "son" (probably a reference to his grandson Joram, not to Ahab) the Moabites were able to free the area of Medeba from Israelite control (see map No. 5 at the end of the study Bible). *after the death of Ahab.* See 1 Ki 22:37.

1:2 *Baal-zebub.* See note on Judg 10:6. *Ekron.* The northernmost of the five major Philistine cities (see Josh 13:3; 1 Sam 5:10 and notes). *whether I shall recover.* Ahaziah appears to have feared that his injury would be fatal. He turned to the pagan deity for a revelatory oracle, not for healing.

1:3 *angel of the LORD.* See 1 Ki 19:7; see also note on Gen 16:7. The Lord usually spoke directly to the consciousness of the prophet (1 Ki 17:2,8; 18:1; 19:9; 21:17). Perhaps the means of revelation was changed in this instance to heighten the contrast between the messengers of Ahaziah (vv. 2–3,5) and the angel (which means "messenger") of the Lord. *Elijah the Tishbite.* See note on 1 Ki 17:1. *king of Samaria.* See note on 1 Ki 21:1.

1:4 *thou . . . shalt surely die.* Ahaziah will receive the oracle he sought, but it will come from the Lord through Elijah, not from Baal-zebub.

1:5 *Why are ye now turned back?* Ahaziah realized the messengers could not have traveled so quickly to Ekron and back.

1:8 *hairy man.* See 1 Ki 19:19. That is, he wore a garment (probably his cloak) made of sheepskin or camel's hair, tied with a simple leather thong (cf. Mat 3:4). His dress contrasted sharply with the fine linen clothing (see Jer 13:1) of his wealthy contemporaries and constituted a protest against the materialistic attitudes of the king and the upper classes (cf. Mat 11:7–8; Luke 7:24–25). *It is Elijah the Tishbite.* Ahaziah was familiar with Elijah's appearance because of the prophet's many encounters with Ahab, his father.

1:9 *the king sent unto him a captain of fifty with his fifty.* The pagan people of that time thought that the magical power of curses could be nullified either by forcing the pronouncer of the curse to retract his statement or by killing him so that his curse would go with him to the netherworld. It appears that Ahaziah shared this view and desired to take Elijah prisoner in order to counteract the pronouncement of his death. *Thou man of God, the king hath said, Come down.* Ahaziah attempted to place the prophet under the authority of the king. This constituted a violation of the covenant nature of Israelite kingship, in which the king's actions were always to be placed under the scrutiny and authority of the word of the Lord spoken by His prophets (see notes on 1 Sam 10:25; 12:23).

1:10 *came down fire from heaven, and consumed him and his fifty.* See 1 Ki 18:38. Another link between the ministries of Elijah and Moses (see Lev 10:2; Num 16:35). At stake in this incident was the question of who was sovereign in Israel. Would Ahaziah recognize that the king in Israel was only a vice-regent under the authority and kingship of the Lord, or would he exercise despotic power, like pagan kings (see notes on 1 Sam 12:14–15)? At mount Carmel the Lord had revealed Himself and authenticated His prophet by fire from heaven (see 1 Ki 18:38–39). Now this previous revelation is confirmed to Ahaziah. Jesus' rebuke of His disciples for suggesting that fire be called down from heaven to destroy the Samaritans (Luke 9:51–56) is not to be understood as a disapproval of Elijah's action, but as an indication that the disciples failed to discern the difference between the issue at stake in Elijah's day and the unbelief of the Samaritans in their own day.

1:11 *Again also he sent unto him another captain of fifty with his fifty.* Ahaziah refused to submit to the word of the Lord in spite of the dramatic revelation of God's power.

1:13 *fell on his knees before Elijah.* The third captain, recognizing that Elijah was the bearer of the word of the Lord, feared

and the life of these fifty thy servants, [a]be precious in thy sight.

14 Behold, there came fire down from heaven, and burnt up the two captains of the former fifties with their fifties: therefore let my life now be precious in thy sight.

15 And the angel of the LORD said unto Elijah, Go down with him: be not afraid of him. And he arose, and went down with him unto the king.

16 And he said unto him, Thus saith the LORD, Forasmuch as thou hast sent messengers to inquire of Baal-zebub the god of Ekron, *is it* not because *there is* no God in Israel to inquire of his word? therefore thou shalt not come down off *that* bed on which thou art gone up, but shalt surely die.

17 So he died according to the word of the LORD which Elijah had spoken. And [1]Jehoram reigned in his stead in the second year of Jehoram the son of Jehoshaphat king of Judah; because he had no son.

18 Now the rest of the acts of Ahaziah which he did, *are* they not written in the book of the chronicles of the kings of Israel?

Elijah taken up to heaven

2 And it came to pass, when the LORD would [a]take up Elijah *into* heaven by a whirlwind, that Elijah went with [b]Elisha from Gilgal.

2 And Elijah said unto Elisha, [a]Tarry here, I pray thee; for the LORD hath sent me to Beth-el. And Elisha said *unto him, As* the LORD liveth, and [b]*as* thy soul liveth, I will not leave thee. So they went down *to* Beth-el.

3 And [a]the sons of the prophets that *were at* Beth-el came forth to Elisha, and said unto him, Knowest thou that the LORD will take away thy master from thy head to day? And he said, Yea, I know *it;* hold you your peace.

1:13 [a]1 Sam. 26:21; Ps. 72:14
1:17 [1][The second year that *Jehoram* was *Prorex,* and the eighteenth of *Jehoshaphat,* ch. 3:1]
2:1 [a]Gen. 5:24 [b]1 Ki. 19:21
2:2 [a]See Ruth 1:15,16 [b]ver. 4,6; 1 Sam. 1:26; ch. 4:30
2:3 [a]ver. 5,7,15; 1 Ki. 20:35; ch. 4:1,38; 9:1

4 And Elijah said unto him, Elisha, tarry here, I pray thee; for the LORD hath sent me *to* Jericho. And he said, *As* the LORD liveth, and *as* thy soul liveth, I will not leave thee. So they came *to* Jericho.

5 And the sons of the prophets that *were* at Jericho came to Elisha, and said unto him, Knowest thou that the LORD will take away thy master from thy head to day? And he answered, Yea, I know *it;* hold you your peace.

6 And Elijah said unto him, Tarry, I pray thee, here; for the LORD hath sent me to Jordan. And he said, *As* the LORD liveth, and *as* thy soul liveth, I will not leave thee. And they two went on.

7 And fifty men of the sons of the prophets went, and stood [1]to view afar off: and they two stood by Jordan.

8 And Elijah took his mantle, and wrapt *it* together, and smote the waters, and [a]they were divided hither and thither, so that they two went over on dry *ground.*

9 And it came to pass, when they were gone over, that Elijah said unto Elisha, Ask what I shall do for thee, before I be taken away from thee. And Elisha said, I pray thee, let a double portion of thy spirit be upon me.

10 And he said, [1]Thou hast asked a hard thing: *nevertheless,* if thou see me *when I am* taken from thee, it shall be so unto thee; but if not, it shall not be *so.*

11 And it came to pass, *as* they still went on, and talked, that behold, *there appeared* [a]a chariot of fire, and horses of fire, and parted them both asunder; and Elijah went up by a whirlwind *into* heaven.

12 And Elisha saw *it,* and he cried, [a]My father, my father, the chariot of Israel, and the horsemen thereof. And he saw him no more: and he took hold of his own clothes, and rent them in two pieces.

2:7 [1]Heb. *in sight,* or, *over against*
2:8 [a]ver. 14; Ex. 14:21; Josh. 3:16
2:10 [1]Heb. *Thou hast done hard in asking*
2:11 [a]ch. 6:17; Ps. 104:4
2:12 [a]ch. 13:14

for his life and bowed before him with a humble request.

1:15 *the angel of the LORD said unto Elijah.* See note on v. 3.

1:17 *died according to the word of the LORD.* In the end Ahaziah was punished for turning away from the God of Israel to a pagan deity, and the word of the Lord was shown to be both reliable and beyond the power of the king to annul. *Jehoram.* Ahaziah's younger brother (see 3:1; 1 Ki 22:51). *second year of Jehoram the son of Jehoshaphat.* Jehoram's reign overlapped that of his father Jehoshaphat from 853 to 848 B.C. (see note on 8:16). The reference here is to the second year of that co-regency. The 18th year of Jehoshaphat (3:1) is therefore the same as the second year of Jehoram's co-regency (852).

1:18 *chronicles of the kings of Israel.* See note on 1 Ki 14:19.

2:2 *I will not leave thee.* Elisha was aware that Elijah's ministry was almost finished and that his departure was near (v. 5). He was determined to accompany him until the moment the Lord took him. His commitment to Elijah and to Elijah's ministry was unfailing (see v. 9; 1 Ki 19:21).

2:3 *sons of.* See note on 1 Ki 20:35. During the days of Elijah and Elisha, companies of prophets were located at Beth-el (here), Jericho (v. 5) and Gilgal (4:38). It appears that Elijah journeyed by divine instruction to Gilgal (v. 1), Beth-el (v. 2) and Jericho (v. 4) for a last meeting with each of these companies.

2:7 *fifty men.* These men were to witness the miracle by which Elijah and Elisha crossed the river.

2:8 *Elijah took his mantle . . . and smote the waters.* Elijah used his cloak much as Moses had used his staff at the time of Israel's passage through the "Red sea" (see Ex 14:16,21,26).

2:9 *let a double portion . . . be upon me.* Elisha was not expressing a desire for a ministry twice as great as Elijah's, but he was using terms derived from inheritance law to express his desire to carry on Elijah's ministry. Inheritance law assigned a double portion of a father's possessions to the firstborn son (see Deut 21:17 and note).

2:10 *hard thing.* Although Elijah had previously been told to anoint Elisha as his successor (1 Ki 19:16,19–21), Elijah's response clearly showed that the issue rested solely with the Lord's sovereign good pleasure. *if thou see me . . . it shall be so . . . but if not, it shall not be so.* Elijah left the answer to Elisha's request in the Lord's hands.

2:11 *chariot of fire, and horses of fire.* The Lord's heavenly host has accompanied and supported Elijah's ministry (as it had that of Moses; see Ex 15:1–10), and now at his departure Elisha is allowed to see it (cf. 6:17). *Elijah went up by a whirlwind into heaven.* Elijah, like Enoch before him (Gen 5:24), was taken up to heaven bodily without experiencing death; like Moses (Deut 34:4–6), he was taken away outside the promised land.

2:12 *chariot of Israel, and the horsemen thereof.* Elisha depict-

13 He took up also the mantle of Elijah that
fell from him, and went back, and stood by the
[1]bank of Jordan;
14 And he took the mantle of Elijah that
fell from him, and smote the waters, and said,
Where *is* the LORD God of Elijah? and when he
also had smitten the waters, [a]they parted hither and thither: and Elisha went over.
15 And when the sons of the prophets
which *were* [a]to view at Jericho saw him, they
said, The spirit of Elijah doth rest on Elisha.
And they came to meet him, and bowed themselves to the ground before him.
16 And they said unto him, Behold now,
there be with thy servants fifty [1]strong men;
let them go, we pray thee, and seek thy master: [a]lest peradventure the spirit of the LORD
hath taken him up, and cast him upon [2]some
mountain, or into some valley. And he said, Ye
shall not send.
17 And when they urged him till *he* was
ashamed, he said, Send. They sent therefore
fifty men; and they sought three days, but
found him not.
18 And when they came again to him, (for
he tarried at Jericho,) he said unto them, Did I
not say unto you, Go not?

Beginning of Elisha's ministry

19 ¶ And the men of the city said unto Elisha, Behold, I pray thee, the situation of *this*
city *is* pleasant, as my lord seeth: but the water *is* naught, and the ground [1]barren.
20 And he said, Bring me a new cruse, and
put salt therein. And they brought *it* to him.
21 And he went forth unto the spring of
the waters, and [a]cast the salt in there, and
said, Thus saith the LORD, I have healed these
waters; there shall not be from thence any
more death or barren *land.*
22 So the waters were healed unto this
day, according to the saying of Elisha which he
spake.
23 ¶ And he went up from thence *unto*
Beth-el: and as he was going up by the way,
there came forth little children out of the city,
and mocked him, and said unto him, Go up,
thou bald head; go up, thou bald head.
24 And he turned back, and looked on
them, and cursed them in the name of the
LORD. And there came forth two she bears out
of the wood, and tare forty and two children of
them.
25 And he went from thence to mount Carmel, and from thence he returned *to* Samaria.

Jehoram's siege against Moab

3 Now Jehoram the son of Ahab *began* to
reign over Israel in Samaria the eighteenth year of Jehoshaphat king of Judah, and
reigned twelve years.
2 And he wrought evil in the sight of the

2:13 [1]Heb. *lip* 2:14 [a]ver. 8 2:15 [a]ver. 7 2:16 [1]Heb. *sons of strength* [2]Heb. *one of the mountains* [a]See 1 Ki. 18:12; Ezek. 8:3; Acts 8:39; ch. 1:17

2:19 [1]Heb. *causing to miscarry* 2:21 [a]See Ex. 15:25; ch. 4:41; 6:6; John 9:6

ed Elijah as embodying the true strength of the nation. He, rather than the apostate king, is the Lord's representative. The same description was later used of Elisha (13:14).

2:13 *He took up also the mantle.* See note on v. 8. Possession of Elijah's cloak symbolized Elisha's succession to Elijah's ministry (see 1 Ki 19:19).

2:14 *when he also had smitten the waters, they parted.* See v. 8. The Lord authenticated Elisha's succession to Elijah's ministry and demonstrated that the same divine power that had accompanied Elijah's ministry was now operative in the ministry of Elisha. In crossing the Jordan as Joshua had before him, Elisha is shown to be Elijah's "Joshua" (Elisha and Joshua are very similar names, Elisha meaning "God saves" and Joshua "The LORD saves").

2:15 *bowed themselves to the ground before him.* Indicated their recognition of Elisha's succession to Elijah's position. Elisha was now the Lord's official representative in this time of royal apostasy.

2:16 *peradventure the spirit of the LORD hath taken him up, and cast him upon.* Obadiah expressed the same idea years earlier (see 1 Ki 18:12). *Ye shall not send.* Elisha knew their search would be fruitless.

2:17 *Send.* When the company of prophets refused to be satisfied with Elisha's answer, he permitted them to go so that the authority and truth of his words would be confirmed to them.

2:19 *city.* Evidently Jericho (see v. 18). *the water is naught, and the ground barren.* The inhabitants of Jericho were experiencing the effects of the covenant curse (contrast Deut 28:15–18 with Ex 23:25–26; Lev 26:9; Deut 28:1–4). See 1 Ki 16:34; Josh 6:26.

2:20 *new cruse.* That which was to be used in the service of the Lord was to be undefiled by profane use (see Lev 1:3,10; Num 19:2; Deut 21:3; 1 Sam 6:7). *put salt therein.* Elisha may have used salt because of its known preservative qualities, but it is more likely that he used it to symbolize the covenant faithfulness of the Lord (see note on Num 18:19; see also 2 Chr 13:5).

2:21 *I have healed these waters.* Any idea of a magical effect of the salt in the purification of the water is excluded by the explicit statement that the Lord Himself healed the water. In this symbolic way Elisha was able, as the first act of his ministry, to proclaim to the people that in spite of their disobedience the Lord was merciful and was still reaching out to them in His grace (see 13:23).

2:23 *Go up.* Since Beth-el was the royal cult center of the northern kings (1 Ki 12:29; Amos 7:13) and Elijah and Elisha were known to frequent Samaria (perhaps even as their main residence; see note on 5:3), the youths from Beth-el no doubt assumed that Elisha was going up to Samaria to continue Elijah's struggle against royal apostasy. (Some believe that the youths, in their mocking, were telling Elisha to ascend to heaven as Elijah had done.) *thou bald head.* Baldness was uncommon among the ancient Jews, and luxuriant hair seems to have been viewed as a sign of strength and vigor (see note on 2 Sam 14:26). By calling Elisha "bald head," the youths from Beth-el expressed that city's utter disdain for the Lord's representative, who, they felt, had no power.

2:24 *cursed them in the name of the LORD.* Elisha pronounced a curse similar to the covenant curse of Lev 26:21–22. The result gave warning of the judgment that would come on the entire nation should it persist in disobedience and apostasy (see 2 Chr 36:16). Thus Elisha's first acts were indicative of his ministry that would follow: God's covenant blessings would come to those who looked to Him (vv. 19–22), but God's covenant curses would fall on those who turned away from Him.

3:1 *Jehoram the son of Ahab began to reign . . . the eighteenth year of Jehoshaphat.* See note on 1:17. *twelve years.* 852–841 B.C.

3:2 *not like his father, and like his mother.* Not as Ahab (see notes

LORD; but not like his father, and like his
mother: for he put away the [1]image of Baal
[a]that his father had made.
3 Nevertheless he cleaved unto [a]the sins of
Jeroboam the son of Nebat, which made Israel
to sin; he departed not therefrom.
4 And Mesha king of Moab was a sheepmaster, and rendered unto the king of Israel an
hundred thousand [a]lambs, and an hundred
thousand rams, *with* the wool.
5 But it came to pass, when [a]Ahab was
dead, that the king of Moab rebelled against
the king of Israel.
6 And king Jehoram went out of Samaria
the same time, and numbered all Israel.
7 And he went and sent to Jehoshaphat the
king of Judah, saying, The king of Moab hath
rebelled against me: wilt thou go with me
against Moab to battle? And he said, I will go
up: [a]I *am* as thou *art*, my people as thy people,
and my horses as thy horses.
8 And he said, Which way shall we go up?
And he answered, The way through the
wilderness of Edom.
9 So the king of Israel went, and the king of
Judah, and the king of Edom: and they fetcht a
compass of seven days' journey: and there was
no water for the host, and for the cattle that
[1]followed them.
10 And the king of Israel said, Alas, that
the LORD hath called these three kings *together*, to deliver them into the hand of Moab.
11 But [a]Jehoshaphat said, *Is there* not here
a prophet of the LORD, that we may inquire of
the LORD by him? And one of the king of Israel's servants answered and said, Here *is* Elisha
the son of Shaphat, which poured water on
the hands of Elijah.
12 And Jehoshaphat said, The word of the
LORD is with him. So the king of Israel and Jehoshaphat and the king of Edom [a]went down
to him.
13 And Elisha said unto the king of Israel,
[a]What have I to do with thee? [b]get thee to
[c]the prophets of thy father, and to the prophets of thy mother. And the king of Israel said
unto him, Nay: for the LORD hath called these
three kings *together*, to deliver them into the
hand of Moab.
14 And Elisha said, [a]*As* the LORD of hosts
liveth, before whom I stand, surely, were it
not that I regard the presence of Jehoshaphat
the king of Judah, I would not look toward
thee, nor see thee.
15 But now bring me [a]a minstrel. And it
came to pass, when the minstrel played, that
[b]the hand of the LORD came upon him.
16 And he said, Thus saith the LORD,
[a]Make this valley full of ditches.
17 For thus saith the LORD, Ye shall not
see wind, neither shall ye see rain; yet that
valley shall be filled *with* water, that ye may
drink, *both* ye, and your cattle, and your
beasts.
18 And this is *but* a light thing in the sight
of the LORD: he will deliver the Moabites also
into your hand.
19 And ye shall smite every fenced city,

3:2 [1]Heb. *statue* [a]1 Ki. 16:31,32
3:3 [a]1 Ki. 12:28,31,32
3:4 [a]See Is. 16:1
3:5 [a]ch. 1:1
3:7 [a]1 Ki. 22:4
3:9 [1]Heb. *at their feet*
3:11 [a]1 Ki. 22:7
3:12 [a]ch. 2:25
3:13 [a]Ezek. 14:3 [b]Judg. 10:14; Ruth 1:15 [c]1 Ki. 18:19
3:14 [a]1 Ki. 17:1; ch. 5:16
3:15 [a]See 1 Sam. 10:5 [b]Ezek. 1:3; 3:14,22; 8:1
3:16 [a]ch. 4:3

on 1 Ki 16:30–34) and Jezebel (see 1 Ki 18:4; 19:1–2; 21:7–15). *image of Baal that his father had made.* Apparently a reference to the stone representation of the male deity (see note on 1 Ki 14:23) that Ahab placed in the temple he had constructed for Jezebel in Samaria (see 1 Ki 16:32–33). From 10:27 it appears that this stone was later reinstated, perhaps by Jezebel.

3:3 *sins of Jeroboam . . . which made Israel to sin.* See note on 1 Ki 14:16.

3:4 *Mesha king of Moab.* See note on 1:1. *an hundred thousand lambs, and an hundred thousand rams, with the wool.* The heavy annual tribute (see Is 16:1) that Israel required from the Moabites as a vassal state.

3:5 *king of Moab rebelled.* See note on 1:1.

3:7 *wilt thou go with me against Moab to battle?* Jehoram wished to attack Moab from the rear (v. 8), but to do that his army had to pass through Judah. *I am as thou art, my people as thy people, and my horses as thy horses.* See 1 Ki 22:4. Jehoshaphat had already been condemned by prophets of the Lord for his alliance with the northern kings Ahab (see 2 Chr 18:1; 19:1–2) and Ahaziah (2 Chr 20:35–37), yet he agreed to join with Jehoram against Moab. Perhaps he was disturbed by the potential danger to Judah posed by the growing strength of Moab (see 2 Chr 20), and he may have considered Jehoram less evil than his predecessors (see v. 2).

3:8 *The way through the wilderness of Edom.* This route of attack took the armies of Israel and Judah south of the Dead Sea, enabling them to circumvent the fortifications of Moab's northern frontier and to avoid the possibility of a rearguard action against them by the Arameans of Damascus. The Edomites, who were subject to Judah, were in no position to resist the movement of Israel's army through their territory.

3:9 *king of Edom.* Although here designated a king, he was in reality a governor appointed by Jehoshaphat (see 8:20; 1 Ki 22:47).

3:11 *Is there not here a prophet of the LORD . . . ?* See 1 Ki 22:7. Only after the apparent failure of their own strategies did the three rulers seek the word of the Lord (v. 12). *Here is Elisha the son of Shaphat.* Since Elijah is reported to have sent a letter to Jehoshaphat's son Jehoram after his father's death (2 Chr 21:12–15), it seems that Elisha accompanied the armies on this campaign as the representative of the aged Elijah. The event is narrated here after the account of Elisha's initiation as Elijah's successor and the two events that foreshadowed the character of his ministry. Following this introduction to Elisha's ministry, the present episode is topically associated with the series of Elisha's acts that now occupies the narrative.

3:13 *get thee to the prophets of thy father and . . . mother.* See 1 Ki 22:6.

3:14 *were it not that I regard . . . Jehoshaphat . . . I would not look toward thee.* Jehoram will share in the blessing of the word of God only because of his association with Jehoshaphat.

3:15 *bring me a minstrel.* To create a disposition conducive to receiving the word of the Lord.

3:16 *this valley.* The Israelite armies were encamped in the broad valley (the Arabah) between the highlands of Moab on the east and those of Judah on the west, just south of the Dead Sea.

3:17 *shall be filled with water.* The word of the Lord contained a promise and a directive. The Lord will graciously provide for His people, but they must respond to His word in faith and obedience (v. 16).

3:19 The two armies will devastate the rebellious country.

and every choice city, and shall fell every good
tree, and stop all wells of water, and [1]mar
every good piece of land with stones.
20 And it came to pass in the morning,
when [a]the meat offering was offered, that behold, there came water by the way of Edom,
and the country was filled with water.
21 ¶ And when all the Moabites heard that
the kings were come up to fight against them,
they [1]gathered all that *were able to* [2]put on armour, and upward, and stood in the border.
22 And they rose up early in the morning,
and the sun shone upon the water, and the
Moabites saw the water on the other side *as*
red as blood:
23 And they said, This *is* blood: the kings
are surely [1]slain, and they have smitten one
another: now therefore, Moab, to the spoil.
24 And when they came to the camp of Israel, the Israelites rose up and smote the Moabites, so that they fled before them: but [1]they
went forward smiting the Moabites, even in
their country.
25 And they beat down the cities, and *on*
every good piece of land cast every man his
stone, and filled it; and they stopped all the
wells of water, and felled all the good trees:
[1]only in [a]Kir-haraseth left *they* the stones
thereof; howbeit the slingers went about *it,*
and smote it.
26 And when the king of Moab saw that
the battle was too sore for him, he took with
him seven hundred men that drew swords, to
break through *even* unto the king of Edom: but
they could not.
27 Then [a]he took his eldest son that
should have reigned in his stead, and offered
him *for* a burnt offering upon the wall. And
there was great indignation against Israel:
[b]and they departed from him, and returned to
their own land.

3:19 [1]Heb. *grieve*
3:20 [a]Ex. 29:39,40
3:21 [1]Heb. *were cried together* [2]Heb. *gird himself with a girdle*
3:23 [1]Heb. *destroyed*
3:24 [1]Or, *they smote in it even smiting*
3:25 [1]Heb. *until he left the stones thereof in Kir-haraseth* [a]Is. 16:7,11
3:27 [a]Amos 2:1 [b]ch. 8:20

The widow's pot of oil

4 Now there cried a certain woman of the
wives of [a]the sons of the prophets unto
Elisha, saying, Thy servant my husband is
dead; and thou knowest that thy servant did
fear the LORD: and the creditor is come [b]to
take unto him my two sons to be bondmen.
2 And Elisha said unto her, What shall I do
for thee? tell me, what hast thou in the house?
And she said, Thine handmaid hath not any
thing in the house, save a pot of oil.
3 Then he said, Go, borrow thee vessels
abroad of all thy neighbours, *even* empty vessels; [a][1]borrow not a few.
4 And when thou art come in, thou shalt
shut the door upon thee and upon thy sons,
and shalt pour out into all those vessels, and
thou shalt set aside *that* which *is* full.
5 So she went from him, and shut the door
upon her and upon her sons, who brought *the*
vessels to her; and she poured out.
6 And it came to pass, when the vessels
were full, that she said unto her son, Bring me
yet a vessel. And he said unto her, *There is* not
a vessel more. And the oil stayed.
7 Then she came and told the man of God.
And he said, Go, sell the oil, and pay thy
[1]debt, and live thou and thy children of the
rest.

The Shunammite's son

8 ¶ And [1]it fell on a day, that Elisha passed
to [a]Shunem, where *was* a great woman; and
she [2]constrained him to eat bread. And *so* it
was, *that* as oft as he passed by, he turned in
thither to eat bread.
9 And she said unto her husband, Behold
now, I perceive that this *is* a holy man of God,
which passeth by us continually.
10 Let us make a little chamber, I pray
thee, on the wall; and let us set for him there
a bed, and a table, and a stool, and a candle-

4:1 [a]1 Ki. 20:35 [b]See Lev. 25:39; Mat. 18:25
4:3 [1]Or, *scant not* [a]See ch. 3:16
4:7 [1]Or, *creditor*
4:8 [1]Heb. *there was a day* [2]Heb. *laid hold on him* [a]Josh. 19:18

3:20 *when the meat offering was offered.* See Ex 29:38–39; Num 28:3–4. *there came water by the way of Edom.* Flash floods in the distant mountains of Edom caused water to flow north through the broad, usually dry, valley that sloped toward the Dead Sea (see note on v. 16).

3:23 *the kings are surely slain . . . smitten one another.* The Moabites would have good reason to suspect that an internal conflict had arisen between the parties of an alliance whose members had previously been mutually hostile.

3:25 *Kir-haraseth.* The capital city of Moab (see Is 16:7,11; Jer 48:31,36), usually identified with present-day Kerak, located about 11 miles east of the Dead Sea and 15 miles south of the Arnon River.

3:26 *break through even unto the king of Edom.* A desperate attempt by the king of Moab to induce Edom to turn against Israel and Judah.

3:27 *offered him for a burnt offering upon the wall.* King Mesha offered his oldest son, the crown prince, as a burnt offering (see 16:3; Jer 7:31) to the Moabite god Chemosh (see 1 Ki 11:7; Num 21:29; Jer 48:46) in an attempt to induce the deity to come to his aid. *there was great indignation against Israel.* The Hebrew underlying this clause would normally refer to a visitation of God's wrath. It may be that just when total victory appeared to be in Israel's grasp, God's displeasure with the Ahab dynasty showed itself in some way that caused the Israelite kings to give up the campaign. Comparing Aramaic and later Hebrew usage, a few scholars suggest that the Hebrew here can be translated, "There was great dismay upon/in Israel."

4:1 *sons of the prophets.* See notes on 2:3; 1 Ki 20:35. *to take unto him my two sons to be bondmen.* Servitude as a means of debt payment by labor was permitted in the Mosaic law (Ex 21:1–2; Lev 25:39–41; Deut 15:1–11). It appears that the practice was much abused (see Neh 5:5,8; Amos 2:6; 8:6), even though the law limited the term of such bondage and required that those so held be treated as hired workers.

4:4 *shut the door upon thee and upon thy sons.* The impending miracle was not intended to be a public sensation but to demonstrate privately God's mercy and grace to this widow (cf. Ps 68:5). She did not hesitate to respond to the instructions of the Lord's prophet in faith and obedience.

4:8 *Shunem.* See note on 1 Ki 1:3.

4:9 *holy man of God.* The woman recognized that Elisha was a person set apart to the Lord's work in a very special sense. Nowhere else in the OT is the term "holy" applied to a prophet.

4:10 *when he cometh to us . . . he shall turn in thither.* By her

stick: and it shall be, when he cometh to us, *that* he shall turn in thither.

11 And it fell on a day, that he came thither, and he turned into the chamber, and lay there.

12 And he said to Gehazi his servant, Call this Shunammite. And when he had called her, she stood before him.

13 And he said unto him, Say now unto her, Behold, thou hast been careful for us with all this care; what *is* to be done for thee? wouldest thou be spoken for to the king, or to the captain of the host? And she answered, I dwell among mine own people.

14 And he said, What then *is* to be done for her? And Gehazi answered, Verily she hath no child, and her husband is old.

15 And he said, Call her. And when he had called her, she stood in the door.

16 And he said, [a]About this [1]season, according to the time of life, thou shalt embrace a son. And she said, Nay, my lord, thou man of God, [b]do not lie unto thine handmaid.

17 And the woman conceived, and bare a son at that season that Elisha had said unto her, according to the time of life.

18 ¶ And when the child was grown, it fell on a day, that he went out to his father to the reapers.

19 And he said unto his father, My head, my head. And he said to a lad, Carry him to his mother.

20 And when he had taken him, and brought him to his mother, he sat on her knees till noon, and *then* died.

21 And she went up, and laid him on the bed of the man of God, and shut *the door* upon him, and went out.

22 And she called unto her husband, and said, Send me, I pray thee, one of the young men, and one of the asses, that I may run to the man of God, and come again.

23 And he said, Wherefore wilt thou go to him to day? *it is* neither new moon, nor sabbath. And she said, *It shall be* [1]well.

24 Then she saddled an ass, and said to her servant, Drive, and go *forward;* [1]slack not *thy* riding for me, except I bid thee.

25 So she went and came unto the man of God [a]to mount Carmel. And it came to pass, when the man of God saw her afar off, that he said to Gehazi his servant, Behold, *yonder is* that Shunammite:

26 Run now, I pray thee, to meet her, and say unto her, *Is it* well with thee? *is it* well with thy husband? *is it* well with the child? And she answered, *It is* well.

27 And when she came to the man of God to the hill, she caught [a][1]him by the feet: but Gehazi came near to thrust her away. And the man of God said, Let her alone; for her soul *is* [b][2]vexed within her: and the LORD hath hid *it* from me, and hath not told me.

28 Then she said, Did I desire a son of my lord? [a]did I not say, Do not deceive me?

29 Then he said to Gehazi, [a]Gird up thy loins, and take my staff in thine hand, and go *thy way:* if thou meet any man, [b]salute him not; and if any salute thee, answer him not *again:* and [c]lay my staff upon the face of the child.

30 And the mother of the child said, [a]*As* the LORD liveth, and *as* thy soul liveth, I will not leave thee. And he arose, and followed her.

31 And Gehazi passed on before them, and

4:16 [1]Heb. *set time* [a]Gen. 18:10,14 [b]ver. 28

4:23 [1]Heb. *peace*
4:24 [1]Heb. *restrain not for me to ride*
4:25 [a]ch. 2:25
4:27 [1]Heb. *by his feet* [2]Heb. *bitter* [a]Mat. 28:9 [b]1 Sam. 1:10
4:28 [a]ver. 16
4:29 [a]1 Ki. 18:46; ch. 9:1 [b]Luke 10:4 [c]See Ex. 7:19; 14:16; ch. 2:8,14; Acts 19:12
4:30 [a]ch. 2:2

hospitality the woman was able to assist in sustaining the proclamation of God's word through Elisha.

4:12 *Gehazi.* Referred to here for the first time; he appears to have served Elisha in some of the same ways as Elisha had served Elijah, though the two men were of drastically different character (see 5:19–27; 6:15).

4:13 *I dwell among mine own people.* The Shunammite woman felt secure and content in the community of her own family and tribe, and she had no need or desire for favors from high government officials.

4:14 *she hath no child, and her husband is old.* A great disappointment because it meant that the family's name would cease and its land and possessions would pass on to others. It was also a great threat to this young wife's future in that she faced the likelihood of many years as a widow with no provider or protector—children were a widow's only social security in old age (see 8:1–6; see also note on 1 Ki 17:22).

4:16 *according to the time of life.* See Gen 17:21; 18:14. *thou man of God, do not lie unto thy handmaid.* The woman's response revealed the depths of her desire for a son and her fear of disappointment more than it showed a lack of confidence in the word of Elisha.

4:17 *that Elisha had said unto her.* The trustworthiness of Elisha's word was confirmed, and the birth of the son was shown to be the result of God's gracious intervention in her behalf.

4:20 *he . . . died.* The child, given as an evidence of God's grace and the reliability of His word, was suddenly taken from the woman in a severe test of her faith. Her subsequent actions demonstrate the strength of her faith in the face of great calamity.

4:21 *laid him on the bed of the man of God.* In this way the woman concealed the child's death from the rest of the household while she went to seek the prophet at whose word the child had been born.

4:23 *Wherefore wilt thou go to him to day?* The question suggests that it was not uncommon for the woman to go to Elisha, but that on this occasion the timing of her visit was unusual. *it is neither new moon, nor sabbath.* The sabbath and new moon were observed by cessation from work (see notes on Gen 2:3; Ex 16:23; 20:9–10; 1 Sam 20:5; see also Lev 23:3).

4:26 *It is well.* The woman was determined to share her distress with no one but the prophet from whom she had received the promise of the birth of her son.

4:28 *did I not say, Do not deceive me?* The woman struggled with the question of why the Lord would take from her that which she had been given as a special demonstration of His grace and the trustworthiness of His word.

4:29 *lay my staff upon the face of the child.* It appears that Elisha expected the Lord to restore the boy's life when the staff was placed on him. This does not suggest that Elisha attributed magical power to the staff, but that he viewed it as a representation of his own presence and a symbol of divine power (see note on 2:8; cf. Ex 14:16; Acts 19:12).

4:30 *I will not leave thee.* The woman was not convinced that Gehazi's mission would be successful and insisted that Elisha himself accompany her to Shunem.

laid the staff upon the face of the child; but
there was neither voice, nor [1]hearing. Wherefore he went again to meet him, and told him,
saying, The child is [a]not awaked.
32 And when Elisha was come into the
house, behold, the child was dead, *and* laid
upon his bed.
33 He [a]went in therefore, and shut the
door upon them twain, [b]and prayed unto the
LORD.
34 And he went up, and lay upon the child,
and put his mouth upon his mouth, and his
eyes upon his eyes, and his hands upon his
hands: and [a]he stretched himself upon the
child; and the flesh of the child waxed warm.
35 Then he returned, and walked in the
house [1]to and fro; and went up, and
[a]stretched himself upon him: and [b]the child
neesed seven times, and the child opened his
eyes.
36 And he called Gehazi, and said, Call this
Shunammite. So he called her. And when she
was come in unto him, he said, Take up thy
son.
37 Then she went in, and fell at his feet,
and bowed herself to the ground, and [a]took up
her son, and went out.

Poisonous food made harmless

38 ¶ And Elisha came again to [a]Gilgal: and
there was a [b]dearth in the land; and the sons
of the prophets *were* [c]sitting before him: and
he said unto his servant, Set on the great pot,
and seethe pottage for the sons of the prophets.
39 And one went out into the field to gather herbs, and found a wild vine, and gathered
thereof wild gourds his lap full, and came and
shred *them* into the pot of pottage: for they
knew *them* not.
40 So they poured out for the men to eat.
And it came to pass, as they were eating of the
pottage, that they cried out, and said, O thou
man of God, *there is* [a]death in the pot. And
they could not eat *thereof.*
41 But he said, Then bring meal. And [a]he
cast *it* into the pot; and he said, Pour out for
the people, that they may eat. And there was
no [1]harm in the pot.

The feeding of the hundred men

42 ¶ And there came a man from [a]Baal-sha-
lisha, [b]and brought the man of God bread of
the firstfruits, twenty loaves of barley, and full
ears of corn [1]in the husk thereof. And he said,
Give unto the people, that they may eat.
43 And his servitor said, [a]What, should I
set this before an hundred men? He said again,
Give the people, that they may eat: for thus
saith the LORD, [b]They shall eat, and shall leave
thereof.
44 So he set *it* before them, and they did
eat, [a]and left *thereof,* according to the word of
the LORD.

The cure of Naaman the leper

5 Now [a]Naaman, captain of the host of the
king of Syria, was [b]a great man [1]with his
master, and [2]honourable, because by him the
LORD had given [3]deliverance unto Syria: he
was also a mighty *man* in valour, *but he was* a
leper.
2 And the Syrians had gone out *by* companies, and had brought away captive out of the
land of Israel a little maid; and she [1]waited on
Naaman's wife.

4:31 [1]Heb. *attention* [a]John 11:11
4:33 [a]ver. 4; Mat. 6:6 [b]1 Ki. 17:20
4:34 [a]1 Ki. 17:21; Acts 20:10
4:35 [1]Heb. *once hither and once thither* [a]1 Ki. 17:21 [b]ch. 8:1,5
4:37 [a]1 Ki. 17:23; Heb. 11:35
4:38 [a]ch. 2:1 [b]ch. 8:1 [c]ch. 2:3; Luke 10:39; Acts 22:3
4:40 [a]Ex. 10:17
4:41 [1]Heb. *evil thing* [a]See Ex. 15:25; ch. 2:21; 5:10; John 9:6
4:42 [1]Or, *in his scrip,* or, *garment* [a]1 Sam. 9:4 [b]1 Sam. 9:7; 1 Cor. 9:11; Gal. 6:6
4:43 [a]Luke 9:13; John 6:9 [b]Luke 9:17; John 6:11
4:44 [a]Mat. 14:20; 15:37; John 6:13
5:1 [1]Heb. *before* [2]Or, *gracious.* Heb. *lifted up,* or, *accepted in countenance* [3]Or, *victory* [a]Luke 4:27 [b]Ex. 11:3
5:2 [1]Heb. *was before*

4:33 *shut the door upon them twain, and prayed.* Just as Elijah had done in a similar situation years before (see 1 Ki 17:20–22), Elisha first turned to the Lord in earnest prayer for restoration of life to the dead child. His prayer is clear evidence that his subsequent actions were not intended as a magical means of restoring life.
4:34 *lay upon the child.* See note on 1 Ki 17:21. Perhaps Elisha was familiar with the earlier similar action of Elijah.
4:37 *fell at his feet, and bowed herself to the ground.* The woman gratefully acknowledged the special favor granted to her by the Lord through Elisha, and silently reaffirmed the verbal confession of the widow of Zarephath (see 1 Ki 17:24).
4:38 *dearth in the land.* Perhaps the same famine mentioned in 8:1. Famine was a covenant curse (see Lev 26:19–20,26; Deut 28:18,23–24; 1 Ki 8:36–37) and evidence of God's anger with His people's disobedience to their covenant obligations. *sons of the prophets.* See note on 2:3.
4:39 *wild vine . . . gourds.* The precise type of plant is not specified.
4:41 *meal.* The flour itself did not make the stew edible (see 2:21 and note). It was simply a means by which the Lord provided for those who were faithful to the covenant, at a time when others suffered under the covenant curse.
4:42 *firstfruits.* Instead of bringing the firstfruits of the new harvest (see Lev 2:14; 23:15–17; Deut 18:3–5) to the apostate priests at Beth-el and Dan (see 1 Ki 12:28–31), godly people in the northern kingdom may have contributed their offerings for the sustenance of Elisha and those associated with him (see note on v. 23). Thus they looked upon Elisha rather than the apostate king and priests as the true representative of their covenant Lord.
4:43 *saith the LORD.* The bread was multiplied at the word of the Lord through Elisha apart from any intermediate means (contrast v. 41; 2:20; cf. Mark 6:35–43).
‡5:1 *king of Syria* [Hebrew *Aram*]. Probably Ben-hadad II (see notes on 8:7; 13:3; 1 Ki 20:1). *the LORD had given deliverance unto Syria.* Probably a reference to an otherwise undocumented Aramean victory over the Assyrians in the aftermath of the battle of Qarqar in 853 B.C. (see note on 1 Ki 22:1). In the narrator's theological perspective, this victory is attributable to the sovereignty of the God of Israel, who is seen as the ruler and controller of the destinies of all nations, not just that of Israel (see Ezek 30:24; Amos 2:1–3; 9:7). *leper.* The Hebrew word was used for various diseases affecting the skin—not necessarily leprosy.
5:2 *gone out by companies.* Although Israel had concluded a peace treaty with the Arameans during the reign of Ahab (see 1 Ki 20:34), minor border skirmishes continued between the two states in the aftermath of the battle for control of Ramoth-gilead, in which Ahab had been killed (see note on 1 Ki 22:4; see also 1 Ki 22:35). *out of the land of Israel a little maid.* In sharp contrast to the Israelite king in Samaria, this young girl held captive in Damascus was very much aware of God's saving presence with His people through His servant Elisha, and she selflessly shared that knowledge with her Aramean captors.

3 And she said unto her mistress, Would God my lord *were* [1]with the prophet that *is* in Samaria; for he would [2]recover him of his leprosy.

4 And *one* went in, and told his lord, saying, Thus and thus said the maid that *is* of the land of Israel.

5 And the king of Syria said, Go to, go, and I will send a letter unto the king of Israel. And he departed, and [a]took [1]with him ten talents of silver, and six thousand *pieces* of gold, and ten changes of raiment.

6 And he brought the letter to the king of Israel, saying, Now when this letter is come unto thee, behold, I have *therewith* sent Naaman my servant to thee, that thou mayest recover him of his leprosy.

7 And it came to pass, when the king of Israel had read the letter, that he rent his clothes, and said, *Am* I [a]God, to kill and to make alive, that this *man* doth send unto me to recover a man of his leprosy? wherefore consider, I pray you, and see how he seeketh a quarrel against me.

8 And it was *so,* when Elisha the man of God had heard that the king of Israel had rent his clothes, that he sent to the king, saying, Wherefore hast thou rent thy clothes? let him come now to me, and he shall know that there is a prophet in Israel.

9 So Naaman came with his horses and with his chariot, and stood *at* the door of the house of Elisha.

5:3 [1]Heb. *before* [2]Heb. *gather in*
5:5 [1]Heb. *in his hand* [a]1 Sam. 9:8; ch. 8:8,9
5:7 [a]Gen. 30:2; Deut. 32:39; 1 Sam. 2:6
5:10 [a]See ch. 4:41; John 9:7
5:11 [1]Heb. [*I*] *said* [2]Or, *I said with myself, He will surely come out, etc.* [3]Heb. *move up and down*
5:12 [1]Or, *Amana*
5:14 [a]Job 33:25 [b]Luke 4:27
5:15 [a]Dan 2:47; 3:29; 6:26,27 [b]Gen. 33:11
5:16 [a]ch. 3:14 [b]Gen. 14:23; See Mat. 10:8; Acts 8:18,20

10 And Elisha sent a messenger unto him, saying, Go and [a]wash in Jordan seven times, and thy flesh shall come again to thee, and thou shalt be clean.

11 But Naaman was wroth, and went away, and said, Behold, [1][2]I thought, He will surely come out to me, and stand, and call on the name of the LORD his God, and [3]strike his hand over the place, and recover the leper.

12 *Are* not [1]Abana and Pharpar, rivers of Damascus, better than all the waters of Israel? may I not wash in them, and be clean? So he turned and went away in a rage.

13 And his servants came near, and spake unto him, and said, My father, *if* the prophet had bid thee *do some* great thing, wouldest thou not have done *it?* how much rather then, when he saith to thee, Wash, and be clean?

14 Then went he down, and dipped *himself* seven times in Jordan, according to the saying of the man of God: and [a]his flesh came again like unto the flesh of a little child, and [b]he was clean.

15 ¶ And he returned to the man of God, he and all his company, and came, and stood before him: and he said, Behold, now I know that *there is* [a]no God in all the earth, but in Israel: now therefore, I pray thee, take [b]a blessing of thy servant.

16 But he said, [a]*As* the LORD liveth, before whom I stand, [b]I will receive none. And he urged him to take *it;* but he refused.

17 And Naaman said, Shall there not then,

5:3 *prophet that is in Samaria.* Elisha, who maintained a residence in Samaria (see v. 9; 2:25; 6:19).

5:5 *I will send a letter unto the king of Israel.* The border skirmishes had not nullified the official peace between the two nations as established by treaty. The king of Israel was Jehoram (see 1:17; 3:1; 9:24). *ten talents of silver.* About 750 pounds of silver. An idea of the relative value of this amount of silver can be seen by comparing it with the price Omri paid for the hill of Samaria (see 1 Ki 16:24).

5:6 *that thou mayest recover him of his leprosy.* Ben-hadad assumed that the prophet described by the Israelite slave girl was subject to the authority of the king and that his services could be bought with a sufficiently large gift. He thought he could buy with worldly wealth one of the chief blessings of God's saving presence among His people.

5:7 *he seeketh a quarrel against me.* Jehoram concluded that the entire incident was an attempt by Ben-hadad to create a pretext for a declaration of war. So blind was the king to God's saving presence through Elisha that he could think only of international intrigue.

5:8 *Wherefore hast thou rent thy clothes?* Elisha chided Jehoram for his fear (see note on 1 Sam 17:11) and for his failure to consult the Lord's prophet (see 3:13–14 for evidence of the tension that existed between Jehoram and Elisha).

5:9 *with his horses and with his chariot.* This proud pagan would command the healing by his lordly presence.

5:10 *wash in Jordan seven times.* The instruction is designed to demonstrate to Naaman that healing would come by the power of the God of Israel, but only if he obeyed the word of the Lord's prophet. The prophet himself was not a healer. Ritual washings were practiced among Eastern religions as a purification rite, and the number seven was generally known as a symbol of completeness. Naaman was to wash in the muddy waters of the Jordan River, demonstrating that there was no natural connection between the washing and the desired healing. Perhaps it also suggested that one needed to pass through the Jordan, as Israel had done (Josh 3–4), in order to obtain healing from the God of Israel.

5:11 *strike his hand over the place, and recover the leper.* Naaman expected to be healed by the magical technique of the prophet rather than by the power of God operative in connection with his own obedient response to God's word.

5:12 *Abana and Pharpar.* The Abanah was termed the Golden River by the Greeks. It is usually identified with the Barada River of today, rising in the Anti-Lebanon mountains and flowing through the city of Damascus. The Pharpar River flows east from mount Hermon just to the south of Damascus.

5:14 *his flesh came again like unto the flesh of a little child, and he was clean.* Physically he was reborn (see also v. 15 and note). As he obeyed God's word, Naaman received the gift of God's grace. Naaman is here a sign to disobedient Israel that God's blessing is found only in the path of trustful obedience. When His own people turn away from covenant faithfulness, God will raise up those who will follow His word from outside the covenant nation (see notes on 1 Ki 17:9–24; see also Mat 8:10–12; Luke 4:27).

5:15 *no God in all the earth, but in Israel.* Naaman's confession put to shame the Israelites who continued to waver in their opinion on whether Baal and the Lord (Yahweh) were both gods, or whether Yahweh alone was God (see note on 1 Ki 18:21).

5:16 *I will receive none.* Elisha did not seek monetary gain for proclaiming the word of the Lord (see Mat 10:8). Naaman was healed solely by divine grace, not by the power of Elisha.

I pray thee, be given to thy servant two mules' burden of earth? for thy servant will henceforth offer neither burnt offering nor sacrifice unto other gods, but unto the LORD.

18 In this thing the LORD pardon thy servant, *that* when my master goeth *into* the house of Rimmon to worship there, and [a]he leaneth on my hand, and I bow myself *in* the house of Rimmon: when I bow down myself *in* the house of Rimmon, the LORD pardon thy servant in this thing.

19 And he said unto him, Go in peace. So he departed from him [1]a little way.

20 ¶ But Gehazi, the servant of Elisha the man of God, said, Behold, my master hath spared Naaman this Syrian, in not receiving at his hands *that* which he brought: but, *as* the LORD liveth, I will run after him, and take somewhat of him.

21 So Gehazi followed after Naaman. And when Naaman saw *him* running after him, he lighted down from the chariot to meet him, and said, [1]*Is all* well?

22 And he said, *All is* well. My master hath sent me, saying, Behold, even now there be come to me from mount Ephraim two young men of the sons of the prophets: give them, I pray thee, a talent of silver, and two changes of garments.

23 And Naaman said, Be content, take two talents. And he urged him, and bound two talents of silver in two bags, with two changes of garments, and laid *them* upon two of his servants; and they bare *them* before him.

24 And when he came to the [1]tower, he took *them* from their hand, and bestowed *them* in the house: and he let the men go, and they departed.

5:18 [a]ch. 7:2,17
5:19 [1]Heb. *a little piece of ground*
5:21 [1]Heb. Is there *peace?*
5:24 [1]Or, *secret place*

5:25 [1]Heb. *not hither or thither*
5:27 [a]1 Tim. 6:10 [b]Ex. 4:6; Num. 12:10; ch. 15:5
6:1 [a]ch. 4:38
6:5 [1]Heb. *iron*
6:6 [a]ch. 2:21

25 But he went in, and stood before his master. And Elisha said unto him, Whence *comest thou,* Gehazi? And he said, Thy servant went [1]no whither.

26 And he said unto him, Went not mine heart *with thee,* when the man turned *again* from his chariot to meet thee? *Is it* a time to receive money, and to receive garments, and oliveyards, and vineyards, and sheep, and oxen, and menservants, and maidservants?

27 The leprosy therefore of Naaman [a]shall cleave unto thee, and unto thy seed for ever. And he went out from his presence [b]a leper *as white* as snow.

Recovery of the lost axe head

6 And [a]the sons of the prophets said unto Elisha, Behold now, the place where we dwell with thee is too strait for us.

2 Let us go, we pray thee, unto Jordan, and take thence every man a beam, and let us make us a place there, where we may dwell. And he answered, Go ye.

3 And one said, Be content, I pray thee, and go with thy servants. And he answered, I will go.

4 So he went with them. And when they came to Jordan, they cut down wood.

5 But as one was felling a beam, the [1]axe head fell into the water: and he cried, and said, Alas, master, for it *was* borrowed.

6 And the man of God said, Where fell it? And he shewed him the place. And [a]he cut down a stick, and cast *it* in thither; and the iron did swim.

7 Therefore said he, Take *it* up to thee. And he put out his hand, and took it.

5:17 *be given to thy servant two mules' burden of earth.* In the ancient world it was commonly thought that a deity could be worshiped only on the soil of the nation to which he was bound (see v. 15). For this reason Naaman wanted to take Israelite soil with him in order to have a place in Damascus for the worship of the Lord.

5:18 *my master.* Ben-hadad, king of Aram. *Rimmon.* Also known as Hadad (and in Canaan and Phoenicia as Baal), this Aramean deity was the god of storm ("Rimmon" means "thunderer") and war. The two names were sometimes combined (see note on Zech 12:11).

5:19 *Go in peace.* Elisha did not directly address Naaman's problem of conscience (v. 18), but commended him to the leading and grace of God as he returned to his pagan environment and official responsibilities.

5:20 *as the LORD liveth.* An oath formula (see note on 1 Sam 14:39).

5:22 *sons of the prophets.* See note on 2:3. *give them, I pray thee, a talent of silver, and two changes of garments.* Gehazi deceived Naaman in order to satisfy his desire for material gain. The evil of his lie was compounded in that it obscured the gracious character of the Lord's work in Naaman's healing and blurred the distinction between Elisha's function as a true prophet of the Lord and the self-serving actions of false prophets and pagan soothsayers.

5:24 *house.* Of Elisha (see v. 9).

5:26 *Is it a time to receive money . . . ?* Gehazi sought to use the grace of God granted to another individual for his own material advantage. This was equivalent to making merchandise of God's grace (see note on 2 Cor 2:17). "Money" here and elsewhere in 2 Kings refers to gold or silver in various weights, not to coins, which were a later invention. *garments . . . maidservants.* Evidently what Gehazi secretly hoped to acquire with the two talents of silver (see note on v. 5).

5:27 *leprosy.* See note on v. 1. *unto thee, and unto thy seed for ever.* For the extension of punishment to the children of an offender of God's law see Ex 20:5 and note; see also note on Josh 7:24. *white as snow.* See Ex 4:6.

6:1 *sons of the prophets.* See note on 2:3.

6:2 *make us a place there, where we may dwell.* Some have suggested that the company of prophets lived in a communal housing structure. The Hebrew for this phrase, however, could be translated "a place there for us to sit," referring to some type of assembly hall. It is implied in 4:1–7 that there were separate dwellings for the members of the prophetic companies (see note on 1 Sam 19:18).

6:5 *it was borrowed.* At that time an iron axe head was a costly tool, too expensive for the members of the prophetic company to purchase. Having lost it, the borrower faced the prospect of having to work off the value as a bondservant.

6:6 *he cut down a stick, and cast it in thither; and the iron did swim.* The Lord demonstrated here His concern for the welfare of His faithful ones.

Elisha strikes the Syrians blind

8 ¶ Then the king of Syria warred against Israel, and took counsel with his servants, saying, In such and such a place *shall be* my [1]camp.

9 And the man of God sent unto the king of Israel, saying, Beware that *thou* pass not such a place; for thither the Syrians are come down.

10 And the king of Israel sent to the place which the man of God told him and warned him of, and saved himself there, not once nor twice.

11 Therefore the heart of the king of Syria was sore troubled for this thing; and he called his servants, and said unto them, Will ye not shew me which of us *is* for the king of Israel?

12 And one of his servants said, [1]None, my lord, O king: but Elisha, the prophet that *is* in Israel, telleth the king of Israel the words that thou speakest in thy bedchamber.

13 And he said, Go and spy where he *is,* that I may send and fetch him. And it was told him, saying, Behold, *he is* in [a]Dothan.

14 Therefore sent he thither horses, and chariots, and a [1]great host: and they came by night, and compassed the city about.

15 And when the [1]servant of the man of God was risen early, and gone forth, behold, a host compassed the city both with horses and chariots. And his servant said unto him, Alas, my master, how shall we do?

16 And he answered, Fear not: for [a]*they* that *be* with us *are* moe than *they* that *be* with them.

17 And Elisha prayed, and said, LORD, I pray thee, open his eyes, that he may see. And the LORD opened the eyes of the young man; and he saw: and behold, the mountain was full *of* [a]horses and chariots of fire round about Elisha.

18 And when they came down to him, Elisha prayed unto the LORD, and said, Smite this people, I pray thee, with blindness. And [a]he smote them with blindness according to the word of Elisha.

19 And Elisha said unto them, This *is* not the way, neither *is* this the city: [1]follow me, and I will bring you to the man whom ye seek. But he led them to Samaria.

20 And it came to pass, when they were come *into* Samaria, that Elisha said, LORD, open the eyes of these *men,* that they may see. And the LORD opened their eyes, and they saw; and behold, *they were* in the midst of Samaria.

21 And the king of Israel said unto Elisha, when he saw them, My father, shall I smite *them?* shall I smite *them?*

22 And he answered, Thou shalt not smite *them:* wouldest thou smite *those* whom thou hast taken captive with thy sword and with thy bow? [a]set bread and water before them, that they may eat and drink, and go to their master.

23 And he prepared great provision for them: and when they had eaten and drunk, he sent them away, and they went to their master. So [a]the bands of Syria came no more into the land of Israel.

Famine in Samaria

24 ¶ And it came to pass after this, that Ben-hadad king of Syria gathered all his host, and went up, and besieged Samaria.

6:8 [1]Or, *encamping*
6:12 [1]Heb. *No*
6:13 [a]Gen. 37:17
6:14 [1]Heb. *heavy*
6:15 [1]Or, *minister*
6:16 [a]2 Chr. 32:7; Ps. 55:18; Rom. 8:31
6:17 [a]ch. 2:11; Ps. 34:7; 68:17; Zech. 1:8; 6:1-7
6:18 [a]Gen. 19:11
6:19 [1]Heb. *come ye after me*
6:22 [a]Rom. 12:20
6:23 [a]ver. 8,9; ch. 5:2

‡6:8 *king of Syria* [Hebrew *Aram*]. Probably Ben-hadad II (see note on 5:1). *warred against Israel.* A reference to border clashes rather than full-scale hostility (see v. 23; see also note on 5:2). Some indication of Israelite weakness and Aramean strength is seen in the ability of the Arameans to send forces to Dothan (only about 11 miles north of Samaria) without apparent difficulty (see vv. 13–14).
6:9 *man of God.* Elisha (see v. 10). *king of Israel.* Probably Jehoram (see 1:17; 3:1; 9:24).
6:11 *which of us is for the king of Israel?* Repeated evidence that Israel possessed advance knowledge of Aramean military plans led the king of Aram to suspect that there was a traitor among his top officials.
6:12 *king of Israel.* Jehoram (see 3:1).
6:13 *fetch him.* The king of Aram thought he could eliminate Elisha's influence by denying him contact with Israel's king. *Dothan.* Located on a hill about halfway between Jezreel and Samaria, where the main royal residences were (see 1:2; 3:1; 8:29; 9:15; 10:1; 1 Ki 21:1).
6:16 *they that be with us are moe* [i.e. more] *than they that be with them.* Elisha knew that there was greater strength in the unseen reality of the hosts of heaven than in the visible reality of the Aramean forces (see 2 Chr 32:7–8; Ps 34:7; 1 John 4:4).
6:17 *he saw . . . the mountain was full of horses and chariots.* In response to Elisha's prayer, his servant was able to see the protecting might of the heavenly hosts gathered about Elisha (see Gen 32:1–2; Ps 34:7; 91:11–12; Mat 18:10; 26:53; see also note on 2 Ki 2:11).
6:18 *Smite this people . . . with blindness.* Elisha had prayed for the eyes of his servant to be opened to the unseen reality of the heavenly hosts; now he prays for the eyes of the Aramean soldiers to be closed to earthly reality (see Gen 19:11).
6:19 *This is not the way, neither is this the city.* Elisha's statement led the Aramean soldiers to believe that they were being directed to the city where Elisha could be found. Technically this statement was not an untruth, since Elisha accompanied them to Samaria, but it was a means of deceiving the Aramean soldiers into a trap inside Samaria, the fortress-like capital city of the northern kingdom (see Ex 1:19–20; Josh 2:6; 1 Sam 16:1–2 for other instances of deception recorded in the OT).
6:20 *they were in the midst of Samaria.* The power of the Lord operative through Elisha turned the intended captors into captives.
6:21 *king of Israel.* Jehoram (see note on v. 9).
6:22 *Thou shalt not smite them.* In reality the Aramean soldiers had been taken captive by the power of the Lord, not by Jehoram's military prowess. The Lord's purpose was to demonstrate to them and their king and to the Israelites and their king that Israel's national security ultimately was grounded in the Lord, not in military forces or strategies.
6:23 *bands of Syria came no more into the land of Israel.* See notes on v. 8; 5:2. Temporarily the Arameans recognized the futility of opposition to the power of the God of Israel.
6:24 *Ben-hadad.* The same Ben-hadad who had besieged Samaria on a previous occasion (see notes on 13:3; 1 Ki 20:1). This siege is probably to be dated c. 850 B.C.

25 And there was a great famine in
Samaria: and behold, they besieged it, until an
ass's head was *sold* for fourscore *pieces* of silver, and the fourth part of a kab of dove's dung
for five *pieces* of silver.
26 And as the king of Israel was passing by
upon the wall, there cried a woman unto him,
saying, Help, my lord, O king.
27 And he said, [1]*If* the LORD do not help
thee, whence shall I help thee? out of the
barnfloor, or out of the winepress?
28 And the king said unto her, What aileth
thee? And she answered, This woman said
unto me, Give thy son, that we may eat him to
day, and we will eat my son to morrow.
29 So [a]we boiled my son, and did eat him:
and I said unto her on the [1]next day, Give thy
son, that we may eat him: and she hath hid
her son.
30 And it came to pass, when the king
heard the words of the woman, that he [a]rent
his clothes; and he passed by upon the wall,
and the people looked, and behold, *he had*
sackcloth within upon his flesh.
31 Then he said, [a]God do so and more also
to me, if the head of Elisha the son of Shaphat
shall stand on him *this* day.

The prophecy of Elisha

32 ¶ But Elisha sat in his house, and [a]the
elders sat with him; and *the king* sent a man
from before him: but ere the messenger came
to him, he said to the elders, [b]See ye how this
son of [c]a murderer hath sent to take away
mine head? look, when the messenger
cometh, shut the door, and hold him fast at the
door: *is* not the sound of his master's feet behind him?
33 And while he yet talked with them, behold, the messenger came down unto him:
and he said, Behold, this evil *is* of the LORD;
[a]what should I wait for the LORD any longer?

6:27 [1] Or, *Let not the LORD save thee*
6:29 [1] Heb. *other* [a] Lev. 26:29; Deut. 28:53,57
6:30 [a] 1 Ki. 21:27
6:31 [a] Ruth 1:17; 1 Ki. 19:2
6:32 [a] Ezek. 8:1; 20:1 [b] Luke 13:32 [c] 1 Ki. 18:4
6:33 [a] Job 2:9

7:1 [a] ver. 18,19
7:2 [1] Heb. *a lord which* belonged *to the king leaning upon his hand* [a] ver. 17,19,20 [b] ch. 5:18 [c] Mal. 3:10
7:3 [a] Lev. 13:46
7:6 [a] 2 Sam. 5:24; ch. 19:7; Job 15:21 [b] 1 Ki. 10:29
7:7 [a] Ps. 48:4-6; Prov. 28:1

7 Then Elisha said, Hear ye the word of the
LORD; Thus saith the LORD, [a]To morrow
about *this* time *shall* a measure of fine flour *be
sold* for a shekel, and two measures of barley
for a shekel, in the gate of Samaria.
2 [a]Then [b][1]a lord on whose hand the king
leaned answered the man of God, and said, Behold, [c]*if* the LORD would make windows in
heaven, might this thing be? And he said, Behold, thou shalt see *it* with thine eyes, but
shalt not eat thereof.
3 ¶ And there were four leprous men [a]*at*
the entering in of the gate: and they said one
to another, Why sit we here until we die?
4 If we say, We will enter *into* the city,
then the famine *is* in the city, and we shall die
there: and if we sit still here, we die also. Now
therefore come, and let us fall unto the host of
the Syrians: if they save us alive, we shall live;
and if they kill us, we shall but die.
5 And they rose up in the twilight, to go
unto the camp of the Syrians: and when they
were come to the uttermost part of the camp
of Syria, behold, *there was* no man there.
6 For the Lord had made the host of the Syrians [a]to hear a noise of chariots, and a noise of
horses, *even* the noise of a great host: and they
said one to another, Lo, the king of Israel hath
hired against us [b]the kings of the Hittites, and
the kings of the Egyptians, to come upon us.
7 Wherefore they [a]arose and fled in the
twilight, and left their tents, and their horses,
and their asses, *even* the camp as it *was,* and
fled for their life.
8 And when these lepers came to the uttermost part of the camp, they went into one
tent, and did eat and drink, and carried thence
silver, and gold, and raiment, and went and
hid *it;* and came again, and entered into another tent, and carried thence *also,* and went
and hid *it.*
9 Then they said one to another, We do not

6:25 *ass's head.* According to Pentateuchal law the donkey was unclean and not to be eaten (see Lev 11:2–7; Deut 14:4–8). The severity of the famine caused the inhabitants of Samaria not only to disregard the laws of uncleanness, but also to place a high value on the least edible part of the donkey. *fourscore pieces of silver.* About two pounds of silver; see also note on 5:5.
6:27 *If the LORD do not help thee, whence shall I help thee?* Jehoram correctly recognized his own inability to assist the woman if the Lord Himself did not act in Israel's behalf, but he wrongly implied that the Lord was to be blamed for a situation brought on by Israel's own disobedience and idolatry.
6:28 *we will eat my son to morrow.* The sins of the king and people were so great that the covenant curses of Lev 26:29 and Deut 28:53,57 were being inflicted (cf. Lam 4:10).
6:30 *rent his clothes.* More an expression of anger toward Elisha and the Lord (see v. 31) than one of repentance and sorrow for the sins that had provoked the covenant curse. *sackcloth.* A coarse cloth usually worn as a sign of mourning (see note on Gen 37:34). It is not clear why Jehoram wore sackcloth hidden under his royal robe. Perhaps it was a testing of the Lord, a private ritual to attempt to gain divine favor.
6:31 *God do so and more also to me.* A curse formula (see note on 1 Sam 3:17). *if the head of Elisha . . . shall stand on him this day.* Joram considered Elisha in some way responsible for the conditions in the city. Cf. Ahab's attitude toward Elijah (1 Ki 18:10,16; 21:20).
6:32 *elders.* Leaders of the city (see notes on Ex 3:16; 2 Sam 3:17). They sit with Elisha rather than with the king.
6:33 *what should I wait for the LORD any longer?* Jehoram felt himself deceived by Elisha and abandoned by the Lord, whom he blamed for the disastrous conditions in the city.
‡7:1 *a measure* [Hebrew *seah*] *of fine flour be sold for a shekel.* A seah was about seven quarts, and a shekel was about two-fifths of an ounce. This was about double the normal cost of flour, but a phenomenal improvement over the highly inflated prices the famine had caused.
7:2 *windows in heaven.* See v. 19; Gen 8:2; Is 24:18.
7:3 *entering in of the gate.* Pentateuchal law excluded persons with skin diseases from residence in the community (Lev 13:46; Num 5:2–3).
7:6 *the LORD had made the . . . Syrians to hear a noise.* See 2 Sam 5:24 and note. *kings of the Hittites and . . . Egyptians.* Kings of small city-states ruled by dynasties of Hittite origin, which had arisen in northern Aram after the fall of the Hittite empire c. 1200 B.C.

well: this day *is* a day of good tidings, and we
hold our peace: if we tarry till the morning
light, [1]*some* mischief will come upon us: now
therefore come, that we may go and tell the
king's household.
10 So they came and called unto the porter
of the city: and they told them, saying, We
came to the camp of the Syrians, and behold,
there was no man there, neither voice of man,
but horses tied, and asses tied, and the tents as
they *were*.
11 And he called the porters; and they told
it to the king's house within.
12 ¶ And the king arose in the night, and
said unto his servants, I will now shew you
what the Syrians have done to us. They know
that we *be* hungry; therefore are they gone out
of the camp to hide themselves in the field,
saying, When they come out of the city, we
shall catch them alive, and get into the city.
13 And one of his servants answered and
said, Let *some* take, I pray thee, five of the
horses that remain, which are left [1]in the city,
(behold, they *are* as all the multitude of Israel
that are left in it: behold, *I say,* they *are even*
as all the multitude of the Israelites that are
consumed:) and let us send and see.
14 They took therefore two chariot horses;
and the king sent after the host of the Syrians,
saying, Go and see.
15 And they went after them unto Jordan:
and lo, all the way *was* full *of* garments and
vessels, which the Syrians had cast away in
their haste. And the messengers returned, and
told the king.
16 And the people went out, and spoiled
the tents of the Syrians. So a measure of fine
flour was *sold* for a shekel, and two measures
of barley for a shekel, [a]according to the word
of the LORD.
17 ¶ And the king appointed the lord on
whose hand he leaned to have the charge of
the gate: and the people trode upon him in the
gate, and he died, [a]as the man of God had said,
who spake when the king came down to him.
18 And it came to pass as the man of God

7:9 [1]Heb. *we shall find punishment*
7:13 [1]Heb. *in it*
7:16 [a]ver. 1
7:17 [a]ver. 2
7:18 [a]ver. 1
8:1 [a]ch. 4:35 [b]Ps. 105:16; Hag. 1:11
8:4 [a]ch. 5:27
8:5 [a]ch. 4:35
8:6 [1]Or, *eunuch*

had spoken to the king, saying, [a]Two measures
of barley for a shekel, and a measure of fine
flour for a shekel, shall be to morrow about
this time in the gate of Samaria:
19 And *that* lord answered the man of God,
and said, Now behold, *if* the LORD should
make windows in heaven, might such a thing
be? And he said, Behold, thou shalt see *it* with
thine eyes, but shalt not eat thereof.
20 And so it fell out unto him: for the people trode upon him in the gate, and he died.

The Shunammite comes home

8 Then spake Elisha unto the woman,
[a]whose son he had restored to life, saying, Arise, and go thou and thine household,
and sojourn wheresoever thou canst sojourn:
for the LORD [b]hath called for a famine; and it
shall also come upon the land seven years.
2 And the woman arose, and did after the
saying of the man of God: and she went with
her household, and sojourned in the land of
the Philistines seven years.
3 And it came to pass at the seven years'
end, that the woman returned out of the land
of the Philistines: and she went forth to cry
unto the king for her house and for her land.
4 And the king talked with [a]Gehazi the servant of the man of God, saying, Tell me, I pray
thee, all the great *things* that Elisha hath done.
5 And it came to pass, *as* he was telling the
king how he had [a]restored a dead *body* to life,
that behold, the woman, whose son he had restored to life, cried to the king for her house
and for her land. And Gehazi said, My lord,
O king, this *is* the woman, and this *is* her son,
whom Elisha restored to life.
6 And when the king asked the woman,
she told him. So the king appointed unto her a
certain [1]officer, saying, Restore all that *was*
hers, and all the fruits of the field since the day
that she left the land, even until now.

Hazael anointed king of Syria

7 ¶ And Elisha came *to* Damascus; and
Ben-hadad the king of Syria was sick; and it

7:12 *what the Syrians have done to us.* Jehoram's unbelief caused him to conclude that the report of the four leprous men was part of an Aramean war strategy rather than an evidence of the fulfillment of Elisha's prophecy (see v. 1).

7:16–20 *according to the word of the LORD ... as the man of God had said ... as the man of God had spoken ... so it fell out unto him.* Emphasizing the trustworthiness of the prophetic word spoken by Elisha. In the fulfillment of Elisha's prophecy Israel was reminded that deliverance from her enemies was a gift of God's grace and that rejection of God's word provoked the wrath of divine judgment.

8:1 *the LORD hath called for a famine.* The famine should have been perceived by the people of the northern kingdom as a covenant curse sent on them because of their sin (see note on 4:38). *seven years.* It is not clear whether this famine began before or after the Aramean siege of Samaria (see 4:38; 6:24–7:20).

8:2 *she went with her household.* Elisha's instruction enabled the woman and her family to escape the privations of the famine.

8:3 *went ... unto the king.* See note on 1 Ki 3:16. *to cry ... for her house and for her land.* Either someone had illegally occupied the woman's property during her absence, or it had fallen to the domain of the king by virtue of its abandonment.

8:4 *Gehazi.* See 5:27. *Tell me ... all the great things that Elisha hath done.* The king's lack of familiarity with Elisha's ministry is perhaps an indication that this incident occurred in the early days of the reign of Jehu rather than in the time of Jehoram, who had had numerous contacts with Elisha (see 3:13–14; 5:7–10; 6:10–23; 6:24–7:20). But see note on 5:7.

8:5 *as he was telling the king.* The woman's approach to the king providentially coincided with Gehazi's story of her son's miraculous restoration to life through the ministry of Elisha.

8:6 *Restore all that was hers.* The widow and her son were living examples of the Lord's provision and blessing for those who were obedient to the word of the Lord through His prophets.

8:7 *Elisha came to Damascus.* The time had come for Elisha to carry out one of the three tasks originally given to Elijah at mount Horeb (see notes on 1 Ki 19:15–16). The annals of the

was told him, saying, The man of God is come
hither.
8 And the king said unto [a]Hazael, [b]Take a
present in thine hand, and go, meet the man
of God, and [c]inquire of the LORD by him, saying, Shall I recover of this disease?
9 So Hazael went to meet him, and took a
present [1]with him, even *of* every good thing
of Damascus, forty camels' burden, and came
and stood before him, and said, Thy son Ben-
hadad king of Syria hath sent me to thee, saying, Shall I recover of this disease?
10 And Elisha said unto him, Go, say unto
him, Thou mayest certainly recover: howbeit
the LORD hath shewed me that [a]he shall surely die.
11 And he settled his countenance [1]sted-
fastly, until *he* was ashamed: and the man of
God [a]wept.
12 And Hazael said, Why weepeth my
lord? And he answered, Because I know [a]the
evil that thou wilt do unto the children of Israel: their strong holds wilt thou set on fire, and
their young *men* wilt thou slay with the
sword, and [b]wilt dash their children, and rip
up their women with child.
13 And Hazael said, But what, [a]*is* thy servant a dog, that he should do this great thing?
And Elisha answered, [b]The LORD hath shewed
me *that* thou *shalt be* king over Syria.
14 So he departed from Elisha, and came to
his master; who said to him, What said Elisha

8:8 [a]1 Ki. 19:15 [b]1 Sam. 9:7; 1 Ki. 14:3; ch. 5:5 [c]ch. 1:2
8:9 [1]Heb. *in his hand*
8:10 [a]ver. 15
8:11 [1]Heb. *and set it* [a]Luke 19:41
8:12 [a]ch. 10:32; 12:17; 13:3,7; Amos 1:3 [b]ch. 15:16; Hos. 13:16; Amos 1:13
8:13 [a]1 Sam. 17:43 [b]1 Ki. 19:15

8:16 [1]Heb. *reigned.* [Began to reign in consort with his father] [a]2 Chr. 21:3
8:17 [a]2 Chr. 21:5
8:18 [a]ver. 26
8:19 [1]Heb. *candle,* or, *lamp* [a]2 Sam. 7:13; 1 Ki. 11:36; 15:4; 2 Chr. 21:7
8:20 [a]Gen. 27:40; ch. 3:27; 2 Chr. 21:8-10 [b]1 Ki. 22:47
8:22 [1][And so fulfilled Gen. 27:40]

to thee? And he answered, He told me *that*
thou shouldest surely recover.
15 And it came to pass on the morrow, that
he took a thick cloth, and dipt *it* in water, and
spread *it* on his face, so that he died: and Hazael reigned in his stead.

Jehoram, king of Judah

16 ¶ And in the fifth year of Joram the son
of Ahab king of Israel, Jehoshaphat *being* then
king of Judah, [a]Jehoram the son of Jehoshaphat king of Judah [1]*began* to reign.
17 [a]Thirty and two years old was he when
he *began* to reign; and he reigned eight years
in Jerusalem.
18 And he walked in the way of the kings
of Israel, as did the house of Ahab: for [a]the
daughter of Ahab was his wife: and he did evil
in the sight of the LORD.
19 Yet the LORD would not destroy Judah
for David his servant's sake, [a]as he promised
him to give to him alway a [1]light, *and* to his
children.
20 In his days [a]Edom revolted from under
the hand of Judah, [b]and made a king over
themselves.
21 So Joram went over to Zair, and all the
chariots with him: and he rose by night, and
smote the Edomites which compassed him
about, and the captains of the chariots: and the
people fled into their tents.
22 [1]Yet Edom revolted from under the

Assyrian ruler Shalmaneser III record Assyrian victories over Ben-hadad (Hadadezer) of Damascus in 846 B.C. and Hazael of Damascus in 842. Elisha's visit to Damascus is to be dated c. 843.

8:8 *inquire of the LORD by him.* In a reversal of the situation described in 1:1–4, a pagan king seeks an oracle from Israel's God. *Shall I recover . . . ?* The question is the same as that of Ahaziah in 1:2.

8:9 *every good thing of Damascus, forty camels' burden.* Damascus was the center for trade between Egypt, Asia Minor and Mesopotamia. Ben-hadad evidently thought a generous gift would favorably influence Elisha's oracle. *Thy son Ben-hadad.* Use of father-son terminology is a tacit acknowledgment by Ben-hadad of Elisha's superiority (see 6:21; 1 Sam 25:8).

8:10 *Thou mayest certainly recover.* An assertion that Ben-hadad's illness was not terminal (see v. 14).

8:12 *evil that thou wilt do unto the children of Israel.* The Lord gave Elisha a clear picture of the severity of the judgment He was about to send on Israel by the hand of Hazael (see 9:14–16; 10:32; 12:17–18; 13:3,22). *set on fire . . . rip up their women with child.* These actions were characteristic of victorious armies at that time (see 15:16; Hos 10:14; 13:16; Amos 1:13). Elisha's words do not sanction such acts but simply describe Hazael's future attacks on Israel.

8:13 *what, is thy servant a dog, that he should do this great thing?* Hazael did not show repulsion at these violent acts but saw no possibility to gain the power necessary to accomplish them (for this metaphorical use of "dog" see note on 2 Sam 9:8). *thou shalt be king over Syria.* Elisha's prophecy suggests that Hazael was not a legitimate successor to Ben-hadad. In an Assyrian inscription Hazael is designated "the son of a nobody" (i.e. a commoner) who usurped the throne.

8:15 *died.* Elisha's prophecy of Hazael's kingship did not legitimize the assassination. Hazael's murder of Ben-hadad as well as his future acts of violence against Israel were wicked acts arising out of his own sinful heart (see Is 10:5–19). His reign extended from c. 842 B.C. to c. 806 or 796, and he was followed by a son he named Ben-hadad (13:24).

8:16 *fifth year of Joram.* 848 B.C. Jehoram had been co-regent with his father since 853 (see note on 1:17), but he now began his reign as sole king.

8:17 *reigned eight years in Jerusalem.* Jehoram's sole reign is to be dated 848–841 B.C.

8:18 *as did the house of Ahab.* Jehoram introduced Baal worship in Judah, as Ahab had done in the northern kingdom (see 11:18). Baal worship now spread to the southern kingdom at the same time it was being restricted in the northern kingdom by Ahab's son Joram (see 3:1–2). *the daughter of Ahab was his wife.* Jehoram's wife was Athaliah, a daughter of Ahab but probably not of Jezebel (see v. 26; 2 Chr 18:1). Athaliah's influence on Jehoram paralleled that of Jezebel on Ahab (see 1 Ki 16:31; 18:4; 19:1–2; 2 Chr 21:6).

8:19 *give to him alway a light.* See note on 1 Ki 11:36; see also Ps 132:17. The Lord spared Judah and its royal house the judgment He brought on the house of Ahab because of the covenant He had made with David (see 2 Sam 7:16,29; 2 Chr 21:7).

8:20 *made a king over themselves.* Previously Edom had been subject to Judah and had been ruled by a deputy (see note on 3:9; see also 1 Ki 22:47).

8:21 *the people fled.* Although Jehoram and his army were able to break through an encirclement by Edomite forces, they were soundly defeated and forced to retreat to their own territory.

8:22 *unto this day.* Until the time of the writing of the account of Jehoram's reign used by the author of 1,2 Kings (see Introduction to 1 Kings: Author, Sources and Date; see also note on 1 Ki 8:8). Later, Amaziah of Judah was able to inflict a serious de-

hand of Judah unto this day. [a]Then Libnah revolted at the same time.

23 And the rest of the acts of Joram, and all that he did, *are* they not written in the book of the chronicles of the kings of Judah?

24 And Joram slept with his fathers, and was buried with his fathers in the city of David: and [a] [1]Ahaziah his son reigned in his stead.

Ahaziah, king of Judah

25 ¶ In the twelfth year of Joram the son of Ahab king of Israel did Ahaziah the son of Jehoram king of Judah *begin* to reign.

26 [a]Two and twenty years old *was* Ahaziah when he *began* to reign; and he reigned one year in Jerusalem. And his mother's name *was* Athaliah, the [1]daughter of Omri king of Israel.

27 [a]And he walked in the way of the house of Ahab, and did evil in the sight of the LORD, as *did* the house of Ahab: for he *was* the son in law of the house of Ahab.

28 And he went [a]with Joram the son of Ahab to the war against Hazael king of Syria in Ramoth-gilead; and the Syrians wounded Joram.

29 And [a]king Joram went back to be healed in Jezreel of the wounds [1]which the Syrians had given him at [2]Ramah, when he fought against Hazael king of Syria. [b]And Ahaziah the son of Jehoram king of Judah went down to see Joram the son of Ahab in Jezreel, because he was [3]sick.

Jehu anointed king of Israel

9 And Elisha the prophet called one of the [a]children of the prophets, and said unto him, [b]Gird up thy loins, and take this box of oil in thine hand, [c]and go *to* Ramoth-gilead:

2 And when thou comest thither, look out there Jehu the son of Jehoshaphat the son of Nimshi, and go in, and make him arise up from among [a]his brethren, and carry him *to* an [1]inner chamber:

3 Then [a]take the box of oil, and pour *it* on his head, and say, Thus saith the LORD, I have anointed thee king over Israel. Then open the door, and flee, and tarry not.

4 So the young man, *even* the young man the prophet, went *to* Ramoth-gilead.

5 And when he came, behold, the captains of the host *were* sitting; and he said, I have an errand to thee, O captain. And Jehu said, Unto which of all us? And he said, To thee, O captain.

6 And he arose, and went into the house; and he poured the oil on his head, and said unto him, [a]Thus saith the LORD God of Israel, I have anointed thee king over the people of the LORD, *even* over Israel.

7 And thou shalt smite the house of Ahab thy master, that I may avenge the blood of my servants the prophets, and the blood of all the servants of the LORD, [a]at the hand of Jezebel.

8 For the whole house of Ahab shall perish: and [a]I will cut off from Ahab [b]*him that* pisseth against the wall, and [c]*him that is* shut up and left in Israel:

9 And I will make the house of Ahab like the house of [a]Jeroboam the son of Nebat, and like the house of [b]Baasha the son of Ahijah:

10 [a]And the dogs shall eat Jezebel in the portion of Jezreel, and *there shall be* none to bury *her*. And he opened the door, and fled.

Jehu kills Joram and Ahaziah

11 ¶ Then Jehu came forth to the servants of his lord: and *one* said unto him, *Is all* well? wherefore came [a]this mad *fellow* to thee? And he said unto them, Ye know the man, and his communication.

12 And they said, *It is* false; tell us now. And he said, Thus and thus spake he to me, saying, Thus saith the LORD, I have anointed thee king over Israel.

13 Then they hasted, and [a]took every man his garment, and put *it* under him on the top of the stairs, and blew with trumpets, saying, Jehu [1]is king.

8:22 [a]2 Chr. 21:10
8:24 [1][Called *Azariah,* 2 Chr. 22:6, and *Jehoahaz,* 2 Chr. 21:17; 25:23] [a]2 Chr. 22:1
8:26 [1][Or, *granddaughter:* See ver. 18] [a]See 2 Chr. 22:2
8:27 [a]2 Chr. 22:3,4
8:28 [a]2 Chr. 22:5
8:29 [1]Heb. *where*with *the Syrians had wounded* [2][Called *Ramoth,* ver. 28] [3]Heb. *wounded* [a]ch. 9:15 [b]ch. 9:16; 2 Chr. 22:6,7
9:1 [a]1 Ki. 20:35 [b]ch. 4:29; Jer. 1:17 [c]ch. 8:28,29
9:2 [1]Heb. *chamber in a chamber* [a]ver. 5,11
9:3 [a]1 Ki. 19:16
9:6 [a]1 Ki. 19:16; 2 Chr. 22:7
9:7 [a]1 Ki. 18:4; 21:15
9:8 [a]1 Ki. 14:10; 21:21 [b]1 Sam. 25:22 [c]Deut. 32:36
9:9 [a]1 Ki. 14:10; 15:29; 21:22 [b]1 Ki. 16:3,11
9:10 [a]ver. 35,36; 1 Ki. 21:23
9:11 [a]Jer. 29:26; John 10:20; Acts 26:24; 1 Cor. 4:10
9:13 [1]Heb. *reigneth* [a]Mat. 21:7

feat on Edom (14:7), and his successor Azariah regained control of the trade route to Elath through Edomite territory (14:22; 2 Chr 26:2). *Libnah revolted at the same time.* Libnah appears to have been located close to the Philistine border near Lachish (see 19:8). It is likely that the revolt of Libnah was connected with that of the Philistines and Arabs described in 2 Chr 21:16–17.

8:23 *the acts of Joram* [Jehoram]. See 2 Chr 21:4–20. *chronicles of the kings of Judah.* See note on 1 Ki 14:29.

8:24 *slept with his fathers.* See notes on 1 Ki 1:21; 2 Chr 21:20.

8:25 *twelfth year of Joram.* 841 B.C. In 9:29 the first year of Joram's reign was counted as his accession year and his second year as the first year of his reign, whereas here his accession year was counted as the first year of his reign (see Introduction to 1 Kings: Chronology).

8:26 *Two and twenty years old . . . when he began to reign.* See note on 2 Chr 22:2. *Athaliah.* See note on v. 18.

8:27 *way of the house of Ahab.* See 2 Chr 22:3–5.

8:28 *he went with Joram . . . to the war against Hazael . . . in Ramoth-gilead.* As Jehoshaphat had joined Ahab in battle against the Arameans at Ramoth-gilead (1 Ki 22), so now Ahaziah joined his uncle Joram in a similar venture. On the previous occasion Ahab met his death (1 Ki 22:37). On this occasion Joram was wounded and, while recuperating in Jezreel (see note on 1 Ki 21:1), both he and his nephew Ahaziah were assassinated by Jehu (see 9:14–28).

‡9:1 *children* [i.e."sons"] *of the prophets.* See note on 2:3.

9:3 *I have anointed thee king.* See notes on 1 Sam 2:10; 9:16; 1 Ki 19:16.

9:7 *smite the house of Ahab.* Jehu learned that he was the divinely appointed agent to inflict the judgment Elijah had pronounced many years earlier in his own hearing against the house of Ahab (see vv. 25–26; 1 Ki 21:21–24). *blood of all the servants of the LORD, at the hand of Jezebel.* A reference to people such as Naboth and his family (1 Ki 21:13), who were unjustly put to death through Jezebel's influence.

9:8 *him that is shut up and left in Israel.* See note on 1 Ki 14:10.

9:9 *like the house of Jeroboam.* See 1 Ki 14:7–11; 15:27–30. *like the house of Baasha.* See 1 Ki 16:1–4,8–12. Elijah had spoken the same words to Ahab years before (see 1 Ki 21:21–24).

9:11 *this mad fellow.* The epithet betrays a scornful attitude on the part of the military officers of the northern kingdom toward members of the prophetic companies.

14 So Jehu the son of Jehoshaphat the son of Nimshi conspired against Joram. (Now Joram had kept Ramoth-gilead, he and all Israel, because of Hazael king of Syria.

15 But [a]king [1]Joram was returned to be healed in Jezreel of the wounds which the Syrians [2]had given him, when he fought with Hazael king of Syria.) And Jehu said, If it be your minds, *then* [3]let none go forth *nor* escape out of the city to go to tell *it* in Jezreel.

16 So Jehu rode *in a chariot,* and went to Jezreel; for Joram lay there. [a]And Ahaziah king of Judah was come down to see Joram.

17 And there stood a watchman on the tower in Jezreel, and he spied the company of Jehu as he came, and said, I see a company. And Joram said, Take a horseman, and send to meet them, and let him say, *Is it* peace?

18 So there went one on horseback to meet him, and said, Thus saith the king, *Is it* peace? And Jehu said, What hast thou to do with peace? turn thee behind me. And the watchman told, saying, The messenger came to them, but he cometh not again.

19 Then he sent *out* a second on horseback, which came to them, and said, Thus saith the king, *Is it* peace? And Jehu answered, What hast thou to do with peace? turn thee behind me.

20 And the watchman told, saying, He came even unto them, and cometh not again: and the [1]driving *is* like the driving of Jehu the son of Nimshi; for he driveth [2]furiously.

21 And Joram said, [1]Make ready. And his chariot was made ready. And [a]Joram king of Israel and Ahaziah king of Judah went out, each in his chariot, and they went out against Jehu, and [2]met him in the portion of Naboth the Jezreelite.

22 And it came to pass, when Joram saw Jehu, that he said, *Is it* peace, Jehu? And he answered, What peace, so long as the whoredoms of thy mother Jezebel and her witchcrafts *are so* many?

23 And Joram turned his hands, and fled, and said to Ahaziah, *There is* treachery, O Ahaziah.

24 And Jehu [1]drew a bow with his full strength, and smote Jehoram between his arms, and the arrow went out at his heart, and he [2]sunk down in his chariot.

9:15 [1]Heb. *Jehoram* [2]Heb. *smote* [3]Heb. *let no escaper go, etc.* [a]ch. 8:29
9:16 [a]ch. 8:29
9:20 [1]Or, *marching* [2]Heb. *in madness*
9:21 [1]Heb. *Bind* [2]Heb. *found* [a]2 Chr. 22:7
9:24 [1]Heb. *filled his hand with a bow* [2]Heb. *bowed*
9:25 [a]1 Ki. 21:29
9:26 [1]Heb. *bloods* [2]Or, *portion*
9:27 [1][In the kingdom of *Samaria,* 2 Chr. 22:9]
9:29 [1][Then he began to reign as viceroy to his father in his sickness, 2 Chr. 21:18,19. But in Joram's 12th year he began to reign alone, ch. 8:25]
9:30 [1]Heb. *put her eyes in painting* [a]Ezek. 23:40
9:31 [a]1 Ki. 16:9-20
9:32 [1]Or, *chamberlains*
9:34 [a]1 Ki. 16:31
9:36 [1]Heb. *by the hand of* [a]1 Ki. 21:23

25 Then said *Jehu* to Bidkar his captain, Take up, *and* cast him in the portion of the field of Naboth the Jezreelite: for remember how that, when I and thou rode together after Ahab his father, [a]the LORD laid this burden upon him;

26 Surely I have seen yesterday the [1]blood of Naboth, and the [1]blood of his sons, saith the LORD; and I will requite thee in this [2]plat, saith the LORD. Now therefore take *and* cast him into the [2]plat *of ground,* according to the word of the LORD.

27 ¶ But when Ahaziah the king of Judah saw *this,* he fled *by* the way of the garden house. And Jehu followed after him, and said, Smite him also in the chariot. *And they did so* at the going up to Gur, which *is* by Ibleam. And he fled *to* [1]Megiddo, and died there.

28 And his servants carried him *in a chariot* to Jerusalem, and buried him in his sepulchre with his fathers in the city of David.

29 And in the eleventh year of Joram the son of Ahab *began* [1]Ahaziah to reign over Judah.

The death of Jezebel

30 ¶ And when Jehu was come to Jezreel, Jezebel heard *of it;* [a]and she [1]painted her face, and tired her head, and looked out at a window.

31 And as Jehu entered in at the gate, she said, [a]*Had* Zimri peace, who slew his master?

32 And he lift up his face to the window, and said, Who *is* on my side? who? And there looked out to him two *or* three [1]eunuchs.

33 And he said, Throw her down. So they threw her down: and *some* of her blood was sprinkled on the wall, and on the horses: and he trode her under foot.

34 And when he was come in, he did eat and drink, and said, Go, see now this cursed *woman,* and bury her: for [a]she *is* a king's daughter.

35 And they went to bury her: but they found no more of her than the skull, and the feet, and the palms of *her* hands.

36 Wherefore they came again, and told him. And he said, This *is* the word of the LORD, which he spake [1]by his servant Elijah the Tishbite, saying, [a]In the portion of Jezreel shall dogs eat the flesh of Jezebel:

9:15 *let none go forth nor escape . . . to go to tell it in Jezreel.* For the success of Jehu's revolt and to avoid a civil conflict it was important to take Joram totally by surprise.
9:16 *Jezreel.* About 45 miles from Ramoth-gilead. *Ahaziah . . . was come down to see Joram.* See 8:29.
9:21 *portion of Naboth.* See notes on 1 Ki 21:2–3,13,19.
9:22 *whoredoms . . . and her witchcrafts.* Both punishable by death (see Deut 13; 18:10–12). As long as these evils were promoted in the northern kingdom, there could be no peace.
9:26 *according to the word of the LORD.* Jehu saw himself providentially placed in the position of fulfilling the prophecy of Elijah given years before (see 1 Ki 21:18–24). Even though Ahab's own blood was not shed on Naboth's field (see 1 Ki 21:29 and note), Jehu saw in Joram's death the fulfillment of Elijah's prophecy (see note on 1 Ki 21:19).
9:27 *fled to Megiddo, and died there.* It may be questioned whether Jehu was justified in extending the purge of Ahab's house (see Hos 1:4) to the descendants of the house of David through Ahab's daughter Athaliah (see 8:18,26).
9:31 *Had Zimri peace, who slew his master?* In bitter sarcasm Jezebel called Jehu by the name Zimri. About 45 years earlier Zimri had seized the throne from Elah by assassination and then had destroyed the whole house of Baasha. He ruled, however, for only seven days before Omri seized power (see 1 Ki 16:8–20).
9:36 *the word of the LORD, which he spake by his servant Elijah.* In the manner of Jezebel's death the word of the Lord was confirmed—the word she had defied during her life (see 1 Ki 21:23).

37 And the carcase of Jezebel shall be [a]as
dung upon the face of the field in the portion
of Jezreel; *so* that they shall not say, This *is* Jezebel.

Ahab's kin destroyed

10 And Ahab had seventy sons in
Samaria. And Jehu wrote letters, and
sent *to* Samaria, unto the rulers of Jezreel, to
the elders, and to [1]them that brought up
Ahab's *children,* saying,
2 Now as soon as this letter cometh to you,
seeing your master's sons *are* with you, and
there are with you chariots and horses, a
fenced city also, and armour;
3 Look even out the best and meetest of
your master's sons, and set *him* on his father's
throne, and fight for your master's house.
4 But they were exceedingly afraid, and
said, Behold, two kings stood not before him:
how then shall we stand?
5 And *he* that *was* over the house, and *he*
that *was* over the city, the elders also, and the
bringers up *of the children,* sent to Jehu, saying, We *are* thy servants, and will do all that
thou shalt bid us; we will not make any king:
do thou *that* which *is* good in thine eyes.
6 Then he wrote a letter the second time to
them, saying, If ye *be* [1]mine, and *if* ye will
hearken unto my voice, take ye the heads of
the men your master's sons, and come to me to
Jezreel by to morrow *this* time. Now the king's
sons, *being* seventy persons, *were* with the
great *men* of the city, which brought them up.
7 And it came to pass, when the letter
came to them, that they took the king's sons,
and [a]slew seventy persons, and put their heads
in baskets, and sent him *them* to Jezreel.
8 And there came a messenger, and told
him, saying, They have brought the heads of
the king's sons. And he said, Lay ye them *in*
two heaps *at* the entering in of the gate until
the morning.
9 And it came to pass in the morning, that
he went out, and stood, and said to all the
people, Ye *be* righteous: behold, [a]I conspired
against my master, and slew him: but who
slew all these?
10 Know now that there shall [a]fall unto the
earth nothing of the word of the LORD, which
the LORD spake concerning the house of Ahab:
for the LORD hath done *that* which he spake
[b][1]by his servant Elijah.
11 So Jehu slew all that remained of the
house of Ahab in Jezreel, and all his great *men,*
and his [1]kinsfolks, and his priests, until *he* left
him none remaining.
12 ¶ And he arose and departed, and came
to Samaria. *And* as he *was at* the [1]shearing
house in the way,
13 [a]Jehu [1]met with the brethren of Ahaziah king of Judah, and said, Who *are* ye? And
they answered, We *are* the brethren of Ahaziah; and we go down [2]to salute the children of
the king and the children of the queen.
14 And he said, Take them alive. And they
took them alive, and slew them at the pit of
the shearing house, *even* two and forty men;
neither left he any of them.
15 And when he was departed thence, he
[1]lighted on [a]Jehonadab the son of [b]Rechab
coming to meet him: and he [2]saluted him, and

9:37 [a]Ps. 83:10
10:1 [1]Heb. *nourishers*
10:6 [1]Heb. *for me*
10:7 [a]1 Ki. 21:21
10:9 [a]ch. 9:14,24
10:10 [1]Heb. *by the hand of* [a]1 Sam. 3:19; Jer. 44:28 [b]1 Ki. 21:19,21,29
10:11 [1]Or, *acquaintance*
10:12 [1]Heb. *house of shepherds binding* sheep
10:13 [1]Heb. *found* [2]Heb. *to the peace of, etc.* [a]ch. 8:29; 2 Chr. 22:8
10:15 [1]Heb. *found* [2]Heb. *blessed* [a]Jer. 35:6 [b]1 Chr. 2:55

10:1 *Ahab had seventy sons.* The number of Ahab's wives is unknown (see 1 Ki 20:5). The 70 presumably included both sons and grandsons. *Samaria.* In order to consolidate his coup and establish control of the northern kingdom, Jehu still faced the formidable problems of taking the nearly impregnable fortress of Samaria (see note on 1 Ki 16:24) and then of completing the destruction of Ahab's house. *rulers.* Officers appointed by the king (see 1 Ki 4:1–6). *elders.* Local leaders by virtue of their position in the tribal and family structure (see notes on Ex 3:16; 2 Sam 3:17). *them that brought up Ahab's children.* Those entrusted with the care and upbringing of the princes in the royal family.
10:3 *fight for your master's house.* Jehu's strategy was to induce the leaders of Samaria into submission to his rule by bluffing a military confrontation.
10:4 *were exceedingly afraid.* The leaders of Samaria were completely intimidated by Jehu's challenge.
10:5 *he that was over the house.* See note on 1 Ki 4:6. *he that was over the city.* Probably an official appointed by the king who served as commander of the militia of the capital city. *the elders also, and the bringers up of the children.* See note on v. 1.
10:6 *take ye the heads of . . . your master's sons, and come to me.* The wording of Jehu's command contains what appears to be a deliberate ambiguity. The "heads of the men your master's sons" could be understood as a reference to the leading figures among the 70 descendants of Ahab, such as the crown prince and several other sons of special ability and standing. On the other hand, the expression could be taken as a reference to the literal heads of all 70 princes.
10:7 *slew seventy persons.* The leaders of the city understood the communiqué in the literal sense, as Jehu most certainly had hoped they would. *put their heads in baskets, and sent him them.* The leaders of Samaria did not carry the heads of the princes to Jezreel themselves as they had been ordered to do by Jehu (see v. 6). It is likely that they feared for their lives.
10:8 *Lay ye them in two heaps at the entering in of the gate.* This gruesome procedure imitated the barbaric practice of the Assyrian rulers Ashurnasirpal and Shalmaneser III, whose reigns were characterized by acts of terror.
10:9 *I conspired . . . and slew him.* Jehu openly confessed his own part in the overthrow of the government of Joram. *who slew all these?* Because of the ambiguous communiqué Jehu sent to the leaders of Samaria (see note on v. 6), he can now deny any personal responsibility for the slaughter of the 70 sons of Ahab and can lay the blame for it on the leaders of Samaria.
10:10 *which he spake by his servant Elijah.* See 1 Ki 21:20–24,29. Jehu implies a divine sanction not only for what had already been done but also for his intent to continue the purge of Ahab's house and associates.
10:11 *all his great men, and his kinfolks, and his priests.* Jehu went beyond the responsibility given to him (see 9:7; Hos 1:4) and acted solely on grounds of political self-interest. Jehu himself had been in the service of Ahab (see 9:25).
10:13 *brethren of Ahaziah.* See 2 Chr 21:17. *children of the king and . . . the queen.* Members of the royal family from Judah who had not yet heard of the deaths of Joram and Jezebel.
10:15 *Jehonadab the son of Rechab.* Jehonadab was the leader of a conservative movement among the Israelites that was char-

said to him, Is thine heart right, as my heart *is*
with thy heart? And Jehonadab answered, It
is. If it be, [c]give *me* thine hand. And he gave
him his hand; and he took him up to him into
the chariot.
16 And he said, Come with me, and see
my [a]zeal for the LORD. So they made him ride
in his chariot.
17 And when he came *to* Samaria, [a]he
slew all that remained unto Ahab in Samaria,
till *he* had destroyed him, according to the saying of the LORD, [b]which he spake to Elijah.

Massacre of Baal worshippers

18 ¶ And Jehu gathered all the people together, and said unto them, [a]Ahab served Baal
a little; *but* Jehu shall serve him much.
19 Now therefore call unto me all the
[a]prophets of Baal, all his servants, and all his
priests; let none be wanting: for I have a great
sacrifice *to do* to Baal; whosoever shall be
wanting, he shall not live. But Jehu did *it* in
subtilty, to the intent that *he* might destroy the
worshippers of Baal.
20 And Jehu said, [1]Proclaim a solemn assembly for Baal. And they proclaimed *it*.
21 And Jehu sent through all Israel: and all
the worshippers of Baal came, so that there
was not a man left that came not. And they
came *into* the [a]house of Baal; and the house of
Baal was [1]full from one end to another.
22 And he said unto *him* that *was* over the
vestry, Bring forth vestments for all the worshippers of Baal. And he brought them forth
vestments.
23 And Jehu went, and Jehonadab the son
of Rechab, *into* the house of Baal, and said unto
the worshippers of Baal, Search, and look that
there be here with you none of the servants of
the LORD, but the worshippers of Baal only.
24 And when they went in to offer sacrifices and burnt offerings, Jehu appointed

10:15 [c]Ezra 10:19
10:16 [a]1 Ki. 19:10
10:17 [a]ch. 9:8; 2 Chr. 22:8 [b]1 Ki. 21:21
10:18 [a]1 Ki. 16:31,32
10:19 [a]1 Ki. 22:6
10:20 [1]Heb. *Sanctify*
10:21 [1]Or, so *full,* that they stood *mouth to mouth* [a]1 Ki. 16:32
10:24 [a]1 Ki. 20:39
10:25 [1]Heb. *the mouth*
10:26 [1]Heb. *statues* [a]1 Ki. 14:23
10:27 [a]Ezra 6:11; Dan. 2:5; 3:29
10:29 [a]1 Ki. 12:28,29
10:30 [a]See ver. 35; ch. 13:1,10; 14:23; 15:8,12
10:31 [1]Heb. *observed not* [a]1 Ki. 14:16
10:32 [1]Heb. *to cut off the ends* [a]ch. 8:12
10:33 [1]Heb. toward *the rising of the sun* [2]Or, *even* to Gilead *and Bashan* [a]Amos 1:3

fourscore men without, and said, *If* any of the
men whom I *have* brought into your hands escape, *he that letteth him go,* [a]his life *shall be*
for the life of him.
25 And it came to pass, as soon as he had
made an end of offering the burnt offering,
that Jehu said to the guard and to the captains,
Go in, *and* slay them; let none come forth.
And they smote them with [1]the edge of the
sword; and the guard and the captains cast
them out, and went to the city of the house of
Baal.
26 And they brought forth the [a][1]images
out of the house of Baal, and burnt them.
27 And they brake down the image of Baal,
and brake down the house of Baal, [a]and made
it a draught house unto *this* day.
28 Thus Jehu destroyed Baal out of Israel.
29 Howbeit *from* the sins of Jeroboam the
son of Nebat, who made Israel to sin, Jehu departed not from after them, *to wit,* [a]the golden
calves that *were in* Beth-el, and that *were* in
Dan.
30 And the LORD said unto Jehu, Because
thou hast done well in executing *that* which *is*
right in mine eyes, *and* hast done unto the
house of Ahab according to all that *was* in
mine heart, [a]thy children of the fourth *generation* shall sit on the throne of Israel.
31 But Jehu [1]took no heed to walk in the
law of the LORD God of Israel with all his heart:
for he departed not from [a]the sins of Jeroboam, which made Israel to sin.
32 ¶ In those days the LORD began [1]to cut
Israel short: and [a]Hazael smote them in all the
coasts of Israel;
33 From Jordan [1]eastward, all the land of
Gilead, the Gadites, and the Reubenites, and
the Manassites, from Aroer, which *is* by the
river Arnon, [2]even [a]Gilead and Bashan.
34 Now the rest of the acts of Jehu, and all
that he did, and all his might, *are* they not

---

acterized by strong opposition to Baalism as well as to various practices of a settled agricultural society, including the building of houses, the sowing of crops and the use of wine. His followers still adhered to these principles over 200 years later and were known as Rechabites (see Jer 35:6–10).

10:16 *made him ride in his chariot.* Public association with Jehonadab gave Jehu added credentials among the rural populace as a follower of the Lord.

10:18 *Ahab served Baal a little; but Jehu shall serve him much.* After settling in Samaria, Jehu gave the appearance of having previously appealed to the word of the Lord as a mere political maneuver.

10:19 *shall not live.* Jehu's reputation made this no idle threat.

10:26 *burnt them.* May refer to the Asherim (see note on 1 Ki 14:15) that usually accompanied a sacred pillar (see 1 Ki 16:32–33).

10:27 *image of Baal.* See note on 1 Ki 14:23. *unto this day.* See note on 8:22.

10:29 *sins of Jeroboam . . . who made Israel to sin.* See 1 Ki 12:26–32; 13:33–34; 14:16.

10:30 *Because thou hast done . . . unto the house of Ahab according to all that was in mine heart.* Jehu was the Lord's instrument to bring judgment on the house of Ahab, for which he was commended. But he was later condemned by the prophet Hosea for the killing of all Ahab's associates, as well as Ahaziah of Judah and the 42 Judahite princes—the "blood of Jezreel" (Hos 1:4). *fourth generation.* The restriction of this blessing to four generations is reflective of the qualified approval given to Jehu's reign. Nevertheless, his dynasty survived longer than any other dynasty of the northern kingdom, lasting nearly 100 years. It included the reigns of Jehoahaz, Jehoash, Jeroboam II and Zechariah (see note on 15:12).

10:31 *took no heed to walk in the law of the LORD . . . with all his heart.* Jehu seems to have been driven more by a political desire to secure his own position on the throne of the northern kingdom than by a desire to serve the Lord. In this he was guilty of using God's judgment on the house of Ahab to satisfy his self-interest.

‡10:32 *the LORD began to cut Israel short.* I.e. He reduced the size of Israel's land. The climax of the covenant curses enumerated in Lev 26 and Deut 28 was Israel's expulsion from Canaan. During the rule of Jehu the northern kingdom experienced the beginnings of this curse (see 17:7–18 for its full realization).

10:33 All the land east of the Jordan was lost to Hazael and the Arameans of Damascus.

10:34 *rest of the acts of Jehu.* The Black Obelisk of the Assyr-

written in the book of the chronicles of the kings of Israel?

35 And Jehu slept with his fathers: and they buried him in Samaria. And Jehoahaz his son reigned in his stead.

36 And [1]the time that Jehu reigned over Israel in Samaria *was* twenty and eight years.

Joash (Jehoash), king of Judah

11 And when [a]Athaliah [b]the mother of Ahaziah saw that her son was dead, she arose and destroyed all the [1]seed royal.

2 But [1]Jehosheba, the daughter of king Joram, sister of Ahaziah, took [2]Joash the son of Ahaziah, and stale him from among the king's sons which were slain; and they hid him, *even* him and his nurse, in the bedchamber from Athaliah, so that he was not slain.

3 And he was with her hid *in* the house of the LORD six years. And Athaliah *did* reign over the land.

4 ¶ And [a]the seventh year Jehoiada sent and fet the rulers over hundreds, with the captains and the guard, and brought them to him *into* the house of the LORD, and made a covenant with them, and took an oath of them in the house of the LORD, and shewed them the king's son.

5 And he commanded them, saying, This *is* the thing that ye shall do; A third *part* of you that enter in [a]on the sabbath shall even be keepers of the watch of the king's house;

6 And a third *part shall be* at the gate of Sur; and a third *part* at the gate behind the guard: so shall ye keep the watch of the house, [1]that it be not broken down.

7 And two [1]parts of all you that go forth on the sabbath, even they shall keep the watch of the house of the LORD about the king.

8 And ye shall compass the king round about, every man with his weapons in his hand: and he that cometh within the ranges, let him be slain: and be ye with the king as he goeth out and as he cometh in.

9 [a]And the captains over the hundreds did according to all *things* that Jehoiada the priest commanded: and they took every man his men that were to come in on the sabbath, with them that should go out on the sabbath, and came to Jehoiada the priest.

10 And to the captains over hundreds did the priest give king David's spears and shields, [a]that *were* in the temple of the LORD.

11 And the guard stood, every man with his weapons in his hand, round about the king, from the right [1]corner of the temple to the left corner of the temple, *along* by the altar and the temple.

12 And he brought forth the king's son, and put the crown upon him, and *gave him* the Testimony; and they made him king, and anointed him; and they clapt their hands, and said, [a][1]God save the king.

13 [a]And when Athaliah heard the noise of the guard *and* of the people, she came to the people *into* the temple of the LORD.

14 And when she looked, behold, the king stood by [a]a pillar, as the manner *was*, and the princes and the trumpeters by the king, and all the people of the land rejoiced, and blew with trumpets: and Athaliah rent her clothes, and cried, Treason, Treason.

15 But Jehoiada the priest commanded the captains of the hundreds, the officers of the

10:36 [1]Heb. *the days were*
11:1 [1]Heb. *seed of the kingdom* [a]2 Chr. 22:10 [b]ch. 8:26
11:2 [1][2 Chr. 22:11, *Jehoshabeath*] [2][Or, *Jehoash*]
11:4 [a]2 Chr. 23:1
11:5 [a]1 Chr. 9:25
11:6 [1]Or, from *breaking up*
11:7 [1]Or, *companies.* Heb. *hands*
11:9 [a]2 Chr. 23:8
11:10 [a]2 Sam. 8:7
11:11 [1]Heb. *shoulder*
11:12 [1]Heb. *Let the king live* [a]1 Sam. 10:24
11:13 [a]2 Chr. 23:12
11:14 [a]ch. 23:3; 2 Chr. 34:31

ian ruler Shalmaneser III informs us that Jehu paid tribute to the Assyrians shortly after coming to the throne of the northern kingdom in 841 B.C. In the Assyrian inscription Jehu is incorrectly called the "son of Omri," but this may simply be Shalmaneser's way of identifying Jehu with Samaria (or Israel). There is no reference to this payment of tribute in the Biblical narratives of Jehu's reign. *chronicles of the kings of Israel.* See note on 1 Ki 14:19.

10:35 *slept with his fathers.* See note on 1 Ki 1:21. *Jehoahaz his son reigned in his stead.* For the reign of Jehoahaz see 13:1–9.

10:36 *twenty and eight years.* 841–814 B.C.

11:1 *Athaliah.* See note on 8:18. *her son was dead.* See 9:27. *destroyed all the seed royal.* To secure the throne in Judah for herself. By this time the royal family in Judah had already been reduced to a mere remnant. Joram, the late husband of Athaliah and the father of Ahaziah, had killed all his brothers when he succeeded his father Jehoshaphat on the throne (see 2 Chr 21:4). Jehu had slain another 42 members of the royal house of Judah, perhaps including many of the sons of Joram's brothers (10:12–14; 2 Chr 22:8–9), and the brothers of Ahaziah had been killed by marauding Arabs (2 Chr 22:1). It is likely that Athaliah's purge focused primarily on the children of Ahaziah, i.e. her own grandchildren. Ahaziah had died at the young age of 22 (see 8:26). This attempt to completely destroy the house of David was an attack on God's redemptive plan—a plan that centered in the Messiah, which the Davidic covenant promised (see notes on 2 Sam 7:11,16; 1 Ki 8:25).

11:2 *daughter of King Joram, sister of Ahaziah.* It is likely that Jehosheba was the daughter of Joram by a wife other than Athaliah, and thus she was a half sister of Ahaziah. She was married to the high priest Jehoiada (see 2 Chr 22:11). *him and his nurse.* The child was not more than a year old and had not yet been weaned (see vv. 3,21).

‡11:4 *seventh year.* Of Athaliah's rule. *rulers over hundreds.* 2 Chr 23:1 lists the names of five commanders, all native Israelites. *captains.* Hebrew *Cari,* i.e. "Carites." These were mercenary soldiers from Caria in southwest Asia Minor who served as royal bodyguards. *brought them to him into the house of the LORD.* 2 Chr 23:2 includes the Levites and family leaders of Judah in the conspiracy.

11:10 *king David's spears and shields, that were in the temple of LORD.* David had probably taken the spears and gold shields as plunder in his battle with Hadadezer and then dedicated them to the Lord (see 2 Sam 8:7–11).

11:12 *Testimony.* Either (1) the ten commandments, (2) the entire Mosaic covenant or (3) a document dealing more specifically with the covenant responsibilities of the king (see Deut 17:14–20; see also note on 1 Sam 10:25). The third option is most likely. *anointed him.* See notes on 1 Sam 2:10; 9:16; 1 Ki 1:39. *God save the king.* See 1 Sam 10:24; 1 Ki 1:34,39.

11:14 *pillar.* Apparently one of the two bronze pillars of the portico of the temple, named Jachin and Boaz (see 23:3; 1 Ki 7:15–22; 2 Chr 23:13). *all the people of the land.* It is likely that Jehoiada had chosen to stage his coup on a sabbath during one of the major religious festivals, when many from the realm who were loyal to the Lord would be in Jerusalem.

host, and said unto them, Have her forth without the ranges: and him that followeth her kill with the sword. For the priest had said, Let her not be slain *in* the house of the LORD.

16 And they laid hands on her; and she went *by* the way by the which the horses came *into* the king's house: and there was she slain.

17 ¶ [a]And Jehoiada made a covenant between the LORD and the king and the people, that *they* should be the LORD'S people; [b]between the king also and the people.

18 And all the people of the land went *into* the [a]house of Baal, and brake it down; his altars and his images [b]brake they in pieces throughly, and slew Mattan the priest of Baal before the altars. And [c]the priest appointed [1]officers over the house of the LORD.

19 And he took the rulers over hundreds, and the captains, and the guard, and all the people of the land; and they brought down the king from the house of the LORD, and came *by* the way of the gate of the guard *to* the king's house. And he sat on the throne of the kings.

20 And all the people of the land rejoiced, and the city was in quiet: and they slew Athaliah with the sword *beside* the king's house.

21 [a]Seven years old *was* Jehoash when he *began* to reign.

Jehoash repairs the temple

12 In the seventh year of Jehu [a]Jehoash *began* to reign; and forty years reigned he in Jerusalem. And his mother's name *was* Zibiah of Beer-sheba.

2 And Jehoash did *that* which *was* right in the sight of the LORD all his days where*in* Jehoiada the priest instructed him.

3 But [a]the high places were not taken away: the people still sacrificed and burnt incense in the high places.

4 And Jehoash said to the priests, [a]All the money of the [1]dedicated *things* that is brought *into* the house of the LORD, *even* [b]the money of every one that passeth *the account,* [2]the money that every man is set at, *and* all the money that [c3]cometh into any man's heart to bring *into* the house of the LORD,

5 Let the priests take *it* to them, every man of his acquaintance: and let them repair the breaches of the house, wheresoever any breach shall be found.

6 But it was *so, that* [1]in the three and twentieth year of king Jehoash [a]the priests had not repaired the breaches of the house.

7 [a]Then king Jehoash called for Jehoiada the priest, and the *other* priests, and said unto them, Why repair ye not the breaches of the house? now therefore receive no *more* money of your acquaintance, but deliver it for the breaches of the house.

8 And the priests consented to receive no *more* money of the people, neither to repair the breaches of the house.

9 But Jehoiada the priest took [a]a chest, and bored a hole in the lid of it, and set it beside the altar, on the right side as one cometh *into* the house of the LORD: and the priests that

11:17 [a]2 Chr. 23:16 [b]2 Sam. 5:3
11:18 [1]Heb. *offices* [a]ch. 10:26 [b]Deut. 12:3; 2 Chr. 23:17 [c]2 Chr. 23:18
11:21 [a]2 Chr. 24:1
12:1 [a]2 Chr. 24:1
12:3 [a]1 Ki. 15:14; 22:43; ch. 14:4
12:4 [1]Or, *holy* things. Heb. *holinesses* [2]Heb. *the money of the souls of his estimation* [3]Heb. *ascendeth upon the heart of a man* [a]ch. 22:4 [b]Ex. 30:13 [c]Ex. 35:5; 1 Chr. 29:9
12:6 [1]Heb. *in the twentieth year and third year* [a]2 Chr. 24:5
12:7 [a]2 Chr. 24:6
12:9 [a]2 Chr. 24:8

11:17 *covenant between the LORD and the king and the people, that they should be the LORD's people.* A renewal of the Mosaic covenant, by which Israel had been constituted as the Lord's people (see Ex 19:5–6; Deut 4:20). The years of apostasy, involving both the royal house and the people of Judah, necessitated a renewal of allegiance to the Lord at the time of an important new beginning for the southern kingdom (see notes on 1 Sam 11:14–15; 12:14–15,24–25). *between the king also and the people.* Defined responsibilities and mutual obligations of king and people that were compatible with Israel's covenant relationship with the Lord (see notes on 1 Sam 10:25; 2 Sam 5:3).
11:18 *images.* Stone pillars (see note on 1 Ki 14:23) and Asherim (see note on 1 Ki 14:15).
‡11:19 *rulers over hundreds, and the captains* [i.e. "Carites"], *and the guard.* See note on v. 4.
11:21 See v. 3. The Lord had preserved a light for David in Jerusalem (see 1 Ki 11:36).
12:1 *seventh year of Jehu.* 835 B.C. (see note on 10:36). *forty years.* 835–796.
12:2 *all his days wherein Jehoiada the priest instructed him.* After Jehoiada died, Jehoash turned away from the Lord (see 2 Chr 24:17–27).
12:3 *high places were not taken away.* These were high places where the Lord was worshiped rather than pagan deities (see note on 1 Ki 15:14). They were nevertheless potential sources for the entrance of pagan practices into Israel's worship (see note on 1 Ki 3:2).
‡12:4 *money of the dedicated things . . . brought into the house of the LORD.* The money was derived from three different sources: 1. *money of every one that passeth the account.* I.e. money collected in the census. At the age of 20, Israelite youths were required to register for military service and to make an offering of half a shekel (see note on 5:26) for use in the service of the central sanctuary (see Ex 30:11–16; 38:25–26; Num 2:32). 2. *money that every man is set at.* I.e. money received from personal vows. Various types of vows and their equivalence in monetary assessments are described in Lev 27:1–25. 3. *money that cometh into any man's heart to bring into the house of the LORD.* I.e. money brought voluntarily to the temple. For voluntary offerings see Lev 22:18–23; Deut 16:10.
12:5 *acquaintance.* Or, more likely, "treasurer," a temple functionary who handled financial matters for the priests relative to the people's sacrifices and offerings. *wheresoever any breach shall be found.* Construction of the temple had been completed 124 years before the beginning of the reign of Jehoash (see notes on v. 1; 1 Ki 6:38). In addition to deterioration due to age, it had fallen into disrepair and abuse during the rule of Athaliah (see 2 Chr 24:7).
12:6 *three and twentieth year of king Jehoash.* Jehoash may have instituted his plan for restoration of the temple a few years before the 23rd year of his reign. Now at age 30 he asserts his royal authority and takes charge of the temple repairs.
12:7 *receive no more money of your acquaintance.* The proceeds from the sources of revenue mentioned in v. 4 were no longer to be given to the priests.
12:8 *priests consented.* Apparently a compromise was reached: The priests would no longer take the money received from the people, but neither would they pay for the temple repairs from the money they had already received.
12:9 *priests that kept the door.* Three high-ranking priests charged with protecting the temple from unlawful (profane)

kept the [1]door put therein all the money that was brought *into* the house of the LORD.

10 And it was *so,* when they saw that *there was* much money in the chest, that the king's [1]scribe and the high priest came up, and they [2]put up *in bags,* and told the money that was found *in* the house of the LORD.

11 And they gave the money, being told, into the hands of *them* that did the work, that had the oversight *of* the house of the LORD: and they [1]laid it out to the carpenters and builders, that wrought upon the house of the LORD,

12 And to masons, and hewers of stone, and to buy timber and hewed stone to repair the breaches of the house of the LORD, and for all that [1]was laid out for the house to repair *it.*

13 Howbeit [a]there were not made *for* the house of the LORD bowls of silver, snuffers, basons, trumpets, any vessels of gold, or vessels of silver, of the money that was brought *into* the house of the LORD:

14 But they gave that to the workmen, and repaired therewith the house of the LORD.

15 Moreover [a]they reckoned not with the men, into whose hand they delivered the money to be bestowed on workmen: for they dealt faithfully.

16 [a]The trespass money and sin money was not brought *into* the house of the LORD: [b]it was the priests'.

17 ¶ Then [a]Hazael king of Syria went up, and fought against Gath, and took it: and [b]Hazael set his face to go up to Jerusalem.

18 And Jehoash king of Judah [a]took all the hallowed *things* that Jehoshaphat, and Jehoram, and Ahaziah, his fathers, kings of Judah, had dedicate, and his own hallowed *things,* and all the gold that was found in the treasures of the house of the LORD, and *in* the king's house, and sent *it* to Hazael king of Syria: and he [1]went away from Jerusalem.

19 And the rest of the acts of Joash, and all that he did, *are* they not written in the book of the chronicles of the kings of Judah?

20 And [a]his servants arose, and made a conspiracy, and slew Joash *in* [1]the house of Millo, which goeth down *to* Silla.

21 For [1]Jozachar the son of Shimeath, and Jehozabad the son of [2]Shomer, his servants, smote him, and he died; and they buried him with his fathers in the city of David: and [a]Amaziah his son reigned in his stead.

Jehoahaz, king of Israel

13 [1]In the three and twentieth year of Joash the son of Ahaziah king of Judah Jehoahaz the son of Jehu *began* to reign over Israel in Samaria, *and reigned* seventeen years.

2 And he did *that* which *was* evil in the sight of the LORD, and [1]followed the sins of Jeroboam the son of Nebat, which made Israel to sin; he departed not therefrom.

3 And [a]the anger of the LORD was kindled against Israel, and he delivered them into the hand of [b]Hazael king of Syria, and into the

12:9 [1]Heb. *threshold*
12:10 [1]Or, *secretary* [2]Heb. *bound up*
12:11 [1]Heb. *brought it forth*
12:12 [1]Heb. *went forth*
12:13 [a]See 2 Chr. 24:14
12:15 [a]ch. 22:7
12:16 [a]Lev. 5:15,18 [b]Lev. 7:7; Num. 18:9
12:17 [a]ch. 8:12 [b]See 2 Chr. 24:23
12:18 [1]Heb. *went up* [a]1 Ki. 15:18; ch. 18:15,16
12:20 [1]Or, *Beth-millo* [a]ch. 14:5; 2 Chr. 24:25
12:21 [1][2 Chr. 24:26, *Zabad*] [2][Or, *Shimrith*] [a]2 Chr. 24:27
13:1 [1]Heb. *In the twentieth year and third year*
13:2 [1]Heb. *walked after*
13:3 [a]Judg. 2:14 [b]ch. 8:12

entry (see 25:18; Jer 52:24). *put therein all the money.* When the people were assured that all their offerings would be used for the temple restoration, they responded with greater generosity. See 22:3–7 for continuation (or renewal) of this practice in the reign of Josiah.

12:10 *king's scribe.* See note on 2 Sam 8:17. Jehoash arranges for direct royal supervision of the temple's monetary affairs.

12:11 *them . . . that had the oversight.* The whole matter is taken out of the hands of the priests.

12:13 *there were not made for the house of the LORD . . . vessels of gold, or . . . silver.* All the money was initially designated for the restoration of the temple. When the restoration was completed, additional funds were used for the acquisition of silver and gold articles for use in the temple service (see 2 Chr 24:14).

12:16 *trespass money and sin money.* See Lev 5:16; 6:5; Num 5:7–10 for references to priestly income in connection with the bringing of a guilt offering. There is no Pentateuchal reference to priestly income in connection with the bringing of a sin offering (but see Lev 7:7).

12:17 *Then.* These events must have taken place toward the end of Jehoash's reign. From 2 Chr 24:17–24 it is clear that the Aramean attack was occasioned by Jehoash's turning away from the Lord after Jehoiada's death. Jehoash's apostasy reached its climax in the stoning of Jehoiada's son Zechariah (2 Chr 24:22). Probably because of Jehoash's earlier zeal for the temple, the author of Kings did not choose to relate these matters. *Hazael.* See 8:7–15; 10:32–33; 13:3,22. *Gath.* One of the major Philistine cities (see Josh 13:3) that David had conquered (1 Chr 18:1) and that continued to be subject to Judah during the reign of Rehoboam (2 Chr 11:8). In the latter years of the reign of Jehoash of Judah (835–796 B.C.) and during the reign of Jehoahaz of Israel (814–798; see 13:3,7), the Arameans had virtually overrun the northern kingdom, enabling them to advance against the Philistines and the kingdom of Judah with little resistance. *Hazael set his face to go up to Jerusalem.* See 2 Chr 24:23–24.

12:18 *hallowed things . . . gold . . . sent it to Hazael.* Years earlier, Asa had sought to secure assistance from the Arameans with a similar gift (see 1 Ki 15:18).

12:19 *chronicles of the kings of Judah.* See note on 1 Ki 14:29. A fuller account of the reign of Joash (Jehoash) is also found in 2 Chr 22:10–24:27.

12:20 *made a conspiracy.* The conspiracy was aroused in response to Joash's murder of Zechariah son of Jehoiada (see 2 Chr 24:25). *house of Millo.* For the meaning of Millo see note on Judg 9:6. Here the reference may be to a building (perhaps a kind of barracks) built on the "Millo" in the old City of David (see 2 Sam 5:9 and note; 1 Ki 11:27). Perhaps the king was staying there temporarily with his troops at the time of his assassination; Chronicles says he was killed "on his bed" (2 Chr 24:25). *Silla.* Perhaps refers to a steep descent from the City of David down into the Kidron Valley.

12:21 *servants.* Sons of Ammonite and Moabite mothers (2 Chr 24:26), suggesting that they may have been mercenary military officers whose services could have been bought by others. *buried him with his fathers.* But see 2 Chr 24:25. *Amaziah his son reigned in his stead.* For the reign of Amaziah see 14:1–22.

13:1 *three and twentieth year of Joash.* 814 B.C. (see note on 12:1; see also Introduction to 1 Kings: Chronology). *seventeen years.* 814–798.

13:2 *sins of Jeroboam.* See 1 Ki 12:26–32; 13:33–34; 14:16.

13:3 *Hazael.* See notes on 8:12,13,15; 10:33. *Ben-hadad.* See v. 24. His reign began in either 806 or 796 B.C.

hand of Ben-hadad the son of Hazael, all *their*
days.
4 And Jehoahaz [a]besought the LORD, and
the LORD hearkened unto him: for [b]he saw the
oppression of Israel, because the king of Syria
oppressed them.
5 ([a]And the LORD gave Israel a saviour, so
that they went out from under the hand of the
Syrians: and the children of Israel dwelt in
their tents, [1]as beforetime.
6 Nevertheless they departed not from the
sins of the house of Jeroboam, who made Israel sin, *but* [1]walked therein: [a]and there [2]re-
mained the grove also in Samaria.)
7 Neither did he leave *of* the people to Jehoahaz but fifty horsemen, and ten chariots,
and ten thousand footmen; for the king of Syria had destroyed them, [a]and had made them
like the dust by threshing.
8 Now the rest of the acts of Jehoahaz, and
all that he did, and his might, *are* they not
written in the book of the chronicles of the
kings of Israel?
9 And Jehoahaz slept with his fathers; and
they buried him in Samaria: and [1]Joash his son
reigned in his stead.

Jehoash, king of Israel

10 ¶ In the thirty and seventh year of Joash
king of Judah *began* [1]Jehoash the son of Jehoahaz to reign over Israel in Samaria, *and*
reigned sixteen years.
11 And he did *that* which *was* evil in the
sight of the LORD; he departed not from all the
sins of Jeroboam the son of Nebat, who made
Israel sin: *but* he walked therein.

13:4 [a]Ps. 78:34 [b]Ex. 3:7; ch. 14:26
13:5 [1]Heb. *as yesterday,* and *third day* [a]See ver. 25; ch. 14:25,27
13:6 [1]Heb. *he walked* [2]Heb. *stood* [a]1 Ki. 16:33
13:7 [a]Amos 1:3
13:9 [1][ver. 10, *Jehoash*]
13:10 [1][In consort with his father, ch. 14:1]

13:12 [a]ch. 14:15 [b]See ver. 14,25 [c]ch. 14:9; 2 Chr. 25:17
13:14 [a]ch. 2:12
13:16 [1]Heb. *Make thine hand to ride*
13:17 [a]1 Ki. 20:26
13:19 [a]ver. 25

12 [a]And the rest of the acts of Joash, and
[b]all that he did, and [c]his might where*with* he
fought against Amaziah king of Judah, *are* they
not written in the book of the chronicles of the
kings of Israel?
13 And Joash slept with his fathers; and
Jeroboam sat upon his throne: and Joash was
buried in Samaria with the kings of Israel.

The death of Elisha

14 ¶ Now Elisha was fallen sick of his sickness whereof he died. And Joash the king of Israel came down unto him, and wept over his
face, and said, O my father, my father, [a]the
chariot of Israel, and the horsemen thereof.
15 And Elisha said unto him, Take bow and
arrows. And he took unto him bow and arrows.
16 And he said to the king of Israel, [1]Put
thine hand upon the bow. And he put his hand
upon it: and Elisha put his hands upon the
king's hands.
17 And he said, Open the window eastward. And he opened *it.* Then Elisha said,
Shoot. And he shot. And he said, The arrow of
the LORD's deliverance, and the arrow of deliverance from Syria: for thou shalt smite the Syrians in [a]Aphek, till *thou* have consumed *them.*
18 And he said, Take the arrows. And he
took *them.* And he said unto the king of Israel,
Smite upon the ground. And he smote thrice,
and stayed.
19 And the man of God was wroth with
him, and said, *Thou* shouldest have smitten
five or six times; then hadst thou smitten Syria till *thou* hadst consumed *it:* [a]whereas now
thou shalt smite Syria *but* thrice.

13:4 *the LORD hearkened unto him.* Although deliverance did not come during the lifetime of Jehoahaz (see v. 22), the Lord was merciful to His people in spite of their sin, because of His covenant with Abraham, Isaac and Jacob (v. 23).

13:5 *Israel a saviour.* Probably either (1) the Assyrian ruler Adadnirari III (810–783 B.C.), whose attacks on the Arameans of Damascus in 806 and 804 enabled the Israelites to break Aramean control over Israelite territory (see v. 25; 14:25), or (2) Jehoash son of Jehoahaz (vv. 17,19,25), or (3) Jeroboam II, who was able to extend Israel's boundaries far to the north (see 14:25,27) after the Assyrians had broken the military power of the Arameans.

‡13:6 *there remained the grove* [Hebrew *Asherah*]. This idol had been set up by Ahab (see 1 Ki 16:33) and had either escaped destruction by Jehu when he purged Baal worship from Samaria (see 10:27–28) or had been reintroduced during the reign of Jehoahaz.

13:7 *ten chariots.* In effect, a small police force. According to the Assyrian annals of Shalmaneser III, Ahab had contributed 2,000 chariots to the coalition of forces that opposed the Assyrians at the battle of Qarqar in 853 B.C. (see note on 1 Ki 22:1). *ten thousand footmen.* At the battle of Qarqar Ahab had supplied 10,000 foot soldiers to the coalition of forces opposing the Assyrians. At that time this would have represented only a contingent of Israel's army, while now it represented the entire Israelite infantry. In 857 Ahab had inflicted 100,000 casualties on the Aramean foot soldiers in one day (see 1 Ki 20:29).

13:8 *chronicles of the kings of Israel.* See note on 1 Ki 14:19.

13:9 *slept with his fathers.* See note on 1 Ki 1:21.

13:10 *thirty and seventh year of Joash.* 798 B.C. (see note on 12:1). *sixteen years.* 798–782.

13:11 *sins of Jeroboam.* See 1 Ki 12:26–32; 13:33–34; 14:16.

13:12 *fought against Amaziah.* See 14:8–14; 2 Chr 25:17–24. *chronicles of the kings of Israel.* See note on 1 Ki 14:19.

13:13 *slept with his fathers.* See note on 1 Ki 1:21. *Jeroboam sat upon his throne.* For the reign of Jeroboam II see 14:23–29.

13:14 *Elisha was fallen sick.* Ch. 9 contains the last previous reference to Elisha. Since Jehu had been anointed in 841 B.C. (see note on 10:36) and Joash began to reign in 798 (see note on v. 10), there is at least a 43-year period in which we are told nothing of Elisha's activities. Based on Elisha's relationship with Elijah, he must have been born prior to 880 and he must have lived to be more than 80 years of age. *the chariot of Israel, and the horsemen thereof.* An expression of recognition by Joash that Elisha was of greater significance for Israel's military success than Israel's military forces were (see notes on 2:12; 6:13,16–23).

13:16 *put his hands upon the king's hands.* By this symbolic act Elisha indicated that Joash was to engage the Arameans in battle with the Lord's blessing on him.

13:17 *window eastward.* Faced across the Jordan, which was controlled by the Arameans (see 10:32–33). *Aphek.* About 60 years earlier Ahab had won a decisive victory at Aphek over the Arameans and Ben-hadad II (see 1 Ki 20:26–30 and note on 1 Ki 20:26).

13:18 *smote thrice, and stayed.* The moderately enthusiastic response to Elisha's directive reflected insufficient zeal for accomplishing the announced task.

13:19 *smite Syria but thrice.* Joash's moderate enthusiasm in

20 And Elisha died, and they buried him.
And the bands of the Moabites invaded the
land *at* the coming in of the year.
21 And it came to pass, as they were burying a man, that behold, they spied a band *of*
men; and they cast the man into the sepulchre
of Elisha: and when the man [1]was let down,
and touched the bones of Elisha, he revived,
and stood up on his feet.
22 ¶ But [a]Hazael king of Syria oppressed Israel all the days of Jehoahaz.
23 And the LORD was gracious unto them,
and had compassion on them, and [a]had respect unto them, [b]because of his covenant
with Abraham, Isaac, and Jacob, and would
not destroy them, neither cast he them from
his [1]presence as yet.
24 So Hazael king of Syria died; and Ben-
hadad his son reigned in his stead.
25 And Jehoash the son of Jehoahaz [1]took
again out of the hand of Ben-hadad the son of
Hazael the cities, which he had taken out of
the hand of Jehoahaz his father by war. [a]Three
times did Joash beat him, and recovered the
cities of Israel.

Amaziah, king of Judah

14 In [a]the second year of Joash son of Jehoahaz king of Israel reigned [b]Ama-
ziah the son of Joash king of Judah.
2 He was twenty and five years old when
he *began* to reign, and reigned twenty and
nine years in Jerusalem. And his mother's
name *was* Jehoaddan of Jerusalem.
3 And he did *that* which *was* right in the
sight of the LORD, yet not like David his father:

13:21 [1]Heb. *went* down
13:22 [a]ch. 8:12
13:23 [1]Heb. *face* [a]Ex. 2:24,25 [b]Ex. 32:13
13:25 [1]Heb. *returned and took* [a]ver. 18,19
14:1 [a]ch. 13:10 [b]2 Chr. 25:1
14:4 [a]ch. 12:3
14:5 [a]ch. 12:20
14:6 [a]Deut. 24:16; Ezek. 18:4,20
14:7 [1]Or, *the rock* [a]2 Chr. 25:11 [b]2 Sam. 8:13; Ps. 60, title [c]Josh. 15:38
14:8 [a]2 Chr. 25:17,18
14:9 [a]See Judg. 9:8 [b]1 Ki. 4:33
14:10 [1]Heb. *at thy house* [a]Deut. 8:14; 2 Chr. 32:25; Ezek. 28:2,5,17; Hab. 2:4

he did according to all *things* as Joash his father did.
4 [a]Howbeit the high places were not taken
away: as yet the people did sacrifice and burnt
incense on the high places.
5 And it came to pass, as soon as the kingdom was confirmed in his hand, that he slew
his servants [a]which had slain the king his father.
6 But the children of the murderers he
slew not: according unto that which is written
in the book of the law of Moses, where*in* the
LORD commanded, saying, [a]The fathers shall
not be put to death for the children, nor the
children be put to death for the fathers; but
every man shall be put to death for his own
sin.
7 [a]He slew *of* Edom in [b]the valley of salt
ten thousand, and took [1]Selah by war, [c]and
called the name of it Joktheel unto this day.
8 ¶ [a]Then Amaziah sent messengers to Jehoash, the son of Jehoahaz son of Jehu, king of
Israel, saying, Come, let us look one another
in the face.
9 And Jehoash the king of Israel sent to
Amaziah king of Judah, saying, [a]The thistle
that *was* in Lebanon sent to the [b]cedar that
was in Lebanon, saying, Give thy daughter to
my son to wife: and there passed by a wild
beast that *was* in Lebanon, and trode down the
thistle.
10 Thou hast indeed smitten Edom, and
[a]thine heart hath lifted thee up: glory *of this,*
and tarry [1]at home: for why shouldest thou
meddle to *thy* hurt, that thou shouldest fall,
even thou, and Judah with thee?

---

striking the ground with arrows symbolized the moderate success he would have against the Arameans. It would be left for Jeroboam II son of Joash to gain complete victory over them (see 14:25,28).

13:21 *when the man . . . touched the bones of Elisha, he revived, and stood up on his feet.* The life-giving power of the God Elisha represented is demonstrated once again in this last OT reference to Elisha (for previous demonstrations of this power see 4:32–37 and 1 Ki 17:17–24; for Elijah's translation to heaven without dying see 2:11–12).

13:23 *would not destroy them, neither cast he them from his presence.* In His mercy and grace the Lord was long-suffering toward His people and refrained from full implementation of the covenant curse of exile from Canaan (see note on 10:32). This postponement of judgment provided Israel with the opportunity to repent and return to covenant faithfulness. *as yet.* Until the time of the writing of the source from which the author derived this account (see note on 1 Ki 8:8; see also Introduction to 1 Kings: Author, Sources and Date).

13:24 *Ben-hadad.* See note on v. 3.

13:25 *cities, which he had taken out of the hand of Jehoahaz.* Probably towns west of the Jordan, since the area east of the Jordan had been lost already in the time of Jehu (see 10:32–33). It was not until the time of Jeroboam II that the area east of the Jordan was fully recovered for Israel (see 14:25). *Three times.* In fulfillment of Elisha's prophecy (v. 19).

14:1 *second year of Joash.* 796 B.C. (see note on 13:10).

14:2 *twenty and nine years.* 796–767. Amaziah's 29-year reign included a 24-year co-regency with his son Azariah (see notes on v. 21; 15:1–2).

14:3 *not like David his father.* Amaziah did not remain completely free from involvement with the worship of pagan deities (see 2 Chr 25:14–16). His loyalty to the Lord fell short of that of Asa and Jehoshaphat before him (see 1 Ki 15:11,14; 22:43; see also 1 Ki 9:4; 11:4).

14:4 *high places were not taken away.* See note on 1 Ki 15:14.

14:7 *slew of Edom . . . ten thousand.* Amaziah was able to regain temporarily (see 2 Chr 28:17) some of Judah's control over the Edomites, which had been lost during the reign of Jehoram (see 8:20–22). *valley of salt.* The same battlefield on which David had defeated the Edomites (see 2 Sam 8:13; 1 Chr 18:12; Ps 60 title), generally identified with the Arabah directly south of the Dead Sea. *Selah.* Means "rock"; often regarded as the Edomite stronghold presently known as Petra (a Greek word meaning "rock"; see Judg 1:36; Is 16:1; 42:11; Obad 3). *unto this day.* Until the time of the writing of the account of Amaziah's reign used by the author (see note on 1 Ki 8:8; see also Introduction to 1 Kings: Author, Sources and Date).

14:8 *let us look one another in the face.* A challenge amounting to a declaration of war. Perhaps it was provoked by the hostile actions of mercenary troops from the northern kingdom after their dismissal from the Judahite army (see 2 Chr 25:10,13) and by the refusal of Jehoash to establish a marriage alliance with Amaziah (see v. 9).

14:9 *Jehoash . . . sent . . . saying.* For his reply Jehoash used a fable (see Judg 9:8–15) in which he represented himself as a strong cedar and Amaziah as an insignificant thistle that could easily be trampled underfoot.

11 But Amaziah would not hear. Therefore Jehoash king of Israel went up; and he and Amaziah king of Judah looked one another *in* the face at [a]Beth-shemesh, which *belongeth* to Judah.

12 And Judah [1]was put to the worse before Israel; and they fled every man to their tents.

13 And Jehoash king of Israel took Amaziah king of Judah, the son of Jehoash the son of Ahaziah, at Beth-shemesh, and came *to* Jerusalem, and brake down the wall of Jerusalem from [a]the gate of Ephraim unto [b]the corner gate, four hundred cubits.

14 And he took all [a]the gold and silver, and all the vessels that were found *in* the house of the LORD, and in the treasures of the king's house, and hostages, and returned to Samaria.

15 [a]Now the rest of the acts of Jehoash which he did, and his might, and how he fought with Amaziah king of Judah, *are* they not written in the book of the chronicles of the kings of Israel?

16 And Jehoash slept with his fathers, and was buried in Samaria with the kings of Israel; and Jeroboam his son reigned in his stead.

17 ¶ [a]And Amaziah the son of Joash king of Judah lived after the death of Jehoash son of Jehoahaz king of Israel fifteen years.

18 And the rest of the acts of Amaziah, *are* they not written in the book of the chronicles of the kings of Judah?

19 Now [a]they made a conspiracy against him in Jerusalem: and he fled to [b]Lachish; but they sent after him to Lachish, and slew him there.

20 And they brought him on horses: and he was buried at Jerusalem with his fathers in the city of David.

21 And all the people of Judah took [1]Azariah, which *was* sixteen years old, and made him king instead of his father Amaziah.

22 He built [a]Elath, and restored it to Judah, after that the king slept with his fathers.

Jeroboam II, king of Israel

23 ¶ In the fifteenth year of Amaziah the son of Joash king of Judah [1]Jeroboam the son of Joash king of Israel *began* to reign in Samaria, *and reigned* forty and one years.

24 And he did *that* which *was* evil in the sight of the LORD: he departed not from all the sins of Jeroboam the son of Nebat, who made Israel to sin.

25 He restored the coast of Israel [a]from the entering of Hamath unto [b]the sea of the plain, according to the word of the LORD God of Israel, which he spake by the hand of his servant [c]Jonah, the son of Amittai, the prophet, which *was* of [d]Gath-hepher.

26 For the LORD [a]saw the affliction of Israel, *that it was* very bitter: for [b]*there was* not any shut up, nor any left, nor any helper for Israel.

14:11 [a]Josh. 19:38; 21:16
14:12 [1]Heb. *was smitten*
14:13 [a]Neh. 8:16; 12:39 [b]Jer. 31:38; Zech. 14:10
14:14 [a]1 Ki. 7:51
14:15 [a]ch. 13:12
14:17 [a]2 Chr. 25:25
14:19 [a]2 Chr. 25:27 [b]Josh. 10:31
14:21 [1][ch. 15:13;] 2 Chr. 26:1, he is called *Uzziah*
14:22 [a]ch. 16:6; 2 Chr. 26:2
14:23 [1][Now he begins to reign alone]
14:25 [a]Num. 13:21; 34:8 [b]Deut. 3:17 [c]Jonah 1:1; Mat. 12:39,40, called *Jonas* [d]Josh. 19:13
14:26 [a]ch. 13:4 [b]Deut. 32:36

14:11 *would not hear.* See 2 Chr 25:20. *Beth-shemesh.* A town about 15 miles west of Jerusalem near the border between Judah and Dan (see Josh 15:10; 1 Sam 6:9).
14:13 *Jehoash . . . took Amaziah.* It is likely that Amaziah was taken back to the northern kingdom as a prisoner, where he remained until being released to return to Judah after the death of Jehoash (see vv. 15–16; see also note on v. 21). *gate of Ephraim unto the corner gate.* The corner gate (see Jer 31:38; Zech 14:10) was at the northwest corner of the wall around Jerusalem. The Ephraim gate was on the north side of Jerusalem (see Neh 12:39), 600 feet east of the corner gate. This northwestern section of the wall of Jerusalem was the point at which the city was most vulnerable to attack.
14:14 *gold and silver, and all the vessels . . . found in the house of the LORD, and . . . the king's house.* The value of the plundered articles was probably not great, because Joash had previously stripped the temple and palace to pay tribute to Hazael of Damascus (see 12:17–18). *hostages.* The hostages were probably intended to secure additional payments of tribute in view of the meager war booty.
14:15 *chronicles of the kings of Israel.* See note on 1 Ki 14:19.
14:16 *slept with his fathers.* See 13:12–13; see also note on 1 Ki 1:21.
14:17 *lived after the death of Jehoash . . . fifteen years.* Jehoash died in 782 B.C. and Amaziah in 767.
14:18 *chronicles of the kings of Judah.* See note on 1 Ki 14:29.
14:19 *conspiracy against him.* 2 Chr 25:27 connects the conspiracy against Amaziah with his turning away from the Lord, but it did not serve the purpose of the author of Kings to note this. *Lachish.* A fortress city in southern Judah 15 miles west of Hebron, presently known as Tell ed-Duweir (see 18:14; 2 Chr 11:9).
14:21 *all the people of Judah took Azariah, which was.* Or "Now all the people of Judah had taken Azariah, when he was." Azariah is also called Uzziah (see 15:13). *made him king instead of his father Amaziah.* It is likely that this occurred after Amaziah had been taken prisoner by Jehoash (see v. 13). Thus Azariah's reign substantially overlapped that of his father Amaziah (see notes on v. 2; 15:2).
14:22 *built Elath, and restored it to Judah.* Azariah extended the subjection of the Edomites begun by his father (see v. 7) and reestablished Israelite control over the important port city on the Gulf of Aqaba (see 1 Ki 9:26).
14:23 *fifteenth year of Amaziah.* 782 B.C. (see note on v. 2). This was the beginning of Jeroboam's sole reign. He had previously served as co-regent with his father Joash. *forty and one years.* 793–753 (including the co-regency with his father).
14:24 *sins of Jeroboam.* See 1 Ki 12:26–32; 13:33–34; 14:16; Amos 3:13–14; 4:4–5; 5:4–6; 7:10–17.
‡14:25 *entering of Hamath.* Jeroboam II was able to free the northern kingdom from the oppression it had suffered at the hands of Hazael and Ben-hadad (see 10:32; 12:17; 13:3,22,25). He also extended Israelite political control over the Arameans of Damascus, an undertaking that had been begun by his father Joash (see 13:25). Assyrian pressure on the Arameans, including attacks on Damascus by Shalmaneser IV in 773 B.C. and Ashur-dan III in 772, had weakened the Arameans enough to enable Jeroboam II to gain the upper hand over them. Meanwhile, Assyria also became too weak to suppress Jeroboam's expansion. *sea of the plain* [Hebrew *Arabah*]. The Dead Sea. According to Amos 6:14 the southern limit of Jeroboam's kingdom east of the Jordan was the "river of the wilderness"—probably to be connected with the valley of salt (see note on v. 7). If so, Jeroboam had also subdued Moab and the Ammonites. *Jonah . . . the prophet . . . of Gath-hepher.* See Jonah 1:1. Gath-hepher was located in the tribe of Zebulun, northeast of Nazareth ("Gittah-hepher," Josh 19:13). This reference to Jonah is of help in dating the ministry of the prophet.
14:26 *affliction.* At the hands of the Arameans (see 10:32–33;

27 [a]And the LORD said not that *he* would blot out the name of Israel from under heaven: but he saved them by the hand of Jeroboam the son of Joash.

28 Now the rest of the acts of Jeroboam, and all that he did, and his might, how he warred, and how he recovered Damascus, and Hamath, [a]*which belonged* to Judah, for Israel, *are* they not written in the book of the chronicles of the kings of Israel?

29 And Jeroboam slept with his fathers, *even* with the kings of Israel; and [1]Zachariah his son reigned in his stead.

Azariah, king of Judah

15 In the [1]twenty and seventh year of Jeroboam king of Israel [a]*began* [b2]Azariah son of Amaziah king of Judah to reign.

2 Sixteen years old was he when he *began* to reign, and he reigned two and fifty years in Jerusalem. And his mother's name *was* Jecholiah of Jerusalem.

3 And he did *that* which *was* right in the sight of the LORD, according to all that his father Amaziah had done;

4 [a]Save that the high places were not removed: the people sacrificed and burnt incense still on the high places.

5 And the LORD [a]smote the king, so that he was a leper unto the day of his death, and [b]dwelt in a several house. And Jotham the king's son *was* over the house, judging the people of the land.

6 And the rest of the acts of Azariah, and all that he did, *are* they not written in the book of the chronicles of the kings of Judah?

7 So Azariah slept with his fathers; and [a]they buried him with his fathers in the city of David: and Jotham his son reigned in his stead.

Zachariah, king of Israel

8 ¶ In the thirty and eighth year of Azariah king of Judah did [1]Zachariah the son of Jeroboam reign over Israel in Samaria six months.

9 And he did *that* which *was* evil in the sight of the LORD, as his fathers had done: he departed not from the sins of Jeroboam the son of Nebat, who made Israel to sin.

10 And Shallum the son of Jabesh conspired against him, and [1]smote him before the people, and slew him, and reigned in his stead.

11 And the rest of the acts of Zachariah, behold, they *are* written in the book of the chronicles of the kings of Israel.

12 This *was* [a]the word of the LORD which he spake unto Jehu, saying, Thy sons shall sit on the throne of Israel unto the fourth *generation.* And so it came to pass.

Shallum, king of Israel

13 ¶ Shallum the son of Jabesh *began* to reign in the nine and thirtieth year of [a1]Uzziah king of Judah; and he reigned [2]a full month in Samaria.

14 For Menahem the son of Gadi went up from [a]Tirzah, and came *to* Samaria, and smote

14:27 [a]ch. 13:5
14:28 [a]2 Sam. 8:6; 1 Ki. 11:24; 2 Chr. 8:3
14:29 [1][After an interregnum of 11 years, ch. 15:8]
15:1 [1][This is the 27th year of Jeroboam's partnership in the kingdom with his father, who made him consort at his going to the Syrian wars. It is the sixteenth year of Jeroboam's monarchy] [2][Called *Uzziah,* ver. 13,30, etc.] [a]ch. 14:21; 2 Chr. 26:1,3,4 [b]2 Chr. 26:1
15:4 [a]ver. 35; ch. 12:3; 14:4
15:5 [a]2 Chr. 26:19-21 [b]Lev. 13:46
15:7 [a]2 Chr. 26:23
15:8 [1][There having been an interregnum for 11 years]
15:10 [1][As prophesied, Amos 7:9]
15:12 [a]ch. 10:30
15:13 [1]Mat. 1.[8,]9, called *Ozias,* [and ver. 1, *Azariah*] [2]Heb. *a month of days*
15:14 [a]1 Ki. 14:17

13:3–7), the Moabites (13:20) and the Ammonites (Amos 1:13). *not any shut up, nor any left.* See note on 1 Ki 14:10.

14:27 *said not.* The sin of the Israelites had not yet reached its full measure, and the Lord mercifully extended to the nation an additional period of grace in which there was opportunity to repent (see note on 13:23). Persistence in apostasy, however, would bring certain judgment (see Amos 4:2–3; 6:14). *saved them by the hand of Jeroboam.* See note on 13:5.

14:28 *all that he did.* During Jeroboam's reign the northern kingdom enjoyed greater material prosperity than at any time since the rule of David and Solomon. Unfortunately, it was also a time of religious formalism and apostasy as well as social injustice (see the books of Amos and Hosea, who prophesied during Jeroboam's reign). *Damascus, and Hamath.* See note on v. 25. *Judah.* Damascus and Hamath were once included in territory ruled by David and Solomon (see 2 Sam 8:6; 2 Chr 8:3). *chronicles of the kings of Israel.* See note on 1 Ki 14:19.

14:29 *slept with his fathers.* See note on 1 Ki 1:21. *Zachariah his son reigned in his stead.* For the reign of Zechariah see 15:8–12.

15:1 *twenty and seventh year of Jeroboam.* 767 B.C., based on dating the beginning of Jeroboam's co-regency with Joash in 793 (see note on 14:23). *began Azariah . . . to reign.* He began his sole reign, after a 24-year co-regency with his father Amaziah (see notes on v. 2; 14:2,21). (His actual years were one less than his official years.)

15:2 *two and fifty years.* 792–740 B.C. (but he was co-regent with his father Amaziah 792–767). See note on v. 1.

15:3 *according to all that his father Amaziah had done.* See note on 14:3.

15:4 *high places were not removed.* See 14:4; see also note on 1 Ki 15:14.

15:5 *smote the king, so that he was a leper.* A punishment for usurping the priestly function of burning incense on the altar in the temple (see 2 Chr 26:16–21; cf. Lev 13:46). *was over the house, judging the people of the land.* Jotham ruled for his father for the remainder of Azariah's life (750–740 B.C.; see note on v. 33).

15:6 *all that he did.* A more detailed account of Azariah's accomplishments is found in 2 Chr 26:1–15. *chronicles of the kings of Judah.* See note on 1 Ki 14:29.

15:7 *slept with his fathers.* See note on 1 Ki 1:21. *Jotham his son reigned in his stead.* For the reign of Jotham see vv. 32–38.

15:8 *thirty and eighth year of Azariah.* 753 B.C. (see note on v. 2).

15:9 *sins of Jeroboam.* See 1 Ki 12:26–32; 13:33–34; 14:16.

15:11 *chronicles of the kings of Israel.* See note on 1 Ki 14:19.

15:12 *the word of the LORD . . . And so it came to pass.* The word was given in 10:30. With the downfall of Jehu's dynasty, the northern kingdom entered a period of political instability (see Hos 1:4). The remaining five kings of the northern kingdom were all assassinated with the exception of Menahem, who reigned ten years, and Hoshea, who was imprisoned by the Assyrians. From the strength and wealth of the reign of Jeroboam II, the decline and fall of the northern kingdom was swift.

15:13 *nine and thirtieth year of Uzziah.* 752 B.C. (see note on v. 2). Uzziah is another name for Azariah (see note on 14:21).

15:14 *Menahem . . . went up from Tirzah . . . to Samaria.* It is likely that Menahem was the commander of a military garrison at Tirzah, the former capital of the northern kingdom (see

Assyrian Campaigns against Israel and Judah

The Assyrian invasions of the eighth century B.C. were the most traumatic political events in the entire history of Israel.

The brutal Assyrian style of warfare relied on massive armies, superbly equipped with the world's first great siege machines manipulated by an efficient corps of engineers.

Psychological terror, however, was Assyria's most effective weapon. It was ruthlessly applied, with corpses impaled on stakes, severed heads stacked in heaps, and captives skinned alive.

The shock of bloody military sieges on both Israel and Judah was profound. The prophets did not fail to scream out against their horror, while at the same time pleading with the people to see God's hand in history, to recognize spiritual causes in the present punishment.

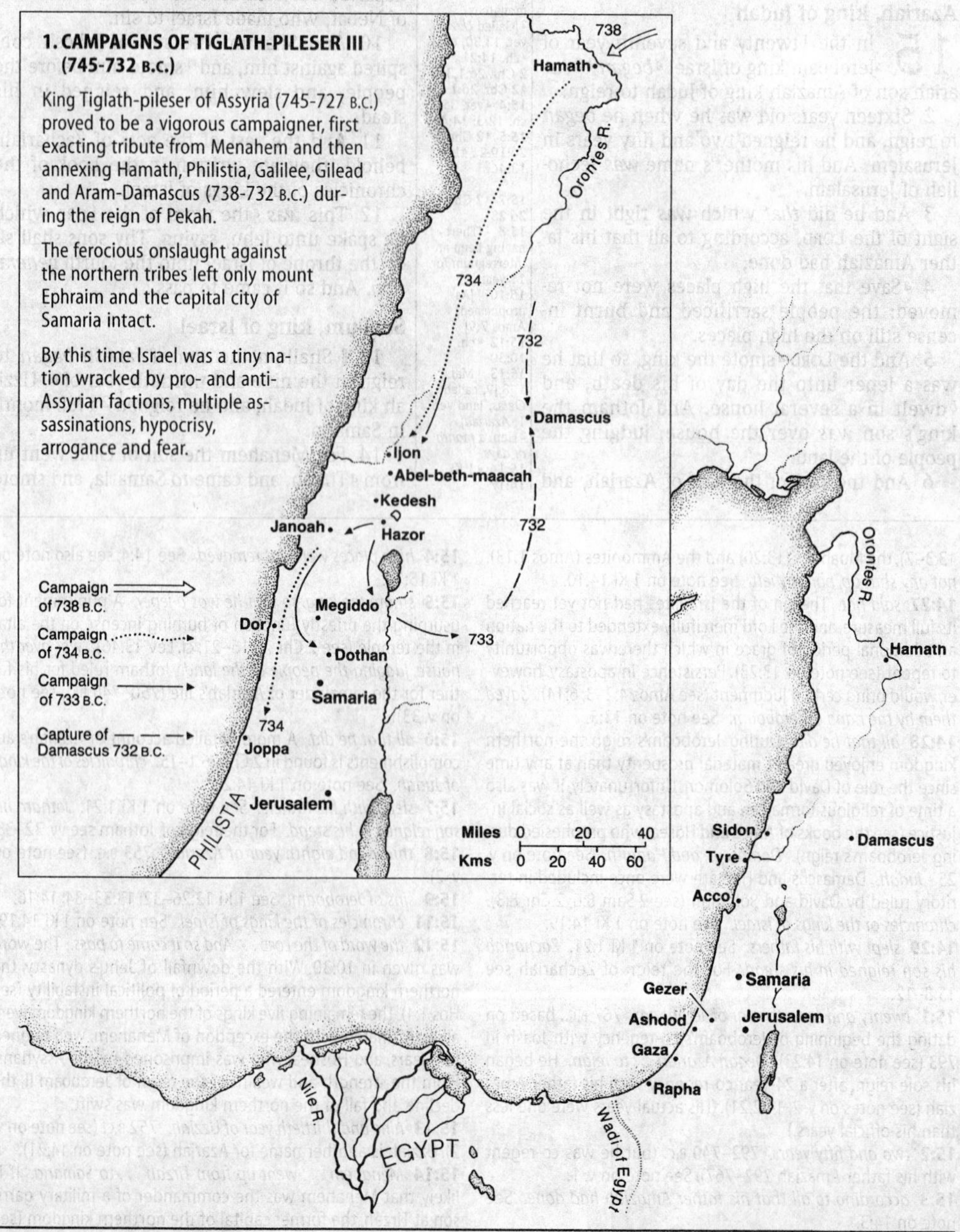

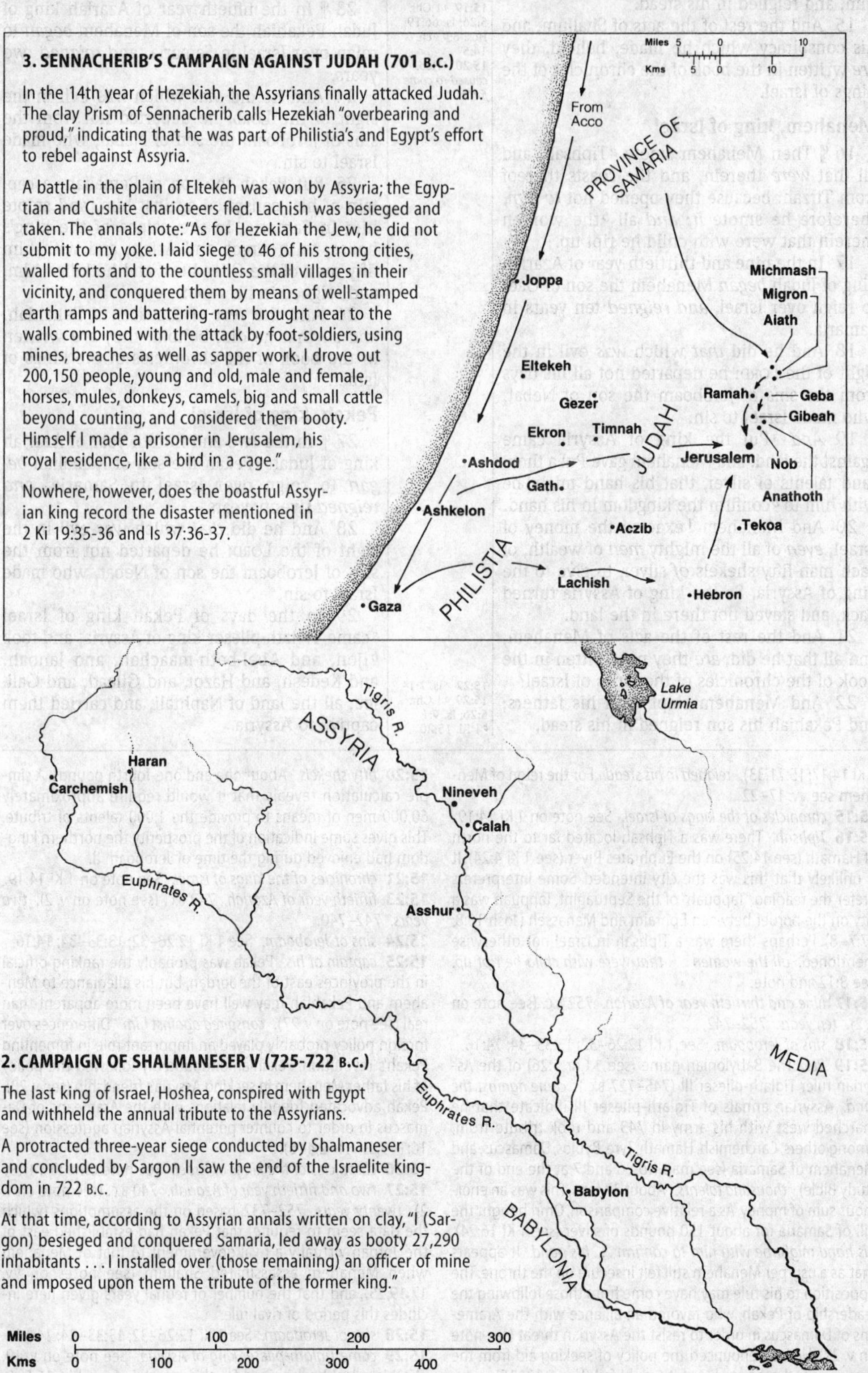

3. SENNACHERIB'S CAMPAIGN AGAINST JUDAH (701 B.C.)
In the 14th year of Hezekiah, the Assyrians finally attacked Judah. The clay Prism of Sennacherib calls Hezekiah "overbearing and proud," indicating that he was part of Philistia's and Egypt's effort to rebel against Assyria.
A battle in the plain of Eltekeh was won by Assyria; the Egyptian and Cushite charioteers fled. Lachish was besieged and taken. The annals note: "As for Hezekiah the Jew, he did not submit to my yoke. I laid siege to 46 of his strong cities, walled forts and to the countless small villages in their vicinity, and conquered them by means of well-stamped earth ramps and battering-rams brought near to the walls combined with the attack by foot-soldiers, using mines, breaches as well as sapper work. I drove out 200,150 people, young and old, male and female, horses, mules, donkeys, camels, big and small cattle beyond counting, and considered them booty. Himself I made a prisoner in Jerusalem, his royal residence, like a bird in a cage."
Nowhere, however, does the boastful Assyrian king record the disaster mentioned in 2 Ki 19:35-36 and Is 37:36-37.
Miles 5 0 10
Kms 5 0 10
From Acco
PROVINCE OF SAMARIA
Joppa
Michmash
Migron
Aiath
Eltekeh
Gezer
Ramah
Geba
Gibeah
JUDAH
Ekron
Timnah
Jerusalem
Ashdod
Nob
Gath
Anathoth
Ashkelon
Aczib
Tekoa
Lachish
PHILISTIA
Gaza
Hebron
Lake Urmia
Tigris R.
ASSYRIA
Haran
Carchemish
Nineveh
Calah
Euphrates R.
Asshur
MEDIA
2. CAMPAIGN OF SHALMANESER V (725-722 B.C.)
The last king of Israel, Hoshea, conspired with Egypt and withheld the annual tribute to the Assyrians. A protracted three-year siege conducted by Shalmaneser and concluded by Sargon II saw the end of the Israelite kingdom in 722 B.C.
At that time, according to Assyrian annals written on clay, "I (Sargon) besieged and conquered Samaria, led away as booty 27,290 inhabitants . . . I installed over (those remaining) an officer of mine and imposed upon them the tribute of the former king."
Euphrates R.
Tigris R.
Babylon
BABYLONIA
Miles 0 100 200 300
Kms 0 100 200 300 400

Shallum the son of Jabesh in Samaria, and slew him, and reigned in his stead.

15 And the rest of the acts of Shallum, and his conspiracy which he made, behold, they *are* written in the book of the chronicles of the kings of Israel.

Menahem, king of Israel

16 ¶ Then Menahem smote [a]Tiphsah, and all that *were* therein, and the coasts thereof from Tirzah: because they opened not *to him,* therefore he smote *it; and* all [b]the women therein that were with child he ript up.

17 In the nine and thirtieth year of Azariah king of Judah *began* Menahem the son of Gadi to reign over Israel, *and reigned* ten years in Samaria.

18 And he did *that* which *was* evil in the sight of the LORD: he departed not all his days from the sins of Jeroboam the son of Nebat, who made Israel to sin.

19 *And* [a]Pul the king of Assyria came against the land: and Menahem gave Pul a thousand talents of silver, that his hand might be with him to [b]confirm the kingdom in his hand.

20 And Menahem [1]exacted the money of Israel, *even* of all the mighty *men* of wealth, of each man fifty shekels *of* silver, to give to the king of Assyria. So the king of Assyria turned back, and stayed not there in the land.

21 And the rest of the acts of Menahem, and all that he did, *are* they not written in the book of the chronicles of the kings of Israel?

22 And Menahem slept with his fathers; and Pekahiah his son reigned in his stead.

15:16 [a]1 Ki. 4:24 [b]ch. 8:12
15:19 [a]1 Chr. 5:26; Is. 66:19; Hos. 8:9 [b]ch. 14:5
15:20 [1]Heb. *caused to come forth*

Pekahiah, king of Israel

23 ¶ In the fiftieth year of Azariah king of Judah Pekahiah the son of Menahem *began* to reign over Israel in Samaria, *and reigned* two years.

24 And he did *that* which *was* evil in the sight of the LORD: he departed not from the sins of Jeroboam the son of Nebat, who made Israel to sin.

25 But Pekah the son of Remaliah, a captain of his, conspired against him, and smote him in Samaria, in the palace of the king's house, with Argob and Arieh; and with him fifty men of the Gileadites: and he killed him, and reigned in his room.

26 And the rest of the acts of Pekahiah, and all that he did, behold, they *are* written in the book of the chronicles of the kings of Israel.

Pekah, king of Israel

27 ¶ In the two and fiftieth year of Azariah king of Judah [a]Pekah the son of Remaliah *began* to reign over Israel in Samaria, *and reigned* twenty years.

28 And he did *that* which *was* evil in the sight of the LORD: he departed not from the sins of Jeroboam the son of Nebat, who made Israel to sin.

29 In the days of Pekah king of Israel [a]came Tiglath-pileser king of Assyria, and took [b]Ijon, and Abel-beth-maachah, and Janoah, and Kedesh, and Hazor, and Gilead, and Galilee, all the land of Naphtali, and carried them captive to Assyria.

15:27 [a]Is. 7:1
15:29 [a]1 Chr. 5:26; Is. 9:1 [b]1 Ki. 15:20

---

1 Ki 14:17; 15:21,33). *reigned in his stead.* For the reign of Menahem see vv. 17–22.

15:15 *chronicles of the kings of Israel.* See note on 1 Ki 14:19.

15:16 *Tiphsah.* There was a Tiphsah located far to the north of Hamath (see 14:25) on the Euphrates River (see 1 Ki 4:24). It is unlikely that this was the city intended. Some interpreters prefer the reading "Tappuah" of the Septuagint. Tappuah was a city on the border between Ephraim and Manasseh (Josh 16:8; 17:7–8). Perhaps there was a Tiphsah in Israel not otherwise mentioned. *all the women . . . that were with child he ript up.* See 8:12 and note.

15:17 *nine and thirtieth year of Azariah.* 752 B.C. (see note on v. 2). *ten years.* 752–742.

15:18 *sins of Jeroboam.* See 1 Ki 12:26–32; 13:33–34; 14:16.

15:19 *Pul.* The Babylonian name (see 1 Chr 5:26) of the Assyrian ruler Tiglath-pileser III (745–727 B.C.). *came against the land.* Assyrian annals of Tiglath-pileser III indicate that he marched west with his army in 743 and took tribute from, among others, Carchemish, Hamath, Tyre, Byblos, Damascus, and Menahem of Samaria (see map Nos. 6 and 7 at the end of the study Bible). *thousand talents.* About 37 tons. This was an enormous sum of money. As a relative comparison, Omri bought the hill of Samaria for about 150 pounds of silver (see 1 Ki 16:24). *his hand might be with him to confirm . . . his hand.* It appears that as a usurper Menahem still felt insecure on the throne. The opposition to his rule may have come from those following the leadership of Pekah, who favored an alliance with the Arameans of Damascus in order to resist the Assyrian threat (see note on v. 27). Hosea denounced the policy of seeking aid from the Assyrians and predicted that it would fail (Hos 5:13–15).

15:20 *fifty shekels.* About one and one-fourth pounds. A simple calculation reveals that it would require approximately 60,000 men of means to provide the 1,000 talents of tribute. This gives some indication of the prosperity the northern kingdom had enjoyed during the time of Jeroboam II.

15:21 *chronicles of the kings of Israel.* See note on 1 Ki 14:19.

15:23 *fiftieth year of Azariah.* 742 B.C. (see note on v. 2). *two years.* 742–740.

15:24 *sins of Jeroboam.* See 1 Ki 12:26–32; 13:33–34; 14:16.

15:25 *captain of his.* Pekah was probably the ranking official in the provinces east of the Jordan, but his allegiance to Menahem and Pekahiah may well have been more apparent than real (see note on v. 27). *conspired against him.* Differences over foreign policy probably played an important role in fomenting Pekah's revolution. Pekahiah undoubtedly followed the policy of his father Menahem in seeking Assyria's friendship (see v. 20). Pekah advocated friendly relations with the Arameans of Damascus in order to counter potential Assyrian aggression (see 16:1–9; Is 7:1–2,4–6).

15:26 *chronicles of the kings of Israel.* See note on 1 Ki 14:19.

15:27 *two and fiftieth year of Azariah.* 740 B.C. (see note on v. 2). *twenty years.* 752–732, based on the assumptions (which the data seem to require) that Pekah had established east of the Jordan virtually a rival government to that of Menahem when Menahem assassinated Shallum (see notes on vv. 17,19,25), and that the number of regnal years given here includes this period of rival rule.

15:28 *sins of Jeroboam.* See 1 Ki 12:26–32; 13:33–34; 14:16.

15:29 *came Tiglath-pileser king of Assyria.* See note on v. 19. The historical background for this attack is found in 16:5–9;

30 And Hoshea the son of Elah made a conspiracy against Pekah the son of Remaliah, and smote him, and slew him, and [1]reigned in his stead, [2]in the twentieth year of Jotham the son of Uzziah.

31 And the rest of the acts of Pekah, and all that he did, behold, they *are* written in the book of the chronicles of the kings of Israel.

Jotham, king of Judah

32 ¶ In the second year of Pekah the son of Remaliah king of Israel *began* [a]Jotham the son of Uzziah king of Judah to reign.

33 Five and twenty years old was he when he *began* to reign, and he reigned sixteen years in Jerusalem. And his mother's name *was* Jerusha, the daughter of Zadok.

34 And he did *that* which *was* right in the sight of the LORD: he did [a]according to all that his father Uzziah had done.

35 [a]Howbeit the high places were not removed: the people sacrificed and burnt incense still in the high places. [b]He built the higher gate of the house of the LORD.

36 Now the rest of the acts of Jotham, and all that he did, *are* they not written in the book of the chronicles of the kings of Judah?

37 [1]In those days the LORD began to send against Judah [a]Rezin the king of Syria, and [b]Pekah the son of Remaliah.

38 And Jotham slept with his fathers, and was buried with his fathers in the city of David his father: and Ahaz his son reigned in his stead.

Ahaz, king of Judah

16 In the seventeenth year of Pekah the son of Remaliah [a]Ahaz the son of Jotham king of Judah *began* to reign.

2 Twenty years old *was* Ahaz when he *began* to reign, and reigned sixteen years in Jerusalem, and did not *that* which *was* right in the sight of the LORD his God, like David his father.

3 But he walked in the way of the kings of Israel, yea, [a]and made his son to pass through the fire, according to the [b]abominations of the heathen, whom the LORD cast out from before the children of Israel.

4 And he sacrificed and burnt incense in the high places, and [a]on the hills, and under every green tree.

15:30 [1][After an anarchy for some years, ch. 17:1; Hos. 10:3,7,15] [2][In the fourth year of Ahaz, in the twentieth year after Jotham had begun to reign: *Ush.*]
15:32 [a]2 Chr. 27:1
15:34 [a]ver. 3
15:35 [a]ver. 4 [b]2 Chr. 27:3
15:37 [1][At the end of Jotham's reign] [a]ch. 16:5; Is. 7:1 [b]ver. 27
16:1 [a]2 Chr. 28:1
16:3 [a]Lev. 18:21; 2 Chr. 28:3; Ps. 106:37,38 [b]Deut. 12:31
16:4 [a]Deut. 12:2; 1 Ki. 14:23

2 Chr 28:16–21; Is 7:1–17. *Ijon . . . Naphtali.* Over 150 years earlier Ben-hadad I of Damascus had taken this same territory from the northern kingdom in response to an appeal by a king of Judah (see notes on 1 Ki 15:19–20). *carried them captive to Assyria.* See 1 Chr 5:26. The forced exile of Israelites from their homeland was a fulfillment of the covenant curse (see note on 10:32).

15:30 *Hoshea . . . made a conspiracy against Pekah.* Hoshea probably represented the faction in the northern kingdom that favored cooperation with Assyria rather than resistance. In one of his annals Tiglath-pileser III claims to have placed Hoshea on the throne of the northern kingdom and to have taken ten talents of gold and 1,000 talents of silver as tribute from him. *twentieth year of Jotham.* 732 B.C. (see notes on vv. 32–33). Reference is to his 20th official year, which was his 19th actual year.

15:31 *chronicles of the kings of Israel.* See note on 1 Ki 14:19.

15:32 *second year of Pekah.* 750 B.C. (see note on v. 27).

15:33 *sixteen years.* 750–735 B.C. Jotham was co-regent with his father 750–740 (see note on v. 5). Jotham's reign was in some sense terminated in 735, and his son Ahaz took over. However, Jotham continued to live until at least 732 (see notes on vv. 30,37).

15:34 *that his father Uzziah had done.* See note on v. 3; see also 2 Chr 27:2.

15:35 *high places were not removed.* See v. 4; see also note on 1 Ki 15:14. *higher gate of the house of the LORD.* See 2 Chr 23:20; Jer 20:2; Ezek 8:3; 9:2. Additional information on Jotham's building activities is given in 2 Chr 27:3–4.

15:36 *the rest of the acts of Jotham.* See 2 Chr 27:1–6. *chronicles of the kings of Judah.* See note on 1 Ki 14:29.

15:37 This parenthetical statement concerning Jotham's reign supports the idea of an overlap between the reigns of Jotham and Ahaz (see note on v. 33), since 16:5–12; 2 Chr 28:5–21; Is 7:1–17 all place the major effort of Rezin and Pekah in the time of Ahaz.

15:38 *slept with his fathers.* See note on 1 Ki 1:21.

16:1 *seventeenth year of Pekah.* 735 B.C. (see note on 15:27). The reign of Ahaz apparently overlapped that of Jotham, with Ahaz serving as a senior partner beginning in 735 (see notes on 15:33,37; see also notes on v. 2; 17:1).

16:2 *Twenty years old . . . when he began to reign.* Perhaps the age at which Ahaz became a senior co-regent with his father Jotham in 735 B.C. (see note on v. 1). Otherwise, according to the ages and dates provided, Ahaz would have been 11 or 12 instead of 14 or 15 years old when his son Hezekiah was born (cf. 18:1–2). *sixteen years.* The synchronizations of the reigns of Ahaz and Hezekiah of Judah with those of Pekah and Hoshea of the northern kingdom present some apparent chronological difficulties (see notes on v. 1; 17:1; 18:1,9–10). It seems best to take the 16 years specified here as the number of years Ahaz reigned after the death of Jotham, thus 732–715 (see notes on 15:30,33). The beginning of his reign appears to be dated in a variety of ways in the Biblical text: (1) in 744/743, which presupposes a co-regency with his grandfather Azariah at the tender age of 11 or 12 (see 17:1); (2) in 735, when he became senior co-regent with Jotham (see v. 1); and (3) in 732, when he began his sole reign after the death of Jotham. *did not that . . . like David his father.* Ahaz does not even receive the qualified approval given to Amaziah (14:3), Azariah (15:3) and Jotham (15:34).

16:3 *way of the kings of Israel.* It is unlikely that Ahaz adhered to the calf worship introduced by Jeroboam I at Beth-el and Dan (see 1 Ki 12:26–32; 13:33–34; 14:16). The reference here is probably to Baal worship in the spirit of Ahab (see notes on 1 Ki 16:31–33; see also 2 Chr 28:2). *made his son to pass through the fire.* Israel had been warned by Moses not to engage in this pagan rite (see Lev 18:21; Deut 18:10). In Israel the firstborn son in each household was to be consecrated to the Lord and redeemed by a payment of five shekels to the priests (see Ex 13:1,11–13; Num 18:16). See also 3:27; 17:17; 21:6; 23:10; 2 Chr 28:3; Jer 7:31; 32:35.

16:4 *high places.* See 15:4,35; see also note on 1 Ki 15:14. These high places appear to be those assimilated from pagan Baal worship and used for the worship of the Lord in a syncretistic fashion. *under every green tree.* Large trees were viewed as symbols of fertility by the pre-Israelite inhabitants of Canaan. Immoral pagan rites were performed at shrines located under such trees. Contrary to the explicit prohibition of the Mosaic covenant, the Israelites adopted this pagan custom (see 17:10; 1 Ki 14:23; Deut 12:2; Jer 2:20; 3:6; 17:2; Ezek 6:13; 20:28; Hos 4:13–14).

5 [a]Then Rezin king of Syria and Pekah son of Remaliah king of Israel came up *to* Jerusalem to war: and they besieged Ahaz, but could not overcome *him.*

6 At that time Rezin king of Syria [a]recovered Elath to Syria, and drave the Jews from [1]Elath: and the Syrians came *to* Elath, and dwelt there unto this day.

7 So Ahaz sent messengers [a]to [1]Tiglath-pileser king of Assyria, saying, I *am* thy servant and thy son: come up, and save me out of the hand of the king of Syria, and out of the hand of the king of Israel, which rise up against me.

8 And Ahaz [a]took the silver and gold that was found *in* the house of the LORD, and in the treasures of the king's house, and sent *it for* a present to the king of Assyria.

9 And the king of Assyria hearkened unto him: for the king of Assyria went up against [1]Damascus, and [2]took it, and carried *the people of* it captive to Kir, and slew Rezin.

10 ¶ And king Ahaz went *to* [1]Damascus to meet Tiglath-pileser king of Assyria, and saw an altar that *was* at Damascus: and king Ahaz sent to Urijah the priest the fashion of the altar, and the pattern of it, according to all the workmanship thereof.

11 And Urijah the priest built an altar according to all that king Ahaz had sent from Damascus: so Urijah the priest made *it* against king Ahaz came from Damascus.

12 And when the king was come from Damascus, the king saw the altar: and [a]the king approached to the altar, and offered thereon.

13 And he burnt his burnt offering and his meat offering, and poured his drink offering, and sprinkled the blood of [1]his peace offerings, upon the altar.

14 And he brought also [a]the brasen altar, which *was* before the LORD, from the forefront of the house, from between the altar and the house of the LORD, and put it on the north side of the altar.

15 And king Ahaz commanded Urijah the priest, saying, Upon the great altar burn [a]the morning burnt offering, and the evening meat offering, and the king's burnt sacrifice, and his meat offering, with the burnt offering of all the people of the land, and their meat offering, and their drink offerings; and sprinkle upon it all the blood of the burnt offering, and all the blood of the sacrifice: and the brasen altar shall be for me to inquire *by.*

16 Thus did Urijah the priest, according to all that king Ahaz commanded.

17 [a]And king Ahaz cut off [b]the borders of the bases, and removed the laver from off them; and took down [c]the sea from off the brasen oxen that *were* under it, and put it upon a pavement of stones.

18 And the covert for the sabbath that they had built in the house, and the king's entry without, turned he *from* the house of the LORD for the king of Assyria.

16:5 [a]Is. 7:1,4
16:6 [1][Heb. *Eloth*] [a]ch. 14:22
16:7 [1][Heb. *Tiglath-peleser.* 1 Chr. 5:26; 2 Chr. 28:20, *Tilgath-pilneser*] [a]ch. 15:29
16:8 [a]ch. 12:18; See 2 Chr. 28:21
16:9 [1]Heb. *Dammesek* [2][Foretold, Amos 1:5]
16:10 [1]Heb. *Dammesek*
16:12 [a]2 Chr. 26:16,19
16:13 [1]Heb. *which* were *his*
16:14 [a]2 Chr. 4:1
16:15 [a]Ex. 29:39-41
16:17 [a]2 Chr. 28:24 [b]1 Ki. 7:27,28 [c]1 Ki. 7:23,25

16:5 *Rezin ... and Pekah ... came up to Jerusalem to war.* See notes on 15:25,37. *could not overcome.* See Is 7:1–17; 2 Chr 28:5–21. Rezin and Pekah desired to replace Ahaz on the throne of the southern kingdom with the son of Tabeel in order to gain another ally in their anti-Assyrian political policy (see notes on 15:19,25). The Lord delivered Judah and Ahaz from this threat in spite of their wickedness because of the promises of the Davidic covenant (see 1 Ki 11:36; 2 Sam 7:13; Is 7:3–7,14).

‡16:6 *Rezin king of Syria recovered Elath.* See note on 14:22. *Syrians came to Elath.* The Hebrew for "Syrians," i.e. "Arameans," can also be read as "Edomites" (see 2 Chr 28:17). The Philistines also took this opportunity to avenge previous defeats (compare 2 Chr 26:5–7 with 2 Chr 28:18). *unto this day.* See note on 1 Ki 8:8.

16:7 *Tiglath-pileser.* See notes on 15:19, 29. *thy servant and thy son.* Ahaz preferred to seek security for Judah by means of a treaty with Assyria rather than by obedience to the Lord and trust in His promises (see Ex 23:22; Is 7:10–16).

16:8 *silver and gold ... in the house of the LORD.* The temple treasure must have been restored to some degree by Jotham (see 12:18; 14:14). The name "Jehoahaz of Judah" (Ahaz) appears on a list of rulers (including those of the Philistines, Ammonites, Moabites and Edomites) who brought tribute to Tiglath-pileser in 734 B.C.

16:9 *went up against Damascus, and took it.* In 732 B.C. Tiglath-pileser III moved against Damascus and destroyed it (see the prophecies of Is 7:16; Amos 1:3–5). *carried the people of it captive to Kir.* The Arameans were sent back to the place from which they had come (Amos 9:7) in fulfillment of the prophecy of Amos (Amos 1:5). The location of Kir is unknown, though it is mentioned in connection with Elam in Is 22:6.

16:10 *Ahaz went to Damascus to meet Tiglath-pileser.* As a vassal king to express his gratitude and loyalty to the victorious Assyrian ruler. *altar ... at Damascus.* Perhaps that of the god Rimmon (see 5:18; 2 Chr 28:23), but more likely a royal altar of Tiglath-pileser. Ahaz's reproduction of such an altar would have been a further sign of submission to the Assyrians.

16:13 *burnt offering ... meat offering ... drink offering ... peace offerings.* With the exception of the drink offering, these same sacrifices were offered at the dedication of the temple (1 Ki 8:64).

16:14 *north side of the altar.* Ahaz removed the bronze altar from its prominent place in front of the temple and gave it a place alongside the new stone altar.

16:15 *great altar.* Even though fire from heaven had inaugurated and sanctioned the use of the bronze altar for the worship of the Lord (see 2 Chr 7:1), Ahaz now replaced it with an altar built on the pattern of the pagan altar from Damascus. Although the bronze altar was quite large (see 2 Chr 4:1), the new altar was larger. *morning burnt offering.* See 3:20; Ex 29:38–39; Num 28:3–4. *evening meat offering.* See note on 1 Ki 18:29. *king's burnt sacrifice, and his meat offering.* There is no other reference to these special offerings of the king in the OT, with the possible exception of Ezekiel's depiction of the offerings of a future prince (Ezek 46:12). *the brasen altar shall be for me to inquire by.* Seeking omens by the examination of the entrails of sacrificed animals is well attested in ancient Near Eastern texts. Here Ahaz states his intention to follow an Assyrian divination technique in an attempt to secure the Lord's guidance.

16:17 *borders of the bases, and removed the laver.* See 1 Ki 7:27–39. *took down the sea from off the brasen oxen.* See 1 Ki 7:23–26. Perhaps the bronze was needed for tribute required by Tiglath-pileser III.

16:18 *for the king of Assyria.* As a vassal of Tiglath-pileser, Ahaz was forced to relinquish some of the symbols of his own royal power.

19 ¶ Now the rest of the acts of Ahaz which he did, *are* they not written in the book of the chronicles of the kings of Judah?

20 And Ahaz slept with his fathers, and [a]was buried with his fathers in the city of David: and Hezekiah his son reigned in his stead.

Samaria captured by Assyria

17 In the twelfth year of Ahaz king of Judah *began* [1]Hoshea the son of Elah to reign in Samaria over Israel nine years.

2 And he did *that* which *was* evil in the sight of the LORD, but not as the kings of Israel that were before him.

3 Against him came up [a]Shalmaneser king of Assyria; and Hoshea became his servant, and [1]gave him [2]presents.

4 And the king of Assyria found conspiracy in Hoshea: for he had sent messengers to So king of Egypt, and brought no [1]present to the king of Assyria, as *he had done* year by year: therefore the king of Assyria shut him up, and bound him *in* prison.

5 Then [a]the king of Assyria came up throughout all the land, and went up *to* Samaria, and besieged it three years.

6 [a]In the ninth year of Hoshea, the king of Assyria took Samaria, and [b]carried Israel away into Assyria, [c]and placed them in Halah and in Habor *by* the river of Gozan, and in the cities of the Medes.

The sins of Israel and Judah

7 ¶ For *so* it was, that the children of Israel had sinned against the LORD their God, which had brought them up out of the land of Egypt, from under the hand of Pharaoh king of Egypt, and had feared other gods,

8 And [a]walked in the statutes of the heathen, whom the LORD cast out from before the children of Israel, and of the kings of Israel, which they had made.

9 And the children of Israel did secretly *those* things that *were* not right against the LORD their God, and they built them high places in all their cities, [a]from the tower of the watchmen to the fenced city.

10 [a]And they set them up [1]images and [b]groves [c]in every high hill, and under every green tree:

11 And there they burnt incense in all the high places, as *did* the heathen whom the LORD carried away before them; and wrought wicked things to provoke the LORD to anger:

12 For they served idols, [a]whereof the LORD had said unto them, [b]Ye shall not do this thing.

13 Yet the LORD testified against Israel, and against Judah, [1]by all the prophets, *and by* all [a]the seers, saying, [b]Turn ye from your evil ways, and keep my commandments *and* my statutes, according to all the law which I com-

16:20 [a]2 Chr. 28:27
17:1 [1][After an interregnum, ch. 15:30]
17:3 [1]Heb. *rendered* [2]Or, *tribute* [a]ch. 18:9
17:4 [1]Or, *tribute*
17:5 [a]ch. 18:9
17:6 [a]ch. 18:10,11; Hos. 13:16, Foretold [b]Lev. 26:32,33; Deut. 28:36,64; 29:27,28 [c]1 Chr. 5:26
17:8 [a]Lev. 18:3; Deut. 18:9; ch. 16:3
17:9 [a]ch. 18:8
17:10 [1]Heb. *statutes* [a]1 Ki. 14:23; Is. 57:5 [b]Ex. 34:13; Deut. 16:21; Mic. 5:14 [c]Deut. 12:2; ch. 16:4
17:12 [a]Ex. 20:3,4; Lev. 26:1; Deut. 5:7,8 [b]Deut. 4:19
17:13 [1]Heb. *by the hand of all* [a]1 Sam. 9:9 [b]Jer. 18:11; 25:5; 35:15

16:19 *rest of the acts of Ahaz.* See 2 Chr 28, where, among other things, it is said that Ahaz even "shut up the doors of the house of the LORD" (2 Chr 28:24). *chronicles of the kings of Judah.* See note on 1 Ki 14:29.

16:20 *slept with his fathers.* See note on 1 Ki 1:21; see also 2 Chr 28:27. *Hezekiah his son reigned in his stead.* For the reign of Hezekiah see 18:1–20:21.

17:1 *twelfth year of Ahaz.* 732 B.C. (see note on 15:30), on the assumption that Ahaz began a co-regency with Azariah in 744/743 (see notes on 16:1–2). Some interpreters prefer to place the beginning of the reign of Ahaz in 735 on the assumption that the "twelfth" year of his reign in this text is a copyist's error for the "fourth" year of his reign (i.e. 732). *nine years.* 732–722 (see Introduction to 1 Kings: Chronology).

17:3 *Shalmaneser.* Hoshea had become a vassal to Assyria under the rule of Tiglath-pileser III (see note on 15:30). The latter was succeeded on the Assyrian throne by Shalmaneser V, who ruled 727–722 B.C.

17:5 *three years.* 725–722 B.C. Samaria was a strongly fortified city and extremely difficult to subdue (see note on 1 Ki 16:24).

17:6 *ninth year of Hoshea.* 722 B.C. (see note on v. 1). *king of Assyria took Samaria.* In the winter (December) of 722–721 Shalmaneser V died (possibly by assassination), and the Assyrian throne was seized by Sargon II (722–705). In his annals Sargon II lays claim to the capture of Samaria at the beginning of his reign, but it was hardly more than a mopping-up operation. *carried Israel away into Assyria.* Because the northern kingdom refused to be obedient to their covenant obligations, the Lord brought on them the judgment pronounced already by Ahijah during the reign of the northern kingdom's first king, Jeroboam I (see note on 1 Ki 14:15). In his annals Sargon II claims to have deported 27,290 Israelites. He then settled other captured people in the vacated towns of the northern kingdom (see v. 24). *Halah.* Location uncertain. *Habor by the river of Gozan.* Or, more likely, "Gozan, on the river of Habor." Gozan was an Assyrian provincial capital located on a tributary of the Euphrates River. *cities of the Medes.* Towns located in the area south of the Caspian Sea and northeast of the Tigris River.

17:7–23 A theological explanation for the downfall of the northern kingdom. Israel had repeatedly spurned the Lord's gracious acts, had refused to heed the prophets' warnings of impending judgment (vv. 13–14,23) and had failed to keep her covenant obligations (v. 15). The result was the implementation of the covenant curse precisely as it had been presented to the Israelites by Moses before they entered into Canaan (Deut 28:49–68; 32:1–47).

17:7 *brought them up out of the land of Egypt.* The deliverance from Egypt was the fundamental redemptive event in Israel's history. She owed her very existence as a nation to this gracious and mighty act of the Lord (see Ex 20:2; Deut 5:15; 26:8; Josh 24:5–7,17; Judg 10:11; 1 Sam 12:6; Neh 9:9–13; Mic 6:4). *feared other gods.* A violation of the most basic obligation of Israel's covenant with the Lord (see v. 35; Deut 5:7; 6:14; Josh 24:14–16,20; Jer 1:16; 2:5–6; 25:6; 35:15).

‡17:8 *statutes of the heathen.* See Deut 18:9; Judg 2:12–13. [statutes] *of the kings of Israel, which they had made.* See, e.g., 10:31 (Jehu); 14:24 (Jeroboam II); 1 Ki 12:28–33 (Jeroboam I); 16:25–26 (Omri); 16:30–34 (Ahab).

17:9 *high places in all their cities.* See 14:4; 15:4,35; see also notes on 16:4; 1 Ki 3:2; 15:14.

17:10 *images.* See note on 1 Ki 14:23. *groves.* See note on 1 Ki 14:15. *in every high hill, and under every green tree.* See 16:4; 1 Ki 14:23; Jer 2:20; 3:6,13; 17:2.

17:11 *wicked things.* Perhaps a reference to ritual prostitution (see note on 1 Ki 14:24; see also Hos 4:13–14).

17:12 *Ye shall not do this thing.* See Ex 20:4–5; see also Ex 23:13; Lev 26:1; Deut 5:6–10.

17:13 *testified against Israel, and against Judah, by all the prophets.* Israel not only violated the requirements of the Sinai covenant, but she also spurned the words of prophets the Lord had

manded your fathers, and which I sent to you [2]by my servants the prophets.

14 Notwithstanding they would not hear, but [a]hardened their necks, like to the neck of their fathers, that did not believe in the LORD their God.

15 And they rejected his statutes, [a]and his covenant that he made with their fathers, and his testimonies which he testified against them; and they followed [b]vanity, and [c]became vain, and *went* after the heathen that *were* round about them, *concerning* whom the LORD had charged them, that *they* should [d]not do like them.

16 And they left all the commandments of the LORD their God, and [a]made them molten images, *even* two calves, [b]and made a grove, and worshipped all the host of heaven, [c]and served Baal.

17 [a]And they caused their sons and their daughters to pass through the fire, and [b]used divination and enchantments, and [c]sold themselves to do evil in the sight of the LORD, to provoke him to anger.

18 Therefore the LORD was very angry with Israel, and removed them out of his sight: there was none left [a]but the tribe of Judah only.

19 Also [a]Judah kept not the commandments of the LORD their God, but walked in the statutes of Israel which they made.

20 And the LORD rejected all the seed of Israel, and afflicted them, and [a]delivered them into the hand of spoilers, until *he* had cast them out of his sight.

21 For [a]he rent Israel from the house of David; and [b]they made Jeroboam the son of Nebat king: and Jeroboam drave Israel from following the LORD, and made them sin a great sin.

22 For the children of Israel walked in all the sins of Jeroboam which he did; they departed not from them;

23 Until the LORD removed Israel out of his sight, [a]as he had said by all his servants the prophets. [b]So was Israel carried away out of their own land to Assyria unto this day.

Israel resettled with Assyrians

24 ¶ [a]And the king of Assyria brought *men* from Babylon, and from Cuthah, and from [1]Ava, and from Hamath, and from Sepharvaim, and placed *them* in the cities of Samaria instead of the children of Israel: and they possessed Samaria, and dwelt in the cities thereof.

25 And *so* it was at the beginning of their dwelling there, *that* they feared not the LORD: therefore the LORD sent lions among them, which slew *some* of them.

26 Wherefore they spake to the king of Assyria, saying, The nations which thou hast removed, and placed in the cities of Samaria, know not the manner of the God of the land: therefore he hath sent lions among them, and behold, they slay them, because they know not the manner of the God of the land.

17:13 [2]Heb. *by the hand of all*
17:14 [a]Deut. 31:27; Prov. 29:1
17:15 [a]Deut. 29:25 [b]Deut. 32:21; 1 Ki. 16:13; 1 Cor. 8:4 [c]Ps. 115:8; Rom. 1:21 [d]Deut. 12:30,31
17:16 [a]Ex. 32:8; 1 Ki. 12:28 [b]1 Ki. 14:15 [c]1 Ki. 16:31; 22:53; ch. 11:18
17:17 [a]Lev. 18:21; ch. 16:3; Ezek. 23:37 [b]Deut. 18:10 [c]1 Ki. 21:20
17:18 [a]1 Ki. 11:13,32
17:19 [a]Jer. 3:8
17:20 [a]ch. 13:3; 15:29
17:21 [a]1 Ki. 11:11,31 [b]1 Ki. 12:20,28
17:23 [a]1 Ki. 14:16 [b]ver. 6
17:24 [1][ch. 18:34, *Ivah*] [a]Ezra 4:2,10

graciously sent to call His people back to the covenant (see, e.g., 1 Ki 13:1–3; 14:6–16; Judg 6:8–10; 1 Sam 3:19–21 as well as the ministries of Elijah, Elisha, Amos and Hosea). *seers.* See note on 1 Sam 9:9.

17:14 *hardened their necks.* A figure derived from the obstinate resistance of an ox to being placed under a yoke (see Deut 10:16; Jer 2:20; 7:26; 17:23; 19:15; Hos 4:16).

17:15 *followed vanity.* See Deut 32:21; Jer 2:5; 8:19; 10:8; 14:22; 51:18.

17:16 *molten images, even two calves.* The golden calves of Beth-el and Dan (see 1 Ki 12:28–30). *grove.* See note on 1 Ki 14:15. *all the host of heaven.* Israel had been commanded not to follow the astral cults of her pagan neighbors (see Deut 4:19; 17:3). Although this form of idolatry is not mentioned previously in 1,2 Kings, the prophet Amos apparently alludes to its practice in the northern kingdom during the reign of Jeroboam II (see note on Amos 5:26). It was later introduced in the southern kingdom during the reign of Manasseh (see 21:3,5) and abolished during the reformation of Josiah (see 23:4–5,12; see also Ezek 8:16).

17:17 *caused their sons and their daughters to pass through the fire.* See note on 16:3. *divination and enchantments.* Such practices were forbidden in the Mosaic covenant (see note on 16:15; see also Lev 19:26; Deut 18:10).

17:18 *removed them out of his sight.* The exile of the northern kingdom (see v. 6; 23:27). *was none left but the tribe of Judah.* The southern kingdom included elements of the tribes of Simeon and Benjamin, but Judah was the only tribe in the south to retain its complete integrity (see notes on 1 Ki 11:31–32; see also note on 2 Ki 19:4).

17:20 *afflicted them, and delivered them into the hand of spoilers.* See 10:32–33; 13:3,20; 24:2; 2 Chr 21:16; 28:18; Amos 1:13.

17:21 *rent Israel from the house of David.* See 1 Ki 11:11,31; 12:24. The division of the kingdom was of the Lord, but it came to the nation as a punishment for their sins. *Jeroboam . . . made them sin a great sin.* See 1 Ki 12:26–32; 13:33–34.

17:23 *had said by all his servants the prophets.* See 1 Ki 14:15–16; Hos 10:1–7; 11:5; Amos 5:27.

17:24 *king of Assyria.* Primarily Sargon II (722–705 B.C.), though later Assyrian rulers, including Esarhaddon (681–669) and Ashurbanipal (669–627), settled additional non-Israelites in Samaria (see Ezra 4:2,9–10). *Babylon . . . Cuthah.* Babylon and Cuthah (located about eight miles northeast of Babylon) were forced to submit to Assyrian rule by Sargon II in 709. *Ava.* Probably the same as Ivah (see 18:34; 19:13). Its association with Hamath, Arpad and Sepharvaim suggests a location somewhere in Aram (Syria). *Hamath.* Located on the Orontes River (see 14:25; 18:34; see also note on Ezek 47:15). In 720 Sargon II made the kingdom of Hamath into an Assyrian province. *Sepharvaim.* Perhaps located in Aramean territory, possibly between Damascus and Hamath. *Samaria.* Here a designation for the entire northern kingdom (see note on 1 Ki 13:32).

17:25 *feared not the LORD.* They worshiped their own national deities. *sent lions among them.* Lions had always been present in Canaan (see 1 Ki 13:24; 20:36; Judg 14:5; 1 Sam 17:34; Amos 3:12). In the aftermath of the disruption and depopulation caused by the conflict with the Assyrians, the lions greatly increased in number (see Ex 23:29). This was viewed by the inhabitants of the land and the writer of Kings as a punishment from the Lord (see Lev 26:21–22).

17:26 *king of Assyria.* Sargon II. *the manner of the God of the land.* According to the religious ideas of that time, each regional deity required special ritual observances, which, if ignored or violated, would bring disaster on the land.

Exile of the Northern Kingdom

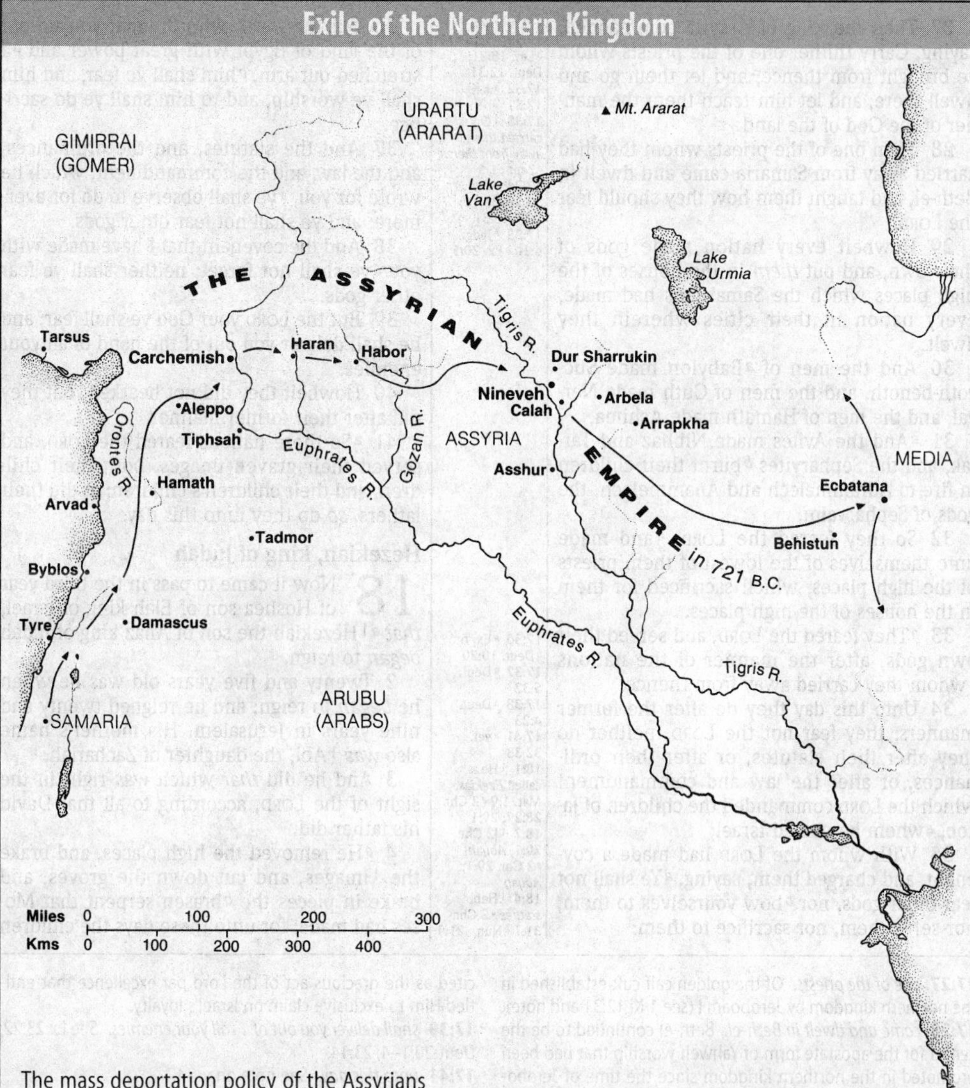

The mass deportation policy of the Assyrians was a companion piece to the brutal and calculated terror initiated by Ashurnasirpal and followed by all his successors. It was intended to forestall revolts but, like all Draconian measures, it merely spread misery and engendered hatred. In the end, it hastened the disintegration of the Assyrian empire.

There is some evidence that Israel experienced its first deportations under Tiglath-pileser III (745-727 B.C.), a cruelty repeated by Sargon II (722-705 B.C.) at the time of the fall of Samaria. The latter king's inscriptions boast of carrying away 27,290 inhabitants of the city "as booty." According to 2 Ki 17:6, they were sent to Assyria, to Halah (Calah?), to Habor on the Gozan River, and apparently to the eastern frontiers of the empire (to the towns of the Medes, most probably somewhere in the vicinity of Ecbatana, the modern Hamadan).

The sequel is provided by the inscriptions of Sargon: "The Arabs who live far away in the desert, who know neither overseers nor officials, and who had not yet brought their tribute to any king, I deported . . . and settled them in Samaria."

Much mythology has developed around the theme of the so-called ten lost tribes of Israel. A close examination of Assyrian records reveals that the deportations approximated only a limited percentage of the population, usually consisting of noble families. Agricultural workers, no doubt the majority, were deliberately left to care for the crops (cf. the Babylonian practice, 2 Ki 24:14; 25:12).

27 Then the king of Assyria commanded, saying, Carry thither one of the priests whom ye brought from thence; and let them go and dwell there, and let him teach them the manner of the God of the land.

28 Then one of the priests whom they had carried away from Samaria came and dwelt in Beth-el, and taught them how they should fear the LORD.

29 Howbeit every nation made gods of their own, and put *them* in the houses of the high places which the Samaritans had made, every nation in their cities wherein they dwelt.

30 And the men of [a]Babylon made Succoth-benoth, and the men of Cuth made Nergal, and the men of Hamath made Ashima,

31 [a]And the Avites made Nibhaz and Tartak, and the Sepharvites [b]burnt their children in fire to Adrammelech and Anammelech, the gods of Sepharvaim.

32 So they feared the LORD, [a]and made unto themselves of the lowest of them priests of the high places, which sacrificed for them in the houses of the high places.

33 [a]They feared the LORD, and served their own gods, after the manner of the nations [1]whom they carried away from thence.

34 Unto this day they do after the former manners: they fear not the LORD, neither do they after their statutes, or after their ordinances, or after the law and commandment which the LORD commanded the children of Jacob, [a]whom he named Israel;

35 With whom the LORD had made a covenant, and charged them, saying, [a]Ye shall not fear other gods, nor [b]bow yourselves to them, nor serve them, nor sacrifice to them:

36 But the LORD, who brought you up out of the land of Egypt with great power and [a]a stretched out arm, [b]him shall ye fear, and him shall ye worship, and to him shall ye do sacrifice.

37 And the statutes, and the ordinances, and the law, and the commandment, which he wrote for you, [a]ye shall observe to do for evermore; and ye shall not fear other gods.

38 And the covenant that I have made with you [a]ye shall not forget; neither shall ye fear other gods.

39 But the LORD your God ye shall fear; and he shall deliver you out of the hand of all your enemies.

40 Howbeit they did not hearken, but they did after their former manner.

41 [a]So these nations feared the LORD, and served their graven images, both their children, and their children's children: as did their fathers, *so* do they unto this day.

Hezekiah, king of Judah

18 Now it came to pass in the third year of Hoshea son of Elah king of Israel, *that* [a][1]Hezekiah the son of Ahaz king of Judah *began* to reign.

2 Twenty and five years old was he when he *began* to reign; and he reigned twenty and nine years in Jerusalem. His mother's name also *was* [1]Abi, the daughter of Zachariah.

3 And he did *that* which *was* right in the sight of the LORD, according to all that David his father did.

4 [a]He removed the high places, and brake the [1]images, and cut down the groves, and brake in pieces the [b]brasen serpent that Moses had made: for unto those days the children

17:30 [a]ver. 24
17:31 [a]Ezra 4:9 [b]Lev. 18:21; Deut. 12:31
17:32 [a]1 Ki. 12:31
17:33 [1]Or, *who carried them away from thence* [a]Zeph. 1:5
17:34 [a]Gen. 32:28; 35:10; 1 Ki. 18:31
17:35 [a]Judg. 6:10 [b]Ex. 20:5
17:36 [a]Ex. 6:6 [b]Deut. 10:20
17:37 [a]Deut. 5:32
17:38 [a]Deut. 4:23
17:41 [a]ver. 32,33
18:1 [1]He is called *Ezekias,* Mat. 1:9 [a]2 Chr. 28:27; 29:1
18:2 [1][2 Chr. 29:1, *Abijah*] [a]2 Chr. 29:1; *Abijah*
18:4 [1]Heb. *statues* [a]2 Chr. 31:1 [b]Num. 21:9

17:27 *one of the priests.* Of the golden calf cult established in the northern kingdom by Jeroboam I (see 1 Ki 12:31 and note).

17:28 *came and dwelt in Beth-el.* Beth-el continued to be the center for the apostate form of Yahweh worship that had been promoted in the northern kingdom since the time of Jeroboam I (see notes on 1 Ki 12:28–30).

17:29 *Samaritans.* The mixed population of the former territory of the northern kingdom. These people of mixed ancestry eventually came to be known as Samaritans. In later times the Samaritans rejected the idolatry of their polytheistic origins and followed the teachings of Moses, including monotheism. In NT times Jesus testified to a Samaritan woman (John 4:4–26), and many Samaritans were converted under the ministry of Philip (Acts 8:4–25).

17:32 *sacrificed for them in the houses of the high places.* See note on 1 Ki 12:31.

17:33 *They feared the LORD, and served their own gods.* A classic statement of syncretistic religion.

17:34 *Unto this day.* Until the time of the writing of 1,2 Kings. *fear not the LORD.* Here used in the sense of faithful worship. In vv. 32–33 "feared the LORD" refers to a paganized worship.

17:35 *Ye shall not fear other gods.* The Mosaic covenant demanded exclusive worship of the Lord (Ex 20:5; Deut 5:9). This was the first and great commandment, and it was to distinguish Israel from all other peoples.

17:36 *the LORD, who brought you up out of the land of Egypt . . . him shall ye fear.* Here, as in v. 7, the deliverance from Egypt is cited as the gracious act of the Lord par excellence that entitled Him to exclusive claim on Israel's loyalty.

17:39 *shall deliver you out of . . . all your enemies.* See Ex 23:22; Deut 20:1–4; 23:14.

17:41 *unto this day.* See note on v. 34.

18:1 *third year of Hoshea . . . Hezekiah . . . began to reign.* 729 B.C. (see 17:1). Hezekiah was co-regent with his father Ahaz from 729 to 715 (see note on 16:2 and Is 36:1).

18:2 *began to reign.* Became sole king of Judah. *twenty and nine years.* 715–686 B.C. See also 2 Chr 29–32 and Is 36–39 for a description of the events of his reign, including a more detailed account of the reformation he led (2 Chr 29–31). One of his first acts was to reopen the temple, which had been closed by his father Ahaz (see note on 16:19; see also 2 Chr 29:3).

18:3 *right . . . according to all that David his father did.* Hezekiah is one of the few kings who is compared favorably with David. The others are Asa (1 Ki 15:11), Jehoshaphat (1 Ki 22:43) and Josiah (2 Ki 22:2). A qualification is introduced, however, with both Asa and Jehoshaphat: They did not remove the high places (see 1 Ki 15:14; 22:43).

18:4 *removed the high places.* Hezekiah was not the first king to destroy high places (see notes on 1 Ki 3:2; 15:14), but he was the first to destroy high places dedicated to the worship of the Lord (see 12:3; 14:4; 15:4,35; 17:9; 1 Ki 22:43). This became known even to the Assyrian king, Sennacherib (see v. 22). *images.* See 3:2; 10:26–27; 17:10; see also note on 1 Ki 14:23. *groves.* See 13:6; 17:10,16; 1 Ki 16:23; see also note on 1 Ki

of Israel did burn incense to it: and he called it
[2]Nehushtan.
5 He [a]trusted in the LORD God of Israel; [b]so
that after him was none like him among all the
kings of Judah, nor *any* that were before him.
6 For he [a]clave to the LORD, *and* departed
not [1]from following him, but kept his commandments, which the LORD commanded Moses.
7 And the LORD [a]was with him; *and* he
[b]prospered whithersoever he went forth: and
he [c]rebelled against the king of Assyria, and
served him not.
8 [a]He smote the Philistines, *even* unto
[1]Gaza, and the borders thereof, [b]from the
tower of the watchmen to the fenced city.
9 ¶ And [a]it came to pass in the fourth year
of king Hezekiah, which *was* the seventh year
of Hoshea son of Elah king of Israel, *that* Shalmaneser king of Assyria came up against
Samaria, and besieged it.
10 And at the end of three years they took
it: *even* in the sixth year of Hezekiah, that *is*
[a]the ninth year of Hoshea king of Israel,
Samaria was taken.
11 [a]And the king of Assyria did carry away
Israel unto Assyria, and put them [b]in Halah
and in Habor *by* the river of Gozan, and in the
cities of the Medes:
12 Because they obeyed not the voice of
the LORD their God, but transgressed his covenant, *and* all that Moses the servant of the

18:4 [2][That is, *A piece of brass*]
18:5 [a]ch. 19:10; Job 13:15; Ps. 13:5 [b]ch. 23:25
18:6 [1]Heb. *from after him* [a]Deut. 10:20; Josh. 23:8
18:7 [a]2 Chr. 15:2 [b]1 Sam. 18:5,14; Ps. 60:12 [c]ch. 16:7
18:8 [1]Heb. *Azzah* [a]1 Chr. 4:41; Is. 14:29 [b]ch. 17:9
18:9 [a]ch. 17:3
18:10 [a]ch. 17:6
18:11 [a]ch. 17:6 [b]1 Chr. 5:26
18:13 [1]Heb. *Sanherib* [a]2 Chr. 32:1; Is. 36:1
18:15 [a]ch. 16:8
18:16 [1]Heb. *them*
18:17 [1]Heb. *heavy* [a]Is. 7:3

LORD commanded, and would not hear *them,*
nor do *them.*
13 ¶ Now [a]in the fourteenth year of king
Hezekiah did [1]Sennacherib king of Assyria
come up against all the fenced cities of Judah,
and took them.
14 And Hezekiah king of Judah sent to the
king of Assyria to Lachish, saying, I have offended; return from me: *that* which thou
puttest on me will I bear. And the king of Assyria appointed unto Hezekiah king of Judah
three hundred talents of silver and thirty talents of gold.
15 And Hezekiah [a]gave *him* all the silver
that was found *in* the house of the LORD, and
in the treasures of the king's house.
16 At that time did Hezekiah cut off *the gold*
from the doors of the temple of the LORD, and
from the pillars which Hezekiah king of Judah
had overlaid, and gave [1]it to the king of Assyria.

The Assyrian threats

17 ¶ And the king of Assyria sent Tartan
and Rabsaris and Rab-shakeh from Lachish to
king Hezekiah with a [1]great host *against* Jerusalem. And they went up and came *to* Jerusalem. And when they were come up, they came
and stood by the conduit of the upper pool,
[a]which *is* in the highway of the fuller's field.
18 And when they had called to the king,
there came out to them Eliakim the son of Hilkiah, which *was* over the household, and

14:15. *children of Israel did burn incense to it.* It is unlikely that the brasen serpent had been an object of worship all through the centuries of Israel's existence as a nation. Just when an idolatrous significance was attached to it is not known, but perhaps it occurred during the reign of Hezekiah's father Ahaz (see ch. 16). Snake worship of various types was common among ancient Near Eastern peoples.

18:5 *after him was none like him ... nor any that were before him.* A difference of emphasis is to be seen in this statement when compared to that of 23:25. Hezekiah's uniqueness is to be found in his trust in the Lord, while Josiah's uniqueness is to be found in his scrupulous observance of the Mosaic law.

18:7 *rebelled against the king of Assyria.* Judah had become a vassal to Assyria under Ahaz (see 16:7)—which required at least formal recognition of Assyrian deities. Hezekiah reversed the policy of his father Ahaz and sought independence from Assyrian dominance. It is likely that sometime shortly after 705 B.C., when Sennacherib replaced Sargon II on the Assyrian throne, Hezekiah refused to pay the annual tribute due the Assyrians.

18:8 *smote the Philistines.* In a reversal of the conditions existing during the time of Ahaz, in which the Philistines captured Judahite cities in the hill country and Negev (see 2 Chr 28:18), Hezekiah was able once again to subdue the Philistines. Probably Hezekiah tried to coerce the Philistines into joining his anti-Assyrian policy. In one of his annals Sennacherib tells of forcing Hezekiah to release Padi, king of the Philistine city of Ekron, whom Hezekiah held prisoner in Jerusalem. This occurred in connection with Sennacherib's military campaign in 701 B.C.

18:9 *fourth year of king Hezekiah.* 725 B.C., the fourth year of Hezekiah's co-regency with Ahaz (see notes on v. 1; 17:1).

18:10 *three years.* See note on 17:5. *ninth year of Hoshea.* See note on 17:6.

18:11 *king of Assyria did carry away Israel.* See note on 17:6.

18:12 *transgressed his covenant.* See 17:7–23.

18:13 *fourteenth year.* Of Hezekiah's sole reign: 701 B.C. (see note on v. 2). *Sennacherib ... come up against.* Verses 13–16 correspond very closely with Sennacherib's own account of his 701 campaign against Phoenicia, Judah and Egypt. *took them.* In his annals, Sennacherib claims to have captured 46 of Hezekiah's fortified cities, as well as numerous open villages, and to have taken 200,150 of the people captive. He says he made Hezekiah "a prisoner in Jerusalem his royal residence, like a bird in a cage," but he does not say he took Jerusalem.

18:14 *three hundred talents of silver and thirty talents of gold.* About eleven tons of silver and one ton of gold. The Assyrian and Biblical reports of the amount of tribute paid by Hezekiah to Sennacherib agree with respect to the 30 talents of gold, but Sennacherib claims to have received 800 talents of silver rather than the 300 specified in the Biblical text. This discrepancy may be the result of differences in the weight of Assyrian and Israelite silver talents, or it may simply be due to the Assyrian propensity for exaggeration. For the relative value of this amount of silver and gold see note on 15:19.

18:15 *silver ... in the house of the LORD, and in the treasures of the king's house.* See 12:10,18; 14:14; 16:8; 1 Ki 7:51; 14:26; 15:18.

18:17–19:37 See Is 36–37; cf. 2Ch 32.

18:17 *Lachish.* See note on Is 36:2. *conduit ... field.* See note on Is 7:3. It is ironic that the Assyrian officials demand Judah's surrender on the very spot where Isaiah had warned Ahaz to trust in the Lord rather than in an alliance with Assyria for deliverance from the threat against him from Aram and the northern kingdom of Israel (see 16:5–10; Is 7:1–17).

18:18 *over the household.* See note on 1 Ki 4:6. *scribe.* See note on 2 Sam 8:17. *recorder.* See note on 2 Sam 8:16.

Shebna the [1]scribe, and Joah the son of Asaph
the recorder.
19 And Rab-shakeh said unto them, Speak
ye now to Hezekiah, Thus saith the great king,
the king of Assyria, [a]What confidence *is* this
where*in* thou trustest?
20 Thou [1]sayest, (but *they are but* [2]vain
words,) [3]*I have* counsel and strength for the
war. Now on whom dost thou trust, that thou
rebellest against me?
21 [a]Now behold, thou [1]trustest upon the
staff of this bruised reed, *even* upon Egypt, on
which if a man lean, it will go into his hand,
and pierce it: so *is* Pharaoh king of Egypt unto
all that trust on him.
22 But if ye say unto me, We trust in the
LORD our God: *is* not *that* he, [a]whose high
places and whose altars Hezekiah hath taken
away, and hath said to Judah and Jerusalem,
Ye shall worship before this altar in Jerusalem?
23 Now therefore, I pray thee, give
[1]pledges to my lord the king of Assyria, and I
will deliver thee two thousand horses, if thou
be able on thy part to set riders upon them.
24 How then wilt thou turn away the face
of one captain of the least of my master's servants, and put thy trust on Egypt for chariots
and for horsemen?
25 Am I now come up without the LORD
against this place to destroy it? The LORD said
to me, Go up against this land, and destroy it.
26 ¶ Then said Eliakim the son of Hilkiah,
and Shebna, and Joah, unto Rab-shakeh,
Speak, I pray thee, to thy servants in the Syrian language; for we understand *it:* and talk not
with us in the Jews' language in the ears of the
people that *are* on the wall.
27 But Rab-shakeh said unto them, Hath
my master sent me to thy master, and to thee,
to speak these words? *hath he* not *sent me* to
the men which sit on the wall, that *they* may
eat their own dung, and drink [1]their own piss
with you?
28 Then Rab-shakeh stood and cried with a
loud voice in the Jews' language, and spake,
saying, Hear the word of the great king, the
king of Assyria:
29 Thus saith the king, [a]Let not Hezekiah
deceive you: for he shall not be able to deliver
you out of his hand:
30 Neither let Hezekiah make you trust in
the LORD, saying, The LORD will surely deliver
us, and this city shall not be delivered into the
hand of the king of Assyria.
31 Hearken not to Hezekiah: for thus saith
the king of Assyria, [1]Make *an agreement* with
me *by* a present, and come out to me, and *then*
eat ye every man of his own vine, and every
one of his fig tree, and drink ye every one the
waters of his [2]cistern:
32 Until I come and take you away to a
land like your own land, [a]a land of corn and
wine, a land of bread and vineyards, a land of
oil olive and of honey, that ye may live, and
not die: and hearken not unto Hezekiah, when
he [1]persuadeth you, saying, The LORD will deliver us.
33 [a]Hath any of the gods of the nations delivered at all his land out of the hand of the
king of Assyria?
34 [a]Where *are* the gods of Hamath, and of

18:18 [1] Or, *secretary*
18:19 [a] 2 Chr. 32:10
18:20 [1] Or, *talkest* [2] Heb. *word of the lips* [3] Or, but *counsel and strength* are *for the war*
18:21 [1] Heb. *trustest thee* [a] Ezek. 29:6,7
18:22 [a] ver. 4; 2 Chr. 31:1; 32:12
18:23 [1] Or, *hostages*
18:27 [1] Heb. *the water of their feet*
18:29 [a] 2 Chr. 32:15
18:31 [1] Or, *Seek my favour.* Heb. *Make with me a blessing* [2] Or, *pit*
18:32 [1] Or, *deceiveth* [a] Deut. 8:7,8
18:33 [a] ch. 19:12; 2 Chr. 32:14; Is. 10:10,11
18:34 [a] ch. 19:13

18:19 *saith.* The following address is a masterpiece of calculated intimidation and psychological warfare designed to break the resistance of the inhabitants of Jerusalem (see vv. 26–27). *great king.* A frequently used title of the Assyrian rulers—and occasionally of the Lord (Ps 47:2; 48:2; 95:3; Mal 1:14; Mat 5:35).

18:21 *trustest upon . . . Egypt.* See 19:9; Is 30:1–5; 31:1–3.

18:22 *is not that he, whose high places and whose altars Hezekiah hath taken away . . . ?* The Assyrians cleverly attempted to drive a wedge between Hezekiah and the people. They attempted to exploit any resentment that may have existed among those who opposed Hezekiah's reformation and his destruction of the high places (see note on v. 4).

18:23 *if thou be able . . . to set riders upon them.* With this sarcastic taunt, the Assyrians undoubtedly accurately suggest that the Judahites were so weak in military personnel that they could not even take advantage of such a generous offer. In contrast with the Assyrians, the army of Judah at the time consisted largely of foot soldiers. The city under siege would have contained few chariots, and it is not known whether the Israelites ever employed mounted men in combat.

18:25 *The LORD said to me.* Possibly Assyrian spies had informed Sennacherib of the prophecies of Isaiah and Micah.

‡18:26 *Syrian.* Hebrew *Aramith,* i.e. Aramaic. It had become the international language of the Near East, known and used by those experienced in diplomacy and commerce. It is surprising that the Assyrian officials were able to speak the Hebrew dialect of the common people of Judah (see 2 Chr 32:18).

18:27 *men which sit on the wall.* The Assyrian strategy was to negotiate in the hearing of the people in order to demoralize them and turn them against Hezekiah. *eat their own dung, and drink . . .* A vivid portrayal of the potential hardship of a prolonged siege.

18:29 *Thus saith the king.* The Assyrian officials now address their remarks directly to the populace rather than to the officials of Hezekiah, as in vv. 19–27. *Let not Hezekiah deceive you.* Here and in vv. 30–31 the people are urged three times to turn against Hezekiah.

18:30 *this city shall not be delivered into the hand of the king of Assyria.* Hezekiah could say this on the basis of God's promise to him (see 20:6; see also note on Is 38:6).

18:31 *eat ye every man of his own vine, and every one of his fig tree, and drink . . . of his cistern.* Depicting peaceful and prosperous times (see 1 Ki 4:25; Mic 4:4; Zech 3:10).

18:32 *until I come and take you away to a land like your own.* Ultimately surrender meant deportation, but Sennacherib pictured it as something desirable. *that ye may live, and not die.* The alternatives depicted for the people are: (1) Trust in the Lord and Hezekiah and die, or (2) trust in the Assyrians and enjoy prosperity and peace. These words directly contradict the alternatives placed before Israel by Moses in Deut 30:15–20.

18:33–35 *Hath any of the gods of the nations delivered at all his land out of the hand of the king of Assyria? Who are they . . . that the LORD should deliver Jerusalem out of mine hand?* The flaw in the Assyrian reasoning was to equate the one true and living God with the no-gods (Deut 32:21) of the pagan peoples the Assyrians had defeated (see 19:4,6; 2 Chr 32:13–19; Is 10:9–11).

18:34 *Hamath.* See notes on 14:25; 17:24. *Arpad.* A city lo-

Arpad? where *are* the gods of Sepharvaim,
Hena, and [1]Ivah? have they delivered Samaria
out of mine hand?
35 Who *are they* among all the gods of the
countries, that have delivered their country
out of mine hand, [a]that the LORD should deliver Jerusalem out of mine hand?
36 But the people held their peace, and answered him not a word: for the king's commandment was, saying, Answer him not.
37 Then came Eliakim the son of Hilkiah,
which *was* over the household, and Shebna
the scribe, and Joah the son of Asaph the
recorder, to Hezekiah [a]with *their* clothes rent,
and told him the words of Rab-shakeh.

Hezekiah sends to Isaiah

19 And [a]it came to pass, when king
Hezekiah heard *it,* that he rent his
clothes, and covered himself with sackcloth,
and went *into* the house of the LORD.
2 And he sent Eliakim, which *was* over the
household, and Shebna the scribe, and the
elders of the priests, covered with sackcloth,
to [a]Esai the prophet the son of Amoz.
3 And they said unto him, Thus saith Hezekiah, This day *is* a day of trouble, and of rebuke, and [1]blasphemy: for the children are
come to the birth, and *there is* not strength to
bring forth.
4 [a]It may be the LORD thy God will hear all
the words of Rab-shakeh, [b]whom the king of
Assyria his master hath sent to reproach the
living God; and will [c]reprove the words which
the LORD thy God hath heard: wherefore lift up
thy prayer for the remnant that are [1]left.
5 So the servants of king Hezekiah came to
Isaiah.
6 [a]And Isaiah said unto them, Thus shall ye
say to your master, Thus saith the LORD, Be not
afraid of the words which thou hast heard,
with which the [b]servants of the king of Assyria have blasphemed me.
7 Behold, I will send [a]a blast upon him,
and he shall hear a rumour, and shall return to
his own land; and I will cause him to fall by
the sword in his own land.
8 ¶ So Rab-shakeh returned, and found the
king of Assyria warring against Libnah: for he
had heard that he was departed [a]from Lachish.
9 And [a]when he heard say of Tirhakah king
of Ethiopia, Behold, he is come out to fight
against thee: he sent messengers again unto
Hezekiah, saying,
10 Thus shall ye speak to Hezekiah king of
Judah, saying, Let not thy God [a]in whom thou
trustest deceive thee, saying, Jerusalem shall
not be delivered into the hand of the king of
Assyria.
11 Behold, thou hast heard what the kings
of Assyria have done to all lands, by destroying
them utterly: and shalt thou be delivered?
12 [a]Have the gods of the nations delivered
them which my fathers have destroyed; *as* Gozan, and Haran, and Rezeph, and the children
of [b]Eden which *were* in Thelasar?
13 [a]Where *is* the king of Hamath, and the
king of Arpad, and the king of the city of
Sepharvaim, *of* Hena, and Ivah?

Hezekiah's prayer

14 ¶ [a]And Hezekiah received the letter of
the hand of the messengers, and read it: and
Hezekiah went up *into* the house of the LORD,
and spread it before the LORD.
15 And Hezekiah prayed before the LORD,

18:34 [1][ch. 17:24, *Ava*] 18:35 [a]Dan. 3:15 18:37 [a]Is. 33:7 19:1 [a]Is. 37:1 19:2 [a]Luke 3:4, called *Esaias* 19:3 [1]Or, *provocation* 19:4 [1]Heb. *found* [a]2 Sam. 16:12 [b]ch. 18:35 [c]Ps. 50:21

19:6 [a]Is. 37:6 [b]ch. 18:17 19:7 [a]ver. 35-37; Jer. 51:1 19:8 [a]ch. 18:14 19:9 [a]See 1 Sam. 23:27 19:10 [a]ch. 18:5 19:12 [a]ch. 18:33,34 [b]Ezek. 27:23 19:13 [a]ch. 18:34 19:14 [a]Is. 37:14

cated near Hamath and taken by the Assyrians in 740 B.C. (see 19:13; Is 10:9; Jer 49:23). *Sepharvaim.* See note on 17:24. *Hena.* Probably located in the vicinity of the other cities mentioned. *Ivah.* See note on 17:24.

18:36 *for the king's commandment was . . . Answer him not.* The Assyrian attempt to stir up a popular revolt against the leadership and authority of Hezekiah had failed.

18:37 *clothes rent.* An expression of great emotion (see 6:30; 1 Ki 21:27). Perhaps in this instance it was motivated by the Assyrian blasphemy against the true God (see 19:4,6; Mat 26:65; Mark 14:63–64).

19:1 *sackcloth.* See note on 6:30.

‡19:2 *over the household.* See note on 1 Ki 4:6. *scribe.* See note on 2 Sam 8:17. *elders of the priests.* Probably the oldest members of various priestly families (see Jer 19:1). The crisis involved not only the city of Jerusalem, but also the temple. *Esai* [i.e. Isaiah] *the prophet.* The first reference to Isaiah in the book of Kings, though he had been active in the reigns of Uzziah, Jotham and Ahaz (see Isa 1:1).

19:3 *for the children are come to the birth, and there is not strength to bring forth.* Depicts the critical nature of the threat facing the city.

19:4 *living God.* In contrast to the no-gods of 18:33–35. See 1 Sam 17:26,36,45 for another example of ridiculing the living and true God. *lift up thy prayer.* Intercessory prayer was an important aspect of the ministry of the prophets (see, e.g., the intercession of Moses and Samuel: Ex 32:31–32; 33:12–17; Num 14:13–19; 1 Sam 7:8–9; 12:19, 23; Ps 99:6; Jer 15:1). *remnant.* Those left in Judah after Sennacherib's capture of many towns and numerous people (see note on 18:13; cf. Is 10:28–32). Archaeological evidence reveals that many Israelites fled the northern kingdom during the Assyrian assaults and settled in Judah, so that the nation of Judah became the remnant of all Israel.

‡19:7 *blast* [Hebrew "spirit"]. Of insecurity and fear. *rumour.* Some interpreters link this "rumor" with the challenge to Sennacherib from Tirhakah of Egypt (v. 9). Others regard it as disturbing information from Sennacherib's homeland. *fall by the sword.* See v. 37. Here the eventual murder of Sennacherib is connected with his blasphemy against the living God.

19:8 *Libnah.* See note on 8:22. *Lachish.* See 18:17 (see also note on Is 36:2).

‡19:9 *Tirhakah.* See note on Is 37:9. *Ethiopia* [Hebrew *Cush*]. The upper Nile region.

19:12 *Gozan.* See note on 17:6. *Haran.* See note on Gen 11:31. It is not known just when Haran was taken by the Assyrians. *Rezeph.* Located south of the Euphrates River and northeast of Hamath. *Eden.* See Ezek 27:23; Amos 1:5; a district along the Euphrates River south of Haran. It was incorporated into the Assyrian empire by Shalmaneser III in 855 B.C. *Thelasar.* Location unknown.

19:13 *Hamath . . . Ivah.* See note on 18:34.

19:14 *letter.* See 2 Chr 32:17.

and said, O LORD God of Israel, [a]which
dwellest *between* the cherubims, [b]thou *art* the
God, *even* thou alone, of all the kingdoms of
the earth; thou hast made heaven and earth.
16 LORD, [a]bow down thine ear, and hear:
[b]open, LORD, thine eyes, and see: and hear the
words of Sennacherib, [c]which hath sent him
to reproach the living God.
17 Of a truth, LORD, the kings of Assyria
have destroyed the nations and their lands,
18 And have [1]cast their gods into the fire:
for they *were* no gods, but [a]the work of men's
hands, wood and stone: therefore they have
destroyed them.
19 Now therefore, O LORD our God, I beseech thee, save *thou* us out of his hand, [a]that
all the kingdoms of the earth may know that
thou *art* the LORD God, *even* thou only.

The divine deliverance

20 ¶ Then Isaiah the son of Amoz sent to
Hezekiah, saying, Thus saith the LORD God of Israel, [a]*That* which thou hast prayed to me against
Sennacherib king of Assyria [b]I have heard.
21 This *is* the word that the LORD hath
spoken concerning him;

The virgin [a]the daughter of Zion hath
despised thee, *and* laughed thee to
scorn;
The daughter of Jerusalem [b]hath
shaken her head at thee.
22 Whom hast thou reproached and
blasphemed?
And against whom hast thou exalted
thy voice,
And lift up thine eyes on high?
Even against [a]the Holy One of Israel.
23 [a][1]By thy messengers thou hast
reproached the Lord, and hast said,
[b]With the multitude of my chariots I
am come up
To the height of the mountains, *to* the
sides of Lebanon,

19:15 [a]Ps. 80:1 [b]Is. 44:6
19:16 [a]Ps. 31:2 [b]2 Chr. 6:40 [c]ver. 4
19:18 [1]Heb. *given* [a]Jer. 10:3
19:19 [a]Ps. 83:18
19:20 [a]Is. 37:21 [b]Ps. 65:2
19:21 [a]Lam. 2:13 [b]Ps. 22:7,8
19:22 [a]Jer. 51:5
19:23 [1]Heb. *By the hand of* [a]ch. 18:17 [b]Ps. 20:7

19:23 [2]Heb. *the tallness, etc.* [3]Or, *the forest* and *his fruitful field*
19:24 [1]Or, *fenced*
19:25 [1]Or, *Hast thou not heard* how *I have made it long ago,* and *formed it of ancient times? should I now bring it to be laid waste,* and *fenced cities* to be *ruinous heaps?* [a]Is. 45:7 [b]Is. 10:5
19:26 [1]Heb. *short of hand* [a]Ps. 129:6
19:27 [1]Or, *sitting* [a]Ps. 139:1
19:28 [a]Ezek. 29:4 [b]ver. 33,36

And will cut down [2]the tall cedar trees
thereof, *and* the choice fir trees
thereof:
And I will enter *into* the lodgings of his
borders, *and into* [3]the forest of his
Carmel.
24 I have digged and drunk strange
waters,
And with the sole of my feet have I
dried up all the rivers of [1]besieged
places.
25 [1]Hast thou not heard long ago *how* [a]I
have done it,
And of ancient times that I have
formed it?
Now have I brought it to pass, that
[b]thou shouldest be to lay waste
Fenced cities *into* ruinous heaps.
26 Therefore their inhabitants *were* [1]of
small power,
They were dismayed and confounded;
They were *as* the grass of the field, and
as the green herb,
As [a]the grass on the housetops, and *as*
corn blasted before it be grown up.
27 But [a]I know thy [1]abode, and thy going
out, and thy coming in,
And thy rage against me.
28 Because thy rage against me and thy
tumult is come up into mine ears,
Therefore [a]I will put my hook in thy
nose, and my bridle in thy lips,
And I will turn thee back [b]by the way
by which thou camest.
29 And this *shall be* a sign unto thee,
Ye shall eat *this* year such things as
grow of themselves,
And in the second year that which
springeth of the same;
And in the third year sow ye, and reap,
And plant vineyards, and eat the fruits
thereof.

19:15 *dwelleth between the cherubims.* See notes on Ex 25:18; 1 Sam 4:4. *thou art the God, even thou alone.* See notes on 18:33–35; Deut 6:4.
19:18 *work of men's hands.* For the foolishness and futility of idolatry see Ps 115:3–8; 135:15–18; Is 2:20; 40:19–20; 41:7; 44:9–20.
19:20 *I have heard.* On this occasion Isaiah's message to Hezekiah was unsolicited by the king (contrast v. 2).
19:21–28 The arrogance of the Assyrians and their ridicule of the Israelites and their God are countered with a derisive pronouncement of judgment (cf. Ps 2) on the misconceived Assyrian pride (see Is 10:5–34).
19:21 *virgin the daughter of Zion.* A personification of Jerusalem and its inhabitants.
19:22 *Holy One of Israel.* A designation of the God of Israel characteristic of Isaiah (see note on Is 1:4).
19:24 *dried up all the rivers of beseiged places.* A presumptuous boast for one who had not even conquered Egypt.
19:25 *I have formed it . . . Now have I brought it to pass.* The God of Israel is the ruler of all nations and history. The Assyrians attributed their victories to their own military superiority. However, Isaiah said that God alone ordained these victories (see Is 10:5–19; cf. Ezek 30:24–26).
19:27 *I know.* See Ps 121:8.
19:28 *hook in thy nose.* At the top of an Assyrian obelisk an Assyrian king (probably Esarhaddon, 681–669 B.C.) is pictured holding ropes attached to rings in the noses of four of his enemies. Here Isaiah portrays the same thing happening to Sennacherib (see note on Is 37:29; cf. Ezek 38:4; Amos 4:2).
19:29 *Ye shall eat this year such things as grow of themselves.* Sennacherib had apparently either destroyed or confiscated the entire harvest that had been sown the previous fall. The people would only have use of the later, second growth that came from seeds dropped from the previous year's harvest (see Lev 25:5). This suggests that Sennacherib came to Judah in March or April about the time of harvest. *the second year that which springeth of the same.* Sennacherib's departure would be too late in the fall (October) for new crops to be planted for the coming year. In the Holy Land crops are normally sown in September and October. *in the third year sow ye, and reap.* The routine times for sowing and harvesting could be observed in the following year. The third year is likely a reference to the third year of harvests detrimentally affected by the Assyrian presence.

30 [a]And [1]the remnant that is escaped of
the house of Judah
Shall *yet* again take root downward,
and bear fruit upward.
31 For out of Jerusalem shall go forth a
remnant,
And [1]they that escape out of mount
Zion:
[a]The zeal of the LORD *of hosts* shall do
this.
32 Therefore thus saith the LORD
concerning the king of Assyria,
He shall not come into this city,
Nor shoot an arrow there,
Nor come before it *with* shield,
Nor cast a bank against it.
33 By the way that he came, *by the same*
shall he return,
And shall not come into this city, saith
the LORD.
34 For [a]I will defend this city, to save it,
For mine own sake, and [b]for my
servant David's sake.
35 And [a]it came to pass that night, that the
angel of the LORD went out, and smote in the
camp of the Assyrians an hundred fourscore
and five thousand: and when they arose early
in the morning, behold, they *were* all dead
corpses.
36 So Sennacherib king of Assyria departed,
and went and returned, and dwelt at [a]Nineveh.
37 And it came to pass, as he was worshipping
in the house of Nisroch his god, that
[a]Adrammelech and Sharezer *his sons* [b]smote
him with the sword: and they escaped *into* the
land of [1]Armenia. And [c]Esarhaddon his son
reigned in his stead.

19:30 [1]Heb. *the escaping of the house of Judah that remaineth* [a]2 Chr. 32:22
19:31 [1]Heb. *the escaping* [a]Is. 9:7
19:34 [a]ch. 20:6 [b]1 Ki. 11:12
19:35 [a]Is. 37:36
19:36 [a]Gen. 10:11
19:37 [1]Heb. *Ararat* [a]2 Chr. 32:21 [b]ver. 7 [c]Ezra 4:2
20:1 [1]Heb. *Give charge concerning thine house* [a]Is. 38:1
20:3 [1]Heb. with *a great weeping* [a]Neh. 13:22
20:4 [1]Or, *city*
20:5 [a]1 Sam. 9:16; 10:1 [b]ch. 19:20; Ps. 65:2 [c]Ps. 39:12; 56:8
20:6 [a]ch. 19:34
20:7 [a]Is. 38:21
20:8 [a]See Judg. 6:17,37,39; Is. 7:11,14; 38:22
20:9 [a]See Is. 38:7,8

The sickness of Hezekiah

20 In [a]those days was Hezekiah sick
unto death. And the prophet Isaiah
the son of Amoz came to him, and said unto
him, Thus saith the LORD, [1]Set thine house in
order; for thou shalt die, and not live.
2 Then he turned his face to the wall, and
prayed unto the LORD, saying,
3 I beseech thee, O LORD, [a]remember now
how I have walked before thee in truth and
with a perfect heart, and have done *that* which
is good in thy sight. And Hezekiah wept [1]sore.
4 And it came to pass, afore Isaiah was
gone out *into* the middle [1]court, that the word
of the LORD came to him, saying,
5 Turn again, and tell Hezekiah [a]the captain
of my people, Thus saith the LORD, the
God of David thy father, [b]I have heard thy
prayer, I have seen [c]thy tears: behold, I will
heal thee: on the third day thou shalt go up
unto the house of the LORD.
6 And I will add unto thy days fifteen years;
and I will deliver thee and this city out of the
hand of the king of Assyria; and [a]I will defend
this city for mine own sake, and for my servant
David's sake.
7 And [a]Isaiah said, Take a lump of figs. And
they took and laid *it* on the boil, and he recovered.
8 And Hezekiah said unto Isaiah, [a]What
shall be the sign that the LORD will heal me,
and *that* I shall go up *into* the house of the
LORD the third day?
9 And Isaiah said, [a]This sign shalt thou
have of the LORD, that the LORD will do the
thing that he hath spoken: shall the shadow go
forward ten degrees, or go back ten degrees?

19:30–31 *remnant.* See note on v. 4. For use of the term "remnant" as a designation for those who will participate in the future unfolding of God's redemptive program see Is 11:11,16; 28:5; Mic 4:7; Rom 11:5.
19:32 *not come into this city.* Sennacherib, who was presently at Libnah (see v. 8; see also note on 8:22), would not be able to carry out his threats against Jerusalem (see note on 18:13).
19:34 *for my servant David's sake.* See note on 1 Ki 11:13.
19:35 *angel of the LORD.* See note on Gen 16:7. *an hundred fourscore and five thousand.* See Is 37:36.
19:36 *Nineveh.* The capital of the Assyrian empire.
‡19:37 *Nisroch.* The name of this deity does not appear in preserved Assyrian records. *Adrammelech and Sharezer his sons.* Ancient records refer to the murder of Sennacherib by an unnamed son on the 20th of the month of Tebet in the 23rd year of Sennacherib's reign. *Armenia* [Hebrew *Ararat*]. See note on Gen 8:4. *Esarhaddon his son reigned in his stead.* And reigned 681–669 B.C. Assyrian inscriptions speak of a struggle among Sennacherib's sons for the right of succession to the Assyrian throne. Sennacherib's designation of Esarhaddon as heir apparent, even though he was younger than several of his brothers, may have sparked the abortive attempt at a coup by Adrammelech and Sharezer.
20:1 *In those days.* Hezekiah's illness (vv. 1–11) as well as his reception of envoys from Babylon (vv. 12–19) must have preceded the Assyrian campaign in 701 B.C. (see v. 6; see also notes on vv. 12–13). Babylonian records indicate that Berodach-baladan (v. 12) died in Elam after being expelled from Babylon in 703. *Set thine house in order.* Arrangements of a testamentary nature needed to be made, especially with respect to throne succession. *thou shalt die.* Assuming that Hezekiah was 25 years old in 715 when he began his sole reign (see 18:2) and that his illness occurred a little more than 15 years prior to his death (see note on v. 6), he would have been about 37 or 38 years old at this time.
20:3 *walked before thee in truth . . . and have done that which is good.* Hezekiah's prayer is not an appeal for divine favor that is based on good works, but it expresses the realization that the Lord graciously favors those who earnestly serve Him (see note on 2 Sam 22:21).
20:5 *I will heal thee.* God is the one who sovereignly ordains all that comes to pass (Ps 139:16; Eph 1:11). Hezekiah's petition and God's response demonstrate that (1) divine sovereignty does not make prayer inappropriate but, on the contrary, it establishes it, and (2) both prayer and the divine response to prayer are to be included in one's conception of God's sovereign plan (see 1 Ki 21:29; Ezek 33:13–16).
20:6 *add unto thy days fifteen years.* Hezekiah died in 686 B.C. The beginning of the extension of his life is thus to be placed no later than 702. *for mine own sake, and for my servant David's sake.* See 19:34; see also note on 1 Ki 11:13.
20:7 *lump.* The Lord healed Hezekiah (see v. 5), but divine healing does not necessarily exclude the use of known remedies.
20:9 *degrees.* Hebrew "stairs," or "steps." See v. 11 (see also note on Is 38:8).

10 And Hezekiah answered, It is a light thing for the shadow to go down ten degrees: nay, but let the shadow return backward ten degrees.

11 And Isaiah the prophet cried unto the LORD: and [a]he brought the shadow ten degrees backward, by which it had gone down in the [1]dial of Ahaz.

Hezekiah's foolishness

12 ¶ [a]At that time [1]Berodach-baladan, the son of Baladan, king of Babylon, sent letters and a present unto Hezekiah: for he had heard that Hezekiah had been sick.

13 And [a]Hezekiah hearkened unto them, and shewed them all the house of his [1]precious things, the silver, and the gold, and the spices, and the precious ointment, and all the house of his [2]armour, and all that was found in his treasures: there was nothing in his house, nor in all his dominion, that Hezekiah shewed them not.

14 Then came Isaiah the prophet unto king Hezekiah, and said unto him, What said these men? and from whence came they unto thee? And Hezekiah said, They are come from a far country, *even* from Babylon.

15 And he said, What have they seen in thine house? And Hezekiah answered, [a]All *the things* that *are* in mine house have they seen: there is nothing among my treasures that I have not shewed them.

16 And Isaiah said unto Hezekiah, Hear the word of the LORD.

20:11 [1]Heb. *degrees* [a]See Is. 38:8
20:12 [1][Or, *Merodach-baladan*] [a]Is. 39:1
20:13 [1]Or, *spicery* [2]Or, *jewels.* Heb. *vessels* [a]2 Chr. 32:27,31
20:15 [a]ver. 13
20:17 [a]ch. 24:13; 25:13; Jer. 27:21; 52:17
20:18 [1][Fulfilled, Dan. 1:3] [a]ch. 24:12; 2 Chr. 33:11
20:19 [1]Or, *Shall there not be peace and truth, etc.* [a]1 Sam. 3:18; Job 1:21; Ps. 39:9
20:20 [a]2 Chr. 32:32 [b]Neh. 3:16 [c]2 Chr. 32:30
20:21 [a]2 Chr. 32:33
21:1 [a]2 Chr. 33:1
21:2 [a]ch. 16:3
21:3 [a]ch. 18:4

17 Behold, the days come, that all that *is* in thine house, and *that* which thy fathers have laid up in store unto this day, [a]shall be carried unto Babylon: nothing shall be left, saith the LORD.

18 And of thy sons that shall issue from thee, which thou shalt beget, [a]shall they take *away;* [1]and they shall be eunuchs in the palace of the king of Babylon.

19 Then said Hezekiah unto Isaiah, [a]Good *is* the word of the LORD which thou hast spoken. And he said, [1]*Is it* not *good,* if peace and truth be in my days?

20 [a]And the rest of the acts of Hezekiah, and all his might, and how he [b]made a pool, and a conduit, and [c]brought water into the city, *are* they not written in the book of the chronicles of the kings of Judah?

21 And [a]Hezekiah slept with his fathers: and Manasseh his son reigned in his stead.

Manasseh, king of Judah

21 Manasseh [a]*was* twelve years old when he *began* to reign, and reigned fifty and five years in Jerusalem. And his mother's name *was* Hephzi-bah.

2 And he did *that* which *was* evil in the sight of the LORD, [a]after the abominations of the heathen, whom the LORD cast out before the children of Israel.

3 For he built *up* again the high places [a]which Hezekiah his father had destroyed; and he reared up altars for Baal, and made a

---

‡20:12 *Berodach-baladan.* Some manuscripts and ancient versions read "Merodach-baladan" (see Is 39:1).The name means "(The god) Marduk has given me a son." He ruled in Babylon 721–710 B.C. before being forced to submit to Assyrian domination by Sargon II of Assyria. Sometime after Sargon's death in 705, Berodach-baladan briefly reestablished Babylonian independence and ruled in Babylon until Sennacherib forced him to flee in 703 (see note on v. 1). *sent letters and a present unto Hezekiah.* See 2 Chr 32:31; Is 39. It is likely that Berodach-baladan was attempting to draw Hezekiah into an alliance against Assyria. Although Hezekiah rejected the pro-Assyrian policies of his father Ahaz (see 16:7) and rebelled against Assyria (see 18:7), he erred in seeking to strengthen Israel's security by friendship with Babylon and Egypt (see 2 Chr 32:31; Is 30–31; see also notes on 1 Sam 17:11; 1 Ki 15:19).
20:13 *hearkened unto them, and shewed them all.* Hezekiah's reception of the delegation from Babylon was overly hospitable. Perhaps it was an attempt to bolster Judah's security by impressing the Babylonians with the wealth and power of his kingdom as a basis for mutual cooperation against the Assyrians. In principle this was a denial of the covenantal nature of the royal office in Israel (see note on 2 Sam 24:1). *silver . . . ointment.* The presence of these treasures in Jerusalem is evidence that this incident occurred before the payment of tribute to Sennacherib in 701 B.C. (see 18:15–16).
20:14 *What said these men . . . ?* Hezekiah gave no response to Isaiah's question concerning the diplomatic purpose of the Babylonian envoys.
20:17 *carried unto Babylon.* Hezekiah's reception of the Babylonians would bring the exact opposite of what he desired and expected. Isaiah's prediction of Babylonian exile at least 115 years before it happened is all the more remarkable because, when he spoke, it appeared that Assyria rather than Babylon was the world power from whom Judah had the most to fear.
20:18 *of thy sons . . . shall they take away.* Hezekiah's own son Manasseh was taken by the Assyrians and held prisoner for a while in Babylon (see 2 Chr 33:11); later, many more from the house of David were to follow (see 24:15; 25:7; Dan 1:3).
20:19 *Good is the word.* Although it is possible to understand Hezekiah's statement as a selfish expression of relief that he himself would not experience the announced adversity, it seems better to take it as a humble acceptance of the Lord's judgment (see 2 Chr 32:26) and as gratefulness for the intervening time of peace that the Lord in His mercy was granting to His people.
20:20 *a pool, and a conduit.* Hezekiah built a tunnel from the Gihon spring (see 1 Ki 1:33,38) to a cistern (2 Chr 32:30) inside the city's walls (see diagram No. 8 at the end of the study Bible). This greatly reduced Jerusalem's vulnerability to siege by guaranteeing a continuing water supply. In 1880 an inscription (the Siloam inscription; see chart, p. xix) was found in the rock wall at the entrance to this tunnel, describing the method of its construction. The tunnel, cut through solid rock, is over 1,700 feet long; its height varies from 3 2/3 feet to 11 1/2 feet and it averages 2 feet in width. *chronicles of the kings of Judah.* See note on 1 Ki 14:29.
20:21 *slept with his fathers.* See note on 1 Ki 1:21.
21:1 *twelve years old.* Manasseh was born after Hezekiah's serious illness (see 20:6). *fifty and five years.* 697–642 B.C., including a ten-year co-regency (697–686) with his father Hezekiah. This was the longest reign of any king in either Israel or Judah.
21:2 *abominations.* Manasseh reversed the religious policies of his father Hezekiah (see 18:3–5) and reverted to those of Ahaz (see 16:3).
21:3 *high places . . . Hezekiah . . . had destroyed.* See note on

grove, [b]as did Ahab king of Israel; and [c]worshipped all the host of heaven, and served them.

4 And [a]he built altars in the house of the LORD, of which the LORD said, [b]In Jerusalem will I put my name.

5 And he built altars for all the host of heaven in the two courts of the house of the LORD.

6 [a]And he made his son pass through the fire, and observed [b]times, and used enchantments, and dealt with familiar spirits and wizards: he wrought much wickedness in the sight of the LORD, to provoke *him* to anger.

7 And he set a graven image of the grove that he had made in the house, of which the LORD said to David, and to Solomon his son, [a]In this house, and in Jerusalem, which I have chosen out of all tribes of Israel, will I put my name for ever:

8 [a]Neither will I make the feet of Israel move any more out of the land which I gave their fathers; only if they will observe to do according to all that I have commanded them, and according to all the law that my servant Moses commanded them.

9 But they hearkened not: and Manasseh [a]seduced them to do more evil than did the nations whom the LORD destroyed before the children of Israel.

10 ¶ And the LORD spake by his servants the prophets, saying,

11 [a]Because Manasseh king of Judah hath done these abominations, [b]*and* hath done wickedly above all that the Amorites did, which *were* before him, and [c]hath made Judah also to sin with his idols:

12 Therefore thus saith the LORD God of Israel, Behold, I *am* bringing *such* evil upon Jerusalem and Judah, that whosoever heareth of it, both [a]his ears shall tingle.

13 And I will stretch over Jerusalem [a]the line of Samaria, and the plummet of the house of Ahab: and I will wipe Jerusalem as *a man* wipeth a dish, [1]wiping *it,* and turning *it* upside down.

14 And I will forsake the remnant of mine inheritance, and deliver them into the hand of their enemies; and they shall become a prey and a spoil to all their enemies;

15 Because they have done *that* which *was* evil in my sight, and have provoked me to anger, since the day their fathers came forth out of Egypt, even unto this day.

16 ¶ [a]Moreover Manasseh shed innocent blood very much, till he had filled Jerusalem [1]from one end to another; beside his sin where*with* he made Judah to sin, in doing *that* which *was* evil in the sight of the LORD.

17 Now [a]the rest of the acts of Manasseh, and all that he did, and his sin that he sinned, *are* they not written in the book of the chronicles of the kings of Judah?

18 And [a]Manasseh slept with his fathers, and was buried in the garden of his own house, in the garden of Uzza: and Amon his son reigned in his stead.

Amon, king of Judah

19 ¶ [a]Amon *was* twenty and two years old when he *began* to reign, and he reigned two years in Jerusalem. And his mother's name *was* Meshullemeth, the daughter of Haruz of Jotbah.

20 And he did *that* which *was* evil in the sight of the LORD, [a]as his father Manasseh did.

21 And he walked in all the way that his father walked *in,* and served the idols that his father served, and worshipped them:

22 And he [a]forsook the LORD God of his fathers, and walked not in the way of the LORD.

21:3 [b]1 Ki. 16:32 [c]Deut. 4:19; 17:3; ch. 17:16
21:4 [a]Jer. 32:34 [b]2 Sam. 7:13; 1 Ki. 8:29; 9:3
21:6 [a]Lev. 18:21; 20:2; ch. 16:3; 17:17 [b]Lev. 19:26,31; Deut. 18:10,11; ch. 17:17
21:7 [a]2 Sam. 7:13; 1 Ki. 8:29; 9:3; ch. 23:27; Jer. 32:34
21:8 [a]2 Sam. 7:10
21:9 [a]Prov. 29:12
21:11 [a]ch. 23:26,27; 24:3,4; Jer. 15:4 [b]1 Ki. 21:26 [c]ver. 9
21:12 [a]1 Sam. 3:11; Jer. 19:3
21:13 [1]Heb. *he wipeth and turneth* it *upon the face thereof* [a]See Is. 34:11; Lam. 2:8; Amos 7:7,8
21:16 [1]Heb. from *mouth to mouth* [a]ch. 24:4
21:17 [a]2 Chr. 33:11-19
21:18 [a]2 Chr. 33:20
21:19 [a]2 Chr. 33:21-23
21:20 [a]ver. 2
21:22 [a]1 Ki. 11:33

18:4; see also 2 Chr 31:1. *grove.* See 1 Ki 14:15,23; 15:13; 16:33. *as did Ahab.* Manasseh was the Ahab of Judah (see 1 Ki 16:30–33). *worshipped all the host of heaven.* See note on 17:16.

21:4 *In Jerusalem will I put My name.* See 1 Ki 8:20,29; 9:3.

21:6 *made his son pass through the fire.* See note on 16:3; see also 17:17. *observed times, and used enchantments.* See notes on 16:15; 17:17. *dealt with familiar spirits and wizards.* See Lev 19:31; Deut 18:11; 1 Sam 28:3,7–9 and notes.

21:7 *graven image of the grove.* See note on 1 Ki 14:15. *David.* See 2 Sam 7:13. *Solomon.* See 1 Ki 9:3. *chosen out of all tribes.* See 1 Ki 11:13,32,36.

21:9 *nations whom the LORD destroyed.* See 1 Ki 14:24; Deut 12:29–31; 31:3.

21:10 *his servants the prophets.* See 2 Chr 33:10,18.

21:11 *done wickedly above all that the Amorites did.* See note on 1 Ki 21:26.

21:12 *whosoever heareth of it, both his ears shall tingle.* See Jer 19:3.

21:13 *line . . . plummet.* Instruments normally associated with construction are used here as symbols of destruction (see Is 34:11; Amos 7:7–9,17).

21:14 *I will forsake.* In the sense of giving over to judgment (see Jer 12:7), not in the sense of abrogation of the covenant (see 1 Sam 12:22; Is 43:1–7). *remnant of mine inheritance.* Upon the destruction of the northern kingdom, Judah had become the remnant of the Lord's inheritance (see 1 Ki 8:51; Deut 4:20; 1 Sam 10:1; Ps 28:9; see also note on 2 Ki 19:4).

21:15 The history of Israel was a history of covenant breaking. With the reign of Manasseh the cup of God's wrath overflowed, and the judgment of exile from the land of promise (see note on 17:7–23) became inevitable (see 24:1–4).

21:16 *innocent blood.* A reference to godly people and perhaps even prophets who were martyred for opposition to Manasseh's evil practices (see vv. 10–11). According to a Jewish tradition (not otherwise substantiated) Isaiah was sawed in two during Manasseh's reign (cf. Heb 11:37).

21:17 *rest of the acts of Manasseh.* See 2 Chr 33:12–19. *chronicles of the kings of Judah.* See note on 1 Ki 14:29.

21:18 *slept with his fathers.* See note on 1 Ki 1:21. *Uzza.* Probably a shortened form of Uzziah (see 14:21–22 and 15:1–7, Azariah; 2 Chr 26, Uzziah).

21:19 *two years.* 642–640 B.C. *Jotbah.* Some identify it with the Jotbathah of Num 33:33–34 and Deut 10:7, near Ezion-geber. Others, including the church father Jerome, have located it in Judah.

21:20 *did . . . evil.* Amon did not share in the change of heart that characterized his father Manasseh in the last days of his life (see 2 Chr 33:12–19). He must have restored the idolatrous practices that Manasseh abolished because these were again in existence in the time of Josiah (see 23:5–7,12).

23 [a]And the servants of Amon conspired against him, and slew the king in his own house.

24 And the people of the land slew all them that had conspired against king Amon; and the people of the land made Josiah his son king in his stead.

25 Now the rest of the acts of Amon which he did, *are* they not written in the book of the chronicles of the kings of Judah?

26 And he was buried in his sepulchre in the garden of Uzza: and [a]Josiah his son reigned in his stead.

The book of the law found

22 Josiah [a]*was* eight years old when he *began* to reign, and he reigned thirty and one years in Jerusalem. And his mother's name *was* Jedidah, the daughter of Adaiah of [b]Boscath.

2 And he did *that* which *was* right in the sight of the LORD, and walked in all the way of David his father, and [a]turned not aside *to* the right hand or *to* the left.

3 [a]And it came to pass in the eighteenth year of king Josiah, *that* the king sent Shaphan the son of Azaliah, the son of Meshullam, the scribe, *to* the house of the LORD, saying,

4 Go up to Hilkiah the high priest, that he may sum the silver which is [a]brought *into* the house of the LORD, which [b]the keepers of the [1]door have gathered of the people:

5 And let them [a]deliver it into the hand of the doers of the work, that have the oversight of the house of the LORD: and let them give it to the doers of the work which *is* in the house of the LORD, to repair the breaches of the house,

6 Unto carpenters, and builders, and masons, and to buy timber and hewn stone to repair the house.

7 Howbeit [a]there was no reckoning made with them of the money that was delivered into their hand, because they dealt faithfully.

8 ¶ And Hilkiah the high priest said unto Shaphan the scribe, [a]I have found the book of the law in the house of the LORD. And Hilkiah gave the book to Shaphan, and he read it.

9 And Shaphan the scribe came to the king, and brought the king word again, and said, Thy servants have [1]gathered the money that was found in the house, and have delivered it into the hand of them that do the work, that have the oversight *of* the house of the LORD.

10 And Shaphan the scribe shewed the king, saying, Hilkiah the priest hath delivered me a book. And Shaphan read it before the king.

11 And it came to pass, when the king had heard the words of the book of the law, that he rent his clothes.

12 And the king commanded Hilkiah the priest, and Ahikam the son of Shaphan, and [1]Achbor the son of [2]Michaiah, and Shaphan the scribe, and Asahiah a servant of the king's, saying,

13 Go ye, inquire of the LORD for me, and for the people, and for all Judah, concerning the words of this book that is found: for great *is* [a]the wrath of the LORD that is kindled against us, because our fathers have not hearkened unto the words of this book, to do according unto all that which is written concerning us.

14 So Hilkiah the priest, and Ahikam, and Achbor, and Shaphan, and Asahiah, went unto Huldah the prophetess, the wife of Shallum the

21:23 [a]2 Chr. 33:24,25
21:26 [a]Mat. 1:10, called *Josias*
22:1 [a]2 Chr. 34:1 [b]Josh. 15:39
22:2 [a]Deut. 5:32
22:3 [a]2 Chr. 34:8
22:4 [1]Heb. *threshold* [a]ch. 12:4 [b]ch. 12:9
22:5 [a]ch. 12:11,12,14
22:7 [a]ch. 12:15
22:8 [a]Deut. 31:24; 2 Chr. 34:14
22:9 [1]Heb. *melted*
22:12 [1][*Abdon*, 2 Chr. 34:20] [2][Or, *Micah*]
22:13 [a]Deut. 29:27

21:23 *conspired against him.* Whether this palace revolt was motivated by religious or political considerations is not known.
21:24 *people of the land.* The citizenry in general (see 11:14,18; 14:21; 23:30). *slew all them that had conspired against king Amon.* It is not clear whether this counterinsurgency was motivated simply by loyalty to the house of David or by other factors.
21:25 *chronicles of the kings of Judah.* See note on 1 Ki 14:29.
21:26 *Uzza.* See note on v. 18.
22:1 *thirty and one years.* 640–609 B.C. (see note on 21:19). *Boscath.* Located in Judah in the vicinity of Lachish (see Josh 15:39).
22:2 *way of David his father.* See note on 18:3. Josiah was the last godly king of the Davidic line prior to the exile. Jeremiah, who prophesied during the time of Josiah (see Jer 1:2), spoke highly of him (Jer 22:15–16). Zephaniah also prophesied in the early days of his reign (Zeph 1:1).
22:3 *eighteenth year.* 622 B.C. Josiah was then 26 years old (see v. 1). He had begun to serve the Lord faithfully at the age of 16 (the 8th year of his reign, 2 Chr 34:3). When he was 20 years old (the 12th year of his reign, 2 Chr 34:3), he had already begun to purge the land of its idolatrous practices. *the scribe.* Probably refers back to Shaphan (see v. 12). For the duties of such a scribe see note on 2 Sam 8:17. Two additional individuals are mentioned as accompanying Shaphan in 2 Chr 34:8.
22:4 *Hilkiah.* Father of Azariah and grandfather of Seraiah, the high priest executed at the time of the destruction of Jerusalem by the Babylonians (see 25:18–20). It is unlikely that this Hilkiah was also the father of Jeremiah (see Jer 1:1). *silver ... the keepers of the door have gathered.* Josiah used the method devised by Joash for collecting funds for the restoration of the temple (see 12:1–16; 2 Chr 34:9).
22:5 *doers of the work, that have the oversight.* See 2 Chr 34:12–13.
22:8 *book of the law.* Some interpreters hold that this refers to a copy of the entire Pentateuch, while others understand it as a reference to a copy of part or all of Deuteronomy alone (see Deut 31:24,26; 2 Chr 34:14).
22:11 *rent his clothes.* See note on 18:37; contrast Josiah's reaction with that of Jehoiakim to the words of the scroll written by Jeremiah (see Jer 36:24). Perhaps the covenant curses of Lev 26 and/or Deut 28, climaxing with the threat of exile, were the statements that especially disturbed Josiah.
22:12 *Ahikam.* Father of Gedaliah, who was later to be appointed governor of Judah by Nebuchadnezzar (see 25:22; Jer 39:14). He was also the protector of Jeremiah when his life was threatened during the reign of Jehoiakim (see Jer 26:24). *Achbor.* His son Elnathan is mentioned in 24:8; Jer 26:22; 36:12. *Shaphan the scribe.* See note on v. 3.
‡22:14 *Huldah the prophetess.* Why the delegation sought out Huldah rather than Jeremiah or Zephaniah is not known. Perhaps it was merely a matter of her accessibility in Jerusalem.

son of [1]Tikvah, the son of [2]Harhas, keeper of the [3]wardrobe; (now she dwelt in Jerusalem [4]in the college;) and they communed with her.

15 And she said unto them, Thus saith the LORD God of Israel, Tell the man that sent you to me,

16 Thus saith the LORD, Behold, [a]I will bring evil upon this place, and upon the inhabitants thereof, *even* all the words of the book which the king of Judah hath read:

17 [a]Because they have forsaken me, and have burnt incense unto other gods, that they might provoke me to anger with all the works of their hands; therefore my wrath shall be kindled against this place, and shall not be quenched.

18 But to [a]the king of Judah which sent you to inquire of the LORD, thus shall ye say to him, Thus saith the LORD God of Israel, *As touching* the words which thou hast heard;

19 Because thine [a]heart was tender, and thou hast [b]humbled thyself before the LORD, when thou heardest what I spake against this place, and against the inhabitants thereof, that *they* should become [c]a desolation and [d]a curse, and hast rent thy clothes, and wept before me; I also have heard *thee,* saith the LORD.

20 Behold therefore, I will gather thee unto thy fathers, and thou [a]shalt be gathered into thy grave in peace; and thine eyes shall not see all the evil which I will bring upon this place. And they brought the king word again.

The renewal of the covenant

23 And [a]the king sent, and they gathered unto him all the elders of Judah and of Jerusalem.

2 And the king went up *into* the house of the LORD, and all the men of Judah and all the inhabitants of Jerusalem with him, and the priests, and the prophets, and all the people, [1]both small and great: and he read in their ears all the words of the book of the covenant [a]which was found in the house of the LORD.

3 And the king [a]stood by a pillar, and made a covenant before the LORD, to walk after the LORD, and to keep his commandments and his testimonies and his statutes with all *their* heart and all *their* soul, to perform the words of this covenant that were written in this book. And all the people stood to the covenant.

4 And the king commanded Hilkiah the high priest, and the priests of the second order; and the keepers of the door, to bring forth out of the temple of the LORD all the vessels that were made for Baal, and for [a]the grove, and for all the host of heaven: and he burnt them without Jerusalem in the fields of Kidron, and carried the ashes of them *unto* Beth-el.

5 And he [1]put down the [2]idolatrous priests, whom the kings of Judah had ordained to burn incense in the high places in the cities of Judah, and in the places round about Jerusalem; them also that burnt incense unto Baal, to the sun, and to the moon, and to the [3]planets, and to [a]all the host of heaven.

6 And he brought out the [a]grove from the house of the LORD, without Jerusalem, unto the brook Kidron, and burnt it at the brook Kidron, and stampt *it* small to powder, and cast the powder thereof upon [b]the graves of the children of the people.

7 And he brake down the houses [a]of the sodomites, that *were* by the house of the LORD, [b]where the women wove [1]hangings for the grove.

22:14 [1][*Tikvath,* 2 Chr. 34:22] [2][Or, *Hasrah*] [3]Heb. *garments* [4]Or, *in the second part*
22:16 [a]Deut. 29:27; Dan. 9:11-14
22:17 [a]Deut. 29:25-27
22:18 [a]2 Chr. 34:26
22:19 [a]Ps. 51:17; Is. 57:15 [b]1 Ki. 21:29 [c]Lev. 26:31,32 [d]Jer. 26:6; 44:22
22:20 [a]Ps. 37:37; Is. 57:1,2
23:1 [a]2 Chr. 34:29,30
23:2 [1]Heb. *from small even unto great* [a]ch. 22:8
23:3 [a]ch. 11:14,17
23:4 [a]ch. 21:3,7
23:5 [1]Heb. *caused to cease* [2]Heb. *Chemarim* [Hos. 10:5; Foretold, Zeph. 1:4] [3]Or, *twelve signs,* or, *constellations* [a]ch. 21:3
23:6 [a]ch. 21:7 [b]2 Chr. 34:4
23:7 [1]Heb. *houses* [a]1 Ki. 14:24; 15:12 [b]Ezek. 16:16

Shallum . . . keeper of the wardrobe. Perhaps the same Shallum who was the uncle of Jeremiah (see Jer 32:7). *college.* Lit. "in the second [quarter]." A section of the city probably located in a newly developed area between the first and second walls in the northwest part of Jerusalem (see 2 Chr 33:14; Zeph 1:10).

22:16 *this place.* Jerusalem.

22:19 *thine heart was tender.* See v. 11.

22:20 *gather thee unto thy fathers.* See note on 1 Ki 1:21. *thou shalt be gathered into thy grave in peace.* This prediction refers to Josiah's death before God's judgment on Jerusalem through Nebuchadnezzar and so is not contradicted by his death in battle with Pharaoh Neco of Egypt (see 23:29–30). Josiah was assured that the final judgment on Judah and Jerusalem would not come in his own days.

23:1 *elders.* See note on 10:1.

23:2 *book of the covenant.* Although this designation is used in Ex 24:7 with reference to the contents of Ex 20–23, it is here applied to either all or part of the book of Deuteronomy or the entire Mosaic law. Whatever else the scroll contained, it clearly included the covenant curses of Lev 26 and/or Deut 28 (see notes on v. 21; 22:8,11).

23:3 *pillar.* See note on 11:14. *made a covenant.* Josiah carries out the function of covenant mediator; cf. Moses (Ex 24:3–8; Deut 1–34), Joshua (Josh 24), Samuel (1 Sam 11:14–12:25) and Jehoiada (2 Ki 11:17). *walk after the LORD.* See notes on 1 Sam 12:14,20. *stood to the covenant.* It is likely that some sort of ratification rite was performed, in which the people participated and pledged by oath to be loyal to their covenant obligations. Whether this was done symbolically (see Jer 34:18) or verbally (see Deut 27:11–26) is not clear.

23:4 *keepers of the door.* See 12:9. *Baal, and for the grove.* See note on 1 Ki 14:15. *host of heaven.* See note on 17:16. *carried ashes of them unto Beth-el.* See vv. 15–16. Beth-el was located just over the border between Judah and the former northern kingdom in territory nominally under Assyrian control. With a decline in Assyrian power, Josiah was able to exert his own influence in the north. He apparently deposited the ashes at Beth-el in order to desecrate (see note on v. 14) the very place where golden calf worship had originally polluted the land (see notes on 1 Ki 12:28–30).

23:5 *idolatrous priests.* See Hos 10:5; Zeph 1:4. *kings of Judah.* A reference to Manasseh and Amon, and perhaps to Ahaz before them. *high places.* See note on 18:4.

23:6 *grove.* See note on 1 Ki 14:15. The Asherah destroyed by Hezekiah (18:4) was reintroduced by Manasseh (21:7). When Manasseh turned to the Lord, it is likely that he too got rid of the Asherah (see 2 Chr 33:15) and that it was then again reintroduced by Amon (2 Ki 21:21; 2 Chr 33:22). *cast the powder thereof upon the graves of the children of the people.* Intended as a defilement of the goddess, not as a desecration of the graves of the poor (see Jer 26:23).

23:7 *sodomites.* I.e. male cult prostitutes. See note on 1 Ki 14:24.

8 And he brought all the priests out of the
cities of Judah, and defiled the high places
where the priests had burnt incense, from
[a]Geba to Beer-sheba, and brake down the high
places of the gates that *were in* the entering in
of the gate of Joshua the governor of the city,
which *were* on a man's left hand at the gate of
the city.
9 [a]Nevertheless the priests of the high
places came not up to the altar of the LORD in
Jerusalem, [b]but they did eat of the unleavened
bread among their brethren.
10 And he defiled [a]Topheth, which *is* in
[b]the valley of the children of Hinnom, [c]that no
man might make his son or his daughter to
pass through the fire to Molech.
11 And he took away the horses that the
kings of Judah had given to the sun, at the entering in of the house of the LORD, by the
chamber of Nathan-melech the [1]chamberlain,
which *was* in the suburbs, and burnt the chariots of the sun with fire.
12 And the altars that *were* [a]on the top of
the upper chamber of Ahaz, which the kings
of Judah had made, and the altars which [b]Ma-
nasseh had made in the two courts of the
house of the LORD, did the king beat down,
and [1]brake *them* down from thence, and cast
the dust of them into the brook Kidron.
13 And the high places that *were* before Jerusalem, which *were* on the right hand of [1]the
mount of corruption, which [a]Solomon the
king of Israel had builded for Ashtoreth the
abomination of the Zidonians, and for Chemosh the abomination of the Moabites, and
for Milcom the abomination of the children of
Ammon, did the king defile.
14 And he [a]brake in pieces the [1]images,
and cut down the groves, and filled their
places *with* the bones of men.
15 ¶ Moreover the altar that *was* at Beth-el,
and the high place [a]which Jeroboam the son of
Nebat, who made Israel to sin, had made, both
that altar and the high place he brake down,
and burnt the high place, *and* stampt *it* small
to powder, and burnt the grove.
16 And as Josiah turned himself, he spied
the sepulchres that *were* there in the mount,
and sent, and took the bones out of the sepulchres, and burnt *them* upon the altar, and polluted it, according to the [a]word of the LORD
which the man of God proclaimed, who proclaimed these words.
17 Then he said, What title *is* that that I
see? And the men of the city told him, *It is*
[a]the sepulchre of the man of God, which came
from Judah, and proclaimed these things that
thou hast done against the altar of Beth-el.
18 And he said, Let him alone; let no man
move his bones. So they let his bones [1]alone,
with the bones of [a]the prophet that came out
of Samaria.
19 And all the houses also of the high
places that *were* [a]in the cities of Samaria,
which the kings of Israel had made to provoke
the LORD to anger, Josiah took away, and did to
them according to all the acts that he had done
in Beth-el.
20 And [a]he [b][1]slew all the priests of the
high places that *were* there upon the altars,
and [c]burnt men's bones upon them, and returned *to* Jerusalem.
21 ¶ And the king commanded all the people, saying, [a]Keep the passover unto the LORD

23:8 [a]1 Ki. 15:22
23:9 [a]See Ezek. 44:10-14 [b]1 Sam. 2:36
23:10 [a]Is. 30:33; Jer. 7:31; 19:6,11-13 [b]Josh. 15:8 [c]Lev. 18:21; Deut. 18:10; Ezek. 23:37,39
23:11 [1]Or, *eunuch,* or, *officer*
23:12 [1]Or, *ran from thence* [a]See Jer. 19:13; Zeph. 1:5 [b]ch. 21:5
23:13 [1]That is, the mount of Olives [a]1 Ki. 11:7
23:14 [1]Heb. *statues* [a]Ex. 23:24; Deut. 7:5,25
23:15 [a]1 Ki. 12:28,33
23:16 [a]1 Ki. 13:2
23:17 [a]1 Ki. 13:1,30
23:18 [1]Heb. *to escape* [a]1 Ki. 13:31
23:19 [a]See 2 Chr. 34:6,7
23:20 [1]Or, *sacrificed* [a]1 Ki. 13:2 [b]Ex. 22:20; 1 Ki. 18:40; ch. 11:18 [c]2 Chr. 34:5
23:21 [a]2 Chr. 35:1

23:8 *defiled the high places.* See note on 18:4. *Geba to Beer-sheba.* Geba was on the northern border of the southern kingdom (see 1 Ki 15:22), and Beer-sheba was on its southern border (see note on 1 Sam 3:20).

23:9 *did eat of the unleavened bread among their brethren.* Although not permitted to serve at the temple altar, these priests were to be sustained by a share of the priestly provisions (see Lev 2:10; 6:16–18). They occupied a status similar to that of priests with physical defects (see Lev 21:16–23).

23:10 *Topheth.* The name of an area in the valley of Hinnom where altars used for child sacrifice were located (see Is 30:33; Jer 7:31; 19:5–6). *make his son or his daughter to pass through the fire.* See 17:17; 21:6; see also note on 16:3. *Molech.* See note on 1 Ki 11:5.

23:11 *horses . . . given to the sun.* If live, the horses may have been used to pull chariots bearing images of a sun-god in religious processions. Small images of horses have recently been found in a cult place just outside one of the ancient walls of Jerusalem. *Nathan-melech.* Perhaps the official in charge of the chariots.

23:12 *altars . . . on the top.* Altars dedicated to the worship of all the starry hosts (see Jer 19:13; Zeph 1:5)—erected by Ahaz (2 Ki 16:3–4,10–16), Manasseh (21:3) and Amon (21:21–22).

23:13 *high places . . . Solomon . . . had builded.* See note on 1 Ki 11:5.

23:14 *filled their places with the bones of men.* The bones would defile these sites and make them unsuitable for cultic use in the future (see Num 19:16).

23:15 *altar that was at Beth-el.* See 1 Ki 12:32–33. Nothing is said of the golden calf, which undoubtedly had been sent to Assyria as tribute at the time of the captivity of the northern kingdom (see Hos 10:5–6).

23:16 *sepulchres.* Of the priests of the Beth-el sanctuary (see 1 Ki 13:2). *burnt them upon the altar, and polluted it.* See notes on vv. 6,14. *the man of God . . . who proclaimed these words.* See 1 Ki 13:1–2,32.

23:18 *prophet that came out of Samaria.* See 1 Ki 13:31–32. Samaria is here not to be understood as the city by that name since the prophet came from Beth-el (see 1 Ki 13:11), and the city Samaria did not yet exist (see 1 Ki 16:24). Rather, it is to be taken as a designation for the entire area of the former northern kingdom (see notes on 17:24,29; 1 Ki 13:32).

23:20 *he slew all the priests of the high places.* These were non-Levitical priests of the apostate worship practiced in the area of the former northern kingdom (see notes on 17:27–28, 33–34). They were treated like the pagan priests of Judah (see v. 5) in contrast to Josiah's treatment of the priests at the high places in Judah (see vv. 8–9). Josiah's actions in this matter conformed to the requirements of Deut 13; 17:2–7.

23:21 *Keep the passover.* A more complete description of this observance is found in 2 Chr 35:1–19. *as it is written in the book of this covenant.* See note on v. 2. This appears to refer to Deut 16:1–8, where the passover is described in a communal setting at a sanctuary (see Ex 23:15–17; 34:23–24; Lev 23:4–14) rather than in the family setting of Ex 12:1–14,43–49.

your God, [b]as it is written in the book of this covenant.

22 Surely [a]there was not holden such a passover from the days of the judges that judged Israel, nor *in* all the days of the kings of Israel, nor of the kings of Judah;

23 But in the eighteenth year of king Josiah, *wherein* this passover was holden to the LORD in Jerusalem.

24 Moreover the *workers with* familiar spirits, and the wizards, and the [a][1]images, and the idols, and all the abominations that were spied in the land of Judah and in Jerusalem, did Josiah put away, that he might perform the words of [b]the law which were written in the book that Hilkiah the priest found *in* the house of the LORD.

25 [a]And like unto him was there no king before him, that turned to the LORD with all his heart, and with all his soul, and with all his might, according to all the law of Moses; neither after him arose there *any* like him.

26 Notwithstanding the LORD turned not from the fierceness of his great wrath, wherewith his anger was kindled against Judah, [a]because of all the [1]provocations that Manasseh had provoked him withal.

27 And the LORD said, I will remove Judah also out of my sight, as [a]I have removed Israel, and will cast off this city Jerusalem which I have chosen, and the house of which I said, [b]My name shall be there.

28 Now the rest of the acts of Josiah, and all that he did, *are* they not written in the book of the chronicles of the kings of Judah?

23:21 [b]Ex. 12:3; Lev. 23:5; Num. 9:2; Deut. 16:2
23:22 [a]2 Chr. 35:18,19
23:24 [1]Or, *teraphim* [a]Gen. 31:19 [b]Lev. 19:31; 20:27; Deut. 18:11
23:25 [a]ch. 18:5
23:26 [1]Heb. *angers* [a]ch. 21:11,12; 24:3,4; Jer. 15:4
23:27 [a]ch. 17:18,20; 18:11; 21:13 [b]1 Ki. 8:29; 9:3; ch. 21:4,7
23:29 [a]2 Chr. 35:20 [b]Zech. 12:11 [c]ch. 14:8
23:30 [a]2 Chr. 35:24 [b]2 Chr. 36:1
23:31 [1][Called *Shallum,* 1 Chr. 3:15; Jer. 22:11] [a]ch. 24:18
23:33 [1]Or, *because he reigned* [2]Heb. *set a mulct upon the land* [a]ch. 25:6; Jer. 52:27 [b]2 Chr. 36:3
23:34 [a]2 Chr. 36:4 [b]ch. 24:17; Dan. 1:7 [c]Mat. 1:11, called *Jakim* [d]Jer. 22:11; Ezek. 19:3
23:35 [a]ver. 33

29 [a]In his days Pharaoh-nechoh king of Egypt went up against the king of Assyria to the river Euphrates: and king Josiah went against him; and he slew him at [b]Megiddo, when he [c]had seen him.

30 [a]And his servants carried him *in a chariot* dead from Megiddo, and brought him *to* Jerusalem, and buried him in his own sepulchre. And [b]the people of the land took Jehoahaz the son of Josiah, and anointed him, and made him king in his father's stead.

Jehoahaz, king of Judah

31 ¶ [1]Jehoahaz *was* twenty and three years old when he *began* to reign; and he reigned three months in Jerusalem. And his mother's name *was* [a]Hamutal, the daughter of Jeremiah of Libnah.

32 And he did *that* which *was* evil in the sight of the LORD, according to all that his fathers had done.

33 And Pharaoh-nechoh put him in bands [a]at Riblah in the land of Hamath, [1]that *he* might not reign in Jerusalem; and [b][2]put the land to a tribute of an hundred talents of silver, and a talent of gold.

34 And [a]Pharaoh-nechoh made Eliakim the son of Josiah king in the room of Josiah his father, and [b]turned his name *to* [c]Jehoiakim, and took Jehoahaz *away:* [d]and he came *to* Egypt, and died there.

35 And Jehoiakim gave [a]the silver and the gold to Pharaoh; but he taxed the land to give the money according to the commandment of Pharaoh: he exacted the silver and the gold of

23:22 The uniqueness of Josiah's passover celebration seems to be in the fact that all the passover lambs were slaughtered exclusively by the Levites (see 2 Chr 35:1–19; cf. 2 Chr 30:2–3, 17–20 for the passover observed in the time of Hezekiah).
23:23 *eighteenth year.* See note on 22:3.
‡23:24 *images.* Hebrew *teraphim.* See note on Gen 31:19. *words of the law.* See notes on v. 2; 22:8.
23:25 *like unto him was there no king.* See note on 18:5. *with all his heart . . . soul, and . . . might.* See Dt 6:5.
23:26 *Notwithstanding the LORD turned not from the fierceness of his great wrath.* The judgment against Judah and Jerusalem was postponed but not rescinded because of Josiah's reformation (see notes on 21:15; 22:20).
23:27 *as I have removed Israel.* See 17:18–23. *this city Jerusalem which I have chosen.* See 21:4,7,13. *the house of which I said, My name shall be there.* See note on 1 Ki 8:16.
23:28 *chronicles of the kings of Judah.* See note on 1 Ki 14:29.
‡23:29 *Pharaoh-nechoh king of Egypt.* Ruled 610–595 B.C. *went up against* [better translated "to"] *the king of Assyria.* Pharaoh Neco intended to help Ashur-uballit II, the last Assyrian king, in his struggle against the rising power of Babylon under Nabopolassar. The Assyrian capital, Nineveh, had already fallen to the Babylonians and Medes in 612 (see the book of Nahum). The remaining Assyrian forces had regrouped at Haran, but in 609 they were forced west of the Euphrates. It appears to be at this time that the Egyptians under Neco were coming to the Assyrians' aid. *king Josiah went against him.* Perhaps Josiah opposed the passage of Neco's army through the pass at Megiddo (see 2 Chr 35:20–24) because he feared that the growth of either Egyptian or Assyrian power would have adverse results for the continued independence of Judah.
23:30 *buried him in his own sepulchre.* See 2 Chr 35:24–25. *people of the land.* See note on 21:24. *Jehoahaz the son of Josiah.* Jehoahaz's name was originally Shallum (see 1 Chr 3:15; Jer 22:11), which was probably changed to Jehoahaz at the time of his accession to the throne. Perhaps Jehoahaz was chosen by the people over Jehoiakim because it was known that Jehoiakim favored a pro-Egyptian policy instead of the anti-Egyptian policy of Josiah and Jehoahaz. *anointed him.* See note on 1 Sam 9:16.
23:31 *three months.* In 609 B.C. *Jeremiah.* Not the prophet (see Jer 1:1). *Libnah.* See note on 8:22.
23:32 *evil . . . according to . . . his fathers.* See 16:3; 21:2,21; Ezek 19:3.
23:33 *put him in bands at Riblah.* By either deception or overt force the Egyptians were able to take Jehoahaz captive and impose tribute on Judah (see 2 Chr 36:3). Jehoahaz was imprisoned at Neco's military headquarters established at Riblah on the Orontes River. Nebuchadnezzar was later to make his headquarters at the same place (see 25:6,20).
23:34 *Eliakim the son of Josiah.* Eliakim was an older brother of Jehoahaz (see 1 Chr 3:15). Perhaps he had been bypassed earlier as a successor to Josiah because of a pro-Egyptian political stance. *turned his name to Jehoiakim.* The meaning of these two names is similar (Eliakim, "God has established"; Jehoiakim, "Yahweh has established"). Perhaps Neco wanted to use the name change to imply that his actions were sanctioned by Yahweh, the God of Judah (see 18:25; 2 Chr 35:21). In any case, the change in name indicated that Jehoiakim was subject to Neco's authority. *took Jehoahaz . . . to Egypt, and died there.* See 2 Chr 36:4; Jer 22:10–12.

the people of the land, of every one according
to his taxation, to give *it* unto Pharaoh-
nechoh.

Jehoiakim, king of Judah

36 ¶ [a]Jehoiakim *was* twenty and five year
old when he *began* to reign; and he reigned
eleven years in Jerusalem. And his mother's
name *was* Zebudah, the daughter of Pedaiah of
Rumah.
37 And he did *that* which *was* evil in the
sight of the LORD, according to all that his fathers had done.
24 In [a]his days Nebuchadnezzar king of
Babylon came up, and Jehoiakim became his servant three years: then he turned
and rebelled against him.
2 [a]And the LORD sent against him bands of
the Chaldees, and bands of the Syrians, and
bands of the Moabites, and bands of the children of Ammon, and sent them against Judah
to destroy it, [b]according to the word of the
LORD, which he spake [1]by his servants the
prophets.
3 Surely at the commandment of the LORD
came *this* upon Judah, to remove *them* out of
his sight, [a]for the sins of Manasseh, according
to all that he did;
4 [a]And also *for* the innocent blood that he
shed: for he filled Jerusalem *with* innocent
blood; which the LORD would not pardon.
5 Now the rest of the acts of Jehoiakim,
and all that he did, *are* they not written in the
book of the chronicles of the kings of Judah?
6 [a]So Jehoiakim slept with his fathers: and
Jehoiachin his son reigned in his stead.
7 And [a]the king of Egypt came not again
any more out of his land: for [b]the king of Babylon had taken from the river of Egypt unto
the river Euphrates all that pertained to the
king of Egypt.

Jehoiachin, king of Judah

8 ¶ [a][1]Jehoiachin *was* eighteen years old
when he *began* to reign, and he reigned in Jerusalem three months. And his mother's name
was Nehushta, the daughter of Elnathan of Jerusalem.
9 And he did *that* which *was* evil in the
sight of the LORD, according to all that his father had done.
10 [a]At that time the servants of Nebuchadnezzar king of Babylon came up *against* Jerusalem, and the city [1]was besieged.
11 And Nebuchadnezzar king of Babylon
came against the city, and his servants *did* besiege it.
12 [a]And Jehoiachin the king of Judah went
out to the king of Babylon, he, and his mother,
and his servants, and his princes, and his [1]of-
ficers: [b]and the king of Babylon [c]took him [d]in
the eighth year of [2]his reign.
13 [a]And he carried out thence all the treasures of the house of the LORD, and the trea-

23:36 [a]2 Chr. 36:5
24:1 [a]2 Chr. 36:6; Jer. 25:1,9; Dan. 1:1
24:2 [1]Heb. *by the hand of* [a]Jer. 25:9; 32:28; Ezek. 19:8 [b]ch. 20:17; 21:12-14; 23:27
24:3 [a]ch. 21:2,11; 23:26
24:4 [a]ch. 21:16
24:6 [a]See 2 Chr. 36:6,8; Jer. 22:18; 36:30
24:7 [a]Jer. 37:5,7 [b]Jer. 46:2
24:8 [1][Called *Jeconiah,* 1 Chr. 3:16; Jer. 24:1. And *Coniah,* Jer. 22:24,28] [a]2 Chr. 36:9
24:10 [1]Heb. *came into siege* [a]Dan. 1:1
24:12 [1]Or, *eunuchs* [2][*Nebuchadnezzar's* eighth year, Jer. 25:1] [a]Jer. 24:1; 29:1,2; Ezek. 17:12 [b]*Nebuchadnezzar's* eighth year; Jer. 25:1 [c]ch. 25:27 [d]Jer. 52:28
24:13 [a]ch. 20:17; Is. 39:6

23:35 *of the people of the land.* The tribute for Neco was raised by a graduated tax placed on the very people who had supported the kingship of Jehoahaz (see v. 30). Menahem of the northern kingdom had used a similar method of raising funds for tribute (see 15:20).

23:36 *eleven years.* 609–598 B.C.

23:37 *did . . . evil in the sight of the LORD.* Jehoiakim was responsible for the murder of the prophet Uriah from Kirjath-jearim (Jer 26:20–24), and his rule was characterized by dishonesty, oppression and injustice (see Jer 22:13–19). He reintroduced idolatrous worship in the temple (see Ezek 8:5–17) and refused to accept the word of the Lord through Jeremiah (see Jer 36). *his fathers.* Manasseh (21:1–18) and Amon (21:19–26).

24:1 *Nebuchadnezzar.* Means "O (god) Nabu, protect my son!" He was the son of Nabopolassar (see note on 23:29) and the most powerful king of the Neo-Babylonian empire (612–539 B.C.), reigning 605–562 (see Dan 1–4). *came up.* In 605 Nebuchadnezzar, the crown prince and commander of the Babylonian army, defeated Pharaoh Neco and the Egyptians at the battle of Carchemish and again at Hamath (see 23:29; Jer 46:2). These victories had far-reaching implications in the geopolitical power structure of the eastern Mediterranean world. Nebuchadnezzar went on to conquer all of the "Hatti-country," which, according to Babylonian records, included the "city of Judah." Daniel was among the Judahite hostages taken at this time (see Dan 1:1). Perhaps as early as Sept. 6, 605, Nebuchadnezzar acceded to the Babylonian throne upon the death of his father. *three years.* Probably 604–602. In 604 Nebuchadnezzar returned to the west and took tribute from "all the kings of Hatti-land." It is likely that Jehoiakim was included among these kings. *turned and rebelled.* In 601 Nebuchadnezzar again marched west against Egypt and was repulsed by strong Egyptian resistance. This may have encouraged Jehoiakim's rebellion, even though Jeremiah had warned against it (see Jer 27:9–11).

24:2 *the LORD sent against him . . . Chaldees . . . Syrians . . . Moabites . . . Ammon.* Reaction to Jehoiakim's rebellion was swift. Babylonian (Chaldean) troops, perhaps garrisoned in Aram, along with troops of other loyal vassals, were sent to put down the Judahite rebellion.

24:3 *sins of Manasseh.* See 21:11–12; 23:26–27; Jer 15:3–4.

24:4 *innocent blood.* See note on 21:16. *would not pardon.* See 22:17.

24:5 *chronicles of the kings of Judah.* See note on 1 Ki 14:29.

24:6 *slept with his fathers.* See note on 1 Ki 1:21. Jehoiakim died shortly before Jerusalem fell to the Babylonian siege (see vv. 8–12). Whether his death was due to natural causes or political intrigue is not indicated.

24:7 *the king of Egypt came not again any more out of his land.* This was due to the Egyptian defeat at Carchemish (see Jer 46:2) in 605 B.C., and it explains why Jehoiakim received no help from Egypt in his rebellion against the Babylonians. *river of Egypt.* See note on 1 Ki 8:65.

24:8 *three months.* In 598–597 B.C. Babylonian records place the fall of Jerusalem to Nebuchadnezzar on Mar. 16, 597. This means that the three-month and ten-day reign (see 2 Chr 36:9–10) of Jehoiachin began in December, 598.

24:9 *according to all that his father had done.* See 23:37; Jer 22:20–30.

24:11 *Nebuchadnezzar king . . . came against the city.* Babylonian records say that Nebuchadnezzar "encamped against the city of Judah, and on the second day of the month of Addaru [i.e. Mar. 16, 597 B.C.] he seized the city and captured the king."

24:12 *eighth year.* April, 597 B.C. (see 2 Chr 36:10; see also note on Jer 52:28, where a different system of dating is reflected).

sures of the king's house, and [b]cut in pieces all
the vessels of gold which Solomon king of Israel had made in the temple of the LORD, [c]as
the LORD had said.
14 And [a]he carried away all Jerusalem, and
all the princes, and all the mighty *men* of valour, [b]*even* ten thousand captives, and [c]all the
craftsmen and smiths: none remained, save
[d]the poorest sort of the people of the land.
15 And [a]he carried away Jehoiachin to
Babylon, and the king's mother, and the king's
wives, and his [1]officers, and the mighty of the
land, *those* carried he *into* captivity from Jerusalem to Babylon.
16 And [a]all the men of might, *even* seven
thousand, and craftsmen and smiths a thousand, all *that were* strong *and* apt for war, even
them the king of Babylon brought captive to
Babylon.
17 And [a]the king of Babylon made Mattaniah [b]his father's brother king in his stead,
and [c]changed his name *to* Zedekiah.

Zedekiah, king of Judah

18 ¶ [a]Zedekiah *was* twenty and one years
old when he *began* to reign, and he reigned
eleven years in Jerusalem. And his mother's
name *was* [b]Hamutal, the daughter of Jeremiah
of Libnah.
19 [a]And he did *that* which *was* evil in the
sight of the LORD, according to all that Jehoiakim had done.
20 For through the anger of the LORD it
came to pass in Jerusalem and Judah, until he
had cast them out from his presence, [a]that
Zedekiah rebelled against the king of Babylon.

24:13 [b]Dan. 5:2,3 [c]Jer. 20:5
24:14 [a]Jer. 24:1 [b]Jer. 52:28 [c]1 Sam. 13:19, 22 [d]ch. 25:12
24:15 [1]Or, *eunuchs* [a]2 Chr. 36:10; Esth. 2:6; Jer. 22:24
24:16 [a]Jer. 52:28
24:17 [a]Jer. 37:1 [b]1 Chr. 3:15; 2 Chr. 36:10 [c]2 Chr. 36:4
24:18 [a]2 Chr. 36:11; Jer. 52:1 [b]ch. 23:31
24:19 [a]2 Chr. 36:12
24:20 [a]2 Chr. 36:13; Ezek. 17:15
25:1 [a]2 Chr. 36:17; Jer. 34:2; Ezek. 24:1
25:3 [a]Jer. 39:2
25:4 [a]Jer. 39:2 [b]Jer. 39:4-7; Ezek. 12:12
25:6 [1]Heb. *spake judgment with him* [a]ch. 23:33; Jer. 52:9
25:7 [1]Heb. *made blind* [a]Jer. 39:7
25:8 [1]Or, *chief marshal* [a]Jer. 52:12 [b]ch. 24:12 [c]Jer. 39:9
25:9 [a]2 Chr. 36:19 [b]Jer. 39:8; Amos 2:5

Jerusalem destroyed

25 And it came to pass [a]in the ninth
year of his reign, in the tenth month,
in the tenth *day* of the month, *that* Nebuchadnezzar king of Babylon came, he, and all his
host, against Jerusalem, and pitched against it;
and they built forts against it round about.
2 And the city was besieged unto the
eleventh year of king Zedekiah.
3 And on the ninth *day* of the [a]*fourth*
month the famine prevailed in the city, and
there was no bread for the people of the land.
4 And [a]the city was broken up, and all the
men of war *fled* by night *by* the way of the gate
between two walls, which *is* by the king's garden: (now the Chaldees *were* against the city
round about:) and [b]*the king* went the way toward the plain.
5 And the army of the Chaldees pursued after the king, and overtook him in the plains of
Jericho: and all his army were scattered from
him.
6 So they took the king, and brought him
up to the king of Babylon [a]to Riblah; and they
[1]gave judgment upon him.
7 And they slew the sons of Zedekiah before his eyes, and [a][1]put out the eyes of Zedekiah, and bound him with fetters of brass, and
carried him *to* Babylon.
8 ¶ And in the fifth month, [a]on the seventh
day of the month, which *is* [b]the nineteenth
year of king Nebuchadnezzar king of Babylon,
[c]came Nebuzar-adan, [1]captain of the guard, a
servant of the king of Babylon, *unto* Jerusalem:
9 [a]And he burnt the house of the LORD,
[b]and the king's house, and all the houses of

24:13 *as the LORD had said.* See 20:13,17.
24:14 *ten thousand.* This figure may include the 7,000 fighting men and 1,000 craftsmen mentioned in v. 16 (see note on Jer 52:28, where a different number of captives is mentioned).
24:15 *carried away Jehoiachin to Babylon.* Fulfilling Jeremiah's prophecy (Jer 22:24–27; see 2 Ki 25:27–30).
24:17 *Mattaniah his father's brother.* Mattaniah was a son of Josiah (see 1 Chr 3:15; Jer 1:3) and brother of Jehoiachin's father, Jehoiakim. *changed his name to Zedekiah.* Mattaniah's name (meaning "gift of Yahweh") was changed to Zedekiah ("righteousness of Yahweh"). Perhaps Nebuchadnezzar wanted to imply that his actions against Jerusalem and Jehoiachin were just. In any case, the name change signified subjection to Nebuchadnezzar (see note on 23:34).
24:18 *eleven years.* 597–586 B.C. *Jeremiah.* See note on 23:31. *Libnah.* See note on 8:22.
24:19 *did . . . evil . . . according to all that Jehoiakim had done.* See note on 23:37. During Zedekiah's reign idolatrous practices continued to increase in Jerusalem (see 2 Chr 36:14; Ezek 8–11). He was a weak and indecisive ruler (see Jer 38:5,19), who refused to heed the word of the Lord given through Jeremiah (2 Chr 36:12).
24:20 *Zedekiah rebelled.* Most interpreters link Zedekiah's revolt with the succession to the Egyptian throne in 589 B.C. of the ambitious pharaoh Apries (Hophra). Zedekiah had sworn allegiance to Nebuchadnezzar (Ezek 17:13), he had sent envoys to Babylon (see Jer 29:3), and he had made a personal visit (see Jer 51:59). However, he seems to have capitulated to the seductive propaganda of the anti-Babylonian and pro-Egyptian faction in Jerusalem (see Jer 37:5; Ezek 17:15–16) in a tragically miscalculated effort to gain independence from Babylon.
25:1 *ninth year . . . tenth month . . . tenth day.* Jan. 15, 588 B.C. (see Jer 39:1; 52:4; Ezek 24:1–2). *Nebuchadnezzar . . . came . . . against Jerusalem.* Earlier, Nebuchadnezzar had subdued all the fortified cities in Judah except Lachish and Azekah (see Jer 34:7). A number of Hebrew inscriptions on potsherds were found at Lachish in 1935 and 1938. These Lachish ostraca (or letters; see chart, p. xix) describe conditions at Lachish and Azekah during the Babylonian siege.
25:2–3 *eleventh year . . . ninth day . . . fourth month.* July 18, 586 B.C. (see Jer 39:2; 52:5–7). Some scholars follow a different dating system and place the fall of Jerusalem in the summer of 587.
25:3 *famine prevailed in the city.* See Jer 38:2–9.
25:6 *king of Babylon to Riblah.* See note on 23:33; see also Jer 39:5; 52:9.
25:7 *slew the sons of Zedekiah . . . put out the eyes of Zedekiah . . . carried him to Babylon.* See Jer 32:4–5; 34:2–3; 38:18; 39:6–7; 52:10–11. Ezekiel (12:13) had predicted that Zedekiah would be brought to Babylon, but that he would not see it. Zedekiah could have spared his own life and prevented the destruction of Jerusalem if he had listened to Jeremiah (see Jer 38:14–28).
25:8 *fifth month . . . seventh day . . . nineteenth year.* Aug. 14, 586 B.C. (see Jer 52:12).
25:9 *burnt the house of the LORD.* See 2 Chr 36:19; Jer 39:8; 52:13.

Nebuchadnezzar's Campaigns against Judah

605–586 B.C.

Events in Judah moved swiftly following the death of Josiah. Pharaoh Neco pressed his advantage by deporting the new ruler and appointing a second son of Josiah, Jehoiakim, as king.

The Persian conquest of Lydia in 546 B.C. brought the Greeks into conflict with Persia, a series of events chronicled in great detail by Herodotus.

The prophet Jeremiah was taken to Egypt by Judahite refugees fleeing from Babylonian-controlled territory. They brought him to Tahpanhes, where he continued his prophecies.

LYDIA
Great Sea
Haran
Tiphsah
Hamath
Riblah
Sidon
Tyre
Tahpanhes
Migdol
JUDAH
AMMON
Jerusalem
KEDAR
EDOM
Brook of Egypt
On
Memphis
EGYPT

CONQUEST OF JERUSALEM 597 B.C.

Route of main Babylonian army
Captives deported
Raids by Babylonian allies 602 B.C.

Sea of Galilee
Megiddo
Samaria
Shechem
Shiloh
Great Sea
Mizpah
Gibeon
Ramah
Jerusalem
Azekah
Lachish
Hebron
Dead Sea

Miles 10 5 0 10 20
Kms 10 5 0 10 20 30

Soon a stronger power appeared in the north in the person of Nebuchadnezzar, king of the Chaldeans (Neo-Babylonians), who determined to follow the fierce policies of his Assyrian predecessors.

The tribute of Jehoiakim was paid at a distance when he heard of Nebuchadnezzar's approach. After three years as a Babylonian vassal, he rebelled, bringing a rapid response in the form of small-scale raids from Babylonians, Arameans, Moabites and Ammonites (c. 602 B.C.). Finally, Nebuchadnezzar's forces controlled all of the coastal territory north of the brook of Egypt.

When 18-year-old Jehoiachin had ruled just three months (597 B.C.), the main Babylonian army struck, capturing Jerusalem and exiling the king as a captive in Babylon. Ten thousand persons were deported.

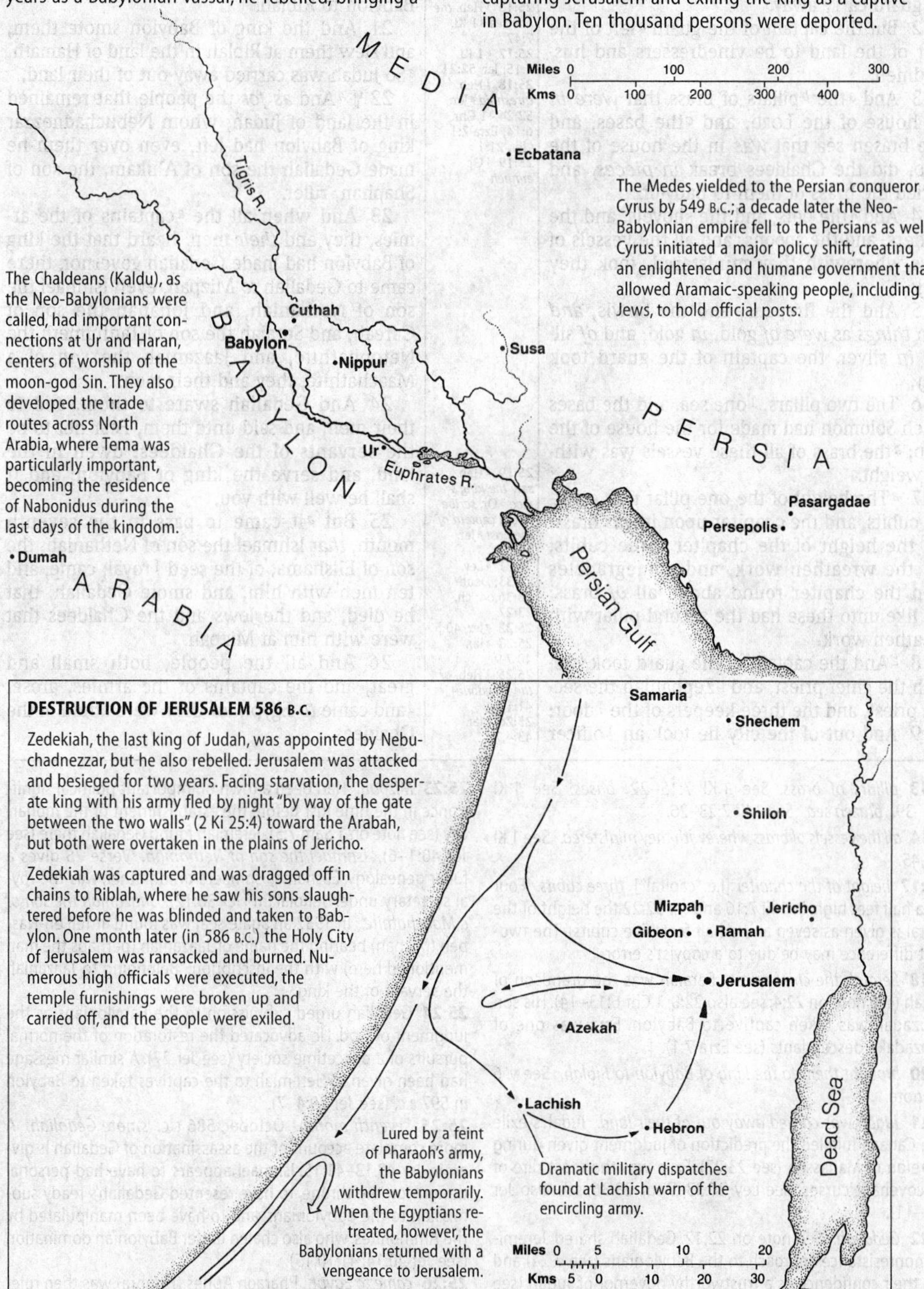

MEDIA
BABYLON
PERSIA
ARABIA
Miles 0 100 200 300
Kms 0 100 200 300 400
Tigris R.
Euphrates R.
Persian Gulf
Ecbatana
Cuthah
Babylon
Nippur
Susa
Ur
Pasargadae
Persepolis
Dumah
The Medes yielded to the Persian conqueror Cyrus by 549 B.C.; a decade later the Neo-Babylonian empire fell to the Persians as well. Cyrus initiated a major policy shift, creating an enlightened and humane government that allowed Aramaic-speaking people, including Jews, to hold official posts.
The Chaldeans (Kaldu), as the Neo-Babylonians were called, had important connections at Ur and Haran, centers of worship of the moon-god Sin. They also developed the trade routes across North Arabia, where Tema was particularly important, becoming the residence of Nabonidus during the last days of the kingdom.
DESTRUCTION OF JERUSALEM 586 B.C.
Zedekiah, the last king of Judah, was appointed by Nebuchadnezzar, but he also rebelled. Jerusalem was attacked and besieged for two years. Facing starvation, the desperate king with his army fled by night "by way of the gate between the two walls" (2 Ki 25:4) toward the Arabah, but both were overtaken in the plains of Jericho. Zedekiah was captured and was dragged off in chains to Riblah, where he saw his sons slaughtered before he was blinded and taken to Babylon. One month later (in 586 B.C.) the Holy City of Jerusalem was ransacked and burned. Numerous high officials were executed, the temple furnishings were broken up and carried off, and the people were exiled.
Samaria
Shechem
Shiloh
Mizpah
Jericho
Gibeon
Ramah
Jerusalem
Azekah
Lachish
Hebron
Dead Sea
Lured by a feint of Pharaoh's army, the Babylonians withdrew temporarily. When the Egyptians retreated, however, the Babylonians returned with a vengeance to Jerusalem.
Dramatic military dispatches found at Lachish warn of the encircling army.
Miles 0 5 10 20
Kms 5 0 10 20 30

Jerusalem, and every great *man's* house burnt
he with fire.
10 And all the army of the Chaldees, that
were with the captain of the guard, [a]brake
down the walls of Jerusalem round about.
11 [a]Now the rest of the people that were
left in the city, and the [1]fugitives that fell away
to the king of Babylon, with the remnant of
the multitude, did Nebuzar-adan the captain of
the guard carry away.
12 But the captain of the guard [a]left of the
poor of the land to be vinedressers and husbandmen.
13 And [a]the [b]pillars of brass that *were in*
the house of the LORD, and [c]the bases, and
[d]the brasen sea that *was* in the house of the
LORD, did the Chaldees break *in pieces,* and
carried the brass of them to Babylon.
14 And [a]the pots, and the shovels, and the
snuffers, and the spoons, and all the vessels of
brass wherewith they ministered, took they
away.
15 And the firepans, and the bowls, *and*
such *things* as *were of* gold, *in* gold, and *of* silver, *in* silver, the captain of the guard took
away.
16 The two pillars, [1]one sea, and the bases
which Solomon had made for the house of the
LORD; [a]the brass of all these vessels was without weight.
17 [a]The height of the one pillar *was* eighteen cubits, and the chapiter upon it *was* brass:
and the height of the chapiter three cubits;
and the wreathen work, and pomegranates
upon the chapiter round about, all *of* brass:
and like unto these had the second pillar with
wreathen work.
18 [a]And the captain of the guard took [b]Se-
raiah the chief priest, and [c]Zephaniah the second priest, and the three keepers of the [1]door:
19 And out of the city he took an [1]officer
that was set over the men of war, and [a]five
men of them that [2]were in the king's presence, which were found in the city, and the
[3]principal scribe of the host, which mustered
the people of the land, and threescore men of
the people of the land that were found in the
city:
20 And Nebuzar-adan captain of the guard
took these, and brought them to the king of
Babylon to Riblah:
21 And the king of Babylon smote them,
and slew them at Riblah in the land of Hamath.
[a]So Judah was carried away out of their land.
22 ¶ [a]And *as for* the people that remained
in the land of Judah, whom Nebuchadnezzar
king of Babylon had left, even over them he
made Gedaliah the son of Ahikam, the son of
Shaphan, ruler.
23 And when all the [a]captains of the armies, they and *their* men, heard that the king
of Babylon had made Gedaliah governor, there
came to Gedaliah *to* Mizpah, even Ishmael the
son of Nethaniah, and Johanan the son of
Careah, and Seraiah the son of Tanhumeth the
Netophathite, and Jaazaniah the son of a
Maachathite, they and their men.
24 And Gedaliah sware to them, and to
their men, and said unto them, Fear not to be
the servants of the Chaldees: dwell in the
land, and serve the king of Babylon; and it
shall be well with you.
25 But [a]it came to pass in the seventh
month, *that* Ishmael the son of Nethaniah, the
son of Elishama, of the seed [1]royal, came, and
ten men with him, and smote Gedaliah, that
he died, and the Jews and the Chaldees that
were with him at Mizpah.
26 And all the people, both small and
great, and the captains of the armies, arose,
[a]and came *to* Egypt: for they were afraid of the
Chaldees.

25:10 [a]Neh. 1:3; Jer. 52:14
25:11 [1]Heb. *fallen away* [a]Jer. 39:9
25:12 [a]ch. 24:14
25:13 [a]Jer. 27:19; 52:17 [b]1 Ki. 7:15 [c]1 Ki. 7:27 [d]1 Ki. 7:23
25:14 [a]Ex. 27:3; 1 Ki. 7:45
25:16 [1]Heb. *the one sea* [a]1 Ki. 7:47
25:17 [a]1 Ki. 7:15; Jer. 52:21
25:18 [1]Heb. *threshold* [a]Jer. 52:24 [b]1 Chr. 6:14; Ezra 7:1 [c]Jer. 21:1
25:19 [1]Or, *eunuch*
25:19 [2]Heb. *saw the king's face* [3]Or, *scribe of the captain of the host* [a]Jer. 52:25
25:21 [a]Lev. 26:33; Deut. 28:36,64; ch. 23:27
25:22 [a]Jer. 40:5
25:23 [a]Jer. 40:7-9
25:25 [1]Heb. *of the kingdom* [a]Jer. 41:1,2
25:26 [a]Jer. 43:4,7

25:13 *pillars of brass.* See 1 Ki 7:15–22. *bases.* See 1 Ki 7:27–39. *brazen sea.* See 1 Ki 7:23–26.

25:14 *all the vessels of brass wherewith they ministered.* See 1 Ki 7:40,45.

‡25:17 *height of the chapiter* [i.e."capital"] *three cubits.* Four and a half feet high. In 1 Ki 7:16 and Jer 52:22 the height of the capital is given as seven and a half feet (five cubits). The two-cubit difference may be due to a copyist's error.

25:18 *Seraiah the chief priest.* Seraiah was the grandson of Hilkiah (see note on 22:4; see also 22:8; 1 Chr 6:13–14). His son Jehozadak was taken captive to Babylon. Ezra was one of Jehozadak's descendants (see Ezra 7:1).

25:20 *brought them to the king of Babylon to Riblah.* See v. 6 and note.

25:21 *Judah was carried away out of their land.* Judah's exile from Canaan fulfilled the prediction of judgment given during the reign of Manasseh (see 23:27). Exile was the most dire of the covenant curses (see Lev 26:33; Deut 28:36; see also Jer 25:8–11).

25:22 *Gedaliah.* See note on 22:12. Gedaliah shared Jeremiah's nonresistance approach to the Babylonians (see v. 24) and won their confidence as a trustworthy governor of Judah (see Jer 41:10).

25:23 *Mizpah.* Had been a town of important political significance in the time just before the establishment of the monarchy (see note on 1 Sam 7:5). Jeremiah found Gedaliah there (see Jer 40:1–6). *Ishmael the son of Nethaniah.* Verse 25 gives a fuller genealogy. Elishama, Ishmael's grandfather, was the royal secretary under Jehoiakim (Jer 36:12). *Jaazaniah the son of a Maachathite.* In 1932 an agate seal was found at Tell en-Nasbeh (Mizpah) bearing the name of Jaazaniah (perhaps the man mentioned here) with the inscription: "Belonging to Jaazaniah the servant of the king."

25:24 Gedaliah urged submission to the Babylonians as the judgment of God. He advocated the restoration of the normal pursuits of a peacetime society (see Jer 27). A similar message had been given by Jeremiah to the captives taken to Babylon in 597 B.C. (see Jer 29:4–7).

25:25 *seventh month.* October, 586 B.C. *smote Gedaliah.* A more complete account of the assassination of Gedaliah is given in Jer 40:13–41:15. Ishmael appears to have had personal designs on the throne, to have resented Gedaliah's ready submission to the Babylonians, and to have been manipulated by the Ammonites, who also chafed under Babylonian domination (see Jer 40:14; 41:10,15).

25:26 *came to Egypt.* Pharaoh Apries (Hophra) was then ruler in Egypt (see note on 24:20).

Jehoiachin in captivity

27 ¶ [a]And it came to pass in the seven and
thirtieth year of the captivity of Jehoiachin
king of Judah, in the twelfth month, on the
seven and twentieth *day* of the month, *that*
Evil-merodach king of Babylon, in the year
that he *began* to reign, [b]did lift up the head of
Jehoiachin king of Judah out of prison;
28 And he spake [1]kindly to him, and set
his throne above the throne of the kings that
were with him in Babylon;
29 And changed his prison garments: and
he did [a]eat bread continually before him all
the days of his life.
30 And his allowance was a continual allowance given him of the king, a daily rate for
every day, all the days of his life.

25:27 [a]Jer. 52:31 [b]See Gen. 40:13,20
25:28 [1]Heb. *good things with him*
25:29 [a]2 Sam. 9:7

25:27 *seven and thirtieth year . . . twelfth month . . . seven and twentieth day.* Mar. 22, 561 B.C. *in the year that he began to reign.* 561 (some scholars place Evil-merodach's succession to the throne in October, 562; see note on 24:1). His name means "man of (the god) Marduk." *did lift up the head of Jehoiachin . . . out of prison.* Babylonian administrative tablets (see chart, p. xix), recording the payment of rations in oil and barley to prisoners held in Babylon, mention Yaukin (Jehoiachin) king of Iahudu (Judah) and five of his sons (cf. 24:15). No reason is given for Jehoiachin's release. Perhaps it was part of a general amnesty proclaimed at the beginning of Evil-merodach's reign.
25:28 *spake kindly to him, and set his throne above the throne of the kings.* The book of Kings ends on a hopeful note. The judgment of exile will not destroy the people of Israel or the line of David. God's promise concerning David's house remains (see 2 Sam 7:14–16).

Exile of the Southern Kingdom

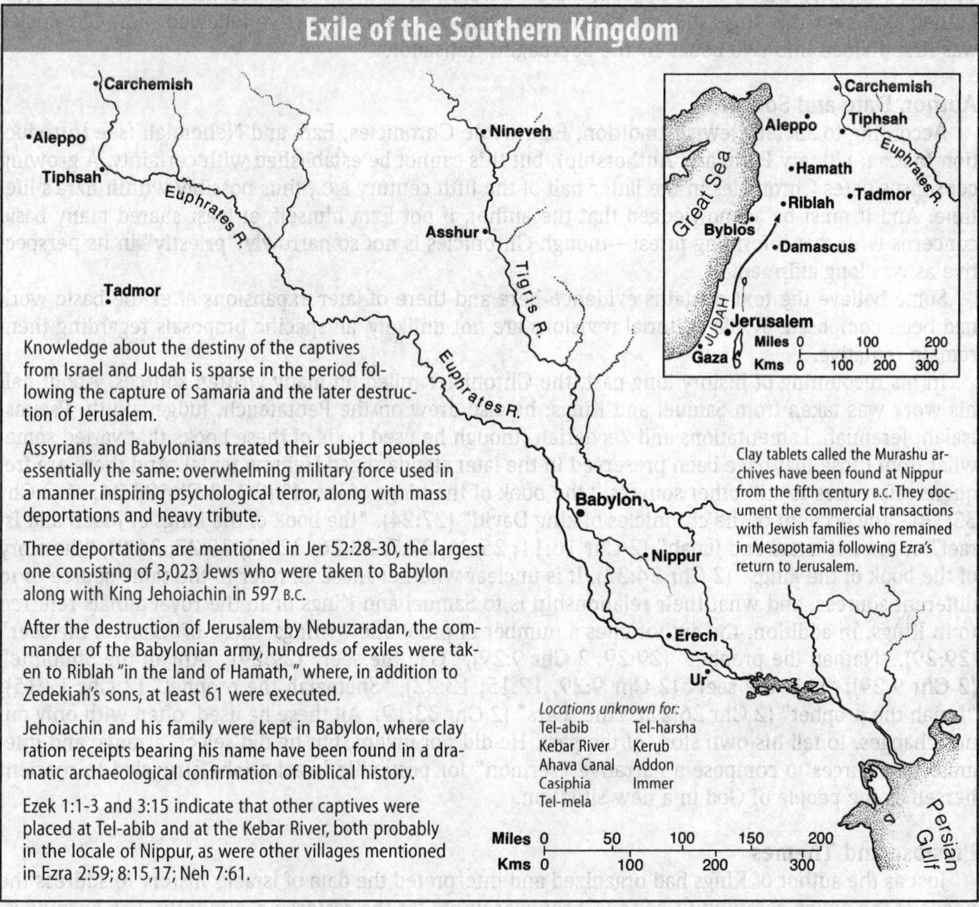

Knowledge about the destiny of the captives from Israel and Judah is sparse in the period following the capture of Samaria and the later destruction of Jerusalem.

Assyrians and Babylonians treated their subject peoples essentially the same: overwhelming military force used in a manner inspiring psychological terror, along with mass deportations and heavy tribute.

Three deportations are mentioned in Jer 52:28-30, the largest one consisting of 3,023 Jews who were taken to Babylon along with King Jehoiachin in 597 B.C.

After the destruction of Jerusalem by Nebuzaradan, the commander of the Babylonian army, hundreds of exiles were taken to Riblah "in the land of Hamath," where, in addition to Zedekiah's sons, at least 61 were executed.

Jehoiachin and his family were kept in Babylon, where clay ration receipts bearing his name have been found in a dramatic archaeological confirmation of Biblical history.

Ezek 1:1-3 and 3:15 indicate that other captives were placed at Tel-abib and at the Kebar River, both probably in the locale of Nippur, as were other villages mentioned in Ezra 2:59; 8:15,17; Neh 7:61.

The First Book of the
Chronicles

INTRODUCTION

Title

The Hebrew title (*dibre hayyamim*) can be translated "the events (or annals) of the days (or years)." The same phrase occurs in references to sources used by the author or compiler of Kings (translated "chronicles" in, e.g., 1 Ki 14:19,29; 15:7,23,31; 16:5,14,20,27; 22:45). The Septuagint translators (who translated the OT into Greek) called the book "the things omitted," indicating that they regarded it as a supplement to Samuel and Kings. Jerome (A.D. 347–420), translator of the Latin Vulgate, suggested that a more appropriate title would be "chronicle of the whole sacred history." Luther took over this suggestion in his German version, and others have followed him. Chronicles was first divided into two books by the Septuagint translators.

Author, Date and Sources

According to ancient Jewish tradition, Ezra wrote Chronicles, Ezra and Nehemiah (see Introduction to Ezra: Literary Form and Authorship), but this cannot be established with certainty. A growing consensus dates Chronicles in the latter half of the fifth century B.C., thus possibly within Ezra's lifetime. And it must be acknowledged that the author, if not Ezra himself, at least shared many basic concerns with that reforming priest—though Chronicles is not so narrowly "priestly" in its perspective as was long affirmed.

Some believe the text contains evidence here and there of later expansions after the basic work had been composed. While editorial revisions are not unlikely, all specific proposals regarding them remain tentative.

In his recounting of history long past, the Chronicler relied on many written sources. About half his work was taken from Samuel and Kings; he also drew on the Pentateuch, Judges, Ruth, Psalms, Isaiah, Jeremiah, Lamentations and Zechariah (though he used texts of these books that varied somewhat from those that have been preserved in the later standardized Hebrew texts). And there are frequent references to still other sources: "the book of the kings of Israel" (9:1; 2 Chr 20:34; cf. 2 Chr 33:18), "the account of the chronicles of king David" (27:24), "the book of the kings of Judah and Israel" or ". . . of Israel and Judah" (2 Chr 16:11; 25:26; 27:7; 28:26; 32:32; 35:27; 36:8), "the story of the book of the kings" (2 Chr 24:27). It is unclear whether these all refer to the same source or to different sources, and what their relationship is to Samuel and Kings or to the royal annals referred to in Kings. In addition, the author cites a number of prophetic writings: those of "Samuel the seer" (29:29), "Nathan the prophet" (29:29; 2 Chr 9:29), "Gad the seer" (29:29), "Ahijah the Shilonite" (2 Chr 9:29), "Iddo the seer" (2 Chr 9:29; 12:15; 13:22), "Shemaiah the prophet" (2 Chr 12:15), "Isaiah the prophet" (2 Chr 26:22), "the seers" (2 Chr 33:19). All these he used, often with only minor changes, to tell his own story of the past. He did not invent, but he did select, arrange and integrate his sources to compose a narrative "sermon" for postexilic Israel as she struggled to reorient herself as the people of God in a new situation.

Purpose and Themes

Just as the author of Kings had organized and interpreted the data of Israel's history to address the needs of the exiled community, so the Chronicler wrote for the restored community. The burning issue was the question of continuity with the past: Is God still interested in us? Are His covenants still in force? Now that we have no Davidic king and are subject to Persia, do God's promises to David still have meaning for us? After the great judgment (the dethroning of the house of David, the destruction of the nation, of Jerusalem and of the temple, and the exile to Babylon), what is our relationship to Israel of old? Several elements go into the Chronicler's answer:

1. Continuity with the past is signified by the temple in Jerusalem, rebuilt by the Lord's sovereign influence on a Persian imperial edict (2 Chr 36:22–23). For a generation that had no independent po-

litical status and no Davidic king the author takes great pains to show that the temple of the Lord and its service (including its book of prayer and praise, an early edition of the Psalms) are supreme gifts of God given to Israel through the Davidic dynasty. For that reason his account of the reigns of David and Solomon is largely devoted to David's preparation for and Solomon's building of the temple and David's instructions for the temple service (with the counsel of Gad the seer and Nathan the prophet, 2 Chr 29:25, and also of the Levites Asaph, Heman and Jeduthun, 2 Chr 35:15). See also the Chronicler's accounts of the reigns of Asa, Jehoshaphat, Joash, Hezekiah and Josiah. The temple of the Lord in the ancient holy city and its service (including the Psalms) were the chief legacy left to the restored community by the house of David.

2. The value of this legacy is highlighted by the author's emphasis on God's furtherance of His gracious purposes toward Israel through His sovereign acts of election: (1) of the tribe of Levi to serve before the ark of God (15:2; see 23:24–32), (2) of David to be king over Israel (28:4; 2 Chr 6:6), (3) of Solomon his son to be king and to build the temple (28:5–6,10; 29:1), (4) of Jerusalem (2 Chr 6:6,34,38; 12:13; 33:7) and (5) of the temple (2 Chr 7:12,16; 33:7) to be the place where God's Name would be present among His people. These divine acts give assurance to postexilic Israel that her rebuilt temple in Jerusalem and its continuing service mark her as God's people whose election has not been annulled.

3. In addition to the temple, Israel has the law and the prophets as a major focus of her covenant life under the leadership of the house of David. Neither the Davidic kings nor the temple had in themselves assured Israel's security and blessing. All had been conditional on Israel's and the king's faithfulness to the law (28:7; 2 Chr 6:16; 7:17; 12:1; 33:8). In the Chronicler's account, a primary feature of the reign of every faithful Davidic king was his attempt to bring about compliance with the law: David (6:49; 15:13,15; 16:40; 22:12–13; 29:19), Asa (2 Chr 14:4; 15:12–14), Jehoshaphat (2 Chr 17:3–9; 19:8–10), Joash (2 Chr 24:6,9), Hezekiah (2 Chr 29:10,31; 30:15–16; 31:3–4,21), Josiah (2 Chr 34:19–21, 29–33; 35:6,12,26). And to heed God's prophetic word was no less crucial. The faithful kings, such as David, Asa, Jehoshaphat, Hezekiah and Josiah—and even Rehoboam (2 Chr 11:4; 12:6) and Amaziah (2 Chr 25:7–10)—honored it; the unfaithful kings disregarded it to their destruction (Jehoram, 2 Chr 21:12–19; Joash, 2 Chr 24:19–25; Amaziah, 2 Chr 25:15–16,20; Manasseh, 2 Chr 33:10–11; see 36:15–16). Chronicles, in fact, notes the ministries of more prophets than do Samuel and Kings. Jehoshaphat's word to Israel expresses the Chronicler's view succinctly: "Believe in the LORD your God, so shall you be established; believe his prophets, so shall ye prosper" (2 Chr 20:20). In the Chronicler's account of Israel's years under the kings, her response to the law and the prophets was more decisive for her destiny than the reigns of kings.

Thus the law and the prophets, like the temple, are more crucial to Israel's continuing relationship with the Lord than the presence or absence of a king, the reigns of the Davidic kings themselves being testimony.

4. The Chronicler further underscores the importance of obedience to the law and the prophets by emphasizing the theme of immediate retribution. See the express statements of David (28:9), of the Lord (2 Chr 7:14) and of the prophets (2 Chr 12:5; 15:2,7; 16:7,9; 19:2–3; 21:14–15; 24:20; 25:15–16; 28:9; 34:24–28). In writing his accounts of individual reigns, he never tires of demonstrating how sin always brings judgment in the form of disaster (usually either illness or defeat in war), whereas repentance, obedience and trust yield peace, victory and prosperity.

5. Clearly the author of Chronicles wished to sustain Israel's hope for the promised Messiah, son of David, in accordance with the Davidic covenant (2 Sam 7) and the assurances of the prophets, including those near to him (Haggai, Zechariah and Malachi). He was careful to recall the Lord's pledge to David (1 Chr 17) and to follow this with many references back to it (see especially his account of Solomon's reign and also 2 Chr 13:5; 21:7; 23:3). But perhaps even more indicative are his idealized depictions of David, Solomon, Asa, Jehoshaphat, Hezekiah and Josiah. While not portrayed as flawless, these kings are presented as prime examples of the Messianic ideal, i.e., as royal servants of the Lord whose reigns promoted godliness and covenant faithfulness in Israel. They were crowned with God's favor toward His people in the concrete forms of victories, deliverances and prosperity. They sat, moreover, on the "throne of the LORD" (29:23; see 28:5; 2 Chr 9:8) and ruled over the Lord's kingdom (17:14; 2 Chr 13:8). Thus they served as types, foreshadowing the David to come of whom the prophets had spoken, and their remembrance nurtured hope in the face of much discouragement (see the book of Malachi). See further the next section on "Portrait of David and Solomon."

6. Yet another major theme of the Chronicler's history is his concern with "all Israel" (see, e.g., 9:1; 11:1–4; 12:38–40; 16:1–3; 18:14; 21:1–5; 28:1–8; 29:21–26; 2 Chr 1:1–3; 7:8–10; 9:30;

10:1–3,16; 12:1; 18:16; 28:23; 29:24; 30:1–13,23–27; 34:6–9,33). As a matter of fact, he viewed the restored community as the remnant of all Israel, both north and south (9:2–3). This was more than a theological conceit. His narrative makes frequent note of movements of godly people from Israel to Judah for specifically religious reasons. The first were Levites in the time of Rehoboam (2 Chr 11:14). In the reign of Asa others followed from Ephraim and Manasseh (2 Chr 15:9). Shortly after the Assyrian destruction of the northern kingdom, many from that devastated land resettled in Judah at Hezekiah's invitation (2 Chr 30). Presumably not all who came for Hezekiah's great passover remained, but archaeology has shown a sudden large increase in population in the region around Jerusalem at this time, and the Chronicler specifically mentions "children of Israel . . . that dwelt in the cities of Judah" (2 Chr 31:6). He also speaks of the people of "Manasseh and Ephraim, and of all the remnant of Israel" who joined with the people of "Judah and Benjamin" and the inhabitants of Jerusalem in restoring the temple in the days of Josiah (2 Chr 34:9). These were also present at Josiah's passover (2 Chr 35:17–18). So the kingdom of "Judah" had absorbed many from the northern kingdom through the years, and the Chronicler viewed it as the remnant of all Israel from the time of Samaria's fall.

7. The genealogies also demonstrate continuity with the past. To the question "Is God still interested in us?" the Chronicler answers, "He has always been." God's grace and love for the restored community did not begin with David or the conquest or the exodus—but with creation (1:1). For the genealogies see below.

8. The Chronicler often introduces speeches not found in Samuel and Kings, using them to convey some of his main emphases. Of the 165 speeches in Chronicles of varying lengths, only 95 are found in the parallel texts of Samuel and Kings. Cf., e.g., the speeches of Abijah (2 Chr 13:4–12), Asa (2 Chr 14:11) and Jehoshaphat (2 Chr 20:5–12).

Portrait of David and Solomon

The bulk of the Chronicler's history is devoted to the reigns of David (chs. 11—29) and Solomon (2 Chr 1—9). His portraits of these two kings are quite distinctive and provide a key to his concerns:

1. The Chronicler has idealized David and Solomon. Anything in his source material (mainly Samuel and Kings) that might tarnish his picture of them is omitted. He makes no reference to the seven-year reign in Hebron before the uniting of the kingdom, the wars between Saul's house and David, the negotiations with Abner, the difficulties over David's wife Michal, or the murders of Abner and Ish-bosheth (2 Sam 1—4). The Chronicler presents David as being immediately anointed king over all Israel after the death of Saul (ch. 11) and enjoying the total support of the people (11:10—12:40; see note on 3:1–9). Subsequent difficulties for David are also not recounted. No mention is made of David's sin with Bath-sheba, the crime and death of Amnon, the fratricide by Absalom and his plot against his father, the flight of David from Jerusalem, the rebellions of Sheba and Shimei, and other incidents that might diminish the glory of David's reign (2 Sam 11—20). David is presented without blemish, apart from the incident of the census (the Chronicler had a special purpose for including it; see ch. 21 and notes).

The Chronicler handles Solomon similarly. Solomon is specifically named in a divine oracle as David's successor (22:7–10; 28:6). His accession to the throne is announced publicly by David and is greeted with the unanimous support of all Israel (chs. 28—29). No mention is made of the bedridden David, who must overturn the attempted coup by Adonijah at the last moment to secure the throne for Solomon. Nor is there mention that the military commander Joab and the high priest Abiathar supported Adonijah's attempt (1 Ki 1). Solomon's execution of those who had wronged David (1 Ki 2) is also omitted. The accession of Solomon is without competition or detracting incident. The account of his reign is devoted almost wholly to the building of the temple (2 Chr 2—8), and no reference to his failures is included. No mention is made of his idolatry, his foreign wives or the rebellions against his rule (1 Ki 11). Even the blame for the schism is removed from Solomon (1 Ki 11:26–40; 12:1–4) and placed on the scheming of Jeroboam. Solomon's image in Chronicles is such that he can be paired with David in the most favorable light (2 Chr 11:17).

The David and Solomon of the Chronicler, then, must be seen not only as the David and Solomon of history, but also as typifying the Messianic king of the Chronicler's expectation.

2. Not only is there idealization of David and Solomon, but the author also appears to consciously adopt the account of the succession of Moses and Joshua as a model for the succession of David and Solomon:

a. Both David and Moses fail to attain their goals—one to build the temple and the other to enter

the promised land. In both cases the divine prohibition is related to the appointment of a successor (22:5–13; 28:2–8; Deut 1:37–38; 31:2–8).

b. Both Solomon and Joshua bring the people of God into rest (22:8–9; Josh 11:23; 21:44).

c. There are a number of verbal parallels in the appointments of Solomon and Joshua (compare 22:11–13,16; 28:7–10,20; 2 Chr 1:1 with Deut 31:5–8,23; Josh 1:5,7–9).

d. There are both private and public announcements of the appointment of the successors: private (22:6; Deut 31:23); public (28:8; Deut 31:7—both "in the sight of all Israel").

e. Both enjoy the immediate and wholehearted support of the people (29:23–24; Deut 34:9; Josh 1:16–18).

f. It is twice reported that God "magnified" or "maginified . . . exceedingly" Solomon and Joshua (29:25; 2 Chr 1:1; Josh 3:7; 4:14).

The Chronicler also uses other models from Pentateuchal history in his portrayal of David and Solomon. Like Moses, David received the plans for the temple from God (28:11–19; Ex 25:9) and called on the people to bring voluntary offerings for its construction (29:1–9; Ex 25:1–7). Solomon's relationship to Huram-abi, the craftsman from Tyre (2 Chr 2:13–14), echoes the role of Bezaleel and Aholiab in the building of the tabernacle (Ex 35:30—36:7). See note on 2 Chr 1:5.

Genealogies

Analysis of genealogies, both inside and outside the Bible, has disclosed that they serve a variety of functions (with different principles governing the lists), that they vary in form (some being segmented, others linear) and depth (number of generations listed), and that they are often fluid (subject to change).

There are three general areas in which genealogies function: the familial or domestic, the legal-political, and the religious. In the domestic area an individual's social status, privileges and obligations may be reflected in his placement in the lineage (see 7:14–19); the rights of the firstborn son and the secondary status of the children of concubines are examples from the Bible. In the political sphere genealogies substantiate claims to hereditary office or settle competing claims when the office is contested. Land organization and territorial groupings of social units may also be determined by genealogical reckoning—e.g., the division of the land among the 12 tribes. In Israel military levies also proceeded along genealogical lines; several of the genealogies in Chronicles reflect military conscription (5:1–26; 7:1–12,30–40; 8:1–40). Genealogies function in the religious sphere primarily by establishing membership among the priests and Levites (6:1–30; 9:10–34; Neh 7:61–65).

As to form, some genealogical lists trace several lines of descent (segmented genealogies) while others are devoted to a single line (linear genealogies).

Comparison of genealogical lists of the same tribal or family line often brings to light surprising differences. This fluidity of the lists may reflect variation in function. But sometimes changes in the status or relations of social structures are reflected in genealogies by changes in the relationships of names in the genealogy (see notes on 1:35–42; 6:22,27) or by the addition of names or segments to a lineage (see notes on 5:11–22; 6:27; 7:6–12). The most common type of fluidity in Biblical materials is telescoping, the omission of names from the list. Unimportant names are left out in order to relate an individual to a prominent ancestor, or possibly to achieve the desired number of names in the genealogy. Some Biblical genealogies, for example, omit names to achieve multiples of 7: For the period from David to the exile Matthew gives 14 generations (2 times 7), while Luke gives 21 (3 times 7), and the same authors give similar multiples of 7 for the period from the exile to Jesus (Matt 1:1–17; Luke 3:23–38).

The genealogies of Chronicles show variation in all these properties; the arrangements often reflect the purpose for which the genealogies were composed prior to their being adopted by the Chronicler as part of his record.

Outline

- I. Genealogies: Creation to Restoration (1 Chr 1—9)
  - A. The Patriarchs (ch. 1)
  - B. The 12 Sons of Jacob/Israel (2:1–2)
  - C. The Family of Judah (2:3—4:23)
  - D. The Sons of Simeon (4:24–43)
  - E. Reuben, Gad and the Half Tribe of Manasseh (ch. 5)
  - F. Levi and Families (ch. 6)

- G. Issachar, Benjamin, Naphtali, Manasseh, Ephraim and Asher (chs. 7—9)

II. The Reign of David (1 Chr 10—29)

- A. Death of Saul (ch. 10)
- B. Capture of Jerusalem; David's Power Base (chs. 11—12)
- C. Return of the Ark; Establishment of David's Kingdom (chs. 13—16)
- D. Dynastic Promise (ch. 17)
- E. David's Conquests (chs. 18—20)
- F. The Census (ch. 21)
- G. Preparations for the Temple (ch. 22)
- H. Organization of the Temple Service (chs. 23—26)
- I. Administrative Structures of the Kingdom (ch. 27)
- J. David's Final Preparations for Succession and the Temple (28:1—29:20)
- K. Succession of Solomon; Death of David (29:21–30)

III. The Reign of Solomon (2 Chr 1—9)

- A. The Gift of Wisdom (ch. 1)
- B. Building the Temple (2:1—5:1)
- C. Dedication of the Temple (5:2—7:22)
- D. Solomon's Other Activities (ch. 8)
- E. Solomon's Wisdom, Splendor and Death (ch. 9)

IV. The Schism, and the History of the Kings of Judah (2 Chr 10—36)

- A. Rehoboam (chs. 10—12)
- B. Abijah (13:1—14:1)
- C. Asa (14:2—16:14)
- D. Jehoshaphat (17:1—21:3)
- E. Jehoram and Ahaziah (21:4—22:9)
- F. Joash (22:10—24:27)
- G. Amaziah (ch. 25)
- H. Uzziah (ch. 26)
- I. Jotham (ch. 27)
- J. Ahaz (ch. 28)
- K. Hezekiah (chs. 29—32)
- L. Manasseh (33:1–20)
- M. Amon (33:21–25)
- N. Josiah (34:1—36:1)
- O. Josiah's Successors (36:2–14)
- P. Exile and Restoration (36:15–23)

Descendants of the patriarchs

1 Adam, [a]Sheth, Enosh,
2 Kenan, Mahalaleel, Jered,
3 Henoch, Methuselah, Lamech,
4 Noah, Shem, Ham, and Japheth.
5 ¶ [a]The sons of Japheth; Gomer, and Magog, and Madai, and Javan, and Tubal, and Meshech, and Tiras.
6 And the sons of Gomer; Ashchenaz, and
[1]Riphath, and Togarmah.
7 And the sons of Javan; Elishah, and Tarshish, Kittim, and [1]Dodanim.
8 ¶ [a]The sons of Ham; Cush, and Mizraim,
Put, and Canaan.
9 And the sons of Cush; Seba, and Havilah,
and Sabta, and Raamah, and Sabtecha. And the
sons of Raamah; Sheba, and Dedan.
10 And Cush [a]begat Nimrod: he began to
be mighty upon the earth.
11 And Mizraim begat Ludim, and
Anamim, and Lehabim, and Naphtuhim,
12 And Pathrusim, and Casluhim, (of
whom came the Philistines,) and [a]Caph-
thorim.
13 And [a]Canaan begat Zidon his firstborn,
and Heth,
14 The Jebusite also, and the Amorite, and
the Girgashite,
15 And the Hivite, and the Arkite, and the
Sinite,
16 And the Arvadite, and the Zemarite,
and the Hamathite.
17 ¶ The sons of [a]Shem; Elam, and Asshur,
and Arphaxad, and Lud, and Aram, and Uz,
and Hul, and Gether, and [1]Meshech.
18 And Arphaxad begat Shelah, and Shelah
begat Eber.
19 And unto Eber were born two sons: the
name of the one *was* [a1]Peleg; because in his
days the earth was divided: and his brother's
name *was* Joktan.
20 And [a]Joktan begat Almodad, and Sheleph, and Hazarmaveth, and Jerah,
21 Hadoram also, and Uzal, and Diklah,
22 And Ebal, and Abimael, and Sheba,
23 And Ophir, and Havilah, and Jobab. All
these *were* the sons of Joktan.
24 ¶ [a]Shem, Arphaxad, Shelah,
25 [a]Eber, Peleg, Rehu,
26 Serug, Nahor, Terah,
27 [a]Abram; the same *is* Abraham.
28 The sons of Abraham; [a]Isaac, and [b]Ish-
mael.
29 ¶ These *are* their generations: The
[a]firstborn of Ishmael, Nebajoth; then Kedar,
and Adbeel, and Mibsam,
30 Mishma, and Dumah, Massa, [1]Hadad,
and Tema,
31 Jetur, Naphish, and Kedemah. These *are*
the sons of Ishmael.
32 ¶ Now [a]the sons of Keturah, Abraham's
concubine: she bare Zimran, and Jokshan, and
Medan, and Midian, and Ishbak, and Shuah.
And the sons of Jokshan; Sheba, and Dedan.
33 And the sons of Midian; Ephah, and
Epher, and Henoch, and Abida, and Eldaah. All
these *are* the sons of Keturah.
34 ¶ And [a]Abraham begat Isaac. [b]The sons
of Isaac; Esau and Israel.
35 ¶ The sons of [a]Esau; Eliphaz, Reuel, and
Jeush, and Jaalam, and Korah.
36 The sons of Eliphaz; Teman, and Omar,
[1]Zephi, and Gatam, Kenaz, and Timna, and
Amalek.

1:1 [a]Gen. 4:25,26; 5:3,9
1:5 [a]Gen. 10:2
1:6 [1]Or, *Diphath,* as it is in some copies
1:7 [1]Or, *Rodanim,* according to some copies
1:8 [a]Gen. 10:6
1:10 [a]Gen. 10:8,13
1:12 [a]Deut. 2:23
1:13 [a]Gen. 10:15
1:17 [1]Or, *Mash,* Gen. 10:23 [a]Gen. 10:22; 11:10
1:19 [1]That is, *division* [a]Gen. 10:25
1:20 [a]Gen. 10:26
1:24 [a]Gen. 11:10; Luke 3:36
1:25 [a]Gen. 11:15
1:27 [a]Gen. 17:5
1:28 [a]Gen. 21:2 [b]Gen. 16:11,15
1:29 [a]Gen. 25:13-16
1:30 [1]Or, *Hadar,* Gen. 25:15
1:32 [a]Gen. 25:1
1:34 [a]Gen. 21:2 [b]Gen. 25:25,26
1:35 [a]Gen. 36:9,10
1:36 [1]Or, *Zepho,* Gen. 36:11

1:1–9:44 The genealogies succinctly show the restored community's continuity with the past. The great deeds of God on Israel's behalf prior to the rise of David are passed over in silence, but the genealogies serve as a skeleton of history to show that the Israel of the restoration stands at the center of the divine purpose from the beginning (from Adam, v. 1). And the genealogies also serve the very practical purpose of legitimizing the present. They provide the framework by which the ethnic and religious purity of the people can be maintained. They also establish the continuing line of royal succession and the legitimacy of the priests for the postexilic temple service. (See Introduction: Genealogies.)

1:1–2:1 The Chronicler here covers the period from Adam to Jacob, and the materials are drawn almost entirely from Genesis. The subsidiary lines of descent are presented first: Japheth and Ham (vv. 5–16) are given before Shem (vv. 17–27), the sons of Shem other than those in Abraham's ancestry (vv. 17–23) before that line (vv. 24–27), the sons of Abraham's concubines (vv. 28–33) before Isaac's line (v. 34), the descendants of Esau and the Edomite ruling houses (vv. 35–54) before the sons of Israel (2:1). In each case the elect lineage is given last.

Several features of this genealogy are striking when compared with non-Biblical materials. The genealogy begins without an introduction. Two sections of the genealogy have no kinship terms and are only lists of names: the first 13 names (vv. 1–4; see note on v. 4) and vv. 24–27. In vv. 5–16 (and following v. 27) kinship terms are used. Both segmented (those tracing several lines of descent) and linear (those tracing a single line) genealogies are included. This identical structure is found in a copy of the Assyrian King List: There is no introduction, and the scribe has drawn lines across the tablet dividing it into four sections, two of which are lists of names without kinship terms, alternating with two lists in which relations are specified; both segmented and linear genealogies are used. This suggests that the Chronicler was following a known literary pattern for his composition.

1:1–4 From creation to the flood. This list is taken from Gen 5:1–32 (see notes there). The omission of Cain and Abel demonstrates the Chronicler's interest in the chosen line (see Gen 4:17–25).

1:4 *Noah.* Shem, Ham, and Japheth were the sons of Noah. The Chronicler's readers would have known this and would not have needed a kinship notice in the text; the Septuagint (the Greek translation of the OT) and some modern translations read "the sons of Noah" to clarify the relationship of the four names.

1:5–23 This genealogy is drawn from the table of nations in Gen 10:2–29 (see notes there). The arrangement is primarily geographical and cultural rather than biological. Omitting the Philistines (v. 12) as a parenthesis, a total of 70 nations is achieved: Japheth, 14; Ham, 30; Shem, 26 (see note on Gen 10:2)—an example of a genealogy telescoped to attain multiples of 7 (see Introduction: Genealogies).

1:24–27 See notes on 1:1–2:1; Gen 11:10–26.

1:28–34 See notes on Gen 25:1–18.

1:35–42 See Gen 36:10–28 and notes.

1:36 *sons of Eliphaz.* These correspond to Gen 36:11–12, but

37 The sons of Reuel; Nahath, Zerah, Shammah, and Mizzah.

38 ¶ And [a]the sons of Seir; Lotan, and Shobal, and Zibeon, and Anah, and Dishon, and Ezer, and Dishan.

39 And the sons of Lotan; Hori, and [1]Homam: and Timna *was* Lotan's sister.

40 The sons of Shobal; [1]Alian, and Manahath, and Ebal, [2]Shephi, and Onam. And the sons of Zibeon; Aiah, and Anah.

41 The sons of Anah; [a]Dishon. And the sons of Dishon; [1]Amram, and Eshban, and Ithran, and Cheran.

42 The sons of Ezer; Bilhan, and Zavan, *and* [1]Jakan. The sons of Dishan; Uz, and Aran.

The kings of Edom

43 ¶ Now these *are* the [a]kings that reigned in the land of Edom before *any* king reigned over the children of Israel; Bela the son of Beor: and the name of his city *was* Dinhabah.

44 And when Bela was dead, Jobab the son of Zerah of Bozrah reigned in his stead.

45 And when Jobab was dead, Husham of the land of the Temanites reigned in his stead.

46 And when Husham was dead, Hadad the son of Bedad, which smote Midian in the field of Moab, reigned in his stead: and the name of his city *was* Avith.

47 And when Hadad was dead, Samlah of Masrekah reigned in his stead.

48 [a]And when Samlah was dead, Shaul of Rehoboth *by* the river reigned in his stead.

49 And when Shaul was dead, Baal-hanan the son of Achbor reigned in his stead.

50 And when Baal-hanan was dead, [1]Hadad reigned in his stead: and the name of his city *was* [2]Pai; and his wife's name *was* Mehetabel, the daughter of Matred, the daughter of Mezahab.

51 Hadad died also. And the [a]dukes of Edom were; duke Timnah, duke [1]Aliah, duke Jetheth,

52 Duke Aholibamah, duke Elah, duke Pinon,

53 Duke Kenaz, duke Teman, duke Mibzar,

54 Duke Magdiel, duke Iram. These *are* the dukes of Edom.

From Israel to David

2 These *are* the sons of [1]Israel; [a]Reuben, Simeon, Levi, and Judah, Issachar, and Zebulun,

2 Dan, Joseph, and Benjamin, Naphtali, Gad, and Asher.

3 ¶ The sons of [a]Judah; Er, and Onan, and Shelah: *which* three were born unto him of the daughter of [b]Shua the Canaanitess. And [c]Er, the firstborn of Judah, was evil in the sight of the LORD; and he slew him.

4 And [a]Tamar his daughter in law bare him Pharez and Zerah. All the sons of Judah *were* five.

5 The sons of [a]Pharez; Hezron, and Hamul.

6 ¶ And the sons of Zerah; [1]Zimri, [a]and Ethan, and Heman, and Calcol, and [2]Dara: five of them in all.

7 And the sons of [a]Carmi; [1]Achar, the troubler of Israel, who transgressed in the thing [b]accursed.

8 And the sons of Ethan; Azariah.

9 ¶ The sons also of Hezron, that were born unto him; Jerahmeel, and [1]Ram, and [2]Chelubai.

1:38 [a]Gen. 36:20 **1:39** [1]Or, *Heman,* Gen. 36:22 **1:40** [1]Or, *Alvan,* Gen. 36:23 [2]Or, *Shepho,* Gen. 36:23 **1:41** [1]Or, *Hemdan,* Gen. 36:26 [a]Gen. 36:25 **1:42** [1]Or, *Akan,* Gen. 36:27 **1:43** [a]Gen. 36:31 **1:48** [a]Gen. 36:37 **1:50** [1]Or, *Hadar,* Gen. 36:39 **1:50** [2]Or, *Pau,* Gen. 36:39 **1:51** [1][Or, *Alvah*] [a]Gen. 36:40 **2:1** [1]Or, *Jacob* [a]Gen. 29:32; 30:5; 35:18,22; 46:8 **2:3** [a]Gen. 38:3; 46:12; Num. 26:19 [b]Gen. 38:2 [c]Gen. 38:7 **2:4** [a]Gen. 38:29,30 **2:5** [a]Gen. 46:12; Ruth 4:18 **2:6** [1]Or, *Zabdi,* Josh. 7:1 [2]Or, *Darda* [a]1 Ki. 4:31 **2:7** [1]Or, *Achan* [a]See ch. 4:1 [b]Josh. 6:18; 7:1 **2:9** [1]Or, *Aram,* Mat. 1:3,4 [2]Or, *Caleb,* ver. 18,42

with one difficulty: Listing Timna and Amalek as sons of Eliphaz is in apparent conflict with Gen 36:12, where Timna is the concubine of Eliphaz and mother of Amalek. The Septuagint (the Greek translation of the OT) assumes a mistake in the Hebrew text and lists Amalek as Eliphaz's son by Timna. Perhaps the Chronicler has once again omitted kinship terminology (see notes on 1:1–2:1; v. 4). Alternatively, some regard this as an example of genealogical fluidity (see Introduction: Genealogies): Since the name Timna also became the name of a chiefdom in Edom (v. 51; Gen 36:40), during the course of time Timna was "promoted" in the Edomite genealogies to the position of a son of Eliphaz and brother of Amalek.

1:43–54 See Gen 36:31–43. The Chronicler continues with extensive coverage of Edom. This is striking in contrast to his omission of the line of Cain and the brief treatment of the line of Ishmael. It probably reflects the fact that the Edomites were important in the Chronicler's own day (see 18:11–13; 2 Chr 8:17; 21:8; 25:20; 28:17).

2:1–2 Although there are numerous lists of the 12 tribes in the OT, only four are given in genealogical form: (1) Gen 29:31–30:24; 35:16–20; (2) Gen 35:22–26; (3) Gen 46:8–27; (4) here. Other lists of the tribes are found in 12:24–37; 27:16–22; Ex 1:2–5; Deut 27:12–13; 33; Ezek 48:31–34. In other lists the tribe of Levi is omitted, and the number 12 is achieved by dividing Joseph into the tribes of Ephraim and Manasseh (Num 1:5–15; 1:20–43; 2:3–31; 7:12–83; 10:14–28; 13:4–15; 26:5–51). In this passage the Chronicler appears to follow Gen 35:22–26 except for the position of the tribe of Dan, which is found in seventh instead of ninth place. The list here does not set the order in which the Chronicler will take up the tribes; rather, he moves immediately to his major concern with the house of David and the tribe of Judah (2:3–4:23), even though Judah is fourth in the genealogy. In the lists of these chapters the Chronicler maintains the number 12, but with the following names: Judah, Simeon, Reuben, Gad, half of Manasseh, Levi, Issachar, Benjamin, Naphtali, Ephraim, Manasseh and Asher. Zebulun and Dan are omitted.

2:3–9 The lineage of Judah is traced to Hezron's sons (v. 9), whose descendants are given in 2:10–3:24. Of Judah's five sons, the first two (Er and Onan) died as the result of sin recorded in Gen 38. The lineage of the third son, Shelah, is taken up in 4:21; this section focuses on the remaining two (see Gen 46:12; Num 26:19–22).

2:6 *Ethan, and Heman, and Calcol, and Dara.* Not immediate descendants of Zerah; rather, they are from the later period of the reign of Solomon (1 Ki 4:31). A Heman and an Ethan were David's musicians (see 15:19; Ps 88–89 titles), but whether these are the same individuals is uncertain. If they are the same, the fact that in 6:33–42 and 15:19 Heman and Ethan are assigned to the tribe of Levi may be another example of genealogical fluidity, where these men's musical skills brought them into the Levitical lineage. Or the reverse may have occurred: As Levites associated with Judah, they were brought into that lineage.

2:7 *Achar.* Achar (meaning "trouble") is called Achan in Josh 7; 22:20. The change from Achan to Achar is probably a play on words reflecting the trouble Achan brought to Israel.

10 And Ram [a]begat Amminadab; and Amminadab begat Nahshon, [b]prince of the children of Judah;

11 And Nahshon begat [1]Salma, and Salma begat Boaz,

12 And Boaz begat Obed, and Obed begat Jesse,

13 [a]And Jesse begat his firstborn Eliab, and Abinadab the second, and [1]Shimma the third,

14 Nethaneel the fourth, Raddai the fifth,

15 Ozem the sixth, David the seventh:

16 Whose sisters *were* Zeruiah, and Abigail. [a]And the sons of Zeruiah; Abishai, and Joab, and Asahel, three.

17 And [a]Abigail bare Amasa: and the father of Amasa *was* [1]Jether the Ishmeelite.

18 ¶ And Caleb the son of Hezron begat *children* of Azubah *his* wife, and of Jerioth: her sons *are* these; Jesher, and Shobab, and Ardon.

19 And when Azubah was dead, Caleb took unto him [a]Ephrath, which bare him Hur.

20 And Hur begat Uri, and Uri begat [a]Bezaleel.

21 ¶ And afterward Hezron went in to the daughter of [a]Machir the father of Gilead, whom he [1]married when he *was* threescore years old; and she bare him Segub.

22 And Segub begat Jair, who had three and twenty cities in the land of Gilead.

23 [a]And he took Geshur, and Aram, with the towns of Jair, from them, with Kenath, and the towns thereof, *even* threescore cities. All these *belonged to* the sons of Machir the father of Gilead.

24 And after that Hezron was dead in Caleb-ephratah, then Abiah Hezron's wife bare him [a]Ashur the father of Tekoa.

25 ¶ And the sons of Jerahmeel the firstborn of Hezron were, Ram the firstborn, and Bunah, and Oren, and Ozem, *and* Ahijah.

2:10 [a]Ruth 4:19,20; Mat. 1:4 [b]Num. 1:7; 2:3
2:11 [1][Or, *Salmon,* Ruth 4:21; Mat. 1:4]
2:13 [1]Or, *Shammah* [a]1 Sam. 16:6
2:16 [a]2 Sam. 2:18
2:17 [1][2 Sam. 17:25, *Ithra an Israelite*] [a]2 Sam. 17:25
2:19 [a]ver. 50
2:20 [a]Ex. 31:2
2:21 [1]Heb. *took* [a]Num. 27:1
2:23 [a]Num. 32:41; Deut. 3:14; Josh. 13:30
2:24 [a]ch. 4:5
2:31 [a]See ver. 34,35
2:36 [a]ch. 11:41

26 Jerahmeel had also another wife, whose name *was* Atarah; she *was* the mother of Onam.

27 And the sons of Ram the firstborn of Jerahmeel were, Maaz, and Jamin, and Eker.

28 And the sons of Onam were, Shammai, and Jada. And the sons of Shammai; Nadab, and Abishur.

29 And the name of the wife of Abishur *was* Abihail, and she bare him Ahban, and Molid.

30 And the sons of Nadab; Seled, and Appaim: but Seled died without children.

31 And the sons of Appaim; Ishi. And the sons of Ishi; Sheshan. And [a]the children of Sheshan; Ahlai.

32 And the sons of Jada the brother of Shammai; Jether, and Jonathan: and Jether died without children.

33 And the sons of Jonathan; Peleth, and Zaza. These were the sons of Jerahmeel.

34 Now Sheshan had no sons, but daughters. And Sheshan had a servant, an Egyptian, whose name *was* Jarha.

35 And Sheshan gave his daughter to Jarha his servant to wife; and she bare him Attai.

36 And Attai begat Nathan, and Nathan begat [a]Zabad,

37 And Zabad begat Ephlal, and Ephlal begat Obed,

38 And Obed begat Jehu, and Jehu begat Azariah,

39 And Azariah begat Helez, and Helez begat Eleasah,

40 And Eleasah begat Sisamai, and Sisamai begat Shallum,

41 And Shallum begat Jekamiah, and Jekamiah begat Elishama.

42 ¶ Now the sons of Caleb the brother of Jerahmeel *were,* Mesha his firstborn, which *was* the father of Ziph; and the sons of Mareshah the father of Hebron.

2:10–3:24 That the Chronicler's primary concern in the genealogy of Judah is with the line of David is seen in his arrangement of this section's material as an inversion:

- Descendants of Ram (David's ancestry), 2:10–17
- Descendants of Caleb, 2:18–24
- Descendants of Jerahmeel, 2:25–33
- Supplementary material on Jerahmeel, 2:34–41
- Supplementary material on Caleb, 2:42–55
- Supplementary material on Ram (David's descendants), ch. 3

The Chronicler has structured this central portion of the Judah genealogy to highlight the Davidic ancestry and descent, which frame this section and emphasize the position of David—in line with the Chronicler's interests in the historical portions that follow (see note on 4:1–23).

2:10–17 Verses 10–12 are a linear genealogy from Ram to Jesse; then Jesse's lineage is segmented, reminiscent of 1 Sam 16:1–13. The source for most of the material is Ruth 4:19–22. In 1 Sam 16:10–13 David was the eighth of Jesse's sons to appear before Samuel; in this passage only seven are named, enabling David to occupy the favored place of the seventh son (v. 15; see Introduction: Genealogies). David was the half-uncle of his famous warriors Abishai, Joab, Asahel and Amasa (11:6,20,26; 2 Sam 2:13,18; 17:25; 19:13).

2:18–24 For the Chronicler the important name in this genealogy of the Calebites is Bezaleel (v. 20), the wise master craftsman who supervised the building of the tabernacle (Ex 31:1–5). He is mentioned in the Bible only in Exodus and Chronicles. The Chronicler uses Bezaleel and Aholiab (Ex 31:6) as a model for his portrait of Solomon and Huram in the building of the temple (see note on 2 Chr 1:5). By inserting a reference to the builder of the tabernacle next to the genealogy of David in vv. 10–17, the Chronicler characteristically juxtaposes the themes of king and temple—so important to his historical narrative.

2:25–33 This section is identified as a separate entity from the supplementary material by its opening and closing formulas: "the sons of Jerahmeel" (v. 25) and "These were the sons of Jerahmeel" (v. 33). Verses 25–41 are the only genealogical materials on the Jerahmeelites in the Bible. 1 Sam 27:10 and 30:27–29 place their settlements in the Negev.

2:34–41 Supplementary material on the line of Sheshan (v. 31); it is a linear genealogy to a depth of 13 generations. The generation of Elishama (v. 41) would be the 23rd since Judah, if there has been no telescoping in this lineage. If no names are omitted, Elishama would likely be contemporary with David, though we know nothing of him.

2:42–55 The same opening and closing formulas noted in vv. 25,33 occur in vv. 42,50a: "Now the sons of Caleb . . . These were

43 And the sons of Hebron; Korah, and Tappuah, and Rekem, and Shema.

44 And Shema begat Raham, the father of Jorkoam: and Rekem begat Shammai.

45 And the son of Shammai *was* Maon: and Maon *was* the father of Beth-zur.

46 And Ephah, Caleb's concubine, bare Haran, and Moza, and Gazez: and Haran begat Gazez.

47 And the sons of Jahdai; Regem, and Jotham, and Geshan, and Pelet, and Ephah, and Shaaph.

48 Maachah, Caleb's concubine, bare Sheber, and Tirhanah.

49 She bare also Shaaph the father of Madmannah, Sheva the father of Machbenah, and the father of Gibea: and the daughter of Caleb *was* [a]Achsah.

50 ¶ These were the sons of Caleb the son of Hur, the firstborn of [1]Ephratah; Shobal the father of Kirjath-jearim,

51 Salma the father of Beth-lehem, Hareph the father of Beth-gader.

52 And Shobal the father of Kirjath-jearim had sons; [1]Haroeh, *and* [2]half of the Manahethites.

53 And the families of Kirjath-jearim; the Ithrites, and the Puhites, and the Shumathites, and the Mishraites; of them came the Zareathites, and the Eshtaulites.

54 The sons of Salma; Beth-lehem, and the Netophathites, [1]Ataroth, the house of Joab, and half of the Manahethites, the Zorites.

55 And the families of the scribes which dwelt at Jabez; the Tirathites, the Shimeathites, *and* Suchathites. These *are* the [a]Kenites that came of Hemath, the father of the house of [b]Rechab.

The family of David

3 Now these were the sons of David, which were born unto him in Hebron; the firstborn [a]Amnon, of Ahinoam the [b]Jezreelitess; the second [1]Daniel, of Abigail the Carmelitess:

2 The third, Absalom the son of Maachah the daughter of Talmai king of Geshur: the fourth, Adonijah the son of Haggith:

3 The fifth, Shephatiah of Abital: the sixth, Ithream by [a]Eglah his wife.

4 *These* six were born unto him in Hebron; and [a]there he reigned seven years and six months: and [b]in Jerusalem he reigned thirty and three years.

5 [a]And these were born unto him in Jerusalem; [1]Shimea, and Shobab, and Nathan, and [b]Solomon, four, of [2]Bath-shua the daughter of [3]Ammiel:

6 Ibhar also, and [1]Elishama, and Eliphelet,

7 And Nogah, and Nepheg, and Japhia,

8 And Elishama, and [1]Eliada, and Eliphelet, [a]nine.

9 *These were* all the sons of David, beside the sons of the concubines, and [a]Tamar their sister.

The family of Solomon

10 ¶ And Solomon's son *was* [a]Rehoboam, [1]Abia his son, Asa his son, Jehoshaphat his son,

11 Joram his son, [1]Ahaziah his son, Joash his son,

12 Amaziah his son, [1]Azariah his son, Jotham his son,

13 Ahaz his son, Hezekiah his son, Manasseh his son,

14 Amon his son, Josiah his son.

15 And the sons of Josiah *were,* the firstborn [1]Johanan, the second [2]Jehoiakim, the third [3]Zedekiah, the fourth Shallum.

2:49 [a]Josh. 15:17
2:50 [1][Or, *Ephrath,* ver. 19]
2:52 [1]Or, *Reaiah,* ch. 4:2 [2]Or, *half of the Menuchites,* or, *Hatsi-hammenuchoth*
2:54 [1]Or, *Atarites,* or, *crowns of the house of Joab*
2:55 [a]Judg. 1:16 [b]Jer. 35:2
3:1 [1]Or, *Chileab,* 2 Sam. 3:3 [a]2 Sam. 3:2 [b]Josh. 15:56
3:3 [a]2 Sam. 3:5
3:4 [a]2 Sam. 2:11 [b]2 Sam. 5:5
3:5 [1]Or, *Shammua,* 2 Sam. 5:14 [2]Or, *Bath-sheba,* 2 Sam. 11:3 [3]Or, *Eliam,* 2 Sam. 11:3 [a]ch. 14:4 [b]2 Sam. 12:24
3:6 [1]Or, *Elishua,* 2 Sam. 5:15
3:8 [1]Or, *Beeliada,* ch. 14:7 [a]See 2 Sam. 5:14-16
3:9 [a]2 Sam. 13:1
3:10 [1]Or, *Abijam,* 1 Ki. 15:1 [a]1 Ki. 11:43
3:11 [1]Or, *Azariah,* 2 Chr. 22:6; [or, *Jehoahaz* in 2 Chr.] 21:17
3:12 [1]Or, *Uzziah,* 2 Ki. 15:30
3:15 [1]Or, *Jehoahaz,* 2 Ki. 23:30 [2]Or, *Eliakim,* 2 Ki. 23:34 [3]Or, *Mattaniah,* 2 Ki. 24:17

---

the sons of Caleb." The list in this section is a mixture of personal and place-names; the phrase "father of" can be understood not only as ancestor or predecessor, but also (as likely here) as "founder of" or "leader of" a city.

2:50b–55 Resumes the genealogy of Hur (v. 20). The same formulas for identifying the genealogical sections in vv. 25,33 and in vv. 42,50a are used in v. 50b and 4:4: "the son[s] of Hur . . . These are the sons of Hur." The presence of these formulas suggests that this section and 4:1–4 were once a unit; the Chronicler has inserted his record of the Davidic descent (ch. 3) into the middle of this other genealogy, apparently to balance the sections of his material (see notes on 2:10–3:24; 4:1–23). Otherwise the disruption of the genealogy of Hur may have already occurred in the Chronicler's sources.

2:55 *Tirathites, the Shimeathites, and Suchathites.* May refer to three families, as translated here, or possibly to three different classes of scribes, perhaps those who (1) read, (2) copied and (3) checked the work. *Kenites.* Originally a foreign people, many of the Kenites were incorporated into Judah (see Num 10:29–32; Judg 1:16; 4:11).

3:1–24 See note on 2:10–3:24.

3:1–9 This list of David's children is largely drawn from 2 Sam 3:2–5; 5:13–16; 13:1 (see notes there). The sons born in Jerusalem are repeated in 1 Chr 14:3–7. The name Eliphelet occurs twice (vv. 6,8); in 14:5,7 two spellings of the name are given (only one son having this name is mentioned in 2 Sam 5:14–16). The reference to David's seven-year rule in Hebron (v. 4) is repeated in 29:27, though the Chronicler does not deal with this period in his narrative. The references to Absalom, Tamar, Adonijah, Amnon and Bath-sheba all recall unhappy incidents in the life of David, incidents the Chronicler has omitted from his later narrative (see 2 Sam 11–15; 17–18; 1 Ki 1).

3:10 *Rehoboam.* See 2 Chr 10–12. *Abia.* See 2 Chr 13:1–14:1. *Asa.* See 2 Chr 14–16. *Jehoshaphat.* See 1 Ki 22.

3:11 *Joram.* See 2 Chr 21.

3:13 *Ahaz.* See 2 Chr 28. *Hezekiah.* See 2 Chr 29–32. *Manasseh.* See 2 Chr 33:1–20.

3:14 *Amon.* See 2 Chr 33:21–25. *Josiah.* See 2 Ki 22:1–23:30; 2 Chr 34:1–36:1.

3:15–16 "the firstborn Johanan" is not mentioned elsewhere and may have died before Josiah. The genealogy is segmented at this point, instead of linear as in vv. 10–14. Since Josiah's other three sons would all occupy the throne, the succession was not uniformly father to son. Shallum/Jehoahaz (2 Chr 36:2–4; 2 Ki 23:30–35) was replaced by Jehoiakim (2 Chr 36:5–8; 2 Ki 23:34–24:6); Jehoiakim was succeeded by his son Jehoiachin (2 Chr 36:9–10; 2 Ki 24:8–16). After Jehoiachin was taken captive to Babylon by Nebuchadnezzar, Josiah's son Zedekiah (2 Ki 24:17–25:7; 2 Chr 36:11–14) became the last king of Judah.

3:17–20 Seven sons are attributed to Jeconiah (Jehoiachin),

16 And the sons of [a]Jehoiakim: [1]Jeconiah his son, Zedekiah [b]his son.

17 ¶ And the sons of Jeconiah; Assir, [1]Salathiel [a]his son,

18 Malchiram also, and Pedaiah, and Shenazar, Jecamiah, Hoshama, and Nedabiah.

19 And the sons of Pedaiah *were,* Zerubbabel, and Shimei: and the son of Zerubbabel; Meshullam, and Hananiah, and Shelomith their sister:

20 And Hashubah, and Ohel, and Berechiah, and Hasadiah, Jushabhesed, five.

21 And the sons of Hananiah; Pelatiah, and Jesaiah: the sons of Rephaiah, the sons of Arnan, the sons of Obadiah, the sons of Shechaniah.

22 And the sons of Shechaniah; Shemaiah: and the sons of Shemaiah; [a]Hattush, and Igeal, and Bariah, and Neariah, and Shaphat, six.

23 And the sons of Neariah; Elioenai, and [1]Hezekiah, and Azrikam, three.

24 And the sons of Elioenai *were,* Hodaiah, and Eliashib, and Pelaiah, and Akkub, and Johanan, and Dalaiah, and Anani, seven.

The family of Judah

4 The sons of Judah; [a]Pharez, Hezron, and [1]Carmi, and Hur, and Shobal.

2 And [1]Reaiah the son of Shobal begat Jahath; and Jahath begat Ahumai, and Lahad. These *are* the families of the Zorathites.

3 And these *were of* the father of Etam; Jezreel, and Ishma, and Idbash: and the name of their sister *was* Hazelelponi:

4 And Penuel the father of Gedor, and Ezer the father of Hushah. These *are* the sons of [a]Hur, the firstborn of Ephratah, the father of Beth-lehem.

5 ¶ And [a]Ashur the father of Tekoa had two wives, Helah and Naarah.

6 And Naarah bare him Ahuzam, and Hepher, and Temeni, and Haahashtari. These *were* the sons of Naarah.

7 And the sons of Helah *were,* Zereth, and Jezoar, and Ethnan.

8 And Coz begat Anub, and Zobebah, and the families of Aharhel the son of Harum.

9 ¶ And Jabez was [a]more honourable than his brethren: and his mother called his name [1]Jabez, saying, Because I bare *him* with sorrow.

10 And Jabez called on the God of Israel, saying, [1]Oh that thou wouldest bless me indeed, and enlarge my coast, and that thine hand might be with me, and that thou wouldest [2]keep *me* from evil, that it may not grieve me. And God granted *him that* which he requested.

11 ¶ And Chelub the brother of Shuah begat Mehir, which *was* the father of Eshton.

12 And Eshton begat Beth-rapha, and Paseah, and Tehinnah the father of [1]Irnahash. These *are* the men of Rechah.

13 And the sons of Kenaz; [a]Othniel, and Seraiah: and the sons of Othniel; [1]Hathath.

3:16 [1]Or, *Jehoiachin,* 2 Ki. 24:6; or, *Coniah,* Jer. 22:24 [a]Mat. 1:11 [b]2 Ki. 24:17, being his uncle
3:17 [1]Heb. *Shealtiel* [a]Mat. 1:12
3:22 [a]Ezra 8:2
3:23 [1]Heb. *Hiskijah*
4:1 [1]Or, *Chelubai,* ch. 2:9; or, *Caleb,* ch. 2:18 [a]Gen. 46:12
4:2 [1]Or, *Haroeh,* ch. 2:52
4:4 [a]ch. 2:50
4:5 [a]ch. 2:24
4:9 [1]That is, *sorrowful* [a]Gen. 34:19
4:10 [1]Heb. *If thou wilt, etc.* [2]Heb. *do me*
4:12 [1]Or, *the city of Nahash*
4:13 [1]Or, *Hathath, and Meonothai,* who *begat, etc.* [a]Josh. 15:17

but not one succeeded him (see notes on vv. 15–16; Jer 22:30). Tablets found in Babylon dating from the 10th to the 35th year of Nebuchadnezzar (595–570 B.C.) and listing deliveries of rations mention Jeconiah and five sons as well as other Judahites held in Babylon. Jeconiah received similar largess from Nebuchadnezzar's successor Evil-merodach (562–560 B.C.; see 2 Ki 25:27–30).

3:18 *Shenazar.* May be another spelling of the name Sheshbazzar. If so, the treasures of the temple were consigned to his care for return to Judah (Ezra 1:11). He also served for a short time as the first governor of the returnees and made an initial attempt at rebuilding the temple (Ezra 5:14–16). Little is known of him; he soon disappeared from the scene and was overshadowed by his nephew Zerubbabel, who assumes such importance in Ezra, Haggai and Zechariah. But see note on Ezra 1:8.

3:19 *Pedaiah.* Other texts name Shealtiel ("Salathiel," v. 17) as Zerubbabel's father (Ezra 3:2,8; Neh 12:1; Hag 1:12,14; 2:2,23). Suggestions offered to resolve this difficulty are: 1. Shealtiel may have died early, and Pedaiah became the head of the family. 2. Pedaiah may have married the childless widow of Shealtiel; Zerubbabel would then be regarded as the son of Shealtiel according to the law of levirate marriage (Deut 25:5–6). In Luke 3:27 Neri instead of Jehoiachin ("Jeconiah," v. 17) is identified as the father of Shealtiel. Similar suggestions to those above could be made in this instance as well. It is also interesting to note that the genealogies of Jesus in Mat 1 and Luke 3 both trace his descent to Zerubbabel, but that none of the names subsequent to Zerubbabel (v. 19–24) is found in the NT genealogies.

3:20 *five.* May have been sons of Zerubbabel, but no kinship terms are provided. Since the sons of Hananiah (v. 19) are specified in v. 21, they could also be the sons of Meshullam (v. 19).

3:21 *sons of Rephaiah . . . Shechaniah.* Probably other Davidic families at the time of Zerubbabel (v. 19) or Pelatiah and Jesaiah. If they are understood as contemporary with Zerubbabel, his genealogy was carried only two generations (his sons and grandsons) and a date for Chronicles as early as 450 B.C. is possible (see Introduction: Author, Date and Sources).

3:22 *six.* Perhaps a copyist accidentally omitted one name.

4:1–23 None of the genealogies of Judah in this section appears elsewhere in Scripture. Although the section may have the appearance of miscellaneous notes, the careful shaping of the Chronicler is evident in light of the overall inverted structure of the genealogies of Judah:

2:3	Shelah
2:4–8	Pharez
2:9—3:24	Hezron
4:1–20	Pharez
4:21–23	Shelah

This balancing of the material in inverse order shows the centrality of the section of the lineage of Hezron and the house of David; the same balancing in inverse order is observed within the Hezron section (see note on 2:10–3:24). The record of Judah's oldest surviving son, Shelah, frames the entire genealogy of Judah. There are 15 fragmentary genealogies in this section, with two to six generations in each.

4:1–2 The descendants of Judah here are not brothers; rather, the genealogy is linear.

4:1 *Carmi.* Either a scribal confusion or an alternative name for Chelubai (2:9); the confusion may have been induced by 2:7.

4:2 *Reaiah.* A variant of Haroeh (2:52).

4:5–8 Supplementary to 2:24.

4:9–10 The practice of inserting short historical notes into genealogical records is amply attested in non-Biblical genealogical texts from the ancient Near East as well as in other Biblical genealogies (Gen 4:19–24; 10:8–12).

4:13 *Othniel.* The first of Israel's judges (Josh 15:17; Judg 1:13; 3:9–11).

14 And Meonothai begat Ophrah: and Seraiah begat Joab, the father of [a]the [1]valley of [2]Charashim; for they were craftsmen.

15 And the sons of Caleb the son of Jephunneh; Iru, Elah, and Naam: and the sons of Elah, [1]even Kenaz.

16 And the sons of Jehaleleel; Ziph, and Ziphah, Tiria, and Asareel.

17 And the sons of Ezra *were,* Jether, and Mered, and Epher, and Jalon: and she bare Miriam, and Shammai, and Ishbah the father of Eshtemoa.

18 And his wife [1]Jehudijah bare Jered the father of Gedor, and Heber the father of Socho, and Jekuthiel the father of Zanoah. And these *are* the sons of Bithiah the daughter of Pharaoh, which Mered took.

19 And the sons of *his* wife [1]Hodiah the sister of Naham, the father of Keilah the Garmite, and Eshtemoa the Maachathite.

20 And the sons of Shimon *were,* Amnon, and Rinnah, Ben-hanan, and Tilon. And the sons of Ishi *were,* Zoheth, and Ben-zoheth.

21 ¶ The sons of Shelah [a]the son of Judah *were,* Er the father of Lecah, and Laadah the father of Mareshah, and the families of the house of them that wrought fine linen, of the house of Ashbea,

22 And Jokim, and the men of Chozeba, and Joash, and Saraph, who had the dominion in Moab, and Jashubi-lehem. And *these are* ancient things.

23 These *were* the potters, and those that dwelt amongst plants and hedges: there they dwelt with the king for his work.

The family of Simeon

24 ¶ The sons of Simeon *were,* [1]Nemuel, and Jamin, [2]Jarib, Zerah, *and* Shaul:

25 Shallum his son, Mibsam his son, Mishma his son.

26 And the sons of Mishma; Hamuel his son, Zacchur his son, Shimei his son.

27 And Shimei had sixteen sons and six daughters; but his brethren had not many children, neither did all their family multiply, [1]like to the children of Judah.

28 And they dwelt at [a]Beer-sheba, and Moladah, and Hazar-shual,

29 And at [1]Bilhah, and at Ezem, and at [2]Tolad,

30 And at Bethuel, and at Hormah, and at Ziklag,

31 And at Beth-marcaboth, and [1]Hazar-susim, and at Beth-birei, and at Shaaraim. These *were* their cities unto the reign of David.

32 And their villages *were,* [1]Etam, and Ain, Rimmon, and Tochen, and Ashan, five cities:

33 And all their villages that *were* round about the same cities, unto [1]Baal. These *were* their habitations, and [2]their genealogy.

34 ¶ And Meshobab, and Jamlech, and Joshah the son of Amaziah,

35 And Joel, and Jehu the son of Josibiah, the son of Seraiah, the son of Asiel,

36 And Elioenai, and Jaakobah, and Jeshohaiah, and Asaiah, and Adiel, and Jesimiel, and Benaiah,

37 And Ziza the son of Shiphi, the son of Allon, the son of Jedaiah, the son of Shimri, the son of Shemaiah;

38 These [1]mentioned by *their* names *were* princes in their families: and the house of their fathers increased greatly.

39 And they went to the entrance of Gedor, *even* unto the east *side* of the valley, to seek pasture for their flocks.

40 And they found fat pasture and good, and the land *was* wide, and quiet, and peaceable; for *they* of Ham had dwelt there of old.

41 And these written by name came in the days of Hezekiah king of Judah, and [a]smote their tents, and the habitations that were found there, and destroyed them utterly unto this day, and dwelt in their rooms: because *there was* pasture there for their flocks.

42 And *some* of them, *even* of the sons of Simeon, five hundred men, went to mount Seir, having for their captains Pelatiah, and Neariah, and Rephaiah, and Uzziel, the sons of Ishi.

43 And they smote [a]the rest of the Amalekites that were escaped, and dwelt there unto this day.

The family of Reuben

5 Now the sons of Reuben the firstborn of Israel, (for [a]he *was* the firstborn; but, forasmuch as he [b]defiled his father's bed, [c]his

4:14 [1]Or, inhabitants *of the valley* [2]That is, *craftsmen* [a]Neh. 11:35
4:15 [1]Or, *Uknaz*
4:18 [1]Or, *the Jewess*
4:19 [1]Or, *Jehudijah,* mentioned before
4:21 [a]Gen. 38:1,5
4:24 [1]Or, *Jemuel,* Gen. 46:10 [2][Or, *Jachin, Zohar*]
4:27 [1]Heb. *unto*
4:28 [a]Josh. 19:2
4:29 [1]Or, *Balah,* Josh. 19:3 [2]Or, *Eltolad,* Josh. 19:4
4:31 [1]Or, *Hazar-susah,* Josh. 19:5
4:32 [1]Or, *Ether,* Josh. 15:42
4:33 [1]Or, *Baalath-beer,* Josh. 19:8 [2]Or, *as they divided themselves by nations among them*
4:38 [1]Heb. *coming*
4:41 [a]2 Ki. 18:8
4:43 [a]See 1 Sam. 15:8; 30:17; 2 Sam. 8:12
5:1 [a]Gen. 29:32; 49:3 [b]Gen. 35:22; 49:4 [c]Gen. 48:15,22

4:16–20 This portion of the genealogy is from preexilic times; several of the places named were not included in the province of Judah in the restoration period (e.g., Ziph and Eshtemoa).

4:18 *Bithiah the daughter of Pharaoh, which Mered took.* Mered is otherwise unknown; the fact that he married a daughter of Pharaoh suggests his prominence. The event may be associated with the fortunes of Israel in Egypt under Joseph.

4:21,23 This section accurately reflects a feature of ancient Near Eastern society. Clans were often associated not only with particular localities but also with special trades or guilds, such as linen workers (v. 21), potters (v. 23), royal patronage (v. 23) and scribes (2:55).

4:24–43 The genealogy of Simeon is also found in Gen 46:10; Ex 6:15; Num 26:12–13. Simeon settled in part of the territory of Judah; the list of occupied towns should be compared with Josh 15:26–32,42; 19:2–7. Since Simeon occupied areas allotted to Judah, this tribe was politically incorporated into Judah and appears to have lost much of its own identity in history (see Gen 34:24–31; 49:5–7; see also notes on Gen 34:25; 49:7). Geographical and historical notes are inserted in the genealogy (see note on vv. 9–10). Apparently two genealogies are included here: vv. 24–33—ending with the formula, "and their genealogy"—and vv. 34–43. Overpopulation (v. 38) caused them to expand toward Gedor and east toward Edom at the time of Hezekiah (vv. 39–43). The long hostility between Israel and Amalek surfaced once again (v. 43; cf. Ex 17:8–16; Deut 25:17–19; 1 Sam 15; see Introduction to Esther: Purpose, Themes and Literary Features).

5:1–26 The genealogical records of the tribes east of the Jordan: Reuben, Gad and half of Manasseh (see Num 32:33–42). The Chronicler's concern with "all Israel" includes incorporating the genealogical records of these tribes that were no longer

birthright was given unto the sons of Joseph
the son of Israel: and the genealogy is not to be
reckoned after the birthright.
2 For [a]Judah prevailed above his brethren,
and of him *came* the [b1]chief ruler; but the
birthright *was* Joseph's:)
3 The sons, *I say,* of [a]Reuben the firstborn
of Israel *were,* Hanoch, and Pallu, Hezron, and
Carmi.
4 The sons of Joel; Shemaiah his son, Gog
his son, Shimei his son,
5 Micah his son, Reaia his son, Baal his
son,
6 Beerah his son, whom [1]Tilgath-pilneser
king of Assyria carried away captive: he *was*
prince of the Reubenites.
7 And his brethren by their families,
[a]when the genealogy of their generations was
reckoned, *were* the chief, Jeiel, and Zechariah,
8 And Bela the son of Azaz, the son of
[1]Shema, the son of Joel, who dwelt in [a]Aroer,
even unto Nebo and Baal-meon:
9 And eastward he inhabited unto the entering in of the wilderness from the river Euphrates: because their cattle were multiplied
[a]in the land of Gilead.
10 And in the days of Saul they made war
[a]with the Hagarites, who fell by their hand:
and they dwelt in their tents [1]throughout all
the east *land* of Gilead.

The family of Gad

11 ¶ And the children of Gad dwelt over
against them, in the land of [a]Bashan unto
Salchah:
12 Joel the chief, and Shapham the next,
and Jaanai, and Shaphat in Bashan.
13 And their brethren of the house of their
fathers *were,* Michael, and Meshullam, and
Sheba, and Jorai, and Jachan, and Zia, and Heber, seven.
14 These *are* the children of Abihail the
son of Huri, the son of Jaroah, the son of Gilead, the son of Michael, the son of Jeshishai,
the son of Jahdo, the son of Buz;

5:2 [1]Or, *prince* [a]Gen. 49:8,10; Ps. 60:7; 108:8 [b]Mic. 5:2; Mat. 2:6
5:3 [a]Gen. 46:9; Ex. 6:14; Num. 26:5
5:6 [1]Or, *Tiglath-pileser,* 2 Ki. 15:29
5:7 [a]See ver. 17
5:8 [1]Or, *Shemaiah,* ver. 4 [a]Josh. 13:15,16
5:9 [a]Josh. 22:9
5:10 [1]Heb. *upon all the face of the east* [a]Gen. 25:12
5:11 [a]Josh. 13:11,24
5:16 [1]Heb. *their goings forth* [a]ch. 27:29
5:17 [a]2 Ki. 15:5,32 [b]2 Ki. 14:16,28
5:18 [1]Heb. *sons of valour*
5:19 [a]Gen. 25:15; ch. 1:31
5:20 [a]See ver. 22 [b]Ps. 22:4,5
5:21 [1]Heb. *led captive* [2]Heb. *souls of men:* as Num. 31:35
5:22 [a]2 Ki. 15:29; 17:6
5:24 [1]Heb. *men of names*
5:25 [a]2 Ki. 17:7

15 Ahi the son of Abdiel, the son of Guni,
chief of the house of their fathers.
16 And they dwelt in Gilead in Bashan,
and in her towns, and in all the suburbs of
[a]Sharon, upon [1]their borders.
17 All these were reckoned by genealogies
in the days of [a]Jotham king of Judah, and in
the days of [b]Jeroboam king of Israel.

The half tribe of Manasseh

18 ¶ The sons of Reuben, and the Gadites,
and half the tribe of Manasseh, of [1]valiant
men, men *able to* bear buckler and sword, and
to shoot with bow, and skilful in war, *were*
four and forty thousand seven hundred and
threescore, that went out *to* the war.
19 And they made war with the Hagarites,
with [a]Jetur, and Nephish, and Nodab.
20 And [a]they were helped against them,
and the Hagarites were delivered into their
hand, and all that *were* with them: for they
cried to God in the battle, and he was intreated of them; because they [b]put their trust in
him.
21 And they [1]took away their cattle; *of*
their camels fifty thousand, and *of* sheep two
hundred and fifty thousand, and *of* asses two
thousand, and *of* [2]men an hundred thousand.
22 For there fell down many slain, because
the war *was* of God. And they dwelt in their
steads until [a]the captivity.
23 And the children of the half tribe of Manasseh dwelt in the land: they increased from
Bashan unto Baal-hermon and Senir, and *unto*
mount Hermon.
24 And these *were* the heads of the house
of their fathers, even Epher, and Ishi, and Eliel, and Azriel, and Jeremiah, and Hodaviah,
and Jahdiel, mighty *men* of valour, [1]famous
men, *and* heads of the house of their fathers.
25 And they transgressed against the God
of their fathers, and went [a]a whoring after the
gods of the people of the land, whom God destroyed before them.
26 And the God of Israel stirred up the

significant entities in Israel's life in the restoration period, having been swept away in the Assyrian conquests.

5:1–10 The necessity to explain why the birthright of the firstborn did not remain with Reuben (see Gen 35:22; 49:4 for Reuben's sin) interrupts the initial statement (v. 1), which is then repeated after the explanation (v. 3). The parenthetical material (vv. 1–2) shows the writer's partiality for Judah, even though Joseph received the double portion (Ephraim and Manasseh) of the firstborn. The Hebrew term translated "chief ruler" (v. 2) is used of David in 11:2; 17:7; 2 Sam 5:2; 6:21; 7:8; cf. 1 Chr 28:4. The use of military titles (vv. 6–7) and a battle account (v. 10) suggest that this genealogy may have functioned in military organization (see Introduction: Genealogies). The source for some of this material on Reuben is Num 26:5–11. The Chronicler has omitted reference to Eliab and his three sons who perished in the rebellion of Korah (see Num 26:8–10) and so were not relevant to his purpose.

5:6 *Tilgath-pilneser.* A variant of Tiglath-pileser. This Assyrian king (745–727 B.C.) attacked Israel (v. 26; 2 Ki 15:29) and also imposed tribute on Ahaz of Judah (2 Chr 28:19–20; 2 Ki 16:7–10).

5:10 *Hagarites.* See vv. 19–22. Named among the enemies of Israel (Ps 83:6), this tribe is apparently associated with Hagar, the mother of Ishmael (Gen 16), but see note on Ps 83:6.

5:11–22 The materials in this list for the tribe of Gad have no parallels in the Bible. The other genealogies of Gad are organized around his seven sons (Gen 46:16; Num 26:15–18); here four names are given, none found in the other lists. The Chronicler states (v. 17) that these records came from the period of Jotham of Judah (750–732 B.C.) and Jeroboam of Israel (793–753). The presence of military titles and narratives (vv. 12,18–22) suggests that this genealogy originated as part of a military census. The territory of Gad is delineated in Deut 3:12.

5:18–22 The first example of the Chronicler's theme of immediate retribution (see Introduction: Purpose and Themes). Success in warfare is attributed to their crying out to God (v. 20; cf. 2 Chr 6:24–25,34–39; 12:7–12; 13:13–16; 14:9–15; 18:31; 20:1–30; 32:1–23).

5:23–26 Manasseh is treated further in 7:14–19; the half tribe that settled east of the Jordan is dealt with here since it shared the same fate as Reuben and Gad, and possibly also so that the

spirit of [a]Pul king of Assyria, and the spirit of
[b]Tilgath-pilneser king of Assyria, and he carried them away, even the Reubenites, and the
Gadites, and the half tribe of Manasseh, and
brought them unto [c]Halah, and Habor, and
Hara, and to the river Gozan, unto this day.

The family of Levi

6 The sons of Levi; [a][1]Gershon, Kohath,
and Merari.
2 And the sons of Kohath; Amram, [a]Izhar,
and Hebron, and Uzziel.
3 And the children of Amram; Aaron, and
Moses, and Miriam. The sons also of Aaron;
[a]Nadab, and Abihu, Eleazar, and Ithamar.
4 ¶ Eleazar begat Phinehas, Phinehas begat
Abishua,
5 And Abishua begat Bukki, and Bukki begat Uzzi,
6 And Uzzi begat Zerahiah, and Zerahiah
begat Meraioth,
7 Meraioth begat Amariah, and Amariah
begat Ahitub,
8 And [a]Ahitub begat Zadok, and [b]Zadok
begat Ahimaaz,
9 And Ahimaaz begat Azariah, and Azariah
begat Johanan,
10 And Johanan begat Azariah, (he *it is*
[a]that executed the priest's office [1]in the [b]temple that Solomon built in Jerusalem:)
11 And [a]Azariah begat Amariah, and Amariah begat Ahitub,
12 And Ahitub begat Zadok, and Zadok begat [1]Shallum,
13 And Shallum begat Hilkiah, and Hilkiah
begat Azariah,
14 And Azariah begat [a]Seraiah, and Seraiah begat Jehozadak,
15 And Jehozadak went *into captivity,*
[a]when the LORD carried away Judah and Jerusalem by the hand of Nebuchadnezzar.
16 ¶ The sons of Levi; [a][1]Gershom, Kohath,
and Merari.
17 And these *be* the names of the sons of
Gershom; Libni, and Shimei.
18 And the sons of Kohath *were,* Amram,
and Izhar, and Hebron, and Uzziel.
19 The sons of Merari; Mahli, and Mushi.
And these *are* the families of the Levites according to their fathers.
20 ¶ Of Gershom; Libni his son, Jahath his
son, [a]Zimmah his son,
21 [1]Joah his son, [2]Iddo his son, Zerah his
son, [3]Jeaterai his son.
22 ¶ The sons of Kohath; [1]Amminadab his
son, Korah his son, Assir his son,
23 Elkanah his son, and Ebiasaph his son,
and Assir his son,

5:26 [a]2 Ki. 15:19 [b]2 Ki. 15:29 [c]2 Ki. 17:6; 18:11
6:1 [1]Or, *Gershom* [a]Gen. 46:11; Ex. 6:16; Num. 26:57; ch. 23:6
6:2 [a]See ver. 22
6:3 [a]Lev. 10:1
6:8 [a]2 Sam. 8:17 [b]2 Sam. 15:27
6:10 [1]Heb. *in the house* [a]See 2 Chr. 26:17,18 [b]1 Ki. 6; 2 Chr. 3
6:11 [a]See Ezra 7:3
6:12 [1]Or, *Meshullam,* ch. 9:11
6:14 [a]Neh. 11:11
6:15 [a]2 Ki. 25:18
6:16 [1]Or, *Gershon,* ver. 1 [a]Ex. 6:16
6:20 [a]ver. 42
6:21 [1]Or, *Ethan,* ver. 42 [2]Or, *Adaiah,* ver. 41 [3][Or, *Ethni,* ver. 41]
6:22 [1]Or, *Izhar,* ver. 2,18,38

Chronicler could keep the total of 12 for his tribal genealogies (see note on 2:1–2). Again immediate retribution is apparent: Just as trust in God can bring victory (vv. 18–22), so also defeat comes to the unfaithful (vv. 25–26). The use of the retributive theme in these two accounts argues for the unity of the genealogies with the historical portions of Chronicles. The list of names given here is not properly a genealogy but a list of clans. Since they are described as brave warriors in connection with a battle report (vv. 24–26), this section too is likely derived from records of military conscription (see note on vv. 1–10; see also 2 Ki 15:19,29; 17:6; 18:11).

5:26 *Pul.* Probably Tilgath-pilneser's (Tiglath-pileser's) throne name in Babylon (the Babylonians called him Pulu).

6:1–81 This chapter is devoted to a series of lists, all pertaining to the tribe of Levi. The first section (vv. 1–15) records the line of the high priests down to the exile; the clans of Levi follow (vv. 16–30). David's appointees as temple musicians came from the three clans of Levi: Gershon (Gershom), Kohath and Merari (vv. 31–47). The generations between Aaron and Ahimaaz are given a separate listing (vv. 49–53), reinforcing the separate duties of priests and Levites (see note on Ex 32:26). The listing of the Levitical possessions among the tribes concludes the chapter (vv. 54–81).

6:1–3 A short segmented genealogy narrows the descendants of Levi to the lineage of Eleazar, in whose line the high priests are presented in linear form (vv. 4–15). The sons of Levi (v. 1) always appear in this order, based on age (v. 16; Gen 46:11; Ex 6:16; Num 3:17; 26:57). Of Aaron's four sons (v. 3), the first two died as a result of sacrilege (Lev 10:2; Num 26:61); succeeding generations of priests would trace their lineage to either Eleazar or Ithamar.

6:4–15 This list of high priests from the time of Eleazar to the exile has been sharply telescoped. The following high priests known from the OT are not mentioned: Jehoiada (2 Ki 12:2), Urijah (2 Ki 16:10–16), possibly two other Azariahs (2 Chr 26:17,20; 31:10–13), Eli (1 Sam 1:9; 14:3) and Abiathar (2 Sam 8:17). The list is repeated with some variation in Ezra 7:1–5 (see notes there).

6:8 *Ahitub begat Zadok.* This Zadok was one of David's two priests (18:16; 2 Sam 8:17). When David's other priest, Abiathar (see note on vv. 4–15), supported the rebellion of Adonijah, Zadok supported Solomon (1 Ki 1). After the expulsion of Abiathar (1 Ki 2:26–27), Zadok alone held the office (1 Chr 29:22), which continued in his line (1 Ki 4:2). The Ahitub mentioned here should not be confused with the priest who was the grandson of Eli (1 Sam 14:3) and grandfather of Abiathar (1 Sam 22:20); the line of Zadok replaced the line of Eli (1 Sam 2:27–36; 1 Ki 2:26–27). For the importance of the line of Zadok see Ezek 40:46; 43:19; 44:15; 48:11. Ezra was concerned to trace his own priestly lineage to this house (Ezra 7:1–5).

6:13 *Hilkiah.* Discovered the book of the law in the temple at the time of Josiah (2 Ki 22; 2 Chr 34).

6:14 *Seraiah.* Executed by the Babylonians after the conquest of Jerusalem in 586 B.C. (2 Ki 25:18–21). *Jehozadak.* Father of Jeshua, the high priest in the first generation of the restoration. His name is spelled "Jozadak" in Ezra 3:2,8; 5:2; 10:18; Neh 12:26 and "Josedech" elsewhere (see Hag 1:1; 2:2; Zech 6:11).

6:16–19a Repeated from Ex 6:16–19; Num 3:17–20; 26:57–61.

6:22 *Amminadab.* The almost parallel genealogy later in this chapter lists Izhar in the place of Amminadab—who is nowhere else listed as a son of Kohath, while every other list includes Izhar (vv. 2,37–38; Ex 6:18,21). Either Amminadab is an otherwise unattested alternative name of Izhar, or he is an otherwise unknown son. Or this may be another example of genealogical fluidity in which the Levites are linked with the tribe of Judah and the lineage of David (see Ruth 4:18–22; see also Mat 1:4; Luke 3:33) in view of Aaron's marriage to the daughter of Amminadab of Judah (Ex 6:23; see 1 Chr 2:10).

6:22–23 *Assir . . . Elkanah . . . Ebiasaph.* Ex 6:24 names these men as sons of Korah, but here they are presented in the form ordinarily used for a linear genealogy of successive generations (see vv. 20–21,25–26,29–30). Either this is another example of

24 Tahath his son, [1]Uriel his son, Uzziah his son, and Shaul his son.

25 And the sons of Elkanah; [a]Amasai, and Ahimoth.

26 *As for* Elkanah: the sons of Elkanah; [1]Zophai his son, and [2]Nahath his son,

27 [1]Eliab his son, Jeroham his son, Elkanah his son.

28 And the sons of Samuel; the firstborn [1]Vashni, and Abiah.

29 ¶ The sons of Merari; Mahli, Libni his son, Shimei his son, Uzza his son,

30 Shimea his son, Haggiah his son, Asaiah his son.

31 ¶ And these *are they* whom David set over the service of song *in* the house of the LORD, after that the [a]ark had rest.

32 And they ministered before the dwelling place of the tabernacle of the congregation with singing, until Solomon had built the house of the LORD in Jerusalem: and *then* they waited on their office according to their order.

33 And these *are* they that [1]waited with their children.

¶ Of the sons of the Kohathites: Heman a singer, the son of Joel, the son of Shemuel,

34 The son of Elkanah, the son of Jeroham, the son of Eliel, the son of [1]Toah,

35 The son of [1]Zuph, the son of Elkanah, the son of Mahath, the son of Amasai,

36 The son of Elkanah, the son of [1]Joel, the son of Azariah, the son of Zephaniah,

37 The son of Tahath, the son of Assir, the son of [a]Ebiasaph, the son of Korah,

38 The son of Izhar, the son of Kohath, the son of Levi, the son of Israel.

39 ¶ And his brother Asaph, who stood on his right hand, *even* Asaph the son of Berachiah, the son of Shimea,

40 The son of Michael, the son of Baaseiah, the son of Malchiah,

41 The son of [a]Ethni, the son of Zerah, the son of Adaiah,

42 The son of Ethan, the son of Zimmah, the son of Shimei,

43 The son of Jahath, the son of Gershom, the son of Levi.

44 ¶ And their brethren the sons of Merari *stood* on the left hand: [1]Ethan the son of [2]Kishi, the son of Abdi, the son of Malluch,

45 The son of Hashabiah, the son of Amaziah, the son of Hilkiah,

46 The son of Amzi, the son of Bani, the son of Shamer,

47 The son of Mahli, the son of Mushi, the son of Merari, the son of Levi.

The family of Aaron

48 ¶ Their brethren also the Levites *were* appointed unto all *manner of* service of the tabernacle of the house of God.

49 But Aaron and his sons offered [a]upon the altar of the burnt offering, and [b]on the altar of incense, *and were appointed* for all the work of the *place* most holy, and to make an atonement for Israel, according to all that Moses the servant of God had commanded.

50 And these *are* the sons of Aaron; Eleazar his son, Phinehas his son, Abishua his son,

51 Bukki his son, Uzzi his son, Zerahiah his son,

52 Meraioth his son, Amariah his son, Ahitub his son,

53 Zadok his son, Ahimaaz his son.

54 ¶ [a]Now these *are* their dwelling places throughout their castles in their coasts, of the sons of Aaron, of the families of the Kohathites: for theirs was the lot.

55 [a]And they gave them Hebron in the land of Judah, and the suburbs thereof round about it.

56 [a]But the fields of the city, and the villages thereof, they gave to Caleb the son of Jephunneh.

57 And [a]to the sons of Aaron they gave the cities of Judah, *namely,* Hebron, *the city* of refuge, and Libnah with her suburbs, and Jattir, and Eshtemoa, with their suburbs,

58 And [1]Hilen with her suburbs, Debir with her suburbs,

59 And [1]Ashan with her suburbs, and Beth-shemesh with her suburbs:

60 And out of the tribe of Benjamin; Geba with her suburbs, and [1]Alemeth with her suburbs, and Anathoth with her suburbs. All their cities throughout their families *were* thirteen cities.

6:24 [1][Or, *Zephaniah, Azariah, Joel,* ver. 36] **6:25** [a]See ver. 35,36 **6:26** [1]Or, *Zuph,* ver. 35 [2][ver. 34, *Toah*] **6:27** [1][ver. 34, *Eliel*] **6:28** [1]Called also *Joel,* ver. 33 **6:31** [a]ch. 16:1 **6:33** [1]Heb. *stood* **6:34** [1][ver. 26, *Nahath*] **6:35** [1][Or, *Zophai*] **6:36** [1][ver. 24, *Shaul, Uzziah, Uriel*] **6:37** [a]Ex. 6:24 **6:41** [a]See ver. 21 **6:44** [1][Called *Jeduthun,* ch. 9:16?; 25:1,3,6] [2]Or, *Kushaiah,* Comp. 2 Chr. 29:12; ch. 15:17 **6:49** [a]Lev. 1:9 [b]Ex. 30:7 **6:54** [a]Josh. 21 **6:55** [a]Josh. 21:11,12 **6:56** [a]Josh. 14:13; 15:13 **6:57** [a]Josh. 21:13 **6:58** [1]Or, *Holon,* Josh. 15:51 **6:59** [1]Or, *Ain,* Josh. 21:16 **6:60** [1]Or, *Almon,* Josh. 21:18

genealogical fluidity, or one must understand "his son" as referring to Kohath and not to the immediately preceding name.

6:24 *Uriel.* Possibly the one who led the Kohathites in David's day (15:5).

6:26–27 *Zophai . . . Nahath . . . Eliab.* Apparently variant names for Zuph, Toah and Eliel (vv. 34–35).

6:28 *Samuel.* His lineage is also given in 1 Sam 1:1, where his family is identified as Ephraimite (see note there). Either this is an example of genealogical fluidity, in which Samuel's involvement in the tabernacle (1 Sam 3) and performance of priestly duties (9:22; 1 Sam 2:18; 3:1) resulted in his incorporation into the Levites, or the term "Ephraimite" is to be understood as a place of residence, not as a statement of lineage.

6:31–48 Each of the three Levitical clans contributed musicians for the temple: Heman from the family of Kohath, Asaph from Gershom, and Ethan from Merari. The Chronicler makes frequent reference to the appointment of the musical guilds by David (15:16,27; 25:1–31; 2 Chr 29:25–26; see Neh 12:45–47). The frequent mention of the role of the Levites has led many to assume that the author was a member of the musicians. Non-Biblical literature also attests to guilds of singers and musicians in Canaanite temples. This genealogy appears to function as a means of legitimizing the Levites of the restoration period (Ezra 2:40–41; Neh 7:43–44; 10:9–13, 28–29; 11:15–18; 12:24–47).

6:49–53 Repeats vv. 4–8 but presumably serves a different function: to legitimize the line of Zadok, which is traced down to Solomon's time, as the only Levitical division authorized to offer sacrifices.

6:54–81 This list of Levitical possessions is taken from Josh 21 with only minor differences (see notes there). The Levites, who were given no block of territory of their own, were distributed throughout Israel.

61 ¶ And unto the sons of Kohath, [a]which were left of the family of *that* tribe, *were cities given* out of the half tribe, *namely, out of* the half *tribe* of Manasseh, [b]by lot, ten cities.

62 And to the sons of Gershom throughout their families out of the tribe of Issachar, and out of the tribe of Asher, and out of the tribe of Naphtali, and out of the tribe of Manasseh in Bashan, thirteen cities.

63 Unto the sons of Merari *were given* by lot, throughout their families, out of the tribe of Reuben, and out of the tribe of Gad, and out of the tribe of Zebulun, [a]twelve cities.

64 And the children of Israel gave to the Levites *these* cities with their suburbs.

65 And they gave by lot out of the tribe of the children of Judah, and out of the tribe of the children of Simeon, and out of the tribe of the children of Benjamin, these cities, which are called by *their* names.

66 And [a]*the residue* of the families of the sons of Kohath had cities of their coasts out of the tribe of Ephraim.

67 [a]And they gave unto them, *of* the cities of refuge, Shechem in mount Ephraim with her suburbs; *they gave* also Gezer with her suburbs,

68 And [1]Jokmeam with her suburbs, and Beth-horon with her suburbs,

69 And Aijalon with her suburbs, and Gath-rimmon with her suburbs:

70 And out of the half tribe of Manasseh; Aner with her suburbs, and Bileam with her suburbs, for the family of the remnant of the sons of Kohath.

71 ¶ Unto the sons of Gershom *were given* out of the family of the half tribe of Manasseh, Golan in Bashan with her suburbs, and [a]Ashtaroth with her suburbs:

72 And out of the tribe of Issachar; [a]Kedesh with her suburbs, Daberath with her suburbs,

73 And Ramoth with her suburbs, and Anem with her suburbs:

74 And out of the tribe of Asher; Mashal with her suburbs, and Abdon with her suburbs,

75 And Hukok with her suburbs, and Rehob with her suburbs:

76 And out of the tribe of Naphtali; Kedesh in Galilee with her suburbs, and Hammon with her suburbs, and Kirjathaim with her suburbs.

77 ¶ Unto the rest of the children of Merari *were given* out of the tribe of Zebulun, Rimmon with her suburbs, Tabor with her suburbs:

78 And on the *other* side Jordan *by* Jericho, on the east *side* of Jordan, *were given them* out of the tribe of Reuben, Bezer in the wilderness with her suburbs, and Jahzah with her suburbs,

79 Kedemoth also with her suburbs, and Mephaath with her suburbs:

80 And out of the tribe of Gad; Ramoth in Gilead with her suburbs, and Mahanaim with her suburbs,

81 And Heshbon with her suburbs, and Jazer with her suburbs.

6:61 [a]ver. 66 [b]Josh. 21:5
6:63 [a]Josh. 21:7,34
6:66 [a]ver. 61
6:67 [a]Josh. 21:21
6:68 [1][See Josh. 21:22-35, where many of these cities have other names]
6:71 [a]Josh. 21:27, *Beeshterah*
6:72 [a]Josh. 21:28, *Kishon*

The family of Issachar

7 Now the sons of Issachar *were,* [a]Tola, and [1]Puah, Jashub, and Shimron, four.

2 And the sons of Tola; Uzzi, and Rephaiah, and Jeriel, and Jahmai, and Jibsam, and Shemuel, heads of their fathers' house, *to wit,* of Tola: *they were* valiant *men* of might in their generations; [a]whose number *was* in the days of David two and twenty thousand and six hundred.

3 And the sons of Uzzi; Izrahiah: and the sons of Izrahiah; Michael, and Obadiah, and Joel, Ishiah, five: all of them chief *men.*

4 And with them, by their generations, after the house of their fathers, *were* bands of soldiers for war, six and thirty thousand *men:* for they had many wives and sons.

5 And their brethren among all the families of Issachar *were* men of might, reckoned in all by their genealogies fourscore and seven thousand.

The family of Benjamin

6 ¶ *The sons of* [a]Benjamin; Bela, and Becher, and Jediael, three.

7 And the sons of Bela; Ezbon, and Uzzi, and Uzziel, and Jerimoth, and Iri, five; heads of the house of *their* fathers, mighty *men* of valour; and were reckoned by their genealogies twenty and two thousand and thirty and four.

8 And the sons of Becher; Zemira, and Joash, and Eliezer, and Elioenai, and Omri, and Jerimoth, and Abiah, and Anathoth, and Alameth. All these *are* the sons of Becher.

9 And the number of them, after their genealogy by their generations, heads of the house of their fathers, mighty *men* of valour, *was* twenty thousand and two hundred.

10 The sons also of Jediael; Bilhan: and the sons of Bilhan; Jeush, and Benjamin, and Ehud, and Chenaanah, and Zethan, and Tharshish, and Ahishahar.

11 All these the sons of Jediael, by the heads of *their* fathers, mighty *men* of valour, *were* seventeen thousand and two hundred *soldiers, fit to* go out *for* war and battle.

12 [1]Shuppim also, and Huppim, the children of [2]Ir, *and* Hushim, the sons of [3]Aher.

7:1 [1][*Phuvah, Job*] [a]Gen. 46:13; Num. 26:23
7:2 [a]2 Sam. 24:1,2; ch. 27:1
7:6 [a]Gen. 46:21; Num. 26:38; ch. 8:1
7:12 [1][Num. 26:39, *Shupham,* and *Hupham*] [2]Or, *Iri,* ver. 7 [3]Or, *Ahiram,* Num. 26:38

7:1–5 Parts of the genealogy of Issachar are taken from Gen 46:13; Num 1:28; 26:23–25, though many of the names are otherwise unattested. This list of the clans appears to come from a military muster (vv. 2,4–5) from the time of David (v. 2), perhaps reflecting the census of ch. 21 and 2 Sam 24.

7:6–12 There is considerable fluidity among the Biblical sources listing the sons of Benjamin. This list gives three sons; Gen 46:21 records ten; Num 26:38–39 and 1 Chr 8:1–2 both list five (the only name appearing in all these sources is Bela, the firstborn). The variations reflect different origins and functions for these genealogies. The list here appears to function in the military sphere (vv. 7,9,11).

The family of Naphtali

13 ¶ The sons of Naphtali; Jahziel, and Guni,
and Jezer, and [1]Shallum, the sons of Bilhah.
14 ¶ The sons of Manasseh; Ashriel, whom
she bare: (*but* his concubine the Aramitess
bare Machir the father of Gilead:
15 And Machir took to wife *the sister* of
Huppim and Shuppim, whose sister's name
was Maachah;) and the name of the second *was*
Zelophehad: and Zelophehad had daughters.
16 And Maachah the wife of Machir bare a
son, and she called his name Peresh; and the
name of his brother *was* Sheresh; and his sons
were Ulam and Rakem.
17 And the sons of Ulam; [a]Bedan. These
were the sons of Gilead, the son of Machir, the
son of Manasseh.
18 And his sister Hammoleketh bare Ishod,
and [a] [1] Abiezer, and Mahalah.
19 And the sons of Shemida were, Ahian,
and Shechem, and Likhi, and Aniam.

The family of Ephraim

20 ¶ And [a]the sons of Ephraim; Shuthelah,
and Bered his son, and Tahath his son, and
Eladah his son, and Tahath his son,
21 And Zabad his son, and Shuthelah his
son, and Ezer, and Elead, whom the men of
Gath that were born in *that* land slew, because
they came down to take *away* their cattle.
22 And Ephraim their father mourned many
days, and his brethren came to comfort him.
23 And when he went in to his wife, she
conceived, and bare a son, and he called his
name Beriah, because it went evil with his
house.
24 (And his daughter *was* Sherah, who
built Beth-horon the nether, and the upper,
and Uzzen-sherah.)
25 And Rephah *was* his son, also Resheph,
and Telah his son, and Tahan his son,
26 Laadan his son, Ammihud his son,
Elishama his son,
27 [1]Non his son, Jehoshua his son.

7:13 [1] [Gen. 46:24, *Shillem*] 7:17 [a] 1 Sam. 12:11 7:18 [1] [Num. 26:30, *Jeezer*] [a] Num. 26:30; *Jeezer* 7:20 [a] Num. 26:35 7:27 [1] Or, *Nun*, Num. 13:8,16

7:28 [1] Heb. *daughters* [2] Josh. 16:7, [*Naarath*] [3] Or, *Adassa* 7:29 [1] Heb. *daughters* [a] Josh. 17:7 [b] Josh. 17:11 7:30 [a] Gen. 46:17; Num. 26:44 7:32 [1] [ver. 34, *Shamer*] 7:34 [1] [ver. 32, *Shomer*] 8:1 [a] Gen. 46:21; Num. 26:38; ch. 7:6

28 ¶ And their possessions and habitations
were, Beth-el and the [1]towns thereof, and
eastward [2]Naaran, and westward Gezer, with
the [1]towns thereof; Shechem also and the
[1]towns thereof, [5]unto Gaza and the [1]towns
thereof:
29 And by the borders of the children of
[a]Manasseh, Beth-shean and her [1]towns, Taanach and her [1]towns, [b]Megiddo and her
[1]towns, Dor and her [1]towns. In these dwelt
the children of Joseph the son of Israel.

The family of Asher

30 ¶ [a]The sons of Asher; Imnah, and Isuah,
and Ishuai, and Beriah, and Serah their sister.
31 And the sons of Beriah; Heber, and
Malchiel, who *is* the father of Birzavith.
32 And Heber begat Japhlet, and [1]Shomer,
and Hotham, and Shua their sister.
33 And the sons of Japhlet; Pasach, and
Bimhal, and Ashvath. These *are* the children
of Japhlet.
34 And the sons of [1]Shamer; Ahi, and Roh-
gah, Jehubbah, and Aram.
35 And the son of his brother Helem; Zophah, and Imna, and Shelesh, and Amal.
36 The sons of Zophah; Suah, and
Harnepher, and Shual, and Beri, and Imrah,
37 Bezer, and Hod, and Shamma, and Shil-
shah, and Ithran, and Beera.
38 And the sons of Jether; Jephunneh, and
Pispah, and Ara.
39 And the sons of Ulla; Arah, and Haniel,
and Rezia.
40 All these *were* the children of Asher,
heads of *their* fathers' house, choice *and*
mighty *men* of valour, chief of the princes.
And the number throughout the genealogy of
them *that were apt* to the war *and* to battle
was twenty and six thousand men.

The family of Benjamin

8 Now Benjamin begat [a]Bela his firstborn,
Ashbel the second, and Aharah the third,

7:13 Repeats Gen 46:24; Num 26:48–50. *sons of Bilhah.* Dan and Naphtali were the actual "sons" of Jacob's concubine Bilhah (Gen 30:3–8), so Naphtali's sons are Bilhah's "descendants."

7:14–19 See note on 5:23–26. The sources for this genealogy are Num 26:29–34; Josh 17:1–18. The daughters of Zelophehad (v. 15) prompted the rulings on the inheritance rights of women (Num 26:29–34; 27:1–11; 36:1–12; Josh 17:3–4). Of the 13 different clans of the tribe of Manasseh known from these genealogies, seven are mentioned in the Samaria ostraca (about 65 inscribed potsherds containing records of deliveries of wine, oil, barley and other commodities in the eighth century B.C.). The prominence of women in this genealogy is unusual; this suggests that it may have functioned in the domestic sphere, perhaps as a statement of the social status of the various clans of Manasseh (see Introduction: Genealogies).

7:20–29 The source for part of the genealogy of Ephraim is Num 26:35. If Rephah (v. 25) is the grandson of Ephraim, ten generations are recorded from Ephraim to Joshua, a number that fits very well the 400-year interval when Israel was in Egypt. Joshua's Ephraimite ancestry is also mentioned in Num 13:8 (where he is called "Oshea"; see Num 13:16). The raid against Gath (vv. 21–22) must have taken place well before the conquest of Canaan and must have originated in Egypt. The list of settlements (vv. 28–29) summarizes Josh 16–17.

7:30–40 The genealogy of Asher follows Gen 46:17 for the first three generations; it is also parallel to Num 26:44–46, except that the name Isuah (v. 30) is missing there. This genealogy too reflects a military function (v. 40).

8:1–40 The inclusion of a second and even more extensive genealogy of Benjamin (see note on 7:6–12) reflects both the importance of this tribe and the Chronicler's interest in Saul. Judah, Simeon and part of Benjamin had composed the southern kingdom (1 Ki 12:1–21), and their territory largely comprised the restoration province of Judah in the Chronicler's own time. The genealogy of Benjamin is more extensive than that of all the other tribes except Judah and Levi. The Chronicler is also concerned with the genealogy of Saul (vv. 29–38) in order to set the stage for the historical narrative that begins with the end of his reign (ch. 10); Saul's genealogy is repeated in 9:35–44. Several references suggest that this genealogy also originated in the military sphere (vv. 6,10,13,28,40).

8:1–5 Cf. the lists in 7:6–12; Gen 46:21–22; Num 26:38–41.

2 Nohah the fourth, and Rapha the fifth.
3 And the sons of Bela were, [1]Addar, and
Gera, and Abihud,
4 And Abishua, and Naaman, and Ahoah,
5 And Gera, and [1]Shephuphan, and Huram.
6 And these *are* the sons of Ehud: these *are*
the heads of the fathers of the inhabitants of
Geba, and they removed them to [a]Manahath:
7 And Naaman, and Ahiah, and Gera, he
removed them, and begat Uzza, and Ahihud.
8 And Shaharaim begat *children* in the
country of Moab, after he had sent them away;
Hushim and Baara *were* his wives.
9 And he begat of Hodesh his wife, Jobab,
and Zibia, and Mesha, and Malcham,
10 And Jeuz, and Shachia, and Mirma.
These *were* his sons, heads of the fathers.
11 And of Hushim he begat Abitub, and Elpaal.
12 The sons of Elpaal; Eber, and Misham,
and Shamed, who built Ono, and Lod, with
the towns thereof:
13 Beriah also, and [a]Shema, who *were*
heads of the fathers of the inhabitants of Aijalon, who drove away the inhabitants of Gath:
14 And Ahio, Shashak, and Jeremoth,
15 And Zebadiah, and Arad, and Ader,
16 And Michael, and Ispah, and Joha, the
sons of Beriah;
17 And Zebadiah, and Meshullam, and
Hezeki, and Heber,
18 Ishmerai also, and Jezliah, and Jobab,
the sons of Elpaal;
19 And Jakim, and Zichri, and Zabdi,
20 And Elienai, and Zilthai, and Eliel,
21 And Adaiah, and Beraiah, and Shim-
rath, the sons of [1]Shimhi;
22 And Ishpan, and Heber, and Eliel,
23 And Abdon, and Zichri, and Hanan,
24 And Hananiah, and Elam, and Antothi-
jah,
25 And Iphedeiah, and Penuel, the sons of
Shashak;
26 And Shamsherai, and Shehariah, and
Athaliah,
27 And Jaresiah, and Eliah, and Zichri, the
sons of Jeroham.
28 These *were* heads of the fathers, by
their generations, chief *men.* These dwelt in
Jerusalem.

29 ¶ And at Gibeon dwelt the [1]father of
Gibeon; whose [a]wife's name *was* Maachah:
30 And his firstborn son Abdon, and Zur,
and Kish, and Baal, and Nadab,
31 And Gedor, and Ahio, and [1]Zacher.
32 And Mikloth begat [1]Shimeah. And
these also dwelt with their brethren in Jerusalem, over against them.
33 ¶ And [a]Ner begat Kish, and Kish begat
Saul, and Saul begat Jonathan, and Malchishua, and [1]Abinadab, and [2]Eshbaal.
34 And the son of Jonathan *was* [1]Merib-
baal; and Merib-baal begat [a]Micah.
35 And the sons of Micah *were,* Pithon,
and Melech, and [1]Tarea, and Ahaz.
36 And Ahaz begat [1]Jehoadah; and Jehoa-
dah begat Alemeth, and Azmaveth, and Zimri;
and Zimri begat Moza,
37 And Moza begat Binea: [1]Rapha *was* his
son, Eleasah his son, Azel his son:
38 And Azel had six sons, whose names
are these, Azrikam, Bocheru, and Ishmael, and
Sheariah, and Obadiah, and Hanan. All these
were the sons of Azel.
39 And the sons of Eshek his brother *were,*
Ulam his firstborn, Jehush the second, and
Eliphelet the third.
40 And the sons of Ulam were mighty men
of valour, archers, and had many sons, and
sons' sons, an hundred and fifty. All these *are*
of the sons of Benjamin.

Inhabitants in Jerusalem

9 So [a]all Israel were reckoned by genealogies; and behold, they *were* written in
the book of the kings of Israel and Judah, *who*
were carried away to Babylon for their transgression.
2 ¶ [a]Now the first inhabitants that *dwelt* in
their possessions in their cities *were,* the Israelites, the priests, Levites, and [b]the Nethinims.
3 And in [a]Jerusalem dwelt of the children
of Judah, and of the children of Benjamin, and
of the children of Ephraim, and Manasseh;
4 Uthai the son of Ammihud, the son of
Omri, the son of Imri, the son of Bani, of the
children of Pharez the son of Judah.
5 And of the Shilonites; Asaiah the firstborn, and his sons.

8:3 [1]Or, *Ard,* Gen. 46:21
8:5 [1]Or, *Shupham,* Num. 26:39
8:6 [a]ch. 2:52
8:13 [a]ver. 21
8:21 [1]Or, *Shema,* ver. 13
8:29 [1]Called *Jehiel,* ch. 9:35 [a]ch. 9:35
8:31 [1]Or, *Zechariah,* ch. 9:37
8:32 [1]Or, *Shimeam,* ch. 9:38
8:33 [1][1 Sam. 14:49, *Ishui*] [2]Or, *Ish-bosheth* [a]1 Sam. 14:51
8:34 [1]Or, *Mephibosheth* [a]2 Sam. 9:12
8:35 [1]Or, *Tahrea,* ch. 9:41
8:36 [1][*Jarah,* ch. 9:42]
8:37 [1][ch. 9:43, *Rephaiah*]
9:1 [a]Ezra 2:59
9:2 [a]Ezra 2:70; Neh. 7:73 [b]Josh. 9:27; Ezra 2:43; 8:20
9:3 [a]Neh. 11:1

8:6–27 Unique to Chronicles.
8:29–38 Essentially the same as the list in 9:35–44.
‡8:33 For the sons of Saul see 1 Sam 14:49; 31:2. *Jonathan.* The firstborn and the best known of the sons of Saul, both for his military prowess and for his friendship with David (1 Sam 13–14; 18:1–4; 19:1–7; 20:1–42; 23:16–18; 2 Sam 21:13–14). *Eshbaal.* Ish-bosheth in 2 Sam 2:8. See also note on 2 Sam 2:8.
‡8:34 *Merib-baal.* Mephibosheth in 2 Sam 4:4. See also note on 2 Sam 4:4.
9:1 *all Israel.* The Chronicler's concern with "all Israel" is one key to why he included the genealogies (see Introduction: Purpose and Themes).
9:2–34 This list of the members of the restored community reflects the Chronicler's concern with the institutions of his own day, especially the legitimacy of officeholders. He lists laity ("Israelites," v. 2) in vv. 3–9, priests in vv. 10–13 and Levites in vv. 14–34. He mentions a fourth class of returnees—the temple servants ("Nethinims," v. 2)—but does not give them separate listing in the material that follows. They may have been originally foreigners who were incorporated into the Levites (Josh 9:23; Ezra 8:20) and so are not listed apart from that tribe. A similar office is known in the temple at ancient Ugarit. The list here is related to the one in Neh 11, but less than half the names are the same in the two lists.
9:3 *Ephraim, and Manasseh.* Again reflecting his concern with "all Israel," the Chronicler shows that the returnees were not only from Judah and Benjamin but also from the northern tribes.
9:4–6 See 2:3–6; 4:21. The returnees of Judah are traced to Judah's sons Perez, Zerah and Shelah—if the word "Shilonites"

6 And of the sons of Zerah; Jeuel, and their brethren, six hundred and ninety.

7 And of the sons of Benjamin; Sallu the son of Meshullam, the son of Hodaviah, the son of Hasenuah,

8 And Ibneiah the son of Jeroham, and Elah the son of Uzzi, the son of Michri, and Meshullam the son of Shephathiah, the son of Reuel, the son of Ibnijah;

9 And their brethren, according to their generations, nine hundred and fifty and six. All these men *were* chief of the fathers in the house of their fathers.

10 ¶ [a]And of the priests; Jedaiah, and Jehoiarib, and Jachin,

11 And [1]Azariah the son of Hilkiah, the son of Meshullam, the son of Zadok, the son of Meraioth, the son of Ahitub, the ruler of the house of God;

12 And Adaiah the son of Jeroham, the son of Pashur, the son of Malchijah, and Maasiai the son of Adiel, the son of Jahzerah, the son of Meshullam, the son of Meshillemith, the son of Immer;

13 And their brethren, heads of the house of their fathers, a thousand and seven hundred and threescore; [1]very able men *for* the work of the service of the house of God.

14 ¶ And of the Levites; Shemaiah the son of Hasshub, the son of Azrikam, the son of Hashabiah, of the sons of Merari;

15 And Bakbakkar, Heresh, and Galal, and Mattaniah the son of Micah, the son of Zichri, the son of Asaph;

16 And Obadiah the son of Shemaiah, the son of Galal, the son of Jeduthun, and Berechiah the son of Asa, the son of Elkanah, that dwelt in the villages of the Netophathites.

17 And the porters *were,* Shallum, and Akkub, and Talmon, and Ahiman, and their brethren: Shallum *was* the chief;

18 Who hitherto *waited* in the king's gate eastward: they *were* porters in the companies of the children of Levi.

19 And Shallum the son of Kore, the son of Ebiasaph, the son of Korah, and his brethren, of the house of his father, the Korahites, *were* over the work of the service, keepers of the [1]gates of the tabernacle: and their fathers, *being* over the host of the LORD, *were* keepers of the entry.

9:10 [a]Neh. 11:10
9:11 [1][Neh. 11:11, *Seraiah*]
9:13 [1]Heb. *mighty* men *of valour*
9:19 [1]Heb. *thresholds*

9:20 [a]Num. 31:6
9:22 [1]Heb. *founded* [2]Or, *trust* [a]ch. 26:1,2 [b]1 Sam. 9:9
9:25 [a]2 Ki. 11:5
9:26 [1]Or, *trust* [2]Or, *storehouses*
9:28 [1]Heb. *bring them in by tale, and carry them out by tale*
9:29 [1]Or, *vessels*
9:30 [a]Ex. 30:23
9:31 [1]Or, *trust* [2]Or, *on flat plates,* or, *slices* [a]Lev. 2:5; 6:21
9:32 [1]Heb. *bread of ordering* [a]Lev. 24:8
9:33 [1]Heb. *upon them* [a]ch. 6:31; 25:1

20 And [a]Phinehas the son of Eleazar was the ruler over them in time past, *and* the LORD *was* with him.

21 *And* Zechariah the son of Meshelemiah *was* porter of the door of the tabernacle of the congregation.

22 All these which were chosen to be porters in the gates *were* two hundred and twelve. These were reckoned by their genealogy in their villages, whom [a]David and Samuel [b]the seer [1]did ordain in their [2]set office.

23 So they and their children had the oversight of the gates of the house of the LORD, *namely,* the house of the tabernacle, by wards.

24 In four quarters were the porters, toward the east, west, north, and south.

25 And their brethren, *which were* in their villages, *were* to come [a]after seven days from time to time with them.

26 For these Levites, the four chief porters, *were* in *their* [1]set office, and were over the [2]chambers and treasuries of the house of God.

27 And they lodged round about the house of God, because the charge *was* upon them, and the opening *thereof* every morning pertained to them.

28 And *certain* of them had the charge of the ministering vessels, that they should [1]bring them in and out by tale.

29 *Some* of them also *were* appointed to oversee the vessels, and all the [1]instruments of the sanctuary, and the fine flour, and the wine, and the oil, and the frankincense, and the spices.

30 And *some* of the sons of the priests made [a]the ointment of the spices.

31 And Mattithiah, *one* of the Levites, who *was* the firstborn of Shallum the Korahite, had the [1]set office [a]over the things that were made [2]in the pans.

32 And *other* of their brethren, of the sons of the Kohathites, [a]*were* over the [1]shewbread, to prepare *it* every sabbath.

33 And these *are* [a]the singers, chief of the fathers of the Levites, *who remaining* in the chambers *were* free: for [1]they were employed in *that* work day and night.

34 These chief fathers of the Levites *were* chief throughout their generations; these dwelt at Jerusalem.

(v. 5) is read as "Shelanites" (Num 26:20). If the reading "Shilonites" is retained, the reference is to Shiloh, the important sanctuary city (Judg 18:31; Jer 7:12–14; 26:9).

9:10–13 The list of priests is essentially the same as that in Neh 11:10–14. Since it is tied to the list of priests earlier in the genealogies (6:1–15,50–53), contemporary Israel's continuity with her past is shown.

9:15–16 *Asaph . . . Jeduthun.* Leaders of musical groups (6:39; 16:41). Later the Chronicler also lists the musicians (ch. 25) before the gatekeepers (ch. 26).

9:16 *Netophathites.* See note on Neh 12:28.

9:17–21 The Chronicler gives the names of four gatekeepers, while Neh 11:19 mentions only two. The chief of the gatekeepers had the honor of responsibility for the gate used by the king (Ezek 46:1–2). The gatekeepers are also listed in ch. 26; Ezra 2:42. These officers traced their origin to Phinehas (v. 20; 6:4; Num 3:32; 25:6–13).

9:22–27 Twenty-four guard stations were manned in three shifts around the clock; 72 men would be needed for each week. With a total of 212 men, each would have a tour of duty approximately every three weeks (26:12–18).

9:28–34 The Levites not only were responsible for the temple precincts and for opening the gates in the morning, but they also had charge of the chambers and supply rooms (23:28; 26:20–29) as well as the implements, supplies and furnishings (28:13–18; Ezra 1:9–11). In addition they were responsible for the preparation of baked goods (Ex 25:30; Lev 2:5–7; 7:9). The priests alone prepared the perfumed anointing oil and spices (Ex 30:23–33).

The family of Saul

35 ¶ And in Gibeon dwelt the father of Gibeon, Jehiel, whose wife's name *was* [a]Maachah:

36 And his firstborn son Abdon, then Zur, and Kish, and Baal, and Ner, and Nadab,

37 And Gedor, and Ahio, and Zechariah, and Mikloth.

38 And Mikloth begat Shimeam. And they also dwelt with their brethren at Jerusalem, over against their brethren.

39 ¶ [a]And Ner begat Kish; and Kish begat Saul; and Saul begat Jonathan, and Malchi-shua, and Abinadab, and Eshbaal.

40 And the son of Jonathan *was* Merib-baal: and Merib-baal begat Micah.

41 And the sons of Micah *were,* Pithon, and Melech, and Tahrea, [a]*and Ahaz.*

42 And Ahaz begat Jarah; and Jarah begat Alemeth, and Azmaveth, and Zimri; and Zimri begat Moza;

43 And Moza begat Binea; and Rephaiah his son, Eleasah his son, Azel his son.

44 And Azel had six sons, whose names *are* these, Azrikam, Bocheru, and Ishmael, and Sheariah, and Obadiah, and Hanan: these *were* the sons of Azel.

Saul killed on mount Gilboa

10 Now [a]the Philistines fought against Israel; and the men of Israel fled from before the Philistines, and fell down [1]slain in mount Gilboa.

2 And the Philistines followed hard after Saul, and after his sons; and the Philistines slew Jonathan, and [1]Abinadab, and Malchi-shua, the sons of Saul.

3 And the battle went sore against Saul, and the [1]archers [2]hit him, and he was wounded of the archers.

4 Then said Saul to his armourbearer, Draw thy sword, and thrust me through therewith; lest these uncircumcised come and [1]abuse me. But his armourbearer would not; for he was sore afraid. So Saul took a sword, and fell upon it.

5 And when his armourbearer saw that Saul was dead, he fell likewise on the sword, and died.

6 So Saul died, and his three sons, and all his house died together.

7 ¶ And when all the men of Israel that *were* in the valley saw that they fled, and that Saul and his sons were dead, then they forsook their cities, and fled: and the Philistines came and dwelt in them.

8 And it came to pass on the morrow, when the Philistines came to strip the slain, that they found Saul and his sons fallen in mount Gilboa.

9 And when they had stripped him, they took his head, and his armour, and sent into the land of the Philistines round about, to carry tidings unto their idols, and to the people.

10 [a]And they put his armour *in* the house of their gods, and fastened his head *in* the temple of Dagon.

11 And when all Jabesh-gilead heard all that the Philistines had done to Saul,

12 They arose, all the valiant men, and took away the body of Saul, and the bodies of his sons, and brought them to Jabesh, and buried their bones under the oak in Jabesh, and fasted seven days.

13 So Saul died for his transgression which he [1]committed against the LORD, [a]*even* against the word of the LORD, which he kept not, and also for asking *counsel* of *one that had* a familiar spirit, [b]to inquire *of it;*

14 And inquired not of the LORD: therefore he slew him, and [a]turned the kingdom unto David the son of [1]Jesse.

David, king of all Israel

11 Then [a]all Israel gathered themselves to David unto Hebron, saying, Behold, we *are* thy bone and thy flesh.

2 *And* moreover [1]in time past, even when Saul was king, thou *wast* he that leddest out and broughtest in Israel: and the LORD thy God said unto thee, Thou shalt [a][2]feed my people Israel, and thou shalt be ruler over my people Israel.

3 Therefore came all the elders of Israel to the king to Hebron; and David made a covenant with them in Hebron before the LORD; and [a]they anointed David king over Israel, according to the word of the LORD [1]by [b]Samuel.

9:35 [a]ch. 8:29
9:39 [a]ch. 8:33
9:41 [a]ch. 8:35
10:1 [1]Or, *wounded* [a]1 Sam. 31:1,2
10:2 [1]Or, *Ishui,* 1 Sam. 14:49
10:3 [1]Heb. *shooters with bows* [2]Heb. *found him*
10:4 [1]Or, *mock me*
10:10 [a]1 Sam. 31:10
10:13 [1]Heb. *transgressed* [a]1 Sam. 13:13; 15:23 [b]1 Sam. 28:7
10:14 [1]Heb. *Isai* [a]1 Sam. 15:28; 2 Sam. 3:9,10; 5:3
11:1 [a]2 Sam. 5:1
11:2 [1]Heb. *both yesterday and the third day* [2]Or, *rule* [a]Ps. 78:71
11:3 [1]Heb. *by the hand of* [a]2 Sam. 5:3 [b]1 Sam. 16:1,12,13

9:35–44 The genealogy of Saul is duplicated here (see 8:29–38) as a transition to the short account of his reign that begins the Chronicler's narration (ch. 10).

10:2 For the strategy of pursuing the king in battle see note on 1 Ki 22:31.

10:6 *his three sons.* See v. 2 (Ish-bosheth survived; see note on 1 Sam 31:2). *all his house.* His three sons and his chief officials (his official "house"), not all his descendants (see 8:33–34 and notes; 1 Sam 31:6).

10:13–14 These verses are not paralleled in the Samuel account; they were put here by the Chronicler in line with his concern with immediate retribution (see Introduction: Purpose and Themes). Seeking mediums was forbidden (Deut 18:9–14) and brought death to Saul. The Chronicler is obviously writing to an audience already familiar with Samuel and Kings, and he frequently assumes that knowledge. Here the consultation with the medium at En-dor is alluded to (see 1 Sam 28), but the Chronicler does not recount the incident.

11:1–2 Chr 9:31 See Introduction: Portrait of David and Solomon.

11:1–3 The material here parallels that in 2 Sam 5:1–3, but is recast by the Chronicler in accordance with his emphasis on the popular support given David by "all Israel" (v. 1). While the Chronicler twice mentions the seven-year reign at Hebron before the death of Ish-bosheth and the covenant with the northern tribes (3:4; 29:27), these incidents are bypassed in the narrative portion of the book. Most striking is the elimination at this point of the information in 2 Sam 5:4–5. Rather, the Chronicler paints a picture of immediate accession over "all Israel," followed by the immediate conquest of Jerusalem (see Introduction: Portrait of David and Solomon). The author once again assumes the reader's knowledge of the parallel account.

4 ¶ And David and all Israel [a]went *to* Jerusalem, which *is* Jebus; [b]where the Jebusites *were,* the inhabitants of the land.

5 And the inhabitants of Jebus said to David, Thou shalt not come hither. Nevertheless David took the castle of Zion, which *is* the city of David.

6 And David said, Whosoever smiteth the Jebusites first shall be [1]chief and captain. So Joab the son of Zeruiah went first up, and was chief.

7 And David dwelt in the castle; therefore they called [1]it the city of David.

8 And he built the city round about, even from Millo round about: and Joab [1]repaired the rest of the city.

9 So David [1]waxed greater and greater: for the LORD of hosts *was* with him.

David's mighty men

10 ¶ [a]These also *are* the chief of the mighty *men* whom David had, who [1]strengthened themselves with him in his kingdom, *and* with all Israel, to make him king, according to [b]the word of the LORD concerning Israel.

11 And this *is* the number of the mighty *men* whom David had; Jashobeam, [1]a Hachmonite, the chief of the captains: he lift up his spear against three hundred slain *by him* at one time.

12 And after him *was* Eleazar the son of Dodo, the Ahohite, who *was one* of the three mighties.

13 He was with David at [1]Pas-dammim, and there the Philistines were gathered together to battle, where was a parcel of ground full *of* barley; and the people fled from before the Philistines.

14 And they [1]set themselves in the midst of *that* parcel, and delivered it, and slew the Philistines; and the LORD saved *them by* a great [a2]deliverance.

15 Now [1]three of the thirty captains [a]went down to the rock to David, into the cave of Adullam; and the host of the Philistines encamped [b]in the valley of Rephaim.

16 And David *was* then in the hold, and the Philistines' garrison *was* then at Beth-lehem.

17 And David longed, and said, Oh that one would give me drink *of* the water of the well of Beth-lehem, that *is* at the gate.

18 And the three brake through the host of the Philistines, and drew water out of the well of Beth-lehem, that *was* by the gate, and took *it,* and brought *it* to David: but David would not drink *of* it, but poured it out to the LORD,

11:4 [a]2 Sam. 5:6 [b]Judg. 1:21; 19:10
11:6 [1]Heb. *head*
11:7 [1]That is, *Zion,* 2 Sam. 5:7
11:8 [1]Heb. *revived*
11:9 [1]Heb. *went in going and increasing*
11:10 [1]Or, *held strongly with him* [a]2 Sam. 23:8 [b]1 Sam. 16:1,12
11:11 [1]Or, *son of Hachmoni*
11:13 [1]Or, *Ephes-dammim,* 1 Sam. 17:1
11:14 [1]Or, *stood* [2]Or, *salvation* [a]Judg. 1:21; 19:10
11:15 [1]Or, *three captains over the thirty* [a]2 Sam. 23:13 [b]ch. 14:9
11:19 [1]Heb. *with their lives?*
11:20 [a]2 Sam. 23:18
11:21 [a]2 Sam. 23:19
11:22 [1]Heb. *great of deeds* [a]2 Sam. 23:20
11:23 [1]Heb. *a man of measure*
11:26 [a]2 Sam. 23:24
11:27 [1][Or, *Shammah*] [2]Or, *Harodite,* 2 Sam. 23:25 [3][Or, *Paltite,* 2 Sam. 23:26]
11:29 [1][Or, *Mebunnai*] [2][Or, *Zalmon*]
11:30 [1][Or, *Heleb*]
11:32 [1][Or, *Hiddai*] [2][Or, *Abi-albon*]
11:34 [1][Or, *Jashen*]
11:35 [1][Or, *Sharar*] [2][Or, *Eliphelet*] [3][Or, *Ahasbai*]
11:37 [1][Or, *Hezrai*] [2][Or, *Paarai the Arbite*]

19 And said, My God forbid it me, that *I* should do this *thing:* shall I drink the blood of these men [1]that have put their lives in jeopardy? for with *the jeopardy of* their lives they brought it. Therefore he would not drink it. These *things* did *these* three mightiest.

20 [a]And Abishai the brother of Joab, he was chief of the three: for lifting up his spear against three hundred, he slew *them,* and had a name among the three.

21 [a]Of the three, he was more honourable than the two; for he was their captain: howbeit he attained not to the *first* three.

22 Benaiah the son of Jehoiada, the son of a valiant man of Kabzeel, [1]who had done many acts; [a]he slew two lionlike men of Moab: also he went down and slew a lion in a pit in a snowy day.

23 And he slew an Egyptian, [1]a man of *great* stature, five cubits *high;* and in the Egyptian's hand *was* a spear like a weaver's beam; and he went down to him with a staff, and pluckt the spear out of the Egyptian's hand, and slew him with his own spear.

24 These *things* did Benaiah the son of Jehoiada, and had the name among the three mighties.

25 Behold, he was honourable among the thirty, but attained not to the *first* three: and David set him over his guard.

26 ¶ Also the valiant *men* of the armies *were,* [a]Asahel the brother of Joab, Elhanan the son of Dodo of Beth-lehem,

27 [1]Shammoth the [2]Harorite, Helez the [3]Pelonite,

28 Ira the son of Ikkesh the Tekoite, Abiezer the Antothite,

29 [1]Sibbecai the Hushathite, [2]Ilai the Ahohite,

30 Maharai the Netophathite, [1]Heled the son of Baanah the Netophathite,

31 Ithai the son of Ribai of Gibeah, that pertained to the children of Benjamin, Benaiah the Pirathonite,

32 [1]Hurai of the brooks of Gaash, [2]Abiel the Arbathite,

33 Azmaveth the Baharumite, Eliahba the Shaalbonite,

34 The sons of [1]Hashem the Gizonite, Jonathan the son of Shage the Hararite,

35 Ahiam the son of [1]Sacar the Hararite, [2]Eliphal the son of [3]Ur,

36 Hepher the Mecherathite, Ahijah the Pelonite,

37 [1]Hezro the Carmelite, [2]Naarai the son of Ezbai,

11:4–9 See 2 Sam 5:6–10 and notes. The "all Israel" theme appears in v. 4 as a substitute for "the king and his men" (2 Sam 5:6).

11:10–41a See 2 Sam 23:8–39 and notes. In the Samuel account this list of David's mighty men is given near the end of his reign. The Chronicler has moved the list to the beginning of his reign and has greatly expanded it (11:41b–12:40), again as part of his emphasis on the broad support of "all Israel" for the kingship of David (v. 10).

11:11 *three hundred.* Actually 800 (see 2 Sam 23:8), 300 here apparently being a copyist's mistake, perhaps influenced by the same number in v. 20.

11:12–14 See 2 Sam 23:9b–11a.

11:15–19 David recognizes that he is not worthy of such devotion and makes the water a drink offering to the Lord (see Gen 35:14; 2 Ki 16:13; Jer 7:18; Hos 9:4).

38 Joel the brother of Nathan, Mibhar [1] the son of Haggeri,

39 Zelek the Ammonite, Naharai the Berothite, the armourbearer of Joab the son of Zeruiah,

40 Ira the Ithrite, Gareb the Ithrite,

41 Uriah the Hittite, Zabad the son of Ahlai,

42 Adina the son of Shiza the Reubenite, a captain of the Reubenites, and thirty with him,

43 Hanan the son of Maachah, and Joshaphat the Mithnite,

44 Uzzia the Ashterathite, Shama and Jehiel the sons of Hothan the Aroerite,

45 Jediael the [1] son of Shimri, and Joha his brother, the Tizite,

46 Eliel the Mahavite, and Jeribai, and Joshaviah, the sons of Elnaam, and Ithmah the Moabite,

47 Eliel, and Obed, and Jasiel the Mesobaite.

David's supporters

12 Now [a] these *are* they that came to David to [b] Ziklag, [1] while he yet kept himself close because of Saul the son of Kish: and they *were* among the mighty *men,* helpers of the war.

2 *They were* armed with bows, and could use both the right hand and [a] the left in *hurling* stones and *shooting* arrows out of a bow, *even* of Saul's brethren of Benjamin.

3 The chief *was* Ahiezer, then Joash, the sons of [1] Shemaah the Gibeathite; and Jeziel, and Pelet, the sons of Azmaveth; and Berachah, and Jehu the Antothite,

4 And Ismaiah the Gibeonite, a mighty *man* among the thirty, and over the thirty; and Jeremiah, and Jahaziel, and Johanan, and Josabad the Gederathite,

5 Eleuzai, and Jerimoth, and Bealiah, and Shemariah, and Shephatiah the Haruphite,

6 Elkanah, and Jesiah, and Azareel, and Joezer, and Jashobeam, the Korhites,

7 And Joelah, and Zebadiah, the sons of Jeroham of Gedor.

8 And of the Gadites there separated themselves unto David into the hold to the wilderness men of might, *and* men [1] of war *fit* for the battle, that could handle shield and buckler, whose faces *were like* the faces of lions, and *were* [a] [2] as swift as the roes upon the mountains:

9 Ezer the first, Obadiah the second, Eliab the third,

10 Mishmannah the fourth, Jeremiah the fifth,

11 Attai the sixth, Eliel the seventh,

12 Johanan the eighth, Elzabad the ninth,

13 Jeremiah the tenth, Machbanai the eleventh.

14 These *were* of the sons of Gad, captains of the host: [1] one of the least *was* over an hundred, and the greatest over a thousand.

15 These *are* they that went over Jordan in the first month, when it had [1] overflown all his [a] banks; and they put to flight all *them of* the valleys, *both* toward the east, and toward the west.

16 And there came of the children of Benjamin and Judah to the hold unto David.

17 And David went out [1] to meet them, and answered and said unto them, If ye be come peaceably unto me to help me, mine heart shall [2] be knit unto you: but if *ye be come* to betray me to mine enemies, seeing *there is* no [3] wrong in mine hands, the God of our fathers look *thereon,* and rebuke *it.*

18 Then [a] [1] the spirit came upon [b] Amasai, *who was* chief of the captains, *and he said,*

Thine *are we,* David,
And on thy side, thou son of Jesse:
Peace, peace *be* unto thee,
And peace *be* to thine helpers;
For thy God helpeth thee.

Then David received them, and made them captains of the band.

19 And there fell *some* of Manasseh to David, [a] when he came with the Philistines against Saul to battle: but they helped them not: for the lords of the Philistines upon advisement sent him away, saying, [b] He will fall to his master Saul [1] to *the jeopardy of* our heads.

20 As he went to Ziklag, there fell to him of Manasseh, Adnah, and Jozabad, and Jediael, and Michael, and Jozabad, and Elihu, and Zilthai, captains of the thousands that *were* of Manasseh.

21 And they helped David [1] against [a] the band *of the rovers:* for they *were* all mighty *men* of valour, and were captains in the host.

22 For at *that* time day by day there came to David to help him, until it was a great host, like the host of God.

The number of David's men

23 ¶ And these *are* the numbers of the [1] bands that were ready armed to the war, *and* [a] came to David to Hebron, to [b] turn the kingdom of Saul to him, [c] according to the word of the LORD.

11:38 [1] Or, *the Haggerite*
11:45 [1] Or, *Shimrite*
12:1 [1] Heb. being *yet shut up* [a] 1 Sam. 27:2 [b] 1 Sam. 27:6
12:2 [a] Judg. 20:16
12:3 [1] Or, *Hasmaah*
12:8 [1] Heb. *of the host* [2] Heb. *as the roes upon the mountains to make haste* [a] 2 Sam. 2:18
12:14 [1] Or, *one that was least could resist an hundred, and the greatest a thousand*
12:15 [1] Heb. *filled over* [a] Josh. 3:15
12:17 [1] Heb. *before them* [2] Heb. *be one* [3] Or, *violence*
12:18 [1] Heb. *the spirit clothed Amasai* [a] Judg. 6:34 [b] 2 Sam. 17:25
12:19 [1] Heb. *on our heads* [a] 1 Sam. 29:2 [b] 1 Sam. 29:4
12:21 [1] Or, *with a band* [a] 1 Sam. 30:1,9,10
12:23 [1] Or, *captains,* or, *men.* Heb. *heads* [a] 2 Sam. 2:3 [b] ch. 10:14 [c] 1 Sam. 16:1

11:41b–12:40 See note on vv. 10–41a. The list in 2 Sam 23 ends with Uriah the Hittite (2 Sam 11); the source for the additional names is not known. The emphasis continues to be on the support of "all Israel"—even Saul's own kinsmen recognized the legitimacy of David's kingship before Saul's death (12:1–7, 16–18,23,29).

12:1 The Chronicler assumes the reader's knowledge of the events at Ziklag (1 Sam 27); see vv. 19–20.

12:8–15 The men of Gad were from across the Jordan. Melting snows to the north would have brought the Jordan to flood stage in the first month (March-April) at the time of their crossing (v. 15). The most appropriate time for this incident would have been in the period of David's wandering in the region of the Dead Sea (1 Sam 23:14; 24:1; 25:1; 26:1).

12:23–37 The emphasis remains on "all Israel" (v. 38). Though 13 tribes are named, they are grouped in order to maintain the traditional number of 12 (see note on 2:1–2). The northernmost tribes and those east of the Jordan send the largest number of men (vv. 33–37), reinforcing the degree of support that David enjoyed not only in Judah and Benjamin but throughout the

24 The children of Judah that bare shield and spear *were* six thousand and eight hundred, ready [1]armed to the war.

25 Of the children of Simeon, mighty *men* of valour for the war, seven thousand and one hundred.

26 Of the children of Levi four thousand and six hundred.

27 And Jehoiada *was* the leader of the Aaronites, and with him *were* three thousand and seven hundred;

28 And [a]Zadok, a young man mighty of valour, and *of* his father's house twenty and two captains.

29 And of the children of Benjamin, the [1]kindred of Saul, three thousand: for hitherto [a2]the greatest part of them had kept the ward of the house of Saul.

30 And of the children of Ephraim twenty thousand and eight hundred, mighty *men* of valour, [1]famous throughout the house of their fathers.

31 And of the half tribe of Manasseh eighteen thousand, which were expressed by name, to come and make David king.

32 And of the children of Issachar, [a]*which were men* that had understanding of the times, to know what Israel ought to do; the heads of them *were* two hundred; and all their brethren *were* at their commandment.

33 Of Zebulun, such as went forth to battle, [1]expert in war, with all instruments of war, fifty thousand, which could [2]keep rank: *they were* [a3]not of double heart.

34 And of Naphtali a thousand captains, and with them with shield and spear thirty and seven thousand.

35 And of the Danites expert in war twenty and eight thousand and six hundred.

36 And of Asher, such as went forth to battle, [1]expert in war, forty thousand.

12:24 [1]Or, *prepared*
12:28 [a]2 Sam. 8:17
12:29 [1]Heb. *brethren* [2]Heb. *a multitude of them* [a]2 Sam. 2:8,9
12:30 [1]Heb. *men of names*
12:32 [a]Esth. 1:13
12:33 [1]Or, *rangers of battle,* or, *ranged in battle* [2]Or, *set the battle in array* [3]Heb. *without a heart and a heart* [a]Ps. 12:2
12:36 [1]Or, *keeping their rank*

12:40 [1]Or, *victual of meal*
13:2 [1]Heb. *let us break forth* and *send* [2]Heb. *in the cities of their suburbs* [a]1 Sam. 31:1; Is. 37:4
13:3 [1]Heb. *bring about* [a]1 Sam. 7:1,2
13:5 [a]1 Sam. 7:5 [b]Josh. 13:3

37 And on the *other* side of Jordan, of the Reubenites, and the Gadites, and of the half tribe of Manasseh, with all *manner of* instruments of war for the battle, an hundred and twenty thousand.

38 All these men of war, that could keep rank, came with a perfect heart to Hebron, to make David king over all Israel: and all the rest also of Israel *were of* one heart to make David king.

39 And there they were with David three days, eating and drinking: for their brethren had prepared for them.

40 Moreover they *that were* nigh them, *even* unto Issachar and Zebulun and Naphtali, brought bread on asses, and on camels, and on mules, and on oxen, *and* [1]meat, meal, cakes *of figs,* and bunches of raisins, and wine, and oil, and oxen, and sheep abundantly: for *there was* joy in Israel.

The ark taken to Obed-edom

13 And David consulted with the captains of thousands and hundreds, *and* with every leader.

2 And David said unto all the congregation of Israel, If *it seem* good unto you, and *that it be* of the LORD our God, [1]let us send abroad unto our brethren every where, that are [a]left in all the land of Israel, and with them *also to* the priests and Levites *which are* [2]in their cities *and* suburbs, that they may gather themselves unto us:

3 And let us [1]bring again the ark of our God to us: [a]for we inquired not *at* it in the days of Saul.

4 And all the congregation said that *they* would do so: for the thing was right in the eyes of all the people.

5 So [a]David gathered all Israel together, from [b]Shihor of Egypt even unto the entering

other tribes as well. The numbers in this section seem quite high. Essentially two approaches are followed on this question: 1. It is possible to explain the numbers so that a lower figure is actually attained. The Hebrew word for "thousand" may represent a unit of a tribe, each having its own commander (13:1; see Num 31:14,48,52,54). In this case the numbers would be read not as a total figure, but as representative commanders. For example, the 6,800 from Judah (v. 24) would be read either as six commanders of 1,000 and eight commanders of 100 (see 13:1), or possibly as six commanders of thousands and 800 men. Reducing the numbers in this fashion fits well with 13:1 and with the list of commanders alone found for Zadok's family (v. 28) and the tribe of Issachar (v. 32). Taking the numbers as straight totals would require the presence of 340,800 persons in Hebron for a feast at the same time. 2. Another approach is to allow the numbers to stand and to view them as hyperbole on the part of the Chronicler to achieve a number "like the host of God" (v. 22). This approach would fit well with the Chronicler's glorification of David and with the banquet scene that follows.

12:38–40 The Chronicler's portrait of David is influenced by his Messianic expectations (see Introduction: Purpose and Themes). In the presence of a third of a million people (see note on vv. 23–37) David's coronation banquet typifies the future Messianic feast (Is 25:6–8). The imagery of the Messianic banquet became prominent in the intertestamental literature (*Apocalypse of Baruch* 29:4–8; *Enoch* 62:14) and in the NT (see Mat 8:11–12 and Luke 13:28–30; Mat 22:1–10 and Luke 14:16–24; see also Mat 25:1–13; Luke 22:28–30; Rev 19:7–9). The Lord's supper anticipates that coming banquet (Mat 26:29; Mark 14:25; Luke 22:15–18; 1 Cor 11:23–26).

13:1–14 See 2 Sam 6:1–11 and notes. The author abandons the chronological order as given in 2 Sam 5–6 and puts the transfer of the ark first, delaying his account of the palace building and the Philistine campaign until later (ch. 14). This is in accordance with his portrayal of David; David's concern with the ark was expressed immediately upon his accession—his consultation with the leaders appears to be set in the context of the coronation banquet (12:38–40).

13:1–4 These verses are not found in Samuel and reflect the Chronicler's own concerns with "all Israel." The semi-military expedition to retrieve the ark in 2 Sam 6:1 is here broadened by consultation with and support from the whole assembly of Israel, "all the land" (v. 2), including the priests and Levites—an important point for the Chronicler since only they are allowed to move the ark (15:2,13; 23:25–27; Deut 10:8).

13:3 *we inquired not at it in the days of Saul.* 1 Sam 14:18 may be an exception (but see note there).

‡13:5–6 The emphasis remains on the united action of "all

of Hemath, to bring the ark of God [c]from Kirjath-jearim.
6 And David went up, and all Israel, to [a]Ba-
alah, *that is,* to Kirjath-jearim, which *belonged*
to Judah, to bring up thence the ark of God the
LORD, [b]that dwelleth *between* the cherubims,
whose name is called *on it.*
7 And they [1]carried the ark of God [a]in a
new cart [b]out of the house of Abinadab: and
Uzza and Ahio drave the cart.
8 [a]And David and all Israel played before
God with all *their* might, and with [1]singing,
and with harps, and with psalteries, and with
timbrels, and with cymbals, and with trumpets.
9 And when they came unto the threshingfloor of [1]Chidon, Uzza put forth his hand to
hold the ark; for the oxen [2]stumbled.
10 And the anger of the LORD was kindled
against Uzza, and he smote him, [a]because he
put his hand to the ark: and there he [b]died before God.
11 And David was displeased, because the
LORD had made a breach upon Uzza: wherefore that place is called [1]Perez-uzza to this
day.
12 And David was afraid of God that day,
saying, How shall I bring the ark of God *home*
to me?
13 So David [1]brought not the ark *home* to
himself to the city of David, but carried it aside
into the house of Obed-edom the Gittite.
14 [a]And the ark of God remained with the
family of Obed-edom in his house three
months. And the LORD blessed [b]the house of
Obed-edom, and all that he had.

13:5 [c]1 Sam. 6:21; 7:1
13:6 [a]Josh. 15:9,60 [b]1 Sam. 4:4; 2 Sam. 6:2
13:7 [1]Heb. *made the ark to ride* [a]See Num. 4:15 [b]1 Sam. 7:1
13:8 [1]Heb. *songs* [a]2 Sam. 6:5
13:9 [1]Called *Nachon,* 2 Sam. 6:6 [2]Or, *shook* it
13:10 [a]Num. 4:15; ch. 15:13,15 [b]Lev. 10:2
13:11 [1]That is, *breach of Uzza*
13:13 [1]Heb. *removed*
13:14 [a]2 Sam. 6:11 [b]As Gen. 30:27; ch. 26:5

14:1 [a]2 Sam. 5:11
14:3 [1]Heb. *yet*
14:4 [a]ch. 3:5
14:7 [1]Or, *Eliada,* 2 Sam. 5:16
14:8 [a]2 Sam. 5:17
14:9 [a]ch. 11:15
14:11 [1]That is, *a place of breaches*

David defeats the Philistines

14 Now [a]Hiram king of Tyre sent messengers to David, and timber of
cedars, with masons and carpenters, to build
him a house.
2 And David perceived that the LORD had
confirmed him king over Israel, for his kingdom *was* lift up on high, because of his people
Israel.
3 ¶ And David took [1]moe wives at Jerusalem: and David begat moe sons and daughters.
4 Now [a]these *are* the names of *his* children
which he had in Jerusalem; Shammua, and
Shobab, Nathan, and Solomon,
5 And Ibhar, and Elishua, and Elpalet,
6 And Nogah, and Nepheg, and Japhia,
7 And Elishama, and [1]Beeliada, and Eliphalet.
8 ¶ And when the Philistines heard that
[a]David was anointed king over all Israel, all
the Philistines went up to seek David. And David heard *of it,* and went out against them.
9 And the Philistines came and spread
themselves [a]in the valley of Rephaim.
10 And David inquired of God, saying,
Shall I go up against the Philistines? and wilt
thou deliver them into mine hand? And the
LORD said unto him, Go up; for I will deliver
them into thine hand.
11 So they came up to Baal-perazim; and
David smote them there. Then David said,
God hath broken in upon mine enemies by
mine hand like the breaking forth of waters:
therefore they called the name of that place
[1]Baal-perazim.
12 And when they had left their gods

Israel." Israelites came to participate in this venture all the way from the entrance of Hemath in the north and from the Shihor River in the south.

13:5 *Shihor.* An Egyptian term meaning "the pool of Horus." It appears to be a part of the Nile or one of the major canals of the Nile (see Josh 13:3; Is 23:3; Jer 2:18 and notes).

‡13:6 *Baalah.* The Canaanite name for Kirjath-jearim, also known as Kirjath-baal (Josh 18:14). The Chronicler assumes that his readers are familiar with the account of how the ark came to be at Kirjath-jearim (1 Sam 6:1–7:1).

13:7 *Uzza and Ahio.* Sons or descendants of Abinadab (2 Sam 6:3).

13:10 *because he put his hand to the ark.* The ark was to be moved only by Levites, who carried it with poles inserted through rings in the sides of the ark (Ex 25:12–15). None of the holy things was to be touched, on penalty of death (Num 4:15). These strictures were observed in the second and successful attempt to move the ark to Jerusalem (15:1–15). It cannot be known whether Uzza and Ahio were Levites—the Samuel account does not mention the presence of Levites, but the Chronicler's careful inclusion of Levites in this expedition suggests that they were present (see note on vv. 1–4). In any case, the ark should not have been moved on a cart (as done by the Philistines, 1 Sam 6) or touched.

13:13 *Obed-edom.* Perhaps the same man mentioned in 15:18,21,24. In 26:4 God's blessing on Obed-edom included numerous sons. This reference also establishes that Obed-edom was a Levite and that the ark was properly left in his care.

14:1–17 The Chronicler backtracks to pick up material from 2 Sam 5 deferred to this point (see note on 13:1–14). The three-month period that the ark remained with Obed-edom (13:14) was filled with incidents showing God's blessing on David: the building of his royal house (vv. 1–2), his large family (vv. 3–7) and his success in warfare (vv. 8–16)—all because of the Lord's blessing (vv. 2,17).

14:1–2 See 2 Sam 5:11–12 and notes.

14:1 *Hiram.* Later provided materials and labor for building the temple (2 Chr 2). His mention here implies international recognition of David as king over Israel and a treaty between David and Hiram.

14:3–7 See 3:5–9; 2 Sam 5:13–16. David's children born in Hebron are omitted (3:1–4; 2 Sam 3:2–5; see note on 11:1–3).

14:7 *Beeliada.* Eliada in 3:8; 2 Sam 5:16.

14:8–12 See 2 Sam 5:17–21 and notes.

‡14:11 *broken in . . . Baal-perazim.* The Hebrew underlying the name of this place where the Lord broke out against the Philistines is literally "master of the breakthrough." It is the same as that underlying the word used in 13:11 when the Lord broke out against Uzza. Perez-uzza means "breakthrough of Uzza."

14:12 *gave a commandment, and they were burnt.* 2 Sam 5:21 does not mention burning but says that David and his men carried the idols away. Many have seen here an intentional change on the part of the Chronicler in order to bring David's actions into strict conformity with the law, which required that pagan idols be burned (Deut 7:5,25). However, some Septuagint (the Greek translation of the OT) manuscripts of Samuel agree with Chronicles that David burned the idols. This would indicate that the Chronicler was not innovating for theological reasons but

there, David gave a commandment, and they were burnt with fire.

13 [a]And the Philistines yet again spread themselves abroad in the valley.

14 Therefore David inquired again of God; and God said unto him, Go not up after them; turn away from them, [a]and come upon them over against the mulberry trees.

15 And it shall be, when thou shalt hear a sound of going in the tops of the mulberry trees, *that* then thou shalt go out to battle: for God is gone forth before thee to smite the host of the Philistines.

16 David therefore did as God commanded him: and they smote the host of the Philistines from [1]Gibeon even to Gazer.

17 And [a]the fame of David went out into all lands; and the LORD [b]brought the fear of him upon all nations.

The ark brought to Jerusalem

15 And *David* made him houses in the city of David, and prepared a place for the ark of God, [a]and pitched for it a tent.

2 Then David said, [1]None ought to carry the [a]ark of God but the Levites: for them hath the LORD chosen to carry the ark of God, and to minister unto him for ever.

3 And David [a]gathered all Israel together to Jerusalem, to bring up the ark of the LORD unto his place, which he had prepared for it.

4 And David assembled the children of Aaron, and the Levites:

5 Of the sons of Kohath; Uriel the chief, and his [1]brethren an hundred and twenty:

6 Of the sons of Merari; Asaiah the chief, and his brethren two hundred and twenty:

7 Of the sons of Gershom; Joel the chief, and his brethren an hundred and thirty:

8 Of the sons of [a]Elizaphan; Shemaiah the chief, and his brethren two hundred:

9 Of the sons of [a]Hebron; Eliel the chief, and his brethren fourscore:

10 Of the sons of Uzziel; Amminadab the chief, and his brethren an hundred and twelve.

11 ¶ And David called for Zadok and Abiathar the priests, and for the Levites, for Uriel, Asaiah, and Joel, Shemaiah, and Eliel, and Amminadab,

12 And said unto them, Ye *are* the chief of the fathers of the Levites: sanctify yourselves, *both* ye and your brethren, that you may bring up the ark of the LORD God of Israel unto *the place that* I have prepared for it.

13 For [a]because ye *did it* not at the first, [b]the LORD our God made a breach upon us, for that we sought him not after the due order.

14 So the priests and the Levites sanctified themselves to bring up the ark of the LORD God of Israel.

15 And the children of the Levites bare the ark of God upon their shoulders with the staves thereon, as [a]Moses commanded according to the word of the LORD.

16 And David spake to the chief of the Levites to appoint their brethren *to be* the singers with instruments of musick, psalteries and harps and cymbals, sounding, by lifting up the voice with joy.

17 So the Levites appointed [a]Heman the son of Joel; and of his brethren, [b]Asaph the son of Berechiah; and of the sons of Merari their brethren, [c]Ethan the son of Kushaiah;

18 And with them their brethren of the second degree, Zechariah, Ben, and Jaaziel, and Shemiramoth, and Jehiel, and Unni, Eliab, and Benaiah, and Maaseiah, and Mattithiah, and Elipheleh, and Mikneiah, and Obed-edom, and Jeiel, the porters.

19 So the singers, Heman, Asaph, and Ethan, *were appointed* to sound with cymbals of brass;

20 And Zechariah, and [1]Aziel, and Shemiramoth, and Jehiel, and Unni, and Eliab, and Maaseiah, and Benaiah, with psalteries [a]on Alamoth;

21 And Mattithiah, and Elipheleh, and Mikneiah, and Obed-edom, and Jeiel, and Azaziah, with harps [a][1]on the Sheminith to excel.

22 And Chenaniah, chief of the Levites, [1]*was* for [2]song: he instructed about the song, because he *was* skilful.

23 And Berechiah and Elkanah *were* doorkeepers for the ark.

24 And Shebaniah, and Jehoshaphat, and Nethaneel, and Amasai, and Zechariah, and Benaiah, and Eliezer, the priests, [a]did blow with the trumpets before the ark of God: and

14:13 [a]2 Sam. 5:22
14:14 [a]2 Sam. 5:23
14:16 [1][2 Sam. 5:25, *Geba*]
14:17 [a]Josh. 6:27; 2 Chr. 26:8 [b]Deut. 2:25; 11:25
15:1 [a]ch. 16:1
15:2 [1]Heb. It is *not to carry the ark of God, but for the Levites* [a]Num. 4:2,15; Deut. 10:8; 31:9
15:3 [a]1 Ki. 8:1; ch. 13:5
15:5 [1]Or, *kinsmen*
15:8 [a]Ex. 6:22
15:9 [a]Ex. 6:18
15:13 [a]2 Sam. 6:3; ch. 13:7 [b]ch. 13:10,11
15:15 [a]Ex. 25:14; Num. 4:15; 7:9
15:17 [a]ch. 6:33 [b]ch. 6:39 [c]ch. 6:44
15:20 [1][ver. 18 *Jaaziel*] [a]Ps. 46, title
15:21 [1]Or, *on the eighth to oversee* [a]Ps. 6, title
15:22 [1]Or, was *for the carriage: he instructed about the carriage* [2]Heb. *lifting up*
15:24 [a]Num. 10:8; Ps. 81:3

was carefully reproducing the text he had before him, which differed from the Masoretic (traditional Hebrew) text of Samuel.

14:13–16 See 2 Sam 5:22–25 and notes.

14:17 *the LORD brought the fear of him upon all nations.* Here and elsewhere the Chronicler uses an expression that refers to an incapacitating terror brought on by the sense that the awful power of God is present in behalf of His people (see Ex 15:16). Thus David is seen by the nations as the very representative of God (similarly Asa, 2 Chr 14:14; Jehoshaphat, 2 Chr 17:10; 20:29).

15:1–16:3 This account of the successful attempt to move the ark to Jerusalem is greatly expanded over the material in 2 Samuel. Only 15:25–16:3 has a parallel (2 Sam 6:12–19); the rest of the material is unique to the Chronicler and reflects his own interests, especially in the Levites and cultic musicians (vv. 3–24; see Introduction: Purpose and Themes). Ps 132 should also be read in connection with this account.

15:1 *made him houses.* See 14:1–2 and note on 13:1–14.

15:2–3 See note on 13:10.

15:4–10 The three clans of Levi are represented (Kohath, Merari and Gershom), as well as three distinct subgroups within Kohath (Elizaphan, Hebron and Uzziel)—862 in all.

15:12 *sanctify yourselves.* Through ritual washings and avoidance of ceremonial defilement (Ex 29:1–37; 30:19–21; 40:31–32; Lev 8:5–35).

15:13–15 The Chronicler provides the explanation for the failure in the first attempt to move the ark, an explanation not found in the Samuel account (see note on 13:10).

15:18,21,24 *Obed-edom.* See note on 13:13.

15:24 *priests, did blow with the trumpets.* See 16:6; Num 10:1–10.

Obed-edom and Jehiah *were* doorkeepers for
the ark.
25 ¶ So [a]David, and the elders of Israel, and
the captains over thousands, went to bring up
the ark of the covenant of the LORD out of the
house of Obed-edom with joy.
26 And it came to pass, when God helped
the Levites that bare the ark of the covenant of
the LORD, that they offered seven bullocks and
seven rams.
27 And David *was* clothed with a robe of
fine linen, and all the Levites that bare the ark,
and the singers, and Chenaniah the master of
the [1]song *with* the singers: David also *had*
upon him an ephod of linen.
28 [a]Thus all Israel brought up the ark of
the covenant of the LORD with shouting, and
with sound of the cornet, and with trumpets,
and with cymbals, making a noise with psalteries and harps.
29 And it came to pass, [a]*as* the ark of the
covenant of the LORD came to the city of David, that Michal the daughter of Saul looking
out at a window saw king David dancing and
playing: and she despised him in her heart.

16 So [a]they brought the ark of God, and
set it in the midst of the tent that David had pitched for it: and they offered burnt
sacrifices and peace offerings before God.
2 And when David had made an end of offering the burnt offerings and the peace offerings, he blessed the people in the name of the
LORD.
3 And he dealt to every one of Israel, both
man and woman, to every one a loaf of bread,
and a good piece *of flesh,* and a flagon *of wine.*
4 And he appointed *certain* of the Levites
to minister before the ark of the LORD, and to
[a]record, and to thank and praise the LORD God
of Israel:
5 Asaph the chief, and next to him
Zechariah, Jeiel, and Shemiramoth, and Jehiel, and Mattithiah, and Eliab, and Benaiah,
and Obed-edom: and Jeiel [1]with psalteries
and with harps; but Asaph made a sound with
cymbals;
6 Benaiah also and Jahaziel the priests with
trumpets continually before the ark of the covenant of God.

15:25 [a]2 Sam. 6:12,13; 1 Ki. 8:1
15:27 [1]Or, *carriage*
15:28 [a]ch. 13:8
15:29 [a]2 Sam. 6:16
16:1 [a]2 Sam. 6:17-19
16:4 [a]Ps. 38; 70, title
16:5 [1]Heb. *with instruments of psalteries and harps*
16:7 [a]See 2 Sam. 23:1
16:8 [a]Ps. 105:1-15
16:16 [a]Gen. 17:2; 26:3; 28:13; 35:11
16:18 [1]Heb. *The cord*
16:19 [1]Heb. *men of number* [a]Gen. 34:30
16:21 [a]Gen. 12:17; 20:3; Ex. 7:15-18
16:22 [a]Ps. 105:15
16:23 [a]Ps. 96:1

David's psalm of gratitude

7 ¶ Then on that day David delivered [a]first
this psalm to thank the LORD into the hand of
Asaph and his brethren.
8 [a]Give thanks unto the LORD, call upon
his name,
Make known his deeds among the
people.
9 Sing unto him, sing psalms unto him,
Talk you of all his wondrous works.
10 Glory ye in his holy name:
Let the heart of them rejoice that seek
the LORD.
11 Seek the LORD and his strength,
Seek his face continually.
12 Remember his marvellous works that
he hath done,
His wonders, and the judgments of his
mouth;
13 O ye seed of Israel his servant,
Ye children of Jacob, his chosen *ones.*
14 He *is* the LORD our God;
His judgments *are* in all the earth.
15 Be ye mindful always of his covenant;
The word *which* he commanded to a
thousand generations;
16 *Even of the* [a]*covenant* which he made
with Abraham,
And of his oath unto Isaac;
17 And hath confirmed the same to Jacob
for a law,
And to Israel *for* an everlasting
covenant,
18 Saying, Unto thee will I give the land
of Canaan,
[1]The lot of your inheritance;
19 When ye were *but* [1]few,
[a]Even a few, and strangers in it.
20 And *when* they went from nation to
nation,
And from *one* kingdom to another
people;
21 He suffered no man to do them wrong:
Yea, he [a]reproved kings for their sakes,
22 *Saying,* [a]Touch not mine anointed,
And do my prophets no harm.
23 [a]Sing unto the LORD, all the earth;
Shew forth from day to day his
salvation.

15:27 Both 2 Sam 6:14 and the Chronicler mention David's wearing a linen ephod, a garment worn by priests (1 Sam 2:18; 22:18). The Chronicler adds, however, that David (as well as the rest of the Levites in the procession) was wearing a robe of fine linen, further associating him with the dress of the cultic functionaries. Apparently the Chronicler viewed David as a priest-king, a kind of Messianic figure (see Ps 110; Zech 6:9–15).

15:29 Parallel to 2 Sam 6:16, but the Chronicler omits the remainder of this incident recorded there (2 Sam 6:20–23). Some interpreters regard this omission as part of the Chronicler's positive view of David, so that a possibly unseemly account is omitted. On the other hand, it is equally plausible that the Chronicler here simply assumes the reader's knowledge of the other account (see notes on 10:13–14; 11:1–3; 12:1; 13:6).

16:1–3 David is further associated with the priests in his supervision of the sacrifices and his exercising the priestly prerogative of blessing the people (Num 6:22–27; see note on 15:27). The baked goods provided by David were for the sacrificial meal following the peace offerings (Lev 3:1–17; 7:11–21, 28–36).

16:8–36 Similar to various parts of the book of Psalms (for vv. 8–22 see Ps 105:1–15; for vv. 23–33, Ps 96; for vv. 34–36, Ps 106:1,47–48). This psalm is not found in the Samuel account. The use of the lengthy historical portion from Ps 105 emphasizing the promises to Abraham would be particularly relevant to the Chronicler's postexilic audience, for whom the faithfulness of God was a fresh reality in their return to the land. The citation from Ps 106 would also be of immediate relevance to the Chronicler's audience as those who had been gathered and delivered from the nations (v. 35).

24 Declare his glory among the heathen;
His marvellous works among all nations.
25 For great *is* the LORD, and greatly to be praised:
He also *is* to be feared above all gods.
26 For all the gods [a]of the people *are* idols:
But the LORD made the heavens.
27 Glory and honour *are* in his presence;
Strength and gladness *are* in his place.
28 Give unto the LORD, ye kindreds of the people,
Give unto the LORD glory and strength.
29 Give unto the LORD the glory due unto his name:
Bring an offering, and come before him:
Worship the LORD in the beauty of holiness.
30 Fear before him, all the earth:
The world also shall be stable, that it be not moved.
31 Let the heavens be glad, and let the earth rejoice:
And let *men* say among the nations,
The LORD reigneth.
32 Let the sea roar, and the fulness thereof:
Let the fields rejoice, and all that *is* therein.
33 Then shall the trees of the wood sing out at the presence of the LORD,
Because he cometh to judge the earth.
34 [a]O give thanks unto the LORD; for *he is* good;
For his mercy *endureth* for ever.
35 [a]And say ye,
Save us, O God of our salvation,
And gather us together, and deliver us from the heathen,
That *we* may give thanks to thy holy name,
And glory in thy praise.
36 [a]Blessed *be* the LORD God of Israel for ever and ever.

And all [b]the people said, Amen, and praised the LORD.

37 ¶ So he left there before the ark of the covenant of the LORD Asaph and his brethren, to minister before the ark continually, as every day's work required:

38 And Obed-edom with their brethren, threescore and eight; Obed-edom also the son of Jeduthun and Hosah to be porters:

39 And Zadok the priest, and his brethren the priests, [a]before the tabernacle of the LORD [b]in the high place that *was* at Gibeon,

40 To offer burnt offerings unto the LORD upon the altar of the burnt offering continually [a][1]morning and evening, and *to do* according to all that is written in the law of the LORD, which he commanded Israel;

41 And with them Heman and Jeduthun, and the rest that were chosen, who were expressed by name, to give thanks to the LORD, [a]because his mercy *endureth* for ever;

42 And with them Heman and Jeduthun *with* trumpets and cymbals for those that should make a sound, and with musical instruments of God. And the sons of Jeduthun *were* [1]porters.

43 [a]And all the people departed every man to his house: and David returned to bless his house.

Nathan's warning to David

17 Now [a]it came to pass, as David sat in his house, that David said to Nathan the prophet, Lo, I dwell in a house of cedars, but the ark of the covenant of the LORD *remaineth* under curtains.

2 Then Nathan said unto David, Do all that *is* in thine heart; for God *is* with thee.

3 And it came to pass the same night, that the word of God came to Nathan, saying,

4 Go and tell David my servant, Thus saith the LORD, Thou shalt not build me a house to dwell in:

5 For I have not dwelt in a house since the day that I brought up Israel unto this day; but [1]have gone from tent to tent, and from *one* tabernacle *to another.*

6 Wheresoever I have walked with all Israel, spake I a word to any of the judges of Israel, whom I commanded to feed my people, saying, Why have ye not built me a house of cedars?

7 Now therefore thus shalt thou say unto my servant David, Thus saith the LORD of hosts, I took thee from the sheepcote, *even* [1]from following the sheep, that *thou* shouldest be ruler over my people Israel:

8 And I have been with thee whithersoever thou hast walked, and have cut off all thine enemies from before thee, and have made

16:26 [a]Lev. 19:4
16:34 [a]Ps. 106:1; 107:1; 118:1; 136:1
16:35 [a]Ps. 106:47,48
16:36 [a]1 Ki. 8:15 [b]Deut. 27:15
16:39 [a]ch. 21:29; 2 Chr. 1:3 [b]1 Ki. 3:4
16:40 [1]Heb. *in the morning, and in the evening* [a]Ex. 29:38; Num. 28:3
16:41 [a]ver. 34; 2 Chr. 5:13; 7:3; Ezra 3:11; Jer. 33:11
16:42 [1]Heb. *for the gate*
16:43 [a]2 Sam. 6:19,20
17:1 [a]2 Sam. 7:1
17:5 [1]Heb. *have been*
17:7 [1]Heb. *from after*

16:29 *beauty of holiness.* See note on Ps 29:2.
16:39 *tabernacle . . . at Gibeon.* The tabernacle remained at Gibeon until Solomon's construction of the temple in Jerusalem (2 Chr 1:13; 5:5), when it was stored within the temple. The existence of these two shrines—the tabernacle and the temporary structure for the ark in Jerusalem (v. 1)—accounts for the two high priests: Zadok serving in Gibeon and Abiathar in Jerusalem (18:16; 27:34; see note on 6:8).
16:42 *trumpets . . . make a sound.* See Num 10:1–10.
17:1–27 See 2 Sam 7 and notes.
17:1,10 In these verses the Chronicler omits the statement that David had rest from his enemies (2 Sam 7:1,11). Several factors may be at work in this omission: 1. The account of David's major wars is yet to come (chs. 18–20). Chronologically, this passage should follow the account of the wars (v. 8), but the author has placed it here to continue his concern with the ark and the building of the temple (vv. 4–6,12). 2. The Chronicler also views David as a man of war through most of his life (22:6–8), in contrast to Solomon, who is the man of "rest" (22:9) and who will build the temple (22:10). For the Chronicler, David has rest from enemies only late in his life (22:18). 3. As part of his concern to parallel David and Solomon to Moses and Joshua, Solomon (like Joshua) brings the people to rest from enemies (see Introduction: Portrait of David and Solomon).

thee a name like the name of the great *men* that *are* in the earth.

9 Also I will ordain a place for my people Israel, and will plant them, and they shall dwell in their place, and shall be moved no more; neither shall the children of wickedness waste them any more, as at the beginning,

10 And since the time that I commanded judges *to be* over my people Israel. Moreover I will subdue all thine enemies. Furthermore I tell thee that the LORD will build thee a house.

11 And it shall come to pass, when thy days be expired that *thou* must go *to be* with thy fathers, that I will raise up thy seed after thee, which shall be of thy sons; and I will stablish his kingdom.

12 He shall build me a house, and I will stablish his throne for ever.

13 [a]I will be his father, and he shall be my son: and I will not take my mercy away from him, as I took *it* from *him* that was before thee:

14 But [a]I will settle him in mine house and in my kingdom for ever: and his throne shall be established for evermore.

15 According to all these words, and according to all this vision, so did Nathan speak unto David.

David's prayer

16 ¶ [a]And David the king came and sat before the LORD, and said, Who *am* I, O LORD God, and what *is* mine house, that thou hast brought me hitherto?

17 And *yet* this was a small thing in thine eyes, O God; for thou hast *also* spoken of thy servant's house for a great while to come, and hast regarded me according to the estate of a man of high degree, O LORD God.

18 What can David *speak* more to thee for the honour of thy servant? for thou knowest thy servant.

19 O LORD, for thy servant's sake, and according to thine own heart, hast thou done all this greatness, in making known all *these* [1]great things.

20 O LORD, *there is* none like thee, neither *is there any* God besides thee, according to all that we have heard with our ears.

21 And what one nation in the earth *is* like thy people Israel, whom God went to redeem *to be* his own people, to make thee a name of greatness and terribleness, by driving out nations from before thy people, whom thou hast redeemed out of Egypt?

22 For thy people Israel didst thou make thine own people for ever; and thou, LORD, becamest their God.

23 Therefore now, LORD, let the thing that thou hast spoken concerning thy servant and concerning his house be established for ever, and do as thou hast said.

24 Let it even be established, that thy name may be magnified for ever, saying, The LORD of hosts *is* the God of Israel, *even* a God to Israel: and *let* the house of David thy servant *be* established before thee.

25 For thou, O my God, [1]hast told thy servant that *thou* wilt build him a house: therefore thy servant hath found *in his heart* to pray before thee.

26 And now, LORD, thou *art* God, and hast promised this goodness unto thy servant:

27 Now therefore [1]let it please thee to bless the house of thy servant, that *it* may be before thee for ever: for thou blessest, O LORD, and *it shall be* blessed for ever.

David's victories

18 Now after this [a]it came to pass, that David smote the Philistines, and subdued them, and took Gath and her towns out of the hand of the Philistines.

2 And he smote Moab; and the Moabites became David's servants, and brought gifts.

3 And David smote [1]Hadarezer king of Zobah unto Hamath, as he went to stablish his dominion by the river Euphrates.

17:13 [a]2 Sam. 7:14,15
17:14 [a]Luke 1:33
17:16 [a]2 Sam. 7:18

17:19 [1]Heb. *greatnesses*
17:25 [1]Heb. *hast revealed the ear of thy servant*
17:27 [1]Or, *it hath pleased thee*
18:1 [a]2 Sam. 8:1
18:3 [1]Or, *Hadadezer,* in 2 Sam. 8:3

17:12–14 Though in this context these words refer to Solomon, the NT applies them to Jesus (Mark 1:11; Luke 1:32–33; Heb 1:5).

‡17:13 The Chronicler omits from his source (2 Sam 7:14) any reference to "chastening with the rod" or "stripes of the children of men" as discipline for Solomon. This omission reflects his idealization of Solomon as a Messianic figure, for whom such punishment would not be appropriate (see Introduction: Portrait of David and Solomon).

17:14 The Chronicler introduces his own concerns by the changes in the pronouns found in his source (2 Sam 7:16); instead of "thine house and thy kingdom," the Chronicler reads "mine house and in my kingdom." This same emphasis on theocracy (God's rule) is found in several other passages unique to Chronicles (28:5–6; 29:23; 2 Chr 1:11; 9:8; 13:4–8).

17:16 *sat.* Aside from its parallel in 2 Sam 7:18, the only other reference in the OT to sitting as a posture for prayer is 1 Ki 19:4.

17:21–22 The references to the exodus from Egypt would remind the Chronicler's audience of the second great exodus, the release of the restoration community from the period of Babylonian captivity.

18:1–20:8 The accounts of David's wars serve to show the blessing of God on his reign; God keeps His promise to subdue David's enemies (17:10). These accounts are also particularly relevant to a theme developed in the postexilic prophets: that the silver and gold of the nations would flow to Jerusalem; the tribute of enemy peoples builds the temple of God (18:7–8,11; 22:2–5,14–15; cf. Hag 2:1–9,20–23; Zech 2:7–13; 6:9–15; 14:12–14). While this passage of Chronicles portrays God's blessing on David, it simultaneously explains the Chronicler's report later (22:6–8; 28:3) that David could not build the temple because he was a man of war. The material in these chapters essentially follows the Chronicler's source in 2 Samuel. The major differences are not changes the Chronicler introduces into the text, but items he chooses not to deal with—in particular 2 Sam 9; 11:2–12:25, where accounts not compatible with his portrait of David occur.

18:1–13 See 2 Sam 8:1–14 and notes.

18:2 The Chronicler omits the harsh treatment of the Moabites recorded in 2 Sam 8:2, perhaps so that no unnecessary cruelty or brutality would tarnish his portrait of David.

4 And David took from him a thousand
chariots, and [1]seven thousand horsemen, and
twenty thousand footmen: David also houghed
all the chariot *horses,* but reserved of them an
hundred chariots.
5 And when the Syrians of [1]Damascus
came to help Hadarezer king of Zobah, David
slew of the Syrians two and twenty thousand
men.
6 Then David put *garrisons* in Syria-damas-
cus; and the Syrians became David's servants,
and brought gifts. Thus the LORD preserved
David whithersoever he went.
7 And David took the shields of gold that
were on the servants of Hadarezer, and
brought them *to* Jerusalem.
8 Likewise from [1]Tibhath, and from Chun,
cities of Hadarezer, brought David very much
brass, wherewith [a]Solomon made the brasen
sea, and the pillars, and the vessels of brass.
9 Now when [1]Tou king of Hamath heard
how David had smitten all the host of Hadarezer king of Zobah;
10 He sent [1]Hadoram his son to king David, [2]to inquire of his welfare, and [3]to congratulate him, because he had fought against
Hadarezer, and smitten him; (for Hadarezer
[4]had war with Tou;) and *with him* all *manner*
of vessels of gold and silver and brass.
11 Them also king David dedicated unto
the LORD, with the silver and the gold that he
brought from all *these* nations; from Edom, and
from Moab, and from the children of Ammon,
and from the Philistines, and from Amalek.
12 Moreover [1]Abishai the son of Zeruiah
slew of the Edomites in the valley of salt
[a]eighteen thousand.
13 [a]And he put garrisons in Edom; and all
the Edomites became David's servants. Thus
the LORD preserved David whithersoever he
went.
14 So David reigned over all Israel, and executed judgment and justice among all his people.
15 And Joab the son of Zeruiah *was* over
the host; and Jehoshaphat the son of Ahilud,
[1]recorder.
16 And Zadok the son of Ahitub, and
[1]Abimelech the son of Abiathar, *were* the
priests; and [2]Shavsha *was* scribe;
17 [a]And Benaiah the son of Jehoiada *was*
over the Cherethites and the Pelethites; and
the sons of David *were* chief [1]about the king.

David and the children of Ammon

19 Now [a]it came to pass after this, that
Nahash the king of the children of
Ammon died, and his son reigned in his stead.
2 And David said, I will shew kindness
unto Hanun the son of Nahash, because his father shewed kindness to me. And David sent
messengers to comfort him concerning his father. So the servants of David came into the
land of the children of Ammon to Hanun, to
comfort him.
3 But the princes of the children of Ammon said to Hanun, [1]Thinkest thou that David
doth honour thy father, that he hath sent comforters unto thee? are not his servants come
unto thee for to search, and to overthrow, and
to spy out the land?
4 Wherefore Hanun took David's servants,
and shaved them, and cut off their garments in
the midst hard by *their* buttocks, and sent
them away.
5 Then there went *certain,* and told David
how the men were served. And he sent to
meet them: for the men were greatly
ashamed. And the king said, Tarry at Jericho
until your beards be grown, and *then* return.
6 And when the children of Ammon saw
that they had made themselves [1]odious to Da-

18:4 [1][2 Sam. 8:4, *seven hundred*]
18:5 [1]Heb. *Darmesek*
18:8 [1]Called in the book of Samuel *Betah, and Berothai* [a]1 Ki. 7:15,23; 2 Chr. 4:12,15,16
18:9 [1]Or, *Toi,* 2 Sam. 8:9
18:10 [1]Or, *Joram,* 2 Sam. 8:10 [2]Or, *to salute* [3]Heb. *to bless* [4]Heb. *was the man of wars*
18:12 [1][Heb. *Abshai*] [a]2 Sam. 8:13
18:13 [a]2 Sam. 8:14
18:15 [1]Or, *remembrancer*
18:16 [1]Called *Ahimelech,* in 2 Sam. 8:17 [2]Called *Seraiah,* in 2 Sam. 8:17; and *Shisha,* 1 Ki. 4:3
18:17 [1]Heb. *at the hand of the king* [a]2 Sam. 8:18
19:1 [a]2 Sam. 10:1
19:3 [1]Heb. *In thine eyes doth David, etc.*
19:6 [1]Heb. *to stink*

18:5 *Syrians.* Mentioned also among the enemies of Saul (1 Sam 14:47, "Zobah"). By the time of David they were united north (Zobah) and south (Beth-rehob, 2 Sam 10:6) under Hadarezer. They persisted as a foe of Israel for two centuries until they fell to Assyria shortly before the northern kingdom likewise fell (2 Ki 16:7–9).

18:8 *Tibhath, and from Chun.* Located in the valley between the Lebanon and Anti-Lebanon mountain ranges. *wherewith Solomon made the brasen . . . vessels.* See 2 Chr 4:2–5,18.

18:12 *Abishai.* 2 Sam 8:13 speaks only of David (see 1 Ki 11:15–16; Ps 60 title).

18:15–17 The titles and duties of these officers at David's court appear to be modeled on the organization of Egyptian functionaries serving Pharaoh.

18:15 For the account of how Joab attained his position over the army see 11:4–6; 2 Sam 5:6–8.

18:16 *Zadok . . . Abimelech the son of Abiathar.* See notes on 6:8; 16:39; 2 Sam 8:17.

18:17 *Cherethites and the Pelethites.* Apparently a group of foreign mercenaries who constituted part of the royal bodyguard (2 Sam 8:18; 20:23; see note on 1 Sam 30:14). They remained loyal to David at the time of the rebellions of Absalom (2 Sam 15:18) and Sheba (2 Sam 20:7) and supported the succession of Solomon against his rival Adonijah (1 Ki 1:38,44). *chief.* The earlier narrative at this point uses the Hebrew term ordinarily translated "priests" (see note on 2 Sam 8:18). The Chronicler has used a term for civil service instead of sacral service. Two approaches to this passage are ordinarily followed: 1. Some scholars see here an attempt by the Chronicler to keep the priesthood restricted to the Levitical line as part of his larger concern with legitimacy of cultic institutions in his own day. 2. Others argue that the Hebrew term used in 2 Sam 8:18 could earlier have had a broader meaning than "priest" and could be used of some other types of officials (cf. 2 Sam 20:26; 1 Ki 4:5). The Chronicler used an equivalent term, since by his day the Hebrew term for "priest" was restricted to cultic functionaries. The Septuagint, Targum, Old Latin and Josephus all translate the term in Samuel by some word other than "priest."

19:1–20:3 The Chronicler follows 2 Sam 10–12 closely (see notes there), apart from his omission of the account of David's sin with Bath-sheba (11:2–12:25). The Ammonites were a traditional enemy of Israel (2 Chr 20:1–2,23; 27:5; Judg 3:13; 10:7–9; 10:17–11:33; 1 Sam 11:1–13; 14:47; 2 Ki 10:32–33; Jer 49:1–6; Zeph 2:8–11). Even during the postexilic period Tobiah the Ammonite troubled Jerusalem (Neh 2:19; 4:3,7; 6:1,12,14; 13:4–9).

19:1 *Nahash.* Possibly the same as Saul's foe (1 Sam 11:1), or perhaps his descendant.

vid, Hanun and the children of Ammon sent a thousand talents of silver to hire them chariots and horsemen out of Mesopotamia, and out of Syria-maachah, [a]and out of Zobah.

7 So they hired thirty and two thousand chariots, and the king of Maachah and his people; who came and pitched before Medeba. And the children of Ammon gathered themselves together from their cities, and came to battle.

8 And when David heard *of it,* he sent Joab, and all the host *of* the mighty *men.*

9 And the children of Ammon came out, and put the battle in array *before* the gate of the city: and the kings that were come *were* by themselves in the field.

10 Now when Joab saw that [1]the battle was set against him before and behind, he chose out of all the [2]choice of Israel, and put *them* in array against the Syrians.

11 And the rest of the people he delivered unto the hand of [1]Abishai his brother, and they set *themselves* in array against the children of Ammon.

12 And he said, If the Syrians be too strong for me, then thou shalt help me: but if the children of Ammon be too strong for thee, then I will help thee.

13 Be of good courage, and let us behave ourselves valiantly for our people, and for the cities of our God: and let the LORD do *that* which *is* good in his sight.

14 So Joab and the people that *were* with him drew nigh before the Syrians unto the battle; and they fled before him.

15 And when the children of Ammon saw that the Syrians were fled, they likewise fled before Abishai his brother, and entered into the city. Then Joab came *to* Jerusalem.

16 ¶ And when the Syrians saw that they were put to the worse before Israel, they sent messengers, and drew forth the Syrians that *were* beyond the [1]river: and [2]Shophach the captain of the host of Hadarezer *went* before them.

17 And it was told David; and he gathered all Israel, and passed over Jordan, and came upon them, and set *the battle* in array against them. So when David had put the battle in array against the Syrians, they fought with him.

19:6 [a]ch. 18:5,9
19:10 [1]Heb. *the face of the battle was* [2]Or, *young men*
19:11 [1]Heb. *Abshai*
19:16 [1]That is, *Euphrates* [2]Or, *Shobach,* 2 Sam. 10:16

20:1 [1]Heb. *at the return of the year* [a]2 Sam. 11:1 [b]2 Sam. 12:26
20:2 [1]Heb. *the weight of* [a]2 Sam. 12:30,31
20:4 [1]Or, *continued.* Heb. *stood* [2]Or, *Gob* [3][Or, *Saph,* 2 Sam. 21:18] [4]Or, *Rapha* [a]2 Sam. 21:18 [b]ch. 11:29
20:5 [1]Called also *Jaare-oregim,* 2 Sam. 21:19
20:6 [1]Heb. *a man of measure* [2]Heb. *born to the giant,* or, *Rapha* [a]2 Sam. 21:20
20:7 [1]Or, *reproached* [2]Called *Shammah,* 1 Sam. 16:9

18 But the Syrians fled before Israel; and David slew of the Syrians seven thousand *men which fought in* chariots, and forty thousand footmen, and killed Shophach the captain of the host.

19 And when the servants of Hadarezer saw that they were put to the worse before Israel, they made peace with David, and became his servants: neither would the Syrians help the children of Ammon any more.

War with the Philistines

20 And [a]it came to pass, that [1]after the year was expired, at the time that kings go out *to battle,* Joab led forth the power of the army, and wasted the country of the children of Ammon, and came and besieged Rabbah. But David tarried at Jerusalem. And [b]Joab smote Rabbah, and destroyed it.

2 And David [a]took the crown of their king from off his head, and found it [1]to weigh a talent of gold, and *there were* precious stones in it; and it was *set* upon David's head: and he brought also exceeding much spoil *out* of the city.

3 And he brought out the people that *were* in it, and cut *them* with saws, and with harrows of iron, and with axes. Even so dealt David with all the cities of the children of Ammon. And David and all the people returned *to* Jerusalem.

4 ¶ And it came to pass after this, [a]that there [1]arose war at [2]Gezer with the Philistines; at which time [b]Sibbechai the Hushathite slew [3]Sippai, *that was* of the children of [4]the giant: and they were subdued.

5 And there was war again with the Philistines; and Elhanan the son of [1]Jair slew Lahmi the brother of Goliath the Gittite, whose spear staff *was* like a weaver's beam.

6 And yet again [a]there was war at Gath, where was [1]a man of *great* stature, whose fingers and toes *were* four and twenty, six *on each hand,* and six *on each foot:* and he also was [2]the son of the giant.

7 But when he [1]defied Israel, Jonathan the son of [2]Shimea David's brother slew him.

8 These were born unto the giant in Gath; and they fell by the hand of David, and by the hand of his servants.

19:6 *Mesopotamia, and out of Syria-maachah, and out of Zobah.* 2 Sam 10:6 also mentions Beth-rehob and Tob. All these states were north and northeast of Israel and formed a solid block from the region of Lake Huleh through the Anti-Lebanons to beyond the Euphrates.

19:7 *Medeba.* A town in Moab apparently in the hands of Ammon.

19:9 *the city.* The capital city, Rabbah, to which Joab would lay siege the following year (20:1–3).

19:18 *seven thousand.* 2 Sam 10:18 has 700, which is evidently a copyist's mistake.

20:1 *at the time that kings go out to battle.* Immediately following the spring harvest when there was some relaxation of agricultural labors and armies on the move could live off the land. *Rabbah.* See note on 19:9. Rabbah is the site of modern Amman, Jordan.

20:2–3 The Chronicler assumes that the reader is familiar with 2 Sam 12:26–29; he does not offer an explanation of how David, who had remained in Jerusalem (v. 1), came to be at Rabbah.

20:4 *Sibbechai.* See 11:29; 27:11. *giant.* See Gen 14:5; Deut 2:10–11; see also note on 2 Sam 21:16.

20:5 See note on 2 Sam 21:19. *weaver's beam.* See 11:23; 1 Sam 17:7.

20:6 *the giant.* See note on 2 Sam 21:16.

21:1–22:1 See 2 Sam 24 and notes. Although the story of David's census is quite similar in both narratives, the two accounts function differently. In Samuel the account belongs to the ap-

David's census

21 And [a]Satan stood *up* against Israel,
and provoked David to number Israel.
2 And David said to Joab and to the rulers
of the people, Go, number Israel from Beer-
sheba even to Dan; [a]and bring the number of
them to me, that I may know *it.*
3 And Joab answered, The LORD make his
people an hundred times so many moe as they
be: but, my lord the king, *are* they not all my
lord's servants? why *then* doth my lord require
this *thing?* why will he be a cause of trespass
to Israel?
4 Nevertheless the king's word prevailed
against Joab. Wherefore Joab departed, and
went throughout all Israel, and came *to* Jerusalem.
5 And Joab gave the sum of the number of
the people unto David. And all *they of* Israel
were a thousand thousand and an hundred
thousand men that drew sword: and Judah
was four hundred threescore and ten thousand
men that drew sword.
6 [a]But Levi and Benjamin counted he not
among them: for the king's word was abominable to Joab.
7 ¶ [1]And God was displeased with this
thing; therefore he smote Israel.
8 And David said unto God, [a]I have sinned
greatly, because I have done this thing: [b]but
now, I beseech thee, do away the iniquity of
thy servant; for I have done very foolishly.
9 And the LORD spake unto Gad, David's
[a]seer, saying,
10 Go and tell David, saying, Thus saith
the LORD, I [1]offer thee three *things:* choose
thee one of them, that I may do *it* unto thee.
11 So Gad came to David, and said unto
him, Thus saith the LORD, [1]Choose thee
12 [a]Either three years' famine; or three
months to be destroyed before thy foes, while
that the sword of thine enemies overtaketh
thee; or else three days the sword of the LORD,
even the pestilence, in the land, and the angel
of the LORD destroying throughout all the coasts
of Israel. Now therefore advise thyself what
word I shall bring again to him that sent me.
13 And David said unto Gad, I am in a
great strait: let me fall now into the hand of
the LORD; for very [1]great *are* his mercies: but
let me not fall into the hand of man.
14 So the LORD sent pestilence upon Israel:
and there fell of Israel seventy thousand men.
15 ¶ And God sent an [a]angel unto Jerusalem to destroy it: and as *he* was destroying, the
LORD beheld, and [b]he repented him of the evil,
and said to the angel that destroyed, *It is*
enough, stay now thine hand. And the angel of
the LORD stood by the threshingfloor of [1]Or-
nan the Jebusite.
16 And David lift up his eyes, and [a]saw the
angel of the LORD stand between the earth and
the heaven, having a drawn sword in his hand
stretched out over Jerusalem. Then David and
the elders *of Israel, who were* clothed in sackcloth, fell upon their faces.
17 And David said unto God, *Is it* not I *that*
commanded the people to be numbered? even
I *it is* that have sinned and done evil indeed;
but *as for* these sheep, what have they done?
let thine hand, I pray thee, O LORD my God, be
on me, and on my father's house; but not on
thy people, that *they* should be plagued.
18 Then the [a]angel of the LORD commanded Gad to say to David, that David should go
up, and set up an altar unto the LORD in the
threshingfloor of Ornan the Jebusite.
19 And David went up at the saying of
Gad, which he spake in the name of the LORD.
20 [1]And Ornan turned back, and saw the
angel; and his four sons with him hid themselves. Now Ornan was threshing wheat.
21 And as David came to Ornan, Ornan
looked and saw David, and went out of the

21:1 [a]2 Sam. 24:1
21:2 [a]ch. 27:23
21:6 [a]ch. 27:24
21:7 [1]Heb. *And it was evil in the eyes of the LORD concerning this thing*
21:8 [a]2 Sam. 24:10 [b]2 Sam. 12:13
21:9 [a]See 1 Sam. 9:9
21:10 [1]Heb. *stretch out*
21:11 [1]Heb. *Take to thee*
21:12 [a]2 Sam. 24:13
21:13 [1]Or, *many*
21:15 [1]Or, *Araunah,* 2 Sam. 24:16,18 [a]2 Sam. 24:16 [b]See Gen. 6:6
21:16 [a]2 Chr. 3:1
21:18 [a]2 Chr. 3:1
21:20 [1]Or, *When Ornan turned back and saw the angel,* then he *and his four sons with him hid themselves*

pendix (2 Sam 21–24), which begins and ends with accounts of the Lord's anger against Israel during the reign of David because of actions by her kings (in ch. 21, an act of Saul; in ch. 24, an act of David). See note on 2 Sam 21:1–24:25. The Chronicler appears to include it in order to account for the purchase of the ground on which the temple would be built. The additional material in Chronicles that is not found in Samuel (21:28–22:1) makes this interest clear. The census is the preface to David's preparations for the temple (chs. 22–29).

21:1 See note on 2 Sam 24:1. *Satan.* Satan means "accuser" (see Job 1:6; Zech 3:1 and notes).

21:4 The Chronicler abridges the more extensive account of Joab's itinerary found in 2 Sam 24:4–8; he does not mention that the census required nine months and 20 days (2 Sam 24:8).

21:5 *all they of Israel were a thousand thousand and an hundred thousand men . . . Judah was four hundred threescore and ten thousand.* 2 Sam 24:9 has 800,000 in Israel and 500,000 (which could be a round number for 470,000) in Judah. The reason for the difference is unclear. Perhaps it is to be related to the unofficial and incomplete nature of the census (see 27:23–24), with the differing figures representing the inclusion or exclusion of certain unspecified groupings among the people (see v. 6). Or perhaps it is simply due to a copyist's mistake.

21:6 The Chronicler adds the note that Joab exempted Levi and Benjamin from the counting. This additional note reflects the Chronicler's concern with the Levites and with the worship of Israel. The tabernacle in Gibeon and the ark in Jerusalem both fell within the borders of Benjamin.

21:9 *Gad.* A longtime friend of David, having been with him when he was a fugitive from Saul (1 Sam 22:3–5; cf. 1 Chr 29:29; 2 Chr 29:25).

21:12 *three years' famine.* 2 Sam 24:13 reads "seven years of famine," but the Septuagint reads "three years" there.

21:16 The verse has no parallel in the traditional Hebrew text of 2 Sam 24, so some scholars regard it as an addition by the Chronicler reflecting the more developed doctrine of angels in the postexilic period. However, a fragmentary Hebrew text of Samuel from the third century B.C., discovered at Qumran, contains the verse. It now appears that the Chronicler was carefully copying the Samuel text at his disposal, which differed in some respects from the Masoretic (traditional Hebrew) text. Josephus, who appears to be following the text of Samuel, also reported this information. Presumably, he too used a text of Samuel similar to that followed by the Chronicler.

21:20–21 The Chronicler reports that Ornan (a variant of Araunah; see 2 Sam 24:16) was threshing wheat as the king ap-

threshingfloor, and bowed himself to David
with his face to the ground.
22 Then David said to Ornan, [1]Grant me
the place of *this* threshingfloor, that I may
build an altar therein unto the LORD: thou shalt
[2]grant it me for the full price: that the plague
may be stayed from the people.
23 And Ornan said unto David, Take *it* to
thee, and let my lord the king do *that* which *is*
good in his eyes: lo, I give *thee* the oxen *also*
for burnt offerings, and the threshing instruments for wood, and the wheat for the meat
offering; I give *it* all.
24 And king David said to Ornan, Nay; but
I will verily buy *it* for the full price: for I will
not take *that* which *is* thine for the LORD, nor
offer burnt offerings without cost.
25 So [a]David gave to Ornan for the place
six hundred shekels of gold *by* weight.
26 And David built there an altar unto the
LORD, and offered burnt offerings and peace offerings, and called upon the LORD; and [a]he answered him from heaven by fire upon the altar
of burnt offering.
27 And the LORD commanded the angel;
and he put up his sword again into the sheath
thereof.

Preparing to build the temple

28 ¶ At that time when David saw that the
LORD had answered him in the threshingfloor
of Ornan the Jebusite, then he sacrificed there.
29 [a]For the tabernacle of the LORD, which
Moses made in the wilderness, and the altar of
the burnt offering, *were* at that season in the
high place at [b]Gibeon.
30 But David could not go before it to inquire of God: for he was afraid because of the
sword of the angel of the LORD.

21:22 [1]Heb. *Give* [2]Heb. *give*
21:25 [a]2 Sam. 24:24
21:26 [a]Lev. 9:24; 2 Chr. 3:1; 7:1
21:29 [a]ch. 16:39 [b]1 Ki. 3:4; ch. 16:39; 2 Chr. 1:3

22:1 [a]Deut. 12:5; 2 Sam. 24:18; ch. 21:18, 19,26,28; 2 Chr. 3:1
22:2 [a]1 Ki. 9:21
22:3 [a]ver. 14; 1 Ki. 7:47
22:4 [a]1 Ki. 5:6
22:5 [a]ch. 29:1
22:7 [a]2 Sam. 7:2; 1 Ki. 8:17; ch. 17:1; 28:2 [b]Deut. 12:5,11
22:8 [a]1 Ki. 5:3
22:9 [1]That is, *peaceable* [a]ch. 28:5 [b]1 Ki. 4:25; 5:4
22:10 [a]2 Sam. 7:13; 1 Ki. 5:5; ch. 17:12,13; 28:6 [b]Heb. 1:5

22 Then David said, [a]This *is* the house
of the LORD God, and this *is* the altar
of the burnt offering for Israel.
2 And David commanded to gather togeth-
er [a]the strangers that *were* in the land of Israel; and he set masons to hew wrought stones
to build the house of God.
3 And David prepared iron in abundance
for the nails for the doors of the gates, and for
the joinings; and brass in abundance [a]without
weight;
4 Also cedar trees in abundance: for the
[a]Zidonians and they of Tyre brought much
cedar wood to David.
5 And David said, [a]Solomon my son *is*
young and tender, and the house *that is* to be
builded for the LORD *must be* exceeding magnifical, of fame and of glory throughout all
countries: I will *therefore* now make preparation for it. So David prepared abundantly before his death.
6 ¶ Then he called for Solomon his son, and
charged him to build a house for the LORD God
of Israel.
7 And David said to Solomon, My son, *as
for* me, [a]it was in my mind to build a house
[b]unto the name of the LORD my God:
8 But the word of the LORD came to me,
saying, [a]Thou hast shed blood abundantly, and
hast made great wars: thou shalt not build a
house unto my name, because thou hast shed
much blood upon the earth in my sight.
9 [a]Behold, a son *shall be* born to thee, who
shall be a man of rest; and I will give him [b]rest
from all his enemies round about: for his name
shall be [1]Solomon, and I will give peace and
quietness unto Israel in his days.
10 [a]He shall build a house for my name;
and [b]he shall be my son, and I *will be* his fa-

proached—information not found in 2 Sam 24:20. However, Josephus and the fragmentary text of Samuel from Qumran both mention this information (see note on v. 16).

21:25 *six hundred shekels of gold.* 2 Sam 24:24 says 50 shekels of silver were paid for the threshingfloor and oxen. The difference has been explained by some as the Chronicler's attempt to glorify David and the temple by inflating the price. However, the difference is more likely explained by the Chronicler's statement that this was the price for the "site," i.e., for a much larger area than the threshingfloor alone.

21:26 *from heaven by fire.* Underscores the divine approval and the sanctity of the site (see 2 Chr 7:1; Lev 9:24; 1 Ki 18:37–38).

21:28–22:1 This material is not found in 2 Sam 24. It reflects the Chronicler's main concern in reporting this narrative (see note on 21:1–22:1).

21:30 *it.* The tabernacle.

22:1–29:30 This material is unique to Chronicles and displays some of the Chronicler's most characteristic interests: the preparations for the building of the temple, the legitimacy of the priests and Levites, and the royal succession. The chapters portray a theocratic "Messianic" kingdom as it existed under David and Solomon.

22:1 David dedicates this property (21:18–30) as the site for the temple (see vv. 2–6). See note on Ps 30 title.

22:2–19 Solomon's appointment to succeed David was twofold: (1) a private audience, with David and some leaders in attendance (vv. 17–19), and (2) a public announcement to the people (ch. 28), similar to when Joshua succeeded Moses (see Introduction: Portrait of David and Solomon).

22:2 *strangers . . . masons.* 2 Sam 20:24 confirms the use of forced labor by David, but does not specify that these laborers were aliens, not Israelites. Solomon used Israelites in conscripted labor (1 Ki 5:13–18; 9:15–23; 11:28), but the Chronicler mentions only his use of aliens (2 Chr 8:7–10). Though they were personally free, aliens were without political rights and could be easily exploited. The OT frequently warns that they were not to be oppressed (Ex 22:21; 23:9; Lev 19:33; Deut 24:14; Jer 7:6; Zech 7:10). Isaiah prophesies the participation of foreigners in the building of Jerusalem's walls in the future (Is 60:10–12).

22:3 *brass.* See note on 18:8.

22:5 *young.* Solomon's age at the time of his accession is not known with certainty. He came to the throne in 970 B.C. and was likely born c. 991.

22:8–9 See note on 17:1. In 1 Ki 5:3 Solomon explains that David could not build the temple because he was too busy with wars. The Chronicler's nuance is slightly different—not just that wars took so much of his time, but that David was in some sense defiled by them because of the bloodshed. A pun on Solomon's name is woven into the divine oracle ("Solomon" sounds like and may be derived from the Hebrew word for "peace").

22:10 See note on 17:12–14.

ther; and I will establish the throne of his
kingdom over Israel for ever.
11 Now, my son, [a]the LORD be with thee;
and prosper thou, and build the house of the
LORD thy God, as he hath said of thee.
12 Only the LORD [a]give thee wisdom and
understanding, and give thee charge concerning Israel, that *thou* mayest keep the law of the
LORD thy God.
13 [a]Then shalt thou prosper, if thou takest
heed to fulfil the statutes and judgments
which the LORD charged Moses with concerning Israel: [b]be strong, and of good courage;
dread not, nor be dismayed.
14 Now behold, [1]in my trouble I have prepared for the house of the LORD an hundred
thousand talents *of* gold, and a thousand thousand talents *of* silver; and of brass and iron
[a]without weight; for it is in abundance: timber
also and stone have I prepared; and thou
mayest add thereto.
15 Moreover *there are* workmen with thee
in abundance, hewers and [1]workers of stone
and timber, and all *manner of* cunning *men* for
every *manner of* work.
16 Of the gold, the silver, and the brass, and
the iron, *there is* no number. Arise *therefore,*
and be doing, and [a]the LORD be with thee.
17 ¶ David also commanded all the princes
of Israel to help Solomon his son, *saying,*
18 *Is* not the LORD your God with you?
[a]and hath he *not* given you rest on every side?
for he hath given the inhabitants of the land
into mine hand; and the land is subdued before the LORD, and before his people.
19 Now set your heart and your soul to
seek the LORD your God; arise therefore, and
build ye the sanctuary of the LORD God, to
[a]bring the ark of the covenant of the LORD, and
the holy vessels of God, into the house that is
to be built [b]to the name of the LORD.
23 So when David was old and full *of*
days, he made [a]Solomon his son king
over Israel.

Priests and Levites assembled

2 ¶ And he gathered together all the
princes of Israel, with the priests and the Levites.
3 Now the Levites were numbered from
the age of [a]thirty years and upward: and their
number by their polls, man by man, was thirty
and eight thousand.
4 Of which, twenty and four thousand
were [1]to set forward the work of the house of
the LORD; and six thousand *were* [a]officers and
judges:
5 Moreover four thousand *were* porters;
and four thousand praised the LORD with the
instruments [a]which I made, *said David,* to
praise *therewith.*
6 And [a]David divided them *into* [1]courses
among the sons of Levi, *namely,* Gershon, Kohath, and Merari.
7 ¶ Of the [a]Gershonites *were,* [1]Laadan,
and Shimei.
8 The sons of Laadan; the chief *was* Jehiel,
and Zetham, and Joel, three.
9 The sons of Shimei; Shelomith, and Haziel, and Haran, three. These *were* the chief of
the fathers of Laadan.
10 And the sons of Shimei *were,* Jahath,
[1]Zina, and Jeush, and Beriah. These four *were*
the sons of Shimei.
11 And Jahath was the chief, and Zizah the
second: but Jeush and Beriah [1]had not many
sons; therefore they were in one reckoning,
according to *their* father's house.
12 ¶ [a]The sons of Kohath; Amram, Izhar,
Hebron, and Uzziel, four.
13 The sons of [a]Amram; Aaron and Moses:
and [b]Aaron was separated, that he should
sanctify the most holy *things,* he and his sons
for ever, [c]to burn incense before the LORD, [d]to
minister unto him, and [e]to bless in his name
for ever.
14 Now *concerning* Moses the man of God,
[a]his sons were named of the tribe of Levi.
15 [a]The sons of Moses *were,* Gershom,
and Eliezer.
16 *Of* the sons of Gershom, [a][1]Shebuel *was*
the chief.
17 And the sons of Eliezer *were,* [a]Rehabiah
[1]the chief. And Eliezer had none other sons;
but the sons of Rehabiah [2]were very many.
18 *Of* the sons of Izhar; [1]Shelomith the
chief.
19 [a]*Of* the sons of Hebron; Jeriah the first,
Amariah the second, Jahaziel the third, and
Jekameam the fourth.

22:11 [a]ver. 16
22:12 [a]1 Ki. 3:9,12
22:13 [a]Josh. 1:7,8; ch. 28:7 [b]Deut. 31:7,8; Josh. 1:6,7,9; ch. 28:20
22:14 [1]Or, *in my poverty* [a]As ver. 3
22:15 [1]That is, *masons and carpenters*
22:16 [a]ver. 11
22:18 [a]Deut. 12:10; Josh. 22:4; 2 Sam. 7:1; ch. 23:25
22:19 [a]2 Chr. 5:7 [b]1 Ki. 5:3
23:1 [a]1 Ki. 1:33
23:3 [a]Num. 4:3
23:4 [1]Or, *to oversee* [a]Deut. 16:18; 2 Chr. 19:8
23:5 [a]2 Chr. 29:25,26
23:6 [1]Heb. *divisions* [a]Ex. 6:16; Num. 26:57; 2 Chr. 8:14
23:7 [1]Or, *Libni,* ch. 6:17 [a]ch. 26:21
23:10 [1]Or, *Zizah,* ver. 11
23:11 [1]Heb. *did not multiply sons*
23:12 [a]Ex. 6:18
23:13 [a]Ex. 6:20 [b]Ex. 28:1; Heb. 5:4 [c]Ex. 30:7; 1 Sam. 2:28 [d]Deut. 21:5 [e]Num. 6:23
23:14 [a]ch. 26:23
23:15 [a]Ex. 18:3,4
23:16 [1][*Shubael,* ch. 24:20] [a]ch. 26:24
23:17 [1]Or, *the first* [2]Heb. *were highly multiplied* [a]ch. 26:25
23:18 [1][*Shelomoth,* ch. 24:22]
23:19 [a]ch. 24:23

22:12–13 See Introduction: Portrait of David and Solomon.
22:19 See 2 Chr 5:1–7.
23:1–27:34 David's preparations for the temple were not restricted to amassing materials for the building; he also arranged for its administration and worship. Unique to Chronicles (see note on 22:1–29:30), these details of the organization of the theocracy (God's kingdom) were of vital concern in the Chronicler's own day. Characteristically for the Chronicler, details about religious and cultic matters (chs. 23–26) take precedence over those that are civil and secular (ch. 27). David's arrangements provided the basis and authority for the practices of the restored community.
23:1 *made Solomon his son king.* The account of Solomon's succession is resumed in chs. 28–29. The Chronicler omits the accounts of disputed succession and bloody consolidation recorded in 1 Ki 1–2 (see note on 28:1–29:30) since these would not be in accord with his overall portrait of David and Solomon (see Introduction: Portrait of David and Solomon).
23:2–5 The Levites were not counted in the census that had provoked the wrath of God (21:6–7).
23:3 *Levites . . . from the age of thirty years and upward.* The census of Levites was made first in accordance with the Mosaic prescription (Num 4:1–3). Apparently soon after this count, David instructed that the age be lowered to 20 years (vv. 24,27); a similar adjustment to age 25 had been made under Moses (Num 8:23–24, but see note on Num 8:24).
23:6 *Gershon, Kohath, and Merari.* The Levites were organized by their three clans (ch. 6; Ex 6:16–19; Num 3). This list parallels those in 6:16–30; 24:20–30.

20 *Of* the sons of Uzziel; Michah the first, and Jesiah the second.

21 ¶ [a]The sons of Merari; Mahli, and Mushi. The sons of Mahli; Eleazar, and [b]Kish.

22 And Eleazar died, and [a]had no sons, but daughters: and their [1]brethren the sons of Kish [b]took them.

23 [a]The sons of Mushi; Mahli, and Eder, and Jeremoth, three.

The duties of the Levites

24 ¶ These *were* the sons of [a]Levi after the house of their fathers; *even* the chief of the fathers, as they were counted by number of names by their polls, that did the work for the service of the house of the LORD, from the age of [b]twenty years and upward.

25 For David said, The LORD God of Israel [a]hath given rest unto his people, [1]that they may dwell in Jerusalem for ever:

26 And also unto the Levites; *they* shall no *more* [a]carry the tabernacle, nor any vessels of it for the service thereof.

27 For by the last words of David, the Levites *were* [1]numbered from twenty years old and above:

28 Because [a][1]their office *was* to wait on the sons of Aaron for the service of the house of the LORD, in the courts, and in the chambers, and in the purifying of all holy *things,* and the work of the service of the house of God;

29 Both for [a]the shewbread, and for [b]the fine flour for meat offering, and for [c]the unleavened cakes, and for [d]*that which is baked in* the [1]pan, and for that which is fried, and for all *manner of* [e]measure and size;

30 And to stand every morning to thank and praise the LORD, and likewise at even;

31 And to offer all burnt sacrifices unto the LORD [a]in the sabbaths, in the new moons, and on the [b]set feasts, by number, according to the order commanded unto them, continually before the LORD:

32 And that they should [a]keep the charge of the tabernacle of the congregation, and the charge of the holy *place,* and [b]the charge of the sons of Aaron their brethren, in the service of the house of the LORD.

23:21 [a]ch. 24:26 [b]ch. 24:29
23:22 [1]Or, *kinsmen* [a]ch. 24:28 [b]Num. 36:6
23:23 [a]ch. 24:30
23:24 [a]Num. 10:17,21 [b]Num. 1:3; Ezra 3:8
23:25 [1]Or, *and he dwelleth in Jerusalem, etc.* [a]ch. 22:18
23:26 [a]Num. 4:5
23:27 [1]Heb. *number*
23:28 [1]Heb. *their station* was *at the hand of the sons of Aaron* [a]Neh. 11:24
23:29 [1]Or, *flat plate* [a]Ex. 25:30 [b]Lev. 6:20 [c]Lev. 2:4 [d]Lev. 2:5,7 [e]Lev. 19:35
23:31 [a]Num. 10:10 [b]Lev. 23:4
23:32 [a]Num. 1:53 [b]Num. 3:6-9
24:1 [a]Lev. 10:1,6; Num. 26:60
24:2 [a]Num. 3:4; 26:61
24:6 [1]Heb. *house of the father*
24:10 [a]Neh. 12:4,17; Luke 1:5

The division of the priests

24 Now *these are* the divisions of the sons of Aaron. [a]The sons of Aaron; Nadab, and Abihu, Eleazar, and Ithamar.

2 But [a]Nadab and Abihu died before their father, and had no children: therefore Eleazar and Ithamar executed the priest's office.

3 And David distributed them, both Zadok of the sons of Eleazar, and Ahimelech of the sons of Ithamar, according to their offices in their service.

4 And there were moe chief men found of the sons of Eleazar than of the sons of Ithamar; and *thus* were they divided. Among the sons of Eleazar *there were* sixteen chief *men* of the house of *their* fathers, and eight among the sons of Ithamar according to the house of their fathers.

5 Thus were they divided by lot, one *sort* with another; for the governors of the sanctuary, and governors *of the house* of God, were of the sons of Eleazar, and of the sons of Ithamar.

6 And Shemaiah the son of Nethaneel the scribe, *one* of the Levites, wrote them before the king, and the princes, and Zadok the priest, and Ahimelech the son of Abiathar, and *before* the chief of the fathers of the priests and Levites: one [1]principal household being taken for Eleazar, and *one* taken for Ithamar.

7 Now the first lot came forth to Jehoiarib, the second to Jedaiah,

8 The third to Harim, the fourth to Seorim,

9 The fifth to Malchijah, the sixth to Mijamin,

10 The seventh to Hakkoz, the eighth to [a]Abijah,

11 The ninth to Jeshua, the tenth to Shecaniah,

12 The eleventh to Eliashib, the twelfth to Jakim,

13 The thirteenth to Huppah, the fourteenth to Jeshebeab,

14 The fifteenth to Bilgah, the sixteenth to Immer,

15 The seventeenth to Hezir, the eighteenth to Aphses,

16 The nineteenth to Pethahiah, the twentieth to Jehezekel,

23:24,27 *twenty years and upward.* See note on v. 3.

23:28–32 See note on 9:28–34. The function of the Levites was to assist the priests. In addition to the care of the precincts and implements, baked goods and music (mentioned as Levitical duties in 9:22–34), the Chronicler adds details on the role of the Levites assisting in sacrifices.

23:30 *morning . . . even.* See Ex 29:38–41; Num 28:3–8.

24:1–19 There are several lists of priests from the postexilic period (see 6:3–15; 9:10–13; Ezra 2:36–39; Neh 10:1–8; 11:10–12; 12:1–7,12–21).

24:2 *Nadab and Abihu died.* The Chronicler alludes to the events recorded in Lev 10:1–3 (see note on 6:1–3).

24:3 *Zadok . . . Ahimelech.* Zadok and Abiathar had served as David's high priests. Here, late in David's life, Abiathar's son Ahimelech appears to have taken over some of his father's duties (see note on 6:8), but see note on 2 Sam 8:17.

24:4 *sixteen . . . eight.* A total of 24 divisions was selected by lot. This would allow for service either in monthly shifts, as was done by priests in Egyptian mortuary temples, or for two-week shifts once each year as found in NT times. The names of the first, second, fourth, ninth and 24th divisions have been found in a Dead Sea scroll from the fourth cave at Qumran (see essay, p. 1356).

24:7 *Jehoiarib.* Mattathias, father of the Maccabees, was a member of the Jehoiarib division (in the Apocrypha see 1 Maccabees 2:1).

24:10 *Abijah.* The father of John the Baptist was "of the course of Abia" (Luke 1:5).

24:15 *Hezir.* The division from the family of Hezir was prominent in intertestamental times; the name appears on one of the large tombs in the Kidron Valley, east of Jerusalem.

17 The one and twentieth to Jachin, the
two and twentieth to Gamul,
18 The three and twentieth to Delaiah, the
four and twentieth to Maaziah.
19 These *were* the orderings of them in
their service [a]to come into the house of the
LORD, according to their manner, under Aaron
their father, as the LORD God of Israel had commanded him.
20 ¶ And the rest of the sons of Levi *were*
these: Of the sons of Amram; [1]Shubael: of the
sons of Shubael; Jehdeiah.
21 Concerning [a]Rehabiah: of the sons of
Rehabiah, the first *was* Isshiah.
22 Of the Izharites; [1]Shelomoth: of the
sons of Shelomoth; Jahath.
23 And the sons *of* [a]*Hebron;* Jeriah *the*
first, Amariah the second, Jahaziel the third,
Jekameam the fourth.
24 *Of* the sons of Uzziel; Michah: of the
sons of Michah; Shamir.
25 The brother of Michah *was* Isshiah: of
the sons of Isshiah; Zechariah.
26 [a]The sons of Merari *were* Mahli and
Mushi: the sons of Jaaziah; Beno.
27 The sons of Merari by Jaaziah; Beno,
and Shoham, and Zaccur, and Ibri.
28 Of Mahli *came* Eleazar, [a]who had no
sons.
29 Concerning Kish: the son of Kish *was*
Jerahmeel.
30 [a]The sons also of Mushi; Mahli, and
Eder, and Jerimoth. These *were* the sons of the
Levites after the house of their fathers.
31 These likewise cast lots over against
their brethren the sons of Aaron in the presence of David the king, and Zadok, and Ahimelech, and the chief of the fathers of the
priests and Levites, *even* the principal fathers
over against their younger brethren.

The arrangements for music

25 Moreover David and the captains of
the host separated to the service of
the sons of [a]Asaph, and of Heman, and of Jeduthun, who should prophesy with harps,
with psalteries, and with cymbals: and the
number of the workmen according to their
service was:
2 Of the sons of Asaph; Zaccur, and Joseph,
and Nethaniah, and [1]Asarelah, the sons of
Asaph under the hands of Asaph, which
prophesied [a2]according to the order of the
king.
3 Of Jeduthun: the sons of Jeduthun; Gedaliah, and [1]Zeri, and Jeshaiah, Hashabiah, and
Mattithiah, [2]six, under the hands of their father Jeduthun, who prophesied with a harp, to
give thanks and to praise the LORD.
4 Of Heman: the sons of Heman; Bukkiah,
Mattaniah, [1]Uzziel, [2]Shebuel, and Jerimoth,
Hananiah, Hanani, Eliathah, Giddalti, and Romamti-ezer, Joshbekashah, Mallothi, Hothir,
and Mahazioth:
5 All these *were* the sons of Heman the
king's seer in the [1]words of God, to lift up the
horn. And God gave to Heman fourteen sons
and three daughters.
6 All these *were* under the hands of their
father for song *in* the house of the LORD, with
cymbals, psalteries, and harps, for the service
of the house of God, [a1]according to the king's
order *to* Asaph, Jeduthun, and Heman.
7 So the number of them, with their brethren *that were* instructed in the songs of the
LORD, *even* all that were cunning, was two
hundred fourscore and eight.
8 ¶ And they cast lots, ward against *ward,*
as well the small as the great, [a]the teacher as
the scholar.
9 Now the first lot came forth for Asaph to
Joseph: the second *to* Gedaliah, who with his
brethren and sons *were* twelve:
10 The third *to* Zaccur, *he,* his sons, and
his brethren, *were* twelve:
11 The fourth *to* Izri, *he,* his sons, and his
brethren, *were* twelve:
12 The fifth *to* Nethaniah, *he,* his sons, and
his brethren, *were* twelve:
13 The sixth *to* Bukkiah, *he,* his sons, and
his brethren, *were* twelve:
14 The seventh *to* Jesharelah, *he,* his sons,
and his brethren, *were* twelve:
15 The eighth *to* Jeshaiah, *he,* his sons,
and his brethren, *were* twelve:
16 The ninth *to* Mattaniah, *he,* his sons,
and his brethren, *were* twelve:
17 The tenth *to* Shimei, *he,* his sons, and
his brethren, *were* twelve:
18 The eleventh *to* Azareel, *he,* his sons,
and his brethren, *were* twelve:
19 The twelfth to Hashabiah, *he,* his sons,
and his brethren, *were* twelve:
20 The thirteenth *to* Shubael, *he,* his sons,
and his brethren, *were* twelve:
21 The fourteenth *to* Mattithiah, *he,* his
sons, and his brethren, *were* twelve:
22 The fifteenth to Jeremoth, *he,* his sons,
and his brethren, *were* twelve:

24:19 [a]ch. 9:25 **24:20** [1][ch. 23:16, *Shebuel*] **24:21** [a]ch. 23:17 **24:22** [1][ch. 23:18, *Shelomith*] **24:23** [a]ch. 23:19; 26:31 **24:26** [a]Ex. 6:19; ch. 23:21 **24:28** [a]ch. 23:22 **24:30** [a]ch. 23:23 **25:1** [a]ch. 6:33,39,44 **25:2** [1]Otherwise called *Jesharelah,* ver. 14 [2]Heb. *by the hands of the king* [a]ver. 6

25:3 [1]Or, *Izri,* ver. 11 [2]With Shimei mentioned, ver. 17 **25:4** [1]Or, *Azareel,* ver. 18 [2]Or, *Shubael,* ver. 20 **25:5** [1]Or, *matters* **25:6** [1]Heb. *by the hands of the king* [a]ver. 2 **25:8** [a]2 Chr. 23:13

24:20–31 This list supplements 23:7–23 by extending some of the lines mentioned there.
25:1 *captains of the host.* David often sought the counsel of military leaders (11:10; 12:32; 28:1), even in cultic affairs (13:1; 15:25). *Asaph . . . Heman . . . Jeduthun.* See note on 6:31–48. *prophesy.* There are several passages in Chronicles, largely in portions unique to these books, where cultic personnel are designated prophets (here; 2 Chr 20:14–17; 29:30; 35:15; cf. 2 Ki 23:2; 2 Chr 34:30). Zechariah the priest also appears to function as a prophet, though he is not so named (2 Chr 24:19–22). This may reflect postexilic interest in the prophet-priest-king figure of Messianic expectation: In Chronicles not only do priests prophesy, but kings also function as priests (see notes on 15:27; 16:1–3). David's organizing of the temple musicians may reflect his overall interest in music (1 Sam 16:23; 18:10; 19:9; 2 Sam 1:17–27; 6:5,14).
25:5 *fourteen sons and three daughters.* Numerous progeny are a sign of divine blessing (see Job 1:2; 42:13). This is specifically stated for Heman as the result of the promises of God to exalt him. See 3:1–9; 14:2–7; 26:4–5; 2 Chr 11:18–21; 13:21; 21:2; 24:3.

23 The sixteenth to Hananiah, *he,* his sons, and his brethren, *were* twelve:

24 The seventeenth to Joshbekashah, *he,* his sons, and his brethren, *were* twelve:

25 The eighteenth to Hanani, *he,* his sons, and his brethren, *were* twelve:

26 The nineteenth to Mallothi, *he,* his sons, and his brethren, *were* twelve:

27 The twentieth to Eliathah, *he,* his sons, and his brethren, *were* twelve:

28 The one and twentieth to Hothir, *he,* his sons, and his brethren, *were* twelve:

29 The two and twentieth to Giddalti, *he,* his sons, and his brethren, *were* twelve:

30 The three and twentieth to Mahazioth, *he,* his sons, and his brethren, *were* twelve:

31 The four and twentieth to Romamti-ezer, *he,* his sons, and his brethren, *were* twelve.

The arrangements for porters

26 Concerning the divisions of the porters: Of the Korhites *was* [1]Meshelemiah the son of Kore, of the sons of [2]Asaph.

2 And the sons of Meshelemiah *were,* Zechariah the firstborn, Jediael the second, Zebadiah the third, Jathniel the fourth,

3 Elam the fifth, Jehohanan the sixth, Elioenai the seventh.

4 Moreover the sons of Obed-edom *were,* Shemaiah the firstborn, Jehozabad the second, Joah the third, and Sacar the fourth, and Nethaneel the fifth,

5 Ammiel the sixth, Issachar the seventh, Peulthai the eighth: for God blessed [1]him.

6 Also unto Shemaiah his son were sons born, that ruled throughout the house of their father: for they *were* mighty *men* of valour.

7 The sons of Shemaiah; Othni, and Rephael, and Obed, Elzabad, whose brethren *were* strong men, Elihu, and Semachiah.

8 All these of the sons of Obed-edom: they and their sons and their brethren, able men for strength for the service, *were* threescore and two of Obed-edom.

9 And Meshelemiah had sons and brethren, strong men, eighteen.

10 Also [a]Hosah, of the children of Merari, had sons; Simri the chief, (for *though* he was not the firstborn, yet his father made him the chief;)

11 Hilkiah the second, Tebaliah the third, Zechariah the fourth: all the sons and brethren of Hosah *were* thirteen.

12 Among these *were* the divisions of the porters, *even* among the chief men, *having* wards one against another, to minister in the house of the LORD.

13 ¶ And they cast lots, [1]as well the small as the great, according to the house of their fathers, for every gate.

14 And the lot eastward fell to [1]Shelemiah. Then *for* Zechariah his son, a wise counseller, they cast lots; and his lot came out northward.

15 To Obed-edom southward; and to his sons the house of [1]Asuppim.

16 To Shuppim and Hosah *the lot came forth* westward, with the gate Shallecheth, by the causeway of the going [a]up, ward against ward.

17 Eastward *were* six Levites, northward four a day, southward four a day, and toward Asuppim two *and* two.

18 At Parbar westward, four at the causeway, *and* two at Parbar.

19 These *are* the divisions of the porters among the sons of Kore, and among the sons of Merari.

The arrangements for treasures

20 ¶ And *of* the Levites, Ahijah *was* [a]over the treasures of the house of God, and over the treasures of the [1]dedicate *things.*

21 *As concerning* the sons of [1]Laadan; the sons of the Gershonite Laadan, chief fathers, *even* of Laadan the Gershonite, *were* [2]Jehieli.

22 The sons of Jehieli; Zetham, and Joel his brother, *which were* over the treasures of the house of the LORD.

23 Of the Amramites, *and* the Izharites, the Hebronites, *and* the Uzzielites:

24 And [a]Shebuel the son of Gershom, the son of Moses, *was* ruler of the treasures.

25 And his brethren by Eliezer; Rehabiah his son, and Jeshaiah his son, and Joram his

26:1 [1]Or, *Shelemiah,* ver. 14 [2]Or, *Ebiasaph,* ch. 6:23,37
26:5 [1]That is, Obed-edom, as ch. 13:14
26:10 [a]ch. 16:38
26:13 [1]Or, *as well for the small as for the great*
26:14 [1]Called *Meshelemiah,* ver. 1
26:15 [1]Heb. *gatherings*
26:16 [a]1 Ki. 10:5; 2 Chr. 9:4
26:20 [1]Heb. *holy* things [a]ch. 28:12; Mal. 3:10
26:21 [1]Or, *Libni,* ch. 6:17 [2]Or, *Jehiel,* ch. 23:8
26:24 [a]ch. 23:16

26:1–19 The most extensive of the Chronicler's lists of porters (see 9:17–27; 16:37–38). A list of porters in the postexilic period is found in Ezra 2:42 (Neh 7:45).

26:1 *Asaph.* This name appears to be an abbreviation of Ebiasaph (6:23; 9:19); he should not be confused with the temple musician (25:1–2,6).

26:4–5 Numerous sons are again a sign of divine blessing (see note on 25:5).

26:4 *Obed-edom.* Had cared for the ark when it was left at his house (see note on 13:13).

‡26:12 *wards* [i.e."duties"]. Elaborated in 9:22–29.

26:14 *eastward.* The east gate was the main entrance; it had six guard posts, as opposed to four at the other gates (v. 17).

26:15 *southward.* The palaces of David and Solomon were south of the temple mount. The southern gate would be the main one used by the king, and this assignment probably reflects a particular honor for Obed-edom (see notes on 26:4–5; see also Ezek 46:1–10).

26:16 *gate Shallecheth.* The only reference to a gate by this name; presumably it was on the western side. The Chronicler writes to an audience familiar with these topographical details.

26:20 *treasures of the house of God.* The Levites in charge of these treasuries received the offerings of the people and cared for the valuable temple equipment (9:28–29). *treasures of the dedicate things.* The plunder from warfare (vv. 27–28). Texts from Mesopotamian temples confirm the presence of temple officers who served as assayers to handle and refine the precious metals received as revenue and offerings. The procedure with reference to the offerings of the people may be seen in the reign of Joash (2 Chr 24:4–14; 2 Ki 12:4–16). Numerous passages reflect on the wealth collected in the temple (see, e.g., 29:1–9; 2 Chr 4:1–22; 34:9–11; 36:7,10,18–19; 1 Ki 14:25–28; 15:15,18; 2 Ki 12:4–18; 14:14; 16:8; 25:13–17).

son, and Zichri his son, and [a]Shelomith his
son.
26 Which Shelomith and his brethren *were*
over all the treasures of the dedicate *things,*
which David the king, and the chief fathers,
the captains over thousands and hundreds,
and the captains of the host, had dedicated.
27 [1]Out of the spoils won in battles did
they dedicate to maintain the house of the
LORD.
28 And all that Samuel [a]the seer, and Saul
the son of Kish, and Abner the son of Ner, and
Joab the son of Zeruiah, had dedicated; *and*
whosoever had dedicated *anything, it was* under the hand of Shelomith, and of his brethren.
29 Of the Izharites, Chenaniah and his
sons *were* for the outward business over Israel, for [a]officers and judges.
30 *And* of the Hebronites, Hashabiah and
his brethren, men of valour, a thousand and
seven hundred, *were* [1]officers among them of
Israel on *this* side Jordan westward in all the
business of the LORD, and in the service of the
king.
31 Among the Hebronites *was* [a]Jerijah the
chief, *even* among the Hebronites, according
to the generations of his fathers. In the fortieth
year of the reign of David they were sought
for, and there were found among them mighty
men of valour [b]at Jazer of Gilead.
32 And his brethren, men of valour, *were*
two thousand and seven hundred chief fathers, whom king David made rulers over the
Reubenites, the Gadites, and the half tribe of
Manasseh, for every matter pertaining to God,
and [a][1]affairs of the king.

Military and civil officials

27 Now the children of Israel after their
number, *to wit,* the chief fathers and
captains of thousands and hundreds, and their
officers that served the king in any matter of
the courses, which came in and went out
month by month throughout all the months of
the year, *of* every course *were* twenty and four
thousand.

26:25 [a]ch. 23:18
26:27 [1]Heb. *Out of the battles and spoils*
26:28 [a]1 Sam. 9:9
26:29 [a]ch. 23:4
26:30 [1]Heb. *over the charge*
26:31 [a]ch. 23:19 [b]See Josh. 21:39
26:32 [1]Heb. *thing* [a]2 Chr. 19:11
27:2 [a]2 Sam. 23:8; ch. 11:11
27:4 [1]Or, *Dodo,* ch. 11:12
27:5 [1]Or, *principal officer*
27:6 [a]2 Sam. 23:20,22,23; ch. 11:22
27:7 [a]2 Sam. 23:24; ch. 11:26
27:9 [a]ch. 11:28
27:10 [a]ch. 11:27
27:11 [a]2 Sam. 21:18
27:12 [a]ch. 11:28
27:13 [a]2 Sam. 23:28; ch. 11:30
27:14 [a]ch. 11:31

2 Over the first course for the first month
was [a]Jashobeam the son of Zabdiel: and in his
course *were* twenty and four thousand.
3 Of the children of Perez *was* the chief of
all the captains of the host for the first month.
4 And over the course of the second month
was [1]Dodai an Ahohite, and *of* his course *was*
Mikloth also the ruler: in his course likewise
were twenty and four thousand.
5 The third captain of the host for the third
month *was* Benaiah the son of Jehoiada, a
[1]chief priest: and in his course *were* twenty
and four thousand.
6 This *is that* Benaiah, *who was* [a]mighty
among the thirty, and above the thirty: and *in*
his course *was* Ammizabad his son.
7 The fourth *captain* for the fourth month
was [a]Asahel the brother of Joab, and Zebadiah
his son after him: and in his course *were* twenty and four thousand.
8 The fifth captain for the fifth month *was*
Shamhuth the Izrahite: and in his course *were*
twenty and four thousand.
9 The sixth *captain* for the sixth month
was [a]Ira the son of Ikkesh the Tekoite: and in
his course *were* twenty and four thousand.
10 The seventh *captain* for the seventh
month *was* [a]Helez the Pelonite, of the children of Ephraim: and in his course *were* twenty and four thousand.
11 The eighth *captain* for the eighth
month *was* [a]Sibbecai the Hushathite, of the
Zarhites: and in his course *were* twenty and
four thousand.
12 The ninth *captain* for the ninth month
was [a]Abiezer the Anetothite, of the Benjamites: and in his course *were* twenty and
four thousand.
13 The tenth *captain* for the tenth month
was [a]Maharai the Netophathite, of the
Zarhites: and in his course *were* twenty and
four thousand.
14 The eleventh *captain* for the eleventh
month *was* [a]Benaiah the Pirathonite, of the
children of Ephraim: and in his course *were*
twenty and four thousand.

26:26 *dedicate things, which David . . . had dedicated.* See note on 18:1–20:8; see also 2 Chr 5:1.

26:27 *Out of the spoils won in battles did they dedicate.* Cf. Gen 14:17–20.

26:29–32 These verses designate the 6,000 officials and judges (23:4) who would work outside Jerusalem; they are drawn from two sub-clans of Kohath (6:18). Deut 17:8–13 envisages a judicial function for the priests and Levites (see 2 Chr 19:4–11).

26:30,32 *in all the business of the LORD, and in the service of the king . . . pertaining to God, and affairs of the king.* In the theocracy (kingdom of God) there is no division between secular and sacred, no tension in serving God and the king (cf. Mat 22:15–22; Luke 16:10–13; Rom 13:1–7; 1 Tim 2:1–4; 1 Pet 2:13–17).

26:31 *fortieth year.* The last year of David's reign.

27:1–15 The names of the commanders of David's army are the same as those found in the list of his mighty men (see 11:11–47; see also 2 Sam 23:8–39 and notes). Those who had served David while he fled from Saul became commanders in the regular army.

27:1 *twenty and four thousand.* See note on 12:23–37. Although a national militia consisting of 12 units of 24,000 each (a total of 288,000) is not unreasonable, the stress in this passage on unit commanders and divisions suggests that here too the Hebrew word for "1,000" should perhaps be taken as the designation of a military unit. To designate a division as "1,000" would be to give the upper limit of the number of men in such a unit, though such units would ordinarily not have a full complement of men. If this approach is followed, the figures in the following verses would be read as "24 units" instead of 24,000.

27:2 *Jashobeam.* See 11:11.

27:4 *Dodai.* See 11:12.

27:5 *Benaiah.* See 11:22–25; 18:17.

27:7 *Asahel.* See 11:26; 2 Sam 2:18–23.

27:9–15 The remainder of the commanders were selected from among the thirty (see 11:25 and the names listed in 11:27–31).

15 The twelfth *captain* for the twelfth month *was* [1]Heldai the Netophathite, of Othniel: and in his course *were* twenty and four thousand.

16 ¶ Furthermore over the tribes of Israel: the ruler of the Reubenites *was* Eliezer the son of Zichri: of the Simeonites, Shephatiah the son of Maachah:

17 Of the Levites, [a]Hashabiah the son of Kemuel: of the Aaronites, Zadok:

18 Of Judah, [a1]Elihu, *one* of the brethren of David: of Issachar, Omri the son of Michael:

19 Of Zebulun, Ishmaiah the son of Obadiah: of Naphtali, Jerimoth the son of Azriel:

20 Of the children of Ephraim, Hoshea the son of Azaziah: of the half tribe of Manasseh, Joel the son of Pedaiah:

21 Of the half *tribe* of Manasseh in Gilead, Iddo the son of Zechariah: of Benjamin, Jaasiel the son of Abner:

22 Of Dan, Azareel the son of Jeroham. These *were* the princes of the tribes of Israel.

23 ¶ But David took not the number of them from twenty years old and under: because [a]the LORD had said *he* would increase Israel like to the stars of the heavens.

24 Joab the son of Zeruiah began to number, but he finished not, because [a]there fell wrath for it against Israel; neither [1]was the number put in the account of the chronicles of king David.

25 ¶ And over the king's treasures *was* Azmaveth the son of Adiel: and over the storehouses in the fields, in the cities, and in the villages, and in the castles, *was* Jehonathan the son of Uzziah:

26 And over them that did the work of the field for tillage of the ground *was* Ezri the son of Chelub:

27:15 [1]Or, *Heled,* ch. 11:30
27:17 [a]ch. 26:30
27:18 [1][1 Sam. 16:6, *Eliab*] [a]1 Sam. 16:6; *Eliab*
27:23 [a]Gen. 15:5
27:24 [1]Heb. *ascended* [a]2 Sam. 24:15; ch 21:7
27:27 [1]Heb. *over that which* was *of the vineyards*
27:32 [1]Or, *secretary* [2]Or, *Hachmonite*
27:33 [a]2 Sam. 15:12 [b]2 Sam. 15:37; 16:16
27:34 [a]1 Ki. 1:7 [b]ch. 11:6
28:1 [1]Or, *cattle* [2][Or, *and his sons*] [3]Or, *eunuchs* [a]ch. 27:16 [b]ch. 27:1,2 [c]ch. 27:25 [d]ch. 11:10

27 And over the vineyards *was* Shimei the Ramathite: [1]over the increase of the vineyards for the wine cellars *was* Zabdi the Shiphmite:

28 And over the olive trees and the sycomore trees that *were* in the low plains *was* Baal-hanan the Gederite: and over the cellars of oil *was* Joash:

29 And over the herds that fed in Sharon *was* Shitrai the Sharonite: and over the herds *that were* in the valleys *was* Shaphat the son of Adlai:

30 Over the camels also *was* Obil the Ishmaelite: and over the asses *was* Jehdeiah the Meronothite:

31 And over the flocks *was* Jaziz the Hagerite. All these *were* the rulers of the substance which *was* king David's.

32 Also Jonathan David's uncle *was* a counseller, a wise man, and a [1]scribe: and Jehiel the [2]son of Hachmoni *was* with the king's sons:

33 And [a]Ahithophel *was* the king's counseller: and [b]Hushai the Archite *was* the king's companion:

34 And after Ahithophel *was* Jehoiada the son of Benaiah, and [a]Abiathar: and the general of the king's army *was* [b]Joab.

David's instructions to Solomon

28 And David assembled all the princes of Israel, [a]the princes of the tribes, and [b]the captains of the companies that ministered to the king by course, and the captains over the thousands, and captains over the hundreds, and [c]the stewards over all the substance and [1]possession of the king, [2]and of his sons, with the [3]officers, and *with* [d]the mighty *men,* and with all the valiant men, unto Jerusalem.

27:16–22 The Chronicler's interest in "all Israel" appears in this list of officers who were over the 12 tribes (see Introduction: Purpose and Themes). The number is kept at 12 by omitting Gad and Asher (see note on 2:1–2).

27:17 *Zadok.* See note on 6:8; see also 12:28; 16:39.

27:18 *Elihu.* Not named elsewhere among the brothers of David. Perhaps he is the unnamed son from the list in 2:10–17 (see note there). Elihu could also be a variant of the name of Jesse's oldest son, Eliab, or the term "brother" could be taken in the sense of "relative," in which case Elihu would be a more distant kinsman.

27:21 *Abner.* A relative of King Saul (see 26:28; 1 Sam 14:50–51; 17:55–58; 26:5–16; 2 Sam 2:8–4:1).

27:23–24 *took not the number ... the number.* Refers to the census narrative in ch. 21 (2 Sam 24).

27:23 *twenty years old and under.* The figures reported in ch. 21 and 2 Sam 24 were the numbers of those older than 20 years. *said he would increase Israel like to the stars.* The patriarchal promises of numerous descendants (Gen 12:2; 13:16; 15:5; 22:17) appear to have been the basis for the objections of Joab (v. 24) to the taking of a census (21:3; 2 Sam 24:3).

27:24 *finished not.* Joab did not count those under age 20, nor did he include the tribes of Levi and Benjamin (21:6).

27:25–31 A list of the administrators of David's property (v. 31). The large cities of the ancient Near East had three basic economic sectors: (1) royal, (2) temple and (3) private. There is no evidence of direct taxation during the reign of David; his court appears to have been financed by extensive landholdings, commerce, plunder from his many wars, and tribute from subjugated kingdoms.

27:32–34 A list of David's cabinet members, supplementary to that in 18:14–17.

27:33 *Ahithophel.* Was replaced after he committed suicide, following his support of Absalom's rebellion (2 Sam 15:12, 31–37; 16:20–17:23).

27:34 *Benaiah.* See v. 5.

28:1–29:30 The account of the transition from the reign of David to that of Solomon is one of the clearest demonstrations of the Chronicler's idealization of their reigns when it is compared with the succession account in 1 Ki 1–2. The Chronicler makes no mention of the infirmities of the aged David (1 Ki 1:1–4), the rebellion of Adonijah and the king's sons (1 Ki 1:5–10), the court intrigue to secure Solomon's succession (1 Ki 1:11–31) or David's charge to Solomon to punish his enemies after his death (1 Ki 2:1–9). His selection of material presents a transition of power that is smooth and peaceful and receives the support of "all Israel" (29:25), the officials and the people (28:1–2; 29:6–9,21–25). Instead of the bedridden David who sends others to anoint Solomon (1 Ki 1:32–35), David himself is present and in charge of the ceremonies (see 23:1 and note).

28:1 The assembly is composed largely of the groups named in ch. 27. This public announcement (v. 5) follows the private announcement of Solomon's succession in ch. 22 (see note on 22:2–19).

2 Then David the king stood up upon his feet, and said, Hear me, my brethren, and my people: *As for me,* [a]I *had* in mine heart to build a house of rest for the ark of the covenant of the LORD, and for [b]the footstool of our God, and had made ready for the building:

3 But God said unto me, [a]Thou shalt not build a house for my name, because thou *hast been* a man of war, and hast shed [1]blood.

4 Howbeit the LORD God of Israel [a]chose me before all the house of my father to be king over Israel for ever: for he hath chosen [b]Judah to be the ruler; and of the house of Judah, [c]the house of my father; and [d]among the sons of my father he liked me to make *me* king over all Israel:

5 [a]And of all my sons, (for the LORD hath given me many sons,) [b]he hath chosen Solomon my son to sit upon the throne of the kingdom of the LORD over Israel.

6 And he said unto me, [a]Solomon thy son, he shall build my house and my courts: for I have chosen him to be my son, and I will be his father.

7 Moreover I will establish his kingdom for ever, [a]if he be [1]constant to do my commandments and my judgments, as *at* this day.

8 Now therefore in the sight of all Israel the congregation of the LORD, and in the audience of our God, keep and seek for all the commandments of the LORD your God: that ye may possess *this* good land, and leave *it* for an inheritance for your children after you for ever.

9 And thou, Solomon my son, [a]know thou the God of thy father, and serve him [b]with a perfect heart and with a willing mind: for [c]the LORD searcheth all hearts, and understandeth all the imaginations of the thoughts: [d]if thou seek him, he will be found of thee; but if thou forsake him, he will cast thee off for ever.

10 Take heed now; [a]for the LORD hath chosen thee to build a house for the sanctuary: be strong, and do *it.*

11 ¶ Then David gave to Solomon his son [a]the pattern of the porch, and of the houses thereof, and of the treasuries thereof, and of the upper chambers thereof, and of the inner parlours thereof, and of the place of the mercy seat,

12 And the pattern [1]of all that he had by the spirit, of the courts of the house of the LORD, and of all the chambers round about, [a]of the treasuries of the house of God, and of the treasuries of the dedicate *things:*

28:2 [a]2 Sam. 7:2 [b]Ps. 99:5; 132:7
28:3 [1]Heb. *bloods* [a]2 Sam. 7:5,13; 1 Ki. 5:3; ch. 17:4; 22:8
28:4 [a]1 Sam. 16:7-13 [b]Gen. 49:8; ch. 5:2 [c]1 Sam. 16:1 [d]1 Sam. 16:12,13
28:5 [a]ch. 3:1; 23:1 [b]ch. 22:9
28:6 [a]2 Sam. 7:13,14; ch. 22:9,10; 2 Chr. 1:9
28:7 [1]Heb. *strong* [a]ch. 22:13
28:9 [a]Jer. 9:24; Hos. 4:1; John 17:3 [b]2 Ki. 20:3 [c]1 Sam. 16:7; 1 Ki. 8:39; ch. 29:17; Jer. 11:20; 17:10; 20:12; Rev. 2:23 [d]2 Chr. 15:2
28:10 [a]ver. 6
28:11 [a]ver. 19; See Ex. 25:40
28:12 [1]Heb. *of all that was with him* [a]ch. 26:20
28:18 [a]Ex. 25:18-22; 1 Sam. 4:4; 1 Ki. 6:23
28:19 [a]ver. 11,12; See Ex. 25,40
28:20 [a]Deut. 31:7,8; Josh. 1:6,7,9; ch. 22:13 [b]Josh. 1:5
28:21 [a]ch. 24; 25; 26 [b]Ex. 35:25,26
29:1 [a]1 Ki. 3:7; ch. 22:5; Prov. 4:3

13 Also for the courses of the priests and the Levites, and for all the work of the service of the house of the LORD, and for all the vessels of service in the house of the LORD.

14 *He gave* of gold by weight for *things of* gold, for all instruments of all manner of service; *silver also* for all instruments of silver by weight, for all instruments of every kind of service:

15 Even the weight for the candlesticks of gold, and *for* their lamps of gold, by weight for every candlestick, and *for* the lamps thereof: and for the candlesticks of silver by weight, *both* for the candlestick, and *also for* the lamps thereof, according to the use of every candlestick.

16 And *by* weight *he gave* gold for the tables of shewbread, for every table; and *likewise* silver for the tables of silver:

17 Also pure gold *for* the fleshhooks, and the bowls, and the cups: and for the golden basons *he gave gold* by weight for every bason; and *likewise silver* by weight for every bason of silver:

18 And for the altar of incense refined gold by weight; and gold for the pattern of the chariot of the [a]cherubims, that spread out *their wings,* and covered the ark of the covenant of the LORD.

19 All *this, said David,* [a]the LORD made me understand in writing by *his* hand upon me, *even* all the works of *this* pattern.

20 And David said to Solomon his son, [a]Be strong and of good courage, and do *it:* fear not, nor be dismayed: for the LORD God, *even* my God, *will be* with thee; [b]he will not fail thee, nor forsake thee, until *thou* hast finished all the work for the service of the house of the LORD.

21 And behold, [a]the courses of the priests and the Levites, *even they shall be with thee* for all the service of the house of God: and *there shall be* with thee for all *manner of* workmanship [b]every willing skilful *man,* for any *manner of* service: also the princes and all the people *will be* wholly at thy commandment.

David invites the people to give

29 Furthermore David the king said unto all the congregation, Solomon my son, whom alone God hath chosen, *is yet* [a]young and tender, and the work *is* great: for the palace *is* not for man, but for the LORD God.

2 Now I have prepared with all my might

28:3 *thou hast been a man of war, and hast shed blood.* See note on 22:8–9.

28:5 *chosen Solomon my son.* See vv. 6,10; 29:1. These are the only uses in the OT of the Hebrew verb for "chosen" with reference to any king after David (see Introduction: Purpose and Themes). The Chronicler's application of this term to Solomon is consistent with his depiction of that king. *kingdom of the LORD.* See note on 17:14.

28:6 *to be my son.* See 17:12–14 and note; see also 22:10.

28:8–9 See Introduction: Portrait of David and Solomon.

28:12 David provides Solomon with the plans for the temple. This reflects the Chronicler's modeling David after Moses: Just as Moses received the plans for the tabernacle from God (Ex 25–30), so also David received the plans for the temple.

28:19 *in writing by his hand upon me.* The Chronicler may intend no more than the ordinary process of inspiration whereby David wrote under divine influence. On the other hand, he may imply a parallel with Moses, who also received documents from the hand of the Lord (Ex 25:40; 27:8; 31:18; 32:16).

28:20 See Introduction: Portrait of David and Solomon.

29:1 *chosen.* See note on 28:5. *young.* See note on 22:5.

29:2–9 After donating his personal fortune to the construc-

for the house of my God the gold for *things to be made of* gold, and the silver for *things of* silver, and the brass for *things of* brass, the iron for *things of* iron, and wood for *things of* wood; [a]onyx stones, and *stones* to be set, glistering stones, and of divers colours, and all *manner of* precious stones, and marble stones in abundance.

3 Moreover, because I have set my affection to the house of my God, I have of mine own proper good, *of* gold and silver, *which* I have given to the house of my God, over and above all *that* I have prepared for the holy house,

4 *Even* three thousand talents of gold, of the gold of [a]Ophir, and seven thousand talents of refined silver, to overlay the walls of the houses *withal:*

5 The gold for *things of* gold, and the silver for *things of* silver, and for all *manner of* work *to be made* by the hands of artificers. And who *then* is willing [1]to consecrate his service *this* day unto the LORD?

6 ¶ Then [a]the chief of the fathers and princes of the tribes of Israel, and the captains of thousands and of hundreds, with [b]the rulers over the king's work, offered willingly,

7 And gave for the service of the house of God *of* gold five thousand talents and ten thousand drams, and *of* silver ten thousand talents, and *of* brass eighteen thousand talents, and one hundred thousand talents *of* iron.

8 And they with whom *precious* stones were found gave *them* to the treasure of the house of the LORD, by the hand of [a]Jehiel the Gershonite.

9 Then the people rejoiced, for that they offered willingly, because with perfect heart they [a]offered willingly to the LORD: and David the king also rejoiced *with* great joy.

David's prayer

10 ¶ Wherefore David blessed the LORD before all the congregation: and David said, Blessed *be* thou, LORD God of Israel our father, for ever and ever.

11 [a]Thine, O LORD, *is* the greatness, and the power, and the glory, and the victory, and the majesty: for all *that is* in the heaven and in the earth *is thine;* thine *is* the kingdom, O LORD, and *thou* art exalted as head above all.

12 [a]Both riches and honour *come* of thee, and thou reignest over all; and in thine hand *is* power and might; and in thine hand *it is* to make great, and to give strength unto all.

29:2 [a]See Is. 54:11,12; Rev. 21:18
29:4 [a]1 Ki. 9:28
29:5 [1]Heb. *to fill his hand*
29:6 [a]ch. 27:1 [b]ch. 27:25
29:8 [a]ch. 26:21
29:9 [a]2 Cor. 9:7
29:11 [a]Mat. 6:13; 1 Tim. 1:17; Rev. 5:13
29:12 [a]Rom. 11:36

29:14 [1]Heb. *retain,* or, *obtain strength* [2]Heb. *of thine hand*
29:15 [1]Heb. *expectation* [a]Ps. 39:12; Heb. 11:13; 1 Pet. 2:11 [b]Job 14:2; Ps. 90:9
29:17 [1]Heb. *found* [a]1 Sam. 16:7; ch. 28:9 [b]Prov. 11:20
29:18 [1]Or, *stablish*
29:19 [a]Ps. 72:1 [b]ver. 2; ch. 22:14
29:22 [a]1 Ki. 1:35,39
29:24 [1]Heb. *gave the hand under Solomon* [a]2 Chr. 30:8; Eccl. 8:2; Ezek. 17:18

13 Now therefore, our God, we thank thee, and praise thy glorious name.

14 But who *am* I, and what *is* my people, that we should [1]be able to offer *so* willingly after this *sort?* for all *things come* of thee, and [2]of thine own have we given thee.

15 For [a]we *are* strangers before thee, and sojourners, as *were* all our fathers: [b]our days on the earth *are* as a shadow, and *there is* none [1]abiding.

16 O LORD our God, all this store that we have prepared to build thee a house for thine holy name *cometh* of thine hand, and *is* all thine own.

17 I know also, my God, that thou [a]triest the heart, and [b]hast pleasure in uprightness. *As for* me, in the uprightness of mine heart I have willingly offered all these *things:* and now have I seen with joy thy people, which are [1]present here, to offer willingly unto thee.

18 O LORD God of Abraham, Isaac, and of Israel, our fathers, keep this for ever in the imagination of the thoughts of the heart of thy people, and [1]prepare their heart unto thee:

19 And [a]give unto Solomon my son a perfect heart, to keep thy commandments, thy testimonies, and thy statutes, and to do all *these things,* and to build the palace, *for* the which [b]I have made provision.

Solomon made king

20 ¶ And David said to all the congregation, Now bless the LORD your God. And all the congregation blessed the LORD God of their fathers, and bowed down their heads, and worshipped the LORD, and the king.

21 And they sacrificed sacrifices unto the LORD, and offered burnt offerings unto the LORD, on the morrow after that day, *even* a thousand bullocks, a thousand rams, *and* a thousand lambs, with their drink offerings, and sacrifices in abundance for all Israel:

22 And did eat and drink before the LORD on that day with great gladness. And they made Solomon the son of David king the second time, and [a]anointed *him* unto the LORD to be the chief governor, and Zadok to be priest.

23 Then Solomon sat on the throne of the LORD as king instead of David his father, and prospered; and all Israel obeyed him.

24 And all the princes, and the mighty *men,* and all the sons likewise of king David, [a][1]submitted themselves unto Solomon the king.

---

tion of the temple, David appeals to the people for their voluntary gifts. The Chronicler again appears to be modeling his account of David on events from the life of Moses (Ex 25:1–8; 35:4–9,20–29). The willing response of the people aided the building of both tabernacle and temple.

‡29:7 *drams* [i.e. "darics"]. The daric was a Persian coin, apparently named for Darius I (522–486 B.C.) in whose reign it first appears (see Ezra 8:27). Since the Chronicler's readers were familiar with it, he could use it as an up-to-date standard of value for an earlier treasure of gold.

29:22 *did eat and drink.* See 12:38–40 and note. The anointing of both Solomon and Zadok portrays the harmony between them (see Zech 4:14; 6:13 and notes). *second time.* Perhaps the first time was Solomon's anointing recorded in 1 Ki 1:32–36, but omitted by the Chronicler (see note on 28:1–29:30). However, the phrase "second time" is missing in the Septuagint, suggesting that it may have been an addition to the Hebrew text of this passage by an ancient scribe after the Septuagint had already been translated, in order to harmonize the Chronicles account with Kings. Multiple anointings are found in the cases of both Saul (1 Sam 10:1,24; 11:14–15) and David (1 Sam 16:13; 2 Sam 2:4; 5:3).

29:24 *all the princes . . . submitted themselves unto Solomon the*

25 And the LORD magnified Solomon exceedingly in the sight of all Israel, and [a]bestowed upon him *such* royal majesty as had not been on any king before him in Israel.

The death of David

26 ¶ Thus David the son of Jesse reigned over all Israel.

27 [a]And the time that he reigned over Israel *was* forty years; [b]seven years reigned he in Hebron, and thirty and three *years* reigned he in Jerusalem.

28 And he [a]died in a good old age, [b]full of days, riches, and honour: and Solomon his son reigned in his stead.

29 Now the acts of David the king, first and last, behold, they *are* written in the [1]book of Samuel the seer, and in the [1]book of Nathan the prophet, and in the [1]book of Gad the seer,

30 With all his reign and his might, [a]and the times that went over him, and over Israel, and over all the kingdoms of the countries.

29:25 [a]1 Ki. 3:13; 2 Chr. 1:12; Eccl. 2:9
29:27 [a]2 Sam. 5:4; 1 Ki. 2:11 [b]2 Sam. 5:5
29:28 [a]Gen. 25:8 [b]ch. 23:1
29:29 [1]Or, *history.* Heb. *words*
29:30 [a]Dan. 2:21

king. But compare the rebellion of Adonijah, in which the officers and sons of the king had assisted the attempted coup (1 Ki 1:9,19,25). Again the Chronicler has bypassed a negative event that would tarnish his image of David and Solomon.

29:25 *all Israel.* See 11:1,10; 12:38–40; see also Introduction: Purpose and Themes.

29:27 See note on 3:1–9.

29:28 *full of days, riches, and honour.* As a feature of the Chronicler's theme of immediate retribution (see Introduction: Purpose and Themes), the righteous enjoy these blessings (cf. Ps 128; Prov 3:2,4,9–10,16,22,33–35).

29:29 See Introduction: Author, Date and Sources.

29:30 *all the kingdoms of the countries.* Those immediately surrounding David's kingdom.

The Second Book of the Chronicles

INTRODUCTION

See Introduction to 1 Chronicles.

The Building of the Temple in Chronicles

The Chronicler has used the Pentateuchal history as a model for his account of the reigns of David and Solomon. Similarly, the Pentateuchal record of the building of the tabernacle affects his account of the building of the temple:

1. The building of the tabernacle was entrusted to Bezaleel and Aholiab (Ex 35:30—36:7), and they provide the Chronicler's model for the relationship of Solomon and Huram (2 Chr 2:13). It is significant that the only references to Bezaleel outside the book of Exodus are in Chronicles (1 Chr 2:20; 2 Chr 1:5).

Solomon is the new Bezaleel: (1) Both Solomon and Bezaleel are designated by name for their tasks by God; they are the only workers on their projects to be chosen by name (Ex 31:2; 35:30—36:2; 38:22–23; 1 Chr 28:6). (2) Both are from the tribe of Judah (Ex 31:2; 35:30; 1 Chr 2:20; 3:10). (3) Both receive the Spirit to endow them with wisdom (Ex 31:3; 35:30–31; 2 Chr 1:1–13), and Solomon's vision at Gibeon (2 Chr 1:3–13) dominates the preface to the account of the temple construction (2 Chr 2—7). (4) Both build a brasen altar for the sanctuary (2 Chr 1:5; 4:1; 7:7)—significantly, the brasen altar is not mentioned in the summary list of Huram's work (4:12–16). (5) Both make the sanctuary furnishings (Ex 31:1–10; 37:10–29; 2 Chr 4:19–22).

Similarly, Huram becomes the new Aholiab: (1) In the account of the temple building in Kings, Huram is not mentioned until after the story of the main construction of temple and palace has been told (1 Ki 7:13–45); in Chronicles he is introduced as being involved in the building work from the beginning, just as Aholiab worked on the tabernacle from the beginning (Ex 31:6; 2 Chr 2:13). (2) Kings speaks only of Huram's skill in works of brass (1 Ki 7:14); in Chronicles, however, his list of skills is the same as Aholiab's (Ex 31:1–6; 35:30–36:2; 38:22–23; 2 Chr 2:14). (3) Kings reports that the mother of Huram was a widow from the tribe of Naphtali (1 Ki 7:14); Chronicles, however, states that she was a widow from the tribe of Dan (2 Chr 2:14), thus giving Huram the same ancestry as Aholiab (Ex 31:6; 35:34; 38:23). See note on 2 Chr 2:13.

2. The plans for both tabernacle and temple are given by God (Ex 25:1—30:37; see Ex 25:9,40; 27:8; see also 1 Chr 28:11–19—not mentioned in Samuel and Kings).

3. The spoils of war are used as building materials for both tabernacle and temple (Ex 3:21–22; 12:35–36; see 1 Chr 18:6–11—not mentioned in Samuel and Kings).

4. The people contribute willingly and generously for both structures (Ex 25:1–7; 36:3–7; see 1 Chr 29:1–9—not mentioned in Samuel and Kings).

5. The glory cloud appears at the dedication of both structures (Ex 40:34–35; 2 Chr 7:1–3).

Solomon asks for wisdom

1 And [a]Solomon the son of David was
strengthened in his kingdom, and [b]the
LORD his God *was* with him, and [c]magnified
him exceedingly.
2 Then Solomon spake unto all Israel, to
[a]the captains of thousands and of hundreds,
and to the judges, and to every governor in all
Israel, the chief of the fathers.
3 So Solomon, and all the congregation
with him, went to the high place that *was* at
[a]Gibeon; for there was the tabernacle of the
congregation of God, which Moses the servant
of the LORD had made in the wilderness.
4 [a]But the ark of God had David brought
up from Kirjath-jearim to *the place which* David had prepared for it: for he had pitched a
tent for it at Jerusalem.
5 Moreover [a]the brasen altar, that [b]Beza-
leel the son of Uri, the son of Hur, had made,
[1]he put before the tabernacle of the LORD: and
Solomon and the congregation sought *unto* it.
6 And Solomon went up thither to the
brasen altar before the LORD, which *was* at the
tabernacle of the congregation, and [a]offered a
thousand burnt offerings upon it.
7 ¶ [a]In that night did God appear unto Solomon, and said unto him, Ask what I shall give
thee.
8 And Solomon said unto God, Thou hast
shewed great mercy unto David my father, and
hast made me [a]to reign in his stead.
9 Now, O LORD God, let thy promise unto
David my father be established: [a]for thou hast
made me king over a people [1]like the dust of
the earth in multitude.
10 [a]Give me now wisdom and knowledge,
that I may [b]go out and come in before this people: for who can judge this thy people, *that is
so* great?
11 [a]And God said to Solomon, Because this
was in thine heart, and thou hast not asked
riches, wealth, or honour, nor the life of thine
enemies, neither yet hast asked long life; but
hast asked wisdom and knowledge for thyself,
that thou mayest judge my people, over whom
I have made thee king:
12 Wisdom and knowledge *is* granted unto
thee; and I will give thee riches, and wealth,
and honour, such as [a]none of the kings have
had that *have been* before thee, neither shall
there any after thee have the like.
13 ¶ Then Solomon came *from his journey*
to the high place that *was* at Gibeon *to* Jerusalem, from before the tabernacle of the congregation, and reigned over Israel.
14 [a]And Solomon gathered chariots and
horsemen: and he had a thousand and four
hundred chariots, and twelve thousand horsemen, which he placed in the chariot cities,
and with the king at Jerusalem.
15 [a]And the king [1]made silver and gold at
Jerusalem *as plenteous* as stones, and cedar
trees made he as the sycomore trees that *are*
in the vale for abundance.
16 [a]And [1]Solomon had horses brought out
of Egypt, and linen yarn: the king's merchants
received the linen yarn at a price.
17 And they fetcht up, and brought forth
out of Egypt a chariot for six hundred *shekels*
of silver, and a horse for an hundred and fifty:
and so brought they out *horses* for all the kings
of the Hittites, and *for* the kings of Syria, [1]by
their means.

2 And Solomon [a]determined to build a
house for the name of the LORD, and a
house for his kingdom.
2 And [a]Solomon told out threescore and ten
thousand men to bear burdens, and fourscore
thousand to hew in the mountain, and three
thousand and six hundred to oversee them.

Preparing to build the temple

3 ¶ And Solomon sent to [1]Huram the king

1:1 [a]1 Ki. 2:46 [b]Gen. 39:2 [c]1 Chr. 29:25
1:2 [a]1 Chr. 27:1
1:3 [a]1 Ki. 3:4; 1 Chr. 16:39; 21:29
1:4 [a]2 Sam. 6:2,17; 1 Chr. 15:1
1:5 [1]Or, was *there* [a]Ex. 27:1,2; 38:1,2 [b]Ex. 31:2
1:6 [a]1 Ki. 3:4
1:7 [a]1 Ki. 3:5
1:8 [a]1 Chr. 28:5
1:9 [1]Heb. *much as the dust of the earth* [a]1 Ki. 3:7,8
1:10 [a]1 Ki. 3:9 [b]Num. 27:17; Deut. 31:2
1:11 [a]1 Ki. 3:11-13
1:12 [a]1 Chr. 29:25; ch. 9:22; Eccl. 2:9
1:14 [a]1 Ki. 4:26; 10:26; ch. 9:25
1:15 [1]Heb. *gave* [a]1 Ki. 10:27; ch. 9:27; Job 22:24
1:16 [1]Heb. *the going forth of the horses which* was *Solomon's* [a]1 Ki. 10:28; ch. 9:28
1:17 [1]Heb. *by their hand*
2:1 [a]1 Ki. 5:5
2:2 [a]ver. 18; 1 Ki. 5:15
2:3 [1]Or, *Hiram,* 1 Ki. 5:1

1:1–9:31 The account of the reign of Solomon is primarily devoted to his building of the temple (chs. 2–7); his endowment with wisdom is mainly to facilitate the building work. Much of the material in Kings that does not bear on building the temple is omitted by the Chronicler; e.g., he does not mention the judgment between the prostitutes (1 Ki 3:16–28) or the building of the royal palace (1 Ki 7:1–12).

1:1 *was strengthened.* This expression, or a variation of it, is common in Chronicles (12:13; 13:7–8,21; 15:8; 16:9; 17:1; 21:4; 23:1; 25:11; 27:6; 32:5; 1 Chr 11:10; 19:13). Here and in 21:4 it includes the elimination of enemies and rivals to the throne (see 1 Ki 2, especially v. 46).

1:2–13 See 1 Ki 3:4–15 and notes. Verses 2–6 are largely unique to Chronicles and show some of the writer's concerns: 1. The support of "all Israel" (v. 2) is emphasized (see Introduction to 1 Chronicles: Purpose and Themes). 2. While the writer of Kings is somewhat apologetic about Solomon's visit to a high place (1 Ki 3:3), the Chronicler adds the note that this was the location of the tabernacle made by Moses in the wilderness (v. 3), bringing Solomon's action into line with the provisions of the law (Lev 17:8–9).

1:5 *Bezaleel.* See Introduction: The Building of the Temple in Chronicles. It is specifically in connection with his offering on the altar built by Bezaleel (Ex 31:1–11; 38:1–2) that Solomon receives the wisdom from God to reign. In the account that follows, Solomon devotes his gift of wisdom primarily to building the temple, just as Bezaleel had been gifted by God to serve as the master craftsman of the tabernacle.

1:7 *God . . . said unto him.* Both David and Solomon function as prophets (7:1; 29:25; 1 Chr 22:8; 28:6,19).

1:9 *like the dust of the earth in multitude.* In provisional fulfillment of the promise to Abraham (Gen 13:16; 22:17; see note on 1 Chr 27:23; cf. Gen 28:14).

1:14–17 The Chronicler does not include the material in 1 Ki 3:16–4:34. He moves rather to the account of Solomon's wealth in 1 Ki 10:26–29; part of this material is repeated in 2 Chr 9:25–28. Recounting Solomon's wealth at this point shows the fulfillment of God's promise (v. 12).

1:16 *Egypt.* See note on 1 Ki 10:29.

2:1 *house for his kingdom.* Although the Chronicler frequently mentions the palace Solomon built (7:11; 8:1; 9:11), he gives no details of its construction (see 1 Ki 7:1–12).

2:2 See vv. 17–18.

2:3–10 The Chronicler's theological interests appear in his handling of Solomon's correspondence with Huram (a variant of Hiram) of Tyre. In the Kings account the correspondence was

of Tyre, saying, [a]As thou didst deal with David
my father, and didst send him cedars to build
him a house to dwell therein, *even so deal*
with me.
4 Behold, [a]I build a house to the name of
the LORD my God, to dedicate *it* to him, *and*
[b]to burn before him [1]sweet incense, and *for*
[c]the continual shewbread, and *for* [d]the burnt
offerings morning and evening, on the sabbaths, and on the new moons, and on the
solemn feasts of the LORD our God. This *is an*
ordinance for ever to Israel.
5 And the house which I build *is* great: for
[a]great *is* our God above all gods.
6 [a]But who [1]is able to build him a house,
seeing the heaven and heaven of heavens cannot contain him? who *am* I then, that I should
build him a house, save only to burn sacrifice
before him?
7 Send me now therefore a man cunning to
work in gold, and in silver, and in brass, and in
iron, and in purple, and crimson, and blue,
and that can skill [1]to grave with the cunning
men that *are* with me in Judah and in Jerusalem, [a]whom David my father did provide.
8 [a]Send me also cedar trees, fir trees, and
[1]algum trees, out of Lebanon: for I know that
thy servants can skill to cut timber in Lebanon; and behold, my servants *shall be* with thy
servants,
9 Even to prepare me timber in abundance: for the house which I am about to build
shall be [1]wonderful great.
10 [a]And behold, I will give to thy servants,
the hewers that cut timber, twenty thousand
measures of beaten wheat, and twenty thousand measures of barley, and twenty thousand
baths of wine, and twenty thousand baths of
oil.
11 ¶ Then Huram the king of Tyre answered in writing, which he sent to Solomon,
[a]Because the LORD hath loved his people, he
hath made thee king over them.
12 Huram said moreover, [a]Blessed *be* the
LORD God of Israel, [b]that made heaven and
earth, who hath given to David the king a wise
son, [1]endued with prudence and understanding, that might build a house for the LORD, and
a house for his kingdom.
13 And now I have sent a cunning man,
endued with understanding, of Huram my father's,
14 [a]The son of a woman of the daughters
of Dan, and his father *was* a man of Tyre, skilful to work in gold, and in silver, in brass, in
iron, in stone, and in timber, in purple, in
blue, and in fine linen, and in crimson; also to
grave any *manner of* graving, and to find out
every device which shall be put to him, with
thy cunning *men,* and with the cunning *men*
of my lord David thy father.
15 Now therefore the wheat, and the barley, the oil, and the wine, which [a]my lord hath
spoken of, let him send unto his servants:
16 [a]And we will cut wood out of Lebanon,
[1]as much as thou shalt need: and we will bring
it to thee *in* flotes by sea *to* [2]Joppa; and thou
shalt carry it up *to* Jerusalem.
17 ¶ [a]And Solomon numbered all [1]the
strangers that *were* in the land of Israel, after
the numbering where*with* [b]David his father
had numbered them; and they were found an
hundred and fifty thousand and three thousand and six hundred.
18 And he set [a]threescore and ten thousand of them *to be* bearers of burdens, and
fourscore thousand *to be* hewers in the mountain, and three thousand and six hundred
overseers to set the people a work.

3 Then [a]Solomon began to build the house
of the LORD at [b]Jerusalem in mount Moriah, [1]where *the LORD* appeared unto David

2:3 [a]1 Chr. 14:1
2:4 [1]Heb. *incense of spices* [a]ver. 1 [b]Ex. 30:7 [c]Ex. 25:30; Lev. 24:8 [d]Num. 28:3,9,11
2:5 [a]Ps. 135:5
2:6 [1]Heb. *hath retained,* or, *obtained strength* [a]1 Ki. 8:27; Is. 66:1
2:7 [1]Heb. *to grave gravings* [a]1 Chr. 22:15
2:8 [1]Or, *almuggim,* 1 Ki. 10:11 [a]1 Ki. 5:6
2:9 [1]Heb. *great and wonderful*
2:10 [a]1 Ki. 5:11
2:11 [a]1 Ki. 10:9; ch. 9:8
2:12 [1]Heb. *knowing prudence and understanding* [a]1 Ki. 5:7 [b]Gen. 1; 2; Acts 4:24; 14:15; Rev. 10:6
2:14 [a]1 Ki. 7:13
2:15 [a]ver. 10
2:16 [1]Heb. *according to all thy need* [2]Heb. *Japho* [a]1 Ki. 5:8,9
2:17 [1]Heb. *the men the strangers* [a]As ver. 2; 1 Ki. 5:13; ch. 8:7,8 [b]1 Chr. 22:2
2:18 [a]As it is; ver. 2
3:1 [1]Or, *which was seen of David his father* [a]1 Ki. 6:1 [b]Gen. 22:2

initiated by Huram ("Hiram," 1 Ki 5:1). The Chronicler omits this (and also the material in 1 Ki 5:3–5) but adds his own material, reflecting his concerns with the temple worship in vv. 3–7.

2:4 See 1 Chr 23:28–31.

2:7 See Introduction: The Building of the Temple in Chronicles. In the Kings account Solomon's request for a master craftsman is found late in the narrative (1 Ki 7:13); to carry out his parallel between Aholiab and Huram, the Chronicler includes it in the initial correspondence. Furthermore, here and in vv. 13–14 the list of Huram's skills is expanded and matches that of Bezaleel and Aholiab (Kings is concerned only with casting bronze, or "brass").

2:10 The payment here differs from that reported in 1 Ki 5:11, but the texts speak of two different payments: In Kings the payment is an annual sum delivered to the royal household of Hiram, while Chronicles speaks of one payment to the woodsmen. The goods paid are also not identical; the oil specified in Kings is of a finer quality.

2:11–16 See 1 Ki 5:7–9; 7:13–14 and notes.

‡2:13 *Huram my father's.* Can be rendered as personal name, "Huram-abi." See note on v. 7. Kings reports that the ancestry of Huram was through a widow of Naphtali (1 Ki 7:14); Chronicles strengthens the parallel between Huram and Aholiab by assigning him Danite ancestry. These statements are not necessarily contradictory: (1) The mother's ancestry may have been Danite, though she lived in the territory of Naphtali; or (2) her parents may have been from Dan and Naphtali, allowing her descent to be reckoned to either. The Danites had been previously associated with the Phoenicians (Judg 18:7).

2:17–18 See 1 Ki 5:13–18 and notes. The Chronicler specifies that this levy of forced laborers was from aliens ("strangers") resident in the land, not from Israelites. This is not stated in the parallel passage in Kings, though 1 Ki 9:20–22 confirms that alien labor was used (see 8:8).

2:18 *three thousand and six hundred overseers.* See v. 2. The number given in 1 Ki 5:16 is 3,300; however, some manuscripts of the Septuagint (the Greek translation of the OT) also have 3,600. The Chronicler may have been following a different text of Kings from the present Masoretic (traditional Hebrew) text at this point (but see note on 1 Ki 5:16).

3:1–17 The Chronicler has considerably curtailed the description of the temple's construction found in Kings, omitting completely 1 Ki 6:4–20. This abridgment probably indicates that the Chronicler's audience was familiar with the details of the earlier history and that the temple of the restoration period was less elaborate than the original Solomonic structure (Hag 2:3). On the other hand, the Chronicler goes into more detail on the furnishings and implements (3:6–9; 4:1,6–9).

his father, in the place that David had prepared in the threshingfloor of [c][2]Ornan the Jebusite.

2 And he began to build in the second *day* of the second month, in the fourth year of his reign.

Building the temple

3 ¶ Now these *are the things* [a]*wherein* Solomon was [1]instructed for the building of the house of God. The length *by* cubits after the first measure *was* threescore cubits, and the breadth twenty cubits.

4 And the [a]porch that *was* in the front *of the house,* the length *of it was* according to the breadth of the house, twenty cubits, and the height *was* an hundred and twenty: and he overlaid it within with pure gold.

5 And [a]the greater house he cieled with fir tree, which he overlaid with fine gold, and set thereon palm trees and chains.

6 And he [1]garnished the house with precious stones for beauty: and the gold *was* gold of Parvaim.

7 He overlaid also the house, the beams, the posts, and the walls thereof, and the doors thereof, with gold; and graved cherubims on the walls.

8 And he made the most holy house, the length whereof *was* according to the breadth of the house, twenty cubits, and the breadth thereof twenty cubits: and he overlaid it with fine gold, *amounting* to six hundred talents.

9 And the weight of the nails *was* fifty shekels of gold. And he overlaid the upper chambers with gold.

10 ¶ [a]And in the most holy house he made two cherubims [1]of image work, and overlaid them with gold.

11 And the wings of the cherubims *were* twenty cubits long: *one* wing of the one *cherub was* five cubits, reaching to the wall of the house: and the other wing *was likewise* five cubits, reaching to the wing of the other cherub.

12 And *one* wing of the other cherub *was* five cubits, reaching to the wall of the house: and the other wing *was* five cubits *also,* joining to the wing of the other cherub.

13 The wings of these cherubims spread themselves forth twenty cubits: and they stood on their feet, and their faces *were* [1]inward.

14 ¶ And he made the [a]vail *of* blue, and purple, and crimson, and fine linen, and [1]wrought cherubims thereon.

15 Also he made before the house [a]two pillars of thirty and five cubits [1]high, and the chapiter that *was* on the top *of each* of them *was* five cubits.

16 And he made chains, *as* in the oracle, and put *them* on the heads of the pillars; and made [a]an hundred pomegranates, and put *them* on the chains.

17 And he [a]reared up the pillars before the temple, one on the right hand, and the other on the left; and called the name of *that on* the right hand [1]Jachin, and the name of *that on* the left [2]Boaz.

The furnishings of the temple

4 Moreover he made [a]an altar of brass, twenty cubits the length thereof, and twenty cubits the breadth thereof, and ten cubits the height thereof.

2 ¶ [a]Also he made a molten sea of ten cubits [1]from brim to brim, round in compass, and five cubits the height thereof; and a line of thirty cubits did compass it round about.

3 [a]And under it *was* the similitude of oxen,

3:1 [2]Or, *Araunah,* 2 Sam. 24:18 [c]1 Chr. 21:18; 22:1
3:3 [1]Heb. *founded* [a]1 Ki. 6:2
3:4 [a]1 Ki. 6:3
3:5 [a]1 Ki. 6:15
3:6 [1]Heb. *covered*
3:10 [1]Or, (as some think) *of moveable work* [a]1 Ki. 6:23
3:13 [1]Or, *toward the house*
3:14 [1]Heb. *caused to ascend* [a]Ex. 26:31; Mat. 27:51; Heb. 9:3
3:15 [1]Heb. *long* [a]1 Ki. 7:15; Jer. 52:21
3:16 [a]1 Ki. 7:20
3:17 [1]That is, *He shall establish* [2]That is, *In it is strength* [a]1 Ki. 7:21
4:1 [a]Ex. 27:1,2; 2 Ki. 16:14; Ezek. 43:13,16
4:2 [1]Heb. *from his brim to his brim* [a]1 Ki. 7:23
4:3 [a]1 Ki. 7:24-26

3:1 *mount Moriah.* The only passage in the OT where mount Zion is identified with mount Moriah, the place where Abraham was commanded to offer Isaac (Gen 22:2,14). *the place that David had prepared.* See 1 Chr 21:18–22:1.

3:2 *second month, in the fourth year.* In the spring of 966 B.C. (see note on 1 Ki 6:1).

3:4 *overlaid.* Or "inlaid," which perhaps gives a more correct picture: not that the entire interior was covered with gold leaf, but that designs (palm trees, chains) were inlaid with gold leaf (v. 5).

3:6 *Parvaim.* Designates either the source of the gold (perhaps southeast Arabia) or a particular quality of fine gold.

3:7 *cherubims.* See vv. 10–14; see also notes on Gen 3:24; Ezek 1:5.

3:8 *length whereof was . . . twenty cubits, and the breadth . . . twenty cubits.* It was also 20 cubits high (1 Ki 6:20), making the dimensions of the most holy place a perfect cube, as probably also in the tabernacle. In the new Jerusalem there is no temple (Rev 21:22); rather, the whole city is in the shape of a cube (Rev 21:16), for the whole city becomes the "most holy place."

3:9 *nails . . . of gold.* The fact that gold is such a soft metal would make it unlikely that nails were made of this substance. It is probable that this small amount (only 1 1/4 pounds) represents gold leaf or sheeting used to gild the nail heads.

3:10–13 See 1 Ki 6:23–27 and notes.

3:14 *vail.* Also separated the two rooms of the tabernacle (Ex 26:31). Wooden doors could also be closed across the opening (4:22; 1 Ki 6:31–32; cf. Mat 27:51; Heb 9:8).

3:15 *thirty and five cubits high.* Since 1 Ki 7:15 indicates the pillars were each 18 cubits high (confirmed by 2 Ki 25:17; Jer 52:21, though the Septuagint at Jer 52:21 has 35), 35 here probably refers to the combined height of both. Alternatively, 35 may be the result of a copyist's mistake.

3:17 *pillars.* Remains of such pillars have been found in the excavations of numerous temples in the Holy Land. Cf. Rev 3:12. *Jachin . . . Boaz.* Jachin probably means "He establishes," and Boaz probably means "in Him is strength."

4:1 *altar of brass.* The parallel text in Kings does not mention the main altar of the temple described here (1 Ki 7:22–23), though several other passages in Kings do refer to it (1 Ki 8:64; 9:25; 2 Ki 16:14). The main altar of Solomon's temple was similar to the altar with steps that is described in Ezek 43:13–17.

4:2 *molten sea.* Replaced the brass laver of the tabernacle (Ex 30:18); it was used by the priests for their ceremonial washing (v. 6; Ex 30:21). The NT views these rituals as foreshadowing the cleansing provided by Christ (Tit 3:5; Heb 9:11–14). In the temple of Ezekiel, the sea, which was on the south side in front of the temple (v. 10), has been replaced by a life-giving river that flows from the south side of the temple (Ezek 47:1–12; cf. Joel 3:18; Zech 14:8; John 4:9–15; Rev 22:1–2).

4:3 *oxen.* 1 Ki 7:24 has "knops." The Hebrew for the two words

which did compass it round about: ten in a cubit, compassing the sea round about. Two rows
of oxen *were* cast, when it was cast.
4 It stood upon twelve oxen, three looking
toward the north, and three looking toward
the west, and three looking toward the south,
and three looking toward the east: and the sea
was set above upon them, and all their hinder
parts *were* inward.
5 And the thickness of it *was* a handbreadth, and the brim of it like the work of the
brim of a cup, [1]*with* flowers of lilies; *and* it received and held [a]three thousand baths.
6 ¶ He made also [a]ten lavers, and put five
on the right hand, and five on the left, to wash
in them: [1]such things as they offered for the
burnt offering they washed in them; but the
sea *was* for the priests to wash in.
7 [a]And he made ten candlesticks of gold
[b]according to their form, and set *them* in the
temple, five on the right hand, and five on the
left.
8 [a]He made also ten tables, and placed
them in the temple, five on the right side, and
five on the left. And he made an hundred [1]ba-
sons of gold.
9 Furthermore [a]he made the court of the
priests, and the great court, and doors for the
court, and overlaid the doors of them with
brass.
10 And [a]he set the sea on the right side of
the east end, over against the south.
11 ¶ And [a]Huram made the pots, and the
shovels, and the [1]basons. And Huram [2]fin-
ished the work that he was to make for king
Solomon for the house of God;
12 *To wit,* the two pillars, and [a]the pommels, and the chapiters *which were* on the top
of the two pillars, and the two wreaths to cover the two pommels of the chapiters which
were on the top of the pillars;
13 And [a]four hundred pomegranates on
the two wreaths; two rows *of* pomegranates
on each wreath, to cover the two pommels of
the chapiters which *were* [1]upon the pillars.
14 He made also [a]bases and [1]lavers made
he upon the bases;
15 One sea, and twelve oxen under it.

4:5 [1]Or, *like a lilyflower* [a]See 1 Ki. 7:26
4:6 [1]Heb. *the work of burnt offering* [a]1 Ki. 7:38
4:7 [a]1 Ki. 7:49 [b]Ex. 25:31; 1 Chr. 28:12,19
4:8 [1]Or, *bowls* [a]1 Ki. 7:48
4:9 [a]1 Ki. 6:36
4:10 [a]1 Ki. 7:39
4:11 [1]Or, *bowls* [2]Heb. *finished to make* [a]See 1 Ki. 7:40
4:12 [a]1 Ki. 7:41
4:13 [1]Heb. *upon the face* [*of the pillars*] [a]See 1 Ki. 7:20
4:14 [1]Or, *caldrons* [a]1 Ki. 7:27,43
4:16 [1]Heb. *made bright,* or, *scoured* [a]1 Ki. 7:14,45
4:17 [1]Heb. *thicknesses of the ground* [a]1 Ki. 7:46
4:18 [a]1 Ki. 7:47
4:19 [a]1 Ki. 7:48-50 [b]Ex. 25:30
4:20 [a]Ex. 27:20,21
4:21 [1]Heb. *perfections of gold* [a]Ex. 25:31
4:22 [1]Or, *bowls*
5:1 [a]1 Ki. 7:51
5:2 [a]1 Ki. 8:1 [b]2 Sam. 6:12
5:3 [a]1 Ki. 8:2 [b]See ch. 7:8-10

16 The pots also, and the shovels, and the
fleshhooks, and all their instruments, did [a]Hu-
ram his father make to king Solomon for the
house of the LORD *of* [1]bright brass.
17 [a]In the plain of Jordan did the king cast
them, in the [1]clay ground between Succoth
and Zeredathah.
18 [a]Thus Solomon made all these vessels
in great abundance: for the weight of the brass
could not be found out.
19 And [a]Solomon made all the vessels that
were for the house of God, the golden altar
also, and the tables whereon [b]the shewbread
was set;
20 Moreover the candlesticks with their
lamps, that they should burn [a]after the manner before the oracle, *of* pure gold;
21 And [a]the flowers, and the lamps, and the
tongs, *made he of* gold, *and* that [1]perfect gold;
22 And the snuffers, and the [1]basons, and
the spoons, and the censers, of pure gold: and
the entry of the house, the inner doors thereof
for the most holy *place,* and the doors of the
house of the temple, *were of* gold.
5 Thus [a]all the work that Solomon made
for the house of the LORD was finished:
and Solomon brought in *all the things* that David his father had dedicated; and the silver,
and the gold, and all the instruments, put he
among the treasures of the house of God.

Bringing the ark to the temple

2 ¶ [a]Then Solomon assembled the elders of
Israel, and all the heads of the tribes, the chief
of the fathers of the children of Israel, unto Jerusalem, to bring up the ark of the covenant of
the LORD [b]out of the city of David, which *is*
Zion.
3 [a]Wherefore all the men of Israel assembled themselves unto the king [b]in the feast
which *was in* the seventh month.
4 And all the elders of Israel came; and the
Levites took up the ark.
5 And they brought up the ark, and the
tabernacle of the congregation, and all the
holy vessels that *were* in the tabernacle, these
did the priests *and* the Levites bring up.
6 Also king Solomon, and all the congrega-

is very similar, so the difference may well be due to a copyist's mistake.

4:4 *twelve oxen.* Possibly symbolic of the 12 tribes, which also encamped three on each side of the tabernacle during the wilderness journeys (Num 2; cf. Ezek 48:30–35).

4:5 *three thousand baths.* 1 Ki 7:26 has 2,000 baths. These figures could easily have been misread by the ancient scribes.

4:6 *ten lavers.* See 1 Ki 7:38–39.

‡4:7 *ten candlesticks* [i.e., lampstands] *of gold.* Instead of one, as in the tabernacle (Ex 25:31–40). *according to their form.* See 1 Chr 28:15. These lamps were not necessarily of the same shape as described in Ex 25:31–40, but could have resembled the style of lamp depicted in Zech 4:2–6.

4:8 *ten tables.* Instead of one, as in the tabernacle (Ex 25:23–30; 40:4; Lev 24:5–9; 1 Sam 21:1–6; Ezek 41:22; Heb 9:2; cf. 2 Chr 13:11; 29:18).

4:11–16 See 1 Ki 7:40–45.

4:17–22 See 1 Ki 7:46–50.

4:17 *clay ground.* The clay beds of the Jordan plain made it possible to dig molds for these bronze ("brass") castings.

5:1 *things that David his father had dedicated.* See notes on 1 Chr 18:1–20:8; 22:2–16; 29:2–5; see also 1 Chr 26:26.

5:2–14 See 1 Ki 8:1–11 and notes.

5:2 *ark.* Had been in a tent provided for it 40 years earlier when David brought it to Jerusalem (1 Chr 15:1–16:6).

5:3 *feast . . . in the seventh month.* The feast of tabernacles. The month is designated by its Canaanite name Ethanim in 1 Ki 8:2; the Hebrew name is Tishri. According to 1 Ki 6:38 the temple was completed in the eighth month of Solomon's 11th year, i.e. September-October, 959 B.C. This celebration of dedication took place either a month before the completion of the work or 11 months after, probably the latter (see note on 1 Ki 8:2).

5:6 Cf. David's bringing of the ark to Jerusalem (1 Chr 15:26; 16:1–3).

tion of Israel that were assembled unto him before the ark, sacrificed sheep and oxen, which could not be told nor numbered for multitude.

7 And the priests brought in the ark of the covenant of the LORD unto his place, to the oracle of the house, into the most holy *place,* even under the wings of the cherubims:

8 For the cherubims spread forth *their* wings over the place of the ark, and the cherubims covered the ark and the staves thereof above.

9 And they drew out the staves *of the ark,* that the ends of the staves were seen from the ark before the oracle; but they were not seen without. And [1]there it is unto this day.

10 *There was* nothing in the ark save the two tables which Moses [a]put *therein* at Horeb, [1]when the LORD made *a covenant* with the children of Israel, when they came out of Egypt.

11 And it came to pass, when the priests were come out of the holy *place:* (for all the priests that were [1]present were sanctified, *and* did not *then* wait by course:

12 [a]Also the Levites *which were* the singers, all of them of Asaph, of Heman, of Jeduthun, with their sons and their brethren, *being* arrayed in white linen, having cymbals and psalteries and harps, stood *at* the east *end* of the altar, [b]and with them an hundred and twenty priests sounding with trumpets:)

13 It came even to pass, as the trumpeters and singers *were* as one, to make one sound to be heard in praising and thanking the LORD; and when *they* lift up *their* voice with the trumpets and cymbals and instruments of musick, and praised the LORD, *saying,* [a]For *he is* good; for his mercy *endureth* for ever: that *then* the house was filled *with* a cloud, *even* the house of the LORD;

14 So that the priests could not stand to minister by reason of the cloud: [a]for the glory of the LORD had filled the house of God.

6 Then [a]said Solomon, The LORD hath said that *he* would dwell in the [b]thick darkness.

2 But I have built a house of habitation for thee, and a place for thy dwelling for ever.

3 And the king turned his face, and blessed the whole congregation of Israel: and all the congregation of Israel stood.

4 And he said, Blessed *be* the LORD God of Israel, who hath with his hands fulfilled *that* which he spake with his mouth to my father David, saying,

5 Since the day that I brought forth my people out of the land of Egypt I chose no city among all the tribes of Israel to build a house *in,* that my name might be there; neither chose I any man to be a ruler over my people Israel:

6 [a]But I have chosen Jerusalem, that my name might be there; and [b]have chosen David to be over my people Israel.

7 Now [a]it was in the heart of David my father to build a house for the name of the LORD God of Israel.

8 But the LORD said to David my father, Forasmuch as it was in thine heart to build a house for my name, thou didst well *in* that it was in thine heart:

9 Notwithstanding thou shalt not build the house; but thy son which shall come forth out of thy loins, he shall build the house for my name.

10 The LORD therefore hath performed his word that he hath spoken: for I am risen up in the room of David my father, and am set on the throne of Israel, as the LORD promised, and have built the house for the name of the LORD God of Israel.

11 And in it have I put the ark, [a]wherein *is* the covenant of the LORD, that he made with the children of Israel.

Solomon's prayer of dedication

12 ¶ [a]And he stood before the altar of the LORD in the presence of all the congregation of Israel, and spread forth his hands:

13 For Solomon had made a brasen scaffold, of five cubits [1]long, and five cubits broad, and three cubits high, and had set it in the midst of the court: and upon it he stood, and kneeled *down* upon his knees before all the congregation of Israel, and spread forth his hands towards heaven,

14 And said, O LORD God of Israel, [a]*there is* no God like thee in the heaven, nor in the earth; which keepest covenant, and *shewest* mercy unto thy servants, that walk before thee with all their hearts:

15 [a]Thou which hast kept with thy servant David my father *that* which thou hast promised him; and spakest with thy mouth, and

5:9 [1]Or, *they are there,* as 1 Ki. 8:8
5:10 [1]Or, *where* [a]Deut. 10:2,5; ch. 6:11
5:11 [1]Heb. *found*
5:12 [a]1 Chr. 25:1 [b]1 Chr. 15:24
5:13 [a]Ps. 136; See 1 Chr. 16:34,41
5:14 [a]Ex. 40:35; ch. 7:2
6:1 [a]1 Ki. 8:12 [b]Lev. 16:2
6:6 [a]ch. 12:13 [b]1 Chr. 28:4
6:7 [a]2 Sam. 7:2; 1 Chr. 17:1; 28:2
6:11 [a]ch. 5:10
6:12 [a]1 Ki. 8:22
6:13 [1]Heb. *the length thereof, etc.*
6:14 [a]Ex. 15:11; Deut. 4:39; 7:9
6:15 [a]1 Chr. 22:9

5:9 *there it is unto this day.* See note on 1 Ki 8:8; see also 8:8; 10:19; 20:26; 21:10; 35:25; 1 Chr 4:41,43; 5:26; 13:11; 17:5.

5:10 *two tables.* See Ex 31:18 and note; see also Ex 32:15–16. The ark had earlier contained also the pot of manna (Ex 16:32–34) and Aaron's rod (Num 17:10–11; Heb 9:4). These items were presumably lost, perhaps while the ark was in Philistine hands.

5:12 *white linen.* See 1 Chr 15:27 and note.

5:14 *cloud . . . glory of the LORD.* Cf. 7:1–3. The glory cloud represented the presence of God. It had guided Israel out of Egypt and through the wilderness, and was present above the tabernacle (Ex 13:21–22; 40:34–38; cf. Ezek 43:1–5; Hag 2:9; Zech 1:16; 2:10; 8:3).

6:1–11 See notes on 1 Ki 8:12–21.

6:8–9 Cf. David's speech in 1 Chr 28:2–3.

6:12–21 See notes on 1 Ki 8:22–30.

6:13 Not in 1 Ki 8. Some think that the Chronicler may have wished to clarify the fact that Solomon was not "before the altar" (v. 12) exercising priestly duties. On the other hand, the verse may have been dropped from Kings by a copying error: The phrase "spread forth his hands" occurs in vv. 12–13; it is possible that the scribe copying Kings looked back to the second occurrence of the phrase, thus omitting the verse. The verse would then be present in Chronicles because it was in the particular text of Kings used by the Chronicler.

hast fulfilled *it* with thine hand, as *it is* this
day.
16 Now therefore, O LORD God of Israel,
keep with thy servant David my father *that*
which thou hast promised him, saying,
[a][1]There shall not fail thee a man in my sight to
sit upon the throne of Israel; [b]yet so that thy
children take heed to their way to walk in my
law, as thou hast walked before me.
17 Now then, O LORD God of Israel, let thy
word be verified, which thou hast spoken unto
thy servant David.
18 ¶ But will God in very deed dwell with
men on the earth? [a]behold, heaven and the
heaven of heavens cannot contain thee; how
much less this house which I have built?
19 Have respect therefore to the prayer of
thy servant, and to his supplication, O LORD
my God, to hearken unto the cry and the
prayer which thy servant prayeth before thee:
20 That thine eyes may be open upon this
house day and night, upon the place whereof
thou hast said that *thou* wouldest put thy
name there; to hearken unto the prayer which
thy servant prayeth [1]towards this place.
21 Hearken therefore unto the supplications of thy servant, and of thy people Israel,
which they shall [1]make towards this place:
hear thou from thy dwelling place, *even* from
heaven; and when thou hearest, forgive.
22 ¶ If a man sin against his neighbour,
[1]and an oath be laid upon him to make him
swear, and the oath come before thine altar in
this house;
23 Then hear thou from heaven, and do,
and judge thy servants, by requiting the
wicked, by recompensing his way upon his
own head; and by justifying the righteous, by
giving him according to his righteousness.
24 ¶ And if thy people Israel [1]be put to the
worse before the enemy, because they have
sinned against thee; and shall return and confess thy name, and pray and make supplication
before thee [2]in this house;
25 Then hear thou from the heavens, and
forgive the sin of thy people Israel, and bring
them again unto the land which thou gavest to
them and to their fathers.
26 ¶ When the [a]heaven is shut up, and
there is no rain, because they have sinned
against thee; *yet* if they pray towards this
place, and confess thy name, *and* turn from
their sin, when thou dost afflict them;
27 Then hear thou *from* heaven, and forgive the sin of thy servants, and of thy people
Israel, when thou hast taught them the good
way, wherein they should walk; and send rain
upon thy land, which thou hast given unto thy
people for an inheritance.
28 ¶ If there [a]be dearth in the land, if there
be pestilence, if there be blasting, or mildew,
locusts, or caterpillars; if their enemies besiege them [1]in the cities of their land; whatsoever sore or whatsoever sickness *there be:*
29 *Then* what prayer *or* what supplication
soever shall be *made* of any man, or of all thy
people Israel, when every one shall know his
own sore and his own grief, and shall spread
forth his hands [1]in this house:
30 Then hear thou from heaven thy
dwelling place, and forgive, and render unto
every man according unto all his ways, whose
heart thou knowest; (for thou only [a]knowest
the hearts of the children of men:)
31 That they may fear thee, to walk in thy
ways, [1]so long as they live [2]in the land which
thou gavest unto our fathers.
32 ¶ Moreover concerning the stranger,
[a]which *is* not of thy people Israel, but is come
from a far country for thy great name's sake,
and thy mighty hand, and thy stretched out
arm; if they come and pray in this house;
33 Then hear thou from the heavens, *even*
from thy dwelling place, and do according to
all that the stranger calleth to thee for; that all
people of the earth may know thy name, and
fear thee, as *doth* thy people Israel, and may
know that [1]this house which I have built is
called by thy name.
34 ¶ If thy people go out to war against
their enemies by the way that thou shalt send
them, and they pray unto thee toward this city
which thou hast chosen, and the house which
I have built for thy name;
35 Then hear thou from the heavens their
prayer and their supplication, and maintain
their [1]cause.
36 If they sin against thee, (for *there is* [a]no
man which sinneth not,) and thou be angry
with them, and deliver them *over* before *their*
enemies, and [1]they carry them away captives
unto a land far off or near;
37 *Yet* if they [1]bethink themselves in the
land whither they are carried captive, and turn
and pray unto thee in the land of their captivity, saying, We have sinned, we have done
amiss, and have dealt wickedly;
38 If they return to thee with all their
heart and with all their soul in the land of
their captivity, whither they have carried them
captives, and pray toward their land, which
thou gavest unto their fathers, and *toward* the
city which thou hast chosen, and toward the
house which I have built for thy name:

6:16 [1]Heb. *There shall not a man be cut off* [a]2 Sam. 7:12,16; 1 Ki. 2:4; 6:12; ch. 7:18 [b]Ps. 132:12
6:18 [a]ch. 2:6; Is. 66:1; Acts 7:49
6:20 [1]Or, *in this place*
6:21 [1]Heb. *pray*
6:22 [1]Heb. *and he require an oath of him*
6:24 [1]Or, *be smitten* [2]Or, *towards*
6:26 [a]1 Ki. 17:1
6:28 [1]Heb. *in the land of their gates* [a]ch. 20:9
6:29 [1]Or, *toward this house*
6:30 [a]1 Chr. 28:9
6:31 [1]Heb. *all the days which* [2]Heb. *upon the face of the land*
6:32 [a]John 12:20; Acts 8:27
6:33 [1]Heb. *thy name is called upon this house*
6:35 [1]Or, *right*
6:36 [1]Heb. *they that take them captives carry them away* [a]Prov. 20:9; Eccl. 7:20; Jas. 3:2; 1 John 1:8
6:37 [1]Heb. *bring back to their heart*

6:18 Cf. 2:6.
6:22–39 See notes on 1 Ki 8:31–46.
6:22–23 See Ex 22:10–11; Lev 6:3–5.
6:24–25 See Lev 26:17,23; Deut 28:25,36–37,48–57,64; Josh 7:11–12.
6:26–27 See Lev 26:19; Deut 11:10–15; 28:18,22–24.
6:28–31 See Lev 26:16,20,25–26; Deut 28:20–22,27–28,35,42.
6:32–33 The prophets also envisaged the Gentiles as coming to Jerusalem to worship the Lord (Is 56:6–8; Zech 8:20–23; 14:16–21; cf. Ps 87).
6:34–35 See Lev 26:7–8; Deut 28:6–7. The Chronicler repeatedly demonstrates God's answer to prayer in time of battle (ch. 13; 14:9–15; 18:31; 20:1–29; 25:5–13; 32:20–22).
6:36 *no man which sinneth not.* See Jer 13:23; Rom 3:23. *captives unto a land far off.* See 36:15–20; Lev 26:33,44–45; Deut 28:49–52; 2 Ki 17:7–20; 25:1–21.

39 Then hear thou from the heavens, *even* from thy dwelling place, their prayer and their supplications, and maintain their [1]cause, and forgive thy people which have sinned against thee.

40 ¶ Now, my God, let, I beseech thee, thine eyes be open, and *let* thine ears *be* attent [1]unto the prayer *that is made* in this place.

41 Now [a]therefore arise, O LORD God, into thy [b]resting place, thou, and the ark of thy strength: let thy priests, O LORD God, be clothed *with* salvation, and let thy saints [c]rejoice in goodness.

42 O LORD God, turn not away the face of thine anointed: [a]remember the mercies of David thy servant.

Dedicating the house of God

7 Now [a]when Solomon had made an end of praying, the [b]fire came down from heaven, and consumed the burnt offering and the sacrifices; and [c]the glory of the LORD filled the house.

2 [a]And the priests could not enter into the house of the LORD, because the glory of the LORD had filled the LORD's house.

3 And when all the children of Israel saw how the fire came down, and the glory of the LORD upon the house, they bowed themselves *with their* faces to the ground upon the pavement, and worshipped, and praised the LORD, [a]*saying,* For *he is* good; [b]for his mercy *endureth* for ever.

4 ¶ [a]Then the king and all the people offered sacrifices before the LORD.

5 And king Solomon offered a sacrifice of twenty and two thousand oxen, and an hundred and twenty thousand sheep: so the king and all the people dedicated the house of God.

6 [a]And the priests waited on their offices: the Levites also with instruments of musick of the LORD, which David the king had made to praise the LORD, because his mercy *endureth* for ever, when David praised [1]by their ministry; and [b]the priests sounded trumpets before them, and all Israel stood.

7 Moreover [a]Solomon hallowed the middle of the court that *was* before the house of the LORD: for there he offered burnt offerings, and the fat of the peace offerings, because the brasen altar which Solomon had made was not able to receive the burnt offerings, and the meat offerings, and the fat.

8 [a]Also at the same time Solomon kept the feast seven days, and all Israel with him, a very great congregation, from the entering in of Hamath unto [b]the river of Egypt.

9 And in the eighth day they made [1]a solemn assembly: for they kept the dedication of the altar seven days, and the feast seven days.

10 And [a]on the three and twentieth day of the seventh month he sent the people away into their tents, glad and merry in heart for the goodness that the LORD had shewed unto David, and to Solomon, and to Israel his people.

The LORD's promise to Solomon

11 ¶ Thus [a]Solomon finished the house of the LORD, and the king's house: and all that came into Solomon's heart to make in the house of the LORD, and in his own house, he prosperously effected.

12 And the LORD appeared to Solomon by night, and said unto him, I have heard thy prayer, [a]and have chosen this place to myself for a house of sacrifice.

13 [a]If I shut up heaven that there be no rain, or if I command the locusts to devour the land, or if I send pestilence among my people;

14 If my people, [1]which are called by my name, shall [a]humble themselves, and pray, and seek my face, and turn from their wicked ways; [b]then will I hear from heaven, and will forgive their sin, and will heal their land.

15 Now [a]mine eyes shall be open, and mine ears attent [1]unto the prayer *that is made* in this place.

16 For now have [a]I chosen and sanctified this house, that my name may be there for

6:39 [1]Or, *right*
6:40 [1]Heb. *to the prayer of this place*
6:41 [a]Ps. 132:8-10,16 [b]1 Chr. 28:2 [c]Neh. 9:25
6:42 [a]Ps. 132:1; Is. 55:3
7:1 [a]1 Ki. 8:54 [b]Lev. 9:24; Judg. 6:21; 1 Ki. 18:38; 1 Chr. 21:26 [c]1 Ki. 8:10,11
7:2 [a]ch. 5:14
7:3 [a]ch. 5:13; Ps. 136:1 [b]1 Chr. 16:41; ch. 20:21
7:4 [a]1 Ki. 8:62,63
7:6 [1]Heb. *by their hand* [a]1 Chr. 15:16
7:6 [b]ch. 5:12
7:7 [a]1 Ki. 8:64
7:8 [a]1 Ki. 8:65 [b]Josh. 13:3
7:9 [1]Heb. *a restraint*
7:10 [a]1 Ki. 8:66
7:11 [a]1 Ki. 9:1
7:12 [a]Deut. 12:5
7:13 [a]ch. 6:26,28
7:14 [1]Heb. *upon whom my name is called* [a]Jas. 4:10 [b]ch. 6:27,30
7:15 [1]Heb. *to the prayer of this place* [a]ch. 6:40
7:16 [a]1 Ki. 9:3; ch. 6:6

6:40–42 The Chronicler replaces the ending of Solomon's prayer in Kings (1 Ki 8:50–53) with a repetition of Ps 132:8–10, a psalm that deals with bringing the ark to the temple, the theme of this section in Chronicles (5:2–14). The prayer in Kings ends with an appeal to the exodus deliverance under Moses, while in Chronicles the appeal is on the basis of the eternal promises to David.

7:1–22 See 1 Ki 8:54–9:9 and notes.

7:1–3 Not found in 1 Ki 8. The addition of the fire descending from heaven to consume the sacrifices provides the same sign of divine acceptance as was given at the dedication of the tabernacle (Lev 9:23–24) and David's offering at the threshingfloor of Ornan (a variant of Araunah; see 2 Sam 24:16) the Jebusite (1 Chr 21:26; cf. 1 Ki 18:38). While vv. 1–3 are unique to Chronicles, the Chronicler has omitted Solomon's blessing of the congregation (1 Ki 8:55–61).

7:1 *glory of the LORD.* See 5:14 and note.

7:3 *he is good . . . for ever.* See v. 6; 5:13.

7:6 The verse is unique to Chronicles and reflects the author's overall interest in the Levites, especially the musicians (cf. 29:26–27; see note on 1 Chr 6:31–48). *all Israel.* See Introduction to 1 Chronicles: Purpose and Themes.

7:8 *from the entering in of Hamath unto the river of Egypt.* Not only were the patriarchal promises of descendants provisionally fulfilled under David and Solomon (see 1:9; 1 Chr 27:23–24 and notes), but also the promises of land (Gen 15:18–21).

7:9 *eighth day.* The final day of the feast of tabernacles (see 5:3 and note; Lev 23:36; Num 29:35). *seven days . . . seven days.* The dedication had run from the 8th to the 14th day of the month, and the feast of tabernacles from the 15th to the 22nd day. The day of atonement was on the 10th day of the 7th month (Lev 16; cf. 1 Ki 8:65–66).

7:12 *appeared to Solomon.* The second time God appeared to Solomon; the first was at Gibeon (1:3–13; 1 Ki 9:2).

7:13–15 Unique to Chronicles. These verses illustrate the writer's emphasis on immediate retribution (see Introduction to 1 Chronicles: Purpose and Themes). The Chronicler subsequently portrays the kings in a way that demonstrates this principle (see v. 22).

7:14 See, e.g., 12:6–7,12.

ever: and mine eyes and mine heart shall be there perpetually.

17 [a]And *as for* thee, if thou wilt walk before me, as David thy father walked, and do according to all that I have commanded thee, and shalt observe my statutes and my judgments;

18 Then will I stablish the throne of thy kingdom, according as I have covenanted with David thy father, saying, [a][1]There shall not fail thee a man *to be* ruler in Israel.

19 [a]But if ye turn away, and forsake my statutes and my commandments, which I have set before you, and shall go and serve other gods, and worship them;

20 Then will I pluck them up by the roots out of my land which I have given them; and this house, which I have sanctified for my name, will I cast out of my sight, and will make it to be a proverb and a byword among all nations.

21 And this house, which is high, shall be an astonishment to every one that passeth by it; so that he shall say, [a]Why hath the LORD done thus unto this land, and unto this house?

22 And it shall be answered, Because they forsook the LORD God of their fathers, which brought them forth out of the land of Egypt, and laid hold on other gods, and worshipped them, and served them: therefore hath he brought all this evil upon them.

Solomon's other achievements

8 And [a]it came to pass at the end of twenty years, wherein Solomon had built the house of the LORD, and his own house,

2 That the cities which Huram had restored to Solomon, Solomon built them, and caused the children of Israel to dwell there.

3 And Solomon went *to* Hamath-zobah, and prevailed against it.

4 [a]And he built Tadmor in the wilderness, and all the store cities, which he built in Hamath.

5 Also he built Beth-horon the upper, and Beth-horon the nether, fenced cities, *with* walls, gates, and bars;

6 And Baalath, and all the store cities that Solomon had, and all the chariot cities, and the cities of the horsemen, and [1]all that Solomon desired to build in Jerusalem, and in Lebanon, and throughout all the land of his dominion.

7 [a]*As for* all the people that were left of the Hittites, and the Amorites, and the Perizzites, and the Hivites, and the Jebusites, which *were* not of Israel,

8 *But* of their children, who were left after them in the land, whom the children of Israel consumed not, them did Solomon make to pay tribute until this day.

9 But of the children of Israel did Solomon make no servants for his work; but they *were* men of war, and chief of his captains, and captains of his chariots and horsemen.

10 And these *were* the chief of king Solomon's officers, *even* [a]two hundred and fifty, that bare rule over the people.

11 And Solomon [a]brought up the daughter of Pharaoh out of the city of David unto the house that he had built for her: for he said, My wife shall not dwell in the house of David king of Israel, because *the places are* [1]holy, whereunto the ark of the LORD hath come.

12 ¶ Then Solomon offered burnt offerings unto the LORD on the altar of the LORD, which he had built before the porch,

13 Even after a certain rate [a]every day, offering according to the commandment of Moses, on the sabbaths, and on the new moons, and on the solemn feasts, [b]three times in the year, *even* in the feast of unleavened bread, and in the feast of weeks, and in the feast of tabernacles.

14 And he appointed, according to the order of David his father, the [a]courses of the priests to their service, and [b]the Levites to their charges, to praise and minister before the priests, as the duty of every day required: the [c]porters also by their courses at every gate: for [1]so had David the man of God commanded.

15 And they departed not *from* the commandment of the king unto the priests and Levites concerning any matter, or concerning the treasures.

7:17 [a]1 Ki. 9:4
7:18 [1]Heb. *There shall not be cut off to thee* [a]ch. 6:16
7:19 [a]Lev. 26:14,33; Deut. 28:15,36,37
7:21 [a]Deut. 29:24
8:1 [a]1 Ki. 9:10
8:4 [a]1 Ki. 9:17
8:6 [1]Heb. *all the desire of Solomon which he desired to build*
8:7 [a]1 Ki. 9:20
8:10 [a]See 1 Ki. 9:23
8:11 [1]Heb. *holiness* [a]1 Ki. 3:1; 7:8; 9:24
8:13 [a]Ex. 29:38; Num. 28:3,9,11, 26; 29:1 [b]Ex. 23:14; Deut. 16:16
8:14 [1]Heb. *so was the commandment of David the man of God* [a]1 Chr. 24:3 [b]1 Chr. 25:1 [c]1 Chr. 9:17; 26:1

7:17–18 See 1 Ki 9:4–5. Such words as these reinforced ancient Israel's Messianic hopes.

7:19–22 See 1 Ki 9:6–9.

8:1–18 See 1 Ki 9:10–18 and notes. Verses 13–16 are unique to Chronicles and underscore the Chronicler's concern to show continuity with the past and his association of David with Moses (see Introduction to 1 Chronicles: Purpose and Themes).

8:1–2 In 1 Ki 9:10–14 the cities were given to Hiram ("Huram" in Chronicles) by Solomon, whereas in Chronicles the reverse is true. Perhaps as part of his effort to idealize Solomon, the Chronicler does not record the fact that Hiram found these cities unacceptable payment (1 Ki 9:11–13); he mentions only the sequel to the story, the return of the cities to Solomon and their subsequent improvement. They may also have served as a kind of collateral against the monies owed Hiram, who returned them when the debt was satisfied (see note on 1 Ki 9:11). The Chronicler also says nothing about Pharaoh's gift of Gezer to Solomon (1 Ki 9:16).

8:3–4 The Chronicler records an additional military campaign to the north, not mentioned in Kings. David had also campaigned in the north against Zobah (1 Chr 18:3–9; 19:6; 2 Sam 8:3–12; 10:6–8; cf. 1 Ki 11:23–24).

8:5 The two Beth-horons were situated on a strategic road from the coastal plain to the area just north of Jerusalem.

8:7 *not of Israel.* See 2:17; 1 Chr 22:2; 1 Ki 9:21.

8:8 *until this day.* See note on 5:9.

8:11 *holy.* Both 1 Ki 9:24 and Chronicles record the transfer of Pharaoh's daughter to special quarters, but only Chronicles adds the reason: Not only the temple but also David's palace was regarded as holy, because of the presence of the ark.

8:12–16 In line with his overall interests, the Chronicler considerably elaborates on the sacrificial and temple provisions made by Solomon. While 1 Ki 9:25 mentions only the sacrifices at the three annual feasts, the Chronicler adds the offerings on sabbaths and new moons to conform these provisions fully to Mosaic prescription (Lev 23:1–37; Num 28–29).

16 Now all the work of Solomon was prepared unto the day of the foundation of the house of the LORD, and until it was finished. *So* the house of the LORD was perfected.

17 ¶ Then went Solomon to [a]Ezion-geber, and to [1]Eloth, at the sea side in the land of Edom.

18 [a]And Huram sent him by the hands of his servants ships, and servants that had knowledge of the sea; and they went with the servants of Solomon to Ophir, and took thence four hundred and fifty talents of gold, and brought *them* to king Solomon.

The visit of the queen of Sheba

9 And [a]when the queen of Sheba heard of the fame of Solomon, she came to prove Solomon with hard questions at Jerusalem, with a very great company, and camels that bare spices, and gold in abundance, and precious stones: and when she was come to Solomon, she communed with him of all that was in her heart.

2 And Solomon told her all her questions: and there was nothing hid from Solomon which he told her not.

3 And when the queen of Sheba had seen the wisdom of Solomon, and the house that he had built,

4 And the meat of his table, and the sitting of his servants, and the attendance of his ministers, and their apparel; his [1]cupbearers also, and their apparel; and his ascent *by* which he went up *into* the house of the LORD; there was no more spirit in her.

5 And she said to the king, *It was* a true [1]report which I heard in mine own land of thine [2]acts, and of thy wisdom:

6 Howbeit I believed not their words, until I came, and mine eyes had seen *it:* and behold, *the one* half of the greatness of thy wisdom was not told me: *for* thou exceedest the fame that I heard.

7 Happy *are* thy men, and happy *are* these thy servants, which stand continually before thee, and hear thy wisdom.

8 Blessed be the LORD thy God, which delighted in thee to set thee on his throne, to be king for the LORD thy God: because thy God loved Israel, to establish them for ever, therefore made he thee king over them, to do judgment and justice.

9 And she gave the king an hundred and twenty talents of gold, and of spices great abundance, and precious stones: neither was there any such spice as the queen of Sheba gave king Solomon.

10 And the servants also of Huram, and the servants of Solomon, [a]which brought gold from Ophir, brought [1]algum trees and precious stones.

11 And the king made *of* the algum trees [1]terraces to the house of the LORD, and to the king's palace, and harps and psalteries for singers: and there were none such seen before in the land of Judah.

12 And king Solomon gave to the queen of Sheba all her desire, what*soever* she asked, besides *that* which she had brought unto the king. So she turned, and went away to her own land, she and her servants.

Solomon's wealth and wisdom

13 ¶ Now the weight of gold that came to Solomon in one year was six hundred and threescore and six talents of gold;

14 Besides *that which* chapmen and merchants brought. And all the kings of Arabia and [1]governors of the country brought gold and silver to Solomon.

15 And king Solomon made two hundred targets *of* beaten gold: six hundred *shekels* of beaten gold went to one target.

16 And three hundred shields *made he of* beaten gold: three hundred *shekels* of gold went to one shield. And the king put them in the house of the forest of Lebanon.

17 Moreover the king made a great throne of ivory, and overlaid it with pure gold.

18 And *there were* six steps to the throne, with a footstool of gold, *which were* fastened to the throne, and [1]stays on each side of the sitting place, and two lions standing by the stays:

19 And twelve lions stood there on the one side and on the other upon the six steps. There was not the like made in any kingdom.

20 And all the drinking vessels of king Solomon *were of* gold, and all the vessels of the house of the forest of Lebanon *were of* [1]pure gold: [2]none *were of* silver; it was *not* any thing accounted of in the days of Solomon.

21 For the king's ships went *to* Tarshish with the servants of Huram: every three years once came the ships of Tarshish bringing gold, and silver, [1]ivory, and apes, and peacocks.

22 And king Solomon passed all the kings of the earth in riches and wisdom.

8:17 [1]Or, *Elath* [a]1 Ki. 9:26
8:18 [a]1 Ki. 9:27; ch. 9:10,13
9:1 [a]1 Ki. 10:1; Mat. 12:42; Luke 11:31
9:4 [1]Or, *butlers*
9:5 [1]Heb. *word* [2]Or, *sayings*
9:10 [1][1 Ki. 10:11, *almug trees*] [a]ch. 8:18
9:11 [1]Or, *stairs.* Heb. *highways*
9:14 [1]Or, *captains*
9:18 [1]Heb. *hands*
9:20 [1]Heb. *shut up* [2]Or, there was *no silver* in them
9:21 [1]Or, *elephants' teeth*

8:17–18 See 1 Ki 9:26–28. This joint venture between Solomon and Huram secured for these kings the lucrative trade routes through the Mediterranean to the south Arabian peninsula; Solomon became the middleman between these economic spheres.
8:18 *Huram sent him . . . ships.* Presumably ships crafted in Phoenicia and assembled at the port of Ezion-geber after being shipped overland (see 9:21).
9:1–12 See 1 Ki 10:1–13 and notes. The visit of the queen of Sheba portrays the fulfillment of God's promise to give Solomon wisdom and wealth (1:12). Although the themes of Solomon's wisdom and wealth are here put to the fore, a major motive for the queen's visit may have been commercial, perhaps prompted by Solomon's naval operations toward south Arabia (8:17–18).
9:1 *Sheba.* See note on 1 Ki 10:1; see also Job 1:15; 6:19; Ps 72:10–11,15; Is 60:6; Jer 6:20; Ezek 27:22; 38:13; Joel 3:8.
9:8 *his throne.* The most significant variation from the account of the queen's visit in 1 Kings (10:9) is found here. The queen's speech becomes the vehicle for the Chronicler's conviction that the throne of Israel is the throne of God, for whom the king ruled (see 13:18; see also note on 1 Chr 17:14).

23 And all the kings of the earth sought the presence of Solomon, to hear his wisdom, that God had put in his heart.

24 And they brought every man his present, vessels of silver, and vessels of gold, and raiment, harness, and spices, horses, and mules, a rate year by year.

25 And Solomon [a]had four thousand stalls for horses and chariots, and twelve thousand horsemen; whom he bestowed in the chariot cities, and with the king at Jerusalem.

26 [a]And he reigned over all the kings [b]from the [1]river even unto the land of the Philistines, and to the border of Egypt.

27 [a]And the king [1]made silver in Jerusalem as stones, and cedar trees made he as the sycomore trees that *are* in the low plains in abundance.

28 [a]And they brought unto Solomon horses out of Egypt, and out of all lands.

Solomon's death and successor

29 ¶ [a]Now the rest of the acts of Solomon, first and last, *are* they not written in the [1]book of Nathan the prophet, and in the prophecy of [b]Ahijah the Shilonite, and in the visions of [c]Iddo the seer against Jeroboam the son of Nebat?

30 [a]And Solomon reigned in Jerusalem over all Israel forty years.

31 And Solomon slept with his fathers, and he was buried in the city of David his father: and Rehoboam his son reigned in his stead.

Rehoboam's harsh rule

10 And [a]Rehoboam went to Shechem: for *to* Shechem were all Israel come to make him king.

2 And it came to pass, when Jeroboam the son of Nebat, who *was* in Egypt, [a]whither he had fled from the presence of Solomon the king, heard *it,* that Jeroboam returned out of Egypt.

3 And they sent and called him. So Jeroboam and all Israel came and spake to Rehoboam, saying,

4 Thy father made our yoke grievous: now therefore ease thou somewhat the grievous servitude of thy father, and his heavy yoke that he put upon us, and we will serve thee.

5 And he said unto them, Come again unto me after three days. And the people departed.

6 And king Rehoboam took counsel with the old men that had stood before Solomon his father while he *yet* lived, saying, What counsel give ye *me* to return answer to this people?

7 And they spake unto him, saying, If thou be kind to this people, and please them, and speak good words to them, they will be thy servants for ever.

8 But he forsook the counsel which the old men gave him, and took counsel with the young men that were brought up with him, that stood before him.

9 And he said unto them, What advice give ye that we may return answer to this people, which have spoken to me, saying, Ease somewhat the yoke that thy father did put upon us?

10 And the young men that were brought up with him spake unto him, saying, Thus shalt thou answer the people that spake unto thee, saying, Thy father made our yoke heavy, but make thou *it* somewhat lighter for us; thus shalt thou say unto them, My little *finger* shall be thicker than my father's loins.

11 For whereas my father [1]put a heavy yoke upon you, I will put more to your yoke: my father chastised you with whips, but I *will chastise you* with scorpions.

12 So Jeroboam and all the people came to Rehoboam on the third day, as the king bade, saying, Come again to me on the third day.

13 And the king answered them roughly; and king Rehoboam forsook the counsel of the old men,

14 And answered them after the advice of the young men, saying, My father made your yoke heavy, but I will add thereto: my father chastised you with whips, but I *will chastise you* with scorpions.

15 So the king hearkened not unto the people: [a]for the cause was of God, that the LORD might perform his word, which he spake by the [b]hand of Ahijah the Shilonite to Jeroboam the son of Nebat.

16 ¶ And when all Israel saw that the king would not hearken unto them, the people answered the king, saying,

What portion have we in David?

9:25 [a]1 Ki. 4:26; 10:26; ch. 1:14
9:26 [1]That is, *Euphrates* [a]1 Ki. 4:21 [b]Gen. 15:18; Ps. 72:8
9:27 [1]Heb. *gave* [a]1 Ki. 10:27; ch. 1:15
9:28 [a]1 Ki. 10:28; ch. 1:16
9:29 [1]Heb. *words* [a]1 Ki. 11:41 [b]1 Ki. 11:29 [c]ch. 12:15; 13:22
9:30 [a]1 Ki. 11:42,43
10:1 [a]1 Ki. 12:1
10:2 [a]1 Ki. 11:40
10:11 [1]Heb. *laded*
10:15 [a]1 Sam. 2:25; 1 Ki. 12:15,24 [b]1 Ki. 11:29

9:26 See 7:8 and note.
9:27 See 1:15.
9:28 The Chronicler omits the accounts of Solomon's wives and the rebellions at the end of his reign (1 Ki 11:1–40), both of which would detract from his uniformly positive portrayal of Solomon. *horses . . . Egypt.* See note on 1:16.
9:29–31 See 1 Ki 11:41–43.
10:1–36:23 The material covering the divided monarchy in Chronicles is considerably shorter than that in Kings: 27 chapters compared to 36 (1 Ki 12–2 Ki 25). Moreover, about half of this material is unique to Chronicles and shows no dependence on Kings. The most obvious reason for this is that the Chronicler has written a history of the Davidic dynasty in Judah; the history of the northern kingdom is passed over in silence except where it impinges on that of Judah. At least two considerations prompt this treatment of the divided kingdom: 1. The Chronicler is concerned to trace God's faithfulness to His promise to give David an unbroken line of descent on the throne of Israel. 2. At the time of the Chronicler the restored community was confined to the returnees of the kingdom of Judah, who were actually the remnant of all Israel (see Introduction to 1 Chronicles: Purpose and Themes).
10:1–19 See 1 Ki 12:1–20 and notes. Somewhat in line with his idealization of Solomon, the Chronicler places most of the blame for the schism on the rebellious Jeroboam (cf. 13:6–7).
10:1 *Rehoboam.* Reigned 930–913 B.C.
10:2 *Jeroboam.* His second mention in Chronicles (see 9:29). The Chronicler assumes the reader's familiarity with 1 Ki 11:26–40.
10:15 *Ahijah.* The Chronicler assumes the reader's familiarity with 1 Ki 11:29–33.

And *we have* none inheritance in the
son of Jesse:
Every man to your tents, O Israel:
And now, David, see to thine own
house.
So all Israel went to their tents.
17 But *as for* the children of Israel that
dwelt in the cities of Judah, Rehoboam reigned
over them.
18 Then king Rehoboam sent Hadoram
that *was* over the tribute; and the children of
Israel stoned him with stones, that he died.
But king Rehoboam [1]made speed to get *him*
up to *his* chariot, to flee *to* Jerusalem.
19 [a]And Israel rebelled against the house
of David unto this day.

Rehoboam builds strongholds

11 And [a]when Rehoboam was come *to*
Jerusalem, he gathered *of* the house
of Judah and Benjamin an hundred and
fourscore thousand chosen *men,* which were
warriors, to fight against Israel, that *he* might
bring the kingdom again to Rehoboam.
2 But the word of the LORD came [a]to Shemaiah the man of God, saying,
3 Speak unto Rehoboam the son of Solomon, king of Judah, and to all Israel in Judah
and Benjamin, saying,
4 Thus saith the LORD, Ye shall not go up,
nor fight against your brethren: return every
man to his house, for this thing is done of me.
And they obeyed the words of the LORD, and
returned from going against Jeroboam.
5 ¶ And Rehoboam dwelt in Jerusalem, and
built cities for defence in Judah.
6 He built even Beth-lehem, and Etam, and
Tekoa,
7 And Beth-zur, and Shoco, and Adullam,
8 And Gath, and Mareshah, and Ziph,

10:18 [1]Heb. *strengthened himself*
10:19 [a]1 Ki. 12:19
11:1 [a]1 Ki. 12:21
11:2 [a]ch. 12:15

11:13 [1]Heb. *presented themselves to him*
11:14 [a]Num. 35:2 [b]ch. 13:9
11:15 [a]1 Ki. 12:31; 13:33; 14:9; Hos. 13:2 [b]Lev. 17:7; 1 Cor. 10:20 [c]1 Ki. 12:28
11:16 [a]See ch. 15:9; 30:11,18
11:17 [a]ch. 12:1
11:20 [a]1 Ki. 15:2; She is called Michaiah the daughter of Uriel, ch. 13:2

9 And Adoraim, and Lachish, and Azekah,
10 And Zorah, and Aijalon, and Hebron,
which *are* in Judah and in Benjamin, fenced
cities.
11 And he fortified the strong holds, and
put captains in them, and store of victual, and
of oil and wine.
12 And in every several city *he put* shields
and spears, and made them exceeding strong,
having Judah and Benjamin on his side.
13 And the priests and the Levites that
were in all Israel [1]resorted to him out of all
their coasts.
14 For the Levites left [a]their suburbs and
their possession, and came to Judah and Jerusalem: for [b]Jeroboam and his sons had cast
them off from executing the priest's office
unto the LORD:
15 [a]And he ordained him priests for the
high places, and for [b]the devils, and for [c]the
calves which he had made.
16 [a]And after them out of all the tribes of
Israel such as set their hearts to seek the LORD
God of Israel came *to* Jerusalem, to sacrifice
unto the LORD God of their fathers.
17 So they [a]strengthened the kingdom of
Judah, and made Rehoboam the son of Solomon strong, three years: for three years they
walked in the way of David and Solomon.

Rehoboam's many wives

18 ¶ And Rehoboam took him Mahalath
the daughter of Jerimoth the son of David *to*
wife, *and* Abihail the daughter of Eliab the son
of Jesse;
19 Which bare him children; Jeush, and
Shamariah, and Zaham.
20 And after her he took [a]Maachah the
daughter of Absalom; which bare him Abijah,
and Attai, and Ziza, and Shelomith.

‡10:18 *Hadoram . . . over the tribute* [i.e. the forced labor]. Had held the same office under Solomon (see 1 Ki 4:6; 5:14, where he is called Adoniram).

10:19 *unto this day.* See note on 5:9.

11:1–23 Verses 1–4 are parallel to 1 Ki 12:21–24; vv. 5–23 are largely unique to Chronicles. The Chronicler's account of Rehoboam is a good example of his emphasis on immediate retribution (see Introduction to 1 Chronicles: Purpose and Themes). Ch. 11 traces the rewards for obedience to the command of God (vv. 1–4): Rehoboam enjoys prosperity and power (vv. 5–12), popular support (vv. 13–17) and progeny (vv. 18–23). Ch. 12 demonstrates the reverse: Disobedience brings judgment.

11:2 *Shemaiah.* The function of the prophets as guardians of the theocracy (God's kingdom) is prominent in Chronicles; most of Judah's kings are portrayed as receiving advice from prophets (see Introduction to 1 Chronicles: Purpose and Themes).

11:3 *all Israel in Judah and Benjamin.* A variation from the wording found in 1 Ki 12:23, in accordance with the Chronicler's interest in "all Israel."

11:4 *of me.* See 10:15.

11:5–10 This list of cities is not found in Kings. Rehoboam fortified his eastern, western and southern borders, but not the north, perhaps demonstrating his hope of reunification of the kingdoms, as well as the threat of invasion from Egypt.

11:13–17 The Chronicler assumes the reader's familiarity with 1 Ki 12:26–33. This material is unique to Chronicles and reflects the author's concern both with the temple and its personnel and with showing that the kingdom of Judah was the remnant of all Israel.

‡11:14 *suburbs* [i.e. pasture lands] *and their possession.* See 1 Chr 6:54–80; Lev 25:32–34; Num 35:1–5; see also Introduction to 1 Chronicles: Purpose and Themes.

‡11:15 *devils* [i.e, goat idols]*, and . . . calves.* The account in Kings mentions only the golden calves (for the worship of "devils" or satyrs see Lev 17:7).

11:17 *three years.* See note on 12:2. *way of David and Solomon.* Characteristic of the Chronicler's idealization of Solomon; contrast the portrait of Solomon in 1 Ki 11:1–13.

11:18–22 The report on the size of Rehoboam's family is placed here as part of the Chronicler's effort to show God's blessing on his obedience (see note on 11:1–23). The material is not in chronological sequence with the surrounding context but summarizes events throughout his reign. The Chronicler uses numerous progeny as a sign of divine blessing (see 13:21; see also notes on 21:2; 1 Chr 25:5).

11:20 *Maachah the daughter of Absalom.* See note on 1 Ki 15:2. She was likely the granddaughter of Absalom, through his daughter Tamar (2 Sam 14:27; 18:18), who was married to Uriel (2 Chr 13:2).

21 And Rehoboam loved Maachah the daughter of Absalom above all his wives and his concubines: (for he took eighteen wives, and threescore concubines; and begat twenty and eight sons, and threescore daughters.)

22 And Rehoboam [a]made Abijah the son of Maachah the chief, to be ruler among his brethren: for *he thought* to make him king.

23 And he dealt wisely, and dispersed of all his children throughout all the countries of Judah and Benjamin, unto every fenced city: and he gave them victual in abundance. And he desired [1]many wives.

Egyptians raid Jerusalem

12 And [a]it came to pass, when Rehoboam had established the kingdom, and had strengthened himself, [b]he forsook the law of the LORD, and all Israel with him.

2 [a]And it came to pass, *that* in the fifth year of king Rehoboam Shishak king of Egypt came up against Jerusalem, because they had transgressed against the LORD,

3 With twelve hundred chariots, and threescore thousand horsemen: and the people *were* without number that came with him out of Egypt; [a]the Lubims, the Sukkiims, and the Ethiopians.

4 And he took the fenced cities which *pertained* to Judah, and came to Jerusalem.

5 Then came [a]Shemaiah the prophet to Rehoboam, and *to* the princes of Judah, that were gathered together to Jerusalem because of Shishak, and said unto them, Thus saith the LORD, Ye have forsaken me, and *therefore* have I also left you in the hand of Shishak.

6 Whereupon the princes of Israel and the king [a]humbled themselves; and they said, [b]The LORD *is* righteous.

7 And when the LORD saw that they humbled themselves, [a]the word of the LORD came to Shemaiah, saying, They have humbled themselves; *therefore* I will not destroy them, but I will grant them [1]some deliverance; and my wrath shall not be poured out upon Jerusalem by the hand of Shishak.

8 Nevertheless [a]they shall be his servants; that they may know [b]my service, and the service of the kingdoms of the countries.

9 [a]So Shishak king of Egypt came up against Jerusalem, and took away the treasures of the house of the LORD, and the treasures of the king's house; he took all: he carried away also the shields of gold which Solomon had [b]made.

10 Instead of which king Rehoboam made shields of brass, and committed *them* [a]to the hands of the chief of the guard, that kept the entrance of the king's house.

11 And when the king entered *into* the house of the LORD, the guard came and fet them, and brought them again into the guard chamber.

12 And when he humbled himself, the wrath of the LORD turned from him, that *he* would not destroy *him* altogether: [a][1]and also in Judah things went well.

13 ¶ So king Rehoboam strengthened himself in Jerusalem, and reigned: for [a]Rehoboam *was* one and forty years old when he *began* to reign, and he reigned seventeen years in Jerusalem, [b]the city which the LORD had chosen out of all the tribes of Israel, to put his name there. And his mother's name *was* Naamah an Ammonitess.

14 And he did evil, because he [1]prepared not his heart to seek the LORD.

15 Now the acts of Rehoboam, first and last, *are* they not written in the [1]book of Shemaiah the prophet, [a]and of Iddo the seer concerning genealogies? [b]And *there were* wars between Rehoboam and Jeroboam continually.

16 And Rehoboam slept with his fathers, and was buried in the city of David: and [1]Abijah his son reigned in his stead.

Abijah, king of Judah

13 Now [a]in the eighteenth year of king Jeroboam *began* Abijah to reign over Judah.

11:22 [a]See Deut. 21:15-17
11:23 [1]Heb. *a multitude of wives*
12:1 [a]ch. 11:17 [b]1 Ki. 14:22-24
12:2 [a]1 Ki. 14:24,25
12:3 [a]ch. 16:8
12:5 [a]ch. 11:2
12:6 [a]Jas. 4:10 [b]Ex. 9:27
12:7 [1]Or, *a little while* [a]1 Ki. 21:28,29
12:8 [a]See Is. 26:13 [b]Deut. 28:47,48
12:9 [a]1 Ki. 14:25,26 [b]1 Ki. 10:16,17; ch. 9:15,16
12:10 [a]1 Ki. 14:27
12:12 [1]Or, *and yet in Judah there were good things* [a]Gen. 18:24; 1 Ki. 14:13; ch. 19:3
12:13 [a]1 Ki. 14:21 [b]ch. 6:6
12:14 [1]Or, *fixed*
12:15 [1]Heb. *words* [a]ch. 9:29; 13:22 [b]1 Ki. 14:30
12:16 [1][1 Ki. 14:31, *Abijam*]
13:1 [a]1 Ki. 15:1

11:21–22 These verses explain why the eldest son was not appointed Rehoboam's successor.

11:23 *dispersed of all his children.* Rehoboam may have sought to secure the succession of Abijah by assigning other sons to outlying posts, perhaps to avoid the difficulties faced by David, whose sons at court (Adonijah and Absalom) had attempted to seize power.

12:1–14 See note on 11:1–23. Whereas obedience to the prophetic word (11:1–4) had brought blessing (11:5–23), now the prophet comes to announce judgment for disobedience (see 1 Ki 14:25–28). While the writer of Kings also reports the attack of Shishak, the Chronicler alone adds the rationale that the invasion was because of forsaking the commands of God (vv. 1–2,5).

12:1 *forsook.* The opposite of seeking the LORD (v. 14); see v. 5; see also note on 24:18,20,24. *all Israel.* Used in a variety of ways in 2 Chronicles: (1) of both kingdoms (9:30), (2) of the northern kingdom (10:16; 11:13) or (3) of the southern kingdom alone (as here; 11:3).

12:2 *fifth year.* 925 B.C. The Chronicler often introduces chronological notes not found in Kings (e.g., 11:17; 15:10,19; 16:1, 12–13; 17:7; 21:20; 24:15,17,23; 26:16; 27:5,8; 29:3; 34:3; 36:21). These become a vehicle for his emphasis on immediate retribution by dividing the reigns of individual kings into cycles of obedience-blessing and disobedience-punishment. This sequence is clear for Rehoboam: Three years of obedience and blessing (11:17) are followed by rebellion, presumably in the fourth year (12:1), and punishment in the fifth (here). *Shishak.* Founder of the 22nd dynasty of Egypt, he ruled c. 945–924 B.C. The Bible mentions this invasion only as it affected Jerusalem, but Shishak's own inscription on the wall of the temple of Amun at Karnak (Thebes) indicates that his armies also swept as far north as the plain of Jezreel and Megiddo.

12:3 *Sukkiims.* Probably a group of mercenary soldiers of Libyan origin who are known from Egyptian texts.

12:5 See notes on vv. 1–14; v. 1.

12:6–7 See v. 12. The Chronicler has in mind God's promise in 7:14.

12:13 *seventeen years.* See note on 10:1.

12:15–16 See 1 Ki 14:29–31.

13:1–14:1 The Chronicler's account of Abijah's reign is about three times longer than that in 1 Ki 15:1–8, largely due to Abi-

2 He reigned three years in Jerusalem. His
mother's name also *was* [a]Michaiah the daughter of Uriel of Gibeah. And there was war between Abijah and Jeroboam.
3 And Abijah [1]set the battle in array with
an army of valiant *men* of war, *even* four hundred thousand chosen men: Jeroboam also set
the battle in array against him with eight hundred thousand chosen men, *being* mighty *men*
of valour.
4 ¶ And Abijah stood up upon mount [a]Zem-
araim, which *is* in mount Ephraim, and said,
Hear me, *thou* Jeroboam, and all Israel;
5 Ought you not to know that the LORD
God of Israel [a]gave the kingdom over Israel to
David for ever, *even* to him and to his sons [b]*by*
a covenant of salt?
6 Yet Jeroboam the son of Nebat, the servant of Solomon the son of David, is risen up,
and hath [a]rebelled against his lord.
7 And there are gathered unto him [a]vain
men, the children of Belial, and have strengthened themselves against Rehoboam the son of
Solomon, when Rehoboam was young and tender hearted, and could not withstand them.
8 And now ye think to withstand the kingdom of the LORD in the hand of the sons of David; and ye *be* a great multitude, and *there are*
with you golden calves, which Jeroboam
[a]made you for gods.
9 [a]Have ye not cast out the priests of the
LORD, the sons of Aaron, and the Levites, and
have made you priests after the manner of the
nations of *other* lands? [b]so that whosoever
cometh [c1]to consecrate himself with a young
bullock and seven rams, *the same* may be a
priest of *them that are* no gods.
10 But *as for* us, the LORD *is* our God, and
we have not forsaken him; and the priests,
which minister unto the LORD, *are* the sons of
Aaron, and the Levites *wait* upon *their* business:
11 [a]And they burn unto the LORD every
morning and every evening burnt sacrifices
and sweet incense: the [b]*shew*bread also *set
they* in order upon the pure table; and the
candlestick of gold with the lamps thereof, [c]to
burn every evening: for we keep the charge of
the LORD our God; but ye have forsaken him.
12 And behold, God *himself is* with us for
our captain, [a]and his priests with sounding
trumpets to cry alarm against you. O children
of Israel, fight ye not against the LORD God of
your fathers; for you shall not prosper.
13 ¶ But Jeroboam caused an ambushment to
come about behind them: so they were before
Judah, and the ambushment *was* behind them.
14 And when Judah looked back, behold,
the battle *was* before and behind: and they
cried unto the LORD, and the priests sounded
with the trumpets.
15 Then the men of Judah gave a shout:
and as the men of Judah shouted, it came to
pass, that God [a]smote Jeroboam and all Israel
before Abijah and Judah.
16 And the children of Israel fled before Judah: and God delivered them into their hand.
17 And Abijah and his people slew them
with a great slaughter: so there fell down slain
of Israel five hundred thousand chosen men.
18 Thus the children of Israel were
brought under at that time, and the children of
Judah prevailed, [a]because they relied upon the
LORD God of their fathers.
19 And Abijah pursued after Jeroboam, and
took cities from him, Beth-el with the towns
thereof, and Jeshanah with the towns thereof,
and [a]Ephrain with the towns thereof.
20 Neither did Jeroboam recover strength
again in the days of Abijah: and the LORD
[a]struck him, and [b]he died.
21 But Abijah waxed mighty, and married
fourteen wives, and begat twenty and two
sons, and sixteen daughters.
22 And the rest of the acts of Abijah, and
his ways, and his sayings, *are* written in the
[1]story of the prophet [a]Iddo.

14 So Abijah slept with his fathers, and
they buried him in the city of David:
and [a]Asa his son reigned in his stead. In his
days the land was quiet ten years.

13:2 [a]See ch. 11:20
13:3 [1]Heb. *bound together*
13:4 [a]Josh. 18:22
13:5 [a]2 Sam. 7:12,13,16 [b]Num. 18:19
13:6 [a]1 Ki. 11:26; 12:20
13:7 [a]Judg. 9:4
13:8 [a]1 Ki. 12:28; 14:9; Hos. 8:6
13:9 [1]Heb. *to fill his hand* [a]ch. 11:14,15 [b]Ex. 29:35 [c]Ex. 29:1; Lev. 8:2
13:11 [a]ch. 2:4 [b]Lev. 24:6
13:11 [c]Ex. 27:20,21; Lev. 24:2,3
13:12 [a]Num. 10:8
13:15 [a]ch. 14:12
13:18 [a]1 Chr. 5:20; Ps. 22:5
13:19 [a]Josh. 15:9
13:20 [a]1 Sam. 25:38 [b]1 Ki. 14:20
13:22 [1]Or, *commentary* [a]ch. 12:15
14:1 [a]1 Ki. 15:8

jah's lengthy speech (13:4–12; see note on 28:1–27). The most striking difference in the accounts of Abijah's reign in Kings and in Chronicles is the evaluation given in each: Kings offers a negative evaluation (1 Ki 15:3), for which there was no doubt warrant, while the assessment in Chronicles is positive, in view of what the Chronicler is able to report of him. The kings' reigns, like the lives of common people, were often a mixture of good and evil.

13:2 *three years.* 913–910 B.C. *Michaiah.* A variant of Maachah (see note on 11:20).

13:3 *four hundred thousand . . . eight hundred thousand.* Surprisingly large figures but in line with those in 1 Chr 21:5 (see note there). Apparently this was all-out war.

13:4 *mount Zemaraim.* Location uncertain. The town Zemaraim was in the territory of Benjamin (Josh 18:22); presumably the battle was along the common border of Benjamin and Israel. *all Israel.* See note on 12:1; here and in v. 15 the reference is to the northern kingdom.

13:5 See 7:17–18; 1 Chr 17:13–14. *covenant of salt.* See notes on Num 18:19; 2 Ki 2:20.

13:6 See note on 10:1–19.

‡13:7 Not all in the northern kingdom are rebuked, only the leadership—a subtle appeal to those in the north who had been led into rebellion. *children of Belial* [i.e. worthless men]. See note on Deut 13:13. *young and tender hearted.* Cf. 1 Chr 22:5; 29:1. Rehoboam was 41 years old at the time of the schism (12:13).

13:8 *kingdom of the LORD.* The house of David represents the kingdom of God (see 9:8 and note).

13:9 See 1 Ki 12:25–33. *consecrate himself.* Cf. Ex 29:1.

13:10–12 The Chronicler's concern with acceptable worship focuses on the legitimate priests and the observance of prescribed worship (cf. 1 Chr 23:28–31).

13:21 See note on 11:18–22.

14:1 *quiet ten years.* For the Chronicler peace and prosperity go hand in hand with righteous rule. This first decade of Asa's reign (910–900 B.C.) preceded the invasion by Zerah (14:9–15) and was followed by 20 more years of peace, from the 15th (15:10) to the 35th years (15:19). Contrast this account with the statement that there was war between Asa and Baasha

Asa, king of Judah

2 ¶ And Asa did *that* which *was* good and
right in the eyes of the LORD his God:
3 For he took away the altars of the strange
gods, and [a]the high places, and [b]brake down
the [1]images, [c]and cut down the groves:
4 And commanded Judah to seek the LORD
God of their fathers, and to do the law and the
commandment.
5 Also he took away out of all the cities of
Judah the high places and the [1]images: and
the kingdom was quiet before him.
6 And he built fenced cities in Judah: for
the land had rest, and he had no war in those
years; because the LORD had given him rest.
7 Therefore he said unto Judah, Let us
build these cities, and make about *them* walls,
and towers, gates, and bars, *while* the land *is*
yet before us; because we have sought the
LORD our God, we have sought *him,* and he
hath given us rest on every side. So they built
and prospered.
8 And Asa had an army *of men* that bare
targets and spears, out of Judah three hundred
thousand; and out of Benjamin, that bare
shields and drew bows, two hundred and
fourscore thousand: all these *were* mighty *men*
of valour.
9 ¶ [a]And there came out against them Zerah the Ethiopian with a host of a thousand
thousand, and three hundred chariots; and
came unto [b]Mareshah.
10 Then Asa went out against him, and
they set the battle in array in the valley of
Zephathah at Mareshah.
11 And Asa [a]cried unto the LORD his God,
and said, LORD, *it is* [b]nothing with thee to
help, *whether* with many, *or* with *them that*
have no power: help us, O LORD our God; for
we rest on thee, and [c]in thy name we go
against this multitude. O LORD, thou *art* our
God; let not [1]man prevail against thee.
12 So the LORD [a]smote the Ethiopians before Asa, and before Judah; and the Ethiopians
fled.
13 And Asa and the people that *were* with
him pursued them unto [a]Gerar: and the Ethiopians were overthrown, that they could not recover themselves; for they were [1]destroyed
before the LORD, and before his host; and they
carried away very much spoil.
14 And they smote all the cities round
about Gerar; for [a]the fear of the LORD came
upon them: and they spoiled all the cities; for
there was *exceeding* much spoil in them.
15 They smote also the tents of cattle, and
carried away sheep and camels in abundance,
and returned *to* Jerusalem.

Asa's reform movement

15 And [a]the spirit of God came upon
Azariah the son of Oded:
2 And he went out [1]to meet Asa, and said
unto him, Hear ye me, Asa, and all Judah and
Benjamin; [a]The LORD *is* with you, while ye be
with him; and [b]if ye seek him, he will be
found of you; but [c]if ye forsake him, he will
forsake you.
3 Now [a]for a long season Israel *hath been*
without the true God, and without [b]a teaching
priest, and without law.
4 But [a]when they in their trouble did turn

14:3 [1]Heb. *statues* [a]See 1 Ki. 15:14; ch. 15:17 [b]Ex. 34:13 [c]1 Ki. 11:7
14:5 [1]Heb. *sun images*
14:9 [a]ch. 16:8 [b]Josh. 15:44
14:11 [a]Ex. 14:10; ch. 13:14; Ps. 22:5
14:11 [1]Or, *mortal man* [b]1 Sam. 14:6 [c]1 Sam. 17:45; Prov. 18:10
14:12 [a]ch. 13:15
14:13 [1]Heb. *broken* [a]Gen. 10:19; 20:1
14:14 [a]Gen. 35:5; ch. 17:10
15:1 [a]Num. 24:2; Judg. 3:10; ch. 20:14
15:2 [1]Heb. *before Asa* [a]Jas. 4:8 [b]ver. 4,15; 1 Chr. 28:9; ch. 33:12,13; Jer. 29:13; Mat. 7:7 [c]ch. 24:20
15:3 [a]Hos. 3:4 [b]Lev. 10:11
15:4 [a]Deut. 4:29

throughout their reigns (see 1 Ki 15:16 and note). The tensions between the two kingdoms may have accounted for Asa's fortifications (14:7–8), though actual combat was likely confined to raids until the major campaign was launched in Asa's 36th year (16:1). See 15:8 and note.

14:2–16:14 The account of Asa's reign (910–869 B.C.) here is greatly expanded over the one in 1 Ki 15:9–24. The expansions characteristically express the Chronicler's view concerning the relationship between obedience and blessing, disobedience and punishment. The author introduces chronological notes into his account to divide Asa's reign into these periods (see note on 12:2): For ten years Asa did what was right and prospered (14:1–7), and an invasion by a powerful Cushite (Ethiopian) force was repulsed because he called on the Lord (14:8–15). There followed further reforms (15:1–9) and a covenant renewal in Asa's 15th year (15:10–18), and so he enjoyed peace until his 35th year (15:19). But then came a change: When confronted by an invasion from the northern kingdom in his 36th year (16:1), he hired Aramean reinforcements rather than trusting in the Lord (16:2–6), and imprisoned the prophet who rebuked him (16:7–10). In his 39th year he was afflicted with a disease (16:12), but still steadfastly refused to seek the Lord. In his 41st year he died (16:13).

‡14:3 *images.* See note on 1 Ki 14:23. *groves* [Hebrew *Asherim*]. Wooden symbols of the goddess Asherah (here and throughout 2 Chronicles).

14:5 *took away . . . the high places.* 1 Ki 15:14 states that Asa did not remove the high places. This difficulty is best resolved by the Chronicler's own statement in 15:17, which is properly parallel to 1 Ki 15:14: Early in his reign Asa did attempt to remove the high places, but pagan worship was extremely resilient, and ultimately his efforts were unsuccessful (15:17). Statements that the high places both were and were not removed are also found in the reign of Jehoshaphat (17:6; 20:33). Cf. Deut 12:2–3.

14:7 *rest on every side.* See note on 20:30.

14:9 *Zerah the Ethiopian.* Lit. "Zerah the Cushite." Many identify him with Pharaoh Osorkon I, second pharaoh of the 22nd Egyptian dynasty. However, since he is not called "king" or "pharaoh," and is known as the "Cushite" or "Nubian," some prefer to identify him as an otherwise unknown general serving the pharaoh. The invasion appears to have been an attempt to duplicate the attack of Shishak 30 years earlier (12:1–12), but the results against Asa were quite different.

14:10 *valley of Zephathah.* Marked the entrance to a road leading to the hills of Judah and Jerusalem. *Mareshah.* Earlier fortified by Rehoboam (11:8) to protect the route mentioned here.

14:13 *Gerar.* See note on Gen 20:1. *spoil.* Much of this booty (v. 14) made its way to the storehouses of the temple (15:18; see note on 1 Chr 18:1–20:8).

14:14 *fear of the LORD.* See note on 1 Chr 14:17.

15:1–19 This chapter appears to recount a second stage in the reforms introduced by Asa, beginning with the victory over Zerah and encouraged by the preaching of Azariah (v. 1).

15:3 *teaching priest.* The duties of the priests were not only to officiate at the altar, but also to teach the law (see 17:7–9; Lev 10:11).

unto the LORD God of Israel, and sought him, he was found of them.

5 And in those times *there was* no peace to him that went out, nor to him that came in, but great vexations *were* upon all the inhabitants of the countries.

6 [a]And nation was [1]destroyed of nation, and city of city: for God did vex them with all adversity.

7 Be ye strong therefore, and let not your hands be weak: for your work shall be rewarded.

8 ¶ And when Asa heard these words, and the prophecy *of* Oded the prophet, he took courage, and put away the [1]abominable idols out of all the land of Judah and Benjamin, and out of the cities [a]which he had taken from mount Ephraim, and renewed the altar of the LORD, that *was* before the porch of the LORD.

9 And he gathered all Judah and Benjamin, and [a]the strangers with them out of Ephraim and Manasseh, and out of Simeon: for they fell to him out of Israel in abundance, when they saw that the LORD his God *was* with him.

10 So they gathered themselves together *at* Jerusalem in the third month, in the fifteenth year of the reign of Asa.

11 [a]And they offered unto the LORD [1]the same time, of [b]the spoil *which* they had brought, seven hundred oxen and seven thousand sheep.

12 And they [a]entered into a covenant to seek the LORD God of their fathers with all their heart and with all their soul;

13 [a]That whosoever would not seek the LORD God of Israel [b]should be put to death, whether small or great, whether man or woman.

14 And they sware unto the LORD with a loud voice, and with shouting, and with trumpets, and with cornets.

15 And all Judah rejoiced at the oath: for they had sworn with all their heart, and [a]sought him with their whole desire; and he was found of them: and the LORD gave them rest round about.

16 ¶ And also *concerning* [a]Maachah the [1]mother of Asa the king, he removed her from *being* queen, because she had made an [2]idol in a grove: and Asa cut down her idol, and stamped *it,* and burnt *it* at the brook Kidron.

17 But [a]the high places were not taken away out of Israel: nevertheless the heart of Asa was perfect all his days.

18 And he brought *into* the house of God *the things* that his father had dedicated, and that he himself had dedicated, silver, and gold, and vessels.

19 And there was no *more* war unto the five and thirtieth year of the reign of Asa.

The end of Asa's reign

16 In the six and thirtieth year of the reign of Asa [a]Baasha king of Israel came up against Judah, and built Ramah, [b]to the intent that *he* might let none go out or come in to Asa king of Judah.

2 Then Asa brought out silver and gold out of the treasures of the house of the LORD and of the king's house, and sent to Ben-hadad king of Syria, that dwelt at [1]Damascus, saying,

3 *There is* a league between me and thee, as *there was* between my father and thy father: behold, I have sent thee silver and gold; go, break thy league with Baasha king of Israel, that he may depart from me.

4 And Ben-hadad hearkened unto king Asa, and sent the captains of [1]his armies against the cities of Israel; and they smote Ijon, and Dan, and Abel-maim, and all the store cities of Naphtali.

5 And it came to pass, when Baasha heard *it,* that he left off building of Ramah, and let his work cease.

15:6 [1]Heb. *beaten in pieces* [a]Mat. 24:7
15:8 [1]Heb. *abominations* [a]ch. 13:19
15:9 [a]ch. 11:16
15:11 [1]Heb. *in that day* [a]ch. 14:15 [b]ch. 14:13
15:12 [a]2 Ki. 23:3; ch. 34:31; Neh. 10:29
15:13 [a]Ex. 22:20 [b]Deut. 13:5,9,15
15:15 [a]ver. 2
15:16 [1][That is, *grandmother,* 1 Ki. 15:2,10] [2]Heb. *horror* [a]1 Ki. 15:13
15:17 [a]ch. 14:3,5; 1 Ki. 15:14
16:1 [a]1 Ki. 15:17 [b]ch. 15:9
16:2 [1]Heb. *Darmesek*
16:4 [1]Heb. *which were his*

15:8 *cities which he had taken from . . . Ephraim.* A tacit admission that there had been some fighting between Baasha and Asa prior to Asa's 36th year (16:1); see 17:1.

15:9 *they fell to him . . . in abundance.* Cf. the defection from the northern kingdom that also occurred under Rehoboam (11:13–17).

15:10 *third month, in the fifteenth year.* Spring, 895 B.C., the year after Zerah's invasion (v. 19). The feast of weeks (or Pentecost) was held in the third month (Lev 23:15–21) and may have been the occasion for this assembly.

15:12 *covenant.* A renewal of the covenant made at Sinai, similar to the covenant renewals in the land of Moab (Deut 29:1), at mount Ebal (Josh 8:30–35), at Shechem (Josh 24:25) and at Gilgal (1 Sam 11:14; see note there). Later the priest Jehoiada (23:16), as well as Hezekiah (29:10) and Josiah (34:31), would also lead in renewals of the covenant—events of primary significance in the view of the Chronicler.

15:13 *would not seek the LORD.* Would turn to other gods. *should be put to death.* In accordance with basic covenant law (Ex 22:20; Deut 13:6–9).

15:15 *rest.* See note on 20:30.

‡15:16 *Maachah . . . made an idol in a grove.* Lit. "Maachah made for Asherah a horrid thing." See note on 14:3.

15:17 *high places were not taken away.* See 14:5 and note.

16:1 *six and thirtieth year of the reign of Asa Baasha.* According to Kings, Baasha ruled for 24 years and was succeeded by Elah in the 26th year of Asa (1 Ki 15:33; 16:8). Obviously Baasha could not have been alive in the 36th year of Asa, where this passage places him—he had been dead for a decade. In order to solve this difficulty, some suggest that the Chronicler here and in 15:19 is dating from the schism in Israel rather than from the year number of Asa's reign: Since Rehoboam had reigned 17 years and Abijah 3, 20 years are deducted with the result that the 35th and 36th years of Asa are in fact the 15th and 16th years of his reign. This would make Baasha's attack come as a possible response to the defections from the northern kingdom (15:9). While this solution may be possible, it has not met with general acceptance. The action described here is not dated in 1 Ki 15:17. Perhaps the dates here and in 15:19 are the result of a copyist's error (possibly for an original 25th and 26th).

16:2–9 Hiring foreign troops brought Asa into a foreign alliance, which showed lack of trust in the Lord. Other examples of condemned foreign alliances are found in the reigns of Jehoshaphat (20:35–37), Ahaziah (22:1–9) and Ahaz (28:16–21). By hiring Ben-hadad to the north, Asa opened a two-front war for Baasha and forced his withdrawal.

6 Then Asa the king took all Judah; and they carried away the stones of Ramah, and the timber thereof, where*with* Baasha was a building; and he built therewith Geba and Mizpah.

7 ¶ And at that time [a]Hanani the seer came to Asa king of Judah, and said unto him, [b]Because thou hast relied on the king of Syria, and not relied on the LORD thy God, therefore is the host of the king of Syria escaped out of thine hand.

8 Were not [a]the Ethiopians and [b]the Lubims [1]a huge host, with very many chariots and horsemen? yet, because thou didst rely on the LORD, he delivered them into thine hand.

9 [a]For the eyes of the LORD run to and fro throughout the whole earth, [1]to shew himself strong in the behalf of *them* whose heart *is* perfect towards him. Herein [b]thou hast done foolishly: therefore from henceforth [c]thou shalt have wars.

10 Then Asa was wroth with the seer, and [a]put him *in* a prison house; for *he was* in a rage with him because of this *thing.* And Asa [1]oppressed *some* of the people the same time.

11 ¶ [a]And behold, the acts of Asa, first and last, lo, they *are* written in the book of the kings of Judah and Israel.

12 And Asa in the thirty and ninth year of his reign was diseased in his feet, until his disease *was* exceeding *great:* yet in his disease he [a]sought not *to* the LORD, but to the physicians.

13 [a]And Asa slept with his fathers, and died in the one and fortieth year of his reign.

14 And they buried him in his own sepulchres, which he had [1]made for himself in the city of David, and laid him in the bed which was filled [a]*with* sweet odours and divers kinds *of spices* prepared by the apothecaries' art: and they made [b]a very great burning for him.

Jehoshaphat, king of Judah

17 And [a]Jehoshaphat his son reigned in his stead, and strengthened himself against Israel.

2 And he placed forces in all the fenced cities of Judah, and set garrisons in the land of Judah, and in the cities of Ephraim, [a]which Asa his father had taken.

3 And the LORD was with Jehoshaphat, because he walked in the first ways [1]of his father David, and sought not unto Baalim;

4 But sought to the *LORD* God of his father, and walked in his commandments, and not after [a]the doings of Israel.

5 Therefore the LORD stablished the kingdom in his hand; and all Judah [a][1]brought to Jehoshaphat presents; [b]and he had riches and honour in abundance.

6 And his heart [1]was lift up in the ways of the LORD: moreover [a]he took away the high places and groves out of Judah.

7 Also in the third year of his reign he sent to his princes, *even* to Ben-hail, and to Obadiah, and to Zechariah, and to Nethaneel, and to Michaiah, [a]to teach in the cities of Judah.

8 And with them *he sent* Levites, *even* Shemaiah, and Nethaniah, and Zebadiah, and Asahel, and Shemiramoth, and Jehonathan, and Adonijah, and Tobijah, and Tob-adonijah, Levites; and with them Elishama and Jehoram, priests.

9 [a]And they taught in Judah, and *had* the book of the law of the LORD with them, and went about throughout all the cities of Judah, and taught the people.

10 ¶ And [a]the fear of the LORD [1]fell upon all the kingdoms of the lands that *were* round about Judah, so that they made no war against Jehoshaphat.

11 Also *some* of the Philistines [a]brought Jehoshaphat presents, and tribute silver; and the Arabians brought him flocks, seven thousand and seven hundred rams, and seven thousand and seven hundred he goats.

12 And Jehoshaphat waxed great exceedingly; and he built in Judah [1]castles, and cities of store.

13 And he had much business in the cities of Judah: and the men of war, mighty *men* of valour, *were* in Jerusalem.

14 And these *are* the numbers of them according to the house of their fathers: Of Judah, the captains of thousands; Adnah the chief,

16:7 [a]1 Ki. 16:1; ch. 19:2 [b]Is. 31:1; Jer. 17:5
16:8 [1]Heb. *in abundance* [a]ch. 14:9 [b]ch. 12:3
16:9 [1]Or, *strongly to hold with* them, etc. [a]Job 34:21; Prov. 5:21; 15:3; Jer. 16:17; 32:19; Zech. 4:10 [b]1 Sam. 13:13 [c]1 Ki. 15:32
16:10 [1]Heb. *crushed* [a]ch. 18:26; Jer. 20:2; Mat. 14:3
16:11 [a]1 Ki. 15:23
16:12 [a]Jer. 17:5
16:13 [a]1 Ki. 15:24
16:14 [1]Heb. *digged* [a]Gen. 50:2; Mark 16:1; John 19:39,40 [b]ch. 21:19; Jer. 34:5
17:1 [a]1 Ki. 15:24
17:2 [a]ch. 15:8
17:3 [1][Or, *of his father,* and *of David*]
17:4 [a]1 Ki. 12:28
17:5 [1]Heb. *gave* [a]1 Sam. 10:27; 1 Ki. 10:25 [b]1 Ki. 10:27; ch. 18:1
17:6 [1]That is, *was encouraged* [a]1 Ki. 22:43; ch. 15:17; 19:3; 20:33
17:7 [a]ch. 15:3
17:9 [a]ch. 35:3; Neh. 8:7
17:10 [1]Heb. *was* [a]Gen. 35:5
17:11 [a]2 Sam. 8:2
17:12 [1]Or, *palaces*

16:12 *diseased in his feet.* For other examples of disease as punishment for sin see 21:16–20; 26:16–23; Acts 12:23. Cf. 2 Ki 15:5.

17:1–21:3 The Chronicler's account of Jehoshaphat's reign is more than twice as long as that in Kings, where the interest in Ahab and Elijah overshadows the space allotted to Jehoshaphat (1 Ki 22:1–46). The Chronicler has also used Jehoshaphat's reign to emphasize immediate retribution. This theme is specifically announced in 19:10 and is illustrated in the blessing of Jehoshaphat's obedient faith and in the reproof for his wrongdoing (19:2–3; 20:35–37). Jehoshaphat reigned 872–848 B.C., from 872 to 869 likely as co-regent with his father Asa (see 20:31 and note). The details of his reign may not be in chronological order; the teaching mission of 17:7–9 may have been part of the reforms noted in 19:4–11.

17:2 *cities of Judah . . . cities of Ephraim.* See note on 15:8. Abijah (13:19), Asa (15:8) and now Jehoshaphat had managed to hold these cities; they would be lost under Amaziah (25:17–24).

‡17:6 *took away the high places.* Just as his father Asa had attempted to remove the high places, only to have them be restored (14:5; 15:17), so also Jehoshaphat removed them initially, only to have them revive and persist (20:33; cf. 1 Ki 22:43). But see notes on 1 Ki 3:2; 15:14. *groves.* Hebrew *Asherim.* See note on 14:3.

17:7–9 This incident may be part of the reform more fully detailed in 19:4–11. In the theocracy, the law of the Lord was supposed to be an integral part of the law of the land; the king and his officials, as well as the priests and prophets, were representatives of the Lord's kingship over His people.

17:7 *third year.* Perhaps the first year of his sole reign after a co-regency of three years with his father Asa (see 20:31 and note).

17:10–11 See note on 1 Chr 18:1–20:8.

17:10 *fear of the LORD.* See note on 1 Chr 14:17.

17:14–18 *three hundred thousand . . . two hundred and fourscore thousand . . . two hundred thousand . . . two hundred*

and with him mighty *men* of valour three hundred thousand.

15 And [1]next to him *was* Jehohanan the captain, and with him two hundred and fourscore thousand.

16 And next him *was* Amasiah the son of Zichri, [a]who willingly offered himself unto the LORD; and with him two hundred thousand mighty *men* of valour.

17 And of Benjamin; Eliada a mighty *man* of valour, and with him armed *men* with bow and shield two hundred thousand.

18 And next him *was* Jehozabad, and with him an hundred and fourscore thousand ready prepared for the war.

19 These waited on the king, besides [a]*those* whom the king put in the fenced cities throughout all Judah.

The prophecy against Ahab

18 Now Jehoshaphat [a]had riches and honour in abundance, and [b]joined affinity with Ahab.

2 [a]And [1]after *certain* years he went down to Ahab to Samaria. And Ahab killed sheep and oxen for him in abundance, and for the people that *he had* with him, and persuaded him to go up *with him* to Ramoth-gilead.

3 And Ahab king of Israel said unto Jehoshaphat king of Judah, Wilt thou go with me *to* Ramoth-gilead? And he answered him, I *am* as thou *art,* and my people as thy people; and *we will be* with thee in the war.

4 And Jehoshaphat said unto the king of Israel, [a]Inquire, I pray thee, at the word of the LORD to day.

5 Therefore the king of Israel gathered together *of* prophets four hundred men, and said unto them, Shall we go to Ramoth-gilead to battle, or shall I forbear? And they said, Go up; for God will deliver *it* into the king's hand.

6 But Jehoshaphat said, *Is there* not here a prophet of the LORD [1]besides, that we might inquire of him?

7 And the king of Israel said unto Jehoshaphat, *There is* yet one man, by whom *we* may inquire of the LORD: but I hate him; for he never prophesied good unto me, but always evil: the same *is* Micaiah the son of Imla. And Jehoshaphat said, Let not the king say so.

8 And the king of Israel called for one *of his* [1]officers, and said, [2]Fetch quickly Micaiah the son of Imla.

9 And the king of Israel and Jehoshaphat king of Judah sat either of them on his throne, clothed in *their* robes, and they sat in a [1]void place *at* the entering in of the gate of Samaria; and all the prophets prophesied before them.

10 And Zedekiah the son of Chenaanah had made him horns of iron, and said, Thus saith the LORD, With these thou shalt push Syria until [1]they be consumed.

11 And all the prophets prophesied so, saying, Go up *to* Ramoth-gilead, and prosper: for the LORD shall deliver *it* into the hand of the king.

12 ¶ And the messenger that went to call Micaiah spake to him, saying, Behold, the words of the prophets *declare* good to the king [1]with one assent; let thy word therefore, I pray thee, be like one of theirs, and speak thou good.

13 And Micaiah said, *As* the LORD liveth, [a]even what my God saith, that will I speak.

14 And when he was come to the king, the king said unto him, Micaiah, shall we go to Ramoth-gilead to battle, or shall I forbear? And he said, Go ye up, and prosper, and they shall be delivered into your hand.

15 And the king said to him, How many times shall I adjure thee that thou say nothing but the truth to me in the name of the LORD?

16 Then he said, I did see all Israel scattered upon the mountains, as sheep that have no shepherd: and the LORD said, These have no master; let them return *therefore* every man to his house in peace.

17 And the king of Israel said to Jehoshaphat, Did I not tell thee *that* he would not prophesy good unto me, [1]but evil?

18 Again he said, Therefore hear the word of the LORD; I saw the LORD sitting upon his throne, and all the host of heaven standing on his right hand and *on* his left.

19 And the LORD said, Who shall entice Ahab king of Israel, that he may go up and fall at Ramoth-gilead? And one spake saying after this manner, and another saying after that manner.

20 Then there came out a [a]spirit, and stood before the LORD, and said, I will entice him. And the LORD said unto him, Wherewith?

21 And he said, I will go out, and be a lying spirit in the mouth of all his prophets. And *the LORD* said, Thou shalt entice *him,* and thou shalt also prevail: go out, and do *even* so.

17:15 [1]Heb. *at his hand,* ver. 16,18
17:16 [a]Judg. 5:2,9
17:19 [a]ver. 2
18:1 [a]ch. 17:5 [b]2 Ki. 8:18
18:2 [1]Heb. *at the end of years* [a]1 Ki. 22:2
18:4 [a]1 Sam. 23:2,4,9; 2 Sam. 2:1
18:6 [1]Heb. *yet,* or, *more*
18:8 [1]Or, *eunuchs* [2]Heb. *Hasten*
18:9 [1]Or, *floor*
18:10 [1]Heb. thou *consume them*
18:12 [1]Heb. with *one mouth*
18:13 [a]Num. 22:18,20,35; 23:12,26; 24:13; 1 Ki. 22:14
18:17 [1]Or, *but for evil?*
18:20 [a]Job 1:6

thousand . . . an hundred and fourscore thousand. Or "300 units . . . 280 units . . . 200 units . . . 200 units . . . 180 units" (see notes on 1 Chr 12:23–37; 27:1).

18:1–19:3 See 1 Ki 22:1–40 and notes. To conform with his interest in the southern kingdom and Jehoshaphat, the Chronicler omits elaboration on the death of Ahab and his succession (1 Ki 22:36–40) and adds the material on the prophetic condemnation of Jehoshaphat's involvement (19:1–3).

‡18:1 Not found in 1 Ki 22. The verse enhances the status of Jehoshaphat by mentioning the blessing of wealth for his fidelity, and also sets the stage for an entangling foreign alliance condemned by the prophet in 19:2–3. *joined affinity with Ahab.* An alliance by marriage. This marriage alliance to Athaliah, daughter of Ahab, resulted later in an attempt to exterminate the Davidic line (22:10–23:21).

18:2 The Chronicler further enhances the status of Jehoshaphat by noting the large number of animals Ahab slaughtered in his honor, a note not found in 1 Ki 22. *persuaded him.* Also not found in the parallel text. The Hebrew for this verb is often used in the sense of inciting to evil (e.g., 1 Chr 21:1) and may express the Chronicler's attitude toward Jehoshaphat's involvement.

18:4 *Inquire . . . at the word of the LORD to day.* This request fits the Chronicler's overall positive portrait of Jehoshaphat.

22 Now therefore behold, [a]the LORD hath
put a lying spirit in the mouth of these thy
prophets, and the LORD hath spoken evil
against thee.
23 Then Zedekiah the son of Chenaanah
came near, and [a]smote Micaiah upon the
cheek, and said, Which way went the spirit of
the LORD from me to speak unto thee?
24 And Micaiah said, Behold, thou shalt
see on that day when thou shalt go [1]into an inner chamber to hide thyself.
25 Then the king of Israel said, Take ye Micaiah, and carry him back to Amon the governor of the city, and to Joash the king's son;
26 And say, Thus saith the king, [a]Put this
fellow in the prison, and feed him with bread
of affliction and with water of affliction, until I
return in peace.
27 And Micaiah said, If thou certainly return in peace, *then* hath not the LORD spoken
by me. And he said, Hearken, all ye people.

The defeat and death of Ahab

28 ¶ So the king of Israel and Jehoshaphat
the king of Judah went up to Ramoth-gilead.
29 And the king of Israel said unto Jehoshaphat, I will disguise myself, and will go to the
battle; but put thou on thy robes. So the king
of Israel disguised himself; and they went to
the battle.
30 Now the king of Syria had commanded
the captains of the chariots that *were* with
him, saying, Fight ye not with small or great,
save only with the king of Israel.
31 And it came to pass, when the captains
of the chariots saw Jehoshaphat, that they
said, It *is* the king of Israel. Therefore they
compassed about him to fight: but Jehoshaphat
cried out, and the LORD helped him; and God
moved them *to depart* from him.
32 For it came to pass, that when the captains of the chariots perceived that it was not
the king of Israel, they turned back *again*
[1]from pursuing him.
33 And a *certain* man drew a bow [1]at a venture, and smote the king of Israel [2]between the
joints of the harness: therefore he said to *his*
chariot man, Turn thine hand, that thou mayest
carry me out of the host; for I am [3]wounded.

18:22 [a]Job 12:16; Is. 19:14; Ezek. 14:9
18:23 [a]Jer. 20:2; Mark 14:65; Acts 23:2
18:24 [1]Or, from *chamber to chamber.* Heb. *chamber in a chamber*
18:26 [a]ch. 16:10
18:32 [1]Heb. *from after him*
18:33 [1]Heb. *in his simplicity* [2]Heb. *between the joints and between the breastplate* [3]Heb. *made sick*

34 And the battle increased that day: howbeit the king of Israel stayed *himself* up in *his*
chariot against the Syrians until the even: and
about the time of the sun going down he died.

Reforms by Jehoshaphat

19 And Jehoshaphat the king of Judah
returned to his house in peace to Jerusalem.
2 And Jehu the son of Hanani [a]the seer
went out to meet him, and said to king Jehoshaphat, Shouldest thou help the ungodly,
and [b]love them that hate the LORD? therefore
is [c]wrath upon thee from before the LORD.
3 Nevertheless there are [a]good things
found in thee, in that thou hast taken away the
groves out of the land, and hast [b]prepared
thine heart to seek God.
4 And Jehoshaphat dwelt at Jerusalem: and
[1]he went out again through the people from
Beer-sheba to mount Ephraim, and brought
them back unto the LORD God of their fathers.
5 And he set judges in the land throughout
all the fenced cities of Judah, city by city,
6 And said to the judges, Take heed what
ye do: for [a]ye judge not for man, but for the
LORD, [b]who *is* with you [1]in the judgment.
7 Wherefore now let the fear of the LORD
be upon you; take heed and do *it:* for [a]*there is*
no iniquity with the LORD our God, nor [b]re-
spect of persons, nor taking of gifts.
8 Moreover in Jerusalem did Jehoshaphat
[a]set of the Levites, and *of* the priests, and of
the chief of the fathers of Israel, for the judgment of the LORD, and for controversies, when
they returned *to* Jerusalem.
9 And he charged them, saying, Thus shall
ye do [a]in the fear of the LORD, faithfully, and
with a perfect heart.
10 [a]And what cause soever shall come to
you of your brethren that dwell in their cities,
between blood and blood, between law and
commandment, statutes and judgments, ye
shall even warn them that they trespass not
against the LORD, and *so* [b]wrath come upon
[c]you, and upon your brethren: this do, and ye
shall not trespass.
11 And behold, Amariah the chief priest *is*
over you [a]in all matters of the LORD; and Zeba-

19:2 [a]1 Sam. 9:9 [b]Ps. 139:21 [c]ch. 32:25
19:3 [a]ch. 17:4,6 [b]ch. 30:19; Ezra 7:10
19:4 [1]Heb. *he returned and went out*
19:6 [1]Heb. *in the matter of judgment* [a]Deut. 1:17 [b]Ps. 82:1; Eccl. 5:8
19:7 [a]Deut. 32:4; Rom. 9:14 [b]Deut. 10:17; Job 34:19; Acts 10:34; Rom. 2:11; Gal. 2:6; Eph. 6:9; Col. 3:25
19:8 [a]Deut. 16:18; ch. 17:8
19:9 [a]2 Sam. 23:3
19:10 [a]Deut. 17:8 [b]Num. 16:46 [c]Ezek. 3:18
19:11 [a]1 Chr. 26:30

18:29 The fact that Ahab disguises himself while directing Jehoshaphat into battle in royal regalia, thus making Jehoshaphat the logical target for attack, is consistent with Israel's dominant position at this time.

18:31 *the LORD helped him; and God moved them to depart from him.* Not found in 1 Ki 22:32. However, some Septuagint (the Greek translation of the OT) manuscripts of Kings do contain the statement that "the LORD helped him," suggesting that the Chronicler was following a Hebrew text of Kings that had these words.

19:1–3 Not found in 1 Ki 22.

19:2 *Shouldest thou help the ungodly . . . ?* Jehu's father Hanani had earlier given Jehoshaphat's father Asa the same warning (see 16:7–9). Jehoshaphat later committed the same sin again and suffered for it (20:35–37).

‡19:3 *groves.* Hebrew *Asheroth.* See note on 14:3.

19:4 *Jehoshaphat . . . went . . . through the people.* The king traveled throughout the realm personally to promote religious reformation.

19:5 *set judges.* The name Jehoshaphat (meaning "The LORD judges") is appropriate for the king who instituted this judicial reform. The arrangement of the courts under Jehoshaphat (vv. 5–11) would be of particular interest to the Chronicler's audience in the postexilic period, when the courts of the restored community would have their own existence and structure legitimized by this precedent.

19:6 Cf. Deut 16:18–20; 17:8–13.

19:7 *let the fear of the LORD be upon you.* Let a terrifying sense of God's presence restrain you from any injustice (see note on 1 Chr 14:17).

19:8 *Levites, and of the priests . . . for the judgment of the LORD.* See note on 1 Chr 26:29–32. One effect of this judicial reform appears to be the bringing of the traditional system of justice

diah the son of Ishmael, the ruler of the house of Judah, for all the king's matters: also the Levites *shall be* officers before you. [1]Deal courageously, and the LORD shall be [b]with the good.

Moab and Ammon defeated

20 It came to pass after this also, *that* the children of Moab, and the children of Ammon, and with them *other* beside the Ammonites, came against Jehoshaphat to battle.

2 Then there came *some* that told Jehoshaphat, saying, There cometh a great multitude against thee from beyond the sea on this side Syria; and behold, they *be* [a]in Hazazon-tamar, which *is* [b]En-gedi.

3 And Jehoshaphat feared, and set [1]himself to [a]seek the LORD, and [b]proclaimed a fast throughout all Judah.

4 And Judah gathered themselves together, to ask *help* of the LORD: even out of all the cities of Judah they came to seek the LORD.

5 And Jehoshaphat stood in the congregation of Judah and Jerusalem, in the house of the LORD, before the new court,

6 And said, O LORD God of our fathers, *art* not thou [a]God in heaven? and [b]rulest *not* thou over all the kingdoms of the heathen? and [c]in thine hand *is there not* power and might, so that none is able to withstand thee?

7 *Art* not thou [a]our God, [1]who [b]didst drive out the inhabitants of this land before thy people Israel, and gavest it to the seed of Abraham [c]thy friend for ever?

8 And they dwelt therein, and have built thee a sanctuary therein for thy name, saying,

9 [a]If, *when* evil cometh upon us, *as* the sword, judgment, or pestilence, or famine, we stand before this house, and in thy presence, (for thy [b]name *is* in this house,) and cry unto thee in our affliction, then thou wilt hear and help.

10 And now behold, the children of Ammon and Moab and mount Seir, whom thou [a]wouldest not let Israel invade, when they came out of the land of Egypt, but [b]they turned from them, and destroyed them not;

11 Behold, I say, *how* they reward us, [a]to come to cast us out of thy possession, which thou hast given us to inherit.

12 O our God, wilt thou not [a]judge them? for we have no might against this great company that cometh against us; neither know we what to do: but [b]our eyes *are* upon thee.

13 And all Judah stood before the LORD, with their little ones, their wives, and their children.

14 ¶ Then upon Jahaziel the son of Zechariah, the son of Benaiah, the son of Jeiel, the son of Mattaniah, a Levite of the sons of Asaph, [a]came the spirit of the LORD in the midst of the congregation;

15 And he said, Hearken ye, all Judah, and ye inhabitants of Jerusalem, and thou king Jehoshaphat, Thus saith the LORD unto you, [a]Be not afraid nor dismayed by reason of this great multitude; for the battle *is* not yours, but God's.

16 To morrow go ye down against them: behold, they come up by the [1]cliff of Ziz; and ye shall find them at the end of the [2]brook, before the wilderness of Jeruel.

17 [a]Ye shall not need to fight in this *battle:* set yourselves, stand ye *still,* and see the salvation of the LORD with you, O Judah and Jerusalem: fear not, nor be dismayed; to morrow go out against them: [b]for the LORD *will be* with you.

18 And Jehoshaphat [a]bowed his head *with his* face to the ground: and all Judah and the inhabitants of Jerusalem fell before the LORD, worshipping the LORD.

19 And the Levites, of the children of the Kohathites, and of the children of the Korhites, stood up to praise the LORD God of Israel with a loud voice on high.

19:11 [1]Heb. *Take courage and do* [b]ch. 15:2
20:2 [a]Gen. 14:7 [b]Josh. 15:62
20:3 [1]Heb. *his face* [a]ch. 19:3 [b]Ezra 8:21; Jer. 36:9; Jonah 3:5
20:6 [a]Deut. 4:39; Josh. 2:11; 1 Ki. 8:23; Mat. 6:9 [b]Ps. 47:2,8; Dan. 4:17 [c]1 Chr. 29:12; Ps. 62:11; Mat. 6:13
20:7 [1]Heb. *thou* [a]Gen. 17:7; Ex. 6:7 [b]Ps. 44:2 [c]Is. 41:8; Jas. 2:23
20:9 [a]1 Ki. 8:33,37; ch. 6:28-30 [b]ch. 6:20
20:10 [a]Deut. 2:4,9,19 [b]Num. 20:21
20:11 [a]Ps. 83:12
20:12 [a]1 Sam. 3:13 [b]Ps. 25:15; 121:1,2; 123:1,2; 141:8
20:14 [a]Num. 11:25,26; 24:2; ch. 15:1
20:15 [a]Ex. 14:13,14; Deut. 1:29,30; 31:6,8; ch. 32:7
20:16 [1]Heb. *ascent* [2]Or, *valley*
20:17 [a]Ex. 14:13,14 [b]Num. 14:9; ch. 15:2; 32:8
20:18 [a]Ex. 4:31

administered by the elders of the city under closer royal and priestly supervision.

19:11 *all matters of the LORD . . . all the king's matters.* This division into the affairs of religion and the affairs of the king reflects the postexilic structure of the Chronicler's day. Cf. the anointing of Solomon and Zadok (1 Chr 29:22) and the administration of the postexilic community by Zerubbabel, a Davidic descendant, and Joshua, the high priest (Zech 4:14; 6:9–15).

‡20:1–30 This episode held special interest for the Chronicler since the restored community was being harassed by the descendants of these same peoples (see Neh 2:19; 4:1–3,7–9; 6:1–4; 13). He uses it to encourage his contemporaries to trust in the Lord and His prophets, as Jehoshaphat son of David had exhorted (v. 20). The account is significantly structured. Apart from the outer frame, which highlights the reversal of circumstances (vv. 1–4,28–30), it falls into three divisions: (1) Jehoshaphat's prayer (vv. 5–13), (2) the Lord's response (vv. 14–19), (3) the great victory (vv. 20–27). At the center of each is its crucial statement, and these are all linked by a key word: v. 9, "we stand before this house, and in thy presence"; v. 17, "stand ye still, and see the salvation of the LORD with you"; v. 23, "the children of Ammon and Moab stood up against the inhabitants of mount Seir, utterly to slay and destroy them."

‡20:1 *other beside the Ammonites.* Better rendered "Meunites." A people from the region of mount Seir in Edom (26:7; 1 Chr 4:41; cf. 2 Chr 20:10,22–23).

‡20:2 *Syria. Most* Hebrew manuscripts *Aram*; one Hebrew manuscript *Edom*. The Arameans are well to the north and not mentioned among the attackers named in v. 1, so "Edom" may be the correct reading. The difference between "Aram" and "Edom" in Hebrew is only one letter, which is very similar in shape and was often confused in the process of copying manuscripts.

20:5–12 Jehoshaphat's prayer shows him to be a true theocratic king, a worthy son of David and type (foreshadowing) of the awaited Messiah (see Introduction to 1 Chronicles: Purpose and Themes).

20:9 An apparent reference to Solomon's prayer and the divine promise of response (6:14–42; 7:12–22).

20:15 See Ex 14:13–14.

‡20:16 *cliff* [i.e. "ascent"] *of Ziz.* Began seven miles north of En-gedi and wound inland, emerging west of Tekoa. *Jeruel.* Southeast of Tekoa.

20:19 *Levites.* The Chronicler's interest in the priests and Levites is apparent throughout the account (vv. 14,21–22,28).

20 ¶ And they rose early in the morning, and went forth into the wilderness of Tekoa: and as they went forth, Jehoshaphat stood and said, Hear me, O Judah, and ye inhabitants of Jerusalem; [a]Believe in the LORD your God, so shall you be established; believe his prophets, so shall ye prosper.

21 And when he had consulted with the people, he appointed singers unto the LORD, [a]and [1]that should praise the beauty of holiness, as *they* went out before the army, and to say, [b]Praise the LORD; [c]for his mercy *endureth* for ever.

22 [1]And when they began [2]to sing and to praise, [a]the LORD set ambushments against the children of Ammon, Moab, and mount Seir, which were come against Judah; and [3]they were smitten.

23 For the children of Ammon and Moab stood up against the inhabitants of mount Seir, utterly to slay and destroy *them:* and when they had made an end of the inhabitants of Seir, every one helped [1]to destroy another.

24 And when Judah came toward the watch tower in the wilderness, they looked unto the multitude, and behold, they *were* dead bodies fallen to the earth, and [1]none escaped.

25 And when Jehoshaphat and his people came to take away the spoil of them, they found among them in abundance both riches with the dead bodies, and precious jewels, which they stript off for themselves, more than they could carry away: and they were three days in gathering of the spoil, it was so much.

26 And on the fourth day they assembled themselves in the valley of [1]Berachah; for there they blessed the LORD: therefore the name of the same place was called, The valley of Berachah, unto *this* day.

27 Then they returned, every man of Judah and Jerusalem, and Jehoshaphat in the [1]forefront of them, to go again to Jerusalem with joy; for the LORD had [a]made them to rejoice over their enemies.

28 And they came *to* Jerusalem with psalteries and harps and trumpets unto the house of the LORD.

29 And [a]the fear of God was on all the kingdoms of *those* countries, when they had heard that the LORD fought against the enemies of Israel.

30 So the realm of Jehoshaphat was quiet: for his [a]God gave him rest round about.

The death of Jehoshaphat

31 ¶ [a]And Jehoshaphat reigned over Judah: *he was* thirty and five years old when he *began* to reign, and he reigned twenty and five years in Jerusalem. And his mother's name *was* Azubah the daughter of Shilhi.

32 And he walked in the way of Asa his father, and departed not from it, doing *that* which *was* right in the sight of the LORD.

33 Howbeit [a]the high places were not taken away: for as yet the people had not [b]prepared their hearts unto the God of their fathers.

34 Now the rest of the acts of Jehoshaphat, first and last, behold they *are* written in the [1]book of Jehu the son of Hanani, [a]who [2]is mentioned in the book of the kings of Israel.

35 And after this [a]did Jehoshaphat king of Judah join himself with Ahaziah king of Israel, who did very wickedly:

36 [1]And he joined himself with him to make ships to go *to* Tarshish: and they made the ships in Ezion-geber.

37 Then Eliezer the son of Dodavah of Mareshah prophesied against Jehoshaphat, saying, Because thou hast joined thyself with Ahaziah, the LORD hath broken thy works. [a]And the ships were broken, that they were not able to go [b]to Tarshish.

Jehoram, king of Judah

21 Now [a]Jehoshaphat slept with his fathers, and was buried with his fathers in the city of David. And Jehoram his son [1]reigned in his stead.

2 And he had brethren the sons of Jehoshaphat, Azariah, and Jehiel, and Zechariah, and

20:20 [a]Is. 7:9
20:21 [1]Heb. *praisers* [a]1 Chr. 16:29 [b]1 Chr. 16:34; Ps 136:1 [c]1 Chr. 16:41; ch. 5:13
20:22 [1]Heb. *And in the time* that *they, etc.* [2]Heb. *in singing and praise* [3]Or, *they smote one another* [a]Judg. 7:22; 1 Sam. 14:20
20:23 [1]Heb. *for the destruction*
20:24 [1]Heb. there was *not an escaping*
20:26 [1]That is, *blessing*
20:27 [1]Heb. *head* [a]Neh. 12:43
20:29 [a]ch. 17:10
20:30 [a]ch. 15:15; Job 34:29
20:31 [a]1 Ki. 22:41
20:33 [a]See ch. 17:6 [b]ch. 12:14; 19:3
20:34 [1]Heb. *words* [2]Heb. *was made to ascend* [a]1 Ki. 16:1,7
20:35 [a]1 Ki. 22:48,49
20:36 [1][At first Jehoshaphat was unwilling, 1 Ki. 22:49]
20:37 [a]1 Ki. 22:48 [b]ch. 9:21
21:1 [1][Alone] [a]1 Ki. 22:50

20:20 *Believe in the LORD your God . . . believe his prophets.* A particularly apt word for the Chronicler's contemporaries to hear from this son of David—at a time when their only hope for the future lay with the Lord and the reassuring words of His prophets.

20:21 *beauty of holiness.* See note on Ps 29:2.

20:22 *ambushments.* The nature of this "ambush" is indicated in v. 23: Israel's foes destroyed each other in the confusion of battle, similar to the victory under Gideon (Judg 7:22).

20:26 *unto this day.* See note on 5:9.

20:29 *the fear of God.* See note on 1 Chr 14:17.

20:30 *rest round about.* Rest from enemies is part of God's blessing for obedience in Chronicles (14:5–7; 15:15; 1 Chr 22:8–9,18). Righteous kings have victory in warfare (Abijah, Asa, Jehoshaphat, Uzziah, Hezekiah), while wicked rulers experience defeat (Jehoram, Ahaz, Joash, Zedekiah).

20:31 *twenty and five years.* Kings reports 22 (18 in 2 Ki 3:1, and 4 more in 8:16). These figures are reconciled by suggesting a co-regency with his father Asa for three years, probably due to the severity of his father's illness and the need to arrange for a secure succession (16:10–14). The author of Kings speaks only of his years of sole reign after his father's death.

20:33 *high places were not taken away.* See note on 17:6.

20:34 *Jehu the son of Hanani.* See note on 19:2.

20:35–37 See 1 Ki 22:48–49. The lucrative maritime trade through the Gulf of Aqaba no doubt tempted Jehoshaphat to enter into this improper alliance (see 19:2 and note). Solomon's earlier alliance for the same purpose had been with a non-Israelite king (8:17–18).

20:35 *Ahaziah.* Reigned 853–852 B.C. (see 1 Ki 22:51–2 Ki 1:18 for the account of his reign).

21:2 *sons of Jehoshaphat.* The Chronicler shows the blessing of God on Jehoshaphat by mentioning his large family, particularly his seven sons (see 11:18–22; 1 Chr 25:5 and notes). Jehoshaphat's large number of sons is in striking contrast to the wicked Jehoram who, after murdering his brothers (v. 4), is left with but one son (v. 17). Jehoram's wife Athaliah would later perform a similar slaughter (22:10).

Azariah, and Michael, and Shephatiah: all these *were* the sons of Jehoshaphat king of Israel.

3 And their father gave them great gifts of silver, and of gold, and of precious things, with fenced cities in Judah: but the kingdom gave he to [1]Jehoram; because he *was* the firstborn.

4 Now when Jehoram was risen up to the kingdom of his father, he strengthened himself, and slew all his brethren with the sword, and *divers* also of the princes of Israel.

5 ¶ Jehoram *was* thirty and two years old when he [1]*began* to reign, and he reigned eight years in Jerusalem.

6 And he walked in the way of the kings of Israel, like as did the house of Ahab: for he had the daughter of [a]Ahab to wife: and he wrought *that* which *was* evil in the eyes of the LORD.

7 Howbeit the LORD would not destroy the house of David, because of the covenant that he had made with David, and as he promised to give a [1]light to him and to his [a]sons for ever.

8 [a]In his days the Edomites revolted from under the [1]dominion of Judah, and made themselves a king.

9 Then Jehoram went forth with his princes, and all *his* chariots with him: and he rose up by night, and smote the Edomites which compassed him in, and the captains of the chariots.

10 So the Edomites revolted from under the hand of Judah unto this day. The same time also did Libnah revolt from under his hand; because he had forsaken the LORD God of his fathers.

11 Moreover he made high places in the mountains of Judah, and caused the inhabitants of Jerusalem to [a]commit fornication, and compelled Judah *thereto*.

12 ¶ And there came a [1]writing to him from Elijah the prophet, saying, Thus saith the LORD God of David thy father, Because thou hast not walked in the ways of Jehoshaphat thy father, nor in the ways of Asa king of Judah,

13 But hast walked in the way of the kings of Israel, and hast [a]made Judah and the inhabitants of Jerusalem to [b]go a whoring, like to the [c]whoredoms of the house of Ahab, and also hast [d]slain thy brethren of thy father's house, *which were* better than thyself:

14 Behold, *with* [1]a great plague will the LORD smite thy people, and thy children, and thy wives, and all thy goods:

15 And thou *shalt* have great sickness by [a]disease of thy bowels, until thy bowels fall out by reason of the sickness day by day.

16 Moreover the LORD stirred up against Jehoram the spirit of the Philistines, and of the Arabians, that *were* near the Ethiopians:

17 And they came up into Judah, and brake into it, and [1]carried away all the substance that was found in the king's house, and [a]his sons also, and his wives; so that there was never a son left him, save [2]Jehoahaz, the youngest of his sons.

18 [1]And after all this the LORD smote him [a]in his bowels with an incurable disease.

19 And it came to pass, that in process of time, after the end of two years, his bowels fell out by reason of his sickness: so he died of sore diseases. And his people made no burning for him, like [a]the burning of his fathers.

20 Thirty and two *years* old was he when he *began* to reign, and he reigned in Jerusalem eight years, and departed [1]without being desired. Howbeit they buried him in the city of David, but not in the sepulchres of the kings.

Ahaziah, king of Judah

22 And the inhabitants of Jerusalem made [a]Ahaziah his youngest son king

21:3 [1] [Jehoram made partner of the kingdom with his father, 2 Ki. 8:16]
21:5 [1] [In consort, 2 Ki. 8:17]
21:6 [a] ch. 22:2
21:7 [1] Heb. *lamp*, or, *candle* [a] 2 Sam. 7:12,13; 1 Ki. 11:36; 2 Ki. 8:19; Ps. 132:11
21:8 [1] Heb. *hand* [a] 2 Ki. 8:20
21:11 [a] Lev. 20:5
21:12 [1] [Which was writ before his death, 2 Ki. 2:1]
21:13 [a] ver. 11 [b] Ex. 34:15; Deut. 31:16 [c] 1 Ki. 16:31-33; 2 Ki. 9:22 [d] ver. 4
21:14 [1] Heb. *a great stroke*
21:15 [a] ver. 18,19
21:17 [1] Heb. *carried captive* [2] Or, *Ahaziah*, ch. 22:1; or, *Azariah*, ch. 22:6 [a] ch. 24:7
21:18 [1] [His son, *Ahaziah Prorex*, 2 Ki. 9:29, soon after] [a] ver. 15
21:19 [a] ch. 16:14
21:20 [1] Heb. *without desire*
22:1 [a] ver. 6; ch. 21:17

21:3 Cf. the similar actions of Rehoboam (11:23).

21:4–20 See 2 Ki 8:16–24.

21:4 This bloody assassination of all potential rivals is not reported in Kings, but it fits the pattern of the northern kings (see v. 6). The princes of Israel were probably leading men in the southern kingdom who opposed having a king married to a daughter of Ahab. For this use of "Israel" see note on 12:1.

21:5 *eight years.* 848–841 B.C. The period 853–848 was probably a co-regency of Jehoram with his father Jehoshaphat—Jehoshaphat's 18th year was also Jehoram's second year (cf. 2 Ki 1:17; 3:1).

21:6 *he had the daughter of Ahab to wife.* Probably the marriage referred to in 18:1, used to cement the alliance between Jehoshaphat and Ahab. Such political marriages were common. Many of Solomon's marriages sealed international relationships, as did Ahab's marriage to Jezebel.

21:8–10 The pious Jehoshaphat had enjoyed victory over Edom (see note on 20:2), while the wicked Jehoram is defeated in his attempt to keep Edom in subjection to Judah (see note on 20:30).

21:10 *unto this day.* See note on 5:9. *Libnah.* Located between Judah and Philistia. *because he had forsaken the LORD.* Not found in 2 Ki 8:22. The Chronicler introduces this judgment as an indication of immediate retribution (see notes on 12:1–14; 12:2; see also Introduction to 1 Chronicles: Purpose and Themes).

21:12–20a Not found in the parallel text in 2 Ki 8.

21:12–15 This reference to a letter from Elijah is the only mention in Chronicles of that prophet, to whom the books of Kings give so much attention (1 Ki 17–2 Ki 2). Elijah's letter specifically announces the immediate consequences of Jehoram's disobedience—further defeat in war, which will cost Jehoram his wives and sons; and disease, which will lead to his death (see note on 16:12). Cf. also the foot disease of Asa (16:12–14) and the leprosy of Uzziah (26:16–23). Kings does not mention the nature of Jehoram's death. Some have argued that this letter could not be authentic because, they claim, Elijah was taken to heaven before Jehoram became king. But this is not a necessary conclusion (see 2 Ki 1:17; see also note on 2 Ki 3:11). Elijah's translation may well have taken place as late as 848 B.C.

21:16 *Ethiopians.* Lit. "Cushites," people from the upper Nile region.

21:20 *eight years.* See note on v. 5. This is the first time that the Chronicler does not refer his readers to other sources for additional details on the reign of a king. *not in the sepulchres of the kings.* Only the Chronicler mentions the refusal of the people to accord Jehoram the customary burial honors of a tomb with the other kings of Judah (cf. 24:25).

in his stead: for the band *of men* that came
with the Arabians to the camp had slain all the
[b]eldest. So Ahaziah the son of Jehoram king of
Judah reigned.
2 [a]Forty and two years old *was* Ahaziah
when he *began* to reign, and he reigned one
year in Jerusalem. His mother's name also *was*
[b]Athaliah the daughter of Omri.
3 He also walked in the ways of the house
of Ahab: for his mother was his counseller to
do wickedly.
4 Wherefore he did evil in the sight of the
LORD, like the house of Ahab: for they were his
counsellers after the death of his father to his
destruction.
5 He walked also after their counsel, and
[a]went with Jehoram the son of Ahab king of Israel to war against Hazael king of Syria at Ramoth-gilead: and the Syrians smote Joram.
6 [a]And he returned to be healed in Jezreel
because of the wounds [1]which were given
him at Ramah, when he fought with Hazael
king of Syria. And [2]Azariah the son of Jehoram
king of Judah went down to see Jehoram the
son of Ahab at Jezreel, because he was sick.
7 And the [1]destruction of Ahaziah [a]was of
God by coming to Joram: for when he was
come, he [b]went out with Jehoram against Jehu
the son of Nimshi, [c]whom the LORD had
anointed to cut off the house of Ahab.
8 And it came to pass, that when Jehu was
[a]executing judgment upon the house of Ahab,
and [b]found the princes of Judah, and the sons
of the brethren of Ahaziah, that ministered to
Ahaziah, he slew them.
9 [a]And he sought Ahaziah: and they caught
him, (for he *was* hid in [1]Samaria,) and brought
him to Jehu: and when they had slain him,
they buried him: Because, said they, he *is* the
son of Jehoshaphat, who [b]sought the LORD
with all his heart. So the house of Ahaziah had
no power to keep still the kingdom.

The murder of the royal family

10 ¶ [a]But when Athaliah the mother of
Ahaziah saw that her son was dead, she arose
and destroyed all the seed royal of the house of
Judah.
11 But [1]Jehoshabeath, the daughter of the
king, took Joash the son of Ahaziah, and stole
him from among the king's sons that were
slain, and put him and his nurse in a bedchamber. So Jehoshabeath, the daughter of
king Jehoram, the wife of Jehoiada the priest,
(for she was the sister of Ahaziah,) hid him
from Athaliah, so that she slew him not.
12 And he was with them hid in the house
of God six years: and Athaliah reigned over
the land.
23 And [a]in the seventh year Jehoiada
strengthened himself, and took the
captains of hundreds, Azariah the son of Jero-

22:1 [b]ch. 21:17
22:2 [a]2 Ki. 8:26 [b]ch. 21:6
22:5 [a]2 Ki. 8:28
22:6 [1]Heb. *wherewith they wounded him* [2]Otherwise called *Ahaziah,* ver. 1, and *Jehoahaz,* ch. 21:17 [a]2 Ki. 9:15
22:7 [1]Heb. *treading down* [a]Judg. 14:4; 1 Ki. 12:15; ch. 10:15 [b]2 Ki. 9:21 [c]2 Ki. 9:6,7
22:8 [a]2 Ki. 10:10,11 [b]2 Ki. 10:13,14
22:9 [1][At *Megiddo* in the kingdom of *Samaria*] [a]2 Ki. 9:27 [b]ch. 17:4
22:10 [a]2 Ki. 11:1
22:11 [1][2 Ki. 11:2, *Jehosheba*]
23:1 [a]2 Ki. 11:4

22:1–9 The Chronicler's account of Ahaziah's reign is much shorter than the parallel in 2 Ki 8:24–9:29, probably due to the fact that the Kings account focuses on the rebellion of Jehu and the downfall of the dynasty of Omri (see 2 Ki 8:26; see also 1 Ki 16:21–28)—events in the northern kingdom, in which the Chronicler is not interested. The Chronicler's account again shows his interest in immediate retribution: Ahaziah's personal wickedness and his involvement in a foreign alliance result in immediate judgment and a reign of only one year (see note on 16:2–9; see also Introduction to 1 Chronicles: Purpose and Themes).
22:1 *had slain all the eldest.* Emphasizes divine retribution: Jehoram, who murdered all his brothers, had to watch the death of his own sons (21:4,13,16–17).
‡22:2 *Forty and two.* The Septuagint reads "twenty-two." The Hebrew reading of "forty two" would make Ahaziah older than his father (21:20). *one year.* 841 B.C.
22:3–4 The great influence of the dynasty of Omri in Judah is indicated by the power of Athaliah and the presence of advisers from the northern kingdom (see note on 18:29).
22:5 *went with Jehoram . . . to war.* An action similar to that for which Jehoshaphat had been rebuked (see 19:2 and note). *Hazael.* Had been anointed by Elisha; he later killed his master in a coup to seize the throne (2 Ki 8:13–15; cf. 1 Ki 19:15 and note). *Ramoth-gilead.* Located in the across the Jordan border area between Israel and Aram. More than ten years earlier Jehoshaphat had participated with Ahab in a battle there that cost Ahab his life (ch. 18; 1 Ki 22).
22:6 *returned to . . . Jezreel.* Jehoram apparently recovered Ramoth-gilead and left Jehu in charge (2 Ki 8:28–9:28).
22:7 *destruction of Ahaziah was of God.* The Chronicler assumes that the reader is familiar with the account of Jehu's anointing and the additional details of the coup, which resulted in the deaths of Jehoram and Ahaziah (2 Ki 8:28–9:28). While the writer of Kings primarily portrays the end of the dynasty of Omri as a result of the judgment of God (1 Ki 21:20–29; 2 Ki 9:24–10:17), the Chronicler notes that the assassination of Ahaziah was also brought about by God.
22:9 The account of Ahaziah's death appears to be somewhat different in the two histories (cf. 2 Ki 9:21–27; 10:12–14). Since the writer of Chronicles presumes the reader's familiarity with the other account (see note on v. 7), it is best to take the details of Chronicles as supplementary to Kings, not contradictory, though it is difficult to know the precise sequence and location of events. Apart from the Chronicler's statement that Ahaziah received a decent burial because of his father's piety rather than his own, the apparent differences in the two accounts do not appear to be theologically motivated. There is no summary statement about the reign of Ahaziah in either history.
22:10–12 See 2 Ki 11:1–3. In the history of Judah, Athaliah represents the only break in the continuity of the Davidic dynasty; she is the only queen of Judah to rule in her own name (841–835 B.C.). Her attempt to wipe out the royal family repeated the action of her husband Jehoram (21:4). It threatened the continuity of the Davidic dynasty, and if she had succeeded, Judah may have been claimed by the dynasty of Omri in the north since Athaliah was from that dynasty and had no living son and heir.
22:11 *wife of Jehoiada the priest.* Not noted in Kings.
23:1–24:27 See 2 Ki 11:4–12:21 and notes. The Chronicler divides the reign of Joash (835–796 B.C.) into three parts: (1) the recovery of the throne for the house of David (ch. 23); (2) Joash and Jehoiada—the good years (24:1–16); (3) Joash alone—the bad years (24:17–27). The last section is largely unique to Chronicles and further develops the theme of immediate retribution: Once again chronological notes provide the framework for cycles of obedience and disobedience (24:15–17,23); see notes on 12:2; 14:2–16:14.

ham, and Ishmael the son of Jehohanan, and
Azariah the son of Obed, and Maaseiah the
son of Adaiah, and Elishaphat the son of
Zichri, into covenant with him.
2 And they went about in Judah, and gathered the Levites out of all the cities of Judah,
and the chief of the fathers of Israel, and they
came to Jerusalem.
3 And all the congregation made a covenant
with the king in the house of God. And he said
unto them, Behold, the king's son shall reign,
as the LORD hath [a]said of the sons of David.
4 This *is* the thing that ye shall do; A third
part of you [a]entering on the sabbath, of the
priests and of the Levites, *shall be* porters of
the [1]doors;
5 And a third *part shall be* at the king's
house; and a third *part* at the gate of the foundation: and all the people *shall be* in the courts
of the house of the LORD.
6 But let none come *into* the house of the
LORD, save the priests, and [a]they that minister
of the Levites; they shall go in, for they *are*
holy: but all the people shall keep the watch of
the LORD.
7 And the Levites shall compass the king
round about, every man with his weapons in
his hand; and whosoever *else* cometh into the
house, he shall be put to death: but be you
with the king when he cometh in, and when
he goeth out.
8 So the Levites and all Judah did according
to all *things* that Jehoiada the priest had commanded, and took every man his men that
were to come in on the sabbath, with them
that were to go out on the sabbath: for Jehoiada the priest dismissed not [a]the courses.
9 Moreover Jehoiada the priest delivered to
the captains of hundreds spears, and bucklers,
and shields, that *had been* king David's, which
were in the house of God.
10 And he set all the people, every man
having his weapon in his hand, from the right
[1]side of the [2]temple to the left side of the
[2]temple, *along* by the altar and the [2]temple,
by the king round about.
11 Then they brought out the king's son,
and put upon him the crown, and [a]*gave him*
the Testimony, and made him king. And Jehoiada and his sons anointed him, and said, [1]God
save the king.
12 Now when Athaliah heard the noise of
the people running and praising the king, she
came to the people *into* the house of the LORD:
13 And she looked, and behold, the king
stood at his pillar at the entering in, and the
princes and the trumpets by the king: and all
the people of the land rejoiced, and sounded
with trumpets, also the singers with instruments of musick, and [a]such as taught to *sing*
praise. Then Athaliah rent her clothes, and
said, [1]Treason, Treason.
14 Then Jehoiada the priest brought out
the captains of hundreds that were set over
the host, and said unto them, Have her forth of
the ranges: and whoso followeth her, let him
be slain with the sword. For the priest said,
Slay her not *in* the house of the LORD.
15 So they laid hands on her; and when
she was come to the entering [a]of the horse
gate *by* the king's house, they slew her there.
16 ¶ And Jehoiada made a covenant between him, and between all the people, and
between the king, that *they* should be the
LORD's people.
17 Then all the people went *to* the house
of Baal, and brake it down, and brake his altars
and his images in pieces, and [a]slew Mattan
the priest of Baal before the altars.
18 Also Jehoiada appointed the offices of
the house of the LORD by the hand of the
priests the Levites, whom David had [a]distrib-
uted in the house of the LORD, to offer the
burnt offerings of the LORD, as it is written in
the [b]law of Moses, with rejoicing and with
singing, [1]as it was ordained [c]by David.
19 And he set the [a]porters at the gates of
the house of the LORD, that none *which was*
unclean in any thing should enter in.
20 [a]And he took the captains of hundreds,
and the nobles, and the governors of the people, and all the people of the land, and brought
down the king from the house of the LORD: and
they came through the high gate *into* the
king's house, and set the king upon the throne
of the kingdom.

23:3 [a]2 Sam. 7:12; 1 Ki. 2:4; 9:5; ch. 6:16; 7:18; 21:7
23:4 [1]Heb. *thresholds* [a]1 Chr. 9:25
23:6 [a]1 Chr. 23:28,29
23:8 [a]See 1 Chr. 24; 25
23:10 [1]Heb. *shoulder* [2]Heb. *house*
23:11 [a]Deut. 17:18

23:11 [1]Heb. *Let the king live*
23:13 [1]Heb. *Conspiracy* [a]1 Chr. 25:8
23:15 [a]Neh. 3:28
23:17 [a]Deut. 13:9
23:18 [1]Heb. *by the hands of David* [a]1 Chr. 23:6,30,31; 24:1 [b]Num. 28:2 [c]1 Chr. 25:2,6
23:19 [a]1 Chr. 26:1
23:20 [a]2 Ki. 11:19

23:1–21 See 2 Ki 11:4–20. The Chronicler has followed his source rather closely but has introduced material reflecting his own concerns in three areas: 1. The account in Kings has more to say about the participation of the military in the coup; the Chronicler adds material emphasizing the presence of temple officials and their role (vv. 2,6,8,13,18–19). 2. The Chronicler stresses the widespread popular support for the coup by mentioning the presence of large groups of people, such as "all the congregation," "all the people" or "all Judah" (vv. 3,5–6,8, 10,16–17). 3. The Chronicler shows additional concern for the sanctity of the temple area by inserting notes showing the steps taken to ensure that only qualified personnel enter the temple precincts (vv. 5–6,19).

23:1 *Azariah . . . Elishaphat.* The Chronicler names the commanders, which was not done in Kings, but he does not mention the Carites, mercenaries who served as a royal guard (see note on "captains," 2 Ki 11:4). Verse 20 exhibits the same omission (cf. 2 Ki 11:19), the motive for which may have been the Chronicler's concern that only authorized persons enter the temple precincts.

23:2 *the Levites . . . and the chief of the fathers of Israel.* Reflects both the Chronicler's concerns with the temple personnel and the widespread support for the coup against Athaliah.

23:3 *as the LORD hath said.* See 2 Sam 7:11–16.

23:11 *the Testimony.* May refer to the covenant sworn by the assembly (vv. 1,3; cf. v. 16) or to the law of God, by which the king was to rule (see Deut 17:18–20). See note on 2 Ki 11:12.

23:13 *singers with instruments of musick.* The Chronicler adds a note (not found in 2 Ki 11:14) about the presence of Levitical musicians, who were leading the praises (see note on 1 Chr 6:31–48).

23:18–19 The Chronicler adds information on the cultic ritual and the guards at the gates (see note on vv. 1–21).

23:20 See note on v. 1.

21 And all the people of the land rejoiced: and the city was quiet, after that they had slain Athaliah with the sword.

Joash restores the temple

24 Joash [a]*was* seven years old when he *began* to reign, and he reigned forty years in Jerusalem. His mother's name also *was* Zibiah of Beer-sheba.

2 And Joash [a]did *that* which *was* right in the sight of the LORD all the days of Jehoiada the priest.

3 And Jehoiada took for him two wives; and he begat sons and daughters.

4 And it came to pass after this, *that* Joash was minded [1]to repair the house of the LORD.

5 And he gathered together the priests and the Levites, and said to them, Go out unto the cities of Judah, and [a]gather of all Israel money to repair the house of your God from year to year, and *see that* ye haste the matter. Howbeit the Levites hastened *it* not.

6 [a]And the king called for Jehoiada the chief, and said unto him, Why hast thou not required of the Levites to bring in out of Judah and out of Jerusalem the collection, *according to the commandment* of [b]Moses the servant of the LORD, and of the congregation of Israel, for the [c]tabernacle of Witness?

7 For [a]the sons of Athaliah, *that* wicked woman, had broken up the house of God; and also all the [b]dedicate *things* of the house of the LORD did they bestow upon Baalim.

8 And at the king's commandment [a]they made a chest, and set it without at the gate of the house of the LORD.

9 And they made [1]a proclamation through Judah and Jerusalem, to bring in to the LORD [a]the collection that Moses the servant of God laid upon Israel in the wilderness.

10 And all the princes and all the people rejoiced, and brought in, and cast into the chest, until *they* had made an end.

11 Now it came to pass, that at *what* time the chest was brought unto the king's office by the hand of the Levites, and [a]when they saw that *there was* much money, the king's scribe and the high priest's officer came and emptied the chest, and took it, and carried it to his place again. Thus they did day by day, and gathered money in abundance.

12 And the king and Jehoiada gave it to such as did the work of the service of the house of the LORD, and hired masons and carpenters to repair the house of the LORD, and also such as wrought iron and brass to mend the house of the LORD.

13 So the workmen wrought, and [1]the work was perfected by them, and they set the house of God in his state, and strengthened it.

14 And when they had finished *it,* they brought the rest of the money before the king and Jehoiada, [a]whereof were made vessels for the house of the LORD, *even* vessels to minister, and [1]to offer *withal,* and spoons, and vessels of gold and silver. And they offered burnt offerings in the house of the LORD continually all the days of Jehoiada.

15 ¶ But Jehoiada waxed old, and was full *of* days when he died; an hundred and thirty years old *was he* when he died.

16 And they buried him in the city of David among the kings, because he had done good in Israel, both towards God, and *towards* his house.

17 Now after the death of Jehoiada came the princes of Judah, and made obeisance to the king. Then the king hearkened unto them.

18 And they left the house of the LORD God of their fathers, and served [a]groves and idols: and [b]wrath came upon Judah and Jerusalem for this their trespass.

19 Yet he [a]sent prophets to them, to bring them again unto the LORD; and they testified against them: but they would not give ear.

20 And the spirit of God [a][1]came upon Zechariah the son of Jehoiada the priest, which stood above the people, and said unto

24:1 [a]2 Ki. 11:21; 12:1
24:2 [a]See ch. 26:5
24:4 [1]Heb. *to renew*
24:5 [a]2 Ki. 12:4
24:6 [a]2 Ki. 12:7 [b]Ex. 30:12-14,16 [c]Num. 1:50; Acts 7:44
24:7 [a]ch. 21:17 [b]2 Ki. 12:4
24:8 [a]2 Ki. 12:9
24:9 [1]Heb. *a voice* [a]ver. 6
24:11 [a]2 Ki. 12:10
24:13 [1]Heb. *the healing went up upon the work*
24:14 [1]Or, *pestils* [a]See 2 Ki. 12:13
24:18 [a]1 Ki. 14:23 [b]Judg. 5:8; ch. 19:2; 28:13; 29:8; 32:25
24:19 [a]ch. 36:15; Jer. 7:25,26; 25:4
24:20 [1]Heb. *clothed* [a]Judg. 6:34

24:1–14 See 2 Ki 12:1–17.
24:1 *forty years.* 835–796 B.C.
24:2 Provides the outline for the Chronicler's treatment of Joash—the good years while Jehoiada was alive (vv. 1–16), and the turn to evil after his death (vv. 17–27). See note on 25:2.
24:3 Another expression of the Chronicler's conviction that large families represent the blessing of God (see v. 27; see also note on 1 Chr 25:5).
24:4 *repair the house of the LORD.* The vandalism and atrocities of Athaliah (v. 7) required the refurbishing of the temple.
24:5 The writer of 2 Kings speaks of three different sources of revenue (2 Ki 12:4–5), whereas the Chronicler mentions only the census tax (see Ex 30:14; 38:26; Mat 17:24). The reason for the tardiness of the priests is not stated (see 2 Ki 12:6–8). The writer of Kings notes that the audience with the priests takes place in the 23rd year of Joash's reign, when he is presumably no longer the ward of Jehoiada. Resistance on the part of the priests to the reassignment of the temple revenues for repair work may be the underlying cause.
24:8 *chest.* Mesopotamian texts speak of a similar offering box placed in temples. Representatives of both the king and the temple officials administered temple revenues (see note on 1 Chr 26:20).
24:14 See 2 Ki 12:13–14. *all the days of Jehoiada.* An additional note on the part of the Chronicler to introduce the turn to the worse in the reign of Joash upon Jehoiada's death (vv. 15–16).
24:15–22 This section is unique to the Chronicler and shows his emphasis on immediate retribution (see note on 23:1–24:27). After a period of righteous rule until the death of Jehoiada, Joash turns to idolatry and murders Jehoiada's son. In the following year he is invaded and defeated by Aram because Judah, under his leadership, "had forsaken the LORD" (v. 24).
24:18,20,24 *left*... *forsaken*... *forsaken*... *forsaken.* The Hebrew word is the same in these verses; it is a verb frequently used by the Chronicler to denote the reason for divine punishment (see note on 12:1; see also 7:19,22; 12:5; 13:10–11; 15:2; 21:10; 24:18,20,24; 28:6; 29:6; 34:25; 1 Chr 28:9,20).
24:19 *Yet he sent prophets.* Israel's failure to heed the Lord's prophets ultimately led to her destruction (see 36:16; cf. 20:20; see also Introduction to 1 Chronicles: Purpose and Themes).
24:20 *Zechariah.* See note on Mat 23:35.

them, Thus saith God, [b]Why transgress ye the commandments of the LORD, that ye cannot prosper? [c]because ye have forsaken the LORD, he hath also forsaken you.

21 And they conspired against him, and [a]stoned him *with* stones at the commandment of the king in the court of the house of the LORD.

22 Thus Joash the king remembered not the kindness which Jehoiada his father had done to him, but slew his son. And when he died, he said, The LORD look upon *it,* and require *it.*

The defeat and death of Joash

23 ¶ And it came to pass [1]at the end of the year, *that* [a]the host of Syria came up against him: and they came to Judah and Jerusalem, and destroyed all the princes of the people from among the people, and sent all the spoil of them unto the king of [2]Damascus.

24 For the army of the Syrians [a]came with a small *company* of men, and the LORD [b]delivered a very great host into their hand, because they had forsaken the LORD God of their fathers. So they [c]executed judgment against Joash.

25 And when they were departed from him, (for they left him in great diseases,) [a]his own servants conspired against him for the blood of the [b]sons of Jehoiada the priest, and slew him on his bed, and he died: and they buried him in the city of David, but they buried him not in the sepulchres of the kings.

26 And these *are* they that conspired against him; [1]Zabad the son of Shimeath an Ammonitess, and Jehozabad the son of [2]Shimrith a Moabitess.

27 Now *concerning* his sons, and the greatness of [a]the burdens *laid* upon him, and the [1]repairing of the house of God, behold they *are* written in the [2]story of the book of the kings. [b]And Amaziah his son reigned in his stead.

24:20 [b]Num. 14:41 [c]ch. 15:2 **24:21** [a]Mat. 23:35; Acts 7:58,59 **24:23** [1]Heb. *in the revolution of the year* [2]Heb. *Darmesek* [a]2 Ki. 12:17 **24:24** [a]Lev. 26:8; Deut. 32:30; Is. 30:17 [b]Lev. 26:25; Deut. 28:25 [c]ch. 22:8; Is. 10:5 **24:25** [a]2 Ki. 12:20 [b]ver. 21 **24:26** [1]Or, *Jozachar* [2]Or, *Shomer* **24:27** [1]Heb. *founding* [2]Or, *commentary* [a]2 Ki. 12:18 [b]2 Ki. 12:21

25:1 [a]2 Ki. 14:1 **25:2** [a]ver. 14; See 2 Ki. 14:4 **25:3** [1]Heb. *confirmed upon him* [a]2 Ki. 14:5 **25:4** [a]Deut. 24:16; 2 Ki. 14:6; Jer. 31:30; Ezek. 18:20 **25:5** [a]Num. 1:3 **25:8** [a]ch. 20:6 **25:9** [1]Heb. *band* [a]Prov. 10:22

Amaziah, king of Judah

25 Amaziah [a]*was* twenty and five years old *when* he *began* to reign, and he reigned twenty and nine years in Jerusalem. And his mother's name *was* Jehoaddan of Jerusalem.

2 And he did *that* which *was* right in the sight of the LORD, [a]but not with a perfect heart.

3 [a]Now it came to pass, when the kingdom was [1]established to him, that he slew his servants that had killed the king his father.

4 But he slew not their children, but *did* as it is written in the law in the book of Moses, where the LORD commanded, saying, [a]The fathers shall not die for the children, neither shall the children die for the fathers, but every man shall die for his own sin.

5 ¶ Moreover Amaziah gathered Judah together, and made them captains over thousands, and captains over hundreds, according to the houses of *their* fathers, throughout all Judah and Benjamin: and he numbered them [a]from twenty years old and above, and found them three hundred thousand choice *men, able to* go forth *to* war, that could handle spear and shield.

6 He hired also an hundred thousand mighty *men* of valour out of Israel for an hundred talents of silver.

7 But there came a man of God to him, saying, O king, let not the army of Israel go with thee; for the LORD *is* not with Israel, *to wit, with* all the children of Ephraim.

8 But if thou *wilt* go, do *it,* be strong for the battle: God shall make thee fall before the enemy: for God hath [a]power to help, and to cast down.

9 And Amaziah said to the man of God, But what *shall we* do for the hundred talents which I have given to the [1]army of Israel? And the man of God answered, [a]The LORD is able to give thee much more than this.

10 Then Amaziah separated them, to wit,

24:24 *small company of men.* Just as God had helped the small army of Judah against overwhelming odds when the king and people were faithful to Him (14:8–9; 20:2,12), so now in their unfaithfulness they are defeated by a much smaller force of invaders (see note on 20:30).

24:25 *servants . . . for the blood of the sons . . . slew him.* Only the Chronicler mentions that this assassination was revenge for the murder of Zechariah. *buried him not in the sepulchres of the kings.* Burial in the tombs of the kings was an honor accorded to Jehoiada (v. 16), but withheld from his rebellious ward Joash (see note on 21:20).

24:26 *an Ammonitess. . . a Moabitess.* Information not given in Kings but important to the Chronicler (see note on 20:1–30).

25:1–28 Typically, the Chronicler has divided the reign of Amaziah into two parts: (1) the good years, marked by obedience, divine blessing and victory (vv. 1–13), and (2) the bad years of idolatry, defeat and regicide (vv. 14–28). See 2 Ki 14:1–20 and notes.

25:1 *twenty and nine years.* 796–767 B.C.

25:2 The Chronicler does not indicate that Amaziah failed to remove the high places, which continued to be used as places for sacrifice by the people (see 2 Ki 14:4). Also compare 24:2 with 2 Ki 12:4, and 26:4 with 2 Ki 15:4. The writer appears to be motivated by his outline, which covered the good years first and then the reversion to evil. Negative comments about these kings are held to the second half of the account of their reigns, whereas in Kings the summary judgment about their reigns and the high places is given immediately.

25:5–16 An expansion of 2 Ki 14:7. The author of Kings mentions the successful war with Edom only as a prelude to Amaziah's challenge to Joash, but the Chronicler sets it in the framework of his emphasis on immediate retribution: Obedience brings victory over Edom, while the subsequent idolatry (vv. 14–16) brings defeat in the campaign against Israel. By expanding his account the Chronicler gives the theological reason for both the victory over Edom and the defeat before Israel.

25:7 *let not the army of Israel go with thee.* Another instance of the Chronicler's condemnation of alliances that imply lack of trust in the Lord (see notes on 16:2–9; 22:5). Cf. other prophetic speeches that call on the people to trust in God (20:15–17,20; 32:7–8).

the army that was come to him out of Ephraim, to go [1]home *again:* wherefore their anger was greatly kindled against Judah, and they returned home [2]in great anger.

11 And Amaziah strengthened himself, and led forth his people, and went *to* [a]the valley of salt, and smote *of* the children of Seir ten thousand.

12 And *other* ten thousand *left* alive did the children of Judah carry away captive, and brought them unto the top of the rock, and cast them down from the top of the rock, that they all were broken in pieces.

13 But [1]the soldiers of the army which Amaziah sent back, that *they* should not go with him to battle, fell upon the cities of Judah, from Samaria even unto Beth-horon, and smote three thousand of them, and took much spoil.

14 ¶ Now it came to pass, after that Amaziah was come from the slaughter of the Edomites, that [a]he brought the gods of the children of Seir, and set them up to be [b]his gods, and bowed down himself before them, and burned incense unto them.

15 Wherefore the anger of the LORD was kindled against Amaziah, and he sent unto him a prophet, which said unto him, Why hast thou sought after [a]the gods of the people, which [b]could not deliver their own people out of thine hand?

16 And it came to pass, as he talked with him, that *the king* said unto him, Art thou made of the king's counsel? forbear; why shouldest thou be smitten? Then the prophet forbare, and said, I know that God hath [a][1]determined to destroy thee, because thou hast done this, and hast not hearkened unto my counsel.

17 ¶ Then [a]Amaziah king of Judah took advice, and sent to Joash, the son of Jehoahaz, the son of Jehu, king of Israel, saying, Come, let us see one another *in* the face.

18 And Joash king of Israel sent to Amaziah king of Judah, saying, The [1]thistle that *was* in Lebanon sent to the cedar that *was* in Lebanon, saying, Give thy daughter to my son to wife: and there passed by [2]a wild beast that *was* in Lebanon, and trode down the thistle.

19 Thou sayest, Lo, thou hast smitten the Edomites; and thine heart lifteth thee up to boast: abide now at home; why shouldest thou meddle to *thine* hurt, that thou shouldest fall, *even* thou, and Judah with thee?

20 But Amaziah would not hear; for [a]it *came* of God, that *he* might deliver them into the hand *of their enemies,* because they [b]sought after the gods of Edom.

21 So Joash the king of Israel went up; and they saw one another *in* the face, *both* he and Amaziah king of Judah, at Beth-shemesh, which *belongeth* to Judah.

22 And Judah was [1]put to the worse before Israel, and they fled every man to his tent.

23 And Joash the king of Israel took Amaziah king of Judah, the son of Joash, the son of [a]Jehoahaz, at Beth-shemesh, and brought him *to* Jerusalem, and brake down the wall of Jerusalem from the gate of Ephraim to [1]the corner gate, four hundred cubits.

24 And *he took* all the gold and the silver, and all the vessels that were found in the house of God with Obed-edom, and the treasures of the king's house, the hostages also, and returned *to* Samaria.

25 ¶ [a]And Amaziah the son of Joash king of Judah lived after the death of Joash son of Jehoahaz king of Israel fifteen years.

26 Now the rest of the acts of Amaziah, first and last, behold, *are* they not written in the book of the kings of Judah and Israel?

27 Now after the time that Amaziah did turn away [1]from following the LORD they [2]made a conspiracy against him in Jerusalem; and he fled to Lachish: but they sent to Lachish after him, and slew him there.

28 And they brought him upon horses, and buried him with his fathers in the city of [1]Judah.

26 Then all the people of Judah took [a][1]Uzziah, who *was* sixteen years old, and made him king in the room of his father Amaziah.

25:10 [1]Heb. *to their place* [2]Heb. *in heat of anger*
25:11 [a]2 Ki. 14:7
25:13 [1]Heb. *the sons of the band*
25:14 [a]See ch. 28:23 [b]Ex. 20:3,5
25:15 [a]Ps. 96:5 [b]ver. 11
25:16 [1]Heb. *counselled* [a]1 Sam. 2:25
25:17 [a]2 Ki. 14:8,9
25:18 [1]Or, *furre bush,* or, *thorn*
25:18 [2]Heb. *a beast of the field*
25:20 [a]1 Ki. 12:15; ch. 22:7 [b]ver. 14
25:22 [1]Heb. *smitten*
25:23 [1]Heb. *the gate of it that looketh* [a]See ch. 21:17; 22:1,6
25:25 [a]2 Ki. 14:17
25:27 [1]Heb. *from after* [2]Heb. *conspired a conspiracy*
25:28 [1]That is, *the city of David,* as it is 2 Ki. 14:20
26:1 [1]Or, *Azariah* [a]2 Ki. 14:21,22; 15:1

25:13 This may be the inciting incident for the later war with the north. *Samaria.* A town by this name in the southern kingdom is not otherwise known. The reference may be a copyist's error.

25:14–25 The Chronicler's account of the war with the north is close to the parallel in 2 Ki 14:8–14, except for some additions in line with his theme of immediate retribution. The Chronicler mentions Amaziah's foolish idolatry and the prophetic speech of judgment, neither of which is found in Kings. He also adds notes in vv. 20,27 to emphasize that the idolatry of Amaziah was being punished.

25:18 Cf. the parable in Judg 9:7–15.

25:23 *gate of Ephraim to the corner gate.* Both gates were located in the northern wall of the city, the Ephraim gate at the northwest and the corner gate at the northeast.

25:24 The family of Obed-edom was the Levitical family into whose care the temple storehouse had been entrusted (1 Chr 26:15).

25:27 See note on vv. 14–25.

26:1–23 See 2 Ki 15:1–7 and notes. The Chronicler has characteristically divided his account of Uzziah's reign into two parts: the good years, then the bad; cf. his treatment of Uzziah's father Amaziah and his grandfather Joash (see notes on 24:2; 25:1–28). The Chronicler elaborates on the blessings and divine help that flowed from Uzziah's obedience and fidelity (vv. 4–15), whereas the author of Kings only alludes to his fidelity (2 Ki 15:3). Where Kings only mentions Uzziah's leprosy (2 Ki 15:5), the Chronicler gives additional details to show that the disease was a result of unfaithfulness (vv. 16–21). Under Uzziah and his contemporary in the north, Jeroboam II, the borders of Israel and Judah briefly reached the extent they had attained under David and Solomon (vv. 6–8; 2 Ki 14:25). In part, this flourishing of the two kingdoms was facilitated by the removal of the Aramean threat by Assyria under Adadnirari III (802 B.C.), following which Assyria herself went into a period of weakness.

26:1 *Uzziah.* Also called Azariah (see, e.g., 2 Ki 15:6–7; 1 Chr 3:12). It is likely that Uzziah was a throne name, while Azariah was his personal name.

2 He built Eloth, and restored it to Judah,
after that the king slept with his fathers.

Uzziah, king of Judah

3 ¶ Sixteen years old *was* Uzziah when he
began to reign, and he reigned fifty and two
years in Jerusalem. His mother's name also
was Jecoliah of Jerusalem.
4 And he did *that* which *was* right in the
sight of the LORD, according to all that his father Amaziah did.
5 And [a]he sought God in the days of
Zechariah, who [b]had understanding [1]in the visions of God: and as long as he sought the
LORD, God made him to prosper.
6 And he went forth and [a]warred against
the Philistines, and brake down the wall of
Gath, and the wall of Jabneh, and the wall of
Ashdod, and built cities [1]about Ashdod, and
among the Philistines.
7 And God helped him against [a]the Philistines, and against the Arabians that dwelt in
Gur-baal, and the Mehunims.
8 And the Ammonites [a]gave gifts to Uzziah: and his name [1]spread abroad even to the
entering in of Egypt: for he strengthened *himself* exceedingly.
9 Moreover Uzziah built towers in Jerusalem at the [a]corner gate, and at the valley gate,
and at the turning *of the wall,* and [1]fortified
them.
10 Also he built towers in the desert, and
[1]digged many wells: for he had much cattle,
both in the low country, and in the plains: husbandmen *also,* and vinedressers in the mountains, and in [2]Carmel: for he loved [3]husbandry.
11 Moreover Uzziah had a host of fighting
men, that went out to war by bands, according
to the number of their account by the hand of
Jeiel the scribe and Maaseiah the ruler, under
the hand of Hananiah, *one* of the king's captains.
12 The whole number of the chief of the
fathers of the mighty *men* of valour *were* two
thousand and six hundred.
13 And under their hand *was* [1]an army,
three hundred thousand and seven thousand
and five hundred, that made war with mighty
power, to help the king against the enemy.
14 And Uzziah prepared for them throughout all the host shields, and spears, and helmets, and habergeons, and bows, and [1]slings
to cast stones.
15 And he made in Jerusalem engines, invented by cunning *men,* to be on the towers
and upon the bulwarks, to shoot arrows and
great stones withal. And his name [1]spread far
abroad; for he was marvellously helped, till he
was strong.
16 ¶ But [a]when he was strong, his heart
was [b]lifted up to *his* destruction: for he transgressed against the LORD his God, and [c]went
into the temple of the LORD to burn incense
upon the altar of incense.
17 And [a]Azariah the priest went in after
him, and with him fourscore priests of the
LORD, *that were* valiant men:
18 And they withstood Uzziah the king,
and said unto him, *It* [a]*pertaineth* not unto
thee, Uzziah, to burn incense unto the LORD,
but to the [b]priests the sons of Aaron, that are
consecrated to burn incense: go out of the
sanctuary; for thou hast trespassed; neither
shall it be for thine honour from the LORD God.
19 Then Uzziah was wroth, and *had* a
censer in his hand to burn incense: and while
he was wroth with the priests, [a]the leprosy
even rose up in his forehead before the priests
in the house of the LORD, from beside the incense altar.
20 And Azariah the chief priest, and all the
priests, looked upon him, and behold, he *was*
leprous in his forehead, and they thrust him
out from thence; yea, himself [a]hasted also to
go out, because the LORD had smitten him.
21 [a]And Uzziah the king was a leper unto
the day of his death, and dwelt *in* a [b][1]several

26:5 [1]Heb. *in the seeing of God* [a]See ch. 24:2 [b]Gen. 41:15; Dan. 1:17; 10:1
26:6 [1]Or, *in the country of Ashdod* [a]Is. 14:29
26:7 [a]ch. 21:16
26:8 [1]Heb. *went* [a]2 Sam. 8:2; ch. 17:11
26:9 [1]Or, *repaired* [a]2 Ki. 14:13; Neh. 3:13,19,32; Zech. 14:10
26:10 [1]Or, *cut out many cisterns* [2]Or, *fruitful fields* [3]Heb. *ground*
26:13 [1]Heb. *the power of an army*
26:14 [1]Heb. *stones of slings*
26:15 [1]Heb. *went forth*
26:16 [a]Deut. 32:15 [b]Deut. 8:14; ch. 25:19 [c]2 Ki. 16:12,13
26:17 [a]1 Chr. 6:10
26:18 [a]Num. 16:40; 18:7 [b]Ex. 30:7,8
26:19 [a]Num. 12:10; 2 Ki. 5:27
26:20 [a]As Esth. 6:12
26:21 [1]Heb. *free* [a]2 Ki. 15:5 [b]Lev. 13:46; Num. 5:2

26:3 *fifty and two years.* 792–740 B.C., including a co-regency with Amaziah from 792 to 767.
26:4 The Chronicler has constructed his account of Uzziah's reign to give it the same outline as that for Amaziah and Joash (see note on vv. 1–23). He has also once again bypassed the statement in the parallel account that the king did not remove the high places (2 Ki 15:4), just as he did in the accounts of the other two kings (see note on 25:2).
26:5 *days of Zechariah.* The author again uses chronological notes to portray the cycles of blessing and judgment associated with the individual king's response to God's commands (see note on 12:2).
26:6–8 Uzziah's conquests were toward the southeast and the southwest; Israel's powerful Jeroboam II was in control to the north of Judah.
‡26:7 *Mehunims* [or "Meunites"]. See note on 20:1.
26:9 *corner gate . . . valley gate.* Found at the northeast and southwest portions of the walls. *fortified.* This construction along the wall of Jerusalem may reflect, in part, repair of the damage done by Joash during the reign of Amaziah (25:23).
‡26:10 *towers . . . wells* [i.e. "cisterns"]. Towers and cisterns have been found in several excavations (Qumran, Gibeah, Beersheba). A seal bearing Uzziah's name has been found in a cistern at Tell Beit Mirsim.
26:11 *Uzziah had a host of fighting men.* Tiglath-pileser III of Assyria states that he was opposed in his advance toward the west (743 B.C.) by a coalition headed by "Azriau of Yaudi," perhaps Azariah (Uzziah) of Judah.
26:15 *engines . . . to shoot arrows and great stones.* Since the catapult was not known in the military technology of the period, and since torsion-operated devices for shooting arrows did not appear for approximately another three centuries, the devices mentioned here may refer to defensive constructions to protect those shooting arrows and hurling stones from the tops of the walls.
26:16 *when he was strong.* See note on v. 5.
26:19 *leprosy.* For disease as a punishment for sin see notes on 16:12; 21:12–15.
‡26:21 *his death.* See Is 6:1 and note. *a several* [i.e. "separate"] *house.* Or "house where he was relieved of responsibilities"; the same phrase in the Canaanite texts from Ugarit suggests a kind of quarantine or separation.

house, *being* a leper; for he was cut off from the house of the LORD: and Jotham his son *was* over the king's house, judging the people of the land.

22 Now the rest of the acts of Uzziah, first and last, did [a]Isaiah the prophet, the son of Amoz, write.

23 [a]So Uzziah slept with his fathers, and they buried him with his fathers in the field of the burial which *belonged* to the kings; for they said, He *is* a leper: and Jotham his son reigned in his stead.

Jotham, king of Judah

27 Jotham [a]*was* twenty and five years old when he *began* to reign, and he reigned sixteen years in Jerusalem. His mother's name also *was* Jerushah, the daughter of Zadok.

2 And he did *that* which *was* right in the sight of the LORD, according to all that his father Uzziah did: howbeit he entered not into the temple of the LORD. And [a]the people did yet corruptly.

3 He built the high gate of the house of the LORD, and on the wall of [1]Ophel he built much.

4 Moreover he built cities in the mountains of Judah, and in the forests he built castles and towers.

5 He fought also with the king of the Ammonites, and prevailed against them. And the children of Ammon gave him the same year an hundred talents of silver, and ten thousand measures of wheat, and ten thousand of barley. [1]So much did the children of Ammon pay unto him, both the second year, and the third.

6 So Jotham became mighty, because he [1]prepared his ways before the LORD his God.

26:22 [a]Is. 1:1
26:23 [a]2 Ki. 15:7; Is. 6:1
27:1 [a]2 Ki. 15:32
27:2 [a]2 Ki. 15:35
27:3 [1]Or, *the tower,* 2 Ki. 5:24
27:5 [1]Heb. *This*
27:6 [1]Or, *established*
27:9 [a]2 Ki. 15:38
28:1 [a]2 Ki. 16:2
28:2 [a]Ex. 34:17; Lev. 19:4 [b]Judg. 2:11
28:3 [1]Or, *offered sacrifice* [a]2 Ki. 23:10 [b]Lev. 18:21; 2 Ki. 16:3; ch. 33:6
28:5 [1]Heb. *Darmesek* [a]Is. 7:1 [b]2 Ki. 16:5,6
28:6 [1]Heb. *sons of valour* [a]2 Ki. 15:27

7 Now the rest of the acts of Jotham, and all his wars, and his ways, lo they *are* written in the book of the kings of Israel and Judah.

8 He was five and twenty years old when he *began* to reign, and reigned sixteen years in Jerusalem.

9 [a]And Jotham slept with his fathers, and they buried him in the city of David: and Ahaz his son reigned in his stead.

Ahaz, king of Judah

28 Ahaz [a]*was* twenty years old when he *began* to reign, and he reigned sixteen years in Jerusalem: but he did not *that* which *was* right in the sight of the LORD, like David his father:

2 For he walked in the ways of the kings of Israel, and made also [a]molten images for [b]Baalim.

3 Moreover he [1]burnt incense in [a]the valley of the son of Hinnom, and burnt [b]his children in the fire after the abominations of the heathen whom the LORD had cast out before the children of Israel.

4 He sacrificed also and burnt incense in the high places, and on the hills, and under every green tree.

5 Wherefore [a]the LORD his God delivered him into the hand of the king of Syria; and they [b]smote him, and carried away a great multitude of them captives, and brought *them to* [1]Damascus. And he was also delivered into the hand of the king of Israel, who smote him *with* a great slaughter.

6 For [a]Pekah the son of Remaliah slew in Judah an hundred and twenty thousand in one day, *which were* all [1]valiant men; because they had forsaken the LORD God of their fathers.

26:22 *did Isaiah . . . write.* Not a reference to the canonical book but to some other work no longer in existence.
26:23 *buried . . . in the field . . . which belonged to the kings.* Cf. 2 Ki 15:7. Apparently due to his leprosy, Uzziah was buried in a cemetery belonging to the kings, though not in the tombs of the kings.
27:1–9 See 2 Ki 15:32–38 and notes.
27:1 *sixteen years.* 750–735 B.C., including a co-regency with Uzziah (750–740). His reign also overlapped that of his successor Ahaz from 735 to 732.
27:2 *entered not into the temple.* The Chronicler commends Jotham for not making the same error Uzziah did (26:16). *did . . . corruptly.* Appears to refer to the flourishing high places (2 Ki 15:35).
27:3–6 Unique to the Chronicler and an elaboration of his thesis that fidelity to God's commands brings blessing: in construction, military victory and prosperity—all "because he prepared his ways before the LORD" (v. 6). Judah's relationship with the Ammonites held particular interest for the Chronicler (see notes on 20:1–30; 24:26).
27:7 *all his wars.* See, e.g., 2 Ki 15:37.
28:1–27 See 2 Ki 16:1–20 and notes, though only the introduction and conclusion in the two accounts are strictly parallel. The reign of Ahaz is the only one for which the Chronicler does not mention a single redeeming feature. In his account the Chronicler appears to adopt explicit parallels from the speech of Abijah condemning the northern kingdom (ch. 13) in order to show that under Ahaz the southern kingdom had sunk to the same depths of apostasy. Judah's religious fidelity, of which Abijah had boasted, was completely overthrown under Ahaz.
28:1 *sixteen years.* 732–715 B.C., not including the co-regency with Jotham (735–732).
28:2 *made also molten images.* Cf. 13:8.
‡28:3 *valley of the son of Hinnom* [or "valley of Ben-hinnom"]. Cf. 33:6. Josiah put an end to the pagan practices observed there (2 Ki 23:10). *burnt his children in the fire.* See Lev 20:1–5; Jer 7:31–32. 2 Ki 16:3 has the singular "son." Some have regarded the plural as a deliberate inflation on the part of the Chronicler to heighten the wickedness of Ahaz. However, some manuscripts of the Septuagint (the Greek translation of the OT) also have a plural in 2 Ki 16:3, suggesting that the Chronicler may have faithfully copied the text before him.
28:5 Cf. 13:16–17. *God delivered him into the hand of.* According to the Chronicler's view on immediate retribution, defeat in war is one of the results of disobedience (see note on 20:30). *also delivered into the hand of the king of Israel.* 2 Ki 16:5–6 and Is 7 make it clear that Rezin (king of Aram) and Pekah acted together against Judah. The Chronicler has chosen either to treat them separately or to report on two different episodes of the Aram-Israel coalition.
28:6 *Pekah.* Reigned over the northern kingdom 752–732 B.C. (see 2 Ki 15:27–31). *had forsaken the LORD.* The same charge Abijah made against the northern kingdom (13:11).

7 And Zichri, a mighty *man* of Ephraim, slew Maaseiah the king's son, and Azrikam the governor of the house, and Elkanah *that was* [1]next to the king.

8 And the children of Israel carried away captive of their [a]brethren two hundred thousand, women, sons, and daughters, and took also away much spoil from them, and brought the spoil to Samaria.

9 But a prophet of the LORD was there, whose name *was* Oded: and he went out before the host that came to Samaria, and said unto them, Behold, [a]because the LORD God of your fathers was wroth with Judah, he hath delivered them into your hand, and ye have slain them in a rage *that* [b]reacheth up unto heaven.

10 And now ye purpose to keep under the children of Judah and Jerusalem for [a]bondmen and bondwomen unto you: but *are there* not *with* you, *even* with you, sins against the LORD your God?

11 Now hear me therefore, and deliver the captives again, which ye have taken captive of your brethren: [a]for the fierce wrath of the LORD *is* upon you.

12 Then certain of the heads of the children of Ephraim, Azariah the son of Johanan, Berechiah the son of Meshillemoth, and Jehizkiah the son of Shallum, and Amasa the son of Hadlai, stood up against them that came from the war,

13 And said unto them, Ye shall not bring in the captives hither: for whereas we have offended against the LORD *already,* ye intend to add *more* to our sins and to our trespass: for our trespass is great, and *there is* fierce wrath against Israel.

14 So the armed men left the captives and the spoil before the princes and all the congregation.

15 And the men [a]which were expressed by name rose up, and took the captives, and with the spoil clothed all *that were* naked among them, and arrayed them, and shod them, and [b]gave them to eat and to drink, and anointed them, and carried all the feeble of them upon asses, and brought them *to* Jericho, [c]the city of palm trees, to their brethren: then they returned *to* Samaria.

16 ¶ [a]At that time did king Ahaz send unto the kings of Assyria to help him.

17 For again the Edomites had come and smitten Judah, and carried away [1]captives.

18 [a]The Philistines also had invaded the cities of the low country, and of the south of Judah, and had taken Beth-shemesh, and Ajalon, and Gederoth, and Shocho with the villages thereof, and Timnah with the villages thereof, Gimzo also and the villages thereof: and they dwelt there.

19 For the LORD brought Judah low because of Ahaz king of [a]Israel; for he [b]made Judah naked, and transgressed sore against the LORD.

20 And [a]Tilgath-pilneser king of Assyria came unto him, and distressed him, but strengthened him not.

21 For Ahaz took away a portion *out* of the house of the LORD, and *out* of the house of the king, and of the princes, and gave *it* unto the king of Assyria: but he helped him not.

22 ¶ And in the time of his distress did he trespass yet more against the LORD: this *is that* king Ahaz.

23 For [a]he sacrificed unto the gods of [1]Damascus, which smote him: and he said, Because the gods of the kings of Syria help them, *therefore* will I sacrifice to them, that [b]they may help me. But they were the ruin of him, and of all Israel.

24 And Ahaz gathered together the vessels of the house of God, and cut in pieces the vessels of the house of God, [a]and shut up the doors of the house of the LORD, and he made him altars in every corner of Jerusalem.

25 And in every several city of Judah he made high places [1]to burn incense unto other gods, and provoked to anger the LORD God of his fathers.

26 [a]Now the rest of his acts and of all his

28:7 [1]Heb. *the second to the king*
28:8 [a]ch. 11:4
28:9 [a]Is. 10:5; 47:6; Ezek. 25:12,15; 26:2; Obad. 10; Zech. 1:15 [b]Ezra 9:6; Rev. 18:5
28:10 [a]Lev. 25:39,42, 43,46
28:11 [a]Jas. 2:13
28:15 [a]ver. 12
28:15 [b]2 Ki. 6:22; Luke 6:27; Rom. 12:20 [c]Deut. 34:3; Judg. 1:16
28:16 [a]2 Ki. 16:7
28:17 [1]Heb. *a captivity*
28:18 [a]Ezek. 16:27,57
28:19 [a]ch. 21:2 [b]Ex. 32:25
28:20 [a]2 Ki. 15:29; 16:7-9
28:23 [1]Heb. *Darmesek* [a]See ch. 25:14 [b]Jer. 44:17,18
28:24 [a]See ch. 29:3,7
28:25 [1]Or, *to offer*
28:26 [a]2 Ki. 16:19,20

28:9–15 The kindness of the northern captors to their captives from Judah, especially as recorded in vv. 14–15, may be the background for Jesus' parable of the Good Samaritan (Luke 10:25–37). Oded's attitude to the north is shown by his willingness to call them "brethren" (v. 11). In this case, too, the record of ch. 13 has been reversed: The northern tribes are more righteous than the south.

28:17–18 *Edomites . . . smitten Judah . . . Philistines also had invaded.* Foreign alliances (v. 16) led to further defeats for Ahaz (see note on 16:2–9).

28:19 *the LORD brought Judah low because of Ahaz.* The same formula used to describe the defeat of the northern tribes in 13:18, though under Ahaz it is Judah that is subdued.

28:20 *Tilgath-pilneser.* A variant of Tiglath-pileser, king of Assyria 745–727 B.C. (see 1 Chr 5:26 and note). *distressed him, but strengthened him not.* Appears on the surface to contradict the statement in 2 Ki 16:9 that Tiglath-pileser III responded to Ahaz's request by attacking and capturing Damascus, exiling its population and killing Rezin. The Chronicler assumes the reader's familiarity with the other account and knows of the temporary respite for Judah gained by Assyrian intervention against Damascus and the northern kingdom of Israel. But he focuses on the long-range results, in which Judah herself was reduced to vassalage to Assyria.

28:22–23 The Chronicler presumes the reader's familiarity with Ahaz's trip to Damascus and his copying of the altar and practices there (2 Ki 16:10–16).

28:24–25 Additional details on Ahaz's alterations are found in 2 Ki 16:17–18. The Chronicler also adds details in his description of Hezekiah's reforming activities to correct some of the abuses under Ahaz: Not only had the doors been shut, but also the lamps were put out and offerings were not made at the sanctuary (29:7); the altar and utensils were desecrated, and the table for the consecrated bread was neglected (29:18–19). It is precisely these accoutrements of proper temple service about which Abijah had boasted when he proclaimed the faithfulness of Judah in contrast to that of the northern kingdom (13:11). Now these orthodox furnishings are lacking under Ahaz and make the southern kingdom just like the north (see note on vv. 1–27).

ways, first and last, behold, they *are* written in the book of the kings of Judah and Israel.

27 And Ahaz slept with his fathers, and they buried him in the city, *even* in Jerusalem: but they brought him not into the sepulchres of the kings of Israel: and Hezekiah his son reigned in his stead.

Hezekiah cleanses the temple

29 Hezekiah [a]*began* to reign *when he was* five and twenty years old, and he reigned nine and twenty years in Jerusalem. And his mother's name *was* Abijah, the daughter [b]of Zechariah.

2 And he did *that* which *was* right in the sight of the LORD, according to all that David his father had done.

3 He in the first year of his reign, in the first month, [a]opened the doors of the house of the LORD, and repaired them.

4 And he brought in the priests and the Levites, and gathered them together into the east street,

5 And said unto them, Hear me, ye Levites, [a]sanctify now yourselves, and sanctify the house of the LORD God of your fathers, and carry forth the filthiness out of the holy *place.*

6 For our fathers have trespassed, and done *that* which *was* evil in the eyes of the LORD our God, and have forsaken him, and have [a]turned away their faces from the habitation of the LORD, and [1]turned *their* backs.

7 [a]Also they have shut up the doors of the porch, and put out the lamps, and have not burnt incense nor offered burnt offerings in the holy *place* unto the God of Israel.

8 Wherefore the [a]wrath of the LORD was upon Judah and Jerusalem, and he hath delivered them to [b][1]trouble, to astonishment, and to [c]hissing, as ye see with your eyes.

9 For lo, [a]our fathers have fallen by the sword, and our sons and our daughters and our wives *are* in captivity for this.

10 Now *it is* in mine heart to make [a]a covenant with the LORD God of Israel, that his fierce wrath may turn away from us.

11 My sons, [1]be not now negligent: for the LORD hath [a]chosen you to stand before him, to serve him, and that *you* should minister unto him, and [2]burn incense.

12 ¶ Then the Levites arose, Mahath the son of Amasai, and Joel the son of Azariah, of the sons of the Kohathites: and of the sons of Merari, Kish the son of Abdi, and Azariah the son of Jehalelel: and of the Gershonites; Joah the son of Zimmah, and Eden the son of Joah:

13 And of the sons of Elizaphan; Shimri, and Jeiel: and of the sons of Asaph; Zechariah, and Mattaniah:

14 And of the sons of Heman; Jehiel, and Shimei: and of the sons of Jeduthun; Shemaiah, and Uzziel.

15 And they gathered their brethren, and [a]sanctified themselves, and came, according to the commandment of the king, [b][1]by the words of the LORD, [c]to cleanse the house of the LORD.

16 And the priests went into the inner part *of* the house of the LORD, to cleanse *it,* and brought out all the uncleanness that they found in the temple of the LORD into the court of the house of the LORD. And the Levites took *it,* to carry *it* out abroad into the brook Kidron.

17 Now they began on the first *day* of the first month to sanctify, and on the eighth day of the month came they to the porch of the LORD: so they sanctified the house of the LORD

29:1 [a]2 Ki. 18:1 [b]ch. 26:5
29:3 [a]ver. 7; See ch. 28:24
29:5 [a]1 Chr. 15:12; ch. 35:6
29:6 [1]Heb. *given the neck* [a]Jer. 2:27; Ezek. 8:16
29:7 [a]ch. 28:24
29:8 [a]ch. 24:18

29:8 [1]Heb. *commotion,* Is. 28:19 [b]Deut. 28:25 [c]1 Ki. 9:8; Jer. 18:16; 19:8; 25:9,18; 29:18
29:9 [a]ch. 28:5,6,8,17
29:10 [a]ch. 15:12
29:11 [1]Or, *be not now deceived* [2]Or, *offer sacrifice* [a]Num. 3:6; 8:14; 18:2,6
29:15 [1]Or, *in the business of the LORD* [a]ver. 5 [b]ch. 30:12 [c]1 Chr. 23:28

28:27 *brought him not into the sepulchres of the kings.* The third king whose wickedness resulted in the loss of this honor at death. The others were Jehoram (21:20) and Joash (24:25). Uzziah's sin and leprosy brought the same result, though it is not reported in exactly the same terms (26:23). Cf. also Manasseh (33:20).

29:1–32:33 The Chronicler devotes more attention to Hezekiah than to any other post-Solomonic king. Although the parallel text (2 Ki 18–20) has about the same amount of material, only about a fourth of the total relates the same or similar material; only a few verses are strict literary parallels (29:1–2; 32:32–33). In Kings preeminence among the post-Solomonic kings is given to Josiah (2 Ki 22–23; cf. 1 Ki 13:2), and the record of Hezekiah is primarily devoted to his confrontation with Sennacherib of Assyria. By contrast, the Chronicler highlights almost exclusively Hezekiah's religious reform and his devotion to matters of ceremony and ritual. The parallel passage (2 Ki 18:1–6) touches the religious reform only briefly. The numerous parallels in these chapters with the account of Solomon's reign suggest that the Chronicler viewed Hezekiah as a "second Solomon" in his celebration of the passover (30:2,5,23,25–26), his cultic arrangements (29:7,18,35; 31:2–3), his wealth (32:27–29), the honor accorded him by the Gentiles (32:23) and the extent of his dominion (30:25).

29:1 *nine and twenty years.* 715–686 B.C. (but see note on Is 36:1), including a 15-year extension of life granted by God (2 Ki 20:6) but not mentioned by the Chronicler.

29:3–30:27 Not found in Kings.

29:3 *first year.* 715 B.C., another example of the Chronicler's practice of introducing chronological materials into his narrative (see note on 12:2). *opened the doors of the house of the LORD.* Necessary after the actions of Ahaz (28:24). *repaired them.* The repairs to the doors included new gold overlay (2 Ki 18:16).

29:5–11 Hezekiah's speech demonstrates again the Chronicler's convictions about the coherence of action and effect: The sins of the past brought difficulty and judgment, but renewed fidelity brings relief.

29:7 Hezekiah reinstitutes these temple arrangements—following the pattern of Solomon (2:4; 4:7).

29:8 *deliverd them to trouble, to astonishment, and to hissing.* Echoes the language of the prophets, especially Jeremiah (see Jer 19:8; 25:9,18; 29:18; 51:37). Reference is to the Assyrian devastation of the northern kingdom and much of Judah.

29:12 *Kohathites . . . sons of Merari . . . Gershonites.* The three clans of Levi (1 Chr 6:1).

29:13 *Elizaphan.* A leader of the Kohathites (Num 3:30), whose family had achieved status almost as a sub-clan (see 1 Chr 15:8 and note on 1 Chr 15:4–10).

29:13–14 *Asaph . . . Heman . . . Jeduthun.* Founders of the three families of Levitical musicians (1 Chr 6:31–48; 25:1–31).

29:16 *carry it out . . . into the brook Kidron.* Asa also burned pagan cult objects there (15:16; cf. 30:14).

in eight days; and in the sixteenth day of the first month they made an end.

18 Then they went in to Hezekiah the king, and said, We have cleansed all the house of the LORD, and the altar of burnt offering, with all the vessels thereof, and the shewbread table, with all the vessels thereof.

19 Moreover all the vessels, which king Ahaz in his reign did [a]cast away in his transgression, have we prepared and sanctified, and behold, they *are* before the altar of the LORD.

20 Then Hezekiah the king rose early, and gathered the rulers of the city, and went up *to* the house of the LORD.

21 And they brought seven bullocks, and seven rams, and seven lambs, and seven he goats, for a [a]sin offering for the kingdom, and for the sanctuary, and for Judah. And he commanded the priests the sons of Aaron to offer *them* on the altar of the LORD.

22 So they killed the bullocks, and the priests received the blood, and [a]sprinkled *it* on the altar: likewise, when they had killed the rams, they sprinkled the blood upon the altar: they killed also the lambs, and they sprinkled the blood upon the altar.

23 And they brought [1]forth the he goats for the sin offering before the king and the congregation; and laid their [a]hands upon them:

24 And the priests killed them, and they made reconciliation with their blood upon the altar, [a]to make an atonement for all Israel: for the king commanded *that* the burnt offering and the sin offering *should be made* for all Israel.

25 [a]And he set the Levites *in* the house of the LORD with cymbals, with psalteries, and with harps, [b]according to the commandment of David, and of [c]Gad the king's seer, and Nathan the prophet: [d]for *so was* the commandment [1]of the LORD [2]by his prophets.

26 And the Levites stood with the instruments [a]of David, and the priests with [b]the trumpets.

27 And Hezekiah commanded to offer the burnt offering upon the altar. And [1]when the burnt offering began, [a]the song of the LORD began *also* with the trumpets, and with [2]the instruments ordained by David king of Israel.

28 And all the congregation worshipped, and the [1]singers sang, and the trumpeters sounded: *and* all *this continued* until the burnt offering was finished.

29 And when *they* had made an end of offering, [a]the king and all that were [1]present with him bowed themselves, and worshipped.

30 Moreover Hezekiah the king and the princes commanded the Levites to *sing* praise unto the LORD with the words of David, and of Asaph the seer. And they *sang* praises with gladness, and they bowed their heads and worshipped.

31 Then Hezekiah answered and said, Now ye have [a][1]consecrated yourselves unto the LORD, come near and bring sacrifices and [b]thank offerings into the house of the LORD. And the congregation brought in sacrifices and thank offerings; and as many as were of a free heart burnt offerings.

32 And the number of the burnt offerings, which the congregation brought, was threescore and ten bullocks, an hundred rams, *and* two hundred lambs: all these *were* for a burnt offering to the LORD.

33 And the consecrated *things were* six hundred oxen and three thousand sheep.

34 But the priests were *too* few, so that they could not flay all the burnt offerings: wherefore [a]their brethren the Levites [1]did help them, till the work was ended, and until the *other* priests had sanctified themselves: [b]for the Levites *were* more [c]upright in heart to sanctify themselves than the priests.

35 And also the burnt offerings *were* in abundance, with [a]the fat of the peace offerings, and [b]the drink offerings for *every* burnt offering. So the service of the house of the LORD was set in order.

36 And Hezekiah rejoiced, and all the people, that God had prepared the people: for the thing was *done* suddenly.

The observance of the passover

30 And Hezekiah sent to all Israel and Judah, and wrote letters also to Ephraim and Manasseh, that *they* should come to the house of the LORD at Jerusalem, to keep the passover unto the LORD God of Israel.

2 For the king had taken counsel, and his princes, and all the congregation in Jerusalem, to keep the passover in the second [a]month.

29:19 [a]ch. 28:24
29:21 [a]Lev. 4:3,14
29:22 [a]Lev. 8:14,15,19,24; Heb. 9:21
29:23 [1]Heb. *near* [a]Lev. 4:15,24
29:24 [a]Lev. 14:20
29:25 [1]Heb. *by the hand of the LORD* [2]Heb. *by the hand of* [a]1 Chr. 16:4; 25:6 [b]1 Chr. 23:5; 25:1; ch. 8:14 [c]2 Sam. 24:11 [d]ch. 30:12
29:26 [a]1 Chr. 23:5; Amos 6:5 [b]Num. 10:8,10; 1 Chr. 15:24; 16:6
29:27 [1]Heb. *in the time* [2]Heb. *hands of instruments* [a]ch. 23:18
29:28 [1]Heb. *song*
29:29 [1]Heb. *found* [a]ch. 20:18
29:31 [1]Or, *filled your hand*, ch. 13:9 [a]ch. 13:9 [b]Lev. 7:12
29:34 [1]Heb. *strengthened them* [a]ch. 35:11 [b]ch. 30:3 [c]Ps. 7:10
29:35 [a]Lev. 3:16 [b]Num. 15:5,7,10
30:2 [a]Num. 9:10,11

29:18 These actions under Hezekiah mirror those of Solomon (2:4).
29:21 *sin offering.* See Lev 4:1–5:13.
29:22 *sprinkled the blood.* See Lev 17:6; Num 18:17.
29:23 *laid their hands upon them.* See Lev 4:13–15; 8:14–15; Num 8:12.
29:25 *David, and of Gad . . . and Nathan . . . his prophets.* The Chronicler considers David among the prophets (see notes on 1:7; 1 Chr 28:19).
29:26 *instruments of David.* See 1 Chr 23:5.
29:35 *burnt offerings were in abundance . . . peace offerings . . . drink offerings.* Reminiscent of the dedication of the temple under Solomon (7:4–6). For the laws regarding the peace offerings see Lev 3; 7:11–21; for the drink offerings see Num 15:1–12. *service of the house of the LORD was set in order.* Similar to the formula used in 8:16 with reference to Solomon's work.
30:1–27 Unique to the Chronicler; cf. the famous passover under Josiah (35:1–19; 2 Ki 23:21–23). Hezekiah allowed two deviations from the law (Ex 12; Deut 16:1–8) in this observance: (1) the date in the second month (v. 2) and (2) exemption from some ritual requirements (vv. 18–19).
30:1 *all Israel and Judah.* See Introduction to 1 Chronicles: Purpose and Themes. With the northern kingdom now ended as the result of the Assyrian invasion and deportation (which surprisingly is not mentioned), the Chronicler shows "all Israel" once again united around the Davidic king and the temple (see vv. 5,18–19,25).
30:2 *second month.* After the division of the kingdom, Jeroboam deferred the sacral calendar of the northern kingdom by

3 For they could not keep it [a]at that time, [b]because the priests had not sanctified themselves sufficiently, neither had the people gathered themselves together to Jerusalem.

4 And the thing [1]pleased the king and all the congregation.

5 So they established a decree to make proclamation throughout all Israel, from Beer-sheba even to Dan, that *they* should come to keep the passover unto the LORD God of Israel at Jerusalem: for they had not done *it* of a long *time in such sort* as it was written.

6 So the posts went with the letters [1]from the king and his princes throughout all Israel and Judah, and according to the commandment of the king, saying, Ye children of Israel, [a]turn again unto the LORD God of Abraham, Isaac, and Israel, and he will return to the remnant of you, that are escaped out of the hand of [b]the kings of Assyria.

7 And be not ye [a]like your fathers, and like your brethren, which trespassed against the LORD God of their fathers, *who* therefore [b]gave them up to desolation, as ye see.

8 Now [1]be ye not [a]stiffnecked, as your fathers *were, but* [b2]yield yourselves unto the LORD, and enter into his sanctuary, which he hath sanctified for ever: and serve the LORD your God, [c]that the fierceness of his wrath may turn away from you.

9 For if ye turn again unto the LORD, your brethren and your children *shall find* [a]compassion before them that lead them captive, so that *they shall* come again into this land: for the LORD your God *is* [b]gracious and merciful, and will not turn away *his* face from you, if ye [c]return unto him.

10 So the posts passed from city to city through the country of Ephraim and Manasseh even unto Zebulun: but [a]they laughed them to scorn, and mocked them.

11 Nevertheless [a]divers of Asher and Manasseh and of Zebulun humbled themselves, and came to Jerusalem.

12 Also in Judah [a]the hand of God was to give them one heart to do the commandment of the king and of the princes, [b]by the word of the LORD.

13 ¶ And there assembled *at* Jerusalem much people to keep the feast of unleavened bread in the second month, a very great congregation.

14 And they arose and took away the [a]altars that *were* in Jerusalem, and all the altars for incense took they away, and cast *them* into the brook Kidron.

15 Then they killed the passover on the fourteenth *day* of the second month: and the priests and the Levites were [a]ashamed, and sanctified themselves, and brought in the burnt offerings *into* the house of the LORD.

16 And they stood in [1]their place after their manner, according to the law of Moses the man of God: the priests sprinkled the blood, *which they received* of the hand of the Levites.

17 For *there were* many in the congregation that were not sanctified: [a]therefore the Levites had the charge of the killing of the passovers for every one *that was* not clean, to sanctify *them* unto the LORD.

18 For a multitude of the people, *even* [a]many of Ephraim, and Manasseh, Issachar, and Zebulun, had not cleansed themselves, [b]yet did they eat the passover otherwise than it was written. But Hezekiah prayed for them, saying, The good LORD pardon every one

19 *That* [a]prepareth his heart to seek God, the LORD God of his fathers, though *he be* not *cleansed* according to the purification of the sanctuary.

20 And the LORD hearkened to Hezekiah, and healed the people.

21 And the children of Israel that were

30:3 [a]Ex. 12:6,18 [b]ch. 29:34
30:4 [1]Heb. *was right in the eyes of the king*
30:6 [1]Heb. *from the hand* [a]Jer. 4:1; Joel 2:13 [b]2 Ki. 15:19
30:7 [a]Ezek. 20:18 [b]ch. 29:8
30:8 [1]Heb. *harden not your necks* [2]Heb. *give the hand* [a]Deut. 10:16 [b]1 Chr. 29:24; Ezra 10:19 [c]ch. 29:10
30:9 [a]Ps. 106:46 [b]Ex. 34:6 [c]Is. 55:7
30:10 [a]ch. 36:16
30:11 [a]ver. 18,21; ch. 11:16
30:12 [a]Phil. 2:13 [b]ch. 29:25
30:14 [a]ch. 28:24
30:15 [a]ch. 29:34
30:16 [1]Heb. *their standing*
30:17 [a]ch. 29:34
30:18 [a]ver. 1,11 [b]Ex. 12:43
30:19 [a]ch. 19:3

one month (1 Ki 12:32), possibly to further wean the subjects in the north away from devotion to Jerusalem. By delaying the celebration of passover one month, Hezekiah not only allows time for the priests to consecrate themselves (v. 3) and for the people to gather (vv. 3,13), but also achieves unity between the kingdoms on the date of the passover for the first time since the schism more than two centuries earlier. Delaying the date reflects Hezekiah's concern to involve "all Israel." For the first time since Solomon the entire nation observes passover together, reflecting the Chronicler's view that Hezekiah is a "second Solomon." passover was prescribed for the 14th day of the first month (Ex 12:2,6; Deut 16:1–8), but could not be celebrated at that time due to the defilement of the temple and the purification rites under way (29:3,17). For celebration of passover by the restored community shortly after the dedication of the rebuilt temple see Ezra 6:16–22.

‡30:5 *of a long time.* Lit. "for great." Probably referring to "great numbers." Another comparison with the time of Solomon (see v. 26). At the time of its inception, passover was primarily a family observance (Ex 12). It later became a national celebration at the temple (v. 8; see Deut 16:1–8).

30:8 *enter into his sanctuary.* passover was one of three annual pilgrim feasts requiring attendance at the temple (see Num 28:9–29:39).

30:9 *find compassion before them that lead them captive.* In Solomon's prayer in 6:39 the Chronicler omitted the phrase found in the parallel account (1 Ki 8:50) that their conquerors would "have compassion on them." Here the phrase is found in the speech of Hezekiah, again portraying him as a kind of "second Solomon" (see Lev 26:40–42). *shall come again into this land.* Those who repent will have hope of return, even those from the Assyrian captivity.

30:14 *cast them into the brook Kidron.* See 29:16 and note.

30:15 *the priests and the Levites . . . sanctified themselves.* The reproach previously directed against the priests (v. 3; 29:34) is here broadened to include also the Levites—an exhortation to the priests and Levites of the restored community to be faithful.

30:17 *Levites had the charge of the killing of the passovers.* See Ex 12:6; Deut 16:6. According to the law the heads of families were to slay the passover sacrifice. The Levites perhaps acted for the recent arrivals from the northern kingdom who were not ceremonially clean. Cf. John 11:55.

30:18–19 Faith and obedience take precedence over ritual (see Mark 7:1–23; John 7:22–23; 9:14–16).

30:20 The response to Hezekiah's prayer recalls the prayer of Solomon (7:14).

[1]present at Jerusalem kept [a]the feast of unleavened bread seven days with great gladness: and the Levites and the priests praised the LORD day by day, *singing* with [2]loud instruments unto the LORD.

22 And Hezekiah spake [a1]comfortably unto all the Levites [b]that taught the good knowledge of the LORD: and they did eat throughout the feast seven days, offering peace offerings, and [c]making confession to the LORD God of their fathers.

23 And the whole assembly took counsel to keep [a]other seven days: and they kept *other* seven days *with* gladness.

24 For Hezekiah king of Judah [a1]did give to the congregation a thousand bullocks and seven thousand sheep; and the princes [1]gave to the congregation a thousand bullocks and ten thousand sheep: and a great number of priests [b]sanctified themselves.

25 And all the congregation of Judah, with the priests and the Levites, and all the congregation [a]that came out of Israel, and the strangers that came out of the land of Israel, and that dwelt in Judah, rejoiced.

26 So there was great joy in Jerusalem: for since the time of Solomon the son of David king of Israel *there was* not the like in Jerusalem.

27 Then the priests the Levites arose and [a]blessed the people: and their voice was heard, and their prayer came *up* to [b1]his holy dwelling place, *even* unto heaven.

Hezekiah's reforms

31 Now when all this was finished, all Israel that were [1]present went out to the cities of Judah, and [a]brake the [b2]images *in pieces,* and cut down the groves, and threw down the high places and the altars out of all Judah and Benjamin, in Ephraim also and Manasseh, [3]until *they* had utterly destroyed *them all.* Then all the children of Israel returned, every man to his possession, into their own cities.

2 And Hezekiah appointed [a]the courses of the priests and the Levites after their courses, every man according to his service, the priests and Levites [b]for burnt offerings and for peace offerings, to minister, and to give thanks, and to praise in the gates of the tents of the LORD.

3 *He appointed* also the king's portion of his substance for the burnt offerings, *to wit,* for the morning and evening burnt offerings, and the burnt offerings for the sabbaths, and for the new moons, and for the set feasts, as it is written in [a]the law of the LORD.

4 Moreover he commanded the people that dwelt in Jerusalem to give the [a]portion of the priests and the Levites, that they might be encouraged in [b]the law of the LORD.

5 And as soon as the commandment [1]came abroad, the children of Israel brought in abundance [a]the firstfruits of corn, wine, and oil, and [2]honey, and of all the increase of the field; and the tithe of all *things* brought they in abundantly.

6 And *concerning* the children of Israel and Judah, that dwelt in the cities of Judah, they also brought in the tithe of oxen and sheep, and the [a]tithe of holy *things* which were consecrated unto the LORD their God, and laid *them* [1]by heaps.

7 In the third month they began to lay the foundation of the heaps, and finished *them* in the seventh month.

8 And when Hezekiah and the princes came and saw the heaps, they blessed the LORD, and his people Israel.

9 Then Hezekiah questioned with the priests and the Levites concerning the heaps.

10 And Azariah the chief priest of the house of Zadok answered him, and said, [a]Since *the people* began to bring the offerings *into* the house of the LORD, *we* have had enough to eat, and have left plenty: for the LORD hath blessed his people; and that which is left *is* this great store.

11 Then Hezekiah commanded to prepare [1]chambers in the house of the LORD; and they prepared *them,*

12 And brought in the offerings and the

30:21 [1]Heb. *found* [2]Heb. *instruments of strength* [a]Ex. 12:15; 13:6
30:22 [1]Heb. *to the heart of all, etc.* [a]Is. 40:2 [b]Deut. 33:10; ch. 17:9; 35:3 [c]Ezra 10:11
30:23 [a]See 1 Ki. 8:65
30:24 [1]Heb. *lifted up,* or, *offered* [a]ch. 35:7,8 [b]ch. 29:34
30:25 [a]ver. 11,18
30:27 [1]Heb. *the habitation of his holiness* [a]Num. 6:23 [b]Ps. 68:5
31:1 [1]Heb. *found* [2]Heb. *statues* [3]Heb. *until to make an end* [a]2 Ki. 18:4 [b]ch. 30:14
31:2 [a]1 Chr. 23:6; 24:1
31:2 [b]1 Chr. 23:30,31
31:3 [a]Num. 28; 29
31:4 [a]Num. 18:8; Neh. 13:10 [b]Mal. 2:7
31:5 [1]Heb. *brake forth* [2]Or, *dates* [a]Ex. 22:29; Neh. 13:12
31:6 [1]Heb. *heaps, heaps* [a]Lev. 27:30; Deut. 14:28
31:10 [a]Mal. 3:10
31:11 [1]Or, *storehouses*

30:23 *other seven days.* The festival was observed for two weeks, just as the observance of the dedication of Solomon's temple had been (7:8–9).

30:26 *since the time of Solomon.* An explicit indication of the Chronicler's modeling of the reign of Hezekiah after that of Solomon (see note on 29:1–32:33).

30:27 *prayer came up to his holy dwelling place, even unto heaven.* Another echo of Solomon's dedication prayer (6:21,30, 33,39).

31:1–21 Apart from the first verse, which parallels 2 Ki 18:4, the material of this chapter is unique to the Chronicler, whose interest in the Levites and the temple predominates. Hezekiah's efforts to ensure the material support of the Levites (v. 4) probably had relevance to the postexilic audience for whom the Chronicler wrote.

‡31:1 *all Israel . . . all the children of Israel.* The Chronicler's interest in "all Israel" as united under Hezekiah is again apparent. *images.* See note on 1 Ki 14:23. *groves.* Hebrew *Asherim.* See note on 14:3.

31:2 Echoes 8:14. The Chronicler continues to model Hezekiah as a "second Solomon" (see notes on 29:7,18).

31:3 *appointed also the king's portion.* The king's giving from his own wealth prompted a generous response from the people, as it had also under David (1 Chr 29:3–9).

31:5–6 See Deut 12:5–19; 14:22–27. The grain ("corn"), new wine and oil had to be brought to the temple (Deut 12:17). Those coming from a distance, however, could bring the value of their offerings and purchase them on arrival (Deut 14:24). Only those who actually lived in Judah brought the tithe of their herds and flocks, a difficult procedure for those who lived farther away. For the restored community's commitment to bring their firstfruits, tithes and offerings see Neh 10:35–39. For their failure to do so see Neh 13:10–13; Mal 3:8–10.

31:7 *third month.* May-June, the time of the feast of weeks and the corn harvest. *seventh month.* September-October, the time of the feast of tabernacles and the fruit and vine harvest (see Ex 23:16).

tithes and the dedicate *things* faithfully: [a]over which Cononiah the Levite *was* ruler, and Shimei his brother *was* the next.

13 And Jehiel, and Azaziah, and Nahath, and Asahel, and Jerimoth, and Jozabad, and Eliel, and Ismachiah, and Mahath, and Benaiah, *were* overseers [1]under the hand of Cononiah and Shimei his brother, at the commandment of Hezekiah the king, and Azariah the ruler of the house of God.

14 And Kore the son of Imnah the Levite, the porter toward the east, *was* over the freewill offerings of God, to distribute the oblations of the LORD, and the most holy *things.*

15 And [1]next him *were* Eden, and Miniamin, and Jeshua, and Shemaiah, Amariah, and Shecaniah, in [a]the cities of the priests, in *their* [2]set office, to give to their brethren by courses, as well *to* the great as *to* the small:

16 Beside their genealogy of males, from three years old and upward, *even* unto every one that entereth into the house of the LORD, *his* daily portion for their service in their charges according to their courses;

17 Both *to* the genealogy of the priests by the house of their fathers, and the Levites [a]from twenty years old and upward, in their charges by their courses;

18 And to the genealogy of all their little ones, their wives, and their sons, and their daughters, through all the congregation: for in their [1]set office they sanctified themselves *in* holiness:

19 Also of the sons of Aaron the priests, *which were* in [a]the fields of the suburbs of their cities, in every several city, the men that were [b]expressed by name, to give portions to all the males among the priests, and to all that were reckoned by genealogies among the Levites.

20 And thus did Hezekiah throughout all Judah, and [a]wrought *that* which *was* good and right and truth before the LORD his God.

21 And in every work that he began in the service of the house of God, and in the law, and in the commandments, to seek his God, he did *it* with all his heart, and prospered.

The defeat of Sennacherib

32 After [a]these things, and the establishment *thereof,* Sennacherib king of Assyria came, and entered into Judah, and encamped against the fenced cities, and thought [1]to win them for himself.

2 And when Hezekiah saw that Sennacherib was come, and that [1]he was purposed to fight against Jerusalem,

3 He took counsel with his princes and his mighty *men* to stop the waters of the fountains which *were* without the city: and they did help him.

4 So there was gathered much people together, who stopt all the fountains, and the brook that [1]ran through the midst of the land, saying, Why should the kings of Assyria come, and find much water?

5 Also [a]he strengthened himself, [b]and built up all the wall that was broken, and raised *it* up to the towers, and another wall without, and repaired [c]Millo *in* the city of David, and made [1]darts and shields in abundance.

6 And he set captains of war over the people, and gathered them together to him in the street of the gate of the city, and [a][1]spake comfortably to them, saying,

7 [a]Be strong and courageous, [b]be not afraid nor dismayed for the king of Assyria, nor for all the multitude that *is* with him: for [c]*there be* moe with us than with him:

8 With him *is* an [a]arm of flesh; but [b]with us *is* the LORD our God to help us, and to fight our battles. And the people [1]rested themselves upon the words of Hezekiah king of Judah.

9 ¶ [a]After this did Sennacherib king of Assyria send his servants to Jerusalem, (but he *himself laid siege* against Lachish, and all his [1]power with him,) unto Hezekiah king of Judah, and unto all Judah that *were* at Jerusalem, saying,

10 [a]Thus saith Sennacherib king of Assyria, Whereon do ye trust, that ye abide [1]in the siege in Jerusalem?

11 Doth not Hezekiah persuade you to give over yourselves to die by famine and by thirst, saying, [a]The LORD our God shall deliver us out of the hand of the king of Assyria?

12 [a]Hath not the same Hezekiah taken away his high places and his altars, and commanded Judah and Jerusalem, saying, Ye shall worship before one altar, and burn incense upon it?

31:12 [a]Neh. 13:13
31:13 [1]Heb. *at the hand*
31:15 [1]Heb. *at his hand* [2]Or, *trust* [a]Josh. 21:9
31:17 [a]1 Chr. 23:24,27
31:18 [1]Or, *trust*
31:19 [a]Lev. 25:34; Num. 35:2 [b]ver. 12-15
31:20 [a]2 Ki. 20:3
32:1 [a]2 Ki. 18:13; Is. 36:1
32:1 [1]Heb. *to break them up*
32:2 [1]Heb. *his face* was *to war*
32:4 [1]Heb. *overflowed*
32:5 [1]Or, *swords,* or, *weapons* [a]Is. 22:9,10 [b]ch. 25:23 [c]2 Sam. 5:9; 1 Ki. 9:24
32:6 [1]Heb. *he spake to their heart* [a]ch. 30:22; Is. 40:2
32:7 [a]Deut. 31:6 [b]ch. 20:15 [c]2 Ki. 6:16
32:8 [1]Heb. *leaned* [a]Jer. 17:5; 1 John 4:4 [b]ch. 13:12; Rom. 8:31
32:9 [1]Heb. *dominion* [a]2 Ki. 18:17
32:10 [1]Or, *in the strong hold* [a]2 Ki. 18:19
32:11 [a]2 Ki. 18:30
32:12 [a]2 Ki. 18:22

31:16 *three years.* Though all ancient manuscripts read "three years," that is probably a copyist's mistake for "30 years," the age at which duties were assigned in the temple (1 Chr 23:3).
31:20–21 Another brief indication of the Chronicler's emphasis on immediate retribution: Not only does disobedience bring immediate chastening, but obedience and seeking God bring prosperity.
32:1–23 The record of Sennacherib's invasion is much more detailed in 2 Kings and Isaiah (see note on 29:1–32:33).
32:1 The Chronicler omits the date of the invasion (701 B.C., Hezekiah's 14th year; see 2 Ki 18:13; Is 36:1).
32:2–8 Unique to the Chronicler, but normal preparations for invasion.
32:3–4 See v. 30.
32:9 The Chronicler bypasses 2 Ki 18:14–16, which records Hezekiah's suit for peace with its accompanying bribe stripped from the temple treasures. These acts were apparently out of accord with the Chronicler's portrait of Hezekiah. He also omits 2 Ki 18:17b–18.
32:10 The Chronicler omits 2 Ki 18:20–21 (and Is 36:5–6), containing a portion of the Assyrian commander's speech ridiculing Hezekiah and the citizens of Jerusalem for trusting in Egypt and Pharaoh. This, too, may be theologically motivated, in light of the Chronicler's attitude toward foreign alliances (see note on 16:2–9). The same concern with foreign alliances is also likely the reason for the omission of the material in 2 Ki 18:23–27 (and Is 36:8–12), where mention is again made of the hope of Egyptian intervention (see 2 Ki 19:9 for the incursion of Tirhakah).

13 Know ye not what I and my fathers have done unto all the people of *other* lands? [a]were the gods of the nations of *those* lands any ways able to deliver their lands out of mine hand?

14 Who *was there* among all the gods of those nations that my fathers utterly destroyed, that could deliver his people out of mine hand, that your God should be able to deliver you out of mine hand?

15 Now therefore [a]let not Hezekiah deceive you, nor persuade you on this *manner,* neither yet believe him: for no god of any nation or kingdom was able to deliver his people out of mine hand, and out of the hand of my fathers: how much less shall your God deliver you out of mine hand?

16 And his servants spake yet *more* against the LORD God, and against his servant Hezekiah.

17 [a]He wrote also letters to rail on the LORD God of Israel, and to speak against him, saying, [b]As the gods of the nations of *other* lands have not delivered their people out of mine hand, so shall not the God of Hezekiah deliver his people out of mine hand.

18 [a]Then they cried with a loud voice in the Jews' speech unto the people of Jerusalem that *were* on the wall, to affright them, and to trouble them; that they might take the city.

19 And they spake against the God of Jerusalem, as against the gods of the people of the earth, *which were* [a]the work of the hands of man.

20 [a]And for this *cause* Hezekiah the king, and [b]the prophet Isaiah the son of Amoz, prayed and cried *to* heaven.

21 [a]And the LORD sent an angel, which cut off all the mighty *men* of valour, and the leaders and captains in the camp of the king of Assyria. So he returned with shame of face to his own land. And when he was come *into* the house of his god, they that came forth of his own bowels [1]slew him there with the sword.

22 Thus the LORD saved Hezekiah and the inhabitants of Jerusalem from the hand of Sennacherib the king of Assyria, and from the hand of all *other,* and guided them on every side.

23 And many brought gifts unto the LORD to Jerusalem, and [a][1]presents to Hezekiah king of Judah: so that he was [b]magnified in the sight of all nations from thenceforth.

Hezekiah's sickness and death

24 ¶ [a]In those days Hezekiah was sick to the death, and prayed unto the LORD: and he spake unto him, and he [1]gave him a sign.

25 But Hezekiah [a]rendered not again according to the benefit *done* unto him; for [b]his heart was lifted up: [c]therefore there was wrath upon him, and upon Judah and Jerusalem.

26 [a]Notwithstanding Hezekiah humbled himself for [1]the pride of his heart, *both* he and the inhabitants of Jerusalem, so that the wrath of the LORD came not upon them [b]in the days of Hezekiah.

27 And Hezekiah had exceeding much riches and honour: and he made himself treasuries for silver, and for gold, and for precious stones, and for spices, and for shields, and for all *manner of* [1]pleasant jewels;

28 Storehouses also for the increase of corn, and wine, and oil; and stalls for all *manner of* beasts, and cotes for flocks.

29 Moreover he provided him cities, and possessions of flocks and herds in abundance: for [a]God had given him substance very much.

30 [a]This same Hezekiah also stopped the upper watercourse of Gihon, and brought it straight down to the west *side* of the city of David. And Hezekiah prospered in all his works.

31 Howbeit in *the business of* the [1]ambassadors of the princes of Babylon, who [a]sent unto him to inquire of the wonder that was *done* in the land, God left him, to [b]try him, that *he* might know all *that was* in his heart.

32 Now the rest of the acts of Hezekiah, and his [1]goodness, behold, they *are* written in [a]the vision of Isaiah the prophet, the son of Amoz, *and* in the [b]book of the kings of Judah and Israel.

33 [a]And Hezekiah slept with his fathers, and they buried him in the [1]chiefest of the sepulchres of the sons of David: and all Judah and the inhabitants of Jerusalem did him [b]honour at his death. And Manasseh his son reigned in his stead.

32:13 [a]2 Ki. 18:33-35
32:15 [a]2 Ki. 18:29
32:17 [a]2 Ki. 19:9 [b]2 Ki. 19:12
32:18 [a]2 Ki. 18:28
32:19 [a]2 Ki. 19:18
32:20 [a]2 Ki. 19:15 [b]2 Ki. 19:2,4
32:21 [1]Heb. *made him fall* [a]2 Ki. 19:35

32:23 [1]Heb. *precious things* [a]ch. 17:5 [b]ch. 1:1
32:24 [1]Or, *wrought a miracle for him* [a]2 Ki. 20:1; Is. 38:1
32:25 [a]Ps. 116:12 [b]ch. 26:16; Hab. 2:4 [c]ch. 24:18
32:26 [1]Heb. *the lifting up* [a]Jer. 26:18 [b]2 Ki. 20:19
32:27 [1]Heb. *instruments of desire*
32:29 [a]1 Chr. 29:12
32:30 [a]Is. 22:9,11
32:31 [1]Heb. *interpreters* [a]2 Ki. 20:12; Is. 39:1 [b]Deut. 8:2
32:32 [1]Heb. *kindnesses* [a]Is. 36; 37; 38; 39 [b]2 Ki. 18; 19; 20
32:33 [1]Or, *highest* [a]2 Ki. 20:21 [b]Prov. 10:7

32:16 *spake yet more.* The Chronicler appears to assume his reader's familiarity with the longer account of the Assyrian taunts found in Kings and Isaiah.

32:18 *cried with a loud voice in the Jews' speech.* Assumes knowledge of the fuller story (2 Ki 18:26–28; Is 36:11–13).

32:20 This brief reference to the prayers of Hezekiah and Isaiah abridges the much longer narrative in 2 Ki 19:1–34 (and Is 37:1–35).

32:21 See 2 Ki 19:35–37; Is 37:36–38. The Chronicler and the parallel accounts telescope events somewhat: Sennacherib's invasion of Judah was in 701 B.C., while his death at the hand of his sons was in 681.

32:23 *magnified in the sight of all nations.* Another effort to compare Hezekiah with Solomon (see 9:23–24).

32:24 The Chronicler again abridges the narrative in 2 Ki 20:1–11 (and Is 38:1–8), assuming the reader's familiarity with the role of Isaiah and the miraculous sign of the shadow reversing ten steps.

32:25–30 Not found in the parallel texts.

32:25–26 *heart was lifted up . . . pride.* The Chronicler does not specify the nature of Hezekiah's pride (however, see v. 31; 2 Ki 20:12–13; Is 39:1–2). Even for a "second Solomon" like Hezekiah, disobedience brings anger from the Lord.

32:27–29 The Chronicler likens Hezekiah to Solomon also by recounting his wealth (9:13–14).

32:30 See vv. 2–4; 2 Ki 20:20.

32:31 See v. 25. The Chronicler assumes the reader's knowledge of the fuller account in 2 Ki 20:12–19 (and Is 39:1–8). The envoys from Babylon were apparently interested in joint efforts against the Assyrians, hoping to open two fronts against them simultaneously.

Manasseh, king of Judah

33 Manasseh [a]*was* twelve years old
when he *began* to reign, and he
reigned fifty and five years in Jerusalem:
2 But did *that* which *was* evil in the sight of
the LORD, like unto the [a]abominations of the
heathen, whom the LORD had cast out before
the children of Israel.
3 For [1]he built again the high places which
Hezekiah his father had [a]broken down, and he
reared up altars for Baalim, and [b]made groves,
and worshipped [c]all the host of heaven, and
served them.
4 Also he built altars in the house of the
LORD, whereof the LORD had said, [a]In Jerusalem shall my name be for ever.
5 And he built altars for all the host of
heaven [a]in the two courts of the house of the
LORD.
6 [a]And he caused his children to pass
through the fire in the valley of the son of
Hinnom: also he observed times, and used enchantments, and used witchcraft, and [b]dealt
with a familiar spirit, and with wizards: he
wrought much evil in the sight of the LORD, to
provoke him to anger.
7 And [a]he set a carved image, the idol
which he had made, in the house of God, of
which God had said to David and to Solomon
his son, In this house, and in Jerusalem, which
I have chosen before all the tribes of Israel,
will I put my name for ever:
8 [a]Neither will I any more remove the foot
of Israel from out of the land which I have appointed for your fathers; so that they will take
heed to do all that I have commanded them,
according to the whole law and the statutes
and the ordinances by the hand of Moses.
9 So Manasseh made Judah and the inhabitants of Jerusalem to err, *and* to do worse than
the heathen, whom the LORD had destroyed
before the children of Israel.
10 ¶ And the LORD spake to Manasseh, and
to his people: but they would not hearken.
11 [a]Wherefore the LORD brought upon
them the captains of the host [1]of the king of
Assyria, which took Manasseh among the
thorns, and [b]bound him with [2]fetters, and carried him to Babylon.
12 And when he was in affliction, he besought the LORD his God, and [a]humbled himself greatly before the God of his fathers,
13 And prayed unto him: and he was [a]intreated of him, and heard his supplication, and
brought him again *to* Jerusalem into his kingdom. Then Manasseh [b]knew that the LORD he
was God.
14 Now after this he built a wall without
the city of David, on the west *side* of [a]Gihon,
in the valley, even to the entering in at the fish
gate, and compassed [b]about [1]Ophel, and
raised it up a very great height, and put captains of war in all the fenced cities of Judah.
15 And he took away [a]the strange gods,
and the idol out of the house of the LORD, and
all the altars that he had built in the mount of
the house of the LORD, and in Jerusalem, and
cast *them* out of the city.
16 And he repaired the altar of the LORD,
and sacrificed thereon peace offerings and
[a]thank offerings, and commanded Judah to
serve the LORD God of Israel.
17 [a]Nevertheless the people did sacrifice
still in the high places, *yet* unto the LORD their
God only.
18 Now the rest of the acts of Manasseh,
and his prayer unto his God, and the words of
[a]the seers that spake to him in the name of the

33:1 [a]2 Ki. 21:1
33:2 [a]Deut. 18:9; 2 Chr. 28:3
33:3 [1]Heb. *he returned and built* [a]2 Ki. 18:4; ch. 30:14; 31:1 [b]Deut. 16:21 [c]Deut. 17:3
33:4 [a]Deut. 12:11; 1 Ki. 8:29; 9:3; ch. 6:6; 7:16
33:5 [a]ch. 4:9
33:6 [a]Lev. 18:21; Deut. 18:10; 2 Ki. 23:10; ch. 28:3; Ezek. 23:37,39 [b]2 Ki. 21:6
33:7 [a]2 Ki. 21:7
33:8 [a]2 Sam. 7:10
33:11 [1]Heb. *which* were *the king's* [2]Or, *chains* [a]Deut. 28:36 [b]Job 36:8; Ps. 107:10,11
33:12 [a]1 Pet. 5:6
33:13 [a]1 Chr. 5:20; Ezra 8:23 [b]Ps. 9:16; Dan. 4:25
33:14 [1]Or, *the tower* [a]1 Ki. 1:33 [b]ch. 27:3
33:15 [a]ver. 3,5,7
33:16 [a]Lev. 7:12
33:17 [a]ch. 32:12
33:18 [a]1 Sam. 9:9

33:1–20 See 2 Ki 21:1–18 and notes. Manasseh had the longest reign of any of the kings of Judah, a total of 55 years (v. 1). The emphasis in the two accounts differs: While both histories report at length the evil done in Manasseh's reign, only the Chronicler mentions his journey to Babylon and his repentance and restoration to rule. For the writer of Kings, the picture is only a bad one in which Manasseh could be considered almost single-handedly the cause of the exile (2 Ki 21:10–15; 23:26). Some scholars regard the record of Manasseh's repentance in Chronicles as motivated by the author's emphasis on immediate retribution: Length of reign is viewed as a blessing for obedience, so that the Chronicler deliberately records some good in Manasseh as a ground for his long reign. However, it must be noted that length of reign is not elsewhere used by the Chronicler as an indication of divine blessing. The usual indicators for such blessing in his account are peace and prosperity, building projects, success in warfare and large families.
33:1 *fifty and five years.* 697–642 B.C.
‡33:3 *groves.* Hebrew *Asheroth.* See note on 14:3.
33:6 *caused his children to pass through the fire.* See 28:3–4.
33:10 See note on vv. 1–20. The Chronicler abridges what the Lord said to Manasseh and the people through the prophets; the fuller record is found in 2 Ki 21:10–15.
33:11–17 Unique to the Chronicler, showing his stress on immediate retribution: Manasseh's evil brings invasion and defeat, while his repentance brings restoration to rule.
33:11 *carried him to Babylon.* In extant non-Biblical records there is no reference as yet to Manasseh being taken to Babylon by an Assyrian king. Esarhaddon (681–669 B.C.) lists him among 22 kings required to forward materials for his building projects, and Ashurbanipal (669–627) names him as one of a number of vassals supporting his campaign against Egypt. The fact that an Assyrian king would have him taken to Babylon suggests that this incident may have taken place during the rebellion of Shamash-shum-ukin against his brother and overlord Ashurbanipal. This rebellion lasted from 652 to 648, and Manasseh may have joined or at least have been suspected of assisting in the Babylonian defection from Assyria. Manasseh may have been found innocent, or he may have been pardoned on the basis of a renewed pledge of loyalty. Egypt had also bolted from the Assyrian yoke under the new 26th dynasty, and the return of Manasseh to rule may reflect the Assyrian need of a vassal near the border of Egypt.
33:12 The language is reminiscent of Solomon's prayer (7:14).
33:14 *built a wall without the city.* I.e. an outer wall. For the Chronicler such building programs are a sign of divine blessing (8:1–6; 11:5–12; 14:6–7; 26:9–10,14–15; 32:1–5,27–30; 1 Chr 11:7–9; 15:1).
33:15–16 Whatever the precise nature of Manasseh's reforms, Josiah would later still need to remove "the altars which Manasseh had made in the two courts of the house of the LORD" (2 Ki 23:12).

LORD God of Israel, behold, they *are written* in
the book of the kings of Israel.
19 His prayer also, and *how God* was intreated of him, and all his sin, and his trespass, and the places wherein he built high places, and set up groves and graven images, before he was humbled: behold, they *are* written among the sayings of [1] the seers.
20 [a] So Manasseh slept with his fathers, and they buried him *in* his own house: and Amon his son reigned in his stead.

Amon, king of Judah

21 ¶ [a] Amon *was* two and twenty years old when he *began* to reign, and reigned two years in Jerusalem.
22 But he did *that* which *was* evil in the sight of the LORD, as did Manasseh his father: for Amon sacrificed unto all the carved images which Manasseh his father had made, and served them;
23 And humbled not himself before the LORD, [a] as Manasseh his father had humbled himself; but Amon [1] trespassed more and more.
24 [a] And his servants conspired against him, and slew him in his own house.
25 But the people of the land slew all them that had conspired against king Amon; and the people of the land made Josiah his son king in his stead.

Josiah repairs the temple

34 Josiah [a] *was* eight years old when he *began* to reign, and he reigned in Jerusalem one and thirty years.

33:19 [1] Or, *Hosai*
33:20 [a] 2 Ki. 21:18
33:21 [a] 2 Ki. 21:19
33:23 [1] Heb. *multiplied trespass* [a] ver. 12
33:24 [a] 2 Ki. 21:23,24
34:1 [a] 2 Ki. 22:1

34:3 [a] ch. 15:2 [b] 1 Ki. 13:2 [c] ch. 33:17,22
34:4 [1] Or, *sun images* [2] Heb. *face of the graves* [a] Lev. 26:30; 2 Ki. 23:4 [b] 2 Ki. 23:6
34:5 [a] 1 Ki. 13:2
34:6 [1] Or, *mauls*
34:7 [1] Heb. *to make powder* [a] Deut. 9:21
34:8 [a] 2 Ki. 22:3

2 And he did *that* which *was* right in the sight of the LORD, and walked in the ways of David his father, and declined neither *to* the right hand, nor *to* the left.
3 For in the eighth year of his reign, while he was yet young, he began to [a] seek after the God of David his father: and in the twelfth year he began [b] to purge Judah and Jerusalem [c] from the high places, and the groves, and the carved images, and the molten images.
4 [a] And they brake down the altars of Baalim in his presence; and the [1] images, that *were* on high above them, he cut down; and the groves, and the carved images, and the molten images, he brake *in pieces,* and made dust *of them,* [b] and strowed *it* upon the [2] graves of them that had sacrificed unto them.
5 And he [a] burnt the bones of the priests upon their altars, and cleansed Judah and Jerusalem.
6 And *so did he* in the cities of Manasseh, and Ephraim, and Simeon, even unto Naphtali, with their [1] mattocks round about.
7 And when he had broken down the altars and the groves, and had [a] beaten the graven images [1] into powder, and cut down all the idols throughout all the land of Israel, he returned to Jerusalem.
8 ¶ Now [a] in the eighteenth year of his reign, when he had purged the land, and the house, he sent Shaphan the son of Azaliah, and Maaseiah the governor of the city, and Joah the son of Joahaz the recorder, to repair the house of the LORD his God.

‡33:19 *groves.* Hebrew *Asherim.* See note on 14:3.
33:20 *buried him in his own house.* Cf. 2 Ki 21:18. His burial in the palace garden makes Manasseh the fifth king the Chronicler names who was not buried in the tombs of the kings (see note on 28:27).
33:21–25 See 2 Ki 21:19–26. The Chronicler's account of the reign of Amon (642–640 B.C.) is quite similar to that in Kings, apart from (1) the additional note that Amon was not repentant like his father Manasseh, a note based on a passage unique to the Chronicler (vv. 12–13), and (2) the absence of the death formula.
34:1–36:1 See 2 Ki 22:1–23:30 and notes. Both accounts of Josiah's reign are about the same length and treat the same subjects, but with considerable variation in emphasis. Both deal with three different aspects of Josiah's reform: (1) the removal of foreign cults, (2) the finding of the book of the law and the covenant renewal that followed and (3) the celebration of passover. On the second item the two histories are quite similar. On the first item the writer of Kings goes to great lengths (2 Ki 23:4–20), while the Chronicler summarizes it only briefly (34:3–7,33). The account of the passover is greatly expanded in Chronicles (35:1–19), while only alluded to in 2 Kings (23:21–23). Not only are these items treated at different lengths, but the order is also changed. In Kings the finding of the book of the law in the temple in Josiah's 18th year is the first incident mentioned. The writer appears to have organized his material geographically, i.e. beginning with the temple and spreading through the city, then into the rest of the nation. The Chronicler, on the other hand, has arranged the incidents in order of their occurrence and has characteristically introduced a number of chronological notes into the text: 34:3 (two notes without parallel in Kings); 34:8 (see 2 Ki 22:3); 35:19 (see 2 Ki 23:23; see also note on 2 Chr 12:2). Chronicles makes it clear that the reform began in Josiah's 12th year (34:3), six years before the discovery of the book of the law.
34:1–2 See 2 Ki 22:1–2.
34:1 *one and thirty years.* 640–609 B.C.
34:3–7 The writer of Kings covers this aspect of Josiah's reform in much greater detail (2 Ki 23:4–20). He also delays his account of the removal of pagan cults until after the discovery of the book of the law, while the Chronicler places it before.
‡34:3 Some scholars have sought to tie the events of Josiah's 8th (v. 3), 12th (v. 3) and 18th (v. 8) years to stages in the progressive decline and fall of the Assyrian empire, which had dominated the area for about two centuries. The demise of Assyrian control in Aram and Israel undoubtedly facilitated and encouraged Josiah's reassertion of Davidic authority over former Assyrian provinces (vv. 6–7). However, one must not undercut religious motives in Josiah's reforms. Otherwise, the reform is reduced to merely a religious expression of an essentially political rebellion. *groves.* Hebrew *Asherim.* See note on 14:3.
34:6 *Manasseh, and Ephraim, and Simeon, even unto Naphtali.* The Chronicler's concern for "all Israel" (see Introduction to 1 Chronicles: Purpose and Themes) is apparent in his recording the involvement of the northern tribes in Josiah's reform (see also vv. 9,21,33). The Chronicler again shows all Israel united under a Davidic king, just as he did under Hezekiah (see note on 30:1). *Simeon.* Perhaps some Simeonites had migrated from Judah to the north.
34:7 *throughout all the land of Israel.* Defined by the list of tribes in v. 6.
34:8–21 See 2 Ki 22:3–13 and notes.

9 And when they came to Hilkiah the high priest, they delivered [a]the money that was brought *into* the house of God, which the Levites that kept the doors had gathered of the hand of Manasseh and Ephraim, and of all the remnant of Israel, and of all Judah and Benjamin; and they returned *to* Jerusalem.

10 And they put *it* in the hand of the workmen that had the oversight of the house of the LORD, and they gave it *to* the workmen that wrought in the house of the LORD, to repair and mend the house:

11 Even to the artificers and builders gave they *it,* to buy hewn stone, and timber for couplings, and [1]to floor the houses which the kings of Judah had destroyed.

12 And the men did the work faithfully: and the overseers of them *were* Jahath and Obadiah, the Levites, of the sons of Merari; and Zechariah and Meshullam, of the sons of the Kohathites, to set *it* forward; and *other of* the Levites, all that could skill of instruments of musick.

13 Also *they were* over the bearers of burdens, and *were* overseers of all that wrought the work in any manner of service: [a]and of the Levites *there were* scribes, and officers, and porters.

Discovery of the book of the law

14 ¶ And when they brought out the money that was brought *into* the house of the LORD, Hilkiah the priest [a]found a book of the law of the LORD *given* [1]by Moses.

15 And Hilkiah answered and said to Shaphan the scribe, I have found the book of the law in the house of the LORD. And Hilkiah delivered the book to Shaphan.

16 And Shaphan carried the book to the king, and brought the king word back again, saying, All that was committed [1]to thy servants, they do *it.*

17 And they have [1]gathered together the money that was found in the house of the LORD, and have delivered it into the hand of the overseers, and to the hand of the workmen.

18 Then Shaphan the scribe told the king, saying, Hilkiah the priest hath given me a book. And Shaphan read [1]it before the king.

19 And it came to pass, when the king had heard the words of the law, that he rent his clothes.

20 And the king commanded Hilkiah, and Ahikam the son of Shaphan, and [1]Abdon the son of Micah, and Shaphan the scribe, and Asaiah a servant of the king's, saying,

21 Go, inquire of the LORD for me, and for them that are left in Israel and in Judah, concerning the words of the book that is found: for great *is* the wrath of the LORD that is poured out upon us, because our fathers have not kept the word of the LORD, to do after all that is written in this book.

22 And Hilkiah, and *they* that the king *had appointed,* went to Huldah the prophetess, the wife of Shallum the son of [a]Tikvath, the son of [1]Hasrah, keeper of the [2]wardrobe; (now she dwelt in Jerusalem [3]in the college:) and they spake to her to that *effect.*

23 And she answered them, Thus saith the LORD God of Israel, Tell ye the man that sent you to me,

24 Thus saith the LORD, Behold, I will bring evil upon this place, and upon the inhabitants thereof, *even* all the curses that are written in the book which they have read before the king of Judah:

25 Because they have forsaken me, and have burned incense unto other gods, that *they* might provoke me to anger with all the works of their hands; therefore my wrath shall be poured out upon this place, and shall not be quenched.

26 And as for the king of Judah, who sent you to inquire of the LORD, so shall ye say unto him, Thus saith the LORD God of Israel *concerning* the words which thou hast heard;

27 Because thine heart was tender, and thou didst humble thyself before God, when thou heardest his words against this place, and against the inhabitants thereof, and humbledst thyself before me, and didst rend thy clothes, and weep before me; I have even heard *thee* also, saith the LORD.

28 Behold, I will gather thee to thy fathers, and thou shalt be gathered to thy grave in peace, neither shall thine eyes see all the evil that I will bring upon this place, and upon the inhabitants of the same. So they brought the king word again.

29 ¶ [a]Then the king sent and gathered together all the elders of Judah and Jerusalem.

30 And the king went up *into* the house of the LORD, and all the men of Judah, and the inhabitants of Jerusalem, and the priests, and the Levites, and all the people, [1]great and small: and he read in their ears all the words of the book of the covenant that was found *in* the house of the LORD.

31 And the king stood in [a]his place, and made a covenant before the LORD, to walk after the LORD, and to keep his commandments, and his testimonies, and his statutes, with all his heart, and with all his soul, to perform the words of the covenant which are written in this book.

34:9 [a]See 2 Ki. 12:4
34:11 [1]Or, *to rafter*
34:13 [a]1 Chr. 23:4,5
34:14 [1]Heb. *by the hand of* [a]2 Ki. 22:8
34:16 [1]Heb. *to the hand of*
34:17 [1]Heb. *poured out,* or, *melted*
34:18 [1]Heb. *in it*
34:20 [1]Or, *Achbor,* 2 Ki. 22:12,14
34:22 [1]Or, *Harhas,* 2 Ki. 22:14 [2]Heb. *garments* [3]Or, *in the school,* or, *in the second part* [a]2 Ki. 22:14
34:29 [a]2 Ki. 23:1
34:30 [1]Heb. *from great even to small*
34:31 [a]2 Ki. 11:14; 23:3; ch. 6:13

34:9 *Manasseh and Ephraim, and of all the remnant of Israel.* Again as part of his concern with "all Israel," the Chronicler notes that worshipers from the north also brought gifts to the temple (not explicitly indicated in 2 Ki 22:4).

34:10–13 Cf. 24:8–12.

34:22–28 See 2 Ki 22:14–20 and notes.

34:28 *gathered to thy grave in peace.* See the death and burial account (35:20–25).

34:29–31 See 2 Ki 23:1–3.

34:30 *the priests, and the Levites.* Cf. 2 Ki 23:2, which has "the priests, and the prophets."

32 And he caused all that were [1]present in
Jerusalem and Benjamin to stand *to it.* And the
inhabitants of Jerusalem did according to the
covenant of God, the God of their fathers.
33 And Josiah took away all the [a]abomina-
tions out of all the countries that *pertained* to
the children of Israel, and made all that were
[1]present in Israel to serve, *even* to serve the
LORD their God. [b]*And* all his days they departed not [2]from following the LORD, the God of
their fathers.

Observance of the passover

35 Moreover [a]Josiah kept a passover
unto the LORD in Jerusalem: and they
killed the passover on the [b]fourteenth *day* of
the first month.
2 And he set the priests in their [a]charges,
and [b]encouraged them to the service of the
house of the LORD,
3 And said unto the Levites [a]that taught all
Israel, which were holy unto the LORD, [b]Put
the holy ark [c]in the house which Solomon the
son of David king of Israel did build; *it shall*
not *be* a burden upon your shoulders: serve
now the LORD your God, and his people Israel,
4 And prepare *yourselves* [a]by the houses of
your fathers, after your courses, according to
the [b]writing of David king of Israel, and according to the [c]writing of Solomon his son.
5 And [a]stand in the holy *place* according to
the divisions of [1]the families of the fathers of
your brethren [2]the people, and *after* the division of the families of the Levites.
6 So kill the passover, and [a]sanctify yourselves, and prepare your brethren, that *they*
may do according to the word of the LORD by
the hand of Moses.
7 And Josiah [a][1]gave to the people, *of* the
flock, lambs and kids, all for the passover *offerings,* for all that were present, to the number of thirty thousand, and three thousand
bullocks: these *were* of the king's substance.
8 And his princes [1]gave willingly unto the
people, to the priests, and to the Levites: Hilkiah and Zechariah and Jehiel, rulers of the
house of God, gave unto the priests for the
passover *offerings* two thousand and six hundred *small cattle,* and three hundred oxen.
9 Conaniah also, and Shemaiah and Nethaneel, his brethren, and Hashabiah and Jeiel
and Jozabad, chief of the Levites, [1]gave unto
the Levites for passover *offerings* five thousand *small cattle,* and five hundred oxen.
10 So the service was prepared, and the
priests [a]stood in their place, and the Levites in
their courses, according to the king's commandment.
11 And they killed the passover, and the
priests [a]sprinkled *the blood* from their hands,
and the Levites [b]flayed *them.*
12 And they removed the burnt offerings,
that they might give according to the divisions
of the families of the people, to offer unto the
LORD, as it is written [a]in the book of Moses.
And so *did they* with the oxen.
13 And they [a]roasted the passover with
fire according to the ordinance: but the *other*
holy *offerings* [b]sod they in pots, and in caldrons, and in pans, and [1]divided *them* speedily among all the people.
14 And afterward they made ready for
themselves, and for the priests: because the
priests the sons of Aaron *were busied* in offering of burnt offerings and the fat until night;
therefore the Levites prepared for themselves,
and for the priests the sons of Aaron.
15 And the singers the sons of Asaph *were*
in their [1]place, according to the [a]command-
ment of David, and Asaph, and Heman, and Jeduthun the king's seer; and the porters [b]*waited* at every gate; they might not depart from
their service; for their brethren the Levites
prepared for them.
16 So all the service of the LORD was prepared the same day, to keep the passover, and
to offer burnt offerings upon the altar of the
LORD, according to the commandment of king
Josiah.
17 And the children of Israel that were
[1]present kept the passover at that time, and
the feast of [a]unleavened bread seven days.
18 And [a]there was no passover like to that,
kept in Israel from the days of Samuel the prophet; neither did all the kings of Israel keep such a
passover as Josiah kept, and the priests, and the
Levites, and all Judah and Israel that were [1]pres-
ent, and the inhabitants of Jerusalem.
19 In the eighteenth year of the reign of Josiah was this passover kept.

The death of Josiah

20 ¶ [a]After all this, when Josiah had prepared the [1]temple, Necho king of Egypt came

34:32 [1]Heb. *found*
34:33 [1]Heb. *found* [2]Heb. *from after* [a]1 Ki. 11:5 [b]Jer. 3:10
35:1 [a]2 Ki. 23:21,22 [b]Ex. 12:6; Ezra 6:19
35:2 [a]ch. 23:18; Ezra 6:18 [b]ch. 29:5,11
35:3 [a]Deut. 33:10 [b]See ch. 34:14 [c]ch. 5:7
35:4 [a]1 Chr. 9:10 [b]1 Chr. 23; 24; 25; 26 [c]ch. 8:14
35:5 [1]Heb. *the house of the fathers* [2]Heb. *the sons of the people* [a]Ps. 134:1
35:6 [a]ch. 29:5,15
35:7 [1]Heb. *offered* [a]ch. 30:24
35:8 [1]Heb. *offered*
35:9 [1]Heb. *offered*
35:10 [a]Ezra 6:18
35:11 [a]ch. 29:22 [b]See ch. 29:34
35:12 [a]Lev. 3:3
35:13 [1]Heb. *made* them *run* [a]Ex. 12:8,9; Deut. 16:7 [b]1 Sam. 2:13-15
35:15 [1]Heb. *station* [a]1 Chr. 25:1 [b]1 Chr. 9:17,18; 26:14
35:17 [1]Heb. *found* [a]Ex. 12:15; 13:6; ch. 30:21
35:18 [1]Heb. *found* [a]2 Ki. 23:22,23
35:20 [1]Heb. *house* [a]2 Ki. 23:29

34:33 *all the countries that pertained to the children of Israel . . . all that were present in Israel.* See note on v. 6.
35:1–19 The Chronicler gives much more extensive coverage to Josiah's passover celebration than is found in the brief allusion in Kings (2 Ki 23:21–23).
35:1 *first month.* The traditional month; contrast the passover of Hezekiah (see note on 30:2).
35:3 *Put the holy ark in the house.* Implies that it had been removed, perhaps for protection during the evil reigns of Manasseh and Amon, who preceded Josiah.
35:4 *David . . . Solomon.* The Chronicler specifically parallels David and Solomon in three cases: 7:10 (contrast 1 Ki 8:66, where only David is mentioned); 11:17; and here. This tendency reflects his glorification and idealization of both (see Introduction to 1 Chronicles: Portrait of David and Solomon).
35:7–9 The emphasis in Chronicles on voluntary and joyful giving (24:8–14; 29:31–36; 31:3–21; 1 Chr 29:3–9) presumably had direct relevance to the postexilic readers for whom the Chronicler wrote.
35:18 *from the days of Samuel the prophet.* Instead of "from the days of the judges" (2 Ki 23:22).
35:19 *eighteenth year.* The same year as the discovery of the book of the law (34:8,14).
‡35:20–27 See 2 Ki 23:28–30. In 609 B.C. Pharaoh-necho "went up against the king of Assyria to the river Euphrates" (2 Ki 23:29, see note) against the Babylonians.

up to fight against Carchemish by Euphrates:
and Josiah went out against him.
21 But he sent ambassadors to him, saying,
What have I to do with thee, thou king of Judah? *I come* not against thee *this* day, but
against [1]the house wherewith I have war: for
God commanded me to make haste: forbear
thee from meddling with God, who *is* with
me, that he destroy thee not.
22 Nevertheless Josiah would not turn his
face from him, but disguised himself, that *he*
might fight with him, and hearkened not unto
the words of Necho from the mouth of God,
and came to fight in the valley of Megiddo.
23 And the archers shot at king Josiah; and
the king said to his servants, Have me away;
for I am sore [a][1]wounded.
24 [a]His servants therefore took him out of
that chariot, and put him in the second chariot that he had; and they brought him *to* Jerusalem, and he died, and was buried [1]in *one of*
the sepulchres of his fathers. And [b]all Judah
and Jerusalem mourned for Josiah.
25 And Jeremiah [a]lamented for Josiah: and
[b]all the singing *men* and the singing *women*
spake of Josiah in their lamentations to *this* day,
[c]and made them an ordinance in Israel: and behold, they *are* written in the lamentations.
26 Now the rest of the acts of Josiah, and
his [1]goodness, according to that which was
written in the law of the LORD,
27 And his deeds, first and last, behold,
they *are* written in the book of the kings of Israel and Judah.

From Josiah to the captivity

36 Then [a]the people of the land took Jehoahaz the son of Josiah, and made
him king in his father's stead in Jerusalem.

35:21 [1]Heb. *the house of my war* 35:23 [1]Heb. *made sick* [a]1 Ki. 22:34 35:24 [1]Or, *among the sepulchres* [a]2 Ki. 23:30 [b]Zech. 12:11 35:25 [a]Lam. 4:20 [b]See Mat. 9:23 [c]Jer. 22:20 35:26 [1]Heb. *kindnesses* 36:1 [a]2 Ki. 23:30

36:3 [1]Heb. *removed him* [2]Heb. *mulcted* 36:5 [a]2 Ki. 23:36,37 36:6 [1]Or, *chains* [a]2 Ki. 24:1; Foretold, Hab. 1:6 [b]Jer. 36:30 36:7 [a]2 Ki. 24:13; Dan. 1:1,2 36:8 [1]Or, *Jeconiah,* 1 Chr. 3:16; or, *Coniah,* Jer. 22:24 36:9 [a]2 Ki. 24:8 36:10 [1]Heb. *at the return of the year* [2]Heb. *vessels of desire* [3]Or, *Mattaniah,* [*his father's brother*] [a]2 Ki. 24:10-17 [b]Dan. 1:1,2 [c]Jer. 37:1 [d]2 Ki. 24:17 36:11 [a]2 Ki. 24:18; Jer. 52:1

2 Jehoahaz *was* twenty and three years old
when he *began* to reign, and he reigned three
months in Jerusalem.
3 And the king of Egypt [1]put him down at
Jerusalem, and [2]condemned the land in an
hundred talents of silver and a talent of gold.
4 And the king of Egypt made Eliakim his
brother king over Judah and Jerusalem, and
turned his name *to* Jehoiakim. And Necho took
Jehoahaz his brother, and carried him to Egypt.
5 ¶ [a]Jehoiakim *was* twenty and five years
old when he *began* to reign, and he reigned
eleven years in Jerusalem: and he did *that*
which *was* evil in the sight of the LORD his
God.
6 [a]Against him came up Nebuchadnezzar
king of Babylon, and bound him in [1]fetters, to
[b]carry him to Babylon.
7 [a]Nebuchadnezzar also carried of the vessels of the house of the LORD to Babylon, and
put them in his temple at Babylon.
8 Now the rest of the acts of Jehoiakim,
and his abominations which he did, and that
which was found in him, behold, they *are*
written in the book of the kings of Israel and
Judah: and [1]Jehoiachin his son reigned in his
stead.
9 ¶ [a]Jehoiachin *was* eight years old when
he *began* to reign, and he reigned three
months and ten days in Jerusalem: and he did
that which *was* evil in the sight of the LORD.
10 And [1]when the year was expired, [a]king
Nebuchadnezzar sent, and brought him to
Babylon, [b]with the [2]goodly vessels of the
house of the LORD, and made [c][3]Zedekiah [d]his
brother king over Judah and Jerusalem.

Defeat and exile to Babylon

11 ¶ [a]Zedekiah *was* one and twenty years

‡35:20 *against Carchemish.* Better rendered as "at Carchemish." Not found in Kings.

35:21–22 Unique to the Chronicler, showing his view on retribution once again: Josiah's death in battle comes as a result of his disobedience to the word of God as heard even in the mouth of the pagan pharaoh.

35:21 *house wherewith I have war.* A reference to the Babylonians; Nabopolassar was on the throne of Babylon, while his son Nebuchadnezzar was commanding the armies in the field. Nebuchadnezzar would succeed his father after another battle at Carchemish against Egypt in 605 B.C. Josiah may have been an ally of Babylon (see 32:31; 33:11 and notes).

35:22 *disguised himself.* Cf. Ahab and Jehoshaphat (see 18:29 and note). *valley of Megiddo.* See note on Judg 5:19.

35:24b–25 Unique to Chronicles.

35:25 *Jeremiah lamented for Josiah.* Jeremiah held Josiah in high esteem (Jer 22:15–16). The laments he composed are no longer extant. The statement that he composed laments is one of the reasons the book of Lamentations has been traditionally associated with him. *to this day.* See note on 5:9.

36:2–14 Josiah is the only king of Judah to be succeeded by three of his sons (Jehoahaz, Jehoiakim and Zedekiah). The Chronicler's account of the reigns of the remaining kings of Judah is quite brief.

36:2 See 2 Ki 23:31–35. With the death of Josiah at the hands of Pharaoh-necho, Judah slipped into a period of Egyptian domination (vv. 3–4). *three months.* In 609 B.C. Necho's assertion of authority over Judah ended the brief 20 years of Judahite independence under Josiah. The Chronicler makes no moral judgment on this brief reign, though the author of Kings does (2 Ki 23:32).

36:4 Just as Necho took Jehoahaz into captivity and replaced him with Eliakim, whose name he changed to Jehoiakim, so also Nebuchadnezzar would later take Jehoiachin to Babylon, replacing him with Mattaniah, whose name he changed to Zedekiah (2 Ki 24:15–17). Each conqueror wanted to place his own man on the throne; the change of name implied authority over him.

36:5–8 See 2 Ki 23:36–24:7. Jehoiakim persecuted the prophets and is the object of scathing denunciation by Jeremiah (Jer 25–26; 36). After the Egyptian defeat at Carchemish (Jer 46:2) in 605 B.C., Jehoiakim transferred allegiance to Nebuchadnezzar of Babylon. When he later rebelled and again allied himself with Egypt, Nebuchadnezzar sent a punitive army against him. But Jehoiakim died before the army arrived, and Nebuchadnezzar took his son Jehoiachin into captivity.

36:5 *eleven years.* 609–598 B.C.

36:9–10 See 2 Ki 24:8–17; see also Jer 22:24–28; 24:1; 29:2; 52:31. Although Jehoiachin was taken into captivity (597 B.C.) with a large retinue, including the queen mother and high officials, and was succeeded by Zedekiah, the exiles continued to date in terms of his reign (Jer 52:31; Ezek 1:2; cf. Esth 2:5–6).

36:9 *three months and ten days.* 598–597 B.C.

old when he *began* to reign, and reigned eleven years in Jerusalem.

12 And he did *that* which *was* evil in the sight of the LORD his God, *and* humbled not himself before Jeremiah the prophet *speaking* from the mouth of the LORD.

13 And he also rebelled against king Nebuchadnezzar, who had made him swear by God: but he [a]stiffened his neck, and hardened his heart from turning unto the LORD God of Israel.

14 Moreover all the chief of the priests, and the people, transgressed very much after all the abominations of the heathen; and polluted the house of the LORD which he had hallowed in Jerusalem.

15 [a]And the LORD God of their fathers sent to them [1]by his messengers, rising up [2]betimes, and sending; because he had compassion on his people, and on his dwelling place:

16 But [a]they mocked the messengers of God, and [b]despised his words, and [c]misused his prophets, until the [d]wrath of the LORD arose against his people, till *there was* no [1]remedy.

17 [a]Therefore he brought upon them the king of the Chaldees, who [b]slew their young men with the sword in the house of their sanctuary, and had no compassion upon young man or maiden, old man, or him that stooped for age: he gave *them* all into his hand.

18 [a]And all the vessels of the house of God, great and small, and the treasures of the house of the LORD, and the treasures of the king, and of his princes; all *these* he brought *to* Babylon.

19 [a]And they burnt the house of God, and brake down the wall of Jerusalem, and burnt all the palaces thereof with fire, and destroyed all the goodly vessels thereof.

20 And [a][1]them that had escaped from the sword carried he away to Babylon; [b]where they were servants to him and his sons until the reign of the kingdom of Persia:

21 To fulfil the word of the LORD by the mouth of [a]Jeremiah, until the land [b]had enjoyed her sabbaths: *for* as long as *she* lay desolate [c]she kept sabbath, to fulfil threescore and ten years.

Cyrus promises end of captivity

22 ¶ [a]Now in the first year of Cyrus king of Persia, that the word of the LORD *spoken* by the mouth of [b]Jeremiah might be accomplished, the LORD stirred up the spirit of [c]Cyrus king of Persia, that he made a proclamation throughout all his kingdom, and *put it* also in writing, saying,

23 [a]Thus saith Cyrus king of Persia, All the kingdoms of the earth hath the LORD God of heaven given me; and he hath charged me to build him a house in Jerusalem, which *is* in Judah. Who *is there* among you of all his people? The LORD his God *be* with him, and let him go up.

36:13 [a]2 Ki. 17:14
36:15 [1]Heb. *by the hand of his messengers* [2]That is, *continually and carefully* [a]Jer. 25:3,4
36:16 [1]Heb. *healing* [a]Jer. 5:12 [b]Prov. 1:25 [c]Jer. 38:6; Mat. 23:34 [d]Ps. 79:5
36:17 [a]Deut. 28:49; 2 Ki. 25:1; Ezra 9:7 [b]Ps. 74:20
36:18 [a]2 Ki. 25:13
36:19 [a]2 Ki. 25:9; Ps. 79:1,7
36:20 [1]Heb. *the remainder from the sword* [a]2 Ki. 25:11 [b]Jer. 27:7
36:21 [a]Jer. 26:6,7 [b]Lev. 26:34; Dan. 9:2 [c]Lev. 25:4,5
36:22 [a]Ezra 1:1 [b]Jer. 29:10 [c]Is. 44:28
36:23 [a]Ezra 1:2,3

36:11–14 See 2 Ki 24:18–20; Jer 52:1–3. Verses 13b–14 are unique to the Chronicler (cf. Jer 1:3; 21:1–7; 24:8; 27:1–15; 32:1–5; 34:1–7,21; 37:1–39:7). Zedekiah succumbed to the temptation to look to Egypt for help and rebelled against Nebuchadnezzar. Babylonian reaction was swift. Jerusalem was besieged (Jer 21:3–7) in 588 B.C. and held out for over two years before being destroyed in the summer of 586.

36:11 *eleven years.* 597–586 B.C.

36:15–16 See 24:19 and note.

36:20–21 The conclusion of the two Biblical histories is interestingly different: The writer(s) of Samuel and Kings had sought to show why the exile occurred and had traced the sad history of Israel's disobedience to the exile, the time in which the writer(s) of those books lived. With the state at an end, he could still show God's faithfulness to His promises to David (2 Ki 25:27–30) by reporting the favor bestowed on his descendants. The Chronicler, whose vantage point was after the exile, was able to look back to the exile not only as judgment, but also as containing hope for the future. For him the purified remnant had returned to a purified land (vv. 22–23), and a new age was beginning. The exile was not judgment alone, but also blessing, for it allowed the land to catch up on its sabbath rests (Lev 26:40–45). And God had remembered His covenant (Lev 26:45) and restored His people to the land (see next note).

36:22–23 The writer of Kings concluded his history before the restoration; so this text is not paralleled in his account. It is repeated, however, at the beginning of Ezra (1:1–4), which resumes the history at the point where Chronicles ends—indicating that Chronicles and Ezra may have been written by the same author. See the prophecy of Jeremiah (Jer 25:1–14; cf. Dan 9). Cyrus also issued decrees for other captive peoples, allowing them to return to their lands. Under God's sovereignty, this effort by a Persian king to win the favor of peoples treated harshly by the Babylonians also inaugurated the restoration period. See notes on Ezra 1:1–4.

Ezra

INTRODUCTION

Ezra and Nehemiah

Although the caption to Neh 1:1, "The words of Nehemiah the son of Hachaliah," indicates that Ezra and Nehemiah were originally two separate compositions, they were combined as one in the earliest Hebrew manuscripts. Josephus (c. A.D. 37–100) and the Jewish Talmud refer to the book of Ezra but not to a separate book of Nehemiah. The oldest manuscripts of the Septuagint (the Greek translation of the OT) also treat Ezra and Nehemiah as one book.

Origen (A.D. 185–253) is the first writer known to distinguish between two books, which he called I Ezra and II Ezra. In translating the Latin Vulgate (A.D. 390–405), Jerome called Nehemiah the second book of Esdrae (Ezra). The English translations by Wycliffe (1382) and Coverdale (1535) also called Ezra "I Esdras" and Nehemiah "II Esdras." The same separation first appeared in a Hebrew manuscript in 1448.

Literary Form and Authorship

As in the closely related books of 1 and 2 Chronicles, one notes the prominence of various lists in Ezra and Nehemiah, which have evidently been obtained from official sources. Included are lists of (1) the temple vessels (Ezra 1:9–11), (2) the returned exiles (Ezra 2, which is virtually the same as Neh 7:6–73), (3) the genealogy of Ezra (Ezra 7:1–5), (4) the heads of the clans (Ezra 8:1–14), (5) those involved in mixed marriages (Ezra 10:18–43), (6) those who helped rebuild the wall (Neh 3), (7) those who sealed the covenant (Neh 10:1–27), (8) residents of Jerusalem and other towns (Neh 11:3–36) and (9) priests and Levites (Neh 12:1–26).

Also included in Ezra are seven official documents or letters (all in Aramaic except the first, which is in Hebrew): (1) the decree of Cyrus (1:2–4), (2) the accusation of Rehum and others against the Jews (4:11–16), (3) the reply of Artaxerxes I (4:17–22), (4) the report from Tatnai (5:7–17), (5) the memorandum of Cyrus's decree (6:2b-5), (6) Darius's reply to Tatnai (6:6–12) and (7) the authorization given by Artaxerxes I to Ezra (7:12–26). The documents compare favorably with contemporary non-Biblical documents of the Persian period.

Certain materials in Ezra are first-person extracts from his memoirs: 7:27–28; 8:1–34; 9. Other sections are written in the third person: 7:1–26; 10; see also Neh 8. Linguistic analysis has shown that the first-person and third-person extracts resemble each other, making it likely that the same author wrote both.

Most scholars conclude that the author/compiler of Ezra and Nehemiah was also the author of 1,2 Chronicles. This viewpoint is based on certain characteristics common to both Chronicles and Ezra-Nehemiah. The verses at the end of Chronicles and at the beginning of Ezra are virtually identical. Both Chronicles and Ezra-Nehemiah exhibit a fondness for lists, for the description of religious festivals and for such phrases as "chief of the fathers" and "the house of God." Especially striking in these books is the prominence of Levites and temple personnel. The words for "singer," "porter" and "Nethinims" [i.e. "temple servants"] are used almost exclusively in Ezra-Nehemiah and Chronicles. See Introduction to 1 Chronicles: Author, Date and Sources.

Date

We may date the composition of Ezra c. 440 B.C. and the Nehemiah memoirs c. 430.

The Order of Ezra and Nehemiah

According to the traditional view, Ezra arrived in Jerusalem in the seventh year (Ezra 7:8) of Artaxerxes I (458 B.C.), followed by Nehemiah, who arrived in the king's 20th year (445; Neh 2:1).

Some have proposed a reverse order in which Nehemiah arrived in 445 B.C., while Ezra arrived

in the seventh year of Artaxerxes II (398). By amending "seventh" (Ezra 7:8) to either "27th" or "37th," others place Ezra after Nehemiah but maintain that they were contemporaries.

These alternative views, however, present more problems than the traditional position. As the text stands, Ezra arrived before Nehemiah and they are found together in Neh 8:9 (at the reading of the law) and Neh 12:26,36 (at the dedication of the wall). See chart, p. 635.

Languages

Ezra and Nehemiah were written in a form of late Hebrew with the exception of Ezra 4:8—6:18; 7:12–26, which were written in Aramaic, the international language during the Persian period. Of these 67 Aramaic verses, 52 are in records or letters. Ezra evidently found these documents in Aramaic and copied them, inserting connecting verses in Aramaic.

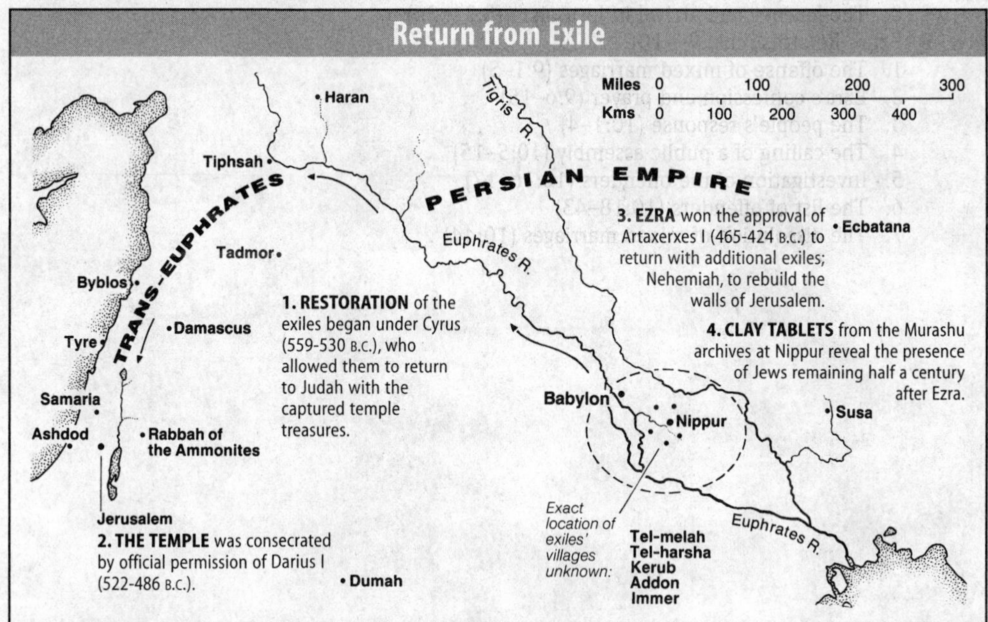
Return from Exile
Miles 0 100 200 300
Kms 0 100 200 300 400
Haran
Tigris R.
Tiphsah
PERSIAN EMPIRE
TRANS-EUPHRATES
Tadmor
Euphrates R.
3. EZRA won the approval of Artaxerxes I (465-424 B.C.) to return with additional exiles; Nehemiah, to rebuild the walls of Jerusalem.
Ecbatana
Byblos
1. RESTORATION of the exiles began under Cyrus (559-530 B.C.), who allowed them to return to Judah with the captured temple treasures.
Tyre
Damascus
4. CLAY TABLETS from the Murashu archives at Nippur reveal the presence of Jews remaining half a century after Ezra.
Samaria
Babylon
Nippur
Susa
Ashdod
Rabbah of the Ammonites
Jerusalem
2. THE TEMPLE was consecrated by official permission of Darius I (522-486 B.C.).
Exact location of exiles' villages unknown:
Tel-melah
Tel-harsha
Kerub
Addon
Immer
Euphrates R.
Dumah

Outline

I. First Return from Exile and Rebuilding of the Temple (chs. 1—6)
- A. First Return of the Exiles (ch. 1)
  1. The edict of Cyrus (1:1–4)
  2. The return under Sheshbazzar (1:5–11)
- B. List of Returning Exiles (ch. 2)
- C. Revival of Temple Worship (ch. 3)
  1. The rebuilding of the altar (3:1–3)
  2. The feast of tabernacles (3:4–6)
  3. The beginning of temple reconstruction (3:7–13)
- D. Opposition to Rebuilding (4:1–23)
  1. Opposition during the reign of Cyrus (4:1–5)
  2. Opposition during the reign of Ahasuerus (4:6)
  3. Opposition during the reign of Artaxerxes (4:7–23)
- E. Completion of the Temple (4:24—6:22)
  1. Resumption of work under Darius (4:24)
  2. A new beginning inspired by Haggai and Zechariah (5:1–2)
  3. Intervention of the governor, Tatnai (5:3–5)
  4. Report to Darius (5:6–17)
  5. Search for the decree of Cyrus (6:1–5)
  6. Darius's order for the rebuilding of the temple (6:6–12)

7. Completion of the temple (6:13–15)
8. Dedication of the temple (6:16–18)
9. Celebration of passover (6:19–22)

II. Ezra's Return and Reforms (chs. 7—10)

A. Ezra's Return to Jerusalem (chs. 7—8)

1. Introduction (7:1–10)
2. The authorization by Artaxerxes (7:11–26)
3. Ezra's doxology (7:27–28)
4. List of those returning with Ezra (8:1–14)
5. The search for Levites (8:15–20)
6. Prayer and fasting (8:21–23)
7. The assignment of the sacred vessels (8:24–30)
8. The journey and arrival in Jerusalem (8:31–36)

B. Ezra's Reforms (chs. 9—10)

1. The offense of mixed marriages (9:1–5)
2. Ezra's confession and prayer (9:6–15)
3. The people's response (10:1–4)
4. The calling of a public assembly (10:5–15)
5. Investigation of the offenders (10:16–17)
6. The list of offenders (10:18–43)
7. The dissolution of mixed marriages (10:44)

The proclamation of Cyrus

1 Now in the first year of Cyrus king of
Persia, that the word of the LORD [a]by the
mouth of Jeremiah might be fulfilled, the LORD
stirred up the spirit of Cyrus king of Persia,
[b]that he [1]made a proclamation throughout all
his kingdom, and *put it* also in writing, saying,
2 Thus saith Cyrus king of Persia, The LORD
God of heaven hath given me all the kingdoms
of the earth; and he hath [a]charged me to build
him a house at Jerusalem, which *is* in Judah.
3 Who *is there* among you of all his people?
his God be with him, and let him go up to Jerusalem, which *is* in Judah, and build the
house of the LORD God of Israel, ([a]he *is* the
God,) which *is* in Jerusalem.
4 And whosoever remaineth in any place
where he sojourneth, let the men of his place
[1]help him with silver, and with gold, and with
goods, and with beasts, besides the freewill offering for the house of God that *is* in Jerusalem.
5 ¶ Then rose up the chief of the fathers of
Judah and Benjamin, and the priests, and the
Levites, with all *them* whose spirit [a]God had
raised, to go up to build the house of the LORD
which *is* in Jerusalem.
6 And all *they that were* about them
[1]strengthened their hands with vessels of silver, with gold, with goods, and with beasts,
and with precious things, beside all *that* was
willingly offered.
7 [a]Also Cyrus the king brought forth the
vessels of the house of the LORD, [b]which Nebuchadnezzar had brought forth out of Jerusalem,
and had put them in the house of his gods;
8 Even those did Cyrus king of Persia bring
forth by the hand of Mithredath the treasurer,
and numbered them unto [a]Sheshbazzar, the
prince of Judah.
9 And this *is* the number of them: thirty
chargers of gold, a thousand chargers of silver,
nine and twenty knives,
10 Thirty basons of gold, silver basons of a
second sort four hundred and ten, *and* other
vessels a thousand.
11 All the vessels of gold and of silver *were*
five thousand and four hundred. All *these* did
Sheshbazzar bring up with *them of* [1]the captivity that were brought up from Babylon unto
Jerusalem.

1:1 [1]Heb. *caused a voice to pass* [a]2 Chr. 36:22,23 [b]ch. 5:13,14
1:2 [a]Is. 44:28; 45:1,13
1:3 [a]Dan. 6:26
1:4 [1]Heb. *lift him up*
1:5 [a]Phil. 2:13
1:6 [1]That is, *helped them*
1:7 [a]ch. 5:14; 6:5 [b]2 Ki. 24:13; 2 Chr. 36:7
1:8 [a]See ch. 5:14
1:11 [1]Heb. *the transportation*

1:1–3a Virtually identical with the last two verses of 2 Chronicles. This fact has been used to argue that Chronicles and Ezra-Nehemiah were written and/or edited by the same person, the so-called Chronicler. However, the repetition may have been a device of the author of Chronicles (or less probably of Ezra) to dovetail the narratives chronologically.

1:1 *first year.* Of the reign of Cyrus over Babylon, beginning in March, 538 B.C., after he captured Babylon in October, 539. Cyrus, the founder of the Persian empire, reigned over the Persians from 559 until 530. Is 44:28; 45:1 speak of him as the Lord's "shepherd" and His "anointed." *that the word of the LORD by the mouth of Jeremiah might be fulfilled.* Jeremiah prophesied a 70-year Babylonian captivity (Jer 25:11–12; 29:10). The first deportation began in 605, the third year of Jehoiakim (Dan 1:1); in 538, approximately 70 years later, the people began to return.

1:2–4 This oral proclamation of Cyrus's decree was written in Hebrew, the language of the Israelite captives, in contrast to the copy of the decree in 6:3–5, which was an Aramaic memorandum for the archives.

1:2 *God of heaven.* Of the 22 OT occurrences of the phrase, 17 occur in Ezra, Nehemiah and Daniel. *house at Jerusalem.* Jerusalem and the house of God are prominent subjects in Ezra and Nehemiah.

1:3 Cyrus instituted the policy of placating the gods of his subject peoples instead of carrying off their cult images as the Assyrians and the Babylonians had done earlier. His generosity to the Jews was paralleled by his benevolence to the Babylonians.

1:4 *whosoever remaineth in any place where he sojourneth.* Probably designates the many Jews who did not wish to leave Mesopotamia. *freewill offering.* A key to the restoration of God's temple and its services (see 2:68; 3:5; 8:28).

1:5 *chief of the fathers.* In ancient times families were extended families—more like clans than modern nuclear families. The authority figure was the patriarch, who was the "head of the household." See 10:16; see also 2:59; Neh 7:61; 10:34. *Judah and Benjamin.* The two main tribes of the kingdom of Judah, which the Babylonians had exiled. *Levites.* See Introduction to Leviticus: Title.

1:7 It was the custom for conquerors to carry off the images of the gods of conquered cities. Since the Jews did not have an image of the Lord (see note on Ex 20:4), Nebuchadnezzar carried away only the temple articles.

1:8 *Mithredath.* A Persian name meaning "given by/to Mithra," a Persian god who became popular among Roman soldiers in the second century A.D. *Sheshbazzar.* A Babylonian name meaning either "Sin, protect the father" or "Shamash/Shashu, protect the father." Sin was the moon-god, and Shamash (Shashu is a variant) was the sun-god. In spite of his Babylonian name, Sheshbazzar was probably a Jewish official who served as a deputy governor of Judah under the satrap in Samaria (see 5:14). Some believe that Sheshbazzar and Zerubbabel were the same person and give the following reasons: 1. Both were governors (5:14; Hag 1:1; 2:2). 2. Both are said to have laid the foundation of the temple (3:2–8; 5:16; Hag 1:14–15; Zech 4:6–10). 3. Jews in Babylon were often given "official" Babylonian names (cf. Dan 1:7). 4. Josephus (*Antiquities,* 11.1.3) seems to identify Sheshbazzar with Zerubbabel.

Others point out, however, that the Apocrypha distinguishes between the two men (1 Esdras 6:18). Furthermore, it is likely that Sheshbazzar was an elderly man at the time of the return, while Zerubbabel was probably a younger contemporary. Sheshbazzar also may have been viewed as the official governor, while Zerubbabel served as the popular leader (3:8–11). Whereas the high priest Jeshua is associated with Zerubbabel, no priest is associated with Sheshbazzar. Although Sheshbazzar presided over the foundation of the temple in 536 B.C., so little was accomplished that Zerubbabel had to preside over a second foundation some 16 years later (see Hag 1:14–15; Zech 4:6–10).

Still others hold that Sheshbazzar is to be identified with Shenazar (1 Chr 3:18), the fourth son of King Jeconiah. Zerubbabel would then have been Sheshbazzar's nephew (compare 3:2 with 1 Chr 3:18).

1:9–11 When Assyrian and Babylonian conquerors carried off plunder, their scribes made a careful inventory of all the goods seized. The total of the figures in vv. 9–10 adds up to 2,499 rather than the 5,400 of v. 11. It may be that only the larger and more valuable vessels were specified.

1:11 We are not told anything about the details of Sheshbazzar's journey, which probably took place in 537 B.C. Judging from

The people who returned

2 Now [a]these *are* the children of the province that went up out of the captivity, *of* those which had been carried away, [b]whom Nebuchadnezzar the king of Babylon had carried away unto Babylon, and came again unto Jerusalem and Judah, every one unto his city;

2 Which came with Zerubbabel: Jeshua, Nehemiah, [1]Seraiah, [2]Reelaiah, Mordecai, Bilshan, [3]Mizpar, Bigvai, [4]Rehum, Baanah.

¶ The number of the men of the people of Israel:

3 The children of Parosh, two thousand an hundred seventy and two.

4 The children of Shephatiah, three hundred seventy and two.

5 The children of Arah, [a]seven hundred seventy and five.

6 The children of [a]Pahath-moab, of the children of Jeshua *and* Joab, two thousand eight hundred and twelve.

7 The children of Elam, a thousand two hundred fifty and four.

8 The children of Zattu, nine hundred forty and five.

9 The children of Zaccai, seven hundred and threescore.

10 The children of [1]Bani, six hundred forty and two.

11 The children of Bebai, six hundred twenty and three.

12 The children of Azgad, a thousand two hundred twenty and two.

13 The children of Adonikam, six hundred sixty and six.

14 The children of Bigvai, two thousand fifty and six.

15 The children of Adin, four hundred fifty and four.

16 The children of Ater of Hezekiah, ninety and eight.

17 The children of Bezai, three hundred twenty and three.

18 The children of [1]Jorah, an hundred and twelve.

19 The children of Hashum, two hundred twenty and three.

20 The children of [1]Gibbar, ninety and five.

21 The children of Beth-lehem, an hundred twenty and three.

22 The men of Netophah, fifty and six.

23 The men of Anathoth, an hundred twenty and eight.

24 The children of [1]Azmaveth, forty and two.

25 The children of Kirjath-arim, Chephirah, and Beeroth, seven hundred and forty and three.

26 The children of Ramah and Gaba, six hundred twenty and one.

27 The men of Michmas, an hundred twenty and two.

28 The men of Beth-el and Ai, two hundred twenty and three.

29 The children of Nebo, fifty and two.

30 The children of Magbish, an hundred fifty and six.

31 The children of the other [a]Elam, a thousand two hundred fifty and four.

32 The children of Harim, three hundred and twenty.

33 The children of Lod, [1]Hadid, and Ono, seven hundred twenty and five.

2:1 [a]Neh. 7:6 [b]2 Ki. 24:14-16; 25:11; 2 Chr. 36:20
2:2 [1]Or, *Azariah* [2][Or, *Raamiah*] [3][Or, *Mispereth*] [4][Or, *Nehum*]
2:5 [a]See Neh. 7:10
2:6 [a]Neh. 7:11
2:10 [1]Or, *Binnui*
2:18 [1]Or, *Hariph,* Neh. 7:24
2:20 [1]Or, *Gibeon,* Neh. 7:25
2:24 [1]Or, *Beth-azmaveth,* Neh. 7:28
2:31 [a]See ver. 7
2:33 [1]Or, *Harid,* as it is in some copies

Ezra's later journey (7:8–9), the trip took about four months. See map No. 7b at the end of the study Bible; see also map, p. 631.

2:1–70 The list of returning exiles in ch. 2 almost exactly parallels the list in Neh 7:6–73 (see also 1 Esdras 5:4–46 in the Apocrypha). The list of localities indicates that people retained the memories of their homes and that exiles from a wide background of tribes, villages and towns returned. In comparing the list here with that in Neh 7, one notes many differences in the names and numbers listed. About 20 percent of the numbers, e.g., are not the same in Ezra and Nehemiah. Many of these differences may be explained, however, by assuming that a cipher notation was used with vertical strokes for units and horizontal strokes for tens, which led to copying errors.

2:1 *province.* Probably Judah (cf. 5:8, where the Aramaic word for "province" occurs; see also Neh 1:3).

2:2 *Zerubbabel.* See notes on 3:2; 5:2. *Jeshua.* Means "The LORD saves" and is an Aramaic variant of Hebrew "Joshua." The Greek form is "Jesus" (see note on Mat 1:21). Jeshua is the same as the Joshua of Hag 1:1, the son of the high priest Jehozadak (Jozadak, Ezra 3:2), who was taken into exile (1 Chr 6:15). *Nehemiah.* Not the Nehemiah of the book by that name. *Mordecai.* A Babylonian name based on that of Marduk the god of Babylon (cf. Jer 50:2). Esther's cousin had the same name (Esth 2:7).

2:3 *Parosh.* Means "flea" (Israelites were often named after insects and animals). Members of this family, as well as of several other families named in vv. 6–14, also returned with Ezra (8:3–14).

2:5 *Arah.* Probably means "wild ox." Since the name is rare in the OT and has been found in documents from Mesopotamia, it may have been adopted during the exile.

2:6 *Pahath-moab.* Means "governor of Moab" and may have once designated an official title.

2:12 *Azgad.* Cf. 8:12; means "Gad is strong." It is a reference either to Gad (the god of fortune, referred to in Is 65:11) or to the tribe of Gad, east of the Jordan.

2:16 *Ater.* Means "left-handed," as in Judg 3:15; 20:16.

2:21–35 Whereas the names in vv. 3–20 are of families, vv. 21–35 present a series of villages and towns, many of which were in Benjamite territory north of Jerusalem. It is significant that there are no references to towns in the Negev, south of Judah. When Nebuchadnezzar overran Judah in 597 B.C. (Jer 13:19), the Edomites (see the book of Obadiah) took advantage of the situation and occupied that area.

2:21 *children of Beth-lehem.* The ancestors of Jesus may have been among the returnees (see 1 Sam 17:12; 20:6; Mic 5:2; Luke 2:4).

2:23 *Anathoth.* See note on Jer 1:1.

2:28 *Beth-el.* See note on Gen 12:8. Towns such as Beth-el, Mizpah, Gibeon and Gibeah seem to have escaped the Babylonian assault. Beth-el, however, was destroyed in the transition between the Babylonian and Persian periods. Archaeological excavations reveal that there was a small town on the site in Ezra's day.

2:31 See v. 7.

2:33 *Lod.* Modern Lydda.

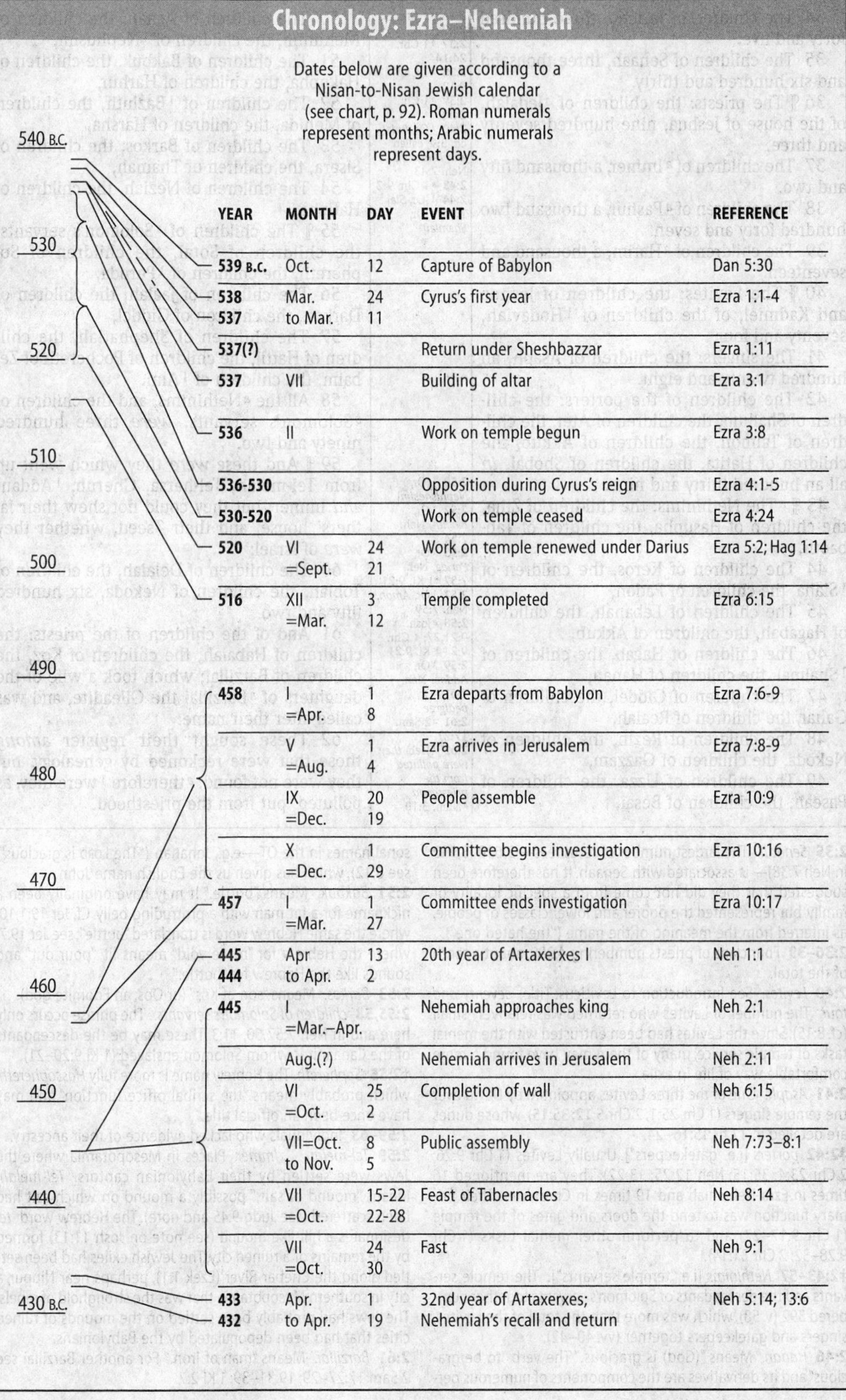

Chronology: Ezra–Nehemiah

Dates below are given according to a Nisan-to-Nisan Jewish calendar (see chart, p. 92). Roman numerals represent months; Arabic numerals represent days.

YEAR	MONTH	DAY	EVENT	REFERENCE
539 B.C.	Oct.	12	Capture of Babylon	Dan 5:30
538 537	Mar. to Mar.	24 11	Cyrus's first year	Ezra 1:1-4
537(?)			Return under Sheshbazzar	Ezra 1:11
537	VII		Building of altar	Ezra 3:1
536	II		Work on temple begun	Ezra 3:8
536-530			Opposition during Cyrus's reign	Ezra 4:1-5
530-520			Work on temple ceased	Ezra 4:24
520	VI =Sept.	24 21	Work on temple renewed under Darius	Ezra 5:2; Hag 1:14
516	XII =Mar.	3 12	Temple completed	Ezra 6:15
458	I =Apr.	1 8	Ezra departs from Babylon	Ezra 7:6-9
	V =Aug.	1 4	Ezra arrives in Jerusalem	Ezra 7:8-9
	IX =Dec.	20 19	People assemble	Ezra 10:9
	X =Dec.	1 29	Committee begins investigation	Ezra 10:16
457	I =Mar.	1 27	Committee ends investigation	Ezra 10:17
445 444	Apr to Apr.	13 2	20th year of Artaxerxes I	Neh 1:1
445	I =Mar.–Apr.		Nehemiah approaches king	Neh 2:1
	Aug.(?)		Nehemiah arrives in Jerusalem	Neh 2:11
	VI =Oct.	25 2	Completion of wall	Neh 6:15
	VII=Oct. to Nov.	8 5	Public assembly	Neh 7:73–8:1
	VII =Oct.	15-22 22-28	Feast of Tabernacles	Neh 8:14
	VII =Oct.	24 30	Fast	Neh 9:1
433 432	Apr. to Apr.	1 19	32nd year of Artaxerxes; Nehemiah's recall and return	Neh 5:14; 13:6

34 The children of Jericho, three hundred forty and five.

35 The children of Senaah, three thousand and six hundred and thirty.

36 ¶ The priests: the children of [a]Jedaiah, of the house of Jeshua, nine hundred seventy and three.

37 The children of [a]Immer, a thousand fifty and two.

38 The children of [a]Pashur, a thousand two hundred forty and seven.

39 The children of [a]Harim, a thousand and seventeen.

40 ¶ The Levites: the children of Jeshua and Kadmiel, of the children of [1]Hodaviah, seventy and four.

41 The singers: the children of Asaph, an hundred twenty and eight.

42 The children of the porters: the children of Shallum, the children of Ater, the children of Talmon, the children of Akkub, the children of Hatita, the children of Shobai, *in* all an hundred thirty and nine.

43 ¶ [a]The Nethinims: the children of Ziha, the children of Hasupha, the children of Tabbaoth,

44 The children of Keros, the children of [1]Siaha, the children of Padon,

45 The children of Lebanah, the children of Hagabah, the children of Akkub,

46 The children of Hagab, the children of [1]Shalmai, the children of Hanan,

47 The children of Giddel, the children of Gahar, the children of Reaiah,

48 The children of Rezin, the children of Nekoda, the children of Gazzam,

49 The children of Uzza, the children of Paseah, the children of Besai,

50 The children of Asnah, the children of Mehunim, the children of [1]Nephusim,

51 The children of Bakbuk, the children of Hakupha, the children of Harhur,

52 The children of [1]Bazluth, the children of Mehida, the children of Harsha,

53 The children of Barkos, the children of Sisera, the children of Thamah,

54 The children of Neziah, the children of Hatipha.

55 ¶ The children of [a]Solomon's servants: the children of Sotai, the children of Sophereth, the children of [1]Peruda,

56 The children of Jaalah, the children of Darkon, the children of Giddel,

57 The children of Shephatiah, the children of Hattil, the children of Pochereth of Zebaim, the children of [1]Ami.

58 All the [a]Nethinims, and the children of [b]Solomon's servants, *were* three hundred ninety and two.

59 ¶ And these *were* they which went up from Tel-melah, Tel-harsa, Cherub, [1]Addan, *and* Immer: but they could not shew their fathers' house, and their [2]seed, whether they *were* of Israel:

60 The children of Delaiah, the children of Tobiah, the children of Nekoda, six hundred fifty and two.

61 And of the children of the priests: the children of Habaiah, the children of Koz, the children of Barzillai; which took a wife of the daughters of [a]Barzillai the Gileadite, and was called after their name:

62 These sought their register *among* those that were reckoned by genealogy, but they were not found: [a]therefore [1]were they, as polluted, put from the priesthood.

2:36 [a]1 Chr. 24:7
2:37 [a]1 Chr. 24:14
2:38 [a]1 Chr. 9:12
2:39 [a]1 Chr. 24:8
2:40 [1]Or, *Judah,* ch. 3:9; called also *Hodevah,* Neh. 7:43
2:43 [a]1 Chr. 9:2
2:44 [1][Or, *Sia*]
2:46 [1][Or, *Shamlai*]
2:50 [1][Or, *Nephishesim*]
2:52 [1]Or, *Bazlith,* Neh. 7:54
2:55 [1]Or, *Perida,* Neh. 7:57 [a]1 Ki. 9:21
2:57 [1]Or, *Amon,* Neh. 7:59
2:58 [a]Josh. 9:21,27; 1 Chr. 9:2 [b]1 Ki. 9:21
2:59 [1]Or, *Addon,* Neh. 7:61 [2]Or, *pedigree*
2:61 [a]2 Sam. 17:27
2:62 [1]Heb. *they were polluted from the priesthood* [a]Num. 3:10

2:35 *Senaah.* The largest number of returnees—3,630 (3,930 in Neh 7:38)—is associated with Senaah. It has therefore been suggested that they did not come from a specific locality or family, but represented the poorer and lower classes of people, as inferred from the meaning of the name ("the hated one").

2:36–39 Four clans of priests numbering 4,289, about a tenth of the total.

2:40 *Levites.* See Introduction to Leviticus: Title. *seventy and four.* The number of Levites who returned was relatively small (cf. 8:15). Since the Levites had been entrusted with the menial tasks of temple service, many of them may have found a more comfortable way of life in exile.

2:41 *Asaph.* One of the three Levites appointed by David over the temple singers (1 Chr 25:1; 2 Chr 5:12; 35:15), whose duties are detailed in 1 Chr 15:16–24.

‡2:42 *porters* [i.e. "gatekeepers"]. Usually Levites (1 Chr 9:26; 2 Chr 23:4; 35:15; Neh 12:25; 13:22). They are mentioned 16 times in Ezra-Nehemiah and 19 times in Chronicles. Their primary function was to tend the doors and gates of the temple (1 Chr 9:17–27) and to perform other menial tasks (1 Chr 9:28–32; 2 Chr 31:14).

‡2:43–57 *Nethinims* [i.e. "temple servants"]. The temple servants and the descendants of Solomon's servants together numbered 392 (v. 58), which was more than the total of the Levites, singers and gatekeepers together (vv. 40–42).

2:46 *Hanan.* Means "(God) is gracious." The verb "to be gracious" and its derivatives are the components of numerous personal names in the OT—e.g., Johanan ("The LORD is gracious"; see 8:12), which has given us the English name John.

2:51 *Bakbuk.* Means "bottle." It may have originally been a nickname for a fat man with a protruding belly. Cf. Jer 19:1,10, where the same Hebrew word is translated "bottle"; see Jer 19:7, where the Hebrew for "make void" means lit. "pour out" and sounds like the Hebrew for "bottle."

2:53 *Barkos.* Means "son of Kos" (or Qos, an Edomite god).

2:55,58 *children of Solomon's servants.* The phrase occurs only here and in Neh 7:57,60; 11:3. These may be the descendants of the Canaanites whom Solomon enslaved (1 Ki 9:20–21).

‡2:55 *Sophereth.* The Hebrew name is more fully *Hassophereth,* which probably means "the scribal office/function" and may have once been an official title.

2:59–63 Individuals who lacked evidence of their ancestry.

2:59 *Tel-melah . . . Immer.* Places in Mesopotamia where the Jews were settled by their Babylonian captors. *Tel-melah.* Means "mound of salt," possibly a mound on which salt had been scattered (see Judg 9:45 and note). The Hebrew word *tel* designates a hill-like mound (see note on Josh 11:13) formed by the remains of a ruined city. The Jewish exiles had been settled along the Chebar River (Ezek 1:1), perhaps near Nippur, a city in southern Mesopotamia that was the stronghold of rebels. The Jews had probably been settled on the mounds of ruined cities that had been depopulated by the Babylonians.

2:61 *Barzillai.* Means "man of iron." For another Barzillai see 2 Sam 17:27–29; 19:31–39; 1 Ki 2:7.

63 And the [1]Tirshatha said unto them, that they [a]should not eat of the most holy *things* till there stood *up* a priest with [b]Urim and with Thummim.

64 ¶ [a]The whole congregation together *was* forty *and* two thousand three hundred *and* threescore,

65 Beside their servants and their maids, of whom *there were* seven thousand three hundred thirty and seven: and *there were* among them two hundred singing *men* and singing *women.*

66 Their horses *were* seven hundred thirty and six; their mules, two hundred forty and five;

67 Their camels, four hundred thirty and five; *their* asses, six thousand seven hundred and twenty.

68 ¶ [a]And *some* of the chief of the fathers, when they came to the house of the LORD which *is* at Jerusalem, offered freely for the house of God to set it up in his place:

69 They gave after their ability unto the [a]treasure of the work threescore and one thousand drams *of* gold, and five thousand pound *of* silver, and one hundred priests' garments.

70 [a]So the priests, and the Levites, and *some* of the people, and the singers, and the porters, and the Nethinims, dwelt in their cities, and all Israel in their cities.

The altar rebuilt

3 And when the seventh month was come, and the children of Israel *were* in the cities, the people gathered themselves together as one man to Jerusalem.

2 Then stood up [1]Jeshua the son of Jozadak, and his brethren the priests, and [2]Zerubbabel the son of [3]Shealtiel, and his brethren, and builded the altar of the God of Israel, to offer burnt offerings thereon, as it is [a]written in the law of Moses the man of God.

3 And they set the altar upon his bases; for fear *was* upon them because of the people of *those* countries: and they offered burnt offerings thereon unto the LORD, *even* [a]burnt offerings morning and evening.

4 [a]They kept also the feast of tabernacles, [b]as it is written, and [c]*offered* the daily burnt offerings by number, according to the custom, [1]as the duty of every day required;

5 And afterward *offered* the [a]continual burnt offering, both of the new moons, and of all the set feasts of the LORD that were consecrated, and of every one that willingly offered a freewill offering unto the LORD.

6 From the first day of the seventh month began they to offer burnt offerings unto the LORD. But [1]the foundation of the temple of the LORD was not *yet* laid.

7 They gave money also unto the masons, and to the [1]carpenters; and [a]meat, and drink, and oil, unto them of Zidon, and to them of Tyre, to bring cedar trees from Lebanon to the sea of [b]Joppa, [c]according to the grant that they had of Cyrus king of Persia.

2:63 [1]Or, *governor* [a]Lev. 22:2,10,15,16 [b]Ex. 28:30; Num. 27:21
2:64 [a]Neh. 7:66
2:68 [a]Neh. 7:70
2:69 [a]1 Chr. 26:20
2:70 [a]ch. 6:16,17; Neh. 7:73
3:2 [1]Or, *Joshua* [2]Mat. 1:12; Luke 3:27, called *Zorobabel* [3]Mat. 1:12; Luke 3:27, called *Salathiel* [a]Deut. 12:5
3:3 [a]Num. 28:3
3:4 [1]Heb. *the matter of the day in his day* [a]Neh. 8:14; Zech. 14:16 [b]Ex. 23:16 [c]Num. 29:12
3:5 [a]Ex. 29:38; Num. 28:3, 11,19,26
3:6 [1]Heb. *the temple of the* LORD *was not* yet *founded*
3:7 [1]Or, *workmen* [a]1 Ki. 5:6,9; 2 Chr. 2:10; Acts 12:20 [b]2 Chr. 2:16; Acts 9:36 [c]ch. 6:3

‡2:63 *Tirshatha.* Transliteration of the Hebrew word for "governor." It probably refers to either Sheshbazzar or Zerubbabel (see note on 1:8). *Urim and . . . Thummim.* See note on Ex 28:30.
2:64 *forty and two thousand three hundred and threescore.* Considerably more than the sum of the other figures given:

Categories	*Ezra*	*Nehemiah*	*1 Esdras*
Men of Israel	24,144	25,406	25,947
Priests	4,289	4,289	5,288
Levites, singers, gatekeepers	341	360	341
Temple servants, descendants of Solomon's servants	392	392	372
Men of unproven origin	652	642	652
Totals	29,818	31,089	32,600

It is difficult to account for the difference of about 10,000–12,000. The figure may refer to an unspecified 10,000–12,000 women and/or children, and it doubtless includes the priests of unproven origin referred to in vv. 61–63. Some suggest that the groups explicitly counted were returnees from Judah and Benjamin, while the remainder were from other tribes.
2:65 *their servants and their maids.* The ratio of servants to others (one to six) is relatively high. The fact that so many returned with their masters speaks highly of the benevolent treatment of servants by the Jews. *singing men and singing women.* The men and women singers listed here may be secular singers who sang at social events such as weddings and funerals (2 Chr 35:25), as distinct from the temple singers of v. 41, who were all male.
2:66 *horses.* Perhaps a donation from Cyrus for the nobility. *mules.* Often used by royalty and the wealthy (1 Ki 1:33; Is 66:20).
2:67 *asses.* Were used to carry loads, women or children. Sheep, goats and cattle are not mentioned. They would have slowed the caravan.
2:68 *came . . . Jerusalem.* For the route of the return from exile see map No. 7b at the end of the study Bible.
‡2:69 The parallel passage (Neh 7:70–72) gives a fuller description than the account in Ezra. In Ezra the gifts come from the heads of the families (v. 68), while in Nehemiah the gifts are credited to three sources: the governor, the heads of the families, and the rest of the people. *drams* [i.e. "drachmas"]. The drachma was a Greek silver coin. Some believe that the coin intended here was the Persian daric, a gold coin. *pound* [lit. "minas"]. In the sexagesimal system (based on the number 60) that originated in Mesopotamia, there were 60 shekels in a mina and 60 minas in a talent. A shekel, which was about two-fifths of an ounce of silver, was the average wage for a month's work. Thus a mina would be the equivalent of five years' wages, and a talent would be 300 years' wages.
2:70 Later, Nehemiah (11:1–2) would be compelled to move people by lot to reinforce the population of Jerusalem.
3:1 *seventh month.* Tishri (September-October), about three months after the arrival of the exiles in Judah (in 537 B.C.). Tishri was one of the most sacred months of the Jewish year (see Lev 23:23–43 and notes).
3:2 *Jeshua . . . Zerubbabel.* The priest takes precedence over the civil leader in view of the nature of the occasion (contrast 3:8; 4:3; 5:2; Hag 1:1).
3:4 *feast of tabernacles.* See Lev 23:33–43 and notes.
3:5 *new moons.* See note on 1 Sam 20:5. *feasts . . . that were consecrated.* See note on Lev 23:2. *freewill offering.* See note on 1:4. It is noteworthy that the restoration of the sacrifices preceded the erection of the temple itself.
3:7 *cedar trees.* As in the case of the first temple, the Phoenicians cooperated by sending timber and workmen (1 Ki 5:6–12).

Rebuilding of the temple begun

8 ¶ Now in the second year of their coming unto the house of God at Jerusalem, in the second month, began Zerubbabel the son of Shealtiel, and Jeshua the son of Jozadak, and the remnant of their brethren the priests and the Levites, and all they that were come out of the captivity *unto* Jerusalem; [a]and appointed the Levites from twenty years old and upward, to set forward the work of the house of the LORD.

9 Then stood [a]Jeshua *with* his sons and his brethren, Kadmiel and his sons, the sons of [1]Judah, [2]together, to set forward the workmen in the house of God: the sons of Henadad, *with* their sons and their brethren the Levites.

10 And when the builders laid the foundation of the temple of the LORD, [a]they set the priests in their apparel with trumpets, and the Levites the sons of Asaph with cymbals, to praise the LORD, after the [b]ordinance of David king of Israel.

11 [a]And they sung together by course in praising and giving thanks unto the LORD; [b]because *he is* good, [c]for his mercy *endureth* for ever towards Israel. And all the people shouted *with* a great shout, when they praised the LORD, because the foundation of the house of the LORD was laid.

3:8 [a]1 Chr. 23:24,27
3:9 [1]Or, *Hodaviah,* ch. 2:40 [2]Heb. *as one* [a]ch. 2:40
3:10 [a]1 Chr. 16:5 [b]1 Chr. 6:31; 16:4; 25:1
3:11 [a]Ex. 15:21; 2 Chr. 7:3; Neh. 12:24 [b]1 Chr. 16:34; Ps. 136:1 [c]1 Chr. 16:41; Jer. 33:11

3:8 *second year.* Since the Jews probably returned to Judah in the spring of 537 B.C., the second year would be the spring of 536. *second month.* The same month (April-May) in which Solomon had begun his temple (1 Ki 6:1). *twenty years.* In earlier times the lower age limit for Levites was 30 (Num 4:3) or 25 years (Num 8:24). It was later reduced to 20 (1 Chr 23:24,27; 2 Chr 31:17), probably because there were so few Levites.
3:10 *trumpets.* Made of hammered silver (see Num 10:2 and note). According to Josephus (*Antiquities,* 3.12.6—written c. A.D. 93), the trumpet was "in length a little short of a cubit; it is a narrow tube, slightly thicker than a flute." With the possible exception of their use at the coronation of Joash (2 Ki 11:14; 2 Chr 23:13), the trumpets were always blown by priests. They were most often used on joyous occasions, such as here and at the dedication of the rebuilt walls of Jerusalem (Neh 12:35; cf. 2 Chr 5:13; Ps 98:6). *cymbals.* The Hebrew for this word occurs 13 times in the OT, all in Chronicles except here and Neh 12:27.
3:11 *sung.* May mean "sang responsively," referring to antiphonal singing by a choir divided into two groups. *he is good . . . his mercy endureth for ever.* See, e.g., 1 Chr 16:34; 2 Chr 5:13; Ps 100:5. *great shout.* See Josh 6:5,20; 1 Sam 4:5; Ps 95:1.

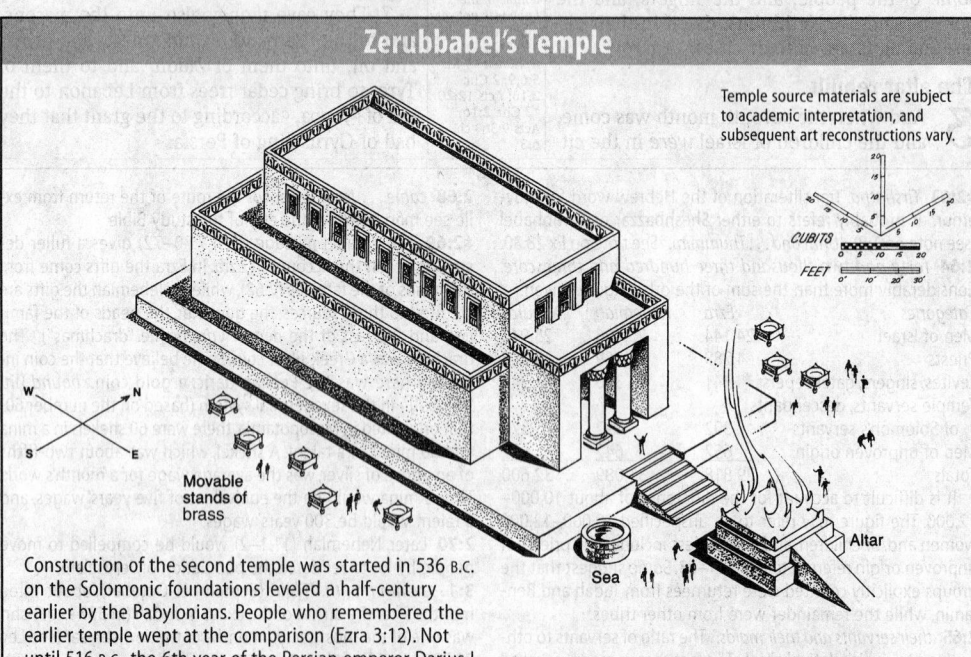

Zerubbabel's Temple

Temple source materials are subject to academic interpretation, and subsequent art reconstructions vary.

CUBITS
FEET
W N S E
Movable stands of brass
Altar
Sea

Construction of the second temple was started in 536 B.C. on the Solomonic foundations leveled a half-century earlier by the Babylonians. People who remembered the earlier temple wept at the comparison (Ezra 3:12). Not until 516 B.C., the 6th year of the Persian emperor Darius I (522-486), was the temple finally completed at the urging of Haggai and Zechariah (Ezra 6:13-15).

Archaeological evidence confirms that the Persian period in the Holy Land was a comparatively impoverished one in terms of material culture. Later Aramaic documents from Elephantine in Upper Egypt illustrate the official process of gaining permission to construct a Jewish place of worship, and the opposition engendered by the presence of various foes during this period.

Of the temple and its construction, little is known. Among the few contemporary buildings, the Persian palace at Lachish and the Tobiad monument at Iraq el-Amir may be compared in terms of technique.

Unlike the more famous structures razed in 586 B.C. and A.D. 70, the temple begun by Zerubbabel suffered no major hostile destruction, but was gradually repaired and reconstructed over a long period. Eventually it was replaced entirely by Herod's magnificent edifice.

12 But many of the priests and Levites and
chief of the fathers, *who were* ancient men
that had seen the first house, when the foundation of this house was laid before their eyes,
wept with a loud voice; and many shouted
aloud for joy:
13 So that the people could not discern the
noise of the shout of joy from the noise of the
weeping of the people: for the people shouted
with a loud shout, and the noise was heard
afar off.

Adversaries of Judah

4 Now *when* [a]the adversaries of Judah and
Benjamin heard that [1]the children of the
captivity builded the temple unto the LORD
God of Israel;
2 Then they came to Zerubbabel, and to
the chief of the fathers, and said unto them,
Let us build with you: for we seek your God, as
ye *do;* and we do sacrifice unto him since [a]the
days of Esar-haddon king of Assur, which
brought us up hither.
3 But Zerubbabel, and Jeshua, and the rest
of the chief of the fathers of Israel, said unto
them, [a]You have nothing to do with us to build
a house unto our God; but we ourselves together will build unto the LORD God of Israel,
as [b]king Cyrus the king of Persia hath commanded us.
4 Then [a]the people of the land weakened
the hands of the people of Judah, and troubled
them in building,
5 And hired counsellers against them, to
frustrate their purpose, all the days of Cyrus
king of Persia, even until the reign of Darius
king of Persia.
6 And in the reign of [1]Ahasuerus, in the
beginning of his reign, wrote they *unto him* an
accusation against the inhabitants of Judah and
Jerusalem.
7 And in the days of Artaxerxes wrote
[1]Bishlam, Mithredath, Tabeel, and the rest of
their [2]companions, unto Artaxerxes king of
Persia; and the writing of the letter *was* written in the Syrian tongue, and interpreted in
the Syrian tongue.

The letter to Artaxerxes

8 ¶ Rehum the chancellor and Shimshai the
[1]scribe wrote a letter against Jerusalem to Artaxerxes the king in this sort:
9 Then *wrote* Rehum the chancellor, and
Shimshai the scribe, and the rest of their
[1]companions; [a]the Dinaites, the Apharsath-
chites, the Tarpelites, the Apharsites, the
Archevites, the Babylonians, the Susanchites,
the Dehavites, *and* the Elamites,
10 [a]And the rest of the nations whom the
great and noble Asnappar brought over, and
set in the cities of Samaria, and the rest *that
are on this* side the river, [b]and [1]at such a time.

4:1 [1]Heb. *the sons of the transportation* [a]See ver. 7-9
4:2 [a]ver. 10; 2 Ki. 17:24,32,33; 19:37
4:3 [a]Neh. 2:20 [b]ch. 1:1-3
4:4 [a]ch. 3:3
4:6 [1]Heb. *Ahashverosh*
4:7 [1]Or, *in peace* [2]Heb. *societies*
4:8 [1]Or, *secretary*
4:9 [1]Chald. *societies* [a]2 Ki. 17:30,31
4:10 [1]Chald. *Cheeneth* [a]ver. 1 [b]ver. 11,17; ch 7:12

3:13 *shout of joy . . . noise of the weeping.* The people of Israel were accustomed to showing their emotions in visible and audible ways (10:1; Neh 1:4; 8:9). The same God who had permitted judgment had now brought them back and would enable them to complete the project. A Babylonian cornerstone reads: "I started the work weeping, I finished it rejoicing." Cf. Ps 126:5–6.

4:1–23 A summary of various attempts to thwart the efforts of the Jews. In vv. 1–5 the author describes events in the reign of Cyrus (559–530 B.C.), in v. 6 the reign of Ahasuerus (486–465) and in vv. 7–23 the reign of Artaxerxes I (465–424). He then reverts in v. 24 to the time of Darius I (522–486), during whose reign the temple was completed (see 5:1–2; 6:13–15; Haggai; Zech 1:1–17; 4:9).

4:1 *adversaries.* The people who offered their "help" (v. 2) were from Samaria. *Judah and Benjamin.* See notes on 1:5; 1 Ki 12:21.

4:2 After the fall of Samaria in 722–721 B.C., the Assyrian kings brought in people from Mesopotamia and Aram. These people served their own gods but also took up the worship of the Lord as the god of the land (2 Ki 17:24–41). *Esar-haddon.* See note on 2 Ki 19:37.

4:4 *people of the land.* Josephus (*Antiquities,* 11.2.1) singles out especially the Cutheans (see 2 Ki 17:24,30). *troubled them.* The Hebrew for this verb often describes the fear aroused in a battle situation (Judg 20:41; 2 Sam 4:1; 2 Chr 32:18).

4:5 *hired.* Cf. the hiring of Balaam (Deut 23:4–5; Neh 13:2) and the hiring of a prophet to intimidate Nehemiah (Neh 6:12–13).

4:6 *Ahasuerus.* See the book of Esther. When Darius died in 486 B.C., Egypt rebelled, and Ahasuerus, the son of Darius, had to march west to suppress the revolt.

‡4:7 *Artaxerxes.* Three Persian kings bore this name: Artaxerxes I (465–424 B.C.), II (404–358) and III (358–338). The king here is Artaxerxes I. *wrote.* Near Eastern kings employed an elaborate system of informers and spies. Egyptian sources speak of the "ears and eyes" of Pharaoh. Sargon II of Assyria had agents in Urartu whom he ordered: "Write me whatever you see and hear." The King's Eye and the King's Ear were these officials who reported to the Persian monarch. *Mithredath.* See 1:8 and note. *Tabeel.* An Aramaic name (see Is 7:6 and note).

4:8–6:18 For this passage the author draws upon Aramaic documents. In the original text of Ezra, this section is written in Aramaic; a further Aramaic section is 7:12–26.

4:8 *chancellor.* An official who had the role of a commanding officer or commissioner. Perhaps Rehum dictated, and Shimshai wrote the letter in Aramaic. (Alternatively, Shimshai may have been a high official rather than a scribe.) The letter would then be read in a Persian translation before the king (v. 18). According to Herodotus (3.128), royal scribes were attached to each governor to report directly to the Persian king.

‡4:9 *companions.* See vv. 17,23; 5:3,6; 6:6,13. One of the striking characteristics of Persian bureaucracy was that each responsibility was shared among colleagues. *Archevites.* I.e. men of Erech. See note on Gen 10:10. *Babylonians.* During the reign of the Assyrian king Ashurbanipal (669–627 B.C.), a major revolt had taken place (652–648), involving Shamash-shum-ukin, the brother of the king and the ruler over Babylonia. After a long siege Shamash-shum-ukin hurled himself into the flames. Doubtless these men of Babylon and the other cities mentioned were the descendants of the rebels, whom the Assyrians deported to the west. *Susanchites.* I.e. men of Susa, the major city of Elam (in southwest Iran). Because of Susa's part in the revolt, Ashurbanipal brutally destroyed it in 640 (two centuries before Rehum's letter).

‡4:10 *Asnappar.* A variant of "Ashurbanipal," the last great Assyrian king, famed for his library at Nineveh. He is not named elsewhere in the Bible, but he is probably the king who freed Manasseh from exile (2 Chr 33:11–13). *brought over.* Ashurba-

11 This *is* the copy of the letter that they sent unto him, *even* unto Artaxerxes the king: ¶ Thy servants the men *on this* side the river, and at such a time.

12 Be it known unto the king, that the Jews which came up from thee to us are come unto Jerusalem, building the rebellious and the bad city, and have [1]set up the walls *thereof,* and [2]joined the foundations.

13 Be it known now unto the king, that, if this city be builded, and the walls set up *again, then* will they not [1]pay [a]toll, tribute, and custom, and *so* thou shalt endamage the [2]revenue of the kings.

14 Now because [1]we have maintenance from *the king's* palace, and *it was* not meet for us to see the king's dishonour, therefore have we sent and certified the king;

15 That search may be made in the book of the records of thy fathers: so shalt thou find in the book of the records, and know that this city *is* a rebellious city, and hurtful unto kings and provinces, and that they have [1]moved sedition [2]within the same of old time: for which *cause* was this city destroyed.

16 We certify the king that, if this city be builded *again,* and the walls thereof set up, by this means thou shalt have no portion on *this* side the river.

17 ¶ *Then* sent the king an answer unto Rehum the chancellor, and *to* Shimshai the scribe, and *to* the rest of their [1]companions that dwell in Samaria, and *unto* the rest beyond the river: ¶ Peace, and at such a time.

18 The letter which ye sent unto us *hath been* plainly read before me.

19 And [1]I commanded, and search hath been made, and it is found that this city of old time *hath* [2]made insurrection against kings, and *that* rebellion and sedition *have been* made therein.

20 There have been mighty kings also over Jerusalem, which have [a]ruled over all *countries* [b]beyond the river; and toll, tribute, and custom, *was* paid unto them.

21 [1]Give ye now commandment to cause these men to cease, and *that* this city be not builded, until *another* commandment shall be [2]given from me.

22 Take heed now that ye fail not to do this: why should damage grow to the hurt of the kings?

23 ¶ Now when the copy of king Artaxerxes' letter *was* read before Rehum, and Shimshai the scribe, and their companions, they went up in haste to Jerusalem unto the Jews, and made them to cease [1]by force and power.

24 Then ceased the work of the house of the God which *is* at Jerusalem. So it ceased unto the second year of the reign of Darius king of Persia.

Zerubbabel begins to build again

5 Then the prophets, [a]Haggai the prophet, and [b]Zechariah the son of Iddo, prophesied unto the Jews that *were* in Judah and Jeru-

4:12 [1]Or, *finished* [2]Chald. *sewed together*
4:13 [1]Chald. *give* [2]Or, *strength* [a]ch. 7:24
4:14 [1]Chald. *we are salted* with *the salt of the palace*
4:15 [1]Chald. *made* [2]Chald. *in the midst thereof*
4:17 [1]Chald. *societies*
4:19 [1]Chald. *by me a decree* is *set* [2]Chald. *lifted up itself*
4:20 [a]1 Ki. 4:21; Ps. 72:8 [b]Gen. 15:18; Josh. 1:4
4:21 [1]Chald. *Make a decree* [2]Chald. *make a decree*
4:23 [1]Chald. *by arm and power*
5:1 [a]Hag. 1:1 [b]Zech. 1:1

nipal may be the unnamed Assyrian king who brought people to Samaria according to 2 Ki 17:24. It is characteristic of such deportations that the descendants of populations that had been removed from their homelands nearly two centuries earlier should still stress their origins. *Samaria.* The murder of Amon king of Judah (642–640 B.C.; see 2 Ki 21:23; 2 Chr 33:24) was probably the result of an anti-Assyrian movement inspired by the revolt in Elam and Babylonia. The Assyrians may then have deported the rebellious Samaritans and replaced them with the rebellious Elamites and Babylonians. *that are on this side the river.* Lit. "beyond the river" (i.e. the Euphrates River). From Israel's point of view the land "beyond the river" was Mesopotamia (Josh 24:2–3,14–15; 2 Sam 10:16). From the Mesopotamian point of view the land "beyond the river" included the areas of Aram, Phoenicia and Israel (1 Ki 4:24). The Persians also called this area Athura.

4:12 *set up the walls . . . and joined the foundations.* As Isaiah had foretold (see Is 58:12 and note).

4:13 Most of the gold and silver coins that came into Persia's treasury were melted down to be stored as bullion. Very little of the taxes returned to benefit the provinces.

4:14 *we have maintenance from the king's palace.* Lit. "we eat the salt of the palace." Salt was made a royal monopoly by the Ptolemies in Egypt, and perhaps by the Persians as well.

4:15 *book of the records.* See 5:17; 6:1; Esth 2:23; 6:1–2. There were several repositories of such documents at the major capitals. These royal archives preserved documents for centuries. In the third century B.C. the Babylonian priest Berossus made use of the Babylonian Chronicles in his history of Babylon, which covered events from the Assyrian to the Hellenistic (beginning with Alexander's conquest of Babylon in 330 B.C.) eras.

4:18 *been plainly read.* I.e. translated from Aramaic into Persian (see note on 4:8–6:18). *read.* Since the king probably could not read Aramaic, he would have had the document read to him.

4:19 *rebellion.* There is some truth in the accusation. Jerusalem had rebelled against the Assyrians in 701 B.C. (2 Ki 18:7) and against the Babylonians in 600 and 589 (2 Ki 24:1,20).

4:21–23 As a result of the intervention of the provincial authorities, Artaxerxes I (see v. 11 and note on v. 7) ordered that the Jews stop rebuilding the walls of Jerusalem (see note on Neh 1:3). The events of vv. 7–23 probably occurred prior to 445 B.C.. The forcible destruction of these recently rebuilt walls rather than the destruction by Nebuchadnezzar would then be the basis of the report made to Nehemiah (Neh 1:3).

4:24 After this long digression describing the opposition to Jewish efforts, the writer returns to his original subject of the rebuilding of the temple (vv. 1–5). *second year of the reign of Darius.* According to Persian reckoning, the second regnal year of Darius I began on Nisan 1 (Apr. 3), 520 B.C., and lasted until Feb. 21, 519. In that year the prophet Haggai (Hag 1:1–5) exhorted Zerubbabel to begin rebuilding the temple on the first day of the sixth month (Aug. 29). Work began on the temple on the 24th day of the month, Sept. 21 (Hag 1:15). During his first two years, Darius had to establish his right to the throne by fighting numerous rebels, as recounted in his famous Behistun (Bisitun) inscription. It was only after the stabilization of the Persian empire that efforts to rebuild the temple could be permitted.

5:1 *Haggai . . . Zechariah.* Beginning on Aug. 29, 520 B.C. (Hag 1:1), and continuing until Dec. 18 (Hag 2:1,10,20), the prophet Haggai delivered a series of messages to stir up the people to

salem in the name of the God of Israel, *even* unto them.

2 Then rose up [a]Zerubbabel the son of Shealtiel, and Jeshua the son of Jozadak, and began to build the house of God which *is* at Jerusalem: and with them *were* the prophets of God helping them.

3 ¶ At the same time came to them [a]Tatnai, governor on *this* side the river, and Shethar-boznai, and their companions, and said thus unto them, [b]Who hath commanded you to build this house, and to make up this wall?

4 [a]Then said we unto them after this manner, What are the names of the men [1]that make this building?

5 But [a]the eye of their God was upon the elders of the Jews, that they could not cause them to cease, till the matter came to Darius: and then they returned [b]answer by letter concerning this *matter.*

6 The copy of the letter that Tatnai, governor on *this* side the river, and Shethar-boznai, [a]and his companions the Apharsachites, which *were* on *this* side the river, sent unto Darius the king:

7 They sent a letter unto him, [1]wherein *was* written thus:

¶ Unto Darius the king, all peace.

8 Be it known unto the king, that we went into the province of Judea, to the house of the great God, which *is* builded *with* [1]great stones, and timber *is* laid in the walls, and this work goeth fast on, and prospereth in their hands.

9 Then asked we those elders, *and* said unto them thus, [a]Who commanded you to build this house, and to make up these walls?

10 We asked their names also, to certify thee, that we might write the names of the men that *were* the chief of them.

11 And thus they returned us answer, saying, We are the servants of the God of heaven and earth, and build the house that was builded these many years ago, which a great king of Israel builded [a]and set up.

12 But [a]after that our fathers had provoked the God of heaven unto wrath, he gave them into the hand of [b]Nebuchadnezzar the king of Babylon, the Chaldean, who destroyed this house, and carried the people away into Babylon.

13 But in the first year of [a]Cyrus the king of Babylon *the same* king Cyrus made a decree to build this house of God.

14 And [a]the vessels also of gold and silver of the house of God, which Nebuchadnezzar took out of the temple that *was* in Jerusalem, and brought them into the temple of Babylon, those did Cyrus the king take out of the temple of Babylon, and they *were* delivered unto *one,* [b]whose name *was* Sheshbazzar, whom he had made [1]governor;

15 And said unto him, Take these vessels, go, carry them into the temple that *is* in Jerusalem, and let the house of God be builded in his place.

16 Then came the same Sheshbazzar, *and* [a]laid the foundation of the house of God which *is* in Jerusalem: and since that time even until now *hath it been* in building, and [b]*yet it is* not finished.

17 Now therefore, if *it seem* good to the king, [a]let there be search made in the king's treasure house, which *is* there at Babylon, whether it be *so,* that a decree *was* made of Cyrus the king to build this house of God at Jerusalem, and let the king send his pleasure to us concerning this *matter.*

5:2 [a]ch. 3:2
5:3 [a]ver. 6; ch. 6:6 [b]ver. 9
5:4 [1]Chald. *that build this building?* [a]ver. 10
5:5 [a]See ch. 7:6,28; Ps. 33:18 [b]ch. 6:6
5:6 [a]ch. 4:9
5:7 [1]Chald. *in the midst whereof*
5:8 [1]Chald. *stones of rolling*
5:9 [a]ver. 3,4
5:11 [a]1 Ki. 6:1
5:12 [a]2 Chr. 36:16,17 [b]2 Ki. 24:2; 25:8,9,11
5:13 [a]ch. 1:1
5:14 [1]Or, *deputy* [a]ch. 1:7,8; 6:5 [b]Hag. 1:14; 2:2,21
5:16 [a]ch. 3:8,10 [b]ch. 6:15
5:17 [a]ch. 6:1,2
6:1 [1]Chald. *books* [2]Chald. *made to descend* [a]ch. 5:17
6:2 [1]Or, *Ecbatana,* or, *in a coffer*

Darius' search and reply

6 Then Darius the king made a decree, [a]and search was made in the house of the [1]rolls, where the treasures were [2]laid up in Babylon.

2 And there was found at [1]Achmetha, in the palace that *is* in the province of the

resume work on the temple. Two months after Haggai's first speech, Zechariah joined him (Zech 1:1).

5:2 *Zerubbabel.* A Babylonian name meaning "offspring of Babylon," referring to his birth in exile. He was the son of Shealtiel and the grandson of Jeconiah (1 Chr 3:17), the next-to-last king of Judah. Zerubbabel was the last of the Davidic line to be entrusted with political authority by the occupying powers. He was also an ancestor of Jesus (Mat 1:12–13; Luke 3:27). *Jeshua.* See note on 2:2.

5:3 *Tatnai.* Probably a Babylonian name. *Shethar-boznai.* Perhaps a Persian official.

5:5 *cause them to cease.* The Persian governor gave the Jews the benefit of the doubt by not stopping the work while the inquiry was proceeding.

5:6–7 *sent unto Darius the king . . . unto him.* Texts found in the royal city of Persepolis vividly confirm that such inquiries were sent directly to the king himself, revealing the close attention he paid to minute details.

5:8 *timber.* May refer to interior paneling (1 Ki 6:15–18) or to logs alternating with the brick or stone layers in the walls (see note on 6:4).

5:11 *great king of Israel.* According to 1 Ki 6:1 Solomon began building the temple in the fourth year of his reign (966 B.C.). The project lasted seven years (1 Ki 6:38).

5:12 *Chaldean.* The Chaldeans were the inhabitants of the southern regions of Mesopotamia who established the Neo-Babylonian empire (612–539 B.C.). Their origins are obscure. In the late seventh century B.C. the Chaldeans, led by Nebuchadnezzar's father Nabopolassar, overthrew the Assyrians.

5:14 *Sheshbazzar . . . governor.* See note on 1:8.

6:1 *house of the rolls, where the treasures were laid up in Babylon.* Many documents have also been found in the so-called "treasury" area of Persepolis (see map, p. 545).

‡6:2 *Achmetha.* [i.e. Ecbatana]. One of the four capitals (along with Babylon, Persepolis and Susa) of the Persian empire. Located in what is today the Iranian city of Hamadan, its remains have not yet been excavated. This is the only reference to the site in the OT, though there are numerous references in the Apocryphal books (Judith 1:1–4; Tobit 3:7; 7:1; 14:12–14; 2 Maccabees 9:3). *Medes.* People whose homeland is Media, in northwestern Iran. The Medes were an Indo-European tribe related to the Persians. After the rise of Cyrus in 550 B.C., they became subordinate to the Persians. The name of the area was retained as late as the NT era (Acts 2:9).

Medes, a roll, and therein *was* a record thus
written:
3 ¶ In the first year of Cyrus the king *the*
same Cyrus the king made a decree *concerning*
the house of God at Jerusalem, Let the house
be builded, the place where they offered sacrifices, and *let* the foundations thereof *be* strongly laid; the height thereof threescore cubits,
and the breadth thereof threescore cubits;
4 [a]*With* three rows of great stones, and a
row of new timber: and let the expences be
given out of the king's house:
5 And also let [a]the golden and silver vessels of the house of God, which Nebuchadnezzar took forth out of the temple which *is* at Jerusalem, and brought unto Babylon, be
restored, and [1]brought *again* unto the temple
which *is* at Jerusalem, *every one* to his place,
and place *them* in the house of God.
6 [a]Now *therefore,* Tatnai, governor beyond
the river, Shethar-boznai, and [1]your companions the Apharsachites, which *are* beyond the
river, be ye far from thence:
7 Let the work of this house of God alone;
let the governor of the Jews and the elders of
the Jews build this house of God in his place.
8 Moreover [1]I make a decree what ye shall
do to the elders of these Jews for the building
of this house of God: that of the king's goods,
even of the tribute beyond the river, forthwith
expences be given unto these men, that *they*
be not [2]hindered.

6:4 [a]1 Ki. 6:36
6:5 [1]Chald. *go* [a]ch. 1:7,8; 5:14
6:6 [1]Chald. *their societies* [a]ch. 5:3
6:8 [1]Chald. *by me a decree is made* [2]Chald. *made to cease*
6:10 [1]Chald. *of rest* [a]ch. 7:23
6:11 [1]Chald. *let him be destroyed* [a]Dan. 2:5; 3:29
6:12 [a]1 Ki. 9:3
6:14 [1]Chald. *decree* [a]ch. 5:1,2

9 And that which *they* have need of, both
young bullocks, and rams, and lambs, for the
burnt offerings of the God of heaven, wheat,
salt, wine, and oil, according to the appointment of the priests which *are* at Jerusalem, let
it be given them day by day without fail:
10 [a]That they may offer sacrifices [1]of
sweet savours unto the God of heaven, and
pray for the life of the king, and of his sons.
11 Also I have made a decree, that whosoever shall alter this word, let timber be pulled
down from his house, and being set up, [1]let
him be hanged thereon; [a]and let his house be
made a dunghill for this.
12 And the God that hath caused his
[a]name to dwell there destroy all kings and
people, that shall put to their hand to alter *and*
to destroy this house of God which *is* at Jerusalem. I Darius have made a decree; let it be
done with speed.

The temple rebuilt and dedicated

13 ¶ Then Tatnai, governor on *this* side the
river, Shethar-boznai, and their companions,
according to that which Darius the king had
sent, so they did speedily.
14 [a]And the elders of the Jews builded,
and they prospered through the prophesying
of Haggai the prophet and Zechariah the son of
Iddo. And they builded, and finished *it,* according to the [1]commandment of the God of
Israel, and according to the [1]commandment of

6:3–5 Compare this Aramaic memorandum of the decree of Cyrus with the Hebrew version in 1:2–4. The Aramaic is written in a more sober administrative style without any reference to the Lord (Yahweh). A similar memorandum dealing with permission to rebuild the Jewish temple at Elephantine in Upper Egypt was found among fifth-century B.C. Aramaic papyri recovered at that site.

6:3 *height thereof threescore cubits, and the breadth thereof threescore cubits.* These dimensions, which contrast with those of Solomon's temple (see 1 Ki 6:2 and note), are probably not specifications of the temple as built but of the outer limits of a building the Persians were willing to subsidize. The second temple was not as grandiose as the first (3:12; Hag 2:3).

6:4 *great stones . . . timber.* See 5:8. The same kind of construction is mentioned in 1 Ki 6:36; 7:12. Such a design was possibly intended to cushion the building against earthquake shocks. *let the expences be given out of the king's house.* In 1973 archaeologists discovered at Xanthos in southwest Turkey a religious foundation charter from the late Persian period that provides some striking parallels with this decree of Cyrus. As in Ezra, amounts of sacrifices, names of priests and the responsibility for the upkeep of the cult are specified. The Persian king seems to have known details of the cult.

6:8 *of the king's goods . . . expences be given.* It was a consistent policy of Persian kings to help restore sanctuaries in their empire. For example, a memorandum concerning the rebuilding of the Jewish temple at Elephantine was written by the Persian governors of Judah and Samaria. Also from non-Biblical sources we learn that Cyrus repaired temples at Uruk (Erech) and Ur. Cambyses, successor to Cyrus, gave funds for the temple at Sais in Egypt. The temple of Amun in the Khargah Oasis was rebuilt by order of Darius.

6:9 That the Persian monarchs were interested in the details of foreign religions is shown clearly by the ordinances of Cambyses and Darius I, regulating the temples and priests in Egypt. On the authority of Darius II (423–404 B.C.) a letter was written to the Jews at Elephantine concerning the keeping of the feast of unleavened bread.

6:10 *pray for the life of the king, and of his sons.* In the inscription on the Cyrus Cylinder (made of baked clay), the king asks: "May all the gods whom I have resettled in their sacred cities ask Bel and Nebo daily for a long life for me." The Jews of Elephantine offered to pray for the Persian governor of Judah. The daily synagogue services included a prayer for the royal family (cf. 1 Tim 2:1–2).

‡6:11 *whosoever shall alter this word.* It was customary at the end of decrees and treaties to append a long list of curses against anyone who might disregard them. *hanged thereon.* Or "impaled." According to Herodotus (3.159), Darius I impaled 3,000 Babylonians when he took the city of Babylon. See Esth 2:23 and note.

6:12 *the God . . . destroy all kings and people.* At the end of his famous Behistun (Bisitun) inscription Darius I warned: "If you see this inscription or these sculptures, and destroy them and do not protect them as long as you have strength, may Ahuramazda strike you, and may you not have a family, and what you do . . . may Ahuramazda utterly destroy." *caused his name to dwell.* See note on Deut 12:5.

6:13–14 Work on the temple had made little progress not only because of opposition but also because of the preoccupation of the returnees with their own homes (Hag 1:2–9). Because they had placed their own interests first, God sent them famine as a judgment (Hag 1:5–6,10–11). Spurred by the preaching of Haggai and Zechariah, and under the leadership of Zerubbabel and Jeshua, a new effort was begun (Hag 1:12–15).

[b]Cyrus, and [c]Darius, and [d]Artaxerxes king of
Persia.
15 And this house was finished on the
third day of the month Adar, which *was in* the
sixth year of the reign of Darius the king.
16 And the children of Israel, the priests,
and the Levites, and the rest of [1]the children
of the captivity, kept [a]the dedication of this
house of God with joy,
17 And [a]offered at the dedication of this
house of God an hundred bullocks, two hundred rams, four hundred lambs; and for a sin
offering for all Israel, twelve he goats, according to the number of the tribes of Israel.
18 And they set the priests in their [a]divi-
sions, and the Levites in their [b]courses, for the
service of God, which *is* at Jerusalem; [c1]as it is
written in the book of Moses.
19 ¶ And the children of the captivity kept
the passover [a]upon the fourteenth *day* of the
first month.
20 For the priests and the Levites were
[a]purified together, all of them *were* pure, and
[b]killed the passover for all the children of the

6:14 [b]ver. 3; ch. 1:1; 5:13 [c]ch. 4:24 [d]ch. 7:1
6:16 [1]Chald. *the sons of the transportation* [a]1 Ki. 8:63; 2 Chr. 7:5
6:17 [a]ch. 8:35
6:18 [1]Chald. *according to the writing* [a]1 Chr. 24:1 [b]1 Chr. 23:6 [c]Num. 3:6; 8:9
6:19 [a]Ex. 12:6
6:20 [a]2 Chr. 30:15 [b]2 Chr. 35:11
6:21 [a]ch. 9:11
6:22 [a]Ex. 12:15; 13:6; 2 Chr. 30:21; 35:17 [b]Prov. 21:1 [c]2 Ki. 23:29; 2 Chr. 33:11; ch. 1:1
7:1 [a]Neh. 2:1 [b]1 Chr. 6:14

captivity, and for their brethren the priests,
and for themselves.
21 And the children of Israel, which were
come again out of captivity, and all such as had
separated themselves unto them from the
[a]filthiness of the heathen of the land, to seek
the LORD God of Israel, did eat,
22 And kept the [a]feast of unleavened bread
seven days with joy: for the LORD had made
them joyful, and [b]turned the heart [c]of the king
of Assyria unto them, to strengthen their
hands in the work of the house of God, the
God of Israel.

Ezra's genealogy and career

7 Now after these things, in the reign of [a]Ar-
taxerxes king of Persia, Ezra [b]the son of
Seraiah, the son of Azariah, the son of Hilkiah,
2 The son of Shallum, the son of Zadok, the
son of Ahitub,
3 The son of Amariah, the son of Azariah,
the son of Meraioth,
4 The son of Zerahiah, the son of Uzzi, the
son of Bukki,

6:14 *Artaxerxes.* The reference to him seems out of place, because he did not contribute to rebuilding the temple. He may have been inserted here since he contributed to the work of the temple at a later date under Ezra (7:21–24).

6:15 *house was finished.* On Mar. 12, 516 B.C., almost 70 years after its destruction. The renewed work on the temple had begun on Sept. 21, 520 (Hag 1:15), and sustained effort had continued for almost three and a half years. According to Hag 2:3, the older members who could remember the splendor of Solomon's temple were disappointed when they saw the smaller size of Zerubbabel's temple (cf. Ezra 3:12). Yet in the long run the second temple, though not as grand as the first, enjoyed a much longer life. The general plan of the second temple was similar to that of Solomon's, but the most holy place was left empty because the ark of the covenant had been lost through the Babylonian conquest. According to Josephus, on the day of atonement the high priest placed his censer on the slab of stone that marked the former location of the ark. The holy place was furnished with a table for the shewbread, the incense altar, and one candlestick (in the Apocrypha cf. 1 Maccabees 1:21–22; 4:49–51) instead of Solomon's ten (1 Ki 7:49).

6:16 *children of the captivity . . . dedication.* Cf. the dedication of Solomon's temple (1 Ki 8). The leaders of those who returned from exile were responsible for the completion of the temple. "Dedication" translates the Aramaic word *ḥanukkah.* The Jewish holiday in December that celebrates the recapture of the temple from the Seleucids and its rededication (165 B.C.) is also known as Hanukkah.

6:17 *an hundred . . . two hundred . . . four hundred.* The number of animals sacrificed was small in comparison with similar services in the reigns of Solomon (1 Ki 8:5,63), Hezekiah (2 Chr 30:24) and Josiah (2 Chr 35:7), when thousands rather than hundreds were offered.

6:18 *divisions.* The priests were separated into 24 divisions (1 Chr 24:1–19), each of which served at the temple for a week at a time (cf. Luke 1:5,8). In 1962 fragments of a synagogue inscription listing the 24 divisions were found at Caesarea. *written in the book of Moses.* Perhaps referring to such passages as Ex 29; Lev 8; Num 3; 8:5–26; 18.

6:19 *passover upon the fourteenth day of the first month.* The date would have been about Apr. 21, 516 B.C.

6:20 *purified together . . . pure.* See note on Lev 4:12. Priests and Levites had to be ceremonially clean to fulfill their ritual functions.

6:21 *all such as had separated themselves.* The returning exiles were willing to accept those who separated themselves from the paganism of the foreigners who had been introduced into the area by the Assyrians.

6:22 *king of Assyria.* A surprising title for Darius, the Persian king. But even after the fall of Nineveh in 612 B.C., the term "Assyria" continued to be used for former territories the Assyrians had occupied (even Syria is an abbreviation of Assyria). Persian kings adopted a variety of titles, including "king of Babylon" (cf. 5:13; Neh 13:6).

7:1–5 The genealogy of Ezra given here lists 16 ancestors back to Aaron, the brother of Moses.

7:1 *after these things.* The events of the preceding chapter concluded with the completion of the temple in 516 B.C. *Artaxerxes.* The identity of the king mentioned in this chapter has been disputed. If this was Artaxerxes I, which seems likely, Ezra would have arrived in Judah in 458, and there would be a gap of almost 60 years between the events of ch. 6 and those of ch. 7. The only recorded event during this interval is the opposition to the rebuilding of Jerusalem in the reign of Ahasuerus (486–465) in 4:6. *Ezra.* Perhaps a shortened form of Azariah, a name that occurs twice in the list of his ancestors. The Greek form is Esdras, as in the Apocrypha. *Seraiah.* Means "The LORD is prince." He was the high priest under Zedekiah who was killed in 586 by Nebuchadnezzar (2 Ki 25:18–21) some 128 years before Ezra's arrival. He was therefore the ancestor rather than the father of Ezra; "son" often means "descendant" (see 1 Chr 6:14–15). *Azariah.* Means "The LORD helps." *Hilkiah.* Means "My portion is the LORD." He was the high priest under Josiah (2 Ki 22:4).

7:2 *Zadok.* Means "righteous." He was a priest under David (2 Sam 8:17). Solomon appointed Zadok as high priest in place of Abiathar, who supported the rebel Adonijah (1 Ki 1:7–8; 2:35). Ezekiel regarded the Zadokites as free from idolatry (Ezek 44:15). They held the office of high priest until 171 B.C. The Sadducees may have been named after Zadok, and the Qumran community (see essay, p. 1344) looked for the restoration of the Zadokite priesthood. *Ahitub.* Probably means "My (divine) brother is good." He was actually the grandfather of Zadok (Neh 11:11).

5 The son of Abishua, the son of Phinehas, the son of Eleazar, the son of Aaron the chief priest:

6 This Ezra went up from Babylon; and he *was* [a]a ready scribe in the law of Moses, which the LORD God of Israel had given: and the king granted him all his request, [b]according to the hand of the LORD his God upon him.

7 [a]And there went up *some* of the children of Israel, and of the priests, and [b]the Levites, and the singers, and the porters, and [c]the Nethinims, unto Jerusalem, in the seventh year of Artaxerxes the king.

8 And he came *to* Jerusalem in the fifth month, which *was in* the seventh year of the king.

9 For upon the first *day* of the first month [1]began he to go up from Babylon, and on the first *day* of the fifth month came he to Jerusalem, [a]according to the good hand of his God upon him.

10 For Ezra had prepared his heart to [a]seek the law of the LORD, and to do *it,* and to [b]teach in Israel statutes and judgments.

11 Now this *is* the copy of the letter that the king Artaxerxes gave unto Ezra the priest, the scribe, *even* a scribe of the words of the commandments of the LORD, and of his statutes to Israel.

Ezra's letter from Artaxerxes

12 ¶ Artaxerxes, [a]king of kings, [1]unto Ezra the priest, a scribe of the law of the God of heaven, perfect *peace,* [b]and at such a time.

13 I make a decree, that all they of the people of Israel, and *of* his priests and Levites, in my realm, *which are* minded of their own freewill to go *up* to Jerusalem, go with thee.

14 Forasmuch as *thou art* sent [1]of the king, and of his [a]seven counsellers, to inquire concerning Judah and Jerusalem, according to the law of thy God which *is* in thine hand;

15 And to carry the silver and gold, which the king and his counsellers have freely offered unto the God of Israel, [a]whose habitation *is* in Jerusalem,

16 [a]And all the silver and gold that thou canst find in all the province of Babylon, with the freewill offering of the people, and of the priests, [b]offering willingly for the house of their God which *is* in Jerusalem:

17 That thou mayest buy speedily with this money bullocks, rams, lambs, with their [a]meat offerings and their drink offerings, and [b]offer them upon the altar of the house of your God which *is* in Jerusalem.

18 And whatsoever shall seem good to thee, and to thy brethren, to do with the rest of the silver and gold, *that* do after the will of your God.

19 The vessels also that *are* given thee for the service of the house of thy God, *those* deliver thou before the God of Jerusalem.

20 And whatsoever more *shall be* needful

7:6 [a]ver. 11,12 [b]ch. 8:22
7:7 [a]ch. 8:1 [b]See ch. 8:15 [c]ch. 2:43; 8:20
7:9 [1]Heb. was *the foundation of the going up* [a]Neh. 2:8,18
7:10 [a]Ps. 119:45 [b]ver. 6,25; Deut. 33:10; Neh. 8:1-8; Mal. 2:7
7:12 [1]Or, *to Ezra the priest, a perfect scribe of the law of the God of heaven,* peace, etc. [a]Ezek. 26:7; Dan. 2:37

7:12 [b]ch. 4:10
7:14 [1]Chald. *from before the king* [a]Esth. 1:14
7:15 [a]2 Chr. 6:2; Ps. 135:21
7:16 [a]ch. 8:25 [b]1 Chr. 29:6,9
7:17 [a]Num. 15:4-13 [b]Deut. 12:5,11

7:5 *Eleazar.* Means "God helps." The Greek form of the name is Lazarus (John 11:1).

7:6 *ready.* The Hebrew for this phrase is translated "diligent" in Prov 22:29. *scribe.* See Neh 8:1,4,9,13; 12:26,36. Earlier, scribes served kings as secretaries, such as Seraiah under David (2 Sam 8:17, where the Hebrew word for "scribe" is translated "secretary"; see note there). Other scribes took dictation—such as Baruch, who wrote down what Jeremiah spoke (Jer 36:32). From the exilic period on, the "scribes" were scholars who studied and taught the Scriptures (cf. the "teachers of the law" and "scribes" in the NT; see notes on Mat 2:4; Luke 5:17). In the NT period they were addressed as "rabbis" (cf. Mat 23:7). *hand of the LORD.* For this striking description of God's power and favor cf. also vv. 9,28; 8:18,22,31; Neh 2:8,18.

7:7–9 *seventh year . . . first day of the first month . . . first day of the fifth month.* Ezra began his journey on the first of Nisan (Apr. 8, 458 B.C.) and arrived in Jerusalem on the first of Ab (Aug. 4, 458). The journey took four months, including an 11-day delay indicated by the comparison of v. 9 with 8:31. The spring was the most auspicious time for such journeys; most armies went on campaigns at this time of the year. Although the actual distance between Babylon and Jerusalem is about 500 miles, the travelers had to cover a total of about 900 miles, going northwest along the Euphrates River and then south. The relatively slow pace was caused by the presence of the elderly and the children. See map No. 7b at the end of the study Bible.

7:10 *seek the law . . . do it . . . teach.* See Neh 8.

7:11 *letter.* Many regard the letter of Artaxerxes I as the beginning point of Daniel's first 69 "weeks" (Dan 9:24–27). Others regard the commission of Nehemiah by the same king as the starting point of this prophecy (Neh 1:1,11; 2:1–8). By using either a solar calendar with the former date (458 B.C.) or a lunar calendar with the latter date (445), one can arrive remarkably close to the date of Jesus' public ministry.

7:12 The text of vv. 12–26 is in Aramaic (see note on 4:18–6:18). *king of kings.* The phrase was originally used by Assyrian kings, since their empires incorporated many kingdoms. It was then used by the later Babylonian (Ezek 26:7; Dan 2:37) and Persian kings. Cf. 1 Tim 6:15; Rev 17:14; 19:16.

7:13 *people of Israel.* It is noteworthy that "Israel" is used rather than "Judah." It was Ezra's aim to make one Israel of all who returned. The markedly Jewish coloring of this decree may have resulted from the king's use of Jewish officials, quite possibly Ezra himself, to help him compose it.

7:14 *seven counsellers.* Cf. Esth 1:14, which refers to the seven princes who "had access to the king's presence." This corresponds with Persian practice as reported by the early Greek historians Herodotus and Xenophon. *law of thy God.* Perhaps the complete Pentateuch (the five books of Moses) in its present form (see v. 6).

7:15 *silver and gold.* Cf. Hag 2:8. *freely offered.* The Persian treasury had ample funds, and benevolence was a well-attested policy of Persian kings.

7:16 *offering of the people.* The custom of sending gifts to Jerusalem from the Jews who lived outside the Holy Land continued until the Jewish-Roman War, when the Romans forced the Jews to send such contributions to the temple of Jupiter instead (Josephus, *Antiquities,* 18.9.1). There are close parallels to such directives in the contemporary letters from the Jewish garrison at Elephantine in Egypt, including a papyrus in which Darius II ordered: "Let grain offering, incense and burnt offering be offered" on the altar of the god Yahu "in your name."

7:20 *bestow it out of the king's treasure house.* Texts from the treasury at Persepolis also record the disbursement of supplies and funds from the royal purse.

for the house of thy God, which thou shalt
have occasion to bestow, bestow *it* out of the
king's treasure house.
21 And I, *even* I Artaxerxes the king, do
make a decree to all the treasurers which *are*
beyond the river, that whatsoever Ezra the
priest, the scribe of the law of the God of heav-
en, shall require of you, *it* be done speedily,
22 Unto an hundred talents *of* silver, and to
an hundred [1] measures *of* wheat, and to an hundred baths *of* wine, and to an hundred baths *of*
oil, and salt without prescribing *how much.*
23 [1] Whatsoever *is* commanded by the God
of heaven, let it be diligently done for the
house of the God of heaven: for why should
there be wrath against the realm of the king
and his sons?
24 Also *we* certify you, that *touching* any
of the priests and Levites, singers, porters,
Nethinims, or ministers of this house of God,
it *shall* not *be* lawful to impose toll, tribute, or
custom, upon them.
25 And thou, Ezra, after the wisdom of thy
God, that *is* in thine hand, [a] set magistrates
and judges, which may judge all the people
that *are* beyond the river, all such as know the
laws of thy God; and [b] teach ye them that
know *them* not.
26 And whosoever will not do the law of
thy God, and the law of the king, let judgment
be executed speedily upon him, whether *it be*
unto death, or [1] to banishment, or to confiscation of goods, or to imprisonment.
27 ¶ [a] Blessed *be* the LORD God of our fathers, [b] which hath put *such a thing* as this in
the king's heart, to beautify the house of the
LORD which *is* in Jerusalem:
28 And [a] hath extended mercy unto me before the king, and his counsellers, and before
all the king's mighty princes. And I was
strengthened as [b] the hand of the LORD my God
was upon me, and I gathered together out of
Israel chief *men* to go up with me.

People returning with Ezra

8 These *are* now the chief of their fathers,
and *this is* the genealogy of them that
went up with me from Babylon, in the reign of
Artaxerxes the king.
2 Of the sons of Phinehas; Gershom: of the
sons of Ithamar; Daniel: of the sons of David;
[a] Hattush.
3 Of the sons of Shechaniah, of the sons of
[a] Pharosh; Zechariah: and with him were reckoned by genealogy of the males an hundred
and fifty.
4 Of the sons of Pahath-moab; Elihoenai
the son of Zerahiah, and with him two hundred males.
5 Of the sons of Shechaniah; the son of Jahaziel, and with him three hundred males.
6 Of the sons also of Adin; Ebed the son of
Jonathan, and with him fifty males.
7 And of the sons of Elam; Jeshaiah the son
of Athaliah, and with him seventy males.
8 And of the sons of Shephatiah; Zebadiah
the son of Michael, and with him fourscore
males.

7:22 [1] Chald. *cors*
7:23 [1] Chald. *Whatsoever* is *of the decree*
7:25 [a] Ex. 18:21,22; Deut. 16:18 [b] ver. 10; 2 Chr. 17:7; Mal. 2:7; Mat. 23:2,3
7:26 [1] Chald. *to rooting out*
7:27 [a] 1 Chr. 29:10
7:27 [b] ch. 6:22
7:28 [a] ch. 9:9 [b] ver. 6,9; See ch. 5:5; 8:18
8:2 [a] 1 Chr. 3:22
8:3 [a] ch. 2:3

‡7:22 *hundred talents.* An enormous amount (about three and three-fourths tons). *hundred measures.* The total was relatively small (about 600 bushels). The wheat would be used in grain offerings. *salt without prescribing how much.* See note on 4:14. A close parallel is the benefaction of Antiochus III as recorded by Josephus (*Antiquities,* 12.3.3): "In the first place we have decided, on account of their piety, to furnish for their sacrifices an allowance of sacrificial animals, wine, oil and frankincense to the value of 20,000 pieces of silver, and sacred artabae of fine flour in accordance with their native law, and 1,460 medimni of wheat and 375 medimni of salt."

7:23 *wrath against the realm of the king.* Egypt had revolted against the Persians in 460 B.C. and had expelled the Persians with the help of the Athenians in 459. In 458, when Ezra traveled to Jerusalem, the Persians were involved in suppressing this revolt. *his sons.* We do not know how many sons the king had at this time, but he ultimately had 18, according to Ctesias (a Greek physician who wrote an extensive history of Persia).

7:24 *priests . . . ministers . . . not . . . to impose toll . . . or custom.* Priests and other temple personnel were often given exemptions from enforced labor or taxes. A close parallel is found in the Gadates Inscription of Darius I to a governor in western Turkey, granting exemptions to the priests of Apollo. Antiochus III granted similar exemptions to the Jews: "The priests, the scribes of the temple and the temple singers shall be relieved from the poll tax, the crown tax and the salt tax that they pay" (Josephus, *Antiquities,* 12.3.3).

7:26 *whosoever will not do . . . let judgment be executed.* The extensive powers given to Ezra are striking and extend to secular fields. Perhaps the implementation of these provisions involved Ezra in a great deal of traveling, which would explain the silence about his activities between his arrival and the arrival of Nehemiah 13 years later. A close parallel to the king's commission of Ezra may be found in an earlier commission by Darius I, who sent Udjahorresenet, a priest and scholar, back to Egypt. He ordered the codification of the Egyptian laws by the chief men of Egypt—a task that took from 518 to 503 B.C.

7:28 *me.* The first occurrence of the first person for Ezra—a trait that characterizes the "Ezra Memoirs," which begin in v. 27 and continue to the end of ch. 9.

8:1–21 In vv. 1–14 Ezra lists those who accompanied him in his return from Mesopotamia, including the descendants of 15 individuals. The figures of the men given total 1,496 in addition to the individuals named. There were also women and children (see note on v. 21). About 40 Levites (vv. 18–19) are also included, as are 220 temple servants ("Nethinims," v. 20).

8:2 *Gershom.* Also the name of the firstborn son of Moses and Zipporah. "Gershom" sounds like the Hebrew for "a stranger here" (see Ex 2:22). *Ithamar.* Also the name of the fourth son of Aaron (Ex 6:23).

8:3 *Zechariah.* Cf. v. 11. The name means "The LORD remembers"; it was the name of about 30 individuals mentioned in the Bible, including both the OT prophet and the father of John the Baptist (Luke 1:5–67).

8:4 *Elihoenai.* Means "On the LORD are my eyes"; the name occurs only here and in 1 Chr 26:3. Cf. Ps 25:15.

8:6 *Ebed.* May be a shortened form of Obadiah (cf. v. 9), meaning "servant of the LORD." *Jonathan.* Means "The LORD gives"; it was the name of 15 OT individuals.

8:7 *Athaliah.* Also the name of a famous queen, daughter of Ahab (2 Ki 11).

8:8 *Michael.* Means "Who is like God?" It was the name of ten

9 Of the sons of Joab; Obadiah the son of
Jehiel, and with him two hundred and eighteen males.
10 And of the sons of Shelomith; the son of
Josiphiah, and with him an hundred and threescore males.
11 And of the sons of Bebai; Zechariah the
son of Bebai, and with him twenty and eight
males.
12 And of the sons of Azgad; Johanan [1]the
son of Hakkatan, and with him an hundred
and ten males.
13 And of the last sons of Adonikam,
whose names *are* these, Eliphelet, Jeiel, and
Shemaiah, and with them threescore males.
14 Of the sons also of Bigvai; Uthai, and
[1]Zabbud, and with them seventy males.

The return to Jerusalem

15 ¶ And I gathered them together to the
river that runneth to Ahava; and there [1]abode
we in tents three days: and I viewed the people, and the priests, and found there none of
the [a]sons of Levi.
16 Then sent I for Eliezer, for Ariel, for
Shemaiah, and for Elnathan, and for Jarib, and
for Elnathan, and for Nathan, and for Zechariah, and for Meshullam, chief *men;* also for Joiarib, and for Elnathan, *men* of understanding.
17 And I sent them with commandment
unto Iddo the chief at the place Casiphia, and
[1]I told them what they should say unto Iddo,
and to his brethren the Nethinims, at the
place Casiphia, that *they* should bring unto us
ministers for the house of our God.
18 And by the good hand of our God upon
us they [a]brought us a man of understanding, of
the sons of Mahli, the son of Levi, the son of
Israel; and Sherebiah, with his sons and his
brethren, eighteen;
19 And Hashabiah, and with him Jeshaiah
of the sons of Merari, his brethren and their
sons, twenty;
20 [a]Also of the Nethinims, whom David
and the princes had appointed for the service
of the Levites, two hundred and twenty
Nethinims: all of them were expressed by
name.
21 Then I [a]proclaimed a fast there, at the
river Ahava, that *we* might [b]afflict ourselves
before our God, to seek of him a [c]right way for
us, and for our little ones, and for all our substance.
22 For [a]I was ashamed to require of the
king a band *of soldiers* and horsemen to help
us against the enemy in the way: because we
had spoken unto the king, saying, [b]The hand
of our God *is* upon all them for [c]good that seek
him; but his power and his wrath *is* [d]against
all them that [e]forsake him.
23 So we fasted and besought our God for
this: and he was [a]intreated of us.
24 ¶ Then I separated twelve of the chief of
the priests, Sherebiah, Hashabiah, and ten of
their brethren with them,
25 And weighed unto them [a]the silver, and
the gold, and the vessels, *even* the offering of
the house of our God, which the king, and his
counsellers, and his lords, and all Israel *there*
present, had offered:
26 I even weighed unto their hand six hundred and fifty talents *of* silver, and silver vessels an hundred talents, *and of* gold an hundred talents;

8:12 [1]Or, *the youngest son*
8:14 [1]Or, *Zaccur,* as some read
8:15 [1]Or, *pitched* [a]See ch. 7:7
8:17 [1]Heb. *I put words in their mouth*
8:18 [a]Neh. 8:7; 9:4,5
8:20 [a]See ch. 2:43
8:21 [a]2 Chr. 20:3 [b]Lev. 16:29; 23:29; Is. 58:3,5 [c]Ps. 5:8
8:22 [a]1 Cor. 9:15 [b]ch. 7:6,9,28 [c]Ps. 33:18,19; 34:15,22; Rom. 8:28 [d]Ps. 34:16 [e]2 Chr. 15:2
8:23 [a]1 Chr. 5:20; 2 Chr. 33:13; Is. 19:22
8:25 [a]ch. 7:15,16

other Biblical personages, including the archangel (Dan 10:13; Jude 9; Rev 12:7).

8:10 *Shelomith.* Although it is a feminine form (see also note on Sol 6:13), it is often a man's name, as here. The Greek equivalent is Salome.

8:12 *Azgad.* See note on 2:12. *Johanan.* See note on 2:46. *Hakkatan.* Means "the little one"; the name occurs only here.

8:15 *river that runneth to Ahava.* Probably a canal that flows into either the Euphrates or the Tigris (the Chebar "River" in Ezek 1:1 was also a canal). *three days.* Perhaps from the 9th to the 12th day of Nisan; the journey began on the 12th (see v. 31). *found there none of the sons of Levi.* Since they were entrusted with many menial tasks, they may have found a more comfortable way of life in exile. A rabbinic midrash (comment) on Ps 137 relates the legend that Levites were in the caravan but that they were not qualified to officiate because when Nebuchadnezzar had ordered them to sing for him the songs of Zion, "they refused and bit off the ends of their fingers, so that they could not play on the harps." In the Hellenistic era (following Alexander's conquest of the Holy Land in 333 B.C.) the role of the Levites declined sharply, though the "Temple Scroll" among the Dead Sea Scrolls from Qumran (see essay, p. 1344) assigns important roles to them.

8:16 *Ariel.* Means "lion of God" or "altar hearth" (see note on Is 29:1,2,7). It occurs only here as a personal name. *Meshullam.* Perhaps means "rewarded." Some assume that he is the same as the Meshullam who opposed the marriage reforms (10:15). *men of understanding.* Lit. "those who cause to understand." The Hebrew for this word is also used in Neh 8:7.

8:17 *Casiphia.* Some have located it at the site that was later to become the Parthian capital of Ctesiphon on the Tigris River, north of Babylon.

8:18–19 *eighteen . . . twenty.* Only about 40 Levites from two families were found who were willing to join Ezra's caravan.

8:20 *Nethinims.* See note on 2:43–57.

8:21 *right way.* Lit. "straight way"—unimpeded by obstacles and dangers (see v. 31; cf. Prov 3:6). *substance.* The vast treasures they were carrying with them offered a tempting bait for robbers.

8:22 *I was ashamed.* Scripture speaks often of unholy shame (Jer 48:13; 49:23; Mic 3:7) and on occasion, as here, of holy shame. Ezra was quick to blush with such shame (see also 9:6). Having proclaimed his faith in God's ability to protect the caravan, he was embarrassed to ask for human protection. Grave dangers faced travelers going the great distance between Mesopotamia and the Holy Land. Some 13 years later Nehemiah was accompanied by an armed escort. The difference, however, does not mean that Nehemiah was a man of lesser faith (see note on Neh 2:9).

8:23 *fasted and besought our God.* For the association of fasting and prayer see Neh 1:4; Dan 9:3; Mat 17:21; Acts 14:23.

8:25 *offering.* Lit. "what is lifted," i.e. dedicated (cf. Ex 25:2; 35:5; Lev 7:14). In Deut 12:6 the Hebrew for this word is translated "the offerings of your hand."

8:26 *six hundred and fifty talents . . . hundred talents.* Enormous sums, worth millions of dollars today. See also note on 7:22.

27 Also twenty basons of gold, of a thousand drams; and two vessels of [1]fine copper,
[2]precious as gold.
28 And I said unto them, Ye *are* [a]holy unto
the LORD; the vessels *are* [b]holy also; and the
silver and the gold *are* a freewill offering unto
the LORD God of your fathers.
29 Watch ye, and keep *them,* until ye weigh
them before the chief of the priests and the Levites, and chief of the fathers of Israel, at Jerusalem, *in* the chambers of the house of the LORD.
30 So took the priests and the Levites the
weight of the silver, and the gold, and the vessels, to bring *them* to Jerusalem unto the
house of our God.
31 ¶ Then we departed from the river of
Ahava on the twelfth *day* of the first month, to
go *unto* Jerusalem: and [a]the hand of our God
was upon us, and he delivered us from the
hand of the enemy, and of such as lay in wait
by the way.
32 And we [a]came *to* Jerusalem, and abode
there three days.
33 Now on the fourth day was the silver
and the gold and the vessels [a]weighed in the
house of our God by the hand of Meremoth
the son of Uriah the priest; and with him *was*
Eleazar the son of Phinehas; and with them
was Jozabad the son of Jeshua, and Noadiah
the son of Binnui, Levites;
34 By number *and* by weight of every one:
and all the weight was written at that time.
35 *Also* the children of those that had been
carried away, which were come out of the captivity, [a]offered burnt offerings unto the God of
Israel, twelve bullocks for all Israel, ninety and
six rams, seventy and seven lambs, twelve he
goats *for* a sin offering: all *this was* a burnt offering unto the LORD.
36 And they delivered the king's [a]commis-
sions unto the king's lieutenants, and *to* the
governors on *this* side the river: and they fur-
thered the people, and the house of God.

8:27 [1]Heb. *yellow,* or, *shining brass* [2]Heb. *desirable*
8:28 [a]Lev. 21:6-8; Deut. 33:8 [b]Lev. 22:2,3; Num. 4:4,15,19,20
8:31 [a]ch. 7:6,9,28
8:32 [a]Neh. 2:11
8:33 [a]ver. 26,30
8:35 [a]ch. 6:17
8:36 [a]ch. 7:21
9:1 [a]ch. 6:21; Neh. 9:2 [b]Deut. 12:30,31
9:2 [a]Ex. 34:16; Deut. 7:3 [b]Ex. 22:31; Deut. 7:6 [c]2 Cor. 6:14
9:3 [a]Job 1:20 [b]Ps. 143:4
9:4 [a]ch. 10:3 [b]Ex. 29:39

Ezra's prayer

9 Now when these *things* were done, the
princes came to me, saying, The people
of Israel, and the priests, and the Levites, have
not [a]separated themselves from the people of
the lands, [b]*doing* according to their abominations, *even* of the Canaanites, the Hittites, the
Perizzites, the Jebusites, the Ammonites, the
Moabites, the Egyptians, and the Amorites.
2 For they have [a]taken of their daughters
for themselves, and for their sons: so that the
[b]holy seed have [c]mingled themselves with
the people of *those* lands: yea, the hand of the
princes and rulers hath been chief in this trespass.
3 And when I heard this thing, [a]I rent my
garment and my mantle, and pluckt off the
hair of my head and of my beard, and sat down
[b]astonied.
4 Then were assembled unto me every one
that [a]trembled at the words of the God of Israel, because of the transgression of those that
had been carried away; and I sat astonied until
the [b]evening sacrifice.

---

‡8:27 *thousand drams.* About 19 pounds. The word occurs only here and in 1 Chr 29:7 (but see note on 2:69). *fine copper.* See KJV marg. This kind of metal may have been orichalc, a bright yellow (the Hebrew for "yellow" in Lev 13:30,32,36 is related to the Hebrew here) alloy of copper, which resembles gold and was highly prized in ancient times.
8:31 *twelfth.* See notes on v. 15; 7:7–9.
8:32 *abode there three days.* Nehemiah also took a similar rest period after his arrival in Jerusalem (Neh 2:11).
8:33 *Meremoth the son of Uriah.* Probably the same as the man who repaired two sections of the wall (Neh 3:4,21).
8:34 *written.* According to Babylonian practice (e.g., in the Code of Hammurapi; see chart, p. xix) almost every transaction, including sales and marriages, had to be recorded in writing. Ezra may have had to send back to Artaxerxes a signed certification of the delivery of the treasures.
8:35 *offered.* Except for the identical number of male goats, the offerings here were far fewer than those presented by the returnees under Zerubbabel (6:17), who brought with him a far greater number of families.
9:1 *when these things were done . . . have not separated themselves.* Ezra had reached Jerusalem in the fifth month (7:9). The measures dealing with the problem of intermarriage were announced in the ninth month (10:9), or four months after his arrival. Those who brought Ezra's attention to the problem were probably the ordinary members of the community rather than the leaders, who were themselves guilty (v. 2). Malachi, who prophesied about the same time as Ezra's mission, indicates that some Jews had broken their marriages to marry daughters of a foreign god (Mal 2:10–16), perhaps the daughters of influential landholders. One of the reasons for such intermarriages may have been the shortage of returning Jewish women who were available. What happened to a Jewish community that was lax concerning intermarriage can be seen in the example of the Elephantine settlement in Egypt, which was contemporary with Ezra and Nehemiah. There the Jews who married pagan spouses expressed their devotion to pagan gods in addition to the Lord. The Elephantine community was gradually assimilated and disappeared. *people of the lands.* The eight groups mentioned are representative of the original inhabitants of Canaan before the Israelite conquest (see note on Ex 3:8). Only the Ammonites, Moabites and Egyptians were still living there in the postexilic period (cf. 2 Chr 8:7–8). *Canaanites.* See note on Gen 10:6. *Hittites.* See note on Gen 10:15. *Perizzites.* See note on Gen 13:7. *Jebusites.* See note on Gen 10:16. *the Ammonites, the Moabites.* See note on Gen 19:36–38. *Amorites.* See note on Gen 10:16.
‡9:2 *holy seed.* The phrase appears also in Is 6:13. *been chief.* In the wrong direction (see 10:18). *trespass.* See 10:6; Josh 22:16; Dan 9:7. Marrying those who did not belong to the Lord was an act of infidelity for the people of Israel.
9:3 *rent my garment and my mantle.* A common way to express grief or distress (see v. 5; Gen 37:29,34; Josh 7:6; Judg 11:35; 2 Sam 13:19; 2 Chr 34:27; Esth 4:1; Job 1:20; Is 36:22; Jer 41:5; Mat 26:65). *pluckt off the hair of my head and of my beard.* Unique in the Bible. Elsewhere we read about the shaving of one's head and/or beard (Job 1:20; Jer 41:5; 47:5; Ezek 7:18; Amos 8:10). When Nehemiah was confronted with the same problem of intermarriage, instead of pulling out his own hair he pulled out the hair of the offending parties (Neh 13:25).
9:4 *every one that trembled.* Cf. Ex 19:16; Is 66:2; Heb 12:21. *astonied.* Or "appalled." See v. 3; cf. Dan 4:19; 8:27. *evening*

5 And at the evening sacrifice I arose up from my [1]heaviness; and having rent my garment and my mantle, I fell upon my knees, and [a]spread out my hands unto the LORD my God,

6 And said,

¶ O my God, I am [a]ashamed and blush to lift up my face to thee, my God: for [b]our iniquities are increased over *our* head, and our [1]trespass is [c]grown up unto the heavens.

7 Since the days of our fathers *have* [a]we *been* in a great trespass unto this day; and for our iniquities have [b]we, our kings, *and* our priests, been delivered into the hand of the kings of the lands, to the sword, to captivity, and to a spoil, and to [c]confusion of face, as *it is* this day.

8 And now for a little [1]space grace hath been *shewed* from the LORD our God, to leave us a remnant to escape, and to give us [a2]a nail in his holy place, that our God may [b]lighten our eyes, and give us a little reviving in our bondage.

9 [a]For we *were* bondmen; [b]yet our God hath not forsaken us in our bondage, but [c]hath extended mercy unto us in the sight of the kings of Persia, to give us a reviving, to set up the house of our God, and [1]to repair the desolations thereof, and to give us [d]a wall in Judah and in Jerusalem.

10 And now, O our God, what shall we say after this? for we have forsaken thy commandments,

11 Which thou hast commanded [1]by thy servants the prophets, saying, The land, *unto* which ye go to possess it, *is* an unclean land with the filthiness of the people of the lands, with their abominations, which have filled it [a2]from one end to another with their uncleanness.

12 Now therefore [a]give not your daughters unto their sons, neither take their daughters unto your sons, [b]nor seek their peace or their wealth for ever: that ye may be strong, and eat the good of the land, and [c]leave *it* for an inheritance to your children for ever.

13 And after all that is come upon us for our evil deeds, and for our great trespass, seeing that thou our God [a1]hast punished us less than our iniquities *deserve,* and hast given us *such* deliverance as this;

14 Should we [a]again break thy commandments, and [b]join in affinity with the people of these abominations? wouldest thou not be [c]angry with us till *thou* hadst consumed *us,* so that *there should be* no remnant nor escaping?

15 O LORD God of Israel, [a]thou *art* righteous: for we remain *yet* escaped, as *it is* this day: behold, we *are* [b]before thee [c]in our trespasses: for *we* cannot stand before thee because of this.

The people's confession

10 Now [a]when Ezra had prayed, and when he had confessed, weeping and casting himself down [b]before the house of God, there assembled unto him out of Israel a very great congregation *of* men and women and children: for the people [1]wept very sore.

2 And Shechaniah the son of Jehiel, *one* of

9:5 [1]Or, *affliction* [a]Ex. 9:29
9:6 [1]Or, *guiltiness* [a]Dan. 9:7,8 [b]Ps. 38:4 [c]2 Chr. 28:9; Rev. 18:5
9:7 [a]Ps. 106:6; Dan. 9:5,6 [b]Deut. 28:36; Neh. 9:30 [c]Dan. 9:7,8
9:8 [1]Heb. *moment* [2]Or, a *pin:* that is, a *constant and sure abode* [a]Is. 22:23 [b]Ps. 34:5
9:9 [1]Heb. *to set up* [a]Neh. 9:36 [b]Ps. 136:23 [c]ch. 7:28 [d]Is. 5:2
9:11 [1]Heb. *by the hand of thy servants*
9:11 [2]Heb. *from mouth to mouth* [a]2 Ki. 21:16
9:12 [a]Ex. 23:32; Deut. 7:3 [b]Deut. 23:6 [c]Prov. 20:7
9:13 [1]Heb. *hast withheld beneath our iniquities* [a]Ps. 103:10
9:14 [a]John 5:14; 2 Pet. 2:20 [b]Neh. 13:23 [c]Deut. 9:8
9:15 [a]Neh. 9:33; Dan. 9:14 [b]Rom. 3:19 [c]1 Cor. 15:17
10:1 [1]Heb. *wept a great weeping* [a]Dan. 9:20 [b]2 Chr. 20:9

sacrifice. See Ex 12:6. The informants had probably visited Ezra in the morning, so that he must have sat appalled for many hours. The time of the evening sacrifice, usually about 3:00 P.M., was also the appointed time for prayer and confession (Acts 3:1).

9:5 *heaviness.* The Hebrew for this word later meant "fasting." See note on Lev 16:29,31. *fell upon my knees.* Cf. 1 Ki 8:54; Ps 95:6; Dan 6:10. *spread out my hands.* See note on Ex 9:29. Ezra's prayer (vv. 6–15) may be compared with those of Nehemiah (Neh 9:5–37) and Daniel (Dan 9:4–19).

9:6 *ashamed and blush.* See 8:22 and note; Luke 18:13. Ezra felt both an inner shame before God and an outward humiliation before people for his own sins and the sins of his people. The two Hebrew verbs often occur together; see Ps 35:4; Is 45:16; Jer 31:19 ("ashamed" and "confounded"). *our iniquities . . . our trespass.* Cf. also vv. 7,13,15; 10:10,19; 1 Chr 21:3; 2 Chr 24:18; Ps 38:4. *is grown up unto the heavens.* But God's love is more than a match for our guilt (Ps 103:11–12).

‡9:7 *Since the days of our fathers.* Israelites were conscious of their corporate solidarity with their ancestors. *sword.* Cf. Neh 4:13. In Ezek 21 "the sword of the king of Babylon" (21:19) is described as an instrument of divine judgment. *confusion of face.* Lit. "shame of faces"; cf. Dan 9:7–8; 2 Chr 32:21.

‡9:8 *remnant.* See Gen 45:7; Is 1:9; 10:20–22 and notes. *nail.* Like a nail driven into a wall (see Is 22:23 and note) or a stake driven into the ground (Is 33:20; 54:2). *lighten our eyes.* An increase in light means vitality and joy (Ps 13:3; 19:8; Eccl 8:1).

9:9 *kings of Persia.* The Achaemenid Persian kings were favorably disposed to the Jews: Cyrus (539–530 B.C.) gave them permission to return (ch. 1); his son Cambyses (530–522), though not named in the Bible, also favored the Jews, as we learn from Elephantine papyri; Darius I (522–486) renewed the decree of Cyrus (ch. 6); his son Ahasuerus (486–465) granted privileges and protection to Jews (Esth 8–10); his son Artaxerxes I (465–424) gave authorizations to Ezra (ch. 7) and to Nehemiah (Neh 2). *repair the desolations thereof.* Isaiah had prophesied that the Lord would restore Jerusalem's ruins (Is 44:26), which would burst into singing (Is 52:9; cf. 58:12; 61:4). *wall.* Used of a city wall only in Mic 7:11. The use here is metaphorical (cf. Zech 2:4–5).

9:11–12 The references are not to a single OT passage but to several passages, such as Deut 11:8–9; Is 1:19; Ezek 37:25.

9:11 *thy servants the prophets.* See notes on Jer 7:25; Zech 1:6. *filthiness.* Of Canaanite idolatry and the immoral practices associated with it (Lev 18:3; 2 Chr 29:5; Lam 1:17; Ezek 7:20; 36:17). The degrading practices and beliefs of the Canaanites are described in texts from ancient Ugarit (see chart, p. xix).

9:14 *be angry.* God's anger came upon the Israelites because they had violated His covenant with them (Deut 7:4; 11:16–17; 29:26–28; Josh 23:16; Judg 2:20).

9:15 *thou art righteous.* See note on Ps 4:1. *our trespasses.* A proper sense of God's holiness makes us aware of our unworthiness. See Is 6:1–5; Luke 5:8. For comparable passages of national lament see Ps 44; 60; 74; 79–80; 83; 85; 90; 108; 126; 129; 137.

10:1 *weeping.* Not silently but out loud (see 3:13 and note; Neh 1:4; Joel 2:12). *casting himself down.* The prophets and other leaders used object lessons, even bizarre actions, to attract people's attention (Is 7:3; 8:1–4,18; Jer 13:1–11; 19; 27:2–12; Ezek 4:1–5:4).

10:2 Ezra, as a wise teacher, waited for his audience to draw

the sons of Elam, answered and said unto
Ezra, We have [a]trespassed against our God,
and have taken strange wives of the people of
the land: yet now there is hope in Israel concerning this *thing.*
3 Now therefore let us make [a]a covenant
with our God [1]to put away all the wives, and
such as are born of them, according to the
counsel of my lord, and of those that [b]tremble
at [c]the commandment of our God; and let it be
done according to the law.
4 Arise; for *this* matter *belongeth* unto
thee: we also *will be* with thee: [a]be of good
courage, and do *it.*
5 Then arose Ezra, and made the chief
priests, the Levites, and all Israel, [a]to swear
that *they* should do according to this word.
And they sware.
6 Then Ezra rose up from before the house
of God, and went into the chamber of Johanan
the son of Eliashib: and *when* he came thither,
he [a]did eat no bread, nor drink water: for he
mourned because of the transgression of them
that had been carried away.
7 And they made proclamation throughout
Judah and Jerusalem unto all the children of
the captivity, that *they* should gather themselves together *unto* Jerusalem;
8 And *that* whosoever would not come
within three days, according to the counsel of
the princes and the elders, all his substance
should be [1]forfeited, and himself separated

10:2 [a]Neh. 13:27
10:3 [1]Heb. *to bring forth* [a]2 Chr. 34:31 [b]ch. 9:4 [c]Deut. 7:2,3
10:4 [a]1 Chr. 28:10
10:5 [a]Neh. 5:12
10:6 [a]Deut. 9:18
10:8 [1]Heb. *devoted*
10:9 [1]Heb. *the showers* [a]See 1 Sam. 12:18
10:10 [1]Heb. *have caused to dwell,* or, *have brought back*
10:11 [a]Josh. 7:19; Prov. 28:13 [b]ver. 3
10:13 [1]Or, *we have greatly offended in this thing*
10:14 [1]Or, *till this matter* be dispatched [a]2 Chr. 30:8

from the congregation of those that had been
carried away.
9 ¶ Then all the men of Judah and Benjamin gathered themselves together *unto* Jerusalem within three days. It *was* the ninth month,
on the twentieth *day* of the month; and [a]all
the people sat in the street of the house of
God, trembling because of *this* matter, and for
[1]the great rain.
10 And Ezra the priest stood up, and said
unto them, Ye have transgressed, and [1]have
taken strange wives, to increase the trespass of
Israel.
11 Now therefore [a]make confession unto
the LORD God of your fathers, and do his pleasure: and [b]separate yourselves from the people
of the land, and from the strange wives.
12 Then all the congregation answered and
said *with* a loud voice, As thou hast said, so
must we do.
13 But the people *are* many, and *it is* a time
of much rain, and *we are* not able to stand
without, neither *is this* a work of one day or
two: for [1]we are many that have transgressed
in this thing.
14 Let now our rulers of all the congregation stand, and let all *them* which have taken
strange wives in our cities come at appointed
times, and with them the elders of every city,
and the judges thereof, until [a]the fierce wrath
of our God [1]for this matter be turned from us.
15 Only Jonathan the son of Asahel and Ja-

their own conclusions about what should be done. *Shecaniah.* Perhaps his father Jehiel is the Jehiel mentioned in v. 26 since he was also of the family of Elam. If so, Shecaniah was doubtless grieved that his father had married a non-Jewish woman. Six members of the clan of Elam were involved in intermarriage (v. 26).

10:3 *make a covenant.* Lit. "cut a covenant" (see note on Gen 15:18). *wives, and such as are born of them.* Mothers were given custody of their children when marriages were dissolved. When Hagar was dismissed, Ishmael was sent with her (Gen 21:14). In Babylonia divorced women were granted their children and had to wait for them to grow up before remarrying, according to the Code of Hammurapi (see chart, p. xix). In Greece, however, children from broken homes remained with their fathers.

10:4 *Arise.* Cf. David's exhortation (1 Chr 22:16).

10:5 *to swear.* The implied curse attendant upon nonfulfillment of a Biblical oath is often expressed in the vague statement, "God do so to thee, and more also, if . . ." (see note on 1 Sam 3:17). On rare occasions the full implications of the curse are spelled out (Num 5:19–22; Job 31; Ps 7:4–5; 137:5–6).

10:6 *chamber.* Such temple chambers were used as storerooms (8:29; Neh 13:4–5). *did eat no bread, nor drink water.* Complete fasting from both food and drink was rare. Moses did it twice (Ex 34:28; Deut 9:18), and the Ninevites also did it (Jonah 3:7). Ordinarily, fasting involved abstaining only from eating (1 Sam 1:7; 2 Sam 3:35). *mourned.* The Hebrew for this word often describes the reaction of those aware of the threat of deserved judgment (Ex 33:4; Num 14:39).

10:7–8 While Ezra continued to fast and pray, the officials and elders ordered all the exiles to assemble in Jerusalem. Although Ezra had been invested with great authority (7:25–26), he used it sparingly and influenced the people by his example.

10:8 *within three days.* Since the territory of Judah had been much reduced, the most distant people would not be more than 50 miles from Jerusalem. The borders were Beth-el in the north, Beer-sheba in the south, Jericho in the east and Ono in the west (cf. Neh 7:26–38; 11:25–35). *forfeited.* The Hebrew for this word means "to ban from profane use and to devote to the Lord," either by destruction (see Ex 22:20; Num 21:2; Deut 2:34; 13:12–18 and notes) or by giving it to the Lord's treasury (cf. Lev 27:28; Josh 6:19; 7:1–15).

10:9,16–17 See chart, p. 637.

‡10:9 *Judah and Benjamin.* See note on 1:5. *street.* Refers either to the outer court of the temple or the open space before the water gate (Neh 8:1). *rain.* The Hebrew for this word is a plural of intensity, indicating heavy torrential rains. The ninth month, Kislev (November-December), is in the middle of the rainy season (see v. 13), which begins with light showers in October and lasts to mid-April. December and January are also cold months, with temperatures in the 50s and even 40s in Jerusalem. The people shivered not only because they were drenched, but perhaps also because they sensed divine displeasure in the heavy rains (see 1 Sam 12:17–18; Ezek 13:11,13).

10:10 *increase the trespass of Israel.* See Ex 9:34; Judg 3:12; 4:1; 2 Chr 28:13. The sins and failures of the exiles were great enough, but they added insult to injury by marrying pagan women.

10:11 *separate yourselves.* See Num 16:21; 2 Cor 6:14.

10:12 *with a loud voice.* See Neh 9:4.

10:14 *elders of every city, and the judges.* See Deut 16:18; 19:12; 21:3,19; Ruth 4:2.

10:15 Perhaps these four men opposed the measure because they wanted to protect themselves or their relatives, or they may have viewed it as being too harsh. *Jahaziah.* Means "May the LORD see" (the name is found only here). *Tikvah.* Means

haziah the son of Tikvah [1]were employed about this *matter:* and Meshullam and Shabbethai the Levite helped them.

16 And the children of the captivity did so. And Ezra the priest, *with* certain chief of the fathers, after the house of their fathers, and all of them by *their* names, were separated, and sat down in the first day of the tenth month to examine the matter.

17 And they made an end with all the men that had taken strange wives by the first day of the first month.

Priests with foreign wives

18 ¶ And among the sons of the priests there were found that had taken strange wives: *namely,* of the sons of Jeshua the son of Jozadak, and his brethren; Maaseiah, and Eliezer, and Jarib, and Gedaliah.

19 And they [a]gave their hands that *they* would put away their wives; and *being* [b]guilty, *they offered* a ram of the flock for their trespass.

20 And of the sons of Immer; Hanani, and Zebadiah.

21 And of the sons of Harim; Maaseiah, and Elijah, and Shemaiah, and Jehiel, and Uzziah.

22 And of the sons of Pashur; Elioenai, Maaseiah, Ishmael, Nethaneel, Jozabad, and Elasah.

23 ¶ Also of the Levites; Jozabad, and Shimei, and Kelaiah, (the same *is* Kelita,) Pethahiah, Judah, and Eliezer.

24 Of the singers also; Eliashib: and of the porters; Shallum, and Telem, and Uri.

25 ¶ Moreover of Israel: of the sons of Parosh; Ramiah, and Jeziah, and Malchiah, and Miamin, and Eleazar, and Malchijah, and Benaiah.

26 And of the sons of Elam; Mattaniah, Zechariah, and Jehiel, and Abdi, and Jeremoth, and Eliah.

27 And of the sons of Zattu; Elioenai, Eliashib, Mattaniah, and Jeremoth, and Zabad, and Aziza.

28 Of the sons also of Bebai; Jehohanan, Hananiah, Zabbai, *and* Athlai.

29 And of the sons of Bani; Meshullam, Malluch, and Adaiah, Jashub, and Sheal, and Ramoth.

30 And of the sons of Pahath-moab; Adna, and Chelal, Benaiah, Maaseiah, Mattaniah, Bezaleel, and Binnui, and Manasseh.

31 And *of* the sons of Harim; Eliezer, Ishijah, Malchiah, Shemaiah, Shimeon,

32 Benjamin, Malluch, *and* Shemariah.

33 Of the sons of Hashum; Mattenai, Mattathah, Zabad, Eliphelet, Jeremai, Manasseh, *and* Shimei.

34 Of the sons of Bani; Maadai, Amram, and Uel,

35 Benaiah, Bedeiah, Chelluh,

36 Vaniah, Meremoth, Eliashib,

37 Mattaniah, Mattenai, and Jaasau,

38 And Bani, and Binnui, Shimei,

39 And Shelemiah, and Nathan, and Adaiah,

40 [1]Machnadebai, Shashai, Sharai,

41 Azareel, and Shelemiah, Shemariah,

42 Shallum, Amariah, *and* Joseph.

43 Of the sons of Nebo; Jeiel, Mattithiah, Zabad, Zebina, Jadau, and Joel, Benaiah.

44 All these had taken strange wives: and *some* of them had wives by *whom* they had children.

10:15 [1] Heb. *stood*
10:19 [a] 2 Ki. 10:15; 1 Chr. 29:24; 2 Chr. 30:8 [b] Lev. 6:4,6
10:40 [1] Or, *Mabnadebai,* according to some copies

"hope" (found elsewhere only in 2 Ki 22:14). *Meshullam.* See note on 8:16. If he is the Meshullam of v. 29, he himself had married a pagan wife. *Shabbethai.* Occurs only here and in Neh 8:7; 11:16; perhaps means "one born on the sabbath."

10:16–17 The committee completed its work in three months, discovering that about 110 men were guilty of marrying pagan wives.

10:18–22 See 2:36–39.

10:19 *gave their hands.* For the symbolic use of the handshake see 2 Ki 10:15; Ezek 17:18. *ram.* Trespass offerings were to be made for sins committed unintentionally (Lev 5:14–19) as well as intentionally (Lev 6:1–7), and a ram was the appropriate offering in either case (Lev 5:15; 6:6).

10:24 It is striking that only one singer and three gatekeepers were involved. No temple servants (2:43–54) or descendants of Solomon's servants (2:55–57) sinned through intermarriage.

10:25–43 See 2:3–20.

10:30 *Bezaleel.* Cf. Ex 31:2.

10:31 *Shimeon.* Probably means "one who hears." The Hebrew for this name is the same as that for Simeon, Jacob's second son. In Greek the name became Simon (e.g., Mat 4:18).

10:43 *Nebo.* The Hebrew equivalent of the name of the Babylonian god Nabu (see Is 46:1); found only here as a personal name.

10:44 Some of the marriages had produced children, but this was not accepted as a reason for halting the divorce proceedings.

The Book of
Nehemiah

INTRODUCTION

See Introduction to Ezra.

Outline

I. Nehemiah's First Administration (chs. 1—12)
   A. Nehemiah's Response to the Situation in Jerusalem (ch. 1)
      1. News of the plight of Jerusalem (1:1–4)
      2. Nehemiah's prayer (1:5–11)
   B. Nehemiah's Journey to Jerusalem (ch. 2)
      1. The king's response (2:1–8)
      2. The journey itself (2:9–10)
      3. Nehemiah's nocturnal inspection of the walls (2:11–16)
      4. His exhortation to rebuild (2:17–18)
      5. The opposition of Sanballat, Tobiah and Geshem (2:19–20)
   C. List of the Builders of the Wall (ch. 3)
      1. The northern section (3:1–7)
      2. The western section (3:8–13)
      3. The southern section (3:14)
      4. The eastern section (3:15–32)
   D. Opposition to Rebuilding the Wall (ch. 4)
      1. The derision of Sanballat and Tobiah (4:1–5)
      2. The threat of attack (4:6–15)
      3. Rebuilding the wall (4:16–23)
   E. Social and Economic Problems (ch. 5)
      1. The complaints of the poor (5:1–5)
      2. The cancellation of debts (5:6–13)
      3. Nehemiah's unselfish example (5:14–19)
   F. The Wall Rebuilt Despite Opposition (ch. 6)
      1. Attempts to snare Nehemiah (6:1–9)
      2. The hiring of false prophets (6:10–14)
      3. The completion of the wall (6:15–19)
   G. List of Exiles (7:1–73a)
      1. Provisions for the protection of Jerusalem (7:1–3)
      2. Nehemiah's discovery of the list of returnees (7:4–5)
      3. The returnees delineated (7:6–72)
      4. Settlement of the exiles (7:73a)
   H. Ezra's Preaching and the Outbreak of Revival (7:73b—10:39)
      1. The public exposition of the Scriptures (7:73b—8:12)
      2. The feast of tabernacles (8:13–18)
      3. A day of fasting, confession and prayer (9:1–5a)
      4. A recital of God's dealings with Israel (9:5b-31)
      5. Confession of sins (9:32–37)
      6. A binding agreement (9:38)
      7. A list of those who sealed it (10:1–29)
      8. Provisions of the agreement (10:30–39)
   I. New Residents of Judah and Jerusalem (ch. 11)
      1. New residents for Jerusalem (11:1–24)
         a. Introductory remarks (11:1–4a)

- b. Residents from Judah (11:4b-6)
- c. From Benjamin (11:7–9)
- d. From the priests (11:10–14)
- e. From the Levites (11:15–18)
- f. From the temple staff (11:19–24)

2. New residents for Judah (11:25–36)
   - a. Places settled by those from Judah (11:25–30)
   - b. Places settled by those from Benjamin (11:31–35)
   - c. Transfer of Levites from Judah to Benjamin (11:36)

J. Lists of Priests and the Dedication of the Wall (ch. 12)
1. Priests and Levites from the first return (12:1–9)
2. High priests and Levites since Joiakim (12:10–26)
3. Dedication of the wall of Jerusalem (12:27–43)
4. Regulation of the temple offerings and services (12:44–47)

II. Nehemiah's Second Administration (ch. 13)

A. Abuses during His Absence (13:1–5)
1. Mixed marriages (13:1–3)
2. Tobiah's occupation of the temple quarters (13:4–5)

B. Nehemiah's Return (13:6–9)
1. His arrival (13:6–7)
2. His expulsion of Tobiah (13:8–9)

C. Reorganization and Reforms (13:10–31)
1. Offerings for the temple staff (13:10–14)
2. The abuse of the sabbath (13:15–22)
3. Mixed marriages (13:23–29)
4. Provisions of wood and firstfruits (13:30–31)

Nehemiah's prayer for Israel

1 The words of [a]Nehemiah the son of
Hachaliah. And it came to pass in the
month Chisleu, *in* the twentieth year, as I was
in Shushan the palace,
2 That Hanani, one of my brethren, came,
he and *certain* men of Judah; and I asked them
concerning the Jews that had escaped, which
were left of the captivity, and concerning Jerusalem.
3 And they said unto me, The remnant that
are left of the captivity there in the province
are in great affliction and reproach: [a]the wall
of Jerusalem also [b]*is* broken down, and the
gates thereof are burnt with fire.
4 And it came to pass, when I heard these
words, *that* I sat down and wept, and mourned
certain days, and fasted, and prayed before the
God of heaven,
5 And said, I beseech thee, [a]O LORD God of
heaven, the great and terrible God, [b]that keepeth covenant and mercy for them that love
him and observe his commandments:
6 Let thine ear now be attentive, and
[a]thine eyes open, that *thou* mayest hear the
prayer of thy servant, which I pray before thee
now, day and night, for the children of Israel
thy servants, and [b]confess the sins of the children of Israel, which we have sinned against
thee: both I and my father's house have
sinned.
7 [a]We have dealt very corruptly against
thee, and have [b]not kept the commandments,
nor the statutes, nor the judgments, which
thou commandedst thy servant Moses.
8 Remember, I beseech thee, the word that
thou commandedst thy servant Moses, saying,
[a]*If* ye transgress, I will scatter you abroad
among the nations:
9 [a]But *if* ye turn unto me, and keep my
commandments, and do them; [b]though there
were of you cast out unto the uttermost part of
the heaven, *yet* will I gather them from
thence, and will bring them unto the place
that I have chosen to set my name there.
10 [a]Now these *are* thy servants and thy
people, whom thou hast redeemed by thy
great power, and by thy strong hand.
11 O Lord, I beseech thee, [a]let now thine
ear be attentive to the prayer of thy servant,
and to the prayer of thy servants, who [b]desire
to fear thy name: and prosper, I pray thee, thy
servant *this* day, and grant him mercy in the
sight of this man. For I was the king's [c]cup-
bearer.

1:1 [a]ch. 10:1
1:3 [a]ch. 2:17 [b]2 Ki. 25:10
1:5 [a]Dan. 9:4 [b]Ex. 20:6
1:6 [a]1 Ki. 8:28,29; 2 Chr. 6:40; Dan. 9:17, 18
1:6 [b]Dan. 9:20
1:7 [a]Ps. 106:6; Dan. 9:5 [b]Deut. 28:15
1:8 [a]Lev. 26:33; Deut. 4:25-27; 28:64
1:9 [a]Lev. 26:39; Deut. 4:29-31; 30:2 [b]Deut. 30:4
1:10 [a]Deut. 9:29; Dan. 9:15
1:11 [a]ver. 6 [b]Is. 26:8; Heb. 13:18 [c]ch. 2:1

---

‡1:1 *The words of.* Originally an introduction to the title of a separate composition (see Jer 1:1; Amos 1:1), though the books of Ezra and Nehemiah appear as a single work from earliest times (see Introduction to Ezra: Ezra and Nehemiah). *Nehemiah.* Means "The LORD comforts." *Hachaliah.* Perhaps means "Wait for the LORD," though an imperative in a Hebrew name is quite unusual. The name occurs only here and in 10:1. *Chisleu . . . twentieth year.* November-December, 445 B.C. See chart, p. 635. *Shushan* [i.e. Susa]. See note on Ezra 4:9.

1:2 *Hanani.* Probably a shortened form of Hananiah, which means "The LORD is gracious." *one of my brethren.* See 7:2. The Elephantine papyri mention a Hananiah who was the head of Jewish affairs in Jerusalem. Many believe that he is to be identified with Nehemiah's brother, and that he may have governed between Nehemiah's first and second terms (see note on 7:2). *Jews that had escaped.* See Ezra 9:8 and notes on Gen 45:7; 2 Ki 19:30–31; Is 1:9; 10:20–22.

1:3 *province.* See note on Ezra 2:1. *wall of Jerusalem also is broken down.* The lack of a city wall meant that the people were defenseless against their enemies. Thucydides (1.89) describes the comparable condition of Athens after its devastation by the Persians in 480–479 B.C. Excavations at Jerusalem during 1961–67 revealed that the lack of a wall on the eastern slopes also meant the disintegration of the terraces there. When Nebuchadnezzar assaulted Jerusalem, he battered and broke down the walls around it (2 Ki 25:10). Most, however, do not believe that Nehemiah's distress was caused by Nebuchadnezzar's destruction in 586 but by the episode of Ezra 4:7–23. The Jews had attempted to rebuild the walls earlier in the reign of Artaxerxes I; but after the protest of Rehum and Shimshai, the king ordered the Jews to desist. See note on Ezra 4:21–23.

1:4 *sat down.* Cf. Ezra 9:3; Job 2:13. *wept.* See 8:9; Ezra 3:13 and note; 10:1; Esth 8:3. *mourned.* See Ezra 10:6; Dan 10:2. *fasted, and prayed.* See note on Ezra 8:23. During the exile, fasting became a common practice, including solemn fasts to commemorate the fall of Jerusalem and the murder of Gedaliah (see note on Zech 8:19; see also Esth 4:16; Dan 9:3; 10:3; Zech 7:3–7). *God of heaven.* See note on Ezra 1:2.

‡1:5 *mercy.* Or "faithful love," the quality that honors a covenant through thick and thin.

1:6 *pray before thee now, day and night.* Cf. Ps 42:3; 88:1; Jer 9:1; 14:17; Lam 2:18; Luke 2:37; 1 Thes 3:10; 1 Tim 5:5; 2 Tim 1:3. *sins . . . I and my father's house.* Nehemiah does not exclude himself or members of his own family in his confession of sins. A true sense of the awesome holiness of God reveals the depths of our own sinfulness (Is 6:1–5; Luke 5:8).

1:7 *commandments . . . statutes . . . judgments.* See note on Gen 26:5. *Moses.* For the prominence of the law of Moses in Ezra and Nehemiah see Ezra 3:2; 6:18; 7:6; Neh 1:8; 8:1,14; 9:14; 10:29; 13:1.

1:8 *Remember.* See note on 13:31; a key word in the book (4:14; 5:19; 6:14; 13:14,22,29,31). *transgress . . . scatter.* Dispersion was the inescapable consequence of the people's unfaithfulness. By the NT period there were still more Jews in the Diaspora (dispersion) than in the Holy Land.

1:9 *will I gather them.* See Deut 30:1–5; a frequent promise, especially in the prophets (e.g., Is 11:12; Jer 23:3; 31:8–10; Ezek 20:34,41; 36:24; Mic 2:12). *chosen to set my name there.* See Deut 12:5 and note; Ps 132:13.

1:10 *thy people . . . thou hast redeemed.* Although they had sinned and failed, they were still God's people by virtue of His redeeming them (see Deut 4:34; 9:29).

1:11 *prosper . . . thy servant this day.* Cf. Gen 24:12. *cupbearer.* Lit. "one who gives (someone) something to drink." The Hebrew for this word occurs 11 other times in the OT in the sense of "cupbearer" (Gen 40:1–2,5,9,13,20–21,23; 41:9; 1 Ki 10:5; 2 Chr 9:4). According to the Greek historian Xenophon (*Cyropaedia,* 1.3.9), one of the cupbearer's duties was to choose and taste the king's wine to make certain that it was not poisoned (see 2:1). Thus Nehemiah had to be a man who enjoyed the unreserved confidence of the king. The need for trustworthy court attendants is underscored by the intrigues that characterized the Achaemenid court of Persia. Ahasuerus, the father of Artaxerxes I, was killed in his own bedchamber by a courtier.

Nehemiah's request

2 And it came to pass in the month Nisan, *in* the twentieth year of [a]Artaxerxes the king, *that* wine *was* before him: and [b]I took up the wine, and gave *it* unto the king. Now I had not been *beforetime* sad in his presence.

2 Wherefore the king said unto me, Why *is* thy countenance sad, seeing thou *art* not sick? this *is* nothing *else* but [a]sorrow of heart. Then I was very sore afraid,

3 And said unto the king, [a]Let the king live for ever: why should not my countenance be sad, when [b]the city, the place of my fathers' sepulchres, *lieth* waste, and the gates thereof are consumed with fire?

4 Then the king said unto me, For what dost thou make request? So I prayed to the God of heaven.

5 And I said unto the king, If it please the king, and if thy servant have found favour in thy sight, that thou wouldest send me unto Judah, unto the city of my fathers' sepulchres, that I may build it.

2:1 [a]Ezra 7:1 [b]ch. 1:11
2:2 [a]Prov. 15:13
2:3 [a]1 Ki. 1:31; Dan. 2:4; 5:10; 6:6,21 [b]ch. 1:3
2:6 [1]Heb. *wife* [a]ch. 5:14; 13:6
2:8 [a]ch. 3:7 [b]ver. 18; Ezra 5:5; 7:6,9,28

6 And the king said unto me, (the [1]queen also sitting by him,) For how long shall thy journey be? and when wilt thou return? So it pleased the king to send me; and I set him [a]a time.

7 Moreover I said unto the king, If it please the king, let letters be given me to the governors beyond the river, that they may convey me over till I come into Judah;

8 And a letter unto Asaph the keeper of the king's forest, that he may give me timber to make beams for the gates of the palace which *appertained* [a]to the house, and for the wall of the city, and for the house that I shall enter into. And the king granted me, [b]according to the good hand of my God upon me.

Nehemiah's inspection of the walls

9 ¶ Then I came to the governors beyond the river, and gave them the king's letters. Now the king had sent captains of the army and horsemen with me.

10 When Sanballat the Horonite, and Tobiah the servant, the Ammonite, heard *of it,*

2:1 *Nisan . . . twentieth year.* March-April, 444 B.C. (see chart, p. 635). There was a delay of four months from Chislev, when Nehemiah first heard the news (1:1), to Nisan, when he approached the king. Various reasons have been suggested: 1. The king may have been in his other winter palace at Babylon. 2. Perhaps the king was not in the right mood. 3. Even though Nehemiah was a favorite of the king, he would not have rashly blurted out his request. *sad in his presence.* No matter what one's personal problems were, the king's servants were expected to keep their feelings to themselves and to display a cheerful disposition before him.

2:3 *Let the king live for ever.* A common form of address to kings. *city.* Nehemiah does not mention Jerusalem by name (see v. 5); he may have wished to arouse the king's sympathy by stressing first the desecration of ancestral tombs.

2:4 *I prayed to the God of heaven.* Before turning to answer the king, Nehemiah utters a brief, spontaneous prayer to God. One of Nehemiah's striking characteristics is his frequent recourse to prayer (1:4; 4:4,9; 5:19; 6:9,14; 13:14,22,29,31).

2:6 *queen.* The Hebrew for this word is used only here and in Ps 45:9. It is a loanword from Akkadian and means lit. "(woman) of the palace." The Aramaic equivalent is found only in Dan 5:2–3,23, where it is translated "wives." Ctesias, a Greek who lived at the Achaemenid court, informs us that the name of Artaxerxes's queen was Damaspia and that he had at least three concubines. Like Esther, Damaspia may have used her influence with the king (Esth 5). The Achaemenid court was notorious for the great influence exercised by the royal women. Especially domineering was Amestris, the cruel wife of Ahasuerus and mother of Artaxerxes I. *For how long shall thy journey be?* Nehemiah probably asked for a brief leave of absence, which he then had extended. We can infer from 5:14 that he spent 12 years on his first term as governor of Judah. In the 32nd year of Artaxerxes, Nehemiah returned to report to the king and then came back to Judah for a second term (13:6–7).

2:7 *letters.* A contemporary document from Arsames, the satrap of Egypt who was at the Persian court, to one of his officers who was returning to Egypt orders Persian officials to provide him with food and drink on the stages of his journey. *beyond the river.* See note on Ezra 4:10.

2:8 *forest.* The Hebrew for this word is *pardes,* a loanword from Old Persian meaning "enclosure," a pleasant retreat or park. The word occurs elsewhere in the OT only in Eccl 2:5 and Sol 4:13 ("orchard"). In the Septuagint (the Greek translation of the OT) the Greek transliteration *paradeisos* is used here. In the period between the OT and the NT, the word acquired the sense of the abode of the blessed dead, i.e. "paradise." It appears three times in the NT (Luke 23:43; 2 Cor 12:4; Rev 2:7). As to the location of the "king's forest," some believe that it was in Lebanon, which was famed for its forests of cedars and other coniferous trees (see notes on Judg 9:15; Ezra 3:7). But a more plausible suggestion is that it should be identified with Solomon's gardens at Etham, about six miles south of Jerusalem (see Josephus, *Antiquities,* 8.7.3). For city gates, costly imported cedars from Lebanon would not be used but rather indigenous oak, poplar or terebinth (Hos 4:13). *palace.* Probably refers to the fortress north of the temple, the forerunner of the Antonia fortress built by Herod the Great (Josephus, *Antiquities,* 15.11.4; see Acts 21:34,37; 22:24).

2:9 *captains of the army and horsemen.* In striking contrast to Ezra (see note on Ezra 8:22), Nehemiah was accompanied by an armed escort since he was officially Judah's governor.

2:10 *Sanballat.* A Babylonian name, meaning "Sin (the moon-god) has given life." *Horonite.* Identifies him as coming from (1) Hauran (Ezek 47:16,18), east of the sea of Galilee, (2) Horonaim, in Moab (Jer 48:34), or, most probably, (3) either Upper or Lower Beth Horon, two key cities 12 miles northwest of Jerusalem, which guarded the main road to Jerusalem (Josh 10:10; 16:3,5; 1 Maccabees 3:16; 7:39). Sanballat was the chief political opponent of Nehemiah (v. 19; 4:1,7; 6:1–2,5,12,14; 13:28). He held the position of governor over Samaria (cf. 4:1–2). An Elephantine papyrus letter of the late fifth century B.C. to Bagohi (Bigvai), governor of Judah, refers to "Delaiah and Shelemiah, the sons of Sanballat, governor of Samaria." In 1962 a fourth-century B.C. papyrus was found in a cave north of Jericho, listing the name Sanballat, probably a descendant of Nehemiah's contemporary. *Tobiah.* Means "The LORD is good." He was probably a worshiper of the Lord (Yahweh), as indicated not only by his name but also by that of his son Johanan (6:17–18), meaning "The LORD is gracious." Johanan was married to the daughter of Meshullam son of Berechiah, the leader of one of the groups repairing the wall (3:4,30; 6:18). Tobiah also had a close relationship with Eliashib the priest (13:4–7). *Ammonite.* See Ezra 9:1; see also note on Gen 19:36–38. Tobiah

grieved them exceedingly that there was come
a man to seek the welfare of the children of Israel.
11 So I [a]came to Jerusalem, and was there
three days.
12 And I arose in the night, I and *some* few
men with me; neither told I *any* man what my
God had put in my heart to do at Jerusalem:
neither *was there any* beast with me, save the
beast that I rode upon.
13 And I went out by night [a]by the gate of
the valley, even before the dragon well, and to
the dung port, and viewed the walls of Jerusalem, which were [b]broken down, and the gates
thereof were consumed with fire.
14 Then I went on to the [a]gate of the fountain, and to the king's pool: but *there was* no
place for the beast *that was* under me to pass.
15 Then went I up in the night by the
[a]brook, and viewed the wall, and turned back,
and entered by the gate of the valley, and *so*
returned.
16 And the rulers knew not whither I
went, or what I did; neither had I as yet told *it*
to the Jews, nor to the priests, nor to the nobles, nor to the rulers, nor to the rest that did
the work.
17 Then said I unto them, Ye see the distress that we *are* in, how Jerusalem *lieth*
waste, and the gates thereof are burnt with
fire: come, and let us build *up* the wall of Jerusalem, that we be no more [a]a reproach.

2:11 [a]Ezra 8:32 **2:13** [a]2 Chr. 26:9; ch. 3:13 [b]ver. 17; ch. 1:3 **2:14** [a]ch. 3:15 **2:15** [a]2 Sam. 15:23; Jer. 31:40 **2:17** [a]ch. 1:3; Ps. 44:13; 79:4; Jer. 24:9; Ezek. 5:14,15; 22:4

was probably governor of the area east of the Jordan under the Persians. In later generations a prominent family bearing the name of Tobiah was sometimes associated with the region of Ammon in non-Biblical texts. *grieved them exceedingly.* The reasons for the opposition of Sanballat and Tobiah were not basically religious but political. The authority of the Samaritan governor in particular was threatened by Nehemiah's arrival.

2:11 *three days.* See note on Ezra 8:32.

2:12 Nehemiah was cautious and discreet as he inspected the city's fortifications. *beast that I rode upon.* Probably a mule or donkey.

2:13 Nehemiah did not make a complete circuit of the walls, but only of the southern area (see map below). Jerusalem was always attacked from the north because it was most vulnerable there, so the walls had probably been completely destroyed in that part of the city. *gate of the valley.* See 3:13. According to 2 Chr 26:9 Uzziah fortified towers in the west wall, which overlooked the Tyropoeon Valley, i.e. the central valley between the Hinnom and Kidron valleys. Excavations in 1927–28 uncovered the remains of a gate from the Persian period, which has been identified as the valley gate. *dragon well.* Many scholars suggest that this was En-rogel (Josh 15:7–8; 18:16; 2 Sam 17:17; 1 Ki 1:9), a well situated at the junction of the Hinnom and Kidron valleys, 250 yards south of the southeast ridge of Jerusalem. Others suggest that it was the pool of Siloam. *dung port.* Perhaps the gate leading to the rubbish dump in the Hinnom Valley (cf. 3:13–14; 12:31; 2 Ki 23:10). It was situated about 500 yards south of the valley gate (3:13).

2:14 *gate of the fountain.* Possibly in the southeast wall facing toward En-rogel (see 3:15; 12:37). *king's pool.* Hezekiah may have diverted the overflow from his Siloam tunnel (cf. 2 Ki 20:20; 2 Chr 32:30) to irrigate the royal gardens (2 Ki 25:4) located outside the city walls at the junction of the Kidron and Hinnom valleys. The king's pool was probably therefore the pool of Siloam ("Siloah," 3:15) or the adjacent Birket el-Hamra. *no place . . . to pass.* Possibly because of the collapse of the supporting terraces (cf. 2 Sam 5:9; 1 Ki 9:15,24) on the east side of the city.

2:15 *brook.* The Kidron.

2:16 *nobles.* The Hebrew root for this word means "free" (see 4:14,19; 5:7; 6:17; 7:5; 13:17; see also note on 3:5).

2:17 *lieth waste.* The condition of the walls and gates of the city since their destruction by Nebuchadnezzar in 586 B.C., in spite of abortive attempts to rebuild them. The leaders and people had evidently become reconciled to this sad state of affairs. It took an outsider to assess the situation and to rally them to renewed efforts.

Jerusalem of the Returning Exiles

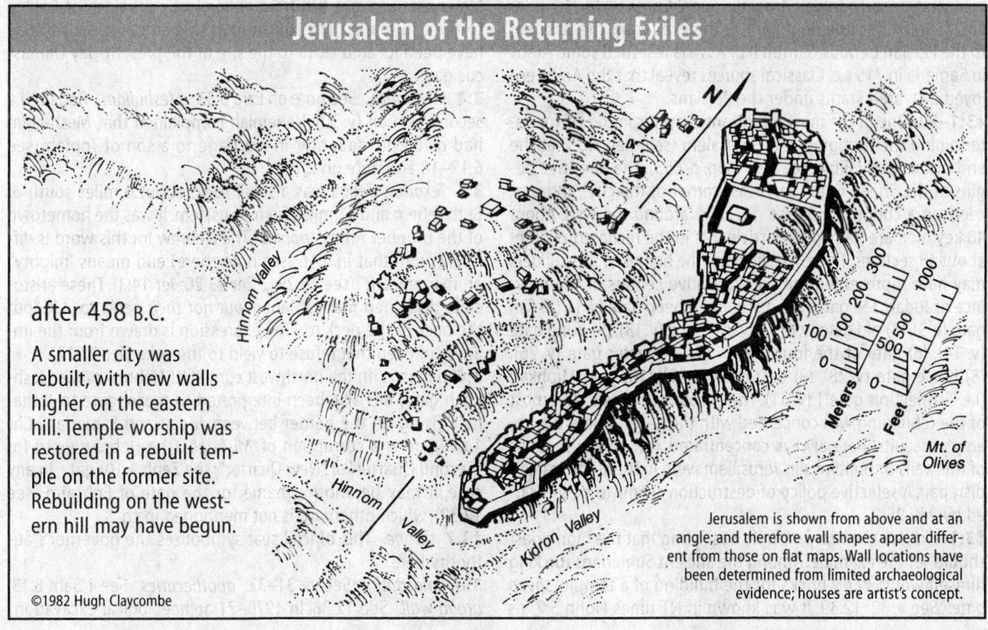

after 458 B.C.

A smaller city was rebuilt, with new walls higher on the eastern hill. Temple worship was restored in a rebuilt temple on the former site. Rebuilding on the western hill may have begun.

Jerusalem is shown from above and at an angle; and therefore wall shapes appear different from those on flat maps. Wall locations have been determined from limited archaeological evidence; houses are artist's concept.

18 Then I told them of [a]the hand of my
God which was good upon me; as also the
king's words that he had spoken unto me. And
they said, Let us rise up and build. So they
[b]strengthened their hands for *this* good *work.*
19 But when Sanballat the Horonite, and
Tobiah the servant, the Ammonite, and Geshem the Arabian, heard *it,* they laughed us to
scorn, and despised us, and said, What *is* this
thing that ye do? [a]will ye rebel against the
king?
20 Then answered I them, and said unto
them, The God of heaven, he will prosper us;
therefore we his servants will arise and build:
[a]but you have no portion, nor right, nor memorial, in Jerusalem.

The rebuilding begun

3 Then [a]Eliashib the high priest rose up
with his brethren the priests, [b]and they
built the sheep gate; they sanctified it, and set
up the doors of it; [c]even unto the tower of
Meah they sanctified it, unto the tower of
[d]Hananeel.
2 And [1]next unto him builded [a]the men of
Jericho. And next to them builded Zaccur the
son of Imri.
3 [a]But the fish gate did the sons of Hasse-
naah build, who *also* laid the beams thereof,
and [b]set up the doors thereof, the locks thereof, and the bars thereof.
4 And next unto them repaired Meremoth
the son of Urijah, the son of Koz. And next
unto them repaired Meshullam the son of
Berechiah, the son of Meshezabeel. And next
unto them repaired Zadok the son of Baana.
5 And next unto them the Tekoites repaired; but their nobles put not their necks to
[a]the work of their Lord.
6 Moreover [a]the old gate repaired Jehoiada
the son of Paseah, and Meshullam the son of
Besodeiah; they laid the beams thereof, and
set up the doors thereof, and the locks thereof,
and the bars thereof.
7 And next unto them repaired Melatiah
the Gibeonite, and Jadon the Meronothite, the
men of Gibeon, and of Mizpah, unto the
[a]throne of the governor on *this* side the river.
8 Next unto him repaired Uzziel the son of
Harhaiah, *of* the goldsmiths. Next unto him
also repaired Hananiah the son of *one of* the
apothecaries, and they [1]fortified Jerusalem
unto the [a]broad wall.
9 And next unto them repaired Rephaiah

2:18 [a]ver. 8 [b]2 Sam. 2:7
2:19 [a]ch. 6:6
2:20 [a]Ezra 4:3
3:1 [a]ch. 12:10 [b]John 5:2 [c]ch. 12:39 [d]Jer. 31:38; Zech. 14:10
3:2 [1]Heb. *at his hand* [a]Ezra 2:34
3:3 [a]2 Chr. 33:14; ch. 12:39; Zeph. 1:10 [b]See ch. 6:1; 7:1
3:5 [a]Judg. 5:23
3:6 [a]ch. 12:39
3:7 [a]ch. 2:8
3:8 [1]Or, *left Jerusalem unto the broad wall* [a]ch. 12:38

2:18 *my God . . . also the king's words.* Nehemiah could personally attest that God was alive and active in his behalf and that he (Nehemiah) had come with royal sanction and authority.

2:19 *Sanballat . . . Tobiah.* See note on v. 10. *Geshem.* Inscriptions from Dedan in northwest Arabia and from Tell el-Maskhutah near Ismailia in Egypt bear the name of Geshem, who may have been in charge of a north Arabian confederacy that controlled vast areas from northeast Egypt to northern Arabia, including the southern part of the Holy Land. Geshem may have been opposed to Nehemiah's development of an independent kingdom because he feared that it might interfere with his lucrative spice trade. *Arabian.* See 2 Chr 9:14; Is 21:13; Jer 25:24. Arabs became dominant in this area from the Assyrian to the Persian periods. Sargon II of Assyria resettled some Arabs in Samaria in 715 B.C. Classical sources reveal that the Arabs enjoyed a favored status under the Persians.

‡3:1–32 One of the most important chapters in the OT for determining the topography of Jerusalem (see map No. 8 at the end of the study Bible; see also map, p. 655). The narrative begins at the Sheep Gate (northeast corner of the city) and proceeds in a counterclockwise direction around the wall. About 40 key men are named as participants in the reconstruction of about 45 sections. The towns listed as the homes of the builders may have represented the administrative centers of the province of Judah. Ten gates are named: (1) sheep gate (v. 1), (2) fish gate (v. 3), (3) old gate (v. 6), (4) valley gate (v. 13), (5) dung gate (v. 14), (6) gate of the fountain (v. 15), (7) water gate (v. 26), (8) horse gate (v. 28), (9) east gate (v. 29), (10) gate Miphkad [i.e. "inspection gate"] (v. 31). The account suggests that most of the rebuilding was concerned with the gates, where the enemy's assaults were always concentrated. Not all the sections of the walls or buildings in Jerusalem were in the same state of disrepair. A selective policy of destruction seems to be indicated by 2 Ki 25:9.

‡3:1 *Eliashib the high priest.* It was fitting that the high priest should set the example. Among the ancient Sumerians the king himself would carry bricks for the building of a temple. *sheep gate.* See v. 32; 12:39. It was known in NT times (John 5:2) as located near the Bethesda Pool (in the northeast corner of Jerusalem). Even today a sheep market is held periodically near this area. The sheep gate may have replaced the earlier gate of Benjamin (Jer 37:13; 38:7; Zech 14:10). *tower of Meah* [Hebrew for "hundred"]. "Hundred" may refer to (1) its height (100 cubits), (2) the number of its steps or (3) a military unit (cf. Deut 1:15). *tower of Hananeel.* The towers were associated with the "palace which appertained to the house [i.e. 'temple']" (2:8) in protecting the vulnerable northern approaches to the city.

3:3 *fish gate.* See 12:39. During the days of the first temple, it was one of Jerusalem's main entrances (2 Chr 33:14; Zeph 1:10). Merchants brought fish from either Tyre or the sea of Galilee to the fish market (13:16) through this entrance, which may have been located close to the site of the present-day Damascus gate.

3:4 *Meremoth.* See note on Ezra 8:33. *Meshullam.* Repaired a second section (v. 30). Nehemiah complained that Meshullam had given his daughter in marriage to a son of Tobiah (see 6:17–18 and note on 2:10).

3:5 *Tekoites.* Tekoa was a small town about 6 miles south of Beth-lehem and 11 miles from Jerusalem. It was the hometown of the prophet Amos. *nobles.* The Hebrew for this word is different from that in 2:16 (see note there) and means "mighty" or "magnificent" (see 10:29; 2 Chr 23:20; Jer 14:3). These aristocrats disdained manual labor. *put not their necks to.* Lit. "put the back of the neck to." The expression is drawn from the imagery of oxen that refuse to yield to the yoke (Jer 27:12).

3:6 *old gate.* In the northwest corner. Its Hebrew name (Jeshanah gate) has also been interpreted to mean "gate to Jeshanah" (lying on the border between Judah and Samaria, 2 Chr 13:19), or as a corruption of *Mishneh* (the Hebrew word for "Second Quarter" or "New Quarter"; see Zeph 1:10) gate. In any case, it may be another name for the gate of Ephraim (see 12:39), which otherwise is not mentioned in ch. 3.

‡3:7 *throne.* This official seat symbolizes the governor's authority here.

3:8 *goldsmiths.* See vv. 31–32. *apothecaries.* See 1 Sam 8:13. *broad wall.* See 12:38. In 1970–71 archaeological excavations

the son of Hur, the ruler of the half part of Jerusalem.
10 And next unto them repaired Jedaiah
the son of Harumaph, even over against his
house. And next unto him repaired Hattush
the son of Hashabniah.
11 Malchijah the son of Harim, and
Hashub the son of Pahath-moab, repaired the
[1]other piece, [a]and the tower of the furnaces.
12 And next unto him repaired Shallum
the son of Hallohesh, the ruler of the half part
of Jerusalem, he and his daughters.
13 [a]The valley gate repaired Hanun, and
the inhabitants of Zanoah; they built it, and set
up the doors thereof, the locks thereof, and
the bars thereof, and a thousand cubits on the
wall unto [b]the dung gate.
14 But the dung gate repaired Malchiah
the son of Rechab, the ruler of part of Beth-
haccerem; he built it, and set up the doors
thereof, the locks thereof, and the bars thereof.
15 But [a]the gate of the fountain repaired
Shallun the son of Col-hozeh, the ruler of part
of Mizpah; he built it, and covered it, and set
up the doors thereof, the locks thereof, and
the bars thereof, and the wall of the pool of
[b]Siloah by the king's garden, and unto the
stairs that go down from the city of David.
16 After him repaired Nehemiah the son of
Azbuk, the ruler of the half part of Beth-zur,
unto *the place* over against the sepulchres of
David, and to the [a]pool that was made, and
unto the house of the mighty.
17 After him repaired the Levites, Rehum
the son of Bani. Next unto him repaired Hashabiah, the ruler of the half part of Keilah, in his
part.
18 After him repaired their brethren, Bavai
the son of Henadad, the ruler of the half part
of Keilah.
19 And next to him repaired Ezer the son
of Jeshua, the ruler of Mizpah, another piece
over against the going up to the armoury *at* the
[a]turning *of the wall.*
20 After him Baruch the son of [1]Zabbai
earnestly repaired the other piece, from the
turning *of the wall* unto the door of the house
of Eliashib the high priest.
21 After him repaired Meremoth the son of
Urijah the son of Koz another piece, from the
door of the house of Eliashib even to the end
of the house of Eliashib.
22 And after him repaired the priests, the
men of the plain.
23 After him repaired Benjamin and
Hashub over against their house. After him repaired Azariah the son of Maaseiah the son of
Ananiah by his house.
24 After him repaired Binnui the son of
Henadad another piece, from the house of Azariah unto [a]the turning *of the wall,* even unto
the corner.
25 Palal the son of Uzai, over against the
turning *of the wall,* and the tower which lieth
out from the king's high house, that *was* by the
[a]court of the prison. After him Pedaiah the son
of Parosh.
26 Moreover [a]the Nethinims [1]dwelt in
[b][2]Ophel, unto *the place* over against [c]the wa-

3:11 [1] Heb. *second measure* [a] ch. 12:38
3:13 [a] ch. 2:13 [b] ch:2:13
3:15 [a] ch. 2:14 [b] John 9:7
3:16 [a] 2 Ki. 20:20; Is. 22:11
3:19 [a] 2 Chr. 26:9
3:20 [1] Or, *Zaccai*
3:24 [a] ver. 19
3:25 [a] Jer. 32:2; 33:1; 37:21
3:26 [1] [Or, which *dwelt in Ophel,* repaired *unto*] [2] Or, *the tower* [a] Ezra 2:43; ch. 11:21 [b] 2 Chr. 27:3 [c] ch. 8:1,3; 12:37

in Jerusalem uncovered such a wall west of the temple area. It is dated to the early seventh century B.C. and was probably built by Hezekiah (2 Chr 32:5). The expansion to and beyond the broad wall may have become necessary because of the influx of refugees fleeing from the fall of Samaria in 722–721.

3:10 *repaired Jedaiah . . . over against his house.* See vv. 23,28–30. It made sense to have him and others repair the sections of the wall nearest their homes.

3:11 *tower of the furnaces.* It was on the western wall, perhaps in the same location as one built by Uzziah (2 Chr 26:9). The furnaces may have been those situated in the "bakers' street" (Jer 37:21).

3:12 *daughters.* A unique reference to women working on the wall. When the Athenians attempted to rebuild their walls after the Persians had destroyed them, it was decreed that "the whole population of the city—men, women and children—should take part in the wall-building" (Thucydides, 1.90.3).

3:13 *valley gate.* See note on 2:13. *a thousand cubits.* Five hundred yards, an extraordinary length; probably most of the section was relatively intact. *dung gate.* See note on 2:13.

3:14 *Beth-haccerem.* Means "house of the vineyard." It was a fire-signal point (Jer 6:1) and is identified with Ramat Rahel, two miles south of Jerusalem. It may have been the residence of a district governor in the Persian period.

‡3:15 *gate of the fountain.* See note on 2:14. *pool of Siloah.* A variant of *Shiloah* [i.e. "Siloam"], perhaps the lower pool of Is 22:9 (see note on Is 8:6). *king's garden.* See note on 2:14. *city of David.* See 12:37; see also note on 2 Sam 5:7.

3:16 *Beth-zur.* A district capital, 13 miles south of Jerusalem. Excavations in 1931 and 1957 revealed that occupation was sparse during the early Persian period but was resumed in the fifth century B.C. *sepulchres of David.* Cf. 2:5. David was buried in the city area (1 Ki 2:10; 2 Chr 21:20; 32:33; Acts 2:29). The so-called Tomb of David on mount Zion venerated today by Jewish pilgrims is in the Coenaculum building, erected in the 14th century A.D. Such a site for David's tomb is mentioned no earlier than the ninth century A.D. *house of the mighty.* May have been the house of David's mighty men (see 2 Sam 23:8–39), which perhaps served later as the barracks or armory.

3:17–18 *Keilah.* Located about 15 miles southwest of Jerusalem, it played an important role in David's early history (1 Sam 23:1–13).

3:19 *armoury.* See note on v. 16.

3:20–21 The residences of the high priest and his fellow priests were located inside the city along the eastern wall.

3:25 *king's high house.* Perhaps the old palace of David (see 12:37). Like Solomon's palace, it would have had a guardhouse (Jer 32:2).

‡3:26 *Ophel.* See v. 27. The word means "swelling" or "bulge," hence a "hill" (as in Mic 4:8), specifically the northern part of the southeastern hill of Jerusalem, which formed the original City of David, just south of the temple area (2 Chr 27:3). *water gate.* So called because it led to the main source of Jerusalem's water, the Gihon spring. It must have opened onto a large area, for the reading of the Law took place there (8:1,3,16; 12:37). *tower that lieth out.* I.e. a "projecting" tower, such as the large tower whose ruins were discovered by archaeologists on the crest of the Ophel hill in 1923–25. Excavations at the base of the tower in 1978 revealed a level dating to the Persian era.

ter gate toward the east, and the tower that lieth out.

27 After them the Tekoites repaired another piece, over against the great tower that lieth out, even unto the wall of Ophel.

28 From above the [a]horse gate repaired the priests, every one over against his house.

29 After them repaired Zadok the son of Immer over against his house. After him repaired also Shemaiah the son of Shechaniah, the keeper of the east gate.

30 After him repaired Hananiah the son of Shelemiah, and Hanun the sixth son of Zalaph, another piece. After him repaired Meshullam the son of Berechiah over against his chamber.

31 After him repaired Malchiah the goldsmith's son unto the place of the Nethinims, and *of* the merchants, over against the gate Miphkad, and to the [1]going up of the corner.

32 And between the [1]going up of the corner unto the sheep gate repaired the goldsmiths and the merchants.

Defence against a conspiracy

4 But it came to pass, [a]that when Sanballat heard that we builded the wall, he was wroth, and took great indignation, and mocked the Jews.

2 And he spake before his brethren and the army of Samaria, and said, What do *these* feeble Jews? will they [1]fortify themselves? will they sacrifice? will they make an end in a day? will they revive the stones out of the heaps of the rubbish which are burnt?

3 Now [a]Tobiah the Ammonite *was* by him, and he said, Even *that* which they build, if a fox go up, he shall even break down their stone wall.

4 [a]Hear, O our God; for we are [1]despised: and [b]turn their reproach upon their own head, and give them for a prey in the land of captivity:

5 And [a]cover not their iniquity, and let not their sin be blotted out from before thee: for they have provoked *thee* to anger before the builders.

3:28 [a]2 Ki. 11:16; 2 Chr. 23:15; Jer. 31:40
3:31 [1]Or, *corner chamber*
3:32 [1]Or, *corner chamber*
4:1 [a]ch. 2:10,19
4:2 [1]Heb. *leave to themselves*
4:3 [a]ch. 2:10,19
4:4 [1]Heb. *despite* [a]Ps. 123:3,4 [b]Ps. 79:12; Prov. 3:34
4:5 [a]Ps. 69:27,28; 109:14,15; Jer. 18:23
4:7 [1]Heb. *ascended* [a]ver. 1
4:8 [1]Heb. *to make an error to it* [a]Ps. 83:3-5
4:9 [a]Ps. 50:15
4:12 [1]Or, *That from all places ye must return to us*
4:13 [1]Heb. *from the lower parts of the place, etc.*
4:14 [a]Num. 14:9; Deut. 1:29 [b]Deut. 10:17 [c]2 Sam. 10:12
4:15 [a]Job 5:12

6 So built we the wall; and all the wall was joined together unto the half thereof: for the people had a mind to work.

7 ¶ But it came to pass, *that* [a]when Sanballat, and Tobiah, and the Arabians, and the Ammonites, and the Ashdodites, heard that the walls of Jerusalem [1]were made up, *and* that the breaches began to be stopped, then they were very wroth,

8 And [a]conspired all of them together to come *and* to fight against Jerusalem, and [1]to hinder it.

9 Nevertheless [a]we made our prayer unto our God, and set a watch against them day and night, because of them.

10 And Judah said, The strength of the bearers of burdens is decayed, and *there is* much rubbish; so that we are not able to build the wall.

11 And our adversaries said, They shall not know, neither see, till we come in the midst among them, and slay them, and cause the work to cease.

12 And it came to pass, that when the Jews which dwelt by them came, they said unto us ten times, [1]From all places whence ye shall return unto us *they will be upon you.*

13 Therefore set I [1]in the lower places behind the wall, *and* on the higher places, I even set the people after *their* families with their swords, their spears, and their bows.

14 And I looked, and rose up, and said unto the nobles, and to the rulers, and to the rest of the people, [a]Be not ye afraid of them: remember the Lord, *which is* [b]great and terrible, and [c]fight for your brethren, your sons, and your daughters, your wives, and your houses.

15 And it came to pass, when our enemies heard that it was known unto us, [a]and God had brought their counsel to nought, that we returned all of us to the wall, every one unto his work.

16 And it came to pass from that time forth, *that* the half of my servants wrought in

---

3:27 *Tekoites.* The common people of Tekoa did double duty, whereas the nobles of Tekoa shirked their responsibility (see note on v. 5).

3:28 *horse gate.* Where Athaliah was slain (2 Chr 23:15). It may have been the easternmost point in the city wall—a gate through which one could reach the Kidron Valley (Jer 31:40).

3:29 *east gate.* May have been the predecessor of the present Golden Gate.

‡3:31 *goldsmith's son.* See v. 8. *gate Miphkad.* The inspection gate in the northern part of the eastern wall.

3:32 *sheep gate.* Back to the point of departure (see v. 1).

4:2 *he spake . . . said.* Disputes between rival Persian governors were frequent. Sanballat asked several derisive questions to taunt the Jews and to discourage them in their efforts. *burnt.* Fire had damaged the stones, which were probably limestone, and had caused many of them to crack and crumble.

4:3 *fox.* See Judg 15:4; Sol 2:15. The Hebrew for this word may also mean "jackal." The jackal normally hunts in packs, whereas the fox is usually a nocturnal and solitary animal.

4:4–5 As in the so-called imprecatory psalms (Ps 79:12; 83; 94:1–3; 109:14; 137:7–9), Nehemiah does not himself take action against his opponents but calls down on them redress from God. In v. 5 Nehemiah's prayer echoes the language of Jer 18:23.

4:7 *Ashdodites.* See note on Is 20:1. Ashdod became a district capital under Persian rule.

4:9 *made our prayer . . . set a watch.* Prayer and watchfulness blend faith and action, and also emphasize both the divine side and the human side.

4:10 *decayed.* The picture is of a worker staggering under the weight of his load and ready to fall at any step.

4:11 *our adversaries said.* Either Nehemiah had friendly informants, or the enemy was spreading unsettling rumors.

4:12 *ten times.* Many times.

4:13 *lower places . . . higher places.* Nehemiah posted men conspicuously in the areas that were the most vulnerable along the wall. *spears.* Used as thrusting weapons (Num 25:7–8; 1 Ki 18:28).

4:14 *Be not ye afraid of them: remember the Lord.* See note on 1:8. The best way to dispel fear is to remember the Lord, who alone is to be feared (see Deut 3:22; 20:3; 31:6).

the work, and the *other* half of them held both the spears, the shields, and the bows, and the habergeons; and the rulers *were* behind all the house of Judah.

17 They which builded on the wall, and they that bare burdens, *with* those that laded, *every one* with one of his hands wrought in the work, and with the other *hand* held a weapon.

18 For the builders, every one had his sword girded [1]by his side, and *so* builded. And he that sounded the trumpet *was* by me.

19 And I said unto the nobles, and to the rulers, and to the rest of the people, The work *is* great and large, and we *are* separated upon the wall, one far from another.

20 In what place *therefore* ye hear the sound of the trumpet, resort ye thither unto us: [a]our God shall fight for us.

21 So we laboured in the work: and half of them held the spears from the rising of the morning till the stars appeared.

22 Likewise at the same time said I unto the people, Let every one with his servant lodge within Jerusalem, that in the night they may be a guard to us, and labour on the day.

23 So neither I, nor my brethren, nor my servants, nor the men of the guard which followed me, none of us put off our clothes, [1]*saving that* every one put them off *for* washing.

Poverty and famine

5 And there was a great [a]cry of the people and of their wives against their [b]brethren the Jews.

2 For there were that said, We, our sons, and our daughters, *are* many: therefore we take up corn *for them,* that we may eat, and live.

3 *Some* also there were that said, We *have* mortgaged our lands, vineyards, and houses, that we might buy corn, because of the dearth.

4 There were also that said, We have borrowed money for the king's tribute, *and that upon* our lands and vineyards.

5 Yet now [a]our flesh *is* as the flesh of our brethren, our children as their children: and lo, we [b]bring into bondage our sons and our daughters to be servants, and *some* of our daughters are brought unto bondage *already:* neither *is it* in our power *to redeem them;* for other men have our lands and vineyards.

4:18 [1]Heb. *on his loins*
4:20 [a]Ex. 14:14,25; Deut. 1:30; 3:22; 20:4; Josh. 23:10
4:23 [1]Or, *every one* went with *his weapon* for *water*
5:1 [a]Is. 5:7 [b]Lev. 25:35-37; Deut. 15:7
5:5 [a]Is. 58:7 [b]Ex. 21:7; Lev. 25:39

4:16 *shields.* Made primarily of wood or wickerwork and therefore combustible (Ezek 39:9). *habergeons.* The Hebrew for this word designated primarily a breastplate of metal or a coat of mail (see 2 Chr 18:33).

4:17 *with one of his hands wrought in the work, and with the other hand held a weapon.* Means either that the workers carried their materials with one hand and their weapons with the other, or simply that the weapons were kept close at hand.

4:18 *he that sounded the trumpet.* See note on Is 18:3; see also Josh 6:4,6,8,13.

4:20 *our God shall fight for us.* For the concept of holy war, in which God fights for His people, see Josh 10:14,42; Judg 4:14; 20:35; 2 Sam 5:24; see also essay, p. 272.

4:21 *till the stars appeared.* Indicates the earnestness of their efforts, since the usual time to stop working was at sunset (Deut 24:15; Mat 20:8).

4:22 *in the night they may be a guard.* Even men from outside Jerusalem stayed in the city at night so that some of them could serve as sentries.

4:23 Constant preparedness was the rule. According to Josephus (*Antiquities,* 11.5.8), Nehemiah "himself made the rounds of the city by night, never tiring either through work or lack of food and sleep, neither of which he took for pleasure but as a necessity."

5:1–19 During his major effort to rebuild the walls of Jerusalem, Nehemiah faced an economic crisis. Since the building of the wall took only 52 days (6:15), it is surprising that Nehemiah called a "great assembly" (v. 7) in the midst of such a project. Perhaps the economic pressures created by the rebuilding program brought to light problems that had long been simmering and that had to be dealt with before work could proceed. Among the classes affected by the economic crisis were (1) the landless, who were short of food (v. 2); (2) the landowners, who were compelled to mortgage their properties (v. 3); (3) those forced to borrow money at exorbitant interest rates and sell their children into slavery (vv. 4–5).

5:1 *wives.* The situation was so serious that the wives joined in the protest as they ran short of funds and supplies to feed their families. They complained not against the foreign authorities but against their own countrymen who were taking advantage of their poorer brothers at a time when all were needed for the defense of the country.

‡5:2 *corn* [i.e. grain]. About six to seven bushels would be needed for a man to feed his family for a month.

5:3 *mortgaged.* Even those who had considerable property were forced to mortgage it, benefiting the wealthy few (cf. Is 5:8). In times of economic stress the rich got richer, and the poor got poorer. *dearth.* The economic situation was aggravated by the natural conditions that had produced a famine. Some 75 years earlier the prophet Haggai had referred to a time of drought, when food was insufficient (Hag 1:5–11). Such times of distress were considered to be expressions of God's judgment (Is 51:19; Jer 14:13–18; Amos 4:6). Famines were common in Canaan. They occurred in the time of Abraham (Gen 12:10), Isaac (Gen 26:1), Joseph (Gen 41:27,54), Ruth (Ruth 1:1), David (2 Sam 21:1), Elijah (1 Ki 18:2), Elisha (2 Ki 4:38) and Claudius (Acts 11:28).

5:4 *tribute.* It is estimated that the Persian king collected the equivalent of 20 million darics a year in taxes. Little was ever returned to benefit the provinces, because most of it was melted down and stored as bullion. Alexander the Great found at Susa alone 9,000 talents (about 340 tons) of coined gold and 40,000 talents (about 1,500 tons) of silver stored as bullion. As coined money was increasingly taken out of circulation by taxes, poverty increased dramatically. The acquisition of land by the Persians and its removal from production also helped produce a 50 percent rise in prices during the Persian period.

5:5 *servants.* In times of economic distress families would borrow funds, using family members as collateral. If a man could not repay the loan and its interest, his children, his wife, or even the man himself could be sold into bondage. An Israelite who fell into debt, however, would serve his creditor as a "hired servant" (Lev 25:39–40). He was to be released in the seventh year (Deut 15:12–18), unless he chose to stay voluntarily. During the seven-year famine in Egypt, Joseph was approached by people who asked him to accept their land and their bodies in exchange for food (Gen 47:18–19). The irony for the Israelites was that at least as exiles in Mesopotamia their families were together, but now, because of dire economic necessity, their children were being sold into slavery.

6 And I was very angry when I heard their cry and these words.

7 Then [1]I consulted with myself, and I rebuked the nobles, and the rulers, and said unto them, [a]You exact usury, every one of his brother. And I set a great assembly against them.

8 And I said unto them, We after our ability have [a]redeemed our brethren the Jews, which were sold unto the heathen; and will you even sell your brethren? or shall they be sold unto us? Then held they their peace, and found nothing *to answer.*

9 Also I said, It *is* not good that ye do: ought ye not to walk [a]in the fear of our God [b]because of the reproach of the heathen our enemies?

10 I likewise, *and* my brethren, and my servants, *might* exact of them money and corn: I pray you, let us leave off this usury.

11 Restore, I pray you, to them, even *this* day, their lands, their vineyards, their oliveyards, and their houses, also the hundredth *part* of the money, and *of* the corn, the wine, and the oil, that ye exact of them.

12 Then said they, We will restore *them,* and will require nothing of them; so will we do as thou sayest. Then I called the priests, [a]and took an oath of them, that *they* should do according to this promise.

13 Also [a]I shook my lap, and said, So God shake out every man from his house, and from his labour, that performeth not this promise, even thus be he shaken out, and [1]emptied. And all the congregation said, Amen, and praised the LORD. [b]And the people did according to this promise.

14 ¶ Moreover from the time that I was appointed to be their governor in the land of Judah, from the twentieth year [a]even unto the two and thirtieth year of Artaxerxes the king, *that is,* twelve years, I and my brethren have not [b]eaten the bread of the governor.

15 But the former governors that *had been* before me were chargeable unto the people, and had taken of them bread and wine, beside forty shekels of silver; *yea,* even their servants bare rule over the people: but [a]so did not I, because of the [b]fear of God.

16 Yea also I continued in the work of this wall, neither bought we *any* land: and all my servants *were* gathered thither unto the work.

17 Moreover *there were* [a]at my table an hundred and fifty of the Jews and rulers, besides those that came unto us from among the heathen that *are* about us.

18 Now *that* [a]which was prepared *for me* daily *was* one ox *and* six choice sheep; also fowls were prepared for me, and once in ten days store of all *sorts of* wine: yet for *all* this [b]required not I the bread of the governor, because the bondage was heavy upon this people.

5:7 [1]Heb. *my heart consulted in me* [a]Ex. 22:25; Lev. 25:36; Ezek. 22:12
5:8 [a]Lev. 25:48
5:9 [a]Lev. 25:36 [b]2 Sam. 12:14; Rom. 2:24; 1 Pet. 2:12
5:12 [a]Ezra 10:5; Jer. 34:8,9
5:13 [a]Mat. 10:14; Acts 13:51; 18:6
5:13 [1]Heb. *empty,* or, *void* [b]2 Ki. 23:3
5:14 [a]ch. 13:6 [b]1 Cor. 9:4,15
5:15 [a]2 Cor. 11:9; 12:13 [b]ver. 9
5:17 [a]2 Sam. 9:7; 1 Ki. 18:19
5:18 [a]1 Ki. 4:22 [b]ver. 14,15

5:6 *I was very angry.* Sometimes it becomes necessary to express indignation against social injustice (cf. Mark 11:15–18; Eph 4:26).

5:7 *usury.* See notes on Ex 22:25–27; Lev 25:36; Deut 23:20. Josephus (*Antiquities,* 4.8.25) explains: "Let it not be permitted to lend upon usury to any Hebrew either meat or drink; for it is not just to draw a revenue from the misfortunes of a fellow countryman. Rather, in consoling him in his distress, you should reckon as gain the gratitude of such persons and the recompense that God has in store for an act of generosity."

5:8 *brethren the Jews, which were sold.* An impoverished brother could be hired as a servant, but he was not to be sold as a slave (Lev 25:39–42). *unto the heathen.* The sale of fellow Hebrews as slaves to foreigners was forbidden (Ex 21:8). *held they their peace.* Their guilt was so obvious that they had no rebuttal or excuse (cf. John 8:7–10).

5:9 *not good.* Failure to treat others, especially fellow believers, with compassion is an insult to our Maker and a blot on our testimony (cf. Prov 14:31; 1 Pet 2:12–15).

5:10 *let us leave off this usury.* The OT condemns the greed that seeks a profit at the expense of people (Ps 119:36; Is 56:9–12; 57:17; Jer 6:13; 8:10; 22:13–17; Ezek 22:12–13; 33:31). In view of the economic crisis facing his people, Nehemiah urges the creditors to relinquish their rights to repayment with interest.

5:11 *corn, the wine, and the oil.* See notes on 10:37; Deut 7:13.

5:13 *shook my lap.* Symbolizing the solemnity of an oath and reinforcing the attendant curses for its nonfulfillment. *Amen.* See 8:6; Num 5:22; see also note on Deut 27:15.

5:14 *two and thirtieth year.* From Apr. 1, 433 B.C., to Apr. 19, 432. Nehemiah served his first term as governor for 12 years before being recalled to court (13:6), after which he returned to Jerusalem (13:7) for a second term whose length cannot be determined. *bread of the governor.* See v. 18. Provincial governors normally assessed the people in their provinces for their support. But Nehemiah, like Paul (1 Cor 9; 2 Thes 3:8–9), sacrificed even what was normally his in order to serve as an example to the people.

5:15 *governors.* The Hebrew for this word is used of Sheshbazzar (Ezra 5:14) and Zerubbabel (Hag 1:1,14; 2:2) as well as of various Persian officials (Ezra 5:3,6; 6:6–7,13; 8:36; Neh 2:7,9; 3:7). Nehemiah was not referring here to men of the caliber of Zerubbabel. Some believe that Judah did not have governors before Nehemiah and that the reference here is to governors of Samaria. But new archaeological evidence, in the form of seals and seal impressions, confirms the reference to the previous governors of Judah. *chargeable unto the people.* It was customary Persian practice to exempt temple personnel from taxation, which increased the burden on lay people. *servants.* If the governors themselves used extortion, their underlings often proved even more oppressive (cf. Mat 18:21–35; 20:25–28). *fear of God.* Those in high positions are in danger of abusing their authority over their subordinates if they forget that they themselves are servants of a superior "Master in heaven" (Col 4:1; cf. Gen 39:9; 2 Cor 5:11).

5:16 *neither bought we any land.* Nehemiah's behavior as governor was guided by principles of service rather than by opportunism.

5:17 *at my table.* As part of his social responsibility, a ruler or governor was expected to entertain lavishly. A text found at Nimrud has Ashurnasirpal II feeding 69,574 guests at a banquet for ten days. When Solomon dedicated the temple, he sacrificed 22,000 cattle and 120,000 sheep and goats, and held a great festival for the assembly for 14 days (1 Ki 8:62–65). We are not told how many he fed (cf. 1 Ki 4:27).

5:18 *daily.* The meat listed here would provide one meal for 600–800 persons, including the 150 Jews and officials of v. 17. Cf. Solomon's provisions for one day (1 Ki 4:22–23). *choice sheep.* Cf. Mal 1:8. *fowls.* Poultry. Chickens were domesticated

19 [a]Think upon me, my God, for good, *according to* all that I have done for this people.

False rumours about Nehemiah

6 Now it came to pass, [a]when Sanballat, and Tobiah, and [1]Geshem the Arabian, and the rest of our enemies, heard that I had builded the wall, and *that* there was no breach left therein; ([b]though at that time I had not set up the doors upon the gates;)

2 That Sanballat and Geshem [a]sent unto me, saying, Come, let us meet together in *some one of* the villages in the plain of [b]Ono. But they [c]thought to do me mischief.

3 And I sent messengers unto them, saying, I *am* doing a great work, so that I cannot come down: why should the work cease, whilst I leave it, and come down to you?

4 Yet they sent unto me four times after this sort; and I answered them after the same manner.

5 Then sent Sanballat his servant unto me in like manner the fifth time with an open letter in his hand;

6 Wherein *was* written, *It is* reported among the heathen, and [1]Gashmu saith *it*, [a]*that* thou and the Jews think to rebel: for which cause thou buildest the wall, that thou mayest be their king, according to these words.

7 And thou hast also appointed prophets to preach of thee at Jerusalem, saying, *There is* a king in Judah: and now shall it be reported to the king according to these words. Come now therefore, and let us take counsel together.

8 Then I sent unto him, saying, There are no such things *done* as thou sayest, but thou feignest them out of thine own heart.

9 For they all made us afraid, saying, Their hands shall be weakened from the work, that it be not done. Now therefore, *O God,* strengthen my hands.

10 Afterward I came *unto* the house of Shemaiah the son of Delaiah the son of Mehetabeel, who *was* shut up; and he said, Let us meet together in the house of God, within the temple, and let us shut the doors of the temple: for they will come to slay thee; yea, in the night will they come to slay thee.

11 And I said, Should such a man as I flee? and who *is there,* that, *being* as I *am,* would go into the temple to save his life? I will not go in.

12 And lo, I perceived that God had not sent him; but *that* [a]he pronounced *this* prophecy against me: for Tobiah and Sanballat had hired him.

13 Therefore *was* he hired, that I should be afraid, and do so, and sin, and *that* they might have *matter* for an evil report, that they might reproach me.

14 [a]My God, think thou upon Tobiah and Sanballat according to these their works, and

5:19 [a]ch. 13:22
6:1 [1][Or, *Gashmu*, ver. 6] [a]ch. 2:10,19 [b]ch. 3:1,3
6:2 [a]Prov. 26:24,25 [b]1 Chr. 8:12; ch. 11:35 [c]Ps. 37:12,32
6:6 [1]Or, *Geshem*, ver. 1,2 [a]ch. 2:19
6:12 [a]Ezek. 13:22
6:14 [a]ch. 13:29

in the Indus River Valley by 2000 B.C. and were brought to Egypt by the time of Thutmose III (15th century B.C.). They were known in Mesopotamia and in Greece by the eighth century B.C. The earliest inscriptional evidence for poultry in the land of Canaan is the seal of Jaazaniah (dated c. 600 B.C.), which depicts a fighting rooster.

5:19 *Think upon me.* See note on 1:8; cf. Heb 6:10. Perhaps Nehemiah's memoirs (see Introduction to Ezra: Literary Form and Authorship) were inscribed as a memorial that was set up in the temple. A striking parallel to Nehemiah's prayer is found in a prayer of Nebuchadnezzar: "O Marduk, my lord, do remember my deeds favorably as good [deeds]; may (these) my good deeds be always before your mind."

6:1 *Sanballat, and Tobiah, and Geshem.* See notes on 2:10,19.

6:2 *Ono.* Located about seven miles southeast of Joppa near Lod (Lydda; see note on Ezra 2:33), in the westernmost area settled by the returning Jews (Neh 7:37; 11:35). It may have been proposed as neutral territory, but Nehemiah recognized the invitation as a trap (cf. Gen 4:8; Jer 41:1–3).

6:3 Nehemiah's sharp reply may seem like a haughty response to a reasonable invitation, but he correctly discerned the insincerity of his enemies. He refused to be distracted by matters that would divert his energies from rebuilding Jerusalem's wall.

6:4 *four times.* Nehemiah's foes were persistent, but he was equally persistent in resisting them.

6:5 *open letter.* During this period a letter was ordinarily written on a papyrus or leather sheet, which was rolled up, tied with a string and sealed with a clay bulla (seal impression) to guarantee the letter's authenticity. Sanballat apparently wanted the contents of his letter to be made known to the public at large.

6:6 *their king.* The Persian kings did not tolerate the claims of pretenders to kingship, as we can see from the Behistun (Bisitun) inscription of Darius I. In NT times the Roman emperor was likewise suspicious of any unauthorized claims to royalty (John 19:12; cf. Mat 2:1–13).

6:8 *such things . . . thou feignest them.* Nehemiah does not mince words. He calls the report a lie. He may have sent his own messenger to the Persian king to assure him of his loyalty.

6:9 *Their hands shall be weakened from the work.* Lit. "Their hands will get too weak for the work," figurative language to express the idea of discouragement. The Hebrew for this phrase is used also in Ezra 4:4; Jer 38:4, as well as on an ostracon from Lachish dated c. 588 B.C.

6:10 *Shemaiah . . . was shut up.* Perhaps as a symbolic action to indicate that his own life was in danger and to suggest that both Nehemiah and he must flee to the temple (for other symbolic actions see 1 Ki 22:11; Is 20:2–4; Jer 27:2–7; 28:10–11; Ezek 4:1–17; 12:3–11; Acts 21:11). Since Shemaiah had access to the temple, he may have been a priest. He was clearly a friend of Tobiah (cf. v. 12), and therefore Nehemiah's enemy. It was at least credible for Shemaiah to propose that Nehemiah take refuge in the temple area at the altar of asylum (see Ex 21:13–14 and notes), but not in the "house of God," the temple building itself.

6:11 Even if the threat against his life was real, Nehemiah was not a coward who would run into hiding. Nor would he transgress the law to save his life. As a layman, he was not permitted to enter the sanctuary (Num 18:7). When King Uzziah entered the temple to burn incense, he was punished by being afflicted with leprosy (2 Chr 26:16–21).

6:12 The fact that Shemaiah proposed a course of action contrary to God's word revealed him as a false prophet (cf. Deut 18:20; Is 8:19–20; see note on Deut 13:1–5).

6:13 If Nehemiah had wavered in the face of the threat against him, his leadership would have been discredited and morale among the people would have plummeted.

6:14 *think thou.* I.e. "remember." See note on 1:8. *prophetess.* See note on Ex 15:20.

on the [b]prophetess Noadiah, and the rest of the prophets, that would have put me in fear.

Building of the walls finished

15 ¶ So the wall was finished in the twenty and fifth *day* of *the month* Elul, in fifty and two days.

16 And it came to pass, that [a]when all our enemies heard *thereof,* and all the heathen that *were* about us saw *these things,* they were much cast down in their own eyes: for [b]they perceived that this work was wrought of our God.

17 Moreover in those days the nobles of Judah [1]sent many letters unto Tobiah, and *the letters* of Tobiah came unto them.

18 For *there were* many in Judah sworn unto him, because he *was* the son in law of Shechaniah the son of Arah; and his son Johanan had taken the daughter of Meshullam the son of Berechiah.

19 Also they reported his good deeds before me, and uttered my [1]words to him. *And* Tobiah sent letters to put me in fear.

7 Now it came to pass, when the wall was built, and I had [a]set up the doors, and the porters and the singers and the Levites were appointed,

2 That I gave my brother Hanani, and Hananiah the ruler [a]of the palace, charge over Jerusalem: for he *was* a faithful man, and [b]feared God above many.

3 And I said unto them, Let not the gates of Jerusalem be opened until the sun be hot; and while they stand by, let them shut the doors, and bar *them:* and appoint watches of the inhabitants of Jerusalem, every one in his watch, and every one *to be* over against his house.

4 Now the city *was* [1]large and great: but the people *were* few therein, and the houses *were* not builded,

List of those who returned

5 ¶ And my God put into mine heart to gather together the nobles, and the rulers, and the people, that *they* might be reckoned by genealogy. And I found a register of the genealogy of them which came up at the first, and found written therein,

6 ¶ [a]These *are* the children of the province, that went up out of the captivity, *of* those that had been carried away, whom Nebuchadnezzar the king of Babylon had carried away, and came again to Jerusalem and to Judah, every one unto his city;

7 Who came with Zerubbabel, Jeshua, Nehemiah, [1]Azariah, Raamiah, Nahamani, Mordecai, Bilshan, Mispereth, Bigvai, Nehum, Baanah. The number, *I say,* of the men of the people of Israel *was this:*

8 ¶ The children of Parosh, two thousand an hundred seventy and two.

9 The children of Shephatiah, three hundred seventy and two.

10 The children of Arah, six hundred fifty and two.

11 The children of Pahath-moab, of the children of Jeshua and Joab, two thousand and eight hundred *and* eighteen.

12 The children of Elam, a thousand two hundred fifty and four.

13 The children of Zattu, eight hundred forty and five.

14 The children of Zaccai, seven hundred and threescore.

15 The children of [1]Binnui, six hundred forty and eight.

16 The children of Bebai, six hundred twenty and eight.

17 The children of Azgad, two thousand three hundred twenty and two.

18 The children of Adonikam, six hundred threescore and seven.

19 The children of Bigvai, two thousand threescore and seven.

20 The children of Adin, six hundred fifty and five.

21 The children of Ater of Hezekiah, ninety and eight.

22 The children of Hashum, three hundred twenty and eight.

23 The children of Bezai, three hundred twenty and four.

24 The children of [1]Hariph, an hundred *and* twelve.

25 The children of [1]Gibeon, ninety and five.

26 The men of Beth-lehem and Netophah, an hundred fourscore and eight.

27 The men of Anathoth, an hundred twenty and eight.

28 The men of [1]Beth-azmaveth, forty and two.

29 The men of [1]Kirjath-jearim, Chephirah, and Beeroth, seven hundred forty and three.

6:14 [b]Ezek. 13:17
6:16 [a]ch. 2:10; 4:1,7; 6:1 [b]Ps. 126:2
6:17 [1]Heb. *multiplied* [*their*] *letters passing to Tobiah*
6:19 [1]Or, *matters*
7:1 [a]ch. 6:1
7:2 [a]ch. 2:8 [b]Ex. 18:21
7:4 [1]Heb. *broad in spaces*
7:6 [a]Ezra 2:1

7:7 [1]Or, *Seraiah*
7:15 [1]Or, *Bani*
7:24 [1]Or, *Jorah*
7:25 [1]Or, *Gibbar*
7:28 [1]Or, *Azmaveth*
7:29 [1]Or, *Kirjath-arim*

6:15 *twenty and fifth day of the month Elul.* Oct. 2, 444 B.C. *fifty and two days.* The walls that lay in ruins for nearly a century and a half were rebuilt in less than two months once the people were galvanized into action by Nehemiah's leadership. Archaeological investigations have shown that the circumference of the wall in Nehemiah's day was much reduced. Josephus states (*Antiquities,* 11.5.8) that the rebuilding of the wall took two years and four months, but he is doubtless including such additional tasks as further strengthening of various sections, embellishing and beautifying, and the like. The dedication of the wall is described in 12:27–47.

6:17–18 Tobiah was related to an influential family in Judah, since his son Johanan was married to the daughter of Meshullam, who had helped repair the wall of Jerusalem (3:4,30).

7:2 *my brother Hanani, and Hananiah.* Or "Hanani my brother, that is, Hananiah" (see note on 1:2). *palace.* See notes on 2:8;3:1. *charge over Jerusalem.* Over Rephaiah and Shallum, who were over sections of the city (3:9,12).

7:3 *until the sun be hot.* Normally the gates would be opened at dawn, but their opening was to be delayed until the sun was high in the heavens to prevent the enemy from making a surprise attack before most of the people were up.

7:6–73 Essentially the same as Ezra 2. See notes there for the nature of the list and the reasons for the numerous variations in names and numbers between the two lists.

7:7 *Nahamani.* Does not occur in Ezra 2:2.

30 The men of Ramah and Geba, six hundred twenty and one.

31 The men of Michmas, an hundred and twenty and two.

32 The men of Beth-el and Ai, an hundred twenty and three.

33 The men of the other Nebo, fifty and two.

34 The children of the other [a]Elam, a thousand two hundred fifty and four.

35 The children of Harim, three hundred and twenty.

36 The children of Jericho, three hundred forty and five.

37 The children of Lod, Hadid, and Ono, seven hundred twenty and one.

38 The children of Senaah, three thousand nine hundred and thirty.

39 ¶ The priests: the children of [a]Jedaiah, of the house of Jeshua, nine hundred seventy and three.

40 The children of [a]Immer, a thousand fifty and two.

41 The children of [a]Pashur, a thousand two hundred forty and seven.

42 The children of [a]Harim, a thousand *and* seventeen.

43 ¶ The Levites: the children of Jeshua, of Kadmiel, *and* of the children of [1]Hodevah, seventy and four.

44 The singers: the children of Asaph, an hundred forty and eight.

45 The porters: the children of Shallum, the children of Ater, the children of Talmon, the children of Akkub, the children of Hatita, the children of Shobai, an hundred thirty and eight.

46 ¶ The Nethinims: the children of Ziha, the children of Hashupha, the children of Tabbaoth,

47 The children of Keros, the children of [1]Sia, the children of Padon,

48 The children of Lebana, the children of Hagaba, the children of [1]Shalmai,

49 The children of Hanan, the children of Giddel, the children of Gahar,

50 The children of Reaiah, the children of Rezin, the children of Nekoda,

51 The children of Gazzam, the children of Uzza, the children of Phaseah,

52 The children of Besai, the children of Meunim, the children of [1]Nephishesim,

53 The children of Bakbuk, the children of Hakupha, the children of Harhur,

54 The children of [1]Bazlith, the children of Mehida, the children of Harsha,

55 The children of Barkos, the children of Sisera, the children of Tamah,

56 The children of Neziah, the children of Hatipha.

57 ¶ The children of Solomon's servants: the children of Sotai, the children of Sophereth, the children of [1]Perida,

58 The children of Jaala, the children of Darkon, the children of Giddel,

59 The children of Shephatiah, the children of Hattil, the children of Pochereth Zebaim, the children of [1]Amon.

60 All the Nethinims, and the children of Solomon's servants, *were* three hundred ninety and two.

61 ¶ [a]And these *were* they which went up *also* from Tel-melah, Tel-haresha, Cherub, [1]Addon, and Immer: but they could not shew their fathers' house, nor their [2]seed, whether they *were* of Israel.

62 The children of Delaiah, the children of Tobiah, the children of Nekoda, six hundred forty and two.

63 And of the priests: the children of Habaiah, the children of Koz, the children of Barzillai, which took *one* of the daughters of Barzillai the Gileadite *to* wife, and was called after their name.

64 These sought their register *among* those that were reckoned by genealogy, but it was not found: therefore were they, as polluted, put from the priesthood.

65 And [1]the Tirshatha said unto them, that they should not eat of the most holy *things,* till there stood *up* a priest with Urim and Thummim.

66 ¶ The whole congregation together *was* forty *and* two thousand three hundred and threescore,

67 Beside their manservants and their maidservants, of whom *there were* seven thousand three hundred thirty and seven: and they had two hundred forty and five singing *men* and singing *women.*

68 Their horses, seven hundred thirty and six: their mules, two hundred forty and five:

69 *Their* camels, four hundred thirty and five: six thousand seven hundred and twenty asses.

70 ¶ And [1]some of the chief of the fathers gave unto the work. [a]The Tirshatha gave to the treasure a thousand drams *of* gold, fifty basons, five hundred and thirty priests' garments.

71 And *some* of the chief of the fathers gave to the treasure of the work [a]twenty thousand drams *of* gold, and two thousand and two hundred pound *of* silver.

72 And *that* which the rest of the people gave *was* twenty thousand drams *of* gold, and two thousand pound *of* silver, and threescore and seven priests' garments.

73 So the priests, and the Levites, and the porters, and the singers, and *some* of the people, and the Nethinims, and all Israel, dwelt in their cities; [a]and when the seventh month came, the children of Israel *were* in their cities.

7:34 [a]See ver. 12
7:39 [a]1 Chr. 24:7
7:40 [a]1 Chr. 24:14
7:41 [a]See 1 Chr. 9:12; 24:9
7:42 [a]1 Chr. 24:8
7:43 [1]Or, *Hodaviah,* Ezra 2:40; or, *Judah,* Ezra 3:9
7:47 [1][Or, *Siaha*]
7:48 [1][Or, *Shamlai*]
7:52 [1][Or, *Nephusim*]
7:54 [1][Or, *Bazluth*]
7:57 [1][Or, *Peruda*]
7:59 [1]Or, *Ami*
7:61 [1][Or, *Addan*] [2]Or, *pedigree* [a]Ezra 2:59
7:65 [1]Or, *the governor,* ver. 70
7:70 [1]Heb. *part* [a]ch. 8:9
7:71 [a]Ezra 2:69
7:73 [a]Ezra 3:1

7:43 *seventy and four.* See note on Ezra 2:40.
7:70 *drams.* See note on Ezra 2:69.
7:73 *dwelt in their cities.* See note on Ezra 2:70. *seventh month.* October-November, 444 B.C.

The law read and explained

8 And all [a]the people gathered themselves together as one man into the street that *was* [b]before the water gate; and they spake unto Ezra the [c]scribe to bring the book of the law of Moses, which the LORD had commanded to Israel.

2 And Ezra the priest brought [a]the law before the congregation both of men and women, and all [1]that could hear with understanding, [b]upon the first day of the seventh month.

3 And he read therein before the street that *was* before the water gate [1]from the morning until midday, before the men and the women, and those that could understand; and the ears of all the people *were attentive* unto the book of the law.

4 And Ezra the scribe stood upon a [1]pulpit of wood, which they had made for the purpose; and beside him stood Mattithiah, and Shema, and Anaiah, and Urijah, and Hilkiah, and Maaseiah, on his right hand; and on his left hand, Pedaiah, and Mishael, and Malchiah, and Hashum, and Hashbadana, Zechariah, *and* Meshullam.

5 And Ezra opened the book in the [1]sight of all the people; (for he was above all the people;) and when he opened *it,* all the people [a]stood *up:*

6 And Ezra blessed the LORD, the great God. And all the people [a]answered, Amen, Amen, with [b]lifting up their hands: and they [c]bowed their heads, and worshipped the LORD *with their* faces to the ground.

7 Also Jeshua, and Bani, and Sherebiah, Jamin, Akkub, Shabbethai, Hodijah, Maaseiah, Kelita, Azariah, Jozabad, Hanan, Pelaiah, and the Levites, [a]caused the people to understand the law: and the people *stood* in their place.

8 So they read in the book in the law of God distinctly, and gave the sense, and caused *them* to understand the reading.

9 ¶ [a]And Nehemiah, which *is* [1]the Tirshatha, and Ezra the priest the scribe, and the Levites that taught the people, said unto all the people, [b]*This* day *is* holy unto the LORD your God; [c]mourn not, nor weep. For all the people wept, when they heard the words of the law.

10 Then he said unto them, Go *your way,* eat the fat, and drink the sweet, [a]and send portions unto *them* for whom nothing is prepared: for *this* day *is* holy unto our Lord: neither be ye sorry; for the joy of the LORD *is* your strength.

11 So the Levites stilled all the people, saying, Hold your peace, for the day *is* holy; neither be ye grieved.

12 And all the people went *their way* to eat, and to drink, and to [a]send portions, and to make great mirth, because they had [b]understood the words that were declared unto them.

8:1 [a]Ezra 3:1 [b]ch. 3:26 [c]Ezra 7:6
8:2 [1]Heb. *that understood in hearing* [a]Deut. 31:11,12 [b]Lev. 23:24
8:3 [1]Heb. *from the light*
8:4 [1]Heb. *tower of wood*
8:5 [1]Heb. *eyes* [a]Judg. 3:20
8:6 [a]1 Cor. 14:16
8:6 [b]Lam. 3:41; 1 Tim. 2:8 [c]Ex. 4:31; 12:27; 2 Chr. 20:18
8:7 [a]Lev. 10:11; Deut. 33:10; 2 Chr. 17:7; Mal. 2:7
8:9 [1]Or, *the governor* [a]Ezra 2:63; ch. 7:65; 10:1 [b]Lev. 23:24; Num. 29:1 [c]Deut. 16:14; Eccl. 3:4
8:10 [a]Esth. 9:19; Rev. 11:10
8:12 [a]ver. 10 [b]ver. 7,8

8:1–18 According to the traditional view, the reading of the law by Ezra would be the first reference to him in almost 13 years since his arrival in 458 B.C. Since he was commissioned to teach the law (Ezra 7:6,10,14,25–26), it is surprising that there was such a long delay in its public proclamation.

8:1 *all the people gathered.* See Ezra 3:1, which also refers to an assembly called in the seventh month (Tishri), the beginning of the civil year (see chart, p. 92). *street . . . before the water gate.* See vv. 3,16; see also notes on 3:26; Ezra 10:9. Squares were normally located near a city gate (2 Chr 32:6). *scribe.* See note on Ezra 7:6. *book of the law of Moses.* Cf. vv. 2–3,5, 8–9,13–15,18. Four views have been proposed concerning the extent of this book: (1) a collection of legal materials, (2) the priestly laws of Exodus and Leviticus, (3) the laws of Deuteronomy, (4) the Pentateuch. Surely Ezra could have brought back with him the Torah, i.e. the entire Pentateuch.

8:2 *women.* See 10:28. Women did not usually participate in assemblies (see note on Ex 10:11), but were brought, together with children, on such solemn occasions (Deut 31:12; Josh 8:35; 2 Ki 23:2). *first day of the seventh month.* Oct. 8, 444 B.C.; the New Year's Day of the civil calendar (see note on Lev 23:24), celebrated as the feast of trumpets (Num 29:1–6), with cessation of labor and a sacred assembly.

8:3 *read therein.* See Ex 24:7; Acts 8:30. *from the morning until midday.* The people evidently stood (vv. 5,7) for five or six hours, listening attentively to the reading and exposition (vv. 7–8,12) of the Scriptures.

8:5 *book.* Scroll (see note on Ex 17:14). *all the people stood up.* The rabbis deduced from this verse that the congregation should stand for the reading of the Torah. It is customary in Eastern Orthodox churches for the congregation to stand throughout the service.

8:6 *Amen, Amen.* See notes on Deut 27:15; Rom 1:25. The repetition conveys the intensity of feeling behind the affirmation (for other repetitions see Gen 22:11 and note; cf. 2 Ki 11:14; Luke 23:21). *lifting up their hands.* See Ex 9:29 and note; Ps 28:2; 134:2; 1 Tim 2:8. *worshipped.* In its original sense the Hebrew for this verb meant "to prostrate oneself on the ground," as the frequently accompanying phrase "to the ground" indicates. Private acts of worship often involved prostration "to the ground," as in the case of Abraham's servant (Gen 24:52), Moses (Ex 34:8), Joshua (Josh 5:14) and Job (Job 1:20). There are three cases of spontaneous communal worship in Exodus (4:31; 12:27; 33:10). In 2 Chr 20:18 Jehoshaphat and the people "fell before the LORD, worshipping the LORD" when they heard His promise of victory.

8:7 *caused . . . to understand.* See v. 8; Ezra 8:16 and note; Ps 119:34,73,130; Is 40:14.

‡8:8 *read.* See note on v. 3. *read . . . distinctly.* Rabbinic tradition understands the Hebrew for this expression as referring to translation from Hebrew into an Aramaic Targum. But there is no evidence of Targums (free Aramaic translations of OT books or passages) from such an early date. The earliest extensive Targum is one on Job from Qumran, dated c. 150–100 B.C. Targums exist for every book of the OT except Daniel and Ezra-Nehemiah. *understand.* See v. 12.

8:9 *Nehemiah . . . Ezra.* An explicit reference showing that they were contemporaries (see 12:26,36). *mourn not.* See Ezra 10:6 and note; Esth 9:22; Is 57:18–19; Jer 31:13. *weep.* See 1:4; Ezra 3:13 and note; 10:1.

8:10 *eat the fat.* Delicious festive food prepared with much fat. The fat of sacrificial animals was offered to God as the tastiest element of the burnt offering (Lev 1:8,12), the peace offering (Lev 3:9–10), the sin offering (Lev 4:8–10) and the trespass offering (Lev 7:3–4). The fat was not to be eaten in these cases. *send portions unto them for whom nothing is prepared.* It was customary for God's people to remember the less fortunate on joyous occasions (2 Sam 6:19; Esth 9:22; contrast 1 Cor 11:20–22; Jas 2:14–16).

13 And on the second day were gathered together the chief of the fathers of all the people, the priests, and the Levites, unto Ezra the scribe, even [1]to understand the words of the law.

14 And they found written in the law which the LORD had commanded [1]by Moses, that the children of Israel should dwell in [a]booths in the feast of the seventh month:

15 And [a]that they should publish and proclaim in all their cities, and [b]in Jerusalem, saying, Go forth *unto* the mount, and [c]fetch olive branches, and pine branches, and myrtle branches, and palm branches, and branches of thick trees, to make booths, as it is written.

16 So the people went forth, and brought *them,* and made themselves booths, every one upon the [a]roof of his house, and in their courts, and in the courts of the house of God, and in the street of the [b]water gate, [c]and in the street of the gate of Ephraim.

17 And all the congregation of them that were come again out of the captivity made booths, and sat under the booths: for since the days of Jeshua the son of Nun unto that day had not the children of Israel done so. And there was very [a]great gladness.

18 Also [a]day by day, from the first day unto the last day, he read in the book of the law of God. And they kept the feast seven days; and on the eighth day *was* [1]a solemn assembly, [b]according unto the manner.

8:13 [1] Or, *that they might instruct in the words of the law*
8:14 [1] Heb. *by the hand of* [a] Lev. 23:34,42; Deut. 16:13
8:15 [a] Lev. 23:4 [b] Deut. 16:16 [c] Lev. 23:40
8:16 [a] Deut. 22:8 [b] ch. 12:37 [c] 2 Ki. 14:13; ch. 12:39
8:17 [a] 2 Chr. 30:21
8:18 [1] Heb. *a restraint* [a] Deut. 31:10 [b] Lev. 23:36; Num. 29:35
9:1 [a] ch. 8:2 [b] Josh. 7:6; 1 Sam. 4:12; 2 Sam. 1:2; Job 2:12
9:2 [1] Heb. *strange children* [a] Ezra 10:11; ch. 13:3,30
9:3 [a] ch. 8:7,8
9:4 [1] Or, *scaffold*
9:5 [a] 1 Chr. 29:13
9:6 [a] 2 Ki. 19:15,19; Ps. 86:10; Is. 37:16,20 [b] Gen. 1:1; Ex. 20:11; Rev. 14:7 [c] Deut. 10:14; 1 Ki. 8:27 [d] Gen. 2:1 [e] Ps. 36:6

Ezra's prayer

9 Now in the twenty and fourth day of [a]this month the children of Israel were assembled with fasting, and with sackclothes, [b]and earth upon them.

2 And [a]the seed of Israel separated themselves from all [1]strangers, and stood and confessed their sins, and the iniquities of their fathers.

3 And they stood up in their place, and [a]read in the book of the law of the LORD their God *one* fourth *part* of the day; and *another* fourth *part* they confessed, and worshipped the LORD their God.

4 Then stood up upon the [1]stairs of the Levites, Jeshua, and Bani, Kadmiel, Shebaniah, Bunni, Sherebiah, Bani, *and* Chenani, and cried with a loud voice unto the LORD their God.

5 Then the Levites, Jeshua and Kadmiel, Bani, Hashabniah, Sherebiah, Hodijah, Shebaniah, *and* Pethahiah, said,

¶ Stand up *and* bless the LORD your God for ever and ever: and blessed be [a]thy glorious name, which *is* exalted above all blessing and praise.

6 [a]Thou, *even* thou, *art* LORD alone; [b]thou hast made heaven, [c]the heaven of heavens, with [d]all their host, the earth, and all *things* that *are* therein, the seas, and all that *is* therein, and thou [e]preservest them all; and the host of heaven worshippeth thee.

7 Thou *art* the LORD the God, who didst

8:14 *booths.* See notes on Ex 23:16; Lev 23:34,42; John 7:37.
8:15 *olive.* Widespread in Mediterranean countries. It was growing in Canaan before the conquest (Deut 8:8). Because it takes an olive tree 30 years to mature, its cultivation requires peaceful conditions. *pine branches.* Lit. "tree of oil," commonly regarded as the wild olive tree. But this is questionable since the "tree of oil" was used as timber (1 Ki 6:23,31–33), whereas the wood of the wild olive tree would have been of little value for use in the temple's furniture. Also, the wild olive tree contains very little oil. The phrase may refer to a resinous tree like the fir. *myrtle.* Evergreen bushes with a pleasing odor (Is 41:19; 55:13; Zech 1:8,10–11). *palm.* The date palm was common around Jericho (Deut 34:3; 2 Chr 28:15). *thick trees.* Cf. Ezek 6:13; 20:28. Later Jewish celebrations of the feast of tabernacles include waving the *lulav* (made of branches of palms, myrtles and willows) with the right hand and holding branches of the *ethrog* (a citrus native to Canaan) in the left.
8:16 *courts of the house of God.* See note on 13:7. The temple that Ezekiel saw in his visions had an outer and an inner court (see diagram, p. 1202). Ezekiel's temple was to some extent patterned after Solomon's, which had an inner court of priests and an outer court (1 Ki 6:36; 7:12; 2 Ki 21:5; 23:12; 2 Chr 4:9; 33:5). The temple of the NT era had a court of the Gentiles and an inner court, which was subdivided into courts of the women, of Israel and of the priests. The Temple Scroll from Qumran has God setting forth in detail an ideal temple. Columns 40–46 describe the outer court as follows: "On the roof of the third story are columns for the constructing of booths for the Feast of Tabernacles, to be occupied by the elders, tribal chieftains and commanders of thousands and hundreds." *gate of Ephraim.* A gate of the oldest rampart of Jerusalem (see note on 3:6; see also 2 Ki 14:13). It was restored by Nehemiah (12:39).
8:17 *since the days of Jeshua . . . unto that day.* The phrase does not mean that the feast of booths (i.e. tabernacles) had not been celebrated since Joshua's time, because such celebrations took place after the dedication of Solomon's temple (2 Chr 7:8–10) and after the return of the exiles (Ezra 3:4). What apparently is meant is that the feast had not been celebrated before with such great joy (cf. 2 Chr 30:26; 35:18).
8:18 *assembly.* See Num 29:35.
9:1–37 The ninth chapters of Ezra, Nehemiah and Daniel are devoted to confessions of national sin and to prayers for God's grace.
9:1 *twenty and fourth day.* Oct. 30, 444 B.C.; a day of penance in the spirit of the day of atonement, which was held on the tenth day (Lev 16:29–30). *fasting . . . sackclothes . . . earth.* See notes on Gen 37:34; Ezra 8:23; 10:6; Joel 1:13–14.
9:3 *fourth part of the day.* About three hours.
9:5–37 One of the most beautiful prayers outside the Psalms, it reviews God's grace and power (1) in creation (v. 6), (2) in the Abrahamic covenant (vv. 7–8), (3) in Egypt and at the Red sea (vv. 9–11), (4) in the wilderness and at Sinai (vv. 12–21), (5) during the conquest of Canaan (vv. 22–25), (6) through the judges ("saviours," vv. 26–28), (7) through the prophets (vv. 29–31) and (8) in the present situation (vv. 32–37). Cf. Ps 78; 105–106.
9:6 *Thou, even thou, art LORD alone.* Though not in the words of Deut 6:4, which expresses the central monotheistic conviction of Israel's faith, the prayer begins with a similar affirmation (cf. 2 Ki 19:15; Ps 86:10). *heaven of heavens.* See Deut 10:14; 1 Ki 8:27; 2 Chr 2:6; Ps 148:4. *host of heaven worshippeth thee.* See Ps 89:5–7.

choose [a]Abram, and broughtest him forth out
of Ur of the Chaldees, and gavest him the
name of [b]Abraham;
8 And foundest his heart [a]faithful before
thee, and madest a [b]covenant with him to give
the land of the Canaanites, the Hittites, the
Amorites, and the Perizzites, and the Jebusites, and the Girgashites, to give *it, I say,* to
his seed, and [c]hast performed thy words; for
thou *art* righteous:
9 [a]And didst see the affliction of our fathers in Egypt, and [b]heardest their cry by the
Red sea;
10 And [a]shewedst signs and wonders upon
Pharaoh, and on all his servants, and on all the
people of his land: for thou knewest that they
[b]dealt proudly against them. So didst thou [c]get
thee a name, as *it is* this day.
11 [a]And thou didst divide the sea before
them, so that they went through the midst of
the sea on the dry *land;* and their persecutors
thou threwest into the deeps, [b]as a stone into
the mighty waters.
12 Moreover thou [a]leddest them in the day
by a cloudy pillar; and in the night by a pillar
of fire, to give them light in the way wherein
they should go.
13 [a]Thou camest down also upon mount
Sinai, and spakest with them from heaven,
and gavest them [b]right judgments, and [1]true
laws, good statutes and commandments:
14 And madest known unto them thy [a]holy
sabbath, and commandedst them precepts,
statutes, and laws, by the hand of Moses thy
servant:
15 And [a]gavest them bread from heaven
for their hunger, and [b]broughtest forth water
for them out of the rock for their thirst, and
promisedst them that *they* should [c]go in to
possess the land [d][1]which thou hadst sworn to
give them.
16 [a]But they and our fathers dealt proudly,
and [b]hardened their necks, and hearkened not
to thy commandments,

9:7 [a]Gen. 11:31 [b]Gen. 17:5
9:8 [a]Gen. 15:6 [b]Gen. 15:18 [c]Josh. 23:14
9:9 [a]Ex. 2:25 [b]Ex. 14:10
9:10 [a]Ex. 7-10,12,14 [b]Ex. 18:11 [c]Jer. 32:20
9:11 [a]Ex. 14:21; Ps. 78:13 [b]Ex. 15:5
9:12 [a]Ex. 13:21
9:13 [1]Heb. *laws of truth* [a]Ex. 20:1 [b]Rom. 7:12
9:14 [a]Gen. 2:3; Ex. 20:8
9:15 [1]Heb. *which thou hadst lift up thine hand to give them* [a]Ex. 16:14; John 6:31 [b]Ex. 17:6 [c]Deut. 1:8 [d]Num. 14:30
9:16 [a]Ps. 106:6 [b]Deut. 31:27
9:17 [1]Heb. *a God of pardons* [a]Ps. 78:11 [b]Num. 14:4 [c]Joel 2:13
9:18 [a]Ex. 32:4
9:19 [a]Ps. 106:45 [b]1 Cor. 10:1
9:20 [a]Num. 11:17; Is. 63:11 [b]Ex. 16:15; Josh. 5:12 [c]Ex. 17:6
9:21 [a]Deut. 2:7 [b]Deut. 8:4; 29:5
9:22 [a]Num. 21:21
9:23 [a]Gen. 22:17
9:24 [1]Heb. *according to their will* [a]Josh. 1:2 [b]Ps. 44:2,3
9:25 [1]Or, *cisterns* [a]Num. 13:27 [b]Deut. 6:11

17 And refused to obey, [a]neither were
mindful of thy wonders that thou didst among
them; but hardened their necks, and in their
rebellion appointed [b]a captain to return to
their bondage: but thou *art* [1]a God ready to
pardon, [c]gracious and merciful, slow to anger,
and of great kindness, and forsookest them not.
18 Yea, [a]when they had made them a
molten calf, and said, This *is* thy God that
brought thee up out of Egypt, and had wrought
great provocations;
19 Yet thou in thy [a]manifold mercies forsookest them not in the wilderness: the [b]pillar
of the cloud departed not from them by day, to
lead them in the way; neither the pillar of fire
by night, to shew them light, and the way
wherein they should go.
20 Thou gavest also thy [a]good spirit to instruct them, and withheldest not thy [b]manna
from their mouth, and gavest them [c]water for
their thirst.
21 Yea, [a]forty years didst thou sustain
them in the wilderness, *so that* they lacked
nothing; their [b]clothes waxed not old, and
their feet swelled not.
22 Moreover thou gavest them kingdoms
and nations, and didst divide them into corners: so they possessed the land of [a]Sihon, and
the land of the king of Heshbon, and the land
of Og king of Bashan.
23 [a]Their children also multipliedst thou
as the stars of heaven, and broughtest them
into the land, *concerning* which thou hadst
promised to their fathers, that *they* should go
in to possess *it.*
24 So [a]the children went in and possessed
the land, and [b]thou subduedst before them the
inhabitants of the land, the Canaanites, and
gavest them into their hands, with their kings,
and the people of the land, that *they* might do
with them [1]as they would.
25 And they took strong cities, and a [a]fat
land, and possessed [b]houses full *of* all goods,
[1]wells digged, vineyards, and oliveyards, and

9:7 *Ur of the Chaldees.* See note on Gen 11:28. *gavest him the name of Abraham.* See note on Gen 17:5.
9:8 *faithful.* Compare Rom 4:16–22 with Jas 2:21–23. *madest a covenant with him.* See note on Gen 15:18. *Canaanites . . . Girgashites.* See notes on Gen 10:6,15–18; 13:7; Ex 3:8; Ezra 9:1.
9:9 *Red sea.* See notes on Ex 13:18; 14:2.
9:11 *divide the sea.* See Ex 14:21–22; 1 Cor 10:1.
9:13 *laws.* The singular form of the Hebrew for this word is *Torah,* which means "instruction," "law," and later the Pentateuch, the five books of Moses.
9:14 *holy sabbath.* According to the rabbis, "the sabbath outweighs all the commandments of the Torah." See 10:31–33; 13:15–22.
9:15 *bread from heaven.* See note on Ex 16:4. *water . . . out of the rock.* See note on Ex 17:6. *sworn.* See Gen 14:22 and note; 22:15–17; Ex 6:8; Ezek 20:6; 47:14.
9:16 *hardened their necks.* I.e. they became stubborn. See vv. 17,29; see also notes on 3:5; Ex 32:9.
9:17 *appointed a captain.* Their intention to do so is recorded in Num 14:4. *gracious . . . great kindness.* See note on Ex 34:6–7.
9:18 *provocations.* See v. 26; Ex 32:4; Ezek 35:12.
9:19 *manifold mercies.* See vv. 27–28; a tender, maternal kind of love (see note on Zech 1:16).
9:20 *spirit to instruct.* See Ex 31:3.
9:21 *clothes waxed not old.* Evidence of the special providence of God (see Deut 8:4; 29:5; contrast Josh 9:13). *swelled.* Or "blistered"; the Hebrew for this word occurs only here and in Deut 8:4.
9:22 *Sihon . . . Og.* See Num 21:21–35.
9:23 *multipliedst . . . as the stars.* See notes on Gen 13:16; 15:5; 22:17.
9:25 See Deut 6:10–12 and note; Josh 24:13. *fat* [i.e. fertile]. See v. 35; cf. Num 14:7; Deut 8:7; Josh 23:13. *wells digged.* Because of the lack of rainfall during much of the year, almost every house had its own well or cistern in which to store water from the rainy seasons (2 Ki 18:31; Prov 5:15). By 1200 B.C. the technique of waterproofing cisterns was developed, permitting greater occupation of the central hills of Judah. *vineyards, and oliveyards, and fruit trees.* Cf. Deut 8:8. The Egyptian story of Sinuhe (c. 2000 B.C.) describes Canaan as follows: "Figs were in it, and grapes. It had more wine than water. Plentiful was its honey, abundant its olives. Every (kind of) fruit was on

[2]fruit trees in abundance: so they did eat, and were filled, and [c]became fat, and delighted themselves in thy great [d]goodness.

26 Nevertheless they [a]were disobedient, and rebelled against thee, and [b]cast thy law behind their backs, and slew thy [c]prophets which testified against them to turn them to thee, and they wrought great provocations.

27 [a]Therefore thou deliveredst them into the hand of their enemies, who vexed them: and in the time of their trouble, when they cried unto thee, thou [b]heardest *them* from heaven; and according to thy manifold mercies [c]thou gavest them saviours, who saved them out of the hand of their enemies.

28 But after they had rest, [a][1]they did evil again before thee: therefore leftest thou them in the hand of their enemies, so that they had the dominion over them: yet when they returned, and cried unto thee, thou heardest *them* from heaven; and [b]many times didst thou deliver them according to thy mercies;

29 And testifiedst against them, that *thou* mightest bring them again unto thy law: yet they dealt proudly, and hearkened not unto thy commandments, but sinned against thy judgments, ([a]which if a man do, he shall live in them;) and [b][1]withdrew the shoulder, and hardened their neck, and would not hear.

30 Yet many years didst thou [1]forbear them, and testifiedst [a]against them by thy spirit [b][2]in thy prophets: yet would they not give ear: [c]therefore gavest thou them into the hand of the people of the lands.

31 Nevertheless for thy great mercies' sake [a]thou didst not utterly consume them, nor forsake them; for thou *art* a gracious and merciful God.

32 Now therefore, our God, the great, the [a]mighty, and the terrible God, who keepest covenant and mercy, let not all the [1]trouble seem little before thee, [2]that hath come upon us, on our kings, on our princes, and on our priests, and on our prophets, and on our fathers, and on all thy people, [b]since the time of the kings of Assyria unto this day.

33 Howbeit [a]thou *art* just in all that is brought upon us; for thou hast done right, but [b]we have done wickedly:

34 Neither have our kings, our princes, our priests, nor our fathers, kept thy law, nor hearkened unto thy commandments and thy testimonies, where*with* thou didst testify against them.

35 For they have [a]not served thee in their kingdom, and in thy great goodness that thou gavest them, and in the large and fat land which thou gavest before them, neither turned they from their wicked works.

36 Behold, [a]we *are* servants *this* day, and *for* the land that thou gavest unto our fathers to eat the fruit thereof and the good thereof, behold, we *are* servants in it:

37 And [a]it yieldeth much increase unto the kings whom thou hast set over us because of our sins: also they have [b]dominion over our bodies, and over our cattle, at their pleasure, and we *are* in great distress.

38 And because of all this we [a]make a sure covenant, and write *it;* and our princes, Levites, *and* priests, [1]seal *unto it.*

The covenant signed

10 Now [1]those that sealed *were,* Nehemiah, [2]the Tirshatha, [a]the son of Hachaliah, and Zidkijah,
2 [a]Seraiah, Azariah, Jeremiah,
3 Pashur, Amariah, Malchijah,
4 Hattush, Shebaniah, Malluch,
5 Harim, Meremoth, Obadiah,
6 Daniel, Ginnethon, Baruch,
7 Meshullam, Abijah, Mijamin,
8 Maaziah, Bilgai, Shemaiah: these *were* the priests.

9 And the Levites: both Jeshua the son of Azaniah, Binnui of the sons of Henadad, Kadmiel;
10 And their brethren, Shebaniah, Hodijah, Kelita, Pelaiah, Hanan,
11 Micha, Rehob, Hashabiah,
12 Zaccur, Sherebiah, Shebaniah,
13 Hodijah, Bani, Beninu.

14 The chief of the people; [a]Parosh, Pahath-moab, Elam, Zatthu, Bani,
15 Bunni, Azgad, Bebai,
16 Adonijah, Bigvai, Adin,
17 Ater, Hizkijah, Azzur,
18 Hodijah, Hashum, Bezai,
19 Hariph, Anathoth, Nebai,
20 Magpiash, Meshullam, Hezir,
21 Meshezabeel, Zadok, Jaddua,
22 Pelatiah, Hanan, Anaiah,
23 Hoshea, Hananiah, Hashub,
24 Hallohesh, Pileha, Shobek,
25 Rehum, Hashabnah, Maaseiah,
26 And Ahijah, Hanan, Anan,
27 Malluch, Harim, Baanah.

28 ¶ [a]And the rest of the people, the

9:25 [2]Heb. *tree of food* [c]Deut. 32:15 [d]Hos. 3:5 9:26 [a]Judg. 2:11 [b]1 Ki. 14:9; Ps. 50:17 [c]1 Ki. 18:4 9:27 [a]Judg. 2:14; Ps. 106:41 [b]Ps. 106:44 [c]Judg. 2:18 9:28 [1]Heb. *they returned to do evil* [a]Judg. 3:11 [b]Ps. 106:43 9:29 [1]Heb. *they gave a withdrawing shoulder* [a]Lev. 18:5; Rom. 10:5; Gal. 3:12 [b]Zech. 7:11 9:30 [1]Heb. *protract over them* [2]Heb. *in the hand of thy prophets* [a]2 Ki. 17:13; 2 Chr. 36:15; Jer. 7:25 [b]Acts 7:51; 1 Pet. 1:11; 2 Pet. 1:21 [c]Is. 5:5 9:31 [a]Jer. 4:27 9:32 [1]Heb. *weariness* [2]Heb. *that hath found us* [a]Ex. 34:6,7 [b]2 Ki. 17:3 9:33 [a]Ps. 119:137; Dan. 9:14 [b]Ps. 106:6; Dan. 9:5,6,8

9:35 [a]Deut. 28:47 9:36 [a]Deut. 28:48; Ezra 9:9 9:37 [a]Deut. 28:33,51 [b]Deut. 28:48 9:38 [1]Heb. are *at the sealing,* or, *sealed* [a]2 Ki. 23:3; 2 Chr. 29:10; Ezra 10:3 10:1 [1]Heb. *at the sealings* [2]Or, *the governor* [a]ch. 1:1 10:2 [a]ch. 12:1-21 10:14 [a]Ezra 2:3; ch. 7:8 10:28 [a]Ezra 2:36-43

its trees." *became fat.* Elsewhere the Hebrew for this word always implies physical fullness and spiritual insensitivity.

9:26–28 See note on Judg 2:6–3:6.

9:27 *saviours.* See Introduction to Judges: Title.

9:29 *if a man do, he shall live in them.* See note on Lev 18:5. *withdrew the shoulder.* See Zech 7:11; cf. the similar expressions in v. 16; 3:5; Hos 4:16.

9:32 *kings of Assyria.* Including Tiglath-pileser III, also known as Pul (1 Chr 5:26); Shalmaneser V (2 Ki 18:9); Sargon II (Is 20:1); Sennacherib (2 Ki 18:13); Esarhaddon (Ezra 4:2); and Ashurbanipal ("Asnappar," Ezra 4:10).

9:37 *dominion over our bodies.* See 1 Sam 8:11–13. The Persian rulers drafted their subjects into military service. Some Jews may have accompanied Xerxes on his invasion of Greece in 480 B.C.

10:1–27 A legal list, bearing the official seal and containing a roster of 84 names.

10:2–8 About half of these names occur again in 12:1–7.

10:9–13 Most of these names appear also in the lists of Levites in 8:7; 9:4–5.

10:14–27 Almost half of the names in this category are also found in the lists of 7:6–63; Ezra 2:1–61.

priests, the Levites, the porters, the singers,
the Nethinims, [b]and all they that had separated themselves from the people of the lands
unto the law of God, their wives, their sons,
and their daughters, every one having knowledge, *and* having understanding;
29 They clave to their brethren, their nobles, [a]and entered into a curse, and into an
oath, [b]to walk in God's law, which was given
[1]by Moses the servant of God, and to observe
and do all the commandments of the LORD our
Lord, and his judgments and his statutes;
30 And that we would not give [a]our daughters unto the people of the land, nor take their
daughters for our sons:
31 [a]And *if* the people of the land bring
ware or any victuals on the sabbath day to sell,
that we would not buy *it* of them on the sabbath, or on the holy day: and *that* we would
leave the [b]seventh year, and the [c]exaction of
[1]every debt.
32 Also we made ordinances for us, to
charge ourselves yearly with the third *part* of a
shekel for the service of the house of our God;
33 For [a]the shewbread, and *for* the [b]con-
tinual meat offering, and for the continual
burnt offering, of the sabbaths, of the new
moons, for the set feasts, and for the holy
things, and for the sin offerings to make an
atonement for Israel, and *for* all the work of
the house of our God.
34 And we cast the lots *among* the priests,
the Levites, and the people, [a]for the wood offering, to bring *it* into the house of our God, after the houses of our fathers, at times appointed year by year, to burn upon the altar of the
LORD our God, [b]as it is written in the law:
35 And [a]to bring the firstfruits of our
ground, and the firstfruits of all fruit of all
trees, year by year, unto the house of the LORD:
36 Also the firstborn of our sons, and of
our cattle, as it is written [a]in the law, and the
firstlings of our herds and of our flocks, to
bring to the house of our God, unto the priests
that minister in the house of our God:
37 [a]And *that* we should bring the firstfruits
of our dough, and our offerings, and the fruit
of all *manner of* trees, of wine and of oil, unto
the priests, to the chambers of the house of
our God; and [b]the tithes of our ground unto
the Levites, that the same Levites *might* have
the tithes in all the cities of our tillage.
38 And the priest the son of Aaron shall be
with the Levites, [a]when the Levites take
tithes: and the Levites shall bring up the tithe
of the tithes unto the house of our God, to
[b]the chambers, into the treasure house.
39 For the children of Israel and the children of Levi [a]shall bring the offering of the
corn, of the new wine, and the oil, unto the
chambers, where *are* the vessels of the sanctuary, and the priests that minister, and the
porters, and the singers: [b]and we will not forsake the house of our God.

The repeopling of Jerusalem

11 And the rulers of the people dwelt at
Jerusalem: the rest of the people also
cast lots, to bring one of ten to dwell in Jerusa-

10:28 [b]Ezra 9:1; ch. 13:3
10:29 [1]Heb. *by the hand of* [a]Deut. 29:12; Ps. 119:106 [b]2 Ki. 23:3; 2 Chr. 34:31
10:30 [a]Ex. 34:16; Deut. 7:3; Ezra 9:12
10:31 [1]Heb. *every hand* [a]Ex. 20:10; Lev. 23:3; Deut. 5:12 [b]Ex. 23:10; Lev. 25:4 [c]Deut. 15:1; ch. 5:12
10:33 [a]Lev. 24:5; 2 Chr. 2:4 [b]See Num. 28; 29
10:34 [a]ch. 13:31; Is. 40:16
10:34 [b]Lev. 6:12
10:35 [a]Ex. 23:19; Lev. 19:23; Num. 18:12
10:36 [a]Ex. 13:2,12,13; Lev. 27:26,27; Num. 18:15,16
10:37 [a]Lev. 23:17; Num. 15:19; 18:12; Deut. 18:4; 26:2 [b]Lev. 27:30; Num. 18:21
10:38 [a]Num. 18:26 [b]1 Chr. 9:26; 2 Chr. 31:11
10:39 [a]Deut. 12:6,11; 2 Chr. 31:12; ch. 13:12 [b]ch. 13:10,11

10:28 *Levites.* See Introduction to Leviticus:Title. *porters.* See note on Ezra 2:42. *wives . . . sons . . . daughters.* See note on 8:2.
10:31–33 Perhaps a code drawn up by Nehemiah to correct the abuses listed in 13:15–22.
‡10:31 *on the sabbath day to sell.* Though Ex 20:8–11; Deut 5:12–15 do not explicitly prohibit trading on the sabbath, see Jer 17:19–27; Amos 8:5 and note. *leave the seventh year . . . every debt.* I.e. forego working the land every seventh year; see note on Lev 25:4. The Romans misrepresented the sabbath and the sabbath year as caused by laziness. According to Tacitus, the Jews "were led by the charms of indolence to give over the seventh year as well to inactivity."
10:32 *third part of a shekel.* Ex 30:13–14 speaks of "half a shekel" as an "offering to the LORD" from each man who was 20 years old or more as a symbolic ransom. Later Joash used the annual contributions for the repair of the temple (2 Chr 24:4–14). In the NT period Jewish men from everywhere sent an offering of a half shekel (actually two drachmas, its equivalent; see Josephus, *Antiquities,* 3.8.2) for the temple in Jerusalem (Mat 17:24). The pledge of a third of a shekel in Nehemiah's time may have been due to economic circumstances.
10:33 *shewbread.* See note on Lev 24:8.
10:34 *cast the lots.* See notes on 11:1; Jonah 1:7. *wood offering.* Though there is no specific reference to a wood offering in the Pentateuch, the perpetual burning of fire on the sanctuary altar (Lev 6:12–13) would have required a continual supply of wood. Josephus mentions "the festival of wood offering" on the 14th day of the fifth month (Ab). The Jewish Mishnah (rabbinic interpretations and applications of Pentateuchal laws) lists nine times when certain families brought wood, and stipulates that all kinds of wood were suitable except the vine and the olive. The Temple Scroll from Qumran describes the celebration of a wood offering festival for six days following a new oil festival.
10:35 *firstfruits.* Brought to the sanctuary to support the priests and Levites (Ex 23:19; Num 18:13; Deut 26:1–11; Ezek 44:30).
10:36 *firstborn.* See note on Ex 13:13.
10:37 *wine.* See note on Deut 7:13. Though the Hebrew for this term can refer to freshly pressed grape juice (Is 65:8; Mic 6:15), it can also be used of intoxicating wine (Hos 4:11). *chambers.* Rooms in the courts of the temple were used as storage areas for silver, gold and sacred articles (cf. vv. 38–39; 12:44; 13:4–5,9; Ezra 8:28–30). *tithes.* See notes on Gen 14:20; 28:22; Lev 27:30; Amos 4:4. *Levites.* Tithes were meant for their support (13:12–13; Num 18:21–32).
10:39 See 13:11. *we will not forsake.* Haggai (Hag 1:4–9) had accused the people of neglecting the temple.
11:1 *cast lots.* See 10:34. Lots were usually made out of small stones or pieces of wood. Sometimes arrows were used (Ezek 21:21). *one of ten to dwell in Jerusalem.* Josephus (*Antiquities,* 11.5.8) asserts: "But Nehemiah, seeing that the city had a small population, urged the priests and Levites to leave the countryside and move to the city and remain there, for he had prepared houses for them at his own expense." The practice of redistributing populations was also used to establish Greek and Hellenistic cities. It involved the forcible transfer from rural settlements to urban centers. Tiberias on the sea of Galilee was populated with Gentiles by such a process by Herod Antipas in A.D. 18. *holy city.* See Is 48:2 and note; Dan 9:24; Mat 4:5; 27:53; Rev 11:2; cf. Joel 3:17.

lem [a]the holy city, and nine parts *to dwell* in *other* cities.

2 And the people blessed all the men, that [a]willingly offered themselves to dwell at Jerusalem.

3 [a]Now these *are* the chief of the province that dwelt in Jerusalem: but in the cities of Judah dwelt every one in his possession in their cities, *to wit,* Israel, the priests, and the Levites, and [b]the Nethinims, and [c]the children of Solomon's servants.

4 And [a]at Jerusalem dwelt *certain* of the children of Judah, and of the children of Benjamin. Of the children of Judah; Athaiah the son of Uzziah, the son of Zechariah, the son of Amariah, the son of Shephatiah, the son of Mahalaleel, of the children of [1]Perez;

5 And Maaseiah the son of Baruch, the son of Col-hozeh, the son of Hazaiah, the son of Adaiah, the son of Joiarib, the son of Zechariah, the son of Shiloni.

6 All the sons of Perez that dwelt at Jerusalem *were* four hundred threescore and eight valiant men.

7 And these *are* the sons of Benjamin; Sallu the son of Meshullam, the son of Joed, the son of Pedaiah, the son of Kolaiah, the son of Maaseiah, the son of Ithiel, the son of Jesaiah.

8 And after him Gabbai, Sallai, nine hundred twenty and eight.

9 And Joel the son of Zichri *was* their overseer: and Judah the son of Senuah *was* second over the city.

10 ¶ [a]Of the priests: Jedaiah the son of Joiarib, Jachin,

11 Seraiah the son of Hilkiah, the son of Meshullam, the son of Zadok, the son of Meraioth, the son of Ahitub, *was* the ruler of the house of God.

12 And their brethren that did the work of the house *were* eight hundred twenty and two: and Adaiah the son of Jeroham, the son of Pelaliah, the son of Amzi, the son of Zechariah, the son of Pashur, the son of Malchiah,

13 And his brethren, chief of the fathers, two hundred forty and two: and Amashai the son of Azareel, the son of Ahasai, the son of Meshillemoth, the son of Immer,

14 And their brethren, mighty *men* of valour, an hundred twenty and eight: and their overseer *was* Zabdiel, [1]the son of *one of* the great *men.*

15 ¶ Also of the Levites: Shemaiah the son of Hashub, the son of Azrikam, the son of Hashabiah, the son of Bunni;

16 And Shabbethai and Jozabad, of the chief of the Levites, [1]had the oversight of [a]the outward business of the house of God.

17 And Mattaniah the son of Micha, the son of Zabdi, the son of Asaph, *was* the principal to begin the thanksgiving in prayer: and Bakbukiah the second among his brethren, and Abda the son of Shammua, the son of Galal, the son of Jeduthun.

18 All the Levites in [a]the holy city *were* two hundred fourscore and four.

19 Moreover the porters, Akkub, Talmon, and their brethren that kept [1]the gates, *were* an hundred seventy and two.

20 ¶ And the residue of Israel, of the priests, *and* the Levites, *were* in all the cities of Judah, every one in his inheritance.

21 [a]But the Nethinims dwelt in [1]Ophel: and Ziha and Gispa *were* over the Nethinims.

22 The overseer also of the Levites at Jerusalem *was* Uzzi the son of Bani, the son of Hashabiah, the son of Mattaniah, the son of Micha. Of the sons of Asaph, the singers *were* over the business of the house of God.

23 For [a]*it was* the king's commandment concerning them, that [1]a certain portion *should be* for the singers, due for every day.

24 And Pethahiah the son of Meshezabeel, of the children of [1]Zerah the son of Judah, *was* [a]at the king's hand in all matters concerning the people.

The villages outside Jerusalem

25 ¶ And for the villages, with their fields, *some* of the children of Judah dwelt at [a]Kirjath-

11:1 [a]ver. 18; Mat. 4:5; 27:53
11:2 [a]Judg. 5:9
11:3 [a]1 Chr. 9:2,3 [b]Ezra 2:43 [c]Ezra 2:55
11:4 [1][Gen. 38:29, *Pharez*] [a]1 Chr. 9:3
11:10 [a]1 Chr. 9:10
11:14 [1]Or, *the son of Haggedolim*
11:16 [1]Heb. *were over* [a]1 Chr. 26:29
11:18 [a]ver. 1
11:19 [1]Heb. *at the gates*
11:21 [1]Or, *the tower* [a]See ch. 3:26
11:23 [1]Or, *a sure ordinance* [a]See Ezra 6:8,9; 7:20
11:24 [1][Gen. 38:30, *Zarah*] [a]1 Chr. 18:17; 23:28
11:25 [a]Josh. 14:15

11:2 In addition to those chosen by lot (v. 1), some volunteered out of a sense of duty. But evidently most preferred to stay in their hometowns.

11:3–19 A census roster that parallels 1 Chr 9:2–21, a list of the first residents in Jerusalem after the return from Babylonia. About half the names in the two lists are the same.

11:8 *nine hundred twenty and eight.* The men of Benjamin provided twice as many men as Judah (v. 6) to live in and protect the city of Jerusalem.

‡11:9 *second.* The Hebrew for this word is better translated "Second [Quarter]." See note on 2 Ki 22:14.

11:16 *outward business.* Duties outside the temple (cf. 1 Chr 26:29) but connected with it.

11:17 *Asaph.* See note on Ezra 2:41; see also titles of Ps 50; 73–83. *Jeduthun.* See 1 Chr 16:42; 25:1,3; 2 Chr 5:12; titles of Ps 39; 62; 77.

11:18 *two hundred fourscore and four.* The relatively small number of Levites, compared with 1,192 priests (the total of 822, 242 and 128 in vv. 12–13), is striking (see note on Ezra 2:40).

11:20 *his inheritance.* Ancestral property—including land, buildings and movable goods—acquired by either conquest or inheritance (Gen 31:14; Num 18:21; 27:7; 34:2; 36:3; 1 Ki 21:1–4).

11:21 *Ophel.* See note on 3:26.

11:23 *the king's commandment.* David had regulated the services of the Levites, including the singers (1 Chr 25). The Persian king, Darius I, gave a royal stipend so that the Jewish elders might "pray for the life of the king, and of his sons" (Ezra 6:10). Artaxerxes I may have done much the same for the Levite choir.

11:25–30 An important list, corresponding to earlier lists of towns in Judah. All these names also appear in Josh 15 with the exception of Dibon, Jekabzeel (but see Kabzeel in Josh 15:21), Jeshua, Meconah and En-rimmon (but see Ain and Rimmon in Josh 15:32). The list, however, is not comprehensive, since a number of towns listed in ch. 3; Ezra 2:21–22 are lacking. No Judean coins have been found outside the area designated by vv. 25–30.

11:25 *Kirjath-arba.* See note on Gen 23:2. In the Hellenistic era it fell to the Idumeans, together with other Judean towns.

arba, and *in* the villages thereof, and at Dibon,
and *in* the villages thereof, and at Jekabzeel,
and *in* the villages thereof,
26 And at Jeshua, and at Moladah, and at
Beth-phelet,
27 And at Hazar-shual, and at Beer-sheba,
and *in* the villages thereof,
28 And at Ziklag, and at Mekonah, and in
the villages thereof,
29 And at En-rimmon, and at Zareah, and
at Jarmuth,
30 Zanoah, Adullam, and *in* their villages,
at Lachish, and the fields thereof, *at* Azekah,
and *in* the villages thereof. And they dwelt
from Beer-sheba unto the valley of Hinnom.
31 The children also of Benjamin [1]from
Geba *dwelt* [2]*at* Michmash, and Aija, and Beth-
el, and *in* their villages,
32 *And at* Anathoth, Nob, Ananiah,
33 Hazor, Ramah, Gittaim,
34 Hadid, Zeboim, Neballat,
35 Lod, and Ono, [a]the valley of craftsmen.
36 And of the Levites *were* divisions *in* Judah, *and* in Benjamin.

Priests and Levites

12 Now these *are* the [a]priests and the
Levites that went up with Zerubba-

11:31 [1] Or, *of Geba*, See Josh. 18:24 [2] Or, to *Michmash*, See 1 Sam. 13:2
11:35 [a] 1 Chr. 4:14
12:1 [a] Ezra 2:1,2
12:1 [b] See ch. 10:2-8
12:2 [1] Or, *Melicu*, ver. 14
12:3 [1] Or, *Shebaniah*, ver. 14 [2] Or, *Harim*, ver. 15 [3] Or, *Meraioth*, ver. 15
12:4 [1] Or, *Ginnethon*, ver. 16 [a] Luke 1:5
12:5 [1] Or, *Miniamin*, ver. 17 [2] Or, *Moadiah*, ver. 17
12:7 [1] Or, *Sallai*, ver. 20 [a] Ezra 3:2; Hag. 1:1; Zech. 3:1
12:8 [1] That is, *the psalms of thanksgiving* [a] ch. 11:17

bel the son of Shealtiel, and Jeshua: [b]Seraiah,
Jeremiah, Ezra,
2 Amariah, [1]Malluch, Hattush,
3 [1]Shechaniah, [2]Rehum, [3]Meremoth,
4 Iddo, [1]Ginnetho, [a]Abijah,
5 [1]Miamin, [2]Maadiah, Bilgah,
6 Shemaiah, and Joiarib, Jedaiah,
7 [1]Sallu, Amok, Hilkiah, Jedaiah. These
were the chief of the priests and of their brethren in the days of [a]Jeshua.
8 Moreover the Levites: Jeshua, Binnui,
Kadmiel, Sherebiah, Judah, *and* Mattaniah,
[a]*which was* over [1]the thanksgiving, he and his
brethren.
9 Also Bakbukiah and Unni, their brethren,
were over against them in the watches.
10 ¶ And Jeshua begat Joiakim, Joiakim also
begat Eliashib, and Eliashib begat Joiada,
11 And Joiada begat Jonathan, and Jonathan begat Jaddua.
12 ¶ And in the days of Joiakim were
priests, the chief of the fathers: of Seraiah, Me-
raiah; of Jeremiah, Hananiah;
13 Of Ezra, Meshullam; of Amariah, Jehohanan;
14 Of Melicu, Jonathan; of Shebaniah, Joseph;
15 Of Harim, Adna; of Meraioth, Helkai;

11:26 *Moladah.* Near Beer-sheba; later occupied by the Idumeans. *Beth-phelet.* Means "house of refuge," a site near Beer-sheba.
11:27 *Hazar-shual.* Means "enclosure of a fox" (see 1 Chr 4:28). *Beer-sheba.* See note on Gen 21:31. Archaeological excavations reveal that the city was destroyed by Sennacherib in 701 B.C. and only resettled in the Persian period.
11:28 *Ziklag.* Given to David by Achish, king of Gath (1 Sam 27:6), and taken by the Amalekites (1 Sam 30:1); see Josh 15:31.
‡11:29 *En-rimmon.* Means "spring of the pomegranate," probably Khirbet Umm er-Ramamin, nine miles north-northeast of Beer-sheba (see Josh 15:32). *Zareah* [i.e. Zorah]. See note on Judg 13:2. *Jarmuth.* Eight miles north-northeast of Eleutheropolis (Beit Jibrin), it was one of five Canaanite cities in the south that attempted to halt Joshua's invasion (Josh 10:3–5).
11:30 *Zanoah.* A village in the Shephelah district of low hills between Judah and Philistia. The men of Zanoah repaired the valley gate (3:13). The site has been identified with Khirbet Zanu, three miles south-southeast of Beth-shemesh. *Adullam.* See note on Gen 38:1. *Lachish.* See Josh 10:3; see also notes on Is 36:2; Mic 1:13. *Azekah.* See note on Jer 34:7. *Hinnom.* The valley west and south of Jerusalem; Gehenna in the NT.
11:31–35 Most of the Benjamite towns listed here appear also in 7:26–38; Ezra 2:23–35.
11:31 *Geba.* See 12:29; see also note on 1 Sam 13:3. *Michmash.* See note on 1 Sam 13:2. *Aija.* An alternate name for Ai (see note on Josh 7:2). *Beth-el.* See notes on Gen 12:8; Josh 7:2; Ezra 2:28; Amos 4:4.
11:32 *Anathoth.* See note on Jer 1:1. *Nob.* See note on 1 Sam 21:1. *Ananiah.* Probably Bethany, meaning "house of Ananiah" (see note on Mat 21:17).
11:33 *Gittaim.* Its location is not known.
11:34 *Hadid.* Three to four miles northeast of Lod (see 7:37; Ezra 2:33).
11:35 *Lod.* See note on Ezra 2:33. *Ono.* See note on 6:2. *valley of craftsmen.* Hebrew *Ge-harashim* (see 1 Chr 4:14). It may be the broad valley between Lod and Ono. The name may preserve the memory of the Philistine iron monopoly (1 Sam 13:19–20).
12:1 *Zerubbabel the son of Shealtiel.* See Ezra 3:2,8; 5:2; see also note on Hag 1:1. *Jeshua.* Returned from Babylonian exile in 538 B.C. (see vv. 10,26; 7:7; Ezra 2:2 and note; Hag 1:1; Zech 3:1 and note). *Ezra.* Not the Ezra of the book, who was the leader of the exiles who returned 80 years later.
12:7 *chief of the priests.* The rotation of 24 priestly houses was established at the time of David (1 Chr 24:3,7–19). Twenty-two heads of priestly houses are mentioned in vv. 1–7. Inscriptions listing the 24 divisions of the priests probably hung in many synagogues in the Holy Land. So far, only fragments of two such inscriptions have been recovered—from Ashkelon in the 1920s and from Caesarea in the 1960s (dated to the third and fourth centuries A.D.).
‡12:9 *over against them.* See v. 24; Ezra 3:11 and note; cf. 2 Chr 7:6. The singing was antiphonal, with two sections of the choir standing opposite each other. *watches* [i.e. "service divisions"]. The Hebrew for this word (*Mishmarot*) is the title of a work from Qumran, which discusses in detail the rotation of the priestly families' service in the temple according to the sect's solar calendar and synchronized with the conventional lunar calendar.
12:10 *Jeshua.* See note on v. 1. *Joiakim.* See vv. 12,26. *Eliashib.* See vv. 22–23; the high priest who assisted in rebuilding the wall (3:1,20–21; 13:28). A priest named Eliashib was guilty of defiling the temple by assigning rooms to Tobiah the Ammonite (13:4,7). It is not known whether this Eliashib was the same as the high priest.
12:11 *Jonathan.* Since v. 22 mentions a Johanan after Joiada and before Jaddua, and v. 23 identifies Johanan as "son" of Eliashib, some believe that "Jonathan" is an error for "Johanan." Further complicating the identification are attempts to identify this high priest with a "Johanan" mentioned in the Elephantine papyri and in Josephus (*Antiquities,* 11.7.1). Such an identification, however, is disputable.
12:12–21 All but one (Hattush, v. 2) of the 22 priestly families listed in vv. 1–7 are repeated (Rehum, v. 3, is a variant of Harim, v. 15; Miamin, v. 5, is a variant of Miniamin, v. 17) in this later list,

16 Of Iddo, Zechariah; of Ginnethon, Meshullam;

17 Of Abijah, Zichri; of Miniamin, of Moadiah, Piltai;

18 Of Bilgah, Shammua; of Shemaiah, Jehonathan;

19 And of Joiarib, Mattenai; of Jedaiah, Uzzi;

20 Of Sallai, Kallai; of Amok, Eber;

21 Of Hilkiah, Hashabiah; of Jedaiah, Nethaneel.

22 ¶ The Levites in the days of Eliashib, Joiada, and Johanan, and Jaddua, *were* recorded chief of the fathers: also the priests, to the reign of Darius the Persian.

23 The sons of Levi, the chief of the fathers, *were* written in the book of the [a]chronicles, even until the days of Johanan the son of Eliashib.

24 And the chief of the Levites: Hashabiah, Sherebiah, and Jeshua the son of Kadmiel, with their brethren over against them, to praise *and* to give thanks, [a]according to the commandment of David the man of God, [b]ward over against ward,

25 Mattaniah, and Bakbukiah, Obadiah, Meshullam, Talmon, Akkub, *were* porters keeping the ward at the [1]thresholds of the gates.

26 These *were* in the days of Joiakim the son of Jeshua, the son of Jozadak, and in the days of Nehemiah [a]the governor, and of Ezra the priest, [b]the scribe.

Dedication of the city walls

27 ¶ And at [a]the dedication of the wall of Jerusalem they sought the Levites out of all their places, to bring them to Jerusalem, to keep the dedication with gladness, [b]both with thanksgivings, and with singing, *with* cymbals, psalteries, and with harps.

28 And the sons of the singers gathered themselves together, both out of the plain country round about Jerusalem, and from the villages of Netophathi;

29 Also from the house of Gilgal, and out of the fields of Geba and Azmaveth: for the singers had builded them villages round about Jerusalem.

30 And the priests and the Levites purified themselves, and purified the people, and the gates, and the wall.

31 Then I brought up the princes of Judah upon the wall, and appointed two great *companies of them that gave* thanks, whereof [a]*one* went on the right hand upon the wall [b]toward the dung gate:

32 And after them went Hoshaiah, and half of the princes of Judah,

33 And Azariah, Ezra, and Meshullam,

34 Judah, and Benjamin, and Shemaiah, and Jeremiah,

35 And *certain* of the priests' sons [a]with trumpets; *namely,* Zechariah the son of Jonathan, the son of Shemaiah, the son of Mattaniah, the son of Michaiah, the son of Zaccur, the son of Asaph:

36 And his brethren, Shemaiah, and Azarael, Milalai, Gilalai, Maai, Nethaneel, and Judah, Hanani, with [a]the musical instruments of David the man of God, and Ezra the scribe before them.

37 [a]And at the fountain gate, which *was* over against them, they went up by [b]the stairs of the city of David, at the going up of the wall, above the house of David, even unto [c]the water gate east*ward.*

38 [a]And the other *company of them that gave* thanks went over against *them,* and I after them, and the half of the people upon the

12:23 [a]1 Chr. 9:14
12:24 [a]1 Chr. 23; 25; 26 [b]Ezra 3:11
12:25 [1]Or, *treasuries,* or, *assemblies*
12:26 [a]ch. 8:9 [b]Ezra 7:6,11
12:27 [a]Deut. 20:5; Ps. 30, title [b]1 Chr. 25:6; 2 Chr. 5:13; 7:6
12:31 [a]See ver. 38 [b]ch. 2:13; 3:13
12:35 [a]Num. 10:2,8
12:36 [a]1 Chr. 23:5
12:37 [a]ch. 2:14; 3:15 [b]ch. 3:15 [c]ch. 3:26; 8:1,3,16
12:38 [a]See ver. 31

which dates to the time of Joiakim (v. 12), high priest in the late sixth and/or early fifth centuries B.C.

12:22 *Darius the Persian.* Either Darius II Nothus (423–404 B.C.) or Darius III Codomannus (336–331).

12:23 *book of the chronicles.* Cf. 7:5. This may have been the official temple chronicle, containing various lists and records. Cf. the annals of the Persian kings (Ezra 4:15; Esth 2:23; 6:1; 10:2); cf. also the "book of the chronicles of the kings," mentioned frequently in 1, 2 Kings.

12:26 *Nehemiah . . . Ezra.* See note on 8:9.

‡12:27 *dedication.* See note on Ezra 6:16. *cymbals.* See note on Ezra 3:10. Cymbals were used in religious ceremonies (1 Chr 16:42; 25:1; 2 Chr 5:12; 29:25). Ancient examples have been found at Beth-shemesh and Tell Abu Hawam. *psalteries.* Better understood as "harps." See note on Gen 31:27; used mainly in religious ceremonies (1 Sam 10:5; 2 Sam 6:5; Ps 150:3). Ancient harps have been reconstructed from information derived from the remains of harps at Ur, pictures of harps, and cuneiform texts describing in detail the tuning of harps. *harps* [i.e. "lyres"]. The instrument had strings of the same length but of different diameters and tensions (see 1 Chr 15:16; Dan 3:5).

12:28 *Netophathi.* From Netophah, a town near Beth-lehem (7:26).

‡12:29 *house of Gilgal.* Hebrew *Beth-gilgal.* Perhaps the Gilgal near Jericho (see note on Josh 4:19), or the Gilgal of Elijah (2 Ki 2:1), about seven miles north of Beth-el.

12:30 *purified.* See note on Lev 4:12. The Levites are said to have purified all that was sacred in the temple (1 Chr 23:28) and the temple itself (2 Chr 29:15) during times of revival. Ritual purity was intended to teach God's holiness and moral purity (Lev 16:30).

12:31 *two great companies.* See note on v. 38. The two great processions probably started from the area of the valley gate (2:13,15; 3:13) near the center of the western section of the wall. The first procession, led by Ezra (v. 36), moved in a counterclockwise direction upon the wall; the second, with Nehemiah (v. 38), moved in a clockwise direction. Both met between the water gate (v. 37) and the prison gate (v. 39), then entered the temple area. Cf. Ps 48:12–13. *on the right hand.* Or "to the south." The Semite oriented himself facing east, so the right hand represented the south (see Josh 17:7; 1 Sam 23:24; Job 23:9). *dung gate.* See note on 2:13.

12:35 *trumpets.* See note on Ezra 3:10. Each choir had priests blowing trumpets, as well as Levites playing other musical instruments. *Asaph.* See note on 11:17.

12:36 *Ezra the scribe.* See notes on Ezra 7:1,6.

12:37 *fountain gate.* See note on 2:14. *city of David.* See 3:15; see also note on 2 Sam 5:7. *water gate.* See note on 3:26.

12:38 *company of them that gave thanks.* Lit. "thanks," i.e.

wall, from beyond [b]the tower of the furnaces even unto [c]the broad wall;

39 [a]And from above the gate of Ephraim, and above [b]the old gate, and above [c]the fish gate, [d]and the tower of Hananeel, and the tower of Meah, even unto [e]the sheep gate: and they stood still in [f]the prison gate.

40 So stood the two *companies of them that gave* thanks in the house of God, and I, and the half of the rulers with me:

41 And the priests; Eliakim, Maaseiah, Miniamin, Michaiah, Elioenai, Zechariah, *and* Hananiah, with trumpets;

42 And Maaseiah, and Shemaiah, and Eleazar, and Uzzi, and Jehohanan, and Malchijah, and Elam, and Ezer. And the singers [1]sang loud, with Jezrahiah *their* overseer.

43 Also that day they offered great sacrifices, and rejoiced: for God had made them rejoice *with* great joy: the wives also and the children rejoiced: so that the joy of Jerusalem was heard even afar off.

44 ¶ [a]And at that time were some appointed over the chambers for the treasures, for the offerings, for the firstfruits, and for the tithes, to gather into them out of the fields of the cities the portions [1]of the law for the priests and Levites: [2]for Judah rejoiced for the priests and for the Levites [3]that waited.

45 And both the singers and the porters kept the ward of their God, and the ward of the purification, [a]according to the commandment of David, *and* of Solomon his son.

46 For in the days of David [a]and Asaph of old *there were* chief of the singers, and songs of praise and thanksgiving unto God.

47 And all Israel in the days of Zerubbabel, and in the days of Nehemiah, gave the portions of the singers and the porters, every day his portion: [a]and they [1]sanctified *holy things* unto the Levites; [b]and the Levites sanctified *them* unto the children of Aaron.

Nehemiah's reforms

13 On that day [a][1]they read in the book of Moses in the [2]audience of the people; and therein was found written, [b]that the Ammonite and the Moabite should not come into the congregation of God for ever;

2 Because they met not the children of Israel with bread and with water, but [a]hired Balaam against them, that *he* should curse them: [b]howbeit our God turned the curse into a blessing.

3 Now it came to pass, when they had heard the law, [a]that they separated from Israel all the mixed multitude.

4 ¶ And before this, Eliashib the priest, [a][1]having the oversight of the chamber of the house of our God, *was* allied unto Tobiah:

5 And he had prepared for him a great chamber, [a]where aforetime they laid the meat offerings, the frankincense, and the vessels, and the tithes of the corn, the new wine, and the oil, [b][1]which was commanded *to be given* to the Levites, and the singers, and the porters; and the offerings of the priests.

6 But in all this *time* was not I at Jerusalem: [a]for in the two and thirtieth year of Artaxerxes king of Babylon came I unto the king, and [1]after certain days [2]obtained I *leave* of the king:

7 And I came to Jerusalem, and understood of the evil that Eliashib did for Tobiah, in [a]preparing him a chamber in the courts of the house of God.

8 And it grieved me sore: therefore I cast forth all the household stuff of Tobiah out of the chamber.

9 Then I commanded, and they [a]cleansed

12:38 [b]ch. 3:11 [c]ch. 3:8
12:39 [a]2 Ki. 14:13; ch. 8:16 [b]ch. 3:6 [c]ch. 3:3 [d]ch. 3:1 [e]ch. 3:32 [f]Jer. 32:2
12:42 [1]Heb. *made* their voice *to be heard*
12:44 [1]That is, *appointed by the law* [2]Heb. *for the joy of Judah* [3]Heb. *that stood* [a]2 Chr. 31:11,12; ch. 13:5, 12,13
12:45 [a]1 Chr. 25; 26
12:46 [a]1 Chr. 25:1
12:47 [1]That is, *set apart* [a]Num. 18:21,24
12:47 [b]Num. 18:26
13:1 [1]Heb. *there was read* [2]Heb. *ears* [a]Deut. 31:11,12; 2 Ki. 23:2; ch. 8:3,8; 9:3; Is. 34:16 [b]Deut. 23:3,4
13:2 [a]Num. 22:5; Josh. 24:9,10 [b]Num. 23:11; 24:10; Deut. 23:5
13:3 [a]ch. 9:2; 10:28
13:4 [1]Heb. *being set over* [a]ch. 12:44
13:5 [1]Heb. *the commandment of the Levites* [a]ch. 12:44 [b]Num. 18:21,24
13:6 [1]Heb. *at the end of days* [2]Or, *I earnestly requested* [a]ch. 5:14
13:7 [a]ver. 1,5
13:9 [a]2 Chr. 29:5

"thanksgiving choir" (see v. 40). *tower of the furnaces.* See note on 3:11. *broad wall.* See note on 3:8.
12:39 *gate of Ephraim.* See notes on 3:6; 8:16. *old gate.* See note on 3:6. *fish gate.* See note on 3:3. *tower of Hananeel . . . tower of Meah . . . sheep gate.* See note on 3:1. *prison gate.* Cf. Jer 32:2.
12:43 *God had made them rejoice with great joy.* See 1 Chr 29:9; Jonah 4:6. *wives.* See 8:2; Ex 15:20 and notes. *heard even afar off.* See note on Ezra 3:13; cf. 1 Ki 1:40; 2 Ki 11:13.
12:44 *Judah rejoiced.* The people cheerfully contributed their offerings to support the priests and Levites (cf. 2 Cor 9:7). *that waited.* See Deut 10:8.
12:46 *Asaph.* See note on 11:17.
12:47 *gave.* The Hebrew for this verb implies continued giving.
13:1–2 See Deut 23:3–6.
13:2 *Balaam.* See note on Num 22:5. An Aramaic inscription of the sixth century B.C. found at Deir 'Alla east of the Jordan refers to Balaam.
13:4 *Eliashib.* See note on 12:10. *Tobiah.* See note on 2:10.
13:5 *prepared for him a great chamber.* During Nehemiah's absence from the city to return to the Persian king's court, Tobiah, one of his archenemies, had used his influence with Eliashib to gain entrance into a chamber ordinarily set aside for the storage of tithes and other offerings (see 10:37 and note; cf. Num 18:21–32; Deut 14:28–29; 26:12–15). Elsewhere we read of the chamber of Meshullam (3:30) and of Johanan (Ezra 10:6).
13:6 *two and thirtieth year of Artaxerxes.* See note on 5:14. *king of Babylon.* The title was assumed by Cyrus after his conquest of Babylon (see Ezra 5:13) and was adopted by subsequent Achaemenid (Persian) kings.
13:7 *came to Jerusalem.* Nehemiah's second term must have ended before 407 B.C., when Bagohi (Bigvai) was governor of Judah according to the Elephantine papyri. Some have suggested that after Nehemiah's first term he was succeeded by his brother Hanani (see note on 1:2). *courts.* See note on 8:16. Zerubbabel's temple had two courtyards (Zech 3:7; cf. Is 62:9).
13:8 *grieved me sore . . . cast forth.* Nehemiah expressed his indignation by taking action (cf. vv. 24–25; 5:6–7). Contrast the reaction of Ezra, who "sat down astonied" (Ezra 9:3). Nehemiah's action reminds us of Christ's expulsion of the moneychangers from the temple area (Mat 21:12–13).
13:9 *chambers.* Though only a single chamber was mentioned in vv. 5–8, additional rooms were involved. A parallel to the occupation and desecration of the temple by Tobiah comes from a century earlier in Egypt, where Greek mercenaries had occupied the temple of Neith at Sais. Upon the appeal of the Egyptian priest, Udjahorresnet, the Persian king had the squatters driven out and the temple's ceremonies, processions and revenues restored: "And His Majesty commanded that all the foreigners who had settled in the temple of Neith should be driv-

the chambers: and thither brought I again the vessels of the house of God, with the meat offering and the frankincense.

10 ¶ And I perceived that the portions of the Levites had [a]not been given *them:* for the Levites and the singers, that did the work, were fled every one to [b]his field.

11 Then [a]contended I with the rulers, and said, [b]Why is the house of God forsaken? And I gathered them together, and set them in their [1]place.

12 [a]Then brought all Judah the tithe of the corn and the new wine and the oil unto the [1]treasuries.

13 [a]And I made treasurers over the [1]treasuries, Shelemiah the priest, and Zadok the scribe, and of the Levites, Pedaiah: and [2]next to them *was* Hanan the son of Zaccur, the son of Mattaniah: for they were counted [b]faithful, and [3]their office *was* to distribute unto their brethren.

14 [a]Remember me, O my God, concerning this, and wipe not out my [1]good deeds that I have done for the house of my God, and for the [2]offices thereof.

15 ¶ In those days saw I in Judah *some* treading wine presses [a]on the sabbath, and bringing in sheaves, and lading asses; as also wine, grapes, and figs, and all *manner of* burdens, [b]which they brought *into* Jerusalem on the sabbath day: and I testified *against them* in the day wherein they sold victuals.

16 There dwelt men of Tyre also therein, which brought fish, and all *manner of* ware, and sold on the sabbath unto the children of Judah, and in Jerusalem.

13:10 [a]Mal. 3:8 [b]Num. 35:2
13:11 [1]Heb. *standing* [a]ver. 17,25 [b]ch. 10:39
13:12 [1]Or, *storehouses* [a]ch. 10:38
13:13 [1]Or, *storehouses* [2]Heb. *at their hand* [3]Heb. it was *upon them* [a]2 Chr. 31:12; ch. 12:44 [b]1 Cor. 4:2
13:14 [1]Heb. *kindnesses* [2]Or, *observations* [a]ch. 5:19
13:15 [a]Ex. 20:10 [b]ch. 10:31; Jer. 17:21
13:18 [a]Jer. 17:21
13:19 [a]Lev. 23:32 [b]Jer. 17:21
13:21 [1]Heb. *before the wall?*
13:22 [1]Or, *multitude* [a]ch. 12:30
13:23 [1]Heb. *had made to dwell* with them [a]Ezra 9:2
13:24 [1]Heb. *they discerned not to speak* [2]Heb. *of people and people*

17 Then I contended with the nobles of Judah, and said unto them, What evil thing *is* this that ye do, and profane the sabbath day?

18 [a]Did not your fathers thus, and *did not* our God bring all this evil upon us, and upon this city? yet ye bring more wrath upon Israel by profaning the sabbath.

19 And it came to pass, that when the gates of Jerusalem [a]began to be dark before the sabbath, I commanded that the gates should be shut, and charged that they should not be opened till after the sabbath: [b]and *some* of my servants set I at the gates, *that* there should no burden be brought in on the sabbath day.

20 So the merchants and sellers of all *kind of* ware lodged without Jerusalem once or twice.

21 Then I testified against them, and said unto them, Why lodge ye [1]about the wall? if ye do *so* again, I will lay hands on you. From that time forth came they no *more* on the sabbath.

22 And I commanded the Levites that [a]they should cleanse themselves, and *that* they should come *and* keep the gates, to sanctify the sabbath day. Remember me, O my God, *concerning* this also, and spare me according to the [1]greatness of thy mercy.

23 ¶ In those days also saw I Jews *that* [a][1]had married wives of Ashdod, of Ammon, *and* of Moab:

24 And their children spake half in the speech of Ashdod, and [1]could not speak in the Jews' language, but according to the language [2]of each people.

---

en out and that all their houses and all their superfluities that were in this temple should be thrown down, and that all their own baggage should be carried for them outside the wall of this temple."

13:10 Nehemiah was apparently correcting an abuse of long standing. Strictly speaking, the Levites had no holdings (Num 18:20,23–24; Deut 14:29; 18:1), but some may have had private income (Deut 18:8). Therefore the Levites were dependent on the faithful support of the people. This may explain the reluctance of great numbers of Levites to return from exile (see Ezra 8:15–20). For the complaints of those who found little material advantage in serving the Lord see Mal 2:17; 3:13–15.

13:11 *forsaken.* See note on 10:39.

13:12 *tithe.* See 12:44. Temples in Mesopotamia also levied tithes for the support of their personnel.

13:13 Of the four treasurers, one was a priest, one a Levite, one a scribe and one a layman of rank. *faithful.* Nehemiah appointed honest men to make sure that supplies were distributed equitably, just as the church appointed deacons for this purpose (Acts 6:1–5).

13:15 *treading wine presses.* See notes on Is 5:2; 16:10. *sabbath.* The temptation to violate the sabbath rest was especially characteristic of non-Jewish merchants (see 10:31; Is 56:1–8). On the other hand, the high regard that many had for the sabbath was expressed by parents who called their children Shabbethai (see 8:7; 11:16; Ezra 10:15).

13:16 *Tyre.* See note on Is 23:1. *fish.* Most of the fish exported by the Tyrians (Ezek 26:4–5,14) was dried, smoked or salted. Fish, much of it from the sea of Galilee, was an important part of the Israelites' diet (Lev 11:9; Num 11:5; Mat 15:34; Luke 24:42; John 21:5–13). It was sold at the market near the fish gate (see note on 3:3).

13:17 *contended with the nobles.* Because they were the leaders. *profane.* Turning what is sacred into common use and so profaning it (see Mal 2:10–11).

13:19 *began to be dark.* Before sunset, when the sabbath began. The Israelites, like the Babylonians, counted their days from sunset to sunset (the Egyptians reckoned theirs from dawn to dawn). The precise moment when the sabbath began was heralded by the blowing of a trumpet by a priest. According to the Jewish Mishnah, "On the eve of sabbath they used to blow six more blasts, three to cause the people to cease from work and three to mark the break between the sacred and the profane." Josephus (*Jewish Wars,* 4.9.12) speaks of the location on the parapet of the temple where the priests "gave a signal beforehand, with a trumpet, at the beginning of every seventh day, in the evening twilight, and also at the evening when that day was finished, announcing to the people the respective hours for ceasing work and for resuming their labors." Excavators at the temple mount recovered a stone from the southwest corner of the parapet, which had fallen to the ground in Tit's siege, with the inscription "for the place of the blowing (of the trumpet)."

13:22 *Remember me.* See note on 1:8.

13:23 Ezra had dealt with the same problem of intermarriage some 25 years before (see note on Ezra 9:1). *Ashdod.* See 4:7; Is 20:1 and notes. *Ammon, and of Moab.* See note on Gen 19:36–38.

13:24 The Israelites recognized other people as foreigners by

25 And I [a]contended with them, and
[1]cursed them, and smote certain of them, and
pluckt off their hair, and made them [b]swear by
God, *saying,* Ye shall not give your daughters
unto their sons, nor take their daughters unto
your sons, or for yourselves.
26 [a]Did not Solomon king of Israel sin by
these *things?* yet among many nations was
there no king like him, [b]who was beloved of
his God, and God made him king over all Israel: [c]*nevertheless* even him did outlandish
women cause to sin.
27 Shall we then hearken unto you to do
all this great evil, to [a]transgress against our
God in marrying strange wives?
28 And *one* of the sons [a]of Joiada, the son
of Eliashib the high priest, *was* son in law to
Sanballat the Horonite: therefore I chased him
from me.
29 [a]Remember them, O my God, [1]be-
cause they have defiled the priesthood, and
[b]the covenant of the priesthood, and of the
Levites.
30 [a]Thus cleansed I them from all
strangers, and [b]appointed the wards of the
priests and the Levites, every one in his business;
31 And for [a]the wood offering, at times appointed, and for the firstfruits. [b]Remember
me, O my God, for good.

13:25 [1]Or, *reviled them* [a]Prov. 28:4 [b]Ezra 10:5; ch. 10:29
13:26 [a]1 Ki. 11:1 [b]2 Sam. 12:24 [c]1 Ki. 11:4
13:27 [a]Ezra 10:2
13:28 [a]ch. 12:10,22
13:29 [1]Heb. *for the defilings* [a]ch. 6:14 [b]Mal. 2:4,11,12
13:30 [a]ch. 10:30 [b]ch. 12:1
13:31 [a]ch. 10:34 [b]ver. 14,22

their languages (see Deut 3:9; Judg 12:6; Ps 114:1; Is 33:19; Ezek 3:5–6).

13:25 *pluckt off their hair.* See Ezra 9:3; Is 50:6 and notes. *Ye shall not give.* Nehemiah's action was designed to prevent future intermarriages, whereas Ezra dissolved the existing unions.

13:26 *Solomon.* Israel's outstanding king in terms of wealth and political achievements (1 Ki 3:13; 2 Chr 1:12). Solomon began his reign by humbly asking for wisdom from the Lord (1 Ki 3:5–9). *even him . . . cause to sin.* In later years his foreign wives led him to worship other gods, so that he built a high place for Chemosh, the god of the Moabites (1 Ki 11:7).

13:28 *son in law to Sanballat.* According to Lev 21:14 the high priest was not to marry a foreigner. The expulsion of Joiada's son followed either this special ban or the general prohibition against intermarriage. The union described in this verse was especially rankling to Nehemiah in the light of Sanballat's enmity (see 2:10). Josephus (*Antiquities,* 11.7.2) records that an almost identical episode, involving a marriage between the daughter of a Sanballat of Samaria and the brother of the Jewish high priest, took place a little over a century later in the time of Alexander the Great.

13:30 *wards.* Or "divisions," referring to the assignment of particular duties to groups of priests and Levites, possibly on a rotating basis (see note on 12:9).

13:31 *wood offering.* See note on 10:34. *firstfruits.* See note on 10:35. *Remember me . . . for good.* The last recorded words of Nehemiah recapitulate a theme running through the final chapter (vv. 14,22; see note on 1:8). His motive throughout his ministry was to please and to serve his divine Sovereign.

Esther

INTRODUCTION

Author and Date

Although we do not know who wrote the book of Esther, from internal evidence it is possible to make some inferences about the author and the date of composition. It is clear that the author was a Jew, both from his emphasis on the origin of a Jewish festival and from the Jewish nationalism that permeates the story. The author's knowledge of Persian customs, the setting of the story in the city of Susa and the absence of any reference to the land of Judah or to Jerusalem suggest that he was a resident of a Persian city. The earliest date for the book would be shortly after the events narrated, i.e., c. 460 B.C. (before Ezra's return to Jerusalem; see note on 8:12). Internal evidence also suggests that the festival of Purim had been observed for some time prior to the writing of the book (9:19). Several scholars have dated the book in the Hellenistic period; the absence of Greek words and the style of the author's Hebrew dialect, however, suggest that the book must have been written before the Persian empire fell to Greece in 331.

Purpose, Themes and Literary Features

The author's central purpose was to record the institution of the annual festival of Purim and to keep alive for later generations the memory of the great deliverance of the Jewish people during the reign of Ahasuerus. The book accounts for both the initiation of that observance and the obligation for its perpetual commemoration (see 3:7; 9:24,28–32; see also chart, p. 164).

Throughout much of the story the author calls to mind the ongoing conflict of Israel with the Amalekites (see notes on 2:5; 3:1–6; 9:5–10), a conflict that began during the exodus (Ex 17:8–16; Deut 25:17–19) and continued through Israel's history (1 Sam 15; 1 Chr 4:43; and, of course, Esther). As the first to attack Israel after their deliverance from Egypt, the Amalekites were viewed—and the author of Esther views them—as the epitome of all the powers of the world arrayed against God's people (see Num 24:20; 1 Sam 15:1–3; 28:18). Now that Israel has been released from captivity, Haman's edict is the final major effort in the OT period to destroy them.

Closely associated with the conflict with the Amalekites is the rest that is promised to the people of God (see Deut 25:19). With Haman's defeat the Jews enjoy rest from their enemies (9:16,22).

The author also draws upon the remnant motif that recurs throughout the Bible (natural disasters, disease, warfare or other calamities threaten God's people; those who survive constitute a remnant). Events in the Persian city of Susa threatened the continuity of God's purposes in redemptive history. The future existence of God's chosen people, and ultimately the appearance of the Redeemer-Messiah, were jeopardized by Haman's edict to destroy the Jews. The author of Esther patterned much of his material on the events of the Joseph story (see notes on 2:3–4,9,21–23; 3:4; 4:14; 6:1,8, 14; 8:6), in which the remnant motif is also central to the narrative (Gen 45:7).

Feasting is another prominent theme in Esther, as shown in the outline below. Banquets provide the setting for important plot developments. There are ten banquets: (1) 1:3–4, (2) 1:5–8, (3) 1:9, (4) 2:18, (5) 3:15, (6) 5:1–8, (7) 7:1–10, (8) 8:17, (9) 9:17, (10) 9:18–32. The three pairs of banquets that mark the beginning, middle and end of the story are particularly prominent: the two banquets given by Ahasuerus, the two prepared by Esther and the double celebration of Purim.

Recording duplications appears to be one of the favorite compositional techniques of the writer. In addition to the three groups of banquets that come in pairs there are two lists of the king's servants (1:10,14), two reports that Esther concealed her identity (2:10,20), two gatherings of the women (2:8,19), two houses for the women (2:12–14), two fasts (4:3,16), two consultations of Haman with his wife and friends (5:14; 6:13), two unscheduled appearances of Esther before the king (5:2; 8:3), two investitures for Mordecai (6:7–11; 8:15), two coverings of Haman's face (6:12; 7:8), two references to Haman's sons (5:11; 9:6–10, 13–14), two appearances of Harbona (1:10; 7:9), two royal edicts (3:12–14; 8:1–13), two references to the subsiding of the king's anger (2:1; 7:10), two

references to the irrevocability of the Persian laws (1:19; 8:8), two days for the Jews to take vengeance (9:5–15) and two letters instituting the commemoration of Purim (9:20–32).

An outstanding feature of this book—one that has given rise to considerable discussion—is the complete absence of any explicit reference to God, worship, prayer, or sacrifice. This "secularity" has produced many detractors who have judged the book to be of little religious value. However, it appears that the author has deliberately refrained from mentioning God or any religious activity as a literary device to heighten the fact that it is God who controls and directs all the seemingly insignificant coincidences (see, e.g., note on 6:1) that make up the plot and issue in deliverance for the Jews. God's sovereign rule is assumed at every point (see note on 4:12–16), an assumption made all the more effective by the total absence of reference to Him.

Outline

- I. The Feasts of Ahasuerus (1:1—2:18)
  - A. Vashti Deposed (ch. 1)
  - B. Esther Made Queen (2:1–18)
- II. The Feasts of Esther (2:19—7:10)
  - A. Mordecai Uncovers a Plot (2:19–23)
  - B. Haman's Plot (ch. 3)
  - C. Mordecai Persuades Esther to Help (ch. 4)
  - D. Esther's Request to the King: The First Banquet (5:1–8)
  - E. A Sleepless Night (5:9—6:14)
  - F. Haman Hanged: The Second Banquet (ch. 7)
- III. The Feasts of Purim (chs. 8—10)
  - A. The King's Edict in Behalf of the Jews (ch. 8)
  - B. The Institution of Purim (ch. 9)
  - C. The Promotion of Mordecai (ch. 10)

The removal of queen Vashti

1 Now it came to pass in the days of [a]Ahasuerus, (this *is* Ahasuerus which reigned, [b]from India even unto Ethiopia, [c]*over* an hundred and seven and twenty provinces:)

2 *That* in those days, when the king Ahasuerus [a]sat on the throne of his kingdom, which *was* in [b]Shushan the palace,

3 In the third year of his reign, he [a]made a feast unto all his princes and his servants; the power of Persia and Media, the nobles and princes of the provinces, *being* before him:

4 When he shewed the riches of his glorious kingdom and the honour of his excellent majesty many days, *even* an hundred and fourscore days.

5 And when these days were expired, the king made a feast unto all the people that were [1]present in Shushan the palace, both unto great and small, seven days, in the court of the garden of the king's palace;

6 *Where were* white, green, and [1]blue *hangings,* fastened with cords of fine linen and purple to silver rings and pillars of marble: [a]the beds *were of* gold and silver, upon a pavement [2]of red, and blue, and white, and black marble.

7 And *they* gave *them* drink in vessels of gold, (the vessels being diverse one from another,) and [1]royal wine in abundance, [2]according to the state of the king.

8 And the drinking *was* according to the law; none did compel: for so the king had appointed to all the officers of his house, that *they* should do according to every man's pleasure.

9 Also Vashti the queen made a feast for the women *in* the royal house which *belonged* to king Ahasuerus.

10 ¶ On the seventh day, when the heart of the king was merry with wine, he commanded Mehuman, Biztha, [a]Harbona, Bigtha, and Abagtha, Zethar, and Carcas, the seven [1]chamberlains that served in the presence of Ahasuerus the king,

11 To bring Vashti the queen before the king with the crown royal, to shew the people and the princes her beauty: for she *was* [1]fair to look on.

12 But the queen Vashti refused to come at the king's commandment [1]by *his* chamberlains: therefore was the king very wroth, and his anger burned in him.

13 Then the king said to the [a]wise *men,* [b]which knew the times, (for so *was* the king's manner towards all that knew law and judgment:

14 And the next unto him *was* Carshena, Shethar, Admatha, Tarshish, Meres, Marsena, *and* Memucan, the [a]seven princes of Persia and Media, [b]which saw the king's face, *and* which sat the first in the kingdom;)

15 [1]What shall *we* do unto the queen Vashti according to law, because she hath not performed the commandment of the king Ahasuerus by the chamberlains?

16 And Memucan answered before the king and the princes, Vashti the queen hath not done wrong to the king only, but *also* to all the princes, and to all the people that *are* in all the provinces of the king Ahasuerus.

17 For *this* deed of the queen shall come abroad unto all women, so that *they* shall [a]despise their husbands in their eyes, when it shall be reported, The king Ahasuerus commanded Vashti the queen to be brought in before him, but she came not.

18 Likewise shall the ladies of Persia and Media say this day unto all the king's princes, which have heard of the deed of the queen. Thus *shall there arise* too much contempt and wrath.

1:1 [a]Ezra 4:6; Dan. 9:1 [b]ch. 8:9 [c]Dan. 6:1
1:2 [a]1 Ki. 1:46 [b]Neh. 1:1
1:3 [a]Gen. 40:20; ch. 2:18
1:5 [1]Heb. *found*
1:6 [1]Or, *violet* [2]Or, *of porphyre, and marble, and alabaster, and stone of blue colour* [a]ch. 7:8; Amos 2:8; 6:4
1:7 [1]Heb. *wine of the kingdom* [2]Heb. *according to the hand of the king*
1:10 [1]Or, *eunuchs* [a]ch. 7:9
1:11 [1]Heb. *good of countenance*
1:12 [1]Heb. *which was by the hand of his eunuchs*
1:13 [a]Jer. 10:7; Dan. 2:12; Mat. 2:1 [b]1 Chr. 12:32
1:14 [a]Ezra 7:14 [b]2 Ki. 25:19
1:15 [1]Heb. *What to do*
1:17 [a]Eph. 5:33

1:1 *Ahasuerus.* Also known as "Xerxes," a Greek form of the Persian name Khshayarshan. Ahasuerus succeeded his father Darius and ruled 486–465 B.C. *hundred and seven and twenty provinces.* See 8:9. The Greek historian Herodotus (3.89) records that Ahasuerus's father Darius had organized the empire into 20 satrapies. (Satraps, the rulers of the satrapies, are mentioned in 3:12; 8:9; 9:3.) The provinces were smaller administrative units.

‡1:2 *Shushan the palace.* The fortified acropolis and palace complex; it is distinguished from the surrounding city in 3:15; 4:1–2,6; 8:15. Several archaeological investigations have been made at the site since the mid-19th century. Ahasuerus had made extensive renovations in the palace structures. *Shushan* [i.e. Susa]. The winter residence of the Persian kings; the three other capitals were Ecbatana (Ezra 6:2), Babylon and Persepolis. One of Daniel's visions was set in Susa (Dan 8:2); Nehemiah also served there (Neh 1:1).

1:3–4 The year (483–482 B.C.), the persons in attendance and the length of the meeting suggest that the purpose of the gathering may have been to plan for the disastrous campaigns of 482–479 against Greece. Herodotus (7.8) possibly describes this assembly.

1:3 *feast.* Feasting is a prominent theme in Esther (see Introduction: Purpose, Themes and Literary Features).

1:5–6 The excavations at Susa have unearthed a text in which Ahasuerus's father Darius describes in some detail the building of his palace. Ahasuerus continued the work his father had begun.

1:9 *Vashti the queen.* Deposed in 484/483 B.C.; Esther became queen in 479/478 (2:16–17). The Greek historians call Ahasuerus's queen Amestris; they record her influence during the early part of his reign and as queen mother during the following reign of her son Artaxerxes (Ezra 7:1,7,11–12,21; 8:1; Neh 2:1; 5:14; 13:6) until the time of her own death c. 424. Artaxerxes came to the throne when he was 18 years old; therefore he was born c. 484/483, approximately at the time of Vashti's deposal. Since he was the third son of Amestris, the name Amestris cannot be identified with Esther and must be viewed as a Greek version of the name Vashti. Comparatively little is known of the late portions of Ahasuerus's reign, nor is it possible to determine the subsequent events of the life of Esther. Apparently after Esther's death or her fall from favor, Vashti was able to reassert her power and to exercise a controlling influence over her son.

1:13–14 Ezra 7:14 and the Greek historian Herodotus indicate that seven men functioned as the immediate advisers to the king.

1:13 *wise men, which knew the times.* Court astrologers.

19 [1]If it please the king, let there go a royal commandment [2]from him, and let it be written among the laws of the Persians and the Medes, [a][3]that it be not altered, That Vashti come no *more* before king Ahasuerus; and let the king give her royal estate [4]unto another *that is* better than she.

20 And when the king's decree which he shall make shall be published throughout all his empire, (for it *is* great,) all the wives shall [a]give to their husbands honour, both to great and small.

21 And the saying [1]pleased the king and the princes; and the king did according to the word of Memucan:

22 For he sent letters into all the king's provinces, [a]into every province according to the writing thereof, and to every people after their language, that every man should [b]bear rule in his own house, and [1]that it should be published according to the language of every people.

Esther chosen to be queen

2 After these things, when the wrath of king Ahasuerus was appeased, he remembered Vashti, and what she had done, and [a]what was decreed against her.

2 Then said the king's servants that ministered unto him, Let there be fair young virgins sought for the king:

3 And let the king appoint officers in all the provinces of his kingdom, that they may gather together all the fair young virgins unto Shushan the palace, to the house of the women, [1]unto the custody of [2]Hege the king's chamberlain, keeper of the women; and let their things for purification be given *them:*

4 And let the maiden which pleaseth the king be queen instead of Vashti. And the thing pleased the king; and he did so.

5 ¶ *Now* in Shushan the palace there was a certain Jew, whose name *was* Mordecai, the son of Jair, the son of Shimei, the son of Kish, a Benjamite;

6 [a]Who had been carried away from Jerusalem with the captivity which had been carried away with [1]Jeconiah king of Judah, whom Nebuchadnezzar the king of Babylon had carried away.

7 And he [1]brought up Hadassah, that *is,* Esther, [a]his uncle's daughter: for she had neither father nor mother, and the maid *was* [2]fair and beautiful; whom Mordecai, when her father and mother were dead, took for his own daughter.

8 So it came to pass, when the king's commandment and his decree was heard, and when many maidens were [a]gathered together unto Shushan the palace, to the custody of Hegai, that Esther was brought *also* unto the king's house, to the custody of Hegai, keeper of the women.

9 And the maiden pleased him, and she obtained kindness of him; and he speedily gave

1:19 [1] Heb. *If it be good with the king* [2] Heb. *from before him* [3] Heb. *that it pass not away* [4] Heb. *unto her companion* [a] ch. 8:8; Dan. 6:8
1:20 [a] Eph. 5:33; Col. 3:18; 1 Pet. 3:1
1:21 [1] Heb. *was good in the eyes of the king*
1:22 [1] Heb. *that* one *should publish* it *according to the language of his people* [a] ch. 8:9 [b] Eph. 5:22-24; 1 Tim. 2:12
2:1 [a] ch. 1:19,20
2:3 [1] Heb. *unto the hand* [2] Or, *Hegai,* ver. 8,15
2:6 [1] [Or, *Jehoiachin,* 2 Ki. 24:6] [a] 2 Ki. 24:14,15; 2 Chr. 36:10,20; Jer. 24:1
2:7 [1] Heb. *nourished* [2] Heb. *fair of form, and good of countenance* [a] ver. 15
2:8 [a] ver. 3

1:19 *be not altered.* The irrevocability of the Persian laws is mentioned in 8:8 and Dan 6:8. *come no more before.* The punishment corresponds to the crime: Since Vashti refused to appear before the king, it is decreed that she never appear before him again. Furthermore, from this point on she is no longer given the title "Queen" in the book of Esther.

1:22 *that . . . people.* The king's example of deposing Vashti, plus the elevation of the husband's language in ethnically mixed marriages, served to strengthen the husband's role as ruler in the home and reinforced the common language base in the empire (see Neh 13:23–24).

2:1 *After these things.* Esther was taken to Ahasuerus "in the seventh year of his reign" (v. 16), i.e. in December, 479 B.C., or January, 478. The Greek wars intervened before a new queen was sought (see note on 1:3–4).

2:2 *virgins . . . for the king.* To add to his harem.

2:3–4 The phraseology here is similar to that in Gen 41:34–37. This and numerous other parallels suggest that the author of Esther modeled his work after the Joseph story. Both accounts are set in the courts of foreign monarchs and portray Israelite heroes who rise to prominence and provide the means by which their people are saved (see notes on vv. 9,21–23; 3:4; 4:14; 6:1,8,14; 8:6).

2:5 *in Shushan the palace . . . Jew.* As far back as the fall of the northern kingdom in 722–721 B.C. Israelites had been exiled among the cities of the Medes (2 Ki 17:6). After the conquest of Babylon by King Cyrus of Persia in 539, some of the Jewish population taken there by the Babylonians (605–586) probably moved eastward into the cities of Medo-Persia. Only 50,000 returned to Israel in the restoration of 538 (Ezra 2:64–67). The presence of a large Jewish population in Medo-Persia is confirmed by the discovery of an archive of texts in Nippur (southern Mesopotamia) from the period of Artaxerxes I (465–424) and Darius II (424–405). This archive contains the names of about 100 Jews who lived in that city. Some had attained positions of importance and wealth. Similar Jewish populations are probable in many other Medo-Persian cities. *Mordecai.* The name is derived from that of the Babylonian deity Marduk. There are numerous examples in the Bible of Jews having double names—a Hebrew name and a "Gentile" name. Mordecai likely had a Hebrew name, as did Esther (v. 7), Daniel and his friends (Dan 1:6–7), Joseph (Gen 41:45) and others, but the text does not mention Mordecai's Hebrew name. A cuneiform tablet from Borsippa near Babylon mentions a scribe by the name of Mardukaya; he was an accountant or minister at the court of Susa in the early years of Ahasuerus. Many scholars identify him with Mordecai. *son of Jair, the son of Shimei, the son of Kish.* The persons named could be immediate ancestors, in which case Mordecai would be the great-grandson of Kish, who was among the exiles with Jehoiachin in 597 B.C. It is more likely, however, that the names refer to remote ancestors in the tribe of Benjamin (see 2 Sam 16:5–14 for Shimei, 1 Sam 9:1 for Kish). This association with the tribe and family of King Saul sets the stage for the ongoing conflict between Israel and the Amalekites (see notes on 3:1–6). If the names are those of remote ancestors, the clause "who had been carried away" [i.e. into exile] (v. 6) would not apply to Mordecai, who would have been over 100 years old in that case; rather, it would have to be taken as an elliptical construction in the sense "whose family had been taken into exile."

2:6 *Jeconiah king of Judah.* See 2 Ki 24:8–17; 2 Chr 36:9–10.

2:7 *Hadassah.* Esther's Hebrew name, meaning "myrtle." The name Esther is likely derived from the Persian word for "star," though some derive it from the name of the Babylonian goddess Ishtar (see note on Jer 7:18).

2:8 *Esther was brought.* Neither she nor Mordecai would have had any choice in the matter (cf. 2 Sam 11:4).

her her [a]things for purification, with [1]such
things as belonged to her, and seven maidens,
which were meet to be given her, out of the
king's house: and [2]he preferred her and her
maids unto the best *place* of the house of the
women.
10 [a]Esther had not shewed her people nor
her kindred: for Mordecai had charged her
that she should not shew *it.*
11 And Mordecai walked every day before
the court of the women's house, [1]to know how
Esther did, and what should become of her.
12 Now when every maid's turn was come
to go in to king Ahasuerus, after that she had
been twelve months, according to the manner
of the women, (for so were the days of their
purifications accomplished, *to wit,* six months
with oil of myrrh, and six months with sweet
odours, and with *other* things for the purifying
of the women;)
13 Then thus came *every* maiden unto the
king; whatsoever she desired was given her to
go with her out of the house of the women
unto the king's house.
14 In the evening she went, and on the
morrow she returned into the second house of
the women, to the custody of Shaashgaz, the
king's chamberlain, which kept the concubines: she came in unto the king no more, except the king delighted in her, and *that* she
were called by name.
15 Now when the turn of Esther, [a]the
daughter of Abihail the uncle of Mordecai,
who had taken *her* for his daughter, was come
to go in unto the king, she required nothing
but what Hegai the king's chamberlain, the
keeper of the women, appointed. And Esther
obtained favour in the sight of all them that
looked upon her.
16 So Esther was taken unto king Ahasuerus into his house royal in the tenth month,
which *is* the month Tebeth, in the seventh
year of his reign.
17 And the king loved Esther above all the
women, and she obtained grace and [1]favour
[2]in his sight more than all the virgins; so that
he set the royal crown upon her head, and
made her queen instead of Vashti.
18 Then the king [a]made a great feast unto
all his princes and his servants, *even* Esther's
feast; and he made a [1]release to the provinces,
and gave gifts, according to the state of the
king.

The plot to kill Ahasuerus fails

19 ¶ And when the virgins were gathered
together the second time, then Mordecai sat
[a]in the king's gate.
20 [a]Esther had not *yet* shewed her kindred
nor her people; as Mordecai had charged her:
for Esther did the commandment of Mordecai,
like as when she was brought up with him.
21 ¶ In those days, while Mordecai sat in
the king's gate, two of the king's chamberlains,
[1]Bigthan and Teresh, of those which kept [2]the
door, were wroth, and sought to lay hand on
the king Ahasuerus.
22 And the thing was known to Mordecai,
[a]who told *it* unto Esther the queen; and Esther
certified the king *thereof* in Mordecai's name.
23 And when inquisition was made of the
matter, it was found out; therefore they were
both hanged on a tree: and it was written in
[a]the book of the chronicles before the king.

2:9 [1]Heb. *her portions* [2]Heb. *he changed her* [a]ver. 3,12
2:10 [a]ver. 20
2:11 [1]Heb. *to know the peace*
2:15 [a]ver. 7
2:17 [1]Or, *kindness* [2]Heb. *before him*
2:18 [1]Heb. *rest* [a]ch. 1:3
2:19 [a]ver. 21; ch. 3:2
2:20 [a]ver. 10
2:21 [1]Or, *Bigthana,* ch. 6:2 [2]Heb. *the threshold*
2:22 [a]ch. 6:2
2:23 [a]ch. 6:1

‡2:9 *such things as belonged to her.* Lit. "her portions" [i.e. her food]. Unlike Daniel and his friends (Dan 1:5–10), Esther does not observe the dietary laws, perhaps in part to conceal her Jewish identity (vv. 10,20). Giving such portions is a sign of special favor (1 Sam 9:22–24; 2 Ki 25:29–30; Dan 1:1–10; negatively, Jer 13:25); in the Joseph narrative cf. Gen 43:34. The motif of giving portions appears later as a practice in observing Purim (9:19,22).
2:10 The fact that Esther concealed her identity is reported twice—here and in v. 20 (for the author's use of duplications see Introduction: Purpose, Themes and Literary Features).
2:14 *into the second house of the women.* To the chambers of the concubines.
2:16 *tenth month . . . seventh year.* December, 479 B.C., or January, 478 (see notes on 1:3–4; 2:1). Esther's tenure as queen continued through the events of the book, i.e. through 473 (see 3:7 and note; see also 8:9–13; 9:1). She may have died or fallen from favor shortly thereafter (see note on 1:9).
2:18 *release.* The Hebrew for this word, unique to this verse, may imply a remission of taxes, an emancipation of slaves, a cancellation of debts or a remission of obligatory military service.
2:19 See Introduction: Purpose, Themes and Literary Features. The enlargement of the harem apparently continued unabated. Perhaps there is a causal connection between the second gathering of women and the assassination plot (vv. 21–23); some have suggested that it reflects palace intrigue in support of the deposed Vashti. *king's gate.* The gate of an ancient city was its major commercial and legal center. Markets were held in the gate; the court sat there to transact its business (see Deut 21:18–20; Josh 20:4; Ruth 4:1–11; Ps 69:12). A king might hold an audience at the gate (see 2 Sam 19:8; 1 Ki 22:10). Daniel was at the king's gate as ruler over all Babylon (Dan 2:48–49). Mordecai's sitting at the king's gate confirms his holding a high position in the civil service of the empire (see note on v. 5). From this vantage point he might overhear plans for the murder of the king.
2:21–23 Another point of comparison with the Joseph narrative is the involvement of two chamberlains (Gen 40:1–3; see note on vv. 3–4).
2:23 *hanged on a tree.* Or "impaled on poles." Among the Persians this form of execution was impalement, as is confirmed in pictures and statues from the ancient Near East and in the comments of the Greek historian Herodotus (3.125,129; 4.43). According to Herodotus (3.159) Darius I impaled 3,000 Babylonians when he took Babylon, an act that Darius himself recorded in his Behistun (Bisitun) inscription. In Israelite and Canaanite practice, hanging was an exhibition of the corpse and not the means of execution itself (Deut 21:22–23; Josh 8:29; 10:26; 1 Sam 31:8–10; 2 Sam 4:12; 21:9–10). The execution of a chamberlain in the Joseph narrative also appears to have been by impalement (Gen 40:19). The sons of Haman were killed by the sword, and then their corpses were displayed in this way (9:5–14). *chronicles.* The concern of the author of Esther with rhetorical symmetry is seen in the fact that the chronicles are mentioned in the beginning (here), middle (6:1) and end (10:2) of the narrative. The episode dealing with the plot of Bigthan

Haman's plot against the Jews

3 After these things did king Ahasuerus
promote Haman the son of Hammedatha
the [a]Agagite, and advanced him, and set his
seat above all the princes that *were* with him.
2 And all the king's servants, that *were* [a]in
the king's gate, bowed, and reverenced Haman: for the king had so commanded concerning him. But Mordecai [b]bowed not, nor did
him reverence.
3 Then the king's servants, which *were* in
the king's gate, said unto Mordecai, Why
transgressest thou the [a]king's commandment?
4 Now it came to pass, when they spake
daily unto him, and he hearkened not unto
them, that they told Haman, to see whether
Mordecai's matters would stand: for he had
told them that he *was* a Jew.
5 And when Haman saw that Mordecai
[a]bowed not, nor did him reverence, *then* was
Haman [b]full *of* wrath.
6 And he thought scorn to lay hands on
Mordecai alone; for they had shewed him the
people of Mordecai: wherefore Haman
[a]sought to destroy all the Jews that *were*
throughout the whole kingdom of Ahasuerus,
even the people of Mordecai.
7 ¶ In the first month, that *is,* the month
Nisan, in the twelfth year of king Ahasuerus,
[a]they cast Pur, that *is,* the lot, before Haman
from day to day, and from month to month, *to*
the twelfth *month,* that *is,* the month Adar.
8 And Haman said unto king Ahasuerus,
There is a certain people scattered abroad and
dispersed among the people in all the
provinces of thy kingdom; and [a]their laws *are*
diverse from all people; neither keep they the
king's laws: therefore it *is* not [1]for the king's
profit to suffer them.
9 If it please the king, let it be written
[1]that they may be destroyed: and I will [2]pay
ten thousand talents of silver to the hands of
those that have the charge of the business, to
bring *it* into the king's treasuries.
10 And the king [a]took [b]his ring from his
hand, and gave it unto Haman the son of
Hammedatha the Agagite, the Jews' [1]enemy.
11 And the king said unto Haman, The silver *is* given to thee, the people also, to do with
them as it seemeth good to thee.
12 [a]Then were the king's [1]scribes called
on the thirteenth day of the first month, and
there was written according to all that Haman
had commanded unto the king's lieutenants,
and to the governors that *were* over every
province, and to the rulers of every people of
every province [b]according to the writing
thereof, and *to* every people after their language; [c]in the name of king Ahasuerus was it
written, and sealed with the king's ring.
13 And the letters were [a]sent by posts into

3:1 [a]Num. 24:7; 1 Sam. 15:8
3:2 [a]ch. 2:19 [b]ver. 5; Ps. 15:4
3:3 [a]ver. 2
3:5 [a]ver. 2; ch. 5:9 [b]Dan. 3:19
3:6 [a]Ps. 83:4
3:7 [a]ch. 9:24
3:8 [1]Heb. *meet,* or, *equal* [a]Ezra 4:13; Acts 16:20
3:9 [1]Heb. *to destroy them* [2]Heb. *weigh*
3:10 [1]Or, *oppressor* [a]Gen. 41:42 [b]ch. 8:2,8
3:12 [1]Or, *secretaries* [a]ch. 8:9 [b]ch. 1:22 [c]1 Ki. 21:8; ch. 8:8,10
3:13 [a]ch. 8:10

and Teresh is a good example of the many "coincidences" in the book that later take on crucial significance for the story.

3:1 *After these things.* Four years have elapsed since Esther's selection as queen (v. 7; 2:16–17). The fact that no reason is given for the promotion of Haman provides an ironic contrast between the unrewarded merit of Mordecai (2:21–23; see 6:3) and the unmerited reward of Haman. *son of Hammedatha the Agagite.* There is some debate about the ancestry of Haman. The name Hammedatha appears to be Persian and probably refers to an immediate ancestor. The title "Agagite" could refer to some other immediate ancestor or to an unknown place; however, it is far more likely that it refers to Agag, king of Amalek (1 Sam 15:20). The Amalekites had attacked Israel after she fled from Egypt (Ex 17:8–16; 1 Sam 14:47–48); for this reason the Lord would have "war with Amalek from generation to generation" (Ex 17:16). Israel was not to forget, but must "blot out the remembrance of Amalek from under heaven" (Deut 25:17–19). Saul's attack on Amalek (1 Sam 15) resulted in the death of most, though not all (1 Chr 4:42–43), of the city's population and later in the death of King Agag. In Esther, about 500 years after the battle led by the Benjamite Saul, the Benjamite Mordecai (see note on 2:5) continues the war with the Amalekites.

3:2–6 Obedience to the second commandment (Ex 20:4) is not the issue in Mordecai's refusal to bow down to Haman, for the Jews were willing to bow down to kings (see 1 Sam 24:8; 2 Sam 14:4; 1 Ki 1:16) and to other persons (see Gen 23:7; 33:3; 44:14). Only the long-standing enmity between the Jews and the Amalekites accounts both for Mordecai's refusal and for Haman's intent to destroy all the Jews (vv. 5–6). The threat against the Jews "throughout the whole kingdom" (v. 6) is a threat against the ultimate issue of redemptive history (see Introduction: Purpose, Themes and Literary Features).

3:4 Compare the phraseology with that in the Joseph story (Gen 39:10).

3:7 *first month . . . twelfth year.* April or May, 474 B.C., the fifth year of Esther's reign. *cast.* Perhaps by the astrologers who assisted Haman (5:10,14; 6:12–13). *Pur.* See 9:24,26. This word is found in Akkadian texts with the meaning "lot" (as here). The celebration known as Purim takes its name from the plural of this noun (see 9:23–32). There is irony in the fact that the month of the Jews' celebration of the passover deliverance from Egypt is also the month that Haman begins plotting their destruction (Ex 12:1–11). *twelfth month.* An 11-month delay is contemplated between the securing of the decree and the execution of it in the month Adar (February-March).

3:8–9 The name of the people Haman wishes to destroy is slyly omitted in this blend of the true and the false: The Jews did have their own customs and laws, but they were not disobedient to the king (Jer 29:7).

3:8 *scattered abroad and dispersed.* See 8:11,17; 9:2, 12,16,19–20,28.

3:9 *ten thousand talents.* Herodotus (3.95) records that the annual income of the Persian empire was 15,000 talents. If this figure is correct, Haman offers two-thirds of that amount—a huge sum. Presumably the money would have come from the plundered wealth of the victims of the decree. Verse 13 implies that those who would take part in the massacre were to be allowed to keep the plunder, perhaps adding financial incentive to the execution of the decree since Ahasuerus disavows taking the money (v. 11). On the other hand, 4:7 and 7:4 may imply that the king had planned on collecting some of the money. *those that have the charge of the business.* This clause may represent the title of revenue officers who would bring the money to the treasury, or it could refer to those who carry out the decree. The Amalekites had once before plundered Israel (see note on v. 1); Haman plans a recurrence.

3:12 *thirteenth day . . . first month.* In the 12th year of Ahasuerus's reign (v. 7), i.e. Apr. 17, 474 B.C.

all the king's provinces, to destroy, to kill, and
to cause to perish, all Jews, both young and
old, little children and women, [b]in one day,
even upon the thirteenth *day* of the twelfth
month, which *is* the month Adar, and [c]*to take*
the spoil of them for a prey.
14 [a]The copy of the writing for a commandment to be given in every province *was*
published unto all people, that *they* should be
ready against that day.
15 The posts went out, being hastened by
the king's commandment, and the decree was
given in Shushan the palace. And the king and
Haman sat down to drink; but [a]the city
Shushan was perplexed.

Mordecai asks Esther for help

4 When Mordecai perceived all that was
done, Mordecai [a]rent his clothes, and
put on sackcloth [b]with ashes, and went out
into the midst of the city, and [c]cried *with* a
loud and a bitter cry;
2 And came even before the king's gate: for
none might enter into the king's gate clothed
with sackcloth.
3 And in every province, whithersoever
the king's commandment and his decree
came, *there was* great mourning among the
Jews, and fasting, and weeping, and wailing;
and [1]many lay in sackcloth and ashes.
4 So Esther's maids and her [1]chamberlains
came and told *it* her. Then was the queen exceedingly grieved; and she sent raiment to
clothe Mordecai, and to take away his sackcloth from him: but he received *it* not.
5 Then called Esther for Hatach, *one* of the
king's chamberlains, [1]whom he had appointed
to attend upon her, and gave him a commandment to Mordecai, to know what it *was,* and
why it *was.*
6 So Hatach went forth to Mordecai unto
the street of the city, which *was* before the
king's gate.
7 And Mordecai told him of all that had
happened unto him, and of [a]the sum of the
money that Haman had promised to pay to the
king's treasuries for the Jews, to destroy them.
8 Also he gave him [a]the copy of the writing
of the decree that was given at Shushan to destroy them, to shew *it* unto Esther, and to declare *it* unto her, and to charge her that *she*
should go in unto the king, to make supplication unto him, and to make request before him
for her people.
9 And Hatach came and told Esther the
words of Mordecai.
10 Again Esther spake unto Hatach, and
gave him commandment unto Mordecai:
11 All the king's servants, and the people
of the king's provinces, do know, that whosoever, *whether* man or woman, shall come unto
the king into [a]the inner court, who is not
called, [b]*there is* one law of his to put *him* to
death, except such [c]to whom the king shall
hold out the golden sceptre, that he may live:
but I have not been called to come in unto the
king these thirty days.
12 And they told to Mordecai Esther's
words.
13 Then Mordecai commanded to answer
Esther, Think not with thyself that *thou* shalt
escape *in* the king's house, more than all the
Jews.
14 For if thou altogether holdest thy peace
at this time, *then* shall there [1]enlargement
and deliverance arise to the Jews from another
place; but thou and thy father's house shall be
destroyed: and who knoweth whether thou art
come to the kingdom for *such* a time as this?
15 Then Esther bade *them* return Mordecai *this answer:*
16 Go, gather together all the Jews that are
[1]present in Shushan, and fast ye for me, and
neither eat nor drink [a]three days, night or day;
I also and my maidens will fast likewise; and

3:13 [b]ch. 8:12 [c]ch. 8:11
3:14 [a]ch. 8:13,14
3:15 [a]See ch. 8:15; Prov. 29:2
4:1 [a]2 Sam. 1:11 [b]Josh. 7:6; Ezek. 27:30 [c]Gen. 27:34
4:3 [1]Heb. *sackcloth and ashes were laid under many*
4:4 [1]Heb. *eunuchs*
4:5 [1]Heb. *whom he had set before her*
4:7 [a]ch. 3:9
4:8 [a]ch. 3:14,15
4:11 [a]ch. 5:1 [b]Dan. 2:9 [c]ch. 5:2; 8:4
4:14 [1]Heb. *respiration*
4:16 [1]Heb. *found* [a]See ch. 5:1

3:13 Haman's decree against Israel is the same destruction that had earlier been decreed against Amalek (1 Sam 15:3). *thirteenth day . . . twelfth month.* Mar. 7, 473 B.C. (see 8:12).

3:15 Haman and the king will drink together again in the story when the fate of the Jews is once again being decided (7:1–2), but then it will be at the dissolution of their relationship and the reversal of the decree here celebrated. The celebration here is in sharp contrast to the fasting and mourning of the Jews (4:1–3,15–16).

4:2 *king's gate.* See note on 2:19.

4:3 See note on 3:15. The prominence of feasting throughout the book of Esther sets the fasts of vv. 3,16 in sharp relief; a pair of fasts matches the prominent pairs of banquets (see Introduction: Purpose, Themes and Literary Features; see also note on 9:31).

4:4–12 The fact that the dialogue of Esther and Mordecai is mediated by Hatach reflects the prohibition against Mordecai's entering the royal citadel dressed in mourning (v. 2) and the isolation of Esther in the harem quarters.

4:7 See note on 3:9. That Mordecai is aware of the amount Haman promised to the king is a reminder of his high position in the bureaucracy at Susa (2:21–23).

4:11 Herodotus (3.118,140) also notes that anyone approaching the Persian king unsummoned would be killed unless the king gave immediate pardon.

4:12–16 The themes of the book of Esther are most clearly expressed in this passage. Mordecai's confidence for the Jews' deliverance is based on God's sovereignty in working out His purposes and fulfilling His promises. Their deliverance will come, even if through some means other than Esther. Yet that sovereignty is not fatalistic: Unless Esther exercises her individual responsibility, she and her family will perish. Cf. Mat 26:24; Acts 2:23 for similar treatments of the relationship between divine sovereignty and human responsibility.

4:14 *such a time as this.* Cf. Gen 45:5–7 in the Joseph narrative.

4:16 *fast.* See note on v. 3. Prayer, which usually accompanied such fasting, was presumably a part of this fast as well (see Judg 20:26; 1 Sam 7:6; 2 Sam 12:16; Ezra 8:21–23; Neh 9:1–3; Is 58:3; Jer 14:12; Joel 1:14; 2:12–17; Jonah 3:6–9). The omission of any reference to prayer or to God is consistent with the author's intention; absence of any distinctively religious concepts or vocabulary is a rhetorical device used to heighten the fact that it is indeed God who has been active in the whole narrative (see Introduction: Purpose, Themes and Literary Features). *I also and*

so will I go in unto the king, which *is* not according to the law: [b]and if I perish, I perish.
17 So Mordecai [1]went his way, and did according to all that Esther had commanded
him.

Esther's intervention

5 Now it came to pass [a]on the third day,
that Esther put on *her* royal *apparel,* and
stood in [b]the inner court of the king's house,
over against the king's house: and the king sat
upon his royal throne in the royal house, over
against the gate of the house.
2 And it was *so,* when the king saw Esther
the queen standing in the court, *that* [a]she obtained favour in his sight: and [b]the king held
out to Esther the golden sceptre that *was* in
his hand. So Esther drew near, and touched
the top of the sceptre.
3 Then said the king unto her, What wilt
thou, queen Esther? and what *is* thy request?
[a]it shall be even given thee to the half of the
kingdom.
4 And Esther answered, If *it seem* good
unto the king, let the king and Haman come
this day unto the banquet that I have prepared
for him.
5 Then the king said, Cause Haman to
make haste, that *he* may do as Esther hath
said. So the king and Haman came to the banquet that Esther had prepared.
6 [a]And the king said unto Esther at the
banquet of wine, [b]What *is* thy petition? and it
shall be granted thee: and what *is* thy request?
even to the half of the kingdom it shall be performed.
7 Then answered Esther, and said, My petition and my request *is;*
8 If I have found favour in the sight of the
king, and if it please the king to grant my petition, and [1]to perform my request, let the king
and Haman come to the banquet that I shall
prepare for them, and I will do to morrow as
the king hath said.

4:16 [b]See Gen. 43:14
4:17 [1]Heb. *passed*
5:1 [a]See ch. 4:16 [b]See ch. 4:11; 6:4
5:2 [a]Prov. 21:1 [b]ch. 4:11; 8:4
5:3 [a]Mark 6:23
5:6 [a]ch. 7:2 [b]ch. 9:12
5:8 [1]Heb *to do*

Haman has gallows made

9 ¶ Then went Haman forth that day joyful
and with a glad heart: but when Haman saw
Mordecai in the king's gate, [a]that he stood not
up, nor moved for him, he was full *of* indignation against Mordecai.
10 Nevertheless Haman [a]refrained himself: and when he came home, he sent and
[1]called for his friends, and Zeresh his wife.
11 And Haman told them of the glory of his
riches, and [a]the multitude of his children, and
all *the things* where*in* the king had promoted
him, and how he had advanced him above the
princes and servants of the king.
12 Haman said moreover, Yea, Esther the
queen did let no *man* come in with the king
unto the banquet that she had prepared but
myself; and to morrow *am* I invited unto her
also with the king.
13 Yet all this availeth me nothing, so long
as I see Mordecai the Jew sitting at the king's
gate.
14 Then said Zeresh his wife and all his
friends unto him, Let a [a][1]gallows be made of
fifty cubits high, and to morrow [b]speak thou
unto the king that Mordecai may be hanged
thereon: then go thou in merrily with the king
unto the banquet. And the thing pleased Haman; and he caused [c]the gallows to be made.

Mordecai honoured

6 On that night [1]could not the king sleep,
and he commanded to bring [a]the book of
records of the chronicles; and they were read
before the king.
2 And it was found written, that Mordecai
had told of [1]Bigthana and Teresh, two of the
king's chamberlains, the keepers of the [2]door,
who sought to lay hand on the king Ahasuerus.
3 And the king said, What honour and dignity hath been done to Mordecai for this?
Then said the king's servants that ministered
unto him, There is nothing done for him.
4 And the king said, Who *is* in the court?

5:9 [a]ch. 3:5
5:10 [1]Heb. *caused to come* [a]2 Sam. 13:22
5:11 [a]ch. 9:7
5:14 [1]Heb. *tree* [a]ch. 7:9 [b]ch. 6:4 [c]ch. 7:10
6:1 [1]Heb. *the king's sleep fled away* [a]ch. 2:23
6:2 [1]Or, *Bigthan,* ch. 2:21 [2]Heb. *threshold*

my maidens will fast. Note the rhetorical symmetry: Where once Esther and her maids had received special foods (2:9), now they share a fast. *if I perish.* Cf. the similar formulation in the Joseph narrative (Gen 43:14).

5:2 See Prov 21:1.

5:6–7 One can only speculate regarding Esther's reasons for delaying her answer to the king's question until he had asked it a third time (vv. 3,6; 7:2). The author uses these delays as plot retardation devices that sustain the tension and permit the introduction of new material on Haman's self-aggrandizement (vv. 11–12) and Mordecai's reward (6:6–11).

5:9 Haman's rage is kindled when Mordecai does not rise in his presence—an ironic contrast to his earlier refusal to bow (3:2–6).

5:11 *the multitude of his children.* Haman had ten sons (9:7–10). Herodotus (1.136) reports that the Persians prized a large number of sons second only to valor in battle; the Persian king sent gifts to the subject with the most sons (cf. Ps 127:3–5).

5:12–13 See Prov 16:18; 29:23.

5:14 *fifty cubits high.* There may be a note of hyperbole in the height of the gallows (75 feet). Others have suggested that the gallows was erected atop some other structure to achieve this height, e.g., the city wall (see 1 Sam 31:10). *hanged.* See note on 2:23.

6:1 This verse marks the literary center of the narrative. When things could not look worse, a series of seemingly trivial coincidences marks a critical turn that brings resolution to the story. The king's inability to sleep, his requesting the reading of the chronicles, the reading of the passage reporting Mordecai's past kindness, Haman's noisy carpentry in the early hours of the morning (5:14), his sudden entry into the outer court and his assumption that he was the man the king wished to honor—all are events testifying to the sovereignty of God over the events of the narrative. Circumstances that seemed incidental earlier in the narrative take on crucial significance. Just as in the Joseph story (Gen 41:1–45), the hero's personal fortunes are reversed because of the monarch's disturbed sleep (cf. Dan 2:1; 6:18).

‡6:2 The scribe was reading at the time from the chronicles that recorded events five years earlier (compare 3:7, the king's "twelfth year," with 2:16, his "seventh" year").

6:4–6 Again, the irony is evident: Just as Haman had withheld from the king the identity of the "certain people" (3:8), so now

Now Haman was come into [a]the outward court of the king's house, [b]to speak unto the king to hang Mordecai on the gallows that he had prepared for him.

5 And the king's servants said unto him, Behold, Haman standeth in the court. And the king said, Let him come in.

6 So Haman came in. And the king said unto him, What shall be done unto the man [1]whom the king delighteth to honour? Now Haman thought in his heart, To whom would the king delight to do honour more than to myself?

7 And Haman answered the king, *For* the man [1]whom the king delighteth to honour,

8 [1]Let the royal apparel be brought [2]which the king *useth* to wear, and [a]the horse that the king rideth upon, and the crown royal which is set upon his head:

9 And let *this* apparel and horse be delivered to the hand of one of the king's most noble princes, that they may array the man *withal* whom the king delighteth to honour, and [1]bring him on horseback through the street of the city, [a]and proclaim before him, Thus shall it be done to the man whom the king delighteth to honour.

10 Then the king said to Haman, Make haste, *and* take the apparel and the horse, as thou hast said, and do *even* so to Mordecai the Jew, that sitteth at the king's gate: [1]let nothing fail of all that thou hast spoken.

11 Then took Haman the apparel and the horse, and arrayed Mordecai, and brought him on horseback through the street of the city, and proclaimed before him, Thus shall it be done unto the man whom the king delighteth to honour.

12 And Mordecai came again to the king's gate. But Haman [a]hasted to his house mourning, [b]and having his head covered.

13 And Haman told Zeresh his wife and all his friends every *thing* that had befallen him. Then said his wise *men* and Zeresh his wife unto him, If Mordecai *be* of the seed of the Jews, before whom thou hast begun to fall, thou shalt not prevail against him, but shalt surely fall before him.

14 And while they *were* yet talking with him, came the king's chamberlains, and hasted to bring Haman unto [a]the banquet that Esther had prepared.

The downfall of Haman

7 So the king and Haman came [1]to banquet with Esther the queen.

2 And the king said again unto Esther on the second day [a]at the banquet of wine, What *is* thy petition, queen Esther? and it shall be granted thee: and what *is* thy request? and it shall be performed, *even* to the half of the kingdom.

3 Then Esther the queen answered and said, If I have found favour in thy sight, O king, and if it please the king, let my life be given me at my petition, and my people at my request:

4 For we are [a]sold, I and my people, [1]to be destroyed, to be slain, and to perish. But if we had been sold for bondmen and bondwomen, I had held my tongue, although the enemy could not countervail the king's damage.

5 Then the king Ahasuerus answered and said unto Esther the queen, Who *is* he, and where *is* he, [1]that durst presume in his heart to do so?

6 And Esther said, [1]The adversary and enemy *is* this wicked Haman. Then Haman was afraid [2]before the king and the queen.

7 And the king arising from the banquet of wine in his wrath *went* into the palace garden: and Haman stood *up* to make request for his life to Esther the queen; for he saw that there was evil determined against him by the king.

8 Then the king returned out of the palace garden into the place of the banquet of wine; and Haman was fallen upon [a]the bed whereon Esther *was*. Then said the king, Will he force the queen also [1]before me in the house? As the word went out of the king's mouth, they [b]covered Haman's face.

9 And [a]Harbonah, one of the chamber-

6:4 [a]See ch. 5:1 [b]ch. 5:14
6:6 [1]Heb. *in whose honour the king delighteth*
6:7 [1]Heb. *in whose honour the king delighteth*
6:8 [1]Heb. *Let them bring the royal apparel* [2]Heb. *wherewith the king clotheth* himself [a]1 Ki. 1:33
6:9 [1]Heb. *cause him to ride* [a]Gen. 41:43
6:10 [1]Heb. *suffer not a whit to fall*
6:12 [a]2 Chr. 26:20 [b]2 Sam. 15:30; Jer. 14:3,4
6:14 [a]ch. 5:8
7:1 [1]Heb. *to drink*
7:2 [a]ch. 5:6
7:4 [1]Heb. *that* they *should destroy,* and *kill, and cause to perish* [a]ch. 3:9
7:5 [1]Heb. *whose heart hath filled him*
7:6 [1]Heb. *The man adversary* [2]Or, *at the presence of*
7:8 [1]Heb. *with me* [a]ch. 1:6 [b]Job 9:24
7:9 [a]ch. 1:10

---

the king unintentionally keeps from Haman the identity of the "man whom the king delighteth to honour" (v. 6).

6:8 *royal apparel . . . which the king useth to wear.* See 8:15; see also Introduction: Purpose, Themes and Literary Features. Cf. in the Joseph story Gen 41:41–43. Great significance was attached to the king's garment in ancient times; wearing his garments was a sign of unique favor (1 Sam 18:4). To wear another's garments was to partake of his power, stature, honor or sanctity (2 Ki 2:13–14; Is 61:3,10; Zech 3; Mark 5:27). Haman's suggestion is not only a great honor to the recipient, but it is also considerably flattering to the king: Wearing his garment was chosen instead of wealth.

6:13 See Introduction: Purpose, Themes and Literary Features.

6:14 Guests were usually escorted to feasts (see in the Joseph narrative Gen 43:15–26; cf. Mat 22:1–14).

7:2 See 5:3,6.

7:3 See 2:15,17.

‡7:4 *sold.* Esther refers to the bribe Haman offered to the king (3:9; 4:7); she also paraphrases Haman's edict (3:13). *enemy . . . king's damage.* The Hebrew word translated "enemy" can also mean "distress," perhaps a better rendering here. The statement probably means either (1) that the affliction of the Jews would be less injurious to the king if slavery was all that was involved, or (2) that Esther would not trouble the king if slavery was the only issue.

7:8 *was fallen upon the bed whereon Esther was.* Meals were customarily taken reclining on a couch (Amos 6:4–7; John 13:23). It is ironic that Haman, who became angry when the Jew Mordecai would not bow down (which set the whole story in motion), now falls before the Jewess Esther (see 6:13). The king's leaving the room sets the stage for the final twist that would seal Haman's fate. *covered Haman's face.* See 6:12; see also Introduction: Purpose, Themes and Literary Features.

7:9 Before this moment there is no evidence that Esther had known of Mordecai's triumph earlier in the day (ch. 6); she has pleaded for the life of her people. Harbona's reference to the gallows in effect introduces a second charge against Haman—his attempt to kill the king's benefactor. *Harbonah.* See Intro-

lains, said before the king, Behold also, [b]the
[1]gallows fifty cubits high, which Haman had
made for Mordecai, who had spoken good for
the king, standeth in the house of Haman.
Then the king said, Hang him thereon.
10 So [a]they hanged Haman on the gallows
that he had prepared for Mordecai. Then was
the king's wrath pacified.

The decree is revoked

8 On that day did the king Ahasuerus give
the house of Haman the Jews' enemy
unto Esther the queen. And Mordecai came
before the king; for Esther had told [a]what he
was unto her.
2 And the king took off [a]his ring, which he
had taken from Haman, and gave it unto Mordecai. And Esther set Mordecai over the house
of Haman.
3 And Esther spake yet again before the
king, and fell down at his feet, [1]and besought
him with tears to put away the mischief of Haman the Agagite, and his device that he had
devised against the Jews.
4 Then [a]the king held out the golden sceptre toward Esther. So Esther arose, and stood
before the king,
5 And said, If it please the king, and if I
have found favour in his sight, and the thing
seem right before the king, and I *be* pleasing
in his eyes, let it be written to reverse the letters [1]devised by Haman the son of Hammedatha the Agagite, [2]which he wrote to destroy
the Jews which *are* in all the king's provinces:
6 For how can I [1]endure to see [a]the evil
that shall come unto my people? or how can I
[1]endure to see the destruction of my kindred?
7 Then the king Ahasuerus said unto Esther the queen and to Mordecai the Jew, Behold, [a]I have given Esther the house of Haman, and him they have hanged upon the
gallows, because he laid his hand upon the
Jews.
8 Write ye also for the Jews, as it liketh
you, in the king's name, and seal *it* with the
king's ring: for the writing which *is* written in
the king's name, and sealed with the king's
ring, [a]may no man reverse.
9 [a]Then were the king's scribes called at
that time in the third month, that *is,* the
month Sivan, on the three and twentieth *day*
thereof; and it was written according to all
that Mordecai commanded unto the Jews,
and to the lieutenants, and the deputies and
rulers of the provinces which *are* [b]from India
unto Ethiopia, an hundred twenty and seven
provinces, *unto* every province [c]according to
the writing thereof, and *unto* every people after their language, and to the Jews according
to their writing, and according to their language.
10 [a]And he wrote in the king Ahasuerus'
name, and sealed *it* with the king's ring, and
sent letters by posts on horseback, *and* riders
on mules, camels, *and* young dromedaries:
11 Where*in* the king granted the Jews
which *were* in every city to gather themselves
together, and to stand for their life, to destroy,
to slay, and to cause to perish, all the power of
the people and province that would assault
them, *both* little ones and women, and [a]*to
take* the spoil of them for a prey,
12 [a]Upon one day in all the provinces of
king Ahasuerus, *namely,* upon the thirteenth
day of the twelfth month, which *is* the month
Adar.
13 [a]The copy of the writing for a commandment to be given in every province *was*
[1]published unto all people, and that the Jews
should be ready against that day to avenge
themselves on their enemies.
14 *So* the posts that rode upon mules *and*
camels went out, being hastened and pressed
on by the king's commandment, and the decree was given at Shushan the palace.
15 And Mordecai went out from the presence of the king in royal apparel *of* [1]blue and
white, and *with* a great crown of gold, and
with a garment of fine linen and purple: and
[a]the city of Shushan rejoiced and was glad.

7:9 [1]Heb. *tree* [b]ch. 5:14; Ps. 7:16; Prov. 11:5,6
7:10 [a]Ps. 37:35,36; Dan. 6:24
8:1 [a]ch. 2:7
8:2 [a]ch. 3:10
8:3 [1]Heb. *and she wept, and besought him*
8:4 [a]ch. 4:11; 5:2
8:5 [1]Heb. *the device* [2]Or, *who wrote*
8:6 [1]Heb. *be able that I may see* [a]Neh. 2:3; ch. 7:4
8:7 [a]ver. 1; Prov. 13:22
8:8 [a]See ch. 1:19; Dan. 6:8,12,15
8:9 [a]ch. 3:12 [b]ch. 1:1 [c]ch. 1:22; 3:12
8:10 [a]1 Ki. 21:8; ch. 3:12,13
8:11 [a]See ch. 9:10,15,16
8:12 [a]ch. 3:13; 9:1
8:13 [1]Heb. *revealed* [a]ch. 3:14,15
8:15 [1]Or, *violet* [a]See ch. 3:15; Prov. 29:2

duction: Purpose, Themes and Literary Features. He had been sent earlier to bring Vashti and thus set in motion the events that would lead to her fall and the choice of Esther (1:10); now he is instrumental in the fall of Haman and the rise of Mordecai.

7:10 *pacified.* See 2:1; see also Introduction: Purpose, Themes and Literary Features.

8:1–17 The author achieves considerable literary symmetry by recapitulating much of 3:1–4:3 in almost identical terms.

8:1 *give the house of Haman . . . unto Esther the Queen.* Herodotus (3.128–129) and Josephus (*Antiquities,* 11.17) confirm that the property of a traitor reverted to the crown; Ahasuerus presents Haman's wealth (5:11) to Esther.

8:2 Cf. 3:10, where the king's offer of his ring includes Haman's keeping the money; here Mordecai receives the office and the estate of Haman.

8:3–6 Esther and Mordecai are secure (7:4–5), but the irrevocable decree is still a threat to the rest of the Jews.

8:3 *Agagite.* See note on 3:1.

8:5 *favour.* See 4:11; 5:2.

8:6 Cf. the Joseph story (Gen 44:34).

8:8 See 1:19; see also Introduction: Purpose, Themes and Literary Features. The dilemma is the same as the one that confronted Darius the Mede in Daniel (Dan 6:8,12,15). The solution is to issue another decree that in effect counters the original decree of Haman without formally revoking it (see note on 9:2–3).

8:9–13 The phraseology is taken from the parallel in 3:12–14. The extent of the destruction is the same as that earlier decreed against Amalek (see note on 3:13).

8:9 *third month . . . three and twentieth day.* In Ahasuerus's 12th year, i.e. June 25, 474 B.C., two months and ten days after the proclamation of Haman's edict (see note on 3:13).

8:12 *thirteenth day . . . twelfth month.* Mar. 7, 473 B.C. (see 3:13). Some 15 years after this first Purim, Ezra would lead his expedition to Jerusalem (Ezra 7:9).

8:14–17 The phraseology is taken from 3:15–4:3.

8:15 *royal apparel.* Mordecai's second investiture (see Introduction: Purpose, Themes and Literary Features; see also note on 6:8).

16 The Jews had [a]light, and gladness, and
joy, and honour.
17 And in every province, and in every
city, whithersoever the king's commandment
and his decree came, the Jews had joy and
gladness, a feast [a]and a good day. And many of
the people of the land [b]became Jews; for [c]the
fear of the Jews fell upon them.

The victory of the Jews

9 Now [a]in the twelfth month, that *is,* the
month Adar, on the thirteenth day of the
same, [b]when the king's commandment and
his decree drew near to be put in execution, in
the day that the enemies of the Jews hoped to
have power over them, (though it was turned
to the contrary, that the Jews [c]had rule over
them that hated them;)
2 The Jews [a]gathered themselves together
in their cities throughout all the provinces of
the king Ahasuerus, to lay hand on such as
[b]sought their hurt: and no man could withstand them; for [c]the fear of them fell upon all
people.
3 And all the rulers of the provinces, and
the lieutenants, and the deputies, and [1]offi-
cers of the king, helped the Jews; because the
fear of Mordecai fell upon them.
4 For Mordecai *was* great in the king's
house, and his fame went out throughout all
the provinces: for *this* man Mordecai [a]waxed
greater and greater.
5 Thus the Jews smote all their enemies
with the stroke of the sword, and slaughter,
and destruction, and did [1]what they would
unto those that hated them.
6 And in Shushan the palace the Jews slew
and destroyed five hundred men.
7 And Parshandatha, and Dalphon, and As-
patha,
8 And Poratha, and Adalia, and Aridatha,
9 And Parmashta, and Arisai, and Aridai,
and Vajezatha,
10 [a]The ten sons of Haman the son of
Hammedatha, the enemy of the Jews, slew
they; [b]but on the spoil laid they not their hand.

8:16 [a]Ps. 97:11
8:17 [a]1 Sam. 25:8 [b]Ps. 18:43 [c]Gen. 35:5; Ex. 15:16; Deut. 2:25; 11:25; ch. 9:2
9:1 [a]ch. 8:12 [b]ch. 3:13 [c]2 Sam. 22:41
9:2 [a]ver. 16; ch. 8:11 [b]Ps. 71:13,24 [c]ch. 8:17
9:3 [1]Heb. *those which did the business that* belonged *to the king*
9:4 [a]2 Sam. 3:1; 1 Chr. 11:9; Prov. 4:18
9:5 [1]Heb. *according to their will*
9:10 [a]ch. 5:11; Job 18:19; 27:13-15; Ps. 21:10 [b]See ch. 8:11
9:11 [1]Heb. *came*
9:12 [a]ch. 5:6; 7:2
9:13 [1]Heb. *let men hang* [a]ch. 8:11 [b]2 Sam. 21:6,9
9:15 [a]ver. 2; ch. 8:11 [b]ver. 10
9:16 [a]ver. 2; ch. 8:11 [b]See ch. 8:11
9:17 [1]Heb. *in it*
9:18 [a]ver. 11,15
9:19 [a]Deut. 16:11,14 [b]ch. 8:17 [c]ver. 22; Neh. 8:10,12

11 ¶ On that day the number of those that
were slain in Shushan the palace [1]was brought
before the king.
12 And the king said unto Esther the
queen, The Jews have slain and destroyed five
hundred men in Shushan the palace, and the
ten sons of Haman; what have they done in the
rest of the king's provinces? now [a]what *is* thy
petition? and it shall be granted thee: or what
is thy request further? and it shall be done.
13 Then said Esther, If it please the king,
let it be granted to the Jews which *are* in
Shushan to do to morrow also [a]according unto
this day's decree, and [1]let Haman's ten sons
[b]be hanged upon the gallows.
14 And the king commanded it so to be
done: and the decree was given at Shushan;
and they hanged Haman's ten sons.
15 For the Jews that *were* in Shushan
[a]gathered themselves together on the fourteenth day also of the month Adar, and slew
three hundred men at Shushan; [b]but on the
prey they laid not their hand.
16 But the other Jews that *were* in the
king's provinces [a]gathered themselves together, and stood for their lives, and had rest from
their enemies, and slew of their foes seventy
and five thousand, [b]but they laid not their
hands on the prey,
17 On the thirteenth day of the month
Adar; and on the fourteenth day [1]of the same
rested they, and made it a day of feasting and
gladness.
18 But the Jews that *were* at Shushan assembled together [a]on the thirteenth *day*
thereof, and on the fourteenth thereof; and on
the fifteenth *day* of the same they rested, and
made it a day of feasting and gladness.
19 Therefore the Jews of the villages, that
dwelt in the unwalled towns, made the fourteenth day of the month Adar [a]*a day of* gladness and feasting, [b]and a good day, and *of*
[c]sending portions one to another.

The feast of Purim instituted

20 ¶ And Mordecai wrote these things, and

9:1 See notes on 8:9–13. The Jews carry out the edict of Mordecai eight months and 20 days later. *turned to the contrary.* The statement that the opposite happened points to the author's concern with literary symmetry: He balances most of the details from the first half of the story with their explicit reversal in the second half.

9:2–3 An illustration of Gen 12:3. Confronted with two conflicting edicts issued in the king's name—the edict of Haman and the edict of Mordecai—the governors follow the edict of the current regime.

9:5–10 The Jews attend to the unfinished business of "blotting out the name of the Amalekites" (Ex 17:16; Deut 25:17–19; see notes on 3:1–6). This incident is presented as the antithesis of 1 Sam 15: The narrator is emphatic that the Jews did not take plunder, in spite of the king's permission to do so (8:11). Seizing the plunder 500 years earlier in the battle against Amalek had cost Saul his kingship (1 Sam 15:17–19); here, not taking the plunder brings royal power to Mordecai (vv. 20–23). See vv. 15–16; cf. Gen 14:22–24.

9:10 *sons of Haman.* The second reference to Haman's sons (see 5:11; see also Introduction: Purpose, Themes and Literary Features).

9:12 See 5:3,6; 7:2.

9:13 The reference to hanging in this case is to the display of the corpses, not to the means of the execution (see vv. 7–10 and note on 2:23).

9:15–16 See note on vv. 5–10.

9:16,22 *had rest from their enemies.* Closely associated with the vengeance on their enemies is the rest promised to Israel (Deut 25:19). The defeat of Haman brings rest to the Jews. Cf. 1 Chr 22:6–10; Ps 95:8–11; Is 32:18; Heb 3:11–4:11.

9:18–19 The author accounts for the tradition of observing Purim on two different days: It is observed on the 14th in most towns, but the Jews of Susa observed it on the 15th. Today it is observed on the 14th except in Jerusalem, where it is observed on the 15th.

9:20 *Mordecai wrote these things.* Some take this as indicating that Mordecai wrote the book of Esther; however, the more

sent letters unto all the Jews that *were* in all the provinces of the king Ahasuerus, *both* nigh and far,

21 To stablish *this* among them, that they should keep the fourteenth day of the month Adar, and the fifteenth day of the same, yearly,

22 As the days wherein the Jews rested from their enemies, and the month which was turned unto them from sorrow to joy, and from mourning into a good day: that *they* should make them days of feasting and joy, and of [a]sending portions one to another, and gifts to the poor.

23 And the Jews undertook to do as they had begun, and as Mordecai had written unto them;

24 Because Haman the son of Hammedatha, the Agagite, the enemy of all the Jews, [a]had devised against the Jews to destroy them, and had cast Pur, that *is,* the lot, to [1]consume them, and to destroy them;

25 But [a][1]when *Esther* came before the king, he commanded by letters *that* his wicked device, which he devised against the Jews, should [b]return upon his own head, and that he and his sons should be hanged on the gallows.

26 Wherefore they called these days Purim after the name of [1]Pur. Therefore for all the words of [a]this letter, and *of that* which they had seen concerning this *matter,* and which had come unto them,

27 The Jews ordained, and took upon them, and upon their seed, and upon all such as [a]joined themselves unto them, so as it should not [1]fail, that they would keep these two days according to their writing, and according to their *appointed* time every year;

9:22 [a]ver. 19; Neh. 8:10
9:24 [1]Heb. *crush* [a]ch. 3:6,7
9:25 [1]Heb. *when she came* [a]ver. 13,14; ch. 7:5; 8:3 [b]ch. 7:10; Ps. 7:16
9:26 [1]That is, *lot* [a]ver. 20
9:27 [1]Heb. *pass* [a]ch. 8:17; Is. 56:3,6; Zech. 2:11

9:28 [1]Heb. *pass* [2]Heb. *be ended*
9:29 [1]Heb. *all strength* [a]ch. 2:15 [b]See ch. 8:10; ver. 20
9:30 [a]ch. 1:1
9:31 [1]Heb. *for their souls* [a]ch. 4:3,16
10:1 [a]Gen. 10:5; Ps. 72:10; Is. 24:15
10:2 [1]Heb. *made him great* [a]ch. 8:15; 9:4
10:3 [a]Gen. 41:40; 2 Chr. 28:7 [b]Neh. 2:10; Ps. 122:8,9

28 And *that* these days *should be* remembered and kept throughout every generation, every family, every province, and every city; and *that* these days of Purim should not [1]fail from among the Jews, nor the memorial of them [2]perish from their seed.

29 Then Esther the queen, [a]the daughter of Abihail, and Mordecai the Jew, wrote with [1]all authority, to confirm this [b]second letter of Purim.

30 And he sent the letters unto all the Jews, to [a]the hundred twenty and seven provinces of the kingdom of Ahasuerus, *with* words of peace and truth,

31 To confirm these days of Purim in their times *appointed,* according as Mordecai the Jew and Esther the queen had enjoined them, and as they had decreed [1]for themselves and for their seed, the matters of [a]the fastings and their cry.

32 And the decree of Esther confirmed these matters of Purim; and *it was* written in the book.

The greatness of Mordecai

10 And the king Ahasuerus laid a tribute upon the land, and *upon* [a]the isles of the sea.

2 And all the acts of his power and of his might, and the declaration of the greatness of Mordecai, [a]where*unto* the king [1]advanced him, *are* they not written in the book of the chronicles of the kings of Media and Persia?

3 For Mordecai the Jew *was* [a]next unto king Ahasuerus, and great among the Jews, and accepted of the multitude of his brethren, [b]seeking the wealth of his people, and speaking peace to all his seed.

natural understanding is that he recorded the events in the letters he sent.

‡9:22 *portions* [of food]. See note on 2:9; cf. Neh 8:10,12.

9:24,26 *Pur.* See note on 3:7.

9:27 *all such as joined themselves unto them.* Some refer this phrase to a period of Jewish proselytism and regard it as important to dating the book. It is more likely that it refers to those mentioned in 8:17.

9:31 *fastings.* See notes on 4:3,16. No date is assigned for this fast. Jews traditionally observe the 13th of Adar, Haman's propitious day (see 3:7,13), as a fast ("the fast of Esther") before the celebration of Purim. These three days of victory celebration on the 13th–15th days of Adar rhetorically balance the three days of Esther's fasting prior to interceding with the king (4:16).

10:1–2 The reference to this taxation may represent material in the author's source, to which he directs the reader for additional information and confirmation (see note on 2:23).

Wisdom Literature

The Jews sometimes speak of the OT as the Law, the Prophets and the Writings. Included within the third division are Psalms and wisdom materials such as Job, Proverbs and Ecclesiastes. These wisdom books are associated with a class of people called "wise men" or "sages" who are listed with priests and prophets as an important force in Israelite society (Jer 18:18). Wise men were called on to give advice to kings and to instruct the young. Whereas the priests and prophets dealt more with the religious side of life, wise men were concerned about practical and philosophical matters. Some of their writings, like Proverbs, were optimistic, as they showed the young how to behave in order to live prosperous and happy lives. Other materials, such as Job and Ecclesiastes, were more pessimistic as they wrestled with difficult philosophical and theological questions such as the problem of evil and the prosperity of the wicked (see also Ps 37; 73). Both viewpoints—the optimistic and the pessimistic—are also found in the literature of other nations in the ancient Near East.

Because of the nature of Proverbs, we must not interpret it as prophecy or its statements about certain effects and results as promises. For instance, 10:27 says that the years of the wicked are cut short, while the righteous live long and prosperous lives (see 3:2 and note). The righteous have abundant food (10:3), but the wicked will go hungry (13:25). While such verses are generally true, there are enough exceptions to indicate that sometimes the righteous suffer and the wicked prosper. Normally the righteous and wicked are "recompensed in the earth" (11:31), but at other times reward and punishment lie beyond the grave.

The Book of
Job

INTRODUCTION

Author

Although most of the book consists of the words of Job and his counselors, Job himself was not the author. We may be sure that the author was an Israelite, since he (not Job or his friends) frequently uses the Israelite covenant name for God (*Yahweh;* "LORD"). In the prologue (chs. 1—2), divine discourses (38:1—42:6) and epilogue (42:7–17) "LORD" occurs a total of 25 times, while in the rest of the book (chs. 3—37) it appears only once (12:9).

The unknown author probably had access to oral and/or written sources from which, under divine inspiration, he composed the book that we now have. Of course the subject matter of the prologue had to be divinely revealed to him, since it contains information only God could know. While the author preserves much of the archaic and non-Israelite flavor in the language of Job and his friends, he also reveals his own style as a writer of wisdom literature. The literary structures and the quality of the rhetoric used display the author's literary genius.

Date

Two dates are involved: (1) the date of the man Job and his historical setting, and (2) the date of the inspired writer who composed the book. The latter could be dated anytime from the reign of Solomon to the exile. Although the writer was an Israelite, he mentions nothing of Israelite history. He had a written and/or oral account about the non-Israelite sage Job (1:1), whose setting appears to be during the second millennium B.C. (2000–1000), and probably late in that millennium (see note on 19:24). Like the Hebrew patriarchs, Job lived more than 100 years (42:16). His wealth was measured in livestock (1:3), and he acted as priest for his family (1:5). The raiding of Sabean (1:15) and Chaldean (1:17) tribes fits the second millennium, as does the mention of the *qesitah,* a "piece of money," in 42:11 (see Gen 33:19; Josh 24:32). The discovery of a Targum (Aramaic paraphrase) on Job from the first or second century B.C. (the earliest written Targum) makes a very late date for authorship highly unlikely.

Language and Text

In many places Job is difficult to translate because of its many unusual words and its style. For that reason, modern translations frequently differ widely. Even the early translator(s) of Job into Greek (the Septuagint) seems often to have been perplexed. The Septuagint of Job is about 400 lines shorter than the accepted Hebrew text, and it may be that the translator(s) simply omitted lines he (they) did not understand. The early Syriac (Peshitta), Aramaic (Targum) and Latin (Vulgate) translators had similar difficulties.

Theme and Message

The book provides a profound statement on the subject of theodicy (the justice of God in light of human suffering). But the manner in which the problem of theodicy is conceived and the solution offered (if it may be called that) is uniquely Israelite. The theodicy question in Greek and later Western thought has been: How can the justice of an almighty God be defended in the face of evil, especially human suffering—and, even more particularly, the suffering of the innocent? In this form of the question, three possible assumptions are left open: (1) that God is not almighty, (2) that God is not just (that there is a "demonic" element in His being) and (3) that man may be innocent. In ancient Israel, however, it was indisputable that God is almighty, that He is perfectly just and that no human is wholly innocent in His sight. These three assumptions were also fundamental to the theology of Job and his friends. Simple logic then dictated the conclusion: Every person's suffering is indicative of the measure of his guilt in the eyes of God. In the abstract, this conclusion appeared inescapable, logically

imperative and theologically satisfying. Hence, in the context of such a theology, theodicy was not a problem because its solution was self-evident.

But what was thus theologically self-evident and unassailable in the abstract was often, as in the case of Job, in radical tension with actual human experience. There were those whose godliness was genuine, whose moral character was upright and who, though not sinless, had kept themselves from great transgression, but who nonetheless were made to suffer bitterly. For these the self-evident theology brought no consolation and offered no guidance. It only gave rise to a great enigma. And the God to whom the sufferer was accustomed to turn in moments of need and distress became Himself the overwhelming enigma. In the speeches of chs. 3—37, we hear on the one hand the flawless logic but wounding thrusts of those who insisted on the "orthodox" theology, and on the other hand the writhing of soul of the righteous sufferer who struggles with the great enigma. In addition he suffers from the wounds inflicted by his well-intended friends (see note on 5:27). Here, then, we have a graphic portrayal of the unique form of the problem of theodicy as experienced by righteous sufferers within orthodox Israel.

The "solution" offered is also uniquely Israelite—or, better said, Biblical. The relationship between God and man is not exclusive and closed. A third party intrudes, the great adversary (see chs. 1—2). Incapable of contending with God hand to hand, power pitted against power, he is bent on frustrating God's enterprise embodied in the creation and centered on the God-man relationship. As tempter he seeks to alienate man from God (see Gen 3; Mat 4:1); as accuser (one of the names by which he is called, *śaṭan,* means "accuser") he seeks to alienate God from man (see Zech 3:1; Rev 12:9–10). His all-consuming purpose is to drive an irremovable wedge between God and man, to effect an alienation that cannot be reconciled.

In the story of Job, the author portrays the adversary in his boldest and most radical assault on God and the godly man in the special and intimate relationship that is dearest to them both. When God calls up the name of Job before the accuser and testifies to the righteousness of this one on the earth—this man in whom God delights—Satan attempts with one crafty thrust both to assail God's beloved and to show up God as a fool. True to one of his modes of operation, he accuses Job before God. He charges that Job's godliness is evil. The very godliness in which God takes delight is void of all integrity; it is a terrible sin. Job's godliness is self-serving; he is righteous only because it pays. If God will only let Satan tempt Job by breaking the link between righteousness and blessing, he will expose the righteous man for the sinner he is.

It is the adversary's ultimate challenge. For if the godliness of the righteous man in whom God delights can be shown to be a terrible sin, then a chasm of alienation stands between them that cannot be bridged. Then even redemption is unthinkable, for the godliest of men will be shown to be the most ungodly. God's whole enterprise in creation and redemption will be shown to be radically flawed, and God can only sweep it all away in awful judgment.

The accusation, once raised, cannot be removed, not even by destroying the accuser. So God lets the adversary have his way with Job (within specified limits) so that God and the righteous Job may be vindicated and the great accuser silenced. Thus comes the anguish of Job, robbed of every sign of God's favor so that God becomes for him the great enigma. Also his righteousness is assailed on earth through the logic of the "orthodox" theology of his friends. Alone he agonizes. But he knows in his heart that his godliness has been authentic and that someday he will be vindicated (see 13:18; 14:13–17; 16:19; 19:25–27). And in spite of all, though he may curse the day of his birth (ch. 3) and chide God for treating him unjustly (9:28–35)—the uncalculated outcry of a distraught spirit—he will not curse God (as his wife, the human nearest his heart, proposes; see 2:9). In fact, what pains him most is God's apparent alienation from him.

In the end the adversary is silenced. And the astute theologians, Job's friends, are silenced. And Job is silenced. But God is not. And when He speaks, it is to Job that He speaks, bringing the silence of regret for hasty speech in days of suffering and the silence of repose in the ways of the Almighty (see 38:1—42:6). Furthermore, as his heavenly friend, God hears Job's intercessions for his associates (42:8–10), and He restores Job's beatitude (42:10–17).

In summary, the author's pastoral word to the godly sufferer is that his righteousness has such supreme value that God treasures it more than all. And the great adversary knows that if he is to thwart the purposes of God he must assail the righteousness of man (see 1:21–22; 2:9–10; 23:8, 10; cf. Gen 15:6). At stake in the suffering of the truly godly is the outcome of the struggle in heaven between the great adversary and God, with the all-encompassing divine purpose in the balance. Thus

the suffering of the righteous has a meaning and value commensurate with the titanic spiritual struggle of the ages.

Literary Form and Structure

Like some other ancient compositions, the book of Job has a sandwich literary structure: prologue (prose), main body (poetry), and epilogue (prose), revealing a creative composition, not an arbitrary compilation. Some of Job's words are lament (cf. ch. 3 and many shorter poems in his speeches), but the form of lament is unique to Job and often unlike the regular format of most lament psalms (except Ps 88). Much of the book takes the form of legal disputation. Although the friends come to console him, they end up arguing over the reason for Job's suffering. The argument breaks down in ch. 27, and Job then proceeds to make his final appeal to God for vindication (chs. 29—31). The wisdom poem in ch. 28 appears to be the words of the author, who sees the failure of the dispute as evidence of a lack of wisdom. So in praise of true wisdom he centers his structural apex between the three cycles of dialogue-dispute (chs. 3—27) and the three monologues: Job's (chs. 29—31), Elihu's (chs. 32—37) and God's (38:1—42:6). Job's monologue turns directly to God for a legal decision: that he is innocent of the charges his counselors have leveled against him. Elihu's monologue—another human perspective on why people suffer—rebukes Job but moves beyond the punishment theme to the value of divine chastening and God's redemptive purpose in it. God's monologue gives the divine perspective: Job is not condemned, but neither is a logical or legal answer given to why Job has suffered. That remains a mystery to Job, though the reader is ready for Job's restoration in the epilogue because he has had the heavenly vantage point of the prologue all along. So the literary structure and the theological significance of the book are beautifully tied together.

Outline

- I. Prologue (chs. 1—2)
  - A. Job's Happiness (1:1–5)
  - B. Job's Testing (1:6—2:13)
    1. Satan's first accusation (1:6–12)
    2. Job's faith despite loss of family and property (1:13–22)
    3. Satan's second accusation (2:1–6)
    4. Job's faith during personal suffering (2:7–10)
    5. The coming of the three friends (2:11–13)
- II. Dialogue-Dispute (chs. 3—27)
  - A. Job's Opening Lament (ch. 3)
  - B. First Cycle of Speeches (chs. 4—14)
    1. Eliphaz (chs. 4—5)
    2. Job's reply (chs. 6—7)
    3. Bildad (ch. 8)
    4. Job's reply (chs. 9—10)
    5. Zophar (ch. 11)
    6. Job's reply (chs. 12—14)
  - C. Second Cycle of Speeches (chs. 15—21)
    1. Eliphaz (ch. 15)
    2. Job's reply (chs. 16—17)
    3. Bildad (ch. 18)
    4. Job's reply (ch. 19)
    5. Zophar (ch. 20)
    6. Job's reply (ch. 21)
  - D. Third Cycle of Speeches (chs. 22—26)
    1. Eliphaz (ch. 22)
    2. Job's reply (chs. 23—24)
    3. Bildad (ch. 25)
    4. Job's reply (ch. 26)
  - E. Job's Closing Discourse (ch. 27)
- III. Interlude on Wisdom (ch. 28)
- IV. Monologues (29:1—42:6)
  - A. Job's Call for Vindication (chs. 29—31)

1. His past honor and blessing (ch. 29)
2. His present dishonor and suffering (ch. 30)
3. His protestations of innocence and final oath (ch. 31)

B. Elihu's Speeches (chs. 32—37)

1. Introduction (32:1–5)
2. The speeches themselves (32:6—37:24)
   a. First speech (32:6—33:33)
   b. Second speech (ch. 34)
   c. Third speech (ch. 35)
   d. Fourth speech (chs. 36—37)

C. Divine Discourses (38:1—42:6)

1. God's first discourse (38:1—40:2)
2. Job's response (40:3–5)
3. God's second discourse (40:6—41:34)
4. Job's repentance (42:1–6)

V. Epilogue (42:7–17)

A. God's Verdict (42:7–9)

B. Job's Restoration (42:10–17)

Job and his background

1 There was a man [a]in the land of Uz,
whose name *was* [b]Job; and that man was
[c]perfect and upright, and one that [d]feared
God, and eschewed evil.
2 And there were born unto him seven
sons and three daughters.
3 His [1]substance also was seven thousand
sheep, and three thousand camels, and five
hundred yoke of oxen, and five hundred she
asses, and a very great [2]household; so that this
man was the greatest of all the [3]men of the
east.
4 And his sons went and feasted *in their*
houses, every one his day; and sent and called
for their three sisters to eat and to drink with
them.
5 And it was so, when the days of *their*
feasting were gone about, that Job sent and
sanctified them, and rose up early in the
morning, [a]and offered burnt offerings *accord-*
ing to the number of them all: for Job said, It
may be that my sons have sinned, and [b]cursed
God in their hearts. Thus did Job [1]continually.

Satan permitted to tempt Job

6 ¶ Now [a]there was a day when the sons of
God came to present themselves before the
LORD, and [1]Satan came also [2]among them.
7 And the LORD said unto Satan, Whence
comest thou? Then Satan answered the LORD,
and said, From [a]going to and fro in the earth,
and from walking up and down in it.
8 And the LORD said unto Satan, [1]Hast thou
considered my servant Job, that *there is* none
like him in the earth, a perfect and an upright
man, one that feareth God, and escheweth
evil?
9 Then Satan answered the LORD, and said,
Doth Job fear God for nought?
10 [a]Hast not thou made a hedge about
him, and about his house, and about all that he
hath on every side? [b]thou hast blessed the
work of his hands, and his [1]substance is increased in the land.
11 [a]But put forth thine hand now, and
touch all that he hath, [1]and he will [b]curse
thee to thy face.
12 And the LORD said unto Satan, Behold,
all that he hath *is* in thy [a1]power; only upon
himself put not forth thine hand. So Satan
went forth from the presence of the LORD.
13 ¶ And there was a day [a]when his sons
and his daughters *were* eating and drinking
wine in their eldest brother's house:
14 And there came a messenger unto Job,
and said, The oxen were plowing, and the asses feeding beside them:
15 And the Sabeans fell *upon them,* and
took them away; yea, they have slain the servants with the edge of the sword; and I only
am escaped alone to tell thee.
16 While he *was* yet speaking, there came
also another, and said, [1]The fire of God is fall-
en from heaven, and hath burnt up the sheep,
and the servants, and consumed them; and I
only am escaped alone to tell thee.
17 While he *was* yet speaking, there came
also another, and said, The Chaldeans made
out three bands, and [1]fell upon the camels,

1:1 [a]1 Chr. 1:17 [b]Ezek. 14:14; Jas. 5:11 [c]Gen. 17:1 [d]Prov. 16:6
1:3 [1]Or, *cattle* [2]Or, *husbandry* [3]Heb. *sons of the east*
1:5 [1]Heb. *all the days* [a]ch. 42:8 [b]1 Ki. 21:10
1:6 [1]Heb. *the adversary* [2]Heb. *in the midst of them* [a]ch. 2:1
1:7 [a]1 Pet. 5:8
1:8 [1]Heb. *Hast thou set thy heart on*
1:10 [1]Or, *cattle* [a]Ps. 34:7; Is. 5:2 [b]Ps. 128:1,2; Prov. 10:22
1:11 [1]Heb. *if he curse thee not to thy face* [a]ch. 2:5; 19:21 [b]Is. 8:21; Mal. 3:13,14
1:12 [1]Heb. *hand* [a]Gen. 16:6
1:13 [a]Eccl. 9:12
1:16 [1]Or, *A great fire*
1:17 [1]Heb. *rushed*

1:1 *land of Uz.* A large territory east of the Jordan (see v. 3), which included Edom in the south (see Gen 36:28; Lam 4:21) and the Aramean lands in the north (see Gen 10:23; 22:21). *perfect and upright.* Spiritually and morally upright. This does not mean that Job was sinless. He later defends his moral integrity but also admits he is a sinner (see 6:24; 7:21). *feared God.* See 28:28; Prov 3:7; see also note on Gen 20:11.

1:2 *seven sons.* An ideal number, signifying completeness (see note on Ruth 4:15).

‡1:3 *seven thousand sheep.* See note on 42:12. Job's enormous wealth was in livestock, not land (see Gen 12:16; 13:2; 26:14). *she asses.* Donkeys that produced offspring were very valuable. *men of the east.* The Hebrew for this phrase is translated "people of the east" in Gen 29:1 and "children of the east" in Judg 6:3 (see note there).

1:5 *days of their feasting.* On special occasions, feasts might last a week (see Gen 29:27; Judg 14:12). *sanctified them.* Make them ceremonially clean in preparation for the sacrifices he offered for them (see Ex 19:10,14). *offered burnt offerings.* Before the ceremonial laws of Moses were introduced, the father of the household acted as priest (see Gen 15:9–10).

1:6 *sons of God came to present themselves.* Angels who came as members of the heavenly council who stand in the presence of God (see 1 Ki 22:19; Ps 89:5–7; Jer 23:18,22). *Satan.* Lit. "the adversary/accuser" (see Rev 12:10). In Job the Hebrew for this word is always preceded by the definite article. In the Hebrew of 1 Chr 21:1 the article is not used, because by then "Satan" had become a proper name.

1:7 *the LORD.* The Israelite covenant name for God (see Introduction: Author; see also note on Gen 2:4).

1:8 *Hast thou considered . . . Job?* The Lord, not Satan, initiates the dialogue that leads to the testing of Job. He holds up Job as one against whom "the accuser" can lodge no accusation. *my servant.* See 42:7–8 and note; a designation for one who stands in a special relationship with God and is loyal in service (e.g., Moses, Num 12:7; David, 2 Sam 7:5; see Is 42:1; 52:13; 53:11).

1:9 "The accuser" boldly accuses the man God commends: He says Job's righteousness, in which God delights, is self-serving—the heart of Satan's attack on God and His faithful servant in the book of Job.

1:10 *hedge.* Symbolizes protection (see Is 5:5; contrast Job 3:23).

1:11 *put forth thine hand now, and touch.* See 4:5.

1:12 Satan, the accuser, is given power to afflict (v. 12a) but is kept on a leash (v. 12b). In all his evil among men (vv. 15,17) or in nature (vv. 16,19), Satan is under God's power (compare 1 Chr 21:1 with 2 Sam 24:1; see 1 Sam 16:14; 2 Sam 24:16; 1 Cor 5:5; 2 Cor 12:7; Heb 2:14). The contest, however, is not a sham. Will Job curse God to His face? If Job does not, the accuser will be proven false and God's delight in Job vindicated.

‡1:15 *Sabeans.* Probably south Arabians from Sheba, whose descendants became wealthy traders in spices, gold and precious stones (see the account of the queen of Sheba in 1 Ki 10:1–13; see also Ps 72:10,15; Is 60:6; Jer 6:20; Ezek 27:22; Joel 3:8). Job 6:19 calls the Sabeans "companies" (of travelers) and associates them with Tema (about 350 miles southeast of Jerusalem).

1:16 *fire of God.* Lightning (see Num 11:1; 1 Ki 18:38; 2 Ki 1:12).

1:17 *Chaldeans.* A people who were Bedouin until c. 1000 B.C., when they settled in southern Mesopotamia and later became the nucleus of Nebuchadnezzar's Babylonian empire.

and have carried them away, yea, and slain the servants with the edge of the sword; and I only am escaped alone to tell thee.

18 While he *was* yet speaking, there came also another, and said, [a]Thy sons and thy daughters *were* eating and drinking wine in their eldest brother's house:

19 And behold, there came a great wind [1]from the wilderness, and smote the four corners of the house, and it fell upon the young men, and they are dead; and I only am escaped alone to tell thee.

20 Then Job arose, [a]and rent his [1]mantle, and shaved his head, and [b]fell down upon the ground, and worshipped,

21 And said,

[a]Naked came I out of my mother's
womb,
And naked shall I return thither:
The LORD [b]gave, and the LORD hath
[c]taken *away;*
[d]Blessed be the name of the LORD.

22 [a]In all this Job sinned not, nor [1]charged God foolishly.

Satan's second request of God

2 Again [a]there was a day when the sons of God came to present themselves before the LORD, and Satan came also among them to present himself before the LORD.

2 And the LORD said unto Satan, From whence comest thou? And [a]Satan answered the LORD, and said, From going to and fro in the earth, and from walking up and down in it.

3 And the LORD said unto Satan, Hast thou considered my servant Job, that *there is* none like him in the earth, [a]a perfect and an upright man, one that feareth God, and escheweth evil? and still he [b]holdeth fast his integrity, although thou movedst me against him, [c1]to destroy him without cause.

4 And Satan answered the LORD, and said, Skin for skin, yea, all that a man hath will he give for his life.

5 [a]But put forth thine hand now, and touch his [b]bone and his flesh, and he will curse thee to thy face.

6 [a]And the LORD said unto Satan, Behold, he *is* in thine hand; [1]but save his life.

7 So went Satan forth from the presence of the LORD, and smote Job with sore boils [a]from the sole of his foot unto his crown.

8 And he took him a potsherd to scrape himself withal; [a]and he sat down among the ashes.

9 Then said his wife unto him, Dost thou still retain thine integrity? curse God, and die.

10 But he said unto her, Thou speakest as one of the foolish *women* speaketh. What? [a]shall we receive good at the hand of God, and shall we not receive evil? [b]In all this did not Job [c]sin with his lips.

The friends of Job

11 ¶ Now when Job's three friends heard of all this evil that was come upon him, they came every one from his own place; Eliphaz the [a]Temanite, and Bildad the [b]Shuhite, and Zophar the Naamathite: for they had made an appointment together to come [c]to mourn with him and to comfort him.

12 And when they lift up their eyes afar off, and knew him not, they lifted up their voice, and wept; and they rent every one his mantle, and [a]sprinkled dust upon their heads toward heaven.

1:18 [a]ver. 4,13
1:19 [1]Heb. *from aside, etc.*
1:20 [1]Or, *robe* [a]Gen. 37:29; Ezra 9:3 [b]1 Pet. 5:6
1:21 [a]Ps. 49:17; Eccl. 5:15; 1 Tim. 6:7 [b]Eccl. 5:19; Jas. 1:17 [c]Gen. 31:16 [d]Eph. 5:20; 1 Thes. 5:18
1:22 [1]Or, *attributed folly to God* [a]ch. 2:10
2:1 [a]ch. 1:6
2:2 [a]ch. 1:7
2:3 [a]ch. 1:1,8
2:3 [1]Heb. *to swallow him up* [b]ch. 27:5,6 [c]ch. 9:17
2:5 [a]ch. 1:11 [b]ch. 19:20
2:6 [1]Or, *only* [a]ch. 1:12
2:7 [a]Is. 1:6
2:8 [a]2 Sam. 13:19; ch. 42:6; Ezek. 27:30; Mat. 11:21
2:10 [a]ch. 1:21; Heb. 12:6; Jas. 5:10,11 [b]ch. 1:22 [c]Ps. 39:1
2:11 [a]Gen. 36:11; Jer. 49:7 [b]Gen. 25:2 [c]ch. 42:11; Rom. 12:15
2:12 [a]Neh. 9:1; Lam. 2:10; Ezek. 27:30

1:19 *great wind.* Tornado.
1:20 *Then Job arose.* He is silent until his children are killed. *rent his mantle, and shaved his head.* In mourning (see notes on Gen 37:34; Is 15:2).
1:21 *shall I return thither.* See Gen 2:7; 3:19 and note. *The LORD gave, and the LORD hath taken away.* Job's faith leads him to see the sovereign God's hand at work, and that gives him repose even in the face of calamity.
2:1–3 Except for the final sentence, this passage is almost identical to 1:6–8. He who accused Job of having a deceitful motive is now shown to have a deceitful motive himself: to discredit the Lord through Job.
2:3 *thou movedst me against him.* God cannot be stirred up to do things against His will. Though it is not always clear how, everything that happens is part of His divine purpose (see 38:2).
2:4 *Skin for skin.* No doubt a proverb—perhaps originally an expression of willingness to barter one animal skin for another of equal value.
2:5 *touch his bone and his flesh.* See 1:11–12; cf. Gen 2:23; Luke 24:39.
2:6 *save his life.* Satan is still limited by God. Should Job die, neither God nor Job could be vindicated.
2:7 The precise nature of Job's sickness is uncertain, but its symptoms were painful festering sores over the whole body (7:5), nightmares (7:14), scabs that peeled and became black (30:28,30), disfigurement and revolting appearance (2:12; 19:19), bad breath (19:17), excessive thinness (17:7; 19:20), fever (30:30) and pain day and night (30:17). *boils.* See Ex 9:9; Lev 13:18; 2 Ki 20:7.
‡2:8 *potsherd.* A piece of broken pottery. *ashes.* Symbolic of mourning (see 42:6; Esth 4:3; cf. Jonah 3:6, which speaks of sitting in dust).
2:9 *curse God.* The Hebrew for this expression here and in 1:5 employs a euphemism (lit. "Bless God"). Satan is using Job's wife to tempt Job as he used Eve to tempt Adam. *and die.* Since nothing but death is left for Job, his wife wants him to provoke God to administer the final stroke due to all who curse Him (Lev 24:10–16).
2:10 *shall we receive good at the hand of God, and shall we not receive evil?* A key theme of the book: Trouble and suffering are not merely punishment for sin; for God's people they may serve as a trial (as here) or as a discipline that culminates in spiritual gain (see 5:17; Deut 8:5; 2 Sam 7:14; Ps 94:12; Prov 3:11–12; 1 Cor 11:32; Heb 12:5–11).
2:11 *three friends.* Older than Job (see 15:10). *Eliphaz.* An Edomite name (see Gen 36:11). *Temanite.* Teman was a village in Edom, south of the Dead Sea (see Gen 36:11; Jer 49:7; Ezek 25:13; Amos 1:12; Obad 9). *Shuhite.* Bildad may have been a descendant of Shuah, the youngest son of Abraham and Keturah (Gen 25:2). *Naamathite.* Apart from 11:1; 20:1; 42:9, this word does not occur elsewhere in the Bible.
‡2:12 *knew him not.* Did not recognize him. Cf. Is 52:14; 53:3. *rent . . . his mantle and, sprinkled dust upon their heads.* Visible signs of mourning (see note on 1:20).

13 So they sat down with him upon the ground [a]seven days and seven nights, and none spake a word unto him: for they saw that *his* grief was very great.

The speech of Job

3 After this opened Job his mouth, and cursed his day.
2 And Job [1]spake, and said,

3 [a]Let the day perish wherein I was born,
And the night *in which it was* said,
There is a man child conceived.
4 Let that day be darkness;
Let not God regard it from above,
Neither let the light shine upon it.
5 Let darkness and [a]the shadow of death [1]stain it;
Let a cloud dwell upon it;
[2]Let the blackness of the day terrify it.

6 *As for* that night, let darkness seize upon it;
[1]Let it not be joined unto the days of the year,
Let it not come into the number of the months.
7 Lo, let that night be solitary,
Let no joyful voice come therein.
8 Let them curse it that curse the day,
[a]Who are ready to raise up [1]their mourning.
9 Let the stars of the twilight thereof be dark;
Let it look for light, but *have* none;
Neither let it see [1]the dawning of the day:

10 Because it shut not up the doors of my *mother's* womb,
Nor hid sorrow from mine eyes.
11 [a]Why died I not from the womb?
Why did I *not* give up the ghost when I came out of the belly?

2:13 [a]Gen. 50:10
3:2 [1]Heb. *answered*
3:3 [a]Jer. 20:14
3:5 [1]Or, *challenge it* [2]Or, *Let them terrify it, as those who have a bitter day* [a]ch. 10:21; Jer. 13:16; Amos 5:8
3:6 [1]Or, *Let it not rejoice among the days*
3:8 [1]Or, *leviathan* [a]Jer. 9:17
3:9 [1]Heb. *the eyelids of the morning*
3:11 [a]ch. 10:18
3:12 [a]Gen. 30:3
3:14 [a]ch. 15:28
3:16 [a]Ps. 58:8
3:17 [1]Heb. *wearied in strength*
3:18 [a]ch. 39:7
3:20 [a]Jer. 20:18 [b]2 Ki. 4:27
3:21 [1]Heb. *wait* [a]Rev. 9:6 [b]Prov. 2:4
3:23 [a]Lam. 3:7
3:24 [1]Heb. *before my meat*

12 [a]Why did the knees prevent me?
Or why the breasts that I should suck?

13 For now should I have lien *still* and been quiet,
I should have slept: then had I been at rest,
14 With kings and counsellers of the earth,
Which [a]built desolate places for themselves;
15 Or with princes that had gold,
Who filled their houses *with* silver:
16 Or [a]as a hidden untimely birth I had not been;
As infants *which* never saw light.

17 There the wicked cease *from* troubling;
And there the [1]weary be at rest.
18 *There* the prisoners rest together;
[a]They hear not the voice of the oppressor.
19 The small and great *are* there;
And the servant *is* free from his master.

20 [a]Wherefore is light given to him that is in misery,
And life unto the [b]bitter in soul;
21 Which [a] [1]long for death, but it *cometh* not;
And dig for it more than [b]for hid treasures;
22 Which rejoice exceedingly,
And are glad, when they can find the grave?
23 *Why is light given* to a man whose way is hid,
[a]And whom God hath hedged in?

24 For my sighing cometh [1]before I eat,
And my roarings are poured out like the waters.

2:13 *sat down with him upon the ground.* See Ezek 3:15; possibly an expression of sympathy. *seven.* See Gen 50:10; 1 Sam 31:13; the number of completeness (see 1:2; see also note on Ruth 4:15). *none spake a word unto him.* A wiser response than their later speeches would prove to be (see 16:2–3).

‡3:1 *cursed his day.* Cursed the day of his birth, wishing he had never been born.

3:3 *Let the day perish wherein I was born.* Job's very existence, which has been a joy to him because of God's favor, is now his intolerable burden. He is as close as he will ever come to cursing God, but he does not do it.

3:4 *Let that day be darkness.* God had said in Gen 1:3, "Let there be light." Job, using similar language, would negate God's creative act.

‡3:8 *them . . . that curse the day.* Eastern soothsayers, like Balaam (see Num 22–24), who pronounced curses on people, objects and days. *raise up their mourning.* Lit. "raise up leviathan." Leviathan is the name of a sea monster from Canaanite mythology (see note on Is 27:1). Using vivid, figurative language, Job wishes that "them . . . that curse the day" would arouse leviathan to swallow the day-night of his birth.

3:11–12,16,20–23 A series of rhetorical questions, in which Job again states his wish that he had never been born or that he could die now and be out of his misery.

‡3:13–19 If Job had died at birth, he would then have lived only in the grave (or Sheol), which he envisions as a place of peace and rest (see note on Gen 37:35).

‡3:14–15 If dead, Job envisions that he would be in peaceful repose with the kings and rulers of the past. Cf. Is 14:9-20 for Sheol as the abode of dead kings. *built desolate places.* The tombs of the kings (cf. "houses" in v. 15). Kings often built elaborate tombs and monuments for themselves, and Job longs for their carefree existence in luxurious surroundings.

3:16 *untimely birth.* Since in fact his birth had taken place, the next possibility would have been a stillbirth. Such a situation would be much better than his present intolerable condition, in which he can find neither peace nor rest (v. 26).

3:18 *voice of the oppressor.* As in Egypt (see Ex 5:13–14).

3:21–22 Death has become desirable for Job.

3:23 *whom God hath hedged in.* God, who had put a hedge of protection around him (see 1:10 and note), has now, he feels, hemmed him in with turmoil (see v. 26).

25 For [1]the thing which I greatly feared is
come upon me,
And *that* which I was afraid of is come
unto me.
26 I was not in safety, neither had I rest,
neither was I quiet;
Yet trouble came.

The speech of Eliphaz

4 Then Eliphaz the Temanite answered
and said,
2 *If we* assay [1]to commune with thee,
wilt thou be grieved?
But [2]who can withhold himself from
speaking?
3 Behold, thou hast instructed many,
And thou [a]hast strengthened the weak
hands.
4 Thy words have upholden him that
was falling,
And thou [a]hast strengthened [b1]the
feeble knees.
5 But now it is come upon thee, and
thou faintest;
It toucheth thee, and thou art troubled.

6 *Is* not *this* [a]thy fear, [b]thy confidence,
Thy hope; and the uprightness of thy
ways?
7 Remember, I pray thee, [a]who *ever*
perished, being innocent?
Or where were the righteous cut off?
8 Even as I have seen, [a]they that plow
iniquity,
And sow wickedness, reap the same.
9 By the blast of God they perish,
And [1]by the breath of his nostrils are
they consumed.
10 The roaring of the lion, and the voice
of the fierce lion,

3:25 [1]Heb. *I feared a fear, and it came upon me*
4:2 [1]Heb. *a word* [2]Heb. *who can refrain from words?*
4:3 [a]Is. 35:3
4:4 [1]Heb. *the bowing knees* [a]Is. 35:3 [b]Heb. 12:12
4:6 [a]ch. 1:1 [b]Prov. 3:26
4:7 [a]Ps. 37:25
4:8 [a]Prov. 22:8
4:9 [1]That is, *by his anger:* as Is. 30:33

4:10 [a]Ps. 58:6
4:11 [a]Ps. 34:10
4:12 [1]Heb. *by stealth*
4:13 [a]ch. 33:15
4:14 [1]Heb. *met me* [2]Heb. *the multitude of my bones* [a]Hab. 3:16
4:16 [1]Or, *I heard a still voice*
4:18 [1]Or, *Nor in his angels,* in whom *he put light* [a]ch. 15:15
4:20 [1]Heb. *beaten in pieces* [a]Ps. 90:5,6

And [a]the teeth of the young lions, are
broken.
11 [a]The old lion perisheth for lack of prey,
And the stout lion's whelps are
scattered abroad.

12 Now a thing was [1]secretly brought to
me,
And mine ear received a little thereof.
13 [a]In thoughts from the visions of the
night,
When deep sleep falleth on men.
14 Fear [1]came upon me, and [a]trembling,
Which made [2]all my bones to shake.
15 Then a spirit passed before my face;
The hair of my flesh stood up:
16 It stood still, but I could not discern
the form thereof:
An image *was* before mine eyes,
[1]*There was* silence, and I heard a
voice, *saying,*

17 Shall mortal man be more just than
God?
Shall a man be more pure than his
Maker?
18 Behold, he [a]put no trust in his
servants;
[1]And his angels he charged with folly:
19 How much less *in* them that dwell in
houses of clay,
Whose foundation *is* in the dust,
Which are crushed before the moth?
20 [a]They are [1]destroyed from morning to
evening:
They perish for ever without *any*
regarding *it.*
21 Doth not their excellency *which is* in
them go away?
They die, even without wisdom.

4:1 *Eliphaz the Temanite.* See note on 2:11. Teman was an Edomite town noted for wisdom (see Jer 49:7). The speeches of Job's three friends contain elements of truth, but they must be carefully interpreted in context. The problem is not so much with what the friends knew but with what they did not know: God's high purpose in allowing Satan to buffet Job.
‡4:2 *assay to commune.* Dare to speak, after remaining silent for seven days and listening to Job's complaint. Eliphaz seems to be genuinely concerned with Job's well-being and offers a complimentary word (vv. 3–4). *grieved.* Or "impatient." See note on 9:2–3.
4:5 *toucheth thee.* See 1:11; 2:5; 19:21.
‡4:6–7 Eliphaz counsels Job to be confident that his piety will count with God, that though God is now chastening him for some sin, it is to a good end (see v. 17; 5:17), and he can be assured that God will not destroy him along with the wicked. Job's friends begin with an assumption of his innocence and only later change their perspective to say that Job is suffering because of personal sin.
‡4:6 *fear.* See note on 1:1. The word is used only by Eliphaz (see 15:4; 22:4). Job's piety is based on a conviction that God rewards the righteous and punishes the wicked (vv. 7-9). Job enters his ordeal with the same perspective as his friends.
4:7–9 If Job is truly innocent, he will not be destroyed.
4:8–11 Just as the strongest lions eventually die (vv. 10–11), so the wicked are eventually destroyed (vv. 8–9).
4:9 *blast of God . . . breath of his nostrils.* See Ex 15:7–8. God's judgment is fearfully severe.
4:12–21 Eliphaz tells of a hair-raising (see v. 15), mystical experience mediated through a dream (see v. 13), through which he claims to have received divine revelation and on which he bases his advice to Job.
4:13 *In . . . visions . . . When deep sleep falleth on men.* Eliphaz's words are echoed by Elihu in 33:15.
4:14 *all my bones to shake.* A sign of great distress (see Jer 23:9; Hab 3:16).
4:17–21 All mortals are sinful; therefore God has a right to punish them. Job should be thankful for the correction God is giving him (see 5:17).
4:18–19 If the angels, who are not made of dust, can be guilty in God's sight, how much more man (see 15:15–16)!
4:18 *servants.* Angels.
4:19 *houses of clay.* Bodies made of dust (see 10:9; 33:6; see also note on Gen 2:7). *moth.* A symbol of fragility (cf. 27:18).
‡4:20 *from morning to evening.* Alive in the morning, but dead by evening. A vivid picture of the shortness of life.
‡4:21 *Doth not their excellency . . . go away?* Lit. "Is not their tent cord pulled up?" A tent was a temporary home, like the human

5 Call now, if there be *any* that will
answer thee;
And to which of the saints wilt thou
[1]turn?
2 For wrath killeth the foolish man,
And [1]envy slayeth the silly one.
3 [a]I have seen the foolish taking root:
But suddenly I cursed his habitation.
4 His children are far from safety,
And they are crushed in the gate,
neither *is there* any to deliver *them.*
5 Whose harvest the hungry eateth up,
And taketh it *even* out of the thorns,
And the robber swalloweth up their
substance.

6 Although [1]affliction cometh not forth
of the dust,
Neither doth trouble spring out of the
ground;
7 Yet man is born unto [1]trouble,
As [2]the sparks fly upward.
8 I would seek unto God,
And unto God would I commit my
cause:
9 Which doeth great *things* [1]and
unsearchable;
Marvellous *things* [2]without number:
10 Who giveth rain upon the earth,
And sendeth waters upon the [1]fields:
11 [a]To set up on high those that be low;
That those which mourn may be
exalted *to* safety.

12 [a]He disappointeth the devices of the
crafty,
So that their hands [1]cannot perform
their enterprise.
13 He taketh the wise in their own
craftiness:
And the counsel of the froward is
carried headlong.

5:1 [1]Or, *look?*
5:2 [1]Or, *indignation*
5:3 [a]Jer. 12:2,3
5:6 [1]Or, *iniquity*
5:7 [1]Or, *labour* [2]Heb. *the sons of the burning coal lift up to fly*
5:9 [1]Heb. *and* there is *no search* [2]Heb. *till* there be *no number*
5:10 [1]Heb. *outplaces*
5:11 [a]Ps. 113:7
5:12 [1]Or, *cannot perform any thing* [a]Neh. 4:15

5:14 [1]Or, *run into*
5:15 [a]Ps. 35:10
5:16 [a]1 Sam. 2:8
5:17 [a]Ps. 94:12
5:18 [a]1 Sam. 2:6
5:19 [a]Ps. 34:19 [b]Ps. 91:10
5:20 [1]Heb. *from the hands* [a]Ps. 33:19
5:21 [1]Or, *when the tongue scourgeth* [a]Ps. 31:20
5:22 [a]Is. 11:9
5:23 [a]Ps. 91:12
5:24 [1]Or, *that peace is thy tabernacle* [2]Or, *err*

14 They [1]meet with darkness in the
daytime,
And grope in the noonday as in the
night.
15 But [a]he saveth the poor from the
sword,
From their mouth, and from the hand
of the mighty.
16 [a]So the poor hath hope,
And iniquity stoppeth her mouth.

17 [a]Behold, happy *is* the man whom God
correcteth:
Therefore despise not thou the
chastening of the Almighty:
18 [a]For he maketh sore, and bindeth up:
He woundeth, and his hands make
whole.
19 [a]He shall deliver thee in six troubles:
Yea, in seven [b]there shall no evil touch
thee.
20 [a]In famine he shall redeem thee from
death:
And in war [1]from the power of the
sword.
21 [a]Thou shalt be hid [1]from the scourge
of the tongue:
Neither shalt thou be afraid of
destruction when it cometh.

22 At destruction and famine thou shalt
laugh:
[a]Neither shalt thou be afraid of the
beasts of the earth.
23 [a]For thou shalt be in league with the
stones of the field:
And the beasts of the field shall be at
peace with thee.
24 And thou shalt know [1]that thy
tabernacle *shall be in* peace;
And thou shalt visit thy habitation, and
shalt not [2]sin.

body (see 2 Cor 5:1,4; 2 Pet 1:13). *without wisdom.* Needlessly and senselessly (see v. 20).
‡5:1 *to which . . . wilt thou turn?* To plead your case with God. The idea of a mediator, someone to arbitrate between God and Job, is an important motif in the book (see 9:33; 16:19–20; see also note on 19:25). *saints.* Or "holy ones," referring to holy angels, the "sons of God" in the prologue (see 1:6 and note; 2:1).
5:2 Without mentioning him, Eliphaz implies that Job is resentful against God and that harm will follow. *foolish man.* One who pays no attention to God. The Hebrew for "fool" or "foolish" denotes moral deficiency.
5:3 *the foolish taking root.* A wicked man prospering like a tree taking root (see Ps 1:3).
‡5:4–5 Different forms of calamity that God brings upon the wicked as punishment for their sins.
5:6 Unlike a weed, trouble must be sown and cultivated.
5:7 *man is born unto trouble.* See 14:1; proof that no one is righteous in the eyes of God (see 4:17–19). Job should stop behaving like a fool (see vv. 1–7) and should humble himself. Then God would bless, and injustice would shut its mouth (see v. 16). *sparks.* Lit. "sons of Resheph." In Canaanite mythology, Resheph was a god of plague and destruction. "(Sons of) Resheph" is used as a poetic image in the OT for fire (Sol 8:6), bolts of lightning (Ps 78:48) and pestilence (Deut 32:24; Hab 3:5).
5:9 Repeated in 9:10.
5:13 Quoted in part in 1 Cor 3:19 (the only clear quotation of Job in the NT).
5:17–26 While the preceding hymn (vv. 8–16) spoke of God's goodness and justice, this poem celebrates the blessedness of the man whom God disciplines (see Prov 1:2,7; 3:12; 23:13,23). Eliphaz believed that discipline is temporary and is followed by healing (v. 18), and that the good man will always be rescued. But with Job's wealth gone and his children dead, these words about security (v. 24) and children (v. 25) must have seemed cruel indeed to him.
5:17 *Almighty.* The first of 31 times that the Hebrew word *Shaddai* is used in Job (see note on Gen 17:1).
5:18–19 See Hos 6:1–2.
5:19 *six . . . seven.* See 33:29; 40:5; Prov 6:16; 30:15,18,21,29; Eccl 11:2; Amos 1:3,6,9,11,13; 2:1,4,6; Mic 5:5. Normally, such number patterns are not to be taken literally but are a poetic way of saying "many."
5:23 *in league with the stones.* A figurative way of saying that stones will "be at peace with you" and will not ruin the crops (see 2 Ki 3:19; Is 5:2; Mat 13:5).
‡5:24 *thy tabernacle.* Job's tent or household.

25 Thou shalt know also that [a]thy seed
shall be [1]great,
And thine offspring [b]as the grass of the
earth.
26 [a]Thou shalt come to *thy* grave in a full
age,
Like as a shock of corn [1]cometh in in
his season.
27 Lo this, we have [a]searched it, so it *is;*
Hear it, and know thou *it* [1]for thy
good.

Job's reply

6 But Job answered and said,
2 Oh that my grief were throughly
weighed,
And my calamity [1]laid in the balances
together!
3 For now it would be heavier than the
sand of the sea:
Therefore [1]my words are swallowed up.
4 [a]For the arrows of the Almighty *are*
within me,
The poison whereof drinketh up my
spirit:
[b]The terrors of God do set *themselves*
in array *against* me.
5 Doth the wild ass bray [1]when he hath
grass?
Or loweth the ox over his fodder?
6 Can that which is unsavoury be eaten
without salt?
Or is there *any* taste in the white of an
egg?
7 The things *that* my soul refused to
touch
Are as my sorrowful meat.
8 O that I might have my request;
And *that* God would grant *me* [1]the
thing that I long for!
9 Even *that* it would please God to
destroy me;
That he would let loose his hand, and
cut me off!
10 Then should I yet have comfort;
Yea, I would harden myself in sorrow;
let him not spare:
For [a]I have not concealed the words of
[b]the Holy One.
11 What *is* my strength, that I should
hope?
And what *is* mine end, that I should
prolong my life?
12 *Is* my strength the strength of stones?
Or *is* my flesh [1]of brass?
13 *Is* not my help in me?
And is wisdom driven *quite* from me?
14 [a][1]To him that is afflicted pity *should be*
shewed from his friend;
But he forsaketh the fear of the
Almighty.
15 [a]My brethren have dealt deceitfully as
a brook,
And [b]as the stream of brooks they pass
away;
16 Which are blackish by reason of the ice,
And wherein the snow is hid:
17 What time they wax warm, [1]they
vanish:
[2]When it is hot, they are [3]consumed
out of their place.
18 The paths of their way are turned aside;
They go to nothing, and perish.
19 The troops of [a]Tema looked,
The companies of [b]Sheba waited for
them.
20 They were [a]confounded because they
had hoped;
They came thither, and were ashamed.
21 [1]For now [a]ye are [2]nothing;
Ye see *my* casting down, and [b]are
afraid.
22 Did I say, Bring unto me?
Or, Give a reward for me of your
substance?

5:25 [1]Or, *much* [a]Ps. 112:2 [b]Ps. 72:16
5:26 [1]Heb. *ascendeth* [a]Prov. 10:27
5:27 [1]Heb. *for thyself* [a]Ps. 111:2
6:2 [1]Heb. *lifted up*
6:3 [1]That is, *I want words to express my grief*
6:4 [a]Ps. 38:2 [b]Ps. 88:15
6:5 [1]Heb. *at grass*
6:8 [1]Heb. *my expectation*
6:10 [a]Acts 20:20 [b]Lev. 19:2; Is. 57:15
6:12 [1]Heb. *brasen?*
6:14 [1]Heb. *To him that melteth* [a]Prov. 17:17
6:15 [a]Ps. 38:11 [b]Jer. 15:18
6:17 [1]Heb. *they are cut off* [2]Heb. *In the heat thereof* [3]Heb. *extinguished*
6:19 [a]Gen. 25:15 [b]Ps. 72:10
6:20 [a]Jer. 14:3
6:21 [1]Or, *For now ye are like to them.* Heb. *to it* [2]Heb. *not* [a]ch. 13:4 [b]Ps. 38:11

5:25 *as the grass.* As numerous as blades of grass (see note on Gen 13:16).
5:26 Eliphaz's prediction was more accurate than he realized (see 42:16–17).
5:27 *know thou it for thy good.* Eliphaz's conclusion: Job must turn from unrighteousness (4:7) and resentment against God (v. 2) to humility (v. 11) and the acceptance of God's righteous discipline (v. 17). Eliphaz's purpose is to offer theological comfort and counsel to Job (2:11), but instead he wounds him with false accusation.
6:2–3 Job appeals for a sympathetic understanding of the harsh words he spoke in ch. 3.
6:4 *arrows of the Almighty.* Job shares Eliphaz's "orthodox" theology and believes that God is aiming His arrows of judgment at him—though he does not know why (see 7:20; 16:12–13; see also Lam 3:12; cf. Deut 32:23; Ps 7:13; 38:2).
6:5–6 Job claims the right to bray and bellow, since he has been wounded by God and offered tasteless food (words) by his friends.
6:8–9 Job repeats the thoughts of ch. 3.
6:10 *Then.* Job has the joy of knowing that he has remained true to God.
6:11–13 With no human resources left, Job considers his condition hopeless.
6:11 *prolong my life.* See note on 9:2–3.
‡6:13 *Is not my help . . . wisdom driven quite from me?* Job questions whether he has the ability to withstand his trial now that the wisdom that made him successful in the past has escaped him.
‡6:14–18 See Gal 6:1. Job needs spiritual help, but his friends are proving to be undependable. In vv, 15-17, Job's friends are compared to overflowing brooks in the winter that dry up in the heat of summer when their refreshing waters are needed.
6:15 *brethren.* By calling his friends his "brethren," Job makes their callousness stand out more sharply.
6:19 *Tema.* See note on Is 21:14. *Sheba.* See note on 1:15.
6:22–23 Job has not asked them for anything except what will cost them nothing: their friendship and counsel.

23 Or, Deliver me from the enemy's hand?
Or, Redeem me from the hand of the mighty?
24 Teach me, and I will hold my tongue:
And cause me to understand wherein I have erred.
25 How forcible are right words!
But what doth your arguing reprove?
26 Do ye imagine to reprove words,
And the speeches of one that is desperate, *which are* as wind?
27 Yea, [1]ye overwhelm the fatherless,
And you [a]dig *a pit* for your friend.

28 Now therefore be content, look upon me;
For *it is* [1]evident unto you if I lie.
29 [a]Return, I pray you, let it not be iniquity;
Yea, return again, my righteousness *is* [1]in it.
30 Is there iniquity in my tongue?
Cannot [1]my taste discern perverse things?

7 *Is there* not [a][1]an appointed time to man upon earth?
Are not his days also like the days of a hireling?
2 As a servant [1]earnestly desireth the shadow,
And as a hireling looketh for the reward of his work:
3 So am I made to possess [a]months of vanity,
And wearisome nights are appointed to me.

4 [a]When I lie down, I say,
When shall I arise, and [1]the night be gone?
And I am full *of* tossings to and fro unto the dawning of the day.
5 My flesh is [a]clothed with worms and clods of dust;
My skin is broken, and become loathsome.
6 [a]My days are swifter than a weaver's shuttle,
And are spent without hope.

7 O remember that [a]my life *is* wind:
Mine eye [1]shall no more [2]see good.
8 [a]The eye of him that hath seen me shall see me no *more:*
Thine eyes *are* upon me, and [1]I *am* not.
9 *As* the cloud is consumed and vanisheth away:
So [a]he that goeth down *to* the grave shall come up no *more.*
10 He shall return no more to his house,
[a]Neither shall his place know him any more.
11 Therefore I will [a]not refrain my mouth;
I will speak in the anguish of my spirit;
I will [b]complain in the bitterness of my soul.

12 *Am* I a sea, or a whale,
That thou settest a watch over me?
13 [a]When I say, My bed shall comfort me,
My couch shall ease my complaint;
14 Then thou scarest me with dreams,
And terrifiest me through visions:
15 So that my soul chooseth strangling,
And death rather [1]than my life.
16 [a]I loathe *it;* I would not live alway:
[b]Let me alone; for [c]my days *are* vanity.

17 [a]What *is* man, that thou shouldest magnify him?

6:27 [1]Heb. *ye cause to fall upon* [a]Ps. 57:6
6:28 [1]Heb. *before your face*
6:29 [1]That is, *in this matter* [a]ch. 17:10
6:30 [1]Heb. *my palate*
7:1 [1]Or, *a warfare* [a]ch. 14:5
7:2 [1]Heb. *gapeth after*
7:3 [a]ch. 29:2
7:4 [1]Heb. *the evening be measured?* [a]Deut. 28:67
7:5 [a]Is. 14:11
7:6 [a]ch. 9:25
7:7 [1]Heb. *shall not return* [2]*to see,* that is, *to enjoy* [a]Ps. 78:39
7:8 [1]That is, *I can live no longer* [a]ch. 20:9
7:9 [a]2 Sam. 12:23
7:10 [a]ch. 8:18
7:11 [a]Ps. 39:1,9 [b]1 Sam. 1:10
7:13 [a]ch. 9:27
7:15 [1]Heb. *than my bones*
7:16 [a]ch. 10:1 [b]ch. 14:6 [c]Ps. 62:9
7:17 [a]Ps. 8:4

6:25 *right words.* Job is referring to his own words.
‡6:26 *speeches of one that is desperate . . . as wind.* They ignore Job's painful words and treat them as wind. Cf. 8:2 where Job refers to their counsel as "wind."
6:27 In addition to dishonesty, Job accuses his friends of heartless cruelty.
‡6:29 Job softens his tone, pleading that his friends take back their harsh words. *Return.* Or "Turn back" or "Stop." *let it not be iniquity.* Do not accuse me unjustly. *my righteousness is in it.* Job asserts that he is innocent of wrongdoing and will ultimately be vindicated.
7:1–21 Having replied to Eliphaz, Job now addresses his complaint toward God.
‡7:1 *an appointed time.* Of forced labor. See 14:14. The Hebrew for this expression sometimes implies military service (see KJV marg.). It is also used in reference to the Babylonian exile in Is 40:2 (see note there).
‡7:2 *shadow.* See KJV marg. End of the workday.
7:5 See note on 2:7.
7:7 *my life is wind.* As a chronic sufferer he has lost all sense of purpose in life (see v. 3; see also Ps 144:3–4). He does not anticipate healing and sees death as his only escape.
7:8 *Thine eyes are upon me, and I am not.* See v. 21.
‡7:9 *he that goeth down to the grave shall come up no more.* Such statements are based on common observation and are not meant to dogmatize about what happens after death. Mesopotamian descriptions of the netherworld refer to it similarly as the "land of no return" (see note on v. 21). For the OT perspective on life after death, see Ps 6:5 and note.
7:11 *not refrain my mouth.* Job is determined to cry out against the apparent injustice of God who, it seems, will not leave him alone (vv. 17–20). *speak in . . . anguish.* See Jer 4:19. *bitterness of my soul.* See 10:1; 21:25; 27:2.
‡7:12 *whale.* Or "sea monster." Like "leviathan," the Hebrew *tannin* is the name of a mythological sea serpent. In the Babylonian creation myth, the god Marduk must defeat the sea monster "Tiamat." This boisterous sea monster was a symbol of chaos (see Ps 74:13–14 and note; Is 27:1; 51:9), and Job objects to being treated like him.
7:13–14 He thinks that even the nightmares that disturb his much-needed sleep are from God.
‡7:16 *I loathe it.* See note on 9:21. *my days are vanity.* His life is but a vapor, without purpose or meaning. Cf. v. 7 and the perspective of the Preacher in Ecclesiastes that "all is vanity" (Eccl 1:2).
7:17 *What is man, that thou shouldest magnify him?* See Ps 144:3; cf. Ps 8:4–8, where the answer is given that man is created in God's image to have dominion over the world (see Gen 1:27–28). Job's words (vv. 18–21) are a parody on this theme—

And that thou shouldest set thine heart
upon him?
18 And *that* thou shouldest visit him
every morning,
And try him every moment?
19 How long wilt thou not depart from me,
Nor let me alone till I swallow down
my spittle?

20 I have sinned; what shall I do unto thee,
[a]O thou preserver of men?
Why [b]hast thou set me as a mark
against thee,
So that I am a burden to myself?
21 And why dost thou not pardon my
transgression,
And take away mine iniquity?
For now shall I sleep in the dust;
And thou shalt seek me in the
morning, but I *shall* not *be.*

The speech of Bildad

8 Then answered Bildad the Shuhite, and
said,

2 How long wilt thou speak these *things?*
And *how long shall* the words of thy
mouth *be like* a strong wind?
3 [a]Doth God pervert judgment?
Or doth the Almighty pervert justice?
4 If [a]thy children have sinned against
him,
And he have cast them away [1]for their
transgression;
5 [a]If thou wouldest seek unto God
betimes,
And make thy supplication to the
Almighty;
6 If thou *wert* pure and upright;
Surely now he would awake for thee,
And make the habitation of thy
righteousness prosperous.
7 Though thy beginning was small,
Yet thy latter end should greatly
increase.

8 [a]For inquire, I pray thee, of the former
age,
And prepare *thyself* to the search of
their fathers:
9 (For [a]we *are but of* yesterday, and
know [1]nothing,
Because our days upon earth *are* a
shadow:)
10 Shall not they teach thee, *and* tell thee,
And utter words out of their heart?

11 Can the rush grow up without mire?
Can the flag grow without water?
12 [a]Whilst it *is* yet in his greenness, *and*
not cut down,
It withereth before any *other* herb.
13 So *are* the paths of all that forget God;
And the [a]hypocrite's hope shall perish:
14 Whose hope shall be cut off,
And whose trust *shall be* [a][1]a spider's
web.
15 [a]He shall lean upon his house, but it
shall not stand:
He shall hold it fast, but it shall not
endure.
16 He *is* green before the sun,
And his branch shooteth forth in his
garden,
17 His roots are wrapped about the heap,
And seeth the place of stones.
18 [a]If he destroy him from his place,
Then *it* shall deny him, *saying,* I have
not seen thee.
19 Behold, this *is* the joy of his way,

7:20 [a]Ps. 36:6 [b]Ps. 21:12; Lam. 3:12
8:3 [a]Gen. 18:25
8:4 [1]Heb. *in the hand of their transgression* [a]ch. 1:5,18
8:5 [a]ch. 11:13
8:8 [a]Deut. 4:32
8:9 [1]Heb. *not* [a]Gen. 47:9; 1 Chr. 29:15; ch. 7:6
8:12 [a]Ps. 129:6; Jer. 17:6
8:13 [a]ch. 11:20; Prov. 10:28
8:14 [1]Heb. *a spider's house* [a]Is. 59:5,6
8:15 [a]ch. 27:18
8:18 [a]ch. 7:10; Ps. 37:36

as if God's only interest in man is to scrutinize him unmercifully and take quick offense at his slightest fault.

7:19 *till I swallow down my spittle.* Job's words suggest he is never free from God's gaze—not even long enough to "swallow."

‡7:20 *I have sinned; what shall I do unto thee . . . ?* I have not been perfect, but what terrible sin have I committed that deserves this kind of suffering? *preserver.* Or "watcher." The Hebrew for this word is used in a favorable sense in Deut 32:10 (God kept Israel), but here Job complains that God is too critical. *set me as a mark against thee.* Made a target out of me. See note on 6:4. *burden to myself.* Ancient Hebrew scribes report that a change in the text had been made from "you" to "myself" because the reading "you" involved too presumptuous a questioning of God's justice.

7:21 *transgression . . . iniquity.* Job confesses that he is a sinner, but he cannot understand why God refuses to forgive him. *sleep in the dust.* Of the netherworld, as in Mesopotamian descriptions of it (see note on v. 9).

8:2 *How long . . . ?* See 18:2. In contrast to the older Eliphaz, Bildad is impatient.

8:3 *Doth God pervert judgment . . . justice?* But Job has not yet blatantly accused God of injustice.

8:5–6 Bildad reasons as follows: God cannot be unjust, so Job and his family must be suffering as a result of sinfulness. Job should plead for mercy, and if he has been upright, God will restore him.

8:6 *If thou wert pure and upright.* We know God's verdict about Job (see 1:8; 2:3), but Bildad is confident that Job is a hypocrite (see v. 13).

‡8:7 Bildad asserts that God would make Job prosperous if he were truly righteous. See v. 21. He spoke more accurately than he realized (see 42:10–17).

‡8:8 *inquire . . . of the former age.* Eliphaz appealed to revelation from the spirit world (see 4:12–21), while Bildad appeals to the accumulated wisdom of tradition of previous generations.

8:9 *days upon earth are a shadow.* A common motif in wisdom literature (see 14:2; 1 Chr 29:15; Ps 102:11; 144:4; Eccl 6:12; 8:13).

8:11–19 A practical wisdom poem, giving words of instruction learned from the fathers. It is introduced in v. 10 and applied to Job in vv. 20–22.

‡8:11 *rush . . . flag.* The papyrus and the reed. Bildad uses these plants as an example of the fate of the wicked. They grow tall in a short time but wither just as quickly.

‡8:16–19 Bildad uses more plant imagery to show the temporary prosperity of the wicked. Vv. 16-17 picture the thriving of the plant; vv. 18-19, its demise.

‡8:18 *If he destroy him from his place.* The plant is uprooted.

‡8:19 *joy of his way . . . shall others grow.* Like the wicked, the

And [a]out of the earth shall others
grow.
20 Behold, God will not cast away a
perfect *man,*
Neither will he [1]help the evil doers:
21 Till he fill thy mouth *with* laughing,
And thy lips *with* [1]rejoicing.
22 They that hate thee shall be [a]clothed
with shame;
And the dwelling place of the wicked
[1]shall come to nought.

Job's reply

9 Then Job answered and said,
2 I know *it is* so of a truth:
But how should [a]man be just [1]with
God?
3 If he will contend with him,
He cannot answer him one of a
thousand.
4 [a]*He is* wise in heart, and mighty in
strength:
Who hath hardened *himself* against
him, and hath prospered?
5 Which removeth the mountains, and
they know not:
Which overturneth them in his anger.
6 Which [a]shaketh the earth out of her
place,
And [b]the pillars thereof tremble.
7 Which commandeth the sun, and it
riseth not;
And sealeth up the stars.
8 [a]Which alone spreadeth out the
heavens,
And treadeth upon the [1]waves of the
sea.
9 [a]Which maketh [1]Arcturus, Orion,
And Pleiades, and the chambers of the
south.
10 [a]Which doeth great *things* past finding
out;
Yea, and wonders without number.
11 [a]Lo, he goeth by me, and I see *him*
not:
He passeth on also, but I perceive him
not.
12 [a]Behold, he taketh away, [b1]who can
hinder him?
Who will say unto him, What dost
thou?
13 *If* God will not withdraw his anger,
[a]The [1]proud helpers do stoop under
him.
14 How much less shall I answer him,
And choose out my words *to reason*
with him?
15 [a]Whom, though I were righteous, *yet*
would I not answer,
But I would make supplication to my
judge.
16 If I had called, and he had answered
me;
Yet would I not believe that he had
hearkened unto my voice.
17 For he breaketh me with a tempest,
And multiplieth my wounds [a]without
cause.
18 He will not suffer me to take my breath,

8:19 [a]Ps. 113:7
8:20 [1]Heb. *take the ungodly by the hand*
8:21 [1]Heb. *shouting for joy*
8:22 [1]Heb. shall *not be* [a]Ps. 35:26; 109:29
9:2 [1]Or, *before God?* [a]Ps. 143:2; Rom. 3:20
9:4 [a]ch. 36:5
9:6 [a]Is. 2:19,21; Hag. 2:6; Heb. 12:26 [b]ch. 26:11
9:8 [1]Heb. *heights* [a]Gen. 1:6; Ps. 104:2,3
9:9 [1]Heb. *Ash, Cesil, and Cimah* [a]Gen. 1:16; Amos 5:8
9:10 [a]Ps. 71:15
9:11 [a]ch. 23:8,9
9:12 [1]Heb. *who can turn him away?* [a]Is. 45:9; Jer. 18:6; Rom. 9:20 [b]ch. 11:10
9:13 [1]Heb. *helpers of pride,* or, *strength* [a]ch. 26:12
9:15 [a]ch. 10:15
9:17 [a]ch. 2:3

plant only temporarily thrives before being forgotten and replaced by others.

8:20 Bildad is blunt about Job's being an evildoer, whereas Eliphaz had resorted to insinuation (see 4:7–9).

8:21 See note on v. 7.

9:2–3 Job does not believe that he is sinless, but he wishes to have his day in court so that he can prove he is innocent of the kind of sin that deserves the suffering he endures. In his despair he voices awful complaints against God (see vv. 16–20,22–24, 29–35; 10:1–7,13–17). Yet he does not abandon God; he does not curse Him (see 10:2,8–12), as Satan said he would (see 1:11; 2:5). Ch. 42 implies that Job persevered, but chs. 9–10 show that he did so with impatience (see 4:2; 6:11; 21:4).

9:3 *contend.* See v. 14. Job's speech is filled with the imagery of the courtroom: "answer him" (vv. 3,14,32), "righteous . . . supplication . . . judge" (v. 15), "plead" (v. 19), "prove me perverse" (v. 20), "judges" (v. 24), "judgment" (v. 32), "contendest with me" (10:2), "witnesses" (10:17). Job argues his innocence, but he feels that because God is so great there is no use in contending with Him (v. 14). Job's innocence does him no good (v. 15).

9:5–10 A beautiful hymn about God's greatness. But Job is not blessed by it, for he does not see that God's power is controlled by goodness and justice.

9:6 *pillars.* See 26:11. The metaphor of the earth resting on a foundation (see 38:6; 1 Sam 2:8; Ps 75:3; 104:5) is changed in 26:7 to a description of the earth suspended over nothing.

9:8 *spreadeth out the heavens.* Either (1) creates the heavens (see Is 44:24), or perhaps (2) causes the dawn to spread, like a man stretching out a tent (see Ps 104:2). *treadeth upon the waves.* Canaanite texts describe the goddess Asherah as walking on the sea (or sea-god) to subdue it. Similarly, God "treadeth upon the waves" to control the boisterous sea.

‡9:9 *Arcturus, Orion . . . Pleiades.* "Arcturus" = "the Bear." These three constellations are mentioned again in 38:31–32, and the last two are mentioned in Amos 5:8 (see note there). Despite their limited knowledge of astronomy, the ancient Israelites were awed by the fact that God had created the constellations.

9:10 The same words are spoken by Eliphaz in 5:9.

9:12 *who can hinder him?* Job argues that God has an unchallengeable, sovereign freedom that works to accomplish everything He pleases.

‡9:13 *proud helpers.* Lit. "helpers of Rahab." Rahab is not the prostitute Rahab of Josh 2 but another mythical sea monster (see 26:12), elsewhere used as symbolic of Egypt (see Is 30:7 and note). See 3:8; 7:12 and notes.

9:15 *judge.* God's fairness is unimpeachable (see Gen 18:25 and note).

‡9:16 *would I not believe . . . hearkened unto my voice.* Job believes in God's justice but is not hopeful of having the chance to present his case to God.

9:17 Job does not know that God has allowed Satan to crush him for a high purpose.

But filleth me *with* bitterness.
19 If *I speak* of strength, lo, *he is* strong:
And if of judgment, who shall set me a time *to plead?*
20 If I justify myself, mine own mouth shall condemn me:
If I say, I *am* perfect, it shall also prove me perverse.
21 *Though* I *were* perfect, *yet* would I not know my soul:
I would despise my life.
22 This *is* one *thing,* therefore I said *it,*
[a]He destroyeth the perfect and the wicked.
23 If the scourge slay suddenly,
He will laugh at the trial of the innocent.
24 The earth is given into the hand of the wicked:
He covereth the faces of the judges thereof;
If not, where, *and* who *is* he?

25 Now [a]my days are swifter than a post:
They flee away, they see no good.
26 They are passed away as the [1][2]swift ships:
[a]As the eagle *that* hasteth to the prey.
27 [a]If I say, I will forget my complaint,
I will leave off my heaviness, and comfort myself:
28 [a]I am afraid of all my sorrows,
I know that thou [b]wilt not hold me innocent.

29 *If* I be wicked,
Why then labour I in vain?
30 [a]If I wash myself with snow water,
And make my hands never so clean;
31 Yet shalt thou plunge me in the ditch,
And mine own clothes shall [1]abhor me.

9:22 [a]Eccl. 9:2,3; Ezek. 21:3
9:25 [a]ch. 7:6,7
9:26 [1]Heb. *ships of desire* [2]Or, *ships of Ebeh* [a]Hab. 1:8
9:27 [a]ch. 7:13
9:28 [a]Ps. 119:120 [b]Ex. 20:7
9:30 [a]Jer. 2:22
9:31 [1]Or, *make me to be abhorred*

9:32 [a]Eccl. 6:10; Is. 45:9; Rom. 9:20
9:33 [1]Heb. *one that should argue* [2]Or, *umpire* [a]1 Sam. 2:25
9:34 [a]ch. 13:20; Ps. 39:10
9:35 [1]Heb. *But I* am *not so with myself*
10:1 [1]Or, *cut off while I live* [a]1 Ki. 19:4; Jonah 4:3 [b]ch. 7:11
10:3 [1]Heb. *the labour of thine hands*
10:4 [a]1 Sam. 16:7
10:7 [1]Heb. It is *upon thy knowledge*
10:8 [1]Heb. *took pains about me* [a]Ps. 119:73

32 For [a]*he is* not a man, as I *am, that* I should answer him,
And we should come together in judgment.
33 [a]Neither is there [1]*any* [2]daysman betwixt us,
That might lay his hand upon us both.
34 [a]Let him take his rod away from me,
And let not his fear terrify me:
35 *Then* would I speak, and not fear him;
[1]But *it is* not so with me.

10 My [a]soul is [1]weary of my life;
I will leave my complaint upon myself;
[b]I will speak in the bitterness of my soul.
2 I will say unto God, Do not condemn me;
Shew me wherefore thou contendest with me.
3 *Is it* good unto thee that thou shouldest oppress,
That thou shouldest despise [1]the work of thine hands,
And shine upon the counsel of the wicked?
4 Hast thou eyes of flesh?
Or [a]seest thou as man seeth?
5 *Are* thy days as the days of man?
Are thy years as man's days,
6 That thou inquirest after mine iniquity,
And searchest after my sin?
7 [1]Thou knowest that I am not wicked;
And *there is* none that can deliver out of thine hand.

8 [a]Thine hands [1]have made me and fashioned me
Together round about; yet thou dost destroy me.

9:20 *mouth shall condemn me.* See 15:6.

‡9:21 *would I not know my soul . . . despise my life.* Even if Job is right, he is to the point where he does not care about his own soul. See 7:16; words of despairing resignation that would be partially echoed in Job's final outpouring of repentance (see 42:6).

9:22–24 God has become Job's great enigma. Job describes a phantom God—one who does not exist, except in Job's mind. The God of the Bible is not morally indifferent (cf. God's words in 38:2; 40:2 and Job's response in 42:3).

‡9:24 *covereth the faces of the judges.* Statues of Lady Justice are blindfolded, implying that she will judge partially. But Job's accusation against God is that He has blindfolded the judges so that they see neither crimes nor innocence. *If not, where, and who is he?* If God is not ultimately responsible for the injustices in the world, then who is?

‡9:26 *swift ships.* Or "reed boats." See note on Ex 2:3.

9:28 *thou wilt not hold me innocent.* Job wants to stand before God as an innocent man—not sinless, but innocent of any sin commensurate with his suffering.

9:29 *be wicked.* As appears from the bitter suffering he is enduring.

‡9:30 *snow water.* Or "soap." A vegetable alkali used as a cleansing agent. The Hebrew underlying this word is translated "sope" (soap) in Jer 2:22; Mal 3:2.

‡9:33 *daysman betwixt us.* Or "an umpire/mediator between us." See note on 5:1. God is so immense that Job feels he needs someone who can help him, someone who can argue his case in court. Job's call is not directly predicting the mediatorship of Christ, for Job is not looking for one to forgive him but for one who can testify to his innocence (see 16:20–21; 19:25–26).

9:34 See 13:21. *his rod.* Symbolic of divine judgment and wrath (see, e.g., Ps 89:32; Lam 3:1).

10:1 *weary of my life.* See note on 9:21. *bitterness of my soul.* Because Job is so bitter, his mind has conjured up a false picture of God.

10:3 Job imagines that God is angry with him, an innocent man (see 9:28 and note), and that He takes delight in the wicked. Such words are a reminder that the sickroom is not the place to argue theology; in times of severe suffering, people may say things that require a response of love and understanding. Job himself will eventually repent, and God will forgive (42:1–6).

10:4 *eyes of flesh.* Imperfect vision, like that of a man.

10:8–17 Job continues to question God as if He were his adversary in court. He wants to know how God, who so wonderfully formed him in the womb, could all the while have planned (see v. 13) to punish him—even though he may be innocent.

10:8–11 A poetic description of God making a baby in the womb (see Ps 139:13–16).

9 Remember, I beseech thee, that [a]thou hast made me as the clay;
And wilt thou bring me into dust again?
10 [a]Hast thou not poured me out as milk,
And cruddled me like cheese?
11 Thou hast clothed me with skin and flesh,
And hast [1]fenced me with bones and sinews.
12 Thou hast granted me life and favour,
And thy visitation hath preserved my spirit.

13 And these *things* hast thou hid in thine heart:
I know that this *is* with thee.
14 If I sin, then [a]thou markest me,
And thou wilt not acquit me from mine iniquity.
15 If I be wicked, [a]woe unto me;
[b]And *if* I be righteous, *yet* will I not lift up my head.
I am full of confusion; therefore [c]see thou mine affliction;
16 For it increaseth. [a]Thou huntest me as a fierce lion:
And again thou shewest thyself marvellous upon me.
17 Thou renewest [a] [1]thy witnesses against me,
And increasest thine indignation upon me;
Changes and war *are* against me.

18 [a]Wherefore then hast thou brought me forth out of the womb?
Oh that I had given up the ghost, and no eye had seen me!
19 I should have been as though I had not been;
I should have been carried from the womb to the grave.
20 [a]*Are* not my days few? cease then,
And [b]let me alone, that I may take comfort a little,
21 Before I go whence I shall not return,
[a]*Even* to the land of darkness [b]and the shadow of death;
22 A land of darkness, as darkness itself;
And of the shadow of death, without any order,
And *where* the light is as darkness.

10:9 [a]Gen. 2:7; Is. 64:8
10:10 [a]Ps. 139:14-16
10:11 [1]Heb. *hedged*
10:14 [a]Ps. 139:1
10:15 [a]Is. 3:11 [b]ch. 9:12,15 [c]Ps. 25:18
10:16 [a]Is. 38:13; Lam. 3:10
10:17 [1]That is, *thy plagues* [a]Ruth 1:21
10:18 [a]ch. 3:11
10:20 [a]Ps. 39:5 [b]ch. 7:16,19
10:21 [a]Ps. 88:12 [b]Ps. 23:4

The speech of Zophar

11 Then answered Zophar the Naamathite, and said,

2 Should not the multitude of words be answered?
And should [1]a man full of talk be justified?
3 Should thy [1]lies make men hold their peace?
And when thou mockest, shall no man make *thee* ashamed?
4 For [a]thou hast said, My doctrine *is* pure,
And I am clean in thine eyes.
5 But O that God would speak,
And open his lips against thee;
6 And that he would shew thee the secrets of wisdom,
That *they are* double to that which is.
Know therefore that [a]God exacteth of thee *less* than thine iniquity *deserveth.*

7 [a]Canst thou *by* searching find out God?
Canst thou find out the Almighty unto perfection?
8 *It is* [1]as high as heaven; what canst thou do?
Deeper than hell; what canst thou know?

11:2 [1]Heb. *a man of lips*
11:3 [1]Or, *devices*
11:4 [a]ch. 6:30
11:6 [a]Ezra 9:13
11:7 [a]Eccl. 3:11
11:8 [1]Heb. *the heights of heaven*

10:8 See Ps 119:73.
10:9 *made me as the clay.* See note on 4:19. *bring me into dust.* See note on Gen 3:19.
‡10:10 Job compares his development in the womb to the process of curdling milk into cheese.
‡10:13 *these things . . . thou hid in thine heart.* Job charges that God has secretly planned his affliction from the very beginning.
10:15–16 Job says that whether he is guilty or innocent, the all-powerful God will not treat him justly.
‡10:16 *shewest thyself marvellous upon me.* God has unleashed his awesome power to destroy Job.
10:17 *witnesses against me.* See note on 9:3.
10:18–22 See notes on ch. 3.
10:21 *shall not return.* See note on 7:9. *land of darkness and the shadow of death.* See 38:17. Ancient Mesopotamian documents refer to the netherworld as the "house of darkness."
11:1–20 Like Eliphaz (see 4:7–11) and Bildad (see 8:3–6), Zophar claims that Job's sins have caused his troubles.
11:2–3 Zophar's failure to put himself in Job's place before condemning him shows a lack of compassion. Nor is Zophar entirely correct in his condemnation: Job has sincerely challenged what he perceives to be God's unjust actions (see 9:14–24), but he has not mocked God (as Zophar accuses him of having done).
‡11:4 *I am clean.* In 10:7,15 Job had disclaimed being guilty, and in 9:21 he said he was "perfect" (a spiritually upright person), the word God used to describe him in 1:8; 2:3. Zophar, however, implies that Job was claiming absolute purity (sinless perfection), but Job nowhere uses such terms of himself.
11:5 Zophar thought God should speak against Job, but eventually God spoke against Zophar himself (see 42:7).
‡11:6 *secrets of wisdom . . . they are double.* Wisdom has two sides and is difficult to fully grasp. OT wisdom literature (especially Proverbs) makes abundant use of the term *mashal* ("proverb," "riddle," "parable"), which often had a hidden as well as an obvious meaning. Zophar thinks Job is shallow and lacks an understanding of the true nature of God (see vv. 7–9).
11:7 Unwittingly, Zophar anticipates the Lord's discourses in 38:1–42:6.
11:8–9 In the same way that Zophar speaks of the height, depth, length and width of God's knowledge, Paul speaks of Christ's love (see Eph 3:18).
11:8 *what canst thou do?* Can you climb into the heavens and explore God's knowledge?

9 The measure thereof *is* longer than the earth,
And broader than the sea.
10 [a]If he [1]cut off, and shut up, or gather together,
Then [2]who can hinder him?
11 For [a]he knoweth vain men:
He seeth wickedness also; will he not then consider *it?*
12 For [a][1]vain man would be wise,
Though man be born *like* a wild ass's colt.

13 If thou [a]prepare thine heart,
And [b]stretch out thine hands toward him;
14 If iniquity *be* in thine hand, put it far away,
And [a]let not wickedness dwell in thy tabernacles.
15 [a]For then shalt thou lift up thy face without spot;
Yea, thou shalt be steadfast, and shalt not fear.

16 Because thou shalt [a]forget *thy* misery,
And remember *it* as waters *that* pass away:
17 And *thine* age [a][1]shall be clearer than the noonday;
Thou shalt shine forth, thou shalt be as the morning.
18 And thou shalt be secure, because there is hope;
Yea, thou shalt dig *about thee, and* [a]thou shalt take thy rest in safety.
19 Also thou shalt lie down, and none shall make *thee* afraid;
Yea, many shall [1]make suit unto thee.
20 But [a]the eyes of the wicked shall fail,
And [1]they shall not escape,
And [b]their hope *shall be as* [2]the giving up of the ghost.

11:10 [1]Or, *make a change* [2]Heb. *who can turn him away?* [a]ch. 9:12; Rev. 3:7
11:11 [a]Ps. 10:14
11:12 [1]Heb. *empty* [a]Rom. 1:22
11:13 [a]1 Sam. 7:3 [b]Ps. 88:9
11:14 [a]Ps. 101:3
11:15 [a]ch. 22:26; Ps. 119:6; 1 John 3:21
11:16 [a]Is. 65:16
11:17 [1]Heb. *shall arise above the noonday* [a]Ps. 37:6; Prov. 4:18; Is. 58:8,10
11:18 [a]Lev. 26:5,6; Ps. 3:5; Prov. 3:24
11:19 [1]Heb. *intreat thy face*
11:20 [1]Heb. *flight shall perish from them* [a]Lev. 26:16; Deut. 28:65
11:20 [2]Or, *a puff of breath* [b]ch. 18:14; Prov. 11:7
12:3 [1]Heb. *a heart* [2]Heb. *I fall not lower than you* [3]Heb. *with whom are not such as these?*
12:4 [a]ch. 21:3 [b]Ps. 91:15
12:5 [a]Prov. 14:2
12:6 [a]Jer. 12:1; Mal. 3:15
12:10 [1]Or, *life* [2]Heb. *all flesh of man*

Job's reply

12 And Job answered and said,
2 No doubt but ye *are* the people,
And wisdom shall die with you.
3 But I have [1]understanding as well as you;
[2]I *am* not inferior to you:
Yea, [3]who knoweth not such *things* as these?

4 [a]I am *as* one mocked of his neighbour,
Who [b]calleth upon God, and he answereth him:
The just upright *man is* laughed to scorn.
5 [a]He that is ready to slip with *his* feet
Is as a lamp despised in the thought of him that is at ease.
6 [a]The tabernacles of robbers prosper,
And they that provoke God are secure;
Into whose hand God bringeth *abundantly.*

7 But ask now the beasts, and they shall teach thee;
And the fowls of the air, and they shall tell thee:
8 Or speak to the earth, and it shall teach thee:
And the fishes of the sea shall declare unto thee.
9 Who knoweth not in all these
That the hand of the LORD hath wrought this?
10 In whose hand *is* the [1]soul of every living *thing,*
And the breath of [2]all mankind.

‡11:11–12 *he knoweth vain men . . . He seeth wickedness.* Job may have fooled others, but God knows what he is like. *vain man would be wise . . . man be born like a wild ass's colt.* It would take a miracle on par with a donkey giving birth to a man for Job to become wise.
‡11:13–20 Zophar assumes that Job's problems are rooted in his sin; all Job has to do is to repent, and then his life will become blessed and happy. But God nowhere guarantees a life "clearer than the noonday" (v. 17) simply because we are His children. He has higher purposes for us than our physical prosperity, or people courting our favor (v. 19). Zophar's philosophy is in conflict with Ps 73.
11:13 *stretch out thine hands toward him.* For help (see Prov 1:24; Lam 1:17).
‡11:15 *lift up thy face without spot.* God will remove Job's shameful expression. Zophar echoes Job's thought in 10:15.
‡11:18 *thou shalt dig about thee.* The Hebrew verb "to dig" can also mean "to search" (cf. "seeketh" in 39:29). Job will "search about" and dwell securely in God's blessing and protection.
‡11:19 *many shall make suit unto thee.* Lit. "many will make soft your face" (to petition or entreat a superior). Cf. Prov 19:6 where the phrase is translated as "intreat the favour of."
11:20 Bildad ended his speech in a similar way (see 8:22).
‡12:1–14:22 As before, Job's reply is divided into two parts: He speaks to his three friends (12:2–13:19), then to God (13:20–14:22). Job responds to the attacks of his friends with a speech that is much longer than either of his first two.
12:2 For the first time, Job reacts with sarcasm to the harshness of his counselors (see v. 20).
12:3 *who knoweth not . . . ?* See v. 9. The advice of Job's friends is trivial and commonplace.
‡12:4 *I am as one mocked . . . he answereth him.* Contrasts Job's present condition with his status in the days before his suffering began and God responded to his requests (contrast 9:16).
12:5 The prosperous despise those who, like Job, have trouble.
12:6 Such statements conerning the prosperity of the wicked (see 9:21–24) irked the counselors and made them brand Job as a man whose feet were slipping (see v. 5).
12:7–12 Job appeals to all creation to prove that God does what He pleases—that He does not use a person's piety as the sole basis for granting freedom from affliction.
‡12:7 *they shall teach thee.* Even dumb animals are smart enough to know that the righteous suffer and the evil are secure.
12:9 *LORD.* The only place in Job's and his friends' speeches (chs. 3–37) where the divine name "LORD" (Hebrew *Yahweh*) is used (see Introduction: Author).

11 Doth not the ear try words?
And the [a] [1] mouth taste his meat?
12 With the ancient *is* wisdom;
And *in* length of days understanding.
13 [1] With him *is* wisdom and strength,
He hath counsel and understanding.

14 Behold, he breaketh down, and it cannot be built *again:*
He shutteth [1] up a man, and there can be no opening.
15 Behold, he [a] withholdeth the waters, and they dry up:
Also he [b] sendeth them out, and they overturn the earth.
16 With him *is* strength and wisdom:
The deceived and the deceiver *are* his.

17 He leadeth counsellers away spoiled,
And maketh the judges fools.
18 He looseth the bond of kings,
And girdeth their loins with a girdle.
19 He leadeth princes away spoiled,
And overthroweth the mighty.
20 [a] He removeth away [1] the speech of the trusty,
And taketh *away* the understanding of the aged.
21 [a] He poureth contempt upon princes,
And [1] weakeneth the strength of the mighty.

22 He discovereth deep *things* out of darkness,
And bringeth out to light the shadow of death.
23 [a] He increaseth the nations, and destroyeth them:
He enlargeth the nations, and [1] straiteneth them *again.*

12:11 [1] Heb. *palate* [a] ch. 6:30
12:13 [1] That is, *With God*
12:14 [1] Heb. *upon*
12:15 [a] 1 Ki. 8:35 [b] Gen. 7:11
12:20 [1] Heb. *the lip of the faithful* [a] ch. 32:9
12:21 [1] Or, *looseth the girdle of the strong* [a] Ps. 107:40; Dan. 2:21
12:23 [1] Heb. *leadeth in* [a] Ps. 107:38; Is. 9:3
12:24 [a] Ps. 107:4
12:25 [1] Heb. *wander* [a] ch. 5:14 [b] Ps. 107:27
13:2 [a] ch. 12:3
13:3 [a] ch. 23:3
13:4 [a] ch. 6:21
13:5 [a] Prov. 17:28
13:7 [a] ch. 36:4

24 He taketh away the heart of the chief of the people of the earth,
And [a] causeth them to wander in a wilderness *where there is* no way.
25 [a] They grope *in* the dark without light,
And he maketh them to [b] [1] stagger like a drunken *man.*

13 Lo, mine eye hath seen all *this,*
Mine ear hath heard and understood it.
2 [a] What ye know, *the same* do I know also.
I *am* not inferior unto you.

3 [a] Surely I would speak to the Almighty,
And I desire to reason with God.
4 But ye *are* forgers of lies,
[a] Ye *are* all physicians of no value.
5 O that you would altogether hold your peace,
And [a] it should be your wisdom.
6 Hear now my reasoning,
And hearken to the pleadings of my lips.

7 [a] Will you speak wickedly for God?
And talk deceitfully for him?
8 Will ye accept his person?
Will ye contend for God?
9 *Is it* good that he should search you out?
Or as *one* man mocketh another, do ye *so* mock him?
10 He will surely reprove you,
If ye do secretly accept persons.
11 Shall not his excellency make you afraid?
And his dread fall upon you?

12 Your remembrances *are* like unto ashes,
Your bodies to bodies of clay.

‡12:11–12 Job sarcastically chides his counselors for being elders and yet lacking in true wisdom. *ear . . . mouth.* The ear hears and discerns truth by listening in the same way that the mouth tastes food, but Job's friends, who are so eager to speak, have not listened enough to learn anything. Job's words in v. 11 are echoed by Elihu in 34:3. *With the ancient is wisdom . . . understanding.* Job's friends are lacking the wisdom they should have in their advanced years.
12:13–25 The theme of this section is stated in v. 13: God is sovereign in the created world, and especially in history. The rest of the poem dwells on the negative aspects of God's power and wisdom—e.g., the destructive forces of nature (vv. 14–15), how judges become fools (v. 17), how priests become humiliated (v. 19), how trusted advisers are silenced and elders deprived of good sense (v. 20). Contrast the claim of Eliphaz that God always uses His power in ways that make sense (5:10–16).
12:20 See note on v. 2.
12:21a,24b The Hebrew text of these lines is repeated verbatim in Ps 107:40.
‡12:22 *shadow of death.* Or "deep darkness." Like "darkness" in the first half of the verse, the phrase refers to the deepest recesses of the human soul. God knows and exposes the secret, evil plans devised by sinful humans.
‡12:24 *taketh away the heart . . . causeth them to wander.* God deprives even the powerful of their reason and renders them void of understanding. *wilderness.* This Hebrew word is translated "without form" in Gen 1:2.
12:25 *grope in the dark.* Job concludes this section with a parody of Eliphaz's confident assertion in 5:14.
13:1–12 Job feels that his counselors have become completely untrustworthy (see v. 12). He calls them quacks (see v. 4; see also 16:2) and accuses them of showing partiality to God (since God is stronger than Job) by telling lies about Job (see vv. 7–8). Someday God will examine and punish them for their deception (see vv. 9–11).
13:1 *all this.* God's sovereign actions as described in ch. 12.
13:2 See 15:9. *I am not inferior unto you.* Repeated from 12:3.
13:5 See v. 13. The friends' silent presence had ministered to Job earlier (see 2:13), but Job's current retort is intended as sarcasm (cf. Prov 17:28).
‡13:8 *accept his person.* Show favoritism, take God's side. Job is having enough trouble contending with God without his friends opposing him as well.
‡13:9 *Is it good . . . search you out?* How would you fare if God were to examine your life the way he has examined mine?
13:12 *remembrances.* Arguments in their defense of God's judgment.

13 [1]Hold your peace, let me alone, that I
may speak,
And let come on me what *will.*
14 Wherefore [a]do I take my flesh in my
teeth,
And put my life in mine hand?
15 [a]Though he slay me, *yet* will I trust in
him:
[b]But I will [1]maintain mine own ways
before him.
16 He also *shall be* my salvation:
For a hypocrite shall not come before
him.

17 Hear diligently my speech,
And my declaration with your ears.
18 Behold now, I have ordered *my* cause;
I know that I shall be justified.
19 [a]Who *is* he *that* will plead with me?
For now, if I hold my tongue, I shall
give up the ghost.

20 [a]Only do not two *things* unto me:
Then will I not hide myself from thee.
21 [a]Withdraw thine hand far from me:
And let not thy dread make me afraid.
22 Then call thou, and I will answer:
Or let me speak, and answer thou me.

23 How many *are* mine iniquities and sins?
Make me to know my transgression
and my sin.
24 [a]Wherefore hidest thou thy face,
And [b]holdest me for thine enemy?
25 [a]Wilt thou break a leaf driven to and
fro?
And wilt thou pursue the dry stubble?

26 For thou writest bitter *things* against me,
And [a]makest me to possess the
iniquities of my youth.

13:13 [1] Heb. *Be silent from me*
13:14 [a] ch. 18:4
13:15 [1] Heb. *prove,* or, *argue* [a] Ps. 23:4; Prov. 14:32 [b] ch. 27:5
13:19 [a] Is. 50:8
13:20 [a] ch. 9:34
13:21 [a] Ps. 39:10
13:24 [a] Deut. 32:20; Is. 8:17 [b] Deut. 32:42; ch. 16:9; Lam. 2:5
13:25 [a] Is. 42:3
13:26 [a] ch. 20:11; Ps. 25:7

13:27 [1] Heb. *observest* [2] Heb. *roots* [a] ch. 33:11
14:1 [1] Heb. *short of days* [a] Eccl. 2:23
14:2 [a] ch. 8:9; Ps. 90:5,6
14:3 [a] Ps. 144:3 [b] Ps. 143:2
14:4 [1] Heb. *Who will give* [a] Ps. 51:2,5,10; John 3:6; Rom. 5:12; Eph. 2:3
14:5 [a] ch. 7:1
14:6 [1] Heb. *cease* [a] ch. 7:16,19; Ps. 39:13 [b] ch. 7:1

27 [a]Thou puttest my feet also in the stocks,
And [1]lookest narrowly unto all my
paths;
Thou settest a print upon the [2]heels of
my feet.
28 And he, as a rotten thing, consumeth,
As a garment that is moth-eaten.

14 Man *that is* born of a woman
Is [1]of few days, and [a]full of trouble.
2 [a]He cometh forth like a flower, and is
cut down:
He fleeth also as a shadow, and
continueth not.
3 And [a]dost thou open thine eyes upon
such a one,
And [b]bringest me into judgment with
thee?

4 [1]Who [a]can bring a clean *thing* out of
an unclean?
Not one.
5 [a]Seeing his days *are* determined,
The number of his months *are* with
thee,
Thou hast appointed his bounds that
he cannot pass;
6 [a]Turn from him, that he may [1]rest,
Till he shall accomplish, [b]as a hireling,
his day.

7 For there is hope of a tree,
If it be cut down, that it will sprout
again,
And that the tender branch thereof will
not cease.
8 Though the root thereof wax old in the
earth,
And the stock thereof die in the ground;
9 *Yet* through the sent of water it will bud,
And bring forth boughs like a plant.

13:15 No matter what happens, Job intends to seek vindication from God and believes that he will receive it (see v. 18).
13:16 *be my salvation.* See Phil 1:19 (perhaps Paul was reflecting on Job's experience).
13:17 Job asks his friends to listen to what he is going to say to God in 13:20–14:22.
‡13:19 Job states that he will be silent and die if anyone can contend with him and prove that he is guilty of wrongdoing.
13:20 *two things.* Job wants God (1) to withdraw His hand of punishment (v. 21), and (2) to start communicating with him (v. 22).
13:21 See 9:34.
13:23 Job's words are based on the counselors' point that suffering always implies sinfulness. He does not yet understand that God has a higher purpose in his suffering. *iniquities . . . sins . . . transgression.* The three most important Hebrew terms for sin lie behind these translations (see Ex 34:7; Is 59:12 and note).
13:24 *hidest thou thy face.* Withhold Your blessing (see note on Ps 13:1).
13:25 *leaf driven . . . dry stubble.* See note on Ps 1:4.
13:26 *writest . . . things against me.* See Ps 130:3; Hos 13:12; contrast 1 Cor 13:5. *iniquities of my youth.* Since Job feels that he is not presently guilty of a sinful life, God must still be holding the sins of his youth against him.
‡13:27 *lookest narrowly . . . my paths.* You watch my every move as if I am a prisoner trying to escape. Elihu later quotes Job's words (see 33:11). *settest a print . . . feet.* The Babylonian Code of Hammurapi (18th century B.C.) attests to the practice of putting marks on slaves. Job feels that he is being harassed by a God who has taken him captive and is tormenting him (see v. 25).
13:28–14:1 The introduction to ch. 14, expressing the pessimistic theme that man's legacy is trouble and his destiny is death.
13:28 *garment that is moth-eaten.* See Mat 6:19–20; Luke 12:33.
14:1 See 5:7.
14:2–6 A symmetrical poem centered around v. 4; v. 2 corresponds to v. 5, and v. 3 to v. 6. Job expostulates with God: Given man's insignificance and inherited impurity, why do You take him so seriously (see 13:25)?
14:2 *He . . . cut down.* Life at best is brief and fragile (see 8:9; Ps 37:2; Is 40:7,24). *as a shadow.* See note on 8:9.
14:7–12 Man is like a flower that lives its short life and is gone (v. 2), not like a tree that revives even after it has been cut down.
14:7 *sprout.* The Hebrew root underlying this word is translated "change" in v. 14.
‡14:9 *sent.* Or "scent." The tree only needs a sniff of water to revive itself.

10 But man dieth, and [1]wasteth away:
Yea, man giveth up the ghost, and where *is* he?
11 *As* the waters fail from the sea,
And the flood decayeth and drieth up:
12 So man lieth down, and riseth not:
[a]Till the heavens *be* no more, they shall not awake,
Nor be raised out of their sleep.

13 O that thou wouldest hide me in the grave,
That thou wouldest keep me secret, until thy wrath be past,
That thou wouldest appoint me a set time, and remember me.
14 If a man die, shall he live *again?*
All the days of my appointed time [a]will I wait,
Till my change come.
15 [a]Thou shalt call, and I will answer thee:
Thou wilt have a desire to the work of thine hands.
16 [a]For now thou numberest my steps:
Dost thou not watch over my sin?

17 [a]My transgression *is* sealed up in a bag,
And thou sewest up mine iniquity.
18 And surely the mountain falling [1]cometh to nought,
And the rock is removed out of his place.
19 The waters wear the stones:
Thou [1]washest away the things which grow out of the dust of the earth;
And thou destroyest the hope of man.

20 Thou prevailest for ever against him, and he passeth:
Thou changest his countenance, and sendest him away.
21 His sons come to honour, and [a]he knoweth *it* not;
And they are brought low, but he perceiveth *it* not of them.
22 But his flesh upon him shall have pain,
And his soul within him shall mourn.

14:10 [1]Heb. *is weakened,* or, *cut off*
14:12 [a]Is. 51:6; Acts 3:21; Rom. 8:20; 2 Pet. 3:7; Rev. 20:11; 21:1
14:14 [a]ch. 13:15
14:15 [a]ch. 13:22
14:16 [a]ch. 10:6,14; Prov. 5:21; Jer. 32:19
14:17 [a]Deut. 32:34; Hos. 13:12
14:18 [1]Heb. *fadeth*
14:19 [1]Heb. *overflowest*
14:21 [a]Eccl. 9:5; Is. 63:16

Eliphaz responds

15 Then answered Eliphaz the Temanite, and said,

2 Should a wise *man* utter [1]vain knowledge,
And fill his belly *with* the east wind?
3 Should he reason *with* unprofitable talk?
Or *with* speeches wherewith he can do no good?
4 Yea, [1]thou castest off fear,
And restrainest [2]prayer before God.
5 For thy mouth [1]uttereth thine iniquity,
And thou choosest the tongue of the crafty.
6 [a]Thine own mouth condemneth thee, and not I;
Yea, thine own lips testify against thee.

7 *Art* thou the first man *that* was born?
[a]Or wast thou made before the hills?
8 [a]Hast thou heard the secret of God?
And dost thou restrain wisdom to thyself?
9 [a]What knowest thou, that we know not?
What understandest thou, which *is* not in us?
10 [a]With us *are* both the grayheaded and very aged men,
Much elder than thy father.
11 *Are* the consolations of God small with thee?
Is there *any* secret thing with thee?
12 Why doth thine heart carry thee away?
And what do thine eyes wink at,
13 That thou turnest thy spirit against God,
And lettest *such* words go out of thy mouth?

15:2 [1]Heb. *knowledge of wind*
15:4 [1]Heb. *thou makest void* [2]Or, *speech*
15:5 [1]Heb. *teacheth*
15:6 [a]Luke 19:22
15:7 [a]Ps. 90:2; Prov. 8:25
15:8 [a]Rom. 11:34; 1 Cor. 2:11
15:9 [a]ch. 13:2
15:10 [a]ch. 32:6,7

14:13–17 Job's spirit now appears to rise above the despair engendered by his rotting body. Although resurrection in the fullest sense is not taught here, Job is saying that if God so desires He is able to hide Job in the grave, then raise him back to life at a time when the divine anger is past.

14:14 *appointed time.* See note on 7:1.

14:18–22 Job's pessimism arises not from skepticism about the possibility of resurrection from the dead but rather from God's apparent unwillingness to do something immediately for a person like him, whose life has become a nightmare of pain and mourning.

‡14:18–19 Human hope disintegrates like a crumbling mountain, eroding rocks, and plants washed away by the rain.

15:1–6 Up to this point Eliphaz has been the most sympathetic of the three counselors, but now he has run out of patience with Job and denounces him more severely than before.

15:2 *vain knowledge.* The Hebrew word is also used in 16:3, where Job hurls Eliphaz's charges back at him. *east wind.* See 27:21; 38:24; the sirocco that blows in from the desert (see notes on Gen 41:6; Jer 4:11).

‡15:4 *casteth off fear.* Accuses Job of irreverence toward God. See note on 4:6.

15:5 See Mat 15:11,17–18.

15:6 *mouth condemneth thee.* See 9:20.

15:7–10 Job, says Eliphaz, presumes to be wise enough to sit among the members of God's council in heaven (see note on 1:6) when in reality he is no wiser than ordinary elders and sages on earth.

‡15:7 *first man . . . made before the hills.* Cf. the description of wisdom in Prov 8:23-26, which was present before the earth was created. Job is acting as if he is wisdom personified.

‡15:8 *restrain wisdom to thyself.* Job thinks that he has an exclusive hold on the truth.

15:10 Age, with its tested experience, was equated with wisdom in ancient times—a truism denied by Elihu (see 32:6–9).

15:11–13 Eliphaz chides Job for replying in rage to his friends' attempts to console him with gentle words, which Eliphaz believes come from God Himself (v. 11). But Eliphaz has been guilty of cruel insinuation (ch. 5), and the other two counselors have

14 [a]What *is* man, that he should be clean?
And *he which is* born of a woman, that he should be righteous?
15 [a]Behold, he putteth no trust in his saints;
Yea, the heavens are not clean in his sight.
16 [a]How much more abominable and filthy
Is man, [b]which drinketh iniquity like water?

17 I will shew thee, hear me;
And that which I have seen I will declare;
18 Which wise *men* have told
[a]From their fathers, and have not hid *it:*
19 Unto whom alone the earth was given,
And [a]no stranger passed among them.

20 The wicked *man* travaileth with pain all his days,
[a]And the number of years is hidden to the oppressor.
21 [1]A dreadful sound *is* in his ears:
[a]In prosperity the destroyer shall come *upon* him.
22 He believeth not that *he* shall return out of darkness,
And he *is* waited for of the sword.
23 He [a]wandereth abroad for bread, *saying,* Where *is it?*
He knoweth that [b]the day of darkness is ready at his hand.
24 Trouble and anguish shall make him afraid;
They shall prevail against him, as a king ready to the battle.

25 For he stretcheth out his hand against God,
And strengtheneth himself against the Almighty.
26 He runneth upon him, *even* on *his* neck,
Upon the thick bosses of his bucklers:
27 [a]Because he covereth his face with his fatness,
And maketh collops of fat on *his* flanks.
28 And he dwelleth in desolate cities,
And in houses which no man inhabiteth,
Which are ready to become heaps.
29 He shall not be rich, neither shall his substance continue,
Neither shall he prolong the perfection thereof upon the earth.
30 He shall not depart out of darkness;
The flame shall dry up his branches,
And by the breath of his mouth shall he go away.

31 Let not him that is deceived [a]trust in vanity:
For vanity shall be his recompence.
32 It shall be [1]accomplished [a]before his time,
And his branch shall not be green.
33 He shall shake off his unripe grape as the vine,
And shall cast off his flower as the olive.
34 For the congregation of hypocrites *shall be* desolate,
And fire shall consume the tabernacles of bribery.
35 [a]They conceive mischief, and bring forth [1]vanity,
And their belly prepareth deceit.

Job answers

16 Then Job answered and said,
2 I have heard many such *things:*
[a][1]Miserable comforters *are* ye all.
3 Shall [1]vain words have an end?
Or what emboldeneth thee that thou answerest?

15:14 [a]ch. 14:4; Prov. 20:9; Eccl. 7:20; 1 John 1:8,10
15:15 [a]ch. 4:18; 25:5
15:16 [a]ch. 4:19; Ps. 14:3; 53:3 [b]ch. 34:7; Prov. 19:28
15:18 [a]ch. 8:8
15:19 [a]Joel 3:17
15:20 [a]Ps. 90:12
15:21 [1]Heb. *A sound of fears* [a]1 Thes. 5:3
15:23 [a]Ps. 59:15; 109:10 [b]ch. 18:12
15:27 [a]Ps. 17:10
15:31 [a]Is. 59:4
15:32 [1]Or, *cut off* [a]ch. 22:16; Ps. 55:23
15:35 [1]Or, *iniquity* [a]Ps. 7:14; Is. 59:4; Hos. 10:13
16:2 [1]Or, *Troublesome* [a]ch. 13:4
16:3 [1]Heb. *words of wind*

been even more malicious. Genuine words of comfort for Job have been few indeed (see 4:2–6).

15:14–16 See 25:4–6. Eliphaz repeats what he had already said in 4:17–19, perhaps because he thought the earlier words had come to him through divine revelation (see note on 4:12–21).

15:14 *born of a woman.* An echo of Job's words in 14:1.

‡15:15 *saints.* Or "holy ones," referring to angels (see note on 5:1).

15:16 *drinketh iniquity like water.* See Elihu's description of Job in 34:7.

15:17–26 Eliphaz now bolsters his earlier advice with traditional wisdom: The wicked man (a caricature of Job) can never escape the suffering he deserves.

15:19 *no stranger passed among them.* He teaches wisdom uncorrupted by strange or foreign influences.

15:20–35 A poem on the fate of the wicked (see 8:11–19). Eliphaz's caricature continues with a variety of figures: a belligerent sinner who attacks God (vv. 24–26); a fat, rich wicked man who finally gets what he deserves (vv. 27–32); a grapevine stripped before the fruit is ripe (v. 33a); an olive tree shedding its blossoms (v. 33b). As long as Eliphaz rejects Job's insistence that the wicked go on prospering, he does not have to wrestle with the disturbing corollary: the mystery of why the innocent sometimes suffer.

15:23,30 *darkness.* Death, characterized by the journey to the netherworld (see note on 10:21).

‡15:26 *runneth upon him . . . on his neck.* Lit. "runneth upon him . . . with his neck" describing the firmly set neck of a running warrior on the attack. *thick bosses of his bucklers.* Or "his thick-bossed shields," an embossed shield that provides the warrior with a sense of invincibility.

‡15:27 *covereth his face . . . fatness . . . maketh collops of fat . . . flanks.* Well-fed, with a puffy face and heavy thighs.

15:35 *They conceive mischief, and bring forth vanity.* Repeated in Is 59:4 (see note there). Once initiated, sinful thoughts develop quickly into evil acts.

16:2–5 Helpful advice is usually brief and encouraging, not lengthy and judgmental.

16:2 *Miserable comforters.* See note on 13:1–12. Job would eventually be comforted, but not by his three friends (see 42:11).

16:3 *vain.* See note on 15:2.

4 I also could speak as ye *do:*
If your soul were in my soul's stead,
I could heap up words against you,
And [a]shake mine head at you.
5 *But* I would strengthen you with my
mouth,
And the moving of my lips should
asswage *your grief.*

6 Though I speak, my grief is not
asswaged:
And *though* I forbear, [1]what am I
eased?
7 But now he hath made me weary:
Thou hast made desolate all my
company.
8 And thou hast filled me with wrinkles,
which is a witness *against me:*
And my leanness rising up in me
Beareth witness to my face.
9 [a]He teareth *me in* his wrath, who
hateth me:
He gnasheth upon me with his
teeth;
[b]Mine enemy sharpeneth his eyes
upon me.

10 They have [a]gaped upon me with their
mouth;
[b]They have smitten me upon the
cheek reproachfully;
They have gathered themselves
together against me.
11 God [a][1]hath delivered me to the
ungodly,
And turned me over into the hands of
the wicked.
12 I was at ease, but he hath broken me
asunder:
He hath also taken *me* by my neck, and
shaken me to pieces,
And [a]set me up for his mark.

16:4 [a]Ps. 22:7; 109:25; Lam. 2:15
16:6 [1]Heb. *what goeth from me?*
16:9 [a]ch. 10:16,17 [b]ch. 13:24
16:10 [a]Ps. 22:13 [b]Lam. 3:30; Mic. 5:1
16:11 [1]Heb. *hath shut me up* [a]ch. 1:15,17
16:12 [a]ch. 7:20

16:15 [a]ch. 30:19; Ps. 7:5
16:18 [a]ch. 27:9; Ps. 66:18
16:19 [1]Heb. *in the high places* [a]Rom. 1:9
16:20 [1]Heb. are *my scorners*
16:21 [1]Or, *friend* [a]ch. 31:35; Eccl. 6:10; Is. 45:9; Rom. 9:20
16:22 [1]Heb. *years of number* [a]Eccl. 12:5
17:1 [1]Or, *My spirit is spent* [a]Ps. 88:3,4
17:2 [1]Heb. *lodge* [a]1 Sam. 1:6
17:3 [a]Prov. 17:18

13 His archers compass me round about,
He cleaveth my reins asunder, and
doth not spare;
He poureth out my gall upon the
ground.
14 He breaketh me *with* breach upon
breach,
He runneth upon me like a giant.

15 I have sewed sackcloth upon my skin,
And [a]defiled my horn in the dust.
16 My face is foul with weeping,
And on mine eyelids *is* the shadow of
death;
17 Not for *any* injustice in mine hands:
Also my prayer is pure.
18 O earth, cover not thou my blood,
And [a]let my cry have no place.
19 Also now, behold [a]my witness *is* in
heaven,
And my record *is* [1]on high.
20 My friends [1]scorn me:
But mine eye poureth out *tears* unto
God.
21 [a]O that *one* might plead for a man
with God,
As a man *pleadeth* for his [1]neighbour.
22 When [1]a few years are come,
Then I shall [a]go the way *whence* I
shall not return.

17 [1]My breath is corrupt,
My days are extinct,
[a]The graves *are ready* for me.
2 *Are there* not mockers with me?
And *doth not* mine eye [1]continue in
their [a]provocation?

3 Lay down now, put me in a surety with
thee;
Who *is* he *that* [a]will strike hands with
me?

16:4 *shake . . . head.* A gesture of insult and scorn (see Ps 22:7; Jer 48:27; Mat 27:39).

‡16:7 *made desolate all my company.* Wiped out my entire household.

‡16:8 *filled me with wrinkles.* Shriveled me to nothing.

16:9 The figure here is graphic and disturbing: God, like a ferocious lion (see 10:16), attacks and tears at Job's flesh. *enemy.* Cf. 19:11.

16:10–14 Job sees himself as God's target and views his situation as the reverse of Eliphaz's description in 15:25–26.

‡16:10 *gaped upon me . . . mouth.* Jeer or taunt with an open mouth.

16:12 *I was at ease, but he . . . asunder.* See 2:3 and note. *set me up for his mark.* Has made me a target. See note on 6:4.

‡16:13 *cleaveth my reins asunder.* God pierces Job's vital organs (lit. "kidneys") with his arrows. God has delivered a mortal wound to Job.

‡16:14 *breaketh me . . . upon breach.* The threefold repetition of the Hebrew root *parats* (lit. "he breaches me with breach upon breach") conveys the picture of a severe beating.

16:15–17 Job summarizes his misery: Though innocent, he continues to suffer.

16:15 *sackcloth . . . dust.* Signs of mourning (see notes on Gen 37:34; Jonah 3:5–6).

‡16:16 *foul.* Lit. "reddened," from weeping. *mine eyelids . . . shadow of death.* Dark circles from grief and sleeplessness.

16:18–21 Verse 18 (see v. 22; 17:1) indicates that Job does not think he will live long enough to be vindicated before his peers. His only hope is that in heaven he has a "witness" (v. 19), one who will plead with God on his behalf (v. 21; see 9:33 and note).

16:18 *blood . . . cry.* Job felt that his blood, like Abel's (see Gen 4:10 and note), was innocent and would therefore cry out from the ground after his death.

‡16:19 *my record.* Or "my advocate." Parallel to "witness" in preceding line.

‡16:22 *When a few years are come.* Job does not expect his death immediately. *go the way . . . I shall not return.* Will go down to the netherworld (see notes on 7:9; 10:21).

17:1 *The graves are ready for me.* See note on vv. 10–16.

‡17:2 *mine eye . . . provocation.* Job is forced to continually look at and endure hostile words of his accusers.

‡17:3 *Lay down . . . put me in a surety with thee.* Job is asking God for a guarantee that he is right, that he is not guilty of sins that deserve punishment (as his counselors have said). *Who is he . . . ?* Who else does Job have to turn to?

4 For thou hast hid their heart from understanding:
Therefore shalt thou not exalt *them.*
5 He *that* speaketh flattery to *his* friends,
Even the eyes of his children shall fail.

6 He hath made me also [a]a byword of the people;
And [1]aforetime I was *as* a tabret.
7 [a]Mine eye also is dim by reason of sorrow,
And all [1]my members *are* as a shadow.
8 Upright *men* shall be astonied at this,
And the innocent shall stir up himself against the hypocrite.
9 The righteous also shall hold on his way,
And he that hath [a]clean hands [1]shall be stronger and stronger.
10 But *as for* you all, [a]do you return, and come now:
For I cannot find *one* wise *man* among you.

11 [a]My days are past,
My purposes are broken off,
Even [1]the thoughts of my heart.
12 They change the night into day:
The light *is* [1]short, because of darkness.
13 If I wait, the grave *is* mine house:
I have made my bed in the darkness.
14 I have [1]said to corruption, Thou *art* my father:
To the worm, *Thou art* my mother, and my sister.
15 And where *is* now my hope?
As for my hope, who shall see it?
16 They shall go down [a]*to* the bars of the pit,
When *our* [b]rest together *is* in the dust.

Bildad reproves Job

18 Then answered Bildad the Shuhite, and said,

2 How long *will it be ere* you make an end of words?
Mark, and afterwards we will speak.
3 Wherefore are we counted [a]as beasts,
And reputed vile in your sight?

4 [a]He teareth [1]himself in his anger:
Shall the earth be forsaken for thee?
And shall the rock be removed out of his place?
5 Yea, [a]the light of the wicked shall be put out,
And the spark of his fire shall not shine.
6 The light shall be dark in his tabernacle,
[a]And his [1]candle shall be put out with him.
7 The steps of his strength shall be straitened,
And [a]his own counsel shall cast him down.

8 For [a]he is cast into a net by his own feet,
And he walketh upon a snare.
9 The grin shall take *him* by the heel,
And [a]the robber shall prevail against him.
10 The snare *is* [1]laid for him in the ground,
And a trap for him in the way.
11 [a]Terrors shall make him afraid on every side,
And shall [1]drive him to his feet.

12 His strength shall be hunger-bitten,
And [a]destruction *shall be* ready at his side.
13 It shall devour the [1]strength of his skin:
Even the firstborn of death shall devour his strength.
14 [a]His confidence shall be rooted out of his tabernacle,

17:6 [1]Or, *before them* [a]ch. 30:9
17:7 [1]Or, *my thoughts* [a]Ps. 6:7; 31:9
17:9 [1]Heb. *shall add strength* [a]Ps. 24:4
17:10 [a]ch. 6:29
17:11 [1]Heb. *the possessions* [a]ch. 7:6
17:12 [1]Heb. *near*
17:14 [1]Heb. *cried,* or, *called*
17:16 [a]Jonah 2:6 [b]ch. 3:17-19
18:3 [a]Ps. 73:22
18:4 [1]Heb. *his soul* [a]ch. 13:14
18:5 [a]Prov. 13:9
18:6 [1]Or, *lamp* [a]ch. 21:17; Ps. 18:28
18:7 [a]ch. 5:13
18:8 [a]ch. 22:10; Ps. 9:15; 35:8
18:9 [a]ch. 5:5
18:10 [1]Heb. *hidden*
18:11 [1]Heb. *scatter him* [a]ch. 20:25; Jer. 6:25; 20:3,4
18:12 [a]ch. 15:23
18:13 [1]Heb. *bars*
18:14 [a]ch. 11:20; Ps. 112:10; Prov. 10:28

17:4 *their heart.* Those of his three friends.
17:5 Job quotes a proverb to counter the false accusations of his friends.
17:6–9 The guarantee Job asked for is not provided, so he feels that God is responsible for making him an object of scorn. If the tone of vv. 8–9 is intended as sarcastic (as v. 10 would seem to indicate), the "Upright" and "innocent" are the counselors (v. 8).
‡17:6 *byword.* See 30:9; an object of scorn and ridicule (see the covenant curse in Deut 28:37). *aforetime I was as a tabret.* Lit. "as one in whose face people spit," an object of derision. See 30:10.
17:7 *members are as a shadow.* See note on 2:7.
17:10–16 Zophar had promised that Job's repentance would turn his darkness into light (11:17). Job now makes a parody on such advice (vv. 12–16). His only hope is the grave (see v. 1), which will not be as his home had been (vv. 13–15).
17:13 *house.* See Eccl 12:5. *darkness.* See 18:18; the netherworld (see note on 10:21).
17:14 In the grave, one's family consists only of decomposition and maggots.
17:15 *where is now my hope?* See 14:19.
‡17:16 *bars of the pit.* Sheol (the grave). See 38:17; Mat 16:18. See note on Gen 37:35. *dust.* See note on 7:21.
18:1–4 Bildad resents what he perceives to be a belittling attitude. He considers Job's emotional reaction as self-centered and irrational.
18:5–21 Another poem on the fate of the wicked (see 8:11–19; 15:20–35). Bildad wants to convince Job that he is wrong when he claims that the righteous suffer and the wicked prosper. Bildad is absolutely certain that every wicked person gets paid in full, in this life, for his wicked deeds.
18:5 *the light of the wicked shall be put out.* See 21:17; repeated in Prov 13:9. Life, symbolized by light, is extinguished.
‡18:9 *The grin.* I.e. "a trap."
‡18:11 *drive him to his feet.* Lit. "scatter his feet," harrassing and bothering him at every step.
18:13 *firstborn of death.* See 5:7.

And it shall bring him to the king of terrors.
15 It shall dwell in his tabernacle, because *it is* none of his:
Brimstone shall be scattered upon his habitation.

16 [a]His roots shall be dried up beneath,
And above shall his branch be cut off.
17 [a]His remembrance shall perish from the earth,
And he shall have no name in the street.
18 [1]He shall be driven from light into darkness,
And chased out of the world.
19 [a]He shall neither have son nor nephew among his people,
Nor *any* remaining in his dwellings.

20 They that come after *him* shall be astonied at his day,
As they that [1]went before [2]were affrighted.
21 Surely such *are* the dwellings of the wicked,
And this *is* the place *of him that* [a]knoweth not God.

Job's response

19 Then Job answered and said,
2 How long will ye vex my soul,
And break me in pieces with words?
3 These ten times have ye reproached me:
You are not ashamed *that* you [1]make yourselves strange to me.
4 And be it indeed *that* I have erred,
Mine error remaineth with myself.
5 If indeed ye will [a]magnify *yourselves* against me,
And plead against me my reproach:
6 Know now that God hath overthrown me,
And hath compassed me with his net.

7 Behold, I cry out *of* [1]wrong, but I am not heard:
I cry aloud, but *there is* no judgment.
8 He hath fenced up my way that I cannot pass,
And he hath set darkness in my paths.
9 He hath stript me of my glory,
And taken the crown *from* my head.
10 He hath destroyed me on every side, and I am gone:
And mine hope hath he removed like a tree.
11 He hath also kindled his wrath against me,
And [a]he counteth me unto him as *one of* his enemies.
12 His troops come together,
And raise up their way against me,
And encamp round about my tabernacle.

13 He hath put my brethren far from me,
And mine acquaintance are verily estranged from me.
14 My kinsfolk have failed,
And my familiar friends have forgotten me.
15 They that dwell in mine house, and my maidens,
Count me for a stranger:
I am an alien in their sight.
16 I called my servant, and he gave *me* no answer;

18:16 [a]ch. 29:19; Is. 5:24; Amos 2:9; Mal. 4:1
18:17 [a]Ps. 34:16; 109:13; Prov. 2:22; 10:7
18:18 [1]Heb. *They shall drive him*
18:19 [a]Is. 14:22; Jer. 22:30
18:20 [1]Or, *lived with him* [2]Heb. *laid hold on horror*
18:21 [a]Jer. 9:3; 1 Thes. 4:5
19:3 [1]Or, *harden yourselves against me*
19:5 [a]Ps. 38:16
19:7 [1]Or, *violence*
19:11 [a]ch. 13:24

18:14 *king of terrors.* A vivid figure of speech referring to death, which is personified in v. 13. Canaanite literature pictured death as the devouring god Mot. Isaiah reverses the figure and envisions the Lord as swallowing up death forever (Is 25:8; see 1 Cor 15:54).
‡18:15 *It shall dwell . . . none of his.* Or "There dwells in his tent nothing of his." A slight variation in the Hebrew text could render, "Fire dwells in his tent." Vv. 13-14 also point to the fact that death visits the home of the wicked. *Brimstone.* Reminiscent of the destruction of Sodom and Gomorrah (see Gen 19:24).
18:16 *roots . . . And . . . branch.* Cf. Amos 2:9; figurative for descendants (see, e.g., Is 11:1,10) and/or ancestors (see, e.g., Judg 5:14; Is 14:29).
18:17 *His remembrance shall perish.* Apparently Bildad knows nothing of punishment in the realm of death. The only retribution beyond the grave is having one's memory (name) cut off by not leaving any heirs (see v. 19).
18:18 *darkness.* See 17:13; the netherworld (see note on 10:21).
‡18:20 *astonied at his day.* Astonished or appalled at his fate.
18:21 *the wicked . . . knoweth not God.* Having no intimate knowledge of God is synonymous with being wicked (see Hos 4:1–2,6).
‡19:3 *ten times.* Several times. Ten is often used as a round number (see, e.g., Gen 31:41; 1 Sam 1:8). *you make yourselves strange to me.* Lit. "you deal harshly with me." See KJV marg.
19:4 *remaineth with myself.* If Job has erred, it is his responsibility. His friends have no right to interfere or to behave as if they were God (see v. 22).
‡19:6 *overthrown.* Or "treated wrongly." Cf. 40:8. The Hebrew for this verb is twice translated "pervert" in 8:3, where Bildad denied that God perverts justice. But Job, struggling with the enigma of his suffering, can only conclude that God is his enemy, though in fact He is his friend who delights in him (see 1:8; 2:3). Job's true enemy, of course, is Satan. *compassed me with his net.* The wicked may get themselves into trouble, as Bildad had pointed out (see 18:8–10), but Job here attributes his suffering to God.
‡19:7 *I cry out of wrong.* Or "I cry out, 'This is wrong.'" See Hab 1:2.
19:8–12 In Job's mind, God is at war with him (see 16:12–14).
19:10 *hope hath he removed like a tree.* See 24:20; unlike 14:7–9, where Job had used as a symbol of hope a tree that is cut down but later sprouts again.
19:12 *their way.* See 30:12.
19:13–19 See Jer 12:6. Nothing in life hurts more than rejection by one's family and friends. Job's children are gone, and his wife, brothers, friends and servants find him repulsive.

I intreated him with my mouth.
17 My breath is strange to my wife,
Though I intreated for the children's *sake* of [1] mine *own* body.
18 Yea, [a] [1] young children despised me;
I arose, and they spake against me.
19 [a] All [1] my inward friends abhorred me:
And they whom I loved are turned against me.
20 [a] My bone cleaveth to my skin [1] and to my flesh,
And I am escaped with the skin of my teeth.
21 Have pity upon me, have pity upon me, O ye my friends;
For the hand of God hath touched me.
22 Why do ye [a] persecute me as God,
And are not satisfied with my flesh?

23 [1] O that my words were now written!
O that they were printed in a book!
24 That they were graven with an iron pen and lead
In the rock for ever!
25 For I know *that* my Redeemer liveth,
And *that* he shall stand *at* the latter *day* upon the earth:
26 [1] And *though* after my skin *worms* destroy this *body,*
Yet [a] in my flesh shall I see God:
27 Whom I shall see for myself,
And mine eyes shall behold, and not [1] another;
[2] *Though* my reins be consumed [3] within me.
28 But ye should say, Why persecute we him?
[1] Seeing the root of the matter is found in me;
29 Be ye afraid of the sword:
For wrath *bringeth* the punishments of the sword,
That ye may know *there is* a judgment.

Zophar's speech

20 Then answered Zophar the Naamathite, and said,

2 Therefore do my thoughts cause me to answer,
And for *this* [1] I make haste.
3 I have heard the check of my reproach,
And the spirit of my understanding causeth me to answer.
4 Knowest thou *not* this of old,
Since man was placed upon earth,
5 [a] That the triumphing of the wicked *is* [1] short,
And the joy of the hypocrite *but* for a moment?

6 [a] Though his excellency mount up to the heavens,
And his head reach unto the [1] clouds;
7 *Yet* he shall perish for ever like his own dung:

19:17 [1] Heb. *my belly* 19:18 [1] Or, *the wicked* [a] 2 Ki. 2:23 19:19 [1] Heb. *the men of my secret* [a] Ps. 55:13 19:20 [1] Or, *as* [a] Ps. 102:5 19:22 [a] Ps. 69:26 19:23 [1] Heb. *Who will give, etc.* 19:26 [1] Or, *After I shall awake, though this* body *be destroyed, yet out of my flesh shall I see God* [a] Ps. 17:15; 1 Cor. 13:12 19:27 [1] Heb. *a stranger*

19:27 [2] [Or, *My reins within me are consumed with earnest desire* [for that day]] [3] Heb. *in my bosom* 19:28 [1] Or, *And* what *root of matter is found in me?* 20:2 [1] Heb. *my haste* is *in me* 20:5 [1] Heb. *from near* [a] Ps. 37:35 20:6 [1] Heb. *cloud* [a] Is. 14:13,14; Obad. 3,4

19:17 *breath is strange.* See note on 2:7.
19:18 *young children despised me.* An intolerable insult in a patriarchal society, where one's elders were to be honored and respected (see Ex 20:12 and note).
19:20 *my skin and to my flesh.* See note on 2:7. *skin of my teeth.* It is possible that the Hebrew for "the skin of my teeth" refers to gums ("with only my gums"), implying that Job's teeth are gone.
19:21 *hand of God hath touched me.* See 1:11; 2:4–6; see also note on v. 6.
19:23–27 Probably the best-known and most-loved passage in the book of Job, reaching a high point in Job's understanding of his own situation and of his relationship to God. Its position between two sections in which Job pleads with (vv. 21–22) and then warns (vv. 28–29) his friends causes it to stand out even more boldly.
19:23 *my words.* Job would have his complaint and defense recorded so that even after his death they would endure until he is finally vindicated. *book.* See note on Ex 17:14.
19:24 *iron.* See also 20:24; 28:2; 40:18; 41:27. Iron did not come into common use in the ancient Near East until the 12th century B.C.
‡19:25 *I know that my Redeemer liveth.* This staunch confession of faith has been appropriated by generations of Christians, especially through the medium of Handel's *Messiah.* Although in other contexts Job desires a defender as an advocate in heaven who would plead with God on his behalf (see 9:33–34; 16:18–21 and notes; see also note on 5:1), here the Redeemer seems to be none other than God Himself (see note on Ruth 2:20). Job expresses confidence that ultimately God will vindicate His faithful servants in the face of all false accusations. *he shall stand.* To defend and vindicate me (see 42:7–10). *at the latter day.* Lit. "afterward" (after Job's life has ended).
‡19:26 *after my skin worms destroy this body.* Job senses that the ravages of his disease will eventually bring about his death. *shall I see God.* He is absolutely certain, however, that death is not the end of existence and that someday he will stand in the presence of his Redeemer and see Him with his own eyes (see v. 27; see also Mat 5:8; 1 John 3:2). See note on 42:5. Job affirms his belief in the resurrection of the body.
‡19:28–29 Job's tirade against the counselors is being resumed after the intervening section (vv. 23–27). Job warns his friends that they should fear God's judgment if they continue to make false accusations against him. *Seeing the root of the matter . . . in me.* Can be read as a question (see KJV marg.). They want to find the evidence that proves their charges against Job.
20:1–29 Yet another poem on the fate of the wicked as held by the "orthodox" theology of Job's friends (see 8:11–19; 15:20–35; 18:5–21).
20:2–3 Zophar takes Job's words, especially his closing words in 19:28–29, as a personal affront. Job has dared to assert that on Zophar's theory of retribution Zophar himself is due for punishment.
20:4–11 Zophar is proud that he is a healthy and prosperous man, for, in his view, that in itself is proof of his goodness and righteousness. But the joy and vigor of the wicked will always be brief and elusive (see Ps 73:18–20 and note).
‡20:6 *excellency.* Pride. *mount up to the heavens.* See Gen 11:4 and note.
‡20:7 *dung.* A graphic symbol of what is temporary and worthless (see 1 Ki 14:10).

They which have seen him shall say,
Where *is* he?
8 He shall fly away [a]as a dream, and shall
not be found:
Yea, he shall be chased away as a
vision of the night.
9 The eye also *which* saw him shall *see*
him no more;
Neither shall his place any more
behold him.
10 [1]His children shall *seek to* please the
poor,
And his hands shall restore their goods.
11 His bones are full *of* [a]*the sin of* his
youth,
[b]Which shall lie down with him in the
dust.

12 Though wickedness be sweet in his
mouth,
Though he hide it under his tongue;
13 *Though* he spare it, and forsake it not;
But keep it still [1]within his mouth:
14 *Yet* his meat in his bowels is turned,
It is the gall of asps within him.
15 He hath swallowed down riches, and
he shall vomit them up again:
God shall cast them out of his belly.
16 He shall suck the poison of asps:
The viper's tongue shall slay him.

17 He shall not see [a]the rivers,
[1]The floods, the brooks of honey and
butter.
18 That which he laboured for shall he
restore, and shall not swallow *it*
down:
[1]According to *his* substance *shall* the
restitution *be,* and he shall not
rejoice *therein.*
19 Because he hath [1]oppressed *and* hath
forsaken the poor;
Because he hath violently taken away a
house which he builded not;
20 [a]Surely he shall not [1]feel quietness in
his belly,
He shall not save of that which he
desired.

20:8 [a]Ps. 73:20
20:10 [1]Or, *The poor shall oppress his children*
20:11 [a]ch. 13:26 [b]ch. 21:26
20:13 [1]Heb. *in the midst of his palate*
20:17 [1]Or, *Streaming brooks* [a]Ps. 36:8; Jer. 17:8
20:18 [1]Heb. *According to the substance of his exchange*
20:19 [1]Heb. *crushed*
20:20 [1]Heb. *know* [a]Eccl. 5:13

20:21 [1]Or, There shall be *none left for his meat*
20:22 [1]Or, *troublesome*
20:24 [a]Is. 24:18; Amos 5:19
20:25 [a]ch. 16:13 [b]ch. 18:11
20:26 [a]Ps. 21:9
20:29 [1]Heb. *of his decree from God* [a]ch. 27:13
21:3 [a]ch. 16:10
21:4 [1]Heb. *shortened?*
21:5 [1]Heb. *Look unto me* [a]Judg. 18:19; ch. 40:4

21 [1]*There shall* none of his meat *be* left;
Therefore shall no *man* look for his
goods.
22 In the fulness of his sufficiency he shall
be in straits:
Every hand of the [1]wicked shall come
upon him.
23 *When* he is about to fill his belly,
God shall cast the fury of his wrath
upon him,
And shall rain *it* upon him while he is
eating.
24 [a]He shall flee from the iron weapon,
And the bow of steel shall strike him
through.
25 It is drawn, and cometh out of the body;
Yea, [a]the glistering sword cometh out
of his gall:
[b]Terrors *are* upon him.

26 All darkness *shall be* hid in his secret
places:
[a]A fire not blown shall consume him;
It shall go ill with him that is left in his
tabernacle.
27 The heaven shall reveal his iniquity;
And the earth shall rise up against him.
28 The increase of his house shall depart,
And his goods shall flow away in the
day of his wrath.
29 [a]This *is* the portion of a wicked man
from God,
And the heritage [1]appointed unto him
by God.

Job disagrees with his friends

21 But Job answered and said,
2 Hear diligently my speech,
And let this be your consolations.
3 Suffer me that I may speak;
And after that I have spoken, [a]mock
on.
4 *As for* me, *is* my complaint to man?
And if *it were so,* why should not my
spirit be [1]troubled?
5 [1]Mark me, and be astonished,
[a]And lay *your* hand upon *your* mouth.

20:10,19 Oppression of the poor is the mark of the truly wicked (see, e.g., Amos 2:6–8; 8:4–8). On this subject, Job had no quarrel with Zophar (see 31:16–23).
20:11 *dust.* See note on 7:21.
20:12–15 An evil man's wicked deeds are like tasty food that pleases his palate but turns sour in his stomach.
20:15 *He hath swallowed down riches.* After taking what belonged to the poor (see note on vv. 10,19).
20:18 *That which he laboured for . . . he shall not rejoice therein.* A common theme in wisdom literature (see, e.g., Eccl 2:18–23).
20:20–25 Although a wicked man may fill his belly, when God vents His anger against him there will be nothing for him to eat.
20:24 *iron.* See note on 19:24.
‡20:26 *All darkness . . . his secret places.* Lit. "All darkness shall hide his treasures." Death will prevent him from enjoying his ill-gotten gain. *darkness.* See note on 10:21.
20:27 See Deut 30:19 and note.
20:29 Like Bildad in 18:21, Zophar concludes his speech with a summary statement in which he claims that all he has said is in accord with God's plans for judging sinners. *This is the portion of a wicked man from God.* Repeated almost verbatim by Job in 27:13.
‡21:2 *consolations.* Job will be comforted if Zophar will hear him out. Contrast v. 34 ("comfort ye me in vain"), which, with v. 2, frames Job's reply to Zophar.
‡21:4 *is my complaint to man?* No, says Job, I am complaining to God, because He is responsible for my condition—at least Job so perceived it. *And if it were so . . . spirit be troubled?* Since my complaint is not with man but God, do I not have a reason to be impatient?" *troubled.* See KJV marg., which implies impatience. See note on 9:2–3.
‡21:5 *Mark me.* Job addresses his three friends and says, "Look at me."

6 Even when I remember I am afraid,
And trembling taketh hold on my flesh.

7 [a]Wherefore do the wicked live,
Become old, yea, are mighty *in* power?
8 Their seed is established in their sight
with them,
And their offspring before their eyes.
9 Their houses [1]*are* safe from fear,
[a]Neither *is* the rod of God upon them.
10 Their bull gendereth, and faileth not;
Their cow calveth, and [a]casteth not
her calf.
11 They send forth their little ones like a
flock,
And their children dance.

12 They take the timbrel and harp,
And rejoice at the sound of the organ.
13 They [a]spend their days [1]in wealth,
And in a moment go down *to* the
grave.
14 [a]Therefore they say unto God, Depart
from us;
For we desire not the knowledge of thy
ways.
15 [a]What *is* the Almighty, that we should
serve him?
And [b]what profit should we have, if
we pray unto him?
16 Lo, their good *is* not in their hand:
[a]The counsel of the wicked is far from
me.
17 How oft is the [1]candle of the wicked
put out!
And *how oft* cometh their destruction
upon them!
God [a]distributeth sorrows in his anger.
18 [a]They are as stubble before the wind,
And as chaff that the storm [1]carrieth
away.
19 God layeth up [1]his iniquity [a]for his
children:
He rewardeth him, and he shall
know *it*.

21:7 [a]ch. 12:6; Ps. 73:3,12; Jer. 12:1
21:9 [1]Heb. are *peace from fear* [a]Ps. 73:5
21:10 [a]Ex. 23:26
21:13 [1]Or, *in mirth* [a]ch. 36:11
21:14 [a]ch. 22:17
21:15 [a]Ex. 5:2 [b]Mal. 3:14
21:16 [a]Ps. 1:1; Prov. 1:10
21:17 [1]Or, *lamp* [a]Luke 12:46
21:18 [1]Heb. *stealeth away* [a]Ps. 1:4
21:19 [1]That is, *the punishment of his iniquity* [a]Ex. 20:5
21:20 [a]Ps. 75:8; Is. 51:17
21:22 [a]Is. 40:13
21:23 [1]Heb. *in his very perfection*, or, *in the strength of his perfection*
21:24 [1]Or, *milk pails*
21:26 [a]Eccl. 9:2
21:28 [1]Heb. *the tent of the tabernacles of the wicked*
21:30 [1]Heb. *the day of wraths* [a]Prov. 16:4
21:32 [1]Heb. *graves* [2]Heb. *watch in the heap*
21:33 [a]Heb. 9:27

20 His eyes shall see his destruction,
And [a]he shall drink of the wrath of the
Almighty.
21 For what pleasure hath he in his house
after him,
When the number of his months is cut
off in the midst?

22 [a]Shall *any* teach God knowledge?
Seeing he judgeth those that are high.
23 One dieth [1]in his full strength,
Being wholly at ease and quiet.
24 His [1]breasts are full *of* milk,
And his bones are moistened with
marrow.
25 And another dieth in the bitterness of
his soul,
And never eateth with pleasure.
26 They shall [a]lie down alike in the dust,
And the worms shall cover them.

27 Behold, I know your thoughts,
And the devices *which* ye wrongfully
imagine against me.
28 For ye say, Where *is* the house of the
prince?
And where *are* [1]the dwelling places of
the wicked?
29 Have ye not asked them that go by the
way?
And do ye not know their tokens,
30 [a]That the wicked is reserved to the day
of destruction?
They shall be brought forth to [1]the day
of wrath.
31 Who shall declare his way to his face?
And who shall repay him *what* he hath
done?

32 Yet shall he be brought to the [1]grave,
And shall [2]remain in the tomb.
33 The clods of the valley shall be sweet
unto him,
And [a]every man shall draw after him,
As *there are* innumerable before him.

21:6 *when I remember.* His complaint to God (see note on v. 4). *I am afraid.* To contemplate the morally upside-down situation in which the wicked flourish.
21:7–15 Job's counselors have elaborated on the fate of the wicked (see 8:11–19; 15:20–35; 18:5–21; ch. 20), but Job insists that experience shows just the reverse of what his friends have said. The wicked, who want to know nothing of God's ways and who even consider prayer a useless exercise (vv. 14–15), flourish in all they do. Far from dying prematurely, as Zophar assumed concerning them (see 20:11), they live long and increase in power (v. 7). Bildad's claim that the wicked have no offspring or descendants (see 18:19) Job flatly denies (vv. 8,11).
21:9 *rod of God.* See note on 9:34.
21:13 *in a moment.* Or "quietly." The Hebrew root underlying this word is translated "them that are quiet" in Ps 35:20.
21:16 See 22:18. Job disavows the unholy counsel of the wicked and knows that God is in control (see v. 17), but such knowledge makes God all the more of an enigma to him.
21:17 *candle of the wicked put out.* See 18:5 and note.
21:18 *stubble . . . chaff.* See 13:25; see also note on Ps 1:4.
‡21:19 *He rewardeth him, and he shall know it.* What Job desires for the wicked is that they receive the punishment for their sins, not their children. This thought continues into v. 20.
21:20 *drink . . . wrath of the Almighty.* See note on Is 51:17.
21:22 *Shall any teach God . . . ?* See Is 40:14. On the contrary, God is the one who does the teaching (see 35:11; 36:22; chs. 38–41).
21:26 *dust.* See note on 7:21.
‡21:28–29 Job anticipates his friends saying that wicked people do not prosper. But Job asks if his friends have ever listened to the "tokens" (eyewitness accounts) of travelers ("them that go by the way") that attest to the wicked thriving.
‡21:30–33 Job acknowledges that the wicked die but sees even their death as a positive experience. They do not have to answer for their actions (v. 31) and they are placed in a comfortable grave (vv. 32-33) where they will be at rest ("The clods of the valley shall be sweet"). Job's words confirm that there is no justice in the universe apart from the final judgment that awaits every individual (cf. Heb 9:27).

34 How then comfort ye me in vain,
Seeing *in* your answers there
remaineth [1] falsehood?

Eliphaz accuses Job again

22 Then Eliphaz the Temanite answered
and said,

2 [a] Can a man be profitable unto God,
[1] As he that is wise may be profitable
unto himself?
3 *Is it any* pleasure to the Almighty, that
thou art righteous?
Or *is it* gain *to him,* that thou makest
thy ways perfect?
4 Will he reprove thee for fear of thee?
Will he enter with thee into judgment?

5 *Is* not thy wickedness great?
And thine iniquities infinite?
6 For thou hast [a] taken a pledge from thy
brother for nought,
And [1] stripped the naked of their
clothing.
7 Thou hast not given water to the weary
to drink,
And thou [a] hast withholden bread from
the hungry.
8 But *as for* [1] the mighty man, he had the
earth;
And the [2] honourable *man* dwelt in it.
9 Thou hast sent widows away empty,
And the arms of the fatherless have
been broken.

10 Therefore snares *are* round about thee,
And sudden fear troubleth thee;

21:34 [1] Heb. *transgression?*
22:2 [1] Or, *If he may be profitable,* doth his *good success* depend *thereon?* [a] Ps. 16:2
22:6 [1] Heb. *stripped the clothes of the naked* [a] Ex. 22:26
22:7 [a] Deut. 15:7
22:8 [1] Heb. *the man of arm* [2] Heb. *eminent,* or, *accepted for countenance*
22:11 [a] Ps. 69:1,2
22:12 [1] Heb. *the head of the stars*
22:13 [1] Or, *What* [a] Ps. 73:11
22:16 [1] Heb. *A flood was poured* upon *their foundation* [a] ch. 15:32
22:17 [1] Or, *to them?* [a] ch. 21:14
22:19 [a] Ps. 58:10
22:20 [1] Or, *estate* [2] Or, *their excellency*
22:21 [1] That is, *with God* [a] Is. 27:5
22:22 [a] Ps. 119:11

11 Or darkness, *that* thou canst not see;
And abundance of [a] waters cover thee.

12 *Is* not God *in* the height of heaven?
And behold [1] the height of the stars,
how high they are.
13 And thou sayest, [a] [1] How doth God know?
Can he judge through the dark *cloud?*
14 Thick clouds *are* a covering to him,
that he seeth not;
And he walketh *in* the circuit of heaven.

15 Hast thou marked the old way
Which wicked men have trodden?
16 Which [a] were cut down out of time,
[1] Whose foundation was overflown
with a flood:
17 [a] Which said unto God, Depart from us:
And what can the Almighty do [1] for
them?
18 Yet he filled their houses *with* good
things:
But the counsel of the wicked is far
from me.

19 [a] The righteous see *it,* and are glad:
And the innocent laugh them to scorn.
20 Whereas our [1] substance is not cut
down,
But [2] the remnant of them the fire
consumeth.

21 Acquaint now thyself [1] with him, and
[a] be at peace:
Thereby good shall come *unto* thee.
22 Receive, I pray thee, the law from his
mouth,
And [a] lay up his words in thine heart.

21:34 *How then comfort ye me . . . ?* See 16:2 and note.

22:1–26:14 The third cycle of speeches, unlike the first (chs. 4–14) and second (chs. 15–21), is truncated and abbreviated. Bildad's speech is very brief (25:1–6), and Zophar does not speak at all. The dialogue between Job and his friends comes to an end because the friends cannot convince Job of his guilt—Job cannot acknowledge what is not true.

22:2–4 Eliphaz's odd reasoning is as follows: Since all things have their origin in God, man's giving back what God has given him does not enhance God in any way. Indeed, God is indifferent to man's goodness, because goodness is expected of him. It is when man becomes wicked that God is aroused (v. 4).

‡22:4 *Will he reprove . . . fear of thee?* Is God judging you for your piety? See note on 4:6. *enter with thee into judgment.* See note on 9:3.

22:5–11 In his earlier speeches, Eliphaz was the least caustic and at first even offered consolation (4:6; 5:17). But despite what he said in 4:3–4, Eliphaz now reprimands Job for gross social sins against the needy, who are naked and hungry (vv. 6–7), and against widows and the fatherless (v. 9). The only proof Eliphaz has for Job's alleged wickedness is his present suffering (vv. 10–11). In ch. 29 Job emphatically denies the kind of behavior of which Eliphaz accuses him.

22:6 *taken a pledge . . . stripped the naked.* Sins condemned by the prophets (see, e.g., Amos 2:8 and note).

‡22:8 *the mighty man . . . the honourable man.* What Job was before his calamity, a wealthy and powerful landowner.

‡22:9 *widows . . . fatherless.* See 24:3; Is 1:17 and note; Jas 1:27.

22:10 *snares.* See 19:6 and note.

22:11 *darkness . . . abundance of waters.* Two common figures of trouble and distress (see Ps 42:7 and note; Is 8:7–8,22; 43:2).

‡22:12–20 Eliphaz finally appears to support the argument of Bildad and Zophar, who were fully convinced that Job was a wicked man. Eliphaz makes a severe accusation: Job follows the path of the ungodly (v. 15), who defy God's power and say, "what can the Almighty do" (v. 17; see vv. 13–14). They even have contempt for God's goodness (v. 18).

‡22:13–14 Does Job think that God is hiding behind the clouds and unable to see his wickedness?

‡22:16 *out of time.* Or "before their time."

22:18 See 21:16 and note.

22:21–30 Eliphaz makes one last attempt to reach Job. In many ways it is a commendable call to repentance: Submit to God (v. 21), establish God's words in your heart (v. 22), return to the Almighty and forsake wickedness (v. 23), find your delight in God rather than in gold (vv. 24–26), pray and obey (v. 27) and become concerned about sinners (vv. 29–30). But Eliphaz's advice assumes (1) that Job is a very wicked man and (2) that Job's major concern is the return of his prosperity (see v. 21). Job had already made it clear in 19:25–27 that he deeply yearned to see God and be His friend.

22:22 See Job's response in 23:12. *lay up his words in thine heart.* See Ps 119:11.

23 If thou return to the Almighty, thou
shalt be built *up,*
Thou shalt put away iniquity far from
thy tabernacles.
24 Then shalt thou [a]lay up gold [1]as dust,
And *the gold of* Ophir as the stones of
the brooks.
25 Yea, the Almighty shall be thy
[1]defence,
And thou shalt have [2]plenty of silver.

26 For then shalt thou have thy [a]delight
in the Almighty,
And shalt lift up thy face unto God.
27 [a]Thou shalt make thy prayer unto him,
and he shall hear thee,
And thou shalt pay thy vows.
28 Thou shalt also decree a thing, and it
shall be established unto thee:
And the light shall shine upon thy
ways.
29 When *men* are cast down, then thou
shalt say, *There is* lifting up;
And [a]he shall save [1]the humble
person.
30 [1]He shall deliver the island of the
innocent:
And it is delivered by the pureness of
thine hands.

22:24 [1]Or, *on the dust* [a]2 Chr. 1:15
22:25 [1]Or, *gold* [2]Heb. *silver of strength*
22:26 [a]ch. 27:10
22:27 [a]Is. 58:9
22:29 [1]Heb. *him that hath low eyes* [a]1 Pet. 5:5
22:30 [1]Or, *The innocent shall deliver the island*
23:2 [1]Heb. *My hand*

Job's response to Eliphaz

23 Then Job answered and said,
2 Even to day *is* my complaint bitter:
[1]My stroke is heavier than my
groaning.
3 O that I knew where I might find him!
That I might come *even* to his seat!
4 I would order *my* cause before him,
And fill my mouth *with* arguments.
5 I would know the words *which* he
would answer me,
And understand what he would say
unto me.
6 [a]Will he plead against me with *his*
great power?
No; but he would put *strength* in me.
7 There the righteous *might* dispute with
him;
So should I be delivered for ever from
my judge.
8 [a]Behold, I go forward, but he *is* not
there;
And backward, but I cannot perceive
him:
9 *On* the left hand, where he doth work,
but I cannot behold *him:*
He hideth *himself on* the right hand,
that I cannot see *him:*

10 But he [a]knoweth [1]the way that I take:
When [b]he hath tried me, I shall come
forth as gold.
11 [a]My foot hath held his steps,
His way have I kept, and not declined.
12 Neither have I gone back from the
commandment of his lips;
[a][1]I have esteemed the words of his
mouth more than [2]my necessary
food.
13 But he *is* in one *mind,* and who can
turn him?
And *what* [a]his soul desireth, even *that*
he doeth.

14 For he performeth the thing that is
[a]appointed for me:
And many such *things are* with him.
15 Therefore am I troubled at his presence:
When I consider, I am afraid of him.
16 For God [a]maketh my heart soft,
And the Almighty troubleth me:
17 Because I was not cut off before the
darkness,
Neither hath he covered the darkness
from my face.

24 Why, seeing [a]times are not hidden
from the Almighty,

23:6 [a]Is. 57:16
23:8 [a]ch. 9:11
23:10 [1]Heb. *the way that is with me* [a]Ps. 139:1-3 [b]Ps. 17:3; 66:10; Jas. 1:12
23:11 [a]Ps. 44:18
23:12 [1]Heb. *I have hid,* or, *laid up* [2]Or, *my appointed portion* [a]John 4:32,34
23:13 [a]Ps. 115:3
23:14 [a]1 Thes. 3:3
23:16 [a]Ps. 22:14
24:1 [a]Acts 1:7

22:24 *gold of Ophir.* See 28:16; the finest gold (see notes on 1 Ki 9:28; 10:11; Ps 45:9; Is 13:12).
22:28 *light shall shine upon thy ways.* Through obedience to the word of God (see vv. 22,27; 29:3; Ps 119:105).
‡22:30 *island of the innocent.* Lit. "the not-innocent." God forgives the sinful when they turn to him. *pureness of thine hands.* See note on Ps 24:4.
‡23:2 *my complaint.* See 21:4 and note. *My stroke.* Lit. "My hand." Some of the ancient versions read, "His [God's] hand," which seems to fit better. See 33:7; see also note on 1 Sam 5:6.
23:3 *where I might find him.* See note on vv. 8–9.
‡23:4 *order my cause.* Present my case.
‡23:6 *put strength in me.* Lit. "establish me" (rule in my favor). Job is seeking a fair trial. In 9:14–20 Job was fearful that he could not find words to argue with God. Now he is confident that if God would give him a hearing, he would be acquitted (see 13:13–19; see also Ps 17:1–3; 26:1–3 and notes).
23:8–9 *forward . . . backward . . . left . . . right.* Whatever direction Job went, he could not find God (contrast Ps 139:7–10).
23:8,10 *I cannot perceive him . . . But he knoweth the way that I take.* Job is frustrated over his apparent inability to have an audience with God, who knows that he is an upright man. Job is here answering Eliphaz's admonition beginning in 22:21: "Acquaint now thyself with him, and be at peace." Job replies that this is what he has always done (vv. 11–12). He treasures God's words more than his daily food. He admits that God is testing him—not to purge away his sinful dross, but to show that Job is pure gold (see Ps 119:11,101,168; 1 Pet 1:7).
23:12 Job's response to the advice offered by Eliphaz in 22:22. *words . . . more than my necessary food.* See Deut 8:3.
23:13 *he is in one mind.* Lit. "He is one." Though Job is not an Israelite, he worships the one true God—there is no other (see Deut 6:4 and note). *what his soul desireth, even that he doeth.* He is sovereign (see Ps 115:3; 135:6; Luke 10:21).
23:15 *troubled at his presence.* See note on 21:6. A necessary part of Job's faith is fear of a God who does what He pleases. By contrast, the counselors tried to make God predictable.
‡23:16 *soft.* "Weak" or "timid" ("faint" in Deut 20:3).
23:17 *I was not cut off before the darkness.* Job responds to Eliphaz's accusation in 22:11 (see note there).

Do they that know him not see his days?
2 *Some* remove the [a]landmarks;
They violently take away flocks, and [1]feed *thereof.*
3 They drive away the ass of the fatherless,
They [a]take the widow's ox for a pledge.
4 They turn the needy out of the way:
[a]The poor of the earth hide themselves together.

5 Behold, *as* wild asses in the desert,
Go they forth to their work; rising betimes for a prey:
The wilderness *yieldeth* food for them *and* for *their* children.
6 They reap *every one* his [1]corn in the field:
And [2]they gather the vintage of the wicked.
7 They [a]cause the naked to lodge without clothing,
That *they have* no covering in the cold.
8 They are wet with the showers of the mountains,
And [a]embrace the rock for want of a shelter.

9 They pluck the fatherless from the breast,
And take a pledge of the poor.
10 They cause *him* to go naked without clothing,
And they take away the sheaf *from* the hungry;
11 *Which* make oil within their walls,
And tread *their* winepresses, and suffer thirst.
12 Men groan from out of the city,
And the soul of the wounded crieth out:
Yet God layeth not folly *to them.*

13 They are of those that rebel against the light;
They know not the ways thereof,
Nor abide in the paths thereof.
14 [a]The murderer rising with the light
Killeth the poor and needy,
And in the night is as a thief.
15 [a]The eye also of the adulterer waiteth for the twilight,
[b]Saying, No eye shall see me:
And [1]disguiseth *his* face.
16 In the dark *they* dig *through* houses,
Which they had marked for themselves in the daytime:
[a]They know not the light.
17 For the morning *is* to them even as the shadow of death:
If *one* know *them, they are in* the terrors of the shadow of death.

18 He *is* swift as the waters;
Their portion is cursed in the earth:
He beholdeth not the way of the vineyards.
19 Drought and heat [1]consume the snow waters:
So doth the grave *those which* have sinned.
20 The womb shall forget him; the worm shall feed sweetly on him;
[a]He shall be no more remembered;
And wickedness shall be broken as a tree.
21 He evil entreateth the barren *that* beareth not:
And doeth not good to the widow.

22 He draweth also the mighty with his power:
He riseth up, and [1]no *man* is sure of life.

24:2 [1]Or, *feed them* [a]Deut. 19:14; 27:17; Prov. 22:28; 23:10; Hos. 5:10
24:3 [a]Deut. 24:6,10,12,17; ch. 22:6
24:4 [a]Prov. 28:28
24:6 [1]Heb. *mingled corn,* or, *dredge* [2]Heb. *the wicked gather the vintage*
24:7 [a]Ex. 22:26; Deut. 24:12,13; ch. 22:6
24:8 [a]Lam. 4:5
24:14 [a]Ps. 10:8
24:15 [1]Heb. *setteth his face in secret* [a]Prov. 7:9 [b]Ps. 10:11
24:16 [a]John 3:20
24:19 [1]Heb. *violently take*
24:20 [a]Prov. 10:7
24:22 [1]Or, *he trusteth not his own life*

24:1–12 Job describes the terrible injustice that often exists in the world. Robbery of both the "haves" (see v. 2) and the "have-nots" (see vv. 3–4) is equally obnoxious to him. But perhaps his suffering has enabled him to empathize with the poor, who must forage for food (v. 5) and "reap . . . corn in the field" (v. 6). The scene he depicts is heart-rending: The naked shiver in the cold of night (vv. 7–8), fatherless infants are snatched from the breast (v. 9), field hands harvest food but go hungry (v. 10), vineyard workers make wine but suffer thirst (v. 11), groans rise from the dying and wounded (v. 12). Job cannot understand why God is silent and indifferent (vv. 1,12) in the face of such misery, but the fact that God waits disproves the counselors' theory of suffering. Job is no more out of God's favor as one of the victims than the criminal in vv. 13–17 is in God's favor because of God's inaction.

‡24:1 See note on vv. 21–24. Job raises the question: "Why is God silent when injustice occurs?"

24:2 *remove the landmarks.* A serious crime in ancient times (see note on Deut 19:14).

24:3 *fatherless . . . widow's.* See 22:9; Is 1:17 and note; Jas 1:27.

24:5 *wild asses.* See 39:5–8.

24:6 *reap.* See note on Ruth 1:22.

24:7,10 Job implicitly denies the accusation of Eliphaz (see 22:6).

24:13–17 A description of those who cause the suffering depicted in vv. 2–12: the murderer (v. 14), the adulterer (v. 15), the robber (v. 16). Darkness is their element, the medium in which they thrive (see vv. 14–17). By contrast, God's law is the light against which they rebel (see v. 13; see also note on 22:28).

‡24:18–20 Job seems to agree with the counselors here. But it is also legitimate to translate the verses as Job's call for redress against evildoers: "May their portion be cursed in the earth . . . may the grave consume . . . May the womb (their mother) forget them; may the worm feed sweetly till they are no more remembered and their wickedness is broken as a tree."

‡24:18 *He is swift as the waters.* Pictures the wicked being swept away by a powerful river or flood.

24:20 *worm shall feed sweetly.* See 21:26; Is 14:11. *broken as a tree.* See note on 19:10.

24:21–24 By way of summary, Job says that God judges the wicked, but He does so in His own good time. Job wishes, however, that God would give the righteous the satisfaction of seeing it happen (v. 1).

‡24:21 *He evil entreateth the barren.* The wicked mistreat barren women who are all alone.

‡22:22 *He draweth also the mighty.* God "drags away" the wicked in judgment.

23 *Though* it be given him *to be* in safety,
whereon he resteth;
Yet [a]his eyes *are* upon their ways.
24 They are exalted for a little while, but
[1]are gone
And brought low, they are [2]taken out
of the way as all *other,*
And cut off as the tops of the ears of
corn.
25 And if *it be* not *so* now, who will make
me a liar,
And make my speech nothing worth?

Bildad answers

25 Then answered Bildad the Shuhite,
and said,

2 Dominion and fear *are* with him,
He maketh peace in his high places.
3 Is there *any* number of his armies?
And upon whom doth not [a]his light
arise?
4 [a]How then can man be justified with
God?
Or how can he be clean *that is* born of
a woman?
5 Behold *even* to the moon, and it
shineth not;
Yea, the stars are not pure in his sight.
6 How much less man, *that is* [a]a worm?
And the son of man, *which is* a worm?

Job's final speech

26 But Job answered and said,

2 How hast thou helped *him that is*
without power?
How savest thou the arm *that hath* no
strength?
3 How hast thou counselled *him that*
hath no wisdom?
And *how* hast thou plentifully declared
the thing as it is?
4 To whom hast thou uttered words?
And whose spirit came from thee?

5 Dead *things* are formed
From under the waters, [1]and the
inhabitants thereof.
6 [a]Hell *is* naked before him,
And destruction hath no covering.
7 [a]He stretcheth out the north over the
empty place,
And hangeth the earth upon nothing.

8 [a]He bindeth up the waters in his thick
clouds;
And the cloud is not rent under them.
9 He holdeth back the face of *his* throne,
And spreadeth his cloud upon it.
10 [a]He hath compassed the waters with
bounds,
[1]Until the day and night come to an
end.

11 The pillars of heaven tremble
And are astonished at his reproof.
12 [a]He divideth the sea with his power,
And by his understanding he smiteth
through [1]the proud.
13 [a]By his spirit he hath garnished the
heavens;
His hand hath formed [b]the crooked
serpent.

14 Lo, these *are* parts of his ways:
But how little a portion is heard of
him?

24:23 [a]Ps. 11:4; Prov. 15:3
24:24 [1]Heb. are *not* [2]Heb. *closed up*
25:3 [a]Jas. 1:17
25:4 [a]ch. 4:17; 15:14
25:6 [a]Ps. 22:6
26:5 [1]Or, *with the inhabitants*
26:6 [a]Ps. 139:8; Prov. 15:11; Heb. 4:13
26:7 [a]ch. 9:8; Ps. 24:2; 104:2
26:8 [a]Prov. 30:4
26:10 [1]Heb. *Until the end of light with darkness* [a]ch. 38:8; Ps. 33:7; 104:9
26:12 [1]Heb. *pride* [a]Ex. 14:21; Is. 51:15; Jer. 31:35
26:13 [a]Ps. 33:6 [b]Is. 27:1

24:24 *cut off as the tops of the ears of corn.* A symbol of judgment (see note on Is 17:5).
25:1–6 See note on 22:1–26:14. Bildad adds nothing new here, and Zophar, who has already admitted how emotionally disturbed he was (see 20:2), doesn't even comment.
25:2 *maketh peace in his high places.* Bildad apparently considered heaven as a place of warfare, where God must use His celestial troops (see v. 3) to establish order.
25:3 *armies.* Angels. *his light.* The sun. All that is under God's dominion pales before Him.
25:4–6 Bildad echoes Eliphaz's earlier statements about human depravity (4:17–19; 15:14–16).
‡25:5 *moon . . . stars.* If the heavenly lights pale in comparison to God's glory, what hope is there for man?
26:2–4 With biting sarcasm, Job responds to Bildad alone (the Hebrew for the word "you" in these verses is singular rather than plural), indicating that Eliphaz and Zophar have already been silenced.
26:2 *savest thou the arm that hath no strength.* See 4:3–4; Is 35:3; Heb 12:12.
26:5–14 Job's poem about the vast power of God, the theme of Bildad's final speech (ch. 25), is written in colorful language that is often highly figurative.
‡26:5 *Dead things.* The Hebrew for this expression is translated "the dead" or "dead" in Prov 2:18; Is 14:9 and 26:14. The term is used figuratively of the deceased who inhabit the netherworld (see 3:13–15, 17–19; see also note on 3:16). *are formed.* Lit. "tremble." They are in anguish. *waters.* Part of the world inhabited by living beings, and therefore above the netherworld.
‡26:6 *Hell.* Or "Sheol," the grave. Personified elsewhere as the "king of terrors" (see 18:14 and note). *destruction.* Hebrew *Abaddon.* See 28:22; 31:12; Prov 15:11. In Rev 9:11, Abaddon is the name of the "angel of the bottomless pit" (see note there). *hath no covering.* Is exposed before God.
26:7 *He.* God. *stretcheth out the north.* See 37:18. *empty place.* The Hebrew for this word is translated "without form" in Gen 1:2. *nothing.* See note on 9:6.
‡26:8 *cloud is not rent under them.* Does not break under the weight of the water they contain.
‡26:9 *holdeth back the face of his throne.* Or "covers" his heavenly throne with a cloud.
26:11 *pillars of heaven.* See note on 9:6.
26:12 *the proud.* Hebrew *Rahab* (the sea monster). See note on 9:13.
26:13 *crooked serpent.* A description of the sea monster Leviathan (see notes on 3:8; Is 27:1).
‡26:14 *these are parts of his ways.* Lit. "these are the edges of his ways." What God has revealed of His dominion over natural and supernatural forces amounts to no more than a whisper. Job is impressed with the severely limited character of human understanding. Zophar had chided Job about his inability to fathom the mysteries of God (11:7–9), but the knowledge pos-

But the thunder of his power who can
understand?

27

Moreover Job [1] continued his parable, and said,

2 *As* God liveth, [a] *who* hath taken away
my judgment;
And the Almighty, *who* hath [b] [1] vexed
my soul;
3 All the while my breath *is* in me,
And [1] the spirit of God *is* in my
nostrils;
4 My lips shall not speak wickedness,
Nor my tongue utter deceit.
5 God forbid that I should justify you:
Till I die [a] I will not remove my
integrity from me.
6 My righteousness I [a] hold fast, and will
not let it go:
[b] My heart shall not reproach *me* [1] so
long as I live.
7 Let mine enemy be as the wicked,
And he that riseth up against me as the
unrighteous.

8 [a] For what *is* the hope of the hypocrite,
though he hath gained,
When God taketh away his soul?
9 [a] Will God hear his cry
When trouble cometh upon him?
10 [a] Will he delight himself in the
Almighty?
Will he always call upon God?
11 I will teach you [1] by the hand of God:
That which *is* with the Almighty will I
not conceal.
12 Behold, all ye yourselves have seen *it;*
Why then are ye thus altogether vain?

27:1 [1] Heb. *added to take up*
27:2 [1] Heb. *made my soul bitter* [a] ch. 34:5 [b] Ruth 1:20; 2 Ki. 4:27
27:3 [1] That is, *the breath which God gave him*
27:5 [a] ch. 2:9; 13:15
27:6 [1] Heb. *from my days* [a] ch. 2:3 [b] Acts 24:16
27:8 [a] Mat. 16:26; Luke 12:20
27:9 [a] ch. 35:12; Prov. 1:28; 28:9; Is. 1:15; Jer. 14:12; Ezek. 8:18; Mic. 3:4; John 9:31; Jas. 4:3
27:10 [a] See ch. 22:26,27
27:11 [1] Or, being *in the hand, etc.*

27:13 [a] ch. 20:29
27:14 [a] Deut. 28:41; Esth. 9:10; Hos. 9:13
27:15 [a] Ps. 78:64
27:17 [a] Prov. 28:8; Eccl. 2:26
27:18 [a] Is. 1:8; Lam. 2:6
27:20 [a] ch. 18:11
27:22 [1] Heb. *In fleeing he would flee*
28:1 [1] Or, *a mine*
28:2 [1] Or, *dust*

13 [a] This *is* the portion of a wicked man
with God,
And the heritage of oppressors, *which*
they shall receive of the Almighty.
14 [a] If his children be multiplied, *it is* for
the sword:
And his offspring shall not be satisfied
with bread.
15 Those that remain of him shall be
buried in death:
And [a] his widows shall not weep.
16 Though he heap up silver as the dust,
And prepare raiment as the clay;
17 He may prepare *it,* but [a] the just shall
put *it* on,
And the innocent shall divide the silver.
18 He buildeth his house as a moth,
And [a] as a booth *that* the keeper maketh.
19 The rich *man* shall lie down, but he
shall not be gathered:
He openeth his eyes, and he *is* not.
20 [a] Terrors take hold on him as waters,
A tempest stealeth him away in the
night.
21 The east wind carrieth him away, and
he departeth:
And as a storm hurleth him out of his
place.
22 For *God* shall cast upon him, and not
spare:
[1] He would fain flee out of his hand.
23 *Men* shall clap their hands at him,
And shall hiss him out of his place.

28

Surely there is [1] a vein for the silver,
And a place for gold *where* they
fine *it.*
2 Iron is taken out of the [1] earth,
And brass *is* molten *out of* the stone.

---

sessed by Job's friends was not superior to that of Job himself (see 12:3; 13:2). *thunder of his power.* If it is difficult for us to comprehend the little that we know about God, how much more impossible it would be to understand the full extent of His might!

27:1–23 The dialogue-dispute section of the book begins with Job's opening lament (ch. 3), continues with the three cycles of speeches (chs. 4–14; 15–21; 22–26) and concludes with Job's closing discourse (ch. 27), in which he reasserts his own innocence (vv. 2–6) and eloquently describes the ultimate fate of the wicked (vv. 13–23).

‡27:2 *As God liveth.* The most solemn of oaths (see note on Gen 42:15). Job's faith in God continued despite his perception of denied justice. *taken away my judgment.* Denied justice to me.

27:5 *you.* The Hebrew for this word is plural. In his summary statement, Job once again speaks to his three friends as a group.

27:6 *My righteousness I hold fast.* God had spoken similarly of Job (see 2:3).

27:7 *Let mine enemy be as the wicked.* Job calls for his friends, who had falsely accused him of being wicked, to be treated as though they themselves were wicked men (cf. Ps 109:6–15; 137:8–9).

27:11 *I will teach you.* Job is about to remind his counselors about an issue on which they all agree: that the truly wicked deserve God's wrath (vv. 13–23). The three friends had falsely put Job in that category.

27:13–23 A poem that dramatizes the effect of Job's earlier call for redress (v. 7).

27:13 Job echoes the words of Zophar in 20:29 (see note there).

27:18 *house as a moth . . . booth.* Symbols of fragility (see note on 4:19; Is 1:8 and note; 24:20).

27:21 *east wind.* See note on 15:2.

‡28:1–28 Job's friends' application of traditional wisdom to human suffering has been even more unsatisfactory than Job's untraditional response. Both attempts to penetrate the mystery have failed, and the dialogue has come to an unsatisfactory conclusion. Therefore Job, or perhaps the unknown author of the book, inserts a striking wisdom poem that answers the question, "Where shall wisdom be found?" (v. 12; see v. 20). The poem consists of three parts: (1) precious stones and metals are found in the deepest mines (vv. 1–11); (2) wisdom is not found in mines, nor can it be bought with precious stones or metals (vv. 12–19); (3) wisdom is found only in God and in the fear of Him (vv. 20–28). The chapter, then, anticipates the theme of God's speeches (38:1–42:6): God alone is the answer to the mystery that Job and his friends have sought to fathom.

28:1–11 A fascinating, lyrical description of ancient mining techniques.

‡28:2 *Iron.* See note on 19:24. *brass.* Or "copper."

3 He setteth an end to darkness,
And searcheth out all perfection,
The stones of darkness, and the shadow of death.
4 The flood breaketh out from the inhabitant;
Even the waters forgotten of the foot:
They are dried up, they are gone away from men.

5 *As for* the earth, out of it cometh bread:
And under it is turned up as it were fire.
6 The stones of it *are* the place of sapphires:
And it hath [1] dust of gold.
7 *There is* a path which no fowl knoweth,
And which the vulture's eye hath not seen:
8 The lion's whelps have not trodden it,
Nor the fierce lion passed by it.

9 He putteth forth his hand upon the [1] rock;
He overturneth the mountains by the roots.
10 He cutteth out rivers among the rocks;
And his eye seeth every precious thing.
11 He bindeth the floods [1] from overflowing;
And the thing that is hid bringeth he forth *to* light.
12 [a] But where shall wisdom be found?
And where *is* the place of understanding?

13 Man knoweth not the [a] price thereof;
Neither is it found in the land of the living.
14 [a] The depth saith, It *is* not in me:
And the sea saith, *It is* not with me.
15 [1] It [a] cannot be gotten for gold,
Neither shall silver be weighed *for* the price thereof.

28:6 [1] Or, *gold ore*
28:9 [1] Or, *flint*
28:11 [1] Heb. *from weeping*
28:12 [a] Eccl. 7:24
28:13 [a] Prov. 3:15
28:14 [a] ver. 22; Rom. 11:33
28:15 [1] Heb. *Fine gold shall not be given for it* [a] Prov. 3:13-15; 8:10,11,19
28:17 [1] Or, *vessel of fine gold*
28:18 [1] Or, *Ramoth*
28:20 [a] ver. 12
28:21 [1] Or, *heaven*
28:22 [a] ver. 14
28:24 [a] Prov. 15:3
28:25 [a] Ps. 135:7
28:26 [a] ch. 38:25
28:27 [1] Or, *did number it*
28:28 [a] Deut. 4:6; Prov. 1:7
29:1 [1] Heb. *added to take up*

16 It cannot be valued with the gold of Ophir,
With the precious onyx, or the sapphire.

17 The gold and the crystal cannot equal it:
And the exchange of it *shall not be for* [1] jewels of fine gold.
18 No mention shall be made of [1] coral, or of pearls:
For the price of wisdom *is* above rubies.
19 The topaz of Ethiopia shall not equal it,
Neither shall it be valued with pure gold.

20 [a] Whence then cometh wisdom?
And where *is* the place of understanding?
21 Seeing it is hid from the eyes of all living,
And kept close from the fowls of the [1] air.
22 [a] Destruction and death say,
We have heard the fame thereof with our ears.
23 God understandeth the way thereof,
And he knoweth the place thereof.
24 For he looketh to the ends of the earth,
And [a] seeth under the whole heaven;

25 [a] To make the weight for the winds;
And he weigheth the waters by measure.
26 When he [a] made a decree for the rain,
And a way for the lightning of the thunder:
27 Then did he see it, and [1] declare it;
He prepared it, yea, and searched it out.
28 And unto man he said, Behold, [a] the fear of the Lord, that *is* wisdom;
And to depart from evil *is* understanding.

29

Moreover Job [1] continued his parable, and said,

‡28:3 *setteth an end to darkness.* By using an artificial source of light, such as a torch or lamp. *searcheth out all perfection . . . shadow of death.* Explores the deepest recesses of the earth.
‡28:4 *The flood breaketh out . . . inhabitant.* Or "A flood (shaft) is cut out far from human habitation." For "flood" as a mining shaft, cf. "rivers" in v. 10 and "floods" in v. 11. *dried up . . . gone away.* Lit. "they dangle away from men as they swing back and forth," which describes the difficult and dangerous work of mining. Men will hazard everything to dig the earth's treasures.
28:6 *sapphires.* See v. 16; see also notes on Sol 5:14; Is 54:11.
28:9 *mountains by the roots.* A poetic expression emphasizing great depth (cf. Jonah 2:6).
‡28:10 *cutteth out rivers among the rocks.* Makes tunnels. An eighth-century B.C. inscription found at Jerusalem's Pool of Siloam testifies to the sophistication of ancient tunneling technology.
28:12 The questions, repeated almost verbatim in v. 20, are answered in v. 28.
28:16 *gold of Ophir.* See 22:24 and note.
28:18 *the price of wisdom is above rubies.* Cf. the value of a "virtuous woman" (Prov 31:10), who fears the Lord (Prov 31:30) and is therefore wise (see v. 28).
28:19 *Ethiopia.* The Hebrew term (Cush) actually includes the entire upper Nile region, south of Egypt.
‡28:21 *kept close from the fowls.* Hidden from the birds, as are precious stones and metals (see v. 7).
‡28:22 *Destruction and death.* See note on 26:6. Sheol is located in the depths of the earth (cf. Ps 139:8), but wisdom is in such a remote place that even death and destruction have only heard of its "fame" (rumor/reputation).
28:25–27 Wisdom has been with God from the time of creation itself (see Prov 8:22–31).
28:28 *fear of the Lord . . . depart from evil.* See the description of Job's character in 1:1,8; 2:3. *that is wisdom.* "The fear of the LORD is the beginning of wisdom" (Ps 111:10; Prov 9:10; see Prov 1:7).
29:1–31:40 Like a lawyer submitting his final brief, Job pre-

2 O that I were as *in* months past,
As *in* the days *when* God preserved me;
3 [a]When his [1]candle shined upon my head,
And when by his light I walked *through* darkness;
4 As I was in the days of my youth,
When [a]the secret of God *was* upon my tabernacle;
5 When the Almighty *was* yet with me,
When my children *were* about me;
6 When [a]*I* washed my steps with butter,
And [b]the rock poured [1]me out rivers of oil;

7 When I went out *to* the gate through the city,
When I prepared my seat in the street;
8 The young men saw me, and hid themselves:
And the aged arose, *and* stood *up.*
9 The princes refrained talking,
And [a]laid *their* hand on their mouth.
10 [1]The nobles held their peace,
And their [a]tongue cleaved to the roof of their mouth.

11 When the ear heard *me,* then it blessed me;
And when the eye saw *me,* it gave witness to me:
12 Because [a]I delivered the poor that cried,
And the fatherless, and *him that had* none to help him.
13 The blessing of him that was ready to perish came upon me:
And I caused the widow's heart to sing for joy.
14 [a]I put on righteousness, and it clothed me:
My judgment *was* as a robe and a diadem.
15 I was [a]eyes to the blind,
And feet *was* I to the lame.
16 I *was* a father to the poor:
And [a]the cause *which* I knew not I searched out.
17 And I brake [a][1]the jaws of the wicked,
And [2]pluckt the spoil out of his teeth.

18 Then I said, [a]I shall die in my nest,
And I shall multiply *my* days as the sand.
19 [a]My root *was* [1]spread out [b]by the waters,
And the dew lay all night upon my branch.
20 My glory *was* [1]fresh in me,
And my [a]bow was [2]renewed in my hand.

21 Unto me *men* gave ear, and waited,
And kept silence at my counsel.
22 After my words they spake not again;
And my speech dropped upon them.
23 And they waited for me as for the rain;
And they opened their mouth wide *as* for [a]the latter rain.
24 *If* I laughed on them, they believed *it* not;
And the light of my countenance they cast not down.
25 I chose out their way, and sat chief,
And dwelt as a king in the army,
As *one that* comforteth the mourners.

30 But now *they that are* [1]younger than I have me in derision,
Whose fathers I would have disdained
To have set with the dogs of my flock.
2 Yea, whereto *might* the strength of their hands profit me,

29:3 [1]Or, *lamp* [a]ch. 18:6
29:4 [a]Ps. 25:14
29:6 [1]Heb. *with me* [a]Gen. 49:11; Deut. 32:13; ch. 20:17 [b]Ps. 81:16
29:9 [a]ch. 21:5
29:10 [1]Heb. *The voice of the nobles was hid* [a]Ps. 137:6
29:12 [a]Ps. 72:12; Prov. 21:13; 24:11
29:14 [a]Deut. 24:13; Is. 59:17; 61:10; Eph. 6:14; 1 Thes. 5:8
29:15 [a]Num. 10:31
29:16 [a]Prov. 29:7
29:17 [1]Heb. *the jaw teeth,* or, *the grinders* [2]Heb. *I cast* [a]Ps. 58:6; Prov. 30:14
29:18 [a]Ps. 30:6
29:19 [1]Heb. *opened* [a]ch. 18:16 [b]Ps. 1:3; Jer. 17:8
29:20 [1]Heb. *new* [2]Heb. *changed* [a]Gen. 49:24
29:23 [a]Zech. 10:1
30:1 [1]Heb. *of fewer days than I*

sents a three-part summation: Part one (ch. 29) is a nostalgic review of his former happiness, wealth and honor; part two (ch. 30) is a lament over the loss of everything, especially his honor; part three (ch. 31) is a final protestation of his innocence.

29:1–25 A classic example of Semitic rhetoric, using the following symmetrical pattern: blessing (vv. 2–6), honor (vv. 7–10), benevolence (vv. 11–17), blessing (vv. 18–20), honor (vv. 21–25).

29:2–6 Words charged with emotion. In earlier days, God had been Job's friend and companion.

29:3 *by his light I walked.* See note on 22:28.

29:4 *When the secret of God was upon my tabernacle.* Lit. "When God's council was by my tent," or "When God was an intimate in my tent." The clause evokes a situation similar to that in Gen 18, where God and two members of His heavenly council eat and drink at Abraham's tent—and there God discloses to His friend the imminent birth of the promised son and God's intentions concerning Sodom and Gomorrah.

29:5 *my children were about me.* See 1:2.

29:6 *butter . . . oil.* Symbols of richness and luxury (see 20:17; Ezek 16:19).

‡29:7 *gate through the city.* The city gate was where the most important business was conducted and the most significant legal cases were tried (see note on Ruth 4:1). *prepared my seat.* Or "took my seat," as a city elder, a member of the ruling council (see note on Gen 19:1).

29:12–13 *I delivered . . . the fatherless . . . caused the widow's heart to sing.* Implicitly responding to Eliphaz's accusation in 22:9, Job expresses his concern for the helpless and unfortunate (see 24:9; 31:16–18,21).

29:14 *I put on righteousness . . . judgment was as a robe.* For similar imagery see Is 59:17; 61:10; Eph 6:14,17.

29:18 *I said.* Job muses on what might have been the course of his life.

29:21–25 His counsel was valued (vv. 21–23), his approval sought (v. 24) and his civic leadership accepted with gratitude (v. 25).

‡29:24 *If I laughed . . . believed it not.* Were astonished when someone as important as Job would smile at them.

30:1–31 In contrast to the positive notes of blessing and honor sounded in ch. 29, Job now bemoans the suffering and dishonor he has been forced to undergo. God has heaped overwhelming terrors on him (v. 15). His final, forlorn lament (see v. 31) over his condition shows that his rage has not yet subsided.

‡30:1,9 *now . . . their song.* The young and old who deferred to him in the past now taunt him (see 29:8–11,21–25).

In whom old age was perished?
3 For want and famine *they were*
[1]solitary;
Flying *into* the wilderness
[2]In former time desolate and waste.
4 Who cut up mallows by the bushes,
And juniper roots *for* their meat.
5 They were driven forth from among
men,
(They cried after them as *after* a thief;)
6 To dwell in the clifts of the valleys,
In [1]caves of the earth, and *in* the
rocks.
7 Among the bushes they brayed;
Under the nettles they were gathered
together.
8 *They were* children of fools, yea,
children of [1]base men:
They were viler than the earth.

9 [a]And now am I their song,
Yea, I am their byword.
10 They abhor me, they flee far from me,
[1]And spare not [a]to spit in my face.
11 Because he [a]hath loosed my cord, and
afflicted me,
They have also let loose the bridle
before me.
12 Upon *my* right hand rise the youth;
They push away my feet,
And [a]they raise up against me the
ways of their destruction.
13 They mar my path,
They set forward my calamity,
They have no helper.
14 They came *upon me* as a wide
breaking in *of waters:*
In the desolation they rolled
themselves *upon me.*
15 Terrors are turned upon me:
They pursue [1]my soul as the wind:
And my welfare passeth away as a
cloud.

16 [a]And now my soul is poured out upon
me;
The days of affliction have taken hold
upon me.

30:3 [1]Or, *dark as the night* [2]Heb. *Yesternight*
30:6 [1]Heb. *holes*
30:8 [1]Heb. *men of no name*
30:9 [a]ch. 17:6; Ps. 35:15; 69:12; Lam. 3:14
30:10 [1]Heb. *And withhold not spittle from my face* [a]Num. 12:14; Deut. 25:9; Is. 50:6; Mat. 26:67; 27:30
30:11 [a]See ch. 12:18
30:12 [a]ch. 19:12
30:15 [1]Heb. *my principal one*
30:16 [a]Ps. 42:4

30:21 [1]Heb. *turned to be cruel* [2]Heb. *the strength of thy hand*
30:22 [1]Or, *wisdom*
30:23 [a]Heb. 9:27
30:24 [1]Heb. *heap*
30:25 [1]Heb. *for him that was hard of day?* [a]Ps. 35:13; Rom. 12:15
30:26 [a]Jer. 8:15
30:28 [a]Ps. 42:9
30:29 [1]Or, *ostriches* [a]Ps. 102:6; Mic. 1:8
30:30 [a]Ps. 119:83; Lam. 4:8 [b]Ps. 102:3

17 My bones are pierced in me in the
night season:
And my sinews take no rest.
18 By the great force *of my disease* is my
garment changed:
It bindeth me about as the collar of my
coat.
19 He hath cast me into the mire,
And I am become like dust and ashes.

20 I cry unto thee, and thou dost not hear
me:
I stand *up,* and thou regardest me *not.*
21 Thou art [1]become cruel to me:
With [2]thy strong hand thou opposest
thyself against me.
22 Thou liftest me up to the wind; thou
causest me to ride *upon it,*
And dissolvest my [1]substance.
23 For I know *that* thou wilt bring me *to*
death,
And *to* the house [a]appointed for all
living.

24 Howbeit *he* will not stretch out *his*
hand to the [1]grave,
Though *they* cry in his destruction.
25 [a]Did not I weep [1]for him that was in
trouble?
Was *not* my soul grieved for the poor?
26 [a]When I looked for good, then evil
came *unto me:*
And when I waited for light, there
came darkness.
27 My bowels boiled, and rested not:
The days of affliction prevented me.

28 [a]I went mourning without the sun:
I stood up, *and* I cried in the
congregation.
29 [a]I am a brother to dragons,
And a companion to [1]owls.
30 [a]My skin is black upon me,
And [b]my bones are burnt with heat.
31 My harp also is *turned* to mourning,
And my organ into the voice of them
that weep.

---

‡30:2 In his prime, Job viewed those who now condemn him as weak and decrepit.
‡30:4 *mallows.* Probably saltwort, which grows in otherwise infertile areas, including the regions east of Sinai where Job and his friends lived. Cf. 39:6. *juniper roots.* Or "broom shrubs," large bushes that grow in the deserts of the Middle East (see 1 Ki 19:4; Ps 120:4).
30:9 *byword.* See note on 17:6.
‡30:11 *he hath loosed my cord.* Unstrung my bow; decimated my strength. Cf. 29:20. *They . . . let loose the bridle before me.* People who once respected Job now have no restraint in their attacks against him.
30:12 *ways of their destruction.* See 19:12.
‡30:14 *wide breaking in.* A breach in a city wall.
30:15 *pursue my soul as the wind.* See v. 22.
‡30:17 *bones are pierced . . . sinews take no rest.* Job feels continual pain. See note on 2:7.
‡30:18 Job's affliction is like a garment that is about to choke him to death.
30:19 *dust and ashes.* Symbolic of humiliation and insignificance (see note on Gen 18:27). Job would someday use "dust and ashes" to symbolize repentance (42:6).
30:20–23 Job now directs his thoughts away from men and toward God. He accuses God of abusing His power by attacking him despite his pleas for mercy.
‡30:22 God has tossed Job about with a violent wind.
‡30:24 *he will not stretch out his hand . . . grave.* It appears that God refuses to help even though Job is at the point of death.
30:26 Cf. Is 5:2,7.
30:28 *mourning.* See v. 30; see also note on 2:7.
‡30:29 *brother to dragons . . . companions to owls.* "Dragons" = "jackals;" "owls" = "ostriches." The prophet Micah uses similar imagery of himself in Mic 1:8.
‡30:30 *heat.* Or "fever." See note on 2:7.

31 I made a covenant with mine [a]eyes;
Why then should I think upon a maid?
2 For what [a]portion of God *is there* from above?
And *what* inheritance of the Almighty from on high?
3 *Is* not destruction to the wicked?
And a strange punishment to the workers of iniquity?
4 [a]Doth not he see my ways,
And count all my steps?

5 If I have walked with vanity,
Or *if* my foot hath hasted to deceit;
6 [1]Let me be weighed in an even balance,
That God may know mine integrity.
7 If my step hath turned out of the way,
And [a]mine heart walked after mine eyes,
And *if any* blot hath cleaved to my hands;
8 *Then* [a]let me sow, and let another eat;
Yea, let my offspring be rooted out.

9 If mine heart have been deceived by a woman,
Or *if* I have laid wait at my neighbour's door;
10 *Then* let my wife grind unto [a]another,
And let others bow down upon her.
11 For this *is* a heinous crime;
Yea, [a]it *is* an iniquity *to be punished by* the judges.
12 For it *is* a fire *that* consumeth to destruction,
And would root out all mine increase.

13 If I did despise the cause of my manservant or of my maidservant,
When they contended with me;
14 What then shall I do when [a]God riseth up?
And when he visiteth, what shall I answer him?
15 [a]Did not he that made me in the womb make him?
And [1]did not one fashion us in the womb?

16 If I have withheld the poor from *their* desire,
Or have caused the eyes of the widow to fail;
17 Or have eaten my morsel myself alone,
And the fatherless hath not eaten thereof;
18 (For from my youth he was brought up *with* me, as *with* a father,
And I have guided [1]her from my mother's womb;)
19 If I have seen *any* perish for want of clothing,
Or *any* poor without covering;
20 If his loins have not [a]blessed me,
And *if* he were *not* warmed with the fleece of my sheep;
21 If I have lift up my hand [a]against the fatherless,
When I saw my help in the gate:
22 *Then* let mine arm fall from *my* shoulder blade,
And mine arm be broken from [1]the bone.
23 For [a]destruction from God *was* a terror to me,
And by reason of his highness I could not endure.

24 [a]If I have made gold my hope,
Or have said to the fine gold, *Thou art* my confidence;
25 [a]If I rejoiced because my wealth *was* great,

31:1 [a]Mat. 5:28
31:2 [a]ch. 20:29
31:4 [a]2 Chr. 16:9; Prov. 5:21; Jer. 32:19
31:6 [1]Heb. *Let him weigh me in balances of justice*
31:7 [a]See Num. 15:39; Eccl. 11:9; Ezek. 6:9; Mat. 5:29
31:8 [a]Lev. 26:16; Deut. 28:30,38
31:10 [a]2 Sam. 12:11; Jer. 8:10
31:11 [a]Gen. 38:24; Lev. 20:10; See ver. 28
31:14 [a]Ps. 44:21
31:15 [1]Or, *did he not fashion us in one womb?* [a]ch. 34:19
31:18 [1]That is, *the widow*
31:20 [a]Deut. 24:13
31:21 [a]ch. 22:9
31:22 [1]Or, *the chanelbone*
31:23 [a]Is. 13:6
31:24 [a]Mark 10:24
31:25 [a]Ps. 62:10

31:1–40 The climactic section of Job's three-part summation (see note on 29:1–31:40). It is negative in the sense that Job denies all the sins listed, but it has the positive purpose of attesting loyalty to God as his sovereign Lord. In the strongest legal terms, using a series of self-maledictory oaths, Job completes his defense. No more can be said (v. 40). He now affixes his signature to the document (v. 35), and the burden of proof that he is a wretched sinner rests with God. Job's call for vindication had reached a climax in 27:2–6. Now he amplifies that statement with the details of his godly life. Each disavowal (vv. 5–7,9,13,16–21,24–27,29–34,38–39) is accompanied by an oath that calls for the punishment the offense deserves (vv. 8,10–12,14–15,22–23,28,40). The principle at work is the so-called "law of retaliation" (see Ex 21:23–25 and note).
‡31:1–12 Job begins with sins of the heart, especially sexual lust (vv. 1–4), cheating in business (vv. 5–8) and marital infidelity (vv. 9–12). Sixteen verses in this chapter begin with "if," raising a series of hypothetical questions.
‡31:1 *think upon a maid.* To think lustful thoughts about a virgin, which Jesus labels as sin (see Mat 5:28).
31:4 Echoed by Elihu in 34:21.
‡31:6 *Let me be weighed in an even balance.* With the accurate scales of justice. See 6:2; Prov 16:12; 21:2; 24:12. *integrity.* Does not imply sinless perfection (see note on 1:1).
‡31:7 *blot . . . to my hands.* Pictures guilt for sin as a stain on the hands.
‡31:9 *deceived by a woman.* Enticed into an illicit relationship.
‡31:10 *grind unto another.* Grind meal for another man's food. *bow down upon her.* Sleep with her.
‡31:12 *destruction.* Hebrew *Abaddon.* See note on 26:6.
31:13–23 Job reveals genuine understanding concerning matters of social justice: Human equality is based on creation (vv. 13–15), compassion toward those in need is essential (vv. 16–20), and power and influence must not be abused (vv. 21–23).
31:16–17 *widow . . . fatherless.* See note on 29:12–13.
‡31:17 *eaten my morsel . . . alone.* Refused to share my food with the needy.
‡31:20 *loins have not blessed me.* Personifies the loins as thankful because they are kept warm by clothing Job has provided ("the fleece of my sheep").
31:24–28 Covetous greed (vv. 24–25) and idolatry (vv. 26–27) are equally reprehensible in the eyes of God (v. 28; see Mat 6:19–24; Col 3:5).
31:25 *my wealth was great.* See 1:3,10.

And because mine hand had [1]gotten much;
26 [a]If I beheld [1]the sun when it shined,
Or the moon walking [2]*in* brightness;
27 And my heart hath been secretly enticed,
Or [1]my mouth hath kissed my hand:
28 This also *were* an iniquity *to be punished by* the judge:
For I should have denied the God *that is* above.

29 [a]If I rejoiced at the destruction of him that hated me,
Or lift up myself when evil found him:
30 ([a]Neither have I suffered [1]my mouth to sin
By wishing a curse to his soul.)

31 If the men of my tabernacle said not,
O that we had of his flesh! we cannot be satisfied.
32 [a]The stranger did not lodge in the street:
But I opened my doors [1]to the traveller.
33 If I covered my transgressions [a][1]as Adam,
By hiding mine iniquity in my bosom:
34 Did I fear a great [a]multitude,
Or did the contempt of families terrify me,
That I kept silence, *and* went not out *of* the door?

35 O that one would hear me!
[1]Behold, my desire *is,* [a]*that* the Almighty would answer me,
And *that* mine adversary had written a book.
36 Surely I would take it upon my shoulder,
And bind it *as* a crown to me.
37 I would declare unto him the number of my steps;
As a prince would I go near unto him.

38 If my land cry against me,
Or that the furrows likewise thereof [1]complain;
39 If [a]I have eaten [1]the fruits thereof without money,
Or [b]have [2]caused the owners thereof to lose their life:
40 Let [a]thistles grow instead of wheat,
And [1]cockle instead of barley.

¶ The words of Job are ended.

Elihu declares his opinion

32 So these three men ceased [1]to answer Job, because he *was* [a]righteous
in his own eyes.
2 Then was kindled the wrath of Elihu the
son of Barachel the Buzite, of the kindred of
Ram: against Job was his wrath kindled, because he justified [1]himself rather than God.
3 Also against his three friends was his
wrath kindled, because they had found no answer, and *yet* had condemned Job.
4 Now Elihu had [1]waited till Job had spoken, because they *were* [2]elder than he.
5 When Elihu saw that *there was* no answer in the mouth of *these* three men, then
his wrath was kindled.

6 ¶ And Elihu the son of Barachel the Buzite answered and said,

31:25 [1]Heb. *found much*
31:26 [1]Heb. *the light* [2]Heb. *bright* [a]Ezek. 8:16
31:27 [1]Heb. *my hand hath kissed my mouth*
31:29 [a]Prov. 17:5
31:30 [1]Heb. *my palate* [a]Mat. 5:44
31:32 [1]Or, *to the way* [a]Gen. 19:2,3
31:33 [1]Or, *after the manner of men* [a]Prov. 28:13
31:34 [a]Ex. 23:2
31:35 [1]Or, *Behold, my sign* is that *the Almighty will answer me* [a]ch. 13:22
31:38 [1]Heb. *weep*
31:39 [1]Heb. *the strength thereof* [2]Heb. *caused the soul of the owners thereof to expire,* or, *breathe out* [a]Jas. 5:4 [b]1 Ki. 21:19
31:40 [1]Or, *noisome weeds* [a]Gen. 3:18
32:1 [1]Heb. *from answering* [a]ch. 33:9
32:2 [1]Heb. *his soul*
32:4 [1]Heb. *expected Job in words* [2]Heb. *elder for days*

31:26–28 The sun and moon are not to be objects of worship (see Deut 4:19; 17:3; Ezek 8:16–17).
31:27 *kissed my hand.* An ancient gesture of worship (see 1 Ki 19:18; Hos 13:2).
31:29–32 The sin of gloating over one's enemy was condemned by Moses (Ex 23:4–5) and by Christ (Mat 5:43–47).
‡31:31 *O . . . cannot be satisfied.* Read as a question, "Can you find anyone who has not been satisfied . . . ? Job's servants always had plenty to eat.
31:33–34 A strong denial of hypocrisy.
31:33 *as Adam.* See Gen 3:8–10; Hos 6:7.
31:35–37 Job's final call for justice. His signature endorses every word of the oaths he has just taken.
31:35 *one would hear me.* See notes on 5:1; 9:33; 16:18–21; 19:25. *that the Almighty would answer me.* See note on 38:1. *adversary.* The Hebrew for this word is not the same as that for "Satan" (see note on 1:6). Here Job's accuser is either (1) a human adversary (perhaps one of the three friends) or (2) God Himself. In any event, Job assumes that accusations have been lodged against him before the court of heaven to which God has responded with judgments.
31:36 *shoulder.* Inscriptions were sometimes worn on the shoulder as a perpetual reminder of their importance (see Ex 28:12).
‡31:37 *declare unto him . . . my steps.* Give an account of my every action.
31:38–40 A climactic oath that completes an earlier theme and creates a unique emphasis. Job calls for a curse on his land if he has not been fully committed to social justice (see also vv. 13–15).
31:40 *The words of Job are ended.* His complaints and arguments are now over. He will only make brief statements of contrition (40:4–5; 42:2–6) following the divine discourses.
32:1–37:24 A fourth counselor, named Elihu and younger than the other three (32:4,6–7,9), has been standing on the sidelines, giving deference to age and listening to the dialogue-dispute. But now he declares himself ready to show that both Job and the three other counselors are in the wrong. Elihu's four poetic speeches (32:5–33:33; ch. 34; ch. 35; chs. 36–37) are preceded by a prose introduction (32:1–4) written by the author of the book.
32:1 *righteous in his own eyes.* He insisted on his innocence in spite of the terrible suffering that he was experiencing.
‡32:2–3 *wrath.* Elihu considers Job's emphasis on vindicating himself rather than God reprehensible, but he also believes that the friends' inability to refute Job was tantamount to condemning God. Elihu felt compelled to speak up for two reasons: (1) Job "justified himself," (2) his friends had "no answer." Neither had properly understood what was really at stake in this discussion.
32:2 *Buzite.* An inhabitant of Buz, a desert region in the east (see Jer 25:23).

I *am* [1]young, and ye *are* very old;
Wherefore I was afraid, and [2]durst not shew you mine opinion.
7 I said, Days should speak,
And multitude of years should teach wisdom.
8 But *there is* a spirit in man:
And [a]the inspiration of the Almighty giveth them understanding.
9 [a]Great men are not *always* wise:
Neither do the aged understand judgment.
10 Therefore I said, Hearken to me;
I also will shew mine opinion.

11 Behold, I waited for your words;
I gave ear to your [1]reasons,
Whilst you searched out [2]what to say.
12 Yea, I attended unto you,
And behold, *there was* none of you that convinced Job,
Or that answered his words:
13 [a]Lest ye should say, We have found out wisdom:
God thrusteth him down, not man.
14 Now he hath not [1]directed *his* words against me:
Neither will I answer him with your speeches.

15 They were amazed, they answered no more:
[1]They left off speaking.
16 When I had waited, (for they spake not,
But stood still, *and* answered no more:)
17 *I said,* I will answer also my part,
I also will shew mine opinion.
18 For I am full *of* [1]matter,
[2]The spirit within me constraineth me.
19 Behold, my belly *is* as wine *which* [1]hath no vent;
It is ready to burst like new bottles.
20 I will speak, [1]that I may be refreshed:
I will open my lips and answer.
21 Let me not, I pray you, accept *any* man's person,
Neither let me give flattering titles unto man.
22 For I know not to give flattering titles;
In so doing my Maker would soon take me away.

33 Wherefore, Job, I pray thee, hear my speeches,
And hearken to all my words.
2 Behold now I have opened my mouth,
My tongue hath spoken [1]in my mouth.
3 My words *shall be of* the uprightness of my heart:
And my lips shall utter knowledge clearly.
4 [a]The Spirit of God hath made me,
And the breath of the Almighty hath given me life.
5 If thou canst, answer me,
Set *thy words* in order before me, stand up.
6 [a]Behold, I *am* [1]according to thy wish in God's stead:
I also am [2]formed out of the clay.
7 [a]Behold, my terror shall not make thee afraid,
Neither shall my hand be heavy upon thee.

8 Surely thou hast spoken [1]in mine hearing,

32:6 [1]Heb. *few of days* [2]Heb. *I feared [to]*
32:8 [a]Prov. 2:6
32:9 [a]1 Cor. 1:26
32:11 [1]Heb. *understandings* [2]Heb. *words*
32:13 [a]Jer. 9:23
32:14 [1]Or, *ordered his words*
32:15 [1]Heb. *They removed speeches from themselves*
32:18 [1]Heb. *words*
32:18 [2]Heb. *The spirit of my belly*
32:19 [1]Heb. *is not opened*
32:20 [1]Heb. *that I may breathe*
33:2 [1]Heb. *in my palate*
33:4 [a]Gen. 2:7
33:6 [1]Heb. *according to thy mouth* [2]Heb. *cut out of the clay* [a]ch. 9:32,33
33:7 [a]ch. 9:34
33:8 [1]Heb. *in mine ears*

32:6 *young . . . afraid.* See Jer 1:6–8; 1 Tim 4:12; 2 Tim 1:7.
‡32:6,10 *shew . . . mine opinion.* See v. 17. Elihu overcomes his hesitance to speak and is now eager to share his thoughts and assumes that he can communicate them effectively (see note on 36:4).
32:8 *inspiration of the Almighty.* See 33:4.
32:14 *Neither will I answer him with your speeches.* Elihu feels that something important has been left out and, where the wisdom of age has failed, he has the understanding to supply the right answers.
32:15–22 Elihu delivers a soliloquy to himself, but it is also for the benefit of those who may be listening.
32:15–16 *They left off speaking . . . answered no more.* See v. 5. The breakdown of the third cycle in the dialogue-dispute cut short Bildad's last word and left Zophar without a third speech (see note on 22:1–26:14).
‡32:18 *full of matter.* See KJV marg. Elihu's speeches continue unabated through ch. 37 and he comes across as somewhat verbose. His speeches are longer than the combined speeches of any of Job's other friends. He has a genuine contribution to make, however, to the problems Job is facing. He does not stoop to false accusation about Job's earlier life but usually confines his criticism of Job to quotations from Job himself. This is perhaps the reason that God, in the epilogue, does not condemn Elihu along with Job's three friends (see 42:7).
‡32:19 *wine which hath no vent.* Like unopened wine. *ready to burst like new bottles.* Old wineskins might be expected to crack or break (see Mat 9:17), but not new ones. Elihu is obviously eager to speak and feels compelled to share his insights (cf. Jer 20:9).
32:21 *Let me not . . . accept any man's person.* Refuse to speak the truth out of respect for either Job or his friends.
33:1–33 Elihu turns to Job and speaks directly to him. Unlike the three friends, he addresses Job by name (vv. 1,31; see 37:14).
33:1 *hear my speeches.* He is thoroughly convinced of the importance and wisdom of the advice he is about to give (see vv. 31,33).
33:4 *Spirit of God hath made me.* See Gen 1:2 and note. *breath of the Almighty.* See 32:8. *given me life.* See 27:3; see also Gen 2:7 and note.
‡33:5 *If thou canst, answer me.* He opens and closes his speech (see v. 32) with the same plea to refute any flaws in his thinking. His attitude of superiority shows through.
‡33:6 *I am according to thy wish . . . stead.* Lit. "I am like your mouth before God." My words carry just as much weight with God as yours. *I also am formed out of the clay.* See note on 4:19.
33:7 *shall my hand be heavy upon thee.* The idiom is elsewhere used only of God (see 23:2; see also note on 1 Sam 5:6).
33:8 *Surely thou hast spoken.* Elihu's method is to quote Job (vv. 9–11; 34:5–6,9; 35:2–3) and then show him where and how he is wrong. The quotations are not always verbatim, which in-

And I have heard the voice of *thy* words, *saying,*
9 [a]I am clean without transgression,
I *am* innocent; neither *is there* iniquity in me.
10 Behold, he findeth occasions against me,
[a]He counteth me for his enemy,
11 [a]He putteth my feet in the stocks,
He marketh all my paths.
12 Behold, *in* this thou art not just: I will answer thee,
That God is greater than man.

13 Why dost thou [a]strive against him?
For [1]he giveth not account of any of his matters.
14 [a]For God speaketh once,
Yea twice, *yet man* perceiveth it not.
15 [a]In a dream, *in* a vision of the night,
When deep sleep falleth upon men,
In slumberings upon the bed;
16 [a]Then [1]he openeth the ears of men,
And sealeth their instruction.
17 That *he* may withdraw man *from his* [1]purpose,
And hide pride from man.
18 He keepeth back his soul from the pit,
And his life [1]from perishing by the sword.

19 He is chastened also with pain upon his bed,
And the multitude of his bones *with* strong *pain:*
20 [a]So that his life abhorreth bread,
And his soul [1]dainty meat.
21 His flesh is consumed away, that it cannot be seen;
And his bones *that* were not seen stick out.
22 Yea, his soul draweth near unto the grave,
And his life to the destroyers.

23 If there be a messenger with him, an interpreter,
One among a thousand,
To shew unto man his uprightness:
24 Then he is gracious unto him, and saith,
Deliver him from going down *to* the pit:
I have found [1]a ransom.

25 His flesh shall be fresher [1]than a child's:
He shall return to the days of his youth:
26 He shall pray unto God, and he will be favourable unto him:
And he shall see his face with joy:
For he will render unto man his righteousness.
27 [1]He looketh upon men, and *if any* [a]say,
I have sinned, and perverted *that which was* right,
And it [b]profited me not;
28 [1]He will [a]deliver his soul from going into the pit,
And his life shall see the light.

29 Lo, all these *things* worketh God
[1]Oftentimes with man,
30 [a]To bring back his soul from the pit,
To be enlightened with the light of the living.

33:9 [a]ch. 10:7
33:10 [a]ch. 16:9
33:11 [a]ch. 13:27
33:13 [1]Heb. *he answereth not* [a]Is. 45:9
33:14 [a]Ps. 62:11
33:15 [a]Num. 12:6
33:16 [1]Heb. *he revealeth,* or, *uncovereth* [a]ch. 36:10,15
33:17 [1]Heb. *work*
33:18 [1]Heb. *from passing by the sword*
33:20 [1]Heb. *meat of desire* [a]Ps. 107:18
33:24 [1]Or, *an atonement*
33:25 [1]Heb. *than childhood*
33:27 [1]Or, *He shall look upon men, and say, I have sinned, etc.* [a]2 Sam. 12:13; Prov. 28:13; Luke 15:21; 1 John 1:9 [b]Rom. 6:21
33:28 [1]Or, *He hath delivered my soul, etc., and my life* [a]Is. 38:17
33:29 [1]Heb. *Twice* and *thrice*
33:30 [a]Ps. 56:13

dicates that Elihu is content simply to repeat the substance of Job's arguments.

33:11 Elihu quotes Job's words almost verbatim here (see 13:27).

‡33:12 *thou art not just.* Elihu feels that Job needs to be corrected. Certainly Job's perception of God as his enemy (see v. 10; 13:24; 19:11) is wrong, but Elihu is also offended by what he considers Job's claim to purity (see v. 9). Job, however, had never claimed to be "clean without transgression," though some of his words were also understood that way by Eliphaz (see 15:14–16). Job admits being a sinner (7:21; 13:26) but disclaims the outrageous sins for which he thinks he is being punished. His complaints about God's silence (see v. 13) are also an offense to Elihu. But he imputes to Job the blanket statement that God never speaks to man, whereas Job's point is that God is silent in his present experience.

33:15 *In a dream . . . When deep sleep falleth upon men.* Elihu echoes Eliphaz (see 4:13).

‡33:17 *withdraw man from his purpose.* God speaks to men in order to deter them from their sinful intentions.

‡33:18 *from the pit . . . by the sword.* Listening to God's warnings will protect against an early death. *pit.* See vv. 22,24,28,30; a metaphor for the grave, as often in the Psalms.

33:19 *He is chastened also with pain upon his bed.* Dreams and visions (see v. 15) are not the only ways in which God speaks. He can talk to us in ways that we do not perceive (see v. 14). Elihu rightly states that God speaks to man in order to turn him from sin. But he overlooks Job's reason for wanting an audience with God: to find out what sins he is being accused of (see 13:22–23).

33:23–28 Having emphasized the importance of the chastening aspect of suffering, a point mentioned only briefly by Eliphaz (see 5:17), Elihu now moves on to the possibility of redemption based on a mediator (see note on 5:1). He further allows for God's gracious response of forgiveness where sincere repentance is present (vv. 27–28). But Elihu is still ignorant of the true nature of Job's relationship to God, known only in the divine council (chs. 1–2).

‡33:23 *a messenger . . . interpreter.* An angel who serves as Job's mediator. Refuting Job's claim that no such person exists (cf. 9:33).

33:24 *Deliver him from going down to the pit.* See Is 38:17. *ransom.* See Ps 49:7–9 and note.

33:25 *flesh shall be fresher than a child's . . . return.* Similar phrases are used in 2 Ki 5:14 with reference to healing from leprosy.

33:26 *see his face.* Not literally (see note on Gen 16:13).

33:30 *To bring back his soul from the pit.* Elihu teaches that God's apparent cruelty in chastening human beings is in reality an act of love, since man is never punished in this life in keeping with what he fully deserves (see v. 27). *light of the living.* Spiritual well-being (see Ps 49:19; see also Ps 27:1 and note). In some contexts, the phrase refers to resurrection (see note on Is 53:11).

31 Mark well, O Job, hearken unto me:
Hold thy peace, and I will speak.
32 If *thou* hast any thing to say, answer me:
Speak, for I desire to justify thee.
33 If not, [a]hearken unto me:
Hold thy peace, and I shall teach thee wisdom.

34 Furthermore Elihu answered and said,

2 Hear my words, O ye wise *men;*
And give ear unto me, ye that have knowledge.
3 [a]For the ear trieth words,
As the [1]mouth tasteth meat.
4 Let us choose to us judgment:
Let us know among ourselves what *is* good.

5 For Job hath said, [a]I am righteous:
And [b]God hath taken away my judgment.
6 [a]Should I lie against my right?
[1]My wound *is* incurable without transgression.
7 What man *is* like Job,
[a]*Who* drinketh up scorning like water?
8 Which goeth in company with the workers of iniquity,
And walketh with wicked men.
9 For [a]he hath said, It profiteth a man nothing
That he should delight himself with God.

10 Therefore hearken unto me, ye [1]men of understanding:
[a]Far be it from God, *that he should do* wickedness;
And *from* the Almighty, *that he should commit* iniquity.
11 [a]For the work of a man shall he render unto him,
And cause every man to find according to *his* ways.

12 Yea, surely God will not do wickedly,
Neither will the Almighty [a]pervert judgment.
13 Who hath given him a charge over the earth?
Or who hath disposed [1]the whole world?
14 If he set his heart [1]upon *man,*
If he [a]gather unto himself his spirit and his breath;
15 [a]All flesh shall perish together,
And man shall turn again unto dust.

16 If now *thou hast* understanding, hear this:
Hearken to the voice of my words.
17 [a]Shall even he that hateth right [1]govern?
And wilt thou condemn him that is most just?
18 [a]*Is it fit* to say to a king, *Thou art* wicked?
And to princes, *Ye are* ungodly?
19 *How much less to him* that [a]accepteth not the persons of princes,
Nor regardeth the rich more than the poor?
For [b]they all *are* the work of his hands.
20 *In* a moment shall they die,
And the people shall be troubled [a]at midnight, and pass away:
And [1]the mighty shall be taken away without hand.

33:33 [a]Ps. 34:11
34:3 [1]Heb. *palate* [a]ch. 6:30; 12:11
34:5 [a]ch. 33:9 [b]ch. 27:2
34:6 [1]Heb. *Mine arrow* [a]ch. 9:17
34:7 [a]ch. 15:16
34:9 [a]Mal. 3:14
34:10 [1]Heb. *men of heart* [a]ch. 8:3
34:11 [a]Ps. 62:12; Prov. 24:12; Mat. 16:27
34:12 [a]ch. 8:3
34:13 [1]Heb. *all of it?*
34:14 [1]Heb. *upon him* [a]Ps. 104:29
34:15 [a]Gen. 3:19
34:17 [1]Heb. *bind?* [a]2 Sam. 23:3
34:18 [a]Ex. 22:28
34:19 [a]Deut. 10:17 [b]ch. 31:15
34:20 [1]Heb. *they shall take away the mighty* [a]Ex. 12:29

33:32 *I desire to justify thee.* But this will happen, Elihu insists, only if Job repents.
34:1–37 The second of Elihu's four speeches (see note on 32:1–37:24), divided into three sections: (1) addressed to a group of wise men (vv. 2–15), doubtless including the three friends; (2) addressed to Job (vv. 16–33); (3) addressed to himself (vv. 34–37), as in 32:15–22 (see note there).
34:2,10 *Hear my words . . . hearken unto me.* Although it is possible that Elihu is overly impressed with his own wisdom, it is more likely that he considered himself a messenger of God (see 32:8; 33:4), especially in the light of his humble attitude in v. 4.
34:2 *wise men . . . ye that have knowledge.* Also referred to as "men of understanding" (vv. 10,34).
34:3 Elihu echoes the words of Job in 12:11 (see note there).
34:5,9 *Job hath said . . . For he hath said.* Elihu again quotes Job and then goes on to defend God's justice against what he considers to be Job's false theology (e.g., 9:14–24; 16:11–17; 19:7; 21:17–18; 24:1–12; 27:2). The substance of the quotation in v. 5 is accurate (cf. 12:4; 13:18; 27:6), and much of v. 6 represents Job fairly (see 21:34; 27:5; see also 6:4 and note)—though Job had never claimed to be completely guiltless. Verse 9 is not a direct quotation from Job, who had only imagined the wicked saying something similar (see 21:15). But perhaps Elihu derives it from Job's repeated statement that God treats the righteous and the wicked in the same way (cf. 9:22; 21:17; 24:1–12), leading to the conclusion that it does not pay to please God.
34:7 *drinketh up scorning like water.* See Eliphaz's description of man in 15:16.
34:10 *Far be it from God, that he should do wickedness.* See Gen 18:25 and note. Elihu's concern that Job was making God the author of evil is commendable. Job, in his frustration, has come perilously close to charging God with wrongdoing (12:4–6; 24:1–12). He has suggested that this is the only conclusion he can reach on the basis of his knowledge and experience (9:24).
34:11 See 2 Cor 5:10.
34:13–15 Elihu is zealous for God's glory as the sovereign Sustainer who demonstrates His grace every moment by granting life and breath to man.
‡34:14 *If he gather . . . his spirit and his breath.* If God withdrew a person's spirit and breath.
34:15 *turn again unto dust.* See Eccl 12:7; see also Gen 3:19 and note.
34:16 *hear . . . Hearken to.* The Hebrew for these verbs is singular, addressed to Job. Elihu is concerned that Job's attitude about God's justice be corrected (see v. 17), so he stresses God's impartial rule as Lord of all, especially in meting out justice to the wicked in high places (see vv. 18–20).
34:18 *Thou art wicked.* See note on Deut 13:13.

21 [a]For his eyes *are* upon the ways of
man,
And he seeth all his goings.
22 [a]*There is* no darkness, nor shadow of
death,
Where the workers of iniquity may
hide themselves.
23 For he will not lay upon man more
than right;
That *he* should [1]enter into judgment
with God.

24 [a]He shall break in pieces mighty *men*
[1]without number,
And set others in their stead.
25 Therefore he knoweth their works,
And he overturneth *them* in the night,
so that they are [1]destroyed.
26 He striketh them as wicked *men*
[1]In the open sight of others;
27 Because they [a]turned back [1]from him,
And [b]would not consider any of his
ways:
28 So that *they* [a]cause the cry of the poor
to come unto him,
And he [b]heareth the cry of the
afflicted.

29 When he giveth quietness, who then
can make trouble?
And when he hideth *his* face, who
then can behold him?
Whether *it be done* against a nation,
Or against a man only:
30 That the hypocrite reign not,
Lest [a]the people be ensnared.
31 Surely it is *meet to be* said unto God,
I have borne *chastisement,* I will not
offend *any more:*
32 *That which* I see not teach thou me:
If I have done iniquity, I will do no
more.

33 [1]*Should it be* according to thy mind?
he will recompense it,
Whether thou refuse, or whether thou
choose; and not I:

34:21 [a]ch. 31:4
34:22 [a]Ps. 139:12; Amos 9:2,3
34:23 [1]Heb. *go*
34:24 [1]Heb. *without searching out* [a]Dan. 2:21
34:25 [1]Heb. *crushed*
34:26 [1]Heb. *In the place of beholders*
34:27 [1]Heb. *from after him* [a]1 Sam. 15:11 [b]Ps. 28:5; Is. 5:12
34:28 [a]Jas. 5:4 [b]Ex. 22:23
34:30 [a]1 Ki. 12:28,30
34:33 [1]Heb. Should it be *from with thee?*
34:34 [1]Heb. *of heart*
34:35 [a]ch. 35:16
34:36 [1]Or, *My father, let Job be tried*
35:3 [1]Or, by it *more than by my sin?* [a]ch. 21:15
35:4 [1]Heb. *I will return to thee words* [a]ch. 34:8
35:5 [a]ch. 22:12
35:6 [a]Prov. 8:36; Jer. 7:19
35:7 [a]Ps. 16:2; Prov. 9:12
35:9 [a]ch. 34:28
35:10 [a]Is. 51:13 [b]Ps. 42:8; Acts 16:25

Therefore speak what thou knowest.
34 Let men [1]of understanding tell me,
And let a wise man hearken unto me.
35 [a]Job hath spoken without knowledge,
And his words *were* without wisdom.
36 [1]My desire *is that* Job may be tried
unto the end
Because of *his* answers for wicked men.
37 For he addeth rebellion unto his sin,
He clappeth *his hands* amongst us,
And multiplieth his words against God.

35 Elihu spake moreover, and said,
2 Thinkest thou this to be right,
That thou saidst, My righteousness *is*
more than God's?
3 For [a]thou saidst, What advantage will
it be unto thee?
And, What profit shall I have, [1]*if I be
cleansed* from my sin?
4 [1]I will answer thee,
And [a]thy companions with thee.

5 [a]Look unto the heavens, and see;
And behold the clouds *which* are
higher than thou.
6 If thou sinnest, what doest thou
[a]against him?
Or *if* thy transgressions be multiplied,
what doest thou unto him?
7 [a]If thou be righteous, what givest thou
him?
Or what receiveth he of thine hand?
8 Thy wickedness *may hurt* a man as
thou *art;*
And thy righteousness *may profit* the
son of man.

9 [a]By reason of the multitude of
oppressions they make *the oppressed*
to cry:
They cry out by reason of the arm of
the mighty.
10 But none saith, [a]Where *is* God my
Maker,
[b]Who giveth songs in the night;

34:21–28 God's omniscience guarantees that He will not make any mistakes when He punishes evildoers. It is not necessary for Him to set times to examine people for judgment (see v. 23; contrast 24:1).

34:21 Elihu echoes the words of Job in 31:4.

34:29 *When he giveth quietness, who then can make trouble?* Elihu attempts to answer Job's complaint about God's silence (ch. 23). God watches over men and nations to see that right is done (vv. 29–30).

34:31–33 First indirectly (vv. 31–32) and then more directly (v. 33), Elihu condemns Job and calls for his repentance.

‡34:33 *Should it be . . . he will recompense it.* Job needs to understand that God rewards on his own terms, not Job's.

34:35 *Job hath spoken without knowledge.* A motif in the first discourse of the Lord (see 38:2) and the final response of Job (see 42:3).

35:1–16 Elihu's third speech (see note on 32:1–37:24), addressed to Job.

35:2 *My righteousness.* Elihu thinks that it is unjust and inconsistent for Job to expect vindication from God and at the same time imply that God does not care whether we are righteous (see v. 3). But allowance must be made for a person to express his feelings. The psalmist who thirsted for God (Ps 42:1–2) also questioned why God had forgotten him (Ps 42:9) and rejected him (Ps 43:2).

35:5 *Look unto the heavens, and see.* Elihu asserts that God is so far above man that there is really nothing man can do, good or bad, that will affect God's essential nature (see v. 6).

35:9 *They cry out.* Elihu states that those like Job who pray for help when suffering innocently never seem to get around to trusting the justice and goodness of their Maker, who is also the author of wisdom and joy (see vv. 10–11). Such failure is a sign of arrogance (see v. 12), so Job's complaint against God's justice and about God's silence is meaningless talk (see vv. 13–16).

‡35:10–11 *giveth songs . . . teacheth . . . maketh us wiser.* God chooses to condescend, to reach out to humanity in love.

11 Who [a]teacheth us more than the
beasts of the earth,
And maketh us wiser than the fowls of
heaven?
12 [a]There they cry, but none giveth
answer,
Because of the pride of evil men.
13 [a]Surely God will not hear vanity,
Neither will the Almighty regard it.
14 [a]Although thou sayest thou shalt not
see him,
Yet judgment *is* before him; therefore
[b]trust thou in him.
15 But now, because *it is* not *so,* [1]he hath
[a]visited *in* his anger;
Yet [2]he knoweth *it* not in great
extremity:
16 [a]Therefore doth Job open his mouth in
vain;
He multiplieth words without
knowledge.

36 Elihu also proceeded, and said,
2 Suffer me a little, and I will shew thee
[1]That *I have* yet to speak on God's
behalf.
3 I will fetch my knowledge from afar,
And will ascribe righteousness to my
Maker.
4 For truly my words *shall* not *be* false:
He that is perfect in knowledge *is* with
thee.
5 Behold, God *is* mighty, and despiseth
not *any:*
[a]*He is* mighty in strength *and*
[1]wisdom.
6 He preserveth not the life of the
wicked:
But giveth right to the [1]poor.
7 [a]He withdraweth not his eyes from the
righteous:
But [b]with kings *are they* on the throne;
Yea, he doth establish them for ever,
and they are exalted.
8 And [a]if *they be* bound in fetters,
And be holden in cords of affliction;
9 Then he sheweth them their work,
And their transgressions that they have
exceeded.
10 [a]He openeth also their ear to
discipline,
And commandeth that they return
from iniquity.
11 If they obey and serve *him,*
They shall [a]spend their days in
prosperity,
And their years in pleasures.
12 But if they obey not,
[1]They shall perish by the sword,
And they shall die without knowledge.
13 But the hypocrites in heart [a]heap up
wrath:
They cry not when he bindeth them.
14 [a] [1]They die in youth,
And their life *is* among the [2]unclean.
15 He delivereth the [1]poor in his
affliction,
And openeth their ears in oppression.
16 Even so would he have removed thee
out of the strait
[a]*Into* a broad place, where *there is* no
straitness;
And [b] [1]that which should be set on thy
table *should be* full of [c]fatness.
17 But thou hast fulfilled the judgment of
the wicked:
[1]Judgment and justice take hold on
thee.
18 Because *there is* wrath, *beware* lest he
take thee away with *his* stroke:
Then [a]a great ransom cannot [1]deliver
thee.

35:11 [a]Ps. 94:12
35:12 [a]Prov. 1:28
35:13 [a]Is. 1:15; Jer. 11:11
35:14 [a]ch. 9:11 [b]Ps. 37:5,6
35:15 [1]That is, *God* [2]That is, *Job* [a]Ps. 89:32
35:16 [a]ch. 34:35
36:2 [1]Heb. *That* there are *yet words for God*
36:5 [1]Heb. *heart* [a]ch. 9:4
36:6 [1]Or, *afflicted*
36:7 [a]Ps. 33:18 [b]Ps. 113:8
36:8 [a]Ps. 107:10
36:10 [a]ch. 33:16
36:11 [a]ch. 21:13; Is. 1:19,20
36:12 [1]Heb. *They shall pass away by the sword*
36:13 [a]Rom. 2:5
36:14 [1]Heb. *Their soul dieth* [2]Or, *sodomites* [a]Ps. 55:23
36:15 [1]Or, *afflicted*
36:16 [1]Heb. *the rest of thy table* [a]Ps. 18:19; 31:8 [b]Ps. 23:5 [c]Ps. 36:8
36:17 [1]Or, *Judgment and justice should uphold* thee
36:18 [1]Heb. *turn thee aside* [a]Ps. 49:7

35:12 Since men are arrogant, God does not listen (see v. 13). Job himself might not be wicked, but he shares their arrogance. He too receives no answer, because he does not ask rightly (see v. 14).
35:16 The reference here to Job in the third person does not necessarily mean that someone other than Job is being addressed (see note on vv. 1–16). *multiplieth words.* Against God (see 34:37). *without knowledge.* See 38:2 and note.
36:1–37:24 Elihu's fourth and final (see 36:2) speech (see note on 32:1–37:24), addressed for the most part to Job (but see note on 37:2).
36:2–4 Elihu desires to strengthen the case for God's goodness and justice.
36:4 *perfect in knowledge.* Here Elihu applies the phrase to himself, while in 37:16 he applies it to God—thus appearing to make himself equal to God. But the Hebrew for "knowledge" is not quite the same here as in 37:16. Elihu is probably referring to his ability as a communicator, i.e. he claims perfection in the knowledge of speech (see note on 32:6,10,17).
36:5 God's power assures the fulfillment of His purpose.
36:6–9 A classic statement of God's justice in rewarding the righteous and punishing sinners (in contrast to what Job has been claiming). In v. 7 Elihu perhaps has in mind Job's complaint that God will not leave him alone (see 7:17–19), and in v. 9 he may be thinking of Job's charge that God will not present His indictment against him (see 31:35–36).
36:10 *openeth also their ear to discipline.* Elihu states that God uses trouble to gain man's attention.
36:12 See note on 33:18.
36:13–15 Elihu understands that the basic spiritual need of man stems from his hardness of heart—his refusal to yield to God, to cry out to God in his distress (see Ps 107), or to hear the voice of God in suffering.
‡36:14 *the unclean.* Lit. "cult prostitutes." See note on 1 Ki 14:24.
36:16–21 Elihu warns Job to respond to God's discipline by turning away from evil (see v. 21). Verse 16 shows that he still views Job as a man for whom there is hope.
‡36:16 The promise of what will happen if Job repents—God will remove him from his difficult situation and restore his prosperity.

19 [a]Will he esteem thy riches? *no,* not gold,
Nor all the forces of strength.
20 Desire not the night,
When people are cut off in their place.
21 Take heed, [a]regard not iniquity:
For [b]this hast thou chosen rather than affliction.

22 Behold, God exalteth by his power:
[a]Who teacheth like him?
23 [a]Who hath enjoined him his way?
Or [b]who can say, Thou hast wrought iniquity?
24 Remember that thou [a]magnify his work,
Which men behold.
25 Every man may see it;
Man may behold *it* afar off.

26 Behold, God *is* great, and we [a]know *him* not,
[b]Neither can the number of his years be searched out.
27 For he [a]maketh small the drops of water:
They pour down rain according to the vapour thereof:
28 [a]Which the clouds do drop
And distil upon man abundantly.
29 Also can *any* understand the spreadings of the clouds,
Or the noise of his tabernacle?

30 Behold, he [a]spreadeth his light upon it,
And covereth [1]the bottom of the sea.
31 For [a]by them judgeth he the people;
He [b]giveth meat in abundance.
32 [a]With clouds he covereth the light;
And commandeth it *not to shine* by *the cloud* that cometh betwixt.
33 [a]The noise thereof sheweth concerning it,
The cattle also concerning [1]the vapour.

36:19 [a]Prov. 11:4
36:21 [a]Ps. 66:18 [b]Heb. 11:25
36:22 [a]Is. 40:13; 1 Cor. 2:16
36:23 [a]ch. 34:13 [b]ch. 34:10
36:24 [a]Ps. 92:5; Rev. 15:3
36:26 [a]1 Cor. 13:12 [b]Ps. 90:2; Heb. 1:12
36:27 [a]Ps. 147:8
36:28 [a]Prov. 3:20
36:30 [1]Heb. *the roots* [a]ch. 37:3
36:31 [a]ch. 37:13 [b]Acts 14:17
36:32 [a]Ps. 147:8
36:33 [1]Heb. that *which goeth up* [a]1 Ki. 18:41

37:2 [1]Heb. *Hear in hearing*
37:3 [1]Heb. *light* [2]Heb. *wings of the earth*
37:4 [a]Ps. 29:3
37:5 [a]ch. 5:9
37:6 [1]Heb. *And* to *the shower of rain, and to the showers of rain of his strength* [a]Ps. 147:16
37:7 [a]Ps. 109:27
37:8 [a]Ps. 104:22
37:9 [1]Heb. *Out of the chamber* [2]Heb. *scattering* winds
37:10 [a]Ps. 147:17
37:11 [1]Heb. *the cloud of his light*
37:12 [a]Ps. 148:8

37 At this also my heart trembleth,
And is moved out of his place.
2 [1]Hear attentively the noise of his voice,
And the sound *that* goeth out of his mouth.
3 He directeth it under the whole heaven,
And his [1]lightning unto the [2]ends of the earth.
4 After it [a]a voice roareth:
He thundereth with the voice of his excellency;
And he will not stay them when his voice is heard.
5 God thundereth marvellously with his voice;
[a]Great *things* doeth he, which we cannot comprehend.

6 For [a]he saith to the snow, Be thou *on* the earth;
[1]Likewise *to* the small rain,
And *to* the great rain of his strength.
7 He sealeth up the hand of every man;
[a]That all men may know his work.
8 Then the beasts [a]go into dens,
And remain in their places.
9 [1]Out of the south cometh the whirlwind:
And cold out of the [2]north.
10 [a]By the breath of God frost is given:
And the breadth of the waters is straitened.
11 Also by watering he wearieth the thick cloud:
He scattereth [1]his bright cloud:
12 And it is turned round about by his counsels:
That they may [a]do whatsoever he commandeth them
Upon the face of the world in the earth.

‡36:20 Job should stop longing for the "night" of death and instead focus on making things right with God (cf. 3:20-23). For the darkness of night as a picture for death, see 10:21 and note; 17:12-13.
36:21 *Take heed, regard not iniquity.* Elihu's evaluation of Job is the opposite of God's (see 1:8; 2:3).
36:22–33 Elihu anticipates some of God's statements in the discourses of chs. 38–41.
‡36:25 God's power and glory as reflected in creation are evident to all people (cf. Ps 19:1-6; Rom 1:18-32).
36:26 *we know him not.* See 37:5. That God's ways and thoughts are infinitely higher than ours is an important theme in chs. 38–41.
36:29–30 *noise of his tabernacle . . . spreadeth his light.* Thunder and lightning. *coveteth the bottom of the sea.* The lightning God sends is so powerful that it even lights up the depths of the sea.
36:31 *judgeth.* The verb can be translated "nourishes," meaning the Lord nourishes the peoples with the showers mentioned in vv. 27–30.
‡36:32 *With clouds he covereth the light.* Lit. "he lifts up the lightning with both hands." God is a powerful warrior who works with equal effectiveness with either hand (cf. 1 Chr 12:2). *commandeth it not to shine . . . betwixt.* God hurls the lightning with such precision that it strikes the exact mark he has chosen.
37:1–13 A continuation of Elihu's hymnic description of God's marvels exhibited in the earth's atmosphere, beginning in 36:27. His heart pounds at the awesome display (see v. 1). The passage reveals a sophisticated observation of atmospheric conditions and their effects: the evaporation and distillation of water for rain (see 36:27), the clouds as holders of moisture (see 36:28; 37:11) and the cyclonic behavior of clouds (see v. 12). Such forces originate from God's command and always perform His will for mankind, whether for good or for ill (v. 13).
37:2 *Hear.* The Hebrew for this verb is plural, indicating that others (including the three friends) besides Job are being addressed here (see note on 36:1–37:24). *noise of his voice . . . sound.* Thunder (see v. 4).
37:5 *we cannot comprehend.* See note on 36:26.
‡37:7 Heavy rain or snowfall forces men to cease from their normal activities, giving them a chance to reflect on God's power revealed in the storm.
37:10 *breath of God.* Here a metaphor for a chilling wind.

13 [a]He causeth it to come, whether for
[1]correction,
Or [b]for his land, or [c]for mercy.

Consider his wondrous works

14 Hearken unto this, O Job:
Stand still, and [a]consider the wondrous
works of God.
15 Dost thou know when God disposed
them,
And caused the light of his cloud to
shine?
16 [a]Dost thou know the balancings of the
clouds,
The wondrous works of [b]*him which is*
perfect in knowledge?
17 How thy garments *are* warm,
When he quieteth the earth by the
south *wind?*
18 Hast thou with him [a]spread out the sky,
Which is strong, *and* as a molten
looking glass?
19 Teach us what we shall say unto him;
For we cannot order *our speech* by
reason of darkness.
20 Shall it be told him that I speak?
If a man speak, surely he shall be
swallowed up.
21 And now *men* see not the bright light
Which *is* in the clouds:
But the wind passeth, and cleanseth
them.
22 [1]Fair weather cometh out of the north:
With God *is* terrible majesty.

37:13 [1]Heb. *a rod* [a]Ex. 9:18 [b]ch. 38:26 [c]2 Sam. 21:10; 1 Ki. 18:45
37:14 [a]Ps. 111:2
37:16 [a]ch. 36:29 [b]ch. 36:4
37:18 [a]Gen. 1:6; Is. 44:24
37:22 [1]Heb. *Gold*
37:23 [a]1 Tim. 6:16 [b]ch. 36:5
37:24 [a]Mat. 10:28 [b]Mat. 11:25
38:1 [a]Ex. 19:16
38:2 [a]ch. 34:35 [b]1 Tim. 1:7
38:3 [1]Heb. *make me know* [a]ch. 40:7
38:4 [1]Heb. *if thou knowest understanding* [a]Ps. 104:5; Prov. 8:29
38:6 [1]Heb. *sockets* [2]Heb. *made to sink?*
38:7 [a]ch. 1:6
38:8 [a]Gen. 1:9

23 *Touching* the Almighty, [a]we cannot
find him out: [b]*he is* excellent in
power,
And *in* judgment, and *in* plenty of
justice: he will not afflict.
24 Men do therefore [a]fear him:
He respecteth not any *that are* [b]wise of
heart.

The LORD speaks

38 Then the LORD answered Job [a]out of
the whirlwind, and said,
2 [a]Who *is* this that darkeneth counsel
By [b]words without knowledge?
3 [a]Gird up now thy loins like a man;
For I will demand of thee, and [1]answer
thou me.

4 [a]Where wast thou when I laid the
foundations of the earth?
Declare, [1]if thou hast understanding.
5 Who hath laid the measures thereof, if
thou knowest?
Or who hath stretched the line
upon it?
6 Whereupon are the [1]foundations
thereof [2]fastened?
Or who laid the corner stone thereof;
7 When the morning stars sang together,
And all [a]the sons of God shouted for
joy?

8 [a]Or *who* shut up the sea with doors,
When it brake forth, *as if* it had issued
out of the womb?

37:14–18 Job is challenged to ponder God's power over the elements. The question format is also used in the divine discourses (chs. 38–41).
37:16 *perfect in knowledge.* See note on 36:4.
37:18 *spread out the sky.* See 26:7. *strong, and as a molten looking glass.* Ancient mirrors were made out of bronze, so they were very hard. In Deut 28:23, a bronze sky symbolizes unremitting heat (see note there; see also Deut 28:22).
37:19 *we cannot order our speech.* Job had dared to sign his defense and call for an audience with God (see 31:35). For this, Elihu seeks to shame him. But he softens his tone by including himself as one equally vulnerable to God's majesty.
‡37:22 *Fair weather cometh out of the north.* Lit. "from the north he comes as gold" (with golden splendor). For the significance of "the north," see note on Ps 48:2. *terrible majesty.* Elihu prepares Job for the appearance of God in the storm (chs. 38–41).
‡37:24 *fear.* See 28:28; Gen 20:11 and notes. *He respecteth not any . . . wise of heart.* God's decisions and actions are not influenced by people like Job who think they are wise enough to argue with Him.
38:1–42:6 The theophany (appearance of God) to Job, consisting of two discourses by the Lord (38:1–40:2; 40:6–41:34), each of which receives a brief response from Job (40:3–5; 42:1–6).
‡38:1 *the LORD.* The Israelite covenant name for God (see Introduction: Author). *whirlwind.* See 40:6. Elihu had imagined the appearance of the divine presence as a display of "terrible majesty" (37:22). He also had anticipated the storm or whirlwind (see note on 37:22), from which Job would hear the voice of God. Job had said his wish was "that the Almighty would answer me" (31:35).
38:2 See 35:16. In 42:3, Job echoes the Lord's words. God states that Job's complaining and raging against Him are unjustified and proceed from limited understanding.
38:3 Repeated in 40:7 (see also 42:4). The format of God's response is to ply Job with rhetorical questions, to each of which Job must plead ignorance. God says nothing about Job's suffering, nor does He address Job's problem about divine justice. Job gets neither a bill of indictment nor a verdict of innocence. But, more important, God does not humiliate or condemn him—which surely would have been the case if the counselors had been right. So by implication Job is vindicated, and later his vindication is directly affirmed (see 42:7–8). The divine discourses, then, succeed in bringing Job to complete faith in God's goodness without his receiving a direct answer to his questions.
38:4–38 Inanimate creation testifies to God's sovereignty and power (the earth, vv. 4–7,18; the sea, vv. 8–11,16; the sun, vv. 12–15; the netherworld, v. 17; light and darkness, vv. 19–20; the weather, vv. 22–30,34–38; the constellations, vv. 31–33). See note on 38:39–39:30.
38:4–5 See the similar questions of Agur, and the similar irony in his demand for a response (Prov 30:4).
38:7 See Ps 148:2–3; see also note on Ps 65:13. When the earth was created, the angels were there to sing the praises of the Creator, but Job was not (see vv. 4–5). He should therefore not expect to be able to understand even lesser aspects of God's plans for the world and for mankind. *sons of God.* See 1:6 and note.
‡38:8–11 The defeat of the sea and the forces of chaos repre-

9 When I made the cloud the garment
thereof,
And thick darkness a swaddling band
for it,
10 And [a] [1] brake up for it my decreed
place,
And set bars and doors,
11 And said, Hitherto shalt thou come,
but no further:
And here shall [1] thy proud waves [a] be
stayed?
12 Hast thou [a] commanded the morning
since thy days;
And caused the dayspring to know his
place;
13 That *it* might take hold of the [1] ends of
the earth,
That [a] the wicked might be shaken out
of it?
14 It is turned as clay *to* the seal;
And they stand as a garment.
15 And from the wicked their [a] light is
withholden,
And [b] the high arm shall be broken.
16 Hast thou [a] entered into the springs of
the sea?
Or hast thou walked in the search of
the depth?
17 Have [a] the gates of death been opened
unto thee?
Or hast thou seen the doors of the
shadow of death?
18 Hast thou perceived the breadth of the
earth?
Declare if thou knowest it all.
19 Where *is* the way *where* light
dwelleth?
And *as for* darkness, where *is* the place
thereof,
20 That thou shouldest take it [1] to the
bound thereof,
And that thou shouldest know the
paths to the house thereof?
21 Knowest thou *it,* because thou wast
then born?
Or *because* the number of thy days *is*
great?

38:10 [1] Or, *established my decree upon it* [a] ch. 26:10
38:11 [1] Heb. *the pride of thy waves* [a] Ps. 89:9
38:12 [a] Ps. 148:5
38:13 [1] Heb. *wings* [a] Ps. 104:35
38:15 [a] ch. 18:5 [b] Ps. 10:15
38:16 [a] Ps. 77:19
38:17 [a] Ps. 9:13
38:20 [1] Or, *at*
38:22 [a] Ps. 135:7
38:23 [a] Ex. 9:18; Josh. 10:11; Is. 30:30; Ezek. 13:11,13; Rev. 16:21
38:25 [a] ch. 28:26
38:27 [a] Ps. 107:35
38:28 [a] Ps. 147:8; Jer. 14:22
38:29 [a] Ps. 147:16
38:30 [1] Heb. *is taken* [a] ch. 37:10
38:31 [1] Or, *the seven stars* [2] Heb. *Cimah* [3] Heb. *Cesil?* [a] ch. 9:9; Amos 5:8
38:32 [1] Or, *the twelve signs* [2] Heb. *guide them*
38:33 [a] Jer. 31:35
38:35 [1] Heb. *Behold us?*

22 Hast thou entered into [a] the treasures
of the snow?
Or hast thou seen the treasures of the
hail,
23 [a] Which I have reserved against the
time of trouble,
Against the day of battle and war?
24 By what way is the light parted,
Which scattereth the east wind upon
the earth?
25 Who [a] hath divided a watercourse for
the overflowing of waters,
Or a way for the lightning of thunder;
26 To cause it to rain on the earth, *where*
no man *is;*
On the wilderness, wherein *there is* no
man;
27 [a] To satisfy the desolate and waste
ground;
And to cause the bud of the tender
herb to spring forth?
28 [a] Hath the rain a father?
Or who hath begotten the drops of dew?
29 Out of whose womb came the ice?
And the [a] hoary frost of heaven, who
hath gendered it?
30 The waters are hid as *with* a stone,
And the face of the deep [1] is [a] frozen.
31 Canst thou bind the sweet influences
of [a] [1] [2] Pleiades,
Or loose the bands of [3] Orion?
32 Canst thou bring forth [1] Mazzaroth in
his season?
Or canst thou [2] guide Arcturus with his
sons?
33 Knowest thou [a] the ordinances of
heaven?
Canst thou set the dominion thereof in
the earth?
34 Canst thou lift up thy voice to the
clouds,
That abundance of waters may cover
thee?
35 Canst thou send lightnings, that they
may go,
And say unto thee, [1] Here we *are?*

sented by the sea is a major motif in ancient Near Eastern myths. See 7:12 and note; Ps 74:13-14 and note. The sea was a formidable foe, but here God's power is such that the sea is nothing more than a helpless baby. God wraps a cloud around the sea as a diaper (v. 9) and confines the sea so that it is unable to cross its boundaries and wreak havoc (vv. 10-11).

38:10–11 See Ps 33:7; Jer 5:22.

38:11 *And said.* God the Father controls the sea by speaking to it, as does God the Son (see Luke 8:24–25).

38:12–13 The arrival of the dawn sends the wicked scurrying for cover.

‡38:14 *clay to the seal.* Either a cylinder seal (see note on Gen 38:18) or a stamp seal. With the morning light, the earth's features become visible like the impressions made on a clay seal. *they stand as a garment.* The light causes the earth to appear as a beautifully designed garment.

38:15 *their light.* The night is when the wicked are active (see John 3:19; for the imagery cf. Luke 11:35). *high arm shall be broken.* See 22:9 and note.

38:16 *springs of the sea.* See Gen 7:11; 8:2.

38:17 *gates of death.* See note on 17:16; see also 26:5–6.

‡38:22–23 *hail . . . Against the day of battle.* God stores the natural elements as ammunition against his enemies. See, e.g., Josh 10:11; Is 28:2 and note.

38:24 *east wind.* See note on 15:2.

‡38:31–32 *Pleiades . . . Orion . . . Arcturus.* See note on 9:9. *Mazzaroth.* Word used only here and meaning unclear. Likely a name for one of the constellations.

‡38:33 *ordinances of heaven.* The principles controlling the movements of the stars and planets. *set the dominon thereof.* Is Job able to determine how the heavenly bodies regulate life on earth?

36 [a]Who hath put wisdom in the inward
parts?
Or who hath given understanding to
the heart?
37 Who can number the clouds in
wisdom?
Or [1]who can stay the bottles of
heaven,
38 [1]When the dust [2]growth into
hardness,
And the clods cleave fast together?

39 [a]Wilt thou hunt the prey for the lion?
Or fill [1]the appetite of the young lions,
40 When they couch in *their* dens,
And abide in the covert to lie in wait?
41 [a]Who provideth for the raven his food?
When his young ones cry unto God,
They wander for lack of meat.

39 Knowest thou the time when the
wild goats of the rock bring forth?
Or canst thou mark when [a]the hinds
do calve?
2 Canst thou number the months *that*
they fulfil?
Or knowest thou the time when they
bring forth?
3 They bow themselves, they bring forth
their young ones,
They cast out their sorrows.
4 Their young ones are in good liking,
they grow up with corn;
They go forth, and return not unto
them.

5 Who hath sent out the wild ass free?
Or who hath loosed the bands of the
wild ass?
6 [a]Whose house I have made the
wilderness,
And the [1]barren *land* his dwellings.
7 He scorneth the multitude of the city,
Neither regardeth he the crying [a][1]of
the driver.
8 The range of the mountains *is* his
pasture,
And he searcheth after every green
thing.

9 Will the [a]unicorn be willing to serve
thee,
Or abide by thy crib?
10 Canst thou bind the unicorn *with* his
band in the furrow?
Or will he harrow the valleys after
thee?
11 Wilt thou trust him, because his
strength *is* great?
Or wilt thou leave thy labour to him?
12 Wilt thou believe him, that he will
bring home thy seed,
And gather *it into* thy barn?

13 *Gavest thou* the goodly wings unto the
peacocks?
Or [1]wings and feathers *unto* the
ostrich?
14 Which leaveth her eggs in the earth,
And warmeth them in dust,
15 And forgetteth that the foot may crush
them,
Or *that* the wild beast may break them.
16 She is [a]hardened against her young
ones, as though *they were* not hers:
Her labour *is* in vain without fear;
17 Because God hath deprived her of
wisdom,
Neither hath he [a]imparted to her
understanding.
18 What time she lifteth up herself on high,
She scorneth the horse and his rider.

19 Hast thou given the horse strength?
Hast thou clothed his neck with
thunder?

38:36 [a]ch. 32:8; Ps. 51:6; Eccl. 2:26
38:37 [1]Heb. *who can cause to lie down*
38:38 [1]Or, *When the dust is turned into mire* [2]Heb. *is poured*
38:39 [1]Heb. *the life* [a]Ps. 104:21; 145:15
38:41 [a]Ps. 147:9; Mat. 6:26
39:1 [a]Ps. 29:9
39:6 [1]Heb. *salt places* [a]ch. 24:5; Jer. 2:24; Hos. 8:9
39:7 [1]Heb. *of the exactor* [a]ch. 3:18
39:9 [a]Num. 23:22; Deut. 33:17
39:13 [1]Or, *the feathers of the stork and ostrich*
39:16 [a]Lam. 4:3
39:17 [a]ch. 35:11

38:36 *inward parts . . . heart.* It is possible that the first word should be translated "ibis" and the second "rooster," two birds whose habits were sometimes observed by people who wished to forecast the weather. If so, the words would serve as a transition to the next major section of the first divine discourse.
‡38:37 *bottles of heaven.* Jars that contain rain water.
‡38:38 Pictures conditions of drought. God knows the places on earth that are in need of rain.
‡38:39–39:30 Animate creation testifies to God's sovereignty, power and loving care (the lion, 38:39–40; the raven, 38:41; the wild goat, 39:1–4; the wild ass, vv. 5–8; the unicorn (wild ox), vv. 9–12; the ostrich, vv. 13–18; the horse, vv. 19–25; the hawk, v. 26; the eagle, vv. 27–30). See note on 38:4–38.
38:41 *provideth for the raven his food.* God cares for and feeds all the birds, of which the raven is representative (e.g., compare Luke 12:24 with Mat 6:26).
39:5 *wild ass.* See 24:5; see also the description of Ishmael in Gen 16:12 and note there.
39:9–12 *unicorn.* Or the "wild ox." As there was an implied contrast between the wild donkey and the domestic donkey (see v. 7), here there is a more explicit contrast between the wild ox and the domestic ox.
39:11 *strength is great.* In the OT, the wild ox (the now virtually extinct aurochs) often symbolizes strength (see, e.g., Num 23:22; 24:8; Deut 33:17; Ps 29:6). Next to the elephant and rhinoceros, the wild ox was the largest and most powerful land animal of the OT world.
39:13–18 This stanza is unique in the discourses, because in it the Lord asks Job no questions. Could it be because the ostrich is so amusing? The oddity of the ostrich highlights God's wisdom—what human would ever think of creating such a strange bird?
‡39:13 *peacocks.* Lit. "bird of piercing cries," the "ostrich." *wings and feathers unto the ostrich.* The name of the bird here is from the Hebrew word *hesed* ("kindness"), referring to the stork, known for its tender care of its young (Deut 14:18; Jer. 8:7). A stork's wings were also particularly impressive (cf. Zec 5:9).
‡39:18 The ostrich cannot fly but is able to run faster than a horse. *horse and his rider.* Forms a transition to the next paragraph.
39:19–25 The horse is the only domestic animal in the discourses. This fact, though unexpected, serves the Lord's purpose, since it is specifically the war horse that is in view.

20 Canst thou make him afraid as a grasshopper?
The glory of his nostrils *is* [1] terrible.
21 [1] He paweth in the valley, and rejoiceth in *his* strength.
[a] He goeth on to meet [2] the armed men.
22 He mocketh at fear, and is not affrighted;
Neither turneth he back from the sword.
23 The quiver rattleth against him,
The glittering spear and the shield.
24 He swalloweth the ground with fierceness and rage:
Neither believeth he that *it is* the sound of the trumpet.
25 He saith among the trumpets, Ha, ha;
And he smelleth the battle afar off,
The thunder of the captains, and the shouting.

26 Doth the hawk fly by thy wisdom,
And stretch her wings toward the south?
27 Doth the eagle mount up [1] at thy command,
And [a] make her nest on high?
28 She dwelleth and abideth on the rock,
Upon the crag of the rock, and the strong place.
29 From thence she seeketh the prey,
And her eyes behold afar off.
30 Her young ones also suck up blood:
And [a] where the slain *are,* there *is* she.

40 Moreover the LORD answered Job, and said,

2 Shall he that [a] contendeth with the Almighty instruct *him?*
He that reproveth God, let him answer it.

3 ¶ Then Job answered the LORD, and said,

4 [a] Behold, I am vile; what shall I answer thee?
[b] I will lay my hand upon my mouth.
5 Once have I spoken; but I will not answer:
Yea, twice; but I will proceed no further.

6 ¶ [a] Then answered the LORD unto Job out of the whirlwind, and said,

7 [a] Gird up thy loins now like a man:
[b] I will demand of thee, and declare thou unto me.
8 [a] Wilt thou also disannul my judgment?
Wilt thou condemn me, that thou mayest be righteous?
9 Hast thou an arm like God?
Or, canst thou thunder with [a] a voice like him?

10 [a] Deck thyself now with majesty and excellency;
And array thyself with glory and beauty.
11 Cast abroad the rage of thy wrath:
And behold every one *that is* proud, and abase him.
12 Look on every one *that is* [a] proud, *and* bring him low;
And tread down the wicked in their place.
13 Hide them in the dust together;
And bind their faces in secret.
14 Then will I also confess unto thee
That thine own right hand can save thee.

15 Behold now [1] behemoth,
Which I made with thee;
He eateth grass as an ox.
16 Lo now, his strength *is* in his loins,
And his force *is* in the navel of his belly.
17 [1] He moveth his tail like a cedar:
The sinews of his stones are wrapt together.

39:20 [1] Heb. *terror* 39:21 [1] Or, His feet *dig* [2] Heb. *the armour* [a] Jer. 8:6 39:27 [1] Heb. *by thy mouth* [a] Jer. 49:16; Obad. 4 39:30 [a] Mat. 24:28; Luke 17:37 40:2 [a] ch. 33:13 40:4 [a] Ezra 9:6; ch. 42:6; Ps. 51:4 40:4 [b] ch. 29:9; Ps. 39:9 40:6 [a] ch. 38:1 40:7 [a] ch. 38:3 [b] ch. 42:4 40:8 [a] Ps. 51:4; Rom. 3:4 40:9 [a] ch. 37:4; Ps. 29:3,4 40:10 [a] Ps. 93:1; 104:1 40:12 [a] Is. 2:12; Dan. 4:37 40:15 [1] Or, *the elephant,* as some think 40:17 [1] Or, *He setteth up*

‡39:20 *afraid as a grasshopper.* Or "leap like a locust," focusing on agility, not fear. Horses and locusts are compared also in Jer 51:27; Rev 9:7; cf. Joel 2:4.
39:26 *hawk.* The sparrow hawk, not resident to the Holy Land, stops there in its migration south for the winter.
39:27 *eagle.* Or possibly "vulture" (see v. 30).
40:1–2 The conclusion of the first divine discourse. Once again, God challenges Job to answer Him.
40:3–5 Job, duly chastened and no longer "as a prince" (31:37), is unwilling to speak another word of complaint.
40:4 *vile.* The Hebrew for this word can also mean "small" or "unworthy."
40:5 *Once . . . twice.* See note on 5:19.
40:6 See 38:1 and note.
40:7 Repeated from 38:3 (see note there).
40:8–14 The prologue to the second divine discourse, which ends at 41:34. Unlike the first discourse, God here addresses the issues of His own justice and Job's futile attempt at self-justification. In chs. 21 and 24, Job had complained about God's indifference toward the wickedness of evil men. Here the Lord asserts His ability and determination to administer justice—a matter over which Job has no control. Therefore by implication Job is admonished to leave all this, including his own vindication (see v. 14), under the power of God's strong arm (see v. 9).
40:10 *Deck thyself now with majesty and excellency.* The Hebrew underlying this clause describes God in Ps 104:1: "Thou art clothed with honour and majesty." The Lord here challenges Job to take on the appearance of deity—if he can.
40:11–12 See Is 13:11, where the Lord describes Himself as doing these things.
40:13 *dust.* See note on 7:21.
40:14 *That thine own right hand can save thee.* Contrast Ps 49:7–9 (see note there).
40:15–24 The first of two poems (ch. 41 constitutes the second) in this discourse, each describing a huge beast and resuming the animal theme of ch. 39.
40:15 *behemoth.* The word is Hebrew and means "beast par excellence," referring to a large land animal (possibly the hippopotamus or the elephant). Much of the language used to describe him in vv. 16–24 is highly poetic and hyperbolic. *Which I made.* He is one of God's creatures, not a mythical being.

18 His bones *are as* strong pieces of brass;
His bones *are* like bars of iron.

19 He *is* the chief of the ways of God:
He that made him can make his sword
to approach *unto him.*
20 Surely the mountains [a]bring him forth
food,
Where all the beasts of the field play.
21 He lieth under the shady trees,
In the covert of the reed, and fens.
22 The shady trees cover him *with* their
shadow;
The willows of the brook compass him
about.
23 Behold, [1]he drinketh up a river, *and*
hasteth not:
He trusteth that he can draw up Jordan
into his mouth.
24 [1]He taketh it with his eyes:
His nose pierceth through snares.

41 Canst thou draw out [a][1]leviathan
with a hook?
Or his tongue with a cord [2]*which* thou
lettest down?
2 Canst thou [a]put a hook into his nose?
Or bore his jaw through with a thorn?
3 Will he make many supplications unto
thee?
Will he speak soft *words* unto thee?
4 Will he make a covenant with thee?
Wilt thou take him for a servant for
ever?
5 Wilt thou play with him as *with* a bird?
Or wilt thou bind him for thy maidens?

6 Shall the companions make a banquet
of him?
Shall they part him among the
merchants?
7 Canst thou fill his skin with barbed
irons?
Or his head with fish spears?
8 Lay thine hand upon him,
Remember the battle, do no more.
9 Behold, the hope of him is in vain:
Shall *not one* be cast down even at the
sight of him?

10 None *is so* fierce that dare stir him up:
Who then is able to stand before me?
11 [a]Who hath prevented me, that I should
repay *him?*
[b]*Whatsoever is* under the whole
heaven *is* mine.

12 I will not conceal his parts,
Nor *his* power, nor his comely
proportion.
13 Who can discover the face of his
garment?
Or who can come *to him* [1]with his
double bridle?
14 Who can open the doors of his face?
His teeth *are* terrible round about.

15 *His* [1]scales *are his* pride,
Shut up *together as with* a close seal.
16 One is so near to another,
That no air can come between them.
17 They are joined one to another,
They stick together, that they cannot
be sundered.
18 *By* his neesings a light doth shine,
And his eyes *are* like the eyelids of the
morning.
19 Out of his mouth go burning lamps,
And sparks of fire leap out.
20 Out of his nostrils goeth smoke,
As *out of* a seething pot or caldron.
21 His breath kindleth coals,
And a flame goeth out of his mouth.

22 In his neck remaineth strength,
And [1]sorrow is turned into joy before
him.
23 [1]The flakes of his flesh are joined
together:
They are firm in themselves; they
cannot be moved.
24 His heart is as firm as a stone;
Yea, as hard as a piece of the nether
millstone.
25 When he raiseth up *himself,* the
mighty are afraid:
By reason of breakings they purify
themselves.

40:20 [a]Ps. 104:14
40:23 [1]Heb. *he oppresseth*
40:24 [1]Or, *Will any take him in his sight,* or *bore his nose with a gin?*
41:1 [1]That is, *a whale,* or, *a whirlpool* [2]Heb. which *thou drownest?* [a]Ps. 104:26; Is. 27:1
41:2 [a]Is. 37:29
41:11 [a]Rom. 11:35 [b]Ex. 19:5; Deut. 10:14; Ps. 24:1; 50:12; 1 Cor. 10:26,28
41:13 [1]Or, *within*
41:15 [1]Heb. *strong pieces of shields*
41:22 [1]Heb. *sorrow rejoiceth*
41:23 [1]Heb. *The fallings*

40:18 *iron.* See note on 19:24.

‡40:19 *chief of the ways of God.* The Hebrew underlying this phrase is translated "beginning of his way" in Prov 8:22 with reference to the creation of wisdom. Here the descriptive phrase stresses the importance of the behemoth as an example of a huge animal under the control of a sovereign God. *He . . . can make his sword approach unto him.* Only God would ever think of engaging this creature in battle.

40:21–23 *reed, and fens . . . willows . . . Jordan.* The area described is probably the Huleh region, north of the sea of Galilee.

41:1–34 The second of two poems in the Lord's final discourse (see note on 40:15–24).

41:1 *leviathan.* The OT uses the word in both a figurative and a literal sense. For its figurative usage see note on 3:8. Literally, the leviathan was a large marine animal (see KJV marg.; see also Ps 104:26), here perhaps a crocodile. His description in ch. 41 indicates that he is even more terrifying than the behemoth in ch. 40.

41:10 The leviathan is mighty, but God is infinitely more powerful.

41:11 Perhaps alluded to, though not directly quoted, by Paul in Rom 11:35.

41:14–15 *doors of his face . . . teeth . . . scales.* Characteristic of the crocodile (see note on v. 1).

‡41:18–21 Highly figurative, exaggerated poetic imagery describing the crocodile with the features of a mythical dragon.

‡41: 18 *neesings.* His sneezing.

‡41:23 *flakes of his flesh.* The folds of his skin.

‡41:24 *nether millstone.* The lower millstone.

26 The sword of him that layeth at him
cannot hold:
The spear, the dart, nor the
[1]habergeon.
27 He esteemeth iron as straw,
And brass as rotten wood.
28 The arrow cannot make him flee:
Slingstones are turned with him into
stubble.
29 Darts are counted as stubble:
He laugheth at the shaking of a spear.

30 [1]Sharp stones *are* under him:
He spreadeth sharp pointed *things*
upon the mire.
31 He maketh the deep to boil like a pot:
He maketh the sea like a pot of
ointment.
32 He maketh a path to shine after him;
One would think the deep to be hoary.
33 Upon earth there is not his like,
[1]Who is made without fear.
34 He beholdeth all high *things:*
He *is* a king over all the children of
pride.

Job repents in dust and ashes

42 Then Job answered the LORD, and
said,

2 I know that thou [a]canst do every *thing,*
And *that* [1]no thought can be
withholden from thee.
3 [a]Who *is* he that hideth counsel
Without knowledge?
Therefore have I uttered that I
understood not;
[b]*Things* too wonderful for me, which I
knew not.

41:26 [1]Or, *breastplate*
41:30 [1]Heb. *Sharp pieces of the potsherd*
41:33 [1]Or, *Who behave themselves without fear*
42:2 [1]Or, *no thought of thine can be hindered* [a]Gen. 18:14; Mat. 19:26; Mark 10:27; 14:36; Luke 18:27
42:3 [a]ch. 38:2 [b]Ps. 40:5; 131:1; 139:6
42:4 [a]ch. 38:3; 40:7
42:6 [a]Ezra 9:6; ch. 40:4
42:8 [1]Heb. *his face,* or, *person* [a]Num. 23:1 [b]Mat. 5:24 [c]Gen. 20:17; Jas. 5:15,16; 1 John 5:16
42:9 [1]Heb. *the face of Job*
42:10 [1]Heb. *added* [all that had been] *to Job unto the double* [a]Ps. 14:7; 126:1 [b]Is. 40:2
42:11 [a]See ch. 19:13
42:12 [a]ch. 8:7; Jas. 5:11

4 Hear, I beseech thee, and I will speak:
[a]I will demand of thee, and declare
thou unto me.
5 I have heard of thee by the hearing of
the ear:
But now mine eye seeth thee.
6 Wherefore I [a]abhor *myself,* and repent
In dust and ashes.

Job's fortunes restored

7 ¶ And it was *so,* that after the LORD had
spoken these words unto Job, the LORD said to
Eliphaz the Temanite, My wrath is kindled
against thee, and against thy two friends: for
ye have not spoken of me *the thing that is*
right, as my servant Job *hath.*
8 Therefore take unto you now [a]seven bullocks and seven rams, and [b]go to my servant
Job, and offer up for yourselves a burnt offering; and my servant Job shall [c]pray for you: for
[1]him will I accept: lest *I* deal with you *after*
your folly, in that ye have not spoken of me *the*
thing which is right, like my servant Job.
9 So Eliphaz the Temanite and Bildad the
Shuhite *and* Zophar the Naamathite went, and
did according as the LORD commanded them:
the LORD also accepted [1]Job.
10 [a]And the LORD turned the captivity of
Job, when he prayed for his friends: also the
LORD [1]gave Job [b]twice as much as he had before.
11 Then came there unto him [a]all his
brethren, and all his sisters, and all *they that*
had been of his acquaintance before, and did
eat bread with him in his house: and they be-
moaned him, and comforted him over all the
evil that the LORD had brought upon him:
every man also gave him a piece of money, and
every one an earring of gold.
12 ¶ So the LORD blessed [a]the latter end of

41:27 *iron.* See note on 19:24.

‡41:30 *Sharp stones.* Broken pottery fragments. *spreadeth sharp pointed things . . . mire.* Like a threshing machine.

41:34 *king over all the children of pride.* The Lord alone can humble such creatures. Job cannot be expected to do so, though God challenges him to attempt it—if he so desires (see 40:11–12).

42:1–6 Job's last recorded words are his response to the Lord's second discourse.

42:2 Job finally sees that God and His purposes are supreme.

42:3 Job quotes the Lord's words in 38:2.

42:4 Job quotes the Lord's words in 38:3; 40:7.

42:5 Job—and his three friends, and Elihu—had only heard of God, but now Job has seen God (see Is 6:5) with the eyes of faith and spiritual understanding. He can therefore accept God's plan for his life (see v. 2)—which includes suffering. *mine eye seeth thee.* A down payment on the hope expressed in 19:26 (see note there).

42:6 *I abhor myself . . . repent.* See note on 9:21. To his humility (see 40:4–5) Job adds repentance for the presumptuous words he had spoken to God. *dust and ashes.* See 30:19 and note.

42:7–9 Despite Job's mistakes in word and attitude while he suffered, he is now commended and the counselors are rebuked. Why? Because even in his rage, even when he challenged God, he was determined to speak honestly before Him. The counselors, on the other hand, mouthed many correct and often beautiful creedal statements, but without living knowledge of the God they claimed to honor. Job spoke to God; they only spoke about God. Even worse, their spiritual arrogance caused them to claim knowledge they did not possess. They presumed to know why Job was suffering.

42:7–8 *my servant Job.* The phrase is used four times in these two verses (see note on 1:8).

42:10 Job's prayer for those who had abused him is a touching OT illustration of the high Christian virtue our Lord taught in Mat 5:44. Job's prayer marked the turning point back to prosperity for him.

42:11 Contrast 16:2; 19:13. *piece of money.* The Hebrew for this phrase is found elsewhere in the OT only in Gen 33:19 (see note there); Josh 24:32.

42:12–16 The cosmic contest with the accuser is now over, and Job is restored. No longer is there a reason for Job to experience suffering—unless he was sinful and deserved it, which is not the case. God does not allow us to suffer for no reason, and even though the reason may be hidden in the mystery of His divine purpose (see Is 55:8–9)—never for us to know in this life—we must trust in Him as the God who does only what is right.

Job more than his beginning: for he had [b]fourteen thousand sheep, and six thousand camels, and a thousand yoke of oxen, and a thousand she asses.

13 [a]He had also seven sons and three daughters.

14 And he called the name of the first, Jemima; and the name of the second, Kezia; and the name of the third, Keren-happuch.

42:12 [b]See ch. 1:3
42:13 [a]ch. 1:2
42:16 [a]ch. 5:26; Prov. 3:16
42:17 [a]Gen. 25:8

15 And in all the land were no women found *so* fair as the daughters of Job: and their father gave them inheritance among their brethren.

16 After this [a]lived Job an hundred and forty years, and saw his sons, and his sons' sons, *even* four generations.

17 So Job died, *being* old and [a]full of days.

42:12 The number of animals is in each case twice as many (see v. 10) as Job had owned before (see 1:3).
42:13 *seven sons and three daughters.* To replace the children he had lost earlier (see 1:2,18–19).
42:14 *Jemima.* Means "dove." *Kezia.* Means "cinnamon." *Keren-happuch.* Means "container of antimony," a highly prized eyeshadow (see note on Jer 4:30).
42:15 *gave them inheritance among their brethren.* Contrast Num 27:8.
42:16 *an hundred and forty years.* The longevity of a true patriarch (see note on Ex 6:16). *saw . . . four generations.* See Gen 50:23.
42:17 *old and full of days.* See 5:26 and note; Gen 25:8.

The Book of Psalms

INTRODUCTION

Title

The titles "Psalms" and "Psalter" come from the Septuagint (the Greek translation of the OT), where they originally referred to stringed instruments (such as harp, lyre and lute), then to songs sung with their accompaniment. The traditional Hebrew title is *tehillim* (meaning "praises"; see note on Ps 145 title), even though many of the psalms are *tephillot* (meaning "prayers"). In fact, one of the first collections included in the book was titled "the prayers of David the son of Jesse" (72:20).

Collection, Arrangement and Date

The Psalter is a collection of collections and represents the final stage in a process that spanned centuries. It was put into its final form by postexilic temple personnel, who completed it probably in the third century B.C. As such, it served as the prayer book (book of prayer, praise and religious instruction) for the second (Zerubbabel's and Herod's) temple and for use in the synagogues. By the first century A.D. it was referred to as the "book of Psalms" (Luke 20:42; Acts 1:20). At that time also Psalms was used as a title for the entire section of the Hebrew OT canon known as the "Writings" (see Luke 24:44).

Many collections preceded this final compilation of the Psalms. In fact, the formation of psalters probably goes back to the early days of the first (Solomon's) temple (or even to the time of David), when the temple liturgy began to take shape. Reference has already been made to "the prayers of David." Additional collections expressly referred to in the present Psalter titles are: (1) the songs and/or psalms "for the sons of Korah" (Ps 42—49; 84—85; 87—88), (2) the psalms and/or songs "of Asaph" (Ps 50; 73—83) and (3) the songs "of degrees" (The Ascent Psalms, Ps 120—134).

Other evidence points to further compilations. Ps 1—41 (Book 1) make frequent use of the divine name *Yahweh* ("the LORD"), while Ps 42—72 (Book 2) make frequent use of *Elohim* ("God"). The reason for the *Elohim* collection in distinction from the *Yahweh* collection remains unexplained, but both of them date, at least essentially in their present form, from the period of the monarchy. Moreover, Ps 93—100 appear to be a traditional collection (see "The LORD reigneth" in 93:1; 96:10; 97:1; 99:1). Other apparent groupings include Ps 111—118 (a series of Hallelujah, "Praise the LORD" psalms), Ps 138—145 (all of which include "David" in their titles) and Ps 146—150 (with their frequent "Praise the LORD"; see note on 111:1). Whether the "Great Hallel" (Ps 120—136) was already a recognized unit is not known. (The seven "penitential psalms" get their name from Christian liturgical usage and so were never a unit in the Jewish Psalter tradition; see introduction to Ps 6.)

In its final edition, the Psalter contained 150 psalms. On this the Septuagint and Hebrew texts agree, though they arrive at this number differently. The Septuagint has an extra psalm at the end (but not numbered separately as Ps 151); it also unites Ps 9—10 (see note on Ps 9) and Ps 114—115 and divides Ps 116 and Ps 147 each into two psalms. Strangely, both the Septuagint and Hebrew texts number Ps 42—43 as two psalms whereas they were evidently originally one (see note on Ps 42—43).

The Psalter was divided into five Books (Ps 1—41; 42—72; 73—89; 90—106; 107—150), and each was provided with an appropriate concluding doxology (see 41:13; 72:18–19; 89:52; 106:48; 150). The first two of these Books, as already noted, were probably preexilic. The division of the remaining psalms into three Books, thus attaining the number five, was possibly in imitation of the five books of Moses (otherwise known simply as the Law). At least one of these divisions (between Ps 106—107) seems arbitrary (see introduction to Ps 107). In spite of this five-book division, the Psalter was clearly thought of as a whole, with an introduction (Ps 1—2) and a conclusion (Ps 146—150). Notes throughout the Psalms give additional indications of conscious arrangement.

Authorship and Titles (or Superscriptions)

Of the 150 psalms, only 34 lack superscriptions of any kind (only 17 in the Septuagint). These so-called "orphan" psalms are found mainly in Books 3–5, where they tend to occur in clusters: Ps 91; 93—97; 99; 104—107; 111—119; 135—137; 146—150. (In Books 1–2, only Ps 1—2; 10; 33; 43; 71 lack titles, and Ps 10; 43 are actually continuations of the preceding psalms.)

The contents of the superscriptions vary but fall into a few broad categories: (1) author, (2) name of collection, (3) type of psalm, (4) musical notations, (5) liturgical notations and (6) brief indications of occasion for composition. For details see notes on the titles of the various psalms.

Students of the Psalms are not agreed on the antiquity and reliability of these superscriptions. That many of them are at least preexilic appears evident from the fact that the Septuagint translators were no longer clear as to their meaning. Furthermore, the practice of attaching titles, including the name of the author, is ancient. On the other hand, comparison between the Septuagint and the Hebrew texts shows that the content of some titles was still subject to change well into the postexilic period. Most discussion centers on categories 1 and 6 above.

As for the superscriptions regarding occasion of composition, many of these brief notations of events read as if they had been taken from 1,2 Samuel. Moreover, they are sometimes not easily correlated with the content of the psalms they head. The suspicion therefore arises that they are later attempts to fit the psalms into the real-life events of history. But then why the limited number of such notations, and why the apparent mismatches? The arguments cut both ways.

Regarding authorship, opinions are even more divided. The notations themselves are ambiguous since the Hebrew phraseology used, meaning in general "belonging to," can also be taken in the sense of "concerning" or "for the use of" or "dedicated to." The name may refer to the title of a collection of psalms that had been gathered under a certain name (as "Of Asaph" or "for the sons of Korah"). As for Davidic authorship, there can be little doubt that the Psalter contains psalms composed by that noted singer and musician and that there was at one time a "Davidic" psalter. This, however, may have also included psalms written concerning David, or concerning one of the later Davidic kings, or even psalms written in the manner of those he authored. It is also true that the tradition as to which psalms are "Davidic" remains somewhat indefinite, and some "Davidic" psalms seem clearly to reflect later situations (see, e.g., Ps 30 title—but see also note there; and see introduction to Ps 69 and note on Ps 122 title). Moreover, "David" is sometimes used elsewhere as a collective for the kings of his dynasty, and this could also be true in the psalm titles.

The word *Selah* is found in 39 psalms, all but two of which (Ps 140; 143, both "Davidic") are in Books 1–3. It is also found in Hab 3, a psalm-like poem. Suggestions as to its meaning abound, but honesty must confess ignorance. Most likely, it is a liturgical notation. The common suggestions that it calls for a brief musical interlude or for a brief liturgical response by the congregation are plausible (the former may be supported by the Septuagint rendering). In some instances its present placement in the Hebrew text is highly questionable.

Psalm Types

Superscriptions to the Psalms acquaint us with an ancient system of classification: (1) *mizmor* ("psalm"); (2) *Shiggaion* (see note on Ps 7 title); (3) *Michtam* (see note on Ps 16 title); (4) *shir* ("song"); (5) *Maschil* (see note on Ps 32 title); (6) *tephillah* ("prayer"); (7) *tehillah* ("praise"); (8) *lehazkir* ("to bring to remembrance"—i.e., before God, a petition); (9) *letodah* ("of praise"); (10) *lelammed* ("to teach"); and (11) *shir yedidot* ("Song of loves"—i.e., a wedding song). The meaning of many of these terms, however, is uncertain. In addition, some titles contain two of these (especially *mizmor* and *shir*), indicating that the types are diversely based and overlapping.

Analysis of content has given rise to a different classification that has proven useful for study of the Psalms. The main types that can be identified are: (1) prayers of the individual (e.g., Ps 3; 7–8); (2) praise from the individual for God's saving help (e.g., Ps 30; 34); (3) prayers of the community (e.g., Ps 12; 44; 79); (4) praise from the community for God's saving help (e.g., Ps 66; 75); (5) confessions of confidence in the Lord (e.g., Ps 11; 16; 52); (6) hymns in praise of God's majesty and virtues (e.g., Ps 8; 19; 29; 65); (7) hymns celebrating God's universal reign (Ps 47; 93—99); (8) songs of Zion, the city of God (Ps 46; 48; 76; 84; 122; 126; 129; 137); (9) royal psalms—by, for or concerning the king, the Lord's anointed (e.g., Ps 2; 18; 20; 45; 72; 89; 110); (10) pilgrimage songs (Ps 120—134); (11) liturgical songs (e.g., Ps 15; 24; 68); (12) didactic (instructional) songs (e.g., Ps 1; 34; 37; 73; 112; 119; 128; 133).

This classification also involves some overlapping. For example, "prayers of the individual" may

include prayers of the king (in his special capacity as king) or even prayers of the community speaking in the collective first person singular. Nevertheless, it is helpful to study a psalm in conjunction with others of the same type. Attempts to fix specific liturgical settings for each type have not been very convincing. For those psalms about which something can be said in this regard see the introductions to the individual psalms.

Of all these psalm types, the prayers (both of the individual and of the community) are the most complex. Several modes of speech combine to form these appeals to God: (1) address to God: "O Lord," "my God," "my redeemer"; (2) initial appeal: "Arise," "Answer me," "Help," "Save me"; (3) description of distress: "Many are they that rise up against me," "[The wicked] attack," "I am in trouble"; (4) complaint against God: "Why hast thou forsaken me?" "Why hidest thou thyself in times of trouble?"; (5) petition: "Be not be far from me," "Preserve me"; (6) motivation for God to hear: "For there is none to help," "for thy name's sake"; (7) accusation against the adversary: "Whose mouth speaketh vanity," "oppressors seek after my soul" ("the wicked" are often quoted); (8) call for redress: "Let the wicked be ashamed and let them be silent in the grave"; (9) claims of innocence: "Judge me . . . according to my righteousness, And according to mine integrity," "Princes have persecuted me without a cause"; (10) confessions of sin: "Against thee . . . have I sinned," "I will declare mine iniquity"; (11) professions of trust: "thou . . . art a shield for me," "The LORD is my shepherd; I shall not want"; (12) vows to praise for deliverance: "We will rejoice in thy salvation," "my mouth shall praise thee with joyful lips"; (13) calls to praise: "O magnify the LORD with me," "Praise ye the LORD"; (14) motivations for praise: "For he hath delivered me out of all trouble," "For the LORD heareth the poor."

Though not all these appear in every prayer, they all belong to the conventions of prayer in the Psalter, with petition itself being but one (usually brief) element among the rest. On the whole they reflect the conventions of the court, the psalmist(s) presenting his/their case before the heavenly King/Judge. When beset by wicked adversaries, the petitioner describes his situation, pleads his innocence ("righteousness"), lodges accusation against his adversaries, and appeals for deliverance and judicial redress. When suffering at the hands of God (when God is his adversary), he confesses his guilt and pleads for mercy. Giving attention to the various modes of speech in the prayers and to their functions in the judicial appeals they present will significantly aid the reader.

Literary Features

The Psalter is from first to last poetry, even though it contains many prayers and not all OT prayers were poetic (see 1 Ki 8:23–53; Ezra 9:6–15; Neh 9:5–37; Dan 9:4–19)—nor was all praise poetic, for that matter (see 1 Ki 8:15–21). The Psalms are impassioned, vivid and concrete; they are rich in images, in simile and metaphor. Assonance, alliteration and wordplays abound in the Hebrew text. Effective use of repetition and the piling up of synonyms and complements to fill out the picture are characteristic. Key words frequently highlight major themes in prayer or song. Enclosure (repetition of a significant word or phrase at the end that occurs at the beginning) frequently wraps up a composition or a unit within it. The notes on the structure of the individual psalms often call attention to literary frames within which the psalm has been set.

Hebrew poetry lacks rhyme and regular meter. Its most distinctive and pervasive feature is parallelism. Most poetic lines are composed of two (sometimes three) balanced segments (the balance is often loose, with the second segment commonly somewhat shorter than the first). The second segment either echoes (synonymous parallelism), contrasts (antithetic parallelism) or syntactically completes (synthetic parallelism) the first. These three types are generalizations and are not wholly adequate to describe the rich variety that the creativity of the poets has achieved within the basic two-segment line structure. They can serve, however, as rough distinctions that will assist the reader.

Determining where the Hebrew poetic lines or line segments begin or end (scanning) is sometimes an uncertain matter. Even the Septuagint at times scans the lines differently from the way the Hebrew texts now available to us do. It is therefore not surprising that modern translations occasionally differ.

A related problem is the extremely concise, often elliptical writing style of the Hebrew poets. The syntactical connection of words must at times be inferred simply from context. Where more than one possibility presents itself, the translator is confronted with ambiguity. He is not always sure with which line segment a border word or phrase is to be read.

The stanza structure of Hebrew poetry is also a matter of dispute. Occasionally, recurring refrains mark off stanzas, and Ps 119 devotes eight lines to each letter of the Hebrew alphabet. For the most

part, however, no such obvious indicators are present. The KJV has used spaces to mark off poetic paragraphs (called "stanzas" in the notes). Usually this could be done with some confidence, and the reader is advised to be guided by them. But there are a few places where these divisions are questionable—and are challenged in the notes.

Close study of the Psalms discloses that the authors often composed with an overall design in mind. This is true of the alphabetic acrostics, in which the poet devoted to each letter of the Hebrew alphabet one line segment (as in Ps 111—112), or a single line (as in Ps 25; 34; 145), or two lines (as in Ps 37), or eight lines (as in Ps 119). In addition Ps 33; 38; 103 each have 22 lines in the Hebrew, no doubt because of the number of letters in the Hebrew alphabet (see Introduction to Lamentations: Literary Features). The oft-voiced notion that this device was used as a memory aid seems culturally prejudiced and quite unwarranted. Actually people of that time were able to memorize far more readily than most people today. It is much more likely that the alphabet—which was relatively recently invented as a simple system of symbols capable of representing in writing the rich and complex patterns of human speech and therefore of inscribing all that man can put into words (one of the greatest intellectual achievements of all time)—commended itself as a framework on which to hang significant phrases.

Other forms were also used. Ps 44 is a prayer fashioned after the design of a ziggurat (a Babylonian stepped pyramid; see note on Gen 11:4). A sense of symmetry is pervasive. Many Psalms begin and end with the same call to praise ("Praise ye the LORD," Ps 113; 135; "O LORD, our Lord . . . ," Ps 8). A particularly interesting device is to place a key thematic line at the very center, sometimes constructing the whole or part of the poem around that center (see note on 6:6). Still other design features are pointed out in the notes. The authors of the psalms crafted their compositions very carefully. They were heirs of an ancient art (in many details showing that they had inherited a poetic tradition that goes back hundreds of years), and they developed it to a state of high sophistication. Their works are best appreciated when carefully studied and pondered.

Theology

The Psalter is for the most part a book of prayer and praise. It speaks to God in prayer and it speaks of God in praise—also in professions of faith and trust. Although occasionally didactic (instructional) in form and purpose (teaching the way of godliness), the Psalter is not a catechism of doctrine. Its "theology" is therefore not abstract or systematic but confessional and doxological. So a summation of that "theology" impoverishes it by translating it into an objective mode.

Furthermore, any summation faces a still greater problem. The Psalter is a large collection of independent pieces of many kinds, serving different purposes and written over the course of many centuries. Not only must a brief summary of its "theology" be selective and incomplete; it will also of necessity be somewhat artificial. It will suggest that each psalm reflects or at least presupposes the "theology" outlined, that there is no "theological" tension or progression within the Psalter. Manifestly this is not so.

Still, the final editors of the Psalter were obviously not eclectic in their selection. They knew that many voices from many times spoke here, but none that in their judgment was incompatible with the Law and the Prophets. No doubt they also assumed that each psalm was to be understood in the light of the collection as a whole. That assumption we may share. Hence something, after all, can be said concerning major theological themes that, while admittedly a bit artificial, need not seriously distort and can be helpful to the student of the Psalms.

At the core of the theology of the Psalter is the conviction that the gravitational center of life (of right human understanding, trust, hope, service, morality, adoration), but also of history and of the whole creation (heaven and earth), is God (*Yahweh,* "the LORD"). He is the Great King over all, the One to whom all things are subject. He created all things and preserves them; they are the robe of glory with which He has clothed Himself. Because He ordered them, they have a well-defined and "true" identity (no chaos there). Because He maintains them, they are sustained and kept secure from disruption, confusion or annihilation. Because He alone is the sovereign God, they are governed by one hand and held in the service of one divine purpose. Under God creation is a cosmos—an orderly and systematic whole. What we distinguish as "nature" and history had for them one Lord, under whose rule all things worked together. Through the creation the Great King's majestic glory is displayed. He is good (wise, righteous, faithful, amazingly benevolent and merciful—evoking trust), and He is great (His knowledge, thoughts and works are beyond human comprehension—evoking reverent awe). By His good and lordly rule He is shown to be the Holy One.

As the Great King by right of creation and enduring absolute sovereignty, He ultimately will not tolerate any worldly power that opposes or denies or ignores Him. He will come to rule the nations so that all will be compelled to acknowledge Him. This expectation is no doubt the root and broadest scope of the psalmists' long view of the future. Because the Lord is the Great King beyond all challenge, His righteous and peaceable kingdom will come, overwhelming all opposition and purging the creation of all rebellion against His rule—such will be the ultimate outcome of history.

As the Great King on whom all creatures depend, He opposes the "proud," those who rely on their own resources (and/or the gods they have contrived) to work out their own destiny. These are the ones who ruthlessly wield whatever power they possess to attain worldly wealth, status and security; who are a law to themselves and exploit others as they will. In the Psalter, this kind of "pride" is the root of all evil. Those who embrace it, though they may seem to prosper, will be brought down to death, their final end. The "humble," the "poor and needy," those who acknowledge their dependence on the Lord in all things—these are the ones in whom God delights. Hence the "fear of the LORD"—i.e., humble trust in and obedience to the Lord—is the "beginning" of all wisdom (111:10). Ultimately, those who embrace it will inherit the earth. Not even death can hinder their seeing the face of God.

The psalmists' hope for the future—the future of God and His kingdom and the future of the godly—was firm, though somewhat generalized. None of the psalmists gives expression to a two-age vision of the future (the present evil age giving way to a new age of righteousness and peace on the other side of a great eschatological divide). Such a view began to appear in the intertestamental literature—a view that had been foreshadowed by Daniel (see especially 12:2–3) and by Isaiah (see 65:17–25; 66:22–24)—and it later received full expression in the teaching of Jesus and the apostles. But this revelation was only a fuller development consistent with the hopes the psalmists lived by.

Because God is the Great King, He is the ultimate Executor of justice among men (to avenge oneself is an act of the "proud"). God is the court of appeal when persons are threatened or wronged—especially when no earthly court that He has established has jurisdiction (as in the case of international conflicts) or is able to judge (as when one is wronged by public slander) or is willing to act (out of fear or corruption). He is the mighty and faithful Defender of the defenseless and the wronged. He knows every deed and the secrets of every heart. There is no escaping His scrutiny. No false testimony will mislead Him in judgment. And He hears the pleas brought to Him. As the good and faithful Judge, He delivers those who are oppressed or wrongfully attacked and redresses the wrongs committed against them (see note on 5:10). This is the unwavering conviction that accounts for the psalmists' impatient complaints when they boldly, yet as "poor and needy," cry to Him, "Why (have you not yet delivered me)?" "How long, O LORD (before you act)?"

As the Great King over all the earth, the Lord has chosen Israel to be His servant people, His "inheritance" among the nations. He has delivered them by mighty acts out of the hands of the world powers, He has given them a land of their own (territory that He took from other nations to be His own "inheritance" in the earth), and He has united them with Himself in covenant as the initial embodiment of His redeemed kingdom. Thus both their destiny and His honor came to be bound up with this relationship. To them He also gave His word of revelation, which testified of Him, made specific His promises and proclaimed His will. By God's covenant, Israel was to live among the nations, loyal only to her heavenly King. She was to trust solely in His protection, hope in His promises, live in accordance with His will and worship Him exclusively. She was to sing His praises to the whole world—which in a special sense revealed Israel's anticipatory role in the evangelization of the nations.

As the Great King, Israel's covenant Lord, God chose David to be His royal representative on earth. In this capacity, David was the Lord's "servant"—i.e., a member of the Great King's administration. The Lord Himself anointed him and adopted him as His royal "son" to rule in His name. Through him God made His people secure in the promised land and subdued all the powers that threatened them. What is more, He covenanted to preserve the Davidic dynasty. Henceforth the kingdom of God on earth, while not dependent on the house of David, was linked to it by God's decision and commitment. In its continuity and strength lay Israel's security and hope as she faced a hostile world. And since the Davidic kings were God's royal representatives in the earth, in concept seated at God's right hand (110:1), the scope of their rule was potentially worldwide (see Ps 2).

The Lord's anointed, however, was more than a warrior king. He was to be endowed by God to govern His people with godlike righteousness: to deliver the oppressed, defend the defenseless, suppress the wicked, and thus bless the nation with internal peace and prosperity. He was also an inter-

cessor with God in behalf of the nation, the builder and maintainer of the temple (as God's earthly palace and the nation's house of prayer) and the foremost voice calling the nation to worship the Lord. It is perhaps with a view to these last duties that he is declared to be not only king, but also "priest" (see Ps 110 and notes).

As the Great King, Israel's covenant Lord, God (who had chosen David and his dynasty to be His royal representatives) also chose Jerusalem (the city of David) as His own royal city, the earthly seat of His throne. Thus Jerusalem (Zion) became the earthly capital (and symbol) of the kingdom of God. There in His palace (the temple) He sat enthroned among His people. There His people could meet with Him to bring their prayers and praise, and to see His power and glory. From there He brought salvation, dispensed blessings and judged the nations. And with Him as the city's great Defender, Jerusalem was the secure citadel of the kingdom of God, the hope and joy of God's people.

God's goodwill and faithfulness toward His people were most strikingly symbolized by His pledged presence among them at His temple in Jerusalem, the "city of the great King" (48:2). But no manifestation of His benevolence was greater than His readiness to forgive the sins of those who humbly confessed them and whose hearts showed Him that their repentance was genuine and that their professions of loyalty to Him had integrity. As they anguished over their own sinfulness, the psalmists remembered the ancient testimony of their covenant Lord: I am *Yahweh* ("the LORD"), "the LORD God, compassionate and gracious, slow to anger, and abounding in lovingkindness and truth, who keeps lovingkindness for thousands, forgives inquity, transgression and sin" (Ex 34:6–7). Only so did they dare to submit to Him as His people, to "fear" Him (see 130:3–4).

Unquestionably the supreme kingship of Yahweh (in which He displays His transcendent greatness and goodness) is the most basic metaphor and most pervasive theological concept in the Psalter—as in the OT generally. It provides the fundamental perspective in which man is to view Himself, the whole creation, events in "nature" and history, and the future. The whole creation is His one kingdom. To be a creature in the world is to be a part of His kingdom and under His rule. To be a human being in the world is to be dependent on and responsible to Him. To proudly deny that fact is the root of all wickedness—the wickedness that now pervades the world.

God's election of Israel and subsequently of David and Zion, together with the giving of His word, represent the renewed inbreaking of God's righteous kingdom into this world of rebellion and evil. It initiates the great divide between the righteous nation and the wicked nations, and on a deeper level between the righteous and the wicked, a more significant distinction that cuts even through Israel. In the end this divine enterprise will triumph. Human pride will be humbled, and wrongs will be redressed. The humble will be given the whole earth to possess, and the righteous and peaceable kingdom of God will come to full realization. These theological themes, of course, have profound religious and moral implications. Of these, too, the psalmists spoke.

One question that ought yet to be addressed is: Do the Psalms speak of the Christ? Yes, but in a variety of ways—and not as the prophets do. The Psalter is not a book of prophetic oracles and was never numbered among the prophetic books.

‡When the Psalms speak of the king on David's throne, they speak of the king who is being crowned (as in Ps 2; 72; 110—though some think 110 is an exception) or is reigning (as in Ps 45) at the time. They proclaim his status as God's anointed and declare what God will accomplish through him and his dynasty. Thus they also speak of the sons of David to come—and in the exile and the postexilic era, when there was no reigning king, they spoke to Israel only of the great Son of David whom the prophets had announced as the one in whom God's covenant with David would yet be fulfilled. So the NT quotes these psalms as testimonies to Christ, which in their unique way they are. In Him they are truly fulfilled. Thus, they are often called "Messianic psalms," since they portray aspects of the coming Messiah.

When in the Psalms righteous sufferers—who are "righteous" because they are innocent, not having provoked or wronged their adversaries, and because they are among the "humble" (or "poor") who trust in the Lord—cry out to God in their distress (as in Ps 22; 69), they give voice to the sufferings of God's servants in a hostile and evil world.

These cries became the prayers of God's oppressed "saints," and as such they were taken up into Israel's book of prayers. When Christ came in the flesh, He identified Himself with God's "humble" people in the world. He became for them God's righteous servant par excellence, and He shared their sufferings at the hands of evil men. Thus these prayers became His prayers also—uniquely His prayers. In Him the suffering and deliverance of which these prayers speak are fulfilled (though they continue to be the prayers also of those who take up their cross and follow Him).

Similarly, in speaking of God's covenant people, of the city of God, and of the temple in which God dwells, the Psalms ultimately speak of Christ's church. The Psalter is not only the prayer book of the second temple; it is also the enduring prayer book of the people of God. Now, however, it must be used in the light of the new era of redemption that dawned with the first coming of the Messiah and that will be consummated at His second coming.

Psalm 1

1 Blessed [a]*is* the man
That walketh not in the counsel of the [1]ungodly,
Nor standeth in the way of sinners,
[b]Nor sitteth in the seat of the scornful.
2 But [a]his delight *is* in the law of the LORD;
[b]And in his law doth he meditate day and night.
3 And he shall be like a tree [a]planted by the rivers of water,
That bringeth forth his fruit in his season;
His leaf also shall not [1]wither;
And whatsoever he doeth shall [b]prosper.
4 The ungodly *are* not so:
But *are* [a]like the chaff which the wind driveth away.
5 Therefore the ungodly shall not stand in the judgment,
Nor sinners in the congregation of the righteous.
6 For [a]the LORD knoweth the way of the righteous:
But the way of the ungodly shall perish.

Psalm 2

1 [a]Why do the heathen [1]rage,
And the people [2]imagine a vain *thing?*
2 The kings of the earth set themselves,
And the rulers take counsel together,
Against the LORD, and against his [a]anointed, *saying,*
3 [a]Let us break their bands asunder,
And cast away their cords from us.
4 He that sitteth in the heavens [a]shall laugh:
The LORD shall have them in derision.
5 Then shall he speak unto them in his wrath,
And [1]vex them in his sore displeasure.

1:1 [1]Or, *wicked* [a]Prov. 4:14 [b]Ps. 26:4; Jer. 15:17
1:2 [a]Ps. 119:35 [b]Josh. 1:8; Ps. 119:1
1:3 [1]Heb. *fade* [a]Jer. 17:8; Ezek. 47:12 [b]Gen. 39:3; Is. 3:10
1:4 [a]Job 21:18; Is. 17:13
1:6 [a]Ps. 37:18; 2 Tim. 2:19
2:1 [1]Or, *tumultuously assemble* [2]Heb. *meditate* [a]Acts 4:25
2:2 [a]John 1:41
2:3 [a]Luke 19:14
2:4 [a]Ps. 37:13; Prov. 1:26
2:5 [1]Or, *trouble*

Ps 1 Author and date unknown. Godly wisdom here declares the final outcome of the two "ways": "the way of sinners" (v. 1) and "the way of the righteous" (v. 6). See 34:19–22; 37; essay, p. 687. As an introduction to the book, this psalm reminds the reader (1) that those of whom the Psalms speak (using various terms) as the people of God, those whom He receives in His presence and favors with His salvation and blessing, must be characterized by righteousness—sinners have no place among them (v. 5; see Ps 15; 24)—and (2) that the godly piety that speaks in the Psalms is a faithful response to God's revealed (and written) directives for life—which is the path that leads to blessedness.

1:1 Speaks progressively of association with the ungodly and participation in their ungodly ways. *Blessed.* The happy condition of those who revere the Lord and do His will (see 94:12; 112:1; 119:1–2; 128:1; Prov 29:18; cf. Ps 41:1; 106:3; Prov 14:21; Is 56:2), who put their trust in Him (see 40:4; 84:5,12; 144:15; 146:5; Prov 16:20; Is 30:18; Jer 17:7; cf. Ps 2:12; 34:8), and so are blessed by God (see especially 41:1–3; 144:12–14; see also Mat 5:3–12). The Psalter begins by proclaiming the blessedness of the godly and ends by calling all living things to praise God in His earthly and heavenly sanctuaries (Ps 150). *walketh not.* Does not order his life according to. *counsel.* Deliberations and advice (see Prov 1:10–19). *standeth.* Station oneself. *sinners.* See v. 5; those for whom evil is habitual, for whom wickedness is a way of life. *sitteth.* Settle oneself. *scornful.* Those who ridicule God and defiantly reject His law (see Prov 1:22).

1:2 *in his law doth he meditate.* Seeking guidance for life in God's law rather than in the deliberations of the wicked. *day and night.* See Josh 1:8.

1:3 *like a tree . . . shall not wither.* See Jer 17:8; a simile of the blessedness of the righteous. Such a tree withstands the buffeting of the winds and, flourishing, it blesses man, animals and birds with its unfailing fruit and shade.

1:4 *like the chaff . . . driveth away.* A simile of the wretchedness of the wicked. Chaff is carried away by the lightest wind, and its removal brings about cleansing by extracting what is utterly useless (see note on Ruth 1:22).

1:5 *shall not stand in the judgment.* Will not be able to withstand God's wrath when He judges (see 76:7; 130:3; Ezra 9:15; Mal 3:2; Mat 25:31–46; Rev 6:17). *congregation.* The worshiping assembly at God's sanctuary (as in 22:25; 26:12; 35:18; 40:9–10; 111:1; 149:1; see Ps 15; 24). *righteous.* One of several terms in the OT for God's people; it presents them as those who honor God and order their lives in all things according to His will. In every human relationship they faithfully fulfill the obligations that the relationship entails, remembering that power and authority (of whatever sort: domestic, social, political, economic, religious, intellectual) are to be used to bless, not to exploit.

1:6 *way . . . way.* Implicit in the destinies of the two lifestyles are also the destinies of those who choose them.

Ps 2 Author and date unknown (Peter and John ascribed it to David in Acts 4:25—possibly in accordance with the Jewish practice of honoring David as the primary author of the Psalter). A royal psalm, it was originally composed for the coronation of Davidic kings, in light of the Lord's covenant with David (see 2 Sam 7). Later, prophetic words of judgment against the house of David and announcements of God's future redemption of His people through an exalted royal son of David highlighted the Messianic import of this psalm. As the second half of a two-part introduction to the Psalms, it proclaims the blessedness of all who acknowledge the lordship of God and His anointed and "put their trust in him" (v. 12; see note on 1:1)—as does the godly piety that speaks in the Psalms. This psalm is frequently quoted in the NT, where it is applied to Christ as the great Son of David and God's Anointed.

2:1–3 The nations rebel. In the ancient Near East the coronation of a new king was often the occasion for the revolt of peoples and kings who had been subject to the crown. The newly anointed king is here pictured as ruler over an empire.

2:1–2 For a NT application see Acts 4:25–28.

2:1 *Why . . . ?* A rhetorical question that implies "How dare they!"

‡2:2 *LORD . . . his anointed.* To rebel against the Lord's Anointed is also to rebel against the One who anointed Him. *anointed.* The psalm refers to the Davidic king and is ultimately fulfilled in Christ. The English word "Messiah" comes from the Hebrew word for "anointed one," and the English word "Christ" from the Greek word (*christos*) for "anointed one."

2:4–6 The Lord mocks the rebels. With derisive laughter the Lord meets the confederacy of rebellious world powers with the sovereign declaration that it is He who has established the Davidic king in His own royal city of Zion (Jerusalem).

2:4 See 59:8.

2:5 *wrath . . . sore displeasure.* God's anger is always an expression of His righteousness (see 7:11; see also note on 4:1).

6 Yet have I [1]set my king
[a][2]Upon my holy hill of Zion.
7 I will declare [1]the decree:
The LORD hath said unto me, [a]Thou *art* my Son;
This day have I begotten thee.
8 [a]Ask of me,
And I shall give *thee* the heathen *for* thine inheritance,
And the uttermost parts of the earth *for* thy possession.
9 [a]Thou shalt break them with a rod of iron;
Thou shalt dash them in pieces like a potter's vessel.
10 Be wise now therefore, O ye kings:
Be instructed, ye judges of the earth.
11 [a]Serve the LORD with fear,
And rejoice [b]with trembling.
12 [a]Kiss the Son, lest he be angry,
And ye perish *from* the way,
When [b]his wrath is kindled but a little:
[c]Blessed *are* all they that put their trust in him.

2:6 [1]Heb. *anointed* [2]Heb. *Upon Zion, the hill of my holiness* [a]2 Sam. 5:7
2:7 [1]Or, *for a decree* [a]Acts 13:33
2:8 [a]Ps. 22:27
2:9 [a]Ps. 89:23; Rev. 2:27
2:11 [a]Heb. 12:28 [b]Phil. 2:12
2:12 [a]John 5:23 [b]Rev. 6:16 [c]Ps. 34:8; Is. 30:18; Rom. 9:33

3:T [a]2 Sam. 15-18
3:1 [a]2 Sam. 15:12
3:2 [a]Ps. 71:11
3:3 [1]Or, *about* [a]Ps. 28:7 [b]Ps. 27:6
3:4 [a]Ps. 34:4 [b]Ps. 2:6
3:5 [a]Lev. 26:6; Prov. 3:24
3:6 [a]Ps. 27:3
3:7 [a]Job 16:10; Lam. 3:30

Psalm 3

A Psalm of David, [a]when he fled from Absalom his son.

1 LORD, [a]how are they increased that trouble me!
Many *are* they that rise up against me.
2 Many *there be* which say of my soul,
[a]*There is* no help for him in God.
Selah.
3 But thou, O LORD, *art* [a]a shield [1]for me;
My glory, and [b]the lifter up of mine head.
4 I cried unto the LORD *with* my voice,
And [a]he heard me out of his [b]holy hill.
Selah.
5 [a]I laid me down and slept;
I awaked; for the LORD sustained me.
6 [a]I will not be afraid of ten thousands of people,
That have set *themselves* against me round about.
7 Arise, O LORD; save me, O my God:
[a]For thou hast smitten all mine enemies *upon* the cheek bone;

2:6 *holy hill.* The site of the Jerusalem temple (see 2 Chr 33:15); see also 3:4; 15:1; 43:3; 99:9.
2:7–9 The Lord's Anointed proclaims the Lord's coronation decree. For NT application to Jesus' resurrection see Acts 13:33; to His superiority over angels see Heb 1:5; to His appointment as high priest see Heb 5:5.
‡2:7 *Son . . . begotten thee.* In the ancient Near East the relationship between a great king and one of his subject kings, who ruled by his authority and owed him allegiance, was expressed not only by the words "lord" and "servant" but also by "father" and "son." The Davidic king was the Lord's "servant" and His "son" (2 Sam 7:5,14). The word "begotten" indicates the initiation of this relationship on the day of the king's coronation. This passage does not teach that Jesus the Son is "begotten" (created/born) of the Father or that the Father eternally generates the Son.
2:8 *thine inheritance.* Your domain—as the promised land was the Lord's "inheritance" (Ex 15:17; see Josh 22:19; Ps 28:9; 79:1; 82:8). *uttermost parts of the earth.* Ultimately the rule of Christ will extend as far as the rule of God Himself.
2:9 According to Rev 12:5; 19:15 this word will be fulfilled in the triumphant reign of Christ; in Rev 2:26–27 Christ declares that He will appoint those who remain faithful to Him to share in His subjugating rule over the nations. *dash them . . . potter's vessel.* See Jer 19:11.
2:10–12 The rebellious rulers are warned.
2:11 *rejoice.* Hail the Lord as King with joy. *trembling.* Awe and reverence.
‡2:12 *Kiss the son.* As a sign of honor and submission (see 1 Sam 10:1; 1 Ki 19:18; Hos 13:2; see also note on Gen 41:40). Submission to an ancient king was often expressed by kissing his feet. *perish from the way.* See 1:6 and note. *Blessed.* See 1:1 and note.
Ps 3 Though threatened by many foes, the psalmist prays confidently to the Lord. Ps 3 and 4 are linked by references to glory (see v. 3; 4:2) and to the psalmist's sleep at night (see v. 5; 4:8). In v. 5 David speaks of the assurance of his waking in the morning because the Lord will keep him while he sleeps; in 4:8 he speaks of the inner quietness with which he goes to sleep because of the Lord's care. This juxtaposition of prayers with references to waking (morning) and sleeping (evening) at the beginning of the Psalter suggests that God's faithful care sustains the godly day and night whatever the need or circumstances, many of which will be mentioned in this book of prayers.
3 title *when he fled.* See 2 Sam 15:13–17:22. References to events in David's life stand in the superscriptions of 13 psalms (3; 7; 18; 34; 51–52; 54; 56–57; 59–60; 63; 142), all but one (Ps 142) in Books 1 and 2. See Introduction: Authorship and Titles (or Superscriptions).
3:1–2 David's need: threatened by many foes.
3:2 See 22:7–8; 71:10–11. The psalmists frequently quote their wicked oppressors in order to portray how they mock (see note on 1:1) God and His servants (see note on 10:11). *Selah.* A word of uncertain meaning, occurring frequently in the Psalms—possibly a musical term; see Introduction: Authorship and Titles (or Superscriptions).
3:3–4 David's confidence in God, who does not fail to answer his prayers.
3:3 *shield.* That one's king is his shield (protector) was a common concept in ancient Israel (see 7:10; 47:9; 59:11; 84:9; 89:18; Gen 15:1). That the Lord is the shield of His people is frequently asserted (see 84:11; 91:4; 115:9–11; Deut 33:29; Prov 30:5) or claimed (see 18:2,30; 28:7; 33:20; 119:114; 144:2). *My glory.* The psalmist rejoices in the Lord as his royal provider and protector (see note on 2:11). *lifter up of mine head.* In victory over his enemies (see 110:7).
3:4 *holy hill.* The place of the Lord's sanctuary, the earthly counterpart of His heavenly throne room (see note on 2:6).
3:5–6 David's sense of security.
3:5 Even while his own watchfulness is surrendered to sleep, the watchful Lord preserves him (see 4:8).
3:7–8 David's prayer.
3:7 *Arise . . . save.* Hebrew idiom frequently prefaces an imperative calling for immediate action with the call to arise (see Ex 12:31; Deut. 2:13, "rise up"; Judg 7:9, "Arise"). In poetry the two imperatives of the idiom are often distributed between the two halves of the poetic line. Hence the psalmist's prayer is: "Arise (and) save me." *LORD . . . my God.* That is, LORD my God; the two elements of a compound divine name are also frequently distributed between the two halves of a poetic line. *broken the teeth.* Probably likening the enemies to wild animals (see note on 7:2).

Thou hast broken the teeth of the
ungodly.
8 [a]Salvation *belongeth* unto the LORD:
Thy blessing *is* upon thy people. Selah.

Psalm 4

To the [1]chief Musician on Neginoth,
A Psalm of David.

1 Hear me when I call, O God of my
righteousness:
Thou hast enlarged me *when I was* in
distress;
[1]Have mercy upon me, and hear my
prayer.
2 O ye sons of men, how long *will ye
turn* my glory into shame?
How long will ye love vanity, *and* seek
after leasing? Selah.
3 But know that [a]the LORD hath set apart
him that is godly for himself:
The LORD will hear when I call unto
him.
4 [a]Stand in awe, and sin not:
[b]Commune with your own heart upon
your bed, and be still. Selah.
5 Offer [a]the sacrifices of righteousness,
And [b]put your trust in the LORD.
6 *There be* many that say, Who will shew
us *any* good?
[a]LORD, lift thou up the light of thy
countenance upon us.
7 Thou hast put [a]gladness in my heart,
More than *in* the time *that* their corn
and their wine increased.
8 [a]I will both lay me down in peace, and
sleep:
[b]For thou, LORD, only makest me dwell
in safety.

Psalm 5

To the chief Musician upon Nehiloth,
A Psalm of David.

1 Give ear to my words, O LORD,
Consider my meditation.
2 Hearken unto the [a]voice of my cry, my
King, and my God:
For unto thee will I pray.
3 [a]My voice shalt thou hear *in* the
morning, O LORD;
In the morning will I direct *my prayer*
unto thee, and will look up.
4 For thou *art* not a God that hath
pleasure in wickedness:
Neither shall evil dwell *with* thee.
5 The foolish shall not stand [1]in thy
sight:
Thou hatest all workers of iniquity.
6 [a]Thou shalt destroy them that speak
leasing:
[b]The LORD will abhor [1]the bloody and
deceitful man.
7 But *as for* me, I will come *into* thy
house in the multitude of thy mercy:

3:8 [a]Is. 43:11
4:T [1]Or, *overseer*
4:1 [1]Or, *Be gracious unto me*
4:3 [a]2 Tim. 2:19; 2 Pet. 2:9
4:4 [a]Eph. 4:26 [b]Ps. 77:6
4:5 [a]Deut. 33:19; Ps. 50:14 [b]Ps. 37:3
4:6 [a]Num. 6:26
4:7 [a]Is. 9:3
4:8 [a]Ps. 3:5 [b]Lev. 25:18
5:2 [a]Ps. 3:4
5:3 [a]Ps. 30:5
5:5 [1]Heb. *before thine eyes*
5:6 [1]Heb. *the man of bloods and deceit* [a]Rev. 21:8 [b]Ps. 55:23

3:8 *Salvation belongeth unto the LORD.* A common feature in the prayers of the Psalter is a concluding expression of confidence that the prayer will be or has been heard (as in 6:8–10; 7:10–17; 10:16–18; 12:7; 13:5–6 and often elsewhere; see note on 12:5–6). Here David's confidence becomes a testimony to God's people. *Thy blessing is upon thy people.* See 25:22; 28:8–9; 51:18. The psalmists stood before God, the royal King, as His servants responsible for the well-being of His people.

Ps 4 Perhaps a prayer for relief when some calamity (possibly drought; see v. 7) has fallen and many are turning from the Lord to the gods of Canaan, from whom they hope to receive better. See introduction to Ps 3.

4 title See Hab 3:19. *To the chief Musician.* Probably a liturgical notation, indicating either that the psalm was to be added to the collection of works to be used by the choir director in Israel's worship services, or that when the psalm was used in the temple worship it was to be spoken by the leader of the Levitical choir—or by the choir itself (see 1 Chr 23:5,30; 25; Neh 11:17). In this liturgical activity the Levites functioned as representatives of the worshiping congregation. Following their lead the people probably responded with "Amen" and "Praise the LORD" (Hallelujah); see 1 Chr 16:36; Neh 5:13; cf. 1 Cor 14:16; Rev 5:14; 7:12; 19:4. *on Neginoth.* See Ps 6; 54–55; 61; 67; 76 titles. This is a liturgical notation, indicating that the Levites (see previous note) were to accompany the psalm with harp and lyre (see 1 Chr 23:5; 25:1,3,6; cf. Ps 33:2; 43:4; 71:22; see also notes on Ps 39; 42 titles).

4:1 Initial request to be heard. *Thou hast enlarged me.* Lit. "You have made a spacious place for me" (see 18:19 and note).

4:2–3 David rebukes those who turn away from his God to seek relief from the counterfeit gods; he assures them that the Lord will hear him.

4:2 *how long . . . ?* See Introduction: Theology; see also note on 6:3. *my glory.* David's special relationship with the Lord is the source of his glory. *Selah.* See note on 3:2; see also Introduction: Authorship and Titles (or Superscriptions).

‡4:3 *godly.* Hebrew *ḥasid,* is one of several Hebrew words for God's people, referring to them as people who are or should be devoted to God and faithful to Him. Often translated as "saint" in the KJV.

4:4–5 An exhortation not to give way to exasperation or anxiety but to look to the Lord.

4:4 *Stand in awe, and sin not.* Paul uses these words in a different context (see Eph 4:26).

4:6 In the face of widespread uncertainty, David prays for the Lord to bless. *Who . . . ?* Which of the gods . . . ? *countenance upon us.* See note on 13:1; a common expression for favor, reminiscent of the Aaronic benediction (see Num 6:25–26).

4:7–8 David's confidence (see note on 3:8).

‡4:7 *heart.* In Biblical language the center of the human spirit, from which spring emotions, thought, motivations, courage and action—"the issues of life" (Prov 4:23).

4:8 See 3:5–6. *in peace.* Without anxiety.

Ps 5 This morning prayer, perhaps offered at the time of the morning sacrifice, is the psalmist's cry for help when his enemies spread malicious lies to destroy him.

‡5 title *To the chief Musician.* See note on Ps 4 title. *Nehiloth.* The Hebrew for this word occurs only here; meaning uncertain, perhaps "flute."

5:1–3 Initial appeal to be heard.

5:2 *King.* See Introduction: Theology.

5:4–6 An appeal to the righteousness of God's rule over mankind.

‡5:6 *leasing.* Lies, falsehood.

And in thy fear will I worship toward
[1]thy holy temple.
8 [a]Lead me, O LORD, in thy
righteousness because of [1]mine
enemies;
Make thy way straight before my face.
9 For *there is* no [1]faithfulness [2]in their
mouth;
Their inward *part is* [3]very wickedness;
[a]Their throat *is* an open sepulchre;
[b]They flatter with their tongue.
10 [1]Destroy thou them, O God;
Let them fall [2]by their own counsels;
Cast them out in the multitude of their
transgressions;
For they have rebelled against thee.
11 But let all those that put their trust in
thee [a]rejoice:
Let them ever shout for joy, because
[1]thou defendest them:
Let them also that love thy name be
joyful in thee.
12 For thou, LORD, wilt bless the righteous;
With favour wilt thou [1]compass him as
with a shield.

5:7 [1]Heb. *the temple of thy holiness*
5:8 [1]Heb. *those which observe me* [a]Ps. 25:5
5:9 [1]Or, *stedfastness* [2]Heb. *in his mouth,* that is, *in the mouth of any of them* [3]Heb. *wickednesses* [a]Luke 11:44; Rom. 3:13 [b]Ps. 62:4
5:10 [1]Or, *Make them guilty* [2]Or, *from their counsels*
5:11 [1]Heb. *thou coverest over,* or, *protectest them* [a]Is. 65:13
5:12 [1]Heb. *crown him*

Psalm 6

To the chief Musician on Neginoth [a][1]upon
Sheminith, A Psalm of David.

1 O LORD, rebuke me not in thine anger,
Neither chasten me in thy hot
displeasure.
2 Have mercy upon me, O LORD; for I *am*
weak:
O LORD, [a]heal me; for my bones are
vexed.
3 My soul is also sore vexed:
But thou, O LORD, how long?

6:T [1]Or, *upon the eighth* [a]1 Chr. 15:21; Ps. 12, title 6:2 [a]Hos. 6:1

5:7–8 The psalmist presents his plea to the Lord in humble reverence (v. 7), trusting in the Lord's great mercy (v. 7) and righteousness (v. 8).

5:7 *multitude of thy mercy.* See note on 6:4.

5:8 *Lead me.* As a shepherd (see 23:3). *thy righteousness.* Very often the "righteousness" of God in the Psalms (and frequently elsewhere in the OT) refers to the faithfulness with which He acts. This faithfulness is in full accordance with His commitments (both expressed and implied) to His people and with His status as the divine King—to whom the powerless may look for protection, the oppressed for redress and the needy for help. *Make thy way straight.* May the way down which You lead me be straight, level and smooth, free from obstacles and temptations. The psalmist prays that God will so direct him that his enemies will have no grounds for their malicious accusations (see 25:4; 27:11; 139:24; 143:8–10).

5:9–10 Accusation against his enemies (a common element in the prayers of the Psalter) and a call for redress.

5:9 *in their mouth.* In what they say about him. The most frequent weapon used against the psalmists is the tongue (for a striking example see Ps 12; see also note on 10:7). The psalmists experienced that the tongue is as deadly as the sword (see 57:4; 64:3–4). Perhaps appeals to God against those who maliciously wield the tongue are frequent in the Psalms because only in God's courtroom can a person experience redress for such attacks. *inward part.* See note on 4:7. *throat . . . sepulchre.* See note on 49:14. *They flatter.* For the plots and intrigues of enemies, usually involving lies to discredit the king and bring him down, see Ps 17; 25; 27–28; 31; 35; 41; 52; 54–57; 59; 63–64; 71; 86; 109; 140–141—all ascribed to David. Frequently such attacks came when the king was "low" and seemingly abandoned by God (as in Ps 25; 35; 41; 71; 86; 109). In that case he was viewed as no longer fit to be king—God was no longer with him (and so he could no longer secure the safety of the nation; see 1 Sam 8:20; 11:12; 12:12; 25:28; 2 Sam 3:18; 7:9–11). In any event, he was an easy prey (see 3:2; 22:7–8; 71:11). See note on 86:17. See also Paul's use of this verse in Rom 3:13.

5:10 The presence of so-called "imprecations" (curses) in the Psalms has occasioned endless discussion and has caused many Christians to wince, in view of Jesus' instructions to turn the other cheek and to pray for one's enemies (see Mat 5:39,44), and His own example on the cross (see Luke 23:34). Actually, these "imprecations" are not that at all; rather, they are appeals to God to redress wrongs perpetrated against the psalmists by imposing penalties commensurate with the violence done (see 28:4)—in accordance also with normal judicial procedure in human courts (see Deut 25:1–3). The psalmists knew that he who has been wronged is not to right that wrong by his own hand but is to leave redress to the Lord, who says, "To me belongeth vengeance, and recompense" (Deut 32:35; see Prov 20:22; Rom 12:19). Therefore they appeal their cases to the divine Judge (see Jer 15:15). *Cast them out.* From God's presence, thus from the source of blessing and life (see Gen 3:23). *rebelled against thee.* By their attacks on the psalmist. When they attack the Lord's anointed, it is as if they are attacking the Lord himself.

5:11 The psalmist expands his prayer to include all the godly (see note on 3:8). *thy name.* The name of the Lord is the manifestation of His character (see notes on Ex 3:14–15; 34:6–7). It has no separate existence apart from the Lord, but is synonymous with the Lord Himself in His gracious manifestation and accessibility to His people. Hence the Jerusalem temple is the earthly residence of His name among His people (see 74:7; Deut 12:5,11; 2 Sam 7:13), and His people can pray to Him by calling on His name (see 79:6; 80:18; 99:6; 105:1; 116:4,13,17). The name of the Lord defends (see 20:1; Prov 18:10); the Lord saves by His name (see 54:1); and His saving acts testify that His name is good (see 52:9). Accordingly, the godly trust in His name (20:7; 33:21), hope in His name (see 52:9), "sing praise" to His name (7:17; 9:2; 18:49) and "rejoice" in His name (89:16). Both the "love" and the "fear" that belong alone to God are similarly directed toward His name (love: 69:36; 119:132; fear: 61:5; 86:11; 102:15).

5:12 See note on 3:8. *righteous.* See note on 1:5.

Ps 6 A prayer in time of severe illness, an occasion seized upon by David's enemies to vent their animosity. In early Christian liturgical tradition it was numbered with the seven penitential psalms (the others: Ps 32; 38; 51; 102; 130; 143).

6 title See note on Ps 4 title. *Sheminith.* A musical term, perhaps referring to an eight-stringed lyre. Occurs also in Ps 12 title and in 1 Chr 15:21.

6:1–3 Initial appeal for mercy. Though the Lord has sent him illness to chastise him for his sin (see 32:3–5; 38:1–8,17–18), the psalmist asks that God would not in anger impose the full measure of the penalty for sin, for then death must come (see v. 5; see also 130:3).

‡6:1 Ps 38 begins similarly. *rebuke . . . chasten.* See 39:11; see also note on 3:7. *anger . . . displeasure.* See note on 2:5.

6:2 *bones.* As the inner skeleton, they here represent the whole body.

6:3 *soul.* Not a spiritual aspect in distinction from the physical, nor the psalmist's "inner" being in distinction from his "outer" being, but his very self as a living, conscious, personal be-

4 Return, O LORD, deliver my soul:
O save me for thy mercy's sake.
5 [a]For in death *there is* no remembrance
of thee:
In the grave who shall give thee
thanks?
6 I am weary with my groaning;
[1]All the night make I my bed to swim;
I water my couch with my tears.
7 [a]Mine eye is consumed because of
grief;
It waxeth old because of all mine
enemies.
8 [a]Depart from me, all ye workers of
iniquity;
For the LORD hath [b]heard the voice of
my weeping.
9 The LORD hath heard my supplication;
The LORD will receive my prayer.
10 Let all mine enemies be ashamed and
sore vexed:
Let them return *and* be ashamed
suddenly.

6:5 [a]Ps. 30:9
6:6 [1]Or, *Every night*
6:7 [a]Job 17:7
6:8 [a]Mat. 25:41 [b]Ps. 3:4
7:T [1]Or, *business* [a]Hab. 3:1 [b]2 Sam. 16
7:1 [a]Ps. 31:15
7:2 [1]Heb. *not a deliverer* [a]Is. 38:13 [b]Ps. 50:22
7:3 [a]2 Sam. 16:7 [b]1 Sam. 24:11
7:4 [a]1 Sam. 24:7

Psalm 7

[a]Shiggaion of David, which he sang unto the LORD, [b]concerning the [1]words of Cush the Benjamite.

1 O LORD my God, in thee do I put my
trust:
[a]Save me from all them that persecute
me, and deliver me:
2 [a]Lest he tear my soul like a lion,
[b]Rending *it* in pieces, while *there is*
[1]none to deliver.
3 O LORD my God, [a]if I have done this;
If there be [b]iniquity in my hands;
4 If I have rewarded evil *unto* him that
was at peace with me;
(Yea, [a]I have delivered him that
without cause is mine enemy:)
5 Let the enemy persecute my soul, and
take *it;*
Yea, let him tread down my life upon
the earth,
And lay mine honour in the dust. Selah.
6 Arise, O LORD, in thine anger,

ing. Its use in conjunction with "bones" (also in 35:9–10: "soul" and "All my bones") did not for the Hebrew writer involve reference to two distinct entities but constituted for him two ways of referring to himself, as is the case also in the combination "soul" and "belly" (31:9) "soul" and "flesh" (63:1). *But thou . . . how long?* See Introduction: Theology. Such language of impatience and complaint is found frequently in the prayers of the Psalter (usually "how long?" or "when?" or "why?"). It expresses the anguish of relief not (yet) granted and exhibits the boldness with which the psalmists wrestled with God on the basis of their relationship with Him and their conviction concerning His righteousness (see note on 5:8).

6:4–5 Earnest prayer for deliverance from death.

‡6:4 *mercy's.* "Mercy" in Hebrew denotes befriending and can be translated "lovingkindness" or "unfailing love." Appeal to God's mercy is frequent in the OT since it summarizes all that the Lord covenanted to show to Israel (see Deut 7:9,12) as well as to David and his dynasty (see 89:24,28,33; 2 Sam 7:15; Is 55:3).

6:5 The psalmist urges that God's praise is at stake. It is the living, not the dead, who remember God's mercies and celebrate His deliverances. The Israelites usually viewed death as they saw it—the very opposite of life. And resurrection was not yet a part of their communal experience with God. The grave brought no escape from God (see 139:8), but just how they viewed the condition of the godly dead is not clear. (Non-Biblical documents from the ancient Near East indicate a general conception that immortality was reserved for the gods but that the dead continued to have some kind of shadowy existence in the dismal netherworld.) The OT writers knew that man was created for life, that God's will for His people was life and that He had power over death. They also knew that death was every man's lot, and at its proper time the godly rested in God and accepted it with equanimity (see Gen 15:15; 25:8; 47:30; 49:33; 1 Ki 2:2). Death could even be a blessing for the righteous, affording escape from the greater evil that would overtake the living (see 2 Ki 22:20; Is 57:1–2). Furthermore, the death of the righteous was reputedly better than that of the wicked (see Num 23:10). It seems clear that there was even an awareness that death (as observed) was not the end of hope for the righteous, that God had more in store for them (see especially 16:9–11; 17:15; 49:14–15; 73:24; see also note on Gen 5:24). But when the psalmists wrestled with God for the preservation of life, it was death as they saw it, in its radical contradiction to life, that was evoked.

6:6–7 Anguish at night because of the prolongation of the illness and the barbs of the enemies.

6:6 *I am weary with my groaning.* The very center of the poem—thus underscoring the pathos of this prayer. This literary device—of placing a key thematic line at the very center of the psalm—was frequently used (see notes on 8:4; 21:7; 23:4; 34:8–14; 42:8; 47:5–6; 48:8; 54:4; 71:14; 74:12; 76:7; 82:5a; 86:9; 92:8; 97:7; 113:5; 138:4–5; 141:5; see also Introduction: Literary Features).

6:7 *eye is consumed . . . old.* In the vivid language of the OT the eyes are dimmed by failing strength (see 38:10; 1 Sam 14:27,29; Jer 14:6), by grief (often associated with affliction: 31:9; 88:9; Job 17:7; Lam 2:11) and by longings unsatisfied or hope deferred (see 69:3; 119:82,123; Deut 28:32; Is 38:14). *because of all mine enemies.* See note on 5:9.

6:8–10 Concluding expression of buoyant confidence (see note on 3:8).

6:10 At the psalmist's restoration, his enemies will be disgraced.

Ps 7 An appeal to the Lord's court of justice when enemies attack.

‡7 title *Shiggaion.* The word occurs only here (but see its plural in Hab 3:1). Perhaps indicates a song of deep passion or a rhythm associated with the lament. *Cush.* Not otherwise known, but as a Benjamite he was probably a supporter of Saul. Hence the title associates the psalm with Saul's determined attempts on David's life. See Introduction: Authorship and Titles (or Superscriptions).

7:1–2 Initial summation of David's appeal.

7:2 *like a lion.* As a young shepherd, David had been attacked by lions (see 1 Sam 17:34–35). But it is also a convention in the Psalms to liken the attack of enemies to that of ferocious animals, especially the lion (see 10:9; 17:12; 22:12–13,16,20–21; 35:17; 57:4; 58:6; 124:6).

7:3–5 David pleads his own innocence; he has given his enemy no cause to attack him.

7:5 *my soul.* Lit. "my glory," a way of referring to the core of one's being (see 16:9; 30:12; 57:8; 108:1 and notes).

7:6–9 An appeal to the Judge of all the earth to execute His

[a] Lift up thyself because of the rage of
mine enemies:
And [b] awake for me *to* the judgment
that thou hast commanded.
7 So shall the congregation of the people
compass thee about:
For their sakes therefore return thou
on high.
8 The LORD shall judge the people:
Judge me, O LORD, [a] according to my
righteousness,
And according to mine integrity *that is*
in me.
9 O let the wickedness of the wicked
come to an end; but establish the just:
[a] For the righteous God trieth the
hearts and reins.
10 [1] My defence *is* of God,
Which saveth the [a] upright in heart.
11 [1] God judgeth the righteous,
And God is angry *with the wicked*
every day.
12 If he turn not, he will [a] whet his sword;
He hath bent his bow, and made it
ready.
13 He hath also prepared for him the
instruments of death;
He ordaineth his arrows against the
persecutors.
14 [a] Behold, he travaileth with iniquity,
And hath conceived mischief,
And brought forth falsehood.

7:6 [a] Ps. 94:2 [b] Ps. 44:23
7:8 [a] Ps. 18:20
7:9 [a] 1 Sam. 16:7
7:10 [1] Heb. *My buckler is upon God* [a] Ps. 125:4
7:11 [1] Or, *God is a righteous judge*
7:12 [a] Deut. 32:41
7:14 [a] Job 15:35
7:15 [1] Heb. *He hath digged a pit* [a] Job 4:8
7:16 [a] Esth. 9:25
8:T [a] Ps. 81, title; 84, title
8:1 [a] Ps. 148:13 [b] Ps. 113:4
8:2 [1] Heb. *founded* [a] 1 Cor. 1:27 [b] Ps. 44:16
8:3 [a] Ps. 111:2
8:4 [a] Job 7:17

15 [1] He made a pit, and digged it,
[a] And is fallen into the ditch *which* he
made.
16 [a] His mischief shall return upon his
own head,
And his violent dealing shall come
down upon his own pate.
17 I will praise the LORD according to his
righteousness:
And will sing *praise* to the name of the
LORD most High.

Psalm 8

To the chief Musician [a] upon Gittith,
A Psalm of David.

1 O LORD our Lord,
How [a] excellent *is* thy name in all the
earth!
Who [b] hast set thy glory above the
heavens.
2 [a] Out of the mouth of babes and
sucklings hast thou [1] ordained strength
Because of thine enemies,
That *thou* mightest still [b] the enemy
and the avenger.
3 When I [a] consider thy heavens, the
work of thy fingers,
The moon and the stars, which thou
hast ordained;
4 [a] What *is* man, that thou art mindful of
him?

judgment over all peoples, and particularly to adjudicate David's cause.
7:6 *Arise . . . Lift up.* See note on 3:7. *anger.* See v. 11 and note on 2:5. *awake for me.* The Lord does not sleep (see 121:4) while evil triumphs and the oppressed cry to Him in vain (as they do to Baal; see 1 Ki 18:27). But the psalmists' language of urgent prayer vividly expresses their anguished impatience with God's inaction in the face of their great need (see 80:2; see also 78:65; Is 51:9).
7:8 *my righteousness.* See vv. 3–5.
7:9 *the just.* See note on 1:5. *righteous.* See note on 5:8. *hearts and reins.* Or, "hearts and minds," lit. "hearts and kidneys." The Israelites used the words as virtual synonyms (but "heart" most often) to refer to man's innermost center of conscious life (see note on 4:7). To search mind and heart was a conventional expression for God's examination of man's hidden character and motives (see Jer 11:20; 17:10; 20:12).
7:10–13 David's confidence that his prayer will be heard (see note on 3:8).
‡7:10 *defence.* Or, "shield." See note on 3:3. *heart.* See note on 4:7.
7:11 *every day.* God's judgments are not all kept in store for some future day.
7:14–16 David comforts himself with the common wisdom that under God's rule "crime does not pay."
7:17 A vow to praise. Many prayers in the Psalter include such vows in anticipation of the expected answer to prayer. They reflect Israel's religious consciousness that praise must follow deliverance as surely as prayer springs from need—if God is to be truly honored. Such praise was usually offered with thank offerings and involved celebrating God's saving act in the presence of those assembled at the temple (see 50:14–15,23; see also note on 9:1). *name of the LORD.* See note on 5:11. *most High.* See note on Gen 14:19.
Ps 8 In praise of the Creator (not of man—as is evident from the doxology that encloses it, vv. 1,9; see also note on 9:1) out of wonder over His sovereign ordering of the creation. Gen 1 (particularly vv. 26–28) clearly provides the spectacles, but David speaks out of his present experience of reality (perhaps on a bright, clear night when the vast host of the heavenly lights, stretching from horizon to horizon, erased from his musings small everyday affairs and engaged his mind with deeper thoughts). Two matters especially impressed him: (1) the glory of God reflected in the starry heavens, and (2) the astonishing condescension of God to be mindful of puny man, to crown him with glory almost godlike and to grant him lordly power over His creatures.
8 title *To the chief Musician.* See note on Ps 4 title. *upon.* See note on Ps 6 title. *Gittith.* See Ps 81; 84 titles. The Hebrew word perhaps refers to either the winepress ("song of the winepress") or the Philistine city of Gath ("Gittite lyre or music"; see 2 Sam 15:18).
8:1a *name.* See note on 5:11.
8:1b–2 The mighty God, whose glory is displayed across the face of the heavens, appoints (and evokes) the praise of little children to silence the dark powers arrayed against Him (for a NT application see Mat 21:16).
8:2 *the avenger.* See 44:16; one who strikes back in malicious revenge (not as in 9:12).
8:3–5 The vastness and majesty of the heavens as the handiwork of God (see 19:1–6; 104:19–23) evoke wonder for what their Maker has done for little man, who is here today and gone tomorrow (see 144:3–4). (See Job 7:17–21 for Job's complaint that God takes man too seriously.)
8:3 *fingers.* See note on Ex 8:19.
8:4–6 Heb 2:6–8, quoting the Septuagint (the Greek transla-

And the son of man, that thou visitest him?
5 For thou hast made him a little lower than the angels,
And hast crowned him *with* glory and honour.
6 [a]Thou madest him to have dominion over the works of thy hands;
[b]Thou hast put all *things* under his feet:
7 [1]All sheep and oxen,
Yea, and the beasts of the field;
8 The fowl of the air, and the fish of the sea,
And whatsoever passeth *through* the paths of the seas.
9 [a]O LORD our Lord, how excellent *is* thy name in all the earth!

Psalm 9

To the chief Musician upon Muth-labben,
A Psalm of David.

1 I will praise *thee,* O LORD, with my whole heart;
I will shew forth all thy marvellous works.
2 I will be glad and [a]rejoice in thee:
I will sing *praise* to thy name, [b]O thou most High.
3 When mine enemies are turned back,
They shall fall and perish at thy presence.
4 For [1]thou hast maintained my right and my cause;
Thou satest in the throne judging [2]right.
5 Thou hast rebuked the heathen, thou hast destroyed the wicked,
Thou hast [a]put out their name for ever and ever.
6 [1]O thou enemy, destructions are come to a perpetual end:
And thou hast destroyed cities;
Their memorial is perished *with* them.
7 [a]But the LORD shall endure for ever:
He hath prepared his throne for judgment.

8:6 [a]Gen. 1:26 [b]Heb. 2:8
8:7 [1]Heb. *Flocks and oxen all of them*
8:9 [a]ver. 1
9:2 [a]Ps. 5:11 [b]Ps. 83:18
9:4 [1]Heb. *thou hast made my judgment* [2]Heb. *in righteousness*
9:5 [a]Prov. 10:7
9:6 [1]Or, *The destructions of the enemy are come to a perpetual end: and their cities hast thou destroyed, etc.*
9:7 [a]Heb. 1:11

tion of the OT), applies these verses to Jesus, who as the incarnate Son of God is both the representative man and the one in whom man's appointed destiny will be fully realized. The author of Hebrews thus makes use of the eschatological implications of these words in his testimony to Christ. Paul does the same with v. 6 in 1 Cor 15:27 (see also Eph 1:22).

‡8:4 *What.* The Hebrew for this word is translated "how" in vv. 1,9 and begins the line that serves as the center of the psalm (see note on 6:6). *art mindful of.* Lit. "remember" (see note on Gen 8:1). *son of man.* Often a poetic synonym for "man" (see 80:17; 144:3; see also note on Ezek 2:1). *visitest.* Attends to, takes care of.

8:5 *angels.* The Hebrew can be translated "God" or "angels."

‡8:6–8 See Gen 1:26-27. Man's rule is real—a part of his "glory and honour" (v. 5)—and it is his destiny (the eschatological import drawn on by Paul and the author of Hebrews; see note on vv. 4–6). But it is not absolute or independent. It is participation, as a subordinate, in God's rule; and it is a gift, not a right.

8:9 Repeated verbatim from v. 1a (see note there).

Ps 9 That Ps 9 and 10 were sometimes viewed (or used) as one psalm is known from the Septuagint (the Greek translation of the OT). Whether they were originally composed as one psalm is not known, though a number of indicators point in that direction. Ps 10 is the only psalm from Ps 3 to 32 that has no superscription, and the Hebrew text of the two psalms together appears to reflect an incomplete (or broken) acrostic structure. The first letter of each verse or pair of verses tends to follow the order of the Hebrew alphabet near the beginning of Ps 9 and again near the end of Ps 10. The thoughts also tend to be developed in two-verse units throughout. Ps 9 is predominantly praise (by the king) for God's deliverance from hostile nations (the specific occasion is unknown, but since there is no reference to victories on the part of Israel, God's destruction of the nations may have come by other means). It concludes with a short prayer for God's continuing righteous judgments (see v. 4) on the haughty nations. Ps 10 is predominantly prayer against the rapacity of unscrupulous men within the realm—as arrogant and wicked in their dealings with the "poor" (v. 2) as the nations were in their attacks on Israel (vv. 2–11 can serve equally as a description of both). The conjunction of these two within a single psalm is not unthinkable since the attacks of "the wicked" (9:5; 10:4), whether from within or from without, on the godly community are equally threatening to true Israel. Praise of God's past deliverances is often an integral part of prayer in the Psalter (see 3:3–4,8 and notes; 25:6; 40:1–5), as also in other ancient Near Eastern prayers. Such praise expressed the ground of the psalmist's hope that his present prayer would be heard, and it also functioned to motivate the Lord to act once more in His people's (or His servant's) behalf. For other lengthy prefaces to prayer see Ps 40; 44; 89. Probably Ps 9–10 came to be separated for the purpose of separate liturgical use, as did Ps 42–43 (see introduction there).

9 title *To the chief Musician.* See note on Ps 4 title. *upon.* See titles of Ps 22; 45; 56–60; 69; 75; 80. The Hebrew for this word (also translated "set to," "according to," or "to the tune of") may indicate that the words that follow were tune titles.

9:1–2 Initial announcement of praise.

9:1 *heart.* See note on 4:7. *shew forth.* The praise of God in the Psalter is rarely a private matter between the psalmist and the Lord. It is usually a public (at the temple) celebration of God's holy virtues or of His saving acts or gracious bestowal of blessings. In his praise the psalmist proclaims to the assembled throng God's glorious attributes or His righteous (see note on 5:8) deeds (see, e.g., 22:22–31; 56:12–13; 61:8; 65:1; 69:30–33). To this is usually added a call to praise, summoning all who hear to take up the praise—to acknowledge and joyfully celebrate God's glory, His goodness and all His righteous acts. This aspect of praise in the Psalms has rightly been called the OT anticipation of NT evangelism. *marvellous works.* God's saving acts, sometimes involving miracles—as in the exodus from Egypt, the wilderness wanderings and the entrance into the promised land—and sometimes not, but always involving the manifestation of God's sovereign lordship over events. Here reference is to the destruction of the enemies celebrated in this psalm.

9:2,10 *thy name.* See note on 5:11.

9:2 *most High.* See note on Gen 14:19.

9:3–6 In destroying the enemies, God has redressed the wrongs committed by them against David (and Israel).

9:4 *throne.* See note on v. 7.

9:5 *put out their name.* Blotted out, as if from a register of mankind written on a papyrus scroll (see Num 5:23; see also Deut 9:14; 25:19; 29:20; 2 Ki 14:27).

‡9:6 *destructions . . . to a perpetual end.* Their defeat is irreversible.

8 And [a]he shall judge the world in
righteousness,
He shall minister judgment to the
people in uprightness.
9 [a]The LORD also will be [1]a refuge for
the oppressed,
[2]A refuge in times of trouble.
10 And they that [a]know thy name will put
their trust in thee:
For thou, LORD, hast not forsaken them
that seek thee.
11 Sing *praises* to the LORD, which
dwelleth in Zion:
[a]Declare among the people his doings.
12 [a]When he maketh inquisition for
blood, he remembereth them:
He forgetteth not the cry of the
[1]humble.
13 Have mercy upon me, O LORD;
Consider my trouble *which I suffer* of
them that hate me,
Thou that liftest me up from the gates
of death:
14 That I may shew forth all thy praise
In the gates of the daughter of Zion:
I will [a]rejoice in thy salvation.
15 [a]The heathen are sunk down in the pit
that they made:
In the net which they hid is their own
foot taken.
16 The LORD is [a]known *by* the judgment
which he executeth:
The wicked is snared in the work of
his own hands.
[b][1]Higgaion. Selah.
17 The wicked shall be turned into hell,
And all the nations [a]that forget God.
18 [a]For the needy shall not alway be
forgotten:
[b]The expectation of the poor shall *not*
perish for ever.
19 Arise, O LORD; let not man prevail:
Let the heathen be judged in thy sight.
20 Put them in fear, O LORD:
That the nations may know themselves
to be but men. Selah.

Psalm 10

1 Why standest thou afar off, O LORD?
Why hidest thou *thyself* in times of
trouble?
2 [1]The wicked in *his* pride doth
persecute the poor:
[a]Let them be taken in the devices that
they have imagined.
3 For the wicked [a]boasteth of his
[1]heart's desire,
And [b][2]blesseth the covetous, *whom*
the LORD abhorreth.
4 The wicked, through the pride of his
countenance, will not seek *after God:*
[1]God *is* not *in* all his [a]thoughts.
5 His ways are always grievous;
Thy judgments *are* far above out of his
sight:
As for all his enemies, he puffeth at
them.
6 [a]He hath said in his heart, I shall not
be moved:
[b]For *I shall* [1]never *be* in adversity.
7 [a]His mouth is full *of* cursing and
[1]deceit and fraud:

9:8 [a]Ps. 96:13
9:9 [1]Heb. *a high place* [2]Heb. *A high place* [a]Ps. 32:7
9:10 [a]Ps. 91:14
9:11 [a]Ps. 107:22
9:12 [1]Or, *afflicted* [a]Gen. 9:5
9:14 [a]Ps. 13:5
9:15 [a]Ps. 7:15,16
9:16 [1][That is, *Meditation*] [a]Ex. 7:5 [b]Ps. 92:3
9:17 [a]Job 8:13
9:18 [a]Ps. 12:5 [b]Prov. 23:18
10:2 [1]Heb. *In the pride of the wicked he doth persecute* [a]Ps. 7:16
10:3 [1]Heb. *soul's* [2]Or, *the covetous blesseth* himself, *he abhorreth the* LORD [a]Ps. 94:4 [b]Prov. 28:4
10:4 [1]Or, *All his thoughts* are, There is *no God* [a]Ps. 14:1
10:6 [1]Heb. *unto generation and generation* [a]Eccl. 8:11; Is. 56:12 [b]Rev. 18:7
10:7 [1]Heb. *deceits* [a]Rom. 3:14

9:7–10 Celebration of the righteous rule of God (see note on 5:8), which evokes trust in those who look to the Lord.
9:7 *his throne.* In heaven (see 11:4). See also v. 4.
9:8 See Acts 17:31.
9:11–12 A call to the assembly at the temple to take up the praise of God for His righteous judgments (see note on v. 1).
9:11 *dwelleth in Zion.* God's heavenly throne (see v. 7) has its counterpart on earth in His temple at Jerusalem, from which center He rules the world (see 2:6; 3:4 and notes; 20:2). For God's election of Zion as the seat of His rule see 132:13.
‡9:12 *maketh inquisition for blood.* Lit. "seeks blood." God "seeks" justice for those who "seek" him (v. 10). The Lord functions as the kinsman redeemer who had the responsibility to avenge the death of a family member. See Num 35:9–34.
‡9:13–14 Perhaps a recollection of David's prayer ("the cry of the humble," v. 12), which the Lord has now answered.
9:13 *gates of death.* See Job 17:16 and note.
9:14 *shew forth.* See notes on v. 1; 7:17. *gates.* Having been thrust down by the attacks of his enemies to "the gates of death" (v. 13), David prayed to be lifted up so he could celebrate his deliverance (see note on v. 1) in "the gates of ... Zion." *daughter of Zion.* A personification of Jerusalem and its inhabitants.
9:15–18 Under the Lord's just rule, those who wickedly attack others bring destruction on themselves (see 7:14–16 and note) and their end will be the grave. But those who are attacked ("the needy," v. 18) will not trust in the Lord in vain.
‡9:15, 19 *heathen.* Lit. "nations," as this same Hebrew word is translated in vv. 17,20.
‡9:17 *hell.* Sheol, or "the grave." *forget.* Take no account of.
9:18 *needy ... poor.* In this psalm David and Israel are counted among them because of the threat from the enemies. *not ... forgotten.* Those who forget God will come to nothing, but the needy and afflicted will not be forgotten by God (see v. 12).
9:19–20 A prayer at the conclusion of praise, asking that the Lord may ever rule over the nations as He has done in the event here celebrated—that those who "forget God" (v. 17) may know that they are only men, not gods, and cannot withstand the God of Israel (see 10:18).
9:19 *Arise.* See note on 3:7.
Ps 10 A prayer for rescue from the attacks of unscrupulous men—containing a classic OT portrayal of "the wicked." See introduction to Ps 9.
10:1 See note on 6:3; see also Introduction: Theology.
‡10:2–11 Accusation lodged against the oppressors (see note on 5:9–10). In the Hebrew the interchange of singular and plural indicates that these accusations are being lodged against wicked oppressors in general. Their deeds betray the arrogance (see vv. 2–5) with which they defy God (see vv. 3–4,13; see especially their words in vv. 6,11,13). They greedily seek to glut their unrestrained appetites (see v. 3) by victimizing others, taking account of neither God (see v. 4) nor His judgments (see v. 5).
10:3 *heart's.* See note on 4:7.
10:4 The wicked man does not consider that he has God to contend with (see note on v. 11; see also 14:1; 36:1; 53:1).
‡10:6 See vv. 11,13 and note on 3:2.
10:7 *cursing and deceit and fraud.* The three most common

Under his tongue *is* mischief and [2]vanity.
8 He sitteth in the lurking places of the villages:
In the secret places doth he murder the innocent:
His eyes [1]are privily set against the poor.
9 He lieth in wait [1]secretly as a lion in his den:
He lieth in wait to catch the poor:
He doth catch the poor, when he draweth him into his net.
10 [1]He croucheth, *and* humbleth himself,
That the poor may fall [2]by his strong *ones.*
11 He hath said in his heart, God hath forgotten:
[a]He hideth his face; he will never see *it.*
12 Arise, O LORD; O God, [a]lift up thine hand:
Forget not the [1]humble.
13 Wherefore doth the wicked contemn God?
He hath said in his heart, Thou wilt not require *it.*
14 Thou hast seen *it;* for thou beholdest mischief and spite,
To requite *it* with thy hand:
The poor [a][1]committeth *himself* unto thee;
[b]Thou art the helper of the fatherless.
15 Break thou the arm of the wicked and the evil *man:*
Seek out his wickedness *till* thou find none.
16 [a]The LORD *is* King for ever and ever:
The heathen are perished out of his land.
17 LORD, thou hast heard the desire of the humble:
Thou wilt [1]prepare their heart, thou wilt cause thine ear to hear:
18 To [a]judge the fatherless and the oppressed,
That the man of the earth may no more [1]oppress.

10:7 [2]Or, *iniquity* 10:8 [1]Heb. *hide themselves* 10:9 [1]Heb. *in the secret places* 10:10 [1]Heb. *He breaketh himself* [2]Or, *into his strong* parts 10:11 [a]Job 22:13 10:12 [1]Or, *afflicted* [a]Mic. 5:9 10:14 [1]Heb. *leaveth* [a]2 Tim. 1:12 [b]Ps. 68:5 10:16 [a]Ps. 29:10 10:17 [1]Or, *establish* 10:18 [1]Or, *terrify* [a]Ps. 82:3 11:1 [a]Ps. 56:11 11:2 [1]Heb. *in darkness* [a]Ps. 64:3,4 11:3 [a]Ps. 82:5 11:4 [a]Ps. 33:13; 34:15,16 11:5 [a]Gen. 22:1

Psalm 11

To the chief Musician, *A Psalm* of David.

1 [a]In the LORD put I my trust:
How say ye to my soul,
Flee *as* a bird *to* your mountain?
2 For lo, [a]the wicked bend *their* bow,
They make ready their arrow upon the string,
That *they* may [1]privily shoot at the upright in heart.
3 [a]If the foundations be destroyed,
What can the righteous do?
4 The LORD *is* in his holy temple,
The LORD's throne *is* in heaven:
[a]His eyes behold,
His eyelids try, the children of men.
5 The LORD [a]trieth the righteous:
But the wicked and him that loveth violence his soul hateth.

weapons of the tongue in Israel's experience (see note on 5:9). *cursing.* The ancient Near Eastern peoples thought that by pronouncing curses on someone they could bring down the power of the gods (or other mysterious powers) on that person. They had a large conventional stock of such curses. *deceit.* Slander and false testimony for malicious purposes (see, e.g., 1 Ki 21:8–15).

10:9 See note on 7:2.

10:11 See note on 3:2. The arrogance with which the wicked speak (see 17:10), especially their easy dismissal of God's knowledge of their evil acts and His unfailing prosecution of their malicious deeds, is frequently noted by the psalmists (see v. 13; 12:4; 42:3,10; 59:7; 64:5; 71:11; 73:11; 94:7; 115:2; see also Is 29:15; Ezek 8:12).

10:12–15 Prayer that God will call the wicked to account.

10:12 *Arise.* See note on 3:7. *Forget.* See 9:18. *humble.* Those at the mercy of the oppressors (see v. 9).

‡10:13 *Wherefore . . . ?* Or, "Why?" See note on 6:3. *contemn God.* Show disrespect, have contempt for. *wilt not require it.* Claiming that God will not punish their sinful actions.

10:14 Appeal to God's righteous rule (see 5:4–6).

10:15 *Break thou the arm.* Destroy the power to oppress. *Seek out his wickedness.* Humble his arrogance (see v. 13) with Your righteous judgment.

10:16–18 The psalmist's confidence in the righteous reign of the Lord (see note on 3:8). Reference to the heathen (v. 16) and to the humbling of the oppressor (see v. 18; see also 9:19–20) suggests links with Ps 9. This conclusion to Ps 10 expands the vision of God's just rule to its universal scope and sets the purging of the Lord's land of all nations that do not acknowledge Him (see v. 16) alongside God's judicial dealing with the wicked oppressors. Both belong to God's assertion of His righteous rule in the face of man's arrogant denial of it.

10:18 *man of the earth.* Who is not God and so constitutes no ultimate threat (see 49:12,20; 56:4,11; 62:9; 78:39; 103:14–16; 118:6,8–9; 144:4; Is 31:3; Jer 17:5).

Ps 11 A confession of confident trust in the Lord's righteous rule, at a time when wicked adversaries seem to have the upper hand.

11 title *To the chief Musician.* See note on Ps 4 title.

‡11:1–3 David testifies of his unshakable trust in the Lord (his refuge) to apprehensive people around him. These people, under attack from a powerful and ruthless enemy, fear that the foundations (v. 3) are crumbling and that flight to a mountain refuge is the only recourse. He dismisses their fearful advice with disdain.

‡11:2 It is not clear whether those who wield the bows and arrows are archers or false accusers (see 57:4; 64:4; see also note on 5:9). *privily shoot.* See KJV marg. They ambush the godly. *heart.* See note on 4:7.

11:3 *foundations.* Of the world order (see 82:5). To those who counsel flight, the powerful upsurge of evil appears to indicate that the righteous can no longer count on a world order in which good triumphs over evil. *righteous.* See note on 1:5.

11:4–7 Reply to the fearful: The Lord is still securely on His heavenly throne. And the righteous Lord (see v. 7) discerns the righteous (see v. 5) to give them a place in His presence (see v. 7), while His judgment will "rain" (v. 6) on the wicked.

‡11:4 *The LORD is in his holy temple.* Repeated verbatim in Hab 2:20. Here reference is to His heavenly temple. *His eyelids try.* The Lord examines and judges their character, motives, and actions (see v. 5).

6 Upon the wicked he shall rain [1]snares,
fire and brimstone,
And [2]a horrible tempest: [a]*this shall be*
the portion of their cup.
7 For the righteous LORD [a]loveth
righteousness;
His countenance doth behold the
upright.

Psalm 12

To the chief Musician [a][1]upon Sheminith,
A Psalm of David.

1 [1]Help, LORD; for the godly *man* ceaseth;
For the faithful fail from among the
children of men.
2 [a]They speak vanity every one with his
neighbour:
With flattering lips *and* with [1]a double
heart do they speak.
3 The LORD shall cut off all flattering lips,
And the tongue that speaketh [1]proud
things:
4 Who have said, With our tongue will
we prevail;
Our lips [1]*are* our own: who *is* lord
over us?
5 For the oppression of the poor, for the
sighing of the needy,
Now will I arise, saith the LORD;
I will set *him* in safety *from him that*
[1]puffeth at him.
6 The words of the LORD *are* [a]pure
words:
As silver tried in a furnace of earth,
purified seven times.
7 Thou shalt keep them, O LORD,
Thou shalt preserve [1]them from this
generation for ever.
8 The wicked walk on every side,
When [1]the vilest men are exalted.

Psalm 13

To the [1]chief Musician, A Psalm of David.

1 How long wilt thou forget me, O LORD?
for ever?
[a]How long wilt thou hide thy face from
me?
2 How long shall I take counsel in my
soul,
Having sorrow in my heart daily?
How long shall mine enemy be exalted
over me?
3 Consider *and* hear me, O LORD my
God:
[a]Lighten mine eyes, [b]lest I sleep the
sleep of death;
4 Lest mine enemy say, I have prevailed
against him;

11:6 [1][Or, *quick burning coals*] [2]Or, *a burning tempest* [a]Gen. 43:34; 1 Sam. 1:4; Ps. 75:8
11:7 [a]Ps. 45:7
12:T [1]Or, *upon the eighth* [a]Ps. 6, title
12:1 [1]Or, *Save*
12:2 [1]Heb. *a heart and a heart* [a]Ps. 10:7
12:3 [1]Heb. *great things*
12:4 [1]Heb. are *with us*
12:5 [1]Or, *would ensnare him*
12:6 [a]2 Sam. 22:31; Ps. 18:30; Prov. 30:5
12:7 [1]Heb. *him:* that is, *every one of them*
12:8 [1]Heb. *the vilest of the sons of men are exalted*
13:T [1]Or, *overseer*
13:1 [a]Job 13:24
13:3 [a]Ezra 9:8 [b]Jer. 51:39

‡11:6 Perhaps recalling God's judgment on Sodom and Gomorrah (see Gen 19:24,28; see also Rev 14:10; 20:10; 21:8). *snares.* See KJV marg., which fits better with "fire" and "brimstone." *their cup.* See 75:8 and note on 16:5.
‡11:7 *righteous.* See note on 5:8. *His countenance doth behold the upright.* Lit. "the upright will see his face." The Hebrew for "see the king's face" was an expression denoting access to the king (see Gen 43:3,5; 44:23,26; 2 Sam 3:13;14:24,28,32). Sometimes it referred to those who served before the king (see 2 Ki 25:19; Esth 1:14, "seven princes ... which saw the king's face." Here David speaks of special freedom of access before the heavenly King. Reference is no doubt to His presence at the temple (God's earthly royal house), but that is still the presence of the One who sits on the heavenly throne. Ultimate access to the heavenly temple may also be implied (see 16:11; 17:15; see also 23:6; 140:13). Even the pagan peoples surrounding Israel believed that man continued after death, though only in some kind of shadowy existence in the netherworld (see Is 14:9–17). *the upright.* Those concerning whom the fearful despaired (see v. 2).
Ps 12 A prayer for help when it seems that all men are faithless and every tongue false (see Mic 7:1–7).
12 title *To the chief Musician.* See note on Ps 4 title. *upon.* See note on Ps 6 title.
12:1–2 Initial appeal, with description of the cause of distress.
12:1 *godly.* See note on 4:3. *the faithful.* Those who maintain moral integrity.
12:2 See 5:9 and note.
12:3–4 The prayer.
12:3 *cut off.* Put an end to (physical mutilation is not in view). *speaketh proud things.* See note on 10:2–11.
12:4 See notes on 3:2; 10:11.
12:5–6 A reassuring word from the Lord. Such words of assurance following prayer in the Psalms were perhaps spoken by a priest (see 1 Sam 1:17) or a prophet (see 51:8 and note; 2 Sam 12:13). It may be that abrupt transitions from prayer to confidence in the Psalms (see note on 3:8) presuppose such priestly or prophetic words, even when they are not contained in the psalm. Here it is possible that David merely recalls this appropriate word from the Lord; notice that it is a general reassurance concerning the righteous rule of God (see note on 4:1).
‡12:5 *Now will I arise.* See Is 33:10. *puffeth at him.* With hateful and maligning words.
12:6 *words of the LORD.* Set in sharp contrast with the boastful words of the adversaries; they are as flawless as thoroughly refined silver. *furnace of earth.* See note on Deut 4:20. *seven.* Signifies fullness or completeness—here thoroughness of refining.
12:7–8 Concluding expression of confidence (see note on 3:8).
‡12:8 David is confident, even though at the present time the wicked think they have the upper hand (see vv. 1–4). *wicked walk on every side.* They strut about in their pride and arrogance.
Ps 13 A cry to the Lord for deliverance from a serious illness that threatens death (see v. 3), which would give David's enemies just what they wanted. See introduction to Ps 6.
13 title *To the chief Musician.* See note on Ps 4 title.
13:1–2 An anguished complaint concerning a prolonged serious illness.
13:1 *How long ...?* See note on 6:3; see also Introduction: Theology. *forget.* Ignore. *hide thy face.* For use in combination with "forget" see 44:24. In moments of need the psalmists frequently ask God why He hides His face (see 30:7; 44:24; 88:14), or they plead with Him not to do so (see 27:9; 69:17; 102:2; 143:7). When He does hide His face, those who depend on Him can only despair (see 30:7; 104:29). When His face shines on a person, blessing and deliverance come (see 4:6 and note; 31:16; 67:1; 80:3,7,19; 119:135).
13:2 *heart.* See note on 4:7.
13:3–4 Appeal for deliverance from death.
13:3 *Lighten my eyes.* Restore me (see note on 6:7).

And those that trouble me rejoice
when I am moved.
5 But I have trusted in thy mercy;
My heart shall rejoice in thy salvation.
6 I will sing unto the LORD, because he
hath dealt bountifully with me.

Psalm 14

To the chief Musician, *A Psalm* of David.

1 The [a]fool hath said in his heart, *There is* no God.
They are corrupt, they have done
abominable works,
There is none that doeth good.
2 [a]The LORD looked down from heaven
upon the children of men,
To see if there were *any* that did
understand, *and* seek God.
3 They are all gone aside, they are *all*
together become [1]filthy:
There is none that doeth good, no, not
one.
4 Have all the workers of iniquity no
knowledge?
Who eat up my people *as* they eat
bread,
And [a]call not upon the LORD.
5 There [1]were they in great fear:
For God *is* in the generation of the
righteous.
6 You have shamed the counsel of the
poor,
Because the LORD *is* his [a]refuge.
7 [a] [1]O that the salvation of Israel *were come* out of Zion!
[b]When the LORD bringeth back the
captivity of his people,
Jacob shall rejoice, *and* Israel shall be
glad.

Psalm 15

A Psalm of David.

1 LORD, [a]who shall [1]abide in thy
tabernacle?
Who shall dwell in thy holy hill?
2 He that walketh uprightly, and worketh
righteousness,
And speaketh the truth in his heart.
3 *He that* backbiteth not with his tongue,
Nor doeth evil to his neighbour,
[a]Nor [1]taketh up a reproach against his
neighbour.
4 [a]In whose eyes a vile *person* is
contemned;
But he honoureth them that fear the
LORD.
He that sweareth to *his own* hurt, and
changeth not.
5 *He that* putteth not out his money to
usury,

14:1 [a]Ps. 10:4
14:2 [a]Ps. 33:13
14:3 [1]Heb. *stinking*
14:4 [a]Is. 64:7
14:5 [1]Heb. *they feared a fear*
14:6 [a]Ps. 9:9
14:7 [1]Heb. *Who will give, etc.* [a]Ps. 53:6 [b]Job 42:10
15:1 [1]Heb. *sojourn* [a]Ps. 24:3
15:3 [1]Or, *receiveth,* or, *endureth* [a]Ex. 23:1
15:4 [a]Esth. 3:2

13:4 See notes on 3:2; 5:9. *moved.* Referring to death (as in 18:38; 82:7; 106:26; Judg 5:27; 2 Sam 1:19; Job 18:12).
13:5–6 Concluding expression of confidence (see note on 3:8).
13:5 *mercy.* See note on 6:4. *heart.* See note on 4:7. *shall rejoice.* It is David who will rejoice, not his enemies.
13:6 See note on 7:17.
Ps 14 A testimony concerning the folly of evil men. This psalm has many links with Ps 10; 12. It shares the view of Ps 11 that the righteous Lord is on the throne, and it stands in contrast with Ps 15, which describes those who are acceptable to God. Ps 53 is a somewhat revised duplicate of this psalm.
14 title *To the chief Musician.* See note on Ps 4 title.
14:1–3 Characterization of the wicked. For Paul's use of these verses in a different context see Rom 3:10–12.
‡14:1 Not intended as a definition of the "fool"; see previous note. The Hebrew words rendered "fool" in Psalms denote one who is morally deficient. *hath said.* See note on 3:2. *heart.* See note on 4:7. *no God.* A practical atheism (see 10:4,6,11, 13; 36:1; see also note on 10:4). *none that doeth good.* Mankind in general is corrupt. Here the reference is to those who take no account of God and do not hesitate to show their malice toward "the generation of the righteous" (see vv. 4–5)—as in 9:19–20; 10:2–11,13,18; 12:1–4,7–8 (this is also the situation that Ps 11 describes). Elsewhere the psalmists included themselves among those who are not righteous in God's eyes (see 130:3; 143:2; see also 1 Ki 8:46; Job 9:2; Eccl 7:20).
‡14:2 *The LORD.* Emphatically contrasted with "The fool" (v. 1). *any that . . . seek God.* Those who truly seek God are described in Ps 15.
‡14:3 *gone aside.* Turned away from God and goodness.
14:4–6 The folly of the wicked exposed.
14:4 *eat up . . . call not upon the LORD.* Renewed characterization of the wicked: They live by the violence of their own hands and do not rely on the Lord (see 10:2–4).
‡14:5 The two lines of this verse contrast the wicked and the righteous. The wicked live "in great fear," a dread of God's coming judgment that is real despite their pretense of self-sufficiency. The "generation of the righteous" have no such fears because they know God is with them. *righteous.* See note on 1:5.
14:6 *poor.* God's people as the victims of injustice. *refuge.* See note on 4:1.
14:7 The psalmist longs for Israel's complete deliverance from her enemies—which will come when God deals with the wicked in defense of their victims. For a similar expansion of scope see 10:16–18 and note. *Zion.* See note on 9:11. *Jacob . . . Israel.* Synonyms (see Gen 32:28).
Ps 15 Instruction to those who wish to have access to God at His temple (see 24:3–6; Is 33:14–16). See also introduction to Ps 14.
15:1 *abide . . . dwell in.* Not as a priest but as God's guest in His holy, royal house, the temple (see 23:6; 27:4–6; 61:4; 84:10; 2 Sam 12:20). *holy hill.* See note on 2:6.
15:2–5 Not sacrifices or ritual purity (as among the religions of the ancient Near East) but moral righteousness gives access to the Lord, the God of Israel (see the basic covenantal law: Ex 20:1–17; see also Is 1:10–17; 33:14–16; 58:6–10; Jer 7:2–7; Ezek 18:5–9; Hos 6:6; Amos 5:14–15,21–24; Mic 6:6–8; Zech 7:9–10; 8:16–17).
15:2 *uprightly.* See Gen 17:1 and note. *worketh righteousness.* See note on 1:5. *heart.* See note on 4:7.
‡15:3 *backbiteth.* To slander. *tongue.* See note on 5:9.
‡15:4 *them that fear the LORD.* Those who honor God and order their lives in accordance with His will (see note on Gen 20:11) because of their reverence for Him. *sweareth to his own hurt.* Keeps his promises even when it costs or is inconvenient.

Nor taketh reward against the
innocent.
He that doeth these *things* [a]shall never
be moved.

Psalm 16

[a] [1] Michtam of David.

1 Preserve me, O God: for in thee do I
put my trust.
2 *O my soul,* thou hast said unto the
LORD, Thou *art* my Lord:
[a]My goodness *extendeth* not to thee;
3 *But* to the saints that *are* in the earth,
And *to* the excellent, in whom *is* all
my delight.
4 Their sorrows shall be multiplied *that*
[1]hasten *after* another *god:*
Their drink offerings of blood will I not
offer,
[a]Nor take up their names into my lips.
5 The LORD *is* the portion [1]of mine
inheritance and of my cup:
Thou maintainest my lot.
6 The lines are fallen unto me in
pleasant *places;*
Yea, I have a goodly heritage.
7 I will bless the LORD, who hath given
me counsel:
My reins also instruct me *in* the night
seasons.
8 I have set the LORD always before me:
Because *he is* at my right hand, I shall
not be moved.
9 Therefore my heart is glad, and my
glory rejoiceth:
My flesh also shall [1]rest in hope.
10 [a]For thou wilt not leave my soul in hell;
Neither wilt thou suffer thine Holy
One to see corruption.
11 Thou wilt shew me the [a]path of life:
In thy presence *is* fulness of joy;
At thy right hand *there are* pleasures
for evermore.

Psalm 17

A Prayer of David.

1 Hear [1]the right, O LORD, attend unto
my cry,
Give ear unto my prayer, *that goeth*
[2]not out of feigned lips.
2 Let my sentence come forth from thy
presence;
Let thine eyes behold the things that
are equal.
3 Thou hast proved mine heart; thou
hast visited *me* in the night;

15:5 [a]2 Pet. 1:10
16:T [1]Or, *A golden* Psalm *of David* [a]Ps. 56-60
16:2 [a]Job 35:7
16:4 [1]Or, *give gifts to another* [a]Ex. 23:13
16:5 [1]Heb. *of my part*
16:9 [1]Heb. *dwell confidently*
16:10 [a]Ps. 49:15
16:11 [a]Mat. 7:14
17:1 [1]Heb. *justice* [2]Heb. *without lips of deceit*

‡15:5 *putteth not out . . . to usury.* Does not charge interest on loans. See note on Ex 22:25–27. *be moved.* See note on 10:6.

Ps 16 A prayer for safekeeping (the petition element in prayer psalms is often relatively short; see 3:7; 22:19–21; 44:23–26), pleading for the Lord's protection against the threat of death. It could also be called a psalm of trust.

16 title *Michtam.* The term remains unexplained, though it always stands in the superscription of Davidic prayers occasioned by great danger (see Ps 56–60).

16:1 The petition and the basis for it. The rest of the psalm elaborates on the latter element.

16:2–4 The Lord is David's one and only good thing (see 73:25,28); David will have nothing to do with the counterfeit gods to whom others pour out their libations (see 4:2).

‡16:2 *My goodness extendeth not to thee.* Or, "I have no good apart from you."

16:3 See Ps 101.

16:4 *sorrows shall be multiplied.* In contrast with David's good "portion" (v. 5; see note on 11:6), which affords him much joy (see 73:18–20). *drink offerings of blood.* Blood of sacrifices poured on altars. *take up their names into my lips.* Appeal to or worship them (see Josh 23:7).

16:5–6 Joy over the inheritance received from the Lord. David refers to what the Lord bestowed on His people in the promised land, either to the gift of fields there (see Num 16:14) or to the Lord Himself (as in 73:26; 119:57; 142:5; Lam 3:24), who was the inheritance of the priests (see Num 18:20) and the Levites (see Deut 10:9).

16:5 *cup.* A metaphor referring to what the host offers his guests to drink. To the godly the Lord offers a cup of blessings (see 23:5) or salvation (see 116:13); He makes the wicked drink from a cup of wrath (see Jer 25:15; Rev 14:10; 16:19). *maintainest my lot.* Just as each Israelite's family inheritance in the promised land was to be secure (see Lev 25; Num 36:7).

‡16:6 *lines.* The boundary lines of his inheritance.

16:7–8 Praise of the Lord who counsels and keeps.

16:7 *given me counsel.* Shown the way that leads to life (see v. 11). *reins.* Or, "mind," lit. "kidneys" (see note on 7:9).

16:8 *he is at my right hand.* As sustainer and protector (see 73:23; 109:31; 110:5; 121:5); complemented by the reference to the Lord's right hand in v. 11. *not be moved.* See note on 10:6.

‡16:9–11 Describes the joy of total security. David speaks here, as in the rest of his psalms, first of all of himself and of the life he now enjoys by the gracious provision and care of God. The Lord, in whom the psalmist takes refuge, wills life for him (hence he made known to him the path of life, v. 11) and will not abandon him to the grave, even though his "flesh and . . . heart faileth" (73:26). But implicit in these words of assurance (if not actually explicit) is the confidence that, with the Lord as his refuge, even the grave cannot rob him of life (see 17:15; 73:24; see also note on 11:7). If this could be said of David, how much more of David's promised Son! So Peter quotes vv. 8–11 and declares that with these words David prophesied of Christ and His resurrection (Acts 2:25–28; see Paul's similar use of v. 10b in Acts 13:35). See also note on 6:5.

16:9 *heart.* See note on 4:7. *glory.* See note on 7:5.

‡16:10 *hell.* Sheol, or the grave. *Holy One.* Hebrew *ḥasid* (see note on 4:3). Reference is first of all to David (see note on 2:2), but the psalm is ultimately fulfilled in Christ.

16:11 *path of life.* See Prov 15:24. *thy right hand.* See note on v. 8.

Ps 17 The psalmist appeals to the Lord as Judge, when under attack by ungodly foes. The psalm reflects many of the Hebrew conventions of lodging a judicial appeal before the king.

17 title *A Prayer.* See titles of Ps 86; 90; 102; 142; see also 72:20.

17:1–2 The initial appeal for justice.

‡17:1 *Hear the right . . . my cry.* His case is truly just ("right"), not a clever misrepresentation by deceitful lips (for a similar situation see 1 Sam 24:15).

17:3–5 David's claim of innocence in support of the rightness of his case. He is not guilty of the ungodly ways of his attackers—let God examine him (cf. 139:23–24).

[a]Thou hast tried me, *and* shalt find nothing;
I am purposed *that* my mouth shall not transgress.
4 Concerning the works of men, by the word of thy lips
I have kept *me from* the paths of the destroyer.
5 [a]Hold up my goings in thy paths,
That my footsteps [1]slip not.
6 [a]I have called upon thee, for thou wilt hear me, O God:
Incline thine ear unto me, *and* hear my speech.
7 Shew thy marvellous lovingkindness,
O thou [1]that savest by thy right hand them which put their trust *in thee*
From those that rise up *against them.*
8 Keep me as the apple of the eye,
Hide me under the shadow of thy wings,
9 From the wicked [1]that oppress me,
From [2]my deadly enemies, *who* compass me about.
10 They are inclosed *in* their own fat:
With their mouth they [a]speak proudly.
11 They have now compassed us *in* our steps:
They have set their eyes bowing down to the earth;
12 [1]Like as a lion *that* is greedy of his prey,
And as it were a young lion [2]lurking in secret places.
13 Arise, O LORD, [1]disappoint him, cast him down:
Deliver my soul from the wicked, [2]*which is* thy sword:
14 [1]From men *which are* thy hand, O LORD,
From men of the world, *which have* their portion in *this* life,
And whose belly thou fillest *with* thy hid *treasure:*
[2]They are full *of* children,
And leave the rest of their *substance* to their babes.
15 *As for* me, [a]I will behold thy face in righteousness:
[b]I shall be satisfied, when *I* awake, *with* thy likeness.

17:3 [a]Job 23:10
17:5 [1]Heb. *be not moved* [a]Ps. 119:133
17:6 [a]Ps. 116:2
17:7 [1]Or, *that savest them which trust* in thee *From those that rise up against thy right hand*
17:9 [1]Heb. *that waste me* [2]Heb. *my enemies against the soul*
17:10 [a]1 Sam. 2:3
17:12 [1]Heb. *The likeness of him* (that is, *of every one of them*) is *as a lion* that *desireth to ravin*
17:12 [2]Heb. *sitting*
17:13 [1]Heb. *prevent his face* [2]Or, *by thy sword*
17:14 [1]Or, *From men by thine hand* [2]Or, Their *children are full*
17:15 [a]1 John 3:2 [b]Ps. 4:6,7; 16:11
18:T [a]Ps. 36, title [b]2 Sam. 22
18:1 [a]Ps. 144:1
18:2 [1]Heb. *my rock* [a]Heb. 2:13

Psalm 18

To the chief Musician, *A Psalm* of David, [a]the servant of the LORD, who spake unto the LORD the words of [b]this song in the day *that* the LORD delivered him from the hand of all his enemies, and from the hand of Saul: And he said,

1 [a]I will love thee, O LORD, my strength.
2 The LORD *is* my rock, and my fortress, and my deliverer;
My God, [1]my strength, [a]in whom I will trust;

‡17:3 *proved.* Tested and examined. *heart.* See note on 4:7.
17:4 *word of thy lips.* God's revealed will, by which He has made known the "paths" (v. 5) that people are to walk.
‡17:6–9 The petition: what the Lord is to do for him—motivated by David's trust in Him ("for thou wilt hear me," v. 6) and the Lord's unfailing righteousness (see v. 7).
17:7 *marvellous.* See note on 9:1. *lovingkindness.* See note on 6:4.
17:8 *apple of the eye.* See note on Deut 32:10. *shadow.* A conventional Hebrew metaphor for protection against oppression—as shade protects from the oppressive heat of the hot desert sun. Kings were spoken of as the "shade" of those dependent on them for protection (as in Num 14:9, "defence"—lit. "shade"; Lam 4:20; Ezek 31:6,12,17). Similarly, the Lord is the protective shadow for his people (see 91:1; 121:5; Is 25:4; 49:2; 51:16). *wings.* Metaphor for the protective outreach of God's power (see 36:7; 57:1; 61:4; 63:7; 91:4; Ruth 2:12; see also Mat 23:37).
17:10–12 The accusation lodged against the vicious adversaries (see note on 5:9–10).
‡17:10 *inclosed in their own fat.* Lit. "they have closed their fat," i.e. they have closed their calloused hearts to the Lord. *mouth.* See note on 5:9. *speak proudly.* See note on 10:11.
17:12 *lion.* See note on 7:2.
17:13–14a Petition: how the Lord is to deal with the two parties in the conflict.
17:13 *Arise.* See note on 3:7. *cast him down.* See note on 5:10.
‡17:14 *From men which are thy hand.* See KJV marg. *men.* See 9:19–20; 10:18; 12:1–4,8; 14:1–3.
17:14b–15 Concluding confession of confidence (see note on 3:8).
‡17:15 *behold thy face.* See note on 11:7. *in righteousness.* The righteous Judge (see note on 5:8) will acknowledge and vindicate the innocence (righteousness) of the petitioner. *satisfied . . . with thy likeness.* By seeing God's likeness, as Moses the servant of the Lord had seen it (see Num 12:8). *when I awake.* From the night of death (see note on 11:7)—in radical contrast to the destiny of the "men of the world" (v. 14; see notes on 6:5; 16:9–11).
Ps 18 This song of David occurs also (with minor variations) in 2 Sam 22 (see notes there). In its structure, apart from the introduction (vv. 1–3) and the conclusion (vv. 46–50), the song is composed of three major divisions: (1) the Lord's deliverance of David from his mortal enemies (vv. 4–19); (2) the moral grounds for the Lord's saving help (vv. 20–29); (3) the Lord's help recounted (vv. 30–45).
18 title *To the chief Musician.* See note on Ps 4 title. *servant of the LORD.* See 78:70; 89:3,20,39; 132:10; 144:10. The title designates David in his royal office as, in effect, an official in the Lord's own kingly rule over His people (see 2 Sam 7:5)—as were Moses (see Ex 14:31 and note), Joshua (see Josh 24:29) and the prophets (Elijah, 2 Ki 9:36; Jonah, 2 Ki 14:25; Isaiah, Is 20:3; Daniel, Dan 6:20). *song.* See note on Ps 30 title. *day that the LORD delivered him.* It is possible that David composed his song shortly after his victories over his foreign enemies (2 Sam 8:1–14), but it may have been later in his life.
18:1–3 A prelude of praise.
18:1 Does not occur in 2 Sam 22. *I will love thee.* From an unusual Hebrew expression that emphasizes the fervor of David's love.
‡18:2 *rock.* A common poetic figure for God (or the gods: Deut 32:31,37; Is 44:8), symbolizing His unfailing (see Is 26:4) strength as a fortress refuge (see vv. 31,46; 31:2–3; 42:9; 62:7; 71:3; 94:22; Is 17:10) or as deliverer (see 19:14; 62:2; 78:35; 89:26; 95:1; Deut 32:15). It is a figure particularly appropriate for David's experience (see 1 Sam 23:14,25; 24:2,22; 26:20), for the Lord was his

My buckler, and the horn of my
salvation, *and* my high tower.
3 I will call upon the LORD, [a]who is
worthy to be praised:
So shall I be saved from mine enemies.
4 [a]The [1]sorrows of death compassed me,
And the floods of [2]ungodly men made
me afraid.
5 The [1]sorrows of hell compassed me
about:
The snares of death prevented me.
6 In my distress I called upon the LORD,
And cried unto my God:
He heard my voice out of his temple,
And my cry came before him, *even*
into his ears.
7 [a]Then the earth shook and trembled;
The foundations also of the hills moved
And were shaken, because he was
wroth.
8 There went up a smoke [1]out of his
nostrils,
And fire out of his mouth devoured:
Coals were kindled by it.
9 [a]He bowed the heavens also, and came
down:
And darkness *was* under his feet.
10 [a]And he rode upon a cherub, and did
fly:
Yea, [b]he did fly upon the wings of the
wind.
11 He made darkness his secret place;
[a]His pavilion round about him
Were dark waters *and* thick clouds of
the skies.

18:3 [a]Ps. 76:4
18:4 [1]Or, *cords* [2]Heb. *Belial* [a]Ps. 116:3
18:5 [1]Or, *cords*
18:7 [a]Acts 4:31
18:8 [1]Heb. *by his*
18:9 [a]Ps. 144:5
18:10 [a]Ps. 99:1 [b]Ps. 104:3
18:11 [a]Ps. 97:2

12 [a]At the brightness *that was* before him
his thick clouds passed,
Hail-*stones* and coals of fire.
13 The LORD also thundered in the
heavens,
And the Highest gave [a]his voice;
Hail-*stones* and coals of fire.
14 [a]Yea, he sent out his arrows, and
scattered them;
And he shot out lightnings, and
discomfited them.
15 Then the channels of waters were
seen,
And the foundations of the world were
discovered
At thy rebuke, O LORD,
At the blast of the breath of thy
nostrils.
16 [a]He sent from above, he took me,
He drew me out of [1]many waters.
17 He delivered me from my strong
enemy,
And from them which hated me: for
they were too strong for me.
18 They prevented me in the day of my
calamity:
But the LORD was my stay.
19 [a]He brought me forth also into a large
place;
He delivered me, because he delighted
in me.
20 [a]The LORD rewarded me according to
my righteousness;
According to the cleanness of my
hands hath he recompensed me.

18:12 [a]Ps. 97:3
18:13 [a]Ps. 29:3
18:14 [a]Josh. 10:10; Ps. 144:6; Is. 30:30
18:16 [1]Or, *great waters* [a]Ps. 144:7
18:19 [a]Ps. 31:8; 118:5
18:20 [a]1 Sam. 24:19

true security. *fortress.* See note on 2 Sam 22:2. *strength.* Or, "shield." See note on 3:3. *horn.* Here symbolizes strength (see Deut 33:17; Jer 48:25).

18:4–6 God heard his cry for help.

18:4–5 David depicts his experiences in poetic figures of mortal danger.

‡18:4 *sorrows.* Or, "cords." 2 Sam 22:5 has "waves." *floods.* See note on 30:1.

‡18:5 *sorrows of hell . . . snares of death.* He had, as it were, been snared by death (personified) and bound as a prisoner of the grave (see Job 36:8). *sorrows of hell.* Lit. "cords of Sheol" (the grave). See 116:3.

18:6 *temple.* God's heavenly abode, where He sits enthroned (see 11:4; 113:5; Is 6:1; 40:22).

18:7–15 The Lord came to the aid of His servant—depicted as a fearful theophany (divine manifestation) of the heavenly Warrior descending in wrathful attack upon David's enemies (see 5:4–5; 68:1–8; 77:16–19; Mic 1:3–4; Nah 1:2–6; Hab 3:3–15). He sweeps down upon them like a fierce thunderstorm (see Josh 10:11; Judg 5:20–22; 1 Sam 2:10; 7:10; 2 Sam 5:24; Is 29:6).

18:8 God's fierce majesty is portrayed in terms similar to those applied to the awesome leviathan (Job 41:19–21).

18:9 *bowed the heavens also, and came down.* See Is 64:1 and note.

18:10 *cherub.* A symbol of royalty (see 80:1; 99:1; see also notes on Gen 3:24; Ex 25:18). In Ezek 1; 10, cherubim appear as the bearers of the throne-chariot of God.

‡18:11 *darkness his secret place.* Covered himself with the dark storm clouds.

‡18:13 *Highest.* Cf. "most high" and note on Gen 14:19. *voice.* For thunder as the voice of God see Ps 29; Job 37:2–5.

‡18:14 *arrows.* For shafts of lightning as the arrows of God see 77:17; 144:6; Hab 3:11. *discomfited.* Routed and put into confusion.

18:15 Perhaps recalls the great deed of the heavenly Warrior when He defeated Israel's enemy at the Red sea (see Ex 15:1–12).

18:16–19 The deliverance.

18:16 *many waters.* See note on 32:6.

‡18:18 *prevented.* Attacked.

18:19 *large place.* See 4:1 and note; where he is free to roam unconfined by the threats and dangers that had hemmed him in (vv. 4–6,16–18). To be afflicted or oppressed is like being bound by fetters (Job 36:8,13). To be delivered is to be set free (Job 36:16). *delighted in me.* God was pleased with David as "a man after his own heart" (1 Sam 13:14; see also 1 Sam 15:28; 1 Ki 14:8; 15:5), a man with whom He had made a covenant assuring him of an enduring dynasty (2 Sam 7). The thought is further elaborated in vv. 20–29.

18:20–24 David's righteousness rewarded. David's assertion of his righteousness (like that of Samuel, 1 Sam 12:3; Hezekiah, 2 Ki 20:3; Job, Job 13:23; 27:6; 31; see also Ps 17:3–5; 26; 44:17–18; 101) is not a pretentious boast of sinless perfection (see 51:5). Rather, it is a claim that, in contrast to his enemies, he has devoted himself heart and life to the service of the Lord, that his has been a godliness with integrity—itself the fruit of God's gracious working in his heart (see 51:10–12).

18:20 *rewarded me.* As a king benevolently rewards those who loyally serve him. *my righteousness.* See note on 1:5.

21 For I have kept the ways of the LORD,
And have not wickedly departed from
my God.
22 For all his judgments *were* before me,
And I did not put away his statutes
from me.
23 I was also upright [1]before him,
And I kept myself from mine iniquity.
24 [a]Therefore hath the LORD recompensed
me according to my righteousness,
According to the cleanness of my
hands [1]in his eyesight.
25 [a]With the merciful thou wilt shew
thyself merciful;
With an upright man thou wilt shew
thyself upright;
26 With the pure thou wilt shew thyself
pure;
And [a]with the froward thou wilt
[1]shew thyself froward.
27 For thou wilt save the afflicted people;
But wilt bring down [a]high looks.
28 [a]For thou wilt light my [1]candle:
The LORD my God will enlighten my
darkness.
29 For by thee I have [1]run *through* a
troop;
And by my God have I leaped over a
wall.
30 *As for* God, [a]his way *is* perfect:
[b]The word of the LORD is [1]tried:
He *is* a buckler [c]to all those that trust
in him.
31 [a]For who *is* God save the LORD?
Or who *is* a rock save our God?
32 *It is* God that [a]girdeth me *with*
strength,
And maketh my way perfect.
33 [a]He maketh my feet like hinds' *feet,*
And [b]setteth me upon my high places.
34 [a]He teacheth my hands to war,
So that a bow of steel is broken *by*
mine arms.
35 Thou hast also given me the shield of
thy salvation:
And thy right hand hath holden me up,
And [1]thy gentleness hath made me
great.
36 Thou hast enlarged my steps under me,
[a]That [1]my feet did not slip.
37 I have pursued mine enemies, and
overtaken them:
Neither did I turn again till they were
consumed.
38 I have wounded them that they were
not able to rise:
They are fallen under my feet.
39 For thou hast girded me *with* strength
unto the battle:
Thou hast [1]subdued under me those
that rose up against me.
40 Thou hast also given me the necks of
mine enemies;
That I might destroy them that hate me.
41 They cried, but *there was* none to save
them:
[a]*Even* unto the LORD, but he answered
them not.
42 Then did I beat them small as the dust
before the wind:
I did [a]cast them out as the dirt in the
streets.
43 Thou hast delivered me from the
strivings of the people;
And [a]thou hast made me the head of
the heathen:
[b]A people *whom* I have not known
shall serve me.
44 [1]As soon as they hear *of me,* they shall
obey me:
[2]The strangers shall [3]submit
themselves unto me.
45 [a][1]The strangers shall fade away,
And be afraid out of their close places.
46 The LORD liveth; and blessed *be* my
rock;
And let the God of my salvation be
exalted.
47 *It is* God that [1]avengeth me,
[a]And [2]subdueth the people under me.

18:23 [1]Heb. *with*
18:24 [1]Heb. *before his eyes* [a]1 Sam. 26:23
18:25 [a]1 Ki. 8:32
18:26 [1]Or, *wrestle* [a]Lev. 26:23,24,27,28; Prov. 3:34
18:27 [a]Ps. 101:5; Prov. 6:17
18:28 [1]Or, *lamp* [a]Job 18:6
18:29 [1]Or, *broken*
18:30 [1]Or, *refined* [a]Deut. 32:4; Dan. 4:37; Rev. 15:3 [b]Ps. 12:6; 119:140; Prov. 30:5 [c]Ps. 17:7
18:31 [a]Deut. 32:31,39; 1 Sam. 2:2; Ps. 86:8; Is. 45:5
18:32 [a]Ps. 91:2
18:33 [a]2 Sam. 2:18; Hab. 3:19 [b]Deut. 32:13; 33:29
18:34 [a]Ps. 144:1
18:35 [1]Or, with *thy meekness thou hast multiplied me*
18:36 [1]Heb. *mine ankles* [a]Prov. 4:12
18:39 [1]Heb. *caused to bow*
18:41 [a]Job 27:9; Prov. 1:28; Jer. 11:11
18:42 [a]Zech. 10:5
18:43 [a]2 Sam. 8 [b]Is. 52:15
18:44 [1]Heb. *At the hearing of the ear* [2]Heb. *The sons of the stranger* [3]Or, *yield feigned obedience.* Heb. *lie*
18:45 [1]Heb. *The sons of the stranger* [a]Mic. 7:17
18:47 [1]Heb. *giveth avengements for me* [2]Or, *destroyeth* [a]Ps. 47:3

18:21 *ways of the LORD.* See 25:4 and note.
18:25–29 Because God responds to man in kind (see Job 34:1; Prov 3:34), David has experienced the Lord's favor.
‡18:26 *froward.* Crooked, deviating from the straight path of truth and righteousness. *shew thyself froward.* God responds to their perverse dealings thrust for thrust, like a wrestler countering his opponent.
‡18:27 The thought of this verse fits well with David's and Saul's reversals of status. It also echoes the central theme of Hannah's song, which the author of Samuel uses to highlight a major thesis of his account of the ways of God as He brings about His kingdom. *high looks.* "Haughty eyes," i.e. people of pride.
18:28 *light my candle.* God causes his life and undertakings to flourish (see especially Job 18:5–6; 21:17). *enlighten.* See note on 27:1.
18:30–36 By God's blessing David the king has thrived.
‡18:30 *is perfect.* Does not fail—and so, because of His blessing, David's way has not failed (see v. 32). *word of the LORD.* While the reference is general, it applies especially to God's promise to David (see 2 Sam 7:8–16). *tried.* See note on 12:6. *buckler.* A shield. See note on 3:3.
‡18:33 *like hinds' feet.* Like the feet of deer.
‡18:35 *thy gentleness.* That causes God to care about David's plight.
18:37–42 With God's help David has crushed all his foes.
18:43–45 God has made David the head of nations (see 2 Sam 5; 8; 10)—he who had been, it seemed, on the brink of death (see vv. 4–5), sinking into the depths (see v. 16).
18:43 *strivings of the people.* All the threats he had endured from his own people in the days of Saul, and perhaps also in the time of Absalom's rebellion. *people whom I have not known.* Those with whom he had had no previous relations.
18:46–50 Concluding doxology.
18:46 *The LORD liveth.* God's interventions and blessings in David's behalf have shown Him to be the living God (see Deut 5:26).
18:47 *avengeth me.* Redresses the wrongs committed against me (see Deut 32:41).

48 He delivereth me from mine enemies:
Yea, [a]thou liftest me up above those that rise up against me:
Thou hast delivered me from the [1]violent man.
49 [a]Therefore will I [1]give thanks unto thee, O LORD, among the heathen,
And sing *praises* unto thy name.
50 [a]Great deliverance giveth he to his king;
And sheweth mercy to his anointed,
To David, and to his seed for evermore.

Psalm 19

To the chief Musician, A Psalm of David.

1 The [a]heavens declare the glory of God;
And the firmament sheweth his handywork.
2 Day unto day uttereth speech,
And night unto night sheweth knowledge.
3 *There is* no speech nor language,
[1]*Where* their voice is not heard.
4 [a1]Their line is gone out through all the earth,
And their words to the end of the world.
In them hath he set a tabernacle for the sun,
5 Which *is* as a bridegroom coming out of his chamber,
[a]*And* rejoiceth as a strong *man* to run a race.
6 His going forth *is* from the end of the heaven,
And his circuit unto the ends of it:
And there is nothing hid from the heat thereof.
7 [a]The [1]law of the LORD *is* perfect, [2]converting the soul:
The testimony of the LORD *is* sure, making wise the simple.
8 The statutes of the LORD *are* right, rejoicing the heart:
The commandment of the LORD *is* pure, enlightening the eyes.
9 The fear of the LORD *is* clean, enduring for ever:
The judgments of the LORD *are* [1]true *and* righteous altogether.
10 More to be desired *are they* than gold, yea, than much fine gold:
Sweeter also than honey and [1]the honeycomb.
11 Moreover by them *is* thy servant warned:
And in keeping of them *there is* great reward.
12 Who can understand *his* errors?
Cleanse thou me from secret *faults.*
13 Keep back thy servant also from presumptuous *sins;*
Let them not have dominion over me:
Then shall I be upright,
And I shall be innocent from [1]*the* great transgression.
14 Let the words of my mouth,
And the meditation of my heart, be acceptable in thy sight,
O LORD, [1]my strength, and my [a]redeemer.

18:48 [1]Heb. *man of violence* [a]Ps. 59:1
18:49 [1]Or, *confess* [a]Rom. 15:9
18:50 [a]Ps. 144:10
19:1 [a]Is. 40:22
19:3 [1]Or, *Without these their voice is heard.* Heb. *Without their voice heard*
19:4 [1]Or, *Their rule,* or, *direction* [a]Rom. 10:18
19:5 [a]Eccl. 1:5
19:7 [1]Or, *doctrine* [2]Or, *restoring* [a]Ps. 111:7
19:9 [1]Heb. *truth*
19:10 [1]Heb. *the dropping of honeycombs*
19:13 [1]Or, *much*
19:14 [1]Heb. *my rock* [a]Is. 47:4

18:49 David vows to praise the Lord among the nations (see note on 9:1). *name.* See note on 5:11.

18:50 *his king . . . his anointed.* David views himself as the Lord's chosen and anointed king (see 1 Sam 16:13; see also notes on 1 Sam 10:25; 12:14–15). *sheweth mercy.* David's final words recall the Lord's covenant with him (see 2 Sam 7:8–16). The whole song is to be understood in the context of David's official capacity and the Lord's covenant with him. What David claims in this grand conclusion—as, indeed, in the whole psalm—has been and is being fulfilled in Jesus Christ, David's great descendant.

‡Ps 19 A hymn extolling "the glory of God" (v. 1) as revealed to all by the starry heavens (see vv. 1–6) and "The law of the LORD" (v. 7), which has been given to Israel (see vv. 7–13). Placed next to Ps 18, it completes the cycle of praise—for the Lord's saving acts, for His glory reflected in creation and for His law.

19 title *To the chief Musician.* See note on Ps 4 title.

19:1–4a The silent heavens speak, declaring the glory of their Maker to all who are on the earth (see 148:3). The heavenly lights are not divine (see Deut 4:19; 17:3), nor do they control or disclose man's destiny (see Is 47:13; Jer 10:2; Dan 4:7). Their glory testifies to the righteousness and faithfulness of the Lord who created them (see 50:6; 89:5–8; 97:6; see also Rom 1:19–20).

‡19:1 *handywork.* Work of his hands. Cf. Is 40:12.

19:4 Interpreting this heavenly proclamation eschatologically in the light of Christ, Paul applies this verse to the proclamation of the gospel in his own day (see Rom 10:18). He thus associates these two universal proclamations.

‡19:4b–6 The heavens are the divinely pitched "tabernacle" (tent) for the lordly sun—widely worshiped in the ancient Near East (cf. Deut 4:19; 17:3; 2 Ki 23:5,11; Jer 8:2; Ezek 8:16), but here, as in 136:7–8; Gen 1:16, a mere creature of God. Of the created realm, the sun is the supreme metaphor of the glory of God (see 84:11; Is 60:19–20), as it makes its daily triumphant sweep across the whole extent of the heavens and pours out its heat (felt presence) on every creature.

19:7–10 Stately, rhythmic celebration of the life-nurturing effects of the Lord's revealed law (see Ps 119).

19:7 *the simple.* The childlike, those whose understanding and judgment have not yet matured (see 119:98–100; Prov 1:4; cf. 2 Tim 3:15; Heb 5:13–14).

19:8 *heart.* See note on 4:7.

19:9 *fear of the LORD.* The sum of what the law requires (see note on 15:4).

19:10 *Sweeter also than honey.* By contrast, those who abandon the law turn justice into bitterness (see Amos 5:7; 6:12).

19:11–13 The law marks the way that leads to life (see Deut 5:33). But man's moral consciousness remains flawed and imperfect; hence he errs without realizing it and has reason to seek pardon for hidden faults (v. 12; see Lev 5:2–4). Willful sins (v. 13), however, are open rebellion; they are the great transgression (v. 13) that leads to being cut off from God's people (see Num 15:30–31).

19:11,13 *thy servant.* The psalmist himself.

‡19:14 The psalmist presents this hymn as a praise offering to the Lord. *heart.* See note on 4:7. *strength . . . redeemer.* See 78:35. *strength.* Lit. "rock." See notes on 18:2; Gen 49:24. *redeemer.* See note on Ex 6:6.

Psalm 20

To the chief Musician, A Psalm of David.

1 The LORD hear thee in the day of trouble;
The name of the God of Jacob [1] defend thee;
2 Send [1] thee help from the sanctuary,
And [2] strengthen thee out of Zion;
3 Remember all thy offerings,
And [1] accept thy burnt sacrifice. Selah.
4 Grant thee according to thine own heart,
And fulfil all thy counsel.
5 We will rejoice in thy salvation,
And in the name of our God we will set up *our* banners:
The LORD fulfil all thy petitions.
6 Now know I that the LORD saveth his anointed;
He will hear him [1] from his holy heaven
[2] With the saving strength of his right hand.
7 Some *trust* in chariots, and some in horses:
But we will remember the name of the LORD our God.
8 They are brought down and fallen:
But we are risen, and stand upright.
9 Save, LORD:
Let the king hear us when we call.

20:1 [1] Heb. *set thee on a high place*
20:2 [1] Heb. *thy help* [2] Heb. *support thee*
20:3 [1] Heb. *turn to ashes:* or, *make fat*
20:6 [1] Heb. *from the heaven of his holiness* [2] Heb. *By the strength of the salvation of his right hand*

Psalm 21

To the chief Musician, A Psalm of David.

1 The king shall joy in thy strength, O LORD;
And in thy salvation how greatly shall he rejoice!
2 Thou hast given him his heart's desire,
And hast not withholden the request of his lips. Selah.
3 For thou preventest him *with* the blessings of goodness:
Thou settest a crown of pure gold on his head.
4 [a] He asked life of thee, *and* thou gavest *it* him,
Even length of days for ever and ever.
5 His glory *is* great in thy salvation:
Honour and majesty hast thou laid upon him.
6 For thou hast [a] [1] made him most blessed for ever:
Thou hast [2] made him exceeding glad with thy countenance.
7 For the king trusteth in the LORD,
And through the mercy of the most High he shall not be moved.
8 Thine hand shall find out all thine enemies:
Thy right hand shall find out those that hate thee.

21:4 [a] Ps. 61:5,6
21:6 [1] Heb. *set him to be blessings* [2] Heb. *gladded him with joy* [a] Ps. 72:17

Ps 20 A liturgy of prayer for the king just before he goes out to battle against a threatening force (see 2 Chr 20:1–30).
20 title *To the chief Musician.* See note on Ps 4 title.
20:1–5 The people (perhaps his assembled army) address the king, adding their prayers to his prayer for victory.
20:1 *hear thee.* Hear your prayers, offered in the present distress, accompanied by "offerings" (v. 3); see v. 9. *name.* See vv. 5,7; see also note on 5:11. *Jacob.* See note on 14:7. *defend thee.* Lit. "raise you to a high, secure place."
20:2 *Zion.* See note on 9:11.
‡20:4 *according to thine own heart.* His heart's desire. See note on 4:7.
20:5 *We will rejoice . . . name of our God.* See note on 7:17. *banners.* Probably the troop standards around which the units rallied.
20:6 A participant in the liturgy (perhaps a Levite; see 2 Chr 20:14) announces assurance that the king's prayer will be heard. *his anointed.* The king appointed by the Lord to rule in His name (see 2:2 and note).
20:7–8 The army's confession of trust in the Lord rather than in a chariot corps (cf. 33:16–17)—the enemy perhaps came reinforced by such a prized corps. See David's similar confession of confidence when he faced Goliath (1 Sam 17:45–47).
‡20:9 The army's concluding petition. *the king.* Read with the preceding line ("Save, O LORD, the king"). *hear us.* Asking God, not the king, to answer their petition. See note on v. 1. The psalm ends as it began.
Ps 21 A psalm of praise for victories granted to the king. It is thus linked with Ps 20, but whether both were occasioned by the same events is unknown. Here the people's praise follows that of the king (see v. 1); there (Ps 20) the people's prayer was added to the king's. In its structure, the psalm is framed by vv. 1,13 ("in thy strength, O LORD . . . LORD, in thine own strength") and is centered around v. 7, which proclaims the king's trust in the Lord and the security afforded him by God's unfailing love (see Introduction: Literary Features).
21 title *To the chief Musician.* See note on Ps 4 title.
21:2–6 The people celebrate the Lord's many favors to the king: all "his heart's desire" (v. 2). Verse 2 announces the theme; vv. 3–5 develop the theme; v. 6 climactically summarizes the theme.
21:2 *heart's desire.* See note on 4:7.
‡21:3 *preventest him.* Or, "meet him," and welcome him back from the battles. *settest a crown . . . on his head.* Exchange the warrior's helmet for the ceremonial emblem of royalty—possibly the captured crown of the defeated king (see 2 Sam 12:30).
21:4 The king's life has been spared—to live for ever and ever (see 1 Ki 1:31; Dan 2:4; 3:9; see also 1 Sam 10:24; 1 Ki 1:25,34,39).
21:5 *glory . . . Honour and majesty.* See 45:3; like that of his heavenly Overlord (see 96:3).
‡21:6 *blessed for ever.* Either (1) blessings of enduring value or (2) an unending flow of blessings. *thy countenance.* The favor of God's presence, which is the supreme cause of joy because it is the greatest blessing and the wellspring of all other blessings.
21:7 The center of the psalm (see note on 6:6). A participant in the liturgy (perhaps a priest or Levite) proclaims the reasons for the king's security. *LORD . . . most High.* That is, LORD most High (see 7:17; see also note on 3:7). *mercy.* See note on 6:4. *most High.* See note on Gen 14:19. *moved.* See note on 10:6.
21:8–12 The people hail the future victories of their triumphant king. Verse 8 announces the theme; vv. 9–11 develop the theme; v. 12 summarizes the theme.

9 Thou shalt make them as a fiery oven
in the time of thine anger:
The LORD shall swallow them up in his
wrath, and the fire shall devour
them.
10 Their fruit shalt thou destroy from the
earth,
And their seed from among the
children of men.
11 For they intended evil against thee:
They imagined a mischievous device,
which they are not able *to perform.*
12 Therefore [1]shalt thou make them turn
their [2]back,
When thou shalt make ready *thine
arrows* upon thy strings against the
face of them.
13 Be thou exalted, LORD, in thine own
strength:
So will we sing and praise thy power.

Psalm 22

To the chief Musician upon [1]Aijeleth Shahar,
A Psalm of David.

1 My [a]God, my God, why hast thou
forsaken me?
Why art thou so far [1]from helping me,
and from the words of my roaring?
2 O my God, I cry in the daytime, but
thou hearest not;
And in the night season, and [1]am not
silent.
3 But thou *art* holy, O thou that
inhabitest the [a]praises of Israel.
4 Our fathers trusted in thee:
They trusted, and thou didst deliver
them.

21:12 [1]Or, *thou shalt set them* as *a butt* [2]Heb. *shoulder*
22:T [1]Or, *The hind of the morning*
22:1 [1]Heb. *from my salvation* [a]Mark 15:34
22:2 [1]Heb. there is *no silence to me*
22:3 [a]Deut. 10:21
22:5 [a]Is. 49:23
22:6 [a]Job 25:6 [b]Is. 53:3
22:7 [1]Heb. *open* [a]Mat. 27:39 [b]Job 16:4
22:8 [1]Heb. *He rolled* himself *on the LORD* [2]Or, *if he delight in him* [a]Mat. 27:43 [b]Ps. 91:14
22:9 [1]Or, *keptest me in safety* [a]Ps. 71:6
22:10 [a]Is. 46:3
22:11 [1]Heb. *not a helper*
22:12 [a]Ps. 68:30
22:13 [1]Heb. *opened their mouths against me* [a]Lam. 2:16
22:14 [1]Or, *sundered* [a]Dan. 5:6
22:15 [a]Prov. 17:22 [b]John 19:28

5 They cried unto thee, and were
delivered:
[a]They trusted in thee, and were not
confounded.
6 But I *am* [a]a worm, and no man;
[b]A reproach of men, and despised of
the people.
7 [a]All they that see me laugh me to scorn:
They [1]shoot out the lip, [b]they shake
the head, *saying,*
8 [a][1]He trusted on the LORD *that* he
would deliver him:
[b]Let him deliver him, [2]seeing he
delighted in him.
9 [a]But thou *art* he that took me out of
the womb:
Thou [1]didst make me hope *when I was*
upon my mother's breasts.
10 I was cast upon thee from the womb:
[a]Thou *art* my God from my mother's
belly.
11 Be not far from me; for trouble *is* near;
For *there is* [1]none to help.
12 [a]Many bulls have compassed me:
Strong *bulls* of Bashan have beset me
round.
13 [a]They [1]gaped upon me *with* their
mouths,
As a ravening and a roaring lion.
14 I am poured out like water,
[a]And all my bones are [1]out of joint:
My heart is like wax;
It is melted in the midst of my bowels.
15 [a]My strength is dried up like a
potsherd;
And [b]my tongue cleaveth *to* my jaws;
And thou hast brought me into the
dust of death.

21:9 *The LORD . . . in his wrath.* Credits the king's victories to the Lord's wrath (see note on 2:5).
21:10 The king's royal enemies will be left no descendants to rise against him again.
‡21:13 Conclusion—and return to the beginning: Lord, assert Your strength, in which "The king shall joy" (v. 1; see also v. 7), and we will ever praise Your might.
Ps 22 The anguished prayer of David as a godly sufferer victimized by the vicious and prolonged attacks of enemies whom he has not provoked and from whom the Lord has not (yet) delivered him. It has many similarities with Ps 69, but contains no calls for redress (see note on 5:10) such as are found in 69:22–28. No other psalm fitted quite so aptly the circumstances of Jesus at His crucifixion. Hence on the cross He took it to His lips (see Mat 27:46 and parallels), and the Gospel writers, especially Matthew and John, frequently alluded to it (as they did to Ps 69) in their accounts of Christ's passion (Mat 27:35,39,43; John 19:23–24,28). They saw in the passion of Jesus the fulfillment of this cry of the righteous sufferer. The author of Hebrews placed the words of v. 22 on Jesus' lips (see Heb 2:12 and note). No psalm is quoted more frequently in the NT.
22 title See notes on Ps 4; 9 titles.
22:1 *why . . . ?* See note on 6:3; see also Introduction: Theology.
22:1a Quoted by Jesus in Mat 27:46; Mark 15:34.
22:3–5 Recollection of what the Lord has been for Israel (see note on vv. 9–10).
‡22:3 *inhabitest . . . praises of Israel.* God's presence dwells in the place where God's people praise Him. See note on 9:11. *praises of Israel.* The one Israel praises for His saving acts in her behalf (see 148:14; Deut 10:21; Jer 17:14).
22:6 *a worm, and no man.* See Job 25:6; Is 41:14.
22:7 *shoot out the lip . . . shake the head.* See Mat 27:39; Mark 15:29; see also note on 5:9.
22:8 Quoted in part in Mat 27:43; see note on 3:2.
‡22:9–10 Recollection of what the Lord has been for him (see note on vv. 3–5). *make me hope . . . upon my mother's breast.* Hyperbole, stressing that David has trusted in God all his life.
‡22:12–18 The psalmist's deep distress. In vv. 12–13,16–18 he uses four figures to portray the attacks of his enemies; in vv. 14–15 he describes his inner sense of powerlessness under their fierce attacks. The references to his thirst (v. 15), the piercing of his hands and feet (v. 16), and casting lots for his robe (v. 18) all point prophetically to the crucifixion of Christ ten centuries later.
22:12–13,16 *bulls . . . lion . . . dogs.* Metaphors for the enemies (see note on 7:2).
22:12 *Bashan.* Noted for its good pasturage, and hence for the size and vigor of its animals (see Deut 32:14, Ezek 39:18 and note; Amos 4:1).
22:14 *bones . . . heart.* See note on 102:4. *heart.* See note on 4:7.
22:15 See John 19:28 and note. *dust of death.* See v. 29; see also Job 7:21 and note.

16 For dogs have compassed me:
The assembly of the wicked have inclosed me:
[a]They pierced my hands and my feet.
17 I may tell all my bones:
[a]They look *and* stare upon me.
18 [a]They part my garments among them,
And cast lots upon my vesture.
19 But be not thou far *from me,* O LORD:
O my strength, haste thee to help me.
20 Deliver my soul from the sword;
[a][1]My darling [2]from the power of the dog.
21 [a]Save me from the lion's mouth:
[b]For thou hast heard me from the horns of the unicorns.
22 [a]I will declare thy name unto [b]my brethren:
In the midst of the congregation will I praise thee.
23 [a]Ye that fear the LORD, praise him;
All ye the seed of Jacob, glorify him;
And fear him, all ye the seed of Israel.
24 For he hath not despised nor abhorred the affliction of the afflicted;
Neither hath he hid his face from him;
But [a]when he cried unto him, he heard.
25 [a]My praise *shall be* of thee in the great congregation:
[b]I will pay my vows before them that fear him.

22:16 [a]Mat. 27:35
22:17 [a]Luke 23:27,35
22:18 [a]Luke 23:34
22:20 [1]Heb. *My only one* [2]Heb. *from the hand* [a]Ps. 35:17
22:21 [a]2 Tim. 4:17 [b]Is. 34:7
22:22 [a]Heb. 2:12 [b]Rom. 8:29
22:23 [a]Ps. 135:19
22:24 [a]Heb. 5:7
22:25 [a]Ps. 35:18 [b]Eccl. 5:4
22:28 [a]Mat. 6:13
22:29 [a]Ps. 45:12 [b]Is. 26:19
22:30 [a]Ps. 87:6
22:31 [a]Ps. 78:6
23:1 [a]Is. 40:11; John 10:11 [b]Phil. 4:19
23:2 [1]Heb. *pastures of tender grass* [2]Heb. *waters of quietness* [a]Ezek. 34:14 [b]Rev. 7:17

26 The meek shall eat and be satisfied:
They shall praise the LORD that seek him:
Your heart shall live for ever.
27 All the ends of the world shall remember and turn unto the LORD:
And all the kindreds of the nations shall worship before thee.
28 [a]For the kingdom *is* the LORD's:
And *he is* the governor among the nations.
29 [a]All *they that be* fat upon earth shall eat and worship:
[b]All they that go down to the dust shall bow before him:
And none can keep alive his own soul.
30 A seed shall serve him;
[a]It shall be accounted to the Lord for a generation.
31 [a]They shall come, and shall declare his righteousness
Unto a people that *shall be* born, that he hath done *this.*

Psalm 23

A Psalm of David.

1 The LORD *is* [a]my shepherd; [b]I shall not want.
2 [a]He maketh me to lie down in [1]green pastures:
[b]He leadeth me beside the [2]still waters.

22:16 *pierced my hands and my feet.* The dogs and/or evil men wound his limbs as he seeks to ward off their attacks. But see also Is 53:5; Zech 12:10; John 19:34,37.
22:17 *I may tell all my bones.* Perhaps better, "I must display all my bones." The figure may be of one attacked by highway robbers or enemy soldiers, who strip him of his garments (see v. 18; see also note on vv. 20–21).
22:18 See introduction to this psalm; see also John 19:23–24.
‡22:20–21 The psalmist's prayer recalls in reverse order the four figures by which he portrayed his attackers in vv. 12–13,16–18:"sword,""dog,""lion,""unicorns" (i.e. wild oxen, corresponding to the "strong bulls" in v. 12). Here "sword" may evoke the scene described in vv. 16b–18, and thus many interpret it as an attack by robbers or enemy soldiers, though "sword" is often used figuratively of any violent death.
‡22:21 *thou hast heard me.* The psalmist experiences the assurance of having been heard. The sense is: You have heard my petition and will answer me by delivering me from death at the hands of my enemies (see note on 3:8). *unicorns* [i.e. "wild oxen]. Aurochs, wild ancestors of domestic cattle; or possibly oryxes, large straight-horned antelopes.
22:22–31 Vows to praise the Lord when the Lord's sure deliverance comes (see note on 7:17). The vows proper appear in vv. 22,25. Verses 23–24 anticipate the calls to praise that will accompany the psalmist's praise (see note on 9:1). Verses 26–31 describe the expanding company of those who will take up the praise—a worldwide company of persons from every station in life and continuing through the generations. No psalm or prophecy contains a grander vision of the scope of the throng of worshipers who will join in the praise of God's saving acts.
22:22 See Heb 2:12 and note. *name.* See note on 5:11.
22:23 *fear the LORD.* See v. 25; see also note on 15:4.
22:25 *congregation.* See note on 1:5.
22:26 *shall eat and be satisfied.* As they share in the ceremonial festival of praise (see Lev 7:11–27).
22:27 *All the ends of the world.* They too will be told of God's saving acts (see 18:49 and note on 9:1). The good news that the God of Israel hears the prayers of His people and saves them will move them to turn from their idols to the true God.
22:28 The rule of the God of Israel is universal, and the nations will come to recognize that fact through what He does in behalf of His people (see Ps 47; Gen 12:2–3; see also Deut 32:21; Rom 10:19; 11:13–14).
22:29 *they that be fat . . . they that go down to the dust.* The most prosperous and those on the brink of death, and all those whose life situation falls in between these two extremes. *dust.* See v. 15; see also Job 7:21 and note.
22:31 *righteousness.* See note on 4:1.
‡Ps 23 A profession of joyful trust in the Lord as the good Shepherd-King. The psalm may have accompanied a festival of praise at "the house of the LORD" (v. 6) following a deliverance, such as is contemplated in 22:25–31 (see note on 7:17).
23:1 *shepherd.* A widely used metaphor for kings in the ancient Near East, and also in Israel (see 78:71–72; 2 Sam 5:2; Is 44:28; Jer 3:15; 23:1–4; Mic 5:4). For the Lord as the shepherd of Israel see 28:9; 79:13; 80:1; 95:7; 100:3; Gen 48:15; Is 40:11; Jer 17:16; 31:10; 50:19; Ezek 34:11–16. Here David the king acknowledges that the Lord is his Shepherd-King. For Jesus as the shepherd of His people see John 10:11,14; Heb 13:20; 1 Pet 5:4; Rev 7:17. *not want.* On the contrary, he will enjoy "goodness" all his life (v. 6).
23:2 *lie down.* For flocks lying down in contented and secure rest see Is 14:30; 17:2; Jer 33:12; Ezek 34:14–15; Zeph 2:7; 3:13. *green pastures.* Metaphor for all that makes life to flourish (see Ezek 34:14; John 10:9). *leadeth me.* Like a shepherd (see Is 40:11). *still waters.* Lit. "waters of resting places," i.e. restful

3 He restoreth my soul:
[a]He leadeth me in the paths of righteousness for his name's sake.
4 Yea, though I walk through the valley of [a]the shadow of death,
[b]I will fear no evil: [c]for thou *art* with me;
Thy rod and thy staff they comfort me.
5 Thou preparest a table before me in the presence of mine enemies:
Thou [a][1]anointest my head with oil; my cup runneth over.
6 Surely goodness and mercy shall follow me all the days of my life:
And I will dwell in the house of the LORD [1]for ever.

23:3 [a]Ps. 5:8 23:4 [a]Job 10:21,22; Ps. 44:19 [b]Ps. 3:6 [c]Is. 43:2 23:5 [1]Heb. *makest fat* [a]Ps. 92:10 23:6 [1]Heb. *to length of days* 24:1 [a]Ex. 9:29; Job 41:11

Psalm 24

A Psalm of David.

1 The [a]earth *is* the LORD's, and the fulness thereof;
The world, and they that dwell therein.
2 For he hath founded it upon the seas,
And established it upon the floods.
3 [a]Who shall ascend into the hill of the LORD?
And who shall stand in his holy place?
4 [1]He that hath [a]clean hands, and [b]a pure heart;
Who hath not lift up his soul unto vanity,
Nor [c]sworn deceitfully.
5 He shall receive the blessing from the LORD,
And righteousness from the God of his salvation.
6 This *is* the generation of them that seek him,
That [a]seek thy face, [1]O Jacob. Selah.
7 [a]Lift up your heads, O ye gates;
And be ye lift up, ye everlasting doors;
[b]And the King of glory shall come in.
8 Who *is* this King of glory?
The LORD strong and mighty,

24:3 [a]Ps. 15:1 24:4 [1]Heb. *The clean of hands* [a]Job 17:9; 1 Tim. 2:8 [b]Mat. 5:8 [c]Ps. 15:4 24:6 [1]Or, O God of *Jacob* [a]Ps. 27:8 24:7 [a]Is. 26:2 [b]Ps. 97:6; Hag. 2:7; Mal. 3:1

waters—waters that provide refreshment and well-being (see Is 49:10).

23:3 *restoreth my soul.* Revives me, refreshes my spirit (see 19:7; Ruth 4:15; Prov 25:13; Lam 1:16). *leadeth me in the paths of righteousness.* As a shepherd leads his sheep (see 77:20; 78:72) in paths that offer safety and well-being, so David's Shepherd-King guides him in ways that cause him to be secure and prosperous. For this meaning of "righteousness" see Prov 8:18; 21:21; Is 48:18; see also Prov 8:20–21. It is also possible that "paths of righteousness" refers to the paths that conform to God's moral will. *for his name's sake.* The prosperity of the Lord's servant brings honor to the Lord's name (see 1 Ki 8:41–42; Is 48:9; Jer 14:21; Ezek 20:9,14,22).

‡23:4 *for thou . . . comfort me.* The very center of the psalm, which introduces a transition from the shepherd-sheep motif in vv. 1–3 to the direct address ("thou") of the Shepherd-King in vv. 5–6. *with me.* See 16:8 and note; see also Deut 31:6,8; Mat 28:20. *rod.* Instrument of authority (as in 2:9; 45:6; Ex 21:20; 2 Sam 7:14; Job 9:34); used also by shepherds for counting, guiding, rescuing and protecting sheep (see Lev 27:32; Ezek 20:37). *staff.* Instrument of support (as in Ex 21:19; Judg 6:21; 2 Ki 4:29; Zech 8:4). *comfort me.* Reassure me (as in 71:21; 86:17; Ruth 2:13; Is 12:1; 40:1; 49:13).

23:5 The heavenly Shepherd-King receives David at His table as his vassal king and takes him under His protection. In the ancient Near East, covenants were often concluded with a meal expressive of the bond of friendship (see 41:9; Gen 31:54; Obad 7); in the case of vassal treaties or covenants, the vassal was present as the guest of the overlord (see Ex 24:8–12). *anointest my head with oil.* Customary treatment of an honored guest at a banquet (see Luke 7:46; see also 2 Sam 12:20; Eccl 9:8; Dan 10:3). *cup.* Of the Lord's banquet (see note on 16:5).

23:6 *goodness and mercy.* Both frequently refer to covenant benefits (see note on 6:4); here they are personified (see 25:21; 43:3; 79:8; 89:14). *follow.* Lit. "pursue." *dwell in the house of the LORD.* See note on 15:1. *for ever.* The Hebrew suggests "throughout the years." But see also notes on 11:7; 16:9–11.

Ps 24 A processional liturgy (see Ps 47; 68; 118; 132) celebrating the Lord's entrance into Zion—composed either for the occasion when David brought the ark to Jerusalem (see 2 Sam 6) or for a festival commemorating the event. It was probably placed next to Ps 23 because it prescribes who may enter the sanctuary (see 23:6). The church has long used this psalm in celebration of Christ's ascension into the heavenly Jerusalem—and into the sanctuary on high (see introduction to Ps 47).

24:1–2 The prelude (perhaps spoken by a Levite), proclaiming the Lord as the Creator, Sustainer and Possessor of the whole world, and therefore worthy of worship and reverent loyalty as "the King of glory" (vv. 7–10; see Ps 29; 33:6–11; 89:5–18; 93; 95:3–5; 104).

‡24:1 *The earth . . . and the fulness thereof.* The earth and all that it contains. For Paul's use of this declaration see 1 Cor 10:25–26.

24:2 An echo of Gen 1:1–10. *founded . . . established.* A metaphor taken from the founding of a city (see Josh 6:26; 1 Ki 16:24; Is 14:32) or of a temple (see 1 Ki 5:17; 6:37; Ezra 3:6–12; Is 44:28; Hag 2:18; Zech 4:9; 8:9). Like a temple, the earth was depicted as having foundations (see 18:15; 82:5; 1 Sam 2:8; Prov 8:29; Is 24:18) and pillars (see 75:3; Job 9:6). In the ancient Near East, temples were thought of as microcosms of the created world, so language applicable to a temple could readily be applied to the earth. *upon.* Or "above" (see 104:5–9; Gen 1:9; 49:25; Ex 20:4; Deut 33:13).

24:3–6 Instruction concerning those who may enter the sanctuary (probably spoken by a priest); see Ps 15 and introduction.

24:3 *hill of the LORD.* See 2:6 and note.

‡24:4 *clean hands.* Guiltless actions. *pure heart.* Right attitudes and motives. Jesus said that the "pure in heart . . . shall see God" (Mat 5:8). *heart.* See note on 4:7. *lift up his soul unto.* Worshiped or put his trust in (see 25:1–2). *soul.* See note on 6:3. *vanity.* What is "false," i.e. false gods, idols. *sworn deceitfully.* Thus it includes perjury (for the same concern see Ex 20:16; Lev 19:12; Jer 5:2; 7:9; Zech 5:4; Mal 3:5).

24:5 *righteousness.* That is, the fruits of vindication, such as righteous treatment from a faithful God; hence, here a synonym of "blessing" (see 23:3 and note).

24:6 *generation.* See note on 78:8. *Jacob.* See note on 14:7.

‡24:7–10 Heralding the approach of the King of glory (perhaps spoken by the king at the head of the assembled Israelites, with responses by the keepers of the gates). The Lord's arrival at His sanctuary in Zion completes His march from Egypt. "The LORD of hosts" (v. 10), "the LORD mighty in battle" (v. 8; see Ex 15:1–18), has triumphed over all His enemies and comes now in victory to His own city (see Ps 46; 48; 76; 87), His place of "rest" (132:8,14; see 68:7–8; Judg 5:4–5; Hab 3:3–7). Henceforth Jerusalem is the royal city of the kingdom of God (see note on 9:11).

24:7 *Lift up your heads . . . be ye lift up.* In jubilant reception of

The LORD mighty *in* battle.
9 Lift up your heads, O ye gates;
Even lift *them* up, ye everlasting doors;
And the King of glory shall come in.
10 Who is this King of glory?
The LORD of hosts, he *is* the King of glory. Selah.

Psalm 25

A Psalm of David.

1 Unto [a]thee, O LORD, do I lift up my soul.
2 O my God, I [a]trust in thee: let me not be ashamed,
[b]Let not mine enemies triumph over me.
3 Yea, let none that wait on thee be ashamed:
Let them be ashamed which transgress without cause.
4 [a]Shew me thy ways, O LORD;
Teach me thy paths.
5 Lead me in thy truth, and teach me:
For thou *art* the God of my salvation;
On thee do I wait all the day.
6 Remember, O LORD, [a][1]thy tender mercies and thy lovingkindnesses;
For they *have been* ever of old.
7 Remember not [a]the sins of my youth, nor my transgressions:
[b]According to thy mercy remember thou me
For thy goodness' sake, O LORD.
8 Good and upright *is* the LORD:
Therefore will he teach sinners in the way.
9 The meek will he guide in judgment:
And the meek will he teach his way.
10 All the paths of the LORD *are* mercy and truth
Unto such as keep his covenant and his testimonies.
11 [a]For thy name's sake, O LORD,
Pardon mine iniquity; [b]for it *is* great.
12 What man *is* he that feareth the LORD?
[a]Him shall he teach in the way *that* he shall choose.
13 [a]His soul [1]shall dwell at ease;
And [b]his seed shall inherit the earth.
14 [a]The secret of the LORD *is* with them that fear him;
[1]And he will shew them his covenant.
15 [a]Mine eyes *are* ever towards the LORD;
For he shall [1]pluck my feet out of the net.
16 [a]Turn thee unto me, and have mercy upon me;
For I *am* desolate and afflicted.
17 The troubles of my heart are enlarged:
O bring thou me out of my distresses.
18 [a]Look upon mine affliction and my pain;
And forgive all my sins.

25:1 [a]Ps. 86:4
25:2 [a]Ps. 34:8; Is. 28:16 [b]Ps. 13:4
25:4 [a]Ex. 33:13; Ps. 5:8
25:6 [1]Heb. *thy bowels* [a]Ps. 103:17; Is. 63:15
25:7 [a]Job 13:26; Jer. 3:25 [b]Ps. 51:1
25:11 [a]Ps. 31:3; 79:9 [b]Rom. 5:20
25:12 [a]Ps. 37:23
25:13 [1]Heb. *shall lodge in goodness* [a]Prov. 19:23 [b]Ps. 37:11
25:14 [1]Or, *And his covenant to make them know it* [a]Prov. 3:32; John 7:17
25:15 [1]Heb. *bring forth* [a]Ps. 141:8
25:16 [a]Ps. 69:16
25:18 [a]2 Sam. 16:12

the victorious King of glory (see 3:3; 27:6; 110:7). *gates.* Reference could be to the gates of either the city or the sanctuary. *doors.* A synonym for "gates," not in this case the doors of the gates (as in Judg 16:3; 1 Sam 21:13). The gates are personified for dramatic effect, as in Is 14:31.

24:10 *LORD of hosts.* See note on 1 Sam 1:3. Here it stands in climactic position.

‡Ps 25 The psalmist prays for God's covenant mercies when suffering affliction for sins and when enemies seize the occasion to attack, perhaps by trying to discredit the king through false accusations (see note on 5:9). Appealing to God's covenant benevolence (His compassion, lovingkindess, goodness, uprightness, truth and grace; see vv. 6–8,10,16) and to his own reliance on the Lord (see vv. 1,5,15,20–21), he prays for deliverance from his enemies (see vv. 2,19), for guidance in God's will (see vv. 4–5,21; see also vv. 8–10,12), for the forgiveness of his sins (see vv. 7,11,18) and for relief from his affliction (see vv. 2,16–18,20). These are related: God's forgiveness will express itself in removing his affliction, and then his enemies will no longer have occasion to slander him. And with God guiding him in "his way" (v. 9)—i.e., in "his covenant and his testimonies" (v. 10)—he will no longer wander into "transgressions" (v. 7). This psalm is linked with Ps 24 by its reference to "lifting up the soul" in reliance on God (see v. 1; 24:4). Structurally, the psalm is an alphabetic acrostic (somewhat irregular, with an additional, concluding verse that extends the lines beyond the alphabet).

25:1–3 Prayer for relief from distress or illness and the slander of his enemies that it occasions.

25:3 *without cause.* David has given no cause for the hostility of his adversaries.

25:4–7 Prayer for guidance and pardon.

‡25:4 *thy ways . . . thy paths.* Metaphors for "his covenant and his testimonies" (v. 10; see Deut 8:6; 10:12–13; 26:17; 30:16; Josh 22:5; see also vv. 8–9; 18:21; 51:13; 81:13; 95:10; 119:3,15; 128:1).

25:5 *thy truth.* A life of faithfulness to the Lord.

‡25:6–7 *Remember . . . Remember not.* Remember your long-standing ("ever of old") "tender mercies and . . . lovingkindnesses," but do not remember my long-standing sins (those "of my youth"). *lovingkindness.* See v. 10 and note on 6:4.

25:8–15 Confidence in the Lord's covenant favors. In this context of prayer for pardon, David implicitly identifies himself with sinners (v. 8) as well as with the meek (v. 9)—those who keep God's covenant (see vv. 10,14) and those who fear the Lord (see vv. 12,14). As sinner he is in need of forgiveness; as humble servant of the Lord he hopefully awaits God's pardon and guidance in covenant faithfulness.

25:9 *meek.* Those who acknowledge that they are without resources.

25:10 *paths of the LORD.* The Lord's benevolent dealings (see 103:7; 138:5) with those who are true to His ways (see note on v. 4).

25:11 *For thy name's sake.* See note on 23:3; see also 1 John 2:12. *name's.* See note on 5:11.

‡25:12 *the way that he shall choose.* Or "the way chosen for him"; the lifestyle that God sets forth in his commandments.

25:13 *inherit the earth.* Retain their family portion in the promised land (see 37:9,11,18,22,29,34; 69:36; Is 60:21).

25:14 *secret of the LORD.* The Lord takes into His confidence as friends those who fear Him (see Gen 18:17–19; Job 29:4). *fear.* See note on 15:4.

25:16–21 Prayer for relief from distress or illness and the attacks of his enemies.

25:17 *heart.* See note on 4:7.

19 Consider mine enemies; for they are
many;
And they hate me *with* [1] cruel hatred.
20 O keep my soul, and deliver me:
Let me not be ashamed; for I put my
trust in thee.
21 Let integrity and uprightness preserve
me;
For I wait on thee.
22 [a] Redeem Israel, O God, out of all his
troubles.

Psalm 26

A Psalm of David.

1 Judge [a] me, O LORD; for I have [b] walked
in mine integrity:
[c] I have trusted also in the LORD;
therefore I shall not slide.
2 [a] Examine me, O LORD, and prove me;
Try my reins and my heart.
3 For thy lovingkindness *is* before mine
eyes:
And [a] I have walked in thy truth.
4 [a] I have not sat with vain persons,
Neither will I go in with dissemblers.
5 I have [a] hated the congregation of
evildoers;
[b] And will not sit with the wicked.
6 [a] I will wash mine hands in innocency:
So will I compass thine altar, O LORD:
7 That *I* may publish with the voice of
thanksgiving,
And tell of all thy wondrous works.
8 LORD, [a] I have loved the habitation of
thy house,
And the place [1] where thine honour
dwelleth.
9 [a] [1] Gather not my soul with sinners,
Nor my life with [2] bloody men:
10 In whose hands *is* mischief,
And their right hand is [1] full *of* [a] bribes.
11 But *as for* me, I will walk in mine
integrity:
Redeem me, and be merciful unto me.
12 [a] My foot standeth in an [b] even place:
[c] In the congregations will I bless the
LORD.

Psalm 27

A Psalm of David.

1 The LORD *is* [a] my light and [b] my
salvation; whom shall I fear?
[c] The LORD *is* the strength of my life; of
whom shall I be afraid?

25:19 [1] Heb. *hatred of violence* 25:22 [a] Ps. 130:8 26:1 [a] Ps. 7:8 [b] 2 Ki. 20:3 [c] Ps. 28:7; Prov. 29:25 26:2 [a] Ps. 17:3 26:3 [a] 2 Ki. 20:3 26:4 [a] Ps. 1:1 26:5 [a] Ps. 31:6

26:5 [b] Ps. 1:1 26:6 [a] Ps. 73:13 26:8 [1] Heb. *of the tabernacle of thy honour* [a] Ps. 27:4 26:9 [1] Or, *Take not away* [2] Heb. *men of blood* [a] Ps. 28:3 26:10 [1] Heb. *filled* with [a] 1 Sam. 8:3 26:12 [a] Ps. 40:2 [b] Ps. 27:11 [c] Ps. 111:1 27:1 [a] Is. 60:19 [b] Ex. 15:2 [c] Ps. 62:2

‡25:21 *integrity and uprightness.* Personified virtues (see 23:6 and note). Pardon is not enough; David prays that God will enable him to live a life of unmarred moral rectitude—even as God is "good and upright" (v. 8; see 51:10–12).
25:22 A concluding prayer in behalf of all God's people (see 3:8 and note). *Redeem.* Here, as often, a synonym for "deliver."
‡Ps 26 A prayer for God's discerning mercies—to spare His faithful and godly servant from the death that overtakes the wicked and ungodly. The prayer for vindication (see v. 1) suggests that the king is threatened by the "vain persons" (v. 4) and "bloody men" (v. 9) to whom he refers (as in Ps 23; 25; 27–28). This psalm is linked with Ps 27–28 (see also Ps 23–24) by the theme of the Lord's house: Here David's love (v. 8) for the temple ("the habitation of thy house") testifies to the authenticity of his piety; in Ps 27 the Lord's temple is David's sanctuary from his enemies; in Ps 28 David directs his cry for help to the Lord's throne room (see 28:2 and note) in the temple.
26:1–8 An appeal for God to take account of David's moral integrity, his unwavering trust and his genuine delight in the Lord—not a boast of self-righteousness, such as that of the Pharisee (Luke 18:9–14).
26:1 *walked in mine integrity.* See v. 11 and note; a claim of moral integrity (see vv. 2–5), not sinless perfection (see 7:8; 41:12; 101:2; and especially 1 Ki 9:4). *trusted.* Obedience and trust are the two sides of godliness, as the Abraham story exemplifies (see Gen 12:4 and note; 22:12; see also Ps 34:8–14 and note).
26:2 *reins . . . heart.* See note on 7:9.
‡26:3 *thy lovingkindness . . . thy truth.* That is, your lovingkindness-and-truth (see 40:10). David keeps his eye steadfastly on the Lord's lovingkindness (see note on 6:4) and truth (faithfulness; see 25:10), which are pledged to those who "keep his covenant and his testimonies" (25:10). *have walked.* In order to receive the covenant benefits.
‡26:4–5 *sat with.* David refuses to settle in or associate himself with that company he describes as "vain persons," "dissemblers," "evildoers," "the wicked" (see 1:1 and note; see also Ps 101).
26:4 *vain persons . . . dissemblers.* Those who speak and deal fraudulently—or people like those described in Prov 6:12–14.
‡26:6 *wash mine hands in innocency.* Reference appears to be to a ritual claiming innocence. "Clean hands" and "a pure heart" are requisite for those who come to God (see 24:4 and note). *compass thine altar.* To vocally celebrate God's saving acts beside His altar was a public act of devotion in which one also invited all the assembled worshipers to praise (see 43:4).
26:7 *publish with . . . thanksgiving . . . tell of . . . wondrous works.* See note on 9:1.
26:8 *where thine honour dwelleth.* The presence of God's glory signaled the presence of God Himself (see Ex 24:16; 33:22). His glory dwelling in the tabernacle (see Ex 40:35), and later the temple (see 1 Ki 8:11), assured Israel of the Lord's holy, yet gracious, presence among them. John 1:14 announces that same presence in the Word who became flesh and who "dwelt among us."
26:9–11 An appeal that God will not bring on David the end (death) that awaits the wicked.
‡26:9 *Gather.* Take away in judgment. *soul.* See note on 6:3.
26:11 *walk in mine integrity.* A return to the appeal with which David began (see v. 1). *Redeem.* See note on 25:22.
26:12 A concluding confession of confidence (see note on 3:8) and a vow to praise (see note on 7:17). *even place.* Where the going is smooth and free from the danger of falling (see 143:10; Is 40:4; 42:16). *congregations.* See note on 1:5. *bless.* That is, "praise" (see note on 9:1).
Ps 27 David's triumphantly confident prayer to God to deliver him from all those who conspire to bring him down. The prayer presupposes the Lord's covenant with David (see 2 Sam 7). Faith's soliloquy (in the first stanza: vv. 1–6), which publicly testifies to the king's confident reliance on the Lord, introduces the prayer of vv. 7–12. The conclusion (vv. 13–14) echoes the confidence of vv. 1–6 and adds faith's dialogue with itself—faith exhorting faith to wait patiently for that which is sure, though not yet seen (see Ps 42–43; Heb 11:1). See further the introduction to Ps 26.
27:1–3 The king's security in the Lord in the face of all that his enemies can do (see Ps 2).
27:1 *light.* Often symbolizes well-being (see 97:11; Job 18:5–6;

2 When the wicked, *even* mine enemies and my foes, [1]came upon me to [a]eat up my flesh,
They stumbled and fell.
3 [a]Though a host should encamp against me, my heart shall not fear:
Though war should rise against me, in this *will* I *be* confident.
4 [a]One *thing* have I desired of the LORD, that will I seek after;
That I may [b]dwell in the house of the LORD all the days of my life,
To behold [c1]the beauty of the LORD, and to inquire in his temple.
5 For [a]in the time of trouble he shall hide me in his pavilion:
In the secret of his tabernacle shall he hide me;
He shall [b]set me up upon a rock.
6 And now shall [a]mine head be lifted up above mine enemies round about me:
Therefore will I offer in his tabernacle sacrifices [1]of joy;
I will sing, yea, I will sing *praises* unto the LORD.

7 Hear, O LORD, *when* I cry *with* my voice:
Have mercy also upon me, and answer me.
8 [1]*When thou saidst,* Seek ye my face; my heart said unto thee,
Thy face, LORD, will I seek.
9 [a]Hide not thy face *far* from me;
Put not thy servant away in anger:
Thou hast been my help; leave me not,
Neither forsake me, O God of my salvation.

27:2 [1]Heb. *approached against me* [a]Ps. 14:4
27:3 [a]Ps. 3:6
27:4 [1]Or, *the delight* [a]Ps. 26:8 [b]Luke 2:37 [c]Ps. 90:17
27:5 [a]Ps. 91:1 [b]Ps. 40:2
27:6 [1]Heb. *of shouting* [a]Ps. 3:3
27:8 [1]Or, *My heart said unto thee, Let my face seek thy face, etc.*
27:9 [a]Ps. 69:17
27:10 [1]Heb. *will gather me* [a]Is. 49:15
27:11 [1]Heb. *a way of plainness* [2]Heb. *those which observe me* [a]Ps. 25:4
27:13 [a]Ezek. 26:20
28:1 [1]Heb. *from me* [a]Ps. 83:1 [b]Ps. 88:4
28:2 [1]Or, *towards the oracle of thy sanctuary* [a]Ps. 5:7 [b]Ps. 138:2
28:3 [a]Ps. 12:2
28:4 [a]Rev. 18:6

10 [a]When my father and my mother forsake me,
Then the LORD [1]will take me up.
11 [a]Teach me thy way, O LORD,
And lead me in [1]a plain path, because of [2]mine enemies.
12 Deliver me not over unto the will of mine enemies:
For false witnesses are risen up against me, and such as breathe out cruelty.
13 *I had fainted,* unless I had believed
To see the goodness of the LORD [a]in the land of the living.
14 Wait on the LORD:
Be of good courage, and he shall strengthen thine heart:
Wait, I say, on the LORD.

Psalm 28

A Psalm of David.

1 Unto thee will I cry, O LORD, my rock;
[a]be not silent [1]to me:
[b]Lest, *if* thou be silent [1]to me, I become like them that go down into the pit.
2 Hear the voice of my supplications, when I cry unto thee,
[a]When I lift up my hands [b1]toward thy holy oracle.
3 Draw me not away with the wicked, and with the workers of iniquity,
[a]Which speak peace to their neighbours, but mischief *is* in their hearts.
4 [a]Give them according to their deeds,
And according to the wickedness of their endeavours:

22:28; 29:3; Prov 13:9; Lam 3:2) or life and salvation (see 18:28; Is 9:2; 49:6; 58:8; 59:9; Jer 13:16; Amos 5:18–20). To say "The LORD is my light" is to confess confidence in Him as the source of these benefits (see Is 10:17; 60:1–2,19–20; Mic 7:8–9). *my salvation.* My Savior (see v. 9).

27:2 *eat up my flesh.* See 7:2 and note.

27:3 *heart.* See note on 4:7.

27:4–6 The Lord's temple (or tabernacle) is the king's stronghold—because the Lord Himself is his stronghold (see v. 1; see notes on 9:11; 18:2).

‡27:4 *dwell in.* See note on 15:1. *beauty of the LORD.* His unfailing benevolence. Cf. 90:17.

‡27:5 *secret of his tabernacle.* His secret hiding place. See 31:20; 32:7; 61:4; 91:1.

27:6 *will I offer . . . sacrifices.* See note on 7:17. *I will sing.* See note on 9:1.

27:7–12 Prayer for deliverance from treacherous enemies. These remain unspecified, whether from inside or outside the kingdom or both. Their chief weapon is false charges intent on discrediting the king (see note on 5:9).

27:9 *Hide not thy face.* See note on 13:1. *anger.* See note on 2:5. *Thou hast been my help.* Or "Be my helper."

27:10 *the LORD will take me up.* Or "may the LORD receive me."

27:11 *Teach me thy way.* Only those who know and do the Lord's will can expect to receive favorable response to their prayers (see Ps 24–26; see also 2 Sam 7:14). *lead me in a plain path.* See 5:8 and note.

27:13–14 Concluding note of confidence (see note on 3:8).

27:13 *goodness of the LORD.* The "good" things promised in the Lord's covenant with David (see 2 Sam 7:28; see also 31:19 and note). *land of the living.* This life.

27:14 *Wait on the LORD.* Faith encouraging faith (see 42:5,11; 43:5; 62:5).

‡Ps 28 A prayer for deliverance from deadly peril at the hands of malicious and God-defying enemies. As with Ps 25, the prayer ends with intercession for all the people of the Lord (see 3:8 and note). Reference in the last verse to the Lord as the shepherd of His people ("Feed them") connects this psalm with Ps 23 and probably marks off Ps 23–28 as a collection linked by many common themes. See introductions to Ps 26; 29.

28:1–2 Initial appeal to be heard.

28:1 *rock.* See note on 18:2. *be silent to me.* Do not act in my behalf. *pit.* Metaphor for the grave (see note on 30:1).

‡28:2 *lift up my hands.* In worship and prayer (see 63:4; 134:2; 141:2). *thy holy oracle.* Lit. "your holy sanctuary." The inner sanctuary of the temple (see 1 Ki 6:5), was where the ark of the covenant stood (see 1 Ki 8:6–8); it was God's throne room on earth.

28:3–5 Prayer for the Lord, enthroned in the temple, to deliver His servant and deal in judgment with those who harbor malice toward the king and God's people and defy God Himself.

28:3 *mischief is in their hearts.* See note on 5:9. *hearts.* See note on 4:7.

‡28:4 *Give them.* Pay them back. See note on 5:10; see also Mat 16:27; 2 Tim 4:14; Rev 20:12–13; 22:12.

Give them after the work of their hands;
Render to them their desert.
5 Because [a]they regard not the works of the LORD,
Nor the operation of his hands,
He shall destroy them, and not build them up.

6 Blessed *be* the LORD, because he hath heard the voice of my supplications.
7 The LORD *is* [a]my strength and my shield;
My heart [b]trusted in him, and I am helped:
Therefore my heart greatly rejoiceth;
And with my song will I praise him.
8 The LORD *is* [1]their strength,
And he *is* the [a2]saving strength of his anointed.
9 Save thy people,
And bless [a]thine inheritance:
[1]Feed them also, [b]and lift them up for ever.

Psalm 29

A Psalm of David.

1 [a]Give unto the LORD, O [1]ye mighty,
Give unto the LORD glory and strength.
2 Give unto the LORD [1]the glory due unto his name;
Worship the LORD [2]in [a]the beauty of holiness.
3 The voice of the LORD *is* upon the waters:
[a]The God of glory thundereth:
The LORD *is* upon [1]many waters.
4 The voice of the LORD *is* [1]powerful;
The voice of the LORD *is* [2]full of majesty.
5 The voice of the LORD breaketh the cedars;
Yea, the LORD breaketh [a]the cedars of Lebanon.
6 [a]He maketh them also to skip like a calf;
Lebanon and [b]Sirion like a young unicorn.
7 The voice of the LORD [1]divideth the flames of fire.
8 The voice of the LORD shaketh the wilderness;
The LORD shaketh the wilderness of [a]Kadesh.
9 The voice of the LORD maketh the hinds [1]to calve,
And discovereth the forests:
And in his temple [2]doth every one speak of *his* glory.

28:5 [a]Is. 5:12
28:7 [a]Ps. 18:2 [b]Ps. 13:5
28:8 [1]Or, *his strength* [2]Heb. *strength of salvations* [a]Ps. 20:6
28:9 [1]Or, *Rule* [a]Deut. 9:29 [b]Ezra 1:4
29:1 [1]Heb. *ye sons of the mighty* [a]1 Chr. 16:28
29:2 [1]Heb. *the honour of his name* [2]Or, *in his glorious sanctuary* [a]2 Chr. 20:21
29:3 [1]Or, *great waters* [a]Job 37:4,5
29:4 [1]Heb. *in power* [2]Heb. *in majesty*
29:5 [a]Is. 2:13
29:6 [a]Ps. 114:4 [b]Deut. 3:9
29:7 [1]Heb. *cutteth out*
29:8 [a]Num. 13:26
29:9 [1]Or, *to be in pain* [2]Or, *every whit of it uttereth, etc.*

‡28:5 *works of the LORD.* His redemption of Israel, the establishment of Israel as His kingdom (by covenant, Ex 19–24), and the appointment of the house of David (also by covenant, 2 Sam 7) as His earthly regent over His people. *operation of his hands.* God's works or deeds. By "the work of their hands" (v. 4), "the wicked" (v. 3) show that they do not acknowledge Israel and David's regency as the work of God's hands. *He shall destroy.* Or "May He destroy."
28:6–7 Joyful praise, in confidence of being heard (see note on 3:8).
28:7 *shield.* See note on 3:3. *heart.* See note on 4:7. *will I praise him.* See note on 7:17.
28:8–9 The Lord and His people (see note on 3:8).
‡28:9 *Save . . . bless.* God's two primary acts by which He effects His people's well-being: He saves from time to time as circumstances require; He blesses day by day to make their lives and labors fruitful. *thine inheritance.* See Deut 9:29. *Feed.* Or "Shepherd." See introduction; see also 80:1; Is 40:11; Jer 31:10; Ezek 34; Mic 5:4. The answer to this prayer—the last, full answer—has come in the ministry of the "good shepherd" (John 10:11,14).
‡Ps 29 A hymn in praise of the King of creation, whose majesty and power are trumpeted by the thunderbolts of the rainstorm—as the storm rose above the Mediterranean ("thundereth . . . upon many waters," v. 3), swept across the Lebanon range (see vv. 5–6) and rolled over the wilds of Kadesh (northern Kadesh, on the upper reaches of the Orontes River, v. 8). The glory of the Lord is not only visible in the creation (19:1–6; 104 and often elsewhere); it is also audible in creation's most awesome voice. This hymn to Yahweh ("the LORD") served also as a testimony and protest against the worship of the Canaanite god Baal, who was thought to be the divine power present in the thunderstorm. Its climactic word (that "in his temple doth every one speak of his glory") suggests that in its present location it was intended to serve as a conclusion to the small collection, Ps 23–28 (see introductions to Ps 26; 28). In its structure, a two-verse introduction and a two-verse conclusion enclose the seven-verse body of the psalm. In both the introduction and the conclusion the name Yahweh ("the LORD") is sounded four times; in the body of the psalm it is heard ten times. "The voice of the LORD" is repeated seven times—the seven thunders of God. (The numbers four, seven and ten often signified completeness in OT number symbolism.)
29:1–2 A summons to all beings in the divine realm (see note on v. 1) to worship the Lord—adapted from a conventional call to praise in the liturgy of the temple (see 96:7–9; 1 Chr 16:28–29).
29:1 *mighty.* Lit. "sons of god(s)." Perhaps reference is to the angelic host (see 103:20; 148:2; Job 1:6 and note; 2:1; Is 6:2), or possibly to all those foolishly thought to be gods—as in Ps 97 (see v. 7), which has several thematic links with this psalm. The Lord alone must be acknowledged as the divine King.
‡29:2 *name.* See note on 5:1. *in the beauty of holiness.* It is uncertain whether the phrase describes God Himself or the sanctuary or the (priestly) garb the worshipers are to wear when they approach God. The use of an almost identical Hebrew phrase in 110:3 (translated "in the beauties of holiness") may give support for the last alternative.
29:3–9 Praise of the Lord, whose voice the crashing thunder is (see 68:4,33). The sound and fury of creation's awesome displays of power proclaim the glory of Israel's God.
29:5 *cedars of Lebanon.* The mightiest of trees (see Is 2:13 and note).
‡29:6 *skip.* See 114:4 and note. *unicorn.* See note on 22:21.
‡29:7 *divideth the flames of fire.* Sends the forked lightning across the sky.
‡29:9 *discovereth.* Lit. "strips or lays bare." *temple.* A primary thematic link with Ps 23–28. Reference may be to the temple in Jerusalem or to God's heavenly temple, where He sits enthroned (see 2:4; 11:4; 113:5; Is 6:1; 40:22) as the Lord of all creation. But perhaps it is the creation itself that here is named

10 The LORD sitteth upon the flood;
Yea, [a]the LORD sitteth King for ever.
11 [a]The LORD will give strength unto his people;
The LORD will bless his people with peace.

Psalm 30

A Psalm *and* Song [a]*at* the dedication of the house of David.

1 I will extol thee, O LORD; for thou hast [a]lifted me up,
And hast not made my foes to [b]rejoice over me.
2 O LORD my God, I cried unto thee, and thou hast healed me.
3 O LORD, [a]thou hast brought up my soul from the grave:
Thou hast kept me alive, that I should not go down *to* the pit.
4 Sing unto the LORD, O ye saints of his,
And give thanks [1]at the remembrance of his holiness.
5 For [a][1]his anger *endureth but* a moment; [b]in his favour *is* life:
Weeping may endure [2]for a night, but [3]joy *cometh* in the morning.
6 And in my prosperity I said,
I shall never be moved.
7 LORD, by thy favour thou hast [1]made my mountain to stand strong:
[a]Thou didst hide thy face, *and* I was troubled.
8 I cried to thee, O LORD;
And unto the LORD I made supplication.
9 What profit *is there* in my blood, when I go down to the pit?
[a]Shall the dust praise thee? shall it declare thy truth?
10 Hear, O LORD, and have mercy upon me:
LORD, be thou my helper.
11 Thou hast turned for me my mourning into dancing:
Thou hast put off my sackcloth, and girded me *with* gladness;
12 To the end that [a][1]*my* glory may sing *praise* to thee, and not be silent.
O LORD my God, I will give thanks unto thee for ever.

29:10 [a]Ps. 10:16
29:11 [a]Ps. 28:8
30:T [a]Deut. 20:5
30:1 [a]Ps. 28:9 [b]Ps. 25:2
30:3 [a]Ps. 86:13
30:4 [1]Or, *to the memorial*
30:5 [1]Heb. there is but *a moment in his anger* [a]Ps. 103:9 [b]Ps. 63:3
30:5 [2]Heb. *in the evening* [3]Heb. *singing*
30:7 [1]Heb. *settled strength for my mountain* [a]Ps. 104:29
30:9 [a]Ps. 6:5
30:12 [1]That is, my *tongue*, or, my *soul* [a]Ps. 57:8

God's temple (see note on 24:2). Then the "every one" which declares God's "glory" is absolutely all—all creation shouts His praise (cf. 150:6). *glory.* See note on 26:8.

29:10–11 The Lord's absolute and everlasting rule is committed to His people's complete salvation and unmixed blessedness—the crowning comfort in a world where threatening tides seem to make everything uncertain.

29:10 *upon the flood.* As the One who by His word brought the ordered creation out of the formless "deep" (Gen 1:2,6–10); or the reference may be to the Noahic flood (see Gen 6:17).

‡Ps 30 A song of praise publicly celebrating the Lord's deliverance from the threat of death, probably brought on by illness ("thou hast healed me" v. 2; see note on 7:17). The psalm is framed by commitments to praise (see vv. 1,12).

‡30 title *Song.* See titles of Ps 18; 45–46; 48; 65–68; 75–76; 83; 87–88; 92; 108—all psalms of praise except 83; 88. In addition there are the songs "of degrees" (or "of ascents") (Ps 120–134). *at the dedication of the house of David.* If "of David" indicates authorship, the most probable occasion for the psalm is recorded in 1 Chr 21:1–22:6. In 1 Chr 22:1–6 David dedicated both property and building materials for the temple, and he may well have intended that Ps 30 be used at the dedication of the temple itself. If this is the case, vv. 2–3 would refer to David's predicament in 1 Chr 21:17–30. The "favour" of v. 5 would be an echo of the "mercies" of 1 Chr 21:13, and v. 6 would refer to his sin of misplaced trust in a large, superior army (see 1 Chr 21:1–8). Later, the psalm came to be applied to the exile experience of Israel. In Jewish liturgical practice dating from Talmudic times it is chanted at Hanukkah, the feast that celebrates the rededication of the temple by Judas Maccabeus (165 B.C.) after its desecration by Antiochus Epiphanes (168). In such communal use, the "I" of the psalm becomes the corporate "person" of Israel—a common mode of speaking in the OT.

30:1–3 Introductory announcement of the occasion for praise.

30:1 *lifted me up.* The vivid imagery that associates distress with the need to be "lifted" out of trouble—so expressive of universal human experience—is common in OT poetry (see 69:2,15; 71:20; 88:6; 130:1; Lam 3:55; Jonah 2:2). The depths are often linked, as here, with Sheol and "the pit" (v. 3), together with a cluster of related associations: silence (see 31:17; 94:17; 115:17; 1 Sam 2:9), darkness (see 88:6,12; 143:3; Job 10:21–22; 17:13; Eccl 6:4; Lam 3:6), death and destruction (see v. 9; 18:4; 55:23, 88:11; Is 38:17; Hos 13:14), dust (see v. 9; 7:5; 22:15,29; Job 17:16; 40:13; Is 26:19; 29:4), mire (see 40:2; 69:2,14; 40:2) and clay (see 40:2; Job 30:19). See also note on 49:14. *my foes to rejoice over me.* See introduction to Ps 6.

‡30:3 *the grave.* Or "Sheol." Figurative of a "brink-of-death" experience, as in 18:5; Jonah 2:2. *pit.* See note on 28:1.

30:4–5 Call to the gathered worshipers to take up the praise of God (see note on 9:1).

‡30:4 *saints.* Lit. "godly ones." See note on 4:3. *remembrance.* Lit. "memorial" (see Is 26:8; Hos 12:5).

30:5 *anger.* See note on 2:5. *but a moment.* See Is 54:7. *endure for a night.* Lit. "come in at evening to lodge." The figure is that of a guest lodging for only one night.

30:6–10 Expanded recollection of the Lord's gracious deliverance.

30:6–7 In his security he had grown arrogant, forgetful of who had made his "mountain to stand strong," but the Lord reminded him.

30:6 *never be moved.* He spoke as do the wicked (see 10:6), hence lost the blessing of the righteous (see 15:5). *moved.* See note on 10:6.

30:7 *made my mountain to stand strong.* Reference may be to David's security in his mountain fortress, Zion; or that mountain fortress may here serve as a metaphor for David's state as a vigorous and victorious king, the "mountain" on which he sat with such secure confidence in God. *hide thy face.* See note on 13:1.

30:8–10 Shattered strength swept away all self-reliance; at the brink of death his cries for God's mercy rose.

‡30:9 See note on 6:5. *thy truth.* Faithfulness to your covenant.

30:11–12 God answered—and David vows to prolong his praise forever (see note on 7:17). Dancing and joy replace wailing and sackcloth so that songs of praise, not silence, may attend the acts of God.

30:11 *sackcloth.* A symbol of mourning (see 35:13; Gen 37:34).

‡30:12 *my glory.* See note on 7:5.

Psalm 31

To the chief Musician, A Psalm of David.

1 [a]In thee, O LORD, do I put my trust;
Let me never be ashamed:
Deliver me in thy righteousness.
2 [a]Bow down thine ear to me; deliver me speedily:
Be thou [1]my strong rock,
For a house of defence to save me.
3 [a]For thou *art* my rock and my fortress;
Therefore [b]for thy name's sake lead me, and guide me.
4 Pull me out of the net that they have laid privily for me:
For thou *art* my strength.
5 [a]Into thine hand I commit my spirit:
Thou hast redeemed me, O LORD God of truth.
6 I have hated them [a]that regard lying vanities:
But I trust in the LORD.
7 I will be glad and rejoice in thy mercy:
For thou hast considered my trouble;
Thou hast [a]known my soul in adversities;
8 And hast not [a]shut me up into the hand of the enemy:
Thou hast set my feet in a large room.
9 Have mercy upon me, O LORD, for I am in trouble:
[a]Mine eye is consumed with grief, *yea,* my soul and my belly.
10 For my life is spent with grief, and my years with sighing:
My strength faileth because of mine iniquity, and my bones are consumed.
11 [a]I was a reproach among all mine enemies,
But [b]especially among my neighbours, and a fear to mine acquaintance:
[c]They that did see me without fled from me.
12 [a]I am forgotten as a dead man out of mind:
I am like [1]a broken vessel.
13 [a]For I have heard the slander of many:
[b]Fear *was* on every side:
While they [c]took counsel together against me,
They devised to take away my life.
14 But I trusted in thee, O LORD:
I said, Thou *art* my God.
15 My times *are* in thy hand:
Deliver me from the hand of mine enemies, and from them that persecute me.
16 [a]Make thy face to shine upon thy servant:
Save me for thy mercy's sake.
17 [a]Let me not be ashamed, O LORD; for I have called upon thee:
Let the wicked be ashamed, *and* [b][1]let them be silent in the grave.
18 [a]Let the lying lips be put to silence;
Which [b]speak [1]grievous things proudly and contemptuously against the righteous.
19 [a]O how great *is* thy goodness, which thou hast laid up for them that fear thee;

31:1 [a]Ps. 22:5
31:2 [1]Heb. *to me for a rock of strength* [a]Ps. 71:2
31:3 [a]Ps. 18:2 [b]Ps. 23:3
31:5 [a]Luke 23:46
31:6 [a]Jonah 2:8
31:7 [a]John 10:27
31:8 [a]Deut. 32:30
31:9 [a]Ps. 6:7
31:11 [a]Is. 53:4 [b]Job 19:13 [c]Ps. 64:8
31:12 [1]Heb. *a vessel that perisheth* [a]Ps. 88:4,5
31:13 [a]Jer. 20:10 [b]Lam. 2:22 [c]Mat. 27:1
31:16 [a]Ps. 4:6
31:17 [1]Or, *let them be cut off for the grave* [a]Ps. 25:2 [b]Ps. 115:17
31:18 [1]Heb. *a hard* thing [a]Ps. 120:2 [b]Ps. 94:4
31:19 [a]Is. 64:4

Ps 31 A prayer for deliverance when confronted by a conspiracy so powerful and open that all David's friends abandoned him. According to Luke 23:46, Jesus on the cross applied Ps 31:5 to His own circumstances; thus those who share in His sufferings at the hands of anti-Christian forces are encouraged to hear and use this psalm in a new light (see Acts 7:59; 1 Pet 4:19). No psalm expresses a more sturdy trust in the Lord when powerful human forces threaten. The heart of the prayer itself is found in vv. 9–18, which is both preceded and followed by eight Hebrew poetic lines that resound with the theme of trust (see v. 14). Verse 13, at the center of the psalm, expresses most clearly the prayer's occasion.

31 title *To the chief Musician.* See note on Ps 4 title.

31:1–5 Initial appeal to the Lord, the faithful refuge.

31:1 *righteousness.* See note on 4:1.

31:2 *rock.* See note on 18:2.

31:3 *for thy name's sake.* God's honor is at stake in the safety of His servant now under attack (see note on 23:3). *name's.* See note on 5:11. *lead me, and guide me.* As a shepherd (see 23:2–3 and notes).

31:4 *net . . . laid privily for me.* By his enemies (see v. 11).

‡31:5 *Into thine hand I commit my spirit.* The climactic expression of trust in the Lord—quoted by Jesus in Luke 23:46. *commit.* Lit. "deposit" (cf. "laid up" in Jer 36:20), here in the very hands of God, thus entrusting to God's care (see Lev 6:4; 1 Ki 14:27). *my spirit.* His very life. *redeemed.* See note on 25:22. *God of truth.* The faithful, trustworthy God (see note on 30:9).

31:6–8 Confession of loyal trust in the Lord, whose past mercies to David when enemies threatened are joyfully recalled.

31:6 *hated.* Refused to be associated with.

31:7 *mercy.* See vv. 16,21; see also note on 6:4. *soul.* See note on 6:3.

31:8 *large room.* See note on 18:19.

31:9–13 The distress described: He is utterly drained physically and emotionally (see vv. 9–10; see also 22:14–15); all his friends have abandoned him like a piece of broken pottery (see vv. 11–12); and all this because the conspiracy against him is so strong (v. 13).

31:9 *eye is consumed.* See note on 13:3. *soul.* See note on 6:3.

31:10 *bones.* See note on 6:2.

31:11–12 Abandonment by friends was a common experience at a time when God seemed to have withdrawn His favor (see 38:11; 41:9; 69:8; 88:8,18; Job 19:13–19; Jer 12:6; 15:17).

31:13 *slander.* See note on 5:9. *Fear was on every side.* See notes on Jer 6:25; 20:3.

31:14–18 His trust in the Lord is unwavering; his defense against his powerful enemies is his reliance on God's faithfulness and discerning judgment.

31:14 Cf. v. 22.

31:15 *My times are in thy hand.* All the events and circumstances of life are in the hands of the Lord, "my God" (v. 14).

31:16 *face to shine.* See note on 13:1.

31:17–18 *Let the wicked . . . be silent.* See note on 5:10.

31:18 *lying lips.* See note on 5:9. *righteous.* See note on 1:5.

31:19–20 Confident anticipation of God's saving help (see note on 3:8).

31:19 *laid up.* David deposits his life in the hands of God to share in the covenant benefits that God has stored up for His

Which thou hast wrought for them that
trust in thee
Before the sons of men!
20 [a]Thou shalt hide them in the secret of
thy presence from the pride of man:
[b]Thou shalt keep them secretly in a
pavilion from the strife of tongues.
21 Blessed *be* the LORD: for [a]he hath
shewed me his marvellous kindness
[b]in a [1]strong city.
22 For [a]I said in my haste, [b]I am cut off
from before thine eyes:
Nevertheless thou heardest the voice
of my supplications when I cried
unto thee.
23 [a]O love the LORD, all ye his saints:
For the LORD preserveth the faithful,
And plentifully rewardeth the proud
doer.
24 [a]Be of good courage, and he shall
strengthen your heart,
All ye that hope in the LORD.

Psalm 32

[1]*A Psalm* of David, Maschil.

1 Blessed *is he whose* [a]transgression *is*
forgiven, whose sin *is* covered.
2 Blessed *is* the man unto whom the
LORD [a]imputeth not iniquity,
And [b]in whose spirit *there is* no guile.
3 When I kept silence, my bones waxed
old
Through my roaring all the day long.
4 For day and night thy [a]hand was heavy
upon me:
My moisture is turned into the drought
of summer. Selah.
5 I acknowledged my sin unto thee,
And mine iniquity have I not hid.
[a]I said, I will confess my transgressions
unto the LORD;
And thou forgavest the iniquity of my
sin. Selah.
6 [a]For this shall every one *that is* godly
[b]pray unto thee [1]in a time when
thou mayest be found:
Surely in the floods of great waters
they shall not come nigh unto him.
7 [a]Thou *art* my hiding place; thou shalt
preserve me from trouble;
Thou shalt compass me about *with*
[b]songs of deliverance. Selah.
8 I will instruct thee and teach thee in
the way which thou shalt go:
[1]I will guide thee with mine eye.

31:20 [a]Ps. 27:5 [b]Job 5:21
31:21 [1]Or, *fenced city* [a]Ps. 17:7 [b]1 Sam. 23:7
31:22 [a]Ps. 116:11 [b]Lam. 3:54
31:23 [a]Ps. 34:9
31:24 [a]Ps. 27:14
32:T [1]Or, A Psalm *of David giving instruction*
32:1 [a]Ps. 85:2
32:2 [a]2 Cor. 5:19 [b]John 1:47
32:4 [a]Job 33:7
32:5 [a]Prov. 28:13
32:6 [1]Heb. *in a time of finding* [a]1 Tim. 1:16 [b]Is. 55:6
32:7 [a]Ps. 9:9 [b]Ex. 15:1
32:8 [1]Heb. *I will counsel* thee, *mine eye* shall be *upon thee*

faithful servants ("goodness"; see Ex 18:9; Num 10:29,32; Deut 26:11; Josh 21:45; 23:14–15; 2 Chr 6:41; Neh 9:25,35; Is 63:7; Jer 31:12, 14; 33:9). *fear.* See note on 15:4. *wrought . . . Before the sons of men.* Thus showing the Lord's approval of and His standing with His faithful servants in contrast to the accusations of their adversaries (see 86:17).

31:20 *secret of thy presence.* See note on 27:5. *strife of tongues.* See "slander" (v. 13) and "lying lips" (v. 18).

31:21–22 Praise anticipating deliverance (see note on 12:5–6).

‡31:21 *strong city.* Or "besieged city," a metaphor for the threat he had experienced.

31:22 *cut off from before thine eyes.* See note on 13:1.

31:23–24 Praise culminates by encouraging the saints (see 62:8).

31:23 *saints.* See note on 4:3. *the faithful.* Those who maintain moral integrity. *the proud.* Those who refuse to live in humble reliance on the Lord. They arrogantly try to make their way in the world either as a law to themselves (see, e.g., v. 18; 10:2–11; 73:6; 94:2–7; Deut 8:14; Is 2:17; Ezek 28:2,5; Hos 13:6) or by relying on false gods (see Jer 13:9–10). Hence "the proud" is often equivalent to "the wicked."

Ps 32 A grateful testimony of joy for God's gift of forgiveness toward those who with integrity confess their sins and are receptive to God's rule in their lives. The psalm appears to be a liturgical dialogue between David and God in the presence of the worshipers at the sanctuary. In vv. 1–2 and again in v. 11 David speaks to the assembly; in vv. 3–7 he speaks to God (in their hearing); in vv. 8–10 he is addressed by one of the Lord's priests (but see note on vv. 8–10). In traditional Christian usage the psalm has been numbered among the penitential psalms (see introduction to Ps 6).

‡32 title *Maschil.* Occurs also in the titles of Ps 42; 44–45; 52–55; 74; 78; 88–89; 142. The Hebrew word perhaps indicates that these psalms contain instruction in godliness (see 41:1, "he that considereth"; 14:2; 53:2, "any that did understand"; 47:7, "with understanding").

32:1–2 Exuberant proclamation of the happy state of those who experience God's forgiveness. *Blessed . . . Blessed.* See note on 1:1. Repetition underscores. *is forgiven . . . is covered . . . imputeth not.* Repetition with variation emphasizes and illumines. For Paul's use of these verses see Rom 4:6–8.

32:2 *in whose spirit there is no guile.* Only those honest with God receive pardon.

32:3–5 Testimony to a personal experience of God's pardon. God's heavy hand, brought down "day and night" on the stubborn silence of unacknowledged sin, filled life with groaning, but full confession brought blessed relief. Neither the sin nor the form of suffering is identified, other than that the latter was physically and psychologically devastating. But it would be uncharacteristic of the Psalms to speak of mere emotional disturbance brought on by suppressed guilt. Some affliction, perhaps illness, was the instrument of God's chastisement (see Ps 38).

32:4 *My moisture . . . drought of summer.* Under God's heavy hand he wilted like a plant in the heat of summer.

32:5 Again repetition is used (see note on vv. 1–2). *sin . . . iniquity . . . transgressions.* See 51:1–2; the three most common OT words for evil thoughts and actions (see Is 59:12 and note). *confess.* See Ps 51; 2 Sam 12:13.

32:6–7 A chastened confession that life is secure only with God.

‡32:6 Though addressed to God as confession, it is also intended for the ears of the fellow worshipers. He admonishes them to "seek ye the LORD while he may be found . . . while he is near" (Is 55:6) and not to foolishly provoke His withdrawal—and the coming near of His heavy hand—as David had done. A God who forgives is a God to whom one can entrust and devote his life (see 130:4). *godly.* See note on 4:3. *floods of great waters.* Powerful imagery for threatening forces or circumstances. This and related imagery was borrowed from ancient Near Eastern creation myths. In many of these a primal mass of chaotic waters (their threatening and destructive forces were often depicted as a many-headed monster of the deep; see 74:13–14 and note) had to be subdued by the creator-god before he could fashion the world and/or rule as the divine king over the earth. Though in these myths the chaotic waters were subdued when the present world was created, they remained

9 [a]Be ye not as the horse,
Or as the mule, *which have* [b]no understanding:
Whose mouth must be held in with bit and bridle,
Lest *they* come near unto thee.
10 [a]Many sorrows *shall be* to the wicked:
But [b]he that trusteth in the LORD, mercy shall compass him about.

11 [a]Be glad in the LORD, and rejoice, ye righteous:
And shout for joy, all *ye that are* upright in heart.

Psalm 33

1 Rejoice [a]in the LORD, O ye righteous:
For [b]praise is comely for the upright.
2 Praise the LORD with harp:
Sing unto him with the psaltery [a]*and* an instrument of ten strings.
3 [a]Sing unto him a new song;
Play skilfully with a loud noise.
4 For the word of the LORD *is* right;
And all his works *are done* in truth.
5 [a]He loveth righteousness and judgment:
[b]The earth is full *of* the [1]goodness of the LORD.
6 [a]By the word of the LORD were the heavens made;
And all the host of them [b]by the breath of his mouth.
7 [a]He gathereth the waters of the sea together as a heap:
He layeth up the depth in storehouses.
8 Let all the earth fear the LORD:
Let all the inhabitants of the world stand in awe of him.
9 For [a]he spake, and it was *done;*
He commanded, and it stood fast.
10 [a]The LORD [1]bringeth the counsel of the heathen to nought:
He maketh the devices of the people of none effect.
11 [a]The counsel of the LORD standeth for ever,
The thoughts of his heart [1]to all generations.

32:9 [a]Prov. 26:3 [b]Job 35:11
32:10 [a]Rom. 2:9 [b]Prov. 16:20
32:11 [a]Ps. 64:10
33:1 [a]Ps. 32:11 [b]Ps. 147:1
33:2 [a]Ps. 92:3
33:3 [a]Ps. 96:1

33:5 [1]Or, *mercy* [a]Ps. 11:7 [b]Ps. 119:64
33:6 [a]Heb. 11:3 [b]Job 26:13
33:7 [a]Job 26:10
33:9 [a]Gen. 1:3
33:10 [1]Heb. *maketh frustrate* [a]Is. 8:10
33:11 [1]Heb. *to generation and generation* [a]Job 23:13

a constant threat to the security and well-being of the present order in the earth (the world in which man lives). Hence by association they were linked with anything that in human experience endangered or troubled that order. They were also associated with the sea, whose angry waves seemed determined at times to engulf the land. Since in Canaanite mythology Sea and Death were the two great enemies of Baal ("lord" of earth), imagery drawn from both realms was used by OT poets, sometimes side by side, to depict threats and distress (see 18:4–5,16; 42:7; 65:7; 74:12–14; 77:16,19; 89:9–10; 93:3–4; 124:4–5; 144:7–8; Job 7:12; 26:12; 38:8–11; Is 5:30; 8:7–8; 17:12–14; 51:9–10; Jer 5:22; 47:2; 51:55; Hab 3:8–10; see also note on Sol 8:7). For imagery associated with the realm of death see notes on 30:1; 49:14.

32:7 *compass me about with songs of deliverance.* Because of Your help, I will be surrounded by people celebrating Your acts of deliverance, as I bring my thank offerings to You (see notes on 7:17; 9:1; see also 35:27; 51:8).

32:8–10 A priestly word of godly instruction, either to David (do not be foolish toward God again) or to those who have just been exhorted to trust in the Lord (to trust add obedience). Some believe that the psalmist himself here turns to others to warn them against the ways into which he had fallen (see 51:13).

32:9 God's servant must be wiser than beasts, more open to God's will than horses and mules are to the will of their masters (see Is 1:3).

32:10 *mercy.* See note on 6:4.

32:11 A final word to the assembled worshipers—let the praise of God resound (see note on 9:1). See also note on 1:5. *heart.* See note on 4:7.

Ps 33 A liturgy in praise of the Lord, the sovereign God of Israel. In the Psalms, calls to praise (as in vv. 1–3) and motivations for praise (as in vv. 4–19) belong to the language of praise (see note on 9:1). Most likely the voices of the Levitical choir (see 1 Chr 16:7–36; 25:1) are heard in this psalm. Perhaps the choir leader spoke vv. 1–3, the choir vv. 4–19, and the people responded with the words of vv. 20–22. The original occasion is unknown, but reference to a "new song" (see note on v. 3) suggests a national deliverance, such as Judah experienced in the time of Jehoshaphat (see 2 Chr 20) or Hezekiah (see 2 Ki 19); see vv. 10–11,16–17. Along with Ps 1–2; 10 (but see introduction to Ps 9), this is one of the only four psalms in Book I without a superscription. Although structurally not an alphabetic acrostic like the psalm that follows it, the length of the psalm (22 verses) has been determined by the length of the Hebrew alphabet (22 letters); see Ps 38; 103; Lam 5. The body of the psalm is framed by a three-verse introduction (call to praise) and a three-verse conclusion (response to praise). In vv. 4–19 are heard the praise of the Lord, developed in two parts of eight verses each (vv. 4–11, 12–19).

33:1–3 The call to praise. Cf. Eph 5:19.

‡33:1 *righteous.* The assembly of worshipers (see note on 1:5). *praise is comely for the upright.* It is fitting for godly people to praise the Lord.

33:3 *new song.* Celebrating God's saving act, as in 40:3; 96:1; 98:1; 144:9; 149:1; see Is 42:10; Rev 5:9; 14:3; see also note on 7:17.

33:4–19 The praise, in two eight-verse parts.

33:4–11 Because the Lord is the Creator, who by His power imposed His order on the creation (see Gen 1), no power or combination of powers can thwart His plan and purpose to save His people. (Hence His chosen people are the blessed nation; see vv. 12–19.)

33:4 *word.* God's royal word by which He governs all things (see 107:20; 147:15,18). *right.* Not chaotic, devious or erratic. Under the Lord's rule in the creation there is goodness, order and dependability.

33:5 *loveth.* Delights in doing. *righteousness and judgment.* See note on 5:8. *goodness of the LORD.* Here, His goodness to all His creatures (see 36:5–9; 104:27–28; see also note on 6:4).

33:6 *word.* God's creating word (see v. 9; 104:7; 119:89; Gen 1; Job 38:8–11; Heb 11:3).

33:7 *as a heap . . . storehouses.* Like a householder storing up his olive oil and grain (see 104:9; Gen 1:9–10; Job 38:8–11; Prov 8:29; Jer 5:22).

33:8 *all the earth . . . all the inhabitants.* Not only Israel, but all mankind, for all experience the goodness of His sovereign rule (see note on 9:1)—but He foils all their contrary designs (vv. 10–11). *fear the LORD.* See v. 18; see also note on 15:4.

33:11 *heart.* See note on 4:7.

12 Blessed *is* the nation whose God *is* the LORD;
And the people *whom* he hath [a]chosen for his own inheritance.
13 [a]The LORD looketh from heaven;
He beholdeth all the sons of men.
14 From the place of his habitation he looketh
Upon all the inhabitants of the earth.
15 He fashioneth their hearts alike;
[a]He considereth all their works.
16 [a]There is no king saved by the multitude of a host:
A mighty *man* is not delivered by much strength.
17 [a]A horse *is* a vain thing for safety:
Neither shall he deliver *any* by his great strength.
18 [a]Behold, the eye of the LORD *is* [b]upon them that fear him,
Upon them that hope in his mercy;
19 To deliver their soul from death,
And [a]to keep them alive in famine.
20 [a]Our soul waiteth for the LORD:
He *is* our help and our shield.
21 For our [a]heart shall rejoice in him,
Because we have trusted in his holy name.
22 Let thy mercy, O LORD, be upon us,
According as we hope in thee.

33:12 [a]Ex. 19:5; Deut. 7:6
33:13 [a]Job 28:24; Ps. 11:4
33:15 [a]Jer. 32:19
33:16 [a]Ps. 44:6
33:17 [a]Ps. 20:7; Prov. 21:31
33:18 [a]Job 36:7; Ps. 34:15 [b]Ps. 147:11
33:19 [a]Job 5:20
33:20 [a]Ps. 130:6
33:21 [a]John 16:22
34:T [1]Or, *Achish*
34:1 [a]Eph. 5:20
34:2 [a]Jer. 9:24 [b]Ps. 119:74
34:3 [a]Luke 1:46
34:4 [a]Mat. 7:7
34:5 [1]Or, *they flowed* unto him
34:6 [a]Ps. 3:4 [b]ver. 17,19
34:7 [a]Dan. 6:22 [b]2 Ki. 6:17
34:8 [a]1 Pet. 2:3 [b]Ps. 2:12

Psalm 34

A Psalm of David, when he changed his behaviour before [1]Abimelech; who drove him away, and he departed.

1 I will [a]bless the LORD at all times:
His praise *shall* continually *be* in my mouth.
2 My soul shall make her [a]boast in the LORD:
[b]The humble shall hear *thereof,* and be glad.
3 O [a]magnify the LORD with me,
And let us exalt his name together.
4 I [a]sought the LORD, and he heard me,
And delivered me from all my fears.
5 They looked unto him, and [1]were lightened:
And their faces were not ashamed.
6 [a]This poor *man* cried, and the LORD heard *him,*
And [b]saved him out of all his troubles.
7 [a]The angel of the LORD [b]encampeth
Round about them that fear him, and delivereth them.
8 O [a]taste and see that the LORD *is* good:
[b]Blessed *is* the man *that* trusteth in him.
9 O fear the LORD, ye his saints:
For *there is* no want to them that fear him.
10 The young lions do lack, and suffer hunger:

33:12–19 Israel is safe and secure under God's protective rule.

33:12 *Blessed.* See note on 1:1. *people whom he hath chosen for his own inheritance.* Israel (see Deut 9:29).

33:16 *king.* Nation (see v. 12) and king constitute an organic social unit (see 28:8 and note).

33:18–19 The concluding couplet of the second eight-verse stanza of praise contrasts with the concluding couplet of the first (vv. 10–11); both are climactic and together they voice the heart of the praise.

33:18,22 *mercy.* Here, His covenant favor toward Israel (see note on 6:4).

33:20–22 The people's response: faith's commitment expressed in confession (vv. 20–21) and petition (v. 22).

33:20 *shield.* See note on 3:3.

33:21 *heart.* See note on 4:7. *name.* See note on 5:11.

Ps 34 Praise of the Lord for deliverance in answer to prayer, and instruction in godliness. In the Psalms, praise commonly leads to a call to praise, as in v. 3 (see note on 9:1). Here, uniquely (but see also Ps 92), praise (vv. 1–7) leads into godly instruction (vv. 8–22) in the manner of the wisdom teachers (see essay, p. 687). Structurally, the psalm is a somewhat irregular alphabetic acrostic (it lacks a verse for one Hebrew letter and adds a verse at the end). It develops four major themes (see following notes).

‡34 title The superscription assigns this psalm to the occasion in David's life (see note on Ps 3 title) narrated in 1 Sam 21:10–15—but note "Abimelech" rather than "Achish" (perhaps Abimelech was a traditional dynastic name or title for Philistine kings; see Gen 20; 21:22–34; 26).

34:1–7 Praise for the Lord's deliverance in answer to prayer.

34:1–3 Commitment to continual praise—to the encouragement of the godly who are afflicted (v. 2; see the instruction in vv. 8–22).

34:2 *soul.* See note on 6:3.

34:3 *name.* See note on 5:11.

34:4–7 The occasion: God's saving answer to prayer.

‡34:5 *lightened.* Radiant with joy (see Is 60:5).

34:6 *poor.* Here, as often in the Psalms, "poor" characterizes not necessarily one who has no possessions, but one who is (and recognizes that he is) without resources to effect his own deliverance (or secure his own life, safety or well-being)—and so is dependent on God.

34:7 *angel of the LORD.* God's heavenly representative, His "messenger," sent to effect His will on earth (see 35:5–6; see also note on Gen 16:7). *encampeth Round about.* The line speaks of the security with which the Lord surrounds His people, individually and collectively; it does not teach a doctrine of individual "guardian angels." *them that fear him.* Those described in vv. 8–14.

34:8–14 Instruction in "the fear of the LORD." The title line (v. 11) is at the center of the psalm Hebrew authors often centered key lines (see note on 6:6). Note the pattern of the imperatives: "taste" (v. 8), "fear" (v. 9), "Come" (v. 11), "Keep" (v. 13), "Depart" (v. 14). A symmetrical development of the theme "good" dominates the stanza: Because the Lord is good (v. 8), those who trust in Him will lack nothing good (v. 10); but in order to experience good days (v. 12), they must shun evil and do good (v. 14). To trust and obey—that is "the fear of the LORD." On the instruction of vv. 8–14 see Ps 37. For Peter's use of vv. 12–16 see 1 Pet 3:8–12.

34:8 *Blessed.* See note on 1:1.

34:9 *fear the LORD.* See v. 11; see also note on 15:4. *saints.* See note on 4:3.

[a]But they that seek the LORD shall not
want any good *thing.*
11 Come, ye children, hearken unto me:
[a]I will teach you the fear of the LORD.
12 [a]What man *is he that* desireth life,
And loveth *many* days, that *he* may see
good?
13 Keep thy tongue from evil,
And thy lips from speaking guile.
14 [a]Depart from evil, and do good;
[b]Seek peace, and pursue it.
15 [a]The eyes of the LORD *are* upon the
righteous,
And his ears *are open* unto their cry.
16 [a]The face of the LORD *is* against them
that do evil,
[b]To cut off the remembrance of them
from the earth.
17 *The righteous* cry, and [a]the LORD
heareth,
And delivereth them out of all their
troubles.
18 [a]The LORD *is* nigh [b1]unto them that
are of a broken heart;
And saveth such as be [2]of a contrite
spirit.
19 [a]Many *are* the afflictions of the
righteous:
[b]But the LORD delivereth him out of
them all.
20 He keepeth all his bones:
[a]Not one of them is broken.
21 [a]Evil shall slay the wicked:
And they that hate the righteous [1]shall
be desolate.
22 The LORD [a]redeemeth the soul of his
servants:
And none of them that trust in him
[1]shall be desolate.

34:10 [a]Ps. 84:11
34:11 [a]Ps. 32:8
34:12 [a]1 Pet. 3:10
34:14 [a]Ps. 37:27 [b]Heb. 12:14
34:15 [a]Job 36:7
34:16 [a]Lev. 17:10 [b]Prov. 10:7
34:17 [a]Ps. 145:19
34:18 [1]Heb. *to the broken of heart* [2]Heb. *contrite of spirit* [a]Ps. 145:18 [b]Is. 57:15
34:19 [a]Prov. 24:16 [b]ver. 6,17
34:20 [a]John 19:36
34:21 [1]Or, *shall be guilty* [a]Ps. 94:23
34:22 [1]Or, *shall be guilty* [a]1 Ki. 1:29; Ps. 71:23

35:1 [a]Ps. 43:1 [b]Ex. 14:25
35:2 [a]Is. 42:13
35:4 [a]Ps. 70:2,3
35:5 [a]Job 21:18; Ps. 1:4
35:6 [1]Heb. *darkness and slipperiness* [a]Ps. 73:18
35:7 [a]Ps. 9:15
35:8 [1]Heb. which *he knoweth not of* [a]1 Thes. 5:3
35:10 [a]Ex. 15:11

Psalm 35

A Psalm of David.

1 Plead [a]*my cause,* O LORD, with them
that strive with me:
[b]Fight against them that fight against
me.
2 [a]Take hold of shield and buckler,
And stand up for mine help.
3 Draw out also the spear, and stop *the
way* against them that persecute me:
Say unto my soul, I *am* thy salvation.
4 [a]Let them be confounded and put to
shame that seek after my soul:
Let them be turned back and brought
to confusion that devise my hurt.
5 [a]Let them be as chaff before the wind:
And let the angel of the LORD chase
them.
6 Let their way be [a1]dark and slippery:
And let the angel of the LORD persecute
them.
7 For without cause have they [a]hid for
me their net *in* a pit,
Which without cause they have digged
for my soul.
8 Let [a]destruction come upon him [1]at
unawares;
And let his net that he hath hid catch
himself:
Into that *very* destruction let him fall.
9 And my soul shall be joyful in the LORD:
It shall rejoice in his salvation.
10 All my bones shall say,
LORD, [a]who *is* like unto thee,
Which deliverest the poor from him
that is too strong for him,
Yea, the poor and the needy from him
that spoileth him?

34:11 *Come, ye children.* Conventional language of the wisdom teachers (see Introduction to Proverbs: Purpose and Teaching).
34:13 See 15:2–3; Jas 3:5–10. For the tongue as a weapon see note on 5:9.
34:14 *Seek peace.* See 37:37; 120:7; Prov 12:20; Zech 8:19 (also Zech 8:16–17); Mat 5:9; Rom 12:18; 1 Cor 7:15; 2 Cor 13:11; 1 Thes 5:13; Heb 12:14; Jas 3:17–18.
34:15–18 Assurance that the Lord hears the prayers of the righteous. He so thoroughly thwarts those who do evil that they are forgotten (v. 16).
34:15 *righteous.* See vv. 8–14; see also note on 1:5.
34:16 *face of the LORD.* See note on 13:1.
34:17–18 See especially 51:17.
34:19–22 Assurance that the Lord is the unfailing deliverer of the righteous—and condemns the wicked for their hostility toward the righteous (see v. 21).
34:20 *all his bones.* His whole being (see note on 6:2). *Not one of them is broken.* It appears that John's Gospel applies this word to Jesus (John 19:36; see also Ex 12:46; Num 9:12)—as the one above all others who could be called "righteous" (v. 19).
‡34:21–22 *shall be desolate.* Lit. "shall be guilty," and thus dealt with as guilty.
34:22 *redeemeth.* See note on 25:22.
Ps 35 An appeal to the heavenly King, as divine Warrior and Judge, to come to the defense of "his servant" (v. 27) who is being maliciously slandered by those toward whom he had shown only the most tender friendship. The attack seems to have been occasioned by some "hurt" (v. 26) that had overtaken the king (see vv. 15,19,21,25), perhaps an illness (see v. 13; see also introduction to Ps 6). Ps 35 exemplifies such a "cry" to the Lord in expectation of vindication as that spoken of in 34:15–22—except that here the author does not expressly identify himself as one of the "righteous" (34:21); he appeals to the Lord rather as innocent victim of an unmotivated attack. Regarding structure, after an initial appeal to the Lord as divine Warrior (vv. 1–3) there follows a threefold elaboration of David's petition to the divine Judge, each concluding with a vow to praise (vv. 4–10, 11–18, 19–28); see note on 7:17.
35:1–3 Appeal to the Lord as Warrior-King (see Ex 15:1–18), David's Overlord.
35:2 *stand up.* See note on 3:7.
35:3 *soul.* See note on 6:3.
35:4–10 Appeal to the Lord to deal with the attackers, matching judgment with their violent intent (see note on 5:10).
‡35:4 *Let them be confounded.* Lit. "let them be humiliated," through their judgment and the psalmist's vindication. *devise my hurt.* See note on 5:9.
35:5–6 *angel of the LORD.* See 34:7 and note.
35:5 *as chaff.* See note on 1:4.
35:9–10 See note on 7:17.
35:9 *soul.* See note on 6:3.
35:10 *poor and . . . needy.* See 34:6 and note.

11 [1]False witnesses did rise up;
[2]They laid to my charge *things* that I knew not.
12 [a]They rewarded me evil for good
To the [1]spoiling of my soul.
13 But *as for* me, [a]when they were sick, my clothing *was* sackcloth:
I [1]humbled my soul with fasting;
And my prayer returned into mine own bosom.
14 I [1]behaved myself [2]as though *he had been* my friend *or* brother:
I bowed down heavily, as one that mourneth for his mother.
15 But in mine [1]adversity they rejoiced, and gathered themselves together:
Yea, [a]the abjects gathered themselves together against me, and I knew *it* not;
They did [b]tear *me,* and ceased not:
16 With hypocritical mockers in feasts,
[a]*They* gnashed upon me *with* their teeth.
17 Lord, how long wilt thou [a]look on?
Rescue my soul from their destructions,
[b][1]My darling from the lions.
18 I will give thee thanks in the great congregation:
I will praise thee among [1]much people.
19 [a]Let not them that are mine enemies [b][1]wrongfully rejoice over me:
Neither [c]let them wink *with* the eye
[d]that hate me without a cause.
20 For they speak not peace:
But they devise deceitful matters against *them that are* quiet in the land.

35:11 [1]Heb. *Witnesses of wrong* [2]Heb. *They asked me* 35:12 [1]Heb. *depriving* [a]John 10:32 35:13 [1]Or, *afflicted* [a]Job 30:25 35:14 [1]Heb. *walked* [2]Heb. *as a friend, as a brother to me* 35:15 [1]Heb. *halting* [a]Job 30:1,8 [b]Job 16:9 35:16 [a]Job 16:9; Lam. 2:16 35:17 [1]Heb. *My only one* [a]Hab. 1:13 [b]Ps. 22:20 35:18 [1]Heb. *strong* 35:19 [1]Heb. *falsely* [a]Ps. 13:4 [b]Ps. 38:19 [c]Job 15:12 [d]Ps. 69:4

21 Yea, they [a]opened their mouth wide against me,
And said, [b]Aha, aha, our eye hath seen *it.*
22 *This* thou hast [a]seen, O LORD: [b]keep not silence:
O Lord, be not [c]far from me.
23 [a]Stir up thyself, and awake to my judgment,
Even unto my cause, my God and my Lord.
24 Judge me, O LORD my God, [a]according to thy righteousness;
And let them not rejoice over me.
25 Let them not say in their hearts, [1]Ah, so would we have it:
Let them not say, [a]We have swallowed him up.
26 Let them be ashamed and brought to confusion together that rejoice at mine hurt:
Let them be [a]clothed with shame and dishonour that magnify *themselves* against me.
27 [a]Let them shout for joy, and be glad, that favour [1]my righteous cause:
Yea, let them say continually, Let the LORD be magnified,
Which hath pleasure in the prosperity of his servant.
28 And my tongue shall speak of thy righteousness
And of thy praise all the day long.

35:21 [a]Ps. 22:13 [b]Ps. 40:15 35:22 [a]Ex. 3:7 [b]Ps. 28:1 [c]Ps. 10:1 35:23 [a]Ps. 44:23 35:24 [a]2 Thes. 1:6 35:25 [1]Heb. *Ah, ah, our soul* [a]Lam. 2:16 35:26 [a]Ps. 109:29 35:27 [1]Heb. *my righteousness* [a]Rom. 12:15

Psalm 36

To the chief Musician, *A Psalm* of David the servant of the LORD.

1 The transgression of the wicked saith within my heart,

35:11–18 The accusation—they repaid my friendship with malicious slander—with a renewed petition (v. 17) and a vow to praise (v. 18).
‡35:12 *spoiling.* Lit."bereavement."This word is used elsewhere for the loss of children (cf. Is 47:8–9). *soul.* See note on 6:3.
‡35:13–14 The psalmist provides a living example of Jesus' command to "pray for them which despitefully use you" (Mat 5:44).
35:13 *sackcloth.* A symbol of mourning (see 30:11; Gen 37:34). *fasting.* An act of mourning (see 69:10).
‡35:15 *the abjects.* His wicked oppressors.
‡35:16 *With hypocritical mockers in feasts.* The enemies of the psalmist are like drunkards at a pagan feast as they heap their vicioius and profane derision upon him. *gnashed . . . their teeth.* In malice (see 37:12; Lam 2:16).
‡35:17 *how long . . . ?* See note on 6:3 (see also Introduction: Theology). *my darling.* Lit."my only one," my soul, my life. *lions.* See note on 7:2.
35:18 *congregation.* See note on 1:5.
35:19–28 Renewed appeal for judgment, with a concluding vow to praise (v. 28).
‡35:19 *mine enemies wrongfully.* See vv. 11–17; an experience frequently reflected also elsewhere in the Psalter (see 38:19; 69:4; 109:3; 119:78,86,161). See also Lam 3:52. *wink with the eye.* A gesture which signals others involved in the conspiracy; cf. Prov 6:13 and note. *hate me without a cause.* See 69:4. It is not known which of these passages is referred to in John 15:25. Both psalms reflect circumstances applicable also to Jesus' experience (but see introduction to Ps 69).
35:21 *Aha, aha.* See v. 25; see also note on 3:2.
35:22 *keep not silence.* Do not remain inactive (see 28:1 and note; 83:1; 109:1).
35:23 *Stir up thyself.* See note on 7:6. *awake.* See note on 3:7.
35:24 *righteousness.* See note on 4:1.
‡35:25 *so would we have it.* Or, "this is just what we wanted." *swallowed.* See 124:3.
35:26 Once again: May their judgment match their evil intent (see vv. 4–10).
35:27 May all who are faithful supporters of the Lord's "servant" (here no doubt equivalent to His "anointed"; see note on 2:2) have reason to rejoice and praise the Lord.
35:28 *righteousness.* See note on 4:1.
Ps 36 A prayer for God's unfailing protection, as the psalmist reflects on the godlessness of the wicked and the goodness of God. In Jewish practice, vv. 7–10 form part of the morning prayer.
36 title *To the chief Musician.* See note on Ps 4 title. *servant of the LORD.* His royal servant (see notes on Ps 18 title; 35:27; see also 2 Sam 7:20).
36:1–4 The foolish and haughty godlessness of the wicked.
‡36:1 *The transgression . . . within my heart.* Or "an oracle con-

That [a]*there is* no fear of God before his eyes.
2 For he flattereth himself in his own eyes,
[1]Until his iniquity be found to be hateful.
3 The words of his mouth *are* iniquity and deceit:
[a]He hath left off to be wise, *and* to do good.
4 [a]He deviseth [1]mischief upon his bed;
He setteth himself [b]in a way *that is* not good;
He abhorreth not evil.
5 Thy mercy, O LORD, *is* in the heavens;
And thy faithfulness *reacheth* unto the clouds.
6 Thy righteousness *is* like [1]the great mountains;
[a]Thy judgments *are* a great deep:
O LORD, thou preservest man and beast.
7 How [1]excellent *is* thy lovingkindness, O God!
Therefore the children of men [a]put their trust under the shadow of thy wings.
8 [a]They shall be [1]abundantly satisfied with the fatness of thy house;
And thou shalt make them drink *of* [b]the river of thy pleasures.
9 [a]For with thee *is* the fountain of life:
[b]In thy light shall we see light.
10 O [1]continue thy lovingkindness unto them that know thee;
And thy righteousness to the upright in heart.
11 Let not the foot of pride come against me,
And let not the hand of the wicked remove me.
12 There are the workers of iniquity fallen:
They are cast down, and shall not be able to rise.

Psalm 37

A Psalm of David.

1 Fret [a]not thyself because of evildoers,
Neither be thou envious against the workers of iniquity.

36:1 [a]Rom. 3:18
36:2 [1]Heb. *To find his iniquity to hate*
36:3 [a]Jer. 4:22
36:4 [1]Or, *vanity* [a]Prov. 4:16 [b]Is. 65:2
36:6 [1]Heb. *the mountains of God* [a]Rom. 11:33
36:7 [1]Heb. *precious* [a]Ps. 17:8
36:8 [1]Heb. *watered* [a]Ps. 65:4 [b]Job 20:17; Rev. 22:1
36:9 [a]Jer. 2:13 [b]1 Pet. 2:9
36:10 [1]Heb. *drawn out at length*
37:1 [a]Ps. 73:3; Prov. 23:17

cerning the rebellion of the wicked is in my heart." *heart.* See note on 4:7. *no fear of God.* See 55:19. They take no account of His all-seeing eye, His righteous judgment and His power to deal with them (see note on 10:11). For Paul's use of this verse see Rom 3:18.

‡36:2 *flattereth himself.* Out of the smug, conceited notion that he is accountable to no one. *Until his iniquity . . . hateful.* Lit. "to find his iniquity to hate." Reflects the degree of his conceit; he is unable to recognize and hate the sinfulness in his own heart.

‡36:3 *words of his mouth.* See note on 5:9. *hath left off to be wise.* Has stopped even trying to do what is right. See 94:8–11; Prov 2:9–11. *do good.* See 34:8–14 and note.

36:4 *upon his bed.* When one's thoughts are free to range, and to set the course for the activities of the day. The wicked do not meditate on God's law "day and night" (1:2; see 119:55), or let a godly heart instruct them at night (see 16:7), or at night commune with God (see 42:8), think of Him (see 63:6) and reflect on His promises (see 119:148).

36:5–9 The goodness of the Lord—His benevolence toward all His creatures (see 33:4–5).

36:5 *mercy . . . faithfulness.* That is, lovingkindness-and-faithfulness (as in 57:3; 61:7; 85:10; 86:15; 89:14; 115:1; 138:2; Prov 3:3; 14:22; 16:6; 20:28; see note on 3:7). *is in the heavens . . . unto the clouds.* Encompasses all the realms of creaturely existence (see 57:10; 108:4).

36:6 *righteousness . . . judgments.* That is, righteousness-and-judgments (as in 33:5; 89:14; 97:2; Hos 2:19; see also Is 9:7; 33:5; Jer 9:24). *righteousness.* See note on 5:8. *great mountains . . . great deep.* As high as the mountains, as deep as the sea.

36:7 *lovingkindness.* See v. 5; see also note on 6:4. *children of men.* All categories of men. *shadow of thy wings.* See 17:8 and note.

‡36:8 *abundantly satisfied . . . drink.* Pictures God's blessing as rich food and life-giving water. *house.* Here, God's whole estate or realm—i.e., the earth, from which springs the abundance of food for all living things (see note on 24:2). *river.* The "watercourse," i.e. "channel" (Job 38:25) by which God brings forth the rain out of His "storehouses" (33:7; see Job 38:8–11, 22,37; Jer 10:13) in His "chambers" (104:13; see 65:9; Is 30:25 and the references to "blessings" from heaven in Gen 49:25; Deut 33:23). This vivid imagery, depicting God's control over, and gift of, the waters from heaven, which feed the rivers and streams of earth to give life and health wherever they flow, is the source of the symbol of the "river of water of life" that flows from the temple of God (Rev 22:1–2; see also Ezek 47:1–12). *of thy pleasures.* Furnishing many sources of joy.

36:9 The climax and summation of vv. 5–9. *fountain of life.* See Jer 2:13; 17:13. Ultimately, for sinners, God provides the water of life through Jesus Christ (John 4:10,14). *thy light.* See 27:1 and note. *see.* Experience, have, enjoy, as in 16:10; 27:13; 34:8,12; 49:9,19; 89:48; 90:15; 106:5; Job 9:25; 42:5; Eccl 3:13; 8:16; Is 53:10; Lam 3:1. *light.* Life in its fullness as it was created to be. For the association of light with life see 49:19; 56:13; Job 3:20; 33:30.

‡36:10–11 The prayer: Show Your "mercy" (v. 5) and "righteousness" (v. 6), which you display in all creation, to all who know (acknowledge) You and are upright (the people of God). But keep the wicked, "foot" and "hand," from success against me (the king; see note on 33:16).

36:10 *lovingkindness.* See note on 6:4. *righteousness.* See note on 4:1.

36:11 *pride.* See note on 31:23.

36:12 Confidence (see note on 3:8). *fallen.* Perhaps in death (see note on 13:4).

‡Ps 37 Instruction in godly wisdom. (For other "wisdom" psalms see 34:8–22; 49; 112; others closely related are Ps 1; 73; 91; 92:6–9,12–15; 111; 119; 127–128; 133; see essay, p. 687.) This psalm's dominant theme is related to the contrast between the wicked and the righteous reflected in Ps 36. The central issue addressed is: Who will "inherit the earth" (vv. 9,11,22,29), i.e. live on to enjoy the blessings of the Lord in the promised land? Will the wicked, who plot (v. 12), scheme (vv. 7,32), default on debts (v. 21), use raw power to gain advantage (v. 14) and seem thereby to flourish (vv. 7,16,35)? Or will the righteous, who trust in the Lord (vv. 3,5,7,34) and are humble (v. 11), blameless (vv. 18,37), generous (vv. 21,26), upright (v. 37) and peaceable (v. 37), and from whose mouth is heard the moral wisdom that reflects meditation on God's law (vv. 30–31)? For a similar characterization of the wicked see 10:2–11; 73:4–12. For a similar characterization of the righteous see Ps 112. For a similar state-

2 For they shall soon be cut down [a]like
the grass,
And wither as the green herb.

3 Trust in the LORD, and do good;
So shalt thou dwell in the land, and
[1]verily thou shalt be fed.
4 [a]Delight thyself also in the LORD;
And he shall give thee the desires of
thine heart.

5 [a][1]Commit thy way unto the LORD;
Trust also in him; and he shall bring *it*
to pass.
6 [a]And he shall bring forth thy
righteousness as the light,
And thy judgment as the noonday.

7 [1]Rest in the LORD, [a]and wait patiently
for him:
Fret not thyself because of him who
prospereth *in* his way,
Because of the man who bringeth
wicked devices to pass.

8 Cease from anger, and forsake wrath:
[a]Fret not thyself in any wise to do evil.
9 For evildoers shall be cut off:
But those that wait upon the LORD,
they shall [a]inherit the earth.
10 For [a]yet a little while, and the wicked
shall not *be:*
Yea, [b]thou shalt diligently consider his
place, and it *shall* not *be.*
11 [a]But the meek shall inherit the earth;
And shall delight themselves in the
abundance of peace.

12 The wicked [1]plotteth against the just,
[a]And gnasheth upon him *with* his
teeth.
13 [a]The Lord shall laugh at him:
For he seeth that [b]his day is coming.

14 The wicked have drawn out the sword,
and have bent their bow,
To cast down the poor and needy,
And to slay [1]such as be of upright
conversation.
15 [a]Their sword shall enter into their own
heart,
And their bows shall be broken.

16 [a]A little that a righteous *man* hath
Is better than the riches of many
wicked.
17 For [a]the arms of the wicked shall be
broken:
But the LORD upholdeth the righteous.

18 The LORD [a]knoweth the days of the
upright:
And their inheritance shall be [b]for
ever.

19 They shall not be ashamed in the evil
time:
And [a]in the days of famine they shall
be satisfied.

20 But the wicked shall perish,
And the enemies of the LORD *shall be*
as [1]the fat of lambs:
They shall consume; [a]into smoke shall
they consume *away.*

37:2 [a]Ps. 90:5,6
37:3 [1]Heb. in *truth,* or, *stableness*
37:4 [a]Is. 58:14
37:5 [1]Heb. *Roll thy way upon the LORD* [a]Ps. 55:22; Mat. 6:25
37:6 [a]Job 11:17
37:7 [1]Heb. *Be silent to the LORD* [a]Lam. 3:26
37:8 [a]Ps. 73:3; Eph. 4:26
37:9 [a]Is. 57:13
37:10 [a]Heb. 10:36 [b]Job 7:10
37:11 [a]Mat. 5:5
37:12 [1]Or, *practiseth* [a]Ps. 35:16
37:13 [a]Ps. 2:4 [b]1 Sam. 26:10
37:14 [1]Heb. *the upright of way*
37:15 [a]Ps. 9:16
37:16 [a]Prov. 15:16
37:17 [a]Ps. 10:15
37:18 [a]Ps. 1:6 [b]Is. 60:21
37:19 [a]Ps. 33:19
37:20 [1]Heb. *the preciousness of lambs* [a]Ps. 102:3

ment concerning the transitoriness of the wicked see Ps 49; 73:18–20. Structurally, in this alphabetic acrostic, two verses are devoted to each letter of the alphabet, though with some irregularity. The main theme is developed in vv. 1–11, then further elaborated in the rest of the psalm. The whole is framed by statements contrasting the brief career of the wicked (vv. 1–2) and the Lord's sustaining help of the righteous (vv. 39–40).
‡37:1–2 See v. 7; Ps 73. This psalm begins by urging the reader not to worry, but to "trust" and "delight" in the Lord and "commit" your way unto Him.
37:2 See note on v. 20.
37:3 See 34:8–14 and note.
37:4 *heart.* See note on 4:7.
37:5 *Commit.* See 1 Pet 5:7.
‡37:6 *righteousness . . . judgment.* That is, righteousness-and-judgment (see note on 36:6). *righteousness.* See note on 1:5. *light . . . noonday.* They will shine brightly for everyone to see.
37:8 *anger . . . wrath.* Evidence of fretting over the wicked's prosperity, gained to the disadvantage of and even at the expense of the righteous.
‡37:9 *inherit the earth.* Or "inherit the land" (the word for "earth" and "land" is the same in Hebrew). They will receive from the Lord secure entitlement (for them and their children) to the promised land as the created and redeemed sphere and bountiful source of provision for the life of God's people. Those who hope in the Lord—i.e., trustfully look to Him to bestow life and its blessings as a gift—will inherit the land, not those who apart from God and by evil means try to take possession of it and its wealth (see vv. 11,22,29; cf. Josh 7).
‡37:10 *a little while.* Shortness of time is here a figure for certainty of event (see 58:9; Job 20:5–11; Hag 2:6). *thou shalt diligently consider his place . . . not be.* Will not be found even with a careful search because God will completely destroy.
37:11 See Mat 5:5. *meek.* Those who humbly acknowledge their dependence on the goodness and grace of God and betray no arrogance toward their fellowman. *abundance of peace.* Unmixed blessedness.
37:12 *just.* See note on 1:5. *gnasheth . . . his teeth.* See 35:16 and note.
‡37:13 *Lord shall laugh.* See 2:4. *seeth that his day is coming.* Strikingly, the psalmist nowhere speaks of God's active involvement in bringing the wicked down—though he hints at it in v. 22. The certainty that the life of the wicked "shall be cut off" is frequently asserted (vv. 9,22,28,34,38; cf. vv. 2,8,10,15, 17,20,36,38)—and the Lord also knows it—but God's positive action is here reserved for His care for and protection of the righteous. *his day.* The time for each of them, when he will be "cut off," as in 1 Sam 26:10; Job 18:20.
37:14 *poor and needy.* See 34:6 and note.
37:15 *enter . . . heart.* See 45:5.
37:16–17 *righteous.* See note on 1:5.
37:18 *upright.* See v. 37; 15:2; see also note on 26:1.
‡37:19 *evil time.* A time of disaster or personal calamity.
37:20 *fat of lambs.* Or, the "beauty of the fields," i.e. the grass and flowers (cf. v. 2; 90:5–6; 102:11; 103:15–16; Job 14:2; Is 40:6–8; see Jas 1:10–11).

21 The wicked borroweth, and payeth not again:
But [a]the righteous sheweth mercy, and giveth.
22 [a]For such as be blessed of him shall inherit the earth;
And they that be cursed of him shall be cut off.

23 [a]The steps of a *good* man are [1]ordered by the LORD:
And he delighteth in his way.
24 [a]Though he fall, he shall not be utterly cast down:
For the LORD upholdeth *him with* his hand.

25 I have been young, and *now* am old;
Yet have I not seen the righteous forsaken,
Nor his seed [a]begging bread.
26 [a]*He is* [1]ever merciful, and lendeth;
And his seed *is* blessed.

27 [a]Depart from evil, and do good;
And dwell for evermore.
28 For the LORD [a]loveth judgment,
And forsaketh not his saints;

They are preserved for ever:
[b]But the seed of the wicked shall be cut off.
29 [a]The righteous shall inherit the land,
And dwell therein for ever.

30 [a]The mouth of the righteous speaketh wisdom,
And his tongue talketh of judgment.
31 [a]The law of his God *is* in his heart;
None of his [1]steps shall slide.

32 The wicked [a]watcheth the righteous,
And seeketh to slay him.
33 The LORD [a]will not leave him in his hand,
Nor [b]condemn him when he is judged.

34 [a]Wait on the LORD, and keep his way,
And he shall exalt thee to inherit the land:
[b]When the wicked are cut off, thou shalt see *it.*

35 [a]I have seen the wicked in great power,
And spreading himself like [1]a green bay tree.
36 Yet he [a]passed away, and lo, he *was* not:
Yea, I sought him, but he could not be found.

37 Mark the perfect *man,* and behold the upright:
For [a]the end of *that* man *is* peace.
38 [a]But the transgressors shall be destroyed together:
The end of the wicked shall be cut off.

39 But [a]the salvation of the righteous *is* of the LORD:
He is their strength [b]in the time of trouble.
40 And [a]the LORD shall help them, and deliver them:
He shall deliver them from the wicked,
And save them, [b]because they trust in him.

Psalm 38

A Psalm of David, [a]to bring to remembrance.

1 [a]O LORD, rebuke me not in thy wrath:
Neither chasten me in thy hot displeasure.

37:21 [a]Ps. 112:5,9
37:22 [a]Prov. 3:33
37:23 [1]Or, *established* [a]1 Sam. 2:9
37:24 [a]Prov. 24:16
37:25 [a]Job 15:23
37:26 [1]Heb. *all the day* [a]Deut. 15:8
37:27 [a]Ps. 34:14
37:28 [a]Is. 30:18 [b]Ps. 21:10
37:29 [a]Prov. 2:21
37:30 [a]Mat. 12:35
37:31 [1]Or, *goings* [a]Deut. 6:6
37:32 [a]Ps. 10:8
37:33 [a]2 Pet. 2:9 [b]Ps. 109:31
37:34 [a]Ps. 27:14 [b]Ps. 52:5,6
37:35 [1]Or, *a green tree that groweth in his own soil* [a]Job 5:3
37:36 [a]Job 20:5
37:37 [a]Is. 32:17
37:38 [a]Ps. 1:4
37:39 [a]Ps. 3:8 [b]Ps. 9:9
37:40 [a]Is. 31:5 [b]1 Chr. 5:20
38:T [a]Ps. 70, title
38:1 [a]Ps. 6:1

37:21 See Deut 15:6; 28:12,44).
37:24 See Prov 24:16.
‡37:25 *righteous forsaken . . . his seed begging bread.* The psalmist's observation provides a promise that God never abandons the righteous but does not give a guarantee that they will never experience difficulties and suffering. Paul, for example, suffered physical hunger because he made the righteous choice to be a messenger of Christ (cf. 1 Cor 4:11; 2 Cor 11:27; Phil 4:12).
37:26 See note on v. 21.
‡37:28 *judgment.* Or "justice." God always does what is right. *saints.* See note on 4:3.
37:29 *for ever.* They and their children and children's children, in contrast to the wicked (see v. 28).
37:30 *wisdom.* See 119:98,130; Deut 4:6.
37:31 *heart.* See note on 4:7. *None . . . shall slide.* From the right path (see 17:5).
‡37:32 *watcheth.* Or "spies upon." See 10:8–9; see also note on 7:2. *seeketh to slay him.* Attempting to seize by false charges at court (see v. 33) the very livelihood of their intended victims.
‡37:33 *will not leave him in his hand.* Will not leave the righteous in the hand of the wicked and will not allow a miscarriage of justice.
37:35–36 Cf. vv. 25–26.
37:37–38 The great contrast: hope for the one, no hope for the other.
37:37 *perfect.* Blameless or upright. See note on v. 18.
37:39–40 *the righteous . . . them.* They are not at the mercy of the wicked: The Lord is their refuge, and in spite of all that the wicked do, the Lord makes secure their inheritance in the promised land.
Ps 38 An urgent appeal for relief from a severe and painful illness, God's "rebuke" for a sin David has committed. Neither the specific occasion nor the illness can be identified. David's suffering is aggravated by the withdrawal of his friends (see v. 11) and the unwarranted efforts of his enemies to seize this opportunity to bring him down (vv. 12,16,19–20). See introductions to Ps 39–41. In traditional Christian usage, this is one of seven penitential psalms (see introduction to Ps 6). Like Ps 33 (see introductory note on its structure), its length (22 verses) is based on the number of letters in the Hebrew alphabet. The psalm can be analyzed as composed of five stanzas of four verses each, with a two-verse conclusion.
38 title *to bring to remembrance.* Occurs elsewhere only in the title of Ps 70.
38:1–4 Plea for relief from the Lord's rebuke.
38:1 *rebuke . . . chasten.* That is, rebuke-and-chasten (see

2 For [a]thine arrows stick fast in me,
And [b]thy hand presseth me sore.
3 *There is* no soundness in my flesh
because of thine anger;
[a]Neither *is there any* [1]rest in my
bones because of my sin.
4 For [a]mine iniquities are gone *over*
mine head:
As a heavy burden they are too [b]heavy
for me.
5 My wounds stink *and* are corrupt
Because of my foolishness.
6 I am [1]troubled; [a]I am bowed down
greatly;
[b]I go mourning all the day long.
7 For my loins are filled *with* a
[a]loathsome *disease:*
And *there is* no soundness in my flesh.
8 I am feeble and sore broken:
[a]I have roared by reason of the
disquietness of my heart.
9 Lord, all my desire *is* before thee;
And my groaning is not hid from thee.
10 My heart panteth, my strength faileth
me:
As for [a]the light of mine eyes, it also
[1]is gone from me.
11 [a]My lovers and my friends [b]stand aloof
from my [1]sore;
And [2]my kinsmen [c]stand afar off.
12 They also that seek after my life [a]lay
snares *for me:*
And they that seek my hurt [b]speak
mischievous things,
And imagine deceits all the day long.
13 But [a]I, as a deaf *man,* heard not;
[b]And *I was* as a dumb *man that*
openeth not his mouth.
14 Thus I was as a man that heareth not,
And in whose mouth *are* no reproofs.
15 For [1]in thee, O LORD, [a]do I hope:
Thou wilt [2]hear, O Lord my God.
16 For I said, *Hear me,* [a]lest *otherwise*
they should rejoice over me:
When my foot slippeth, they [b]magnify
themselves against me.
17 For I *am* ready [1]to halt,
And my sorrow *is* continually before
me.
18 For I will [a]declare mine iniquity;
I will be [b]sorry for my sin.
19 But mine enemies [1]*are* lively, *and* they
are strong:
And they that hate me wrongfully are
multiplied.
20 They also [a]that render evil for good are
mine adversaries;
Because I follow *the thing that* good *is.*
21 Forsake me not, O LORD:
O my God, [a]be not far from me.
22 Make haste [1]to help me,
O Lord my salvation.

Psalm 39

To the chief Musician, *even* to [a]Jeduthun,
A Psalm of David.

1 I said, I will [a]take heed to my ways,
That *I* sin not with my tongue:
I will keep [1]my mouth with a bridle,
While the wicked *is* before me.

38:2 [a]Job 6:4 [b]Ps. 32:4
38:3 [1]Heb. *peace,* or, *health* [a]Ps. 6:2
38:4 [a]Ezra 9:6 [b]Mat. 11:28
38:6 [1]Heb. *wried* [a]Ps. 35:14 [b]Job 30:28
38:7 [a]Job 7:5
38:8 [a]Job 3:24
38:10 [1]Heb. is *not with me* [a]Ps. 6:7
38:11 [1]Heb. *stroke* [2]Or, *my neighbours* [a]Ps. 31:11 [b]Luke 10:31 [c]Luke 23:49
38:12 [a]2 Sam. 17:1 [b]2 Sam. 16:7
38:13 [a]2 Sam. 16:10
38:13 [b]Ps. 39:2,9
38:15 [1]Or, *thee do I wait for* [2]Or, *answer* [a]Ps. 39:7
38:16 [a]Ps. 13:4 [b]Ps. 35:26
38:17 [1]Heb. *for halting*
38:18 [a]Prov. 28:13 [b]2 Cor. 7:9
38:19 [1]Heb. being *living, are strong*
38:20 [a]Ps. 35:12
38:21 [a]Ps. 35:22
38:22 [1]Heb. *for my help*
39:T [a]1 Chr. 16:41; Ps. 62, title; 77, title
39:1 [1]Heb. *a bridle,* or, *muzzle for my mouth* [a]1 Ki. 2:4

39:11; see also note on 3:7). *wrath . . . displeasure.* See note on 2:5.

38:2 *arrows.* A vivid metaphor for God's blows (see Job 6:4; 34:6; Lam 3:12; Ezek 5:16). *thy hand presseth me sore.* See 32:4 and note on 32:3–5.

38:3 *bones.* See note on 6:2.

38:4 *burden.* Not only a psychological "burden of guilt," but the heavy burden of suffering described in vv. 5–8.

38:5–8 The devastating physical and psychological effects of his illness.

‡38:5 *My wounds stink and are corrupt.* His body is covered with festering sores.

‡38:7 *loathsome disease.* Or "burning pain."

‡38:8 *roared.* Or "groaned" in agony. *heart.* See note on 4:7.

38:9–12 Renewed appeal, with further elaboration of his troubles: his illness (v. 10), abandonment by his friends (v. 11) and the hostility of his enemies (v. 12).

38:10 *light of mine eyes . . . is gone from me.* See note on 13:3.

‡38:11 See note on 31:11–12. *sore.* Wound or affliction.

38:12 See note on 5:9.

38:13–16 Let the Lord answer (v. 15) my enemies. Like a deaf-mute, David will not reply to his enemies (vv. 13–14); he waits for the Lord to act in his behalf (vv. 15–16). See 1 Sam 25:32–39; 2 Sam 16:10,12.

38:16 *When my foot slippeth.* When he experiences a personal blow to health or circumstance—here referring to his illness (see 66:9; 94:18; 121:3).

38:17–20 As health declines, the vigor of his many enemies increases.

‡38:17 *ready to halt.* About to collapse; death seems near (see note on 13:4).

38:18 See vv. 3–4; Ps 32.

38:19–20 He has sinned against the Lord, but he is innocent of any wrong against those attacking him (see note on 35:19).

38:20 *Because.* Or "though." *good.* Morally good (see 34:14).

38:21–22 In conclusion, a renewed appeal.

‡Ps 39 The poignant prayer of a soul deeply troubled by the fragility of human life. He is reminded of this by the present illness through which God is rebuking him (vv. 10–11) for his "transgressions" (v. 8). Ps 38 speaks of silence before the enemy, Ps 39 of silence before God. Both are prayers in times of illness (God's "rebukes," v. 11; 38:1); both acknowledge sin, and both express deep trust in God. See introduction to Ps 40. In addition, this psalm has many links with Ps 90; see also Ps 49.

39 title *To the chief Musician.* See note on Ps 4 title. *Jeduthun.* One of David's three choir leaders (1 Chr 16:41–42; 25:1,6; 2 Chr 5:12; called his "seer" in 2 Chr 35:15). Jeduthun is probably also the Ethan of 1 Chr 6:44; 15:19; if so, he represented the family of Merari, even as Asaph did the family of Gershon and Heman the family of Kohath, the three sons of Levi (see 1 Chr 6:16,33,39,43–44). See titles of Ps 62; 77; 89.

39:1–3 Introduction: Having determined to keep silent, he could finally no longer suppress his anguish.

39:1 He had kept a muzzle on his mouth for fear that rebellious words would escape in the hearing of the wicked (see Ps 73).

2 [a]I was dumb *with* silence, I held my
peace, *even* from good;
And my sorrow was [1]stirred.
3 My heart was hot within me,
While I was musing the fire burned:
Then spake I with my tongue,

4 LORD, make me to know mine end,
And the measure of my days, what it *is;*
That I may know [1]how frail I *am.*
5 Behold, thou hast made my days *as* a
handbreadth;
And mine age *is* as nothing before thee:
Verily every man [1]at his best state *is*
altogether vanity. Selah.

6 Surely every man walketh in [1]a vain
shew:
Surely they are disquieted in vain:
[a]He heapeth up *riches,* and knoweth
not who shall gather them.
7 And now, Lord, what wait I for?
My hope *is* in thee.
8 Deliver me from all my transgressions:
Make me not [a]the reproach of the
foolish.
9 [a]I was dumb, I opened not my mouth;
Because [b]thou didst *it.*
10 Remove thy stroke away from me:
I am consumed by the [1]blow of thine
hand.
11 When thou with rebukes dost correct
man for iniquity,
Thou makest [1]his beauty [a]to consume
away like a moth:
Surely every man *is* vanity. Selah.

12 Hear my prayer, O LORD,
And give ear unto my cry;
Hold not thy peace at my tears:
For I *am* a stranger with thee,
And a sojourner, [a]as all my fathers *were.*
13 [a]O spare me, that I may recover
strength,
Before I go hence, and [b]be no more.

39:2 [1]Heb. *troubled* [a]Ps. 38:13
39:4 [1]Or, *what time I* have here
39:5 [1]Heb. *settled*
39:6 [1]Heb. [*an*] *image* [a]Luke 12:20
39:8 [a]Ps. 44:13
39:9 [a]Lev. 10:3 [b]Job 2:10
39:10 [1]Heb. *conflict*
39:11 [1]Heb. *that which is to be desired in him to melt away* [a]Job 13:28
39:12 [a]Gen. 47:9
39:13 [a]Job 10:20 [b]Job 14:10
40:1 [1]Heb. In *waiting I waited* [a]Ps. 27:14
40:2 [1]Heb. *a pit of noise* [a]Ps. 69:2,14 [b]Ps. 27:5
40:3 [a]Ps. 33:3
40:4 [a]Ps. 34:8
40:5 [1]Or, *None can order them unto thee* [a]Job 9:10 [b]Is. 55:8

Psalm 40

To the chief Musician, A Psalm of David.

1 [a]I [1]waited patiently for the LORD;
And he inclined unto me, and heard
my cry.
2 He brought me up also out of [1]a
horrible pit, out of [a]the miry clay,
And [b]set my feet upon a rock, *and*
established my goings.
3 [a]And he hath put a new song in my
mouth, *even* praise unto our God:
Many shall see *it,* and fear, and shall
trust in the LORD.
4 [a]Blessed *is that* man that maketh the
LORD his trust,
And respecteth not the proud, nor
such as turn aside to lies.
5 [a]Many, O LORD my God, *are* thy
wonderful works *which* thou hast
done,
[b]And thy thoughts *which are* to us-
ward:
[1]They cannot be reckoned up in order
unto thee:
If I would declare and speak *of them,*
They are moe than can be numbered.

39:2–3 Suppressed anguish only intensified the agony (see Jer 20:9).

39:4–6 A prayer for understanding and patient acceptance of the brief span of human life.

‡39:4 *how frail I am.* How brief and transient life really is. See 78:39 and note on 37:20.

‡39:5 *a handbreadth.* The length of four fingers, one of the smallest measures in Hebrew, and thus an extreme example of the brevity of life. Cf. Jer 52:21 ("thickness . . . was four fingers"). *as nothing before thee.* See 90:4. *altogether vanity.* Or "only a breath." See v. 11; 144:4; Job 14:2; Eccl 6:12.

‡39:6 Could almost serve as a summary of Ecclesiastes. *walketh in a vain shew.* Or "walks around like a shadowy image." *disquieted in vain.* They hurry and worry over things that do not ulimately matter.

39:7–11 A modest prayer: Only grant me relief from your present rebuke.

39:8 *Deliver me.* As from an enemy. *reproach of the foolish.* If the Lord does not restore him, he will be mocked (see 22:7–8; 69:6–12) by godless fools (see 14:1).

39:10 *blow of thine hand.* See 32:4; 38:2.

39:11 *with rebukes dost correct.* See 6:1; 38:1. *vanity.* See note on v. 5.

39:12–13 The modest prayer repeated even more modestly.

39:12 *a stranger . . . a sojourner.* He lives this life before God only as a pilgrim passing through.

‡39:13 *be no more.* Here there is no glimpse of what lies beyond the horizon of death (see note on 6:5).

Ps 40 A prayer for help when troubles abound. The causes of distress are not specified, but David acknowledges that they are occasioned by his sin (see v. 12), as in Ps 38–39; 41 (see introductions to Ps 39; 41). They are aggravated by the gloating of his enemies, a theme also present in Ps 38–39; 41 (see introduction to Ps 6). The prayer begins with praise of God for His past mercies (vv. 1–5) and a testimony to the king's own faithfulness to the Lord (vv. 6–10). These form the grounds for his present appeal for help (vv. 11–17). See also the lengthy prefaces to prayer in Ps 44; 89. Ps 70 is a somewhat revised duplicate of vv. 13–17 of this psalm.

40 title *To the chief Musician.* See note on Ps 4 title.

40:1–5 Praise of the Lord for past mercies (see introduction to Ps 9).

40:1–3 David's experience of God's past help in time of trouble, which moved him to praise and others to faith (see notes on 7:17; 9:1).

40:2 See 30:1 and note.

40:3 *new song.* See note on 33:3. *Many shall see.* As a result of David's praise (see 18:49; 22:22–31; see also note on 9:1). *fear.* See note on 34:8–14.

40:4–5 The Lord's benevolence to others: to all who trust in the Lord (v. 4), and to His people Israel (v. 5).

40:4 See Jer 17:7; praise of the Lord for the blessedness of those who trust in Him (see 32:1–2; 146:5). *Blessed.* See note on 1:1. *proud.* See note on 31:23.

40:5 *wonderful works.* See note on 9:1. *thoughts . . . to usward.* God's actions in behalf of Israel are according to His predetermined purpose (see Is 25:1; 46:10–11).

6 Sacrifice and offering thou didst not
desire;
Mine ears hast thou [1] opened:
Burnt offering and sin offering hast
thou not required.
7 Then said I, Lo, I come:
In the volume of the book *it is* written
of me,
8 [a] I delight to do thy will, O my God:
Yea, thy law *is* [b1] within my heart.
9 [a] I have preached righteousness in the
great congregation:
Lo, [b] I have not refrained my lips,
O LORD, thou knowest.
10 [a] I have not hid thy righteousness
within my heart;
I have declared thy faithfulness and thy
salvation:
I have not concealed thy
lovingkindness and thy truth from
the great congregation.
11 Withhold not thou thy tender mercies
from me, O LORD:
[a] Let thy lovingkindness and thy truth
continually preserve me.
12 For innumerable evils have compassed
me about:
[a] Mine iniquities have taken hold upon
me, so that I am not able to look *up;*
They are moe than the hairs of mine
head: therefore my heart [1] faileth me.
13 [a] Be pleased, O LORD, to deliver me:
O LORD, make haste to help me.
14 [a] Let them be ashamed and confounded
together that seek after my soul to
destroy it;
Let them be driven backward and put
to shame that wish me evil.
15 Let them be [a] desolate for a reward of
their shame
That say unto me, Aha, aha!
16 [a] Let all those that seek thee rejoice
and be glad in thee:
Let such as love thy salvation [b] say
continually, The LORD be magnified.
17 [a] But I *am* poor and needy; *yet* the Lord
thinketh upon me:
Thou *art* my help and my deliverer;
Make no tarrying, O my God.

Psalm 41

To the chief Musician, A Psalm of David.

1 Blessed *is* he that considereth [1] the
poor:
The LORD will deliver him [2] in time of
trouble.
2 The LORD will preserve him, and keep
him alive;
And he shall be blessed upon the
earth:
[a] And [1] thou wilt not deliver him unto
the will of his enemies.
3 The LORD will strengthen him upon the
bed of languishing:

40:6 [1] Heb. *digged*
40:8 [1] Heb. *in the midst of my bowels* [a] John 4:34 [b] Ps. 37:31; Jer. 31:33
40:9 [a] Ps. 22:22 [b] Ps. 119:13
40:10 [a] Acts 20:20
40:11 [a] Ps. 43:3
40:12 [1] Heb. *forsaketh* [a] Ps. 38:4
40:13 [a] Ps. 70:1
40:14 [a] Ps. 35:4
40:15 [a] Ps. 73:19
40:16 [a] Ps. 70:4 [b] Ps. 35:27
40:17 [a] Ps. 70:5
41:1 [1] Or, *the weak,* or, *sick* [2] Heb. *in the day of evil*
41:2 [1] Or, *do not thou deliver* [a] Ps. 27:12

40:6–8 David's commitment to God's will. Heb 10:5–10 applies these verses to Christ (see notes there).

40:6 *didst not desire . . . not required.* More important is obedience (see 1 Sam 15:22), especially to God's moral law (see Is 1:10–17; Amos 5:21–24; Mic 6:6–8)—i.e., the ten basic commandments of His covenant (see Ex 20:3–17; Deut 5:7–21). *opened.* Translated "opened," it refers to ears made able and eager to hear God's law (see Prov 28:9; Is 48:8; 50:4–5). If, however, it is translated "pierced," it probably refers to the sign by which a servant pledged lifelong service to his beloved master (see Ex 21:6; Deut 15:17).

‡40:7 *Lo, I come.* Probably refers to David's commitment to the Lord at the time of his enthronement. *In the volume . . . it is written of me.* Some take this to be a reference to a prophecy, perhaps Deut 17:14–15. The context, however, strongly suggests that the "volume" (or "scroll") refers to the personal copy of the law that the king is to take at the time of his enthronement to serve as the covenant charter of his administration (see Deut 17:18–20; 2 Ki 11:12; cf. 1 Ki 2:3).

40:8 *I delight.* I desire whatever is in full accord with God's "desire" (v. 6)—a claim that frames vv. 6–8.

40:9–10 David's life is filled with praise, proclaiming God's faithful and loving acts in behalf of His people. This, too, God desires more than animal sacrifices (see 50:7–15,23).

‡40:9 *preached.* See 68:11; 96:2; proclaimed as good tidings (see 1 Ki 1:42; Is 40:9; 41:27; 52:7; 61:1). *righteousness.* See note on 5:8. *in the great congregation.* See notes on 1:5; 9:1. *not refrained my lips.* He is not silent about God's praise (see 38:13–16; 39:1 and notes).

‡40:10 *I have not hid.* Have not kept a secret. *heart.* See note on 4:7. *thy lovingkindness and thy truth.* See note on 26:3.

40:11–17 The prayer for help.

40:11 *thy lovingkindness and thy truth.* Which he has been proclaiming to all at the temple (see v. 10 and note).

‡40:12 *iniquities have taken hold upon me.* In the form of the "innumerable evils" that burden him (see Ps 38–39 and their introductions). *not able to look up.* See note on 13:3. *moe* [i.e. "more"] *than the hairs of mine head.* See Mat 10:30; Luke 12:7. *heart.* See note on 4:7.

40:14–15 In the midst of his troubles his enemies harass him, as in 38:12; 39:8; 41:5,7 and often in the Psalms (see note on 5:9). May those who wish to put him to shame be put to shame themselves (see note on 5:10).

40:15 *Aha, aha!* See note on 3:2.

40:17 *poor and needy.* In need of God's help (see note on 34:6).

‡Ps 41 David's prayer for mercy when seriously ill. He acknowledges that his illness is related to his sin (v. 4). See the introductions to Ps 38–40. His enemies greet the prospect of his death with malicious glee (see note on 5:9), and even his "familiar friend" (v. 9) betrays his friendship (see note on 31:11–12). This psalm concludes a collection of four psalms connected by common themes, and also forms the conclusion to Book 1. (Book 1 begins and ends with a "Blessed" psalm.) In its structure, the psalm is very symmetrical. The first and last sections (vv. 1–3, vv. 10–12) frame the prayer with a note of confidence; the middle verses elaborate the prayer. Verse 13 is actually not part of the psalm but the doxology that closes Book 1 (see note on v. 13).

41 title *To the chief Musician.* See note on Ps 4 title.

41:1–3 Confidence that the Lord will restore.

41:1 *Blessed is he that considereth the poor.* Especially if he is king, whose duty it is to defend the powerless (see 72:2,4, 12–14; 82:3–4; Prov 29:14; 31:8–9; Is 11:4; Jer 22:16). *Blessed.* See note on 1:1.

Thou wilt [1]make all his bed in his
sickness.
4 I said, LORD, be merciful unto me:
Heal my soul; for I have sinned against
thee.
5 Mine enemies speak evil of me,
When shall he die, and his name
perish?
6 And if he come to see *me,* he speaketh
vanity:
His heart gathereth iniquity to itself;
When he goeth abroad, he telleth *it.*
7 All that hate me whisper together
against me:
Against me do they devise [1]my hurt.
8 [1]An evil disease, *say they,* cleaveth fast
unto him:
And *now* that he lieth he shall rise up
no more.
9 [a]Yea, [1]mine own familiar friend, in
whom I trusted,
[b]Which did eat *of* my bread,
Hath [2]lift up *his* heel against me.
10 But thou, O LORD, be merciful unto me,
And raise me up, that I may requite
them.

41:3 [1]Heb. *turn*
41:7 [1]Heb. *evil to me*
41:8 [1]Heb. *A thing of Belial*
41:9 [1]Heb. *the man of my peace* [2]Heb. *magnified* [a]2 Sam. 15:12; Job 19:19; Ps. 55:12 [b]Obad. 7; John 13:18
41:12 [a]Job 36:7; Ps. 34:15
41:13 [a]Ps. 106:48
42:T [1]Or, A Psalm *giving instruction of the sons, etc.*
42:1 [1]Heb. *brayeth*
42:2 [a]Ps. 63:1
42:3 [a]Ps. 80:5

11 By this I know that thou favourest me,
Because mine enemy doth not triumph
over me.
12 And *as for* me, thou upholdest me in
mine integrity,
And [a]settest me before thy face for ever.

13 [a]Blessed *be* the LORD God of Israel
from everlasting, and to everlasting.
Amen, and Amen.

Psalm 42

To the chief Musician, [1]Maschil,
for the sons of Korah.

1 As the hart [1]panteth after the water
brooks,
So panteth my soul after thee, O God.
2 [a]My soul thirsteth for God, for the
living God:
When shall I come and appear before
God?
3 [a]My tears have been my meat day and
night,
While *they* continually say unto me,
Where *is* thy God?

---

‡41:3 *make all his bed . . . sickness.* Or "restore him from his sickbed."
41:4–6 Prayer for God to show mercy and to heal.
41:4 *sinned.* See note on 32:3–5.
41:5 *When shall he die . . . ?* See note on 3:2. *his name perish.* See note on 9:5.
‡41:6 *he.* Any of his enemies. *see me.* Visit him in his sickness. *speaketh vanity.* Speaks falsely as if he were a friend. *heart.* See note on 4:7.
41:7–9 His enemies and his friend.
41:9 *familiar friend . . . Which did eat of my bread.* One who shared the king's table—i.e., was an honored, as well as trusted, friend (see note on 31:11–12). Reference may be to one who had sealed his friendship by a covenant (see note on 23:5). For Jesus' use of this verse in application to Himself see John 13:18. In fulfilling the role of His royal ancestor as God's anointed king over Israel, the great Son of David also experienced the hostility of men and the betrayal of a trusted associate, and thus fulfilled His forefather's lament.
41:10–12 Prayer, with confidence.
41:10 *that I may requite them.* That I (as king) may call them to account and pay them back for their evil.
‡41:12 *settest.* Establishes. *before thy face.* Or "in your presence," as the royal servant of Israel's heavenly King. (For the idiom see 101:7; 1 Sam 16:22, "stand before me"; 1 Ki 10:8, "before thee"; 17:1, "before whom I stand.") *for ever.* Never to be rejected (see 2 Sam 7:15–16).
41:13 The doxology with which the worshiping community is to respond to the contents of Book 1 (see 72:18–19; 89:52; 106:48; 150).
Ps 42–43 A prayer for deliverance from the "oppression of the enemy" (42:9; 43:2) and for restoration to the presence of God at His temple. That these two psalms form a single prayer (though they are counted as two psalms also in the Septuagint) is evident from its unique structure (see below) and the development of common themes. Ps 43 may have come to be separated from Ps 42 for a particular liturgical purpose (see introduction to Ps 9). The speaker may have been a leading member of the Korahites whose normal duties involved him in the liturgical activities of the temple (see especially 42:4 and note on Ps 42 title). It may be that the "ungodly nation" (43:1) referred to was the Arameans of Damascus and that the author had been taken captive by the Arameans during one of their incursions into Judah, such as that of Hazael (see 2 Ki 12:17–18). (This attack by Hazael affected especially the area in which the Korahites, descendants of Kohath, had been assigned cities; see Josh 21:4,9–19.) See also notes below. This psalm begins Book 2 of the Psalter, a collection that is distinguished from Book 1 primarily by the fact that the Hebrew word for "God" (*Elohim*) predominates, whereas in the first book the Hebrew word for "the LORD" (*Yahweh*) predominates.

Structurally, the stanzas of this psalm are followed by the same refrain (42:5,11; 43:5). The middle stanza, however, has a verse (42:8) that interrupts the developing thought and injects a note of confidence, such as comes to expression also in the threefold refrain. Apart from the refrains, the prayer is framed by an expression of longing for God's presence (42:1) and a vow to praise God at His altar (43:4). For other psalms with recurring refrains see Ps 46; 49; 59; 80; 107.
42 title *To the chief Musician.* See note on Ps 4 title. *Maschil.* See note on Ps 32 title. *for the sons of Korah.* "Sons of Korah" refers to the Levitical choir made up of the descendants of Korah appointed by David to serve in the temple liturgy. The Korahites represented the Levitical family of Kohath son of Levi. Their leader in the days of David was Heman (see Ps 88 title)—just as Asaph led the choir of the Gershonites and Jeduthun (Ethan) the choir of the Merarites (see 1 Chr 6:31–47 and note on Ps 39 title). This is the first of a collection of seven psalms ascribed to the "sons of Korah" (Ps 42–49); four more occur in Book 3 (Ps 84–85; 87–88).
42:1–4 Longing to be with God at the temple.
42:1 *hart panteth after . . . water.* Because its life depends on water—especially when being pressed by hunters, as the psalmist was by his oppressors. *soul.* See note on 6:3.
42:2 *living God.* See Deut 5:26. *When . . . ?* Circumstances (see v. 9; 43:1–2) now prevent him from being at the temple. *appear before God.* Enter His presence to commune with Him (see Ex 19:17; 29:42–43; 30:6,36).
42:3 *day and night.* See vv. 8,10. *Where is thy God?* See note on 10:11.

4 When I remember these *things,* [a]I
pour out my soul in me:
For I had gone with the multitude, [b]I
went with them to the house of God,
With the voice of joy and praise, *with* a
multitude that kept holyday.
5 [a]Why art thou [1]cast down, O my soul?
and *why* art thou disquieted in me?
[b]Hope thou in God: for I shall yet
[2]praise him
[3]*For* the help of his countenance.

6 O my God, my soul is cast down
within me: therefore will I
remember thee
From the land of Jordan, and of the
Hermonites, from [1]the hill Mizar.
7 Deep calleth unto deep at the noise of
thy waterspouts:
[a]All thy waves and thy billows are
gone over me.
8 *Yet* the LORD will command his
lovingkindness in the daytime,
And [a]in the night his song *shall be*
with me,
And my prayer unto the God of my life.
9 I will say unto God my rock, Why hast
thou forgotten me?
[a]Why go I mourning because of the
oppression of the enemy?
10 *As* with a [1]sword in my bones, mine
enemies reproach me;
[a]While they say daily unto me, Where
is thy God?

42:4 [a]Job 30:16 [b]Is. 30:29
42:5 [1]Heb. *bowed down* [2]Or, *give thanks* [3]Or, *His presence* is *salvation* [a]ver. 11 [b]Lam. 3:24
42:6 [1]Or, *the little hill*
42:7 [a]Ps. 88:7
42:8 [a]Job 35:10
42:9 [a]Ps. 38:6
42:10 [1]Or, *killing* [a]Joel 2:17; Mic. 7:10
42:11 [a]Ps. 43:5
43:1 [1]Or, *unmerciful* [2]Heb. *from a man of deceit and iniquity* [a]Ps. 26:1 [b]Ps. 35:1
43:2 [a]Ps. 42:9
43:3 [a]Ps. 40:11; 57:3 [b]Ps. 3:4
43:4 [1]Heb. *the gladness of my joy*
43:5 [a]Ps. 42:5,11

11 [a]Why art thou cast down, O my soul?
and why art thou disquieted within
me?
Hope thou in God: for I shall yet praise
him,
Who is the health of my countenance,
and my God.

Psalm 43

1 [a]Judge me, O God, and [b]plead my
cause against an [1]ungodly nation:
O deliver me [2]from the deceitful and
unjust man.
2 For thou *art* the God of my strength:
why dost thou cast me off?
[a]Why go I mourning because of the
oppression of the enemy?
3 [a]O send out thy light and thy truth: let
them lead me;
Let them bring me unto [b]thy holy hill,
and to thy tabernacles.
4 Then will I go unto the altar of God,
Unto God [1]my exceeding joy:
Yea, upon the harp will I praise thee,
O God my God.
5 [a]Why art thou cast down, O my soul?
and why art thou disquieted within
me?
Hope in God: for I shall yet praise
him,
Who is the health of my countenance,
and my God.

‡42:4 The psalmist remembers the past processions to Jerusalem on the holy feast days. His current situation (see note on Ps 42–43) prevents him from being part of such celebrations. *soul.* See note on 6:3.
‡42:5 The refrain: faith encouraging faith (see 27:13–14 and introduction to Ps 27). *praise him.* For His saving help (see notes on 7:17; 9:1; see also 43:4). *For the help of his countenance.* Or, "his presence is salvation." For the significance of God's "countenance/face," cf. 13:1 and note; 41:12 and note.
42:6–10 The cause and depth of the trouble of his soul.
‡42:6 *soul is cast down.* See vv. 5,11; 43:5. *therefore will I remember thee.* As he remembers (v. 4) in his exile the joy of his past intimacy with God, so now in his exile he remembers God and painfully wonders (vv. 7,9–10), yet not without hope (v. 8). *From the land . . . from the hill Mizar.* Probably indicating that the author speaks from exile outside the contemporary boundaries of Israel and Judah. It appears that the author locates himself at mount Mizar (a small peak or village, not otherwise known) on the flanks of mount Hermon somewhere near the headwaters of the Jordan.
‡42:7 *Deep calleth . . . noise of thy waterspouts.* Often taken to be an allusion to the cascading waters of the upper Jordan as they rush down from mount Hermon. It is more likely, however, that this is a literary allusion to the "waterspouts" (or "waterfalls") by which the waters from God's storehouse of water above (see note on 36:8)—the "Deep" above—pour down into the streams and rivers that empty into the seas—the "deep" below. It pictures the great distress the author suffers, and the imagery is continued in the following reference to God's "waves" and "billows" sweeping over him (see 69:1–2; 88:7; Jonah 2:3,5; see also note on 32:6). God's hand is involved in the psalmist's suffering, at least to the extent that He has allowed this catastrophe. He seems to the psalmist to have "forgotten" (v. 9)—to have "cast [him] off" (43:2). But he makes no link between this and any sin in his life (see Ps 44; 77).
‡42:8 The center: confession of hope in all the trouble. That is, "Daytime-and-night [cf. v. 3] the LORD directs his love, and his song is with me" (see note on 3:7). *the LORD.* Only here at the center in this psalm (see introduction). *command his lovingkindness.* Send forth His love, like a messenger to do His will (see 43:3). *lovingkindness.* See note on 6:4. *his song.* A song concerning Him. *prayer.* Praise and prayer belong together in the thought of the psalmist.
42:9 Echoed in 43:2. *rock.* See note on 18:2. *Why . . . ? Why . . . ?* See note on 6:3 (see also Introduction: Theology).
42:10 See v. 3. *bones.* See note on 6:2.
‡42:11 *health of my countenance.* See v. 5 and note.
43:1–4 Prayer for deliverance from the enemy and for restoration to God's presence.
43:1 A plea in the language of the court (see introduction to Ps 17).
43:2 Echoes 42:9.
43:3 *thy light and thy truth.* Personified as God's messengers who work out (1) His salvation (light; see note on 27:1) and (2) His faithful care in behalf of His own (truth; see 26:3; 30:9; 40:10). May these guide me back to Your temple. *holy hill.* See note on 2:6.
43:4 See note on 7:17. *unto the altar.* See 26:6 and note.
‡43:5 *health of my countenance.* See 42:5 and note.

Psalm 44

To the chief Musician for
the sons of Korah, Maschil.

1 We have heard with our ears, O God,
[a]Our fathers have told us,
What work thou didst in their days, in
the times of old.
2 *How* [a]thou didst drive out the heathen
with thy hand, and plantedst them;
How thou didst afflict the people, and
cast them out.
3 For [a]they got not the land in
possession by their own sword,
Neither did their own arm save them:
But thy right hand, and thine arm, and
the light of thy countenance,
[b]Because thou hadst a favour unto them.
4 [a]Thou *art* my King, O God:
Command deliverances for Jacob.
5 Through thee [a]will we push down our
enemies:
Through thy name will we tread them
under that rise up against us.
6 For [a]I will not trust in my bow,
Neither shall my sword save me.
7 But thou hast saved us from our
enemies,
And hast [a]put them to shame that
hated us.
8 [a]In God we boast all the day long,
And praise thy name for ever. Selah.

9 But [a]thou hast cast off, and put us to
shame;
And goest not forth with our armies.
10 Thou makest us to [a]turn back from the
enemy:
And they which hate us spoil for
themselves.
11 [a]Thou hast given us [1]like sheep
appointed for meat;
And hast [b]scattered us among the
heathen.
12 [a]Thou sellest thy people [1]for nought,
And dost not increase *thy wealth* by
their price.
13 [a]Thou makest us a reproach to our
neighbours,
A scorn and a derision to them that are
round about us.
14 [a]Thou makest us a byword among the
heathen,
A [b]shaking of the head among the
people.
15 My confusion *is* continually before me,
And the shame of my face hath
covered me,
16 For the voice of him that reproacheth
and blasphemeth;
[a]By reason of the enemy and avenger.
17 [a]All this is come upon us; yet have we
not forgotten thee,
Neither have we dealt falsely in thy
covenant.
18 Our heart is not turned back,
[a]Neither have our [1]steps declined from
thy way;
19 Though thou hast sore broken us in
[a]the place of dragons,
And covered us [b]with the shadow of
death.
20 If we have forgotten the name of our
God,
Or [a]stretched out our hands to a
strange god;

44:1 [a]Ex. 12:26; Ps. 78:3
44:2 [a]Ex. 15:17; Deut. 7:1; Ps. 80:8
44:3 [a]Deut. 8:17; Josh. 24:12 [b]Deut. 7:7,8
44:4 [a]Ps. 74:12
44:5 [a]Dan. 8:4
44:6 [a]Ps. 33:16
44:7 [a]Ps. 40:14
44:8 [a]Ps. 34:2; Jer. 9:24
44:9 [a]Ps. 60:1
44:10 [a]Lev. 26:17; Deut. 28:25
44:11 [1]Heb. *as sheep of meat* [a]Rom. 8:36 [b]Deut. 28:64; Ps. 60:1
44:12 [1]Heb. *without riches* [a]Is. 52:3,4; Jer. 15:13
44:13 [a]Deut. 28:37
44:14 [a]Jer. 24:9 [b]Job 16:4; Ps. 22:7
44:16 [a]Ps. 8:2
44:17 [a]Dan. 9:13
44:18 [1]Or, *goings* [a]Job 23:11
44:19 [a]Is. 34:13 [b]Ps. 23:4
44:20 [a]Deut. 6:14; Ps. 88:9

Ps 44 Israel's cry for help after suffering a devastating defeat at the hand of an enemy. In the light of vv. 17–22, it is difficult to associate this psalm with any of those defeats announced by the prophets as judgments on Israel's covenant unfaithfulness. It probably relates to an experience of the kingdom of Judah (which as a nation did not break covenant with the Lord until late in her history), perhaps during the reign of Jehoshaphat or Hezekiah. Structurally, three thematic developments rise one upon the other as the psalm advances to the prayer in the closing verses. Its structure is like the stages of a ziggurat (a stepped pyramidal structure that the Babylonians built as a mountain-like base for some of their temples; see Gen 11:4 and note) leading to the temple that crowns it. First there is praise of the Lord for past victories (vv. 1–8), second a description of the present defeat and its consequences (vv. 9–16), third a plea of innocence (vv. 17–22), then finally the prayer (vv. 23–26). Each of the themes (recalling of past mercies, description of the present distress, and claim of covenant loyalty) in its own way functions as a ground for the appeal for help (see Ps 40 and its introduction; see also the lengthy prefaces to prayer in Ps 40; 89).

44 title See note on Ps 42 title.

44:1–8 Praise to God for past victories: (1) those by which Israel became established in the land (vv. 1–3); (2) those by which Israel has been kept secure in the land (vv. 4–8).

44:1 See 78:3.

44:3 *light of thy countenance.* See notes on 4:6; 13:1.

44:4 *my.* Here and elsewhere in this psalm the first-person singular pronoun refers to the nation corporately (see note on Ps 30 title). *Jacob.* See note on 14:7.

44:5,8 *thy name.* See v. 20; see also note on 5:11.

44:9–16 But now You have forsaken us: (1) You have caused us to suffer defeat (vv. 9–12); (2) You have shamed us before our enemies (vv. 13–16).

44:11 *given us like sheep . . . for meat.* Have not protected us as our Shepherd-King (see v. 4 and note on 23:1).

44:12 *sellest thy people.* Like chattel no longer valued (see Deut 32:30; Judg 2:14). *for nought.* For nothing of value (see Is 52:3; Jer 15:13; cf. Is 43:3–4).

‡44:14 *A shaking of the head.* A gesture of contempt. See 64:8.

‡44:15 *My confusion.* Lit. "my reproach."

‡44:16 *For.* Because of. *avenger.* See 8:2 and note.

44:17–22 And we have not been disloyal to You: (1) We have not been untrue to Your covenant (vv. 17–19); (2) You are our witness that we have not turned to another god (vv. 20–22).

44:17 *thy covenant.* See Ex 19–24.

44:18 *heart.* See note on 4:7. *thy way.* The way marked out in God's covenant (see note on 5:8).

‡44:19 *thou hast sore broken us.* You have crushed us, but that cannot be used as evidence that we have been disloyal. *place of dragons.* Or "place of jackals," a desolate place, uninhabited by man (see Is 13:22; Jer 9:11). *shadow of death.* The absence of all that was associated with the metaphor "light" (see notes on 30:1; 36:9).

44:20 *stretched out our hands.* Prayed (see Ex 9:29).

21 [a]Shall not God search this out?
For he knoweth the secrets of the heart.
22 [a]Yea, for thy sake are we killed all the day long;
We are counted as sheep for the slaughter.
23 [a]Awake, why sleepest thou, O Lord?
Arise, cast *us* not off for ever.
24 [a]Wherefore hidest thou thy face,
And forgettest our affliction and our oppression?
25 For [a]our soul is bowed down to the dust:
Our belly cleaveth unto the earth.
26 Arise [1]for our help,
And redeem us for thy mercy's sake.

Psalm 45

To the chief Musician [a]upon Shoshannim, for the sons of Korah, [1]Maschil, A Song of loves.

1 My heart [1]is inditing a good matter:
I speak of the things which I have made touching *the* king:
My tongue *is* the pen of a ready writer.
2 Thou art fairer than the children of men:
[a]Grace is poured into thy lips:
Therefore God hath blessed thee for ever.
3 Gird thy [a]sword upon *thy* thigh,
[b]O *most* mighty,
With thy glory and thy majesty.
4 [a]And *in* thy majesty [1]ride prosperously
Because of truth and meekness *and* righteousness;
And thy right hand shall teach thee terrible *things.*
5 Thine arrows *are* sharp
In the heart of the king's enemies;
Whereby the people fall under thee.
6 [a]Thy throne, O God, *is* for ever and ever:
The sceptre of thy kingdom *is* a right sceptre.
7 [a]Thou lovest righteousness, and hatest wickedness:

44:21 [a]Job 31:14; Ps. 139:1
44:22 [a]Rom. 8:36
44:23 [a]Ps. 7:6
44:24 [a]Job 13:24; Ps. 13:1
44:25 [a]Ps. 119:25
44:26 [1]Heb. *a help for us*
45:T [1]Or, *of instruction* [a]Ps. 69, title; 80, title
45:1 [1]Heb. *boileth,* or, *bubbleth up*
45:2 [a]Luke 4:22
45:3 [a]Is. 49:2; Heb. 4:12; Rev. 1:16 [b]Is. 9:6
45:4 [1]Heb. *prosper thou, ride thou* [a]Rev. 6:2
45:6 [a]Ps. 93:2; Heb. 1:8
45:7 [a]Ps. 33:5

44:22 *Yea.* Or "As a matter of fact" or "As you, O God, know." From the time of her stay in Egypt (see Ex 1), Israel has suffered the hostility of the nations because of her relationship with the Lord (see Mat 10:34). For Paul's application of this verse to the Christian community in the light of Christ's death and resurrection see Rom 8:36.

44:23–26 The appeal for help: (1) Awake to our need (vv. 23–24); (2) arise to our help (vv. 25–26; see introduction to Ps 16).

44:23 *Awake.* See note on 7:6. *why . . . ?* See note on 6:3 (see also Introduction: Theology).

44:24 *hidest . . . thy face.* See note on 13:1.

44:25 *bowed down to the dust.* Is about to sink into death (see 22:29 and note; see also note on 30:1).

44:26 *Arise.* See note on 3:7. *redeem.* See note on 25:22. *mercy's sake.* See note on 6:4.

Ps 45 A song in praise of the king on his wedding day (see title). He undoubtedly belonged to David's dynasty, and the song was probably used at more than one royal wedding. Since the bride is a foreign princess (see vv. 10,12), the wedding reflects the king's standing as a figure of international significance (see note on v. 9). Accordingly he is addressed as one whose reign is to be characterized by victories over the nations (vv. 3–5; cf. Ps 2; 110). As a royal son of David, he is a type (foreshadowing) of Christ. After the exile this psalm was applied to the Messiah, the promised Son of David who would sit on David's throne (for the application of vv. 6–7 to Christ see Heb 1:8–9). The superscription implies that it was composed and sung by a member of the Levitical temple choir, a fact not surprising in view of the close link between the temple (housing the earthly throne room of Israel's heavenly King) and the Davidic dynasty (the Lord's appointed regents over His people, described throughout the books of Samuel, Kings and Chronicles). As a word from one of the temple personnel, the song was no doubt received as a word from the temple—and from the One who sat enthroned there. In its structure, the song is framed by vv. 1,17 while vv. 2,16 constitute a secondary frame within them—all addressed to the king. The body of the song falls into two parts: (1) words addressed to the king (vv. 3–9) and (2) words addressed to the royal bride (vv. 10–15). These in turn each contain two parts, reflecting a similar pattern: (1) (a) exhortations to the king (vv. 3–5), (b) the glory of the king (vv. 6–9); (2) (a) exhortations to the bride (vv. 10–11), (b) the glory of the bride (vv. 12–15).

‡45 title *To the chief Musician.* See note on Ps 4 title. *upon.* See note on Ps 9 title. *Shoshannim.* Means "Lilies" (see Ps 69 title). "Lilies" may be an abbreviated form of "The Lily (Lilies) of the Covenant" found in the titles of Ps 60; 80 ("Shushan-eduth"). *for the sons of Korah.* See note on Ps 42 title. *Maschil.* See note on Ps 32 title. *Song.* See note on Ps 30 title.

‡45:1 See v. 17, where the speaker pledges (perhaps by means of this song) to perpetuate the king's memory throughout the generations and awaken the praise of the nations. *heart.* See note on 4:7. *is inditing.* Is stirred up, bubbling up. *things which I have made . . . king.* Verses I have composed for the king.

45:2 *fairer than the children of men.* One who excels in manly traits and beauty, as a king should (see 1 Sam 9:2; 16:18)—but he is so beyond ordinary men as to be almost Godlike (see note on v. 6). *Grace is poured into thy lips.* See Prov 22:11; Eccl 10:12; cf. Is 50:4; Luke 4:22; see also v. 16, where it is suggested that such a king will be perpetuated in his sons. *for ever.* See note on v. 6.

45:3–5 Go forth with your sword victoriously in the service of all that is right, and clothe yourself thereby with glory—make your reign adorn you more truly than the wedding garb with which you are now arrayed (v. 8).

45:3 *glory and . . . majesty.* See 21:5 and note.

‡45:4 *righteousness.* See note on 1:5. *thy right hand . . . terrible things.* Or "let your right hand do awesome deeds." See 66:5; 106:22; 145:6. For the warrior's "right hand" as a symbol of strength, cf. Ex 15:6, 12.

45:5 *people fall under thee.* See 2:8–9; 110:1–2,5–6.

45:6–9 The glory of the king's reign: justice and righteousness (see Ps 72).

‡45:6 *O God.* Possibly the king's throne is called God's throne because he is God's appointed regent. But it is also possible that the king himself is addressed as "god." The Davidic king (the "LORD's anointed," 2 Sam 19:21), because of his special relationship with God, was called at his enthronement the "son" of God (see 2:7; 2 Sam 7:14; 1 Chr 28:6; cf. 89:27). In this psalm, which praises the king and especially extols his "glory and . . . majesty" (v. 3), it is not unthinkable that he was called "god" as a title of honor (cf. Is 9:6). Such a description of the Davidic king attains its fullest meaning when applied to Christ, as the author of Hebrews does (Heb 1:8–9). (The pharaohs of Egypt were sometimes addressed as "my god" by their vassal kings in Canaan, as evidenced by the Amarna letters; see chart, p.

Therefore [b] [1] God, thy God, [c] hath
anointed thee
With the oil [d] of gladness above thy
fellows.
8 [a] All thy garments *smell of* myrrh, and
aloes, *and* cassia,
Out of the ivory palaces, *where*by they
have made thee glad.
9 Kings' daughters *were* among thy
honourable *women:*
[a] Upon thy right hand did stand the
queen in gold of Ophir.
10 Hearken, O daughter, and consider,
and incline thine ear;
[a] Forget also thine own people, and thy
father's house;
11 So shall the king greatly desire thy
beauty:
[a] For he *is* thy Lord; and worship thou
him.
12 And the daughter of Tyre *shall be there*
with a gift;
Even [a] the rich among the people shall
intreat [1] thy favour.
13 [a] The king's daughter *is* all glorious
within:
Her clothing *is* of wrought gold.
14 [a] She shall be brought unto the king in
raiment of needlework:
The virgins her companions that follow
her *shall be* brought unto thee.
15 With gladness and rejoicing shall they
be brought:
They shall enter into the king's palace.
16 Instead of thy fathers shall be thy
children,
[a] Whom thou mayest make princes in
all the earth.
17 I will make thy name to be
remembered in all generations:
Therefore shall the people praise thee
for ever and ever.

45:7 [1] [Or, *O God*] [b] Is. 61:1 [c] 1 Ki. 1:39; Ps. 79:4 [d] Ps. 21:6
45:8 [a] Sol. 1:3
45:9 [a] 1 Ki. 2:19
45:10 [a] See Deut. 21:13
45:11 [a] Ps. 95:6; Is. 54:5
45:12 [1] Heb. *thy face* [a] Is. 49:23
45:13 [a] Is. 61:10
45:14 [a] Sol. 1:4
45:16 [a] 1 Pet. 2:9; Rev. 1:6; 20:6
46:T [1] Or, *of* [a] Ps. 48; 66 [b] 1 Chr. 15:20
46:1 [a] Deut. 4:7
46:2 [1] Heb. *the heart of the seas*
46:3 [a] Ps. 93:3,4

Psalm 46

To the chief Musician [1] for the sons of Korah,
[a] A Song [b] upon Alamoth.

1 God *is* our refuge and strength,
[a] A very present help in trouble.
2 Therefore will not we fear, though the
earth be removed,
And though the mountains be carried
into [1] the midst of the sea;
3 [a] *Though* the waters thereof roar *and*
be troubled,
Though the mountains shake with the
swelling thereof. Selah.

xix.) *for ever and ever.* See vv. 2,17. Such was the language used with respect to kings (see note on 21:4). It here gains added significance in the light of God's covenant with David (see 89:4,29,36; 132:12; 2 Sam 7:16). In Christ, the Son of David, it is fulfilled. *a right sceptre.* Or "a sceptre which works justice."

45:7 *oil of gladness.* God has anointed him with a more delightful oil than the aromatic oils with which his head and body were anointed on his wedding day—namely, with joy (see 23:5; Is 61:3). *fellows.* The noble guests of the king, perhaps from other lands.

45:8–9 The glory of the king's wedding.

45:8 *myrrh.* See notes on Gen 37:25; Sol 1:13. *aloes.* See note on Sol 4:14. *cassia.* See note on Ex 25:6. *ivory palaces.* See 1 Ki 22:39; Amos 3:15; 6:4.

45:9 *Kings' daughters.* Whether members of his royal harem (see 1 Ki 11:1–3) or guests at his wedding, they represent international recognition of the king. *in gold of Ophir.* Adorned with jewels of finest gold (see notes on Gen 10:29; 1 Ki 9:28) and all the finery associated with it.

45:10–15 The word to the royal bride.

45:10–11 Be totally loyal to your adoring king.

45:12–15 The royal bride's glory.

45:12 *daughter of Tyre.* A personification of the city of Tyre and its inhabitants (see note on 2 Ki 19:21). The king of Tyre was the first foreign ruler to recognize the Davidic dynasty (see 2 Sam 5:11), and Solomon maintained close relations with that city-state (see 1 Ki 5; 9:10–14,26–28). As a great trading center on the Mediterranean coast, Tyre was world-renowned for its wealth (see Is 23; Ezek 26:1–28:19). *the rich.* Such as those from your homeland. *intreat thy favour.* Desire to be in your good graces as the wife of this king.

45:14 *virgins her companions.* She too has "fellows" (see v. 7), perhaps her permanent attendants. *unto thee.* To the king.

‡45:16 *Instead of thy fathers . . . children.* Expresses confidence that God will continue the family line of the king (dynastic succession). Perhaps it is also hinted that the sons to come will surpass the fathers in honor (see note on v. 2).

45:17 See note on v. 1. *for ever and ever.* See note on v. 6.

Ps 46 A celebration of the security of Jerusalem as the city of God (the inspiration of Martin Luther's great hymn, "A Mighty Fortress Is Our God"). Thematically this psalm is closely related to Ps 48 (see also Ps 76; 87), while Ps 47 celebrates God's victorious reign over all the earth. It probably predates the exile. However, as a song concerning the "city of God" (v. 4), the royal city of His kingdom on earth (see Ps 48), it remained for Israel a song of hope celebrating the certain triumph of God's kingdom. It was originally liturgical and sung at the temple: The citizens of Jerusalem (or the Levitical choir in their stead) apparently sang the opening stanza (vv. 1–3) and the responses (vv. 7,11), while the Levitical leader of the liturgy probably sang the second and third stanzas (vv. 4–6,8–10). In its structure, apart from the refrains (vv. 7,11), the psalm is composed of three symmetrical stanzas, each containing three verses. For other psalms with recurring refrains see introduction to Ps 42–43.

‡46 title *To the chief Musician.* See note on Ps 4 title. *for the sons of Korah.* See note on Ps 42 title. *A Song.* See note on Ps 30 title. *upon.* See note on Ps 6 title. *Alamoth.* Probably a musical term. Since the Hebrew word appears to mean "maidens," the phrase "upon Alamoth" may refer to the "maidens playing tambourines" who accompanied the singers as the liturgical procession made its way to the temple (68:25).

46:1–3 A triumphant confession of fearless trust in God, though the continents break up and sink beneath the resurging waters of the seas—i.e., though the creation itself may seem to become uncreated (see 104:6–9; Gen 1:9–10) and all may appear to be going down before the onslaught of the primeval deep. The described upheaval is probably imagery for great threats to Israel's existence (see note on 32:6), especially from her enemies (see vv. 6,8–10; 65:5–8).

4 *There is* [a]a river, the streams whereof
shall make glad [b]the city of God,
The holy *place* of the tabernacles of the
most High.
5 God *is* [a]in the midst of her; she shall
not be moved:
God shall help her, [1]*and that* right early.
6 [a]The heathen raged, the kingdoms
were moved:
He uttered his voice, [b]the earth
melted.
7 The LORD of hosts *is* with us;
The God of Jacob *is* [a 1]our refuge. Selah.

8 [a]Come, behold the works of the LORD,
What desolations he hath made in the
earth.
9 [a]He maketh wars to cease unto the
end of the earth;
[b]He breaketh the bow, and cutteth the
spear in sunder;
[c]He burneth the chariot in the fire.
10 Be still, and know that I *am* God:
[a]I will be exalted among the heathen,
I will be exalted in the earth.
11 The LORD of hosts *is* with us;
The God of Jacob *is* our refuge. Selah.

Psalm 47

To the chief Musician, A Psalm
[1]for the sons of Korah.

1 [a]O clap *your* hands, all ye people;
Shout unto God with the voice of
triumph.
2 For the LORD most High *is* [a]terrible;
[b]*He is* a great King over all the earth.
3 [a]He shall subdue the people under us,
And the nations under our feet.
4 He shall choose our [a]inheritance for us,
The excellency of Jacob whom he
loved. Selah.

5 [a]God is gone up with a shout,

46:4 [a]See Is. 8:7 [b]Ps. 48:1,8; Is. 60:14
46:5 [1]Heb. *when the morning appeareth* [a]Is. 12:6; Ezek. 43:7
46:6 [a]Ps. 2:1 [b]Josh. 2:9
46:7 [1]Heb. *a high place for us* [a]Ps. 9:9
46:8 [a]Ps. 66:5
46:9 [a]Is. 2:4 [b]Ps. 76:3 [c]Ezek. 39:9
46:10 [a]Is. 2:11,17
47:T [1]Or, *of*
47:1 [a]Is. 55:12
47:2 [a]Deut. 7:21; Ps. 76:12 [b]Mal. 1:14
47:3 [a]Ps. 18:47
47:4 [a]1 Pet. 1:4
47:5 [a]Ps. 68:33

46:4–6 A description of blessed Zion—a comforting declaration of God's mighty, sustaining presence in His city.
‡46:4 *river.* Jerusalem had no river, unlike Thebes (Nah 3:8), Damascus (2 Ki 5:12), Nineveh (Nah 2:6,8) or Babylon (137:1), yet she had a "river." Here the "river" of 36:8 (see note there) serves as a metaphor for the continual outpouring of the sustaining and refreshing blessings of God, which make the city of God like the Garden of Eden (see Gen 2:10; Is 33:21; 51:3; cf. also Ezek 31:4–9). *city of God.* See v. 5; see especially Ps 48. *God . . . most High.* That is, God most High (see 57:2; see also note on 3:7). *tabernacles.* Dwelling places. See note on 9:11. *most High.* See note on Gen 14:19.
‡46:5 *right early.* Lit. "at the turning of the morning," i.e. at dawn, when attacks against cities were likely to be launched. His help brings on the dawn of deliverance, dispelling the night of danger (see 44:19 and note; cf. Is 37:36 for an example).
46:6 *heathen . . . moved.* Because of God's victory (see vv. 8–9; 48:4–7). *raged.* See v. 3 and note on vv. 1–3; see also 2:1–3; Rev 11:18. *uttered his voice.* See 2:5; 9:5; Jer 25:30; Amos 1:2; see also 104:7. God's thunder is evoked (see introduction to Ps 29), the thunder of His wrath (see 18:13; Is 2:10). *earth melted.* As though struck by lightning (see 97:4–5).
46:7 The people's glad response (also v. 11). *LORD of hosts.* See note on 1 Sam 1:3. *Jacob.* See note on 14:7.
46:8–10 A declaration of the blessed effects of God's triumph over the nations.
46:8 *Come, behold.* An invitation to see God's victories in the world (see 48:8 and note). *the LORD.* Emphatic because of its rare use in Book 2 of the Psalter. *in the earth.* Among the hostile nations.
46:9 No more attacks against His city. The verse probably speaks of universal peace (see note on 65:6–7). *breaketh . . . cutteth . . . burneth.* See 76:3; see also 1 Sam 2:4. For the Messiah's universal victory over Israel's enemies see Is 9:2–7.
‡46:10 God's voice breaks through, as He addresses the nations (see v. 6)—the climax. *Be still.* Here, the Hebrew for this phrase probably means "Enough!" as in 1 Sam 15:16 ("Stay"). God instructs the people to cease from seeking to find security in their own actions and strength and to look to Him. *know.* Acknowledge. *I will be exalted . . . in the earth.* God's mighty acts in behalf of His people will bring Him universal recognition, a major theme in the Psalter (see 22:27; 47:9; 57:5,11; 64:9; 65:8; 66:1–7; 67:2–5; 86:9; 98:2–3; 99:2–3; 102:15) and elsewhere in the OT (see Ex 7:5; 14:4,18; Lev 26:45; Num 14:15; 1 Sam 17:46; 1 Ki 8:41–43; 2 Ki 19:19; Ezek 20:41; 28:25; 36:23; Hab 2:14). This has proven to be supremely true of God's climactic saving act in the birth, life, death, resurrection and glorification of Jesus Christ—yet to be brought to complete fruition at His return.
46:11 See note on v. 7.
Ps 47 Celebration of the universal reign of Israel's God: a testimony to the nations. This psalm belongs to a group of hymns to the Great King found elsewhere clustered in Ps 92–100. Here it serves to link Ps 46 and 48, identifying the God who reigns in Zion as "a great King over all the earth" (v. 2; see v. 7; 48:2). It dates from the period of the monarchy and was composed for use in the temple liturgy on one of the high festival days. The specific setting is perhaps the feast of tabernacles (see Lev 23:34), which was also the festival for which Solomon waited to dedicate the temple (see 1 Ki 8:2). A liturgical procession is presupposed (v. 5), similar to that indicated in Ps 24; 68. Later Jewish usage employed this psalm in the synagogue liturgy for *Rosh Hashanah* (the New Year festival). The Christian church has appropriately employed it in the celebration of Christ's ascension (see v. 5). Structurally, vv. 5–6 form a centered (see note on 6:6) couplet between two four-line stanzas (in Hebrew). This center may represent a different voice in the liturgy.
47 title See note on Ps 42 title.
47:1–4 The nations are called to rejoice in the God of Israel, the Lord over all the earth—OT anticipation of the evangelization of the nations (see notes on v. 9; 9:1).
47:1 *clap your hands.* As at the enthronement of a king (see 2 Ki 11:12; see also 98:8) or at other times of rejoicing (see Is 55:12). *voice of triumph.* See 1 Ki 1:40; 2 Ki 11:14.
47:2–3 The Lord of all the earth has shaped the destiny of His people Israel (see 105:6; 135:4; Ex 9:29; 15:1–18; 19:5–6; Deut 7:6; 14:2; Is 41:8).
‡47:2 *most High.* See note on Gen 14:19. *great King.* A title often used by the imperial rulers of Assyria (see note on 2 Ki 18:19). *terrible.* Awesome and to be feared. See 68:35; 89:7; 99:3; 111:9; see also note on 45:4.
47:3 See 2 Sam 5:17–25; 8:1–14; 10.
‡47:4 *He shall choose.* The Lord affirms His past decrees each time He gives Israel victory over its enemies. *inheritance.* The promised land (see Gen 12:7; 17:8; Ex 3:8; Deut 1:8; Jer 3:18). *excellency.* That in which Jacob took supreme delight. *Jacob.* See note on 14:7.
47:5–6 The center of the poem (see note on 6:6). These verses

The LORD with the sound of a trumpet.
6 Sing *praises* to God, sing *praises:*
Sing *praises* unto our King, sing *praises.*
7 [a]For God *is* the King of all the earth:
[b]Sing ye *praises* [1]with understanding.
8 [a]God reigneth over the heathen:
God sitteth upon the throne of his holiness.
9 [1]The princes of the people are gathered together,
Even the people of the God of Abraham:
[a]For the shields of the earth *belong* unto God:
He is greatly exalted.

47:7 [1]Or, every one *that hath understanding* [a]Zech. 14:9 [b]1 Cor. 14:15
47:8 [a]1 Chr. 16:31; Ps. 93:1; Rev. 19:6
47:9 [1]Or, *The voluntary of the people are gathered* unto *the people of the God of Abraham* [a]Ps. 89:18

Psalm 48

A Song *and* Psalm [1]for the sons of Korah.

1 Great *is* the LORD, and greatly to be praised
[a]In the city of our God, *in* the [b]mountain of his holiness.
2 [a]Beautiful for situation, the joy of the whole earth, *is* mount Zion,
[b]*On* the sides of the north, [c]the city of the great King.
3 God is known in her palaces for a refuge.
4 For lo, [a]the kings were assembled, they passed by together.
5 They saw *it, and* so they marvelled;
They were troubled, *and* hasted away.
6 Fear [a]took hold upon them there,
And pain, as of a woman in travail.
7 Thou [a]breakest the ships of Tarshish
[b]with an east wind.
8 As we have heard, so have we seen
In the city of the LORD of hosts, in the city of our God:
God will establish it for ever. Selah.
9 We have thought of [a]thy lovingkindness, O God,
In the midst of thy temple.
10 According to [a]thy name, O God, so *is* thy praise unto the ends of the earth:
Thy right hand is full *of* righteousness.

48:T [1]Or, *of*
48:1 [a]Ps. 46:4 [b]Is. 2:2,3; Mic. 4:1; Zech. 8:3
48:2 [a]Ps. 50:2; Jer. 3:19 [b]Is. 14:13 [c]Mat. 5:35
48:4 [a]2 Sam. 10:6, 14,16, 18,19
48:6 [a]Ex. 15:15
48:7 [a]Ezek. 27:26 [b]Jer. 18:17
48:9 [a]Ps. 26:3
48:10 [a]Deut. 28:58

portray the liturgical ascension of God to the temple—perhaps represented by the processional bearing of the ark into the temple. The ark is symbolic of God's throne; the temple is the earthly symbol of His heavenly palace (see Ps 24; 68).

47:5 *a shout . . . sound of a trumpet.* See note on v. 1. *trumpet.* The ram's horn, here announcing the presence of God as King (see 98:6; Ex 19:16,19; Josh 6:4).

47:7–9 The liturgical enthronement of God as world ruler.

‡47:7 *God is the King of all the earth.* See 2 Sam 15:10; 2 Ki 9:13; Is 52:7. *with understanding.* Hebrew *Maschil* (see note on Ps 32 title).

47:8 *sitteth upon the throne of his holiness.* In the most holy place of the temple, where He takes the reins of world rule into His hands (see Jer 17:12). This verse is frequently echoed in Revelation (see Rev 4:9,10; 5:1,7,13; 6:16; 7:10,15; 19:4).

‡47:9 The nations acknowledge the God of Israel to be the Great King—anticipated as the final effect of God's rule (see note on 46:10). *Even.* Or, "as." *Even the people of the God of Abraham.* The "princes" of the nations becoming the people of Abraham's God fulfills the covenant promises made to Abraham (see Gen 12:2–3; 17:4–6; 22:17–18). *shields.* See note on 3:3; cf. Is 2:2; 56:7.

Ps 48 A celebration of the security of Zion (as viewed with the eyes of faith) in that it is the city of the great King (see introductions to Ps 46–47). It may have been sung by the Levitical choir on behalf of the assembled worshipers at the temple. Structure and theme are beautifully matched. The first and last verses combine to frame the whole with a comforting confession concerning Zion's God. The center, v. 8 (see note on 6:6), summarizes the main theme of the body of the psalm. The Hebrew follows a symmetrical pattern: three lines, four lines, four lines, three lines, and develops the theme: (1) the beauty of Zion as God's impregnable citadel (vv. 2–3); (2) the futility of all enemy attacks (vv. 4–7); (3) Zion's joy over God's saving acts (vv. 9–11)—related to the second section; (4) Zion as impregnable citadel (vv. 12–13)—related to the first section. Regularly distributed between the four main sections are allusions to the four primary directions (see notes on vv. 2,7,10,13)—suggesting that the city is secure from all points of attack.

48 title *Song.* See note on Ps 30 title. *for the sons of Korah.* See note on Ps 42 title.

48:1 *In the city of our God, in the mountain of his holiness.* See 46:4. *our God.* Occurs in this psalm only here, in the center (v. 8) and at the end (v. 14). *mountain of his holiness.* See 43:3; see also note on 2:6.

48:2–3 Describes the lofty impregnability of mount Zion.

‡48:2 *Beautiful.* Its loftiness and secure position are its beauty (see note on 27:4). *for situation.* Or "in elevation." Although not the highest ridge in its environment, in its significance as the mountain of God it is the "highest" mountain in the world (see 68:15–16 and note; Is 2:2). *joy of the whole earth.* Perhaps referring to admiration from other nations, like that expressed by the queen of Sheba (see 1 Ki 10:1–13). *great King.* See note on 47:2.

48:3 God Himself, not her walls, was Zion's defense, a fact on which the next section elaborates (see note on vv. 12–13). *her palaces.* See v. 13.

48:4–7 The futile attacks of hostile nations—they fled in panic when they saw that the great King was in Zion. Such events as the destruction of the confederacy in the days of Jehoshaphat (see 2 Chr 20) or the slaughter of the Assyrians in the time of Hezekiah (see 2 Ki 19:35–36) may have been in the psalmist's mind.

48:7 *Thou breakest . . . with an east wind.* See Acts 27:14; see also 1 Ki 22:48. *ships of Tarshish.* Great merchant ships of the Mediterranean (see 1 Ki 10:22 and note). *east.* See introduction above.

‡48:8 The central verse and theme (see note on 6:6). *heard . . . seen.* "Seen" is climactic, as in Job 42:5. They had heard because "Our fathers have told us what work thou didst in their days" (44:1; see 78:3), but now in the liturgical experience of God at His temple they have "seen" how secure the city of God is. *LORD of hosts.* See note on 1 Sam 1:3. *our God.* See note on v. 1.

48:9–11 The worshipers meditate at the temple with joy because of God's mighty acts in Zion's behalf.

48:9 *lovingkindness.* See note on 6:4. As is clear from vv. 10–11, reference here is to God's saving acts by which He has expressed His covenant love for His people (see 31:21; 40:9–10). *In the midst of thy temple.* In the temple courts.

48:10 *name.* See note on 5:11. *so is thy praise.* Praise of God reaches from the temple to the ends of the earth (see 9:11; 22:27). *right hand.* In Hebrew idiom a subtle reference to the

11 Let mount Zion rejoice,
Let the daughters of Judah be glad,
Because of thy judgments.
12 Walk about Zion, and go round about
her: tell the towers thereof.
13 [1]Mark ye well her bulwarks, [2]consider
her palaces;
That ye may tell *it* to the generation
following.
14 For this God *is* our God for ever and
ever:
He will be our guide *even* unto death.

Psalm 49

To the chief Musician, A Psalm
[1]for the sons of Korah.

1 Hear this, all ye people;
Give ear, all ye inhabitants of the
world:
2 Both low and high,
Rich and poor, together.
3 My mouth shall speak of wisdom;
And the meditation of my heart *shall
be of* understanding.
4 [a]I will incline mine ear to a parable:
I will open my dark saying upon the
harp.
5 Wherefore should I fear in the days of
evil,
When the iniquity of my heels shall
compass me about?
6 They that [a]trust in their wealth,
And boast themselves in the multitude
of their riches;
7 None *of them* can by any means
redeem *his* brother,
Nor [a]give to God a ransom for him:
8 (For [a]the redemption of their soul is
precious,
And it ceaseth for ever:)
9 That he should still live for ever,
And [a]not see corruption.
10 For he seeth *that* [a]wise *men* die,
Likewise the fool and the brutish
person perish,
[b]And leave their wealth to others.
11 Their inward *thought is, that* their
houses *shall continue* for ever,
And their dwelling places [1]to all
generations;
They [a]call *their* lands after their own
names.
12 Nevertheless man *being* in honour
abideth not:
He is like the beasts *that* perish.
13 This their way *is* their [a]folly:
Yet their posterity [1]approve their
sayings. Selah.
14 Like sheep they are laid in the grave;
Death shall feed *on* them;

48:13 [1]Heb. *Set your heart to her bulwarks* [2]Or, *raise up*
49:T [1]Or, *of*
49:4 [a]Ps. 78:2; Mat. 13:35
49:6 [a]Mark 10:24
49:7 [a]Job 36:18
49:8 [a]Mat. 16:26
49:9 [a]Ps. 89:48
49:10 [a]Eccl. 2:16 [b]Eccl. 2:18
49:11 [1]Heb. *to generation and generation* [a]Gen. 4:17
49:13 [1]Heb. *delight in their mouth* [a]Luke 12:20

south. *righteousness.* Righteous acts (see 40:9–10 and note; see also note on 4:1).

48:11 *judgments.* God's righteous judgments by which He has acted in defense of Zion.

‡48:12–13 The people contemplate Zion's defense, viewed from the perspective of what they have "seen" (v. 8) at the temple. The strength of Zion's "towers," "bulwarks" and "palaces" is the presence of God.

‡48:13 *generation following.* In Hebrew idiom, the word for "following" (or "behind") is a subtle reference to the west.

48:14 *our God.* See note on v. 1. *guide.* See notes on 23:1,3.

‡Ps 49 A word of instruction from the temple following upon Ps 46–48 (see introductions to those psalms). It concerns rich fools who proudly rely on their great wealth and on themselves to assure their security in the world (see Ps 52). The Levitical author knows what it is to be without wealth (see Num 18:21–24; Deut 14:27–29) and has observed the attitudes of many of the rich (see vv. 5–6). He has seen through their folly, however, and offers his wisdom for all to hear (vv. 1–2), so that those who are awed by the rich may be freed from their spell. Inescapable death is their undoing and their destiny, and in the end the "upright shall have dominion over them" (v. 14). The date of this psalm may well be postexilic. See introduction to Ps 37.

49 title See note on Ps 42 title.

49:1–4 Introduction.

49:1–2 More like the address of the prophets (see 1 Ki 22:28; Is 34:1; Mic 1:2) than that of the wisdom teachers (see 34:11; Prov 1:8,10; 2:1).

49:3 See Mat 12:34. *wisdom.* See essay, p. 687. *heart.* See note on 4:7.

‡49:4 *incline mine ear.* The wisdom he is about to speak first had to be "heard" by him—all true wisdom is from God (see Job 28). *dark saying.* Or "a riddle" (cf. Judg 14:12). *upon the harp.* Another hint of the author's sense of inspiration (see 1 Sam 10:5–6; 2 Ki 3:15).

49:5–11 Those of little means or power need not be unsettled when surrounded by rich fools who threaten and strut; death is their destiny.

‡49:5 *Wherefore . . . ?* Or Why . . . ?

49:7–9 Wealth cannot buy escape from death—not even one's "redeemer" can accomplish it (cf. Ex 21:30; Lev 25:47–49). Only God Himself can redeem a life from the grave (see v. 15 and note).

‡47:8 *it ceaseth for ever.* Or "no amount could ever be enough."

49:10 Anyone whose "eyes are in his head" (Eccl 2:14) can see that even the wise die (see Eccl 7:2; 9:5) and leave their wealth to others (see Eccl 2:18,21). How much more the fool (see 73:18–20; 92:6–7)! See also 89:48; Job 30:23; Eccl 2:14–16. *wise men . . . fool.* Essentially the "righteous" and the "wicked" of Ps 37. *wealth.* Often gotten by devious means that their foolish "wisdom" had contrived (v. 5). *to others.* But not to their children (see note on 37:29; see also 39:6; Luke 12:20–21).

‡49:11 Fools refuse to accept the inevitability of death or attempt to perpetuate their memory by attaching their names to their large landholdings (see Num 32:41). Contrast the perspective of a wise person in 90:10–12. The bitter irony is that their only "dwelling places" that will "continue for ever" and "to all generations" are their graves (cf. "his long home" in Eccl 12:5).

49:12 The epitaph of the fool (see note on 10:18; see also Eccl 3:19; 7:2) and the psalm's refrain (see introduction to Ps 42–43).

49:13–15 Their fate and mine—so "Wherefore should I fear?" (v. 5).

‡49:13 *folly.* Because they trust in themselves and their wealth and think that they are secure (see v. 6).

‡49:14 *Like sheep.* Death is already their shepherd, "guiding" them to the grave. *Death shall feed on them.* For the imagery of death (or the grave) as an insatiable monster feeding on its

And [a]the upright shall have dominion
over them in the morning;
[b]And their [1]beauty shall consume [2]*in*
the grave from their dwelling.
15 But God [a]will redeem my soul [1]from
the power of [2]the grave:
For he shall receive me. Selah.
16 Be not thou afraid when one is made
rich,
When the glory of his house is
increased;
17 For when he dieth he shall carry
nothing away:
His glory shall not descend after him.
18 Though [1]whiles he lived [a]he blessed
his soul:
And *men* will praise thee, when thou
doest well to thyself.
19 [1]He shall go to the generation of his
fathers;
They shall never see [a]light.
20 Man *that is* in honour, and
understandeth not,
[a]Is like the beasts *that* perish.

Psalm 50

A Psalm [a] [1] of Asaph.

1 The [a]mighty God, *even* the LORD, hath
spoken, and called the earth
From the rising of the sun unto the
going down thereof.
2 Out of Zion, the perfection of beauty,
[a]God hath shined.
3 Our God shall come, and shall not
keep silence:
[a]A fire shall devour before him,
And it shall be very tempestuous round
about him.
4 [a]He shall call to the heavens from
above,
And to the earth, that *he* may judge his
people.
5 Gather [a]my saints together unto me;
[b]Those that have made a covenant
with me by sacrifice.
6 And the heavens shall declare his
righteousness:
For [a]God *is* judge himself. Selah.

49:14 [1] Or, *strength* [2] Or, *the grave* being a *habitation to every one of them* [a] Ps. 47:3; Dan. 7:22; Mal. 4:3 [b] Job 4:21
49:15 [1] Heb. *from the hand of the grave* [2] Or, *hell* [a] Hos. 13:14
49:18 [1] Heb. *in his life* [a] Deut. 29:19
49:19 [1] Heb. The soul *shall go* [a] Job 33:30
49:20 [a] Eccl. 3:19
50:T [1] Or, *for Asaph* [a] 1 Chr. 15:17; 2 Chr. 29:30
50:1 [a] Is. 9:6
50:2 [a] Ps. 80:1
50:3 [a] Ps. 97:3; Dan. 7:10
50:4 [a] Deut. 4:26
50:5 [a] Deut. 33:3 [b] Ex. 24:7
50:6 [a] Ps. 75:7

victims see 69:15; 141:7; Prov 1:12; 27:20; 30:15–16; Is 5:14; Jonah 2:2 ("belly of hell"); Hab 2:5. The imagery is borrowed from Canaanite mythology, which so depicts the god Mot (death). As one Canaanite document reads, "Do not approach divine Mot, lest he put you like a lamb into his mouth." *have dominion over.* See Lev 26:17; Is 14:2; perhaps "prevail over" in contrast to the situation referred to in v. 5. *in the morning.* See vv. 15,19 and notes on 6:5; 11:7; 16:9–11; 17:15. But see also introduction to Ps 57.

49:15 See note on vv. 7–9. *redeem my soul from . . . grave.* While this may refer to saving (for a while) from the universal prospect of death (as in Job 5:20; see 116:8), the context strongly suggests that the author, as one of the upright, speaks of his final destiny. Perhaps the thought is of being conveyed into the presence of God in His heavenly temple, analogous to the later Jewish thought of being conveyed to "Abraham's bosom" (Luke 16:22; see notes on 6:5; 11:7; 16:9–11; 17:15). *my soul.* See note on 6:3). *he shall receive me.* See 73:24 and note; see also Gen 5:24 and note.

49:16–19 So do not let the present state of the wealthy captivate you.

49:16 *his house.* His whole estate (see Ex 20:17).

‡49:18 *blessed his soul.* Viewed himself as blessed by God. *men will praise thee.* Others also view the rich as "blessed" with life's ultimate good.

49:19 *light.* See notes on 27:1; Is 53:11.

49:20 The last word. See note on v. 12.

Ps 50 The Lord calls His covenant people to account as they meet before Him in worship at the temple. (Thus the psalm has links with Ps 46–49; see introductions to those psalms.) The psalm appears to have been composed for a temple liturgy in which Israel reaffirms her commitment to God's covenant. A leader of the Levitical choir addresses Israel on behalf of the Lord (see Ps 15; 24, either of which may have been spoken earlier in the same liturgy). This liturgy was possibly related to the feast of tabernacles (see Deut 31:9–13; see also introduction to Ps 47). In its rebuke of a false understanding of sacrifice the psalm has affinity with the prophecies of Amos, Micah and Isaiah and so may date from the late eighth and/or early seventh centuries B.C. Others find a closer relationship with the reformation of Josiah (2 Ki 22:1–23:25) and the ministry of Jeremiah. Structurally, the psalm has three parts: (1) the announcement of the "coming" of Israel's covenant Lord to call His people to account (vv. 1–6); (2) the Lord's words of correction for those of honest intent (vv. 7–15); (3) His sharp rebuke of "the wicked" among them (vv. 16–23).

50 title A traditional ascription of the psalm to Asaph; or it may mean "for Asaph" (see "to Jeduthun" in Ps 39 title) or for the descendants of Asaph who functioned in his place. This psalm may have been separated from the other psalms of Asaph (73–83) because of its thematic links with Ps 46–49. Asaph was one of David's three choir leaders (see note on Ps 39 title).

50:1–6 The Lord comes (v. 3) in the temple worship to correct and rebuke His people: Israel must know that the God of Zion is the God of Sinai (see Ex 19:16–20).

50:1 *The mighty God, even the LORD.* A sequence found elsewhere only in Josh 22:22 (see note there). Ps 50 is noteworthy for its use of numerous names and titles for God (see notes on vv. 6,14,21–22). *the earth.* See "the heavens . . . the earth" (v. 4) and "the heavens" (v. 6). When Moses renewed the covenant between the Lord and Israel on the plains of Moab, he called upon heaven and earth to serve as third-party witnesses to the covenant (Deut 30:19; 31:28). The Lord now summons these to testify that His present word to His people is in complete accord with that covenant (see Is 1:2).

50:2 *perfection of beauty.* Because God resides there (cf. Ezek 27:3–4,11; 28:12). *hath shined.* Manifested His glory as He has come to act (see 80:1; 94:1; Deut 33:2; cf. Ezek 28:7,17), now confronting His people, but not yet announcing judgment as in Is 1 or Mic 1.

50:3 *Our God shall come.* From His enthronement between the cherubim (see 80:1; 99:1; see also 1 Sam 4:4; 2 Sam 6:2; 2 Ki 19:15) in the most holy place of the temple (see note on 28:2; see also Is 26:21; Mic 1:3). *not keep silence.* No longer (see v. 21) will He let their sins go unrebuked. *fire . . . tempestuous.* See Ex 19:16,18.

50:4 *judge.* Call them to account in accordance with His covenant.

50:5 *saints.* See note on 4:3. *by sacrifice.* Sacrifices were a part of the ritual that sealed the covenant (see Ex 24:4–8) and continued to be an integral part of Israel's expression of covenant commitment to the Lord.

50:6 *declare.* See note on v. 1. *righteousness.* See note on 5:8. *judge.* Lord over His people (the Hebrew for "judge" and that

7 Hear, O my people, and I will speak;
O Israel, and I will testify against thee:
[a]I *am* God, *even* thy God.
8 [a]I will not reprove thee [b]for thy sacrifices
Or thy burnt offerings, *to have been* continually before me.
9 [a]I will take no bullock out of thy house,
Nor he goats out of thy folds.
10 For every beast of the forest *is* mine,
And the cattle upon a thousand hills.
11 I know all the fowls of the mountains:
And the wild beasts of the field *are* [1]mine.
12 If I were hungry, I would not tell thee:
[a]For the world *is* mine, and the fulness thereof.
13 Will I eat the flesh of bulls,
Or drink the blood of goats?
14 [a]Offer unto God thanksgiving;
And [b]pay thy vows unto the most High:
15 And [a]call upon me in the day of trouble:
I will deliver thee, and thou shalt [b]glorify me.

16 But unto the wicked God saith,
What hast thou to do to declare my statutes,
Or *that* thou shouldest take my covenant in thy mouth?
17 [a]Seeing thou hatest instruction,
And [b]castest my words behind thee.
18 When thou sawest a thief, then thou [a]consentedst with him,
And [1]hast been [b]partaker with adulterers.
19 [1]Thou givest thy mouth to evil,
And [a]thy tongue frameth deceit.
20 Thou sittest *and* speakest against thy brother;
Thou slanderest thine own mother's son.
21 These *things* hast thou done, [a]and I kept silence;
[b]Thou thoughtest that I was altogether *such a one* as thyself:
But [c]I will reprove thee, and set *them* in order before thine eyes.
22 Now consider this, ye that [a]forget God,
Lest I tear *you* in pieces, and *there be* none to deliver.
23 [a]Whoso offereth praise glorifieth me:
And [b]to him [1]that ordereth *his* conversation *aright*
Will I shew the salvation of God.

50:7 [a]Ex. 20:2
50:8 [a]Jer. 7:22 [b]Hos. 6:6
50:9 [a]Acts 17:25
50:11 [1]Heb. *with me*
50:12 [a]Job 41:11
50:14 [a]Heb. 13:15 [b]Deut. 23:21
50:15 [a]Job 22:27 [b]Ps. 22:23
50:17 [a]Rom. 2:21
50:17 [b]Neh. 9:26
50:18 [1]Heb. *thy portion was with adulterers* [a]Rom. 1:32 [b]1 Tim. 5:22
50:19 [1]Heb. *Thou sendest* [a]Ps. 52:2
50:21 [a]Eccl. 8:11 [b]Ps. 10:11 [c]Ps. 90:8
50:22 [a]Job 8:13; Ps. 9:17; Is. 51:13
50:23 [1]Heb. *that disposeth his way* [a]Ps. 27:6 [b]Gal. 6:16
51:T [a]2 Sam. 12:1; 11:2,4

Psalm 51

To the chief Musician, A Psalm of David, [a]when Nathan the prophet came unto him, after he had gone in to Bath-sheba.

1 Have mercy upon me, O God,
according to thy lovingkindness:

for "king" are sometimes used synonymously; see, e.g., Is 33:22). "Judge" occurs as a title for God (see note on v. 1) in, e.g., 94:2; Gen 18:25; Judg 11:27.

50:7–15 The Lord corrects His people.

50:7 *my people.* "Our God" (v. 3) and "thy God" (here) reflect the covenant bond. *I am God, even thy God.* See Ex 19:3–6; Lev 19:2–4,10,25,31,34,36; 20:7,24; 22:33; 23:22.

50:8–13 Israel had not failed to bring enough sacrifices (v. 8), but she was ever tempted to think that sacrifices were of first importance to God, as though He was dependent on them. This notion was widespread among Israel's pagan neighbors. See note on 40:6.

‡50:8 *to have been.* Or "which have been."

‡50:9–10 God is not dependent on their sacrifices because He already possesses the animals they offer to Him. The sacrifices are more for their benefit than for God's.

50:10 *thousand.* Used here figuratively for a very large number.

50:12 *the world . . . fulness thereof.* See 24:1 and note.

50:14–15 God wants Israel to acknowledge her dependence on Him, by giving thank offerings for His mercies (v. 14) and by praying to Him in times of need (v. 15; see 116:17–19). Those who do so may expect God's gracious answer to their prayers (stated more directly in v. 23). God also desires obedience to His moral law (see vv. 16–21 and note on 40:6).

‡50:14 *God . . . most High.* That is, God most High (see 57:2 and note on 3:7). *thanksgiving.* Thanksgiving offerings; see Lev 7:12–13. *thy vows.* Vows that accompanied prayer in times of need, usually involving thank offerings (see 66:13–15), always involving praise of the Lord for His answer to prayer (see note on 7:17). See also Heb 13:15. *most High.* See note on v. 1; see also note on Gen 14:19.

50:15 *glorify me.* With praise in the fulfillment of the vows (see v. 23)—and, implicitly, with obedience to His covenant law (see following verses).

50:16–23 The Lord's rebuke of the wicked.

‡50:16 *What hast thou to do . . . ?* What right do you have? *declare my statutes.* Apparently a part of the liturgy of covenant commitment. *take my covenant in thy mouth.* Affirm their loyalty to God and claim His covenant blessings but without the conduct that is to characterize a person of covenant faithfulness. The verse rebukes those whose worship is nothing more than empty words.

50:17 *thou hatest instruction.* They formally participate in the holy ritual but reject God's law as the rule for life outside the ritual.

50:19 *givest thy mouth to evil.* See note on 5:9.

50:21 God's merciful and patient "silence" is distorted by the wicked into bad and self-serving theology (see Eccl 8:11; Is 42:14; 57:11). *thoughtest that I was.* Or "thought the 'I AM' was"; see Ex 3:14 and note (see also note on v. 1). *set them in order before thine eyes.* Set forth the particulars of My indictment before your eyes.

50:22 *God.* A relatively rare word for "God" (Hebrew *Eloah*), though common in Job. See note on v. 1.

50:23 See note on vv. 14–15.

Ps 51 David's humble prayer for forgiveness and cleansing. As the prayer of a contrite sinner, it represents a proper response to the Lord's confrontation of His people in Ps 50 (compare v. 16 with 50:8–15). This psalm has many points of contact with Ps 25. In traditional Christian usage it is one of seven penitential psalms (see introduction to Ps 6). The psalm is constructed symmetrically: An introduction (vv. 1–2) balances a two-verse conclusion, and the stanzas in Hebrew consist of five lines, three lines, three lines and five lines respectively. The whole is framed by David's prayer for himself (vv. 1–2) and for Zion (vv. 18–19).

According unto the multitude of thy tender mercies [a]blot out my transgressions.
2 [a]Wash me throughly from mine iniquity,
And cleanse me from my sin.
3 For I acknowledge my transgressions:
And my sin *is* ever before me.
4 [a]Against thee, thee only, have I sinned,
And done *this* evil [b]in thy sight:
[c]That thou mightest be justified when thou speakest,
And be clear when thou judgest.
5 [a]Behold, I was shapen in iniquity;
[b]And in sin did my mother [1]conceive me.
6 Behold, thou desirest truth in the inward parts:
And in the hidden *part* thou shalt make me to know wisdom.
7 [a]Purge me with hyssop, and I shall be clean:
Wash me, and I shall be [b]whiter than snow.
8 Make me to hear joy and gladness;
That the bones *which* thou hast broken [a]may rejoice.
9 [a]Hide thy face from my sins,
And blot out all mine iniquities.
10 [a]Create in me a clean heart, O God;
And renew [1]a right spirit within me.
11 Cast me not away [a]from thy presence;
And take not thy [b]holy Spirit from me.
12 Restore unto me the joy of thy salvation;
And uphold me *with thy* [a]free spirit.
13 *Then* will I teach transgressors thy ways;
And sinners shall be converted unto thee.
14 Deliver me from [a][1]bloodguiltiness, O God, thou God of my salvation:
And [b]my tongue shall sing aloud of thy righteousness.
15 O Lord, open thou my lips;
And my mouth shall shew forth thy praise.

51:1 [a]Is. 43:25; Col. 2:14
51:2 [a]Heb. 9:14; 1 John 1:7
51:4 [a]2 Sam. 12:13 [b]Luke 15:21 [c]Rom. 3:4
51:5 [1]Heb. *warm me* [a]Job 14:4 [b]Job 14:4
51:7 [a]Lev. 14:4; Heb. 9:19 [b]Is. 1:18
51:8 [a]Mat. 5:4
51:9 [a]Jer. 16:17
51:10 [1]Or, *a constant spirit* [a]Ezek. 18:31; Acts 15:19
51:11 [a]Gen 4:14 [b]Luke 11:13; Eph. 4:30
51:12 [a]2 Cor. 3:17
51:14 [1]Heb. *bloods* [a]2 Sam. 12:9 [b]Ps. 35:28

The well-being of the king and the city stand and fall together (see 28:8 and note on 3:8).

51 title *To the chief Musician.* See note on Ps 4 title. *when.* For the event referred to see 2 Sam 11:1–12:25; see also note on Ps 3 title.

‡51:1–2 In mercy grant pardon (see Luke 18:13). Note the piling up of synonyms: mercy, lovingkindness, tender mercies; blot out, wash, cleanse; transgressions, iniquity, sin (for this last triad see note on 32:5).

51:1 *lovingkindness.* See note on 6:4. *blot out.* See v. 9. The image is that of a papyrus scroll (see note on 9:5) on which God had recorded David's deeds. The "blotting out" of sins pictures forgiveness (Jer 18:23; see Is 43:25). For the imagery of God's keeping records of the events in His realm in the way that earthly kings do, see 56:8; 87:6; 130:3; 139:16; Neh 13:14; Dan 7:10; see also Ex 32:32–33.

51:2 See v. 7. *Wash.* As a filthy garment. *cleanse me.* Make me clean in Your sight (see Lev 11:32).

51:3–6 Confession of sin (cf. Prov 28:13; 1 John 1:9).

51:3 *before me.* On my mind.

51:4 *Against thee . . . only.* David acknowledges that his sin was preeminently against God (see 2 Sam 12:13; cf. Gen 20:6; 39:9; Luke 15:18). He had violated specific covenant stipulations (Ex 20:13–14,17). *when thou speakest . . . when thou judgest.* As the Lord did through Nathan the prophet (2 Sam 12:7–12). For a NT application see Rom 3:4.

‡51:5 He cannot plead that this sin was a rare aberration in his life; it sprang from what he is and has been (in his "inward parts," v. 6) from birth (see 58:3; Gen 8:21; cf. John 9:34; Eph 2:3). The apparently similar statements in Job 14:4; 15:14; 25:4–6 rise from a different motivation.

51:6 The great contrast: He has acted absolutely contrary to what God desires and to what God has been teaching him "in the hidden part." But it is just this "desire" of God and this "teaching" of God that are his hope—what he pleads for in vv. 7,10. *truth.* Moral integrity. *inward parts.* See 139:13–16; Job 38:36. *hidden part.* The most secret place within. *wisdom.* Whoever gives himself over to sin is a fool; he who has God's law in his heart is wise (see 37:30–31).

51:7–9 Renewed prayer for pardon.

51:7 *Purge me.* Lit. "Un-sin me." *hyssop.* Used in ritual cleansing; see note on Ex 12:22. *be clean.* The Hebrew root for this phrase is the same as that for "cleanse" in v. 2. *whiter than snow.* Like a filthy garment, he needs washing (see note on v. 2); but if God washes him, he will be so pure that there is no figurative word that can describe him (see Is 1:18; Dan 7:9; Rev 7:14; 19:14).

51:8 *Make me to hear joy.* Let me be surrounded by joy (see 32:7 and note; see also 35:27), or let me hear a prophetic oracle of forgiveness that will result in joy—from the assurance of sins forgiven (see 2 Sam 12:13). *bones.* See note on 6:2.

51:9 *Hide thy face.* From what is "ever before me" (v. 3). *blot out.* See note on v. 1.

51:10–12 Prayer for purity—for a pure heart, a steadfast spirit of faithfulness and a willing spirit of service. These can be his only if God does not reject him and take His holy Spirit from him. If granted, the joy of God's salvation will return to gladden his troubled soul.

51:10 *Create.* As something new, which cannot emerge from what now is (see v. 5), and which only God can fashion (see Gen 1:1; Is 65:17; Jer 31:22). *heart.* See note on 4:7.

51:11 The two requests are essentially one (see 139:7; Ezek 39:29). David's prayer recalls the rejection of Saul (see 1 Sam 16:1,14; 2 Sam 7:15) and pleads for God not to take away His Spirit, by which He had equipped and qualified him for his royal office (see 1 Sam 16:13; cf. 2 Sam 23:1–2). *holy Spirit.* The phrase is found elsewhere in the OT only in Is 63:10–11. By His Spirit, God effected His purposes in creation (see 104:30; Gen 1:2; Job 33:4) and redemption (see Is 32:15; 44:3; 63:11,14; Hag 2:5), equipped His servants for their appointed tasks (see Ex 31:3; Num 11:29; Judg 3:10; 1 Sam 10:6; 16:13; Is 11:2; 42:1), inspired His prophets (see Num 24:2–3; 2 Sam 23:2; Neh 9:30; Is 59:21; 61:1; Ezek 11:5; Mic 3:8; Zech 7:12) and directed their ministries (see 1 Ki 18:12; 2 Ki 2:16; Is 48:16; Ezek 2:2; 3:14). And it is by His Spirit that God gives His people a "new heart and . . . a new spirit" to live by His will (see Ezek 36:26–27; see also Jer 24:7; 32:39; Ezek 11:19; 18:31).

51:13–17 The vow to praise (see note on 7:17).

51:13 His praise for God's forgiveness and purification will be accompanied by instruction for sinners (see Ps 34 and note on 32:8–10). *thy ways.* See 25:4 and note.

51:14 If God will only forgive, praise will follow. *righteousness.* See note on 4:1.

51:15 *open thou my lips.* By granting the forgiveness and cleansing I seek.

16 For [a]thou desirest not sacrifice; [1]else
would I give *it:*
Thou delightest not in burnt offering.
17 [a]The sacrifices of God *are* a broken
spirit:
A broken and a contrite heart, O God,
thou wilt not despise.

18 Do good in thy good pleasure unto Zion:
Build thou the walls of Jerusalem.
19 Then shalt thou be pleased with [a]the
sacrifices of righteousness, with
burnt offering and whole *burnt
offering:*
Then shall they offer bullocks upon
thine altar.

Psalm 52

To the chief Musician, Maschil, *A Psalm* of David, [a]when Doeg the Edomite came and [b]told Saul, and said unto him, David is come to the house of Ahimelech.

1 Why boastest thou thyself in mischief,
[a]O mighty *man?*
The goodness of God *endureth*
continually.
2 [a]Thy tongue deviseth mischiefs;
[b]Like a sharp rasor, working
deceitfully.
3 Thou lovest evil more than good;
And [a]lying rather than to speak
righteousness. Selah.
4 Thou lovest all devouring words,
[1]O thou deceitful tongue.
5 God shall likewise [1]destroy thee for
ever,
He shall take thee away, and pluck
thee out of *thy* dwelling place,
And [a]root thee out of the land of the
living. Selah.
6 [a]The righteous also shall see, and fear,
[b]And shall laugh at him:
7 Lo, *this is* the man *that* made not God
his strength;
But [a]trusted in the abundance of his
riches,
And strengthened himself in his
[1]wickedness.
8 But I *am* [a]like a green olive tree in the
house of God:
I trust in the mercy of God for ever and
ever.
9 I will praise thee for ever, because thou
hast done *it:*
And I will wait on thy name; [a]for *it is*
good before thy saints.

Psalm 53

To the chief Musician upon Mahalath, Maschil, *A Psalm* of David.

1 The fool hath said in his heart, *There is*
no God.
Corrupt are they, and have done
abominable iniquity:
[a]*There is* none that doeth good.
2 God [a]looked down from heaven upon
the children of men,

51:16 [1]Or, *that I should give it* [a]1 Sam. 15:22; Ps. 40:6; Is. 1:11; Jer. 7:22
51:17 [a]Ps. 34:18; Is. 57:15
51:19 [a]Ps. 4:5; Mal. 3:3
52:T [a]1 Sam. 22:9 [b]Ezek. 22:9
52:1 [a]1 Sam. 21:7
52:2 [a]Ps. 50:19 [b]Ps. 57:4
52:3 [a]Jer. 9:4,5
52:4 [1]Or, and *the deceitful tongue*
52:5 [1]Heb. *beat thee down* [a]Prov. 2:22
52:6 [a]Job 22:19; Ps. 37:34; Mal. 1:5 [b]Ps. 58:10
52:7 [1]Or, *substance* [a]Ps. 49:6
52:8 [a]Jer. 11:16; Hos. 14:6
52:9 [a]Ps. 54:6
53:1 [a]Rom. 3:10
53:2 [a]Ps. 33:13

51:16 See note on 40:6.
51:17 *broken spirit: A broken and a contrite heart.* What pleases God more than sacrifices is a humble heart that looks to Him when troubles crush and that penitently pleads for mercy when sin has been committed (see 50:7–15 and notes; see also 34:17–18).
51:18–19 Prayer for Zion (see note on 3:8).
51:19 *sacrifices of righteousness.* Such as are pleasing to God; here, sacrifices accompanied by praise for God's mercies (see 50:14–15 and notes).
Ps 52 Fearless confidence in God when under attack by an arrogant and evil enemy. David stands in the presence of God and from the high tower of that refuge hurls his denunciation (much like the prophetic denunciation in Is 22:15–19) into the face of his attacker. Though not a wisdom psalm, it has much in common with Ps 49. The extended depiction of David's enemy forms a sharp contrast with the spirit of Ps 51. See also David's denunciation of Goliath (1 Sam 17:45–47).
52 title *To the chief Musician.* See note on Ps 4 title. *Maschil.* See note on Ps 32 title. *when.* See note on Ps 3 title. For the event referred to see 1 Sam 22:9–10.
52:1–4 The enemy castigated.
52:1 *Why . . . ?* By what right? See 50:16; Is 3:15. *boastest.* By act as well as by word (see 75:4–5). *mighty man.* In his own estimation (see Is 22:17).
52:2 *Thy tongue.* See v. 4; see also note on 5:9.
‡52:3 Your whole moral sense is perverted (cf. Is 5:20). *Thou lovest.* You prefer.
52:4 *tongue.* See note on v. 2.
52:5–7 The enemy's end announced (implicitly a prayer): God will slay you, and the righteous will mock you.
‡52:5 Note the triple imagery: "destroy thee," "take thee away," "root thee out." The arrogant enemy will meet the same end as the rich fools of Ps 49. *out of thy dwelling place.* See Job 18:14. *root thee out.* Contrast v. 8.
52:6 *righteous.* See note on 1:5. *fear.* Learn from your downfall (see 40:3 and note on 34:8–14).
52:7 See Ps 49.
52:8–9 David's security is God.
52:8 *like a green olive tree.* Which lives for hundreds of years. *green.* See 1:3. It will not be uprooted (see v. 5). *in the house of God.* Olive trees were not planted in the temple courts, but David had access to God's temple as his refuge (see 15:1; 23:6; 27:4; 61:4 and note), where he was kept safe (see 27:5 and note). *mercy.* See note on 6:4.
52:9 A vow to praise (see note on 7:17). *name.* See note on 5:11. *saints.* See note on 4:3.
Ps 53 A testimony concerning the folly of evil men, a somewhat revised duplicate of Ps 14; see introduction there. (The main difference between the two psalms is that here the word "God" is used instead of "the LORD"; see also note on v. 5.) The original psalm may have been revised in the light of an event such as is narrated in 2 Chr 20. Here it also serves as a further commentary on the kind of arrogant fool denounced in Ps 52.
53 title *To the chief Musician.* See note on Ps 4 title. *upon.* See note on Ps 6 title. *Mahalath.* Possibly the name of a tune (see note on Ps 9 title). The Hebrew appears to be the word for "suffering" or "sickness" (see Ps 88 title and note). Perhaps the Hebrew phrase indicates here that the psalm is to be used in a time of affliction, when the godless mock (see Ps 102; see also note on 5:9). *Maschil.* See note on Ps 32 title.
53:1–4 See notes on 14:1–4.

To see if there were *any* that did understand, that did [b]seek God.
3 Every one of them is gone back, they are altogether become filthy;
There is none that doeth good, no, not one.
4 Have the workers of iniquity [a]no knowledge?
Who eat up my people *as* they eat bread:
They have not called upon God.
5 [a]There [1]were they in great fear, *where* no fear was:
For God hath [b]scattered the bones of him that encampeth *against* thee:
Thou hast put *them* to shame, because God hath despised them.

6 [a][1]O that the salvation of Israel *were come* out of Zion!
When God bringeth back the captivity of his people,
Jacob shall rejoice, *and* Israel shall be glad.

Psalm 54

To the chief Musician on Neginoth, Maschil, *A Psalm* of David, [a]when the Ziphims came and said to Saul, Doth not David hide himself with us?

1 Save me, O God, by thy name,
And judge me by thy strength.
2 Hear my prayer, O God;
Give ear to the words of my mouth.
3 For [a]strangers are risen up against me,
And oppressors seek after my soul:

53:2 [b]2 Chr. 15:2
53:4 [a]Jer. 4:22
53:5 [1]Heb. *they feared a fear* [a]Lev. 26:17 [b]Ezek. 6:5
53:6 [1]Heb. *Who will give salvations, etc.* [a]Ps. 14:7
54:T [a]1 Sam. 23:19
54:3 [a]Ps. 86:14
54:4 [a]Ps. 118:7
54:5 [1]Heb. *those that observe me* [a]Ps. 89:49
54:6 [a]Ps. 52:9
54:7 [a]Ps. 59:10
55:2 [a]Is. 38:14
55:3 [a]2 Sam. 16:7,8
55:4 [a]Ps. 116:3
55:5 [1]Heb. *covered me*

They have not set God before them. Selah.
4 Behold, God *is* mine helper:
[a]The Lord *is* with them that uphold my soul.
5 He shall reward evil unto [1]mine enemies:
Cut them off [a]in thy truth.
6 I will freely sacrifice unto thee:
I will praise thy name, O LORD; [a]for *it is* good.
7 For he hath delivered me out of all trouble:
[a]And mine eye hath seen *his desire* upon mine enemies.

Psalm 55

To the chief Musician on Neginoth, Maschil, *A Psalm* of David.

1 Give ear to my prayer, O God;
And hide not thyself from my supplication.
2 Attend unto me, and hear me:
I [a]mourn in my complaint, and make a noise;
3 Because of the voice of the enemy, because of the oppression of the wicked:
[a]For they cast iniquity upon me, and in wrath they hate me.
4 [a]My heart is sore pained within me:
And the terrors of death are fallen upon me.
5 Fearfulness and trembling are come upon me,
And horror hath [1]overwhelmed me.

---

‡53:5 Differs considerably from 14:5–6, though the basic thought remains the same: God overwhelms the godless who attack His people. Here the verbs are in the past tense (perhaps to express the certainty of their downfall). *where no fear was.* They fell victim to fear when, humanly speaking, they were not even threatened. God's curse fell on them rather than on Israel (see Lev 26:36–37; see also Judg 7:21; 2 Ki 3:22–23; 7:6–7; Prov 28:1). *scattered the bones.* Over the battlefield of their defeat, their bodies left unburied like something loathsome (see Is 14:18–20; Jer 8:2 and note). *God hath despised them.* As they had despised Him.
53:6 See note on 14:7.
Ps 54 A prayer for deliverance from enemies who want to have David killed. The prayer is short, like that of Ps 3; 4; 13; yet it is one of the most typical prayers of the Psalter. Completely symmetrical, the prayer is framed by David's cry for vindication (v. 1) and his statement of assurance that he will look in triumph on his foes (v. 7). A confession of confidence (v. 4) centers the prayer (see 42:8 and note on 6:6). Verses 3,5 each form a separate element in the prayer.
54 title *To the chief Musician.* See note on Ps 4 title. *on Neginoth.* See note on Ps 4 title. *Maschil.* See note on Ps 32 title. *when.* For the event referred to see 1 Sam 23:19; see also note on Ps 3 title.
54:1–2 Prayer for God to judge his case (see Ps 17).
54:1 *name.* See v. 6; see also note on 5:11.
54:3 The case against his enemies. *have not set God before them.* Like those of Ps 53.
54:4 The confession of confidence and the center of the poem (see 42:8 and note).
54:5 The call for redress (see note on 5:10).
54:6 The vow to praise (see note on 7:17). *name.* See v. 1; see also note on 5:11.
54:7 Assurance of being heard (see note on 3:8).
Ps 55 A prayer for God's help when threatened by a powerful conspiracy in Jerusalem under the leadership of a former friend. The situation described is like that of Absalom's conspiracy against the king (see 2 Sam 15–17): The city is in turmoil; danger is everywhere; there is uncertainty as to who can be trusted; rumors, false reports and slander are circulating freely. Under such circumstances David longs for a quiet retreat to escape it all (vv. 6–8). That being out of the question, he casts his cares on the Lord, whom he knows he can trust. In its structure, the prayer is framed by a plea for help (v. 1) and a simple confession of faith: "I will trust in thee" (v. 23).
55 title *To the chief Musician.* See note on Ps 4 title. *on Neginoth.* See note on Ps 4 title. *Maschil.* See note on Ps 32 title.
55:1–3 Initial appeal for God to hear.
‡55:3 *cast iniquity upon me.* Bring down evil on me.
55:4–8 His heart's anguish.
55:4–5 Danger is everywhere (see 31:13), a danger so great that it is as if death itself were stalking him (see 18:4–5; 116:3).
55:4 *heart.* See note on 4:7. *terrors of death.* See 1 Sam 5:11; 15:32; 28:5; Job 18:14.

6 And I said, O that I had wings like a dove,
For then would I fly away, and be at rest.
7 Lo, *then* would I wander far off,
And remain in the wilderness. Selah.
8 I would hasten my escape
From the windy storm *and* tempest.

9 Destroy, O Lord, *and* divide their tongues:
For I have seen [a]violence and strife in the city.
10 Day and night they go about it upon the walls thereof:
Mischief also and sorrow *are* in the midst of it.
11 Wickedness *is* in the midst thereof:
Deceit and guile depart not from her streets.
12 [a]For *it was* not an enemy *that* reproached me; then I could have borne *it:*
Neither *was it* he that hated me *that* did [b]magnify *himself* against me; then I would have hid myself from him:
13 But *it was* thou, [1]a man mine equal,
[a]My guide, and mine acquaintance.
14 [1]We took sweet counsel together,
And [a]walked unto the house of God in company.
15 Let death seize upon them,
And let them [a]go down quick *into* [1]hell:
For wickedness *is* in their dwellings, *and* among them.
16 *As for* me, I will call upon God;
And the LORD shall save me.
17 [a]Evening, and morning, and at noon, will I pray, and cry aloud:
And he shall hear my voice.
18 He hath delivered my soul in peace from the battle *that was* against me:
For [a]there were many with me.
19 God shall hear, and afflict them,
[a]Even he that abideth of old. Selah.
[1]Because they have no changes,
Therefore they fear not God.
20 He hath [a]put forth his hands against such as [b]be at peace with him:
[1]He hath broken his covenant.
21 [a]*The words of* his mouth were smoother than butter, but war *was* in his heart:
His words were softer than oil, yet *were* they drawn swords.
22 [a]Cast thy [1]burden upon the LORD, and he shall sustain thee:
[b]He shall never suffer the righteous to be moved.
23 But thou, O God, shalt bring them down into the pit of destruction:
[a 1]Bloody and deceitful men [b 2]shall not live out half their days;
But I will trust in thee.

Psalm 56

To the chief Musician upon Jonath-elem-rechokim, [1]Michtam of David, when the [a]Philistines took him in Gath.

1 Be [a]merciful unto me, O God: for man would swallow me up;
He fighting daily oppresseth me.
2 [1]Mine enemies would daily [a]swallow *me* up:

55:9 [a]Jer. 6:7
55:12 [a]Ps. 41:9 [b]Ps. 35:26
55:13 [1]Heb. *a man according to my rank* [a]2 Sam. 15:12; Ps. 41:9; Jer. 9:4
55:14 [1]Heb. *Who sweetened counsel* [a]Ps. 42:4
55:15 [1]Or, *the grave* [a]Num. 16:30
55:17 [a]Luke 18:1
55:18 [a]2 Chr. 32:7,8
55:19 [1]Or, *with whom* also there be *no changes, yet they fear not God* [a]Deut. 33:27
55:20 [1]Heb. *He hath profaned* [a]Acts 12:1 [b]Ps. 7:4
55:21 [a]Ps. 28:3
55:22 [1]Or, *gift* [a]Ps. 37:5; Mat. 6:25 [b]Ps. 37:24
55:23 [1]Heb. *Men of bloods and deceit* [2]Heb. *shall not half their days* [a]Ps. 5:6 [b]Job 15:32; Prov. 10:27; Eccl. 7:17
56:T [1]Or, *A golden* Psalm *of David* [a]1 Sam. 21:11
56:1 [a]Ps. 57:1
56:2 [1]Heb. *Mine observers* [a]Ps. 57:3

55:6–8 He longs for a quiet retreat, away from treacherous and conniving people (see similarly Jer 9:2–6).
55:9–11 Prayer for God to foil the plots of his enemies.
55:9 *Destroy . . . divide their tongues.* Paralyze the conspirators with conflicting designs, as at Babel (Gen 11:5–9; see 2 Sam 17:1–14). *the city.* See v. 11; Jerusalem.
‡55:10 *Mischief . . . sorrow.* "Mischief" and "sorrow" are like two watchmen who constantly "go about" on the city walls looking for an opportune moment to attack the righteous. See 127:1; 130:6; Sol 5:7.
‡55:11 *Deceit and guile.* The partners of "Mischief" and "sorrow," who patrol through the city streets (see Sol 3:3).
55:12–14 The insults and plots of an enemy can be endured—but those of a treacherous friend?
‡55:13 *a man mine equal.* A man just like me. *My guide, and mine acquaintance.* See v. 20; see also 41:9 and note.
‡55:14 *took sweet counsel.* Or "enjoyed sweet fellowship." *unto the house of God.* Their ties of friendship had been a bond hallowed by common commitment to the Lord and sealed by its public display in the presence of God and the worshipers at the temple.
‡55:15 Prayer for redress (see note on 5:10). *Let death seize upon them.* The conspirators were seeking his death. *quick into hell.* Or "alive into Sheol." May they go to the grave before life has run its normal course. Cf. the experience of Moses' enemies in Num 16:29–33 (see also v. 23; Prov 1:12; Is 5:14).
55:16–19 Assurance of being heard (see note on 3:8).
‡55:17 *Evening, and morning, and at noon, will I pray.* Cf. Dan 6:10.
‡55:19 He who is the eternal King will deal with those who "have no changes" and "fear not God" (see 36:1 and note; see also Ps 14; 53).
55:20–21 Further sorrowful (or angry) reflection over the treachery of his former friend.
55:20 *such as be at peace with him.* See 7:4.
55:21 See 28:3; Prov 5:3–4; see also note on 5:9. *heart.* See note on 4:7.
55:22–23 Once more, assurance of being heard.
55:22 A testimony to all who are assembled at the temple. 1 Pet 5:7 echoes this assurance. *righteous.* See note on 1:5.
55:23 *pit of destruction.* The grave (see note on 30:1). *not live out half their days.* See note on v. 15.
Ps 56 A prayer for help when the psalmist is attacked by enemies and his very life is threatened. It is marked by consoling trust in the face of unsettling fear. Structurally, the prayer is framed by an urgent appeal to God (vv. 1–2) and a word of confident assurance (vv. 12–13). An inner frame, vv. 3–4 and vv. 10–11, confesses a sure trust in God in a form that is almost a refrain. The prayer itself is developed in the intervening verses (vv. 5–9).
‡56 title *To the chief Musician.* See note on Ps 4 title. *upon.* See note on Ps 9 title. *Michtam.* See note on Ps 16 title. *when.* See note on Ps 3 title. For the event referred to see 1 Sam 21:10–15; see also Ps 34 title and note. *took.* Or "were about to take."

For *they be* many that fight against me,
O thou *most* High.
3 *What* time I am afraid,
I will trust in thee.
4 In God I will praise his word,
In God I have put my trust; [a]I will not fear
What flesh can do unto me.

5 Every day they wrest my words:
All their thoughts *are* against me for evil.
6 [a]They gather themselves together, they hide themselves,
They mark my steps,
[b]When they wait for my soul.
7 *Shall* they escape by iniquity?
In *thine* anger cast down the people, O God.
8 Thou tellest my wanderings:
Put thou my tears into thy bottle:
Are they not in thy book?
9 When I cry *unto thee,* then shall mine enemies turn back:
This I know; for [a]God *is* for me.
10 In God will I praise *his* word:
In the LORD will I praise *his* word.
11 In God have I put my trust: I will not be afraid
What man can do unto me.

12 Thy vows *are* upon me, O God:
I will render praises unto thee.

56:4 [a]Ps. 118:6; Is. 31:3
56:6 [a]Ps. 59:3 [b]Ps. 71:10
56:9 [a]Rom. 8:31
56:13 [a]Ps. 116:8 [b]Job 33:30
57:T [1]Or, *Destroy not* [2][*A golden* Psalm] [a]1 Sam. 22:1; Ps. 142, title
57:1 [a]Ps. 17:8 [b]Is. 26:20
57:2 [a]Ps. 138:8
57:3 [1]Or, *He reproacheth him that would swallow me up* [a]Ps. 43:3
57:4 [a]Prov. 30:14
57:5 [a]Ps. 108:5

13 For [a]thou hast delivered my soul from death: *wilt* not *thou deliver* my feet from falling,
That *I* may walk before God in [b]the light of the living?

Psalm 57

To the chief Musician, [1]Al-taschith, [2]Michtam of David, [a]when he fled from Saul in the cave.

1 Be merciful unto me, O God, be merciful unto me:
For my soul trusteth in thee:
[a]Yea, in the shadow of thy wings will I make my refuge,
[b]Until *these* calamities be overpast.
2 I will cry unto God most High;
Unto God [a]that performeth *all things* for me.
3 He shall send from heaven, and save me
[1]*From* the reproach of him that would swallow me up. Selah.
God [a]shall send forth his mercy and his truth.
4 My soul *is* among lions:
And I lie *even among* them that are set on fire, *even* the sons of men,
[a]Whose teeth *are* spears and arrows,
And their tongue a sharp sword.
5 [a]Be thou exalted, O God, above the heavens;
Let thy glory *be* above all the earth.

56:1–2 Initial appeal for God's help.
56:3–4 See vv. 10–11; confession of trust in the face of fear.
56:4 *word.* God's reassuring promise that He will be the God of His people and will come to their aid when they appeal to Him (see 50:15; 91:15; see also 119:74,81; 130:5). *flesh.* Man in his feebleness compared with God's power (see note on 10:18).
56:5–7 Accusation and call for redress (see note on 5:9–10).
‡56:5 *wrest my words.* Distort what I say; see v. 2.
‡56:7 See note on 5:10. *Shall they escape by iniquity?* Will they get away with their wrongdoing? A rhetorical question appealing to God's sense of justice. *anger.* See note on 2:5.
56:8–9 Appeal for God to take special note of the psalmist's troubles.
‡56:8 *tellest my wanderings . . . in thy book.* Recorded my troubles in Your heavenly royal records as matters calling for Your action (see note on 51:1). *Put thou my tears into thy bottle.* Calls for God to preserve his tears in a skin bottle normally used for water, wine or milk. Though the use of "tear bottles" is not attested elsewhere, the picture of tears being stored in the same way as liquids used for drinking in a hot and arid climate is an indication of God's great regard for the cries of His people.
‡56:9 If God takes such note of his tears that He collects them in a bottle and records them in His book, He will surely respond to David's call for help.
56:10–11 Renewed confession of trust in the face of fear (see vv. 3–4).
56:12–13 Assurance of being heard (see note on 3:8).
56:12 *vows are upon me.* Speaking as if his prayer has already been heard, David acknowledges that now he must keep the vows he made to God when he was in trouble (see 66:14 and note on 7:17).
56:13 *my soul.* See note on 6:3. *falling.* See note on 35:15. *before God.* See note on 11:7. *light of the living.* The full blessedness of life (see note on 36:9).
‡Ps 57 A prayer for deliverance when threatened by fierce enemies (it has many links with Ps 56). The psalm appears to reflect the imagery of the night of danger (v. 4: "My soul is among lions") followed by the morning of salvation (v. 8: "I myself will awake early"). For other instances of these associations see 30:5; 46:5; 59:6,14,16; 63:1,6; 90:14. Verses 7–11 are used again in 108:1–5. The psalm is composed of two parts (vv. 1–5 and vv. 6–11) that are alike in structure—both contain three Hebrew couplets and end with an identical refrain. (For the use of refrains elsewhere see introduction to Ps 42–43.)
57 title See note on Ps 56 title. *Al-taschith.* Possibly meaning "Do Not Destroy" (see Ps 58; 59; 75 titles). *when.* For the event referred to see 1 Sam 24:1–3; see also Ps 142 title.
57:1–5 The prayer.
57:1 Initial cry for God's merciful help. *my soul.* See note on 6:3. *shadow of thy wings.* See note on 17:8.
57:2–3 Confidence of being heard.
‡57:2 *most High.* See note on Gen 14:19. *that performeth all things for me.* See 138:8. God will not let David's enemies thwart His divine purposes for anointing him king (see 1 Sam 16:1,12; 2 Sam 7). But the Hebrew can also be translated "who makes an end [of troubles] for me" (see 7:9).
‡57:3 *He shall send.* God sends His mercy and truth (here personified; see note on 23:6) as His messengers from heaven to save His servant (see note on 43:3). *his mercy and his truth.* See note on 26:3. *mercy.* See note on 6:4.
57:4 The threatening situation. *I lie.* As a sheep among lions. *them that are set on fire.* The psalmists often compare their enemies to ferocious beasts (see note on 7:2). (The use of the metaphor here has no connection with the description of Saul and Jonathan in 2 Sam 1:23.) *tongue.* See note on 5:9.
57:5 A prayer for God to show His exalted power and glory

6 [a]They have prepared a net for my steps;
My soul is bowed down:
They have digged a pit before me,
Into the midst whereof they are fallen *themselves.* Selah.
7 [a]My heart is [1]fixed, O God, my heart is fixed:
I will sing and give praise.
8 Awake up, [a]my glory; awake, psaltery and harp:
I *myself* will awake early.
9 [a]I will praise thee, O Lord, among the people:
I will sing unto thee among the nations.
10 [a]For thy mercy *is* great unto the heavens,
And thy truth unto the clouds.
11 [a]Be thou exalted, O God, above the heavens:
Let thy glory *be* above all the earth.

57:6 [a]Ps. 9:15 57:7 [1]Or, *prepared* [a]Ps. 108:1 57:8 [a]Ps. 16:9 57:9 [a]Ps. 108:3 57:10 [a]Ps. 103:11 57:11 [a]ver. 5 58:T [1]Or, *Destroy not, A golden* Psalm *of David* [a]Ps. 57, title

Psalm 58

To the chief Musician, [a][1]Al-taschith, Michtam of David.

1 Do ye indeed speak righteousness, O congregation?
Do ye judge uprightly, O ye sons of men?
2 Yea, in heart you work wickedness;
You weigh the violence of your hands in the earth.
3 [a]The wicked are estranged from the womb:
They go astray [1]as soon as they be born, speaking lies.
4 [a]Their poison *is* [1]like the poison of a serpent:
They are like the deaf [2]adder *that* stoppeth her ear;
5 Which will not hearken to the voice of charmers,
[1]Charming *never so* wisely.
6 [a]Break their teeth, O God, in their mouth:
Break out the great teeth of the young lions, O LORD.
7 Let them melt away as waters *which* run continually:
When he bendeth *his bow to shoot* his arrows, let them be as cut in pieces.
8 As a snail *which* melteth, let *every one of them* pass away:

58:3 [1]Heb. *from the belly* [a]Is. 48:8 58:4 [1]Heb. *according to the likeness* [2]Or, *asp* [a]Eccl. 10:11 58:5 [1]Or, Be *the charmer* never so *cunning* 58:6 [a]Job 4:10

throughout His creation by coming to His servant's rescue (see 7:6–7; 21:13; 46:10; 59:5,8; 113:4–9; cf. Ex 14:4; Is 26:15; 44:23; 59:19; see also note on Ps 46:10).

57:6–11 Praise for God's saving help—confidently anticipating the desired deliverance. For such a sudden transition from prayer to assurance see note on 3:8.

57:6 The threat and its outcome: The enemies suffer the calamity they plotted. *net...pit.* They hunted him as if he were a wild beast, but the "lions" themselves were caught.

‡57:7 All cause for fear has been removed. *heart.* See note on 4:7. *is fixed.* Feels steadfast, secure (see 112:7).

‡57:8 *Awake...awake.* Greet with joy the dawn of the day of deliverance (see Is 51:9,17; 52:1). *glory.* See note on 7:5. *psaltery and harp.* Instruments (here personified) to accompany the praise of the Lord at His temple in celebration of deliverance (see 71:22; 81:2; and note on Ps 4 title). *awake early.* Lit. "I will awaken the dawn." With joyful cries proclaiming God's saving act. (Dawn, too, is here personified—the Canaanites even deified it.)

57:9–10 The vow to praise (see notes on 7:17; 9:1).

‡57:10 *mercy.* See note on 6:4. *mercy...truth.* That is, mercy-and-truth (see v. 3; note on 36:5; see also note on 3:7). *unto the heavens...unto the clouds.* See note on 36:5.

57:11 The refrain (see v. 5), but now as praise (see 18:46; 30:1; 34:3; 35:27; 40:16; 70:4; 92:8; 97:9; 99:2; 113:4; 148:13).

Ps 58 A prayer for God, the supreme Judge, to set right the affairs of men, judging those rulers who corrupt justice, and championing the cause of the righteous. (The psalm was applied by the early church to Jesus' trial before the Sanhedrin; see Mat 26:57–68 and parallels.) Concern for the just use of judicial power is pervasive throughout the OT. This was the primary agency in the administrative structures of the ancient Near East for the protection of the innocent, usually the poor and powerless, against the assaults of unscrupulous men, usually the rich and powerful. Israelite society was troubled with the corruption of this judicial power from the days of Samuel to the end of the monarchy (see, e.g., 1 Sam 8:3; Is 1:23; 5:23; 10:1–2; Ezek 22:6,12; Amos 5:7,10–13; Mic 3:1–3,9–11; 7:2). Even in David's time all was not well (see 2 Sam 15:1–4). For the central concern of this psalm see Ps 82. Structurally, the psalm is framed by a rhetorical address to the wicked judges in their absence (vv. 1–2) and by a reassuring word to "the righteous" (vv. 9–11). The frame also emphasizes the fact that those who do not judge uprightly (v. 1) will be judged by God (v. 11).

58 title *To the chief Musician.* See note on Ps 4 title. *Al-taschith.* See Ps 57; 59; 75 titles. *Michtam.* See note on Ps 16 title.

58:1–5 Accusation against the wicked judges whose mouths, hearts and hands (vv. 1–2) are united in the pursuit of injustice.

‡58:1 *speak righteousness.* Make just judicial pronouncements. *congregation.* Hebrew *'elem* ("gods" or "mighty ones"). This title is applied to those whose administrative positions called upon them to act as earthly representatives of God's heavenly court (see Ex 22:8–9, where the Hebrew for "gods" is translated "judges"; see also Deut 1:17; 2 Chr 19:6).

58:2 *heart.* See note on 4:7. *work wickedness...weigh the violence of your hands.* Issue decisions that result in cruel injustice.

58:3 *The wicked.* See their description in Ps 10. *from the womb ...as soon as they be born.* Their corrupt ways are not sporadic; they act in accordance with their nature (see 51:5). Here reference is to the wicked; the author does not make a general statement about all people, as is the case in Gen 6:5; 8:21; Job 14:4; 15:14–16; 25:4–6. *speaking lies.* They have never been concerned for the truth (see John 8:44).

58:4 *poison.* What issues from their mouths is as cruel and deadly as the venom of snakes (see 140:3; Mat 23:33; Jas 3:8). *stoppeth her ear.* They are incorrigible; nothing—neither appeals nor threats—will move them.

58:6–8 Prayer for God to purge the land of such perverse judges. The author uses imagery drawn from conventional curses of the ancient Near East (see note on 5:10).

58:6 Let the weapons of their mouths (see 57:4) be broken and torn out. *lions.* See note on 7:2.

58:7 *waters which run continually.* And is absorbed by the ground. *arrows.* Malicious pronouncements (see 57:4 and note on 5:9).

[a]*Like* the untimely birth of a woman,
that they may not see the sun.
9 Before your pots can feel the thorns,
He shall take them away [a]as with a
whirlwind, [1]both living, and in *his*
wrath.
10 The righteous shall rejoice when he
seeth the vengeance:
[a]He shall wash his feet in the blood of
the wicked.
11 [a]So that a man shall say, Verily *there is*
[1]a reward for the righteous:
Verily he is a God that judgeth in the
earth.

Psalm 59

To the chief Musician, [a][1]Al-taschith, Michtam of David; [b]when Saul sent, and they watcht the house to kill him.

1 Deliver me from mine enemies, O my
God:
[1]Defend me from them that rise up
against me.
2 Deliver me from the workers of
iniquity,
And save me from bloody men.
3 For lo, they lie in wait for my soul:
[a]The mighty are gathered against me;
Not *for* my transgression, nor *for* my
sin, O LORD.
4 They run and prepare themselves
without *my* fault:
[a]Awake [1]to help me, and behold.
5 Thou therefore, O LORD God *of* hosts,
the God of Israel,
Awake to visit all the heathen:
Be not merciful to any wicked
transgressors. Selah.

6 [a]They return at evening:
They make a noise like a dog,
And go round about the city.
7 Behold, they belch out with their
mouth:
[a]Swords *are* in their lips:
For [b]who, *say they,* doth hear?
8 But [a]thou, O LORD, shalt laugh at them;
Thou shalt have all the heathen in
derision.
9 *Because of* his strength will I wait
upon thee:
[a]For God *is* [1]my defence.
10 The God of my mercy shall [a]prevent me:
God shall let [b]me see *my desire* upon
[1]mine enemies.

58:8 [a]Job 3:16 58:9 [1]Heb. *as living, as wrath* [a]Prov. 10:25 58:10 [a]Ps. 68:23 58:11 [1]Heb. *fruit of the, etc.* [a]Ps. 92:15 59:T [1]Or, *Destroy not, A golden* Psalm *of David* [a]Ps. 57, title [b]1 Sam. 19:11 59:1 [1]Heb. *Set me on high* 59:3 [a]Ps. 56:6

59:4 [1]Heb. *to meet me* [a]Ps. 35:23 59:6 [a]ver. 14 59:7 [a]Ps. 57:4; Prov. 12:18 [b]Ps. 10:11 59:8 [a]Prov. 1:26 59:9 [1]Heb. *my high place* [a]Ps. 62:2 59:10 [1]Heb. *mine observers* [a]Ps. 21:3 [b]Ps. 54:7

‡58:8 *snail.* Or "slug," that appears to dry up to nothing as it moves over a stone in the hot sun. *the untimely birth.* A miscarriage.
58:9–11 Assurance that God will surely judge them (see note on 3:8).
‡58:9 *feel the thorns.* Twigs from wild thorn bushes were used as fuel for quick heat (see 118:12; Eccl 7:6). The idea here is that God's judgment will come more quickly than these thorns can heat a fire for cooking. The speed of God's judgment indicates both its certainty and its severity (see note on 37:10; see also Luke 18:7–8). *take them away.* As by a storm—God's storm (see Job 27:21).
58:10 *righteous.* Here a judicial term for those who are in the right but who have been wronged (see note on 1:5). *when he seeth the vengeance.* When the wrongs committed against them are redressed. *wash his feet in the blood.* Vivid imagery borrowed from the literary conventions of the ancient Near East (see 68:23). Its origin is the exaggerated language of triumphant reports of victory on the battlefield.
‡58:11 The climax: When God has judged the unjust judges (see note on v. 1), all people will see that right ultimately triumphs under God's just rule (see note on 46:10). No more will people despair, like those in Mal 3:15.
‡Ps 59 A prayer for deliverance when endangered by enemy attacks. If originally composed by David under the circumstances noted in the superscription, it must have been revised for use by one of David's royal sons when Jerusalem was under siege by a hostile force made up of troops from many nations—as when Hezekiah was besieged by the Assyrians (see 2 Ki 18:19). (Some, however, ascribe it to Nehemiah; see Neh 4.) The enemy weapon most prominent is the tongue, attacking with slander and curses. In this psalm, too, the imagery of the night of danger (vv. 6,14), followed by the morning of deliverance (v. 16), is evoked (see introduction to Ps 57). Regarding the structure, the two halves of the psalm (vv. 1–9,10–17) each conclude with an almost identical refrain (vv. 9,17), preceded by a characterization of the enemies (vv. 6,14). The first half of the psalm is predominantly prayer, the second half predominantly assurance of deliverance. The whole is framed by a cry for protection (v. 1) and a joyful confession that God is the psalmist's "defence" (v. 17, in Hebrew the same root as that for "Defend me" in v. 1).
59 title See note on Ps 56 title. *Al-taschith.* See Ps 57; 58; 75 titles. *when.* For the event referred to see 1 Sam 19:11.
59:1–2 The cry for deliverance.
59:1 *Defend me.* Lit. "Raise me to a high, secure place."
59:2 *workers of iniquity . . . bloody men.* Common characterizations of those who attack the psalmists out of malice.
59:3–5 By curses and lies (v. 12) the enemies seek to justify their attacks, but the psalmist protests his innocence and pleads with God to judge those who wrong him (see 58:11).
‡59:3 *lie in wait.* Or "set an ambush." See 10:8–9 and note on 7:2.
‡59:4 *without my fault.* He has done nothing to deserve the attacks of his enemies. *Awake.* See note on 3:7.
59:5 *LORD God of hosts.* See note on 1 Sam 1:3. *God of Israel.* This appeal to the Lord as the God of Israel to punish the nations makes clear that the attack on the psalmist involves an attack by the nations on Israel. *Awake.* See note on 7:6. *visit . . . Be not merciful.* See note on 5:10. *wicked transgressors.* Whether Israelites had joined in the attack is not clear; the Hebrew indicates only that the enemies were treacherous.
59:6–8 Confidence: Surely God mocks such a pack of dogs (see 22:16–17).
59:6 *round about the city.* The enemies besiege the city like dogs at night on the prowl for food (see vv. 14–15).
59:7 *Swords are in their lips.* Their "cursing and lying" (v. 12). For the imagery see 57:4; see also note on 5:9. *say they.* See note on 3:2.
‡59:9 *wait upon.* Or "watch for;" Hebrew *shamar* (see note on v. 17). The psalmist watches as one who longingly waits for the morning (of salvation); see 130:6.
59:10–13 The prayer renewed. Confident that the Lord will hear his prayer (v. 10) and will punish the nations (v. 5), the psalmist prays that God will not sweep them away suddenly

11 Slay them not, lest my people forget:
Scatter them by thy power;
And bring them down, O Lord our shield.
12 [a]*For* the sin of their mouth *and* the words of their lips
Let them even be taken in their pride:
And for cursing and lying *which* they speak.
13 Consume *them* in wrath, consume *them,* that they *may* not *be:*
And let them know that God ruleth in Jacob
Unto the ends of the earth. Selah.

14 And [a]at evening let them return;
And let them make a noise like a dog,
And go round about the city.

15 Let them [a]wander up and down [1]for meat,
[2]And grudge if they be not satisfied.
16 But I will sing of thy power;
Yea, I will sing aloud of thy mercy in the morning:
For thou hast been my defence
And refuge in the day of my trouble.
17 Unto thee, [a]O my strength, will I sing:
For God *is* my defence, *and* the God of my mercy.

59:12 [a]Prov. 12:13
59:14 [a]ver. 6
59:15 [1]Heb. *to eat* [2]Or, *If they be not satisfied, then they will stay all night* [a]Job 15:23
59:17 [a]Ps. 18:1
60:T [1]Or, *A golden* Psalm [a]Ps. 80 [b]2 Sam. 8:3; 1 Chr. 18:3
60:1 [1]Heb. *broken* [a]Ps. 44:9
60:2 [a]2 Chr. 7:14
60:3 [a]Ps. 71:20 [b]Jer. 25:15
60:4 [a]Ps. 20:5

Psalm 60

To the chief Musician [a]upon Shushan-eduth, [1]Michtam of David, to teach; [b]when he strove with Aram-naharaim and with Aram-zobah, when Joab returned, and smote of Edom in the valley of salt twelve thousand.

1 O God, [a]thou hast cast us off, thou hast [1]scattered us,
Thou hast been displeased; O turn thyself to us again.
2 Thou hast made the earth to tremble; thou hast broken it:
[a]Heal the breaches thereof; for it shaketh.
3 [a]Thou hast shewed thy people hard *things:*
[b]Thou hast made us to drink the wine *of* astonishment.
4 [a]Thou hast given a banner to them that fear thee,

but will prolong their punishment so that Israel ("my people," v. 11) will not forget God's acts of salvation, as they had done so often before (see 78:11; 106:13). Nevertheless, the psalmist asks God not to allow the enemies to escape the full consequences of their malice (vv. 12–13).

‡59:10 *mercy.* See note on 6:4. *shall prevent me.* Will meet me and come to my aid.

‡59:11 *Scatter them.* Instead of killing them, let them be like vagabonds, with no place to settle (see Gen 4:12; 2 Sam 15:20; Lam 4:15) and having to hunt for food (like dogs, v. 15; see 109:10; Amos 4:8), so that they will be a continual reminder of what happens to those who oppose God and His people. *shield.* See note on 3:3.

59:12 See note on v. 7. *taken in their pride.* Let the pride with which they treacherously attack the Lord's servant and his people be the trap that catches them. *cursing and lying.* See 10:7 and note.

‡59:13 *And let them know.* When God has thus dealt with Israel's enemies, these enemies will acknowledge that the Judge of all the earth (see 58:11) is the God of Israel. *Jacob.* See note on 14:7.

59:14–16 Assurance of being heard (see note on 3:8). Just as God mocks the defiant pack of dogs (vv. 6–8), so the psalmist will sing for joy at God's triumph over them.

‡59:14–15 *let them . . . let them . . . Let them.* Or "they . . . they . . . They," a description of how the enemies are like wild dogs (cf. v. 6) rather than a request or prayer. The severity of their attacks only highlights the confidence of the psalmist in the Lord's protection (v. 17).

59:16 *power . . . mercy . . . defence.* See the refrain (vv. 9,17). *morning.* See introduction.

59:17 The vow to praise (see note on 7:17). *sing.* Hebrew *zamar* (see note on v. 9). The play on words in the refrain marks an advance from watching during the night of danger to singing in the morning of salvation.

‡Ps 60 A national prayer for God's help after suffering a severe blow by a foreign nation, presumably Edom (see v. 9). The prayer leader may have been the king (the "me" in v. 9), as in 2 Chr 20. The lament that God has "cast off" (v. 1) His people and no longer accompanies their armies links the psalm with Ps 44. Verses 5–12 appear again in 108:6–13. As for its structure, the prayer is framed by three verses lamenting God's rejection of His people (vv. 1–3) and three verses expressing confidence that the God who has rejected them will yet give them victory (vv. 10–12). This transition from lament to confidence constitutes the overarching movement of the prayer. Verses 4–8 contain the plea for help (v. 5) and the grounds for confidence (vv. 4,6–8).

60 title See note on Ps 56 title. *Shushan-eduth.* Means "The Lily of the Covenant" (see Ps 80 title and note on Ps 45 title). *to teach.* Only here in the psalm titles. For other songs that Israel was to learn see Deut 31:19,21; 2 Sam 1:18. That it was intended for a variety of uses, especially to convey confidence in times of national threat, is illustrated by its use in Ps 108. *when.* For the events referred to see 2 Sam 8; 1 Chr 18 (perhaps also 2 Sam 10). If the tradition that assigns the prayer to these events is correct, it must be supposed that our knowledge of the events is incomplete, since these accounts do not mention Edom. The Israelite war against Edom at this time of great northern battles may have been occasioned by an attack on the part of Edom trying to take advantage of Israel's preoccupation elsewhere, an attack in which Edom succeeded in overrunning the garrisons that guarded Judah's southern borders.

60:1–3 Lament over God's rejection of His people (see 44:9–16; 89:38–45) and prayer for restoration.

60:1 *cast us off.* At least momentarily (see 30:5). Defeat by the enemy is interpreted as a sign of God's anger (though no reason for that anger is noted, and the bond between Israel and God is not broken). *scattered us.* Like a flood (see 2 Sam 5:20).

60:2 *made the earth to tremble.* As by a devastating earthquake—such as was occasionally experienced in ancient Canaan.

‡60:3 *wine of astonishment.* Or "wine that makes us stagger." God has made them drink from the cup of His wrath rather than from His cup of blessing and salvation (see note on 16:5).

60:4–8 A plea for help, grounded in reasons for confidence.

60:4 *banner.* Banners were used as rallying points for troops in preparation for battle and for leading them into action. This practice is often alluded to in Isaiah (5:26; 11:10,12; 13:2; 18:3; 30:17; 49:22; 62:10) and Jeremiah (4:21, "standard"; 50:2;

That *it* may be displayed because of the
truth. Selah.
5 [a]That thy beloved may be delivered;
Save *with* thy right hand, and hear me.
6 God hath [a]spoken in his holiness;
I will rejoice, I will [b]divide [c]Shechem,
And mete out [d]the valley of Succoth.
7 Gilead *is* mine, and Manasseh *is* mine;
[a]Ephraim also *is* the strength of mine
head;
[b]Judah *is* my lawgiver;
8 Moab *is* my washpot;
Over Edom will I cast out my shoe:
[a]Philistia, [1]triumph thou because of me.

9 Who will bring me *into* the [1]strong
city?
Who will lead me into Edom?
10 *Wilt* not thou, O God, *which* [a]hadst
cast us off?
And *thou,* O God, *which* didst [b]not go
out with our armies?

60:5 [a]Ps. 108:6
60:6 [a]Ps. 89:35 [b]Josh. 1:6 [c]Gen. 12:6 [d]Josh. 13:27
60:7 [a]Deut. 33:17 [b]Gen. 49:10
60:8 [1]Or, *triumph thou over me:* (by an irony) [a]2 Sam. 8:1
60:9 [1]Heb. *city of strength?*
60:10 [a]Ps. 108:11 [b]Josh. 7:12
60:11 [1]Heb. *salvation*
60:12 [a]Num. 24:18
61:3 [a]Prov. 18:10
61:4 [1]Or, *make my refuge* [a]Ps. 91:4

11 Give us help from trouble:
For vain *is* the [1]help of man.
12 Through God [a]we shall do valiantly:
For he *it is that* shall tread down our
enemies.

Psalm 61

To the chief Musician upon Neginah,
A Psalm of David.

1 Hear my cry, O God;
Attend unto my prayer.
2 From the end of the earth will I cry
unto thee, when my heart is
overwhelmed:
Lead me to the rock *that* is higher
than I.
3 For thou hast been a shelter for me,
And [a]a strong tower from the enemy.
4 I will abide in thy tabernacle for ever:
[a]I will [1]trust in the covert of thy
wings. Selah.

51:12,27). The "banner" here must be the reassuring word from God recited in vv. 6–8 (see Ex 17:15). *them that fear thee.* Your people, in distinction from the nations (see 61:5; see also note on Gen 20:11).

60:5 *thy beloved.* The Hebrew for this expression is here a word of special endearment, as in 127:2; 2 Sam 12:25; Jer 11:15.

‡60:6–8 A comforting oracle from the Lord, perhaps recalling an already ancient word from the time of the conquest. If so, it may have been preserved in the "book of the wars of the LORD" (Num 21:14). In any event, the Lord is depicted as Israel's triumphant Warrior-King (see Ex 15:3,13–18).

60:6 *divide . . . mete out.* Divide His conquered territory among His servant people who were with Him in the battles. *Shechem . . . Succoth.* Places representative of the territory west and east of the Jordan taken over by the Lord and Israel (see Gen 33:17–18; 1 Ki 12:25).

‡60:7 Israel is the Lord's kingdom—both the land conquered and His people established within it. *Gilead . . . Manasseh.* Half of Manasseh was established in Gilead, east of the Jordan, and half of it west of the Jordan, just north of Ephraim (see Josh 13:29–31; 17:5–11). This once again showed that the Lord's kingdom included territory both east and west of the Jordan. *Ephraim . . . Judah.* The two leading tribes of Israel, the one representative of the Rachel tribes (Ephraim) in the north, the other of the Leah tribes (Judah) in the south; see Gen 48:13–20; 49:8–12; Num 2:3,18; Josh 15–16. Together they represented all Israel (Is 11:13; Zech 9:13). *strength.* Or "protection"; a helmet. As a powerful and aggressive tribe (Deut 33:17; Judg 7:24–8:3; 12:1), Ephraim figuratively represents the Lord's helmet. *lawgiver.* Or "a scepter." Called such because from Judah would come (Gen 49:10)—and had now come (1 Sam 16:1–13)—the Lord's chosen earthly regent over His people (see 2 Sam 7).

60:8 *Moab . . . Edom . . . Philistia.* Perpetual enemies on Israel's eastern, southern and western borders respectively (see Ex 15:14–15; see also Ex 13:17; Num 20:14–21; 22–24). *is my washpot.* Is reduced to a household vessel in which the Lord washes His feet (Gen 18:4). The metaphor is perhaps suggested by the fact that Moab lay along the east shore of the Dead Sea. *cast out my shoe.* Perhaps refers to the conventional symbolic act by which one claimed possession of land (cf. Ruth 4:7).

60:9 A rhetorical question following the reassuring oracle and leading to the confidence expressed in vv. 10–12. *me . . . me.* Possibly referring to the king (see introduction), though the praying community may be referring to itself collectively (see note on Ps 30 title). *lead me.* As God went before His people into battle in the desert (Ex 13:21) and during the conquest (Ex 23:27–28; 33:2; Deut 9:3; 31:8).

60:10–12 Confidence of victory (see note on 3:8).

60:10 *cast us off.* See v. 1.

60:11 *help.* Lit. "salvation" (see v. 5, "Save"). *of man.* See 33:17.

60:12 *do valiantly.* Lit. "do mighty things." With God's help Israel will achieve in a manner similar to that of the Lord Himself (see 118:15–16) and will triumph over Edom (see Num 24:18). *tread down.* Like a victorious warrior (see Is 14:19, 25; Jer 12:10; Zech 10:5).

Ps 61 A prayer for restoration to God's presence. The circumstances appear to be similar to those referred to in Ps 42–43. Here, however, a king is involved (v. 6), and if the author was David, he may have composed this prayer at the time of his flight from Absalom (see 2 Sam 17:21–29). For another possibility see note on v. 2. Ps 61–64 form a series linked together by the common theme of trust in God when under threat. Structurally, the prayer is framed by a cry to God (v. 1) and a vow to praise (v. 8).

61 title See note on Ps 4 title.

61:1 Initial plea for God to hear.

61:2–3 The prayer.

‡61:2 *end of the earth.* So it seemed (see 42:6). Possibly the phrase here refers to the brink of the netherworld, i.e., the grave (see 63:9); the psalmist feels himself near death. *heart.* See note on 4:7. *Lead me.* See 23:2. *rock.* Secure place (see 27:5; 40:2). *higher than I.* The place of security that he seeks is beyond his reach; only God can bring him to it. Since God is often confessed by the psalmists to be their "rock" ("strong rock" in 31:2; "rock of my refuge" in 94:22; see also 18:2; 62:2,6–7; 71:3), it may be that God Himself is that higher "rock" (the secure refuge) that the psalmist pleads for (see v. 3). Or it may be the secure refuge of God's sanctuary (see v. 4; see also 27:5).

61:3 The reason he appeals to God: God has never failed him as a refuge. *enemy.* If this is a prayer when faced with death, death is the present foe (see 68:20; 141:8; Job 33:22; Is 25:8; 28:15; Jer 9:21; Hos 13:14; see also 1 Cor 15:26). See note on 49:14.

61:4–5 Longing for the security of God's sanctuary (see 27:5 and note).

‡61:4 *abide in.* See note on 15:1. *tabernacle.* Tent of residence (see 2 Sam 6:17; 7:2; 1 Ki 1:39; 2:28–30). *covert of thy wings.* See note on 17:8.

5 For thou, O God, hast heard my vows:
Thou hast given *me* the heritage of
those that fear thy name.
6 [1]Thou wilt prolong the king's life:
And his years [2]as many generations.
7 He shall abide before God for ever:
O prepare mercy [a]and truth, *which*
may preserve him.
8 So will I sing *praise* unto thy name for
ever,
That I may daily perform my vows.

Psalm 62

To the chief Musician, to [a]Jeduthun, A Psalm of David.

1 [1]Truly [a]my soul [2]waiteth upon God:
From him *cometh* my salvation.
2 He only *is* my rock and my salvation;
He is my [a][1]defence; I shall not be
greatly moved.
3 How long will ye imagine mischief
against a man?
Ye shall be slain all of you:
[a]As a bowing wall *shall ye be, and as* a
tottering fence.
4 They only consult to cast *him* down
from his excellency:
They delight in lies:
[a]They bless with their mouth, but they
curse [1]inwardly. Selah.
5 My soul, wait thou only upon God;
For my expectation *is* from him.
6 He only *is* my rock and my salvation:
He is my defence; I shall not be
moved.
7 [a]In God *is* my salvation and my glory:
The rock of my strength, *and* my
refuge, *is* in God.
8 Trust in him at all times; ye people,
[a]Pour out your heart before him:
God *is* a refuge for us. Selah.

9 [a]Surely men of low degree *are* vanity,
and men of high degree *are* a lie:
To be laid in the balance, they *are*
[1]altogether *lighter* than vanity.
10 Trust not in oppression,
And become not vain in robbery:
[a]If riches increase, set not *your* heart
upon them.
11 God hath spoken [a]once;
Twice have I heard this;
That [1]power *belongeth* unto God.
12 Also unto thee, O Lord, *belongeth*
mercy:
For [a]thou renderest to *every* man
according to his work.

61:6 [1]Heb. *Thou shalt add days to the days of the king* [2]Heb. *as generation and generation*
61:7 [a]Ps. 40:11
62:T [a]1 Chr. 25:1
62:1 [1]Or, *Only* [2]Heb. is *silent* [a]Ps. 33:20
62:2 [1]Heb. *high place* [a]Ps. 59:9,17
62:3 [a]Is. 30:13
62:4 [1]Heb. *in their inward parts* [a]Ps. 28:3
62:7 [a]Jer. 3:23
62:8 [a]1 Sam. 1:15; Lam. 2:19
62:9 [1]Or, *alike* [a]Ps. 39:5; Is. 40:17
62:10 [a]Luke 12:15
62:11 [1]Or, *strength* [a]Job 33:14
62:12 [a]Mat. 16:27

‡61:5 The reason for his longing: Either (1) because God has been so responsive to him in the past, or (2) confidence that his longing is about to be satisfied. *my vows.* The vows that accompanied his prayers (see 50:14; 66:14; see also note on 7:17). *heritage.* Or "inheritance;" a place with God's people in the promised land, together with all that the Lord had promised to give and to be to His people (see 16:6; 37:18; 135:12; 136:21–22). *those that fear.* See 60:4 and note. *thy name.* See note on 5:11.
61:6–7 Prayer for the king's long life. The king himself may have made this prayer—such transitions to the third person are known from the literature of the ancient Near East—or it may be the prayer of the people, perhaps voiced by a priest or Levite. Later Jewish interpretations applied these verses to the Messiah. They are fulfilled in Christ, David's great Son.
61:6 May the king live forever (see note on 45:6).
61:7 *abide before God.* See note on 41:12. *mercy and truth.* Personified as God's messengers (see notes on 23:6; 43:3; see also note on 26:3).
61:8 The vow to praise (see note on 7:17).
Ps 62 The psalmist commits himself to God when threatened by the assaults of conspirators who wish to dethrone him. The author surely was a king and, if it was David, the circumstances could well have been the efforts of the family of Saul to topple him. Verse 3 suggests a time of weakness and may indicate advanced age. Implicitly the psalm is an appeal to God to uphold him. No psalm surpasses it in its expression of simple trust in God (see Ps 31 and introduction to Ps 61). The psalm is composed of three parts: vv. 1–4, 5–8, 9–12. The middle stanza (vv. 5–8), which begins by echoing vv. 1–2, constitutes the central expression of trust and hope. The whole is framed by a confession of tranquil resting in God (vv. 1–2) and the reason for such trust (vv. 11–12). The remaining verses (vv. 3–4,9–10) speak of those who threaten.
62 title See note on Ps 39 title.
62:1–4 Confidence in God in the face of conspiracy.
62:1 *my soul.* See note on 6:3. *waiteth upon.* Lit. "is silence," i.e., is in repose.
62:2,6 *moved.* See note on 10:6.
‡62:3 Question to the assailants: Will you never give up? *Ye shall be slain . . . fence.* Reads as a statement of confidence in the ultimate demise of his enemies. However, the context of vv. 3–4 would suggest a descpription of David's fragile condition: "Would you slay him—this bowing wall and tottering fence?" The image of a collapsing wall vividly depicts David's weakened condition.
‡62:4 *excellency.* Exalted position or throne. *lies . . . curse.* See note on 10:7. *bless.* For example, "God save the king" (1 Sam 10:24; 2 Sam 16:16; see also 1 Ki 1:25,34,39).
62:5–8 Trust in God: an exhortation to himself (v. 5) and to the people (v. 8).
62:5 *wait.* See note on v. 1; faith encouraging faith (see 27:13–14; 42:5,11; 43:5).
62:8 Exhortation to God's people (see 31:23–24). *Pour out your heart.* In earnest prayer (see Lam 2:19). *heart.* See note on 4:7.
62:9–12 Frail, misguided man; mighty, trustworthy God.
62:9–10 Man, as a threat, is nothing (see note on 10:18).
62:9 *men of low degree . . . men of high degree.* Persons of every condition. *vanity . . . lie.* People appear to be much more than a puff of wind, especially the rich and powerful.
62:10 A warning to those (including those conspiring against him) who trust in their own devices to get what they want (by fair means or foul) rather than trusting in God to sustain them—a virtual summary of Ps 49. *heart.* See note on 4:7.
62:11–12 The climax: recollection of God's reassuring word to His people. *power . . . mercy.* Able to do all that He has promised; committed to His people's salvation and blessedness.
62:11 *once; Twice.* See note on Amos 1:3.
62:12 *mercy.* See note on 6:4. *For.* Ultimately every person

Psalm 63

A Psalm of David, [a]when he was in the wilderness of Judah.

1 O God, thou *art* my God; early will I
seek thee:
[a]My soul thirsteth for thee,
My flesh longeth for thee,
In a dry and [1]thirsty land, [2]where no
water is;
2 To see [a]thy power and thy glory,
So *as* I have seen thee in the sanctuary.
3 Because thy lovingkindness *is* better
than life,
My lips shall praise thee.
4 Thus will I bless thee while I live:
I will lift up my hands in thy name.
5 My soul shall be satisfied as *with*
[1]marrow and fatness;
And my mouth shall praise *thee with*
joyful lips:
6 When [a]I remember thee upon my bed,
And meditate on thee in the *night*
watches.
7 Because thou hast been my help,
Therefore in the shadow of thy wings
will I rejoice.
8 My soul followeth hard after thee:
Thy right hand upholdeth me.
9 But those *that* seek my soul, to
destroy *it,*
Shall go into the lower parts of the
earth.
10 [1]They shall fall by the sword:
They shall be a portion for foxes.
11 But the king shall rejoice in God;
[a]Every one that sweareth by him shall
glory:
But the mouth of them that speak lies
shall be stopped.

63:T [a]1 Sam. 22:5
63:1 [1]Heb. *weary* [2]Heb. *without water* [a]Ps. 42:2
63:2 [a]Ps. 27:4
63:5 [1]Heb. *fatness*
63:6 [a]Ps. 42:8
63:10 [1]Heb. *They shall make him run out* like water *by the hands of the sword*
63:11 [a]Deut. 6:13
64:3 [a]Ps. 58:7

Psalm 64

To the chief Musician, A Psalm of David.

1 Hear my voice, O God, in my prayer:
Preserve my life from fear of the
enemy.
2 Hide me from the secret counsel of the
wicked;
From the insurrection of the workers
of iniquity:
3 Who whet their tongue like a sword,
[a]*And* bend *their bows to shoot* their
arrows, *even* bitter words:
4 That *they* may shoot in secret at the
perfect:
Suddenly do they shoot at him, and
fear not.

will experience God's righteousness (see note on 5:8). *renderest . . . according to.* See notes on Jer 17:10; 32:19.

Ps 63 A confession of longing for God and for the security His presence offers when deadly enemies threaten. That longing is vividly described by the metaphor of thirst (v. 1) and hunger (v. 5; see 42:1–2). Like Ps 62 this psalm is an implicit prayer. It is linked to that psalm also by the advancement from hearing (62:11) to seeing (v. 2; see 48:8 and note). The imagery of the night of danger (v. 6) and the morning of salvation (see note on v. 1) once more occurs (see introduction to Ps 57). This psalm was prescribed for daily public prayers of the early church. In its structure, the initial expression of longing (v. 1) gives way at the end to the expectation of joy (v. 11)—the literary frame of the psalm. What he has seen in the sanctuary (v. 2) he remembers on his bed at night (v. 6), and that reassures him that his enemies will suffer the end they plot for him (vv. 9–10).

63 title See note on Ps 3 title. *when.* If this tradition is correct, the reference is probably to 2 Sam 15:23–28; 16:2,14; 17:16,29 since the psalmist is referred to as king (see v. 11).

‡63:1 Intense longing for God in a time of need. *early.* Lit. "at dawn," "in the morning." *My soul . . . My flesh.* I, with my whole being (see note on 6:3). *dry and thirsty land.* A metaphor for his situation of need, in which he does not taste "marrow and fatness" (v. 5) supplied by the "river, the streams whereof shall make glad the city of God" (see 46:4 and note).

63:2–5 Comforting reflection on what he had seen in the sanctuary; it awakens joyful expectations.

63:2 See 27:4; 48:8 and notes.

63:3 *lovingkindness.* See note on 6:4.

63:4 *lift up my hands.* In praise. *name.* See note on 5:11.

63:5 *soul.* See note on 6:3.

63:6–8 Night reflections, remembering what he had seen "in the sanctuary" (v. 2).

63:6 *upon my bed.* At night as he expectantly awaits the dawning of the morning of deliverance. *the night watches.* See note on Judg 7:19; see also 119:148; Lam 2:19.

63:7 *shadow of thy wings.* See note on 17:8.

63:9–10 His enemies will get what they deserve; in seeking his life they forfeit their own (see Gen 9:5; Ex 21:23; Deut 19:21; see also note on Ps 5:10).

63:9 *lower parts.* See note on 30:1. *earth.* Here, the netherworld or grave (see note on 61:2).

63:10 *portion for foxes.* Like bodies of enemies left unburied on the battlefield to add to their disgrace (see note on 53:5).

63:11 *Every one that sweareth by him.* Those who revere and trust God (see Deut 6:13). *mouth of them that speak lies.* Those who live by falsehood.

Ps 64 Prayer to God for protection when threatened by a conspiracy. The circumstances may be similar to those reflected in Ps 62 (see introduction to that psalm), but here there is no allusion to the king's weakened condition, and it is not clear whether the conspirators come from within or outside Israel (see note on v. 2). As so often in the prayers of the Psalter, the enemy's tongue is his main weapon (see note on 5:9). The prayer is framed by a plea for protection (vv. 1–2) and a confident word concerning the effects of God's saving action (vv. 9–10). At the center, vv. 5–6 describe the disdainful confidence of the conspirators. Verses 3–4 relate how the enemies attack with their tongues, while vv. 7–8 proclaim how God will turn their tongues against them.

64 title See note on Ps 4 title.

64:1–2 The prayer for protection.

64:1 *Hear.* In Hebrew a wordplay on the word for "be glad" in v. 10 (see note there).

‡64:2 *insurrection.* Views the wicked as an angry mob. The Hebrew root underlying this expression is the same as that for "rage" in 2:1.

64:3–4 The enemy attacks.

64:3 *tongue.* See note on 5:9. *sword . . . arrows.* See 59:7.

64:4 *fear not.* They feel themselves secure from exposure and retaliation, but see vv. 7–8.

5 They encourage themselves *in* an evil
[1] matter:
They commune [2] of laying snares privily;
[a] They say, Who shall see them?
6 They search out iniquities;
[1] They accomplish [2] a diligent search:
Both the inward *thought* of every one
of them, and the heart, *is* deep.
7 But God shall shoot at them *with* an
arrow;
Suddenly [1] shall they be wounded.
8 So they shall make their own tongue to
fall upon themselves:
[a] All that see them shall flee away.
9 And all men shall fear,
And shall [a] declare the work of God;
For they shall wisely consider of his
doing.
10 The righteous shall be glad in the
LORD, and shall trust in him;
And all the upright in heart shall glory.

Psalm 65

To the chief Musician,
A Psalm *and* Song of David.

1 Praise [a] [1] waiteth for thee, O God, in
Zion:
And unto thee shall the vow be
performed.
2 O thou that hearest prayer,
[a] Unto thee shall all flesh come.
3 [1] Iniquities prevail against me:
As for our transgressions, thou shalt
[a] purge them away.
4 [a] Blessed *is the man whom* thou
[b] choosest,
And causest to approach *unto thee,*
that he may dwell *in* thy courts:
[c] We shall be satisfied with the
goodness of thy house,
Even of thy holy temple.

5 *By* terrible *things* in righteousness wilt
thou answer us, O God of our
salvation;
Who art the confidence of all the ends
of the earth, and of them that are
afar off *upon* the sea:
6 Which by his strength setteth fast the
mountains;
[a] *Being* girded with power:
7 [a] Which stilleth the noise of the seas,
The noise of their waves, [b] and the
tumult of the people.
8 They also that dwell in the uttermost
parts are afraid at thy tokens:
Thou makest the outgoings of the
morning and evening [1] to rejoice.

64:5 [1] Or, *speech* [2] Heb. *to hide snares* [a] Ps. 10:11
64:6 [1] Or, *We are consumed* by *that which* they *have thoroughly searched* [2] Heb. *a search searched*
64:7 [1] Heb. *their wound shall be*
64:8 [a] Ps. 31:11
64:9 [a] Jer. 50:28; 51:10
65:1 [1] Heb. is *silent* [a] Ps. 62:1
65:2 [a] Is. 66:23
65:3 [1] Heb. *Words,* or, *Matters of iniquities* [a] Heb. 9:14
65:4 [a] Ps. 33:12 [b] Ps. 4:3 [c] Ps. 36:8
65:6 [a] Ps. 93:1
65:7 [a] Mat. 8:26 [b] Is. 17:13
65:8 [1] Or, *to sing*

64:5–6 The enemies' contemptuous self-confidence.
64:5 *They say.* See notes on 3:2; 10:11.
‡64:6 *heart.* See note on 4:7. *deep.* See Prov 18:4; 20:5. The idea here is that the "deep" thoughts of the wicked are cunning and devious as they plot evil. Depravity has perverted the intellectual capacities that God has given to humanity.
64:7–8 Confidence in God's righteous judgment: He will do to them what they had intended to do to David (see 63:9–10 and note). *shoot . . . arrow, Suddenly . . . tongue.* See vv. 3–4.
64:9–10 The happy effects of God's judgment: All mankind will fear, proclaim, ponder (see note on 46:10); the righteous will rejoice, take refuge, praise.
64:9 See 58:11; see also 40:3; 52:6; 65:8.
64:10 *righteous.* See note on 1:5. *be glad.* In Hebrew this is the first word of this verse, and it is a wordplay on the Hebrew for "Hear," which is the first word of the first verse.
Ps 65 A hymn in praise of God's great goodness to His people. In answer to their prayers (1) He pardons their sins so that they continue to enjoy the "goodness" of fellowship with Him at His temple (vv. 3–4); (2) He orders the affairs of the world so that international turbulence is put to rest and Israel is secure in her land (vv. 5–8); and (3) He turns the promised land into a veritable Garden of Eden (vv. 9–13). This hymn begins a series of four that are linked by many common themes.
65 title See notes on Ps 4; 30 titles.
65:1–2 Introductory commitment to praise.
‡65:1 *waiteth for thee.* Lit. "is silent before you." Perhaps the imagery is that of praise personified as a permanent resident of the temple, lying quietly at rest, whom the people will awaken when they come to make good their vows (see 57:8). *the vow.* Made in conjunction with their prayers in time of need (see 66:14 and note on 7:17).
‡65:2 *all flesh.* In light of vv. 5,8, appears to refer to all peoples (as in 64:9; 66:1,4,8; 67:3–5 and elsewhere), not just Israel. *come.* To praise God as the (only) God who hears and graciously answers prayers.
65:3–4 The first and primary blessing.
65:3 *our transgressions, thou shalt purge them away.* You accept the atonement sacrifices You appointed and so forgive our sins (see 32:1–2; 78:38; 79:9 and notes on Lev 16:20–22; 17:11; Heb 2:17; 9:5,7).
65:4 *Blessed.* See note on 1:1. *the man whom thou choosest, And causest to approach unto thee.* Everyone belonging to Israel as God's chosen people (see, e.g., 33:12; Deut 4:37) and whom God accepts at His temple. *dwell in thy courts.* See note on 15:1; see also 23:6. *goodness of thy house.* All the blessings that flow from God's presence (see 36:8 and note).
65:5–8 God stills the nations and makes Israel secure in answer to her prayers.
‡65:5 *terrible things.* Or "awesome works"; acts of God such as were associated with His deliverance of Israel from Egypt and the conquest of Canaan, acts of power that made Israel's enemies cringe (see 66:3; see also 106:22; 145:6; Deut 10:21; 2 Sam 7:23; Is 64:3). *righteousness.* Saving acts by which God kept His covenanted promises to Israel (see note on 5:8). *confidence of all.* Even though the nations of the world did not yet know it.
65:6–7 The God of creation who by His power brought order to the world out of the earlier chaos (see Gen 1) similarly in the redemption of His people establishes a peaceful order among nations (see Is 2:4; 11:6–9; Mic 4:3–4) so that Israel may be at rest in the promised land (see also Ps 33; 46). God's mighty acts in redemption are often compared by OT poets with His mighty acts in creation (see 74:12–17; 89:9–18; Is 27:1; 40:6–14,21–31; 51:9–11), since His power as Creator guaranteed His power as Redeemer. *setteth fast the mountains . . . stilleth . . . the seas.* Gives order to the whole creation (see 95:4–5).
65:7 *tumult of the people.* God's stilling the turbulence of the nations—which often threatened Israel—is compared to His taming the turbulence of the primeval waters of chaos (see notes on 32:6; 33:7).
‡65:8 All peoples will (ultimately) see God's saving acts in behalf of His people and will be moved to fear (see note on 46:10).

9 Thou visitest the earth, [1]and
[a]waterest it:
Thou greatly enrichest it
[b]*With* the river of God, *which* is full *of*
water:
Thou preparest them corn, when thou
hast so provided for it.
10 *Thou* waterest the ridges thereof
abundantly: [1]*thou* settlest the
furrows thereof:
[2]Thou makest it soft with showers:
thou blessest the springing thereof.
11 Thou crownest [1]the year with thy
goodness;
And thy paths drop fatness.
12 They drop *upon* the pastures of the
wilderness:
And the little hills [1]rejoice on every
side.
13 The pastures are clothed with flocks;
[a]The valleys also are covered over with
corn;
They shout for joy, they also sing.

65:9 [1]Or, *after thou hadst made it to desire* rain [a]Jer. 5:24 [b]Ps. 46:4
65:10 [1]Or, thou *causest* rain to *descend* into the *furrows thereof* [2]Heb. *Thou dissolvest it*
65:11 [1]Heb. *the year of thy goodness*
65:12 [1]Heb. *are girded* with *joy*
65:13 [a]Is. 55:12
66:1 [1]Heb. *all the earth* [a]Ps. 100:1

Psalm 66

To the chief Musician, A Song *or* Psalm.

1 [a]Make a joyful noise unto God, [1]all ye
lands:
2 Sing forth the honour of his name:
Make his praise glorious.
3 Say unto God, How [a]terrible *art thou*
in thy works!
Through the greatness of thy power
shall thine enemies [b1]submit
themselves unto thee.
4 [a]All the earth shall worship thee,
And shall sing unto thee; they shall
sing *to* thy name. Selah.
5 Come and see the works of God:
He is terrible *in his* doing toward the
children of men.
6 [a]He turned the sea into dry *land:*
They went through the flood on foot:
There did we rejoice in him.
7 He ruleth by his power for ever;
His eyes behold the nations:
Let not the rebellious exalt themselves.
Selah.
8 O bless our God, ye people,
And make the voice of his praise to be
heard:
9 Which [1]holdeth our soul in life,
And suffereth not our feet to be
moved.
10 For [a]thou, O God, hast proved us:
[b]Thou hast tried us, as silver is tried.
11 [a]Thou broughtest us into the net;
Thou laidst affliction upon our loins.

66:3 [1]Or, *yield feigned obedience.* Heb. *lie* [a]Ps. 65:5 [b]Ps. 18:44
66:4 [a]Ps. 117:1
66:6 [a]Ex. 14:21
66:9 [1]Heb. *putteth*
66:10 [a]Ps. 17:3; Is. 48:10 [b]Zech. 13:9; 1 Pet. 1:7
66:11 [a]Lam. 1:13

And all creation will rejoice (see v. 13). *tokens.* Or "signs," referring to God's great saving acts, such as those He performed when He delivered Israel out of Egypt (Deut 4:34; see Ps 78:43; 105:27; 135:9). As "tokens" they indicated that God was at work (see John 2:11 and note).

65:9–13 God blesses the promised land with all good things in answer to Israel's prayers.

65:9 *river of God.* See note on 36:8.

‡65:11 *goodness.* See 68:10; see also 31:19 and note. *drop fatness.* Another figure of agricultural bounty (cf. 63:5).

65:13 *They shout for joy, they also sing.* In the exuberant language of the psalmists, all creation—even its inanimate elements—joins the human chorus to celebrate the goodness of God in creation, blessing and redemption (see 89:12; 96:11–13; 98:8–9; 103:22; 145:10; 148:3–4,7–10; see also Job 38:7; Is 44:23; 49:13; 55:12).

Ps 66 A psalm of praise for God's answer to prayer. It seems that God has saved the author, probably a king, from an enemy threat, and his deliverance has involved also that of the whole nation. It has often been suggested that the psalm speaks of Judah's remarkable deliverance from the Assyrians (see 2 Ki 19). The praise is offered at the temple in fulfillment of a vow (vv. 13–14; see note on 7:17). Such praise was often climaxed by a call for others to take up the praise (see note on 9:1). Here the psalmist exuberantly begins with that call and, as often elsewhere (e.g., 67:3–5; 68:32; 98:4; 99:3; 100:1; 117:1), addresses it even to the far corners of the earth. This psalm is the second in a series of four (see introduction to Ps 65). The psalm is framed by a call to praise (vv. 1–2) and a declaration of the present occasion for praise (vv. 19–20, in Hebrew involving a play on words—the Hebrew for "Blessed" and "prayer" sound very much alike). The first line of the first call to praise (v. 5) begins with "Come and see"; the first line of the second (v. 16) begins with "Come and hear."

66 title See notes on Ps 4; 30 titles.

66:1–4 Calling all the earth to joyful praise.

66:1 *all ye lands.* See note on 65:2.

66:2 *name.* See note on 5:11.

‡66:3 *terrible.* Or "awesome." See v. 5; see also note on 65:5. *submit themselves unto thee.* See 81:15.

66:4 See note on 46:10.

66:5–7 Recollection of God's deliverance of Israel at the Red sea as a sign of His power to rule over the nations. The psalmist portrays His deliverance (see introduction above) both as similar to this Red sea rescue in its manifestation of God's saving power (see 65:5–7 for a comparison of God's mighty saving acts with His mighty acts of creation) and as a continuation of God's same saving purposes.

‡66:5 *Come and see.* God's saving acts of old can still be "seen" at His temple, where they are continually celebrated (see 46:8; 48:8–9 and notes). *terrible.* See v. 3. *toward the children of men.* Specifically in behalf of His people.

66:6 *flood.* Or "river," possibly the Jordan, but more likely a parallel reference to the Red sea.

66:7 *rebellious.* Nations that are in revolt against God's rule (see 68:6).

66:8–12 Proclamation in praise of God's new deliverance of His people.

66:8 *people.* Here probably the grateful throng of worshipers (see 2 Chr 20:27–28).

66:9 *feet to be moved.* See note on 38:16.

66:10 *hast proved . . . hast tried.* From one point of view, times of distress constitute a testing of God's people as to their trust in and loyalty to God. The metaphor is borrowed from the technology of refining precious metals, which included heating the metals in a crucible to see if all impurities had been removed (see 12:6; 17:3).

66:11–12 *Thou . . . Thou.* God's rule is all-pervasive; even when enemies for malicious purposes attack His people, God is not a

12 [a]Thou hast caused men to ride over
our heads;
[b]We went through fire and through
water:
But thou broughtest us out into a
[1]wealthy *place.*
13 I will go *into* thy house with burnt
offerings:
[a]I will pay thee my vows,
14 Which my lips have [1]uttered,
And my mouth hath spoken, when I
was in trouble.
15 I will offer unto thee burnt sacrifices of
[1]fatlings,
With the incense of rams;
I will offer bullocks with goats. Selah.
16 Come *and* hear, all ye that fear God,
And I will declare what he hath done
for my soul.
17 I cried unto him *with* my mouth,
And *he was* extolled with my tongue.
18 [a]If I regard iniquity in my heart,
The Lord will not hear *me:*
19 *But* verily God [a]hath heard *me;*
He hath attended to the voice of my
prayer.
20 Blessed *be* God, which hath not turned
away my prayer,
Nor his mercy from me.

Psalm 67

To the chief Musician on Neginoth,
A Psalm *or* Song.

1 God be merciful unto us, and bless us;
And [a]cause his face to shine [1]upon us;
Selah.
2 That [a]thy way may be known upon
earth,
[b]Thy saving health among all nations.
3 Let the people praise thee, O God;
Let all the people praise thee.
4 O let the nations be glad and sing for
joy:
For [a]thou shalt judge the people
righteously,
And [1]govern the nations upon earth.
Selah.
5 Let the people praise thee, O God;
Let all the people praise thee.
6 [a]*Then* shall the earth yield her
increase;
And God, *even* our own God, shall
bless us.
7 God shall bless us;
And all the ends of the earth shall fear
him.

Psalm 68

To the chief Musician,
A Psalm *or* Song of David.

1 Let [a]God arise, let his enemies be
scattered:
Let them also that hate him flee
[1]before him.
2 [a]As smoke is driven away, *so* drive
them away:
[b]As wax melteth before the fire,
So let the wicked perish at the
presence of God.
3 But [a]let the righteous be glad; let them
rejoice before God:
Yea, let them [1]exceedingly rejoice.
4 Sing unto God, sing *praises to* his name:

66:12 [1]Heb. *moist* [a]Is. 51:23 [b]Is. 43:2
66:13 [a]Eccl. 5:4
66:14 [1]Heb. *opened*
66:15 [1]Heb. *marrow*
66:18 [a]Is. 1:15; John 9:31; Jas. 4:3
66:19 [a]Ps. 116:1,2
67:1 [1]Heb. *with us* [a]Num. 6:25; Ps. 4:6
67:2 [a]Acts 18:25 [b]Is. 52:10; Tit. 2:11
67:4 [1]Heb. *lead* [a]Ps. 96:10
67:6 [a]Lev. 26:4; Ps. 85:12; Ezek. 34:27
68:1 [1]Heb. *from his face* [a]Num. 10:35; Is. 33:3
68:2 [a]Is. 9:18; Hos. 13:3 [b]Mic. 1:4
68:3 [1]Heb. *rejoice with gladness* [a]Ps. 32:11

mere passive observer but has His own holy purposes in it (see Is 45:7; Amos 3:6). *net . . . affliction . . . ride over.* Three metaphors describe their suffering: captives thrown into prison, prisoners of war turned into slaves, defeated troops overrun by a chariot force.

66:12 *fire and . . . water.* Conventional metaphors for severe trials (see Is 43:2). *into a wealthy place.* Lit."to an overflowing" (see 23:5). They were brought out of a situation of distress into a situation of overflowing well-being.

66:13–15 Announcement of fulfillment of vows: addressed to God (see note on 7:17; see also 50:14; 116:17–19).

66:13 *I.* The king.

66:16–20 Proclamation of what God has done: in praise of God, addressed to the worshiping congregation.

66:16 *fear God.* See note on Gen 20:11.

66:17 *he was extolled.* Prayer and praise belonged together in the OT (see also Phil 4:6; 1 Tim 2:1).

66:20 *Blessed be God.* See v. 8. *mercy.* See note on 6:4.

Ps 67 A communal prayer for God's blessing. Its content, form and brevity suggest that it served as a liturgical prayer of the people at the conclusion of worship, perhaps just prior to (or immediately after) the priestly benediction (see note on v. 1). God's blessing of His people (as well as His saving acts in their behalf) will catch the attention of the nations and move them to praise (see 65:2). This psalm is the third in a series of four (see introduction to Ps 65). It has a symmetrical structure: Two verses at the beginning contain the prayer, while the two concluding verses speak of the effects of God's answer. In the intervening verses, framed by a refrain (vv. 3,5), the people seek to motivate God's answer by referring to the worldwide praise that His mercies to His people will awaken.

67 title See notes on Ps 4; 30 titles.

67:1–2 The prayer.

67:1 The heart of the prayer, anticipating (or echoing) the priestly benediction (see Num 6:24–26). *cause his face to shine.* See notes on 4:6; 13:1.

67:2 May God's favors to His people be so obvious that all the world takes notice (see note on 46:10).

67:3–5 The motivation. Elaborating on v. 2, the people speak of the worldwide praise that will resound to God when He graciously blesses His people. Their wish is twofold: (1) that God's blessings may be so abundant that the people will be moved to praise, and (2) that the nations may indeed add their praise to that of Israel—an appropriate expression at this climax of the liturgy of worship.

67:4 May the nations rejoice in the Lord when they see how benevolent the rule of God is (see 98:4–6; 100:1).

67:6–7 The effects of God's blessing His people.

67:6 The promised land will yield its abundance (see 65:9–13).

Ps 68 A processional liturgy celebrating the glorious and triumphant rule of Israel's God (see introductions to Ps 24; 47; 118; 132). Verses 1–18 contain many clear references to God's triumphal march from mount Sinai (in the days of Moses) to mount Zion (in the days of David). The events at mount Sinai marked the birth of the kingdom of God among His people; the establishing of the ark of the covenant, symbol of God's throne,

[a]Extol him that rideth upon the
heavens
[b]By his name JAH, and rejoice before
him.
5 [a]A father of the fatherless, and a judge
of the widows,
Is God in his holy habitation.
6 [a]God setteth the solitary [1]in families:
[b]He bringeth out those which are
bound with chains:
But [c]the rebellious dwell *in* a dry *land.*

7 O God, [a]when thou wentest forth
before thy people,
When thou didst march through the
wilderness; Selah.
8 The earth shook, the heavens also
dropped
At the presence of God: *even* Sinai
itself *was moved*
At the presence of God, the God of
Israel.

9 [a]Thou, O God, didst [1]send a plentiful
rain,
Whereby thou didst [2]confirm thine
inheritance, when it was weary.
10 Thy congregation hath dwelt therein:
[a]Thou, O God, hast prepared of thy
goodness for the poor.

11 The Lord gave the word:
Great *was* the [1]company of those that
published *it.*
12 [a]Kings of armies [1]did flee apace:
And she that tarried at home divided
the spoil.
13 [a]Though ye have lien among the pots,
[b]*Yet shall ye be as* the wings of a dove
covered with silver,
And her feathers with yellow gold.
14 [a]When the Almighty scattered kings
[1]in it,
It was *white as* snow in Salmon.

68:4 [a]Deut. 33:26 [b]Ex. 6:3
68:5 [a]Ps. 10:14
68:6 [1]Heb. *in a house* [a]1 Sam. 2:5; Ps. 107:4-7 [b]Acts 12:6 [c]Ps. 107:34
68:7 [a]Ex. 13:21; Judg. 4:14
68:9 [1]Heb. *shake out* [2]Heb. *confirm it* [a]Deut. 11:11
68:10 [a]Deut. 26:5; Ps. 74:19
68:11 [1]Heb. *army*
68:12 [1]Heb. *did flee, did flee* [a]Num. 31:8; Josh. 10:16
68:13 [a]Ps. 81:6 [b]Ps. 105:37
68:14 [1]Or, *for her, she was* [a]Josh. 10:10

in Jerusalem marked the establishment of God's redemptive kingdom in the earth, with Jerusalem as its royal city. The early church, taking its cue from Eph 4:8–13, understood this psalm to foreshadow the resurrection, ascension and present rule of Christ and the final triumph of His church over the hostile world. Ps 68 is the last in a series of four (see introduction to Ps 65).

The psalm is composed of nine (Hebrew) stanzas, with the last line as a concluding doxology. The first (vv. 1–3) indicates the beginning of the liturgical procession, and the last (vv. 32– 35) refers to its conclusion—God enthroned in His sanctuary. The seventh (vv. 24–27) speaks expressly of the procession coming into view and entering the sanctuary. In light of these clear references, the third stanza (vv. 7–10) suggests a stage in the procession recalling the wilderness journey from Sinai to the promised land, while the fifth (vv. 15–18) marks that stage in which the Lord ascends mount Zion. On the other hand, the second stanza (vv. 5–6) reflects on the benevolence of God's rule; the fourth (vv. 11–14) recalls His victories over the kings of Canaan; the sixth (vv. 19–23) speaks reassuringly of God's future victories; and the eighth (vv. 28–31) contains prayers that God may muster His power to subdue the enemy as He had done before.

68 title See notes on Ps 4; 30 titles.

68:1–3 The start of the procession, liturgically recalling the beginning of God's march with his people in army formation from Sinai (see Num 10:33–35).

68:1 *enemies be scattered.* See note on v. 30.

68:3 *righteous.* Israel as the committed people of God in distinction from those opposed to the coming of God's kingdom (the "wicked" of v. 2).

68:4–6 A call to praise God for the benevolence of His rule.

‡68:4 *name.* See note on 5:11. *that rideth upon the heavens.* Lit. "who rides on the clouds." With this reading, an epithet of Baal found in Canaanite literature is used to make the point that the Lord (Yahweh, not Baal) is the exalted One who truly makes the storm cloud His chariot (see v. 33; 18:9; 104:3; Is 19:1; Mat 26:64). *JAH.* Shortened form of Jahweh (Yahweh), the personal name of God, normally translated "LORD." For the significance of this name for God, see Ex. 3:14 and note.

68:5–6 God is the defender of the powerless (see 10:14; 146:7–9; 147:6; Deut 10:18).

‡68:6 *setteth the solitary in families.* Provides them with a home. See Ex 1:21; Ruth 4:14–17; 1 Sam 2:5. *bringeth out those . . . bound with chains.* As He led Israel out of Egypt (see 69:33; 107:10,14). *rebellious.* See notes on v. 18; 66:7. *dry land.* A place utterly barren, lacking even soil for vegetation (see Ezek 26:4,14).

68:7–10 Recollection of God's march through the wilderness from Sinai into the promised land (see Judg 5:4–5; Hab 3:3–6).

‡68:8 *earth shook.* A reference to the quaking of mount Sinai (Ex 19:18). *heavens also dropped.* Dropped rain. The Pentateuch preserves no tradition of rain during the wilderness wanderings, but here (and in Judg 5:4) rain is closely associated with the quaking of the earth as a manifestation of the majesty of God. Perhaps the "thunders and lightnings, and a thick cloud" over mount Sinai (Ex 19:16) were accompanied by rain. But see also v. 9, which suggests rains that refreshed the people on their journey.

68:9 *thine inheritance.* The people of Israel (see Deut 9:29).

‡68:10 *therein.* Probably refers to the promised land. *prepared.* God provided for them from the produce of Canaan (see Josh 5:11–12). *goodness.* See 65:11 and note. *poor.* Israel as a people dependent on God.

68:11–14 Recollection of God's victories over the kings of Canaan.

‡68:11 *gave the word.* God declares beforehand that He would be victorious over the Canaanite kings (see Ex 23:22–23, 27–28,31; Deut 7:10–24; 11:23–25; Josh 1:2–6). *Great . . . those that published it.* A large throne gathers to proclaim and celebrate God's victories (see Ex 15:1–21; 1 Sam 18:6–7; 2 Chr 20:26–28). *published.* See 40:9 and note.

‡68:12 *flee apace.* They flee rapidly because they are no match for the Lord.

‡68:13 *ye have lien among the pots.* Rested by the campfires in the safety of the camp. *wings of a dove covered with silver.* Israel, God's "dove" (see "turtledove" in 74:19 and note; cf. Hos 7:11), is enriched with the silver and gold of plunder from the kings of Canaan even though she still remains in camp. This poetic hyperbole (a figure of speech that uses exaggeration for emphasis) celebrates the fact that God had defeated the kings even before Israel met them in battle (see Josh 2:8–11; 5:1; 6:16; see also 2 Sam 5:24; 2 Ki 7:5–7; 19:35; 2 Chr 20:22–30).

68:14 *Almighty.* Hebrew *Shaddai* (see note on Gen 17:1). *white as snow in Salmon* [i.e. "Zalmon"]. Zalmon was a mountain near Shechem (see Judg 9:46–48), but others identify it here as Jebel Druze, a dark volcanic mountain east of Bashan. Its name appears to mean "the dark one"—in distinction from the Lebanon ("the white one") range, composed of limestone—and the figure may involve the contrast of white snow scattered

15 The hill of God *is as* the hill of Bashan;
A high hill *as* the hill of Bashan.
16 Why leap ye, ye high hills?
[a]*This is* the hill *which* God desireth to dwell in;
Yea, the LORD will dwell *in it* for ever.
17 [a]The chariots of God *are* twenty thousand, [1]*even* thousands of angels:
The Lord *is* among them, *as in* Sinai, in the holy *place*.
18 [a]Thou hast ascended on high, [b]thou hast led captivity captive:
[c]Thou hast received gifts [1]for men;
Yea, *for* [d]the rebellious also, [e]that the LORD God might dwell *among them*.

19 Blessed *be* the Lord,
Who daily loadeth us *with benefits*,
Even the God of our salvation. Selah.
20 *He that is* our God *is* the God of salvation;
And [a]unto GOD the Lord *belong* the issues from death.
21 But [a]God shall wound the head of his enemies,
[b]*And* the hairy scalp of such a one as goeth on still in his trespasses.
22 The Lord said, I will bring [a]again from Bashan,
I will bring *my people* again [b]from the depths of the sea:
23 [a]That thy foot may be [1]dipped in the blood of *thine* enemies,
[b]*And* the tongue of thy dogs in the same.
24 They have seen thy goings, O God;
Even the goings of my God, my King, in the sanctuary.
25 [a]The singers went before, the players on instruments *followed* after;
Among *them were* the damsels playing with timbrels.
26 Bless ye God in the congregations,
Even the Lord, [1]from [a]the fountain of Israel.
27 There *is* [a]little Benjamin *with* their ruler,
The princes of Judah [1]*and* their council,
The princes of Zebulun, *and* the princes of Naphtali.
28 Thy God hath [a]commanded thy strength:
Strengthen, O God, that which thou hast wrought for us.
29 Because of thy temple at Jerusalem
[a]Shall kings bring presents unto thee.
30 Rebuke [1]the company of spearmen,
[a]The multitude of the bulls, with the calves of the people,
Till every one [b]submit himself with pieces of silver:

68:16 [a]Deut. 12:5; 1 Ki. 9:3
68:17 [1]Or, even *many thousands* [a]Deut. 33:2
68:18 [1]Heb. *in the man* [a]Eph. 4:8 [b]Judg. 5:12 [c]Acts 2:4,33 [d]1 Tim. 1:13 [e]Ps. 78:60
68:20 [a]Deut. 32:39
68:21 [a]Hab. 3:13 [b]Ps. 55:23
68:22 [a]Num. 21:33 [b]Ex. 14:22
68:23 [1]Or, *red* [a]Ps. 58:10 [b]1 Ki. 21:19
68:25 [a]1 Chr. 13:8
68:26 [1]Or, ye that are *of the fountain of Israel* [a]Deut. 33:28; Is. 48:1
68:27 [1]Or, with *their company* [a]1 Sam. 9:21
68:28 [a]Ps. 42:8
68:29 [a]Ps. 72:10
68:30 [1]Or, *the beasts of the reeds* [a]Ps. 22:12 [b]2 Sam. 8:2

on "Dark Mountain." The reference may then be to abandoned weapons littering the field from which the kings have fled headlong (see 2 Ki 7:15).

68:15–18 Celebration of God's ascent to mount Zion.

68:15–16 The mountains surrounding Bashan, including the towering mount Hermon, are portrayed as being jealous because God has chosen mount Zion as the seat of His rule, making it the "highest" of mountains (see 48:2 and note).

‡68:16 *Why leap ye . . . ?* Or, Why do you look enviously (at the favor shown to Zion)?

68:17 *chariots of God.* God's great heavenly host, here likened to a vast chariot force (see 2 Ki 6:17; Hab 3:8,15). In the time of the Roman empire Jesus referred to God's host in terms of "legions" (Mat 26:53).

‡68:18 *hast ascended on high.* Have gone up to Your place of enthronement on mount Zion (see 47:5–6 and note; see also 7:7). *led captivity captive . . . received gifts.* Like a victorious king after triumphs on the field of battle. *for the rebellious.* Or "from the rebellious." Those who had opposed the kingdom of God (see v. 6 and note on 66:7) are compelled to submit to Him and bring tribute. *that the LORD God may dwell among them.* Grammatically completes the clause, "Thou hast ascended on high." Paul applies this verse (as translated in the Septuagint) to the ascended Christ (Eph 4:8–13), thereby implying that Christ's ascension was a continuation of, and a fulfillment of, God's establishment of His kingdom in His royal city Jerusalem (see introduction).

68:19–23 Joyous confession of hope that God's victorious campaigns will continue until the salvation of His people is complete.

68:19 *loadeth us with benefits.* The verb here can be translated "bear or carry" (God carries His people or bears their daily burdens; cf. "borne by me" in Is 46:3) or "load or load down" (God loads down His people with blessings; cf. "lade you with a . . . yoke" in 1 Ki 12:11). The Lord receives "gifts" from His vanquished enemies and heaps them upon His people (cf. v. 18).

68:20 *issues from death.* Or "escape from death," at the hand of our enemies—implicitly, perhaps, also from death itself as the last great enemy (see notes on 6:5; 11:7; 16:9–11; 17:15; 49:14–15).

68:21 As God assures the life of His people (see v. 20), so He will crush those who oppose Him. *wound the head.* See Num 24:17.

68:23 See note on 58:10.

68:24–27 The liturgical procession approaches the temple (see Ps 24; 47).

‡68:24 *thy goings . . . the goings . . . in the sanctuary.* God's victory procession into the temple.

68:25 *damsels playing with timbrels.* See note on Jer 31:4.

68:27 All Israel is represented, from little Benjamin to powerful Judah, and tribes from the north as well as the south. *Benjamin with their ruler.* Perhaps reflecting the fact that from the tribe of Benjamin came the first king (Saul), who began the royal victories over Israel's enemies (see 1 Sam 11:11; 14:20–23).

68:28–31 Prayer for God to continue His conquest of the threatening powers.

68:28 *God hath commanded thy strength.* Or, perhaps, "Command Your power to act, O God."

68:29 *Because of thy temple.* Because Your earthly royal house has been established in Jerusalem. *bring presents unto thee.* Acknowledge You by bringing tribute, as subjected kings brought tribute to their conquerers (see 2 Sam 8:2,6,10; 2 Ki 3:4).

‡68:30 *Rebuke.* See note on 76:6. *company of spearmen.* Lit. "the beasts of the reeds," i.e. Pharaoh (see Ezek 29:3). *multitude of the bulls, with the calves.* Powerful princes supporting the pharaoh, and the lesser princes of other nations. Egypt is singled out here as representative of the hostile nations—because

[2]Scatter thou the people *that* delight in war.
31 [a]Princes shall come out of Egypt;
[b]Ethiopia shall soon [c]stretch out her hands unto God.

32 Sing unto God, ye kingdoms of the earth;
O sing *praises unto* the Lord; Selah.
33 To him [a]that rideth upon the heavens of heavens, *which were* of old;
Lo, he doth [1]send out his voice, *and that* a mighty voice.
34 [a]Ascribe ye strength unto God:
His excellency *is* over Israel,
And his strength *is* in the [1]clouds.
35 O God, [a]*thou art* terrible out of thy holy places:
The God of Israel *is* he
That giveth strength and power unto *his* people.
Blessed *be* God.

Psalm 69

To the chief Musician [a]upon Shoshannim, *A Psalm* of David.

1 Save me, O God; for [a]the waters are come in unto *my* soul.
2 [a]I sink in [1]deep mire, where *there is* no standing:
I am come into [2]deep waters, where the floods overflow me.

68:30 [2]Or, *He scattereth*
68:31 [a]Is. 19:21 [b]Is. 45:14 [c]Ps. 44:20
68:33 [1]Heb. *give* [a]Ps. 18:10
68:34 [1]Or, *heavens* [a]Ps. 29:1
68:35 [a]Ps. 76:12
69:T [a]Ps. 45, title
69:1 [a]Jonah 2:5
69:2 [1]Heb. *the mire of depth* [2]Heb. *depth of waters* [a]Ps. 40:2
69:3 [a]Ps. 6:6 [b]Ps. 119:82; Is. 38:14
69:4 [a]Ps. 35:19; John 15:25
69:5 [1]Heb. *guiltiness*
69:8 [a]Is. 53:3
69:9 [a]John 2:17 [b]Rom. 15:3
69:10 [a]Ps. 35:13

3 [a]I am weary of my crying: my throat is dried:
[b]Mine eyes fail while *I* wait for my God.
4 They that [a]hate me without a cause are moe than the hairs of mine head:
They that would destroy me, *being* mine enemies wrongfully, are mighty:
Then I restored *that* which I took not away.
5 O God, thou knowest my foolishness;
And my [1]sins are not hid from thee.
6 Let not them that wait on thee, O Lord God of hosts, be ashamed for my sake:
Let not those that seek thee be confounded for my sake, O God of Israel.
7 Because for thy sake I have borne reproach;
Shame hath covered my face.
8 [a]I am become a stranger unto my brethren,
And an alien unto my mother's children.
9 [a]For the zeal of thine house hath eaten me up;
[b]And the reproaches of them that reproached thee are fallen upon me.
10 [a]When I wept, *and chastened* my soul with fasting,
That was to my reproach.

of Israel's past experiences with that world power and because at the time the psalm was composed it was the one great empire on Israel's immediate horizons. *Scatter thou the people.* See v. 1; so that Israel may have peace (see 46:9; 48:4–7; 65:7; 76:3).

68:32–35 Climax of the liturgical procession: a call for all kingdoms to hail with praise the God of Israel as the God who reigns in heaven and has established His earthly throne in the temple in Jerusalem (see Ps 47).

68:33 See v. 4 and note. *send out his voice . . . a mighty voice.* See note on 29:3–9.

‡68:35 *terrible.* Or "awesome." See 45:4 and note. *giveth strength and power unto his people.* The Lord of all has made Israel His people (His "kingdom"; see Ex 19:5–6), and His rule among them makes them participants in His victorious power (see 29:10–11).

Ps 69 A plea for God to have mercy and to save from a host of enemies: the prayer of a godly king when under vicious attack by a widespread conspiracy at a time when God had "wounded" him (see v. 26) for some sin in his life (see v. 5). If, as tradition claims, David authored the original psalm (see the superscription), the occasion is unknown. In its present form the prayer suggests a later son of David who ruled over the southern kingdom of Judah (see v. 35). That king may have been Hezekiah (see 2 Ki 18–20; 2 Chr 29–32). In themes and language this psalm has many links with Ps 32; 35; 38; 40; 109 (all psalms "of David"; see also Ps 18). It begins a series of three prayers for deliverance when threatened by enemies. The authors of the NT viewed this cry of a godly sufferer as foreshadowing the sufferings of Christ; no psalm, except Ps 22, is quoted more frequently in the NT.

69 title *To the chief Musician.* See note on Ps 4 title. *upon.* See note on Ps 9 title. *Shoshannim.* See note on Ps 45 title.

69:1–4 Initial plea for God to save.

69:1–2 *waters . . . deep mire . . . deep waters . . . floods.* Conventional imagery for great distress (see notes on 30:1; 32:6)—here the results of God's "wounding" (see v. 26), but especially of the attacks of the enemies (see vv. 14–15,29).

69:3 *throat is dried.* See 22:15. *eyes fail.* See 6:7 and note.

‡69:4 *without a cause . . . mine enemies wrongfully.* Those whom he has not wronged are pitted against him (see 35:19 and note). *moe* [i.e."more"] *than the hairs of mine head.* See note on 40:12. *Then I restored . . . away.* Had to pay restitution for that which I did not steal, an illustrative way of saying that his enemies are spreading false accusations about him (see 5:9 and note).

69:5–12 Prayer that God's discipline of His godly servant may not bring disgrace on all those who trustingly look to the Lord. The author acknowledges (v. 5) that God's "wounding" of him (see v. 26) has been occasioned by some sin in his life (but he has not sinned against those who have become his enemies). Because of his present suffering, his enemies mock his deep commitment to the Lord (see 22:6–8; 42:3; 79:10; 115:2; Job 2:9). Implicitly he prays that God will restore him again and vindicate his trust in Him.

69:5 *foolishness.* See note on 14:1.

69:8 Even those nearest him dissociate themselves from him (see 31:11–12 and note).

69:9 *zeal of thine house.* What was true of the author was even more true of Jesus (see John 2:17). *reproaches of them that reproached thee.* Those who mock God also mock His servant who trusts in Him (see 74:18,22–23; 2 Ki 18:31–35)—as Christ also experienced (see Rom 15:3).

‡69:10–11 *wept . . . with fasting . . . made sackcloth also my garment.* As tokens of humbling himself before the Lord in repentance as he prays for God to have mercy and restore him

11 I made sackcloth also my garment;
[a]And I became a proverb to them.
12 They that sit in the gate speak against
me;
And [a]*I was* the song of the [1]drunkards.
13 But *as for* me, my prayer *is* unto thee,
O LORD, [a]*in* an acceptable time:
O God, in the multitude of thy mercy
hear me, in the truth of thy
salvation.
14 Deliver me out of the mire, and let me
not sink:
[a]Let me be delivered from them that
hate me, and out of [b]the deep
waters.
15 Let not the waterflood overflow me,
Neither let the deep swallow me up,
And let not the pit [a]shut her mouth
upon me.
16 Hear me, O LORD; for thy
lovingkindness *is* good:
[a]Turn unto me according to the
multitude of thy tender mercies.
17 And [a]hide not thy face from thy servant;
For I am in trouble: [1]hear me speedily.
18 Draw nigh unto my soul, *and* redeem it:
Deliver me because of mine enemies.

19 Thou hast known [a]my reproach, and
my shame, and my dishonour:
Mine adversaries *are* all before thee.
20 Reproach hath broken my heart; and I
am full of heaviness:
And [a]I looked *for some* [1]to take pity,
but *there was* none;
And for [b]comforters, but I found none.
21 They gave me also gall for my meat;
[a]And in my thirst they gave me vinegar
to drink.
22 [a]Let their table become a snare before
them:
And *that which should have been* for
their welfare, *let it become* a trap.
23 [a]Let their eyes be darkened, that *they*
see not;
And make their loins continually to
shake.
24 [a]Pour out thine indignation upon
them,
And let thy wrathful anger take hold of
them.
25 [a]Let [1]their habitation be desolate;
And [2]let none dwell in their tents.
26 For they persecute [a]*him* whom thou
hast smitten;
And they talk to the grief of [1]those
whom thou hast wounded.
27 [a]Add [1]iniquity unto their iniquity:
[b]And let them not come into thy
righteousness.
28 Let them [a]be blotted out of the book of
the living,
[b]And not be written with the
righteous.
29 But I *am* poor and sorrowful:
Let thy salvation, O God, set me up on
high.
30 [a]I will praise the name of God with a
song;

69:11 [a]Jer. 24:9
69:12 [1]Heb. *drinkers of strong drink* [a]Job 30:9
69:13 [a]Is. 49:8
69:14 [a]Ps. 144:7 [b]ver. 1,2,15
69:15 [a]Num. 16:33
69:16 [a]Ps. 25:16
69:17 [1]Heb. *make haste to hear me* [a]Ps. 27:9
69:19 [a]Ps. 22:6,7; Is. 53:3
69:20 [1]Heb. *to lament* with me [a]Is. 63:5
69:20 [b]Job 16:2
69:21 [a]Mat. 27:34; Mark 15:23; John 19:29
69:22 [a]Rom. 11:9
69:23 [a]Is. 6:9,10; Rom. 11:10
69:24 [a]1 Thes. 2:16
69:25 [1]Heb. *their palace* [2]Heb. *let there not be a dweller* [a]Mat. 23:38
69:26 [1]Heb. *thy wounded* [a]Is. 53:4
69:27 [1]Or, *punishment of iniquity* [a]Rom. 1:28 [b]Is. 26:10
69:28 [a]Ex. 32:32; Phil. 4:3 [b]Ezek. 13:9
69:30 [a]Ps. 28:7

(see 35:13 and note; see also Gen 37:34; 2 Sam 12:16–17; Joel 1:13–14; 2:15–17; Jonah 3:5). *became a proverb.* An object of mocking and ridicule (cf. Deut 28:37; 1 Ki 9:7).

69:12 *They that sit in the gate . . . drunkards.* Everyone, from the elders of the city to the town drunks.

69:13–18 Though they mock, I pray to You.

69:13 *in an acceptable time.* When God is near to save (see 32:6 and note; see also Is 49:8; 61:2; 2 Cor 6:2). *multitude of thy mercy.* See note on 6:4.

69:14–15 *mire . . . deep waters . . . waterflood . . . deep.* See note on vv. 1–2.

69:15 *swallow me.* See note on 49:14. *pit.* See note on 30:1.

69:16 *lovingkindness.* See note on 6:4.

69:17 *hide . . . thy face.* See note on 13:1.

69:18 *redeem.* See note on 25:22.

69:19–21 In my trouble they heaped on scorn instead of bringing comfort (see 35:11–16; see also 142:4; Job 13:4; 16:2; 21:34).

69:20 *heart.* See note on 4:7.

69:21 *gall for my meat . . . vinegar to drink.* Vivid metaphors for the bitter scorn they made him eat and drink when his whole being craved for the nourishment and refreshment of comfort. The authors of the Gospels, especially Matthew, suggest that the suffering expressed in this verse foreshadowed Christ's suffering on the cross (see Mat 27:34,48; Mark 15:23,36; Luke 23:36; John 19:29).

69:22–28 Prayer for God to redress the wrongs committed (see note on 5:10).

69:22–23 For Paul's application of these verses to the Jews who rejected the Christ see Rom 11:9–10.

69:22 They had set his table with "gall" and "vinegar" (v. 21). *their table.* Reference may be to the meal accompanying the sealing of a covenant (see note on 23:5). In that case, this verse alludes to a pact uniting the enemies and calls on God to turn it against them.

69:23 They mocked him for his wound (v. 26); now may they experience the same failing of the eyes (see v. 3 and note on 6:7) and bending of the back (from weakness and pain; see 38:5–8). *make their loins . . . shake.* "Loins" refers to the belly and lower part of the back; they were viewed as the back's center of strength (see 66:11; see also Job 40:16).

‡69:24 *indignation . . . anger.* See note on 2:5.

69:25 They sought to remove him from his place; may they be removed. Cf. Peter's application of this judgment to Judas (Acts 1:20).

69:26 The great wrong committed by his enemies against him and to which reference has repeatedly been made.

69:27 They have falsely charged him with crimes (v. 4); may their real crimes all be charged against them.

69:28 They had plotted his death; may death be their destiny. *book of the living.* God's royal list of the righteous, whom God blesses with life (see 1:3; 7:9; 11:7; 34:12; 37:17,29; 55:22; 75:10; 92:12–14; 140:13). For other references to God's books see notes on 9:5; 51:1. In the NT the "book of life" refers to God's list of those destined for eternal life (see Phil 4:3; Rev 3:5; 13:8; 17:8; 20:12,15; 21:27).

69:29 Renewal of the prayer just prior to the vow to praise.

69:30–33 A vow to praise (see note on 7:17) out of assurance that the prayer will be heard (see note on 3:8).

69:30 *name of God.* See v. 36 and note on 5:11.

And will magnify him with thanksgiving.
31 [a]*This* also shall please the LORD better
than an ox
Or bullock that hath horns *and* hoofs.
32 [a]The [1]humble shall see *this, and* be
glad:
And [b]your heart shall live that seek God.
33 For the LORD heareth the poor,
And despiseth not [a]his prisoners.
34 [a]Let the heaven and earth praise him,
The seas, [b]and every *thing* that
[1]moveth therein.
35 [a]For God will save Zion,
And will build the cities of Judah:
That they may dwell there, and have it
in possession.
36 [a]The seed also of his servants shall
inherit it:
And they that love his name shall
dwell therein.

Psalm 70

To the chief Musician, *A Psalm* of David,
[a]to bring to remembrance.

1 *Make haste,* [a]O God, to deliver me;
Make haste [1]to help me, O LORD.
2 [a]Let them be ashamed and confounded
that seek after my soul:
Let them be turned backward, and put
to confusion, that desire my hurt.
3 [a]Let them be turned back for a reward
of their shame
That say, Aha, aha.
4 Let all those that seek thee rejoice and
be glad in thee:
And let such as love thy salvation say
continually, Let God be magnified.
5 [a]But I *am* poor and needy: [b]make haste
unto me, O God:
Thou *art* my help and my deliverer;
O LORD, make no tarrying.

Psalm 71

1 In [a]thee, O LORD, do I put my trust:
Let me never be put to confusion.
2 [a]Deliver me in thy righteousness, and
cause me to escape:
[b]Incline thine ear unto me, and save
me.
3 [a][1]Be thou my strong habitation,
whereunto *I* may continually resort:
Thou hast given [b]commandment to
save me;
For thou *art* my rock and my fortress.
4 [a]Deliver me, O my God, out of the
hand of the wicked,
Out of the hand of the unrighteous and
cruel *man.*
5 For thou *art* [a]my hope, O Lord GOD:
Thou art my trust from my youth.
6 [a]By thee have I been holden up from
the womb:
Thou art he that took me out of my
mother's bowels:
My praise *shall be* continually of thee.
7 [a]I am as a wonder unto many;
But thou *art* my strong refuge.

69:31 [a]Ps. 50:13
69:32 [1]Or, *meek* [a]Ps. 34:2 [b]Ps. 22:26
69:33 [a]Eph. 3:1
69:34 [1]Heb. *creepeth* [a]Ps. 96:11; 148:1; Is. 44:23 [b]Is. 55:12
69:35 [a]Ps. 51:18; Is. 44:26
69:36 [a]Ps. 102:28
70:T [a]Ps. 38, title
70:1 [1]Heb. *to my help* [a]Ps. 40:13
70:2 [a]Ps. 35:4,26
70:3 [a]Ps. 40:15
70:5 [a]Ps. 40:17 [b]Ps. 141:1
71:1 [a]Ps. 25:2,3
71:2 [a]Ps. 31:1 [b]Ps. 17:6
71:3 [1]Heb. *Be thou to me for a rock of habitation* [a]Ps. 31:2,3 [b]Ps. 44:4
71:4 [a]Ps. 140:1,4
71:5 [a]Jer. 17:7
71:6 [a]Ps. 22:9,10; Is 46:3
71:7 [a]Is. 8:18

69:32 *humble.* See note on 34:6. *shall see this, and be glad.* See 22:26 and note. *heart.* See note on 4:7. *shall live.* Bubble over with the joy of life, because the Lord does hear the prayers of His people in need—contrary to the mocking of scoffers.
69:34–36 A call to praise (see note on 9:1) in the assurance that God will restore Judah and assure His people's inheritance in the promised land. This stanza appears to indicate that in its final form this royal prayer was used at a time when not only the king was in trouble but the kingdom of Judah had also suffered devastating defeat.
69:34 Let all creation praise Him (see 148:1–13; Is 49:13).
69:35–36 *they . . . seed.* God's people and their children through the generations, specifically "they that love his name."
69:35 *Zion.* See note on 9:11.
Ps 70 An urgent prayer for God's help when threatened by enemies—a somewhat revised duplicate of 40:13–17 (see notes there). This is the second in a series of three such prayers; its language has many links with that of Ps 71. The prayer is framed by pleas for God to "make haste" with His help (vv. 1,5). The rest of the prayer focuses on the effects of God's saving help: (1) upon those "that seek after my soul" (vv. 2–3) and (2) for those "that seek thee" (v. 4).
70 title See note on Ps 4 title. *to bring to remembrance.* See note on Ps 38 title.
70:4 God's deliverance of His servant will give joy to all who trust in the Lord, because they see in it the assurance of their own salvation. *Let God be magnified.* Because His saving help is sure and effective (contrast v. 3).
Ps 71 A prayer for God's help in old age when enemies threaten because they see that the king's strength is waning (see note on 5:9). The psalm bears no superscription, but it may well be that Ps 70 was viewed by the editors of the Psalms as the introduction to Ps 71, in which case the psalm is ascribed to David (in his old age; see vv. 9,18). This suggestion gains support from the fact that Ps 72 is identified as a prayer by and/or for King Solomon (see introduction to that psalm). This is the third in a series of three prayers; its dominant theme is hope (see v. 14). Formally symmetrical, the psalm has a five-four-five, five-four-five (in Hebrew) line pattern: vv. 1–4 (five lines), vv. 5–8 (four lines), vv. 9–13 (five lines), vv. 15–18 (five lines), vv. 19–21 (four lines), vv. 22–24 (five lines). At the center (v. 14; see note on 6:6) stands a confident confession of hope. The whole is framed by an appeal for help (vv. 1–4) and a vow to praise in anticipation of deliverance (vv. 22–24). The intervening verses are linked by references to the troubles the king has experienced and references to old age.
71:1–4 The initial appeal for God's help.
‡71:1 *put to confusion.* Or "put to shame."
71:2 *thy righteousness.* See vv. 15–16,19,24; see also note on 5:8.
71:5–8 A confession that the Lord has always been his hope (see vv. 14,19–21).
71:5 *from my youth.* See 22:9.
‡71:6 *bowels.* Or "womb."
‡71:7 *a wonder.* He is a mystery to others because he claims to follow the Lord but experiences "great and sore troubles" in his life (v. 20). While God has not promised to exempt His people from hardship, the psalmist is unshaken in his confidence that God will remain his "strong refuge" in these difficulties.

8 Let [a]my mouth be filled *with* thy praise
And *with* thy honour all the day.
9 [a]Cast me not off in the time of old age;
Forsake me not when my strength
faileth.
10 For mine enemies speak against me;
And they that [1]lay wait for my soul
[a]take counsel together,
11 Saying, God hath forsaken him:
Persecute and take him; for *there is*
none to deliver *him.*
12 [a]O God, be not far from me:
O my God, [b]make haste for my help.
13 [a]Let them be confounded *and*
consumed that are adversaries to my
soul;
Let them be covered *with* reproach and
dishonour that seek my hurt.
14 But I will hope continually,
And will yet praise thee more and more.
15 [a]My mouth shall shew forth thy
righteousness
And thy salvation all the day;
For [b]I know not the numbers *thereof.*
16 I will go in the strength of the Lord
GOD:
I will make mention of thy
righteousness, *even* of thine only.
17 O God, thou hast taught me from my
youth:
And hitherto have I declared thy
wondrous works.
18 [a]Now also [1]when I am old and
grayheaded,
O God, forsake me not;
Until I have shewed [2]thy strength unto
this generation,
And thy power to every one *that* is to
come.
19 [a]Thy righteousness also, O God, *is* very
high,
Who hast done great *things:*
[b]O God, who *is* like unto thee!
20 [a]*Thou,* which hast shewed me great
and sore troubles,
[b]Shalt quicken me again,
And shalt bring me up again from the
depths of the earth.
21 Thou shalt increase my greatness,
And comfort me on every side.
22 I will also praise thee [a][1]with the
psaltery,
Even thy truth, O my God: unto thee
will I sing
With the harp, O thou [b]Holy One of
Israel.
23 My lips shall greatly rejoice when I
sing unto thee;
And [a]my soul, which thou hast
redeemed.
24 My tongue also shall talk of thy
righteousness all the day long:
For they are confounded, for they are
brought unto shame, that seek my
hurt.

Psalm 72

A Psalm [a][1]for Solomon.

1 Give the king thy judgments, O God,
And thy righteousness unto the king's
son.
2 [a]He shall judge thy people with
righteousness,

71:8 [a]Ps. 35:28
71:9 [a]ver. 18
71:10 [1]Heb. *watch,* or, *observe* [a]2 Sam. 17:1; Mat. 27:1
71:12 [a]Ps. 35:22 [b]Ps. 70:1
71:13 [a]ver. 24
71:15 [a]Ps. 35:28 [b]Ps. 40:5
71:18 [1]Heb. *unto old age and gray hairs* [2]Heb. *thine arm* [a]ver. 9
71:19 [a]Ps. 57:10 [b]Ps. 35:10
71:20 [a]Ps. 60:3 [b]Hos. 6:1,2
71:22 [1]Heb. *with the instrument of psaltery* [a]Ps. 92:1-3 [b]2 Ki. 19:22; Is. 60:9
71:23 [a]Ps. 103:4
72:T [1]Or, *of* [a]Ps. 127, title
72:2 [a]Is. 32:1

71:9–13 A prayer for God's continuing help in the waning years of his life.
71:10 *enemies speak against me.* See notes on 3:2; 5:9.
71:13 A plea for redress (see note on 5:10).
71:14 The centered confession of unfaltering hope (see 42:8; see also notes on 6:6; 42:8).
71:15–18 A vow to praise, accompanying the renewal of his prayer (v. 18); see note on 7:17.
‡71:15 *know not the numbers thereof.* He is unable to measure the fullness and richness of God's salvation, the thing that he desires more than anything else.
‡71:16–17 *strength . . . righteousness . . . wondrous works.* The things that the psalmist will speak of when he comes to fulfill his vows. God's strong and powerful works on behalf of His people are expressions of His righteousness; thus they can also be called His "righteousness" (v. 24).
71:16 *I will go.* To the temple, where God's people assemble for worship.
71:19–21 A confession that the Lord is still his hope, in the face of all his troubles (see vv. 5–8,14).
71:19 *very high.* Is as expansive as all space above the earth (see also 36:5 and note). *O God, who is like unto thee!* See Mic 7:18.
71:20 *Shalt quicken me again.* He who gave him life (see v. 6) will renew his life. *depths of the earth.* The realm of the dead, of which the grave is the portal (see note on 30:1).
71:22–24 A vow to praise in confident anticipation of God's saving help (see notes on 3:8; 7:17).
71:22 *psaltery . . . harp.* See note on 57:8. *Holy One of Israel.* See 78:41; 89:18; see also note on Is 1:4.
71:23 *redeemed.* Here, as often, a synonym for "deliver."
71:24 *righteousness.* God's saving acts in behalf of His people according to His covenant promises.
Ps 72 A prayer for the king, a son of David who rules on David's throne as God's earthly regent over His people. It may have been used at the time of the king's coronation (as were Ps 2; 110). Written as a petition, vv. 2–11, 17 express the desire of the nation that the king's reign will, as a consequence of God's endowment of His servant, be characterized by justice and righteousness, the supreme virtues of kingship. The prayer reflects the ideal concept of the king and the glorious effects of his reign. See Jeremiah's indictment of some of the last Davidic kings (e.g., Jer 22:2–3,13,15) and the prophetic announcement of the Messiah's righteous rule (see Is 9:7; 11:4–5; Jer 23:5–6; 33:15–16; Zech 9:9). Later Jewish tradition saw in this psalm a description of the Messiah, as did the early church. The last three verses do not belong to the prayer (see notes there).
72 title *for Solomon.* Either by him or for him—of course, both may be true. Undoubtedly it was also used by Israel (Judah) as a prayer for later Davidic kings.
72:1 The basic prayer. *judgments . . . righteousness.* May the king be endowed with the gift for and the love of justice and righteousness so that his reign reflects the rule of God Himself. Solomon asked for wisdom (see 1 Ki 3:9,11–12; see also Prov 16:12). *righteousness.* See note on 5:8.

And thy poor with judgment.
3 [a]The mountains shall bring peace to the people,
And the little hills, by righteousness.
4 [a]He shall judge the poor of the people,
He shall save the children of the needy,
And shall break in pieces the oppressor.
5 They shall fear thee [a]as long as the sun
And moon endure, throughout all generations.
6 [a]He shall come down like rain upon the mown grass:
As showers that water the earth.
7 In his days shall the righteous flourish;
[a]And abundance of peace [1]so long as the moon endureth.
8 [a]He shall have dominion also from sea to sea,
And from the river unto the ends of the earth.
9 [a]They that dwell in the wilderness shall bow before him;
[b]And his enemies shall lick the dust.
10 [a]The kings of Tarshish and *of* the isles shall bring presents:
The kings of Sheba and Seba shall offer gifts.
11 [a]Yea, all kings shall fall down before him:
All nations shall serve him.
12 For he [a]shall deliver the needy when he crieth;
The poor also, and *him* that hath no helper.
13 He shall spare the poor and needy,
And shall save the souls of the needy.
14 He shall redeem their soul from deceit and violence:
And [a]precious shall their blood be in his sight.
15 And he shall live, and to him [1]shall be given of the gold of Sheba:
Prayer also shall be made for him continually;
And daily shall he be praised.
16 There shall be a handful of corn in the earth upon the top of the mountains;
The fruit thereof shall shake like Lebanon:
[a]And *they* of the city shall flourish like grass of the earth.
17 [a]His name [1]shall endure for ever:
[2]His name shall be continued as long as the sun:
And [b]*men* shall be blessed in him:
[c]All nations shall call him blessed.

18 [a]Blessed *be* the LORD God, the God of Israel,
[b]Who only doeth wondrous *things.*
19 And [a]blessed *be* his glorious name for ever:
[b]And let the whole earth be filled *with* his glory; Amen, and Amen.

20 The prayers of David the son of Jesse are ended.

Psalm 73

[1]A Psalm [a]of Asaph.

1 [1]Truly God *is* good to Israel,
Even to such as are [2]of a clean heart.

72:3 [a]Ps. 85:10; Is. 32:17
72:4 [a]Is. 11:4
72:5 [a]ver. 7:17
72:6 [a]Hos. 6:3
72:7 [1]Heb. *till there be no moon* [a]Is. 2:4; Jer. 33:6; Luke 1:33
72:8 [a]Ex. 23:31; Zech. 9:10
72:9 [a]Ps. 74:14 [b]Is. 49:23
72:10 [a]2 Chr. 9:21
72:11 [a]Is. 49:23
72:12 [a]Job 29:12
72:14 [a]Ps. 116:15
72:15 [1]Heb. one *shall give*
72:16 [a]1 Ki. 4:20
72:17 [1]Heb. *shall be* [2]Heb. *Shall be as a son to continue his father's name for ever* [a]Ps. 89:36 [b]Gen. 12:3; Jer. 4:2 [c]Luke 1:48
72:18 [a]1 Chr. 29:10 [b]Ex. 15:11
72:19 [a]Neh. 9:5 [b]Num. 14:21; Hab. 2:14
73:T [1]Or, *A Psalm for Asaph* [a]Ps. 50, title
73:1 [1]Or, *Yet* [2]Heb. *clean of heart*

72:2–7 The quality of his reign: May it be righteous, prosperous and enduring.
72:3 Righteousness in the realm will be like fertilizing rain on the land, for then the Lord will bless His people with abundance (see vv. 6–7; 5:12; 65:9–13; 133:3; Lev 25:19; Deut 28:8).
72:5 *as long as the sun.* See 21:4 and note.
72:6 See v. 3 and note; see also v. 7. For another vivid metaphor expressive of the significance of the Lord's anointed for the realm see Lam 4:20.
72:7 *righteous.* See note on 1:5. *flourish.* Because the king supports and protects them, but uses all his royal power to suppress the wicked (see Ps 101).
72:8–14 The extent of his domain (vv. 8–11) as the result of his righteous rule (vv. 12–14).
72:8 His kingdom and his authority will extend to all the world (see vv. 9–11). Ideally and potentially, as God's earthly regent, he possesses royal authority that extends on earth as far as God's—an expectation that is fulfilled in Christ. See Zech 9:10 and note.
72:9 The tribes of the Arabian Desert to the east will yield to him. *lick the dust.* See Mic 7:17.
72:10 The kings whose lands border the Mediterranean Sea to the west will acknowledge him as overlord, as will those who rule in south Arabia and along the eastern African coast. *Tarshish.* A distant Mediterranean seaport, perhaps as far west as modern Spain. *Sheba.* See notes on Gen 10:28; 1 Ki 10:1; Joel 3:8. *Seba.* Elsewhere in the OT associated with Cush (Gen 10:7; Is 43:3); it may refer to a region in modern Sudan, south of Egypt.
72:15–17 Concluding summation: May the king enjoy a long, prosperous, world-renowned reign—one that blesses all the nations.
‡72:16 *handful of corn.* Or "an abundance of grain."
72:17 *All nations.* The language recalls the promise to Abraham (see Gen 12:3; 22:18) and suggests that it will be fulfilled through the royal son of David—ultimately the Messiah.
72:18–19 A doxology at the conclusion of Book 2 of the Psalter (see 41:13 and note). It is the people's response, their "Amen," to the contents of Book 2 (see note on Ps 4 title).
72:19 *filled with his glory.* See note on 85:9.
72:20 An editorial notation probably carried over from an earlier collection of psalms ascribed exclusively to David. *prayers of David.* See titles of Ps 86; 142.
Ps 73 A word of godly wisdom concerning the destinies of the righteous and the wicked. The editors of the Psalter placed it at the beginning of Book 3, as they did Ps 1 at the beginning of the whole collection (see introduction to Ps 1). Here is addressed one of the most disturbing problems of the OT saints: How is it that the wicked so often prosper while the godly suffer so much? Thematically the psalm has many links with Ps 49 (see introduction to that psalm; see also Ps 37). Its date may be as late as the postexilic era. Thematic development divides the psalm's structure into two halves of 14 verses each. The whole is framed by the sharply etched contrast of v. 1 and v. 27.

2 But *as for* me, my feet were almost
gone;
My steps had well nigh slipt.
3 [a]For I was envious at the foolish,
When I saw the prosperity of the
wicked.
4 For *there are* no bands in their death:
But their strength *is* [1]firm.
5 [a]They *are* not [1]in trouble *as other* men;
Neither are they plagued [2]like *other*
men.
6 Therefore pride compasseth them
about as a chain;
Violence covereth them [a]*as* a garment.
7 [a]Their eyes stand out with fatness:
[1]They have more than heart could wish.
8 [a]They are corrupt, and speak wickedly
concerning oppression:
They [b]speak loftily.
9 They set their mouth [a]against the
heavens,
And their tongue walketh through the
earth.
10 Therefore his people return hither:
[a]And waters of a full *cup* are wrung
out to them.
11 And they say, [a]How doth God know?
And is there knowledge in the most
High?

73:3 [a]Job 21:7; Ps. 37:1
73:4 [1]Heb. *fat*
73:5 [1]Heb. *in the trouble of* other *men* [2]Heb. *with* [a]Job 21:9
73:6 [a]Ps. 109:18
73:7 [1]Heb. *They pass the thoughts of the heart* [a]Jer. 5:28
73:8 [a]Ps. 53:1 [b]Jude 16
73:9 [a]Rev. 13:6
73:10 [a]Ps. 75:8
73:11 [a]Job 22:13

73:13 [a]Job 34:9; Mal. 3:14 [b]Ps. 26:6
73:14 [1]Heb. *my chastisement* was
73:16 [1]Heb. *It* was *labour in mine eyes* [a]Eccl. 8:17
73:17 [a]Ps. 77:13 [b]Ps. 37:38
73:18 [a]Ps. 35:6
73:20 [a]Job 20:8; Ps. 90:5

12 Behold, these *are* the ungodly,
Who prosper in the world; they
increase *in* riches.
13 [a]Verily I have cleansed my heart *in*
vain,
And [b]washed my hands in innocency.
14 For all the day long have I been
plagued,
And [1]chastened every morning.
15 If I say, I will speak thus;
Behold, I should offend *against* the
generation of thy children.
16 [a]When I thought to know this,
[1]It *was* too painful for me;
17 Until [a]I went into the sanctuary of God;
Then understood I [b]their end.
18 Surely [a]thou didst set them in slippery
places:
Thou castedst them down into
destruction.
19 How are they *brought* into desolation,
as *in* a moment!
They are utterly consumed with terrors.
20 [a]As a dream when *one* awaketh;
So, O Lord, when *thou* awakest, thou
shalt despise their image.
21 Thus my heart was grieved,
And I was pricked *in* my reins.

73 title The psalm is ascribed to Asaph, leader of one of David's Levitical choirs (see notes on Ps 39; 42; 50 titles). It begins a collection of 11 Asaphite psalms (Ps 73–83), to which Ps 50 at one time probably belonged. In view of the fact that the collection clearly contains prayers from a later date (e.g., Ps 74; 79; 83), references to Asaph in these titles must sometimes include descendants of Asaph who functioned in his place (see note on Ps 50 title). The Asaphite psalms are dominated by the theme of God's rule over His people and the nations. Apart from an introductory word of instruction (Ps 73) the collection is bracketed by prayers for God to rescue His people from foreign oppression (Ps 74; 83). The rest of the collection (Ps 75–82) appears to reflect thematic pairing: 1. The God who brings down the wicked and exalts the righteous (Ps 75) is the God and Savior of Israel (Ps 76). 2. God's saving acts in behalf of His people are remembered (Ps 77–78). 3. God is petitioned for help against the devastating attacks of Israel's enemies (Ps 79–80). 4. God is portrayed as presiding in judgment over His people (Ps 81) and over the world powers (Ps 82).

73:1–14 An almost fatal trial of faith: In the midst of his many troubles a godly man lets his eyes become fixed on the prosperity of the wicked.

73:1 *of a clean heart.* See v. 13; see also note on 24:4. *heart.* See note on 4:7.

‡73:2 *feet were almost gone.* Had almost stumbled from the path of truth and godliness (see 37:31 and note).

73:4–12 A description of the prosperous state of the wicked and the haughty self-reliance such prosperity engenders—hardly an objective account; it is rather the exaggerated picture that envious and troubled eyes perceived (see the description of the wicked in 10:2–11; cf. Job's anguished portrayal of the prosperity of the wicked in Job 21).

‡73:4 *bands.* Bonds or fetters as a symbol of pain or difficulty.

‡73:6 *pride compasseth them . . . as a chain.* Their pride is like an expensive necklace that they wear for all to see. Contrast Prov 1:9; 3:3,22.

‡73:7 *eyes stand out with fatness.* Have a full face that shows they are prosperous and well-fed.

‡73:8 *speak wickedly concerning oppression.* Make threats to oppress others.

‡73:9 *tongue walketh through the earth.* Making proud boasts.

‡73:10 *his people return hither.* Difficult phrase, perhaps suggesting that others (perhaps "His" [God's] people) are so impressed by the wicked who prosper that they turn to the wicked, rather than the Lord, as their source of provision. *waters of a full cup.* Contrast the full cup of the wicked with the "overflowing cup" provided by the Lord to those who trust in Him (23:5).

73:11 *God . . . most High.* That is, God most High (see 57:2; see also note on 3:7). *most High.* See note on Gen 14:19.

73:13–14 The thoughts that plagued him when he compared the state of the wicked with his own troubled lot.

73:13 *cleansed my heart.* See note on v. 1.

73:14 *chastened.* As a child by his father to keep him in the right way (see Prov 3:12; 23:13–14).

73:15–28 The renewal of faith: In the temple the godly man sees the destiny God has appointed for the wicked.

‡73:15 *If I say.* Or "If I had said." If he had given public expression to his thoughts as embodying true insight. *I should offend against.* Or "I would have betrayed." *thy children.* Those characterized by a humble reliance on and commitment to God.

73:18–20 Though the wicked seem to prosper, God has made their position precarious, and without warning they are swept away. The psalmist does not reflect on their state after death but leaves it as his final word that the wicked fall utterly and inevitably from their state of proud prosperity (see Ps 49; cf. the final state of the godly in v. 24).

73:20 When God arouses Himself as from sleep (see note on 7:6) and deals with the wicked, they vanish like the shadowy characters of a dream.

73:21 *heart.* See note on 4:7. *in my reins.* Lit. "in my kidneys" [i.e. "my mind"] (see note on 7:9).

22 [a]So foolish *was* I, and [1]ignorant:
I was *as* a beast [2]before thee.
23 Nevertheless I *am* continually with thee:
Thou hast holden *me* by my right hand.
24 [a]Thou shalt guide me with thy counsel,
And afterward receive me *to* glory.
25 [a]Whom have I in heaven *but thee?*
And *there is* none upon earth *that* I desire beside thee.
26 [a]My flesh and my heart faileth:
But God *is* the [1]strength of my heart, and my portion for ever.
27 For lo, [a]they that are far from thee shall perish:
Thou hast destroyed all them that go a whoring from thee.
28 But *it is* good for me to [a]draw near to God:
I have put my trust in the Lord GOD,
That *I* may declare all thy works.

Psalm 74

[1]Maschil of Asaph.

1 O God, why hast thou [a]cast *us* off for ever?
Why doth thine anger [b]smoke against [c]the sheep of thy pasture?
2 Remember thy congregation, *which* thou hast purchased of old;
The [1]rod of thine inheritance, *which* thou hast redeemed;
This mount Zion, wherein thou hast dwelt.
3 Lift up thy feet unto the perpetual desolations;
Even all *that* the enemy hath done wickedly in the sanctuary.
4 Thine enemies roar in the midst of thy congregations;
[a]They set up their ensigns *for* signs.
5 *A man* was famous according as he had lifted up
Axes upon the thick trees.
6 But now they break down the carved work thereof
At once with axes and hammers.
7 [1]They have cast fire into thy sanctuary,
They have defiled *by casting down* the dwelling place of thy name to the ground.
8 [a]They said in their hearts, Let us [1]destroy them together:
They have burnt up all the synagogues of God in the land.
9 We see not our signs:
[a]*There is* no more any prophet:
Neither *is there* among us any that knoweth how long.

73:22 [1]Heb. *I knew not* [2]Heb. *with thee* [a]Ps. 92:6; Prov. 30:2
73:24 [a]Ps. 32:8; 48:14
73:25 [a]Phil. 3:8
73:26 [1]Heb. *rock* [a]Ps. 84:2; 119:81
73:27 [a]Ps. 119:155
73:28 [a]Heb. 10:22
74:T [1]Or, A Psalm *for Asaph to give instruction*
74:1 [a]Ps. 44:9,23; Jer. 31:37 [b]Deut. 29:20 [c]Ps. 95:7
74:2 [1]Or, *tribe*
74:4 [a]Dan. 6:27
74:7 [1]Heb. *They have sent thy sanctuary into the fire*
74:8 [1]Heb. *break* [a]Ps. 83:4
74:9 [a]Amos 8:11

73:22 *a beast.* As stupid as a beast (see Job 18:3).

73:23–26 Although he had (almost) fallen to the level of beastly stupidity, God has not, will not, let him go—ever!

73:24 God's counsel has overcome his folly and will guide him through all the pitfalls of life (see 16:7; 32:8; 48:14). *receive me to glory.* At the end of the believer's pilgrimage (see 49:15 and note).

73:25 Though he has envied the prosperity of the wicked, he now confesses that nothing in heaven or earth is more desirable than God.

73:26 *My flesh . . . heart.* My whole being (see 84:2). *heart.* See note on 4:7. *portion.* Since the psalmist was a Levite, the Lord was his portion in the promised land in that he lived by the people's tithes dedicated to the Lord (see Num 18:21–24; Deut 10:9; 18:1–2). Here he confesses more: The Lord Himself is his sustainer, his preserver—his very life.

73:28 *I may declare all thy works.* A concluding vow to praise God for all His mercies to him (see note on 7:17).

‡Ps 74 A prayer for God to come to the aid of His people and defend His cause in the face of the mocking of the enemies—the Lord's relation to His people is like that of a king to his nation. The psalm dates from the time of the exile when Israel had been destroyed as a nation, the promised land devastated and the temple reduced to ruins (see Ps 79; Lam 2). Its relationship to the ministries of Jeremiah and Ezekiel is uncertain (see note on v. 9). Thematically the psalm divides into two halves of 11 verses each, with v. 12 (the center line; see note there) highlighting the primary thematic element that unifies the prayer. Verses 1–11 are framed by the "why's" of the people's complaint (vv. 1,11); the whole psalm is framed by pleas for God to "remember"(vv. 2,22). Note also that the "they's" of vv. 4–8 have their counterpoint in the "thou's" of vv. 13–17 (highlighted in the Hebrew by seven emphatic pronouns)—the mighty acts of God are appealed to against the destructive and haughty deeds of the enemies.

74 title *Maschil.* See note on Ps 32 title. *Asaph.* See note on Ps 73 title.

74:1–2 Initial complaint and appeal.

74:1 *why . . . ? Why . . . ?* Cf. "how long . . . ?" (v. 10) and "Why . . . ?" (v. 11). See note on 6:3; see also Introduction: Theology. *for ever.* So it seemed, since no relief was in sight. *anger.* See note on 2:5. *sheep of thy pasture.* See note on 23:1.

‡74:2 *purchased.* Or "acquired"; or "created." *rod* Or "tribe," here referring to all Israel. *thine inheritance.* See Deut 9:29. *redeemed.* Here, as often, a synonym for "delivered." *mount Zion.* See note on 9:11. This verse recalls the victory song of Ex 15 (see especially vv. 13–17, and compare the center verse of this psalm, v. 12, with the last verse of the song, Ex 15:18) and thus sets the stage for the other exodus recollections that follow. The Babylonian destruction of Zion seems to be the undoing of God's great victory over Egypt when He redeemed His people.

74:3–8 The Babylonians' high-handed destruction of the Lord's temple.

74:3 *Lift up thy feet unto.* Hurry to restore.

74:4 *ensigns.* Probably troop standards (see Num 1:52; Is 31:9; Jer 4:21). *for signs.* Signifying their triumph.

‡74:5 The Babylonians destroyed the temple like woodcutters chopping trees in the forest.

74:6 *carved work.* See 1 Ki 6:15.

74:7 *thy name.* See note on 5:11.

74:8 *They said.* See note on 10:11. *all the synagogues of God.* The reference is uncertain. At the time of the Babylonian attacks there may have been a number of (illegitimate) places in Judah where people went to worship God (see notes on 1 Ki 3:2; 2 Ki 18:4).

74:9–11 The complaint and prayer renewed (see vv. 1–2).

74:9 *see not our signs.* As we did at the time of the exodus (see vv. 13–15; 78:43). *no . . . prophet.* Jeremiah had been taken to

10 O God, how long shall the adversary reproach?
Shall the enemy blaspheme thy name for ever?
11 [a]Why withdrawest thou thy hand, even thy right hand?
Pluck *it* out of thy bosom.
12 For [a]God *is* my King of old,
Working salvation in the midst of the earth.
13 [a]Thou didst [1]divide the sea by thy strength:
[b]Thou brakest the heads of the [2]dragons in the waters.
14 Thou brakest the heads of leviathan in pieces,
And gavest him [a]*to be* meat to the people inhabiting the wilderness.
15 [a]Thou didst cleave the fountain and the flood:
[b]Thou driedst up [1]mighty rivers.
16 The day *is* thine, the night also *is* thine:
Thou hast prepared the light and the sun.
17 Thou hast set all the borders of the earth:
[a]Thou hast [1]made summer and winter.

74:11 [a]Lam. 2:3 74:12 [a]Ps. 44:4 74:13 [1]Heb. *break* [2]Or, *whales* [a]Ex. 14:21 [b]Is. 51:9,10; Ezek. 29:3 74:14 [a]Num. 14:9 74:15 [1]Heb. *rivers of strength* [a]Ex. 17:5,6; Num. 20:11 [b]Josh. 3:13 74:17 [1]Heb. *made them* [a]Gen. 8:22

18 [a]Remember this, *that* the enemy hath reproached, O LORD,
And *that* [b]the foolish people have blasphemed thy name.
19 O deliver not the soul [a]of thy turtledove unto the multitude *of the wicked:*
[b]Forget not the congregation of thy poor for ever.
20 [a]Have respect unto the covenant:
For the dark places of the earth are full *of* the habitations of cruelty.
21 O let not the oppressed return ashamed:
Let the poor and needy praise thy name.
22 Arise, O God, plead thine own cause:
[a]Remember how the foolish *man* reproacheth thee daily.
23 Forget not the voice of thine enemies:
The tumult of those that rise up against thee [a][1]increaseth continually.

Psalm 75

To the chief Musician, [a][1]Al-taschith,
A Psalm *or* Song [2]of Asaph.

1 Unto thee, O God, do we give thanks, *unto thee* do we give thanks:
For *that* thy name *is* near thy wondrous works declare.

74:18 [a]ver. 22 [b]Ps. 39:8 74:19 [a]Sol. 2:14 [b]Ps. 68:10 74:20 [a]Gen. 17:7,8; Ps. 106:45 74:22 [a]Ps. 89:51 74:23 [1]Heb. *ascendeth* [a]Jonah 1:2 75:T [1]Or, *Destroy not* [2]Or, *for Asaph* [a]Ps. 57, title

Egypt (see Jer 43:6–7), but whether Ezekiel was no longer prophesying is unknown. Perhaps this psalm was composed by an Asaphite who remained in Israel, part of a small group overlooked by Johanan when that army officer led the remnant to Egypt (see Jer 43:4–7).

74:10 *reproach . . . blaspheme thy name.* See v. 18; see also v. 22; 2 Ki 18:32–35; Is 37:6,23.

74:12 The center verse (center line in the Hebrew text; see note on 6:6). The whole psalm presupposes the truth confessed here: God is Israel's King, her hope and Savior; Israel is God's people (kingdom). This accounts for both the complaint and the prayer, and why the destruction of Israel brings with it the mocking of God. *my.* Communal use of the singular pronoun (see note on Ps 30 title). *of old.* From the days of the exodus (see Ex 3:7; 19:5–6).

74:13–17 The Lord is the mighty God of salvation and creation (see 65:6–7 and note).

74:13–14 Recollection of God's mighty acts when He delivered His people from Egypt. The imagery is borrowed from ancient Near Eastern creation myths, in which the primeval chaotic waters were depicted as a many-headed dragon that the creator-god overcame, after which he established the world order (see note on 32:6). The poet here interweaves creation and salvation themes to celebrate the fact that the God of Israel has shown by His saving acts (His opening of the Red sea for His people and His destruction of the Egyptians) that He is able to overcome all hostile powers to redeem His people and establish His new order in the world. For poetic use of this imagery (1) to celebrate God's creation works see 89:10; Job 9:13; 26:12–13; (2) to celebrate the deliverance from Egypt see Is 51:9; (3) to announce a future deliverance of Israel see Is 27:1. Echoes of the same imagery are present in the judgment announced against Egypt in Ezek 29:3–5; 32:2–6.

74:15 Recollection of God's water miracles at the Red sea, in the wilderness and at the Jordan.

74:16–17 God is the One who established the orders of creation; He (alone) is able to effect redemption and establish His kingdom in the world against all creaturely opposition.

74:18–23 A prayer for God to defend His cause and restore His people.

74:18 See vv. 2,10. *foolish people.* The "enemies" of v. 10 are here called fools for their contempt of God (see v. 22; see also note on 14:1).

74:19 *thy turtledove.* Israel—probably a figure of endearment (see Sol 2:14; 5:2; 6:9; see also Ps 68:13 and note).

74:20 *the covenant.* God's covenant to be the God of Israel, who makes them secure and richly blessed in the promised land (see Ex 19:5–6; 23:27–31; 34:10–11; Lev 26:11–12,42,44–45; Deut 28:1–14; see also Ps 105:8–11; 106:45; 111:5,9; Is 54:10; Jer 14:21; Ezek 16:60).

74:21 *poor and needy.* See note on 34:6. *praise thy name.* May they have cause to do so.

74:22 *Arise.* See note on 3:7.

74:23 *voice . . . tumult.* See 64:2.

Ps 75 A song of reassurance when arrogant worldly powers threaten Israel's security. The psalm may date from the time of the Assyrian menace (see 2 Ki 18:13–19:37). See also Ps 11; 76. Thematic parallels to the song of Hannah (1 Sam 2:1–10) are numerous. The worshiping congregation speaks (v. 1), perhaps led in its praise by one of the descendants of Asaph (v. 9). The psalm is framed by thanksgiving (v. 1) and praise (vv. 9–10). Two (Hebrew) stanzas of four lines each form the body of the psalm, and each stanza is composed of two couplets. The first stanza (vv. 2–5) contains a reassuring word from heaven; the second (vv. –8) contains a triumphant response from earth.

75 title *To the chief Musician.* See note on Ps 4 title. *Al-taschith.* See note on Ps 57 title; see also Ps 58; 59 titles. *Song.* See note on Ps 30 title. *Asaph.* See note on Ps 73 title.

75:1 The congregation begins with thanksgiving in the form

2 [1]When I shall receive the congregation
I will judge uprightly.
3 The earth and all the inhabitants
thereof *are* dissolved:
I bear up the pillars of it. Selah.
4 I said unto the fools, Deal not foolishly:
And to the wicked, [a]Lift not up the
horn:
5 Lift not up your horn on high:
Speak *not* with a stiff neck.
6 For promotion *cometh* neither from
the east,
Nor from the west, nor from the
[1]south.
7 But [a]God *is* the judge:
[b]He putteth down one, and setteth up
another.
8 For [a]in the hand of the LORD *there is* a
cup, and the wine is red;
It is [b]full *of* mixture; and he poureth
out of the same:
[c]But the dregs thereof, all the wicked
of the earth shall wring *them* out,
and drink *them.*
9 But I will declare for ever;
I will sing *praises* to the God of Jacob.
10 [a]All the horns of the wicked also will I
cut off;
But [b]the horns of the righteous shall be
exalted.

Psalm 76

To the chief Musician on Neginoth,
A Psalm *or* Song [1]of Asaph.

1 In [a]Judah *is* God known:
His name *is* great in Israel.
2 In Salem also is his tabernacle,
And his dwelling place in Zion.
3 [a]There brake he the arrows of the bow,
The shield, and the sword, and the
battle. Selah.
4 Thou *art* more glorious *and* excellent
[a]than the mountains of prey.
5 [a]The stouthearted are spoiled, [b]they
have slept their sleep:
And none of the men of might have
found their hands.
6 [a]At thy rebuke, O God of Jacob,
Both the chariot and horse *are* cast into
a dead sleep.

75:2 [1]Or, *When I shall take a set time*
75:4 [a]Zech. 1:21
75:6 [1]Heb. *desert*
75:7 [a]Ps. 50:6 [b]1 Sam. 2:7; Dan. 2:21
75:8 [a]Job 21:20; Jer. 25:15; Rev. 14:10; 16:19 [b]Prov. 23:30 [c]Ps. 73:10
75:10 [a]Ps. 101:8; Jer. 48:25 [b]Ps. 89:17; 148:14
76:T [1]Or, *for Asaph*
76:1 [a]Ps. 48:1
76:3 [a]Ps. 46:9; Ezek. 39:9
76:4 [a]Ezek. 38:12
76:5 [a]Is. 46:12 [b]Ps. 13:3; Jer. 51:39
76:6 [a]Ex. 15:1,21; Ezek. 39:20; Nah. 2:13; Zech. 12:4

of praise (see 7:17; 28:7; 30:12; 35:18). *name.* See notes on 5:11; 74:7. *wondrous works.* See note on 9:1.

75:2–5 A reassuring word from above: God will not fail to call the arrogant to account. It is not clear whether a new word from the Lord is heard or whether these verses recall (and perhaps summarize) earlier prophetic words (such as those of Isaiah in 2 Ki 19:21–34).

‡75:2 *When I shall receive the congregation.* Lit. "When I shall set the time." God will not fail to judge—but in His own time.

75:3 When, because of the upsurge of evil powers, the whole moral order of the world seems to have crumbled, God still guarantees its stability (see note on 11:3). *pillars.* A figure for that which stabilizes the world order (see note on 24:2).

75:4 *fools . . . wicked.* To the psalmists the wicked are both arrogant (see especially Ps 10; 73:4–12; 94:4; see also note on 31:23) and foolish (see 14:1; 74:18,22; 92:6; 94:8). *Lift . . . up the horn.* A figure for defiant opposition, based on the action of attacking bulls. "Horn" (see also v. 10) is a common Biblical metaphor for vigor or strength (see note on 18:2).

‡75:5 *stiff neck.* A figure for insolence and pride (cf. Ex 32:9; 33:3,5; 34:9).

75:6–8 Triumphant echo from earth: perhaps spoken by the Levitical song leader in elaboration of the comforting word from God.

‡75:6 *promotion.* Or "exaltation."

75:8 *cup.* See note on 16:5. *full of mixture.* Probably mixed with spices to increase the intoxicating effect (see Prov 9:2,5; 23:29–30; Sol 8:2; Is 65:11). *dregs . . . drink them.* Because God pours it out, they have no choice.

75:9 Concluding vow to praise God forever (see note on 7:17) for His righteous judgments. *I.* Probably the Levitical song leader speaking representatively for the people, but the pronoun may be a communal use of the singular, as in 74:12 (see note on Ps 30 title). *Jacob.* A synonym for Israel (see Gen 32:28).

75:10 *righteous.* See note on 1:5. *exalted.* See v. 7; see also note on v. 4.

Ps 76 A celebration of the Lord's invincible power in defense of Jerusalem, His royal city. The psalm is thematically related to Ps 46; 48; 87 (see introduction to Ps 46). The ancient tradition may well be correct that the psalm was composed after the Lord's destruction of Sennacherib's army when it threatened Jerusalem (see 2 Ki 19:35). Structurally, the opening (vv. 1–3) and closing (vv. 11–12; v. 10 should be read in the middle stanza) stanzas contain the main thematic development. Between them, a seven-verse stanza of praise addressed to God (vv. 4–10) celebrates His awesome act of judgment. The internal structure is notable: Verses 4,7,10 present general reflections, while the intervening verses recall the judgment itself. Verse 7, the center line (see note on 6:6), states the main theme of this stanza.

76 title *To the chief Musician.* See note on Ps 4 title. *on Neginoth.* See note on Ps 4 title. *Song.* See note on Ps 30 title. *Asaph.* See note on Ps 73 title.

76:1–3 God's crushing defeat of the enemy in defense of Zion.

76:1 *is God known.* Now especially—as a result of His marvelous act. *Israel.* The poet probably does not intend to distinguish between the two kingdoms (Judah and Israel) but only, by joining their names together, to refer to the whole of God's covenant people. Moreover, as a result of the Assyrian invasions, many displaced Israelites from the northern kingdom now resided in and around Jerusalem.

‡76:2 *Salem.* Jerusalem, as the parallelism makes clear (see note on Gen 14:18). *tabernacle.* Lit. "booth," referring to the temple. Since the Lord has just achieved a great victory over a menacing army, the poet may have wished to speak of the temple as the Lord's campaign tent (see 2 Sam 11:11; 1 Ki 20:12,16). But see also 18:11 and 31:20 ("pavilion"). *Zion.* See note on 9:11.

76:4–10 Praise of God's awesome majesty, whose mighty judgment evokes fearful reverence (see introduction).

‡76:4 *mountains of prey.* Mountains that are rich with animals to be hunted.

76:5–6 Perhaps echoes also God's victory over the Egyptians at the Red sea (see Ex 14:28,30; 15:4–5,10).

‡76:5 *have slept their sleep.* The sleep of death. *none . . . have found their hands.* Cannot even lift their hands to defend themselves against God's awesome power.

76:6 *rebuke.* This word, when predicated of God, usually refers to either (1) the thunder of His fierce majesty by which He wields His sovereign control over cosmic entities (see 18:15;

7 Thou, *even* thou, *art* to be feared:
And [a]who may stand in thy sight when once thou art angry?
8 [a]Thou didst cause judgment to be heard from heaven;
[b]The earth feared, and was still,
9 When God [a]arose to judgment,
To save all the meek of the earth. Selah.

10 [a]Surely the wrath of man shall praise thee:
The remainder of wrath shalt thou restrain.
11 [a]Vow, and pay unto the LORD your God:
[b]Let all that be round about him bring presents [1]unto him that ought to be feared.
12 He shall cut off the spirit of princes:
[a]*He is* terrible to the kings of the earth.

Psalm 77

To the chief Musician, [a]to Jeduthun, A Psalm [1]of Asaph.

1 [a]I cried unto God *with* my voice,
Even unto God *with* my voice; and he gave ear unto me.
2 [a]In the day of my trouble I [b]sought the Lord:
[1]My sore ran in the night, and ceased not:
My soul refused to be comforted.
3 I remembered God, and was troubled:
I complained, and [a]my spirit was overwhelmed. Selah.

4 Thou holdest mine eyes waking:
I am *so* troubled that I cannot speak.
5 [a]I have considered the days of old,
The years of ancient times.
6 I call to remembrance [a]my song in the night:
[b]I commune with mine own heart:
And my spirit made diligent search.
7 [a]Will the Lord cast off for ever?
And will he [b]be favourable no more?
8 Is his mercy clean gone for ever?
Doth [a]*his* promise fail [1]for evermore?
9 Hath God [a]forgotten to be gracious?
Hath he in anger shut up his tender mercies? Selah.

10 And I said, This *is* [a]my infirmity:
But I will remember the years of the right hand of the most High.
11 [a]I will remember the works of the LORD:
Surely I will remember thy wonders of old.
12 I will meditate also of all thy work,
And talk of thy doings.
13 [a]Thy way, O God, *is* in the sanctuary:
[b]Who *is so* great a God as *our* God?
14 Thou *art* the God that doest wonders:
Thou hast declared thy strength among the people.
15 [a]Thou hast with *thine* arm redeemed thy people,
The sons of Jacob and Joseph. Selah.

76:7 [a]Nah. 1:6
76:8 [a]Ex. 19:10 [b]2 Chr. 20:29,30
76:9 [a]Ps. 9:7-9; 72:4
76:10 [a]Ps. 65:7; Dan. 3:28
76:11 [1]Heb. *to fear* [a]Eccl. 5:4-6 [b]2 Chr. 32:22,23; Ps. 68:29
76:12 [a]Ps. 68:35
77:T [1]Or, *for Asaph* [a]Ps. 39, title; 62, title
77:1 [a]Ps. 3:4
77:2 [1]Heb. *My hand* [a]Ps. 50:15 [b]Is. 26:9,16
77:3 [a]Ps. 143:4
77:5 [a]Deut. 32:7; Ps. 143:5; Is. 51:9
77:6 [a]Ps. 42:8 [b]Ps. 4:4
77:7 [a]Ps. 74:1 [b]Ps. 85:1
77:8 [1]Heb. *to generation and generation?* [a]Rom. 9:6
77:9 [a]Is. 49:15
77:10 [a]Ps. 31:22
77:11 [a]Ps. 143:5
77:13 [a]Ps. 73:17 [b]Ex. 15:11
77:15 [a]Ex. 6:6; Deut. 9:29

104:7; 106:9; Job 26:11; Is 50:2; Nah 1:4) or repulses His enemies (as here; see also 9:5; 68:30; Is 17:13), or (2) the thunder of His wrath (see 80:16; Is 51:20; 54:9; 66:15; Mal 2:3). *God of Jacob.* A link with Ps 75 (see 75:9 and note).
76:7 The thematic center of vv. 4–10 (see note on 6:6).
76:8 *from heaven.* Though God is present in Zion (see v. 2), He sovereignly rules from heaven.
‡76:10 *wrath.* See note on 2:5. *shall praise thee.* When His judgments bring deliverance, those rescued praise Him. When men rise against God's kingdom, He crushes them in wrath to His own praise as Victor and Deliverer. The "remainder of wrath" indicates that particular judgments do not exhaust His wrath; a remainder is left to deal with other hostile powers.
76:11–12 Let Israel acknowledge God's help with grateful vows; let the nations acknowledge His sovereign rule with tribute.
76:11 *Vow.* See note on 50:14.
76:12 *spirit of princes.* Their bold rebelliousness.
Ps 77 Comforting reflections in a time of great distress. The distress appears to be personal rather than national. Comparison of vv. 16–19 with Hab 3:8–10 suggests, but does not prove, a time late in the monarchy. The poetic development advances from anguished bewilderment (vv. 1–9) to comforting recollection (vv. 10–20). A striking and dramatic feature is the insertion of a four-verse section (vv. 16–19) between the third and fourth verses of another four-verse section (vv. 13–15,20).
77 title *To the chief Musician.* See note on Ps 4 title. *Jeduthun.* See note on Ps 39 title. *Asaph.* See note on Ps 73 title.
77:1–9 Anguished perplexity over God's apparent inaction, when He fails to respond to unceasing and urgent prayers.
‡77:2 *My sore ran.* Lit. "my hand was stretched out" (in prayer). *soul.* See note on 6:3.
77:3–6 Remembrance of God's past mercies intensifies the present perplexity (as also in 22:1–11). God's failure to act now is so troubling that the psalmist cannot sleep (cf. 3:5; 4:8) and words fail (but see vv. 10–20).
77:6 *heart.* See note on 4:7.
77:7–9 Though words fail (v. 4), troubled thoughts will not go away.
77:8 *mercy.* See note on 6:4.
77:9 *anger.* See note on 2:5.
77:10–20 Reassuring recollection of God's mighty acts in behalf of Israel in the exodus.
77:10–12 Faith's decision to look beyond the present troubles—and God's bewildering inactivity—to draw hope anew from God's saving acts of old.
‡77:10 *right hand.* For the warrior's "right hand" as a symbol of strength, cf. Ex 15:6,12. *most High.* See note on Gen 14:19.
77:11,14 *wonders.* See note on 9:1.
77:13–20 God's mighty acts in the exodus recalled.
77:13 Appears to echo Ex 15:11. *is in the sanctuary.* Or "is seen in the sanctuary," as Israel rehearses and praises God's great acts of salvation on their behalf (see 63:2).
77:15 *redeemed.* Here, as often, a synonym for "deliver" (see 74:2). *Joseph.* OT authors sometimes refer to the northern kingdom as "Joseph" (or "Ephraim," Joseph's son) in distinction from the southern kingdom of Judah (see 78:67; 2 Sam 19:20; 1 Ki 11:28; Ezek 37:16,19; Amos 5:6,15; 6:6; Zech 10:6). However, here and elsewhere (see 80:1; 81:5; Obad 18) Joseph—the one elevated to the position of firstborn (see Gen 48:5 and note;

16 [a]The waters saw thee, O God, the
waters saw thee; they were afraid:
The depths also were troubled.
17 [1]The clouds poured out water:
The skies sent out a sound:
[a]Thine arrows also went abroad.
18 The voice of thy thunder *was* in the
heaven:
The lightnings lightened the world:
[a]The earth trembled and shook.
19 [a]Thy way *is* in the sea,
And thy path in the great waters,
[b]And thy footsteps are not known.
20 [a]Thou leddest thy people like a flock
By the hand of Moses and Aaron.

Psalm 78

[a][1] Maschil of Asaph.

1 [a]Give ear, O my people, to my law:
Incline your ears to the words of my
mouth.
2 [a]I will open my mouth in a parable:
I will utter dark sayings of old:
3 [a]Which we have heard and known,
And our fathers have told us.
4 [a]We will not hide *them* from their
children,
[b]Shewing to the generation to come
The praises of the LORD, and his
strength,
And his wonderful works that he hath
done.

5 For [a]he established a testimony in
Jacob,
And appointed a law in Israel,
Which he commanded our fathers,
[b]That *they* should make them known
to their children:
6 [a]That the generation to come might
know *them, even* the children *which*
should be born;
Who should arise and declare *them* to
their children:
7 That they might set their hope in God,

77:16 [a]Ex. 14:21
77:17 [1]Heb. *The clouds were poured forth* with *water* [a]2 Sam. 22:15
77:18 [a]2 Sam. 22:8
77:19 [a]Hab. 3:15 [b]Ex. 14:28
77:20 [a]Ex. 13:21; Is. 63:11,12
78:T [1]Or, A Psalm *for Asaph to give instruction* [a]Ps. 74, title
78:1 [a]Is. 51:4
78:2 [a]Mat. 13:35
78:3 [a]Ps. 44:1
78:4 [a]Deut. 6:7; Joel 1:3 [b]Ex. 13:8,14
78:5 [a]Ps. 147:19 [b]Deut. 4:9
78:6 [a]Ps. 102:18

Josh 16:1–4; 1 Chr 5:2; Ezek 47:13)—represents the whole of his generation and thus also all the descendants of Jacob.

77:16–19 A poetically heightened description of the majesty of God displayed when He opened a way through the Red sea. Verses 16,19 speak expressly of that event; the intervening verses (vv. 17–18) evoke the majesty of God displayed in the thunderstorm and earthquake. Ex 14:19 speaks only of God's cloud, not of a thunderstorm or earthquake, but the Hebrew poets often associated either or both with the Lord's coming to effect redemption or judgment—no doubt because these were the two most fearsome displays of power known to them (see 18:12–14; 68:8; Judg 5:4–5; Hab 3:6,10). Here the psalmist declares: It was the God of thunderstorm and earthquake who made His majestic way through the mighty waters of the sea to bring His people out of bondage. For Christians the display of God's power in behalf of His people now includes the resurrection of Jesus Christ from the dead (see Mat 28:2; cf. Eph 1:18–23).

77:17 *arrows.* Lightning bolts.

77:20 Completes the thought of v. 15 (see introduction). *leddest thy people.* Through the wilderness of Sinai.

Ps 78 A psalm of instruction—of warnings not to repeat Israel's sins of the past but to remember God's saving acts and marvelously persistent grace and, remembering, to keep faith with Him and His covenant. Here as elsewhere (pervasively in the OT), trust in and loyalty to God on the part of God's people are covenant matters. They do not spring from abstract principles (such as the formal structure of the God-man relationship) or from general human consciousness (such as feelings of dependence on "God" or a sense of awe in the presence of the "holy"), but they result from remembering God's mighty saving acts. Correspondingly, unfaithfulness is the more blameworthy because it contemptuously disregards all God's wonderful acts in His people's behalf (see Ps 105–106).

The psalm probably dates from the period of the divided monarchy and may have been composed about the time of the prophet Hosea (both Hosea and Isaiah speak frequently of the northern kingdom as Ephraim since it was the dominant tribe of that realm). Israel's unfaithfulness is here epitomized in the sin of Ephraim (v. 9); the psalm concludes by recalling the rejection of "Israel" (v. 59) and the abandonment of Shiloh (v. 60), but the election of Judah and mount Zion (v. 68). Coming, as may be assumed, from the pen of an Asaphite, the psalm was no doubt a warning to worshipers at Jerusalem not to fall away after the manner of their brothers to the north.

By placing this psalm next to Ps 77, the editors of the Psalter ranged David alongside Moses (and Aaron) as the Lord's shepherd over His people (see vv. 70–72; 77:20) who brought the exodus to its (provisionally) climactic fruition by completing the conquest of the promised land—a perspective apparently shared by the author of the psalm.

The psalm is composed of 77 (Hebrew) lines (72 numbered verses) and seven stanzas—with an 11-line introduction. After the introduction, the structure of the stanzas in Hebrew is symmetrical: 8 lines, 16 lines, 9 lines, 16 lines, 9 lines, 8 lines. The two sequences of 16 lines–9 lines constitute a thematic cycle, while the two 8-line stanzas frame the double cycle and underscore the contrast between the sin of Israel ("Ephraim," vv. 9–16) and the unending mercy of God to His people—mercy that is evidenced in His victory over His enemies and His election of Zion (in Judah) and David (vv. 65–72).

78 title *Maschil.* See note on Ps 32 title. *Asaph.* See note on Ps 73 title.

78:1–8 Our children must hear what our fathers have told us, so that they may be faithful to the Lord.

78:1–2 This introduction is written in the style of a wisdom writer (see essay, p. 687; see also Ps 49:1–4).

78:2 *parable . . . dark sayings.* The Hebrew underlying these two expressions occurs in 49:4 and Ezek 17:2 ("riddle," "parable")—which raises the question of whether the author is here influenced by prophetic use of wisdom language. While both terms had specialized uses—those reflected in 49:4—they apparently also became conventionalized more generally for instruction in a wide variety of forms. *of old.* Things for instruction from the past. Mat 13:35 refers to this verse as a prophecy of Jesus' parabolic teaching. Matthew apparently perceived in this psalm a prophetic voice anticipating that of the great Prophet. The "parables" of the psalm are, however, more like the teaching of Stephen (Acts 7) than that of Jesus.

78:4–5 The Lord's saving acts and covenant statutes—both must be taught, and in relationship, for together they remain the focal point for faith and obedience down through the generations (see vv. 7–8).

78:4 *not hide them.* See Job 15:18.

78:5 *make them known to their children.* See, e.g., Ex 10:2; 12:26–27; 13:8,14; Deut 4:9; 6:20–21.

And not forget the works of God,
But keep his commandments:
8 And [a]might not be as their fathers,
[b]A stubborn and rebellious generation;
A generation [c][1]*that* set not their heart aright,
And whose spirit was not stedfast with God.
9 The children of Ephraim, *being* armed, *and* [1]carrying bows,
Turned *back* in the day of battle.
10 [a]They kept not the covenant of God,
And refused to walk in his law;
11 And [a]forgat his works,
And his wonders that he had shewed them.
12 [a]Marvellous things did he in the sight of their fathers,
In the land of Egypt, [b]*in* the field of Zoan.
13 [a]He divided the sea, and caused them to pass through;
And [b]he made the waters to stand as a heap.
14 [a]In the daytime also he led them with a cloud,
And all the night with a light of fire.
15 [a]He clave the rocks in the wilderness,
And gave *them* drink as *out of* the great depths.
16 He brought [a]streams also out of the rock,
And caused waters to run down like rivers.
17 And they sinned yet more against him
By [a]provoking the most High in the wilderness.

78:8 [1]Heb. that *prepared not their heart* [a]2 Ki. 17:14 [b]Ex. 32:9 [c]ver. 37
78:9 [1]Heb. *throwing forth*
78:10 [a]2 Ki. 17:15
78:11 [a]Ps. 106:13
78:12 [a]Ex. 7-12 [b]Num. 13:22
78:13 [a]Ex. 14:21 [b]Ex. 15:8
78:14 [a]Ex. 13:21
78:15 [a]Num. 20:11
78:16 [a]Deut. 9:21
78:17 [a]Heb. 3:16
78:18 [a]Ex. 16:2
78:19 [1]Heb. *order* [a]Num. 11:4
78:20 [a]Num. 20:11
78:21 [a]Num. 11:1
78:22 [a]Heb. 3:18
78:23 [a]Mal. 3:10
78:24 [a]John 6:31
78:25 [1]Or, *Every one did eat the bread of the mighty*
78:26 [1]Heb. *to go* [a]Num. 11:31
78:27 [1]Heb. *fowl of wing*
78:29 [a]Num. 11:20

18 And [a]they tempted God in their heart
By asking meat for their lust.
19 [a]Yea, they spake against God; they said,
Can God [1]furnish a table in the wilderness?
20 [a]Behold, he smote the rock, that the waters gushed out,
And the streams overflowed;
Can he give bread also?
Can he provide flesh for his people?
21 Therefore the LORD heard *this,* and [a]was wroth:
So a fire was kindled against Jacob,
And anger also came up against Israel;
22 Because they [a]believed not in God,
And trusted not in his salvation:
23 Though he had commanded the clouds from above,
[a]And opened the doors of heaven,
24 [a]And had rained down manna upon them to eat,
And had given them *of* the corn of heaven.
25 [1]Man did eat angels' food:
He sent them meat to the full.
26 [a]He caused an east wind [1]to blow in the heaven:
And by his power he brought in the south wind.
27 He rained flesh also upon them as dust,
And [1]feathered fowls like as the sand of the sea:
28 And he let *it* fall in the midst of their camp,
Round about their habitations.
29 [a]So they did eat, and were well filled:
For he gave them their own desire;

78:8 *stubborn and rebellious.* Like a rebellious son (see Deut 9:6–7, 24;31:27). *generation.* A people with certain characteristics (see 24:6; Deut 32:5,20), thus not limited to the exodus generation (see vv. 9–11,56–64). *heart.* See note on 4:7.

78:9–16 The northern kingdom has violated God's covenant, not remembering His saving acts (a message emphasized by the prophets Amos and Hosea). Israel's history with God has been a long series of rebellions on her part (vv. 9–16,32–39, 56–64), beginning already in the wilderness (vv. 17–31,40–55).

78:9 *children of Ephraim.* The northern kingdom, dominated by the tribe of Ephraim (see introduction). *Turned back.* Neither the tribe of Ephraim nor the northern kingdom had a reputation for cowardice or ineffectiveness in battle (see, e.g., Deut 33:17). This verse is best understood as a metaphor for Israel's betrayal of God's covenant (see v. 10), related to the figure of the "deceitful bow" (v. 57).

78:12–16 A summary reference to the plagues in Egypt and to the water miracles at the Red sea and in the wilderness. In the two cycles that follow (vv. 17–39,40–64), further elaboration intensifies the indictment.

78:12 See Ex 7–12. *Zoan.* A city in the northeast part of the Nile delta (see v. 43; see also Num 13:22 and note).

78:13 See Ex 14:1–15:21.

78:15–16 See v. 20; Ex 17:6; Num 20:8,10–11.

78:17–31 Israel's rebelliousness in the wilderness; God's marvelous provision of food—and His anger.

78:17 *sinned yet more.* Although no sin in the wilderness has yet been mentioned, the poet probably expected his readers to recall (in conjunction with the miraculous provisions of water just mentioned) how the people grumbled at Marah because of lack of water (see Ex 15:24). *most High.* See vv. 35,56; see also note on Gen 14:19.

78:18 See Ex 16:2–3. *tempted God.* See vv. 41,56; see also note on Ex 17:2.

78:19 *Can God furnish a table . . . ?* For a different use of the same imagery see 23:5.

78:20 *bread . . . flesh.* The poet is probably combining and compressing two episodes (Ex 16:2–3; Num 11:4).

78:21 *wroth.* See vv. 31,49–50,58–59,62; see also note on 2:5.

78:23 *opened the doors of heaven.* For this imagery see Gen 7:11; 2 Ki 7:2; Mal 3:10.

78:25 *angels' food.* So called because it came down from heaven. *angels'.* Lit. "mighty ones." The Hebrew word is used only here of the angels, but reference is clearly to heavenly beings (see 103:20).

78:26–28 See Ex 16:13; Num 11:31.

78:26 *east wind . . . south wind.* Since the quails were migrating from Egypt at this time, the south wind may have carried them north and the east wind may have diverted them to the wilderness area occupied by the Israelites (the book of Numbers does not provide wind directions).

78:27 *as dust . . . as the sand.* Similes for a huge number (see note on Gen 13:16).

30 They were not estranged from their lust.
But [a]while their meat *was* yet in their
mouths,
31 The wrath of God came upon them,
And slew the fattest of them,
And [1]smote down the [2]chosen *men* of
Israel.
32 For all this [a]they sinned still,
And [b]believed not for his wondrous
works.
33 [a]Therefore their days did he consume
in vanity,
And their years in trouble.
34 [a]When he slew them, then they sought
him:
And they returned and inquired early
after God.
35 And they remembered that [a]God *was*
their rock,
And the high God [b]their redeemer.
36 Nevertheless they did [a]flatter him with
their mouth,
And they lied unto him with their
tongues.
37 For their heart was not right with him,
Neither were they stedfast in his
covenant.
38 [a]But he, *being* full of compassion,
forgave *their* iniquity, and destroyed
them not:
Yea, many a time [b]turned he his anger
away,
[c]And did not stir up all his wrath.
39 For [a]he remembered [b]that they *were*
but flesh;
[c]A wind that passeth away, and cometh
not again.
40 How oft did they [a][1]provoke him in the
wilderness,
And grieve him in the desert!
41 Yea, [a]they turned *back* and tempted
God,
And limited the Holy One of Israel.
42 They remembered not his hand:
Nor the day when he delivered them
[1]from the enemy.
43 How he had [1]wrought his signs in
Egypt,
And his wonders in the field of Zoan:
44 [a]And had turned their rivers into
blood;
And their floods, *that* they could not
drink.
45 [a]He sent divers sorts *of flies* among
them, which devoured them;
And [b]frogs, which destroyed them.
46 He gave also their increase unto the
caterpillar,
And their labour unto the locust.
47 [a]He [1]destroyed their vines with hail,
And their sycomore trees with [2]frost.
48 [a][1]He gave up their cattle also to the
hail,
And their flocks to [2]hot thunderbolts.
49 He cast upon them the fierceness of his
anger,
Wrath, and indignation, and trouble,
By sending evil angels *among them.*
50 [1]He made a way to his anger;
He spared not their soul from death,
But gave [2]their life over to the
pestilence;
51 [a]And smote all the firstborn in Egypt;
The chief of *their* strength in [b]the
tabernacles of Ham:
52 But [a]made his own people to go forth
like sheep,
And guided them in the wilderness
like a flock.
53 And he [a]led them on safely, so that
they feared not:
But the sea [b][1]overwhelmed their
enemies.
54 And he brought them to the border of
his [a]sanctuary,
Even to this mountain, [b]*which* his
right hand had purchased.
55 [a]He cast out the heathen also before
them,

78:30 [a]Num. 11:33
78:31 [1]Heb. *made to bow* [2]Or, *young men*
78:32 [a]Num. 14; 16; 17 [b]ver. 22
78:33 [a]Num. 14:29
78:34 [a]Hos. 5:15
78:35 [a]Deut. 32:4,15,31 [b]Is. 41:14; 63:9
78:36 [a]Ezek. 33:31
78:38 [a]Num. 14:18,20 [b]Is. 48:9 [c]1 Ki. 21:29
78:39 [a]Ps. 103:14 [b]John 3:6 [c]Job 7:7,16
78:40 [1]Or, *rebel against him* [a]Ps. 95:8-10; Heb. 3:16
78:41 [a]Num. 14:22; Deut. 6:16
78:42 [1]Or, *from affliction*
78:43 [1]Heb. *set*
78:44 [a]Ex. 7:20; Ps. 105:29
78:45 [a]Ex. 8:24; Ps. 105:31 [b]Ex. 8:6
78:47 [1]Heb. *killed* [2]Or, *great hailstones* [a]Ex. 9:23,25; Ps. 105:33
78:48 [1]Heb. *He shut up* [2]Or, *lightnings* [a]Ex. 9:23-25
78:50 [1]Heb. *He weighed a path* [2]Or, *their beasts to the murrain*
78:51 [a]Ex. 12:29 [b]Ps. 106:22
78:52 [a]Ps. 77:20
78:53 [1]Heb. *covered* [a]Ex. 14:19 [b]Ex. 14:27
78:54 [a]Ex. 15:17 [b]Ps. 44:3
78:55 [a]Ps. 44:2

78:30–31 See Num 11:33.
‡78:31 *fattest.* Their sturdiest and most vigorous.
78:32–39 Rebelliousness, which became Israel's way of life, showed itself early in the wilderness wandering (vv. 17–31) and continued throughout that journey.
78:32 *believed not.* That God could give them victory over the Canaanites (see Num 14:11).
78:33 The exodus generation was condemned to die in the wilderness (see Num 14:22–23,28–35).
78:34–37 A cycle repeated frequently during the period of the judges.
78:35 *rock.* See note on 18:2. *redeemer.* Deliverer (see note on Ex 6:6).
78:36 See Is 29:13.
78:37 *heart.* See note on 4:7.
78:38 See Ex 32:14; Num 14:20. *forgave.* See note on 65:3.
78:39 See 103:14; see also note on 10:18.
78:40–64 The second cycle (the first is vv. 17–39).
78:40–55 Israel's rebelliousness began in the wilderness; she did not remember how she had been delivered from oppression by God's plagues upon Egypt (see v. 12). Yet He brought them through the sea and the wilderness and established them in the promised land.
78:41 *Holy One of Israel.* See 71:22; 89:18; see also note on Is 1:4.
78:44–51 The plagues upon Egypt (see Ex 7–12): The sequence in Exodus is followed only in the first and last; the third, fifth, sixth and ninth plagues are not mentioned.
78:47 *sycomore trees.* See note on Amos 7:14.
78:49 *evil angels.* The poet personifies God's wrath, indignation and hostility as agents of His anger.
‡78:50 *made a way to his anger.* Made a path or road for His anger to reach them
‡78:51 *tabernacles.* Tents, dwellings. *Ham.* For the association of Ham with Egypt see 105:23,27; 106:21–22; Gen 10:6 and note.
78:53 *sea.* Red sea.
78:55 Summarizes the story told in Joshua.

And [b]divided them an inheritance by line,
And made the tribes of Israel to dwell in their tents.
56 [a]Yet they tempted and provoked the most high God,
And kept not his testimonies:
57 But [a]turned *back,* and dealt unfaithfully like their fathers:
They were turned aside [b]like a deceitful bow.
58 [a]For they provoked him to anger with their [b]high places,
And moved him to jealousy with their graven images.
59 When God heard *this,* he was wroth,
And greatly abhorred Israel:
60 So that he forsook the tabernacle of Shiloh,
The tent *which* he placed among men;
61 [a]And delivered his strength into captivity,
And his glory into the enemy's hand.
62 [a]He gave his people over also unto the sword;
And was wroth with his inheritance.
63 The fire consumed their young men;
And [a]their maidens were not [1]given to marriage.
64 [a]Their priests fell by the sword;
And [b]their widows made no lamentation.
65 Then the Lord awaked as one out of sleep,
And [a]like a mighty *man* that shouteth by reason of wine.
66 And [a]he smote his enemies in the hinder parts:
He put them to a perpetual reproach.
67 Moreover he refused the tabernacle of Joseph,
And chose not the tribe of Ephraim:
68 But chose the tribe of Judah,
The mount Zion [a]which he loved.
69 And he built his sanctuary like high *palaces,*
Like the earth which he hath [1]established for ever.
70 [a]He chose David also his servant,
And took him from the sheepfolds:
71 [1]From following [a]the *ewes* great with young he brought him
[b]To feed Jacob his people,
And Israel his inheritance.
72 So he fed them according to the [a]integrity of his heart;
And guided them by the skilfulness of his hands.

78:55 [b]Josh. 13:7
78:56 [a]Judg. 2:11
78:57 [a]Ezek. 20:27 [b]Hos. 7:16
78:58 [a]Deut. 32:16,21; Judg. 2:12 [b]Deut. 12:2
78:61 [a]Judg. 18:30
78:62 [a]1 Sam. 4:10
78:63 [1]Heb. *praised* [a]Jer. 7:34
78:64 [a]1 Sam. 22:18
78:64 [b]Job 27:15
78:65 [a]Is. 42:13
78:66 [a]1 Sam. 5:6
78:68 [a]Ps. 87:2
78:69 [1]Heb. *founded*
78:70 [a]1 Sam. 16:11,12
78:71 [1]Heb. *From after* [a]Is. 40:11 [b]2 Sam. 5:2
78:72 [a]1 Ki. 9:4

78:56–64 Rebelliousness continued to be Israel's way of life in the promised land (a recurring theme of Judges; see also 1 Sam 2:12–7:2), so God rejected Israel (v. 59; see Jer 7:15).
78:57 *deceitful bow.* See note on v. 9.
78:58 *high places.* See note on 1 Sam 9:12. *jealousy.* God's intense reaction to disloyalty to Him (see note on Ex 20:5).
78:59 *greatly abhorred Israel.* Abandoned her to her enemies. The psalmist does not speak of a permanent casting off of Israel, not even of the ten northern tribes.
78:60 *Shiloh.* The center of worship since the time of Joshua (see Josh 18:1,8; 21:1–2; Judg 18:31; 1 Sam 1:3; Jer 7:12), it was located in Ephraim between Beth-el and Shechem (see Judg 21:19). Apparently it was destroyed by the Philistines when they captured the ark or shortly afterward (see note on Jer 7:12).
78:61 *his strength . . . his glory.* The ark is here so called because it was the sign of God's kingship in Israel and the focal point for the display of His power and glory (see 26:8; 63:2; 1 Sam 4:3,21–22).
78:62,71 *his inheritance.* See Deut 9:29.
‡78:63 *fire.* Often associated with the sword (see vv. 62,64) as the two primary instruments of destruction in ancient warfare. *were not given to marriage.* Lit. "were not praised" (with wedding songs). So great was the catastrophe that both the wedding songs of the brides and the wailing of the widows (see v. 64) were silenced in the land.
78:64 *priests fell by the sword.* See 1 Sam 4:11.
78:65–72 The Lord's election of Judah (instead of Ephraim) as the leading tribe in Israel (anticipated in Jacob's deathbed blessing of his sons, Gen 49:8–12), of mount Zion (instead of Shiloh) as the place of His sanctuary (royal seat), and of David as His regent to shepherd His people. By these acts the Lord established His people securely as His kingdom in the promised land, following the long period of Israel's troubles from the death of Joshua to the death of Saul—by then God's salvation of Israel begun in the exodus had reached its climactic (if provisional) fulfillment (see introduction to Ps 68 and the combination of echoes of God's saving act in the exodus and through David in Isaiah's prophecy of Israel's future deliverance, Is 11:11–16).
78:65 *awakened as one out of sleep.* Poetic hyperbole to highlight the contrast between God's action in behalf of His people in the days of David and the preceding time of Israel's troubles (see note on 7:6).
78:66–72 The saving events noted have two focal points: (1) God's decisive victory over His enemies (thus securing His realm) and the establishment of Zion as His royal city, and (2) the appointment of David to be the shepherd of His people.
78:67 *tabernacle of Joseph.* A figure for the tribe of Ephraim (for the figurative use of "tabernacle," see v. 51; see also 69:25; 83:6; 84:10; 120:5; Gen 9:27; Deut 33:18; 1 Ki 12:16; Job 8:22; 12:6; Hab 3:7; Mal 2:12).
78:68,70 *chose . . . mount Zion . . . chose David.* See Ps 132.
78:69 *high palaces . . . earth.* The verse is subject to two interpretations: (1) The Lord built His sanctuary as impregnable as a mountain fortress and as enduring and unmovable as the age-old earth, or (2) the Lord built His sanctuary as secure and enduring as the heavens and the earth (see note on 24:2) and there manifests Himself as the Lord of glory (see 24:7–10; 26:8; 63:2; 96:6), even as He does in the creation (see 19:1; 29:9; 97:6).
78:70–71 See 1 Sam 16:11–13; 2 Sam 7:8.
78:70 *his servant.* Here an official title marking David as a member of God's royal administration (see notes on Ex 14:31; Ps 18 title; Is 41:8–9; 42:1).
78:71 *feed.* Or "shepherd." See note on 23:1.
78:72 Israel under the care of the Lord's royal shepherd from the house of David was for the prophets the hope of God's people (see Ezek 34:23; 37:24; Mic 5:4—fulfilled in Jesus Christ, Mat 2:6; John 10:11; Rev 7:17).

Psalm 79

A Psalm [1] of Asaph.

1 O God, the heathen are come into
[a] thine inheritance;
Thy holy temple have they defiled;
[b] They have laid Jerusalem on heaps.
2 [a] The dead bodies of thy servants have
they given
To be meat unto the fowls of the
heaven,
The flesh of thy saints unto the beasts
of the earth.
3 Their blood have they shed like water
Round about Jerusalem; and *there was*
none to bury *them.*
4 We are become a reproach to our
neighbours,
A scorn and derision to them that are
round about us.
5 [a] How long, LORD? wilt thou be angry,
for ever?
Shall thy [b] jealousy burn like fire?
6 [a] Pour out thy wrath upon the heathen
that have [b] not known thee,
And upon the kingdoms that have [c] not
called upon thy name.
7 For they have devoured Jacob,
And laid waste his dwelling place.
8 [a] O remember not against us [1] former
iniquities:
Let thy tender mercies speedily
prevent us:
For we are brought very low.
9 Help us, O God of our salvation, for the
glory of thy name:
And deliver us, and purge away our
sins, [a] for thy name's sake.
10 [a] Wherefore should the heathen say,
Where *is* their God?
Let him be known among the heathen
in our sight
By the [1] revenging of the blood of thy
servants which is shed.
11 Let [a] the sighing of the prisoner come
before thee,
According to the greatness of [1] thy
power:
[2] Preserve thou those that are
appointed to die;
12 And render unto our neighbours
[a] sevenfold into their bosom
[b] Their reproach, wherewith they have
reproached thee, O Lord.
13 So [a] we thy people and sheep of thy
pasture

79:T [1] Or, *for Asaph*
79:1 [a] Ps. 74:2 [b] Mic. 3:12
79:2 [a] Jer. 7:33
79:5 [a] Ps. 74:1,9 [b] Zeph. 3:8
79:6 [a] Jer. 10:25; Rev. 16:1 [b] Is. 45:4,5; 2 Thes. 1:8 [c] Ps. 53:4
79:8 [1] Or, *the iniquities of them that were before us* [a] Is. 64:9
79:9 [a] Jer. 14:7
79:10 [1] Heb. *vengeance* [a] Ps. 42:10
79:11 [1] Heb. *thine arm* [2] Heb. *Reserve the children of death* [a] Ps. 102:20
79:12 [a] Gen. 4:15; Is. 65:6,7; Jer. 32:18; Luke 6:38 [b] Ps. 74:18
79:13 [a] Ps. 74:1; 95:7

Ps 79 Israel's prayer for God's forgiveness and help and for His judgment on the nations that have so cruelly destroyed her, showing utter contempt for both the Lord and His people. Like Ps 74, with which it has many thematic links, it dates from the time of the exile. The poignancy of its appeal is heightened by its juxtaposition to Ps 77 (recalling God's saving acts under Moses) and Ps 78 (recalling God's saving acts under David), two psalms with which it is significantly linked by the shepherd-sheep figure and other thematic elements. Israel acknowledges that the Lord has used the nations to punish her for her sins, so she pleads for pardon. But she knows too that the nations have acted out of their hostility to and disdain for God and His people; that warrants her plea for God's judgment on them (see Is 10:5–11; 47:6–7). Daniel's prayer (Dan 9:4–19) contains much that is similar to the elements of penitence in this psalm.

79 title *Asaph.* See note on Ps 73 title.

79:1–4 What the nations have done: They have attacked God's own special domain, violated His temple, destroyed His royal city, slaughtered His people, degraded them in death (by withholding burial—see note on 53:5—and leaving their bodies as carrion for birds and beasts) and reduced them to the scorn of the world.

79:1 *thine inheritance.* Cf. 78:62,71. Here reference is to Israel's homeland as the Lord's domain (see note on 2:8). *holy temple.* See note on 78:69.

79:2 *thy servants.* Though banished from the Lord's land for sins that cannot be denied, the exiles plead their special covenant relationship with God (see "thy saints," here, and "thy people and sheep of thy pasture," v. 13). *saints.* See note on 4:3.

79:3 *blood have they shed . . . Round about Jerusalem.* Cf. 2 Ki 21:16.

79:5–8 A prayer for God to relent and deal with the nations who do not acknowledge Him.

79:5 *How long . . . ?* See note on 6:3 (see also Introduction: Theology). *angry.* See v. 6 ("wrath"); see also note on 2:5. *jealousy.* See note on 78:58. *burn like fire.* See Deut 4:24; 6:15; Zeph 1:18; 3:8.

79:6–7 See Jer 10:25 and note. Perhaps the psalmist is quoting Jeremiah here.

79:6 *Pour out thy wrath.* As they "shed like water" (v. 3) the blood of Your people. The exiles plead with God to redress the wrongs committed against them (see note on 5:10).

79:7 *devoured.* Like wild beasts (see 44:11; 74:19 and note on 7:2). *Jacob.* A synonym for Israel (see Gen 32:28).

‡79:8 *former iniquities.* Lit. "iniquities of them that were before us." Israel suffered exile because of the accumulated sins of the nation (see 2 Ki 17:7–23; 23:26–27; 24:3–4; Dan 9:4–14), from which she did not repent until the judgment of God had fallen on her. The exiles here pray that God will take notice of their penitence and not continue to hold the sins of past generations against His now repentant people. *tender mercies.* Here personified as God's agent sent to bring relief (see notes on 23:6; 43:3).

79:9–11 A prayer for God to help and forgive His people and to redress the violent acts of the enemies.

79:9 *for the glory of thy name.* As the desolation of God's people brings reproach to God (see v. 10), so their salvation and prosperity bring Him glory (see note on 23:3). *purge away.* See note on 65:3.

79:10 *Where is their God?* See note on 3:2. *revenging.* Redress (see Deut 32:35,43).

79:11 *prisoner . . . those that are appointed to die.* The exiles, as imperial captives in Babylonia (see 102:20)—not actually in prisons, but under threat of death should they seek to return to their homeland.

79:12–13 Concluding prayer and vow to praise.

79:12 *render . . . into their bosom.* See note on Jer 32:18. *sevenfold.* In full measure; the number seven symbolized completeness. *reproach . . . reproached thee.* The enemies' violent action against Israel was above all a high-handed reviling of God (see vv. 1,10; 2 Ki 19:10–12,22–23; Is 52:5).

79:13 See note on 7:17. *sheep of thy pasture.* See 74:1; 77:20; 78:72. *to all generations.* See 78:4.

Will give thee thanks for ever:
[b]We will shew forth thy praise [1]to all generations.

Psalm 80

To the chief Musician [a]upon Shoshannim-Eduth,
A Psalm [1]of Asaph.

1 Give ear, O Shepherd of Israel,
Thou that leadest Joseph [a]like a flock;
Thou that dwellest *between* the cherubims, [b]shine forth.
2 Before Ephraim and Benjamin and Manasseh
Stir up thy strength,
And [1]come and save us.
3 [a]Turn us again, O God,
[b]And cause thy face to shine; and we shall be saved.

4 O LORD God *of* hosts,
How long [1]wilt thou be angry against the prayer of thy people?
5 [a]Thou feedest them with the bread of tears;
And givest them tears to drink *in great* measure.
6 Thou makest us a strife unto our neighbours:
And our enemies laugh among themselves.
7 Turn us again, O God *of* hosts,
And cause thy face to shine; and we shall be saved.

8 Thou hast brought [a]a vine out of Egypt:
[b]Thou hast cast out the heathen, and planted it.
9 Thou preparedst *room* before it,
And didst cause it to take deep root, and it filled the land.
10 The hills were covered *with* the shadow of it,
And the boughs thereof *were like* [1]the goodly cedars.
11 She sent out her boughs unto the sea,
And her branches unto the river.

12 Why hast thou *then* [a]broken down her hedges,
So that all they which pass by the way do pluck her?
13 The boar out of the wood doth waste it,
And the wild beast of the field doth devour it.
14 Return, we beseech thee, O God *of* hosts:
[a]Look down from heaven, and behold,

79:13 [1]Heb. *to generation and generation* [b]Is. 43:21
80:T [1]Or, *for Asaph* [a]Ps. 45, title; 69, title
80:1 [a]Ps. 77:20 [b]Deut. 33:2; Ps. 50:2
80:2 [1]Heb. *come for salvation to us*
80:3 [a]Lam. 5:21 [b]Num. 6:25; Ps. 4:6
80:4 [1]Heb. *wilt thou smoke*
80:5 [a]Ps. 42:3; Is. 30:20
80:8 [a]Is. 5:1,7; Jer. 2:21; Ezek. 15:6 [b]Ps. 44:2
80:10 [1]Heb. *the cedars of God*
80:12 [a]Is. 5:5; Nah. 2:2
80:14 [a]Is. 63:15

Ps 80 Israel's prayer for restoration when she had been ravaged by a foreign power. It seems likely that "Ephraim and Benjamin and Manasseh" (v. 2) here represent the northern kingdom. If Jeroboam was indeed given ten tribes (see 1 Ki 11:29–36), leaving only one to Rehoboam—Judah (see 1 Ki 12:20), which was actually two tribes because Simeon was located within Judah (see Josh 19:1–9)—then Benjamin belonged to the northern kingdom. However, part of Benjamin must always have remained with the southern kingdom since its territory actually bordered on Jerusalem itself, and the southern kingdom continued to control Jerusalem's environs (see 1 Ki 12:21). This suggests that the disaster suffered was the Assyrian campaign that swept the northern kingdom away (see 2 Ki 17:1–6). Recent archaeological surveys of the Holy Land have shown that Jerusalem and the surrounding countryside experienced at this time a dramatic increase of population, no doubt the result of a massive influx of displaced persons from the north fleeing the Assyrian beast. This could account for the presence of "Ephraim and Benjamin and Manasseh" at the Jerusalem sanctuary, and for a national prayer for restoration with special focus on these tribes (see notes below).

The prayer has five (Hebrew) stanzas of four lines each. A recurring petition climaxes the first, second and last (for other refrains see introduction to Ps 42–43), with a progressing urgency of appeal: "O God" (v. 3); "O God of hosts" (v. 7); "O LORD God of hosts" (v. 19).

80 title *To the chief Musician.* See note on Ps 4 title. *upon.* See note on Ps 9 title. *Shoshannim-Eduth.* See note on Ps 45 title. *Asaph.* See note on Ps 73 title.

80:1–3 An appeal for God to arouse Himself and go before His people again with all His glory and might as He did in days of old in the wilderness.

80:1 See the shepherd-flock motif in 74:1; 77:20; 78:52,71–72; 79:13. *Joseph.* See note on 77:15. *dwellest between the cherubims.* See note on Ex 25:18. *shine forth.* Let Your glory be seen again, as in the wilderness journey (see Ex 24:16–17; 40:34–35), but now especially through Your new saving act (see 102:15–16; Ex 14:4,17–18; Num 14:22; Is 40:5; 44:23; 60:1–2).

80:2 *Before Ephraim and Benjamin and Manasseh.* March against the nations as You marched in the midst of Your army from Sinai into the promised land (in that march the ark of the covenant advanced in front of the troops of these three tribes; see Num 10:21–24; see also introduction to Ps 68). *Stir up.* See note on 7:6.

80:3 *cause thy face to shine.* See vv. 7,19; an echo of the priestly benediction (see Num 6:25; see also notes on 4:6; 13:1).

80:4–7 A lament over the Lord's severe punishment of His people.

80:4 *LORD . . . of hosts.* See vv. 7,14,19; see also note on 1 Sam 1:3. *How long . . . ?* See note on 6:3 (see also Introduction: Theology). *angry.* See note on 2:5.

80:5 God has now given them tears to eat and tears to drink rather than "angels' food" and water from the rock (see 78:20,25).

‡80:6 *a strife.* Or "a source of strife."

80:8–16 This use of the vine-vineyard metaphor (here to describe Israel's changed condition) is found also in the prophets (see Is 3:14; 5:1–7; 27:2; Jer 2:21; 12:10; Ezek 17:6–8; 19:10–14; Hos 10:1; 14:7; Mic 7:1; see also Gen 49:22; Mat 20:1–16; Mark 12:1–9; Luke 20:9–16; John 15:1–5).

80:8–11 Israel was once God's flourishing transplanted vine.

‡80:8 *brought.* The Hebrew for this verb has the sense of "uprooted" (cf. "removed" in Job 19:10). *cast out the heathen, and planted.* See 44:2. *planted.* Transplanted.

‡80:9 *preparedst room.* Or "cleared the ground." See Is 5:2.

‡80:10 *goodly cedars.* Or "mighty cedars."

80:11 *sea . . . river.* The "sea" is probably the Mediterranean and the "river" the Euphrates (see Ex 23:31 and note).

80:12–15 A prayer for God to renew His care for His ravaged vine.

80:12 *Why . . . ?* Israel's anguished perplexity over God's abandonment (see note on 6:3). *broken down her hedges.* Taken away its defenses.

And visit this vine;
15 And the vineyard which thy right hand
hath planted,
And the branch *that* thou madest
strong for thyself.

16 *It is* burnt with fire, *it is* cut down:
[a]They perish at the rebuke of thy
countenance.
17 [a]Let thy hand be upon the man of thy
right hand,
Upon the son of man *whom* thou
madest strong for thyself.
18 So will not we go *back* from thee:
Quicken us, and we will call upon thy
name.
19 Turn us again, O LORD God *of* hosts,
Cause thy face to shine; and we shall
be saved.

Psalm 81

To the chief Musician [a]upon Gittith,
A Psalm [1]of Asaph.

1 Sing aloud unto God our strength:
Make a joyful noise unto the God of
Jacob.
2 Take a psalm, and bring hither the
timbrel,
The pleasant harp with the psaltery.
3 Blow up the trumpet in the new moon,
In the time appointed, on our solemn
feast day.
4 For this *was* a statute for Israel,
And a law of the God of Jacob.
5 This he ordained in Joseph *for* a
testimony,
When he went out [1]through the land
of Egypt:
[a]*Where* I heard a language *that* I
understood not.

6 I removed his shoulder from the burden:
His hands [1]were delivered from the
pots.
7 [a]Thou calledst in trouble, and I
delivered thee;
[b]I answered thee in the secret place of
thunder:
I [c]proved thee at the waters of
[1]Meribah. Selah.
8 [a]Hear, O my people, and I will testify
unto thee:
O Israel, if thou wilt hearken unto me;

80:16 [a]Ps. 39:11; 76:7
80:17 [a]Ps. 89:21
81:T [1]Or, *for Asaph* [a]Ps. 8, title
81:5 [1]Or, *against* [a]Ps. 114:1
81:6 [1]Heb. *passed away*
81:7 [1]Or, *Strife* [a]Ex. 2:23; Ps. 50:15 [b]Ex. 19:19 [c]Ex. 17:6,7
81:8 [a]Ps. 50:7

‡80:14 *visit.* Take care of or give aid to (cf. "visited" in Ruth 1:6).
‡80:15 *madest strong.* See v. 17; lit. "made vigorous."
80:16–19 Concluding prayer for restoration.
80:16 *rebuke.* See 9:5 and note on 76:6.
‡80:17 *Let thy hand be upon.* Show your favor to (see Ezra 7:6,9,28; 8:18,22,31; Neh 2:8,18). *man of thy right hand.* Reference may be to the Davidic king as the Lord's anointed, seated in the place of honor in God's presence (see 110:1) and the one in whom the hope of the nation rested (see 2:7–9; 72:8–11; 89:21–25). But v. 15 strongly suggests another sense: that "the man" is Jacob/Israel and that he is "of" God's "right hand" in that he has been "planted" and made "strong" by Him.
80:18 A vow to be loyal to God and to trust in Him alone. It occurs in a place where it would be more common to find a vow to praise (see note on 7:17).
Ps 81 A festival song. But it is unclear whether the festival is passover/unleavened bread (v. 5; see Ex 12:14–17) or the Jewish new year (v. 3; see Lev 23:24; Num 29:1) or the feast of tabernacles (v. 3; see Lev 23:34; Num 29:12). It may have been used at all three. But more likely it was composed for use at both new year (the first day of the month, "new moon") and the beginning of tabernacles (the 15th day of the month, full moon); see notes below. Whether the psalm is preexilic or postexilic cannot be determined, but it clearly shows the grand significance of Israel's annual religious festivals (see chart, pp. 166–167). As memorials of God's saving acts they called Israel to celebration, remembrance and recommitment (see Ps 95). In this psalm Israel is addressed by a Levite, speaking (prophetically) on behalf of God.
The psalm's thematic development follows a symmetrical pattern: two verses, three verses; two verses, three verses; two verses, four verses. Note also the contrast between vv. 6–7 and vv. 11–12, and the thematic link between v. 10c and v. 16.
81 title *To the chief Musician.* See note on Ps 4 title. *upon.* See note on Ps 6 title. *Gittith.* See note on Ps 8 title. *Asaph.* See note on Ps 73 title.
81:1–5 A summons to celebrate the appointed sacred feast.
81:1 *Jacob.* A synonym for Israel (see Gen 32:28).
‡81:2 *Take a psalm.* Or "Start the music." *timbrel.* See note on Jer 31:4. *harp with the psaltery.* See note on 57:8.
81:3 *trumpet.* The ram's horn trumpet (see Ex 19:13). *solemn feast day.* Probably the feast of tabernacles, often called simply "the feast" (see 1 Ki 8:2,65; 12:32; 2 Chr 5:3; 7:8; Neh 8:14,18; Ezek 45:25; see also Deut 16:14). As the great seven-day autumn festival, beginning on the 15th of the month (full moon), it followed shortly after the day of atonement (observed on the tenth of the month, Lev 16:29), recalled God's care for His people during the wilderness journey (see Lev 23:43), served as a feast of thanksgiving for the harvest (see Lev 23:39–40; Deut 16:13–15) and marked the conclusion of the annual cycle of religious festivals that began with passover and unleavened bread six months earlier (see Ex 23:14–17; Lev 23; Deut 16:16). Every seventh year at this festival the covenant law was to be read to all the people (see Deut 31:9–13; Neh 8:2,15). The first day of this month (New Moon) was commemorated with trumpets (see Lev 23:24). It later came to be known as New Year since the seventh month marked the end of harvest and the beginning of the rainy season, when the new crops were planted.
81:4–5 *statute . . . law . . . testimony.* See the passages referred to in note on v. 3.
‡81:5 *Joseph.* See note on 77:15. *went out through the land of Egypt.* Some believe this indicates that the festival referred to is passover and unleavened bread (see Ex 12:14,42). More likely it serves as a reference to the whole exodus period, while highlighting especially God's triumph over Egypt by which He had set His people free (see vv. 6–7). *heard a language that I understood not.* Was an alien in a foreign land (see 114:1; see also Deut 28:49; Is 19:18; 33:19; Jer 5:15; Ezek 3:5–6).
81:6–10 God heard and delivered and now summons His people to loyalty.
81:6 *burden . . . pots.* The forced labor to which the Israelites were subjected in Egypt (see Ex 1:11–14).
81:7 *Thou calledst . . . I delivered.* See Ex 3:7–10. *in the secret place of thunder.* See 106:9; Ex 14:21,24; 15:8,10; see also note on 76:6. *I proved thee.* Or "tested you." See Ex 17:1–7.
81:8–10 God heard His people in their distress (vv. 6–7); now they must listen to Him.

9 There shall no [a]strange god be in thee;
Neither shall thou worship *any* strange
god.
10 [a]I *am* the LORD thy God,
Which brought thee out of the land of
Egypt:
[b]Open thy mouth wide, and I will
fill it.
11 But my people would not hearken to
my voice;
And Israel would [a]none of me.
12 [a]So I gave them up [1]unto their own
heart's lust:
And they walked in their own
counsels.
13 [a]O that my people had hearkened unto
me,
And Israel had walked in my ways!
14 I should soon have subdued their
enemies,
And turned my hand against their
adversaries.
15 [a]The haters of the LORD should have
[b1]submitted themselves unto him:
But their time should have endured for
ever.
16 He should [a]have fed them also [1]with
the finest of the wheat:
And *with* honey [b]out of the rock
should I have satisfied thee.

81:9 [a]Deut. 32:12; Is. 43:12
81:10 [a]Ex. 20:2 [b]Ps. 103:5
81:11 [a]Ex. 32:1; Deut. 32:15
81:12 [1]Or, *to the hardness of their hearts*, or, *imagination* [a]Acts 7:42
81:13 [a]Deut. 5:29; 32:29; Is. 48:18
81:15 [1]Or, *yielded feigned obedience*. Heb. *lied* [a]Rom. 1:30 [b]Ps. 18:44
81:16 [1]Heb. *with the fat of wheat* [a]Deut. 32:14
81:16 [b]Job 29:6
82:T [1]Or, *for Asaph*
82:1 [a]2 Chr. 19:6 [b]ver. 6
82:2 [a]Deut. 1:17
82:3 [1]Heb. *Judge* [a]Jer. 22:3
82:4 [a]Job 29:12; Prov. 24:11
82:5 [1]Heb. *moved* [a]Mic. 3:1 [b]Ps. 11:3
82:6 [a]Ex. 22:28; John 10:34
82:7 [a]Ps. 49:12

Psalm 82

A Psalm [1]of Asaph.

1 God [a]standeth in the congregation of
the mighty;
He judgeth among [b]the gods.
2 How long will ye judge unjustly,
And [a]accept the persons of the
wicked? Selah.
3 [1]Defend the poor and fatherless:
[a]Do justice to the afflicted and
needy.
4 [a]Deliver the poor and needy:
Rid *them* out of the hand of the
wicked.
5 They [a]know not, neither will they
understand;
They walk on in darkness:
[b]All the foundations of the earth are
[1]out of course.
6 [a]I have said, Ye *are* gods;
And all of you *are* children of the most
High.
7 But [a]ye shall die like men,
And fall like one of the princes.

81:9–10 See Ex 19:4–5; 20:2–4; Deut 4:15–20.
81:10 *Open thy mouth wide.* Trust in the Lord alone for all of life's needs. *I will fill it.* See v. 16; as He did in the wilderness (see 78:23–29; see also 37:3–4; Deut 11:13–15; 28:1–4).
81:11–16 Israel has not listened—if only they would! See Ezek 18:23,32; 33:11.
81:11 See 78:10,17,32,40,56; Deut 9:7,24; Jer 7:24–26.
‡81:12 It is God who "circumcises" the heart (see Deut 30:6; see also 1 Ki 8:58; Jer 31:33; Ezek 11:19; 36:26). Thus for God to abandon His people to their "heart's lust" (lit. "stubborness of heart") is the most fearful of punishments (see 78:29; Is 6:9–10; 29:10; 63:17; cf. Rom 1:24,26,28). They will have to suffer the consequences of where their stubborn hearts lead them.
‡81:13–16 What Israel could have had if they had followed the Lord instead of going their own way. See the promised covenant blessings outlined in Ex 23:22–27; Lev 26:3–13; Deut 7:12–26; 28:1–14.
81:13 *my ways.* See 25:4 and note.
‡81:15 What God would have done to the enemies of an obedient Israel—would have brought about their submission and destruction.
81:16 *honey out of the rock.* See note on Deut 32:13.
‡Ps 82 A word of judgment on unjust rulers and judges. The Levitical author of this psalm evokes a vision of God presiding over His heavenly court—analogous to the experiences of the prophets (see 1 Ki 22:19–22; Is 6:1–7; Jer 23:18,22; see also Job 15:8). As the Great King (see introduction to Ps 47) and the Judge of all the earth (see 94:2; Gen 18:25; 1 Sam 2:10) who "loveth judgment" (99:4) and judges the nations in righteousness (see 9:8; 96:13; 98:9), he is seen calling to account those responsible for defending the weak and oppressed on earth. An early rabbinic interpretation (see John 10:34–35) understood the "gods" (v. 6) to be unjust rulers and judges in Israel, of whom there were many (see 1 Sam 8:3; Is 1:16–17; 3:13–15; Jer 21:12; 22:3; Ezek 34:4,21; Mic 3:1–3; 7:3). Today many identify the "gods" as the kings of surrounding nations who encouraged the conceit that they were actually or virtually divine beings but who ruled with lofty disregard for justice—though honoring it as a royal ideal. Others hold that the "gods" are the divine beings in whose names the kings claimed to rule (see 95:3). In any event, rulers and judges here are confronted by their King and Judge (see Ps 58). Structurally, the words of the Levite (vv. 1,6) frame the words of God. At the very center (v. 5a; see note on 6:6) stands the most devastating judgment of all.
82 title See note on Ps 73 title.
82:1 *congregation.* The assembly in the great hall of judgment (cf. 1 Ki 7:7) in heaven (see 89:5; 1 Ki 22:19; Job 1:6; 2:1; Is 6:1–4). As if in a vision, the psalmist sees the rulers and judges gathered before the Great King to give account of their administration of justice. *gods.* See also v. 6. In the language of the OT—and in accordance with the conceptual world of the ancient Near East—rulers and judges, as deputies of the heavenly King, could be given the honorific title "god" (see note on 45:6; 58:1) or be called "Son of God" (see 2:7 and note).
‡82:2 *accept the persons.* Show partiality and favoritism.
82:3–4 In the OT a first-order task of kings and judges was to protect the powerless against all who would exploit or oppress them (see 72:2,4,12–14; Prov 31:8–9; Is 11:4; Jer 22:3,16).
‡82:5 *They know not, neither . . . understand.* The center of the poem (see note on 6:6). They ought to have shared in the wisdom of God (see 1 Ki 3:9; Prov 8:14–16; Is 11:2), but they are utterly devoid of true understanding of moral issues or of the moral order that God's rule sustains (see Is 44:19). *foundations . . . are out of course.* Shaken from their foundations. When such men are the wardens of justice, the whole world order crumbles (see 11:3; 75:3 and notes).
‡82:6 *I have said.* Those who rule (or judge) do so by God's appointment (see 2:7; Is 44:28) and thus they are His representatives—whether they acknowledge Him or not (see Ex 9:16; Jer 27:6; Dan 2:21; 4:17,32; 5:18; John 19:11; Rom 13:1). They are accountable to God for how they carry out this important responsibility. *gods.* See note on v. 1. *children of.* See note on v. 1. *most High.* See note on Gen 14:19.
82:7 However exalted their position, these corrupt "gods" will be brought low by the same judgment as other men. *fall.* See note on 13:4.

8 [a]Arise, O God, judge the earth:
[b]For thou shalt inherit all nations.

Psalm 83

A Song *or* Psalm [1]of Asaph.

1 Keep [a]not thou silence, O God:
Hold not thy peace, and be not still, O God.
2 For lo, [a]thine enemies make a tumult:
And they that [b]hate thee have lift up the head.
3 They have taken crafty counsel against thy people,
And consulted [a]against thy hidden ones.
4 They have said, Come, and [a]let us cut them off from *being* a nation;
That the name of Israel may be no more in remembrance.
5 For they have consulted together *with one* [1]consent:
They are confederate against thee:
6 [a]The tabernacles of Edom, and the Ishmaelites;
Of Moab, and the Hagarenes;
7 Gebal, and Ammon, and Amalek;
The Philistines with the inhabitants of Tyre;
8 Assur also is joined with them:
[1]They have holpen the children of Lot. Selah.
9 Do unto them as *unto* the Midianites;
As *to* [a]Sisera, as *to* Jabin, at the brook of Kison:
10 *Which* perished at En-dor:
[a]They became *as* dung for the earth.
11 Make their nobles like Oreb, and like Zeeb:
Yea, all their princes as [a]Zebah, and as Zalmunna:
12 Who said, Let us take to ourselves
The houses of God in possession.
13 [a]O my God, make them like a wheel;
[b]As the stubble before the wind.
14 As the fire burneth a wood,
And as the flame [a]setteth the mountains on fire;
15 So persecute them with thy tempest,
And make them afraid with thy storm.
16 Fill their faces *with* shame;
That they may seek thy name, O LORD.
17 Let them be confounded and troubled for ever;
Yea, let them be put to shame, and perish:
18 [a]That *men* may know that thou, whose [b]name alone *is* JEHOVAH,
Art [c]the most High over all the earth.

82:8 [a]Mic. 7:2,7 [b]Ps. 2:8; Rev. 11:15
83:T [1]Or, *for Asaph*
83:1 [a]Ps. 28:1
83:2 [a]Ps. 2:1 [b]Ps. 81:15
83:3 [a]Ps. 27:5
83:4 [a]Jer. 11:19
83:5 [1]Heb. *heart*
83:6 [a]See 2 Chr. 20:1,10,11
83:8 [1]Heb. *They have been an arm to the children of Lot*
83:9 [a]Judg. 4:15
83:10 [a]Zeph. 1:17
83:11 [a]Judg. 8:12
83:13 [a]Is. 17:13 [b]Ps. 35:5
83:14 [a]Deut. 32:22
83:18 [a]Ps. 59:13 [b]Ex. 6:3 [c]Ps. 92:8

82:8 Having seen the prospect in store, the psalmist prays for God's judgment to hasten and for the perfect reign of God to come quickly to the whole world. *Arise.* See note on 3:7. *inherit.* The nations are Your domain (see note on 79:1).

Ps 83 Israel's prayer for God to crush His enemies when the whole world—or so it seemed—was arrayed against His people. Neither Kings nor Chronicles tells of a confederacy as extensive as that described here. Perhaps only some of the nations mentioned were actually attacking, while the rest of Israel's historic enemies were more passively supporting the campaign. If so, the occasion may have been that reported in 2 Chr 20, when Moab, Ammon, Edom and their allies were invading Judah. In any event, the psalm must date from sometime after the reign of Solomon and before the great thrust of Assyria in the time of king Menahem (see 2 Ki 15:19).

Each of the two main divisions (vv. 1–8, 9–18) consists of two four-verse stanzas in the Hebrew, with the latter division being extended by a two-verse stanza that brings the prayer to its climactic conclusion.

83 title *Song.* See note on Ps 30 title. *Asaph.* See note on Ps 73 title.

83:1–4 An appeal to God to act in the face of Israel's imminent danger.

83:1 *Keep not thou silence.* Do not remain inactive (see 35:22; 109:1).

‡83:2 *lift up the head.* Rear their head in defiance against God.

‡83:3 *thy hidden ones.* Or "Your treasured ones," God's treasured people that He keeps hidden from the enemy.

83:4 *They have said.* See note on 3:2. *let us cut them off.* Israel's very existence is at stake (see v. 12).

83:5–8 The array of nations allied against Israel—threat from every quarter.

‡83:6 *tabernacles.* Tents. *Hagarenes.* Either Ishmaelites (descendants of Hagar) or a group mentioned in Assyrian inscriptions as an Aramean confederacy (see 1 Chr 5:10,18–22; 27:31).

83:7 *Gebal.* See 1 Ki 5:18; Ezek 27:9. Gebal was an important Phoenician city (also called Byblos).

‡83:8 *Assur.* Assyria. Since it is mentioned only as an ally of Moab and Ammon (the descendants of Lot; see note on Gen 19:36–38), Assyria, though distantly active in the region, must not yet have become a major threat in its own right.

83:9–12 A plea for God to destroy His enemies as He did of old in the time of the judges. Those who hurl themselves against the kingdom of God to destroy it from the earth—so that the godless powers are left to shape the destiny of the world as they will—must be crushed if God's kingdom of righteousness and peace is to come and be at rest (see note on 5:10).

83:9 *as unto the Midianites.* In Gideon's great victory (see Judg 7). *As to Sisera, as to Jabin.* In Barak's defeat of the Canaanite coalition (see Judg 4).

83:10 *En-dor.* See Josh 17:11 and note; northeast of where the main battle was fought—apparently where much of the fleeing army was overtaken and decimated.

83:11 *Oreb . . . Zeeb . . . Zebah . . . Zalmunna.* Leaders of the Midianite host destroyed by Gideon.

‡83:12 See v. 4. *houses of God.* Or "pastures of God" (the land of Israel).

83:13–16 The plea renewed, with vivid imagery of fleeing armies and of God's fearsome power.

‡83:13 *like a wheel.* Like tumbleweed blowing in the wind (cf. the parallel line).

83:15 Imagery of the heavenly Warrior attacking His enemies out of the thunderstorm (see 18:7–15; 68:33; 77:17–18; Ex 15:7–10; Josh 10:11; Judg 5:4,20–21; 1 Sam 2:10; 7:10; Is 29:5–6; 33:3). For the storm cloud as God's chariot see 68:4 and note.

83:16 *may seek.* See note on v. 18. *name.* See note on 5:11.

83:17–18 The prayer's climactic conclusion.

‡83:18 The ultimate goal of God's warfare is not merely the security of Israel and the destruction of Israel's (and God's) enemies but the worldwide acknowledgment of the true God and

Psalm 84

To the chief Musician [a]upon Gittith,
A Psalm [1]for the sons of Korah.

1 How [a]amiable *are* thy tabernacles,
O LORD of hosts!
2 [a]My soul longeth, yea, even fainteth
for the courts of the LORD:
My heart and my flesh crieth out for
the living God.
3 Yea, the sparrow hath found a house,
And the swallow a nest for herself,
where she may lay her young,
Even thine altars, O LORD of hosts, my
King, and my God.

4 Blessed *are* they that dwell in thy
house:
They will be still praising thee.
Selah.
5 Blessed *is* the man whose strength *is*
in thee;
In whose heart *are* the ways *of them.*
6 *Who* passing through the valley [a][1]of
Baca make it a well;
The rain also [2]filleth the pools.
7 They go [a][1]from strength to strength,
Every one of them in Zion [b]appeareth
before God.

8 O LORD God *of* hosts, hear my
prayer:
Give ear, O God of Jacob. Selah.
9 Behold, [a]O God our shield,
And look upon the face of thine
anointed.
10 For a day in thy courts *is* better than a
thousand.
[1]I had rather be a doorkeeper in the
house of my God,
Than to dwell in the tents of
wickedness.
11 For the LORD God *is* [a]a sun and
[b]shield:
The LORD will give grace and glory:
[c]No good *thing* will he withhold from
them that walk uprightly.
12 O LORD of hosts,
[a]Blessed *is* the man that trusteth in
thee.

84:T [1]Or, *of* [a]Ps. 8, title
84:1 [a]Ps. 27:4
84:2 [a]Ps. 42:1,2
84:6 [1]Or, *of mulberry trees make him a well, etc.* [a]2 Sam. 5:23
84:6 [2]Heb. *covereth*
84:7 [1]Or, *from company to company* [a]Prov. 4:18 [b]Deut. 16:16
84:9 [a]ver. 11
84:10 [1]Heb. *I would choose rather to sit at the threshold*
84:11 [a]Is. 60:19 [b]Gen. 15:1; Ps. 115:9; Prov. 2:7 [c]Ps. 34:9
84:12 [a]Ps. 2:12

---

of His rule, even to the point of seeking Him as His people do (see v. 16; see also 40:9; 47:9; 58:11; 59:13 and notes). *JEHOVAH.* The LORD ("Yahweh"), the personal name of God (cf. Ex 3:14 and note). *most High.* See note on Gen 14:19.

Ps 84 A prayer of longing for the house of the Lord. In tone and perspective it stands close to Ps 42 and may reflect similar circumstances. If so, the author (presumably a Levite who normally functioned in the temple service), now barred from access to God's house (perhaps when Sennacherib was ravaging Judah; see 2 Ki 18:13–16), gives voice to his longing for the sweet nearness to God in His temple that he had known in the past. Reference to God and His temple and to the "blessedness" (see vv. 4–5,12) of those having free access to both dominates the psalm and highlights its central themes.

The psalm has three main divisions (vv. 1–4, 5–7, 8–11) and a conclusion (v. 12). In the Hebrew text, a six-line unit precedes and follows a three-line reflection on the blessedness of those free to make pilgrimage to Zion. Each of these six-line divisions contains three references to the "LORD," while the seventh reference (symbolizing completeness or perfection) appears in the conclusion.

84 title *To the chief Musician.* See note on Ps 4 title. *upon.* See note on Ps 6 title. *Gittith.* See note on Ps 8 title. *for the sons of Korah.* See note on Ps 42 title.

84:1–4 A confession of deep longing for the house of the Lord.

‡84:1 *How amiable.* Or "How loved." *LORD of hosts.* See vv. 3,8,12; see also note on 1 Sam 1:3.

84:2 *My soul.* I (see note on 6:3). *courts.* Of the temple (see v. 10; 2 Ki 21:5; 23:11–12). *My heart . . . flesh.* My whole being (see 73:26). *heart.* See note on 4:7. *living God.* See Deut 5:26.

84:3 The psalmist is jealous of the small birds that have such unhindered access to the temple and the altar. They are able even to build their nests there for their young—the place where Israel was to have communion with God.

84:4–5,12 *Blessed.* See note on 1:1.

84:4 *that dwell in thy house.* See note on 15:1.

84:5–7 The joyful blessedness of those who are free to make pilgrimage to Zion—them too the psalmist envies.

‡84:5 *the man whose strength is in thee.* The one who has come to know the Lord as his deliverer and the sustainer of his life. *In whose heart are the ways.* The one who has purposed in his heart to travel the highways the Israelites took to observe the religious festivals at Jerusalem (Zion, v. 7). *heart.* See note on 4:7.

‡84:6 *passing.* On their way to the temple. *Baca.* Means either "weeping" or "balsam trees" (common in arid valleys). The place is unknown and may be figurative (see 23:4) for arid stretches the pilgrims had to traverse. *well.* The joyful expectations of the pilgrims transform the difficult ways into places of refreshment. *rain.* Or "early rains," the gentle early showers that are harbingers of the later spring rains (see Joel 2:23). By God's benevolent care over His pilgrims, the vale of weeping (or balsam trees), already transformed by the glad hearts of the expectant wayfarers, is turned into a valley of praise (see 2 Chr 20:26). God's saints on their hopeful way to Zion experience anew the bountiful hand of God as their ancestors did on their way through the wilderness of Sinai to the promised land (see 78:15–16; 105:41; 114:8)—and as their descendants would on their return to Zion from Babylonian exile (see Is 41:17–20; 43:19–20; 49:10).

84:7 *from strength to strength.* Whatever the toils and hardships of the journey (see Is 40:31). *Zion.* See 9:11 and note.

84:8–11 A prayer for the king, and its motivation: Only as God blesses the king in Jerusalem will the psalmist once more realize his great desire to return to his accustomed service in the temple (see introduction).

84:8 *LORD God of hosts . . . God of Jacob.* That is, LORD God of Hosts, the God of Jacob (see 59:5; see also note on 3:7). *Jacob.* A synonym for Israel (see Gen 32:28).

84:9 *our shield.* The king in Jerusalem (see note on 3:3). *thine anointed.* God's earthly regent over His people (from David's line); see note on 2:2.

84:10 *be a doorkeeper.* Perhaps the psalmist's normal (and humble) service at the temple was that of doorkeeper (see 2 Ki 22:4). *dwell in the tents of wickedness.* Share in the life of those who do not honor the God of Zion.

84:11 *sun.* The glorious source of the light of life (see note on 27:1). *shield.* See note on 3:3. *uprightly.* See 15:2 and note on Gen 17:1.

84:12 The sum of it all (see 40:4).

Psalm 85

To the chief Musician, A Psalm [a] [1] for the sons of Korah.

1 LORD, thou hast been [a] [1] favourable unto thy land:
Thou hast [b] brought back the captivity of Jacob.
2 Thou hast forgiven the iniquity of thy people,
Thou hast covered all their sin. Selah.
3 Thou hast taken away all thy wrath:
[1] Thou hast turned *thyself* from the fierceness of thine anger.

4 [a] Turn us, O God of our salvation,
And cause thine anger towards us to cease.
5 [a] Wilt thou be angry with us for ever?
Wilt thou draw out thine anger to all generations?
6 Wilt thou not [a] revive us again:
That thy people may rejoice in thee?
7 Shew us thy mercy, O LORD,
And grant us thy salvation.

8 [a] I will hear what God the LORD will speak:
For [b] he will speak peace unto his people, and to his saints:
But let them not [c] turn *again* to folly.
9 Surely [a] his salvation *is* nigh them that fear him;
[b] That glory may dwell in our land.
10 Mercy and truth are met together;
[a] Righteousness and peace have kissed *each other.*
11 Truth shall spring out of the earth;
And righteousness shall look down from heaven.
12 [a] Yea, the LORD shall give *that which is* good;
And our land shall yield her increase.
13 [a] Righteousness shall go before him;
And shall set *us* in the way of his steps.

Psalm 86

[1] A Prayer of David.

1 Bow down thine ear, O LORD, hear me:
For I *am* poor and needy.

85:T [1] Or, *of* [a] Ps. 42, title
85:1 [1] Or, *well pleased* [a] Ps. 77:7 [b] Ezra 1:11; Jer. 30:18; Ezek. 39:25; Joel 3:1
85:3 [1] Or, *Thou hast turned thine anger from waxing hot*
85:4 [a] Ps. 80:7
85:5 [a] Ps. 79:5
85:6 [a] Hab. 3:2
85:8 [a] Hab. 2:1 [b] Zech. 9:10 [c] 2 Pet. 2:20
85:9 [a] Is. 46:13 [b] Zech. 2:5
85:10 [a] Ps. 72:3; Is. 32:17; Luke 2:14
85:12 [a] Ps. 84:11; Jas. 1:17
85:13 [a] Ps. 89:14
86:T [1] Or, *A Prayer,* being a Psalm *of David*

‡Ps 85 A communal prayer for the renewal of God's mercies to His people at a time when they are once more suffering distress. Many believe that vv. 1–3 refer to the return from exile and that the troubles experienced are those alluded to by Nehemiah and Malachi. Verse 12 suggests that a drought has ravaged the land and may reflect the drought with which the Lord chastened His people in the time of Haggai (see Hag 1:5–11). However, the reference to "captivity" does not necessitate a specific historical event (cf. Job 42:10). The psalmist's purpose is to remind the reader that the God who has delivered His people in the past can do it again.

The psalm has two main divisions of seven (Hebrew) lines each: (1) the prayer (vv. 1–7); (2) a reassuring word (vv. 8–13). Each division contains a three-line stanza followed by a four-line stanza, with the corresponding stanzas of the second half answering to those of the first: Verses 1–3 speak of mercies granted, while vv. 8–9 speak of mercies soon to come; vv. 4–7 voice the prayer, and vv. 10–13 offer the blessed reassurance that the prayer will be heard. Each of the four stanzas contains one reference to the "LORD."

85 title *To the chief Musician.* See note on Ps 4 title. *for the sons of Korah.* See note on Ps 42 title.

‡85:1–7 Prayer for the renewal of God's favor and the revival of God's people.

85:1–3 Israel begins her prayer by appealing to the Lord's past mercies, recalling how He has forgiven and restored them before (perhaps a reference to the restoration from exile).

85:1 *brought back the captivity of Jacob.* Or "restored the fortunes of Jacob" (see Jer 29:14). *Jacob.* A synonym for Israel (see Gen 32:28).

85:3 *wrath . . . anger.* See v. 5; see also note on 2:5.

85:4–7 The prayer acknowledges that the present troubles are indicative of God's displeasure. No confession of sin is expressed, but in the light of v. 3 (and possibly v. 8; see below) it is probably implicit.

‡85:4 *Turn us.* Restore us (the same verb as "brought back" in v. 1).

85:7 *mercy.* See v. 10; see also note on 6:4.

85:8–13 God's reassuring answer to the prayer, conveyed through a priest or Levite, perhaps one of the Korahites (see note on 12:5–6; see also 2 Chr 20:14).

85:8–9 The assurance that God will again bless His people.

85:8 *I will hear.* The speaker awaits the word from the Lord. *speak peace.* The word from the Lord perhaps takes the form of the priestly benediction (see Num 6:22–26). *saints.* See note on 4:3. *But let them not turn again to folly.* And so provoke God's displeasure again. But it is also possible to translate the clause: "and to those who turn from folly." *folly.* See note on 14:1.

85:9 *glory.* Wherever God's saving power is displayed, His glory is revealed (see 57:5,11; 72:18–19; Ex 14:4,17–18; Num 14:22; Is 40:5; 44:23; 66:19; Ezek 39:21).

85:10–13 God's sure mercies to His people spring from His covenant love, to which in His faithfulness and righteousness He remains true, and that assures His people's welfare (peace).

85:10 *Mercy and truth . . . Righteousness and peace.* These expressions of God's favor toward His people are here personified (see note on 23:6), and the vivid portrayal of their meeting and embracing offers one of the most beautiful images in all Scripture of God's gracious dealings with His covenant people. *Righteousness.* See vv. 11,13; see also note on 5:8. *peace.* See note on Num 6:26.

85:11 *Truth shall spring.* As new growth springs from the earth to bless mankind with plenty. *righteousness shall look down.* It shines down benevolently. From heaven and from earth, God's covenant blessings will abound till Israel's cup overflows.

85:12 *that which is good.* See 31:19 and note.

85:13 *Righteousness shall go before.* Again the psalmist personifies. Acting either as herald or guide, righteousness leads the way and marks the course for God's engagement in His people's behalf—and righteousness is God's perfect faithfulness to all His covenant commitments (see note on 5:8).

Ps 86 A prayer for God's help when attacked by enemies, whose fierce onslaughts betray their disdain for the Lord. Whether or not David was the author (see Introduction: Authorship and Titles), the psalmist's identification of himself as God's "servant" (v. 2) suggests his royal status and thus his special relationship with the Lord (see 2 Sam 7:5,8 and note on Ps 18 title). The enemies may then be either those within the kingdom who refuse to acknowledge him as the Lord's anointed, or

2 Preserve my soul; for I *am* [1]holy:
O thou my God, save thy servant that
trusteth in thee.
3 [a]Be merciful unto me, O Lord:
For I cry unto thee [1]daily.
4 Rejoice the soul of thy servant:
[a]For unto thee, O Lord, do I lift up my
soul.
5 [a]For thou, Lord, *art* good, and ready to
forgive;
And plenteous in mercy unto all them
that call upon thee.
6 Give ear, O LORD, unto my prayer;
And attend to the voice of my
supplications.
7 In the day of my trouble I will call
upon thee:
For thou wilt answer me.
8 [a]Among the gods *there is* none like
unto thee, O Lord;
[b]Neither *are there any works* like unto
thy works.
9 [a]All nations whom thou hast made
shall come
And worship before thee, O Lord;
And shall glorify thy name.
10 For thou *art* great, and [a]doest
wondrous *things:*
[b]Thou *art* God alone.
11 [a]Teach me thy way, O LORD; I will walk
in thy truth:
Unite my heart to fear thy name.
12 I will praise thee, O Lord my God,
with all my heart:
And I will glorify thy name for
evermore.
13 For great *is* thy mercy toward me:
And thou hast delivered my soul from
the lowest [1]hell.
14 O God, the proud are risen against me,
And the assemblies of [1]violent *men*
have sought after my soul;
And have not set thee before them.
15 [a]But thou, O Lord, *art* a God full of
compassion, and gracious,
Longsuffering, and plenteous in mercy
and truth.
16 O turn unto me, and have mercy upon
me;
Give thy strength unto thy servant,
And save the son of thine handmaid.
17 Shew me a token for good;
That they which hate me may see *it,*
and be ashamed:
Because thou, LORD, hast holpen me,
and comforted me.

86:2 [1]Or, *one whom thou favourest*
86:3 [1]Or, *all the day* [a]Ps. 56:1; 57:1
86:4 [a]Ps. 25:1; 143:8
86:5 [a]Ps. 130:7; 145:9; Joel 2:13
86:8 [a]Ex. 15:11; Ps. 89:6 [b]Deut. 3:24
86:9 [a]Ps. 22:31; Is. 43:7; Rev. 15:4
86:10 [a]Ex. 15:11; Ps. 72:18 [b]Deut. 6:4; Mark 12:29
86:11 [a]Ps. 25:4
86:13 [1]Or, *grave*
86:14 [1]Heb. *terrible*
86:15 [a]Ex. 34:6; Neh. 9:17; Ps. 103:8; Joel 2:13
87:T [1]Or, *of*

Psalm 87

A Psalm *or* Song [1]for the sons of Korah.

1 His foundation *is* in the holy
mountains.

foreign powers that are attempting to remove him from the international scene.

In the Hebrew the psalm has a symmetrical verse pattern (four, three, three, three, four). The author identifies himself as the Lord's servant in the first and last stanzas, which also contain the prayer for God's mercy and deliverance from the enemy threat. The center stanza (vv. 8–10) hails the Lord as the incomparable, the only God, whom all the nations will someday worship. Verse 9 is the center verse (see note on 6:6).

86 title *Prayer.* See note on Ps 17 title; see also note on 72:20. *of David.* This is the only psalm in Book 3 (Ps 73–89) that is ascribed to David. Perhaps its placement among the Korahite psalms is because those who arranged the Psalter perceived a thematic link between v. 9 and 87:4.

86:1–4 Initial prayer for God to have mercy and protect the life of His servant.

86:1 *poor and needy.* See 35:10; see also 34:6 and note.

86:2 *holy.* The Hebrew for this phrase is *ḥasid* (see note on 4:3). *thou my God.* Not that David has chosen Him, but that He has chosen David to be His servant (see 1 Sam 13:14; 15:28; 16:12; 2 Sam 7:8). David's devotion to God and God's commitment to him are deliberately juxtaposed. *thy servant.* See vv. 4,16; see also introduction.

‡86:4 *Rejoice.* Bring joy to. *my soul.* See note on 6:3.

86:5–7 In his need David prays to the Lord because, out of His kindness and love, God answers prayer.

86:5 *mercy.* See vv. 13,15; see also note on 6:4.

86:8–10 The God to whom David appeals is the only true God. No other "god" acts with such sovereign power (see 115:3–7; 135:13–17)—that is why David appeals to Him and why all the nations will someday worship Him.

86:9 *All nations.* See note on 46:10. This is the center verse of the psalm (see note on 6:6) and contains the psalm's most exalted confession of faith concerning God's sovereign and universal rule. *shall glorify.* As David vows to do (v. 12). *thy name.* See vv. 11–12; see also note on 5:11.

86:10 *wondrous things.* See note on 9:1.

86:11–13 A prayer for godliness and a vow to praise.

86:11 *Teach me . . . Unite my.* What would be the benefit if God saved him from his enemies but abandoned him to his own waywardness? David's dependence on God is complete, and so is his devotion to God—save me from the enemy outside but also from my frailty within (see 25:5; 51:7,10). Only one who is thus devoted to God may expect God's help and will truly fulfill the vow (v. 12). *Unite my heart.* See Ezek 11:19; see also 1 Chr 12:33; 1 Cor 7:35. *heart.* See note on 4:7.

86:12 Vow to praise (see note on 7:17).

‡86:13 David anticipates the answer to his prayer (see note on 3:8). *from the lowest hell.* Or "from the depths of Sheol" (i.e. the grave). See note on 30:1.

86:14–17 Conclusion: the prayer renewed.

86:14 *violent.* The Hebrew for this word suggests also ferocity. *have not set thee before them.* In their arrogance they dismiss the heavenly Warrior, who is David's defender (see note on 10:11; see also Jer 20:11).

86:15 Echoes v. 5, but is even more similar to Ex 34:6 (see note on Ex 34:6–7).

86:16 *Give thy strength.* Exert Your power in my behalf. *son of thine handmaid.* See 116:16.

‡86:17 *token for good.* A sign of Your covenanted favors (see 27:13 and note). *may see it.* May see that You stand with me and help me (see 31:19 and note).

Ps 87 A celebration of Zion as the "city of God" (v. 3), the special object of His love and the royal city of His kingdom (see introductions to Ps 46; 48; 76). According to the ancient and consistent interpretation of Jewish and Christian scholars alike, this psalm stands in lonely isolation in the Psalter (but see 47:9) in that it foresees the ingathering of the nations into Zion as fel-

2 [a]The LORD loveth the gates of Zion
More than all the dwellings of Jacob.
3 [a]Glorious *things* are spoken of thee,
O city of God. Selah.

4 I will make mention of Rahab and
Babylon to them that know me:
Behold Philistia, and Tyre, with
Ethiopia;
This *man* was born there.
5 And of Zion it shall be said, This and
that man was born in her:
And the Highest himself shall establish
her.
6 The LORD shall count, when he
[a]writeth *up* the people,
That this *man* was born there. Selah.
7 As well the singers as the players on
instruments *shall be there:*
All my springs *are* in thee.

87:2 [a]Ps. 78:68
87:3 [a]See Is. 60
87:6 [a]Ezek. 13:9

88:T [1]Or, *of* [2]Or, A Psalm *of Heman the Ezrahite, giving instruction* [a]1 Ki. 4:31; 1 Chr. 2:6
88:1 [a]Ps. 27:9
88:3 [a]Ps. 107:18
88:4 [a]Ps. 28:1
88:5 [1]Or, *by thy hand* [a]Is. 53:8

Psalm 88

A Song *or* Psalm [1]for the sons of Korah. To the chief Musician upon Mahalath Leannoth, [2]Maschil of [a]Heman the Ezrahite.

1 O LORD [a]God of my salvation,
I have cried day *and* night before thee:
2 Let my prayer come before thee:
Incline thine ear unto my cry;
3 For my soul is full of troubles:
And my life [a]draweth nigh unto the
grave.
4 [a]I am counted with them that go down
into the pit:
I am as a man *that hath* no strength:
5 Free among the dead,
Like the slain that lie in the grave,
Whom thou rememberest no more:
And they are [a]cut off [1]from thy hand.
6 Thou hast laid me in the lowest pit,
In darkness, in the deeps.

low citizens with Israel in the kingdom of God—after the manner of such prophetic visions as Is 2:2–4; 19:19–25; 25:6; 45:14,22–24; 56:6–8; 60:3; 66:23; Dan 7:14; Mic 4:1–3; Zech 8:23; 14:16. (Accordingly, some have assigned it to the time of Isaiah and Micah, while others have thought it to be postexilic.) So interpreted, this psalm stands in sharpest possible contrast with the other Zion songs of the Psalter (see Ps 46; 48; 76; 125; 129; 137). The key to its main thrust lies in v. 4.

87 title *Song.* See note on Ps 30 title. *for the sons of Korah.* See note on Ps 42 title.

87:1 *His foundation.* The Lord Himself has laid the foundations of Zion (see Is 14:32) and of the temple as His royal house. *mountains.* Though "Zion" (v. 2) is singular, the Hebrew for this word is plural, emphasizing the majesty of the holy mountain on which God's throne has been set (see 48:2 and note).

87:2 *loveth . . . More than.* As the city of His founding, His chosen seat of rule over His people, Zion is the Lord's most cherished city, even among the towns of Israel (see 9:11; 78:68; 132:12–14). *Jacob.* A synonym for Israel (see Gen 32:28).

87:4 *I will make mention . . . This man was born there.* God will list them in His royal register (see notes on 9:5; 51:1; 69:28) as those who are native (born) citizens of His royal city, having all the privileges and enjoying all the benefits and security of such citizenship. *Rahab.* Whereas elsewhere this name is applied to the mythical monster of the deep (see 89:10; see also notes on 32:6; Job 9:13), here the reference is to Egypt (Rahab was a poetic name for Egypt), as in Is 30:7 (see note there); 51:9. The nations listed are representative of all Gentile peoples. This psalm here foresees a widespread conversion to the Lord from the peoples who from time immemorial had been hostile to Him and to His kingdom (see Is 19:21; 26:18 and note).

87:5 *This and that man.* Wherever they may be dispersed among the nations. *the Highest.* See note on Gen 14:19.

87:7 *All my springs.* All that refreshes them is found in the city of God, a possible allusion to God's "river of thy pleasures" (36:8) whose "streams . . . make glad the city of God" (46:4); see notes on those passages. Alternatively, "springs" may be a metaphor for sources; the sense of the line would then be: We all spring from you. *my.* Communal use of the singular pronoun (see note on Ps 30 title).

‡Ps 88 A cry out of the depths, the prayer of one on the edge of death, whose whole life has been lived, as it were, in the near vicinity of the grave. So troubled have been his years that he seems to have known only the back of God's hand (God's "wrath," v. 7), and even those nearest him have withdrawn themselves as from one with an infectious skin disease (see v. 8). No expressions of hopeful expectation (as in most prayers of the Psalter) burst from these lips. Ending on a despairing note, the last verse says "Lover and friend hast thou put far from me." And yet the prayer begins, "O LORD God of my salvation." The psalm recalls the fact that although sometimes godly persons live lives of unremitting trouble (see 73:14), they can still grasp the hope that God is Savior. In its Hebrew structure, three four-line stanzas (vv. 3–5, 6–9a, 9b–12) are framed by two two-line prayers; to this is appended an additional four-line stanza in which the psalmist complains that his present distress is but characteristic of his whole troubled life.

88 title The psalm bears a double title, perhaps representing two different traditions. *Song.* See note on Ps 30 title. *for the sons of Korah.* See note on Ps 42 title. *To the chief Musician.* See note on Ps 4 title. *upon.* See note on Ps 6 title. *Maschil.* See note on Ps 32 title. *Heman.* See note on Ps 39 title. *Ezrahite.* The reference appears to be to Zerah, one of Judah's sons, who is recorded as having a Heman and an Ethan (see Ps 89 title) among his sons (see 1 Chr 2:6). If so, the title here represents a confusion in the tradition, arising from the similarity between these two Judahite names and those of two famous Korahite choir leaders, Heman and Ethan (Jeduthun; see note on Ps 39 title).

‡88:1–2 Opening appeal to the Lord as the "God of my salvation."

88:3–5 Living on the brink of death. Whether the psalmist lies mortally ill or experiences some analogous trouble or peril cannot be known.

88:3 *my soul.* See note on 6:3.

88:4 *pit.* See note on 30:1.

‡88:5 *Free.* Abandoned or forsaken. *rememberest no more.* From the perspective of this life, death cuts off from God's care; there is no remembering by God of the needy sufferer to rescue and restore (see 25:7; 74:2; 106:4). In his dark mood the author portrays his situation in bleakest colors (see note on 6:5).

88:6–9a You, O God, have done this! The psalmist knows no reason for it (see v. 14), but he knows God's hand is in it (see Ruth 1:20–21; Amos 3:6). That his Savior-God shows him the face of wrath deepens his anguish and helplessness. But he does not try to resolve the dark enigma; he simply pleads his case—and it is to his Savior-God that he can appeal.

88:6 *lowest pit . . . darkness.* See note on 30:1.

7 Thy wrath lieth hard upon me,
And [a]thou hast afflicted *me with* all thy waves. Selah.
8 [a]Thou hast put away mine acquaintance far from me;
Thou hast made me an abomination unto them:
[b]*I am* shut up, and I cannot come forth.
9 [a]Mine eye mourneth by reason of affliction:
LORD, [b]I have called daily upon thee,
[c]I have stretched out my hands unto thee.
10 [a]Wilt thou shew wonders to the dead?
Shall the dead arise *and* praise thee? Selah.
11 Shall thy lovingkindness be declared in the grave?
Or thy faithfulness in destruction?
12 [a]Shall thy wonders be known in the dark?
And thy righteousness in the land of forgetfulness?
13 But unto thee have I cried, O LORD;
And [a]in the morning shall my prayer prevent thee.
14 LORD, why castest thou off my soul?
Why [a]hidest thou thy face from me?
15 I *am* afflicted and ready to die from *my* youth *up:*
While [a]I suffer thy terrors I am distracted.
16 Thy fierce wrath goeth over me;
Thy terrors have cut me off.
17 They came round about me [1]daily like water;
They [a]compassed me about together.
18 [a]Lover and friend hast thou put far from me,
And mine acquaintance *into* darkness.

Psalm 89

[1]Maschil of [a]Ethan the Ezrahite.

1 [a]I will sing of the mercies of the LORD for ever:
With my mouth will I make known thy faithfulness [b][1]to all generations.
2 For I have said, Mercy shall be built up for ever:
[a]Thy faithfulness shalt thou establish in the very heavens.
3 [a]I have made a covenant with my chosen,
I have [b]sworn unto David my servant,
4 Thy seed will I stablish for ever,
And build up thy throne [a]to all generations. Selah.
5 And [a]the heavens shall praise thy wonders, O LORD:

88:7 [a]Ps. 42:7
88:8 [a]Job 19:13 [b]Lam. 3:7
88:9 [a]Ps. 38:10 [b]Ps. 86:3 [c]Ps. 143:6
88:10 [a]Ps. 6:5; Is. 38:18
88:12 [a]Job 10:21
88:13 [a]Ps. 5:3
88:14 [a]Job 13:24; Ps. 13:1
88:15 [a]Job 6:4
88:17 [1]Or, *all the day* [a]Ps. 22:16
88:18 [a]Job 19:13
89:T [1]Or, A Psalm *for Ethan the Ezrahite, to give instruction* [a]1 Ki. 4:31; 1 Chr. 2:6
89:1 [1]Heb. *to generation and generation* [a]Ps. 101:1 [b]ver. 4; Ps. 119:90
89:2 [a]Ps. 119:89
89:3 [a]1 Ki. 8:16; 1 Chr. 28:4 [b]2 Sam. 7:13
89:4 [a]Luke 1:33
89:5 [a]Ps. 19:1

88:7 *wrath.* See v. 16; see also note on 2:5. *all thy waves.* See note on 32:6.
88:8 *mine acquaintance.* See v. 18 and note on 31:11–12.
88:9 *eye mourneth.* See note on 6:7.
88:9b–12 Appeal to God to help before the psalmist sinks into "the land of forgetfulness" (see note on v. 5).
88:10,12 *wonders.* God's saving acts in behalf of His people (see note on 9:1).
88:10 *arise.* In the realm of the dead (not in the resurrection); see Is 14:9.
88:11 *lovingkindness . . . faithfulness.* That is, lovingkindness-and-faithfulness (see note on 36:5; see also note on 3:7). *lovingkindness.* See note on 6:4.
88:12 *righteousness.* See note on 71:24.
88:13–14 Concluding prayer.
88:14 *why . . . ?* See note on 6:3; see also Introduction: Theology. *hidest thou thy face.* See note on 13:1.
88:15–18 The psalmist has been no stranger to trouble; all his life he has suffered the terrors of God.
88:17 *like water.* See v. 7; see also note on 32:6.
Ps 89 A prayer that mourns the downfall of the Davidic dynasty and pleads for its restoration. The bitter shock of that event (reflected partially in the sudden transition of v. 38) is almost unbearable—that God, the faithful and almighty One, has abandoned His anointed and made him the mockery of the nations, in seeming violation of His firm covenant with David—and it evokes from the psalmist a lament that borders on reproach (vv. 38–45). The event may have been the attack on Jerusalem by Nebuchadnezzar and the exile of King Jehoiachin in 597 B.C. (see 2 Ki 24:8–17).

As with Ps 44 (see introduction to that psalm), a massive foundation is laid for the prayer with which the psalm concludes. An introduction (vv. 1–4) sings of God's love and faithfulness (vv. 1–2) and His covenant with David (vv. 3–4). These two themes are then jubilantly expanded in order: vv. 5–18, God's love and faithfulness; vv. 19–37, His covenant with David. Suddenly jubilation turns to lament, and the psalmist recounts in detail how God has rejected His anointed (vv. 38–45). Thus he comes to his prayer, impatient and urgent, that God will remember once more His covenant with David (vv. 46–51). (Verse 52 concludes not the psalm but Book 3 of the Psalter.)
89 title *Maschil.* See note on Ps 32 title. *Ethan.* Jeduthun (see note on Ps 39 title). The author was no doubt a Levite (perhaps a descendant of Jeduthun) who voiced this agonizing prayer as spokesman for the nation. *Ezrahite.* See note on Ps 88 title.
89:1–2 God's love and faithfulness celebrated.
‡89:1 *mercies . . . faithfulness.* See vv. 2,33,49; that is, mercies-and-faithfulness (see v. 14); see note on 36:5. *mercies.* See vv. 2,14,24,28,33,49; see also note on 6:4. It is God's love and faithfulness that appear to have failed in His rejection (see vv. 38–45) of the Davidic king. The author repeats each of these words precisely seven times.
89:2 *in the very heavens.* God's love and faithfulness have been made sure in the highest seat of power and authority (see vv. 5–8).
‡89:3–4 God's covenant with David celebrated (see 2 Sam 7:8–16). It is clearly distinguished as an eternal covenant that will last forever.
89:3 *servant.* See vv. 20,39,50; here an official title (see note on 78:70).
89:5–8 The Lord's faithfulness and awesome power set Him apart among all the powers in the heavenly realm, and they acknowledge Him with praise and reverence.
‡89:5 *the heavens.* All beings belonging to the divine realm in the heavens. *wonders.* God's mighty acts in creation and redemption (see note on 9:1). *congregation of the saints.* Lit.

Thy faithfulness also in the congregation of the saints.
6 For who in the heaven can be compared unto the LORD?
Who among the sons of the mighty can be likened unto the LORD?
7 [a]God *is* greatly to be feared in the assembly of the saints,
And to be had in reverence of all them that are about him.
8 O LORD God of hosts,
Who *is* a strong LORD like unto thee?
Or *to* thy faithfulness round about thee?
9 [a]Thou rulest the raging of the sea:
When the waves thereof arise, thou stillest them.
10 [a]Thou hast broken [1]Rahab in pieces, as one that is slain;
Thou hast scattered thine enemies [2]with thy strong arm.
11 [a]The heavens *are* thine, the earth also *is* thine:
As for the world and the fulness thereof, thou hast founded them.
12 The north and the south thou hast created them:
[a]Tabor and [b]Hermon shall rejoice in thy name.
13 Thou hast [1]a mighty arm:
Strong is thy hand, *and* high is thy right hand.
14 Justice and judgment *are* the [1]habitation of thy throne:
Mercy and truth shall go before thy face.
15 Blessed *is* the people that know the [a]joyful sound:
They shall walk, O LORD, in the light of thy countenance.
16 In thy name shall they rejoice all the day:
And in thy righteousness shall they be exalted.
17 For thou *art* the glory of their strength:
And in thy favour our horn shall be exalted.
18 For [a1]the LORD *is* our defence;
And the Holy One of Israel *is* our king.
19 Then thou spakest in vision to thy holy one,
And saidst, I have laid help upon *one that is* mighty;
I have exalted *one* [a]chosen out of the people.
20 [a]I have found David my servant;
With my holy oil have I anointed him:
21 [a]With whom my hand shall be established:
Mine arm also shall strengthen him.
22 [a]The enemy shall not exact upon him;
Nor the son of wickedness afflict him.
23 [a]And I will beat down his foes before his face,
And plague them that hate him.
24 But [a]my faithfulness and my mercy *shall be* with him:
And in my name shall his horn be exalted.
25 I will set his hand also in the sea,
And his right hand in the rivers.
26 He shall cry unto me, Thou *art* [a]my Father,
My God, and [b]the rock of my salvation.
27 Also I will make him [a]*my* firstborn,
[b]Higher than the kings of the earth.
28 [a]My mercy will I keep for him for evermore,

89:7 [a]Ps. 76:7,11
89:9 [a]Ps. 65:7
89:10 [1]Or, *Egypt* [2]Heb. *with the arm of thy strength* [a]Ps. 87:4
89:11 [a]Gen. 1:1
89:12 [a]Josh. 19:22 [b]Josh. 12:1
89:13 [1]Heb. *an arm with might*
89:14 [1]Or, *establishment*
89:15 [a]Ps. 98:6
89:18 [1]Or, *our shield* is *of the* LORD, *and our king* is *of the Holy One of Israel* [a]Ps. 47:9
89:19 [a]1 Ki. 11:34
89:20 [a]1 Sam. 16:1
89:21 [a]Ps. 80:17
89:22 [a]2 Sam. 7:10
89:23 [a]2 Sam. 7:9
89:24 [a]2 Sam. 7:15
89:26 [a]1 Chr. 22:10 [b]2 Sam. 22:47
89:27 [a]Col. 1:15 [b]Num. 24:7
89:28 [a]Is. 55:3

"assembly of the holy ones," the divine council in heaven (see "sons of the mighty" in v. 6 and "the assembly of the saints" who are "about him" in v. 7; see also note on 82:1).

89:6 *sons of the mighty.* Lit. "sons of god(s)" (see 29:1 and note).

‡89:8 *LORD . . . of hosts.* See note on 1 Sam 1:3. *thy faithfulness round about thee.* God's faithfulness surrounds Him as an essential attribute. It also surrounds this stanza (see v. 5).

89:9–13 The Lord's power as Creator—and creation's joy in Him.

89:9–10 Poetic imagery borrowed from ancient Near Eastern myths of creation, here celebrating God's power in ordering the primeval chaotic waters so that the creation order could be established (see Gen 1:6–10; see also notes on 65:6–7; 74:13–14).

89:10 *Rahab.* Mythical monster of the deep (see notes on 32:6; 87:4), probably another name for leviathan (see 74:14; 104:26). The last half of this verse is probably echoed in Luke 1:51.

‡89:12 *The north and the south.* Reference may be to two mountains, here parallel to Tabor and Hermon: mount Zaphon ("north"; see note on Is 14:13) and mount Amana (see Sol 4:8). *Tabor.* See note on Judg 4:6. *Hermon.* See note on Deut 3:8. *name.* See vv. 16,24; see also note on 5:11.

89:14–18 The Lord's righteousness and faithfulness in His rule in behalf of His people—and their joy in Him.

‡89:14 Righteousness and justice are the foundation stones of God's throne; mercy and truth are personified as angelic attendants that herald His royal movements (see note on 23:6).

89:17 *horn.* King ("horn" here symbolizes "strong one"; see also v. 18).

89:18 *Holy One of Israel.* See note on Is 1:4.

89:19–29 The Lord's election of David to be His regent over His people, and His everlasting covenant with him. The thought is developed by couplets: (1) introduction (v. 19); (2) I have anointed David as My servant and will sustain him (vv. 20–21); (3) I will crush all his foes (vv. 22–23); (4) I will extend his realm (vv. 24–25); (5) I will make him first among the kings (vv. 26–27); (6) I will cause his dynasty to endure forever (vv. 28–29)—a promise fulfilled in the eternal reign of Jesus Christ (see John 12:34).

‡89:19 *vision.* Reference is to the revelation to Samuel (see 1 Sam 16:12) and/or to Nathan (see 2 Sam 7:4–16). *holy one.* See note on "godly" (same word) in 4:3.

89:25 *sea . . . rivers.* David's rule will reach from the Mediterranean Sea to the Euphrates River (see 72:8; 80:11 and note on Ex 23:31). But the author uses imagery that underscores the fact that, as His royal son (see v. 26) and regent, David's rule will be a reflection of God's (see vv. 9–10 and notes; also compare v. 23 with v. 10).

89:27 *firstborn.* The royal son of highest privilege and position in the kingdom of God (see 2:7–12; 45:6–9; 72:8–11; 110), thus the most exalted of the kings of the earth (see Rev 1:5). So the words may speak of universal rule—ultimately fulfilled in Christ.

And my covenant *shall* stand fast with
him.
29 His seed also will I make *to endure* for
ever,
[a]And his throne [b]as the days of heaven.
30 [a]If his children [b]forsake my law,
And walk not in my judgments;
31 If they [1]break my statutes,
And keep not my commandments;
32 Then [a]will I visit their transgression
with the rod,
And their iniquity with stripes.
33 [a]Nevertheless my lovingkindness [1]will
I not utterly take from him,
Nor suffer my faithfulness [2]to fail.
34 My covenant will I not break,
Nor alter the thing that is gone out of
my lips.
35 Once have I sworn [a]by my holiness
[1]That I will not lie unto David.
36 [a]His seed shall endure for ever,
And his throne [b]as the sun before me.
37 It shall be established for ever as the
moon,
And *as* a faithful witness in heaven.
Selah.

38 But thou hast [a]cast off and [b]abhorred,
Thou hast been wroth with thine
anointed.
39 Thou hast made void the covenant of
thy servant:
[a]Thou hast profaned his crown *by
casting it* to the ground.
40 Thou hast broken down all his hedges;
Thou hast brought his strong holds to
ruin.
41 All that pass by the way spoil him:
He is [a]a reproach to his neighbours.
42 Thou hast set up the right hand of his
adversaries;
Thou hast made all his enemies to
rejoice.

89:29 [a]Jer. 33:17 [b]Deut. 11:21
89:30 [a]2 Sam. 7:14 [b]Ps. 119:53; Jer. 9:13
89:31 [1]Heb. *profane my statutes*
89:32 [a]2 Sam. 7:14
89:33 [1]Heb. *I will not make void from him* [2]Heb. *to lie* [a]2 Sam. 7:15
89:35 [1]Heb. *If I lie* [a]Amos 4:2
89:36 [a]Luke 1:33 [b]Ps. 72:17
89:38 [a]1 Chr. 28:9 [b]Deut. 32:19
89:39 [a]Lam. 5:16
89:41 [a]Ps. 44:13
89:44 [1]Heb. *brightness*
89:46 [a]Ps. 79:5
89:47 [a]Job 7:7
89:48 [a]Ps. 49:9 [b]Heb. 11:5
89:49 [a]2 Sam. 7:15 [b]Ps. 54:5
89:50 [a]Ps. 69:9,19
89:51 [a]Ps. 74:22
89:52 [a]Ps. 41:13
90:T [1]Or, *A Prayer,* being a Psalm *of Moses* [a]Deut. 33:1
90:1 [1]Heb. *in generation and generation* [a]Ezek. 11:16

43 Thou hast also turned the edge of his
sword,
And hast not made him to stand in the
battle.
44 Thou hast made his [1]glory to cease,
And cast his throne down to the ground.
45 The days of his youth hast thou
shortened:
Thou hast covered him with shame.
Selah.

46 [a]How long, LORD? wilt thou hide
thyself, for ever?
Shall thy wrath burn like fire?
47 [a]Remember how short my time is:
Wherefore hast thou made all men in
vain?
48 [a]What man *is he that* liveth, and shall
not [b]see death?
Shall he deliver his soul from the hand
of the grave? Selah.

49 Lord, where *are* thy former
lovingkindnesses,
Which thou [a]swarest unto David [b]in
thy truth?
50 Remember, Lord, the reproach of thy
servants;
[a]*How* I do bear in my bosom *the
reproach of* all the mighty people;
51 [a]Wherewith thine enemies have
reproached, O LORD;
Wherewith they have reproached the
footsteps of thine anointed.

52 [a]Blessed *be* the LORD for evermore.
Amen, and Amen.

Psalm 90

[1]A Prayer [a]of Moses the man of God.

1 Lord, [a]thou hast been our dwelling
place [1]in all generations.

89:29 *as the days of heaven.* See vv. 36–37.
89:30–37 The Lord's covenant with David and his dynasty (see chart, p. 16) was everlasting (see v. 28) and unconditional—though if any of his royal descendants is unfaithful, he will individually suffer under God's rod (to the detriment of the entire nation).
89:38–45 God's present rejection of David's son, and all its fearful consequences—the undoing of all that had been promised and assured by covenant (see especially vv. 19–29).
89:46–51 The prayer, an appeal—in spite of all—to God's faithfulness to His covenant with David. In this dark hour, that remains the psalmist's hope.
89:46 *How long . . . ?* See note on 6:3; see also Introduction: Theology. *wrath.* See note on 2:5.
89:50 *Remember.* See v. 47.
89:52 A brief doxology with which the final editors concluded Book 3 of the Psalter (see note on 41:13).
Ps 90 A prayer to the everlasting God to have compassion on His servants, who live their melancholy lives under the rod of divine wrath and under His sentence of death—a plea that God will yet show them His love, give them cause for joy and bless their labors with enduring worth. No other psalm depicts so poignantly the dismal state of man before the face of God, holy and eternal. Yet there is neither defiance nor despair; honesty acknowledges guilt (God's anger is warranted), and faith knows of God's "mercy" (v. 14) to which appeal can confidently be made. That Israel's 40 years of enforced sojourn in the "great and terrible wilderness" (Deut 8:15) on its pilgrimage to the promised land (see Num 14:26–35) should evoke such a prayer ought not be surprising.

Two passages descriptive of the human condition under God's aggrieved anger (vv. 3–6, 7–10) are framed by two couplets (vv. 1–2, 11–12) that, by their implicit contrasts, highlight the major polarities over which the intervening stanzas brood: 1. The Lord, who has ever been our "dwelling place" (v. 1), has shown us the power of His wrath (v. 7). 2. God is the Everlasting One (v. 2), while we must come to terms with the small number of our days (v. 12). These reflections lead to the prayer with which the psalm concludes (vv. 13–17).
90 title *A Prayer.* See note on Ps 17 title. *man of God.* A phrase normally applied in the OT to prophets (see note on 1 Sam 2:27), including Moses (see, e.g., Josh 14:6).
90:1 *dwelling place.* See 91:9. The Hebrew for this phrase is translated "habitation" in 71:3.

2 [a]Before the mountains were brought
forth,
Or ever thou hadst formed the earth
and the world,
Even from everlasting to everlasting,
thou *art* God.
3 Thou turnest man to destruction;
And sayest, [a]Return, ye children of men.
4 [a]For a thousand years in thy sight
Are but as yesterday [1]when it is past,
And *as* a watch in the night.
5 Thou carriest them away as with a
flood; [a]they are *as* a sleep:
In the morning [b]*they are* like grass
which [1]groweth up.
6 In the morning it flourisheth, and
groweth up;
In the evening it is cut down, and
withereth.
7 For we are consumed by thine anger,
And by thy wrath are we troubled.
8 [a]Thou hast set our iniquities before
thee,
Our [b]secret *sins* in the light of thy
countenance.
9 For all our days are [1]passed away in
thy wrath:
We spend our years [2]as a tale *that is
told.*
10 [1]The days of our years *are* threescore
years and ten;
And if by reason of strength *they be*
fourscore years,

90:2 [a]Prov. 8:25
90:3 [a]Gen. 3:19
90:4 [1]Or, *when he hath passed* them [a]2 Pet. 3:8
90:5 [1]Or, *is changed* [a]Ps. 73:20 [b]Is. 40:6
90:8 [a]Ps. 50:21 [b]Ps. 19:12
90:9 [1]Heb. *turned away* [2]Or, *as a meditation*
90:10 [1]Heb. As for *the days of our years, in them* are *seventy years*

90:12 [1]Heb. *cause to come* [a]Ps. 39:4
90:13 [a]Deut. 32:36; Ps. 135:14
90:14 [a]Ps. 85:6
90:16 [a]Hab. 3:2
90:17 [a]Ps. 27:4 [b]Is. 26:12
91:1 [a]Ps. 31:20

Yet *is* their strength labour and sorrow;
For it is soon cut off, and we fly away.
11 Who knoweth the power of thine
anger?
Even according to thy fear, *so is* thy
wrath.
12 [a]So teach *us* to number our days,
That we may [1]apply *our* hearts *unto*
wisdom.
13 Return, O LORD, how long?
And let it [a]repent thee concerning thy
servants.
14 O satisfy us early *with* thy mercy;
[a]That we may rejoice and be glad all
our days.
15 Make us glad according to the days
wherein thou hast afflicted us,
And the years *wherein* we have seen
evil.
16 Let [a]thy work appear unto thy
servants,
And thy glory unto their children.
17 [a]And let the beauty of the LORD our
God be upon us:
And [b]establish thou the work of our
hands upon us;
Yea, the work of our hands establish
thou it.

Psalm 91

1 He [a]that dwelleth in the secret place of
the most High

90:3–6 Man lives under God's sentence of death.
‡90:3 *destruction.* Lit."dust"; cf."dust . . . unto dust" in Gen 3:19.
‡90:4–5 *For . . . Thou.* Perhaps better "Though . . . , Thou": Though for God 1,000 years are like a watch in the night, which man sleeps through with no sense of the passage of time, He cuts man's life short like new grass that shows itself at dawn's light but is withered away by the hot Canaanite sun before evening falls.
90:4 *watch in the night.* See note on Judg 7:19.
90:7–10 Even life's short span is filled with trouble, as God ferrets out man's every sin and makes him feel His righteous anger.
90:7 *anger . . . wrath.* See vv. 9,11; see also note on 2:5.
90:8 *light of thy countenance.* The holy light of God that illumines the hidden corners of the heart and exposes its dark secrets.
‡90:10 *threescore . . . fourscore.* 70 . . . 80. *fourscore.* Hebrew poetic convention called for 80 following 70 in parallel construction (see note on Amos 1:3). *their strength.* What people prize and accomplish in their years of life. The thought could be: All their health, joys, riches and honor are soured by trouble and sorrow. *sorrow.* Or "emptiness."
90:11–12 *Who knoweth . . . ? . . . teach us.* No one has taken the measure of God's anger. But everyone ought to know the measure of his (few) days or he will play the arrogant fool, with no thought of his mortality or of his accountability to God (see Ps 49; 73:4–12).
‡90:11 *according to thy fear, so is thy wrath.* The more one grasps the power of God's wrath, the more one is able to give God the "fear" (reverence, awe) He deserves. See Gen 20:11 and note.
‡90:12 *That we may apply our hearts.* Or "so that our hearts might obtain." *hearts.* See note on 4:7.

90:13–17 Prayer for God's compassion—from Him come also joy and gladness.
90:13 *Return.* Lit. "turn" (cf. v. 3). *how long?* See note on 6:3 (see also Introduction: Theology).
‡90:14 *early.* Or "in the morning." Let there be for us a dawning of Your love to relieve this long, dark night of Your anger. Perhaps Moses (see title) pleads for the promised rest of the promised land (see Ex 33:14; Deut 12:9). The final answer to his prayer comes with the resurrection (see Rom 5:2–5; 8:18; 2 Cor 4:16–18). *mercy.* See note on 6:4.
‡90:16 *work . . . glory.* That is, work-of-glory (see 111:3; see also note on 3:7). For a fuller description of such works see the whole of Ps 111. *unto their children.* As to past generations (v. 1).
90:17 *beauty.* See 27:4 and note. *establish.* As You only have been our security in the world (see v. 1), so also make our labors to be effective and enduring—though we are so transient.
‡Ps 91 A glowing testimony to the security of those who trust in God. It was probably written by one of the temple personnel (a priest or Levite) as a word of assurance to godly worshipers. Because the "thee" of vv. 3–13 applies to any of the godly who make "the most High, thy habitation" (v. 9; see 90:1), the devil applied vv. 11–12 to Jesus (see Mat 4:6; Luke 4:10–11). Thematically, the psalm is divided into two halves. The opening couplet of the second half (vv. 9–10) echoes the theme of vv. 1–2. In the first half, the godly are assured of security from four threats (vv. 5–6)—though thousands fall (v. 7). In the second half, they are assured of triumphing over four menacing beasts (v. 13). The oracle of vv. 14–16 offers climactic assurance.
‡91:1 *secret place.* Or "hiding place," referring to the temple (as in 27:5; 31:20; see also 23:6; 27:4), where the godly find safety under the protective wings of the Lord (see v. 4; 61:4). *most*

Shall [1] abide [b] under the shadow of the
Almighty.
2 [a] I will say of the LORD, *He is* my refuge
and my fortress:
My God; in him will I trust.
3 Surely [a] he shall deliver thee from the
snare of the fowler,
And from the noisome pestilence.
4 [a] He shall cover thee with his feathers,
And under his wings shalt thou trust:
His truth *shall be thy* shield and buckler.
5 [a] Thou shalt not be afraid for the terror
by night;
Nor for the arrow *that* flieth by day;
6 *Nor* for the pestilence *that* walketh in
darkness;
Nor for the destruction *that* wasteth at
noonday.
7 A thousand shall fall at thy side,
And ten thousand at thy right hand;
But it shall not come nigh thee.
8 Only [a] with thine eyes shalt thou behold
And see the reward of the wicked.
9 Because thou hast made the LORD,
which is [a] my refuge,
Even the most High, [b] thy habitation;
10 [a] There shall no evil befall thee,
Neither shall *any* plague come nigh thy
dwelling.
11 [a] For he shall give his angels charge
over thee,
To keep thee in all thy ways.
12 They shall bear thee up in *their* hands,
[a] Lest thou dash thy foot against a
stone.
13 Thou shalt tread upon the lion and
[1] adder:
The young lion and the dragon shalt
thou trample under feet.
14 Because he hath set his love upon me,
therefore will I deliver him:
I will set him on high, because he hath
[a] known my name.
15 [a] He shall call upon me, and I will
answer him:
[b] I *will be* with him in trouble;
I will deliver him, and [c] honour him.
16 *With* [a] [1] long life will I satisfy him,
And shew him my salvation.

91:1 [1] Heb. *lodge* [b] Ps. 17:8
91:2 [a] Ps. 142:5
91:3 [a] Ps. 124:7
91:4 [a] Ps. 17:8
91:5 [a] Job 5:19; Ps. 112:7; Prov. 3:23; Is. 43:2
91:8 [a] Mal. 1:5
91:9 [a] ver. 2 [b] Ps. 90:1
91:10 [a] Prov. 12:21
91:11 [a] Ps. 34:7; 71:3; Mat. 4:6; Luke 4:10; Heb. 1:14
91:12 [a] Job 5:23; Ps. 37:24
91:13 [1] Or, *asp*
91:14 [a] Ps. 9:10
91:15 [a] Ps. 50:15 [b] Is. 43:2 [c] 1 Sam. 2:30
91:16 [1] Heb. *length of days* [a] Prov. 3:2
92:1 [a] Ps. 147:1
92:2 [1] Heb. *in the nights* [a] Ps. 89:1
92:3 [1] Or, *Upon the solemn sound with the harp* [2] Heb. *Higgaion* [a] 1 Chr. 23:5; Ps. 33:2

Psalm 92

A Psalm *or* Song for the sabbath day.

1 *It is a* [a] good *thing* to give thanks unto
the LORD,
And to sing *praises* unto thy name,
O most High:
2 To [a] shew forth thy lovingkindness in
the morning,
And thy faithfulness [1] every night,
3 [a] Upon an instrument of ten strings,
and upon the psaltery;
[1] Upon the harp with [2] a solemn sound.

High. See v. 9; see also note on Gen 14:19. *shadow.* See note on 17:8. *Almighty.* Hebrew *Shaddai* (see note on Gen 17:1).

‡91:3 *snare of the fowler.* The hunter's trap is a metaphor for danger from an enemy (see 124:7). *noisome pestilence.* Or "deadly plague." These two threats are further elaborated in vv. 5–6.

‡91:4 *with his feathers.* See note on 17:8. *shield and buckler.* See note on 3:3.

91:5 *terror.* As in 64:1 ("fear"), reference is to attack by enemies; thus it is paired with "arrow." These two references to threats from war are arrayed alongside "pestilence" and "destruction" (v. 6), two references to mortal diseases that often reached epidemic proportions. *night . . . day.* At whatever time of day or night the threat may come, you will be kept safe—the time references are not specific to their respective phrases (see also v. 6).

91:7 *ten thousand.* Hebrew poetic convention called for 10,000 following 1,000 in parallel construction (see notes on 90:10; Amos 1:3). Cf. 1 Sam 18:7.

‡91:8 *reward.* Or "recompense" (i.e. their punishment).

91:9 *habitation.* See 90:1 and note.

91:11–12 Quoted by Satan in Mat 4:6; Luke 4:10–11.

91:11 *his angels.* See note on 34:7.

91:12 *against a stone.* On the stony trails of Canaan (see Prov 3:23).

91:13 *lion . . . adder . . . young lion . . . dragon.* These double references to lions and to poisonous snakes ("dragon"= "serpent") balance the double references of vv. 5–6, and complete the illustrative roster of mortal threats (see Amos 5:19).

91:14–16 Employing the form of a prophetic oracle, the author (see introduction) supports his testimony by assuring the godly that it is confirmed by all the promises of God to those who truly love and trust Him.

‡91:14 *I will set him on high.* Protect him or put him in a secure place. *my name.* See note on 5:11.

Ps 92 A joyful celebration of the righteous rule of God. Its testimony to the prosperity of the righteous, "planted in the house of the LORD" (v. 13), links it thematically with Ps 91, while its joy over God's righteous reign relates it to the cluster of psalms that follow (Ps 93–100; see especially Ps 94). In fact, celebration of God's love and faithfulness as characteristic of His reign (see v. 2; 100:5) may have served for the editors of the Psalter as a frame enclosing the collection. The psalmist here may have been the king (see vv. 10–11). Following the introduction on praise (vv. 1–3), vv. 4–5 offer the motivation for the praise ("me," "I"), which is picked up again in vv. 10–11 ("my," "I," "Mine," "my," "mine," "my," "me"). Verses 6–9 expound the folly and destiny of evildoers, while vv. 12–15 expound the prosperity of the righteous. Notice also the link between v. 7 and v. 13.

92 title *Song.* See note on Ps 30 title. *for the sabbath day.* In the postexilic liturgy of the temple, this psalm came to be sung at the time of the morning sacrifice on the sabbath. (The rest of the weekly schedule was: first day, Ps 24; second day, Ps 48; third day, Ps 82; fourth day, Ps 94; fifth day, Ps 81; sixth day, Ps 93.)

92:1–3 Hymnic introduction.

92:1 *LORD . . . most High.* That is, LORD most High (see 7:17; see also note on 3:7). *name.* See note on 5:11. *most High.* See note on Gen 14:19.

92:2 *lovingkindness . . . faithfulness.* That is, lovingkindness-and-faithfulness (see note on 36:5; see also note on 3:7). *lovingkindness.* See note on 6:4. *morning . . . night.* Continuously.

‡92:3 *psaltery . . . harp.* See note on 57:8. *harp.* See note on Gen 31:27. *solemn sound.* Or "resounding music."

4 For thou, LORD, hast made me glad
through thy work:
I will triumph in the works of thy
hands.
5 [a]O LORD, how great are thy works!
And [b]thy thoughts are very deep.
6 [a]A brutish man knoweth not;
Neither doth a fool understand this.
7 When [a]the wicked spring as the grass,
And when all the workers of iniquity
do flourish;
It is that they shall be destroyed for
ever:
8 [a]But thou, LORD, *art most* high for
evermore.
9 For lo, thine enemies, O LORD,
For lo, thine enemies shall perish;
All the workers of iniquity shall [a]be
scattered.
10 But [a]my horn shalt thou exalt like *the
horn of* an unicorn:
I shall be [b]anointed with fresh oil.
11 [a]Mine eye also shall see *my desire* on
mine enemies,
And mine ears shall hear *my desire* of
the wicked that rise up against me.
12 [a]The righteous shall flourish like the
palm tree:
He shall grow like a cedar in Lebanon.
13 Those that be planted in the house of
the LORD

92:5 [a]Ps. 40:5 [b]Is. 28:29; Rom. 11:33
92:6 [a]Ps. 73:22
92:7 [a]Job 12:6; 21:7; Ps. 37:1,2; Jer. 12:1,2; Mal. 3:15
92:8 [a]Ps. 83:18
92:9 [a]Ps. 68:1
92:10 [a]Ps. 89:17 [b]Ps. 23:5
92:11 [a]Ps. 54:7; 59:10
92:12 [a]Ps. 52:8; Is. 65:22; Hos. 14:5,6
92:13 [a]Ps. 100:4
92:14 [1]Heb. *green*
92:15 [a]Deut. 32:4 [b]Rom. 9:14
93:1 [a]Ps. 96:10; 97:1; Is. 52:7; Rev. 19:6 [b]Ps. 104:1 [c]Ps. 65:6
93:2 [1]Heb. *from then* [a]Ps. 45:6; Prov. 8:22
93:4 [a]Ps. 65:7; 89:9
93:5 [1]Heb. *to length of days*
94:1 [1]Heb. *God of revenges* [a]Nah. 1:2

Shall flourish [a]in the courts of our God.
14 They shall still bring forth fruit in old
age;
They shall be fat and [1]flourishing;
15 To shew that the LORD *is* upright:
[a]*He is* my rock, and [b]*there is* no
unrighteousness in him.

Psalm 93

1 The [a]LORD reigneth, [b]he is clothed
with majesty;
The LORD is clothed with strength,
[c]*wherewith* he hath girded himself:
The world also is stablished, *that* it
cannot be moved.
2 [a]Thy throne is established [1]of old:
Thou *art* from everlasting.
3 The floods have lifted up, O LORD,
The floods have lifted up their voice;
The floods lift up their waves.
4 [a]The LORD on high *is* mightier
Than the noise of many waters,
Yea, than the mighty waves of the sea.
5 Thy testimonies are very sure:
Holiness becometh thine house,
O LORD, [1]for ever.

Psalm 94

1 O LORD [1]God, [a]to whom vengeance
belongeth;

92:4–5 Joy over God's saving acts (see vv. 10–11).
‡92:5 *thy thoughts.* As shown by your deeds. Cf. Is 55:8–9.
92:6–9 The fatal folly of evildoers (contrast vv. 12–15).
‡92:6 *brutish man . . . fool.* See note on 14:1; see also 49:10; 94:8–11. They do not know that the Lord rules righteously. They see the wicked flourishing, but do not see the Lord or foresee the end he has appointed for them. The author thus characterizes his "enemies" (v. 11), whom the Lord has routed.
‡92:7 A condensed statement of what is expounded more fully in Ps 73 (see note on 90:4–5). *It is that.* Or "It is so that." Their ultimate demise glorifies God's justice and righteousness.
92:8 *most high for evermore.* God's eternal exaltation assures the destruction of His enemies.
92:9 *enemies.* Here the evildoers, referred to also in v. 7.
‡92:10–11 Joy over God's favors (see vv. 4–5): God has made him triumphant (see 89:24) and anointed him with "the oil of gladness" (45:7; see also 23:5) by giving him victory over all his enemies.
92:12–15 The secure prosperity of the righteous (contrast vv. 6–9).
‡92:13 *planted in the house of the LORD.* Though the wicked may "spring as the grass," their end is sure (see v. 7). But the righteous are planted in a secure place (see Ps 91) and so retain the vigor of youth into old age, rejoicing in God's just discrimination (see v. 15). *courts.* Of the temple (see 84:2,10; 2 Ki 21:5; 23:11–12).
Ps 93 A hymn to the eternal, universal and invincible reign of the Lord, a theme it shares with Ps 47; 94–100. Together they offer a majestic confession of faith in and hope for the kingdom of God on earth. These hymns were composed for the liturgy of a high religious festival in which the kingship of the Lord—over the cosmic order, over the nations and in a special sense over Israel—was annually celebrated (see introduction to Ps 47). And implicitly, where not explicitly, the Lord's kingship is hailed in contrast to the claims of all other gods; He is "a great King above all gods" (95:3). Ps 93–100 may all have been composed by temple personnel and spoken by them in the liturgy. They probably date from the preexilic era. Structurally, in Hebrew the psalm has two short stanzas (vv. 1–2, 3–4) and a conclusion (v. 5).
93:1–2 The Lord's reign, by which the creation order has been and will be secure throughout the ages, is from eternity (see Gen 1:1). Though Israel as a nation has come late on the scene, her God has been King since before the creation of the world.
93:1 *The LORD reigneth.* The ultimate truth, and first article, in Israel's creed (see 96:10; 97:1; 99:1; see also Zech 14:9 and note).
93:3–4 Since His founding of the world, the Lord has shown Himself to be mightier than all the forces of disorder that threaten His kingdom.
93:3 *floods.* Reference is to the primeval chaotic waters, tamed and assigned a place by the Lord's creative word (see 33:7; 104:7–9; Gen 1:6–10; Job 38:8–11). Implicitly they symbolize all that opposes the coming of the Lord's kingdom (see 65:6–7; 74:13–14 and notes).
93:4 The thunder of the chaotic waters is no match for the thunder of the Lord's ordering word (see 104:7).
93:5 *testimonies.* He whose indisputable rule has made the world secure has given His people life directives that are stable and reliable (see 19:7)—and that they must honor (see 95:8–11). *thine house.* His earthly temple—but also the heavenly. *for ever.* Qualifies both clauses.
‡Ps 94 An appeal to the Lord, as "judge of the earth" (v. 2), to redress the wrongs perpetrated against the weak by arrogant and wicked men who occupy seats of power. The psalm has links with Ps 92, but is the voice of the oppressed within Israel (thus not the king), seeking redress at God's throne for injustices done them by those smugly established in the power structures of the nation. Thus it is unique within the Ps 92–100 collection. (See introduction to Ps 93.)

O God, to whom vengeance belongeth,
[2]shew thyself.
2 [a]Lift up thyself, thou [b]judge of the earth:
Render a reward to the proud.

3 LORD, [a]how long shall the wicked,
How long shall the wicked triumph?
4 *How long* shall they [a]utter *and* speak hard *things?*
And all the workers of iniquity boast themselves?
5 They break in pieces thy people, O LORD,
And afflict thine heritage.
6 They slay the widow and the stranger,
And murder the fatherless.
7 [a]Yet they say, The LORD shall not see,
Neither shall the God of Jacob regard *it.*

8 [a]Understand, ye brutish among the people:
And ye fools, when will ye be wise?
9 [a]He that planted the ear, shall he not hear?
He that formed the eye, shall he not see?
10 He that chastiseth the heathen, shall not he correct?
He that [a]teacheth man knowledge, *shall not he know?*
11 [a]The LORD knoweth the thoughts of man,
That they *are* vanity.
12 [a]Blessed *is* the man whom thou chastenest, O LORD,
And teachest him out of thy law;
13 That *thou* mayest give him rest from the days of adversity,
Until the pit be digged for the wicked.
14 [a]For the LORD will not cast off his people,
Neither will he forsake his inheritance.
15 But judgment shall return unto righteousness:
And all the upright in heart [1]shall follow it.

16 Who will rise up for me against the evildoers?
Or who will stand up for me against the workers of iniquity?
17 [a]Unless the LORD *had been* my help,
My soul had [1]almost dwelt *in* silence.
18 When I said, [a]My foot slippeth;
Thy mercy, O LORD, held me up.
19 In the multitude of my thoughts within me
Thy comforts delight my soul.
20 Shall [a]the throne of iniquity have fellowship *with* thee,
Which [b]frameth mischief by a law?
21 [a]They gather themselves together against the soul of the righteous,
And [b]condemn the innocent blood.
22 But the LORD is [a]my defence;
And my God *is* the rock of my refuge.
23 And [a]he shall bring upon them their own iniquity,
And shall cut them off in their own wickedness;
Yea, the LORD our God shall cut them off.

Psalm 95

1 O come, let us sing unto the LORD:
[a]Let us make a joyful noise to [b]the rock of our salvation.

94:1 [2]Heb. *shine forth*
94:2 [a]Ps. 7:6 [b]Gen. 18:25
94:3 [a]Job 20:5
94:4 [a]Ps. 31:18; Jude 15
94:7 [a]Ps. 10:11
94:8 [a]Ps. 73:22; 92:6
94:9 [a]Ex. 4:11
94:10 [a]Job 35:11; Is. 28:26
94:11 [a]1 Cor. 3:20
94:12 [a]Job 5:17; Heb. 12:5
94:14 [a]1 Sam. 12:22; Rom. 11:1
94:15 [1]Heb. shall be *after it*
94:17 [1]Or, *quickly* [a]Ps. 124:1,2
94:18 [a]Ps. 38:16
94:20 [a]Amos 6:3 [b]Is. 10:1
94:21 [a]Mat. 27:1 [b]Prov. 17:15
94:22 [a]Ps. 59:9
94:23 [a]Ps. 7:16; Prov. 2:22
95:1 [a]Ps. 100:1 [b]Deut. 32:15; 2 Sam. 22:47

94:1–3 Initial appeal to God, the Judge.
94:1 *vengeance.* Redress of wrongs (see Deut 32:35,41 and note on Deut 32:35).
94:2 *the proud.* See vv. 4–7 for a description of them.
94:3 *how long . . . ?* See note on 6:3; see also Introduction: Theology.
94:4–7 Indictment of the wicked.
94:4 *hard things . . . boast themselves.* For the arrogance of the wicked see 10:2–11 and notes.
94:5 *thy people . . . thine heritage.* Those among them who are vulnerable (see v. 6).
94:7 *they say.* See notes on 3:2; 10:11. *Jacob.* A synonym for Israel (see Gen 32:28).
‡94:8–11 Warning to the wicked—those "brutish . . . fools" (see 92:6–9; see also note on 14:1).
94:10 *chastiseth.* Keeps them in line by means of punishment (see Lev 26:18; Jer 31:18). *teacheth.* Gives him some knowledge of the creation order (see Is 28:26).
94:11 *The LORD knoweth.* Contrary to their foolish supposition (see v. 7).
94:12–15 Those whose lives are directed by God's law are the blessed ones (see Ps 1)—contrary to the arrogant expectations of the wicked and in spite of their oppressions.
94:12 *Blessed.* See note on 1:1. *chastenest . . . teachest.* See v. 10. Here the author speaks of God's correcting and teaching His people in the ways of His law.
94:14 *people . . . inheritance.* See v. 5. The Lord will not abandon the powerless among His people to the injustice of their oppressors. Paul may be echoing this verse in Rom 11:1–2.
94:15 *return unto righteousness.* Or "restore righteousness." *heart.* See note on 4:7. *shall follow it.* Or "with it." In any event, the author appears to say that God's judgment will restore justice for the upright in heart.
94:16–19 The Lord is the only sure court of appeal.
94:17 *silence.* See note on 30:1. Without God's help the wicked would have silenced the psalmist in the grave, but now it is the wicked for whom the pit will be dug (see v. 13).
‡94:18 *When I said.* As he feels that he is about to be overwhelmed by the wicked (see note on 38:16). *mercy.* See note on 6:4.
94:19 *soul.* See note on 6:3.
94:20–23 Confidence that the Lord's justice will prevail.
‡94:20 *throne of iniquity.* A seat of authority that works mischief. The author speaks of injustice at the center of power. *frameth mischief by a law.* Corrupt leaders abuse their power to pass unjust laws.
94:21 *righteous.* See note on 1:5.
Ps 95 A call to worship the Lord, spoken by a priest or Levite to the assembled Israelites at the temple. (See introduction to Ps 93.) The psalm is composed of two parts: (1) a call to praise the Lord of all the earth (vv. 1–5); (2) a call to acknowledge by submissive attitude and obedient heart the Lord's kingship over

2 Let us [1]come before his presence with
thanksgiving,
And make a joyful noise unto him with
psalms.
3 For [a]the LORD *is* a great God,
And a great King above all gods.
4 [1]In his hand *are* the deep places of the
earth:
[2]The strength of the hills *is* his also.
5 [a][1]The sea *is* his, and he made it:
And his hands formed the dry *land.*
6 O come, let us worship and bow down:
Let [a]us kneel before the LORD our
Maker.
7 For he *is* our God;
And [a]we *are* the people of his pasture,
and the sheep of his hand.

[b]To day if ye will hear his voice,
8 Harden not your heart, [a]as *in* the
[1]provocation,
And as *in* the day of temptation in the
wilderness:
9 When [a]your fathers tempted me,
Proved me, and [b]saw my work.
10 [a]Forty years long was I grieved with
this generation,
And said, It *is* a people that do err in
their heart,
And they have not known my ways:
11 *Unto* whom [a]I sware in my wrath
[1]That they should not enter into my
rest.

95:2 [1] Heb. *prevent his face*
95:3 [a] Ps. 96:4
95:4 [1] Heb. *In whose* [2] Or, *The heights of the hills are his*
95:5 [1] Heb. *Whose the sea* is [a] Gen. 1:9,10
95:6 [a] Phil. 2:10
95:7 [a] Ps. 79:13; 100:3 [b] Heb. 3:7
95:8 [1] Heb. *contention* [a] Ex. 17:2,7
95:9 [a] Ps. 78:18; 1 Cor. 10:9 [b] Num. 14:22
95:10 [a] Heb. 3:10
95:11 [1] Heb. *If they enter into my rest* [a] Heb. 4:3,5
96:1 [a] 1 Chr. 16:23-33
96:4 [a] Ps. 145:3 [b] Ps. 18:3 [c] Ps. 95:3
96:5 [a] Jer. 10:11 [b] Ps. 115:15; Is. 42:5
96:6 [a] Ps. 29:2

Psalm 96

1 [a]O sing unto the LORD a new song:
Sing unto the LORD, all the earth.
2 Sing unto the LORD, bless his name;
Shew forth his salvation from day to day.
3 Declare his glory among the heathen,
His wonders among all people.
4 For [a]the LORD *is* great, and [b]greatly to
be praised:
[c]He *is* to be feared above all gods.
5 For [a]all the gods of the nations *are* idols:
[b]But the LORD made the heavens.
6 Honour and majesty *are* before him:
Strength and [a]beauty *are* in his
sanctuary.

His people (vv. 6–11). Each part also has two subdivisions, the latter of which forms the climax. Cf. the structure of Ps 96.

95:1–2 The call to praise.

95:1 *rock of our salvation.* See note on 18:2.

95:3–5 Why Israel is to praise the Lord—because He is above all gods, and there is no corner of the universe that is not in His hand. The ancient pagan world had different gods for different peoples, different geographical areas, different cosmic regions (heaven, earth, netherworld) and different aspects of life (e.g., war, fertility, crafts).

95:4–5 *deep places . . . strength of the hills . . . sea . . . dry land.* All the world—the extremes and all that lies between and all that is in them.

95:6–11 The exhortation to submit to the Lord with obedient hearts—a bent knee is not enough. For a NT reflection on these verses in the light of the advent of Christ see Heb 3:7–4:13.

95:6–7 The call to confess submission to the Lord by kneeling before him.

95:6 *our Maker.* Both as Creator of all things (see Gen 1) and as Israel's Redeemer, He has "made" her what she is: the people of the Lord in the earth (see Is 45:9–13; 51:12–16).

95:7 *people of his pasture.* See 100:3; Jer 23:1; Ezek 34:21. Since kings were commonly called the "shepherds" of their people (see note on 23:1), their realms could be referred to as their "pastures" (see Jer 25:36; 49:20; 50:45). *if ye will hear his voice.* In the liturgy of the religious festival, possibly in some such manner as Ps 50 and/or 78.

‡95:8 *provocation . . . temptation.* Or the place names, "Meribah" ("quarreling") and "Massah" ("testing"). The leader of the liturgy reminds Israel of times of her rebellion in the wilderness (see Ex 17:7; Num 20:13).

95:9 *saw my work.* In Egypt and at the Red sea—and His provision of food in the wilderness (see Ex 16; see also Num 14:11).

95:10 *Forty years.* The climax of Israel's rebellion came when she faithlessly refused to undertake the conquest of Canaan and considered returning to Egypt (see Num 14:1–4). It was then that God condemned her to a 40-year stay in the wilderness (see Num 14:34). *this generation.* The (adult) Israelites who came out of Egypt and covenanted with God at Sinai (see Num 32:13). *It is a people . . . my ways.* A restatement of the Lord's word in Num 14:11. *heart.* See note on 4:7. *my ways.* See 25:4 and note.

‡95:11 *sware.* See Num 14:28. *not enter into my rest.* The language of Num 14:30 is "ye shall not come into the land," but since the promised land was also called the place where God will give His people "rest" (Josh 1:13,15; see Ex 33:14; Deut 12:10; 25:19), the two statements are equivalent. *rest.* Here a fertile concept indicating Israel's possession of a place with God in the earth where she is secure from all external threats and internal calamities (see 1 Ki 5:4).

Ps 96 A call to all nations to praise the Lord as the only God and to proclaim the glory of His reign throughout the world—an OT anticipation of the world mission of the NT people of God (see Mat 28:16–20). (See introductions to Ps 93; 95.) This psalm appears in slightly altered form in 1 Chr 16:23–33. The psalm is composed of two thematic parts: (1) a call to all nations to sing the praise of the Lord (vv. 1–6); (2) a call to all nations to worship the Lord and to hail throughout the world the glory of His righteous rule (vv. 7–13). Each part has two subdivisions, the last of which forms the climax to the whole psalm. Cf. the structure of Ps 95.

‡96:1–3 The call to all the earth to sing the praise of the Lord among the nations. Triple repetition ("sing . . . Sing . . . Sing") was a common feature in OT liturgical calls to worship (see vv. 7–9 and note; see also 103:20–22; 118:2–4; 135:1; 136:1–3).

96:1 *new song.* See note on 33:3. *all the earth.* See v. 9; or "all the land," in which case the call is addressed to all Israel. However, the worldwide perspective of this psalm (see especially v. 7) suggests that here the psalmist has in view broader horizons (see 97:1; 100:1 and note; 117:1; see also note on 9:1).

96:2 *name.* See v. 8; see also note on 5:11. *Shew forth his salvation.* Proclaim (see 40:9 and note) that deliverance comes from the Lord (see 3:8; see also 85:9).

96:3 *glory.* See note on 85:9. *wonders.* See note on 71:16–17.

96:4–6 Why "all the earth" is to praise the Lord: He alone is God (see Ps 115).

96:4 *feared.* See note on Gen 20:11.

96:5 *made the heavens.* As the Maker of the heavenly realm, in pagan eyes the abode of the gods, the Lord is greater than all the gods (see 97:7).

96:6 *Honour and majesty . . . Strength and beauty.* Two pairs of divine attributes personified as throne attendants whose pres-

7 [a]Give unto the LORD, O ye kindreds of
the people,
Give unto the LORD glory and strength.
8 Give unto the LORD the glory [1]due
unto his name:
Bring an offering, and come into his
courts.
9 O worship the LORD [a][1]in the beauty of
holiness:
Fear before him, all the earth.
10 Say among the heathen *that* [a]the LORD
reigneth:
The world also shall be established *that*
it shall not be moved:
[b]He shall judge the people righteously.
11 [a]Let the heavens rejoice, and let the
earth be glad;
[b]Let the sea roar, and the fulness thereof.
12 Let the field be joyful, and all that *is*
therein:
Then shall all the trees of the wood
rejoice
13 Before the LORD, for he cometh,
For he cometh to judge the earth:
[a]He shall judge the world with
righteousness,
And the people with his truth.

96:7 [a]Ps. 29:1,2 96:8 [1]Heb. *of his name* 96:9 [1]Or, *in the glorious sanctuary* [a]Ps. 29:2 96:10 [a]Ps. 97:1 [b]Ps. 67:4 96:11 [a]Ps. 69:34 [b]Ps. 98:7 96:13 [a]Rev. 19:11

97:1 [1]Heb. *many,* or, *great isles* [a]Ps. 96:10 [b]Is. 60:9 97:2 [1]Or, *establishment* [a]Ps. 18:11 [b]Ps. 89:14 97:3 [a]Ps. 18:8 97:4 [a]Ex. 19:18 97:5 [a]Mic. 1:4 97:6 [a]Ps. 19:1 97:7 [a]Ex. 20:4; Lev. 26:1 [b]Heb. 1:6

Psalm 97

1 The [a]LORD reigneth; let the earth
rejoice;
Let the [1]multitude of [b]isles be glad
thereof.
2 [a]Clouds and darkness *are* round about
him:
[b]Righteousness and judgment *are* the
[1]habitation of his throne.
3 [a]A fire goeth before him,
And burneth up his enemies round
about.
4 [a]His lightnings enlightened the world:
The earth saw, and trembled.
5 [a]The hills melted like wax at the
presence of the LORD,
At the presence of the Lord of the
whole earth.
6 [a]The heavens declare his
righteousness,
And all the people see his glory.
7 [a]Confounded be all they that serve
graven images,
That boast themselves of idols:
[b]Worship him, all ye gods.
8 Zion heard, and was glad,

ence before the Lord heralds the exalted nature of the one, universal King. For similar personifications see 23:6 and note.

‡96:7–9 The call to all nations to worship the Lord (see 29:1–2 and note). The two half-sentences of 29:2 have been expanded in this psalm. The threefold "give" here balances the threefold "sing" of vv. 1–2.

‡96:8 *courts.* Of the temple (see 84:2,10; 2 Ki 21:5; 23:11–12).

96:10–13 The call to all nations to proclaim among the nations the righteous reign of the Lord.

96:10 *the LORD reigneth.* See 93:1 and note. *The world . . . righteously.* In OT perspective, the world order is one, embracing both its physical and moral aspects because both have been established by God as aspects of His one kingdom and both are upheld by His one rule. Therefore God's rule over creation and over the affairs of men (also His acts of creation and redemption) is often spoken of in one breath, and "righteousness," "faithfulness" and "love" are equally ascribable to both. And since the creation order is secure in its "goodness" (see Gen 1), it often serves in OT poetry (as it does here) as a manifest assurance that God's rule over the affairs of men will also be "with righteousness" and "with . . . truth" (v. 13; see 11:3; 33:4–11; 36:5–9; 57:10; 65:6–7; 71:19; 74:13–14,16–17; 75:3; 82:5; 93:3–4; 119:89–91 and notes). *shall judge.* See v. 13 and note.

96:11–12 Because God's kingdom is one (see v. 10 and note), all His creatures will rejoice when God's rule over mankind brings righteousness to full expression in His cosmic kingdom (see note on 65:13; see also 97:7–9). For the present state of the creation as it awaits the fullness of redemption see Rom 8:21–22 and notes.

96:13 *cometh . . . cometh . . . shall judge.* Because God reigns over all things and is the Lord of history, Israel lived in hope (as the prophets announced) of the "coming" of God—His future acts by which He would decisively deal with all wickedness and establish His righteousness in the earth. *righteousness.* See note on 5:8.

Ps 97 A joyful celebration of the Lord's righteous reign over all the earth. (See introductions to Ps 93; 95.) The psalm's two main thematic divisions (vv. 1–6, 8–12) are joined by a centered verse (v. 7; see note on 6:6) that serves as a counterpoint to the main theme. The opening verses of the two main divisions are thematically linked: v. 1, "rejoice . . . be glad"; v. 8, "was glad . . . rejoiced"—in reverse order, a frequent stylistic device in OT poetry.

97:1–6 A testimony to the nations—that they too have seen God's majesty displayed (vv. 2–6) and ought to rejoice with Israel that the Lord reigns supreme.

97:1 *The LORD reigneth.* See 93:1 and note. *earth.* See 96:1; 99:1; 117:1; see also note on 9:1. *multitude of isles.* Even distant lands reached by the far-ranging ships that sail the seas (see 1 Ki 9:26–28; 10:22; Is 60:9; Jonah 1:3).

97:2–6 The Lord's majestic glory revealed in the sky's awesome displays, especially in the thunderstorm (see 18:7–15 and note; see also introduction to Ps 29).

‡97:2 *Clouds and darkness.* The dark storm clouds that hide the sun and cast a veil across the sky are dramatic visual reminders that the fierce heat and brilliance (also metaphors) of God's naked glory must be veiled from creaturely eyes (see Ex 19:9; 1 Ki 8:12). Thus also a curtain closed off the most holy place in the tabernacle and temple (see Ex 26:33; 2 Chr 3:14), veiling it in darkness. *Righteousness.* See v. 6; see also note on 5:8. *habitation of his throne.* Or "foundation (establishment) of his throne." God rules by His power (see 66:7), but His reign is founded on righteousness and justice, which also the heavens proclaim (see v. 6 and note).

97:3 *fire.* Manifested in the storm cloud's lightning bolts (see v. 4), fire often signified God's judicial wrath (see, e.g., 21:9; 50:3; 83:14; Deut 4:24; 9:3; 32:22; 1 Ki 19:12; Is 10:17; 30:27,30).

97:4 *world.* Here probably the physical earth personified.

97:6 *declare his righteousness.* The stable order of the heaven's vast array "speaks" (see 19:1–4); it declares that God's reign similarly upholds the moral order (see note on 96:10). *all the people see.* Verses 2–6 have spoken of general revelation (cf. 19:1–6).

97:7 The center verse (see note on 6:6) and counterpoint of the psalm: joy to all who acknowledge the Lord; shame and disgrace to those who trust in the false gods. *Worship him.* With biting irony the psalm calls on all the gods that people fool-

And the daughters of Judah rejoiced,
Because of thy judgments, O LORD.
9 For thou, LORD, *art* [a]High above all the earth:
[b]Thou art exalted far above all gods.
10 Ye that love the LORD, [a]hate evil:
[b]He preserveth the souls of his saints;
[c]He delivereth them out of the hand of the wicked.
11 [a]Light is sown for the righteous,
And gladness for the upright in heart.
12 [a]Rejoice in the LORD, ye righteous;
[b]And give thanks [1]at the remembrance of his holiness.

Psalm 98

A Psalm.

1 [a]O sing unto the LORD a new song;
For [b]he hath done marvellous *things:*
[c]His right hand, and his holy arm, hath gotten him the victory.
2 [a]The LORD hath made known his salvation:
[b]His righteousness hath he [1]openly shewed in the sight of the heathen.
3 He hath [a]remembered his mercy and his truth toward the house of Israel:

97:9 [a]Ps. 83:18 [b]Ex. 18:11; Ps. 95:3
97:10 [a]Ps. 34:14; Amos 5:15 [b]Prov. 2:8 [c]Ps. 37:39; Dan. 3:28
97:11 [a]Job 22:28; Prov. 4:18
97:12 [1]Or, *to the memorial* [a]Ps. 33:1 [b]Ps. 30:4
98:1 [a]Ps. 96:1; Is. 42:10 [b]Ex. 15:11; Ps. 77:14 [c]Ex. 15:6; Is. 63:5
98:2 [1]Or, *revealed* [a]Is. 52:10; Luke 2:30 [b]Is. 62:2
98:3 [a]Luke 1:54
98:3 [b]Is. 49:6
98:4 [a]Ps. 95:1
98:6 [a]Num. 10:10
98:8 [a]Is. 55:12
98:9 [a]Ps. 96:10
99:1 [1]Heb. *stagger* [a]Ex. 25:22
99:2 [a]Ps. 97:9

[b]All the ends of the earth have seen the salvation of our God.
4 [a]Make a joyful noise unto the LORD, all the earth:
Make a loud noise, and rejoice, and sing *praise.*
5 Sing unto the LORD with the harp;
With the harp, and the voice of a psalm.
6 [a]With trumpets and sound of cornet
Make a joyful noise before the LORD, the King.
7 Let the sea roar, and the fulness thereof;
The world, and they that dwell therein.
8 Let the floods [a]clap *their* hands:
Let the hills be joyful together
9 Before the LORD; [a]for he cometh to judge the earth:
With righteousness shall he judge the world,
And the people with equity.

Psalm 99

1 The LORD reigneth; let the people tremble:
[a]He sitteth *between* the cherubims; let the earth [1]be moved.
2 The LORD *is* great in Zion;
And he *is* [a]high above all the people.

ishly worship to bow in worship before the Lord (see v. 9; see also 29:1 and note).

97:8–12 A declaration of Zion's joy that the Lord reigns (vv. 8–9), and a reminder that only those who hate evil have real cause to rejoice in His righteous rule (vv. 10–12).

‡97:8 *Zion heard.* That "the LORD reigneth" (v. 1) in "righteousness" (v. 6). *judgments.* God's righteous acts in the affairs of mankind (see 105:7; Is 26:9), especially His saving acts in Israel's behalf (see 48:11; 105:5; Deut 33:21).

‡97:9 *art High.* Or "most High." See note on Gen 14:19.

97:10 *saints.* See note on 4:3.

97:11 *Light.* See 27:1 and note; see also 36:9. *righteous.* See v. 12; see also note on 1:5. *heart.* See note on 4:7.

97:12 *remembrance.* See note on 30:4.

‡Ps 98 A call to celebrate with joy the righteous reign of the Lord. Its beginning and end echo Ps 96. (See introductions to Ps 93; 95.) In Hebrew its three stanzas progressively extend the call to ever wider circles: (1) the worshiping congregation at the temple; (2) all the peoples of the earth; (3) the whole creation. The first stanza (vv. 1–3) recalls God's revelation of His righteousness (v. 2) in the past; the last stanza (vv. 7–9) speaks confidently of His coming rule "With righteousness" (v. 9); the middle stanza is enclosed by the jubilant cry, "Make a joyful noise" (vv. 4,6).

98:1–3 The call to celebrate in song God's saving acts in behalf of His people.

98:1 *new song.* See note on 33:3. *marvellous things.* See note on 9:1 ("marvellous works").

98:2 *made known . . . openly shewed . . . in the sight of the heathen.* God's saving acts in behalf of His people are also His self-revelation to the nations; in this sense God is His own evangelist (see note on 46:10; see also Is 52:10). *salvation . . . righteousness.* God's saving acts reveal His righteousness (see notes on 5:8; 71:24).

‡98:3 *mercy . . . truth.* That is, mercy-and-truth (see note on 36:5; see also note on 3:7). This compound expression often sums up God's covenant commitment to His people (see note on 6:4).

98:4–6 The call to all the earth to join in the celebration.

98:4 See 100:1. *all the earth.* The peoples of the earth (see 96:1 and note; see also 99:1).

98:5 *harp.* See note on Gen 31:27.

98:6 *trumpets.* The special long, straight trumpets of the sanctuary (referred to only here in Psalms; see notes on Num 10:2–3,10). *cornet.* The more common trumpet (referred to also in 47:5; 81:3; 150:3; see note on Joel 2:1).

98:7–9 The call to the whole creation to celebrate (see note on 96:11–12).

98:7 *sea . . . world.* The two great regions of creaturely life.

98:8 *floods . . . hills.* From the rivers to the mountains, let every feature of the whole earth clap and sing (see note on 65:13).

98:9 *cometh to judge.* See 96:13 and note. Israel in faith lived between the past (see vv. 1–3) and the future righteous (saving) acts of God.

‡Ps 99 A hymn celebrating the Lord as the great and holy King in Zion. In developing his theme, the poet makes striking use of the symbolic significance (completeness) of the number seven: Seven times he speaks of the "LORD," and seven times he refers to Him by means of independent personal pronouns (Hebrew). (See introduction to Ps 93.) The form is symmetrical, with four stanzas of three (Hebrew) poetic lines and with each of the two main divisions concluded by the major refrain (vv. 5,9). The lesser refrain, "it/he is holy" (vv. 3,5, and expanded in v. 9), probably reflects a traditional threefold liturgical rubric (see Is 6:3; Rev 4:8; see also Ps 96:1–3,7–9 and notes for further evidence of a liturgical penchant for triple repetition). The second half of the psalm develops the theme introduced in the second stanza.

99:1–3 The God enthroned in Zion is ruler over all the nations—let them acknowledge him.

99:1 *The LORD reigneth.* See 93:1 and note. *tremble . . . be moved.* In reverent awe before God. *cherubims.* See 80:1; see also note on Ex 25:18.

3 Let them praise thy great and terrible
name;
For it *is* holy.

4 [a]The king's strength also loveth
judgment;
Thou dost establish equity,
Thou executest judgment and
righteousness in Jacob.
5 Exalt ye the LORD our God,
And worship at [a]his footstool;
For [b1]he *is* holy.

6 [a]Moses and Aaron among his priests,
And Samuel among them that call upon
his name;
They [b]called upon the LORD, and he
answered them.
7 [a]He spake unto them in the cloudy
pillar:
They kept his testimonies, and the
ordinance *that* he gave them.

8 Thou answeredst them, O LORD our
God:
[a]Thou wast a God that forgavest them,
Though [b]thou tookest vengeance of
their inventions.
9 [a]Exalt the LORD our God,
And worship at his holy hill;
For the LORD our God *is* holy.

99:4 [a]Job 36:5-7
99:5 [1]Or, *it is holy* [a]Ps. 132:7 [b]Lev. 19:2
99:6 [a]Jer. 15:1 [b]Ex. 14:15; 1 Sam. 7:9
99:7 [a]Ex. 33:9
99:8 [a]Num. 14:20 [b]Deut. 9:20
99:9 [a]Ps. 34:3

100:T [1]Or, *thanksgiving* [a]Ps. 145, title
100:1 [1]Heb. *all the earth* [a]Ps. 95:1
100:3 [1]Or, *and his we* are [a]Eph. 2:10 [b]Ezek. 34:31
100:4 [a]Ps. 116:17
100:5 [1]Heb. *to generation and generation* [a]Ps. 136:1 [b]Ps. 89:1

Psalm 100

[a]A Psalm of [1]praise.

1 Make [a]a joyful noise unto the LORD,
[1]all ye lands.
2 Serve the LORD with gladness:
Come before his presence with singing.
3 Know ye that the LORD he *is* God:
[a]*It is* he *that* hath made us, [1]and not
we ourselves;
[b]*We are* his people, and the sheep of
his pasture.
4 [a]Enter *into* his gates with thanksgiving,
And into his courts with praise:
Be thankful unto him, *and* bless his
name.
5 For the LORD *is* good; [a]his mercy *is*
everlasting;
And his truth *endureth* [b1]to all
generations.

Psalm 101

A Psalm of David.

1 I will sing of mercy and judgment: unto
thee, O LORD, will I sing.

---

‡99:3 *Let them praise.* As the Great King, He ought to be shown the fear (v. 1) and honor that are His due. *name.* See v. 6; see also note on 5:11. *it is holy.* Or "He is holy." See vv. 5,9; see also Introduction to Leviticus: Themes; note on Lev 11:44.

99:4–5 The Lord has shown the quality of His rule by what He has done for Israel.

‡99:4 See 103:6–12. *strength . . . loveth judgment.* Two chief characteristics of God's reign. God's absolute power is in harmony with His perfect justice. *establish equity.* As a (His) throne (see 9:7–8; 97:2; 2 Sam 7:13). *judgment and righteousness.* See 97:2. Though even the heavens proclaim God's righteousness (see 97:6 and note), it is in the whole complex of His saving acts in and for Israel that the "righteousness" of God's reign is especially disclosed (see 98:2 and note). *Jacob.* A synonym for Israel (see Gen 32:28).

99:5 See also v. 9. For other refrains in the Psalms see introduction to Ps 42–43. *footstool.* God's royal footstool (see 2 Chr 9:18), here a metaphor linking the heavenly throne with the earthly; when God sits on His heavenly throne, His earthly throne is His footstool (here "his holy hill," v. 9; see 132:7; 1 Chr 28:2; Lam 2:1).

99:6–7 In Israel the Lord provided priestly intermediaries, who (1) were appointed to intercede with Him on behalf of His faltering people (v. 6), and (2) were given knowledge of His will so they could instruct Israel.

99:6 *Moses . . . Aaron . . . Samuel.* These three no doubt serve here as representatives of all those the Lord used as intermediaries with His people in times of great crises. *priests . . . that call upon his name.* The priestly function of intercession is highlighted (see Ex 17:11 and note; 32:11–13,31–32; Num 14:13–19; 21:7; 1 Sam 7:5,8–9; 12:19,23; Jer 15:1). *answered them.* See v. 8; see also the Lord's responses to the intercessions referred to in note on vv. 6–7.

99:7 *spake unto them in the cloudy pillar.* Though reference may be to all Israel ("them"), more likely the hymn recalls God's speaking with Moses (see Ex 33:9) and Aaron (see Num 12:5–6). But that special mode of revelation in the wilderness may also be generalized here to include God's revelations to Samuel, who was called to his prophetic ministry at the sanctuary, "where the ark of God was" (1 Sam 3:3; see also 1 Sam 12:23). *They kept.* However imperfectly, it was in Israel that God's righteous statutes and decrees were kept because only in Israel had they been made known (see 147:19–20; Deut 4:5–8).

99:8–9 The justice and righteousness of God's rule in Israel (see v. 4) have been especially shown in the manner in which He has dealt with their sins (see Ex 34:6–7; see also note on 5:8).

99:9 *holy hill.* See v. 5 and note. *the LORD our God is holy.* Climactic expansion of the secondary refrain.

Ps 100 A call to praise the Lord. Whether or not it was composed for that purpose, the final editors of the Psalter here used it to close the series that begins with Ps 93. It has special affinity with 95:1–2,6–7; see also Ps 117. (See introduction to Ps 93.) The second main division (vv. 4–5) parallels the structure of the first (vv. 1–3), namely, a call to praise followed by a declaration of why the Lord is worthy of praise—the corresponding elements of the two divisions are complementary.

‡100 title *praise.* Grateful praise of thanksgiving (see v. 4; see also note on 75:1). Perhaps it indicates that the psalm was to accompany a thank offering (see Lev 7:12).

100:1 *all ye lands.* Though vv. 3,5 clearly speak of God's special relationship with Israel, the call to worship goes out to the whole world, which ought to acknowledge the Lord because of what He has done for His people (see also Ps 98–99; 117).

100:3 *Know.* Acknowledge. *made us.* See 95:6 and note. *not we ourselves.* Or "we are His." *sheep of his pasture.* See 95:7 and note.

100:4 *his gates.* The gates of the temple (see 24:7 and note). *courts.* Of the temple (see 84:2,10; 2 Ki 21:5; 23:11–12).

‡100:5 *the LORD is good.* In that His mercy and truth (see note on 36:5) are unfailing through all time (see 98:3 and note). *mercy.* See note on 6:4.

‡Ps 101 A king's pledge to reign righteously (see 2 Ki 23:3). If authored by David (see title), it may have been composed for

2 I will [a]behave myself wisely in a perfect way. O when wilt thou come unto me?
I will [b]walk within my house with a perfect heart.
3 I will set no [1]wicked thing before mine eyes:
[a]I hate the work of them [b]that turn aside; *it* shall not cleave to me.
4 A froward heart shall depart from me: I will not [a]know a wicked *person.*
5 Whoso privily slandereth his neighbour, him will I cut off:
[a]Him that hath a high look and a proud heart will not I suffer.
6 Mine eyes *shall be* upon the faithful of the land, that *they* may dwell with me:
He that walketh [1]in a perfect way, he shall serve me.
7 He that worketh deceit shall not dwell within my house:
He that telleth lies [1]shall not tarry in my sight.
8 I will [a]early destroy all the wicked of the land;
That *I* may cut off all wicked doers [b]from the city of the LORD.

101:2 [a]1 Sam. 18:14 [b]1 Ki. 11:4
101:3 [1]Heb. *thing of Belial* [a]Ps. 97:10 [b]Josh. 23:6
101:4 [a]Ps. 119:115
101:5 [a]Prov. 6:17
101:6 [1]Or, *perfect in the way*
101:7 [1]Heb. *shall not be established*
101:8 [a]Ps. 75:10; Jer. 21:12 [b]Ps. 48:2,8
102:T [1]Or, *for* [a]Ps. 61:2
102:1 [a]Ps. 18:6

Psalm 102

A Prayer [1]of the afflicted, [a]when he is overwhelmed, and poureth out his complaint before the LORD.

1 Hear my prayer, O LORD,
And let my cry [a]come unto thee.

Solomon's use at his coronation (see 1 Ki 2:2–4; see also 2 Sam 23:1–7 and introduction to Ps 72). Only Christ, the great Son of David, has perfectly fulfilled these commitments. In the final arrangement of the Psalter this psalm, together with Ps 110 (both relating to the king), frames the collection of ten psalms located between the preceding thematic group (Ps 92–100; see introduction to Ps 92) and that which follows (Ps 111–118; see introduction to Ps 111). This little psalter-within-the-Psalter is concentrically arranged: Ps 102 and 109 are individual prayers; Ps 103 and 108 praise the Lord for His "great . . . mercy" (103:11; 108:4) that reaches to the heavens; Ps 104, which celebrates God's many wise and benevolent acts in creation, and Ps 107, which celebrates God's "wonderful works" (107:8,15,21,24,31) for man through His lordship over creation, are complements; and so also are Ps 105, which recites the history of Israel's redemption, and Ps 106, which recites the same history as a history of Israel's rebellion. As a mini-Psalter, it includes most of the forms and themes found in the rest of the Psalter. Its outer frame is devoted to royal psalms and its center pair is devoted to recitals of Israel's history with God—with its themes ranging from creation and God's eternal enthronement to the covenant with Abraham, Isaac and Jacob, the exodus from Egypt and entrance into Canaan, the exile and restoration, and finally the ultimate triumph of the Lord's anointed. The collection bears a distinctive redemption-history stamp and evokes recollection of all the salient elements of the OT message. (For the problem of the Book division at Ps 107 see introduction to that psalm.)

Composed of seven (Hebrew) couplets (the number of completeness), the psalm begins with a twofold introduction (vv. 1–3a; see notes below), followed by an elaboration (vv. 3b–8) of the theme of the second couplet. The middle one (v. 6) speaks of the king's commitment to the "faithful," while the other four (vv. 3b–4, 5, 7, 8) declare His repudiation of all the "wicked" in the land. (See also notes below.) The middle couplet is linked with couplets one and two also by the catchword "perfect." (For centering in the Psalms see note on 6:6.)

101:1–2a Celebration of the pattern of God's reign, which the king makes the model for his own.

101:1 *mercy and judgment.* Two of the chief qualities of God's rule (see 6:4; 99:4 and notes).

‡101:2a *perfect.* Or "blameless," not implying sinless perfection. See vv. 2b,6; see also note on Gen 17:1. *when . . . ?* An urgent prayer for God to come and sustain in him his pledge (see 1 Ki 3:7–9; see also Ps 72).

101:2b–3a The essential commitment. *heart . . . eyes.* In OT understanding, a person follows the dictates of the heart—the inner man (see note on 4:7)—and/or the attractions of the eye—external influences (see 119:37; Judg 14:1–2; 2 Sam 11:2; 2 Ki 16:10; Job 31:1; Prov 4:25; 17:24). For the combination heart-eyes see v. 5; Num 15:39; Job 31:7; Prov 21:4; Eccl 2:10; Jer 22:17.

101:2b *house.* Royal administration (also in v. 7).

101:3a *wicked.* Belial (2 Cor 6:15) is derived from the Hebrew for this word (see note on Deut 13:13).

101:3b–4 A repudiation of evil deeds and those who promote them (see v. 7).

101:3b *them that turn aside.* Those who rebel against what is right (see Hos 5:2, "revolters").

‡101:4 *froward.* Or "perverse," the opposite of "perfect" (see 18:26; Prov 11:20; 19:1; 28:6). A froward heart and a deceitful tongue (see v. 7) are root and fruit (see Prov 17:20).

101:5 A pledge to remove from his presence all slanderous and all arrogant persons (see v. 8). *will I cut off.* See v. 8; 54:5; 94:23). *high look . . . proud heart.* See vv. 2b–3a and note; see also 131:1; Prov 21:4; Is 10:12. The arrogant tend to be ruthless (see Is 10:12) and are a law to themselves (see note on 31:23).

101:6 A pledge to surround himself in his reign with the faithful and blameless. *Mine eyes shall be upon.* I will look with favor on (see 33:18; 34:15). *the faithful.* Those who maintain moral integrity. *shall serve me.* Minister as my servant (see Ex 24:13), personal servant (Gen 39:4; 1 Ki 19:21), attendant (2 Ki 4:43), commanders and officials (1 Chr 27:1; 2 Chr 17:19; Prov 29:12).

101:7 A repudiation of all those who make their way by double-dealing (see vv. 3b–4).

101:8 A pledge to remove all the wicked from the Lord's kingdom (see v. 5). *I will early.* With diligence and persistence (see Jer 21:12; Zeph 3:5). It may have been traditional for kings to hear cases in the morning. *city of the LORD.* See Ps 46; 48; 87; see also note on 3:4.

Ps 102 The prayer of an individual in a time of great distress. It is also one of the traditional penitential psalms (see introduction to Ps 6). Some interpreters believe that the "I" of vv. 1–11,23–24 was originally communal (see note on Ps 30 title; see also note on title below). (See introduction to Ps 101.) The main body of the psalm (vv. 1–22) is developed in four themes (initial appeal for God to hear, vv. 1–2; description of distress, vv. 3–11; assurance that the Lord will surely hear, vv. 12–17; call for the Lord's certain deliverance to be recorded for His enduring praise, vv. 18–22), followed by a concluding recapitulation (vv. 23–28).

102 title Unique in the Psalter (no author named and no liturgical or historical notes), the title identifies only the life situation in which the prayer is to be used, and in accordance with vv. 1–11,23–24 it designates the prayer as that of an individual. But vv. 12–22,28 clearly indicate national involvement in

2 [a]Hide not thy face from me
In the day *when* I am in trouble;
[b]incline thine ear unto me:
In the day *when* I call answer me
speedily.
3 [a]For my days are consumed [1]like
smoke,
And [b]my bones are burnt as a hearth.
4 My heart is smitten, and [a]withered
like grass;
So that I forget to eat my bread.
5 By reason of the voice of my groaning
[a]my bones cleave to my [1]skin.
6 [a]I am like [b]a pelican of the wilderness:
I am like an owl of the desert.
7 I [a]watch, and am as a sparrow [b]alone
upon the housetop.
8 Mine enemies reproach me all the day;
And they that are [a]mad against me are
[b]sworn against me.
9 For I have eaten ashes like bread,
And [a]mingled my drink with weeping,
10 Because of thine indignation and thy
wrath:
For [a]thou hast lifted me up, and cast
me down.
11 [a]My days *are* like a shadow that
declineth;
And [b]I am withered like grass.

12 But [a]thou, O LORD, shalt endure for
ever;
And [b]thy remembrance unto all
generations.
13 Thou shalt arise, *and* [a]have mercy
upon Zion:
For the time to favour her, yea, the
[b]set time, is come.
14 For thy servants take pleasure in [a]her
stones,
And favour the dust thereof.
15 So the heathen shall [a]fear the name of
the LORD,
And all the kings of the earth thy glory.
16 When the LORD shall build up Zion,
[a]He shall appear in his glory.
17 [a]He will regard the prayer of the
destitute,
And not despise their prayer.
18 This shall be [a]written for the
generation to come:
And [b]the people which *shall be*
created shall praise the LORD.
19 For he hath [a]looked down from the
height of his sanctuary;
From heaven did the LORD behold the
earth;
20 [a]To hear the groaning of the prisoner;
To loose [1]those that are appointed to
death;
21 To [a]declare the name of the LORD in
Zion,
And his praise in Jerusalem;

102:2 [a]Ps. 69:17 [b]Ps. 71:2
102:3 [1]Or, (as some read) *into smoke* [a]Jas. 4:14 [b]Job 30:30; Ps. 31:10
102:4 [a]Ps. 37:2
102:5 [1]Or, *flesh* [a]Job 19:20
102:6 [a]Job 30:29 [b]Is. 34:11
102:7 [a]Ps. 77:4 [b]Ps. 38:11
102:8 [a]Acts 26:11 [b]Acts 23:12
102:9 [a]Ps. 42:3
102:10 [a]Ps. 30:7
102:11 [a]Eccl. 6:12 [b]Is. 40:6-8; Jas. 1:10
102:12 [a]Ps. 9:7
102:12 [b]Ps. 135:13
102:13 [a]Is. 60:10 [b]Is. 40:2
102:14 [a]Ps. 79:1
102:15 [a]1 Ki. 8:43
102:16 [a]Is. 60:1,2
102:17 [a]Neh. 1:6
102:18 [a]Rom. 15:4 [b]Ps. 22:31
102:19 [a]Deut. 26:15
102:20 [1]Heb. *the children of death* [a]Ps. 79:11
102:21 [a]Ps. 22:22

the calamity. It may be that the distress suffered by the individual, while its description suggests physical illness, is the result of his sharing in a national disaster such as the exile—a suggestion supported by references to the restoration of Zion. Because of the close relationship of the fortunes of king and nation and because of the many themes shared by this and some of the royal psalms, it has been plausibly suggested that the prayer was originally that of a Davidic king, or of a member of the Davidic royal house, while in Babylonian exile. *Prayer.* See vv. 1,17. *overwhelmed.* See 61:2; 77:3; 142:3; 143:4; see also 107:5; Jonah 2:7. *complaint.* See 64:1; 142:2; Job 7:13; 9:27; 10:1; 21:4.

102:1–2 Initial appeal for God to hear.

102:2 *Hide . . . thy face.* See note on 13:1.

102:3–11 The description of distress—a suffering so great that it withers body and spirit—brought on by a visitation of God's wrath (v. 10) and making him the mockery of his enemies (v. 8).

102:3 *my days.* His life wastes away—a lament that frames the whole stanza (see v. 11). *bones are burnt.* As if a fire is consuming his physical frame (see 31:10; 32:3; 42:10).

102:4 *heart.* See note on 4:7. Here "heart" is used in combination with "bones" (v. 3) to refer to the whole man (body and spirit); see 22:14; Prov 14:30; 15:30; Is 66:14; Jer 20:9; 23:9. *smitten.* Or "scorched" (by the hot sun); see 121:6. *withered.* See v. 11; see also note on 90:4–5.

102:6 *pelican . . . owl.* The owl was associated with wilderness areas and ruins (see Is 34:11,15; Jer 50:39; Zeph 2:14).

‡102:8 *enemies reproach me.* See 109:25; see also notes on 5:9; 39:8. *sworn against me.* Or "used my name as a curse." They say, "May you become like that one (the one named) is."

102:9 *drink . . . weeping.* For tears as food and drink see 42:3; 80:5.

102:10 *wrath.* See note on 2:5.

102:11 A concluding summation of vv. 3–4.

102:12–17 Assurance that the King eternal will surely hear the prayer of the destitute (v. 17) and restore Zion (see note on 3:8).

‡102:12 *shalt endure.* A central theme of the preceding collection (Ps 92–100). Because God reigns forever and remains the same (see v. 27), His mercies to those who look to Him for salvation will not fail. *remembrance.* Or God's "fame" or "renown." For elaborate celebrations of the Lord's renown see Ps 111; 135; 145.

‡102:13 This verse and v. 16 suggest that the psalmist's distress was occasioned by the Babylonian exile. *arise.* See note on 3:7. *set time.* The time set by God for judgment and deliverance (see 75:2; Ex 9:5; 2 Sam 24:15; Dan 11:27,35). Perhaps the psalmist is referring to the prophet Jeremiah's announcements that the the exile would last for a period of 70 years; see Jer 25:11–12; 29:10 and notes).

102:14 *thy servants take pleasure.* If Zion, the city of God (see 46:4; 48:1–2,8; 87:3; 101:8; 132:13), is so loved by the Lord's servants (see Ps 126; 137), how much more is she cherished by the Lord!

102:15 See note on 46:10. *name.* See note on 5:11.

102:18–22 Let God's certain deliverance of His people be recorded for His continual praise.

102:18 *written.* Only here does a psalmist call for memory to be sustained by a written record of God's saving act; usually oral transmission suffices (see 22:30; 44:1; 78:1–4). *created.* Brought into being by God's sovereign act (see 51:10; 104:30; 139:13).

102:20 *prisoner . . . those that are appointed to death.* Perhaps prisoners of war, but more likely the exiles in Babylon (see 79:11 and note).

102:21 *praise.* See note on 9:1.

22 When the people are gathered
together,
And the kingdoms, to serve the LORD.
23 He [1]weakened my strength in the way;
He [a]shortened my days.
24 [a]I said, O my God, take me not away
in the midst of my days:
[b]Thy years *are* throughout all
generations.
25 [a]Of old hast thou laid the foundation of
the earth:
And the heavens *are* the work of thy
hands.
26 [a]They shall perish, but thou shalt
[1]endure:
Yea, all of them shall wax old like a
garment;
As a vesture shalt thou change them,
and they shall be changed:
27 But [a]thou *art* the same,
And thy years shall have no end.
28 [a]The children of thy servants shall
continue,
And their seed shall be established
before thee.

Psalm 103

A Psalm of David.

1 Bless [a]the LORD, O my soul:
And all that is within me, *bless* his
holy name.
2 Bless the LORD, O my soul,
And forget not all his benefits:
3 [a]Who forgiveth all thine iniquities;
Who [b]healeth all thy diseases;
4 Who redeemeth thy life from
destruction;
[a]Who crowneth thee *with*
lovingkindness and tender mercies;
5 Who satisfieth thy mouth with good
things;
So that [a]thy youth is renewed like the
eagle's.
6 The LORD executeth righteousness
And judgment for all that are
oppressed.
7 [a]He made known his ways unto
Moses,
His acts unto the children of Israel.
8 [a]The LORD *is* merciful and gracious,
Slow to anger, and [1]plenteous in
mercy.
9 [a]He will not always chide:
Neither will he keep *his anger* for ever.
10 [a]He hath not dealt with us after our
sins;
Nor rewarded us according to our
iniquities.
11 For [1]as the heaven is high above the
earth,
So great is his mercy toward them that
fear him.
12 As far as the east is from the west,
So far hath he [a]removed our
transgressions from us.
13 [a]Like as a father pitieth *his* children,
So the LORD pitieth them that fear him.
14 For he knoweth our frame;

102:23 [1]Heb. *afflicted* [a]Job 21:21
102:24 [a]Is. 38:10 [b]Ps. 90:2
102:25 [a]Heb. 1:10
102:26 [1]Heb. *stand* [a]Is. 34:4
102:27 [a]Mal. 3:6; Heb. 13:8
102:28 [a]Ps. 69:36
103:1 [a]Ps. 104:1
103:3 [a]Ps. 130:8; Is. 33:24
103:3 [b]Ex. 15:26
103:4 [a]Ps. 5:12
103:5 [a]Is. 40:31
103:7 [a]Ps. 147:19
103:8 [1]Heb. *great of mercy* [a]Ex. 34:6,7
103:9 [a]Ps. 30:5
103:10 [a]Ezra 9:13
103:11 [1]Heb. *according to the height of the heaven*
103:12 [a]Is. 43:25
103:13 [a]Mal. 3:17

102:22 See note on 46:10; see also 47:9 and note; 96; 98; 100. The expectation here expressed may also be influenced by such prophecies as Is 2:2–4; Mic 4:1–3.

102:23–28 Concluding recapitulation.

102:23–24a See vv. 3–11.

102:24b–27 See v. 12 and note. For a NT application of vv. 25–27 to Christ see Heb 1:10–12 and note on Heb 1:10.

102:26 *like a garment.* With His first creation God clothed Himself with the manifestation of His glory (see 8:1,3–4; 19:1; 29:3–9; 104:1,31; Is 6:3; see also Job 38–41, especially 40:10). But He is more enduring than what He has made—and the first creation will give way to a new creation (see Is 65:17; 66:22).

102:28 Because the Lord does not change (see v. 27), Israel's future is secure (see Mal 3:6). *continue.* Or "dwell in the (promised) land" (see 69:36; see also 37:3,29; Is 65:9). *established before thee.* See 2 Sam 7:24.

Ps 103 A hymn to God's love and compassion toward His people. (See introduction to Ps 101.) Calls to praise frame the body of the hymn (vv. 1–2, 20–22) and set its tone. The recital of praise falls into two unequal parts: (1) a three-verse celebration of personal benefits received (vv. 3–5) and (2) a 14-verse recollection of God's mercies to His people Israel (vv. 6–19). The major thematic division (vv. 6–19) is composed of six couplets framed by vv. 6 and 19, which describe the general character of God's reign. Thematic development divides the six couplets into two equal parts (vv. 7–12, 13–18), of which the first celebrates God's compassion on His people as sinners while the second sings of His compassion on them as frail mortals. The two concluding couplets proclaim the vastness of His love (vv. 11–12) and its unending perseverance (vv. 17–18). As with the hymn found in Ps 33, the length of the psalm has been determined by the number of letters in the Hebrew alphabet (see introduction to Ps 33).

103:1–2 Call to praise, directed inward (cf. vv. 20–22).

103:1–2,22 *O my soul.* A conventional Hebrew way of addressing oneself (see 104:1,35; 116:7). *soul.* See note on 6:3.

103:3–5 Recital of personal blessings received.

‡103:4 *redeemeth.* A synonym for "delivers." *destruction.* Or "the pit," a metaphor for the grave (see note on 30:1). *lovingkindness and tender mercies.* The key words of the hymn (see vv. 8,11,13,17). *lovingkindness.* See vv. 8,11,17; see also note on 6:4.

103:5 *like the eagle's.* The vigor of youth is restored to match the proverbial unflagging strength of the eagle (see Is 40:31).

103:6–19 God's love and compassion toward His people.

103:6 Together with v. 19 (the other side of the literary frame) it characterizes the reign of God under which Israel has been so graciously blessed. *righteousness.* See v. 17; see also note on 5:8.

103:7–12 God's compassion on His people as sinners.

103:7–8 See 99:7; Ex 33:13; see also note on Ex 34:6–7.

103:7 *his ways.* See 25:10 and note.

103:9 *anger.* See note on 2:5.

103:11–12 The vastness of God's love is supremely shown in His forgiving Israel's sins.

103:11 See 36:5–9. *So great is.* So prevails. *them that fear him.* See vv. 13,17–18; see also 34:8–14 and note.

103:12 See Is 1:18; 38:17; 43:25; Jer 31:34; 50:20; Mic 7:18–19.

103:13–18 God's compassion on His people as frail mortals; perhaps echoed in Luke 1:50.

He remembereth that we *are* [a]dust.
15 *As for* man, [a]his days *are* as grass:
[b]As a flower of the field, so he flourisheth.
16 For the wind passeth over it, and [1]it is gone;
And [a]the place thereof shall know it no more.
17 But the mercy of the LORD *is* from everlasting to everlasting upon them that fear him,
And his righteousness unto children's children;
18 [a]To such as keep his covenant,
And to those that remember his commandments to do them.

19 The LORD hath prepared his throne in the heavens;
And [a]his kingdom ruleth over all.
20 [a]Bless the LORD, ye his angels,
[1]That excel in strength, that [b]do his commandments,
Hearkening unto the voice of his word.
21 Bless ye the LORD, all ye [a]his hosts;
[b]Ye ministers of his, that do his pleasure.
22 Bless the LORD, all his works
In all places of his dominion:
Bless the LORD, O my soul.

103:14 [a]Eccl. 12:7
103:15 [a]1 Pet. 1:24 [b]Job 14:1,2
103:16 [1]Heb. *it is not* [a]Job 7:10
103:18 [a]Deut. 7:9
103:19 [a]Ps. 47:2; Dan. 4:25
103:20 [1]Heb. *Mighty in strength* [a]Ps. 148:2 [b]Mat. 6:10
103:21 [a]Gen. 32:2 [b]Heb. 1:14

104:1 [a]Ps. 103:1
104:2 [a]Dan. 7:9 [b]Is. 40:22
104:3 [a]Amos 9:6 [b]Is. 19:1 [c]Ps. 18:10
104:4 [a]Heb. 1:7
104:5 [1]Heb. *He hath founded the earth upon her bases* [a]Job 26:7
104:6 [a]Gen. 7:19
104:8 [1]Or, *The mountains ascend, the valleys descend* [a]Gen. 8:5

Psalm 104

1 Bless [a]the LORD, O my soul.
O LORD my God, thou art very great;
Thou art clothed with honour and majesty.
2 [a]Who coverest *thyself with* light as *with* a garment:
[b]Who stretchest out the heavens like a curtain:
3 [a]Who layeth the beams of his chambers in the waters:
[b]Who maketh the clouds his chariot:
[c]Who walketh upon the wings of the wind:
4 [a]Who maketh his angels spirits;
His ministers a flaming fire:
5 [a][1]*Who* laid the foundations of the earth,
That it should not be removed for ever.
6 [a]Thou coveredst it *with* the deep as *with* a garment:
The waters stood above the mountains.
7 At thy rebuke they fled;
At the voice of thy thunder they hasted away.
8 [a][1]They go up *by* the mountains; they go down *by* the valleys
Unto the place which thou hast founded for them.

103:14 *we are dust.* See note on 78:39.
103:17 The infinite span of God's love overarches man's little time (see v. 11). *unto children's children.* See note on 109:12.
103:19 See v. 6 and note; see also 9:4,7; 11:4; 47:2,7–8; 123:1.
103:20–22 Concluding call to praise, directed to all creatures (cf. vv. 1–2). A call to praise is often the climax of praise in the Psalter (as also of the whole collection; see Ps 148–150). See note on 9:1. *Bless . . . Bless . . . Bless.* See note on 96:1–3 (the final line was probably added by the editors of the Psalter; see 104:1,35).
103:20 *that do his commandments.* See 91:11; Heb 1:14.
‡103:21 *his hosts.* Uniquely here and in 148:2 the Hebrew for "hosts" is masculine, and in both places the "hosts" are associated with "angels." *Ye ministers of his.* See notes on 101:6 and 104:4.
103:22 *all his works.* See 65:13; 96:11–12 and notes.
Ps 104 A hymn to the Creator. Obviously influenced by Gen 1, the preexilic author has adapted that account to his different purpose and has subordinated its sequence somewhat to his own design (see next paragraph). Whereas Gen 1 recounts creation as God's first work at the beginning, the poet views the creation displayed before his eyes and sings the glory of its Maker and Sustainer. Surprisingly, he only hints at the angelic world (v. 4) and mentions man only in passing (vv. 14,23); his theme is the visible creation around him, which he views as the radiant and stately robe with which the invisible Creator has clothed Himself to display His glory. (See introduction to Ps 101.)
Following his one-verse introduction, the poet designed the main body of his poem concentrically, with stanzas in Hebrew of three-five-nine-five-three verses. The first stanza speaks of the celestial realm (vv. 2–4) and the fifth of the nautical (vv. 24–26)—the two realms that bracket the "earth" of his experience. The second sings of the earth's solid foundations and secure boundaries (vv. 5–9) and the fourth of the orderly cycles of life on earth governed by sun and moon (vv. 19–23). At the center an eight-verse stanza celebrates the luxuriation of life in the earth (vv. 10–18). To the poem's main body he added a four-verse stanza that recites how God maintains life on earth (vv. 27–30), a two-verse conclusion (vv. 31–32—which together with v. 1 frames the whole), and a three-verse epilogue (vv. 33–35). The outer frame ("Bless the LORD, O my soul") was probably added by the editors of the Psalter when they inserted the Book division after Ps 106—thus concluding Book 4 with doxologies (see the liturgical frames added to Ps 105–106 and the similar conclusion to Book 5: Ps 146–150).
104:1 Introduction: the theme of the hymn. *clothed.* See note on 102:26.
104:2–4 The celestial realm.
104:2 *light.* Cf. the first day of creation in Gen 1. *heavens.* Cf. the second day of creation in Gen 1. *like a curtain.* Over the earth and the luminaries that give it light.
‡104:3 *his chambers.* Vivid imagery for the heavenly abode of God (see v. 13). In the singular, the Hebrew for this phrase usually refers to the upper-level room of a house (as in 1 Ki 17:19; 2 Ki 1:2). *waters.* The waters above the "curtain" (v. 2; see Gen 1:7), from which, in the imagery of the OT, God gives the rain (see v. 13; see also 36:8 and note). *clouds his chariot.* See 18:7–15; 68:4; 77:16–19 and notes.
‡104:4 *spirits . . . flaming fire.* Or "winds . . . flaming fire." The winds and lightning bolts of the thunderstorm are here personified as the agents of God's purposes (see 148:8; cf. 103:21).
104:5–9 The earth realm made secure (vv. 5,9 frame the stanza, highlighting its two main themes).
104:5 *foundations.* See 24:2 and note. *earth.* Land in distinction from sky and seas, not the earth as a planet (see Gen 1:10). *it should not be removed for ever.* Firmly founded (see 93:1; 96:10), it will not give way (cf. v. 9).
104:7 *rebuke.* See note on 76:6. *they fled.* Cf. the third day of creation in Gen 1.

9 [a]Thou hast set a bound *that* they may
not pass over;
[b]*That* they turn not again to cover the
earth.
10 [1]He sendeth the springs into the
valleys,
Which [2]run among the hills.
11 They give drink to every beast of the
field:
The wild asses [1]quench their thirst.
12 By them shall the fowls of the heaven
have their habitation,
Which [1]sing among the branches.
13 [a]He watereth the hills from his
chambers:
The earth is satisfied with [b]the fruit of
thy works.
14 [a]He causeth the grass to grow for the
cattle,
And herb for the service of man:
That *he* may bring forth [b]food out of
the earth;
15 And [a]wine *that* maketh glad the heart
of man,
And [1]oil to make *his* face to shine,
And bread *which* strengtheneth man's
heart.
16 The trees of the LORD are full *of sap;*
The cedars of Lebanon, which he hath
planted;
17 Where the birds make their nests:
As for the stork, the fir trees *are* her
house.
18 The high hills *are* a refuge for the wild
goats;
And the rocks for the conies.
19 [a]He appointed the moon for seasons:
The sun knoweth his going down.
20 [a]Thou makest darkness, and it is night:
Wherein [1]all the beasts of the forest do
creep *forth.*
21 [a]The young lions roar after *their* prey,
And seek their meat from God.

104:9 [a]Job 26:10 [b]Gen. 9:11
104:10 [1]Heb. *Who sendeth* [2]Heb. *walk*
104:11 [1]Heb. *break*
104:12 [1]Heb. *give a voice*
104:13 [a]Ps. 147:8 [b]Jer. 10:13
104:14 [a]Gen. 1:29 [b]Job 28:5; Ps. 136:25
104:15 [1]Heb. *to make* his *face shine with oil,* or, *more than oil* [a]Judg. 9:13
104:19 [a]Gen. 1:14
104:20 [1]Heb. *all the beasts thereof do trample on the forest* [a]Is. 45:7
104:21 [a]Job 38:39
104:23 [a]Gen. 3:19
104:24 [a]Prov. 3:19
104:26 [1]Heb. *formed* [a]Job 41:1
104:27 [a]Ps. 136:25
104:29 [a]Job 34:15; Eccl. 12:7
104:30 [a]Is. 32:15; Ezek. 37:9
104:31 [1]Heb. *shall be* [a]Gen. 1:31
104:32 [a]Hab. 3:10 [b]Ps. 144:5
104:33 [a]Ps. 63:4

22 The sun ariseth, they gather
themselves together,
And lay them down in their dens.
23 Man goeth forth unto [a]his work
And to his labour until the evening.
24 [a]O LORD, how manifold are thy works!
In wisdom hast thou made them all:
The earth is full *of* thy riches.
25 *So is* this great and wide sea,
Wherein *are* things creeping
innumerable,
Both small and great beasts.
26 There go the ships:
There is that [a]leviathan, *whom* thou
hast [1]made to play therein.
27 [a]These wait all upon thee;
That *thou* mayest give *them* their meat
in due season.
28 *That* thou givest them they gather:
Thou openest thine hand, they are
filled *with* good.
29 Thou hidest thy face, they are troubled:
[a]Thou takest away their breath, they
die,
And return to their dust.
30 [a]Thou sendest forth thy spirit, they are
created:
And thou renewest the face of the
earth.
31 The glory of the LORD [1]shall endure for
ever:
The LORD [a]shall rejoice in his works.
32 He looketh on the earth, and it
[a]trembleth:
[b]He toucheth the hills, and they
smoke.
33 [a]I will sing unto the LORD as long as I
live:
I will sing *praise* to my God while I
have my being.
34 My meditation of him shall be sweet:
I will be glad in the LORD.

---

‡104:9 *set a bound.* God has placed boundaries so that the land ("earth") will never be overwhelmed by the sea (cf. v. 5; see 33:7 and note; see also Gen 9:15).
104:10–18 The earth a flourishing garden of life—the center of the psalm and the focal point of the author's contemplation of the creation (the earth, bounded by sky, vv. 2–4, and sea, vv. 24–26). Cf. the third and sixth days of creation in Gen 1.
104:10–12 The gift of water from below—watering the ravines of the Negev.
104:13–15 The gift of water from above—watering the uplands of Israel with their cultivated fields.
104:13 *his chambers.* See v. 3 and note.
104:15 *heart . . . heart.* See note on 4:7. *oil.* Olive oil. *make his face to shine.* As food (see 1 Ki 17:12), causing man's face to glow with health, and/or as cosmetic (see Esth 2:12).
104:16–18 Well-watered Lebanon, with its great trees, its hordes of birds and its alpine animals, the very epitome of God's earthly parkland (see 72:16; 2 Ki 14:9; 19:23; Is 10:34; 35:2; 40:16; 60:13; Jer 22:6; Hos 14:7).
104:19–23 The orderly cycles of life on earth, governed by the moon and sun. Cf. the fourth day of creation in Gen 1.
104:21,23 *lions . . . Man.* The one (representing the animal world), lord of the night; the other, lord of the day.
104:24–26 The nautical realm. Cf. the fifth day of creation in Gen 1. The realm of the sea is structurally balanced with the celestial realm (vv. 2–4) as the other boundary to the realm of earth.
104:24 A pause to recapitulate before treating the sea.
‡104:25 *creeping.* Or "swarming." See Gen 1:20–21.
104:26 *leviathan.* That fearsome mythological monster of the deep (see Job 3:8 and note) is merely God's harmless pet playing in the ocean.
104:27–30 By God's benevolent care this zoological garden flourishes. Cf. the sixth day of creation in Gen 1.
104:29 *hidest thy face.* See note on 13:1.
104:30 *created.* See note on 102:18.
104:31 *glory of the LORD.* Such as is displayed in His creation.
104:32 He is so much greater than His creation that with a look or a touch He could undo it.
104:33–35 Pious epilogue.
104:33 A vow to praise—here attached to a hymn of praise (see note on 7:17).
104:34 *My meditation.* The preceding hymn (see 19:14 and note).

35 Let [a]the sinners be consumed out of
the earth,
And let the wicked be no more.
Bless thou the LORD, O my soul.
Praise ye the LORD.

Psalm 105

1 [a]O give thanks unto the LORD; call
upon his name:
[b]Make known his deeds among the
people.
2 Sing unto him, sing psalms unto him:
[a]Talk ye of all his wondrous works.
3 Glory ye in his holy name:
Let the heart of them rejoice that seek
the LORD.
4 Seek the LORD, and his strength:
[a]Seek his face evermore.
5 [a]Remember his marvellous works that
he hath done;
His wonders, and the judgments of his
mouth;
6 O ye seed of Abraham his servant,
Ye children of Jacob, his chosen.
7 He *is* the LORD our God:
[a]His judgments *are* in all the earth.
8 He hath [a]remembered his covenant for
ever,
The word *which* he commanded to a
thousand generations.
9 [a]Which *covenant* he made with
Abraham,
And his oath unto Isaac;
10 And confirmed the same unto Jacob for
a law,
And to Israel *for* an everlasting
covenant:
11 Saying, [a]Unto thee will I give the land
of Canaan,
[1]The lot of your inheritance:
12 [a]When they were *but a few* men in
number;
Yea, *very* few, [b]and strangers in it.
13 When they went from one nation to
another,
From *one* kingdom to another people;
14 [a]He suffered no man to do them wrong:
Yea, [b]he reproved kings for their sakes;
15 *Saying,* Touch not mine anointed,
And do my prophets no harm.
16 Moreover, [a]he called *for* a famine upon
the land:
He brake the whole [b]staff of bread.
17 [a]He sent a man before them,
Even Joseph, *who* [b]was sold for a
servant:
18 [a]Whose feet they hurt with fetters:
[1]He was laid *in* iron:
19 Until the time that his word came:
[a]The word of the LORD tried him.
20 [a]The king sent and loosed him;
Even the ruler of the people, and let
him go free.
21 [a]He made him lord of his house,
And ruler of all his [1]substance:
22 To bind his princes at his pleasure;
And teach his senators wisdom.

104:35 [a]Ps. 37:38; Prov. 2:22
105:1 [a]1 Chr. 16:8; Is. 12:4 [b]Ps. 145:5
105:2 [a]Ps. 119:27
105:4 [a]Ps. 27:8
105:5 [a]Ps. 77:11
105:7 [a]Is. 26:9
105:8 [a]Luke 1:72
105:9 [a]Gen. 17:2; 22:16
105:11 [1]Heb. *The cord* [a]Gen. 13:15; 15:18
105:12 [a]Gen. 34:30; Deut. 7:7 [b]Heb. 11:9
105:14 [a]Gen. 35:5 [b]Gen. 12:17
105:16 [a]Gen. 41:54 [b]Lev. 26:26; Is. 3:1
105:17 [a]Gen. 45:5 [b]Gen. 37:28
105:18 [1]Heb. *His soul came into iron* [a]Gen. 40:15
105:19 [a]Gen. 41:25
105:20 [a]Gen. 41:14
105:21 [1]Heb. *possession* [a]Gen. 41:40

104:35 May the earth be purged of that which alone mars it (cf. Rev 21:27).

Ps 105 An exhortation to Israel to worship and trust in the Lord because of all His saving acts in fulfillment of His covenant with Abraham to give his descendants the land of Canaan. It was composed to be addressed to Israel by a Levite (see 1 Chr 16:7 and compare vv. 1–15 with 1 Chr 16:8–22) on one of her annual religious festivals (see chart, p. 166), possibly the feast of tabernacles (see Lev 23:34) but more likely the feast of weeks (see Ex 23:16; Lev 23:15–21; Num 28:26; Deut 16:9–12; see also Deut 26:1–11). For other recitals of the same history (but for different purposes) see Ps 78; 106; Josh 24:2–13; Neh 9:7–25.

The introduction is composed of seven verses in two parts: (1) an exhortation (with ten imperatives) to worship the Lord (vv. 1–4); (2) a call to remember what the Lord has done (vv. 5–7). The main body that follows is framed by two four-verse groupings (vv. 8–11, 42–45) that summarize—as introduction and conclusion—its main theme: The Lord has remembered His covenant with Abraham.

105:1–4 The exhortation to worship and trust.

105:1 *give thanks.* Through praise (see note on Ps 100 title). *call upon.* In prayer (see v. 4). The first two imperatives highlight the two themes of the ten imperatives of the exhortation: praise and prayer as expressions of devotion to the Lord (celebration of His past saving acts; trust in Him for future deliverance and blessing). *his name.* See v. 3; see also note on 5:11. *Make known . . . among the people.* As an integral part of praise (see note on 9:1).

‡105:2 *wondrous works.* See note on 9:1.

105:3,25 *heart.* See note on 4:7.

105:5–7 Exhortation to remember God's saving acts.

105:5 *Remember.* As a motivation for and focus of worship and the basis for trust—remember how the Lord has remembered (see vv. 8–11). *judgments.* See v. 7; see also notes on 48:11; 97:8. *of his mouth.* As Lord, He commands and it is done.

105:8–11 The Lord remembers His covenant with Abraham (see vv. 42–45).

105:8 *covenant.* The promissory covenant of Gen 15:9–21. This verse and v. 9 may be echoed in Luke 1:72–73. *thousand generations.* See Ex 20:6; Deut 7:9; 1 Chr 16:15.

105:10 *for a law.* As a fixed policy governing His future actions (see note on v. 45).

105:12–41 A recital of God's saving acts in Israel's behalf from the granting of the covenant (see v. 11; Gen 15:9–20) to its fulfillment (see v. 44; Josh 21:43). Cf. the recital prescribed by Moses in conjunction with the offering of firstfruits (Deut 26:1–11).

105:14–15 See Gen 20:2–7; see also note on Gen 20:7.

‡105:16 *brake the whole staff of bread.* Destroyed the food supply.

105:18 *fetters . . . iron.* That is, shackles of iron (see 149:8; see also note on 3:7). The poet takes the freedom to use a later conventional description of prisoners (see Job 13:27; 33:11). (Shackles are not spoken of in Gen 39:20–23, and iron came into common use for them at a later time—earlier shackles were made of bronze; see Judg 16:21.)

‡105:22 *bind.* Govern or control. He who was himself (v. 18; Hebrew *nephesh*) put in fetters was given authority to "bind" Pharaoh's princes "at his pleasure" (Hebrew "with his *nephesh*"—here meaning his will). *senators.* Or "elders," Pharaoh's counselors, conventionally older men of wide experience and learning (see note on Ex 3:16).

23 [a]Israel also came *into* Egypt;
And Jacob sojourned [b]in the land of
Ham.
24 And [a]he increased his people greatly;
And made them stronger than their
enemies.
25 [a]He turned their heart to hate his
people,
To deal subtilly with his servants.
26 [a]He sent Moses his servant;
And Aaron whom he had chosen.
27 [a]They shewed [1]his signs among them,
[b]And wonders in the land of Ham.
28 [a]He sent darkness, and made it dark;
And [b]they rebelled not against his
word.
29 [a]He turned their waters into blood,
And slew their fish.
30 [a]Their land brought forth frogs in
abundance,
In the chambers of their kings.
31 [a]He spake, and there came divers sorts
of flies,
And lice in all their coasts.
32 [a] [1]He gave them hail *for* rain,
And flaming fire in their land.
33 [a]He smote their vines also and their fig
trees;
And brake the trees of their coasts.
34 [a]He spake, and the locusts came,
And caterpillars, and that without
number,
35 And did eat up all the herbs in their
land,
And devoured the fruit of their ground.
36 [a]He smote also all the firstborn in their
land,
[b]The chief of all their strength.
37 [a]He brought them forth also with silver
and gold:
And *there was* not *one* feeble *person*
among their tribes.
38 [a]Egypt was glad when they departed:
For the fear of them that fell upon them.
39 [a]He spread a cloud for a covering;
And fire to give light in the night.
40 [a]*The people* asked, and he brought
quails,
And [b]satisfied them *with* the bread of
heaven.
41 [a]He opened the rock, and the waters
gushed out;
They ran in the dry *places like* a river.
42 For he remembered [a]his holy promise,
And Abraham his servant.
43 And he brought forth his people with
joy,
And his chosen with [1]gladness:
44 [a]And gave them the lands of the
heathen:
And they inherited the labour of the
people;
45 [a]That they might observe his statutes,
And keep his laws.
[1]Praise ye the LORD.

Psalm 106

1 [1]Praise ye the LORD.
[a]O give thanks unto the LORD; for *he is*
good:

105:23 [a]Gen. 46:6 [b]Ps. 78:51
105:24 [a]Ex. 1:7
105:25 [a]Ex. 1:8
105:26 [a]Ex. 3:10
105:27 [1]Heb. *words of his signs* [a]Ex. 7-12 [b]Ps. 106:22
105:28 [a]Ex. 10:22 [b]Ps. 99:7
105:29 [a]Ex. 7:20; Ps. 78:44
105:30 [a]Ex. 8:6; Ps. 78:45
105:31 [a]Ex. 8:17; Ps. 78:45
105:32 [1]Heb. *He gave their rain, hail* [a]Ex. 9:23; Ps. 78:48
105:33 [a]Ps. 78:47
105:34 [a]Ex. 10:4; Ps. 78:46
105:36 [a]Ex. 12:29; Ps. 78:51 [b]Gen. 49:3
105:37 [a]Ex. 12:35
105:38 [a]Ex. 12:33
105:39 [a]Ex. 13:21; Neh. 9:12
105:40 [a]Ex. 16:12; Ps. 78:18 [b]Ps. 78:24
105:41 [a]Ex. 17:6; Ps. 78:15; 1 Cor. 10:4
105:42 [a]Gen. 15:14
105:43 [1]Heb. *singing*
105:44 [a]Josh. 13:7
105:45 [1][Heb. *Hallelujah*] [a]Deut. 4:1; 6:21-25
106:1 [1]Heb. *Hallelujah* [a]1 Chr. 16:34

105:23,27 *land of Ham.* See 78:51 and note.

105:25 *turned.* In OT perspective God's sovereign control over Israel's destiny is so complete that it governs—mysteriously—even the evil that men commit against her; hence the bold language used here (see Ex 4:21; 7:3; Josh 11:20; 2 Sam 24:1; Is 10:5–7; 37:26–27; Jer 34:22).

105:26,42 *servant.* See 78:70 and note.

105:28–36 Recital of the plagues against Egypt. In this poetic recollection seven plagues (symbolizing completeness) represent the ten plagues of Ex 7–11. Apart from omissions (the plagues of livestock disease and boils) the poet follows the order of Exodus except that he combines the third and fourth plagues (lice and flies)—in reverse order—to stay within the number seven. He also places the ninth plague (darkness) first in order to frame his recital with mention of the two plagues that climaxed the series.

‡105:34 *caterpillars.* Or "locusts," parallel to "locusts" in the preceding line.

105:39 *for a covering.* Elsewhere it is said that the cloud (symbolic of God's presence) served (1) as a guide for Israel in her wilderness journeys (see 78:14; Ex 13:21; Num 9:17; Neh 9:12,19), (2) as a shield of darkness to protect Israel from the pursuing Egyptians (see Ex 14:19–20) and (3) as a covering for the fiery manifestations of God's glorious presence (see Ex 16:10; 24:16; 34:5; 40:34–35,38; Num 11:25; 12:5; 16:42; Deut 31:15; 1 Ki 8:11). The psalmist appears to highlight yet another function: God's protective cover over His people in the wilderness, perhaps as His shading "wings" (17:8; see note there), so that the sun would not harm them by day (see 121:5–6).

105:40 *bread of heaven.* See 78:24–25 and notes.

105:41 *like a river.* Poetically heightened imagery to evoke due wonder for the event. This miracle of the wilderness wanderings concludes the recital and has been placed in climactic position as one of the most striking manifestations of God's redeeming power and benevolence (see 114:8; Is 43:19–20; cf. Is 50:2).

105:42–45 Concluding summary (balancing the introduction to the recital: vv. 8–11).

105:44 *gave them the lands.* See v. 11.

‡105:45 *statutes.* God has kept His "law" (v. 10) so that Israel might keep His "statutes"—the Hebrew word is the same (see note on v. 5: "Remember"). God's redemptive working in fulfillment of His covenant promise has as its goal the creating of a people in the earth who conform their lives to His holy will. Thus the list of appropriate responses begun in v. 1—praise and prayer (trust)—is completed by the third: obedience (see Gen 18:19).

‡Ps 106 A confession of Israel's long history of rebellion and a prayer for God to once again save His people. In length, poetic style and shared themes it has much affinity with Ps 105 even while it contrasts with it by reciting the past as a history of rebellion (see Ps 78; Neh 9:5–37). It was most likely authored by a Levite in Jerusalem sometime after the return of some of the exiles. The first verse and the last two verses seem to have been taken over from an earlier composition (see 1 Chr 16:34–36). These may have been added, along with the "Praise ye the Lord" (Hebrew *Hallelu Yah*), by the editors of the Psalter (borrowing from an earlier Davidic psalter) when they set the Book divisions between Ps 106 and 107. (See introduction to Ps 101.)

Apart from the fact that the psalm has an introduction (vv.

For his mercy *endureth* for ever.
2 Who can utter the mighty acts of the LORD?
Who can shew forth all his praise?
3 Blessed *are* they that keep judgment,
And he that [a]doeth righteousness at [b]all times.
4 [a]Remember me, O LORD, with the favour *that thou bearest* unto thy people:
O visit me with thy salvation;
5 That *I* may see the good of thy chosen,
That *I* may rejoice in the gladness of thy nation,
That *I* may glory with thine inheritance.
6 [a]We have sinned with our fathers,
We have committed iniquity, we have done wickedly.
7 Our fathers understood not thy wonders in Egypt;
They remembered not the multitude of thy mercies;
[a]But provoked *him* at the sea, *even* at the Red sea.
8 Nevertheless he saved them for his name's sake,
[a]That *he* might make his mighty power to be known.
9 [a]He rebuked the Red sea also, and it was dried up:
So [b]he led them through the depths, as *through* the wilderness.
10 And he [a]saved them from the hand of him that hated *them,*
And redeemed them from the hand of the enemy.
11 [a]And the waters covered their enemies:
There was not one of them left.
12 [a]Then believed they his words;
They sang his praise.

106:3 [a]Ps. 15:2 [b]Gal. 6:9
106:4 [a]Ps. 119:132
106:6 [a]Dan. 9:5
106:7 [a]Ex. 14:11
106:8 [a]Ex. 9:16
106:9 [a]Ex. 14:21; Ps. 18:15; Nah. 1:4 [b]Is. 63:11
106:10 [a]Ex. 14:30
106:11 [a]Ex. 14:27
106:12 [a]Ex. 15:1
106:13 [1]Heb. *They made haste, they forgat* [a]Ex. 15:24
106:14 [1]Heb. *lusted a lust* [a]1 Cor. 10:6
106:15 [a]Num. 11:31 [b]Is. 10:16
106:16 [a]Num. 16:1
106:17 [a]Deut. 11:6
106:18 [a]Num. 16:35,46
106:19 [a]Ex. 32:4
106:20 [a]Jer. 2:11; Rom. 1:23
106:21 [a]Ps. 78:11
106:22 [a]Ps. 78:51
106:23 [a]Ex. 32:10; Deut. 9:19 [b]Ezek. 22:30
106:24 [1]Heb. *a land of desire* [a]Deut. 8:7; Ezek. 20:6 [b]Heb. 3:18
106:25 [a]Num. 14:2
106:26 [1]Heb. *To make them fall* [a]Ezek. 20:15 [b]Num. 14:29
106:27 [1]Heb. *To make them fall* [a]Lev. 26:33

13 [a][1]They soon forgat his works;
They waited not for his counsel:
14 [a]But [1]lusted exceedingly in the wilderness,
And tempted God in the desert.
15 [a]And he gave them their request;
But [b]sent leanness into their soul.
16 [a]They envied Moses also in the camp,
And Aaron the saint of the LORD.
17 [a]The earth opened and swallowed up Dathan,
And covered the company of Abiram.
18 [a]And a fire was kindled in their company;
The flame burnt up the wicked.
19 [a]They made a calf in Horeb,
And worshipped the molten image.
20 Thus [a]they changed their glory
Into the similitude of an ox that eateth grass.
21 They [a]forgat God their saviour,
Which had done great *things* in Egypt;
22 Wondrous works in [a]the land of Ham,
And terrible *things* by the Red sea.
23 [a]Therefore he said that *he* would destroy them,
Had not Moses his chosen [b]stood before him in the breach,
To turn away his wrath, lest *he* should destroy *them.*
24 Yea, they despised [a][1]the pleasant land,
They [b]believed not his word:
25 [a]But murmured in their tents,
And hearkened not unto the voice of the LORD.
26 [a]Therefore he lifted up his hand against them,
[b][1]To overthrow them in the wilderness:
27 [a][1]To overthrow their seed also among the nations,
And to scatter them in the lands.

1–5) and a (composite) conclusion (vv. 44–48), the recital character of its main theme (as in Ps 105) controls its basic outline. Beginning with the events at the Red sea (vv. 6–12), the psalm next narrates at length Israel's many rebellions during the wilderness wanderings (vv. 13–33), follows with a summary description of Israel's apostasy in the promised land (vv. 34–39) and completes its recital with a general statement of God's stern measures in the promised land (vv. 40–43).

106:1–5 Introduction.

106:1 *give thanks.* With praise (see note on Ps 100 title); a conventional liturgical call to praise (see 107:1; 118:1,29; 136:1–3). *mercy.* See note on 6:4.

106:2 *Who can . . . ?* With integrity. *his praise.* Praise for His mighty acts (see v. 47; see also note on 9:1).

‡106:3 *Blessed.* See note on 1:1. *judgment . . . righteousness.* That is, judgment (justice)-and-righteousness (see 36:6 and note; see also note on 3:7). This verse answers the question posed in v. 2.

‡106:4 *Remember me.* As one committed to the way of life described in v. 3. *with the favour.* See vv. 44–46. *with thy salvation.* The psalmist prays that God will include him in "the multitude of his mercies" (v. 45), which He shows to His people. Thus the inner logic of the prayer seems to be completed at v. 46. The editors of the Psalter appear to have converted an individual prayer into a communal one by their additions (see introduction).

106:5 *good . . . rejoice . . . glory.* A progressive sequence of cause and effect. *thine inheritance.* See v. 40.

106:6–43 Israel's history of rebellion.

106:6 A general confession of sin introducing the recital. *We.* The author identifies himself with Israel in her rebellion even as he prays for inclusion in God's mercies toward His people (see Ezra 9:6–7).

106:7 *wonders.* For example, the plagues against Egypt (see note on 9:1).

106:10 *redeemed.* Here, as often, a synonym for "delivered."

106:13 *his counsel.* The working out of His plan.

106:16–18 See Num 16:1–35.

106:19 *Horeb.* See note on Ex 3:1.

106:20 *glory.* Glorious One (see 1 Sam 15:29; Jer 2:11).

106:22 *land of Ham.* See 78:51 and note.

106:23 *stood before him in the breach.* See Ex 32:11–14,31–32. *wrath.* See note on 2:5.

106:24 *pleasant land.* So described in Jer 3:19; 12:10; Zech 7:14; see also Deut 8:7–9; Ezek 20:6.

‡106:26–27 *overthrow them.* See note on 13:4 ("moved").

28 [a]They joined themselves also unto
Baal-peor,
And ate the sacrifices of the dead.
29 Thus they provoked *him* to anger with
their inventions:
And the plague brake in upon them.
30 [a]Then stood up Phinehas, and
executed judgment:
And *so* the plague was stayed.
31 And *that* was counted unto him [a]for
righteousness
Unto all generations for evermore.
32 [a]They angered *him* also at the waters
of strife,
So that it went ill with Moses for their
sakes:
33 [a]Because they provoked his spirit,
So that he spake unadvisedly with his
lips.
34 [a]They did not destroy the nations,
[b]*Concerning* whom the LORD
commanded them:
35 [a]But were mingled among the heathen,
And learned their works.
36 And [a]they served their idols:
[b]Which were a snare unto them.
37 Yea, [a]they sacrificed their sons
And their daughters unto [b]devils,
38 And shed innocent blood,
Even the blood of their sons and of
their daughters,
Whom they sacrificed unto the idols of
Canaan:
And [a]the land was polluted with blood.
39 Thus were they [a]defiled with their
own works,
And [b]went a whoring with their own
inventions.
40 Therefore [a]was the wrath of the LORD
kindled against his people,
Insomuch that he abhorred [b]his own
inheritance.
41 And [a]he gave them into the hand of
the heathen;
And they that hated them ruled over
them.
42 Their enemies also oppressed them,
And they were brought into subjection
under their hand.
43 [a]Many times did he deliver them;
But they provoked *him* with their
counsel,
And were [1]brought low for their
iniquity.
44 Nevertheless he regarded their affliction,
When [a]he heard their cry:
45 [a]And he remembered for them his
covenant,
And [b]repented [c]according to the
multitude of his mercies.
46 [a]He made them also to be pitied
Of all those that carried them captives.

47 [a]Save us, O LORD our God,
And gather us from among the heathen,
To give thanks unto thy holy name,

106:28 [a]Hos. 9:10
106:30 [a]Num. 25:7
106:31 [a]Num. 25:11
106:32 [a]Num. 20:3; Ps. 81:7
106:33 [a]Num. 20:10
106:34 [a]Judg. 1:21 [b]Deut. 7:2; Judg. 2:2
106:35 [a]Judg. 3:5,6; Is. 2:6
106:36 [a]Judg. 2:12 [b]Deut. 7:16
106:37 [a]2 Ki. 16:3 [b]Lev. 17:7
106:38 [a]Num. 35:33
106:39 [a]Ezek. 20:18 [b]Lev. 17:7; Num. 15:39; Ezek. 20:30
106:40 [a]Judg. 2:14 [b]Deut. 9:29
106:41 [a]Judg. 2:14; Neh. 9:27
106:43 [1]Or, *impoverished,* or, *weakened* [a]Judg. 2:16; Neh. 9:27
106:44 [a]Judg. 10:10
106:45 [a]Lev. 26:41 [b]Judg. 2:18 [c]Ps. 69:16
106:46 [a]Ezra 9:9; Jer. 42:12
106:47 [a]1 Chr. 16:35

106:28–31 See Num 25.

‡106:29 *their inventions.* Their sinful actions.

‡106:31 *counted unto him for righteousness.* When Abram "believed in the LORD . . . he counted it to him for righteousness" (Gen 15:6). So, says the psalmist, was Phinehas's priestly zeal for the Lord (see Num 25:7–8). *Unto all generations for evermore.* The psalmist refers to the "covenant of an everlasting priesthood" (Num 25:13) that the Lord granted Phinehas as a gracious reward for his zealous act. It was the granting of this promissory covenant that warranted the statement about crediting righteousness, for God's granting of a promissory covenant to Abram had followed upon His crediting Abram's faith to him as righteousness (see Gen 15:9–21). Similarly, God's promissory covenants with Noah (see Gen 9:9–17) and with David (see 2 Sam 7:5–16) followed upon God's testimony to their righteousness (see Gen 7:1; 1 Sam 13:14). See chart, p. 16.

‡106:32 *strife.* Or "Meribah" (which means "strife"). See notes on 95:8 and Ex 17:7.

106:33 *provoked his spirit.* For the Spirit of God present and at work in the wilderness wanderings see Ex 31:3; Num 11:17; 24:2; Neh 9:20; Is 63:10–14.

106:34–39 A general description of the worst of rebellious Israel's sins, applicable from the time of the judges to the Babylonian exile.

106:37 *devils.* The Hebrew for this word occurs elsewhere in the OT only in Deut 32:17, where it refers to false gods. It is related to a Babylonian word referring to (pagan) protective spirits.

106:38 Cf. Jer 19:4–5. *innocent blood.* The blood of anyone not guilty of a capital crime. *polluted.* The very land itself is defiled by the slaughter of innocents (see Num 35:33; Jer 3:2,9).

106:39 *defiled.* See Lev 18:24; Jer 2:23; Ezek 20:30–31; 22:3–4. *went a whoring.* Committed prostitution by joining themselves with false gods (see Ezek 23:3,5–8; Hos 5:3; 6:10; see also note on Judg 2:17).

106:40–43 God's stern measures against His rebellious people—a general description applicable from the days of the judges to the Babylonian exile and focusing particularly on God's most severe form of covenant sanctions (see Lev 26:25–26,33,38–39; Deut 28:25,36–37,48–57,64–68).

106:40 *wrath.* See note on 2:5. *abhorred.* See 5:6.

106:44–46 God's gracious remembering of His covenant—a general description applicable from the days of the judges to the Babylonian exile.

106:44 *heard their cry.* See Ex 2:23; 3:7–9; Num 20:16; Judg 3:9,15; 4:3; 6:6–7; 10:10; 1 Sam 9:16; 2 Chr 20:6–12; Neh 9:27–28.

‡106:45 *remembered . . . his covenant.* See 105:8,42; Ex 2:24; Lev 26:42,45. *repented.* Relented from sending judgment. God does not "repent" in the sense that he alters His decrees out of a limited knowledge of the future. At the same time, God has entered into a give-and-take relationship with human beings so that human responses to Him and His word do have an effect on His decisions and actions. See notes on Jer 18:7–10 and Jonah 3:9. *mercies.* See note on 6:4.

106:46 *pitied . . . those that carried them captives.* Makes clear that the author's recital includes the Babylonian captivity (see 1 Ki 8:50; 2 Chr 30:9; Ezra 9:9; Jer 42:12). Although there were earlier captivities of Israelite communities, no other captive group was said to have been shown pity.

106:47 A communal prayer for deliverance and restoration from dispersion (see introduction and note on v. 4). *name.* See note on 5:11. *triumph in.* Triumphantly celebrate. The Hebrew for this phrase is found elsewhere only in the parallel in 1 Chr 16:35. *praise.* See note on 9:1.

And to triumph in thy praise.

48 [a]Blessed *be* the LORD God of Israel from everlasting to everlasting:
And let all the people say, Amen.
[1]Praise ye the LORD.

Psalm 107

1 [a]O give thanks unto the LORD, for [b]*he is* good:
For his mercy *endureth* for ever.
2 Let the redeemed of the LORD say *so,*
[a]Whom he hath redeemed from the hand of the enemy;
3 And [a]gathered them out of the lands,
From the east, and from the west, from the north, and [1]from the south.

4 They wandered in [a]the wilderness in a solitary way;
They found no city to dwell in.
5 Hungry and thirsty,
Their soul fainted in them.
6 [a]Then they cried unto the LORD in their trouble,
And he delivered them out of their distresses.
7 And he led them forth by the [a]right way,
That *they* might go to a city of habitation.
8 [a]Oh that *men* would praise the LORD *for* his goodness,
And *for* his wonderful works to the children of men!
9 For [a]he satisfieth the longing soul,
And filleth the hungry soul *with* goodness.

10 Such as [a]sit in darkness and in the shadow of death,
Being [b]bound in affliction and iron;
11 Because they [a]rebelled against the words of God,

106:48 [1][Heb. *Hallelujah*] [a]Ps. 41:13
107:1 [a]Ps. 106:1 [b]Ps. 119:68
107:2 [a]Ps. 106:10
107:3 [1]Heb. *from the sea* [a]Ps. 106:47
107:4 [a]Deut. 32:10
107:6 [a]Ps. 50:15; Hos. 5:15
107:7 [a]Ezra 8:21
107:8 [a]ver. 15,21
107:9 [a]Ps. 34:10; Luke 1:53
107:10 [a]Luke 1:79 [b]Job 36:8
107:11 [a]Lam. 3:42

106:48 The doxology for Book 4 (see 41:13 and note). *Amen.* See note on Deut 27:15.

‡Ps 107 An exhortation to praise the Lord for His unfailing love in that He hears the prayers of those in need and saves them (see next paragraph—on structure). It was composed for liturgical use at one of Israel's annual religious festivals. Interpretations vary widely, but the following is most likely: Having experienced anew God's mercies in her return from Babylonian exile (v. 3; see Jer 33:11), Israel is led by a Levite in celebrating God's unfailing benevolence toward those who have cried to Him in the crises of their lives. In its recitational style the psalm is closely related to Ps 104–106, and in its language to Ps 105–106. For that reason it has been seriously proposed that with these last two psalms it forms a trilogy from the same author. Whether or not this is so, its affinity with the preceding psalms strongly suggests that it was associated with them before the insertion of a Book division between Ps 106 and 107 and that it was intended to conclude the little series, Ps 104–107. Its recital of God's "wonderful works to the children of men" (v. 8)—which climaxes Ps 105–106—balances the recital of His many wise works in creation (see 104:2–26) and His benevolent care over the animal world (see 104:27–30). The editors may have inserted a Book division between Ps 106 and 107 with a view to a fivefold division of the Psalter (see Introduction: Collection, Arrangement and Date). (See introduction to Ps 101.)

The introduction (vv. 1–3) and conclusion (v. 43) enclose six thematic stanzas in the Hebrew, of which the last two (vv. 33–38, 39–42) stand apart as an instructive supplement focusing in a more general way on reversals in fortunes—which, however, end up with God restoring the "hungry" (v. 36) and the "poor" (v. 41). Of the four remaining thematic stanzas (marked by recurring refrains: vv. 6,13,19,28; vv. 8,15,21,31), the first and last refer to God's deliverance of those lost in the trackless wilderness (vv. 4–9) and those imperiled on the boisterous sea (vv. 23–32). The two central stanzas celebrate deliverance from the punishment of foreign bondage (vv. 10–16) and from the punishment of disease (vv. 17–22). Of the concluding lines to these four stanzas, the first two (vv. 9,16) and the last two (vv. 22,32) are similar. The verse pattern of these four thematic stanzas (six-seven-six-ten) makes deliberate use of the significant numbers seven and ten.

107:1–3 Introductory call to praise.

107:1 A conventional liturgical call to praise (see 106:1; 118:1,29; 136:1; Jer 33:11). *give thanks.* See vv. 8,15,21,31; see also note on Ps 100 title. *mercy.* See vv. 8,15,21,31,43; see also note on 6:4.

107:2 *redeemed.* Here, as often, a synonym for "delivered."

107:3 *out of the lands.* From the dispersion resulting from the Assyrian (see 2 Ki 17:6) and Babylonian captivities (see 2 Ki 24:14,16; 25:11,26; Jer 52:28–30; see also Neh 1:8; Esth 8:5,9,13; Is 11:12; 43:5–6; Ezek 11:17; 20:34). *south.* Lit. "(the) sea," i.e., the west, as in Is 49:12. But perhaps the final letter of the Hebrew word has been lost, which if supplied yields "south."

107:4–9 Deliverance for those lost in the trackless wilderness. No reference is made to rebellion (as in the third and fourth stanzas), but since Israel had journeyed through the wilderness on her way to Canaan she had firsthand experience of the terrors of the wilderness. She was, moreover, bounded on the east by the great Arabian Desert (as on the west by the Mediterranean Sea; see vv. 23–32), across which her merchant caravans traveled.

107:4,7,36 *city/city of habitation.* Where people live and where a steady supply of food and water makes human life secure.

107:6 *they cried.* The author uses the same Hebrew verb in v. 28 to establish linkage. In vv. 13,19 he uses a different (but similar-sounding) Hebrew verb for the same reason. Just as Israel's history was a history of divine deliverance (see Ps 105) and a history of rebellion (see Ps 106), so also it was a history of crying out to the Lord in distress (see references in note on 106:44).

‡107:7 *right way.* Or "level way." A direct route, clear of dangerous and difficult obstacles.

107:8 For other refrains see introduction to Ps 42–43. *wonderful works.* See vv. 15,21,24,31; see also note on 9:1.

107:9 *satisfieth the longing . . . filleth the hungry soul.* See v. 5; see also 105:40–41.

107:10–16 Deliverance from the punishment of foreign bondage. God even delivers those who cry to Him when their distress is a result of His discipline for their sins (see vv. 17–20, 33–41).

107:10 *sit in darkness . . . shadow of death.* Vivid imagery for distress (see 18:28; Is 5:30; 8:22; 59:9; see also note on 44:19). *bound . . . iron.* While reference is no doubt to foreign bondage, the imagery of being bound was also used by OT poets to refer to other forms of distress (see Job 36:8; Is 28:22; Lam 3:7); so the reference may be deliberately ambiguous.

And contemned [b]the counsel of the
most High:
12 Therefore he brought down their heart
with labour;
They fell down, and *there was* [a]none
to help.
13 Then they cried unto the LORD in their
trouble,
And he saved them out of their
distresses.
14 [a]He brought them out of darkness and
the shadow of death,
And brake their bands in sunder.
15 [a]Oh that *men* would praise the LORD
for his goodness,
And *for* his wonderful works to the
children of men!
16 For he hath [a]broken the gates of brass,
And cut the bars of iron in sunder.

17 Fools [a]because of their transgression,
And because of their iniquities, are
afflicted.
18 [a]Their soul abhorreth all *manner of*
meat;
And they [b]draw near unto the gates of
death.
19 Then they cry unto the LORD in their
trouble,
He saveth them out of their distresses.
20 [a]He sent his word, and [b]healed them,
And [c]delivered *them* from their
destructions.
21 Oh that *men* would praise the LORD *for*
his goodness,
And *for* his wonderful works to the
children of men!
22 [a]And let them sacrifice the sacrifices of
thanksgiving,
And [b]declare his works with
[1]rejoicing.

23 They that go down to the sea in ships,
That do business in great waters;
24 These see the works of the LORD,
And his wonders in the deep.
25 For he commandeth, and [a][1]raiseth the
stormy wind,
Which lifteth up the waves thereof.
26 They mount up *to* the heaven, they go
down *again to* the depths:
[a]Their soul is melted because of
trouble.
27 They reel to and fro, and stagger like a
drunken *man*,
And [1]are at their wit's end.
28 [a]Then they cry unto the LORD in their
trouble,
And he bringeth them out of their
distresses.
29 [a]He maketh the storm a calm,
So that the waves thereof are still.
30 Then are they glad because they be
quiet;
So he bringeth them unto their desired
haven.
31 [a]Oh that *men* would praise the LORD
for his goodness,
And *for* his wonderful works to the
children of men!
32 Let them exalt him also [a]in the
congregation of the people,
And praise him in the assembly of the
elders.

33 He [a]turneth rivers into a wilderness,
And the watersprings into dry ground;
34 A [a]fruitful land into [1]barrenness,

107:11 [b]Ps. 73:24; Luke 7:30; Acts 20:27
107:12 [a]Ps. 22:11; Is. 63:5
107:14 [a]Ps. 68:6; Acts 12:7
107:15 [a]ver. 8,21,31
107:16 [a]Is. 45:2
107:17 [a]Lam. 3:39
107:18 [a]Job 33:20 [b]Job 33:22; Ps. 9:13
107:20 [a]Mat. 8:8 [b]Ps. 30:2; 103:3 [c]Job 33:28; Ps. 30:3; 49:15
107:22 [a]Lev. 7:12; Ps. 116:17; Heb. 13:15
107:22 [1]Heb. *singing* [b]Ps. 9:11; 73:28; 118:17
107:25 [1]Heb. *maketh to stand* [a]Jonah 1:4
107:26 [a]Ps. 22:14
107:27 [1]Heb. *all their wisdom is swallowed up*
107:28 [a]ver. 6,13,19
107:29 [a]Ps. 89:9; Mat. 8:26
107:31 [a]ver. 8,15,21
107:32 [a]Ps. 22:22,25
107:33 [a]1 Ki. 17:1,7
107:34 [1]Heb. *saltness* [a]Gen. 13:10; 14:3; 19:25

107:11 *God . . . most High.* That is, God most High (see Gen 14:19 and note; see also note on 3:7). *counsel.* God's wise directives embodied in His words.
107:12 *brought down their heart with labour.* A labor so burdensome it broke their spirit. *fell down.* Their strength failed (see 31:10; 109:24; Neh 4:10; Is 40:30; Zech 12:8).
107:13 *cried unto.* See note on v. 6.
‡107:16 Either this verse is quoted from Is 45:2, or both verses quote an established saying. *gates of brass.* City gates—normally of wood; here proverbially of "brass," i.e. bronze, the strongest gates then imaginable (see Jer 1:18). *bars of iron.* Bars that secured city gates (see Deut 3:5; Jer 51:30), usually made of wood (see Nah 3:13) but sometimes of bronze (see 1 Ki 4:13).
107:17–22 Deliverance from the punishment of wasting disease (see note on vv. 10–16).
107:17 *Fools.* See note on 14:1; see also Jer 4:22. "Fools despise wisdom and instruction" (Prov 1:7; see v. 43). *because of their iniquities, are afflicted.* See Lev 26:16,25; Deut 28:20–22,35, 58–61.
‡107:18 *soul abhorreth all manner of meat.* Are so afflicted by God's judgment that they do not even want food. *gates of death.* The realm of the dead was sometimes depicted as a netherworld city with a series of concentric walls and gates (seven, each inside the other, according to ancient Near Eastern mythology) to keep those descending there from returning to the land of the living (see 9:13 and note on Job 38:17; see also Mat 16:18).
107:19 *cry unto.* See note on v. 6. *saveth.* See v. 13; cf. vv. 6,28.
107:20 *his word.* His command, here personified as the agent of His purpose (see 147:15,18; see also note on 23:6).
107:22 *sacrifices of thanksgiving.* See Lev 7:12–15; 22:29–30. *declare his works.* See note on 7:17. *rejoicing.* See, e.g., Ps 116.
107:23–32 Deliverance from the perils of the sea (see note on vv. 4–9). Israel's merchants also braved the sea in pursuit of trade (see Gen 49:13; Judg 5:17; 1 Ki 9:26–28; 10:22).
107:23 *great waters.* See 29:3.
107:24 *wonders in the deep.* Since the peoples of the eastern Mediterranean coastlands associated the "great waters" (v. 23) of the sea with the primeval chaotic waters (see note on 32:6), the Lord's total control of them was always for Israel a cause of wonder and of a sense of security. Therefore the terrifying storms that sometimes swept the Mediterranean (see Jonah 1; Acts 27) are here included among His wonderful deeds.
107:30 *haven.* Perhaps trading center.
107:32 See v. 22. *elders.* See note on Ex 3:16.
107:33–42 A twofold instructive supplement recalling how the Lord sometimes disciplined His people by turning the fruitful land (v. 34) into a virtual wilderness (see 1 Ki 17:1–7; 2 Ki 8:1) but then restored the land again (see Ruth 1:6; 1 Ki 18:44–45), so that the hungry (v. 36) could live there and prosper in the midst of plenty. But then He sent powerful armies

For the wickedness of them that dwell therein.
35 [a]He turneth the wilderness into a standing water,
And dry ground into watersprings;
36 And there he maketh the hungry to dwell,
That they may prepare a city for habitation;
37 And sow the fields, and plant vineyards,
Which may yield fruits of increase.
38 [a]He blesseth them also, so that they [b]are multiplied greatly;
And suffereth not their cattle to decrease.
39 Again, they are [a]minished and brought low
Through oppression, affliction, and sorrow.
40 [a]He poureth contempt upon princes,
And causeth them to wander in the [1]wilderness, *where there is* no way.
41 [a]Yet setteth he the poor on high [1]from affliction,
And [b]maketh *him* families like a flock.
42 [a]The righteous shall see *it*, and rejoice:
And all [b]iniquity shall stop her mouth.
43 [a]Whoso *is* wise, and will observe these *things*,
Even they shall understand the lovingkindness of the LORD.

Psalm 108

A Song *or* Psalm of David.

1 [a]O God, my heart is fixed;
I will sing and give praise,
Even *with* my glory.
2 [a]Awake, psaltery and harp:
I *myself* will awake early.
3 I will praise thee, O LORD, among the people:
And I will sing *praises* unto thee among the nations.
4 For thy mercy *is* great above the heavens:
And thy truth *reacheth* unto the [1]clouds.
5 [a]Be thou exalted, O God, above the heavens:
And thy glory above all the earth.

6 [a]That thy beloved may be delivered:
Save *with* thy right hand, and answer me.
7 God hath spoken in his holiness;
I will rejoice, I will divide Shechem,
And mete out the valley of Succoth.
8 Gilead *is* mine; Manasseh *is* mine;
Ephraim also *is* the strength of mine head;
[a]Judah *is* my lawgiver;
9 Moab *is* my washpot;
Over Edom will I cast out my shoe;
Over Philistia will I triumph.

10 [a]Who will bring me *into* the strong city?
Who will lead me into Edom?
11 *Wilt* not *thou*, O God, *who* hast cast us off?
And wilt not thou, O God, go forth with our hosts?
12 Give us help from trouble:
For vain *is* the help of man.
13 [a]Through God we shall do valiantly:
For he *it is that* shall tread down our enemies.

Psalm 109

To the chief Musician, A Psalm of David.

1 Hold [a]not thy peace, O God of my praise;

107:35 [a]Ps. 114:8; Is. 41:18
107:38 [a]Gen. 12:2; 17:16,20 [b]Ex. 1:7
107:39 [a]2 Ki. 10:32
107:40 [1]Or, *void place* [a]Job 12:21,24
107:41 [1]Or, *after* [a]1 Sam. 2:8; Ps. 113:7,8 [b]Ps. 78:52
107:42 [a]Job 5:15,16 [b]Job 5:16; Ps. 63:11; Prov. 10:11; Rom. 3:19
107:43 [a]Ps. 64:9; Jer. 9:12; Hos. 14:9
108:1 [a]Ps. 57:7
108:2 [a]Ps. 57:8-11
108:4 [1]Or, *skies*
108:5 [a]Ps. 57:5,11
108:6 [a]Ps. 60:5
108:8 [a]Gen. 49:10
108:10 [a]Ps. 60:9
108:13 [a]Ps. 60:12
109:1 [a]Ps. 83:1

against them (such as the Assyrians, 2 Ki 17:3–6, and the Babylonians, 2 Ki 24:10–17) that devastated the land once more and deported its people; yet afterward He restored the needy (v. 41). But the poet generalizes upon these experiences in the manner of the wisdom teachers.

107:33–35 The imagery is similar to that found in Is 35:6–7; 41:18; 42:15; 43:19–20; 50:2 and may indicate that the author has been influenced by Isaiah.

‡107:39 *minished.* Or "diminished" (made few in number).

107:40 Perhaps quoted from Job 12:21,24. In their prosperity the people, led by their nobles, grow proud and turn their backs on the God who has blessed them (see Deut 31:20; 32:15), so He returns them to the wilderness (see Deut 32:10; Hos 2:3,14).

107:41 *poor.* Those in need of help (see v. 39; see also 9:18 and note).

‡107:42 Conclusion to the instruction (vv. 33–41); perhaps an echo of Job 5:16. *righteous . . . iniquity.* A frequent contrast in OT wisdom literature (see Prov 2:21–22; 11:6–7; 12:6; 14:11; 15:8; 21:18,29; 29:27—but the Hebrew for "iniquity" here is shared more often with Job).

107:43 Conclusion to the psalm. *Whoso is wise.* See Deut 32:29; Hos 14:9. *these things.* The instruction in vv. 33–42. *understand the lovingkindnesses of the LORD.* The theme of vv. 4–32.

Ps 108 Praise of God's love, and prayer for His help against the enemies—a combination (with very slight modifications) of 57:7–11 and 60:5–12. For a similar composition of a new psalm by combination of portions from several psalms see 1 Chr 16:8–36. The celebration of the greatness of God's love (v. 4) links this psalm thematically with Ps 103 (see 103:11). See introduction to Ps 101.

108 title *Song.* See note on Ps 30 title. *of David.* Both sources (Ps 57; 60) were credited to him.

108:1–5 Praise of God's love, possibly intended to function here as an expression of trust in God (the God of vv. 7–9,11), to whom appeal is to be made (vv. 6,12); see 109:1 and note. For this stanza see notes on 57:7–11.

‡108:1 *glory.* See note on 7:5.

108:6–13 Prayer for God's help against enemies (see notes on 60:5–12).

‡Ps 109 A prayer for God to judge a case of false accusation. The author speaks of his enemies in the singular in vv. 6–19 but in the plural elsewhere. Some therefore suppose that vv. 6–19 contain the enemies' curses pronounced against the author (if so, v. 6 would read, "They say, 'Set thou a wicked man . . .'"). But it is more likely that either (1) the author shifts here to a collective mode of speaking, or (2) the enemies are united under

2 For the mouth of the wicked and the
[1]mouth of the deceitful [2]are opened
against me:
They have spoken against me *with* a
lying tongue.
3 They compassed me about also *with*
words of hatred;
And fought against me [a]without a cause.
4 For my love they are my adversaries:
But I *give myself unto* prayer.
5 And [a]they have rewarded me evil for
good,
And hatred for my love.
6 Set thou a wicked *man* over him:
And let [a][1]Satan stand at his right hand.
7 When he shall be judged, let him [1]be
condemned:
And [a]let his prayer become sin.
8 Let his days be few;
And [a]let another take his [1]office.
9 [a]Let his children be fatherless,
And his wife a widow.
10 Let his children be continually
vagabonds, and beg:
Let them seek *their bread* also out of
their desolate places.
11 [a]Let the extortioner catch all that he
hath;
And let the strangers spoil his labour.
12 Let there be none to extend mercy
unto him:
Neither let there be any to favour his
fatherless children.
13 [a]Let his posterity be cut off;
And in the generation following let
their [b]name be blotted out.
14 [a]Let the iniquity of his fathers be
remembered with the LORD;
And let not the sin of his mother [b]be
blotted out.
15 Let them be before the LORD
continually,
That he may [a]cut off the memory of
them from the earth.
16 Because that he remembered not to
shew mercy,
But persecuted the poor and needy man,
That *he* might even slay the [a]broken in
heart.
17 [a]As he loved cursing, so let it come
unto him:
As he delighted not in blessing, so let
it be far from him.
18 As he clothed himself with cursing like
as with his garment,
So let it [a]come [1]into his bowels like
water,
And like oil into his bones.

109:2 [1]Heb. *mouth of deceit* [2]Heb. *have opened* themselves
109:3 [a]Ps. 35:7; 69:4; John 15:25
109:5 [a]Ps. 35:7,12; 38:20
109:6 [1]Or, *an adversary* [a]Zech. 3:1
109:7 [1]Heb. *go out guilty,* or, *wicked* [a]Prov. 28:9
109:8 [1]Or, *charge* [a]Acts 1:20
109:9 [a]Ex. 22:24
109:11 [a]Job 5:5; 18:9
109:13 [a]Job 18:19; Ps. 37:28 [b]Prov. 10:7
109:14 [a]Ex. 20:5 [b]Neh. 4:5; Jer. 18:23
109:15 [a]Job 18:17; Ps. 34:16
109:16 [a]Ps. 34:18
109:17 [a]Prov. 14:14; Ezek. 35:6
109:18 [1]Heb. *within him* [a]Num. 5:22

a leader whose personal animosity toward the psalmist has fired the antagonism of others and so is singled out for special attention. Traditional attempts to isolate a distinct class of psalms called "imprecatory" (and then identify Ps 109 as the climax of the series) are mistaken (see note on vv. 6–15). This prayer has much affinity with Ps 35. See introduction to Ps 101.

Two (Hebrew) four-line stanzas of petition frame the whole (vv. 1–5, 26–29), followed by a two-line conclusion (vv. 30–31). The remaining 20 lines fall into two main divisions of ten lines each (vv. 6–15, 16–25). Of these, the second is thematically divided into two parts of five lines each, the first of which (vv. 16–20) catalogues what "he" has done while the second (vv. 21–25) describes how "I" am suffering.

109 title See note on Ps 4 title.

109:1–5 Appeal to God to deliver him from false accusers.

‡109:1 *Hold not thy peace.* Do not be (judicially) inactive (see 28:1; 35:22; 50:3,21; 83:1). *God of my praise.* The one he publicly praises as his trustworthy deliverer and defender (see 22:3 and note; see also 35:18; 74:21; 76:10; 79:13; 102:18).

109:2–5 The particulars of his case, which he presents before the heavenly bar of justice (see 35:11–16).

109:2 *mouth . . . are opened against me.* See note on 5:9.

109:4 *But I give myself unto prayer.* In contrast to the enemy (see vv. 16–18). The intent may be: But I have prayed for them (as in 35:13–14).

109:6–15 Appeal for judicial redress—that the Lord will deal with them in accordance with their malicious intent against him, matching punishment with crime (see note on 5:10; see also 35:4–10 and note).

‡109:6 *wicked man . . . Satan.* The psalmist's enemy falsely accused him in order to bring him down; now let the enemy be confronted by an accuser. *Satan.* Lit. "an accuser." The lack of the definite article would seem to indicate that "Satan" himself is not in view, and this would be the only reference to Satan in Ps (but see also Job 1:8 and note).

109:7 *his prayer.* The petitions he offers in his defense.

109:8 *days be few.* The false accuser was no doubt seeking to effect David's death (see 1 Ki 21:8–15). *another take his office.* The enemy held some official position and was perhaps plotting a coup. For a NT application of these words to Judas see Acts 1:20.

109:10–11 May he also be deprived of all his property so that he has no inheritance to pass on to his children.

‡109:12 *none to extend mercy.* See v. 16. *his . . . children.* The close identity of a man with his children and of children with their parents, resulting from the tightly bonded unity of the three- or four-generation households of that ancient society, is alien to the modern reader, whose sense of self is highly individualistic. But that deep, profoundly human bond accounts for the ancient legal principle of "visiting the iniquity of the fathers upon the children unto the third and the fourth generations" (see Ex 20:5; but see also 103:17; Gen 18:19).

109:13 Since a man lived on in his children (see previous note), the focus of judgment remains on the false accuser (see 21:10; 37:28). *name be blotted out.* See note on 9:5.

109:14–15 *iniquity of his fathers . . . sin of his mother . . . them.* These verses return to the theme of vv. 7–8 (and thus form a frame around the section): May the indictment the accuser lodges against him include the sins of his parents (see note on v. 12).

109:15 *cut off the memory of them.* May this slanderer be the last of their family line.

109:16–20 The ruthless character of the enemy—may he be made to suffer the due consequences (see 10:2–15; 59:12–13). Accusation of the adversary is a common feature in psalms that are appeals to the heavenly Judge (see, e.g., 5:9–10; 10:2–11; 17:10–12).

109:17 *cursing.* The enemy added curses to lies (see note on 10:7).

109:18 *into his bowels like water, And like oil into his bones.* Cursing was his food and drink as well as his clothing; he lived by cursing (see Prov 4:17).

19 Let it be unto him as the garment *which* covereth *him*,
And for a girdle where*with* he is girded continually.
20 *Let* this *be* the reward of mine adversaries from the LORD,
And of them that speak evil against my soul.

21 But do thou for me, O GOD the Lord, for thy name's sake:
Because thy mercy *is* good, deliver thou me.
22 For I *am* poor and needy,
And my heart is wounded within me.
23 I am gone [a]like the shadow when it declineth:
I am tossed up and down as the locust.
24 My [a]knees are weak through fasting;
And my flesh faileth of fatness.
25 I became also [a]a reproach unto them:
When they looked upon me [b]they shaked their heads.
26 Help me, O LORD my God:
O save me according to thy mercy:
27 [a]That they may know that this *is* thy hand;
That thou, LORD, hast done it.
28 [a]Let them curse, but bless thou:
When they arise, let them be ashamed; but let [b]thy servant rejoice.

109:23 [a]Ps. 102:11
109:24 [a]Heb. 12:12
109:25 [a]Ps. 22:6,7 [b]Mat. 27:39
109:27 [a]Job 37:7
109:28 [a]2 Sam. 16:11 [b]Is. 65:14

29 [a]Let mine adversaries be clothed with shame,
And let them cover *themselves with* their own confusion, as *with* a mantle.
30 I will greatly praise the LORD with my mouth;
Yea, [a]I will praise him among the multitude.
31 For [a]he shall stand at the right hand of the poor,
To save *him* [1]from those that condemn his soul.

Psalm 110

A Psalm of David.

1 The [a]LORD said unto my Lord,
Sit thou at my right hand,
Until I make thine enemies thy footstool.
2 The LORD shall send the rod of thy strength out of Zion:
Rule thou in the midst of thine enemies.
3 [a]Thy people *shall be* willing in the day of thy power, [b]in the beauties of holiness
[1]From the womb of the morning: thou hast the dew of thy youth.

109:29 [a]Ps. 35:26; 132:18
109:30 [a]Ps. 35:18; 111:1
109:31 [1]Heb. *from the judges of his soul* [a]Ps. 16:8; 73:23
110:1 [a]Mat. 22:44; Mark 12:36; Luke 20:42; Acts 2:34; 1 Cor. 15:25
110:3 [1]Or, *More than the womb of the morning: thou* shalt *have, etc.* [a]Judg. 5:2 [b]Ps. 96:9

109:21–25 The intensity of "my" suffering—Lord, deliver me!
109:21 *for thy name's sake.* See notes on 5:11; 23:3. *mercy.* See v. 26; see also note on 6:4.
109:22 The psalmist's description of his situation echoes the words of v. 16. *poor and needy.* Dependent on the Lord (see note on 34:6). *heart.* See note on 4:7. *is wounded.* The Hebrew for this phrase sounds like the Hebrew for "cursing" in vv. 17–18, a deliberate wordplay—while he lives by cursing, I live with deep inward pain.
‡109:23 *I am gone.* I am fading or passing away. Apparently the psalmist suffers a life-sapping affliction, which is the occasion for his enemies to turn on him (see vv. 24–25; see also note on 5:9). *like the shadow.* See 102:11. *tossed up and down.* Or "shaken out." See Neh 5:13; Job 38:13.
109:26–29 Concluding petition, with many echoes of preceding themes.
109:28 *servant.* Perhaps identifies the psalmist as the Lord's anointed (see title; see also 78:70 and note).
109:30–31 A vow to praise the Lord for His deliverance (see note on 7:17).
Ps 110 Oracles concerning the Messianic King-Priest. This psalm (specifically its two brief oracles, vv. 1,4) is frequently referred to in the NT testimony to Christ. Like Ps 2, it has the marks of a coronation psalm, composed for use at the enthronement of a new Davidic king. Before the Christian era Jews already viewed it as Messianic. Because of the manner in which it has been interpreted in the NT—especially by Jesus (see Mat 22:43–45; Mark 12:36–37; Luke 20:42–44), but also by Peter (see Acts 2:34–36) and the author of Hebrews (see especially Heb 1:13; 5:6–10; 7:11–28)—Christians have generally held that this is the most directly "prophetic" of all the psalms. If so, David, speaking prophetically (see 2 Sam 23:2), composed a coronation psalm for his great future Son, of whom the prophets did not speak until later. It may be, however, that David composed the psalm for the coronation of his son Solomon, that he called him "my Lord" (v. 1) in view of his new status, which placed him above the aged David, and that in so doing he spoke a word that had far larger meaning than he knew. This would seem to be in more accord with what we know of David from Samuel, Kings and Chronicles. See introduction to Ps 101.

The psalm falls into two precisely balanced halves (vv. 1–3, 4–7). Each of the two brief oracles (vv. 1,4) is followed by thematically similar elaboration.
110:1–3 The Lord's decree, establishing His anointed as His regent in the face of all opposition (see 2:7–12).
‡110:1 The first oracle (see note on v. 4). *my Lord.* My sovereign, therefore superior to David (see Mat 22:44–45; Mark 12:36–37; Luke 20:42–44; Acts 2:34–35; Heb 1:13 and their contexts). Jesus specifically used this verse to refer to His divine origin (Mat 22:41–45). *Sit.* Sit enthroned. *right hand.* The place of honor beside a king (see 45:9; 1 Ki 2:19); thus he is made second in authority to God Himself. NT references to Jesus' exaltation to this position are many (see Mat 26:64; Mark 14:62; 16:19; Luke 22:69; Acts 2:33; 5:31; 7:55–56; Rom 8:34; Eph 1:20; Col 3:1; Heb 1:3; 8:1; 10:12; 12:2). *enemies.* See note on 2:1–3. *thy footstool.* See Heb 10:12–13. Ancient kings often had themselves portrayed as placing their feet on vanquished enemies (see Josh 10:24). For a royal footstool as part of the throne see 2 Chr 9:18. For the thought here see 1 Ki 5:3. Paul applies this word to Christ in 1 Cor 15:25; Eph 1:22.
110:2 *send the rod of thy strength.* Expand Your reign in ever widening circles until no foe remains to oppose Your rule. *Zion.* David's royal city (see 2 Sam 5:7,9), but also God's (see 9:11 and note), where He rules as the Great King (see Ps 46; 48; 132:13–18). The Lord's anointed is His regent over His emerging kingdom in the world.
‡110:3 *shall be willing.* Lit. "freewill offerings," i.e., they will offer themselves as dedicated warriors to support You on the bat-

4 The LORD hath sworn, and [a]will not
repent,
Thou *art* a priest for ever
After the order of Melchizedek.
5 The Lord [a]at thy right hand
Shall strike through kings [b]in the day
of his wrath.
6 He shall judge among the heathen, he
shall fill *the places with* the dead
bodies;

110:4 [a]Num. 23:19
110:5 [a]Ps. 16:8 [b]Ps. 2:5,12; Rom. 2:5
110:6 [1]Or, *great* [a]Ps. 68:21; Hab. 3:13
110:7 [a]Is. 53:12
111:1 [1]Heb. *Hallelujah* [a]Ps. 35:18; 89:5; 107:32

[a]He shall wound the heads over [1]many
countries.
7 He shall drink of the brook in the way:
[a]Therefore shall he lift up the head.

Psalm 111

1 [1]Praise ye the LORD.
[a]I will praise the LORD with *my* whole
heart,

tlefield (see Judg 5:2)—as the Israelites offered of their treasures for the building of the tabernacle in the wilderness (see Ex 35:29; 36:3; see also Ezra 1:4; 2:68). Accordingly, Paul speaks of Christ's followers offering their bodies as "a living sacrifice" (Rom 12:1) and of himself as being "offered upon the sacrifice and service of your faith" (Phil 2:17); see also 2 Cor 8:5. *in the beauties of holiness . . . dew.* If this phrase is descriptive of the Lord's anointed, as seems likely, it depicts Him as clothed in the beauty of royal majesty and perpetually preserving the bloom of youth even as the "womb of the morning" gives birth each day to the dew (for a different use of this imagery see Is 26:19). If it speaks of the young warriors who flock to Him, it apparently describes them as dressed in priestly garb, ready for participation in a holy war (see 1 Sam 21:4–5; 25:28; 2 Chr 13:8,12; 20:15,21; Is 13:3–4; Jer 6:4; 51:27), and pouring into His camp morning by morning as copious as the dew (see 2 Sam 17:11–12). *beauties of holiness.* See note on 29:2.

110:4–7 The Lord's oath establishing His anointed as king-priest in Zion and assuring Him victory over all powers that oppose Him.

110:4 The second oracle (see note on v. 1). *hath sworn.* In accordance also with His sworn covenant to maintain David's royal line forever (see 89:35–37). The force of this oath is elaborated by the author of Hebrews (Heb 6:16–18; 7:20–22). *priest . . . order of Melchizedek.* David and his royal sons, as chief representatives of the rule of God, performed many worship-focused activities, such as overseeing the ark of the covenant (see 2 Sam 6:1–15, especially v. 14; 1 Ki 8:1), building and overseeing the temple (see 1 Ki 5–7; 2 Ki 12:4–7; 22:3–7; 23:4–7; 2 Chr 15:8; 24:4–12; 29:3–11; 34:8) and overseeing the work of the priests and Levites and the temple liturgy (see 1 Chr 6:31; 15:11–16; 16:4–42; 23:3–31; 25:1; 2 Chr 17:7–9; 19:8–11; 29:25,30; 31:2; 35:15–16; Ezra 3:10; 8:20; Neh 12:24,36,45). In all these duties they exercised authority over even the high priest. But they could not engage in those specifically priestly functions that had been assigned to the Aaronic priesthood (see 2 Chr 26:16–18). In the present oracle the son of David is installed by God as king-priest in Zion after the manner of Melchizedek, the king-priest of God most High at Jerusalem in the days of Abraham (see Gen 14:18). As such a king-priest, He was appointed to a higher order of priesthood than that of Aaron and his sons. (For the union of king and priest in one person see Zech 6:13.) What this means for Christ's priesthood is the main theme of Heb 7. *for ever.* Permanently and irrevocably; perhaps alluded to in John 12:34.

110:5 *The Lord at thy right hand.* God is near to assist you in your warfare (see v. 2; 109:31). Some take these words as an address to God: The Lord (David's superior son) is at your (God's) right hand (as in v. 1). *in the day of his wrath.* See 2:5 and note.

‡110:6 *He.* The Lord's anointed. *fill the places with dead bodies.* Battlefield imagery (borrowed from David's victories) that depicts the victory of the Lord's anointed over all powers that oppose the kingdom of God (see 2:9; Rev 19:11–21). *wound the heads.* He will destroy the leaders of enemy nations.

110:7 *drink of the brook.* Even in the heat of battle He will find refreshment and lift up His head with undiminished vigor (see note on v. 3).

Ps 111 Praise of God for His unfailing righteousness. The psalm combines hymnic praise with wisdom instruction, as its first and last verses indicate. Close comparison with Ps 112 shows that these two psalms are twins, probably written by the same author and intended to be kept together. The two psalms are most

The Christ of the Psalms

PSALM	PORTRAYAL	FULFILLED	PSALM	PORTRAYAL	FULFILLED
2:7	The Son of God	Mat 3:17	**41:9**	Betrayed by a friend	Luke 22:47
8:2	Praised by children	Mat 21:15,16	**45:6**	His eternal throne	Heb 1:8
8:6	His dominion	Heb 2:8	**68:18**	Ascends to heaven	Acts 1:9-11
16:10	His resurrection	Mat 28:7	**69:9**	Zealous for God's house	John 2:17
22:1	Forsaken by God	Mat 27:46	**69:21**	Given vinegar and gall	Mat 27:34
22:7,8	Derided by enemies	Luke 23:35	**109:4**	Prays for enemies	Luke 23:34
22:16	Hands and feet pierced	John 20:27	**109:8**	His betrayer replaced	Acts 1:20
22:18	Lots cast for clothing	Mat 27:35,36	**110:1**	Rules over his enemies	Mat 22:44
34:20	Bones unbroken	John 19:32,33,36	**110:4**	A priest forever	Heb 5:6
35:11	Accused by false witnesses	Mark 14:57	**118:22**	The head stone of God's building	Mat 21:42
35:19	Hated without cause	John 15:25			
40:7,8	Delights in God's will	Heb 10:7	**118:26**	Comes in the name of the Lord	Mat 21:9

In the assembly of the upright, and *in* the congregation.
2 [a]The works of the LORD *are* great,
[b]Sought out of all them that have pleasure therein.
3 His work *is* [a]honourable and glorious:
And his righteousness endureth for ever.
4 He hath made his wonderful works to be remembered:
[a]The LORD *is* gracious and full of compassion.
5 He hath given [a][1]meat unto them that fear him:
He will ever be mindful of his covenant.
6 He hath shewed his people the power of his works,
That *he* may give them the heritage of the heathen.
7 The works of his hands *are* [a]verity and judgment;
[b]All his commandments *are* sure.
8 [a]They [1]stand fast for ever and ever,
And are [b]done in truth and uprightness.
9 [a]He sent redemption unto his people:
He hath commanded his covenant for ever:
[b]Holy and reverend *is* his name.
10 [a]The fear of the LORD *is* the beginning of wisdom:
[b][1]A good understanding have all they [2]that do *his commandments:*
His praise endureth for ever.

111:2 [a]Job 38-41; Ps. 92:5 [b]Ps. 143:5
111:3 [a]Ps. 145:4
111:4 [a]Ps. 86:5; 103:8
111:5 [1]Heb. *prey* [a]Mat. 6:26
111:7 [a]Rev. 15:3 [b]Ps. 19:7
111:8 [1]Heb. are *stablished* [a]Is. 40:8 [b]Rev. 15:3
111:9 [a]Luke 1:68 [b]Luke 1:49
111:10 [1]Or, *Good success* [2]Heb. *that do them* [a]Eccl. 12:13 [b]Prov. 3:4
112:1 [1]Heb. *Hallelujah* [a]Ps. 119:16
112:2 [a]Ps. 102:28
112:3 [a]Mat. 6:33
112:4 [a]Job 11:17; Ps. 97:11
112:5 [1]Heb. *judgment* [a]Ps. 37:26 [b]Eph. 5:15; Col. 4:5
112:6 [a]Prov. 10:7

Psalm 112

1 [1]Praise ye the LORD.
Blessed *is* the man *that* feareth the LORD,
That [a]delighteth greatly in his commandments.
2 [a]His seed shall be mighty upon earth:
The generation of the upright shall be blessed.
3 [a]Wealth and riches *shall be* in his house:
And his righteousness endureth for ever.
4 [a]Unto the upright there ariseth light in the darkness:
He is gracious, and full of compassion, and righteous.
5 [a]A good man sheweth favour, and lendeth:
He will guide his affairs [b]with [1]discretion.
6 Surely he shall not be moved for ever:
[a]The righteous shall be in everlasting remembrance.

likely postexilic. They introduce a series of Hallelujah psalms (Ps 111–118), but stand apart from them in traditional Jewish liturgical use (see introduction to Ps 113). Structurally, both Ps 111 and Ps 112 are alphabetic acrostics, but unique in that each (Hebrew) half-line advances the alphabet. Both psalms are framed by first and last verses that highlight their primary themes, and in both psalms the main body develops the theme introduced by the first verse, while the closing verse adds a counterpart. In both psalms the main body of eight verses falls thematically into two halves of four verses each, with the corresponding verses of each half containing certain thematic links (compare, e.g., 111:2 and 111:6; also vv. 5 and 9). Corresponding verses of the two psalms also tend to share common themes (compare, e.g., 111:3–5 with 112:3–5).

111:1 *I will praise the LORD.* Introductory to the praise that follows in vv. 2–9. *assembly of the upright.* Probably a more intimate circle than the assembly (see 107:32 for a similar distinction) and referring to those who are truly godly—such as the "upright" of 112:2,4 (see 11:7; 33:1; 49:14; 97:11; 107:42; 140:13). *in the congregation.* See note on 9:1.

‡111:2 *works of the LORD.* The hymn focuses especially on what God has done for His people. Verses 2,9 sum it up. *Sought out.* Reflectively examined (see Ezra 10:16, "examine"; Eccl 1:13, "seek").

111:3 *righteousness.* As embodied in His deeds (see note on 4:1).

111:4 *wonderful works.* See note on 9:1. *gracious and full of compassion.* See Ex 34:6–7 and note.

111:5 *given meat.* The provision of food is illustrative of His bountiful provisions for the daily needs of His people (as in the Lord's prayer: "Give us this day our daily bread," Mat 6:11). *fear.* See v. 10 and note. *his covenant.* See v. 9; see also 105:8–11.

111:6 Cf. v. 2.

‡111:7 *verity and judgment.* Cf. "honourable and glorious" (v. 3). *commandments are sure.* See note on 93:5.

‡111:8 *They.* "The works of his hands" (v. 7). *truth and uprightness.* Cf. "gracious and full of compassion" (v. 4).

‡111:9 *sent redemption.* The other great benefit of God's deeds in behalf of His people (cf. "hath given meat," v. 5). *Holy and reverend.* As shown by His works. *name.* See note on 5:11.

‡111:10 Concluding word of godly wisdom. *The fear of the LORD is the beginning of wisdom.* The classic OT statement concerning the religious basis of what it means to be wise (see Job 28:28; Prov 1:7; 9:10; see also note on Gen 20:11). *that do his commandments.* Lit. "who do them." The plural Hebrew pronoun refers back to "commandments" in v. 7 (see 19:7–9, where "The fear of the LORD" stands parallel to "testimony," "statutes," "commandment," "judgments"; see also 112:1).

Ps 112 A eulogy to the godly man—in the spirit of Ps 1 but formed after the pattern of Ps 111 and likely intended as its complement (see introduction to Ps 111).

112:1 The basic theme, developed more fully in vv. 2–9. Verse 10 states its converse. See 1:1–2; 128:1. *Blessed.* See note on 1:1. *feareth the LORD.* See 34:8–14 and note.

112:2 *seed.* The godly man brings blessing to his children and is himself blessed through them (cf. v. 6; see 37:26; 127:3–5; 128:3; see also note on 109:12). *shall be mighty.* Will be persons of influence and reputation.

‡112:3 *Wealth and riches.* See 1:3; 128:2. *righteousness.* See v. 9; see also note on 1:5. *endureth.* It is not an occasional characteristic of his actions (see "His heart is fixed," v. 7).

112:4 *light.* See note on 27:1. *darkness.* A metaphor for calamitous times (see 107:10 and note). *gracious, and full of compassion.* See Ex 34:6–7 and note.

‡112:5 *sheweth favour, and lendeth.* See v. 9; see also 111:5.

112:6 *moved.* See note on 10:6. *everlasting remembrance.* His righteousness will have erected an enduring memorial of honor in the memory of both God and man (see v. 2 and note).

7 [a]He shall not be afraid of evil tidings:
His [b]heart is fixed, [c]trusting in the LORD.
8 His heart *is* established, [a]he shall not be afraid,
Until he [b]see *his desire* upon his enemies.
9 [a]He hath dispersed, he hath given to the poor;
His righteousness endureth for ever;
[b]His horn shall be exalted with honour.
10 [a]The wicked shall see *it,* and be grieved;
[b]He shall gnash *with* his teeth, and [c]melt away:
[d]The desire of the wicked shall perish.

Psalm 113

1 [1]Praise ye the LORD.
[a]Praise, O ye servants of the LORD,
Praise the name of the LORD.
2 [a]Blessed be the name of the LORD
From this time forth and for evermore.
3 [a]From the rising of the sun unto the going down of the same
The LORD's name *is* to be praised.
4 The LORD *is* [a]high above all nations,
And [b]his glory above the heavens.
5 [a]Who *is* like unto the LORD our God,
Who [1]dwelleth on high,
6 [a]Who humbleth *himself* to behold
The things that are in heaven, and in the earth?
7 [a]He raiseth up the poor out of the dust,
And lifteth the needy out of the dunghill;
8 That *he* may [a]set *him* with princes,
Even with the princes of his people.
9 [a]He maketh the barren *woman* [1]to keep house,
To be a joyful mother of children.
Praise ye the LORD.

Psalm 114

1 When [a]Israel went out of Egypt,
The house of Jacob [b]from a people of strange language;

112:7 [a]Prov. 1:33 [b]Ps. 57:7 [c]Ps. 64:10
112:8 [a]Prov. 1:33 [b]Ps. 59:10; 118:7
112:9 [a]2 Cor. 9:9 [b]Ps. 75:10
112:10 [a]Luke 13:28 [b]Ps. 37:12 [c]Ps. 58:7,8 [d]Prov. 11:7
113:1 [1]Heb. *Hallelujah* [a]Ps. 135:1
113:2 [a]Dan. 2:20
113:3 [a]Is. 59:19; Mal. 1:11
113:4 [a]Ps. 97:9; 99:2 [b]Ps. 8:1
113:5 [1]Heb. *exalteth* himself *to dwell* [a]Ps. 89:6
113:6 [a]Ps. 11:4; 138:6; Is. 57:15
113:7 [a]1 Sam. 2:8; Ps. 107:41
113:8 [a]Job 36:7
113:9 [1]Heb. *to dwell* in *a house* [a]1 Sam. 2:5; Ps. 68:6; Is. 54:1; Gal. 4:27
114:1 [a]Ex. 13:3 [b]Ps. 81:5

112:7 *heart.* See v. 8; see also note on 4:7. *trusting.* His trust in God will be as steadfast as His righteousness is enduring (see v. 3). For trust and obedience to God's righteous will as the sum of true godliness see 34:8–14 and note.

‡112:8 *see his desire.* Cf. "there ariseth light in the darkness" (v. 4). Not a desire for personal revenge, but rather the execution of God's perfect justice.

112:9 *given to the poor.* See v. 5. *exalted with honour.* As God's name is held in holy awe (see 111:9), so the godly man will be held in honor.

112:10 The counterpart. *see it, and be grieved.* That godliness is the way to blessedness is the reverse of the expectations of the wicked (see 10:2–11; 107:42). *gnash with his teeth.* The grinding of the teeth is a figure for the bitter regret of the wicked at their fate. Cf. Mt. 13:42 and note. *shall perish.* See 1:4–6; see also Ps 37; cf. 111:10.

‡Ps 113 A hymn to the Lord celebrating His high majesty and His mercies to the lowly (see 138:6). It was probably composed originally for the temple liturgy. This psalm begins the "Egyptian Hallel" (Ps 113–118), which came to be used in Jewish liturgy at the great religious festivals (passover, weeks, tabernacles, dedication, new moon; see Lev 23; Num 10:10; John 10:22; see also chart, pp. 166–167). At passover, Ps 113 and 114 were sung before the meal and Ps 115–118 after the meal. (See introduction to Ps 111.)

In the Hebrew three precisely balanced thematic stanzas (each having three verses) give the psalm a pleasing symmetry. With seven (the number of completeness) verbs the author celebrates God's praise in stanzas two and three ("is high," "dwelleth on high," "humbleth himself," "raiseth," "lifteth," "set," "maketh ... to keep house")—and note the fourfold praise in the first stanza. At the center (v. 5; see note on 6:6) a rhetorical question focuses and heightens the hymnic theme.

113:1b–3 The fourfold call to praise.

113:1 *name of the LORD.* See vv. 2–3. Triple repetition was a common liturgical convention (see note on 96:1–3). *name.* See note on 5:11.

113:2 *this time forth and for evermore.* The praise of those who truly praise the Lord cannot rest content until it fills all time—and space (v. 3).

113:4–6 The Lord is enthroned on high, exalted over all creation.

113:4 See the refrain in 57:5,11. *above all nations.* And implicitly over all their gods (see 95:3; 96:4–5; 97:9; see also 47:2,7–8). *above the heavens.* Above even the most exalted aspect of the creation (see v. 6).

‡113:5 The rhetorical center (see note on 6:6). *our God.* What grace, that He has covenanted to be "our" God (cf. v. 6—he "humbleth himself to behold ..."; see also Gen 17:7; Ex 19:5–6; 20:2)!

113:7–9 The Lord exalts the lowly—the God of highest majesty does not ally Himself with the high and mighty of the earth but stands with and raises up the poor and needy (see 1 Sam 2:3–8; Luke 1:46–55).

113:7–8 Repeated almost verbatim from 1 Sam 2:8.

113:7 *poor ... needy.* See 9:18; 34:6 and notes. *dust ... dunghill.* Symbolic of a humble status (see Gen 18:27; 1 Ki 16:2), but here probably also of extreme distress and need (see Job 30:19; 42:6; Is 47:1; Jer 25:34).

113:9 *barren woman.* In that ancient society barrenness was for a woman the greatest disgrace and the deepest tragedy (see Gen 30:1; 1 Sam 1:6–7,10); in her old age she would be as desolate as Naomi because she would have no one to sustain her (see Ruth 1:11–13; see also 2 Ki 4:14). *house.* Family circle. *joyful mother.* Because of God's gracious provision, as in the case of Sarah (see Gen 21:2), Rebekah (see Gen 25:21), Rachel (see Gen 30:23), Hannah (see 1 Sam 1:20), the Shunammite (see 2 Ki 4:17) and others. *Praise ye the LORD.* Probably once stood at the beginning of Ps 114, which now lacks a Hallelujah.

Ps 114 A hymnic celebration of the exodus—one of the most exquisitely fashioned songs of the Psalter. It probably dates from the period of the monarchy sometime after the division of the kingdom (see v. 2). No doubt it was composed for liturgical use at the temple during one of the annual religious festivals (see introduction to Ps 113). The theme is progressively developed through four balanced thematic stanzas, reaching its climax in the fourth. The first two stanzas (vv. 1–4) recall the great events of the exodus; the last two (vv. 5–8) celebrate their continuing significance.

114:1–2 The great OT redemptive event.

114:1 *Israel ... house of Jacob.* Synonyms (see Ex 19:3). *went out of Egypt.* Recalls the exodus and all the great events of the wilderness journey.

2 [a]Judah was his sanctuary,
And Israel his dominion.

3 [a]The sea saw *it,* and fled:
[b]Jordan was driven back.
4 [a]The mountains skipped like rams,
And the little hills like lambs.

5 [a]What ailed thee, O thou sea, that thou fleddest?
Thou Jordan, *that* thou wast driven back?
6 Ye mountains, *that* ye skipped like rams;
And ye little hills, like lambs?

7 Tremble, thou earth, at the presence of the Lord,
At the presence of the God of Jacob;
8 [a]Which turned the rock *into* a standing water,
The flint into a fountain of waters.

Psalm 115

1 Not [a]unto us, O LORD, not unto us,
But unto thy name give glory,
For thy mercy, *and* for thy truth's sake.
2 Wherefore should the heathen say,
[a]Where *is* now their God?

3 [a]But our God *is* in the heavens:
He hath done whatsoever he pleased.
4 [a]Their idols *are* silver and gold,
The work of men's hands.
5 They have mouths, but they speak not:
Eyes have they, but they see not:
6 They have ears, but they hear not:
Noses have they, but they smell not:
7 They *have* hands, but they handle not:
Feet *have* they, but they walk not:
Neither speak they through their throat.
8 [a]They that make them are like unto them;
So is every one that trusteth in them.

9 [a]O Israel, trust thou in the LORD:
[b]He *is* their help and their shield.
10 O house of Aaron, trust in the LORD:
He *is* their help and their shield.
11 Ye that fear the LORD, trust in the LORD:
He *is* their help and their shield.

12 The LORD hath been mindful of us: he will bless *us;*
He will bless the house of Israel;
He will bless the house of Aaron.
13 [a]He will bless them that fear the LORD,
Both small [1]and great.
14 The LORD shall increase you more and more,
You and your children.

114:2 [a]Ex. 6:7; Deut. 27:9
114:3 [a]Ex. 14:21; Ps. 77:16 [b]Josh. 3:13
114:4 [a]Ps. 29:6; 68:16
114:5 [a]Hab. 3:8
114:8 [a]Ex. 17:6; Num. 20:11; Ps. 107:35
115:1 [a]Is. 48:11; Ezek. 36:32
115:2 [a]Ps. 42:3,10; 79:10; Joel 2:17
115:3 [a]1 Chr. 16:26; Ps. 135:6; Dan. 4:35
115:4 [a]Deut. 4:28; Ps. 135:15; Jer. 10:3
115:8 [a]Ps. 135:18; Is. 44:9-11
115:9 [a]Ps. 118:2,3 [b]Ps. 33:20
115:13 [1]Heb. *with* [a]Ps. 128:1

‡114:2 *Judah . . . Israel.* The southern and northern kingdoms, viewed here as the one people of God. *was.* The crucial event was the establishment of the covenant at Sinai, where Israel became bound to the Lord as a "kingdom of priests, and a holy nation" (Ex 19:3–6). *his.* The "antecedent" is not expressed until the climax (v. 7). *sanctuary.* His temple in which He took up His residence in the world—symbolized by the tabernacle, later the temple. In Ex 15:17 the promised land is similarly called God's sanctuary. *dominion.* The special realm over which He ruled as King. This, rather than the exodus itself, was the great wonder of God's grace.
114:3–4 The author evokes a fearsome scene such as that portrayed by other poets (see 18:7–15; 68:7–8; 77:16–19; Judg 5:4–5; Hab 3:3–10).
114:3 *sea . . . Jordan.* The Red sea and the Jordan River, through which the Lord brought His people—here they are personified. *saw it, and fled.* Saw the mighty God approach in His awesome pillar of cloud and fled.
114:4 *skipped.* Or "leaped"; the mountains and hills quaked at God's approach (see 29:6).
114:7–8 The Lord of yesterday (vv. 5–6)—the God of Jacob—is still with us.
114:7 *Tremble.* In awesome recognition. *earth.* All creation. *Jacob.* A synonym for Israel (see Gen 32:28).
114:8 *turned the rock into a standing water.* Thus sustaining and refreshing life (see Ex 17:6; Num 20:11).
Ps 115 Praise of the Lord, the one true God, for His love and faithfulness toward His people. It was composed as a liturgy of praise for the temple worship. It may have been written for use at the dedication of the second temple (see Ezra 6:16) when Israel was beginning to revive after the disruption of the exile. See introduction to Ps 113. Structurally, the song advances in five movements involving a liturgical exchange between the people and temple personnel: (1) vv. 1–8: the people; (2) vv. 9–11: Levitical choir leader (the refrain perhaps spoken by the Levitical choir); (3) vv. 12–13: the people; (4) vv. 14–15: the priests; (5) vv. 16–18: the people.
115:1–8 Praise of God's love and faithfulness toward His people, which silences the taunts of the nations.
115:1 *Not unto us . . . not unto us.* Israel's existence, and now her revival, is not her own achievement. *name.* See note on 5:11. *mercy . . . truth's.* The most common OT expression for God's covenant benefits (see note on 26:3). *mercy.* See note on 6:4.
115:2 *Where is . . . God?* The taunt of the nations when Israel is decimated by natural disasters (see Joel 2:17) or crushed by enemies, especially when Judah is destroyed and the temple of God razed (see 79:10; Mic 7:10).
115:3 *is in the heavens.* Sits enthroned (see 113:5) in the heavens (v. 16). *whatsoever he pleased.* If Israel is decimated or destroyed, it is God's doing; it is not His failure or inability to act, nor is it the achievement of the idols the nations worship. And when Israel is revived, that is also God's doing, and no other god can oppose Him.
115:4–7 Whatever glory and power the false gods are thought to have (as symbolized in the images made to represent them), they are mere figments of human imagination and utterly worthless (see 135:15–18; Is 46:1–7).
115:8 *They that make them.* The taunting nations (cf. v. 2). *like unto them.* Powerless and ineffectual. For a graphic elaboration of this truth see Is 44:9–20.
115:9–11 The call to trust in the Lord, not in idols (see v. 8). For triple repetition as a liturgical convention see note on 96:1–3. For the same groupings see 118:2–4; see also 135:19–20.
115:11 *Ye that fear the LORD.* Perhaps proselytes (see 1 Ki 8:41–43; Ezra 6:21; Neh 10:28).
115:12–13 The people's confession of trust.
115:14–15 The priestly blessing.
‡115:14 *shall increase you.* In numbers, wealth and strength (cf. Eccl 2:9: "was great, and increased more than").

15 You *are* [a]blessed of the LORD
[b]Which made heaven and earth.
16 The heaven, *even* the heavens, *are* the LORD'S:
But the earth hath he given to the children of men.
17 [a]The dead praise not the LORD,
Neither any that go down into silence.
18 [a]But we will bless the LORD
From this time forth and for evermore.
Praise the LORD.

Psalm 116

1 [a]I love the LORD, because he hath heard
My voice *and* my supplications.
2 Because he hath inclined his ear unto me,
Therefore will I call upon *him* [1]as long as I live.
3 [a]The sorrows of death compassed me,
And the pains of hell [1]gat hold upon me:
I found trouble and sorrow.
4 Then called I upon the name of the LORD;
O LORD, I beseech thee, deliver my soul.
5 [a]Gracious *is* the LORD, and [b]righteous;
Yea, our God *is* merciful.
6 The LORD preserveth the simple:
I was brought low, and he helped me.
7 Return unto thy [a]rest, O my soul;
For [b]the LORD hath dealt bountifully with thee.
8 [a]For thou hast delivered my soul from death,
Mine eyes from tears,
And my feet from falling.
9 I will walk before the LORD
[a]In the land of the living.
10 [a]I believed, therefore have I spoken:
I was greatly afflicted:
11 [a]I said in my haste,
[b]All men *are* liars.

12 What shall I render unto the LORD
For all his benefits towards me?
13 I will take the cup of salvation,
And call upon the name of the LORD.
14 [a]I will pay my vows unto the LORD
Now in the presence of all his people.
15 [a]Precious in the sight of the LORD
Is the death of his saints.
16 Oh LORD, truly [a]I *am* thy servant;
I *am* thy servant, *and* [b]the son of thy handmaid:
Thou hast loosed my bonds.

115:15 [a]Gen. 14:19 [b]Gen. 1:1; Ps. 96:5
115:17 [a]Ps. 6:5; 88:10-12; Is. 38:18
115:18 [a]Ps. 113:2; Dan. 2:20
116:1 [a]Ps. 18:1
116:2 [1]Heb. *in my days*
116:3 [1]Heb. *found me* [a]Ps. 18:4-6
116:5 [a]Ps. 103:8 [b]Ezra 9:15; Neh. 9:8; Ps. 119:137; 145:17
116:7 [a]Jer. 6:16; Mat. 11:29 [b]Ps. 13:6; 119:17
116:8 [a]Ps. 56:13
116:9 [a]Ps. 27:13
116:10 [a]2 Cor. 4:13
116:11 [a]Ps. 31:22 [b]Rom. 3:4
116:14 [a]ver. 18; Ps. 22:25; Jonah 2:9
116:15 [a]Ps. 72:14
116:16 [a]Ps. 119:125; 143:12 [b]Ps. 86:16

115:16–18 The people's concluding doxology.
115:16 *heaven . . . earth.* The one the exclusive realm of the exalted, all-sovereign God; the other the divinely appointed place for man, where he lives under God's rule and care, enjoys His abundant blessings (vv. 12–13) and celebrates His praise (v. 18).
115:17 *dead praise not.* The dead no longer live in "the earth" (v. 16) but have descended to the silent realm below, where blessings are no longer enjoyed and hence praise is absent (see notes on 6:5; 30:1).
Ps 116 Praise of the Lord for deliverance from death. It may have been written by a king (see v. 16 and note; cf. also Hezekiah's thanksgiving, Is 38:10–20); its language echoes many of the psalms of David. As used in Jewish liturgy (see introduction to Ps 113), the singular personal pronoun must have been used corporately (see note on Ps 30 title), and the references to "death" may have been understood as alluding to the Egyptian bondage and/or the exile. This thanksgiving song falls into three main divisions (vv. 1–6, 7–14, 15–19), each of which contains a unified thematic development.
116:1–6 I love the Lord because He has heard and saved me.
116:2 *will I call upon him.* In Him I will trust and my prayers will ever be to Him—a declaration repeated in each of the main divisions (see vv. 13,17).
116:3–4 See 18:4–6.
116:3 *sorrows of death.* See note on 18:5.
116:5 *our God.* The author is conscious of those about him; he is praising the Lord "in the presence of all his people" (vv. 14,18).
116:6 *simple.* The person who is childlike in his sense of dependence on and trust in the Lord (see note on 19:7).
116:7–14 The Lord's goodness to me and how I will repay Him.
‡116:7 *rest.* A state of unthreatened well-being (cf. Jer 6:16; see 1 Ki 5:4; see also note on 23:2, "still waters"). *O my soul.* See note on 103:1–2,22. *hath dealt bountifully.* The Hebrew underlying this phrase is the same as that underlying "benefits" in v. 12 (see note there) and so marks v. 7 as introductory to vv. 7–14.
116:8 *my soul.* Me (see note on 6:3).
116:10 *I believed.* The author speaks of his faith that moved him to call on the Lord when he was threatened. *I was greatly afflicted.* This and the quotation in v. 11 should perhaps be taken, together with the one in v. 4, as a brief recollection of the prayer offered when the psalmist was in distress. The threat of death from which he had been delivered was brought on by the false accusations of enemies, as in Ps 109 (see notes on 5:9; 10:7). (For another interpretation see following note.)
116:11 *All men are liars.* The heart of the accusation he had lodged against his false accusers (for examples of similar accusations see 5:9–10; 35:11,15; 109:2–4). Others interpret these words as a declaration that all men offer but a false hope for deliverance (see 60:11; 118:8–9)—therefore the psalmist called on the Lord.
‡116:12 *What shall I render . . . ?* Expressions of devotion He desires (compare vv. 13–14,17–18 with 50:14–15,23). *benefits.* The Hebrew for this word occurs only here in the OT, but represents the same basic root as "hath dealt bountifully" in v. 7 (see note there).
116:13 *cup of salvation.* Often thought to be related to the cup of the passover meal referred to in Mat 26:27 and parallels, but far more likely the cup of wine drunk at the festal meal that climaxed a thank offering (cf. 22:26,29; Lev 7:11–21)—called the "cup of salvation" because the thank offering and its meal celebrated deliverance by the Lord. See the parallel with "sacrifice of thanksgiving" in the corresponding series in vv. 17–18.
116:14 *vows.* To praise the Lord (see note on 7:17).
116:15–19 Because God has counted my life precious, I offer Him the expressions of my devotion.
‡116:15 *Precious . . . Is the death.* Not in the sense of highly valued but of that which is carefully watched over; cf. the analogous expression, "precious shall their blood be in his sight" (72:14). *saints.* See note on 4:3.
116:16 *thy servant.* This may identify the psalmist as the Lord's anointed (see 78:70), but in any event as one devoted to the Lord (see 19:11,13). *son of thy handmaid.* See 86:16.

17 I will offer to thee [a]the sacrifice of thanksgiving,
And will call upon the name of the LORD.
18 I will pay my vows unto the LORD
Now in the presence of all his people,
19 In the [a]courts of the LORD's house,
In the midst of thee, O Jerusalem.
Praise ye the LORD.

Psalm 117

1 [a]O praise the LORD, all ye nations:
Praise him, all ye people.
2 For his merciful kindness is great toward us:
And [a]the truth of the LORD *endureth* for ever.
Praise ye the LORD.

Psalm 118

1 [a]O give thanks unto the LORD; for *he is* good:
Because his mercy *endureth* for ever.
2 [a]Let Israel now say,
That his mercy *endureth* for ever.
3 Let the house of Aaron now say,
That his mercy *endureth* for ever.
4 Let them now that fear the LORD say,
That his mercy *endureth* for ever.
5 [a]I called upon the LORD [1]in distress:
The LORD answered me, *and* [b]*set me* in a large place.
6 [a]The LORD *is* [1]on my side; I will not fear:
What can man do unto me?
7 [a]The LORD taketh my part with them that help me:
Therefore shall [b]I see *my desire* upon them that hate me.
8 [a]*It is* better to trust in the LORD
Than to put confidence in man.
9 [a]*It is* better to trust in the LORD
Than to put confidence in princes.
10 All nations compassed me about:
But in the name of the LORD will I [1]destroy them.
11 They [a]compassed me about; yea, they compassed me about:
But in the name of the LORD I will destroy them.
12 They compassed me about [a]like bees;
They are quenched [b]as the fire of thorns:
For in the name of the LORD I will [1]destroy them.
13 Thou hast thrust sore at me that *I* might fall:
But the LORD helped me.

116:17 [a]Lev. 7:12; Ps. 50:14; 107:22
116:19 [a]Ps. 96:8; 100:4
117:1 [a]Rom. 15:11
117:2 [a]Ps. 100:5
118:1 [a]1 Chr. 16:8; Ps. 106:1; 107:1
118:2 [a]Ps. 115:9
118:5 [1]Heb. *out of distress* [a]Ps. 120:1 [b]Ps. 18:19
118:6 [1]Heb. *for me* [a]Ps. 27:1; Heb. 13:6
118:7 [a]Ps. 54:4 [b]Ps. 59:10
118:8 [a]Ps. 40:4; 62:8,9
118:9 [a]Ps. 146:3
118:10 [1]Heb. *cut them off*
118:11 [a]Ps. 88:17
118:12 [1]Heb. *cut down* [a]Deut. 1:44 [b]Eccl. 7:6; Nah. 1:10

116:19 *courts.* Of the temple (see 84:2,10; 2 Ki 21:5; 23:11–12).
Ps 117 The shortest psalm in the Psalter—and the shortest chapter in the Bible—Ps 117 is an expanded Hallelujah (sometimes joined with Ps 118). It may originally have served as the conclusion to the preceding collection of Hallelujah psalms (Ps 111–116)—of which it is the seventh. All nations and peoples are called on to praise the Lord (as in 47:1; 67:3–5; 96:7; 98:4; 100:1; see note on 9:1) for His great love and enduring faithfulness toward Israel (see Is 12:4–6). Thus the Hallelujahs of the OT Psalter, when fully expounded, express that great truth, so often emphasized in the OT, that the destiny of all peoples is involved in what God was doing in and for His people Israel (see, e.g., 2:8–12; 47:9; 67:2; 72:17; 102:15; 110; Gen 12:3; Deut 32:43; 1 Ki 8:41–43; Is 2:2–4; 11:10; 14:2; 25:6–7; 52:15; 56:7; 60:3; 66:18–24; Jer 3:17; 16:19–21; 33:9; Amos 9:11–12; Mic 5:7–9; Zeph 3:8–9; Hag 2:7; Zech 2:10–11; 8:20–23; 9:9–10; 14:2–3; Mal 3:12). See introduction to Ps 113.
117:1 Quoted in Rom 15:11 as proof that the salvation of Gentiles and the glorifying of God by Gentiles was not a divine afterthought.
‡117:2 The reason for the praise. *merciful kindness . . . truth.* That is, merciful kindness-and-truth (see 36:5 and note; also note on 3:7). *merciful kindness.* See note on 6:4.
Ps 118 A hymn of thanksgiving for deliverance from enemies. Of the many interpretations of this psalm, three have gained the most adherents (but with much variation in detail): 1. A Davidic king leads the nation in a liturgy of thanksgiving for deliverance and victory after a hard-fought battle with a powerful confederacy of nations (cf. 2 Chr 20:27–28; see note on v. 19). 2. Israel celebrates—probably at the feast of tabernacles—her deliverance from Egypt and victory over the Canaanites. 3. The postexilic Jews celebrate deliverance from their enemies, either at the dedication of the second temple (see Ezra 6:16) or at the dedication of the rebuilt walls of Jerusalem (see Neh 12:37–43). According to the first interpretation, the speaker in vv. 5–21 is the king; according to the second and third, the speaker is the Levitical (or priestly) leader of the liturgy, speaking (representatively) on behalf of the people. The notes that follow assume the first interpretation. In the postexilic liturgy developed for the annual festivals (see introduction to Ps 113), the song was used as a thanksgiving for national deliverance. As the last song of that liturgy, it may have been the hymn sung by Jesus and His disciples at the conclusion of the Last Supper (see Mat 26:30).

Following a liturgical call to praise (vv. 1–4), the king offers a song of thanksgiving for deliverance and victory in battle (vv. 5–21). In vv. 22–27 the people rejoice over what the Lord has done. Thereafter, the king speaks his final word of praise (v. 28), and a liturgical conclusion (v. 29) repeats the opening call to praise, thus framing the whole service.
118:1–4 The liturgical call to praise.
118:1 A conventional call to praise (shared in whole or in part with Ps 105–107; 136; 1 Chr 16:8,34; 2 Chr 20:21). *give thanks.* See note on Ps 100 title. This, together with vv. 2–4 (except for the refrain) and 29, may have been by the same voice that speaks in vv. 5–21. *mercy.* See vv. 2–4,29; see also note on 6:4.
118:2–4 *Israel . . . house of Aaron . . . them now that fear the LORD.* See 115:9–11 and note. Triple repetition is a common feature in this psalm (see note on 96:1–3).
118:5–21 The king's song of thanksgiving for deliverance and victory.
118:5 *in a large place.* See 18:19 and note ("broad place").
118:7 *shall I see.* Or "I see."
118:8–9 See 33:16–19; see also Ps 62; 146.
118:10 *in the name of the LORD.* See 1 Sam 17:45. *name.* See vv. 11–12,26; see also note on 5:11.
118:12 *as the fire of thorns.* See 58:9 and note.
‡118:13 *Thou hast thrust sore at me.* Addresses the enemy that viciously attacked him. *that I might fall.* I was about to be killed (see vv. 17–18; see also note on 13:4). *But the LORD helped.* Even in its brutality, the strength of the enemy was nothing compared to the Lord's protection.

14 [a]The LORD *is* my strength and song,
And is become my salvation.
15 The voice of rejoicing and salvation *is* in the tabernacles of the righteous:
The right hand of the LORD doeth valiantly.
16 [a]The right hand of the LORD is exalted:
The right hand of the LORD doeth valiantly.
17 [a]I shall not die, but live,
And [b]declare the works of the LORD.
18 The LORD hath [a]chastened me sore:
But he hath not given me over unto death.
19 [a]Open to me the gates of righteousness:
I will go into them, *and* I will praise the LORD:
20 [a]This gate of the LORD,
[b]Into which the righteous shall enter.
21 I will praise thee: for thou hast [a]heard me,
And [b]art become my salvation.
22 [a]The stone *which* the builders refused
Is become the head *stone* of the corner.
23 [1]This is the LORD'S doing;
It is marvellous in our eyes.
24 This *is* the day *which* the LORD hath made;
We will rejoice and be glad in it.
25 Save now, I beseech thee, O LORD:
O LORD, I beseech thee, send now prosperity.
26 [a]Blessed *be* he that cometh in the name of the LORD:
We have blessed you out of the house of the LORD.
27 God *is* the LORD, which hath shewed us [a]light:
Bind the sacrifice with cords,
Even unto the horns of the altar.
28 Thou *art* my God, and I will praise thee:
[a]*Thou art* my God, I will exalt thee.
29 [a]O give thanks unto the LORD; for *he is* good:
For his mercy *endureth* for ever.

118:14 [a]Ex. 15:2; Is. 12:2
118:16 [a]Ex. 15:6
118:17 [a]Ps. 6:5; Hab. 1:12 [b]Ps. 73:28
118:18 [a]2 Cor. 6:9
118:19 [a]Is. 26:2
118:20 [a]Ps. 24:7 [b]Is. 35:8; Rev. 22:14
118:21 [a]Ps. 116:1 [b]ver. 14
118:22 [a]Mat. 21:42; Mark 12:10; Luke 20:17; Acts 4:11
118:23 [1]Heb. *This is from the* LORD
118:26 [a]Mat. 21:9; Mark 11:9; Luke 19:38; See Zech. 4:7
118:27 [a]Esth. 8:16; 1 Pet. 2:9
118:28 [a]Ex. 15:2; Is. 25:1
118:29 [a]ver. 1

Psalm 119

א ALEPH.

1 Blessed *are* the [1]undefiled in the way,
[a]Who walk in the law of the LORD.

119:1 [1]Or, *perfect,* or, *sincere* [a]Ps. 128:1

118:14 Perhaps recalls the triumph song of Ex 15, but more likely the verse had become a widely used testimony of praise (see Is 12:2).

‡118:15 *tabernacles.* Tents or dwellings. *righteous.* Israel as the people (ideally) committed in heart and life to the Lord (see v. 20; see also 68:3 and note). Cf. "the tents of wickedness" (84:10).

118:17 *live, And declare.* See 115:17–18; see also note on 6:5.

118:18 *chastened me.* The king acknowledges that the grave threat through which he has passed has also served God's purpose—to discipline him and teach him humble godliness (see 6:1; 38:1; 94:12; Deut 4:36; 8:5).

‡118:19 *Open to me.* This line suggests a liturgical procession (see v. 27) in which the king approaches the inner court of the temple at the head of the jubilant worshipers (see Ps 24; 68). *gates.* Those leading to the inner temple court. *of righteousness.* Often thought to be the name of a particular gateway, but more likely only descriptive here of the gate through which "the righteous shall enter" (v. 20). It is possible that the procession began outside the city and that "the gates of righteousness" are the gates of Jerusalem, the city of God (see note on 24:7; see also Is 26:2).

118:21 This closing verse of the thanksgiving song echoes the "give thanks" of v. 1, the "answered me" of v. 5 and the testimony of v. 14.

118:22–27 The people's exultation.

‡118:22 *The stone . . . the builders refused.* Most likely a reference to the king (whose deliverance and victory are being celebrated), who had been looked on with disdain by the kings invading his realm—the builders of worldly empires. Others suppose that the stone refers to Israel, a nation held in contempt by the world powers. *head stone of the corner.* Either a capstone over a door (a large stone used as a lintel), or a large stone used to anchor and align the corner of a wall, or the keystone of an arch (see Zech 4:7; 10:4). This stone, disdained by the worldly powers, has become the most important stone in the structure of the new world order that God is bringing about through Israel. Jesus applied this verse (and v. 23) to Himself (see Mat 21:42; Mark 12:10–11; Luke 20:17; see also Acts 4:11; Eph 2:20; 1 Pet 2:7).

‡118:24 *day which the LORD hath made . . . rejoice.* This day of rejoicing was made possible by God's deliverance in the victory being celebrated. Others suppose a reference to passover or the feast of tabernacles. *hath made.* Or "has done it" (see vv. 15–17, 23)—has made the "stone" the "head stone of the corner" (v. 22).

118:25 Prayer for the Lord to continue to save and sustain His people.

118:26 *he that cometh in the name of the LORD.* The one who with God's help had defeated the enemies "in the name of the LORD" (see vv. 10–12). *you.* The plural ("you" is plural in the Hebrew) may have been used to exalt the king (the plural was often used with reference to God), whom God had so singularly blessed (as in 1 Ki 9:6). Alternatively, it may refer to those who have come with the king victoriously from the battle. The crowds who greeted Jesus at His Triumphal Entry into Jerusalem used the words of vv. 25–26 (see John 12:13). *out of the house of the LORD.* From God's very presence (see 134:3).

118:27 *shewed us light.* An echo of the priestly benediction (see Num 6:25). *Bind . . . with cords.* Apparently a call to complete the climax of the liturgy of a thank offering (see Lev 7:11–21), though others suggest the liturgy of the feast of tabernacles.

118:28–29 See introduction.

‡Ps 119 A devotional on the word of God. The author was an Israelite of exemplary piety (probably postexilic) who (1) was passionately devoted to the word of God as the word of life; (2) humbly acknowledged, nevertheless, the errant ways of his heart and life; (3) knew the pain—but also the fruits—of God's corrective discipline; and (4) had suffered much at the hands of those who arrogantly disregarded God's word and made him the target of their hostility, ridicule and slander. It is possible that he was a priest (see notes on vv. 23,57)—and the psalm might well be a vehicle for priestly instruction in godliness. He elaborated on the themes of 19:7–13 and interwove with them many prayers for deliverance, composing a massive alphabetic acrostic (the psalm is an acrostic poem; the verses of each stanza begin with the same letter of the Hebrew alphabet) that de-

2 Blessed *are* they that keep his testimonies,
And *that* seek him with the whole heart.
3 [a]They also do no iniquity:
They walk in his ways.
4 Thou hast commanded *us*
To keep thy precepts diligently.
5 O that my ways were directed
To keep thy statutes!
6 [a]Then shall I not be ashamed,
When I have respect unto all thy commandments.
7 [a]I will praise thee with uprightness of heart,
When I shall have learned [1]thy righteous judgments.
8 I will keep thy statutes:
O forsake me not utterly.

ב BETH.

9 Wherewithal shall a young man cleanse his way?
By taking heed *thereto* according to thy word.
10 With my whole heart have I [a]sought thee:
O let me not [b]wander from thy commandments.

119:3 [a]1 John 3:9; 5:18
119:6 [a]Job 22:26; 1 John 2:28
119:7 [a]ver. 171
119:7 [1]Heb. *judgments of thy righteousness*
119:10 [a]2 Chr. 15:15 [b]ver. 21,118

mands patient, meditative reading. In regard to length, form and type it stands alone in the Psalter. And of all the psalms, this one is the most likely to have been composed originally in writing and intended to be read rather than sung or recited. Most of its lines are addressed to God, mingling prayers with professions of devotion to God's law. Yet, as the opening verses (and perhaps also its elaborate acrostic form) make clear, it was intended for godly instruction (in the manner of Ps 1; see v. 9 and note). It was included in the Psalter no doubt as a model of piety.

Whereas elsewhere in the Psalter the focus falls primarily on God's mighty acts of creation and redemption and His rule over all the world, here devotion to the word of God (and the God of the word) is the dominant theme. The author highlights two aspects of that word: (1) God's directives for life and (2) God's promises—the one calling for obedience, the other for faith (the two elements of true godliness; see 34:8–14 and note). In referring to these, he makes use of eight Hebrew terms supplied him by OT traditions: *torah,* "law"; *'edot,* "testimonies"; *piqqudim,* "precepts"; *miṣwot,* "commandments"; *mishpaṭim,* "judgments" (all shared with 19:7–9; *piqqudim* is translated "statutes" in 19:8); *ḥuqqim,* "statutes"; *dabar,* "word" (sometimes in the sense of "law," sometimes in the sense of "promise"); *'imrah,* "word" (often with the sense of "promise;" cf. v. 76). These terms he distributes throughout the 22 stanzas (using all eight in *He, Vau, Cheth, Jod, Caph, Pe*—never using less than six), employing a different order in each stanza. It may be that the availability of these eight terms determined (in large part) for the author the decision to devote eight verses to each letter of the alphabet. The alphabetic acrostic form, especially one as elaborate as this, may appear arbitrary and artificial to a modern reader (as if the author merely selected a traditional form from the poet's workshop and then labored to fill it with pious sentences), but a sympathetic and reflective reading of this devotional will compel a more favorable judgment. The author had a theme that filled his soul, a theme as big as life, that ranged the length and breadth and height and depth of a person's walk with God. Nothing less than the use of the full power of language would suffice, and of that the alphabet was a most apt symbol.

Apart from the obvious formal structure dictated by the chosen acrostic form, little need (or can) be said. It must be noted, however, that the first three and the last three verses were designed as introduction and conclusion to the whole. The former sets the tone of instruction in godly wisdom; the latter succinctly restates and summarizes the main themes. It may also be observed that the middle of the psalm has been marked by a similar three-verse introduction to the second half (see note on vv. 89–91). For the rest, the thought meanders, turns back upon itself and repeats (with varied nuances). The following notes point out continuities of thought and possible structure within stanzas.

119:1–3 General introduction.
119:1–2 *Blessed.* See note on 1:1.
‡119:1 *undefiled in the way.* This opening general description is further elaborated in the rest of the introduction, which concludes with an equally general statement: "They walk in his ways" (v. 3). See Gen 17:1; cf. Gen 26:5. *law.* Hebrew *torah,* a collective term for God's covenant directives for His people (see Deut 4:44). "Law" often came, especially later, to have a broader reference—the whole Pentateuch (see Luke 24:44) or even the whole OT (see John 15:25; 1 Cor 14:21)—but here it is limited by the synonyms with which it is used interchangeably.
119:2 *testimonies.* Hebrew *'edot,* a specifically covenantal term referring to stipulations laid down by the covenant Lord (see 25:10; Deut 4:45). *heart.* See v. 7; see also note on 4:7.
119:3 *ways.* The Hebrew for this word occurs only rarely in this psalm, but is common in Deuteronomy and elsewhere as a general reference to God's covenant requirements (see note on 25:4)—used here to balance "way" in v. 1.
119:4–8 Those who obey God's law (see vv. 4–5,8) can hope for God's help (see vv. 6–8).
119:4 *precepts.* Hebrew *piqqudim,* covenant regulations laid down by the Lord (see 19:8; 111:7).
119:5 *statutes.* Hebrew *ḥuqqim,* covenant directives (see Deut 6:2; 28:15,45; 30:10,16; 1 Ki 11:11), emphasizing their fixed character.
‡119:6 *not be ashamed.* The psalmist would not suffer poverty or sickness, or humiliation at the hands of his enemies, and so become the object of sneers (see vv. 31,46,80; 25:2–3,20), but he would have reason to praise the Lord (see v. 7) for blessings received and deliverances granted because the Lord does not forsake him (see v. 8). *have respect unto.* See v. 15; 74:20. *commandments.* Hebrew *miṣwot,* covenant directives (see Ex 20:6; 24:12; Deut 4:2), designated specifically as that which God has commanded.
119:7 *righteous.* One of the author's favorite characterizations of God's law (see vv. 62,75,106,123,144,160,164; see also 19:9). *judgments.* Hebrew *mishpaṭim,* covenant directives (see Ex 21:1; 24:3; Deut 4:1), as the laws laid down by a ruler (king).
‡119:8 *forsake me not.* Do not abandon me to poverty, sickness or my enemies.
‡119:9 *young man.* Some have thought this a characterization of the author, but more likely it indicates instruction addressed to the young after the manner of the wisdom teachers (see 34:11; Prov 1:4; Eccl 11:9; 12:1). *cleanse his way.* Be free from all moral taint (see 73:13). *word.* Hebrew *dabar,* a general designation for God's (word) revelation, but here used with special reference to His law (sometimes promises).
119:10 *heart.* See v. 11; see also note on 4:7. *have I sought thee.* The author's devotion is first of all to the God of the law and the promises; they have meaning for him only because they are God's word of life for him.

11 [a]Thy word have I hid in mine heart,
That I might not sin against thee.
12 Blessed *art* thou, O LORD:
[a]Teach me thy statutes.
13 With my lips have I [a]declared
All the judgments of thy mouth.
14 I have rejoiced in the way of thy testimonies,
As *much as* in all riches.
15 I will [a]meditate in thy precepts,
And have respect unto thy ways.
16 I will [a]delight myself in thy statutes:
I will not forget thy word.

ג GIMEL.

17 [a]Deal bountifully with thy servant, *that* I may live,
And keep thy word.
18 [1]Open thou mine eyes,
That I may behold wondrous *things* out of thy law.
19 [a]I *am* a stranger in the earth:
Hide not thy commandments from me.
20 [a]My soul breaketh for the longing
That it hath unto thy judgments at all times.
21 Thou hast rebuked the proud *that are* cursed,
Which do [a]err from thy commandments.
22 [a]Remove from me reproach and contempt;
For I have kept thy testimonies.
23 Princes also did sit *and* speak against me:
But thy servant did [a]meditate in thy statutes.
24 [a]Thy testimonies also *are* my delight
And [1]my counsellers.

ד DALETH.

25 [a]My soul cleaveth unto the dust:
[b]Quicken thou me according to thy word.
26 I have declared my ways, and thou heardest me:
[a]Teach me thy statutes.
27 Make me to understand the way of thy precepts:
So [a]shall I talk of thy wondrous works.
28 [a]My soul [1]melteth for heaviness:
Strengthen thou me according unto thy word.
29 Remove from me the way of lying:
And grant me thy law graciously.
30 I have chosen the way of truth:
Thy judgments have I laid *before me.*
31 I have stuck unto thy testimonies:
O LORD, put me not to shame.
32 I will run the way of thy commandments,
When thou shalt [a]enlarge my heart.

ה HE.

33 [a]Teach me, O LORD, the way of thy statutes;
And I shall keep it [b]*unto* the end.
34 Give me understanding, and I shall keep thy law;

119:11 [a]Ps. 37:31; Luke 2:19
119:12 [a]ver. 26,33; Ps. 25:4
119:13 [a]Ps. 34:11
119:15 [a]ver. 23,48; Ps. 1:2
119:16 [a]Ps. 1:2
119:17 [a]Ps. 116:7
119:18 [1]Heb. *Reveal*
119:19 [a]Gen. 47:9; 1 Chr. 29:15; Ps. 39:12; 2 Cor. 5:6; Heb. 11:13
119:20 [a]Ps. 42:1,2; 63:1; 84:2
119:21 [a]ver. 10,110
119:22 [a]Ps. 39:8
119:23 [a]ver. 15
119:24 [1]Heb. *men of my counsel* [a]ver. 77,92
119:25 [a]Ps. 44:25 [b]Ps. 143:11
119:26 [a]Ps. 25:4; 27:11; 86:11
119:27 [a]Ps. 145:5,6
119:28 [1]Heb. *droppeth* [a]Ps. 107:26
119:32 [a]1 Ki. 4:29; Is. 60:5; 2 Cor. 6:11
119:33 [a]ver. 12 [b]Mat. 10:22; Rev. 2:26

119:11 *word.* Hebrew *'imrah,* a synonym of *dabar* ("word"; see note on v. 9; see also Deut 33:9; Prov 30:5).
119:13 *have I declared.* Either in meditation or in liturgies of covenant commitment to the Lord (see 50:16).
119:14 *As much as in all riches.* See vv. 72,111,162.
‡119:15 *ways.* The Hebrew for this word is a synonym of the Hebrew for "ways" in v. 3 (the two Hebrew words parallel each other in 25:4).
119:17–24 Devotion to God's law marks the Lord's servant, but alienates him from the arrogant (v. 21) of the world.
119:17 *I may . . . keep.* Out of gratitude for God's care and blessing.
119:18 *wondrous things.* Usually ascribed to God's redeeming acts (see 9:1 and note)—but God's law contains matters just as wonderful (see v. 27).
119:19 *stranger in the earth.* As a servant of the Lord, i.e., a citizen of His kingdom, he is not at home in any of the kingdoms of the world (see 39:12 and note; see also note on v. 54).
‡119:20 *My soul breaketh . . . longing.* Or "I am consumed with the passion" (see vv. 28,81; see also note on 6:3).
119:21 *the proud.* Those who are a law to themselves, most fully described in 10:2–11 (see vv. 51,69,78,85,122; see also note on 31:23). The author has suffered much from their hostility because of his zeal for God and His law, as the next two verses and many others indicate. *cursed.* Ripe for God's judgment.
119:22 *reproach and contempt.* Of the arrogant.
‡119:23 *Princes.* Because the author mentions also speaking "before kings" (v. 46) and being persecuted by "princes" (v. 161), it may be that he held some official position, such as priest (one of whose functions it would have been to teach God's law; see Lev 10:11; Ezra 7:6; Neh 8:2–8; Jer 2:8; 18:18; Mal 2:7; see also note on v. 57). (These kings and rulers are probably either Israelite from the time of the monarchy or Persian in the postexilic period.) *sit.* As those securely settled in the world—not as strangers (cf. v. 19). *speak against me.* As they share their worldly counsels, they speak derisively of the one who stands apart because he delights in God's statutes and makes them his "counsellers" (v. 24).
119:25–32 Regardless of his circumstances, he is determined to "cling to" (v. 31) God's word.
119:25 *cleaveth unto the dust.* The author speaks much of his sorrow, suffering and affliction (see vv. 28,50,67,71,75,83,92, 107,143,153). It is likely that the ridicule, slander and persecution from his adversaries are usually occasioned by this suffering of God's devoted servant, who makes God's word (His law and promises) the hope of his life (see vv. 42,51,65,69,78, 85,95,110,134,141,150,154,157,161; see also notes on v. 6; 5:9; 31:11–12). See 44:25 and note. *word.* Especially its promises, as also in vv. 28,37,42,49,65,74,81,107,114,147.
119:27 *wondrous works.* See note on v. 18.
119:29 *way of lying.* The way that seems right but leads to death (see Prov 14:12)—in contrast to the way prescribed by God's law, which is trustworthy (see vv. 86,138) and true (see vv. 142,151,160). *grant me thy law.* By keeping me true to Your law, let me enjoy Your blessings.
119:30 *the way of truth.* See note on v. 29.
119:31 *put me not to shame.* See note on v. 6.
‡119:32 *enlarge my heart.* Or "increase my understanding" (see 1 Ki 4:29, "largeness of heart"). *heart.* See note on 4:7.
119:33–40 Prayer for instruction in God's will as he longs for His precepts.

Yea, I shall observe it with *my* whole
heart.

35 Make me to go in the path of thy
commandments;
For therein do I [a]delight.

36 Incline my heart unto thy testimonies,
And not to [a]covetousness.

37 [a][1]Turn away mine eyes from
[b]beholding vanity;
And quicken thou me in thy way.

38 [a]Stablish thy word unto thy servant,
Who *is devoted* to thy fear.

39 Turn away my reproach which I fear:
For thy judgments *are* good.

40 Behold, I have [a]longed after thy
precepts:
[b]Quicken me in thy righteousness.

ו VAU.

41 [a]Let thy mercies come also *unto* me,
O LORD,
Even thy salvation, according to thy
word.

42 [1]So shall I have wherewith to answer
him that reproacheth me:
For I trust in thy word.

43 And take not the word of truth utterly
out of my mouth;
For I have hoped in thy judgments.

44 So shall I keep thy law continually
For ever and ever.

45 And I will walk [1]at liberty:
For I seek thy precepts.

46 [a]I will speak of thy testimonies also
before kings,
And will not be ashamed.

47 And I will [a]delight myself in thy
commandments,
Which I have loved.

119:35 [a]ver. 16
119:36 [a]Ezek. 33:31; Mark 7:21; Luke 12:15; Heb. 13:5
119:37 [1]Heb. *Make to pass* [a]Is. 33:15 [b]Prov. 23:5
119:38 [a]2 Sam. 7:25
119:40 [a]ver. 20 [b]ver. 25,37
119:41 [a]ver. 77; Ps. 106:4
119:42 [1]Or, *So shall I answer him that reproveth me* in a *thing*
119:45 [1]Heb. *at large*
119:46 [a]Ps. 138:1; Mat. 10:18; Acts 26
119:47 [a]ver. 16
119:48 [a]ver. 15
119:49 [a]ver. 74,81
119:50 [a]Rom. 15:4
119:51 [a]Jer. 20:7 [b]ver. 157; Job 23:11; Ps. 44:18
119:53 [a]Ezra 9:3
119:55 [a]Ps. 63:6
119:57 [a]Ps. 16:5; Jer. 10:16; Lam. 3:24
119:58 [1]Heb. *face* [a]ver. 41
119:59 [a]Luke 15:17

48 My hands also will I lift up unto thy
commandments, which I have loved;
And I will [a]meditate in thy statutes.

ז ZAIN.

49 Remember the word unto thy servant,
Upon which thou hast caused me to
[a]hope.

50 This *is* my [a]comfort in my affliction:
For thy word hath quickened me.

51 The proud have had me greatly [a]in
derision:
Yet have I not [b]declined from thy law.

52 I remembered thy judgments of old,
O LORD;
And have comforted myself.

53 [a]Horror hath taken hold upon me
because of the wicked
That forsake thy law.

54 Thy statutes have been my songs
In the house of my pilgrimage.

55 [a]I have remembered thy name,
O LORD, in the night,
And have kept thy law.

56 This I had,
Because I kept thy precepts.

ח CHETH.

57 [a]*Thou art* my portion, O LORD:
I have said that *I* would keep thy
words.

58 I intreated thy [1]favour with *my* whole
heart:
Be merciful unto me [a]according to thy
word.

59 I [a]thought on my ways,
And turned my feet unto thy
testimonies.

60 I made haste, and delayed not
To keep thy commandments.

119:34 *heart.* See v. 36; see also note on 4:7.
119:36–37 *heart . . . eyes.* See 101:2b–3a and note.
‡119:38 *Stablish thy word.* Fufill the promises found in your word. *Who is devoted to thy fear.* Or "so that [your servant] will have reverence for You." The Lord's saving acts in fulfillment of His promises contribute to the recognition that He is the true God (see 130:4; 2 Sam 7:25–26; 1 Ki 8:39–40; Jer 33:8–9).
119:39 *reproach which I fear.* See notes on vv. 6,25.
119:40 *righteousness.* See note on 4:1.
119:41–48 May the Lord deliver me and not take His truth from my mouth; then I will honor His law in my life and speak of it before kings, for I love His commands.
119:41 *mercies.* See vv. 64,76,88,124,149,159; see also note on 6:4.
119:42 *him that reproacheth me.* See note on v. 25 ("cleaveth unto the dust"). *word.* See note on v. 25.
119:43 *word of truth . . . out of my mouth.* See v. 13 and note; see also v. 46.
119:45 *liberty.* Lit. "a wide space," i.e., unconfined by affliction or oppression (see 18:19 and note).
119:46 *before kings.* Such will be his boldness (see note on v. 23).
119:48 *My hands . . . will I lift up.* An act accompanying praise (as in 63:4; 134:2); so the sense may be: I praise.
119:49–56 God's word is my comfort and my guide whatever my circumstances.
119:49 *word.* See note on v. 25.
‡119:50–51 *in my affliction . . . The proud have had me . . . in derision.* See note on v. 25 ("cleaveth unto the dust").
119:51 *proud.* See note on v. 21.
119:52 *of old.* God's law is not fickle, but it is grounded firmly in His unchanging moral character. This is a major source of the author's comfort and one of the main reasons he cherishes the law so highly (see vv. 89,144,152,160).
119:53 *Horror hath taken hold upon me.* Zeal for God's law (see vv. 136,139) awakens righteous anger against those who reject it (see vv. 113,115,158), and it brings abhorrence of all that is contrary to it (see vv. 104,128,163); but it draws together those who honor it (see v. 63).
119:54 *In the house of my pilgrimage.* Lit. "in my temporary house." The sense may be that of v. 19 (see note there).
119:55 *name.* See note on 5:11.
119:57–64 The Lord is the psalmist's true homestead because it is God's law that fills the earth with all that makes life secure and joyous. So God's promises are his hope, and God's righteous laws his delight.
119:57 *portion.* May identify the author as a priest or Levite (see 73:26 and note).
119:58 *heart.* See note on 4:7.

61 The [1]bands of the wicked have robbed me:
But I have not forgotten thy law.
62 [a]At midnight I will rise to give thanks unto thee
Because of thy righteous judgments.
63 I *am* a companion of all *them* that fear thee,
And of them that keep thy precepts.
64 [a]The earth, O LORD, is full *of* thy mercy:
[b]Teach me thy statutes.

ט TETH.

65 Thou hast dealt well with thy servant,
O LORD, according unto thy word.
66 Teach me good judgment and knowledge:
For I have believed thy commandments.
67 [a]Before I was afflicted I went astray:
But now have I kept thy word.
68 Thou *art* [a]good, and doest good;
[b]Teach me thy statutes.
69 The proud have [a]forged a lie against me:
But I will keep thy precepts with *my* whole heart.
70 [a]Their heart is as fat as grease;
But I [b]delight *in* thy law.
71 [a]*It is* good for me that I have been afflicted;
That I might learn thy statutes.
72 [a]The law of thy mouth *is* better unto me
Than thousands of gold and silver.

י JOD.

73 [a]Thy hands have made me and fashioned me:
[b]Give me understanding, that I may learn thy commandments.
74 [a]They that fear thee will be glad when they see me;
Because [b]I have hoped in thy word.
75 I know, O LORD, that thy judgments *are* [1]right,
And [a]*that* thou *in* faithfulness hast afflicted me.
76 Let, I pray thee, thy merciful kindness be [1]for my comfort,
According to thy word unto thy servant.
77 [a]Let thy tender mercies come *unto* me, that I may live:
For [b]thy law *is* my delight.
78 Let the proud [a]be ashamed; [b]for they dealt perversely with me without a cause:
But I will [c]meditate in thy precepts.
79 Let those that fear thee turn unto me,
And those that have known thy testimonies.
80 Let my heart be sound in thy statutes;
That I be not ashamed.

כ CAPH.

81 [a]My soul fainteth for thy salvation:
But [b]I hope in thy word.
82 [a]Mine eyes fail for thy word,
Saying, When wilt thou comfort me?
83 For [a]I am become like a bottle in the smoke;
Yet do I not forget thy statutes.
84 [a]How many *are* the days of thy servant?

119:61 [1]Or, *companies* 119:62 [a]Acts 16:25 119:64 [a]Ps. 33:5 [b]ver. 12,26 119:67 [a]ver. 71; Jer. 31:18; Heb. 12:11 119:68 [a]Ps. 106:1; 107:1; Mat. 19:17 [b]ver. 12,26 119:69 [a]Job 13:4; Ps. 109:2 119:70 [a]Ps. 17:10; Is. 6:10; Acts 28:27 [b]ver. 35 119:71 [a]ver. 67; Heb. 12:10 119:72 [a]Ps. 19:10; Prov. 8:10,11,19 119:73 [a]Job 10:8; Ps. 100:3; 138:8; 139:14 119:73 [b]ver. 34,144 119:74 [a]Ps. 34:2 [b]ver. 49,147 119:75 [1]Heb. *righteousness* [a]Heb. 12:10 119:76 [1]Heb. *to comfort me* 119:77 [a]ver. 41 [b]ver. 24,47 119:78 [a]Ps. 25:3 [b]ver. 86 [c]ver. 23 119:81 [a]Ps. 73:26; 84:2 [b]ver. 74,114 119:82 [a]ver. 123; Ps. 69:3 119:83 [a]Job 30:30 119:84 [a]Ps. 39:4

‡119:61 *The bands of the wicked . . . robbed me.* The picture of the wicked binding him with cords as a figure for oppression and persecution.
119:62 *give thanks unto thee.* See note on Ps 100 title. *righteous.* See note on v. 7.
119:63 *companion.* See note on v. 53.
119:65–72 Do good to me in accordance with Your goodness, even if that means affliction, because Your affliction is good for me; it teaches me knowledge and good judgment from Your law.
119:65 *dealt well.* Cf. v. 68; see 31:19; 86:17 and notes. *word.* See note on v. 25.
‡119:66 *believed.* Had confidence in; God's commands are not deceitful (see note on v. 29) or fickle (see note on v. 52).
119:67 *afflicted.* At the hands of God (see v. 71; see also note on v. 25, "cleaves to the dust"). *word.* See note on v. 11.
119:69 *proud.* See note on v. 21.
‡119:70 *as fat as grease.* They have a callous disregard for God's law. Similar expressions occur also in Is 6:10; Jer 5:28 (see also 17:10).
119:72 *Than thousands of gold and silver.* See vv. 14,57,111, 162.
119:73–80 Complete Your forming of me by helping me to conform to Your righteous laws so that the arrogant may be put to shame and those who fear You may rejoice with me. (The stanza has a concentric structure; compare vv. 73 and 80, 74 and 79, 75 and 78, 76 and 77.)
119:73 *Give me understanding.* What I need to perfect the work You began when You formed me.
119:74 *fear thee.* See v. 79; see also note on 34:8–14. *will be glad when they see me.* When I am perfectly formed and enjoying the blessings of the godly. *word.* See note on v. 25.
119:75 *judgments.* Here the Hebrew for this word (*mishpaṭim*) may refer to God's just decisions in dealing with His servant, as the rest of the verse implies (see v. 84 and note). *thou . . . hast afflicted me.* See vv. 67,71.
119:76 *merciful kindness.* See note on 6:4. *my comfort.* In my affliction.
119:77 *that I may live.* And not perish in my affliction.
‡119:78 *the proud.* See note on v. 21. *be ashamed.* As they have subjected me to shame (see note on 5:10). *for they dealt perversely with me.* See note on v. 25 ("cleaveth unto the dust").
119:79 *turn unto me.* See v. 63 and note on v. 53.
119:80 *heart.* See note on 4:7. *be not ashamed.* See note on v. 6.
119:81–88 Save me from my affliction and my persecutors, according to Your promises, and I will obey Your statutes. This last stanza of the first half of the psalm, like the closing stanza, is dominated by prayer for God's help (see note on v. 25).
119:81 *soul.* See note on 6:3.
119:82 *Mine eyes fail.* See note on 6:7.
119:83 *like a bottle in the smoke.* As a wineskin hanging in the smoke and heat above a fire becomes smudged and shriveled, so the psalmist bears the marks of his affliction.
119:84 *How many . . . days . . . ?* That is, do not delay the punishment of my persecutors, because my life is short. *execute judgment.* Lit. "effect justice upon" (the Hebrew for "justice" is *mishpaṭ;* see note on v. 7, "judgments"; see also note on 5:10).

[b]When wilt thou execute judgment on
them that persecute me?
85 [a]The proud have digged pits for me,
Which *are* not after thy law.
86 All thy commandments *are* [1]faithful:
[a]They persecute me [b]wrongfully; help
thou me.
87 They had almost consumed me upon
earth;
But I forsook not thy precepts.
88 [a]Quicken me after thy lovingkindness;
So shall I keep the testimony of thy
mouth.

ל LAMED.

89 [a]For ever, O LORD,
Thy word *is* settled in heaven.
90 Thy faithfulness *is* [1]unto all
generations:
Thou hast established the earth, and it
[2]abideth.
91 They continue *this* day according to
[a]thine ordinances:
For all *are* thy servants.
92 Unless [a]thy law *had been* my delights,
I should then have perished in mine
affliction.
93 I will never forget thy precepts:
For with them thou hast quickened
me.
94 I *am* thine, save me;
For I have sought thy precepts.
95 The wicked have waited for me to
destroy me:
But I will consider thy testimonies.
96 [a]I have seen an end of all perfection:
But thy commandment *is* exceeding
broad.

מ MEM.

97 O how love I thy law!
[a]It *is* my meditation all the day.
98 Thou *through* thy commandments hast
made me [a]wiser than mine enemies:
For [1]they *are* ever with me.
99 I have more understanding than all my
teachers:
[a]For thy testimonies *are* my
meditation.
100 [a]I understand more than the ancients,
Because I keep thy precepts.
101 I have [a]refrained my feet from every
evil way,
That I might keep thy word.
102 I have not departed from thy
judgments:
For thou hast taught me.
103 [a]How sweet are thy words unto my
[1]taste!
Yea, sweeter than honey to my mouth!
104 Through thy precepts I get
understanding:
Therefore [a]I hate every false way.

נ NUN.

105 [a]Thy word *is* a [1]lamp unto my feet,
And a light unto my path.
106 [a]I have sworn, and I will perform *it*,
That *I* will keep thy righteous
judgments.
107 I am afflicted very much:
[a]Quicken me, O LORD, according unto
thy word.
108 Accept, I beseech thee, [a]the freewill
offerings of my mouth, O LORD,
And [b]teach me thy judgments.
109 [a]My soul *is* continually in my hand:
Yet do I not forget thy law.

119:84 [b]Rev. 6:10
119:85 [a]Ps. 35:7; Prov. 16:27
119:86 [1]Heb. *faithfulness* [a]ver. 78 [b]Ps. 35:19
119:88 [a]ver. 40
119:89 [a]Ps. 89:2; Mat. 24:34; 1 Pet. 1:25
119:90 [1]Heb. *to generation and generation* [2]Heb. *standeth*
119:91 [a]Jer. 33:25
119:92 [a]ver. 24
119:96 [a]Mat. 5:18
119:97 [a]Ps. 1:2
119:98 [1]Heb. *it is ever with me* [a]Deut. 4:6
119:99 [a]2 Tim. 3:15
119:100 [a]Job 32:7-9
119:101 [a]Prov. 1:15
119:103 [1]Heb. *palate* [a]Ps. 19:10; Prov. 8:11
119:104 [a]ver. 128
119:105 [1]Or, *candle* [a]Prov. 6:23
119:106 [a]Neh. 10:29
119:107 [a]ver. 88
119:108 [a]Hos. 14:2; Heb. 13:15 [b]ver. 12,26
119:109 [a]Job 13:14

‡119:85 *The proud.* See note on v. 21. *digged pits.* Probably referring to slander—public accusations that the psalmist must be guilty of vile sins or he would not be suffering such affliction. *not after thy law.* Not in agreement with. See Ex 20:16.
119:86 *faithful.* See note on v. 29 ("way of lying").
119:88 *lovingkindness.* See note on 6:4.
119:89–91 God's sovereign and unchanging word governs and maintains all creation. (These first three verses of the second half of the psalm teach a general truth; cf. vv. 1–3.)
‡119:89 *Thy word.* Here God's word by which He created, maintains and governs all things (see 33:4,6; 107:20; 147:15,18). *settled in heaven.* The secure order of the heavens and the earth (v. 90) declares (19:1–4) the reassuring truth that God's word (His "ordinances," v. 91), by which He upholds and governs all things, is enduring (eternal) and trustworthy ("Thy faithfulness," v. 90). And that is the larger truth that confirms the godly man's confidence in the trustworthiness of God's word (His laws and promises) of special revelation (see notes on 93:5; 96:10; see also note on v. 29, "way of lying").
119:90 *Thy faithfulness.* An indirect reference to God's word (see v. 89 and note).
119:92 *should then have perished in mine affliction.* Would not have learned the way of life (see v. 93) from your law (see vv. 67,71 and note on vv. 65–72).
‡119:95 *The wicked.* See note on v. 21 ("the proud"). *have waited for me to destroy me.* See note on v. 25 ("cleaveth unto the dust").
119:96 *perfection.* Probably that which has been perfected in the sense of completed, given fixed bounds so that it is no longer open-ended. *exceeding broad.* An inexhaustible source of wise counsel for life (see vv. 97–100).
119:97–104 Meditation on God's law yields the highest wisdom.
119:98 *mine enemies.* Those arrogant ones (see note on v. 21) who place confidence in worldly wisdom. *they.* Your commands.
119:99 *teachers.* Merely human teachers.
119:100 *ancients.* Old men, taught by experience (see note on Ex 3:16).
119:102 *thou hast taught me.* Through Your laws.
119:103 *words.* Perhaps better understood here as "laws" (see vv. 67,133,158,172 and note on v. 11).
119:104 *hate every false way.* See note on v. 53.
119:105 *lamp . . . light.* Apart from which I could only grope about in the darkness.
119:106 *have sworn . . . will perform.* Have covenanted (see Neh 10:29).
119:107 See v. 25 and note.
‡119:109 *My soul is continually in my hand.* Or "I am taking my life into my own hands" (i.e. putting my life at risk) by publicly honoring God's law in the face of threats and hostility (see especially vv. 23,46,161).

110 [a]The wicked have laid a snare for me:
Yet I [b]erred not from thy precepts.
111 [a]Thy testimonies have I taken as an
heritage for ever:
For [b]they *are* the rejoicing of my heart.
112 I have inclined mine heart [1]to perform
thy statutes
Alway, [a]*even unto* the end.

ס SAMECH.

113 I hate *vain* thoughts:
But thy law do I love.
114 [a]Thou *art* my hiding place and my
shield:
[b]I hope in thy word.
115 [a]Depart from me, ye evildoers:
For I will keep the commandments of
my God.
116 Uphold me according unto thy word,
that I may live:
And let me not [a]be ashamed of my
hope.
117 Hold thou me up, and I shall be safe:
And I will have respect unto thy
statutes continually.
118 Thou hast trodden down all them that
[a]err from thy statutes:
For their deceit *is* falsehood.
119 Thou [1]puttest away all the wicked of
the earth [a]*like* dross:
Therefore I love thy testimonies.
120 [a]My flesh trembleth for fear of thee;
And I am afraid of thy judgments.

ע AIN.

121 I have done judgment and justice:
Leave me not to mine oppressors.
122 Be [a]surety for thy servant for good:
Let not the proud oppress me.
123 [a]Mine eyes fail for thy salvation,

119:110 [a]Ps. 140:5 [b]ver. 10,21
119:111 [a]Deut. 33:4 [b]ver. 77,92
119:112 [1]Heb. *to do* [a]ver. 33
119:114 [a]Ps. 32:7 [b]ver. 81
119:115 [a]Ps. 6:8; Mat. 7:23
119:116 [a]Ps. 25:2; Rom. 5:5
119:118 [a]ver. 21
119:119 [1]Heb. *causest to cease* [a]Ezek. 22:18
119:120 [a]Hab. 3:16
119:122 [a]Heb. 7:22
119:123 [a]ver. 81,82
119:124 [a]ver. 12
119:125 [a]Ps. 116:16
119:127 [a]Ps. 19:10
119:128 [a]ver. 104
119:130 [a]Ps. 19:7
119:131 [a]ver. 20
119:132 [1]Heb. *According to the custom towards those, etc.* [a]Ps. 106:4 [b]2 Thes. 1:6
119:133 [a]Ps. 17:5 [b]Ps. 19:13; Rom. 6:12
119:134 [a]Luke 1:74
119:135 [a]Ps. 4:6 [b]ver. 12,26
119:136 [a]Jer. 9:1; Ezek. 9:4

And for the word of thy righteousness.
124 Deal with thy servant according unto
thy mercy,
And [a]teach me thy statutes.
125 [a]I *am* thy servant; give me
understanding,
That I may know thy testimonies.
126 *It is* time for *thee*, LORD, to work:
For they have made void thy law.
127 [a]Therefore I love thy commandments
Above gold; yea, above fine gold.
128 Therefore I esteem all *thy* precepts
concerning all *things to be* right;
And I [a]hate every false way.

פ PE.

129 Thy testimonies *are* wonderful:
Therefore doth my soul keep them.
130 The entrance of thy words giveth
light;
[a]It giveth understanding unto the
simple.
131 I opened my mouth, and panted:
For I [a]longed for thy commandments.
132 [a]Look thou upon me, and be merciful
unto me,
[b1]As thou usest to do unto those that
love thy name.
133 [a]Order my steps in thy word:
And [b]let not any iniquity have
dominion over me.
134 [a]Deliver me from the oppression of
man:
So will I keep thy precepts.
135 [a]Make thy face to shine upon thy
servant;
And [b]teach me thy statutes.
136 [a]Rivers of waters run down mine
eyes,
Because they keep not thy law.

119:110 *laid a snare.* See v. 85 and note.
119:111–112 *heart.* See note on 4:7.
119:111 *taken as an heritage* The possession I have received from God as my homestead and that from which I draw the provisions for my life (see note on vv. 57–64).
‡119:113 *vain thoughts.* Lit. "half-heartedness," i.e. those who are not fully committed to following God's commands. A "double minded man is unstable in all his ways" (Jas 1:8).
119:114 *word.* See note on v. 25.
‡119:118 *their deceit.* Probably their ways, which are deceitful (see note on v. 29).
‡119:119 *dross.* Scum removed from molten ore or metal. The Hebrew for this word is a pun on the word for "err" (i.e. to wander away) in v. 118: Those who wander from the truth are treated like dross.
119:120 *My flesh trembleth.* He quivers out of his deep reverence for God.
‡119:121–128 As Your faithful servant I pray for deliverance from my oppressors—another stanza in which prayer for deliverance is dominant (see vv. 81–88 and note; see also note on v. 25, "cleaveth unto the dust").
119:121 *judgment and justice.* God's law.
‡119:122 The only verse in this psalm that does not have either a direct or an indirect (as in vv. 90,121,132; see note on v. 75) reference to God's word. *Be surety for thy servant.* Take the responsibility to guarantee my safety (cf. Gen 43:9 and how Judah provides "surety" for his younger brother). *the proud.* See note on v. 21.
119:123 *Mine eyes fail.* See note on 6:7.
119:124 *mercy.* See note on 6:4.
‡119:126 *work.* Either in defense of His servant, or in judgment on the lawbreakers, or both. *made void thy law.* Have broken God's commands.
119:127 *Above gold.* See vv. 14,57,72,111.
119:128 *I hate every false way.* See note on v. 53.
119:129 *wonderful.* See v. 18 and note.
‡119:130 *entrance.* Lit. "opening," here meaning the entering of God's words into the heart. *the simple.* See 19:7 and note.
‡119:132 *As thou usest to do.* Lit. "according to the judgment" (*mishpaṭ*); i.e. according to the way that God has customarily acted toward his people. The psalmist recognizes the consistency of God's character and also makes an indirect reference (see note on v. 122) to God's law (see note on v. 7), recognizing God's faithfulness to the "judgments" that He has rendered in His word.
‡119:134 *oppression.* See note on v. 25 ("cleaveth unto the dust").
‡119:135 *thy face to shine.* See note on 13:1 ("hide thy face").
119:136 See v. 53 and note.

צ TZADDI.

137 [a]Righteous *art* thou, O LORD,
And upright *are* thy judgments.
138 [a]Thy testimonies *that* thou hast commanded *are* [1]righteous
And very [2]faithful.
139 [a]My zeal hath [1]consumed me,
Because mine enemies have forgotten thy words.
140 [a]Thy word *is* very [1]pure:
Therefore thy servant loveth it.
141 I *am* small and despised:
Yet do not I forget thy precepts.
142 Thy righteousness *is* an everlasting righteousness,
And thy law *is* [a]the truth.
143 Trouble and anguish have [1]taken hold on me:
Yet thy commandments *are* [a]my delights.
144 The righteousness of thy testimonies *is* everlasting:
[a]Give me understanding, and I shall live.

ק KOPH.

145 I cried with *my* whole heart;
Hear me, O LORD: I will keep thy statutes.
146 I cried unto thee; save me,
[1]And I shall keep thy testimonies.
147 [a]I prevented the dawning of the morning, and cried:
[b]I hoped in thy word.
148 [a]Mine eyes prevent the *night* watches,
That *I* might meditate in thy word.
149 Hear my voice according unto thy lovingkindness:
O LORD, [a]quicken me according to thy judgment.
150 They draw nigh that follow after mischief:
They are far from thy law.
151 Thou *art* [a]near, O LORD;
[b]And all thy commandments *are* truth.
152 Concerning thy testimonies, I have known of old
That thou hast founded them [a]for ever.

ר RESH.

153 [a]Consider mine affliction, and deliver me:
For I do not forget thy law.
154 [a]Plead my cause, and deliver me:
[b]Quicken me according to thy word.
155 [a]Salvation *is* far from the wicked:
For they seek not thy statutes.
156 [1]Great *are* thy tender mercies, O LORD:
[a]Quicken me according to thy judgments.
157 Many *are* my persecutors and mine enemies;
Yet do I not [a]decline from thy testimonies.
158 I beheld the transgressors, and [a]was grieved;
Because they kept not thy word.
159 Consider how I love thy precepts:
[a]Quicken me, O LORD, according to thy lovingkindness.
160 [1]Thy word *is* true *from* the beginning:
And every one of thy righteous judgments *endureth* for ever.

ש SCHIN.

161 [a]Princes have persecuted me without a cause:
But my heart standeth in awe of thy word.
162 I rejoice at thy word,
As one that findeth great spoil.
163 I hate and abhor lying:
But thy law do I love.
164 Seven *times* a day do I praise thee
Because of thy righteous judgments.
165 [a]Great peace have they which love thy law:
And [1]nothing *shall* offend them.
166 [a]LORD, I have hoped for thy salvation,
And done thy commandments.
167 My soul hath kept thy testimonies;
And *I* love them exceedingly.
168 I have kept thy precepts and thy testimonies:
[a]For all my ways *are* before thee.

119:137 [a]Neh. 9:33
119:138 [1]Heb. *righteousness* [2]Heb. *faithfulness* [a]Ps. 19:7-9
119:139 [1]Heb. *cut me off* [a]Ps. 69:9; John 2:17
119:140 [1]Heb. *tried,* or, *refined* [a]Ps. 12:6
119:142 [a]Ps. 19:9
119:143 [1]Heb. *found me* [a]ver. 77
119:144 [a]ver. 34,73
119:146 [1]Or, *That I may keep*
119:147 [a]Ps. 5:3 [b]ver. 74
119:148 [a]Ps. 63:1,6
119:149 [a]ver. 40
119:151 [a]Ps. 145:18 [b]ver. 142
119:152 [a]Luke 21:33
119:153 [a]Lam. 5:1
119:154 [a]1 Sam. 24:15 [b]ver. 40
119:155 [a]Job 5:4
119:156 [1]Or, *Many* [a]ver. 149
119:157 [a]Ps. 44:18
119:158 [a]Ezek. 9:4
119:159 [a]ver. 88
119:160 [1]Heb. *The beginning of thy word is true*
119:161 [a]1 Sam. 24:11
119:165 [1]Heb. *they shall have no stumblingblock* [a]Prov. 3:2; Is. 32:17
119:166 [a]Gen. 49:18
119:168 [a]Prov. 5:21

119:137–144 The Lord and His laws are righteous.
119:137 *Righteous.* See note on 4:1.
‡119:138 *faithful.* True and trustworthy; see v. 142; see also note on v. 29 ("way of lying").
119:139 *My zeal.* See note on v. 53.
119:140 *pure.* Lit. "refined," i.e., God's word contains nothing worthless or useless.
119:141 *small and despised.* Cf. v. 143; see also note on v. 25.
‡119:145–152 Save me, O Lord, and I will keep Your law. As the psalm draws to a close, prayer for deliverance becomes more dominant (see note on v. 25, "cleaveth unto the dust").
‡119:147 *I prevented the dawning of the morning.* I rise up before dawn.
119:148 *the night watches.* See note on Judg 7:19; see also Lam 2:19.
‡119:149 *lovingkindness.* See note on 6:4. *thy judgment.* Or "Your justice" (complementing "thy lovingkindness"); Hebrew *mishpaṭ* (see note on v. 75).
119:150 *far from thy law.* See vv. 21,53,85,118,126,139, 155,158.
119:151 *are truth.* See note on v. 29 ("way of lying").
119:152 *for ever.* See note on v. 52.
119:153–160 See note on vv. 145–152.
‡119:155 *the wicked.* See note on v. 21 ("the proud").
119:156 *thy judgments.* See v. 149 and note.
119:158 *word.* Hebrew *'imrah* (see note on v. 11).
‡119:160 *true.* See note on v. 29 ("way of lying"). *endureth for ever.* See note on v. 52.
119:161–168 See note on vv. 145–152.
119:161 *Princes.* See note on v. 23. *heart.* See note on 4:7.
119:162 *great spoil.* See vv. 14,72,111.
119:163 *I hate.* See note on v. 53. *lying.* Or "that which is (ways that are) deceitful" (see v. 29 and note).
119:164 *Seven.* A number signifying completeness—he praises God throughout the day.
119:165 *Great peace.* Complete security and well-being.

ת TAU.

169 Let my cry come near before thee, O LORD:
[a]Give me understanding according to thy word.
170 Let my supplication come before thee:
Deliver me according to thy word.
171 [a]My lips shall utter praise,
When thou hast taught me thy statutes.
172 My tongue shall speak of thy word:
For all thy commandments *are* righteousness.
173 Let thine hand help me;
For [a]I have chosen thy precepts.
174 [a]I have longed for thy salvation, O LORD;
And [b]thy law *is* my delight.
175 Let my soul live, and it shall praise thee;
And let thy judgments help me.
176 [a]I have gone astray like a lost sheep; seek thy servant;
For I do not forget thy commandments.

Psalm 120

A Song of degrees.

1 In [a]my distress I cried unto the LORD,
And he heard me.
2 Deliver my soul, O LORD, from lying lips,
And from a deceitful tongue.
3 [1]What shall be given unto thee? or what shall be [2]done unto thee,
Thou false tongue?
4 [1]Sharp arrows of the mighty,
With coals of juniper.
5 Woe is me, that I sojourn *in* [a]Mesech,
[b]*That* I dwell in the tents of Kedar!
6 My soul hath long dwelt
With him that hateth peace.
7 I *am* [1]*for* peace: but when I speak,
they *are* for war.

Psalm 121

A Song of degrees.

1 [a][1]I will lift up mine eyes unto the hills,
From whence cometh my help.
2 [a]My help *cometh* from the LORD,
Which made heaven and earth.
3 [a]He will not suffer thy foot to be moved:
[b]He that keepeth thee will not slumber.

119:169 [a]ver. 144
119:171 [a]ver. 7
119:173 [a]Josh. 24:22
119:174 [a]ver. 166 [b]ver. 16,24
119:176 [a]Is. 53:6
120:1 [a]Jonah 2:2
120:3 [1]Or, *What shall* the deceitful tongue *give unto thee?* or, *What shall it profit thee?* [2]Heb. *added*
120:4 [1]Or, It is as *the sharp arrows of the mighty* man, *with coals of juniper*
120:5 [a]Gen. 10:2; Ezek. 27:13 [b]Gen. 25:13; 1 Sam. 25:1; Jer. 49:28
120:7 [1]Or, a man of *peace*
121:1 [1]Or, *Shall I lift up mine eyes to the hills? whence should my help come?* [a]Jer. 3:23
121:2 [a]Ps. 124:8
121:3 [a]1 Sam. 2:9 [b]Ps. 127:1; Is. 27:3

119:169–176 See note on vv. 145–152.
119:171 *utter praise.* Because You have delivered me.
119:172 *righteousness.* See note on v. 7.
119:174–176 The conclusion to the psalm.
119:176 *I have gone astray.* See Is 53:6; the clearest expression of the author's acknowledgment that, for all his devotion to God's law, he has again and again wandered into other (deceitful) ways and, like a lost sheep, must be brought back by his heavenly Shepherd. For one who has made God's law the guide and dearest treasure of his life, the last word can only be such a confession—and such a prayer.
Ps 120 A prayer for deliverance from false accusers. Verse 7 suggests that the speaker is a king, in which case the accusers seek either to discredit him before his people or, more likely, to awaken suspicion concerning him in foreign courts. But if "war" is understood metaphorically, the psalm could be used also by a private individual beset by slanderers.
‡120 title *degrees.* Or "ascents." Some have thought that the Hebrew for this word refers to stairs leading to the temple, hence "a song of the stairs," to be used in the temple liturgy (probably at the feast of tabernacles). Most believe it refers to the annual religious pilgrimages to Jerusalem (see 84:5–7; Ex 23:14–17; Deut 16:16; Mic 4:2; Zech 14:16), which brought the worshipers singing to mount Zion (Is 30:29)—a view that does not exclude the psalm's use also in the temple liturgy. This title, found also at the head of Ps 121–134, no doubt reflects postexilic usage rather than the original purpose of composition and also marks Ps 120–134 as a collection that was taken up as a unit into the final postexilic arrangement of the Psalter. Together with Ps 135–136, it came to be known in Jewish liturgy as the "Great Hallel" (in distinction from the "Egyptian Hallel"; see introduction to Ps 113). The spirit of Ps 84 pervades it (see also Ps 42–43). Whether a thematic (or some other) scheme controls the arrangement of Ps 120–134 is unclear, though it is probably not coincidental that they begin with a prayer that evokes the experience of one far from home and beset by barbarians and end with a call to praise in the sanctuary. See introduction to Ps 122.
120:2 *lying lips . . . deceitful tongue.* See note on 5:9.
120:3–4 Assurance that God will act (see 6:8–10 and note on 3:8).
‡120:4 *Sharp arrows . . . coals.* As a weapon, the tongue is a sharp arrow (see Prov 25:18; Jer 9:8; see also 57:4; 64:3) and a searing fire (see Prov 16:27; Jas 3:6), and God's judgment will answer in kind (see 7:11–13; 11:6; 64:7). For judgment in kind see 63:9–10; 64:7–8 and notes. *juniper.* Or "broom tree." A desert shrub, sometimes large enough to provide shade.
120:5–7 Complaint over prolonged harassment.
120:5 *Mesech . . . Kedar.* The former was in central Asia Minor (see note on Gen 10:2), the latter in Arabia (see note on Is 21:16). Besieged by slanderers, the psalmist feels as if far from home, surrounded by barbarians.
‡Ps 121 A dialogue (perhaps liturgical) of confession and assurance. Its use as a pilgrimage song provides the key to its understanding. Whether the dialogue takes place in a single heart (cf. the refrain in Ps 42–43) or between individuals in the caravan is of no great consequence since all would share the same convictions. The comforting assurance expressed (see Ps 33) is equally appropriate for the pilgrimage to Jerusalem and for the pilgrimage of life to the "glory" into which the faithful will be received (see notes on 49:15; 73:24). The psalm is composed of four (Hebrew) couplets, each having an introductory line, which the rest of the couplet develops. Key terms are "the LORD" and "keep" ("preserve" in vv.7,8), each occurring five times.
121 title See note on Ps 120 title.
121:1–2 Confession of trust in the Lord.
121:1 *hills.* Those in the vicinity of Jerusalem, of which mount Zion is one (125:2), or, if the plural indicates majesty (as in the Hebrew in 87:1; 133:3), mount Zion itself.
121:2 *Which made heaven and earth.* The one true God, the King of all creation (see 124:8; 134:3; see also 33:6; 89:11–13; 96:4–5; 104:2–9; 136:4–9).
121:3–4 Assurance concerning the unsleeping guardian over Israel.
‡121:3 *suffer thy foot to be moved.* Will not allow your foot to slip, not even where the way is treacherous. *not slumber.* Like the pagan god Baal (see 1 Ki 18:27).

4 Behold, he that keepeth Israel
Shall neither slumber nor sleep.
5 The LORD *is* thy keeper:
The LORD *is* [a]thy shade [b]upon thy right
hand.
6 [a]The sun shall not smite thee by day,
Nor the moon by night.
7 The LORD shall preserve thee from all
evil:
He shall [a]preserve thy soul.
8 The LORD shall [a]preserve thy going out
and thy coming in
From this time forth, and *even* for
evermore.

Psalm 122

A Song of degrees of David.

1 I was glad when they said unto me,
[a]Let us go *into* the house of the LORD.
2 Our feet shall stand
Within thy gates, O Jerusalem.
3 Jerusalem *is* builded
As a city that is [a]compact together:
4 [a]Whither the tribes go up, the tribes of
the LORD,
Unto [b]the testimony of Israel,
To give thanks unto the name of the
LORD.
5 [a]For there [1]are set thrones of judgment,
The thrones of the house of David.
6 [a]Pray for the peace of Jerusalem:
They shall prosper that love thee.
7 Peace be within thy walls,
And prosperity within thy palaces.
8 For my brethren and companions'
sakes,
I will now say, Peace *be* within thee.
9 Because of the house of the LORD our
God
I will [a]seek thy good.

Psalm 123

A Song of degrees.

1 Unto thee [a]lift I up mine eyes,
O thou [b]that dwellest in the heavens.
2 Behold, as the eyes of servants *look*
unto the hand of their masters,
And as the eyes of a maiden unto the
hand of her mistress;
So our eyes *wait* upon the LORD our
God,
Until that he have mercy upon us.

121:5 [a]Is. 25:4 [b]Ps. 16:8
121:6 [a]Ps. 91:5; Is. 49:10
121:7 [a]Ps. 41:2
121:8 [a]Deut. 28:6
122:1 [a]Is. 2:3; Zech. 8:21
122:3 [a]See 2 Sam. 5:9
122:4 [a]Ex. 23:17; Deut. 16:16 [b]Ex. 16:34
122:5 [1]Heb. *do sit* [a]Deut. 17:8; 2 Chr. 19:8
122:6 [a]Ps. 51:18
122:9 [a]Neh. 2:10
123:1 [a]Ps. 121:1; 141:8 [b]Ps. 2:4; 11:4; 115:3

121:4 *he that keepeth Israel.* The Lord of all creation and the guardian over Israel—the One in whom the faithful may put unfaltering trust.
121:5–6 Assurance concerning unfailing protection.
121:5 *shade.* See 91:1 ("shadow") and note on 17:8. *upon thy right hand.* See 16:8 and note.
121:6 *sun . . . moon.* Here, in agreement with the "shade" metaphor, these serve as figures for all that distresses or threatens, day or night (see Is 4:6; 25:4–5; 49:10; Jonah 4:8).
121:7–8 Assurance concerning all of life.
121:8 *thy going out and thy coming in.* See 1 Sam 29:6 and 2 Sam 3:25 for the use of the phrase in military contexts. See Deut 28:6 for a context perhaps more like v.8.
Ps 122 A hymn of joy over Jerusalem (see Ps 42–43; 46; 48; 84; 87; 137 and the introductions to those psalms). Sung by a pilgrim in Jerusalem (very likely at one of the three annual festivals, Deut 16:16), it expresses his deep joy over the city and his prayer for its welfare. As the third of the pilgrimage psalms (see introduction to Ps 120), it shares many dominant themes with Ps 132, the third from the end of this collection—possibly a deliberate arrangement. Structurally, a two-verse introduction locates the worshiper with the festival throng in the city of his joy, and the major themes are developed in two stanzas of four (Hebrew) lines each. References to "the house of the LORD" (vv. 1,9) frame the song.
122 title *degrees.* See note on Ps 120 title. *of David.* This element is not present in all ancient witnesses to the text, and the content suggests a later date (see note on v. 1).
122:1–2 Joy for having joined the pilgrimage to Jerusalem.
122:1 *the house of the LORD.* The temple (2 Sam 7:5,13; 1 Ki 5:3,5; 8:10). That Jerusalem became the city of pilgrimage before the dedication of the temple is doubtful in light of 1 Ki 3:4; 8:1–11.
122:2 *gates.* Gateways.
122:3–5 Jerusalem's significance for the faithful.
‡122:3 *compact together.* Perhaps refers to the city's well-knit construction (see Ps 48) and probably recalls the construction of the tabernacle (cf. Ex 26:11, "couple . . . that it may be one"). If so, Jerusalem is being celebrated as the earthly residence of God (see note on 9:11; see also Is 4:5).
122:4 *the testimony of Israel.* See 81:3–5; Deut 16:1–17. *To give thanks.* For God's saving acts in behalf of Israel and His blessings on the nation. *name.* See note on 5:11.
122:5 *there . . . The thrones of the house of David.* Jerusalem is both the city of the Lord and the royal city of His chosen dynasty, through which He (ideally) protects and governs the nation (see 2:2,6–7; 89:3–4,19–37; 110; 2 Sam 7:8–16 and notes). In postexilic times it remained, though now in Messianic hope, the city of David.
122:6–9 Prayers for Jerusalem's peace.
‡122:6 In Hebrew a beautiful wordplay tightly binds together "Pray," "peace," "Jerusalem" and "prosper." *peace.* See vv. 7–8; includes both security and prosperity. *that love thee.* The psalmist, those referred to in vv. 1,8 and all who love Jerusalem because they are devoted to the Lord and His chosen king. These constitute a loving brotherhood, who worship together, pray together and seek each other's welfare as the people of God (see Ps 133).
‡122:7 *walls . . . palaces.* See 48:13 ("bulwarks . . . palaces").
122:8–9 *For my brethren . . . Because of the house of the LORD.* Because Jerusalem is the place supreme where God and His people meet together in fruitful union, the psalmist vows to seek the city's peace.
Ps 123 A prayer of God's humble people for Him to show mercy and so foil the contempt of the proud. See introduction to Ps 124. As to its structure, a one-verse introduction is followed by two couplets, each developing its own theme.
123 title See note on Ps 120 title.
123:1 *thou that dwellest in the heavens.* The same God whose earthly throne is in the temple on mount Zion (see 122:5 and note; see also 2:4; 9:11; 11:4; 80:1; 99:1; 113:5; 132:14).
123:2 *servants . . . maiden.* Similes by which the faithful (men and women alike) present themselves as humbly dependent on God.

3 Have mercy upon us, O LORD, have
mercy upon us:
For we are exceedingly filled *with*
contempt.
4 Our soul is exceedingly filled
With the scorning of those that are at
ease,
And with the contempt of the proud.

Psalm 124

A Song of degrees of David.

1 If *it had* not *been* the LORD who was on
our side,
[a]Now may Israel say;
2 If *it had* not *been* the LORD who was on
our side,
When men rose up against us:
3 Then they had [a]swallowed us up
quick,
When their wrath was kindled
against us:
4 Then the waters had overwhelmed us,
The stream had gone over our soul:
5 Then the proud waters
Had gone over our soul.
6 Blessed *be* the LORD,
Who hath not given us *as* a prey to
their teeth.
7 Our soul is escaped [a]as a bird out of
the snare of the fowlers:
The snare is broken, and we are
escaped.
8 [a]Our help *is* in the name of the LORD,
[b]Who made heaven and earth.

Psalm 125

A Song of degrees.

1 They that trust in the LORD *shall be* as
mount Zion,
Which cannot be removed, *but* abideth
for ever.
2 *As* the mountains *are* round about
Jerusalem,
So the LORD *is* round about his people
From henceforth even for ever.
3 For [a]the rod of [1]the wicked shall not
rest upon the lot of the righteous;
Lest the righteous put forth their hands
unto iniquity.
4 Do good, O LORD, unto *those that be*
good,
And to *them that are* upright in their
hearts.
5 As for such as turn aside *unto* their
[a]crooked ways,
The LORD shall lead them forth with
the workers of iniquity:
But [b]peace *shall be* upon Israel.

Psalm 126

A Song of degrees.

1 When the LORD [a][1]turned again the
captivity of Zion,

124:1 [a]Ps. 129:1
124:3 [a]Ps. 56:1,2; 57:3; Prov. 1:12
124:7 [a]Ps. 91:3; Prov. 6:5
124:8 [a]Ps. 121:2 [b]Gen. 1:1; Ps. 134:3
125:3 [1]Heb. *wickedness* [a]Prov. 22:8; Is. 14:5
125:5 [a]Prov. 2:15 [b]Ps. 128:6
126:1 [1]Heb. *returned the returning of Zion* [a]Ps. 53:6; 85:1; Hos. 6:11; Joel 3:1

123:4 *those . . . at ease, And . . . the proud.* Those who live by their own wits and strength (see notes on 10:2–11; 31:23) pour contempt on those who humbly rely on God, especially when those who rely on God suffer or do not prosper.

Ps 124 Israel's praise of the Lord for deliverance from powerful enemies—an appropriate sequel to Ps 123. Very likely a Levite speaks in vv. 1–5, while the worshipers answer in vv. 6–8. Like Ps 129 it divides into two well-balanced stanzas in Hebrew.

124 title *degrees.* See note on Ps 120 title. *of David.* Not all ancient witnesses to the text contain this element, and both language and theme suggest a postexilic date (see note on Ps 122 title). It may have been assigned to David because of supposed echoes of Ps 18; 69.

124:1–5 Let Israel acknowledge that the Lord alone has saved her from extinction (see 20:7; 94:17).

124:2 *men rose up against us.* Proud and arrogant men (123:4) may attack, but the Lord is Israel's help (v. 8).

124:3 *swallowed us.* Like death (see note on 49:14). But see 69:15.

124:4–5 *waters . . . stream . . . proud waters.* See 18:16; see also 32:6; 69:1–2 and notes.

124:6–8 Response of praise for deliverance—with a vivid enrichment of the imagery.

‡124:6 *prey to their teeth.* Without the Lord's help, their enemies would have torn them like wild beasts (see note on 7:2).

124:7 *escaped as a bird out of the snare of the fowlers.* A most apt figure for Israel's release from Babylonian captivity.

124:8 In climax, the great confession (see 121:2 and note).

Ps 125 Israel's peace: in testimony, prayer and benediction. The psalm is most likely postexilic and was probably spoken in the temple liturgy by a Levite.

125 title See note on Ps 120 title.

125:1–2 The solid security of God's people.

‡125:1 *They that trust in the LORD.* God's "people" (v. 2) are also characterized as "the righteous" (v. 3) and "those that be good," who "are upright in their hearts" (v. 4). For a similar description of the "righteous" see 34:8–14 and note. *as mount Zion.* In their security (see Ps 46; 48).

125:2 *mountains are round about Jerusalem.* Though Jerusalem is not surrounded by a ring of peaks, the city is located in what OT writers called a mountainous region. *So the LORD is round about his people.* As surely, as substantially and as immovably (see 2 Ki 6:17; Zech 2:5).

125:3 Wicked rulers, whether by example or by oppression, tend to corrupt even the righteous, but the Lord will preserve His people also from this corrosive threat. *rod of the wicked.* Probably referring to Persian rule (see Neh 9:36–37) and its invidious underlings, such as those Nehemiah had to contend with (see Neh 2:19; 4:1–3,7–8; 6:1–14,17–19; 13:7–8,28). *lot of the righteous.* The promised land (see 78:55).

125:4–5 To each according as he is and does—that is God's way (see 18:25–27); thus the confident prayer (v. 4) and the equally confident assertion (v. 5).

125:4 *hearts.* See note on 4:7.

125:5 *peace shall be upon Israel.* Perhaps a concise form of the priestly benediction (Num 6:24–26).

‡Ps 126 A song of joy for restoration to Zion. If not composed for those who returned from Babylonian exile (see Ezra and Nehemiah)—the place of exile is not named—it surely served to voice the joy of that restored community (cf. Ps 42–43; 84; 137). The psalm divides into two stanzas of four (Hebrew) lines each with their initial lines sharing the theme of the "turning" of Israel's "captivity" (vv. 1,4). Thematic unity is further served by repetition (cf. vv. 2–3) and other key words ("the LORD," "singing,"

[b]We were like them that dream.
2 Then [a]was our mouth filled *with* laughter,
And our tongue *with* singing:
Then said they among the heathen,
The LORD [1]hath done great things for them.
3 The LORD hath done great things for us;
Whereof we are glad.
4 Turn again our captivity, O LORD,
As the streams in the south.
5 [a]They that sow in tears shall reap in [1]joy.
6 He that goeth forth and weepeth, bearing [1]precious seed,
Shall doubtless come again with rejoicing, bringing his sheaves *with him.*

Psalm 127

A Song of degrees [1]for Solomon.

1 Except the LORD build the house, they labour in vain [1]that build it:
Except [a]the LORD keep the city, the watchman waketh *but* in vain.
2 *It is* vain for you to rise up early, to sit up late,
To [a]eat the bread of sorrows:
For so he giveth his beloved sleep.
3 Lo, [a]children *are* an heritage of the LORD:
And [b]the fruit of the womb *is his* reward.
4 As arrows *are* in the hand of a mighty *man;*
So *are* children of the youth.
5 Happy *is* the man that [1]hath his quiver full of them:
[a]They shall not be ashamed,
But they [2]shall speak with the enemies in the gate.

Psalm 128

A Song of degrees.

1 Blessed [a]*is* every one that feareth the LORD;
That walketh in his ways.
2 [a]For thou shalt eat the labour of thine hands:
Happy *shalt* thou *be,* and *it shall be* well with thee.
3 Thy wife *shall be* [a]as a fruitful vine
By the sides of thine house:
Thy children [b]like olive plants

126:1 [b]Acts 12:9
126:2 [1]Heb. *hath magnified to do with them* [a]Job 8:21
126:5 [1]Or, *singing* [a]See Jer. 31:9
126:6 [1]Or, *seed basket*
127:T [1]Or, *of Solomon*
127:1 [1]Heb. that are *builders of it in it* [a]Ps. 121:3-5
127:2 [a]Gen. 3:17,19
127:3 [a]Gen. 33:5; 48:4; Josh. 24:3,4 [b]Deut. 28:4
127:5 [1]Heb. *hath filled his quiver with them* [2]Or, *shall subdue,* as Ps. 18:47, or, *destroy* [a]Job 5:4; Prov. 27:11
128:1 [a]Ps. 119:1
128:2 [a]Is. 3:10
128:3 [a]Ezek. 19:10 [b]Ps. 52:8; 144:12

"bearing . . . bringing"). References to God's action (vv. 1,3) frame the first stanza, while v. 2 offers exposition.
126 title See note on Ps 120 title.
126:1–3 Joy over restoration experienced.
126:1 *dream.* The wonder and joy of the reality were so marvelous that they hardly dared believe it. It seemed more like the dreams with which they had so long been tantalized.
126:2 The twofold effect: joy for those who returned and honor for God among the nations (see note on 46:10).
126:4–6 Prayer for restoration to be completed.
126:4 *Turn again our captivity.* Either complete the repatriation of exiles or fully restore the security and prosperity of former times. *As the streams in the south.* Which are bone-dry in summer, until the winter rains renew their flow.
126:5–6 An apt metaphorical portrayal of the joy already experienced and the joy anticipated. *in tears . . . weepeth.* Even when sowing is accompanied by trouble or sorrow, harvest brings joy. For a related figure see 20:5.
Ps 127 Godly wisdom concerning home and hearth. Its theme is timeless; it reminded the pilgrims on their way to Jerusalem that all of life's securities and blessings are gifts from God rather than their own achievements (see Deut 28:1–14). Two balanced stanzas develop, respectively, two distinct but related themes.
127 title *degrees.* See note on Ps 120 title. *for Solomon.* If Solomon was not the author (not all witnesses to the text ascribe it to him), it is easy to see why some thought him so.
127:1–2 It is the Lord who provides shelter, security and food.
‡127:1 *house.* Domestic shelter. *they . . . that build it.* The Hebrew here is a pun on that for "children" in v. 3. *keep.* Guards, protects. See 121:3–8. *city.* The center of power, the refuge when enemies invade the land. *watchman.* See 2 Sam 13:34; 18:24–27; Sol 3:3; 5:7.
‡127:2 *giveth his beloved sleep.* Those that trust in the Lord are free of anxiety. A good harvest is not the achievement of endless toil, but it is the result of God's blessing (see Prov 10:22; Mat 6:25–34; 1 Pet 5:7). *his beloved.* See especially Deut 33:12; Jer 11:15.
127:3–5 Children are God's gift and a sign of His favor.
‡127:3 *children.* See note on v. 1. Children too are a gift—not the mere product of virility and fertility (see 113:9 and note; Gen 30:2). *heritage.* Emphasis here is on gift rather than possession. But perhaps more is implied. In the OT economy, an Israelite's "heritage" (inheritance) from the Lord was first of all property in the promised land (Num 26:53; Josh 11:23; Judg 2:6), which provided a sure place in the life and "rest" (Josh 1:13) of the Lord's kingdom. But without children the inheritance in the land would be lost (Num 27:8–11), so that offspring were a heritage in a double sense. *reward.* Bestowed by God on one who stands in His favor because he has been faithful.
127:5 *they shall speak with the enemies in the gate.* Fathers with many sons have many defenders when falsely accused in court. Moreover, the very fact that they have many sons as God's "reward" (v. 3) testifies to God's favor toward them (in effect, they are God-provided character witnesses; see 128:3–4). *in the gate.* For the use of "gate" and "gates" as a judicial site see Deut 17:5; 21:19; 22:15,24; 25:7; Ruth 4:1; Is 29:21; Amos 5:12.
‡Ps 128 The blessedness of the godly man; another word of wisdom concerning hearth and home (see Ps 127). The concluding benediction suggests that the psalm originally served as a Levitical (or priestly) word of instruction to those assembled from their homes to worship in Jerusalem. Its date may well be preexilic. Structurally, the frame ("that feareth the LORD") around vv. 1–4 sets off those verses as the main body of the psalm.
128 title See note on Ps 120 title.
128:1–4 Blessedness affirmed.
128:1 *Blessed.* See note on 1:1. *feareth the LORD.* See note on 34:8–14. *his ways.* See note on 25:4.
128:2 Blessings upon labor.
‡128:3 A faithful and fruitful wife. *vine.* Symbol of fruitfulness (Gen 49:22)—and perhaps also of sexual charms (Sol 7:8–12) and festivity (Judg 9:13). *By the sides of thine house.* She is not like the faithless wife whose "feet abide not in her house" (Prov 7:11). *olive plants.* Ever green and with the promises of both long life and productivity (of staples: wood, fruit, oil). The vine and the olive tree are frequently paired in the OT

Round about thy table.
4 Behold, that thus shall the man be
blessed that feareth the LORD.
5 [a]The LORD shall bless thee out of Zion:
And thou shalt see the good of
Jerusalem
All the days of thy life.
6 Yea, thou shalt [a]see thy children's
children,
And [b]peace upon Israel.

Psalm 129

A Song of degrees.

1 [1]Many a time have they afflicted me
from [a]my youth,
[b]May Israel now say:
2 [1]Many a time have they afflicted me
from my youth:
Yet they have not prevailed against me.
3 The plowers plowed upon my back:
They made long their furrows.
4 The LORD *is* righteous:
He hath cut asunder the cords of the
wicked.
5 Let them all be confounded and turned
back
That hate Zion.
6 Let them be as [a]the grass upon the
housetops,
Which withereth afore it groweth up:
7 Where*with* the mower filleth not his
hand;
Nor he that bindeth sheaves his
bosom.
8 Neither do they which go by say,
[a]The blessing of the LORD *be* upon you:
We bless you in the name of the LORD.

Psalm 130

A Song of degrees.

1 Out [a]of the depths have I cried unto
thee, O LORD.
2 Lord, hear my voice:
Let thine ears be attentive to the voice
of my supplications.
3 [a]If thou, LORD, shouldest mark
iniquities,
O Lord, who shall stand?
4 But *there is* [a]forgiveness with thee,
That [b]thou mayest be feared.
5 [a]I wait for the LORD, my soul doth
wait,
And [b]in his word do I hope.
6 [a]My soul *waiteth* for the Lord
More than they that watch for the
morning:
[1]*I say, more than* they that watch for
the morning.
7 [a]Let Israel hope in the LORD:
For [b]with the LORD *there is* mercy,
And with him *is* plenteous redemption.
8 And [a]he shall redeem Israel
From all his iniquities.

128:5 [a]Ps. 134:3
128:6 [a]Gen. 50:23; Job 42:16 [b]Ps. 125:5
129:1 [1]Or, *Much* [a]Ezek. 23:3; Hos. 2:15 [b]Ps. 124:1
129:2 [1]Or, *Much*
129:6 [a]Ps. 37:2
129:8 [a]Ruth 2:4; Ps. 118:26
130:1 [a]Lam. 3:55; Jonah 2:2
130:3 [a]Ps. 143:2; Rom. 3:20
130:4 [a]Ex. 34:7 [b]1 Ki. 8:40; Ps. 2:11; Jer. 33:8
130:5 [a]Ps. 27:14; Is. 8:17 [b]Ps. 119:81
130:6 [1]Or, *which watch unto the morning* [a]Ps:119:147
130:7 [a]Ps. 131:3 [b]Ps. 86:5; Is. 55:7
130:8 [a]Ps. 103:3,4; Mat. 1:21

(as, e.g., in Ex 23:11). Both were especially long-lived, and they produced the wine and the oil that played such a central role in the lives of the people. *Round about thy table.* Converting each family meal into a banquet of domestic joys.

128:5–6 The benediction pronounced—completing the scope of true blessedness: unbroken prosperity, secure relationship with God and secure national existence (the prosperity of Jerusalem entailed both), and long life.

128:5 *out of Zion.* See 9:11 and note; 20:2; 135:21.

128:6 *peace upon Israel.* See 125:5 and note.

Ps 129 Israel's prayer for the continued withering of all her powerful enemies. The rescue celebrated (v. 4) is probably from Babylonian exile. Against the background of Ps 124–128, this prayer for the withholding of God's blessing is set in sharp relief. Like Ps 124 (with which Ps 129 shares other affinities), the psalm is composed of two nicely balanced stanzas.

129 title See note on Ps 120 title.

129:1–4 The wicked oppressors have not prevailed.

129:1 *from my youth.* From the time Israel was enslaved in Egypt, she has suffered much at the hands of hostile powers.

129:2 *have not prevailed.* Have not succeeded in their efforts to destroy Israel totally or to hold her permanently in bondage.

129:4 *righteous.* See note on 4:1.

129:5–8 May all who hate Zion wither.

129:5 See note on 5:10.

129:6 *as the grass upon the housetops.* May those who would "plow" the backs of Israel (see v. 3) wither like grass that sprouts on the flat, sunbaked housetops, where no plow can prepare a nurturing soil to sustain the young shoots—and so there is no harvest (v. 7).

129:8 *they which go by.* Whoever may pass by the harvesters in the fields will exchange no joyful greetings (Ruth 2:4) because the hands of the harvesters will be empty.

Ps 130 A testimony of trust in the Lord—by one who knows that even though he is a sinner, the Lord hears his cry out of the depths. The language of the psalm suggests a postexilic date. This is the sixth of seven penitential psalms (see introduction to Ps 6). Composed of four thematic couplets, the psalm further divides into two halves of two couplets each.

130 title See note on Ps 120 title.

130:1–4 A prayer for mercy, and grounds for assurance.

130:1 *the depths.* As in 69:2 (see notes on 30:1; 32:6).

‡130:3 *shouldest mark.* Keep a record of.

130:4 *there is forgiveness.* No doubt recalling such reassuring words as Ex 34:6–7. *feared.* Honored, worshiped, trusted and served as the one true God. If God were not forgiving, people could only flee from Him in terror.

130:5–8 Trust in the Lord: a personal testimony, expanding into a reassuring invitation (see 131:3).

130:5 *I wait.* In hopeful expectation. *my soul.* See note on 6:3. *his word.* Especially His covenant promises (see 119:25,28, 37,42,49,65,74,81,107,114,147).

130:6 *they that watch.* See 127:1; 2 Sam 13:34; 18:24–27; Sol 3:3; 5:7. *the morning.* See introduction to Ps 57; see also note on 59:9.

130:7 *mercy.* See note on 6:4.

130:8 *From all his iniquities.* From the root of trouble—but also from all its consequences. This greatest of all hopes has been fulfilled in Christ.

Psalm 131

A Song of degrees of David.

1 LORD, my heart is not haughty, nor mine eyes lofty:
[a]Neither do I [1]exercise myself in great *matters,* or in *things* too [b][2]high for me.

2 Surely I have behaved and quieted [1]myself,
[a]As a child that is weaned of his mother:
My soul *is even* as a weaned child.

3 [a]Let Israel hope in the LORD
[1]From henceforth and for ever.

Psalm 132

A Song of degrees.

1 LORD, remember David,
And all his afflictions:

2 How he sware unto the LORD,
And vowed unto [b]the mighty *God* of Jacob;

3 Surely I will not come into the tabernacle of my house,
Nor go up into my bed;

4 I will [a]not give sleep to mine eyes,
Or slumber to mine eyelids,

5 Until I [a]find out a place for the LORD,
[1]A habitation for the mighty *God* of Jacob.

6 Lo, we heard *of* it [a]at Ephratah:
[b]We found it [c]in the fields of the wood.

7 We will go into his tabernacles:
[a]We will worship at his footstool.

8 [a]Arise, O LORD, into thy rest;
Thou, and [b]the ark of thy strength.

9 Let thy priests [a]be clothed *with* righteousness;
And let thy saints shout for joy.

10 For thy servant David's sake
Turn not away the face of thine anointed.

131:1 [1]Heb. *walk* [2]Heb. *wonderful* [a]Rom. 12:16 [b]Job 42:3; Ps. 139:6
131:2 [1]Heb. *my soul* [a]Mat. 18:3; 1 Cor. 14:20
131:3 [1]Heb. *From now* [a]Ps. 130:7
132:2 [a]Ps. 65:1 [b]Gen. 49:24
132:4 [a]Prov. 6:4
132:5 [1]Heb. *Habitations* [a]Acts 7:46
132:6 [a]1 Sam. 17:12 [b]1 Sam. 7:1 [c]1 Chr. 13:5
132:7 [a]Ps. 5:7; 99:5
132:8 [a]Num. 10:35; 2 Chr. 6:41 [b]Ps. 78:61
132:9 [a]Job 29:14; Is. 61:10

Ps 131 A confession of humble trust in the Lord—appropriately placed next to Ps 130.

131 title *degrees.* See note on Ps 120 title.

131:1 *heart.* See note on 4:7. *haughty . . . lofty.* More than all else, it is human pride that pits man against God (see note on 31:23; cf. 2 Sam 6:21–22). *exercise myself in.* (Presume to) walk among, live among, be party to. *great matters . . . too high for me.* Heroic exploits or achievements to rival, if not substitute for, the mighty works of God. The focus seems to be on not claiming Godlike powers (thus trusting in God for deliverance and blessing) rather than on seeking (or claiming) Godlike understanding.

131:2 *child . . . weaned.* A child of four or five who walks trustingly beside his mother. *soul.* See note on 6:3.

131:3 As he has done, so ought all Israel—for all time.

‡Ps 132 A prayer for God's favor on the son of David who reigns on David's throne—as the structure makes clear (and see note on v. 10). Its language suggests a date early in the monarchy. The venerable belief that it was composed for the dedication of the temple may be correct (compare vv. 8–10 with 2 Chr 6:41–42), but the possibility cannot be ruled out that it was used in the coronation ritual (cf. Ps 2; 72; 110). The author of Chronicles places the prayer (or a portion of it) on the lips of the king himself. In the postexilic liturgy it had Messianic implications.

Two verses of petition (vv. 1,10) are each followed (in Hebrew) by two four-line stanzas, all having an identical form: an introductory line followed by a three-line quotation (see the structure of these quotations). A final couplet brings the prayer to its climactic conclusion. The four thematic stanzas, together with the final couplet, ground the prayer made in vv. 1,10. Verses 2–9 appeal to David's oath to the Lord to find a "place" for the Lord and to his bringing the ark to its place of "rest," while vv. 11–18 appeal to the Lord's oath to David and to His election of Zion as His place of "rest" (but see note on v. 10).

132 title See note on Ps 120 title.

132:1 *remember.* See 20:3; see also 1 Ki 11:12–13; 15:4–5. *afflictions.* The affliction he took on himself in his vow (vv. 2–5; see Num 30:13, where the same technical term for a self-denying oath is used).

132:2 *he sware.* This prayer for David's son is grounded in the special relationship between David and the Lord, as epitomized in their mutual oaths (see vv. 11–12). In 2 Sam 6–7, which narrates the events here recalled, David's oath is not mentioned. *LORD . . . mighty God of Jacob.* See v. 5; Is 1:24; see also note on 3:7. *Jacob.* A synonym for Israel (see Gen 32:28).

‡132:6 *it . . . it.* Often thought to refer to the ark, but more likely it refers to the call to worship that follows (in Hebrew the pronoun is feminine, but the Hebrew for "ark" is masculine). *Ephratah.* The region around Beth-lehem, David's hometown (see Ruth 4:11; Mic 5:2). *fields of the wood.* Or "Kirjath-jearim;" called "Baale of Judah" in 2 Sam 6:2. The call to worship is depicted as emanating from David's city and the city where the ark had been since the days of Samuel (see 1 Sam 7:1). The call appears to come from a time after the temple had been built—thus involving a poetic compression of events.

132:7 *footstool.* See 99:5 and note.

132:8 *Arise.* Although the Hebrew omits (a common feature in Hebrew poetry) an introductory word, such as "saying," vv. 8–9 are probably words on the lips of the worshipers. See introduction to Ps 24. *rest.* As the promised land was Israel's place of rest at the end of her wanderings (see Num 10:33; Josh 1:13; Mic 2:10), so the temple was the Lord's resting place after He had been moving about in a tent (see 2 Sam 7:6; see also 1 Chr 28:2). The expression may suggest that the temple was the place of God's throne (v. 14). *ark of thy strength.* See note on 78:61.

132:9 *clothed with.* Beyond their normal priestly garb—may their ministry bear the character of (see Job 29:14; Prov 31:25), i.e., result in. *righteousness.* Since the corresponding word in v. 16 is "salvation," the same word used by the author of Chronicles when quoting this verse (2 Chr 6:41), and since "righteousness" and "salvation" are often paralleled (40:10; 51:14; 71:15; 98:2; Is 45:8; 46:13; 51:5–6; 56:1; 59:17; 60:17–18; 61:10; 62:1), the reference is clearly to God's righteousness that effects the salvation of His people (see note on 5:8). *saints.* See note on 4:3.

132:10 See v. 1. *thy servant.* See note on Ps 18 title. *Turn not away.* Do not refuse his petitions (as in 1 Ki 2:16–17,20; see 1 Ki 8:59; 2 Chr 6:41–42). If, as some have proposed, the petitions in vv. 1,10 form a frame around the first half of the psalm, the second half offers assurance that the prayer will be heard (perhaps spoken by a priest or Levite). In any event, David's vow to provide the Lord a dwelling place, which would be for His royal sons and for Israel a house of prayer (see 1 Ki 8:27–53; 9:3; 2 Chr 7:15–16; Is 56:7), is made the basis for the appeal that God will hear His anointed's prayer. *thine anointed.* See note on 2:2.

132:11–12 The Lord's covenant with David is recalled, as

11 [a]The LORD hath sworn *in* truth unto
David;
He will not turn from it;
[b]Of the fruit of [1]thy body will I set
upon thy throne.
12 If thy children will keep my covenant
And my testimony that I shall teach
them,
Their children also shall sit upon thy
throne for evermore.
13 [a]For the LORD hath chosen Zion;
He hath desired *it* for his habitation.
14 [a]This *is* my rest for ever:
Here will I dwell; for I have desired it.
15 [a]I will [1]abundantly bless her provision:
I will satisfy her poor *with* bread.
16 [a]I will also clothe her priests with
salvation:
[b]And her saints shall shout aloud for
joy.
17 [a]There will I make the horn of David
to bud:
[b]I have ordained a [1]lamp for mine
anointed.
18 His enemies will I [a]clothe with shame:
But upon himself shall his crown
flourish.

Psalm 133

A Song of degrees of David.

1 Behold, how good and how pleasant
it is
For [a]brethren to dwell [1]together in
unity.
2 *It is* like [a]the precious ointment upon
the head,
That ran down upon the beard, *even*
Aaron's beard:
That went down to the skirts of his
garments;
3 As the dew of [a]Hermon, *and as the*
dew that descended upon the
mountains of Zion:
For [b]there the LORD commanded the
blessing,
Even life for evermore.

Psalm 134

A Song of degrees.

1 Behold, bless ye the LORD, [a]all ye
servants of the LORD,
[b]Which by night stand in the house of
the LORD.
2 [a]Lift up your hands [1]*in* the sanctuary,
And bless the LORD.

3 [a]The LORD that made heaven and
earth
[b]Bless thee out of Zion.

Psalm 135

1 Praise ye the LORD.
Praise ye the name of the LORD;
[a]Praise *him,* O ye servants of the LORD.

132:11 [1]Heb. *thy belly* [a]Ps. 89:3,4 [b]2 Sam. 7:12; 1 Ki. 8:25
132:13 [a]Ps. 48:1,2
132:14 [a]Ps. 68:16
132:15 [1]Or, *surely* [a]Ps. 147:14
132:16 [a]2 Chr. 6:41 [b]Hos. 11:12
132:17 [1]Or, *candle* [a]Ezek. 29:21; Luke 1:69 [b]1 Ki. 11:36
132:18 [a]Ps. 35:26; 109:29
133:1 [1]Heb. *even together* [a]Gen. 13:8; Heb. 13:1
133:2 [a]Ex. 30:25
133:3 [a]Deut. 4:48 [b]Lev. 25:21; Deut. 28:8; Ps. 42:8
134:1 [a]Ps. 135:1,2 [b]1 Chr. 9:33
134:2 [1]Or, in *holiness* [a]1 Tim. 2:8
134:3 [a]Ps. 124:8 [b]Ps. 128:5; 135:21
135:1 [a]Ps. 113:1; 134:1

grounds for the prayer. These and vv. 13–18 are a poetic recollection of 1 Ki 9:1–5 (see 2 Chr 7:11–18).
132:11 *hath sworn.* See v. 2 and note. 2 Sam 7 does not mention an oath, but elsewhere God's promise to David is called a covenant (89:3,28,34,39; 2 Sam 23:5; Is 55:3), and covenants were made on oath. *will not turn from it.* See 110:4.
132:12 *covenant . . . testimony.* The stipulations of the Sinai covenant, which all Israelites were to keep (see 1 Sam 10:25 and note; see also 1 Ki 2:3–4).
132:13–16 The Lord's election of Zion recalled, as grounds for the prayer.
132:13 *desired it for his habitation.* David's and the Lord's desires harmonize (see Deut 12:5–14).
132:15 The Lord enthroned in His resting place (see vv. 8,14) will bless the land, making it a place of rest for His people (see Deut 12:9; Josh 1:13; 1 Ki 5:4).
132:16 See note on v. 9.
132:17–18 Concluding word of assurance, which addresses the petition (vv. 1,10) directly and climactically.
132:17 *horn.* The Lord's anointed. *to bud.* Like a plant or branch. *ordained a lamp for.* See note on 1 Ki 11:36.
132:18 *clothe with shame.* In contrast with v. 16. *shall . . . flourish.* Lit. "blossom"—subtly evoking the imagery: spring forth (v. 17) and blossom.
Ps 133 A song in praise of brotherly unity among the people of God. If David was the author (see title), he may have been moved to write it by some such occasion as when, after many years of conflict, all Israel came to Hebron to make him king (2 Sam 5:1–3). The first and last (Hebrew) lines (vv. 1,3b) frame the whole with the song's main theme. Next to these an inner frame (lines 2,4) elaborates with two striking complementary similes (vv. 2a,3a). The center line (v. 2b) extends the first simile.
133 title *degrees.* See note on Ps 120 title. *of David.* Not all textual sources ascribe the psalm to him.
133:1 *how good and how pleasant.* See 135:3; 147:1.
133:2 *like the precious ointment . . . Aaron's beard . . . down to the skirts of his garment.* The oil of Aaron's anointing (Ex 29:7; Lev 21:10) saturated all the hair of his beard and ran down on his priestly robes, signifying his total consecration to holy service. Similarly, brotherly harmony sanctifies God's people.
133:3 *dew of Hermon . . . upon the mountains of Zion.* A dew as profuse as that of mount Hermon would make the mountains of Zion (or mount Zion) richly fruitful (see Gen 27:28; Hag 1:10; Zech 8:12). So would brotherly unity make Israel richly fruitful. The two similes (vv. 2–3) are well chosen: God's blessings flowed to Israel through the priestly ministrations at the sanctuary (Ex 29:44–46; Lev 9:22–24; Num 6:24–26)—epitomizing God's redemptive mercies—and through heaven's dew that sustained life in the fields—epitomizing God's providential mercies in the creation order. *life.* The great covenant blessing (see Deut 30:15,19–20; 32:47).
‡Ps 134 A liturgy of praise—a brief exchange between the worshipers, as they are about to leave the temple after the evening service, and the Levites, who kept the temple watch through the night. In the Psalter it concludes the "songs of degrees," as Ps 117 concludes a collection of Hallelujah psalms (Ps 111–117). Its date is probably postexilic.
134 title See note on Ps 120 title.
134:1–2 The departing worshipers call on the Levites to continue the praise of the Lord through the night (see 1 Chr 9:33).
134:2 *Lift up your hands.* See 63:4.
134:3 One of the Levites responds with a benediction on the worshipers (see note on 121:2; see also 124:8; 128:5).
Ps 135 A call to praise the Lord—the one true God: Lord of all

2 [a]Ye that stand in the house of the LORD,
In [b]the courts of the house of our God,
3 Praise the LORD; for [a]the LORD *is* good:
Sing *praises* unto his name; [b]for *it is* pleasant.
4 For [a]the LORD hath chosen Jacob unto himself,
And Israel for his peculiar treasure.
5 For I know that [a]the LORD *is* great,
And *that* our Lord *is* above all gods.
6 [a]Whatsoever the LORD pleased,
That did he in heaven, and in earth,
In the seas, and all deep places.
7 [a]He causeth the vapours to ascend from the ends of the earth;
[b]He maketh lightnings for the rain;
He bringeth the wind out of his [c]treasuries.
8 [a]Who smote the firstborn of Egypt,
[1]Both of man and beast.
9 [a]*Who* sent tokens and wonders into the midst of thee, O Egypt,
[b]Upon Pharaoh, and upon all his servants.
10 [a]Who smote great nations,
And slew mighty kings;
11 Sihon king of the Amorites,
And Og king of Bashan,
And [a]all the kingdoms of Canaan:
12 [a]And gave their land *for* an heritage,
An heritage unto Israel his people.
13 [a]Thy name, O LORD, *endureth* for ever;
And thy memorial, O LORD,
[1]throughout all generations.
14 [a]For the LORD will judge his people,
And he will repent himself concerning his servants.
15 [a]The idols of the heathen *are* silver and gold,
The work of men's hands.
16 They have mouths, but they speak not;
Eyes have they, but they see not;
17 They have ears, but they hear not;
Neither is there *any* breath in their mouths.
18 They that make them are like unto them:
So is every one that trusteth in them.
19 [a]Bless the LORD, O house of Israel:
Bless the LORD, O house of Aaron:
20 Bless the LORD, O house of Levi:
Ye that fear the LORD, bless the LORD.
21 Blessed *be* the LORD [a]out of Zion,
which dwelleth *at* Jerusalem.
Praise ye the LORD.

135:2 [a]Luke 2:37 [b]Ps. 116:19 135:3 [a]Ps. 119:68 [b]Ps. 147:1 135:4 [a]Ex. 19:5; Deut. 7:6,7 135:5 [a]Ps. 95:3; 97:9 135:6 [a]Ps. 115:3 135:7 [a]Jer. 10:13 [b]Job 28:25; Zech. 10:1 [c]Job 38:22 135:8 [1]Heb. *From man unto beast* [a]Ex. 12:12; Ps. 78:51 135:9 [a]Ex. 7-10 [b]Ps. 136:15 135:10 [a]Num. 21:24; Ps. 136:17 135:11 [a]Josh. 12:7 135:12 [a]Ps. 78:55; 136:21,22 135:13 [a]Ex. 3:15; Ps. 102:12 135:13 [1]Heb. *to generation and generation* 135:14 [a]Deut. 32:36 135:15 [a]Ps. 115:4-8 135:19 [a]Ps. 115:9 135:21 [a]Ps. 134:3 136:1 [a]Ps. 106:1 [b]1 Chr. 16:34 136:2 [a]Deut. 10:17

Psalm 136

1 [a]O give thanks unto the LORD; for *he is* good:
[b]For his mercy *endureth* for ever.
2 O give thanks unto [a]the God of gods:
For his mercy *endureth* for ever.

creation, Lord over all the nations, Israel's Redeemer. No doubt postexilic, it echoes many lines found elsewhere in the OT. It was clearly composed for the temple liturgy. For its place in the Great Hallel see note on Ps 120 title. Framed with "Praise ye the LORD" (as are also Ps 146–150), its first and last stanzas are also calls to praise. Recital of God's saving acts for Israel in Egypt and Canaan (vv. 8–12) makes up the middle of seven stanzas, while the remaining four constitute two pairs related to each other by theme and language (vv. 3–4, 13–14; vv. 5–7, 15–18).

135:1–2 Initial call to praise, addressed to priests and Levites (see 134:1–2).

135:1,3,13 *name.* See note on 5:11.

135:3–4 A central reason for Israel to praise the Lord (see vv. 13–14).

135:3 *it is pleasant.* See 133:1. Or "He (the Lord) is beautiful" (see 27:4 and note).

‡135:4 *Jacob.* A synonym for Israel (see Gen 32:28). *his peculiar treasure.* His personal and prized possession. See Ex 19:5 and note.

135:5–7 The Lord is great as well as good (v. 3); He is the absolute Lord in all creation (cf. the word about idols in vv. 15–18; see Jer 10:11–16; see also 115:3 and 96:5; 97:7 and notes).

135:6 *Whatsoever the LORD pleased, That did he.* The idols can do nothing (vv. 16–17); they are themselves "done" (made) by their worshipers (v. 18). *heaven . . . earth . . . seas.* The three great domains of the visible creation, as the ancients viewed it (see Gen 1:8–10 and introduction to Ps 104).

135:7 *He causeth the vapours to ascend.* The Lord, not Baal or any other god, causes clouds to bring the life-giving rains (see Ps 29). *wind.* See 104:4; 148:8. The idols do not even have any "wind" (breath) in their mouths (v. 17). *treasuries.* See 33:7 and note; Job 38:22.

135:8–12 The Lord's triumph over Egypt and over the kings whose lands became Israel's inheritance, a concise recollection of Ex 7–14; Num 21:21–35; Joshua.

135:13–14 See vv. 3–4 and note.

‡135:13 *memorial.* God's fame and renown that are perpetuated by the praise of His people.

‡135:14 *judge.* Uphold against all attacks by the world powers both Israel's cause and her claim that the Lord is the only true God. *repent himself.* Or "have compassion on." See Ex 34:6–7. *his servants.* His covenant people.

135:15–18 The powerlessness of the false gods and of those who trust in them (see vv. 5–7 and note; see also 115:4–8 and notes).

135:19–21 Concluding call to praise, addressed to all who are assembled at the temple (see 115:9–11; 118:2–4).

Ps 136 A liturgy of praise to the Lord as Creator and as Israel's Redeemer. Its theme and many of its verses parallel much of Ps 135. Most likely a Levitical song leader led the recital, while the Levitical choir (1 Chr 16:41; 2 Chr 5:13; Ezra 3:11) or the worshipers (2 Chr 7:3,6; 20:21) responded with the refrain (see 106:1; 107:1; 118:1–4,29). This liturgy concludes the Great Hallel (see note on Ps 120 title). Following the initial call to praise (vv. 1–3), the recital devotes six verses to God's creation acts (vv. 4–9), six to His deliverance of Israel out of Egypt (vv. 10–15), one to the wilderness journey (v. 16) and six to the conquest (vv. 17–22). The four concluding verses return to the same basic themes in reverse order: God's action in history in behalf of His people (vv. 23–24), God's action in the creation order (v. 25) and a closing call to praise (v. 26).

136:1–3,26 *give thanks unto.* Or "Praise" (see 7:17 and note).

136:2 *the God of gods.* See Deut 10:17; see also 135:5.

3 O give thanks to the Lord of lords:
For his mercy *endureth* for ever.
4 To him [a]who alone doeth great wonders:
For his mercy *endureth* for ever.
5 [a]To him that by wisdom made the heavens:
For his mercy *endureth* for ever.
6 [a]To him that stretched out the earth above the waters:
For his mercy *endureth* for ever.
7 [a]To him that made great lights:
For his mercy *endureth* for ever:
8 [a]The sun [1]to rule by day:
For his mercy *endureth* for ever:
9 The moon and stars to rule by night:
For his mercy *endureth* for ever.
10 [a]To him that smote Egypt in their firstborn:
For his mercy *endureth* for ever:
11 [a]And brought out Israel from among them:
For his mercy *endureth* for ever:
12 [a]With a strong hand, and with a stretched out arm:
For his mercy *endureth* for ever.
13 [a]To him which divided the Red sea into parts:
For his mercy *endureth* for ever:
14 And made Israel to pass through the midst of it:
For his mercy *endureth* for ever:
15 [a]But [1]overthrew Pharaoh and his host in the Red sea:
For his mercy *endureth* for ever.
16 [a]To him which led his people through the wilderness:
For his mercy *endureth* for ever.
17 [a]To him which smote great kings:
For his mercy *endureth* for ever:
18 [a]And slew famous kings:
For his mercy *endureth* for ever:
19 [a]Sihon king of the Amorites:
For his mercy *endureth* for ever:

136:4 [a]Ps. 72:18
136:5 [a]Gen. 1:1; Prov. 3:19; Jer. 51:15
136:6 [a]Gen. 1:9; Ps. 24:2; Jer. 10:12
136:7 [a]Gen. 1:14
136:8 [1]Heb. *for the ruling by day* [a]Gen. 1:16
136:10 [a]Ex. 12:29; Ps. 135:8
136:11 [a]Ex. 12:51
136:12 [a]Ex. 6:6
136:13 [a]Ex. 14:21; Ps. 78:13
136:15 [1]Heb. *shaked off* [a]Ex. 14:27; Ps. 135:9
136:16 [a]Ex. 13:18
136:17 [a]Ps. 135:10
136:18 [a]Deut. 29:7
136:19 [a]Num. 21:21
136:20 [a]Num. 21:33
136:21 [a]Josh. 12:1; Ps. 135:12
136:23 [a]Gen. 8:1; Deut. 32:36; Ps. 113:7
136:25 [a]Ps. 104:27; 145:15
137:3 [1]Heb. *the words of a song* [2]Heb. *laid us on heaps* [a]Ps. 79:1
137:4 [1]Heb. *land of a stranger?*
137:6 [1]Heb. *the head of my joy* [a]Ezek. 3:26
137:7 [1]Heb. *Make bare* [a]Jer. 49:7; Lam. 4:22; Ezek. 25:12; Obad. 10

20 [a]And Og the king of Bashan:
For his mercy *endureth* for ever:
21 [a]And gave their land for an heritage:
For his mercy *endureth* for ever:
22 *Even* an heritage unto Israel his servant:
For his mercy *endureth* for ever.
23 Who [a]remembered us in our low estate:
For his mercy *endureth* for ever:
24 And hath redeemed us from our enemies:
For his mercy *endureth* for ever.
25 [a]Who giveth food to all flesh:
For his mercy *endureth* for ever.
26 O give thanks unto the God of heaven:
For his mercy *endureth* for ever.

Psalm 137

1 By the rivers of Babylon, there we sat down, yea, we wept,
When we remembered Zion.
2 We hanged our harps
Upon the willows in the midst thereof.
3 For there they that carried us away captive required of us [1]a song;
And they that [a2]wasted us *required of us* mirth,
Saying, Sing us *one* of the songs of Zion.
4 How shall we sing the LORD's song
In a [1]strange land?
5 If I forget thee, O Jerusalem,
Let my right hand forget *her cunning.*
6 If I do not remember thee,
Let my [a]tongue cleave to the roof of my mouth;
If I prefer not Jerusalem above [1]my chief joy.
7 Remember, O LORD, [a]the children of Edom *in* the day of Jerusalem;
Who said, [1]Rase *it,* rase *it, even* to the foundation thereof.

136:5 *by wisdom.* See Prov 3:19; Jer 10:12.
136:6 *above the waters.* See 24:2 and note.
136:7–9 Direct echoes of Gen 1:16.
136:23–24 Probably a concluding summary of the deliverance recalled above, but may allude also to the deliverances experienced during the period of the judges and the reign of David.
136:26 *the God of heaven.* A Persian title for God (see note on Ezra 1:2) found frequently in Ezra, Nehemiah and Daniel. Its intent is similar to that of the language of vv. 2–3.
Ps 137 A plaintive song of the exile—of one who has recently returned from Babylon but in whose soul there lingers the bitter memory of the years in a foreign land and of the cruel events that led to that enforced stay. Here speaks the same deep love of Zion as that found in Ps 42–43; 46; 48; 84; 122; 126. The 12 poetic lines of the Hebrew song divide symmetrically into three stanzas of four lines each: the remembered sorrow and torment (vv. 1–3), an oath of total commitment to Jerusalem (vv. 4–6), a call for retribution on Edom and Babylon (vv. 7–9).
137:1 *rivers.* The Tigris and Euphrates and the many canals associated with them. *we sat.* Again and again the thought of their forced separation from Zion brought them down to the posture of mourning (see Job 2:8,13; Lam 2:10).
‡137:2 *We hanged our harps.* "The joy of the harp ceaseth" (Is 24:8) because the callous Babylonians demanded exotic entertainment with the joyful songs of distant Zion, while the exiles' instruments were only "turned to mourning" (Job 30:31).
137:4–6 Only he whose heart had disowned the Lord and His holy city Jerusalem could play the puppet on a Babylonian stage. But may I never play the harp again or sing another syllable if I am untrue to that beloved city!
137:7–9 Lord, remember Edom; and as for you, Babylon, I bless whoever does to you what you did to Jerusalem: a passionate call for redress from a loyal son of the ravaged city (see note on 5:10).
137:7 *children of Edom.* The agelong animosity of Edom—descendants of Esau, Jacob's brother—showed its most dastardly face in Jerusalem's darkest hour. No doubt the author knew the Lord's judgments against that nation announced by the prophets (Is 63:1–4; Jer 49:7–22; Ezek 25:8,12–14; 35; Obadiah). *Rase it.* Lit. "Strip her"—cities were conventionally portrayed as women. Lam 4:21 anticipates that Edom will be punished by suffering the same humiliation.

8 O daughter of Babylon, [a]who art *to be*
[1]destroyed;
Happy *shall he be,* [b2]that rewardeth
thee
As thou hast served us.
9 Happy *shall he be* that taketh
And [a]dasheth thy little ones against
[1]the stones.

Psalm 138

A Psalm of David.

1 I will praise thee with my whole heart:
[a]Before the gods will I sing *praise* unto
thee.
2 [a]I will worship [b]toward thy holy temple,
And praise thy name for thy
lovingkindness and for thy truth:
For thou hast [c]magnified thy word
above all thy name.
3 In the day when I cried thou
answeredst me,
And strengthenedst me *with* strength
in my soul.
4 [a]All the kings of the earth shall praise
thee, O LORD,
When they hear the words of thy
mouth.
5 Yea, they shall sing in the ways of the
LORD:
For great *is* the glory of the LORD.
6 [a]Though the LORD *be* high, yet [b]hath
he respect unto the lowly:
But the proud he knoweth afar off.
7 [a]Though I walk in the midst of trouble,
thou wilt revive me:
Thou shalt stretch forth thine hand
against the wrath of mine enemies,
And thy right hand shall save me.
8 [a]The LORD will perfect that which
concerneth me:
Thy mercy, O LORD, *endureth* for ever:
[b]Forsake not the works of thine own
hands.

Psalm 139

To the chief Musician, A Psalm of David.

1 O LORD, [a]thou hast searched me, and
known *me.*
2 [a]Thou knowest my downsitting and
mine uprising,
Thou [b]understandest my thought afar
off.
3 [a]Thou [1]compassest my path and my
lying down,
And art acquainted *with* all my ways.
4 For *there is* not a word in my tongue,
But lo, O LORD, [a]thou knowest it
altogether.

137:8 [1]Heb. *wasted* [2]Heb. *that recompenseth unto thee thy deed which thou didst to us* [a]Is. 13:1,6; Jer. 25:12 [b]Jer. 50:15; Rev. 18:6
137:9 [1]Heb. *the rock* [a]Is. 13:16
138:1 [a]Ps. 119:46
138:2 [a]Ps. 28:2 [b]1 Ki. 8:29; Ps. 5:7 [c]Is. 42:21
138:4 [a]Ps. 102:15
138:6 [a]Ps. 113:5,6; Is. 57:15 [b]Prov. 3:34; Jas. 4:6; 1 Pet. 5:5
138:7 [a]Ps. 23:3,4
138:8 [a]Ps. 57:2; Phil. 1:6 [b]Job 10:3,8
139:1 [a]Ps. 17:3; Jer. 12:3
139:2 [a]2 Ki. 19:27 [b]Mat. 9:4; John 2:24
139:3 [1]Or, *winnowest* [a]Job 31:4
139:4 [a]Heb. 4:13

137:8 *daughter.* A personification of Babylon and its inhabitants. *who art to be destroyed.* The author may have known the Lord's announced judgments on this cruel destroyer (Is 13; 21:1–10; 47; Jer 50–51; Hab 2:4–20).
137:9 *thy little ones.* War was as cruel then as now; women and children were not spared (see 2 Ki 8:12; 15:16; Is 13:16,18; Hos 10:14; 13:16; Amos 1:13; Nah 3:10). For the final announcement of the destruction of the "Babylon" that persists in its warfare against the City of God, and the joy with which that announcement is greeted, see Rev 18:1–19:4.
Ps 138 A royal song of praise for God's saving help against threatening foes. In many respects it is like Ps 18, though it is more concise and direct. Two (Hebrew) four-line stanzas (vv. 1–3, 6–8) develop the main theme; at the center a two-line stanza (vv. 4–5) expands the praise of the Lord to a universal company of earth's royalty.
138 title This begins a collection of eight "Davidic" psalms (Ps 138–145): six prayers framed by two psalms of praise.
138:1–3 Praise for God's faithful love shown in answer to prayers for help.
138:1 *heart.* See note on 4:7. *gods.* Either pagan kings (see vv. 4–5) or the gods they claimed to represent (see introduction to Ps 82; see also note on 82:1).
138:2 *thy holy temple.* If David is in fact the author, reference is to the tent he set up for the ark (2 Sam 6:17)—many psalms ascribed to David refer to the "temple" (see, e.g., 5:7; 11:4; 18:6; 27:4; see also Ps 30 title). *name.* See note on 5:11. *lovingkindness and . . . truth.* See note on 36:5. *lovingkindness.* See v. 8; see also note on 6:4. *thy word.* Especially God's promises. God's display of His love and faithfulness in His answers to prayer (v. 3) has made His name and promises more precious than all else that even a king may possess.
138:4–5 The center of the poem (see note on 6:6): a wish and hope that all the kings of earth may come to join him in his praise of the Lord (see note on 9:1).
138:4 *words of thy mouth.* God's grand commitments to His people.
138:5 *ways of the LORD.* See 25:10 and note. God's words and His ways are in harmony, and together they display His great glory (see Ps 145).
138:6–8 A testimony to God's condescending and faithful love, concluded with a prayer.
‡138:6 See 113:4–9 and notes. *hath he respect unto.* With favor. *the proud.* See notes on 31:23; 101:5; 131:1. *knoweth afar off.* Already from a great distance recognizes them for what they are and so does not allow them into His presence (see note on 11:7).
‡138:8 *will perfect that which concerneth me.* Will accomplish or bring about. See note on 57:2. *works of thine own hands.* The king himself, whom the Lord had made. The Hebrew often uses plurals to refer to God or the king.
Ps 139 A prayer for God to examine the heart and see its true devotion. Like Job, the author firmly claims his loyalty to the Lord. Nowhere (outside Job) does one find expressed such profound awareness of how awesome it is to ask God to examine not only one's life but also his soul—God, who knows every thought, word and deed, from whom there is no hiding, who has been privy even to one's formation in the dark concealment of the womb. The thought progresses steadily in four poetic paragraphs of six verses each (vv. 1–6, 7–12, 13–18, 19–24), and each paragraph is concluded with a couplet that elaborates on the unit's central theme. References to God's searching and knowing begin and end the prayer.
139 title *To the chief Musician.* See note on Ps 4 title. *of David.* See note on Ps 138 title.
139:1–6 God, You know me perfectly, far beyond my knowledge of myself: my every action (v. 2a), my every undertaking (v. 3a) and the manner in which I pursue it (v. 3b), even my thoughts before they are fully crystallized (v. 2b) and my words before they are uttered (v. 4).

5 Thou hast beset me behind and before,
And laid thine hand upon me.
6 [a]*Such* knowledge *is* too wonderful for
me;
It is high, I cannot attain unto it.

7 [a]Whither shall I go from thy spirit?
Or whither shall I flee from thy
presence?
8 [a]If I ascend up *into* heaven, thou *art*
there:
[b]If I make my bed in hell, behold, thou
art there.
9 *If* I take the wings of the morning,
And dwell in the uttermost parts of the
sea;
10 Even there shall thy hand lead me,
And thy right hand shall hold me.
11 If I say, Surely the darkness shall cover
me;
Even the night *shall be* light about me.
12 Yea, [a]the darkness [1]hideth not from
thee;
But the night shineth as the day:
[2]The darkness and the light *are* both
alike *to thee.*

13 For thou hast possessed my reins:
Thou hast covered me in my mother's
womb.
14 I will praise thee; for I am fearfully and
wonderfully made:
Marvellous *are* thy works;
And *that* my soul knoweth [1]right well.
15 [a]My [1]substance was not hid from thee,
When I was made in secret,
And curiously wrought in the lowest
parts of the earth.
16 Thine eyes did see my substance, yet
being unperfect;
And in thy book [1]all *my members* were
written,
[2]*Which* in continuance were
fashioned, when *as yet there was*
none of them.
17 [a]How precious also are thy thoughts
unto me, O God:
How great is the sum of them!
18 *If* I should count them, they are moe in
number than the sand:
When I awake, I am still with thee.

19 Surely thou wilt [a]slay the wicked,
O God:
[b]Depart from me therefore, ye bloody
men.

139:6 [a]Job 42:3; Ps. 40:5
139:7 [a]Jer. 23:24; Jonah 1:3
139:8 [a]Amos 9:2 [b]Prov. 15:11
139:12 [1]Heb. *darkeneth not* [2]Heb. *As is the darkness, so is the light* [a]Job 34:22
139:14 [1]Heb. *greatly*
139:15 [1]Or, *strength,* or, *body* [a]Job 10:8,9
139:16 [1]Heb. *all of them* [2]Or, what *days they should be fashioned*
139:17 [a]Ps. 40:5
139:19 [a]Is. 11:4 [b]Ps. 119:115

139:5 *Thou hast beset me behind and before.* To keep me under scrutiny. *laid thine hand upon me.* So that I do not escape You. The figures are different in Job 13:27, but the thought is much the same. *hand.* Or "hands."

139:6 *too wonderful for me.* Yours is a "wonder" knowledge, beyond my human capacity—the Hebrew term regularly applies to God's wondrous acts (see 77:11,14; Ex 15:11).

139:7–12 There is no hiding from You—here no abstract doctrine of divine omnipresence but an awed confession that God cannot be escaped (see Jer 23:23–24).

‡139:7 *thy spirit . . . thy presence.* See 51:11; Is 63:9–10; Ezek 39:29 ("face . . . spirit").

‡139:8 *into heaven . . . in hell.* The two vertical extremes. *hell.* Sheol, or the grave.

139:9 *wings of the morning . . . uttermost parts of the sea.* The two horizontal extremes: east and west (the sea is the Mediterranean). Using a literary figure in which the totality is denoted by referring to its two extremes (merism), vv. 8–9 specify all spatial reality, the whole creation.

139:10 *lead me . . . hold me.* Though this language occurs in 73:23–24 to indicate God's solicitous care, it here denotes God's inescapable supervision, not unlike the thought of v. 5.

139:11–12 Just as the whole creation offers no hiding place (vv. 8–9), neither does even the darkness.

139:13–16 You Yourself put me together in the womb and ordained the span of my life before I was born.

‡139:13 *reins.* Lit. "kidneys"—in Hebrew idiom, the innermost center of emotions and of moral sensitivity—that which God tests and examines when He "trieth" a person (see note on 7:9).

139:14 *fearfully and wonderfully . . . Marvellous.* You know me as the One who formed me (see vv. 15–16), but I cannot begin to comprehend this creature You have fashioned. I can only look upon him with awe and wonder (see note on v. 6)—and praise You (see Eccl 11:5).

‡139:15 *substance.* Lit. "bones." His frame or skeleton, referring to the substantial part of man's physical being. Though not visable to the human eye, it is certainly not hidden from the eyes of God. The poetic terminology clearly indicates God's sovereign activity in human conception. *in secret . . . lowest parts of the earth.* Reference is to the womb: called a "secret" place because it normally conceals (see 2 Sam 12:12), and it shares with "lowest parts of the earth" (see note on 30:1) associations with darkness, dampness and separation from the visible realm of life. Moreover, both phrases refer to the place of the dead (63:9; Job 14:13; Is 44:23; 45:19), with which on one level the womb appears to have been associated: Man comes from the dust and returns to the dust (90:3; Gen 3:19; Eccl 3:20; 12:7), and the womb is the "lowest parts" where he is formed (see Is 44:2,24; 49:5; Jer 1:5).

‡139:16 *substance.* (from the Hebrew, *go lem*) is not the same term translated "substance" in v. 15. This is the only usage of this word in the Hebrew Bible. It refers to something that is "wrapped together" in an unformed mass. The context indicates that the embryonic mass is fashioned daily in fetal form as God's blueprint for life is clearly charted from the moment of conception. *thy book.* The heavenly royal register of God's decisions (see note on 56:8). *all my members were written . . . were fashioned.* Lit. "all were written down, the days that were planned."

139:17 *thy thoughts.* As expressed in His works—and in contrast with "my thought" (v. 2).

139:18 *moe.* More. *When I awake.* The sleep of exhaustion overcomes every attempt to count God's thoughts/works (see 63:6; 119:148), and waking only floods my soul once more with the sense of the presence of this God.

139:19–22 My zeal for You sets me against all Your adversaries.

‡139:19 *Surely thou wilt slay the wicked.* Expressing a desire, "O that . . . ." Jealous impatience with God's patience toward the wicked—whose end will come (Is 11:4). But the psalmist leaves it to God. For the Christian, Jesus has elevated the law of love to the place that we are to pray for our enemies (cf. Mat 5:44), with a recognition that God is "not willing that any should perish" (2 Pet 3:9). At the same time, Christians will rejoice in the fairness and justice of God's judgment when it falls on the wicked (cf. 2 Thes 1:7–10). A failure on God's part to judge the wicked would be the ultimate act of wickedness.

20 For they [a]speak against thee wickedly,
And thine enemies take *thy name* in vain.
21 [a]Do not I hate them, O LORD, that hate thee?
And am not I grieved with those that rise up against thee?
22 I hate them *with* perfect hatred:
I count them mine enemies.
23 [a]Search me, O God, and know my heart:
Try me, and know my thoughts:
24 And see if *there be any* [1]wicked way in me,
And [a]lead me in the way everlasting.

Psalm 140

To the chief Musician, A Psalm of David.

1 Deliver me, O LORD, from the evil man:
Preserve me from the [1]violent man;
2 Which imagine mischiefs in *their* heart;
[a]Continually are they gathered together *for* war.
3 They have sharpened their tongues like a serpent;
[a]Adder's poison *is* under their lips. Selah.

4 [a]Keep me, O LORD, from the hands of the wicked;
Preserve me from the violent man;
Who have purposed to overthrow my goings.
5 [a]The proud have hid a snare for me, and cords;
They have spread a net by the way side;
They have set grins for me. Selah.

6 I said unto the LORD, Thou *art* my God:
Hear the voice of my supplications, O LORD.
7 O GOD the Lord, the strength of my salvation,
Thou hast covered my head in the day of battle.
8 Grant not, O LORD, the desires of the wicked:
Further not his wicked device;
[a][1]*Lest* they exalt themselves. Selah.

9 *As for* the head of those that compass me about,
[a]Let the mischief of their own lips cover them.
10 [a]Let burning coals fall upon them:
Let them be cast into the fire;
Into deep pits, *that* they rise not up again.
11 Let not [1][2]an evil speaker be established in the earth:
Evil shall hunt the violent man to overthrow *him.*

12 I know that the LORD will [a]maintain the cause of the afflicted,
And the right of the poor.
13 Surely the righteous shall give thanks unto thy name:
The upright shall dwell in thy presence.

Psalm 141

A Psalm of David.

1 LORD, I cry unto thee: [a]make haste unto me;
Give ear unto my voice, when I cry unto thee.

139:20 [a]Jude 15
139:21 [a]2 Chr. 19:2
139:23 [a]Job 31:6
139:24 [1]Heb. *way of pain,* or, *grief* [a]Ps. 5:8
140:1 [1]Heb. *man of violences*
140:2 [a]Ps. 56:6
140:3 [a]Ps. 58:4
140:4 [a]Ps. 71:4
140:5 [a]Jer. 18:22
140:8 [1]Or, *Let them not be exalted* [a]Deut. 32:27
140:9 [a]Ps. 7:16
140:10 [a]Ps. 11:6
140:11 [1]Heb. *a man of tongue* [2]Or, *an evil speaker, a wicked man of violence, be established in the earth: Let him be hunted to his overthrow*
140:12 [a]Ps. 9:4
141:1 [a]Ps. 70:5

139:20 *take thy name in vain.* Perhaps by calling down curses on those trying to be the faithful servants of God.
139:21–22 A declaration of loyalty that echoes the pledge required by ancient Near Eastern kings of their vassals (e.g., "With my friend you shall be friend, and with my enemy you shall be enemy," from a treaty between Mursilis II, a Hittite king, and Tette of Nuhassi, 14th century B.C.).
139:23–24 Examine me, see the integrity of my devotion and keep me true (see 17:3–5 and note).
139:23 *heart.* See note on 4:7. *thoughts.* See 94:19. It is no light matter to be examined by God.
139:24 *the way everlasting.* See note on 16:9–11.
‡Ps 140 A prayer for deliverance from the plots and slander of unscrupulous enemies. It recalls Ps 58; 64 but employs a number of words found nowhere else in the OT. The prayer is strikingly rich in physiological allusions: heart, head, tongue, lips, hands—also ears ("Hear," lit. "give ear," v. 6), feet ("goings," i.e. footsteps, v. 4) and teeth (by a wordplay on the Hebrew for "sharpened," v. 3). See Ps 141.
140 title *To the chief Musician.* See note on Ps 4 title. *of David.* See note on Ps 138 title.
‡140:1–3 Rescue me from those "adders."
140:2 *heart.* See note on 4:7.
140:3 *tongues.* See note on 5:9. *Adder's poison.* See 58:4 and note.
140:4–5 Protect me from those proud and wicked hunters (see 10:2–11 and notes).
140:5 *The proud.* See note on 31:23.
140:6–8 Do not let these wicked men attain their evil designs against me.
140:9–11 Let the harm they plot against me recoil on their heads (see note on 5:10).
140:10 *burning coals.* See note on 11:6. *fire . . . deep pits.* This combination, together with the conjunction of fire and darkness in Job 15:30; 20:26, suggests the idea that the fire of God's judgment (see, e.g., 21:9; 97:3; Is 1:31; 26:11; 33:14) reaches even into the realm of the dead (see Job 31:12 and note on Ps 30:1). *that they rise not up again.* See 36:12; Is 26:14.
140:11 *hunt.* May these hunters (vv. 4–5) themselves be hunted by the ruin they intended to bring on me.
140:12–13 Confidence in God's just judgment (see note on 3:8).
140:12 *afflicted . . . poor.* See notes on 9:18; 34:6.
140:13 *the righteous.* See note on 1:5. *shall give thanks.* Having experienced God's help (see notes on 7:17; 9:1). *shall dwell in thy presence.* In contrast to the wicked (v. 10; see notes on 11:7; 16:9–11).
Ps 141 A prayer for deliverance from the wicked and their evil ways. The structure of the first half (two Hebrew lines plus three lines) is repeated in the second half, while at the center a cou-

2 Let [a]my prayer be [1]set forth before
thee [b]*as* incense;
And [c]the lifting up of my hands *as* [d]the
evening sacrifice.
3 Set a watch, O LORD, before my mouth;
Keep the door of my lips.
4 Incline not my heart to *any* evil thing,
To practise wicked works with men
that work iniquity:
[a]And let me not eat of their dainties.

5 [a1]Let the righteous smite me; *it shall*
be a kindness:
And let him reprove me; *it shall be* an
excellent oil,
Which shall not break my head:
For yet my prayer also *shall be* in their
calamities.
6 When their judges are overthrown in
stony places,
They shall hear my words; for they are
sweet.
7 Our bones are scattered at the grave's
mouth,
As when one cutteth and cleaveth
wood upon the earth.

8 But [a]mine eyes *are* unto thee, O GOD
the Lord:
In thee is my trust; [1]leave not my soul
destitute.
9 Keep me from [a]the snare *which* they
have laid for me,
And the grins of the workers of
iniquity.

141:2 [1]Heb. *directed* [a]Rev. 5:8 [b]Rev. 8:3 [c]1 Tim. 2:8 [d]Ex. 29:39
141:4 [a]Prov. 23:6
141:5 [1]Or, *Let the righteous smite me kindly, and reprove me; Let not* their *precious oil break my head, etc.* [a]Prov. 9:8
141:8 [1]Heb. *make not my soul bare* [a]Ps. 25:15
141:9 [a]Ps. 119:110
141:10 [1]Heb. *pass over* [a]Ps. 35:8
142:T [1]Or, A Psalm *of David, giving instruction* [a]Ps. 57, title [b]1 Sam. 22:1
142:2 [a]Is. 26:16
142:3 [a]Ps. 143:4 [b]Ps. 140:5
142:4 [1]Or, *Look on the right hand, and see* [2]Heb. *perished from me* [3]Heb. *No man sought after my soul* [a]Ps. 69:20 [b]Ps. 31:11
142:5 [a]Ps. 46:1 [b]Lam. 3:24 [c]Ps. 27:13
142:6 [a]Ps. 116:6
142:7 [a]Ps. 34:2 [b]Ps. 13:6

10 [a]Let the wicked fall into their own nets,
Whilst that I withal [1]escape.

Psalm 142

[a1]Maschil of David; A Prayer [b]when he was in the cave.

1 I cried unto the LORD *with* my voice;
With my voice unto the LORD did I
make my supplication.
2 [a]I poured out my complaint before him;
I shewed before him my trouble.
3 [a]When my spirit was overwhelmed
within me,
Then thou knewest my path.
[b]In the way wherein I walked
Have they privily laid a snare for me.
4 [a1]I looked *on my* right hand, and
beheld,
But [b]*there was* no man that would
know me:
Refuge [2]failed me;
[3]No man cared for my soul.
5 I cried unto thee, O LORD:
I said, [a]Thou *art* my refuge
And [b]my portion [c]in the land of the
living.
6 Attend unto my cry;
For I am [a]brought very low:
Deliver me from my persecutors;
For they are stronger than I.
7 Bring my soul out of prison,
That *I* may praise thy name:
[a]The righteous shall compass me about;
[b]For thou shalt deal bountifully with me.

---

plet develops a complementary theme (see note on v. 5). Like Ps 140, the prayer is profuse in its physiological allusions: hands, mouth, lips, heart, head, bones, eyes.

141 title See note on Ps 138 title.

141:1–2 Initial appeal for God to hear.

141:3–4 A plea that God will keep him from speaking, desiring or doing what is evil.

141:4 *Incline not my heart.* Keep me from yielding to the example and urgings of the wicked (see Prov 1:10–16). *heart.* See note on 4:7. *their dainties.* The luxuriant tables the wicked set from their unjust gains—keep me from acquiring an appetite for such unholy dainties.

‡141:5 The center of the poem (see note on 6:6). *Let the righteous smite me.* The disciplining blows and rebukes of the righteous are the true "kindness" (Hebrew *ḥesed,* meaning "faithful love"; see Prov 27:6; see also note on 6:4). *oil, Which shall not break my head.* Or "which my head will not refuse." See note on 23:5.

141:6–7 The destiny of the wicked.

141:6 *my words.* Of commitment to righteousness, as in vv. 3–5. *sweet.* Good and right.

141:8–10 A plea that God will deliver from the designs of the wicked.

141:8 *leave not my soul destitute.* As you do the wicked (see v. 7; see also 73:18–20,23–26 and notes).

‡141:9 *snare . . . grins.* Or "snare and traps." Perhaps, as usual, the plots of men to bring him down (as in 38:12; 64:5; 91:3; 140:5; 142:3)—but here reference may be to the enticements to evil that the wicked lay before him (see Ex 23:33; Deut 7:16; Josh 23:13; Judg 2:3).

141:10 *Let the wicked fall.* See note on 5:10.

Ps 142 A plaintive prayer for deliverance from powerful enemies—when powerless, alone and without refuge. Apart from the introduction (vv. 1–2) and conclusion (v. 7b), the prayer (in Hebrew) is composed of two four-line stanzas (vv. 3–7a).

142 title *Maschil.* See note on Ps 32 title. *of David.* See note on Ps 138 title. *A Prayer.* See note on Ps 17 title. *when . . . cave.* See note on Ps 57 title.

142:1–2 Initial appeal—using the formal third person (as was often done when addressing kings), equivalent to: "I cry aloud to You, O LORD."

142:3–4 Description of when he had been "brought very low" (v. 6).

142:3 *When my spirit was overwhelmed.* Because he is overwhelmed by his situation (see 22:14–15). *thou knewest.* And were concerned about (cf. v. 4).

‡142:4 *on my right hand.* Where one's helper or defender stands (see 16:8 and note). *know me.* Have regard or take notice of my situation. In Hebrew a less common synonym of the word for "knewest" in v. 3; see Ruth 2:10,19 ("take knowledge").

142:5–7 Prayer for rescue.

142:5 *portion.* The sustainer and preserver of his life (see 73:26 and note).

142:7 *prison.* Metaphor for the sense of being fettered by affliction (see note on 18:19; see also Job 36:8). *That I may praise thy name.* In celebration of God's saving help (see note on 7:17). *name.* See note on 5:11. *righteous.* See note on 1:5. *shall compass me about.* He will no longer be alone. The conclusion expresses an expectant word of confidence (see note on 3:8).

Psalm 143

A Psalm of David.

1 Hear my prayer, O LORD,
Give ear to my supplications:
[a]In thy faithfulness answer me, *and* in thy righteousness.
2 And [a]enter not into judgment with thy servant:
For [b]in thy sight shall no *man* living be justified.
3 For the enemy hath persecuted my soul;
He hath smitten my life down to the ground;
He hath made me to dwell in darkness, as those that have been long dead.
4 [a]Therefore is my spirit overwhelmed within me;
My heart within me is desolate.
5 [a]I remember the days of old;
I meditate on all thy works;
I muse on the work of thy hands.
6 [a]I stretch forth my hands unto thee:
[b]My soul *thirsteth* after thee, as a thirsty land. Selah.

7 Hear me speedily, O LORD: my spirit faileth:
Hide not thy face from me,
[a][1]Lest I be like unto them that go down into the pit.
8 Cause me to hear thy lovingkindness [a]in the morning;
For in thee do I trust:
Cause me to know the way wherein I should walk;
For [b]I lift up my soul unto thee.
9 Deliver me, O LORD, from mine enemies:
I [1]flee unto thee to hide me.
10 [a]Teach me to do thy will; for thou *art* my God:
[b]Thy spirit *is* good; lead me into [c]the land of uprightness.
11 [a]Quicken me, O LORD, for thy name's sake:
For thy righteousness' sake bring my soul out of trouble.
12 And of thy mercy [a]cut off mine enemies,
And destroy all them that afflict my soul:
For I *am* thy servant.

Psalm 144

A Psalm of David.

1 Blessed *be* the LORD [a][1]my strength,
[b]Which teacheth my hands [2]to war,
And my fingers to fight:
2 [1]My goodness, and my fortress; my high tower, and my deliverer;
My shield, and *he* in whom I trust;
Who subdueth my people under me.

143:1 [a]Ps. 31:1
143:2 [a]Job 14:3 [b]Ex. 34:7
143:4 [a]Ps. 77:3
143:5 [a]Ps. 77:5
143:6 [a]Ps. 88:9 [b]Ps. 63:1
143:7 [1]Or, *For I am become like, etc.* [a]Ps. 28:1
143:8 [a]Ps. 46:5 [b]Ps. 25:1
143:9 [1]Heb. *hide me with thee*
143:10 [a]Ps. 25:4,5 [b]Neh. 9:20 [c]Is. 26:10
143:11 [a]Ps. 119:25
143:12 [a]Ps. 54:5
144:1 [1]Heb. *my rock* [2]Heb. *to the war, etc.* [a]Ps. 18:2,31 [b]2 Sam. 22:35; Ps. 18:34
144:2 [1]Or, *My mercy*

‡Ps 143 A prayer for deliverance from enemies and for divine leading. This is the seventh and final penitential psalm (see introduction to Ps 6). In the first half (vv. 1–6) the psalmist makes his appeal and describes his situation; in the second half (vv. 7–12) he presents his prayer. Appeal to God's righteousness (vv. 1,11) and the author's self-identification as "thy servant" (vv. 2,12) enclose the prayer. See also his appeal to God's faithfulness (v. 1) and mercy (v. 12), which together form a frequent pair (see note on 36:5). For another enclosure see note on v. 7.

143 title See note on Ps 138 title.

143:1–2 Initial appeal.

143:1 *righteousness.* See note on 4:1.

143:2 As he begins his prayer, he pleads that God not sit in judgment over His servant (he knows his own failings) but that He focus His judicial attention on the enemy's harsh and unwarranted attacks.

143:3–4 The distress he suffers.

143:3 The last half of this verse appears almost verbatim in Lam 3:6. *in darkness.* As one cut off from the enjoyments of life (see v. 7; see also notes on 27:1; 30:1).

143:4 *is my spirit overwhelmed.* See note on 142:3. *heart.* See note on 4:7.

143:5–6 Remembrance of God's past acts of deliverance encourages him in his appeal.

143:6 *stretch forth my hands.* In prayer (see 44:20; 88:9; Ex 9:29). *soul.* See v. 8; see also note on 6:3. *thirsteth after thee.* See note on 63:1.

143:7–10 The prayer.

‡143:7 *my spirit faileth.* Or perhaps: "my spirit faints with longing," which parallels that in 119:81; in view of the next line the thought appears closer to that of 104:29. Ultimately, the failing of "my spirit" will be healed by the leading of God's "spirit" (v. 10)—the two references enclose the prayer. *Hide not thy face.* See note on 13:1. *the pit.* See v. 3 and note on 30:1.

‡143:8 *lovingkindness.* See v. 12; see also note on 6:4. *the morning.* Of salvation from the present "darkness" (v. 3; see introduction to Ps 57). *Cause me to know the way.* See v. 10. Deliverance from the enemy is not enough—either for God's "servant" (vv. 2,12) or for entrance into life.

143:10 *land of uprightness.* See note on 26:12.

143:11–12 Concluding summary of the prayer (see introduction).

143:11 *For thy righteousness' sake.* See note on 23:3.

143:12 *destroy all them that afflict my soul.* See note on 5:10.

Ps 144 A royal prayer for victory over treacherous enemies (but see note on vv. 12–15). Verses 1–10 show much affinity with Ps 18; this section begins and ends like that psalm, and vv. 5–7 all appear to be variations on corresponding lines found there (see notes below). The remaining lines of this section contain similar echoes of other psalms, and the author may have drawn directly on them. The main body (vv. 1–10) is fairly typical of the prayers of the Psalter, but the conclusion (vv. 12–15) is unique. Verse 11 appears to be transitional.

144 title See note on Ps 138 title.

144:1–2 Praise of the Lord. As the opening words of a prayer, it seems to function both as an initial appeal (see 143:1–2) and as a confession of confidence that the prayer will be heard. Notice the unusual piling up of epithets for God—all having their counterparts in Ps 18.

‡144:2 *My goodness.* See note on "mercy" in 6:4. God is here called "My goodness" because He is the source of benevolent acts of love that David can count on—just as God can be called "my salvation" because He is the source of salvation (see 27:1; 35:3; 62:2).

3 [a]LORD, what *is* man, that thou takest
knowledge of him?
Or the son of man, that thou makest
account of him?
4 [a]Man is like to vanity:
[b]His days *are* as a shadow that passeth
away.
5 [a]Bow thy heavens, O LORD, and come
down:
[b]Touch the mountains, and they shall
smoke.
6 [a]Cast forth lightning, and scatter
them:
Shoot out thine arrows, and destroy
them.
7 Send thine [1]hand from above;
Rid me, and deliver me out of great
waters,
From the hand of strange children;
8 Whose mouth [a]speaketh vanity,
And their right hand *is* a right hand of
falsehood.
9 I will [a]sing a new song unto thee,
O God:
Upon a psaltery *and* an instrument of
ten strings will I sing *praises* unto
thee.
10 [a]*It is he* that giveth [1]salvation unto
kings:
Who delivereth David his servant from
the hurtful sword.
11 Rid me, and deliver me from the hand
of strange children,
Whose mouth speaketh vanity,
And their right hand *is* a right hand of
falsehood:

12 That our sons *may be* [a]as plants grown
up in their youth;
That our daughters *may be* as corner
stones, [1]polished *after* the similitude
of a palace:
13 *That* our garners *may be* full, affording
[1]all manner of store:
That our sheep may bring forth
thousands and ten thousands in our
streets:
14 *That* our oxen *may be* [1]strong to labour;
That there be no breaking in, nor going
out;
That *there be* no complaining in our
streets.
15 [a]Happy *is that* people, that is in such a
case:
Yea, happy *is that* people, whose God
is the LORD.

Psalm 145

David's [a]*Psalm of* praise.

1 I will extol thee, my God, O king;
And I will bless thy name for ever and
ever.
2 Every day will I bless thee;
And I will praise thy name for ever and
ever.
3 [a]Great *is* the LORD, and greatly to be
praised;
[1]And [b]his greatness *is* unsearchable.
4 [a]One generation shall praise thy works
to another,
And shall declare thy mighty acts.
5 I will speak of the glorious honour of
thy majesty,
And of thy wondrous [1]works.
6 And *men* shall speak of the might of
thy terrible acts:
And I will [1]declare thy greatness.

144:3 [a]Job 7:17; Ps. 8:4; Heb. 2:6
144:4 [a]Job 4:19 [b]Ps. 102:11
144:5 [a]Ps. 18:9 [b]Ps. 104:32
144:6 [a]Ps. 18:13
144:7 [1]Heb. *hands*
144:8 [a]Ps. 12:2
144:9 [a]Ps. 33:2,3
144:10 [1]Or, *victory* [a]Ps. 18:50
144:12 [a]Ps. 128:3
144:12 [1]Heb. *cut*
144:13 [1]Heb *from kind to kind*
144:14 [1]Heb. *able to bear burdens,* or, *loaden* with flesh
144:15 [a]Ps. 33:12
145:T [a]Ps. 100, title
145:3 [1]Heb. *And of his greatness* there is *no search* [a]Ps. 147:5 [b]Rom. 11:33
145:4 [a]Is. 38:9
145:5 [1]Heb. *things,* or, *words*
145:6 [1]Heb. *declare it*

144:3–4 Confession of man's insignificance and of his dependence on God's help.
144:3 A variation of 8:4.
‡144:4 See 39:4–6 and notes. *Man is like to vanity.* A breath or vapor that is here and gone (cf. Job 7:7; Jas 4:14).
144:5–8 Prayer for deliverance.
144:5 See 18:9 and note on 18:7–15.
144:6 See 18:14 and note.
‡144:7 See 18:16–17 and note on 32:6. *strange children.* Foreigners from the bordering kingdoms.
144:8 *mouth.* See note on 5:9. *right hand.* Hand raised to swear a covenant oath of allegiance or submission (see 106:26; Ex 6:8; Deut 32:40).
144:9–10 Vow to praise (see note on 7:17).
144:9 *new song.* See note on 33:3.
144:10 *David his servant.* See note on Ps 18 title.
144:11 Repetition of the prayer in vv. 7–8, apparently to serve as transition to what follows: If God will deliver His servant David, the realm will prosper and be secure.
‡144:12 *daughters . . . as corner stones, polished . . . palace.* Not the cornerstone (the "stone of the corner" in 118:22), but carved and ornately decorated pillars. Temple columns in the shape of women were not uncommon (e.g., on the Acropolis in Athens).
‡144:13 *garners.* Or "barns."
‡144:14 *That our oxen may be strong to labour.* Or "Let our cattle be heavy with flesh" or "Let our cattle be heavy with young." *no breaking in, nor going out.* No "breaking in" of enemy armies, and no "going out" into captivity. *no complaining.* No crying out or distress.
‡144:15 *Happy.* Or "blessed." See note on 1:1.
Ps 145 A hymn to the Lord, the Great King, for His mighty acts and benevolent virtues, which are the glory of His kingly rule. It exploits to the full the traditional language of praise and, as an alphabetic acrostic, reflects the care of studied composition. Between the two-line introduction (vv. 1–2) and one-line conclusion (v. 21), four poetic paragraphs develop as many themes, each introduced with a thematic line (see vv. 3,8, 13b,17).
145 title *David's.* See note on Ps 138 title. *praise.* Hebrew *tehillah,* occurring only here in the psalm titles, but from a plural form (*tehillim*) has come the traditional Hebrew name of the Psalter.
145:1–2 Initial commitment to praise. *name.* See v. 21, thus framing the psalm (see note on 5:11).
145:3–7 Praise of God's mighty acts, which display His greatness (v. 3) and His goodness (v. 7)—as the author underscores by enclosing the paragraph with these two references. For the same combination see 86:10,17; 135:3,5.
145:4 *shall praise . . . shall declare.* See vv. 5–7,10–12,21; see also note on 9:1. *thy wondrous works.* In creation, providence and redemption.
‡145:6 *terrible acts.* Awesome acts of power.

7 They shall abundantly utter the
memory of thy great goodness,
And shall sing of thy righteousness.

8 [a]The LORD *is* gracious, and full of
compassion;
Slow to anger, and [1]of great mercy.
9 [a]The LORD *is* good to all:
And his tender mercies *are* over all his
works.
10 [a]All thy works shall praise thee,
O LORD;
And thy saints shall bless thee.
11 They shall speak of the glory of thy
kingdom,
And talk of thy power;
12 To make known to the sons of men his
mighty acts,
And the glorious majesty of his
kingdom.
13 [a]Thy kingdom *is* [1]an everlasting
kingdom,
And thy dominion *endureth*
throughout all generations.

14 The LORD upholdeth all that fall,
And [a]raiseth up all those that be
bowed down.
15 [a]The eyes of all [1]wait upon thee;
And [b]thou givest them their meat in
due season.
16 Thou openest thine hand,
[a]And satisfiest the desire of every
living thing.
17 The LORD *is* righteous in all his ways,
And [1]holy in all his works.
18 [a]The LORD *is* nigh unto all them that
call upon him,
To all that call upon him [b]in truth.
19 He will fulfil the desire of them that
fear him:
He also will hear their cry, and will
save them.
20 [a]The LORD preserveth all them that
love him:
But all the wicked will he destroy.

145:8 [1]Heb. *great in mercy* [a]Num. 14:18
145:9 [a]Nah. 1:7
145:10 [a]Ps. 19:1
145:13 [1]Heb. *a kingdom of all ages* [a]1 Tim. 1:17
145:14 [a]Ps. 146:8
145:15 [1]Or, *look unto thee* [a]Ps. 104:27 [b]Ps. 136:25
145:16 [a]Ps. 104:21
145:17 [1]Or, *merciful*, or, *bountiful*
145:18 [a]Deut. 4:7 [b]John 4:24
145:20 [a]Ps. 31:23

146:1 [1]Heb. *Hallelujah* [a]Ps. 103:1
146:2 [a]Ps. 104:33
146:3 [1]Or, *salvation* [a]Is. 2:22
146:4 [a]Eccl. 12:7 [b]1 Cor. 2:6
146:5 [a]Jer. 17:7
146:6 [a]Rev. 14:7
146:7 [a]Ps. 103:6 [b]Ps. 107:9 [c]Ps. 107:10
146:8 [a]Mat. 9:30 [b]Luke 13:13
146:9 [a]Deut. 10:18; Ps. 68:5 [b]Ps. 147:6
146:10 [a]Ex. 15:18; Ps. 10:16
147:1 [a]Ps. 92:1

21 My mouth shall speak the praise of the
LORD:
And let all flesh bless his holy name for
ever and ever.

Psalm 146

1 [1]Praise ye the LORD.
[a]Praise the LORD, O my soul.
2 [a]While I live will I praise the LORD:
I will sing *praises* unto my God while I
have *any* being.
3 [a]Put not your trust in princes,
Nor in the son of man, in whom *there*
is no [1]help.
4 [a]His breath goeth forth, he returneth
to his earth;
In that *very* day [b]his thoughts perish.
5 [a]Happy *is he* that *hath* the God of
Jacob for his help,
Whose hope *is* in the LORD his God:
6 [a]Which made heaven, and earth,
The sea, and all that therein is:
Which keepeth truth for ever:
7 [a]Which executeth judgment for the
oppressed:
[b]Which giveth food to the hungry.
[c]The LORD looseth the prisoners:
8 [a]The LORD openeth *the eyes of* the
blind:
[b]The LORD raiseth them that are bowed
down:
The LORD loveth the righteous:
9 [a]The LORD preserveth the strangers;
He relieveth the fatherless and widow:
[b]But the way of the wicked he turneth
upside down.
10 [a]The LORD shall reign for ever,
Even thy God, O Zion, unto all
generations.
Praise ye the LORD.

Psalm 147

1 Praise ye the LORD:
For [a]*it is* good to sing *praises* unto our
God;

145:7 *righteousness.* See v. 17; see also note on 4:1.
145:8–13a Praise of God's benevolent virtues, which move all creatures to celebrate the glory of His kingdom.
145:8 See Ex 34:6–7 and note.
145:10 *All thy works shall praise thee.* See v. 21; see also note on 65:13. *saints.* See note on 4:3.
145:14–16 Praise God's faithfulness.
145:17–20 Praise of God's righteousness.
‡145:18 *nigh.* Near. *in truth.* With godly integrity.
‡145:21 The praise of God must continue, and every creature take it up—forever. *all flesh.* Or perhaps "every human" (cf. 65:2; but see also 150:6).
Ps 146 An exhortation to trust in the Lord, Zion's King. The first of five Hallelujah psalms with which the Psalter closes, its date is probably postexilic. This and the remaining four psalms are all framed with Hallelujahs, which may have been added by the final editors (see Ps 105–106; 111–117).
146:1–2 Initial vow to praise—as long as life continues (see 145:21).
146:1 *Praise the LORD, O my soul.* See the frames around Ps 103–104. *soul.* See note on 6:3.
146:3–4 The call to trust in the Lord (see vv. 5–9) is heightened by contrast.
‡146:4 *breath goeth forth.* Spirit departs from his body in death.
146:5–9 Exhortation to trust in the covenant God of Jacob (see note on 14:7), who as Creator is Lord over all, as the Faithful One defends the defenseless and provides for the needy, and as the Righteous One shows favor to the righteous but checks the wicked in their pursuits.
146:6 *Which made heaven, and earth.* See note on 121:2.
146:8 *righteous.* See note on 1:5.
146:10 Concluding exultant testimony to the citizens of God's royal city. *Zion.* See note on 9:11.
Ps 147 Praise of God, the Creator, for His special mercies to Israel—possibly composed for the Levitical choirs on the joyous occasion of the dedication of the rebuilt walls of Jerusalem (see Neh 12:27–43). The Septuagint (the Greek translation of the OT)

[b]For *it is* pleasant; *and* [c]praise is
comely.
2 The LORD doth [a]build up Jerusalem:
[b]He gathereth together the outcasts of
Israel.
3 [a]He healeth the broken in heart,
And bindeth up their [1]wounds.
4 [a]He telleth the number of the stars;
He calleth them all *by their* names.
5 [a]Great *is* our Lord, and of [b]great
power:
[c][1]His understanding *is* infinite.
6 [a]The LORD lifteth up the meek:
He casteth the wicked down to the
ground.
7 Sing unto the LORD with thanksgiving;
Sing *praise* upon the harp unto our
God:
8 [a]Who covereth the heaven with
clouds,
Who prepareth rain for the earth,
Who maketh grass to grow *upon* the
mountains.
9 [a]He giveth to the beast his food,
And [b]to the young ravens which cry.
10 [a]He delighteth not in the strength of
the horse:
He taketh not pleasure in the legs of a
man.
11 The LORD taketh pleasure in them that
fear him,
In those that hope in his mercy.
12 Praise the LORD, O Jerusalem;
Praise thy God, O Zion.
13 For he hath strengthened the bars of
thy gates;
He hath blessed thy children within
thee.
14 [a][1]He maketh peace *in* thy borders,
And [b]filleth thee *with* the [2]finest of
the wheat.
15 [a]He sendeth forth his commandment
upon earth:
His word runneth very swiftly.
16 [a]He giveth snow like wool:
He scattereth the hoarfrost like ashes.
17 He casteth forth his ice like morsels:
Who can stand before his cold?
18 [a]He sendeth out his word, and melteth
them:
He causeth his wind to blow, *and* the
waters flow.
19 [a]He sheweth [1]his word unto Jacob,
[b]His statutes and his judgments unto
Israel.
20 [a]He hath not dealt so with any nation:
And *as for his* judgments, they have
not known them.
Praise ye the LORD.

Psalm 148

1 [1]Praise ye the LORD.
Praise ye the LORD from the heavens:
Praise him in the heights.
2 Praise ye him, all his angels:
Praise ye him, all his hosts.
3 Praise ye him, sun and moon:
Praise him, all ye stars of light.
4 Praise him, [a]ye heavens of heavens,
And [b]ye waters that *be* above the
heavens.
5 Let them praise the name of the LORD:
For [a]he commanded, and they were
created.
6 [a]He hath also stablished them for ever
and ever:
He hath made a decree which shall not
pass.

147:1 [b]Ps. 135:3 [c]Ps. 33:1 **147:2** [a]Ps. 102:16 [b]Deut. 30:3 **147:3** [1]Heb. *griefs* [a]Ps. 51:17 **147:4** [a]Is. 40:26 **147:5** [1]Heb. *Of his understanding* there is *no number* [a]Ps. 48:1 [b]Nah. 1:3 [c]Is. 40:28 **147:6** [a]Ps. 146:8 **147:8** [a]Job 38:26; Ps. 104:13 **147:9** [a]Job 38:41; Ps. 104:27 [b]Mat. 6:26 **147:10** [a]Ps. 33:16; Hos. 1:7 **147:14** [1]Heb. *Who maketh thy border peace* [a]Is. 60:17,18 **147:14** [2]Heb. *fat of wheat* [b]Ps. 132:15 **147:15** [a]Ps. 107:20 **147:16** [a]Job 37:6 **147:18** [a]Job 37:10 **147:19** [1]Heb. *his words* [a]Deut. 33:4; Ps. 76:1 [b]Mal. 4:4 **147:20** [a]Rom. 3:1,2 **148:1** [1]Heb. *Hallelujah* **148:4** [a]1 Ki. 8:27; 2 Cor. 12:2 [b]Gen. 1:7 **148:5** [a]Gen. 1:1,6; Ps. 33:6,9 **148:6** [a]Ps. 89:37; Jer. 33:25

divides the work into two separate psalms (vv. 1–11, 12–20), but it is actually a three-part song (vv. 1–6, 7–11, 12–20), bound together by the frame (vv. 2–3, 19–20), in which the Lord's unique favors to Israel are celebrated. See introduction to Ps 146.

147:1 See note on 135:3.

147:2 *build up . . . gathereth together.* Refers to the postexilic restoration of Jerusalem and Israel.

147:3 *broken in heart.* Such as the exiles (see Ps 137; cf. Ps 126) and those who struggled in the face of great opposition to rebuild Jerusalem's walls (Neh 2:17–20; 4:1–23).

147:4–6 He whose power and understanding are such that He fixes the number of (or counts) the stars and names them is able to sustain His humble ones and bring the wicked down (see 20:8; 146:9; see also Is 40:26–29).

147:6 *meek.* Those who acknowledge that they are without resources (see 149:4). *ground.* Probably the grave (see note on 61:2).

147:7–11 The God who governs the rain and thus provides food for beast and bird is not pleased by man's reliance on his own capabilities or those of the animals he has domesticated (or the technologies he has developed); He is pleased when people serve Him and trust His loving care.

147:11 *fear.* See note on 34:8–14. *mercy.* See note on 6:4.

147:12–18 The Lord of all creation, Zion's God, secures His people's defenses and prosperity, their peace and abundant provision. The verses mention clouds and rain (v. 8); snow, frost and hail (vv. 16–17); icy winds and warm breezes (vv. 17–18)—the whole range of weather.

147:15 *his commandment . . . His word.* Personified as messengers commissioned to carry out a divine order (see notes on 23:6; 33:4; 104:4).

‡147:19–20 God's most unique gift to Israel: His other word, His redemptive word, by which He makes known His program of salvation and His holy will. Cf. Deut 4:8.

Ps 148 A call to all things in all creation to praise the Lord. Whatever its original liturgical purpose, its placement here serves to complete the scope of the calls to praise with which the Psalter concludes. Two balanced (Hebrew) stanzas of six verses each are followed by a two-verse conclusion. In the first stanza (vv. 1–6) the call goes to all creatures in the heavens, in the second (vv. 7–12) to all beneath the heavens (see 103:20–22). The conclusion (vv. 13–14) focuses on motivation for praise. See introduction to Ps 146.

148:1–6 Let all creatures in the heavens praise the Lord.

148:3 *sun and moon . . . stars of light.* See note on 65:13.

148:4 *waters . . . above the heavens.* The "deep" above (see Gen 1:7; cf. "all deeps" in v. 7; see also note on 42:7).

148:5 *name of the LORD.* See v. 13; see also note on 5:11. They are to praise the Lord because He has created them and made their existence secure.

7 Praise the LORD from the earth,
[a]Ye dragons, and all deeps:
8 Fire, and hail; snow, and vapour;
Stormy wind [a]fulfilling his word:
9 [a]Mountains, and all hills;
Fruitful trees, and all cedars:
10 Beasts, and all cattle;
Creeping things, and [1]flying fowl:
11 Kings of the earth, and all people;
Princes, and all judges of the earth:
12 Both young men, and maidens;
Old men, and children:
13 Let them praise the name of the LORD:
For [a]his name alone *is* [1]excellent;
[b]His glory *is* above the earth and heaven.
14 [a]He also exalteth the horn of his people,
[b]The praise of all his saints;
Even of the children of Israel, [c]a people near unto him.
Praise ye the LORD.

Psalm 149

1 [1]Praise ye the LORD.
[a]Sing unto the LORD a new song,
And his praise in the congregation of saints.
2 Let Israel rejoice in [a]him that made him:
Let the children of Zion be joyful in their [b]King.
3 [a]Let them praise his name [1]in the dance:
Let them sing *praises* unto him with the timbrel and harp.
4 For [a]the LORD taketh pleasure in his people:
[b]He will beautify the meek with salvation.
5 Let the saints be joyful in glory:
Let them [a]sing aloud upon their beds.
6 *Let* the high *praises* of God *be* [1]in their mouth,
And [a]a twoedged sword in their hand;
7 To execute vengeance upon the heathen,
And punishments upon the people;
8 To bind their kings with chains,
And their nobles with fetters of iron;
9 [a]To execute upon them the judgment written:
[b]This honour have all his saints.
Praise ye the LORD.

Psalm 150

1 [1]Praise ye the LORD.
Praise God in his sanctuary:
Praise him in the firmament of his power.

148:7 [a]Is. 43:20
148:8 [a]Ps. 147:15-18
148:9 [a]Is. 44:23
148:10 [1]Heb. *birds of wing*
148:13 [1]Heb. *exalted* [a]Is. 12:4 [b]Ps. 113:4
148:14 [a]Ps. 75:10 [b]Ps. 149:9 [c]Eph. 2:17
149:1 [1]Heb. *Hallelujah* [a]Ps. 33:3; Is. 42:10
149:2 [a]Job 35:10; Ps. 100:3; Is. 54:5
149:2 [b]Zech. 9:9; Mat. 21:5
149:3 [1]Or, *with the pipe* [a]Ps. 81:2
149:4 [a]Ps. 35:27 [b]Ps. 132:16
149:5 [a]Job 35:10
149:6 [1]Heb. *in their throat* [a]Heb. 4:12; Rev. 1:16
149:9 [a]Deut. 7:1,2 [b]Ps. 148:14
150:1 [1]Heb. *Hallelujah*

148:7–12 Let all creatures of earth praise the Lord. ("Heaven and earth" are the sum of all creation; see v. 13; see also 89:11; 113:6; 136:5–6; Gen 2:1,4.)
148:7 *dragons, and all deeps.* Likely with Gen 1 in mind (see Gen 1:7,10,21), the call begins with these and moves toward the human components. This and the pairs that follow employ a figure of speech (merism) that refers to all reality pertaining to the sphere to which they belong—here, all creatures great and small that belong to the realm of lakes and seas.
148:8 *his word.* See 147:15 and note.
148:13–14 Conclusion, with focus on motivation for praise.
148:13 *his name . . . His glory.* As shown in the glory of His creation. *is above.* The glory of the Creator is greater than the glory of the creation.
148:14 *horn.* The Lord's anointed ("horn" here symbolizes strong one, that is, the king; see notes on 2:2; Ps 18 title). It may be, however, that "horn" here represents the strength and vigor of God's people (see 92:10; 1 Sam 2:1; Jer 48:25; Lam 2:17). In any event, reference is to God's saving acts for Israel—God is to be praised for His works in creation and redemption (see note on 65:6–7). *praise.* See 22:3 and note.
‡Ps 149 Praise of God for the high honor bestowed on His people. It is no doubt postexilic. Israel's unique honor has two sides: She has been granted salvation (in fact and in promise), and she has been armed to execute God's sentence of judgment on the world powers that have launched their attacks against the kingdom of God—she is the earthly contingent of the armies of the King of heaven (see 68:17 and note; see also Josh 5:14; 2 Sam 5:23–24; 2 Chr 20:15–17,22; Hab 3:3–15). This next-to-last psalm clearly marks the Psalter as the prayer book (liturgical book of prayer and praise) of OT Israel.

Following an introductory verse, the two main themes are developed in two balanced (Hebrew) stanzas of four verses each. References to God's "saints" enclose the song (see also v. 5). The common pair of synonyms, "glory" (v. 5) and "honour" (v. 9), effectively link the two stanzas (see 8:5; 21:5, "glory . . . majesty"; 104:1,31, "majesty . . . glory"; 145:5, "glorious honour").
‡149:1 *new song.* See note on 33:3. *in the congregation.* See note on 9:1. *saints.* Lit. "godly ones." See vv. 5,9; see also note on 4:3.
149:2–5 Let Israel rejoice in their King, who has crowned them with the honor of salvation.
149:3 *his name.* See note on 5:11.
149:4 *beautify.* Endow with splendor (see Is 55:5; 60:9; 61:3). *meek.* Those who acknowledge that they are without resources (see 147:6).
149:5 *upon their beds.* The salvation (v. 4) so tangible in the daytime evokes songs in the night (see 42:8; 63:6; 77:6).
149:6–9 Let Israel praise their God, who has given them the glory of bearing the sword as His army in service.
149:7 *vengeance.* God's just retribution on those who have attacked His kingdom. Of this divine retribution the OT speaks often: 58:10; 79:10; 94:1; Num 31:2; Deut 32:35,41,43; 2 Ki 9:7; Is 34:8; 35:4; 47:3; 59:17; 61:2; 63:4; Jer 46:10; 50:15,28; 51:6,11,36; Ezek 25:14,17; Mic 5:15; Nah 1:2. In the NT age, however, God's people are armed with the "sword of the Spirit" for overcoming the powers arrayed against God's kingdom (see 2 Cor 6:7; 10:4; Eph 6:12,17; Heb 4:12); their participation in God's retribution on the world awaits the final judgment (see 1 Cor 6:2–3).
149:9 *judgment written.* God's firmly determined judgment (see 139:16 and note).
Ps 150 The final great Hallelujah—perhaps composed specifically to close the Psalter. See the conclusions to the first four Books: 41:13; 72:18–19; 89:52; 106:48. This final call to praise moves powerfully by stages from place to themes to orchestra to choir, framed with Hallelujahs. See introduction to Ps 146.
‡150:1 Where God should be praised. *his sanctuary.* At Jerusalem. *firmament of his power.* See 19:1; Gen 1:6. The fir-

2 [a]Praise him for his mighty acts:
Praise him according to his excellent
[b]greatness.
3 Praise him with the sound of the
[a][1]trumpet:
[b]Praise him with the psaltery and harp.
4 Praise him [a]with the timbrel and
[b][1]dance:
Praise him with [c]stringed instruments
and organs.
5 Praise him upon the loud [a]cymbals:
Praise him upon the high sounding
cymbals.
6 Let every *thing that hath* breath praise
the LORD.
Praise ye the LORD.

150:2 [a]Ps. 145:5 [b]Deut. 3:24
150:3 [1]Or, *cornet* [a]Ps. 98:6 [b]Ps. 81:2
150:4 [1]Or, *pipe* [a]Ex. 15:20 [b]Ps. 149:3 [c]Ps. 33:2; Is. 38:20
150:5 [a]1 Chr. 15:16,19,28

mament is the expanse that displays or symbolizes His power or in which His power resides. Usually thought to refer to God's heavenly temple (see 11:4), it may signify the vaulted ceiling of the visible universe viewed as a cosmic temple.

150:2 Why God should be praised. *his mighty acts.* In creation and redemption.

150:3–5 How God should be praised—with the whole orchestra (eight instruments: wind, string, percussion), with dancing aptly placed at the middle.

150:6 Who should praise God. Finally the choir, with articulate expression, celebrates God's mighty acts and surpassing greatness.

The Proverbs

INTRODUCTION

Authors

Although the book begins with a title ascribing the proverbs to Solomon, it is clear from later chapters that he was not the only author of the book. Prov 22:17 refers to the "words of the wise," and 24:23 introduces additional sayings that are attributed simply "to the wise." The presence of an introduction in 22:17–21 further indicates that these sections stem from a circle of wise men, not from Solomon himself. Ch. 30 is attributed to Agur son of Jakeh and 31:1–9 to king Lemuel, neither of whom is mentioned elsewhere. Lemuel's sayings contain several Aramaic spellings that point to a non-Israelite background.

Most of the book, however, is closely linked with Solomon. The headings in 10:1 and 25:1 again include his name, though 25:1 states that these proverbs were transcribed by the men of Hezekiah. This indicates that a group of wise men or scribes compiled these proverbs as editors and added chs. 25—29 to the earlier collections. Solomon's ability to produce proverbs is specified in 1 Ki 4:32, where 3,000 proverbs are attributed to him. Coupled with the statements about his unparalleled wisdom (1 Ki 4:29–31), it is quite likely that he was the source of most of Proverbs. The book contains a short prologue (1:1–7) and a longer epilogue (31:10–31), which may have been added to the other materials. It is possible that the discourses in the large opening section (1:8—9:18) were the work of a compiler or editor, but the similarities of this section with other chapters (compare 6:1 with 11:15; 17:18; 20:16; 27:13; compare 6:19 with 14:5,25; 19:5) fit a Solomonic origin equally well. The emphasis on the "fear of the LORD" (1:7) throughout the book ties the various segments together.

Date

If Solomon is granted a prominent role in the book, most of Proverbs would stem from the tenth century B.C. during the time of Israel's united kingdom. The peace and prosperity that characterized that era accord well with the development of reflective wisdom and the production of literary works. Moreover, several scholars have noted that the 30 sayings of the wise in 22:17—24:22 contain similarities to the 30 sections of the Egyptian "Wisdom of Amenemope," an instructional piece that is roughly contemporary with the time of Solomon (see chart, p. xix). Likewise, the personification of wisdom so prominent in chs. 1—9 (see 1:20 and note; 3:15–18; 8:1–36) can be compared with the personification of abstract ideas in both Mesopotamian and Egyptian writings of the second millennium B.C.

The role of Hezekiah's men (see 25:1) indicates that important sections of Proverbs were compiled and edited from 715 to 686 B.C. This was a time of spiritual renewal led by the king, who also showed great interest in the writings of David and Asaph (see 2 Chr 29:30). Perhaps it was also at this time that the sayings of Agur (ch. 30) and Lemuel (31:1–9) and the other "words of the wise" (22:17—24:22; 24:23–34) were added to the Solomonic collections, though it is possible that the task of compilation was not completed until after the reign of Hezekiah.

The Nature of a Proverb

The Hebrew word translated "proverb" is also translated "parable" (Num 23:7,18; Ezek 17:2) and "byword" (Ps 44:14); so its meaning is considerably broader than the English term. This may help explain the presence of the longer discourse sections in chs. 1—9. Most proverbs are short, compact statements that express truths about human behavior. Often there is some repetition of a word or sound that aids memorization. In 30:33, e.g., the same Hebrew verb is translated "churning" and "wringing."

In the largest section of the book (10:1—22:16) most of the proverbs are two lines long, and those in chs. 10—15 almost always express a contrast. Sometimes the writer simply makes a general observation, such as "Even in laughter the heart is sorrowful" (14:13), but usually he evaluates conduct:

"Lying lips are abomination to the LORD" (12:22). Many proverbs, in fact, describe the consequences of a particular action or character trait: "A wise son maketh a glad father" (10:1). Since the proverbs were written primarily for instruction, often they are given in the form of commands: "Love not sleep, lest thou come to poverty" (20:13). Even where the imperative form is not used, the desired action is quite clear (see 14:5).

A common feature of the proverbs is the use of figurative language: "As cold waters to a thirsty soul, So is good news from a far country" (25:25). In ch. 25 alone there are 9 verses that use similes introduced by the words "like" or "as." These similes make the proverbs more vivid and powerful. Occasionally the simile is used in a humorous or sarcastic way: "As a jewel of gold in a swine's snout, So is a fair woman which is without discretion" (11:22; cf. 26:9), or, "As the door turneth upon his hinges, So doth the slothful upon his bed" (26:14). Equally effective is the use of metaphors: "The law of the wise is a fountain of life" (13:14), and "A wholesome tongue is a tree of life" (15:4). According to 16:24, "Pleasant words are as a honeycomb." The figure of sowing and reaping is used in both a positive and a negative way (cf. 11:18; 22:8).

In order to develop a proper set of values, a number of proverbs use direct comparisons: "Better is the poor that walketh in his uprightness, Than he that is perverse . . . though he be rich" (28:6). This "better . . . than" pattern can be seen also in 15:16–17; 16:19,32; 17:1; a modified form occurs in 17:12; 22:1. Another pattern found in the book is the so-called numerical proverb. Used for the first time in 6:16 (see note there), this type of saying normally has the number three in the first line and four in the second (cf. 30:15,18,21,29).

The repetition of entire proverbs (compare 6:10–11 with 24:33–34; 14:12 with 16:25; 20:16 with 27:13) or parts of proverbs may serve a poetic purpose. A slight variation allows the writer(s) to use the same image to make a related point (as in 17:3; 27:21) or to substitute a word to achieve greater clarity or a different emphasis (cf. 19:1; 28:6). In 26:4–5 the same line is repeated in a seemingly contradictory way, but this was designed to make two different points (see notes there).

At times the book of Proverbs is very direct and earthy (cf. 6:6; 21:9; 25:16; 26:3,11). This is the nature of wisdom literature as it seeks to drive home truth and to turn sinners from their wicked ways (see essay, p. 687).

Purpose and Teaching

According to the prologue, Proverbs was written to give "subtilty to the simple, To the young man knowledge and discretion" (1:4), and to make wise men wiser (1:5). The frequent references to "My son" (1:8,10; 2:1; 3:1; 5:1) emphasize instructing the young and guiding them into a happy and prosperous life. Acquiring wisdom and knowing how to avoid the pitfalls of folly will lead to health and success. Although Proverbs is a practical book dealing with the art of living, it bases wisdom solidly on the fear of the Lord (1:7). Throughout the book this reverence for God is set forth as the path to life and security (cf. 3:5; 9:10; 22:4). People must trust in the Lord (3:5) and not in themselves (28:26). The references to the "tree of life" (3:18; 11:30; 13:12) recall the joyful bliss of the Garden of Eden and figuratively say that the one who finds wisdom will be greatly blessed.

In chs. 1—9 the writer contrasts the way of wisdom with the path of violence (1:11–18) and immorality (2:16–18). The adulteress with her seductive words tries to lure a young man to her house and ultimately to death (cf. ch. 5; 6:24–35; 7; 9:13–18). Sexual immorality is thus an example of and a symbol for the antithesis of wisdom (cf. 22:14; 23:27; 30:20).

At the same time, Proverbs condemns the quarrelsome wife and her unbearable ways (19:13; 21:9,19). The home is supposed to be a place of love, not dissension (cf. 15:17; 17:1). Quarrelsome, quick-tempered men are also denounced (cf. 14:29; 26:21), and gossiping is viewed as a source of great trouble (11:13; 18:8; 26:22). If anyone is able to control his tongue, he is a man of knowledge (cf. 10:19; 17:27). At the same time, the tongue must be used to instruct one's children (cf. 1:8; 22:6; 31:26), and discipline is necessary for their well-being (see 13:24 and note).

Proverbs strongly encourages diligence and hard work (see 10:4 and note; 31:17–19) and holds the sluggard up to contempt for his laziness (see 6:6 and note). A son "that sleepeth in the harvest . . . causeth shame" (10:5), and those who love sleep are sure to grow poor (cf. 20:13). Generally, wealth is connected to righteousness (cf. 3:16) and poverty to wickedness (cf. 22:16), but some verses link riches with the wicked (15:16; 28:6). Honesty and justice are praised repeatedly, and it is expected that a king will defend the rights of the poor and needy (cf. 31:5). Those who are kind to the needy will be richly blessed (see 14:21 and note), but there are several warnings against putting up security for a neighbor (see 6:1 and note).

The proud and the arrogant are sure to be destroyed (cf. 11:2; 16:18), especially the "scorner" with his insolent pride (see note on 1:22). Drunkards are depicted as the epitome of the fool (cf. 20:1), and their woes and miseries are described in graphic terms in 23:29–35.

Although Proverbs is more practical than theological, God's work as Creator is especially highlighted. The role of wisdom in creation is the subject of 8:22–31 (see notes there), where wisdom as an attribute of God is personified. Twice God is called the Maker of the poor (14:31; 17:5). He also directs the steps of a man (cf. 16:9; 20:24), and his eyes observe all his actions (cf. 5:21; 15:3). God is sovereign over the kings of the earth (21:1), and all history moves forward under his control (see notes on 16:4,33).

Literary Structure

A short prologue (stating the purpose and theme, 1:1–7) opens the book, and a longer epilogue (identifiable by its subject matter and its alphabetic form, 31:10–31) closes it. The first nine chapters contain a series of discourses that contrast the way and benefits of wisdom with the way of the fool. Except for the sections where personified wisdom speaks (1:20; 8:1,22; 9:1), each discourse begins with "My son" or "ye children." These units are similar to the discourses found in Job and Ecclesiastes, which also contain speeches given in poetic form.

A key feature in the introductory discourses of Proverbs is the personification of both wisdom and folly (as women), each of whom (by appeals and warnings on the part of Lady Wisdom, by enticements on the part of Lady Folly) seeks to persuade "simple" youths to follow her ways. These discourses are strikingly organized. Beginning (1:8–33) and ending (chs. 8—9) with direct enticements and appeals, the main body of the discourses is made up of two nicely balanced sections, one devoted to the commendation of wisdom (chs. 2—4) and the other to warnings against folly (chs. 5—7). In these discourses the young man is depicted as being enticed to folly by men who try to get ahead in the world by exploiting others (1:10–19) and by women who seek sexual pleasure outside the bond of marriage (ch. 5; 6:20–25; 7). In the social structures of that day, these were the two great temptations for young men. The second especially functions here as illustrative and emblematic of the appeal of Lady Folly.

The main collection of Solomon's proverbs in 10:1—22:16 consists of individual couplets, many of which express a contrast. On the surface, there does not seem to be any discernible arrangement, though occasionally two or three proverbs deal with the same subject. For example, 11:24–25 deals with generosity, 16:12–15 mentions a king, and 19:4,6–7 talks about friendship. However, there is growing evidence that arrangements of larger units were deliberate. Further study of this possibility is necessary. The second Solomonic collection (chs. 25—29) continues the pattern of two-line verses, but there are also examples of proverbs with three (25:13; 27:10,22) or four (25:4–5,21–22; 26:18–19) lines. The last five verses of ch. 27 (vv. 23–27) present a short discourse on the benefits of raising flocks and herds.

In the "words of the wise" (22:17—24:22) and the collection introduced by "These things also belong to the wise" in 24:23–34, there is a prevalence of two- or three-verse units and something of a return to the style of chs. 1—9 (see 23:29–35 especially). These sections function as an appendix to 10:1—22:16 and contain some similar proverbs (compare 24:6 with 11:14; 24:16 with 11:5). Even stronger are the links with chs. 1—9 (compare 23:27 with 2:16; 24:33–34 with 6:10–11).

The last two chapters serve as an appendix to chs. 25—29. The words of Agur are dominated by the numerical proverb (30:15,18,21,24,29) and include a close parallel to Ps 18:30 in 30:5 (also compare 30:6 with Deut 4:2). After the nine verses attributed to King Lemuel (31:1–9), Proverbs concludes with an epilogue, an impressive acrostic poem honoring a worthy woman. She demonstrates, and thus epitomizes, many of the qualities and values identified with wisdom throughout the book. In view of the fact that Proverbs is primarily addressed to young men on the threshold of mature life, this focus on a worthy woman appears surprising. But its purpose may be twofold: (1) to offer counsel on the kind of wife a young man ought to seek, and (2) in a subtle way to advise the young man (again) to marry Lady Wisdom, thus returning to the theme of chs. 1—9 (as climaxed in ch. 9; compare the description of Lady Wisdom in 9:1–2 with the virtues of the wife of noble character). In any event, the concluding epitomizing of wisdom in the wife of noble character forms a literary frame with the opening discourses, where wisdom is personified as a woman.

Outline

- I. Prologue: Purpose and Theme (1:1–7)
- II. The Superiority of the Way of Wisdom (1:8—9:18)
  - A. Appeals and Warnings Confronting Youth (1:8–33)
    1. Enticements to secure happiness by violence (1:8–19)
    2. Warnings against rejecting wisdom (1:20–33)
  - B. Commendation of Wisdom (chs. 2—4)
    1. Benefits of accepting wisdom's instructions (ch. 2)
    2. Wisdom's instructions and benefits (3:1–20)
    3. Wisdom's instructions and benefits (3:21–35)
    4. Challenge to hold on to wisdom (ch. 4)
  - C. Warnings against Folly (chs. 5—7)
    1. Warning against adultery (ch. 5)
    2. Warning against perverse ways (6:1–19)
    3. Cost of committing adultery (6:20–35)
    4. Warning against the enticements of an adulteress (ch. 7)
  - D. Appeals Addressed to Youth (chs. 8—9)
    1. Wisdom's appeal (ch. 8)
    2. Invitations of wisdom and folly (ch. 9)
- III. The Main Collection of Solomon's Proverbs (10:1—22:16)
- IV. The Thirty Sayings of the Wise (22:17—24:22)
- V. Additional Sayings of the Wise (24:23–34)
- VI. Hezekiah's Collection of Solomon's Proverbs (chs. 25—29)
- VII. The Words of Agur (ch. 30)
- VIII. The Words of King Lemuel (31:1–9)
- IX. Epilogue: The Worthy Woman (31:10–31)

The purpose of Proverbs

1 The [a]proverbs of Solomon the son of David, king of Israel.

2 To know wisdom and instruction;
To perceive the words of understanding;
3 To receive the instruction of wisdom,
Justice, and judgment, and [1]equity;
4 To give subtilty to the simple,
To the young man knowledge and [1]discretion.
5 [a]A wise *man* will hear, and will increase learning;
And a man of understanding shall attain unto wise counsels:
6 To understand a proverb, and [1]the interpretation;
The words of the wise, and their [a]dark sayings.

Warnings against violence

7 [a]The fear of the LORD *is* [1]the beginning of knowledge:
But fools despise wisdom and instruction.
8 [a]My son, hear the instruction of thy father,
And forsake not the law of thy mother:
9 For they *shall be* [1]an ornament of grace unto thy head,
And chains about thy neck.
10 My son, if sinners entice thee,
[a]Consent thou not.
11 If they say, Come with us, let us [a]lay wait for blood,
Let us lurk privily for the innocent without cause:
12 Let us swallow them up alive as the grave;
And whole, [a]as those that go down into the pit:
13 We shall find all precious substance,
We shall fill our houses *with* spoil:
14 Cast in thy lot among us;
Let us all have one purse:
15 My son, [a]walk not thou in the way with them;
[b]Refrain thy foot from their path:
16 [a]For their feet run to evil,
And make haste to shed blood.
17 Surely in vain the net *is* spread [1]in the sight of any bird.
18 And they lay wait for their own blood;
They lurk privily for their own lives.
19 [a]So *are* the ways of every one that is greedy of gain;
Which taketh away the life of the owners thereof.

Result of rejecting wisdom

20 [a][1]Wisdom crieth without;

1:1 [a]1 Ki. 4:32; Eccl. 12:9
1:3 [1]Heb. *equities*
1:4 [1]Or, *advisement*
1:5 [a]ch. 9:9
1:6 [1]Or, *an eloquent speech* [a]Ps. 78:2
1:7 [1]Or, *the principal part* [a]Job 28:28; Ps. 111:10; Eccl. 12:13
1:8 [a]ch. 4:1
1:9 [1]Heb. *an adding*
1:10 [a]Gen. 39:7
1:11 [a]Jer. 5:26
1:12 [a]Ps. 28:1
1:15 [a]Ps. 1:1 [b]Ps. 119:101
1:16 [a]Is. 59:7
1:17 [1]Heb. *in the eyes of every thing that hath a wing*
1:19 [a]1 Tim. 6:10
1:20 [1]Heb. *Wisdoms*, that is, *Excellent wisdom* [a]John 7:37

1:1 *Solomon.* His wisdom and prolific production of proverbs and songs are mentioned in 1 Ki 4:32. His name occurs again in the headings of 10:1 and 25:1. Cf. Eccl 1:1; Sol 1:1.

1:2–4 Verses 2–3 apply to the son (or student); v. 4 refers to the father (or teacher).

1:2 *wisdom.* This key term occurs over 40 times in the book. It includes skill in living—following God's design and thus avoiding moral pitfalls. A craftsman can be called a wise man (Ex 31:3). Proverbs urges people to get wisdom (4:5), for it is worth more than silver or gold (3:13–14). The NT refers to Christ as "wisdom" from God (1 Cor 1:30; cf. Col 2:3).

1:3 *Justice, and judgment, and equity.* See 2:9.

1:4 *subtilty.* Good judgment or good sense (see 15:5; 19:25). Outside Proverbs the Hebrew word is used in a negative sense for craftiness or shrewdness (cf. Gen 3:1; Job 5:13). *simple.* Another key word in Proverbs, occurring some 15 times. It denotes those who are easily persuaded and lacking "understanding" (9:4,16), who are immature, inexperienced and simple (cf. Ps 19:7). Generally speaking, the Hebrew term for "simple" denotes one without moral direction and inclined to evil; see 1:22.

1:6 *dark sayings.* The Hebrew for this word can sometimes refer to riddles or allegories (cf. Ezek 17:2).

1:7 The theme of the book (see 9:10; 31:30; cf. Job 28:28; Ps 111:10). *fear of the LORD.* A loving reverence for God that includes submission to His lordship and to the commands of His word (Eccl 12:13). God is our king (Mal 1:14), but even as we stand in awe of Him we can rejoice (see Ps 2:11; Is 12:6). *fools.* Those who hate knowledge (v. 22) and correction of any kind (12:1), who are ready to argue (20:3) and make no effort to restrain their anger (29:11), who are complacent (1:32) and who trust in themselves (28:26) rather than in God (Ps 14:1). *despise wisdom and instruction.* See 5:12 and note.

1:8 A typical introduction to an instruction speech in Proverbs, evoking a domestic situation of a father preparing his son for life in the world. Here and in 6:20 the mother is also depicted as teacher.

1:9 *ornament . . . chains.* Wisdom is like precious jewelry. Those who follow wisdom add beauty and honor to their lives.

1:11 *lay wait for blood.* Their goal is personal enrichment by theft or oppression (vv. 13,19), even if they have to commit murder. The author uses two major enticements that confronted the young man (in that culture) as examples of the way of folly: (1) to get rich by exploiting others (here) and (2) to be drawn into illicit sexual pleasure by immoral women who fail to honor their marriage vows (5:1–6; 6:24; 7:5; cf. 2:12–19).

1:12 *swallow . . . as the grave.* Vivid poetic imagery for shamelessly victimizing others (see note on Ps 49:14).

1:13 *precious substance.* Ill-gotten gain. By contrast, the book of Proverbs teaches that wisdom brings the greatest riches man could ever gain (3:14–16; 16:16; see also Job 28:12–19).

1:15 *way.* Cf. the destructive paths of the adulteress in 2:18; 7:25.

1:16 The same as the first two lines of Is 59:7 and partially quoted in Rom 3:15. Cf. Prov 6:17–18.

1:17 *net.* Nets were used to catch birds and animals (see 6:5; 7:23; Eccl 9:12; Is 51:20; Jer 5:26).

1:18 *lurk privily for their own lives.* The wicked unintentionally spread a net for their own feet (29:6; Ps 35:8), so they are less intelligent than birds (see 7:22–23). According to Is 17:14, the lot of those who plunder God's people is destruction.

1:19 Cf. Is 17:14. Contrast the long life enjoyed by the one who hates ill-gotten gain (28:16).

1:20 *Wisdom crieth without.* Here and in 3:15–18; 8; 9:1–12 wisdom is personified. This is a poetic device common also in Isaiah (cf. 55:12; 59:14). *streets.* Or in the town square, an open area inside the gate of a fortified city.

She uttereth her voice in the streets:
21 She crieth in the chief place of concourse, in the openings of the gates:
In the city she uttereth her words, *saying,*
22 How long, ye simple ones, will ye love simplicity?
And the scorners delight in their scorning,
And fools hate knowledge?
23 Turn you at my reproof:
Behold, [a]I will pour out my spirit unto you,
I will make known my words unto you.

24 [a]Because I have called, and ye refused;
I have stretched out my hand, and no man regarded;
25 But ye [a]have set at nought all my counsel,
And would none of my reproof:
26 [a]I also will laugh at your calamity;
I will mock when your fear cometh;
27 When [a]your fear cometh as desolation,
And your destruction cometh as a whirlwind;
When distress and anguish cometh upon you:
28 [a]Then shall they call upon me, but I will not answer;
They shall seek me early, but they shall not find me:

1:23 [a]Joel 2:28
1:24 [a]Is. 66:4; Jer. 7:13; Zech. 7:11
1:25 [a]Ps. 107:11; Luke 7:30
1:26 [a]Ps. 2:4
1:27 [a]ch. 10:24
1:28 [a]Job 27:9; Is. 1:15; Jer. 14:12; Ezek. 8:18; Mic. 3:4; Zech. 7:13; Jas. 4:3

1:29 [a]Job 21:14 [b]Ps. 119:173
1:30 [a]Ps. 81:11
1:31 [a]Job 4:8; Is. 3:11; Jer. 6:19
1:32 [1]Or, *ease of the simple*
1:33 [a]Ps. 25:12 [b]Ps. 112:7
2:1 [a]ch. 4:21
2:3 [1]Heb. *givest thy voice*
2:4 [a]ch. 3:14; Mat. 13:44

29 For that they [a]hated knowledge,
And did not [b]choose the fear of the LORD:
30 [a]They would none of my counsel:
They despised all my reproof.
31 Therefore [a]shall they eat of the fruit of their own way,
And be filled with their own devices.
32 For the [1]turning away of the simple shall slay them,
And the prosperity of fools shall destroy them.
33 But [a]whoso hearkeneth unto me shall dwell safely,
And [b]shall be quiet from fear of evil.

The reward of wisdom

2 My son, if thou wilt receive my words,
And [a]hide my commandments with thee;
2 So that *thou* incline thine ear unto wisdom,
And apply thine heart to understanding;
3 Yea, if thou criest after knowledge,
And [1]liftest up thy voice for understanding;
4 [a]If thou seekest her as silver,
And searchest for her as *for* hid treasures;
5 Then shalt thou understand the fear of the LORD,
And find the knowledge of God.

1:21 *gates.* Where the leaders of the city met to hold court (see 31:23; Ruth 4:11; Job 29:7) and where the marketplace was located (2 Ki 7:1). As a young man confronts life in its social context, two voices lure him, appeal for his allegiance, and seek to shape his life: (1) the voice of wisdom (as exemplified in the instructions of the teachers of wisdom) and (2) the voice of folly (as exemplified in the sinners of vv. 10–14 and in the adulteress of 5:3; 6:24; 7:5). Thus in the midst of life the youth must learn to exercise discretion. Here and in chs. 8–9 wisdom makes her appeal. She speaks neither out of heaven (by special revelation, as do the prophets) nor out of the earth (through voices from the dead—necromancy; see Lev 19:31; Deut 18:11; 1 Sam 28:7–19), but out of the center of the life of the city, where man's communal experience of the creation order (established by God's wisdom, 8:22–31) is concentrated (see, e.g., 11:10 and note). And it is there also that the godly, the truly wise, test human experience in the crucible of faith and afterward give divine wisdom a human voice in their wise instructions—as in Proverbs.
1:22 *scorners.* Those who are proud and arrogant (21:24), who are full of insults, hatred and strife (9:7–8; 22:10; 29:8), who resist correction (13:1; 15:12) even though they deserve flogging (19:25; 21:11).
1:23 *pour out my spirit.* Wisdom is like a fountain. Her words would constantly refresh and strengthen (see 18:4).
1:24 *refused.* As God was refused by Israel (see Is 1:4; 5:24) and Jesus by the people of Jerusalem (Mat 23:37). *stretched out my hand.* Cf. Is 65:2, where God held out His hands all day long to a stubborn people.
1:25 *set at nought . . . counsel.* Cf. 8:33.
1:26 *laugh at your calamity.* Not an expression of heartlessness but a reaction to the absurdity of fools, who laugh at wisdom, choose folly and bring disaster on themselves. Cf. the Lord's response to kings who think they can rebel against Him (Ps 2:4). *fear cometh.* The foolish man experiences the calamity that he dreads coming (his worst nightmare). Also the fate of the "wicked man" (6:12–15).
1:27 *as desolation.* See 10:25. *as a whirlwind.* When Job's family was killed by a mighty wind (Job 1:19), his comforters concluded that his wickedness was the cause of the disaster (Job 18:5,12). *distress and anguish.* See Is 8:22.
1:28 *I will not answer.* Just as God refused to listen to Israel when the people sinned (Deut 1:45; Is 1:15). *find me.* Those who find wisdom find life and blessing (see v. 33; 3:13; 8:17,35).
1:29 *fear of the LORD.* See note on v. 7.
1:31 *eat . . . filled with their own devices.* The consequences depend on their actions (18:20; 31:31; Is 3:10). "Whatsoever a man soweth, that shall he also reap" (Gal 6:7).
1:32 *prosperity.* The false sense of security that prosperity provides (see Is 32:9; Amos 6:1; Zeph 1:12).
1:33 *safely . . . quiet.* Words used of places that enjoy God's protection (see Is 32:18; Ezek 34:27).
2:1 *hide . . . with thee.* Just as the psalmist urged young men to avoid sin by hiding God's word in their hearts (Ps 119:11).
2:2 *incline thine ear.* Listening implies attentiveness and obedience (Is 55:3; Jer 13:15). *heart.* The Hebrew word translated "heart" here (and in 4:21; 1 Ki 3:9) can sometimes be translated "mind" or "understanding" (see Job 12:3).
2:4 *silver . . . hid treasures.* Job 28:1–11 describes ancient mining techniques, comparing mining with the search for wisdom (see Job 28:12).
2:5 *fear of the LORD.* See note on 1:7. *knowledge of God.* Involves knowing God as a person (Phil 3:10) and knowing what He is teaching us (v. 6). *God.* Hebrew *Elohim* (see note on Gen 2:4); occurs elsewhere in Proverbs only in v. 17; 3:4; 25:2; 30:9.

6 [a]For the LORD giveth wisdom:
Out of his mouth *cometh* knowledge and understanding.
7 He layeth up sound wisdom for the righteous:
[a]*He is* a buckler to them that walk uprightly.
8 *He* keepeth the paths of judgment,
And [a]preserveth the way of his saints.
9 Then shalt thou understand righteousness, and judgment,
And equity; *yea,* every good path.

10 When wisdom entereth into thine heart,
And knowledge is pleasant unto thy soul;
11 Discretion shall preserve thee,
[a]Understanding shall keep thee:
12 To deliver thee from the way of the evil *man,*
From the man that speaketh froward things;
13 Who leave the paths of uprightness,
To [a]walk in the ways of darkness;
14 Who [a]rejoice to do evil,
And [b]delight in the frowardness of the wicked;
15 [a]Whose ways *are* crooked,
And *they* froward in their paths:
16 To deliver thee from [a]the strange woman,
[b]*Even* from the stranger *which* flattereth with her words;
17 [a]Which forsaketh the guide of her youth,
And forgetteth the covenant of her God.
18 For [a]her house inclineth unto death,
And her paths unto the dead.
19 None that go *unto* her return *again,*
Neither take they hold of the paths of life.
20 That thou mayest walk in the way of good *men,*
And keep the paths of the righteous.
21 [a]For the upright shall dwell *in* the land,
And the perfect shall remain in it.
22 [a]But the wicked shall be cut off from the earth,
And the transgressors shall be [1]rooted out of it.

2:6 [a]1 Ki. 3:9; Jas. 1:5
2:7 [a]Ps. 84:11
2:8 [a]1 Sam. 2:9; Ps. 66:9
2:11 [a]ch. 6:22
2:13 [a]John 3:19
2:14 [a]Jer. 11:15 [b]Rom. 1:32
2:15 [a]Ps. 125:5
2:16 [a]ch. 5:20 [b]ch. 5:3
2:17 [a]See Mal. 2:14,15
2:18 [a]ch. 7:27
2:21 [a]Ps. 37:29
2:22 [1]Or, *pluckt up* [a]Job 18:17; Ps. 37:28
3:1 [a]Deut. 8:1
3:2 [1]Heb. *years of life* [a]Ps. 119:165
3:3 [a]Ex. 13:9; Deut. 6:8 [b]2 Cor. 3:3
3:4 [1]Or, *good success* [a]Rom. 14:18

The blessing of wisdom

3 My son, forget not my law;
[a]But let thine heart keep my commandments:
2 For length of days, and [1]long life,
And [a]peace, shall they add to thee.
3 Let not mercy and truth forsake thee:
[a]Bind them about thy neck;
[b]Write them upon the table of thine heart:
4 [a]So shalt thou find favour and [1]good understanding
In the sight of God and man.

2:7 *buckler.* Or shield. It is associated with victory also in Ps 18:2,35; cf. Prov 30:5. *uprightly.* See 19:1.
2:8 *keepeth . . . preserveth.* See Ps 91:3–7,11–12.
2:9–11 Those who know the Lord and the wisdom He gives will know what course of action to follow (cf. Heb 5:11–14).
2:9 *righteousness and judgment, And equity.* See 1:3; Phil 4:8. *good path.* See "the paths of righteousness" of Ps 23:3.
2:10 *pleasant unto thy soul.* Just as the words of a wise man are "sweet to the soul" of another (16:24; cf. 3:17).
2:11 *preserve . . . keep.* As God guards the faithful (v. 8).
2:12–19 Wisdom will save from the enticements of men to follow perverse ways (vv. 12–15) and from the enticements of the adulteress (vv. 16–19). See note on 1:11.
2:12 *speaketh froward things.* Uses perverse and dishonest speech (cf. v. 14). The deceitfulness of men's speech is also mentioned in 8:13; 10:31–32; 17:20.
2:13 *paths of uprightness.* See 3:6; 9:15–16. *ways of darkness.* Men love darkness instead of light (see John 3:19–21; see also Job 24:15–16; Is 29:15; Rom 13:12).
2:14 *rejoice . . . delight . . . wicked.* Like the sinners of 1:10–16.
2:15 *ways are crooked.* See Is 59:7–8.
2:16 *strange woman . . . stranger.* The Hebrew for these terms occurs again in 5:20 and 7:5. The terms mean lit. "foreigner," implying an "adulteress," because anyone other than one's own wife was to be considered off limits, like a foreigner who worshiped another god (cf. 1 Ki 11:1). "Stranger" is parallel to "evil woman" in 6:24 and "whore" in 23:27. *words.* Equal to the "flattering of the tongue" of 6:24 and the "fair speech" of 7:21. Cf. 5:3.
2:17 *guide of her youth.* Her husband, whom she married when she was a young woman (cf. Is 54:6). *covenant of her God.* Perhaps the marriage covenant, spoken in God's presence (see Ezek 16:8; Mal 2:14). Here, however, the "covenant of her God" more likely refers to the breaking of the seventh commandment (Ex 20:14).
2:18 *inclineth unto death.* A life of immorality leads to the destruction and death of all who are involved (cf. 5:5; 9:18). *the dead.* See Job 26:5 and note. The deceased are in the grave (or Sheol), "the chambers of death" (7:27).
2:21 *dwell in the land.* Israel had been promised the land of Canaan (Gen 17:8; Deut 4:1), and Ps 37:29 says that "The righteous shall inherit the land" (see Ps 37:9,11; Mat 5:5). *perfect.* A person who lives a "blameless" life, not a life of sinless perfection.
2:22 *cut off from the earth . . . rooted out of it.* The Hebrew word for "earth" can also be translated "land" and here refers to removal from the promised land of Israel. In Deut 28:63 God warned that if the people refuse to obey Him, they will be "plucked from off the land." Evil men and their offspring will be cut off (Ps 37:9,28).
3:2 *length of days, and long life . . . shall they add to thee.* Fear of the Lord (10:27; 19:23) brings health to the body (v. 8) and "prolongeth days" (10:27; see also 9:10–11). *peace.* Or "prosperity." When Solomon prayed for wisdom, God promised him riches as well as long life if he obeyed God's commands (1 Ki 3:13–14). Normally the righteous are prosperous and happy (12:21), but sometimes it is the wicked who are strong and prosperous (Ps 73:3,12), temporary though that may be (Ps 73:17–19). Job 1–2 also shows how disaster and death can strike a godly person.
3:3 *Bind . . . neck.* Like a beautiful necklace (cf. 1:9; 3:22). *Write them upon the table of thine heart.* See Jer 31:33.
3:4 *favour.* See 8:35; Gen 6:8. *God and man.* See Luke 2:52; Rom 12:17; 2 Cor 8:21.

5 [a]Trust in the LORD with all thine heart;
[b]And lean not unto thine own understanding.
6 [a]In all thy ways acknowledge him,
And he shall [b]direct thy paths.

7 [a]Be not wise in thine own eyes:
[b]Fear the LORD, and depart from evil.
8 It shall be [1]health to thy navel,
And [a][2]marrow to thy bones.

9 [a]Honour the LORD with thy substance,
And with the firstfruits of all thine increase:
10 [a]So shall thy barns be filled *with* plenty,
And thy presses shall burst out with new wine.

11 [a]My son, despise not the chastening of the LORD;
Neither be weary of his correction:
12 For whom the LORD loveth he correcteth;
[a]Even as a father the son *in whom* he delighteth.

13 [a]Happy *is* the man *that* findeth wisdom,
And [1]the man *that* getteth understanding.
14 [a]For the merchandise of it *is* better than the merchandise of silver,
And the gain thereof than fine gold.
15 She *is* more precious than rubies:
And [a]all the things thou canst desire are not to be compared unto her.
16 [a]Length of days *is* in her right hand;
And in her left hand riches and honour.
17 [a]Her ways *are* ways of pleasantness,
And all her paths *are* peace.
18 She *is* [a]a tree of life to them that lay hold upon her:
And happy *is every one* that retaineth her.
19 [a]The LORD by wisdom hath founded the earth;
By understanding hath he [1]established the heavens.
20 [a]By his knowledge the depths are broken up,
And [b]the clouds drop down the dew.

21 My son, let not them depart from thine eyes:
Keep sound wisdom and discretion:
22 So shall they be life unto thy soul,
And [a]grace to thy neck.
23 [a]Then shalt thou walk *in* thy way safely,
And thy foot shall not stumble.
24 [a]When thou liest down, thou shalt not be afraid:
Yea, thou shalt lie down, and thy sleep shall be sweet.
25 [a]Be not afraid of sudden fear,
Neither of the desolation of the wicked, when it cometh.

3:5 [a]Ps. 37:3,5 [b]Jer. 9:23
3:6 [a]1 Chr. 28:9 [b]Jer. 10:23
3:7 [a]Rom. 12:16 [b]ch. 16:6
3:8 [1]Heb. *medicine* [2]Heb. *watering,* or, *moistening* [a]Job 21:24
3:9 [a]Ex. 22:29
3:10 [a]Deut. 28:8
3:11 [a]Job 5:17; Ps. 94:12
3:12 [a]Deut. 8:5
3:13 [1]Heb. *the man that draweth out understanding* [a]ch. 8:34,35
3:14 [a]Job 28:13; Ps. 19:10
3:15 [a]Mat. 13:44
3:16 [a]1 Tim. 4:8
3:17 [a]Mat. 11:29
3:18 [a]Gen. 2:9
3:19 [1]Or, *prepared* [a]Ps. 104:24
3:20 [a]Gen. 1:9 [b]Deut. 33:28; Job 36:28
3:22 [a]ch. 1:9
3:23 [a]Ps. 37:24
3:24 [a]Lev. 26:6; Ps. 3:5
3:25 [a]Ps. 91:5

3:5 *Trust in the LORD.* Commit your way to the Lord (Ps 37:5), like Israel's forefathers, who trusted in God and were rescued (Ps 22:4–5). *with all thine heart.* Like Caleb (Num 14:24; Deut 1:36) or the godly King Hezekiah (Is 38:3). David challenged Solomon to serve God with wholehearted devotion (1 Chr 28:9).
3:6 *acknowledge him.* Be ever mindful of God and serve Him with a willing and faithful heart (see 1 Chr 28:9; Hos 4:1; 6:6). *direct thy paths.* He will remove the obstacles from your pathway and bring you to your appointed goal (see 11:5; Is 45:13).
3:7 *Fear the LORD, and depart from evil.* Cf. Job, who was a "perfect (blameless) and upright" man (Job 1:1). See note on 1:7.
3:8 *bones.* Elsewhere, good news and pleasant words bring health to the bones (15:30; 16:24; cf. 17:22), which stand here for the whole body.
3:9 *firstfruits of . . . thine increase.* The Israelites were required to give to the priests the first part of the olive oil, wine and grain produced each year (see Lev 23:10; Num 18:12–13).
3:10 *filled with plenty.* For those who bring to the Lord His tithes and offerings, God promises to pour out more blessing than they have room for (see Mal 3:10; see also Deut 28:8,12; 2 Cor 9:8).
3:11–12 A warning that the righteous are not always prosperous (see v. 2 and note). Through times of testing and affliction, God is teaching them (see 12:1; Job 5:17; 36:22; Ps 119:71). Heb 12:5–6 quotes both of these verses to encourage believers to endure hardship (Heb 12:7).
3:12 *as a father.* God disciplined His son Israel by testing the nation in the wilderness 40 years (Deut 8:2–5).
3:13–18 A poem praising wisdom , the first and last verse of which suggest that happiness attends those whose find it.
3:14 *the merchandise of it is better than . . . silver, And . . . gold.* The psalmist makes the same claim for the commands and precepts of the Lord (Ps 19:10; 119:72,127).
3:15–18 Wisdom is personified.
3:15 *rubies.* See Job 28:18, where wisdom is also more valuable than rubies, and Prov 31:10, where the price of a "virtuous woman" is "far above rubies."
3:16 *Length of days.* See note on v. 2. *riches and honour.* See 8:18; 22:4.
3:17 *peace.* Hebrew *shalom* (see v. 2; 16:7; Ps 119:165).
3:18 *tree of life.* Source of life. This figure of speech may allude to the tree in the Garden of Eden (see Gen 2:9 and note; cf. Prov 11:30; 13:12; 15:4).
3:19–20 The role of wisdom in creation is described more fully in 8:22–31. Divine wisdom guided the Creator and now permeates the whole creation. To live by wisdom is to imitate the Lord and conform to the divinely appointed creation order.
3:19 *founded the earth.* God's work in creation is compared to the construction of a building (see 1 Ki 5:17; 6:37; see also 8:29; Job 38:4–6; Ps 104:5; Zech 12:1). *established the heavens.* See Is 42:5; 51:16.
3:20 *broken up.* God opened up springs and streams (see Gen 7:11; 49:25; Ps 74:15). Alternatively, though perhaps less likely, reference is to the dividing of the waters above from the waters below (see Gen 1:7; Ps 42:7 and note). *dew.* Probably also includes rain (see Deut 33:13; 2 Sam 1:21).
3:22 *grace to thy neck.* Like a beautiful necklace (see v. 3).
3:23 *safely, And thy foot shall not stumble.* Cf. 10:9.
3:24 *When thou liest down, thou shalt not be afraid.* Also listed among the covenant blessings (see Lev 26:6; Job 11:18–19; Mic 4:4; Zeph 3:13; see also Prov 1:33). *thy sleep shall be sweet.* See 6:22; Ps 4:8.
3:25 *fear . . . desolation.* The Lord shields the godly from deadly arrows and plagues (see 10:25; Ps 91:3–8; Job 5:21).

26 For the LORD shall be thy confidence,
And shall keep thy foot from being taken.
27 [a]Withhold not good from [1]them to whom it is due,
When it is in the power of thine hand to do *it*.
28 [a]Say not unto thy neighbour,
Go, and come again, and to morrow I will give;
When thou hast it by thee.
29 [1]Devise not evil against thy neighbour,
Seeing he dwelleth securely by thee.
30 [a]Strive not with a man without cause,
If he have done thee no harm.
31 [a]Envy thou not [1]the oppressor,
And choose none of his ways.
32 For the froward *is* abomination to the LORD:
[a]But his secret *is* with the righteous.
33 [a]The curse of the LORD *is* in the house of the wicked:
But [b]he blesseth the habitation of the just.
34 [a]Surely he scorneth the scorners:
But he giveth grace unto the lowly.
35 The wise shall inherit glory:
But shame [1]shall be the promotion of fools.

The command to obtain wisdom

4 Hear, [a]ye children, the instruction of a father,
And attend to know understanding.
2 For I give you good doctrine,
Forsake you not my law.
3 For I was my father's son,
[a]Tender and only *beloved* in the sight of my mother.
4 [a]He taught me also, and said unto me,
Let thine heart retain my words:
[b]Keep my commandments, and live.
5 [a]Get wisdom, get understanding:
Forget *it* not; neither decline from the words of my mouth.
6 Forsake her not, and she shall preserve thee:
[a]Love her, and she shall keep thee.
7 [a]Wisdom *is* the principal thing; *therefore* get wisdom:
And with all thy getting get understanding.
8 [a]Exalt her, and she shall promote thee:
She shall bring thee to honour, when thou dost embrace her.
9 She shall give to thine head [a]an ornament of grace:
[1]A crown of glory shall she deliver *to* thee.

10 Hear, O my son, and receive my sayings;
[a]And the years of thy life shall be many.
11 I have taught thee in the way of wisdom;
I have led thee in right paths.
12 When thou goest [a]thy steps shall not be straitened;
[b]And when thou runnest, thou shalt not stumble.
13 Take fast hold of instruction; let *her* not go:
Keep her; for she *is* thy life.
14 [a]Enter not into the path of the wicked,
And go not in the way of evil *men*.
15 Avoid it, pass not by it,
Turn from it, and pass away.
16 [a]For they sleep not, except they have done mischief;
And their sleep is taken away, unless they cause *some* to fall.
17 For they eat the bread of wickedness,
And drink the wine of violence.

3:27 [1]Heb. *the owners thereof* [a]Rom. 13:7; Gal. 6:10
3:28 [a]Lev. 19:13
3:29 [1]Or, *Practise no evil*
3:30 [a]Rom. 12:18
3:31 [1]Heb. *a man of violence* [a]Ps. 37:1
3:32 [a]Ps. 25:14
3:33 [a]Zech. 5:3,4; Mal. 2:2 [b]Ps. 1:3
3:34 [a]Jas. 4:6; 1 Pet. 5:5
3:35 [1]Heb. *exalteth the fools*
4:1 [a]Ps. 34:11; ch. 1:8
4:3 [a]1 Chr. 29:1
4:4 [a]1 Chr. 28:9; Eph. 6:4 [b]ch. 7:2
4:5 [a]ch. 2:2,3
4:6 [a]2 Thes. 2:10
4:7 [a]Mat. 13:44; Luke 10:42
4:8 [a]1 Sam. 2:30
4:9 [1]Or, *She shall compass thee with a crown of glory* [a]ch. 1:9; 3:22
4:10 [a]ch. 3:2
4:12 [a]Ps. 18:36 [b]Ps. 91:11,12
4:14 [a]Ps. 1:1; ch. 1:10,15
4:16 [a]Ps. 36:4; Is. 57:20

3:26 *keep thy foot from being taken.* Contrast the fate of the fool in 1:18; 7:22–23.
3:27 *Withhold not good.* See Acts 9:36; Gal 6:10; 1 John 3:17–18. *them to whom it is due.* Especially the poor and needy.
3:28 See Luke 11:5–8; Jas 2:15–16.
3:30 *Strive not . . . without cause.* See Job 2:3.
3:31 *Envy thou not.* See 24:19; Ps 37:1,7. *the oppressor.* Like the sinners of 1:10–16 (cf. 16:29).
3:32 *abomination.* A word that elsewhere expresses abhorrence of pagan practices (see Deut 18:9,12) and moral abuses. It is common in Proverbs (e.g., 6:16; 8:7; 11:20). *his secret is with the righteous.* God takes the righteous into his confidence by revealing his plans to them. See Gen 18:17–19; Job 29:4; Ps 25:14; John 15:15.
3:33 This contrast is seen also in Deut 11:26–28. *The curse of the LORD is in the house of the wicked.* See Josh 7:24–25; Zech 5:3–4. *blesseth the habitation of the just.* See Job 42:12–14.
3:34 *scorneth the scorners.* See note on 1:26. *giveth grace.* Shows favor (see v. 4).
4:3 *Tender.* Youthful and inexperienced. Cf. David's words about Solomon (1 Chr 22:5; 29:1). This is part of an autobiographical statement, such as was sometimes used by the wisdom teachers (see 24:30–34; see also the book of Ecclesiastes). *only beloved.* An only son, and thus, deeply loved (cf. Gen 37:3; Zech 12:10).
4:4 *Let thine heart retain.* See note on 3:5.
4:6 *preserve . . . keep.* The Hebrew for these two verbs is used together also in 2:8,11. *Love her.* To love wisdom is to prosper (8:21); to hate wisdom is to "love death" (8:36).
4:7 *with all thy getting get understanding.* Because of its supreme value, make acquiring wisdom the top priority (see also 1:7). Cf. the merchant who sold everything to buy a pearl of great value (Mat 13:45–46).
4:9 *crown of glory.* Wreaths or crowns were worn at joyous occasions, such as weddings or feasts (see Ezek 16:12; 23:42).
4:10 *years . . . shall be many.* See note on 3:2.
4:11 *right paths.* See notes on 3:6; Ps 23:3.
4:12 *thou shalt not stumble.* Because of some obstacle or lack of light (see v. 19; 3:23; 10:9; Ps 18:36; Is 40:30–31).
4:14 *path of the wicked.* Cf. the destructive paths of the adulteress in 2:18; 7:25; see Ps 1:1; 17:4–5.
4:16 *sleep not, except they have done mischief.* See Ps 36:4; Mic 2:1. Contrast the attitude of David, who would not sleep until he found a permanent place for God's house (Ps 132:3–5).
4:17 *eat the bread . . . drink the wine.* They thrive on wickedness and violence (see 13:2; Job 15:16).

18 [a]But the path of the just [b]*is* as the
shining light,
That shineth more and more unto the
perfect day.
19 [a]The way of the wicked *is* as darkness:
They know not at what they stumble.
20 My son, attend to my words;
Incline thine ear unto my sayings.
21 [a]Let them not depart from thine eyes;
[b]Keep them in the midst of thine
heart.
22 For they *are* life unto those that find
them,
And [a] [1]health to all their flesh.
23 Keep thy heart [1]with all diligence;
For out of it *are* the issues of life.
24 Put away from thee [1]a froward mouth,
And perverse lips put far from thee.
25 Let thine eyes look right on,
And let thine eyelids look straight
before thee.
26 Ponder the path of thy feet,
And [1]let all thy ways be established.
27 [a]Turn not *to* the right hand nor *to* the
left:
[b]Remove thy foot from evil.

Warning against unchastity

5 My son, attend unto my wisdom,
And bow thine ear to my understanding:
2 That *thou* mayest regard discretion,
And *that* thy lips may [a]keep
knowledge.
3 [a]For the lips of a strange *woman* drop
as a honeycomb,
And her [1]mouth *is* [b]smoother than oil:
4 But her end is [a]bitter as wormwood,
[b]Sharp as a twoedged sword.
5 [a]Her feet go down *to* death;
Her steps take hold on hell.
6 Lest thou shouldest ponder the path of
life,
Her ways are moveable, *that* thou canst
not know *them.*
7 Hear me now therefore, O ye children,
And depart not from the words of my
mouth.
8 Remove thy way far from her,
And come not nigh the door of her
house:
9 Lest thou give thine honour unto
others,
And thy years unto the cruel:
10 Lest strangers be filled *with* [1]thy wealth;
And thy labours *be* in the house of a
stranger;
11 And thou mourn at the last,
When thy flesh and thy body are
consumed,
12 And say, How have I [a]hated
instruction,
And my heart [b]despised reproof;
13 And have not obeyed the voice of my
teachers,
Nor inclined mine ear to them that
instructed me!
14 I was almost in all evil
In the midst of the congregation and
assembly.
15 Drink waters out of thine own cistern,
And running waters out of thine own
well.

4:18 [a]Mat. 5:14,45; Phil. 2:15 [b]2 Sam. 23:4
4:19 [a]1 Sam. 2:9; Job 18:5,6; Is. 59:9,10; Jer. 23:12; John 12:35
4:21 [a]ch. 3:3,21 [b]ch. 2:1
4:22 [1]Heb. *medicine* [a]ch. 3:8; 12:18
4:23 [1]Heb. *above all keeping*
4:24 [1]Heb. *frowardness of mouth, and perverseness of lips*
4:26 [1]Or, *all thy ways shall be ordered aright*
4:27 [a]Deut. 5:32; 28:14; Josh. 1:7 [b]Is. 1:16; Rom. 12:9
5:2 [a]Mal. 2:7
5:3 [1]Heb. *palate* [a]ch. 2:16; 6:24 [b]Ps. 55:21
5:4 [a]Eccl. 7:26 [b]Heb. 4:12
5:5 [a]ch. 7:27
5:10 [1]Heb. *thy strength*
5:12 [a]ch. 1:29 [b]ch. 1:25; 12:1

4:18 *path of the just is as the shining light.* The godly have all the guidance and protection they need (see vv. 11–12) and are able to lead others to righteousness (Dan 12:3).
4:19 *darkness.* A dangerous path that leads to destruction (see note on 2:13; see also Is 59:9–10; Jer 23:12; John 11:10; 12:35).
4:21 *heart.* See 3:1,3.
4:22 *health.* Physical, psychological and spiritual (see 3:8 and note).
4:23 *issues of life.* If we store up good things (2:1) in our hearts, our words and actions will be good. "For out of the abundance of the heart the mouth speaketh" (Mat 12:34; cf. Mark 7:21).
4:24 *Put away from thee a froward mouth.* Put away lying and deceit. See note on 2:12; see also 19:1. *perverse lips.* Another reference to deceitful speech. See 6:12; 19:28; Eph 4:29; Jas 3:6.
4:25 *Let thine eyes look right on.* Straight ahead, not at worthless things (Ps 119:37).
4:26 *Ponder the path of thy feet.* Pay attention to what is good and remove every moral hindrance (see vv. 11–12; Is 26:7).
4:27 *Turn not to the right hand nor to the left.* A warning found also in Deut 5:32–33; 28:14; Josh 1:7. *foot from evil.* See 1:15.
5:3 *lips . . . drop as a honeycomb.* Probably a reference to the pleasant-sounding talk (cf. 16:24) of the adulteress, though some explain it as kisses (cf. Sol 4:11; 5:13; 7:9). *strange woman.* See note on 2:16. *smoother than oil.* See 2:16. Her words are soothing (see Ps 55:21) but full of flattery (Prov 29:5) and hypocrisy (Ps 5:9).
5:4 *wormwood.* A bitter herb (see Deut 29:18; Lam 3:15,19; Amos 6:12). *twoedged sword.* A lethal weapon (see Judg 3:16; see also Ps 55:21; 149:6; Heb 4:12; Rev 1:16).
5:5 *down to death.* Her immorality hastens her end (see note on 2:18).
5:6 *ways are moveable.* Or shaky and unstable See 2:15; 10:9. *thou canst not know them.* Or the young man refuses to acknowledge her instability.
5:7–14 The father (teacher) warns the son (student) about the price of immorality.
5:8 *far from her.* See Gen 39:12; 2 Tim 2:22. *door of her house.* Cf. 7:25; 9:14.
5:9 *the cruel.* Possibly the vengeful husband (see 6:34–35).
5:10 *strangers be filled with thy wealth.* Contrast the riches and honor that come to the man who embraces wisdom (3:16–18). Immorality eventually reduces one "to a piece of bread" (6:26).
5:11 *flesh and . . . body are consumed.* Possibly because of the debilitating effects of immorality (see 1 Cor 6:18; cf. Prov 3:8; 4:22), but more likely referring to the loss of vigor that accompanies old age.
5:12 *hated instruction . . . despised reproof.* In old age he will look back and sadly acknowledge that he has played the fool (see 1:7,22,29–30).
5:13 *have not obeyed.* In spite of the repeated urging to "hear" or "attend unto" their instruction (1:8; 3:1; 4:1; 5:1).
5:14 *all evil.* Total calamity, physical, financial and social. *In the midst of the congregation.* The offender was subject to "a wound and dishonour" (6:33) or even death (see Deut 22:22).
5:15 *thine own cistern . . . thine own well.* Your own wife (see Sol 4:12,15). Let your own wife be your source of pleasure, as

16 Let thy fountains be dispersed abroad,
And rivers of waters in the streets.
17 Let them be only thine own,
And not strangers' with thee.
18 Let thy fountain be blessed:
And rejoice with [a]the wife of thy youth.
19 [a]*Let her be as* the loving hind and pleasant roe;
Let her breasts [1]satisfy thee at all times;
And [2]be thou ravisht always with her love.
20 And why wilt thou, my son, be ravisht with [a]a strange *woman,*
And embrace the bosom of a stranger?
21 [a]For the ways of man *are* before the eyes of the LORD,
And he pondereth all his goings.
22 [a]His own iniquities shall take the wicked himself,
And he shall be holden with the cords of his [1]sins.
23 [a]He shall die without instruction;
And in the greatness of his folly he shall go astray.

5:18 [a]Mal. 2:14
5:19 [1]Heb. *water thee* [2]Heb. *err thou always in her love* [a]Sol. 2:9; 4:5
5:20 [a]ch. 2:16
5:21 [a]2 Chr. 16:9; Job 31:4; ch. 15:3; Jer. 16:17; Hos. 7:2; Heb. 4:13
5:22 [1]Heb. *sin* [a]Ps. 9:15
5:23 [a]Job 4:21; 36:12
6:1 [a]ch. 11:15

Warnings against idleness

6 My son, [a]if thou be surety for thy friend,
If thou hast stricken thy hand with a stranger,
2 Thou art snared with the words of thy mouth,
Thou art taken with the words of thy mouth,
3 Do this now, my son, and deliver thyself,
When thou art come into the hand of thy friend;
Go, humble thyself, [1]and make sure thy friend.
4 [a]Give not sleep to thine eyes,
Nor slumber to thine eyelids.
5 Deliver thyself as a roe from the hand *of the hunter,*
And as a bird from the hand of the fowler.

6 [a]Go to the ant, thou sluggard;
Consider her ways, and be wise:
7 Which having no guide, overseer, or ruler,
8 Provideth her meat in the summer,
And gathereth her food in the harvest.
9 [a]How long wilt thou sleep, O sluggard?
When wilt thou arise out of thy sleep?
10 *Yet* a little sleep, a little slumber,
A little folding of the hands to sleep:
11 [a]So shall thy poverty come as one that travelleth,
And thy want as an armed man.

Warning against sowing discord

12 A naughty person, a wicked man,
Walketh *with* a froward mouth.
13 [a]He winketh with his eyes,
He speaketh with his feet,
He teacheth with his fingers;

6:3 [1]Or, *so shalt thou prevail with thy friend*
6:4 [a]Ps. 132:4
6:6 [a]Job 12:7
6:9 [a]ch. 24:33
6:11 [a]ch. 10:4
6:13 [a]Job 15:12; ch. 10:10

water refreshes a thirsty man. Wells and cisterns were privately owned and of great value (2 Ki 18:31; Jer 38:6).
5:16 *fountains . . . rivers of water.* Like "cistern" and "well" in v. 15 and "fountain" in v. 18, these also refer to the wife (see Sol 4:12,15). *in the streets.* The wife may become promiscuous if the husband is unfaithful.
5:18 *wife of thy youth.* Chosen by you when you were young.
5:19 *hind . . . roe.* Descriptive of the wife, perhaps because of the delicate beauty of the roe's limbs (see Sol 2:9). *Let her breasts satisfy thee at all times.* See Sol 7:7–8. *satisfy thee.* Or "be intoxicated with," "be captivated by." Marital love is portrayed as better than wine in Sol 4:10 (cf. Sol 7:9).
5:20 *why . . . ?* In light of the sheer joy found within the bonds of marriage and the calamity (v. 14) outside it, why commit adultery? *strange woman.* See v. 3; 2:16 and note.
5:21 *before the eyes of the LORD.* See 15:3; Job 31:4; 34:21; Jer 16:17. *pondereth all his goings.* See Job 7:18; 34:23; Ps 11:4; 26:2; 139:23; Jer 17:10.
5:22 *shall take the wicked.* See 1:18 and note; Deut 7:25; 12:30. In Eccl 7:26 the sinner is captured by a woman "whose heart is snares and nets." *cords of his sins.* See Job 36:8; Eccl 4:12; Is 5:18.
5:23 The death of the fool is described in similar terms in 1:29–32; 7:21–25; cf. Job 36:12. *instruction.* See v. 12.
6:1 *be surety . . . stricken thy hand.* Refers to responsibility for someone else's debt (cf. 22:26) or for some other obligation. It can end in abject poverty (cf. 22:27) or even slavery if you cannot pay. For example, Judah volunteered to personally guarantee the safe return of Benjamin to Jacob (Gen 43:9), and when this seemed impossible, he had to offer himself to Joseph as a slave (Gen 44:32–33). Such an arrangement was sealed by "striking hands," equivalent to our handshake (see 11:15; 17:18; 20:16; 22:26; cf. Job 17:3).
6:2 *snared . . . taken.* Cf. v. 5; 5:22.
6:3 *deliver thyself.* To gain release from the obligation. *come into the hand of thy friend.* Assumed responsibility for his obligation. *make sure thy friend.* Be as persistent as the man in Luke 11:8 in getting out of this responsibility.
6:4 *not sleep . . . Nor slumber.* Like David in Ps 132:4.
6:5 *hand of the fowler.* See Ps 124:7.
6:6 *sluggard.* A lazy individual who refuses to work and whose desires are not met (see 10:26; 13:4; 15:19; 19:24; 22:13; 24:30; 26:13–16).
6:7 *no . . . ruler.* Cf. the locust in 30:27.
6:9 *How long wilt thou sleep, O sluggard?* His love for sleep is described also in 26:14.
6:10–11 Repeated in 24:33–34.
6:11 *poverty . . . want.* Connected with too much sleep also in 10:5; 19:15; 20:13. Hard work is an antidote to poverty (see 12:11; 14:23; 28:19). *as one that travelleth . . . an armed man.* Poverty will come when it is too late to do anything about it (cf. Mat 24:43).
6:12–14 A vivid description of one who uses mouth, eyes, feet and fingers (all a person's means of communication) in devious ways to achieve the deceitful plots of his heart—here especially to spread slander about someone to destroy him.
6:12 *naughty person.* Or a "worthless person." For the use of this term, see Judg 19:22; 1 Sam 25:25; Job 34:18; see also note on Deut 13:13. *froward mouth.* See 19:28; 2:12 and note.
6:13 *winketh with his eyes.* To make insinuations (see 10:10; 16:30).

14 Frowardness *is* in his heart,
[a]He deviseth mischief continually;
[b]He [1]soweth discord.
15 Therefore shall his calamity come
suddenly;
Suddenly shall he [a]be broken [b]without
remedy.

16 These six *things* doth the LORD hate:
Yea, seven *are* an abomination [1]unto
him:
17 [a][1]A proud look, [b]a lying tongue,
And [c]hands that shed innocent blood,
18 [a]A heart that deviseth wicked
imaginations,
[b]Feet that be swift in running to
mischief,
19 [a]A false witness *that* speaketh lies,
And he [b]that soweth discord among
brethren.

Warning against adultery

20 [a]My son, keep thy father's
commandment,
And forsake not the law of thy mother:
21 [a]Bind them continually upon thine
heart,
And tie them about thy neck.
22 [a]When thou goest, it shall lead thee;
When thou sleepest, [b]it shall keep
thee;
And *when* thou awakest, it shall talk
with thee.
23 [a]For the commandment *is* a [1]lamp;
and the law *is* light;
And reproofs of instruction *are* the way
of life:
24 [a]To keep thee from the evil woman,

6:14 [1]Heb. *casteth forth* [a]Mic. 2:1 [b]ver. 19
6:15 [a]Jer. 19:11 [b]2 Chr. 36:16
6:16 [1]Heb. *of his soul*
6:17 [1]Heb. *Haughty eyes* [a]Ps. 101:5 [b]Ps. 120:2,3 [c]Is. 1:15
6:18 [a]Gen. 6:5 [b]Is. 59:7
6:19 [a]Ps. 27:12 [b]ver. 14
6:20 [a]Eph. 6:1
6:21 [a]ch. 3:3
6:22 [a]ch. 3:23 [b]ch. 2:11
6:23 [1]Or, *candle* [a]Ps. 19:8
6:24 [a]ch. 2:16

6:24 [1]Or, *of the strange tongue*
6:25 [a]Mat. 5:28
6:26 [1]Heb. *the woman of a man*, or, *a man's wife* [a]ch. 29:3 [b]Gen. 39:14 [c]Ezek. 13:18
6:31 [a]Ex. 22:1
6:32 [1]Heb. *heart* [a]ch. 7:7
6:35 [1]Heb. *He will not accept the face of any ransom*
7:1 [a]ch. 2:1
7:2 [a]Lev. 18:5; ch. 4:4

From the flattery [1]of the tongue of a
strange *woman.*
25 [a]Lust not after her beauty in thine heart;
Neither let her take thee with her
eyelids.
26 For [a]by means of a whorish woman *a*
man is brought to a piece of bread:
[b]And [1]the adulteress will [c]hunt for the
precious life.
27 Can a man take fire in his bosom,
And his clothes not be burnt?
28 Can one go upon hot coals,
And his feet not be burnt?
29 So he that goeth in to his neighbour's
wife;
Whosoever toucheth her shall not be
innocent.
30 *Men* do not despise a thief, if he steal
To satisfy his soul when he is hungry;
31 But *if* he be found, [a]he shall restore
sevenfold;
He shall give all the substance of his
house.
32 *But* whoso committeth adultery with a
woman [a]lacketh [1]understanding:
He *that* doeth it destroyeth his own soul.
33 A wound and dishonour shall he get;
And his reproach shall not be wiped
away.
34 For jealousy *is* the rage of a man:
Therefore he will not spare in the day
of vengeance.
35 [1]He will not regard any ransom;
Neither will he rest content, though
thou givest many gifts.

7 My son, keep my words,
And [a]lay up my commandments with
thee.
2 [a]Keep my commandments, and live;

6:14 *deviseth mischief.* See v. 18; 3:29; Mic 2:1. *soweth discord.* Through slander he creates distrust that culminates in alienation and conflict.
6:15 *shall his calamity come suddenly.* Usually a sign of God's judgment (see 1:26; 24:22; Job 34:20). *Suddenly . . . be broken without remedy.* He will suffer the same fate he thought to bring upon another—his punishment will fit his crime.
6:16–19 A further elaboration on the theme of vv. 12–15, explaining why "calamity" will come suddenly (v. 15) on the scoundrel described here.
6:16 *six . . . seven.* A way of handling numbers in synonymous parallelism in Hebrew poetry (see Introduction: The Nature of a Proverb). Such catalogues of items are frequent in the wisdom literature of the OT (see 30:15,18,21,29; see also Job 5:19). *abomination.* See 3:32 and note.
6:17 *proud look.* Reflects a proud heart that God will judge (see 21:4; 30:13; Ps 18:27; 101:5). *lying tongue.* See 2:12 and note; 12:19; 17:7; 21:6. *hands that shed innocent blood.* See 1:11,16 and notes; 28:17.
6:18 *heart that deviseth wicked imaginations.* See 1:31; 24:2; Gen 6:5. *Feet that be swift in running to mischief.* See 1:16 and note.
6:19 *false witness.* Proverbs emphasizes the damage done by the false witness (12:17–18; 25:18; see note on Ps 5:9) and the punishment he receives (see note on v. 15; see also 19:5,9; 21:28). *speaketh lies.* See 14:5,25. *soweth discord.* See note on v. 14.
6:20 See 1:8.
6:21 Those who follow wisdom add beauty and honor to their lives.
6:22 *goest . . . sleepest.* Wisdom guides and protects the godly at all times—when awake and when asleep. *When thou sleepest.* See note on 3:24. *it shall keep thee.* See 4:6.
6:23 *lamp . . . light.* Just as the word of God "is a lamp to my feet and a light unto my path" (Ps 119:105; cf. Ps 19:8). *way of life.* See 3:22; 4:22. Contrast the way to death for the one who hates discipline (5:23).
6:24 See notes on 2:16; 5:3.
6:25 *Lust not after.* Jesus shows the close connection between lust and adultery (Mat 5:28; cf. Ex 20:17). *take thee.* See 5:20.
6:26 *brought to a piece of bread.* Both the prostitute (29:3) and the adulteress (5:10) reduce a man to poverty (see 1 Sam 2:36).
6:29 *Whosoever . . . shall not be innocent.* Will not go unpunished; see vv. 33–34 and note on 5:14.
6:31 *sevenfold.* Hebrew law demanded no more than fivefold payment as a penalty for any theft (Ex 22:1–9). The number seven is here symbolic—he will pay in full.
6:32 *destroyeth his own soul.* See 5:14 and note; 7:22–23.
6:33 *dishonour.* Dishonor followed Amnon's raping of Tamar (2 Sam 13:13,22).
6:34 *jealousy.* Its strength is also illustrated in 27:4; Sol 8:6.
7:1 See Ps. 119:11.

[b]And my law as the apple of thine eye.
3 [a]Bind them upon thy fingers,
Write them upon the table of thine heart.
4 Say unto wisdom, Thou *art* my sister;
And call understanding *thy* kinswoman:
5 [a]That *they* may keep thee from the strange woman,
From the stranger *which* flattereth with her words.
6 For at the window of my house
I looked through my casement,
7 And beheld among the simple ones,
I discerned among [1]the youths,
A young man [a]void of understanding,
8 Passing through the street near her corner;
And he went the way to her house,
9 [a]In the twilight, [1]in the evening,
In the black and dark night:
10 And behold, there met him a woman
With the attire of a harlot, and subtil of heart.
11 ([a]She *is* loud and stubborn;
[b]Her feet abide not in her house:
12 Now *is she* without, now in the streets,
And lieth in wait at every corner.)
13 So she caught him, and kissed him,
And [1]with an impudent face said unto him,
14 [1]*I have* peace offerings with me;
This day have I payed my vows.
15 Therefore came I forth to meet thee,
Diligently to seek thy face, and I have found thee.
16 I have deckt my bed *with* coverings of tapestry,
With carved *works, with* [a]fine linen of Egypt.

7:2 [b]Deut. 32:10
7:3 [a]Deut. 6:8; 11:18; ch. 3:3; 6:21
7:5 [a]ch. 2:16; 5:3; 6:24
7:7 [1]Heb. *the sons* [a]ch. 6:32; 9:4,16
7:9 [1]Heb. *in the evening of the day* [a]Job 24:15
7:11 [a]ch. 9:13 [b]1 Tim. 5:13; Tit. 2:5
7:13 [1]Heb. *she strengthened her face, and said*
7:14 [1]Heb. *Peace offerings are upon me*
7:16 [a]Is. 19:9
7:20 [1]Heb. *in his hand* [2]Or, *the new moon*
7:21 [a]ch. 5:3 [b]Ps. 12:2
7:22 [1]Heb. *suddenly*
7:23 [a]Eccl. 9:12
7:26 [a]Neh. 13:26
7:27 [a]ch. 2:18; 5:5; 9:18
8:1 [a]ch. 1:20; 9:3

17 I have perfumed my bed
With myrrh, aloes, and cinnamon.
18 Come, let us take our fill of love until the morning:
Let us solace ourselves with loves.
19 For the goodman *is* not at home,
He is gone a long journey:
20 He hath taken a bag of money [1]with him,
And will come home at [2]the day appointed.
21 With [a]her much fair speech she caused him to yield,
[b]With the flattering of her lips she forced him.
22 He goeth after her [1]straightway,
As an ox goeth to the slaughter,
Or as a fool to the correction of the stocks;
23 Till a dart strike through his liver;
[a]As a bird hasteth to the snare,
And knoweth not that it *is* for his life.

24 Hearken unto me now therefore, O ye children,
And attend to the words of my mouth.
25 Let not thine heart decline to her ways,
Go not astray in her paths.
26 For she hath cast down many wounded:
Yea, [a]many strong *men have been* slain by her.
27 [a]Her house *is* the way to hell,
Going down to the chambers of death.

The call of wisdom

8 Doth not [a]wisdom cry?
And understanding put forth her voice?

7:2 *the apple of thine eye.* The pupil, which is cared for and protected because of its great value (see Deut 32:10 and note).
7:3 *Bind them upon thy fingers.* As a reminder (see 6:21; Deut 6:8). *table of thine heart.* See Jer 31:33.
7:4 *wisdom.* As embodied in the instructions of the wisdom teacher (vv. 1–3). *my sister . . . kinswoman.* Make wisdom your most intimate companion. "Sister" may be used here in the sense of "bride" (see Sol 4:9–10,12; 5:1–2).
7:5 See note on 2:16.
7:7 *simple ones.* See note on 1:4. *void of understanding.* See 6:32; 9:4,16.
7:8 *the way to her house.* See 5:8.
7:9 *black and dark night.* He was hoping no one would see him (see 2:13 and note).
7:10 *the attire of a harlot.* Perhaps dressed in a gaudy manner (see Ezek 16:16) and heavily veiled (see Gen 38:14–15).
7:12 *she . . . lieth in wait.* Ready to catch her prey (see v. 22).
7:13 *kissed him.* A bold greeting (see Gen 29:11).
7:14 *peace offerings.* Part of the meat could be eaten by the one who brought the offering and by his (or her) family (Lev 7:12–15). *This day I have payed my vows.* An offering made as the result of a vow was one of the peace offerings, and the meat had to be eaten on the first or second day (see Lev 7:15–16). So the young man had an opportunity to enjoy a real feast, one that ironically had a religious significance (cf. Amos 5:21–22).
7:16 *fine linen of Egypt.* Linen is associated with the wealthy in 31:22. Egyptian linen was of great value (see Is 19:9; Ezek 27:7).
7:17 *myrrh, aloes, and cinnamon.* Fragrant perfumes that are linked with making love also in Ps 45:8; Sol 4:14; 5:5.
7:18 *take our fill of love.* Making love is compared to eating and drinking also in 9:17; 30:20; Sol 4:16; 5:1.
7:19 *not at home.* So he will never know (cf. 6:34–35). *long journey.* Perhaps he was a wealthy merchant.
7:20 *money.* Pieces of silver of various weights were a common medium of exchange, but not in the form of coins until a later period.
7:21 *fair speech . . . flattering of her lips.* See notes on 2:16; 5:3; see also 6:24; 7:5. *caused him to yield.* Cf. 5:23.
7:22 *As an ox goeth to the slaughter.* Totally oblivious of the fate that awaits him.
7:23 *through his liver.* The terrible fate of the wicked is similarly described in Job 20:24–25. *hasteth to the snare.* See notes on 1:17–18; 5:22.
7:24 See 5:7.
7:25 *her paths.* See 1:15.
7:26 *she hath cast down many wounded.* See 9:18; Is 5:14.
7:27 *way to hell.* See notes on 2:18; 5:5; see also 14:12; 16:25; Mat 7:13; cf. 1 Cor 6:9–10.
8:1–36 Wisdom is personified (see note on 1:20) as she addresses mankind in preparation for the final plea from both "Wisdom" and "Folly" in ch. 9.
8:1 *cry . . . put forth her voice.* See 1:20.

2 She standeth in the top of high places by the way,
In the places of the paths.
3 She crieth at the gates, at the entry of the city,
At the coming in at the doors.
4 Unto you, O men, I call;
And my voice *is* to the sons of man.
5 O ye simple, understand wisdom:
And, ye fools, be ye of an understanding heart.
6 Hear, for I will speak of [a]excellent things;
And the opening of my lips *shall be* right things.
7 For my mouth shall speak truth;
And wickedness *is* [1]an abomination to my lips.
8 All the words of my mouth *are* in righteousness;
There is nothing [1]froward or perverse in them.
9 They *are* all plain to him that understandeth,
And right to them that find knowledge.
10 Receive my instruction, and not silver;
And knowledge rather than choice gold.
11 [a]For wisdom *is* better than rubies;
And all the things that may be desired are not to be compared to it.
12 I wisdom dwell *with* [1]prudence,
And find out knowledge of witty inventions.
13 [a]The fear of the LORD *is* to hate evil:
[b]Pride, and arrogancy, and the evil way,
And [c]the froward mouth, do I hate.

8:6 [a]ch. 22:20
8:7 [1]Heb. *the abomination of my lips*
8:8 [1]Heb. *wreathed*
8:11 [a]Job 28:15; Ps. 19:10; 119:127; ch. 3:14,15; 4:5,7; 16:16
8:12 [1]Or, *subtilty*
8:13 [a]ch. 16:6 [b]ch. 6:17 [c]ch. 4:24

14 Counsel *is* mine, and sound wisdom:
I *am* understanding; [a]I have strength.
15 [a]By me kings reign,
And princes decree justice.
16 By me princes rule,
And nobles, *even* all the judges of the earth.
17 [a]I love them that love me;
And [b]those that seek me early shall find me.
18 [a]Riches and honour *are* with me;
Yea, durable riches and righteousness.
19 [a]My fruit *is* better than gold, yea, than fine gold;
And my revenue than choice silver.
20 I [1]lead in the way of righteousness,
In the midst of the paths of judgment:
21 That *I* may cause those that love me to inherit substance;
And I will fill their treasures.
22 [a]The LORD possessed me *in* the beginning of his way,
Before his works of old.
23 [a]I was set up from everlasting, from the beginning,
Or ever the earth was.
24 When *there were* no depths, I was brought forth;
When *there were* no fountains abounding with water.
25 [a]Before the mountains were settled,
Before the hills was I brought forth:
26 While as yet he had not made the earth, nor the [1]fields,
Nor [2]the highest part of the dust of the world.
27 When he prepared the heavens, I *was* there:

8:14 [a]Eccl. 7:19
8:15 [a]Dan. 2:21; Rom. 13:1
8:17 [a]1 Sam. 2:30; Ps. 91:14; John 14:21 [b]Jas. 1:5
8:18 [a]ch. 3:16; Mat. 6:33
8:19 [a]ver. 10; ch. 3:14
8:20 [1]Or, *walk*
8:22 [a]ch. 3:19
8:23 [a]Ps. 2:6
8:25 [a]Job 15:7,8
8:26 [1]Or, *open places* [2]Or, *the chief part*

8:2–3 See notes on 1:20–21.
8:4 *sons of man.* See v. 31.
8:5 *simple . . . fools.* Both are addressed in wisdom's speech in 1:22,32. *simple, understand wisdom.* See note on 1:4.
8:6 *excellent things . . . right things.* See Phil 4:8.
8:7 *wickedness is an abomination to my lips.* See 3:32; 12:22.
8:8 *froward or perverse.* See Phil 2:15; cf. Prov 2:15.
8:9 *to him that understandeth.* The wiser a person is, the more he appreciates words of wisdom. *that find knowledge.* Especially the knowledge of God (see note on 2:5).
8:10 *silver . . . gold.* See v. 19; 2:4; 3:14 and note.
8:11 Almost identical with 3:15 (see note there).
8:12 *dwell with prudence.* Cf. Job 28:20. *prudence . . . knowledge of witty inventions.* See 1:4 and note.
8:13 *The fear of the LORD is to hate evil.* See 1:7; 3:7 and notes; see also 9:10; 16:6. *Pride, and arrogancy . . . I hate.* See 16:18; 1 Sam 2:3; Is 13:11; see also Ps 10:2–11 and note. *evil way, And the froward mouth.* See note on 2:12; see also 6:12,16–19.
8:14 *Counsel . . . and sound wisdom . . . understanding . . . strength.* These characterize the Lord (2:6–7; Job 12:13,16; Is 40:13–14; Rom 16:27) and the Spirit of the Lord (Is 11:2). *Counsel.* See 1:25; 19:20. *strength.* Cf. Eccl 9:16.
8:15 *By me kings reign.* See 29:4. Solomon prayed for wisdom to govern Israel (see 1 Ki 3:9; 2 Chr 1:10).
8:17 *I love.* I pour out my benefits on (see 4:6 and note; see also John 14:21). *those that seek me early shall find me.* See 2:4–5; Is 55:6; Jas 1:5.
8:18 *Riches and honour.* See 3:16; 22:4.
8:19 *My fruit.* Wisdom is called a "tree of life" in 3:18 (see note there). *fine gold . . . choice silver.* See v. 10; Job 28:15; see also 3:14 and note.
8:20 *way . . . paths.* See 3:17. *judgment.* See v. 15.
8:21 *fill their treasures.* See note on 3:10; see also 24:4.
8:22–31 A hymn describing wisdom's role in creation. Wisdom is here personified, as in 1:20–33; 3:15–18; 9:1–12. Therefore these verses should not be interpreted as a direct description of Christ. Yet they provide part of the background for the NT portrayal of Christ as the divine Word (John 1:1–3) and as the wisdom of God (1 Cor 1:24,30; Col 2:3). Here, wisdom is an attribute of God involved with Him in creation.
8:22 *possessed me.* The Hebrew for this verb is also used in Gen 4:1; 14:19,22. *me.* Wisdom (see 3:19; Ps 104:24). *in the beginning of his way.* Cf. Job's statement about the Behemoth (Job 40:19).
8:23 *from everlasting.* Descriptive also of Christ (see John 1:1; cf. Mic 5:2). *ever the earth was.* Wisdom was already there before God began to create the world (cf. Christ's statement in John 17:5).
8:24 *I was brought forth.* Elsewhere the sea "brake forth" (Job 38:8–9), the hills and mountains "were brought forth" (Ps 90:2). *fountains abounding with water.* See Ps 104:10.
8:25 *mountains.* See Ps 90:2.

When he set [1] a compass upon the face
of the depth:
28 When he established the clouds above:
When *he* strengthened the fountains of
the deep:
29 [a] When he gave to the sea his decree,
That the waters should not pass his
commandment;
When [b] he appointed the foundations
of the earth:
30 [a] Then I was by him, *as* one brought up
with him:
[b] And I was daily *his* delight,
Rejoicing always before him;
31 Rejoicing in the habitable part of his
earth;
And [a] my delights *were* with the sons
of men.

32 Now therefore hearken unto me, O ye
children:
For [a] blessed *are they that* keep my ways.
33 Hear instruction, and be wise,
And refuse *it* not.
34 [a] Blessed *is* the man that heareth me,
Watching daily at my gates,
Waiting at the posts of my doors.
35 For whoso findeth me findeth life,
And shall [a] [1] obtain favour of the LORD.
36 But he that sinneth *against* me
[a] wrongeth his own soul:
All they that hate me love death.

Wisdom and folly contrasted

9 Wisdom hath [a] builded her house,
She hath hewn out her seven pillars:
2 [a] She hath killed [1] her beasts; [b] she hath
mingled her wine;
She hath also furnished her table.
3 She hath [a] sent forth her maidens:
[b] She crieth [c] upon the highest places of
the city,
4 [a] Whoso *is* simple, let him turn in hither:
As for him that wanteth
understanding, she saith to him,
5 [a] Come, eat of my bread,
And drink of the wine *which* I have
mingled.
6 Forsake the foolish, and live;
And go in the way of understanding.
7 He that reproveth a scorner getteth to
himself shame:
And he that rebuketh a wicked *man*
getteth himself a blot.
8 [a] Reprove not a scorner, lest he hate
thee:
[b] Rebuke a wise *man,* and he will love
thee.
9 Give *instruction* to a wise *man,* and he
will be yet wiser:
Teach a just *man,* [a] and he will increase
in learning.
10 [a] The fear of the LORD *is* the beginning
of wisdom:
And the knowledge of the holy *is*
understanding.
11 [a] For by me thy days shall be multiplied,
And the years of thy life shall be
increased.
12 [a] If thou be wise, thou shalt be wise for
thyself:
But *if* thou scornest, thou alone shalt
bear *it.*

8:27 [1] Or, *a circle* 8:29 [a] Gen. 1:9,10; Job 38:10; Jer. 5:22 [b] Job 38:4 8:30 [a] John 1:1,2 [b] Mat. 3:17; Col. 1:13 8:31 [a] Ps. 16:3 8:32 [a] Ps. 119:1,2; Luke 11:28 8:34 [a] ch. 3:13,18 8:35 [1] Heb. *bring forth* [a] ch. 12:2 8:36 [a] ch. 20:2 9:1 [a] Mat. 16:18; Eph. 2:20; 1 Pet. 2:5

9:2 [1] Heb. *her killing* [a] Mat. 22:4 [b] ch. 23:30 9:3 [a] Rom. 10:15 [b] ch. 8:1,2 [c] ver. 14 9:4 [a] Ps. 19:7; ch. 6:32 9:5 [a] Sol. 5:1; Is. 55:1; John 6:27 9:8 [a] Mat. 7:6 [b] Ps. 141:5 9:9 [a] Mat. 13:12 9:10 [a] Job 28:28; ch. 1:7 9:11 [a] ch. 3:2,16 9:12 [a] Job 35:6,7; ch. 16:26

8:27 *prepared the heavens.* See 3:19. *When he set a compass upon the face of the depth.* See Job 26:10.
8:28 *fountains of the deep.* Earth's springs and streams (see note on 3:20; cf. Gen 7:11).
8:29 *the sea his decree.* Established the sea's boundaries. See Gen 1:9; Job 38:10–11; Ps 104:9. *foundations of the earth.* See note on 3:19.
8:30 *as one brought up with him.* Or "as a master workman." A workman was sometimes called a wise man. See, e.g., Bezaleel, who designed and built the tabernacle (Ex 31:3). Here the term stresses the skill demonstrated in creation. *his delight, Rejoicing always.* Cf. the joyful shouts of the angels at the time of creation (Job 38:7).
8:31 *delights were with the sons of men.* Cf. v. 4. Man, made in the image of God, represented the climax of creation (see Gen 1:26–28).
8:32 *blessed.* The blessings associated with gaining wisdom are also given in 3:13–18; see also Ps 119:1–2; 128:1.
8:34 *Watching daily at my gates.* Contrast the warning not to go near the door of the adulteress's house (5:8).
8:35 *findeth life.* See 3:2; 4:22 and notes. *favour.* See 3:4; 12:2; 18:22.
8:36 *All they that hate me love death.* See 1:28–33; 5:12,23; 7:27 and notes.
9:1 *hath builded her house.* Both wisdom and folly have a house to which mankind is invited (see v. 14; 7:8; 8:34), but wisdom has built her house (see note on 14:1)—for her there is no "sitting" (v. 14). Cf. the virtues of the wife of noble character (31:10–27). *seven pillars.* Indicating a large house. Perhaps "seven" refers to seven major aspects of wisdom.
9:2 See v. 17 and note. The banquet prepared by wisdom contrasts with the perfumed bed made ready by the adulteress in 7:17. *mingled her wine.* With spices, to make it tastier (see Sol 8:2).
9:3 *She crieth upon the highest places of the city.* See the description of folly in v. 14; see also 8:1–3.
9:4 The same invitation is given by folly in v. 16. *simple.* See 1:4 and note on 8:5. *wanteth understanding.* See v. 16; 7:7.
9:5 As in v. 2, wisdom's gifts to mankind are described symbolically as a great banquet (see Is 55:1–2; cf. John 6:27,35).
9:6 *Forsake the foolish.* See 1:22. *live.* See v. 11; 8:35; see also note on 3:2.
9:7 *He that reproveth a scorner getteth to himself shame.* See 1:22 and note; cf. 1:30. *getteth himself a blot.* Receives insults from the scorner; cf. 1 Pet 4:4.
9:8 *lest he hate thee.* See 15:12,32. *Rebuke a wise man, and he will love thee.* See 10:8; 17:10.
9:9 *he will be yet wiser.* See 18:15; 21:11.
9:10–12 Wisdom's final words summarize the heart of the message in chs. 1–9.
9:10 *The fear of the LORD is the beginning of wisdom.* See 1:7 and note. *knowledge of the holy.* See note on 2:5.
9:11 *years of thy life shall be increased.* See note on 3:2; see also 3:16; 10:27; 14:27; 19:23.
9:12 *thou shalt be wise for thyself.* The wise person reaps the benefits of wisdom. Some of wisdom's rewards are given in

13 [a]A foolish woman *is* clamorous:
She is simple, and knoweth nothing.
14 For she sitteth at the door of her house,
On a seat [a]in the high places of the city,
15 To call passengers
Who go right *on* their ways:
16 [a]Whoso *is* simple, let him turn in
hither:
And *as for* him that wanteth
understanding, she saith to him,
17 [a]Stolen waters are sweet,
And bread [1]*eaten* in secret is pleasant.
18 But he knoweth not that [a]the dead *are*
there;
And that her guests *are* in the depths
of hell.

9:13 [a]ch. 7:11
9:14 [a]ver. 3
9:16 [a]ch. 7:7,8
9:17 [1]Heb. *of secrecies* [a]ch. 20:17
9:18 [a]ch. 2:18
10:1 [a]ch. 15:20
10:2 [a]Ps. 49:6; Luke 12:20 [b]Dan. 4:27
10:3 [1]Or, *the wicked* for their *wickedness* [a]Ps. 10:14

Proverbs of Solomon

10 The proverbs of Solomon.
[a]A wise son maketh a glad father:
But a foolish son *is* the heaviness of his
mother.
2 [a]Treasures of wickedness profit
nothing:
[b]But righteousness delivereth from
death.
3 [a]The LORD will not suffer the soul of
the righteous to famish:
But he casteth away [1]the substance of
the wicked.

10:4 [a]ch. 19:15 [b]ch. 13:4
10:5 [a]ch. 19:26
10:6 [a]ver. 11
10:7 [a]Ps. 112:6; Eccl. 8:10
10:8 [1]Heb. *a fool of lips* [2]Or, *shall be beaten* [a]ver. 10
10:9 [a]Ps. 23:4; ch. 28:18; Is. 33:15,16
10:10 [1]Or, *shall be beaten* [a]ch. 6:13 [b]ver. 8
10:11 [a]Ps. 37:30 [b]Ps. 107:42
10:12 [a]1 Cor. 13:7; 1 Pet. 4:8

4 [a]*He becometh* poor that dealeth *with* a
slack hand:
But [b]the hand of the diligent maketh
rich.
5 He that gathereth in summer *is* a wise
son:
But he that sleepeth in harvest *is* [a]a
son that causeth shame.
6 Blessings *are* upon the head of the just:
But [a]violence covereth the mouth of
the wicked.
7 [a]The memory of the just *is* blessed:
But the name of the wicked shall rot.
8 The wise in heart will receive
commandments:
[a]But [1]a prating fool [2]shall fall.
9 [a]He that walketh uprightly walketh
surely:
But he that perverteth his ways shall
be known.
10 [a]He that winketh *with* the eye causeth
sorrow:
[b]But a prating fool [1]shall fall.
11 [a]The mouth of a righteous *man is* a
well of life:
But [b]violence covereth the mouth of
the wicked.
12 Hatred stirreth up strifes:
But [a]love covereth all sins.
13 In the lips of him that hath
understanding wisdom is found:

3:16–18; 4:22; 8:35; 14:14. *scornest.* See v. 7; see note on 1:22. *shalt bear it.* See 1:26; 19:29.

9:13 *A foolish woman is clamorous.* "Clamorous" links the personified "folly" with the adulteress, the wayward wife of 2:16 and 7:11. *simple, and knoweth nothing.* She lacks good judgment, prudence and the fear of the Lord (see 1:3–4,22,29; 5:6).

9:14 *sitteth.* Cf. wisdom's building her house (v. 1). *at the door of her house.* See 5:8; 8:34. *in the high places of the city.* Cf. the position of wisdom in v. 3; 8:2.

9:15 *To call.* Cf. the appeal of wisdom in v. 3; 8:1,4.

9:16 Her invitation is identical to wisdom's (v. 4; see note on 1:21).

9:17 *Stolen waters . . . bread eaten in secret.* The "banquet" prepared by "folly" seems poorer than the wine and meat of wisdom (v. 2). And it was stolen at that! This "meal" refers to stolen pleasures, exemplified by the illicit sex offered by the adulteress (see 7:18 and note; cf. 5:15–16). *sweet.* But see Job 20:12–14.

9:18 *the dead are there . . . her guests are in the depths of hell.* Similar to 2:18; 5:5; 7:27 (see notes).

10:1 *The proverbs of Solomon.* The title of a collection of individual proverbs that extends through 22:16. The numerical values of the consonants in the Hebrew word for "Solomon" total 375—the exact number of verses in 10:1–22:16; 375 of Solomon's proverbs were selected from a much larger number (cf. 1 Ki 4:32). *wise son.* See v. 5; 15:20; 17:21,25; 29:3,15. In later collections he is described as "righteous" (23:24–25) and as one "who keepeth the law" (28:7).

10:2 *Treasures of wickedness profit nothing.* Ill-gotten gain. These treasures are fleeting (21:6) and result in God's judgment (see 1:19 and note; 10:16; Ezek 7:19). *righteousness delivereth from death.* See 2:16–18; 3:2; 13:21.

10:3 *will not suffer the soul of the righteous to famish.* Will not allow the righteous to go hungry; see 13:25; 28:25; Ps 34:9–10; 37:19,25. But see note on Prov 3:2. *casteth away the substance of the wicked.* Does not give the wicked their desires; see Num 11:34; Ps 112:10.

10:4 Many proverbs praise diligence and the profit it brings, and they condemn laziness as a cause of hunger and poverty (see 6:6–11 and notes; 12:11,24,27; 13:4; 14:23; 18:9; 27:23–27; 28:19).

10:5 *sleepeth in harvest.* Sleeping when there is work to be done is condemned also in 6:9–11; 19:15; 20:13. *son that causeth shame.* See 17:2; 19:26; 28:7; 29:15.

10:6 *Blessings.* God's gifts and favors (see 3:13–18; 28:20; Gen 49:26; Deut 33:16). *are upon the head.* See 11:26. *violence covereth the mouth of the wicked.* The trouble caused by their lips will eventually ruin them (see Ps 140:9; Hab 2:17; but cf. Prov 2:11).

10:7 *memory of the just.* Remembering the righteous (see 22:1).

10:8 *The wise . . . receive commandments.* See 9:8–9. *prating fool.* Lit. "a fool of lips," a person who babbles on without wisdom; see vv. 10,14,18,19.

10:9 *He that walketh uprightly walketh surely.* See 2:7; 3:23; 13:6; Ps 23:4; Is 33:15–16. *he that perverteth his ways shall be known.* His wicked ways will be exposed; see 26:26; Luke 8:17; 1 Tim 5:24–25; 2 Tim 3:9.

10:10 *winketh with the eye.* See note on 6:13. *prating fool.* See v. 8.

10:11 *well of life.* A source of life-giving wisdom (see 13:14; 14:27; 16:22; see also Ps 37:30). *violence covereth.* The wicked may disguise their ill intent by their words (see v. 6 and note).

10:12 *stirreth up strifes.* See note on 6:14. *covereth all sins.* Promotes forgiveness (see 17:9). This line is quoted in Jas 5:20; 1 Pet 4:8.

10:13 *rod is for the back.* See 14:3; 19:29.

But [a]a rod *is* for the back of him that is
void of [1]understanding.

14 Wise *men* lay up knowledge:
But [a]the mouth of the foolish *is* near
destruction.

15 [a]The rich *man's* wealth *is* his strong
city:
The destruction of the poor *is* their
poverty.

16 The labour of the righteous *tendeth* to
life:
The fruit of the wicked to sin.

17 He *is in* the way of life that keepeth
instruction:
But he that refuseth reproof [1]erreth.

18 He that hideth hatred *with* lying lips,
And [a]he that uttereth a slander, *is* a
fool.

19 [a]In the multitude of words there
wanteth not sin:
But [b]he that refraineth his lips *is* wise.

20 The tongue of the just *is as* choice
silver:
The heart of the wicked *is* little worth.

21 The lips of the righteous feed many:
But fools die for want [1]of wisdom.

22 [a]The blessing of the LORD, it maketh
rich,
And he addeth no sorrow with it.

23 [a]*It is* as sport to a fool to do mischief:
But a man of understanding hath
wisdom.

24 [a]The fear of the wicked, it shall come
upon him:
But [b]the desire of the righteous shall
be granted.

25 As the whirlwind passeth, [a]so *is* the
wicked no *more:*
But [b]the righteous *is* an everlasting
foundation.

26 As vinegar to the teeth, and as smoke
to the eyes,
So *is* the sluggard to them that send
him.

27 [a]The fear of the LORD [1]prolongeth days:
But [b]the years of the wicked shall be
shortened.

28 The hope of the righteous *shall be*
gladness:
But the [a]expectation of the wicked
shall perish.

29 The way of the LORD *is* strength to the
upright:
[a]But destruction *shall be* to the
workers of iniquity.

30 [a]The righteous shall never be removed:
But the wicked shall not inhabit the
earth.

31 [a]The mouth of the just bringeth forth
wisdom:
But the froward tongue shall be cut
out.

32 The lips of the righteous know what is
acceptable:
But the mouth of the wicked *speaketh*
[1]frowardness.

11

[a] [1] A false balance *is* abomination to
the LORD:
But [2]a just weight *is* his delight.

10:13 [1] Heb. *heart* [a] ch. 26:3
10:14 [a] ch. 18:7
10:15 [a] Job 31:24; 1 Tim. 6:17
10:17 [1] Or, *causeth to err*
10:18 [a] Ps. 15:3
10:19 [a] Eccl. 5:3 [b] Jas. 3:2
10:21 [1] Heb. *of heart*
10:22 [a] Gen. 24:35; Ps. 37:22
10:23 [a] ch. 15:21
10:24 [a] Job 15:21
10:24 [b] Ps. 145:19; Mat. 5:6; 1 John 5:14
10:25 [a] Ps. 37:9,10 [b] Ps. 15:5; Mat. 16:18
10:27 [1] Heb. *addeth* [a] ch. 9:11 [b] Job 15:32
10:28 [a] Job 8:13
10:29 [a] Ps. 1:6
10:30 [a] Ps. 37:22
10:31 [a] Ps. 37:30
10:32 [1] Heb. *frowardnesses*
11:1 [1] Heb. *Balances of deceit* [2] Heb. *a perfect stone* [a] Lev. 19:35; Deut. 25:13

10:14 *lay up knowledge.* Rather than babbling folly—and so the wise prosper. See 2:1 and note. *is near destruction.* Quick with his mouth, the fool only brings ruin on himself (see vv. 8,10; 13:3).

10:15 An observation about wealth and poverty. *wealth is his strong city.* Wealth brings friends (14:20; 19:4) and power (18:23; 22:7)—but ultimate security is found only in God (Ps 52:7). *destruction of the poor is their poverty.* Poverty has no influence (18:23), no friends (19:4,7), no security. See v. 4 and note.

10:16 *the labour of the righteous tendeth to life.* Not wealth (v. 15) but righteousness assures life (see note on 3:2; see also 3:16; 4:22). *fruit of the wicked to sin.* Or to the personal calamity that results from their sin; see 1:13,31 and notes. "The wages of sin is death" (Rom 6:23).

10:17 *way of life.* See note on 6:23. *he that refuseth reproof.* See 5:12; 15:10.

10:18 *hideth hatred with lying lips.* By pretending friendliness (see 26:24,26,28).

10:20 *choice silver.* What the righteous say has great value (see 3:14; 8:10; 25:11). *heart of the wicked.* Their thoughts and schemes (see 6:14,18).

10:21 *feed many.* See v. 11 and note. *die for want of wisdom.* See 5:23 and note; see also 7:7; 9:16.

10:22 *blessing of the LORD, it maketh rich.* Wealth is a gift from God, not a product of human attainment (see notes on v. 6; 3:10; see also 8:21; Gen 24:35; 26:12). *addeth no sorrow with it.* Unlike the "treasures of wickedness" of v. 2 (see note); cf. 15:6.

10:23 *It is as sport to a fool to do mischief.* See 2:14; 15:21; 26:19.

10:24 *The fear of the wicked.* The calamity and distress that the wicked person dreads (see 1:26–27; 3:25; Job 15:21; Is 66:4). *the desire of the righteous.* See Ps 37:4; 145:19; Mat 5:6; 1 John 5:14–15.

10:25 Cf. the wise man who built his house on a rock, and the foolish man who built his on the sand (Mat 7:24–27). *so is the wicked no more.* See Ps 37:10; Is 28:18. *the righteous . . . foundation.* Unshakable, unmovable (see 3:25 and note; see also 12:3,7; 14:11; Ps 15:5; 1 Cor 15:58).

10:26 *vinegar.* See 25:20; Ps 69:21. *sluggard.* See note on 6:6. *them that send him.* As a messenger (cf. 25:13; 26:6) or worker.

10:27 *fear of the LORD.* See note on 1:7. *prolongeth days.* See note on 3:2. *years . . . shall be shortened.* See Job 22:16; Ps 37:36; 55:23.

10:28 *hope of the righteous.* See v. 24 and note; Ps 9:18. *gladness.* Of fulfillment (cf. 11:23). *expectation of the wicked shall perish.* See 11:7,23.

10:29 *way of the LORD.* The way He prescribes, the life of wisdom (see Ps 27:11; 143:8; Mat 22:16; Acts 18:25). *destruction . . . to the workers of iniquity.* Since judgment comes to those who refuse God's way (see 21:15; 2 Cor 2:15–16; 2 Pet 2:21).

10:30 *shall never be removed.* Or shaken from their security. See 2:21 and note; 10:25; 12:3; Ps 125:1. *not inhabit the earth.* Or dwell in the promised land. See note on 2:22.

10:31 *froward tongue.* See note on 2:12. *cut out.* See Ps 12:3; cf. Mat 5:30.

11:1 *false balance is abomination.* Similar denunciation is found in the law (see Lev 19:35 and note) and the prophets (Amos 8:5; Mic 6:11). See also 16:11; 20:10,23. *just weight.* See KJV marg. Silver was weighed on scales balanced against a stone weight. Weights with dishonest labels were used for cheating.

2 [a]*When* pride cometh, then cometh
shame:
But with the lowly *is* wisdom.
3 [a]The integrity of the upright shall
guide them:
But the perverseness of transgressors
shall destroy them.
4 [a]Riches profit not in the day of wrath:
But [b]righteousness delivereth from
death.
5 The righteousness of the perfect shall
[1]direct his way:
But the wicked shall fall by his own
wickedness.
6 The righteousness of the upright shall
deliver them:
But [a]transgressors shall be taken in
their own naughtiness.
7 [a]When a wicked man dieth, *his*
expectation shall perish:
And the hope of unjust *men* perisheth.
8 [a]The righteous is delivered out of
trouble,
And the wicked cometh in his stead.
9 A hypocrite with *his* mouth destroyeth
his neighbour:
But through knowledge shall the just
be delivered.
10 [a]When it goeth well with the
righteous, the city rejoiceth:
And when the wicked perish, *there is*
shouting.
11 [a]By the blessing of the upright the city
is exalted:
But it is overthrown by the mouth of
the wicked.
12 He that is [1]void of wisdom despiseth
his neighbour:
But a man of understanding holdeth his
peace.
13 [a][1]A talebearer revealeth secrets:
But he that is of a faithful spirit
concealeth the matter.
14 [a]Where no counsel *is,* the people fall:
But in the multitude of counsellers
there is safety.
15 [a]He that is surety for a stranger [1]shall
smart *for it:*
And he that hateth [2]suretiship *is* sure.
16 [a]A gracious woman retaineth honour:
And strong *men* retain riches.
17 [a]The merciful man doeth good to his
own soul:
But *he that is* cruel troubleth his own
flesh.
18 The wicked worketh a deceitful work:
But [a]*to* him that soweth righteousness
shall be a sure reward.
19 As righteousness *tendeth* to life:
So he that pursueth evil *pursueth it* to
his own death.
20 *They that are* of a froward heart *are*
abomination unto the LORD:
But *such as are* upright in *their* way
are his delight.
21 [a]*Though* hand *join* in hand, the wicked
shall not be unpunished:
But [b]the seed of the righteous shall be
delivered.
22 *As* a jewel of gold in a swine's snout,
So is a fair woman which [1]is without
discretion.
23 The desire of the righteous *is* only
good:
But the expectation of the wicked [a]*is*
wrath.

11:2 [a]ch. 16:18 11:3 [a]ch. 13:6 11:4 [a]Ezek. 7:19; Zeph. 1:18 [b]Gen. 7:1 11:5 [1]Heb. *rectify* 11:6 [a]Eccl. 10:8 11:7 [a]ch. 10:28 11:8 [a]ch. 21:18 11:10 [a]Esth. 8:15 11:11 [a]ch. 29:8 11:12 [1]Heb. *destitute of heart* 11:13 [1]Heb. *He that walketh, being a talebearer* [a]Lev. 19:16; ch. 20:19 11:14 [a]1 Ki. 12:1 11:15 [1]Heb. *shall be sore broken* [2]Heb. *those that strike hands* [a]ch. 6:1 11:16 [a]ch. 31:30 11:17 [a]Mat. 5:7 11:18 [a]Hos. 10:12 11:21 [a]ch. 16:5 [b]Ps. 112:2 11:22 [1]Heb. *departeth from* 11:23 [a]Rom. 2:8,9

11:2 *When pride cometh, then cometh shame.* Along with destruction (see 16:18; cf. the humbling of proud Assyria in Is 10:12; cf. also Is 14:13–15). *with the lowly is wisdom.* Along with honor (see note on 15:33).
11:3 *integrity . . . shall guide them.* Cf. the actions of Joseph in Gen 39:6–12. *perverseness . . . shall destroy them.* See 2:22 and note; see also 19:3. *perverseness.* Cf. Luke 20:23.
11:4 *day of wrath.* The day of judgment (see Is 10:3; Zeph 1:18). *righteousness delivereth from death.* See 2:16–18; 3:2; 10:2; 13:21.
11:5 *perfect.* See 2:21. *shall direct his way.* Will enable him to reach his goals (see note on 3:6; see also v. 3; 10:9).
11:6 *righteousness . . . shall deliver them.* See vv. 3–4. *taken.* See 5:22 and note.
11:7 *his expectation shall perish.* See v. 23; 10:28.
11:8 Cf. the rescue of Mordecai and the execution of Haman in Esth 5:14; 7:10.
11:9 *destroyeth his neighbour.* By spreading slander (cf. 10:18). *through knowledge.* Perhaps the knowledge of the schemes and distortions of the godless (cf. John 2:25).
11:10 *city rejoiceth.* See 28:12; 29:2. Thus life in the city is itself a teacher of wisdom (see note on 1:21). *there is shouting.* Cf. the joy at the fall of Assyria (Is 30:32; Nah 3:19; cf. 2 Chr 21:20).
11:11 *blessing of the upright.* Their good influence and desire for justice as well as their prosperity (v. 10) bring honor to the city. *mouth of the wicked.* Their deceit, dishonesty and sowing of discord (see v. 9; 6:12–14).
‡11:12 *despiseth his neighbour.* Shows his contempt openly (see 10:18; 14:21). *holdeth his peace.* He keeps silent. See 10:19.
11:14 See the close parallels in 15:22; 20:18; 24:6. *counsellers.* See 2 Sam 16:23; Is 1:26.
11:15 See note on 6:1.
11:16 Assuming that "a good name is rather to be chosen than great riches" (22:1) this verse observes that a woman, if she is kindhearted, will be accorded more respect than wealthy men if they are "strong" [i.e. "ruthless"]. *gracious woman.* See 31:28,30.
‡11:17 *doeth good to his own soul.* Or "benefits himself." See Mat 5:7. *troubleth his own flesh.* Or "does himself harm." See Gen 34:25–30; 49:7.
‡11:18 *worketh a deceitful work.* Receives deceptive rewards for wrongdoing because the benefits do not last (see notes on 10:2,16; see also Hag 1:6). *shall be a sure reward.* See 10:24; Gal 6:8–9; Jas 3:18.
11:19 *tendeth to life.* See 10:16; see also 12:28; 19:23. *pursueth it to his own death.* See 5:23; 21:16; Rom 6:23; Jas 1:15.
11:20 *froward heart . . . abomination.* See 3:32 and note; 16:5. *upright.* See note on 2:7.
11:21 *shall not be unpunished.* See 6:29. *shall be delivered.* See Ps 118:5.
11:22 *jewel of gold.* Commonly worn by women on their noses (see Gen 24:47; Ezek 16:12). *without discretion.* Abigail was praised by David for her display of discernment (1 Sam 25:33).
11:23 See 10:24,28. *wrath.* Judgment (see v. 4; Is 10:3; Zeph 1:18; Rom 2:8–9).

24 There is that [a]scattereth, and yet increaseth;
And *there is* that withholdeth more than is meet, but *it tendeth* to poverty.
25 [a] [1]The liberal soul shall be made fat:
[b]And he that watereth shall be watered also himself.
26 [a]He that withholdeth corn, the people shall curse him:
But [b]blessing *shall be* upon the head of him that selleth *it.*
27 He that diligently seeketh good procureth favour:
[a]But he that seeketh mischief, it shall come *unto* him.
28 [a]He that trusteth in his riches shall fall:
But [b]the righteous shall flourish as a branch.
29 He that troubleth his own house [a]shall inherit the wind:
And the fool *shall be* servant to the wise of heart.
30 The fruit of the righteous *is* a tree of life;
And [a]he that [1]winneth souls *is* wise.
31 [a]Behold, the righteous shall be recompensed in the earth:
Much more the wicked and the sinner.

12 Whoso loveth instruction loveth knowledge:
But he that hateth reproof *is* brutish.
2 A good *man* obtaineth favour of the LORD:
But a man of wicked devices will he condemn.
3 A man shall not be established by wickedness:
But the [a]root of the righteous shall not be moved.
4 [a]A virtuous woman *is* a crown to her husband:
But she that maketh ashamed *is* [b]as rottenness in his bones.
5 The thoughts of the righteous *are* right:
But the counsels of the wicked *are* deceit.
6 [a]The words of the wicked *are* to lie in wait *for* blood:
[b]But the mouth of the upright shall deliver them.
7 [a]The wicked *are* overthrown, and *are* not:
But the house of the righteous shall stand.
8 A man shall be commended according to his wisdom:
[a]But he that is [1]of a perverse heart shall be despised.
9 [a]*He that is* despised, and hath a servant, *is* better
Than he that honoureth himself, and lacketh bread.
10 [a]A righteous *man* regardeth the life of his beast:
But the [1]tender mercies of the wicked *are* cruel.
11 [a]He that tilleth his land shall be satisfied *with* bread:
But he that followeth vain *persons* [b]*is* void of understanding.

11:24 [a]Ps. 112:9
11:25 [1]Heb. *The soul of blessing* [a]2 Cor. 9:6 [b]Mat. 5:7
11:26 [a]Amos 8:5,6 [b]Job 29:13
11:27 [a]Esth. 7:10; Ps. 7:15,16
11:28 [a]Job 31:24; Mark 10:24; Luke 12:21; 1 Tim. 6:17 [b]Ps. 1:3; Jer. 17:8
11:29 [a]Eccl. 5:16
11:30 [1]Heb. *taketh* [a]Dan. 12:3; Jas. 5:20
11:31 [a]Jer. 25:29
12:3 [a]ch. 10:25
12:4 [a]1 Cor. 11:7 [b]ch. 14:30
12:6 [a]ch. 1:11,18 [b]ch. 14:3
12:7 [a]Ps. 37:36
12:8 [1]Heb. *perverse of heart* [a]1 Sam. 25:17
12:9 [a]ch. 13:7
12:10 [1]Or, *bowels* [a]Deut. 25:4
12:11 [a]Gen. 3:19; ch. 28:19 [b]ch. 6:32

11:24 Generosity is the path to blessing and further prosperity (see 3:9–10 and notes; Eccl 11:1–2 and notes; Ps 112:9; 2 Cor 9:6–9). By contrast, the stingy person does not make any friends and hurts himself in the long run (21:13).
‡11:25 *The liberal soul shall be made fat.* A generous person will experience prosperity. "He which soweth bountifully shall reap also bountifully" (2 Cor 9:6; cf. Luke 6:38). *be watered.* See Rom 15:32.
11:26 *withholdeth corn* [i.e. grain]. Probably in times of scarcity to raise the price. *blessing shall be upon the head.* See 10:6. *him that selleth it.* Like Joseph during the famine in Egypt (Gen 41:53–57).
‡11:27 *He that diligently seeketh good procureth favour.* He reaps what he sows, like the man in v. 25 (cf. Mat 7:12). *he that seeketh mischief, it shall come unto him.* His wicked schemes will backfire (see v. 8 and note; 1:18).
‡11:28 *He that trusteth in his riches.* Usually said of the wicked (Ps 49:6; 62:10; but see Mark 10:25; 1 Tim 6:17). *flourish as a branch.* He is like a healthy tree sprouting vegetation, cf. Ps. 1:3.
11:29 *He that troubleth his own house shall inherit the wind.* The inheritance of Levi and Simeon was affected because of their cruelty against Shechem (Gen 34:25–30; 49:7). See 15:27 and note. *servant to the wise of heart.* As the evil man serves the good (14:19; cf. 17:2).
11:30 *fruit of the righteous.* What a wise man produces (8:18–19). *tree of life.* See note on 3:18. *winneth souls.* Wins people over to wisdom and righteousness (see Dan 12:3; 1 Cor 9:19–22; Jas 5:20). However, the Hebrew for this expression is unusual so that its translation is somewhat uncertain.
‡11:31 *the righteous shall be recompensed in the earth.* Even Moses and David were punished for their sins (see Num 20:11–12; 2 Sam 12:10). *Much more the wicked and the sinner.* See 1:18,31 and notes; Ps 11:6; 73:18–19; 1 Pet. 4:17.
‡12:1 *loveth instruction loveth knowledge.* See 1:7; 10:17; see also 6:23 and note. *hateth reproof is brutish.* The person who hates correction is foolish. See 1:22; 5:12 and note.
12:2 *obtaineth favour.* See 3:4; 8:35. *a man of wicked devices will he condemn.* Cf. Job 5:12–13; 1 Cor 3:19.
‡12:3 *shall not be established.* See 11:5. *root of the righteous shall not be moved.* See 2:21; see also notes on 10:25,30; 12:12.
12:4 *virtuous woman.* Someone like Ruth (Ruth 3:11). Such a woman is fully described in 31:10–31. *crown to her husband.* She brings him honor and joy (see 4:9 and note). *rottenness.* See Hab 3:16. *his bones.* See note on 3:8.
12:5 *counsels of the wicked are deceit.* See Ps 1:1.
12:6 *lie in wait for blood.* See note on 1:11; see also 1:16. *mouth of the upright shall deliver them.* See 11:3–4,6,9.
12:7 See 10:25 and note.
12:8 *commended according to his wisdom.* See 3:4 and note. *he that is of a perverse heart shall be despised.* See Deut 32:5; Tit 3:11.
12:9 *hath a servant.* Even people of moderate means had servants (see Judg 6:15,27). *honoureth himself.* Cf. 13:7.
12:10 *regardeth the life of his beast.* See 27:23; Deut 25:4; see also chart, p. 256. *the tender mercies of the wicked are cruel.* Probably to both man and beast.
‡12:11 Repeated with slight variation in 28:19. *followeth vain persons.* The Hebrew reads, "follows vain [worthless] things." The verse is contrasting the honest pursuits of the wise with the dishonest schemes of the fool.

12 The wicked desireth [1]the net of evil *men:*
But the root of the righteous yieldeth *fruit.*
13 [a][1]The wicked is snared by the transgression of *his* lips:
[b]But the just shall come out of trouble.
14 [a]A man shall be satisfied *with* good by the fruit of *his* mouth:
[b]And the recompence of a man's hands shall be rendered unto him.
15 [a]The way of a fool *is* right in his own eyes:
But he that hearkeneth unto counsel *is* wise.
16 [a]A fool's wrath is [1]presently known:
But a prudent *man* covereth shame.
17 [a]*He that* speaketh truth sheweth forth righteousness:
But a false witness deceit.
18 [a]There is that speaketh like the piercings of a sword:
But the tongue of the wise *is* health.
19 The lip of truth shall be established for ever:
[a]But a lying tongue *is* but for a moment.
20 Deceit *is* in the heart of them that imagine evil:
But to the counsellers of peace *is* joy.
21 There shall no evil happen to the just:
But the wicked shall be filled *with* mischief.
22 [a]Lying lips *are* abomination to the LORD:
But they that deal truly *are* his delight.

12:12 [1]Or, *the fortress*
12:13 [1]Heb. *The snare of the wicked* is *in the transgression of lips* [a]ch. 18:7 [b]2 Pet. 2:9
12:14 [a]ch. 13:2 [b]Is. 3:10,11
12:15 [a]Luke 18:11
12:16 [1]Heb. *in* that *day* [a]ch. 29:11
12:17 [a]ch. 14:5
12:18 [a]Ps. 57:4; 64:3
12:19 [a]ch. 19:5,9
12:22 [a]Rev. 22:15
12:23 [a]ch. 13:16
12:24 [1]Or, *deceitful* [a]ch. 10:4
12:25 [a]ch. 15:13 [b]Is. 50:4
12:26 [1]Or, *abundant*
13:1 [a]Is. 28:15
13:2 [a]ch. 12:14
13:3 [a]Ps. 39:1; ch. 21:23; Jas. 3:2
13:4 [a]ch. 10:4

23 [a]A prudent man concealeth knowledge:
But the heart of fools proclaimeth foolishness.
24 [a]The hand of the diligent shall bear rule:
But the [1]slothful shall be under tribute.
25 [a]Heaviness in the heart of man maketh it stoop:
But [b]a good word maketh it glad.
26 The righteous *is* more [1]excellent than his neighbour:
But the way of the wicked seduceth them.
27 The slothful *man* roasteth not that which he took in hunting:
But the substance of a diligent man *is* precious.
28 In the way of righteousness *is* life;
And *in* the pathway *thereof there is* no death.

13 A wise son *heareth his* father's instruction:
[a]But a scorner heareth not rebuke.
2 [a]A man shall eat good by the fruit of *his* mouth:
But the soul of the transgressors *shall eat* violence.
3 [a]He that keepeth his mouth keepeth his life:
But he that openeth wide his lips shall have destruction.
4 [a]The soul of the sluggard desireth, and *hath* nothing:
But the soul of the diligent shall be made fat.
5 A righteous *man* hateth lying:

‡12:12 *desireth the net of evil men.* The hunting net used to trip the righteous—the wicked desire ill-gotten gain. See 1:13 and note; 21:10. *root of the righteous yieldeth fruit.* Like firmly rooted trees (see vv. 3,7; 11:30; Ps 1:3; see also 10:25 and note).
12:13 *snared by the transgression of his lips.* See 1:18 and note; 29:6. *just shall come out of trouble.* See 11:8–9 and notes; 21:23; 2 Pet 2:9.
12:14 A man who speaks with wisdom will reap a harvest from his words, just as a farmer enjoys the crops he planted (see 1:31 and note; Job 34:11).
12:15 *is right.* But ends in death (see 1:25,30; 14:12; 16:25).
‡12:16 *covereth shame.* Has good self-control that keeps him from doing shameful things (see 29:11; 2 Sam 16:11–12).
12:17 *false witness deceit.* See note on 6:19.
‡12:18 *There is that speaketh like the piercings of a sword.* The words of the wicked hurt and injure like a sword piercing the body. Cf. Ps 106:33. See note on Ps 5:9. *tongue of the wise is health.* Promotes healing by speaking soothing, comforting words (see 4:22; 15:4).
12:19 *is but for a moment.* The lies will be refuted and the liar punished (see 19:9; Ps 52:4–5).
12:20 *Deceit is in the heart.* See 6:14 and note; see also 1:31; 24:2; Gen 6:5. *to the counsellers of peace is joy.* "Blessed are the peacemakers" (Mat 5:9).
‡12:21 *No evil.* The righteous do not experience calamity. See 1:33 and note; 2:8; Ps 91:10–12; 121:7. *filled with mischief.* See 1:31 and note; 11:5,8; 22:8; Job 4:8.
12:22 Compare the structure of this verse with that of 11:1,20. *abomination.* See note on 3:32. *they that deal truly.* See 16:13.
12:23 *concealeth knowledge.* Stores up knowledge (see 10:14). *proclaimeth foolishness.* See v. 16; 13:16; 15:2; 29:11.
‡12:24 *hand of the diligent . . . slothful.* Contrasted also in 10:4 (see note there). *shall bear rule.* Cf. 17:2. *under tribute.* Subjected to forced labor. See Judg 1:28; see also note on 2 Sam 20:24.
‡12:25 *Heaviness in . . . heart.* The effect of anxiety. See Ps 94:19. *good word maketh it glad.* See 15:23.
‡12:26 *seduceth them.* Leads them down the wrong path. See 5:23; 14:22.
12:27 *roasteth not that which he took in hunting.* And is too lazy to lift the food from the dish to his mouth (19:24).
12:28 *is life.* Cf. 3:2; 11:4. *no death.* The way or path of righteousness does not lead to death. Cf. the identification of wisdom with the "tree of life" (3:18 and note; cf. 14:32).
13:1 *heareth his father's instruction.* See 1:8; 4:1. *scorner heareth not rebuke.* See 1:22; 9:7–8 and notes.
13:2 See 12:14 and note. *soul . . . eat violence.* See 4:17 and note.
13:3 *keepeth his mouth keepeth his life.* The ability to control the tongue is one of the clearest marks of wisdom. "Death and life are in the power of the tongue" (18:21; see 10:19; 21:23; Jas 3:2). *he that openeth wide his lips shall have destruction.* See 12:18 and note; see also 10:14; 18:7; 2 Tim 3:3–4.
13:4 *sluggard.* See 6:6 and note. *desireth, and hath nothing.* Is never satisfied, yet refuses to work (see 21:25–26). *soul of the*

But a wicked *man* is loathsome, and
cometh to shame.
6 [a]Righteousness keepeth *him that is*
upright in the way:
But wickedness overthroweth [1]the
sinner.
7 [a]There is that maketh himself rich, yet
hath nothing:
There is that maketh himself poor, yet
hath great riches.
8 The ransom of a man's life *are* his riches:
But the poor heareth not rebuke.
9 The light of the righteous rejoiceth:
[a]But the [1]lamp of the wicked shall be
put out.
10 Only by pride cometh contention:
But with the well advised *is* wisdom.
11 [a]Wealth *gotten* by vanity shall be
diminished:
But he that gathereth [1]by labour shall
increase.
12 Hope deferred maketh the heart sick:
But [a]*when* the desire cometh, *it is* a
tree of life.
13 Whoso [a]despiseth the word shall be
destroyed:
But he that feareth the commandment
[1]shall be rewarded.
14 [a]The law of the wise *is* a fountain of life,
To depart from [b]the snares of death.
15 Good understanding giveth favour:
But the way of transgressors *is* hard.
16 [a]Every prudent *man* dealeth with
knowledge:
But a fool [1]layeth open *his* folly.
17 A wicked messenger falleth into
mischief:
But [a] [1]a faithful ambassador *is* health.
18 Poverty and shame *shall be to* him that
refuseth instruction:
But [a]he that regardeth reproof shall be
honoured.
19 [a]The desire accomplished is sweet to
the soul:
But *it is* abomination to fools to depart
from evil.
20 He that walketh with wise *men* shall
be wise:
But a companion of fools [1]shall be
destroyed.
21 [a]Evil pursueth sinners:
But to the righteous good shall be
repayed.
22 A good *man* leaveth an inheritance to
his children's children:
And [a]the wealth of the sinner *is* laid
up for the just.
23 [a]Much food *is in* the tillage of the poor:
But there is *that is* destroyed for want
of judgment.
24 [a]He that spareth his rod hateth his son:
But he that loveth him chasteneth him
betimes.
25 [a]The righteous eateth to the satisfying
of his soul:
But the belly of the wicked shall want.

14 Every wise woman buildeth her
house:
But the foolish plucketh it down with
her hands.

13:6 [1]Heb. *sin* [a]ch. 11:3,5,6
13:7 [a]ch. 12:9
13:9 [1]Or, *candle* [a]Job 18:5,6; 21:17; ch. 24:20
13:11 [1]Heb. *with the hand* [a]ch. 10:2; 20:21
13:12 [a]ver. 19
13:13 [1]Or, *shall be in peace* [a]2 Chr. 36:16
13:14 [a]ch. 10:11; 14:27; 16:22 [b]2 Sam. 22:6
13:16 [1]Heb. *spreadeth* [a]ch. 12:23; 15:2
13:17 [1][Heb. *an ambassador of faithfulness*] [a]ch. 25:13
13:18 [a]ch. 15:5,31
13:19 [a]ver. 12
13:20 [1]Heb. *shall be broken*
13:21 [a]Ps. 32:10
13:22 [a]Job 27:17; ch. 28:8; Eccl. 2:26
13:23 [a]ch. 12:11
13:24 [a]ch. 19:18; 22:15; 23:13; 29:15,17
13:25 [a]Ps. 34:10; 37:3

diligent shall be made fat. Diligence yields a profit (see 6:6; see also notes on 10:4,24).

13:5 *is loathsome, and cometh to shame.* Like a lazy or ungrateful son (10:5; 19:26).

13:6 This contrast repeats the thought of 2:21–22; 10:9; 11:3,5 (see notes); cf. 21:12; Ps 25:21.

13:7 Both pretenses are folly and lead to folly (see 14:8 and note; see also 11:24; 12:9).

13:8 *ransom of a man's life.* He has the means to pay off robbers or enemies (see 10:15 and note; Jer 41:8). *poor heareth not rebuke.* Even poverty has its advantages.

13:9 *light . . . lamp.* Symbols of life (cf. Job 3:20). *rejoiceth.* There is joy and prosperity (see note on 4:18). *lamp of the wicked shall be put out.* His life will end (see 20:20; 24:20; Job 18:5; 21:17).

13:10 *pride.* See 11:2 and note.

13:11 *Wealth . . . by vanity shall be diminished.* Such as wealth gained by extortion (Ps 62:10) or deceit (Prov 21:6). See note on 10:2; see also Jer 17:11. *shall increase.* See note on 10:4.

13:12 *Hope deferred maketh the heart sick.* Cf. Gen 30:1. *when the desire cometh, it is a tree of life.* It revives and strengthens (see note on 3:18; see also 10:28; 13:19).

13:13 *Whoso despiseth the word shall be destroyed.* See 1:29–31; see also 5:12 and note. *he that feareth the commandment shall be rewarded.* With the benefits wisdom gives (see 3:2 and note; 3:16–18; 13:21).

13:14 *fountain of life.* See note on 10:11. *from the snares of death.* See notes on 1:17; 5:22; see also 7:23; 22:5.

13:15 *giveth favour.* See 3:4; 8:35. *is hard.* See v. 13 and note.

13:16 See 12:23 and note.

13:17 *falleth into mischief.* Perhaps by misrepresenting those who sent him. *a faithful ambassador is health.* His tactful, honest approach benefits both parties (see 25:13; cf. 12:18; 15:4).

13:18 *Poverty and shame.* See 5:10–12 and notes. *he that regardeth reproof shall be honoured.* See v. 1; 3:16–18; 8:35; 10:17.

13:19 *desire accomplished.* See v. 12. *abomination . . . to depart from evil.* Cf. their hatred of correction in 5:12.

13:20 *He that walketh with wise men shall be wise.* Choose your friends with care (see 2:20; 12:26). *companion of fools shall be destroyed.* See 1:10,18; 2:12; 16:29; 22:24–25.

13:21 See v. 13 and note.

13:22 *is laid up for the just.* Job agrees that this is often what happens to a wicked man's possessions (Job 27:16–17; cf. Prov 28:8).

‡13:23 *there is that is destroyed for want of judgment.* Or, "it is swept away by injustice." Referring to the food the poor man has earned by his hard work; a case of the rich and powerful oppressing the poor (cf. Ps 35:10).

‡13:24 *spareth his rod hateth his son.* Parents are encouraged to apply the rod of punishment to drive out folly (22:15) so that the child will not follow a path of destruction (19:18; 23:13–14). "The rod and reproof give wisdom" (29:15) and promote a healthy and happy family (29:17). Discipline is rooted in love (see 3:11–12 and note). *rod.* A figure of speech for loving and corrective discipline of any kind.

13:25 States more specifically the teaching of vv. 13,18,21; see 10:3 and note.

14:1 *wise woman buildeth her house.* She is a source of strength and an example of diligence for her family (see 31:10–31). Cf. the house built by wisdom in 9:1.

2 He that walketh in his uprightness
feareth the LORD:
[a]But he that is perverse in his ways
despiseth him.
3 In the mouth of the foolish *is* a rod of
pride:
[a]But the lips of the wise shall preserve
them.
4 Where no oxen *are,* the crib *is* clean:
But much increase *is* by the strength of
the ox.
5 [a]A faithful witness will not lie:
But a false witness will utter lies.
6 A scorner seeketh wisdom, and *findeth*
it not:
But [a]knowledge *is* easy unto him that
understandeth.
7 Go from the presence of a foolish man,
When thou perceivest not *in him* the
lips of knowledge.
8 The wisdom of the prudent *is* to
understand his way:
But the folly of fools *is* deceit.
9 [a]Fools make a mock at sin:
But among the righteous *there is* favour.
10 The heart knoweth [1]his own
bitterness;
And a stranger doth not intermeddle
with his joy.
11 [a]The house of the wicked shall be
overthrown:
But the tabernacle of the upright shall
flourish.
12 [a]There is a way which seemeth right
unto a man,
But [b]the end thereof *are* the ways of
death.

14:2 [a]Rom. 2:4
14:3 [a]ch. 12:6
14:5 [a]ver. 25; Ex. 20:16; 23:1; ch. 6:19; 12:17
14:6 [a]ch. 8:9; 17:24
14:9 [a]ch. 10:23
14:10 [1]Heb. *the bitterness of his soul*
14:11 [a]Job 8:15
14:12 [a]ch. 16:25 [b]Rom. 6:21
14:13 [a]ch. 5:4; Eccl. 2:2
14:14 [a]ch. 1:31; 12:14
14:16 [a]ch. 22:3
14:20 [1]Heb. *many* are *the lovers of the rich* [a]ch. 19:7
14:21 [a]Ps. 41:1; 112:9
14:25 [a]ver. 5

13 Even in laughter the heart is sorrowful;
And [a]the end of that mirth *is* heaviness.
14 The backslider in heart shall be [a]filled
with his own ways:
And a good man *shall be satisfied* from
himself.
15 The simple believeth every word:
But the prudent *man* looketh well to
his going.
16 [a]A wise *man* feareth, and departeth
from evil:
But the fool rageth, and *is* confident.
17 *He that is* soon angry dealeth foolishly:
And a man of wicked devices is hated.
18 The simple inherit folly:
But the prudent are crowned *with*
knowledge.
19 The evil bow before the good;
And the wicked at the gates of the
righteous.
20 [a]The poor is hated even of his own
neighbour:
But [1]the rich *hath* many friends.
21 He that despiseth his neighbour
sinneth:
[a]But he that hath mercy on the poor,
happy *is* he.
22 Do they not err that devise evil?
But mercy and truth *shall be to* them
that devise good.
23 In all labour there is profit:
But the talk of the lips *tendeth* only to
penury.
24 The crown of the wise *is* their riches:
But the foolishness of fools *is* folly.
25 [a]A true witness delivereth souls:
But a deceitful *witness* speaketh lies.

14:2 *feareth the LORD.* See note on 1:7.
‡14:3 *rod of pride.* His proud and arrogant words get him into trouble. See 10:13; 19:29; 26:3.
14:4 Perhaps the thought is that men need to take good care of their oxen (the means of production) if they expect an abundant harvest (see 12:10).
14:5 See note on 6:19.
14:6 *scorner.* See 1:22 and note. *seeketh wisdom, and findeth it not.* Because he refuses to fear the Lord or accept any correction.
14:8 *folly of fools is deceit.* What a fool believes to be prudent (but is really folly) does not bring success; instead, it tends toward his ruin.
14:9 *among the righteous . . . favour.* See 11:27.
‡14:10 *knoweth his own bitterness.* See 1 Ki 8:38. Cf. the experience of Hannah (1 Sam 1:10) and Peter (Mat 26:75). *intermeddle with his joy.* Both sorrow and joy have a personal dimension that cannot be fully shared with another individual. Cf. Mat 13:44; 1 Pet 1:8.
14:11 See 10:25 and note.
14:12 *the end thereof are the ways of death.* See 5:4,23; 7:21–27; Mat 7:13–14.
‡14:13 *in laughter the heart is sorrowful.* One can never fully escape the harsh realities of life in a fallen world. Cf. Ezra 3:11–12. *end of that mirth is heaviness.* As the death of Rachel in childbirth (Gen 35:17–18).
14:14 See 1:31; 12:14 and notes; see also 11:5,8; 18:20; 22:8; Job 4:8.
‡14:15 *simple.* See note on 1:4. *looketh well to his going.* Approaches life with caution and discernment. See 4:26 and note; 21:29.
‡14:16 *feareth, and departeth from evil.* He avoids sin because he fears the consequences of his actions. See also notes on 1:7; 3:7. *rageth.* Cf. 21:24. *confident.* Has a presumptous confidence that causes him to be careless in words (12:18; 13:3) and actions (Judg 9:4).
‡14:17 *soon angry.* Quick-tempered. See Tit 1:7. *wicked devices.* Cf. 12:2; Job 5:12–13; 1 Cor 3:19.
14:18 *crowned with knowledge.* Adorned and blessed with knowledge (see note on 4:9; see also v. 24; 12:4; Ps 103:4).
14:19 *evil bow before the good.* Cf. 17:2. *at the gates of the righteous.* Perhaps to beg for some favor (cf. 1 Sam 2:36).
14:20 *hated even of his own neighbor.* And sometimes by his relatives (see 19:7).
14:21 *he that hath mercy on the poor, happy is he.* Sharing food (22:9), lending money (28:8) and defending rights (31:9) are ways one can show kindness. Such a person honors God (v. 31; cf. 17:5) and will lack nothing (28:27). Cf. 21:13; Ps 41:1.
14:22 *err.* See 5:23; 12:26. *devise evil.* See 3:29; 6:14,18; Mic 2:1. *mercy and truth . . . to them.* They receive the support and care of faithful friends (cf. 3:3; 16:6; 20:28)—perhaps God's support and care are also implied here.
14:23 *In all labour there is profit.* See note on 10:4; see also 21:5.
14:24 *crown of the wise is . . . riches.* The wise obtain wealth, and it adorns them like a crown (see 10:22).
14:25 See v. 5; 12:17; see also note on 6:19.

26 In the fear of the LORD *is* strong
confidence:
And his children shall have a place of
refuge.
27 [a]The fear of the LORD *is* a fountain of
life,
To depart from the snares of death.
28 In the multitude of people *is* the king's
honour:
But in the want of people *is* the
destruction of the prince.
29 [a]*He that is* slow to wrath *is* of great
understanding:
But *he that is* [1]hasty of spirit exalteth
folly.
30 A sound heart *is* the life of the flesh:
But [a]envy [b]the rottenness of the bones.
31 [a]He that oppresseth the poor
reproacheth [b]his Maker:
But he that honoureth him hath mercy
on the poor.
32 The wicked is driven away in his
wickedness:
But [a]the righteous hath hope in his
death.
33 Wisdom resteth in the heart of him
that hath understanding:
But [a]*that which is* in the midst of fools
is made known.
34 Righteousness exalteth a nation:
But sin *is* a reproach [1]to any people.
35 [a]The king's favour *is* toward a wise
servant:
But his wrath is *against* him that
causeth shame.

15 [a]A soft answer turneth away wrath:
But [b]grievous words stir up anger.
2 The tongue of the wise useth
knowledge aright:
[a]But the mouth of fools [1]poureth out
foolishness.
3 [a]The eyes of the LORD *are* in every
place,
Beholding the evil and the good.
4 [1]A wholesome tongue *is* a tree of life:
But perverseness therein *is* a breach in
the spirit.
5 [a]A fool despiseth his father's
instruction:
[b]But he that regardeth reproof is
prudent.
6 *In* the house of the righteous *is* much
treasure:
But in the revenues of the wicked *is*
trouble.
7 The lips of the wise disperse
knowledge:
But the heart of the foolish *doeth*
not so.
8 [a]The sacrifice of the wicked *is* an
abomination to the LORD:
But the prayer of the upright *is* his
delight.
9 The way of the wicked *is* an
abomination unto the LORD:
But he loveth him that [a]followeth after
righteousness.
10 [1]Correction *is* [a]grievous unto him that
forsaketh the way:
And [b]he that hateth reproof shall die.
11 [a]Hell and destruction *are* before the
LORD:
How much more then [b]the hearts of
the children of men?

14:27 [a]ch. 13:14
14:29 [1]Heb. *short of spirit* [a]Jas. 1:19
14:30 [a]Ps. 112:10 [b]ch. 12:4
14:31 [a]ch. 17:5; Mat. 25:40 [b]ch. 22:2
14:32 [a]Job 13:15; Ps. 23:4; 2 Cor. 1:9; 2 Tim. 4:18
14:33 [a]ch. 12:16
14:34 [1]Heb. *to nations*
14:35 [a]Mat. 24:45
15:1 [a]ch. 25:15 [b]1 Sam. 25:10
15:2 [1]Heb. *belcheth,* or, *bubbleth* [a]ch. 12:23
15:3 [a]Job 34:21; Heb. 4:13
15:4 [1]Heb. *The healing of the tongue*
15:5 [a]ch. 10:1 [b]ch. 13:18
15:8 [a]Is. 1:11; Jer. 6:20; Amos 5:22
15:9 [a]ch. 21:21; 1 Tim. 6:11
15:10 [1]Or, *Instruction* [a]1 Ki. 22:8 [b]ch. 5:12
15:11 [a]Job 26:6; Ps. 139:8 [b]2 Chr. 6:30; John 2:24

14:26 *fear of the LORD.* See 1:7; 3:7 and notes. *strong confidence . . . refuge.* Means either that the father's godliness will result in blessing for himself and his children (see 20:7) or that the "fear of the LORD" will be a strong tower where the children also can find refuge (see 18:10; Ps 71:7; Is 33:6).
14:27 See note on 10:11; see also 13:14.
14:29 *He that is slow to wrath.* See 15:18; 16:32; 19:11; Jas 1:19.
‡14:30 *life of the flesh.* Brings health to the body; cf. the healthy effects of fearing the Lord and walking in wisdom in 3:7–8, 16–18. *envy the rottenness of the bones.* Envy leaves physical and emotional scars. See note on 3:8; see also 12:4; Ps 37:7–8.
‡14:31 *reproacheth his Maker.* Because God created both the rich and the poor in His image (see 22:2; Job 31:15; Jas 3:9). *he that honoureth him hath mercy on the poor.* Practicing generosity honors God and in a sense is giving to God Himself (see 19:17; Mat 25:40). See note on v. 21.
14:32 *wicked is driven away.* See 1:26–27 and note; 11:5; 24:16. *righteous hath hope in his death.* His faith in God gives him hope beyond the grave (see note on 12:28; see also Ps 49:14–15; 73:24).
‡14:33 *that which is in the midst of fools is made known.* A foolish person's lack of wisdom is reflected in their words and actions.
‡14:34 *Righteousness exalteth a nation.* See note on 11:11. Israel was promised prosperity and prestige if she obeyed God's laws (see Deut 28:1–14). In the context of wisdom literature, this basic principle applies to all nations. *sin is a reproach to any people.* The Canaanites were driven out because of their terrible sin (Lev 18:24–25), and Israel later received the same curse (Deut 28:15–68; cf. 2 Sam 12:10).
14:35 *his wrath is against him.* See 16:14; 19:12; Dan 2:12.
15:1 *soft answer turneth away wrath.* Cf. the way Gideon calmed the anger of the men of Ephraim in Judg 8:1–3 (cf. also Prov 15:18; Eccl 10:4). *grievous words stirs up anger.* Nabal's sarcastic response put David in a fighting mood (1 Sam 25:10–13).
‡15:2 *poureth out foolishness.* See KJV marg. See also vv. 7, 28; 12:23; 13:16.
15:3 *eyes of the LORD are in every place.* See 5:21; Job 31:4; 34:21; Jer 16:17.
‡15:4 *wholesome tongue.* See note on 12:18. *tree of life.* See note on 3:18. *perverseness therein is a breach in the spirit.* Wicked speech hurts others, especially false testimony in court (see 6:19; 22:22), or slander in the community.
15:6 See 10:2,16,22 and notes. *much treasure.* See 8:18,21; 24:4; Zech 8:12; see also note on 3:10.
15:8 *sacrifice of the wicked is an abomination.* Those whose hearts are not right with God gain nothing by offering sacrifices (see 21:3,27; Eccl 5:1; Is 1:11–15; Jer 6:20). *prayer of the upright.* See 3:32.
15:9 *followeth after righteousness.* See 21:21; 1 Tim 6:11.
15:10 *the way.* The right path (see 2:13). *he that hateth reproof shall die.* See 5:12,23 and notes.
15:11 *Hell and destruction are before the LORD.* Not even the grave, the netherworld, is inaccessible to God (see Job 26:6; Ps 139:8). Therefore He knows the secrets of man's innermost being (cf. 1 Sam 16:7).

12 [a]A scorner loveth not one that reproveth him:
Neither will he go unto the wise.
13 [a]A merry heart maketh a cheerful countenance:
But [b]by sorrow of the heart the spirit *is* broken.
14 The heart of him that hath understanding seeketh knowledge:
But the mouth of fools feedeth on foolishness.
15 All the days of the afflicted *are* evil:
[a]But *he that is* of a merry heart *hath* a continual feast.
16 [a]Better *is* little with the fear of the LORD
Than great treasure and trouble therewith.
17 [a]Better *is* a dinner of herbs where love is,
Than a stalled ox and hatred therewith.
18 [a]A wrathful man stirreth up strife:
But *he that is* slow to anger appeaseth strife.
19 [a]The way of the slothful *man is* as a hedge of thorns:
But the way of the righteous [1]*is* made plain.
20 [a]A wise son maketh a glad father:
But a foolish man despiseth his mother.
21 [a]Folly *is* joy to *him that is* [1]destitute of wisdom:
[b]But a man of understanding walketh uprightly.
22 [a]Without counsel purposes *are* disappointed:
But in the multitude of counsellers *they* are established.
23 A man hath joy by the answer of his mouth:
And [a]a word *spoken* [1]in due season, how good *is it!*
24 [a]The way of life *is* above to the wise,
That *he* may depart from hell beneath.
25 [a]The LORD will destroy the house of the proud:
But [b]he will establish the border of the widow.
26 [a]The thoughts of the wicked *are* an abomination to the LORD:
[b]But *the words of* the pure *are* [1]pleasant words.
27 [a]He that is greedy of gain troubleth his own house;
But he that hateth gifts shall live.
28 The heart of the righteous [a]studieth to answer:
But the mouth of the wicked poureth out evil *things.*
29 [a]The LORD *is* far from the wicked:
But [b]he heareth the prayer of the righteous.
30 The light of the eyes rejoiceth the heart:
And a good report maketh the bones fat.
31 [a]The ear that heareth the reproof of life
Abideth among the wise.
32 He that refuseth [1]instruction despiseth his own soul:
But he that [2]heareth reproof [3]getteth understanding.
33 [a]The fear of the LORD *is* the instruction of wisdom;
And [b]before honour *is* humility.

15:12 [a]Amos 5:10; 2 Tim. 4:3
15:13 [a]ch. 17:22 [b]ch. 12:25
15:15 [a]ch. 17:22
15:16 [a]Ps. 37:16; 1 Tim. 6:6
15:17 [a]ch. 17:1
15:18 [a]ch. 26:21
15:19 [1]Heb. is *raised up as a causey* [a]ch. 22:5
15:20 [a]ch. 10:1
15:21 [1]Heb. *void of heart* [a]ch. 10:23 [b]Eph. 5:15
15:22 [a]ch. 11:14
15:23 [1]Heb. *in his season* [a]ch. 25:11
15:24 [a]Phil. 3:20; Col. 3:1,2
15:25 [a]ch. 12:7 [b]Ps. 68:5,6
15:26 [1]Heb. *words of pleasantness* [a]ch. 6:16,18 [b]Ps. 37:30
15:27 [a]Is. 5:8
15:28 [a]1 Pet. 3:15
15:29 [a]Ps. 10:1; 34:16 [b]Ps. 145:18
15:31 [a]ver. 5
15:32 [1]Or, *correction* [2]Or, *obeyeth* [3]Heb. *possesseth a heart*
15:33 [a]ch. 1:7 [b]ch. 18:12

15:12 See 1:30; 10:8; 13:1; 17:10. *scorner.* See note on 1:22.
15:13 *merry heart maketh a cheerful countenance.* Cf. 14:30. *by sorrow of the heart . . . spirit is broken.* Cf. the great sorrow of Job (Job 3) and David (Ps 51:8,10).
15:15 *he that is of a merry heart hath a continual feast.* Life is as joyful and satisfying as the days of a festival (see v. 13; 14:30; cf. Lev 23:39–41).
15:16 *great treasure and trouble.* The ill-gotten gains of 10:2.
‡15:17 *stalled ox.* A fattened cow. Such meat was something of a luxury, reserved for special occasions (cf. 7:14; Mat 22:4; Luke 15:23).
15:18 *stirreth up strife.* See note on 6:14. *slow to anger.* See 14:29; 16:32; 19:11; Jas 1:19.
‡15:19 *slothful.* See note on 6:6. *as a hedge of thorns.* Mainly because he was too lazy to remove them (see 24:30–31; Hos 2:6). *way . . . made plain.* Lit. "lifted up" like a smooth path or highway, meaning that the upright are able to make progress and reach their goals (see note on 3:6).
15:20 See 10:1 and note.
15:21 A variation of 10:23.
15:22 See the close parallel in 11:14; 20:18; 24:6.
‡15:23 *answer of his mouth.* When he speaks in the right way; cf. Is 50:4. *word . . . due season, how good is it!* Cf. 24:26.
15:24 *is above.* Leads upward along the highway (v. 19), the straight course (v. 21) that leads to life. *he may depart from hell beneath.* See note on 2:18.
15:25 *destroy the house of the proud.* See 2:22; 14:11; see also 10:25 and note. *establish the border of the widow.* In ancient times boundary stones marked a person's property. Anyone who moved such a stone was, in effect, stealing land (see 22:28; Job 24:2; Ps 68:5; see also Deut 19:14 and note).
15:26 *thoughts of the wicked are an abomination.* Cf. vv. 8–9. *words of the pure are pleasant words.* See 22:11; Ps 24:4.
15:27 *He that is greedy of gain troubleth his own house.* See 1:19; 11:29; 28:25. Achan's whole family perished because of his greed at Jericho (Josh 7:24–26). *he that hateth gifts shall llive.* Referring to bribes. See 17:8; 28:16; Deut 16:19; 1 Sam 12:3; Eccl 7:7; 1 Tim 6:10.
‡15:28 *studieth to answer.* Thinks before speaking; cf. 10:32; 1 Pet 3:15. *poureth out evil things.* See v. 2; see also v. 7; 12:23.
15:29 *far from the wicked.* See 1:28 and note.
‡15:30 *The light of the eyes rejoiceth the heart.* A cheerful attitude brings joy. Cf. v. 13; 16:15; Job 29:24. *a good report maketh the bones fat.* See 3:8 and note; see also Phil 2:19.
15:31 *The ear that heareth the reproof of life.* See 1:23; 6:23 and note.
15:32 *He that refuseth instruction despiseth his own soul.* See note on 5:12; see also 1:7; 5:23; 8:36. *he that heareth reproof.* Cf. vv. 5,31.
15:33 *fear of the LORD.* See note on 1:7. *before honour is humility.* See 22:24; 25:6–7; Mat 23:12; Luke 14:11; 18:14; 1 Pet 5:6. Wisdom also comes with humility (11:2; 13:10).

16 The [a] [1] preparations of the heart in man,
[b] And the answer of the tongue, *is* from the LORD.
2 [a] All the ways of a man *are* clean in his own eyes;
But [b] the LORD weigheth the spirits.
3 [a] [1] Commit thy works unto the LORD,
And thy thoughts shall be established.
4 [a] The LORD hath made all *things* for himself:
[b] Yea, even the wicked for the day of evil.
5 [a] Every one *that is* proud in heart *is* an abomination to the LORD:
[b] *Though* hand *join* in hand, he shall not be [1] unpunished.
6 [a] By mercy and truth iniquity is purged:
And [b] by the fear of the LORD *men* depart from evil.
7 When a man's ways please the LORD,
He maketh even his enemies to be at peace with him.
8 [a] Better *is* a little with righteousness
Than great revenues without right.
9 [a] A man's heart deviseth his way:
[b] But the LORD directeth his steps.
10 [1] A divine sentence *is* in the lips of the king:
His mouth transgresseth not in judgment.

16:1 [1] Or, *disposings* [a] Jer. 10:23 [b] Mat. 10:19
16:2 [a] ch. 21:2 [b] 1 Sam. 16:7
16:3 [1] Heb. *Roll* [a] Ps. 37:5
16:4 [a] Is. 43:7 [b] Job 21:30
16:5 [1] Heb. *held innocent* [a] ch. 8:13 [b] ch. 11:21
16:6 [a] Dan. 4:27 [b] ch. 14:16
16:8 [a] Ps. 37:16
16:9 [a] ch. 19:21 [b] Jer. 10:23
16:10 [1] Heb. *Divination*

16:11 [1] Heb. *All the stones* [a] Lev. 19:36
16:12 [a] ch. 25:5
16:13 [a] ch. 14:35
16:14 [a] ch. 19:12
16:15 [a] ch. 19:12 [b] Job 29:23
16:16 [a] ch. 8:11, 19
16:20 [1] Or, *He that understandeth a matter*

11 [a] A just weight and balance *are* the LORD'S:
[1] All the weights of the bag *are* his work.
12 *It is* an abomination to kings to commit wickedness:
For [a] the throne is established by righteousness.
13 [a] Righteous lips *are* the delight of kings;
And *they* love him that speaketh right.
14 [a] The wrath of a king *is as* messengers of death:
But a wise man will pacify it.
15 In the light of the king's countenance *is* life;
And [a] his favour *is* [b] as a cloud of the latter rain.
16 [a] How much better *is it* to get wisdom than gold!
And to get understanding rather to be chosen than silver!
17 The highway of the upright *is* to depart from evil:
He that keepeth his way preserveth his soul.
18 Pride *goeth* before destruction,
And a haughty spirit before a fall.
19 Better *it is to be* of an humble spirit with the lowly,
Than to divide the spoil with the proud.
20 [1] He that handleth a matter wisely shall find good:

16:1 *the answer of the tongue, is from the LORD.* God must give the ability to articulate and accomplish those plans (cf. 19:21).
‡16:2 *are clean.* See 14:12. *the LORD weigheth the spirits.* God examines the motives behind the actions. See 24:12; Ps 139:23; 1 Cor 4:4–5; Heb 4:12.
‡16:3 *Commit.* See 1 Pet 5:7. *thy thoughts shall be established.* Goals and plans will be reached (see 3:5–6 and notes; Ps 1:3; 55:22; 90:17).
‡16:4 *hath made all things for himself.* God is sovereign in every life and in all of history (see Eccl 7:14; Rom 8:28). *the wicked for the day of evil.* Even through wicked men God displays His power (cf. Ex 9:16), and all evil will be judged (cf. Ezek 38:22–23; Rom 2:5–11). The passage is not teaching that God is the author or creator of evil.
16:5 See 11:20–21 and notes.
‡16:6 *By mercy and truth iniquity is purged.* The moral quality of conduct that God desires is sometimes summed up by two Hebrew terms often translated as "mercy and truth" (3:3; Hos 4:1). When His people repent of sin and bring their lives into accord with His will, God forgives and withdraws His judgment (see Is 1:18–19; 55:7; Jer 3:22; Ezek 18:23,30–32; 33:11–12, 14–16; Hos 14:1–2,4). Thus it can be said that mercy and truth, in a manner of speaking, "purge" sin, i.e. they turn away God's wrath against it. *fear of the LORD.* See note on 1:7.
16:7 *maketh even his enemies to be at peace with him.* As in the reigns of godly Asa and Jehoshaphat (2 Chr 14:6–7; 17:10). *peace.* See 3:17 and note; Rom 12:18; Heb 12:14.
16:8 See 10:2 and note.
16:9 *the LORD directeth his steps.* Verses 1,3–4 (see notes) also emphasize God's control of men's lives (see 19:21; 20:24; Ps 37:23; Jer 10:23).
16:10 *divine sentence . . . lips of the king.* In judging cases brought before him, a king functioned as God's representative (see Deut 1:17). Therefore he needed the divine gift of wisdom to discern between right and wrong in order to render God's judgment (see 1 Ki 3:9). When he did so, his judgment was tantamount to a divine oracle for the people (see 1 Ki 3:28; see also 2 Sam 14:17,20; 19:27).
16:11 See note on 11:1. *just weight and balance . . . the LORD's.* Cf. 21:2; 24:12; Job 6:2; 31:6. *All the weights of the bag.* Merchants carried stones of different sizes with them to weigh and measure quantities of silver for payment (cf. Mic 6:11).
16:12 *throne is established by righteousness.* When the king "faithfully judgeth the poor" (29:14), refuses to take bribes (29:4) and removes any wicked advisers (25:5). See 14:34; Deut 17:19–20; Is 16:5; Rom 13:3.
16:13 *Righteous lips.* Rather than flattering lips (cf. 20:28).
16:14 *messengers of death.* Any angry king can pronounce death quickly and effectively (see 19:12; Esth 7:7–10; Mat 22:7; Luke 19:27). *wise man will pacify it.* Cf. Daniel's response to the rage of Nebuchadnezzar (Dan 2:12–16).
‡16:15 *light of the king's countenance.* Referring to the king's favorable disposition toward a person. Cf. Num 6:25. *his favor is as a cloud of the latter rain.* The spring rain was essential for the full development of barley and wheat; it was therefore a sign of good things to come. Cf. the "dew" of 19:12; see Ps 72:6.
16:16 See 3:14 and note; 8:10,19.
16:17 *highway of the upright.* See note on 15:19. *depart from evil.* Cf. the thorns and snares in the paths of the wicked (22:5).
16:18 See 11:2 and note.
16:19 *Better it is to be of an humble spirit.* See 3:34; Is 57:15; Mat 5:3. *divide the spoil with the proud.* See 1:13–14; Judg 5:30.
16:20 *find good.* See 13:13 and note. *whoso trusteth in the LORD, happy is he.* See v. 3; 3:5–6; 28:25; Ps 34:8; 37:4–5.

And whoso [a]trusteth in the LORD,
happy *is* he.
21 The wise in heart shall be called
prudent:
And the sweetness of the lips
increaseth learning.
22 [a]Understanding *is* a wellspring of life
unto him that hath it:
But the instruction of fools *is* folly.
23 The heart of the wise [1]teacheth his
mouth,
And addeth learning to his lips.
24 Pleasant words *are as* a honeycomb,
Sweet to the soul, and health to the
bones.
25 [a]There is a way that seemeth right
unto a man,
But the end thereof *are* the ways of
death.
26 [a] [1]He that laboureth laboureth for
himself;
For his mouth [2]craveth it of him.
27 [1]An ungodly man diggeth up evil:
And in his lips *there is* as a burning fire.
28 [a]A froward man [1]soweth strife:
And [b]a whisperer separateth chief
friends.
29 A violent man [a]enticeth his neighbour,
And leadeth him into the way *that is*
not good.
30 He shutteth his eyes to devise froward
things:
Moving his lips he bringeth evil to pass.
31 [a]The hoary head *is* a crown of glory,
If it be found in the way of
righteousness.

16:20 [a]Ps. 34:8
16:22 [a]ch. 13:14
16:23 [1]Heb. *maketh wise*
16:25 [a]ch. 14:12
16:26 [1]Heb. *The soul of him that laboureth* [2]Heb. *boweth unto him* [a]Eccl. 6:7
16:27 [1]Heb. *A man of Belial*
16:28 [1]Heb. *sendeth forth* [a]ch. 15:18 [b]ch. 17:9
16:29 [a]ch. 1:10
16:31 [a]ch. 20:29
16:32 [a]ch. 19:11
17:1 [1]Or, *good cheer* [a]ch. 15:17
17:2 [a]ch. 10:5
17:3 [a]Jer. 17:10
17:5 [1]Heb. *held innocent* [a]ch. 14:31
17:7 [1]Heb. *A lip of excellency* [2]Heb. *a lip of lying*
17:8 [1]Heb. *a stone of grace*

32 [a]*He that is* slow to anger *is* better than
the mighty;
And he that ruleth his spirit than he
that taketh a city.
33 The lot is cast into the lap;
But the whole disposing thereof *is* of
the LORD.

17 Better *is* [a]a dry morsel, and
quietness therewith,
Than a house full *of* [1]sacrifices with
strife.
2 A wise servant shall have rule over [a]a
son that causeth shame,
And shall have part of the inheritance
among the brethren.
3 The fining pot *is* for silver, and the
furnace for gold:
[a]But the LORD trieth the hearts.
4 A wicked doer giveth heed to false lips;
And a liar giveth ear to a naughty
tongue.
5 [a]Whoso mocketh the poor reproacheth
his Maker:
And he that is glad at calamities shall
not be [1]unpunished.
6 Children's children *are* the crown of
old men;
And the glory of children *are* their
fathers.
7 [1]Excellent speech becometh not a fool:
Much less do [2]lying lips a prince.
8 A gift *is as* [1]a precious stone in the
eyes of him that hath it:
Whithersoever it turneth, it
prospereth.

‡16:21 *sweetness of the lips increaseth learning.* People are more willing to listen to someone who uses pleasant speech. Cf. the last line of v. 23. "Sweetness" is expanded in v. 24. Cf. the persuasive but destructive words of the adulteress in 7:21.
16:22 *wellspring of life.* See note on 10:11. *instruction of fools.* See 13:13 and note; see also 7:22; 13:15; 15:10.
16:23 *teacheth his mouth.* See 22:17–18.
16:24 *Pleasant words are as a honeycomb.* They are good for you (see 24:13–14), and they taste good (cf. 2:10; Ps 19:10). *health to the bones.* See notes on 4:22; 12:18; 15:30. *bones.* See note on 3:8.
16:25 *end thereof are the ways of death.* See 5:4,23; 7:21–27; Mat 7:13–14.
16:26 Cf. 2 Thes 3:10: ". . . if any would not work, neither should he eat"; see also Eccl 6:7; Eph 4:28.
16:27 *ungodly man.* See 6:12 and note; see also note on Deut 13:13. *diggeth up evil.* See 3:29; 6:14; Mic 2:1. *burning fire.* His speech is inflammatory and destructive (see Jas 3:6).
‡16:28 *soweth strife.* See note on 6:14. *whisperer.* One who whispers slander and gossip about others. See 11:13.
‡16:30 *shutteth his eyes.* His winking eye signals his insincerity. See note on 6:13. *Moving his lips.* Thereby making insinuations (see note on 6:12–14).
‡16:31 *hoary head is a crown of glory.* The gray-haired person. The elderly were to receive deep respect (see Lev 19:32). *in the way of righteousness.* See 3:1–2,16.
16:32 *that is slow to anger is . . . mighty.* See 14:29; 15:18; 19:11; Jas 1:19. "Wisdom is better than weapons of war" (Eccl 9:18). *he that ruleth his spirit than he that taketh a city.* Although one who practices patience and self-control receives far less attention and acclaim than a warrior who takes a city, he accomplishes better things.
16:33 *The lot is cast into the lap.* Here the lot may have been several pebbles held in the fold of a garment and then drawn out or shaken to the ground. It was commonly used to make decisions (see notes on Ex 28:30; Num 26:53; Neh 11:1; Jonah 1:7; Acts 1:26; see also Ps 22:18). *the whole disposing thereof is of the LORD.* God, not chance, is in control (see vv. 1,3–4,9).
17:2 *A wise servant shall have rule over a son.* See 11:29 and note. *son that causeth shame.* See 10:5; 19:26; 28:7; 29:15.
17:3 *The fining pot . . . the furnace.* Silver and gold were refined to remove their impurities (cf. Is 1:25; Mal 3:3). *trieth the hearts.* See 15:11; 16:2 and notes; Jer 17:10.
17:5 *Whoso mocketh the poor reproacheth his Maker.* See 14:31 and note. *he that is glad at calamities shall not be unpunished.* The people of Edom in particular were condemned for gloating over the collapse of "brother" Israel ("Jacob," Obad 10; see Ezek 35:12,15; see also Prov 24:17).
17:6 *crown of old men.* Cf. the "hoary head" of 16:31. To live to see one's grandchildren was considered a great blessing (see Gen 48:11; Ps 128:5–6). *the glory of children are their fathers.* See Gen 47:7.
17:7 For the structure of this verse cf. 19:10; 26:1. *lying lips a prince.* His right to rule depends on honesty and justice (see 12:22; 16:12–13).
‡17:8 *A gift is as a precious stone.* Greed brings people under the influence of bribery, a sad commentary on human behavior (see 18:16; 21:14; Eccl 10:19). Elsewhere, bribes are condemned

9 [a]He that covereth a transgression
[1]seeketh love;
But [b]he that repeateth a matter
separateth very friends.
10 [1]A reproof entereth more into a wise
man
Than an hundred stripes into a fool.
11 An evil *man* seeketh only rebellion:
Therefore a cruel messenger shall be
sent against him.
12 *Let* [a]a bear robbed of her whelps meet
a man,
Rather than a fool in his folly.
13 Whoso [a]rewardeth evil for good,
Evil shall not depart from his house.
14 The beginning of strife *is as* when one
letteth out water:
Therefore [a]leave off contention, before
it be meddled with.
15 [a]He that justifieth the wicked, and he
that condemneth the just,
Even they both *are* abomination to the
LORD.
16 Wherefore *is there* a price in the hand
of a fool
To get wisdom, [a]seeing *he hath* no
heart *to it?*
17 [a]A friend loveth at all times,
And a brother is born for adversity.
18 [a]A man void of [1]understanding
striketh hands,
And becometh surety in the presence
of his friend.
19 He loveth transgression that loveth
strife:
And [a]he that exalteth his gate seeketh
destruction.
20 [1]He that hath a froward heart findeth
no good:
And he that hath [a]a perverse tongue
falleth into mischief.
21 [a]He that begetteth a fool *doeth it* to his
sorrow:
And the father of a fool hath no joy.
22 [a]A merry heart doeth good [1]*like* a
medicine:
[b]But a broken spirit drieth the bones.
23 A wicked *man* taketh a gift out of the
bosom
[a]To pervert the ways of judgment.
24 [a]Wisdom *is* before him that hath
understanding;
But the eyes of a fool *are* in the ends of
the earth.
25 [a]A foolish son *is* a grief to his father,
And bitterness to her that bare him.
26 Also [a]to punish the just *is* not good,
Nor to strike princes for equity.
27 [a]He that hath knowledge spareth his
words:
And a man of understanding is of [1]an
excellent spirit.
28 [a]Even a fool, when he holdeth his
peace, is counted wise:
And he that shutteth his lips *is*
esteemed a man of understanding.

18 [1]Through desire a man, having
separated himself, seeketh
And intermeddleth with all wisdom.
2 A fool hath no delight in understanding,
But that his heart may discover itself.

17:9 [1]Or, *procureth* [a]ch. 10:12 [b]ch. 16:28
17:10 [1]Or, *A reproof aweth more a wise* man, *than to strike a fool an hundred* times
17:12 [a]Hos. 13:8
17:13 [a]Ps. 109:4,5; Jer. 18:20
17:14 [a]ch. 20:3
17:15 [a]Ex. 23:7; Is. 5:23
17:16 [a]ch. 21:25,26
17:17 [a]Ruth 1:16
17:18 [1]Heb. *heart* [a]ch. 6:1
17:19 [a]ch. 16:18
17:20 [1]Heb. *The froward of heart* [a]Jas. 3:8
17:21 [a]ch. 10:1
17:22 [1]Or, *to a medicine* [a]ch. 12:25 [b]Ps. 22:15
17:23 [a]Ex. 23:8
17:24 [a]Eccl. 2:14
17:25 [a]ch. 10:1
17:26 [a]ch. 18:5
17:27 [1]Or, *a cool spirit* [a]Jas. 1:19
17:28 [a]Job 13:5
18:1 [1]Or, *He that separateth himself seeketh according to* his *desire,* And *intermeddleth in every business*

(see v. 23; 15:27; 28:16; Deut 16:19; 1 Sam 12:3; Eccl 7:7; Is 1:23; Amos 5:12; 1 Tim 6:10).

17:9 *He that covereth a transgression seeketh love.* See 10:12 and note.

‡17:10 *reproof entereth more into a wise man.* One only has to speak to get the attention of a wise person. See 9:8–9. *an hundred stripes into a fool.* Fools deserved and received flogging (cf. 10:13; 19:25,29; 26:3; Deut 25:3).

17:11 *cruel messenger.* Cf. the dispatching of Abishai and Joab to end Sheba's rebellion against David (2 Sam 20:1–22; see 1 Ki 2:25,29,46; Prov 16:14).

17:12 *bear robbed of her whelps.* Sure to attack you and rip you open (see 2 Sam 17:8; Hos 13:8; cf. the raging of the fool in 29:9).

17:13 *rewardeth evil for good.* Like Nabal, who refused to pay David's men (1 Sam 25:21; see Ps 109:5; Rom 12:17–21). *Evil shall not depart from his house.* The fate of David's family after his affair with Bathsheba and the murder of Uriah (2 Sam 12:10; cf. Jer 18:20–23).

17:15 *justifieth the wicked.* Perhaps because of a bribe (see v. 8; 24:24).

17:16 *price in the hand of a fool.* Perhaps to pay the fee for his schooling.

17:17 *friend loveth at all times.* Cf. David's friendship with Jonathan (2 Sam 1:26; see 18:24; Ruth 1:16; 1 Cor 13:4–7).

17:18 See 6:1 and note.

17:19 *He loveth transgression that loveth strife.* A hot-tempered man commits many sins (29:22). *exalteth his gate.* Out of pride (cf. 16:18; 29:23). Or "gate" (lit. "opening") in this context may be a figure for the mouth ("he who opens his mouth wide"), meaning "he brags too much" and so "seeketh destruction," including his own.

17:20 *findeth no good.* Contrast 16:20. *perverse tongue.* See note on 2:12.

17:21 *sorrow . . . no joy.* See v. 25; 19:13.

17:22 *merry heart.* See 14:30; 15:13,30; 16:15; Job 29:24. *broken spirit drieth the bones.* See note on 3:8; see also 12:4; 14:30; Ps 32:3; 37:7–8.

‡17:23 *taketh a gift.* Receives a bribe. See note on v. 8.

17:24 *are in the ends of the earth.* He chases fantasies and is interested in everything except wisdom (see 12:11; cf. Deut 30:11–14).

17:25 See v. 21. *bitterness.* See 14:10 and note.

17:26 *punish the just.* See v. 15 and note. *strike princes.* Cf. the beating and disgrace endured by Jeremiah (Jer 20:2; see v. 10 and note).

‡17:27 *spareth his words.* See 10:19. *an excellent spirit.* Not a "hot-tempered" person (see KJV marg.). See also 16:32.

‡17:28 *a fool, when he holdeth his peace, is counted wise.* A fool who keeps quiet does not expose his lack of wisdom. Cf. Job's sarcastic comment in Job 13:5.

‡18:1 *Through desire a man, having separated himself.* Refers to a person who alienates himself from others because of his selfish desires. *intermeddleth with all wisdom.* The selfish person rejects wisdom and has an argumentative spirit.

‡18:2 *no delight . . . But that his heart may discover itself.* The fool has no desire for wisdom but is only driven by the selfish desires of his heart. Cf. Eccl 10:3.

3 When the wicked cometh, *then*
cometh also contempt,
And with ignominy reproach.
4 [a]The words of a man's mouth *are as*
deep waters,
[b]*And* the wellspring of wisdom *as* a
flowing brook.
5 [a]*It is* not good to accept the person of
the wicked,
To overthrow the righteous in
judgment.
6 A fool's lips enter into contention,
And his mouth calleth for strokes.
7 [a]A fool's mouth *is* his destruction,
And his lips *are* the snare of his soul.
8 [a]The words of a [1]talebearer *are* [2]as
wounds,
And they go down *into* the [3]innermost
parts of the belly.
9 He also that is slothful in his work
Is [a]brother to him that is a great waster.
10 [a]The name of the LORD *is* a strong
tower:
The righteous runneth into it, and [1]is
safe.
11 [a]The rich *man's* wealth *is* his strong
city,
And as a high wall in his own conceit.
12 [a]Before destruction the heart of man is
haughty,
And before honour *is* humility.
13 He that [1]answereth a matter [a]before
he heareth *it,*
It *is* folly and shame unto him.
14 The spirit of a man will sustain his
infirmity;
But a wounded spirit who can bear?
15 The heart of the prudent getteth
knowledge;

18:4 [a]ch. 10:11 [b]Jas. 3:17
18:5 [a]Lev. 19:15
18:7 [a]ch. 10:14
18:8 [1]Or, *whisperer* [2]Or, *like as when* men *are wounded* [3]Heb. *chambers* [a]ch. 12:18
18:9 [a]ch. 28:24
18:10 [1]Heb. *is set aloft* [a]2 Sam. 22:3
18:11 [a]ch. 10:15
18:12 [a]ch. 16:18
18:13 [1]Heb. *returneth a word* [a]John 7:51
18:16 [a]Gen. 32:20; 1 Sam. 25:27
18:20 [a]ch. 12:14
18:21 [a]Mat. 12:37
18:22 [a]ch. 31:10
18:23 [a]Jas. 2:3
18:24 [a]ch. 17:17
19:1 [a]ch. 28:6

And the ear of the wise seeketh
knowledge.
16 [a]A man's gift maketh room for him,
And bringeth him before great *men.*
17 *He that is* first in his own cause
seemeth just;
But his neighbour cometh and
searcheth him.
18 The lot causeth contentions to cease,
And parteth between the mighty.
19 A brother offended *is harder to be won*
than a strong city:
And *their* contentions *are* like the bars
of a castle.
20 [a]A man's belly shall be satisfied with
the fruit of his mouth;
And with the increase of his lips shall
he be filled.
21 [a]Death and life *are* in the power of the
tongue:
And they that love it shall eat the fruit
thereof.
22 [a]*Whoso* findeth a wife findeth a good
thing,
And obtaineth favour of the LORD.
23 The poor useth intreaties;
But the rich answereth [a]roughly.
24 A man that hath friends must shew
himself friendly:
[a]And there is a friend *that* sticketh
closer than a brother.

19 Better [a]*is* the poor that walketh in
his integrity,
Than *he that is* perverse in his lips,
and *is* a fool.
2 Also, *that* the soul *be* without
knowledge, *it is* not good;
And he that hasteth with *his* feet,
sinneth.

18:3 *contempt . . . ignominy reproach.* Cf. 3:35; 6:33; 10:5; 11:2; Ps 31:17; Is 22:18.
18:4 *deep waters.* Profound or obscure (cf. 20:5). *wellspring of wisdom as a flowing brook.* A wise man's words are refreshing and a source of life (see 1:23; 13:14; see also 10:11 and note).
‡18:5 *to accept the person of the wicked.* To show partiality to the ungodly person. See 17:15 and note. Favoritism of any kind was condemned in the law (see Lev 19:15; Deut 1:17; 16:19). *To overthrow the righteous in judgment.* See 17:26; 31:5; Mal 3:5.
18:6 *contention.* A fool is quick to quarrel (see 17:14,19; 20:3). *calleth for strokes.* By a rod on his back (see 10:13; 19:29).
18:7 See 10:14 and note.
‡18:8 *words of a talebearer.* Words of a gossip are as pleasant as a wise man's words (cf. 16:21,23), but they promote dissension (see 11:13; 26:20,22). *as wounds.* Lit. "as bits greedily swallowed." Gossip is like tasty food but has disastrous consequences. *they go down into the innermost parts of the belly.* Where they are thoroughly digested and so are carried about and live on and on.
18:9 *He . . . that is slothful in his work.* See 10:4 and note.
18:10 *name of the LORD.* The "name" equals the person, since it expresses his nature and qualities (see Ex 3:14–15 and notes). *strong tower.* See Ps 18:2; 91:2; 144:2. *safe.* See 29:25; Ps 27:5.
18:11 *wealth is his strong city.* Identical to 10:15 (see note there). *high wall.* But God can bring it down (see Is 25:12).
18:12 See 15:33 and note.
18:14 See 15:13; 17:22 and notes.
18:16 *A man's gift maketh room for him.* A reference to the effectiveness of a bribe (see note on 17:8).
18:17 A warning to judges to hear both sides of a case (cf. Deut 1:16), but applicable to many situations.
‡18:18 *The lot causeth contentions to cease.* Reaching a decision through the casting of lots was one way of settling a dispute. See note on 16:33. Cf. Mat 27:35.
18:19 *A brother offended.* Cf. Esau's anger because of the blessing Jacob received from Isaac (Gen 27:41).
18:20 See 12:14 and note.
18:21 *Death and life are in the power of the tongue.* See note on 13:3. *fruit.* See v. 20.
18:22 *Whoso findeth a wife findeth a good thing.* See 12:4 and note; 19:14. *obtaineth favour of the LORD.* Identical to 8:35, where finding wisdom brought such favor.
‡18:24 *A man that hath friends must shew himself friendly.* Lit. "a man of many [companions] comes to ruin." One must choose friends carefully (see 12:26 and note; 17:17). *a friend that sticketh closer than a brother.* True friends do not turn away in tough times. It is better to have a true friend than many false friends.
19:1 *in his integrity.* See note on 2:7. *Than he that is perverse.* Even if he becomes rich (see 28:6).
‡19:2 *be without knowledge.* Cf. Rom 10:2. *hasteth with his feet.* Haste can lead to poverty (21:5) or folly (29:20).

3 The foolishness of man perverteth his
way:
[a]And his heart fretteth against the LORD.
4 [a]Wealth maketh many friends;
But the poor is separated from his
neighbour.
5 [a]A false witness shall not be
[1]unpunished,
And *he that* speaketh lies shall not
escape.
6 [a]Many will intreat the favour of the
prince:
And [b]every *man is* a friend to [1]him
that giveth gifts.
7 [a]All the brethren of the poor do hate
him:
How much more do his friends go [b]far
from him!
He pursueth *them with* words, *yet* they
are wanting *to him.*
8 He that getteth [1]wisdom loveth his
own soul:
He that keepeth understanding [a]shall
find good.
9 [a]A false witness shall not be
unpunished,
And *he that* speaketh lies shall perish.
10 Delight *is* not seemly for a fool;
Much less [a]for a servant to have rule
over princes.
11 [a]The [1]discretion of a man deferreth his
anger;
[b]And *it is* his glory to pass over a
transgression.
12 [a]The king's wrath *is* as the roaring of a
lion;
But his favour *is* [b]as dew upon the grass.
13 [a]A foolish son *is* the calamity of his
father:
[b]And the contentions of a wife *are* a
continual dropping.
14 [a]House and riches *are* the inheritance
of fathers:

19:3 [a]Ps. 37:7
19:4 [a]ch. 14:20
19:5 [1]Heb. *held innocent* [a]Ex. 23:1
19:6 [1]Heb. *a man of gifts* [a]ch. 29:26 [b]ch. 17:8
19:7 [a]ch. 14:20 [b]Ps. 38:11
19:8 [1]Heb. *a heart* [a]ch. 16:20
19:9 [a]ver. 5
19:10 [a]ch. 30:22
19:11 [1]Or, *prudence* [a]Jas. 1:19 [b]ch. 16:32
19:12 [a]ch. 16:14 [b]Hos. 14:5
19:13 [a]ch. 10:1 [b]ch. 21:9,19
19:14 [a]2 Cor. 12:14 [b]ch. 18:22
19:15 [a]ch. 6:9 [b]ch. 10:4
19:16 [a]Luke 10:28
19:17 [1]Or, *his deed* [a]2 Cor. 9:6
19:18 [1]Or, *to his destruction:* or, *to cause him to die* [a]ch. 13:24
19:19 [1]Heb. *add*
19:20 [a]Ps. 37:37
19:21 [a]Heb. 6:17
19:23 [a]1 Tim. 4:8
19:24 [a]ch. 15:19
19:25 [1]Heb. *will be cunning* [a]Deut. 13:11 [b]ch. 9:8
19:26 [a]ch. 17:2

And [b]a prudent wife *is* from the LORD.
15 [a]Slothfulness casteth into a deep sleep;
And an idle soul shall [b]suffer hunger.
16 [a]He that keepeth the commandment
keepeth his own soul;
But he that despiseth his ways shall die.
17 [a]He that hath pity upon the poor
lendeth unto the LORD;
And [1]that which he hath given will he
pay him again.
18 [a]Chasten thy son while there is hope,
And let not thy soul spare [1]for his
crying.
19 *A man* of great wrath *shall* suffer
punishment:
For if thou deliver *him,* yet thou must
[1]do *it* again.
20 Hear counsel, and receive instruction,
That thou mayest be wise [a]in thy latter
end.
21 *There are* many devices in a man's
heart;
[a]Nevertheless the counsel of the LORD,
that shall stand.
22 The desire of a man *is* his kindness:
And a poor *man is* better than a liar.
23 [a]The fear of the LORD *tendeth* to life:
And *he that hath it* shall abide
satisfied;
He shall not be visited *with* evil.
24 [a]A slothful *man* hideth his hand in *his*
bosom,
And will not so much as bring it to his
mouth again.
25 Smite a scorner, and the simple [a][1]will
beware:
And [b]reprove one that hath
understanding, *and* he will
understand knowledge.
26 He that wasteth *his* father, *and* chaseth
away *his* mother,
Is [a]a son that causeth shame, and
bringeth reproach.

‡19:3 *his heart fretteth against the LORD.* Rages in anger as he blames God for his troubles (see Gen 4:5; Is 8:21; cf. Lam 3:39).
19:4 See v. 7; 14:20.
19:5 See 6:19 and note.
19:6 *intreat the favour.* Cf. Job 11:19. *friend to him that giveth gifts.* Generosity (v. 4) or bribery (18:16) could be in view.
19:7 *brethren of the poor do hate him.* See v. 4; 14:20; Job 19:19; Ps 38:11.
19:8 *loveth his own soul.* Cf. 8:35–36. *shall find good.* See 13:13 and note.
19:10 *Delight is not seemly for a fool.* Nor is honor (26:1). *for a servant to have rule over princes.* Because of his lack of wisdom and tendency to become a tyrant (see 17:2; 29:2; Is 3:4).
19:11 *deferreth his anger.* See 14:29; 15:18; 16:32; Eccl 7:9; Jas 1:19. *pass over a transgression.* He has good self-control (see 12:16; 29:11; 2 Sam 16:11–12).
19:12 *The king's wrath is as the roaring of a lion.* See 16:14 and note. *his favour is as dew.* See 16:15 and note.
19:13 *foolish son.* See 17:21,25. *contentions of a wife.* Also denounced in 21:9,19; 25:24; 27:15. Stirring up dissension is condemned throughout Proverbs (see 6:14 and note).
19:14 *prudent wife.* See 12:4 and note; see also 18:22.
19:15 See 6:11; 10:4 and notes.
19:16 See 13:13; 15:10; 16:17 and notes.
19:17 *hath pity upon the poor.* See note on 14:21; see also 14:31. *lendeth unto the LORD.* The Lord regards it as a gift to Him (cf. Mat 25:40).
‡19:18 *Chasten thy son . . . spare for his crying.* False pity should not keep a parent from disciplining a child.
19:19 *man of great wrath.* Cf. 14:16–17,29; 15:18.
19:21 See 16:1,9 and notes.
‡19:22 *The desire of a man is his kindness.* A good-hearted person desires to practice kindness to others, but such goodness is difficult to find (cf. 3:3; 14:22). *a poor man is better than a liar.* See vv. 1,28; 6:12.
19:23 *fear of the LORD.* See note on 1:7. *tendeth to life.* See note on 10:11. *visited with evil.* See 3:2; 14:26 and notes.
19:24 *slothful man.* See note on 6:6.
19:25 *Smite a scorner.* See v. 29; 14:3; see also notes on 1:22; 17:10. *simple.* Not to be confused with the mocker (see note on 1:4).
‡19:26 *wasteth his father, and chaseth away his mother.* They steal from and are abusive toward their parents. Children were expected to take care of their parents when they were sick or

27 Cease, my son, to hear the instruction
That causeth to err from the words of
knowledge.
28 [1] An ungodly witness scorneth
judgment:
And [a] the mouth of the wicked
devoureth iniquity.
29 Judgments are prepared for scorners,
[a] And stripes for the back of fools.

20 Wine [a] *is* a mocker, strong drink *is*
raging:
And whosoever is deceived thereby is
not wise.
2 [a] The fear of a king *is* as the roaring of
a lion:
Whoso provoketh him to anger
[b] sinneth *against* his own soul.
3 [a] *It is* an honour for a man to cease
from strife:
But every fool will be meddling.
4 [a] The sluggard will not plow by reason
of the [1] cold;
[b] Therefore shall he beg in harvest, and
have nothing.
5 Counsel in the heart of man *is like*
deep water;
But a man of understanding will draw
it out.
6 [a] Most men will proclaim every one his
own [1] goodness:
But [b] a faithful man who can find?
7 [a] The just *man* walketh in his integrity:
[b] His children *are* blessed after him.
8 [a] A king that sitteth in the throne of
judgment
Scattereth *away* all evil with his eyes.
9 [a] Who can say, I have made my heart
clean,
I am pure from my sin?

19:28 [1] Heb. *A witness of Belial* [a] Job 15:16
19:29 [a] ch. 26:3
20:1 [a] Gen. 9:21
20:2 [a] ch. 19:12 [b] ch. 8:36
20:3 [a] ch. 17:14
20:4 [1] Or, *winter* [a] ch. 10:4 [b] ch. 19:15
20:6 [1] Or, *bounty* [a] Mat. 6:2; Luke 18:11 [b] Luke 18:8
20:7 [a] 2 Cor. 1:12 [b] Ps. 37:26
20:8 [a] ver. 26
20:9 [a] 1 Ki. 8:46
20:10 [1] Heb. *A stone and a stone* [2] Heb. *an ephah and an ephah* [a] Deut. 25:13
20:11 [a] Mat. 7:16
20:12 [a] Ex. 4:11
20:13 [a] Rom. 12:11
20:15 [a] ch. 3:15
20:16 [a] ch. 22:26
20:17 [1] Heb. *Bread of lying*, or, *falsehood* [a] ch. 9:17
20:18 [a] ch. 24:6 [b] Luke 14:31
20:19 [1] Or, *enticeth* [a] ch. 11:13 [b] Rom. 16:18
20:20 [1] Or, *candle* [a] Mat. 15:4 [b] Job 18:5,6
20:21 [a] ch. 28:20

10 [a] [1] Divers weights, *and* [2] divers measures,
Both of them *are* alike abomination to
the LORD.
11 Even a child is [a] known by his doings,
Whether his work *be* pure, and
whether *it be* right.
12 [a] The hearing ear, and the seeing eye,
The LORD hath made even both of them.
13 [a] Love not sleep, lest thou come to
poverty;
Open thine eyes, *and* thou shalt be
satisfied *with* bread.
14 *It is* naught, *it is* naught, saith the
buyer:
But when he is gone his way, then he
boasteth.
15 There is gold, and a multitude of rubies:
But [a] the lips of knowledge *are* a
precious jewel.
16 [a] Take his garment that is surety *for* a
stranger:
And take a pledge of him for a strange
woman.
17 [a] [1] Bread of deceit *is* sweet to a man;
But afterwards his mouth shall be filled
with gravel.
18 [a] Every purpose is established by
counsel:
[b] And with good advice make war.
19 [a] He that goeth about *as* a talebearer
revealeth secrets:
Therefore meddle not with him [b] that
[1] flattereth *with* his lips.
20 [a] Whoso curseth his father or his
mother,
[b] His [1] lamp shall be put out in obscure
darkness.
21 [a] An inheritance *may be* gotten hastily
at the beginning;

elderly (cf. Is 51:18). Robbing them (cf. Judg 17:1–2) and attacking them (Ex 21:15,17) were serious crimes. *shame . . . reproach.* See 10:5; 13:5.

19:27 See 5:1–2.

19:28 *ungodly witness.* See v. 5; see also note on 6:19. *devoureth iniquity.* Cf. the description of man as one who "drinketh iniquity like water" (Job 15:16; see Job 34:7).

19:29 *Judgments . . . for scorners.* See v. 25. *stripes for the back of fools.* See 10:13; 14:3; 26:3.

‡20:1 *Wine is a mocker, strong drink is raging.* Those who overindulge become mockers and brawlers (see Hos 7:5). Proverbs associates drunkenness with poverty (23:20–21), strife (23:29–30) and injustice (31:4–5). *deceived.* The person who becomes drunk. See Gen 9:21; Is 28:7.

20:2 See 16:14 and note.

‡20:3 *will be meddling.* The fool is quarrelsome and argumentative. See 6:14; 17:14,19; 18:6.

20:4 *sluggard.* See note on 6:6. *and have nothing.* See 13:4; 21:25–26.

‡20:5 *Counsel.* Refers to "plans" or "motives" behind the plans (cf. 16:1–2). *deep water.* Cf. 18:4. *will draw it out.* As if from a well.

‡20:6 *goodness.* Or, his loyalty. See note on 19:22. *a faithful man who can find?* Cf. Eccl 7:28–29.

20:7 *walketh in his integrity.* See note on 2:7. *His children are blessed.* See 13:22; see also note on 14:26.

20:8 *Scattereth away all evil.* See 16:10; Ps 11:4.

20:9 *clean . . . pure from my sin.* No one is without sin (cf. Job 14:4; Rom 3:23)—but those whose sins have been forgiven have "clean hands and a pure heart" (Ps 24:4; see also 51:1–2, 9–10).

20:10 See note on 11:1; cf. 16:11.

20:13 *sleep . . . come to poverty.* See 24:33–34.

20:14 *naught . . . naught.* Prices were often agreed upon by bargaining, so the buyer is questioning the quality of the article in order to buy it more cheaply.

20:15 *gold . . . rubies.* Earlier, wisdom itself was valued more highly than gold or jewels (3:14–15; 8:10–11).

20:16 See note on 6:1. *Take his garment.* A garment could be taken as security for a debt (Deut 24:10–13). Anyone who foolishly assumes responsibility for the debt of a stranger, whose reliability is unknown, or of a wayward woman, whose unreliability is known, ought to be held accountable, even to the degree of taking his garment as a pledge.

20:17 *is sweet to a man.* Cf. the sweet "bread" prepared by the adulteress in 9:17. Zophar observes that evil is sweet in the mouth of a wicked man, but it turns sour in his stomach (Job 20:12–18). See note on 10:2.

20:18 *counsel . . . advice.* See 15:22; Luke 14:31.

20:20 *curseth his father or his mother.* Punishable by death (see Lev 20:9; cf. Prov 30:11,17). *lamp shall be put out.* He will die (see note on 13:9).

20:21 *An inheritance may be gotten hastily . . . shall not be*

[b]But the end thereof shall not be
blessed.
22 [a]Say not thou, I will recompense evil;
But [b]wait on the LORD, and he shall
save thee.
23 [a]Divers weights *are* an abomination
unto the LORD;
And [1]a false balance *is* not good.
24 [a]Man's goings *are* of the LORD;
How can a man then understand his
own way?
25 *It is* a snare to the man *who* devoureth
that which is holy,
And [a]after vows to make inquiry.
26 [a]A wise king scattereth the wicked,
And bringeth the wheel over them.
27 [a]The spirit of man *is* the [1]candle of the
LORD,
Searching all the inward parts of the
belly.
28 [a]Mercy and truth preserve the king:
And his throne is upholden by mercy.
29 The glory of young men *is* their
strength:
And [a]the beauty of old men *is* the gray
head.
30 The blueness of a wound [1]cleanseth
away evil:
So *do* stripes the inward parts of the
belly.

21 The king's heart *is* in the hand of
the LORD, *as* the rivers of water:
He turneth it whithersoever he will.
2 [a]Every way of a man *is* right in his
own eyes:
[b]But the LORD pondereth the hearts.

20:21 [b]Hab. 2:6
20:22 [a]Rom. 12:17 [b]2 Sam. 16:12
20:23 [1]Heb. *balances of deceit* [a]ver. 10
20:24 [a]Ps. 37:23
20:25 [a]Eccl. 5:4,5
20:26 [a]Ps. 101:8
20:27 [1]Or, *lamp* [a]1 Cor. 2:11
20:28 [a]Ps. 101:1
20:29 [a]ch. 16:31
20:30 [1]Heb. *is a purging medicine against evil*
21:2 [a]ch. 16:2 [b]ch. 24:12; Luke 16:15
21:3 [a]1 Sam. 15:22
21:4 [1]Heb. *Haughtiness of eyes* [2]Or, *the light of the wicked* [a]ch. 6:17
21:5 [a]ch. 10:4
21:6 [a]2 Pet. 2:3
21:7 [1]Heb. *saw them,* or, *dwell with them*
21:9 [1]Heb. *a woman of contentions* [2]Heb. *a house of society*
21:10 [1]Heb. *is not favoured* [a]Jas. 4:5
21:11 [a]ch. 19:25
21:13 [a]Mat. 7:2

3 [a]To do justice and judgment
Is more acceptable to the LORD than
sacrifice.
4 [a][1]A high look, and a proud heart,
And [2]the plowing of the wicked, *is* sin.
5 [a]The thoughts of the diligent *tend* only
to plenteousness;
But *of* every one that is hasty only to
want.
6 [a]The getting of treasures by a lying
tongue
Is a vanity tossed to and fro of them
that seek death.
7 The robbery of the wicked shall
[1]destroy them;
Because they refuse to do judgment.
8 The way of man *is* froward and
strange:
But *as for* the pure, his work *is* right.
9 *It is* better to dwell in a corner of the
housetop,
Than with [1]a brawling woman in [2]a
wide house.
10 [a]The soul of the wicked desireth evil:
His neighbour [1]findeth no favour in his
eyes.
11 [a]When the scorner is punished, the
simple is made wise:
And when the wise is instructed, he
receiveth knowledge.
12 The righteous *man* wisely considereth
the house of the wicked:
But God overthroweth the wicked for
their wickedness.
13 [a]Whoso stoppeth his ears at the cry of
the poor,

---

blessed. Cf. 19:26; cf. also the sad experience of the son who "wasted his substance with riotous living" (Luke 15:12–13).

20:22 *I will recompense evil.* Vengeance was God's prerogative. He would repay the wicked for their actions (see Deut 32:35; Ps 94:1). *wait on the LORD.* See Ps 27:14; 37:34.

20:23 See v. 10; see also note on 11:1.

20:24 See notes on 3:5–6; 16:9.

‡20:25 *It is a snare . . . that which is holy.* Lit. "It is a snare for a man to vow rashly." The vow was a promise to make a special gift to the Lord if He answered an earnest request (see Lev 27:1–25; Deut 23:21; Judg 11:30–31,34–35; 1 Sam 1:11). Sometimes such a vow was made hastily and was not carried out (cf. Eccl 5:4–6).

20:26 *bringeth the wheel.* The wheel of the threshing cart that separated the grain from the husk (cf. Is 28:27–28). The wicked will be separated from the righteous and duly punished.

‡20:27 *The spirit of man is the candle of the LORD.* The soul of man has a God-consciousness and moral awareness of right and wrong. Cf. Rom. 2:14–15. *Searching all the inward parts of the belly.* See note on 15:11.

20:28 *Mercy and truth preserve the king . . . mercy.* Kindness and moral uprightness endear a king to his people and encourage them to be loyal subjects (cf. 3:3; 14:22; 16:12; 29:14).

20:29 *their strength.* Cf. Jer 9:23. *beauty of old men is the gray head.* See note on 16:31.

‡20:30 *blueness of a wound.* The bruises caused by a beating as the punishment for a crime. Stern punishment is necessary to restrain evil. Several verses refer to fools whose backs are beaten (10:13; 14:3; 19:29), but even then, because they are fools, they may not change their ways (cf. 17:10; 27:22).

21:1 *king's heart is . . . in the hand of the LORD.* God controls the lives and actions even of kings, such as Nebuchadnezzar (Dan 4:31–32,35) and Cyrus (Is 45:1–3; cf. Ezra 6:22). *turneth it whithersoever he will.* See 16:9; see also 16:1; 19:21; 20:24.

21:2 *is right.* See 14:12; 16:2. *pondereth the hearts.* See 24:12; Job 31:6; Ps 139:23; 1 Cor 4:4–5; Heb 4:12.

21:3 *more acceptable . . . than sacrifice.* A theme also found in the prophets (Hos 6:6; Mic 6:7–8). See v. 27; see also note on 15:8.

‡21:4 *high look.* A proud and haughty look. See note on 6:17; see also 16:5,18.

21:5 *The thoughts of the diligent tend . . . to plenteousness.* See note on 10:4. *hasty.* Either rash actions (19:2) or a desire to get rich quick (see 13:11 and note; 20:21; 28:20).

‡21:6 *treasures by a lying tongue.* See note on 10:2; cf. 19:1. *vanity.* Like a vapor that is here and gone. See 13:11 and note; Eccl 1:14. *seek death.* Cf. 5:22; 7:23.

21:7 *robbery of the wicked shall destroy them.* See 1:18–19 and notes.

21:9 *corner of the housetop.* Roofs were flat, and small rooms could be built there (see Deut 22:8; 2 Ki 4:10). *brawling woman.* See note on 19:13.

21:10 *desireth evil.* See 4:16; 10:23. *His neighbour findeth no favour.* Cf. 14:21.

21:11 See 19:25 and note.

21:12 *house of the wicked . . . overthroweth.* See 10:25 and note; 14:11.

‡21:13 *cry of the poor.* See note on 14:21; see also 28:27. *He*

He also shall cry himself, but shall not
be heard.
14 A gift in secret pacifieth anger:
And a reward in the bosom strong
wrath.
15 *It is* joy to the just to do judgment:
But destruction *shall be* to the workers
of iniquity.
16 The man that wandereth out of the
way of understanding
Shall remain in the congregation of the
dead.
17 He that loveth [1] pleasure *shall be* a
poor man:
He that loveth wine and oil shall not
be rich.
18 The wicked *shall be* a ransom for the
righteous,
And the transgressor for the upright.
19 *It is* better to dwell [1] in the wilderness,
Than with a contentious and an angry
woman.
20 [a] *There is* treasure to be desired and oil
in the dwelling of the wise;
But a foolish man spendeth it up.
21 [a] He that followeth after righteousness
and mercy
Findeth life, righteousness, and
honour.
22 [a] A wise *man* scaleth the city of the
mighty,
And casteth down the strength of the
confidence thereof.
23 [a] Whoso keepeth his mouth and his
tongue
Keepeth his soul from troubles.

21:17 [1] Or, *sport*
21:19 [1] Heb. *in the land of the desert*
21:20 [a] Ps. 112:3; Mat. 25:3,4
21:21 [a] Mat. 5:6
21:22 [a] Eccl. 9:14
21:23 [a] ch. 12:13; Jas. 3:2
21:24 [1] Heb. *in the wrath of pride*
21:27 [1] Heb. *in wickedness?* [a] Jer. 6:20
21:28 [1] Heb. *A witness of lies*
21:29 [1] Or, *considereth*
21:30 [a] Is. 8:9,10; Jer. 9:23; Acts 5:39
21:31 [1] Or, *victory* [a] Ps. 3:8
22:1 [1] Or, *favour is better than, etc.* [a] Eccl. 7:1
22:4 [1] Or, *The reward of humility, etc.*

24 Proud *and* haughty scorner *is* his
name,
Who dealeth [1] in proud wrath.
25 The desire of the slothful killeth him;
For his hands refuse to labour.
26 He coveteth greedily all the day long:
But the righteous giveth and spareth
not.
27 [a] The sacrifice of the wicked *is*
abomination:
How much more, *when* he bringeth it
[1] with a wicked mind?
28 [1] A false witness shall perish:
But the man that heareth, speaketh
constantly.
29 A wicked man hardeneth his face:
But *as for* the upright, he [1] directeth
his way.
30 [a] *There is* no wisdom nor
understanding
Nor counsel against the LORD.
31 The horse *is* prepared against the day
of battle:
But [a] [1] safety *is* of the LORD.

22

[a] A *good* name *is* rather to be chosen
than great riches,
And [1] loving favour rather than silver
and gold.
2 The rich and poor meet together:
The LORD *is* the Maker of them all.
3 A prudent *man* foreseeth the evil, and
hideth himself:
But the simple pass on, and are
punished.
4 [1] By humility *and* the fear of the LORD
Are riches, and honour, and life.

also shall cry himself, but shall not be heard. The punishment fits the crime. See note on 1:28. Cf. the fate of the rich man (Luke 16:19–31) and the unmerciful servant (Mat 18:23–34).

21:14 *gift . . . reward.* See note on 17:8; see also 18:16; 19:6. *pacifieth anger . . . wrath.* Perhaps that of an offended party (see 6:34–35).

21:15 *joy to the just.* See 11:10 and note. *destruction . . . to the workers of iniquity.* See 10:29 and note; Rom 13:3.

21:16 Graphically illustrated by the man who succumbed to the adulteress (see 2:18; 5:23; 7:22–23; 9:18).

21:17 *wine and oil.* Both were associated with lavish feasting (see 23:20–21; Amos 6:6). Oil was used in various lotions or perfumes, some of which were very expensive (John 12:5).

21:18 *The wicked shall be a ransom for the righteous.* Close to the thought of 11:8. In Is 43:3–4 God gave three nations to Persia in exchange for Persia's willingness to release the exiles of Judah (see note on Is 43:4).

21:19 See 19:13 and note.

21:20 *treasure . . . oil in the dwelling of the wise.* See 3:10 and note; 8:21. *oil.* Olive oil (see note on v. 17; see also Deut 7:13).

21:21 *followeth after righteousness.* See 15:9. *life, righteousness, and honour.* Benefits for those who seek wisdom (see note on 3:2; see also 3:16; 8:18; cf. 22:4).

21:22 *wise man scaleth . . . of the mighty.* Probably another way of saying, "Wisdom is better than strength" (Eccl 9:16). Cf. 24:5; 2 Cor 10:4, where spiritual weapons are "mighty through God to the pulling down of strong holds."

21:23 See 13:3 and note; 18:21.

21:24 *Proud . . . scorner is his name.* See note on 1:22. God mocks and punishes him for his "proud wrath" (cf. 3:34; 19:25, 29; 21:11).

21:25 *desire of the slothful.* See notes on 6:6; 13:4.

21:26 *giveth and spareth not.* The righteous are prosperous, so they can share with those in need (see Ps 37:26; 112:9; cf. Eph 4:28).

21:27 *The sacrifice of the wicked is abomination.* See notes on v. 3; 15:8.

21:28 *false witness shall perish.* See 19:5,9; see also note on 6:19.

‡21:29 *hardeneth his face.* He has a defiant attitude. Cf. the behavior of the adulteress in 7:13.

21:30 *Nor counsel against the LORD.* Because He is sovereign and controls people and nations (see 16:4,9 and notes; 19:21; 21:1; 1 Cor 3:19–20).

‡21:31 *horse.* Many times God cautions against trusting in horses and chariots for victory (e.g., Ps 20:7; Hos 1:7; cf. Deut 17:16). *safety is of the LORD.* Victory in battle. See 1 Sam 17:47; Ps 3:8.

22:1 *good name.* Its value is recognized also in 3:4; 10:7; Eccl 7:1. *rather than silver and gold.* Like the possession of wisdom (see 3:14; 16:16).

22:2 *Maker of them all.* See 14:31 and note.

22:3 *prudent . . . hideth himself.* Cf. 14:8. *the simple.* See note on 1:4; see also 9:16.

22:4 See 18:12. *humility and the fear of the LORD.* Associated also in 15:33 (see note on 1:7). *riches, and honour, and life.* Benefits for those who seek wisdom (see note on 3:2; see also 3:16; 8:18; cf. 21:21).

5 Thorns *and* snares *are* in the way of
the froward:
He that doth keep his soul shall be far
from them.
6 [a][1]Train up a child [2]in the way he
should go:
And when he is old, he will not depart
from it.
7 The rich ruleth over the poor,
And the borrower *is* servant [1]to the
lender.
8 He that soweth iniquity shall reap
vanity:
[1]And the rod of his anger shall fail.
9 [a][1]He that hath a bountiful eye shall be
blessed;
For he giveth of his bread to the poor.
10 [a]Cast out the scorner, and contention
shall go out;
Yea, strife and reproach shall cease.
11 [a]He that loveth pureness of heart,
[1]*For* the grace of his lips the king *shall
be* his friend.
12 The eyes of the LORD preserve
knowledge,
And he overthroweth [1]the words of
the transgressor.
13 [a]The slothful *man* saith, *There is* a lion
without,
I shall be slain in the streets.
14 [a]The mouth of strange *women is* a
deep pit:
[b]He that is abhorred of the LORD shall
fall therein.
15 Foolishness *is* bound in the heart of a
child;
But [a]the rod of correction shall drive it
far from him.
16 He that oppresseth the poor to increase
his *riches,*
And he that giveth to the rich, *shall*
surely *come* to want.

Hear the words of the wise

17 Bow down thine ear, and hear the
words of the wise,
And apply thine heart unto my
knowledge.
18 For *it is* a pleasant *thing* if thou keep
them [1]within thee;
They shall withal be fitted in thy lips.
19 That thy trust may be in the LORD,
I have made known to thee *this* day,
[1]even *to* thee.
20 Have not I written to thee excellent
things
In counsels and knowledge,
21 [a]That *I* might make thee know the
certainty of the words of truth;
[b]That *thou* mightest answer the words
of truth [1]to them that send *unto* thee?
22 Rob not the poor, because he *is* poor:
Neither oppress the afflicted in the gate:
23 [a]For the LORD will plead their cause,
And spoil the soul of those that spoiled
them.
24 Make no friendship with an angry man;
And with a furious man thou shalt
not go:
25 Lest thou learn his ways,
And get a snare to thy soul.

22:6 [1]Or, *Catechise* [2]Heb. *in his way* [a]Eph. 6:4; 2 Tim. 3:15
22:7 [1]Heb. *to the man that lendeth*
22:8 [1]Or, *And with the rod of his anger he shall be consumed*
22:9 [1]Heb. *Good of eye* [a]2 Cor. 9:6
22:10 [a]Ps. 101:5
22:11 [1]Or, And hath *grace in his lips* [a]Ps. 101:6
22:12 [1]Or, *the matters*
22:13 [a]ch. 26:13
22:14 [a]ch. 2:16; 5:3; 7:5 [b]Eccl. 7:26
22:15 [a]ch. 13:24
22:18 [1]Heb. *in thy belly*
22:19 [1]Or, trust *thou also*
22:21 [1]Or, *to those that send thee?* [a]Luke 1:3,4 [b]1 Pet. 3:15
22:23 [a]1 Sam. 24:12; Ps. 12:5

22:5 *Thorns and snares.* Evil (cf. 15:19). *shall be far from them.* By taking the "highway of the upright" (16:17).
22:6 *Train.* Or "Dedicate," as in 1 Ki 8:63; or "Start." Instruction (1:8) and discipline (22:15) are primarily involved. *way he should go.* The right way, the way of wisdom (see 4:11 and note). *old.* Or "grown."
22:7 *The rich.* See note on 10:15. *the borrower is servant to the lender.* One of the reasons why putting up security for someone else (v. 26) was frowned upon (cf. Neh 5:4–5).
22:8 *soweth iniquity shall reap vanity.* See 12:21. *rod of his anger.* His ability to oppress others (see Ps 125:3; Is 14:5–6).
22:9 *He that hath a bountiful eye shall be blessed.* See note on 11:25. *giveth of his bread.* See note on 14:21; see also Deut 15:8–11.
22:10 *Cast out the scorner.* See note on 1:22; cf. Gen 21:9–10. *contention shall go out.* Cf. 17:14; 18:3; 20:3.
‡22:11 *pureness of heart.* Cf. Ps 24:4. *the grace of his lips.* Gracious speech is characteristic of the wise man in Eccl 10:12. *king shall be his friend.* Cf. v. 29.
22:12 *The eyes of the LORD preserve.* See 5:21; 15:3; Job 31:4; 34:21; Jer 16:17; Heb 4:13. *knowledge.* God protects those who have knowledge (cf. Ps 1:6; 34:15). *overthroweth . . . the words of the transgressor.* Overrules their plans and desires (see 16:9; see also note on 21:30).
22:13 The sluggard (see note on 6:6) creates excuses to avoid work.
‡22:14 *The mouth of strange women.* The seductive speech of the adultress (see note on 5:3; see also 2:16; 7:5). *deep pit.* Perhaps a well or a hunter's trap (see 5:22 and note; 7:22).
22:15 *rod of correction.* See note on 13:24.
22:16 *He that oppresseth the poor.* Condemned also in 14:31; 28:3. *giveth to the rich.* Perhaps bribes (see 17:8; 18:16; 19:6). *want.* See 21:5; 28:22.
22:17–24:22 A new section that returns more to the style of chs. 1–9. Verses 17–21 form the introduction to these 30 sayings (see Introduction: Date). The 30 sayings are (1) 22:22–23; (2) 22:24–25; (3) 22:26–27; (4) 22:28; (5) 22:29; (6) 23:1–3; (7) 23:4–5; (8) 23:6–8; (9) 23:9; (10) 23:10–11; (11) 23:12; (12) 23:13–14; (13) 23:15–16; (14) 23:17–18; (15) 23:19–21; (16) 23:22–25; (17) 23:26–28; (18) 23:29–35; (19) 24:1–2; (20) 24:3–4; (21) 24:5–6; (22) 24:7; (23) 24:8–9; (24) 24:10; (25) 24:11–12; (26) 24:13–14; (27) 24:15–16; (28) 24:17–18; (29) 24:19–20; (30) 24:21–22.
22:17 *Bow down thine ear, and hear.* See 4:20; 5:1. *words of the wise.* A title, like "proverbs of Solomon" in 10:1.
22:18 *it is a pleasant thing.* See 2:10; 16:24.
22:19 *That thy trust may be in the LORD.* See note on 3:5.
22:21 *mightest answer the words of truth.* See 1 Pet 3:15. *to them that send unto thee.* Possibly a parent or guardian.
22:22 *Rob not the poor.* See v. 16; 14:31. *Neither oppress the afflicted in the gate.* See Is 1:17.
‡22:23 *the LORD will plead their cause.* See 23:11; Ps 12:5; 140:12; Is 3:13–15; Mal 3:5. *spoil the soul of those that spoiled them.* The Lord will put to death those that oppress the poor. See Ex 22:22–24.
22:24 *Make no friendship with.* Cf. 12:26. *an angry man.* His characteristics are given in 14:16–17; 15:18; 29:22.
22:25 *get a snare.* See note on 5:22; see also 12:13; 13:14; 29:6.

26 [a]Be not thou *one* of them that strike
hands,
Or of them that are sureties for debts.
27 If thou hast nothing to pay,
Why should he take away thy bed from
under thee?
28 [a]Remove not the ancient [1]landmark,
Which thy fathers have set.

29 Seest thou a man diligent in his
business?
He shall stand before kings;
He shall not stand before [1]mean *men.*

23 When thou sittest to eat with a
ruler,
Consider diligently what *is* before thee:
2 And put a knife to thy throat,
If thou *be* a man given to appetite.
3 Be not desirous of his dainties:
For they *are* deceitful meat.
4 [a]Labour not to be rich:
[b]Cease from thine own wisdom.
5 [1]Wilt thou set thine eyes upon that
which is not?
For *riches* certainly make themselves
wings;
They fly away as an eagle *toward*
heaven.

6 Eat thou not the bread of *him that hath*
[a]an evil eye,
Neither desire thou his dainty meats:
7 For as he thinketh in his heart, so *is* he:
Eat and drink, [a]saith he to thee;
But his heart *is* not with thee.
8 The morsel *which* thou hast eaten shalt
thou vomit up,
And lose thy sweet words.
9 [a]Speak not in the ears of a fool:
For he will despise the wisdom of thy
words.
10 Remove not the old [1]landmark;
And enter not into the fields of the
fatherless:
11 [a]For their Redeemer *is* mighty;
He shall plead their cause with thee.
12 Apply thine heart unto instruction,
And thine ears to the words of
knowledge.
13 [a]Withhold not correction from the child:
For *if* thou beatest him with the rod,
he shall not die.
14 Thou shalt beat him with the rod,
And shalt deliver his soul from hell.

15 My son, if thine heart be wise,
My heart shall rejoice, [1]even mine.
16 Yea, my reins shall rejoice,
When thy lips speak right things.
17 [a]Let not thine heart envy sinners:
But [b]*be thou* in the fear of the LORD all
the day long.
18 [a]For surely there is an [1]end;
And thine expectation shall not be cut
off.
19 Hear thou, my son, and be wise,
And guide thine heart in the way.
20 [a]Be not amongst winebibbers;
Amongst riotous eaters [1]of flesh:
21 For the drunkard and the glutton shall
come to poverty:
And drowsiness shall clothe *a man*
with rags.

22 [a]Hearken unto thy father that begat
thee,
And despise not thy mother when she
is old.

22:26 [a]ch. 11:15
22:28 [1]Or, *bound* [a]Deut. 19:14
22:29 [1]Heb. *obscure* men
23:4 [a]1 Tim. 6:9 [b]Rom. 12:16
23:5 [1]Heb. *Wilt thou cause thine eyes to fly upon*
23:6 [a]Deut. 15:9
23:7 [a]Ps. 12:2
23:9 [a]ch. 9:8; Mat. 7:6
23:10 [1]Or, *bound*
23:11 [a]ch. 22:23
23:13 [a]ch. 13:24
23:15 [1]Or, *even I* will rejoice
23:17 [a]Ps. 37:1 [b]ch. 28:14
23:18 [1]Or, *reward* [a]Ps. 37:37
23:20 [1]Heb. *of their flesh* [a]Is. 5:22
23:22 [a]ch. 1:8; Eph. 6:1,2

22:26 See note on 6:1.
22:27 *take away thy bed from under thee.* You will be reduced to poverty.
22:28 *ancient landmark.* See note on 15:25; see also 23:10.
‡22:29 *a man diligent in his business.* He works hard and is skilled in his craft. Craftsmen were considered to be wise (see note on 8:30; see also Ex 35:30–35). *stand before kings.* Like Joseph, an administrator (Gen 41:46); David, a musician (1 Sam 16:21–23); and Hiram, a worker in bronze (1 Ki 7:13–14).
23:2 *given to appetite.* Cf. the similar warning in vv. 20–21.
‡23:3 *Be not desirous of his dainties.* Lavish foods served at the king's table. Repeated in a different context in v. 6. *deceitful.* Perhaps the meaning is that the ruler wants to obligate you in some way, even to influence you to support a wicked scheme (cf. Ps 141:4).
23:4 *Labour not to be rich.* The desire to get rich can ruin a person physically and spiritually. "For the love of money is the root of all evil" (1 Tim 6:10; cf. 15:27; 28:20; Heb 13:5).
23:5 *They fly away.* Our trust must be in God, not in riches (see Jer 17:11; Luke 12:21; 1 Tim 6:17).
‡23:6 *him . . . evil eye.* A selfish man who is eager to get rich (see 28:22).
23:7 *his heart is not with thee.* Cf. 26:24–25.
23:8 *vomit.* Out of disgust at the attitude of the host.
23:9 *despise the wisdom of thy words.* Fools despise wisdom (1:7) and hate knowledge and correction (1:22; 12:1). They heap abuse on one who rebukes them (9:7).
‡23:10 *old landmark.* Boundary stones. See note on 15:25; see also 22:28. *fatherless.* Oppressing the widow and the fatherless is strongly denounced (see Is 10:2; Jer 22:3; Zech 7:10).
23:11 *Redeemer.* Kinsman-Redeemer, someone who helped a close relative regain land (see Lev 25:25 and note) or who avenged his death (Num 35:12,19). God is a "father of the fatherless, and a judge of the widows" (Ps 68:5). See notes on Ruth 2:20; Jer 31:11; see also Jer 50:34. *shall plead their cause.* See Ps 12:5; 140:12; Is 3:13–15; Mal 3:5.
23:13–14 See 13:24 and note.
23:15 See 10:1 and note; see also v. 24; 27:11; 29:3. *My son.* See 1:8,10.
23:17 *Let not . . . envy sinners.* See 3:31; 24:1,19. *fear of the LORD.* See notes on 1:7; 3:7.
‡23:18 *end.* A future when God will reward the person who fears Him. See Ps 37:37; Jer 29:11.
23:19 *the way.* Cf. 4:25–26.
‡23:20 *Be not amongst.* See 1:15; 12:26. *winebibbers.* Heavy drinkers. Drunkenness is also condemned in vv. 29–35; 20:1 (see note there); cf. Deut 21:20; Mat 24:49; Luke 21:34; Rom 13:13; Eph 5:18; 1 Tim 3:3.
23:21 *glutton.* See v. 2; 28:7; cf. Mat 11:19. *come to poverty.* See 21:17. *drowsiness.* Cf. the poverty that overtakes the sluggard in 6:9–11.
23:22 *despise not thy mother.* Cf. 15:20; 30:17.

23 [a]Buy the truth, and sell *it* not;
Also wisdom, and instruction, and understanding.
24 [a]The father of the righteous shall greatly rejoice:
And he that begetteth a wise *child* shall have joy of him.
25 Thy father and thy mother shall be glad,
And she that bare thee shall rejoice.
26 My son, give me thine heart,
And let thine eyes observe my ways.
27 [a]For a whore *is* a deep ditch;
And a strange *woman is* a narrow pit.
28 [a]She also lieth in wait [1]as *for* a prey,
And increaseth the transgressors among men.
29 [a]Who hath woe? who hath sorrow?
Who hath contentions? who hath babbling?
Who hath wounds without cause?
Who [b]hath redness of eyes?
30 [a]They that tarry long at the wine;
They that go to seek [b]mixt wine.
31 Look not thou upon the wine when it is red,
When it giveth his colour in the cup,
When it moveth itself aright.
32 At the last it biteth like a serpent,
And stingeth like [1]an adder.
33 Thine eyes shall behold strange *women,*
And thine heart shall utter perverse things.
34 Yea, thou shalt be as he that lieth down [1]in the midst of the sea,
Or as he that lieth upon the top of a mast.
35 [a]They have stricken me, *shalt thou say, and* I was not sick;
They have beaten me, *and* [b] [1]I felt *it* not:
When shall I awake?
I will seek it yet again.

23:23 [a]Mat. 13:44
23:24 [a]ch. 10:1
23:27 [a]ch. 22:14
23:28 [1]Or, *as a robber* [a]ch. 7:12; Eccl. 7:26
23:29 [a]Is. 5:11,22 [b]Gen. 49:12
23:30 [a]Eph. 5:18 [b]Ps. 75:8
23:32 [1]Or, *a cockatrice*
23:34 [1]Heb. *in the heart of the sea*
23:35 [a]Jer. 5:3
23:35 [1]Heb. *I knew* it *not* [b]Eph. 4:19
24:1 [a]Ps. 37:1; 73:3; ch. 3:31
24:5 [1]Heb. is *in strength* [2]Heb. *strengtheneth might* [a]ch. 21:22
24:6 [a]Luke 14:31
24:7 [a]Ps. 10:5
24:8 [a]Rom. 1:30
24:10 [1]Heb. *narrow*
24:11 [a]Ps. 82:4; Is. 58:6,7; 1 John 3:16
24:12 [a]ch. 21:2 [b]Ps. 62:12

24

Be not thou [a]envious against evil men,
Neither desire to be with them.
2 For their heart studieth destruction,
And their lips talk of mischief.
3 Through wisdom is a house builded;
And by understanding it is established:
4 And by knowledge shall the chambers be filled
With all precious and pleasant riches.
5 [a]A wise man [1]*is* strong;
Yea, a man of knowledge [2]increaseth strength.
6 [a]For by wise counsel thou shalt make thy war:
And in multitude of counsellers *there is* safety.
7 [a]Wisdom *is too* high for a fool:
He openeth not his mouth in the gate.
8 He that [a]deviseth to do evil
Shall be called a mischievous person.
9 The thought of foolishness *is* sin:
And the scorner *is* an abomination to men.
10 *If* thou faint in the day of adversity,
Thy strength *is* [1]small.
11 [a]If thou forbear to deliver *them that are* drawn unto death,
And *those that are* ready to be slain;
12 If thou sayest, Behold, we knew it not;
Doth not [a]he that pondereth the heart consider *it?*
And he that keepeth thy soul, doth *not* he know *it?*
And shall *not* he render to *every* man [b]according to his works?

23:23 *Buy the truth . . . Also wisdom . . . understanding.* See 4:5; see also 4:7 and note.
23:24–25 See v. 15; 27:11; see also 10:1 and note.
23:27 *deep ditch.* See note on 22:14. *strange woman.* See note on 2:16; see also 5:20; 7:17–23.
23:28 *lieth in wait.* See 6:26; 7:12; Eccl 7:26. *increaseth the transgressors.* Cf. 7:26.
23:29–35 A vivid description of the physical and psychological effects of drunkenness.
23:29 *Who hath woe?* Cf. the woes pronounced on drunkards in Is 5:11,22. *contentions.* See 20:1. *wounds.* Cf. the "stripes for the back of fools" in 19:29.
23:30 *tarry long at the wine.* See 1 Sam 25:36. *mixt wine.* Probably with spices (see 9:2; Ps 75:8).
23:32 *biteth like a serpent.* Death will be the result (cf. Num 21:6).
‡23:33 *behold strange women.* Or "strange things" (the noun is not supplied in the original). Perhaps a reference to the delirium that afflicts the alcoholic.
23:34 *thou shalt be as he that lieth down in the midst of the sea.* Your head will be spinning.
‡23:35 *They have stricken me . . . I was not sick.* The drunken person is not even aware of the injuries he received from the beating. Cf. the condition of Israel in Jer 5:3. *I will seek it yet again.* The woe and misery do not prevent him from repeating his folly (cf. 26:11; 27:22; Is 56:12).
24:1 *Be not thou envious.* See v. 19; Ps 37:1. *Neither desire to be with them.* See 1:15; 12:26; 23:20.
‡24:2 *studieth destruction.* Plans and devises violence. See 1:10–11; 6:14; Job 15:35; Ps 38:12.
24:3 *house.* Symbolic of the life of an individual or a family. *builded.* Cf. the similar expression in 9:1.
24:4 *precious and pleasant riches.* Wisdom promises to bestow wealth on those who love her (8:21).
24:5 *is strong.* See note on 21:22.
24:7 *in the gate.* The normal meeting place for official business (see note on 1:21).
24:8 *deviseth to do evil.* See v. 2; see also 1:10–11; 6:14; Job 15:35; Ps 38:12. *mischievous person.* A schemer; called a "man of wicked devices" in 12:2,14:17.
‡24:9 *The thought of foolishness is sin.* The plotting to do evil. Cf. 1:11–16; 9:13–18. *scorner is an abomination to men.* Because he is proud, dishonoring (9:7) and contentious (22:10). See note on 1:22.
24:10 Cf. Jer 12:5; Gal 6:9.
24:11 *them that are drawn unto death.* Perhaps innocent men condemned to die (cf. 17:15; Is 58:6–7).
24:12 *Doth not he that pondereth the heart consider it?* God knows even our thoughts and motives (see 16:2; 21:2; Ps 94:9–11).

13 My son, [a]eat thou honey, because *it is* good;
And the honeycomb, *which is* sweet [1]to thy taste:
14 [a]So shall the knowledge of wisdom be unto thy soul:
When thou hast found *it,* then there shall be a reward,
And thy expectation shall not be cut off.
15 Lay not wait, O wicked *man,* against the dwelling of the righteous;
Spoil not his resting place:
16 [a]For a just *man* falleth seven *times,* and riseth up *again:*
[b]But the wicked shall fall into mischief.
17 [a]Rejoice not when thine enemy falleth,
And let not thine heart be glad when he stumbleth:
18 Lest the LORD see *it,* and [1]it displease him,
And he turn away his wrath from him.
19 [a1]Fret not thyself because of evil *men,*
Neither be thou envious at the wicked;
20 For there shall be no reward to the evil *man;*
The [1]candle of the wicked shall be put out.
21 My son, [a]fear thou the LORD and the king:
And meddle not with [1]them that are given to change:
22 For their calamity shall rise suddenly;
And who knoweth the ruin of them both?

Sayings of the wise

23 ¶ These *things* also *belong* to the wise.

[a]*It is* not good to have respect of persons in judgment.
24 [a]He that saith unto the wicked, Thou *art* righteous;
Him shall the people curse, nations shall abhor him:
25 But to them that rebuke *him* shall be delight,
And [1]a good blessing shall come upon them.
26 *Every man* shall kiss *his* lips
[1]That giveth a right answer.
27 [a]Prepare thy work without,
And make it fit for thyself in the field;
And afterwards build thine house.
28 [a]Be not a witness against thy neighbour without cause;
And deceive not with thy lips.
29 [a]Say not, I will do so to him as he hath done to me:
I will render to the man according to his work.

30 I went by the field of the slothful,
And by the vineyard of the man void of understanding;
31 And lo, [a]it was all grown over *with* thorns,
And nettles had covered the face thereof,
And the stone wall thereof was broken down.
32 Then I saw, *and* [1]considered *it* well:
I looked upon *it, and* received instruction.
33 [a]*Yet* a little sleep, a little slumber,
A little folding of the hands to sleep:
34 So shall thy poverty come *as* one that travelleth;
And thy want as [1]an armed man.

More proverbs of Solomon

25 [a]These *are* also proverbs of Solomon, which the men of Hezekiah king of Judah copied out.

24:13 [1]Heb. *upon thy palate* [a]Sol. 5:1
24:14 [a]Ps. 19:10
24:16 [a]Ps. 34:19; Mic. 7:8 [b]Esth. 7:10; Amos 5:2
24:17 [a]Job 31:29; Obad. 12
24:18 [1]Heb. *it be evil in his eyes*
24:19 [1]Or, *Keep not company with the wicked* [a]Ps. 37:1
24:20 [1]Or, *lamp*
24:21 [1]Heb. *changers* [a]Rom. 13:7; 1 Pet. 2:17
24:23 [a]Lev. 19:15; Deut. 16:19
24:24 [a]Is. 5:23
24:25 [1]Heb. *a blessing of good*
24:26 [1]Heb. *That answereth right words*
24:27 [a]1 Ki. 5:17
24:28 [a]Eph. 4:25
24:29 [a]Mat. 5:39
24:31 [a]Gen. 3:18
24:32 [1]Heb. *set my heart*
24:33 [a]ch. 6:9
24:34 [1]Heb. *a man of shield*
25:1 [a]1 Ki. 4:32

‡24:14 *the knowledge of wisdom . . . unto thy soul.* It nourishes and brings healing (see 16:24 and note). *expectation.* Hope for the future. See Ps 9:18; 37:37; Jer 29:11.
24:15 *Lay not wait.* Cf. 1:11; 12:6; Ps 10:9–10.
24:16 *seven times.* Many times (see 6:16; Job 5:19 and note). *riseth up again.* God promises to uphold and rescue the righteous (cf. Ps 34:19; 37:24; Mic 7:8). *wicked shall fall into mischief.* See v. 22; 4:19; 6:15; 11:3,5.
24:17 *Rejoice not.* See 17:5 and note.
24:18 *turn away his wrath from him.* Edom was made desolate because she rejoiced over Israel's destruction (see Ezek 35:15).
24:19 Almost identical to Ps 37:1; see v. 1; 23:17.
24:20 *no reward.* For himself or his posterity (see Ps 37:2,28,38; contrast v. 14; 23:18). *candle . . . shall be put out.* See note on 13:9.
24:21 *fear thou the LORD and the king.* Submission to civil authority is also commanded in Eccl 8:2–5. 1 Pet 2:17 says, "Fear God. Honour the king," and Rom 13:1–7 urges the same obedience. These passages all view the king as a terror to the wicked (cf. 20:8,26).
24:22 *calamity shall rise suddenly; And . . . ruin.* God's judgment is more common (see 6:15; 11:3,5), but the power of the king is seen in 20:26. *them both.* God and the king.
24:23–34 An appendix to 22:17–24:22, giving a few additional sayings of the wise.
‡24:23 *It is not good . . . respect of persons.* To show favoritism or partiality. See 18:5 and note.
24:24 *Thou art righteous.* See 17:15. *Him shall the people curse.* Just as they curse the man who "withholdeth corn" (11:26).
24:25 *good blessing.* See 10:6; Deut 16:20.
24:26 *kiss his lips.* Cf. the "pleasant words" that are "sweet to the soul" in 16:24. *right answer.* Cf. 16:13.
24:27 *make it fit . . . in the field.* Plan carefully and acquire the means as you build your house. *house.* See note on v. 3.
24:28 *witness . . . without cause.* See 3:30. *deceive not with thy lips.* See 6:19 and note; 12:17; 25:18.
24:29 *I will do so to him.* A spirit of revenge is discouraged also in 20:22 (see note there); cf. 25:21–22; Mat 5:43–45; Rom 12:17.
24:30 *slothful.* See note on 6:6; see also 20:4.
24:31 *thorns . . . nettles.* Cf. 15:19; Is 34:13.
24:33–34 See 6:10–11 and note on 6:11.
25:1–29:27 Another collection of Solomon's proverbs similar to 10:1–22:16.
25:1 *proverbs of Solomon.* See notes on 1:1; 10:1. *men of Hezekiah . . . copied out.* There was a great revival in the reign of

2 [a]*It is* the glory of God to conceal a thing:
But the honour of kings *is* [b]to search out a matter.
3 The heaven for height, and the earth for depth,
And the heart of kings [1]*is* unsearchable.
4 [a]Take away the dross from the silver,
And there shall come forth a vessel for the finer.
5 [a]Take away the wicked *from* before the king,
And [b]his throne shall be established in righteousness.
6 [1]Put not forth thyself in the presence of the king,
And stand not in the place of great *men:*
7 [a]For better *it is* that it be said unto thee, Come up hither;
Than that thou shouldest be put lower in the presence of the prince
Whom thine eyes have seen.
8 [a]Go not forth hastily to strive,
Lest *thou know not* what to do in the end thereof,
When thy neighbour hath put thee to shame.
9 [a]Debate thy cause with thy neighbour *himself;*
And [1]discover not a secret *to* another:
10 Lest he that heareth *it* put thee to shame,
And thine infamy turn not away.

11 [a]A word [1]fitly spoken
Is like apples of gold in pictures of silver.

25:2 [a]Rom. 11:33 [b]Job 29:16
25:3 [1]Heb. there is *no searching*
25:4 [a]2 Tim. 2:21
25:5 [a]ch. 20:8 [b]ch. 16:12
25:6 [1]Heb. *Set not out thy glory*
25:7 [a]Luke 14:10
25:8 [a]Mat. 5:25
25:9 [1]Or, *discover not the secret of another* [a]Mat. 5:25
25:11 [1]Heb. *spoken upon his wheels* [a]ch. 15:23
25:13 [a]ch. 13:17
25:14 [1]Heb. *in a gift of falsehood* [a]ch. 20:6 [b]Jude 12
25:15 [a]ch. 15:1
25:16 [a]ver. 27
25:17 [1]Or, *Let thy foot be seldom in thy neighbour's house* [2]Heb. *full of thee*
25:18 [a]Ps. 57:4
25:20 [a]Dan. 6:18

12 *As* an earring of gold, and an ornament of fine gold,
So is a wise reprover upon an obedient ear.
13 [a]As the cold of snow in the time of harvest,
So is a faithful messenger to them that send him:
For he refresheth the soul of his masters.
14 [a]Whoso boasteth himself [1]of a false gift
Is like [b]clouds and wind without rain.
15 [a]By long forbearing is a prince persuaded,
And a soft tongue breaketh the bone.
16 [a]Hast thou found honey? eat so much as is sufficient for thee,
Lest thou be filled there*with,* and vomit it.
17 [1]Withdraw thy foot from thy neighbour's house;
Lest he be [2]weary *of* thee, and *so* hate thee.
18 [a]A man that beareth false witness against his neighbour
Is a maul, and a sword, and a sharp arrow.
19 Confidence in an unfaithful *man* in time of trouble
Is like a broken tooth, and a foot out of joint.
20 *As* he that taketh away a garment in cold weather,
And as vinegar upon nitre,
So *is* he that [a]singeth songs to a heavy heart.

Hezekiah (c. 715–686 B.C.), and the king restored the singing of hymns to its proper place (2 Chr 29:30). His interest in the words of David corresponds to his support of a compilation of Solomon's proverbs. Solomon was the last king to rule over all Israel during the united monarchy; Hezekiah was the first king to rule over all Israel (now restricted to the southern kingdom) after the destruction of the divided monarchy's northern kingdom.

25:2 *to conceal a thing.* God gets glory because man cannot understand His universe or the way He rules it (see Deut 29:29; Job 26:14 and note; Is 40:12–24; Rom 11:33–36). *to search out a matter.* A king gets glory if he can uncover the truth and administer justice (see 1 Ki 3:9; 4:34).

25:3 *is unsearchable.* Cannot be understood; like the four things in 30:18–19. Yet God controls the hearts of kings (see note on 21:1).

25:4 *Take away the dross from the silver.* A process compared to the purification of society in general and rulers in particular in Is 1:22–25; Ezek 22:18; Mal 3:2–3.

25:5 *his throne shall be established in righteousness.* See note on 16:12; see also 20:26.

‡25:6 *Put not forth thyself in the presence of the king.* Probably at a feast (cf. 23:1). Jesus gives a smiliar warning about taking the place of honor at a wedding feast (Luke 14:7–11).

25:7 *Come up hither.* Cf. "Friend, go up higher" (Luke 14:10); contrast Is 22:15–19.

‡25:8 *Go not forth hastily to strive.* A warning about the seriousness of disputes (see 17:14) and the need to exercise caution in initiating a dispute (see 24:28).

25:9 *discover not a secret.* If you do, you are a gossip (see 11:13; 20:19).

‡25:10 *thine infamy.* A gossip gets a bad reputation, a serious issue because a good name is one of life's most valuable possessions (see 22:1 and note).

25:11 *gold . . . silver.* Cf. the fruit of wisdom in 8:19.

25:12 *earring of gold.* Comparable to the beautiful wreath and necklace that represent the adornment of wisdom and sound teaching (see 1:9; 3:22; 4:9). *wise reprover.* Cf. the "reproof of life" in 15:31.

25:13 *cold of snow.* Probably a drink cooled by snow from the mountains; it did not snow at harvest time. See 26:1; contrast 10:26. *faithful messenger.* See 13:17 and note.

25:14 *like clouds . . . without rain.* An image applied to unproductive men in Jude 12.

25:15 *By long forbearing is a prince persuaded.* Cf. 14:29. *soft tongue.* See note on 15:1.

25:18 *false witness.* See note on 6:19; see also 24:28; Ex 20:16. *maul . . . sword . . . arrow.* Cf. Ps 57:4; Jer 9:8.

25:19 *broken tooth . . . foot out of joint.* Relying on Egypt was like leaning on a crushed reed (Is 36:6).

25:20 *nitre.* Probably sodium carbonate, natron (see Jer 2:22). There is a vigorous reaction when vinegar is poured on it. *singeth songs to a heavy heart.* The exiles were reluctant to sing the songs of Zion (Ps 137:3–4).

25:21–22 Quoted in Rom 12:20 as a way to overcome evil with good.

21 [a]If thine enemy *be* hungry, give him
bread to eat;
And if he *be* thirsty, give him water to
drink:
22 For thou shalt heap coals of fire upon
his head,
[a]And the LORD shall reward thee.
23 [a][1]The north wind driveth away rain:
So *doth* an angry countenance [b]a
backbiting tongue.
24 [a]*It is* better to dwell in a corner of the
housetop,
Than with a brawling woman and in a
wide house.
25 *As* cold waters to a thirsty soul,
So *is* good news from a far country.
26 A righteous *man* falling down before
the wicked
Is as a troubled fountain, and a corrupt
spring.
27 [a]*It is* not good to eat much honey:
So *for men* [b]to search their own glory
is not glory.
28 [a]He that *hath* no rule over his own spirit
Is like a city *that is* broken down, *and*
without walls.

26

As snow in summer, [a]and as rain in
harvest,
So honour *is* not seemly for a fool.
2 As the bird by wandering, as the
swallow by flying,
So [a]the curse causeless shall not come.
3 [a]A whip for the horse, a bridle for the
ass,
And a rod for the fools' back.
4 Answer not a fool according to his folly,
Lest thou also be like unto him.
5 [a]Answer a fool according to his folly,
Lest he be wise in [1]his own conceit.
6 He that sendeth a message by the hand
of a fool
Cutteth off the feet, *and* drinketh
[1]damage.
7 The legs of the lame [1]are not equal:
So *is* a parable in the mouth of fools.
8 [1]As *he that* bindeth a stone in a sling,
So *is* he that giveth honour to a fool.
9 *As* a thorn goeth up into the hand of a
drunkard,
So *is* a parable in the mouth of fools.
10 [1]The great *God* that formed all *things*
Both rewardeth the fool, and
rewardeth transgressors.
11 [a]As a dog returneth to his vomit,
[b]*So* a fool [1]returneth to his folly.
12 [a]Seest thou a man wise in his own
conceit?
There is more hope of a fool than of him.
13 The slothful *man* saith, *There is* a lion
in the way;
A lion *is* in the streets.
14 *As* the door turneth upon his hinges,
So *doth* the slothful upon his bed.
15 The slothful hideth his hand in *his*
bosom;
[1]It grieveth him to bring it again to his
mouth.
16 The sluggard *is* wiser in his own conceit
Than seven *men* that can render a
reason.

17 He that passeth by, *and* [1]meddleth
with strife *belonging* not to him,
Is like one that taketh a dog by the ears.

25:21 [a]Mat. 5:44
25:22 [a]2 Sam. 16:12
25:23 [1]Or, *The north wind bringeth forth rain: So* doth a *backbiting tongue an angry countenance* [a]Job 37:22 [b]Ps. 101:5
25:24 [a]ch. 19:13
25:27 [a]ver. 16 [b]ch. 27:2
25:28 [a]ch. 16:32
26:1 [a]1 Sam. 12:17
26:2 [a]Deut. 23:5
26:3 [a]Ps. 32:9
26:5 [1]Heb. *his own eyes* [a]Mat. 16:1-4
26:6 [1]Or, *violence*
26:7 [1]Heb. *are lifted up*
26:8 [1]Or, *As* he that *putteth a* precious *stone in a heap of stones*
26:10 [1]Or, *A great* man *grieveth all, And he hireth the fool, he hireth also transgressors*
26:11 [1]Heb. *iterateth his folly* [a]2 Pet. 2:22 [b]Ex. 8:15
26:12 [a]Rev. 3:17
26:15 [1]Or, *He is weary*
26:17 [1]Or, *is enraged*

25:21 Kindness to one's enemy is encouraged in 20:22; Ex 23:4–5. *give him bread . . . water.* At Elisha's request, a trapped Aramean army was given a great feast and then sent home (2 Ki 6:21–23; cf. 2 Chr 28:15).

25:22 *heap coals of fire upon his head.* Horrible punishment reserved for the wicked (see Ps 140:10). Here, however, it is kindness that will hurt the enemy (cf. the broken bone of v. 15) but perhaps win him over. Alternatively, the expression may reflect an Egyptian expiation ritual, in which a guilty person, as a sign of his repentance, carried a basin of glowing coals on his head. The meaning here, then, would be that in returning good for evil and so being kind to your enemy, you may cause him to repent or change. *LORD shall reward thee.* Even if the enemy remains hostile (cf. 11:18; 19:17).

25:23 *north.* Perhaps northwest (cf. Luke 12:54). *backbiting tongue.* One that spreads slander (cf. 10:18).

25:25 *good news from a far country.* See Gen 45:25–28.

25:26 *troubled fountain.* Cf. Ezek 34:18–19.

‡25:27 *to search their own glory.* To seek glory for oneself. See vv. 6–7 and notes.

‡25:28 *He that hath no rule over his own spirit.* One who is lacking self-control. See 16:32 and note. *city that is . . . without walls.* Defenseless and disgraced (cf. Neh 1:3).

26:1 *rain in harvest.* It rarely rains in the Holy Land from June through September, but see 1 Sam 12:17–18. *honour is not seemly for a fool.* See v. 8; 30:22.

‡26:2 *the curse causeless shall not come.* A curse without basis. When David was cursed by Shimei, he realized that the curse would not take effect because he was innocent of the charge of murdering members of Saul's family (2 Sam 16:8,12).

26:3 *rod for the fools' back.* See 14:3; 19:29.

26:4 *Answer not a fool according to his folly.* Do not stoop to his level (see 23:9; Mat 7:6).

26:5 *Answer a fool according to his folly.* Sometimes folly must be plainly exposed and denounced.

26:6 *drinketh damage.* See 4:17; Job 34:7.

26:7 *a parable in the mouth of fools.* He will likely misrepresent the one who sends him, or in some other manner frustrate the sender's purpose (see 13:17).

26:8 *As he that bindeth a stone in a sling.* A fool with authority wields a formidable weapon, but it is useless in his hands—as useless as a stone that is tied, not placed, in the sling.

26:9 A fool reciting a proverb will do as much damage to himself and others as a drunkard wielding a thorn bush.

‡26:11 *As a dog returneth to his vomit.* Quoted in 2 Pet 2:22 with reference to false teachers. *fool returneth to his folly.* He repeats the same foolish actions, like the drunkard who returns to his drink (23:35).

26:12 *wise in his own conceit.* This conceit is applied to the sluggard in v. 16 and the rich in 28:11; cf. 26:5.

26:13 See 22:13 and note.

26:14 The sluggard loves to sleep and seems to be attached to his bed as a door to its hinges.

26:16 *wiser in his own conceit.* See v. 12 and note.

26:17 *taketh a dog by the ears.* To do so is to immediately create a disturbance.

18 As a mad *man* who casteth [1]firebrands,
arrows, and death,
19 So *is* the man *that* deceiveth his
neighbour,
And saith, [a]Am not I in sport?
20 [1]Where no wood is, *there* the fire
goeth out:
So where *there is* no [2]talebearer, the
strife [3]ceaseth.
21 [a]*As* coals *are* to burning coals, and
wood to fire;
So *is* a contentious man to kindle
strife.
22 The words of a talebearer *are* as
wounds,
And they go down *into* the [1]innermost
parts of the belly.
23 Burning lips and a wicked heart
Are like a potsherd covered with silver
dross.
24 He that hateth [1]dissembleth with his
lips,
And layeth up deceit within him;
25 [a]When he [1]speaketh fair, believe him
not:
For *there are* seven abominations in
his heart.
26 *Whose* [1]hatred is covered by deceit,
His wickedness shall be shewed before
the *whole* congregation.
27 [a]Whoso diggeth a pit shall fall therein:
And he that rolleth a stone, it will
return upon him.
28 A lying tongue hateth *those that are*
afflicted by it;
And a flattering mouth worketh ruin.

27 Boast not thyself of [1]to morrow;
For thou knowest not what a day
may bring forth.
2 Let another *man* praise thee, and not
thine own mouth;
A stranger, and not thine own lips.
3 A stone *is* [1]heavy, and the sand
weighty;
But a fool's wrath *is* heavier than them
both.
4 [1]Wrath *is* cruel, and anger *is*
outrageous;
But who is able to stand before [2]envy?
5 Open rebuke *is* better than secret love.
6 Faithful *are* the wounds of a friend;
But the kisses of an enemy *are*
[1]deceitful.
7 The full soul [1]loatheth a honeycomb;
But *to* the hungry soul every bitter
thing is sweet.
8 As a bird that wandereth from her
nest,
So *is* a man that wandereth from his
place.
9 Ointment and perfume rejoice the
heart:
So *doth* the sweetness of a man's
friend [1]by hearty counsel.
10 Thine own friend, and thy father's
friend, forsake not;
Neither go *into* thy brother's house in
the day of thy calamity:
For [a]better *is* a neighbour *that is* near
than a brother far off.

11 My son, be wise, and make my heart
glad,
[a]That I may answer him that
reproacheth me.
12 A prudent *man* foreseeth the evil, *and*
hideth himself;
But the simple pass on, *and* are
punished.
13 Take his garment that is surety *for* a
stranger,
And take a pledge of him for a strange
woman.

26:18 [1]Heb. *flames, or, sparks* 26:19 [a]Eph. 5:4 26:20 [1]Heb. *Without wood* [2]Or, *whisperer* [3]Heb. *is silent* 26:21 [a]ch. 15:18 26:22 [1]Heb. *chambers* 26:24 [1]Or, *is known* 26:25 [1]Heb. *maketh his voice gracious* [a]Ps. 28:3 26:26 [1]Or, *hatred is covered in secret* 26:27 [a]Ps. 7:15 27:1 [1]Heb. *to morrow day*

27:3 [1]Heb. *heaviness* 27:4 [1]Heb. *Wrath is cruelty, and anger an overflowing* [2]Or, *jealousy?* 27:6 [1]Or, *earnest,* or, *frequent* 27:7 [1]Heb. *treadeth under foot* 27:9 [1]Heb. *from the counsel of the soul* 27:10 [a]ch. 17:17 27:11 [a]Ps. 127:5

26:18 *As a mad man who casteth.* Cf. the archer in v. 10. *firebrands.* Could easily ignite sheaves of grain (cf. Zech 12:6).
‡26:19 *Am not I in sport?* Claims that he is joking or playing a prank.
26:21 *kindle strife.* See 6:14 and note.
26:22 See 18:8 and note.
26:23 *Burning lips and a wicked heart.* The speech of the adulteress is seductive (2:16; 5:3). *silver dross.* Or "glaze." Cf. the clean outside of the cup and dish (Luke 11:39; cf. Mat 23:27).
26:24 *layeth up deceit within him.* See 12:20.
‡26:25 *he speaketh fair.* He uses gracious speech to deceive. See Jer 9:8. *seven.* Many (see note on Job 5:19). For seven things the Lord detests see 6:16–19.
26:26 *shall be shewed before the whole congregation.* See 5:14; Luke 8:17.
26:27 *Whoso diggeth a pit shall fall therein.* "His mischief shall return upon his own head" (Ps 7:16). See 1:18 and note; 28:10; 29:6; Esth 7:10; Ps 7:15; Eccl 10:8–9.
26:28 *lying tongue hateth those that are afflicted by it.* See 10:18. *flattering mouth worketh ruin.* See 29:5; cf. 16:13.
27:1 Cf. the words of the rich fool in Luke 12:19–20; see Prov 16:9; Is 56:12.
27:2 *Let another man praise thee.* See 2 Cor 10:12,18.
27:4 *who is able to stand before envy?* See 6:34; Sol 8:6.
27:5 *Open rebuke.* Called the "reproof of life" in 15:31; cf. Gal 2:14.
27:6 *Faithful are the wounds of a friend.* Called a sign of kindness in Ps 141:5. *kisses of an enemy.* See 5:3–4; Mat 26:49.
27:7 *loatheth a honeycomb.* Cf. 25:16,27.
‡27:8 *man that wandereth from his place.* By leaving home, he has lost his security and may be vulnerable to temptation (cf. 7:21–23).
27:9 *Ointment.* See note on 21:17. *perfume.* Cf. the one "perfumed with myrrh and frankincense" (Sol 3:6). *sweetness of a man's friend.* Cf. 16:21,24.
27:10 Do not fail a friend in need; when in need rely on friendship rather than on mere family relationships. *brother far off.* Either physically or emotionally.
27:11 *My son, be wise.* See 10:1 and note. *That I may answer him that reproacheth me.* A wise son (or student) serves as a powerful testimony that the father (or teacher) who has shaped him has shown himself to be a man of worth.
‡27:12 *the simple.* See note on 1:4. *pass on, and are punished.* They go their own way and disregard wise counsel. See 7:22–23; 9:16–18.
27:13 A repetition of 20:16 (see note there).

14 He that blesseth his friend with a loud
voice, rising early in the morning,
It shall be counted a curse to him.
15 A continual dropping in a very rainy
day
And a contentious woman are alike.
16 Whosoever hideth her, hideth the
wind,
And the ointment of his right hand,
which bewrayeth *itself.*
17 Iron sharpeneth iron;
So a man sharpeneth the countenance
of his friend.
18 [a]Whoso keepeth the fig tree shall eat
the fruit thereof:
So he that waiteth on his master shall
be honoured.
19 As *in* water face *answereth* to face,
So the heart of man to man.
20 [a]Hell and destruction are [1]never full;
So [b]the eyes of man are never satisfied.
21 [a]*As* the fining pot for silver, and the
furnace for gold;
So *is* a man to his praise.
22 [a]Though thou shouldest bray a fool in a
mortar among wheat with a pestle,
Yet will not his foolishness depart from
him.

23 Be thou diligent to know the state of
thy flocks,
And [1]look well to thy herds.
24 For [1]riches *are* not for ever:
And doth the crown *endure* [2]to every
generation?

27:18 [a]1 Cor. 9:7
27:20 [1]Heb. *not*
[a]Hab. 2:5 [b]Eccl. 1:8
27:21 [a]ch. 17:3
27:22 [a]Jer. 5:3
27:23 [1]Heb. *set thy heart*
27:24 [1]Heb. *strength* [2]Heb. *to generation and generation?*

27:25 [a]Ps. 104:14
27:27 [1]Heb. *life*
28:1 [a]Ps. 53:5
28:2 [1]Or, *by men of understanding* and *wisdom shall they likewise be prolonged*
28:3 [1]Heb. *without food*
[a]Mat. 18:28
28:4 [a]Rom. 1:32
[b]1 Ki. 18:18
28:5 [a]Ps. 92:6
[b]John 7:17
28:6 [a]ch. 19:1
28:7 [1]Or, *feedeth gluttons*
[a]ch. 29:3

25 [a]The hay appeareth, and the tender
grass sheweth itself,
And herbs of the mountains are
gathered.
26 The lambs *are* for thy clothing,
And the goats *are* the price of the field.
27 And *thou shalt have* goats' milk enough
for thy food,
For the food of thy household,
And *for* the [1]maintenance for thy
maidens.

28 The [a]wicked flee when no man
pursueth:
But the righteous are bold as a lion.
2 For the transgression of a land many
are the princes thereof:
But [1]by a man of understanding *and*
knowledge the state *thereof* shall be
prolonged.
3 [a]A poor man that oppresseth the poor
Is like a sweeping rain [1]which leaveth
no food.
4 [a]They that forsake the law praise the
wicked:
[b]But such as keep the law contend
with them.
5 [a]Evil men understand not judgment:
But [b]they that seek the LORD
understand all *things.*
6 [a]Better *is* the poor that walketh in his
uprightness,
Than *he that is* perverse in *his* ways,
though he *be* rich.
7 [a]Whoso keepeth the law *is* a wise son:
But he that [1]is a companion of riotous
men shameth his father.

27:14 *blesseth his friend.* Perhaps to win his favor (cf. Ps 12:2).
27:15 See 19:13 and note.
27:17 *sharpeneth the countenance of his friend.* Develops and molds his character.
27:18 *shall eat the fruit thereof.* Cf. 2 Tim 2:6. *shall be honoured.* Cf. Gen 39:4; see also Mat 25:21; Luke 12:42–44; John 12:26.
‡27:19 *the heart of man to man.* The condition of a man's heart indicates his true character like the reflection of one's face in a pool of water (see Mat 5:8).
27:20 *Hell and destruction.* See note on Job 26:6; see also 15:11. *are never full.* Their appetite is insatiable (see Is 5:14). *So the eyes of man.* See Eccl 4:8.
‡27:21 *fining pot . . . gold.* Silver and gold were refined to remove their impurities (cf. Is 1:25; Mal 3:3). *So is a man to his praise.* How a person responds to praise is a reflection of one's character. One must not become proud, and one must be wary of flattery (cf. 12:8; Luke 6:26).
27:22 *mortar.* A bowl (see Num 11:8). *pestle.* A club-like tool for pounding grain in a mortar. *will not his foolishness depart from him.* In spite of severe punishment, fools refuse to change (see note on 20:30; see also 26:11; Jer 5:3).
27:23–27 A section praising the basic security afforded by agricultural pursuits—reflecting the agricultural base of the ancient economy.
27:23 *Be thou diligent . . . herds.* Like Jacob, with Laban's flocks (Gen 31:38–40).
‡27:24 *riches are not for ever.* See note on 23:5. *doth the crown endure to every generation?* A rhetorical question expecting a negative answer. Even kings may lose their wealth and power (see Job 19:9; Lam 5:16).
27:25 *The hay appeareth . . . grass sheweth itself.* This began in March or April.
27:26 *price of the field.* See 31:16. Sheep and goats sometimes also served as tribute payments (see 2 Ki 3:4).
27:27 *goats' milk.* Commonly drunk along with cows' milk (see Deut 32:13–14; Is 7:21–22). *maidens.* See 31:15.
28:1 *wicked flee.* See Lev 26:17,36; Ps 53:5. *bold as a lion.* Like David in 1 Sam 17:46; cf. Ps 18:33–38.
28:2 *many are the princes thereof.* Israel's rebellion often brought rapid change in leadership (see 1 Ki 16:8–28; 2 Ki 15:8–15). *by a man of understanding . . . shall be prolonged.* A wise ruler will be successful (see 8:15–16; 24:5; 29:4).
28:3 *that oppresseth the poor.* See 14:31. *sweeping rain.* Describes the destructive power of Assyria's army in Is 28:2. The gentle rain is compared to a righteous king in Ps 72:6–7.
28:4 *law.* Either the teachings of wisdom (3:1; 7:2) or the law of Moses (Ps 119:53). *praise the wicked.* Cf. Rom 1:32. *such as keep the law.* See v. 7; 29:18; cf. v. 9. *contend with them.* See Eph 5:11; cf. Rom 1:32.
‡28:5 *they that seek the LORD.* Who fear Him (see note on 1:7). *understand all things.* All things that are necessary to live a godly and successful life. They know "righteousness, and justice, and equity" (2:9).
28:6 *walketh in his uprightness.* See 2:7 and note.
‡28:7 *Whoso keepeth the law.* See note on v. 4. *companion of riotous men.* Persons who pursue a hedonistic lifestyle without regard for God. See notes on 23:20–21.

8 [a]He that by usury and [1]unjust gain
increaseth his substance,
He shall gather it for him that will pity
the poor.
9 He that turneth away his ear from
hearing the law,
[a]Even his prayer *shall be* abomination.
10 [a]Whoso causeth the righteous to go
astray in an evil way,
He shall fall himself into his own pit:
[b]But the upright shall have good *things*
in possession.
11 The rich man *is* wise [1]in his own
conceit;
But the poor that hath understanding
searcheth him out.
12 [a]When righteous *men* do rejoice, *there*
is great glory:
But when the wicked rise, a man is
[1]hidden.
13 [a]He that covereth his sins shall not
prosper:
But whoso confesseth and forsaketh
them shall have mercy.
14 Happy *is* the man [a]that feareth alway:
[b]But he that hardeneth his heart shall
fall into mischief.
15 [a]*As* a roaring lion, and a ranging bear;
[b]*So is* a wicked ruler over the poor
people.
16 The prince that wanteth understanding
is also a great oppressor:
But he that hateth covetousness shall
prolong *his* days.
17 [a]A man that doeth violence to the
blood of *any* person
Shall flee to the pit; let no man stay him.
18 [a]Whoso walketh uprightly shall be
saved:
But [b]*he that is* perverse in *his* ways
shall fall at once.
19 [a]He that tilleth his land shall have
plenty *of* bread:
But he that followeth after vain
persons shall have poverty enough.
20 A faithful man shall abound with
blessings:
[a]But he that maketh haste to be rich
shall not be [1]innocent.
21 [a]To have respect of persons *is* not good:
For [b]for a piece of bread *that* man will
transgress.
22 [a][1]He that hasteth to be rich *hath* an
evil eye,
And considereth not that poverty shall
come *upon* him.
23 [a]He that rebuketh a man, afterwards
shall find more favour
Than he that flattereth with the tongue.
24 Whoso robbeth his father or his
mother,
And saith, *It is* no transgression;
The same [a]*is* the companion of [1]a
destroyer.
25 [a]He that is of a proud heart stirreth up
strife:
[b]But he that putteth his trust in the
LORD shall be made fat.
26 He that trusteth in his own heart *is* a
fool:
But whoso walketh wisely, he shall be
delivered.

28:8 [1]Heb. *by increase* [a]ch. 13:22
28:9 [a]Ps. 66:18
28:10 [a]ch. 26:27 [b]Mat. 6:33
28:11 [1]Heb. *in his eyes*
28:12 [1]Or, *sought for* [a]ch. 11:10
28:13 [a]Ps. 32:3,5
28:14 [a]Ps. 16:8 [b]Rom. 2:5
28:15 [a]1 Pet. 5:8 [b]Mat. 2:16
28:17 [a]Gen. 9:6
28:18 [a]ch. 10:9,25 [b]ver. 6
28:19 [a]ch. 12:11
28:20 [1]Or, *unpunished* [a]1 Tim. 6:9
28:21 [a]ch. 18:5 [b]Ezek. 13:19
28:22 [1]Or, *He that hath an evil eye hasteth to be rich* [a]ver. 20
28:23 [a]ch. 27:5,6
28:24 [1]Heb. *a man destroying* [a]ch. 18:9
28:25 [a]ch. 13:10 [b]1 Tim. 6:6

28:8 *usury and unjust gain.* Prohibited in Ex 22:25; Lev 25:35–37; Deut 23:19–20; Ezek 22:12. *gather it for him.* See 13:22 and note. *that will pity the poor.* See 14:31; see also note on 14:21.

28:9 *law.* See note on v. 4. *his prayer shall be abomination.* Like the sacrifice of the wicked in 15:8 (see note on 3:32; see also Ps 66:18; Is 1:15; 59:1–2).

28:10 *into his own pit.* See note on 26:27. *upright.* See note on 2:7. *shall have good things.* See 3:35; Heb 6:12; 1 Pet 3:9.

28:11 *rich man is wise in his own conceit.* Like the fool (26:5) or the sluggard (26:16).

‡28:12 *there is great glory.* See 11:10 and note. *a man is hidden.* He hides to avoid the tyranny of the wicked ruler. Obadiah hid 100 prophets during the reign of Ahab (1 Ki 18:13), and Joash was hidden for six years while the wicked Athaliah ruled (2 Ki 11:2–3).

‡28:13 *He that covereth his sins shall not prosper.* Tries to hide his wrongdoing. Note the physical and psychological pain referred to in 3:7–8; Ps 32:3. *whoso confesseth and forsaketh them shall have mercy.* Note the joy of forgiveness in Ps 32:5,10–11.

28:14 *feareth alway.* See note on 1:7; see also 23:17. *he that hardeneth his heart.* Like Pharaoh (Ex 7:13), and the Israelites who tested the Lord at Horeb (Ex 17:7; cf. Ps 95:8; Rom 2:5).

‡28:15 *roaring lion.* Full of rage and murderous intent (cf. 19:12; Mat 2:16; 1 Pet 5:8). *ranging bear.* An angry bear on the attack. See 17:12 and note. *wicked ruler.* See v. 12.

28:16 *he that hateth covetousness shall prolong his days.* Unlike those who love such gain (see 1:19).

‡28:17 *A man that doeth violence to the blood.* A murderer. *Shall flee to the pit.* Will experience an early death himself as punishment for his sin. Murder was punishable by death (see Gen 9:6; Ex 21:14).

28:18 *uprightly . . . perverse.* Contrasted also in v. 6; 19:1. *shall fall at once.* Cf. 11:5.

‡28:19 *followeth after vain persons.* Lit. "follows after unprofitable [things]" (the noun is not supplied). Probably referring here to schemes for making easy money.

‡28:20 *abound with blessings.* With God's gifts and favors (see 3:13–18; 10:6; Gen 49:26; Deut 33:16). *he that maketh haste to be rich shall not be innocent.* He will not go unpunished for his wrongdoing. Cf. similar warnings in 20:21; 23:4 (see notes).

28:21 *To have respect of persons is not good.* See 18:5 and note; 24:23. *for a piece of bread that man will transgress.* Perhaps a reference to a bribe, however small (cf. Ezek 13:19).

‡28:22 *hasteth to be rich.* A warning to him is given in v. 20 (cf. similar warnings in 20:21; 23:4). *hath an evil eye.* He has impure motives. See 23:6. *poverty shall come upon him.* Because it is the generous man who prospers (see note on 11:25).

28:23 *He that rebuketh a man.* See Gal 2:14; cf. 15:31; 25:12. *Than he that flattereth with the tongue.* Cf. 16:13; 26:28; 29:5.

28:24 *Whoso robbeth his father or his mother.* See note on 19:26; cf. Mat 15:4–6; Mark 7:10–12.

‡28:25 *stirreth up strife.* See note on 6:14. *shall be made fat.* Will become prosperous, as will also the generous person (11:25) and the one who is diligent (13:4, "the soul of the diligent shall be made fat").

28:26 *whoso walketh wisely.* Equals "whoso putteth his trust in the LORD" in 29:25; cf. 3:5.

27 [a]He that giveth unto the poor *shall* not
lack:
But he that hideth his eyes shall have
many a curse.
28 [a]When the wicked rise, [b]men hide
themselves:
But when they perish, the righteous
increase.

29 [a][1]He, that being often reproved
hardeneth *his* neck,
Shall suddenly be destroyed, and that
without remedy.
2 [a]When the righteous are [1]in authority,
the people rejoice:
But when the wicked beareth rule,
[b]the people mourn.
3 [a]Whoso loveth wisdom rejoiceth his
father:
[b]But he that keepeth company with
harlots spendeth *his* substance.
4 The king by judgment stablisheth the
land:
But [1]he that receiveth gifts
overthroweth it.
5 A man that flattereth his neighbour
Spreadeth a net for his feet.
6 In the transgression of an evil man
there is a snare:
But the righteous doth sing and rejoice.
7 [a]The righteous considereth the cause
of the poor:
But the wicked regardeth not to know *it.*
8 [a]Scornful men [1]bring a city into a
snare:
But wise *men* [b]turn away wrath.
9 If a wise man contendeth with a
foolish man,
[a]Whether he rage or laugh, *there is* no
rest.
10 [a][1]The bloodthirsty hate the upright:
But the just seek his soul.
11 A [a]fool uttereth all his mind:
But a wise *man* keepeth it in *till*
afterwards.
12 If a ruler hearken to lies,
All his servants *are* wicked.
13 The poor and [1]the deceitful man meet
together:
[a]The LORD lighteneth both their eyes.
14 [a]The king that faithfully judgeth the
poor,
His throne shall be established for ever.
15 The rod and reproof give wisdom:
But [a]a child left *to himself* bringeth his
mother to shame.
16 When the wicked are multiplied,
transgression increaseth:
[a]But the righteous shall see their fall.
17 [a]Correct thy son, and he shall give
thee rest;
Yea, he shall give delight unto thy soul.
18 [a]Where *there is* no vision, the people
[1]perish:
But [b]he that keepeth the law, happy *is*
he.
19 A servant will not be corrected by
words:
For though he understand he will not
answer.
20 Seest thou a man that is hasty [1]in his
words?
[a]*There is* more hope of a fool than of
him.
21 He that delicately bringeth up his
servant from a child

28:27 [a]Deut. 15:7
28:28 [a]ver. 12 [b]Job 24:4
29:1 [1]Heb. *A man of reproofs* [a]2 Chr. 36:16
29:2 [1]Or, *increased* [a]Esth. 8:15 [b]Esth. 3:15
29:3 [a]ch. 10:1 [b]Luke 15:13
29:4 [1]Heb. *a man of oblations*
29:7 [a]Job 29:16; Ps. 41:1
29:8 [1]Or, *set a city on fire* [a]ch. 11:11 [b]Ezek. 22:30
29:9 [a]Mat. 11:17
29:10 [1]Heb. *Men of blood* [a]1 John 3:12
29:11 [a]ch. 12:16
29:13 [1]Or, *the usurer* [a]Mat. 5:45
29:14 [a]ch. 20:28
29:15 [a]ch. 17:21,25
29:16 [a]Ps. 37:36
29:17 [a]ch. 19:18
29:18 [1]Or, *is made naked* [a]1 Sam. 3:1; Amos 8:11 [b]John 13:17
29:20 [1]Or, *in his matters?* [a]ch. 26:12

‡28:27 *giveth unto the poor.* See note on 14:21. *shall not lack.* Generosity is the path to blessing (see 11:24 and note; 14:21; 19:17). *hideth his eyes.* From the needs of the poor. See 21:13.
28:28 *men hide themselves.* See v. 12 and note. *righteous increase.* See 11:10; 29:2.
29:1 *being often reproved hardeneth his neck.* Eli's sons died because of their stubbornness (see 1 Sam 2:25; cf. Deut 9:6,13). *Shall suddenly be destroyed, and that without remedy.* Cf. the fate of the mockers in 1:22–27.
29:2 *When the righteous are in authority, the people rejoice.* See 11:10 and note. *when the wicked beareth rule, the people mourn.* See 28:12 and note; see also Judg 2:18. The Israelites groaned in Egypt (Ex 2:23–24).
‡29:3 *Whoso loveth wisdom rejoiceth his father.* Brings joy to his father. See 10:1 and note. *he that keepeth company with harlots spendeth his substance.* Wastes his money. See 5:10; 6:26 and notes.
‡29:4 *The king by judgment stablisheth the land.* The king brings stability through the practice of justice. See 16:12 and note. *gifts.* See 17:8 and note.
29:6 *In the transgression . . . snare.* See 1:18 and note; 22:5.
29:7 *The righteous considereth . . . the poor.* Like Job (Job 29:16); cf. v. 14; 19:17; 22:22.
29:8 *Scornful men . . . snare.* See notes on 6:14; 11:11; see also 26:21. *Scornful men.* See 1:22 and note. *wise men turn away wrath.* See Jas 3:17–18.
‡29:9 *Whether he rage or laugh.* The fool will go from anger to ridicule in his attempt to disrupt justice. *rage.* Like an angry bear (17:12) or the tossing sea (Is 57:20-21).
29:10 *The bloodthirsty hate the upright.* Their schemes are described in 1:11–16; cf. Ps 5:6.
‡29:11 *uttereth all his mind.* Says whatever he feels when losing his temper. See v. 9; 14:16–17. *keepeth it in till afterwards.* See 16:32 and note.
29:12 *All his servants are wicked.* Cf. Is 1:23.
29:14 See note on 16:12; see also v. 4; Is 9:7.
29:15 *rod.* See note on 13:24.
29:16 *When the wicked are multiplied.* See v. 2; 11:11; 28:12,28. *righteous shall see their fall.* See 10:25 and note; 14:11; 21:12.
29:17 *Correct thy son.* Teach him and train him (see 13:24 and note; 22:6).
‡29:18 *vision.* A message from God given through a prophet; a prophetic vision (see 1 Sam 3:1; Is 1:1; Amos 8:11–12). *perish.* Lit."are unrestrained."The people act without the moral restraint of God's Word. Possibly an allusion to the sinful actions of the Israelites while Moses was on mount Sinai (see Ex 32:25 and note). *he that keepeth the law, happy is he.* See 28:4 and note; see also 8:32; 28:14.
29:19 *will not be corrected by words.* Servants, like sons (vv. 15,17), must be disciplined (see note on 22:6).
29:20 *hasty in his words.* See 10:19; 17:27–28; Jas 1:19. *There is more hope of a fool than of him.* Identical to 26:12.
‡29:21 *delicately bringeth up his servant.* Pampers his servant. See v. 19. *Shall have him . . . son at the length.* The Hebrew lit.

Shall have him become *his* son at the
length.
22 [a]An angry man stirreth up strife,
And a furious man aboundeth in
transgression.
23 [a]A man's pride shall bring him low:
But honour shall uphold the humble in
spirit.
24 Whoso is partner with a thief hateth
his own soul:
[a]He heareth cursing, and bewrayeth *it*
not.
25 [a]The fear of man bringeth a snare:
But whoso putteth his trust in the LORD
[1]shall be safe.
26 [a]Many seek [1]the ruler's favour;
But *every* man's judgment *cometh* from
the LORD.
27 An unjust man is an abomination to
the just:
And *he that is* upright in the way *is*
abomination to the wicked.

Observations of Agur

30 The words of Agur the son of Jakeh,
even the prophecy: the man spake
unto Ithiel, even unto Ithiel and Ucal.

2 [a]Surely I *am* more brutish than *any*
man,
And have not the understanding of a
man.
3 I neither learned wisdom,
Nor [1]have the knowledge of the holy.
4 [a]Who hath ascended up *into* heaven,
or descended?
[b]Who hath gathered the wind in his
fists?
Who hath bound the waters in a
garment?
Who hath established all the ends of
the earth?
What *is* his name, and what *is* his son's
name, if thou canst tell?

5 [a]Every word of God *is* [1]pure:
[b]He *is* a shield unto them that put
their trust in him.
6 [a]Add thou not unto his words,
Lest he reprove thee, and thou be
found a liar.

7 Two *things* have I required of thee;
[1]Deny me *them* not before I die:
8 Remove far from me vanity and lies:
Give me neither poverty nor riches;
[a]Feed me with food [1]convenient for
me:
9 [a]Lest I be full, and [1]deny *thee,*
And say, Who *is* the LORD?
Or lest I be poor, and steal,
And take the name of my God *in vain.*

10 [1]Accuse not a servant unto his master,
Lest he curse thee, and thou be found
guilty.
11 *There is* a generation *that* curseth their
father,
And doth not bless their mother.
12 *There is* a generation [a]*that are* pure in
their own eyes,
And *yet* is not washed from their
filthiness.
13 *There is* a generation, O how [a]lofty are
their eyes!
And their eyelids are lifted up.

29:22 [a]ch. 26:21
29:23 [a]Job 22:29; Is. 66:2; Dan. 4:30; Mat. 23:12
29:24 [a]Lev. 5:1
29:25 [1]Heb. *shall be set on high* [a]Gen. 12:12
29:26 [1]Heb. *the face of a ruler* [a]Ps. 20:9
30:2 [a]Ps. 73:22
30:3 [1]Heb. *know*
30:4 [a]John 3:13 [b]Job 38:4; Ps. 104:3; Is. 40:12
30:5 [1]Heb. *purified* [a]Ps. 12:6 [b]Ps. 18:30
30:6 [a]Deut. 4:2; Rev. 22:18
30:7 [1]Heb. *Withhold not from me*
30:8 [1]Heb. *of my allowance* [a]Mat. 6:11
30:9 [1]Heb. *belie thee* [a]Deut. 8:12
30:10 [1]Heb. *Hurt not with thy tongue*
30:12 [a]Luke 18:11
30:13 [a]Ps. 131:1; ch. 6:17

reads, "the end shall be trouble." The word translated "trouble" appears only here.
29:22 *angry man stirreth up strife.* See note on 6:14; see also 15:18.
29:23 See 15:33 and note; see also 18:12.
‡29:24 *cursing.* The swearing of an oath in the courtroom to tell the truth. *and bewrayeth it not.* He will be held responsible for failing to testify against his partner in crime (cf. Lev 5:1).
29:25 *fear of man.* Cf. 1 Sam 15:24; Is 51:12; John 12:42–43. *whoso putteth his trust in the LORD shall be safe.* See 18:10 and note; cf. 3:5–6.
29:26 *Many seek the ruler's favour.* See 2 Sam 14:22; 16:4; Esth 4:8; 5:2; 7:3; 8:5. *every man's judgment cometh from the LORD.* God controls a king's actions (see note on 21:1) and defends the cause of the poor and the just (cf. Job 36:6).
30:1–33 The first of two chapters that serve as an appendix to Proverbs.
30:1 *Agur the son of Jakeh.* Probably a wise man like Ethan and Heman (1 Ki 4:31). *prophecy.* Usually the message of a prophet (see note on Is 13:1). If "prophecy" is taken as the place name "Massa" (that is, "Jakeh of Massa"), Agur would then be associated with an Ishmaelite people (cf. Gen 25:13–14). *Ithiel . . . Ucal.* Perhaps students of Agur.
‡30:2 *I am more brutish than any man.* An exaggerated expression of his ignorance as an expression of humility. Paul described himself as the "chief" of sinners (1 Tim 1:16).
‡30:3 *knowledge of the holy.* Or, of the "Holy One" (God). See note on 2:5. This phrase occurs elsewhere in Proverbs only in 9:10.
‡30:4 The use of rhetorical questions to express God's greatness as Creator occurs also in Job 38:4–11; Is 40:12. *gathered the wind.* Cf. Ps 135:7. *bound the waters in a garment.* See Job 26:8; 38:8–9. *if thou canst tell.* "Do you know?" God similarly challenged Job (Job 38:4).
30:5 Almost identical to Ps 18:30. *shield.* See note on 2:7. *them that put their trust in him.* See 14:32; 18:10.
30:6 *Add thou not unto his words.* Cf. Moses' warning to the Israelites in Deut 4:2.
30:7 *Two things.* The use of lists characterizes Agur's sayings (see vv. 15,18,21,24,29).
‡30:8 *food convenient for me.* Ration or portion of daily food. Cf. Job 23:12 and the Lord's prayer (Mat 6:11).
30:9 *Lest I be full, and deny thee.* Moses predicted that Israel would forget God when their food was plentiful and their herds large (Deut 8:12–17; 31:20). *Who is the LORD?* Or, Why should I serve Him (see Job 21:14–16)? *lest I be poor, and steal.* Cf. 6:30.
30:10 *thou be found guilty.* Since the accusation is false, the servant's curse will be effective (cf. 26:2)—so do not suppose you can take advantage of a servant's lowly position.
30:11 *curseth their father.* Punishable by death (see Ex 21:17; Lev 20:9; cf. v. 17).
30:12 *pure in their own eyes.* Like the Pharisees (Luke 18:11; cf. Is 65:5).
30:13 *how lofty are their eyes!* See note on 6:17; see also Is 3:16.

14 [a]*There is* a generation, whose teeth *are*
as swords,
And their jaw teeth *as* knives,
[b]To devour the poor from off the earth,
And the needy from *among* men.

15 The horseleach hath two daughters,
crying, Give, give.

There are three *things that* are never
satisfied,
Yea, four *things* say not, [1]*It is* enough:
16 [a]The grave; and the barren womb;
The earth *that* is not filled *with* water;
And the fire *that* saith not, *It is*
enough.

17 [a]The eye *that* mocketh at *his* father,
And despiseth to obey *his* mother,
The ravens of [1]the valley shall pick it
out,
And the young eagles shall eat it.

18 There be three *things which* are too
wonderful for me,
Yea, four which I know not:
19 The way of an eagle in the air;
The way of a serpent upon a rock;
The way of a ship in the [1]midst of the
sea;
And the way of a man with a maid.
20 Such *is* the way of an adulterous
woman;
She eateth, and wipeth her mouth,
And saith, I have done no wickedness.

21 For three *things* the earth is
disquieted,
And for four *which* it cannot bear:
22 [a]For a servant when he reigneth;
And a fool when he is filled *with* meat;

30:14 [a]Job 29:17; Ps. 52:2 [b]Ps. 14:4; Amos 8:4
30:15 [1]Heb. *Wealth*
30:16 [a]ch. 27:20; Hab. 2:5
30:17 [1]Or, *the brook* [a]Gen. 9:22; Lev. 20:9; ch. 20:20; 23:22
30:19 [1]Heb. *heart*
30:22 [a]ch. 19:10; Eccl. 10:7
30:24 [1]Heb. *wise made wise*
30:25 [a]ch. 6:6
30:26 [a]Ps. 104:18
30:27 [1]Heb. *gathered together*
30:31 [1]Or, *horse* [2]Heb. *girt in the loins*
30:32 [a]Job 21:5; 40:4; Mic. 7:16

23 For an odious *woman* when she is
married;
And a handmaid that is heir to her
mistress.

24 There be four *things which are* little
upon the earth,
But they *are* [1]exceeding wise:
25 [a]The ants *are* a people not strong,
Yet they prepare their meat in the
summer;
26 [a]The conies *are but* a feeble folk,
Yet make they their houses in the
rocks;
27 The locusts have no king,
Yet go they forth all of them [1]by bands;
28 The spider taketh hold with her hands,
And *is* in kings' palaces.

29 There be three *things* which go well,
Yea, four are comely in going:
30 A lion *which is* strongest among beasts,
And turneth not away for any;
31 A [1][2]greyhound; a he goat also;
And a king, against whom *there is* no
rising up.

32 If thou hast done foolishly in lifting up
thyself,
Or if thou hast thought evil,
[a]*Lay thine* hand upon thy mouth.
33 Surely the churning of milk bringeth
forth butter,
And the wringing of the nose bringeth
forth blood:
So the forcing of wrath bringeth forth
strife.

Words of king Lemuel

31 The words of king Lemuel, the prophecy that his mother taught him.

30:14 *whose teeth are as swords . . . as knives.* The wicked are like ravenous beasts that devour the prey (see Job 29:17). *To devour the poor . . . the needy.* Cf. Ps 14:4; Mic 3:2–3.
30:15,18,21,29 *three . . . four.* See note on 6:16.
30:16 *The grave.* Its appetite is never satisfied (Is 5:14; Hab 2:5). *barren womb.* In ancient Israel, a wife without children was desolate, even desperate (cf. Gen 16:2; 30:1; Ruth 1:11–13,20–21; 1 Sam 1:6,10–11; 2 Ki 4:14).
30:17 *The eye.* Haughty and disdainful (see v. 13). *mocketh at his father, And despiseth to obey his mother.* See v. 11 and note; 15:20. *The ravens . . . shall pick it out, And the young eagles.* The loss of an eye was a terrible curse (see the story of Samson in Judg 16:21). Since vultures normally devoured the dead (see Jer 16:4; Mat 24:28), the meaning may be that the body of a disgraceful son will lie unburied and exposed.
30:18–19 It is difficult to understand the four "ways" because there are no tracks that can be readily followed.
30:19 *way of an eagle.* Soaring and swooping majestically (cf. Job 39:27; Jer 48:40; 49:22). *way of a man with a maid.* Probably a reference to the mystery of courting and how it leads to consummation.
30:20 *adulterous.* See 2:16 and note. *She eateth, and wipeth her mouth.* Making love is compared to eating food also in 9:17 (see note there; see also 7:18 and note).
30:22 *servant when he reigneth.* See 19:10 and note.
‡30:23 *an odious woman when she is married.* Probably one of several wives, who is miserable because her husband does not love her (cf. Leah in Gen 29:31–32). *handmaid that is heir to her mistress.* She replaces the wife in the affections of the husband, perhaps because she was able to bear a child, whereas the wife was barren (cf. Hagar and Sarah in Gen 16:1–6).
‡30:26 *conies.* The hyrax, or the rock badger. *in the rocks.* Which provide a refuge for them (see Ps 104:18).
30:27 *locusts have no king.* Cf. 6:7. *go they forth . . . by bands.* Locusts are portrayed as a mighty army in Joel 2:3–9.
‡30:28 *in kings' palaces.* Spiders climb stone walls easily.
30:30 *lion . . . strongest among beasts.* See 2 Sam 1:23; Mic 5:8.
‡30:31 *greyhound.* The Hebrew is uncertain. Some translators interpret it "rooster"; see also KJV marg. *he goat.* Goats were used to lead flocks of sheep (see Jer 50:8; Dan 8:5).
30:32 *lifting up thyself.* Pride is condemned in 8:13; 11:2; 16:18. *thought evil.* Cf. 6:14; 16:27. *Lay thine hand upon thy mouth.* Stop your plotting immediately (cf. Job 21:5; 40:4).
30:33 *forcing of wrath bringeth forth strife.* See notes on 6:14; 15:1; see also 29:22.
31:1–9 This brief section is also of non-Israelite origin. King Lemuel is otherwise unknown.
31:1 *prophecy.* See note on 30:1. *his mother.* This entire chap-

2 What, my son? and what, [a]the son of
my womb?
And what, the son of my vows?
3 [a]Give not thy strength unto women,
Nor thy ways [b]to *that which* destroyeth
kings.
4 [a]*It is* not for kings, O Lemuel, *it is* not
for kings to drink wine;
Nor for princes strong drink:
5 [a]Lest they drink, and forget the law,
And [1]pervert the judgment [2]of any of
the afflicted.
6 [a]Give strong drink unto him that is
ready to perish,
And wine unto those that be [1]of heavy
hearts.
7 Let him drink, and forget his poverty,
And remember his misery no more.
8 [a]Open thy mouth for the dumb
In the cause of all [1]such as are
appointed to destruction.
9 Open thy mouth, [a]judge righteously,
And [b]plead the cause of the poor and
needy.

The virtuous woman

10 [a]Who can find a virtuous woman?
For her price *is* far above rubies.
11 The heart of her husband doth *safely*
trust in her,
So that he shall have no need of spoil.
12 She will do him good and not evil
All the days of her life.
13 She seeketh wool, and flax,
And worketh willingly with her hands.
14 She is like the merchant's ships;
She bringeth her food from afar.
15 [a]She riseth also while *it is* yet night,
And [b]giveth meat to her household,
And a portion to her maidens.
16 She considereth a field, and [1]buyeth it:
With the fruit of her hands she
planteth a vineyard.
17 She girdeth her loins with strength,
And strengtheneth her arms.
18 [1]She perceiveth that her merchandise
is good:
Her candle goeth not out by night.
19 She layeth her hands to the spindle,
And her hands hold the distaff.
20 [a][1]She stretcheth out her hand to the
poor;
Yea, she reacheth forth her hands to
the needy.
21 She is not afraid of the snow for her
household:
For all her household *are* clothed with
[1]scarlet.
22 She maketh herself coverings of
tapestry;
Her clothing *is* silk and purple.
23 [a]Her husband is known in the gates,
When he sitteth among the elders of
the land.
24 She maketh fine linen, and selleth *it;*
And delivereth girdles unto the
merchant.
25 Strength and honour *are* her
clothing;
And she shall rejoice in time to come.
26 She openeth her mouth with
wisdom;
And in her tongue *is* the law of
kindness.
27 She looketh well to the ways of her
household,

31:2 [a]Is. 49:15
31:3 [a]ch. 5:9 [b]Deut. 17:17; Neh. 13:26; ch. 7:26; Hos. 4:11
31:4 [a]Eccl. 10:17
31:5 [1]Heb. *alter* [2]Heb. *of all the sons of affliction* [a]Hos. 4:11
31:6 [1]Heb. *bitter of soul* [a]Ps. 104:15
31:8 [1]Heb. *the sons of destruction* [a]See Job 29:15,16
31:9 [a]Lev. 19:15; Deut. 1:16 [b]Job 29:12; Is. 1:17; Jer. 22:16
31:10 [a]ch. 12:4; 18:22; 19:14
31:15 [a]Rom. 12:11
31:15 [b]Luke 12:42
31:16 [1]Heb. *taketh*
31:18 [1]Heb. *She tasteth*
31:20 [1]Heb. *She spreadeth* [a]Eph. 4:28; Heb. 13:16
31:21 [1]Or, *double garments*
31:23 [a]ch. 12:4

ter emphasizes the role and significance of wise women. The queen mother was an influential figure (see 1 Ki 1:11–13; 15:13).

31:2 *son of my vows?.* Hannah made a vow as she prayed for a son (1 Sam 1:11). *vows.* See 20:25 and note.

31:3 *strength unto women.* A warning against a large harem and sexual immorality (see 5:9–11 and notes; 1 Ki 11:1; Neh 13:26).

31:4 *It is not for kings . . . to drink wine.* Woe to the land whose rulers are drunkards (Eccl 10:16–17; see 20:1 and note; Hos 7:5).

31:5 *pervert the judgment of any of the afflicted.* See 30:14 and note; see also 17:15; Is 5:23; 10:2.

31:8–9 The king represents God as the defender of the poor and needy (see 16:10; Ps 82:3; cf. Lev 19:15; Job 29:12–17; Is 1:17).

31:10–31 The epilogue: an acrostic poem (each verse begins with a successive letter of the Hebrew alphabet) praising the "virtuous woman" (v. 10). It corresponds to 1:1–7 (the prologue) as it describes a "woman that feareth the LORD" (v. 30; see note on 1:7). Such a wife is almost a personification of wisdom. Like wisdom, "her price is far above rubies" (v. 10; 3:15; 8:11), and he who finds her "obtains favour of the LORD" (8:35; 18:22). See Introduction: Literary Structure.

31:10 *virtuous woman.* Like Ruth (Ruth 3:11). She is "the crown to her husband" (12:4).

31:12 *She will do him good.* See 18:22; 19:14.

31:13 *flax.* Its fibers were made into linen (see vv. 19,22,24; cf. Is 19:9).

31:14 *like the merchant's ships.* She is an enterprising person (see v. 18).

31:15 *She riseth also while it is yet night.* She is the opposite of the sluggard (see 6:9–10; 20:13). *a portion to her maidens.* See 27:27; Luke 12:42.

31:16 *considereth a field . . . planteth a vineyard.* She shows good judgment—unlike the sluggard, whose vineyard is overgrown with thorns and weeds (24:30–31).

31:17 *girdeth her loins with strength.* See 10:4 and note.

‡31:18 *her merchandise is good.* Her profit or value. Like wisdom, "her price is far above rubies" (v. 10; 3:15; 8:11). The profit of wisdom "is better than the merchandise of silver" (3:14).

31:19 *spindle . . . distaff.* Spinning thread was women's work.

31:20 *stretcheth out her hand to the poor.* See note on 14:21; see also 22:9; Job 31:16–20.

31:21 *clothed with scarlet.* Of high quality, probably made of wool (cf. 2 Sam 1:24; Rev 18:16).

31:22 *silk.* Associated with nobility (see note on 7:16; see also Gen 41:42). *purple.* Linked with kings (Judg 8:26; Sol 3:10) or the rich (Luke 16:19; Rev 18:16).

31:23 *in the gates.* The court (see note on 1:21).

31:24 *fine linen.* See Judg 14:12–13; Is 3:23. *merchant.* Cf. v. 18.

‡31:25 *Strength and honour are her clothing.* See Is 52:1; 1 Tim 2:9–10. The opposite is to be "clothed with shame and dishonour" (Ps 35:26). *she shall rejoice in time to come.* She is free of anxiety and worry concerning the future (cf. Job 39:7).

31:26 *law of kindness.* Given to her children and friends. She is a wise and loving counselor (see 1:8; 6:20).

And eateth not the bread of idleness.
28 Her children arise up, and call her blessed;
Her husband *also,* and he praiseth her.
29 Many daughters [1] have done virtuously,
But thou excellest them all.
30 Favour *is* deceitful, and beauty *is* vain:
But a woman that feareth the LORD, she shall be praised.
31 Give her of the fruit of her hands;
And let her own works praise her in the gates.

31:29 [1] Or, *have gotten riches*

31:28 *call her blessed.* Because of the happy environment she creates and the joy she radiates to others. See Gen 30:13; Ps 72:17; Sol 6:9; Mal 3:12; cf. Ruth 4:14–15.

31:29 *done virtuously.* See Is 32:8.

31:30 *Favour is deceitful.* Cf. 5:3. *beauty is vain.* Cf. Job 14:2; 1 Pet 3:3–5. *that feareth the LORD.* See note on 1:7.

31:31 *fruit of her hands.* See 12:14 and note. *praise her.* Honor comes through "humility and the fear of the LORD" (22:4). *in the gates.* See v. 23; see also note on 1:21.

Ecclesiastes
or the Preacher

INTRODUCTION

Author and Date

No time period or writer's name is mentioned in the book, but several passages strongly suggest that king Solomon is the author (1:1,12,16; 2:4–9; 7:26–29; 12:9; cf. 1 Ki 2:9; 3:12; 4:29–34; 5:12; 10:1–8). On the other hand, the writer's title ("Preacher," Hebrew *qoheleth;* see note on 1:1), his unique style of Hebrew and his attitude toward rulers (suggesting that of a subject rather than a monarch—see, e.g., 4:1–2; 5:8–9; 8:2–4; 10:20) may point to another person and a later period.

Purpose and Method

With his life largely behind him, the author takes stock of the world as he has experienced it between the horizons of birth and death—the latter a horizon beyond which man cannot see. The world is seen as being full of enigmas, the greatest of which is man himself.

From the perspective of his own understanding, the Preacher takes measure of man, examining his capabilities. He discovers that human wisdom, even that of a godly person, has limits (1:13,16–18; 7:24; 8:16–17). It cannot find out the larger purposes of God or the ultimate meaning of man's existence.

As the author looks about at the human enterprise, he sees man in mad pursuit of one thing and then another—laboring as if he could master the world, lay bare its secrets, change its fundamental structures, break through the bounds of human limitations and master his own destiny. He sees man vainly pursuing hopes and expectations that in reality are "vanity and vexation of spirit" (1:14; 2:11,17,26; 4:4,16; 6:9; cf. 1:17; 4:6).

But faith teaches him that God has ordered all things according to His own purposes (3:1–15; 5:19; 6:1–2; 9:1) and that man's role is to accept these, including his own limitations, as God's appointments. Man, therefore, should be patient and enjoy life as God gives it. He should know his own limitations and not vex himself with unrealistic expectations. He should be prudent in everything, living carefully before God and the king and, above all, fearing God and keeping His commandments (12:13).

Teaching

Life not centered on God is purposeless and meaningless (see notes on 1:2; 2:24–25). Without Him, nothing else can satisfy (2:25). With Him, all of life and His other good gifts are to be gratefully received (see Jas 1:17) and used and enjoyed to the full (2:26; 11:8). The book contains the philosophical and theological reflections of an old man (12:1–7), most of whose life was meaningless because he had not himself relied on God as he should have.

Outline

I. Author (1:1)
II. Theme: The vanity of man's efforts on earth apart from God (1:2)
III. Introduction: The profitlessness of working to accumulate things to achieve happiness (1:3–11)
IV. Discourse, Part 1: In spite of life's apparent enigmas and vanity, it is to be enjoyed as a gift from God (1:12—11:6)
V. Discourse, Part 2: Since old age and death will soon come, man should enjoy life in his youth, remembering that God will judge (11:7—12:7)
VI. Theme Repeated (12:8)
VII. Conclusion: Reverently trust in and obey God (12:9–14)

Vanity of human wisdom

1 The words [a]of the Preacher, the son of
David, king in Jerusalem.
2 ¶ [a]Vanity of vanities, saith the Preacher,
vanity of vanities; [b]all *is* vanity.
3 [a]What profit hath a man of all his labour
which he taketh under the sun?
4 ¶ *One* generation passeth away, and *another* generation cometh: [a]but the earth
abideth for ever.
5 [a]The sun also ariseth, and the sun goeth
down, and [1]hasteth to his place where he
arose.
6 [a]The wind goeth toward the south, and
turneth about unto the north; it whirleth
about continually, and the wind returneth
again according to his circuits.
7 [a]All the rivers run into the sea; yet the
sea *is* not full; unto the place from whence the
rivers come, thither they [1]return again.
8 All things *are* full of labour; man cannot
utter *it:* [a]the eye is not satisfied with seeing,
nor the ear filled with hearing.
9 [a]The thing that hath been, *it is* that
which shall be; and that which is done *is* that
which shall be done: and *there is* no new
thing under the sun.
10 Is there *any* thing whereof it may be
said, See, this *is* new? it hath been already of
old time, which was before us.
11 *There is* no remembrance of former
things; neither shall there be *any* remembrance of *things* that are to come with *those*
that shall come after.
12 ¶ [a]I the Preacher was king over Israel in
Jerusalem.
13 And I gave my heart to seek and search
out by wisdom concerning all *things* that are
done under heaven: [a]this sore travail hath
God given to the sons of man [1]to be exercised
therewith.
14 I have seen all the works that are done
under the sun; and behold, all *is* vanity and
vexation of spirit.
15 [a]*That which is* crooked cannot be made
straight: and [1]that which is wanting cannot be
numbered.
16 I communed with mine own heart, saying, Lo, I am come to great estate, and have gotten [a]more wisdom than all *they* that have been
before me in Jerusalem: yea, my heart [1]had
great experience of wisdom and knowledge.
17 [a]And I gave my heart to know wisdom,
and to know madness and folly: I perceived
that this also *is* vexation of spirit.
18 For [a]in much wisdom *is* much grief: and
he that increaseth knowledge increaseth sorrow.

Vanity of pleasure and wealth

2 [a]I said in mine heart, Go to now, I will
prove thee with mirth, therefore enjoy
pleasure: and behold, [b]this also *is* vanity.

1:1 [a]ver. 12; ch. 7:27; 12:8-10
1:2 [a]Ps. 39:5,6; 62:9; 144:4; ch. 12:8 [b]Rom. 8:20
1:3 [a]ch. 2:22
1:4 [a]Ps. 104:5; 119:90
1:5 [1]Heb. *panteth* [a]Ps. 19:4-6
1:6 [a]John 3:8
1:7 [1]Heb. *return to go* [a]Ps. 104:8,9; Jer. 5:22
1:8 [a]Prov. 27:20
1:9 [a]ch. 3:15
1:12 [a]ver. 1
1:13 [1]Or, *to afflict* them [a]Gen. 3:19; ch. 3:10
1:15 [1]Heb. *defect* [a]ch. 7:13
1:16 [1]Heb. *had seen much* [a]1 Ki. 3:12,13
1:17 [a]ch. 2:3,12
1:18 [a]ch. 12:12
2:1 [a]Luke 12:19 [b]ch. 1:2

1:1 *Preacher.* The preacher of wisdom (12:9). The Hebrew term for "Preacher" (*qoheleth*) is related to that for "assembly" (possibly meaning "leader of the assembly"; also in vv. 2,12; Ex 16:3; Num 16:3). Perhaps the Preacher, whose work is described in 12:9–10, also held an office in the assembly. The Septuagint (the Greek translation of the OT) word for "Preacher" is *ekklesiastes,* from which most English titles of the book are taken, and from which such English words as "ecclesiastical" are derived. *son of David.* Suggests Solomon, though his name occurs nowhere in the book. The Hebrew word for "son" can refer to a descendant (even many generations removed)—or even to someone who follows in the footsteps of another (see Gen 4:21; see also Introduction: Author and Date).

1:2 Briefly states the author's theme (see 12:8). *Vanity.* This key term is translated "vanity" or "vanities" about 22 times in Ecclesiastes and only a few other places in the OT (see 2 Ki 17:15; Ps 62:9; Is 49:4). The Hebrew for it originally meant "breath" (see Ps 39:5,11; 62:9; 144:4). The basic thrust of Ecclesiastes is that all of life is meaningless, useless, hollow, futile and vain if it is not rightly related to God. Only when based on God and His word is life worthwhile. *all.* See v. 8; whatever man undertakes apart from God.

1:3–11 In this section the author elaborates his theme that human effort appears to be without benefit or purpose.

1:3 Jesus expands on this question in Mark 8:36–38. *under the sun.* Another key expression (used 29 times), which refers to this present world and the limits of what it offers. "Under heaven," though it occurs less frequently (v. 13; 2:3; 3:1), is used synonymously.

1:4 *earth abideth for ever.* By contrast, man's life is fleeting.

1:8 *All things.* Everything mentioned in vv. 4–7 (see note on v. 2).

1:10 *new.* Many things seem to be new simply because the past is easily and quickly forgotten. The old ways reappear in new guises.

1:12–18 Having set forth his theme that all human striving seems futile (see especially vv. 3,11, which frame the section), the Preacher shows that both human endeavor (vv. 12–15; cf. 2:1–11) and the pursuit of human wisdom (vv. 16–18; cf. 2:12–17) are futile and meaningless.

1:12 *I.* The author shifts to the first person, returning to the third person only in the conclusion (12:9–14).

1:13 *God.* The only Hebrew word the writer uses for God is *Elohim* (used almost 30 times), which emphasizes His absolute sovereignty. He does not use the covenant name, *Yahweh* (translated "LORD"; see note on Ex 3:15).

1:14 *vexation of spirit.* Lit. "a striving after wind," a graphic illustration of futility and meaninglessness (see Introduction: Purpose and Method). These words are used nine times in the first half of the discourse (here; v. 17; 2:11,17,26; 4:4,6,16; 6:9; see also 5:16).

1:15 See 7:13 and note. Because of the unalterableness of events, human effort is meaningless and hopeless. We should therefore learn to happily accept things the way they are and to accept our divinely appointed lot in life, as the Preacher later counsels.

1:16 *than all they that have been before me in Jerusalem.* See 2:7,9. This does not necessarily exclude Solomon as the Preacher. The reference could include kings prior to David, such as Melchizedek (Gen 14:18), Adoni-zedek (Josh 10:1) and Abdi-khepa (mentioned in the Amarna letters from Egypt; see chart, p. xix).

1:18 Humanistic wisdom—wisdom without God—leads to grief and sorrow.

2:1–11 The Preacher now shows that mere pleasure cannot give meaning or satisfaction (see 1:12–15; see also note on 1:12–18).

2:1 *I said in mine heart.* See v. 15; 1:16.

2 I said of laughter, *It is* mad: and of mirth, What doeth it?

3 [a]I sought in mine heart [1]to give myself unto wine, (yet acquainting mine heart with wisdom) and to lay hold on folly, till I might see what *was* that good for the sons of men, which they should do under the heaven [2]all the days of their life.

4 I made me great works; I builded me houses; I planted me vineyards:

5 I made me gardens and orchards, and I planted trees in them of all *kind of* fruits:

6 I made me pools of water, to water therewith the wood that bringeth forth trees:

7 I got *me* servants and maidens, and had [1]servants born in *my* house; also I had great possessions of great and small cattle above all that were in Jerusalem before me:

8 [a]I gathered me also silver and gold, and the peculiar treasure of kings and of the provinces: I gat me *men* singers and *women* singers, and the delights of the sons of men, *as* [1]musical instruments, and that of all sorts.

9 So I was great, and increased more than all that were before me in Jerusalem: also my wisdom remained with me.

10 And whatsoever mine eyes desired I kept not from them, I withheld not my heart from any joy; for my heart rejoiced in all my labour: and [a]this was my portion of all my labour.

11 Then I looked on all the works that my hands had wrought, and on the labour that I had laboured to do: and behold, all *was* [a]vanity and vexation of spirit, and *there was* no profit under the sun.

The fool and the wise must die

12 ¶ And I turned myself to behold wisdom, [a]and madness, and folly: for what *can* the man *do* that cometh after the king? [1]*even* that which hath been already done.

13 Then I saw [1]that wisdom excelleth folly, as far as light excelleth darkness.

14 [a]The wise *man's* eyes *are* in his head; but the fool walketh in darkness: and I myself perceived also that [b]one event happeneth to them all.

15 Then said I in my heart, As it happeneth to the fool, so it [1]happeneth even to me; and why was I then more wise? Then I said in my heart, that this also *is* vanity.

16 For *there is* no remembrance of the wise more than of the fool for ever; seeing *that* which now *is, in* the days to come shall all be forgotten. And how dieth the wise *man?* as the fool.

17 Therefore I hated life; because the work that is wrought under the sun *is* grievous unto me: for all *is* vanity and vexation of spirit.

18 Yea, I hated all my labour which I *had* [1]taken under the sun: because [a]I should leave it unto the man that shall be after me.

19 And who knoweth whether he shall be a wise *man* or a fool? yet shall he have rule over all my labour where*in* I have laboured, and where*in* I have shewed myself wise under the sun. This *is* also vanity.

20 Therefore I went about to cause my heart to despair of all the labour which I took under the sun.

21 For there is a man whose labour *is* in wisdom, and in knowledge, and in equity; yet to a man that hath not laboured therein shall he [1]leave it *for* his portion. This also *is* vanity and a great evil.

22 [a]For what hath man of all his labour, and of the vexation of his heart, wherein he *hath* laboured under the sun?

23 For all his days *are* [a]sorrows, and his travail grief; yea, his heart taketh not rest in the night. This *is* also vanity.

24 ¶ [a]*There is* nothing better for a man, *than* that he should eat and drink, and *that* he [1]should make his soul enjoy good in his labour. This also I saw, that it *was* from the hand of God.

25 For who can eat, or who else can hasten *hereunto,* more than I?

26 For *God* giveth to a man that *is* good [1]in his sight wisdom, and knowledge, and joy: but to the sinner he giveth travail, to gather and to heap up, that [a]*he* may give to *him that is* good before God. This also *is* vanity and vexation of spirit.

2:3 [1]Heb. *to draw my flesh with wine* [2]Heb. *the number of the days of their life* [a]ch. 1:17
2:7 [1]Heb. *sons of* my *house*
2:8 [1]Heb. *musical instrument and instruments* [a]1 Ki. 9:28; 10:10,14,21
2:10 [a]ch. 3:22; 5:18; 9:9
2:11 [a]ch. 1:3,14
2:12 [1]Or, *in those* things *which have been already done* [a]ch. 1:17; 7:25
2:13 [1]Heb. *that there is an excellency in wisdom more than in folly, etc.*
2:14 [a]Prov. 17:24; ch. 8:1 [b]Ps. 49:10; ch. 9:2,3,11
2:15 [1]Heb. *happeneth to me, even to me*
2:18 [1]Heb. *laboured* [a]Ps. 49:10
2:21 [1]Heb. *give*
2:22 [a]ch. 1:3; 3:9
2:23 [a]Job 5:7; 14:1
2:24 [1]Or, *delight his senses* [a]ch. 3:12,13,22; 5:18; 8:15
2:26 [1]Heb. *before him* [a]Job 27:16,17; Prov. 28:8

2:3 *yet acquainting mine heart with wisdom.* From first to last (v. 9) the author used wisdom to discover the good (v. 1) and the worthwhile (v. 3).

2:4–9 See 1 Ki 4–11, which tells of Solomon's splendor and of his wives.

2:8 *and that of all sorts.* The Hebrew for this word occurs only here in Scripture, and its meaning is uncertain. The meaning seems to be indicated in an early Egyptian letter that uses a similar Canaanite term for concubines. It fits the situation of Solomon, who had 300 concubines in addition to 700 wives (1 Ki 11:3).

2:10 *labour. . . labour.* A key thought in Ecclesiastes is the vanity (v. 11), apart from God, of toil, labor, work—words that occur more than 25 times.

2:12–17 The Preacher returns to the folly of trying to find satisfaction in merely human wisdom (see 1:16–18; see also note on 1:12–18).

2:13 *wisdom excelleth folly.* Even secular wisdom is better than folly, but in the end it is of no value, since "one fate befalls them both" (i.e. befalls both the wise believer and the foolish unbeliever, v. 14; see Ps 49:10).

2:14 *eyes.* Understanding.

2:16 People tend to soon forget even the greatest leaders and heroes (see 1:11).

2:18 *leave it unto the man that shall be after me.* See v. 21; Ps 39:6; Luke 12:20.

2:19 *who knoweth . . . ?* For a more searching "Who knoweth . . . ?" for secular man see 3:21.

2:24–25 The heart of Ecclesiastes, a theme repeated in 3:12–13,22; 5:18–20; 8:15; 9:7 and climaxed in 12:13. Only in God does life have meaning and true pleasure. Without Him nothing satisfies, but with Him we find satisfaction and enjoyment. True pleasure comes only when we acknowledge and revere God (12:13).

2:26 *but to the sinner.* For exceptions to this general principle see 8:14; Ps 73:1–12.

A time for everything

3 To every *thing there is* a season, and a [a]time to every purpose under the heaven:
2 A time [1]to be born, and [a]a time to die;
A time to plant, and a time to pluck up *that which is* planted;
3 A time to kill, and a time to heal;
A time to break down, and a time to build *up;*
4 A time to weep, and a time to laugh;
A time to mourn, and a time to dance;
5 A time to cast away stones, and a time to gather stones together;
A time to embrace, and [a]a time [1]to refrain from embracing;
6 A time to [1]get, and a time to lose;
A time to keep, and a time to cast away;
7 A time to rent, and a time to sew;
[a]A time to keep silence, and a time to speak;
8 A time to love, and a time to [a]hate;
A time of war, and a time of peace.

9 ¶ [a]What profit *hath* he that worketh in
that where*in* he laboureth?
10 ¶ [a]I have seen the travail, which God
hath given to the sons of men to be exercised
in it.
11 He hath made every *thing* beautiful in
his time: also he hath set the world in their
heart, so that [a]no man can find out the work
that God maketh from the beginning to the
end.
12 I know that *there is* no good in them,
but for *a man* to rejoice, and to do good in his
life.
13 And also [a]that every man should eat
and drink, and enjoy the good of all his labour,
it *is* the gift of God.
14 I know that, whatsoever God doeth, it
shall be for ever: [a]nothing can be put to it, nor
any thing taken from it: and God doeth *it,* that
men should fear before him.

3:1 [a]ver. 17; ch. 8:6
3:2 [1]Heb. *to bear* [a]Heb. 9:27
3:5 [1]Heb. *to be far from* [a]Joel 2:16; 1 Cor. 7:5
3:6 [1]Or, *seek*
3:7 [a]Amos 5:13
3:8 [a]Luke 14:26
3:9 [a]ch. 1:3
3:10 [a]ch. 1:13
3:11 [a]ch. 8:17; Rom. 11:33
3:13 [a]ch. 2:24
3:14 [a]Jas. 1:17
3:15 [1]Heb. *that which is driven away* [a]ch. 1:9
3:16 [a]ch. 5:8
3:17 [a]Rom. 2:6-8; 2 Cor. 5:10; 2 Thes. 1:6 [b]ver. 1
3:18 [1]Or, *that they might clear God, and see, etc.*
3:19 [a]Ps. 49:12,20; 73:22; ch. 2:16
3:20 [a]Gen. 3:19
3:21 [1]Heb. *of the sons of man* [2]Heb. is *ascending* [a]ch. 12:7
3:22 [a]ver. 12; ch. 2:24; 5:18; 11:9 [b]ch. 2:10 [c]ch. 6:12; 8:7; 10:14
4:1 [1]Heb. *hand* [a]ch. 3:16; 5:8
4:2 [a]Job 3:17
4:3 [a]Job 3:11,16,21; ch. 6:3

15 [a]That which hath been, *is* now; and
that which *is* to be hath already been; and God
requireth [1]that which is past.

The vanity of all life

16 ¶ And moreover [a]I saw under the sun
the place of judgment, *that* wickedness *was*
there; and the place of righteousness, *that* iniquity *was* there.
17 I said in mine heart, [a]God shall judge the
righteous and the wicked: for *there is* [b]a time
there for every purpose and for every work.
18 ¶ I said in my heart concerning the estate of the sons of men, [1]that God might manifest them, and that *they* might see that they
themselves are beasts.
19 [a]For that which befalleth the sons of
men befalleth beasts; even one thing befalleth
them: as the one dieth, so dieth the other; yea,
they have all one breath; so that a man hath no
preeminence above a beast: for all *is* vanity.
20 All go unto one place; [a]all are of the
dust, and all turn to dust again.
21 [a]Who knoweth the spirit [1]of man that
[2]goeth upward, and the spirit of the beast that
goeth downward to the earth?
22 [a]Wherefore I perceive that *there is*
nothing better, than that a man should rejoice
in his own works; for [b]that *is* his portion: [c]for
who shall bring him to see what shall be after
him?

4 So I returned, and considered all the [a]op-
pressions that *are* done under the sun:
and behold, the tears of such as were oppressed, and they had no comforter; and on
the [1]side of their oppressors *there was* power;
but they had no comforter.
2 [a]Wherefore I praised the dead which are
already dead more than the living which are
yet alive.
3 [a]Yea, better *is he* than both they, which
hath not yet been, who hath not seen the evil
work that is done under the sun.

3:1–22 The Preacher shows that we are subject to times and changes over which we have little or no control, and contrasts this state with God's eternity and sovereignty. God sovereignly predetermines all of life's activities (e.g., the 14 opposites of vv. 2–8).
3:1 Cf. 8:6. *under the heaven.* See note on 1:3.
3:2 *A time.* Divinely appointed (see Ps 31:15; Prov 16:1–9).
3:11 The chapter summarized: God's beautiful but tantalizing world is too big for us, yet its satisfactions are too small. Since we were made for eternity, the things of time cannot fully and permanently satisfy.
3:12–13 A pointer to the book's conclusion. God's people find meaning in life when they cheerfully accept it from the hand of God.
3:14 *for ever.* In this word the "eternity" of v. 11 becomes clearer. *fear.* Sums up the message of the book (cf. 12:13).
3:15 See 1:9.
3:17 *judge.* God's true judgments are the answer to human cynicism about man's injustices. "That which hath been" (v. 15) is not meaningless (as people dismiss it as being, 1:11), and God will override the perverse judgments (v. 16) of men (see 12:14).
3:18 *beasts.* Man "under the sun" (man on his own) is as mortal as any animal; but, unlike them, he must be made to see this condition and, through his dim awareness of eternity (v. 11), be distressed.
3:19 *one breath.* See Ps 104:27–30.
3:20 *unto one place.* Not heaven or hell but man's observable destination, which is a return to dust, just like the animals. Death is the great leveler of all living things (see Gen 3:19; Ps 103:14).
3:21 *Who knoweth . . . ?* See 2:19 and note; cf. 12:7. Man on his own cannot know; he can only guess. The answer, revealed at first in glimpses (e.g., Ps 16:9–11; 49:15; 73:23–26; Is 26:19; Dan 12:2–3), was brought fully "to light through the gospel" (2 Tim 1:10).
3:22 *there is nothing better.* As an end in itself, work too is meaningless (see 4:4; 9:9). Only receiving it as a gift from God (v. 13) gives it enduring worth (v. 14).
4:1 *oppressions.* A theme already touched on (3:16) and another ingredient in the human tragedy. To find life meaningless is sad enough, but to taste its cruelty is bitter beyond words.
4:2 *more than the living.* See Job 3; Jer 20:14–18. For faith that sees a bigger picture see Rom 8:35–39.
‡4:3 *better . . . than.* The author introduces a series of comparisons reminding the reader that despite the difficulties of

Travail of the wise and foolish

4 ¶ Again, I considered all travail, and [1]every right work, that [2]for this a man is envied of his neighbour. This *is* also vanity and vexation of spirit.

5 [a]The fool foldeth his hands together, and eateth his own flesh.

6 [a]Better *is* a handful *with* quietness, than both the hands full *with* travail and vexation of spirit.

7 ¶ Then I returned, and I saw vanity under the sun.

8 There is one *alone,* and *there is* not a second; yea, he hath neither child nor brother: yet *is there* no end of all his labour; neither is his [a]eye satisfied *with* riches; [b]neither *saith he,* For whom do I labour, and bereave my soul of good? This *is* also vanity, yea, it *is* a sore travail.

9 Two *are* better than one; because they have a good reward for their labour.

10 For if they fall, the one will lift up his fellow: but woe to him *that is* alone when he falleth; for *he hath* not another to help him up.

11 Again, if two lie together, then they have heat: but how can one be warm *alone?*

12 And if one prevail against him, two shall withstand him; and a threefold cord is not quickly broken.

13 ¶ Better *is* a poor and a wise child than an old and foolish king, [1]who will no more be admonished.

14 For out of prison he cometh to reign; whereas also *he that is* born in his kingdom becometh poor.

15 I considered all the living which walk under the sun, with the second child that shall stand *up* in his stead.

16 *There is* no end of all the people, *even* of all that have been before them: they also that come after shall not rejoice in him. Surely this also *is* vanity and vexation of spirit.

The vanity of vows

5 Keep [a]thy foot when thou goest to the house of God, and *be* more ready to hear, [b]than to give the sacrifice of fools: for they consider not that *they* do evil.

2 Be not rash with thy mouth, and let not thine heart be hasty to utter *any* [1]thing before God: for God *is* in heaven, and thou upon earth: therefore let thy words [a]be few.

3 For a dream cometh through the multitude of business; and [a]a fool's voice *is known* by multitude of words.

4 [a]When thou vowest a vow unto God, defer not to pay it; for *he hath* no pleasure in fools: pay that which thou hast vowed.

5 [a]Better *is it* that thou shouldest not vow, than that thou shouldest vow and not pay.

6 Suffer not thy mouth to cause thy flesh to sin; [a]neither say thou before the angel, that it *was* an error: wherefore should God be angry at thy voice, and destroy the work of thine hands?

7 For in the multitude of dreams and many words *there are* also *divers* vanities: but [a]fear thou God.

The vanity of riches

8 ¶ If thou [a]seest the oppression of the poor, and violent perverting of judgment and justice in a province, marvel not [1]at the matter: for [b]*he that is* higher than the highest regardeth; and *there be* higher than they.

9 ¶ Moreover the profit of the earth *is* for all: the king *himself* is served by the field.

10 He that loveth silver shall not be satisfied *with* silver; nor he that loveth abundance *with* increase: this *is* also vanity.

11 When goods increase, they are increased that eat them: and what good *is there* to the owners thereof, saving the beholding *of them* with their eyes?

12 The sleep of a labouring *man is* sweet, whether he eat little or much: but the abundance of the rich will not suffer him to sleep.

13 ¶ [a]There is a sore evil *which* I have seen under the sun, *namely,* riches kept for the owners thereof to their hurt.

14 But those riches perish by evil travail:

4:4 [1]Heb. *all the rightness of work* [2]Heb. *this is the envy of a man from his neighbour*
4:5 [a]Prov. 6:10; 24:33
4:6 [a]Prov. 15:16,17; 16:8
4:8 [a]Prov. 27:20; 1 John 2:16 [b]Ps. 39:6
4:13 [1]Heb. *who knoweth not to be admonished*
5:1 [a]See Ex. 3:5; Is. 1:12
5:1 [b]1 Sam. 15:22; Ps. 50:8; Prov. 15:8; 21:27; Hos. 6:6
5:2 [1]Or, *word* [a]Prov. 10:19; Mat. 6:7
5:3 [a]Prov. 10:19
5:4 [a]Num. 30:2; Deut. 23:21
5:5 [a]Prov. 20:25; Acts 5:4
5:6 [a]1 Cor. 11:10
5:7 [a]ch. 12:13
5:8 [1]Heb. *at the will,* or, *purpose* [a]ch. 3:16 [b]Ps. 12:5; 58:11; 82:1
5:13 [a]ch. 6:1

life, some things are better than others. This is his first indication that all may not be hopeless after all.

4:4–6 Neither hard work (motivated by envy) nor idleness brings happiness, meaning or fulfillment.

4:4 *all travail, and every right work.* This too is meaningless unless done with God's blessing (see 3:13; cf. the selfless success of Joseph, Gen 39).

4:5 The ruin of the idle person is vividly pictured in 10:18; Prov 6:6–11; 24:30–34.

4:6 *quietness.* See Prov 30:7–9. Paul says the last word on this subject (Phil 4:11–13).

4:7–12 The loner, too, has a meaningless and difficult life if he is an unbeliever.

4:12 *two . . . threefold.* A climactic construction.

4:13–16 Advancement without God is another example of the vanity of secularism.

5:1–7 The theme of this section is the vanity of superficial religion, as reflected in making rash vows.

5:1 *Keep thy foot.* Think about what you ought to say and do. *hear.* Obey. 1 Sam 15:22 uses the same Hebrew verb and makes the same contrast between real and superficial worship. *sacrifice.* Probably connected with the vow of vv. 4–6.

5:2 *rash with thy mouth.* As in a rash vow.

5:3 A proverb. In the context it suggests that in the midst of cares a person dreams of bliss (as a starving man dreams of a banquet), and in anticipation may offer rash vows ("multitude of words") to God (see v. 7).

5:4 *vow.* See Deut 23:21–23; 1 Sam 1:11, 24–28. *no pleasure in fools.* In Scripture the fool is not one who cannot learn, but one who refuses to learn due to moral deficiency (see Prov 1:7,20–27).

5:6 *angel.* Or messenger; see Mal 2:7.

5:8 *marvel not.* For other frank appraisals of human society see 4:1–3. This teacher, like Jesus, who "knew what was in man" (John 2:25), had no illusions or utopian schemes.

5:10 Greater wealth does not bring satisfaction (see 1 Tim 6:9–10).

5:11–12 Greater wealth brings greater anxiety.

5:13 *hurt.* Including worry about his possessions.

and he begetteth a son, and *there is* nothing in
his hand.
15 [a]As he came forth of his mother's
womb, naked shall he return to go as he came,
and shall take nothing of his labour, which he
may carry away in his hand.
16 And this also *is* a sore evil, *that* in all
points as he came, so shall he go: and [a]what
profit hath he [b]that hath laboured for the wind?
17 All his days also [a]he eateth in darkness,
and *he hath* much sorrow and wrath with his
sickness.
18 ¶ Behold *that* which I have seen: [a] [1]*it is*
good and comely *for one* to eat and to drink,
and to enjoy the good of all his labour that he
taketh under the sun [2]all the days of his life,
which God giveth him: [b]for it *is* his portion.
19 [a]Every man also to whom God hath giv-
en riches and wealth, and hath given him power to eat thereof, and to take his portion, and to
rejoice in his labour; this *is* the gift of God.
20 [1]For he shall not much remember the
days of his life; because God answereth *him* in
the joy of his heart.

6 [a]There is an evil which I have seen under the sun, and it *is* common among
men:
2 A man to whom God hath given riches,
wealth, and honour, [a]so that he wanteth nothing for his soul of all that he desireth, [b]yet God
giveth him not power to eat thereof, but a
stranger eateth it: this *is* vanity, and it *is* an
evil disease.
3 If a man beget an hundred *children,* and
live many years, so that the days of his years
be many, and his soul be not filled with good,
and [a]also *that* he have no burial; I say, *that* [b]an
untimely birth *is* better than he.
4 For he cometh in with vanity, and departeth in darkness, and his name shall be covered with darkness.
5 Moreover he hath not seen the sun, nor
known *any thing:* this hath more rest than the
other.
6 Yea, though he live a thousand years
twice *told,* yet hath he seen no good: do not all
go to one place?
7 ¶ [a]All the labour of man *is* for his mouth,
and yet the [1]appetite is not filled.
8 For what hath the wise more than the

5:15 [a]Job 1:21; Ps. 49:17; 1 Tim. 6:7
5:16 [a]ch. 1:3 [b]Prov. 11:29
5:17 [a]Ps. 127:2
5:18 [1]Heb. there is *a good which is comely, etc.* [2]Heb. *the number of the days* [a]ch. 2:24; 3:12,13; 9:7; 11:9; 1 Tim. 6:17 [b]ch. 2:10; 3:22
5:19 [a]ch. 2:24; 3:13
5:20 [1]Or, *Though* he give *not much, yet he remembereth, etc.*
6:1 [a]ch. 5:13
6:2 [a]Job 21:10; Ps. 17:14; 73:7 [b]Luke 12:20
6:3 [a]2 Ki. 9:35; Is. 14:19,20; Jer. 22:19 [b]Job 3:16; Ps. 58:8; ch. 4:3
6:7 [1]Heb. *soul* [a]Prov. 16:26
6:9 [1]Heb. *than the walking of the soul*
6:10 [a]Job 9:32; Is. 45:9; Jer. 49:19
6:12 [1]Heb. *the number of the days of the life of his vanity* [a]Ps. 102:11; 144:4; Jas. 4:14 [b]Ps. 39:6; ch. 8:7
7:1 [a]Prov. 22:1
7:3 [1]Or, *Anger* [a]2 Cor. 7:10
7:5 [a]Ps. 141:5; Prov. 15:31
7:6 [1]Heb. *sound* [a]ch. 2:2
7:7 [a]Ex. 23:8; Deut. 16:19
7:8 [a]Prov. 14:29
7:9 [a]Prov. 14:17; Jas. 1:19
7:10 [1]Heb. *out of wisdom*
7:11 [1]Or, *as good as an inheritance, yea, better* too [a]ch. 11:7
7:12 [1]Heb. *shadow*

fool? what hath the poor, that knoweth to walk
before the living?
9 Better *is* the sight of the eyes [1]than the
wandering of the desire: this *is* also vanity and
vexation of spirit.
10 That which hath been is named already,
and *it is* known that it *is* man: [a]neither may he
contend with him that *is* mightier than he.
11 Seeing there be many things that increase vanity, what *is* man the better?
12 For who knoweth what *is* good for man
in *this* life, [1]all the days of his vain life which
he spendeth as [a]a shadow? for [b]who can tell a
man what shall be after him under the sun?

Choosing wisdom

7 [a]A *good* name *is* better than precious
ointment; and the day of death than the
day of one's birth.
2 *It is* better to go to the house of mourning, than to go to the house of feasting: for that
is the end of all men; and the living will lay *it*
to his heart.
3 [1]Sorrow *is* better than laughter: [a]for by
the sadness of the countenance the heart is
made better.
4 The heart of the wise *is* in the house of
mourning; but the heart of fools *is* in the
house of mirth.
5 [a]*It is* better to hear the rebuke of the
wise, than for a man to hear the song of fools.
6 [a]For as the [1]crackling of thorns under a
pot, so *is* the laughter of the fool: this also *is*
vanity.
7 ¶ Surely oppression maketh a wise *man*
mad; [a]and a gift destroyeth the heart.
8 Better *is* the end of a thing than the beginning thereof: *and* [a]the patient in spirit *is*
better than the proud in spirit.
9 [a]Be not hasty in thy spirit to be angry: for
anger resteth in the bosom of fools.
10 Say not thou, What is *the cause* that the
former days were better than these? for thou
dost not inquire [1]wisely concerning this.
11 Wisdom *is* [1]good with an inheritance:
and *by it there is* profit [a]to them that see the
sun.
12 For wisdom *is* a [1]defence, *and* money *is*
a [1]defence: but the excellency of knowledge
is, that wisdom giveth life to them that have it.

5:15 *shall take nothing.* Monetary riches have no value after death. See Luke 12:14–21.

5:18–20 See note on 2:24–25.

6:2 *a stranger eateth it.* Comparing v. 2 with 5:19 demonstrates that the ability to enjoy God's blessings is a bonus—a gift of God, not a right or guarantee (see also vv. 3,6). God calls the person who forgets this truth a fool (Luke 12:20).

6:3 *have no burial.* Dies unlamented or dishonored, like king Jehoiakim (Jer 22:18–19). *an untimely birth.* For the secularist, life is a pointless journey to extinction, to which miscarriage is the quickest and easiest route (cf. Job 3:16; Ps 58:8).

6:6 *to one place.* Still talking in terms of what we can observe (that all men die), not of what lies beyond death (see v. 12; 3:21).

6:7–12 In confronting complacency, the Preacher gives several causes for concern: the short-lived (v. 7), debatable (v. 8) and elusive (v. 9) rewards of life; the limits of our creativity, power and wisdom (vv. 10–11); and the unreliability of merely human values and predictions (v. 12).

6:10 *named.* Predetermined by God. *known.* Foreknown by God. *him that is mightier than he.* Especially if the "mightier" (stronger) one is God.

6:12 *as a shadow.* See 1 Chr 29:15.

7:1 *day of death than . . . birth.* The Christian has ample reason to say this (2 Cor 5:1–10; Phil 1:21–23). But the Preacher's point is valid, as explained in vv. 2–6, namely, that happy times generally teach us less than hard times.

7:7 *gift.* See Mat 28:11–15; Luke 22:4–6.

7:9 *anger.* See, e.g., Prov 16:32; 17:14; 1 Cor 13:4–5.

7:12 *giveth life.* See Prov 3:13–18; 13:14.

13 Consider the work of God: for [a]who can make *that* straight, which he hath made crooked?

14 [a]In the day of prosperity be joyful, but in the day of adversity consider: God also hath [1]set the one over against the other, to the end that man should find nothing after him.

15 ¶ All *things* have I seen in the days of my vanity: [a]there is a just *man* that perisheth in his righteousness, and there is a wicked *man* that prolongeth *his life* in his wickedness.

16 [a]Be not righteous over much; [b]neither make thyself over wise: why shouldest thou [1]destroy thyself?

17 Be not over much wicked, neither be thou foolish: [a]why shouldest thou die [1]before thy time?

18 *It is* good that thou shouldest take hold of this; yea, also from this withdraw not thine hand: for he that feareth God shall come forth of them all.

19 [a]Wisdom strengtheneth the wise more than ten mighty *men* which are in the city.

20 [a]For *there is* not a just man upon earth, that doeth good, and sinneth not.

21 Also [1]take no heed unto all words that are spoken; lest thou hear thy servant curse thee:

22 For oftentimes also thine own heart knoweth that thou thyself likewise hast cursed others.

23 ¶ All this have I proved by wisdom: [a]I said, I will be wise; but it *was* far from me.

24 [a]That which is far off, and [b]exceeding deep, who can find it out?

25 [a1]I applied mine heart to know, and to search, and to seek out wisdom, and the reason *of things,* and to know the wickedness of folly, even of foolishness *and* madness:

26 [a]And I find more bitter than death the woman, whose heart *is* snares and nets, *and* her hands *as* bands: [1]whoso pleaseth God shall escape from her; but the sinner shall be taken by her.

27 Behold, this have I found, saith [a]the Preacher, [1]*counting* one by one, to find out the account:

28 Which yet my soul seeketh, but I find not: [a]one man among a thousand have I found; but a woman among all those have I not found.

29 Lo, this only have I found, [a]that God hath made man upright; but [b]they have sought out many inventions.

Obedience to authority

8 Who *is* as the wise *man?* and who knoweth the interpretation of a thing? [a]a man's wisdom maketh his face to shine, and [b1]the boldness of his face shall be changed.

2 I *counsel thee* to keep the king's commandment, [a]and *that* in regard of the oath of God.

3 [a]Be not hasty to go out of his sight: stand not in an evil thing; for he doeth whatsoever pleaseth him.

4 Where the word of a king *is, there is* power: and [a]who may say unto him, What doest thou?

5 Whoso keepeth the commandment [1]shall feel no evil thing: and a wise *man's* heart discerneth *both* time and judgment.

6 ¶ Because [a]to every purpose there is time and judgment, therefore the misery of man *is* great upon him.

7 [a]For he knoweth not that which shall be: for who can tell him [1]when it shall be?

8 [a]*There is* no man that hath power over the spirit to retain the spirit; neither *hath he* power in the day of death: and *there is* no [1]discharge in *that* war; neither shall wickedness deliver those that are given to it.

9 All this have I seen, and applied my heart unto every work that is done under the sun: *there is* a time wherein one man ruleth over another to his own hurt.

10 And so I saw the wicked buried, who had come and gone from the place of the holy, and they were forgotten in the city where they had so done: this *is* also vanity.

11 ¶ [a]Because sentence *against* an evil work is not executed speedily, therefore the heart of the sons of men is fully set in them to do evil.

12 [a]Though a sinner do evil an hundred

7:13 [a]Job 12:14; ch. 1:15
7:14 [1]Heb. *made* [a]Deut. 28:47
7:15 [a]ch. 8:14
7:16 [1]Heb. *be desolate?* [a]Prov. 25:16 [b]Rom. 12:3
7:17 [1]Heb. *not in thy time?* [a]Job 15:32; Ps. 55:23
7:19 [a]Prov. 21:22; ch. 9:16,18
7:20 [a]1 Ki. 8:46; 2 Chr. 6:36; Prov. 20:9; 1 John 1:8
7:21 [1]Heb. *give not thine heart*
7:23 [a]Rom. 1:22
7:24 [a]Job 28:12; 1 Tim. 6:16 [b]Rom. 11:33
7:25 [1]Heb. *I and mine heart compassed* [a]ch. 1:17
7:26 [1]Heb. he that is *good before God* [a]Prov. 5:3,4
7:27 [1]Or, weighing *one* thing *after another, to find out the reason* [a]ch. 1:1,2
7:28 [a]Job 33:23; Ps. 12:1
7:29 [a]Gen. 1:27 [b]Gen. 3:6,7
8:1 [1]Heb. *the strength* [a]Prov. 4:8,9; Acts 6:15 [b]Deut. 28:50
8:2 [a]1 Chr. 29:24; Ezek. 17:18
8:3 [a]ch. 10:4
8:4 [a]Job 34:18
8:5 [1]Heb. *shall know*
8:6 [a]ch. 3:1
8:7 [1]Or, *how it shall be?* [a]Prov. 24:22; ch. 6:12; 9:12; 10:14
8:8 [1]Or, *casting* of weapons [a]Ps. 49:6,7
8:11 [a]Ps. 10:6; 50:21; Is. 26:10
8:12 [a]Is. 65:20; Rom. 2:5

7:13 *who can make that straight . . . ?* Not fatalism, but a reminder of who is God. Man cannot change what God determines (see note on 1:15).

7:14 *hath set the one over against the other.* God uses both prosperity and adversity in our lives to accomplish his purposes; cf. Rom 8:28–29. *man should find nothing after him.* No one knows the future, whether it will hold prosperity or adversity.

7:15 *just man that perisheth . . . righteousness.* Righteousness is no sure protection against hard times or an early death.

7:16 *not righteous over much . . . over wise.* If true righteousness and wisdom do not necessarily prevent ruin, then extreme, legalistic righteousness and wisdom will surely not help.

7:17 *over much wicked.* Extreme wickedness is even more foolhardy.

7:20 *not a just man upon earth.* A sober Biblical truth (see Rom 3:10–20).

7:24 See Job 28:12–28; 1 Cor 2:9–16.

7:26 See Prov 7:6–27.

7:27 *Preacher.* See note on 1:1. *counting one by one, to find out the account.* This inductive method can never be complete, nor can we reliably interpret all that we manage to observe (3:11b). Human wisdom and understanding must always yield to revealed truth.

7:29 *God hath made man upright; but . . . inventions.* See Gen 3:1–6; Rom 5:12.

8:2 *king's commandment.* Both principle (v. 2) and prudence (vv. 3–6) set limits on our freedom. *the oath.* Of loyalty to the king (as seen, e.g., in 1 Chr 29:24).

8:4 *who may say . . . , "What doest thou?"* Cf. Is 45:9; Rom 9:20.

8:6 *the misery of man.* One should put the king's command above his own misery.

8:7–8 *he knoweth not . . . . no man that hath power.* See Ps 31:15; 2 Cor 5:1–10; Jas 4:13–16.

8:10 *the wicked buried.* In this context it implies undeserved respect (see note on 6:3; cf. Job 21:28–33; Luke 16:22).

8:11 Delayed punishment tends to induce more wrongdoing.

times, and his *days* be prolonged, yet surely I
know that [b]it shall be well with them that fear
God, which fear before him:
13 But it shall not be well with the wicked,
neither shall he prolong *his* days, *which are* as
a shadow; because he feareth not before God.
14 ¶ There is a vanity which is done upon
the earth; that there be just *men,* unto whom
it [a]happeneth according to the work of the
wicked; again, there be wicked *men,* to whom
it happeneth according to the work of the righteous: I said that this also *is* vanity.
15 [a]Then I commended mirth, because a
man hath no better *thing* under the sun, than
to eat, and to drink, and to be merry: for that
shall abide with him of his labour the days of
his life, which God giveth him under the sun.
16 ¶ When I applied mine heart to know
wisdom, and to see the business that is done
upon the earth: (for also *there is that* neither
day nor night seeth sleep with his eyes:)
17 Then I beheld all the work of God, that
[a]a man cannot find out the work that is done
under the sun: because though a man labour
to seek *it* out, yet he shall not find *it;* yea further, though a wise *man* think to know *it,* yet
shall he not be able to find *it.*

Make the best of this life

9 For all this [1]I considered in my heart
even to declare all this, [a]that the righteous, and the wise, and their works, *are* in
the hand of God: no man knoweth either love
or hatred *by* all *that is* before them.
2 [a]All *things come* alike to all: *there is* one
event to the righteous, and to the wicked; to
the good and to the clean, and to the unclean;
to him that sacrificeth, and to him that sacrificeth not: as *is* the good, so *is* the sinner; *and*
he that sweareth, as he that feareth an oath.
3 This *is* an evil among all *things* that are
done under the sun, that *there is* one event
unto all: yea, also the heart of the sons of men
is full *of* evil, and madness *is* in their heart
while they live, and after that *they go* to the
dead.
4 For to him that is joined to all the living
there is hope: for a living dog *is* better than a
dead lion.
5 For the living know that they shall die:
but [a]the dead know not any thing, neither
have they any more a reward; for [b]the memory of them is forgotten.
6 Also their love, and their hatred, and
their envy, is now perished; neither have they
any more a portion for ever in any *thing* that is
done under the sun.
7 ¶ Go *thy way,* [a]eat thy bread with joy, and
drink thy wine with a merry heart; for God
now accepteth thy works.
8 Let thy garments be always white; and let
thy head lack no ointment.
9 [1]Live joyfully with the wife whom thou
lovest all the days of the life of thy vanity,
which he hath given thee under the sun, all
the days of thy vanity: [a]for that *is* thy portion
in *this* life, and in thy labour which thou takest under the sun.
10 Whatsoever thy hand findeth to do, do
it with thy might; for *there is* no work, nor device, nor knowledge, nor wisdom, in the
grave, whither thou goest.
11 ¶ I returned, [a]and saw under the sun,
that the race *is* not to the swift, nor the battle
to the strong, neither yet bread to the wise,
nor yet riches to men of understanding, nor
yet favour to men of skill; but time and chance
happeneth to them all.
12 For [a]man also knoweth not his time: as
the fishes that are taken in an evil net, and as
the birds that are caught in the snare; so *are*
the sons of men [b]snared in an evil time, when
it falleth suddenly upon them.

The wise man and the fool

13 ¶ This wisdom have I seen also under
the sun, and it *seemed* great unto me:
14 [a]*There was* a little city, and few men
within it; and there came a great king against
it, and besieged it, and built great bulwarks
against it:
15 Now there was found in it a poor wise
man, and he by his wisdom delivered the city;
yet no man remembered that *same* poor man.

8:12 [b]Ps. 37:11,18,19; Prov. 1:32,33; Is. 3:10,11; Mat. 25:34,41
8:14 [a]Ps. 73:14; ch. 2:14; 7:15; 9:1-3
8:15 [a]ch. 2:24; 3:12,22; 5:18; 9:7
8:17 [a]Job 5:9; ch. 3:11; Rom. 11:33
9:1 [1]Heb. *I gave,* or, *set to my heart* [a]ch. 8:14
9:2 [a]Job 21:7; Ps. 73:3,12,13; Mal. 3:15
9:5 [a]Job 14:21; Is. 63:16 [b]Job 7:8-10; Is. 26:14
9:7 [a]ch. 8:15
9:9 [1]Heb. *See,* or, *Enjoy life* [a]ch. 2:10,24; 3:13,22; 5:18
9:11 [a]Amos 2:14,15; Jer. 9:23
9:12 [a]ch. 8:7 [b]Prov. 29:6; Luke 12:20,39; 17:26; 1 Thes. 5:3
9:14 [a]See 2 Sam. 20:16-22

8:12 *I know.* Here the Preacher speaks from mature faith, not as one who "seeketh" without coming to the truth (7:28). For similar declarations see 3:17; 11:9; 12:14.
8:14 Job 21–24 enlarges on this; Ps 73 draws the sting of it; and John 5:28–29 gives the final explanation.
8:15 *eat . . . drink . . . be merry.* Spoken gratefully (see 5:19; 9:7; Deut 8). For such words spoken arrogantly see Luke 12:19–20; 1 Cor 15:32.
8:17 *man cannot find out.* Deut 29:29 sums up what we are allowed and not allowed to know.
9:1 *either love or hatred.* The future is under God's control, and no one knows whether that future will be good or bad.
9:2 *alike to all.* Not only the wise and foolish (2:14), but also the good and the bad are seen leveled, in the sense noted at 3:20. For the Preacher's conviction (beyond mere observation) that God ultimately will see justice done see note on 8:12.
9:3 *evil . . . evil.* The apparently common destiny (both the righteous and the wicked die) encourages some people to sin.
9:5 *neither . . . any more a reward.* The dead have lost all opportunity in this life for enjoyment and reward from labor (see v. 6).
9:7–9 The Babylonian *Epic of Gilgamesh* contains a section (10.3.6–14) remarkably similar to this passage, illustrating the international flavor of ancient wisdom literature (see chart, p. xix).
9:7 See note on 8:15.
9:10 Cf. Col 3:23.
9:11 *time and chance.* Success is uncertain—more evidence that man does not ultimately control events.
9:12 *time.* Of disaster. *so are . . . men snared.* Success is unpredictable, because man is not wise enough to know when misfortune may overtake him.
9:15 *yet no man remembered.* Further warning against placing too high hopes on one's wisdom. Its reputation fades, its good is soon undone (v. 18b), and it has no answer to death (2:15–16).

16 [a]Then said I, Wisdom *is* better than strength: nevertheless [b]the poor *man's* wisdom *is* despised, and his words *are* not heard.

17 The words of wise *men are* heard in quiet, more than the cry of him that ruleth among fools.

18 [a]Wisdom *is* better than weapons of war: but [b]one sinner destroyeth much good.

10 [1]Dead flies cause the ointment of the apothecary to send forth a stinking savour: *so doth* a little folly *him that is* in reputation for wisdom *and* honour.

2 ¶ A wise *man's* heart *is* at his right hand; but a fool's heart at his left.

3 Yea also, when he that is a fool walketh by the way, [1]his wisdom faileth *him,* [a]and he saith to every one *that* he *is* a fool.

4 ¶ If the spirit of the ruler rise up against thee, [a]leave not thy place; for [b]yielding pacifieth great offences.

5 ¶ There is an evil *which* I have seen under the sun, as an error *which* proceedeth [1]from the ruler:

6 [a]Folly is set [1]in great dignity, and the rich sit in low place.

7 I have seen servants [a]upon horses, and princes walking as servants upon the earth.

8 ¶ [a]He that diggeth a pit shall fall into it; and whoso breaketh a hedge, a serpent shall bite him.

9 Whoso removeth stones shall be hurt therewith; *and* he that cleaveth wood shall be endangered thereby.

10 ¶ If the iron be blunt, and he do not whet the edge, then must he put to more strength: but wisdom *is* profitable to direct.

11 ¶ Surely the serpent will bite [a]without enchantment; and [1]a babbler is no better.

12 [a]The words of a wise *man's* mouth *are* [1]gracious; but [b]the lips of a fool will swallow up himself.

13 The beginning of the words of his mouth *is* foolishness: and the end of [1]his talk *is* mischievous madness.

14 [a]A fool also [1]is full of words: a man cannot tell what shall be; and [b]what shall be after him, who can tell him?

15 The labour of the foolish wearieth every one of them, because he knoweth not how to go to the city.

16 ¶ [a]Woe to thee, O land, when thy king *is* a child, and thy princes eat in the morning.

17 Blessed *art* thou, O land, when thy king *is* the son of nobles, and [a]thy princes eat in due season, for strength, and not for drunkenness.

18 ¶ By much slothfulness the building decayeth; and through idleness of the hands the house droppeth through.

19 ¶ A feast is made for laughter, and [a]wine [1]maketh merry: but money answereth all *things.*

20 ¶ [a]Curse not the king, no not in thy [1]thought; and curse not the rich in thy bedchamber: for a bird of the air shall carry the voice, and that which hath wings shall tell the matter.

The investment of a life

11 Cast thy bread [a][1]upon the waters: [b]for thou shalt find it after many days.

2 [a]Give a portion [b]to seven, and also to eight; [c]for thou knowest not what evil shall be upon the earth.

3 If the clouds be full *of* rain, they empty *themselves* upon the earth: and if the tree fall toward the south, or toward the north, *in* the place where the tree falleth, there it shall be.

4 He that observeth the wind shall not sow; and he that regardeth the clouds shall not reap.

5 As [a]thou knowest not what *is* the way of the spirit, [b]*nor* how the bones *do grow* in the womb of her that is with child: even so thou knowest not the works of God who maketh all.

6 In the morning sow thy seed, and in the evening withhold not thine hand: for thou knowest not whether [1]shall prosper, either this or that, or whether they both *shall be* alike good.

7 ¶ Truly the light *is* sweet, and a pleasant *thing it is* for the eyes [a]to behold the sun:

8 But if a man live many years, *and* rejoice in them all; yet let him remember the days of darkness; for they shall be many. All that cometh *is* vanity.

9:16 [a]ver. 18; Prov. 21:22; 24:5; ch. 7:19 [b]Mark 6:2
9:18 [a]ver. 16 [b]Josh. 7:1
10:1 [1]Heb. *Flies of death*
10:3 [1]Heb. *his heart* [a]Prov. 13:16; 18:2
10:4 [a]ch. 8:3 [b]1 Sam. 25:24; Prov. 25:15
10:5 [1]Heb. *from before*
10:6 [1]Heb. *in great heights* [a]Esth. 3:1
10:7 [a]Prov. 19:10; 30:22
10:8 [a]Ps. 7:15; Prov. 26:27
10:11 [1]Heb. *the master of the tongue* [a]Ps. 58:4,5; Jer. 8:17
10:12 [1]Heb. *grace* [a]Prov. 10:32 [b]Prov. 10:14
10:13 [1]Heb. *his mouth*
10:14 [1]Heb. *multiplieth words* [a]Prov. 15:2 [b]ch. 3:22; 8:7
10:16 [a]Is. 3:4,5; 5:11
10:17 [a]Prov. 31:4
10:19 [1]Heb. *maketh glad the life* [a]Ps. 104:15
10:20 [1]Or, *conscience* [a]Ex. 22:28; Acts 23:5
11:1 [1]Heb. *upon the face of the waters* [a]See Is. 32:20 [b]Deut. 15:10; Prov. 19:17; Mat. 10:42
11:2 [a]Ps. 112:9; 1 Tim. 6:18 [b]Mic. 5:5 [c]Eph. 5:16
11:5 [a]John 3:8 [b]Ps. 139:14
11:6 [1]Heb. *shall be right*
11:7 [a]ch. 7:11

10:2 *at his right hand . . . at his left.* These can stand for the greater and the lesser good (cf. Gen 48:13–20); or perhaps here, as in some later Jewish writings, for good and evil.

10:5 *error . . . from the ruler.* For the Preacher's observations on human regimes see vv. 4,6–7,16–17,20; 3:16; 4:1–3,13–16; 5:8–9; 8:2–6,10–11; 9:17.

10:12 *words.* A favorite topic in wisdom literature (see, e.g., Prov 15).

10:15 *knoweth not how to go to the city.* Since in Scripture a fool is one who refuses God's teaching (see note on 5:4), this caustic saying (probably proverbial) refers to more than mere stupidity.

10:16 *king is a child.* A small-minded upstart, not a "poor and a wise child" as in 4:13. See 2 Ki 15:8–25; Hos 7:3–7, which portray some of the short-lived usurpers and vicious courtiers who hastened the downfall of Israel.

10:18 *slothfulness . . . idleness.* See note on 4:5.

10:19 *money answereth all things.* Stating the great versatility of money (cf. Luke 16:9), not that weath is the ultimate good or the solution to all problems.

11:1 *Cast thy bread upon the waters.* Be adventurous, like those who accept the risks and reap the benefits of seaborne trade. Do not always play it safe (see Prov 11:24).

11:2 *Give a portion to seven.* Be generous while you have plenty; unforeseen disasters may make you dependent on the generosity of others.

11:3–6 *clouds . . . tree . . . wind . . . seed.* Do not toy with maybes and might-have-beens. Start where you can, and recognize how limited your role (or knowledge) is.

11:5 *way of the spirit.* The way that the spirit enters the body at the beginning point of life.

11:7–10 Live life to the fullest.

11:8,10 *vanity . . . vanity.* Warns against letting the wonder-

9 ¶ Rejoice, O young man, in thy youth;
and let thy heart cheer thee in the days of thy
youth, [a]and walk in the ways of thine heart,
and in the sight of thine eyes: but know thou,
that for all these *things* [b]God will bring thee
into judgment.
10 Therefore remove [1]sorrow from thy
heart, and [a]put away evil from thy flesh: [b]for
childhood and youth *are* vanity.

The span of a life

12 Remember [a]now thy Creator in the
days of thy youth, while the evil days
come not, nor the years draw nigh, [b]when
thou shalt say, I have no pleasure in them;
2 While the sun, or the light, or the moon,
or the stars, be not darkened, nor the clouds
return after the rain:
3 In the day when the keepers of the house
shall tremble, and the strong men shall bow
themselves, and [1]the grinders cease because
they are few, and those that look out of the
windows be darkened,
4 And the doors shall be shut in the
streets, when the sound of the grinding is
low, and he shall rise up at the voice of the
bird, and all [a]the daughters of musick shall be
brought low;
5 Also *when* they shall be afraid of *that*
which is high, and fears *shall be* in the way,
and the almond tree shall flourish, and the
grasshopper shall be a burden, and desire shall
fail: because man goeth to [a]his long home, and
[b]the mourners go about the streets:
6 Or ever the silver cord be loosed, or the
golden bowl be broken, or the pitcher be broken at the fountain, or the wheel broken at the
cistern.
7 [a]Then shall the dust return to the earth
as it was: [b]and the spirit shall return unto God
[c]who gave it.
8 ¶ [a]Vanity of vanities, saith the Preacher;
all *is* vanity.

The whole duty of man

9 ¶ And [1]moreover, because the Preacher
was wise, he still taught the people knowledge; yea, he gave good heed, and sought out,
and [a]set in order many proverbs.
10 The Preacher sought to find out [1]ac-
ceptable words: and *that which was* written
was upright, *even* words of truth.
11 The words of the wise *are* as goads, and
as nails fastened *by* the masters of assemblies,
which are given from one shepherd.
12 And further, by these, my son, be admonished: of making many books *there is* no end;
and [a]much [1]study *is* a weariness of the flesh.
13 ¶ [1]Let us hear the conclusion of the
whole matter: [a]Fear God, and keep his commandments: for this *is* the whole *duty of* man.
14 For [a]God shall bring every work into
judgment, with every secret *thing,* whether *it*
be good, or whether *it be* evil.

11:9 [a]Num. 15:39 [b]ch. 12:14
11:10 [1]Or, *anger* [a]2 Cor. 7:1 [b]Ps. 39:5
12:1 [a]Lam. 3:27 [b]2 Sam. 19:35
12:3 [1]Or, *the grinders fail, because they grind little*
12:4 [a]2 Sam. 19:35
12:5 [a]Job 17:13 [b]Jer. 9:17
12:7 [a]Gen. 3:19 [b]ch. 3:21 [c]Num. 16:22; Job 34:14; Zech. 12:1
12:8 [a]Ps. 62:9
12:9 [1]Or, *the more wise the Preacher was, etc.* [a]1 Ki. 4:32
12:10 [1]Heb. *words of delight*
12:12 [1]Or, *reading* [a]ch. 1:18
12:13 [1]Or, *The end of the matter, even all that hath been heard,* is [a]Deut. 10:12
12:14 [a]Mat. 12:36

ful gifts mentioned in vv. 7–10 dazzle and distract us. Verse 9 sets us on the true course.

11:9 *judgment.* See 12:14 and note. The prospect of divine praise or blame makes every detail of life significant rather than meaningless. To know this gives direction to our heart and discrimination to our eyes. The stage is set for ch. 12.

12:2–5 A graphic description of man's progressive deterioration; an allegory of aging.

12:3 *keepers of the house.* This and the other metaphors may refer to parts of the body (hands, legs, etc.). But the imagery should not be pressed to the extent that it destroys the poetry, which moves freely between figures such as darkness, storm, a house in decline and a deserted well, and such literal descriptions as in v. 5a.

12:5 *almond tree.* Its pale blossom possibly suggests the white hair of age. *grasshopper.* Normally agile, its slow movements on a cold morning (cf. Nah 3:17) recall the stiffness of old age. *long home.* Lit. "his eternal home." In context, probably points simply to the grave, not beyond it (cf. Job 10:21; 17:13).

12:6 *silver cord . . . golden bowl.* A hanging lamp suspended by a silver chain. If only one link snaps, this light and beauty will perish, suggesting how fragile life is.

12:8 *Vanity.* Such is life "under the sun" (on earth, apart from God), ending in brokenness. But with a relationship to our Creator already demanded (v. 1), and with the fact of His judgment affirmed (11:9), vanity is not the last word. *Preacher.* See note on 1:1.

12:9 *gave good heed, and sought out, and set in order.* The rigorous process on man's side, with no pains spared in seeking truth and comprehension.

‡12:11 *goads . . . nails.* Lit. "prods" . . . "pegs." Wisdom both prods us to seek for truth and serves as a peg on which to hang our thoughts. *given from one shepherd.* The other side of the matter, recognizing that Scripture is in a class of its own, as v. 12 insists.

12:13–14 The chief end of man.

12:13 *Fear God.* Loving reverence is the foundation of wisdom (Ps 111:10; Prov 1:7; 9:10), as well as its content (Job 28:28) and its goal and conclusion. *this is the whole duty of man.* To "fear God" is our fulfillment, our all—a far cry from "vanity."

12:14 *every work into judgment.* Glimpses of this truth are given at intervals in the book: 3:17; 8:12–13; 11:9 and note; see Mat 12:36; 1 Cor 3:12–15; 2 Cor 5:9–10; Heb 4:12–13. *every secret thing.* See Rom 2:16.

Song of Solomon

INTRODUCTION

Title

The title in the Hebrew text is "Solomon's Song of Songs," meaning a song by, for, or about Solomon. The phrase "Song of Songs" means the greatest of songs (cf. Deut 10:17, "God of gods, and Lord of lords"; 1 Tim 6:15, "King of kings").

Author and Date

Verse 1 appears to ascribe authorship to Solomon (see note on 1:1; but see also Title above). Solomon is referred to seven times (1:1,5; 3:7,9,11; 8:11–12), and several verses speak of the "king" (1:4,12; 7:5), but whether he was the author remains an open question.

To date the Song in the tenth century B.C. during Solomon's reign is not impossible. In fact, mention of Tirzah and Jerusalem in one breath (6:4) has been used to prove a date prior to king Omri (885–874 B.C.; see 1 Ki 16:23–24), though the reason for Tirzah's mention is not clear. On the other hand, many have appealed to the language of the Song as proof of a much later date, but on present evidence the linguistic data are ambiguous.

Consistency of language, style, tone, perspective and recurring refrains seems to argue for a single author. However, many who have doubted that the Song came from one pen, or even from one time or place, explain this consistency by ascribing all the Song's parts to a single literary tradition, since Near Eastern traditions were very careful to maintain stylistic uniformity.

Interpretation

To find the key for unlocking the Song, interpreters have looked to prophetic, wisdom and apocalyptic passages of Scripture, as well as to ancient Egyptian and Babylonian love songs, traditional Semitic wedding songs and songs related to ancient Mesopotamian fertility cults. The closest parallels appear to be those found in Proverbs (see Prov 5:15–20; 6:24–29; 7:6–23). The description of love in 8:6–7 (cf. the descriptions of wisdom found in Prov 1—9 and Job 28) seems to confirm that the Song belongs to Biblical wisdom literature and that it is wisdom's description of an amorous relationship. The Bible speaks of both wisdom and love as gifts of God, to be received with gratitude and celebration.

This understanding of the Song contrasts with the long-held view that the Song is an allegory of the love relationship between God and Israel, or between Christ and the church, or between Christ and the soul (the NT nowhere quotes from or even alludes to the Song). It is also distinct from more modern interpretations of the Song, such as that which sees it as a poetic drama celebrating the triumph of a maiden's pure, spontaneous love for her rustic shepherd lover over the courtly blandishments of Solomon, who sought to win her for his royal harem. Rather, it views the Song as a linked chain of lyrics depicting love in all its spontaneity, beauty, power and exclusiveness—experienced in its varied moments of separation and intimacy, anguish and ecstasy, tension and contentment. The Song shares with the love poetry of many cultures its extensive use of highly sensuous and suggestive imagery drawn from nature.

Theme and Theology

In ancient Israel everything human came to expression in words: reverence, gratitude, anger, sorrow, suffering, trust, friendship, commitment, loyalty, hope, wisdom, moral outrage, repentance. In the Song, it is love that finds words—inspired words that disclose its exquisite charm and beauty as one of God's choicest gifts. The voice of love in the Song, like that of wisdom in Prov 8:1—9:12, is a woman's voice, suggesting that love and wisdom draw men powerfully with the subtlety and mystery of a woman's allurements.

This feminine voice speaks profoundly of love. She portrays its beauty and delights. She claims its

exclusiveness ("My beloved is mine, and I am his," 2:16) and insists on the necessity of its pure spontaneity ("stir not up, nor awake my love, till he please," 2:7). She also proclaims its overwhelming power—it rivals that of the fearsome enemy, death; it burns with the intensity of a blazing fire; it is unquenchable even by the ocean depths (8:6–7a). She affirms its preciousness: All a man's possessions cannot purchase it, nor (alternatively) should they be exchanged for it (8:7b). She hints, without saying so explicitly (see 8:6), that it is a gift of the Lord to man.

God intends that such love—grossly distorted and abused by both ancient and modern people—be a normal part of marital life in His good creation (see Gen 1:26–31; 2:24).

Literary Features

No one who reads the Song with care can question the artistry of the poet. The subtle delicacy with which he evokes intense sensuous awareness while avoiding crude titillation is one of the chief marks of his achievement. This he accomplishes largely by indirection, by analogy and by bringing to the foreground the sensuous in the world of nature (or in food, drink, cosmetics and jewelry). To liken a lover's enjoyment of his beloved to one who "feedeth among the lilies" (2:16), or her breasts to two fawns that "feed among the lilies" (4:5), or the beloved herself to a garden filled with choice fruits inviting the lover to feast (4:12–16)—these combine exquisite artistry and fine sensitivity.

Whether the Song has the unity of a single dramatic line linking all the subunits into a continuing story is a matter of ongoing debate among interpreters. There do appear to be connected scenes in the love relationship (see Outline).

Virtually all agree that the literary climax of the Song is found in 8:6–7, where the unsurpassed power and value of love—the love that draws man and woman together—are finally expressly asserted. Literary relaxation follows the intenseness of that declaration. A final expression of mutual desire between the lovers brings the Song to an end, suggesting that love goes on. This last segment (8:8–14) is in some sense also a return to the beginning, as references to the beloved's brothers, to her vineyard and to Solomon (the king) link 8:8–12 with 1:2–6.

In this song of love the voice of the beloved is dominant. It is her experience of love, both as the one who loves and as the one who is loved, that is most clearly expressed. The Song begins with her wish for the lover's kiss and ends with her urgent invitation to him for love's intimacy.

Outline

I. Title (1:1)
II. The First Meeting (1:2—2:7)
III. The Second Meeting (2:8—3:5)
IV. The Third Meeting (3:6—5:1)
V. The Fourth Meeting (5:2—6:3)
VI. The Fifth Meeting (6:4—8:4)
VII. The Literary Climax (8:5–7)
VIII. The Conclusion (8:8–14)

1 The [a]song of songs, which *is* Solomon's.

In the chambers of the king

2 Let him kiss me with the kisses of his mouth:
[a]For [1]thy love *is* better than wine.
3 Because of the savour of thy good ointments
Thy name *is as* ointment poured forth,
Therefore do the virgins love thee.
4 [a]Draw me, [b]we will run after thee:
The king [c]hath brought me *into* his chambers:
We will be glad and rejoice in thee,
We will remember thy love more than wine:
[1]The upright love thee.
5 I *am* black, but comely, O ye daughters of Jerusalem,
As the tents of Kedar, as the curtains of Solomon.
6 Look not upon me, because I *am* black,
Because the sun hath looked upon me:
My mother's children were angry with me;
They made me the keeper of the vineyards;
But mine own vineyard have I not kept.
7 Tell me, O thou whom my soul loveth,
Where thou feedest, where thou makest *thy flock* to rest at noon:
For why should I be [1]as one that turneth aside by the flocks of thy companions?

8 If thou know not, [a]O thou fairest among women,
Go thy way forth by the footsteps of the flock,
And feed thy kids beside the shepherds' tents.
9 I have compared thee, [a]O my love,
[b]To a company of horses in Pharaoh's chariots.
10 [a]Thy cheeks are comely with rows *of jewels,*
Thy neck with chains *of gold.*
11 We will make thee borders of gold
With studs of silver.

12 While the king *sitteth* at his table,
My spikenard sendeth forth the smell thereof.
13 A bundle of myrrh *is* my well-beloved unto me;
He shall lie all night betwixt my breasts.
14 My beloved *is* unto me *as* a cluster of [a][1]camphire
In the vineyards of En-gedi.

15 [a]Behold, thou *art* fair, [1]my love;
behold, thou *art* fair;
Thou *hast* doves' eyes.

1:1 [a]1 Ki. 4:32
1:2 [1]Heb. *thy loves* [a]ch. 4:10
1:4 [1]Or, *They love thee uprightly* [a]Hos. 11:4; John 6:44; 12:32 [b]Phil. 3:12-14 [c]Ps. 45:14,15; John 14:2; Eph. 2:6
1:7 [1]Or, *as one that is vailed*
1:8 [a]ch. 5:9
1:9 [a]ch. 2:2,10, 13; 4:1,7; John 15:14 [b]2 Chr. 1:16
1:10 [a]Ezek. 16:11
1:14 [1]Or, *cypress* [a]ch. 4:13
1:15 [1]Or, *my companion* [a]ch. 4:1; 5:12

1:1 *song of songs.* Greatest of songs (see Introduction: Title). 1 Ki 4:32 says that Solomon wrote 1,005 songs. *Solomon's.* See Introduction: Title; Author and Date.

1:2–3 *kisses . . . thy love . . . thy good ointments.* Cf. 4:10–11, "thy love . . . thine ointments . . . Thy lips."

1:2 *him . . . his . . . thy.* These pronouns all refer to the same person, the lover (Solomon). *love.* Expressions of love—caresses, embraces and consummation (see v. 4; 4:10; 7:12; see also Prov 7:18; Ezek 16:8; 23:17). *better than wine.* See v. 4. In 4:10 the lover speaks similarly of the beloved's love.

1:3 *savour . . . ointments.* Aromatic spices and gums blended in cosmetic oil. *Thy name.* The very mention of the lover's name fills the air as with a pleasant aroma. The Hebrew words for "name" and "savour" sound alike. *virgins.* Probably young women of the court or of the royal city (see 6:8–9).

1:4 *king.* Solomon. *his chambers.* The king's private quarters. *We.* Probably the maidens of v. 3. *remember thy love more than wine.* For the reason given in v. 2.

‡1:5 *black.* Deeply browned by the sun (see v. 6); *daughters of Jerusalem.* Probably the maidens of v. 3. *tents . . . curtains.* Handwoven from black goat hair. *Kedar.* See note on Is 21:16.

1:6 *mine own vineyard.* Her body, as in 8:12 (see 2:15). Vineyard is an apt metaphor since it yields wine, and the excitements of love are compared with those produced by wine (see note on v. 2). The beloved is also compared to a garden, yielding precious fruits for the lover (see note on 4:12).

1:7 *whom my soul loveth.* See 3:1. *Where thou feedest . . . thy flock.* The lover is portrayed as a shepherd. In v. 8 the beloved is depicted as a shepherdess. *noon.* A time of rest in warm climates. *one that turneth aside by the flocks.* Prostitute (see Gen 38:14–15). The beloved does not wish to look for her lover among the shepherds, appearing as though she were a prostitute.

1:8 *fairest among women.* The beloved; also in v. 15; 2:10,13; 4:1,7; 5:9; 6:1,4,10. The lover is called "fair" in v. 16 (the masculine form of the same Hebrew word). *thy kids.* The beloved is pictured as a shepherdess (see v. 7). *beside the shepherds' tents.* The beloved is instructed to learn where the lover is by joining the shepherds in the fields.

1:9 *my love.* Used only of the beloved (see note on v. 13). *a company of horses.* A flattering comparison, similar to Theocritus's praise of the beautiful Helen of Troy (*Idyl,* 18.30–31). *in Pharaoh's chariots.* Her beauty attracts attention the way a mare would among the Egyptian chariot stallions. According to 1 Ki 10:28, Solomon imported horses from Egypt.

1:11 *We.* Perhaps the "daughters of Jerusalem" (v. 5).

1:12 *king.* Solomon. *at his table.* Reclining on his couch at the table. *My spikenard.* Nard is an aromatic oil extracted from the roots of a perennial herb that grows in India (see 4:13–14; Mark 14:3; John 12:3).

1:13 *myrrh.* An aromatic gum exuding from the bark of a balsam tree that grows in Arabia, Ethiopia and India. It was commonly used as an alluring feminine perfume (Esth 2:12; Prov 7:17). It was also used to perfume royal nuptial robes (Ps 45:8). The wise men brought myrrh to the young Jesus as a gift fit for a king (Mat 2:2,11). Myrrh was an ingredient in the holy anointing oil (Ex 30:23). *my well-beloved.* Used only of the lover (see note on v. 9).

1:14 *camphire.* A shrub of the Holy Land (perhaps the cypress) with tightly clustered, aromatic blossoms. *En-gedi.* An oasis watered by a spring, located on the west side of the Dead Sea. David sought refuge there from king Saul (1 Sam 24:1).

1:15 *thou art fair, my love.* See 4:1; 6:4; cf. v. 16. *my love.* See note on v. 9. *doves' eyes.* See 4:1.

16 Behold, thou *art* fair, my beloved, yea, pleasant:
Also our bed *is* green.
17 The beams of our house *are* cedar,
And our [1] rafters of fir.

The rose of Sharon

2 I am the rose of Sharon,
And the lily of the valleys.

2 As the lily among thorns,
So *is* my love among the daughters.

3 As the apple tree among the trees of the wood,
So *is* my beloved among the sons.
[1] I sat down under his shadow with great delight,
[a] And his fruit *was* sweet to my [2] taste.
4 He brought me to the [1] banqueting house,
And his banner over me *was* love.
5 Stay me with flagons, [1] comfort me with apples:
For I *am* sick of love.
6 [a] His left hand *is* under my head,
And his right hand doth embrace me.
7 [a] [1] I charge you, O ye daughters of Jerusalem,
By the roes, and by the hinds of the field,
That ye stir not up, nor awake *my* love, till he please.

8 The voice of my beloved! behold, he cometh
Leaping upon the mountains, skipping upon the hills.
9 [a] My beloved *is* like a roe or a young hart:
Behold, he standeth behind our wall,
He looketh forth at the windows,
[1] Shewing himself through the lattice.
10 My beloved spake, and said unto me,
[a] Rise up, my love, my fair one, and come away.
11 For lo, the winter is past,
The rain is over *and* gone;
12 The flowers appear on the earth;
The time of the singing *of birds* is come,
And the voice of the turtle is heard in our land;
13 The fig tree putteth forth her green figs,
And the vines *with* the tender grape give a *good* smell.
[a] Arise, my love, my fair one, and come away.
14 O my dove, *that art* in the clefts of the rock, in the secret places of the stairs,
Let me see thy countenance, [a] let me hear thy voice;
For sweet *is* thy voice, and thy countenance *is* comely.
15 Take us [a] the foxes,
The little foxes, that spoil the vines:
For our vines *have* tender grapes.
16 [a] My beloved *is* mine, and I *am* his:
He feedeth among the lilies.
17 [a] Until the day break, and the shadows flee away,
Turn, my beloved,
And be thou [b] like a roe or a young hart
Upon the mountains [1] of Bether.

The maiden's search

3 By [a] night on my bed I sought *him* whom my soul loveth:
I sought him, but I found him not.
2 I will rise now, and go about the city
In the streets and in the broad ways,
I will seek *him* whom my soul loveth:
I sought him, but I found him not.
3 [a] The watchmen that go about the city found me:

1:17 [1] Or, *galleries*
2:3 [1] Heb. *I delighted and sat down, etc.* [2] Heb. *palate* [a] Rev. 22:1,2
2:4 [1] Heb. *house of wine*
2:5 [1] Heb. *straw me with apples*
2:6 [a] ch. 8:3
2:7 [1] Heb. *I adjure you* [a] ch. 3:5; 8:4
2:9 [a] ver. 17
2:9 [1] Heb. *Flourishing*
2:10 [a] ver. 13
2:13 [a] ver. 10
2:14 [a] ch. 8:13
2:15 [a] Ps. 80:13; Ezek. 13:4; Luke 13:32
2:16 [a] ch. 6:3
2:17 [1] Or, *of division* [a] ch. 4:6 [b] ver. 9; ch. 8:14
3:1 [a] Is. 26:9
3:3 [a] ch. 5:7

1:16 *our bed is green.* Or "luxuriant." The lovers lie together in the field under the trees.
2:1 *rose.* Possibly a member of the crocus family (see also Is 35:1–2). *Sharon.* The fertile coastal plain south of mount Carmel (see map No. 2 at the end of the study Bible). *lily.* Probably either lotus or anemone.
2:2 *my love.* See note on 1:9.
2:3 *apple tree.* The precise nature of this fruit tree is uncertain.
2:4 *banner.* See 6:4; Num 2:2; Ps 20:5. The king's love for her is displayed for all to see, like a large military banner.
2:5 *flagons.* Raisin cakes. *apples.* With the "flagons" a metaphor for caresses and embraces.
‡2:7 *charge.* Place under oath. *daughters of Jerusalem.* See note on 1:5. *roes . . . hinds.* Perhaps in the imaginative language of love the roes (or gazelles) and hinds are portrayed as witnesses to the oath. This would be in harmony with the author's frequent reference to nature. *stir not up.* A recurring refrain in the Song (see 3:5; 8:4; cf. 5:8). It is always spoken by the beloved and always in a context of physical intimacy with her lover. It is best translated, "do not arouse love until it is proper." *till he please.* Out of the beloved's experience of love comes wise admonition that love is not to be artificially stimulated; utter spontaneity is essential to its genuine truth and beauty.
2:9 *roe.* Celebrated for its form and beauty. *young hart.* Or "deer," an apt simile for youthful vigor (cf. Is 35:6). *looketh . . . windows.* The eager lover tries to catch sight of the beloved while she is still preparing herself for their meeting.
2:10 *Rise up . . . come away.* See v. 13; cf. 7:11–13. *my fair one.* See note on 1:8.
2:11–13 The first signs of spring appear (see 6:11; 7:12)—the time of love.
2:14 *dove . . . secret places of the stairs.* Cf. Ps 55:6–8; Jer 48:28.
2:15 Perhaps spoken by the beloved. *vines.* As in 1:6 ("mine own vineyard"), probably a metaphor for the lovers' physical beauty. Thus the desire is expressed that the lovers be kept safe from whatever ("foxes") might mar their mutual attractiveness. *have tender grapes.* Their attractiveness is in its prime.
2:16 *My beloved is mine, and I am his.* See 6:3; 7:10. They belong to each other exclusively in a relationship that allows no intrusion. *He feedeth among the lilies.* The lover is compared to a "roe" (see vv. 9, 17). The pasturing is a metaphor for the lover's intimate enjoyment of her charms (see 6:2–3).
3:1 This verse begins a new moment in love's experience. *By night.* Night, with its freedom from the distractions of the day, allows the heart to be filled with its own preoccupations.
3:3 *watchmen.* Were stationed at the city gates (see Neh 3:29;

To whom I said, Saw ye *him* whom my
soul loveth?
4 *It was* but a little that I passed from
them,
But I found *him* whom my soul loveth:
I held him, and would not let him go,
Until I had brought him into my
mother's house,
And into the chamber of her that
conceived me.
5 [a]I charge you, O ye daughters of
Jerusalem,
By the roes, and by the hinds of the
field,
That ye stir not up, nor awake *my* love,
till he please.

6 [a]Who *is* this that cometh out of the
wilderness like pillars of smoke,
Perfumed *with* myrrh and
frankincense,
With all powders of the merchant?
7 Behold his bed, which *is* Solomon's;
Threescore valiant *men are* about it,
Of the valiant of Israel.
8 They all hold swords, *being* expert in
war:
Every man *hath* his sword upon his
thigh because of fear in the night.
9 King Solomon made himself [1]a chariot
of the wood of Lebanon.
10 He made the pillars thereof *of* silver,
The bottom thereof *of* gold,
The covering of it *of* purple,
The midst thereof being paved *with*
love, for the daughters of Jerusalem.
11 Go forth, O ye daughters of Zion, and
behold king Solomon
With the crown where*with* his mother
crowned him
In the day of his espousals,
And in the day of the gladness of his
heart.

3:5 [a]ch. 2:7; 8:4
3:6 [a]ch. 8:5
3:9 [1]Or, *a bed*

The king offers his love

4 Behold, [a]thou *art* fair, my love; behold,
thou *art* fair;
Thou *hast* doves' eyes within thy locks:
Thy hair *is* as a [b]flock of goats, [1]that
appear from mount Gilead.
2 [a]Thy teeth *are* like a flock of *sheep*
that are even shorn, which came up
from the washing;
Whereof every one beareth twins, and
none *is* barren among them.
3 Thy lips *are* like a thread of scarlet, and
thy speech *is* comely:
[a]Thy temples *are* like a piece of a
pomegranate within thy locks.
4 [a]Thy neck *is* like the tower of David
Builded [b]for an armoury,
Whereon there hang a thousand
bucklers, all shields of mighty *men.*
5 [a]Thy two breasts *are* like two young
roes *that are* twins,
Which feed among the lilies.

6 [a]Until the day [1]break, and the shadows
flee away,
I will get me to the mountain of myrrh,
and to the hill of frankincense.

7 [a]Thou *art* all fair, my love; *there is* no
spot in thee.
8 Come with me from Lebanon, *my*
spouse, with me from Lebanon:

4:1 [1]Or, *that eat of, etc.* [a]ch. 1:15; 5:12 [b]ch. 6:5
4:2 [a]ch. 6:6
4:3 [a]ch. 6:7
4:4 [a]ch. 7:4 [b]Neh. 3:19
4:5 [a]See Prov. 5:19; ch:7:3
4:6 [1]Heb. *breathe* [a]ch. 2:17
4:7 [a]Eph. 5:27

11:19; 13:22) and on the walls (see 5:7; 2 Sam 13:34; 18:24–27; 2 Ki 9:17–20; Ps 127:1; Is 52:8; 62:6). Apparently they also patrolled the streets at night (see 5:7).

3:4 *mother's.* Mothers are referred to frequently in the Song; fathers are never mentioned.

3:5 See note on 2:7. Once again the charge occurs at the moment of intimacy.

3:6–11 Perhaps spoken by friends (see 8:5). If so, this section probably portrays the wedding procession of Solomon and his bride approaching the city.

3:6 This verse begins a new moment in the relationship. *Who . . . wilderness.* See 8:5, where the reference is to the beloved. *wilderness.* Uncultivated seasonal grasslands. *smoke.* Incense (see note on Ex 30:34). *of the merchant.* Imported.

3:7 *bed.* A richly adorned royal conveyance, a palanquin (see vv. 9–10).

3:8 *fear in the night.* See Ps 91:5.

3:10 *pillars.* Supporting the canopy. *silver . . . gold.* Probably metals that overlay the Lebanon wood. *purple.* See notes on 7:5; Ex 25:4.

3:11 *daughters of Zion.* Elsewhere "daughters of Jerusalem" (see note on 1:5). *crown.* A wedding wreath (see Is 61:10). *mother.* See note on v. 4. Here the reference is to Bath-sheba.

4:1–7 For other exuberant descriptions of the beloved's beauty see 6:4–9; 7:1–7.

4:1b–2 See 6:5b–6.

4:1 *thou art fair, my love.* See 1:15 and note. *doves'.* See 1:15 and note. *eyes within thy locks.* With the rest of her face concealed by a veil, the lover's attention is focused on the beloved's eyes. *flock of goats.* The goats of Canaan were usually black (see note on 1:5). The lover's hair was also black (5:11). *that appear from mount Gilead.* The beloved's black tresses flowing from her head remind the lover of a flock of sleek black goats streaming down one of the hills of Gilead (noted for its good pasturage).

4:2 *that are even shorn.* Clean and white. *came up from the washing.* Still wet, like moistened teeth.

4:3 *Thy lips . . . scarlet.* Perhaps the beloved painted her lips, like Egyptian women. *temples . . . within thy locks.* See note on v. 1. *piece of a pomegranate.* Round and blushed with red.

4:4 The beloved's erect, bespangled neck is like a tower on the city wall adorned with warriors' shields (cf. 7:4).

4:5 See 7:3. *young roes.* Or fawns, representing tender, delicate beauty, and promise rather than full growth (cf. 8:8). The simile of the "roe" (gazelle) is used of the lover in 2:9. *feed among the lilies.* For a different use of this phrase see 2:16 and note.

4:6 *Until . . . shadows flee away.* See 2:17. *mountain of myrrh . . . hill of frankincense.* Metaphors for lovers' intimacy.

4:8 To the lover the beloved seems to have withdrawn as if to a remote mountain. *Lebanon . . . Amana . . . Hermon.* Mountain peaks on the northern horizon. *Shenir.* Amorite name for mount Hermon (Deut 3:9).

Look from the top of Amana, from the
top of Shenir [a] and Hermon,
From the lions' dens, from the
mountains of the leopards.
9 Thou hast [1] ravished my heart, my
sister, *my* spouse;
Thou hast [1] ravished my heart with one
of thine eyes,
With one chain of thy neck.
10 How fair is thy love, my sister, *my*
spouse!
[a] How much better is thy love than
wine!
And the smell of thine ointments than
all spices!
11 Thy lips, O *my* spouse, drop *as* the
honeycomb:
[a] Honey and milk *are* under thy tongue;
And the smell of thy garments *is* [b] like
the smell of Lebanon.
12 A garden [1] inclosed *is* my sister, *my*
spouse;
A spring [1] shut up, a fountain sealed.
13 Thy plants *are* an orchard of
pomegranates, with pleasant fruits;
[1] Camphire, with spikenard,
14 Spikenard and saffron;
Calamus and cinnamon, with all trees
of frankincense;
Myrrh and aloes, with all the chief
spices:
15 A fountain of gardens, a well of [a] living
waters,
And streams from Lebanon.

4:8 [a] Deut. 3:9
4:9 [1] Or, *taken away my heart*
4:10 [a] ch. 1:2
4:11 [a] Prov. 24:13,14; ch. 5:1 [b] Gen. 27:27; Hos. 14:6,7
4:12 [1] Heb. *barred*
4:13 [1] Or, *Cypress*
4:15 [a] John 4:10; 7:38

16 Awake, O north wind; and come thou
south;
Blow upon my garden, *that* the spices
thereof may flow out.
[a] Let my beloved come into his garden,
And eat his pleasant fruits.

5 [a] I am come into my garden, my sister,
my spouse:
I have gathered my myrrh with my spice;
[b] I have eaten my honeycomb with my
honey;
I have drunk my wine with my milk:
Eat, [c] O friends; drink, [1] yea, drink
abundantly, O beloved.

The torment of separation

2 I sleep, but my heart waketh:
It is the voice of my beloved [a] that
knocketh *saying,*
Open to me, my sister, my love, my
dove, my undefiled:
For my head is filled *with* dew,
And my locks *with* the drops of the
night.
3 I have put off my coat; how shall I put
it on?
I have washed my feet; how shall I
defile them?
4 My beloved put in his hand by the hole
of the door,
And my bowels were moved [1] for him.
5 I rose up to open to my beloved;
And my hands dropped *with* myrrh,
And my fingers *with* [1] sweet smelling
myrrh,
Upon the handles of the lock.

4:16 [a] ch. 5:1
5:1 [1] Or, *and be drunken* with *loves* [a] ch. 4:16 [b] ch. 4:11 [c] Luke 15:7,10
5:2 [a] Rev. 3:20
5:4 [1] Or, (as some read) *in me*
5:5 [1] Heb. *passing,* or, *running about*

4:9 *my sister.* For lovers to address each other as "brother" and "sister" was common in the love poetry of the ancient Near East (see vv. 10,12; 5:1). *with one of thine eyes.* With a single glance (cf. 6:5 and note).
4:10 *better . . . than wine.* See note on 1:2. *smell of thine ointments.* See 1:3. *spices.* See v. 14; 5:1,13; 6:2; 8:14. Spice was an imported luxury item (see 1 Ki 10:2,10,25; Ezek 27:22). Spices were used for fragrance in the holy anointing oil (Ex 25:6; 30:23–25; 35:8) and for fragrant incense (Ex 25:6; 35:8) as well as for perfume.
4:11 *Thy lips . . . drop as the honeycomb.* They drip with honey. The beloved speaks to him of love (cf. Prov 5:3; 16:24). People in the ancient Near East associated sweetness with the delights of love. *Honey and milk.* Perhaps reminiscent of the description of the promised land (see note on Ex 3:8). *under thy tongue.* See Job 20:12; Ps 10:7.
4:12 *garden.* A place of sensual delights (see v. 16; 5:1; 6:2; see also note on 1:6). *inclosed . . . shut up . . . sealed.* Metaphors for the beloved's virginity—or perhaps for the fact that she keeps herself exclusively for her husband. *spring . . . fountain.* Sources of refreshment; metaphors for the beloved as a sexual partner, as in Prov 5:15–20.
4:13–15 Verses 13–14 elaborate on the garden metaphor of v. 12a, and v. 15 on the fountain metaphor of v. 12b. The trees and spices in vv. 13–14 are mostly exotic, referring to the beloved's charms.
4:13 *Thy plants.* All the beloved's features that delight the lover. *orchard.* Hebrew *pardes* (from which the English word "paradise" comes), a loanword from Old Persian meaning "enclosure" or "park." In Neh 2:8 and Eccl 2:5 it refers to royal parks and forests. *Camphire.* See note on 1:14. *spikenard.* See note on 1:12.
4:14 *saffron.* A plant of the crocus family bearing purple or white flowers, parts of which, when dried, were used as a cooking spice. *Calamus.* An imported (see Jer 6:20), aromatic spice cane, used also in the holy anointing oil and incense ("cane" in Ex 30:23,25; Is 43:23–24). *cinnamon.* Used in the holy anointing oil (Ex 30:23,25). *Myrrh.* See note on 1:13. *aloes.* Aromatic aloes, used to perfume royal nuptial robes (Ps 45:8). Prov 7:17 says that the adulteress perfumed her bed "with myrrh, aloes and cinnamon."
4:15 *living waters.* Fresh, not stagnant. *streams from Lebanon.* Cool, sparkling water from the snowfields on the Lebanon mountains.
4:16 May the fragrance of my charms be wafted about to draw my lover to me so that we may enjoy love's intimacies. *his garden.* She belongs to him and she yields herself to her lover (see 6:2).
5:1 The lover claims the beloved as his garden and enjoys all her delights. *my sister.* See note on 4:9. *Eat, O friends.* The friends of the lovers applaud their enjoyment of love.
5:2–8 See 3:1–5 and note on 3:1.
5:2 *I sleep, but my heart waketh.* Love holds sway even in sleep—just as a new mother sleeps with an ear open to her baby's slightest whimper.
5:3 Instinctive reaction raises a foolish complaint before the language of love takes over.
5:5 *fingers . . . sweet smelling myrrh.* Love's eager imagination extravagantly lotioned the beloved's hands with perfume.

6 I opened to my beloved;
But my beloved had withdrawn
himself, *and* was gone:
My soul failed when he spake:
[a]I sought him, but I could not find him;
I called him, but he gave me no answer.
7 [a]The watchmen that went about the
city found me,
They smote me, they wounded me;
The keepers of the walls took away my
vail from me.
8 I charge you, O daughters of Jerusalem,
If ye find my beloved, [1]that ye tell him,
That I *am* sick of love.

9 What *is* thy beloved more than *another*
beloved, [a]O thou fairest among
women?
What *is* thy beloved more than *another*
beloved, that thou dost so charge us?

10 My beloved *is* white and ruddy,
[1]The chiefest among ten thousand.
11 His head *is as* the most fine gold,
His locks *are* [1]bushy, *and* black as a
raven.
12 [a]His eyes *are* as *the eyes of* doves by
the rivers of waters,
Washed with milk, *and* [1]fitly set.
13 His cheeks *are* as a bed of spices, *as*
[1]sweet flowers:
His lips *like* lilies, dropping sweet
smelling myrrh.
14 His hands *are as* gold rings set with the
beryl:
His belly *is as* bright ivory overlaid
with sapphires.
15 His legs *are as* pillars of marble, set
upon sockets of fine gold:

5:6 [a]ch. 3:1
5:7 [a]ch. 3:3
5:8 [1]Heb. *what*
5:9 [a]ch. 1:8
5:10 [1]Heb. *A standard-bearer*
5:11 [1]Or, *curled*
5:12 [1]Heb. *sitting in fulness, that is, fitly placed, and set as a precious stone in the foil of a ring* [a]ch. 1:15; 4:1
5:13 [1]Or, *towers of perfumes*

5:16 [1]Heb. *His palate*
6:1 [a]ch. 1:8
6:3 [a]ch. 2:16; 7:10
6:4 [a]ver. 10
6:5 [1]Or, *they have puffed me up* [a]ch. 4:1
6:6 [a]ch. 4:2
6:7 [a]ch. 4:3

His countenance *is* as Lebanon,
excellent as the cedars.
16 [1]His mouth *is* most sweet: yea, he *is*
altogether lovely.
This *is* my beloved, and this *is* my
friend, O daughters of Jerusalem.

6 Whither is thy beloved gone, [a]O thou
fairest among women?
Whither is thy beloved turned aside?
that we may seek him with thee.

2 My beloved is gone down into his
garden, to the beds of spices,
To feed in the gardens, and to gather
lilies.
3 [a]I *am* my beloved's, and my beloved *is*
mine:
He feedeth among the lilies.

The maiden's beauty

4 Thou *art* beautiful, O my love, as Tirzah,
Comely as Jerusalem,
[a]Terrible as *an army* with banners.
5 Turn away thine eyes from me, for
[1]they have overcome me:
Thy hair *is* [a]as a flock of goats that
appear from Gilead.
6 [a]Thy teeth *are* as a flock of sheep
which go up from the washing,
Whereof every one beareth twins, and
there is not one barren among them.
7 [a]As a piece of a pomegranate *are* thy
temples within thy locks.
8 There *are* threescore queens, and
fourscore concubines,
And virgins without number.
9 My dove, my undefiled *is but* one;
She *is* the *only* one of her mother,

5:9 The friends' question provides an opportunity for the beloved to describe the beauty of her lover—which she does only here.
5:10 *ruddy.* See 1 Sam 16:12.
5:11 *black.* The beloved's hair was also black (see note on 4:1).
5:12 *doves.* See note on 1:15. *by the rivers of waters.* The lover's eyes sparkle. *Washed with milk.* Describing the white of the eye.
5:13 *spices . . . lilies.* These similes probably compare sensuous effects rather than appearances, as do the following similes and metaphors, at least in part. *lilies.* See note on 2:1. *dropping . . . myrrh.* Love's pleasant excitements are aroused by the lover's lips.
5:14 *beryl.* See note on Ezek 1:16. *sapphires.* Hebrew *sappir* (from which the English word "sapphire" comes).
5:15 *countenance is as Lebanon.* Awesome and majestic. *excellent as the cedars.* The cedars of Lebanon were renowned throughout the ancient Near East, and their wood was desired for adorning temples and palaces.
5:16 *mouth.* The lover's kisses and loving speech. *daughters of Jerusalem.* See note on 1:5.
6:1 The question asked by the friends forms a transition from the beloved's description of the lover to her delighted acknowledgment of his intimacy with her and the exclusiveness of their relationship.
6:2 *his garden.* The beloved. *beds of spices.* Her sensuous attractions (cf. 5:13). *gather lilies.* See note on 2:1. The lover, enjoying intimacies with the beloved, is compared to a graceful gazelle (see notes on 2:7,9) nibbling from lily to lily in undisturbed enjoyment of exotic delicacies.
6:3 *I . . . mine.* See note on 2:16. Notice the reversal; here her yielding to her lover is emphasized.
6:4 *Tirzah.* An old Canaanite city in the middle of the land (see Josh 12:24). It was chosen by Jeroboam I (930–909 B.C.) as the first royal city of the northern kingdom (see 1 Ki 14:17; see also 1 Ki 15:21; 16:23–24). The meaning of its name ("pleasure, beauty") suggests that it was a beautiful site, perhaps explaining why the author here sets it alongside Jerusalem (though what constituted the beauty of Tirzah is not known). Comparison of the beloved's beauty to that of cities was perhaps not so unusual in the ancient Near East, since cities were regularly depicted as women (see note on 2 Ki 19:21). *Terrible.* Or awesome, (cf. v. 10). *as an army with banners.* The beloved's noble beauty evoked in the lover emotions like those aroused by a troop marching under its banners.
6:5–7 See 4:1–3 and notes.
6:5 *thine eyes . . . have overcome me.* The beloved's eyes awaken in the lover such intensity of love that he is held captive (see 4:9).
6:8 *queens . . . concubines . . . virgins.* The reference is either to Solomon's harem or to all the beautiful women of the realm.
6:9 *my undefiled.* See 5:2. *only one of her mother.* Not literal-

She *is* the choice one of her that bare her.
The daughters saw her, and blessed her;
Yea, the queens and the concubines, and they praised her.
10 Who *is* she that looketh forth as the morning,
Fair as the moon, clear as the sun,
[a]*And* terrible as *an army* with banners?

11 I went down into the garden of nuts to see the fruits of the valley,
And [a]to see whether the vine flourished, *and* the pomegranates budded.
12 [1]Or ever I was aware,
My soul [2]made me *like* the chariots of Ammi-nadib.

13 Return, return, O Shulamite;
Return, return, that we may look upon thee.

What will ye see in the Shulamite?
As it were the company [1]of two armies.

7 How beautiful are thy feet with shoes,
[a]O prince's daughter!
The joints of thy thighs *are* like jewels,
The work of the hands of a cunning workman.
2 Thy navel *is like* a round goblet, *which* wanteth not [1]liquor:
Thy belly *is like* a heap of wheat set about with lilies.
3 [a]Thy two breasts *are* like two young roes *that are* twins.
4 [a]Thy neck *is* as a tower of ivory;
Thine eyes *like* the *fish*pools in Heshbon, by the gate of Bath-rabbim:
Thy nose *is* as the tower of Lebanon which looketh toward Damascus.
5 Thine head upon thee *is* like [1]Carmel,
And the hair of thine head like purple;
The king *is* [2]held in the galleries.
6 How fair and how pleasant art thou, O love, for delights!
7 This thy stature is like to a palm tree,
And thy breasts to clusters *of grapes.*
8 I said, I will go up to the palm tree,
I will take hold of the boughs thereof:
Now also thy breasts shall be as clusters of the vine,
And the smell of thy nose like apples;
9 And the roof of thy mouth like the best wine,
For my beloved, that goeth *down* [1]sweetly,
Causing the lips [2]of *those that are* asleep to speak.

The maiden desires her beloved

10 [a]I *am* my beloved's, and [b]his desire *is* towards me.
11 Come, my beloved, let us go forth *into* the field;
Let us lodge in the villages.
12 Let us get up early to the vineyards;
Let us [a]see if the vine flourish,
whether the tender grape [1]appear,
And the pomegranates bud forth:
There will I give thee my loves.
13 The [a]mandrakes give a smell,
And at our gates [b]*are* all *manner of* pleasant *fruits,*
New and old,
Which I have laid up for thee, O my beloved.

6:10 [a]ver. 4
6:11 [a]ch. 7:12
6:12 [1]Heb. *I knew not* [2]Or, *set me on the chariot[s] of my willing people*
6:13 [1]Or, *of Mahanaim*
7:1 [a]Ps. 45:13
7:2 [1]Heb. *mixture*
7:3 [a]ch. 4:5
7:4 [a]ch. 4:4
7:5 [1]Or, *crimson* [2]Heb. *bound*
7:9 [1]Heb. *straightly* [2]Or, *of the ancient*
7:10 [a]ch. 2:16; 6:3 [b]Ps. 45:11
7:12 [1]Heb. *open* [a]ch. 6:11
7:13 [a]Gen. 30:14 [b]Mat. 13:52

ly an only child, but the one uniquely loved (cf. Gen 22:2; Judg 11:34; Prov 4:3). *daughters . . . blessed her.* All the other women praised her beauty (see 1:8; 5:9; 6:1).
6:10 See 5:9; 6:1.
6:11 *nuts.* Perhaps walnuts. *see . . . the valley.* For the first signs of spring (see note on 2:11–13).
6:12 *chariots.* Solomon was famous for his chariots (1 Ki 10:26).
6:13 *Shulamite.* The beloved. It is either a variant of "Shunammite" (see 1 Ki 1:3), i.e. a young woman from Shunem (see Josh 19:18), or a feminine form of the word "Solomon," meaning "Solomon's girl." In ancient Semitic languages the letters *l* and *n* were sometimes interchanged.
7:1–7 Here the description moves up from the feet rather than down from the head (cf. 5:11–15).
7:1 Cf. v. 6. *prince's daughter.* Alludes to the nobility of her beauty (see Ps 45:13).
7:2 *goblet.* A large, two-handled, ring-based bowl (see Ex 24:6; Is 22:24; see also Amos 6:6). *set about with lilies.* The beloved perhaps wore a loose garland of flowers around her waist.
7:3 See note on 4:5.
7:4 *tower of ivory.* Mixed imagery, referring to shape as well as to color and texture. *fishpools.* The beloved's eyes reflect like the surface of a pool; or the imagery may depict serenity and gentleness. *Heshbon.* Once the royal city of king Sihon (Num 21:26), it was blessed with an abundant supply of spring water. *Bath-rabbim.* Means "daughter of many"; perhaps a popular name for Heshbon. *tower of Lebanon.* Perhaps a military tower on the northern frontier of Solomon's kingdom, but more likely the beautiful, towering Lebanon mountain range.
7:5 *Carmel.* A promontory midway along the western coast of the kingdom, with a wooded top and known for its beauty. *purple.* A reference to purple, royal cloth, as in 3:10 (see note on Ex 25:4). *king.* Solomon. *held in the galleries.* Lit. "bound by the locks"; captivated by the beauty of her hair.
7:7 *palm.* The stately date palm.
7:8 *apples.* Perhaps the fragrance of apple blossoms (but see note on 2:3).
7:9 *that goeth down sweetly.* The beloved offers the wine (see 5:1) of her love to her lover.
7:10 *I am my beloved's.* See notes on 2:16; 6:3. *desire.* Cf. Gen 3:16.
7:11–12 In 2:10–13 the beloved reports a similar invitation from her lover.
7:12 *give thee my loves.* She offers herself completely to her lover.
7:13 *mandrakes.* Short-stemmed herbs associated with fertility (see note on Gen 30:14). The odor of its blossom is pungent. *at our gates.* The gates where the lovers meet. *pleasant fruits.* Metaphor for the delights the beloved has for her lover from her "garden" (cf. 4:13–14). *New and old.* Those already shared and those still to be enjoyed.

8 O that thou *wert* as my brother, that
sucked the breasts of my mother!
When I should find thee without, I
would kiss thee;
Yea, [1]I should not be despised.
2 I would lead thee, *and* bring thee into
my mother's house, *who* would
instruct me:
I would cause thee to drink of [a]spiced
wine, of the juice of my pomegranate.
3 [a]His left hand *should be* under my head,
And his right hand should embrace me.
4 [a]I charge you, O daughters of
Jerusalem,
[1]That ye stir not up, nor awake *my*
love, until he please.

5 [a]Who *is* this that cometh up from the
wilderness,
Leaning upon her beloved?

I raised thee up under the apple tree:
There thy mother brought thee forth:
There she brought *thee* forth *that* bare
thee.
6 [a]Set me as a seal upon thine heart,
As a seal upon thine arm:
For love *is* strong as death;
Jealousy *is* [1]cruel as the grave:
The coals thereof *are* coals of fire,
Which hath a most vehement flame.
7 Many waters cannot quench love,
Neither can the floods drown it:
[a]If a man would give all the substance
of his house for love,
It would utterly be contemned.
8 [a]We have a little sister, and she hath
no breasts:
What shall we do for our sister in the
day when she shall be spoken for?
9 If she *be* a wall, we will build upon her
a palace of silver:
And if she *be* a door, we will inclose
her with boards of cedar.

10 I *am* a wall, and my breasts like towers:
Then was I in his eyes as one that
found [1]favour.
11 Solomon had a vineyard at Baal-hamon;
[a]He let out the vineyard unto keepers;
Every one for the fruit thereof was to
bring a thousand *pieces* of silver.

12 My vineyard, which *is* mine, *is* before
me:

Thou, O Solomon, *must have* a
thousand,
And those that keep the fruit thereof
two hundred.
13 Thou that dwellest in the gardens,
The companions hearken to thy voice:
[a]Cause me to hear *it.*

14 [a][1]Make haste, my beloved,
And [b]be thou like to a roe or to a
young hart
Upon the mountains of spices.

8:1 [1]Heb. *they should not despise me*
8:2 [a]Prov. 9:2
8:3 [a]ch. 2:6
8:4 [1]Heb. *Why should ye stir up, or why, etc.* [a]ch. 2:7; 3:5
8:5 [a]ch. 3:6
8:6 [1]Heb. *hard* [a]Is. 49:16; Jer. 22:24; Hag. 2:23
8:7 [a]Prov. 6:35
8:8 [a]Ezek. 23:33
8:10 [1]Heb. *peace*
8:11 [a]Mat. 21:33
8:13 [a]ch. 2:14
8:14 [1]Heb. *Flee away* [a]See Rev. 22:17,20 [b]ch. 2:17

8:1 *I should not be despised.* The beloved could openly show affection without any public disgrace.
8:2 *I would cause thee to drink.* She would offer her lover the delights of her love. *juice.* The Hebrew for this word refers to intoxicating juices.
8:4 See 2:7 and note.
8:5 *Who . . . wilderness.* See 3:6. *under the apple tree.* In the ancient world, sexual union and birth were often associated with fruit trees.
8:6–7 *love is . . . death . . . The coals . . . fire . . . Many waters . . . drown it.* These three wisdom statements (see essay, p. 687) characterize marital love as the strongest, most unyielding and invincible force in human experience. With these statements the Song reaches its literary climax and discloses its purpose.
8:6 *seal.* Seals were precious to their owners, as personal as their names (see note on Gen 38:18). *arm.* Probably a poetic synonym for "hand." *strong as death.* As the grave will not give up the dead, so love will not surrender the loved one.
8:7 *Many waters.* Words that suggest not only the ocean depths (see Ps 107:23) but also the primeval waters that the people of the ancient Near East regarded as a permanent threat to the world (see note on Ps 32:6). The waters were also associated with the realm of the dead (see note on Ps 30:1). *If a man . . . contemned.* A fourth wisdom statement (see note on vv. 6–7), declaring love's unsurpassed worth. Riches are "contemned" (despised) in comparison to love.
8:8–14 In the closing lines of the Song, the words of the brothers (vv. 8–9), the beloved's reference to her own vineyard (v. 12) and her final reference to Solomon (vv. 11–12) suggest a return to the beginning of the Song (see 1:2–7). The lines may recall the beloved's development into the age for love and marriage and the blossoming of her relationship with her lover.
8:8 In the ancient Near East, brothers often were guardians of their sisters, especially in matters pertaining to marriage (see Gen 24:50–60; 34:13–27). *in the day when she shall be spoken for.* Marriage was often contracted at an early age.
8:9 This imaginative verse probably expresses the brothers' determination to defend their young sister (the beloved) until her proper time for love and marriage has come. Or it may mean that the brothers are concerned to see that she is properly adorned for marriage before she is spoken for.
8:10 *I . . . like towers.* In contrast to the time when she was watched over by her brothers, the beloved rejoices in her maturity (see Ezek 16:7–8). *his.* The lover's.
8:11–12 *thousand pieces of silver . . . two hundred.* Whether these figures are to be taken literally (see Is 7:23) is uncertain.
8:11 *Baal-hamon.* Location unknown. The Hebrew *hamon* sometimes means "wealth" or "abundance"; hence Baal (i.e. "lord") Hamon could mean "lord of abundance," bringing to mind Solomon's great wealth.
8:12 *My vineyard.* Her body (see note on 1:6). *is mine.* As Solomon is master of his vineyard, so the beloved is mistress of her attractions to dispense them as she will. She offers Solomon the owner's portion of her vineyard.
8:13 *in the gardens.* In 7:11–12 the beloved invites her lover to accompany her to the countryside and the vineyards. Here the imagery places her appropriately in a garden. *companions.* Male; perhaps the companions of the lover (see 1:7). *Cause me to hear it.* See 2:14.
8:14 *be thou like to a roe or . . . hart.* Display your virile strength and agility for my delight (see note on 2:9). *Upon the mountains of spices.* Cf. 2:17.

The Book of the Prophet
Isaiah

INTRODUCTION

Author

Isaiah son of Amoz is often thought of as the greatest of the writing prophets. His name means "The LORD saves." He was a contemporary of Amos, Hosea and Micah, beginning his ministry in 740 B.C., the year King Uzziah died (see note on 6:1). According to an unsubstantiated Jewish tradition (*The Ascension of Isaiah*), he was sawed in half during the reign of Manasseh (cf. Heb 11:37). Isaiah was married and had at least two sons, Shear-jashub (7:3) and Maher-shalal-hash-baz (8:3). He probably spent most of his life in Jerusalem, enjoying his greatest influence under King Hezekiah (see 37:1–2). Isaiah is also credited with writing a history of the reign of King Uzziah (2 Chr 26:22).

Many scholars today challenge the claim that Isaiah wrote the entire book that bears his name. Yet his is the only name attached to it (see 1:1; 2:1; 13:1). The strongest argument for the unity of Isaiah is the expression "the Holy One of Israel," a title for God that occurs 12 times in chs. 1—39 and 13 times in chs. 40—66. Outside Isaiah it appears in the OT only 6 times. There are other striking verbal parallels between chs. 1—39 and chs. 40—66. Compare the following verses:

1:2	66:24
1:5–6	53:4–5
5:27	40:30
6:1	52:13; 57:15
6:11–12	62:4
11:1	53:2
11:6–9	65:25
11:12	49:22
35:10	51:11

Altogether, there are at least 25 Hebrew words or forms found in Isaiah (i.e. in both major divisions of the book) that occur in no other prophetic writing.

Isaiah's use of fire as a figure of punishment (see 1:31; 10:17; 26:11; 33:11–14; 34:9–10; 66:24), his references to the "mountain of the LORD" of Jerusalem (see note on 2:2–4) and his mention of the highway to Jerusalem (see note on 11:16) are themes that recur throughout the book.

The structure of Isaiah also argues for its unity. Chs. 36—39 constitute a historical interlude, which concludes chs. 1—35 and introduces chs. 40—66 (see note on 36:1).

Several NT verses refer to the prophet Isaiah in connection with various parts of the book: Mat 12:17–21 (Is 42:1–4); Mat 3:3 and Luke 3:4 (Is 40:3); Rom 10:16,20 (Is 53:1; 65:1); see especially John 12:38–41 (Is 53:1; 6:10).

Date

Most of the events discussed in chs. 1—39 occurred during Isaiah's ministry (see 6:1; 14:28; 36:1), so it is likely that these chapters were completed not long after 701 B.C., the year the Assyrian army was destroyed (see note on 10:16). The prophet lived until at least 681 (see note on 37:38) and may have written chs. 40—66 during his later years. In his message to the exiles of the sixth century B.C., Isaiah was projected into the future, just as the apostle John was in Rev 4—22.

Background

Isaiah wrote during the stormy period marking the expansion of the Assyrian empire and the decline of Israel. Under King Tiglath-pileser III (745–727 B.C.) the Assyrians swept westward into Aram (Syria) and Canaan. About 733 the kings of Aram and Israel tried to pressure Ahaz king of Judah into joining a coalition against Assyria. Ahaz chose instead to ask Tiglath-pileser for help, a decision condemned by Isaiah (see note on 7:1). Assyria did assist Judah and conquered the northern kingdom in 722–721. This made Judah even more vulnerable, and in 701 King Sennacherib of Assyria threat-

ened Jerusalem itself (see 36:1 and note). The godly King Hezekiah prayed earnestly, and Isaiah predicted that God would force the Assyrians to withdraw from the city (37:6–7).

Nevertheless Isaiah warned Judah that her sin would bring captivity at the hands of Babylon. The visit of the Babylonian king's envoys to Hezekiah set the stage for this prediction (see 39:1,6 and notes). Although the fall of Jerusalem would not take place until 586 B.C., Isaiah assumes the demise of Judah and proceeds to predict the restoration of the people from captivity (see 40:2–3 and notes). God would redeem His people from Babylon just as He rescued them from Egypt (see notes on 35:9; 41:14). Isaiah predicts the rise of Cyrus the Persian, who would unite the Medes and Persians and conquer Babylon in 539 (see 41:2 and note). The decree of Cyrus would allow the Jews to return home in 538, a deliverance that prefigured the greater salvation from sin through Christ (see 52:7 and note).

Themes and Theology

Isaiah is a book that unveils the full dimensions of God's judgment and salvation. God is "the Holy One of Israel" (see 1:4; 6:1 and notes) who must punish His rebellious people (1:2) but will afterward redeem them (41:14,16). Israel is a nation blind and deaf (6:9–10; 42:7), a vineyard that will be trampled (5:1–7), a people devoid of justice or righteousness (5:7; 10:1–2). The awful judgment that will be unleashed upon Israel and all the nations that defy God is called "the day of the LORD." Although Israel has a foretaste of that day (5:30; 42:25), the nations bear its full power (see 2:11,17,20 and note). It is a day associated in the NT with Christ's second coming and the accompanying judgment (see 24:1,21; 34:1–2 and notes). Throughout the book, God's judgment is pictured as a consuming fire (see 1:31; 30:33 and notes). He is the "Lord GOD" (see note on 25:8), far above all nations and rulers (40:15–24).

Yet God will have compassion on His people (14:1–2) and will rescue them from both political and spiritual oppression. Their restoration is like a new exodus (43:2,16–19; 52:10–12) as God redeems them (see 35:9; 41:14 and notes) and saves them (see 43:3; 49:8 and notes). Israel's mighty Creator (40:21–22; 48:13) will make streams spring up in the desert (32:2) as He graciously leads them home. The theme of a highway for the return of exiles is a prominent one (see 11:16; 40:3 and notes) in both major parts of the book. The Lord raises an "ensign" (banner) to summon the nations to bring Israel home (see 5:26 and note).

Peace and safety mark this new Messianic age (11:6–9). A king descended from David will reign in righteousness (9:7; 32:1), and all nations will stream to the holy mountain of Jerusalem (see 2:2–4 and note). God's people will no longer be oppressed by wicked rulers (11:14; 45:14), and Jerusalem will truly be the "city of the LORD" (60:14).

The Lord calls the Messianic King "my servant" in chs. 42—53, a term also applied to Israel as a nation (see 41:8–9; 42:1 and notes). It is through the suffering of the servant that salvation in its fullest sense is achieved. Cyrus was God's instrument to deliver Israel from Babylon (41:2), but Christ delivered mankind from the prison of sin (52:13—53:12). He became a "light of [to] the Gentiles" (42:6), so that those nations that faced judgment (chs. 13—23) could find salvation (55:4–5). These Gentiles also became "servants of the LORD" (see 54:17 and note).

The Lord's kingdom on earth, with its righteous Ruler and His righteous subjects, is the goal toward which the book of Isaiah steadily moves. The restored earth and the restored people will then conform to the divine ideal, and all will result in the praise and glory of the Holy One of Israel for what He has accomplished.

Literary Features

Isaiah contains both prose and poetry; the beauty of its poetry is unsurpassed in the OT. The main prose material is found in chs. 36—39, the historical interlude that unites the two parts of the book (see Author). The poetic material includes a series of oracles in chs. 13—23. A taunting song against the king of Babylon is found in 14:4–23. Chs. 24—27 comprise an apocalyptic section stressing the last days (see note on 24:1—27:13). A wisdom poem is found in 28:23–29 (also cf. 32:5–8). The parable of the vineyard (5:1–7) begins as a love song as Isaiah describes God's relationship with Israel. Hymns of praise are given in 12:1–6 and 38:10–20, and a national lament occurs in 63:7—64:12. The poetry is indeed rich and varied, as is the prophet's vocabulary (e.g., he uses nearly 2,200 different Hebrew words—more than any other OT writer).

One of Isaiah's favorite techniques is personification. The sun is ashamed and the moon con-

founded (24:23), while the wilderness and desert rejoice (see 35:1 and note) and the mountains and forests burst into song (44:23). The trees "clap their hands" (55:12). A favorite figure is the vineyard, which represents Israel (5:7). Treading the winepress is a picture of judgment (see 63:3 and note), and to drink God's "cup of . . . fury" is to stagger under His punishment (see 51:17 and note). Isaiah uses the name "rock" to describe God (17:10), and animals such as Leviathan and Rahab represent nations (see 27:1; 51:9).

The power of Isaiah's imagery is seen in 30:27–33, and he makes full use of sarcasm in his denunciation of idols in 44:9–20. A forceful example of wordplay appears in 5:7 (see note there), and one finds chiasm (inversion) in 6:10 (see note there; see also note on 16:7) and alliteration and assonance in 24:17 (see note there). The "overflowing scourge" of 28:15,18 is an illustration of mixed metaphor.

Isaiah often alludes to earlier events in Israel's history, especially the exodus from Egypt. The crossing of the Red sea forms the background for 11:15 and 43:2,16–17, and other allusions occur in 4:5–6; 31:5; 37:36 (see notes on these verses). The overthrow of Sodom and Gomorrah is referred to in 1:9, and Gideon's victory over Midian is mentioned in 9:4; 10:26 (see also 28:21). Several times Isaiah draws upon the song of Moses in Deut 32 (cf. 1:2 and Deut 32:1; 30:17 and Deut 32:30; 43:11,13 and Deut 32:39). Isaiah, like Moses, called the nation to repentance and to faith in a holy, all-powerful God. See also note on 49:8.

Outline

Part 1: The Book of Judgment (chs. 1—39)

I. Messages of Rebuke and Promise (chs. 1—6)
   A. Introduction: Charges against Judah for Breaking the Covenant (ch. 1)
   B. The Future Discipline and Glory of Judah and Jerusalem (chs. 2—4)
      1. Jerusalem's future blessings (2:1–5)
      2. The Lord's discipline of Judah (2:6—4:1)
      3. The restoration of Zion (4:2–6)
   C. The Nation's Judgment and Exile (ch. 5)
   D. Isaiah's Unique Commission (ch. 6)
II. Prophecies Occasioned by the Aramean and Israelite Threat against Judah (chs. 7—12)
   A. Ahaz Warned Not to Fear the Aramean and Israelite Alliance (ch. 7)
   B. Isaiah's Son and David's Son (8:1—9:7)
   C. Judgment against Israel (9:8—10:4)
   D. The Assyrian Empire and the Davidic Kingdom (10:5—12:6)
      1. The destruction of Assyria (10:5–34)
      2. The establishment of the Davidic king and his kingdom (ch. 11)
      3. Songs of joy for deliverance (ch. 12)
III. Judgment against the Nations (chs. 13—23)
   A. Against Assyria and Its Ruler (13:1—14:27)
   B. Against Philistia (14:28–32)
   C. Against Moab (chs. 15—16)
   D. Against Aram and Israel (ch. 17)
   E. Against Cush (Ethiopia) (ch. 18)
   F. Against Egypt and Cush (Ethiopia) (chs. 19—20)
   G. Against Babylon (21:1–10)
   H. Against Dumah (Edom) (21:11–12)
   I. Against Arabia (21:13–17)
   J. Against the Valley of Vision (Jerusalem) (ch. 22)
   K. Against Tyre (ch. 23)
IV. Judgment and Promise (the Lord's Kingdom) (chs. 24—27)
   A. Universal Judgments for Universal Sin (ch. 24)
   B. Deliverance and Blessing (ch. 25)
   C. Praise for the Lord's Sovereign Care (ch. 26)
   D. Israel's Enemies Punished but Israel's Remnant Restored (ch. 27)
V. Six Woes: Five on the Unfaithful in Israel and One on Assyria (chs. 28—33)
   A. Woe to Ephraim (Samaria)—and to Judah (ch. 28)

B. Woe to David's City, Jerusalem (29:1–14)
C. Woe to Those Who Rely on Foreign Alliances (29:15–24)
D. Woe to the Obstinate Nation (ch. 30)
E. Woe to Those Who Rely on Egypt (chs. 31—32)
F. Woe to Assyria—but Blessing for God's People (ch. 33)

VI. More Prophecies of Judgment and Promise (chs. 34—35)
A. The Destruction of the Nations and the Avenging of God's People (ch. 34)
B. The Future Blessings of Restored Zion (ch. 35)

VII. A Historical Transition from the Assyrian Threat to the Babylonian Exile (chs. 36—39)
A. Jerusalem Preserved from the Assyrian Threat (chs. 36—37)
1. The siege of Jerusalem by Sennacherib and the Assyrian army (ch. 36)
2. The Lord's deliverance of Jerusalem (ch. 37)
B. The Lord's Extension of Hezekiah's Life (ch. 38)
C. The Babylonian Exile Predicted (ch. 39)

Part 2: The Book of Comfort (chs. 40—66)

VIII. The Deliverance and Restoration of Israel (chs. 40—48)
A. The Coming of the Victorious God (40:1–26)
B. Unfailing Strength for the Weary Exiles (40:27–31)
C. The Lord of History (41:1—42:9)
D. Praise and Exhortation (42:10–25)
E. The Regathering and Renewal of Israel (43:1—44:5)
F. The Only God (44:6—45:25)
G. The Lord's Superiority over Babylon's Gods (ch. 46)
H. The Fall of Babylon (ch. 47)
I. The Lord's Exhortations to His People (ch. 48)

IX. The Servant's Ministry and Israel's Restoration (chs. 49—57)
A. The Call and Mission of the Servant (49:1–13)
B. The Repopulation of Zion (49:14–26)
C. Israel's Sin and the Servant's Obedience (ch. 50)
D. The Remnant Comforted Because of Their Glorious Prospect (51:1—52:12)
E. The Sufferings and Glories of the Lord's Righteous Servant (52:13—53:12)
F. The Future Glory of Zion (ch. 54)
G. The Lord's Call to Salvation and Covenant Blessings (55:1—56:8)
H. The Condemnation of the Wicked in Israel (56:9—57:21)

X. Everlasting Deliverance and Everlasting Judgment (chs. 58—66)
A. False and True Worship (ch. 58)
B. Zion's Confession and Redemption (ch. 59)
C. Zion's Peace and Prosperity (ch. 60)
D. The Lord's Favor (ch. 61)
E. Zion's Restoration and Glory (62:1—63:6)
F. Prayer for Divine Deliverance (63:7—64:12)
G. The Lord's Answer: Mercy and Judgment (ch. 65)
H. Judgment for False Worshipers and Blessing for True Worshipers (ch. 66)

1 The [a]vision of Isaiah the son of Amoz, which he saw concerning Judah and Jerusalem in the days of Uzziah, Jotham, Ahaz, *and* Hezekiah, kings of Judah.

Israel's rebellion

2 [a]Hear, O heavens, and give ear, O earth:
For the LORD hath spoken,
I have nourished and brought up children,
And they have rebelled against me.
3 [a]The ox knoweth his owner,
And the ass his master's crib:
But Israel [b]doth not know,
My people doth not consider.
4 Ah sinful nation, a people [1]laden with iniquity,
[a]A seed of evildoers, children that are corrupters:
They have forsaken the LORD,
They have provoked the Holy One of Israel unto anger,
They are [2]gone away backward.
5 [a]Why should ye be stricken any more?
Ye will [1]revolt more and more:
The whole head *is* sick, and the whole heart faint.
6 From the sole of the foot even unto the head *there is* no soundness in it;
But wounds, and bruises, and putrifying sores:
They have not been closed, neither bound up, neither mollified with [1]ointment.
7 [a]Your country *is* desolate,
Your cities *are* burnt *with* fire:
Your land, strangers devour it in your presence,
And *it is* desolate, [1]as overthrown by strangers.
8 And the daughter of Zion is left [a]as a cottage in a vineyard,
As a lodge in a garden of cucumbers,
[b]As a besieged city.
9 [a]Except the LORD of hosts had left unto us a very small remnant,
We should have been as [b]Sodom,
And we should have been like unto Gomorrah.

10 Hear the word of the LORD, ye rulers [a]of Sodom;
Give ear unto the law of our God, ye people of Gomorrah.
11 To what purpose *is* the multitude of your [a]sacrifices unto me? saith the LORD:
I am full *of* the burnt offerings of rams, and the fat of fed beasts;
And I delight not in the blood of bullocks, or of lambs, or of [1]he goats.
12 When ye come [a][1]to appear before me,
Who hath required this at your hand, to tread my courts?
13 Bring no more [a]vain oblations; incense *is* an abomination unto me;
The new moons and sabbaths, [b]the calling of assemblies, I cannot away with;
It is [1]iniquity, even the solemn meeting.
14 Your [a]new moons and your [b]appointed feasts my soul hateth:

1:1 [a]Num. 12:6
1:2 [a]Jer. 2:12
1:3 [a]Jer. 8:7 [b]Jer. 9:3,6
1:4 [1]Heb. *of heaviness* [2]Heb. *alienated,* or, *separated* [a]Mat. 3:7
1:5 [1]Heb. *increase revolt* [a]ch. 9:13
1:6 [1]Or, *oil*
1:7 [a]Deut. 28:51
1:7 [1]Heb. *as the overthrow of strangers*
1:8 [a]Job 27:18 [b]Jer. 4:17
1:9 [a]Lam. 3:22 [b]Gen. 19:24
1:10 [a]Deut. 32:32
1:11 [1]Heb. *great he goats* [a]1 Sam. 15:22
1:12 [1]Heb. *to be seen* [a]Ex. 23:17
1:13 [1]Or, *grief* [a]Mat. 15:9 [b]Joel 1:14
1:14 [a]Num. 28:11 [b]Lam. 2:6

1:1–31 Compare the indictment of ch. 1 with that of ch. 5; the two enclose the first series of oracles. Ch. 1 also serves as an introduction to the whole book.

1:1 The title of the book. Other headings occur in 2:1; 13:1; 14:28; 15:1; 17:1; 19:1; 21:1,11,13; 22:1; 23:1. *vision.* In the sense of "revelation" or "prophecy" (see 1 Sam 3:1; Prov 29:18; Obad 1). *Amoz.* Not to be confused with the prophet Amos. *Uzziah, Jotham, Ahaz and Hezekiah.* These kings reigned from 792 to 686 B.C. None of the kings of Israel is mentioned since Isaiah ministered primarily to the southern kingdom (Judah).

‡1:2 Isaiah begins and ends (66:24) with a condemnation of those who rebel against God. The prophet depicts a courtroom scene charging Israel with covenant unfaithfulness and calls on heaven and earth to testify to the truth of God's accusation against Israel and the rightness of His judgment—since they were witnesses of His covenant (see Deut 30:19; 31:28; 32:1).

1:3 *crib.* Feeding trough. *doth not know.* Refusal to know and understand God later resulted in Judah's exile from her land (5:13).

1:4 *Holy One of Israel.* Occurs 25 times in Isaiah (see especially 5:24) and only 6 times elsewhere in the OT (see Introduction: Author).

1:5–6 The pitiable moral and spiritual condition of Israel is transferred to the suffering servant in 53:4–5. The Hebrew words for "stricken," "sick" and "bruises" correspond to those for "smitten," "griefs" and "stripes."

1:6 The disease ravages the entire body, as with Job (2:7). *ointment.* Commonly used for treating wounds (see Luke 10:34).

1:7–9 The desolation of the land of Judah is the result of foreign invasion: e.g., by Aram, the northern kingdom of Israel, Edom and Philistia (2 Chr 28:5–18); later (701 B.C.), by King Sennacherib and the Assyrian army (36:1–2); still later (605–586), by King Nebuchadnezzar and the Neo-Babylonian army.

‡1:8 *daughter of Zion.* A personification of Jerusalem and its inhabitants. *cottage . . . lodge.* Temporary structures (a shelter or hut) used by watchmen (Job 27:18), who were on the lookout for thieves and intruders. Thus Jerusalem was not very defensible.

1:9–10 *Sodom . . . Gomorrah.* Classic examples of sinful cities that were completely destroyed (see 3:9; Gen 13:13; 18:20–21; 19:5,24–25). Just as Jesus addressed Peter as though he were Satan (Mat 16:23), so Isaiah addresses his countrymen as though they were the rulers of Sodom and the people of Gomorrah.

1:9 Quoted in Rom 9:29, where it is linked with Is 10:22–23. Isaiah often refers to the remnant that will survive God's judgment on the nation and take possession of the land (see 4:3; 10:20–23; 11:11,16; 46:3).

1:11–15 The sincerity of the worshiper, not the number of his religious activities, is most important (see 66:3; Jer 7:21–26; Hos 6:6; Amos 5:21–24; Mic 6:6–8).

‡1:11 *fed beasts.* Cattle kept in confinement for special feeding.

1:14 *new moons.* Celebrated on the first day of each Hebrew month. Special sacrifices and feasts were part of the observance (see Num 28:11–15). *appointed feasts.* Included the annual feasts, such as passover, weeks (Pentecost) and tabernacles (Ex 23:14–17; 34:18–25; Lev 23; Deut 16:1–17).

They are a trouble unto me;
[c]I am weary to bear *them.*
15 And [a]when ye spread forth your hands,
I will hide mine eyes from you:
[b]Yea, when ye [1]make many prayers, I
will not hear:
Your hands are full *of* [2]blood.

16 [a]Wash ye, make you clean; put away
the evil of your doings from before
mine eyes;
[b]Cease to do evil;
17 Learn to do well;
Seek judgment, [1]relieve the oppressed,
Judge the fatherless, plead for the
widow.
18 Come now, and [a]let us reason together,
saith the LORD:
Though your sins be as scarlet, [b]they
shall be as white as snow;
Though they be red like crimson, they
shall be as wool.
19 If ye be willing and obedient, ye shall
eat the good of the land:
20 But if ye refuse and rebel,
Ye shall be devoured *with* the sword:
[a]For the mouth of the LORD hath
spoken *it.*

21 [a]How is the faithful city become a
harlot!
It was full of judgment; righteousness
lodged in it;
But now murderers.
22 [a]Thy silver is become dross,
Thy wine mixt with water:
23 [a]Thy princes *are* rebellious, and
[b]companions of thieves:
[c]Every one loveth gifts, and followeth
after rewards:
They [d]judge not the fatherless,

1:14 [c]ch. 43:24
1:15 [1]Heb. *multiply prayer* [2]Heb. *bloods* [a]Prov. 1:28; Mic. 3:4 [b]Ps. 66:18
1:16 [a]Jer. 4:14 [b]Rom. 12:9
1:17 [1]Or, *righten*
1:18 [a]ch. 43:26 [b]Ps. 51:7; Rev. 7:14
1:20 [a]Tit. 1:2
1:21 [a]Jer. 2:20
1:22 [a]Jer. 6:28
1:23 [a]Hos. 9:15 [b]Prov. 29:24 [c]Jer. 22:17; Ezek. 22:12 [d]Jer. 5:28; Zech. 7:10

1:24 [a]Deut. 28:63
1:25 [1]Heb. *according to pureness* [a]Mal. 3:3
1:26 [a]Jer. 33:7 [b]Zech. 8:3
1:27 [1]Or, *they that return of her*
1:28 [1]Heb. *breaking* [a]Job 31:3
1:29 [a]ch. 57:5 [b]ch. 65:3
1:31 [1]Or, *And his work* [a]Ezek. 32:21 [b]ch. 43:17
2:2 [a]Mic. 4:1 [b]Gen. 49:1; Jer. 23:20

Neither doth the cause of the widow
come unto them.
24 Therefore saith the Lord, the LORD of
hosts, the mighty One of Israel,
Ah, [a]I will ease me of mine
adversaries,
And avenge me of mine enemies:
25 And I will turn my hand upon thee,
And [a][1]purely purge away thy dross,
And take away all thy tin:
26 And I will restore thy judges [a]as at the
first,
And thy counsellers as at the
beginning:
Afterward [b]thou shalt be called,
The city of righteousness, the faithful
city.
27 Zion shall be redeemed with judgment,
And [1]her converts with righteousness.
28 And the [a][1]destruction of the
transgressors and of the sinners *shall
be* together,
And they that forsake the LORD shall be
consumed.
29 For they shall be ashamed of [a]the oaks
which ye have desired,
[b]And ye shall be confounded for the
gardens that ye have chosen.
30 For ye shall be as an oak whose leaf
fadeth,
And as a garden that hath no water.
31 [a]And the strong shall be [b]as tow,
[1]And the maker of it as a spark,
And they shall both burn together, and
none shall quench *them.*

God's kingdom to triumph

2 The word that Isaiah the son of Amoz
saw concerning Judah and Jerusalem.
2 And [a]it shall come to pass [b]in the last
days,

1:15 *hide mine eyes.* In 8:17; 59:2 God hides His face from Israel (see also Mic 3:4).
1:17 See Jer 22:16; Jas 1:27. *fatherless . . . widow.* Represented the weak and often oppressed part of society. Rulers were warned not to take advantage of them (see v. 23; 10:2; Jer 22:3).
1:18 *scarlet . . . crimson.* Refers to the blood that has stained the hands of murderers (see vv. 15,21). *white as snow.* A powerful figurative description of the result of forgiveness (see Ps 51:7). This offer of forgiveness is conditioned on the reformation of life called for in v. 19.
1:19–20 *eat . . . be devoured.* The vivid contrast is stressed by the use of the same Hebrew verb.
‡1:21 Jerusalem (representing all Judah) has been an unfaithful wife to the Lord. By following idols and foreign gods she has become a harlot in a spiritual sense (see v. 4; Jer 3:6–14; Ezek 16:25–26). One of the important themes in Isaiah is the transformation of Zion from an unfaithful harlot to the pure and holy wife of the Lord (cf. Is. 54:4–8; 62:3–5).
1:24 *the LORD of hosts, the mighty One of Israel.* Stressing God's authority as Judge.
1:25–26 *turn . . . restore.* The use of the same Hebrew verb emphasizes the contrast (see note on vv. 19–20).
1:25 *purge away thy dross.* Purifying fire is also mentioned in 4:4; 48:10.
1:26 *faithful city.* See v. 21. Using a related Hebrew noun, Zech 8:3 similarly refers to the future Jerusalem as the "city of truth."
1:27–28 This contrast between the redemption of Zion (Jerusalem) as a whole and the perishing of individuals who refuse to repent is developed in 65:8–16.
1:29 *oaks . . . gardens.* Pagan sacrifices were offered and sexual immorality occurred at such places (see 65:3; 66:17).
1:31 *the strong shall be as tow.* Self-reliant people will be consumed by God's judgment like tinder that quickly burns. *burn.* Fire is often a figure of punishment (see 33:11–14; 34:9–10).
2:1 A second introduction, probably relating to chs. 2–4 or to chs. 2–12 (see 13:1).
2:2–5 See note on 4:2–6.
‡2:2–4 Almost identical to Mic 4:1–3. The theme of the "mountain of the LORD" (mount Zion) is common in Isaiah; it occurs in passages that depict the coming of both Jews and Gentiles to Jerusalem (Zion) in the last days (see 11:9; 27:13; 56:7; 57:13; 65:25; 66:20; see also 60:3–5; Zech 14:16).
2:2 *the last days.* Can refer to the future generally (see Gen 49:1), but usually it seems to have in view the Messianic era. In a real sense the last days began with the first coming of Christ (see Acts 2:17; Heb 1:2) and will be fulfilled at His second coming.
2:4 *swords into plowshares.* The reverse process occurs in Joel

[c]*That* the mountain of the LORD's
house shall be [1]established in the
top of the mountains,
And *shall be* exalted above the hills;
[d]And all nations shall flow unto it.
3 And many people shall go and say,
[a]Come ye, and let us go up to the
mountain of the LORD,
To the house of the God of Jacob;
And he will teach us of his ways,
And we will walk in his paths:
[b]For out of Zion shall go forth the law,
And the word of the LORD from
Jerusalem.
4 And he shall judge among the nations,
And shall rebuke many people:
And [a]they shall beat their swords into
plowshares,
And their spears into [1]pruninghooks:
Nation shall not lift up sword against
nation,
[b]Neither shall they learn war any more.

The day of the LORD

5 O house of Jacob, come ye,
And let us [a]walk in the light of the
LORD.
6 Therefore thou hast forsaken thy
people the house of Jacob,
Because they be replenished [a][1]from
the east,
And [b]*are* soothsayers like the
Philistines,
[c]And they [2]please themselves in the
children of strangers.
7 [a]Their land also is full *of* silver and
gold,
Neither *is there any* end of their
treasures;
Their land is also full *of* horses,
Neither *is there any* end of their
chariots:
8 [a]Their land is also full *of* idols;
They worship the work of their own
hands,
That which their own fingers have
made:

2:2 [1]Or, *prepared* [c]Ps. 68:15 [d]Ps. 72:8
2:3 [a]Jer. 50:5; Zech. 8:21 [b]Luke 24:47
2:4 [1]Or, *sythes* [a]Ps. 46:9 [b]Ps. 72:3,7
2:5 [a]Eph. 5:8
2:6 [1]Or, *more than the east* [2]Or, *abound with the children, etc.* [a]Num. 23:7 [b]Deut. 18:14 [c]Ps. 106:35; Jer. 10:2
2:7 [a]Deut. 17:16
2:8 [a]Jer. 2:28

2:10 [a]Rev. 6:15
2:11 [a]ch. 5:15 [b]Hos. 2:16; Zech. 9:16
2:13 [a]ch. 14:8; Ezek. 31:3; Zech. 11:1
2:14 [a]ch. 30:25
2:16 [1]Heb. *pictures of desire* [a]1 Ki. 10:22
2:17 [a]ver. 11 [b]ver. 11
2:18 [1]Or, *the idols shall utterly pass away*
2:19 [1]Heb. *the dust* [a]Hos. 10:8; Rev. 9:6 [b]2 Thes. 1:9 [c]Hag. 2:6,21
2:20 [1]Heb. *the idols of his silver, etc.* [2]Or, *Which they made for him*

9 And the mean man boweth down,
And the great man humbleth himself;
Therefore forgive them not.
10 [a]Enter into the rock, and hide thee in
the dust,
For fear of the LORD, and for the glory
of his majesty.
11 The [a]lofty looks of man shall be
humbled,
And the haughtiness of men shall be
bowed down,
And the LORD alone shall be exalted
[b]in that day.
12 For the day of the LORD of hosts *shall*
be upon every one *that is* proud and
lofty,
And upon every one that is lifted up;
and he shall be brought low:
13 And upon all [a]the cedars of Lebanon,
that are high and lifted up,
And upon all the oaks of Bashan,
14 And [a]upon all the high mountains,
And upon all the hills that are lifted up,
15 And upon every high tower,
And upon every fenced wall,
16 [a]And upon all the ships of Tarshish,
And upon all [1]pleasant pictures.
17 [a]And the loftiness of man shall be
bowed down,
And the haughtiness of men shall be
made low:
And the LORD alone shall be exalted
[b]in that day.
18 And [1]the idols he shall utterly abolish.
19 And they shall go into the [a]holes of the
rocks,
And into the caves of [1]the earth,
[b]For fear of the LORD, and for the glory
of his majesty,
When he ariseth [c]to shake terribly the
earth.
20 In that day a man shall cast [1]his idols
of silver, and his idols of gold,
[2]Which they made *each one* for
himself to worship,
To the moles and to the bats;

3:10. What is here called a plowshare was actually an iron point mounted on a wooden beam. Ancient plows did not have a plowshare proper.

2:6 *east.* Probably means Aram (Syria) and Mesopotamia. *soothsayers like the Philistines.* See 1 Sam 6:2; see also Deut 18:10–11 for a description of such practices.

2:7 *silver and gold . . . horses.* Accumulating large quantities of these was forbidden to the king (Deut 17:16–17). They usually led to a failure to trust in God (see 31:1).

2:10,19,21 These verses contain a refrain that builds to a climax in v. 21.

2:10 *rock . . . dust.* During times of severe oppression the Israelites took refuge in caves and holes in the ground (see Judg 6:1–2; 1 Sam 13:6). *majesty.* The Hebrew for this word is translated "pride" when used of man. Pride is an attempt by man to be his own god (see 14:13–14).

2:11,17,20 *in that day.* The phrase occurs seven times in chs. 2–4 (see 3:7, 18; 4:1–2). The day of the Lord (see also v. 12) is a time of judgment and/or blessing as God intervenes decisively in the affairs of the nations (see Zeph 1:14–2:3). Assyria and Babylon would bring the terror of judgment upon Judah in Isaiah's day (5:30).

2:13 *cedars of Lebanon.* Even inanimate things that people stand in awe of will be humbled so that "the LORD alone shall be exalted" (v. 11). *Bashan.* A region east of the Jordan River and north of Gilead. It was famous for its oaks (Ezek 27:6) and its animals (Ezek 39:18).

‡2:16 *ships of Tarshish.* Large vessels such as those used by Solomon (1 Ki 10:22) and the Phoenicians (Is 23:1,14) to ply the sea in far-flung commercial ventures. For the location of Tarshish see notes on 23:6; Ezek 27:12. Jonah attempted to flee from God on a ship bound for Tarshish (cf. Jonah 1:3).

2:20 The futility of worshiping idols is repeatedly noted by Isaiah (see, e.g., 30:22; 31:7; 40:19–20; 44:9–20). See also note on 40:18–20.

21 [a]To go into the clifts of the rocks,
And into the tops of the ragged rocks,
[b]For fear of the LORD, and for the glory of his majesty,
When he ariseth to shake terribly the earth.

22 [a]Cease ye from man, whose [b]breath *is* in his nostrils:
For wherein is he *to be* accounted of?

The judgment of the LORD

3 For behold, the Lord, the LORD of hosts,
[a]Doth take away from Jerusalem and from Judah [b]the stay and the staff,
The whole stay of bread, and the whole stay of water,
2 [a]The mighty *man,* and the man of war,
The judge, and the prophet, and the prudent, and the ancient,
3 The captain of fifty, and [1]the honourable *man,*
And the counseller, and the cunning artificer, and the [2]eloquent orator.
4 And I will give [a]children *to be* their princes,
And babes shall rule over them.
5 And the people shall be oppressed, every one by another, and every one by his neighbour:
The child shall behave himself proudly against the ancient,
And the base against the honourable.
6 When a man shall take hold of his brother *of* the house of his father, *saying,*
Thou hast clothing, be thou our ruler,
And *let* this ruin *be* under thy hand:
7 In that day shall he [1]swear, saying,
I will not be a [2]healer;
For in my house *is* neither bread nor clothing:
Make me not a ruler of the people.

8 For [a]Jerusalem is ruined, and Judah is fallen:
Because their tongue and their doings *are* against the LORD,
To provoke the eyes of his glory.
9 The shew of their countenance doth witness against them;
And they declare their sin as [a]Sodom, they hide *it* not.
Woe unto their soul! for they have rewarded evil unto themselves.
10 Say ye *to* the righteous, [a]that *it shall be* well *with him:*
[b]For they shall eat the fruit of their doings.
11 Woe unto the wicked! [a]*it shall be* ill *with him:*
For the reward of his hands shall be [1]given him.
12 *As for* my people, [a]children *are* their oppressors,
And women rule over them.
O my people, [b1]they which lead thee cause *thee* to err,
And [2]destroy the way of thy paths.

13 The LORD standeth *up* [a]to plead,
And standeth to judge the people.
14 The LORD will enter into judgment with the ancients of his people, and the princes thereof:
For ye have [1]eaten up [a]the vineyard;
The spoil of the poor *is* in your houses.
15 What mean ye *that* ye [a]beat my people to pieces,
And grind the faces of the poor?
Saith the Lord GOD of hosts.

16 Moreover the LORD saith,
Because the daughters of Zion are haughty,
And walk with stretched forth necks and [1]wanton eyes,
Walking and [2]mincing *as* they go,
And making a tinkling with their feet:

2:21 [a]ver. 19 [b]ver. 10,19
2:22 [a]Ps. 146:3 [b]Job 27:3
3:1 [a]Jer. 37:21 [b]Lev. 26:26
3:2 [a]2 Ki. 24:14
3:3 [1]Heb. *a man eminent in countenance* [2]Or, *skilful of speech*
3:4 [a]Eccl. 10:16
3:7 [1]Heb. *lift up the hand* [2]Heb. *binder up*
3:8 [a]Mic. 3:12
3:9 [a]Gen. 13:13
3:10 [a]Eccl. 8:12 [b]Ps. 128:2
3:11 [1]Heb. *done to him* [a]Ps. 11:6
3:12 [1]Or, *they which call thee blessed* [2]Heb. *swallow up* [a]ver. 4 [b]ch. 9:16
3:13 [a]Mic. 6:2
3:14 [1]Or, *burnt* [a]Mat. 21:33
3:15 [a]Mic. 3:2,3
3:16 [1]Heb. *deceiving with their eyes* [2]Or, *tripping nicely*

---

‡2:22 *Cease ye from man.* Stop putting your trust in man as your ultimate source of security. The verb here describes the rejection of the Messiah in 53:3 ("he was despised"). Ironically, the one Man who should have been trusted and "esteemed" (equals "to be accounted of" here) was "forsaken," "given up on" by men. He alone was worthy of the esteem wrongly given to frail leaders.

3:1–3 Leaders would be taken away by either death or deportation (see 2 Ki 24:14; 25:18–21).

‡3:2–3 *prudent . . . eloquent orator.* Terms that in Hebrew refer to occult practitioners and snake charmers (see Deut 18:10; Jer 8:17), whose activities were condemned. Both legitimate and illegitimate kinds of assistance would be removed or deported (see 2 Ki 24:14–16; Hos 3:4).

3:3 *captain of fifty.* A company of 50 was a common military unit (see 2 Ki 1:9). It was also used for civil groupings (Ex 18:25).

‡3:6 Normally it was unnecessary to force anyone to be a leader. In 4:1 the same social upheaval is seen as seven women "take hold of" one man. *Thou hast clothing.* There will be such extreme poverty in the aftermath of God's judgment that the one brother who has a cloak will be placed in a position of leadership. *ruin.* Probably Jerusalem (v. 8).

3:7,18 *that day.* See note on 2:11,17,20.

3:8 *Judah is fallen.* A prophecy not completely fulfilled until almost 150 years later.

‡3:9 *The shew of their countenance.* The defiant looks on their faces show their contempt for God. *Sodom.* See note on 1:9–10.

3:12 In the Near East, neither the rule of the young nor that of women was looked on with favor.

3:14 *vineyard.* Represents Israel (see 5:1).

3:15 The leaders were grinding the poor, as men grind grain between two millstones.

3:16–24 For a NT warning against overemphasis on outward adornment see 1 Pet 3:3–4.

‡3:16 *Walking and mincing.* In the Near East the way one walked communicated specific attitudes. Ornaments on ankles made short steps necessary. *making a tinkling with their feet.* The sound of the ornaments on their ankles as they walked.

17 Therefore the Lord will smite with [a]a
scab the crown of the head of the
daughters of Zion,
And the LORD will [b][1]discover their
secret parts.
18 In that day the Lord will take away the
bravery of *their* tinkling ornaments
about their feet,
And *their* [1]cauls, and *their* [a]round tires
like the moon,
19 The [1]chains, and the bracelets, and the
[2]mufflers,
20 The bonnets, and the ornaments of the
legs, and the headbands,
And the [1]tablets, and the earrings,
21 The rings, and nose jewels,
22 The changeable suits of apparel, and
the mantles,
And the wimples, and the crisping pins,
23 The glasses, and the fine linen,
And the hoods, and the vails.
24 And it shall come to pass, *that* instead
of sweet smell there shall be stink;
And instead of a girdle a rent;
And instead of well set hair [a]baldness;
And instead of a stomacher a girding of
sackcloth;
And burning instead of beauty.
25 Thy men shall fall by the sword,
And thy [1]mighty in the war.
26 [a]And her gates shall lament and mourn;
And she *being* [1][2]desolate [b]shall sit
upon the ground.

4 And [a]in that day seven women shall
take hold of one man, saying,
We will [b]eat our own bread, and wear
our own apparel:
Only [1]let us be called by thy name,
[2]To take away [c]our reproach.

3:17 [1]Heb. *make naked* [a]Deut. 28:27 [b]Jer. 13:22
3:18 [1]Or, *networks* [a]Judg. 8:21
3:19 [1]Or, *sweet balls* [2]Or, *spangled ornaments*
3:20 [1]Heb. *houses of the soul*
3:24 [a]ch. 22:12
3:25 [1]Heb. *might*
3:26 [1]Or, *emptied* [2]Heb. *cleansed* [a]Jer. 14:2 [b]Lam. 2:10
4:1 [1]Heb. *let thy name be called upon us* [2]Or, *Take thou away* [a]ch. 2:11,17 [b]2 Thes. 3:12 [c]Luke 1:25
4:2 [1]Heb. *beauty and glory* [2]Heb. *For the escaping of Israel* [a]Jer. 23:5
4:3 [1]Or, *to life* [a]ch. 60:21 [b]Phil. 4:3
4:4 [a]Mal. 3:2,3
4:5 [1]Or, *above* [2]Heb. *a covering* [a]Ex. 13:21 [b]Zech. 2:5
4:6 [a]ch. 25:4
5:1 [1]Heb. *the horn of the son of oil* [a]Ps. 80:8; Jer. 2:21; Mat. 21:33; Mark 12:1

Blessings under the Messiah

2 In that day shall [a]the branch of the
LORD be [1]beautiful and glorious,
And the fruit of the earth *shall be*
excellent and comely
[2]For them that are escaped of Israel.
3 And it shall come to pass, *that* he that
is left in Zion,
And he that remaineth in Jerusalem,
[a]Shall be called holy,
Even every one that is [b]written
[1]among the living in Jerusalem:
4 When [a]the Lord shall have washed
away the filth of the daughters of
Zion,
And shall have purged the blood of
Jerusalem from the midst thereof
By the spirit of judgment, and by the
spirit of burning.
5 And the LORD will create upon every
dwelling place of mount Zion,
And upon her assemblies,
[a]A cloud and smoke by day,
And [b]the shining of a flaming fire by
night:
For [1]upon all the glory *shall be* [2]a
defence.
6 And there shall be a tabernacle for a
shadow in the daytime from the
heat,
And [a]for a place of refuge, and for a
covert from storm and from rain.

The parable of the vineyard

5 Now will I sing to my wellbeloved a
song of my beloved touching [a]his
vineyard.
My wellbeloved hath a vineyard in [1]a
very fruitful hill:

‡3:17 *And the LORD will discover their secret parts.* The Lord will shame them by exposing their nakedness as they are led away as captives.
‡3:18 *cauls . . . round tires like the moon.* Round and crescent-shaped jewelry, indicating their veneration of the sun and moon.
3:20 *bonnets.* Perhaps a kind of turban (see Ezek 24:17,23).
3:21 *rings.* Contained a seal and were a mark of authority (see Gen 41:42 and note). *nose jewels.* Sometimes made of gold and worn by brides.
‡3:24 *girdle . . . burning.* Instead of wearing their expensive clothing, the women of Zion will be taken away as captives and treated like cattle. They will be led away by ropes and branded.
3:26 *her gates.* The gates are personified, as in Ps 24:7,9. They will lament because the crowds that used to assemble there are gone.
4:1–2 *in that day.* See notes on 2:2 and 2:11,17,20. After judgment comes salvation.
4:1 See note on 3:6. War will decimate the male population (3:25; see 13:12), leaving many women with the double disgrace of being widows and childless. See 54:4.
4:2–6 An oracle of redemption just before the long message of indictment and judgment in ch. 5. It balances that found in 2:2–5, which immediately follows the long message of indictment and judgment in ch. 1 (see note on 1:1–31). These two oracles of redemption were intended to complement each other.
4:2–3 *escaped . . . left.* See note on 1:9.
‡4:2 *branch.* A Messianic title related to the "rod" and "Branch" (11:1; 53:2cf. Jer 23:5-6) descended from David—but some believe that here "branch" refers to Judah. *excellent.* Translated "pride" elsewhere (cf. 9:9); here a legitimate pride in the fruitfulness of the land that will characterize the Messiah's reign (see Ps 72:3,6,16). Contrast the pride of 2:11,17. *excellent and comely.* Here the fruitfulness of the land will be Israel's glory; in 46:13 God's salvation will be her glory; in 60:19 God Himself will be her glory.
4:3 *holy.* Means "set apart" to God. See 1:26; 6:13; see also Zech 14:20.
4:4 *judgment . . . burning.* Purifying fire is also mentioned in 1:25; 48:10.
4:5–6 *cloud . . . fire . . . shadow.* These words recall Israel's wilderness wanderings, when the pillar of cloud and fire guided and protected the people (Ex 13:21–22; 14:21–22). Isaiah often refers to the time of the exodus (see 11:15–16; 31:5; 51:10).
4:5 *the glory.* The manifestation of God's presence represented by a glow of flaming fire (see Ex 16:10; 24:17; 40:34–35). *defence.* The cloud of smoke.
4:6 God's presence in cloud and fire will protect and preserve redeemed Zion (cf. Ps 121:5–6).
5:1–30 See note on 1:1–31.
5:1 *wellbeloved.* God. *vineyard.* Israel (see v. 7; 3:14; Ps 80:8–16). Jesus' parable of the tenants (Mat 21:33–44; Mark

2 And he [1]fenced it, and gathered out
the stones thereof,
And planted it *with* the choicest vine,
And built a tower in the midst of it,
And also [2]made a winepress therein:
[a]And he looked that *it* should bring
forth grapes,
And it brought forth wild grapes.
3 And now, O inhabitants of Jerusalem,
and men of Judah,
[a]Judge, I pray you, betwixt me and my
vineyard.
4 What could have been done more to
my vineyard,
That I have not done in it?
Wherefore, when I looked that *it*
should bring forth grapes,
Brought it forth wild grapes?
5 And now go to, I will tell you what I
will do to my vineyard:
[a]I *will* take away the hedge thereof,
and it shall be eaten up;
And break down the wall thereof, and
it shall be [1]trodden down:
6 And I will lay it waste:
It shall not be pruned, nor digged;
But there shall come up briers and
thorns:
I will also command the clouds that
they rain no rain upon it.
7 For the vineyard of the LORD of hosts *is*
the house of Israel,
And the men of Judah [1]his pleasant
plant:
And he looked for judgment, but
behold [2]oppression;
For righteousness, but behold a cry.

God's judgment against Judah

8 Woe unto them that join [a]house to
house,
That lay field to field, till *there be* no
place,
That [1]they may be placed alone in the
midst of the earth!
9 [a][1]In mine ears *said* the LORD of hosts,
[2]Of a truth many houses shall be
desolate,
Even great and fair, without inhabitant.
10 Yea, ten acres of vineyard shall yield
one [a]bath,
And the seed of a homer shall yield an
ephah.
11 [a]Woe unto them that rise up early in
the morning, *that* they may follow
strong drink;
That continue until night, *till* wine
[1]inflame them!
12 And [a]the harp, and the viol, the tabret,
and pipe,
And wine, are *in* their feasts:
But [b]they regard not the work of the
LORD,
Neither consider the operation of his
hands.
13 [a]Therefore my people are gone into
captivity, because *they have* no
knowledge:
And [1]their honourable men *are*
famished,
And their multitude dried up with thirst.
14 Therefore hell hath enlarged herself,
And opened her mouth without
measure:
And their glory, and their multitude,
and their pomp,
And he that rejoiceth, shall descend
into it.
15 And [a]the mean man shall be brought
down,
And the mighty man shall be humbled,
And the eyes of the lofty shall be
humbled:
16 But the LORD of hosts shall be exalted
in judgment,
And [1][2]God that is holy shall be
sanctified in righteousness.

5:2 [1]Or, *made a wall about it* [2]Heb. *hewed* [a]Deut. 32:6
5:3 [a]Rom. 3:4
5:5 [1]Heb. *for a treading* [a]Ps. 80:12
5:7 [1]Heb. *plant of his pleasures* [2]Heb. *a scab*
5:8 [a]Mic. 2:2
5:8 [1][Heb. *ye*]
5:9 [1]Or, This is *in mine ears,* saith *the LORD, etc.* [2]Heb. *If not, etc.* [a]ch. 22:14
5:10 [a]Ezek. 45:11
5:11 [1]Or, *pursue them* [a]Prov. 23:29
5:12 [a]Amos 6:5 [b]Job 34:27; Ps. 28:5
5:13 [1]Heb. *their glory* are *men of famine* [a]Hos. 4:6
5:15 [a]ch. 2:9,11
5:16 [1]Or, *the holy God* [2]Heb. *the God the holy*

12:1–11; Luke 20:9–18) is probably based on this song. See John 15:1–17.

‡5:2 *tower.* Contrast the more modest "cottage" (shelter) of 1:8. God's vineyard had every advantage (see Mat 21:33). *winepress.* A trough into which the grape juice flowed (see 16:10). *he looked . . . And.* Expresses a contrast between the return that God expected from his investment in the people of Israel and what he actually received. The same expression appears in v. 7 ("he looked for . . . but").

5:6 *briers and thorns.* This pair occurs five more times (7:23–25; 9:18; 27:4). *rain no rain.* The withholding of rain constituted a curse on the land. See Deut 28:23–24; 2 Sam 1:21; 1 Ki 17:1.

‡5:7 The song of the vineyard (vv. 1–6) is now interpreted. A powerful play on words makes the point: The words for "judgment" (justice) and "opression" (*mishpaṭ* and *miśpaḥ*) sound alike, as do those for "righteousness" (*ṣedaqah*) and "cry" (*ṣe'aqah*).

‡5:8–23 A series of six woes are pronounced (vv. 8, 11–12, 18–19, 20, 21, 22–23), followed by three judgment sections (vv. 9–10, 13–15, 24–25). The word "woe" was used in Israel to introduce a lament for the dead (cf. "alas" in 1 Ki 13:30; Jer 22:18; "Ah" in Jer 34:5). By using this word, the prophet is, in effect, inviting Israel to listen in on their own funeral. It is another reminder that "the wages of sin is death" (Rom 6:23).

5:8 *house to house . . . field to field.* Land in Israel could only be leased, never sold, because parcels had been permanently assigned to individual families (see Num 27:7–11; 1 Ki 21:1–3).

5:9 *many houses shall be desolate . . . without inhabitant.* When God judges, the punishment fits the crime. The people will forfeit the houses and lands they have acquired through oppression and dishonesty.

5:10 *bath.* About six gallons. *ephah.* A tenth of a homer. Meager crops often accompanied national sin (Deut 28:38–39; Hag 2:16–17). The amount of wine and grain is only a tiny fraction of what a ten-acre vineyard and a homer of seed would normally produce.

5:11–13 See Amos 4:1–3; 6:6–7, where a style of life characterized by drunkenness and revelry is likewise condemned.

5:14 *hell.* Hebrew "Sheol" or the grave. See note on Gen 37:35. The grave has an insatiable appetite (see Ps 49:14 and note; Hab 2:5).

17 Then shall the lambs feed after their
manner,
And the waste places of [a]the fat ones
shall strangers eat.
18 Woe unto them that draw iniquity with
cords of vanity,
And sin as it were with a cart rope:
19 [a]That say, Let him make speed, *and*
hasten his work,
That we may see *it:*
And let the counsel of the Holy One of
Israel draw nigh and come,
That we may know *it!*

20 Woe unto them [1]that call evil good,
and good evil;
That put darkness for light, and light
for darkness;
That put bitter for sweet, and sweet for
bitter!

21 Woe unto *them that are* [a]wise in their
own eyes,
And prudent [1]in their own sight!
22 Woe unto *them that are* mighty to
drink wine,
And men of strength to mingle strong
drink:
23 Which [a]justify the wicked for reward,
And take away the righteousness of the
righteous from him.

24 Therefore [a]as [1]the fire devoureth the
stubble,
And the flame consumeth the chaff,
So [b]their root shall be as rottenness,
And their blossom shall go up as dust:
Because they have cast away the law of
the LORD of hosts,
And despised the word of the Holy
One of Israel.
25 [a]Therefore is the anger of the LORD
kindled against his people,
And he hath stretched forth his hand
against them, and hath smitten them:
And [b]the hills did tremble, and their
carcases were [1]torn in the midst of
the streets.
[c]For all this his anger is not turned
away,
But his hand *is* stretched out still.

26 [a]And he will lift up an ensign to the
nations from far,
And will [b]hiss unto them from [c]the
end of the earth:
And behold, [d]they shall come with
speed swiftly:
27 None *shall be* weary nor stumble
amongst them;
None shall slumber nor sleep;
Neither [a]shall the girdle of their loins
be loosed,
Nor the latchet of their shoes be
broken:
28 [a]Whose arrows *are* sharp, and all their
bows bent,
Their horses' hoofs shall be counted
like flint,
And their wheels like a whirlwind:
29 Their roaring *shall be* like a lion,
They shall roar like young lions:
Yea, they shall roar, and lay hold of the
prey,
And shall carry *it* away safe, and none
shall deliver *it.*
30 And in that day they shall roar against
them like the roaring of the sea:
And if *one* [a]look unto the land, behold
darkness *and* [1]sorrow,
[2]And the light is darkened in the
heavens thereof.

Isaiah commissioned

6 In the year that king Uzziah died I [a]saw also the Lord sitting upon a throne, high and lifted up, and [1]his train filled the temple.

5:17 [a]ch. 10:16
5:19 [a]Jer. 17:15; Amos 5:18
5:20 [1]Heb. *that say concerning evil, It is good, etc.*
5:21 [1]Heb. *before their face* [a]Rom. 1:22
5:23 [a]Prov. 17:15
5:24 [1]Heb. *the tongue of fire* [a]Ex. 15:7 [b]Job 18:16
5:25 [a]2 Ki. 22:13
5:25 [1]Or, *as dung* [b]Jer. 4:24 [c]ch. 9:12,17
5:26 [a]ch. 11:12 [b]ch. 7:18 [c]Mal. 1:11 [d]Joel 2:7
5:27 [a]Dan. 5:6
5:28 [a]Jer. 5:16
5:30 [1]Or, *distress* [2]Or, *When it is light, it shall be dark in the destructions thereof* [a]ch. 8:22
6:1 [1]Or, *the skirts thereof* [a]John 12:41

5:18 Contrast Hos 11:4, where God leads His people with "cords of . . . love."
5:19 The Hebrew for the words "make speed" and "hasten" corresponds to that of the first and third elements of the name "Maher-shalal-hash-baz" (meaning, "In making speed to the spoil he hasteneth the prey"; see KJV marg. on 8:1). When Isaiah named his son (8:3), he may have been responding to the sarcastic taunts of these sinners. God did bring swift judgment, according to v. 26. *Holy One of Israel.* See 1:4 and note.
5:22 *mingle strong drink.* Spices were added to beer and wine (see Prov 23:30).
5:23 See 1:23; 10:1–2.
5:24 *despised . . . the Holy One of Israel.* See v. 19; see also 1:4 and note.
5:25 *And . . . stretched forth.* A refrain repeated in 9:12,17,21; 10:4. *the hills did tremble.* When God takes action, even the mountains tremble (see 64:3; Jer 4:24–26). This is the language of theophany (a manifestation or appearance of God).
5:26 *lift up an ensign.* A pole with a banner was often placed on a hill as a signal for gathering troops (13:2) or for summoning the nations to bring Israel back home (11:10,12; 49:22; 62:10). *nations from far.* Such as Assyria, whose armies struck Israel and Judah in 722 and 701 B.C., and Babylon, which began its invasions in 605. *from the end of the earth.* Nations like Egypt and Assyria.
5:27 *None shall be weary nor stumble.* Cf. the use of these terms in 40:29–31.
5:30 *in that day.* See note on 2:11,17,20. *darkness and sorrow.* Similar words describe the horrors of war in 8:22.
6:1 *the year that King Uzziah died.* 740 B.C. Isaiah's commission probably preceded his preaching ministry; the account was postponed to serve as a climax to the opening series of oracles and to provide warrant for the shocking announcements of judgment they contain. The people had mocked the "Holy One of Israel" (5:19), and now He has commissioned Isaiah to call them to account. Uzziah reigned from 792 to 740 and was a godly and powerful king. When he insisted on burning incense in the temple, however, he was struck with leprosy and remained leprous until his death (2 Chr 26:16–21). He was also called Azariah (2 Ki 14:21; 2 Chr 26:1). *I saw.* Probably in a vision in the temple. *the Lord.* The true King (see v. 5). *high and lifted up.* The same Hebrew words are applied to God in 57:15,

2 Above it stood the seraphims: each one
had six wings; with twain he covered his face,
and [a]with twain he covered his feet, and with
twain he did fly.
3 And [1]one cried unto another, and said,
[a]Holy, holy, holy, *is* the LORD of hosts:
[b][2]The whole earth *is* full of his glory.
4 ¶ And the posts of the [1]door moved at the
voice of him that cried, and the house was
filled *with* smoke.
5 Then said I, Woe *is* me! for I am [1]un-
done; because I *am* a man of unclean lips, and
I dwell in the midst of a people of unclean lips:
for mine eyes have seen the King, the LORD of
hosts.
6 Then flew one of the seraphims unto me,
[1]having a live coal in his hand, *which* he had
taken with the tongs from off [a]the altar:
7 And he [a][1]laid *it* upon my mouth, and
said, Lo, this hath touched thy lips; and thine
iniquity is taken away, and thy sin purged.
8 Also I heard the voice of the Lord, saying,
Whom shall I send, and who will go for [a]us?
Then I said, [1]Here *am* I; send me.
9 And he said, Go, and tell this people,
[1]Hear ye [2]indeed, but understand not;
And see ye [3]indeed, but perceive not.
10 Make [a]the heart of this people fat,
And make their ears heavy, and shut
their eyes;
[b]Lest they see with their eyes, and
hear with their ears,
And understand *with* their heart, and
convert, and be healed.
11 Then said I, Lord, how long? And he
answered,
[a]Until the cities be wasted without
inhabitant,
And the houses without man,
And the land be [1]utterly desolate,
12 [a]And the LORD have removed men far
away,
And *there be* a great forsaking in the
midst of the land.
13 But yet in it *shall be* a tenth, [1]and *it*
shall return, and shall be eaten:
As a teil tree, and as an oak, whose
[2]substance *is* in them, when they
cast *their leaves:*
So [a]the holy seed *shall be* the
[2]substance thereof.

6:2 [a]Ezek. 1:11
6:3 [1]Heb. *this cried to this* [2]Heb. *His glory is the fulness of the whole earth* [a]Rev. 4:8 [b]Ps. 72:19
6:4 [1]Heb. *thresholds*
6:5 [1]Heb. *cut off*
6:6 [1]Heb. *and in his hand a live coal* [a]Rev. 8:3
6:7 [1]Heb. *caused* it *to touch* [a]Jer. 1:9
6:8 [1]Heb. *Behold me* [a]Gen. 1:26
6:9 [1]Heb. *hear ye in hearing, etc.* [2]Or, *without ceasing, etc.* [3][Heb. *in seeing*]
6:10 [a]Ps. 119:70
6:10 [b]Jer. 5:21
6:11 [1]Heb. *desolate* with *desolation* [a]Mic. 3:12
6:12 [a]2 Ki. 25:21
6:13 [1]Or, *when* it *is returned, and hath been broused* [2]Or, *stock*, or, *stem* [a]Ezra 9:2
7:2 [1]Heb. *resteth on Ephraim*

The sign of Immanuel

7 And it came to pass in the days of Ahaz
the son of Jotham, the son of Uzziah king
of Judah, *that* Rezin the king of Syria, and Pekah the son of Remaliah, king of Israel, went
up *towards* Jerusalem to war against it, but
could not prevail against it.
2 And it was told the house of David, saying, Syria [1]is confederate with Ephraim. And

and similar terms are used of the suffering servant in 52:13. *his train.* A long, flowing garment. Cf. the robe of the "Son of man" in Rev 1:13. *temple.* Probably the heavenly temple, with which the earthly temple was closely associated. John's vision of God on His throne is similar (Rev 4:1–8).

6:2 *seraphims.* See v. 6; angelic beings not mentioned elsewhere. The Hebrew root underlying this word means "burn," perhaps to indicate their purity as God's ministers. (It refers to venomous snakes in 14:29; 30:6; see Num 21:6.) They correspond to the "four beasts" of Rev 4:6–9, each of whom also had six wings. *covered his face.* Apparently the seraphim could not gaze directly at the glory of God.

6:3 *Holy, holy, holy.* The repetition underscores God's infinite holiness. Note the triple use of "the temple of the LORD" in Jer 7:4 to stress the people's confidence in the security of Jerusalem because of the presence of that sanctuary. *full of his glory.* In Num 14:21–22; Ps 72:18–19 the worldwide glory of God is linked with His miraculous signs.

‡6:4 *posts . . . moved . . . filled with smoke.* Similarly the power of God's voice terrified the Israelites at mount Sinai, and the mountain was covered with smoke (see Ex 19:18–19; 20:18–19). This same power of God resided with the corporate church at prayer in Acts 4:23–31.

6:5 *eyes have seen the King.* Isaiah was dismayed because anyone who saw God expected to die immediately (see Gen 16:13; 32:30 and notes; Ex 33:20).

6:6 *live coal.* Coals of fire were taken inside the most holy place on the day of atonement (Lev 16:12), when sacrifice was made to atone for sin. See note on 1:25.

‡6:7 *laid it upon my mouth.* When God commissioned Jeremiah, His hand touched the prophet's mouth (Jer 1:9). The fire purifies Isaiah's "unclean lips" so that he can speak for God.

6:8–10 Isaiah's prophetic commission will have the ironic but justly deserved effect of hardening the callous hearts of rebellious Israel—and so rendering the warnings of judgment sure (see vv. 11–13). See also Jer 1:8,19; Ezek 2:3–4.

‡6:8 *for us.* The heavenly King speaks in the divine assembly of the angels. As a true prophet, Isaiah is made privy to that council, as were Micaiah (1 Ki 22:19–20) and Jeremiah (23:18, 22). Cf. Gen 1:26; 11:7; Amos 3:7. *Here am I.* See note on Gen 22:1.

6:9–10 Quoted by Jesus in the parable of the sower (Mat 13:14–15; Mark 4:12; Luke 8:10). See also Rom 11:7–10,25.

6:10 *heart . . . ears . . . eyes . . . eyes . . . ears . . . heart.* The *a-b-c/c-b-a* inversion is called a "chiastic" arrangement, a common literary device in the OT. *ears heavy . . . shut their eyes.* Israel's deafness and blindness are also mentioned in 29:9; 42:18; 43:8. One day, however, the nation will be able to see and hear (29:18; 35:5).

6:12 *far away.* See 5:13.

‡6:13 *a tenth.* A remnant—even it will be laid waste. *holy seed.* The few who are faithful in Israel (cf. 1 Ki 19:18; see note on 1:9). *substance.* Lit. "stump." The tree of Israel will be reduced to a stump, out of which the nation will grow again. For a similar use of this imagery see 11:1.

7:1–12:6 The second section of Isaiah's prophecies, climaxing in the songs of praise found in ch. 12.

7:1 The invasion of Rezin and Pekah (probably in 735/734 B.C.) is known as the Syro-Ephraimite War. Aram (Syria) and Israel (Ephraim; see note on v. 2) were trying unsuccessfully to persuade Ahaz to join a coalition against Assyria, which had strong designs on lands to the west. Isaiah was trying to keep Ahaz from forming a counteralliance with Assyria (see 2 Ki 16:5–18; 2 Chr 28:16–21). *Pekah.* Ruled 752–732 B.C. (see 2 Ki 15:27–31).

‡7:2 *house of David.* A reference to Ahaz, who belonged to David's dynasty (see 2 Sam 7:8–11). *Ephraim.* Another name for Israel, the northern kingdom. *heart was moved.* Ahaz trembled

his heart was moved, and the heart of his people, as the trees of the wood are moved with the wind.

3 Then said the LORD unto Isaiah, Go forth now to meet Ahaz, thou, and [1]Shear-jashub thy son, at the end of the conduit of the upper pool in the [2]highway of the fuller's field;

4 And say unto him,
Take heed, and be quiet;
Fear not, [1]neither be fainthearted
For the two tails of these smoking firebrands,
For the fierce anger of Rezin with Syria, and of the son of Remaliah.
5 Because Syria, Ephraim, and the son of Remaliah,
Have taken evil counsel against thee, saying,
6 Let us go up against Judah, and [1]vex it,
And let us make a breach therein for us,
And set a king in the midst of it, *even* the son of Tabeal:
7 Thus saith the Lord GOD,
[a]It shall not stand, neither shall it come to pass.
8 [a]For the head of Syria *is* Damascus,
And the head of Damascus *is* Rezin;
And within threescore and five years shall Ephraim be broken, [1]that *it be* not a people.

7:3 [1]That is, *The remnant shall return* [2]Or, *causeway*
7:4 [1]Heb. *let not thy heart be tender*
7:6 [1]Or, *waken*
7:7 [a]ch. 8:10
7:8 [1]Heb. *from a people* [a]2 Sam. 8:6
7:9 [1]Or, *Do ye not believe?* it is *because ye are not stable* [a]2 Chr. 20:20
7:10 [1]Heb. *And the LORD added to speak*
7:11 [1]Or, *Make thy petition deep* [a]Mat. 12:38
7:14 [1]Or, *thou, O virgin, shalt call* [a]Mat. 1:23 [b]ch. 9:6 [c]ch. 8:8
7:16 [a]See ch. 8:4 [b]2 Ki. 15:30
7:17 [a]2 Chr. 28:19

9 And the head of Ephraim *is* Samaria,
And the head of Samaria *is* Remaliah's son.
[a][1]If ye will not believe, surely ye shall not be established.

10 ¶ [1]Moreover the LORD spake again unto Ahaz, saying,

11 [a]Ask thee a sign of the LORD thy God;
[1]Ask it either in the depth, or in the height above.

12 ¶ But Ahaz said, I will not ask, neither will I tempt the LORD.

13 And he said,
Hear ye now, O house of David;
Is it a small thing for you to weary men, but will ye weary my God also?
14 Therefore the Lord himself shall give you a sign;
[a]Behold, a Virgin shall conceive, and bear [b]a Son,
And [1]shall call his name [c]Immanuel.
15 Butter and honey shall he eat,
That he may know to refuse the evil, and choose the good.
16 [a]For before the child shall know to refuse the evil, and choose the good,
The land that thou abhorrest shall be forsaken of [b]both her kings.

17 [a]The LORD shall bring upon thee,

in fear because he had been defeated by Aram and Israel earlier (2 Chr 28:5–8).

‡7:3 *Shear-jashub.* The name means "The remnant shall return;" see also 10:21–22. Isaiah gave each of his sons symbolic names (see 8:1,3,18). *conduit of the upper pool.* Location unknown. Ahaz was probably inspecting the city's water supply to see if Jerusalem could survive a long siege. *fuller's field.* Clothes were cleaned by trampling on them in cold water and using a kind of soap (soda) or bleach (see Mal 3:2; Mark 9:3).

‡7:4 *two tails . . . smoking.* Smoldering embers that are about to be snuffed out. Damascus (Aram's capital; see v. 8) was crushed by Tiglath-pileser III in 732 B.C., and Israel was soundly defeated the same year. It is foolish for Ahaz not to trust God because the enemies he fears are not going to be around for very long.

‡7:6 *Tabeal.* The name means "good for nothing." The enemies of Judah want to install a puppet ruler who will do their bidding and support their cause.

‡7:8 *within threescore and five years.* 65 years. By c. 670 B.C. Esarhaddon (and, shortly after him, Ashurbanipal) king of Assyria settled foreign colonists in Israel. Their intermarriage with the few Israelites who had not been deported resulted in the "Samaritans" (see 2 Ki 17:24–34 and note on 2 Ki 17:29) and marked the end of Ephraim as a separate nation.

‡7:9 *Remaliah's son.* Pekah was a usurper and hardly worthy to challenge Ahaz, a son of David. Aram ("Syria," v. 8) and Israel ("Ephraim," v. 9) had human heads. Judah had a divine head; God was with them (v. 14; 8:8,10). *believe . . . established.* These two verbs are from the same Hebrew word, giving the sense, "If you have a firm faith, then your kingdom will be firmly established." The repetition of this Hebrew verb emphasizes the seriousness of the Lord's warning (see 1:19–20,25–26 and notes).

7:11 *a sign.* God was willing to strengthen the faith of Ahaz through a sign (see Ex 3:12).

7:13 *house of David.* See note on v. 2.

‡7:14 *sign.* A sign was a miraculous event that signified God's intervention in human history. *a Virgin.* Or, "the Virgin." The prophet has a specific virgin in view. Isaiah uses the unique word *'almah* to specify an unmarried young woman. *Bethulah* is the more common word, but in at least two passages it refers to a young widow (Deut 22:19; Joel 1:8). In Gen 24:43 the same Hebrew word *('almah)* refers to a woman about to be married (see also Prov 30:19). Mat 1:23 apparently understood the virgin to be the Virgin Mary. *Immanuel.* The name "God is with us" was meant to convince Ahaz that God could rescue him from his enemies. See Num 14:9; 2 Chr 13:12; Ps 46:7. The Hebrew for "Immanuel" is used again in 8:8,10 and refers to the Messianic claim of Immanuel over the land of Judah. Jesus was the final fulfillment of this prophecy, for He was miraculously born of a virgin and was "God with us" in the fullest sense (Mat 1:23; cf. Is 9:6–7).

‡7:15 *Butter and honey.* Butter, or curds (a kind of yogurt), and honey meant a return to the simple diet of those who lived off the land. The Assyrian invasion would devastate the countryside and make farming impossible. (See vv. 22–25 for the significance of the expression.) *That he may know to refuse the evil . . . good.* Refers to the time when the child reaches the age of moral determination and responsibility under the law—most likely 12 or 13 years of age. When this boy born during the time of Ahaz is 12 or 13 (722/721 B.C.), he will be eating curds and honey instead of agricultural products—due to the devastation of Israel by Assyria. Some believe that this expression involves a shorter period of time, identical to that in v. 16 and 8:4.

‡7:16 *before the child shall know . . . land . . . forsaken.* See note on v. 4; cf. 8:4. "Before" the boy is 12 or 13 years old, Aram and Israel will be plundered. This happened in 732 B.C., when the boy was about two years old. The tragedy is that Ahaz would have had complete deliverance from his enemies in a very short time if he had trusted God.

And upon thy people, and upon thy
father's house,
Days that have not come,
From the day that [b]Ephraim departed
from Judah;
Even the king of Assyria.
18 And it shall come to pass in that day,
That the LORD [a]shall hiss for the fly
that *is* in the uttermost part of the
rivers of Egypt,
And for the bee that *is* in the land of
Assyria.
19 And they shall come, and shall rest all
of them
In the desolate valleys, and in [a]the
holes of the rocks,
And upon all thorns, and upon all
[1]bushes.
20 In the same day shall the Lord shave
with a [a]rasor that is hired,
Namely, by them beyond the river, by
the king of Assyria,
The head, and the hair of the feet:
And it shall also consume the beard.
21 And it shall come to pass in that day,
That a man shall nourish a young cow,
and two sheep;
22 And it shall come to pass, for the
abundance of milk *that they* shall
give he shall eat butter:
For butter and honey shall every one
eat that is left [1]in the land.
23 And it shall come to pass in that day,
That every place shall be,
Where there were a thousand vines at
a thousand silverlings,
[a]It shall *even* be for briers and thorns.

7:17 [b]1 Ki. 12:16
7:18 [a]ch. 5:26
7:19 [1]Or, *commendable trees* [a]Jer. 16:16
7:20 [a]2 Ki. 16:7
7:22 [1]Heb. *in the midst of the land*
7:23 [a]ch. 5:6

8:1 [1]Heb. *In making speed to the spoil he hasteneth the prey,* or, *Make speed, etc.* [a]Hab. 2:2
8:2 [a]2 Ki. 16:10
8:3 [1]Heb. *approached unto*
8:4 [1]Or, *he that is before the king of Assyria shall take away the riches, etc.* [a]ch. 7:16 [b]2 Ki. 15:29
8:6 [a]John 9:7 [b]ch. 7:1,2

24 With arrows and with bows shall *men*
come thither;
Because all the land shall become
briers and thorns.
25 And *on* all hills that shall be digged
with the mattock,
There shall not come thither the fear of
briers and thorns:
But it shall be for the sending forth of
oxen,
And for the treading of lesser cattle.

The coming war and deliverer

8 Moreover the LORD said unto me, Take
thee a great roll, and [a]write in it with a
man's pen concerning [1]Maher-shalal-hash-baz.
2 And I took unto me faithful witnesses to
record, [a]Uriah the priest, and Zechariah the
son of Jeberechiah.
3 And I [1]went unto the prophetess; and
she conceived, and bare a son. Then said the
LORD to me, Call his name Maher-shalal-hash-
baz.
4 [a]For before the child shall have knowledge to cry, My father, and my mother, [b1]the
riches of Damascus and the spoil of Samaria
shall be taken away before the king of Assyria.
5 ¶ The LORD spake also unto me again, saying,
6 Forsomuch as this people refuseth the
waters of [a]Shiloah that go softly,
And rejoice [b]in Rezin and Remaliah's
son;
7 Now therefore behold, the Lord
bringeth up upon them
The waters of the river, strong and
many,

‡7:17 *Ephraim departed from Judah.* Almost two centuries earlier (see 1 Ki 12:19–20). *king of Assyria.* Ahaz's appeal to Assyria would bring temporary relief (2 Ki 16:8–9), but eventually Assyria would attack Judah (see 8:7–8; 36:1). Looking to anyone or anything other than God as our ultimate source of security always has disastrous consequences.
7:18,20,23 *in that day.* Their difficulties will be a foretaste of the "day of the LORD." See note on 2:11,17,20.
7:18 *fly . . . bee.* See Ex 23:28 and note.
7:19 *holes of the rocks.* See note on 2:10. It will be impossible to escape from the invaders.
7:20 *shave . . . head . . . beard.* The forcible shaving of the beard was considered a great insult (2 Sam 10:4–5). In times of mourning, a man would shave his own head and beard (see 15:2; see also note on 3:17).
‡7:23 *a thousand silverlings.* Lit. "a thousand silver" (a thousand shekels), an indication of great value and wealth. *briers and thorns.* See note on 5:6. The destruction of the vineyards and the farmlands would fulfill 5:5–6.
‡8:1–2 *roll . . . witnesses.* The witnesses would attest to a legal transaction, either the marriage of Isaiah (see note on 7:14) or a symbolic deed connected with Maher-shalal-hash-baz. The Hebrew word for "roll" (tablet) is related to the word for an "open" (unsealed) document in Jer 32:11.
8:2 *Uriah the priest.* Served under King Ahaz (see 2 Ki 16:10–11).
8:3–10 See 7:14–17.
‡8:3 *prophetess . . . son.* Probably the initial fulfillment of 7:14. Note the repetition of "conceive," "son," and "call his name" from 7:14. The fact that this child is given a different name from "Immanuel" is not an argument against this child being part of the fulfillment of 7:14, because Jesus Himself was given a name other than Immanuel (cf. Mat 1:21,23). This is the only known case of a prophetess (see note on Ex 15:20) marrying a prophet. But the young woman may be called a prophetess here because she had become the wife of a prophet. *Maher-shalal-hash-baz.* This symbolic name (KJV marg., v. 1) meant that Ahaz's enemies would be plundered (see v. 4 and note on 7:4), but it also implied that Judah would suffer (see vv. 7–8).
8:4 *shall have knowledge to cry.* At about age two. The time period is identical to that in 7:16 (see notes on 7:4,16). *spoil of Samaria shall be taken away.* The first stage of the destruction of the northern kingdom (see note on 7:4), which was not completed until 722–721 B.C. (see note on 7:15).
‡8:6 *waters of Shiloah.* The waters in Jerusalem that flow from the Gihon spring (see 2 Chr 32:30) to the pool of Siloam (see John 9:7) may be intended (see Neh 3:15). Here they symbolize the sustaining power of the Lord (cf. Ps 46:4). *rejoice in Rezin and Remaliah's son.* Rezin and Pekah both died in 732 B.C. (see 2 Ki 16:9; see note on Is 7:1). The people would be rejoicing that Ahaz's alliance with Assyria had brought about the fall of their enemies without seeing that the failure of Ahaz to trust in God would bring devastating judgment on Jerusalem as well.
8:7–8 *waters . . . strong . . . overflow.* Mighty rivers were often used to symbolize a powerful invading army (see 28:17–19).

Even the king of Assyria, and all his
glory:
And he shall come up over all his
channels,
And go over all his banks:
8 And he shall pass through Judah;
He shall overflow and go over,
[a]He shall reach *even* to the neck;
And [1]the stretching out of his wings
shall fill the breadth of thy land,
[b]O Immanuel.
9 [a]Associate yourselves, O ye people,
[1]and ye shall be broken in pieces;
And give ear, all ye of far countries:
Gird yourselves, and ye shall be broken
in pieces;
Gird yourselves, and ye shall be broken
in pieces.
10 [a]Take counsel together, and it shall
come to nought;
Speak the word, [b]and it shall not stand:
[c]For God *is* with us.

11 For the LORD spake thus to me [1]with a
strong hand,
And instructed me that *I* should not
walk in the way of this people, saying,
12 Say ye not, A confederacy,
To all *them to* whom [a]this people shall
say, A confederacy;
[b]Neither fear ye their fear, nor be afraid.
13 [a]Sanctify the LORD of hosts himself;
And [b]*let* him *be* your fear, and *let* him
be your dread.
14 And [a]he shall be for a sanctuary;
But for [b]a stone of stumbling and for a
rock of offence to both the houses of
Israel,
For a gin and for a snare to the
inhabitants of Jerusalem.

8:8 [1]Heb. *the fulness of the breadth of thy land shall be the stretchings out of his wings* [a]ch. 30:28 [b]ch. 7:14
8:9 [1]Or, *yet* [a]Joel 3:9
8:10 [a]Job 5:12 [b]ch. 7:7 [c]ch. 7:14; Rom. 8:31
8:11 [1]Heb. *in strength of hand*
8:12 [a]ch. 7:2 [b]1 Pet. 3:14
8:13 [a]Num. 20:12 [b]Ps. 76:7; Luke 12:5
8:14 [a]Ezek. 11:16 [b]Luke 2:34; Rom. 9:33; 1 Pet. 2:8
8:15 [a]Mat. 21:44; Luke 20:18; Rom. 11:25
8:17 [a]ch. 54:8 [b]Hab. 2:3; Luke 2:25
8:18 [a]Heb. 2:13 [b]Ps. 71:7; Zech. 3:8
8:19 [a]1 Sam. 28:8 [b]ch. 29:4 [c]Ps. 106:28
8:20 [1]Heb. *no morning* [a]Luke 16:29 [b]Mic. 3:6
8:21 [a]Rev. 16:11
8:22 [a]ch. 5:30 [b]ch. 9:1

15 And many among them shall [a]stumble,
and fall, and be broken,
And be snared, and be taken.

Command to trust the LORD

16 Bind up the testimony, seal the law
among my disciples.
17 And I will wait upon the LORD,
That [a]hideth his face from the house of
Jacob,
And I [b]will look for him.
18 [a]Behold, I and the children whom the
LORD hath given me
[b]*Are* for signs and for wonders in Israel
From the LORD of hosts, which
dwelleth in mount Zion.

19 And when they shall say unto you,
[a]Seek unto them that have familiar
spirits,
And unto wizards [b]that peep, and that
mutter:
Should not a people seek unto their
God?
For the living [c]to the dead?
20 [a]To the law and to the testimony:
If they speak not according to this
word,
It is because [b]*there is* [1]no light in them.
21 And they shall pass through it, hardly
bestead and hungry:
And it shall come to pass, that when
they shall be hungry, they shall fret
themselves,
And [a]curse their king and their God,
and look upward.
22 And [a]they shall look unto the earth;
And behold trouble and darkness,
[b]dimness of anguish;
And *they shall be* driven *to* darkness.

8:8 *even to the neck.* Sennacherib's invasion in 701 B.C. overwhelmed all the cities of Judah except Jerusalem (see 1:7–9). *stretching out of its wings.* The figure changes to a bird of prey, perhaps the eagle, renowned for its speed. *Immanuel.* All seems lost, but "God is with us" (v. 10) and defeats the enemy (see note on 7:14).

8:9 *people . . . be broken in pieces.* Just as Aram and Israel would be shattered (7:7–9), so Assyria and Babylon would eventually fall.

‡8:10 *it shall not stand.* Only God's plans and purposes will last (cf. Ps 2:2–6).

8:11 *with a strong hand.* See Ezek 1:3; 37:1; 40:1. The prophets were conscious of God's presence in and control over their lives.

‡8:12 *confederacy.* Or "conspiracy." Isaiah's warning against relying on Assyria was considered treason (see note on 7:1; cf. Jer 37:13–14).

8:13 *let him be your fear.* See 7:2; Prov 1:7.

8:14 *sanctuary . . . stone of stumbling . . . offence.* Either the Lord is the cornerstone of our lives (see 28:16) or He is a rock over which we fall. See Rom 9:33; 1 Pet 2:6–8 for an application to Christ. *both the houses.* The northern and southern kingdoms, Israel and Judah.

8:16 Perhaps a reference to the legal transaction connected with vv. 1–2 (see note there). *testimony.* See v. 20. By preserving Isaiah's teaching ("the law"), his disciples could later prove that his predictions had come true. This term occurs elsewhere only in Ruth 4:7 ("this was a testimony in Israel"). *law.* The Hebrew for this word can also mean "teaching" or "instruction." The legal document containing Isaiah's teaching about Assyria's invasion was tied and sealed and then given to the prophet's followers, who were to preserve it until the time of its fulfillment, when God would authenticate it by the events of history (see Jer 32:12–14,44).

8:17–18 In Heb 2:13 these verses are applied to Christ.

8:17 *hideth his face.* See 1:15; 59:2; Mic 3:4.

8:18 *signs and . . . wonders.* See notes on 7:3,14; cf. 20:3.

8:19 *familiar spirits . . . wizards.* In the present crisis, people were turning to the spirits of the dead (necromancy), as King Saul did when he went to a medium to contact the spirit of Samuel (1 Sam 28:8–11) and learn about the future. See note on 3:2–3.

8:20 *the law . . . the testimony.* See v. 16 and note. Only by heeding the Lord's word through Isaiah—reinforced by the "signs and . . . wonders" (v. 18) that Isaiah and his sons represented—would the light dawn for Israel.

8:21–22 The Assyrian invasion would bring deep distress on all Israel.

8:21 *curse . . . king and . . . God.* Because of their terrible suffering (cf. Prov 19:3)—but severe punishment awaited anyone who cursed God or a ruler (Ex 22:28; Lev 24:15–16).

The birth of the messianic king

9 Nevertheless [a]the dimness *shall* not *be*
such as *was* in her vexation,
When at the [b]first he lightly afflicted
the land of Zebulun and the land of
Naphtali,
And [c]afterward did more grievously
afflict *her by* the way of the sea,
Beyond Jordan, in Galilee [1]of the
nations.
2 [a]The people that walked in darkness
have seen a great light:
They that dwell in the land of the
shadow of death, upon them hath
the light shined.
3 Thou hast multiplied the nation, *and*
[1]not increased the joy:
They joy before thee according to the
joy in harvest,
And as *men* rejoice [a]when they divide
the spoil.
4 [1]For thou hast broken the yoke of his
burden, and [a]the staff of his
shoulder,
The rod of his oppressor, as *in* the day
of [b]Midian.
5 [1]For every battle of the warrior *is* with
confused noise,
And garments rolled in blood;
[a][2]But *this* shall be with burning *and*
[3]fuel of fire.
6 [a]For unto us a child is born, unto us a
[b]Son is given:
And [c]the government shall be upon his
shoulder:
And his name shall be called
[d]Wonderful, Counseller, [e]The mighty
God,
The everlasting Father, [f]The Prince of
Peace.
7 Of the increase of *his* government and
peace [a]*there shall be* no end,
Upon the throne of David, and upon
his kingdom,
To order it, and to stablish it with
judgment and with justice
From henceforth even for ever.
The [b]zeal of the LORD of hosts will
perform this.

The LORD's anger against Israel

8 The Lord sent a word into Jacob,
And it hath lighted upon Israel.
9 And all the people shall know,
Even Ephraim and the inhabitant of
Samaria,
That say in the pride and stoutness of
heart,
10 The bricks are fallen down, but we will
build *with* hewn stones:
The sycomores are cut down, but we
will change *them into* cedars.
11 Therefore the LORD shall set up the
adversaries of Rezin against him,
And [1]join his enemies together;
12 The Syrians before, and the Philistines
behind;
And they shall devour Israel [1]with
open mouth.
[a]For all this his anger is not turned
away,
But his hand *is* stretched out still.
13 For [a]the people turneth not unto him
that smiteth them,
Neither do they seek the LORD of hosts.

9:1 [1]Or, *populous* [a]ch. 8:22 [b]2 Ki. 15:29; 2 Chr. 16:4 [c]Lev. 26:24; 2 Ki. 17:5; 1 Chr. 5:26
9:2 [a]Mat. 4:16; Eph. 5:8,14
9:3 [1]Or, *to him* [a]Judg. 5:30
9:4 [1]Or, *When thou brakest* [a]ch. 10:5 [b]Judg. 7:22; Ps. 83:9
9:5 [1]Or, *When the whole battle of the warrior* was, etc. [2]Or, *And it was, etc.* [3]Heb. *meat* [a]ch. 66:15
9:6 [a]ch. 7:14; Luke 2:11 [b]John 3:16 [c]Mat. 28:18; 1 Cor. 15:25 [d]Judg. 13:18 [e]Tit. 2:13
9:6 [f]Eph. 2:14
9:7 [a]Dan. 2:44; Luke 1:32 [b]ch. 37:32
9:11 [1]Heb. *mingle*
9:12 [1]Heb. *with whole mouth* [a]Jer. 4:8
9:13 [a]Jer. 5:3

‡9:1 *Naphtali.* This tribe in northern Israel suffered greatly when the Assyrian Tiglath-pileser III attacked in 734 and 732 B.C. (2 Ki 15:29).

‡9:2 *people that walked in darkness.* There would be a special blessing upon the people of Galilee who experienced such devastating judgment during the days of Isaiah. This prophecy was fufilled when Jesus lived and ministered in Galilee during his earthly ministry (cf. Mat 4:13–15). *great light.* Jesus and His salvation would be a "light of /to the Gentiles" (42:6; 49:6).

9:4 *day of Midian.* Gideon defeated the hordes of Midian and broke their domination over Israel (Judg 7:22–25). *yoke . . . staff.* In 10:26–27 Isaiah predicts that God will destroy the Assyrian army and their oppressive yoke. This was fulfilled in 701 B.C. (see 37:36–38).

‡9:5 *every battle . . . rolled in blood.* Describes the violence that the enemy armies inflicted on Israel during the time of God's punishment. *But this shall be . . . burning and fuel of fire.* A promise of Israel's deliverence from its enemies and a time of universal peace. Even the uniforms used in warfare ("garments rolled in blood") will be burned because there will no longer be a need for military garb and equipment. See notes on 2:2–4.

‡9:6 *Son.* A royal son, a son of David (see v. 7; see also 2 Sam 7:14; Ps 2:7; Mat 1:1; 3:17; Luke 1:32). *Wonderful, Counseller.* Or "Wonderful counseller," with "wonderful" describing the kind of "Counseller" that Messiah will be. Each of the four throne names of the Messiah would then consist of two elements. Unlike Immanuel (see note on 7:14), these titles were not like normal OT personal names. "Counseller" points to the Messiah as a king (see Mic 4:9) who determines upon and carries out a program of action (see 14:27, "purposed"; Ps 20:4, "counsel"). As Wonderful counseller, the coming Son of David will carry out a royal program that will cause all the world to marvel. What that program will be is spelled out in ch. 11, and more fully in chs. 24–27 (see 25:1—"done wonderful things, Thy counsels of old"). *mighty God.* See 10:21. His divine power as a warrior is stressed. *everlasting Father.* He will be an everlasting, compassionate provider and protector (cf. 40:9–11). *Prince of Peace.* His rule will bring wholeness and well-being to individuals and to society (see 11:6–9).

9:7 *throne of David . . . justice . . . for ever.* In spite of the sins of kings like Ahaz, Christ will be a descendant of David who will rule in righteousness forever (see 11:3–5; 2 Sam 7:12–13,16; Jer 33:15,20–22). *The zeal . . . this.* God is like a jealous lover who will not abandon His people.

9:9 *Ephraim.* See note on 7:2.

9:10 *bricks are fallen down.* Bricks made of clay and dried by the sun crumbled easily. *hewn stones.* Amos denounces the stone mansions of the wicked (Amos 5:11). *cedars.* The cedars of Lebanon provided the most valuable wood in the ancient Near East (see 1 Ki 7:2–3).

9:12,17,21 *For all this . . . stretched out still.* See 5:25. This refrain is repeated in 10:4, where the anger of the Lord reaches a climax in the captivity of His people.

14 Therefore the LORD will cut off from
Israel head and tail,
Branch and rush, [a]*in* one day.
15 The ancient and honourable, he *is* the
head;
And the prophet that teacheth lies, he
is the tail.
16 For [a] [1]the leaders of this people cause
them to err;
And [2]*they that are* led of them *are*
[3]destroyed.
17 Therefore the Lord [a]shall have no joy
in their young men,
Neither shall have mercy on their
fatherless and widows:
For every one *is* a hypocrite and an
evildoer,
And every mouth speaketh [1]folly.
[b]For all this his anger is not turned
away,
But his hand *is* stretched out still.
18 For wickedness [a]burneth as the fire:
It shall devour the briers and thorns,
And shall kindle in the thickets of the
forest,
And they shall mount up *like* the lifting
up of smoke.
19 Through the wrath of the LORD of hosts
is [a]the land darkened,
And the people shall be as the [1]fuel of
the fire:
[b]No man shall spare his brother.
20 And he shall [1]snatch on the right
hand, and be hungry;
And he shall eat on the left hand, [a]and
they shall not be satisfied:
[b]They shall eat every man the flesh of
his own arm:
21 Manasseh, Ephraim; and Ephraim,
Manasseh:
And they together *shall be* against Judah.
[a]For all this his anger is not turned
away,
But his hand *is* stretched out still.

10 Woe unto them that [a]decree
unrighteous decrees,
And [1]that write grievousness *which*
they have prescribed;
2 To turn aside the needy from judgment,
And to take away the right from the
poor of my people,
That widows may be their prey,
And *that* they may rob the fatherless.
3 And [a]what will ye do in [b]the day of
visitation,
And in the desolation *which* shall come
from far?
To whom will ye flee for help?
And where will ye leave your glory?
4 Without me they shall bow down
under the prisoners,
And they shall fall under the slain.
[a]For all this his anger is not turned
away,
But his hand *is* stretched out still.

Assyria to be destroyed

5 [1]O [2]Assyrian, [a]the rod of mine anger,
[3]And the staff in their hand *is* mine
indignation.
6 I will send him against [a]a hypocritical
nation,
And against the people of my wrath
will I [b]give him a charge,
To take the spoil, and to take the prey,
And [1]to tread them down like the mire
of the streets.
7 [a]Howbeit he meaneth not so,
Neither doth his heart think so;
But *it is* in his heart to destroy
And cut off nations not a few.
8 [a]For he saith, *Are* not my princes
altogether kings?
9 *Is* not [a]Calno [b]as Carchemish?
Is not Hamath as Arpad?
Is not Samaria [c]as Damascus?
10 As my hand hath found the kingdoms
of the idols,
And whose graven images did excel
them of Jerusalem and *of* Samaria;
11 Shall I not, as I have done unto
Samaria and her idols,

9:14 [a]Rev. 18:8
9:16 [1]Or, *they that call them blessed* [2]Or, *they that are called blessed of them* [3]Heb. *swallowed up* [a]ch. 3:12
9:17 [1]Or, *villany* [a]Ps. 147:10 [b]ch. 5:25
9:18 [a]Mal. 4:1
9:19 [1]Heb. *meat* [a]ch. 8:22 [b]Mic. 7:2,6
9:20 [1]Heb. *cut* [a]Lev. 26:26 [b]Jer. 19:9
9:21 [a]ver. 12,17
10:1 [a]Ps. 58:2
10:1 [1]Or, *to the writers* that *write grievousness*
10:3 [a]Job 31:14 [b]Hos. 9:7
10:4 [a]ch. 5:25
10:5 [1]Or, *Woe to the Assyrian* [2]Heb. *Asshur* [3]Or, *Though* [a]Jer. 51:20
10:6 [1]Heb. *to lay them a treading* [a]ch. 9:17 [b]Jer. 34:22
10:7 [a]Gen. 50:20
10:8 [a]2 Ki. 19:10
10:9 [a]Amos 6:2 [b]2 Chr. 35:20 [c]2 Ki. 16:9

9:14 *head and tail . . . Branch and rush.* The leaders of Israel (see also 3:1–3). These two pairs refer to Egyptian leaders in 19:15.

9:17 *fatherless and widows.* They often suffered at the hands of the powerful (see note on 1:17), but now even they are wicked.

9:18 *briers and thorns.* See note on 5:6.

9:19 *fuel of the fire.* Contrast v. 5.

9:21 *Manasseh, Ephraim.* These two prominent tribes in the northern kingdom were descended from the two sons of Joseph (see Gen 46:20; see also Gen 48:5–6 and notes). They had fought each other centuries earlier (Judg 12:4).

10:1 *Woe.* Cf. the series of woes in 5:8–23.

10:2 *widows . . . fatherless.* See notes on 1:17; 9:17.

10:4 *prisoners . . . slain.* Jer 39:6–7 similarly describes the plight of Judah's rulers when Nebuchadnezzar captured Jerusalem in 586 B.C. *For all this . . . stretched out still.* See note on 9:12,17,21.

10:5 *rod . . . staff.* See 9:4 and note. Babylon also was a hammer or club used by God to punish other nations (Jer 50:23; 51:20; Hab 1:6).

‡10:6 *hypocritical nation.* Lit. "a godless nation," referring to Judah (see v. 10). *spoil . . . prey.* The last part of the fulfillment symbolized by Maher-shalal-hash-baz ("spoil" here is the translation of Hebrew *shalal,* and "prey" is the translation of *baz*). See 8:1–4 and note on 8:3.

10:9 *Calno.* A region in northern Aram (Syria). See Calneh in Amos 6:2. *Carchemish.* The great fortress on the Euphrates River east of Calno (see Jer 46:2). *Hamath.* A city on the Orontes River that marked the northern extent of Solomon's rule (2 Chr 8:4). See note on 2 Ki 17:24. *Arpad.* A city near Hamath and just south of Calno. All these areas submitted to Assyria by c. 717 B.C. (see 36:19).

10:10 *images . . . of Jerusalem and of Samaria.* No Israelite was supposed to worship idols, but the land was full of them (2:8). Samaria fell to Shalmaneser V (2 Ki 17:3–6) and Sargon II in 722–721 B.C.

So do to Jerusalem and her idols?
12 Wherefore it shall come to pass, *that* when the Lord hath performed his whole work
[a]Upon mount Zion and on Jerusalem,
[b]I will [1]punish the fruit [2]of the stout heart of the king of Assyria,
And the glory of his high looks.
13 [a]For he saith, By the strength of my hand I have done *it,*
And by my wisdom; for I am prudent:
And I have removed the bounds of the people,
And have robbed their treasures,
And I have put down the inhabitants [1]like a valiant *man:*
14 And [a]my hand hath found as a nest the riches of the people:
And as *one* gathereth eggs *that are* left,
Have I gathered all the earth;
And there was none that moved the wing,
Or opened the mouth, or peeped.

15 Shall [a]the axe boast itself against him that heweth therewith?
Or shall the saw magnify itself against him that shaketh it?
[1]As if the rod should shake *itself against* them that lift it up,
Or as if the staff should lift up [2]*itself, as if it were* no wood.
16 Therefore shall the Lord, the Lord of hosts,
Send among his fat ones leanness;
And under his glory he shall kindle a burning
Like the burning of a fire.
17 And the light of Israel shall be for a fire,
And his Holy One for a flame:
[a]And it shall burn and devour his thorns and his briers in one day;

10:12 [1]Heb. *visit upon* [2]Heb. *of the greatness of the heart* [a]2 Ki. 19:31 [b]Jer. 50:18
10:13 [1]Or, *like many people* [a]Is. 37:24
10:14 [a]Job 31:25
10:15 [1]Or, *As if a rod should shake them that lift it up* [2]Or, that which is *not wood* [a]Jer. 51:20
10:17 [a]ch. 9:18
10:18 [1]Heb. *From the soul, and even to the flesh* [a]2 Ki. 19:23
10:19 [1]Heb. *number*
10:20 [a]2 Ki. 16:7
10:22 [1]Heb. *in,* or, *amongst* [2]Or, in [a]Rom. 9:27 [b]ch. 6:13
10:23 [a]Dan. 9:27; Rom. 9:28
10:24 [1]Or, *But he shall lift up his staff for thee* [a]ch. 37:6 [b]Ex. 14
10:25 [a]Dan. 11:36
10:26 [a]2 Ki. 19:35 [b]ch. 9:4

18 And shall consume the glory of his forest, and of [a]his fruitful field,
[1]Both soul and body:
And they shall be as when a standard-bearer fainteth.
19 And the rest of the trees of his forest shall be [1]few,
That a child may write them.

A remnant of Israel to be saved

20 And it shall come to pass in that day,
That the remnant of Israel,
And such as are escaped of the house of Jacob,
[a]Shall no more again stay upon him that smote them;
But shall stay upon the LORD,
The Holy One of Israel, in truth.
21 The remnant shall return, *even* the remnant of Jacob,
Unto the mighty God.
22 [a]For though thy people Israel be as the sand of the sea,
[b]*Yet* a remnant [1]of them shall return:
The consumption decreed shall overflow [2]*with* righteousness.
23 [a]For the Lord GOD of hosts shall make a consumption, even determined,
In the midst of all *the land.*
24 Therefore thus saith the Lord GOD of hosts,
O my people that dwellest in Zion,
[a]Be not afraid of the Assyrian:
He shall smite thee with a rod,
[1]And shall lift up his staff against thee, after the manner of [b]Egypt.
25 For yet a very little while, [a]and the indignation shall cease,
And mine anger in their destruction.
26 And the LORD of hosts shall stir up [a]a scourge for him
According to the slaughter of [b]Midian at the rock Oreb:

‡10:12 *stout heart.* Or "arrogant heart." Judgment against the proud was announced in 2:11,17. The Lord uses even pagan kings and nations to carry out his purposes but also holds them accountable for their cruel and wicked behavior.

10:13–14 *my . . . I.* The king of Assyria boastfully refers to himself eight times. Cf. 14:13–14; Ezek 28:2–5.

10:15 *axe . . . saw . . . rod . . . staff.* See v. 5; 9:4 and notes.

‡10:16 *the Lord, the Lord of hosts.* See 1:24 and note. *fat ones.* The mighty warriors of the Assyrian army. *leanness.* When the angel put to death 185,000 soldiers of the Assyrian king Sennacherib in 701 B.C., he may have used a rapidly spreading plague (see note on 37:36; see also 2 Sam 24:15–16; 1 Chr 21:22,27).

10:17,20 *Holy One.* See note on 1:4.

10:18–19 *forest.* A reference to the Assyrian army. See vv. 33–34.

10:19 Probably fulfilled between 612 B.C. (fall of Nineveh) and 605 (battle of Carchemish).

10:20,27 *in that day.* The day of victory and joy, the positive aspect of the "day of the LORD" (see notes on 2:11,17,20; 9:4). Israel is restored and the people praise God. Ch. 11 connects this "day" with the Messianic age (see 11:10–11; see also 12:1,4).

10:20–22 *remnant.* See note on 1:9. "The remnant shall return" was the name of Isaiah's first son (see note on 7:3). A faithful remnant led by Hezekiah survived the Assyrian invasion of 701 B.C. (see 37:4). Later, a remnant returned from Babylonian exile.

10:20 *him that smote them.* The king of Assyria (see note on 7:17).

10:21 *mighty God.* See note on 9:6.

‡10:22 *the sand of the sea.* See notes on Gen 13:16; 22:17. *consumption decreed.* Because of Israel's sin, God would punish the nation through foreign invaders. *shall overflow with righteousness.* God's judgment of His sinful people is perfectly just.

‡10:23–24 *the Lord GOD of hosts.* See 1:24 and note. *after the manner of Egypt.* Both the oppression and ultimate deliverance (cf. v. 26; 11:4) of Israel will be like the first exodus. See note on 4:5–6.

10:24 *rod . . . staff.* See v. 5; 9:4 and notes.

10:26–27 *Midian . . . burden . . . yoke.* See note on 9:4.

10:26 *Oreb.* One of the Midianite leaders (Judg 7:25). *the sea . . . of Egypt.* When Moses stretched out his hand over the Red sea, the waters engulfed the chariots of Pharaoh (see Ex 14:26–28).

And [c]*as* his rod *was* upon the sea,
So shall he lift it up after the manner of
Egypt.
27 And it shall come to pass in that day,
That his burden [1]shall be taken away
from off thy shoulder,
And his yoke from off thy neck,
And the yoke shall be destroyed
because of [a]the anointing.

28 He is come to Aiath, he is passed to
Migron;
At Michmash he hath laid up his
carriages:
29 They are gone over [a]the passage: they
have taken up their lodging at Geba;
Ramah is afraid; [b]Gibeah of Saul is
fled.
30 [1]Lift up thy voice, O daughter [a]of
Gallim:
Cause *it* to be heard unto [b]Laish,
O poor Anathoth.
31 [a]Madmenah is removed;
The inhabitants of Gebim gather
themselves to flee.
32 As yet shall *he* remain [a]at Nob *that*
day:
He shall [b]shake his hand *against* the
mount of [c]the daughter of Zion,
The hill of Jerusalem.
33 Behold, the Lord, the LORD of hosts,
Shall lop the bough with terror:
And [a]the high ones of stature *shall be*
hewn down,
And the haughty shall be humbled.
34 And he shall cut down the thickets of
the forest with iron,
And Lebanon shall fall [1]by a mighty
one.

10:26 [c]Ex. 14:26
10:27 [1]Heb. *shall remove* [a]Ps. 105:15; 1 John 2:20
10:29 [a]1 Sam. 13:23 [b]1 Sam. 11:4
10:30 [1]Heb. *Cry shrill with thy voice* [a]1 Sam. 25:44 [b]Judg. 18:7
10:31 [a]Josh. 15:31
10:32 [a]1 Sam. 21:1; Neh. 11:32 [b]ch. 13:2 [c]ch. 37:22
10:33 [a]Amos 2:9
10:34 [1]Or, *mightily*
11:1 [a]Zech. 6:12; Rev. 5:5 [b]Acts 13:23 [c]ch. 4:2
11:2 [a]ch. 61:1; John 1:32
11:3 [1]Heb. *sent*, or, *smell*
11:4 [1]Or, *argue* [a]Rev. 19:11 [b]Job 4:9; Mal. 4:6; 2 Thes. 2:8
11:6 [a]Hos. 2:18

The branch out of Jesse

11 And [a]there shall come forth a rod
out of the stem of [b]Jesse,
And [c]a Branch shall grow out of his
roots:
2 [a]And the Spirit of the LORD shall rest
upon him,
The spirit of wisdom and understanding,
The spirit of counsel and might,
The spirit of knowledge and of the fear
of the LORD;
3 And shall make him of [1]quick
understanding in the fear of the LORD:
And he shall not judge after the sight
of his eyes,
Neither reprove after the hearing of his
ears:
4 But [a]with righteousness shall he judge
the poor,
And [1]reprove with equity for the meek
of the earth:
And he shall [b]smite the earth with the
rod of his mouth,
And with the breath of his lips shall he
slay the wicked.
5 And righteousness shall be the girdle of
his loins,
And faithfulness the girdle of his reins.
6 [a]The wolf also shall dwell with the
lamb,
And the leopard shall lie down with
the kid;
And the calf and the young lion and
the fatling together;
And a little child shall lead them.
7 And the cow and the bear shall feed;
Their young ones shall lie down
together:
And the lion shall eat straw like the ox.

‡10:27 *anointing.* The Hebrew reads "fatness" here. The idea is that like a sturdy animal, Israel is able to break off the yoke of oppression.

10:28–32 As if seeing a vision, Isaiah describes the approach of the Assyrian army to Jerusalem from about ten miles north of the city.

10:28 *Michmash.* Located about seven miles north of Jerusalem.

10:29 *Ramah.* The home of Samuel. It was about five miles from Jerusalem (1 Sam 7:17). *Gibeah of Saul.* About three miles from Jerusalem. It had been the capital of Israel's first king (see 1 Sam 10:26).

10:30 *poor Anathoth.* Jeremiah's hometown (see Jer 1:1). The Hebrew for "poor" sounds like the word "Anathoth," thus a wordplay.

10:32 *Nob.* Perhaps on present-day mount Scopus, on the outskirts of Jerusalem. *daughter of Zion.* A personification of Jerusalem and its inhabitants.

‡10:33 *the Lord, the LORD of hosts.* See 1:24 and note. *bough . . . high ones of stature.* Sennacherib and his armies will fall (see vv. 16–19 and notes) in spite of their impressive military strength.

10:34 *Lebanon.* Refers to the famed cedars of Lebanon (see note on 2:13).

11:1 *rod . . . stem.* The Assyrians all but destroyed Judah, but it was the Babylonian exile that brought the kingdom of Judah to an end in 586 B.C. The Messiah will grow as a shoot from that stump of David's dynasty. See 6:13 and note. *Jesse.* David's father (see 1 Sam 16:10–13). *Branch.* See notes on 4:2; Mat 2:23.

11:2 *the Spirit . . . shall rest upon him.* The Messiah, like David (1 Sam 16:13), will be empowered by the Holy Spirit. *counsel and might.* The Spirit will endow Him with the wisdom to undertake wise purposes and with the power to carry them out (see note on 9:6). *fear of the LORD.* See Prov 1:7 and note.

‡11:3 *shall make him of quick understanding . . . fear of the LORD.* Lit. "His delight (will be) in the fear of the LORD." See John 8:29.

11:4 *righteousness . . . equity.* The rulers of Isaiah's day lacked these qualities (see 1:17; 5:7; see also note on 9:7). *rod of his mouth.* Assyria was God's rod in 10:5,24, but the Messiah will rule the nations with an iron scepter (Ps 2:9; Rev 19:15).

‡11:5 *girdle.* His belt. When a man prepared for vigorous action, he tied up his loose, flowing garments with a belt (see 5:27).

‡11:6–9 The peace and safety of the Messianic age are reflected in the fact that little children will be unharmed as they play with formerly ferocious animals. Such conditions are a description of the future consummation of the Messianic kingdom. The description is literal in that it portrays the transformation of nature that will occur and figurative in that it portrays the conditions of peace and security that will exist in the kingdom. See 2:2–4 and notes; 35:9; 65:20–25; Ezek 34:25–29.

8 And the sucking child shall play on the
hole of the asp,
And the weaned child shall put his
hand on the [1] cockatrice' den.
9 [a] They shall not hurt nor destroy in all
my holy mountain:
For [b] the earth shall be full *of* the
knowledge of the LORD,
As the waters cover the sea.
10 [a] And in that day [b] there shall be a root
of Jesse,
Which shall stand for an ensign of the
people;
To it shall the [c] Gentiles seek:
And his rest shall be [1] glorious.
11 And it shall come to pass in that day,
That the Lord shall set his hand again
the second time
To recover the remnant of his people,
Which shall be left [a] from Assyria,
And from Egypt, and from Pathros,
And from Cush, and from Elam, and
from Shinar,
And from Hamath, and from the
islands of the sea.
12 And he shall set up an ensign for the
nations,
And shall assemble the outcasts of Israel,
And gather together the [a] dispersed of
Judah
From the four [1] corners of the earth.
13 [a] The envy also of Ephraim shall depart,
And the adversaries of Judah shall be
cut off:
Ephraim shall not envy Judah,
And Judah shall not vex Ephraim.
14 But they shall fly upon the shoulders of
the Philistines toward the west;
They shall spoil [1] them of the east
together:
[a 2] They shall lay their hand upon Edom
and Moab;
And [3] the children of Ammon shall
obey them.
15 And the LORD [a] shall utterly destroy the
tongue of the Egyptian sea;
And with his mighty wind shall he
shake his hand over the river,
And shall smite it in *the* seven streams,
[b] And make *men* go over [1] dryshod.
16 And [a] there shall be a highway for the
remnant of his people,
Which shall be left from Assyria;
[b] Like as it was to Israel
In the day that he came up out of the
land of Egypt.

11:8 [1] Or, *adder's*
11:9 [a] Job 5:23 [b] Hab. 2:14
11:10 [1] Heb. *glory* [a] ch. 2:11 [b] Rom. 15:12 [c] Rom. 15:10
11:11 [a] Zech. 10:10
11:12 [1] Heb. *wings* [a] John 7:35
11:13 [a] Jer. 3:18; Ezek. 37:16, 17,22
11:14 [1] Heb. *the children of the east* [2] Heb. *Edom and Moab* shall be *the laying on of their hand* [3] Heb. *the children of Ammon their obedience* [a] Dan. 11:41
11:15 [1] Heb. *in shoes* [a] Zech. 10:11 [b] Rev. 16:12
11:16 [a] ch. 19:23 [b] Ex. 14:29
12:1 [a] ch. 2:11
12:2 [a] Ps. 83:18 [b] Ex. 15:2; Ps. 118:14
12:3 [a] John 4:10

Thanksgiving for God's salvation

12 And [a] in that day thou shalt say,
O LORD, I will praise thee: though
thou wast angry with me,
Thine anger is turned away, and thou
comfortedst me.
2 Behold, God *is* my salvation;
I will trust, and not be afraid:
For the LORD [a] JEHOVAH *is* my
[b] strength and *my* song;
He also is become my salvation.
3 Therefore with joy shall ye draw
[a] water out of the wells of salvation.

‡**11:8** *cockatrice.* Or, "poisonous snake"; see KJV marg.
11:9 *my holy mountain.* See 2:2–4 and note. *full of the knowledge.* See 2:3, where the word of the Lord is taught in Jerusalem. Cf. Hab 2:14.
‡**11:10** *in that day.* See note on 10:20,27. *root of Jesse.* A Messianic title closely connected with v. 1 (see also 53:2; Rom 15:12; Rev 5:5; 22:16). *ensign.* A banner or flag. See 5:26 and note.
‡**11:11** *second time.* The first time was the exodus from Egypt (see v. 16). The initial fulfillment in the immediate future is the return from Assyrian and Babylonian exile, but the ultimate fulfillment refers to the regathering of Israel to take place at Christ's second coming. For the future regathering/salvation of Israel, see 52:9–10; 54:6–8; Amos 9:1–15; Zeph 3:14–20; Rom 11:26–27. *remnant.* See notes on 1:9; 10:20–22. *Egypt.* The delta region of the Nile, in the north. *Pathros.* Southern Egypt, upstream from the delta. *Elam.* The land northeast of the lower Tigris Valley (see 21:2; Jer 49:34–39; Dan 8:2). *Hamath.* See note on 10:9. *islands of the sea.* The coastlands and islands of the Mediterranean are probably intended (see 41:1,5; 42:4; Gen 10:5).
11:12 *assemble the outcasts.* See 27:13; 49:22; 56:8; 62:10; 66:20. *four corners.* Lit. "four wings." "Four corners of the earth" is equivalent to "the uttermost part of the earth" (see 24:16; Job 37:3).
11:13 *envy also of Ephraim.* See note on 7:2. Prior to the exile, Ephraim and Judah were frequently fighting each other (see 9:21).
11:14 *them of the east.* Perhaps the Midianites, who plundered Israel, along with other eastern peoples (see 9:4). *Edom . . . Moab . . . children of Ammon.* After the exodus, Israel did not attack these nations (see Judg 11:14–18). Israel's future political domination is also referred to in 14:2; 49:23; 60:12 (see also 25:10; 34:5).
11:15 *destroy . . . the Egyptian sea.* An allusion to the drying up of the Red sea during the exodus (see Ex 14:21–22). *tongue.* See "bay" in Josh 15:2,5. *the river.* Rev 16:12 refers to the drying up of the Euphrates, perhaps symbolizing the removal of barriers preventing the coming of "the kings from the east."
11:16 *highway.* The removal of obstacles and the building of a highway leading to Jerusalem are also described in 35:8; 57:14; 62:10 (cf. 40:3–4).
12:1–6 Two short psalms of praise for deliverance (vv. 1–3, 4–6) climax chs. 7–11 (see note on 7:1–12:6; see also note on 6:1).
‡**12:1** *in that day.* Also in v. 4. See note on 10:20,27. *I will praise thee.* The "I" is probably the nation, praising the Lord for the deliverance He is sure to bring. *Thine anger is turned away.* See note on 9:12,17,21. After God punishes Israel, His anger will be directed against nations like Assyria and Babylon.
‡**12:2** *the LORD JEHOVAH.* Two Hebrew forms for the personal name of God are given: The first is "Yah." The name JEHOVAH was probably pronounced "Yahweh." See note on Ex 3:15. *the LORD . . . salvation.* These lines quote Ex 15:2, a verse commemorating the defeat of the Egyptians at the Red sea. See also Ps 118:14.
12:3 *wells.* Perhaps an allusion to God's abundant provision of water for Israel during the wilderness wanderings (cf. Ex 15:25,27). But here God's future saving act is itself the "well" from which Israel will draw life-giving water (see Ps 36:9; Jer 2:13; John 4:10).

4 And in that day shall ye say,
[a]Praise the LORD, [1]call upon his name,
[b]Declare his doings among the people,
Make mention that his [c]name *is* exalted.
5 [a]Sing unto the LORD; for he hath done excellent things:
This *is* known in all the earth.
6 [a]Cry out and shout, thou [1]inhabitant of Zion:
For great *is* [b]the Holy One of Israel in the midst of thee.

The doom of Babylon

13 The [a]burden of Babylon, which Isaiah the son of Amoz did see.
2 [a]Lift ye up a banner [b]upon the high mountain,
Exalt the voice unto them, [c]shake the hand,
That they may go *into* the gates of the nobles.
3 I have commanded my sanctified ones,
I have also called [a]my mighty ones for mine anger,
Even them that [b]rejoice in my highness.
4 The noise of a multitude in the mountains, [1]like as of a great people;
A tumultuous noise of the kingdoms of nations gathered together:
The LORD of hosts mustereth the host of the battle.
5 They come from a far country, from the end of the heaven,
Even the LORD, and the weapons of his indignation,
To destroy the whole land.
6 Howl ye; [a]for the day of the LORD *is* at hand;
[b]It shall come as a destruction from the Almighty.
7 Therefore shall all hands [1]be faint,
And every man's heart shall melt:
8 And they shall be afraid: [a]pangs and sorrows shall take hold of *them;*
They shall be in pain as a woman that travaileth:
They shall [1]be amazed [2]one at another;
Their faces *shall be as* [3]flames.
9 Behold, [a]the day of the LORD cometh,
Cruel both *with* wrath and fierce anger,
To lay the land desolate:
And he shall destroy [b]the sinners thereof out of it.
10 For the stars of heaven and the constellations thereof shall not give their light:
The sun shall be [a]darkened in his going forth,
And the moon shall not cause her light to shine.
11 And I will punish the world for *their* evil,
And the wicked for their iniquity;
[a]And I will cause the arrogancy of the proud to cease,

12:4 [1]Or, *proclaim his name* [a]1 Chr. 16:8; Ps. 105:1 [b]Ps. 145:4-6 [c]Ps. 34:3
12:5 [a]Ex. 15:1; Ps. 98:1
12:6 [1]Heb. *inhabitress* [a]Zeph. 3:14 [b]Ps. 89:18
13:1 [a]Jer. 50; 51
13:2 [a]ch. 18:3 [b]Jer. 51:25 [c]ch. 10:32
13:3 [a]Joel 3:11 [b]Ps. 149:2
13:4 [1]Heb. *the likeness of*
13:6 [a]Zeph. 1:7; Rev. 6:17 [b]Job 31:23; Joel 1:15
13:7 [1]Or, *fall down*
13:8 [1]Heb. *wonder* [2]Heb. *every man at his neighbour* [3]Heb. *faces of the flames* [a]Ps. 48:6
13:9 [a]Mal. 4:1 [b]Ps. 104:35; Prov. 2:22
13:10 [a]Ezek. 32:7; Joel 2:31; Mat. 24:29; Mark 13:24
13:11 [a]ch. 2:17

12:6 *Cry out and shout.* These two imperatives occur again in 54:1, where Zion rejoices over the restoration of her people. *Holy One of Israel.* See notes on 1:4; 6:1.

13:1–23:18 A series of prophecies against the nations (see also Jer 46–51; Ezek 25–32; Amos 1–2; Zeph 2:4–15). They begin with Babylon (13:1–14:23) and Assyria (14:24–27) before moving on to smaller nations. God's judgment on His people does not mean that the pagan nations will be spared (see Jer 25:29). In fact, God's judgments on the nations are often a part of His salvation of His people (see, e.g., 10:12).

13:1–14:27 This prophecy concerns Babylon during the Assyrian empire rather than during the Neo-Babylonian empire. Thus the prophecy is actually against the Assyrian empire, Babylon being its most important city. From 729 B.C. on, the kings of Assyria also assumed the title "king of Babylon." Note that there is no new "burden" heading at 14:24, even though 14:24–27 clearly pertains to Assyria; so 13:1–14:27 forms a unit.

13:1 See note on 1:1. *burden.* The Hebrew for this word is related to a Hebrew verb meaning "to lift up, carry" and is possibly to be understood as either lifting up one's voice or carrying a burden. Such a "burden" often contains a message of doom. *Babylon.* See 21:1–9; 46:1–2; 47:1–15; Jer 50–51. Its judgment is announced first because of the present Assyrian threat and because Babylon would later bring about the downfall of Judah and Jerusalem between 605 and 586 B.C. Babylon was conquered by Cyrus the Persian (see 45:1; 47:1) in 539. Subsequently it came to symbolize the world powers arrayed against God's kingdom (cf. 1 Pet 5:13), and its final destruction is announced in Rev 14:8; 16:19; 17–18. Here, however, Babylon is still part of the Assyrian empire (see 14:24–27; see also note on 13:1–14:27).

13:2 *Lift ye up a banner.* See note on 5:26.

‡13:3 *my sanctified ones.* Those set apart to carry out God's will. Cf. 10:5, where the Lord calls Assyria "the rod of mine anger"; see also 45:1. The Lord is calling out an unidentified army from a distant nation to bring judgment upon Babylon. *anger.* God's anger is no longer turned against Israel (see 5:25; 9:12,17,21; 10:4) but against her enemies (see vv. 5,9,13; cf. 30:27). God must punish sin, particularly arrogance (see v. 11).

13:4 *The LORD of hosts mustereth the host of the battle.* See note on 1 Sam 1:3. The Hebrew for "army" is the singular form of the word for "hosts." God is the head of the armies of Israel (1 Sam 17:45), of angelic powers (1 Ki 22:19; Luke 2:13) and, here, of the armies that will destroy Babylon.

13:5 *weapons of his indignation.* Assyria was the club in God's hand during Isaiah's day, and Babylon itself would later serve as God's weapon (see 10:5 and note).

13:6,9 *day of the LORD.* See note on 2:11,17,20.

13:6 *destruction.* Hebrew *shod,* forming a wordplay on "Almighty" (Hebrew *Shaddai*)—as also in Joel 1:15. See note on 5:7. For *Shaddai* see note on Gen 17:1.

‡13:7 *shall all hands be faint.* Hands will fall limp as courage will fail. See Jer 6:24.

13:8 *afraid.* Holy war usually brings panic to the enemy (see Ex 15:14–16; Judg 7:21–22). *pain . . . travaileth.* The prophets often compare the suffering of judgment and war with the pain and anguish that frequently accompany childbirth (see 26:17; Jer 4:31; 6:24).

13:10 *stars . . . sun . . . moon.* Cosmic darkness is associated with the day of the Lord also in Joel 2:10,31; Rev 6:12–13. Cf. Judg 5:20.

13:11 *arrogancy . . . haughtiness.* Cf. 2:9,11,17; 5:15.

And will lay low the haughtiness of the terrible.
12 I will make a man more precious than fine gold;
Even a man than the golden wedge of Ophir.
13 [a]Therefore I will shake the heavens,
And the earth shall remove out of her place,
In the wrath of the LORD of hosts,
And in [b]the day of his fierce anger.
14 And it shall be as the chased roe,
And as a sheep that no *man* taketh up:
[a]They shall every man turn to his own people,
And flee every one into his own land.
15 Every one that is found shall be thrust through;
And every one that is joined *unto them* shall fall by the sword.
16 Their children also shall be [a]dashed to pieces before their eyes;
Their houses shall be spoiled, and their wives ravished.
17 [a]Behold, I will stir up the Medes against them,
Which shall not regard silver;
And *as for* gold, they shall not delight in it.
18 *Their* bows also shall dash the young men to pieces;
And they shall have no pity on the fruit of the womb;
Their eye shall not spare children.
19 [a]And Babylon, the glory of kingdoms,
The beauty of the Chaldees' excellency,
Shall be [1]as when God overthrew
[b]Sodom and Gomorrah.
20 [a]It shall never be inhabited,
Neither shall it be dwelt in from generation to generation:
Neither shall the Arabian pitch tent there;
Neither shall the shepherds make their fold there.
21 [a]But [1]wild beasts of the desert shall lie there;
And their houses shall be full *of* [2]doleful creatures;
And [3][4]owls shall dwell there,
And satyrs shall dance there.
22 And [1]the wild beasts of the islands shall cry in their [2]desolate houses,
And dragons in *their* pleasant palaces:
[a]And her time *is* near to come,
And her days shall not be prolonged.

14 For the LORD [a]will have mercy on Jacob,
And [b]will yet choose Israel,
And set them in their own land:
[c]And the strangers shall be joined with them,
And they shall cleave to the house of Jacob.
2 And the people shall take them, [a]and bring them to their place:
And the house of Israel shall possess them in the land of the LORD
For servants and handmaids:
And they shall take them captives,
[1]whose captives they were;
[b]And they shall rule over their oppressors.

3 ¶ And it shall come to pass in the day that
the LORD shall give thee rest from thy sorrow,
and from thy fear, and from the hard bondage
wherein thou wast made to serve,

13:13 [a]Hag. 2:6 [b]Ps. 110:5; Lam. 1:12
13:14 [a]Jer. 50:16
13:16 [a]Ps. 137:9; Nah. 3:10; Zech. 14:2
13:17 [a]Jer. 51:11; Dan. 5:28
13:19 [1]Heb *as the overthrowing* [a]ch. 14:4 [b]Gen. 19:24; Deut. 29:23; Jer. 50:40
13:20 [a]Jer. 50:3
13:21 [1]Heb. *Ziim* [2]Heb. *Ochim* [3]Or, *ostriches* [4]Heb. *daughters of the owl* [a]ch. 34:11
13:22 [1]Heb. *Iim* [2]Or, *palaces* [a]Jer. 51:33
14:1 [a]Ps. 102:13 [b]Zech. 1:17 [c]ch. 60:4,5,10
14:2 [1]Heb. *that had taken them captives* [a]ch. 49:22; 60:9; 66:20 [b]ch. 60:14

13:12 *more precious than fine gold.* War will reduce the male population drastically (see 4:1 and note). *golden wedge of Ophir.* Solomon imported large quantities of gold from this place (see 1 Ki 9:28; 10:11 and notes).
13:13 *shake the heavens . . . earth . . . remove out of her place.* Thunderstorms and earthquakes often accompany the powerful presence of the Lord (see notes on v. 10; 34:4; Ex 19:16). Hail may also be involved (cf. 30:30; Josh 10:11).
13:14 *flee.* From parts of the Assyrian empire.
13:16 *children . . . dashed to pieces.* Invading armies often slaughtered infants and children; thus there would be no future warriors, nor would there be a remnant through which the city (or country or people) might be revived (see Ps 137:8–9; Hos 10:14; Nah 3:10). *wives ravished.* Women also suffered greatly in war. With their husbands killed, they were often used as prostitutes (see note on Amos 7:17).
13:17 *the Medes.* Located in what is today northwestern Iran. There was conflict between Assyria and Media during the eighth century B.C. Some, however, relate the fulfillment of this verse to the period when the Medes joined the Babylonians in defeating Assyria in 612–609 but later united with Cyrus to conquer Babylon in 539. See Jer 51:11,28; Dan 5:31; 6:28.
13:19 *glory . . . excellency.* Babylon with its temples and palaces became a very beautiful city (see Dan 4:29–30). The hanging gardens of Nebuchadnezzar were one of the seven wonders of the ancient world. In 4:2 the Hebrew words for "glory" and "excellency" were used to describe the "branch of the LORD." *Chaldees.* The Neo-Babylonian empire of 612–539 B.C. was led by the Chaldean people of southern Babylonia. Nabopolassar welded the tribes together c. 626, and his son Nebuchadnezzar became their most powerful ruler (605–562). *Sodom and Gomorrah.* Previously Isaiah compared Judah to these cities (see 1:9–10 and note).
13:20–22 See the similar description of the desolation of Edom in 34:10–15. Cf. Rev 18:2.
13:20 *never be inhabited.* Babylon was completely deserted by the seventh century A.D.
13:21 *satyrs.* This term is connected with demons in Lev 17:7 ("goat idols") and 2 Chr 11:15 ("devils"). In Rev 18:2 fallen Babylon is described as a home for demons and evil spirits.
14:1 *will have mercy . . . And set them.* Babylon's fall will be linked with Israel's restoration. God's compassion on His people is the theme of chs. 40–66 (see 40:1–2). *in their own land.* See 2:2–4; 11:10–12 and notes. *strangers shall be joined with them.* See 11:10; 56:6–7; 60:3.
14:2 *people . . . place.* See note on 5:26. *shall possess them.* See note on 11:14.
14:3–21 However exalted (and almost divine) the king of Babylon may have thought himself (see vv. 12–14), he will go the way of all world rulers—down to the grave.
14:3 *sorrow . . . made to serve.* The Babylonian captivity was much like Israel's experience in Egypt (cf. Ex 1:14).

4 That thou [a]shalt take up this [1]proverb
against the king of Babylon, and say,
How hath the oppressor ceased! the
[b2]golden city ceased!
5 The LORD hath broken [a]the staff of the
wicked, *and* the sceptre of the rulers.
6 He who smote the people in wrath
with [1]a continual stroke,
He that ruled the nations in anger, *is*
persecuted, *and* none hindereth.
7 The whole earth is at rest, *and* is quiet:
they break forth *into* singing.
8 [a]Yea, the fir trees rejoice at thee, *and*
the cedars of Lebanon, *saying,*
Since thou art laid down, no feller is
come up against us.
9 [a1]Hell from beneath is moved for thee
to meet *thee at* thy coming:
It stirreth up the dead for thee, *even* all
the [2]chief ones of the earth;
It hath raised up from their thrones all
the kings of the nations.
10 All they shall speak and say unto thee,
Art thou also become weak as we? art
thou become like unto us?
11 Thy pomp is brought down *to* the
grave, *and* the noise of thy viols:
The worm is spread under thee, and
the worms cover thee.

12 [a]How art thou fallen from heaven,
[1]O Lucifer, son of the morning!
How art thou cut down to the ground,
which didst weaken the nations!
13 For thou hast said in thine heart, [a]I
will ascend *into* heaven,
[b]I will exalt my throne above the stars
of God:
I will sit also upon the mount of the
congregation, [c]in the sides of the
north:
14 I will ascend above the heights of the
clouds; [a]I will be like the most High.
15 Yet thou [a]shalt be brought down to
hell, to the sides of the pit.

16 They that see thee shall narrowly look
upon thee, *and* consider thee, *saying,*
Is this the man that made the earth to
tremble, that did shake kingdoms;
17 *That* made the world as a wilderness,
and destroyed the cities thereof;
That [1]opened not the house of his
prisoners?
18 All the kings of the nations, *even* all of
them,
Lie in glory, every one in his own
house.
19 But thou art cast out of thy grave like
an abominable branch,
And as the raiment of those that are
slain, thrust through with a sword,
That go down to the stones of the pit;
as a carcase trodden under feet.
20 Thou shalt not be joined with them in
burial,
Because thou hast destroyed thy land,
and slain thy people:
[a]The seed of evildoers shall never be
renowned.
21 Prepare slaughter for his children [a]for
the iniquity of their fathers;

14:4 [1]Or, *taunting speech* [2]Or, *exactress of gold* [a]ch. 13:19; Hab. 2:6 [b]Rev. 18:16
14:5 [a]Ps. 125:3
14:6 [1]Heb. *a stroke without removing*
14:8 [a]ch. 55:12; Ezek. 31:16
14:9 [1]Or, *The grave* [2]Heb. *leaders,* or, *great goats* [a]Ezek. 32:21
14:12 [1]Or, *O day star* [a]ch. 34:4
14:13 [a]Mat. 11:23
14:13 [b]Dan. 8:10 [c]Ps. 48:2
14:14 [a]ch. 47:8; 2 Thes. 2:4
14:15 [a]Mat. 11:23
14:17 [1]Or, *did not let his prisoners loose homeward?*
14:20 [a]Job 18:19; Ps. 21:10; 37:28; 109:13
14:21 [a]Ex. 20:5; Mat. 23:35

‡14:4 *proverb.* A taunt. Cf. the taunts against Babylon in Rev 18. *king of Babylon.* Another title used by the king of Assyria at this time.
14:5 *staff . . . sceptre.* See 10:5 and note; see also 10:24.
‡14:7 *break forth into singing.* The nations are celebrating the death of the king of Babylon.
14:8 *fir trees . . . cedars.* Isaiah often personified nature. The trees along with the mountains burst into song in 44:23 (cf. 55:12). *cedars of Lebanon.* These highly prized timbers were hauled away by the kings of Assyria and Babylon for centuries.
14:9 *chief ones.* Lit. "goats"; a goat often led a flock of sheep (see Jer 50:8). In Zech 10:3 the term is parallel to "shepherds." *raised up from their thrones.* Conditions among the dead are described in terms of their roles on earth.
‡14:11 *pomp . . . grave.* Cf. 5:14. *noise of thy viols.* The music of their harps. Music is sometimes a sign of luxury and pleasure (see Amos 6:5–6). *worm . . . cover thee.* The king of Babylon is pictured as a rotting corpse covered with maggots.
‡14:12–15 Some believe that Isaiah is giving a description of the fall of Satan (cf. Luke 10:18—where, however, Jesus seems to be referring to an event contemporary with Himself). But the context of the passage clearly refers to the king of Babylon. While Satan is not specifically in view here, the Bible teaches that evil world leaders are under Satanic and demonic control (cf. Dan. 10:13,20). The king of Babylon is also later used as a type (prefiguration) of the "beast" who will lead the Babylon of the last days (see Rev 13:4; 17:3). Cf. the description of the king of Tyre in Ezek 28.
‡14:12 *Lucifer, son of the morning.* The name "Lucifer" comes from the translation of the Latin Vulgate. The Hebrew for "Lucifer" is literally "shining one." The king of Babylon is compared to the morning star (Venus) that appears in the sky but then is extinguished by the sun before reaching its zenith. The king of Babylon, like Satan, appears to be great but will have a sudden fall.
‡14:13 *of the north.* Most likely referring to mount Zaphon, also called mount Casius, which was about 25 miles northeast of Ugarit in Syria. The Canaanites considered it the home and meeting place of the gods, much like mount Olympus for the Greeks (see Ps 48:2 and note). Cf. Ps 82:1. The king of Babylon committed the ultimate sin of thinking himself to be like God (cf. Gen 3:5).
14:16–20a These verses seem to take place on earth, not in the realm of the dead (Sheol)—probably also vv. 9–10.
‡14:16 *shall narrowly look upon thee.* The people of earth will stare in amazement when the powerful king of Babylon goes down to the grave.
14:17 *opened not the house of his prisoners.* Babylon, like Assyria, deported large segments of defeated populations to subdue the rebellious among them (see 2 Ki 24:14–16).
‡14:19 *cast out of thy grave.* A proper burial was considered important for an ordinary individual, and especially so for a king. To have one's body simply discarded was a terrible fate. *like an abominable branch.* Contrast the fate of the king of Babylon with the glory awaiting the Messianic "Branch" in 4:2; 11:1. *carcase trodden under feet.* A trampled corpse; see 5:25.
14:21 *Prepare slaughter for his children.* A man's children, as

That they do not rise, nor possess the land,
Nor fill the face of the world *with* cities.
22 For I will rise up against them, saith the LORD of hosts,
And cut off from Babylon [a]the name, and [b]remnant,
[c]And son, and nephew, saith the LORD.
23 [a]I will also make it a possession for the bittern, and pools of water:
And I will sweep it with the besom of destruction, saith the LORD of hosts.

The overthrow of Assyria

24 The LORD of hosts hath sworn, saying,
Surely as I have thought, so shall it come to pass;
And as I have purposed, *so* shall it stand:
25 That *I* will break the Assyrian in my land,
And upon my mountains tread him under foot:
Then shall [a]his yoke depart from off them,
And his burden depart from off their shoulders.
26 This *is* the purpose that is purposed upon the whole earth:
And this *is* the hand that is stretched out upon all the nations.
27 For the LORD of hosts hath [a]purposed, and who shall disannul *it?*
And his hand *is* stretched out, and who shall turn it back?

14:22 [a]Prov. 10:7; Jer. 51:62 [b]1 Ki. 14:10 [c]Job 18:19
14:23 [a]ch. 34:11; Zeph. 2:14
14:25 [a]ch. 10:27
14:27 [a]2 Chr. 20:6; Job 9:12; 23:13; Ps. 33:11; Prov. 19:21; 21:30; ch. 43:13; Dan. 4:31,35

14:28 [a]2 Ki. 16:20
14:29 [1]Or, *adder* [a]2 Chr. 26:6 [b]2 Ki. 18:8
14:31 [1]Or, he shall *not be alone* [2]Or, *assemblies*
14:32 [1]Or, *betake themselves unto it* [a]Ps. 87:1,5 [b]Zech. 11:11
15:1 [1]Or, *cut off* [a]Jer. 48:1 [b]Num. 21:28

A burden about Palestina

28 ¶ In the year that [a]king Ahaz died was this burden.
29 Rejoice not thou, whole Palestina,
[a]Because the rod of him that smote thee is broken:
For out of the serpent's root shall come forth a [1]cockatrice,
[b]And his fruit *shall be* a fiery flying serpent.
30 And the firstborn of the poor shall feed,
And the needy shall lie down in safety:
And I will kill thy root with famine,
And he shall slay thy remnant.
31 Howl, O gate; cry, O city;
Thou, whole Palestina, *art* dissolved:
For there shall come from the north a smoke,
And [1]none *shall be* alone in his [2]appointed times.
32 What shall *one* then answer the messengers of the nation?
That [a]the LORD hath founded Zion,
And [b]the poor of his people shall [1]trust in it.

Moab's devastation

15 The [a]burden of Moab.
Because in the night [b]Ar of Moab is laid waste, *and* [1]brought to silence;
Because in the night Kir of Moab is laid waste, *and* [1]brought to silence;
2 He is gone up *to* Bajith, and *to* Dibon, the high places, to weep:

well as his tombstone, were his memorial (cf. 2 Sam 18:18). The king of Babylon would have neither (cf. 47:9).

14:22–23 The taunt is extended to include Babylon itself (see note on vv. 3–21); fulfilled, at least partially, through Sennacherib's destruction of Babylon in 689 B.C.—ultimately by the Medes and Persians after they took Babylon in 539.

14:22 *remnant.* Israel will survive through a remnant (see 10:20–22; 11:11,16), but Babylon will not.

‡14:23 See 13:20–22 and notes. *bittern.* A porcupine. *pools of water.* Babylon will be turned into swamp land. Southern Babylonia, where the Chaldean tribes once lived, was a region of marshlands.

14:24–27 See Zeph 2:13–15; see also note on 13:1–14:27.

14:24 *so shall it stand.* See 8:10 and note. God's sovereign purposes regarding Assyria and Babylon will be carried out.

14:25 *yoke . . . burden.* See 9:4 and note.

14:26 *hand . . . stretched out.* See 9:12; 12:1 and notes. God's hand was stretched out against Egypt at the Red sea (see Ex 15:12).

14:28–32 See Jer 47; Ezek 25:15–17; Amos 1:6–8; Zeph 2:4–7.

14:28 *the year.* Perhaps 715 B.C. The occasion appears to be the Philistine revolt against Assyria while King Sargon (see 20:1) was too preoccupied with serious revolts elsewhere to give much attention to Canaan. *burden.* See note on 13:1.

‡14:29 *Palestina.* The Philistines. See note on Gen 10:14. Philistine territory was vulnerable to attack by the great empires (Egypt and Assyria) since it lay along the main route from Egypt to Mesopotamia. *the rod.* Probably Sargon of Assyria. *is broken.* If the rod was Sargon, reference is to the threats to his empire by a series of revolts in Babylonia and Asia Minor. *root . . . fruit.* A figure of speech that refers to the whole (tree) by speaking of its two extremes. After Sargon will come other Assyrian kings: Sennacherib, Esarhaddon, Ashurbanipal. *cockatrice.* See 11:8 and note. The kings that come after Sargon are going to bring even more severe devastation upon Israel.

14:30 *poor . . . needy.* Israelites (see v. 32).

‡14:31 *Howl.* Wailing in grief; cf. the similar reaction in 13:6; 15:2; 16:7; 23:1. *smoke.* The dust raised by the marching feet and the chariots of the Assyrians—who always invaded Canaan from the north. *none shall be alone . . . appointed times.* A powerful army with no stragglers in the ranks; cf. the longer description in 5:26–29.

14:32 *hath founded Zion.* God will protect Jerusalem from the Assyrians (compare 31:4–5 with 2:2).

15:1–16:14 See Jer 48; Ezek 25:8–11; Amos 2:1–3; Zeph 2:8–11.

15:1 *burden.* See note on 13:1. *Moab.* A country east of the Dead Sea that was a perpetual enemy of Israel (see 25:10; 2 Ki 13:20). *Ar.* The location of this city is unknown. *laid waste.* The same Hebrew word describes Isaiah's feelings about himself in 6:5. The destruction of Moab was probably connected with an invasion by Sargon of Assyria in 715/713 B.C. Cf. Jer 48:1–17. *Kir.* Probably Kir Hareseth, 15 miles south of the Arnon River and perhaps the capital of Moab at this time. Kir means "city."

15:2 *Dibon.* Located four miles north of the Arnon River and given to the tribe of Gad at one time (see Num 32:34). *high places.* Shrines originally built on hilltops and usually associated with pagan worship. *Nebo.* North of the Arnon River, perhaps near mount Nebo (Deut 34:1). *Medeba.* About six miles

Moab shall howl over Nebo, and over
Medeba:
[a]On all their heads *shall be* baldness,
and every beard cut off.
3 In their streets they shall gird
themselves with sackcloth:
On the tops of their houses, and in
their streets,
Every one shall howl, [1]weeping
abundantly.
4 And Heshbon shall cry, and Elealeh:
Their voice shall be heard *even* unto
Jahaz:
Therefore the armed soldiers of Moab
shall cry out;
His life shall be grievous unto him.
5 [a]My heart shall cry out for Moab;
[1]His fugitives *shall flee* unto Zoar,
A heifer of three years old:
For [b]*by* the mounting up of Luhith
with weeping shall they go it up;
For *in* the way of Horonaim they shall
raise up a cry of [2]destruction.
6 For the waters [a]of Nimrim shall be
[1]desolate:
For the hay is withered away, the grass
faileth, there is no green thing.
7 Therefore the abundance they have
gotten, and that which they have laid
up,
Shall they carry away to the [1]brook of
the willows.
8 For the cry is gone round about the
borders of Moab;
The howling thereof unto Eglaim, and
the howling thereof *unto* Beer-elim.

15:2 [a]Lev. 21:5
15:3 [1]Heb. *descending into weeping,* or, *coming down with weeping*
15:5 [1]Or, To *the borders thereof,* even *to Zoar,* as *a heifer* [2]Heb. *breaking* [a]Jer. 48:31 [b]Jer. 48:5
15:6 [1]Heb. *desolations* [a]Num. 32:36
15:7 [1]Or, *valley of the Arabians*
15:9 [1]Heb. *additions* [a]2 Ki. 17:25
16:1 [1]Or, *Petra.* Heb. *A rock* [a]2 Ki. 3:4 [b]2 Ki. 14:7
16:2 [1]Or, *a nest forsaken* [a]Num. 21:13
16:3 [1]Heb. *Bring*
16:4 [1]Heb. *wringer* [2]Heb. *The treaders down*
16:5 [1]Or, *prepared* [a]Luke 1:33 [b]Ps. 72:2
16:6 [a]Jer. 48:29

9 For the waters of Dimon shall be full *of*
blood:
For I will bring [1]more upon Dimon,
[a]Lions upon him that escapeth of Moab,
And upon the remnant of the land.

16 Send [a]ye the lamb *to* the ruler of
the land
[b]From [1]Sela to the wilderness,
Unto the mount of the daughter of
Zion.
2 For it shall be, *that,* as a wandering
bird [1]cast out of the nest,
So the daughters of Moab shall be *at*
the fords of [a]Arnon.
3 [1]Take counsel, execute judgment;
Make thy shadow as the night in the
midst of the noonday;
Hide the outcasts; bewray not him that
wandereth.
4 Let mine outcasts dwell with thee,
Moab;
Be thou a covert to them from the face
of the spoiler:
For the [1]extortioner is at an end, the
spoiler ceaseth,
[2]The oppressors are consumed out of
the land.
5 And in mercy [a]shall the throne be
[1]established:
And he shall sit upon it in truth in the
tabernacle of David,
[b]Judging, and seeking judgment, and
hasting righteousness.
6 We have heard of the [a]pride of Moab;
he is very proud:

south of Heshbon (see v. 4) and once captured by Israel from Sihon (see Num 21:26,30). *baldness . . . beard cut off.* Characteristic of intense mourning (Jer 48:37).

15:3 *sackcloth.* The coarse garb of mourners (see Job 16:15; Jer 48:37; Lam 2:10), made of goat hair. *tops of their houses.* Perhaps chosen because incense was sometimes offered there (see Jer 19:13).

15:4 *Heshbon.* Located about 18 miles east of the northern tip of the Dead Sea. See also Jer 48:34. It was King Sihon's capital before Israel captured it (see Num 21:23–26). *Elealeh.* About a mile north of Heshbon and always mentioned with it. *Jahaz.* Just north of the Arnon River and about 20 miles from Heshbon (Num 21:23; Jer 48:34).

‡15:5 *Zoar.* Probably located near the southern end of the Dead Sea. Lot fled there from Sodom (see Gen 14:2; 19:23,30). *A heifer of three years old.* A place name, Eglath-shelishiyah, meaning "three-year old heifer" (cf. 1 Sam 1:24), the location of which is unknown (see also Jer 48:34). *Luhith.* Location unknown (see also Jer 48:5). *Horonaim.* Location unknown (see also Jer 48:3,5,34).

15:6 *waters of Nimrim.* Perhaps to be identified with the Wadi en-Numeirah, ten miles from the southern end of the Dead Sea (cf. Jer 48:34). *hay is withered away.* The advancing enemy may have stopped up the major springs of Moab.

‡15:7 *brook of the willows.* Or the brook of Arabim, probably located at the border between Moab and Edom (see v. 8).

15:8 *Eglaim.* Perhaps near the northern border of Moab. *Beer-elim.* Beer means "well" (cf. Num 21:16). This site may have been close to the southern border.

15:9 *waters of Dimon . . . blood.* The Hebrew for "blood" (*dam*) sounds like "Dimon." This is probably also a wordplay on the name "Dibon" (v. 2), close to the Arnon River. Many Moabites will die in the conflict. *Lions.* A reference to either the Assyrian army (cf. 5:29; Jer 50:17) or actual lions (cf. 13:21–22).

16:1 *Send ye the lamb.* As King Mesha sent 100,000 lambs to King Ahab of Israel each year (see 2 Ki 3:4), so now proud Moab, which has often oppressed Israel, is advised in her crisis to submit to the king in Jerusalem. *Sela.* The naturally fortified capital of the Edomites south of the Dead Sea, situated on a rocky plateau that towers 1,000 feet above the nearby Petra (cf. 42:11). The name means "cliff." The tribute would be sent around the southern end of the Dead Sea. *daughter of Zion.* A personification of Jerusalem and its inhabitants.

16:2 *fords of Arnon.* The women were fleeing south, away from the northern invader.

‡16:3 *Hide the outcasts.* The Moabites are asking Judah for refuge (contrast Ruth 1:1; 1 Sam 22:3–4). *bewray not him . . . wandereth.* A request not to betray those who are fleeing as fugitives.

16:4 *spoiler.* Probably Assyria (see notes on 15:1; 33:1). *extortioner.* Moab.

16:5 *tabernacle of David.* See 9:7; Amos 9:11 and notes. "Tabernacle" (or "tent") equals "dynasty" (see note on 7:2). *Judging . . . and hasting righteousness.* See 11:2–4 and notes. The Messiah is again in view.

16:6 *pride of Moab.* Though a small nation, Moab is proud and defiant like Assyria and Babylon. Cf. 10:12; 14:13; 25:11; Jer 48:42.

Even of his haughtiness, and his pride,
and his wrath:
[b]*But* his lies *shall* not *be* so.
7 Therefore shall Moab [a]howl for Moab,
every one shall howl:
For the foundations [b]of Kir-hareseth
shall ye [1]mourn; surely *they are*
stricken.
8 For [a]the fields of Heshbon languish,
and [b]the vine of Sibmah:
The lords of the heathen have broken
down the principal plants thereof,
They are come *even* unto Jazer, they
wandered *through* the wilderness:
Her branches are [1]stretched out, they
are gone over the sea.
9 Therefore I will bewail with the
weeping of Jazer the vine of Sibmah:
I will water thee *with* my tears,
[a]O Heshbon, and Elealeh:
For [1]the shouting for thy summer
fruits and for thy harvest is fallen.
10 And [a]gladness is taken away, and joy
out of the plentiful field;
And in the vineyards there shall be no
singing, neither shall there be
shouting:
The treaders shall tread out no wine in
their presses;
I have made *their vintage* shouting to
cease.
11 Wherefore [a]my bowels shall sound like
a harp for Moab,
And mine inward parts for Kir-haresh.
12 And it shall come to pass, when it is
seen that Moab is weary on [a]the
high place,
That he shall come to his sanctuary to
pray; but he shall not prevail.

16:6 [b]ch. 28:15
16:7 [1]Or, *mutter* [a]Jer. 48:20 [b]2 Ki. 3:25
16:8 [1]Or, *plucked up* [a]ch. 24:7 [b]ver. 9
16:9 [1]Or, *the alarm is fallen upon, etc.* [a]ch. 15:4
16:10 [a]ch. 24:8; Jer. 48:33
16:11 [a]Jer. 48:36
16:12 [a]ch. 15:2

16:14 [1]Or, *not many* [a]ch. 21:16
17:1 [a]Jer. 49:23; Amos 1:3; Zech. 9:1
17:2 [a]Jer. 7:33
17:3 [a]ch. 7:16; 8:4
17:4 [a]ch. 10:16
17:5 [a]Jer. 51:33
17:6 [a]ch. 24:13

13 This *is* the word that the LORD hath
spoken concerning Moab since that
time.
14 But now the LORD hath spoken, saying,
Within three years, [a]as the years of a
hireling,
And the glory of Moab shall be
contemned, with all *that* great
multitude;
And the remnant *shall be* very small
and [1]feeble.

Crushing of Damascus

17 The [a]burden of Damascus.
Behold, Damascus *is* taken away
from *being* a city,
And it shall be a ruinous heap.
2 The cities of Aroer *are* forsaken:
They shall be for flocks,
Which shall lie down, and [a]none shall
make *them* afraid.
3 [a]The fortress also shall cease from
Ephraim,
And the kingdom from Damascus, and
the remnant of Syria:
They shall be as the glory of the
children of Israel, saith the LORD of
hosts.
4 And in that day it shall come to pass,
That the glory of Jacob shall be made
thin,
And [a]the fatness of his flesh shall wax
lean.
5 [a]And it shall be as when the
harvestman gathereth the corn,
And reapeth the ears *with* his arm;
And it shall be as he that gathereth
ears in the valley of Rephaim.
6 [a]Yet gleaning grapes shall be left in it,
as the shaking of an olive tree,

‡16:7 *Kir-hareseth.* See note on 15:1. The four cities in vv. 7–8 appear in inverted (chiastic) order in vv. 9–11.

‡16:8 *Heshbon.* See note on 15:4. *Sibmah.* Perhaps three miles west of Heshbon. See Jer 48:32. *principal plants.* Or "choice vines." The poet shifts to a metaphor, comparing Moab to a vineyard (see 5:1–7). He returns to a literal description again in v. 10. *Jazer.* Possibly located about 15 miles north of the Dead Sea. *wilderness.* On the eastern edge of Moab. *branches are stretched out.* This is hyperbole, as in Ps 80:11, where Israel is the vineyard. *sea.* Probably the Dead Sea.

16:9–11 *I . . . I . . . I . . . my . . . mine inward parts.* The Lord (and/or Isaiah) weeps and laments over the destruction brought on proud Moab to humble her.

16:9 *Elealeh.* See note on 15:4.

16:10 *treaders shall tread.* The grapes were trampled on, and the juice flowed into the wine vat (see note on 5:2; cf. Jer 48:33; Amos 9:13).

16:11 Cf. Jer 48:36.

16:12 *high place.* See 15:2 and note. *pray . . . not prevail.* Moab's god, Chemosh, was a mere idol (see 44:17–20; 1 Ki 11:7).

16:13–14 An epilogue to 15:1–16:12.

16:14 *Within three years.* Other signs that have a three-year limit are given in 20:3; 37:30; see also notes on 7:14,16. Moab's three years were over by c. 715 B.C. (see note on 15:1). *hireling.* Cf. 21:16–17, where the prophecy against Kedar follows the pattern of this verse.

17:1–14 See Jer 49:23–27; Amos 1:3–5.

17:1 *burden.* See note on 13:1. *Damascus.* The capital of Aram (Syria), located northeast of mount Hermon on strategic trade routes between Mesopotamia, Egypt and Arabia. Since the time of David, the Arameans of Damascus were frequent enemies of Israel (see 2 Sam 8:5; 1 Ki 22:31).

17:2 *Aroer.* About 14 miles east of the Dead Sea on the Arnon River. It marked the southern boundary of Aram's sphere of control (see 2 Ki 10:32–33).

17:3 *Ephraim.* The northern kingdom (see note on 7:2) is mentioned here because of its alliance with Damascus against Assyria (see note on 7:1). *kingdom.* In 732 B.C. Tiglath-pileser III captured Damascus and made it an Assyrian province. Many of the cities of Israel were also captured (see note on 9:1).

17:4–11 The prophet shifts from Damascus to Israel (likely the northern kingdom)—a shift prepared for at the end of v. 3. This association of judgment on Damascus and Israel reflects the same linkage as that in ch. 7.

17:4,7,9 *that day.* See notes on 2:11,17,20; 10:20,27.

17:5 *reapeth the ears.* Harvest can signify a time of judgment (see Joel 3:13). *valley of Rephaim.* A fertile area southwest of Jerusalem (Josh 15:8) and the scene of Philistine raids (1 Chr 14:9).

Two *or* three berries in the top of the
uppermost bough,
Four *or* five in the outmost fruitful
branches thereof,
Saith the LORD God of Israel.
7 At that day shall a man [a]look to his
Maker,
And his eyes shall have respect to the
Holy One of Israel.
8 And he shall not look to the altars, the
work of his hands,
Neither shall respect *that* which his
fingers have made,
Either the groves, or the [1]images.
9 In that day shall his strong cities be
As a forsaken bough, and an uppermost
branch,
Which they left because of the children
of Israel:
And there shall be desolation.
10 Because thou hast forgotten [a]the God
of thy salvation,
And hast not been mindful of the rock
of thy strength,
Therefore shalt thou plant pleasant
plants,
And shalt set it *with* strange slips:
11 In the day shalt thou make thy plant to
grow,
And in the morning shalt thou make
thy seed to flourish:
But the harvest *shall be* [1]a heap in the
day of grief and of desperate sorrow.

12 Woe to the [1]multitude of many people,
Which make a noise [a]like the noise of
the seas;
And to the rushing of nations,
That make a rushing like the rushing of
[2]mighty waters.
13 The nations shall rush like the rushing
of many waters:
But *God* shall [a]rebuke them, and they
shall flee far off,
And [b]shall be chased as the chaff of the
mountains before the wind,
And like [1]a rolling thing before the
whirlwind.
14 And behold at eveningtide trouble;
And before the morning he *is* not.
This *is* the portion of them that
spoil us,
And the lot of them that rob us.

An oracle about Ethiopia

18 Woe [a]to the land shadowing with
wings,
Which *is* beyond the rivers of Ethiopia:
2 That sendeth ambassadors by the sea,
Even in vessels of bulrushes upon the
waters, *saying,*
Go, ye swift messengers,
To [a]a nation [1]scattered and peeled,
To a people terrible from their
beginning hitherto;
[2][3]A nation meted out and trodden
down,
[4]Whose land the rivers have spoiled.
3 All ye inhabitants of the world, and
dwellers on the earth,
See ye, [a]when *he* lifteth up an ensign
on the mountains;
And when *he* bloweth a trumpet,
hear ye.

17:7 [a]Mic. 7:7
17:8 [1]Or, *sun images*
17:10 [a]Ps. 68:19
17:11 [1]Or, *removed in the day of inheritance, and* there shall be *deadly sorrow*
17:12 [1]Or, *noise* [a]Jer. 6:23
17:12 [2]Or, *many*
17:13 [1]Or, *thistledown* [a]Ps. 9:5 [b]Ps. 88:13; Hos. 13:3
18:1 [a]ch. 20:4,5; Ezek. 30:4,5,9; Zeph. 2:12; 3:10
18:2 [1]Or, *outspread and polished* [2]Or, *A nation that meteth out, and treadeth down* [3]Heb. *A nation of line, line, and treading under foot* [4]Or, *Whose land the rivers despise* [a]ver. 7
18:3 [a]ch. 5:26

17:7–8 Cf. 2:20; 10:20.
17:7 *Holy One of Israel.* See note on 1:4.
‡17:8 *altars.* Probably altars for Baal (cf. 1 Ki 16:32). *groves.* Lit. "Asherim" ("sacred tree"), wooden symbols of the goddess Asherah; see notes on Ex 34:13; Judg 2:13. *images.* Or "incense altars," associated with high places in Lev 26:30 and with altars for Baal in 2 Chr 34:4.
17:9 *forsaken bough . . . uppermost branch.* Cf. 7:23–25. *they.* Perhaps the Canaanites, whose religious practices are referred to in v. 8.
‡17:10–11 Moves from speaking about Israel in v. 9 to speaking to Israel in vv. 10–11. Israel is the nation that has "forgotten" their God and "not been mindful" of the Lord. *the rock.* See 26:4; 30:29; 44:8; Deut 32:4,15,18; Ps 19:14. *pleasant plants . . . strange slips.* For Israel as a vineyard, cf. 5:7:18:5; 37:30–31. The planting of "strange slips" (imported vines) probably refers to how Israel has been corrupted as God's vineyard through the worship of foreign gods.
17:11 *grief and . . . desperate sorrow.* Brought by the Assyrian invasions.
17:12–14 The same sequence of a powerful invader that is quickly cut down occurs in 10:28–34. Both passages may refer to Sennacherib's invasion of 701 B.C. (see 37:36–37). But it is more likely that the prophet here speaks more generally of Israel's experience of the world of nations as a perpetual threat to her existence.
‡17:12 *noise of the seas . . . rushing of nations.* "Noise" and "rushing" are from the same Hebrew verb (*hamah*). See Ps 46:3,5, which states that Zion is secure even as the seas "roar" and the nations "rage." The churning sea represents the forces of evil and chaos that oppose God and his people. The underlying promise here is that the Lord has chosen Zion as his dwelling place (Ps 132:13) and will protect the city from its enemies. Assyria is also called "the waters of the river, strong and many" in 8:7.
‡17:13 *chaff . . . rolling thing.* Symbolic of the enemy also in 29:5; 41:15–16; Ps 83:13. The whirlwind of God's judgment will blow away the enemy armies like chaff and dust.
18:1–7 See Zeph 2:12.
‡18:1 *shadowing with wings.* Either a reference to insects (perhaps locusts) or a figurative description of the armies of Ethiopia or Cush (see 7:18–19). *Ethiopia.* Nubia or ancient Ethiopia (not to be confused with modern Ethiopia, which is located farther to the southeast), south of Egypt. In 715 B.C. a Cushite named Shabako gained control of Egypt and founded the 25th dynasty.
‡18:2 *sea.* Perhaps the Nile River (cf. 19:5; Nah 3:8). *vessels of bulrushes.* Lightweight boats made out of papyrus reeds. See note on Ex 2:3. *Go, ye swift messengers.* With the message contained in vv. 3–6. *nation scattered and peeled.* Lit. "tall and smooth." Probably the peoples of Cush and Egypt. Unlike Semites, they were clean-shaven (see note on Gen 41:14). *rivers.* The Nile and its tributaries.
18:3 *All ye inhabitants of the world.* All the nations arrayed against God's people Israel (see 17:12–14 and note). *ensign.* See 5:26 and note. *trumpet.* Used to summon troops.

4 For so the LORD said unto me,
I will take my rest, and I will [1]consider
in my dwelling place
Like a clear heat [2]upon herbs,
And like a cloud of dew in the heat of
harvest.
5 For afore the harvest, when the bud is
perfect,
And the sour grape is ripening in the
flower,
He shall both cut off the sprigs with
pruning hooks,
And take away *and* cut down the
branches.
6 They shall be left together unto the
fowls of the mountains,
And to the beasts of the earth:
And the fowls shall summer upon them,
And all the beasts of the earth shall
winter upon them.
7 In that time [a]shall the present be
brought unto the LORD of hosts
Of a people [b][1]scattered and peeled,
And from a people terrible from their
beginning hitherto;
A nation meted out and trodden under
foot,
Whose land the rivers have spoiled,
To the place of the name of the LORD of
hosts, the mount Zion.

The doom of Egypt

19 The [a]burden of Egypt.
Behold, the LORD [b]rideth upon a swift
cloud, and shall come *into* Egypt:
And [c]the idols of Egypt shall be moved
at his presence,
And the heart of Egypt shall melt in
the midst of it.
2 And I will [a][1]set the Egyptians against
the Egyptians:
And they shall fight every one against
his brother, and every one against his
neighbour;

18:4 [1]Or, *regard my set dwelling* [2]Or, *after rain*
18:7 [1]Or, *outspread and polished, etc.* [a]See Ps. 68:31; 72:10; ch. 16:1; Zeph. 3:10; Mal. 1:11 [b]ver. 2
19:1 [a]Jer. 46:13; Ezek. 29; 30 [b]Ps. 18:10; 104:3 [c]Ex. 12:12; Jer. 43:12
19:2 [1]Heb. *mingle* [a]Judg. 7:22; 1 Sam. 14:16,20; 2 Chr. 20:23
19:3 [1]Heb. *shall be emptied* [2]Heb. *swallow up* [a]ch. 8:19; 47:12
19:4 [1]Or, *shut up* [a]ch. 20:4; Jer. 46:26; Ezek. 29:19
19:5 [a]Jer. 51:36; Ezek. 30:12
19:6 [a]2 Ki. 19:24
19:7 [1]Heb. *and shall not be*
19:9 [1]Or, *white works* [a]1 Ki. 10:28; Prov. 7:16
19:10 [1]Heb. *foundations* [2]Heb. *of living things*
19:11 [a]Num. 13:22

City against city, *and* kingdom against
kingdom.
3 And the spirit of Egypt [1]shall fail in the
midst thereof;
And I will [2]destroy the counsel
thereof:
And they shall [a]seek to the idols, and
to the charmers,
And to them that have familiar spirits,
and to the wizards.
4 And the Egyptians will I [1]give over
[a]into the hand of a cruel lord;
And a fierce king shall rule over them,
Saith the Lord, the LORD of hosts.
5 [a]And the waters shall fail from the sea,
And the river shall be wasted and dried
up.
6 And they shall turn the rivers far away;
And the brooks [a]of defence shall be
emptied and dried up:
The reeds and flags shall wither.
7 The paper reeds by the brooks, by the
mouth of the brooks,
And every thing sown by the brooks,
Shall wither, be driven away, [1]and *be*
no *more.*
8 The fishers also shall mourn,
And all they that cast angle into the
brooks shall lament,
And they that spread nets upon the
waters shall languish.
9 Moreover they that work in [a]fine flax,
And they that weave [1]networks, shall
be confounded.
10 And they shall be broken *in* the
[1]purposes thereof,
All that make sluces *and* ponds [2]for
fish.
11 Surely the princes of [a]Zoan *are* fools,
The counsel of the wise counsellers of
Pharaoh is become brutish:
How say ye unto Pharaoh, I *am* the son
of the wise,

‡18:4 *I will take my rest . . . I will consider.* The Lord responds thoughtfully and deliberately. In the face of the hostility of the nations, the Lord will not act immediately; but when they are in the full growth of summer (v. 5), He will cut them down. *Like a clear heat upon herbs.* Or "like a dazzling heat caused by the sunlight."
18:6 *fowls of the mountains . . . beasts of the earth.* Cf. 56:9; Jer 7:33; Ezek 32:4; 39:17–20.
18:7 See v. 2. *present.* According to 2 Chr 32:23 gifts were brought to Hezekiah after Sennacherib's death. The Moabites were asked to send tribute to mount Zion in 16:1 (cf. 45:14; Zeph 3:10). *place of the name.* See Deut 12:5 and note.
19:1–20:6 See Jer 46; Ezek 29–32.
19:1 *burden.* See note on 13:1. *rideth upon a swift cloud.* A metaphor used also in Ps 68:4; 104:3; cf. Mat 26:64. *idols . . . be moved.* See Jer 50:2. God had also previously judged Egypt's idols during the ten plagues (see Ex 12:12 and note). *heart . . . melt.* See 13:7.
19:2 *Egyptians against the Egyptians.* Cf. 9:21. The Libyan dynasty clashed with the "Ethiopians" (Cushites; see note on 18:1) and with the Saites of Dynasty 24.
‡19:3 *spirit of Egypt shall fail.* The Egyptians will become demoralized. *seek to . . . wizards.* Spiritists who consult the dead. Israel also did so in desperate times (see 8:19 and note).
19:4 *cruel lord.* The king of Assyria (see 20:4). Esarhaddon conquered Egypt in 670 B.C.
19:5 *waters shall fail from the sea.* The Nile was the lifeline of Egypt; its annual flooding provided essential water and produced the only fertile soil there.
‡19:6 *they shall turn the rivers far away.* Lit. "the rivers (or canals) will stink."
19:7 *every thing sown by the brooks.* Egypt's crops were normally abundant, and some were exported.
19:8 *fishers.* Fish were usually plentiful (see Num 11:5).
‡19:9 *they that work in fine flax.* Large amounts of water were needed to process flax. *networks.* White linen, another well-known Egyptian export.
19:11 *Zoan.* A city (possibly Tanis) in the northeastern part of the Nile delta. It would have been familiar to the Israelites enslaved in Egypt (see Num 13:22; Ps 78:12,43). It was the northern capital for the 25th dynasty (see note on 18:1). *son of the wise.* See v. 12. Egypt was famous for its wise men (see 1 Ki 4:30).

The son of ancient kings?
12 [a]Where *are* they? where *are* thy wise
men?
And let them tell thee now,
And let them know what the LORD of
hosts hath purposed upon Egypt.
13 The princes of Zoan are become fools,
[a]The princes of Noph are deceived;
They have also seduced Egypt, *even*
[1 2]*they that are* the stay of the tribes
thereof.
14 The LORD hath mingled [a 1]a perverse
spirit in the midst thereof:
And they have caused Egypt to err in
every work thereof,
As a drunken *man* staggereth in his
vomit.
15 Neither shall there be *any* work for
Egypt,
Which [a]the head or tail, branch or
rush, may do.
16 In that day shall Egypt [a]be like unto
women:
And it shall be afraid and fear
Because of the shaking of the hand of
the LORD of hosts,
[b]Which he shaketh over it.
17 And the land of Judah shall be a terror
unto Egypt,
Every one that maketh mention thereof
shall be afraid in himself,
Because of the counsel of the LORD of
hosts,
Which he hath determined against it.

19:12 [a]1 Cor. 1:20
19:13 [1]Or, *governors* [2]Heb. *corners* [a]Jer. 2:16
19:14 [1]Heb. *a spirit of perversities* [a]1 Ki. 22:22; ch. 29:10
19:15 [a]ch. 9:14
19:16 [a]Jer. 51:30; Nah. 3:13 [b]ch. 11:15
19:18 [1]Heb. *the lip* [2]Or, *of Heres,* or, *of the sun* [a]Zeph. 3:9
19:19 [a]Gen. 28:18; Ex. 24:4; Josh. 22:10,26, 27
19:20 [a]Josh. 4:20; 22:27
19:21 [a]Mal. 1:11
19:23 [a]ch. 11:16

18 In that day shall five cities in the land
of Egypt
[a]Speak [1]the language of Canaan,
And swear to the LORD of hosts:
One shall be called, The city [2]of
destruction.
19 In that day [a]shall there be an altar to
the LORD in the midst of the land of
Egypt,
And a pillar at the border thereof to
the LORD.
20 And [a]it shall be for a sign and for a
witness unto the LORD of hosts in the
land of Egypt:
For they shall cry unto the LORD
because of the oppressors,
And he shall send them a saviour, and
a great one, and he shall deliver
them.
21 And the LORD shall be known to Egypt,
And the Egyptians shall know the LORD
in that day,
And [a]shall do sacrifice and oblation;
Yea, they shall vow a vow unto the
LORD, and perform *it.*
22 And the LORD shall smite Egypt: *he*
shall smite and heal *it:*
And they shall return *even* to the LORD,
and he shall be intreated of them,
and shall heal them.
23 In that day [a]shall there be a highway
out of Egypt to Assyria,
And the Assyrian shall come into
Egypt, and the Egyptian into Assyria,

‡19:13 *Noph.* Memphis, an important city 15 miles south of the delta that was the capital during the Old Kingdom (c. 2686–2160 B.C.). *they that are the stay of the tribes.* Prophets and priests, as well as political leaders (see 9:15–16).
‡19:14 *mingled a perverse spirit . . . As a drunken man staggereth.* The Lord has caused their leaders to stumble and stagger like drunks. Israel's leaders stagger in 28:7–8.
19:15 *head or tail, branch or rush.* Egypt's leaders. The same two pairs are used of Israel's leaders in 9:14–15.
19:16–25 A chain of four announcements of coming events associated with "that day": 1. An act of divine judgment will cause Egypt to "be afraid and fear" (v. 16) and be in terror of Judah (vv. 16–17). 2. "Five cities" in Egypt will "swear" an oath of loyalty to the Lord (v. 18). 3. Because of a divine act of deliverance and healing in Egypt, an altar will be erected in Egypt where Egyptians will offer sacrifices to the Lord (vv. 19–22). 4. Egypt, Assyria and Israel will be linked into one people of the Lord (vv. 23–25). The prophet looks well beyond the present realities in which the world powers do not acknowledge the true God and proudly pursue their own destinies, running roughshod over the people of the Lord. He foresees a series of divine acts that will bring about the conversion of the nations.
19:16,18–19,23–24 *In that day.* The coming day of the Lord (see 10:20,27 and note; cf. 11:10–11).
19:16 *be afraid and fear.* Like the people of Jericho (Josh 2:9,11). *shaking of the hand of the LORD of hosts.* See 14:26–27 and note.
19:17 *land of Judah.* The Egyptians will somehow recognize (perhaps through court contacts with Hezekiah) that it is the God of Judah who has brought judgment upon them.
19:18 *five.* Perhaps in the sense of "many." *Speak the language of Canaan.* Either a symbolic reference to Egypt's allegiance to the Lord (see vv. 21–22,25) or a literal reference to Jews living in Egypt. After the fall of Jerusalem in 586 B.C., many Jews fled to Egypt (Jer 44:1). *city of destruction.* Probably a reference to Heliopolis, city of the sun-god; it was destroyed by Nebuchadnezzar (see Jer 43:12–13). The Hebrew for "destruction" is almost identical to the Hebrew for "sun."
19:19 *altar.* Some relate this to the temple built in Egypt by the Jewish high priest Onias IV, who fled to Egypt in the second century B.C., but the reference appears to be to a conversion to the Lord of a significant number of Egyptians.
19:20 *sign and for a witness.* Cf. the purpose of the altar built by the tribes east of the Jordan River in Josh 22:26–27. *oppressors . . . saviour.* The language of the book of Judges (see Judg 2:18). The "saviour" is the promised Son of the house of David (see 11:1–10).
19:21 *the LORD shall be known.* Cf. Ex 7:5. *shall do sacrifice.* Offerings of foreigners are also mentioned in 56:7; 60:7 (cf. Zech 14:16–19).
19:22 *smite Egypt.* Oppression (see v. 20) and plague were two common forms of divine affliction. Contrast the results of the plague on the firstborn in Ex 12:23. *shall be intreated . . . heal.* Cf. 6:10; here parallel to sending Egypt a "saviour, and a great one" (v. 20). Earlier a hardhearted pharaoh had not turned to the Lord (Ex 9:34–35).
19:23 *highway.* Cf. the highway to Jerusalem in 11:16 (see note there). For centuries Egyptians and Assyrians had fought each other (see 20:4), but in the future they would be linked in a bond of friendship sealed by their common allegiance to the Lord (cf. 25:3). *serve with.* This description of peace and of unity in worship is similar to 2:2–4 (see note there; see also note on v. 21).

And the Egyptians shall serve *with* the
Assyrians.
24 In that day shall Israel be the third
with Egypt and with Assyria,
Even a blessing in the midst of the land:
25 Whom the LORD of hosts shall bless,
saying,
Blessed *be* Egypt my people,
And Assyria [a]the work of my hands,
And Israel mine inheritance.

20 In the year that [a]Tartan came unto
Ashdod, (when Sargon the king of
Assyria sent him,) and fought against Ashdod,
and took it;
2 At the same time spake the LORD [1]by Isaiah the son of Amoz, saying,
Go and loose [a]the sackcloth from off
thy loins,
And put off thy shoe from thy foot.

¶ And he did so, [b]walking naked and barefoot.
3 And the LORD said,
Like as my servant Isaiah hath walked
naked and barefoot
Three years [a]*for* a sign and wonder
Upon Egypt and upon Ethiopia;
4 So shall the king of Assyria lead away
[1]the Egyptians prisoners, and the
Ethiopians captives,
Young and old, naked and barefoot,
[a]Even with *their* buttocks uncovered,
To the [2]shame of Egypt.
5 [a]And they shall be afraid and ashamed
of Ethiopia their expectation,
And of Egypt their glory.

19:25 [a]Ps. 100:3; ch. 29:23; Hos. 2:23; Eph. 2:10
20:1 [a]2 Ki. 18:17
20:2 [1]Heb. *by the hand of Isaiah* [a]Zech. 13:4 [b]1 Sam. 19:24; Mic. 1:8,11
20:3 [a]ch. 8:18
20:4 [1]Heb. *the captivity of Egypt* [2]Heb. *nakedness* [a]2 Sam. 10:4; ch. 3:17; Jer. 13:22; Mic. 1:11
20:5 [a]2 Ki. 18:21
20:6 [1]Or, *country*
21:1 [a]Zech. 9:14
21:2 [1]Heb. *hard* [a]ch. 33:1 [b]ch. 13:17; Jer. 49:34
21:3 [a]ch. 15:5; 16:11 [b]ch. 13:8
21:4 [1]Or, *My mind wandered* [2]Heb. *put* [a]Deut. 28:67
21:5 [a]Dan. 5:5
21:7 [a]ver. 9

6 And the inhabitant of this [1]isle shall
say in that day,
Behold, such *is* our expectation,
Whither we flee for help
To be delivered from the king of Assyria:
And how shall we escape?

Elam and Media defeat Babylon

21 The burden of the desert of the sea.
As [a]whirlwinds in the south pass
through;
So it cometh from the desert, from a
terrible land.
2 A [1]grievous vision is declared unto me;
[a]The treacherous dealer dealeth
treacherously, and the spoiler spoileth.
[b]Go up, O Elam: besiege, O Media;
All the sighing thereof have I made to
cease.
3 Therefore [a]are my loins filled *with* pain:
[b]Pangs have taken hold upon me, as
the pangs of a woman that travaileth:
I was bowed down at the hearing *of it;*
I was dismayed at the seeing *of it.*
4 [1]My heart panted, fearfulness
affrighted me:
[a]The night of my pleasure hath he
[2]turned into fear unto me.
5 [a]Prepare the table, watch *in* the
watchtower, eat, drink:
Arise, ye princes, *and* anoint the shield.
6 For thus hath the Lord said unto me,
Go, set a watchman,
Let him declare what he seeth.
7 [a]And he saw a chariot *with* a couple of
horsemen,
A chariot of asses, *and* a chariot of
camels;

19:25 *shall bless.* A fulfillment of Gen 12:3. *Egypt my people.* Such a universal vision seems possible for Isaiah only in the light of what has been said about the "rod out of the stem of Jesse" (11:1; see 11:1–10). Cf. 45:14; Eph 2:11–13.
20:1–6 An epilogue to chs. 18–19, as 16:13–14 is to 15:1–16:12.
20:1 *the year.* Probably 712 B.C. *Tartan.* Refers to Sargon II, who reigned 721–705 B.C. He is mentioned by name only here in the OT. *Ashdod.* One of the five Philistine cities (see map, p. 313), Ashdod was located near the Mediterranean Sea about 18 miles northeast of Gaza. The city had rebelled against Assyria in 713 under King Azuri. In 1963 three fragments of an Assyrian monument commemorating Sargon's victory and mentioning Sargon by name were discovered at Ashdod.
20:2 *sackcloth.* Normally the garment of mourners (see note on 15:3), but perhaps also the usual garb of prophets (see 2 Ki 1:8; Zech 13:4).
20:3 *my servant.* A title for prophets and others used by God in a special way. *Three years.* See 16:14 and note. *sign and wonder.* See 8:18; see also 7:3,14 and notes. The prophet Ezekiel's behavior also had symbolic significance (Ezek 24:24,27; cf. Zech 3:8). *Egypt . . . Ethiopia.* See 18:1; 19:1.
20:4 *naked and barefoot.* Cf. 2 Chr 28:15; Mic 1:8.
20:5 *Ethiopia their expectation . . . Egypt their glory.* After Assyria conquered the northern kingdom of Israel in 722–721 B.C., King Hezekiah of Judah was under great pressure to make an alliance with Egypt. Isaiah urgently warned against such a policy (cf. 30:1–2; 31:1).

‡21:1 *burden.* See note on 13:1. *desert.* The coming judgment would eventually turn Babylon (see v. 9) into a wasteland (cf. 13:20–22). *the sea.* Refers either to the Persian Gulf, which was just south of Babylon, or to the alluvial plain deposited by the Euphrates and Tigris rivers and their tributaries. *whirlwinds . . . desert.* The wilderness sometimes spawns powerful winds (see Hos 13:15).
‡21:2 *treacherous dealer . . . spoiler spoileth.* Refers to Babylon who has attacked and plundered other nations. *Elam.* See note on 11:11. The Elamites were a perpetual enemy of Assyria and Babylon. Much later, they were part of the Persian army that conquered Babylon under Cyrus in 539 B.C. *Media.* See note on 13:17. *All the sighing . . . have I made to cease.* God promises to put an end to the suffering that Babylon has caused the other nations.
21:3 *filled with pain: Pangs have taken hold upon me.* See Daniel's reaction to visions in Dan 8:27; 10:16–17; but see also notes on 29:9–11.
21:4 *night of my pleasure.* Perhaps the end of the Babylonian empire (see note on v. 12). *turned into fear unto me.* The devastation is beyond even what he had desired.
21:5 *eat, drink.* With the kind of confident assurance reflected in Belshazzar's feast (see Dan 5:1). *Arise.* Rhetorically the prophet, who has seen in a vision the coming attack on Babylon, calls on the officers of Babylon to prepare. *anoint the shield.* See note on 2 Sam 1:21.
21:6 *Go, set a watchman.* Probably on the walls of Jerusalem.
21:7 *chariot . . . asses . . . camels.* Bearing messengers from afar.

And he hearkened diligently *with*
much heed:
8 And [1]he cried, A lion:
My lord, I stand continually upon the
[a]watchtower in the daytime,
And I *am* set in my ward [2]whole nights:
9 And behold, here cometh a chariot of
men, *with* a couple of horsemen.
And he answered and said,
[a]Babylon is fallen, is fallen;
And [b]all the graven images of her gods
he hath broken unto the ground.
10 [a]O my threshing, and the [1]corn of my
floor:
That which I have heard of the LORD of
hosts, the God of Israel,
Have I declared unto you.

11 ¶ [a]The burden of Dumah.
He calleth to me out of Seir,
Watchman, what of the night?
Watchman, what of the night?
12 The watchman said,
The morning cometh, and also the night:
If ye will inquire, inquire ye:
Return, come.

13 ¶ [a]The burden upon Arabia.
In the forest in Arabia shall ye lodge,
O ye travelling companies [b]of Dedanim.
14 The inhabitants of the land of Tema
[1]brought water to him that was thirsty,
They prevented with their bread him
that fled.
15 For they fled [1][2]from the swords,
From the drawn sword, and from the
bent bow,
And from the grievousness of war.

21:8 [1]Or, *cried as a lion* [2]Or, *every night* [a]Hab. 2:1
21:9 [a]Jer. 51:8; Rev. 14:8; 18:2 [b]ch. 46:1; Jer. 50:2; 51:44
21:10 [1]Heb. *son* [a]Jer. 51:33
21:11 [a]1 Chr. 1:30; Jer. 49:7,8; Ezek. 35:2; Obad. 1
21:13 [a]Jer. 49:28 [b]1 Chr. 1:9
21:14 [1]Or, *bring ye*
21:15 [1]Or, *for fear* [2]Heb. *from the face*
21:16 [a]ch. 16:14 [b]Ps. 120:5; ch. 60:7
21:17 [1]Heb. *bows*
22:2 [a]ch. 32:13
22:3 [1]Heb. *of the bow*
22:4 [1]Heb. *I will be bitter in weeping* [a]Jer. 4:19
22:5 [a]ch. 37:3 [b]Lam. 1:5
22:6 [1]Heb. *made naked* [a]Jer. 49:35 [b]ch. 15:1

16 For thus hath the Lord said unto me,
Within a year, [a]according to the years
of a hireling,
And all the glory of [b]Kedar shall fail:
17 And the residue of the number of
[1]archers,
The mighty *men* of the children of
Kedar, shall be diminished:
For the LORD God of Israel hath spoken
it.

A burden about Jerusalem

22 The burden of the valley of vision.
What aileth thee now, that thou art
wholly gone up to the housetops?
2 Thou *that art* full *of* stirs,
A tumultuous city, [a]a joyous city:
Thy slain *men are* not slain with the
sword,
Nor dead in battle.
3 All thy rulers are fled together, they are
bound [1]by the archers:
All that are found in thee are bound
together, *which* have fled from far.
4 Therefore said I, Look away from me;
[a][1]I will weep bitterly,
Labour not to comfort me, because of
the spoiling of the daughter of my
people.
5 [a]For *it is* a day of trouble, and of
treading down, and of perplexity
[b]By the Lord GOD of hosts in the valley
of vision,
Breaking down the walls, and of crying
to the mountains.
6 [a]And Elam bare the quiver
With chariots of men *and* horsemen,
And [b]Kir [1]uncovered the shield.

‡21:8 *he cried, A lion.* Or "he cried out like a lion" (with a loud voice).
21:9 *Babylon is fallen.* See 13:19. Babylon fell in 689 B.C. and again in 539. These words were adapted by John in Rev 14:8; 18:2. *graven images . . . broken unto the ground.* The fall of a kingdom meant the disgrace of its gods (cf. 46:1–2).
‡21:10 *O my threshing.* Refers to Judah who would be punished by the Babylonians and taken into captivity (see 39:5–7). Threshing was a common metaphor for judgment or destruction from war (see Amos 1:3). *corn of my floor.* Lit. "son of my floor." Parallel to the first part of the line in comparing Judah to threshed grain.
21:11–12 See Jer 49:7–22; Ezek 25:12–14; Amos 1:11–12.
21:11 *burden.* See note on 13:1. *Seir.* A synonym for Edom (Gen 32:3), homeland of Esau's descendants, south of the Dead Sea. Edom is dealt with more extensively in 34:5–15 (cf. 63:1).
21:12 *morning . . . and also the night.* Perhaps meaning that the long night of Assyrian oppression is almost over, but only a short "morning" will precede Babylonian domination.
21:13–17 See Jer 49:28–33.
21:13 *burden.* See note on 13:1. *forest.* The caravans had to hide from the invader (cf. Judg 5:6). The Assyrians began to attack the Arabs in 732 B.C., and the Babylonians did the same under Nebuchadnezzar (see Jer 25:17,23–24). *Dedanim.* An Arabian tribe whose merchant activities are mentioned also in Ezek 27:20; 38:13.
21:14 *Tema.* An oasis in northern Arabia about 400 miles southwest of Babylon (cf. Job 6:19; Jer 25:23).
21:15 *sword . . . bow.* The simple bows of the Arabs were ineffective against the swords and composite bows of Assyria.
21:16 *hireling.* See 16:14 and note. *glory.* See 14:11; 16:14. *Kedar.* The home of Bedouin tribes in the Arabian Desert. Kedar was known for its flocks (60:7; Ezek 27:21). Nebuchadnezzar defeated the people of Kedar (Jer 49:28–29; cf. Jer 2:10).
21:17 *residue . . . shall be diminished.* Cf. 10:19; 16:14; 17:6.
22:1–13 The notes on this prophecy assume that it refers primarily to the final Babylonian siege of Jerusalem in 588–586 B.C. But it is also possible that the primary reference is to the siege by the Assyrian king Sennacherib in 701.
22:1 *burden.* See note on 13:1. *valley of vision.* A valley where God revealed Himself in visions, probably one of the valleys near Jerusalem (see note on v. 7). See also v. 5. *housetops.* See 15:3 and note.
22:2 *tumultuous . . . joyous.* See v. 13; 5:11–12; 32:13. Jerusalem is behaving just like Babylon (see 21:5; cf. 23:7). *not slain with the sword.* Perhaps a reference to death from disease and famine when the Babylonians besieged Jerusalem in 586 B.C.
22:3 *rulers are fled together.* King Zedekiah and his army fled Jerusalem but were captured near Jericho (see 2 Ki 25:4–6).
‡22:5 *it is a day.* The "day of the LORD;" see 2:12 and note on 2:11,17,20. Also cf. "in that day" in vv. 8,12. *trouble . . . perplexity.* Conditions of calamity and confusion, a fulfillment of the curse of Deut 28:20.
22:6 *Elam.* See note on 11:11. Elamites probably fought in the

7 And it shall come to pass, *that* [1]thy
choicest valleys shall be full *of*
chariots,
And the horsemen shall set themselves
in array [2]at the gate.
8 And he discovered the covering of
Judah,
And thou didst look in that day to the
armour [a]of the house of the forest.
9 [a]Ye have seen also the breaches of the
city of David, that they are many:
And ye gathered together the waters of
the lower pool.
10 And ye have numbered the houses of
Jerusalem,
And the houses have ye broken down
to fortify the wall.
11 [a]Ye made also a ditch between the two
walls for the water of the old pool:
But ye have not looked unto the Maker
thereof,
Neither had respect unto him that
fashioned it long ago.
12 And in that day did the Lord GOD of
hosts [a]call to weeping, and to
mourning,
And [b]to baldness, and to girding with
sackcloth:
13 And behold joy and gladness,
Slaying oxen, and killing sheep,
Eating flesh, and drinking wine:
[a]Let us eat and drink; for to morrow
we shall die.
14 [a]And it was revealed in mine ears *by*
the LORD of hosts,
Surely this iniquity [b]shall not be
purged from you till ye die,
Saith the Lord GOD of hosts.

15 ¶ Thus saith the Lord GOD of hosts, Go,
get thee unto this treasurer, *even* unto [a]Sheb-
na, which *is* over the house, *and say,*
16 What hast thou here? and whom hast
thou here,
That thou hast hewed thee out a
sepulchre here,
[1]*As* he [a]that heweth him out a
sepulchre on high,
And that graveth a habitation for
himself in a rock?
17 Behold, [1]the LORD will carry thee away
with [2]a mighty captivity,
[a]And will surely cover thee.
18 He will surely violently turn and toss
thee like a ball
Into a [1]large country:
There shalt thou die,
And there the chariots of thy glory
Shall be the shame of thy lord's house.
19 And I will drive thee from thy station,
And from thy state shall he pull thee
down.
20 And it shall come to pass in that day,
That I will call my servant [a]Eliakim the
son of Hilkiah:
21 And I will clothe him with thy robe,
And strengthen him *with* thy girdle,
And I will commit thy government into
his hand:
And he shall be a father to the
inhabitants of Jerusalem,
And to the house of Judah.
22 And the key of the house of David will
I lay upon his shoulder;
So he shall [a]open, and none shall shut;
And he shall shut, and none shall open.
23 And I will fasten him *as* [a]a nail in a
sure place;

22:7 [1]Heb. *the choice of thy valleys* [2]Or, *towards*
22:8 [a]1 Ki. 7:2; 10:17
22:9 [a]2 Ki. 20:20; 2 Chr. 32:4
22:11 [a]Neh. 3:16
22:12 [a]Joel 1:13 [b]See Ezra 9:3; ch. 15:2; Mic. 1:16
22:13 [a]ch. 56:12; 1 Cor. 15:32
22:14 [a]ch. 5:9 [b]1 Sam. 3:14; Ezek. 24:13
22:15 [a]2 Ki. 18:37; ch. 36:3
22:16 [1]Or, *O he* [a]See 2 Sam. 18:18; Mat. 27:60
22:17 [1]Or, *the LORD who covered thee with an excellent covering, and clothed thee gorgeously,* ver. 18, *shall surely, etc.* [2]Heb. *the captivity of a man* [a]Esth. 7:8
22:18 [1]Heb. *large of spaces*
22:20 [a]2 Ki. 18:18
22:22 [a]Job 12:14
22:23 [a]Ezra 9:8

Babylonian army. *Kir.* Perhaps another name for Media (see 21:2).
22:7 *choicest valleys.* The Kidron Valley lay east of Jerusalem (see John 18:1), the Hinnom Valley to the south and west (see Josh 15:8).
22:8 *house of the forest.* Built by King Solomon out of cedars from Lebanon (see 1 Ki 7:2–6; 10:17,21).
22:9 *city of David.* See 2 Sam 5:6–7,9. *lower pool.* Probably the same as the "old pool" of v. 11. Hezekiah made a pool and a tunnel as a precaution against Sennacherib's invasion (see 2 Ki 20:20). The "upper pool" is mentioned in 7:3; 36:2.
22:10 *fortify the wall.* Cf. Hezekiah's preparations in 2 Chr 32:5.
22:11 *ye have not looked unto the Maker.* In 31:1 those who look to horses and chariots rather than to God are similarly condemned.
22:12 *baldness.* The hair was either torn out or shaved off (cf. Jer 16:6; Ezek 27:31).
‡22:13 *joy and gladness.* The people of Jerusalem were celebrating that they had avoided destruction, but this was supposed to be a time to mourn over their sins (Eccl 3:4). See note on v. 2.
‡22:15 *Shebna.* Apparently a foreigner, possibly Egyptian; a contemporary of King Hezekiah. *over the house.* The official in charge of the royal house, a position second only to the king (see note on v. 21; cf. 36:3; 1 Ki 4:6; 2 Ki 15:5).
22:16 *hewed thee out a sepulchre.* One's place of burial was considered very important, and Shebna coveted a tomb worthy of a king (cf. 2 Chr 16:14).
‡22:17 *the LORD will carry . . . captivity.* Lit. "the Lord will violently hurl you, O mighty man." Shebna will not be buried in his tomb because the Lord is going to violently cast him out of the city of Jerusalem; cf. Jer 22:24–26.
‡22:18 *turn and toss thee like a ball.* Repeats idea of previous verse—the Lord will wad Shebna into a ball and throw him out of the city. *There shalt thou die.* Apparently without an honorable burial (see note on 14:19). *chariots.* A sign of luxury and high office (see 2:7; Gen 41:43).
22:20 *in that day.* When the Lord acts in judgment (see vv. 17–19). *my servant.* See note on 20:3. *Eliakim.* See 36:3,11,22; 37:2.
22:21 *commit thy government into his hand.* By 701 B.C. (see 36:3) Eliakim had replaced Shebna, who was demoted to "scribe."
22:22 Quoted in part in Rev 3:7. The mention of "father" (v. 21) and of the responsibility "upon his shoulder" recalls the words about the Messiah in 9:6. *key of the house of David.* The authority delegated to him by the king, who belongs to David's dynasty—perhaps controlling entrance into the royal palace. Cf. the "keys of the kingdom" given to Peter (Mat 16:19).
‡22:23 *nail.* Or "peg." Normally the Hebrew for this word refers to a tent peg, but here to a peg driven into wood (see Ezek 15:3). *glorious throne.* Cf. 1 Sam 2:8.

And he shall be for a glorious throne to
his father's house.
24 And they shall hang upon him all the
glory of his father's house,
The offspring and the issue,
All vessels of small quantity,
From the vessels of cups, even to all
the [1]vessels of flagons.
25 In that day, saith the LORD of hosts,
Shall the nail that is fastened in the
sure place be removed,
And be cut down, and fall;
And the burden that *was* upon it shall
be cut off:
For the LORD hath spoken *it.*

A burden about Tyre

23 The [a]burden of Tyre.
Howl, ye ships of Tarshish;
For it is laid waste, so that *there is* no
house, no entering in:
[b]From the land of Chittim it is revealed
to them.
2 Be [1]still, ye inhabitants of the isle;
Thou whom the merchants of Zidon,
that pass over the sea, have
replenished.
3 And by great waters the seed of Sihor,
The harvest of the river, *is* her
revenue;
And [a]she is a mart of nations.
4 Be thou ashamed, O Zidon: for the sea
hath spoken,
Even the strength of the sea, saying,
I travail not, nor bring forth children,
Neither do I nourish up young men,
nor bring up virgins.
5 [a]As *at* the report concerning Egypt,
So shall they be sorely pained *at* the
report of Tyre.
6 Pass ye over to Tarshish; howl, ye
inhabitants of the isle.
7 *Is* this your [a]joyous *city,* whose
antiquity *is* of ancient days?
Her own feet shall carry her [1]afar off to
sojourn.
8 Who hath taken this counsel against
Tyre, [a]the crowning *city,*
Whose merchants *are* princes, whose
traffickers *are* the honourable of the
earth?
9 The LORD of hosts hath purposed it,
[1]To stain the pride of all glory,
And to bring into contempt all the
honourable of the earth.
10 Pass through thy land as a river,
O daughter of Tarshish:
There is no more [1]strength.
11 He stretched out his hand over the sea,
he shook the kingdoms:
The LORD hath given a commandment
[1]against [2]the merchant *city,* to
destroy the [3]strong holds thereof.
12 And he said, [a]Thou shalt no more
rejoice,
O thou oppressed virgin, daughter of
Zidon:
Arise, [b]pass over *to* Chittim;
There also shalt thou have no rest.
13 Behold the land of the Chaldeans;
This people was not,
Till the Assyrian founded it for [a]them
that dwell in the wilderness:
They set up the towers thereof,
They raised up the palaces thereof;
And he brought it to ruin.
14 Howl, ye ships of Tarshish: for your
strength is laid waste.
15 And it shall come to pass in that day,

22:24 [1]Or, *instruments of viols*
23:1 [a]Jer. 25:22; 47:4; Ezek. 26; 27; 28; Amos 1:9; Zech. 9:2,4 [b]ver. 12
23:2 [1]Heb. *silent*
23:3 [a]Ezek. 27:3
23:5 [a]ch. 19:16
23:7 [1]Heb. *from afar off* [a]ch. 22:2
23:8 [a]See Ezek. 28:2,12
23:9 [1]Heb. *To pollute*
23:10 [1]Heb. *girdle*
23:11 [1]Or, *concerning a merchantman* [2]Heb. *Canaan* [3]Or, *strengths*
23:12 [a]Rev. 18:22 [b]ver. 1
23:13 [a]Ps. 72:9

22:25 *In that day.* Another (unspecified) day when the Lord will come in judgment. *nail . . . be removed.* Eliakim, like Shebna, will eventually fall from power.
23:1–18 See Ezek 26:1–28:19; Amos 1:9–10.
‡23:1 *burden.* See note on 13:1. *Tyre.* The main seaport along the Phoenician coast, about 35 miles north of mount Carmel. Part of the city was built on two rocky islands about half a mile from the shore. King Hiram of Tyre supplied cedars and craftsmen for the temple (see 1 Ki 5:8–9) and sailors for Solomon's commercial fleet (1 Ki 9:27). *Howl, ye ships.* See v. 14. *ships of Tarshish.* Trading ships (see note on 2:16). *laid waste.* Fulfilled through Assyria, Nebuchadnezzar and Alexander. Nebuchadnezzar captured the mainland city in 572 B.C. (see Ezek 26:7–11), but the island fortress was not taken until Alexander the Great destroyed it in 332 (cf. Ezek 26:3–5). *Chittim.* Cyprus, an island that had close ties with Tyre (see Ezek 27:6).
23:2,4,12 *Zidon.* Sidon; see Ezek 28:20–26, the other prominent Phoenician city, about 25 miles north of Tyre.
23:2 *merchants . . . replenished.* Tyre's commercial ventures affected the entire Mediterranean world (see vv. 3,8).
‡23:3 *Sihor.* Appears to refer to the easternmost branch of the Nile River (cf. Josh 13:3; Jer 2:18). *harvest of the river.* See 19:7 and note.
23:4 *the strength of the sea.* Tyre (see note on v. 1). *travail . . . bring forth children.* Contrast 54:1.
23:6 *Tarshish.* Perhaps Tartessus in Spain (see Jonah 1:3 and note), or an island in the western Mediterranean, or a site on the coast of North Africa.
‡23:7 *joyous.* See note on 22:2. *antiquity . . . ancient days.* Tyre was founded before 2000 B.C. *Her own feet . . . sojourn.* Lit. "her own feet carried her to sojourn afar off." Refers to Tyre's colonization of distant lands. Carthage in North Africa was a colony of Tyre. Tarshish may have been another.
23:8–9 *purposed.* See 14:24,26–27; 25:1.
23:8 *the crowning city.* Tyre crowned kings in her colonies. *traffickers are . . . honourable.* See Ezek 28:4–5.
23:9 *pride of all glory.* See Ezek 27:3–4.
23:10 *daughter of Tarshish.* A personification of Tarshish and its inhabitants.
‡23:11 *stretched out his hand.* See note on 14:26–27. *merchant city.* Lit. "Canaan," here roughly the same as modern Lebanon.
23:12 *oppressed.* Sidon was captured by Esarhaddon in the seventh century B.C. and later by Nebuchadnezzar c. 587 (cf. Jer 25:22). *virgin, daughter of Zidon.* See note on v. 10.
23:13 *the Assyrian.* Sennacherib destroyed the city of Babylon in 689 B.C. Phoenicia would look like the Babylon of that time. *them that dwell . . . wilderness.* Cf. 13:21. *towers.* See note on 2 Ki 25:1.
23:14 See v. 1 and note.

That Tyre shall be forgotten seventy
years,
According to the days of one king:
After the end of seventy years [1] shall
Tyre sing as a harlot.
16 Take a harp, go about the city, thou
harlot that hast been forgotten;
Make sweet melody, sing many songs,
that thou mayest be remembered.
17 And it shall come to pass after the end
of seventy years,
That the LORD will visit Tyre,
And she shall turn to her hire,
And [a] shall commit fornication with all
the kingdoms of the world
Upon the face of the earth.
18 And her merchandise and her hire
[a] shall be holiness to the LORD:
It shall not be treasured nor laid up;
For her merchandise shall be for them
that dwell before the LORD,
To eat sufficiently, and for [1] durable
clothing.

Judgment for universal sin

24 Behold, the LORD maketh the earth
empty, and maketh it waste,
And [1] turneth it upside down, and
scattereth abroad the inhabitants
thereof.
2 And it shall be, as *with* the people, so
with the [a] [1] priest;
As *with* the servant, so *with* his master;
As *with* the maid, so *with* her mistress;
[b] As *with* the buyer, so *with* the seller;
As *with* the lender, so *with* the
borrower;
As *with* the taker of usury, so *with* the
giver of usury to him.
3 The land shall be utterly emptied, and
utterly spoiled:
For the LORD hath spoken this word.
4 The earth mourneth *and* fadeth away,
The world languisheth *and* fadeth away,
[1] The haughty people of the earth do
languish.
5 [a] The earth also is defiled under the
inhabitants thereof;
Because they have transgressed the
laws, changed the ordinance,
Broken the everlasting covenant.
6 Therefore hath [a] the curse devoured
the earth,
And they that dwell therein are
desolate:
Therefore the inhabitants of the earth
are burned,
And few men left.
7 [a] The new wine mourneth, the vine
languisheth,
All the merryhearted do sigh.
8 The mirth [a] of tabrets ceaseth, the
noise of them that rejoice endeth,
The joy of the harp ceaseth.
9 They shall not drink wine with a song;
Strong drink shall be bitter to them
that drink it.
10 The city of confusion is broken down:
Every house is shut up, that no *man*
may come in.
11 *There is* a crying for wine in the streets;
All joy is darkened,
The mirth of the land is gone.
12 In the city is left desolation,
And the gate is smitten *with*
destruction.
13 When thus it shall be in the midst of
the land among the people,
[a] *There shall be* as the shaking of an
olive tree,
And as the gleaning grapes when the
vintage is done.
14 They shall lift up their voice, they shall
sing,
For the majesty of the LORD, they shall
cry aloud from the sea.
15 Wherefore glorify ye the LORD in the
[1] fires,

23:15 [1] Heb. *it shall be unto Tyre as the song of a harlot*
23:17 [a] Rev. 17:2
23:18 [1] Heb. *old* [a] Zech. 14:20,21
24:1 [1] Heb. *perverteth the face thereof*
24:2 [1] Or, *prince* [a] Hos. 4:9 [b] Ezek. 7:12,13
24:4 [1] Heb. *The height of the people*
24:5 [a] Gen. 3:17; Num. 35:33
24:6 [a] Mal. 4:6
24:7 [a] ch. 16:8,9; Joel 1:10,12
24:8 [a] Jer. 7:34; 16:9; 25:10; Ezek. 26:13; Hos. 2:11; Rev. 18:22
24:13 [a] ch. 17:5,6
24:15 [1] Or, *valleys*

23:15 *seventy years.* Also the length of the Babylonian captivity (see Jer 25:11; 29:10), and the length of time Sennacherib decreed that Babylon should remain devastated.
23:16 Cf. Prov 7:10–15.
‡23:17 *her hire.* The wages of a prostitute. A "harlot" nation was one that sought to make the highest profits, regardless of the means. Self-gratification was the key (cf. Rev 17:5).
‡23:18 *holiness to the LORD.* Devoted to the Lord. The earnings of a prostitute could not be given to the Lord (Deut 23:18), but the silver and gold of a city devoted to destruction (see note on Deut 2:34) were placed in the Lord's treasury (see Josh 6:17,19; cf. Mic 4:13). *for them.* Israel will one day receive the wealth of the nations (see note on 18:7; cf. 60:5–11; 61:6).
‡24:1–27:13 Chs. 24–27 deal with apocalyptic judgment and blessing in the last days, the time of God's final victory over the forces of evil. These chapters form a conclusion to chs. 13–23 just as chs. 34–35 form a conclusion to chs. 28–33.
24:1 *maketh the earth empty.* Cf. 2:10,19,21; see also 13:13 and note. *scattereth abroad the inhabitants.* See Gen 11:9.
24:2 Social distinctions will provide no escape from the judgment (cf. 3:1–3).
‡24:5 *Broken the everlasting covenant.* Reference is probably to the covenant of Gen 9:8–17 (see Gen 9:11 and note). See also v. 18 and note. This same covenant appears to serve as the basis of the judgment of the nations surrounding Israel in Amos 1–2 (cf. 1:9–10). Although everlasting from the divine viewpoint, God's covenants can be broken by sinful mankind.
24:6 *curse.* Because of the intensification of evil in the world, God's devastating curse will burn up the earth's inhabitants (cf. Gen 8:21–22; cf. also the covenant of Gen 9:8–17).
24:7 *vine languisheth.* See v. 4 and note.
24:8 *mirth . . . ceaseth.* Cf. 22:2,13; 23:7.
24:9 *wine with a song.* Characteristic of Judah in 5:11–13 (see note there).
24:10 *city of confusion.* The same idea appears in 25:2; 26:5 (cf. 17:1; 19:18). It is probably a composite of all the cities opposed to God—such as Babylon, Tyre, Jerusalem and Rome.
24:13 Only a few olives and grapes will be left (see v. 6; 17:6,11).
24:14 *They.* The godly remnant that survives the judgment.
‡24:15 *in the fires.* In the "east" (the land of light). *isles of the sea.* See note on 11:11.

Even [a]the name of the LORD God of
Israel in the isles of the sea.
16 From the [1]uttermost part of the earth
have we heard songs, *even* glory to
the righteous.
But I said, [2]My leanness, my leanness,
woe unto me!
[a]The treacherous dealers have dealt
treacherously;
Yea, the treacherous dealers have dealt
very treacherously.
17 [a]Fear, and the pit, and the snare,
Are upon thee, O inhabitant of the
earth.
18 And it shall come to pass, *that* he who
fleeth from the noise of the fear shall
fall into the pit;
And he that cometh up out of the
midst of the pit shall be taken in the
snare:
For [a]the windows from on high are
open,
And [b]the foundations of the earth do
shake.
19 [a]The earth is utterly broken down,
The earth is clean dissolved,
The earth is moved exceedingly.
20 The earth shall [a]reel to and fro like a
drunkard,
And shall be removed like a cottage;
And the transgression thereof shall be
heavy upon it;
And it shall fall, and not rise again.
21 And it shall come to pass in that day,
That the LORD shall [1]punish the host of
the high ones *that are* on high,
[a]And the kings of the earth upon the
earth.
22 And they shall be gathered together,
[1]*as* prisoners are gathered in the
[2]pit,

24:15 [a]Mal. 1:11
24:16 [1]Heb. *wing* [2]Heb. *Leanness to me,* or, *My secret to me* [a]Jer. 5:11
24:17 [a]See Jer. 48:43,44
24:18 [a]Gen. 7:11 [b]Ps. 18:7
24:19 [a]Jer. 4:23
24:20 [a]ch. 19:14
24:21 [1]Heb. *visit upon* [a]Ps. 76:12
24:22 [1]Heb. with *the gathering of prisoners* [2]Or, *dungeon*

24:22 [3]Or, *found wanting*
24:23 [1]Or, there shall be *glory before his ancients* [a]ch. 13:10; 60:19; Ezek. 32:7; Joel 2:31; 3:15 [b]Rev. 19:4,6 [c]Heb. 12:22
25:1 [a]Ex. 15:2 [b]Ps. 98:1 [c]Num. 23:19
25:2 [a]ch. 21:9; 23:13; Jer. 51:37
25:3 [a]Rev. 11:13
25:4 [a]ch. 4:6
25:6 [a]ch. 2:2,3 [b]Prov. 9:2; Mat. 22:4 [c]Dan. 7:14; Mat. 8:11

And shall be shut up in the prison,
And after many days shall they be
[3]visited.
23 Then the [a]moon shall be confounded,
and the sun ashamed,
When the LORD of hosts shall [b]reign
In [c]mount Zion, and in Jerusalem,
And [1]before his ancients gloriously.

Praise the LORD

25 O LORD, thou *art* my God;
[a]I will exalt thee, I will praise thy
name;
[b]For thou hast done wonderful things;
[c]*Thy* counsels of old *are* faithfulness
and truth.
2 For thou hast made [a]of a city a heap;
Of a defenced city a ruin:
A palace of strangers to be no city;
It shall never be built.
3 Therefore shall the strong people
[a]glorify thee,
The city of the terrible nations shall
fear thee.
4 For thou hast been a strength to the
poor,
A strength to the needy in his distress,
[a]A refuge from the storm, a shadow
from the heat,
When the blast of the terrible ones *is*
as a storm *against* the wall.
5 Thou shalt bring down the noise of
strangers,
As the heat in a dry place;
Even the heat with the shadow of a
cloud:
The branch of the terrible ones shall be
brought low.
6 And in [a]this mountain shall [b]the LORD
of hosts make unto [c]all people
A feast of fat things, a feast of wines on
the lees,

‡**24:16** *uttermost part of the earth.* See note on 11:12. *I.* Probably collective for the godly community that wastes away because of the villainy of the treacherous nations that seek to crush the people of God. *My leanness . . . dealt treacherously.* The prophet expresses deep grief over the devastation that will befall the world as God judges the wicked. In the Hebrew text these last four lines of the verse (*Razi li, razi li! 'Oy li! Bogedim bagadu! Ubeged bogedim bagadu!*) contain a powerful example of alliteration and assonance. *woe unto me!* Isaiah had the same reaction in 6:5 ("Woe is me"). *the treacherous.* The enemies of God's people.

24:17–18 Cf. Amos 5:19.

24:17 *Fear, and the pit, and the snare.* Another example (see note on v. 16) of alliteration and assonance (see note on Jer 48:43). The Hebrew words are *paḥad, paḥat* and *paḥ.*

24:18 *windows from on high.* An echo of Noah's flood (Gen 7:11; 8:2). *foundations . . . shake.* Earthquakes and thunder (see note on 13:13; cf. Joel 3:16).

24:20 *like a drunkard.* Cf. 19:14. *like a cottage.* See 1:8 and note.

24:21 *in that day.* The day of the Lord (see notes on 2:11,17,20; 10:20,27; cf. 25:9; 26:1; 27:1–2,12–13). *host of the high ones.* Satan and the fallen angels (see Eph 6:11–12).

‡**24:22** *shut up in the prison.* Cf. Rev 20:2. *visited.* Sentenced or punished; cf. Rev 20:7–10.

24:23 *moon . . . confounded, and the sun ashamed.* The sun and moon do not shine during judgment (see note on 13:10) or when the Lord is the "everlasting light" (60:19–20; cf. Rev 21:23; 22:5). *reign In mount Zion.* See 2:2–4 and note.

25:1–5 A song of praise celebrating the deliverance brought about by the judgments of ch. 24 (see 24:14–16; see also ch. 12).

25:1 *counsels of old.* See 14:24,26–27; 23:8–9.

25:2 *city a ruin.* See 24:10 and note. *never be built.* Cf. 24:20.

25:3 *strong people . . . terrible nations.* Such as Egypt and Assyria (see 19:18–25 and notes). *glorify thee . . . fear thee.* See 24:15.

25:4–5 *strength . . . strength . . . refuge . . . shadow.* See 4:5–6 and note; cf. 32:2.

‡**25:5** *branch of the terrible ones . . . brought low.* Hebrew reads "songs" instead of "branch." God will put an end to the celebrations of the wicked.

25:6–8 The eschatological feast of God.

25:6–7,10 *this mountain.* mount Zion. See 2:2–4 and note; cf. 24:23.

25:6 *feast of fat things.* Rich food is symbolic of great spiritu-

Of fat things full of marrow, of wines
on the lees well refined.
7 And he will [1]destroy in this mountain
The face of the covering [2]cast over all
people,
And [a]the vail that is spread over all
nations.
8 He will [a]swallow up death in victory;
And the Lord GOD will [b]wipe away
tears from off all faces;
And the rebuke of his people shall he
take away from off all the earth:
For the LORD hath spoken *it.*
9 And it shall be said in that day,
Lo, this *is* our God;
[a]We have waited for him, and he will
save us:
This *is* the LORD; we have waited for
him,
[b]We will be glad and rejoice in his
salvation.
10 For in this mountain shall the hand of
the LORD rest,
And Moab shall be [1]trodden down
under him,
Even as straw is [2]trodden down for the
dunghill.
11 And he shall spread forth his hands in
the midst of them,
As he that swimmeth spreadeth forth
his hands to swim:
And he shall bring down their pride
Together with the spoils of their hands.
12 And the [a]fortress of the high fort of thy
walls shall he bring down,
Lay low, *and* bring to the ground, *even*
to the dust.

Song of rejoicing in Judah

26 In [a]that day shall this song be sung
in the land of Judah;
We have a strong city;
[b]Salvation will *God* appoint *for* walls
and bulwarks.
2 [a]Open ye the gates,
That the righteous nation which
keepeth the [1]truth may enter in.
3 Thou wilt keep *him in* [1]perfect peace,
Whose [2]mind *is* stayed *on thee:*
Because he trusteth in thee.
4 Trust ye in the LORD for ever:
[a]For in the LORD JEHOVAH *is*
[b][1]everlasting strength:
5 For he bringeth down them that dwell
on high;
[a]The lofty city, he layeth it low;
He layeth it low, *even* to the ground;
He bringeth it *even* to the dust.
6 The foot shall tread it down,
Even the feet of the poor, *and* the steps
of the needy.
7 The way of the just *is* uprightness:
[a]Thou, most upright, dost weigh the
path of the just.
8 Yea, [a]*in* the way of thy judgments,
O LORD, have we waited for thee;
The desire of *our* soul *is* to thy name,
and to the remembrance of thee.
9 [a]*With* my soul have I desired thee in
the night;
Yea, *with* my spirit within me will I
seek thee early:
For when thy judgments *are* in the
earth,
The inhabitants of the world will learn
righteousness.
10 [a]Let favour be shewed to the wicked,
yet will he not learn righteousness:
In [b]the land of uprightness will he deal
unjustly,
And will not behold the majesty of the
LORD.
11 LORD, *when* thy hand is lifted up, [a]they
will not see:
But they shall see, and be ashamed for
their envy [1]at the people;
Yea, the fire of thine enemies shall
devour them.

25:7 [1]Heb. *swallow up* [2]Heb. *covered* [a]2 Cor. 3:15; Eph. 4:18
25:8 [a]Hos. 13:14; 1 Cor. 15:54 [b]Rev. 7:17; 21:4
25:9 [a]Gen. 49:18; Tit. 2:13 [b]Ps. 20:5
25:10 [1]Or, *threshed* [2]Or, *threshed in Madmenah*
25:12 [a]ch. 26:5
26:1 [a]ch. 2:11 [b]ch. 60:18
26:2 [1]Heb. *truths* [a]Ps. 118:19,20
26:3 [1]Heb. *peace, peace* [2]Or, *thought,* or, *imagination*
26:4 [1]Heb. *the rock of ages* [a]ch. 45:17 [b]Deut. 32:4
26:5 [a]ch. 25:12; 32:19
26:7 [a]Ps. 37:23
26:8 [a]ch. 64:5
26:9 [a]Ps. 63:6; Sol. 3:1
26:10 [a]Eccl. 8:12; Rom 2:4 [b]Ps. 143:10
26:11 [1]Or, *towards* thy *people* [a]Job 34:27; Ps. 28:5; ch. 5:12

al blessings (see 55:2). A feast is associated with a coronation (1 Ki 1:25) or wedding (Judg 14:10); cf. the "marriage supper of the Lamb" (Rev 19:9). *wines on the lees.* The best wine—aged by being left on its dregs (see Jer 48:11; Zeph 1:12).
25:7 *covering . . . vail.* Used to cover faces in mourning—in any event, the associations are with death.
25:8 Quoted in part in 1 Cor 15:54. *swallow up death.* Death, the great swallower (see Ps 49:14 and note), will be swallowed up. *Lord GOD.* See 7:7; 28:16; 30:15; 40:10; 49:22; 52:4; 61:11; 65:13. *rebuke . . . take away.* See 54:4.
25:9 Another brief song of praise. *in that day.* See 12:1,4; 24:21; see also 10:20,27 and note. *We have waited for him, and he will save.* Cf. Ps 22:4–5. *be glad and rejoice.* Cf. 35:10; 51:11; 66:10.
25:10–12 An elaboration on the theme of judgment.
25:10 *Moab.* Symbolic of all the enemies of God, like Edom in 34:5–17. See note on 15:1.
25:11 *pride.* See note on 16:6.
25:12 *fortress . . . walls.* See v. 2; 2:15; 2 Ki 3:27; Jer 51:58.
26:1–15 Another song of praise for God's deliverance.
26:1 *In that day.* See 12:1,4; 24:21; 25:9; see also note on 10:20,27. *bulwarks.* Sloping fortifications of earth or stone (cf. 2 Sam 20:15).
26:3 See 30:15. *Whose mind is stayed on thee.* Cf. Ps 112:6–8. *trusteth.* Cf. 25:9.
26:5 *lofty city.* See note on 24:10. *layeth it low . . . to the ground.* Cf. 25:2,12.
26:6 *feet of the poor.* The oppressors are humiliated also in 49:24–26; 51:22–23 (contrast 3:14–15).
‡26:7 *way of the just . . . path of the just.* God makes the path of the righteous smooth and straight, a theme found also in 40:3–4; 42:16; 45:13.
26:8 A desire for God to reveal His power in their behalf (see Hos 12:5–6). *name . . . remembrance.* See v. 13; 24:15; 25:1.
26:9 *judgments.* Punishment (cf. 4:4).
26:10 *favour.* Such as the blessings of harvest and general prosperity (cf. Mat 5:45).
‡26:11 *hand is lifted up.* A sign of power. See 9:12,17,21 and note; Ps 89:13. *their envy at the people.* Lit, "jealousy of people," referring to God's zeal for his people, Israel that will bring shame and defeat to the nations. See 9:7 and note; cf. 37:32; 63:15. *fire.* See note on 1:31.

12 LORD, thou wilt ordain peace for us:
For thou also hast wrought all our
works [1] in us.
13 O LORD our God,
[a] *Other* lords besides thee have had
dominion over us:
But by thee only will we make mention
of thy name.
14 *They are* dead, they shall not live;
They are deceased, they shall not rise:
Therefore hast thou visited and
destroyed them,
And made all their memory to perish.
15 Thou hast increased the nation, O LORD,
Thou hast increased the nation: thou
art glorified:
Thou hadst removed *it* far *unto* all the
ends of the earth.

16 LORD, [a] in trouble have they visited thee,
They poured out a [1] prayer *when* thy
chastening *was* upon them.
17 Like as [a] a woman with child, *that*
draweth near the time of her
delivery,
Is in pain, *and* crieth out in her pangs;
So have we been in thy sight, O LORD.
18 We have been with child, we have
been in pain,
We have as it were brought forth wind;
We have not wrought any deliverance
in the earth;
Neither have [a] the inhabitants of the
world fallen.

19 [a] Thy dead *men* shall live,
Together with my dead body shall they
arise.
[b] Awake and sing, ye that dwell in dust:
For thy dew *is as* the dew of herbs,
And the earth shall cast out the dead.

20 Come, my people, [a] enter thou into thy
chambers,
And shut thy doors about thee:
Hide thyself as it were [b] for a little
moment,
Until the indignation be overpast.
21 For behold, the LORD [a] cometh out of
his place
To punish the inhabitants of the earth
for their iniquity:
The earth also shall disclose her
[1] blood,
And shall no more cover her slain.

Israel to be delivered

27 In that day the LORD with his sore
and great and strong sword
Shall punish leviathan the [1] piercing
serpent,
[a] Even leviathan *that* crooked serpent;
And he shall slay [b] the dragon that *is* in
the sea.

2 In that day [a] sing ye unto her,
[b] A vineyard of red wine.
3 [a] I the LORD do keep it;
I will water it every moment:
Lest *any* hurt it, I will keep it night and
day.
4 Fury *is* not in me:
Who would set [a] the briers *and* thorns
against me in battle?
I would [1] go through them, I would
burn them together.
5 Or let him take hold [a] of my strength,
That he may [b] make peace with me;
And he shall make peace with me.
6 He shall cause them that come of Jacob
[a] to take root:
Israel shall blossom and bud,
And fill the face of the world *with* fruit.

26:12 [1] Or, *for us* 26:13 [a] 2 Chr. 12:8 26:16 [1] Heb. *secret speech* [a] Hos. 5:15 26:17 [a] ch. 13:8; John 16:21 26:18 [a] Ps. 17:14 26:19 [a] Ezek. 37:1 [b] Dan. 12:2 26:20 [a] Ex. 12:22,23 [b] Ps. 30:5; ch. 54:7,8; 2 Cor. 4:17 26:21 [1] Heb. *bloods* [a] Mic. 1:3; Jude 14 27:1 [1] Or, *crossing like a bar* [a] Ps. 74:13,14 [b] ch. 51:9; Ezek. 29:3; 32:2 27:2 [a] ch. 5:1 [b] Ps. 80:8; Jer. 2:21 27:3 [a] Ps. 121:4,5 27:4 [1] Or, *march against* [a] 2 Sam. 23:6; ch. 9:18 27:5 [a] ch. 25:4 [b] Job 22:21 27:6 [a] ch. 37:31; Hos. 14:5,6

26:12 *peace.* See v. 3.
26:13 *Other lords.* Foreign rulers, such as those of Egypt or Assyria.
26:14 *dead ... deceased.* Cf. the fate of the king of Babylon in 14:9–10.
26:15 *increased the nation.* Applied to the return from Babylonian exile in 54:2–3; also cf. 9:3.
26:16–18 The prophet speaks to the Lord on behalf of God's people.
‡26:16 *trouble.* Most likely the Assyrian oppression, described in 5:30; 8:21–22.
26:17–18 *time of her delivery ... pain ... her pangs.* See 13:8 and note (cf. 37:3).
26:18 *deliverance in the earth.* Israel was designed to be "a light of the Gentiles" (42:6—see note there; see also 9:2; 49:6 and notes).
26:19–21 The prophet speaks a word of reassurance to God's people.
‡26:19 *dead men shall live ... shall they arise.* A reference to the restoration of Israel (see Ezek 37:11–12)—perhaps including the resurrection of the body (Dan 12:2). Cf. 25:8; contrast 26:14. The verse at least implies that the people of this day were aware of the concept of resurrection. *dew.* A symbol of fruitfulness (see 2 Sam 1:21; Hos 14:5).
26:20–21 See 24:21–22 and note on 2:11,17,20.
26:20 *a little moment ... indignation.* Cf. 10:25; 54:7–8. Assyrian tyranny and Babylonian exile, as well as all other oppressions, will end.
26:21 *punish.* See 66:14–16. *shall disclose ... shall no more cover.* The blood and bodies of the innocent/righteous who have been slaughtered by the oppressive powers will no longer be hidden in the ground, but will be brought forth to testify against their murderers, so that God may in judgment avenge their deaths (see Gen 4:10).
27:1–2,12–13 *In that day.* See 10:20,27 and note; see also 12:1,4; 24:21; 25:9; 26:1.
27:1 The climactic word of judgment. *leviathan ... dragon.* A symbol (drawn from Canaanite myths) of wicked nations, such as Egypt (see 30:7 and note; 51:9; Ezek 29:3; 32:2). *piercing ... crooked serpent.* Cf. Job 3:8; 41:1; Ps 74:14. Such descriptions of leviathan occur outside the Bible as well.
27:2–6 A second vineyard song (see 5:1–7 and notes).
27:2 *vineyard.* Israel.
27:4–5 A picture of Israel's lukewarmness toward the Lord—not "briers and thorns" (v. 4) like the other nations, but not fully trusting in the Lord either (see 29:13).
27:4 *briers and thorns.* See 5:6 and note.
27:6 *take root.* See 11:1,10 and notes. *blossom and bud.* See

7 Hath he smitten him, [1] as he smote
those that smote him?
Or is he slain according to the slaughter
of them that are slain by him?
8 [a] In measure, [1] when it shooteth forth,
thou wilt debate with it:
[b] [2] He stayeth his rough wind in the day
of the east wind.
9 By this therefore shall the iniquity of
Jacob be purged;
And this *is* all the fruit to take away his
sin;
When he maketh all the stones of the
altar as chalkstones that are beaten
in sunder,
The groves and [1] images shall not stand
up.
10 Yet the defenced city *shall be* desolate,
And the habitation forsaken, and left
like a wilderness:
[a] There shall the calf feed, and there
shall he lie down,
And consume the branches thereof.
11 When the boughs thereof are withered,
they shall be broken off:
The women come, *and* set them on
fire:
For [a] it *is* a people of no understanding:
Therefore he that made them will not
have mercy on them,
And [b] he that formed them will shew
them no favour.
12 And it shall come to pass in that day,
That the LORD shall beat off from the
channel of the river unto the stream
of Egypt,
And ye shall be gathered one by one,
O ye children of Israel.
13 [a] And it shall come to pass in that day,
[b] *That* the great trumpet shall be
blown,
And they shall come which were ready
to perish in the land of Assyria,
And the outcasts in the land of Egypt,
And shall worship the LORD in the holy
mount at Jerusalem.

27:7 [1] Heb. *according to the stroke of those* 27:8 [1] Or, *when thou sendest it forth* [2] Or, When *he removeth* it [*with*] [a] Job 23:6; Ps. 6:1; Jer. 10:24; 30:11; 46:28; 1 Cor. 10:13 [b] Ps. 78:38 27:9 [1] Or, *sun images* 27:10 [a] See ch. 17:2; 32:14 27:11 [a] Deut. 32:28; ch. 1:3; Jer. 8:7 [b] Deut. 32:18; ch. 43:1,7; 44:2,21,24 27:13 [a] ch. 2:11 [b] Mat. 24:31; Rev. 11:15

Woe to Ephraim

28 Woe to [a] the crown of pride, to the
drunkards of Ephraim,
Whose [b] glorious beauty *is* a fading
flower,
Which *are* on the head of the fat
valleys of them that are [1] overcome
with wine.
2 Behold, the LORD hath a mighty and
strong one,
[a] *Which* as a tempest of hail *and* a
destroying storm,
As a flood of mighty waters overflowing,
Shall cast down to the earth with the
hand.
3 [a] The crown of pride, the drunkards of
Ephraim,
Shall be trodden [1] under feet:
4 And [a] the glorious beauty, which *is* on
the head of the fat valley, shall be a
fading flower,
And as the hasty fruit before the
summer;
Which *when* he that looketh upon it
seeth,
While it is yet in his hand he [1] eateth
it up.

5 In that day shall the LORD of hosts be
for a crown of glory,
And for a diadem of beauty, unto the
residue of his people,
6 And for a spirit of judgment to him that
sitteth in judgment,

28:1 [1] Heb. *broken* [a] ver. 3 [b] ver. 4 28:2 [a] ch. 30:30; Ezek. 13:11 28:3 [1] Heb. *with feet* [a] ver. 1 28:4 [1] Heb. *swalloweth* [a] ver. 1

4:2 and note. The Messianic age is in view. *fill the face of the world.* Contrast 26:18.
27:7–11 What the Lord is going to do with Israel in the judgments that are about to overtake her in Isaiah's day.
‡27:7 If the people of Israel doubt the promise of v. 6, then they should consider that the punishment they have received from God is not as severe as the one that he pours out on their pagan oppressors (cf. 10:24–26).
‡27:8 *In measure . . . thou wilt debate with it.* The sense is that God measures the judgment that comes against his people and "debates" ("contends") with Israel's oppressors so that the punishment does not become too severe.
27:9 *purged.* Israel (Jacob) will have to atone for her guilt through the coming judgment. *altar . . . groves and images.* See 17:8 and note. *beaten in sunder.* Demolished; see Ex 34:13.
27:10 *defenced city.* Jerusalem. *desolate . . . forsaken.* Cf. 6:11–12. *shall the calf feed.* Cf. 5:5; 7:25.
27:12–13 The redemption that lies beyond the coming judgment.
‡27:12 *the LORD shall beat.* The verb means to "thresh" and refers to judgment on the nations into which Israel has been dispersed (see note on 21:10). The threshing will separate Israelites from Gentiles. *stream of Egypt.* Probably the Wadi el-Arish, the southern border of the promised land (the Euphrates is the northern border). See Gen 15:18 and note; 1 Ki 4:21; 8:65.
27:13 *great trumpet.* Used especially to summon troops (see 1 Sam 13:3). *Assyria . . . Egypt.* See 11:11–12 and notes. *holy mount.* mount Zion (see 2:2–4 and note; see also 24:23; 25:6–7,10 and note).
28:1–35:10 A series of six woes (28:1; 29:1; 29:15; 30:1; 31:1; 33:1), concluded with an announcement of judgment on the nations (ch. 34) and a song celebrating the joy of the redeemed (ch. 35). Cf. the six woes in ch. 5 (see note on 5:8–23).
‡28:1 *crown.* Samaria, the capital of the northern kingdom, was a beautiful city on a prominent hill (see note on 1 Ki 16:24). *pride.* See v. 3 and note on 16:6. *drunkards.* In the eighth century B.C. Samaria was a city of luxury and indulgence. See 5:11–13 and note; Amos 6:4–7. *Ephraim.* See note on 7:2. *fat valleys.* Valleys of fertility; cf. 5:1.
28:2 *mighty and strong one.* The king of Assyria. *tempest of hail . . . waters overflowing.* See v. 17; 8:7–8 and note; 17:12 and note. Cf. 30:30; 32:19.
‡28:5 *In that day.* See 4:1–2; 10:20,27 and note; 12:1,4; 24:21; 25:9; 26:1; 27:1–2,12–13. *glory . . . beauty.* See 4:2. *residue.* Remnant; see note on 1:9.
28:6 *spirit of judgment.* See 11:2–4 and notes. *gate.* The most vulnerable part of a city.

And for strength to them that turn the
battle to the gate.
7 But they also [a]have erred through
wine, and through strong drink are
out of the way;
[b]The priest and the prophet have erred
through strong drink,
They are swallowed up of wine, they are
out of the way through strong drink;
They err in vision, they stumble *in*
judgment.
8 For all tables are full *of* vomit *and*
filthiness,
So that there is no place *clean.*

9 [a]Whom shall he teach knowledge?
And whom shall he make to
understand [1]doctrine?
Them that are weaned from the milk,
And drawn from the breasts.
10 For precept [1]*must be* upon precept,
precept upon precept;
Line upon line, line upon line;
Here a little, *and* there a little:
11 For with [a][1]stammering lips and
another tongue
[2]Will he speak to this people.
12 To whom he said,
This *is* the rest *wherewith* ye may
cause the weary to rest;
And this *is* the refreshing: yet they
would not hear.
13 But the word of the LORD was unto
them
Precept upon precept, precept upon
precept;
Line upon line, line upon line;
Here a little, *and* there a little;
That they might go, and fall backward,
and be broken,
And snared, and taken.

14 Wherefore hear the word of the LORD,
ye scornful men,
That rule this people which *is* in
Jerusalem.
15 Because ye have said, We have made a
covenant with death,
And with hell are we at agreement;
When the overflowing scourge shall
pass through, it shall not come *unto*
us:
[a]For we have made lies our refuge,
And under falsehood have we hid
ourselves:
16 Therefore thus saith the Lord GOD,
Behold, I lay in Zion for a foundation
[a]a stone,
A tried stone, a precious corner *stone,*
a sure foundation:
He that believeth shall not make haste.
17 Judgment also will I lay to the line,
And righteousness to the plummet:
And the hail shall sweep away [a]the
refuge of lies,
And the waters shall overflow the
hiding place.
18 And your covenant with death shall be
disannulled,
And your agreement with hell shall not
stand;
When the overflowing scourge shall
pass through,
Then ye shall be [1]trodden down by it.
19 From the time that it goeth forth it
shall take you:
For morning by morning shall it pass
over, by day and by night:
And it shall be a vexation only [1]*to*
understand the report.
20 For the bed is shorter than that *a man*
can stretch himself *on it:*
And the covering narrower than that
he can wrap himself *in it.*
21 For the LORD shall rise up as *in* mount
[a]Perazim,
He shall be wroth as *in* the valley of
[b]Gibeon,
That *he* may do his work, [c]his strange
work;
And bring to pass his act, his strange
act.

28:7 [a]Prov. 20:1; Hos. 4:11 [b]ch. 56:10,12
28:9 [1]Heb. *the hearing?* [a]Jer. 6:10
28:10 [1]Or, hath been
28:11 [1]Heb. *stammerings of lip* [2]Or, *He hath spoken* [a]1 Cor. 14:21
28:15 [a]Amos 2:4
28:16 [a]Gen. 49:24; Ps. 118:22; Mat. 21:42; Acts 4:11; Rom. 9:33; 10:11; Eph. 2:20; 1 Pet. 2:6-8
28:17 [a]ver. 15
28:18 [1]Heb. *a treading down to it*
28:19 [1]Or, when *he shall make* you to *understand doctrine*
28:21 [a]2 Sam. 5:20; 1 Chr. 14:11 [b]Josh. 10:10,12; 2 Sam. 5:25; 1 Chr. 14:16 [c]Lam. 3:33

28:7 *wine . . . strong drink.* The religious leaders should have been filled with the Spirit, not with wine. See Lev 10:9; Num 11:29; Eph 5:18.

28:8 *vomit.* Cf. Jer 25:16,27.

‡28:9–10 The mocking response of Isaiah's hearers. The monosyllabic words *Sav lasav, sav lasav, Kav lakav, kav lakav* . . . imitate the babbling sounds of a child; cf. the mocking tones of 5:19.

28:11–12 Quoted in part in 1 Cor 14:21.

28:11 *stammering lips.* The language of the Assyrians.

28:12 *rest.* The land given to them by the Lord, in whom they were to trust (see 26:3; 30:15; 40:31; Josh 1:13). *would not hear.* Cf. Jer 6:16.

‡28:13 *was unto them Precept upon precept.* They dismissed the words of the prophet as childish nonsense, so the word of the Lord that he speaks will remain nonsense to them (see 6:9–10 and notes).

28:15,18 *covenant with death.* Possibly an allusion to necromancy and worship of idols (see 8:19). By using a vivid figure of speech, Isaiah mocks their sense of assurance against national calamity, placing on their lips a claim to have a covenant with death that it will not harm them (see Hos 2:18). *overflowing scourge.* A mixed metaphor referring to the armies of Assyria and Babylonia. "Overflowing" pictures an army as a flooding river (see 8:7,8); a "scourge" is a whip (10:26).

28:16 *stone.* The Lord (see 8:14; 17:10 and notes). *corner stone.* Cf. the "head stone of the corner" of Ps 118:22. *foundation.* See 1 Cor 3:11; cf. 1 Pet 2:4–7.

28:17 *line . . . plummet.* The standards and tests the Lord will apply are His justice and righteousness. *hail.* See v. 2; 30:30; 32:19.

28:20 *shorter . . . narrower.* Israel was unprepared both militarily and spiritually.

28:21 *mount Perazim.* Where God "broke forth" against the Philistines (2 Sam 5:20). *valley of Gibeon.* Where God sent hail to demolish the Amorites (Josh 10:10–12). *strange work . . . strange act.* This time God would fight against Israel.

22 Now therefore be ye not mockers,
Lest your bands be made strong:
For I have heard from the Lord GOD of hosts
[a] A consumption, even determined
Upon the whole earth.

23 Give ye ear, and hear my voice;
Hearken, and hear my speech.
24 Doth the plowman plow all day to sow?
Doth he open and break the clods of his ground?
25 When he hath made plain the face thereof,
Doth he not cast abroad the fitches, and scatter the cummin,
And cast in [1] the principal wheat
And the appointed barley and the [2] rye *in* their [3] place?
26 [1] For his God doth instruct him to discretion, *and* doth teach him.
27 For the fitches are not threshed with a threshing *instrument,*
Neither is a cart wheel turned about upon the cummin;
But the fitches are beaten out with a staff,
And the cummin with a rod.
28 Bread *corn* is bruised;
Because he will not ever be threshing it,
Nor break *it with* the wheel of his cart,
Nor bruise it *with* his horsemen.
29 This also cometh forth from the LORD of hosts,
[a] Which is wonderful in counsel, *and* excellent in working.

Doom to the city of Jerusalem

29 [1] Woe [a] to Ariel, to Ariel, [2] the city [b] *where* David dwelt!
Add ye year to year; let them [3] kill sacrifices.
2 Yet I will distress Ariel,
And there shall be heaviness and sorrow:
And it shall be unto me as Ariel.
3 And I will camp against thee round about,
And will lay siege against thee *with* a mount,
And I will raise forts against thee.
4 And thou shalt be brought down, *and* shalt speak out of the ground,
And thy speech shall be low out of the dust,
And thy voice shall be, as of one that hath a familiar spirit, [a] out of the ground,
And thy speech shall [1] whisper out of the dust.
5 Moreover the multitude of thy [a] strangers shall be like small dust,
And the multitude of the terrible ones *shall be* [b] as chaff that passeth away:
Yea, it shall be [c] at an instant suddenly.
6 [a] Thou shalt be visited of the LORD of hosts
With thunder, and with earthquake, and great noise,
With storm and tempest, and the flame of devouring fire.
7 [a] And the multitude of all the nations that fight against Ariel,
Even all that fight against her and her munition, and that distress her,
Shall be [b] as a dream of a night vision.
8 [a] It shall even be as when a hungry *man* dreameth, and behold, he eateth;
But he awaketh, and his soul *is* empty:
Or as when a thirsty *man* dreameth, and behold, he drinketh;
But he awaketh, and behold, *he is* faint, and his soul hath appetite:
So shall the multitude of all the nations be,
That fight against mount Zion.

28:22 [a] ch. 10:22; Dan 9:27
28:25 [1] Or, *the wheat* in the *principal* place, *and barley* in the *appointed* place [2] Or, *spelt* [3] Heb. *border?*
28:26 [1] Or, *And he bindeth it in such sort as [his] God doth teach him*
28:29 [a] Ps. 92:5; Jer. 32:19
29:1 [1] Or, *Oh Ariel,* that is, *the lion of God* [2] Or, *of the city* [3] Heb. *cut off the heads [of]* [a] Ezek. 43:15,16 [b] 2 Sam. 5:9
29:4 [1] Heb. *peep,* or, *chirp* [a] ch. 8:19
29:5 [a] ch. 25:5 [b] Job 21:18; ch. 17:13 [c] ch. 30:13
29:6 [a] ch. 28:2; 30:30
29:7 [a] ch. 37:36 [b] Job 20:8
29:8 [a] Ps. 73:20

‡28:22 *A consumption, even determined.* The judgment God has planned against the nations; see 10:22–23 and note on 10:22.
28:23–29 A wisdom poem (a poetic parable) in two stanzas, each ending in a verse that praises the wisdom of God. In the context, and since "threshing" is emphasized (vv. 27–28), the point may be that though God must punish Israel, His actions will be as measured and as well-timed as a farmer's. See 27:12 and note.
‡28:25 *fitches . . . cummin.* Black cummin and regular cummin, herbs used for seasoning (see Mat 23:23 and note). *rye.* Or "spelt," a kind of wheat (see note on Ex 9:32).
28:27 *rod.* See 10:5 and note.
28:29 *wonderful in counsel.* See 9:6 and note.
‡29:1–2,7 *Ariel.* Jerusalem. Fighting and bloodshed will turn Jerusalem into a virtual "altar hearth" (Hebrew *'ari'el;* the Hebrew for "altar hearth" and for Ariel sound the same). A similar Hebrew word for the same term is used in Ezek 43:15 (see note there). The prophet's warning points out that Israel's sacrificial center is in danger of being sacrificed itself.
‡29:1 *Woe.* See note on 28:1. *city where David dwelt.* See 2 Sam 5:6–9. *year to year . . . kill sacrifices.* Refers to yearly observance of the festivals. God is going to judge Jerusalem even though the people continue to go through the motions of worship. See 1:13–14 and note on 1:14.
‡29:3 *forts.* Siege towers pushed up to the city wall by attackers so they could fight the defenders on the same level.
29:4 *whisper.* Used of mediums and spiritists in 8:19. Judah speaks as from the realm of the dead—so much for their covenant with death (see 28:15,18).
29:5–8 In God's time, those nations that devastate Jerusalem will be devastated (see 10:5–19; 27:1). The sudden destruction of the enemy resembles that of Assyria's army in 701 B.C. (see 10:16 and note).
‡29:5 *multitude . . . dust.* Israel's many enemies will be reduced to nothing. *chaff.* See 17:13; Ps 1:4 and notes.
29:6 *thunder . . . earthquake . . . storm and tempest.* As in Judg 5:4–5; Ps 18:7–15; Hab 3:3–7; see also 28:2; Ps 83:13–15 and notes.
29:9–14 Isaiah speaks again of Israel's spiritual state and warns of the Lord's impending judgment.

9 Stay yourselves, and wonder;
[1]Cry ye out, and cry:
[a]They are drunken, [b]but not *with* wine;
They stagger, but not *with* strong drink.
10 For [a]the LORD hath poured out upon
you the spirit of deep sleep,
And hath [b]closed your eyes:
The prophets and your [1]rulers, [c]the
seers hath he covered.
11 And the vision of all is become unto
you as the words of a [1]book [a]that is
sealed,
Which *men* deliver to one that is
learned,
Saying, Read this, I pray thee:
[b]And he saith, I cannot; for it *is* sealed:
12 And the book is delivered to *him* that
is not learned,
Saying, Read this, I pray thee:
And he saith, I am not learned.
13 Wherefore the Lord said,
[a]Forasmuch as this people draw near
me with their mouth,
And with their lips do honour me,
But have removed their heart far from
me,
And their fear towards me is taught *by*
[b]the precept of men:
14 [a]Therefore, behold, [1]I will proceed to
do a marvellous work amongst this
people,
Even a marvellous work and a wonder:
[b]For the wisdom of their wise *men*
shall perish,
And the understanding of their prudent
men shall be hid.
15 [a]Woe unto them that seek deep to hide
their counsel from the LORD,
And their works are in the dark,
And [b]they say, Who seeth us? and who
knoweth us?
16 Surely your turning *of things* upside
down shall be esteemed as the
potter's clay:
For shall the [a]work say of him that
made it, He made me not?
Or shall the thing framed say of him
that framed it, He had no
understanding?
17 *Is* it not yet a very little while,
And [a]Lebanon shall be turned into a
fruitful field,
And the fruitful field shall be esteemed
as a forest?
18 And [a]in that day shall the deaf hear the
words of the book,
And the eyes of the blind shall see out
of obscurity, and out of darkness.
19 [a]The meek also [1]shall increase *their*
joy in the LORD,
And [b]the poor among men shall rejoice
in the Holy One of Israel.
20 For the terrible one is brought to
nought, and [a]the scorner is
consumed,
And all that [b]watch for iniquity are cut
off:
21 That make a man an offender for a word,
And [a]lay a snare for him that reproveth
in the gate,
And turn aside the just [b]for a thing of
nought.
22 Therefore thus saith the LORD, [a]who
redeemed Abraham, concerning the
house of Jacob,
Jacob shall not now be ashamed,
Neither shall his face now wax pale.
23 But when he seeth his children, [a]the
work of mine hands, in the midst of
him,

29:9 [1]Or, *Take your pleasure, and riot* [a]See ch. 28:7,8 [b]ch. 51:21
29:10 [1]Heb. *heads* [a]Rom. 11:8 [b]Ps. 69:23; ch. 6:10 [c]1 Sam. 9:9
29:11 [1]Or, *letter* [a]ch. 8:16 [b]Dan. 12:4; Rev. 5:1-5,9
29:13 [a]Ezek. 33:31; Mat. 15:8,9; Mark 7:6,7 [b]Col. 2:22
29:14 [1]Heb. *I will add* [a]Hab. 1:5 [b]Jer. 49:7; Obad. 8; 1 Cor. 1:19
29:15 [a]ch. 30:1
29:15 [b]Ps. 94:7
29:16 [a]ch. 45:9; Rom. 9:20
29:17 [a]ch. 32:15
29:18 [a]ch. 35:5
29:19 [1]Heb. *shall add* [a]ch. 61:1 [b]Jas. 2:5
29:20 [a]ch. 28:14,22 [b]Mic. 2:1
29:21 [a]Amos 5:10,12 [b]Prov. 28:21
29:22 [a]Josh. 24:3
29:23 [a]ch. 19:25; 45:11; 60:21; Eph. 2:10

‡29:9 *Cry ye out, and cry.* Lit. "Blind yourself and be blind." The prophet sarcastically commands the people to remain in their blind state because they refuse to believe that God will deliver them from their enemies. *drunken, but not with wine.* Refers to Israel's spiritual stupor caused by their unbelief (see 6:10 and note; cf. 28:1,7).
29:10 Quoted in part in Rom 11:8. *seers.* See 1 Sam 9:9 and note; 2 Ki 17:13.
‡29:11 *vision of all.* The totality of Isaiah's prophetic message. See 1:1 and note. *I cannot.* God's word is a closed book even to the educated.
‡29:13 Quoted in part by Jesus to show the hypocrisy of the Pharisees (Mat 15:8–9). *this people.* Not "my people" (cf. 8:6,11–12; Jer 14:10–11; Hag 1:2). *precept of men.* The nation leans more on human traditions than divine revelation (cf. Mark 7:8–9).
29:14 Quoted in part in 1 Cor 1:19. *marvellous work and a wonder.* He who showed them wonders in the exodus (see Ex 15:11; Ps 78:12) will now show them wonders in judgment. *wisdom . . . shall perish.* Cf. 44:25; Jer 8:9.
29:15 *Woe.* A new woe begins (see note on 28:1–35:10). *their counsel.* Perhaps the alliance between Ahaz and Assyria or between Hezekiah and Egypt (see 30:1–2). *Who seeth us?* See note on Ps 10:11.
29:16 Quoted in part in Rom 9:20. Cf. the creation of Adam in Gen 2:7; also cf. Is 10:15.
29:17–24 Another sudden shift to the theme of redemption, as in 28:5–8.
29:17 *Lebanon.* Perhaps symbolic of Assyria (see 10:34). The forests of Lebanon were unequaled (see 2:13), so "fruitful field" represents a lesser status (see 32:15).
‡29:18 *in that day.* See notes on 10:20,27; 26:1. Beyond the day of Assyria's destruction lies the day of Israel's restoration. *deaf hear . . . blind shall see.* A reversal of the stupor in vv. 9–11. This imagery is linked with the Messianic age in 35:5; contrast 6:9.
29:19 *poor.* See 11:4. *Holy One of Israel.* See note on 1:4.
29:20 *terrible one.* See v. 21. *scorner.* Cf. 28:14,22.
‡29:21 *make a man an offender . . . word.* Use false testimony to indict. *turn aside the just.* To defraud; see 1:17; 9:17 and notes; see also 10:2; Amos 5:10,12.
29:22 *redeemed.* Normally used of the deliverance of Israel from Egypt (see Ex 6:6; 15:13). Cf. 43:1,3,14. But Abraham also had an "exodus" out of a pagan world (see Gen 12:1; Josh 24:2–3,14–15). *be ashamed.* Cf. 45:17; 50:7; 54:4. *wax pale.* From fear of the enemy.
29:23 *seeth his children.* Cf. 49:20–21; 54:1–2. Restoration from exile may be in view. See also 53:10. *children, the work of mine*

They shall sanctify my name,
And sanctify the Holy One of Jacob,
And shall fear the God of Israel.
24 They also [a]that erred in spirit [1]shall
come to understanding,
And they that murmured shall learn
doctrine.

Rebellious Judah to be crushed

30 Woe to the rebellious children, saith
the LORD,
[a]That take counsel, but not of me;
And that cover *with* a covering, but not
of my Spirit,
[b]That *they* may add sin to sin:
2 [a]That walk to go down *into* Egypt,
And [b]have not asked *at* my mouth;
To strengthen themselves in the
strength of Pharaoh,
And to trust in the shadow of Egypt.
3 [a]Therefore shall the strength of
Pharaoh be your shame,
And the trust in the shadow of Egypt
your confusion.
4 For his princes were at [a]Zoan,
And his ambassadors came to Hanes.
5 [a]They were all ashamed of a people
that could not profit them,
Nor be a help nor profit,
But a shame, and also a reproach.

6 [a]The burden of the beasts of the south:
Into the land of trouble and anguish,
From whence *come* the young and old
lion,
[b]The viper and fiery flying serpent,
They will carry their riches upon the
shoulders of young asses,
And their treasures upon the bunches
of camels,
To a people *that* shall not profit *them.*
7 [a]For the Egyptians shall help in vain,
and to no purpose:
Therefore have I cried [1]concerning
this, [b]Their strength *is* to sit still.

8 Now go, [a]write it before them in a
table,
And note it in a book,
That it may be for [1]the time to come
For ever and ever:
9 That [a]this *is* a rebellious people, lying
children,
Children *that* will not hear the law of
the LORD:
10 [a]Which say to the seers, See not;
And to the prophets, Prophesy not
unto us right *things,*
[b]Speak unto us smooth *things,*
Prophesy deceits:
11 Get ye out of the way,
Turn aside out of the path,
Cause the Holy One of Israel to cease
from before us.
12 Wherefore thus saith the Holy One of
Israel,
Because ye despise this word,
And trust in [1]oppression and
perverseness,
And stay thereon:
13 Therefore this iniquity shall be to you
[a]as a breach ready to fall,
Swelling out in a high wall,
Whose breaking [b]cometh suddenly at
an instant.
14 And [a]he shall break it as the breaking
of [1]the potters' vessel
That is broken in pieces; he shall not
spare:

29:24 [1] Heb. *shall know understanding* [a] ch. 28:7
30:1 [a] ch. 29:15 [b] Deut. 29:19
30:2 [a] ch. 31:1 [b] Num. 27:21; Josh. 9:14; 1 Ki. 22:7; Jer. 21:2; 42:2,20
30:3 [a] ch. 20:5; Jer. 37:5,7
30:4 [a] ch. 19:11
30:5 [a] Jer. 2:36
30:6 [a] ch. 57:9; Hos. 8:9; 12:1 [b] Deut. 8:15
30:7 [1] Or, *to her* [a] Jer. 37:7 [b] ver. 15
30:8 [1] Heb. *the latter day* [a] Hab. 2:2
30:9 [a] Deut. 32:20; ch. 1:4
30:10 [a] Jer. 11:21; Amos 2:12; Mic. 2:6 [b] 1 Ki. 22:13; Mic. 2:11
30:12 [1] Or, *fraud*
30:13 [a] Ps. 62:3 [b] ch. 29:5
30:14 [1] Heb. *the bottle of potters* [a] Ps. 2:9; Jer. 19:11

hands. See 45:11 (cf. Eph 2:10). *sanctify . . . fear.* See 8:13. Isaiah's contemporaries showed little respect for the Lord. *Holy One of Jacob.* Cf. v. 19; see note on 1:4.

29:24 *erred in spirit.* See 19:14. *come to understanding.* Contrast 1:3.

‡30:1 *Woe.* See note on 28:1–35:10. *rebellious children.* See 1:2 and note. *counsel, but not of me.* See 29:15 and note. *cover with a covering.* Lit. "pour out a drink offering." Refers to making an alliance with another nation confirmed by a cermony involving a drink offering. After Shabako became pharaoh in 715 B.C., the smaller nations in Aram (Syria) and Canaan sought his help against Assyria. Judah apparently joined them (see 20:5 and note). *my Spirit.* Who spoke through His prophet.

30:2 Hezekiah did this (see 2 Ki 18:21). *shadow.* A metaphor for a king as one who provides protection (see Judg 9:15; Lam 4:20). The Lord should have been Israel's "shadow" (cf. 49:2; 51:16; see Ps 91:1; 121:5).

30:3 *shame . . . confusion.* See also "shame . . . reproach" in v. 5. Cf. 20:4–5; see Judg 9:14–15 and notes.

30:4 *Zoan.* Ironically, where the Israelites once served as slaves; see 19:11 and note. *Hanes.* Possibly Heracleopolis Magna, about 50 miles south of Cairo, or perhaps a city in the Nile delta, close to Zoan.

‡30:6 *burden.* See 13:1 and note. *the south.* The Negev, the dry region in the southern part of the Holy Land (see Gen 12:9 and note; cf. Judg 1:9). *trouble and anguish.* Perhaps it was necessary to use back roads because the Assyrians had control of the main coastal road (see Deut 8:15; Judg 5:6). *flying serpent.* See 14:29.

‡30:7 *Their strength.* Hebrew *rahab;* read as a proper name, "Rahab," the name of a mythical sea monster, here symbolic of Egypt. The name itself means "storm," and also "arrogance." See 27:1 and note. *sit still.* Rahab (Egypt) will be destroyed.

‡30:8 *write it.* Isaiah is to write down the prophecy concerning the destruction of Rahab (Egypt) so that the people will be reminded of its fulfillment when Egypt falls.

30:9 *rebellious people.* See v. 1; see also 1:2 and note.

‡30:10 *seers.* See 1 Sam 9:9 and note; 2 Ki 17:13. *Prophesy not unto us right things.* Cf. Amos 2:12. *Speak unto us smooth things.* The people want a favorable message like the ones they receive from the false prophets (1 Ki 22:13; Jer 6:14; 8:11; 23:17,26).

30:11–12,15 *Holy One of Israel.* See 1:4 and note.

‡30:12 *oppression.* Especially in their domestic policy (see 1:15–17,23; 5:7; 29:21; 58:3–4; 59:3,6–8,13). *perverseness.* Guile and intrigue, especially in their foreign policy (see vv. 1–2; 29:15).

30:13 *as a breach . . . Swelling out in a high wall.* Oppression and perverseness (v. 12) had been the "wall" they built to assure their safety and prosperity, but it will be shattered to pieces.

‡30:14 *sheard . . . pit.* There will not even be shards from the destroyed wall big enough to scoop coals or water.

So that there shall not be found in the
bursting of it a sheard
To take fire from the hearth,
Or to take water *withal* out of the pit.
15 For thus saith the Lord GOD, the Holy
One of Israel;
[a]In returning and rest shall ye be saved;
In quietness and in confidence shall be
your strength:
[b]And ye would not.
16 But ye said, No; for we will flee upon
horses;
Therefore shall ye flee:
And, We will ride upon the swift;
Therefore shall they that pursue you be
swift.
17 [a]One thousand *shall flee* at the rebuke
of one;
At the rebuke of five shall ye flee:
Till ye be left as [1]a beacon upon the
top of a mountain,
And as an ensign on a hill.

18 And therefore will the LORD wait, that
he may be gracious unto you,
And therefore will he be exalted, that
he may have mercy upon you:
For the LORD *is* a God of judgment:
[a]Blessed *are* all they that wait for him.
19 For the people [a]shall dwell in Zion at
Jerusalem:
Thou shalt weep no more:
He will be very gracious unto thee at
the voice of thy cry;
When *he* shall hear it, he will answer
thee.
20 And *though* the Lord give you [a]the
bread of adversity, and the water of
[1]affliction,
Yet shall not [b]thy teachers be removed
into a corner any more,
But thine eyes shall see thy teachers:
21 And thine ears shall hear a word
behind thee, saying,
This *is* the way, walk ye in it,
When ye [a]turn to the right hand, and
when ye turn to the left.
22 [a]Ye shall defile also the covering of
[1]thy graven images of silver,
And the ornament of thy molten
images of gold:
Thou shalt [2]cast them away as a
menstruous cloth;
[b]Thou shalt say unto it, Get thee hence.
23 [a]Then shall he give the rain of thy
seed,
That thou shalt sow the ground withal;
And bread of the increase of the earth,
And it shall be fat and plenteous:
In that day shall thy cattle feed *in* large
pastures.
24 The oxen likewise and the young asses
that ear the ground
Shall eat [1][2]clean provender,
Which hath been winnowed with the
shovel and with the fan.
25 And there shall be [a]upon every high
mountain,
And upon every [1]high hill,
Rivers *and* streams of waters in the day
of the great slaughter,
When the towers fall.
26 Moreover [a]the light of the moon shall
be as the light of the sun,
And the light of the sun shall be
sevenfold,
As the light of seven days,
In the day that the LORD bindeth up
the breach of his people,
And healeth the stroke of their wound.

27 Behold, the name of the LORD cometh
from far,
Burning *with* his anger, [1]and the
burden *thereof is* [2]heavy:
His lips are full *of* indignation,
And his tongue as a devouring fire:
28 And [a]his breath, as an overflowing
stream,
[b]Shall reach to the midst of the neck,

30:15 [a]ch. 7:4 [b]Mat. 23:37
30:17 [1]Or, *a tree bereft of branches,* or, *boughs:* or, *a mast* [a]Lev. 26:8; Deut. 28:25; Josh. 23:10
30:18 [a]Ps. 2:12; 34:8; Prov. 16:20; Jer. 17:7
30:19 [a]ch. 65:9
30:20 [1]Or, *oppression* [a]1 Ki. 22:27; Ps. 127:2 [b]Ps. 74:9; Amos 8:11
30:21 [a]Josh. 1:7
30:22 [1]Heb. *the graven images of thy silver* [2]Heb. *scatter* [a]2 Chr. 31:1; ch. 31:7 [b]Hos. 14:8
30:23 [a]Mat. 6:33; 1 Tim. 4:8
30:24 [1]Or, *savoury* [2]Heb. *leavened*
30:25 [1]Heb. *lifted up* [a]ch. 2:14,15
30:26 [a]ch. 60:19,20
30:27 [1]Or, *and the grievousness of flame* [2]Heb. *heaviness*
30:28 [a]ch. 11:4 [b]ch. 8:8

‡**30:15** See 26:3. *returning and rest.* The true way to salvation and security is turning to God and trusting in his promises.
30:16 *horses.* See Ps 33:17.
30:17 *One thousand shall flee.* A fulfillment of the curse of Deut 32:30. *beacon . . . ensign.* See 5:26 and note (see also 1:8 and note).
‡**30:18** *gracious . . . mercy.* After punishing Israel, God will once again bless them (cf. 40:2). *the LORD is a God of judgment.* A God of justice who does what is right in delivering his people as he has promised.
30:19 *weep no more.* See 25:8 and note. God's response is similar to His zeal for the vineyard (Israel) in 27:2–6.
‡**30:20** *bread of adversity . . . water of affliction.* Prisoners' food (see 1 Ki 22:27). *teachers be removed . . . any more.* True prophets of God will no longer have to hide because of persecution.
30:21 *This is the way.* Contrast the attitude shown in vv. 10–11 (cf. 29:24).
30:22 *defile . . . thy graven images.* In repentance, not in despair as in 2:20 (see note there).
30:23 *rain . . . bread . . . fat and plenteous.* Part of the covenant blessings promised in Deut 28:11–12. See 5:6 and note. *In that day.* Cf. 29:18; see notes on 10:20,27; 26:1. *cattle feed in large pastures.* Cf. 32:20.
‡**30:24** *ear the ground.* Animals that work the soil. *clean provender.* Fodder that is seasoned and tasty.
30:25 *upon every high mountain . . . streams.* Paradise-like conditions will return to the land (see 41:18; Ps 104:13–15). *day of the great slaughter.* Cf. 24:1; 34:2,6. Assyria's fall (v. 31) is one illustration.
‡**30:26** *moon . . . sevenfold.* The darkness will be past: Night will be like the day, and day will be illumined with sevenfold light. *bindeth up the breach . . . healeth the stroke of their wound.* Israel was wounded politically because of the sins of the people (see 1:6; 61:1; Jer 33:6).
‡**30:27** *the name.* The revelation of God, especially His power and glory. *anger . . . devouring fire.* The language of theophany (a manifestation or appearance of God). God is portrayed as coming in a storm (see v. 30; see also 28:2; 29:6; Ps 18:7–15 and notes).
30:28 *reach to . . . the neck.* The army of Assyria was similarly described in 8:8 (see note there). *bridle.* Cf. 37:29.

To sift the nations with the sieve of
vanity:
And *there shall be* [c]a bridle in the jaws
of the people, causing *them* to err.
29 Ye shall have a song, as *in* the night
when a holy solemnity is kept;
And gladness of heart, as when one
goeth with a pipe
To come into [a]the mountain of the
LORD, to the [b][1]mighty One of Israel.
30 [a]And the LORD shall cause [1]his glorious
voice to be heard,
And shall shew the lighting down of
his arm,
With the indignation of *his* anger,
And *with* the flame of a devouring fire,
With scattering, and tempest, [b]and
hailstones.
31 For [a]through the voice of the LORD
shall the Assyrian be beaten down,
[b]*Which* smote with a rod.
32 And [1]*in* every *place* where the
grounded staff shall pass,
Which the LORD shall [2]lay upon him,
It shall be with tabrets and harps:
And in battles of [a]shaking will he fight
[3]with it.
33 [a]For Tophet *is* ordained [1]of old;
Yea, for the king it is prepared;
He hath made *it* deep *and* large:
The pile thereof *is* fire and much wood;
The breath of the LORD, like a stream
of brimstone, doth kindle it.

The folly of reliance upon Egypt

31 Woe to them [a]that go down *to* Egypt
for help;
And [b]stay on horses,
And trust in chariots, because *they are*
many;
And in horsemen, because they are
very strong;
But they look not unto the Holy One of
Israel,
[c]Neither seek the LORD.
2 Yet he also *is* wise, and will bring evil,
And [a]will not [1]call back his words:
But will arise against the house of the
evildoers,
And against the help of them that work
iniquity.
3 Now the Egyptians *are* men, and not
God;
And their horses flesh, and not spirit.
When the LORD shall stretch out his
hand,
Both he that helpeth shall fall, and he
that is holpen shall fall down,
And they all shall fail together.
4 For thus hath the LORD spoken unto
me,
[a]Like as the lion and the young lion
roaring on his prey,
When a multitude of shepherds is
called forth against him,
He will not be afraid of their voice,
Nor abase himself for the [1]noise of
them:
So shall the LORD of hosts come down
To fight for mount Zion, and for the
hill thereof.
5 [a]As birds flying, so will the LORD of
hosts defend Jerusalem;
Defending also he will deliver *it;*
And passing over he will preserve *it.*
6 Turn ye unto *him from* whom the
children of Israel have deeply
revolted.
7 For in that day every man shall [a]cast
away
His idols of silver, and [1]his idols of
gold,
Which your own hands have made
unto you *for* [b]a sin.
8 Then shall the Assyrian [a]fall with the
sword, not of a mighty man;
And the sword, not of a mean man,
shall devour him:
But he shall flee [1]from the sword,
And his young men shall be
[2][3]discomfited.

30:28 [c]ch. 37:29
30:29 [1]Heb. *Rock* [a]ch. 2:3 [b]Deut. 32:4
30:30 [1]Heb. *the glory of his voice* [a]ch. 29:6 [b]ch. 28:2
30:31 [a]ch. 37:36 [b]ch. 10:5,24
30:32 [1]Heb. *every passing of the rod founded* [2]Heb. *cause to rest upon him* [3]Or, *against them* [a]ch. 11:15
30:33 [1]Heb. *from yesterday* [a]Jer. 7:31
31:1 [a]ch. 30:2 [b]Ps. 20:7 [c]Dan. 9:13
31:2 [1]Heb. *remove* [a]Num. 23:19
31:4 [1]Or, *multitude* [a]Amos 3:8
31:5 [a]Deut. 32:11
31:7 [1]Heb. *the idols of his gold* [a]ch. 2:20 [b]1 Ki. 12:30
31:8 [1]Or, *for fear of the sword* [2]Or, *tributary* [3]Heb. *for melting, or, tribute* [a]2 Ki. 19:35,36

‡30:29 *song . . . holy solemnity.* Perhaps the passover, alluded to in 31:5 (cf. Mat 26:30). *mountain of the LORD.* Zion, where the temple was (see 2:2–4 and note).
30:30–31 *voice.* Associated with thunder in Ex 20:18–19; Ps 29:3–4.
30:30 *lighting down . . . arm.* See 9:12,17,21; 51:9 and notes. *scattering . . . hailstones.* See 28:2.
30:31 *voice of the LORD . . . beaten down.* Cf. Ps 29:5–9.
‡30:32 *grounded staff.* Lit. "the appointed staff" that God uses against the nations. See 11:4 and note. *tabrets and harps.* After a great victory the women rejoiced with singing and dancing (see Ex 15:20–21; 1 Sam 18:6).
30:33 *Tophet.* A region outside Jerusalem where children were sacrificed to Molech (see 2 Ki 23:10; Jer 7:31–32; 19:6, 11–14), the god of the Ammonites (see 1 Ki 11:7). Thus it was a place of burning. *king.* Of Assyria. *brimstone.* See 1:31; Gen 19:24 and notes.
31:1 See 30:1 and note. Ch. 31 recapitulates ch. 30. *go down to Egypt.* See Gen 26:2. *horses . . . chariots.* Egypt had large numbers of horses and chariots (see 1 Ki 10:28–29). *Holy One of Israel.* See 1:4 and note.
31:2 *he also is wise.* People had questioned God's wisdom in 29:14–16.
‡31:3 *stretch out his hand.* Cf. the refrain in 5:25; 9:12,17,21; 10:4. *he that is holpen.* Or "the one who is helped" (Israel). *shall fall.* Israel will fall in spite of Egypt's help; cf. 30:3,5.
31:4 *lion.* A simile, but perhaps also an allusion to the Assyrian king (see note on 15:9). *shepherds.* Perhaps an allusion to the rulers of the nations (see Nah 3:18 and note).
31:5 *birds . . . defend.* Cf. Deut 32:10–11. *passing over.* The technical word used of the destroying angel who "passed over" every house in Egypt that had blood on the doorposts (see Ex 12:13,23). Cf. Is 37:35.
31:6 *deeply revolted.* See 1:2 and note.
31:7 *cast away His idols.* See 2:20 and note.
‡31:8 *sword, not of a mighty man.* The angel of the Lord struck down 185,000 soldiers (see 37:36). *shall be discomfited.* Lit. "shall become slave laborers" (as prisoners of war).

9 And [a][1]he shall pass over *to* [2]his strong
hold for fear,
And his princes shall be afraid of the
ensign,
Saith the LORD, whose fire *is* in Zion,
And his furnace in Jerusalem.

Israel's ultimate deliverance

32 Behold, [a]a king shall reign in
righteousness,
And princes shall rule in judgment.
2 And a man shall be as a hiding place
from the wind,
And [a]a covert from the tempest;
As rivers of water in a dry place,
As the shadow of a [1]great rock in a
weary land.
3 And [a]the eyes of them that see shall
not be dim,
And the ears of them that hear shall
hearken.
4 The heart also of the [1]rash shall
understand knowledge,
And the tongue of the stammerers shall
be ready to speak [2]plainly.
5 The vile person shall be no more called
liberal,
Nor the churl said *to be* bountiful.
6 For the vile person will speak villany,
And his heart will work iniquity,
To practise hypocrisy, and to utter error
against the LORD,
To make empty the soul of the hungry,
And he will cause the drink of the
thirsty to fail.
7 The instruments also of the churl *are*
evil:
He deviseth wicked devices
To destroy the poor with lying words,
Even [1]when the needy speaketh right.
8 But the liberal deviseth liberal *things;*
And by liberal *things* shall he [1]stand.

After calamity, restoration

9 Rise up, ye women [a]that are at ease,
hear my voice;
Ye careless daughters, give ear unto my
speech.
10 [1]Many days and years shall ye be
troubled, ye careless *women:*
For the vintage shall fail, the gathering
shall not come.
11 Tremble, ye *women* that are at ease; be
troubled, ye careless ones:
Strip ye, and make ye bare, and gird
sackcloth upon *your* loins.
12 They *shall* lament for the teats,
For [1]the pleasant fields, for the fruitful
vine.
13 [a]Upon the land of my people shall
come up thorns *and* briers;
[1]Yea, upon all the houses of joy *in* [b]the
joyous city:
14 [a]Because the palaces shall be forsaken;
The multitude of the city shall be left;
The [1]forts and towers shall be for dens
for ever,
A joy of wild asses, a pasture of flocks;
15 Until [a]the spirit be poured upon us
from on high,
And [b]the wilderness be a fruitful field,
And the fruitful field be counted for a
forest.
16 Then judgment shall dwell in the
wilderness,
And righteousness remain in the
fruitful field.
17 [a]And the work of righteousness shall
be peace;

31:9 [1]Heb. [*his*] *rock shall pass away for fear* [2]Or, *his strength* [a]ch. 37:37
32:1 [a]Ps. 45:1
32:2 [1]Heb. *heavy* [a]ch. 4:6
32:3 [a]ch. 29:18
32:4 [1]Heb. *hasty* [2]Or, *elegantly*
32:7 [1]Or, *when he speaketh* against *the poor* in *judgment*
32:8 [1]Or, *be established*
32:9 [a]Amos 6:1
32:10 [1]Heb. *Days above a year*
32:12 [1]Heb. *the fields of desire*
32:13 [1]Or, *Burning upon, etc.* [a]Hos. 9:6 [b]ch. 22:2
32:14 [1]Or, *clifts and watchtowers* [a]ch. 27:10
32:15 [a]Joel 2:28 [b]ch. 29:17
32:17 [a]Jas. 3:18

‡31:9 *pass over . . . fear.* The Assyrian king will retreat out of fear but will still not avoid God's judgment. Nineveh was destroyed by the Medes and Babylonians in 612 B.C. (see Nah 3:7). *princes shall be afraid.* Cf. Nah 2:10. *fire . . . furnace.* The Lord's glory resides in Zion, and from that center of His people His fire of judgment breaks out upon the wicked (see 10:17; 30:33; cf. Lev 10:2; Joel 3:16; Amos 1:2).
32:1 *king . . . reign in righteousness.* The Messianic age is again in view (see 9:7; 11:4; 16:5 and notes). Cf. vv. 16–17; 33:17.
32:2 *a man . . . hiding place.* The Lord's redeemed, as sources of protection and blessing, will reflect Him (see the rest of this note; see also vv. 3–8). *hiding place . . . covert . . . shadow.* Similar terms are applied to the Lord in 25:4 (see 4:5–6 and note). *rivers . . . in a dry place.* See 35:6–7; 41:18; 49:10.
32:3 *eyes . . . not be dim . . . ears . . . shall hearken.* See 35:5 and note (contrast 6:9–10).
32:5–8 The redeemed will no longer be among the fools. The contrast between the fool and the wise or noble man is characteristic of wisdom literature (compare Prov 9:1–6 with Prov 9:13–18).
32:6 *vile person will speak villany.* Cf. 9:16–17; Ps 14:1; 53:1.
‡32:7 *churl.* Another word for a fool. *the needy speaketh right.* The fool disregards the truthful words of the needy. See 1:17 and note.
‡32:8 *liberal.* A generous person. *deviseth . . . stand.* See 8:10 and note.
‡32:9 *women.* Cf. 3:16–4:1. *at ease . . . careless.* "Careless" here means "complacent." See v. 11; Amos 6:1. These words are used in a good sense in v. 18 (the Hebrew for "quiet" is the same as that for "careless").
32:10 *the vintage shall fail.* Cf. 37:30. The armies of Assyria would bring widespread destruction, ruining the summer fruit.
32:11 *Strip.* Cf. 47:2–3. *sackcloth.* Cf. 3:24; 22:12; see note on Gen 37:34.
‡32:12 *lament for the teats.* Lit. "[they will be] wailing on their breasts." They will be beating their breasts like the slave girls of Nineveh (Nah 2:7). *for the fruitful vine.* Cf. the Lord's weeping in 16:9.
32:13 *thorns and briers.* See 5:6; 7:23 and notes. *joy . . . joyous.* See 22:2 and note; cf. Jer 16:8–9.
32:14 *palaces . . . multitude of the city.* Assyria's invasion is a warning that Jerusalem (see 24:10 and note) will one day be destroyed. *wild asses . . . flocks.* Cf. 7:25; 13:21–22; 34:13.
32:15 *Until the spirit.* The outpouring of the Spirit is linked with abundance also in 44:3 (see v. 2; 11:2 and notes; see also Joel 2:28–32). *fruitful field . . . forest.* The forest probably stands for Lebanon (see 29:17 and note; cf. 35:1–2).
32:16 *judgment . . . righteousness.* See v. 1 and note.
32:17 *peace.* Cf. 9:7; 11:6–9. *quietness and assurance.* Contrast 30:15.

And the effect of righteousness
quietness and assurance for ever.
18 And my people shall dwell in a
peaceable habitation,
And in sure dwellings,
And in quiet resting places;
19 [a]When it shall hail, coming down [b]*on* the forest;
[1]And the city shall be low in a low
place.
20 Blessed *are* ye that sow beside all
waters,
That send forth *thither* the feet of [a]the
ox and the ass.

The distress of Judah

33 Woe to thee [a]that spoilest, and thou
wast not spoiled;
And dealest treacherously, and they
dealt not treacherously with thee!
[b]When thou shalt cease to spoil, thou
shalt be spoiled;
And when thou shalt make an end to
deal treacherously, they shall deal
treacherously with thee.
2 O LORD, be gracious unto us; [a]we have
waited for thee:
Be thou their arm every morning,
Our salvation also in the time of
trouble.
3 At the noise of the tumult the people
fled;
At the lifting up of thyself the nations
were scattered.
4 And your spoil shall be gathered *like*
the gathering of the caterpillar:
As the running to and fro of locusts
shall he run upon them.
5 [a]The LORD *is* exalted; for he dwelleth
on high:
He hath filled Zion *with* judgment and
righteousness.
6 And wisdom and knowledge shall be
The stability of thy times, *and* strength
of [1]salvation:
The fear of the LORD *is* his treasure.
7 Behold, their [1]valiant ones shall cry
without:
[a]The ambassadors of peace shall weep
bitterly.
8 [a]The highways lie waste, the wayfaring
man ceaseth:
[b]He hath broken the covenant,
He hath despised the cities, he
regardeth no man.
9 [a]The earth mourneth *and* languisheth:
Lebanon is ashamed *and* [1]hewn down:
Sharon is like a wilderness;
And Bashan and Carmel shake off *their*
fruits.

10 [a]Now will I rise, saith the LORD;
Now will I be exalted;
Now will I lift up myself.
11 [a]Ye shall conceive chaff, ye shall bring
forth stubble:
Your breath, *as* fire, shall devour you.
12 And the people shall be *as* the
burnings of lime:
[a]*As* thorns cut up shall they be burnt
in the fire.
13 Hear, [a]ye *that are* far off, what I have
done;
And ye *that are* near, acknowledge my
might.
14 The sinners in Zion are afraid;
Fearfulness hath surprised the
hypocrites.
Who among us shall dwell *with* the
devouring fire?
Who amongst us shall dwell *with*
everlasting burnings?

32:19 [1]Or, *And the city shall be utterly abased* [a]ch. 30:30 [b]Zech. 11:2
32:20 [a]ch. 30:24
33:1 [a]ch. 21:2; Hab. 2:8 [b]Rev. 13:10
33:2 [a]ch. 25:9
33:5 [a]Ps. 97:9
33:6 [1]Heb. *salvations*
33:7 [1]Or, *messengers* [a]2 Ki. 18:18,37
33:8 [a]Judg. 5:6 [b]2 Ki. 18:14-17
33:9 [1]Or, *withered away* [a]ch. 24:4
33:10 [a]Ps. 12:5
33:11 [a]Ps. 7:14; ch. 59:4
33:12 [a]ch. 9:18
33:13 [a]ch. 49:1

32:18 *sure . . . quiet.* See note on v. 9. *resting places.* See 28:12 and note.
32:19 *hail.* Cf. 28:2. *forest.* Probably Assyria. See 10:33–34 and notes. *city.* See 24:10 and note.
32:20 The abundance of the day of the Lord is described (see 30:23–24 and notes).
33:1 *Woe.* See note on 28:1–35:10. *spoilest . . . dealest treacherously.* Probably Assyria—depicted as a deceitful destroyer (see 10:5–6; 16:4; 21:2; 24:16 and notes).
33:2–9 A prayer asking the Lord to bring about the promised destruction of Assyria.
33:2 *be gracious.* See 30:18 and note. *their arm . . . salvation.* See 12:2 and note; cf. 59:16. *trouble.* See 37:3.
33:3 *noise of the tumult.* See 30:30–31 and note. *lifting up . . . scattered.* An allusion to Num 10:35; cf. Ps 68:1.
33:5 *filled . . . righteousness.* See 1:26; 32:1 and note.
33:6 *wisdom and knowledge . . . fear of the LORD.* Terms linked with the Messiah in 11:2. See 9:6; Prov 1:7 and notes.
33:7 *their valiant ones.* The men of Judah, during Sennacherib's invasion of 701 B.C. (see 10:28–34). *ambassadors of peace.* Perhaps the three officials who conferred with the Assyrian field commander (see 36:3,22).
33:8 *highways lie waste.* Travel and trade were impossible, creating economic hardship (see Judg 5:6). *covenant.* Perhaps the agreement made when Hezekiah paid large sums to Sennacherib (2 Ki 18:14).
33:9 *earth . . . languisheth.* Farmland and pastures were ruined by the invaders. See 24:4 and note. *Lebanon.* Renowned for its cedars (2:13) and beasts (40:16). *Sharon.* A plain along the Mediterranean coast north of Joppa, known for its beautiful foliage and superb grazing land (see 35:2; 65:10; 1 Chr 27:29). *wilderness.* Desert land associated with the Jordan River and the Dead Sea (see Deut 1:1; 2:8). *Bashan.* See 2:13 and note. *Carmel.* See note on 1 Ki 18:19; means "fruitful field" (as in 29:17; 32:15) or "plentiful field" (as in 16:10) and is also associated with lush pasturelands (see 35:2; Mic 7:14; Nah 1:4).
33:10 *be exalted.* Through the judgment He brings on His rebellious people (see v. 14 and note).
33:11 *conceive . . . bring forth.* Cf. 26:18. *breath, as fire.* They only produce what results in their destruction.
33:12 *burnings of lime.* The burning will be complete (see Amos 2:1). *thorns.* They burn very quickly (see 27:4; 2 Sam 23:6–7).
33:13 *Hear . . . acknowledge.* Cf. 34:1.
33:14 *sinners in Zion.* See 1:27–28; 4:4. *devouring fire.* The presence of the God of judgment (see 29:6; 30:27,30; Ex 24:17; Deut 4:24; 9:3; 2 Sam 22:9; Ps 18:8; Heb 12:29).

15 He that [a]walketh [1]righteously, and
speaketh [2]uprightly;
He that despiseth the gain of
[3]oppressions,
That shaketh his hands from holding of
bribes,
That stoppeth his ears from hearing of
[4]blood,
And [b]shutteth his eyes from seeing
evil;
16 He shall dwell on [1]high:
His place of defence *shall be* the
munitions of rocks:
Bread *shall be* given him; his waters
shall be sure.

Safety and joy under the Messiah

17 Thine eyes shall see the king in his
beauty:
They shall behold [1]the land that is very
far off.
18 Thine heart shall meditate terror.
[a]Where *is* the scribe? where *is* the
[1]receiver?
Where *is* he that counted the towers?
19 [a]Thou shalt not see a fierce people,
[b]A people of a deeper speech than
thou canst perceive;
Of a [1]stammering tongue, *that thou*
canst not understand.
20 [a]Look upon Zion, the city of our
solemnities:
Thine eyes shall see [b]Jerusalem a quiet
habitation,
A tabernacle *that* shall not be taken
down;
[c]Not one of [d]the stakes thereof shall
ever be removed,
Neither shall any of the cords thereof
be broken.

33:15 [1]Heb. in *righteousnesses* [2]Heb. *uprightnesses* [3]Or, *deceits* [4]Heb. *bloods* [a]Ps. 15:2; 24:4 [b]Ps. 119:37
33:16 [1]Heb. *heights,* or, *high places*
33:17 [1]Heb. *the land of far distances*
33:18 [1]Heb. *weigher?* [a]1 Cor. 1:20
33:19 [1]Or, *ridiculous* [a]2 Ki. 19:32 [b]Deut. 28:49,50; Jer. 5:15
33:20 [a]Ps. 48:12 [b]Ps. 46:5; 125:1,2 [c]ch. 37:33 [d]ch. 54:2
33:21 [1]Heb. *broad of spaces,* or, *hands*
33:22 [1]Heb. *statutemaker* [a]Jas. 4:12 [b]Ps. 89:18
33:23 [1]Or, *They have forsaken thy tacklings*
33:24 [a]Jer. 50:20
34:1 [1]Heb. *the fulness thereof* [a]Ps. 49:1 [b]Deut. 32:1
34:3 [a]Joel 2:20
34:4 [a]Ps. 102:26; Ezek. 32:7,8; Joel 2:31; Mat. 24:29; 2 Pet. 3:10 [b]ch. 14:12

21 But there the glorious LORD *will be*
unto us
A place [1]of broad rivers *and* streams;
Wherein shall go no galley with oars,
Neither shall gallant ship pass thereby.
22 For the LORD *is* our judge, the LORD *is*
our [a]1 lawgiver,
[b]The LORD *is* our king; he will save us.
23 [1]Thy tacklings are loosed;
They could not well strengthen their
mast, they could not spread the sail:
Then is the prey of a great spoil divided;
The lame take the prey.
24 And the inhabitant shall not say, I am
sick:
[a]The people that dwell therein *shall be*
forgiven *their* iniquity.

The judgment on the nations

34 [a]Come near, ye nations, to hear;
And hearken, ye people:
[b]Let the earth hear, and [1]all that is
therein;
The world, and all things that come
forth of it.
2 For the indignation of the LORD *is* upon
all nations,
And *his* fury upon all their armies:
He hath utterly destroyed them, he
hath delivered them to the slaughter.
3 Their slain also shall be cast out,
And [a]their stink shall come up *out of*
their carcases,
And the mountains shall be melted
with their blood.
4 And [a]all the host of heaven shall be
dissolved,
And the heavens shall be rolled
together as a scrole:
[b]And all their host shall fall down,

33:15 Similar requirements are found in Ps 15:2–5; 24:4. *bribes.* See 1:23.
33:16 *rocks.* Symbolic of the security found in God (cf. Ps 18:1–3). *Bread . . . waters.* Cf. 49:10.
33:17 *king.* See 32:1 and note; cf. 6:5. *in his beauty.* Reflecting on the splendor and majesty of a Davidic king; probably a foreshadowing of the Messianic kingdom (cf. 4:2; Ps 45:3–4; contrast Is 53:2). *land that is very far off.* See 26:15 and note.
33:18 *terror.* The Assyrian invasion (see 17:12–14 and note). *the receiver.* Of the forced tribute collected by the Assyrians (see note on v. 8). *towers.* Judah's fortifications were probably under strict Assyrian control (see 2:15).
‡33:19 *shalt not see a fierce people.* Assyria will no longer be a feared nation. *deeper speech . . . stammering tongue.* The Assyrian language was related to Hebrew but was different enough to sound strange to Israelite ears. See 28:11; Deut 28:49.
‡33:20 *Look upon Zion.* The redeemed city, in contrast to the city described in vv. 7–9. *solemnities.* Religious feasts. See 1:14 and note. *quiet habitation.* See 32:17–18 and notes. *tabernacle . . . not be taken down.* Her exile will be over and she will be completely secure. *stakes . . . cords.* Cf. the similar description of Jerusalem in 54:2.
33:21 *glorious LORD.* See 10:34 (cf. Ps 93:4). *broad rivers.* To prevent easy access to her borders—thus like Tyre (23:1) or Thebes (see Nah 3:8).
33:22 *our judge.* See 2:4; 11:4 and note. *our lawgiver.* See 2:3; 51:4; Gen 49:10. *our king.* See v. 17; 32:1 and note; see also Ps 46; 48. *save.* See Judg 2:16.
33:23 *tacklings.* Jerusalem is pictured as a ship, unprepared to sail into battle against Assyria. *Then.* When God strikes down the Assyrian army (see 10:33–34; 37:36). *prey.* See v. 4.
33:24 Looking beyond Isaiah's own day to the physically and spiritually whole Jerusalem of vv. 17,20–22.
34:1–35:10 Chs. 34–35 conclude chs. 28–33 and comprise an eschatological section corresponding to chs. 24–27, which conclude chs. 13–23 (see note on 24:1–27:13).
34:2 *indignation . . . fury.* In the day of the Lord (see 2:11,17,20; 26:20–21 and notes). See also 13:3 and note; 13:13. *utterly destroyed.* The kind of destruction the Canaanites had deserved. The Hebrew term refers to the irrevocable giving over of things or persons to the LORD, often by totally destroying them (see v. 5; see also Josh 6:17). *slaughter.* See 30:25 and note.
34:3 *cast out.* Not to have a proper burial was considered a disgrace (see 14:19 and note).
‡34:4 *host of heaven . . . dissolved.* Disturbances in the heavens characterize the day of the Lord (see 13:10,13 and notes; cf. Ezek 32:7–8). *heavens . . . scrole . . . host shall fall down.* Referred to in Mat 24:29; Rev 6:13–14 in connection with the "great tribulation" (Mat 24:21) and the second coming of Christ to set up his kingdom. *As the leaf falleth off.* Cf. 24:4; 40:7–8.

As the leaf falleth off from the vine,
And as a [c]falling *fig* from the fig tree.
5 For [a]my sword shall be bathed in heaven:
Behold, it [b]shall come down upon Idumea,
And upon the people of my curse, to judgment.
6 The sword of the LORD is filled *with* blood,
It is made fat with fatness,
And with the blood of lambs and goats,
With the fat of the kidneys of rams:
For [a]the LORD hath a sacrifice in Bozrah,
And a great slaughter in the land of Idumea.
7 And the [1]unicorns shall come down with them,
And the bullocks with the bulls;
And their land shall be [2]soaked with blood,
And their dust made fat with fatness.
8 For *it is* the day of the LORD's [a]vengeance,
And the year of recompences for the controversy of Zion.
9 [a]And the streams thereof shall be turned into pitch,
And the dust thereof into brimstone,
And the land thereof shall become burning pitch.
10 It shall not be quenched night nor day;
[a]The smoke thereof shall go up for ever:
[b]From generation to generation it shall lie waste;
None shall pass through it for ever and ever.
11 [a]But the [1]cormorant and the bittern shall possess it;
The owl also and the raven shall dwell in it:
And [b]he shall stretch out upon it the line of confusion, and the stones of emptiness.
12 They shall call the nobles thereof *to* the kingdom, but none *shall be* there,
And all her princes shall be nothing.
13 And [a]thorns shall come up *in* her palaces,
Nettles and brambles in the fortresses thereof:
And [b]it shall be a habitation of dragons,
And a court for [1][2]owls.
14 [1]The wild beasts of the desert shall also meet with [2]the wild beasts of the island,
And the satyr shall cry to his fellow;
The [3]shrich owl also shall rest there,
And find for herself a place of rest.
15 There shall the great owl make her nest, and lay,
And hatch, and gather under her shadow:
There shall the vultures also be gathered,
Every one *with* her mate.
16 Seek ye out of [a]the book of the LORD, and read:
No one of these shall fail,
None shall want her mate:
For my mouth it hath commanded,
And his spirit it hath gathered them.
17 And he hath cast the lot for them,
And his hand hath divided it unto them by line:
They shall possess it for ever,
From generation to generation shall they dwell therein.

The return to Zion promised

35 The [a]wilderness and the solitary place shall be glad *for* them;

34:4 [c]Rev. 6:13
34:5 [a]Jer. 46:10 [b]Jer. 49:7; Mal. 1:4
34:6 [a]Zeph. 1:7
34:7 [1]Or, *rhinocerots* [2]Or, *drunken*
34:8 [a]ch. 63:4
34:9 [a]Deut. 29:23
34:10 [a]Rev. 14:11; 18:18; 19:3 [b]Mal. 1:4
34:11 [1]Or, *pelican* [a]ch. 14:23; Zeph. 2:14; Rev. 18:2
34:11 [b]2 Ki. 21:13; Lam. 2:8
34:13 [1]Or, *ostriches* [2]Heb. *daughters of the owl* [a]ch. 32:13; Hos. 9:6 [b]ch. 13:21
34:14 [1]Heb. *Ziim* [2]Heb. *Ijim* [3]Or, *night monster*
34:16 [a]Mal. 3:16
35:1 [a]ch. 55:12

‡34:5 *bathed.* Cf. Ezek 39:18–20. *Idumea.* Read as "Edom," symbolic of all the enemies of God and His people (cf. Obad 8–9,15–16), like Moab in 25:10–12. See note on 21:11. The Edomites were driven from their homeland by the Nabatean Arabs, perhaps as early as 500 B.C.
34:6 *fat.* Considered the best part of the meat, and therefore offered to the Lord in the sacrifices (see Lev 3:9–11). *lambs and goats.* Symbolizing the people. *sacrifice.* Battles are often compared to sacrifices (see Jer 46:10; 50:27; Ezek 39:17–19). *Bozrah.* An important city of Edom and a sheepherding center, it was located about 25 miles southeast of the southern end of the Dead Sea. The name means "grape-gathering" (cf. 63:1–3).
‡34:7 *unicorns . . . bullocks.* For "unicorns," read "wild oxen." These animals symbolize the troops and/or leaders of the nations. *soaked with blood.* See v. 3.
34:8 *day of the LORD's vengeance.* See 35:4; 61:2. The Edomites opposed Israel at every opportunity (see 2 Sam 8:13–14) and rejoiced when Jerusalem was destroyed (Lam 4:21; Ps 137:7). But Edom's day would come (see 63:4).
34:9 *brimstone.* Edom's destruction is compared with the overthrow of Sodom and Gomorrah (see Jer 49:17–18). See also 1:31; Gen 19:24 and notes.
34:10 *smoke . . . for ever.* Applied to Babylon in Rev 19:3 (see also Rev 14:10–11). *lie waste.* See 13:20–22 and note; Mal 1:3–4.
‡34:11 *cormorant.* Pelican. *cormorant . . . owl . . . raven.* "Unclean" birds (see Deut 14:14–17). Such birds would also live in the ruins of Babylon (13:21) and Nineveh (Zeph 2:14). *line . . . stones.* Used for measuring. See 28:17 and note. *confusion . . . emptiness.* The Hebrew for these words is used in Gen 1:2 (see note there) to describe the earth in its "without form" and "void" state (see also Jer 4:23 and note).
‡34:13 *thorns . . . Nettles.* Cf. 7:24–25. *dragons.* Read "jackal" instead (an animal of the wilderness, cf. 35:7; 43:20; Jer 9:11).
34:14 *beasts of the desert . . . beasts of the island.* See 13:21–22. *satyr.* Sometimes connected with demons (see note on 13:21). *shrich owl.* Outside the Bible a related Semitic word refers to a "night demon."
‡34:15 *vultures.* More likely "hawks" or "kites," ceremonially unclean birds (see v. 11 and note; Deut 14:13,15–17).
34:16 *book.* After the destruction of Edom, people will read this prophecy given by Isaiah. *these.* The creatures just listed.
34:17 *cast the lot for them.* God will give the creatures of vv. 11,13–15 clear title to the land of Edom.
35:1 *wilderness . . . shall be glad.* The personification of nature is common in Isaiah (see 33:9; 44:23; 55:12). *desert.* See note on 33:9. *rose.* See Sol 2:1 and note.

And the desert shall rejoice, and
blossom as the rose.
2 [a]It shall blossom abundantly and rejoice
Even *with* joy and singing:
The glory of Lebanon shall be given
unto it,
The excellency of Carmel and Sharon,
They shall see the glory of the LORD,
And the excellency of our God.

3 [a]Strengthen ye the weak hands,
And confirm the feeble knees.
4 Say to them that are of a [1]fearful heart,
Be strong, fear not:
Behold, your God will come *with*
vengeance,
Even God *with* a recompence;
He will come and save you.
5 Then the [a]eyes of the blind shall be
opened,
And [b]the ears of the deaf shall be
unstopped.
6 Then shall the [a]lame *man* leap as a
hart,
And the [b]tongue of the dumb sing:
For in the wilderness shall [c]waters
break out,
And streams in the desert.
7 And the parched ground shall become
a pool,
And the thirsty land springs of water:
In [a]the habitation of dragons, where
each lay,
Shall be [1]grass with reeds and rushes.
8 And a highway shall be there, and a
way,
And it shall be called The way of
holiness;
[a]The unclean shall not pass over it;
[1]but it *shall be* for those:
The wayfaring men, though fools, shall
not err *therein*.
9 [a]No lion shall be there,
Nor *any* ravenous beast shall go up
thereon,
It shall not be found there;
But the redeemed shall walk *there:*
10 And the [a]ransomed of the LORD shall
return,
And come *to* Zion with songs
And everlasting joy upon their heads:
They shall obtain joy and gladness,
And [b]sorrow and sighing shall flee away.

Sennacherib taunts Hezekiah

36 Now [a]it came to pass in the fourteenth year of king Hezekiah, *that*
Sennacherib king of Assyria came up against
all the defenced cities of Judah, and took them.
2 And the king of Assyria sent Rabshakeh
from Lachish to Jerusalem unto king Hezekiah
with a great army. And he stood by the conduit
of the upper pool in the highway of the fuller's
field.
3 Then came forth unto him Eliakim, Hilkiah's son, which *was* over the house, and Shebna the [1]scribe, and Joah, Asaph's son, the
recorder.
4 [a]And Rabshakeh said unto them, Say ye
now to Hezekiah, Thus saith the great king,
the king of Assyria, What confidence *is* this
where*in* thou trustest?
5 I say, *sayest thou,* (but *they are but* [1]vain
words) [2]*I have* counsel and strength for war:
now on whom dost thou trust, that thou rebellest against me?

35:2 [a]ch. 32:15
35:3 [a]Job 4:3,4; Heb. 12:12
35:4 [1]Heb. *hasty*
35:5 [a]ch. 29:18; Mat. 9:27; 11:5; John 9:6,7 [b]Mat. 11:5
35:6 [a]Mat. 11:5; 15:30; John 5:8,9; Acts 8:7 [b]ch. 32:4; Mat. 9:32; 12:22 [c]ch. 41:18; John 7:38
35:7 [1]Or, *a court for reeds, etc.* [a]ch. 34:13
35:8 [1]Or, *for he shall be with them* [a]ch. 52:1; Rev. 21:27
35:9 [a]Lev. 26:6; ch. 11:9; Ezek. 34:25
35:10 [a]ch. 51:11 [b]ch. 25:8; Rev. 7:17; 21:4
36:1 [a]2 Ki. 18:13,17; 2 Chr. 32:1
36:3 [1]Or, *secretary*
36:4 [a]2 Ki. 18:19
36:5 [1]Heb. *a word of lips* [2]Or, but *counsel and strength* are *for the war*

35:2 *rejoice . . . joy and singing.* See 54:1. *Lebanon . . . Carmel . . . Sharon.* Fertile areas renowned for their beautiful trees and foliage (see note on 33:9). *glory of the LORD.* In the great transformation just announced. See 6:3 and note.

35:4 *Be strong, fear not.* Cf. God's words of encouragement to Joshua in Josh 1:6–7,9,18. *God will come.* Similar language is used of the coming of the Messiah (see 62:11; cf. Rev 22:12). *vengeance . . . recompence.* See note on 34:8.

35:5 *eyes . . . ears.* See 29:18; 32:3; 42:7 and notes. Spiritual and physical healing are also linked together in Christ's ministry (see Mat 11:5).

35:6 *lame man leap . . . tongue of the dumb sing.* Signs of the Messianic age (see Mat 12:22; Acts 3:7–8). *waters . . . streams.* See 32:2 and note. Cf. God's provision of water in Ex 17:6; 2 Ki 3:15–20.

‡35:7 *springs.* Cf. 41:18. *dragons.* See note on 34:13. *reeds and rushes.* Plants that grow in marshes and lakes (cf. 19:6-7).

35:8 *highway.* A road built up to make travel easier (see 11:16; 40:3 and notes). *The way of holiness.* The way set apart for those who are holy; only the redeemed (v. 9) could use it. In ancient times, certain roads between temples were open only to those who were ceremonially pure.

35:9 *lion . . . beast.* Sometimes wild animals made travel dangerous (see Deut 8:15; Judg 14:5). *redeemed.* Those the Lord has delivered from bondage (cf. 1:27; 51:10; 62:12; Lev 25:47–48; Deut 7:8).

‡35:10 Repeated verbatim in 51:11. *come to Zion with songs.* As the Israelites did when they returned from Babylonian exile (see Ps 126). *sorrow . . . shall flee.* Cf. 25:8; 65:19.

36:1–39:8 Much of chs. 36–39 is paralleled, sometimes verbatim, in 2 Ki 18:13–20:19. The compiler of 2 Kings may have used Is 36–39 as one of his sources, or both may have drawn on a common source. Chs. 36–37 describe the fulfillment of many predictions about Assyria's collapse, while chs. 38–39 point toward the Babylonian context of chs. 40–66.

36:1 *fourteenth year of king Hezekiah.* 701 B.C., the 14th year of his sole reign. Hezekiah ruled as sole king from 715 to 686 but was a co-regent from c. 729 (see note on 2 Ki 18:1). *Sennacherib.* Reigned over Assyria from 705 to 681. *all the . . . cities.* In his annals Sennacherib lists 46 such cities (see note on 2 Ki 18:13).

36:2 *Lachish.* An important city about 30 miles southwest of Jerusalem that guarded the main approach to Judah's capital from that quarter (see Jer 34:7). *great army.* Cf. 37:36. *conduit . . . field.* See 7:3 and note; see also note on 2 Ki 18:17.

36:3 *Eliakim.* See 22:20–21 and notes. *over the house.* In charge of the palace (see 22:15 and note). *Shebna.* See 22:15 and note. *scribe.* Perhaps equivalent to secretary of state (see Jer 36:12; see also note on 2 Sam 8:17). *recorder.* An official position also associated elsewhere with "scribe" (see 1 Ki 4:3). See also note on 2 Sam 8:16.

36:4,13 *great king.* See note on 2 Ki 18:19.

36:5 *rebellest.* By refusing to pay the expected tribute (see 2 Ki 17:4; 18:7).

6 Lo, thou trustest in the [a]staff of this broken reed, on Egypt; whereon if a man lean, it will go into his hand, and pierce it: so *is* Pharaoh king of Egypt to all that trust in him.

7 But if thou say to me, We trust in the LORD our God: *is it* not he, whose high places and whose altars Hezekiah hath taken away, and said to Judah and to Jerusalem, Ye shall worship before this altar?

8 Now therefore give [1]pledges, I pray thee, to my master the king of Assyria, and I will give thee two thousand horses, if thou be able on thy part to set riders upon them.

9 How then wilt thou turn away the face of one captain of the least of my master's servants, and put thy trust on Egypt for chariots and for horsemen?

10 And am I now come up without the LORD against this land to destroy it? the LORD said unto me, Go up against this land, and destroy it.

11 ¶ Then said Eliakim and Shebna and Joah unto Rabshakeh, Speak, I pray thee, unto thy servants in the Syrian language; for we understand *it:* and speak not to us in the Jews' language, in the ears of the people that *are* on the wall.

12 But Rabshakeh said, Hath my master sent me to thy master and to thee to speak these words? *hath he* not *sent me* to the men that sit upon the wall, that *they* may eat their own dung, and drink their own piss with you?

13 Then Rabshakeh stood, and cried with a loud voice in the Jews' language, and said, Hear ye the words of the great king, the king of Assyria.

14 Thus saith the king, Let not Hezekiah deceive you: for he shall not be able to deliver you.

15 Neither let Hezekiah make you trust in the LORD, saying, The LORD will surely deliver us: this city shall not be delivered into the hand of the king of Assyria.

16 Hearken not to Hezekiah: for thus saith the king of Assyria, [1]Make *an agreement* with me *by* a present, and come out to me: [a]and eat ye every one *of* his vine, and every one *of* his fig tree, and drink ye every one the waters of his own cistern;

17 Until I come and take you away to a land like your own land, a land of corn and wine, a land of bread and vineyards.

18 *Beware* lest Hezekiah persuade you, saying, The LORD will deliver us. Hath any of the gods of the nations delivered his land out of the hand of the king of Assyria?

19 Where *are* the gods of Hamath and Arphad? where *are* the gods of Sepharvaim? and have they delivered Samaria out of my hand?

20 Who *are they* amongst all the gods of these lands, that have delivered their land out of my hand, that the LORD should deliver Jerusalem out of my hand?

21 But they held their peace, and answered him not a word: for the king's commandment was, saying, Answer him not.

22 Then came Eliakim, the son of Hilkiah, that *was* over the household, and Shebna the scribe, and Joah, the son of Asaph, the recorder, to Hezekiah with *their* clothes rent, and told him the words of Rabshakeh.

Isaiah's message to Hezekiah

37 And [a]it came to pass, when king Hezekiah heard *it,* that he rent his clothes, and covered himself with sackcloth, and went *into* the house of the LORD.

2 And he sent Eliakim, who *was* over the household, and Shebna the scribe, and the

36:6 [a]Ezek. 29:6,7
36:8 [1]Or, *hostages*
36:16 [1]Or, *Seek my favour by a present.* Heb. *Make with me a blessing* [a]Zech. 3:10
37:1 [a]2 Ki. 19:1

36:6 *broken reed.* Egypt is compared to a reed again in Ezek 29:6–7. *Egypt.* Hezekiah had been under pressure to make an alliance with Egypt since 715 B.C. or earlier (see 20:5; 30:1 and notes). *so is Pharaoh.* Cf. 30:3,7.
36:7 *high places and . . . altars.* Hezekiah had destroyed these popular shrines often dedicated to Baal worship (see note on 2 Ki 18:4; see also 2 Chr 31:1). *this altar.* In Solomon's temple.
36:8 *two thousand horses.* A sizable number for any army. Horses and chariots were highly prized (see note on 30:16). *if thou be able . . . to set riders upon them.* See note on 2 Ki 18:23. *riders.* Probably charioteers, since cavalry was not employed by these nations this early (see v. 9).
36:10 *The LORD said unto me.* The Lord had used Assyria to punish Israel (see 10:5–6), but now it was Assyria's turn to be judged. Pharaoh Neco claimed God's approval on his mission according to 2 Chr 35:21.
‡36:11 *Eliakim . . . Joah.* See v. 3 and note. *Syrian language.* Aramaic, the diplomatic language of that day (see note on 2 Ki 18:26). *speak not to us . . . the Jews' language.* The officials feared that the commander's speech might damage the people's morale.
36:12 *eat . . . dung . . . drink . . . piss.* A crude way of describing the horrors of famine if Jerusalem was to be besieged (cf. 2 Ki 6:25). Contrast v. 16.
36:14 *deceive you.* Cf. 37:10.
‡36:16 *Make an agreement . . . present.* The Assyrian king is demanding the surrender of the city and the payment of tribute. *his vine . . . his fig tree.* Symbols of security and prosperity in the best of times (see 1 Ki 4:25; Mic 4:4).
36:17 *come and take you.* The Assyrians deported rebellious peoples to reduce their will to revolt (see 2 Ki 15:29; 17:6). *corn and wine.* Two of the staples of Israel (cf. Deut 28:51; Hag 1:11).
36:18–20 The commander's words echo the boasts of the proud Assyrians in 10:8–11. See note on 2 Ki 18:33–35.
36:19 *Hamath and Arphad.* See 10:9 and note. *Sepharvaim.* Probably located in northern Aram (Syria) not far from Hamath. Residents of Sepharvaim were deported to Samaria, though they still worshiped the gods Adrammelech and Anammelech. See 2 Ki 17:24,31. *Samaria.* The Assyrians assumed that each people had its own gods and so did not associate the God of Judah with that of Samaria.
36:21 *held their peace.* The Assyrians had hoped that the masterful psychology of vv. 4–20 would produce panic.
36:22 See v. 3 and note. *clothes rent.* See note on 2 Ki 18:37.
37:1 *clothes . . . sackcloth.* See Gen 37:34 and note; see also note on 2 Ki 18:37. *house of the LORD.* Designated as a place of prayer by Solomon (see 1 Ki 8:33). The Assyrian references to Hezekiah's dependence on the Lord (36:7,15,18) were true.
37:2 *Eliakim . . . Shebna.* See note on 36:3. *elders of the priests.*

elders of the priests covered with sackcloth,
unto Isaiah the prophet the son of Amoz.
3 And they said unto him, Thus saith Hezekiah, This day *is* a day of trouble, and of rebuke, and of [1]blasphemy: for the children are
come to the birth, and *there is* not strength to
bring forth.
4 It may be the LORD thy God will hear the
words of Rabshakeh, whom the king of Assyria his master hath sent to reproach the living
God, and will reprove the words which the
LORD thy God hath heard: wherefore lift up *thy*
prayer for the remnant that is [1]left.
5 So the servants of king Hezekiah came to
Isaiah.
6 And Isaiah said unto them, Thus shall ye
say unto your master, Thus saith the LORD, Be
not afraid of the words that thou hast heard,
where*with* the servants of the king of Assyria
have blasphemed me.
7 Behold, I will [1]send a blast upon him,
and he shall hear a rumour, and return to his
own land; and I will cause him to fall by the
sword in his own land.
8 ¶ So Rabshakeh returned, and found the
king of Assyria warring against Libnah: for he
had heard that he was departed from Lachish.
9 And he heard say concerning Tirhakah
king of Ethiopia, He is come forth to make war
with thee. And when he heard *it,* he sent messengers to Hezekiah, saying,
10 Thus shall ye speak to Hezekiah king of
Judah, saying, Let not thy God, in whom thou
trustest, deceive thee, saying, Jerusalem shall
not be given into the hand of the king of Assyria.
11 Behold, thou hast heard what the kings
of Assyria have done to all lands by destroying
them utterly; and shalt thou be delivered?
12 Have the gods of the nations delivered
them which my fathers have destroyed, *as* Gozan, and Haran, and Rezeph, and the children
of Eden which *were* in Telassar?
13 Where *is* the king of [a]Hamath, and the
king of Arphad, and the king of the city of
Sepharvaim, Hena, and Ivah?

Hezekiah's prayer to the LORD

14 ¶ And Hezekiah received the letter from
the hand of the messengers, and read it: and
Hezekiah went up *unto* the house of the LORD,
and spread it before the LORD.
15 And Hezekiah prayed unto the LORD,
saying,
16 O LORD of hosts, God of Israel, that
dwellest *between* the cherubims, thou *art* the
God, *even* thou alone, of all the kingdoms of
the earth: thou hast made heaven and earth.
17 [a]Incline thine ear, O LORD, and hear;
open thine eyes, O LORD, and see: and hear all
the words of Sennacherib, which hath sent to
reproach the living God.
18 Of a truth, LORD, the kings of Assyria have
laid waste all the [1]nations, and their countries,
19 And have [1]cast their gods into the fire:
for they *were* no gods, but the work of men's
hands, wood and stone: therefore they have
destroyed them.
20 Now therefore, O LORD our God, save
us from his hand, that all the kingdoms of the
earth may know that thou *art* the LORD, *even*
thou only.

The promise of deliverance

21 ¶ Then Isaiah the son of Amoz sent unto
Hezekiah, saying, Thus saith the LORD God of
Israel, Whereas thou hast prayed to me against
Sennacherib king of Assyria:
22 This *is* the word which the LORD hath
spoken concerning him;

> The virgin, the daughter of Zion, hath
> despised thee, *and* laughed thee to
> scorn;

37:3 [1] Or, *provocation*
37:4 [1] Heb. *found*
37:7 [1] Or, *put a spirit into him*
37:13 [a] Jer. 49:23
37:17 [a] Dan. 9:18
37:18 [1] Heb *lands*
37:19 [1] Heb. *given*

See note on 2 Ki 19:2. *Isaiah . . . son of Amoz.* See note on 1:1. Prophet, priests and king join in supplication.

‡37:3 *day of trouble.* See 5:30; 26:16; 33:2 and notes. *come to the birth.* The child is at the opening of the womb but cannot be born, an even more vivid description than that of the pains of childbirth (see 13:8 and note).

37:4 *reproach.* See vv. 17,23–24. *lift up thy prayer.* See note on 2 Ki 19:4. *remnant.* Jerusalem was left almost alone (see 36:1 and notes on 1:9; 2 Ki 19:4; see also 10:20–22).

37:6 *Be not afraid.* Cf. 7:4; see 35:4 and note.

37:7 *blast.* See KJV marg.; perhaps a compulsion or a disposition (cf. 1 Chr 5:26). *rumour.* See note on 2 Ki 19:7. *return . . . fall by the sword.* See vv. 37–38.

37:8 *Libnah.* See note on 2 Ki 8:22; see also Josh 10:31. *Lachish.* See note on 36:2.

37:9 *Tirhakah king of Ethiopia.* In 701 B.C. he was actually a prince (the brother of the new pharaoh Shebitku, who sent him with an army to help Hezekiah withstand the Assyrian invasion); he did not become king until 690. But this part of Isaiah was not written before 681 (see note on v. 38), so it was natural to speak of Tirhakah as king. See 18:1 and note.

37:10 *God . . . deceive.* See 36:14–15,18. The message of vv. 10–13 is similar to that of 36:18–20 (see note there).

37:12 *Gozan.* A city in northern Mesopotamia to which some of the Israelites had been deported by the Assyrians (see 2 Ki 17:6). *Haran.* A city west of Gozan where Abraham lived for a number of years (see Gen 11:31 and note). *Rezeph.* A city between Haran and the Euphrates River. *Eden.* The state of Bit Adini, located between the Euphrates and Balikh rivers (see note on 2 Ki 19:12).

37:13 *Hamath . . . Arphad.* See 10:9 and note. *Sepharvaim.* See 36:19 and note.

37:14 *house of the LORD.* See v. 1 and note. *spread it before.* Contrast the hypocritical spreading out of hands to pray in 1:15.

37:16 *LORD of hosts.* See 13:4 and note. *dwellest . . . cherubims.* See note on 1 Sam 4:4. *all the kingdoms.* Cf. 40:17. *made heaven and earth.* The role of God as Creator is emphasized also in 40:26,28; 42:5; 45:12.

37:17 *Incline thine ear . . . open thine eyes.* Cf. Solomon's prayer in 1 Ki 8:52; 2 Chr 6:40. *reproach the living God.* See v. 4 and note.

37:19 *no gods.* See 36:19 and note. *wood and stone.* Cf. 2:8; 44:9–20.

37:20 *thou art the LORD, even thou only.* Cf. 43:11; 45:18,21–22.

37:22 *virgin, the daughter of Zion.* A personification of

The daughter of Jerusalem hath shaken
her head at thee.
23 Whom hast thou reproached and
blasphemed?
And against whom hast thou exalted
thy voice,
And lifted up thine eyes on high?
Even against the Holy One of Israel.
24 [1]By thy servants hast thou reproached
the Lord, and hast said,
By the multitude of my chariots am I
come up
To the height of the mountains, *to* the
sides of Lebanon;
And I will cut down [2]the tall cedars
thereof, *and* the choice fir trees
thereof:
And I will enter *into* the height of his
border, *and* [3]the forest of his Carmel.
25 I have digged, and drunk water;
And with the sole of my feet have I
dried up all the rivers of the
[1]besieged *places*.
26 [a][1]Hast thou not heard long ago, *how* I
have done it;
And of ancient times, that I have
formed it?
Now have I brought it to pass, that
thou shouldest be to lay waste
Defenced cities *into* ruinous heaps.
27 Therefore their inhabitants *were* [1]of
small power,
They were dismayed and confounded:
They were *as* the grass of the field, and
as the green herb,
As the grass on the housetops, and *as*
corn blasted before it be grown up.
28 But I know thy [1]abode, and thy going
out, and thy coming in,
And thy rage against me.
29 Because thy rage against me, and thy
tumult, is come up into mine ears,
Therefore [a]will I put my hook in thy
nose, and my bridle in thy lips,
And I will turn thee back by the way
by which thou camest.
30 And this *shall be* a sign unto thee,
Ye shall eat *this* year such as groweth
of itself;
And the second year that which
springeth of the same:
And in the third year sow ye, and reap,
And plant vineyards, and eat the fruit
thereof.
31 And [1]the remnant that is escaped of
the house of Judah
Shall again take root downward, and
bear fruit upward.
32 For out of Jerusalem shall go forth a
remnant,
And [1]they that escape out of mount
Zion:
The [a]zeal of the LORD of hosts shall do
this.
33 Therefore thus saith the LORD
concerning the king of Assyria,
He shall not come into this city,
Nor shoot an arrow there,
Nor come before it *with* [1]shields,
Nor cast a bank against it.
34 By the way that he came, *by the same*
shall he return,
And shall not come into this city, saith
the LORD.
35 For I will [a]defend this city to save it
For mine own sake, and for my servant
David's sake.

36 ¶ Then the [a]angel of the LORD went
forth, and smote in the camp of the Assyrians
an hundred and fourscore and five thousand:
and when they arose early in the morning, behold, they *were* all dead corpses.
37 So Sennacherib king of Assyria departed,
and went and returned, and dwelt at Nineveh.

37:24 [1]Heb. *By the hand of thy servants* [2]Heb. *the tallness of the cedars thereof,* and the *choice of the fir trees thereof* [3]Or, *the forest* and *his fruitful field*
37:25 [1]Or, *fenced and closed*
37:26 [1]Or, *Hast thou not heard* how *I have made it long ago,* and *formed it of ancient times? Should I now bring it to be laid waste,* and *defenced cities* to be *ruinous heaps?* [a]2 Ki. 19:25
37:27 [1]Heb. *short of hand*
37:28 [1]Or, *sitting*
37:29 [a]ch. 30:28; Ezek. 38:4
37:31 [1]Heb. *the escaping of the house of Judah that remaineth*
37:32 [1]Heb. *the escaping* [a]2 Ki. 19:31; ch. 9:7
37:33 [1][Heb. *shield*]
37:35 [a]2 Ki. 20:6; ch. 38:6
37:36 [a]2 Ki. 19:35

Jerusalem and its inhabitants. *shaken her head.* A gesture of mocking (see Ps 22:7; 44:14).
37:23 *lifted up . . . on high.* Assyria's great pride had been condemned earlier (see 10:12 and note). *Holy One of Israel.* A designation of the God of Israel characteristic of Isaiah (see 1:4 and note).
‡37:24 *multitude of my chariots.* See 36:8 and note. *come up To the height.* Cf. the words of the king of Babylon in 14:13–14. *Lebanon.* See 33:9; 35:2 and notes. *cut down . . . cedars.* For many centuries the kings of Mesopotamia had used the cedars of Lebanon in their royal buildings (cf. 1 Ki 5:8–10). *height of his border.* The highest peak of mount Lebanon, a rather bold claim in that chariots were primarily effective for fighting on level land.
‡37:25 *digged.* The digging of wells; even desert lands could not stop him. *dried up all the rivers.* The branches of the Nile were no obstacle either. This boast was almost a claim to deity. See 11:15; 44:27 and notes.
37:26 Cf. 40:21. *Defenced cities into ruinous heaps.* Assyria had been God's tool of judgment against the nations (see 10:5–6).
37:27 See 40:6–8; Ps 37:1–2. *grass on the housetops.* Roofs in the Near East were flat.
37:29 *hook in thy nose.* The Assyrians often led away captives by tying ropes to rings placed in their noses (see note on 2 Ki 19:28). *bridle.* Cf. 30:28.
37:30 *sign.* See 7:11,14 and notes. *such as groweth of itself.* See note on 2 Ki 19:29. *second . . . third year.* See note on 2 Ki 19:29. Probably the second year was to begin shortly, so the total time was less than 36 months. Another three-year sign was given in 20:3. *plant vineyards, and eat.* The response to Assyria's proposal in 36:16 (see note there).
37:31–32 *remnant.* See notes on v. 4; 1:9; 2 Ki 19:4,30–31.
37:31 *take root . . . bear fruit.* See 4:2; 11:1,10; 27:6 and notes.
37:32 *The zeal . . . this.* See 9:7 and note.
‡37:33 *cast a bank.* To put up a siege ramp that would help the invaders bring up battering rams and scale the walls (see 2 Sam 20:15).
37:35 *David's sake.* God had promised David an enduring throne in Jerusalem (see 9:7; 55:3; 2 Sam 7:16).
‡37:36 *angel of the LORD . . . smote.* Cf. the striking down of the firstborn in Egypt (Ex 12:12) and the angel's sword poised against Jerusalem (2 Sam 24:16). The Greek historian Herodotus attributed this destruction to a bubonic plague. In the biblical account, the death of these soldiers is by divine intervention and fulfills the prophecies of 10:33–34; 30:31; 31:8.
37:37 *Nineveh.* The capital of Assyria. See Jonah 1:2.

38 And it came to pass, as he was worshipping *in* the house of Nisroch his god, that Adrammelech and Sharezer his sons smote him with the sword; and they escaped *into* the land of [1]Armenia: and Esar-haddon his son reigned in his stead.

Hezekiah's sickness

38 In [a]those days was Hezekiah sick unto death. And Isaiah the prophet the son of Amoz came unto him, and said unto him, Thus saith the LORD, [b][1]Set thine house in order: for thou shalt die, and not live.

2 Then Hezekiah turned his face toward the wall, and prayed unto the LORD,

3 And said, [a]Remember now, O LORD, I beseech thee, how I have walked before thee in truth and with a perfect heart, and have done *that* which *is* good in thy sight. And Hezekiah wept [1]sore.

4 Then came the word of the LORD to Isaiah, saying,

5 Go and say to Hezekiah, Thus saith the LORD, the God of David thy father, I have heard thy prayer, I have seen thy tears: behold, I will add unto thy days fifteen years.

6 And I will deliver thee and this city out of the hand of the king of Assyria: and [a]I will defend this city.

7 And this *shall be* [a]a sign unto thee from the LORD, that the LORD will do this thing that he hath spoken;

8 Behold, I will bring again the shadow of the degrees, which is gone down in the [1]sun dial of Ahaz, ten degrees backward. So the sun returned ten degrees, by which degrees it was gone down.

9 ¶ The writing of Hezekiah, king of Judah, when he had been sick, and was recovered of his sickness:

10 I said, in the cutting off of my days, I
shall go to the gates of the grave:
I am deprived of the residue of my
years.

11 I said, I shall not see the LORD, *even*
the LORD, [a]in the land of the living:
I shall behold man no more with the
inhabitants of the world.

12 [a]Mine age is departed, and is removed
from me as a shepherd's tent:
I have cut off like a weaver my life: he
will cut me off [1]with pining sickness:
From day *even* to night wilt thou make
an end of me.

13 I reckoned till morning, *that,* as a lion,
so will he break all my bones:
From day *even* to night wilt thou make
an end of me.

14 Like a crane *or* a swallow, so did I
chatter:
[a]I did mourn as a dove:
Mine eyes fail *with looking* upward:
O LORD, I am oppressed; [1]undertake
for me.

15 What shall I say? he hath both spoken
unto me, and himself hath done *it:*
I shall go softly all my years [a]in the
bitterness of my soul.

16 O Lord, by these *things men* live,
And in all these *things is* the life of my
spirit:
So wilt thou recover me, and make me
to live.

17 Behold, [1]for peace I had great
bitterness:
But [2]thou hast in love to my soul
delivered it from the pit of
corruption:
For thou hast cast all my sins behind
thy back.

18 For [a]the grave cannot praise thee,
death can *not* celebrate thee:
They that go down into the pit cannot
hope for thy truth.

37:38 [1]Heb. *Ararat*
38:1 [1]Heb. *Give charge concerning thy house* [a]2 Ki. 20:1; 2 Chr. 32:24 [b]2 Sam. 17:23
38:3 [1]Heb. *with great weeping* [a]Neh. 13:14
38:6 [a]ch. 37:35
38:7 [a]2 Ki. 20:8; ch. 7:11
38:8 [1]Heb. *degrees by,* or, *with the sun*
38:11 [a]Ps. 27:13; 116:9
38:12 [1]Or, *from the thrum* [a]Job 7:6
38:14 [1]Or, *ease me* [a]ch. 59:11
38:15 [a]Job 7:11
38:17 [1]Or, *on my peace came great bitterness* [2]Heb. *thou hast loved my soul from the pit*
38:18 [a]Ps. 6:5; 30:9; 88:11; 115:17; Eccl. 9:10

37:38 *in the house.* Hezekiah had gone to the Lord's temple and gained strength (vv. 1,14). Twenty years later (681 B.C.) Sennacherib went to the temple of his god and was killed. *Armenia.* Urartu, north of Assyria in Armenia (see note on Gen 8:4). *Esar-haddon.* Reigned 681–669. See Ezra 4:2.

38:1 *In those days.* Sometime before Sennacherib's invasion of 701 B.C. (see v. 6). *Isaiah.* He is prominent in this historical interlude (chs. 36–39). *Set thine house in order.* See note on 2 Ki 20:1. *thou shalt die.* Elisha similarly predicted the death of Ben-Hadad (2 Ki 8:9–10). See note on 2 Ki 20:1.

38:2 *wall.* Perhaps of the nearby temple. *prayed.* Hezekiah apparently had no son and successor to the throne yet (cf. 39:7; 2 Ki 21:1).

‡38:3 *perfect heart.* A fully devoted heart. Like David (1 Ki 11:4), Hezekiah was truly faithful (see 36:7; 2 Ki 18:3–5).

38:6 *deliver . . . this city.* See 31:5; 37:35.

38:7 *sign.* See 7:11,14 and notes.

‡38:8 *sun returned ten degrees.* The miracle of the shadow of the sun moving backward perhaps involved the refraction of light. See 2 Ki 20:9–11; Josh 10:12–14.

38:10–20 A hymn of thanksgiving, in structure similar to many of the psalms. Hezekiah was deeply interested in the psalms of David and Asaph (see 2 Chr 29:30).

38:10–14 Hezekiah voices his complaint.

38:11 *the LORD, even the LORD.* See 26:4. *land of the living.* Cf. Ps 27:13.

‡38:12 *Mine age.* Hezekiah's life span. *as a shepherd's tent.* His life ends suddenly like a tent that is folded up and put away. *I have cut off . . . my life.* Lit. "I have rolled up . . . my life"; cf. the rolling up of the sky like a scroll in 34:4 (see also Heb 1:12).

38:13 *break all my bones.* Physical or spiritual distress is often described in terms of aching or broken bones (see Ps 6:2; 32:3).

38:15–20 Hezekiah offers praise for God's healing.

38:15 *What shall I say?* See 2 Sam 7:20. Hezekiah wonders how he can praise God.

38:16 *by these things.* Perhaps referring to God's promises and gracious acts, though His gracious acts can include such experiences as sickness and peril.

38:17 *pit of corruption.* The grave (see Ps 55:23). *all my sins.* Physical and spiritual healing are sometimes linked together (see 53:4–5). *sins behind thy back.* God not only puts our sins out of sight; He also puts them out of reach (Mic 7:19; Ps 103:12), out of mind (Jer 31:34) and out of existence (Is 43:25; 44:22; Ps 51:1,9; Acts 3:19).

38:18 *cannot hope.* Knowledge about the afterlife was limit-

19 The living, the living, he shall praise
thee, as I *do this* day:
[a]The father to the children shall make
known thy truth.
20 The LORD *was ready* to save me:
Therefore we will sing my songs *to* the
stringed instruments
All the days of our life in the house of
the LORD.

21 ¶ For [a]Isaiah had said, Let them take a lump of figs, and lay *it* for a plaister upon the boil, and he shall recover.

22 [a]Hezekiah also had said, What *is* the sign that I shall go up *to* the house of the LORD?

38:19 [a]Deut. 4:9; 6:7; Ps. 78:3,4
38:21 [a]2 Ki. 20:7
38:22 [a]2 Ki. 20:8
39:1 [a]2 Ki. 20:12
39:2 [1]Or, *spicery* [2]Or, *jewels* [3]Heb. *vessels,* or, *instruments* [a]2 Chr. 32:31

Hezekiah's folly and exile

39 At [a]that time Merodach-baladan, the son of Baladan, king of Babylon, sent letters and a present to Hezekiah: for he had heard that he had been sick, and was recovered.

2 [a]And Hezekiah was glad of them, and shewed them the house of his [1]precious things, the silver, and the gold, and the spices, and the precious ointment, and all the house of his [2][3]armour, and all that was found in his treasures: there was nothing in his house, nor in all his dominion, that Hezekiah shewed them not.

3 Then came Isaiah the prophet unto king Hezekiah, and said unto him, What said these men? and from whence came they unto thee? And Hezekiah said, They are come from a far country unto me, *even* from Babylon.

4 Then said he, What have they seen in thine house? And Hezekiah answered, All that *is* in mine house have they seen: there is nothing among my treasures that I have not shewed them.

5 Then said Isaiah to Hezekiah, Hear the word of the LORD of hosts:

6 Behold, the days come, [a]that all that *is* in thine house, and *that* which thy fathers have laid up in store until this day, shall be carried *to* Babylon: nothing shall be left, saith the LORD.

7 And of thy sons that shall issue from thee, which thou shalt beget, shall they take away; and [1]they shall be eunuchs in the palace of the king of Babylon.

8 Then said Hezekiah to Isaiah, [a]Good *is* the word of the LORD which thou hast spoken. He said moreover, For there shall be peace and truth in my days.

39:6 [a]Jer. 20:5
39:7 [1][Fulfilled, Dan. 1:2,3,7]
39:8 [a]1 Sam. 3:18
40:2 [1]Heb. *to the heart* [2]Or, *appointed time* [a]ch. 61:7
40:3 [a]Mat. 3:3 [b]Mal. 3:1 [c]Ps. 68:4

Comfort for God's people

40 Comfort ye, comfort ye my people,
saith your God.
2 Speak ye [1]comfortably to Jerusalem,
and cry unto her,
That her [2]warfare is accomplished,
That her iniquity is pardoned:
[a]For she hath received of the LORD's
hand double for all her sins.

3 [a]The voice of him that crieth in the
wilderness, [b]Prepare ye the way of
the LORD,
[c]Make straight in the desert a highway
for our God.

ed in the OT period, but the gospel of Christ has "brought . . . immortality to light" (2 Tim 1:10).

38:20 *sing . . . to the stringed instruments.* Instrumental music and hymns of praise were closely linked in worship (cf. Ps 33:1–3). *All . . . our life in the house of the LORD.* Hezekiah, like David (Ps 23:6), loved God's house.

‡38:21 *take . . . lay it.* The verbs are plural (probably addressed to the court physicians). *lump of figs.* Figs were used for medicinal purposes in ancient Ugarit. *he shall recover.* Contrast v. 1. God answered Hezekiah's prayer for healing (see v. 5). This instruction also demonstrates that there is nothing inconsistent with a person praying for healing from God and receiving the best possible care from human physicians.

38:22 *sign.* Perhaps the healing of the boil (see v. 21).

39:1 *Merodach-baladan.* Reigned 721–710 B.C. and again later (see note on 2 Ki 20:12). *Babylon.* See note on 13:1. *sent letters and a present.* Merodach-baladan probably wanted Hezekiah's support in a campaign against Assyria. During his career, he organized several revolts against his hated neighbors. See note on 2 Ki 20:12.

39:2 *silver . . . gold . . . treasures.* See 2 Chr 32:27–29,31. Probably Hezekiah was seeking help from the Babylonians against the Assyrian threat (see note on 2 Ki 20:13). But the information gained during this ill-advised tour escorted by Hezekiah would be valuable to Merodach-baladan's powerful successors (vv. 5–7).

39:3 *Isaiah the prophet.* Earlier God had sent Isaiah to confront Ahaz (7:3); cf. also Nathan's rebuke of David (2 Sam 12:1,7).

39:5 *word of the LORD.* Contrast the word of hope in 38:4–6.

39:6 *carried to Babylon.* The first mention of Babylon as Jerusalem's conqueror, though 14:3–4 implied the Babylonian captivity. The wickedness of Hezekiah's son Manasseh was a major cause of the captivity (see 2 Ki 21:11–15). See also note on 2 Ki 20:17.

‡39:7 *thy sons.* Such as King Jehoiachin (2 Ki 24:15). *eunuchs.* See 56:3; see also Esth 2:3, 14–15; Jer 38:7). *king of Babylon.* Nebuchadnezzar.

39:8 *Good is the word.* See note on 2 Ki 20:19. *peace . . . in my days.* See 2 Ki 22:20. "Peace" recurs in a refrain in 48:22; 57:21, dividing the last 27 chapters into 3 sections of 9 chapters each (40–48; 49–57; 58–66).

40:1–66:24 In chs. 1–35 Isaiah prophesied against the backdrop of the Assyrian threat against Judah and Jerusalem, in chs. 36–39 he recorded Assyria's failure and warned about the future rise of Babylon, and in chs. 40–66 he wrote as if the Babylonian exile of Judah was almost over.

40:1 *Comfort ye, comfort ye.* Repeated for emphasis (= "Comfort greatly"). The double imperative is found also in 51:9,17; 52:1,11; 57:14; 62:10.

‡40:2 *Speak ye comfortably.* Lit. "Speak to the heart" ("kindly" or "tenderly"). The Hebrew for this phrase is used also in 2 Chr 32:6, where Hezekiah "spake comfortably" (encouraged) so that Judah would trust in God in spite of the Assyrian invasion. *warfare.* The exile in Babylon (cf. Ps 137:1–6; Lam 1:1–2,9,16–17, 21). *iniquity is pardoned.* By enduring the punishment of captivity (see Lev 26:41). *double.* Full (or enough) punishment. Cf. the "two things" of 51:19.

40:3 *voice.* Three voices are mentioned (vv. 3,6,9), each showing how the comfort of v. 1 will come about. The NT links the voice of v. 3 with John the Baptist in Mat 3:3; Mark 1:3; Luke 3:4; John 1:23. *Prepare ye the way.* Clear obstacles out of the road (cf. 57:14; 62:10). The language of vv. 3–4 has in view the an-

4 Every valley shall be exalted,
And every mountain and hill shall be made low:
[a]And the crooked shall be made [1]straight,
And the rough places [2]plain:
5 And the glory of the LORD shall be revealed,
And all flesh shall see *it* together:
For the mouth of the LORD hath spoken *it.*
6 The voice said, Cry.
And he said, What shall I cry?
[a]All flesh *is* grass,
And all the goodliness thereof *is* as the flower of the field:
7 The grass withereth, the flower fadeth:
Because the spirit of the LORD bloweth upon it:
Surely the people *is* grass.
8 The grass withereth, the flower fadeth:
But [a]the word of our God shall stand for ever.

9 [a][1]O Zion, that bringest good tidings,
get thee up into the high mountain;
[2]O Jerusalem, that bringest good tidings, lift up thy voice with strength;
Lift *it* up, be not afraid;
Say unto the cities of Judah, Behold your God.
10 Behold, the Lord GOD will come [1]with strong *hand,*
And [a]his arm *shall* rule for him:
Behold, [b]his reward *is* with him,
And [c][2]his work before him.
11 He shall [a]feed his flock like a shepherd:
He shall gather the lambs with his arm,
And carry *them* in his bosom,
And shall gently lead those [1]that are with young.

12 [a]Who hath measured the waters in the hollow of his hand,
And meted out heaven with the span,
And comprehended the dust of the earth in [1]a measure,
And weighed the mountains in scales,
And the hills in a balance?
13 [a]Who hath directed the spirit of the LORD,
Or *being* [1]his counseller hath taught him?
14 With whom took he counsel, and *who* [1]instructed him,
And taught him in the path of judgment,
And taught him knowledge,
And shewed to him the way of [2]understanding?
15 Behold, the nations *are* as a drop of a bucket,
And are counted as the small dust of the balance:
Behold, he taketh up the isles as a very little thing.
16 And Lebanon *is* not sufficient to burn,
Nor the beasts thereof sufficient *for* a burnt offering.
17 All nations before him *are* as [a]nothing;
And [b]they are counted to him less than nothing, and vanity.

18 To whom then will ye [a]liken God?

40:4 [1]Or, *a straight place* [2]Or, *a plain place* [a]ch. 45:2
40:6 [a]Job 14:2
40:8 [a]John 12:34
40:9 [1]Or, *O thou that tellest good tidings to Zion* [2]Or, *O thou that tellest good tidings to Jerusalem* [a]ch. 41:27
40:10 [1]Or, *against the strong* [2]Or, *recompence for his work* [a]ch. 59:16 [b]ch. 62:11 [c]ch. 49:4
40:11 [a]Ezek. 34:23; John 10:11; Heb. 13:20; 1 Pet. 2:25
40:11 [1]Or, *that give suck*
40:12 [1]Heb. *a tierce* [a]Prov. 30:4
40:13 [1]Heb. *man of his counsel* [a]Job 21:22; 1 Cor. 2:16
40:14 [1]Heb. *made him understand* [2]Heb. *understandings?*
40:17 [a]Dan. 4:35 [b]Ps. 62:9
40:18 [a]ch. 46:5; Acts 17:29

cient Near Eastern custom of sending representatives ahead to prepare the way for the visit of a monarch. The picture is that of preparing a processional highway for the Lord's coming to Jerusalem. In Mat 3:1–8 John declares that repentance is necessary to prepare the way for Christ. *Make straight . . . a highway.* See 11:16; 35:8 and notes.

40:4 *rough places plain.* See 26:7 and note.

40:5 *glory . . . revealed.* God would redeem Israel from Babylon (see 35:2 and note; 44:23), and all the nations would see the deliverance (52:10; cf. Luke 3:6). Ultimately the glory of the redeeming God would be seen in Jesus Christ (John 1:14; 11:4,40; 17:4; Heb 1:3), especially at His return (Mat 16:27; 24:30; 25:31; Rev 1:7)—but also in the redeemed (see 1 Cor 10:31; 2 Cor 3:18; Eph 3:21). See also Is 6:3 and note.

40:6,8 Quoted in part in 1 Pet 1:24–25.

40:6 *is grass.* See 37:27 and note; 51:12. *all the goodliness . . . field.* Even the power of Assyria and Babylon would soon vanish.

40:8 *word of our God shall stand.* The plans and purposes of the nations will not prevail (see 8:10 and note).

40:9 *good tidings.* The news that God is leading His people back to Judah (vv. 10–11). He cares for His people and will redeem them (52:7–10; 61:1). The NT expands this "good tidings" or "gospel" to refer to the salvation that Christ brings to all people (1 Cor 15:1–4). *Behold your God.* The Lord is returning to Jerusalem (see v. 10). These words apply to the return from exile (52:7–9), the first coming of Christ (Mat 21:5) and the second coming of Christ (62:11; Rev 22:12). See 35:4 and note.

‡40:10 *arm shall rule.* Cf. 51:9; 59:16. He is characterized by both strength and gentleness (v. 11). *reward . . . work.* His delivered people, the flock of v. 11 (see 62:11–12). "Work" here refers to "recompense for work" (parallel to "reward").

40:11 *feed his flock.* Cf. Jer 31:10; Ezek 34:11–16.

40:12–31 Rhetorical questions are used to persuade the people to trust in the Lord, who has the ability to deliver, strengthen and restore His people.

‡40:12–13 Compares the Lord to a wise master craftsman sitting as his work bench and crafting the world; cf. Prov 8:22–31 where wisdom is portrayed as God's companion at the time of creation.

40:12 *measured the waters.* See Job 28:25; 38:8. In Job 38–41 the Lord overwhelms Job with a description of His greatness. *meted out heaven.* See 48:13.

40:13 Quoted in Rom 11:34; 1 Cor 2:16. *counseller.* See 9:6 and note.

40:15 *nations . . . a drop of a bucket.* See note on v. 6. *dust.* See 17:13 and note; 29:5.

40:16 *Lebanon.* The wood of its cedar trees. *beasts thereof.* Cf. Ps 104:16–18. Sacrifices, however numerous, could never do justice to the greatness of God.

40:17 *nothing . . . vanity.* In spite of the temporary splendor they might possess (see 13:19 and note).

40:18–20 More than any other prophet, Isaiah shows the folly of worshiping idols. His sarcastic caricature, satire and

Or what likeness will ye compare unto
him?
19 [a]The workman melteth a graven
image,
And the goldsmith spreadeth it over
with gold,
And casteth silver chains.
20 He that [1]*is* so impoverished that he
hath no oblation chooseth a tree *that*
will not rot;
He seeketh unto him a cunning
workman
[a]To prepare a graven image, *that* shall
not be moved.
21 [a]Have ye not known? have ye not
heard?
Hath it not been told you from the
beginning?
Have ye not understood *from* the
foundations of the earth?
22 [1]*It is* he that sitteth upon the circle of
the earth,
And the inhabitants thereof *are* as
grasshoppers;
That [a]stretcheth out the heavens as a
curtain,
And spreadeth them out as a tent to
dwell in:
23 That bringeth the [a]princes to nothing;
He maketh the judges of the earth as
vanity.
24 Yea, they shall not be planted;
Yea, they shall not be sown:
Yea, their stock shall not take root in
the earth:
And he shall also blow upon them, and
they shall wither,
And the whirlwind shall take them
away as stubble.

40:19 [a]ch. 41:6,7; 44:12; Jer. 10:3
40:20 [1]Heb. is *poor of oblation* [a]ch. 41:7; Jer. 10:4
40:21 [a]Ps. 19:1; Acts 14:17; Rom. 1:19
40:22 [1]Or, *Him that sitteth, etc.* [a]Job 9:8; Ps. 104:2; ch. 42:5; 51:13; Jer. 10:12
40:23 [a]Job 12:21; Ps. 107:40
40:25 [a]ver. 18
40:26 [a]Ps. 147:4
40:28 [a]Ps. 147:5; Rom. 11:33
40:31 [1]Heb. *change* [a]Ps. 103:5
41:1 [a]Zech. 2:13

25 [a]To whom then will ye liken me, or
shall I be equal? saith the Holy One.
26 Lift up your eyes on high,
And behold who hath created these
things,
That bringeth out their host by number:
[a]He calleth them all by names
By the greatness of *his* might, for that
he is strong in power;
Not one faileth.
27 Why sayest thou, O Jacob, and
speakest, O Israel,
My way is hid from the LORD,
And my judgment is passed over from
my God?
28 Hast thou not known? hast thou not
heard,
That the everlasting God, the LORD,
The Creator of the ends of the earth,
Fainteth not, neither is weary?
[a]*There is* no searching of his
understanding.
29 He giveth power to the faint;
And to *them that have* no might he
increaseth strength.
30 Even the youths shall faint and be weary,
And the young men shall utterly fall:
31 But they that wait upon the LORD [a]shall
[1]renew *their* strength;
They shall mount up *with* wings as
eagles;
They shall run, and not be weary;
And they shall walk, and not faint.

God will help Israel

41 [a]Keep silence before me, O islands;
And let the people renew *their*
strength:
Let them come near; then let them
speak:
Let us come near together to judgment.

denunciation of these false gods reach a peak in 44:9–20 (see 41:7,22–24; 42:17; 46:5–7; 48:5).

40:18 *To whom . . . liken God?* See v. 25; 46:5.

40:19 *workman . . . goldsmith.* See 41:7; 44:10–12. *gold . . . silver.* See 2:20; Hab 2:18–19 and notes.

‡40:20 *He . . . oblation.* The person too poor to purchase gold or silver for the making of an idol. *tree.* See 44:14–16,19. *that shall not be moved.* See 41:7; 46:7.

40:21 *from the beginning.* God's work as Creator is emphasized in the rest of the chapter (cf. 37:26; 41:4,26).

40:22 *sitteth upon.* Cf. 66:1; see 37:16 and note. *circle.* Or "horizon." See Job 22:14; Prov 8:27. *stretcheth out the heavens . . . as a tent.* See 42:5; 44:24; 51:13; Ps 19:4; 104:2.

40:23 *princes . . . judges . . . vanity.* See v. 17; 2:22 and notes; cf. Jer 25:17–26; Dan 2:21.

40:24 *whirlwind . . . as stubble.* See 17:13 and note; 41:15–16.

40:25 See v. 18. Apparently some Israelite doubters were comparing their God with the gods of their captors, and they believed that the Lord was failing the test. *Holy One.* See 1:4 and note.

‡40:26 *created.* See vv. 21–22 and notes. *bringeth out.* The Hebrew for this expression is used for bringing forth the constellations in Job 38:32. *their host.* The stars were worshiped by the people (see 47:13; Jer 19:13). *all by names.* See Ps 147:4. *Not one faileth.* None is missing; see 34:16 and note.

40:27–31 As in many psalms of praise, Isaiah now stresses the goodness of God after describing His majesty (vv. 12–26). Such a God is able to deliver and restore His distressed people if they will wait in faith for Him to act. They are to trust in Him and draw strength from Him.

40:27 *way.* Condition. *hid . . . passed over.* Cf. 49:14; 54:8.

40:28 *everlasting God.* See 9:6. *Creator.* See vv. 21–22 and notes. *ends of the earth.* See 11:12 and note; cf. 5:26; 41:9; 43:6. *Fainteth not.* Contrast 44:12.

40:30 *be weary . . . utterly fall.* See note on 5:27.

40:31 *wait upon.* Trust in or look expectantly to (see 5:2; 49:23). *renew.* Lit. "exchange." Their weakness will give way to God's strength (v. 29). The Hebrew for this verb is used of changes of clothes (Gen 35:2; Judg 14:12), which can symbolize strength and beauty (Is 52:1). Paul tells believers to clothe themselves with Christ (Rom 13:14; cf. Eph 4:24; Col 3:10). *eagles.* Known for their vigor (Ps 103:5) and speed (Jer 4:13; 48:40).

41:1,5 *islands/isles.* See 11:11 and note.

41:1 *renew their strength.* See 40:31. The nations and their gods are challenged to display the same power and wisdom as Israel's God (see vv. 21–24).

2 Who raised up [1]the righteous *man*
[a]from the east,
Called him to his foot,
[b]Gave the nations before him, and
made *him* rule over kings?
He gave *them* as the dust *to* his sword,
And as driven stubble *to* his bow.
3 He pursued them, *and* passed [1]safely;
Even by the way *that* he had not gone
with his feet.
4 [a]Who hath wrought and done *it,*
Calling the generations from the
beginning?
I the LORD, the [b]first,
And with the last; I *am* he.
5 The isles saw *it,* and feared;
The ends of the earth were afraid,
Drew near, and came.
6 [a]They helped every one his neighbour;
And *every one* said to his brother, [1]Be
of good courage.
7 [a]So the carpenter encouraged the
[1]goldsmith,
And he that smootheth *with* the
hammer [2]him that smote the anvil,
[3]Saying, It *is* ready for the sodering:
And he fastened it with nails, [b]*that* it
should not be moved.
8 But thou, Israel, *art* my servant,
Jacob whom I have [a]chosen,
The seed of Abraham my [b]friend.
9 *Thou* whom I have taken from the
ends of the earth,
And called thee from the chief men
thereof,
And said unto thee, Thou *art* my
servant;
I have chosen thee, and not cast thee
away.
10 [a]Fear thou not; [b]for I *am* with thee:
Be not dismayed; for I *am* thy God:
I will strengthen thee; yea, I will help
thee;
Yea, I will uphold thee with the right
hand of my righteousness.
11 Behold, all they that were incensed
against thee shall be [a]ashamed and
confounded:
They shall be as nothing; and [1]they
that strive with thee shall perish.
12 Thou shalt seek them, and shalt not
find them, *even* [1]them that
contended with thee:
[2]They that war against thee shall be as
nothing, and as a thing of nought.
13 For I the LORD thy God will hold thy
right hand,
Saying unto thee, Fear not; I will help
thee.
14 Fear not, thou worm Jacob, *and* ye
[1]men of Israel;
I will help thee, saith the LORD,
And thy redeemer, the Holy One of
Israel.
15 Behold, [a]I will make thee a new sharp
threshing instrument having [1]teeth:

41:2 [1]Heb. *righteousness* [a]ch. 46:11 [b]Gen. 14:14; ch. 45:1
41:3 [1]Heb. in *peace*
41:4 [a]ver. 26 [b]ch. 44:6; Rev. 1:17; 22:13
41:6 [1]Heb. *Be strong* [a]ch. 40:19
41:7 [1]Or, *founder* [2]Or, *the smiting* [3]Or, *Saying of the soder, It is good* [a]ch. 40:19 [b]ch. 40:20
41:8 [a]Deut. 7:6; 10:15; Ps. 135:4; ch. 43:1 [b]2 Chr. 20:7; Jas. 2:23
41:10 [a]ver. 13,14; ch. 43:5 [b]Deut. 31:6
41:11 [1]Heb. *the men of thy strife* [a]Ex. 23:22; ch. 45:24; 60:12; Zech. 12:3
41:12 [1]Heb. *the men of thy contention* [2]Heb. *The men of thy war*
41:14 [1]Or, *few men*
41:15 [1]Heb. *mouths* [a]Mic. 4:13; 2 Cor. 10:4

‡41:2 *the righteous man from the east.* Cyrus the Great, king of Persia (559–530 B.C.), who conquered Babylon in 539 (see 13:17 and note) and issued the decree allowing the Jews to return to Jerusalem (see Ezra 1:1–4; 6:3–5). Cyrus is called "righteous," because like the servant of the Lord in 42:6, Cyrus was chosen to carry out God's righteous purposes. Cyrus is referred to also in v. 25; 44:28–45:5,13; 46:11. *Called him to his foot.* Raised up and empowered to rule. *made him rule over kings.* Such as Croesus king of Lydia in Asia Minor. *driven stubble.* See 17:13 and note. *his bow.* The Persians were renowned for their ability as archers.

41:4 *from the beginning.* See 40:21 and note. *the first . . . with the last.* Since the Lord was present when the first generations were called and will still be there with the last of them, He is the eternal Lord of history and nations (see Heb 13:8; Rev 1:8,17; 2:8; 21:6; 22:13).

41:5–7 By 546 B.C. Cyrus had fought his way victoriously to the west coast of Asia Minor, where his leading opponent was Croesus king of Lydia. Sarcasm and satire are used in the description of the frantic efforts in vv. 6–7—all of them futile (cf. 40:19–20).

41:5 *ends of the earth.* See 11:12 and note.

41:6 *Be of good courage.* See 35:4 and note.

41:7 *hammer.* Cf. 44:12. *that it should not be moved.* See 40:18–20 and notes.

41:8–9 *my servant.* A significant term in chs. 41–53, referring sometimes to the nation of Israel and other times to an individual. In these passages the title refers to one who occupies a special position in God's royal administration of His kingdom, as in "his servant Moses" (Ex 14:31; Num 12:7), "my servant David" (2 Sam 3:18; 7:5,8), "my servants the prophets" (2 Ki 17:13; Jer 7:25). See note on 42:1; see also 20:3; 22:20; 42:1,19; 43:10; 44:1–2,21; 45:4; 49:3,5–7; 50:10; 52:13; 53:11.

41:8 *But.* In contrast to the nations of vv. 5–7, Israel does not need to be afraid (v. 10). *my friend.* See Gen 18; 2 Chr 20:7; Jas 2:23. Some believe, however, that here "my friend" refers to "seed" (Israel), thus paralleling "my servant" and "whom I have chosen."

‡41:9 *ends of the earth.* See v. 5; probably a reference to Mesopotamia and Egypt (see Gen 11:31; 12:1; 15:7; Ps 114:1–2; Jer 31:32). *called thee . . . thereof.* Lit. "called thee from its [earth's] borders," parallel to "ends of the earth."

41:10 *Fear not . . . Be not dismayed.* See vv. 13–14; 43:1,5; see also 35:4 and note. *strengthen . . . help thee.* As one called to God's service (see vv. 9,15–16). See also v. 14; 40:29; 44:2; 49:8. *right hand.* A hand of power and salvation (see Ex 15:6,12; Ps 20:6; 48:10; 89:13; 98:1).

41:11 *be ashamed and confounded.* Cf. 45:17; 50:7; 54:4. *shall be as nothing.* See vv. 15–16 and notes.

41:13 *hold thy right hand.* To strengthen them and keep them from stumbling. *Fear not.* See v. 10 and note.

‡41:14 *worm.* A reference to their feeble and despised condition (cf. Job 25:6). *redeemer.* The Hebrew for this word refers to an obligated family protector and thus portrays the Lord as the Family Protector of Israel. He is related to Israel as Father (63:16; 64:8) and Husband (54:5). As Redeemer (or Family Protector), He redeems their property (for He regathers them to their land, 54:1–8), guarantees their freedom (35:9; 43:1–4; 48:20; 52:11–12), avenges them against their tormentors (47:3; 49:25–26; 64:4) and secures their posterity for the future (61:8–9). See note on Ruth 2:20. *Holy One of Israel.* See vv. 16,20; see also 1:4 and note. The title occurs with "redeemer" also in 43:14; 47:4; 48:17; 49:7; 54:5.

41:15 *threshing instrument.* Cf. 28:27; Amos 1:3 and note;

Thou shalt thresh the mountains, and
beat *them* small,
And shalt make the hills as chaff.
16 Thou shalt [a]fan them, and the wind
shall carry them away,
And the whirlwind shall scatter them:
And thou shalt rejoice in the LORD,
And [b]shalt glory in the Holy One of
Israel.
17 *When* the poor and needy seek water,
and *there is* none,
And their tongue faileth for thirst,
I the LORD will hear them,
I the God of Israel will not forsake
them.
18 I will open [a]rivers in high places,
And fountains in the midst of the
valleys:
I will make the [b]wilderness a pool of
water,
And the dry land springs of water.
19 I will plant in the wilderness the cedar,
the shittah tree, and the myrtle, and
the oil tree;
I will set in the desert the fir tree, *and*
the pine, and the box tree together:
20 [a]That they may see, and know, and
consider, and understand together,
That the hand of the LORD hath done
this,
And the Holy One of Israel hath
created it.
21 [1]Produce your cause, saith the LORD;
Bring forth your strong *reasons,* saith
the King of Jacob.
22 [a]Let them bring *them* forth, and shew
us what shall happen:
Let them shew the former *things,* what
they *be,*
That we may [1]consider *them,* and
know the latter end of them;
Or declare us *things* for to come.
23 [a]Shew the *things* that are to come
hereafter,
That we may know that ye *are* gods:
Yea, [b]do good, or do evil,
That we may be dismayed, and behold
it together.
24 Behold, [a]ye *are* [1]of nothing, and your
work [2]of nought:
An abomination *is he that* chooseth
you.
25 I have raised up *one* from the north,
and he shall come:
From the rising of the sun [a]shall he
call upon my name:
[b]And he shall come *upon* princes as
upon morter,
And as the potter treadeth clay.
26 [a]Who hath declared from the
beginning, that we may know?
And beforetime, that we may say, *He is*
righteous?
Yea, *there is* none that sheweth, yea,
there is none that declareth,
Yea, *there is* none that heareth your
words.
27 [a]The first [b]*shall say* to Zion, Behold,
behold them:
And I will give to Jerusalem one that
bringeth good tidings.
28 [a]For I beheld, and *there was* no man;
Even amongst them, and *there was* no
counseller,
That, when I asked of them, could
[1]answer a word.
29 [a]Behold, they *are* all vanity; their
works *are* nothing:
Their molten images *are* wind and
confusion.

41:16 [a]Jer. 51:2 [b]ch. 45:25
41:18 [a]ch. 35:6,7; 43:19; 44:3 [b]Ps. 107:35
41:20 [a]Job 12:9
41:21 [1]Heb. *Cause to come near*
41:22 [1]Heb. *set our heart* upon them [a]ch. 45:21
41:23 [a]ch. 42:9; 44:7,8; 45:3; John 13:19 [b]Jer. 10:5
41:24 [1]Or, worse *than nothing* [2]Or, worse *than of a viper* [a]Ps. 115:8; ch. 44:9; 1 Cor. 8:4
41:25 [a]Ezra 1:2 [b]ver. 2
41:26 [a]ch. 43:9
41:27 [a]ver. 4 [b]ch. 40:9
41:28 [1]Heb. *return* [a]ch. 63:5
41:29 [a]ver. 24

Mic 4:13; Hab 3:12. *mountains . . . hills.* Probably represents the nations. See 2:14. *make . . . as chaff.* See v. 2; 17:13 and note; 29:5–6.

‡41:16 *fan.* Or "winnow," a figure of judgment used also in Jer 51:2. *rejoice.* Cf. 25:9; 35:10; 51:11.

‡41:17 *poor and needy.* Israel in exile or on the way home (cf. v. 14; 32:7). *will hear.* See 30:19 and note. God will provide water for the returning exiles in the same way that he provided water for Israel in the wilderness under Moses (cf. Ex 17:1–7; Nu. 20:2–11; 21:16–18).

41:18 *rivers in high places.* See 30:25 and note. *wilderness a pool . . . springs.* See 32:2; 35:6–7 and notes.

41:19 These trees will beautify the wilderness (cf. 35:1–2). Several are named in 60:13 in connection with adorning the place of God's sanctuary. Acacia wood was used for the tabernacle (Ex 25:5,10,13). The pine tree and myrtle replace thorns and briers in 55:13.

41:20 *created it.* These fruitful conditions are part of God's new creation in behalf of His people (see 48:7; 57:19; 65:17–18).

41:21–22 God takes the nations and their idols to court (see v. 1 and note).

‡41:22 *former things.* Earlier predictions or accomplishments (see 42:9; 43:9,18; 46:9; 48:3). *declare us things for to come.* The Lord is superior to the gods of the nations in his ability to predict the future (cf. 41:2–3,24–26 where the Lord predicts the rise of Cyrus).

41:23 *do good, or do evil.* See note on 40:18–20.

41:24 *nothing . . . nought.* Like the nations that worship them. See 40:17; 44:9; Hos 9:10. *abomination.* Like those who marry idolaters (see Mal 2:11).

‡41:25 *raised up.* See v. 2 and note. *from the north.* Cyrus came from the east (v. 2) but conquered a number of kingdoms north of Babylon early in his reign. From the perspective of a writer in Jerusalem, the north is generally the point of origin for Israel's oppressors (see 14:31; Jer 1:14; 6:1,22; 10:22; 46:20; 50:3,9,41; 51:48). Now, Israel's deliverer comes from the north. *call upon my name.* Cyrus used the Lord's name in his decree (Ezra 1:2) but did not acknowledge Him (see 45:4–5). *come upon . . . morter . . . clay.* Similar to Assyria in 10:6. Cf. Mic 7:10; Nah 3:14.

41:26 *from the beginning.* Before these events began to unfold (cf. v. 4). *your.* Referring to idols or their worshipers.

41:27 *Behold, behold them.* Words about the deliverance from Babylon. *one that bringeth good tidings.* Isaiah. See 40:9; 52:7 and notes.

41:28 *no counseller . . . could answer a word.* See 46:7.

41:29 *vanity.* See v. 24.

The mission of God's servant

42 Behold [a]my servant, whom I uphold;
Mine elect, *in whom* my soul
[b]delighteth;
[c]I have put my spirit upon him:
He shall bring forth judgment to the
Gentiles.
2 He shall not cry, nor lift up,
Nor cause his voice to be heard in the
street.
3 A bruised reed shall he not break,
And the [1]smoking flax shall he not
[2]quench:
He shall bring forth judgment unto
truth.
4 He shall not fail nor be [1]discouraged,
Till he have set judgment in the earth:
[a]And the isles shall wait for his law.

5 Thus saith God the LORD,
[a]He that created the heavens, and
stretched them out;
He that spread forth the earth, and that
which cometh out of it;
[b]He that giveth breath unto the people
upon it,
And spirit to them that walk therein:
6 [a]I the LORD have called thee in
righteousness,
And will hold thine hand, and will
keep thee,
[b]And give thee for a covenant of the
people, for [c]a light of the Gentiles;
7 [a]To open the blind eyes,
To [b]bring out the prisoners from the
prison,
And them that sit in [c]darkness out of
the prison house.
8 I *am* the LORD: that *is* my name:
And my [a]glory will I not give to
another,
Neither my praise to graven images.
9 Behold, the former *things* are come to
pass,
And new *things* do I declare:
Before they spring forth I tell you of
them.

Song of praise to the LORD

10 [a]Sing unto the LORD a new song,
And his praise from the end of the earth,
[b]Ye that go down to the sea, and [1]all
that is therein;
The isles, and the inhabitants thereof.
11 Let the wilderness and the cities
thereof lift up *their voice,*
The villages *that* Kedar doth inhabit:
Let the inhabitants of the rock sing,
Let them shout from the top of the
mountains.
12 Let them give glory unto the LORD,
And declare his praise in the islands.
13 The LORD shall go forth as a mighty *man,*
He shall stir up jealousy like a man of
war:
He shall cry, [a]yea, roar;
He shall [1]prevail against his enemies.
14 I have long time holden my peace;
I have been still, *and* refrained myself:
Now will I cry like a travailing woman;
I will destroy and [1]devour at once.
15 I will make waste mountains and hills,

42:1 [a]ch. 43:10; 49:3,6; Mat. 12:18; Phil. 2:7 [b]Mat. 3:17; 17:5; Eph. 1:6 [c]ch. 11:2; John 3:34
42:3 [1]Or, *dimly burning* [2]Heb. *quench it*
42:4 [1]Heb. *broken* [a]Gen. 49:10
42:5 [a]ch. 44:24; Zech. 12:1 [b]Acts 17:25
42:6 [a]ch. 43:1 [b]ch. 49:8 [c]ch. 49:6; Luke 2:32; Acts 13:47
42:7 [a]ch. 35:5 [b]ch. 61:1; Luke 4:18; 2 Tim. 2:26; Heb. 2:14
42:7 [c]ch. 9:2
42:8 [a]ch. 48:11
42:10 [1]Heb. *the fulness thereof* [a]Ps. 33:3; 40:3; 98:1 [b]Ps. 107:23
42:13 [1]Or, *behave himself mightily* [a]ch. 31:4
42:14 [1]Heb. *swallow, or, sup up*

42:1–4 Quoted in part in Mat 12:18–21 with reference to Christ. There are four "servant songs" in which the servant is the Messiah: 42:1–4 (or 42:1–7 or 42:1–9); 49:1–6 (or 49:1–7 or 49:1–13); 50:4–9 (or 50:4–11); 52:13–53:12. He is "Israel" in its ideal form (49:3). The nation was to be a kingdom of priests (Ex 19:6), but the Messiah would be the high priest who would atone for the sins of the world (53:4–12). Cyrus was introduced in ch. 41 as a deliverer from Babylon, but the servant would deliver the world from the prison of sin (see v. 7).
42:1 *my servant.* See 41:8–9 and note; Zech 3:8. In the royal terminology of the ancient Near East "servant" meant something like "trusted envoy" or "confidential representative." *Mine elect.* See 41:8–9 and note. *delighteth.* Cf. Luke 3:22. *my spirit upon him.* Like the "Branch" of 11:1–2 (see note on 11:2); cf. 61:1. *judgment.* A righteous world order (see v. 4); see also 9:7 and note; 11:4 and note.
‡42:2 *not cry, nor lift up . . . in the street.* The servant will not be a typical ruler who leads by loud proclamations; instead he will bring peace (cf. 9:6)
‡42:3 *bruised reed.* A bent reed, figuarative of someone who is weak (see Ps 72:2,4). The servant will mend broken lives.
42:4 *not fail nor be discouraged.* Cf. 40:28. *judgment.* Perfect order (see v. 1 and note). *isles.* See note on 11:11. *wait for his law.* As do the nations in 2:2–4. The servant will be a new Moses (see Deut 18:15–18; Acts 3:21–23,26).
42:5 *created the heavens . . . stretched.* See 40:22 and note. *giveth breath . . . spirit.* Cf. 57:15.
‡42:6 *called . . . righteousness.* Similar to the call of Cyrus (see 41:2 and note). *hold thine hand.* See 41:13 and note. *covenant.* See 49:8. The Messiah will fulfill the Davidic covenant as king (9:7) and will institute the new covenant by His death (Jer 31:31–34; Heb 8:6–13; 9:15). *people.* Probably the Israelites (see 49:8; Acts 26:17–18). *light.* Parallel to "salvation" in 49:6 (cf. 51:4). *Gentiles.* The work of Messiah will bring blessing to all nations, in fulfillment of the promise to Abraaham in Gen 12:3 (cf. Rom 4:16–17; Gal 3:8–14).
42:7 *open the blind eyes.* See 29:18; 32:3; 35:5 and notes. *bring out . . . prison.* From the prison of Babylon and also from spiritual and moral bondage (compare 61:1 with Luke 4:18).
42:8 *my glory.* See 40:5 and note.
42:9 *former things.* See 41:22 and note. *new things.* The restoration of Israel (43:19). Cf. 48:6.
42:10 *new song.* To celebrate the "new things" of v. 9. *end of the earth.* See 11:12 and note; 41:5. *isles.* See v. 12; 11:11 and note.
‡42:11 *wilderness.* See 35:1 and note. *Kedar.* See note on 21:16. *rock.* Read the place name "Sela"; see note on 16:1.
42:12 *give glory . . . praise.* See 24:14–16.
‡42:13 *mighty man.* A warrior. God will fight as He did at the Red sea (Ex 15:3); see 9:6 and note. *jealousy.* Zeal with which he attacks his enemies; cf. 9:7; 37:32; 59:17; 63:15. *shall cry, yea roar.* Raises a battle cry that causes panic among the enemy (see 1 Sam 4:5–8).
42:14 *long time.* During Israel's humiliation and exile. *refrained myself.* See 63:15; 64:12. The Hebrew verb is also used of Joseph, who controlled his emotions while he tested his brothers (Gen 43:31; 45:1). See 30:18 and note.
42:15 *make waste . . . dry up.* The opposite of 35:1–2; 41:18.

And dry up all their herbs;
And I will make the rivers islands,
And I will dry up the pools.
16 And I will bring the blind by a way
that they knew not;
I will lead them in paths *that* they have
not known:
I will make darkness light before them,
And crooked things [1] straight.
These things will I do unto them, and
not forsake them.
17 They shall be [a] turned back, they shall
be greatly ashamed, that trust in
graven images,
That say to the molten images, Ye *are*
our gods.

The nation's sin and punishment

18 Hear, ye deaf;
And look, ye blind, that *ye* may see.
19 [a] Who *is* blind, but my servant?
Or deaf, as my messenger *that* I sent?
Who *is* blind as he that is perfect,
And blind as the LORD's servant?
20 Seeing many *things,* [a] but thou
observest not;
Opening the ears, but he heareth not.
21 The LORD is well pleased for his
righteousness' sake;
He will magnify the law, and make [1] *it*
honourable.
22 But this *is* a people robbed and spoiled;
[1] *They are* all of them snared in holes,
And they are hid in prison houses:
They are for a prey, and none
delivereth;
[2] *For* a spoil, and none saith, Restore.
23 Who among you will give ear to this?
Who will hearken and hear [1] for the
time to come?

42:16 [1] Heb. *into straightness*
42:17 [a] Ps. 97:7; ch. 1:29; 44:11; 45:16
42:19 [a] ch. 43:8; Ezek. 12:2; See John 9:39,41
42:20 [a] Rom. 2:21
42:21 [1] Or, him
42:22 [1] Or, *In snaring all the young men of them* [2] Heb. *a treading*
42:23 [1] Heb. *for the after* time?

42:25 [a] 2 Ki. 25:9 [b] Hos. 7:9
43:1 [a] ver. 7 [b] ver. 21; ch. 44:2,21 [c] ch. 44:6 [d] ch. 42:6; 45:4
43:2 [a] Ps. 66:12; 91:3 [b] Deut. 31:6 [c] Dan. 3:25
43:3 [a] Prov. 11:8; 21:18
43:4 [1] Or, *person*

24 Who gave Jacob for a spoil, and Israel
to the robbers?
Did not the LORD, he against whom we
have sinned?
For they would not walk in his ways,
Neither were they obedient unto his
law.
25 Therefore he hath poured upon him
the fury of his anger, and the
strength of battle:
[a] And it hath set him on fire round
about, [b] yet he knew not;
And it burned him, yet he laid *it* not to
heart.

God will redeem his people

43 But now thus saith the LORD [a] that
created thee, O Jacob,
[b] And he that formed thee, O Israel,
Fear not: [c] for I have redeemed thee,
[d] I have called *thee* by thy name; thou
art mine.
2 [a] When thou passest through the
waters, [b] I *will be* with thee;
And through the rivers, they shall not
overflow thee:
When thou [c] walkest through the fire,
thou shalt not be burnt;
Neither shall the flame kindle upon
thee.
3 For I *am* the LORD thy God,
The Holy One of Israel, thy Saviour:
[a] I gave Egypt *for* thy ransom,
Ethiopia and Seba for thee.
4 Since thou wast precious in my sight,
Thou hast been honourable, and I have
loved thee:
Therefore will I give men for thee,
And people for thy [1] life.

---

make the rivers islands. Perhaps to make travel easier. See 37:25; 44:27.

42:16 *blind.* Israel (vv. 19–20). *crooked things straight.* See 40:4. *not forsake them.* Cf. 40:27; 49:14; 54:8.

42:18 *deaf . . . blind.* See 6:10 and note.

‡42:19 *my servant.* Israel. See note on 41:8–9. *messenger that I sent.* A term associated with prophets (see Hag 1:13; cf. Is 44:26; Mal 3:1). Israel failed in its mission to be God's messenger to the world, leading the nations to worship the true God.

‡42:21 *magnify the law . . . honourable.* Not a future event but referring to how God honored His law in the past by communicating the law to Moses and the people in the awesome setting of mount Sinai (see Ex 34:29). Israel was supposed to have fulfilled its mission as God's messenger by keeping the law (cf. Deut 4:5–8) and showing the nations the blessings and benefits of living under God's righteous rule.

42:22 *robbed and spoiled.* By the Assyrians (see 10:6 and note) and the Babylonians (see 39:6). *snared in holes . . . prison houses.* See v. 7 and note. Cf. Judg 6:2–4.

42:24 *Who gave Jacob for a spoil . . . ?* Babylon conquered Israel, not because their gods were stronger than the Lord (see 40:17–18; 1 Ki 20:23), but because the Lord was punishing His people.

42:25 *poured upon him . . . anger.* Israel had a foretaste of the day of the Lord (see 5:25; 9:12,17,21; 13:3; 34:2 and notes; cf. Jer 10:25).

43:1 *created . . . formed.* God made the nation Israel as surely as He made the first man (see Gen 1:27; see also Is 43:7,15,21; 44:2,24). *Fear not.* See 41:10 and note. *redeemed thee.* See notes on 35:9; 41:14. The verb is also used in 29:22; 44:22–23; 48:20 (cf. Ex 15:13). *called thee by thy name.* God chose Israel to serve Him in a special way. See 45:3–4 (Cyrus).

43:2 *waters . . . rivers.* Probably an allusion to crossing the Red sea (Ex 14:21–22) and the Jordan River (Josh 3:14–17). Cf. Ps 66:6,12. *walkest through the fire.* Fulfilled literally in the experience of Shadrach, Meshach and Abednego (Dan 3:25–27). Contrast 42:25.

‡43:3 *Holy One of Israel.* See notes on 1:4; 41:14. *Saviour.* Who delivers from the oppression of Egypt or Babylon and from the spiritual oppression of sin (see 19:20 and note; 25:9 and note; 33:22; 35:4 and note; 43:11–12; 45:15,21–22; 49:25; 60:16; 63:8–9). The name "Isaiah" means "The LORD saves." *ransom.* The Persians conquered Egypt, Cush and Seba, and perhaps this was a reward or ransom for Persia's kindness to Israel (see note on 41:2; cf. Ezek 29:19–20). The Lord loves Israel so much that He allows other nations to experience oppression in its place (cf. v. 4). *Ethiopia.* Cush; see note on 18:1. *Seba.* A land near Cush (cf. 45:14) or Sheba (Ps 72:10). It was probably either in south Arabia (see Gen 10:7 and note; see also Ezek 27:21–22) or across the Red sea in Africa.

5 [a]Fear not: for I *am* with thee:
I will bring thy seed from the east,
And gather thee from the west;
6 I will say to the north, Give *up;*
And to the south, Keep not back:
Bring my sons from far,
And my daughters from the ends of the earth;
7 *Even* every one that is [a]called by my name:
For [b]I have created him for my glory,
[c]I have formed him; yea, I have made him.
8 [a]Bring forth the blind people that have eyes,
And the deaf that have ears.
9 Let all the nations be gathered together,
And let the people be assembled:
[a]Who among them can declare this,
And shew us former *things?*
Let them bring forth their witnesses, that they may be justified:
Or let them hear, and say, *It is* truth.
10 [a]Ye *are* my witnesses, saith the LORD,
[b]And my servant whom I have chosen:
That ye may know and believe me,
And understand that I *am* he:
[c]Before me there was [1]no God formed,
Neither shall there be after me.
11 I, *even* I, [a]*am* the LORD;
And beside me *there is* no saviour.
12 I have declared, and have saved, and I have shewed,
When *there was* no [a]strange *god* among you:
[b]Therefore ye *are* my witnesses, saith the LORD, that I *am* God.
13 [a]Yea, before the day *was* I *am* he;
And *there is* none that can deliver out of my hand:
I will work, and who shall [b1]let it?

14 Thus saith the LORD, your redeemer, the Holy One of Israel;
For your sake I have sent to Babylon,
And have brought down all their [1]nobles,
And the Chaldeans, whose cry *is* in the ships.
15 I *am* the LORD, your Holy One,
The creator of Israel, your King.
16 Thus saith the LORD, which [a]maketh a way in the sea,
And a [b]path in the mighty waters;
17 Which [a]bringeth forth the chariot and horse, the army and the power;
They shall lie down together, they shall not rise:
They are extinct, they are quenched as tow.
18 [a]Remember ye not the former *things,*
Neither consider the *things* of old.
19 Behold, I will do a [a]new *thing;*
Now it shall spring forth; shall ye not know it?
[b]I will even make a way in the wilderness,
And rivers in the desert.
20 The beast of the field shall honour me,
The dragons and the [12]owls:
Because [a]I give waters in the wilderness,
And rivers in the desert,
To give drink to my people, my chosen.
21 [a]This people have I formed for myself;
They shall shew forth my praise.

Israel's sin of ingratitude

22 But thou hast not called upon me, O Jacob;

43:5 [a]ch. 41:10; 44:2; Jer. 30:10; 46:27,28 43:7 [a]ch. 63:19; Jas. 2:7 [b]Ps. 100:3; ch. 29:23; John 3:3,5; 2 Cor. 5:17; Eph. 2:10 [c]ver. 1 43:8 [a]ch. 6:9; 42:19; Ezek. 12:2 43:9 [a]ch. 41:21,22,26 43:10 [1]Or, *nothing formed of God* [a]ch. 44:8 [b]ch. 55:4 [c]ch. 44:6 43:11 [a]ch. 45:21; Hos. 13:4 43:12 [a]Deut. 32:16; Ps. 81:9 [b]ch. 44:8 43:13 [a]Ps. 90:2; John 8:58

43:13 [1]Heb. *turn it back?* [b]Job 9:12; ch. 14:27 43:14 [1]Heb. *bars* 43:16 [a]Ex. 14:16; Ps. 77:19; ch. 51:10 [b]Josh. 3:13 43:17 [a]Ex. 14:4-9,25 43:18 [a]Jer. 16:14 43:19 [a]2 Cor. 5:17; Rev. 21:5 [b]Ex. 17:6; Num. 20:11; Deut. 8:15; Ps. 78:16 43:20 [1]Or, *ostriches* [2]Heb. *daughters of the owl* [a]ch. 48:21 43:21 [a]Ps. 102:18; Eph. 1:5,6

43:5 *Fear not.* See 41:10 and note. *east.* Especially Assyria and Babylonia. See 11:11–12 and notes; cf. Ps 107:3. *west.* For example, the "islands" of 11:11 (see also 24:14–15; 49:12).
43:6 *north.* For example, Hamath (see 10:9 and note; 11:11). *south.* Egypt. *ends of the earth.* See note on 11:12 (cf. 41:5; 42:10).
43:7 *called by my name.* People belonging to God. *created . . . formed.* See v. 1 and note.
43:8 *blind . . . deaf.* Probably referring to Israel (see 6:10 and note; 42:18–20).
43:9–13 A court scene; see also 41:21–22.
43:9 *nations . . . people be assembled.* See 41:1 and note. *former things.* See 41:22 and note. *witnesses.* To verify the accuracy of earlier predictions by idols or their worshipers (see 41:26).
43:10 *Ye are my witnesses.* See also v. 12; 44:8. God's work in behalf of Israel is proof of His saving power. *my servant.* See 41:8–9 and note.
43:11 The main thrust is repeated in 44:6,8; 45:5–6,18,21–22; 46:9 (see also Deut 32:39). *saviour.* See v. 3 and note.
43:12 *strange god.* Cf. Deut 32:12,16. Israel repeatedly worshiped other gods (see Judg 2:12–13). *witnesses.* See v. 10 and note.
43:13 See v. 11. *none that can deliver . . . hand.* Quoted verbatim from Deut 32:39.
‡43:14 *redeemer.* See 41:14 and note. *Holy One of Israel.* See 1:4; 41:14 and notes. *Babylon.* See note on 13:1. *brought down all their nobles.* Lit."brought down all of them as fugitives." Babylon will go from being the oppressor to the oppressed. *whose cry is in the ships.* The Babylonians used the Persian Gulf, as well as the Tigris and Euphrates rivers, for trading purposes. But their splendid ships (cf. 2:16) would one day become their means of flight (cf. Jer 51:13).
43:15 *creator.* See v. 1 and note. *King.* God was called "king in Jeshurun" (Israel) in Deut 33:5 (contrast 1 Sam 8:7).
43:16–17 A reference to crossing the Red sea (see v. 2 and note). Pharaoh's chariots and horsemen were destroyed as Israel's God fought against them (see 51:10; Ex 14:28; 15:4).
‡43:17 *quenched as tow.* Extinguished like a candle wick. Contrast 42:3.
‡43:19 *a new thing.* See 42:9 and note. *way in the wilderness.* A road or highway; see 35:8; 40:3 and notes. *rivers in the desert.* See v. 20; 32:2 and note. Contrast 42:15 and note.
‡43:20 *dragons . . . owls.* Probably "jackals" and "ostriches," creatures of the desert (see 13:21–22; 34:13–15; 35:7).
43:21 *people . . . shew forth my praise.* Cf. 42:12.
43:22–24 The Israelites may have brought sacrifices (see 1:11–15 and note), but their hearts were not right with God.

But thou [a]hast been weary of me,
O Israel.
23 [a]Thou hast not brought me the [1]small
cattle of thy burnt offerings;
Neither hast thou honoured me *with*
thy sacrifices.
I have not caused thee to serve with an
offering,
Nor wearied thee with incense.
24 Thou hast bought me no sweet cane
with money,
Neither hast thou [1]filled me *with* the
fat of thy sacrifices:
But thou hast made me to serve with
thy sins,
Thou hast [a]wearied me with thine
iniquities.
25 I, *even* I, *am* he that [a]blotteth out thy
transgressions [b]for mine own sake,
[c]And will not remember thy sins.
26 Put me in remembrance: let us plead
together:
Declare thou, that thou mayest be
justified.
27 Thy first father hath sinned,
And thy [a][1]teachers have transgressed
against me.
28 Therefore [a]I have profaned the
[1]princes of the sanctuary,
[b]And have given Jacob to the curse,
And Israel to reproaches.

God's blessings upon the nation

44 Yet now hear, [a]O Jacob my servant;
And Israel, whom I have chosen:
2 Thus saith the LORD that made thee,
[a]And formed thee from the womb,
which will help thee;
Fear not, O Jacob, my servant;
And *thou,* [b]Jeshurun, whom I have
chosen.

3 For I will [a]pour water upon *him that is*
thirsty,
And floods upon the dry *ground:*
I will pour my spirit upon thy seed,
And my blessing upon thine offspring:
4 And they shall spring up *as* among the
grass,
As willows by the water courses.
5 One shall say, I *am* the LORD's;
And another shall call *himself* by the
name of Jacob;
And another shall subscribe *with* his
hand unto the LORD,
And surname *himself* by the name of
Israel.

Judgment upon idol worship

6 Thus saith the LORD the King of Israel,
And his redeemer the LORD of hosts;
[a]I *am* the first, and I *am* the last;
And besides me *there is* no God.
7 And [a]who, as I, shall call,
And shall declare it, and set it in order
for me,
Since I appointed the ancient people?
And the *things* that are coming, and
shall come, let them shew unto
them.
8 Fear ye not, neither be afraid:
[a]Have not I told thee from that time,
And have declared *it?* [b]ye *are* even my
witnesses.
Is there a God besides me?
Yea, [c]*there is* no [1]God; I know not *any.*
9 [a]They that make a graven image *are* all
of them vanity;
And their [1]delectable *things* shall not
profit;
And they *are* their own witnesses;
[b]They see not, nor know; that they
may be ashamed.

43:22 [a]Mal. 1:13
43:23 [1]Heb. *lambs,* or, *kids* [a]Amos 5:25
43:24 [1]Heb. *made me drunk,* or, *abundantly moistened* [a]ch. 1:14; Mal. 2:17
43:25 [a]ch. 44:22; Jer. 50:20; Acts 3:19 [b]Ezek. 36:22 [c]ch. 1:18; Jer. 31:34
43:27 [1]Heb. *interpreters* [a]Mal. 2:7,8
43:28 [1]Or, *holy princes* [a]ch. 47:6; Lam. 2:2,6 [b]Ps. 79:4; Jer. 24:9; Dan. 9:11; Zech. 8:13
44:1 [a]ver. 21; Jer. 30:10; 46:27,28
44:2 [a]ch. 43:1,7 [b]Deut. 32:15
44:3 [a]ch. 35:7; Joel 2:28; John 7:38; Acts 2:18
44:6 [a]ch. 41:4; Rev. 1:8,17; 22:13
44:7 [a]ch. 41:4,22
44:8 [1]Heb. *rock* [a]ch. 41:22 [b]ch. 43:10 [c]Deut. 4:35; 32:39; 1 Sam. 2:2; 2 Sam. 22:32
44:9 [1]Heb. *desirable* [a]ch. 41:24 [b]Ps. 115:4

43:22 *not called . . . been weary.* Apparently their prayers were halfhearted (contrast Ps 69:3).
43:23 *have not caused thee to serve . . . Nor wearied.* God did not make excessive demands on His people.
43:24 *cane.* Linked with incense (see v. 23) also in Sol 4:14; Jer 6:20. *fat.* See note on 34:6. *made me to serve . . . wearied.* See 1:14.
43:25 *blotteth out thy transgressions.* In spite of the punishment Israel must suffer (v. 28), God is eager to forgive His people (see 1:18; 44:22; see also 40:2 and note).
43:26 *let us plead together.* The Lord takes Israel to court, as He did the nations in 41:21–22.
43:27 *first father.* See 51:2. Even Abraham was a sinner (see Gen 12:18; 20:9). *thy teachers.* Probably the priests and prophets.
‡43:28 *princes of the sanctuary.* The priests; cf. 1 Chr 24:5 ("governors of the sanctuary"). *have given . . . to the curse.* See note on 34:2. Any town of Israel that harbored idolatry was to receive this fate (Deut 13:12–15). Jerusalem suffered destruction at the hands of the Babylonians (2 Ki 25:8–9) because of idolatry (see Ezek 7:15–22).
44:1–2 *my servant.* See 41:8–9 and note.
44:2 *formed thee.* See 43:1 and note. *from the womb.* See v. 24. The tenderness of the Creator is shown (see also 49:5; Jer 1:5). *Fear not.* See v. 8; 41:10 and note. *Jeshurun.* Israel (see v. 1), meaning "the upright one"; found elsewhere only in Deut 32:15; 33:5,26.
44:3 *pour water . . . floods.* See 30:25; 32:2; 35:6–7 and notes; see also 41:18. *pour my spirit.* Associated with the Messianic age in 32:15 (see note there) and Joel 2:28.
44:4 *grass.* A symbol of luxuriant growth also in 35:7 (contrast 37:27; 40:6–8).
‡44:5 *call himself . . . Jacob.* A willingness to identify with Jacob, the Lord's people. See 43:7 and note. *subscribe . . . unto the LORD.* Or "write on his hand, 'To the LORD,'" perhaps a mark of ownership (cf. 49:16; Rev 13:16) or a reminder of one's allegiance (cf. Ex 13:9,16).
44:6 *King.* See 43:15 and note. *redeemer.* See v. 24; 41:14 and note. *first . . . last.* See 41:4 and note. *besides me . . . no God.* See 43:11 and note.
‡44:8 *ye are even my witnesses.* See 43:10 and note. *God.* Lit. "Rock." See 17:10 and note. As in v. 2; 43:11–13, Isaiah may be drawing on the song of Moses, which describes God as "the Rock" (Deut 32:4,15,30–31), but the metaphor is also common in the Psalms (see note on Ps 18:2).
44:9–20 A satire on the folly of idolatry (see 40:18–20 and note).
44:9 *vanity . . . shall not profit.* Like the nations and their idols (see 40:17; 41:24 and notes). *ashamed.* Cf. v. 11; 42:17; 45:16.

10 Who hath formed a god, or molten a
graven image
[a]*That* is profitable for nothing?
11 Behold, all his fellows shall be
[a]ashamed:
And the workmen, they *are* of men:
Let them all be gathered together, let
them stand *up;*
Yet they shall fear, *and* they shall be
ashamed together.
12 [a]The smith [1]*with* the tongs both
worketh in the coals,
And fashioneth it with hammers,
And worketh it with the strength of his
arms:
Yea, he is hungry, and his strength
faileth:
He drinketh no water, and is faint.
13 The carpenter stretcheth out *his* rule;
he marketh it out with a line;
He fitteth it with planes, and he
marketh it out with the compass,
And maketh it after the figure of a man,
according to the beauty of a man;
That it may remain *in* the house.
14 *He* heweth him down cedars, and
taketh the cypress and the oak,
Which [1]he strengtheneth for himself
among the trees of the forest:
He planteth an ash, and the rain doth
nourish *it.*
15 Then shall it be for a man to burn:
For he will take thereof, and warm
himself;
Yea, he kindleth *it,* and baketh bread;
Yea, he maketh a god, and worshippeth
it;
He maketh it a graven image, and
falleth down thereto.
16 He burneth part thereof in the fire;
With part thereof he eateth flesh;
He roasteth roast, and is satisfied:
Yea, he warmeth himself, and saith,
Aha,
I am warm, I have seen the fire:

44:10 [a]Jer. 10:5; Hab. 2:18
44:11 [a]Ps. 97:7; ch. 1:29; 42:17
44:12 [1]Or, with *an axe* [a]ch. 40:19; Jer. 10:3
44:14 [1]Or, *taketh courage*

17 And the residue thereof he maketh a
god, *even* his graven image:
He falleth down unto it, and
worshippeth *it,* and prayeth unto it,
And saith, Deliver me; for thou *art* my
god.
18 [a]They have not known nor understood:
For [b]he hath [1]shut their eyes, that *they*
cannot see;
And their hearts, that *they* cannot
understand.
19 And none [a1]considereth in his heart,
Neither *is there* knowledge nor
understanding to say,
I have burnt part of it in the fire;
Yea, also I have baked bread upon the
coals thereof;
I have roasted flesh, and eaten *it:*
And shall I make the residue thereof
an abomination?
Shall I fall down to [2]the stock of a tree?
20 He feedeth on ashes:
[a]A deceived heart hath turned him
aside,
That he cannot deliver his soul, nor say,
Is there not a lie in my right hand?
21 Remember these, O Jacob
And Israel; for [a]thou *art* my servant:
I have formed thee; thou *art* my
servant:
O Israel, thou shalt not be forgotten of
me.
22 [a]I have blotted out, as a thick cloud,
thy transgressions,
And, as a cloud, thy sins:
Return unto me; for [b]I have redeemed
thee.

23 [a]Sing, O ye heavens; for the LORD hath
done *it:*
Shout, ye lower parts of the earth:
Break forth *into* singing, ye mountains,
O forest, and every tree therein:
For the LORD hath redeemed Jacob,
And glorified himself in Israel.

44:18 [1]Heb. *daubed* [a]ch. 45:20 [b]2 Thes. 2:11
44:19 [1]Heb. *setteth to his heart* [2]Heb. *that which comes of a tree?* [a]ch. 46:8
44:20 [a]Hos. 4:12; Rom. 1:21; 2 Thes. 2:11
44:21 [a]ver. 1,2
44:22 [a]ch. 43:25 [b]ch. 43:1; 1 Cor. 6:20; 1 Pet. 1:18
44:23 [a]Ps. 69:34; ch. 42:10; 49:13; Jer. 51:48; Rev. 18:20

44:11 *workmen.* See 40:19 and note.
44:12–20 Two idols are described: a metal one in v. 12 and a wooden one in vv. 13–20. The latter was more common (see 40:20).
44:12 *strength faileth . . . is faint.* But God never gets tired (40:28).
44:13 *after the figure of a man.* Man was made in the image of God (see Gen 1:26–27 and notes), but an idol is made in the image of man (Deut 4:16; Rom 1:23).
44:14 *cedars . . . cypress . . . oak.* The most valuable kinds of wood then known. See 9:10; 41:19 and notes.
44:15 *worshippeth . . . falleth down.* Repeated in vv. 17,19; see 2:8,20.
44:16 *roasteth roast . . . warmeth himself.* Although wood serves common purposes, it is also made into an idol (see v. 19).
44:17 *Deliver me.* King Amaziah was condemned for worshiping the gods of Seir, a nation he had defeated in battle (2 Chr 25:14–15). Isaiah denounces such idolatry as totally irrational (see 45:20). Whereas those who worshiped idols associated the god with the idol, for Isaiah there was no god for the idol to represent, so he depicts idolatry as worship of a mere "stock of a tree" (v. 19).
44:18 *he hath shut their eyes . . . And their hearts.* Israel's condition in 6:9–10 (see note there). The description ironically characterizes both the idols and those who worship them. See also Ps 82:5.
44:19 *an abomination.* The Lord detests idols (see Deut 27:15). In 1 Ki 11:5,7; 2 Ki 23:13 Molech and Chemosh are called detestable gods and an abomination. Those who worship idols are also called an abomination (see 41:24 and note).
44:20 *feedeth on ashes.* Even devoted worship does not benefit the idolater. Cf. Hos 12:1. *lie.* Or "fraud." See 2 Thes 2:11.
44:21 *my servant.* See vv. 1–2; 41:8–9 and note.
44:22 *blotted out . . . thy transgressions.* As in 40:2 (see note there), the suffering of Israel has paved the way for forgiveness and the restoration of the nation (see 43:25 and note). *Return unto me.* Cf. Jer 31:18; Zech 1:3 and note. *redeemed.* Cf. v. 23; see notes on 35:9; 41:14; 43:1.
44:23 *Sing . . . Shout.* Nature is called on to join in praise (see

Cyrus to restore Jerusalem

24 Thus saith the LORD, [a]thy redeemer,
And [b]he that formed thee from the womb,
I *am* the LORD that maketh all *things;*
[c]That stretcheth forth the heavens alone;
That spreadeth abroad the earth by myself;
25 That [a]frustrateth the tokens [b]of the liars,
And maketh diviners mad;
That turneth wise *men* backward,
[c]And maketh their knowledge foolish;
26 [a]That confirmeth the word of his servant,
And performeth the counsel of his messengers;
That saith to Jerusalem, Thou shalt be inhabited;
And to the cities of Judah, Ye shall be built,
And I will raise up the [1]decayed places thereof:
27 [a]That saith to the deep, Be dry,
And I will dry up thy rivers:
28 That saith of Cyrus, *He is* my shepherd,
And shall perform all my pleasure:
Even saying to Jerusalem, [a]Thou shalt be built;
And *to* the temple, Thy foundation shall be laid.

45 Thus saith the LORD to his anointed, to Cyrus,
Whose [a]right hand I [1]have holden,
[b]To subdue nations before him;
And I will loose the loins of kings,

44:24 [a]ch. 43:14 [b]ch. 43:1 [c]Job 9:8
44:25 [a]ch. 47:13 [b]Jer. 50:36 [c]1 Cor. 1:20
44:26 [1]Heb. *wastes* [a]Zech. 1:6
44:27 [a]Jer. 50:38; 51:32,36
44:28 [a]2 Chr. 36:22; Ezra 1:1; ch. 45:13
45:1 [1]Or, *strengthened* [a]ch. 41:13 [b]Dan. 5:30

45:2 [a]ch. 40:4 [b]Ps. 107:16
45:3 [a]ch. 41:23 [b]Ex. 33:12
45:4 [a]ch. 44:1
45:5 [a]Deut. 4:35; 32:39; ch. 44:8 [b]ver. 14,18 [c]Ps. 18:32
45:6 [a]Ps. 102:15; Mal. 1:11
45:7 [a]Amos 3:6
45:8 [a]Ps. 85:11

To open before him the two leaved gates;
And the gates shall not be shut;
2 I will go before thee,
[a]And make the crooked places straight:
[b]I will break in pieces the gates of brass,
And cut in sunder the bars of iron:
3 And I will give thee the treasures of darkness,
And hidden riches of secret places,
[a]That thou mayest know that I, the LORD, which [b]call *thee* by thy name, *am* the God of Israel.
4 For [a]Jacob my servant's sake, and Israel mine elect,
I have even called thee by thy name:
I have surnamed thee, though thou hast not known me.
5 I [a]*am* the LORD, and [b]*there is* none else,
There is no God besides me:
[c]I girded thee though thou hast not known me:
6 [a]That they may know from the rising of the sun, and from the west,
That *there is* none besides me.
I *am* the LORD, and *there is* none else.
7 I form the light, and create darkness:
I make peace, and [a]create evil:
I the LORD do all these *things.*
8 [a]Drop down, ye heavens, from above,
And let the skies pour down righteousness:
Let the earth open, and let them bring forth salvation,
And let righteousness spring up together;
I the LORD have created it.

---

also 35:1; 49:13). *Break forth . . . ye mountains.* See 49:13; 55:12. *glorified himself.* See 35:2; 40:5 and notes.

44:24 *redeemer.* See 41:14 and note. *stretcheth forth . . . spreadeth abroad.* See 40:22 and note; cf. 51:13.

‡44:25 *frustrateth . . . liars.* God frustrates those who use "tokens" (omens) to predict the future. See Deut 13:1–3. *diviners.* The Hebrew for this word is used of Balaam (Josh 13:22), the witch of Endor (1 Sam 28:8) and false prophets (Jer 27:9). It is linked with soothsaying and sorcery (see 3:2–3 and note; Deut 18:10–11). *turneth wise men backward.* See 29:14 and note.

44:26 *servant . . . messengers.* The true prophets (see 42:19 and note; Jer 7:25). *inhabited . . . built.* See Jer 32:15; cf. Is 58:12; 61:4. *raise up the decayed places.* Contrast 6:11.

44:27 *Be dry.* A reference to the crossing of the Red sea (see 11:15; 37:25; 43:16–17 and notes; cf. 50:2; 51:10).

44:28 *Cyrus.* See 41:2 and note. *shepherd.* Often applied to rulers (see 2 Sam 5:2; Jer 23:2). *Jerusalem . . . temple.* The decree of Cyrus (Ezra 1:2–4; 6:3–5) authorized the rebuilding of the temple, which would lead to a restored Jerusalem (see 45:13).

‡45:1 *anointed.* "Messiah" comes from the Hebrew for this word. Cyrus, a foreign emperor, is called "his anointed" just as he is called "my shepherd" (44:28), because God has appointed him to carry out a divine commission in his role as king. Nebuchadnezzar is similarly called "my servant" (Jer 25:9; 27:6; 43:10). The servant—Christ (see note on 42:1–4)—is called "the Messiah" ("the Anointed One") in Dan 9:25–26 (*Christ* in Greek means "the Anointed One," just as *Messiah* does in Hebrew). See also Ps 2:2 and note. *right hand I have holden.* See 41:13 and note.

45:2 *gates of brass . . . bars of iron.* Normally the doors of city gates were made of wood, and the bars were metal (see Judg 16:3 and note).

45:3 *That thou mayest know.* God's actions reveal His power (cf. Ezek 6:7; 7:27). *call thee by thy name.* To indicate God's control of Cyrus's activities. See v. 4; see also note on 43:1.

‡45:4 *my servant's sake.* See 41:8–9 and note. *I have surnamed thee.* The Lord gives Cyrus a title of honor. *though thou hast not known me.* See v. 5. Cyrus apparently worshiped the chief Babylonian deity, Marduk, whom he praised in his inscriptions.

45:5 *I . . . there is none else.* See vv. 6,14,18,21–22; 43:11 and note.

45:6 *rising of the sun . . . west.* The whole earth (see Mal 1:11 and note).

‡45:7 *darkness.* Such as the darkness that plagued the Egyptians (see Ex 10:21–23; Ps 105:28; cf. Is 47:11; Amos 3:6). *evil.* The word "evil" in Hebrew (*ra'*) can also be translated "calamity" (cf. Ps 49:5; 94:13; Jer 26:3 for this sense of the word). The passage is not teaching that God is responsible for the moral evil in the universe (cf. Jas 1:13)

45:8 *Drop down . . . pour down.* A picture of abundance (see Hos 10:12). *righteousness.* In v. 13; 41:2 Cyrus is mentioned in connection with God's righteousness. God is "making things

9 Woe unto him that striveth with [a]his
maker!
Let the potsherd *strive* with the
potsherds of the earth.
[b]Shall the clay say to him that
fashioneth it, What makest thou?
Or thy work, He hath no hands?
10 Woe unto him that saith unto *his*
father, What begettest thou?
Or to the woman, What hast thou
brought forth?
11 Thus saith the LORD, the Holy One of
Israel, and his maker,
Ask me of *things* to come concerning
[a]my sons,
And concerning [b]the work of my hands
command ye me.
12 [a]I have made the earth,
And [b]created man upon it:
I, *even* my hands, have stretched out
the heavens,
And [c]all their host have I commanded.
13 [a]I have raised him up in righteousness,
And I will [1]direct all his ways:
He shall [b]build my city, and he shall let
go my captives,
[c]Not for price nor reward,
Saith the LORD of hosts.
14 Thus saith the LORD,
[a]The labour of Egypt, and merchandise
of Ethiopia
And of the Sabeans, men of stature,
Shall come over unto thee, and they
shall be thine:
They shall come after thee, [b]in chains
they shall come over,
And they shall fall down unto thee,
they shall make supplication unto
thee, *saying,*
[c]Surely God *is* in thee;
And [d]*there is* none else, *there is* no
God.
15 Verily thou *art* a God [a]that hidest
thyself,

45:9 [a]ch. 64:8 [b]ch. 29:16; Jer. 18:6; Rom. 9:20
45:11 [a]Jer. 31:9 [b]Is. 29:23
45:12 [a]ch. 42:5 [b]Gen. 1:26 [c]Gen. 2:1
45:13 [1]Or, *make straight* [a]ch. 41:2 [b]2 Chr. 36:22 [c]Rom. 3:24
45:14 [a]Ps. 68:31; Zech. 8:22 [b]Ps. 149:8 [c]1 Cor. 14:25 [d]ver. 5
45:15 [a]Ps. 44:24; ch. 57:17
45:16 [a]ch. 44:11
45:17 [a]ch. 26:4
45:18 [a]ch. 42:5 [b]ver. 5
45:19 [a]Deut. 30:11 [b]Ps. 19:8
45:20 [a]ch. 46:7
45:21 [a]ch. 41:22; 43:9 [b]ch. 44:8
45:22 [a]Ps. 22:27; 65:5
45:23 [a]Heb. 6:13

O God of Israel, the saviour.
16 They shall be ashamed, and also
confounded, all of them:
They shall go to confusion together
that are [a]makers of idols.
17 [a]*But* Israel shall be saved in the LORD
with an everlasting salvation:
Ye shall not be ashamed nor
confounded world without end.

18 For thus saith the LORD [a]that created
the heavens;
God himself that formed the earth and
made it; he hath established it,
He created it not in vain, he formed it
to be inhabited:
[b]I *am* the LORD; and *there is* none else.
19 I have not spoken in [a]secret, in a dark
place of the earth:
I said not unto the seed of Jacob, Seek
ye me in vain:
[b]I the LORD speak righteousness, I
declare things that are right.
20 Assemble yourselves and come;
Draw near together, ye *that are*
escaped of the nations:
[a]They have no knowledge that set up
the wood of their graven image,
And pray unto a god *that* cannot save.
21 Tell ye, and bring *them* near;
Yea, let them take counsel together:
[a]Who hath declared this from ancient
time? *who* hath told it from that
time?
Have not I the LORD? [b]and *there is* no
God else beside me;
A just God and a saviour; *there is* none
beside me.
22 [a]Look unto me, and be saved, all
the ends of the earth:
For I *am* God, and *there is* none else.
23 [a]I have sworn by myself,
The word is gone out of my mouth *in*
righteousness, and shall not return,

right" through the Persian king. *bring forth salvation.* God will deliver His people. *righteousness spring up.* Peace and justice will prevail (see 11:4 and note).

45:9 *clay say to him that fashioneth it.* See 29:16 and note; cf. 64:8; Jer 18:6.

45:11 *Holy One of Israel.* See 1:4 and note. *sons . . . work of my hands.* See 29:23 and note.

45:12 *stretched . . . heavens.* See 40:22 and note. *host have I commanded.* See 40:26 and note.

45:13 *him up in righteousness.* See note on 41:2. *direct all his ways.* Enabling him to reach his goals (see v. 2; see also 40:3 and note; cf. Prov 3:6). *build my city.* See note on 44:28. *Not for price nor reward.* Since God had not received a payment when He sold them (see 52:3 and note; contrast note on 43:3).

45:14 *labour . . . merchandise.* See 18:7 and note. *Egypt . . . Ethiopia . . . Sabeans.* See notes on 18:1; 43:3. *come over unto thee . . . fall down.* See Ps 68:31. Israel's future domination over her former enemies has been mentioned in 11:14; 14:1–2 (see note on 14:1); it is also the theme of 49:23; 54:3; 60:11–14. *Surely God is in thee.* One day the nations will acknowledge Israel's God (see v. 23; 19:23–25; Zech 8:20–23 and notes).

45:15 *hidest thyself.* God's plans and actions are a mystery to man (cf. 54:8; 55:8–9). *saviour.* See v. 21 and note on 43:3.

45:16 *shall be ashamed.* See 42:17; 44:9.

‡45:17 *everlasting salvation.* Cf. the "everlasting kindness" of 54:8. *not be ashamed.* See 29:22 and note.

‡45:18 *created . . . formed.* See 40:21–22 and notes. *in vain.* Or "without form" (see Gen 1:2 and note) or "chaotic." *to be inhabited.* The Holy Land was now empty (see 6:11; Jer 4:23–26) and chaotic but would soon have inhabitants (see 44:26,28) and be orderly again.

‡45:19 *in secret, in a dark place.* Probably an allusion to the clandestine ways of mediums and spiritists (see 8:19; 29:4). *Seek ye me in vain.* Cf. Jer 29:13–14.

45:20 *no knowledge . . . save.* See 44:17–18 and notes.

45:21 *Tell ye.* See 41:21–22 and note. *declared . . . told it from that time.* See 41:26 and note.

45:22 *Look unto me . . . saved.* Cf. 49:6 and the invitation of 55:7. *ends of the earth.* See 11:12 and note; 42:10.

‡45:23 *I have sworn by myself.* Explained in Heb 6:13. See also 62:8. *word . . . shall not return.* God will not go back on his promises and his word will not fail to come true. See 55:10–11.

That unto me every [b]knee shall bow,
[c]Every tongue shall swear.
24 [1]Surely, shall *one* say, in the LORD have
I [a2]righteousness and strength:
Even to him shall *men* come;
And [b]all that are incensed against him
shall be ashamed.
25 [a]In the LORD shall all the seed of Israel
be justified, and [b]shall glory.

Babylon's idols and the LORD

46 Bel [a]boweth down, Nebo stoopeth,
Their idols were upon the beasts,
and upon the cattle:
Your carriages *were* heavy loaden;
[b]*They are* a burden to the weary *beast.*
2 They stoop, they bow down together;
They could not deliver the burden,
[a]But [1]themselves are gone into captivity.

3 Hearken unto me, O house of Jacob,
And all the remnant of the house of
Israel,
[a]Which are borne *by me* from the belly,
Which are carried from the womb:
4 And *even* to *your* old age [a]I *am* he;
And *even* to hoar hairs [b]will I carry *you:*
I have made, and I will bear;
Even I will carry, and will deliver *you.*
5 [a]To whom will ye liken me, and make
me equal,
And compare me, that we may be like?
6 [a]They lavish gold out of the bag,
And weigh silver in the balance,
And hire a goldsmith; and he maketh it
a god:
They fall down, yea, they worship.
7 [a]They bear him upon the shoulder,
they carry him,
And set him in his place, and he
standeth;
From his place shall he not remove:

45:23 [b]Phil. 2:10 [c]Ps. 63:11
45:24 [1]Or, *Surely he shall say of me, In the* LORD *is all righteousness and strength* [2]Heb. *righteousnesses* [a]Jer. 23:5; 1 Cor. 1:30 [b]ch. 41:11
45:25 [a]ver. 17 [b]1 Cor. 1:31
46:1 [a]ch. 21:9; Jer. 50:2 [b]Jer. 10:5
46:2 [1]Heb. *their soul* [a]Jer. 48:7
46:3 [a]Deut. 32:11; Ps. 71:6
46:4 [a]Mal. 3:6 [b]Ps. 48:14
46:5 [a]ch. 40:18
46:6 [a]ch. 40:19; 41:6; Jer. 10:3
46:7 [a]Jer. 10:5
46:7 [b]ch. 45:20
46:8 [a]ch. 44:19
46:9 [a]Deut. 32:7 [b]ch. 45:5,21
46:10 [a]ch. 45:21 [b]Ps. 33:11; Prov. 19:21; Acts 5:39; Heb. 6:17
46:11 [1]Heb. *The man of my counsel* [a]ch. 41:2,25 [b]ch. 44:28 [c]Num. 23:19
46:12 [a]Ps. 76:5 [b]Rom. 10:3
46:13 [a]Rom. 1:17 [b]Hab. 2:3 [c]ch. 62:11
47:1 [a]Jer. 48:18 [b]ch. 3:26
47:2 [a]Ex. 11:5; Judg. 16:21; Mat. 24:41
47:3 [a]ch. 3:17; 20:4; Jer. 13:22; Nah. 3:5

Yea, [b]*one* shall cry unto him, yet can
he not answer,
Nor save him out of his trouble.
8 Remember this, and shew yourselves
men:
[a]Bring *it* again to mind, O ye
transgressors.
9 [a]Remember the former *things* of old:
For I *am* God, and [b]*there is* none else;
I am God, and *there is* none like me,
10 [a]Declaring the end from the beginning,
And from ancient times *the things* that
are not *yet* done,
Saying, [b]My counsel shall stand,
And I will do all my pleasure:
11 Calling a ravenous bird [a]from the east,
[1]The man [b]that executeth my counsel
from a far country:
Yea, [c]I have spoken *it,* I will also bring
it to pass;
I have purposed *it,* I will also do it.
12 Hearken unto me, ye [a]stouthearted,
[b]That *are* far from righteousness:
13 [a]I bring near my righteousness; it shall
not be far off,
And my salvation [b]shall not tarry:
And I will place [c]salvation in Zion for
Israel my glory.

Judgment against Babylon

47 Come [a]down, and [b]sit in the dust,
O virgin daughter of Babylon,
Sit on the ground: *there is* no throne,
O daughter of the Chaldeans;
For thou shalt no more be called
tender and delicate.
2 [a]Take the millstones, and grind meal:
Uncover thy locks, make bare the leg,
Uncover the thigh, pass over the
rivers.
3 [a]Thy nakedness shall be uncovered,
yea, thy shame shall be seen:

---

every knee . . . Every tongue. See v. 14 and note. Paul quotes this portion of Isaiah in Rom 14:11 and Phil 2:10–11 to describe Christ's exalted position.
‡45:24 *all . . . shall be ashamed.* Very similar to 41:11 except for "against thee" (Israel).
45:25 *glory.* See 41:16.
46:1 *Bel.* Another name for Marduk, the chief deity of Babylon. The name "Bel" is equivalent to Canaanite "Baal" and means "lord." *boweth down . . . stoopeth.* In disgrace (see v. 2; 21:9 and note). *Nebo.* Nabu, the god of learning and writing who was the son of Marduk.
46:2 *gone into captivity.* The idols join their worshipers in exile (see Jer 48:7; 49:3; Hos 10:5; Amos 1:15).
46:3 *all . . . the house.* The remnant (see 1:9 and note). *from the belly . . . from the womb.* See 44:2 and note.
‡46:4 *old age . . . hoar hairs.* "Hoar" = "gray or white." Cf. Ps 37:25. *bear . . . carry . . . deliver.* Unlike the helpless idols of vv. 1–2. See 41:10,13; 43:1–2 and notes.
46:5–7 See 40:18–20 and note.
46:6 *fall down . . . worship.* See 44:15,17,19.
46:7 *carry.* See v. 1. *Nor save him.* See 44:17 and note.
46:8 *transgressors.* Israel. See 1:2 and note; cf. 1:20,23,28; 30:1; 57:4.
46:9 *former things.* See 41:22 and note. *there is none else.* See 43:11 and note.
‡46:10–11 *My counsel.* Especially God's purposes and plans regarding the future (see 8:9–10; 14:24; 48:14 and notes). Cf. Ps 33:11. God alone can predict the future with accuracy.
46:10 *from the beginning.* See 41:26 and note.
46:11 *a ravenous bird . . . east.* Cyrus king of Persia (see 41:2 and note). The swiftness and power of a bird of prey are in view (see 8:8 and note; Jer 49:22; cf. Dan 8:4).
46:12 *stouthearted.* Or "stubborn-hearted." See v. 8; 48:4; Ezek 2:4.
46:13 *righteousness.* Here equivalent to salvation. See 41:2 and note; 45:8 and note. *salvation.* See note on 43:3. *glory.* See 35:2 and note; 40:5 and note; see also 44:23; 49:3.
47:1 *sit in the dust . . . on the ground.* A sign of mourning (see 3:26). *virgin daughter of Babylon.* A personification of Babylon and its inhabitants.
47:2 *millstones, and grind.* A menial task performed by women (see Ex 11:5 and note; Judg 9:53 and note). *pass over the rivers.* Probably on the way to exile.
47:3 *nakedness shall be uncovered.* See Ezek 16:36. Babylon is no longer a queen (see vv. 5,7); she is reduced to a servant girl or a prostitute (see v. 8). *take vengeance.* See 34:8 and note.

[b]I will take vengeance, and I will not
meet *thee as* a man.
4 *As for* [a]our redeemer, the LORD of hosts
is his name,
The Holy One of Israel.
5 Sit thou [a]silent, and get thee into
darkness, O daughter of the
Chaldeans:
[b]For thou shalt no more be called, The
lady of kingdoms.
6 [a]I was wroth with my people, [b]I have
polluted mine inheritance,
And given them into thine hand:
Thou didst shew them no mercy;
[c]Upon the ancient hast thou very
heavily laid thy yoke.
7 And thou saidst, I shall be [a]a lady for
ever:
So that thou didst not [b]lay these *things*
to thy heart,
[c]Neither didst remember the latter end
of it.
8 Therefore hear now this, *thou that art*
given to pleasures, that dwellest
carelessly,
That sayest in thine heart, [a]I *am,* and
none else besides me;
[b]I shall not sit *as* a widow, neither
shall I know the loss of children:
9 But [a]these two *things* shall come to
thee [b]*in* a moment in one day,
The loss of children, and widowhood:
They shall come upon thee in their
perfection
[c]For the multitude of thy sorceries,
and for the great abundance of thine
enchantments.
10 For thou [a]hast trusted in thy
wickedness: [b]thou hast said, None
seeth me.
Thy wisdom and thy knowledge, it
hath [1]perverted thee;
[c]And thou hast said in thine heart, I
am, and none else besides me.

47:3 [b]Rom. 12:19
47:4 [a]Jer. 50:34
47:5 [a]1 Sam. 2:9 [b]Dan. 2:37
47:6 [a]See 2 Sam. 24:14; 2 Chr. 28:9; Zech. 1:15 [b]ch. 43:28 [c]Deut. 28:50
47:7 [a]Rev. 18:7 [b]ch. 46:8 [c]Deut. 32:29
47:8 [a]Zeph. 2:15 [b]Rev. 18:7
47:9 [a]ch. 51:19 [b]1 Thes. 5:3 [c]Nah. 3:4
47:10 [1]Or, *caused thee to turn away* [a]Ps. 52:7 [b]ch. 29:15; Ezek. 8:12 [c]ver. 8
47:11 [1]Heb. *the morning thereof* [2]Heb. *expiate* [a]1 Thes. 5:3
47:13 [1]Heb. *viewers of the heavens* [2]Heb. *that give knowledge concerning the months* [a]ch. 57:10 [b]Dan. 2:2
47:14 [1]Heb. *their souls* [a]Nah. 1:10; Mal. 4:1
47:15 [a]Rev. 18:11
48:1 [a]Ps. 68:26 [b]Deut. 6:13; Zeph. 1:5 [c]Jer. 4:2
48:2 [a]ch. 52:1

11 Therefore shall evil come upon thee;
thou shalt not know [1]from whence it
riseth:
And mischief shall fall upon thee; thou
shalt not be able to [2]put it off:
And [a]desolation shall come upon thee
suddenly, *which* thou shalt not know.
12 Stand now with thine enchantments,
and with the multitude of thy
sorceries,
Wherein thou hast laboured from thy
youth;
If so be thou shalt be able to profit, if
so be thou mayest prevail.
13 [a]Thou art wearied in the multitude of
thy counsels.
Let now [b]the [1]astrologers, the
stargazers, [2]the monthly
prognosticators,
Stand *up,* and save thee from *these*
things that shall come upon thee.
14 Behold, they shall be [a]as stubble; the
fire shall burn them;
They shall not deliver [1]themselves
from the power of the flame:
There shall not *be* a coal to warm at,
nor fire to sit before it.
15 Thus shall they be unto thee *with*
whom thou hast laboured, *even* [a]thy
merchants, from thy youth:
They shall wander every one to his
quarter; none shall save thee.

Obstinate Israel

48 Hear ye this, O house of Jacob,
Which are called by the name of
Israel,
And [a]are come forth out of the waters
of Judah,
[b]Which swear by the name of the LORD,
And make mention of the God of Israel,
[c]*But* not in truth, nor in righteousness.
2 For they call themselves [a]of the holy
city,

I will not . . . as a man. Lit. "I will not meet/befriend anyone." The Lord will have no mercy on Babylon. See 13:18–20.

47:4 *redeemer.* See note on 41:14. *LORD of hosts.* See 13:4 and note. *Holy One of Israel.* See 1:4; 41:14 and notes.

‡47:5 *The lady of kingdoms.* "Lady" = "queen." Babylon was a very beautiful city (see 13:19 and note).

‡47:6 *wroth . . . polluted mine inheritance.* See 10:5–6 (where Assyria is God's tool); 42:24 and note; 43:28 and note; Lam 2:2. *Upon the ancient.* Israel's suffering fulfilled Moses' curse for covenant disobedience (Deut 28:49–50), but the Babylonians are guilty for their cruel treatment of even the "ancient," or the "elderly."

‡47:7 *I shall be a lady for ever.* See v. 5. Cf. the arrogant words of Nebuchadnezzar in Dan 4:30.

47:8,10 *I am, and none else besides me.* Almost a claim of deity (cf. the Lord's words in 43:11; 45:5–6,18,22). See also 14:12–15 and note.

‡47:8 *dwellest carelessly.* An arrogant and false sense of security. Similar language is used of the complacent women of Jerusalem in 32:9,11. *widow.* Deserted and distressed. *loss of children.* See v. 9; 13:16,18; 14:22.

47:9,12 *sorceries . . . enchantments.* Magical practices to avoid danger and to inflict harm on the enemy (see 3:2–3 and note).

47:10 *None seeth me.* See 29:15 and note.

47:11 *not be able to put it off.* The Medes and Persians would not accept any settlement short of surrender (see 13:17).

47:13 *astrologers . . . monthly prognosticators.* Babylon probably utilized their services more than any other nation (see Dan 2:2,10).

47:14 *stubble.* This will be a rapid, powerful fire. See note on 1:31; cf. Mal 4:1. *shall not deliver themselves.* In contrast to the mighty Savior of Israel (see 43:3 and note), astrologers and sorcerers are as helpless as idols (see 44:17 and note). *not be a coal to warm at.* A subtle reference to firewood, a material from which pagans sometimes made idols (see 44:15).

‡48:1 *called by the name.* They belong to Israel (see 43:7 and note). *Israel.* See Gen 32:28 and note. *waters.* Semen (indicating paternity), or perhaps the picture of a fountain indicating "source." *Judah.* The main tribe of the southern kingdom. See Gen 49:8 and note. *not in truth.* Contrast the oaths of 65:16.

‡48:2 *holy city.* Jerusalem, where the temple was located (see

And [b]stay themselves upon the God of Israel;
The LORD of hosts *is* his name.
3 [a]I have declared the former *things* from the beginning;
And they went forth out of my mouth, and I shewed them;
I did *them* suddenly, [b]and they came to pass.
4 Because I knew that thou *art* [1]obstinate,
And [a]thy neck *is* an iron sinew,
And thy brow brass:
5 [a]I have even from the beginning declared *it* to thee;
Before it came to pass I shewed *it* thee:
Lest thou shouldest say, Mine idol hath done them,
And my graven image, and my molten image, hath commanded them.
6 Thou hast heard, see all this;
And will not ye declare *it?*
I have shewed thee new *things* from this time,
Even hidden *things,* and thou didst not know them.
7 They are created now, and not from the beginning;
Even before the day when thou heardest them not;
Lest thou shouldest say, Behold, I knew them.
8 Yea, thou heardest not; yea, thou knewest not;
Yea, from that time *that* thine ear was not opened:
For I knew *that* thou wouldest deal very treacherously,
And wast called [a]a transgressor from the womb.
9 [a]For my name's sake [b]will I defer mine anger,
And *for* my praise will I refrain for thee,
That *I* cut thee not off.
10 Behold, [a]I have refined thee, but not [1]with silver;
I have chosen thee in the furnace of affliction.
11 [a]For mine own sake, *even* for mine own sake, will I do *it:*
For [b]how should *my name* be polluted?
And [c]I will not give my glory unto another.

The Redeemer of Israel

12 Hearken unto me, O Jacob, and Israel my called;
[a]I *am* he; I *am* the [b]first, I also *am* the last.
13 [a]Mine hand also hath laid the foundation of the earth,
And [1]my right hand hath spanned the heavens:
When [b]I call unto them, they stand *up* together.
14 All ye, assemble yourselves, and hear;
Which among them hath declared these *things?*
[a]The LORD hath loved him:
[b]He will do his pleasure on Babylon,
And his arm *shall be on* the Chaldeans.
15 I, *even* I, have spoken; yea, [a]I have called him:
I have brought him, and he shall make his way prosperous.

16 Come ye near unto me, hear ye this;
[a]I have not spoken in secret from the beginning;
From the time that it was, there *am* I:
And now [b]the Lord GOD, and his Spirit, hath sent me.

48:2 [b]Mic. 3:11; Rom. 2:17 48:3 [a]ch. 44:7,8 [b]Josh. 21:45 48:4 [1]Heb. *hard* [a]Ex. 32:9; Deut. 31:27 48:5 [a]ver. 3 48:8 [a]Ps. 58:3 48:9 [a]Ps. 79:9; 106:8; Ezek. 20:9 [b]Ps. 78:38

48:10 [1]Or, *for silver* [a]Ps. 66:10 48:11 [a]ver. 9 [b]Deut. 32:26; Ezek. 20:9 [c]ch. 42:8 48:12 [a]Deut. 32:39 [b]ch. 44:6; Rev. 22:13 48:13 [1]Or, *the palm of my right hand hath spread out* [a]Ps. 102:25 [b]ch. 40:26 48:14 [a]ch. 45:1 [b]ch. 44:28 48:15 [a]ch. 45:1,2 48:16 [a]ch. 45:19 [b]Zech. 2:8

2:2–4 and note; 52:1; 56:7; 57:13; 64:10–11; 65:11). See also 1:26 and note; 4:3 and note; Dan 9:24. *stay themselves upon . . . God.* They claim to trust the Lord, but their source of security was elsewhere (cf. 31:1; 36:6,9; Ezek 29:6–7). Contrast 10:20 and the true faith that the Lord will instill in his people. *LORD of hosts.* See 13:4 and note.
48:3 *former things.* See 41:22 and note. *they came to pass.* See 42:9.
48:4 *obstinate . . . brass.* See Jer 6:28; cf. Ezek 3:7.
48:5 *Mine idol hath done them.* See Isaiah's harsh words about idolatry in 44:17–20 (see also notes there). *graven image . . . molten image.* See note on 44:12–20.
48:6 *new things.* For example, Israel's restoration (see 42:9 and note). The Messianic age and the new heavens and new earth may also be in view (cf. 65:17). *hidden things.* Cf. Rom 16:25–26.
48:7 *created now.* Now given substance in the prophetic announcement of their coming.
48:8 *heardest not . . . knewest not.* See 1:3. *ear was not opened.* See 6:10 and note. *transgressor.* See 1:2; 46:8 and notes.
48:9 *defer mine anger.* Cf. Ps 78:38. *my praise.* The praise God is worthy of.
‡48:10 *refined . . . chosen.* Images of judgment (see Jer 9:7; Ezek 22:18–22). For "chosen," read "tested." Purifying fire is also mentioned in 1:25; 4:4. *furnace of affliction.* For Israel, Egypt had been an "iron furnace" (Deut 4:20; 1 Ki 8:51; Jer 11:4). The fall of Jerusalem and the Babylonian exile were a similar furnace.
‡48:11 *For . . . polluted.* Or "profaned." Jerusalem's fall and God's scattered people had brought dishonor to God's name (see Ezek 36:20–23). *my glory.* See 40:5 and note.
48:12 *called.* To be God's servant, His chosen people. See 42:6; see also 41:2; 43:1 and notes. *first . . . last.* See 41:4 and note.
48:13 *laid the foundation . . . spanned the heavens.* Isaiah often refers to God as Creator (see 40:21–22; 42:5; 51:13 and notes). Cf. Ps 102:25. *When I call . . . they stand.* All creation does God's bidding (see 40:26 and note; Ps 103:22).
48:14 *Which . . . hath declared.* See 41:21–23,26; 43:9 and notes. *loved him.* Cyrus the Great (see 41:2 and note). *his pleasure.* See 46:10–11 and note. *Babylon.* See 13:1 and note.
48:15 *called him.* Cyrus (see 41:2 and note). *way prosperous.* See 44:28; 45:1–4 and notes.
48:16 *not spoken in secret.* See 45:19 and note. *the beginning.* The prediction about Cyrus and his mission (see 41:25–27 and notes). *his Spirit, hath sent me.* A reference to either Isaiah or the servant of the Lord. The Spirit of the Lord comes upon the servant in 42:1 (see note there) and upon the Messianic prophet of 61:1 (see note there).

17 Thus saith [a]the LORD, thy redeemer,
the Holy One of Israel;
I *am* the LORD thy God which teacheth
thee to profit,
[b]Which leadeth thee by the way *that*
thou shouldest go.
18 [a]O that thou hadst hearkened to my
commandments!
[b]Then had thy peace been as a river,
And thy righteousness as the waves of
the sea:
19 [a]Thy seed also had been as the sand,
And the offspring of thy bowels like
the gravel thereof;
His name should not have been cut off
nor destroyed from before me.

20 [a]Go ye forth of Babylon, flee ye from
the Chaldeans,
With a voice of singing declare ye, tell
this,
Utter it *even* to the end of the earth;
Say ye, The LORD hath [b]redeemed his
servant Jacob.
21 And they [a]thirsted not *when* he led
them through the deserts:
He [b]caused the waters to flow out of
the rock for them:
He clave the rock also, and the waters
gushed out.
22 [a]*There is* no peace, saith the LORD,
unto the wicked.

48:17 [a]ch. 43:14 [b]Ps. 32:8
48:18 [a]Deut. 32:29; Ps. 81:13 [b]Ps. 119:165
48:19 [a]Gen. 22:17; Hos. 1:10
48:20 [a]Jer. 50:8 [b]Ex. 19:4-6
48:21 [a]ch. 41:17,18 [b]Ex. 17:6; Ps. 105:41
48:22 [a]ch. 57:21

49:1 [a]ch. 41:1 [b]Jer. 1:5; Mat. 1:20; John 10:36
49:2 [a]ch. 11:4; Hos. 6:5; Rev. 1:16 [b]ch. 51:16 [c]Ps. 45:5
49:3 [a]ch. 42:1; Zech. 3:8 [b]John 15:8; Eph. 1:6
49:4 [1]Or, *my reward* [a]Ezek. 3:19 [b]ch. 40:10
49:5 [1]Or, *That Israel may be gathered to him, and I may, etc.* [a]ver. 1 [b]Mat. 23:37
49:6 [1]Or, Art thou *lighter than that thou shouldest, etc.* [2]Or, *desolations*

The servant's call

49 Listen, [a]O isles, unto me;
And hearken, ye people, from afar;
[b]The LORD hath called me from the
womb;
From the bowels of my mother hath he
made mention of my name.
2 And he hath made [a]my mouth like a
sharp sword;
[b]In the shadow of his hand hath he hid
me,
And made me [c]a polished shaft;
In his quiver hath he hid me;
3 And said unto me, [a]Thou *art* my
servant,
O Israel, [b]in whom I will be glorified.
4 [a]Then I said, I have laboured in vain,
I have spent my strength for nought,
and in vain:
Yet surely my judgment *is* with the
LORD,
And [b][1]my work with my God.
5 And now, saith the LORD [a]that formed
me from the womb *to be* his servant,
To bring Jacob again to him,
[1]Though Israel [b]be not gathered,
Yet shall I be glorious in the eyes of the
LORD,
And my God shall be my strength.
6 And he said, [1]It is a light thing that
thou shouldest be my servant
To raise up the tribes of Jacob,
And to restore the [2]preserved of Israel:

48:17 *redeemer, the Holy One of Israel.* See 41:14 and note. *teacheth thee . . . the way that thou shouldest go.* Through the prophets (see 30:20–21 and notes; Ps 32:8).
48:18 *peace been as a river . . . righteousness as the waves.* Abundant and overflowing peace and righteousness (see 45:8; Amos 5:24 and notes). Peace (or "well-being") and righteousness are also linked in 9:7; 32:17; 54:13–14; 60:17; Ps 85:10; Heb 7:2.
48:19 *seed . . . as the sand.* See 10:22; see also Gen 13:16 and note; Gen 22:17; Jer 33:22 and note. *name . . . not have been cut off.* Israel's name would not be completely obliterated (see v. 9; 54:3; Jer 31:36).
48:20 *Go ye forth of Babylon, flee.* Although the Jews did not have to flee (see 52:12), they were encouraged to depart quickly because of the judgment coming on Babylon (cf. Rev 18:4). This is the last mention of Babylon by name in Isaiah. *voice of singing.* See 44:23; 49:13; 52:9 and notes. *end of the earth.* See 11:12; 42:10 and notes. *redeemed.* See 43:1 and note. *his servant.* See 41:8–9 and note.
48:21 *they thirsted not . . . waters . . . out of the rock.* A reference to God's provision after the exodus (see Ex 17:6 and note; Num 20:11; see also Is 32:2; 35:6; 43:19; 49:10 and notes). God's people would have water on the way home from Babylonian exile also.
48:22 Repeated almost verbatim in 57:21. *peace.* See 39:8 and note. *wicked.* Those who rebel against the Lord (see note on 1:2).
49:1–6 (or **1–7** or **1–13**) The second of the four servant songs (see note on 42:1–4).
‡49:1 *isles.* Or "coastlands." In 42:4 the islands "wait" for the servant's law. *called me from the womb.* Cf. v. 5. The language is similar to that of the call of the prophet Jeremiah (Jer 1:5) and of the apostle Paul (Gal 1:15). Cf. 41:9. *he made mention of my name.* See 43:1 and note.
‡49:2 *my mouth . . . sharp sword.* See Eph 6:17; Heb 4:12; Rev 1:16; 2:12,16. In 11:4 a powerful rod comes from the mouth of the Messiah. *shadow of his hand.* Descriptive of protection (see 30:2–3; 51:16). *a polished shaft.* A special arrow kept in top condition until time for its use. Arrows are used of God's judgment in Deut 32:23,42, of the deadly words of the wicked in Ps 64:3–4 and of Satan's schemes and temptations in Eph 6:11,16.
‡49:3 *my servant, O Israel.* See notes on 41:8–9; 42:1–4; 42:1. "Servant" here cannot mean literally national Israel, since in v. 5 this servant has a mission to Israel. Rather, the Messianic servant is the ideal Israel through whom the Lord will be glorified. He will succeed where national Israel failed and will ultimately enable Israel to fulfill its "servant" role as God's messenger to the nations (contrast 42:18–22). *I will be glorified.* Through the redemption He will accomplish (see notes on 35:2; 40:5).
‡49:4 *laboured in vain.* Just as the nation Israel had toiled in vain (see 65:23), so Christ would encounter strong opposition during His ministry and would temporarily suffer apparent failure. The "suffering servant" theme is developed in the third and fourth of the four servant songs (50:4–9 or 50:4–11; 52:13–53:12). *my judgment . . . my work.* The reward that is due the servant for his work, perhaps referring to the spiritual offspring of the servant (see 53:10)—Jews and Gentiles alike who believe in Him (vv. 5–6); see 40:10 and note. In any case, He will be vindicated and rewarded (50:8; 53:10–12; 1 Tim 3:16).
49:5 *formed me from the womb.* See v. 1; 44:2 and notes. *bring Jacob again to him.* A prophecy of release from captivity in Babylon (see vv. 9–12,22; 41:2 and note) and from the greater captivity of sin (see 42:7 and note). *my strength.* See 12:2.
‡49:6 Together with Gen 12:1–3; Ex 19:5–6, this verse is some-

I will also give thee for a [a]light to the Gentiles,
That *thou* mayest be my salvation unto the end of the earth.
7 Thus saith the LORD, the redeemer of Israel, *and* his Holy One,
[a][1]To him whom man despiseth, to him whom the nation abhorreth, to a servant of rulers,
[b]Kings shall see and arise,
Princes also shall worship,
Because of the LORD that *is* faithful,
And the Holy One of Israel, and he shall choose thee.

The restoration of Israel

8 Thus saith the LORD,
[a]In an acceptable time have I heard thee,
And in a day of salvation have I helped thee:
And I will preserve thee, [b]and give thee for a covenant of the people,
To [1]establish the earth, to cause to inherit the desolate heritages;
9 That *thou* mayest say [a]to the prisoners, Go forth;
To *them* that *are* in darkness, Shew yourselves.
They shall feed in the ways,
And their pastures *shall be* in all high places.
10 They shall not [a]hunger nor thirst;
[b]Neither shall the heat nor sun smite them:
For he that hath mercy on them [c]shall lead them,
Even by the springs of water shall he guide them.

49:6 [a]Luke 2:32
49:7 [1]Or, *To him that is despised in soul* [a]Mat. 26:67 [b]Ps. 72:10
49:8 [1]Or, *raise up* [a]Ps. 69:13; 2 Cor. 6:2 [b]ch. 42:6
49:9 [a]Zech. 9:12
49:10 [a]Rev. 7:16 [b]Ps. 121:6 [c]Ps. 23:2

49:11 [a]ch. 40:4
49:12 [a]ch. 43:5,6
49:13 [a]ch. 44:23
49:14 [a]ch. 40:27
49:15 [1]Heb. *From having compassion* [a]Ps. 103:13; Mal. 3:17; Mat. 7:11 [b]Rom. 11:29
49:16 [a]Ex. 13:9; Sol. 8:6
49:17 [a]ver. 19
49:18 [a]ch. 60:4 [b]Prov. 17:6

11 [a]And I will make all my mountains a way,
And my highways shall be exalted.
12 Behold, [a]these shall come from far:
And lo, these from the north and from the west;
And these from the land of Sinim.
13 [a]Sing, O heavens; and be joyful, O earth;
And break forth *into* singing, O mountains:
For the LORD hath comforted his people,
And will have mercy upon his afflicted.
14 [a]But Zion said, The LORD hath forsaken me,
And my Lord hath forgotten me.
15 [a]Can a woman forget her sucking child,
[1]That *she* should not have compassion on the son of her womb?
Yea, they may forget,
[b]Yet will I not forget thee.
16 Behold, [a]I have graven thee upon the palms of *my* hands;
Thy walls *are* continually before me.
17 Thy children shall make haste;
[a]Thy destroyers and they that made thee waste shall go forth of thee.
18 [a]Lift up thine eyes round about, and behold:
All these gather themselves together, *and* come to thee.
As I live, saith the LORD, thou shalt surely clothe thee with them all, [b]as with an ornament,
And bind them *on thee,* as a bride *doth.*

times called the "great commission of the OT" and is quoted in part by Paul and Barnabas in Acts 13:47. The fulfillment of this passage begins with the church's preaching of the gospel to all nations and climaxes with the submission of the nations to Christ in his future kingdom (cf. 2:1–4). *light thing . . . tribes of Jacob.* The mission of the servant extends beyond Israel to all nations. *preserved.* Probably referring to the remnant (see 1:9 and note). *light to the Gentiles.* See 42:6 and note; Acts 26:23. Christ is the light of the world (Luke 2:30–32; John 8:12; 9:5), and Christians are to reflect His light (Mat 5:14). *end of the earth.* See 11:12 and note; see also 41:5; 42:10; 48:20.

49:7 *redeemer of Israel . . . Holy One.* See 41:14 and note. *despiseth.* Applied twice to the suffering servant in 53:3. In 60:14 Zion is despised by her enemies. *nation.* Refers to either Israel (1:4) or Gentiles. *Kings shall see . . . worship.* See v. 23. This reaction to the servant is similar to that of 52:15. Former oppressors bow before a restored Jerusalem in 60:14 (cf. 45:14; 60:11–12; 66:23). *choose thee.* See 41:8–9; 42:1 and notes.

49:8 Quoted in part in 2 Cor 6:2. *an acceptable time . . . day of salvation.* The background of this verse is probably the year of jubile (see 61:1–2; Lev 25:10). The return from exile will bring the same restoration of land for the people as that year of liberty did. *preserve thee . . . for a covenant.* See 42:6 and note. *cause . . . the desolate heritages.* See 44:26. It was under Joshua that the land had been divided among individual tribes and families (Josh 14:1–5). The Messianic servant will be a new Joshua—as well as a new Moses (see vv. 9–10, which echo Israel's deliverance from Egypt and her wilderness experiences under Moses during the period of the exodus).

49:9 *prisoners.* The exiles. See 42:7 and note. *high places.* See 41:18 and note.

49:10 *not hunger nor thirst.* See 48:21 and note. *hath mercy.* See 14:1 and note. *shall lead them.* As a shepherd (see 40:11 and note). This whole verse is also a picture of heaven according to Rev 7:16–17.

49:11 *mountains a way.* See 26:7 and note. *highways . . . exalted.* See 11:16; 35:8; 40:3; 62:10 and notes.

49:12 *come from far.* See 11:11 and note; 60:4. *north . . . west.* See 43:5–6 and notes. *Sinim.* See Ezek 29:10; 30:6; located in the most southern part of Egypt (Aswan).

49:13 *Sing . . . O mountains.* Nature is personified often in Isaiah. See 44:23 and note. *comforted his people.* As He redeemed and saved them. Cf. 2 Cor 1:3–4. *will have mercy.* See v. 10 and note; 54:7–10.

49:14 *forsaken . . . forgotten.* See 40:27; 54:7; Lam 5:20–22.

49:15 *Can a woman forget . . . ?* Cf. Ps 27:10.

49:16 *graven thee upon . . . my hands.* As the names of the tribes of Israel were engraved on stones and fastened to the ephod of the high priest as a memorial before the Lord (Ex 28:9–12; cf. Sol 8:6). *continually before me.* Cf. Ps 137:5–6.

49:18 *All these gather.* See vv. 5,12 and notes. *ornament.* Beautiful clothes and jewels symbolize strength and joy.

19 For thy waste and thy desolate places,
and the land of thy destruction,
[a]Shall even now be too narrow by
reason of the inhabitants,
And they that swallowed thee up shall
be far away.
20 [a]The children which thou shalt have,
[b]after thou hast lost the other, shall
say again in thine ears,
The place *is* too strait for me:
Give place to me that I may dwell.
21 Then shalt thou say in thine heart,
Who hath begotten me these,
Seeing I have lost my children, and *am*
desolate,
A captive, and removing to and fro?
And who hath brought up these?
Behold, I was left alone;
These, where *had* they *been?*
22 [a]Thus saith the Lord GOD,
Behold, I will lift up mine hand to the
Gentiles,
And set up my standard to the people:
And they shall bring thy sons in *their*
[1]arms,
And thy daughters shall be carried
upon *their* shoulders.
23 [a]And kings shall be thy [1]nursing
fathers,
And their [2]queens thy nursing
mothers:
They shall bow down to thee *with their*
face *toward* the earth,
And [b]lick up the dust of thy feet;
And thou shalt know that I *am* the
LORD:
For [c]they shall not be ashamed that
wait for me.
24 [a]Shall the prey be taken from the
mighty,
Or [1]the lawful captive delivered?

49:19 [a]ch. 54:1,2; Zech. 10:10
49:20 [a]ch. 60:4 [b]Mat. 3:9; Rom. 11:11
49:22 [1]Heb. *bosom* [a]ch. 60:4
49:23 [1]Heb. *nourishers* [2]Heb. *princesses* [a]Ps. 72:11; ch. 52:15; 60:16 [b]Ps. 72:9; Mic. 7:17 [c]Ps. 34:22; Rom. 5:5; 9:33
49:24 [1]Heb. *the captivity of the just* [a]Mat. 12:29; Luke 11:21,22
49:25 [1]Heb. *captivity*
49:26 [1]Or, *new wine* [a]ch. 9:20 [b]Rev. 14:20; 16:6 [c]Ps. 9:16; ch. 60:16
50:1 [a]Deut. 24:1; Jer. 3:8; Hos. 2:2 [b]2 Ki. 4:1; Mat. 18:25 [c]ch. 52:3
50:2 [a]Prov. 1:24; ch. 65:12; Jer. 35:15 [b]Num. 11:23 [c]Ps. 106:9; Nah. 1:4 [d]Ex. 14:21 [e]Josh. 3:16 [f]Ex. 7:18
50:3 [a]Ex. 10:21 [b]Rev. 6:12

25 But thus saith the LORD,
Even the [1]captives of the mighty shall
be taken away,
And the prey of the terrible shall be
delivered:
For I will contend with him that
contendeth with thee,
And I will save thy children.
26 And I will [a]feed them that oppress
thee with their own flesh;
And they shall be drunken with their
own [b]blood, as with [1]sweet wine:
And all flesh [c]shall know that I the
LORD *am* thy Saviour
And thy redeemer, the mighty One of
Jacob.

Sin separates Israel from God

50 Thus saith the LORD,
Where *is* [a]the bill of your mother's
divorcement, whom I have put away?
Or which of my [b]creditors *is it* to
whom I have sold you?
Behold, for your iniquities [c]have you
sold yourselves,
And for your transgressions *is* your
mother put away.
2 Wherefore, when I came, *was there* no
man?
[a]When I called, *was there* none to
answer?
[b]Is my hand shortened at all, that *it*
cannot redeem?
Or have I no power to deliver?
Behold, [c]at my rebuke I [d]dry up the
sea,
I make the [e]rivers a wilderness:
[f]Their fish stinketh, because *there is*
no water, and dieth for thirst.
3 [a]I clothe the heavens with blackness,
[b]And I make sackcloth their covering.

‡49:19–20 *too narrow.* The restoration of Israel will be astonishing and complete, and Jerusalem will be too small to contain all of its inhabitants. The prophecy was partially fulfilled in the return from Babylon (see note on 11:11) but will have its ultimate fulfillment when Christ returns to establish his kingdom on earth (cf. Zech 2:1–5).
49:19 *waste . . . desolate.* Cf. v. 8; see 44:26 and note.
49:21 *lost my children . . . desolate.* The concept of Israel as a barren woman is stressed in 54:1.
49:22 *set up my standard.* See 5:26 and note; 13:2. *bring thy sons . . . daughters.* See 11:12 and note. The nations bring Israel back also in 14:2; 43:6; 60:9. *in their arms.* Cf. 60:4; see 40:11 and note.
49:23 *kings . . . shall bow down.* See v. 7; 11:14 and notes. *know that I am the LORD.* See v. 26; 60:16; Ezek 12:20; 13:9; 36:38. *shall not be ashamed.* See 29:22 and note. *wait for me.* See 40:31 and note.
49:24 *the mighty.* The Babylonians (see 51:13).
‡49:25 *captives . . . shall be taken.* See Ezra 2:1,64–65; Jer 50:33–34; 52:27–30. *I will contend.* God takes up the case of His people. He will "plead their cause" (Jer 50:34). *I will save.* See 35:4 and note.
49:26 *them that oppress.* See 14:4; 16:4; 51:13. *with their own flesh.* During the siege of Jerusalem its people were reduced to cannibalism (Lam 4:10). *drunken with their own blood.* Cf. 51:22–23. *all flesh shall know.* See v. 23 and note. *Saviour.* See 43:3 and note; 60:16. *redeemer.* See 41:14 and note. *mighty One of Jacob.* See 1:24 and note; 60:16.
50:1 *mother's divorcement.* A husband was required to give this to a wife he wished to divorce (see Deut 24:1,3; Mat 19:7; Mark 10:4). According to Jer 3:8 God gave the northern kingdom of Israel her certificate of divorce, and Is 54:6–7 indicates that God had left Judah (see 62:4). Perhaps Isaiah's point is that God did not initiate the divorce; Judah broke her relationship with Him. The exile, then, was actually a temporary period of separation (see 54:7) rather than a divorce. *my creditors.* If a man's debts were not paid, his children could be sold into slavery (see 2 Ki 4:1). But God has no creditors. *you sold yourselves.* Cf. 45:13; 52:3.
50:2 *I came . . . called.* Through His servants the prophets (see Jer 25:4). *none to answer.* Israel was deaf toward God (see 6:10 and note; 66:4). *hand shortened.* The hand represented power. *dry up the sea.* A reference to crossing the Red sea (see 43:16–17 and notes; Ps 106:9). *rivers a wilderness.* See 42:15 and note. *fish stinketh.* Perhaps a reference to one of the plagues in Egypt (see 19:5–6,8; Ex 7:18).
50:3 *heavens with blackness.* Perhaps an allusion to the plague of darkness (Ex 10:21); but see 13:10 and note.

Obedient response of the servant

4 [a]The Lord GOD hath given me the
tongue of the learned,
That *I* should know how to speak a
word in season to *him that is* [b]weary:
He wakeneth morning by morning,
He wakeneth mine ear to hear as the
learned.
5 The Lord GOD [a]hath opened mine ear,
And I was not [b]rebellious,
Neither turned away back.
6 [a]I gave my back to the smiters,
And [b]my cheeks to them that plucked
off the hair:
I hid not my face from shame and
spitting.
7 For the Lord GOD will help me;
Therefore shall I not be confounded:
Therefore have [a]I set my face like a
flint,
And I know that I shall not be
ashamed.
8 [a]*He is* near that justifieth me;
Who will contend with me? let us
stand together:
Who *is* [1]mine adversary? let him come
near to me.
9 Behold, the Lord GOD will help me;
Who *is* he *that* shall condemn me?
[a]Lo, they all shall wax old as a garment;
[b]the moth shall eat them up.
10 Who *is* among you that feareth the
LORD,
That obeyeth the voice of his servant,
That [a]walketh *in* darkness, and hath no
light?
[b]Let him trust in the name of the
LORD,
And stay upon his God.
11 Behold, all ye that kindle a fire, that
compass *yourselves* about with
sparks:
Walk in the light of your fire, and in
the sparks *that* ye have kindled.
[a]This shall ye have of mine hand;
Ye shall lie down [b]in sorrow.

50:4 [a]Ex. 4:11 [b]Mat. 11:28
50:5 [a]Ps. 40:6-8 [b]Mat. 26:39; John 14:31; Heb. 10:5
50:6 [a]Mat. 26:67 [b]Lam. 3:30
50:7 [a]Ezek. 3:8,9
50:8 [1]Heb. *the master of my cause?* [a]Rom. 8:32
50:9 [a]Job 13:28; Ps. 102:26; ch. 51:6 [b]ch. 51:8
50:10 [a]Ps. 23:4 [b]2 Chr. 20:20; Ps. 20:7
50:11 [a]John 9:39 [b]Ps. 16:4
51:1 [a]Rom. 9:30-32
51:2 [a]Rom. 4:1; Heb. 11:11 [b]Gen. 12:1 [c]Gen. 24:35
51:3 [a]ver. 12; ch. 52:9 [b]Gen. 13:10; Joel 2:3
51:4 [a]ch. 2:3 [b]ch. 42:6

The LORD will deliver his people

51 Hearken to me, [a]ye that follow after
righteousness, ye that seek the
LORD:
Look unto the rock *whence* ye are
hewn,
And to the hole of the pit *whence* ye
are digged.
2 [a]Look unto Abraham your father,
And unto Sarah *that* bare you:
[b]For I called him alone,
And [c]blessed him, and increased him.
3 For the LORD [a]shall comfort Zion:
He will comfort all her waste places;
And he will make her wilderness like
Eden,
And her desert [b]like the garden of the
LORD;
Joy and gladness shall be found
therein,
Thanksgiving, and the voice of melody.
4 Hearken unto me, my people;
And give ear unto me, O my nation:
[a]For a law shall proceed from me,
And I will make my judgment to rest
[b]for a light of the people.

50:4–9 (or **4–11**) The third of the four servant songs (see note on 42:1–4).

50:4–5,7,9 *Lord GOD.* The only uses of this title in the servant songs.

50:4 *how to speak . . . to him that is weary.* In 42:3 the servant assisted the weak (contrast 49:2). Cf. Jer 31:25. *wakeneth mine ear.* Unlike Israel (see v. 2), the servant was responsive to God.

50:5 *opened mine ear.* A sign of obedience (see 1:19; Ps 40:6 and note). *was not rebellious.* Unlike Israel (see 1:2 and note; 1:20).

‡50:6 *my back to the smiters.* Beatings were for criminals or fools (see Prov 10:13; 19:29; 26:3; Mat 27:26; John 19:1). *plucked off the hair.* Plucking the beard was a sign of disrespect and contempt (see 2 Sam 10:4–5; Neh 13:25). *shame and spitting.* To show hatred (Job 30:10) or to insult or disgrace (Deut 25:9; Job 17:6; Mat 27:30). This treatment of the servant anticipates His ultimate suffering in 52:13–53:12.

‡50:7 *help me.* See v. 9; 49:8. *not be confounded . . . not be ashamed.* See 29:22 and note. Ultimately the servant will be honored (see 49:7; 52:13; 53:10–12). *my face like a flint.* Like the prophets, the servant will endure with great determination. Cf. Luke 9:51, where Jesus "steadfastly set his face to go to Jerusalem."

50:8 *justifieth me.* The Lord will find Him righteous (see 45:25; for its ultimate fulfillment see 1 Tim 3:16). *contend with.* See 49:25 and note. Because Christ was sinless, He also nullifies the charges brought against any who believe in Him (see Rom 8:31–34). *Who is mine adversary?* Cf. 54:17.

50:9 *wax old as a garment; the moth.* Those who falsely accuse the righteous succumb to moths in 51:8 (i.e. they will be destroyed).

50:10 *feareth the LORD.* See Gen 20:11; Prov 1:7 and notes. Cf. 25:3; 59:19. *in darkness.* Perhaps trouble or distress, similar to the experience of the servant (cf. 8:22). *trust . . . stay upon.* The Lord encouraged such trust in 12:2; 31:1.

50:11 *kindle a fire . . . sparks.* Perhaps a reference to wicked practices that will ultimately destroy those who engage in them. Fire is a frequent figure of punishment (see 1:31 and note; cf. 9:18; 47:14; Ps 7:13). *sorrow.* Cf. 66:24.

‡51:1 *ye that follow after righteousness.* Cf. v. 7; Deut 16:20; Prov 15:9. *rock.* Abraham (v. 2). Elsewhere God is called "the rock" (see 17:10 and note). *hole of the pit . . . digged.* Pictures Israel as a rock dug from a quarry.

‡51:2 *alone.* When Abraham was one individual and had no heir. See Gen 12:1; Ezek 33:24. If God was able to raise up a great nation from one individual in the past, then he will surely be able to make Israel a great nation in spite of their condition in exile. *blessed him, and increased him.* See Gen 12:2–3; 13:16; 15:5; 17:5; 22:17.

51:3 *comfort . . . comfort.* See 49:13 and note. *wilderness like Eden.* See 35:1–2. The contrast between the lush splendor of Eden and the barrenness of the wilderness is found also in Joel 2:3. Cf. Gen 2:8,10. *Joy and gladness.* See v. 11; 25:9 and note.

51:4 *law . . . my judgment.* The rule of the servant would bring justice also (see 2:2–4; 42:4 and notes). *light of the people.* The servant is the light in 42:6; 49:6.

5 [a]My righteousness *is* near; my
salvation is gone forth,
[b]And mine arms shall judge the people;
[c]The isles shall wait upon me,
And [d]on mine arm shall they trust.
6 [a]Lift up your eyes to the heavens,
And look upon the earth beneath:
For [b]the heavens shall vanish away like
smoke,
[c]And the earth shall wax old like a
garment,
And they that dwell therein shall die in
like manner:
But my salvation shall be for ever,
And my righteousness shall not be
abolished.
7 [a]Hearken unto me, ye that know
righteousness,
The people [b]in whose heart *is* my law;
[c]Fear ye not the reproach of men,
Neither be ye afraid of their revilings.
8 For [a]the moth shall eat them up like a
garment,
And the worm shall eat them like wool:
But my righteousness shall be for ever,
And my salvation from generation to
generation.
9 [a]Awake, awake, [b]put on strength,
O arm of the LORD;
Awake, [c]as *in* the ancient days, *in* the
generations of old.
[d]*Art* thou not it that hath cut [e]Rahab,
and wounded the [f]dragon?
10 *Art* thou not it which hath [a]dried the
sea, the waters of the great deep;
That hath made the depths of the sea a
way for the ransomed to pass over?
11 Therefore [a]the redeemed of the LORD
shall return,
And come with singing *unto* Zion;
And everlasting joy *shall be* upon their
head:
They shall obtain gladness and joy;
And sorrow and mourning shall flee
away.
12 I, *even* I, *am* he [a]that comforteth you:
Who *art* thou, that thou shouldest be
afraid [b]of a man *that* shall die,
And of the son of man *which* shall be
made [c]*as* grass;
13 And forgettest the LORD thy Maker,
[a]That hath stretched forth the heavens,
and laid the foundations of the earth;
And hast feared continually every day
because of the fury of the oppressor,
As if he [1]were ready to destroy?
[b]And where *is* the fury of the
oppressor?
14 The captive exile hasteneth that *he*
may be loosed,
[a]And that he should not die in the pit,
Nor that his bread should fail.
15 But I *am* the LORD thy God,
That [a]divided the sea, whose waves
roared:
The LORD of hosts *is* his name.
16 And [a]I have put my words in thy
mouth,
And [b]have covered thee in the shadow
of mine hand,
[c]That I may plant the heavens, and lay
the foundations of the earth,
And say unto Zion, Thou *art* my
people.

The cup of God's fury

17 [a]Awake, awake, stand up, O Jerusalem,
Which [b]hast drunk at the hand of the
LORD the cup of his fury;
[c]Thou hast drunken the dregs of the
cup of trembling, *and* wrung *them*
out.
18 *There is* none to guide her among all
the sons *whom* she hath brought
forth;

51:5 [a]ch. 46:13; Rom. 1:16 [b]Ps. 67:4 [c]ch. 60:9 [d]Rom. 1:16
51:6 [a]ch. 40:26 [b]Ps. 102:26; Mat. 24:35; 2 Pet. 3:10 [c]ch. 50:9
51:7 [a]ver. 1 [b]Ps. 37:31 [c]Mat. 10:28; Acts 5:41
51:8 [a]ch. 50:9
51:9 [a]Ps. 44:23 [b]Ps. 93:1 [c]Ps. 44:1 [d]Job 26:12 [e]Ps. 87:4; 89:10 [f]Ps. 74:13; Ezek. 29:3
51:10 [a]Ex. 14:21; ch. 43:16
51:11 [a]ch. 35:10
51:12 [a]2 Cor. 1:3 [b]Ps. 118:6 [c]1 Pet. 1:24
51:13 [1]Or, *made* himself *ready* [a]Ps. 104:2 [b]Job 20:7
51:14 [a]Zech. 9:11
51:15 [a]Job 26:12; Ps. 74:13; Jer. 31:35
51:16 [a]Deut. 18:18; ch. 59:21; John 3:34 [b]ch. 49:2 [c]ch. 65:17
51:17 [a]ch. 52:1 [b]Job 21:20; Jer. 25:15 [c]See Deut. 28:28,34; Ps. 60:3; Ezek. 23:32-34

51:5 *righteousness is near.* In the deliverance from exile. Ultimately, salvation through Christ will come to all nations. See 46:13 and note. *arms.* Symbolic of power. *isles.* See 11:11 and note. *wait upon me.* See 40:31 and note; 42:4 and note.
51:6 *Lift . . . to the heavens.* See 40:26. *heavens shall vanish.* See 34:4 and note. *earth shall wax old like a garment.* See 24:4; Heb 1:10–11; cf. Is 50:9. *be for ever.* See v. 8; 45:17. The word of God will also endure forever (see 40:8 and note; Mat 24:35; Luke 21:33).
51:7 *ye that know righteousness.* See v. 1 and note. *in whose heart is my law.* See Ps 37:31; Jer 31:33. *reproach . . . revilings.* Such as those borne by the servant in 50:6–7.
51:8 *moth . . . like a garment.* See 50:9 and note; cf. 51:6.
51:9 *Awake, awake.* See v. 17; 52:1 for the same double command (see also 40:1 and note).
51:9 *put on strength.* Cf. 50:2; see note on 40:31. *arm of the LORD.* Symbol of God's power (cf. v. 5). See 30:30; 50:2 and notes; 52:10; 53:1; 63:12. *Rahab . . . the dragon.* Egypt. See 27:1 and note; 30:7 and note.
51:10 *sea.* The Red sea (see 50:2 and note). *the ransomed.* See 35:9 and note.
51:11 This verse is the same as 35:10 (see note there).
51:12 *he that comforteth.* See v. 3; 49:13 and note. *grass.* See 37:27; 40:6 and notes.
‡51:13 *stretched forth the heavens, and . . . earth.* See v. 16; 48:13 and note. *hast feared continually.* Israel has learned to fear God in a new way through the punishment he has meted out. *fury of the oppressor.* See 49:26 and note. Babylon's wrath was insignificant beside the mighty wrath of God (cf. 13:3,5; 30:27).
‡51:14 *exile . . . loosed.* The exiles in Babylon will soon be set free (see 42:7 and note; 49:9). *in the pit.* In the dungeon or prison; cf. 42:7; Jer 37:16.
51:15 *divided the sea.* Cf. Job 26:12; Ps 107:25; Jer 31:35. *LORD of hosts.* See 13:4 and note.
51:16 *my words.* Primarily the law of Moses, mentioned in v. 7. Like the servant of 49:2, the people are responding to God's word (cf. 59:21; Josh 1:8). *shadow of mine hand.* See 49:2 and note. *plant the heavens . . . earth.* See v. 13 and note.
51:17 *cup of his fury.* See vv. 20–22; 13:3 and note. Experiencing God's judgment is often compared to becoming drunk on strong wine. It is the fate of wicked nations in particular. See 29:9; 63:6; Ps 60:3; 75:8; Jer 25:15–16; Lam 4:21; Ezek 23:32–34; Hab 2:16; Zech 12:2; cf. John 18:11.

Neither *is there any* that taketh her by
the hand of all the sons *that* she hath
brought up.
19 [a]These two *things* [1]are come unto
thee; who shall be sorry for thee?
Desolation, and [2]destruction, and the
famine, and the sword:
[b]*By* whom shall I comfort thee?
20 [a]Thy sons have fainted, they lie at the
head of all the streets, as a wild bull
in a net:
They are full *of* the fury of the LORD,
the rebuke of thy God.
21 Therefore hear now this, thou afflicted,
And drunken, [a]but not with wine:
22 Thus saith thy Lord the LORD,
And thy God [a]*that* pleadeth the cause
of his people,
Behold, I have taken out of thine hand
the cup of trembling,
Even the dregs of the cup of my fury;
Thou shalt no more drink it again:
23 But [a]I will put it into the hand of them
that afflict thee;
[b]Which have said to thy soul, Bow
down, that we may go over:
And thou hast laid thy body as the
ground,
And as the street, to them that went
over.

God will restore Jerusalem

52 Awake, [a]awake; put on thy strength,
O Zion;
Put on thy beautiful garments,
O Jerusalem, [b]the holy city:
For [c]henceforth there shall no more
come into thee the uncircumcised
[d]and the unclean.
2 [a]Shake thyself from the dust; arise, *and*
sit down, O Jerusalem:
[b]Loose thyself from the bands of thy
neck, O captive daughter of Zion.
3 For thus saith the LORD,
[a]Ye have sold yourselves for nought;
And ye shall be redeemed without
money.
4 For thus saith the Lord GOD,
My people went down aforetime *into*
[a]Egypt to sojourn there;
And the Assyrian oppressed them
without cause.
5 Now therefore, what have I here, saith
the LORD,
That my people is taken away for
nought?
They that rule over them make *them* to
howl, saith the LORD;
And my name continually every day *is*
[a]blasphemed.
6 Therefore my people shall know my
name:
Therefore *they shall know* in that day
that I *am* he that doth speak: behold,
it is I.
7 [a]How beautiful upon the mountains
are the feet of him that bringeth
good tidings, that publisheth peace;
That bringeth good tidings of good,
that publisheth salvation;
That saith unto Zion, [b]Thy God
reigneth!
8 Thy watchmen shall lift up the voice;
With the voice together shall they sing:
For they shall see eye to eye,
When the LORD shall bring again Zion.
9 Break forth into joy, sing together, ye
waste places of Jerusalem:
For the LORD hath comforted his
people, he hath redeemed Jerusalem.
10 [a]The LORD hath made bare his holy
arm in the eyes of all the nations;

51:19 [1]Heb. *happened* [2]Heb. *breaking* [a]ch. 47:9 [b]Amos 7:2
51:20 [a]Lam. 2:11
51:21 [a]See ver. 17; Lam. 3:15
51:22 [a]Jer. 50:34
51:23 [a]Jer. 25:17; Zech. 12:2 [b]Ps. 66:11
52:1 [a]ch. 51:9,17
52:1 [b]Neh. 11:1; Mat. 4:5; Rev. 21:2 [c]Nah. 1:15 [d]Rev. 21:27
52:2 [a]ch. 3:26
52:2 [b]Zech. 2:7
52:3 [a]Ps. 44:12
52:4 [a]Gen. 46:6
52:5 [a]Ezek. 36:20
52:7 [a]Rom. 10:15 [b]Ps. 93:1
52:10 [a]Ps. 98:2,3

51:18 Children were expected to take care of parents who were sick or unsteady.
51:19 *who shall be sorry for thee?* A question also asked in Jer 15:5. Contrast v. 3.
51:20 *in a net.* Cf. Prov 7:22. *rebuke.* See 17:13; 54:9; 66:15.
51:21 *thou afflicted.* Jerusalem (see 54:11). *drunken.* On God's wrath (see v. 17 and note).
51:22 *pleadeth the cause of his people.* See 49:25 and note. *cup of my fury.* See v. 17 and note.
‡51:23 *them that afflict thee.* The Babylonians. See vv. 13–14; 14:4. *thy body as the ground.* The picture here is of trampling on an enemy (perhaps figurative, but cf. Josh 10:24).
52:1 *Awake, awake, put on thy strength.* See 51:9,17 and notes. *beautiful garments.* Perhaps the robes of the priests, which belong to Jerusalem as a "holy city." See 49:18 and note. *holy city.* See 48:2 and note. *uncircumcised . . . unclean.* Foreign invaders. See 35:8 and note; Judg 14:3 and note.
52:2 *Shake thyself from the dust.* Contrast the fate of Babylon in 47:1 (see note there). *Loose thyself.* See 42:7 and note; 49:9; 51:14. *daughter of Zion.* A personification of Jerusalem and its inhabitants.
52:3 *sold yourselves for nought.* The enemy paid the Lord nothing for acquiring Jerusalem. See 45:13; 50:1 and notes. *redeemed without money.* See 41:14 and note; 43:1; 45:13.
52:4 *Assyrian oppressed them.* See 9:4 and note.
‡52:5 Quoted in part in Rom 2:24. *for nought.* See v. 3 and note. *my name . . . is blasphemed.* The captivity brought disrespect to God because it appeared that the gods of other nations were more powerful (see Ezek 36:20–23). Cf. Assyria's blasphemy in 37:23–24.
52:6 *know my name.* See 49:26 and note. *in that day.* The day of deliverance from Babylon. See 10:20,27 and note.
52:7 *feet of him that bringeth good tidings.* A reference to a messenger who ran from the scene of a battle to bring news of the outcome to a waiting king and people (see 2 Sam 18:26). Here the news refers to the return from exile (vv. 11–12; see 40:9 and note; 41:27), a deliverance that prefigures Christ's deliverance from sin. See Rom 10:15; Eph 6:15. *salvation.* See 49:8 and note. *Thy God reigneth!* See Ps 96:10. The return of God's people to Jerusalem emphasizes His sovereign rule over the world (see 40:9 and note). God's kingdom will come more fully at the second coming of Christ (see Rev 19:6).
52:8 *watchmen.* Those in Jerusalem watching for the arrival of the messengers (cf. 62:6–7; 2 Sam 18:24–27).
52:9 *Break forth.* See 44:23 and note. *comforted.* See 49:13 and note. *redeemed.* See v. 3 and note.

And [b]all the ends of the earth shall see
the salvation of our God.
11 [a]Depart ye, depart ye, go ye out from
thence, touch no unclean *thing;*
Go ye out of the midst of her; [b]be ye
clean, that bear the vessels of the
LORD.
12 For [a]ye shall not go out with haste,
Nor go by flight:
[b]For the LORD will go before you;
[c]And the God of Israel *will* [1]*be* your
rereward.

The servant of the LORD

13 Behold, [a]my servant shall [b][1]deal
prudently,
[c]He shall be exalted and extolled, and
be very high.
14 As many were astonied at thee;
His [a]visage *was* so marred more than
any man,
And his form more than the sons of
men:
15 [a]So shall he sprinkle many nations;
The kings shall shut their mouths at
him:
For *that* [b]which had not been told
them shall they see;
And *that* which they had not heard
shall they consider.

52:10 [b]Luke 3:6
52:11 [a]ch. 48:20 [b]Lev. 22:2
52:12 [1]Heb. *gather you up* [a]Ex. 12:33 [b]Mic. 2:13 [c]Ex. 14:19
52:13 [1]Or, *prosper* [a]ch. 42:1 [b]Jer. 23:5 [c]Phil. 2:9
52:14 [a]Ps. 22:6,7
52:15 [a]Ezek. 36:25 [b]Eph. 3:5,9
53:1 [1]Or, *doctrine?* [2]Heb. *hearing?* [a]John 12:38; Rom. 10:16
53:3 [1]Or, *he hid as it were his face from us* [2]Heb. *as a hiding of faces from him,* or, *from us* [a]Ps. 22:6 [b]Heb. 4:15 [c]John 1:10
53:4 [a]Mat. 8:17; Heb. 9:28
53:5 [1]Or, *tormented* [2]Heb. *bruise* [a]Rom. 4:25 [b]1 Pet. 2:24

53 Who [a]hath believed our [1][2]report?
And to whom is the arm of the LORD
revealed?
2 For he shall grow up before him as a
tender plant,
And as a root out of a dry ground:
He hath no form nor comeliness;
And when we shall see him, *there is*
no beauty that we should desire him.
3 [a]He is despised and rejected of men;
A man of sorrows, and [b]acquainted
with grief:
And [1][2]we hid as it were *our* faces from
him;
He was despised, and [c]we esteemed
him not.
4 Surely [a]he hath borne our griefs,
And carried our sorrows:
Yet we did esteem him stricken,
Smitten of God, and afflicted.
5 But he *was* [a][1]wounded for our
transgressions,
He was bruised for our iniquities:
The chastisement of our peace *was*
upon him;
And with his [b][2]stripes we are healed.
6 All we like sheep have gone astray;
We have turned every one to his own
way;

52:10 *holy arm.* See 51:9 and note. God's arm is often associated with redemption and salvation (see Ex 6:6). *all the ends of the earth.* Equivalent to "all flesh" in 40:5 (see note there). Cf. 45:22.

52:11 See 2 Cor 6:17. *Depart ye, depart ye.* See note on 40:1. *unclean.* Perhaps referring to pagan religious objects (cf. Gen 31:19; 35:2). *that bear the vessels.* Cyrus allowed the people to take back the articles of the temple seized by Nebuchadnezzar (Ezra 1:7–11). The priests and Levites were responsible for them (see Num 3:6–8; 2 Chr 5:4–7).

‡52:12 *not go out with haste . . . flight.* Israel's future deliverance will be superior to the exodus from Egypt because Israel will not need to hurry from their captors (contrast Ex 12:39; 14:5–8). But, see also 48:20 and note. *go before you . . . be your rereward.* As He did for the Israelites when they were freed from Egypt (see Ex 13:21; 14:19–20; cf. Is 42:16; 49:10; 58:8). *rereward.* Or "rear guard."

52:13–53:12 The fourth and longest of the four servant songs (see note on 42:1–4). It constitutes the central and most important unit in chs. 40–66 as well as in chs. 49–57 (see note on 39:8). In the Hebrew the song contains five stanzas of three numbered verses each. It is quoted in the NT more than any other OT passage and is often referred to as the "gospel in the OT."

‡52:13 *my servant.* See note on 42:1. *shall deal prudently.* Or "shall prosper," a mark of God's blessing (see 1 Sam 18:14) and of obedience to God's word (see Josh 1:8). *exalted and extolled.* Words that describe the Lord in Isaiah's vision (see 6:1 and note; 57:15). Christ's exaltation is referred to in Acts 2:33; 3:13; Eph 1:20–23; Phil 2:9–11 (see also 1 Pet 1:10–11).

‡52:14 *astonied at thee.* Astonished when they saw Christ's suffering on the cross. Cf. the reaction to the ruined city of Tyre (Ezek 27:35). *marred.* A term used of a "corrupt" (blemished) animal which should not be offered to the Lord (Mal 1:14). Cf. the disgraceful treatment of the servant (see 50:6 and note). *more than any man.* Cf. Ps 22:6. His treatment was inhuman.

52:15 *sprinkle many nations.* With the sprinkling of cleansing (see Lev 14:7; Num 8:7; 19:18–19) and/or of consecration (see Ex 29:21; Lev 8:11,30). *kings shall shut their mouths.* In astonishment at the suffering and exaltation of the servant (see 49:6–7 and notes). Cf. Job 21:5. *For that . . . consider.* Quoted in Rom 15:21. Even though they have not heard the prophetic word, kings will understand the mission of the servant when they see His humiliation and exaltation (contrast 6:9–10).

53:1 Quoted in whole or in part in John 12:38; Rom 10:16. *our report.* The good news about salvation, given by the prophets to Israel and the nations (see 52:7,10). *arm of the LORD.* See 51:9 and note.

‡53:2 *tender plant.* The Messiah would grow from the "stem of Jesse." See 4:2; 11:1 and notes. His beginnings would be humble. *root.* See 11:10 and note. *form.* The Hebrew for this word is used of David in 1 Sam 16:18, where it is translated "comely" (handsome). Christ had nothing of the bearing or trappings of royalty.

53:3 *despised.* See 49:7 and note; Ps 22:6. *rejected . . . esteemed him not.* The Hebrew words used here occur together also in 2:22 (see note there). Cf. John 1:10–11. *sorrows.* The Hebrew for this word is used of both physical and mental pain (see v. 4; Ex 3:7). *we hid . . . our faces.* See 1:15 and note; 8:17.

53:4 Quoted in part in Mat 8:17 with reference to Jesus' healing ministry. *griefs.* Diseases often result from sinful living and are ultimately the consequences of original (Adamic) sin. See 1:5–6 and note. *stricken.* With a terrible disease (see Gen 12:17; 2 Ki 15:5). People (Israel in particular) thought the servant was suffering for His own sins. *afflicted.* Or "humbled," or "oppressed" (see v. 7; 58:10).

‡53:5 *wounded.* Or "pierced." See Ps 22:16; Zech 12:10; John 19:34. *bruised.* Crushed in spirit (see Ps 34:18; cf. Is 57:15). The sins of the world weighed heavily upon Him. *healed.* Here probably equivalent to "forgiven" (see 6:10; Jer 30:17; see also note on 1 Pet 2:24), not implying that physical healing is one of the benefits of Christ's atonement.

53:6 *have gone astray.* Cf. Ps 119:176; Jer 50:6; Ezek 34:4–6,16;

And the LORD [1]hath laid on him the
iniquity of us all.
7 He was oppressed, and he was afflicted,
Yet [a]he opened not his mouth:
[b]He is brought as a lamb to the
slaughter,
And as a sheep before her shearers is
dumb,
So he openeth not his mouth.
8 [1]He was taken from prison and from
judgment:
And who shall declare his generation?
For [a]he was cut off out of the land of
the living:
For the transgression of my people
[2]was he stricken.
9 [a]And he made his grave with the
wicked,
And with the rich in his [1]death;
Because he had done no violence,
Neither *was any* [b]deceit in his mouth.
10 Yet it pleased the LORD to bruise him;
he hath put *him* to grief:
[1]When thou shalt make his soul [a]an
offering for sin,
He shall see *his* seed, he shall prolong
his days,
And the pleasure of the LORD shall
prosper in his hand.

53:6 [1]Heb. *hath made the iniquity of us all to meet on him*
53:7 [a]Mat. 26:63 [b]Acts 8:32
53:8 [1]Or, *He was taken away by distress and judgment: but, etc.* [2]Heb. was *the stroke upon him* [a]Dan. 9:26
53:9 [1]Heb. *deaths* [a]Mat. 27:57 [b]1 John 3:5
53:10 [1]Or, *When his soul shall make an offering* [a]2 Cor. 5:21
53:11 [a]1 John 2:1 [b]ch. 42:1 [c]Rom 5:18
53:12 [a]Ps. 2:8 [b]Col. 2:15 [c]Luke 22:37 [d]Luke 23:34
54:1 [a]Gal. 4:27 [b]1 Sam. 2:5
54:2 [a]ch. 49:19,20

11 He shall see of the travail of his soul,
and shall be satisfied:
By his knowledge shall [a]my righteous
[b]servant [c]justify many;
For he shall bear their iniquities.
12 [a]Therefore will I divide him *a portion*
with the great,
[b]And he shall divide the spoil with the
strong;
Because he hath poured out his soul
unto death:
And he was [c]numbered with the
transgressors;
And he bare the sin of many,
And [d]made intercession for the
transgressors.

Blessings through the servant

54 [a]Sing, O barren, thou *that* didst not
bear;
Break forth *into* singing, and cry aloud,
thou *that* didst not travail with child:
For [b]more *are* the children of the
desolate than the children of the
married wife, saith the LORD.
2 [a]Enlarge the place of thy tent,
And let them stretch forth the curtains
of thine habitations:
Spare not, lengthen thy cords, and
strengthen thy stakes;

1 Pet 2:25. *laid on him the iniquity of us all.* Just as the priest laid his hands on the scapegoat and symbolically put Israel's sins on it (Lev 16:21). See 1 Pet 2:24.

53:7–8 Verses read by the Ethiopian eunuch in the presence of Philip (Acts 8:32–33).

53:7 *oppressed.* Like Israel. See 49:26 and note. The Hebrew for this word is translated "taskmasters" in Ex 5:6. *lamb . . . to the slaughter.* Cf. Ps 44:22; Rev 5:6. John the Baptist called Jesus "the Lamb of God" (John 1:29,36). *openeth not his mouth.* Jesus remained silent before the chief priests and Pilate (Mat 27:12–14; Mark 14:60–61; 15:4–5; John 19:8–9) and before Herod (Luke 23:8–9).

‡53:8 *from prison and from judgment.* Lit. "because of oppression and judgment." Jesus was given an unfair trial. *who shall declare his generation?* Or "of his generation, who considered [it]?" For the most part, Jesus' contemporaries did not understand the sacrificial nature of his death.

53:9 *the wicked.* The manner of His death would indicate that, as far as those who condemned Him were concerned, He was to be buried with executed criminals. *with the rich.* Not as a burial with honor. The parallelism (with its effective wordplay in Hebrew) makes clear that Isaiah here associates the rich with the wicked, as do many OT writers—because they acquired their wealth by wicked means and/or trusted in their wealth rather than in God (see, e.g., Ps 37:16,35; Prov 18:23; 28:20; Jer 5:26–27; Mic 6:10,12). According to the Gospels (Mat 27:57–60 and parallels), the wealthy Joseph of Arimathea gave Jesus an honorable burial by placing His body in his own tomb. But this was undoubtedly an act of love growing out of his awareness that he had been forgiven much (see Luke 7:47). Thus the fulfillment fitted but also transcended the prophecy. *he had done no violence, Neither . . . deceit in his mouth.* Peter quotes these lines as he encourages believers to endure unjust suffering (1 Pet 2:22).

53:10 *bruise him.* See v. 5 and note. *an offering for sin.* An offering where restitution was usually required (Lev 5:16; 6:5) and the offender sacrificed a ram (Lev 5:15). *his seed.* Spiritual descendants. *prolong his days.* Christ would live forever (see 9:7 and note). *prosper.* See 52:13.

‡53:11 *be satisfied.* In 1:11, where the same Hebrew word appears, God was "full" (had enough) of innumerable sacrifices that accomplished nothing. Here the one sacrifice of Christ brings perfect satisfaction. *his knowledge.* His true knowledge of the true God (see 1:3; 6:9; 43:10; 45:4–5; 52:6; 56:10). The "spirit of knowledge" (11:2) rested on the Messiah. Cf. 52:13. *my righteous servant.* See 41:8–9; 42:1 and notes. *justify.* Cause many to be declared righteous. See 5:23; Rom 5:19 and note. *many.* See 52:15; Dan 12:3.

53:12 *with the great . . . with the strong.* God will reward His servant as if he was a king sharing in the spoils of a great victory (see 52:15). *divide the spoil.* God's gift to His suffering servant (cf. 9:3). *poured out his soul.* As a sacrifice (see v. 10). *unto death.* See Phil 2:8. *And he was numbered with the transgressors.* Quoted in Luke 22:37 with reference to Jesus. *made intercession.* See Jer 7:16 ("pray"); 27:18. Cf. 59:16; Heb 7:25.

‡54:1—55:13 Celebrates the restoration that is made possible through the sacrifice of the servant in the preceding section and calls upon the nation to enjoy the blessings of this restoration.

54:1 This verse is applied by Paul to Sarah and the covenant of promise, representing the "Jerusalem which is above" (Gal 4:26–27). *Sing . . . Break forth.* See 12:6; 44:23; 52:9 and notes. *O barren.* Jerusalem (representing Israel), especially during the exile (see 49:21). In the Near East, barrenness was considered a disgrace (see 4:1 and note). *more are the children of the desolate.* See 49:19–20 and note. Israel will be restored both physically and spiritually (cf. 62:4). *married wife.* See 50:1 and note. After being both barren and divorced, Israel is now a blessed mother.

‡54:2 See 26:15; 33:20 and notes. *thy tent.* Jerusalem is viewed as a woman living in her own tent. She will need a larger tent because of her many children.

3 For thou shalt break forth *on* the right
hand and *on* the left;
[a]And thy seed shall inherit the Gentiles,
And make the desolate cities to be
inhabited.
4 Fear not; for thou shalt not be ashamed:
Neither be thou confounded; for thou
shalt not be put to shame:
For thou shalt forget the shame of thy
youth,
And shalt not remember the reproach
of thy widowhood any more.
5 [a]For thy Maker *is* thine husband;
The [b]LORD of hosts *is* his name;
And thy redeemer the Holy One of
Israel;
[c]The God of the whole earth shall he
be called.
6 For the LORD [a]hath called thee as a
woman forsaken and grieved in
spirit,
And a wife of youth, when thou wast
refused, saith thy God.
7 [a]For a small moment have I forsaken
thee;
But with great mercies will I gather
thee.
8 In a little wrath I hid my face from
thee for a moment;
[a]But with everlasting kindness will I
have mercy on thee,
Saith the LORD thy redeemer.
9 For this *is as* the waters of [a]Noah unto
me:
For *as* I have sworn that the waters of
Noah should no more go over the
earth;
So have I sworn that *I* would not be
wroth with thee, nor rebuke thee.
10 For [a]the mountains shall depart,
And the hills be removed;
[b]But my kindness shall not depart from
thee,
Neither shall the covenant of my peace
be removed,
Saith the LORD that hath mercy on thee.
11 O thou afflicted, tossed with tempest,
and not comforted,
Behold, I will lay thy stones with [a]fair
colours,
And lay thy foundations with
sapphires.
12 And I will make thy windows *of* agates,
And thy gates of carbuncles,
And all thy borders of pleasant stones.
13 And all thy children *shall be* [a]taught of
the LORD;
And [b]great *shall be* the peace of thy
children.
14 In righteousness shalt thou be
established:
Thou shalt be far from oppression; for
thou shalt not fear:
And from terror; for it shall not come
near thee.
15 Behold, they shall surely gather
together, *but* not by me:
Whosoever shall gather together
against thee shall fall for thy sake.
16 Behold, I have created the smith
That bloweth the coals in the fire,
And that bringeth forth an instrument
for his work;
And I have created the waster to
destroy.
17 No weapon *that* is formed against thee
shall prosper;
And every tongue *that* shall rise against
thee in judgment thou shalt
condemn.

54:3 [a]ch. 55:5 **54:5** [a]Jer. 3:14 [b]Luke 1:32 [c]Zech. 14:9; Rom. 3:29 **54:6** [a]ch. 62:4 **54:7** [a]Ps. 30:5; ch. 26:20; 60:10; 2 Cor. 4:17 **54:8** [a]ch. 55:3; Jer. 31:3 **54:9** [a]Gen. 8:21 **54:10** [a]Ps. 46:2; ch. 51:6; Mat. 5:18 **54:10** [b]Ps. 89:33 **54:11** [a]1 Chr. 29:2; Rev. 21:18 **54:13** [a]ch. 11:9; Jer. 31:34; John 6:45; 1 Cor. 2:10; 1 Thes. 4:9; 1 John 2:20 [b]Ps. 119:165

54:3 *break forth* See 49:19–20 and note; cf. Gen 28:14. *inherit the Gentiles.* See 11:14; 49:7 and notes.

54:4 *not be ashamed . . . confounded.* See 29:22 and note; 45:17. *shame of thy youth.* Probably the period of slavery in Egypt. Cf. Jer 31:19; Ezek 16:60. *reproach of thy widowhood.* Probably referring to the exile, when Israel was alone, like a widow (vv. 6–7).

54:5 *husband.* See 62:4–5. *redeemer the Holy One of Israel.* See 1:4, 41:14 and notes.

54:6–7 *woman forsaken . . . refused.* Israel's experience in exile (see 49:14; 50:1 and note; 62:4).

54:7–8,10 *mercies.* See 14:1; 49:10,13; 51:3.

54:7 *small moment.* The Babylonian exile was relatively brief (see 26:20; 50:1 and notes).

54:8 *a little wrath.* See 9:12,17,21 and note; 60:10. *hid my face.* See 1:15 and note. *everlasting kindness.* See v. 10; 55:3 and note. Cf. 45:17. *redeemer.* See v. 5.

‡54:9 *no more go over the earth.* See Gen 9:11 and note. *not be wroth.* Not be angry. See 12:1 and note.

54:10 *mountains . . . be removed.* Cf. 51:6; Ps 46:2; 102:26–27. *kindness . . . covenant of my peace.* A reference to either the covenant with Israel or the Davidic covenant, described in similar terms in 55:3 (see note there). Cf. Jer 33:20–21; for the language see Num 25:11–13.

54:11–12 A figurative description of restored Jerusalem, echoed in the description of the new Jerusalem in Rev 21:10, 18–21.

‡54:11 *thou afflicted.* Jerusalem. See 51:21. *tossed with tempest.* See 28:2 and note. *stones with fair colours.* Or "stones of antinomy," probably referring to a mosaic pattern of light and dark stones that was also used in Solomon's temple (cf. 1 Chr 29:2). *sapphires.* Cf. the "paved work of a sapphire stone" (of blue color) in Ex 24:10 (see also Ezek 1:26; 10:1).

‡54:12 *windows.* Parapets on the top of walls. *agates.* A precious stone, perhaps referring to jasper or rubies. *carbuncles.* Lit. "stones that sparkle," perhaps referring to crystal. *all thy borders.* The walls surrounding the city; cf. 26:1.

54:13–14 *peace . . . righteousness.* See 48:18 and note.

54:13 *taught of the LORD.* Like the servant of the Lord in 50:4. Cf. Jer 31:34.

54:14 *oppression . . . terror.* Cf. 14:4; 33:18–19.

54:15 *they shall surely gather . . . but not by me.* Any attack on Jerusalem by the nations will not be prompted by the Lord and is thus doomed to failure. *shall fall for thy sake.* See v. 3.

54:16 *created the waster to destroy.* God raised up nations such as Assyria and Babylonia to punish Israel (see 10:5 and note; 33:1 and note).

‡54:17 *every tongue . . . thou shalt condemn.* Just as no legitimate charges could be brought against the servant of 50:8–9. *servants of the LORD.* After ch. 53 the singular "servant" no longer

This *is* the heritage of the servants of
the LORD,
[a]And their righteousness *is* of me,
saith the LORD.

The great invitation

55 Ho, [a]every one that thirsteth, come
ye to the waters,
And he that hath no money;
[b]Come ye, buy, and eat;
Yea, come, buy wine and milk without
money and without price.
2 Wherefore do ye [1]spend money for
that which is not bread?
And your labour for *that which*
satisfieth not?
Hearken diligently unto me, and eat ye
that which is good,
And let your soul delight itself in fatness.
3 Incline your ear, and [a]come unto me:
Hear, and your soul shall live;
[b]And I will make an everlasting
covenant with you,
Even the [c]sure mercies of David.
4 Behold, I have given him *for* [a]a
witness to the people,
[b]A leader and commander to the people.
5 [a]Behold, thou shalt call a nation *that*
thou knowest not,
[b]And nations *that* knew not thee shall
run unto thee
Because of the LORD thy God,
And for the Holy One of Israel; [c]for he
hath glorified thee.

6 [a]Seek ye the LORD while he may be
found,
Call ye upon him while he is near:
7 [a]Let the wicked forsake his way,
And [1]the unrighteous man [b]his
thoughts:
And let him return unto the LORD,
[c]and he will have mercy upon him;
And to our God, for [2]he will
abundantly pardon.
8 [a]For my thoughts *are* not your thoughts,
Neither *are* your ways my ways, saith
the LORD.
9 [a]For *as* the heavens are higher than
the earth,
So are my ways higher than your ways,
And my thoughts than your thoughts.
10 For [a]as the rain cometh down,
And the snow from heaven,
And returneth not thither,
But watereth the earth,
And maketh it bring forth and bud,
That it may give seed to the sower, and
bread to the eater:
11 [a]So shall my word be that goeth forth
out of my mouth:
It shall not return unto me void,
But it shall accomplish that which I
please,
And it shall prosper *in the thing*
whereto I sent it.
12 [a]For ye shall go out with joy,
And be led forth with peace:
The mountains and the hills shall
[b]break forth before you *into* singing,
And [c]all the trees of the field shall clap
their hands.
13 [a]Instead of [b]the thorn shall come up
the fir tree,
And instead of the brier shall come up
the myrtle tree:

54:17 [a]ch. 45:24,25
55:1 [a]John 4:14 [b]Mat. 13:44; Rev. 3:18
55:2 [1]Heb. *weigh*
55:3 [a]Mat. 11:28 [b]ch. 54:8; 61:8; Jer. 32:40 [c]2 Sam. 7:8; Ps. 89:28; Acts 13:34
55:4 [a]John 18:37; Rev. 1:5 [b]Jer. 30:9; Ezek. 34:23; Dan. 9:25; Hos. 3:5
55:5 [a]ch. 52:15; Eph. 2:11 [b]ch. 60:5 [c]ch. 60:9
55:6 [a]Ps. 32:6; Mat. 5:25; 25:11; John 7:34; 8:21; 2 Cor. 6:1; Heb. 3:13
55:7 [1]Heb. *the man of iniquity* [2]Heb. *he will multiply to pardon* [a]ch. 1:16 [b]Zech. 8:17 [c]Ps. 130:7; Jer. 3:12
55:8 [a]2 Sam. 7:19
55:9 [a]Ps. 103:11
55:10 [a]Deut. 32:2
55:11 [a]ch. 54:9
55:12 [a]ch. 35:10 [b]Ps. 98:8 [c]1 Chr. 16:33
55:13 [a]ch. 41:19 [b]Mic. 7:4

occurs in Isaiah. The "servants" (see 63:17; 65:8–9,13–15; 66:14) are true believers—both Jew and Gentile (see 56:6–8)—who are faithful to the Lord. They are in a sense the "seed" of the servant (53:10). See 49:19–20 and note.

55:1 The exiles are summoned to return and be restored. *thirsteth.* Spiritual thirst is primarily in view (see 41:17; 44:3; Ps 42:1–2; 63:1). *waters.* Figurative for spiritual refreshment. Cf. Wisdom's invitation in Prov 9:5. Christ similarly invited people to drink the water of life (John 4:14; 7:37). *no money.* In hard times even water had to be purchased (see Lam 5:4). *wine and milk.* Symbols of abundance, enjoyment and nourishment. *without money.* The death of the servant (53:5–9) paid for the free gift of life (see Rom 6:23).

‡55:2 *that which is not bread.* Perhaps the husks of pagan religious practices. Cf. Deut 8:3. *in fatness.* Great spiritual blessings are compared to a banquet of rich foods (see 25:6 and note; Ps 22:26; 34:8; Jer 31:14).

‡55:3 *everlasting covenant.* David had been promised an unending dynasty, one that would culminate in the Messiah (see 9:7; 54:10; 61:8; 2 Sam 7:14–16 and notes). The Messiah will bring the blessings of the covenant to the whole nation. *sure mercies.* Assuring the continuation of the nation. See 54:8 and note. Christ's resurrection was further proof of God's faithfulness to David (see Acts 13:34, which quotes from this verse).

55:4 *to the people . . . to the people.* Hebrew has "to the peoples" for both, referring to the impact of Messiah's mission on all nations. Just as David exalted the Lord among the nations (Ps 18:43,49–50), so also will David's Son, the Messiah, be a light to the nations (see 42:6; 49:6 and notes). *leader and commander to the people.* Similar titles are used of David (1 Sam 13:14; 25:30) and the Messiah (Dan 9:25).

‡55:5 *thou shalt call a nation.* The attraction of nations to Zion and to the God of Israel is a major Biblical theme (see, e.g., 2:2–4; 45:14; Zech 8:22 and notes). *that thou knowest not.* The reverse of the exile, when Israel was sent to a nation unknown to them (see Deut 28:36). Ruth left Moab to live with a people she "knewest not heretofore" (Ruth 2:11). *Holy One of Israel.* See 1:4; 41:14 and notes. *glorified.* See 4:2; 60:9. The nation will be restored physically and spiritually.

55:6 *Seek ye the LORD.* See Jer 29:13–14; Hos 3:5; Amos 5:4,6,14 (contrast the hypocritical seeking of 58:2).

55:7 *wicked forsake.* See 1:16. *return unto the LORD . . . he will have mercy.* See 43:25 and note; 44:22 and note.

55:9 *my ways higher.* See Ps 145:3.

55:11 *my word.* Especially the promises of vv. 3,5,12. The word is viewed as a messenger also in 9:8; Ps 107:20. Cf. John 1:1. *shall prosper.* See 46:10–11 and note; cf. 40:8; Heb 4:12.

55:12 *go out with joy.* The departure from Babylon provides the background (see 35:10; 52:9–12 and notes). *mountains . . . break forth . . . into singing.* See 44:23 and note. *hands.* Branches. The language is figurative (cf. 1 Chr 16:33; Ps 98:8; 114:3–6).

‡55:13 *thorn . . . fir tree . . . brier . . . myrtle tree.* The reverse of the desolation Isaiah had prophesied about earlier (5:6; 32:13).

And it shall be to the LORD [c]for a name,
For an everlasting sign *that* shall not be
cut off.

Strangers included in the blessing

56 Thus saith the LORD,
Keep ye [1]judgment, and do justice:
[a]For my salvation *is* near to come,
And my righteousness to be revealed.
2 Blessed *is* the man *that* doeth this,
And the son of man *that* layeth hold on
it;
[a]That keepeth the sabbath from
polluting it,
And keepeth his hand from doing any
evil.
3 Neither let [a]the son of the stranger,
that hath joined himself to the LORD,
speak, saying,
The LORD hath utterly separated me
from his people:
Neither let the eunuch say, Behold, I
am a dry tree.
4 For thus saith the LORD unto the
eunuchs that keep my sabbaths,
And choose *the things* that please me,
And take hold of my covenant;
5 Even unto them will I give in [a]mine
house and within my walls
A place [b]and a name better than *of*
sons and *of* daughters:
I will give them an everlasting name,
that shall not be cut off.
6 Also the sons of the stranger, that join
themselves to the LORD,
To serve him, and to love the name of
the LORD,
To be his servants,
Every one that keepeth the sabbath
from polluting it,

55:13 [c]Jer. 13:11
56:1 [1]Or, *equity* [a]Mat. 4:17
56:2 [a]ch. 58:13
56:3 [a]Acts 8:27
56:5 [a]1 Tim. 3:15 [b]1 John 3:1
56:7 [a]ch. 2:2 [b]Rom. 12:1; Heb. 13:15; 1 Pet. 2:5 [c]Mat. 21:13 [d]Mal. 1:11
56:8 [1]Heb. *to his gathered* [a]ch. 11:12 [b]John 10:16
56:9 [a]Jer. 12:9
56:10 [1]Or, *Dreaming,* or, *talking in their sleep* [a]Mat. 15:14 [b]Phil. 3:2
56:11 [1]Heb. *strong of appetite* [2]Heb. *know not to be satisfied* [a]Mic. 3:11 [b]Ezek. 34:2
56:12 [a]Ps. 10:6; Prov. 23:35; Luke 12:19

And taketh hold of my covenant;
7 Even them will I [a]bring to my holy
mountain,
And make them joyful in my house of
prayer:
[b]Their burnt offerings and their
sacrifices *shall be* accepted upon
mine altar;
For [c]mine house shall be called a
house of prayer [d]for all people.
8 The Lord GOD [a]which gathereth the
outcasts of Israel saith,
[b]Yet will I gather *others* to him, [1]besides
those that are gathered unto him.

The failure of Israel's leaders

9 [a]All ye beasts of the field, come to
devour,
Yea, all ye beasts in the forest.
10 His watchmen *are* [a]blind: they are all
ignorant,
[b]They *are* all dumb dogs, they cannot
bark;
[1]Sleeping, lying down, loving to
slumber.
11 Yea, *they are* [a 1]greedy dogs *which*
[b 2]can never have enough,
And they *are* shepherds *that* cannot
understand:
They all look to their own way,
Every one for his gain, from his
quarter.
12 Come ye, *say they,* I will fetch wine,
And we will fill ourselves with strong
drink;
[a]And to morrow shall be as this day,
and much more abundant.

57 The righteous perisheth, and no
man layeth *it* to heart:

For the significance of trees see 35:2; see also 41:19 and note. *to the LORD for a name.* As a continual memorial to God's power and faithfulness, similar to God's fame in the exodus (see 63:12,14). *everlasting sign.* God's deliverance would never be forgotten. Cf. 19:20; 56:5.

56:1 *salvation . . . righteousness.* See 45:8; 46:13; 51:5 and notes.

56:2 *keepeth the sabbath.* See vv. 4,6. Just as the sabbath had been instituted after the exodus from Egypt (see Ex 20:8–11) as a sign of the Mosaic covenant (see Ex 31:13–17), so God's new deliverance (55:12) afforded an opportunity to obey Him fully, an obedience summed up in "keeping the sabbath" (see 58:13; 66:23; Jer 17:21–27; Ezek 20:20–21).

‡56:3 *stranger.* Or "foreigner." See v. 6. Members of certain nations who came to live among the Israelites had been excluded from worship, at least for several generations (see Ex 12:43; Deut 23:3,7–8). But the work of the servant of the Lord would change this (see 49:19–20; 54:17; 60:10 and notes). Cf. 14:1. *eunuch.* See v. 4. Eunuchs were also excluded from the assembly of the Lord (Deut 23:1), but they could still be part of God's offspring (see Acts 8:27,38–40).

56:4 *take hold of my covenant.* Keeping the sabbath was a sign of the covenant (see Ex 31:13–17; Ezek 20:12,20), as was circumcision (see Gen 17:11). See also v.6.

‡56:5 *place.* Absalom built a "place" (or "monument") as a memorial since he had no surviving sons (2 Sam 18:18). *name.* The Hebrew for "a place and a name" (*yad vashem*) was chosen from v. 5 as the name of the main Holocaust monument in Jerusalem in modern Israel. *that shall not be cut off.* An idiom sometimes referring to the preserving of a name through one's descendants.

56:6 *To serve him.* Cf. 60:7,10.

56:7 *my holy mountain.* See 2:2–4 and note. *offerings . . . accepted upon mine altar.* Cf. 60:7; contrast 1:11–13. *house of prayer for all people.* Solomon may have anticipated this in his prayer of dedication for the temple (1 Ki 8:41–43).

56:8 *gathereth the outcasts.* See 11:11–12 and notes. *Yet will I gather others.* Including Gentiles (see v. 3 and note; cf. John 10:16).

56:9–59:15 Many verses in these sections could apply to conditions before or during the Babylonian exile.

56:9 *beasts.* Foreign invaders (see 18:6 and note).

‡56:10 *watchmen.* The prophets (see Hab 2:1). *blind . . . loving to slumber.* Cf. 29:9–10. *dumb dogs.* Mute watchdogs who guarded the sheep (cf. Job 30:1).

56:11 *greedy.* They devour the sheep. See Ezek 34:3. *shepherds.* Rulers may be included. See Ezek 34:1–6.

56:12 *wine . . . strong drink.* Cf. the behavior of priests and prophets in 28:7. *to morrow shall be . . . more abundant.* Cf. the words of the rich fool in Luke 12:19.

And [a][1] merciful men *are* taken away,
[b] none considering
That the righteous is taken away [2] from
the evil *to come.*
2 He shall [a][1] enter *into* peace:
They shall rest in [b] their beds,
Each one walking [2] *in* his uprightness.

3 But draw near hither, [a] ye sons of the
sorceress,
The seed of the adulterer and the
whore.
4 Against whom do ye sport yourselves?
Against whom make ye a wide mouth,
and draw out the tongue?
Are ye not children of transgression, a
seed of falsehood,
5 Inflaming yourselves [1] with idols
[a] under every green tree,
[b] Slaying the children in the valleys
under the clifts of the rocks?
6 Among the smooth *stones* of the
stream *is* thy portion;
They, they *are* thy lot:
Even to them hast thou poured a drink
offering,
Thou hast offered a meat offering.
Should I receive comfort in these?
7 [a] Upon a lofty and high mountain hast
thou set [b] thy bed:
Even thither wentest thou up to offer
sacrifice.
8 Behind the doors also and the posts
hast thou set up thy remembrance:
For thou hast discovered *thyself to
another* than me, and art gone up;
Thou hast enlarged thy bed, and
[1] made thee *a covenant* with them;
[a] Thou lovedst their bed [2] where thou
sawest *it.*
9 And [a][1] thou wentest to the king with
ointment,
And didst increase thy perfumes,
And didst send thy messengers far off,
And didst debase *thyself even* unto
hell.
10 Thou art wearied in the greatness of
thy way;
[a] *Yet* saidst thou not, There is no hope:
Thou hast found the [1] life of thine
hand;
Therefore thou wast not grieved.
11 And [a] of whom hast thou been afraid or
feared, that thou hast lied,
And hast not remembered me, nor laid
it to thy heart?
[b] Have not I held my peace even of old,
And thou fearest me not?
12 I will declare thy righteousness,
And thy works; for they shall not profit
thee.
13 When thou criest, let thy companies
deliver thee;
But the wind shall carry them all away;
vanity shall take *them:*
But he that putteth his trust in me
shall possess the land,
And shall inherit my holy mountain;
14 And shall say, [a] Cast ye up, cast ye up,
prepare the way,
Take up the stumblingblock out of the
way of my people.

Compassion for the repentant

15 For thus saith the high and lofty One
That inhabiteth eternity, [a] whose name
is Holy;

57:1 [1] Heb. *men of kindness,* or, *godliness* [2] Or, *from that which is evil* [a] Ps. 12:1 [b] 1 Ki. 14:13
57:2 [1] Or, *go in peace* [2] Or, *before him* [a] Luke 2:29 [b] 2 Chr. 16:14
57:3 [a] Mat. 16:4
57:5 [1] Or, *among the oaks* [a] 2 Ki. 16:4 [b] Lev. 18:21; 2 Ki. 16:3; Jer. 7:31; Ezek. 16:20
57:7 [a] Ezek. 16:16 [b] Ezek. 23:41
57:8 [1] Or, *hewed it for thyself larger than theirs*
57:8 [2] Or, *thou providest room* [a] Ezek. 16:26
57:9 [1] Or, *thou respectedst the king* [a] Hos. 7:11
57:10 [1] Or, *living* [a] Jer. 2:25
57:11 [a] ch. 51:12 [b] Ps. 50:21
57:14 [a] ch. 40:3
57:15 [a] Job 6:10; Luke 1:49

57:1 *taken away from the evil to come.* Huldah explained that righteous King Josiah would die before disaster struck (2 Ki 22:19–20).
57:2 *peace.* Contrast v. 21. *rest.* Cf. Paul's words in Phil 1:21,23.
57:3 *sorceress.* One who practices soothsaying or magic (see 3:2; 47:12; Deut 18:10). *adulterer and the whore.* Spiritual adultery (idolatry) is in view (see vv. 5–8).
57:4 *sport . . . make ye a wide mouth.* The people mocked Isaiah in 28:9,14. *children of transgression.* See 1:4; 46:8 and note.
‡57:5 *green tree.* Associated with high places of pagan worship in 1 Ki 14:23. Cf. Jer 2:20; 3:13. For sacred trees in pagan worship, see also 1:29 and note. *Slaying the children.* Often associated with the worship of Molech (cf. v. 9; see note on 30:33, "Tophet") or Baal (Jer 19:5). Ps 106:37–38 says that children were sacrificed to idols and demons.
‡57:6 *stones of the stream is thy portion.* The Lord was the "portion" (inheritance) of his people (Ps 73:26; 142:5), but the people have chosen their stone idols to be their "portion." Cf. Rom 1:21–25. When people worship creation more than the Creator, God gives them over to their sinful desires to experience the consequences of their choices. The "stream" in view here is possibly the Hinnom Valley, southwest of Jerusalem, notorious as a place of Molech worship. *drink offering.* This pagan libation was especially popular.
57:7 *lofty and high mountain.* "High places" or "mountain shrines" (see Jer 3:6; Ezek 16:16; 22:9).
‡57:8 *Behind the doors . . . set up thy remembrance.* They have set up their idolatrous altars in a place where they were supposed to have prominently displayed the Lord's commandments (cf. Deut 6:9; 11:20). *them.* Pagan deities or idols.
‡57:9 *ointment.* Used for perfume (see Sol 4:10). *unto hell.* Or "the grave." They have corrupted themselves by consulting the dead. Cf. 8:19.
57:10 *Thou art wearied . . . There is no hope.* The people had chosen the hopeless path of idolatry but refused to acknowledge the futility of their choice. *found the life of thine hand.* No matter how disappointed they were by foreign gods, they found strength to persist in their idolatry. Contrast 40:30–31 and how they could have found true strength by turning to the Lord.
57:11 *of whom . . . afraid or feared.* They feared men (see 51:12). *hast not remembered me.* See 51:13. *held my peace even of old.* God had not acted in judgment (see 42:14 and note).
57:12 *righteousness.* See 58:2–3; 64:6.
‡57:13 *companies deliver thee.* Refers to their collection of idols. See 44:17 and note. *wind shall carry . . . vanity shall take them.* Idols are no stronger than men. *putteth his trust in me.* See 25:4. *possess the land.* See 49:8 and note. *my holy mountain.* See 2:2–4 and note.
‡57:14 *Cast ye up, cast ye up.* A command to build. See note on 40:1. *prepare the way.* See 40:3 and note.
‡57:15 *high and lofty One.* See 6:1; 52:13 and notes; cf. 33:5. *contrite.* Or "bruised" (see 53:5).

[b]I dwell *in* the high and holy *place,*
[c]With him also *that is* of a contrite and
humble spirit,
[d]To revive the spirit of the humble,
And to revive the heart of the contrite
ones.
16 [a]For I will not contend for ever,
Neither will I be always wroth:
For the spirit should fail before me,
And the souls [b]*which* I have made.
17 For the iniquity of [a]his covetousness
was I wroth, and smote him:
[b]I hid me, and was wroth,
[c]And he went on [1]frowardly in the
way of his heart.
18 I have seen his ways, and [a]will heal
him:
I will lead him also, and restore
comforts unto him and to [b]his
mourners.
19 I create [a]the fruit of the lips;
Peace, peace [b]to *him that is* far off, and
to *him that is* near, saith the LORD;
And I will heal him.
20 [a]But the wicked *are* like the troubled
sea,
When it cannot rest,
Whose waters cast up mire and dirt.
21 [a]*There is* no peace, saith my God, to
the wicked.

Right and wrong fasting

58 Cry [1]aloud, spare not,
Lift up thy voice like a trumpet,
And shew my people their
transgression,
And the house of Jacob their sins.
2 Yet they seek me daily,
And delight to know my ways,
As a nation that did righteousness,
And forsook not the ordinance of their
God:
They ask of me the ordinances of justice;
They take delight in approaching to God.
3 [a]Wherefore have we fasted, *say they,*
and thou seest not?
Wherefore have we [b]afflicted our soul,
and thou takest no knowledge?
Behold, in the day of your fast you find
pleasure,
And exact all your [1][2]labours.
4 [a]Behold, ye fast for strife and debate,
And to smite with the fist of
wickedness:
[1]Ye shall not fast as *ye do this* day,
To make your voice to be heard on
high.
5 Is it [a]such a fast that I have chosen?
[b][1]A day for a man to afflict his soul?
Is it to bow down his head as a
bulrush,
And [c]to spread sackcloth and ashes
under him?
Wilt thou call this a fast,
And an acceptable day to the LORD?
6 *Is* not this the fast that I have chosen?
To loose the bands of wickedness,
[a]To undo [1]the heavy burdens,
And [b]to let the [2]oppressed go free,
And *that* ye break every yoke?
7 *Is it* not [a]to deal thy bread to the
hungry,
And that thou bring the poor that are
[1]cast out *to thy* house?
[b]When thou seest the naked, that thou
cover him;
And that thou hide not thyself from
[c]thine own flesh?
8 [a]Then shall thy light break forth as the
morning,

57:15 [b]Zech. 2:13 [c]Ps. 34:18; 51:17 [d]Ps. 147:3; ch. 61:1
57:16 [a]Ps. 85:5; 103:9; Mic. 7:18 [b]Num. 16:22; Job 34:14; Heb. 12:9
57:17 [1]Heb. *turning away* [a]Jer. 6:13 [b]ch. 8:17; 45:15 [c]ch. 9:13
57:18 [a]Jer. 3:22 [b]ch. 61:2
57:19 [a]Heb. 13:15 [b]Acts 2:39; Eph. 2:17
57:20 [a]Job 15:20; Prov. 4:16
57:21 [a]ch. 48:22
58:1 [1]Heb. *with the throat*
58:3 [1]Or, *things wherewith ye grieve others* [2]Heb. *griefs* [a]Mal. 3:14 [b]Lev. 16:29; 23:27
58:4 [1]Or, *Ye fast not as* this *day* [a]1 Ki. 21:9
58:5 [1]Or, *To afflict his soul* for *a day?* [a]Zech. 7:5 [b]Lev. 16:29 [c]Esth. 4:3; Job 2:8; Dan. 9:3
58:6 [1]Heb. *the bundles of the yoke* [2]Heb. *broken* [a]Neh. 5:10 [b]Jer. 34:9
58:7 [1]Or, *afflicted* [a]Ezek. 18:7; Mat. 25:35 [b]Job 31:19 [c]Gen. 29:14; Neh. 5:5
58:8 [a]Job 11:17

57:16 *not contend for ever.* He had taken Israel to court repeatedly (see 3:13–14). *Neither . . . be always wroth.* See 54:9 and note; Jer 3:12.
57:17 *I hid me, and was wroth.* See 54:8; see also 1:15 and note.
57:18 *heal him.* See v. 19; 6:10; 30:26; Jer 3:22. God will forgive and restore His people. *lead.* Cf. 40:11; 42:16; 49:10. *restore comforts.* See 49:13 and note.
‡57:19 *create the fruit of the lips.* God turns the mourning of v. 18 to praise through his great act of salvation (see 66:10). *Peace, peace.* Contrast Jer 6:13–14; 8:10–11. *him that is far off.* Either Gentiles or exiled Jews. Paul probably had this verse in mind in Eph 2:17.
57:20 *like the troubled sea.* See Jer 49:23. *cannot rest.* Contrast v. 2.
57:21 See 39:8; 48:22 and notes.
58:1 *voice like a trumpet.* God's powerful voice is compared to a trumpet blast at mount Sinai (see Ex 19:19; 20:18–19). *transgression.* See 1:2 and note. *sins.* See 1:4; 59:12–13.
58:2 *seek me.* See 55:6 and note. Cf. the frequent sacrifices of 1:11. *delight to know my ways.* The same hypocrisy is mentioned in 29:13 (see note there).
‡58:3 *fasted . . . fast.* See v. 6; a time of self-denial and repentance for sin. After the fall of Jerusalem, the number of fast days increased (see Lev 16:29; see also Zech 7:5; 8:19 and note). *afflicted our soul.* The people have gone through the motions of humbling themselves. Cf. 2 Chr 7:14; 1 Ki 21:29. *thou takest no knowledge.* Wondering why God does not reocgnize their acts of penance. Note the same attitude in Mal 3:14; cf. Luke 18:12. *exact all of your labours.* Lit. "oppress all of your workers." They are pretending to worship God and exploiting their workers all on the same day. See 3:14–15; 10:2.
‡58:4 *ye fast . . . fist of wickedness.* Their worship ends in fights and arguments with each other. *voice to be heard on high.* Hypocritical religious activity is a hindrance to prayer (see 1:15; 59:2).
58:5 *as a bulrush.* A sign of weakness and humility (see 42:3 and note). *sackcloth and ashes.* Cf. 1 Ki 21:27; Jonah 3:5–8. *acceptable.* A term often applied to sacrifices (see 56:7; 60:7; Lev 1:3).
58:6 *bands of wickedness.* During the siege of Jerusalem, Hebrew slaves were rightly released—only to be reclaimed by their masters (see Jer 34:8–11). *oppressed.* See 1:17. *yoke.* See v. 9; 9:4; 10:27, where the yoke imposed by Assyria is mentioned.
58:7 *deal thy bread . . . bring . . . house . . . cover.* The outward evidence of genuine righteousness. See Job 31:17–20; Ezek 18:7,16 and Jesus' identification with the hungry and naked in Mat 25:35–36. *flesh.* Probably refers to close relatives (Gen 37:27), but see 2 Sam 5:1.
58:8 *light.* The joy, prosperity and salvation brought by the Lord (see 9:2; 60:1–3). *health.* See 57:18 and note. *go before*

And thine health shall spring forth
speedily:
And thy righteousness shall go before
thee;
[b]The glory of the LORD [1]shall be thy
rereward.
9 Then shalt thou call, and the LORD shall
answer;
Thou shalt cry, and he shall say, Here I
am.
If thou take away from the midst of
thee the yoke,
The putting forth of the finger, and
[a]speaking vanity;
10 And *if* thou draw out thy soul to the
hungry,
And satisfy the afflicted soul;
Then shall thy light rise in obscurity,
And thy darkness *be* as the noonday:
11 And the LORD shall guide thee
continually,
And satisfy thy soul in [1]drought,
And make fat thy bones:
And thou shalt be like a watered
garden,
And like a spring of water, whose
waters [2]fail not.
12 And *they that shall be* of thee [a]shall
build the old waste places:
Thou shalt raise up the foundations of
many generations;
And thou shalt be called, The repairer
of the breach,
The restorer of paths to dwell in.
13 If [a]thou turn away thy foot from the
sabbath,
From doing thy pleasure on my holy
day;
And call the sabbath a delight,
The holy of the LORD, honourable;
And shalt honour him, not doing thine
own ways,
Nor finding thine own pleasure, nor
speaking *thine own* words:
14 [a]Then shalt thou delight thyself in the
LORD;
And I will cause thee to [b]ride upon the
high places of the earth,
And feed thee with the heritage of
Jacob thy father:
[c]For the mouth of the LORD hath
spoken *it.*

58:8 [1]Heb. *shall gather thee up* [b]Ex. 14:19; ch. 52:12
58:9 [a]Ps. 12:2
58:11 [1]Heb. *droughts* [2]Heb. *lie, or, deceive*
58:12 [a]ch. 61:4
58:13 [a]ch. 56:2
58:14 [a]Job 22:26 [b]Deut. 32:13; 33:29 [c]ch. 1:20; 40:5; Mic. 4:4

Sin, confession and redemption

59 Behold, the LORD's hand is not
[a]shortened, that *it* cannot save;
Neither his ear heavy, that *it* cannot
hear:
2 But your iniquities have separated
between you and your God,
And your sins [1]have hid *his* face from
you, that *he* will not hear.
3 For [a]your hands are defiled with blood,
And your fingers with iniquity;
Your lips have spoken lies,
Your tongue hath muttered
perverseness.
4 None calleth for justice, nor any
pleadeth for truth:
They trust in vanity, and speak lies;
[a]*They* conceive mischief, and bring
forth iniquity.
5 They hatch [1]cockatrice' eggs,
And weave the spider's web:
He that eateth of their eggs dieth,
And [2]that which is crushed breaketh
out *into* a viper.
6 [a]Their webs shall not become
garments,
Neither shall they cover themselves
with their works:
Their works *are* works of iniquity,
And the act of violence *is* in their
hands.

59:1 [a]Num. 11:23; ch. 50:2
59:2 [1]Or, *have made him hide*
59:3 [a]ch. 1:15
59:4 [a]Job 15:35; Ps. 7:14
59:5 [1]Or, *adder's* [2]Or, *that which is sprinkled* is as if *there brake out a viper*
59:6 [a]Job 8:14

thee . . . be thy rereward. See 52:12 and note. The Lord will protect them and guide them. *glory of the LORD.* Probably a reference to the pillar of cloud and fire in the wilderness (see 4:5–6; Ex 13:21; 14:20 and notes).

‡58:9 *LORD shall answer.* See 30:19 and note. *Here I am.* The Lord is quick to respond to a genuine cry of repentance and confession. *take away . . . the yoke.* The oppression of their fellow Israelites. See vv. 3,6. *putting forth of the finger.* A gesture of either contempt (see Prov 6:13) or accusation. *speaking vanity.* See Prov 6:12–14.

58:10 *hungry . . . afflicted.* See vv. 6–7 and notes. *light.* See v. 8 and note.

58:11 *guide thee.* See 57:18 and note. *satisfy thy soul.* With both material and spiritual blessings (see note on 32:2). *drought.* See 35:7; 49:10. *watered garden.* In 1:30 Jerusalem was a garden without water. *waters fail not.* Cf. the "living water" Jesus gives in John 4:10,14.

58:12 *old waste places . . . foundations of many generations.* See 44:26,28 and notes; 61:4; Ezek 36:10; Amos 9:11,14. *repairer of the breach.* Cf. the work of Nehemiah in Neh 2:17.

58:13 *sabbath.* See 56:2 and note. *my holy day.* A day set apart to God (see Ex 3:5 and note). *delight.* They were also to delight themselves in the Lord (Ps 37:4) and in His law (Ps 1:2). *thine own ways.* Perhaps to engage in business (see Amos 8:5).

58:14 *delight thyself in the LORD.* See 61:10. *ride upon the high places.* Thus controlling the land. See 33:16 and note; see also Hab 3:19. *feed thee with the heritage.* Enjoying plentiful food in the promised land (see Deut 32:13–14). *mouth . . . hath spoken it.* See 40:5 and note.

59:1 *hand . . . shortened.* See 51:9 and note. *ear heavy . . . cannot hear.* See 30:19 and note.

59:2 *hid his face . . . he will not hear.* See 1:15 and note.

59:3–4 *lies.* See v. 13; 28:15; Hos 4:2.

59:3 *defiled with blood.* See v. 7; 1:15,21; Ezek 7:23.

‡59:4 *calleth for justice . . . pleadeth for truth.* The poor and helpless could not receive fair trials (see v. 14; 1:17–23; 5:7,23). *They conceive . . . iniquity.* Cf. Is 33:11; Job 15:35; Ps 7:14.

‡59:5 *cockatrice'.* See 11:8 and note. *spider's web.* Verse 6 and Job 8:14–15 stress how fragile it is. *dieth . . . breaketh out into a viper.* Contrast the poison and death created by their injustice with the peace and security brought by the Messiah's reign of justice in 11:8.

‡59:6 *webs . . . garments.* Their acts of injustice and violence for security are as worthless as garments made of spider webs. *act of violence.* See v. 3; Jer 6:7; Ezek 7:11.

7 [a]Their feet run to evil,
And they make haste to shed innocent blood:
Their thoughts *are* thoughts of iniquity;
Wasting and [1]destruction are in their paths.
8 The way of peace they know not;
And *there is* no [1]judgment in their goings:
[a]They have made them crooked paths:
Whosoever goeth therein shall not know peace.

9 Therefore is judgment far from us,
Neither doth justice overtake us:
[a]We wait for light, but behold obscurity;
For brightness, *but* we walk in darkness.
10 [a]We grope for the wall like the blind,
And we grope as if *we had* no eyes:
We stumble at noonday as *in* the night;
We are in desolate places as dead *men.*
11 We roar all like bears,
And [a]mourn sore like doves:
We look for judgment, but *there is* none;
For salvation, *but* it is far off from us.
12 For our transgressions are multiplied before thee,
And our sins testify against us:
For our transgressions *are* with us;
And *as for* our iniquities, we know them;
13 In transgressing and lying against the LORD,
And departing away from our God,
Speaking oppression and revolt,
Conceiving and uttering [a]from the heart words of falsehood.
14 And judgment is turned away backward,
And justice standeth afar off:
For truth is fallen in the street,
And equity cannot enter.
15 Yea, truth faileth;
And he *that* departeth from evil [1]maketh himself a prey:
And the LORD saw *it,* and [2]it displeased him
That *there was* no judgment.
16 [a]And he saw that *there was* no man,
And [b]wondered that *there was* no intercessor:
[c]Therefore his arm brought salvation unto him;
And his righteousness, it sustained him.
17 [a]For he put on righteousness as a breastplate,
And a helmet of salvation upon his head;
And he put on the garments of vengeance *for* clothing,
And was clad with zeal as a cloke.
18 [a]According to *their* [1]deeds, accordingly he will repay,
Fury to his adversaries, recompence to his enemies;
To the islands he will repay recompence.
19 [a]So shall they fear the name of the LORD from the west,
And his glory from the rising of the sun.
When the enemy shall come in [b]like a flood,

59:7 [1]Heb. *breaking* [a]Prov. 1:16; Rom. 3:15
59:8 [1]Or, *right* [a]Ps. 125:5; Prov. 2:15
59:9 [a]Jer. 8:15
59:10 [a]Deut. 28:29; Job 5:14; Amos 8:9
59:11 [a]ch. 38:14; Ezek. 7:16
59:13 [a]Mat. 12:34
59:15 [1]Or, *is accounted mad* [2]Heb. *it was evil in his eyes*
59:16 [a]Ezek. 22:30 [b]Mark 6:6 [c]Ps. 98:1; ch. 63:5
59:17 [a]Eph. 6:14,17; 1 Thes. 5:8
59:18 [1]Heb. *recompences* [a]ch. 63:6
59:19 [a]Ps. 113:3; Mal. 1:11 [b]Rev. 12:15

59:7–8 Quoted in part in Rom 3:15–17 by Paul to show the universality of sin.

59:7 *Their feet run . . . to shed innocent blood.* This sentence appears in Prov 1:16. *thoughts of iniquity.* God's thoughts are different (see 55:7–9). *Wasting and destruction.* Contrast 60:18.

59:8 *way of peace.* Cf. 26:3,12; 57:20–21; Luke 1:79. *crooked paths.* Unsafe (see Judg 5:6 and note).

‡59:9 *us . . . We.* The prophet includes himself with the people. *judgment . . . justice.* Personified here and in v. 14. They live in a society where justice is not practiced. See v. 4 and note; 1:21. *obscurity . . . darkness.* Similar language describes conditions when Assyria invaded Israel (see 5:30; 8:21–22; 9:1–2). Contrast 58:8.

‡59:10 *We grope . . . like the blind . . . at noonday.* The fulfillment of the curse for disobedience in Deut 28:29. Cf. Job 5:14.

59:11 *roar all like bears.* Impatient and frustrated.

59:12 *transgressions are multiplied.* See 58:1. *our iniquities, we know them.* Like Ezra (9:6–7), Isaiah confesses the sins of the nation. In this verse he uses the three most common Hebrew words for evil thoughts and deeds.

59:13 *transgressing and lying.* See 46:8; 48:8 and notes. *departing away from.* See 1:4. *oppression.* See 30:12. *words of falsehood.* See vv. 3–4.

59:14 *judgment . . . truth.* Cf. the personification of wisdom in Prov 8:1–9:12. *justice standeth afar off.* Cf. v. 9; contrast 46:13 and note.

59:15 *truth.* Restored Jerusalem is called the "city of truth" in Zech 8:3 (see 1:21 and note). *maketh himself a prey.* See 32:7.

59:16 *there was no man.* To help (see 63:5, a parallel to the whole verse). Cf. Ezek 22:30. *wondered.* Cf. the reaction to the servant in 52:14. *intercessor.* Cf. the intercession of the servant in 53:12 (see note there). *his arm brought salvation.* See 51:9; 52:10. For the meaning of salvation see 43:3; 49:8; 52:7 and notes. *righteousness.* For the relationship between righteousness and salvation see 45:8; 46:13 and notes.

59:17 *righteousness as a breastplate.* The Lord's armor is compared to the believer's armor in the battle against Satan in Eph 6:14. *garments of vengeance.* Cf. the blood-spattered garments of 63:1–3. God's vengeance is described also in 34:8 (see note there); 63:4. It is part of the day of the Lord (see 34:2 and note). *zeal.* God's jealous love (see 9:7 and note; 37:32; 42:13).

59:18 *adversaries . . . enemies.* God will judge the nations, but He must also punish wicked Israelites (see 65:6–7; 66:6; Jer 25:29). Only the remnant will be blessed (see v. 20; see also 1:9 and note). *islands.* See note on 11:11.

‡59:19 *name.* See 30:27 and note. *from the west . . . rising of the sun.* All nations will see God's saving work in behalf of His people (see 40:5; 45:6; 52:10 and notes). *flood.* The coming of the Lord will be irresistible, like an "overflowing stream" that overwhelms the enemy (see 30:28).

The spirit of the LORD shall [1]lift up a
standard against him.
20 And [a]the redeemer shall come to Zion,
And unto them that turn from
transgression in Jacob, saith the
LORD.
21 [a]As for me, this *is* my covenant with
them, saith the LORD;
My spirit that *is* upon thee,
And my words which I have put in thy
mouth,
Shall not depart out of thy mouth,
Nor out of the mouth of thy seed,
Nor out of the mouth of thy seed's
seed, saith the LORD,
From henceforth and for ever.

The dawn of Zion's glory

60 Arise, [a] [1]shine; for thy light is come,
And [b]the glory of the LORD is risen
upon thee.
2 For behold, the darkness shall cover
the earth,
And gross darkness the people:
But the LORD shall arise upon thee,
And his glory shall be seen upon thee.
3 And the [a]Gentiles shall come to thy
light,
And kings to the brightness of thy rising.
4 [a]Lift up thine eyes round about, and
see:
All they gather themselves together,
[b]they come to thee:
Thy sons shall come from far,
And thy daughters shall be nursed at
thy side.
5 Then thou shalt see, and flow *together,*
And thine heart shall fear, and be
enlarged;
Because [a]the [1]abundance of the sea
shall be converted unto thee,
The [2]forces of the Gentiles shall come
unto thee.
6 The multitude of camels shall cover
thee,
The dromedaries of Midian and
[a]Ephah;
All they from [b]Sheba shall come:
They shall bring [c]gold and incense;
And they shall shew forth the praises
of the LORD.
7 All the flocks of [a]Kedar shall be
gathered together unto thee,
The rams of Nebajoth shall minister
unto thee:
They shall come up with acceptance on
mine altar,
And [b]I will glorify the house of my
glory.
8 Who *are* these *that* fly as a cloud,
And as the doves to their windows?
9 [a]Surely the isles shall wait for me,
And the ships of Tarshish first,
[b]To bring thy sons from far,
[c]Their silver and their gold with them,
[d]Unto the name of the LORD thy God,
And to the Holy One of Israel,
[e]because he hath glorified thee.
10 And [a]the sons of strangers shall build
up thy walls,
[b]And their kings shall minister unto
thee:

59:19 [1]Or, *put him to flight* 59:20 [a]Rom. 11:26 59:21 [a]Heb. 8:10; 10:16 60:1 [1]Or, *be enlightened; for thy light cometh* [a]Eph. 5:14 [b]Mal. 4:2 60:3 [a]ch. 49:6,23; Rev. 21:24 60:4 [a]ch. 49:18 [b]ch. 49:20-22; 66:12

60:5 [1]Or, *noise of the sea shall be turned toward thee* [2]Or, *wealth* [a]Rom. 11:25 60:6 [a]Gen. 25:4 [b]Ps. 72:10 [c]ch. 61:6; Mat. 2:11 60:7 [a]Gen. 25:13 [b]Hag. 2:7,9 60:9 [a]Ps. 72:10; ch. 51:5 [b]Gal. 4:26 [c]Ps. 68:30; Zech. 14:14 [d]Jer. 3:17 [e]ch. 55:5 60:10 [a]Zech. 6:15 [b]ch. 49:23; Rev. 21:24

59:20 *redeemer.* See 41:14 and note. *come to Zion.* In the return from exile, but more fully in the person of Christ. See 35:4; 40:9; 52:7 and notes. Cf. Zech 8:3. *them that turn.* See 1:27–28 and note; 30:15; 31:6; Ezek 18:30–32.

59:21 *covenant.* The description fits the "new covenant" best (see 42:6 and note; Jer 31:31–34). *My spirit.* See 11:2 and note; 32:15; Ezek 36:27; John 16:13. *thee . . . thy . . . thy . . . thy . . . thy.* In Hebrew the pronouns are singular but are probably intended in a collective sense—the citizens of Zion. *my words . . . in thy mouth.* Then Israel will truly be God's people (see 51:16 and note; Jer 31:33). *not depart out of thy mouth.* See Josh 1:8.

60:1–2 *glory.* Probably an allusion to the pillar of cloud, but announcing a new manifestation of God's redeeming glory (see 58:8 and note). See also 35:2 and note.

60:1 *light.* See 58:8 and note. Here the Lord Himself is viewed as the light (see vv. 19–20).

60:2 *darkness.* A symbol of gloom, oppression and sin (see 8:22; 9:2; 59:9).

60:3 *Gentiles shall come.* See vv. 5,10–12 and notes. This theme was first mentioned in 2:2–4 (see note there). *light.* See 42:6; 49:6 and notes.

60:4 The first two lines are almost identical to the beginning of 49:18, the last two to the end of 49:22 (see note there). The setting there was the return from exile, but here much broader implications are involved. *from far.* See v. 9; 49:12 and note.

‡60:5 *flow together.* Lit. "be radiant," as they reflect the glory of God's light to the nations. *heart shall fear, and be enlarged.* Or "heart shall be in awe and enlarged with joy." Positive, not negative—the joy and thrill of experiencing God's blessing. *abundance of the sea.* Jerusalem will be enriched by the wealth of the nations brought as tribute to the Lord (see v. 11; 61:6; 66:12; see also 18:7; 23:18; 45:14 and notes). The contribution of King Darius to Zerubbabel's temple may be a partial fulfillment (Ezra 6:8–9). This verse ultimately refers to the future phase of the Messianic kingdom. See Rev 21:26 (the new Jerusalem); see also Hag 2:7; Zech 14:14 and notes.

60:6 *camels shall cover thee.* As caravans bringing goods. Ironically it was on camels that the Midianites once devastated Israel (see 9:4; Judg 6:1–6). *Midian.* Abraham's son through Keturah (Gen 25:2). The Midianites roamed the deserts east of the Jordan. *Ephah.* A son of Midian (Gen 25:4). *Sheba.* A wealthy land in southern Arabia, perhaps roughly equal to modern Yemen (see Gen 25:3; 1 Ki 10:1–2). *gold and incense.* The queen of Sheba brought gold and spices to Solomon (1 Ki 10:2). Jer 6:20 mentions the incense (frankincense) of Sheba. Cf. Ps 72:10; Mat 2:11. *shew forth the praises.* Cf. the queen's words in 1 Ki 10:9.

60:7 *flocks of Kedar.* See note on 21:16. *Nebajoth.* The firstborn son of Ishmael (Gen 25:13). The name is probably preserved in that of the later Nabatean kingdom. *minister.* See v. 10; 56:6. *come up with acceptance.* See 56:7; 58:5 and notes.

60:9 *isles shall wait for me.* See 11:11 and note. *ships of Tarshish.* See note on 2:16. *bring thy sons.* See 49:22 and note. *silver and . . . gold.* Ships of Tarshish had brought these to Solomon every three years (1 Ki 10:22). *Holy One of Israel.* See v. 14; 1:4 and note. *glorified thee.* See 55:5 and note.

60:10 *strangers . . . kings.* See vv. 12,14; 49:7,23; 61:5. *shall build up thy walls.* In 445 B.C. King Artaxerxes issued the de-

For *c* in my wrath I smote thee,
d But in my favour have I had mercy on
thee.
11 Therefore thy gates *a* shall be open
continually;
They shall not be shut day nor night;
That *men* may bring unto thee the
[1] forces of the Gentiles,
And *that* their kings *may be* brought.
12 *a* For the nation and kingdom that will
not serve thee shall perish;
Yea, *those* nations shall be utterly
wasted.
13 *a* The glory of Lebanon shall come unto
thee,
The fir tree, the pine tree, and the box
together,
To beautify the place of my sanctuary;
And I will make *b* the place of my feet
glorious.
14 The sons also of them that afflicted
thee shall come bending unto thee;
And all they that despised thee shall
a bow themselves down at the soles
of thy feet;
And they shall call thee, The city of the
LORD,
b The Zion of the Holy One of Israel.
15 Whereas thou hast been forsaken and
hated,
So that no man went through *thee,*
I will make thee an eternal excellency,
A joy of many generations.
16 Thou shalt also suck the milk of the
Gentiles,
a And shalt suck the breast of kings:
And thou shalt know that *b* I the LORD
am thy Saviour

60:10 *c* ch. 57:17 *d* ch. 54:7,8
60:11 [1] Or, *wealth* *a* Rev. 21:25
60:12 *a* Zech. 14:17; Mat. 21:44
60:13 *a* ch. 35:2 *b* 1 Chr. 28:2; Ps. 132:7
60:14 *a* ch. 49:23; Rev. 3:9 *b* Heb. 12:22; Rev. 14:1
60:16 *a* ch. 49:23; 61:6 *b* ch. 43:3
60:18 *a* ch. 26:1
60:19 *a* Rev. 21:23 *b* Zech. 2:5
60:20 *a* Amos 8:9
60:21 *a* ch. 52:1; Rev. 21:27 *b* Ps. 37:11; Mat. 5:5 *c* ch. 61:3; Mat. 15:13; John 15:2 *d* ch. 29:23; Eph. 2:10
60:22 *a* Mat. 13:31
61:1 *a* Luke 4:18; John 1:32; 3:34

And thy redeemer, the mighty One of
Jacob.
17 For brass I will bring gold,
And for iron I will bring silver,
And for wood brass,
And for stones iron:
I will also make thy officers peace,
And thine exactors righteousness.
18 Violence shall no more be heard in thy
land,
Wasting nor destruction within thy
borders;
But thou shalt call *a* thy walls Salvation,
And thy gates Praise.
19 The *a* sun shall be no more thy light by
day;
Neither for brightness shall the moon
give light unto thee:
But the LORD shall be unto thee an
everlasting light,
And *b* thy God thy glory.
20 *a* Thy sun shall no more go down;
Neither shall thy moon withdraw itself:
For the LORD shall be thine everlasting
light,
And the days of thy mourning shall be
ended.
21 *a* Thy people also *shall be* all righteous:
b They shall inherit the land for ever,
c The branch of my planting, *d* the work
of my hands, that *I* may be glorified.
22 *a* A little one shall become a thousand,
And a small one a strong nation:
I the LORD will hasten it in his time.

Good tidings of salvation

61 The *a* Spirit of the Lord GOD *is* upon
me;

cree allowing Nehemiah to rebuild the walls of Jerusalem (Neh 2:8). Some also apply the rebuilt walls to the building up of the church through Gentile believers (Acts 15:14–16). *in my wrath I . . . had mercy.* See 54:7–8 and notes.

‡60:11 *gates shall be open continually.* As are the gates of the new Jerusalem (Rev 21:25). *forces.* Or "wealth." See v. 5.

60:12 *nation . . . shall perish.* Israel's future political domination is referred to also in 11:14; 14:2; 49:23 (cf. vv. 10,14).

60:13 *glory of Lebanon.* Its magnificent cedar trees, which were used in the construction of Solomon's temple, along with pine trees (1 Ki 5:10,18). See also 35:2. The glory of Solomon's era would return. *fir tree, the pine . . . box.* See 41:19 and note. Perhaps the trees would be ornamental rather than building material. *beautify . . . sanctuary.* See v. 7. *place of my feet.* The temple, and especially the ark of the covenant, God's "footstool."

60:14 *afflicted . . . come bending.* See 49:7,23 and notes. Cf. vv. 10,12. *The city of the LORD.* Cf. the names for the future Jerusalem in 1:26; 62:4; Ezek 48:35; Zech 8:3; Heb 12:22.

60:15 *forsaken and hated.* See 6:11–12; 62:4; Jer 30:17. *excellency, A joy.* See 4:2 and note.

‡60:16 *suck the breast of kings.* Jerusalem will receive the very best nourishment, the "forces (wealth) of the Gentiles" (v. 5). *And thou . . . Jacob.* For this sentence see 49:26 and note.

60:17 *gold . . . silver.* As in Solomon's day gold and silver were plentiful (1 Ki 10:21,27), so the future Jerusalem will have the most valuable metals as well as the strongest (iron). Cf. 9:10. *peace . . . righteousness.* Both are also present in the rule of the Messianic king in 9:7. See note on 48:18.

60:18 *Violence shall no more be heard.* Cf. 54:14. *Wasting nor destruction.* See 51:19 and note. *walls Salvation.* See 26:1.

60:19 *sun . . . moon.* According to Rev 21:23; 22:5 their light will no longer be needed in the new Jerusalem, since God and the Lamb will be the everlasting "light." *glory.* See vv. 1–2 and note; Zech 2:5.

60:20 *sun shall no more go down.* There will be no night there (cf. Rev 22:5) but only the light of joy and salvation (see 58:8 and note). *mourning shall be ended.* See 25:8; 35:10; 51:11; 65:19; Rev 21:4.

‡60:21 *people . . . shall be all righteous.* Only the redeemed will be there (see 4:3; 35:8; Rev 21:27). *inherit the land for ever.* Enter into full blessing (see 49:8 and note; see also 57:13; 61:7; Ps 37:11,22). Because the "new covenant" will provide perfect obedience to the law of God (cf. Jer 31:33–34), there will be no more need to punish Israel for their sins. *branch of my planting.* Cf. the vineyard of 5:2,7 (see also 11:1). *work of my hands.* God made them as a potter forms clay (see 64:8; see also 29:23; 45:11). *I may be glorified.* They are the evidence of God's redemptive work. See 49:3; 61:3; see also notes on 35:2; 40:5.

60:22 *small one a strong nation.* See 51:2; 54:3 and notes. The blessing of Lev 26:8 is similar.

61:1–2 Jesus applied these verses to Himself in the synagogue at Nazareth (see Luke 4:16–21; cf. Mat 11:5).

‡61:1 *Spirit . . . is upon me.* The statement may refer to Isaiah in a limited sense, but the Messianic servant is the main figure

Because the LORD [b]hath anointed me to
preach good tidings unto the meek;
He hath sent me [c]to bind up the
broken-hearted,
To proclaim [d]liberty to the captives,
And the opening of the prison to *them*
that are bound;
2 [a]To proclaim the acceptable year of the
LORD,
And [b]the day of vengeance of our God;
[c]To comfort all that mourn;
3 To appoint unto them that mourn in
Zion,
[a]To give unto them beauty for ashes,
The oil of joy for mourning,
The garment of praise for the spirit of
heaviness;
That they might be called trees of
righteousness,
[b]The planting of the LORD, [c]that *he*
might be glorified.
4 And they shall [a]build the old wastes,
They shall raise up the former
desolations,
And they shall repair the waste cities,
The desolations of many generations.
5 And [a]strangers shall stand and feed
your flocks,
And the sons of the alien *shall be* your
plowmen and your vinedressers.
6 [a]But ye shall be named the Priests of
the LORD:
Men shall call you the Ministers of our
God:
[b]Ye shall eat the riches of the Gentiles,
And in their glory shall you boast
yourselves.
7 [a]For your shame *you shall have* double;
And *for* confusion they shall rejoice in
their portion:
Therefore in their land they shall
possess the double:
Everlasting joy shall be unto them.
8 For [a]I the LORD love judgment,
[b]I hate robbery for burnt offering;
And I will direct their work in truth,
[c]And I will make an everlasting
covenant with them.
9 And their seed shall be known among
the Gentiles,
And their offspring among the people:
All that see them shall acknowledge
them,
[a]That they *are* the seed *which* the
LORD hath blessed.
10 [a]I will greatly rejoice in the LORD,
My soul shall be joyful in my God;
For [b]he hath clothed me with the
garments of salvation,
He hath covered me with the robe of
righteousness,
[c]As a bridegroom [1]decketh *himself*
with ornaments,
And as a bride adorneth *herself* with
her jewels.
11 For as the earth bringeth forth her bud,
And as the garden causeth the things
that are sown in it to spring forth;
So the Lord GOD will cause
[a]righteousness and [b]praise to spring
forth
Before all the nations.

The restoration of Zion

62 For Zion's sake will I not hold my
peace,

61:1 [b]Ps. 45:7 [c]Ps. 147:3; ch. 57:15 [d]ch. 42:7; Jer. 34:8
61:2 [a]Lev. 25:9 [b]ch. 34:8; Mal. 4:1,3; 2 Thes. 1:7 [c]ch. 57:18; Mat. 5:4
61:3 [a]Ps. 30:11 [b]ch. 60:21 [c]John 15:8
61:4 [a]ch. 49:8; Ezek. 36:33
61:5 [a]Eph. 2:12
61:6 [a]Ex. 19:6; ch. 60:17; 1 Pet. 2:5; Rev. 1:6; 5:10 [b]ch. 60:5
61:7 [a]ch. 40:2; Zech. 9:12
61:8 [a]Ps. 11:7 [b]ch. 1:11,13 [c]ch. 55:3
61:9 [a]ch. 65:23
61:10 [1]Heb. *decketh as a priest* [a]Hab. 3:18 [b]Ps. 132:9,16 [c]ch. 49:18; Rev. 21:2
61:11 [a]Ps. 72:3; 85:11 [b]ch. 60:18; 62:7

intended (cf. what is said of Him in 42:1; see 11:2; 48:16 and notes). *Lord GOD.* See 50:4–5,7,9 and note. *anointed me.* See 45:1 and note. *good tidings.* See 40:9 and note. *meek.* Afflicted or needy. Cf. 11:4; 29:19. *bind up the broken-hearted.* See 30:26 and note. *liberty to the captives.* Freedom is used of the year of jubilee in Lev 25:10 (see 49:8 and note). Release from sin has as its background release from Babylon (see 42:7 and note).

‡61:2 *acceptable year of the LORD.* Corresponds to the "day of salvation" in 49:8 (see note there) and "the year of my redeemed" in 63:4. Christ ended His quotation at this point (Luke 4:19–20), probably because the "day of vengeance" will not occur until His second coming. *day of vengeance.* See 34:2,8 and notes. *comfort all that mourn.* See 49:13; 57:19 and notes; 66:10; Jer 31:13; Mat 5:4.

‡61:3 *beauty.* Or "a crown of beauty." The Hebrew word here refers to a "turban" or "headdress" (cf. the use of this word in the phrase "tire of thine head" in Ezek 24:17). In 3:20 the women of Jerusalem were to lose their beautiful headdresses. *oil of joy.* Anointing with olive oil was common on joyous occasions (see Ps 23:5; 45:7; 104:15; 133:1–2; cf. 2 Sam 14:2). See also 1:6 and note. *garment of praise.* Contrast the "garments of vengeance" in 59:17. *trees of righteousness.* Contrast the tree of 1:30. *planting . . . that he might be glorified.* See 60:21 and note.

61:4 *build the old wastes . . . waste cities.* See 58:12 and note.

61:5 *strangers . . . alien.* See 14:1–2; 56:3; 60:10 and notes.

‡61:6 *Priests of the LORD.* See 66:21. True Israel will be a "kingdom of priests" among the Gentiles (see Ex 19:6 and note), fulfilling God's original design for the nation. Contrrast 42:18–22 where Israel has failed in its mission. *Ministers.* Priests. *riches of the Gentiles.* See 60:5 and note.

61:7 *shame . . . confusion.* See 45:17; 54:4. *double.* The firstborn son received a double share of the inheritance (see Deut 21:17; Zech 9:12). Contrast the "double" punishment Israel received (40:2). *Everlasting joy.* See 35:10; 51:11; cf. Ps 16:11.

‡61:8 *love judgment.* Or "justice." Cf. 30:18; 59:15. *robbery for burnt offering.* Textual evidence favors the reading "robbery and iniquity," referring to how Israel had been mistreated by her conquerors. Cf. 42:24; 59:18. *everlasting covenant.* Probably the new covenant (see 55:3; 59:21 and notes; cf. Jer 31:35–37; 32:40).

61:9 *seed which the LORD hath blessed.* See 44:3; 65:23 and the promises to Abraham in Gen 12:1–3.

61:10 Zion is probably the speaker. *garments of salvation.* See v. 3; 52:1 and note. *decketh himself with ornaments.* Putting on a turban or headband (see note on v. 3). *bride . . . with her jewels.* See 49:18 and note.

61:11 *bud . . . spring forth.* Cf. 55:10. *righteousness and praise to spring forth.* See 45:8 and note.

62:1,6 *I.* The Lord.

‡62:1 *not hold my peace . . . rest.* See v. 6; 42:14; 57:11 and note; 64:12; 65:6; see also Ps 28:1. *righteousness . . . salvation.* See 46:13 and note.

And for Jerusalem's sake I will not rest,
Until the righteousness thereof go forth as brightness,
And the salvation thereof as a lamp *that* burneth.
2 [a]And the Gentiles shall see thy righteousness,
And all kings thy glory:
[b]And thou shalt be called by a new name,
Which the mouth of the LORD shall name.
3 Thou shalt also be [a]a crown of glory in the hand of the LORD,
And a royal diadem in the hand of thy God.
4 [a]Thou shalt no more be termed [b]Forsaken;
Neither shall thy land any more be termed [c]Desolate:
But thou shalt be called [1]Hephzi-bah,
And thy land [2]Beulah:
For the LORD delighteth in thee,
And thy land shall be married.
5 For *as* a young man marrieth a virgin,
So shall thy sons marry thee:
And [1]*as* the bridegroom rejoiceth over the bride,
So [a]shall thy God rejoice over thee.
6 [a]I have set watchmen upon thy walls, O Jerusalem,
Which shall never hold their peace day nor night:
[1]Ye that make mention of the LORD,
Keep not silence,
7 And give him no [1]rest,
Till he establish, and till he make Jerusalem [a]a praise in the earth.
8 The LORD hath sworn by his right hand, and by the arm of his strength,

62:2 [a]ch. 60:3 [b]See ver. 4,12
62:3 [a]Zech. 9:16
62:4 [1]That is, *My delight is in her* [2]That is, *Married* [a]Hos. 1:10 [b]ch. 49:14; 54:6,7 [c]ch. 54:1
62:5 [1]Heb. with *the joy of the bridegroom* [a]ch. 65:19
62:6 [1]Or, *Ye that are the LORD's remembrancers* [a]Ezek. 3:17
62:7 [1]Heb. *silence* [a]ch. 61:11; Zeph. 3:20
62:8 [1]Heb. *If I give, etc.* [a]Deut. 28:31; Jer. 5:17
62:9 [a]See Deut. 12:12; 14:23,26; 16:11,14
62:10 [a]ch. 40:3; 57:14 [b]ch. 11:12
62:11 [1]Or, *recompence* [a]Zech. 9:9; Mat. 21:5; John 12:15 [b]ch. 40:10; Rev. 22:12
62:12 [a]ver. 4
63:1 [1]Heb. *decked*
63:2 [a]Rev. 19:13
63:3 [a]Lam. 1:15; Rev. 14:19,20; 19:15

[1]Surely I will no more [a]give thy corn *to be* meat for thine enemies;
And the sons of the stranger shall not drink thy wine, for the which thou hast laboured:
9 But they that have gathered it shall eat it, and praise the LORD;
And they that have brought it together shall drink it [a]in the courts of my holiness.
10 Go through, go through the gates;
[a]prepare you the way of the people;
Cast up, cast up the highway; gather out the stones;
[b]Lift up a standard for the people.
11 Behold, the LORD hath proclaimed unto the end of the world,
[a]Say ye to the daughter of Zion,
Behold, thy salvation cometh;
Behold, his [b]reward *is* with him,
And his [1]work before him.
12 And they shall call them, The holy people, The redeemed of the LORD:
And thou shalt be called, Sought out, A city [a]not forsaken.

Vengeance and redemption

63 Who *is* this *that* cometh from Edom,
With dyed garments from Bozrah?
This *that is* [1]glorious in his apparel,
Travelling in the greatness of his strength?
I that speak in righteousness, mighty to save.
2 Wherefore [a]*art thou* red in thine apparel,
And thy garments like him that treadeth in the winefat?
3 I have [a]trodden the winepress alone;

62:2 *Gentiles shall see . . . glory.* See 52:10; see also 40:5; 60:3 and notes. *thy.* Jerusalem's (see vv. 1,6). *new name.* To reflect a new status (see vv. 4,12; see also 1:26; 60:14; Gen 32:28 and notes).
62:3 *crown of glory.* In 28:5 the Lord is a "crown of glory" for His people (cf. Zech 9:16).
‡62:4 *Forsaken . . . Desolate.* See 54:6–7; 60:15 and note. *Hephzi-bah.* "My delight is in her," also the name of Hezekiah's wife (2 Ki 21:1). *married.* Israel's relationship with the Lord will be restored and his temporary divorce of Israel reversed. See 50:1 and note.
62:5 *shall thy sons marry thee.* The Israelites will again possess the land once deserted. Cf. 54:1. Or the Hebrew for "sons" could be read as "Builder," referring to God
‡62:6 *watchmen.* Probably those (the prophets especially; see 56:10) waiting for the messenger with good news (see 52:8 and note). *never hold their peace.* They will be praying that God will not be silent (see v. 1) but will restore Jerusalem. God has promised restoration, but his people still have the responsibility to pray for the realization of God's promises. Contrast Ezek 22:30 where God had to destroy Jerusalem because there was no one to intercede for the city. *Keep not silence.* Cf. David's intense prayer as he searched for a home for the ark (Ps 132:1–5).
62:7 *praise in the earth.* Cf. Jer 33:9; Zeph 3:19–20; see 60:3 and note.
62:8 *hath sworn.* Cf. 45:23; 54:9. *arm of his strength.* See 51:9 and note. *corn . . . for thine enemies . . . stranger shall not drink thy wine.* Punishment Moses warned about in Lev 26:16; Deut 28:33. See also 52:1 and note; Jer 5:17.
62:9 *eat it . . . drink it.* See 65:13,21–23. *in the courts of my holiness.* During a festival, or when they brought the tithe to the Lord (Lev 23:39–40; Deut 14:22–26).
62:10 *Go through, go through.* See note on 40:1. *gates.* Probably of Babylon (cf. 48:20; Mic 2:12–13). *prepare you the way . . . cast up the highway.* See 40:3; 49:11 and notes. *gather out the stones.* See 57:14. *standard.* See 5:26 and note.
62:11 *end of the world.* See 11:12; 49:6 and notes. *daughter of Zion.* A personification of Jerusalem and its inhabitants. *thy salvation cometh.* See 40:9 and note; Zech 9:9; Mat 21:5; see also 43:3 and note. *reward . . . his work.* See 40:10 and note.
62:12 *holy people.* See 4:3; Ex 19:6 and notes. *redeemed.* See 35:9 and note. *Sought out, A city not forsaken.* See v. 4.
‡63:1 *Edom.* See 21:11; 34:5 and notes. Edom here symbolizes a world that hates God's people. *Bozrah.* See 34:6 and note. *dyed garments.* "Dyed" = "red" or "crimson." Cf. Christ's robe "dipt in blood" (Rev 19:13) as He wages war at His second coming. *righteousness, mighty to save.* See 45:8; 46:13; 59:16 and notes.
‡63:2 *Wherefore . . . ?* Isaiah responds with a question. *treadeth in the winefat.* Or "winepress." See 16:10 and note.
63:3 *trodden the winepress.* A figure of judgment also in Lam

And of the people *there was* none with
me:
For I will tread them in mine anger,
And trample them in my fury;
And their blood shall be sprinkled
upon my garments,
And I will stain all my raiment.
4 For the [a]day of vengeance *is* in mine
heart,
And the year of my redeemed is come.
5 [a]And I looked, and [b]*there was* none to
help;
And I wondered that *there was* none to
uphold:
Therefore mine own [c]arm brought
salvation unto me;
And my fury, it upheld me.
6 And I will tread down the people in
mine anger,
And make them drunk in my fury,
And I will bring down their strength to
the earth.

Praise to the LORD

7 I will mention the lovingkindnesses of
the LORD, *and* the praises of the
LORD,
According to all that the LORD hath
bestowed on us,
And the great goodness towards the
house of Israel,
Which he hath bestowed on them
according to his mercies,
And according to the multitude of his
lovingkindnesses.
8 For he said, Surely they *are* my people,
Children *that* will not lie:
So he was their Saviour.
9 [a]In all their affliction he was afflicted,
[b]And the angel of his presence saved
them:

63:4 [a]ch. 34:8; 61:2
63:5 [a]ch. 41:28; 59:16 [b]John 16:32 [c]Ps. 98:1; ch. 59:16
63:9 [a]Judg. 10:16; Acts 9:4 [b]Ex. 14:19; Acts 12:11

63:9 [c]Deut. 7:7 [d]Ex. 19:4
63:10 [a]Ex. 15:24; Ps. 95:9 [b]Ps. 78:40; Acts 7:51 [c]Ex. 23:21
63:11 [1]Or, *shepherds,* as Ps. 77:20 [a]Ex. 14:30 [b]Ps. 77:20 [c]Num. 11:17
63:12 [a]Ex. 15:6 [b]Josh. 3:16
63:13 [a]Ps. 106:9
63:14 [a]2 Sam. 7:23
63:15 [1]Or, *The multitude* [a]Deut. 26:15; Ps. 80:14 [b]Ps. 33:14 [c]Jer. 31:20; Hos. 11:8
63:16 [1]Or, *our redeemer from everlasting* is *thy name* [a]Deut. 32:6 [b]Job 14:21

[c]In his love and in his pity he
redeemed them;
And [d]he bare them, and carried them
all the days of old.
10 But they [a]rebelled, and [b]vexed his holy
Spirit:
[c]Therefore he was turned to be their
enemy, *and* he fought against them.
11 Then he remembered the days of old,
Moses, *and* his people, *saying,*
Where *is* he that [a]brought them up out
of the sea with the [b][1]shepherd of his
flock?
[c]Where *is* he that put his holy Spirit
within him?
12 That led *them* by the right hand of
Moses [a]*with* his glorious arm,
[b]Dividing the water before them, to
make himself an everlasting name?
13 [a]That led them through the deep,
As a horse in the wilderness, *that* they
should not stumble?
14 As a beast goeth down into the valley,
The Spirit of the LORD caused him to
rest:
So didst thou lead thy people,
[a]To make thyself a glorious name.

Judah appeals to God

15 [a]Look down from heaven, and behold
[b]From the habitation of thy holiness
and of thy glory:
Where *is* thy zeal and thy strength,
[1]The sounding [c]of thy bowels and of
thy mercies towards me? are they
restrained?
16 [a]Doubtless thou *art* our father,
Though Abraham [b]be ignorant of us,
And Israel acknowledge us not:
Thou, O LORD, *art* our father, [1]our
redeemer;

1:15; Joel 3:13; Rev 14:17–20; 19:15. *in mine anger . . . fury.* The day of the Lord. See v. 6; 13:3; 34:2 and notes.

63:4 *day of vengeance . . . year of my redeemed.* See 61:2 and note. The day of judging the enemy meant at the same time redemption for God's people. See 35:9; 41:14 and notes.

63:5 See 59:16 (a parallel to the whole verse) and note. *fury.* In 59:16 "righteousness" is used. God's righteousness and holiness resulted in His wrath.

‡63:6 *made them drunk.* They drank the "cup of his fury" (see 51:17 and note). *I will bring down . . . to the earth.* Lit. "I will pour out their juice (blood) on the ground." Here the battle is compared to a sacrifice, as in 34:6.

63:7–64:12 A prayer of Isaiah, asking the Lord to bring about the redemption He has promised—as one of the "watchmen" the Lord has posted on the walls of Jerusalem (see 62:6 and note). It is similar to a national lament (see, e.g., Ps 44).

63:7 *lovingkindnesses.* A demonstration of God's unfailing love as He stood true to His covenant with Israel. *great goodness.* Cf. Josh 21:45; 1 Ki 8:66. *mercies.* See 54:7–8,10 and note.

63:8 *my people, Children that will not lie.* But see 1:2–4. *Saviour.* See 43:3 and note.

63:9 *In all their affliction he was afflicted.* The suffering in Egypt and during the period of the judges is probably in view (see Judg 10:16). *angel of his presence.* See Ex 23:20–23; 33:14–15. *redeemed.* See 41:14; 43:1 and notes. *bare . . . carried.* Like a father (see Deut 1:31; 32:10–12).

63:10 *rebelled.* In the wilderness (see 1:2 and note; 30:1; Num 20:10; Ps 78:40). *vexed his holy Spirit.* See Ps 106:33; cf. Is 11:1–2; 42:1. *turned to be their enemy.* See 43:28 and note.

‡63:11 *sea.* The Red sea (see 50:2 and note; 51:10). *shepherd.* Or "shepherds." Moses and Aaron (cf. Ps 77:20). *holy Spirit.* See note on Ps 51:11. The Spirit rested on Moses and 70 elders (Num 11:17,25). See also v. 14.

63:12 *arm.* See 51:9 and note; Ex 15:16. *Dividing the water.* See Ex 14:21; cf. 11:15; 51:10. *everlasting name.* See 55:13 and note.

‡63:13 *deep.* Depths of the Red sea (see Ex 15:5,8; Ps 106:9). But the crossing of the Jordan may be intended as well (see v. 14 and note).

63:14 *into the valley.* To find pasture and water. *caused him to rest.* They found a home in Canaan, the promised land (see Deut 12:9; Josh 1:13; 21:44).

‡63:15 *zeal.* See 9:7; 42:13 and notes. *sounding of thy bowels and . . . mercies.* Lit. "stirring of your inward parts and your compassion." Note God's deep emotional attachment to his people. Cf. Hos 11:8. *restrained.* See 42:14 and note.

63:16 *father.* See 64:8; Deut 32:6. *Abraham be ignorant.* Even if their human fathers abandon them, God will not (see 49:14–15 and notes). *redeemer.* See 41:14 and note.

Thy name *is* from everlasting.
17 O LORD, why hast thou [a]made us to err
from thy ways,
And [b]hardened our heart from thy
fear?
[c]Return for thy servants' sake,
The tribes of thine inheritance.
18 [a]The people of thy holiness have
possessed *it* but a little while:
[b]Our adversaries have trodden down
thy sanctuary.
19 We are *thine:* thou never barest rule
over them;
[1]They were not called by thy name.

64 O that thou wouldest [a]rend the
heavens, that thou wouldest come
down,
That [b]the mountains might flow down
at thy presence,
2 As *when* [1]the melting fire burneth, the
fire causeth the waters to boil,
To make thy name known to thine
adversaries,
That the nations may tremble at thy
presence.
3 When [a]thou didst terrible things *which*
we looked not for,
Thou camest down, the mountains
flowed down at thy presence.
4 For since the beginning of the world
[a]*men* have not heard, nor perceived
by the ear,
Neither hath the eye [1]seen, O God,
besides thee,
What he hath prepared for him that
waiteth for him.
5 Thou meetest him that rejoiceth [a]and
worketh righteousness,
[b]*Those that* remember thee in thy
ways:
Behold, thou art wroth; for we have
sinned:
[c]In those is continuance, and we shall
be saved.
6 But we are all as an unclean *thing,*
And all [a]our righteousnesses *are* as
filthy rags;
And we all do [b]fade as a leaf;
And our iniquities, like the wind, have
taken us away.
7 And *there is* none that calleth upon thy
name,
That stirreth up himself to take hold of
thee:
For thou hast hid thy face from us,
And hast [1]consumed us, [2]because of
our iniquities.
8 [a]But now, O LORD, thou *art* our father;
We *are* the clay, [b]and thou our potter;
And we all *are* [c]the work of thine
hand.
9 Be not [a]wroth very sore, O LORD,
Neither remember iniquity for ever:
Behold, see, we beseech thee, [b]we *are*
all thy people.
10 Thy holy cities are a wilderness,
Zion is a wilderness, [a]Jerusalem a
desolation.
11 [a]Our holy and our beautiful house,
Where our fathers praised thee,
Is burnt up with fire:
And all [b]our pleasant things are laid
waste.
12 [a]Wilt thou refrain thyself for these
things, O LORD?
[b]Wilt thou hold thy peace, and afflict
us very sore?

63:17 [a]Ps. 119:10 [b]ch. 6:10 with John 12:40 [c]Ps. 90:13
63:18 [a]Deut. 7:6 [b]Ps. 74:7
63:19 [1]Heb. *Thy name was not called upon them*
64:1 [a]Ps. 144:5 [b]Mic. 1:4
64:2 [1]Heb. *the fire of meltings*
64:3 [a]Ex. 34:10; Ps. 68:8
64:4 [1]Or, *seen a God besides thee,* which *doeth so for him, etc.* [a]Ps. 31:19; 1 Cor. 2:9
64:5 [a]Acts 10:35 [b]ch. 26:8 [c]Mal. 3:6
64:6 [a]Phil. 3:9 [b]Ps. 90:5,6
64:7 [1]Heb. *melted* [2][Heb. *by the hand:* as Job 8:4]
64:8 [a]ch. 63:16 [b]ch. 29:16 [c]Eph. 2:10
64:9 [a]Ps. 74:1,2 [b]Ps. 79:13
64:10 [a]Ps. 79:1
64:11 [a]Ps. 74:7 [b]Ezek. 24:21
64:12 [a]ch. 42:14 [b]Ps. 83:1

‡**63:17** *made us to err.* When Israel went astray (see 53:6), God let them wander and then caused them to experience the consequences of their choice. *hardened our heart.* The people's hearts were hard (see 6:10; Ps 95:8), and the Lord confirmed that condition (see 6:10; Ex 4:21 and notes). *servants'.* True believers (see 54:17 and note).
63:18 *adversaries.* The Babylonians. *trodden down.* The temple, graphically described in Ps 74:3–7; cf. Is 64:11. Since it was God's sanctuary, His honor was at stake (cf. 48:11).
63:19 *called by thy name.* See 43:7 and note.
64:1 *rend the heavens.* The sky is compared to a tent curtain. For this and the further description of the cosmic effects of God's coming in judgment and redemption see Judg 5:4–5; Ps 18:7–15; 144:5; Nah 1:5; Hab 3:3–7.
64:2 *make thy name known.* See 30:27 and note.
64:3 *terrible things.* Or "awesome deeds." See Ps 66:3,5–6.
‡**64:4** This verse is quoted in 1 Cor 2:9 with reference to the truths that God has revealed through the Holy Spirit. *Neither . . . O God, besides thee.* See 43:11 and note. *waiteth for him.* See 30:18; see also 40:31 and note.
‡**64:5** *worketh righteousness.* See 56:1. God's blessing is conditioned upon obedience. The difference between the old and new covenants is not a lessening of the demand for obedience, but rather the enablement of grace in the new covenant that makes obedience possible (cf. Jer 31:31–34; 2 Cor 3:6–9). *thou art wroth.* See 9:12,17,21 and note. God's anger culminated in the exile. *saved.* Or "delivered" (see 43:3 and note).
64:6 *unclean.* Ceremonially unclean, like a person with a terrible disease (see 6:5; Lev 5:2; 13:45). *righteousnesses.* See 57:12 and note. *filthy rags.* The cloths a woman uses during her period, a time when she is "unclean" (see Lev 15:19–24; Ezek 36:17). *fade as a leaf.* A figure used also in 1:30. *like the wind.* Which blows away the chaff (see 17:13; 40:24 and note).
64:7 *none that calleth upon thy name.* The Lord urges earnest prayer in times of distress (see, e.g., 2 Chr 7:14). *stirreth up himself to take hold of thee.* God expects prayer to be an energetic exercise (cf. Gen 32:24–28; Luke 22:44). *hid thy face.* See 1:15 and note.
64:8 *father.* See 63:16 and note. *clay . . . potter.* See 45:9 and note. *work of thine hand.* See 60:21 and note.
64:9 *Be not wroth.* Cf. the promise to end that anger in 54:7–8 (see notes there). *Neither remember iniquity.* See 43:25 and note; Jer 31:34; Mic 7:18. *thy people.* See 63:17–19; Ps 79:13.
64:10 *holy cities.* Sacred because Israel was the holy land (called "his sanctuary" in Ps 78:54). Jerusalem is often called the "holy city" (see 48:2 and note). *Zion is a wilderness . . . desolation.* See 1:7–9 and note; 6:11; Jer 12:11.
64:11 *holy and our beautiful house.* See 60:7; 63:15. *burnt up with fire.* Isaiah here reaches the climax of his lament. See 63:18 and note.
64:12 *refrain thyself . . . hold thy peace.* See 42:14; 57:11; 62:1,6–7 and notes.

Judgment and salvation

65 [a]I am sought of *them that* asked not
for me:
I am found of *them that* sought me not:
I said, Behold me, behold me,
Unto a nation *that* [b]was not called by
my name.
2 [a]I have spread out mine hands all the
day unto a rebellious people,
Which walketh *in* a way *that was* not
good, after their own thoughts;
3 A people [a]that provoketh me to anger
continually to my face;
[b]That sacrificeth in gardens, and
burneth incense [1]upon altars of
brick;
4 [a]Which remain among the graves,
And lodge in the monuments,
[b]Which eat swine's flesh,
And [1]broth of abominable *things is in*
their vessels;
5 [a]Which say, Stand by thyself,
Come not near to me; for I am holier
than thou.
These *are* a smoke in my [1]nose,
A fire that burneth all the day.
6 Behold, [a]*it is* written before me:
[b]I will not keep silence, [c]but will
recompense,
Even recompense into their bosom,
7 Your iniquities, and [a]the iniquities of
your fathers together, saith the LORD,
[b]Which have burnt incense upon the
mountains,
[c]And blasphemed me upon the hills:
Therefore will I measure their former
work into their bosom.

65:1 [a]Rom. 9:24; Eph. 2:12 [b]ch. 63:19
65:2 [a]Rom. 10:21
65:3 [1]Heb. *upon bricks* [a]Deut. 32:21 [b]ch. 1:29; Lev. 17:5
65:4 [1]Or, *pieces* [a]Deut. 18:11 [b]ch. 66:17
65:5 [1]Or, *anger* [a]Mat. 9:11; Luke 18:11; Jude 19
65:6 [a]Deut. 32:34; Mal. 3:16 [b]Ps. 50:3 [c]Ps. 79:12; Jer. 16:18; Ezek. 11:21
65:7 [a]Ex. 20:5 [b]Ezek. 18:6 [c]Ezek. 20:27
65:8 [a]Joel 2:14
65:9 [a]Mat. 24:22
65:10 [a]ch. 33:9 [b]Josh. 7:24; Hos. 2:15
65:11 [1]Or, *Gad* [2]Or, *Meni* [a]ch. 56:7 [b]Ezek. 23:41; 1 Cor. 10:21
65:12 [a]2 Chr. 36:15,16; Prov. 1:24; Jer. 7:13

8 Thus saith the LORD,
As the new wine is found in the cluster,
And *one* saith, Destroy it not; for [a]a
blessing *is* in it:
So will I do for my servants' sakes,
That *I* may not destroy them all.
9 And I will bring forth a seed out of
Jacob,
And out of Judah an inheritor of my
mountains:
And mine [a]elect shall inherit it,
And my servants shall dwell there.
10 And [a]Sharon shall be a fold of flocks,
And [b]the valley of Achor a place for
the herds to lie down in,
For my people that have sought me.
11 But ye *are* they that forsake the LORD,
That forget [a]my holy mountain,
That prepare [b]a table for *that* [1]troop,
And that furnish the drink offering
unto *that* [2]number.
12 Therefore will I number you to the
sword,
And ye shall all bow down to the
slaughter:
[a]Because when I called, ye did not
answer;
When I spake, ye did not hear;
But did evil before mine eyes,
And did choose *that* wherein I
delighted not.
13 Therefore thus saith the Lord GOD,
Behold, my servants shall eat, but ye
shall be hungry:
Behold, my servants shall drink, but ye
shall be thirsty:

65:1–66:24 The grand conclusion to chs. 58–66, as well as to chs. 40–66 and to the whole book.

‡65:1 *asked not . . . sought me not.* The Lord now proceeds to answer Isaiah's prayer. Israel failed to stay close to the Lord, though they sought Him in a superficial way (see 55:6; 58:2 and notes). *Behold me.* See 58:9. *nation . . . not called by my name.* Or "a nation that did not call on my name." This reading fits better with the context. See also 64:7.

65:2 *rebellious people.* See 1:2; 30:1,9 and notes. *their own thoughts.* See 59:7 and note.

65:3 *provoketh me.* By worshiping idols (see Judg 2:12–13). *to my face.* Defiantly (cf. 3:8–9). *gardens.* See 1:29 and note. *burneth incense.* As when worshiping the queen of Heaven (see Jer 44:17–19).

65:4 *remain among the graves.* Perhaps to consult the dead (see 8:19 and note; 57:9; Deut 18:11). *swine's flesh.* Considered ceremonially unclean (see 66:3,17; Lev 11:7–8).

65:5 *I am holier than thou.* Those who engage in pagan rituals believe they are superior to others (cf. the attitude of the Pharisees in Mat 9:11; Luke 7:39; 18:9–12).

65:6 *not keep silence.* The answer to 64:12. *recompense.* See 59:18 and note.

65:7 *burnt incense upon the mountains.* Offered to Baal on the high places (see 57:7; Hos 2:13). *blasphemed me.* See Ezek 20:27–28.

65:8 *the cluster.* Israel was a vineyard that had produced bad grapes (5:2,4,7). *servants'.* See vv. 9,13–15; 54:17 and note. Here the Lord's servants are equivalent to the remnant (see 1:9 and note).

65:9 *seed.* See Jer 31:36. *Jacob . . . Judah.* The northern and southern kingdoms respectively. *inheritor of my mountains.* See 49:8; 60:21 and notes. "Mountains" refers to the whole land, since so much of it was hilly (see Judg 1:9; Ezek 6:2–3). *elect.* See 41:8–9 and note. *inherit.* See 57:13 and note.

65:10 *Sharon.* See 33:9 and note. *valley of Achor.* A valley near Jericho (see Josh 7:24,26; Hos 2:15). Since Sharon and Achor are on the western and eastern edges of the land respectively, they probably represent the whole country. *sought me.* See v. 1; 51:1 and notes.

‡65:11 *forsake the LORD.* See 1:4. *holy mountain.* See 2:2–4 and note. *prepare a table . . . furnish the drink offering.* A meal and drink offering presented to deities. See note on 5:22; cf. v. 3; Jer 7:18. *troop . . . number.* Hebrew reads *gad* ("Fortune") . . . *meni* ("Fate") generally understood here as proper names for the pagan gods of good fortune and fate. See Josh 11:17, where "gad" may mean "Fortune."

65:12 *sword.* Designed for God's enemies, such as Edom (34:5–6), but the wicked of Israel would also suffer (see 1:20; 59:18 and note; 66:16). *called . . . not answer.* See 50:2 and note; 2 Chr 36:15–16. *choose . . . I delighted not.* Contrast the faithfulness of the eunuchs in 56:4. The last four lines of v. 12 are almost identical to those of 66:4.

65:13 *eat . . . drink.* See 41:17–18; 49:10. *be hungry . . . thirsty.* See 5:13; 8:21. *rejoice.* See 61:7 and note; 66:14. *be ashamed.* See 42:17; 44:9,11.

Behold, my servants shall rejoice, but
ye shall be ashamed:
14 Behold, my servants shall sing for joy
of heart,
But ye shall cry for sorrow of heart,
And [a]shall howl for [1]vexation of spirit.
15 And ye shall leave your name [a]for a
curse unto [b]my chosen:
For the Lord GOD shall slay thee,
And [c]call his servants by another name:
16 [a]That he who blesseth himself in the
earth shall bless himself in the God
of truth;
And [b]he that sweareth in the earth
shall swear by the God of truth;
Because the former troubles are
forgotten,
And because they are hid from mine
eyes.

The joy of the new age

17 For, behold, I create [a]new heavens and
a new earth:
And the former shall not be
remembered, nor [1]come into mind.
18 But be you glad and rejoice for ever *in
that* which I create:
For behold, I create Jerusalem a
rejoicing, and her people a joy.
19 And [a]I will rejoice in Jerusalem, and
joy in my people:
And the [b]voice of weeping shall be no
more heard in her, nor the voice of
crying.
20 There shall be no more thence an
infant of days,
Nor an old man that hath not filled his
days:
For the child shall die an hundred
years old;
[a]But the sinner *being* an hundred years
old shall be accursed.

65:14 [1]Heb. *breaking* [a]Mat. 8:12; Luke 13:28
65:15 [a]Jer. 29:22; Zech. 8:13 [b]ver. 9,22 [c]Acts 11:26
65:16 [a]Ps. 72:17; Jer. 4:2 [b]Deut. 6:13; Zeph. 1:5
65:17 [1]Heb. *come upon the heart* [a]2 Pet. 3:13; Rev. 21:1
65:19 [a]ch. 62:5 [b]ch. 35:10; Rev. 7:17
65:20 [a]Eccl. 8:12
65:22 [1]Heb. *shall make them continue long,* or, *shall wear out* [a]Ps. 92:12 [b]ver. 9,15
65:23 [a]Hos. 9:12 [b]ch. 61:9
65:24 [a]Dan. 9:21
65:25 [a]ch. 11:6 [b]Gen. 3:14
66:1 [a]1 Ki. 8:27; 2 Chr. 6:18; Mat. 5:34; Acts 17:24
66:2 [a]ch. 57:15; 61:1 [b]Ps. 34:18; 51:17

21 And they shall build houses, and
inhabit *them;*
And they shall plant vineyards, and eat
the fruit of them.
22 They shall not build, and another
inhabit;
They shall not plant, and another eat:
For [a]as the days of a tree *are* the days
of my people,
And [b]mine elect [1]shall long enjoy the
work of their hands.
23 They shall not labour in vain,
[a]Nor bring forth for trouble;
For [b]they *are* the seed of the blessed of
the LORD,
And their offspring with them.
24 And it shall come to pass, that [a]before
they call, I will answer;
And whiles they are yet speaking, I
will hear.
25 The [a]wolf and the lamb shall feed
together,
And the lion shall eat straw like the
bullock:
[b]And dust *shall be* the serpent's meat.
They shall not hurt nor destroy in all
my holy mountain, saith the LORD.

Judgment and hope

66 Thus saith the LORD,
[a]The heaven *is* my throne, and the
earth *is* my footstool:
Where *is* the house that ye build unto
me?
And where *is* the place of my rest?
2 For all those *things* hath mine hand
made,
And all those *things* have been, saith
the LORD:
[a]But to this *man* will I look,
[b]*Even* to *him that is* poor and of a
contrite spirit,

‡**65:14** *sing for joy.* See 35:10; 54:1 and notes. *vexation of spirit.* A broken spirit because they had refused God's healing. See 61:1 and note.
65:15 *my chosen.* See v. 9 and note. *for a curse.* The rebellious Israelites will be used as an example when curses are uttered (see Jer 29:22). *another name.* Perhaps the "new name" of 62:2 (see note there).
65:16 *God of truth.* God is true to His promises. The Hebrew word for "truth" here is *amen* (see 2 Cor 1:20; cf. Rev 3:14). *swear by.* See 45:23. Perhaps a contrast is intended with those who took oaths in the name of Baal (see Jer 12:16).
‡**65:17** *new heavens and a new earth.* The climax of the "new things" Isaiah has been promising (see 42:9; 48:6 and notes). *former.* See Rev 21:4, where the "former things" include the pain and sorrow of this life.
65:18 *be you glad and rejoice.* See 66:10; see also 51:3 and note. *create Jerusalem.* John links the notion of a new heaven and a new earth with the "new Jerusalem" (Rev 21:1–2). A restored Jerusalem after the exile and in the Messianic kingdom points toward this greater Jerusalem. See note on 54:11–12.
65:19 *rejoice . . . joy.* See 62:4–5 and notes. *weeping . . . crying.* See 25:8 and note; 35:10.
65:20–25 See 11:6–9 and note.
65:20 *child . . . an hundred years old.* Comparable to the longevity of Adam and his early descendants. See the genealogy of Gen 5 (but see note on Gen 5:5).
65:21–22 Contrast Moses' curse for disobedience in Deut 28:30.
65:21 *plant vineyards.* See 62:8–9.
65:22 *days of a tree.* Compared to the righteous also in Ps 1:3; 92:12–14. *elect.* See 41:8–9 and note. *long enjoy.* Cf. Ps 91:16.
‡**65:23** *labuor in vain.* See 49:4 and note. *bring forth for trouble.* The children they bear will never experience calamities such as death or captivity. *blessed of the LORD.* See 61:9 and note.
65:24 *before they call, I will answer.* See 30:19; 58:9; Mat 6:8.
65:25 *wolf . . . lamb . . . lion.* See 11:6–9 and notes. *dust . . . serpent's meat.* See Gen 3:14 and note. The serpent will be harmless (see 11:8). *They . . . mountain.* Identical to the first part of 11:9.
66:1 *throne . . . footstool.* See 40:22 and note. *Where is the house . . . ?* Solomon realized that God could not be localized in a man-made temple, magnificent though it may be (1 Ki 8:27).
66:2 *all those things . . . made.* See 40:26 and note. *poor and . . . contrite.* See 57:15 and note.

And [c]trembleth at my word.
3 [a]He that killeth an ox *is as if* he slew a man;
He that sacrificeth a [1]lamb, *as if* he [b]cut off a dog's neck;
He that offereth an oblation, *as if he offered* swine's blood;
He that [2]burneth incense, *as if* he blessed an idol.
Yea, they have chosen their own ways,
And their soul delighteth in their abominations.
4 I also will choose their [1]delusions,
And will bring their fears upon them;
[a]Because when I called, none did answer;
When I spake, they did not hear:
But they did evil before mine eyes,
And chose *that* in which I delighted not.

5 Hear the word of the LORD, [a]ye that tremble at his word;
Your brethren that hated you,
That cast you out for my name's sake, said,
[b]Let the LORD be glorified:
But [c]he *shall* appear to your joy, and they shall be ashamed.
6 A voice of noise from the city, a voice from the temple,
A voice of the LORD that rendereth recompence to his enemies.
7 Before she travailed, she brought forth;
Before her pain came, she was delivered of a man child.
8 Who hath heard such *a thing?* who hath seen such *things?*
Shall the earth be made to bring forth in one day?
Or shall a nation be born at once?
For as soon as Zion travailed, she brought forth her children.
9 Shall I bring to the birth, and not [1]cause to bring forth? saith the LORD:
Shall I cause to bring forth, and shut *the womb?* saith thy God.
10 Rejoice ye with Jerusalem, and be glad with her, all ye that love her:
Rejoice for joy with her, all ye that mourn for her:
11 That ye may suck, and be satisfied with the breasts of her consolations;
That ye may milk out, and be delighted with the [1]abundance of her glory.
12 For thus saith the LORD,
Behold, [a]I will extend peace to her like a river,
And the glory of the Gentiles like a flowing stream:
Then shall ye [b]suck, ye shall be [c]borne upon *her* sides,
And be dandled upon *her* knees.
13 As one whom his mother comforteth, so will I comfort you;
And ye shall be comforted in Jerusalem.
14 And when ye see *this,* your heart shall rejoice,
And [a]your bones shall flourish like an herb:
And the hand of the LORD shall be known towards his servants,
And *his* indignation towards his enemies.
15 [a]For behold, the LORD will come with fire,
And with his chariots like a whirlwind,
To render his anger with fury,
And his rebuke with flames of fire.
16 For by fire and by [a]his sword will the LORD plead with all flesh:

66:2 [c]ver. 5; Ezra 9:4; 10:3; Prov. 28:14
66:3 [1]Or, *kid* [2]Heb. *maketh a memorial of* [a]ch. 1:11 [b]Deut. 23:18
66:4 [1]Or, *devices* [a]Prov. 1:24; ch. 65:12; Jer. 7:13
66:5 [a]ver. 2 [b]ch. 5:19 [c]2 Thes. 1:10; Tit. 2:13
66:9 [1]Or, *beget?*
66:11 [1]Or, *brightness*
66:12 [a]ch. 48:18; 60:5 [b]ch. 60:16 [c]ch. 49:22; 60:4
66:14 [a]See Ezek. 37:1
66:15 [a]ch. 9:5
66:16 [a]ch. 27:1

‡66:3 Cf. Isaiah's harsh words about ineffective sacrifices in 1:11–14. *killeth an ox . . . slew a man.* Extreme hyperbole stating that the sacrifice of a sinful person is no better than an act of murder in the eyes of God. *cut off a dog's neck.* The dog was "unclean" and not used in offerings. Cf. the law about breaking a donkey's neck in Ex 13:13. *swine's blood.* See 65:4 and note. The dog and pig are mentioned together also in Mat 7:6; 2 Pet 2:22. *blessed an idol.* See 44:19 and note. *abominations.* Probably idols (see Jer 4:1).

‡66:4 *I also will choose . . . delusions.* The punishment fits the crime because the Lord will punish them with the natural consequences of their own foolish choices. Cf. 65:7. *Because . . . that in which I delighted not.* For these last four lines see 65:12 and note.

‡66:5 *tremble.* See v. 2. *Your brethren.* Fellow Israelites (see Acts 22:1). *Let the LORD be glorified.* Apparently spoken sarcastically, much like 5:19; Ps 22:8. *to your joy.* The righteous will not be disappointed for putting their trust in the Lord.

66:6 *city.* Probably Jerusalem. *rendereth recompence to his enemies.* See 59:18 and note; 65:6–7.

66:7 *Before she travailed.* See 54:1 (and note), where Zion was barren.

‡66:8 *earth . . . in one day . . . nation be born at once.* In the future kingdom, it will be as if Israel is born in one day. See 49:19–20 and note.

‡66:9 *to the birth.* Or "to the point of birth." See 37:3 and note.

66:10 *Rejoice . . . be glad.* See 65:18 and note. *all ye that love her.* Cf. Ps 137:6. *ye that mourn.* See 57:19; 61:2 and notes.

66:11 *suck, and be satisfied.* In 60:16 (see note there) Jerusalem was drinking the milk of nations. Here she is the mother (cf. v. 12; 49:23).

‡66:12 *peace . . . like a river.* See 48:18 and note. *glory of the Gentiles.* See 60:5 and note. *flowing stream.* Contrast the destructive flood of 8:7–8 (see note there). *borne upon her sides.* The picture is of a mother carrying an infant in her arms. See 40:11. *dandled.* The mother playfully bouncing the child on her knee.

66:13 *comforted in Jerusalem.* See 49:13 and note. Cf. 2 Cor 1:3–4.

‡66:14 *heart shall rejoice.* See 60:5. *herb.* Or "grass," usually a symbol of weakness. See 37:27 and note; 51:12; but contrast 44:4. *hand of the LORD.* Cf. Ezra 7:9; 8:31. *servants.* See 54:17 and note. *indignation.* See v. 15; 13:3 and note.

66:15–16 *fire.* A figure of judgment (see 1:31 and note; 30:27).

66:15 *chariots like a whirlwind.* See 5:28; 2 Ki 2:11; 6:17; Ps 68:17. *anger.* See 34:2; 42:25 and notes. *rebuke.* See 51:20 and note.

‡66:16 *sword.* See 27:1; 34:6 and note. *plead.* Or "to carry

And the slain of the LORD shall be
many.
17 [a]They that sanctify themselves, and
purify themselves in the gardens
[1]Behind one *tree* in the midst,
Eating swine's flesh, and the
abomination, and the mouse,
Shall be consumed together, saith the
LORD.
18 For I *know* their works and their
thoughts:
It shall come, that *I* will gather all
nations and tongues;
And they shall come, and see my glory.
19 [a]And I will set a sign among them,
And I will send those that escape of
them unto the nations,
To Tarshish, Pul, and Lud, that draw
the bow,
To Tubal, and Javan, *to* the isles afar
off,
That have not heard my fame, neither
have seen my glory;
[b]And they shall declare my glory
among the Gentiles.
20 And they shall bring all your brethren
[a]*for* an offering unto the LORD out of
all nations

66:17 [1] Or, *One after another* [a] ch. 65:3,4
66:19 [a] Luke 2:34 [b] Mal. 1:11
66:20 [a] Rom. 15:16

66:20 [1] Or, *coaches*
66:21 [a] Ex. 19:6; ch. 61:6; 1 Pet. 2:9; Rev. 1:6
66:22 [a] ch. 65:17; 2 Pet. 3:13; Rev. 21:1
66:23 [1] Heb. *from new moon to his new moon, and from sabbath to his sabbath* [a] Zech. 14:16 [b] Ps. 65:2
66:24 [a] ver. 16 [b] Mark 9:44, 46,48

Upon horses, and in chariots, and in
[1]litters, and upon mules, and upon
swift beasts,
To my holy mountain Jerusalem, saith
the LORD,
As the children of Israel bring an
offering
In a clean vessel *into* the house of the
LORD.
21 And I will also take of them for [a]priests
and for Levites, saith the LORD.
22 For as [a]the new heavens and the new
earth, which I *will* make,
Shall remain before me, saith the LORD,
So shall your seed and your name
remain.
23 And [a]it shall come to pass, *that* [1]from
one new moon to another,
And from one sabbath to another,
[b]Shall all flesh come to worship before
me, saith the LORD.
24 And they shall go forth, and look
Upon [a]the carcases of the men that
have transgressed against me:
For their [b]worm shall not die,
Neither shall their fire be quenched;
And they shall be an abhorring unto all
flesh.

out/enter into judgment." The day of the Lord (see note on 2:11,17,20; cf. Ezek 38:21–22).

66:17 *sanctify . . . and purify themselves.* By special rituals required by their pagan religion. Cf. 2 Chr 30:17. *gardens.* See 1:29 and note. *swine's flesh.* See 65:4 and note.

66:18 *their thoughts.* See 65:2 and note. Wicked Israelites may be the antecedent. *gather all nations.* Cf. Joel 3:2; Zeph 3:8; Zech 14:2. *see my glory.* Usually linked with God's deliverance of His people (see 35:2–4; 40:5 and notes).

‡66:19 *sign.* Possibly the banner of 11:10,12 (see note on 5:26; cf. Ps 74:4). Cf. the "sign of the Son of man" (Mat 24:30) at the second coming. *those that escape.* After the judgment of v. 16. Cf. Zech 14:16. *Tarshish.* See 23:6 and note. *Pul.* People who lived west of Egypt (in Libia). See Nah 3:9. *Lud.* People from either west-central Asia Minor (see Gen 10:13 and note) or Africa. *Tubal.* Usually mentioned with Meshech (see Gen 10:2 and note; Ezek 27:13; 38:2–3; 39:1). It was probably a region southeast of the Black Sea. *Javan.* "Ionia" or "Greece." *isles.* See 11:11 and note. *declare my glory . . . Gentiles.* See 42:12; 1 Chr 16:24.

66:20 *bring all your brethren.* Gentiles will bring back the remnant (see 11:11–12; 49:22; 60:4 and notes). *holy mountain.* See 2:2–4 and note. *offering . . . into the house of the LORD.* As the Israelites were to bring their tithes and offerings (see Deut 12:5–7).

‡66:21 *take of them.* Gentiles will be allowed to serve as Levitical priests, thus indicating their full inclusion in the blessings of the new covenant. Gentile inclusion in the priesthood is a present reality in the church (see 1 Pet 2:5,9 and notes) and will carry over into the Messianic kingdom.

66:22 *new heavens . . . new earth.* See 65:17 and note. *seed . . . your name remain.* See 48:19 and note.

66:23 *new moon.* See 1:14 and note. *all flesh come to worship.* See 19:21; Zech 14:16 and notes.

‡66:24 Quoted in part in Mark 9:48. *go forth, and look.* The Valley of Hinnom (Hebrew *ge' hinnom,* from which the word "Gehenna" comes) was located southwest of Jerusalem and became a picture of hell. See Neh 11:30; Jer 7:32. *carcases.* Or corpses. See 5:25; 34:3. *transgressed.* See 1:2 and note; 24:20. *worm shall not die.* There will be everlasting torment. See 14:11; 48:22; 50:11; 57:21. *fire be quenched.* See 1:31 and note; Mat 3:12. *abhorring.* The Hebrew for this word is translated "contempt" in Dan 12:2. These verses clearly distinguish the eternal destinies of the saved and the unsaved.

The Book of the Prophet Jeremiah

INTRODUCTION

Author and Date

The book preserves an account of the prophetic ministry of Jeremiah, whose personal life and struggles are known to us in greater depth and detail than those of any other OT prophet. The meaning of his name is uncertain. Suggestions include "The LORD exalts" and "The LORD establishes," but a more likely proposal is "The LORD throws," either in the sense of "hurling" the prophet into a hostile world or of "throwing down" the nations in divine judgment for their sins. Jeremiah's prophetic ministry began in 626 B.C. and ended sometime after 586 (see notes on 1:2–3). His ministry was immediately preceded by that of Zephaniah. Habakkuk was a contemporary, and Obadiah may have been also. Since Ezekiel began his ministry in Babylon in 593 he too was a late contemporary of the great prophet in Jerusalem. How and when Jeremiah died is not known; Jewish tradition, however, asserts that while living in Egypt he was put to death by being stoned (cf. Heb 11:37).

Jeremiah was a priest, a member of the household of Hilkiah. His hometown was Anathoth (1:1), so he may have been a descendant of Abiathar (1 Ki 2:26), a priest during the days of King Solomon. The Lord commanded Jeremiah not to marry and raise children because the impending divine judgment on Judah would sweep away the next generation (16:1–4). Primarily a prophet of doom, he attracted only a few friends, among whom were Ahikam (26:24), Gedaliah (Ahikam's son, 39:14) and Ebed-melech (38:7–13; cf. 39:15–18). Jeremiah's closest companion was his faithful secretary, Baruch, who wrote down Jeremiah's words as the prophet dictated them (36:4–32). He was advised by Jeremiah not to succumb to the temptations of ambition but to be content with his lot (ch. 45). He also received from Jeremiah and deposited for safekeeping a deed of purchase (32:11–16), and accompanied the prophet on the long road to exile in Egypt (43:6–7). It is possible that Baruch was also responsible for the final compilation of the book of Jeremiah itself, since no event recorded in chs. 1—51 occurred after 580 B.C. (ch. 52 is an appendix added by a later hand).

Given to self-analysis and self-criticism (10:24), Jeremiah has revealed a great deal about his character and personality. Although timid by nature (1:6), he received the Lord's assurance that he would become strong and courageous (1:18; 6:27; 15:20). In his "confessions" (11:18–23; 12:1–4; 15:10–21; 17:12–18; 18:18–23; 20:7–18) he laid bare the deep struggles of his innermost being, sometimes making startlingly honest statements about his feelings toward God (12:1; 15:18). On occasion, he engaged in calling for redress against his personal enemies (12:1–3; 15:15; 17:18; 18:19–23)—a practice that explains the origin of the English word "jeremiad," referring to a denunciatory tirade or complaint. Jeremiah, so often characterized by anguish of spirit (4:19; 9:1; 10:19–20; 23:9), has often been called the "weeping prophet." It should also be pointed out that his "Book of Comfort" in chs 30–33 is placed in the middle to emphasize his message of hope. It is also true that the memory of his divine call (1:17) and the Lord's frequent reaffirmations of his commissioning as a prophet (see, e.g., 3:12; 7:2,27–28; 11:2,6; 13:12–13; 17:19–20) made Jeremiah fearless in the service of his God (cf. 15:20).

Background

Jeremiah began prophesying in Judah halfway through the reign of Josiah (640–609 B.C.) and continued throughout the reigns of Jehoahaz (609), Jehoiakim (609–598), Jehoiachin (598–597) and Zedekiah (597–586). It was a period of storm and stress when the doom of entire nations—including Judah itself—was being sealed. The smaller states of western Asia were often pawns in the power plays of such imperial giants as Egypt, Assyria and Babylon, and the time of Jeremiah's ministry was no exception. Ashurbanipal, last of the great Assyrian rulers, died in 627. His successors were no match for Nabopolassar, the founder of the Neo-Babylonian empire, who began his rule in 626 (the year of Jeremiah's call to prophesy). Soon after Assyria's capital city Nineveh fell under the onslaught of a coalition of Babylonians and Medes in 612, Egypt (no friend of Babylon) marched northward in

an attempt to rescue Assyria, which was near destruction. King Josiah of Judah made the mistake of trying to stop the Egyptian advance, and his untimely death near Megiddo in 609 at the hands of Pharaoh Neco II was the sad result (2 Chr 35:20–24). Jeremiah, who had found a kindred spirit in the godly Josiah and had perhaps proclaimed the messages recorded in 11:1–8; 17:19–27 during the king's reformation movement, lamented Josiah's death (2 Chr 35:25).

Josiah's son Jehoahaz (his throne name; see note on 22:11), also known as Shallum, is mentioned only briefly in the book of Jeremiah (22:10b-12), and then in an unfavorable way. Neco put Jehoahaz in chains and made Eliakim, another of Josiah's sons, king in his place, renaming him Jehoiakim. Jehoahaz had ruled for a scant three months (2 Chr 36:2), and his reign marks the turning point in the court's attitude toward Jeremiah. Once the king's friend and confidant, the prophet now entered a dreary round of persecution and imprisonment, alternating with only brief periods of freedom (20:1–2; 26:8–9; 32:2–3; 33:1; 36:26; 37:12–21; 38:6–13,28).

Jehoiakim was relentlessly hostile toward Jeremiah. On one occasion, when an early draft of the prophet's writings was being read to Jehoiakim (36:21), the king used a scribe's knife to cut the scroll apart, three or four columns at a time, and threw it piece by piece into the firepot in his winter apartment (vv. 22–23). At the Lord's command, however, Jeremiah simply dictated his prophecies to Baruch a second time, adding "many like words" to them (v. 32).

Just prior to this episode in Jeremiah's life, an event of extraordinary importance took place that changed the course of history: In 605 B.C., the Egyptians were crushed at Carchemish on the Euphrates by Nebuchadnezzar (46:2), the gifted general who succeeded his father Nabopolassar as ruler of Babylon that same year. Neco returned to Egypt with heavy losses, and Babylon was given a virtually free hand in western Asia for the next 70 years. Nebuchadnezzar besieged Jerusalem in 605, humiliating Jehoiakim (Dan 1:1–2) and carrying off Daniel and his three companions to Babylon (Dan 1:3–6). Later, in 598–597, Nebuchadnezzar attacked Jerusalem again, and the rebellious Jehoiakim was heard of no more. His son Jehoiachin ruled Judah for only three months (2 Chr 36:9). Jeremiah foretold the captivity of Jehoiachin and his followers (22:24–30), a prediction that was later fulfilled (24:1; 29:1–2).

Mattaniah, Jehoiachin's uncle and a son of Josiah, was renamed Zedekiah and placed on Judah's throne by Nebuchadnezzar in 597 B.C. (37:1; 2 Chr 36:9–14). Zedekiah, a weak and vacillating ruler, sometimes befriended Jeremiah and sought his advice but at other times allowed the prophet's enemies to mistreat and imprison him. Near the end of Zedekiah's reign, Jeremiah entered into an agreement with him to reveal God's will to him in exchange for his own personal safety (38:15–27). Even then the prophet was under virtual house arrest until Jerusalem was captured in 586 (38:28).

While trying to flee the city, Zedekiah was overtaken by the pursuing Babylonians. In his presence his sons were executed, after which he himself was blinded by Nebuchadnezzar (39:1–7). Nebuzaradan, commander of the imperial guard, advised Jeremiah to live with Gedaliah, whom Nebuchadnezzar had made governor over Judah (40:1–6). After a brief rule Gedaliah was murdered by his opponents (ch. 41). Others in Judah feared Babylonian reprisal and fled to Egypt, taking Jeremiah and Baruch with them (43:4–7). By that time the prophet was probably over 70 years old. His last recorded words are found in 44:24–30, the last verse of which is the only explicit reference in the Bible to Pharaoh-hophra, who ruled Egypt from 589 to 570 B.C.

Themes and Message

Referred to frequently as "Jeremiah the prophet" in the book that bears his name (20:2; 25:2; 28:5,10–12,15; 29:1,29; 32:2; 34:6; 36:8,26; 37:2,3,6; 38:9–10,14; 42:2,4; 43:6; 45:1; 46:1,13; 47:1; 49:34; 50:1) and elsewhere (2 Chr 36:12; Dan 9:2; Mat 2:17; 27:9; see Mat 16:14), Jeremiah was ever conscious of his call from the Lord (1:5; 15:19) to be a prophet. As such, he proclaimed words that were spoken first by God Himself (19:2) and were therefore certain of fulfillment (28:9; 32:24). Jeremiah had only contempt for false prophets (14:13–18; 23:13–40; 27:14–18) like Hananiah (ch. 28) and Shemaiah (29:24–32). Many of his own predictions were fulfilled in the short term (e.g., 16:15; 20:4; 25:11–14; 27:19–22; 29:10; 34:4–5; 43:10–11; 44:30; 46:13), and others were—or will yet be—fulfilled in the long term (e.g., 23:5–6; 30:8–9; 31:31–34; 33:15–16).

As hinted earlier, an aura of conflict surrounded Jeremiah almost from the beginning. He lashed out against the sins of his countrymen (44:23), scoring them severely for their idolatry (16:10–13,20; 22:9; 32:29; 44:2–3,8,17–19,25)—which sometimes even involved sacrificing their children to foreign gods (see 7:30–34 and notes). But Jeremiah loved the people of Judah in spite of their sins, and he prayed for them (14:7,20) even when the Lord told him not to (7:16; 11:14; 14:11).

Judgment is one of the all-pervasive themes in Jeremiah's writings, though he was careful to point out that repentance, if sincere, would postpone the inevitable. His counsel of submission to Babylon and his message of "life as usual" for the exiles of the early deportations branded him as a traitor in the eyes of many. Actually, of course, his advice against rebellion marked him as a true patriot, a man who loved his countrymen too much to stand by silently and watch them destroy themselves. By warning them to submit and not rebel, Jeremiah was revealing God's will to them—always the most sensible prospect under any circumstances.

For Jeremiah, God was ultimate. The prophet's theology conceived of the Lord as the Creator of all that exists (10:12–16; 51:15–19), as all-powerful (32:27; 48:15; 51:57), as everywhere present (23:24). Jeremiah ascribed the most elevated attributes to the God whom he served (32:17–25), viewing Him as the Lord not only of Judah but also of the nations (5:15; 18:7–10; 25:17–28; chs. 46—51).

At the same time, God is very much concerned about individual people and their accountability to Him. Jeremiah's emphasis in this regard (see, e.g., 31:29–30) is similar to that of Ezekiel (see Ezek 18:2–4), and the two men have become known as the "prophets of individual responsibility." The undeniable relationship between sin and its consequences, so visible to Jeremiah as he watched his beloved Judah in her death throes, made him—in the pursuit of his divine vocation—a fiery preacher (5:14; 20:9; 23:29) of righteousness, and his oracles have lost none of their power with the passing of the centuries.

Called to the unhappy task of announcing the destruction of the kingdom of Judah (thoroughly corrupted by the long and evil reign of Manasseh and only superficially affected by Josiah's efforts at reform), it was Jeremiah's commission to lodge God's indictment against His people and proclaim the end of an era. At long last, the Lord was about to inflict on the remnant of His people the ultimate covenant curse (see Lev 26:31–33; Deut 28:49–68). He would undo all that He had done for them since the day He brought them out of Egypt. It would then seem that the end had come, that Israel's stubborn and uncircumcised (unconsecrated) heart had sealed her final destiny, that God's chosen people had been cast off, that all the ancient promises and covenants had come to nothing.

But God's judgment of His people (and the nations), though terrible, was not to be the last word, the final work of God in history. Mercy and covenant faithfulness would triumph over wrath. Beyond the judgment would come restoration and renewal. Israel would be restored, the nations that crushed her would be crushed, and the old covenants (with Israel, David and the Levites) would be honored. God would make a new covenant with His people in which He would write His law on their hearts (31:31–34) and thus consecrate them to His service. The house of David would rule them in righteousness, and faithful priests would serve. God's commitment to Israel's redemption was as unfailing as the secure order of creation (ch. 33).

Jeremiah's message illumined the distant as well as the near horizon. It was false prophets who proclaimed peace to a rebellious nation, as though the God of Israel's peace was indifferent to her unfaithfulness. But the very God who compelled Jeremiah to denounce sin and pronounce judgment was the God who authorized him to announce that the divine wrath had its bounds, its 70 years. Afterward forgiveness and cleansing would come—and a new day, in which all the old expectations, aroused by God's past acts and His promises and covenants, would yet be fulfilled in a manner transcending all God's mercies of old.

Literary Features

Jeremiah is the longest book in the Bible, containing more words than any other book. Although a number of chapters were written mainly in prose (chs. 7; 11; 16; 19; 21; 24—29; 32—45), including the appendix (ch. 52), many sections are predominantly poetic in form. Jeremiah's poetry is as lofty and lyrical as any found elsewhere in Scripture. A creator of beautiful phrases, he has given us an abundance of memorable passages (e.g., 2:13,26–28; 7:4,11,34; 8:20,22; 9:23–24; 10:6–7,10,12–13; 13:23; 15:20; 17:5–9; 20:13; 29:13; 30:7,22; 31:3,15,29–30,31–34; 33:3; 51:10).

Poetic repetition was used by Jeremiah with particular skill (see, e.g., 4:23–26; 51:20–23). He understood the effectiveness of repeating a striking phrase over and over. An example, "by the sword, and by the famine, and by the pestilence," is found in 15 separate verses (14:12; 21:7,9; 24:10; 27:8,13; 29:17–18; 32:24,36; 34:17; 38:2; 42:17,22; 44:13). He made use of cryptograms (see notes on 25:26; 51:1,41) on appropriate occasions. Alliteration and assonance were also a part of his

literary style, examples being *zarim wezeruha* ("fanners, that shall fan her." 51:2) and *paḥad wapaḥat wapaḥ* ("Fear, and the pit, and the snare," 48:43; see note on Is 24:17).

Like Ezekiel, Jeremiah was often instructed to use symbolism to highlight his message: a ruined and useless girdle (13:1–11), a smashed earthen jar (19:1–12), a yoke of straps and crossbars (ch. 27), large stones in a brick pavement (43:8–13). Symbolic value is also seen in the Lord's commands to Jeremiah not to marry and raise children (16:1–4), not to enter a house where there is a funeral meal or where there is feasting (16:5–9), and to buy a field in his hometown, Anathoth (32:6–15). Similarly, the Lord used visual aids in conveying his message to Jeremiah: potter's clay (18:1–10), two baskets of figs (ch. 24).

Outline

Unlike Ezekiel, the oracles in Jeremiah are not arranged in chronological order. Had they been so arranged, the sequence of sections within the book would have been approximately as follows: 1:1—7:15; ch. 26; 7:16—20:18; ch. 25; chs. 46—51; 36:1–8; ch. 45; 36:9–32; ch. 35; chs. 21—24; chs. 27—31; 34:1–7; 37:1–10; 34:8–22; 37:11—38:13; 39:15–18; chs. 32–33; 38:14—39:14; 52:1–30; chs. 40—44; 52:31–34. The outline below represents an analysis of the book of Jeremiah in its present canonical order.

- I. Call of the Prophet (ch. 1)
- II. Warnings and Exhortations to Judah (chs. 2—35)
  - A. Earliest Discourses (chs. 2—6)
  - B. Temple Message (chs. 7—10)
  - C. Covenant and Conspiracy (chs. 11—13)
  - D. Messages concerning the Drought (chs. 14—15)
  - E. Disaster and Comfort (16:1—17:18)
  - F. Command to Keep the Sabbath Holy (17:19–27)
  - G. Lessons from the Potter (chs. 18—20)
  - H. Condemnation of Kings, Prophets and People (chs. 21—24)
  - I. Foretelling the Babylonian Exile (chs. 25—29)
  - J. Promises of Restoration (chs. 30—33)
  - K. Historical Appendix (chs. 34—35)
- III. Sufferings and Persecutions of the Prophet (chs. 36—38)
  - A. Burning Jeremiah's Roll (ch. 36)
  - B. Imprisoning Jeremiah (chs. 37—38)
- IV. The Fall of Jerusalem and Its Aftermath (chs. 39—45)
  - A. The Fall Itself (ch. 39)
  - B. Accession and Assassination of Gedaliah (40:1—41:15)
  - C. Migration to Egypt (41:16—43:13)
  - D. Prophecy against Those in Egypt (ch. 44)
  - E. Historical Appendix: Promise to Baruch (ch. 45)
- V. Judgment against the Nations (chs. 46—51)
  - A. Against Egypt (ch. 46)
  - B. Against Philistia (ch. 47)
  - C. Against Moab (ch. 48)
  - D. Against Ammon (49:1–6)
  - E. Against Edom (49:7–22)
  - F. Against Damascus (49:23–27)
  - G. Against Kedar and Hazor (Arabia) (49:28–33)
  - H. Against Elam (49:34–39)
  - I. Against Babylon (chs. 50—51)
- VI. Historical Appendix (ch. 52)

The prophet's call

1 The words of Jeremiah the son of Hilkiah, of the priests that *were* [a]in Anathoth
in the land of Benjamin:
2 To whom the word of the LORD came in
the days of Josiah the son of Amon king of Judah, [a]in the thirteenth year of his reign.
3 It came also in the days of Jehoiakim the
son of Josiah king of Judah, [a]unto the end of
the eleventh year of Zedekiah the son of Josiah
king of Judah, [b]unto the carrying away of Jerusalem captive [c]in the fifth month.
4 ¶ Then the word of the LORD came unto
me, saying,
5 Before I [a]formed thee in the belly [b]I
knew thee; and before thou camest forth out
of the womb I [c]sanctified thee, *and* I [1]or-
dained thee a prophet unto the nations.
6 Then said I, [a]Ah, Lord GOD, behold, I
cannot speak: for I *am* a child.
7 But the LORD said unto me, Say not, I *am*
a child: for thou shalt go to all that I shall send
thee, and [a]whatsoever I command thee thou
shalt speak.
8 [a]Be not afraid of their faces: for [b]I *am*
with thee to deliver thee, saith the LORD.
9 Then the LORD put forth his hand, and
[a]touched my mouth. And the LORD said unto
me, Behold, I have [b]put my words in thy
mouth.
10 [a]See, I have this day set thee over the
nations and over the kingdoms, to [b]root out,
and to pull down, and to destroy, and to throw
down, to build, and to plant.
11 ¶ Moreover, the word of the LORD came
unto me, saying, Jeremiah, what seest thou?
And I said, I see a rod of an almond tree.

1:1 [a]Josh. 21:18; 1 Chr. 6:60; ch. 32:7,8
1:2 [a]ch. 25:3
1:3 [a]ch. 39:2 [b]ch. 52:12 [c]2 Ki. 25:8
1:5 [1]Heb. *gave* [a]Is. 49:1,5 [b]Ex. 33:12 [c]Luke 1:15; Gal. 1:15
1:6 [a]Ex. 4:10; 6:12,30
1:7 [a]Num. 22:20,38; Mat. 28:20
1:8 [a]Ezek. 2:6; 3:9 [b]Ex. 3:12; Deut. 31:6; Josh. 1:5; ch. 15:20; Acts 26:17; Heb. 13:6
1:9 [a]Is. 6:7 [b]Is. 51:16; ch. 5:14
1:10 [a]1 Ki. 19:17 [b]ch. 18:7; 2 Cor. 10:4

1:1–3 The background and setting of Jeremiah's call are stated concisely but comprehensively.

1:1 *The words of.* See 36:10; see also Neh 1:1; Eccl 1:1; Amos 1:1; cf. Deut 1:1. *Jeremiah.* For the meaning of the name see Introduction: Author and Date. Nine other OT men had the same name (see 1 Chr 5:24; 12:4,10,13; Neh 10:2; 12:1,34), two of whom were the prophet's contemporaries (Jer 35:3; 52:1). *Hilkiah.* Means "The LORD is my portion." For Hilkiah's possible relationship to a priestly house dating back to King Solomon see Introduction: Author and Date. Two other men named Hilkiah (a common OT name) were also Jeremiah's contemporaries (see 29:3; Ezra 7:1 and note). *priests.* Like Ezekiel (Ezek 1:3) and Zechariah (see Introduction to Zechariah: Author), Jeremiah was both prophet and priest. *Anathoth.* See 11:21–23; 32:6–9. The Hebrew word is the plural form of the name of the Canaanite deity Anat(h), goddess of war. Anathoth had had priestly connections in Israel as early as the times of Joshua (Josh 21:18) and Solomon (1 Ki 2:26), and its pagan origins had presumably been almost forgotten by Jeremiah's time. Present-day Anata, three miles northeast of Jerusalem, preserves the ancient name, though the ancient site was about half a mile southwest of Anata. *Benjamin.* Anathoth was one of the four Levitical towns in the tribal territory of Benjamin (Josh 21:17–18), and after the exile Benjamites settled there again (Neh 11:31–32).

1:2 *To whom.* Beginning in v. 4, Jeremiah speaks in the first person (see, e.g., vv. 11,13; 2:1). *the word of the LORD came.* The most common way of introducing a divine oracle at the beginning of a prophetic book (see Ezek 1:3; Jonah 1:1; Hag 1:1; Zech 1:1; cf. Hos 1:1; Joel 1:1; Mic 1:1; Zeph 1:1). *Josiah.* See 3:6; 36:2. He was the last good and godly king of Judah. Jeremiah sympathized with and supported his attempts at spiritual reformation and renewal (see 22:15b–16), which began in earnest in 621 (see 2 Ki 22:3–23:25; 2 Chr 34:8–35:19; cf. 2 Chr 34:3–7). *thirteenth year.* 626 B.C. (see 25:3).

1:3 *Jehoiakim.* His predecessor (Jehoahaz) and successor (Jehoiachin) are not mentioned, since they each reigned only three months. In contrast to his father Josiah, Jehoiakim was a wicked ruler (see 2 Ki 23:36–37; 2 Chr 36:5)—as Jeremiah discovered almost immediately (see Introduction: Background; see also 22:13–15a,17–19; 26:20–23). *eleventh year . . . in the fifth month.* Ab (July-August), 586 B.C. (see 52:12). *Zedekiah.* The last king of Judah (see Introduction: Background), as wicked in his own way as Jehoiakim (see 52:1–2; 2 Chr 36:11–14; see also Jer 24:8; 37:1–2). *captive.* The main captivity of Judah's people coincided with the destruction of Jerusalem and Solomon's temple by Nebuchadnezzar in 586 (see 2 Ki 25:8–11).

1:4–19 The account of Jeremiah's call includes two prophetic visions (vv. 10–16) and some closing words of exhortation and encouragement (vv. 17–19).

1:4 See note on v. 2.

1:5 See Judg 13:5; Gal 1:15. *I formed thee.* See Is 49:5. God's creative act (see Gen 2:7; Ps 119:73) is the basis of His sovereign right (see 18:4–6; Is 43:21) to call Jeremiah into His service. *I knew thee.* In the sense of making Jeremiah the object of His choice. The Hebrew verb used here can be translated "chose" (Gen 18:19); in Amos 3:2 it is rendered "known." *I ordained thee.* The Hebrew for this verb is not the same as that in v. 10, but both refer to the commissioning of the prophet. *prophet.* Lit. "one who has been called" to be God's spokesman (see Ex 7:1–2; 1 Sam 9:9 and notes). *nations.* Although Judah's neighbors are probably the primary focus (see 25:8–38; chs. 46–51), Judah herself is not excluded.

1:6 *I cannot speak* Like Moses (Ex 4:10), Jeremiah claimed inability to be a prophet; God nevertheless made him His spokesman (15:l9) *a child.* See 1 Ki 3:7. Jeremiah's objection is denied immediately by the Lord (v. 7).

1:7 Youth and inexperience do not disqualify when God calls (see 1 Tim 4:12); He equips and sustains those He commissions.

1:8 *Be not afraid.* See 10:5; 30:10; 40:9; 42:11; 46:27–28; 51:46; see also Is 35:4 and note; 41:10. *I am with thee.* See v. 19; 15:20. God's promise of His continuing presence should calm the fears of the most reluctant of prophets (see Ex 3:12; see also note on Gen 26:3). *deliver.* See v. 19; 15:20; 39:17. The Lord does not promise that Jeremiah will not be persecuted or imprisoned, but that no serious physical harm will come to him.

1:9 *touched my mouth.* Either in prophetic vision (see note on v. 11) or figuratively—or both (cf. Is 6:7). *I have put my words in thy mouth.* Continues the figure of speech begun earlier in the verse and provides a classic description of the relationship between the Lord and His prophet (see 5:14; Ex 4:15; Num 22:38; 23:5,12,16; Deut 18:18; Is 51:16; cf. 2 Pet 1:21).

‡1:10 *set thee.* See note on v. 5. *to root out . . . pull down . . . destroy . . . throw down . . . build . . . plant.* See 12:14–15,17; 18:7–10; 24:6; 31:28; 42:10; 45:4. The first two pairs of verbs are negative, stressing the fact that Jeremiah is to be primarily a prophet of doom, while the last pair is positive, indicating that he is also to be a prophet of restoration—even if only secondarily. The first verb ("root out") is the opposite of the last ("plant"), and fully half of the verbs ("pull down," "destroy," "throw down") are the opposite of "build."

1:11 *what seest thou?* Often spoken by the Lord (or His representative) to introduce a prophetic vision (see v. 13; Amos 7:8; 8:2; Zech 4:2; 5:2).

12 Then said the LORD unto me, Thou hast well seen: for I will hasten my word to perform it.

13 And the word of the LORD came unto me the second time, saying, What seest thou? And I said, I see [a]a seething pot; and the face thereof *is* [1]towards the north.

14 Then the LORD said unto me, Out of the [a]north an evil [1]shall break forth upon all the inhabitants of the land.

15 For lo, I will [a]call all the families of the kingdoms of the north, saith the LORD; and they shall come, and they shall [b]set every one his throne *at* the entering of the gates of Jerusalem, and against all the walls thereof round about, and against all the cities of Judah.

16 And I will utter my judgments against them touching all their wickedness, [a]who have forsaken me, and have burnt incense unto other gods, and worshipped the works of their own hands.

17 Thou therefore [a]gird up thy loins, and arise, and speak unto them all that I command thee: [b]be not dismayed at their faces, lest I [1]confound thee before them.

18 For behold, I have made thee *this* day [a]a defenced city, and an iron pillar, and brasen walls against the whole land, against the kings of Judah, against the princes thereof, against the priests thereof, and against the people of the land.

19 And they shall fight against thee; but they shall not prevail against thee; [a]for I *am* with thee, saith the LORD, to deliver thee.

Israel's faithlessness

2 Moreover the word of the LORD came to me, saying,

2 Go and cry in the ears of Jerusalem, saying, Thus saith the LORD; I remember [1]thee, the kindness of thy [a]youth, the love of thine espousals, [b]when thou wentest after me in the wilderness, in a land *that was* not sown.

3 [a]Israel *was* holiness unto the LORD, *and* [b]the firstfruits of his increase: [c]all that devour him shall offend; evil shall come upon them, saith the LORD.

4 Hear ye the word of the LORD, O house of Jacob, and all the families of the house of Israel:

5 Thus saith the LORD, [a]What iniquity have your fathers found in me, that they are gone far from me, [b]and have walked after vanity, and are become vain?

1:13 [1] Heb. *from the face of the north* [a] Ezek. 11:3; 24:3
1:14 [1] Heb. *shall be opened* [a] ch. 6:1
1:15 [a] ch. 6:22 [b] ch. 39:3
1:16 [a] Deut. 28:20; ch. 17:13
1:17 [1] Or, *break to pieces* [a] 2 Ki. 4:29; Job 38:3; Luke 12:35; 1 Pet. 1:13 [b] Ex. 3:12; Ezek. 2:6
1:18 [a] Is. 50:7; ch. 6:27; 15:20
1:19 [a] ver. 8
2:2 [1] Or, *for thy sake* [a] Ezek. 16:8,22,60; 23:3,8; Hos. 2:15 [b] Deut. 2:7
2:3 [a] Ex. 19:5,6 [b] Jas. 1:18; Rev. 14:4 [c] ch. 12:14; See ch. 50:7
2:5 [a] Is. 5:4; Mic. 6:3 [b] 2 Ki. 17:15; Jonah 2:8

‡1:12 *hasten.* The Hebrew for "hasten" sounds like the Hebrew for "almond tree." Just as the almond tree blooms first in the year (and therefore "wakes up" early—the Hebrew word for "hasten" means to be wakeful), so the Lord is ever quick to make sure that His word is fulfilled.

1:13 *pot.* The Hebrew for "pot" stresses its large size (see Job 41:31; Ezek 24:3–5).

‡1:14 *Out of the north an evil.* See note on Is 41:25. *shall break forth.* The Hebrew for this word has a similar sound to that for "seething" in v. 13. *land.* Judah (see v. 15).

1:15 *kingdoms of the north.* Since Assyria posed a minimal threat to Judah after the death of Ashurbanipal in 627 B.C., reference is most likely to Babylon and her allies. *set every one his throne at . . . the gates of Jerusalem.* For the fulfillment see 39:3. Since the gateway of a city was the place where its ruling council sat (see notes on Gen 19:1; Ruth 4:1), the Babylonians replaced Judah's royal authority with their own (cf. 43:10; 49:38).

1:16 *my judgments against them.* God, sovereign over His own, judges His own for their sins, using the Babylonians as His agents of judgment. *burnt incense unto other gods.* A common feature of pagan worship (e.g., 7:9; 11:12–13,17; 18:15; 19:13; 32:29; 44:17). *the works of their own hands.* Idols (see 16:19–20; 25:6; 2 Ki 22:17; 2 Chr 33:22; Is 46:6).

1:17 *gird up thy loins.* Meaning "get yourself ready." For related expressions see Ex 12:11; 1 Ki 18:46; 2 Ki 4:29; 9:1; Job 38:3; 40:7.

‡1:18 *defenced city.* A symbol of security and impregnability (see 5:17; Prov 18:11,19). *iron pillar.* Unique in the OT, the expression signifies dignity and strength. *brasen walls.* See 15:20. Jeremiah would be able to withstand the abuse and persecution that his divine commission would evoke, even though his enemies themselves would be "brass and iron" (6:28). *kings . . . princes . . . priests . . . people.* The whole nation would defy the prophet and his God (see, e.g., 2:26; 23:8; 32:32).

1:19 See note on v. 8; see also 15:20.

2:1–6:30 It is generally agreed that these chapters are among Jeremiah's earliest discourses, delivered during the reign of Josiah (3:6). The basic theme is the virtually total apostasy of Judah (chs. 2–5), leading inevitably to divine retribution through foreign invasion (ch. 6).

2:1–3:5 The wickedness and backsliding of God's people are vividly portrayed in numerous colorful figures of speech.

2:1 See note on 1:2.

‡2:2 *kindness.* Or "devotion," referring to the most intimate degree of loyalty, love and faithfulness that can exist between two people or between an individual and the Lord. *youth . . . thine espousals.* Early in her history, Israel had enjoyed a close and cordial relationship with the Lord, who is often described figuratively as Israel's husband (3:14; 31:32; Is 54:5; Hos 2:16). *love.* But later God's people forsook Him and loved "strangers" (foreign gods, v. 25), tragically abandoning their first love (cf. Rev 2:4). *wentest after me.* But later they followed "vanity" (v. 5) following after "Baalim" (v. 23). *wilderness.* Sinai (see v. 6).

2:3 *holiness unto the LORD.* Set apart to Him and His service (see notes on Ex 3:5; Lev 11:44; Deut 7:6). *the firstfruits.* Just as the "choice firstfruits" of Israel's crops were to be brought to the Lord (Ex 23:19; see Num 18:12; 2 Chr 31:5; Ezek 44:30), so also the people themselves were His first and choicest treasure (cf. Jas 1:18; Rev 14:4). *evil shall come upon them.* See, e.g., Ex 17:8–16.

2:4 *Hear.* A common divine imperative in prophetic writings, summoning God's people—as well as the nations—into His courts to remind them of their legal obligations to Him and, when necessary, to pass judgment on them (see, e.g., 7:2; 17:20; 19:3; 21:11; 22:2,29; 31:10; 42:15; 44:24,26; Is 1:10; Ezek 13:2; Hos 4:1; Amos 7:16).

2:5 *Thus saith the LORD.* The so-called messenger formula, introducing God's word through the prophet. Though frequent in overall occurrence, its use is restricted to Jeremiah, Isaiah (e.g., 7:7), Ezekiel (e.g., 2:4), Amos (e.g., 1:3), Obadiah (1), Micah (3:5), Nahum (1:12), Haggai (e.g., 1:2), Zechariah (e.g., 1:3) and Malachi (1:4). *gone far from.* See 4:1; 23:13,32; 31:19; 50:6; Is 53:6; Ezek 34:4–6,16; 1 Pet 2:25. *walked after vanity.* See vv. 8,23; see also note on v. 2. Jeremiah describes the objects of Israel's idolatry in a variety of ways (8:19; 10:8,15; 14:22; 16:19; 51:18). *are become vain.* See 2 Ki 17:15. Idolaters are no better than the idols they worship (see Ps 115:8).

6 Neither said they, Where *is* the LORD that
[a]brought us up out of the land of Egypt, that
led us through [b]the wilderness, through a land
of deserts and of pits, through a land of
drought, and of the shadow of death, through
a land that no man passed through, and where
no man dwelt?
7 And I brought you into [a][1]a plentiful country, to eat the fruit thereof and the goodness
thereof; but when ye entered, ye [b]defiled my
land, and made mine heritage an abomination.
8 The priests said not, Where *is* the LORD?
and they that handle the [a]law knew me not:
the pastors also transgressed against me, [b]and
the prophets prophesied by Baal, and walked
after *things that* do not profit.
9 Wherefore [a]I will yet plead with you,
saith the LORD, and with your children's children will I plead.
10 For pass [1]over the isles of Chittim, and
see; and send *unto* Kedar, and consider diligently, and see if there be such a *thing.*
11 [a]Hath a nation changed *their* gods,
which *are* [b]yet no gods? [c]but my people have
changed their glory for *that which* doth not
profit.
12 Be astonished, O ye heavens, at this,
and be horribly afraid, be ye very desolate,
saith the LORD.

2:6 [a]Is. 63:9 [b]Deut. 8:15
2:7 [1][Or, *the land of Carmel*] [a]Num. 13:27 [b]Num. 35:33
2:8 [a]Rom. 2:20 [b]ch. 23:13
2:9 [a]Ezek. 20:35,36; Mic. 6:2
2:10 [1]Or, *over to*
2:11 [a]Mic. 4:5 [b]Ps. 115:4; Is. 37:19 [c]Ps. 106:20; Rom. 1:23
2:13 [a]Ps. 36:9; John 4:14
2:14 [1]Heb. *become a spoil?* [a]Ex. 4:22
2:15 [1]Heb. *gave out their voice* [a]Is. 1:7
2:16 [1]Or, *feed on thy crown* [a]ch. 43:7-9
2:17 [a]ch. 4:18 [b]Deut. 32:10
2:18 [a]Is. 30:1,2 [b]Josh. 13:3
2:20 [1]Or, *serve* [a]Judg. 10:16 [b]Deut. 12:2 [c]Ex. 34:15

13 For my people have committed two
evils; they have forsaken me the [a]fountain of
living waters, and hewed them out cisterns,
broken cisterns, that can hold no water.
14 ¶ *Is* Israel [a]a servant? *is* he a homeborn
slave? why is he [1]spoiled?
15 [a]The young lions roared upon him, *and*
[1]yelled, and they made his land waste: his cities are burnt without inhabitant.
16 Also the children of Noph and [a]Taha-
panes [1]have broken the crown of thy head.
17 [a]Hast thou not procured this unto thyself, in that thou hast forsaken the LORD thy
God, when [b]he led thee by the way?
18 And now what hast thou to do [a]in the
way of Egypt, to drink the waters of [b]Sihor? or
what hast thou to do in the way of Assyria, to
drink the waters of the river?
19 Thine own wickedness shall correct
thee, and thy backslidings shall reprove thee:
know therefore and see that *it is* an evil *thing*
and bitter, that thou hast forsaken the LORD
thy God, and *that* my fear *is* not in thee, saith
the Lord GOD of hosts.
20 For of old time I have broken thy yoke,
and burst thy bands; and [a]thou saidst, I will
not [1]transgress; when [b]upon every high hill
and under every green tree thou wanderest,
[c]playing the harlot.

2:6 *LORD . . . brought us up out of . . . Egypt.* The Lord, Israel's Redeemer (see notes on Gen 2:4; Ex 3:15), freed His people from Egyptian bondage so that they might serve Him alone (Ex 20:2–6). *led us.* As a shepherd leads his sheep (see v. 17; Deut 8:15; Ps 23:2–3). *land of deserts . . . land of . . . shadow of death.* The desert often symbolized darkness with its attendant dangers, including death (v. 31; 9:10; 12:12; 17:6; 23:10; Ps 44:19).
2:7 *plentiful.* The Hebrew for this word is *karmel,* translated "plentiful field" in 48:33 and also used as the name of a place (see Is 33:9 and note). Rendered "fruitful place" in 4:26, it is the opposite of a desert. *defiled my land.* Made it ceremonially unclean (see 3:1–2,9; 16:18; see also note on Lev 4:12). *heritage.* The promised land, given by God to Israel as a legacy and often intimately associated with the people themselves (see especially 12:7–9,14–15). *abomination.* See note on Lev 7:21.
2:8 No one consulted the Lord (see v. 6). *priests . . . pastors . . . prophets.* See note on 1:18. *they that handle the law.* Priests (see Deut 31:11 and note). *pastors.* Lit. "shepherds," a term used elsewhere to denote rulers (23:1–4; 49:19; 50:44; see especially Ezek 34:1–10,23–24). *by Baal.* In the name of Baal (cf. 11:21; 14:15; 23:25; 26:9). *that do not profit.* See v. 11.
2:9 *plead with.* See note on v. 4; see also 25:31; Hos 4:1; 12:2; Mic 6:2.
2:10 *Chittim.* Represents the western nations and regions. *Kedar.* Represents the eastern nations and regions (see 49:28; Is 21:16 and note).
2:11 *Hath . . . gods?* A rhetorical question, clearly expecting a negative answer and emphasizing how incredible is Judah's practice of substituting idolatry for the worship of the Lord. *their glory.* God (see Ps 106:20; Hos 4:7; see also 1 Sam 15:29). *that which doth not profit.* See v. 8.
2:12 *Be atonished, O ye heavens.* See note on Is 1:2; see also Mic 6:1–2 and note. The Hebrew for these phrases offers a striking play on words: *shommu shamayim.*
2:13 See 1:16. *me the fountain of living waters.* See 17:13. God Himself provides life-giving power to His people (see Ps 36:9; see also note on John 4:10; Is 55:1 and note; Rev 21:6). *broken cisterns.* Watertight plaster was used to keep cisterns from losing water. Idols, like broken cisterns, will always fail their worshipers; by contrast, God provides life abundant and unfailing.
2:14 *Is . . . servant?* Rhetorical questions (see note on v. 11), again expecting a negative answer in the light of God's redemptive acts during the period of the exodus (see Ex 6:6; 20:2). *spoiled.* To Assyria and Egypt (see vv. 15–16).
2:15 *lions.* Possibly literal (see 2 Ki 17:25–26), though probably here symbolizing Assyria (see v. 18; 50:17; see also notes on 4:7; Is 15:9). *roared . . . yelled.* See Amos 3:4. *made his land waste.* See 4:7; 18:16; 50:3. *cities are burnt.* The Hebrew for this phrase is very similar to that in 4:7, rendered there "cities shall be laid waste, without an inhabitant" (cf. 22:6).
2:16 *Noph.* See 44:1; 46:14,19; see also note on Is 19:13. *Tahapanes.* Probably the city later called Daphnai by the Greeks, located just south of Lake Menzaleh in the eastern delta region of Egypt and known today as Tell Defneh (see 43:7–9; 44:1; 46:14; Ezek 30:18). *broken the crown of thy head.* Figurative for bringing disgrace and devastation (see 47:5; 48:37; see also notes on Is 3:17; 7:20).
2:17 *he led thee.* See note on v. 6. *the way.* See Ex 18:8; 23:20; Deut 1:33.
2:18 See v. 36. The tendency of Israel or Judah to seek help alternately from Egypt and Assyria was not restricted to Jeremiah's time (see, e.g., Hos 7:11; 12:2). *drink the waters.* Provided by enemies, whether national or spiritual, rather than by God (see v. 13; Is 8:6–8 and notes).
2:19 *backslidings.* See 3:22; 5:6; 14:7; repeated apostasy.
2:20–3:6 The rebellion of Judah against God is vividly portrayed by Jeremiah with the use of numerous figures of speech.
2:20 Like a stubborn draft animal (see Hos 4:16), Judah refuses to obey the Lord's commands. *broken thy yoke, and burst thy bands.* See 5:5; see also 31:18; cf. Ps 2:3. Judah has broken God's law and violated His covenant. *upon every high hill and under every green tree.* Locales of pagan worship (see 1 Ki 14:23; 2 Ki

21 Yet I had [a]planted thee a noble vine,
wholly a right seed: how then art thou turned
into [b]the degenerate plant of a strange vine
unto me?
22 For though thou wash thee with nitre,
and take thee much sope, *yet* thine iniquity *is*
marked before me, saith the Lord GOD.
23 [a]How canst thou say, I am not polluted,
I have not gone after Baalim? see thy way in
the valley, know what thou hast done: [1]*thou*
art a swift dromedary traversing her ways;
24 [1]A wild ass [2]used to the wilderness,
that snuffeth up the wind at [3]her pleasure; *in*
her occasion who can [4]turn her away? all they
that seek her will not weary themselves; in
her month they shall find her.
25 Withhold thy foot from being unshod,
and thy throat from thirst: but thou saidst,
[1]There is no hope: no; for I have loved
[a]strangers, and after them will I go.
26 As the thief is ashamed when he is
found, so is the house of Israel ashamed; they,
their kings, their princes, and their priests,
and their prophets,
27 Saying to a stock, Thou *art* my father;
and to a stone, Thou hast [1]brought me forth:
for they have turned [2]*their* back unto me, and
not *their* face: but in the time of their [a]trouble
they will say, Arise, and save us.
28 But [a]where *are* thy gods that thou hast
made thee? let them arise, if they [b]can save
thee in the time of thy [1]trouble: for [c]*accord-*
ing to the number of thy cities are thy gods,
O Judah.
29 Wherefore will ye plead with me? ye all
have transgressed against me, saith the LORD.
30 In vain have I [a]smitten your children;
they received no correction: your own sword
hath [b]devoured your prophets, like a destroying lion.
31 ¶ O generation, see ye the word of the
LORD. Have I been a wilderness unto Israel? a
land of darkness? wherefore say my people,
[1]We are lords; [a]we will come no more unto
thee?
32 Can a maid forget her ornaments, *or* a
bride her attire? yet my people [a]have forgotten
me days without number.
33 Why trimmest thou thy way to seek
love? therefore hast thou also taught the
wicked ones thy ways.
34 Also in thy skirts is found [a]the blood of
the souls of the poor innocents: I have not
found it by [1]secret search, but upon all these.
35 [a]Yet thou sayest, Because I am innocent, surely his anger shall turn from me. Behold, [b]I *will* plead with thee, [c]because thou
sayest, I have not sinned.
36 [a]Why gaddest thou about *so* much to
change thy way? [b]thou also shalt be ashamed
of Egypt, [c]as thou wast ashamed of Assyria.
37 Yea, thou shalt go forth from him, and
[a]thine hands upon thine head: for the LORD

2:21 [a]Ex. 15:17 [b]Is. 5:4
2:23 [1]Or, *O swift dromedary* [a]Prov. 30:12
2:24 [1]Or, *O wild ass, etc.* [2]Heb. *taught* [3]Heb. *the desire of her heart* [4]Or, *reverse it?*
2:25 [1]Or, *Is the case desperate?* [a]ch. 3:13
2:27 [1]Or, *begotten me* [2]Heb. *the hinder part of the neck* [a]Is. 26:16
2:28 [1]Heb. *evil* [a]Judg. 10:14 [b]Is. 45:20 [c]ch. 11:13
2:30 [a]Is. 9:13 [b]Acts 7:52
2:31 [1]Heb. *We have dominion* [a]Deut. 32:15
2:32 [a]Ps. 106:21
2:34 [1]Heb. *digging* [a]Ps. 106:38
2:35 [a]ver. 23,29 [b]ver. 9 [c]Prov. 28:13
2:36 [a]Hos. 12:1 [b]Is. 30:3 [c]2 Chr. 28:16
2:37 [a]2 Sam. 13:19

17:10; Ezek 6:13). *the harlot.* Ritual prostitution was a particularly detestable practice (see, e.g., Hos 4:10–14).

2:21 See Is 5:1–7; see also Ps 80:8–16; Ezek 17:1–10; Hos 10:1–2; cf. John 15:1–8. *noble vine.* See Is 5:2. The Hebrew for this word refers to a grape of exceptional quality. *strange vine.* A vine symbolizing Israel should not be like a vine symbolizing Israel's enemies (see Deut 32:32).

2:22 *nitre . . . sope.* Mineral alkali and vegetable alkali respectively. Sins can be removed and forgiven (see Ps 51:2,7; Is 1:18), but only when the sinner repents and confesses (see Prov 28:13; cf. 1John 1:7,9).

2:23 *polluted.* Ceremonially unclean (see 19:13; see also note on Lev 4:12). *gone after.* See note on v. 2; see also v. 25. *Baalim.* See 9:14; see also note on Judg 2:11. *the valley.* Probably the Hinnom Valley (see note on Josh 15:5), known also as the valley of Ben-hinnom (7:31–32; 19:2,6; 32:35). *traversing her ways.* Instead, the people of Judah should have been obeying the Lord, not turning aside either "to the right or to the left" (Deut 28:14).

2:24 *wild ass.* An unruly (see Gen 16:12) and intractable (see Job 39:5–8) animal. *used to the wilderness.* See 14:6; Job 24:5. *snuffeth up the wind.* The picture is one of active searching, not passive waiting (see Hos 2:7,13).

2:25 *unshod.* You wear out your sandals. *There is no hope.* See 18:12; see also note on Is 57:10. *loved strangers.* As opposed to the love Judah was expected to express toward God under the terms of their covenant relationship (see, e.g., Deut 6:6; 7:7–13; Hos 2:14–3:1). *after them.* See v. 23; see also note on v. 2.

‡2:26 *ashamed when he is found.* See, e.g., Ex 22:3–4. The Hebrew word underlying "ashamed" is often used as a pejorative synonym for the name of Baal, the chief god of Canaan (see 11:13 and note; Hos 9:10; see also note on Judg 6:32). *kings . . . princes . . . priests . . . prophets.* See note on 1:18.

2:27 See Is 44:13–17; contrast Deut 32:6,18; Is 64:8; Mal 2:10. *Arise . . . save.* See v. 28.

2:28 *according to . . . thy cities are thy gods.* See 11:13; cf. 1 Cor 8:5. Every ancient Near Eastern town of any importance had its own patron deity (cf. Acts 19:28,34–35), and many towns were named after deities (see, e.g., note on 1:1).

2:29 *plead with.* Cf. v. 9; see 12:1; Job 33:13.

2:30 *have I smitten your children.* Cf. Heb 12:6. *received no correction.* See 5:3. *sword hath devoured your prophets.* See, e.g., 26:20–23; 2 Ki 21:16; 24:4; see also Neh 9:26.

‡2:31 *generation.* Often has negative connotations (see, e.g., Deut 32:5). *Have I been a wilderness . . . a land of darkness?* On the contrary, the Lord led His people through the wilderness and its darkness (v. 6). The word "darkness" translates the Hebrew for "darkness of the LORD" (i.e., darkness sent by the Lord; cf. 1 Sam 26:12 and "a most vehement flame (of the Lord)" in Sol 8:6).

2:32 See Is 49:15,18 and notes. *maid.* Cf. v. 2. *my people have forgotten me.* See 18:15; see also 3:21; 13:25; Is 17:10; Ezek 22:12; 23:35; Hos 8:14. Israel was always to "remember" the Lord and all that He had done for her (Deut 7:18; 8:18) and so trust and worship Him alone, but she often "forgot" Him—put Him out of mind (see Judg 2:10; Hos 2:13).

2:33 *love.* Here, worship of pagan gods (see note on v. 20).

2:34 See Amos 2:6–8; 4:1; 5:11–12. *I have not found it by secret search.* See Ex 22:2 and note.

2:36 *shalt be ashamed of Egypt . . . of Assyria.* See vv. 15–18 and notes. The days of Ahaz (see 2 Chr 28:21), and perhaps the days of Zedekiah (see 37:7), are in view here.

2:37 *and thine hands upon thine head.* Ancient reliefs depict captives with wrists tied together above their heads. *thy confidences.* Egypt and Assyria.

hath rejected thy confidences, and thou shalt not prosper in them.

3 [1]They say, If a man put away his wife, and she go from him, and become another man's, [a]shall he return unto her again? shall not that [b]land be greatly polluted? but thou hast [c]played the harlot with many lovers; [d]yet return again to me, saith the LORD.

2 Lift up thine eyes unto [a]the high places, and see where thou hast not been lien with. [b]In the ways hast thou sat for them, as the Arabian in the wilderness; [c]and thou hast polluted the land with thy whoredoms and with thy wickedness.

3 Therefore the [a]showers have been withholden, and there hath been no latter rain; and thou hadst a [b]whore's forehead, thou refusedst to be ashamed.

4 Wilt thou not from this time cry unto me, My father, thou *art* [a]the guide of [b]my youth?

5 [a]Will he reserve *his anger* for ever? will he keep *it* to the end? Behold, thou hast spoken and done evil *things* as thou couldest.

6 ¶ The LORD said also unto me in the days of Josiah the king, Hast thou seen *that* which [a]backsliding Israel hath done? she is [b]gone up upon every high mountain and under every green tree, and there hath played the harlot.

7 [a]And I said after she had done all these *things,* Turn thou unto me. But she returned not. And her treacherous [b]sister Judah saw *it.*

8 And I saw, when [a]for all the causes whereby backsliding Israel committed adultery I had [b]put her away, and given her a bill of divorce; [c]yet her treacherous sister Judah feared not, but went and played the harlot also.

9 And it came to pass through the [1]lightness of her whoredom, that she [a]defiled the land, and committed adultery with [b]stones and with stocks.

10 And yet for all this her treacherous sister Judah hath not turned unto me [a]with her whole heart, but [1]feignedly, saith the LORD.

11 And the LORD said unto me, [a]The backsliding Israel hath justified herself more than treacherous Judah.

12 Go and proclaim these words toward [a]the north, and say, Return, thou backsliding Israel, saith the LORD; *and* I will not cause mine anger to fall upon you: for I *am* [b]merciful, saith the LORD, *and* I will not keep *anger* for ever.

13 [a]Only acknowledge thine iniquity, that thou hast transgressed against the LORD thy God, and hast [b]scattered thy ways to the [c]strangers [d]under every green tree, and ye have not obeyed my voice, saith the LORD.

14 Turn, O backsliding children, saith the LORD; [a]for I am married unto you: and I will take you [b]one of a city, and two of a family, and I will bring you *to* Zion:

15 And I will give you [a]pastors according to mine heart, which shall [b]feed you with knowledge and understanding.

16 And it shall come to pass, when ye be multiplied and increased in the land, in those

3:1 [1]Heb. *Saying* [a]Deut. 24:4 [b]ch. 2:7 [c]ch. 2:20; Ezek. 16:26 [d]Zech. 1:3
3:2 [a]Deut. 12:2 [b]Prov. 23:28 [c]ch. 2:7
3:3 [a]Lev. 26:19 [b]Zeph. 3:5
3:4 [a]Prov. 2:17 [b]Hos. 2:15
3:5 [a]Ps. 103:9; Is. 57:16
3:6 [a]ch. 7:24 [b]ch. 2:20
3:7 [a]2 Ki. 17:13 [b]Ezek. 16:46
3:8 [a]Ezek. 23:9 [b]2 Ki. 17:6 [c]Ezek. 23:11
3:9 [1]Or, *fame* [a]ch. 2:7 [b]ch. 2:27
3:10 [1]Heb. *in falsehood* [a]Hos. 7:14
3:11 [a]Ezek. 16:51
3:12 [a]2 Ki. 17:6 [b]Ps. 86:15
3:13 [a]Deut. 30:1 [b]Ezek. 16:15 [c]ch. 2:25 [d]Deut. 12:2
3:14 [a]Hos. 2:19 [b]Rom. 11:5
3:15 [a]Ezek. 34:23; Eph. 4:11 [b]Acts 20:28

3:1 *If . . . polluted?* Cf. Deut 24:1–4. Divorce and remarriage on a widespread scale defiles not only the participants but also the land in which they live (cf. v. 2; Lev 18:25–28). *the harlot.* See note on 2:20. *many.* See note on 2:28. *return again to me.* Repent of your sins against me (see vv. 12–14,22; 4:1).
3:2 *high places.* Places where pagan gods were consulted and worshiped (see v. 21; 12:12; Num 23:3). *been lien with.* Cf. Deut 28:30. *In the ways hast thou sat for them.* See Gen 38:14 and note; Prov 7:10,12. The connection of this imagery with ritual prostitution is made explicit in Ezek 16:25. *as the Arabian in the wilderness.* Waiting in ambush to waylay a traveler (see Luke 10:30). *polluted the land.* See v. 9.
3:3 *showers have been withholden.* See 14:1–6; Amos 4:7–8. This is the reverse of God's gracious response to His people in Hos 2:21; 6:3. *latter rain.* See note on Deut 11:14. *whore's forehead.* A shameless, brazen countenance (see Prov 7:13).
3:4 *My Father.* See v. 19; contrast 2:27 and see note there. Compared to the NT, the title "Father" for God is relatively rare in the OT. However, it often occurs in personal names—compound names that begin with Abi- (e.g., Abinadab and Abiram) refer to God as "(my) Father." *guide.* Claiming intimate association (see Ps 55:13; Prov 16:28; 17:9; Mic 7:5); perhaps even claiming to be the Lord's faithful wife (cf. Prov 2:17). *of my youth.* See note on 2:2.
3:5 *Will he reserve his anger for ever?* Not if God's people repent (vv. 12–13).
3:6–6:30 The unfaithfulness of Judah (3:6–5:31) will ultimately bring the Babylonians as God's instrument of judgment (ch. 6).
3:6 *Josiah the king.* See Introduction: Background; see also note on 1:2. *backsliding Israel.* The northern kingdom, destroyed in 722–721 B.C. (see vv. 8,11–12). *upon every high mountain and under every green tree . . . hath played the harlot.* See note on 2:20.
3:7 *her treacherous sister Judah.* The southern kingdom (see vv. 8,10–11). Samaria (Israel's capital) and Jerusalem (Judah's capital) are similarly compared as adulterous sisters in Ezek 23. *it.* Israel's adultery.
3:8 *put her away.* Into exile in 721 B.C. *bill of divorce.* See v. 1 and note; see also Deut 24:1–14; Is 50:1 and notes. *Judah feared not.* She refused to learn from Israel's tragic experience.
3:9 *committed adultery with stones and with stocks.* Worshiped pagan deities (see 2:27).
3:10 *but feignedly.* Judah's response to Josiah's reform measures (see note on 1:2) was superficial and hypocritical.
3:11 *Israel hath justified herself more than . . . Judah.* See note on v. 8; see also Ezek 16:51–52; 23:11.
3:12 *Go and proclaim.* See 2:2. *north.* Assyria's northern provinces, to which many Israelites had been exiled. *Return.* Repent (see v. 13). *merciful.* The Hebrew for this word is used of God elsewhere only in Ps 145:17, where it is translated "kind." *not keep anger for ever.* See note on v. 5.
3:13 *scattered thy ways.* See Ezek 16:15,33–34. *strangers.* See note on 2:25. *under every green tree.* See note on 2:20.
3:14 *I am married unto you.* See 31:32; Hos 2:16–17. The Hebrew root underlying this word is *ba'al.* Instead of allowing God to be their husband, His people followed "the Baals" (2:23; see note on Judg 2:11). *one . . . two.* A remnant will return (see note on Is 10:20–22). *Zion.* Jerusalem.
3:15 See 23:4. *pastors.* Rulers (see note on 2:8). *according to mine heart.* Like David (see 1 Sam 13:14; see also Ezek 34:23; Hos 3:5).
‡3:16 *ye be multiplied.* See 23:3; Ezek 36:11. For the fuller meaning of the Hebrew underlying this phrase see note on Gen 1:28. *in those days.* The Messianic age (see v. 18; 31:29).

days, saith the LORD, they shall say no more,
The ark of the covenant of the LORD: [a]neither
shall it [1]come to mind: neither shall they remember it; neither shall they visit *it;* neither
shall [2]*that* be done any more.
17 At that time they shall call Jerusalem the
throne of the LORD; and all the nations shall be
gathered unto it, [a]to the name of the LORD, to
Jerusalem: neither shall they [b]walk any more
after the [1]imagination of their evil heart.
18 In those days [a]the house of Judah shall
walk [1]with the house of Israel, and they shall
come together out of the land of [b]the north to
[c]the land that I have [2]given for an inheritance
unto your fathers.
19 But I said, How shall I put thee among
the children, and give thee [a]a [1]pleasant land,
[2]a goodly heritage of the hosts of nations? and
I said, Thou shalt call me, [b]My father; and
shalt not turn away [3]from me.
20 Surely *as* a wife treacherously departeth
from her [1]husband, so [a]have you dealt treacherously with me, O house of Israel, saith the
LORD.
21 ¶ A voice was heard upon [a]the high
places, weeping *and* supplications of the children of Israel: for they have perverted their way,
and they have forgotten the LORD their God.
22 [a]Return, ye backsliding children, *and* [b]I
will heal your backslidings. Behold, we come
unto thee; for thou *art* the LORD our God.
23 [a]Truly in vain *is salvation hoped for*
from the hills, *and from* the multitude of
mountains: [b]truly in the LORD our God *is* the
salvation of Israel.
24 [a]For shame hath devoured the labour of
our fathers from our youth; their flocks and
their herds, their sons and their daughters.
25 We lie down in our shame, and our confusion covereth us: [a]for we have sinned
against the LORD our God, we and our fathers,
from our youth even unto this day, and [b]have
not obeyed the voice of the LORD our God.

3:16 [1]Heb. *come upon the heart* [2]Or, it *be magnified* [a]Is. 65:17
3:17 [1]Or, *stubbornness* [a]Is. 60:9 [b]ch. 11:8
3:18 [1]Or, *to* [2]Or, *caused your fathers to possess* [a]Is. 11:13; Hos. 1:11 [b]ch. 31:8 [c]Amos 9:15
3:19 [1]Heb. *land of desire* [2][Heb. *an heritage of glory,* or, *beauty*] [3]Heb. *from after me* [a]Ps. 106:24 [b]Is. 63:16
3:20 [1]Heb. *friend* [a]Is. 48:8
3:21 [a]Is. 15:2
3:22 [a]ver. 14; Hos. 14:1 [b]Hos. 6:1; 14:4
3:23 [a]Ps. 121:1,2
3:23 [b]Ps. 3:8
3:24 [a]ch. 11:13; Hos. 9:10
3:25 [a]Ezra 9:7 [b]ch. 22:21
4:1 [a]ch. 3:1,22; Joel 2:12
4:2 [a]Deut. 10:20; Is. 45:23; 65:16; See ch. 5:2 [b]Is. 48:1; Zech. 8:8 [c]Gen. 22:18; Ps. 72:17; Gal. 3:8 [d]1 Cor. 1:31
4:3 [a]Hos. 10:12 [b]Mat. 13:7
4:4 [a]Deut. 10:16; ch. 9:26; Rom. 2:28
4:5 [a]ch. 8:14

Judgment from the north

4 If thou wilt return, O Israel, saith the
LORD, [a]return unto me: and if thou wilt
put away thine abominations out of my sight,
then shalt thou not remove.
2 [a]And thou shalt swear, The LORD liveth,
[b]in truth, in judgment, and in righteousness;
[c]and the nations shall bless themselves in
him, and in him shall they [d]glory.
3 For thus saith the LORD to the men of Judah and Jerusalem, [a]Break up your fallow
ground, and [b]sow not among thorns.
4 [a]Circumcise yourselves to the LORD, and
take away the foreskins of your heart, ye men
of Judah and inhabitants of Jerusalem: lest my
fury come forth like fire, and burn that none
can quench *it,* because of the evil of your doings.
5 Declare ye in Judah, and publish in Jerusalem; and say, Blow ye the trumpet in the land:
cry, gather together, and say, [a]Assemble yourselves, and let us go into the defenced cities.

neither shall that be done any more. The ark of the covenant, formerly symbolizing God's royal presence (see 1 Sam 4:3), will be irrelevant when the Messiah comes.

3:17 *throne.* The Lord sat enthroned "above the cherubim" over the ark (see 1 Sam 4:4 and note), but Jerusalem itself would someday be His throne. *all the nations shall be gathered.* See Zech 2:11; see also note on Is 2:2–4. *they.* Israel. *walk any more after the imagination of their evil heart.* A stock phrase referring to Israel's disobedience and often involving the worship of pagan gods (see 9:14; 11:8; 13:10; 16:12; 18:12; 23:17).

3:18 *Judah shall walk with . . . Israel.* In the Messianic age God's divided people will again be united (see, e.g., Is 11:12; Ezek 37:15–23; Hos 1:11). *land of the north.* Where they had been exiles (see note on v. 12; see also 31:8). *land that I have given for an inheritance.* See note on 2:7.

3:19 *children.* Israel was the Lord's firstborn (see Ex 4:22; cf. Hos 11:1). *pleasant land.* See Ps 106:24; Zech 7:14. *goodly heritage.* Judah, Jerusalem, the people themselves—ideally, all were beautiful in God's eyes (see 6:2; 11:16). *father.* See note on v. 4.

3:20 A concise summary of the story told in Hos 1–3.

3:21 *high places.* See note on v. 2. *weeping and supplications.* A description of repentance, verbalized in vv. 22b–25. *forgotten.* See note on 2:32.

3:22 See v. 14. *Return . . . backsliding . . . backslidings.* Each of these three words is derived from the same Hebrew root, producing a striking series of puns. *I will heal your backslidings.* See 30:17; 33:6; Hos 6:1; 14:1,4. *we come unto thee.* The people's repentance begins.

3:23 *the multitude of mountains.* See, e.g., 1 Ki 18:25–29. *in the LORD . . . is . . . salvation.* See Gen 49:18; Ps 3:8; Jonah 2:9 and note.

3:24 *shame hath devoured the labour.* See notes on 2:26; 11:13. False worship is costly, both financially and spiritually. *our youth.* The period of the judges. *sons and . . . daughters.* Often sacrificed to pagan gods (see note on 7:31).

‡3:25 *shame.* The Hebrew for this word can be translated "shameful thing" both here and in v. 24.

4:1 *remove.* The Hebrew for this word implies wandering, as in Gen 4:12,14 (see Gen 4:16 and note).

4:2 *The LORD liveth.* See note on Gen 42:15. *truth . . . judgment . . . righteousness.* The piling up of such words underscores the need for repentance that is sincere and not perfunctory. *nations shall bless themselves in him.* Reflects the language of the seventh of God's great promises to Abram (see Gen 12:2–3 and note). Israel's repentance is a necessary precondition for the ultimate blessing of the nations.

4:3 *Break up your fallow ground.* Probably quoted from Hos 10:12. *sow not among thorns.* See Mat 13:7,22. Openness to the Lord's overtures is necessary, as is total commitment to Him (see Ezek 18:31).

4:4 *take away the foreskins of your heart.* Consecrate your hearts (see 6:10; 9:26; see also Gen 17:10 and note; Deut 10:16; 30:6). *fury come forth . . . burn that none can quench.* See 21:12; see also Is 1:31; Amos 5:6. *because of the evil of your doings.* Probably quoted from Deut 28:20.

4:5–31 The invaders from the north will bring God's judgment against His unrepentant people (see ch. 6).

4:5 *Blow ye the trumpet.* To warn of impending doom (see 6:1; see also note on Joel 2:1). *go into the defenced cities.* See v. 6. To avoid capture by hostile troops, people living in the countryside would take refuge in the nearest walled town (see 5:17; 8:14; 34:7; 48:18).

6 Set up the standard toward Zion: [1]retire,
stay not: for I will bring evil from the [a]north,
and a great [2]destruction.
7 [a]The lion is come up from his thicket,
and [b]the destroyer of the Gentiles is on his
way; he is gone forth from his place [c]to make
thy land desolate; *and* thy cities shall be laid
waste, without an inhabitant.
8 For this [a]gird you with sackcloth, lament
and howl: for the fierce anger of the LORD is
not turned back from us.
9 And it shall come to pass at that day, saith
the LORD, *that* the heart of the king shall perish,
and the heart of the princes; and the priests shall
be astonished, and the prophets shall wonder.
10 (Then said I, Ah, Lord GOD! [a]surely
thou hast greatly deceived this people and Jerusalem, [b]saying, Ye shall have peace; whereas
the sword reacheth unto the soul).
11 At that time shall it be said to this people and to Jerusalem,

[a]A dry wind of the high places in the
wilderness toward the daughter of
my people,
Not to fan, nor to cleanse,
12 *Even* [1]a full wind from those *places*
shall come unto me:
Now also [a]will I [2]give sentence against
them.
13 Behold, he shall come up as clouds,
And [a]his chariots *shall be* as a
whirlwind:
[b]His horses are swifter than eagles.
Woe unto us! for we are spoiled.
14 O Jerusalem, [a]wash thine heart from
wickedness, that thou mayest be
saved.
How long shall thy vain thoughts lodge
within thee?
15 For a voice declareth [a]from Dan,
And publisheth affliction from mount
Ephraim.
16 Make ye mention to the nations;
behold, publish against Jerusalem,
That watchers come from a far country,
And give out their voice against the
cities of Judah.
17 [a]As keepers of a field, are they against
her round about;
Because she hath been rebellious
against me, saith the LORD.
18 [a]Thy way and thy doings have
procured these *things* unto thee;
This *is* thy wickedness, because *it is*
bitter,
Because it reacheth unto thine heart.

19 My [a]bowels, my bowels! I am pained
at [1]my very heart;
My heart maketh a noise in me; I
cannot hold my peace,
Because thou hast heard, O my soul,
the sound of the trumpet, the alarm
of war.
20 [a]Destruction upon destruction is cried;
for the whole land is spoiled:
Suddenly are [b]my tents spoiled, *and*
my curtains in a moment.
21 How long shall I see the standard, *and*
hear the sound of the trumpet?
22 For my people *is* foolish, they have not
known me;
They *are* sottish children, and they
have none understanding:

4:6 [1]Or, *strengthen* [2]Heb. *breaking* [a]ch. 1:13-15; 6:1,22
4:7 [a]2 Ki. 24:1; ch. 5:6; Dan. 7:4 [b]ch. 25:9 [c]Is. 1:7
4:8 [a]Is. 22:12
4:10 [a]Ezek. 14:9; 2 Thes. 2:11 [b]ch. 14:13
4:11 [a]ch. 51:1; Ezek. 17:10; Hos. 13:15
4:12 [1]Or, *a fuller wind than those* [2]Heb. *utter judgments* [a]ch. 1:16
4:13 [a]Is. 5:28 [b]Deut. 28:49; Lam. 4:19; Hos. 8:1; Hab. 1:8
4:14 [a]Is. 1:16; Jas. 4:8
4:15 [a]ch. 8:16
4:17 [a]2 Ki. 25:1
4:18 [a]Ps. 107:17; Is. 50:1; ch. 2:17,19
4:19 [1]Heb. *the walls of my heart* [a]Is. 15:5; 16:11; 21:3; See Luke 19:42
4:20 [a]Ps. 42:7; Ezek. 7:26 [b]ch. 10:20

4:6 See 6:1. *Set up the standard.* See note on Is 5:26. *evil from the north.* The Babylonians (see 1:14; see also note on Is 41:25). *great destruction.* See 6:1; cf. 48:3; 50:22; 51:54.
4:7 *lion.* A symbol of Babylon (see note on 2:15). *destroyer.* Usually refers to Babylon (6:26; 15:8; 48:8,32), but in 51:1,56 it refers to Persia and her allies (see 51:48,53). *cities . . . without an inhabitant.* See note on 2:15; see also v. 25; 46:19.
4:8 *sackcloth.* See note on Gen 37:34. *anger . . . is not turned back.* Contrast 2:35.
4:9 *at that day.* See note on Is 2:11,17,20. *king . . . princes . . . priests . . . prophets.* See note on 1:18.
4:10 *thou hast greatly deceived.* Not directly, but through false prophets (see, e.g., 1 Ki 22:20–23 and note on 1 Ki 22:23). *Ye shall have peace.* Here the words of false prophets, not of God (see 14:13; 23:17; see also 6:13–14; 8:10–11). *soul.* The Hebrew for this word is usually translated "soul" or "life," but originally it had the meaning "throat, neck" (see, e.g., Ps 69:1).
4:11 *dry wind.* The sirocco or khamsin, a hot, dry wind that brings sand and dust (see Ps 11:6; Is 11:15; Jonah 4:8). *fan.* See note on Ruth 1:22.
4:12 *full wind.* Neither winnowing (separating grain from chaff) nor cleansing (blowing dust from the grain), God's judgments will sweep away good and bad alike.
‡4:13 *come up as clouds.* Cf. Ezek 38:16. *chariots shall be as a whirlwind.* See 2 Ki 2:11; 6:17; Ps 68:17; Is 66:15. *horses are swifter than eagles.* See Hab 1:8, where the Babylonians (Hab 1:6) use horses that are "swifter than leopards" and employ cavalry that "fly as the eagle" (see also Deut 28:49). *spoiled.* See v. 20; 9:19; 48:1.
4:14 *wash.* See 2:22 and note. *vain thoughts.* Against other people (see Prov 6:18; Is 59:7).
4:15 *Dan.* Far away, close to the northern border of Israel (see 8:16). *Ephraim.* A few miles north of Jerusalem. The enemy, in the mind's eye of the prophet, is making fearfully rapid progress toward the holy city.
4:16 *watchers.* See Is 1:8. *far country.* Babylon. *give out their voice.* The Hebrew underlying this phrase is translated "roared" in 2:15.
4:17 *against her round about.* See 1:15.
4:19–26 A brief personal interlude, broken only by the divine complaint in v. 22. Jeremiah voices his agony at the approaching destruction of his beloved land and its people.
4:19 See 10:19–20. *pained.* Often associated with labor pangs, as here (see 6:24; 49:24; 50:43). *My heart maketh a noise.* See Job 37:1; Ps 38:10; Hab 3:16. *sound of the trumpet.* See note on v. 5.
4:20 *tents spoiled.* See v. 13; 9:19; 48:1. *curtains.* Tent curtains (see Is 54:2) were usually made of goat hair (see Ex 26:7) and therefore were strong enough to protect from cold and rain (see 10:20).
4:21 *standard . . . sound of the trumpet.* See notes on vv. 5–6.
4:22 The Lord speaks. *foolish.* The Hebrew word refers to one who is morally deficient. *they have not known me.* See 2:8. Leaders and people alike had committed the ultimate sin (see Is 1:3; Hos 4:1). *sottish.* Or "senseless." See 5:21; 10:8,14,21; 51:17. *wise to do evil.* See Mic 7:3.

[a]They *are* wise to do evil, but to do
good they have no knowledge.
23 I [a]beheld the earth, and lo, *it was*
[b]without form, and void;
And the heavens, and they *had* no light.
24 [a]I beheld the mountains, and lo, they
trembled,
And all the hills moved lightly.
25 I beheld, and lo, *there was* no man,
And [a]all the birds of the heavens were
fled.
26 I beheld, and lo, the fruitful place *was*
a wilderness,
And all the cities thereof were broken
down
At the presence of the LORD, *and* by his
fierce anger.

27 For thus hath the LORD said,
The whole land shall be desolate;
[a]Yet will I not make a full end.
28 For this [a]shall the earth mourn, and
[b]the heavens above be black:
Because I have spoken *it,* I have
purposed *it,*
And [c]will not repent, neither will I
turn back from it.
29 The whole city shall flee for the noise
of the horsemen and bowmen;
They shall go into thickets, and climb
up upon the rocks:
Every city *shall be* forsaken, and not a
man dwell therein.
30 And when thou art spoiled, what wilt
thou do?
Though thou clothest thyself with
crimson, though thou deckest thee
with ornaments of gold,

4:22 [a]Rom. 16:19
4:23 [a]Is. 24:19 [b]Gen. 1:2
4:24 [a]Is. 5:25; Ezek. 38:20
4:25 [a]Zeph. 1:3
4:27 [a]ch. 5:10,18; 30:11; 46:28
4:28 [a]Hos. 4:3 [b]Is. 5:30; 50:3 [c]Num. 23:19; ch. 7:16
4:30 [1]Heb. *eyes* [a]2 Ki. 9:30 [b]ch. 22:20,22
4:31 [a]Is. 1:15; Lam. 1:17
5:1 [a]Ezek. 22:30 [b]Gen. 18:23 [c]Gen. 18:26
5:2 [a]Tit. 1:16 [b]ch. 4:2 [c]ch. 7:9
5:3 [a]2 Chr. 16:9 [b]Is. 1:5; 9:13; ch. 2:30 [c]ch. 7:28; Zeph. 3:2
5:4 [a]ch. 8:7
5:5 [a]Mic. 3:1 [b]Ps. 2:3
5:6 [a]ch. 4:7

[a]Though thou rentest thy [1]face with
painting, in vain shalt thou make
thyself fair;
[b]*Thy* lovers will despise thee, they will
seek thy life.
31 For I have heard a voice as of a woman
in travail, *and* the anguish as of her
that bringeth forth her first child,
The voice of the daughter of Zion, *that*
bewaileth herself, *that* [a]spreadeth
her hands,
Saying, Woe *is* me now! for my soul is
wearied because of murderers.

Futile search for an upright man

5 Run ye to and fro through the streets of
Jerusalem, and see now, and know, and
seek in the broad places thereof, [a]if ye can find
a man, [b]if there be *any* that executeth judgment, that seeketh the truth; [c]and I will pardon it.
2 And [a]though they say, [b]The LORD liveth;
surely they [c]swear falsely.
3 O LORD, *are* not [a]thine eyes upon the
truth? thou hast [b]stricken them, but they have
not grieved; thou hast consumed them, *but*
[c]they have refused to receive correction: they
have made their faces harder than a rock; they
have refused to return.
4 Therefore I said, Surely these *are* poor;
they are foolish: for [a]they know not the way of
the LORD, *nor* the judgment of their God.
5 I will get me unto the great men, and will
speak unto them; for [a]they have known the
way of the LORD, *and* the judgment of their
God: but these have altogether [b]broken the
yoke, *and* burst the bonds.
6 Wherefore [a]a lion out of the forest shall

‡4:23–26 The striking repetition of "I" beheld at the beginning of each verse ties this poem together and underscores its visionary character, as the prophet sees his beloved land in ruins after the Babylonian onslaught. Creation, as it were, has been reversed.
4:23 *without form, and void.* The phrase occurs elsewhere only in Gen 1:2 (see note there). In Jeremiah's vision, the primeval chaos has returned. *had no light.* Contrast Gen 1:3.
4:24 See Nah 1:5.
4:25 *there was no man.* The Hebrew underlying this phrase occurs elsewhere only in Gen 2:5. Again, uncreation has replaced creation.
4:26 *fruitful place.* See note on 2:7. *fierce anger.* See v. 8; Is 13:13; Nah 1:6.
4:27 *Yet will I not make a full end.* See 5:10,18; 30:11; 46:28. God's mercy tempers the total judgment envisioned by Jeremiah in vv. 23–26.
‡4:28 *will not repent.* Unless His people repent (see 18:7–8).
4:29 *bowmen.* Babylon's evil deeds against Judah will someday recoil on her (see 50:29). *They shall go.* See Judg 6:2; 1 Sam 13:6; Is 2:19,21. Even people living in fortified towns feel unsafe. *forsaken.* Contrast Is 62:4.
4:30 *painting.* Antimony, a black powder was used to enlarge the eyes and make them more attractive (see 2 Ki 9:30; Ezek 23:40). *lovers.* The Hebrew root underlying this word is found elsewhere only in Ezek 23:5,7,9,12,16,20, where it is used of Samaria and Jerusalem, the adulterous sisters (see notes on 2:20; 3:7) who "lusted" after foreign nations and their gods. *seek thy life.* They are intent only on murdering you (see v. 31).
4:31 *daughter of Zion.* A personification of Jerusalem and its inhabitants (see 6:2,23). *spreadeth her hands.* In prayer for help (see Job 11:13).
5:1–31 Jeremiah resumes his vivid description of the wickedness of the people of Judah and Jerusalem.
5:1 See Zeph 1:12. The Lord challenges anyone to find just one righteous person in Israel—a rhetorical way of charging that corruption pervaded the city (see Ps 14:1–3; Is 64:6–7; Hos 4:1–2; Mic 7:2). *if ye can find . . . I will pardon.* See Gen 18:26–32.
5:2 *The LORD liveth.* See 4:2; see also Gen 42:15 and note. *they swear falsely.* In violation of Lev 19:12 (see note on Ex 20:7). The Hebrew could be translated "swear by false gods."
5:3 *refused . . . correction.* See 2:30. *made their faces harder than a rock.* A striking portrayal of rebellion (see Ezek 3:7–9).
5:4 *poor.* Concerned about basic physical needs (cf. 39:10; 40:7), they are uninformed of God's word and way. *foolish.* See 4:22 and note; see also Num 12:11. *know not . . . judgment of their God.* They are more ignorant than the birds of the heavens (see 8:7).
5:5 *they have known.* Although possessing every advantage, they were no more righteous than the poorest of the common people. *broken . . . bonds.* See note on 2:20.
5:6 *lion . . . wolf . . . leopard.* See Lev 26:22; Ezek 14:15; cf. 2 Ki 17:25–26. *transgressions.* See 2:19; 3:22; 14:7; repeated apostasy.

slay them, [b]*and* a wolf of the [1]evenings shall
spoil them, [c]a leopard shall watch over their
cities: every one that goeth out thence shall be
torn in pieces: because their transgressions are
many, *and* their backslidings [2]are increased.
7 How shall I pardon thee for this? thy children have forsaken me, and [a]sworn by *them*
[b]*that are* no gods: [c]when I had fed them to the
full, they then committed adultery, and assembled themselves by troops *in* the harlots'
houses.
8 [a]They were *as* fed horses in the morning:
every one neighed after his neighbour's wife.
9 [a]Shall I not visit for these *things?* saith
the LORD: [b]and shall not my soul be avenged
on such a nation as this?
10 ¶ [a]Go ye up upon her walls, and destroy; [b]but make not a full end: take away her
battlements; for they *are* not the LORD's.
11 For [a]the house of Israel and the house
of Judah have dealt very treacherously against
me, saith the LORD.
12 [a]They have belied the LORD, and said,
[b]*It is* not he; neither shall evil come upon us;
[c]neither shall we see sword nor famine:
13 And the prophets shall become wind,
and the word *is* not in them: thus shall it be
done unto them.
14 Wherefore thus saith the LORD God of
hosts, Because ye speak this word, [a]behold, I
will make my words in thy mouth fire, and
this people wood, and it shall devour them.
15 Lo, I will bring a [a]nation upon you
[b]from far, O house of Israel, saith the LORD: it
is a mighty nation, it *is* an ancient nation, a nation whose language thou knowest not, neither understandest what they say.
16 Their quiver *is* as an open sepulchre,
they *are* all mighty *men.*
17 And they shall eat up thine [a]harvest,

5:6 [1]Or, *deserts* [2]Heb. *are strong* [b]Ps. 104:20; Hab. 1:8; Zeph. 3:3 [c]Hos. 13:7
5:7 [a]Josh. 23:7; Zeph. 1:5 [b]Deut. 32:21; Gal. 4:8 [c]Deut. 32:15
5:8 [a]Ezek. 22:11
5:9 [a]ver. 29; ch. 9:9 [b]ch. 44:22
5:10 [a]ch. 39:8 [b]ver. 18; ch. 4:27
5:11 [a]ch. 3:20
5:12 [a]2 Chr. 36:16; ch. 4:10 [b]Is. 28:15 [c]ch. 14:13
5:14 [a]ch. 1:9
5:15 [a]Deut. 28:49; Is. 5:26; ch. 1:15; 6:22 [b]Is. 39:3; ch. 4:16
5:17 [a]Lev. 26:16; Deut. 28:31,33
5:18 [a]ch. 4:27
5:19 [a]Deut. 29:24; 1 Ki. 9:8,9; ch. 13:22; 16:10 [b]ch. 2:13 [c]Deut. 28:48
5:21 [1]Heb. *heart* [a]Is. 6:9; Ezek. 12:2; Mat. 13:14; John 12:40; Acts 28:26; Rom. 11:8
5:22 [a]Rev. 15:4 [b]Job 26:10; Prov. 8:29
5:24 [a]Ps. 147:8; Acts 14:17 [b]Joel 2:23 [c]Gen. 8:22
5:25 [a]ch. 3:3
5:26 [1]Or, *they pry as fowlers lie in wait* [a]Prov. 1:11; Hab. 1:15
5:27 [1]Or, *coop*

and thy bread, *which* thy sons and thy daughters should eat: they shall eat up thy flocks and
thine herds: they shall eat up thy vines and thy
fig trees: they shall impoverish thy fenced cities, wherein thou trustedst, with the sword.
18 Nevertheless in those days, saith the
LORD, I [a]will not make a full end with you.
19 ¶ And it shall come to pass, when ye
shall say, [a]Wherefore doth the LORD our God
all these *things* unto us? then shalt thou answer them, Like as ye have [b]forsaken me, and
served strange gods in your land, so [c]shall ye
serve strangers in a land *that is* not yours.
20 Declare this in the house of Jacob, and
publish it in Judah, saying,
21 Hear now this, [a]O foolish people, and
without [1]understanding; which have eyes,
and see not; which have ears, and hear not:
22 [a]Fear ye not me? saith the LORD: will ye
not tremble at my presence, which have
placed the sand *for* the [b]bound of the sea *by* a
perpetual decree, that it cannot pass it: and
though the waves thereof toss themselves, yet
can they not prevail; though they roar, yet can
they not pass over it?
23 But this people hath a revolting and a
rebellious heart; they are revolted and gone.
24 Neither say they in their heart, Let us
now fear the LORD our God, [a]that giveth rain,
both the [b]former and the latter, in his season:
[c]he reserveth unto us the appointed weeks of
the harvest.
25 [a]Your iniquities have turned away these
things, and your sins have withholden good
things from you.
26 For among my people are found wicked
men: [1]they [a]lay wait, as he that setteth snares;
they set a trap, they catch men.
27 As a [1]cage *is* full *of* birds, so *are* their

5:7 *How shall I pardon thee . . . ?* See v. 1. *them that are no gods.* Idols (see 2:11). *when I had fed . . . they.* See Deut 32:15–16; Hos 2:8. *committed adultery.* See note on 2:20.

5:8 Religious prostitution (v. 7; see Amos 2:7) leads quite naturally to literal adultery, the breaking of God's law (see Ex 20:14,17). *fed horses.* See 13:27; 50:11; Ezek 23:20.

‡5:10 *Go.* Addressed to Israel's enemies (see v. 15). *walls.* The Hebrew suggests vine rows as a metaphor for walls. Vines and vineyards are often symbolic of Israel (see notes on 2:21; Is 5:1). *not . . . a full end.* See v. 18; see also note on 4:27. *battlements.* Probably branches; see Is 18:5; John 15:2,6. *are not the LORD's.* See Hos 1:9.

5:11 See note on 3:7.

5:12 *not he.* The Lord will do nothing, either good or bad (see Zeph 1:12). *sword nor famine.* Jeremiah introduces us to the first two elements of his characteristic triad: "sword, famine and pestilence" (see note on 14:12).

5:13 *prophets shall become wind.* Like images of false gods (see Is 41:29). *thus shall it be done unto them.* See note on 4:29; see also Ps 7:16; 54:5.

5:14 *my words in thy mouth fire.* In contrast to the total lack of God's word in the mouths of false prophets (v. 13). *devour.* See note on Is 1:31.

5:15 *nation . . . from far.* See note on 4:16. *mighty . . . ancient nation.* Babylon's history reached back 2,000 years and more. *whose language thou knowest not.* See Deut 28:49 and note.

5:16 *open sepulchre.* Symbolizing insatiability, destruction and death (see Ps 5:9; Prov 30:15–16).

5:17 *eat up . . . thy sons and thy daughters.* Either as sacrifices to pagan gods (see note on 3:24), or as casualties of war (see 10:25). *fenced cities, wherein thou trustedst.* See note on 4:5; see also Deut 28:52.

5:18 See v. 10; see also note on 4:27.

5:21 *Hear now.* See note on 2:4. *foolish people, and without understanding.* See 4:22 and note. *which have eyes . . . and hear not.* See note on Is 6:10; see also Deut 29:4; Ps 115:4–8; 135:15–18.

5:22 *Fear ye not me?* See note on Gen 20:11. *bound of the sea.* See Job 38:8–11; Ps 104:6–9.

5:23 Though the sea never crosses its divinely appointed boundaries, God's people have violated the limits He has set for them.

5:24 *God, that giveth.* See v.7 and note. *former . . . latter.* See 3:3; see also note on Deut 11:14. *appointed weeks of the harvest.* Perhaps the seven weeks between passover and the feast of weeks (see Lev 23:15–16).

5:26 *trap.* Lit. "destroyer" (see, e.g., Ex 12:23) or "destruction" (see, e.g., Ezek 21:31). *men.* Innocent (see Is 29:21), godly, upright people (see Mic 7:2).

5:27 *cage.* A trap woven of wicker; the Hebrew for this word

houses full *of* deceit: therefore they are become great, and waxen rich.
28 They are waxen [a]fat, they shine: yea,
they overpass the deeds of the wicked: they
judge not [b]the cause, the cause of the fatherless, [c]yet they prosper; and the right of the
needy do they not judge.
29 [a]Shall I not visit for these *things?* saith
the LORD: shall not my soul be avenged on
such a nation as this?
30 ¶ [1]A wonderful and [a]horrible thing is
committed in the land;
31 The prophets prophesy [a]falsely, and the
priests [1]bear rule by their means; and my people [b]love *to have it* so: and what will ye do in
the end thereof?

Jerusalem under siege

6 O ye children of Benjamin, gather yourselves to flee out of the midst of Jerusalem, and blow the trumpet in Tekoa, and set
up a sign of fire in [a]Beth-haccerem: [b]for evil
appeareth out of the north, and great destruction.
2 I have likened the daughter of Zion *to* a
[1]comely and delicate *woman.*
3 The shepherds with their flocks shall
come unto her; [a]they shall pitch *their* tents
against her round about; they shall feed every
one *in* his place.
4 [a]Prepare ye war against her; arise, and

5:28 [a]Deut. 32:15 [b]Is. 1:23; Zech. 7:10 [c]Job 12:6; Ps. 73:12
5:29 [a]Mal. 3:5
5:30 [1]Or, *Astonishment and filthiness* [a]Hos. 6:10
5:31 [1]Or, *take into their hands* [a]ch. 14:14; 23:25,26; Ezek. 13:6 [b]Mic. 2:11
6:1 [a]Neh. 3:14 [b]ch. 4:6
6:2 [1]Or, *dwelling at home*
6:3 [a]2 Ki. 25:1
6:4 [a]Joel 3:9

6:4 [b]ch. 15:8
6:6 [1]Or, *pour out the engine of shot*
6:7 [a]Is. 57:20 [b]Ps. 55:9; ch. 20:8; Ezek. 7:11
6:8 [1]Heb. *be loosed,* or, *disjointed* [a]Hos. 9:12
6:10 [a]Acts 7:51; See Ex. 6:12 [b]ch. 20:8
6:11 [a]ch. 20:9 [b]ch. 9:21

let us go up [b]at noon. Woe unto us! for the day
goeth away, for the shadows of the evening are
stretched out.
5 Arise, and let us go by night, and let us
destroy her palaces.
6 For thus hath the LORD of hosts said, Hew
ye down trees, and [1]cast a mount against Jerusalem: this is the city to be visited; she *is*
wholly oppression in the midst of her.
7 [a]As a fountain casteth out her waters, so
she casteth out her wickedness: [b]violence and
spoil is heard in her; before me continually *is*
grief and wounds.
8 Be thou instructed, O Jerusalem, lest [a]my
soul [1]depart from thee; lest I make thee desolate, a land not inhabited.
9 ¶ Thus saith the LORD of hosts, They shall
throughly glean the remnant of Israel as a
vine: turn back thine hand as a grapegatherer
into the baskets.
10 To whom shall I speak, and give warning, that they may hear? behold, their [a]ear *is*
uncircumcised, and they cannot hearken: behold, [b]the word of the LORD is unto them a reproach; they have no delight in it.
11 Therefore I am full *of* the fury of the
LORD; [a]I am weary with holding in: I *will* pour
it out [b]upon the children abroad, and upon the
assembly of young men together: for even the
husband with the wife shall be taken, the aged
with *him that is* full of days.

is translated "basket" in Amos 8:1–2. *deceit.* Riches gained through extortion and deception (see Hab 2:6).

5:28 *fat . . . shine.* Symbolic of prosperity (see Deut 32:15). *they overpass the deeds of the wicked.* See Ps 73:7. *they judge not the cause.* What the wicked will not do, God must do (see Deut 10:18)—and so must those who truly know and serve Him (see 22:16; Jas 1:27).

5:29 Repeated from v. 9.

5:31 See 1:18 and note. *prophesy falsely.* See 20:6 (often, and arrogantly, in God's name; see 23:25; 27:15; 29:9). *people love to have it so.* See note on Amos 4:5.

6:1–30 The prophet envisions the future Babylonian attack on Jerusalem.

6:1 The Lord speaks in vv. 1–3. Verse 1 is strongly reminiscent of 4:6 (see note there). But whereas in 4:6 the command was to seek protection in Jerusalem, in 6:1 the people are to flee from Jerusalem, because no place—not even the holy city itself—will be safe from the invader. *Benjamin.* The tribal territory bordering Judah north of Jerusalem. Jeremiah himself was from Benjamite territory (see 1:1). *blow . . . Tekoa.* In the Hebrew there is a play on these words. Tekoa was the hometown of Amos (see Introduction to Amos: Author). *set up . . . sign.* In the Hebrew there is a play on words, made possible by using a different Hebrew word (found also in Lachish Letter 4:10) for "sign" (caused by the smoke of a fire; see Judg 20:38,40) than the one used in 4:6. *Beth-haccerem.* Mentioned elsewhere only in Neh 3:14 (see note there). *evil . . . out of the north.* See 1:14 and note.

6:2 *delicate.* The Hebrew word is used to describe the city of Babylon in Is 47:1 ("delicate"). *daughter of Zion.* See v. 23; see also note on 4:31.

6:3 See 1:15. *shepherds with their flocks.* Rulers (see note on 2:8) with their troops. *pitch.* The Hebrew for this verb continues the pun on "Tekoa" in v. 1 (see note on v. 8). *feed.* Graze or depasture, and thus destroy. *every one in his place.* The Hebrew for this phrase is used similarly ("every man in his place") in Num 2:17.

6:4 The invaders speak in vv. 4–5. *Prepare.* Lit. "Consecrate" (also in Joel 3:9; Mic 3:5). Since ancient battles had religious connotations, soldiers had to prepare themselves ritually as well as militarily (see Deut 20:2–4; 1 Sam 25:28). *at noon.* To take advantage of the element of surprise, since the usual time of attack was early in the morning.

6:5 *by night.* Since attacking soldiers normally retired for the night and resumed siege the following morning, the phrase underscores their eagerness and determination.

6:6 The Lord addresses the Babylonian troops. *mount.* That is, siege ramps, to help them bring up battering rams and scale Jerusalem's walls (see 33:4). *oppression.* Against its own people (see note on Is 30:12).

6:7 *grief and wounds.* Jerusalem suffers from spiritual decay and disease (see v. 14), and is not aware of it.

6:8 *Be thou instructed.* The better part of wisdom (see v. 10; Ps 2:10). *my soul depart.* In sorrow, but also in disgust. The Hebrew for this phrase continues the pun on "Tekoa" in v. 1 (see note on v. 3). *desolate, a land not inhabited.* See 22:6.

6:9 *throughly.* Stopping just short of complete destruction (see 4:27; 5:10,18; 30:11; 46:28). *glean.* See notes on Ruth 2:2; Is 17:5. *remnant.* See 11:23; 23:3; 31:7; 40:11,15; 42:2,15,19; 43:5; 44:7,12,14, 28; 50:20; see also note on Is 10:20–22. *vine.* Symbolic of Israel (see 2:21 and note; 5:10).

6:10 Jeremiah speaks. *give warning.* See note on v. 8. *their ear is uncircumcised.* See also 4:4 and note. The imagery of uncircumcised ears is found elsewhere only in Acts 7:51.

‡6:11 The prophet speaks, then the Lord resumes His speech (through v. 23). *full of the fury.* See 25:15. *children . . . young men . . . husband . . . wife . . . aged.* All will be judged, from youngest to oldest (see v. 13). *Abroad.* In the streets, where children play (see 9:21; Zech 8:5).

12 And [a]their houses shall be turned unto others, *with their* fields and wives together: for I will stretch out my hand upon the inhabitants of the land, saith the LORD.

13 For from the least of them even unto the greatest of them every one *is* given to [a]covetousness; and from the prophet even unto the priest every one dealeth falsely.

14 They have [a]healed also the [1]hurt of *the daughter of* my people slightly, [b]saying, Peace, peace; when *there is* no peace.

15 Were they [a]ashamed when they had committed abomination? nay, they were not at all ashamed, neither could they blush: therefore they shall fall among them that fall: at the time *that* I visit them they shall be cast down, saith the LORD.

16 Thus saith the LORD, Stand ye in the ways, and see, and ask for the [a]old paths, where *is* the good way, and walk therein, and ye shall find [b]rest for your souls. But they said, We will not walk *therein.*

17 Also I set [a]watchmen over you, *saying,* Hearken to the sound of the trumpet. But they said, We will not hearken.

18 Therefore hear, ye nations, and know, O congregation, what *is* among them.

19 [a]Hear, O earth: behold, I will bring evil upon this people, *even* [b]the fruit of their thoughts, because they have not hearkened unto my words, nor *to* my law, but rejected it.

20 [a]To what purpose cometh there to me incense [b]from Sheba, and the sweet cane from a far country? [c]your burnt offerings *are* not acceptable, nor your sacrifices sweet unto me.

21 Therefore thus saith the LORD, Behold, I will lay stumblingblocks before this people, and the fathers and the sons together shall fall upon them; the neighbour and his friend shall perish.

22 Thus saith the LORD, Behold, a people cometh from the [a]north country, and a great nation shall be raised from the sides of the earth.

23 They shall lay hold on bow and spear; they *are* cruel, and have no mercy; their voice [a]roareth like the sea; and they ride upon horses, set in array as men for war against thee, O daughter of Zion.

24 We have heard the fame thereof: our hands wax feeble: [a]anguish hath taken hold of us, *and* pain, as of a woman in travail.

25 Go not forth *into* the field, nor walk by the way; for the sword of the enemy *and* fear *is* on every side.

26 O daughter of my people, [a]gird *thee* with sackcloth, [b]and wallow thyself in ashes: [c]make thee mourning, *as* for an only *son,* most bitter lamentation: for the spoiler shall suddenly come upon us.

27 I have set thee *for* a tower *and* [a]a fortress among my people, that thou mayest know and try their way.

28 [a]They *are* all grievous revolters, [b]walking with slanders: *they are* [c]brass and iron; they *are* all corrupters.

29 The bellows are burnt, the lead is consumed of the fire; the founder melteth in vain: for the wicked are not plucked away.

6:12 [a]Deut. 28:30; ch. 8:10
6:13 [a]Is. 56:11; ch. 8:10; Mic. 3:5,11
6:14 [1]Heb. *bruise,* or, *breach* [a]ch. 8:11; Ezek. 13:10 [b]ch. 4:10; 23:17
6:15 [a]ch. 3:3
6:16 [a]Is. 8:20; ch. 18:15; Mal. 4:4; Luke 16:29 [b]Mat. 11:29
6:17 [a]Is. 21:11; 58:1; ch. 25:4; Ezek. 3:17; Hab. 2:1
6:19 [a]Is. 1:2 [b]Prov. 1:31
6:20 [a]Ps. 40:6; 50:7-9; Is. 1:11; 66:3; Amos 5:21; Mic. 6:6 [b]Is. 60:6 [c]ch. 7:21
6:22 [a]ch. 1:15; 10:22
6:23 [a]Is. 5:30
6:24 [a]ch. 4:31; 13:21; 49:24; 50:43
6:26 [a]ch. 4:8 [b]ch. 25:34; Mic. 1:10 [c]Zech. 12:10
6:27 [a]ch. 1:18; 15:20
6:28 [a]ch. 5:23 [b]ch. 9:4 [c]Ezek. 22:18

6:12–15 Repeated almost verbatim in 8:10–12.

6:12 *houses . . . fields . . . wives.* See Ex 20:17; Deut 5:21. *turned to others.* As Deut 28:30 warned—one of the covenant curses. *stretch out my hand upon.* To destroy (see 15:6).

6:13 See 1:18 and note.

6:14 *hurt.* See note on v. 7. *Peace . . . no peace.* A common message of false and greedy prophets (see Ezek 13:10; Mic 3:5). The wicked, in any case, cannot expect to enjoy peace (Is 48:22; 57:21).

6:16 *old paths.* The tried and true ways of Judah's godly ancestors (see 18:15; Deut 32:7). *walk therein.* See Is 30:21. *ye shall find rest for your souls.* Quoted by Jesus in Mat 11:29 (see Is 28:12; cf. Ps 119:165).

6:17 *watchmen.* True prophets (see Ezek 3:17; 33:7; Hab 2:1). *sound of the trumpet.* To warn of approaching danger (see v. 1; see also note on Joel 2:1).

6:19 *Hear, O earth.* See Mic 1:2. *nor to my law, but rejected it,* Disobeyed the law of Moses (see 8:8–9).

6:20 *Sheba.* Located in southwestern Arabia, it was the center of the spice trade (see Is 60:6 and note). *sweet cane.* See Ex 30:23; Sol 4:14, "calamus"; Is 43:24. Cane, which probably came from India, was an ingredient in the sacred anointing oil (Ex 30:25). *burnt offerings are not acceptable.* The attitude of one's heart and the manner of one's life are far more important than the ritual of sacrifice (see note on Is 1:11–15).

6:21 *stumblingblocks.* The Babylonian invaders (see v. 22).

6:22–24 Repeated almost verbatim in 50:41–43.

6:22 *the north country.* Babylonia (see 4:6; Is 41:25 and notes). *from the sides of the earth.* See 25:32; 31:8.

6:23 *spear.* The Hebrew for this word is translated "a target of brass" in 1 Sam 17:6. Another possibility is "sword," as attested in *The War of the Sons of Light against the Sons of Darkness,* one of the Dead Sea Scrolls (see essay, p. 1346). *roareth like the sea.* See Is 5:30; see also Is 17:12 and note. *horses.* See note on 4:13; see also 8:16. *daughter of Zion.* A personification of Jerusalem and its inhabitants (see v. 2; 4:31).

6:24–26 The prophet speaks to, and on behalf of, the people of Judah.

6:24 *hands wax feeble.* Courage fails (see Is 13:7). *anguish.* See note on 4:19.

6:25 *fear is on every side.* A favorite expression of Jeremiah (20:10; 46:5; 49:29). The Hebrew for this phrase is used once as a proper name, "Magor-missabib" (20:3; see note there).

6:26 *gird thee with sackcloth.* See 4:8; see also note on Gen 37:34. *wallow thyself in ashes . . . mourning.* See Ezek 27:30–31; cf. Mic 1:10. *only son.* A father's most precious possession (see Gen 22:12,16; Amos 8:10; Zech 12:10; Rom 8:32). *spoiler.* Babylon (see note on 4:7).

6:27–30 The Lord speaks to Jeremiah and appoints him to test the people of Judah as a refiner tests metals (see 9:7; Is 1:25; Mal 3:2–3).

6:27 *tower and . . . fortress.* See Job 23:10.

6:28 *walking with slanders.* Contrary to Lev 19:16. *brass and iron.* Base metals when compared to gold and silver. *are all corrupters.* See Deut 31:29; Is 1:4.

6:29 In ancient times, lead was added to silver ore in the refining process. When the crucible was heated, the lead oxidized and acted as a flux to remove the alloys. Here the process fails because the ore is not pure enough (cf. Ezek 24:11–13).

30 [a][1]Reprobate silver shall *men* call them, because the LORD hath rejected them.

Judah's idolatry and immorality

7 The word that came to Jeremiah from the LORD, saying,

2 [a]Stand in the gate of the LORD's house, and proclaim there this word, and say, Hear the word of the LORD, all *ye of* Judah, that enter in at these gates to worship the LORD.

3 Thus saith the LORD of hosts, the God of Israel, [a]Amend your ways and your doings, and I will cause you to dwell in this place.

4 [a]Trust ye not in lying words, saying, The temple of the LORD, The temple of the LORD, The temple of the LORD, *are* these.

5 For if you throughly amend your ways and your doings; if you throughly [a]execute judgment between a man and his neighbour;

6 *If* ye oppress not the stranger, the fatherless, and the widow, and shed not innocent blood in this place, [a]neither walk after other gods to your hurt:

7 [a]Then will I cause you to dwell in this place, in [b]the land that I gave to your fathers, for ever and ever.

8 ¶ Behold, [a]ye trust in [b]lying words, *that* cannot profit.

9 [a]*Will ye* steal, murder, and commit adultery, and swear falsely, and burn incense unto Baal, and [b]walk after other gods whom ye know not;

10 [a]And come and stand before me in this house, [b][1]which is called by my name, and say, We are delivered to do all these abominations?

11 Is [a]this house, which is called by my name, become a [b]den of robbers in your eyes? Behold, even I have seen *it,* saith the LORD.

12 But go ye now unto [a]my place which *was* in Shiloh, [b]where I set my name at the first, and see [c]what I did to it for the wickedness of my people Israel.

13 And now, because ye have done all these works, saith the LORD, and I spake unto you, [a]rising up early and speaking, but ye heard not; and I [b]called you, but ye answered not;

14 Therefore will I do unto *this* house, which is called by my name, wherein ye trust, and unto the place which I gave to you and to your fathers, as I have done to [a]Shiloh.

15 And I will cast you out of my sight, [a]as I

6:30 [1]Or, *Refuse silver* [a]Is. 1:22
7:2 [a]ch. 26:2
7:3 [a]ch. 18:11; 26:13
7:4 [a]Mic. 3:11
7:5 [a]ch. 22:3
7:6 [a]Deut. 6:14,15; 8:19; ch. 13:10
7:7 [a]Deut. 4:40 [b]ch. 3:18
7:8 [a]ver. 4 [b]ch. 5:31; 14:13,14
7:9 [a]1 Ki. 18:21; Hos. 4:1,2; Zeph. 1:5 [b]Ex. 20:3
7:10 [1]Heb. *whereupon my name is called* [a]Ezek. 23:39 [b]ver. 11,14; ch. 32:34; 34:15
7:11 [a]Is. 56:7 [b]Mat. 21:13; Mark 11:17; Luke 19:46
7:12 [a]Josh. 18:1; Judg. 18:31 [b]Deut. 12:11 [c]1 Sam. 4:10; Ps. 78:60; ch. 26:6
7:13 [a]2 Chr. 36:15; ch. 11:7 [b]Prov. 1:24; Is. 65:12; 66:4
7:14 [a]1 Sam. 4:10; Ps. 78:60
7:15 [a]2 Ki. 17:23

6:30 *men call them.* The "grievous revolters" (v. 28), the "wicked" (v. 29), have failed to pass the Lord's test. Nothing worthwhile can be made of them.

7:1–10:25 A series of temple messages delivered by Jeremiah, perhaps over a period of several years. Since 26:2–6,12–15 is very similar in content to ch. 7, it is possible that chs. 7–10 (or at least ch. 7) date to the reign of Jehoiakim (see 26:1). On the other hand, Jeremiah may have repeated various themes on several occasions during his lengthy ministry. In any event, nothing in chs. 7–10 is inappropriate to the time of King Josiah.

7:1–8:3 The straightforward narrative of this section asserts that Solomon's temple in Jerusalem will not escape the fate of the earlier sanctuary at Shiloh if the people of Judah persist in worshiping false gods.

7:1 *The word that came.* See 1:2 and note; 1:4,11,13; 2:1.

7:2 *gate.* In the wall between the inner and outer courts of the temple, perhaps the so-called "new gate" (26:10; 36:10). *Hear.* See note on 2:4. *all ye . . . that enter . . . to worship.* Perhaps during one of the three annual pilgrimage festivals (see Deut 16:16 and note). *gates.* Leading into the outer court.

7:3 *this place.* The land God had given them (see v. 7; 14:13,15; 24:5–6).

7:4 *lying words.* Spoken by false prophets. The idea that God would not destroy Jerusalem simply because His dwelling, the temple, was located there was a delusion, fostered in part by the miraculous deliverance of the city during the reign of Hezekiah (see 2 Ki 19:32–36; cf. 2 Sam 7:11b–13; Ps 132:13–14). In the light of Judah's sinful rebellion against the Lord such an idea was of "no avail" (v. 8; see Mic 3:11). *temple . . . temple . . . temple.* Vain and repetitious babbling (cf. Mat 6:7). Often such a threefold repeating of a word or phrase is for emphasis (see 22:29; see also note on Is 6:3). *are these.* Lit. "They are," referring to the buildings that constituted the entire temple complex.

7:6 Rulers and people alike needed to hear and act on these prophetic words (see 22:2–3). *stranger . . . fatherless . . . widow.* See Deut 16:11,14; 24:19–21; 26:12–13; 27:19. *innocent blood.* See 19:4; 22:17; 26:15; see also the frightening example of King Manasseh (2 Ki 21:16).

7:7 *land . . . for ever and ever.* See Gen 17:8 and note.

7:8 *lying words.* See note on v. 4.

7:9 This one verse mentions the violation of fully half of the ten commandments (cf. Hos 4:2). *burn incense unto Baal.* See note on 1:16. *walk after other gods whom ye know not.* See 19:4. Tragically, such sins would be the cause of their exile to lands they had not known (see 9:14,16; 16:11,13).

7:10 *house, which is called by my name.* See vv. 11,14,30; 25:29; 32:34; 34:15; 1 Ki 8:43; 2 Chr 6:33; 20:9; Dan 9:18. The "name" of God is equivalent to His gracious presence in such passages (see vv. 12,15). *We are delivered.* See 12:12. *abominations.* See 2:7; see also note on Lev 7:21.

7:11 Together with the last half of Is 56:7, part of this verse is quoted by Jesus in Mat 21:13; Mark 11:17; Luke 19:46. *den of robbers.* As thieves hide in caves and think they are safe, so the people of Judah falsely trust in the temple to protect them in spite of their sins.

7:12 See note on 7:1–8:3. *place . . . in Shiloh . . . see what I did to it.* See v. 14; 26:6,9; Ps 78:60–61. The tabernacle had been set up in Shiloh after the conquest of Canaan (Josh 18:1) and was still there at the end of the period of the judges (see 1 Sam 1:9 and note). Modern Seilun, near a main highway about 18 miles north of Jerusalem, preserves the name of the ancient site. Archaeological excavations there indicate that it was destroyed by the Philistines c. 1050 B.C. The tabernacle itself was not included in that destruction, since it was still in existence at Gibeon during David's reign (see 1 Chr 21:29). One or more auxiliary buildings had apparently been erected at Shiloh near the tabernacle in connection with various aspects of public worship there (cf. the reference to the "doors of the house of the LORD" in 1 Sam 3:15). Such structures would have been destroyed with the city itself, perhaps sometime after the events of 1 Sam 4.

7:13 *rising . . . speaking.* The Hebrew idiom underlying this phrase, suggesting repetition or intensity of action, is found frequently in Jeremiah (v. 25; 11:7; 25:3–4; 26:5; 29:19; 32:33; 35:14–15; 44:4), but appears nowhere else in the OT.

7:15 *cast you out of my sight.* Into exile (see Deut 29:28). *as I have . . . all your brethren.* God sent Israel, the northern kingdom, into captivity in 721 B.C. (see 2 Ki 17:20). *Ephraim.* An-

have cast out all your brethren, [b]*even* the whole seed of Ephraim.

16 Therefore [a]pray not thou for this people, neither lift up cry nor prayer for them, neither make intercession to me: [b]for I *will* not hear thee.

17 Seest thou not what they do in the cities of Judah and in the streets of Jerusalem?

18 [a]The children gather wood, and the fathers kindle the fire, and the women knead *their* dough, to make cakes to the [1]queen of heaven, and to [b]pour out drink offerings unto other gods, that *they* may provoke me to anger.

19 [a]Do they provoke me to anger? saith the LORD: *do they* not *provoke* themselves to the confusion of their own faces?

20 Therefore thus saith the Lord GOD; Behold, mine anger and my fury *shall be* poured out upon this place, upon man, and upon beast, and upon the trees of the field, and upon the fruit of the ground; and it shall burn, and shall not be quenched.

21 ¶ Thus saith the LORD of hosts, the God of Israel; [a]Put your burnt offerings unto your sacrifices, and eat flesh.

22 [a]For I spake not unto your fathers, nor commanded them in the day that I brought them out of the land of Egypt, [1]concerning burnt offerings or sacrifices:

23 But this thing commanded I them, saying, [a]Obey my voice, and [b]I will be your God, and ye shall be my people: and walk ye in all the ways that I have commanded you, that it may be well unto you.

7:15 [b]Ps. 78:67
7:16 [a]Ex. 32:10 [b]ch. 15:1
7:18 [1]Or, *frame,* or, *workmanship of heaven* [a]ch. 44:17 [b]ch. 19:13
7:19 [a]Deut. 32:16,21
7:21 [a]Is. 1:11; Amos 5:21; Hos. 8:13
7:22 [1]Heb. *concerning the matter of* [a]1 Sam. 15:22; Ps. 51:16; Hos. 6:6
7:23 [a]Ex. 15:26; Deut. 6:3 [b]Ex. 19:5; Lev. 26:12
7:24 [1]Or, *stubbornness* [2]Heb. *were* [a]Ps. 81:11 [b]Ps. 81:12 [c]ch. 32:33
7:25 [a]2 Chr. 36:15 [b]ver. 13
7:26 [a]ch. 11:8 [b]Neh. 9:17 [c]ch. 16:12
7:27 [a]Ezek. 2:7
7:28 [1]Or, *instruction* [a]ch. 5:3 [b]ch. 9:3
7:29 [a]Job 1:20; Is. 15:2; Mic. 1:16
7:30 [a]2 Ki. 21:4; 2 Chr. 33:4; Ezek. 7:20; Dan. 9:27
7:31 [1]Heb. *came it upon my heart* [a]2 Ki. 23:10 [b]Ps. 106:38 [c]Deut. 17:3

24 [a]But they hearkened not, nor inclined their ear, but [b]walked in the counsels *and* in the [1]imagination of their evil heart, and [c][2]went backward, and not forward.

25 Since the day that your fathers came forth out of the land of Egypt unto this day, I have even [a]sent unto you all my servants the prophets, [b]daily rising up early and sending *them:*

26 [a]Yet they hearkened not unto me, nor inclined their ear, but [b]hardened their neck: [c]they did worse than their fathers.

27 Therefore [a]thou shalt speak all these words unto them; but they will not hearken to thee: thou shalt also call unto them; but they will not answer thee.

28 But thou shalt say unto them, This *is* a nation that obeyeth not the voice of the LORD their God, [a]nor receiveth [1]correction: [b]truth is perished, and is cut off from their mouth.

The terrible days to come

29 ¶ [a]Cut off thine hair, *O Jerusalem,* and cast *it* away, and take up a lamentation on high places; for the LORD hath rejected and forsaken the generation of his wrath.

30 For the children of Judah have done evil in my sight, saith the LORD: [a]they have set their abominations in the house which is called by my name, to pollute it.

31 And they have built the [a]high places of Tophet, which *is* in the valley of the son of Hinnom, to [b]burn their sons and their daughters in the fire; [c]which I commanded *them* not, neither [1]came it into my heart.

---

other name for Israel (see, e.g., 31:9)—and, ironically, the tribal territory in which Shiloh was located.

7:16 Perhaps the events of ch. 26 belong chronologically between vv. 15 and 16 (see Introduction: Outline). *pray not thou for this people.* As a true prophet would (see 27:18; Ex 32:31–32; 1 Sam 12:23). See 11:14; 14:11. There is virtually no hope for them. On various occasions, however, Jeremiah prayed for his countrymen (see, e.g., 18:20).

7:18 *children . . . fathers . . . women.* Entire families participate in idolatrous worship. *cakes.* See 44:19. *queen of heaven.* A Babylonian title for Ishtar, an important goddess in the Babylonian pantheon (see 44:17–19,25). *drink offerings unto other gods.* And sometimes to the queen of heaven herself (see 44:19,25). *provoke me.* See Deut 31:29.

7:19 *the confusion of their own faces.* See 3:25.

7:20 All nature suffers when God judges sinners (see 5:17; Rom 8:20–22). *burn, and shall not be quenched.* See 4:4; 21:12; see also Is 1:31; Amos 5:6.

7:21 *eat flesh.* Because of your sinful deeds your sacrifices are worthless, so you might as well eat them yourselves.

7:22–23 Sacrifices are valid only when accompanied by sincere repentance and joyful obedience (see 6:20; Is 1:11–15 and note).

7:23 *your God . . . my people.* The most basic summary of the relationship between God and Israel implied in the covenant at Sinai (see Ex 6:7; Lev 26:12 and notes; Deut 26:17–18).

7:24 *walked in . . . evil heart.* See note on 3:17; see also Gen 6:5 and note.

7:25 *sent . . . sending.* See note on v. 13. *my servants the prophets.* See 25:4; 26:5; 29:19; 35:15; 44:4; see also Zech 1:6 and note. God had promised that Moses would be the first in a long line of prophets who would speak in the Lord's name and serve Him faithfully (see Deut 18:15–22 and notes).

7:26 *hardened their neck.* See 17:23; 19:15; see also notes on Ex 32:9; Neh 3:5.

7:28 *not . . . receiveth correction.* See 2:30; 5:3. *truth . . . is cut off from their mouth.* No one seeks the truth (see 5:1 and note).

7:29 Addressed to Jerusalem. *Cut off thine hair.* A sign of mourning (see Job 1:20; Mic 1:16). The Hebrew for the word "hair" is related to the word "Nazarite" (see Num 6:2) and referred originally to the diadem worn by the high priest (see Ex 29:6). The Nazarite's hair was the symbol of his separation or consecration (Num 6:7). As the Nazarite was commanded to cut off his hair when he became ceremonially unclean (Num 6:9), so also Jerusalem must cut off her hair because of her sins. *lamentation on high places.* See 3:21; see also note on 3:2.

7:30 *set their abominations in the house.* Manasseh had put a carved Asherah pole (a wooden symbol of the goddess Asherah; see 2 Ki 13:6 and note) in the temple (2 Ki 21:7). Jeremiah's contemporary, the good King Josiah, removed the pole and other accessories to idol worship (2 Ki 23:4–7). But less than 20 years after Josiah's death, Ezekiel reported that there were numerous idols in the temple courts (see Ezek 8:3,5–6,10,12). *pollute it.* See note on 2:7.

7:31 *high places.* Pagan cult centers, usually (but not here) located on natural heights (see 1 Sam 9:13–14; 10:5; 1 Ki 11:7). *Tophet.* See v. 32; 19:6,11–14; see also note on Is 30:33. The word may be of Aramaic origin with the meaning "fireplace," though in cultures outside Israel it was used as a common noun meaning "place of child sacrifice." Its vocalization was perhaps intentionally conformed to that of Hebrew *bosheth,* "shameful thing" (see note on Judg 6:32), often used in connection with

32 Therefore, behold, [a]the days come, saith the LORD, that it shall no more be called Tophet, nor the valley of the son of Hinnom, but the valley of slaughter: [b]for they shall bury in Tophet, till there be no place.

33 And the [a]carcases of this people shall be meat for the fowls of the heaven, and for the beasts of the earth; and none shall fray *them* away.

34 Then will I cause to [a]cease from the cities of Judah, and from the streets of Jerusalem, the voice of mirth, and the voice of gladness, the voice of the bridegroom, and the voice of the bride: for [b]the land shall be desolate.

8 At that time, saith the LORD, they shall bring out the bones of the kings of Judah, and the bones of his princes, and the bones of the priests, and the bones of the prophets, and the bones of the inhabitants of Jerusalem, out of their graves:

2 And they shall spread them before the sun, and the moon, and all the host of heaven, whom they have loved, and whom they have served, and after whom they have walked, and whom they have sought, and [a]whom they have worshipped: they shall not be gathered, [b]nor be buried; they shall be for dung upon the face of the earth.

3 And [a]death shall be chosen rather than life by all the residue of them that remain of this evil family, which remain in all the places whither I have driven them, saith the LORD of hosts.

7:32 [a]ch. 19:6 [b]2 Ki. 23:10; ch. 19:11
7:33 [a]Deut. 28:26
7:34 [a]Is. 24:7,8; Ezek. 26:13; Hos. 2:11; Rev. 18:23 [b]Lev. 26:33
8:2 [a]2 Ki. 23:5; Ezek. 8:16 [b]ch. 22:19
8:3 [a]Job 3:21; 7:15,16; Rev. 9:6
8:5 [a]ch. 7:24 [b]ch. 9:6 [c]ch. 5:3
8:6 [a]2 Pet. 3:9
8:7 [a]Is. 1:3 [b]Sol. 2:12 [c]ch. 5:4,5
8:8 [1]Or, *the false pen of the scribes worketh for falsehood* [a]Rom. 2:17 [b]Is. 10:1
8:9 [1]Or, *Have they been ashamed, etc.* [2]Heb. *the wisdom of what thing* [a]ch. 6:15
8:10 [a]Zeph. 1:13
8:11 [a]ch. 6:14 [b]Ezek. 13:10

Punishment of sinful Israel

4 ¶ Moreover thou shalt say unto them, Thus saith the LORD; Shall they fall, and not arise? shall he turn away, and not return?

5 Why *then* is this people of Jerusalem [a]slidden back *by* a perpetual backsliding? [b]they hold fast deceit, [c]they refuse to return.

6 [a]I hearkened and heard, *but* they spake not aright: no man repented him of his wickedness, saying, What have I done? every one turned to his course, as the horse rusheth into the battle.

7 Yea, [a]the stork in the heaven knoweth her appointed times; and [b]the turtle and the crane and the swallow observe the time of their coming; but [c]my people know not the judgment of the LORD.

8 How do ye say, We *are* wise, [a]and the law of the LORD *is* with us? Lo, certainly [b][1]in vain made he *it;* the pen of the scribes *is* in vain.

9 [a][1]The wise *men* are ashamed, they are dismayed and taken: lo, they have rejected the word of the LORD; and [2]what wisdom *is* in them?

10 Therefore [a]will I give their wives unto others, *and* their fields to them that *shall* inherit *them:* for every one from the least even unto the greatest is given to covetousness, from the prophet even unto the priest every one dealeth falsely.

11 For they have [a]healed the hurt of the daughter of my people slightly, saying, [b]Peace, peace; when *there is* no peace.

idol worship (see notes on 2:26; 3:25). The OT Topheth had a fire pit (see Is 30:33), into which the hapless children were apparently thrown. *valley of the son of Hinnom.* See v. 32; 19:2,6; 32:35; see also note on Josh 15:5. It was used as a trash dump and also as a place for sacrificing children to pagan gods. From the abbreviated name "valley of Hinnom" (see Neh 11:30 and note), Hebrew *ge' hinnom,* came "Gehenna" (Greek *geenna*), consistently translated in the NT as "hell," the place of eternal, fiery punishment for all who die without having trusted Christ as Savior (see, e.g., Mat 18:9; Mark 9:47–48). *burn their sons and their daughters in the fire.* A horrible ritual, prohibited in the law of Moses (see Lev 18:21 and note; Deut 18:10) but practiced by Ahaz (see 2 Ki 16:2–3) and Manasseh (2 Ki 21:1,6).

7:32 *behold . . . valley of the slaughter.* Repeated almost verbatim in 19:6. Their place of sacrifice would become their cemetery when the people of Judah were slaughtered by the Babylonian invaders.

7:33 The punishment announced here is one of the curses for covenant disobedience (see Deut 28:26). *meat for the fowls . . . of the earth.* See 16:4; 19:7; see also 34:20, where the same judgment is the result of violating God's covenant (34:18–19). To remain unburied was an unspeakable abomination in ancient times.

7:34 See 16:9; 25:10; contrast 33:10–11. *land shall be desolate.* Another covenant curse (Lev 26:31,33).

8:1 *bring out the bones . . . out of their graves.* A gross indignity and sacrilege (see 2 Ki 23:16,18; Amos 2:1 and note). *kings . . . princes . . . priests . . . prophets.* See 2:26; see also note on 1:18.

8:2 *spread them before the sun . . . moon . . . host of heaven.* To hasten their disintegration, and perhaps also to demonstrate that the heavenly bodies, which had been worshiped by some of Judah's kings (see 2 Ki 21:3,5; 23:11), among others, were powerless to help. *loved . . . served . . . walked . . . sought . . . worshipped.* Acts of homage and adoration that should have been given to God alone. *they.* The bones. *not be gathered, nor be buried.* Contrast 2 Sam 21:13–14. *dung.* See 9:22; 16:4; 25:33.

8:3 *the residue of them that remain.* See note on 6:9.

8:4–9:26 In contrast to 7:1–8:3, this section is almost completely in poetic form. Jeremiah resumes his extended commentary on the inevitability of divine judgment against sinners.

8:4 *say unto them.* Connects this section with the previous (see 7:28). *turn away . . . not return.* The Hebrew for these two verbs is identical, forming a play on words.

8:5 The general truths stated in v. 4 are routinely and perversely violated by the people of Jerusalem. *slidden back . . . perpetual . . . return.* Continuing the wordplay of v. 4.

8:6 *I.* The Lord. *turned.* The Hebrew for this word continues the wordplay of vv. 4–5. *his course.* And therefore evil (see 23:10).

8:7 See Is 1:3. Although migratory birds obey their God-given instincts, God's rebellious people refuse to obey His laws. *know not the judgment of the LORD.* See note on 5:4.

8:8–9 *law of the LORD . . . word of the LORD.* Misinterpreting and manipulating the first (the written law of Moses) leads to rejection of the second (God's truth as found in the law and proclaimed by His servants the prophets).

‡8:8 *in vain made he it.* Or, "the scribes have handled it falsely." Contrast 2 Tim 2:15. *the pen . . . is in vain.* Symbolizes mistreatment of the written law. *scribes.* The earliest mention of them as a recognizable group. They were apparently organized on the basis of families (see 1 Chr 2:55; 2 Chr 34:13).

8:9 *rejected . . . wisdom.* Contrast Deut 4:5–6.

8:10–12 See 6:12–15 and notes.

12 Were they [a]ashamed when they had
committed abomination? nay, they were not at
all ashamed, neither could they blush: therefore shall they fall among them that fall: in the
time of their visitation they shall be cast down,
saith the LORD.
13 [1]I will surely consume them, saith the
LORD: *there shall be* no grapes [a]on the vine,
nor figs on the [b]fig tree, and the leaf shall fade;
and *the things that* I have given them shall
pass away from them.
14 Why do we sit still? [a]assemble yourselves, and let us enter into the defenced cities, and let us be silent there: for the LORD our
God hath put us to silence, and given us [b]wa-
ter of [1]gall to drink, because we have sinned
against the LORD.
15 *We* [a]looked for peace, but no good *came;*
and for a time of health, and behold trouble.
16 The snorting of his horses was heard
from [a]Dan: the whole land trembled at the
sound of the neighing of his [b]strong ones; for
they are come, and have devoured the land,
and [1]all that is in it; the city, and those that
dwell therein.
17 For behold, I will send serpents, cocka-
trices, among you, which *will* not *be* [a]charmed,
and they shall bite you, saith the LORD.
18 ¶ *When* I would comfort myself against
sorrow, my heart *is* faint [1]in me.
19 Behold the voice of the cry of the
daughter of my people [1]because of them that
dwell in [a]a far country: *Is* not the LORD in
Zion? *is* not her king in her? Why have they
provoked me to anger with their graven images, *and* with strange vanities?

8:12 [a]ch. 3:3
8:13 [1]Or, *In gathering I will consume* [a]Joel 1:7 [b]Mat. 21:19
8:14 [1]Or, *poison* [a]ch. 4:5 [b]ch. 9:15
8:15 [a]ch. 14:19
8:16 [1]Heb. *the fulness thereof* [a]ch. 4:15 [b]ch. 47:3
8:17 [a]Ps. 58:4,5
8:18 [1]Heb. *upon*
8:19 [1]Heb. *because of the country of them that are far off* [a]Is. 39:3
8:21 [a]ch. 9:1 [b]Joel 2:6
8:22 [1]Heb. *gone up?* [a]ch. 46:11
9:1 [1]Heb. *Who will give my head, etc.* [a]Is. 22:4
9:2 [a]ch. 5:7,8
9:3 [a]Ps. 64:3 [b]1 Sam. 2:12
9:4 [1]Or, *friend* [a]Mic. 7:5,6 [b]ch. 6:28
9:5 [1]Or, *mock*

20 The harvest is past, the summer is ended, and we are not saved.
21 [a]For the hurt of the daughter of my
people am I hurt; I am [b]black; astonishment
hath taken hold on me.
22 *Is there* no [a]balm in Gilead; *is there* no
physician there? why then is not the health of
the daughter of my people [1]recovered?

9 [1]O [a]that my head were waters, and
mine eyes a fountain of tears,
That I might weep day and night for the
slain of the daughter of my people!
2 O that I had in the wilderness a
lodging place of wayfaring men;
That I might leave my people, and go
from them!
For [a]they *be* all adulterers, an assembly
of treacherous *men.*
3 And [a]they bend their tongues *like* their
bow *for* lies:
But they are not valiant for the truth
upon the earth;
For they proceed from evil to evil,
And they [b]know not me, saith the LORD.
4 [a]Take ye heed every one of his
[1]neighbour,
And trust ye not in any brother:
For every brother will utterly supplant,
And every neighbour will [b]walk *with*
slanders.
5 And they will [1]deceive every one his
neighbour,
And will not speak the truth:
They have taught their tongue to speak
lies,

8:13–9:24 This section is read aloud in synagogues every year on the ninth of Ab (see chart, p. 92), the day the temple in Jerusalem was destroyed by the Babylonians in 586 B.C. and by the Romans in A.D. 70.
8:13 *grapes . . . figs.* Symbolic of individual people also in Mic 7:1; see ch. 24. *vine.* Israel (see 2:21 and note). *leaf shall fade.* Contrast 17:8; Ps 1:3.
8:14–16 On behalf of the people the prophet speaks, envisioning the Babylonian invasion.
8:14 *assemble yourselves.* See 4:5. The Hebrew for this phrase forms a wordplay with the Hebrew for "I will surely consume them" in v. 13. *enter into the defenced cities.* See note on 4:5. *water of gall.* The phrase is unique to the prophet Jeremiah (see 9:15; 23:15; cf. 25:15).
8:15 Repeated almost verbatim in 14:19. *peace.* Under the circumstances, a false hope (see notes on 4:10; 6:14). *a time of health.* See note on 6:7.
8:16 *His horses.* See note on 4:13. *Dan.* Far away, close to the northern border of Israel. *strong ones.* Or "stallions"; see 47:3; 50:11.
8:17 *serpents . . . which will not be charmed.* Such are the wicked always (see Ps 58:4–5).
8:18 The prophet speaks. *my heart is faint.* See Lam 1:22; 5:17.
8:19 The prophet speaks in the first part of the verse, the Lord in the last part. *them that dwell in a far country.* Judah in Babylonian exile (see Ps 137:1–4) as Jeremiah envisions the future. *Is not the LORD in Zion?* Cf. Mic 3:11. The people are perplexed at their fate, still wondering how God could have permitted the destruction of His land and temple (see note on 7:4). *King.* God (see Is 33:22). *provoked me.* See 7:18; Deut 31:29. *graven . . . strange vanities.* See note on 2:5.
8:20 The people speak from the hopelessness of their exile. *we are not saved.* We have been captured by the enemy.
8:21 Jeremiah identifies himself with his exiled countrymen. *taken hold of me.* See 6:24.
8:22 *balm in Gilead.* See 46:11; 51:8. The territory of Gilead was an important source of spices and medicinal herbs (see note on Gen 37:25). *not the health . . . recovered.* Contrast 30:17.
9:1–2 The prophet's frustration is highlighted as he speaks of his countrymen with tender sympathy in v. 1 and with indignant disgust in v. 2.
9:1 Jeremiah is often called the "weeping prophet"—a well-deserved title (see v. 10; the book of Lamentations; cf. 2 Sam 18:33; Mat 23:37; Rom 9:2–4; 10:1).
9:2 The prophet wants to get as far away from his wicked countrymen as possible (cf. Ps 55:6–8). *adulterers.* See note on 2:20. *assembly.* The Hebrew for this word is always used elsewhere in the OT in the sense of a solemn religious assembly (see, e.g., Deut 16:8), sometimes perverted by the worshipers and therefore falling under divine judgment (see Is 1:13; Amos 5:21). *treacherous.* Toward God (see note on 3:7).
9:3–9 The Lord speaks.
9:3 *tongues like their bow.* See vv. 5,8; see also Ps 64:3–4; Jas 3:5–12. *know not me.* See v. 6; Judg 2:10; 1 Sam 2:12; Job 18:21; Hos 4:1; Rom 1:28; contrast Hos 6:3.
‡9:4 *brother will utterly supplant.* A deceiving Jacob (Gen 25:26 and note; 27:36; Hos 12:2–3).

And weary themselves to commit
iniquity.
6 Thine habitation *is* in the midst of
deceit;
Through deceit they refuse to know
me, saith the LORD.
7 Therefore thus saith the LORD of hosts,
Behold, [a]I will melt them, and try
them;
[b]For how shall I do for the daughter of
my people?
8 Their tongue *is as* an arrow shot out; it
speaketh [a]deceit:
One speaketh [b]peaceably to his
neighbour with his mouth,
But [c][1]in heart he layeth [2]his wait.
9 [a]Shall I not visit them for these *things?*
saith the LORD:
Shall not my soul be avenged on such a
nation as this?

10 For the mountains will I take up a
weeping and wailing,
And [a]for the [1]habitations of the
wilderness a lamentation,
Because they are [2]burnt up, so that
none can pass through *them;*
Neither can *men* hear the voice of the
cattle;
[b][3]Both the fowl of the heavens and the
beast
Are fled; they are gone.
11 And I will make Jerusalem [a]heaps, *and*
[b]a den of dragons;
And I will make the cities of Judah
[1]desolate, without an inhabitant.
12 [a]Who *is* the wise man, that may
understand this?
And *who is he* to whom the mouth of
the LORD hath spoken, that he may
declare it,
For what the land perisheth
And is burnt up like a wilderness, that
none passeth through?

9:7 [a]Is. 1:25 [b]Hos. 11:8
9:8 [1]Heb. *in the midst of him* [2]Or, *wait for him* [a]Ps. 12:2 [b]Ps. 55:21 [c]Heb. *in the midst of him*
9:9 [a]ch. 5:9,29
9:10 [1]Or, *pastures* [2]Or, *desolate* [3]Heb. *From the fowl even to, etc.* [a]Hos. 4:3 [b]ch. 4:25
9:11 [1]Heb. *desolation* [a]Is. 25:2 [b]Is. 13:22; 34:13
9:12 [a]Hos. 14:9
9:14 [1]Or, *stubbornness* [a]ch. 7:24 [b]Gal. 1:14
9:15 [a]Ps. 80:5 [b]ch. 8:14; Lam. 3:19
9:16 [a]Lev. 26:33; Deut. 28:64 [b]Lev. 26:33; ch. 44:27; Ezek. 5:2
9:17 [a]2 Chr. 35:25; Job 3:8; Eccl. 12:5; Amos 5:16; Mat. 9:23
9:18 [a]ch. 14:17
9:19 [a]Lev. 18:28

13 And the LORD saith, Because they have
forsaken my law which I set before
them,
And have not obeyed my voice, neither
walked therein;
14 But have [a]walked after the
[1]imagination of their own heart,
And after Baalim, [b]which their fathers
taught them:
15 Therefore thus saith the LORD of hosts,
the God of Israel;
Behold, I *will* [a]feed them, *even* this
people, [b]with wormwood,
And give them water of gall to drink.
16 I will [a]scatter them also among the
heathen, whom neither they nor
their fathers have known:
[b]And I will send a sword after them,
till I have consumed them.
17 Thus saith the LORD of hosts,
Consider ye, and call for [a]the mourning
women, that they may come;
And send for cunning *women,* that
they may come:
18 And let them make haste, and take up
a wailing for us,
That [a]our eyes may run down *with*
tears,
And our eyelids gush out with waters.
19 For a voice of wailing is heard out of
Zion, How are we spoiled!
We are greatly confounded, because we
have forsaken the land,
Because [a]our dwellings have cast *us*
out.
20 Yet hear the word of the LORD, O ye
women,
And let your ear receive the word of
his mouth,
And teach your daughters wailing,
And every one her neighbour
lamentation.
21 For death is come up into our windows,
and is entered into our palaces,

---

‡9:6 *refuse to know me.* The situation has deteriorated even further (v. 3 says simply "know not me").

9:7 *melt . . . and try them.* See 6:27–30 and notes. The Lord will test His people "in the furnace of affliction" (see Is 48:10 and note).

9:8 *tongue . . . deceit.* See v. 3 and note. *with his mouth . . . But in heart.* See Ps 55:21. *peaceably.* See 6:14 and note.

9:9 Repeated from 5:9,29.

9:10 The prophet speaks. See 4:23–26 and notes. *weeping and wailing.* See v. 18; see also note on v. 1. *habitations of the wilderness.* Good for poor grazing at best (see 1 Sam 17:28; cf. Ex 3:1). *burnt up.* Parched by the blazing sun. *none can pass.* See v. 12; Ezek 33:28.

‡9:11 The Lord speaks. *den of dragons.* Undesirable creatures. See 10:22; 49:33; 51:37; Ps 44:19; Is 13:21–22; Lam 5:18; Ezek 13:4; Mal 1:3; contrast Is 35:7. *without an inhabitant.* See 2:15; 4:7 and notes.

9:12 The prophet asks a series of questions. *Who is the wise man . . . ?* See Hos 14:9.

9:13 The Lord answers the prophet and then continues to speak through v. 19. *law which I set before them.* In the days of Moses (see Deut 4:8).

9:14 *imagination.* See note on 3:17. *Baalim.* See 2:23; see also note on Judg 2:11.

9:15 *feed them . . . with wormwood . . . water of gall.* Repeated in 23:15; see note on 8:14. Centuries earlier, Moses had warned the Israelites concerning just such a fate (see Deut 29:18).

9:16 *I will scatter them.* See 13:24; 18:17; 30:11; 46:28. This warning was given in Deut 28:64 as one of the covenant curses. *send a sword after them.* See 42:16. *consumed them.* But not to the last man (see note on 4:27; see especially 44:27–28).

9:17 *mourning women.* Professionals, paid to mourn at funerals and other sorrowful occasions (see 2 Chr 35:25; Eccl 12:5; Amos 5:16).

9:18 The purpose of the professional mourners was to arouse the bereaved to weep and lament. *wailing.* See v. 10. *eyes may run down with tears.* See v. 1.

9:19 *How are we spoiled!* See 4:13,20; 48:1.

9:20–21 The prophet speaks.

9:20 The wailing women will have to teach their daughters how to lament, so great will be the need for their services.

9:21 *death.* Personified here (as in Hab 2:5). Canaanite mythol-

To cut off [a]the children from without,
and the young men from the streets.
22 Speak, Thus saith the LORD,
Even the carcases of men shall fall [a]as
dung upon the open field,
And as the handful after the
harvestman, and none shall gather
them.

23 Thus saith the LORD,
[a]Let not the wise *man* glory in his
wisdom,
Neither let the mighty *man* glory in his
might,
Let not the rich *man* glory in his riches:
24 But [a]let him that glorieth glory in this,
That *he* understandeth and knoweth
me,
That I *am* the LORD which exercise
lovingkindness, judgment, and
righteousness, in the earth:
[b]For in these *things* I delight, saith the
LORD.
25 Behold, the days come, saith the LORD,
That [a]I will [1]punish all *them which are*
circumcised with the uncircumcised;
26 Egypt, and Judah, and Edom, and the
children of Ammon, and Moab,
And all *that are* [1]in the [a]utmost
corners, that dwell in the wilderness:
For all *these* nations *are*
uncircumcised,
And all the house of Israel *are*
[b]uncircumcised in the heart.

9:21 [a]ch. 6:11
9:22 [a]ch. 8:2
9:23 [a]Eccl. 9:11
9:24 [a]1 Cor. 1:31; 2 Cor. 10:17 [b]Mic. 7:18
9:25 [1]Heb. *visit upon* [a]Rom. 2:8,9
9:26 [1]Heb. *cut off into corners,* or, *having the corners* of their hair *polled* [a]ch. 25:23 [b]Lev. 26:41; Ezek. 44:7; Rom. 2:28

10:2 [a]Lev. 18:3
10:3 [1]Heb. *statutes,* or, *ordinances* are *vanity* [a]Is. 40:19; 45:20
10:4 [a]Is. 41:7
10:5 [a]Ps. 115:5; Hab. 2:19; 1 Cor. 12:2 [b]Ps. 115:7; Is. 46:1,7 [c]Is. 41:23
10:6 [a]Ex. 15:11; Ps. 86:8,10
10:7 [1]Or, *it liketh thee* [a]Rev. 15:4 [b]Ps. 89:6

The living God and dead gods

10 Hear ye the word which the LORD
speaketh unto you, O house of
Israel:
2 Thus saith the LORD,
[a]Learn not the way of the heathen,
And be not dismayed at the signs of
heaven;
For the heathen are dismayed at them.
3 For the [1]customs of the people *are* vain:
For [a]*one* cutteth a tree out of the forest,
The work of the hands of the
workman, with the axe.
4 They deck it with silver and with gold;
They [a]fasten it with nails and with
hammers, that it move not.
5 They *are* upright as the palm tree, [a]but
speak not:
They must needs be [b]borne, because
they cannot go.
Be not afraid of them; for [c]they cannot
do evil,
Neither also *is it* in them to do good.
6 Forasmuch as *there is* none [a]like unto
thee, O LORD;
Thou *art* great, and thy name *is* great
in might.
7 [a]Who would not fear thee, O King of
nations? for [1]to thee doth it
appertain:
Forasmuch as [b]among all the wise *men*
of the nations, and in all their
kingdoms, *there is* none like unto
thee.

ogy included a deity named Mot (a word related to the Hebrew word for "death"), the god of infertility and the netherworld. *come up into our windows.* Said of enemy soldiers in Joel 2:9. *children . . . young men.* See 6:11.

9:22 *carcases.* See 7:33 and note. *as dung.* See note on 8:2. *harvestman.* The concept of death as the "grim reaper" comes largely from this verse.

9:23 *Let not . . . the rich man glory in his riches.* An almost exact parallel occurs in the Aramaic *Words of Ahiqar,* written about a century after Jeremiah's time: "Let not the rich man say, 'In my riches I am glorious.' "

‡9:24 1 Cor 1:31 summarizes: "He that glorieth, let him glory in the Lord." *this . . . these.* Ultimately, only God and our knowledge of and love for Him are worthwhile. *understandeth and knoweth.* See 3:15; see also note on 4:22. *I am the LORD.* Ex 6:2–8, a key passage on the doctrine of redemption, begins and ends with this statement of divine self-disclosure. *lovingkindness.* The Hebrew for this word is translated "kindness" in 2:2 (see note there). *in these things I delight.* See Ps 11:7; 33:5; 99:4; 103:6; Mic 6:8; 7:18.

9:25–26 See Rom 2:25–29; see also note on Gen 17:10.

9:26 *in the utmost corners, that dwell in the wilderness.* Arab tribes (see 25:23; 49:32), later to be attacked by the Babylonians under Nebuchadnezzar (see 49:28–33). Cf. Lev 19:27. *uncircumcised in the heart.* See 4:4 and note.

10:1–25 Jeremiah concludes his series of temple messages with a poetic section that focuses primarily on the vast difference between idols and the Lord (vv. 2–16). Idols and their worshipers are condemned in vv. 2–5,8–9,11,14–15, while the one true God is praised in the alternate passages (vv. 6–7,10, 12–13,16). See Is 40:18–20; 41:7; 44:9–20; 46:5–7.

10:1 *Hear.* See note on 2:4.

10:2 *Learn not . . . be not dismayed.* See 1:17. *way.* Refers to the religious practices of the nations. The early Christians often called their distinctive beliefs "the Way" (see Acts 9:2; 19:9,23; 22:4; 24:14,22). *signs of heaven.* The heavenly bodies were created by the Lord for purposes other than idolatrous worship (see Gen 1:14–18 and notes). *heathen are dismayed.* Not only by the heavenly bodies themselves but also by unusual phenomena associated with them (such as comets, meteors and eclipses).

10:3 *vain.* A term that Jeremiah often applies to idols (see vv. 8,15; see also note on 2:5). *tree . . . forest.* See Is 44:14–15. *workman.* The word is often used of idol-makers who work usually—but not always (see Is 40:19)—with wood (see Is 41:7). *the axe.* Cf. Is 44:13.

10:4 *with silver and . . . gold.* Wooden idols were plated with precious metals to beautify them (see Is 30:22; 40:19). *fasten it . . . that it move not.* See Is 40:20; 41:7; cf. 46:7; contrast 1 Sam 5:2–4.

‡10:5 The impotence of idols is described in classic form in Ps 115:4–7; 135:15–18. *upright as the palm tree.* Some translate "like a scarecrow." Verse 70 in the Apocryphal *Letter of Jeremiah* uses the same imagery. *must needs be borne.* Usually on the backs of animals. See Is 46:1. *cannot do evil . . . good.* Idols can do nothing at all (see Is 41:23).

10:6 *none.* Among the gods (see Ps 86:8). *thy name is great in might.* See 16:21.

10:7 *King of nations.* See Ps 47:8–9; 96:10. Unlike the tribal deities, limited to their own territories, the Lord is King over all. *it.* Fear, respect. *among all the wise men . . . none like unto thee.* See Is 19:12; 29:14; 1 Cor 1:20.

8 But they are [1]altogether [a]brutish and
foolish:
The stock *is* a doctrine of vanities.
9 Silver spread into plates is brought
from Tarshish,
And [a]gold from Uphaz, the work of the
workman, and of the hands of the
founder:
Blue and purple *is* their clothing:
They *are* all [b]the work of cunning *men.*
10 But the LORD *is* the [a][1]true God,
He *is* [b]the living God, and an
[c][2]everlasting king:
At his wrath the earth shall tremble,
And the nations shall not be able to
abide his indignation.
11 [1]Thus shall ye say unto them, [a]The
gods that have not made the heavens
and the earth, *even* [b]they shall
perish from the earth, and from
under these heavens.
12 He [a]hath made the earth by his power,
He hath [b]established the world by his
wisdom,
And [c]hath stretched out the heavens
by his discretion.
13 [a]When he uttereth his voice, *there is* a
[1]multitude of waters in the heavens,
And [b]he causeth the vapours to ascend
from the ends of the earth;
He maketh lightnings [2]with rain,
And bringeth forth the wind out of his
treasures.
14 [a]Every man [1]is [b]brutish in *his*
knowledge:
[c]Every founder is confounded by the
graven image:
[d]For his molten image *is* falsehood,
and *there is* no breath in them.
15 They *are* vanity, *and* the work of
errors:
In the time of their visitation they shall
perish.
16 [a]The portion of Jacob *is* not like them:
For he *is* the former of all *things;*
And [b]Israel *is* the rod of his
inheritance:
[c]The LORD of hosts *is* his name.

Coming distress

17 [a]Gather up thy wares out of the land,
O [1]inhabitant of the fortress.
18 For thus saith the LORD,
Behold, I will [a]sling out the inhabitants
of the land at this once,
And will distress them, [b]that they may
find *it so.*
19 [a]Woe is me for my hurt! my wound *is*
grievous:
But I said, [b]Truly this *is* a grief, and [c]I
must bear it.
20 [a]My tabernacle is spoiled, and all my
cords are broken:
My children are gone forth *of* me, and
they *are* not:
There is none to stretch forth my tent
any more,
And to set up my curtains.
21 For the pastors are become brutish,
And have not sought the LORD:
Therefore they shall not prosper;
And all their flocks shall be scattered.
22 Behold, the noise of the bruit is come,
And a great commotion out of the
[a]north country,
To make the cities of Judah desolate,
And a [b]den of dragons.
23 O LORD, I know that the [a]way of man
is not in himself:
It is not in man that walketh to direct
his steps.

10:8 [1]Heb. *in one, or, at once* [a]Ps. 115:8; Hab. 2:18
10:9 [a]Dan. 10:5 [b]Ps. 115:4
10:10 [1]Heb. *God of truth* [2]Heb. *king of eternity* [a]Ps. 31:5 [b]1 Tim. 6:17 [c]Ps. 10:16
10:11 [1][In the Chaldean language] [a]Ps. 96:5 [b]Zech. 13:2
10:12 [a]Gen. 1:1,6; Ps. 136:5 [b]Ps. 93:1 [c]Job 9:8; Ps. 104:2; Is. 40:22
10:13 [1]Or, *noise* [2]Or, *for rain* [a]Job 38:34 [b]Ps. 135:7
10:14 [1]Or, *is more brutish than to know* [a]ch. 51:17 [b]Prov. 30:2 [c]Is. 42:17; 44:11 [d]Hab. 2:18
10:16 [a]Lam. 3:24 [b]Deut. 32:9 [c]Is. 47:4; 54:5
10:17 [1]Heb. *inhabitress* [a]ch. 6:1; Ezek. 12:3
10:18 [a]1 Sam. 25:29 [b]Ezek. 6:10
10:19 [a]ch. 8:21 [b]Ps. 77:10 [c]Mic. 7:9
10:20 [a]ch. 4:20
10:22 [a]ch. 5:15 [b]ch. 9:11
10:23 [a]Prov. 16:1

10:8 *brutish and foolish.* See vv. 14,21; 5:21; see also 4:22 and note. *doctrine of vanities.* Contrast Deut 11:2; Job 5:17; Prov 3:11.
10:9 *Silver . . . from Tarshish.* See Ezek 27:12; see also notes on Is 23:6; Jonah 1:3. *Uphaz.* Mentioned only here; location unknown. *workman, and . . . the founder.* See Is 40:19; 41:7. *Blue and purple . . . clothing.* To make the idols look regal. *all.* The idols.
10:10 Everything that idols are not, the Lord is. *true.* See 1 Thes 1:9. *living.* See Deut 5:26. *everlasting.* See Ex 15:18; Ps 10:16; 29:10. *At his wrath.* See Ps 97:5; Nah 1:5.
10:11 The text of this verse is in Aramaic. The other major Aramaic passages in the OT are Ezra 4:8–6:18; 7:12–26; Dan 2:4–7:28. *them.* Pagan idolaters, who would have been more likely to understand Aramaic (the language of diplomacy during this period) than Hebrew.
10:12–16 Repeated almost verbatim in 51:15–19.
10:12 *He hath.* In contrast to the false gods of v. 11. *stretched out the heavens.* Like a tent or canopy (see Ps 104:2; Is 40:22 and note).
10:13 *he causes the vapours . . . out of his treasures.* Repeated in Ps 135:7, where the one true God is contrasted to false gods (see Ps 135:5,15–17); cf. Job 38:22.
10:14 *brutish.* See vv. 8,21; see also note on 4:22. *image.* Cast in metal; the Hebrew for this word is translated "graven image" in Is 48:5. *no breath.* See Ps 135:17.
10:15 *vanity.* See note on v. 3.
10:16 *portion of Jacob.* A title for God, used again only in 51:19 (see Ps 73:26; 119:57; 142:5; Lam 3:24). *rod of his inheritance.* See Is 63:17. *The LORD of hosts is his name.* See Is 54:5; Amos 4:13.
10:17–22 Destruction and exile are imminent.
10:19–20 On behalf of his countrymen, the prophet bemoans their fate and his own (see 4:19–21).
10:20 *children.* The people of Judah and Jerusalem (Jeremiah never married or had children; see 16:2). *curtains.* See note on 4:20.
10:21 *pastors . . . flocks.* Rulers and people (see note on 2:8). *brutish.* See vv. 8,14; see also note on 4:22. *have not sought the LORD.* Instead, they consult the heavenly bodies (see 8:2). *scattered.* See note on 9:16.
10:22 *great commotion.* The sound of the invaders (see 6:23; 8:16). *north country.* Babylonia (see 4:6; 6:22; see also note on Is 41:25). *den of dragons.* See 9:11 and note.
10:23–25 On the people's behalf, the prophet prays for divine justice.
10:23 Only the Lord can direct people's steps (see Ps 37:23; Prov 16:9).

24 O LORD, [a]correct me, but with judgment;
Not in thine anger, lest thou [1]bring me
to nothing.
25 [a]Pour out thy fury upon the heathen
[b]that know thee not,
And upon the families that call not on
thy name:
For they have eaten up Jacob, and
[c]devoured him, and consumed him,
And have made his habitation desolate.

Judah has broken the covenant

11 The word that came to Jeremiah
from the LORD, saying,
2 Hear ye the words of this covenant, and
speak unto the men of Judah, and to the inhabitants of Jerusalem;
3 And say thou unto them, Thus saith the
LORD God of Israel; [a]Cursed *be* the man that
obeyeth not the words of this covenant,
4 Which I commanded your fathers in the
day that I brought them forth out of the land of
Egypt, [a]from the iron furnace, saying, [b]Obey
my voice, and do them, according to all which
I command you: so shall ye be my people, and
I will be your God:
5 That *I* may perform the [a]oath which I
have sworn unto your fathers, to give them a
land flowing with milk and honey, as *it is* this
day. Then answered I, and said, [1]So be it,
O LORD.
6 Then the LORD said unto me, Proclaim all
these words in the cities of Judah, and in the
streets of Jerusalem, saying, Hear ye the words
of this covenant, [a]and do them.
7 For I earnestly protested unto your fathers in the day that I brought them up out of
the land of Egypt, *even* unto this day, [a]rising
early and protesting, saying, Obey my voice.
8 [a]Yet they obeyed not, nor inclined their
ear, but [b]walked every one in the [1]imagina-
tion of their evil heart: therefore I will bring
upon them all the words of this covenant,
which I commanded *them* to do; but they did
them not.
9 And the LORD said unto me, [a]A conspiracy is found among the men of Judah, and
among the inhabitants of Jerusalem.
10 They are turned back to [a]the iniquities
of their forefathers, which refused to hear my
words; and they went after other gods to serve
them: the house of Israel and the house of Judah have broken my covenant which I made
with their fathers.
11 Therefore thus saith the LORD, Behold, I
will bring evil upon them, which they shall not
be able [1]to escape; and [a]though they shall cry
unto me, I will not hearken unto them.
12 Then shall the cities of Judah and inhabitants of Jerusalem go, and [a]cry unto the
gods unto whom they offer incense: but they
shall not save them at all in the time of their
[1]trouble.
13 For *according to* the number of thy [a]cit-
ies were thy gods, O Judah; and *according to*
the number of the streets of Jerusalem have ye
set up altars to *that* [b1]shameful thing, *even* altars to burn incense unto Baal.
14 Therefore [a]pray not thou for this people, neither lift up a cry or prayer for them: for
I will not hear *them* in the time that they cry
unto me for their [1]trouble.

The certainty of doom

15 ¶ [a1]What hath my beloved to do in
mine house, *seeing* she hath [b]wrought lewdness *with* many, and [c]the holy flesh is passed
from thee? [2]when thou doest evil, then thou
[d]rejoicest.
16 The LORD called thy name, [a]A green

10:24 [1]Heb. *diminish me* [a]ch. 30:11
10:25 [a]Ps. 79:6 [b]Job 18:21 [c]ch. 8:16
11:3 [a]Deut. 27:26
11:4 [a]Deut. 4:20 [b]Lev. 26:12; ch. 7:23
11:5 [1]Heb. *Amen* [a]Deut. 7:12; Ps. 105:9
11:6 [a]Rom. 2:13; Jas. 1:22
11:7 [a]ch. 35:15
11:8 [a]ch. 7:26
11:8 [1]Or, *stubbornness* [b]ch. 9:14
11:9 [a]Ezek. 22:25
11:10 [a]Ezek. 20:18
11:11 [1]Heb. *to go forth of* [a]Ps. 18:41; Prov. 1:28
11:12 [1]Heb. *evil* [a]Deut. 32:37
11:13 [1]Heb. *shame* [a]ch. 2:28 [b]ch. 3:24
11:14 [1]Heb. *evil* [a]Ex. 32:10
11:15 [1]Heb. *What is to my beloved in my house* [2]Or, *when thy evil is* [a]Ps. 50:16 [b]Ezek. 16:25 [c]Tit. 1:15 [d]Prov. 2:14
11:16 [a]Ps. 52:8

10:25 Repeated almost verbatim in Ps 79:6–7, where the context (see Ps 79:1–5) shows that the prayer is not vengeful but is an appeal for God's justice. The verse is recited annually by Jews during their passover service.
11:1–13:27 Because of Judah's violations of its covenant obligations, the people will be exiled to Babylonia. The section is perhaps to be dated to the reign of Josiah (but see note on 13:18).
11:1–17 God's people have broken His covenant with them.
11:2 *Hear.* See note on 2:4. *words.* A technical term for covenant stipulations (see vv. 3–4,6; 34:18; see also note on Ex 20:1). *this covenant.* See vv. 3,6,8,10; Deut 29:9. Reference is to the covenant established by God with Israel through Moses at mount Sinai (see v. 4; Ex 19–24). *speak unto.* Periodic public reading of covenants was a common and necessary practice (see Deut 31:10–13; Josh 8:34–35).
11:3 *Cursed be the man.* The phrase ("Cursed be he") appears at the beginning of every verse in Deut 27:15–26 (and "Amen" appears at the end; see note on v. 5). Blessings resulted from obedience to the covenant (see Deut 28:1–14); curses resulted from disobedience (see Deut 28:15–68; see also Deut 11:26–28; 29:20–21).
11:4 *out of . . . Egypt, from the iron furnace.* See note on Deut 4:20. *Obey my voice.* See v. 7; 7:23; Ex 19:5. *shall ye be my people . . . your God.* See note on 7:23.
‡11:5 *perform the oath . . . I have sworn.* See Gen 15:17–18 and notes; Deut 7:8. *land flowing with milk and honey.* See 32:22; see also note on Ex 3:8. *So be it.* Hebrew *Amen,* which appears at the end of every verse in Deut 27:15–26 (and "cursed be the man" appears at the beginning; see note on v. 3).
11:6 *Proclaim.* See 2:2; 3:12.
11:7 *earnestly.* See note on 7:13.
11:8 See 7:24. *the imagination of their evil heart.* See note on 3:17. *therefore I will bring upon them.* See 2 Ki 17:18–23.
11:9 *conspiracy.* Against the intended reforms of Josiah (see Introduction: Background; see also note on 1:2).
11:10 *refused.* Their sin was deliberate (see note on 9:6). *my covenant.* Emphasizing its origin in God Himself.
11:11 *I will bring . . . upon them.* Judah will be judged, just as Israel had been judged earlier (see v. 10; see also 2 Ki 17:18–23).
11:12 *offer incense.* See vv 13,17; see also note on 1:16.
11:13 *the number of thy cities were thy gods.* See note on 2:28. *according to the number of the streets of Jerusalem have ye set up altars.* See 2 Chr 28:24. *shameful thing . . . Baal.* See 3:24; see also notes on 2:26; Judg 6:32.
11:14 *pray not thou for this people.* See note on 7:16; cf. 1 John 5:16.
11:15 See 7:10–11,21–24. *my beloved.* Judah (see 12:7; cf. Deut 33:12, where Benjamin is called the "beloved of the LORD").
11:16 *called thy name . . . olive tree.* See Ps 52:8; 128:3. *tumult.*

olive tree, fair, *and* of goodly fruit: with the
noise of a great tumult he hath kindled fire
upon it, and the branches of it are broken.
17 For the LORD of hosts, [a]that planted
thee, hath pronounced evil against thee, for
the evil of the house of Israel and of the house
of Judah, which they have done against themselves to provoke me to anger in offering incense unto Baal.
18 And the LORD hath given me knowledge
of it, and I know *it:* then thou shewedst me
their doings.
19 But I *was* like a lamb *or* an ox *that* is
brought to the slaughter; and I knew not that
they had devised devices against me, *saying,* Let
us destroy [1]the tree with the fruit thereof, [a]and
let us cut him off from [b]the land of the living,
that his name may be no more remembered.
20 But, O LORD of hosts, that judgest righteously, that [a]triest the reins and the heart, let
me see thy vengeance on them: for unto thee
have I revealed my cause.
21 ¶ Therefore thus saith the LORD of the
men of Anathoth, [a]that seek thy life, saying,
[b]Prophesy not in the name of the LORD, that
thou die not by our hand:
22 Therefore thus saith the LORD of hosts,
Behold, I will [1]punish them: the young men
shall die by the sword; their sons and their
daughters shall die by famine:
23 And there shall be no remnant of them:
for I will bring evil upon the men of Anathoth,
even [a]the year of their visitation.

11:17 [a]Is. 5:2
11:19 [1]Heb. *the stalk with his bread* [a]Ps. 83:4 [b]Ps. 27:13
11:20 [a]1 Chr. 28:9; Ps. 7:9
11:21 [a]ch. 12:5,6 [b]Mic. 2:6
11:22 [1]Heb. *visit upon*
11:23 [a]ch. 23:12

12:1 [1]Or, *let me reason the case with thee* [a]Ps. 51:4 [b]Mal. 3:15
12:2 [1]Heb. *they go on* [a]Mat. 15:8
12:3 [1]Heb. *with thee* [a]Ps. 17:3 [b]ch. 11:20 [c]Jas. 5:5
12:4 [a]Hos. 4:3 [b]Ps. 107:34 [c]ch. 9:10
12:5 [a]Josh. 3:15; 1 Chr. 12:15
12:6 [1]Or, *they cried after thee fully* [2]Heb. *good things* [a]ch. 9:4 [b]Prov. 26:25

Jeremiah's prayer

12 Righteous [a]*art* thou, O LORD, when I
plead with thee: yet [1]let me talk with
thee of *thy* judgments. [b]Wherefore doth the
way of the wicked prosper? *wherefore* are all
they happy that deal very treacherously?
2 Thou hast planted them, yea, they have
taken root: [1]they grow, yea, they bring forth
fruit: [a]thou *art* near in their mouth, and far
from their reins.
3 But thou, O LORD, [a]knowest me: thou
hast seen me, and [b]tried mine heart [1]towards
thee: pull them out like sheep for the slaughter, and prepare them for [c]the day of slaughter.
4 How long shall [a]the land mourn, and the
herbs of every field wither, [b]for the wickedness of them that dwell therein? [c]the beasts
are consumed, and the birds; because they
said, He shall not see our last end.

God's answer

5 ¶ If thou hast run with the footmen, and
they have wearied thee, then how canst thou
contend with horses? and *if* in the land of
peace, *wherein* thou trustedst, *they wearied*
thee, then how wilt thou do in [a]the swelling of
Jordan?
6 For even [a]thy brethren, and the house of
thy father, even they have dealt treacherously
with thee; yea, [1]they have called a multitude
after thee: [b]believe them not, though they
speak [2]fair *words* unto thee.
7 ¶ I have forsaken mine house, I have left

The Hebrew for this word appears elsewhere only in Ezek 1:24, where it refers to the noise made by an army (see Is 13:4). *branches of it are broken.* See Ezek 31:12.

11:17 Fulfilled when Judah was destroyed in 586 B.C. (see 44:2–3). *provoke me.* See 8:19; Deut 31:29.

11:18–23 The first of Jeremiah's six "confessions" (see Introduction: Author and Date).

11:18 *their.* Jeremiah's personal enemies, the "men of Anathoth" (vv. 21,23), his hometown.

11:19 *lamb . . . is brought to the slaughter;* See 51:40; see also Is 53:7 and note. *destroy the tree with the fruit.* Contrast 12:2. *cut him off from the land of the living.* See Is 53:8; contrast Ps 27:13. *name.* Since Jeremiah had no children (see 16:2), his name would die with him. *be no more remembered.* As though he were evil (see Job 24:20; Ezek 21:32).

11:20 Repeated almost verbatim in 20:12; see also 17:10. *O LORD . . . that judgest righteously.* See note on Gen 18:25.

‡11:21 *men of Anathoth, that seek thy life.* See 12:6. "A man's enemies are the men of his own house" (Mic 7:6, quoted by Jesus in Mat 10:36).

11:22 *sword . . . famine.* See note on 5:12.

11:23 *remnant.* See 6:9; Is 10:20–22 and notes. *them.* The conspirators in Anathoth, not its entire population, since 128 men of Anathoth returned to their hometown after the exile (see Ezra 2:23).

12:1–6 The second of Jeremiah's "confessions," continuing (and closely related to) the first (11:18–23). Jeremiah speaks in vv. 1–4, and God responds in vv. 5–6.

‡12:1 *Righteous art thou.* See note on Gen 18:25; see also 11:20; Ps 51:4; Rom 3:4. Because God is righteous, He is a dependable arbiter and judge. He is ready to listen to our questions and complaints. *Wherefore doth the way of the wicked prosper?* The question is not unique to Jeremiah (see, e.g., Job 21:7–15; Mal 3:15). The Lord replies that ultimately the wicked in Judah will perish (vv. 7–13) and that the wicked invaders who destroy them will themselves be destroyed (vv. 14–17).

12:2 *Thou hast planted them.* But a sovereign God can always reconsider His intentions if conditions warrant a change (see 18:9–10). *bring forth fruit.* The wicked flourish, while Jeremiah's fellow citizens plot to destroy his own "fruit" (see 11:19). *near in their mouth, and far from their reins.* Quoted in part by Jesus in Mat 15:8–9.

12:3 *tried mine heart.* See 11:20. *like sheep for the slaughter.* Jeremiah asks that his wicked countrymen receive the fate mentioned for himself in 11:19. His request arises not so much out of a desire for revenge as for the vindication of God's righteousness.

12:4 *mourn . . . wither.* See 23:10; see also 3:3; 14:1. Apparently there was a series of droughts in Judah during Jeremiah's ministry. *He shall not see.* The prophet's enemies do not believe that his predictions will be fulfilled.

‡12:5 The Lord warns Jeremiah that in the future his troubles will increase (see, e.g., 38:4–6). *they wearied thee.* The Hebrew for this word, which usually means "trust" ("If you put your trust in a land of peace"), has a negative meaning in a few passages (see, e.g., Prov 14:16, where it is translated "confident"). *swelling.* Providing cover for lions (see 49:19; 50:44; Zech 11:3). If the Hebrew for this word means "flooding" ("the flooding of the Jordan") here, an ancient example is described in Josh 3:15.

12:6 *house.* Linking this verse verbally with the following context (see v. 7). Apparently, members of Jeremiah's own family were included in the "men of Anathoth" (11:21,23) who wanted to kill him.

mine heritage; I have given [1]the dearly
beloved of my soul into the hand of her enemies.
8 Mine heritage is unto me as a lion in the
forest; it [1][2]crieth out against me: therefore
have I hated it.
9 Mine heritage *is* unto me *as* a [1]speckled
bird, the birds round about *are* against her;
come ye, assemble all the beasts of the field,
[a][2]come to devour.
10 Many [a]pastors have destroyed [b]my
vineyard, they have [c]trodden my portion under foot, they have made my [1]pleasant portion
a desolate wilderness.
11 They have made it desolate, *and being*
desolate [a]it mourneth unto me; the whole
land is made desolate, because [b]no man layeth
it to heart.
12 The spoilers are come upon all high
places through the wilderness: for the sword
of the LORD *shall* devour from the *one* end of
the land even to the *other* end of the land: no
flesh *shall* have peace.
13 [a]They have sown wheat, but shall reap
thorns: they have put themselves to pain, *but*
shall not profit: and [1]they shall be ashamed of
your revenues because of the fierce anger of
the LORD.
14 ¶ Thus saith the LORD against all mine
evil neighbours, that [a]touch the inheritance
which I have caused my people Israel to inherit; Behold, I will [b]pluck them out of their
land, and pluck out the house of Judah from
among them.
15 [a]And it shall come to pass, after that I
have plucked them out, I will return, and have
compassion on them, [b]and will bring them
again, every man to his heritage, and every
man to his land.
16 And it shall come to pass, if they will
diligently learn the ways of my people, [a]to
swear by my name, The LORD liveth; as they
taught my people to swear by Baal; then shall
they be [b]built in the midst of my people.
17 But if they will not [a]obey, I will utterly
pluck up and destroy that nation, saith the
LORD.

The parable of the girdle

13 Thus saith the LORD unto me, Go and
get thee a linen girdle, and put it
upon thy loins, and put it not in water.
2 So I got a girdle, according to the word of
the LORD, and put *it* on my loins.
3 And the word of the LORD came unto me
the second time, saying,
4 Take the girdle that thou hast got, which
is upon thy loins, and arise, go to Euphrates,
and hide it there in a hole of the rock.
5 So I went, and hid it by Euphrates, as the
LORD commanded me.
6 And it came to pass after many days, that
the LORD said unto me, Arise, go to Euphrates,
and take the girdle from thence, which I commanded thee to hide there.
7 Then I went to Euphrates, and digged,
and took the girdle from the place where I had
hid it: and behold, the girdle was marred, it
was profitable for nothing.
8 Then the word of the LORD came unto
me, saying,
9 Thus saith the LORD, After this manner

12:7 [1]Heb. *the love*
12:8 [1]Or, *yelleth* [2]Heb. *giveth out his voice*
12:9 [1]Or, *taloned* [2]Or, *cause them to come* [a]Is. 56:9
12:10 [1]Heb. *portion of desire* [a]ch. 6:3 [b]Is. 5:1,5 [c]Is. 63:18
12:11 [a]ver. 4 [b]Is. 42:25
12:13 [1][Or, *ye*] [a]Lev. 26:16; Deut. 28:38; Mic. 6:15; Hag. 1:6
12:14 [a]Zech. 2:8 [b]Deut. 30:3; ch. 32:37
12:15 [a]Ezek. 28:25
12:15 [b]Amos 9:14
12:16 [a]ch. 4:2 [b]Eph. 2:20,21; 1 Pet. 2:5
12:17 [a]Is. 60:12

12:7–17 The Lord will judge Judah (vv. 7–13) as well as the wicked neighboring nations (vv. 14–17).

12:7 *house.* Judah (see, e.g., 11:17). *heritage.* God's land and people (see vv. 8–9,14–15; see also Ex 15:17 and note; Deut 4:20; Is 19:25; 47:6). *the dearly beloved of my soul.* See note on 11:15.

12:8 *I hated it.* I will withdraw my love from her by giving her "Into the hand of her enemies" (v. 7; see Mal 1:3).

‡12:9 *birds round about . . . beasts of the field.* Judah's enemies (see Is 56:9 and note).

12:10 *pastors.* Rulers (see note on 2:8). *my vineyard.* Judah (see 2:21 and note). *pleasant portion.* See 3:19 and note.

12:11 *it mourneth.* See v. 4 and note. A total of seven *s*-sounds and seven *m*-sounds in the Hebrew of this brief verse provides a striking example of Jeremiah's literary gifts.

12:12 *spoilers.* The Babylonians (see note on 4:7). *high places.* Places of idolatrous worship (see 3:2; Num 23:3). *sword of the LORD.* Symbolizing God's instruments of judgment (see 25:29; 47:6). *from the one end of the land even to the other end.* See 25:33. *no flesh shall have peace.* See 6:14 and note).

12:13 See 14:2–4.

12:14 *evil neighbours.* See, e.g., 2 Ki 24:2. *touch.* Also used in the context of attack and plunder in Zech 2:8. *pluck.* Carry off into exile (see, e.g., 1 Ki 14:15).

12:15 The exiles from Judah, and those from the neighboring nations, will eventually be brought back to their respective lands (see v. 16; 32:37,44; 33:26; 48:47; 49:6).

12:16 See Is 56:6–7. The Messianic age is in view (see Is 2:2–4). *ways.* See note on 10:2.

13:1–27 A series of five warnings, the first two (vv. 1–11, 12–14) originally written in prose and the last three (vv. 15–17, 18–19, 20–27) in poetry.

13:1–11 The story of the ruined, useless girdle (i.e. belt) is the first major example of the Lord's commanding Jeremiah to perform symbolic acts to illustrate his message (see Introduction: Literary Features).

13:1–2,4–7 *Go and get . . . So I got . . . Take the girdle that thou hast got . . . and hide it . . . So I went, and hid it . . . go to Euphrates, and take the girdle . . . Then I went to Euphrates, and digged, and took the girdle . . . .* Like his spiritual ancestor Abraham (see note on Gen 12:4), Jeremiah was characterized by prompt obedience.

13:1 *linen.* The material of which the priests' garments were made (see Ezek 44:17–18), symbolic of Israel's holiness as a "kingdom of priests" (see Ex 19:6 and note). The linen girdle is a symbol of the formerly intimate relationship between God and Judah (see v. 11). *put it not in water.* Do not wash it—symbolic of Judah's sinful pride (see v. 9).

‡13:3 *And.* Lit: "Then," i.e. some time later.

13:4 *Euphrates.* The Euphrates serves as an appropriate symbol of the corrupting Assyrian and Babylonian influence on Judah that began during the reign of Ahaz (see 2 Ki 16).

13:6 *after many days.* Perhaps a reference to the lengthy Babylonian exile.

13:7 *took the girdle.* It had either been buried by the prophet or silted over by the water of the river. *the girdle was marred.* As foreseen in Lev 26:39, God's people in exile would waste away because of their sins and the sins of their ancestors.

[a]will I mar the pride of Judah, and the great
pride of Jerusalem.
10 This evil people, which refuse to hear
my words, which [a]walk in the [1]imagination of
their heart, and walk after other gods, to serve
them, and to worship them, shall even be as
this girdle, which is good for nothing.
11 For as the girdle cleaveth to the loins of
a man, so have I caused to cleave unto me the
whole house of Israel and the whole house of
Judah, saith the LORD; that [a]*they* might be unto
me for a people, and [b]for a name, and for a
praise, and for a glory: but they would not
hear.

The parable of the bottles

12 ¶ Therefore thou shalt speak unto them
this word; Thus saith the LORD God of Israel,
Every bottle shall be filled *with* wine: and they
shall say unto thee, Do we not certainly know
that every bottle shall be filled *with* wine?
13 Then shalt thou say unto them, Thus
saith the LORD, Behold, I *will* fill all the inhabitants of this land, even the kings that sit upon
David's throne, and the priests, and the prophets, and all the inhabitants of Jerusalem, [a]*with*
drunkenness.
14 And [a]I will dash them [1]one against another, even the fathers and the sons together,
saith the LORD: I will not pity, nor spare, nor
have mercy, [2]but destroy them.

The pride and shame of Jerusalem

15 ¶ Hear ye, and give ear; be not proud:
for the LORD hath spoken.
16 Give glory to the LORD your God, before
he cause [a]darkness, and before your feet stumble upon the dark mountains, and, while ye
[b]look for light, he turn it into [c]the shadow of
death, *and* make *it* gross darkness.
17 But if ye will not hear it, my soul shall
weep in secret places for *your* pride; and
[a]mine eye shall weep sore, and run down *with*
tears, because the LORD's flock is carried away
captive.
18 Say unto [a]the king and to the queen,
Humble yourselves, sit down: for your [1]princi-
palities shall come down, *even* the crown of
your glory.
19 The cities of the south shall be shut up,
and none shall open *them:* Judah shall be carried away captive all of it, it shall be wholly
carried away captive.
20 Lift up your eyes, and behold them
[a]that come from the north: where *is* the flock
that was given thee, thy beautiful flock?
21 What wilt thou say when he shall [1]pun-
ish thee? for thou hast taught them *to be* captains, *and* as chief over thee: shall not [a]sor-
rows take thee, as a woman in travail?
22 And if thou say in thine heart, [a]Where-
fore come these *things* upon me? For the
greatness of thine iniquity are [b]thy skirts discovered, *and* thy heels [1]made bare.
23 Can the Ethiopian change his skin, or
the leopard his spots? *then* may ye also do
good, that are [1]accustomed to do evil.
24 Therefore will I scatter them [a]as the
stubble that passeth away by the wind of the
wilderness.
25 [a]This *is* thy lot, the portion of thy measures from me, saith the LORD; because thou
hast forgotten me, and trusted in [b]falsehood.
26 Therefore [a]will I discover thy skirts
upon thy face, that thy shame may appear.
27 I have seen thine adulteries, and thy

13:9 [a]Lev. 26:19
13:10 [1]Or, *stubbornness* [a]ch. 9:14; 11:8; 16:12
13:11 [a]Ex. 19:5 [b]ch. 33:9
13:13 [a]Is. 51:17,21; 63:6; ch. 25:27; 51:7
13:14 [1]Heb. *a man against his brother* [2]Heb. *from destroying them* [a]Ps. 2:9
13:16 [a]Is. 5:30; 8:22; Amos 8:9
13:16 [b]Is. 59:9 [c]Ps. 44:19
13:17 [a]ch. 9:1; 14:17; Lam. 1:2,16; 2:18
13:18 [1]Or, *head tires* [a]2 Ki. 24:12; ch. 22:26
13:20 [a]ch. 6:22
13:21 [1]Heb. *visit upon* [a]ch. 6:24
13:22 [1]Or, *shall be violently taken away* [a]ch. 16:10 [b]Is. 3:17; 47:2,3; Ezek. 16:37-39; Nah. 3:5
13:23 [1]Heb. *taught*
13:24 [a]Ps. 1:4; Hos. 13:3
13:25 [a]Job 20:29; Ps. 11:6 [b]ch. 10:14
13:26 [a]Lam. 1:8; Ezek. 16:37; Hos. 2:10

13:9 *pride . . . great pride.* Contrast 9:23–24. Judah's vaunted pride would be a cause of her downfall and exile (see vv. 15,17), as foreshadowed in Lev 26:19.

13:10 *refuse to hear.* See note on 9:6. *imagination of their heart.* See note on 3:17. *good for nothing.* See 24:8.

13:11 *but they would not hear.* And therefore the promise of Deut 26:19 can no longer be fulfilled in them.

13:12–14 The Lord uses the imagery of filled wineskins to point toward the eventual destruction of Judah's leaders and people.

13:13 *kings . . . priests . . . prophets . . . all the inhabitants of Jerusalem.* See 26:16; see also note on 1:18. *drunkenness.* In a literal sense (see, e.g., Is 28:7), but also symbolizing the effects of the wine of God's wrath (see 25:15–29; Ps 60:3; Is 51:17–20; Ezek 23:32–34).

13:14 *dash them one against another.* The various factions in Judah produced only confusion and chaos in the face of determined outside enemies. *not pity, nor spare, nor have mercy.* See 21:7; see also Ezek 5:11.

13:15–17 Sinful pride carries the seeds of its own destruction, says the prophet.

13:15 *hear ye.* See note on 2:4. *be not proud.* See v. 17; see also note on v. 9.

13:16 *Give glory to . . . God.* An exhortation to speak the truth (see Josh 7:19 and note; John 9:24). *while ye look for light.* Cf. the description of the day of the Lord in Amos 5:18–20; 8:9.

13:17 *my soul shall weep.* See note on 9:1. *pride.* See v. 15; see also note on v. 9. *flock.* People (see v. 20; Zech 10:3; see also notes on 2:8; 10:21). *carried away captive.* Into exile (see v. 19).

13:18–19 The prophet speaks: Exile is imminent.

13:18 *king and . . . queen.* Probably Jehoiachin and Nehushta (2 Ki 24:8). If so, the date is 597 B.C., about 12 years after Josiah's death (see note on 11:1–13:27). *principalities shall come down.* See 22:24–26; 29:2; 2 Ki 24:15.

13:19 *south.* The dry southland (see note on Gen 12:9). *shut up.* Blocked by debris (see Is 24:10). *carried away captive all of it.* See Amos 1:6,9.

13:20–27 First the prophet speaks (vv. 20–23), then the Lord (vv. 24–27). Judah's willful rebellion has made exile inevitable.

13:20 *your . . . thy.* Jerusalem, personified as a woman (see vv. 21–22,26–27), is being addressed. *the north.* Babylonia (see 4:6; see also note on Is 41:25). *flock.* See note on v. 17.

‡13:21 *them.* Perhaps Egypt and Babylon, who alternated in dominating Judah (see Introduction: Background). *as a woman in travail.* See 6:24; 49:24; 50:43.

13:22 *skirts . . . discovered.* Disgraced publicly, like a common prostitute (see vv. 26–27; Is 47:3; Hos 2:3,10).

13:23 A rhetorical question, expecting a negative answer (see 17:9).

13:24 *stubble that passeth away.* The fate of the wicked (see, e.g., Ps 1:4). *wind of the wilderness.* See note on 4:11.

13:25 *forgotten me.* See note on 2:32.

13:26 See v. 22 and note.

[a]neighings, the lewdness of thy whoredom,
and thine abominations [b]on the hills in the
fields. Woe unto thee, O Jerusalem! wilt thou
not be made clean? [1]when *shall it* once *be?*

Judah beyond deliverance

14 The word of the LORD that came to
Jeremiah concerning [1]the dearth.

2 Judah mourneth, and [a]the gates thereof
languish;
They are [b]black unto the ground;
And [c]the cry of Jerusalem is gone up.
3 And their nobles have sent their little
ones to the waters:
They came to the pits, *and* found no
water;
They returned *with* their vessels
empty;
They were [a]ashamed and confounded,
[b]and covered their heads.
4 Because the ground is chapt,
For there was no rain in the earth,
The plowmen were ashamed, they
covered their heads.
5 Yea, the hind also calved in the field,
and forsook *it,*
Because there was no grass.
6 And [a]the wild asses did stand in the
high places,
They snuffed up the wind like dragons;
Their eyes did fail, because *there was*
no grass.

7 ¶ O LORD, though our iniquities testify
against us, do thou *it* [a]for thy name's sake: for
our backslidings are many; we have sinned
against thee.
8 [a]O the hope of Israel, the saviour thereof
in time of trouble, why shouldest thou be as a
stranger in the land, and as a wayfaring man
that turneth aside to tarry for a night?
9 Why shouldest thou be as a man as-
tonied, as a mighty *man* [a]*that* cannot save? yet
thou, O LORD, [b]*art* in the midst of us, and [1]we
are called by thy name; leave us not.
10 Thus saith the LORD unto this people,
[a]Thus have they loved to wander, they have
not refrained their feet, therefore the LORD
doth not accept them; [b]he will now remember
their iniquity, and visit their sins.
11 Then said the LORD unto me, [a]Pray not
for this people for *their* good.
12 [a]When they fast, I will not hear their
cry; and [b]when they offer burnt offering and
an oblation, I will not accept them: but [c]I will
consume them by the sword, and by the
famine, and by the pestilence.
13 ¶ [a]Then said I, Ah Lord GOD! behold,
the prophets say unto them, Ye shall not see
the sword, neither shall ye have famine; but I
will give you [1]assured peace in this place.
14 Then the LORD said unto me, [a]The
prophets prophesy lies in my name: [b]I sent
them not, neither have I commanded them,
neither spake unto them: they prophesy unto
you a false vision and divination, and a thing of
nought, and the deceit of their heart.
15 Therefore thus saith the LORD concerning the prophets that prophesy in my name,
and I sent them not, [a]yet they say, Sword and
famine shall not be in this land; By sword and
famine shall those prophets be consumed.
16 And the people to whom they prophesy
shall be cast out in the streets of Jerusalem because of the famine and the sword; [a]and they
shall have none to bury them, them, their

13:27 [1]Heb. *after when yet?* [a]ch. 5:8 [b]Is. 65:7; ch. 2:20
14:1 [1]Heb. *the words of the dearths,* or, *restraints*
14:2 [a]Is. 3:26 [b]ch. 8:21 [c]1 Sam. 5:12
14:3 [a]Ps. 40:14 [b]2 Sam. 15:30
14:6 [a]ch. 2:24
14:7 [a]Ps. 25:11
14:8 [a]ch. 17:13
14:9 [1]Heb. *thy name is called upon us* [a]Is. 59:1 [b]Ex. 29:45; Lev. 26:11
14:10 [a]See ch. 2:23-25 [b]Hos. 8:13
14:11 [a]Ex. 32:10
14:12 [a]Prov. 1:28; Is. 1:15; Ezek. 8:18; Zech. 7:13 [b]ch. 6:20 [c]ch. 9:16
14:13 [1]Heb. *peace of truth* [a]ch. 4:10
14:14 [a]ch. 27:10 [b]ch. 29:8,9
14:15 [a]ch. 5:12
14:16 [a]Ps. 79:3

13:27 *adulteries, and . . . neighings.* See note on 5:8. *lewdness of . . . whoredom.* See Ezek 16:27. *when shall it once be?* There is yet hope, however slender, to postpone the divine wrath (cf., e.g., 12:14–16).
14:1–15:21 Messages delivered by Jeremiah during an especially severe drought, the date of which is unknown.
14:1–15:9 After an initial vivid description of the drought (14:2–6), Jeremiah alternately prays (14:7–9,13,19–22) and God responds (14:10–12,14–18; 15:1–9).
14:1 *dearth.* Or "drought"; see 17:8. Unlike that in 3:3; 12:4, the suffering is increased because an enemy has invaded the land (see v. 18). Drought was one of the curses threatened (see 23:10) for disobedience to the covenant (see Lev 26:19–20; Deut 28:22–24).
14:2 *gates.* See 15:7; see also note on Gen 22:17.
14:3 *nobles.* A drought is no respecter of class distinctions. *covered their heads.* In mourning (see v. 4; 2 Sam 15:30; cf. 2 Sam 19:4).
14:4 *For there was no rain.* See 1 Ki 17:7. Unlike Egypt, where the mighty Nile waters the ground, the Holy Land depends on adequate rainfall.
‡14:6 *snuffed up.* See this expression in 2:24. There a female wild donkey (Jerusalem) was in the heat of desire, while here the male wild donkeys are panting because of a drought brought on by Judah's sin.
14:7–9 The prophet prays on behalf of the people (see v. 11).
14:7 *for thy name's sake.* See v. 21; Josh 7:9; Is 48:9–11. *backslidings.* See 2:19; 3:22; 5:6.
14:8 *O the hope of Israel.* See v. 22; 17:13; 50:7; Acts 28:20.
14:9 *we are called by thy name.* We belong to you, our ever-present Savior (see note on 7:10).
14:10–12 The Lord responds.
14:10–11 *this people.* God does not acknowledge them as His own (see Is 6:9–10; 8:6,11–12; see also note on Ex 17:4).
14:10 *wander.* After false gods (see 2:23,31). *the LORD doth not accept . . . sins.* The Hebrew is quoted verbatim from Hos 8:13 (cf. Hos 9:9).
14:11 *Pray not.* See note on 7:16; cf. 1 Sam 7:8; 12:19.
14:12 *not accept them.* See v. 10. Sacrifice is to no avail when unaccompanied by repentance (see note on 6:20). *sword . . . famine . . . pestilence.* Curses for violating God's covenant (see Lev 26:25–26); the first occurrence of this triad, which occurs 15 times in Jeremiah (see Introduction: Literary Features).
14:13 Jeremiah reminds the Lord of what the false prophets are saying. *not . . . sword, neither . . . famine.* See 5:12. *assured peace.* Jeremiah's elaboration of the false prophets' "Peace, peace" (see 6:14; 8:11).
14:14–18 The Lord responds.
‡14:14 *lies.* See 5:12. *in my name.* See Deut 18:20,22. *deceit of their heart.* "Delusions of their own minds." See 23:26.
14:15 *those prophets be consumed.* See 28:15–17; Deut 18:20.
14:16 *none to bury them.* See note on 7:33. *wives . . . sons . . . daughters.* All would perish, because all had worshiped false gods (see note on 7:18).

wives, nor their sons, nor their daughters: for
I will pour their wickedness upon them.
17 Therefore thou shalt say this word unto
them;
[a]Let mine eyes run down *with* tears
night and day, and let them not
cease:
[b]For the virgin daughter of my people
is broken *with* a great breach, *with* a
very grievous blow.
18 If I go forth *into* [a]the field, then behold
the slain with the sword:
And if I enter *into* the city, then behold
them that are sick with famine:
Yea, both the prophet and the priest
[b][1]go about into a land that they
know not.
19 [a]Hast thou utterly rejected Judah? hath
thy soul lothed Zion?
Why hast thou smitten us, and [b]*there*
is no healing for us?
[c]*We* looked for peace, and *there is* no
good;
And for the time of healing, and behold
trouble.
20 We acknowledge, O LORD, our
wickedness, *and* the iniquity of our
fathers:
For [a]we have sinned against thee.
21 Do not abhor *us,* for thy name's sake,
Do not disgrace the throne of thy glory:
[a]Remember, break not thy covenant
with us.
22 [a]Are there *any* among [b]the vanities of
the Gentiles that can cause rain?
Or can the heavens give showers?
[c]*Art* not thou he, O LORD our God?
therefore we will wait upon thee:
For thou hast made all these *things.*

15 Then said the LORD unto me,
[a]Though [b]Moses and [c]Samuel stood
before me, *yet* my mind *could* not *be* toward
this people: cast *them* out of my sight, and let
them go forth.
2 And it shall come to pass, if they say unto
thee, Whither shall we go forth? then thou shalt
tell them, Thus saith the LORD; [a]Such as *are* for
death, to death; and such as *are* for the sword,
to the sword; and such as *are* for the famine, to
the famine; and such as *are* for the captivity, to
the captivity.
3 And I will [a]appoint over them four [1]kinds,
saith the LORD: the sword to slay, and the dogs
to tear, and [b]the fowls of the heaven, and the
beasts of the earth, to devour and destroy.
4 And [1]I will cause them to be [a]removed
into all kingdoms of the earth, because of [b]Ma-
nasseh the son of Hezekiah king of Judah, for
that which he did in Jerusalem.
5 For who shall have pity upon thee, O Jerusalem? or who shall bemoan thee? or who
shall go aside [1]to ask how thou doest?
6 [a]Thou hast forsaken me, saith the LORD,
thou art [b]gone backward: therefore will I
stretch out my hand against thee, and destroy
thee; [c]I am weary with repenting.
7 And I will fan them with a fan in the
gates of the land; I will bereave *them* of [1]chil-
dren, I will destroy my people, *sith* they return
not from their ways.
8 Their widows are increased to me above
the sand of the seas: I have brought upon them

14:17 [a]ch. 9:1 [b]ch. 8:21
14:18 [1]Or, *make merchandise against a land, and men acknowledge it not* [a]Ezek. 7:15 [b]ch. 5:31
14:19 [a]Lam. 5:22 [b]ch. 15:18 [c]ch. 8:15
14:20 [a]Ps. 106:6; Dan. 9:8
14:21 [a]Ps. 106:45
14:22 [a]Zech. 10:1 [b]Deut. 32:21
14:22 [c]Ps. 135:7
15:1 [a]Ezek. 14:14 [b]Ex. 32:11; Ps. 99:6 [c]1 Sam. 7:9
15:2 [a]Ezek. 5:2; Zech. 11:9
15:3 [1]Heb. *families* [a]Lev. 26:16 [b]Deut. 28:26
15:4 [1]Heb. *I will give them for a removing* [a]Deut. 28:25 [b]2 Ki. 24:3,4
15:5 [1]Heb. *to ask of thy peace?*
15:6 [a]ch. 2:13 [b]ch. 7:24 [c]Hos. 13:14
15:7 [1]Or, *whatsoever is dear*

14:17 *mine eyes run down with tears.* See 9:18; 13:17. *virgin daughter.* Used of Jerusalem in Is 37:22 (see note there; see also Is 23:12 and note); see 18:13.
14:19–22 The prophet prays on behalf of the people.
14:20 *iniquity of our fathers.* See 2:5–6; 7:25–26. *we have sinned.* Repentance brings restoration (see Deut 30:2–3).
14:21 *throne of thy glory.* The Jerusalem temple (see 17:12; 2 Ki 19:14–15; Ps 99:1–2). *Remember, break not thy covenant.* Jeremiah pleads the ancient promise of God in Lev 26:44–45.
14:22 See Hos 2:8,21–22. *vanities.* See note on 2:5. *Art not thou he . . . ?* Only the Lord (not Baal) can send the showers to end the drought (see v. 1). *we will wait upon thee.* See note on v. 8.
15:1–9 The Lord responds, concluding this section (see note on 14:1–15:9).
15:1 *Moses and Samuel.* Famed for their intercession for sinful Israel (see Ex 32:11–14,30–34; Num 14:13–23; Deut 9:18–20, 25–29; 1 Sam 7:5–9; 12:19–25; Ps 99:6–8). *stood before me.* The posture of God's servants as they are about to pray to Him (see Gen 18:22). *cast them out of my sight.* The people are so wicked that God refuses to hear prayers offered on their behalf. They are beyond divine help (see notes on 7:16; 14:11–12).
15:2 See Ezek 14:21; 33:27. *death.* Probably by plague; see 14:12 (and note), where "sword, famine and pestilence" are God's three agents of destruction, paralleling the first three here.
15:3–4 Foreseen in Deut 28:25–26.
15:3 *four kinds.* Not the same four as in v. 2, but an elaboration of three of the fates awaiting the corpses of those killed by the sword. The seventh-century B.C. vassal treaties of Esarhaddon present similar curses: "May Ninurta, leader of the gods, fell you with his fierce arrow, fill the plain with your corpses, and give your flesh to the eagles and vultures to feed on . . . May dogs and pigs eat your flesh." *dogs.* See 1 Ki 21:23. *beasts of the earth.* See Rev 6:8.
‡15:4 *I will cause them to be removed.* See the parallel passage in Deut 28:25. *Manasseh . . . that which he did in Jerusalem.* Manasseh, good King Josiah's grandfather, was the most wicked king in Judah's long history (see 2 Ki 21:1–11,16). His sins were a primary cause of Judah's eventual destruction (see 2 Ki 21:12–15; 23:26–27; 24:3–4).
15:5–9 A poem concerning the forthcoming destruction of Jerusalem in 586 B.C. (see Lam 1:1,12,21; 2:13,20).
15:5 Cf. Mat 23:37.
15:6 *thou art gone backward.* Cf. 7:24; see note on 2:19.
‡15:7 *fan them.* Or "winnow them." See note on Ruth 1:22. Winnowing as a figure of judgment is found also in 51:2; Prov 20:8,26; Is 41:16. *gates of the land.* The approaches to the land. *bereave . . . my people.* The young men will fall in battle, and Judah and Jerusalem will be left childless (see Ezek 5:17). *return not.* Reminiscent of the refrain in Amos 4:6,8–11: "Yet have ye not returned unto me" where the same Hebrew verb is used (see note on 3:1).
15:8 *widows are increased . . . above the sand of the seas.* A tragic reversal of the covenant promise of innumerable offspring (see Gen 22:17 and note). *spoiler.* Babylon (see note on 4:7). *at noonday . . . suddenly.* Military attacks at noon were unexpected (see note on 6:4). *terrors.* See note on 4:19.

[1]against the mother of the young men a spoiler at noonday: I have caused *him* to fall upon it suddenly, and terrors *upon* the city.

9 [a]She that hath borne seven languisheth: she hath given up the ghost; [b]her sun is gone down while *it was* yet day: she hath been ashamed and confounded: and the residue of them will I deliver to the sword before their enemies, saith the LORD.

10 ¶ [a]Woe is me, my mother, that thou hast borne me a man of strife and a man of contention to the whole earth! I have neither lent on usury, nor *men* have lent to me on usury; *yet* every one of them doth curse me.

11 The LORD said, Verily it shall be well with thy remnant; verily [1]I will cause [a]the enemy to entreat thee *well* in the time of evil, and in the time of affliction.

12 Shall iron break the northern iron and the steel?

13 Thy substance and thy treasures will I give to the [a]spoil without price, and *that* for all thy sins, even in all thy borders.

14 And I will make *thee* to pass with thine enemies [a]into a land *which* thou knowest not: for a [b]fire is kindled in mine anger, *which* shall burn upon you.

15 ¶ O LORD, [a]thou knowest: remember me, and visit me, and [b]revenge me of my persecutors; take me not away in thy longsuffering: know that [c]for thy sake I have suffered rebuke.

16 Thy words were found, and I did [a]eat them; and [b]thy word was unto me the joy and rejoicing of mine heart: for [1]I am called by thy name, O LORD God of hosts.

17 [a]I sat not in the assembly of the mockers, nor rejoiced; I sat alone because of thy hand: for thou hast filled me *with* indignation.

18 Why is my [a]pain perpetual, and my wound incurable, *which* refuseth to be healed? wilt thou be altogether unto me [b]as a liar, *and as* waters *that* [1]fail?

19 ¶ Therefore thus saith the LORD, [a]If thou return, then will I bring thee again, *and* thou shalt [b]stand before me: and if thou [c]take forth the precious from the vile, thou shalt be as my mouth: let them return unto thee; but return not thou unto them.

20 And I will make thee unto this people a fenced brasen wall: and they shall fight against thee, but [a]they shall not prevail against thee: for I *am* with thee to save thee and to deliver thee, saith the LORD.

21 And I will deliver thee out of the hand of the wicked, and I will redeem thee out of the hand of the terrible.

Punishment and promise

16 The word of the LORD came also unto me, saying,

2 Thou shalt not take thee a wife, neither shalt thou have sons nor daughters in this place.

15:8 [1]Or, *against the mother city* a *young man spoiling, etc.,* or, *against the mother* and *the young men*
15:9 [a]1 Sam. 2:5 [b]Amos 8:9
15:10 [a]Job 3:1
15:11 [1]Or, *I will intreat the enemy for thee* [a]ch. 40:4,5
15:13 [a]Ps. 44:12
15:14 [a]ch. 16:13 [b]Deut. 32:22
15:15 [a]ch. 12:3 [b]ch. 20:12 [c]Ps. 69:7
15:16 [1]Heb. *thy name is called upon me* [a]Ezek. 3:1,3; Rev. 10:9 [b]Job 23:12; Ps. 119:72
15:17 [a]Ps. 26:4,5
15:18 [1]Heb. *be not sure?* [a]ch. 30:15 [b]ch. 1:18,19
15:19 [a]Zech. 3:7 [b]ver. 1 [c]Ezek. 22:26
15:20 [a]ch. 20:11

15:9 *seven.* The complete, ideal number of sons (see Ruth 4:15 and note)—soon to be destroyed. *sun is gone down while it was yet day.* See Amos 8:9; cf. Mat 27:45. *the residue of them.* Lit. "remnant" (see note on 6:9). Even they will be put to the sword (see Mic 6:14).

15:10–21 The third of Jeremiah's "confessions" (see Introduction: Author and Date), including in this case two responses by the Lord (vv. 11–14, 19–21).

15:10 See 20:14–15; Job 3:3–10. *mother.* See v. 8. In the OT, adjacent paragraphs are often linked by key words. *have neither lent on usury, nor men have lent.* Have not become involved in matters likely to evoke dispute or difference of opinion.

15:11–14 The Lord speaks, first to Jeremiah (v. 11), then to the people of Judah (vv. 12–14).

15:11 God encourages Jeremiah. *I will cause the enemy to entreat thee well.* Fulfilled, e.g., in 21:1–2; 37:3; 38:14–26; 42:1–3.

15:12 A rhetorical question assuming a negative answer. *iron.* Symbolic of great strength (see 28:13). *the northern iron.* From Babylonia (see note on Is 41:25).

15:13–14 Repeated in large part in 17:3–4.

15:13 Fulfilled in 52:17–23. *without price.* Cf. Is 55:1. People and plunder alike would be free for the taking (see note on Is 52:3).

‡15:14 *a fire is kindled in mine anger.* Quoted verbatim from Deut 32:22, where the Hebrew is translated "For a fire is kindled in my anger."

15:15 *thou knowest.* The Lord is aware of what Jeremiah has suffered (see v. 10). *remember.* Express concern for (see note on Gen 8:1).

15:16 *Thy words . . . I did eat them.* I digested them, I assimilated them, I made them a part of me (see Ezek 2:8–3:3; Rev 10:9–10). *were found.* Perhaps referring to the discovery of the Book of the Law in the temple during the reign of Josiah in 621 B.C. (see 2 Ki 22:13; 23:2; see also note on 1:2). *was unto me . . . rejoicing of mine heart.* See Ps 1:2. *I am called by thy name.* See 14:9. I belong to You (see note on 7:10).

15:17 *sat alone.* Jeremiah never married (see 16:1), and he attracted only a few friends (see Introduction: Author and Date). *thy hand.* Divine constraint (see 2 Ki 3:15; Is 8:11 and note; Ezek 1:3; 3:14,22; 37:1; 40:1). *indignation.* At the sins of Judah (see 6:11).

‡15:18 Two rhetorical questions used by Jeremiah to express his nagging doubts about himself, his mission and God's faithfulness. *pain perpetual . . . wound incurable.* Jerusalem is similarly described in 30:12–15, together with God's promise of healing in 30:17. *wilt thou be altogether unto me.* See Ps 22:1; Mat 27:46. *waters that fail.* See Mic 1:14, where also "lie" probably refers to the kind of intermittent streams described in Job 6:15–20. Jeremiah here accuses God of being undependable, in contrast to the Lord's own earlier description of Himself as a "fountain of living waters" (see 2:13 and note).

15:19–21 The Lord commands Jeremiah to repent, then encourages him and renews his call.

15:19 *return . . . bring thee again . . . return . . . return.* The Hebrew root is the same for all four words (see notes on 3:1; Is 1:25–26). *thou shalt stand before me.* The appropriate posture for the obedient servant (see Num 16:9; Deut 10:8). *my mouth.* Or, "my spokesman" (see 1:9 and note; Ex 4:15–16; see also note on Ex 7:1–2).

15:20 See 1:8,18–19 and notes.

15:21 *deliver thee out of the . . . wicked.* See, e.g., 36:26; 38:6–13.

16:1–17:18 Messages of disaster and comfort, with the note of disaster predominating (16:1–13,16–18; 16:21–17:6; 17:9–13,18). In the Hebrew the first half of the section is prose (16:1–18), the second half poetry (16:19–17:18).

16:2 Jeremiah's ministry was such that he had to face life alone (see note on 15:17), without the comfort and support a family

3 For thus saith the LORD concerning the sons and concerning the daughters that are born in this place, and concerning their mothers that bare them, and concerning their fathers that begat them in this land;

4 They shall die of [a]grievous deaths; they shall not be [b]lamented; neither shall they be buried; *but* they shall be [c]as dung upon the face of the earth: and they shall be consumed by the sword, and by famine; and their [d]carcases shall be meat for the fowls of heaven, and for the beasts of the earth.

5 For thus saith the LORD, [a]Enter not *into* the house of [1]mourning, neither go to lament nor bemoan them: for I have taken away my peace from this people, saith the LORD, *even* lovingkindness and mercies.

6 Both the great and the small shall die in this land: they shall not be buried, [a]neither shall *men* lament for them, nor [b]cut themselves, nor [c]make themselves bald for them:

7 Neither shall *men* [a][1]tear *themselves* for them in mourning, to comfort them for the dead; neither shall *men* give them the cup of consolation to [b]drink for their father or for their mother.

8 Thou shalt not also go *into* the house of feasting, to sit with them to eat and to drink.

9 For thus saith the LORD of hosts, the God of Israel; Behold, [a]I will cause to cease out of this place in your eyes, and in your days, the voice of mirth, and the voice of gladness, the voice of the bridegroom, and the voice of the bride.

10 And it shall come to pass, when thou shalt shew this people all these words, and they shall say unto thee, [a]Wherefore hath the LORD pronounced all this great evil against us? or what *is* our iniquity? or what *is* our sin that we have committed against the LORD our God?

11 Then shalt thou say unto them, [a]Because your fathers have forsaken me, saith the LORD, and have walked after other gods, and have served them, and have worshipped them, and have forsaken me, and have not kept my law;

12 And ye have done [a]worse than your fathers; for behold, [b]ye walk every one after the [1]imagination of his evil heart, that *they* may not hearken unto me:

13 [a]Therefore will I cast you out of this land [b]into a land that ye know not, *neither* ye nor your fathers; and there shall ye serve other gods day and night; where I will not shew you favour.

14 ¶ Therefore behold, the [a]days come, saith the LORD, that it shall no more be said, The LORD liveth, that brought up the children of Israel out of the land of Egypt;

15 But, The LORD liveth, that brought up the children of Israel from the land of the north, and from all the lands whither he had driven them: and [a]I will bring them again into their land that I gave unto their fathers.

16 Behold, I will send for many [a]fishers, saith the LORD, and they shall fish them; and after will I send for many hunters, and they shall hunt them from every mountain, and from every hill, and out of the holes of the rocks.

17 For mine [a]eyes *are* upon all their ways: they are not hid from my face, neither is their iniquity hid from mine eyes.

18 And first I will recompense their iniquity and their sin [a]double; because [b]they have defiled my land, they have filled mine inheritance with the carcases of their detestable and abominable things.

16:4 [a]ch. 15:2 [b]ch. 22:18; 25:33 [c]Ps. 83:10; ch. 8:2; 9:22 [d]Ps. 79:2; ch. 7:33; 34:20
16:5 [1]Or, *mourning feast* [a]Ezek. 24:17,22, 23
16:6 [a]ch. 22:18 [b]Lev. 19:28; Deut. 14:1; ch. 41:5; 47:5 [c]Is. 22:12; ch. 7:29
16:7 [1]Or, *break bread for them,* as [Is. 58:7] [a]Ezek. 24:17; Hos. 9:4; See Deut. 26:14; Job 42:11 [b]Prov. 31:6
16:9 [a]Is. 24:7,8; Ezek. 26:13; Hos. 2:11; Rev. 18:23
16:10 [a]Deut. 29:24; ch. 5:19
16:11 [a]Deut. 29:25; ch. 22:9
16:12 [1]Or, *stubbornness* [a]ch. 7:26 [b]ch. 13:10
16:13 [a]Deut. 4:26; 28:36,63 [b]ch. 15:14
16:14 [a]Is. 43:18; ch. 23:7,8
16:15 [a]ch. 24:6; 30:3; 32:37
16:16 [a]Amos 4:2; Hab. 1:15
16:17 [a]Job 34:21; Prov. 5:21; 15:3; ch. 32:19
16:18 [a]Is. 40:2; ch. 17:18 [b]Ezek. 43:7

can provide. *Thou shalt not.* The Hebrew underlying this phrase is used for the most forceful of negative commands, as, e.g., in the ten commandments (see Ex 20:3–4,7,13–17). *this place.* Judah and Jerusalem, especially the latter (see, e.g., Zeph 1:4).

16:4 *grievous deaths.* Cf. 14:18. *not be lamented . . . buried.* See v. 6; 7:33 and note; 8:2; 14:16; 25:33. *dung.* See 8:2; 9:22; 25:33. *consumed by the sword and by famine.* See 14:15–16; see also note on 5:12. *meat for the fowls . . . for the beasts.* See note on 7:33.

16:5 *Enter not . . . go to lament.* See the similar command of God in Ezek 24:16–17,22–23.

16:6 *cut themselves, nor make themselves bald.* Actions forbidden in the law (see Lev 19:28; 21:5 and note; Deut 14:1 and note), but sometimes practiced by Israelites (see 41:5; Ezek 7:18; Mic 1:16).

16:7 Food was customarily offered to mourners (see 2 Sam 3:35; 12:16–17; Ezek 24:17,22; Hos 9:4). *cup of consolation.* In later Judaism a special cup of wine given to the chief mourner.

16:8 *not also go into the house of.* The present crisis is a time for neither feasting nor mourning (see v. 5).

16:9 See 7:34; 25:10; contrast 33:10–11.

16:10–13 The same question but a more elaborate answer than in 5:19 (see 9:12–16; 22:8–9; Deut 29:24–28; 1 Ki 9:8–9).

16:10 Cf. the similar questions in Mal 1:6–7; 2:17; 3:7–8,13.

16:11 See 11:10, where committing sins like those mentioned here is called breaking the Lord's covenant.

16:12 *done worse than your fathers.* See 1 Ki 14:9. The coming judgment cannot be blamed on the sins of previous generations (see 31:29–30; Ezek 18:2–4). *after the imagination of his evil heart.* See note on 3:17; see also 7:24.

16:13 See Deut 28:36,64. *I will cast you out.* Into exile (see 7:15; 22:26; Deut 29:28). *land . . . ye know not . . . nor your fathers.* Babylonia (see 9:16).

16:14–15 Repeated almost verbatim in 23:7–8, the passage outlines nearly 1,000 years of Israelite history: exodus (c. 1446 B.C.), exile (586), restoration (537). See Is 43:16–21; 48:20–21; 51:9–11. *The LORD liveth.* See note on Gen 42:15.

16:15 *land of the north.* Babylonia (see note on Is 41:25).

16:16 *fishers . . . hunters.* Symbolic of conquerors (see Ezek 12:13; 29:4; Amos 4:2 and note). *mountain, and . . . hill.* To which the people would flee in vain (see 4:29 and note). *holes of the rocks.* The phrase occurs outside Jeremiah only in Is 7:19. The Lord may be recalling here the episode of the ruined linen girdle, hidden in a "hole of the rock" (13:4).

16:17 *mine eyes are upon all their ways.* See 32:19. *their iniquity hid from mine eyes.* See 23:24.

16:18 *recompense . . . double.* See 17:18; Is 40:2 and note. *defiled . . . land.* Made it ceremonially unclean (see 2:7; 3:1–2; see also note on Lev 4:12). *mine inheritance.* God's land (see 17:4; see also note on 2:7). *carcases of their detestable . . . things.* See Lev 26:30. Idols have no life in them (see Ps 115:4–7; 135:15–17). *abominable things.* Detestable in the Lord's eyes (see 2:7; see also note on Lev 7:21).

19 O LORD, [a]my strength, and my fortress, and [b]my refuge in the day of affliction, the Gentiles shall come unto thee from the ends of the earth, and shall say, Surely our fathers have inherited lies, vanity, and *things* [c]wherein *there is* no profit.

20 Shall a man make gods unto himself, and [a]they *are* no gods?

21 Therefore behold, I *will* this once cause them to know, I will cause them to know mine hand and my might; and they shall know that [a]my name *is* [1]The LORD.

God, the hope of Israel

17 The sin of Judah *is* written with a [a]pen of iron, *and* with the [1]point of a diamond: *it is* [b]graven upon the table of their heart, and upon the horns of your altars;

2 Whilst their children remember their altars and their [a]groves by the green trees upon the high hills.

3 O my mountain in the field, I will give thy substance *and* all thy treasures to the spoil, *and* thy high places for sin, throughout all thy borders.

4 And thou, even [1]thyself, shalt discontinue from thine heritage that I gave thee; and I will cause thee to serve thine enemies in [a]the land which thou knowest not: for [b]ye have kindled a fire in mine anger, *which* shall burn for ever.

5 ¶ Thus saith the LORD; [a]Cursed *be* the man that trusteth in man, and maketh [b]flesh his arm, and whose heart departeth from the LORD.

6 For he shall be [a]like the heath in the desert, and [b]shall not see when good cometh; but shall inhabit the parched places in the wilderness, [c]*in* a salt land and not inhabited.

7 [a]Blessed *is* the man that trusteth in the LORD, and whose hope the LORD is.

8 For he shall be [a]as a tree planted by the waters, and *that* spreadeth out her roots by the river, and shall not see when heat cometh, but her leaf shall be green; and shall not be careful in the year of [1]drought, neither shall cease from yielding fruit.

9 ¶ The heart *is* deceitful above all *things*, and desperately wicked: who can know it?

10 I the LORD [a]search the heart, *I* try the reins, [b]even to give every man according to his ways, *and* according to the fruit of his doings.

11 *As* the partridge [1]sitteth *on eggs*, and hatcheth *them* not; *so* he that getteth riches, and not by right, [a]shall leave them in the midst of his days, and at his end shall be [b]a fool.

12 ¶ A glorious high throne from the beginning *is* the place of our sanctuary.

16:19 [a]Ps. 18:2 [b]ch. 17:17 [c]Is. 44:10; ch. 10:5
16:20 [a]Is. 37:19; ch. 2:11; Gal. 4:8
16:21 [1][Or, *JEHOVAH*. Ps. 83:18] [a]Ex. 15:3; ch. 33:2; Amos 5:8
17:1 [1]Heb. *nail* [a]Job 19:24 [b]Prov. 3:3; 2 Cor. 3:3
17:2 [a]Judg. 3:7; 2 Chr. 24:18; 33:3,19; ch. 2:20
17:4 [1]Heb. *in thyself* [a]ch. 16:13 [b]ch. 15:14
17:5 [a]Is. 30:1,2; 31:1 [b]See Is. 31:3
17:6 [a]ch. 48:6 [b]Job 20:17 [c]Deut. 29:23
17:7 [a]Ps. 2:12; 34:8; Prov. 16:20; Is. 30:18
17:8 [1]Or, *restraint* [a]Job 8:16; Ps. 1:3
17:10 [a]1 Sam. 16:7; 1 Chr. 28:9; Ps. 7:9; 139:23,24; Prov. 17:3; ch. 20:12; Rom. 8:27; Rev. 2:23 [b]Ps. 62:12; ch. 32:19; Rom. 2:6
17:11 [1]Or, *gathereth young which she hath not brought forth* [a]Ps. 55:23 [b]Luke 12:20

16:19–20 The prophet interjects a few brief words of hope.
16:19 *strength . . . fortress . . . refuge in the day of affliction.* Such descriptions of God's dependability and protecting power are common in the Psalms (see, e.g., Ps 18:1–2; 28:7–8; 59:9,16–17). *the Gentiles shall come unto thee.* See 4:2 and note; see also Is 2:2–4; 42:4; 45:14; 49:6; Zech 8:20–23; 14:16. *vanity.* See note on 2:5. *things . . . no profit.* See note on 2:8.
16:20 *no gods.* See 5:7.
16:21–17:4 The Lord responds to Jeremiah and continues His solemn warnings that began in v. 1.
16:21 *cause them to know . . . cause them to know . . . shall know.* The same Hebrew root underlies each of these words. God would "cause them to know," and then they would surely "know." *them . . . they.* Probably includes Judah as well as the nations (see Ezek 36:23; 37:14). *know that my name is The LORD.* "Name" often means "person" or "being" in the OT (see note on Ps 5:11). Ezekiel's equivalent of Jeremiah's phrase is "know that I am the LORD," found in his prophecy about 65 times (see Introduction to Ezekiel: Themes; see also note on Ezek 5:13).
17:1 *written with a pen of iron.* The method used to inscribe the most permanent of records (see Job 19:24). *diamond.* Or "flint," which was one of the hardest of stones known to ancient man (see Ezek 3:9; Zech 7:12). *table of their heart.* For the same imagery see Prov 3:3; 7:3. *horns of your altars.* The people of Judah have backslid so badly that their sins are engraved not only on their hearts but also on their altars—to be remembered by God rather than to be atoned for (see Lev 16:18).
17:2 *altars and their groves.* See notes on Ex 34:13; Deut 7:5. *green trees . . . high hills.* See note on 2:20.
17:3–4 Repeated in large part from 15:13–14 (see notes there).
17:3 *my mountain.* mount Zion, the location of the temple in Jerusalem (see Ps 24:3; Is 2:3; Zech 8:3). *high places.* Locales of idolatrous worship.
17:4 *heritage.* The land of Canaan (see 16:18; see also note on 2:7).
17:5–8 See Ps 1 and notes.
17:5 *Cursed.* See note on 11:3. *flesh.* The opposite of "spirit" (see Is 31:3; see also Job 10:4).
‡17:6 *heath.* See 48:6. Apart from these two places in Jeremiah, the Hebrew for this word appears elsewhere in the OT only in Ps 102:17, where it is translated "destitute." *salt land.* An evidence of God's curse also in Deut 29:23.
17:8 *planted.* Or "transplanted." *waters.* See Is 44:4, where the same Hebrew root is used again to illustrate the source of the righteous man's strength. *drought.* See note on 14:1. *yielding fruit.* The Lord's answer to Jeremiah's complaint in 12:1–2 (see notes there).
17:9 The prophet makes an observation, then asks a rhetorical question. *The heart.* The source of the "springs of life," in which wickedness must not be allowed to take root (Prov 4:23). *deceitful.* The Hebrew root for this word is the basis of the name Jacob (see note on Gen 27:36).
17:10 The Lord responds to Jeremiah's question. *search . . . try.* See 11:20; 12:3. *reins.* Or "mind," lit. "kidneys" (see 11:20). *the fruit of his doings.* I.e. "what his deeds deserve" (cf. 6:19).
17:11 The prophet uses a proverb to make his point (as in v. 9); see especially Prov 23:5. *partridge.* Mentioned elsewhere in the OT only in 1 Sam 26:20. *sitteth on eggs.* The Hebrew root underlying this phrase is found again only in Is 34:15. Its Aramaic cognate, however, is used to explain Job 39:14 in the Targum (ancient Aramaic paraphrase). *in the midst of his days.* See Ps 102:24. *fool.* Morally and spiritually reprobate (see note on Prov 1:7).
17:12–18 The fourth of Jeremiah's "confessions" (see Introduction: Author and Date).
17:12 *glorious high throne.* See note on 14:21; see also Is 6:1. The Lord is often represented as sitting on a throne between the cherubim on the ark of the covenant in the temple (see, e.g., Ps 80:1; 99:1) *high.* mount Zion is the "mountain of the height of Israel" (Ezek 20:40). *from the beginning.* From time

13 O LORD, [a]the hope of Israel, [b]all that forsake thee shall be ashamed, and they that depart from me shall be [c]written in the earth,
because they have forsaken the LORD, the
[d]fountain of living waters.
14 Heal me, O LORD, and I shall be healed;
save me, and I shall be saved: for [a]thou *art* my
praise.
15 Behold, they say unto me, [a]Where *is*
the word of the LORD? let it come now.
16 As for me, [a]I have not hastened from *be-*
ing a pastor [1]to follow thee: neither have I desired the woeful day; thou knowest: that which
came out of my lips was right before thee.
17 Be not a terror unto me: [a]thou *art* my
hope in the day of evil.
18 [a]Let them be confounded that persecute me, but [b]let not me be confounded: let
them be dismayed, but let not me be dismayed: bring upon them the day of evil, and
[c][1]destroy them *with* double destruction.

Sabbath observance stressed

19 ¶ Thus said the LORD unto me; Go and
stand in the gate of the children of the people,
whereby the kings of Judah come in, and by
the which they go out, and in all the gates of
Jerusalem;
20 And say unto them, [a]Hear ye the word
of the LORD, ye kings of Judah, and all Judah,
and all the inhabitants of Jerusalem, that enter
in by these gates:
21 Thus saith the LORD; [a]Take heed to
yourselves, and bear no burden on the sabbath
day, nor bring *it* in by the gates of Jerusalem;
22 Neither carry forth a burden out of your
houses on the sabbath day, neither do ye any
work, but hallow ye the sabbath day, as I
[a]commanded your fathers.
23 [a]But they obeyed not, neither inclined
their ear, but made their neck stiff, that *they*
might not hear, nor receive instruction.
24 And it shall come to pass, if ye diligently hearken unto me, saith the LORD, to bring in
no burden through the gates of this city on the
sabbath day, but hallow the sabbath day, to do
no work therein;
25 [a]Then shall there enter into the gates of
this city kings and princes sitting upon the
throne of David, riding in chariots and on
horses, they, and their princes, the men of Judah, and the inhabitants of Jerusalem: and this
city shall remain for ever.
26 And they shall come from the cities of Judah, and from [a]the places about Jerusalem, and
from the land of Benjamin, and from [b]the plain,
and from the mountains, and from [c]the south,
bringing burnt offerings, and sacrifices, and
meat offerings, and incense, and bringing [d]*sac-*
rifices of praise, *unto* the house of the LORD.
27 But if you will not hearken unto me to
hallow the sabbath day, and not to bear a burden, even entering in at the gates of Jerusalem
on the sabbath day; then [a]will I kindle a fire in
the gates thereof, [b]and it shall devour the palaces of Jerusalem, and it shall not be quenched.

17:13 [a]ch. 14:8 [b]Ps. 73:27; Is. 1:28 [c]See Luke 10:20 [d]ch. 2:13
17:14 [a]Deut. 10:21; Ps. 109:1; 148:14
17:15 [a]Is. 5:19; Ezek. 12:22; Amos 5:18; 2 Pet. 3:4
17:16 [1]Heb. *after thee* [a]ch. 1:4
17:17 [a]ch. 16:19
17:18 [1]Heb. *break them* with *a double breach* [a]Ps. 35:4; 70:2 [b]Ps. 25:2 [c]ch. 11:20
17:20 [a]ch. 19:3
17:21 [a]Num. 15:32; Neh. 13:19
17:22 [a]Ex. 20:8; 31:13; Ezek. 20:12
17:23 [a]ch. 7:24,26
17:25 [a]ch. 22:4
17:26 [a]ch. 33:13 [b]Zech. 7:7 [c]Zech. 7:7 [d]Ps. 107:22; 116:17
17:27 [a]ch. 21:14; Lam. 4:11; Amos 1:4,7,10,12 [b]2 Ki. 25:9; ch. 52:13

immemorial, Zion had been chosen by God as the place of His sanctuary (see Ex 15:17).

17:13 *forsaken . . . fountain of living waters.* Contrast 15:18; see note on 2:13.

17:14 *Heal me.* See 15:18; Ps 6:2. *thou art my praise.* Or, "You are the One I praise" (likewise in Deut 10:21).

17:15 See 20:8. Jeremiah's enemies accuse him of being a false prophet (see Deut 18:21–22). The accusation must have been voiced before the first invasion of Judah by the Babylonians in 605 B.C. after the battle of Carchemish (see 46:2; see also Introduction: Background).

17:16 *pastor.* Symbolic of leadership (see note on 2:8), and therefore of Jeremiah's role as a prophet.

17:17 *my hope.* See note on 16:19. *day of evil.* See v. 18; 15:11.

17:18 *that persecute me.* See 15:15. *double.* See 16:18; Is 40:2 and note.

17:19–27 An extended commentary on the sabbath-day commandment (the covenant sign of God's relationship with Israel; see Ex 31:13–17; Ezek 20:12), probably the version recorded in Deut 5:12–15 (see especially note on v. 22 below).

‡17:19 *children of the people.* The Hebrew for this word is translated "common people" in 26:23. The "gate of the children of the people," then, is most likely the east gate of the temple, where the people assembled in large numbers and which the kings would be expected to use frequently.

17:20 *kings of Judah.* The current king and all subsequent ruling members of David's dynasty (see, e.g., v. 25; 1:18; 2:26; 13:13; 19:3).

17:21 *Take heed.* See Josh 23:11. The Hebrew underlying this phrase is also in Deut 4:15, and a similar expression is translated "take heed to your spirit" in Mal 2:15, stressing the urgency and solemnity of the Lord's command.

17:22 See note on 16:2. The Hebrew for the negative expression in this verse is stronger than that in v. 21. *Neither . . . neither do ye any work . . . hallow ye the sabbath day.* Specific references to the sabbath-day commandment of Ex 20:8,10; Deut 5:12,14. *as I commanded.* The Hebrew underlying this phrase is unique to the ten commandments as recorded in Deuteronomy (see Deut 5:12,15–16; see note on vv. 19–27).

17:23 *But they obeyed not . . . made their neck stiff.* Repeated from 7:26 (see note there; see also 11:10). *nor receive instruction.* See 2:30; 5:3.

17:25 Repeated in part in 22:4. King David's dynasty will last forever (see 23:5–6; 30:9; 33:15; 2 Sam 7:12–17), and Jerusalem will be inhabited for all time (Zech 2:2–12; 8:3; 14:11), if the people of Judah obey the Lord (see v. 27)—and they will, according to 31:33–34.

17:26 *land of Benjamin.* Jeremiah's hometown was located there (see 1:1). *plain . . . the mountains.* See note on Deut 1:7. *the south.* See note on Gen 12:9. *sacrifices of praise.* The repetition here of "bringing" from earlier in the verse separates the sacrifices of praise (thank offerings) from the other specific sacrifices mentioned and gives them the more general designation of offerings of thanksgiving (as intended also in 33:11).

17:27 Disobedience will bring disaster and will negate—at least temporarily—the promises of vv. 24–26. *gates of Jerusalem.* The symbols of sabbath violation would be the first structures destroyed. *kindle a fire . . . devour the palaces.* Common prophetic language for divine judgment against rebellious cities (see 49:27; 50:32; Amos 1:4,7,10,12,14; 2:2,5; cf. Jer 21:14).

The parable of potter and clay

18 The word which came to Jeremiah from the LORD, saying,

2 Arise, and go down *to* the potter's house, and there I will cause thee to hear my words.

3 Then I went down *to* the potter's house, and behold, he wrought a work on the [1]wheels.

4 And the vessel [1]that he made of clay was marred in the hand of the potter: so he [2]made it again another vessel, as seemed good to the potter to make *it.*

5 Then the word of the LORD came to me, saying,

6 O house of Israel, [a]cannot I do with you as this potter? saith the LORD. Behold, [b]as the clay *is* in the potter's hand, so *are* ye in mine hand, O house of Israel.

7 *At what* instant I shall speak concerning a nation and concerning a kingdom, to [a]pluck up, and to pull down, and to destroy *it;*

8 [a]If that nation, against whom I have pronounced, turn from their evil, [b]I will repent of the evil that I thought to do unto them.

9 And *at what* instant I shall speak concerning a nation, and concerning a kingdom, to build and to plant *it;*

10 If it do evil in my sight, that *it* obey not my voice, then I will repent of the good, wherewith I said *I* would benefit them.

11 Now therefore go to, speak to the men of Judah, and to the inhabitants of Jerusalem, saying, Thus saith the LORD; Behold, I frame evil against you, and devise a device against you: [a]return ye now every one from his evil way, and make your ways and your doings good.

12 And they said, [a]There is no hope: but we will walk after our own devices, and we will every one do the imagination of his evil heart.

13 Therefore thus saith the LORD; [a]Ask ye now among the heathen, who hath heard such *things:* the virgin of Israel hath done [b]a very horrible thing.

14 Will *a man* leave [1]the snow of Lebanon *which cometh* from the rock of the field? *or* shall the cold flowing waters that come from another place be forsaken?

15 Because my people hath forgotten [a]me, they have burnt incense to vanity, and they have caused them to stumble in their ways *from* the [b]ancient paths, to walk *in* paths, *in* a way not cast up;

16 To make their land [a]desolate, *and* a perpetual [b]hissing; every one that passeth thereby shall be astonished, and wag his head.

17 [a]I will scatter them [b]as *with* an east wind before the enemy; [c]I will shew them the back, and not the face, in the day of their calamity.

18 ¶ Then said they, [a]Come, and let us devise devices against Jeremiah; [b]for the law shall not perish from the priest, nor counsel

18:3 [1]Or, *frames,* or, *seats* 18:4 [1]Or, *that he made was marred, as clay in the hand of the potter* [2]Heb. *returned and made* 18:6 [a]Is. 45:9; Rom. 9:20 [b]Is. 64:8 18:7 [a]ch. 1:10 18:8 [a]Ezek. 18:21; 33:11 [b]ch. 26:3; Jonah 3:10 18:11 [a]2 Ki. 17:13; ch. 7:3 18:12 [a]ch. 2:25 18:13 [a]ch. 2:10; 1 Cor. 5:1 [b]ch. 5:30 18:14 [1]Or, *my fields for a rock,* or for *the snow of Lebanon? shall the running waters be forsaken for the strange cold* waters? 18:15 [a]ch. 2:13,32 [b]ch. 6:16 18:16 [a]ch. 19:8 [b]1 Ki. 9:8; Lam. 2:15; Mic. 6:16 18:17 [a]ch. 13:24 [b]Ps. 48:7 [c]See ch. 2:27 18:18 [a]ch. 11:19 [b]Lev. 10:11; Mal. 2:7; John 7:48

18:1–20:18 Three chapters focusing on lessons the Lord taught Jeremiah at the potter's workshop, probably before 605 B.C. (see note on 17:15).

18:1–17 As the potter controls what he does with the clay, so the Lord is sovereign over the people of Judah.

18:2 *go down.* The potter's workshop was probably located on the slopes of the valley of Ben-hinnom near the east gate (see 19:2 and note).

18:3 *wheels.* Lit. "two stones." Both wheels were attached to a single upright shaft, one end of which was sunk permanently in the ground. The potter would spin the lower wheel with his foot and would work the clay on the upper wheel; the process is described in the Apocryphal book of Ecclesiasticus (38:29–30).

‡18:4 *marred.* The same word appeared in 13:7 with respect to the linen girdle that Jeremiah had hidden (see note there). *as seemed good to the potter.* The flaw was in the clay itself, not in the potter's skill.

18:6 *as the clay . . . so are ye.* Biblical imagery often pictures mankind as made of clay by a potter (see Job 4:19 and note). *potter's.* The Hebrew for this word is translated "former" in 10:16 with reference to God.

18:7–10 The Lord retains the right of limiting His own absolute sovereignty on the basis of human response to His offers of pardon and restoration and His threats of judgment and destruction. *At . . . if . . . at . . . if.* God's promises and threats are conditioned on man's actions. God, who Himself does not change (see Num 23:19; Mal 3:6; Jas 1:17), nevertheless will change His preannounced response to man, depending on what the latter does (see note on 4:28; see also Joel 2:13; Jonah 3:9 and note; Jonah 3:8–4:2; 4:11).

18:7 *pluck up . . . pull down . . . destroy.* See 1:10 and note.

18:8 See 26:3. *evil . . . evil.* The Hebrew is the same for both words (also in v. 11).

18:9 *built . . . plant it.* See 1:10 and note.

‡18:11 *I frame evil.* See note at 18:8. See Esth 8:3; 9:25; Ezek 38:10.

18:12 *There is no hope.* See 2:25; see also note on Is 57:10. *do the imagination of his evil heart.* See note on 3:17.

18:13–17 See 2:10–13.

18:13 *virgin of Israel.* See 14:17 and note. *horrible thing.* See 5:30; 23:14; Hos 6:10.

18:14–15 Although nature is reliable (v. 14), Judah is fickle and unfaithful (v. 15).

18:14 *Lebanon.* One of the highest of the northern mountains (see 22:6), reaching an altitude of over 10,000 feet.

18:15 *my people hath forgotten me.* Repeated from 2:32 (see note there). *burnt incense.* See note on 1:16. *vanity.* Lit. "nothing" (see Ps 31:6). The Hebrew for this phrase is different from that in either 2:5 or 2:8 (see note on 2:8). *they have caused them to stumble.* See 2 Chr 28:23. *ancient paths.* See note on 6:16. *in a way not cast up.* See note on Is 35:8.

18:16 *desolate . . . astonished.* The same Hebrew root underlies both words. *perpetual hissing.* See 19:8; 25:9,18; 29:18; 51:37. The phrase implies hissing or whistling to express shock, ridicule and contempt. *every one . . . astonished.* See 19:8; 1 Ki 9:8. *wag his head.* See 48:27; Job 16:4 and note; see also Ps 44:14; 109:25.

18:17 *east wind.* See note on 4:11; see also Ps 48:7. *shew them the back, and not the face.* As the people themselves had done to God (see 2:27). His face symbolizes His gracious blessing and favor (see Num 6:24–26).

18:18–23 The fifth of Jeremiah's "confessions" (see Introduction: Author and Date).

18:18 *they.* Jeremiah's enemies (see note on 17:15). *devise devices against Jeremiah.* See v. 12; 11:18–23; 12:6; 15:10–11, 15–21. *the law.* Delegated to the priests (see note on Deut 31:11). *priest . . . the wise . . . prophet.* See 8:8–10; see also Ezek

from the wise, nor the word from the prophet.
Come, and let us smite him [1]with the tongue,
and let us not give heed to any of his words.
19 Give heed to me, O LORD, and hearken
to the voice of them that contend with me.
20 [a]Shall evil be recompensed for good? for
[b]they have digged a pit for my soul. Remember
that I stood before thee to speak good for
them, *and* to turn away thy wrath from them.
21 Therefore [a]deliver up their children to
the famine, and [1]pour out their *blood* by the
force of the sword; and let their wives be bereaved of their children, and *be* widows; and
let their men be put to death; *let* their young
men *be* slain by the sword in battle.
22 Let a cry be heard from their houses,
when thou shalt bring a troop suddenly upon
them: for [a]they have digged a pit to take me,
and hid snares for my feet.
23 Yet, LORD, thou knowest all their counsel against me [1]to slay *me:* [a]forgive not their
iniquity, neither blot out their sin from thy
sight, but let them be overthrown before thee;
deal *thus* with them in the time of thine anger.

19 Thus saith the LORD, Go and get a
potter's earthen bottle, and *take* of
the ancients of the people, and of the ancients
of the priests;
2 And go forth unto [a]the valley of the son
of Hinnom, which *is by* the entry of [1]the east
gate, and proclaim there the words that I shall
tell thee,

18:18 [1] Or, *for the tongue*
18:20 [a] Ps. 109:4 [b] ver. 22; Ps. 35:7
18:21 [1] Heb. *pour them out* [a] Ps. 109:9
18:22 [a] ver. 20
18:23 [1] Heb. *for death* [a] Ps. 35:4; 109:14; ch. 11:20
19:2 [1] Heb. *the sun gate* [a] Josh. 15:8; 2 Ki. 23:10
19:3 [a] ch. 17:20 [b] 1 Sam. 3:11; 2 Ki. 21:12
19:4 [a] Deut. 28:20; Is. 65:11 [b] 2 Ki. 21:16; ch. 2:34
19:5 [a] ch. 7:31; 32:35 [b] Lev. 18:21
19:6 [a] Josh. 15:8
19:7 [a] Lev. 26:17; Deut. 28:25 [b] Ps. 79:2; ch. 7:33; 16:4; 34:20
19:8 [a] ch. 18:16; 49:13; 50:13
19:9 [a] Lev. 26:29; Deut. 28:53; Is. 9:20; Lam. 4:10

3 [a]And say, Hear ye the word of the LORD,
O kings of Judah, and inhabitants of Jerusalem; Thus saith the LORD of hosts, the God of
Israel; Behold, I *will* bring evil upon this place,
the which whosoever heareth, his ears shall
[b]tingle.
4 Because they [a]have forsaken me, and
have estranged this place, and have burnt incense in it unto other gods, whom neither
they nor their fathers have known, nor the
kings of Judah, and have filled this place *with*
[b]the blood of innocents;
5 [a]They have built also the high places of
Baal, to burn their sons with fire *for* burnt offerings unto Baal, [b]which I commanded not,
nor spake *it,* neither came *it* into my mind:
6 Therefore behold, the days come, saith
the LORD, that this place shall no more be
called Tophet, nor [a]The valley of the son of
Hinnom, but The valley of slaughter.
7 And I will make void the counsel of Judah
and Jerusalem in this place; [a]and I will cause
them to fall by the sword before their enemies, and by the hands of them that seek their
lives: and their [b]carcases will I give to be meat
for the fowls of the heaven, and for the beasts
of the earth.
8 And I will make this city [a]desolate, and a
hissing; every one that passeth thereby shall
be astonished and hiss because of all the
plagues thereof.
9 And I will cause them to eat the [a]flesh of
their sons and the flesh of their daughters, and

7:26, where the wise are replaced by the elders. *smite him with the tongue.* See note on 9:3.

18:20 *Shall evil be recompensed for good?* See Ps 35:12. *digged a pit.* Symbolic of his enemies' plots against him (see v. 22; Ps 57:6 and note; Prov 22:14; 23:27). *stood before thee.* See note on 15:1. *speak good for them.* See 14:7–9,21.

18:21 *pour out their blood by the force of the sword.* The Hebrew underlying this phrase occurs also in Ps 63:10; Ezek 35:5. *be put to death.* Lit. "be slain by death," probably referring to plague, as in 15:2 (see note there).

18:22–23 See Ps 141:8–10.

18:22 *hid snares.* See Ps 140:5; 142:3.

18:23 *Yet, LORD, thou knowest.* See 12:3; 15:15. *forgive not their iniquity . . . let them be overthrown before thee.* A prayer not for human vengeance but for divine vindication. *blot out.* The Phoenician cognate of the Hebrew for this phrase appears in a ninth-century B.C. inscription on a gateway: "If . . . a man . . . blots out the name of Azitawadda from this gate . . . may (the gods) wipe out . . . that man!"

19:1–15 A bottle deliberately broken by Jeremiah (vv. 1–10) symbolizes the forthcoming destruction of Judah and Jerusalem (vv. 11–15). In ch. 18, the potter's clay was still moist and pliable, making it possible to reshape and rework it (see 18:1–11). In ch. 19, however, the earthen bottle is hard and, if unsuitable for the owner's use, can only be destroyed (see v. 11).

19:1 *bottle.* The Hebrew for this word implies a vessel with a narrow neck, perhaps the water decanter frequently found in excavations and ranging from 5 to 12 inches high. *ancients.* See note on Ex 3:16. *of the people.* See 1 Ki 8:1–3. *ancients of the priests.* See 2 Ki 19:2, "elders of the priests." Elders in Israel were of two kinds, one performing primarily civil functions and the other primarily religious functions.

‡19:2 *the valley of the son of Hinnom.* See note on 7:31. *east gate.* The Hebrew underlying the word "east" is the same as that translated "earthen" in v. 1. The Jerusalem Targum identified the potsherd gate (so called because it overlooked the main dump for broken pottery) with the "dung port" of Neh 2:13 (see note there); 3:13–14; 12:31.

19:3 *kings.* See note on 17:20. *evil . . . ears . . . shall tingle.* Echoed from 2 Ki 21:12 (see 1 Sam 3:11). The phrase refers to the shock of hearing an announcement of threatened punishment.

‡19:4 *they.* All who tried to combine the worship of idols with the worship of the one true God. *this place.* Jerusalem. *burnt incense.* The Hebrew for this phrase is mostly translated this same way elsewhere in Jeremiah (see note on 1:16). *filled this place with the blood of innocents.* The blood of godly people (see 2:34; 7:6; 22:3,17; 26:15), specifically as shed by wicked King Manasseh (see 15:4 and note; see also especially 2 Ki 21:16).

19:5–6 Repeated in large part from 7:31–32 (see notes there).

19:7 *make void.* Lit. "pour out." The Hebrew for "make void" ("pour out") sounds like the Hebrew for "bottle" (see note on v. 1). As Jeremiah was saying this, he may have been pouring water from the bottle to the ground (cf. 2 Sam 14:14). *fall by the sword before their enemies.* The Babylonians are the instruments of the divine threat (see 20:6). *carcases . . . to be meat for the fowls of the heaven.* See 7:33 and note.

19:8 Echoes the language of 18:16 (see note there; see also Ezek 27:35; Zeph 2:15). *desolate . . . astonished.* The same Hebrew root underlies both words.

19:9 One of the covenant curses (see Lev 26:29; Deut 28:53–57). *eat the flesh of their sons and . . . daughters . . . eat every one the flesh of his friend.* When Jerusalem's food supply ran out during the Babylonian siege in 586 B.C., cannibalism re-

they shall eat every one the flesh of his friend in the siege and straitness, wherewith their enemies, and they that seek their lives, shall straiten them.

10 [a]Then shalt thou break the bottle in the sight of the men that go with thee.

11 And shalt say unto them, Thus saith the LORD of hosts; [a]Even so will I break this people and this city, as *one* breaketh a potter's vessel, that cannot [1]be made whole again: and they shall [b]bury *them* in Tophet, till *there be* no place to bury.

12 Thus will I do unto this place, saith the LORD, and to the inhabitants thereof, and *even* make this city as Tophet:

13 And the houses of Jerusalem, and the houses of the kings of Judah, shall be defiled [a]as the place of Tophet, because of all the houses upon whose [b]roofs they have burnt incense unto all the host of heaven, and [c]have poured out drink offerings unto other gods.

14 ¶ Then came Jeremiah from Tophet, whither the LORD had sent him to prophesy; and he stood in [a]the court of the LORD's house; and said to all the people,

15 Thus saith the LORD of hosts, the God of Israel; Behold, I will bring upon this city and upon all her towns all the evil that I have pronounced against it, because [a]they have hardened their necks, that *they* might not hear my words.

19:10 [a]ch. 51:63,64
19:11 [1]Heb. *be healed* [a]Ps. 2:9; Is. 30:14; Lam. 4:2 [b]ch. 7:32
19:13 [a]2 Ki. 23:10 [b]2 Ki. 23:12; ch. 32:29; Zeph. 1:5 [c]ch. 7:18
19:14 [a]See 2 Chr. 20:5
19:15 [a]ch. 7:26; 17:23

20:1 [a]1 Chr. 24:14
20:3 [1]That is, *Fear round about*
20:5 [a]2 Ki. 20:17; 24:12-16; 25:13; ch. 3:24
20:6 [a]ch. 14:13,14; 28:15; 29:21

Jeremiah and Pashur

20 Now Pashur the son of [a]Immer the priest, who *was* also chief governor in the house of the LORD, heard *that* Jeremiah prophesied these things.

2 Then Pashur smote Jeremiah the prophet, and put him in the stocks that *were* in the high gate of Benjamin, which *was* by the house of the LORD.

3 And it came to pass on the morrow, that Pashur brought forth Jeremiah out of the stocks. Then said Jeremiah unto him, The LORD hath not called thy name Pashur, but [1]Magor-missabib.

4 For thus saith the LORD, Behold, I will make thee a terror to thyself, and to all thy friends: and they shall fall by the sword of their enemies, and thine eyes *shall* behold *it;* and I will give all Judah into the hand of the king of Babylon, and he shall carry them captive into Babylon, and shall slay them with the sword.

5 Moreover I [a]will deliver all the strength of this city, and all the labours thereof, and all the precious things thereof, and all the treasures of the kings of Judah will I give into the hand of their enemies, which shall spoil them, and take them, and carry them to Babylon.

6 And thou, Pashur, and all that dwell in thine house shall go into captivity: and thou shalt come *to* Babylon, and there thou shalt die, and shalt be buried there, thou, and all thy friends, to whom thou hast [a]prophesied lies.

---

sulted (see Lam 2:20; 4:10; Ezek 5:10). Such shocking activity was not unprecedented in Israel (see 2 Ki 6:28–29), and it would occur again in A.D. 70 during the Roman siege of Jerusalem (see Zech 11:9 and note): "A woman . . . who . . . had fled to Jerusalem . . . killed her son, roasted him, and ate one half, concealing and saving the rest" (Josephus, *Jewish Wars,* 6.3.4).

19:11 *break this people . . . as one breaketh a potter's vessel.* Egyptians of the 12th Dynasty (1991–1786 B.C.) inscribed the names of their enemies on pottery bowls and then smashed them, hoping to break the power of their enemies by so doing. *cannot be made whole again.* See note on vv. 1–15.

19:13 *shall be defiled as . . . Tophet.* King Josiah had earlier "defiled Topheth" (2 Ki 23:10). *roofs.* See 32:29; see also note on Is 15:3. The kings of Judah had built pagan altars on the roof of the palace in Jerusalem (see 2 Ki 23:12). The Ugaritic Keret epic of the 14th century B.C. (see chart, p. xix) describes a similar practice: "Go to the top of a tower, bestride the top of the wall . . . Honor Baal with your sacrifice . . . Then descend . . . from the housetops." *burnt incense.* See note on 1:16. *host of heaven.* Worship of the sun, moon and stars was common in Judah throughout much of the later history of the monarchy (see, e.g., 2 Ki 17:16; 21:3,5; 23:4–5; Zeph 1:5). *drink offerings unto other gods.* See note on 7:18.

19:14 *all the people.* A much larger audience than the elders of v. 1.

19:15 *all her towns.* The towns of Judah that were dependent on Jerusalem (see 1:15; 9:11). *hardened their necks, that they might not hear my words.* Repeated from 7:26 (see note there; see also 11:10).

20:1–6 Pashur's response to Jeremiah's symbolic act (vv. 1–2), and Jeremiah's rejoinder (vv. 3–6).

20:1 *Pashur.* One or more different men with the same name appear in 21:1; 38:1. *Immer.* Perhaps a descendant of the head of the 16th division of priests in the Jerusalem temple (see 1 Chr 24:14). *chief governor.* The priest in charge of punishing troublemakers, real or imagined, in the temple courts (see v. 2; 29:26). The position was second only to that of the chief priest himself (compare 29:25–26 with 52:24).

20:2 The first of many recorded acts of physical violence against Jeremiah. *the prophet.* The first time Jeremiah is so called in the book (see Introduction: Themes and Message), here to stress the enormity of Pashur's actions. *smote.* Probably in accordance with the Mosaic law of Deut 25:2–3 (see note on Deut 25:3). *stocks.* Lit. "restraint, confinement" (the Hebrew for this word is translated "prison house" in 2 Chr 16:10). *the high gate of Benjamin.* Probably the same as the north gate of the inner court (Ezek 8:3; see 2 Ki 15:35; see also Ezek 9:2). *by the house of the LORD.* This qualifying phrase distinguishes the temple's gate of Benjamin from the "Benjamin Gate" in the city wall (37:13; 38:7). Both gates were in the northern part of the city, facing the territory of Benjamin.

‡20:3 *Magor-missabib.* Means "terror on every side" (see note on 6:25). The phrase "fear round about" (see v. 10) is found in the plural in Lam 2:22 ("terrors round about").

20:4 Pashur's new name symbolizes terror to all Judah, whose people will be exiled to Babylonia or put to death. *friends.* Associates and allies in the sense of covenant partners (see v. 6). *king of Babylon.* Nebuchadnezzar, who acceded to the Babylonian throne in 605 B.C. (see notes on 17:15; 18:1–20:18).

20:5 Fulfilled in 597 B.C. (see 2 Ki 24:13) and in 586 (see 52:17–23; 2 Ki 25:13–17).

20:6 *thou, Pashur . . . shall go into captivity.* Probably in 597 B.C., because shortly after that year (see 29:2) two other men in succession had replaced Pashur as chief governor in the temple (see 29:25–26). The priest Pashur had pretended to be a prophet.

Jeremiah complains to the LORD

7 O LORD, thou hast deceived me, and I
was [1]deceived:
[a]Thou art stronger than I, and hast
prevailed:
[b]I am in derision daily,
Every one mocketh me.
8 For since I spake, I cried out,
[a]I cried violence and spoil;
Because the word of the LORD was
made a reproach unto me,
And a derision, daily.
9 Then I said, I will not make mention of
him,
Nor speak any more in his name.
But *his word* was in mine heart as a
[a]burning fire shut up in my bones,
And I was weary with forbearing, and
[b]I could not stay.
10 [a]For I heard the defaming of many, fear
on every side.
Report, *say they,* and we will report it.
[b][1]All my familiars watched for my
halting, *saying,*
Peradventure he will be enticed, and
we shall prevail against him,
And we shall take our revenge on him.
11 But the LORD *is* with me as a mighty
terrible one:
Therefore my persecutors shall
stumble, and they shall not [a]prevail:
They shall be greatly ashamed: for they
shall not prosper:
Their [b]everlasting confusion shall
never be forgotten.
12 But, O LORD of hosts, that [a]triest the
righteous,
And seest the reins and the heart,
[b]Let me see thy vengeance on them:
For unto thee have I opened my cause.
13 Sing unto the LORD, praise ye the LORD:
For [a]he hath delivered the soul of the
poor from the hand of evildoers.

14 [a]Cursed *be* the day wherein I was born:
Let not the day wherein my mother
bare me be blessed.
15 Cursed *be* the man who brought
tidings to my father, saying,
A man child is born unto thee;
Making him very glad.
16 And let that man be as the cities which
the LORD [a]overthrew, and repented
not:
And let him [b]hear the cry in the
morning, and the shouting at
noontide;
17 [a]Because he slew me not from the
womb;
Or that my mother might have been
my grave,
And her womb *to be* always great *with
me.*
18 [a]Wherefore came I forth out of the
womb
To [b]see labour and sorrow,
That my days should be consumed
with shame?

20:7 [1]Or, *enticed* [a]ch. 1:6,7 [b]Lam. 3:14
20:8 [a]ch. 6:7
20:9 [a]Job 32:18,19; Ps. 39:3 [b]Job 32:18; Acts 18:5
20:10 [1]Heb. *Every man of my peace* [a]Ps. 31:13 [b]Job 19:19; Ps. 41:9; 55:13,14; Luke 11:53,54
20:11 [a]ch. 15:20; 17:18 [b]ch. 23:40
20:12 [a]ch. 11:20; 17:10 [b]Ps. 54:7; 59:10
20:13 [a]Ps. 35:9,10; 109:30,31
20:14 [a]Job 3:3; ch. 15:10
20:16 [a]Gen. 19:25 [b]ch. 18:22
20:17 [a]Job 3:10,11
20:18 [a]Job 3:20 [b]Lam. 3:1

20:7–18 The sixth, last and longest of Jeremiah's "confessions" (see Introduction: Author and Date). In some respects, it is the most daring and bitter of them all.ome respects, it is the most daring and bitter of them all.

20:7 Cf. 15:18. *deceived.* Lit. "seduced" (Ex 22:16) or "enticed" (1 Ki 22:20–22); see v. 10. Jeremiah feels that when the Lord originally called him to be a prophet, He had overly persuaded him (see 1:7–8,17–19; cf. Ezek 14:9).

20:8 Jeremiah attributes his suffering to the Lord's demands on his life. *violence and spoil.* The prophet's message echoes the Lord's word (see 6:7). *reproach.* See Ps 44:13; 79:4.

20:9 A classic description of prophetic reluctance overcome by divine compulsion (see 1:6–8; Amos 3:8; Acts 4:20; 1 Cor 9:16). *in mine heart as a burning fire.* See 5:14; 23:29. The figure is unique to the prophet Jeremiah (see also Lam 1:13).

‡20:10 The Hebrew of the first two lines is identical with that of the first two lines of Ps 31:13. *fear on every side.* See note on 6:25. The phrase is here used as a nickname for Jeremiah in the light of his doleful message. *familiars.* Lit. "men of my peace/welfare" (a similar Hebrew phrase appears in Ps 41:9, where it is translated "familiar friend"). *watched for my halting.* See Ps 35:15; 38:16. *enticed.* See v. 7 and note. *we shall prevail against him.* Or so they think (see v. 11). *take our revenge on him.* His enemies will not give up, no matter what it takes (see 11:19; 12:6; 26:11; cf. Ps 56:5–6; 71:10).

‡20:11 *the LORD is with me.* See 1:8 and note. *mighty . . . one.* See notes on Ex 14:14; 15:3. *terrible one.* The Lord's strength produces dread in His opponents. The Hebrew for this word is translated "terrible" in 15:21, where it describes Jeremiah's enemies. Here it has a different nuance and is applied to God, whose "dread" overcomes all "violence."

20:12 Repeated almost verbatim from 11:20.

20:13 *Sing . . . praise.* See 31:7; see also introduction to Ps 9. *delivered . . . from the hand of evildoers.* See 15:21; 21:12. *poor.* See 22:16. By Jeremiah's time, "poor/needy" had become virtually synonymous with "righteous" (see Amos 2:6; see also notes on Ps 9:18; 34:6).

20:14–18 See Job 3:3–19. From the heights of exultation (v. 13), Jeremiah now sinks to the depths of despair. The irreversibility of his divine call (v. 9), the betrayal of his friends (v. 10), the relentless pursuit of his enemies (vv. 7,11), the negative and condemnatory nature of his message (v. 8)—all have combined to bring to his lips a startling expression of despondency and hopelessness. The passage serves also as a transition to the next major section of the book. Judah and Jerusalem, Jeremiah will soon say, are now irrevocably doomed (see 21:1–10).

20:14 *Cursed be the day wherein I was born.* See note on Job 3:3. The prophet questions the very basis of his divine commission (see 1:5).

20:15 News of the birth of a son, normally a blessing in ancient times (see, e.g., Gen 29:31–35), Jeremiah sees as a curse in his own case. *Cursed be the man.* A rhetorical curse, not directed against the man personally.

20:16 *cities . . . the LORD overthrew.* Sodom and Gomorrah (see Gen 19:24–25,29). By Jeremiah's time, their wickedness had long been proverbial (see 23:14; Deut 29:23; see also note on Is 1:9–10). *cry in the morning.* See 4:19. *at noontide.* See note on 6:4.

20:17 *And her womb to be always great with me.* In his anguish, Jeremiah wishes that his mother's womb, which gave him birth, had been instead his eternal tomb.

Zedekiah's prayer; God's answer

21 The word which came unto Jeremiah
from the LORD, when king Zedekiah
sent unto him [a]Pashur the son of Melchiah,
and [b]Zephaniah the son of Maaseiah the
priest, saying,
2 [a]Inquire, I pray thee, of the LORD for us;
for Nebuchadrezzar king of Babylon maketh
war against us; if so be that the LORD will deal
with us according to all his wondrous works,
that he may go up from us.
3 Then said Jeremiah unto them, Thus
shall ye say to Zedekiah:
4 Thus saith the LORD God of Israel; Behold, I *will* turn back the weapons of war that
are in your hands, wherewith ye fight against
the king of Babylon, and against the
Chaldeans, which besiege you without the
walls, and [a]I will assemble them into the
midst of this city.
5 And I myself will fight against you with
an [a]outstretched hand and with a strong arm,
even in anger, and in fury, and in great wrath.
6 And I will smite the inhabitants of this
city, both man and beast: they shall die of a
great pestilence.
7 And afterward, saith the LORD, [a]I will deliver Zedekiah king of Judah, and his servants,
and the people, and such as are left in this city
from the pestilence, from the sword, and from
the famine, into the hand of Nebuchadrezzar
king of Babylon, and into the hand of their enemies, and into the hand of those that seek
their life: and he shall smite them with the
edge of the sword; [b]he shall not spare them,
neither have pity, nor have mercy.
8 ¶ And unto this people thou shalt say,
Thus saith the LORD; Behold, [a]I set before you
the way of life, and the way of death.
9 He that [a]abideth in this city shall die by
the sword, and by the famine, and by the
pestilence: but he that goeth out, and falleth to
the Chaldeans that besiege you, he shall live,
and [b]his life shall be unto him for a prey.
10 For I have [a]set my face against this city
for evil, and not for good, saith the LORD: [b]it
shall be given into the hand of the king of Babylon, and he shall [c]burn it with fire.
11 And touching the house of the king of
Judah, *say,* Hear ye the word of the LORD.
12 O house of David, thus saith the LORD;
[a] [1]Execute judgment [b]in the morning, and deliver *him that is* spoiled out of the hand of the
oppressor, lest my fury go out like fire, and
burn that none can quench *it,* because of the
evil of your doings.
13 Behold, [a]I *am* against thee, O [1]inhabi-
tant of the valley, *and* rock of the plain, saith

21:1 [a]ch. 38:1 [b]2 Ki. 25:18; ch. 29:25; 37:3
21:2 [a]ch. 37:3,7
21:4 [a]Is. 13:4
21:5 [a]Ex. 6:6
21:7 [a]ch. 37:17; 39:5; 52:9
21:7 [b]Deut. 28:50; 2 Chr. 36:17
21:8 [a]Deut. 30:19
21:9 [a]ch. 38:2,17,18 [b]ch. 39:18; 45:5
21:10 [a]Lev. 17:10; ch. 44:11; Amos 9:4 [b]ch. 38:3 [c]ch. 34:2,22; 37:10; 38:18,23; 52:13
21:12 [1]Heb. *Judge* [a]ch. 22:3; Zech. 7:9 [b]Ps. 101:8
21:13 [1]Heb. *inhabitress* [a]Ezek. 13:8

21:1–24:10 The prophet denounces Judah's rulers (21:1–23:7), false prophets (23:8–40) and sinful people (ch. 24). Although for the most part chs. 1–20 relate events in chronological order, chs. 21–52 are arranged on the basis of subject matter rather than chronology (see 24:1; 25:1; 26:1; 27:1; 29:2; 32:1; 35:1; 36:1; 37:1; 45:1; 49:34; 51:59; 52:4).

21:1–23:7 The rulers of Judah, who bear the primary responsibility for the nation's economic, social and spiritual ills, are the first to be denounced by Jeremiah.

21:1 *The word which came.* The phrase does not appear again until 25:1, suggesting that chs. 21–24 constitute an integral section in the book. *Zedekiah.* Means "The LORD is my righteousness." See Introduction: Background. *Pashur the son of Melchiah.* Not the same as the Pashur of 20:1–6 (see 38:1). *Zephaniah the son of Maaseiah the priest.* Not the same as the prophet Zephaniah (see 29:25,29; 37:3; 52:24; see also Zeph 1:1).

21:2 *Inquire . . . of the LORD.* A request for knowledge or information (see Gen 25:22; 2 Ki 22:13), not necessarily for help. *Nebuchadrezzar.* The name means "O Nabu [a god], protect my son/boundary!" He was the most famous ruler (605–562 B.C.) of the Neo-Babylonian empire (612–539). *maketh war.* About 588, because the brash Zedekiah had rebelled against Babylon (see 52:3). *us.* Jerusalem. *wondrous works.* For example, in the days of Hezekiah (see Is 37:36). *that he may go up from us.* See Is 37:37.

21:4 *turn back the weapons.* Your defense of Jerusalem will fail. *Chaldeans.* See note on Job 1:17. *I will assemble them into . . . this city.* Either (1) the weapons, meaning that Judah's troops would be totally unable to defend the approaches to the city, or (2) the Babylonians, meaning that Jerusalem's defeat is imminent and inevitable.

21:5 *I myself will fight against you.* The Lord, usually His people's defender, will now destroy them and seal their doom. *with an outstretched hand and with a strong arm.* See 27:5; 32:17. A similar phrase is used to describe God's powerful redemption of Israel at the exodus (see 32:21; Deut 4:34; 5:15; 7:19; 26:8), but here God turns His wrath against His own people. *even in anger, and in fury, and in great wrath.* Probably quoted from Deut 29:28, where the Hebrew for this phrase is translated "in anger and in wrath and in great indignation."

21:7 *I will deliver Zedekiah . . . his servants, and the people.* Fulfilled in 52:8–11,24–27 (see Ezek 12:13–14). *pestilence . . . the sword . . . the famine.* See v. 9. For this triad see note on 14:12. *not spare them, neither have pity, nor have mercy.* For this triad see 13:14; see also Ezek 5:11. The three triads here heighten the literary effect of the passage.

21:8–10 See 27:12–13. Similar advice is offered in 38:2–3, 17–18 (see Deut 30:15–20).

21:8 *Behold, I set before you.* See Deut 11:26. The people are offered a choice, but few of them will make the right decision. *the way of life, and the way of death.* See Deut 30:15,19; see also Prov 6:23.

21:9 Repeated almost verbatim in 38:2. Jeremiah's counsel of surrender branded him as a traitor in the eyes of many (see 37:13), but he was in fact a true patriot who wanted to stay in Judah even after Jerusalem was destroyed (see 37:14; 40:6; 42:7–22). *he that . . . falleth to the Chaldeans . . . shall live.* Fulfilled in 39:9; 52:15. *his life shall be unto him.* Lit. "his life will be his (only) booty." The victorious in battle can expect to share plunder; the defeated are fortunate indeed if their lives are spared.

21:10 *set my face.* See 44:11. *evil, and not for good.* See Amos 9:4; contrast 24:6. *it shall be given . . . burn it with fire.* See 34:2.

21:12 *Execute judgment.* See 5:28; 22:16; 1 Ki 3:28; Lam 3:59. The king was obliged and expected to do so, as was the future Messiah (see 23:5; 33:15). *in the morning.* When the mind is clear and the day is cool (court sessions were held outside, at the city gate; see notes on Gen 19:1; Ruth 4:1). *deliver . . . that is spoiled.* Repeated in 22:3. *lest my fury go . . . none can quench.* The Hebrew is repeated verbatim from 4:4 (see Amos 5:6). *fury . . . burn.* See 15:14; 17:4,27.

21:13 *thee . . . which say.* The pronouns are plural in the sec-

the LORD; which say, [b]Who shall come down
against us? or who shall enter into our habitations?

14 But I will [1]punish you according to the
[a]fruit of your doings, saith the LORD: and I will
kindle a fire in the forest thereof, and [b]it shall
devour all things round about it.

A burden about evil kings

22 Thus saith the LORD; Go down *to* the
house of the king of Judah, and speak
there this word,

2 And say, [a]Hear the word of the LORD,
O king of Judah, that sittest upon the throne of
David, thou, and thy servants, and thy people
that enter in by these gates:

3 Thus saith the LORD; [a]Execute ye judgment
and righteousness, and deliver the
spoiled out of the hand of the oppressor; and
do no wrong, do no violence, to the stranger,
the fatherless, nor the widow, neither shed innocent
blood in this place.

4 For if ye do this thing indeed, [a]then shall
there enter in by the gates of this house kings
sitting [1]upon the throne of David, riding in
chariots and on horses, he, and his servants,
and his people.

5 But if ye will not hear these words, [a]I
swear by myself, saith the LORD, that this
house shall become a desolation.

6 For thus saith the LORD unto the king's
house of Judah; Thou *art* Gilead unto me, *and*
the head of Lebanon: *yet* surely I will make

21:13 [b]ch. 49:4
21:14 [1]Heb. *visit upon* [a]Prov. 1:31; Is. 3:10,11 [b]2 Chr. 36:19; ch. 52:13
22:2 [a]ch. 17:20
22:3 [a]ch. 21:12
22:4 [1]Heb. *for David upon his throne* [a]ch. 17:25
22:5 [a]Heb. 6:13,17
22:7 [a]Is. 37:24 [b]ch. 21:14
22:8 [a]Deut. 29:24,25; 1 Ki. 9:8,9
22:9 [a]2 Ki. 22:17; 2 Chr. 34:25
22:10 [a]2 Ki. 22:20 [b]ver. 11
22:11 [a]See 1 Chr. 3:15, with 2 Ki. 23:30 [b]2 Ki. 23:34
22:13 [a]ver. 18; 2 Ki. 23:35 [b]Lev. 19:13; Deut. 24:14,15; Mic. 3:10; Hab. 2:9; Jas. 5:4

thee a wilderness *and* cities *which* are not inhabited.

7 And I will prepare destroyers against
thee, every one with his weapons: and they
shall cut down [a]thy choice cedars, [b]and cast
them into the fire.

8 And many nations shall pass by this city,
and they shall say every man to his neighbour,
[a]Wherefore hath the LORD done thus unto this
great city?

9 Then they shall answer, [a]Because they
have forsaken the covenant of the LORD their
God, and worshipped other gods, and served
them.

10 Weep ye not for [a]the dead, neither
bemoan him:
But weep sore for him [b]that goeth away:
For he shall return no more,
Nor see his native country.

11 ¶ For thus saith the LORD touching
[a]Shallum the son of Josiah king of Judah,
which reigned instead of Josiah his father,
[b]which went forth out of this place; He shall
not return thither any more:

12 But he shall die in the place whither
they have led him captive, and shall see this
land no more.

13 [a]Woe unto him that buildeth his house
by unrighteousness,
And his chambers by wrong;
[b]*That* useth his neighbour's service
without wages,

ond half of the verse (referring to Jerusalem's inhabitants), singular in the first half (referring to Jerusalem personified). *valley.* Jerusalem, surrounded on three sides by valleys (see note on Is 22:7), is called the "valley of vision" in Is 22:1,5. *rock of the plain.* mount Zion. *Who shall come down against us?* The people think that no one can successfully besiege them (see notes on 7:4; 8:19).

21:14 *according to . . . your doings.* See note on 17:10. *kindle a fire . . . devour.* See note on 17:27. *forest.* Perhaps refers figuratively to Jerusalem's royal palace, called the "house of the forest of Lebanon" (1 Ki 7:2; 10:17,21; see Is 22:8) because of the cedar (see 22:7,14,15,23) used in its construction. The palace (see 22:1) is compared to the "summit of Lebanon" in 22:6 (see 22:23 and note).

22:1 *Go down.* The palace was at a lower elevation than the temple (see 26:10; 36:10–12).

22:2 *king of Judah.* Probably Zedekiah (see 21:3,7; compare v. 3 with 21:12), whose predecessors are mentioned in sequence later in the chapter (Josiah, vv. 10a,15b–16; Jehoahaz/Shallum, vv. 10b–12; Jehoiakim, vv. 13–15a,17–19; Jehoiachin/Coniah, vv. 24–30). *throne of David.* Though all the kings of the Davidic dynasty failed to a greater or lesser degree, the victorious Messiah would someday appear as the culmination of David's royal line (see 23:5 and note; 33:15; Ezek 34:23–24; Mat 1:1). *that enter in by these gates.* See 17:25 and note.

22:3 Contrast Is 11:3–5 with Ezek 22:6–7.

22:4 Repeated in part from 17:25.

22:5 See 17:27 and note. *swear by myself.* See notes on Gen 22:16; Is 45:23; see also 49:13; 51:14; cf. 44:26. *become a desolation.* Fulfilled in 52:13 (see 27:17).

22:6 *Gilead . . . Lebanon.* Renowned for their forests. Lebanon in particular supplied cedar for the royal palace (see note on 21:14; see also 1 Ki 5:6,8–10; 7:2–3; 10:27).

22:7 *I will prepare.* Or "consecrate" (see note on 6:4). *destroyers.* The Babylonians (see note on 4:7; see also 12:12). *every one with his weapons.* See Ezek 9:2. *cut down thy . . . cedars.* Cf. Is 10:33–34; cf. especially the vivid description of the Babylonian troops smashing the carved paneling of the Jerusalem temple with their axes and hatchets (Ps 74:3–6).

22:8–9 Echoed in 1 Ki 9:8–9; see Deut 29:24–26.

22:9 *forsaken the covenant . . . worshipped other gods . . . served them.* A gross violation of the first and second stipulations of the Mosaic covenant (see Ex 20:3–5 and notes).

22:10 *Weep ye not for the dead.* Josiah, who was mourned long after his death (see 2 Chr 35:24–25). *him that goeth away.* Jehoahaz/Shallum. In 609 B.C., Pharaoh Neco "brought him to Egypt, and he died there" (2 Ki 23:34).

22:11 *Shallum.* See 1 Chr 3:15. "Shallum" was his personal name, "Jehoahaz" his throne name (the latter means "The LORD seizes").

22:12 *the place whither they have led him captive.* Egypt (see note on v. 10).

22:13–19 A scathing denunciation of King Jehoiakim, who is described in the third person (vv. 13–14), then rhetorically addressed in the second person (vv. 15,17), then identified by name (v. 18), meaning "The LORD raises up." Good King Josiah is referred to in vv. 15b–16 by way of contrast.

22:13 *Woe unto him that buildeth.* See Hab 2:9,12. *by unrighteousness . . . by wrong.* Contrast v. 3; 21:12. *chambers.* See note on Judg 3:20. *useth his neighbour's service without wages.* Contrary to the law (see Lev 25:39; Deut 24:14–15). Jehoiakim's refusal to pay them may have been due partly to inability, since Judah was under heavy tribute to Egypt during the early part of his reign (see 2 Ki 23:35).

And giveth him not *for* his work;
14 That saith, I will build me a wide
house and [1]large chambers,
And cutteth him out [2]windows;
And *it is* cieled with cedar, and painted
with vermilion.
15 Shalt thou reign, because thou closest
thyself in cedar?
Did not thy father eat and drink,
And do judgment and justice,
And then [a]*it was* well with him?
16 He judged the cause of the poor and
needy; then *it was* well *with him:*
Was not this to know me? saith the
LORD.
17 [a]But thine eyes and thine heart *are* not
but for thy covetousness,
And for to shed innocent blood,
And for oppression, and for [1]violence,
to do *it.*
18 Therefore thus saith the LORD
concerning Jehoiakim the son of
Josiah king of Judah;
[a]They shall not lament for him, *saying,*
[b]Ah my brother! or, Ah sister!
They shall not lament for him, *saying,*
Ah lord! or, Ah his glory.
19 [a]He shall be buried *with* the burial of
an ass,
Drawn and cast forth beyond the gates
of Jerusalem.
20 Go up *to* Lebanon, and cry; and lift up
thy voice in Bashan,
And cry from the passages:

22:14 [1]Heb. *through-aired* [2]Or, *my windows* 22:15 [a]Ps. 128:2; Is. 3:10 22:17 [1]Or, *incursion* [a]Ezek. 19:6 22:18 [a]ch. 16:4,6 [b]See 1 Ki. 13:30; Fulfilled 22:19 [a]2 Chr. 36:6; ch. 36:30

22:21 [1]Heb. *prosperities* [a]ch. 3:25; 7:23 22:22 [a]ch. 23:1 22:23 [1]Heb. *inhabitress* [a]ch. 6:24 22:24 [a]See 2 Ki. 24:6,8; 1 Chr. 3:16; ch. 37:1 [b]Sol. 8:6; Hag. 2:23 22:25 [a]ch. 34:20 22:26 [a]2 Ki. 24:15; 2 Chr. 36:10 22:27 [1]Heb. *lift up their mind* 22:28 [a]Ps. 31:12; ch. 48:38; Hos. 8:8

For all thy lovers are destroyed.
21 I spake unto thee in thy [1]prosperity;
But thou saidst, I will not hear.
[a]This *hath been* thy manner from thy
youth,
That thou obeyedst not my voice.
22 The wind shall eat up all [a]thy pastors,
And thy lovers shall go into captivity:
Surely then shalt thou be ashamed and
confounded for all thy wickedness.
23 O [1]inhabitant of Lebanon, that makest
thy nest in the cedars,
How gracious shalt thou be when
pangs come upon thee,
[a]The pain as of a woman in travail.

24 ¶ *As* I live, saith the LORD, [a]though Coniah the son of Jehoiakim king of Judah [b]were
the signet upon my right hand, yet would I
pluck thee thence;
25 [a]And I will give thee into the hand of
them that seek thy life, and into the hand *of*
them whose face thou fearest, even into the
hand of Nebuchadrezzar king of Babylon, and
into the hand of the Chaldeans.
26 [a]And I will cast thee out, and thy mother that bare thee, into another country, where
ye were not born; and there shall ye die.
27 But to the land whereunto they [1]desire
to return, thither shall they not return.
28 *Is* this man Coniah a despised broken
idol? *is he* [a]a vessel wherein *is* no pleasure?
wherefore are they cast out, he and his seed,
and are cast into a land which they know not?

22:14 *windows.* The windows described here may well be the same as those found in the ruins of Beth-hakkerem (see 6:1; see also note on Neh 3:14) by archaeologists in the early 1960s. *is cieled.* Or "paneled." Haggai similarly deplores the use of paneling as an extravagant and unneeded luxury in certain situations (see Hag 1:4).
22:15 *thy father.* Josiah. *eat and drink.* Enjoy life (see Eccl 2:24–25; 3:12–13). *do judgment and justice.* Like his ancestor David (see 2 Sam 8:15); contrast v. 13 (see note there).
22:16 James defines a proper relationship to God in similar terms (see Jas 1:27); contrast 5:28 (see note there). *poor and needy.* See note on 20:13. *to know me.* To love God fully, which results in living a pious life and serving those in need (see Deut 10:12–13; Hos 6:6; Mic 6:8).
22:17 *thine.* Jehoiakim's (see v. 18). *covetousness.* See 6:13; 8:10. *shed innocent blood.* See note on 19:4; for an illustration of Jehoiakim's cruelty in this regard see 26:20–23. *oppression.* See v. 3; 6:6; 21:12.
22:18 Contrast 2 Chr 35:24–25. *They shall not lament for him . . . Ah, my brother.* Contrast 1 Ki 13:30.
22:19 *burial of an ass.* Tantamount to no burial at all (see 36:30); fulfilled in 2 Ki 24:6, where no burial is described and where it says that Jehoiakim "slept with his fathers," a euphemism for dying (see notes on Gen 25:8; 1 Ki 1:21). *Drawn.* See 15:3.
22:20–23 The Lord speaks to Jerusalem, which is personified as a woman (see v. 23).
22:20 *Lebanon . . . Bashan . . . the passages.* Mountainous regions (see v. 6; Num 27:12; 33:47–48; Deut 32:49; Judg 3:3; Ps 68:15), the first two in the north and the third in the south, suitable heights from which the whole land of Israel could be rhetorically addressed. *lovers.* See 4:30 and note. "Lovers" here refers to nations joined together by treaty. Judah's onetime allies included Egypt, Assyria (see 2:36), Edom, Moab, Ammon and Phoenicia (see 27:3), all of whom had been—or soon would be—conquered by Babylonia (see 27:6–7; 28:14). *destroyed.* See 14:17.
22:21 *not hear . . . obeyedst not my voice.* See 7:22–26; 11:7–8. *thy youth.* The days of Israel's early history in Egypt (see 2:2 and note; Hos 2:15).
‡22:22 *shall eat up . . . pastors . . . wickedness.* The Hebrew root is the same for the first two words, and that of the third is very similar. For "pastors" see 2:8 and note; 10:21; 23:1–4. The initial fulfillment of this verse took place in 597 B.C. (see 2 Ki 24:12–16). *wind shall eat up all.* See 13:24; Job 27:21; Is 27:8.
22:23 *Lebanon.* The palace in Jerusalem (see 1 Ki 7:2). See also 21:14 and note; Ezek 17:3–4,12. *pain as of a woman in travail.* See 4:31; 6:24; 13:21; see also note on 4:19.
22:24–30 A prophecy against King Jehoiachin (fulfilled in 24:1; 29:2), who was also known as Coniah (vv. 24, 28), a shortened form of Jeconiah (24:1); see Introduction: Background. All three forms of the name mean "The LORD establishes."
22:24 *As I live.* See note on Gen 42:15. *though Coniah . . . were the signet.* The curse on Coniah is apparently reversed in Hag 2:23 (see note there).
22:25 *I will give thee into the hand of them . . . them . . . thou fearest.* Contrast 39:17.
22:26 Fulfilled in 597 B.C. (see 29:2; 2 Ki 24:15). *cast thee . . . into another country.* Send into exile in Babylonia (see 7:15; 16:13; Deut 29:28). *and thy mother that bare thee.* Coniah and Nehushta (see note on 13:18).
22:28 Rhetorical questions, answered in v. 30. *broken idol . . .*

29 [a]O earth, earth, earth, hear the word of
the LORD.
30 Thus saith the LORD, Write ye this man
[a]childless, a man *that* shall not prosper in his
days: for no man of his seed shall prosper, [b]sit-
ting upon the throne of David, and ruling any
more in Judah.

The remnant and the true king

23 Woe [a]be unto *the* pastors that destroy and scatter the sheep of my pasture! saith the LORD.
2 Therefore thus saith the LORD God of Israel against the pastors that feed my people; Ye
have scattered my flock, and driven them
away, and have not visited them: [a]behold, I
will visit upon you the evil of your doings,
saith the LORD.
3 And [a]I will gather the remnant of my
flock out of all countries whither I have driven
them, and will bring them again to their folds;
and they shall be fruitful and increase.
4 And I will set up [a]shepherds over them
which shall feed them: and they shall fear no
more, nor be dismayed, neither shall they be
lacking, saith the LORD.
5 ¶ Behold, [a]the days come, saith the LORD,
that I will raise unto David a righteous Branch,
and a King shall reign and prosper, [b]and shall
execute judgment and justice in the earth.

22:29 [a]Deut. 32:1; Is. 1:2; 34:1; Mic. 1:2
22:30 [a]See 1 Chr. 3:16,17; Mat. 1:12 [b]ch. 36:30
23:1 [a]ch. 10:21; 22:22; Ezek. 34:2
23:2 [a]Ex. 32:34
23:3 [a]ch. 32:37; Ezek. 34:13
23:4 [a]ch. 3:15; Ezek. 34:23
23:5 [a]Is. 4:2; 11:1; 40:10,11; ch. 33:14; Dan. 9:24; Zech. 6:12; John 1:45 [b]Ps. 72:2; Is. 9:7; 32:1,18
23:6 [1]Heb. *Jehovah-tsidkenu* [a]Deut. 33:28; Zech. 14:11 [b]ch. 32:37 [c]ch. 33:16; 1 Cor. 1:30
23:7 [a]ch. 16:14
23:8 [a]Is. 43:5,6
23:9 [a]See Hab. 3:16
23:10 [1]Or, *cursing* [2]Or, *violence* [a]ch. 9:2 [b]Hos. 4:2,3 [c]ch. 9:10

6 [a]In his days Judah shall be saved, and Israel [b]shall dwell safely: and [c]this *is* his name
whereby he shall be called, [1]THE LORD OUR
RIGHTEOUSNESS.
7 Therefore behold, [a]the days come, saith
the LORD, that they shall no more say, The
LORD liveth, which brought up the children of
Israel out of the land of Egypt;
8 But, The LORD liveth, which brought up
and which led the seed of the house of Israel
out of the north country, [a]and from all countries whither I had driven them; and they shall
dwell in their own land.

False prophets

9 Mine heart within me is broken
because of the prophets;
[a]All my bones shake;
I am like a drunken man,
And like a man whom wine hath
overcome,
Because of the LORD, and because of
the words of his holiness.
10 For [a]the land is full *of* adulterers;
For [b]because of [1]swearing the land
mourneth;
[c]The pleasant places of the wilderness
are dried up,
And their [2]course is evil, and their
force *is* not right.

cast out. Coniah and his descendants, like Judah itself (see 19:10–11), are under God's judgment. *he and his seed.* Though Coniah was only 18 years old at the time of his exile (see 2 Ki 24:8), he already had more than one wife (see 2 Ki 24:15) and therefore probably one or more children.

22:29 *earth, earth, earth.* The repetition implies the strongest possible emphasis and intensity (see 7:4; 23:30–32; Ezek 21:27; see also note on Is 6:3).

22:30 *no man of his seed.* Not in the sense of Coniah's having no children at all (he had at least seven; see 1 Chr 3:17–18), but of having none to sit on the throne of David in Judah. Coniah's grandson Zerubbabel (1 Chr 3:17–19; Mat 1:12) became governor of Judah (see Hag 1:1), but not king. Zedekiah was a son of Josiah (see 37:1), not of Coniah, and he and his sons died before the latter (see 52:10–11). Coniah therefore was Judah's last surviving Davidic king—until Christ.

23:1–8 A summary statement (probably dating to Zedekiah's reign; see note on v. 6) that includes God's intention to judge the wicked rulers and leaders of Judah (vv. 1–2), to ultimately bring His people back from exile (vv. 3–4,7–8), and to raise up an ideal Davidic King (vv. 5–6).

23:1 See 10:21 and note. *sheep.* The people of Judah (see v. 2).

‡23:2 *not visited them . . . will visit upon you.* The same Hebrew root underlies both phrases. See v. 4 and note. What Judah's rulers had failed to do is summarized in Ezek 34:4.

23:3 *remnant.* See notes on 6:9; Is 10:20–22. *I have driven.* Although Judah's sins and the sins of their leaders had caused them to be "driven . . . away" (v. 2) into exile, the Lord Himself ultimately carried out the results of His people's repeated violations of their covenant commitments. *be fruitful and increase.* See note on Gen 1:28.

23:4 *fear no more, nor be dismayed.* The absence of a concerned shepherd invites attacks by wild animals (see Ezek 34:8). *be lacking.* See Num 31:49. The Hebrew root underlying this phrase is the same as that for "visited" and "visited upon" in v. 2 (see note there).

23:5–6 One of the most important Messianic passages in Jeremiah, echoed in 33:15–16.

23:5 *raise unto.* See 2 Sam 7:12; see also 30:9; Ezek 34:23–24; 37:24. *unto David.* See Mat 1:1; 1:17 and note. The Messiah, unlike any previous descendant of David, would be the ideal King. He would sum up in Himself all the finest qualities of the best rulers, and infinitely more. *Branch.* A Messianic title (see notes on Is 4:2; Zech 3:8; 6:12). The Targum (ancient Aramaic paraphrase) reads "Messiah" here. *reign . . . prosper.* See note on Is 52:13. *shall execute judgment and justice.* See 22:3,15; said also of King David (see 2 Sam 8:15).

‡23:6 *Judah . . . and Israel.* God's reunited people will be restored (see Ezek 37:15–22). *be saved . . . dwell safely.* The deliverance will be both spiritual and physical (see Deut 33:28–29). *THE LORD OUR RIGHTEOUSNESS.* Although Zedekiah did not live up to the meaning of his name, "The LORD is my righteousness," Jesus the Messiah would bestow on His people the abundant blessings (see Ezek 34:25–31) that come from the hands of a King who brings "judgment and justice" (v. 5).

23:7–8 Repeated almost verbatim from 16:14–15 (see notes there).

23:9–40 False prophets denounced (see 2:8; 4:9; 5:30–31; 6:13–15; 8:10–12; 14:13–15; 18:18–23; 26:8,11,16; 27–28; Is 28:7–13; Ezek 13; Mic 3:5–12).

‡23:9 *words of his holiness.* Contrast the unholy words of the false prophets (see vv. 16–18).

23:10 See Is 24:4–6. *adulterers.* See 5:7–8; 9:2; see also note on 2:20. *swearing.* Brought on by violating the Lord's covenant (see 11:3 and note; 11:8). *mourneth . . . dried up.* See 12:4 and note. To worship other gods is to deny to the land the fertility

11 For [a]both prophet and priest are
profane;
Yea, [b]in my house have I found their
wickedness, saith the LORD.
12 [a]Wherefore their way shall be unto
them as slippery *ways* in the darkness:
They shall be driven on, and fall
therein:
For I [b]will bring evil upon them, *even*
the year of their visitation, saith the
LORD.
13 And I have seen [1 2]folly in the prophets
of Samaria;
[a]They prophesied in Baal,
And [b]caused my people Israel to err.
14 I have seen also in the prophets of
Jerusalem [1]a horrible thing:
[a]*They* commit adultery, and [b]walk in
lies:
They [c]strengthen also the hands of
evildoers,
That none doth return from his
wickedness:
They are all of them unto me as
[d]Sodom,
And the inhabitants thereof as
Gomorrah.
15 ¶ Therefore thus saith the LORD of hosts
concerning the prophets; Behold, I will feed
them with [a]wormwood, and make them drink
the water of gall: for from the prophets of Jerusalem is [1]profaneness gone forth into all the
land.
16 Thus saith the LORD of hosts, Hearken
not unto the words of the prophets that prophesy unto you: they make you vain: [a]they speak
a vision of their own heart, *and* not out of the
mouth of the LORD.
17 They say still unto them that despise
me, The LORD hath said, [a]Ye shall have peace;
and they say *unto* every one that walketh after
the [1]imagination of his own heart, [b]No evil
shall come upon you.
18 For [a]who hath stood in the [1]counsel of
the LORD, and hath perceived and heard his
word? who hath marked his word, and heard *it?*
19 Behold, a [a]whirlwind of the LORD is
gone forth *in* fury, even a grievous whirlwind:
it shall fall grievously upon the head of the
wicked.
20 The [a]anger of the LORD shall not return,
until he have executed, and till he have performed the thoughts of his heart: [b]in the latter
days ye shall consider it perfectly.
21 [a]I have not sent *these* prophets, yet
they ran: I have not spoken to them, yet they
prophesied.
22 But if they had [a]stood in my counsel,
and had caused my people to hear my words,
then they should have [b]turned them from their
evil way, and from the evil of their doings.
23 *Am* I a God at hand, saith the LORD, and
not a God afar off?
24 Can any [a]hide himself in secret places
that I shall not see him? saith the LORD. [b]Do
not I fill heaven and earth? saith the LORD.
25 I have heard what the prophets said,
that prophesy lies in my name, saying, I have
dreamed, I have dreamed.
26 How long shall *this* be in the heart of
the prophets that prophesy lies? yea, *they are*
prophets of the deceit of their own heart;
27 Which think to cause my people to forget my name by their dreams which they tell
every man to his neighbour, [a]as their fathers
have forgotten my name for Baal.
28 The prophet [1]that hath a dream, let him
tell a dream; and he that hath my word, let

23:11 [a]Zeph. 3:4 [b]ch. 7:30; Ezek. 8:11; 23:39
23:12 [a]Ps. 35:6; Prov. 4:19; ch. 13:16 [b]ch. 11:23
23:13 [1]Or, *an absurd thing* [2]Heb. *unsavoury* [a]ch. 2:8 [b]Is. 9:16
23:14 [1]Or, *filthiness* [a]ch. 29:23 [b]ver. 26 [c]Ezek. 13:22 [d]Is. 1:9,10
23:15 [1]Or, *hypocrisy* [a]ch. 9:15
23:16 [a]ch. 14:14
23:17 [1]Or, *stubbornness* [a]ch. 8:11; Ezek. 13:10; Zech. 10:2 [b]Mic. 3:11
23:18 [1]Or, *secret* [a]Job 15:8; 1 Cor. 2:16
23:19 [a]ch. 25:32; 30:23
23:20 [a]ch. 30:24 [b]Gen. 49:1
23:21 [a]ch. 14:14
23:22 [a]ver. 18 [b]ch. 25:5
23:24 [a]Ps. 139:7; Amos 9:2,3 [b]1 Ki. 8:27; Ps. 139:7
23:27 [a]Judg. 3:7
23:28 [1]Heb. *with whom is*

that only the Lord can bring (see Hos 2:5–8,21–22; Amos 4:4–9). *places of the wilderness.* See note on 9:10. *course is evil.* Evil because it is their own and not God's (see 8:6).

23:11 *Yea, in my house . . . wickedness.* For examples see 32:34; 2 Ki 16:10–14; 21:5; Ezek 8:5,10,14,16.

23:12 *their way . . . in the darkness.* See Ps 35:5–6; see also Ps 73:18.

23:13 *prophesied in Baal.* See 2:8 and note; see also 1 Ki 18:19–40.

‡23:14 *walk in lies* See 14:13. *strengthen also the hands of.* The Hebrew underlying this phrase can also be translated "encouraged." *none doth return from his wickedness.* See Ezek 13:22. *as Sodom . . . as Gomorrah.* See note on 20:16.

23:15 *make them drink the water of gall.* Repeated almost verbatim from 9:15 (see note there). *profaneness.* See v. 11.

23:16 *vision.* "Revelation" or "prophecy" (see 1 Sam 3:1; Prov 29:18; Is 1:1; Obad 1 and notes). *of their own heart.* See v. 26; 14:14. False prophets are like preachers of a "different gospel" (Gal 1:6–9).

23:17 *Ye shall have peace.* The essential message of the false prophets (see 6:14 and note; 8:11; 14:13 and note; cf. 28:8–9). *imagination of his own heart.* See note on 3:17.

‡23:18 *counsel of the LORD.* God's heavenly confidants (see v. 22; Job 15:7–10 and note; see also 1 Ki 22:19–22; Job 1:6; 2:1; 29:4 and note; Ps 89:7) In Amos 3:7 the Hebrew for "counsel" is used in the sense of "plan," for the purposes that God has promised to reveal to his chosen servants (see v. 20).

23:19–20 Repeated almost verbatim in 30:23–24.

23:19 *whirlwind . . . grievous whirlwind.* A vivid image of God's wrath.

23:20 *ye shall consider it perfectly.* Unlike the false prophets, who continued to mislead their hearers even in Babylonia after the exile of 597 B.C. (see 29:20–23).

23:21 *I have not sent.* See v. 32; 29:9; contrast 1:7; Is 6:8; Ezek 3:5. *have not spoken to them.* See 29:23.

23:22 *my counsel.* See note on v. 18.

‡23:23 *a God at hand . . . not a God afar off.* God is both transcendent and immanent; He lives "in the high and holy place, with him . . . of a contrite and humble spirit" (Is 57:15).

23:24 *hide . . . that I shall not see him.* See Job 26:6; Ps 139:7–12; Amos 9:2–4. *fill heaven and earth.* See Is 66:1.

23:25 *prophesy lies.* See 5:12. *in my name.* See Deut 18:20,22. *dreamed.* Usually dreams are not a means of divine revelation to a true prophet (see 27:9; Deut 13:1–3; 1 Sam 28:6; Zech 10:2; but cf. Num 12:6; Joel 2:28).

23:26 *their own heart.* See note on v. 16.

23:27 *my name.* To forget the Lord's name is tantamount to forgetting Him. *forgotten . . . for Baal.* When Judah's ancestors forgot God, they began to serve Baal (see Judg 3:7; 1 Sam 12:9–10).

‡23:28–29 The true word of God is symbolized in three figures of speech (wheat, fire, hammer).

him speak my word faithfully. What *is* the chaff to the wheat? saith the LORD.
29 *Is* not my word like as a fire? saith the
LORD; and like a hammer *that* breaketh the rock in pieces?
30 Therefore behold, [a]I *am* against the prophets, saith the LORD, that steal my words every one from his neighbour.
31 Behold, I *am* against the prophets, saith
the LORD, [1]that use their tongues, and say, He saith.
32 Behold, I *am* against them that prophesy false dreams, saith the LORD, and do tell them, and cause my people to err by their lies, and by [a]their lightness; yet I sent them not, nor commanded them: therefore they shall not profit this people at all, saith the LORD.

The burden of the LORD

33 ¶ And when this people, or the prophet,
or a priest, shall ask thee, saying, What *is* [a]the burden of the LORD? thou shalt then say unto them, What burden? [b]I will even forsake you, saith the LORD.
34 And *as for* the prophet, and the priest,
and the people, that shall say, The burden of the LORD, I will even [1]punish that man and his house.
35 Thus shall ye say every one to his neigh-
bour, and every one to his brother, What hath the LORD answered? and, What hath the LORD spoken?
36 And the burden of the LORD shall ye
mention no more: for every man's word shall be his burden; for ye have perverted the words of the living God, of the LORD of hosts our God.
37 Thus shalt thou say to the prophet,
What hath the LORD answered thee? and, What hath the LORD spoken?

23:30 [a]Deut. 18:20; ch. 14:14,15
23:31 [1]Or, *that smooth their tongues*
23:32 [a]Zeph. 3:4
23:33 [a]Mal. 1:1 [b]ver. 39
23:34 [1]Heb. *visit upon*
23:39 [a]Hos. 4:6 [b]ver. 33
23:40 [a]ch. 20:11
24:1 [a]Amos 7:1,4; 8:1 [b]2 Ki. 24:12; 2 Chr. 36:10 [c]See ch. 22:24; 29:2
24:2 [1]Heb. *for badness*
24:5 [1][Heb. *the captivity*]
24:6 [a]ch. 12:15; 29:10 [b]ch. 32:41; 33:7; 42:10

38 But sith ye say, The burden of the LORD;
therefore thus saith the LORD; Because you say this word, The burden of the LORD, and I have sent unto you, saying, Ye shall not say, The burden of the LORD;
39 Therefore behold, I, even I, [a]will utter-
ly forget you, and [b]I will forsake you, and the city that I gave you and your fathers, *and cast you* out of my presence:
40 And I will bring [a]an everlasting re-
proach upon you, and a perpetual shame, which shall not be forgotten.

Sign of the good and evil figs

24 The [a]LORD shewed me, and behold,
two baskets of figs *were* set before the temple of the LORD, after that Nebuchadrezzar [b]king of Babylon had carried away captive [c]Jeconiah the son of Jehoiakim king of Judah, and the princes of Judah, with the carpenters and smiths, from Jerusalem, and had brought them *to* Babylon.
2 One basket *had* very good figs, *even* like
the figs *that are* first ripe: and the other basket *had* very naughty figs, which could not be eaten, [1]they were so bad.
3 Then said the LORD unto me, What seest
thou, Jeremiah? And I said, Figs; the good figs, very good; and the evil, very evil, that cannot be eaten, they are so evil.
4 Again the word of the LORD came unto
me, saying,
5 Thus saith the LORD, the God of Israel;
Like these good figs, so will I acknowledge [1]them that are carried away captive of Judah, whom I have sent out of this place *into* the land of the Chaldeans for *their* good.
6 For I will set mine eyes upon them for
good, and [a]I will bring them again to this land: and [b]I will build them, and not pull *them*

23:28 *chaff . . . wheat.* Of the two, only grain can feed and nourish (see note on 15:16).
23:29 *like as a fire.* See note on 20:9. The fire of the divine word ultimately tests the quality of each man's work (1 Cor 3:13). *like a hammer.* Similarly, the divine word works relentlessly, like a sword or hammer, to judge "the thoughts and intents of the heart" (Heb 4:12).
23:30–32 *I am against.* The threefold statement is for emphasis (see note on 22:29).
23:31 *prophets . . . that . . . say.* False prophets are claiming that their own prophecies are the oracles of God. The Hebrew for this verb is used only here with someone other than God as the subject. The phrase "declares the LORD" or its equivalent occurs hundreds of times in the OT, more frequently in Jeremiah (over 175 times) than in any other book.
23:32 *I sent them not.* See v. 21 and note.
23:33 *burden.* The Hebrew for this word may refer to a burdensome message from the Lord (see, e.g., Nah 1:1).
23:36 The three divine titles at the end of the verse enhance the solemnity of what is being said. *living God.* See 10:10; Deut 5:26.
‡23:39 *forget.* The Hebrew for this word is a pun on the Hebrew for the word "burden" in vv. 33–34,36,38. *the city.* Jerusalem.
23:40 Echoed from 20:11.

24:1–10 See Amos 8:1–3. Having denounced Judah's leaders (21:1–23:8) and false prophets (23:9–40), Jeremiah now describes the division of Judah's people into good and bad (24:1–3) and summarizes the Lord's determination to restore the good (vv. 4–7) but destroy the bad (vv. 8–10).
24:1 *The LORD shewed me.* A common way of introducing prophetic visions (see Amos 7:1,4,7). *figs.* See note on 8:13. *set.* The Hebrew root underlying this word is translated "meet" in Ex 29:42–43. As the Lord desired to "meet" with the Israelites at the entrance to the tabernacle, so the figs (symbolizing the people of Judah) would be "met" by him in front of the Jerusalem temple. *Jeconiah . . . and the princes . . . to Babylon.* In 597 B.C. *carpenters and smiths.* See 29:2; 2 Ki 24:14,16. Only the poorest and weakest people were left behind in Judah (see 2 Ki 24:14).
24:2 *very good figs . . . figs that are first ripe.* The first figs in June are especially juicy and delicious (see Is 28:4; Hos 9:10; Mic 7:1; Nah 3:12).
24:3 *What seest thou . . . ?* See note on 1:11.
24:5–6 Just as good figs should be protected and preserved by their owner, so also the exiles of 597 B.C., who were the best of Judah's leaders and craftsmen (see 2 Ki 24:14–16), would be watched over and cared for by the Lord (see 29:4–14).
24:6 *I will set mine eyes upon them for good.* Contrast Amos 9:4. *bring them again.* In 538 B.C. *build them . . . pull them down*

down; and I will plant them, and not pluck
them up.
7 And I will give them [a]a heart to know
me, that I *am* the LORD: and they shall be [b]my
people, and I will be their God: for they shall
return unto me [c]with their whole heart.
8 And as the evil [a]figs, which cannot be
eaten, they are so evil; surely thus saith the
LORD, So will I give Zedekiah the king of Judah,
and his princes, and the residue of Jerusalem,
that remain in this land, and [b]them that dwell
in the land of Egypt:
9 And I will deliver them [1]to [a]be removed
into all the kingdoms of the earth for *their*
hurt, [b]to be a reproach and a proverb, a taunt
and a curse, in all places whither I shall drive
them.
10 And I will send the sword, the famine,
and the pestilence, among them, till they be
consumed from off the land that I gave unto
them and to their fathers.

Judah's captivity

25 The word that came to Jeremiah concerning all the people of Judah [a]in
the fourth year of Jehoiakim the son of Josiah
king of Judah, that *was* the first year of Nebuchadrezzar king of Babylon;
2 The which Jeremiah the prophet spake
unto all the people of Judah, and to all the inhabitants of Jerusalem, saying,
3 [a]From the thirteenth year of Josiah the
son of Amon king of Judah, even unto this day,
that *is* the three and twentieth year, the word
of the LORD hath come unto me, and I have
spoken unto you, rising early and speaking;
[b]but ye have not hearkened.
4 And the LORD hath sent unto you all his
servants the prophets, [a]rising early and sending *them;* but ye have not hearkened, nor inclined your ear to hear.
5 *They* said, [a]Turn ye again now every one
from his evil way, and from the evil of your doings, and dwell in the land that the LORD hath
given unto you and to your fathers for ever and
ever:
6 And go not after other gods to serve
them, and to worship them, and provoke me
not to anger with the works of your hands; and
I will do you no hurt.
7 Yet ye have not hearkened unto me, saith
the LORD; that *ye* might [a]provoke me to anger
with the works of your hands to your own hurt.
8 ¶ Therefore thus saith the LORD of hosts;
Because ye have not heard my words,
9 Behold, I will send and take [a]all the families of the north, saith the LORD, and Nebuchadrezzar the king of Babylon, [b]my servant,
and will bring them against this land, and
against the inhabitants thereof, and against all
these nations round about, and will utterly destroy them, and [c]make them an astonishment,
and a hissing, and perpetual desolations.
10 Moreover [1]I will take from them the
[a]voice of mirth, and the voice of gladness, the
voice of the bridegroom, and the voice of
the bride, [b]the sound of the millstones, and
the light of the candle.
11 And this whole land shall be a desolation, *and* an astonishment; and these nations
shall serve the king of Babylon seventy years.

24:7 [a]Deut. 30:6; ch. 32:39; Ezek. 11:19; 36:26,27 [b]ch. 30:22; 31:33; 32:38 [c]ch. 29:13
24:8 [a]ch. 29:17 [b]See ch. 43; 44
24:9 [1]Heb. *for removing,* or, *vexation* [a]Deut. 28:25,37; 1 Ki. 9:7; 2 Chr. 7:20; ch. 15:4; 29:18; 34:17 [b]Ps. 44:13,14
25:1 [a]ch 36:1
25:3 [a]ch. 1:2 [b]ch. 7:13; 11:7,8,10
25:4 [a]ch. 7:13,25
25:5 [a]ch. 18:11; Jonah 3:8
25:7 [a]Deut. 32:21
25:9 [a]ch. 1:15 [b]ch. 27:6; Is. 45:1 [c]ch. 18:16
25:10 [1]Heb. *I will cause to perish from them* [a]Is. 24:7; Hos. 2:11; Rev. 18:23 [b]Eccl. 12:4

. . . *plant . . . pluck.* See 1:10 and note.
24:7 *a heart to know me.* For a more comprehensive prediction including the same promise see 31:31–34. *my people . . . their God.* The classic statement of covenant relationship (see 31:33; 32:38; see also notes on Gen 17:7; Zech 8:8). *with their whole heart.* See 29:13.
24:8 *dwell in . . . Egypt.* Perhaps those deported with Jehoahaz in 609 B.C. (see 22:10b–12 and notes; 2 Ki 23:31–34) and/or those who fled to Egypt after the Babylonians defeated the Egyptians in the battle of Carchemish in 605 (see 46:2).
24:9 *removed . . . into all the kingdoms.* See 34:17. *reproach . . . taunt.* See Deut 28:37. *proverb.* See notes on 1 Ki 9:7; Job 17:6.
24:10 *sword, the famine, and the pestilence.* See note on 14:12. *consumed from off the land.* In 586 B.C. (see 52:4–27).
25:1–29:32 The dominant theme in chs. 25–29 is the forthcoming destruction of Jerusalem and exile to Babylonia in 586 B.C. (hinted at briefly in 24:10).
25:1–38 Divine judgment will descend not only on Judah but on "all . . . nations round about" (v. 9) as well.
25:1 *fourth year of Jehoiakim . . . first year of Nebuchadrezzar.* The synchronism yields the date 605 B.C. (see note on Dan 1:1).
25:3 *thirteenth year of Josiah.* 626 B.C. (or possibly as early as 627); see 1:2. *three and twentieth year.* Nineteen under Josiah and four under Jehoiakim (see v. 1). *rising . . . speaking.* See v. 4; see also note on 7:13. *ye have not hearkened.* Jeremiah, now halfway through his prophetic ministry, had been warned at the time of his call that the people of Judah would oppose him (see 1:17–19).
25:4 Echoed from 7:25–26; see also 35:15. *his servants the prophets.* See note on 7:25.
25:5 *dwell in the land . . . LORD hath given . . . your fathers for ever.* Echoed from 7:7; see Gen 17:8 and note.
25:6 *provoke me not to anger.* See 7:18; Deut 31:29. *the works of your hands.* Idols (see note on 1:16).
25:7 *to your own hurt.* See 7:6.
25:9 *families of the north.* Babylonia and her allies (see 1:15 and note). *Nebuchadrezzar . . . my servant.* See 27:6; 43:10. "Servant" is used here not in the sense of "worshiper" but of "vassal" or "agent of judgment," just as the pagan ruler Cyrus is called the Lord's "shepherd" in Is 44:28 and His "anointed" in Is 45:1. *this land.* Judah. *nations round about.* Named in vv. 19–26. *utterly destroy.* The Hebrew term refers to the irrevocable giving over of things to the Lord, often by totally destroying them. See 50:21,26; 51:3; see also note on Deut 2:34. *an astonishment, and a hissing.* See note on 18:16. *perpetual desolations.* See 49:13; Ps 74:3; Is 58:12 and note.
25:11–12 *seventy years.* See 29:10. This round number (as in Ps 90:10; Is 23:15) probably represents the period from 605 (see notes on v. 1; Dan 1:1) to 538 B.C., which marked the beginning of Judah's return from exile (see 2 Chr 36:20–23; see also notes on Dan 9:1–2). The 70 years of Zech 1:12 are not necessarily the same as those here and in 29:10. They probably represent the period from 586 (when Solomon's temple was destroyed) to 516 (when Zerubbabel's temple was completed). See note on Zech 7:5; see also Ezra 1:1 and note.
25:11 *this . . . land . . . and these nations.* Judah and the nations named in vv. 19–26.

12 And it shall come to pass, [a]when seventy years are accomplished, *that* I will [1]punish the king of Babylon, and that nation, saith the LORD, for their iniquity, and the land of the Chaldeans, [b]and will make it perpetual desolations.

13 And I will bring upon that land all my words which I have pronounced against it, *even* all that is written in this book, which Jeremiah hath prophesied against all the nations.

14 [a]For many nations [b]and great kings shall [c]serve themselves of them also: [d]and I will recompense them according to their deeds, and according to the works of their own hands.

The cup of fury

15 ¶ For thus saith the LORD God of Israel unto me; Take the [a]wine cup of this fury at mine hand, and cause all the nations, to whom I send thee, to drink it.

16 And [a]they shall drink, and be moved, and be mad, because of the sword that I will send among them.

17 Then took I the cup at the LORD's hand, and made all the nations to drink, unto whom the LORD had sent me:

18 *To wit,* Jerusalem, and the cities of Judah, and the kings thereof, *and* the princes thereof, to make them [a]a desolation, an astonishment, a hissing, and [b]a curse; as *it is* this day;

19 Pharaoh king of Egypt, and his servants, and his princes, and all his people;

20 And all the mingled people, and all the kings of [a]the land of Uz, and all the kings of the land of the Philistines, and Ashkelon, and Azzah, and Ekron, and [b]the remnant of Ashdod:

21 [a]Edom, and Moab, and the children of Ammon,

22 And all the kings of [a]Tyrus, and all the kings of Zidon, and the kings of the [1]isles which *are* beyond the [b]sea,

23 [a]Dedan, and Tema, and Buz, and all *that are* [1]in the utmost corners,

24 And all the kings of Arabia, and all the kings of the [a]mingled people that dwell in the desert,

25 And all the kings of Zimri, and all the kings of Elam, and all the kings of the Medes,

26 [a]And all the kings of the north, far and near, one with another, and all the kingdoms of the world, which *are* upon the face of the earth: and the king of Sheshach shall drink after them.

27 Therefore thou shalt say unto them, Thus saith the LORD of hosts, the God of Israel; [a]Drink ye, and [b]be drunken, and spue, and fall, and rise no more, because of the sword which I will send among you.

25:12 [1]Heb. *visit upon* [a]2 Chr. 36:21, 22; Ezra 1:1; Dan. 9:2 [b]Is. 21:1; ch. 50:3
25:14 [a]ch. 50:9; 51:27,28 [b]ch. 51:27 [c]ch. 27:7 [d]ch. 50:29; 51:6,24
25:15 [a]Job 21:20; Ps. 75:8; Is. 51:17; Rev. 14:10
25:16 [a]ch. 51:7; Ezek. 23:34; Nah. 3:11
25:18 [a]ver. 9,11 [b]ch. 24:9
25:20 [a]Job 1:1 [b]Is. 20:1
25:21 [a]ch. 49:7
25:22 [1]Or, *region by the sea side* [a]ch. 47:4 [b]ch. 49:23
25:23 [1]Heb. *cut off into corners,* or, *having the corners* of the hair *polled,* ch. 9:26; 49:32 [a]ch. 49:8
25:24 [a]Ezek. 30:5
25:26 [a]ch. 50:9
25:27 [a]Hab. 2:16 [b]Is. 63:6

25:12 *punish the king . . . and that nation.* See 50:18. The city of Babylon was captured by the Medes and Persians in 539 B.C. (near the end of Jeremiah's 70 years; see note on vv. 11–12). *for their iniquity.* See 50:11,31–32; 51:6,49,53,56; Is 13:19. *perpetual desolations.* See 50:12–13; 51:26; see also note on Is 13:20.
25:13 *book.* After this word, the Septuagint (the Greek translation of the OT) inserts the material found in chs. 46–51, though rearranged.
25:14 *many nations.* Media, Persia and their allies. *great kings.* Cyrus and his associates. *recompense them according to their deeds.* See 50:29; 51:24.
25:15 *wine cup of this fury.* Symbolic of divine judgment, especially against wicked nations (see Is 51:17 and note; see also 51:7; Rev 18:6). *nations, to whom I send thee.* See 1:5 and note.
25:16 *be moved, and be mad.* See 13:12–14 and notes; Rev 14:8. *because of the sword.* As the sting of wine causes people to stagger, so the stroke of the sword causes them to fall, never to rise again (see v. 27).
25:17 A symbolic description of Jeremiah's announcement of divine judgment against the nations.
25:18 *Jerusalem, and . . . Judah.* God's own people are to be judged first (see v. 29; see also Ezek 9:6; 1 Pet 4:17). *kings.* See note on 17:20. *desolation . . . astonishment . . . hissing . . . curse.* See vv. 9,11; 18:16; 19:8.
25:19–26 The roster of nations begins with Egypt and ends with Babylon, as in chs. 46–51; but Damascus (see 49:23–27) is omitted, and a few other regions are added.
25:19 *Egypt.* See 46:2–28.
25:20 *mingled people.* See v. 24; Neh 13:3. *Uz.* See note on Job 1:1. *Philistines.* See ch. 47; see also note on Gen 10:14. *Ashkelon, and Azzah, and Ekron.* See note on Judg 1:18 and map, p. 313. *remnant of Ashdod.* According to the Greek historian Herodotus (2.157), the Egyptian pharaoh Psammetichus I (664–610 B.C.) destroyed Ashdod after a long siege. By Nehemiah's time, it was inhabited again (see note on Neh 4:7). The fifth main Philistine city, Gath (see Josh 13:3), though important earlier (see, e.g., 1 Sam 21:10–12), was destroyed and apparently not rebuilt (in later centuries it is not mentioned with the other four cities; see Amos 1:6–8; Zeph 2:4; Zech 9:5–6).
25:21–22 See 27:3–5.
25:21 *Edom.* See 49:7–22; see also note on Gen 36:1. *Moab, and . . . Ammon.* See 48:1–49:6; see also note on Gen 19:36–38.
25:22 *Tyrus . . . Zidon.* Tyre and Sidon. See 47:4; see also notes on Is 23:1–2,4,12. *isles . . . beyond the sea.* Island and maritime regions, some of them Phoenician colonies, located to the west and northwest of Tyre and Sidon (see notes on Ezek 27:15; Dan 11:18).
‡**25:23** *Dedan.* See 49:8; see also notes on Is 21:13; Ezek 25:13. *Tema.* See note on Is 21:14. *Buz.* A desert region in the east. *in the utmost corners.* See 9:26 and note.
‡**25:24** *Arabia.* See 49:28–33; see also 3:2. *mingled people.* See v. 20; Neh 13:3. The same Hebrew root underlies "Arabia" and "mingled people."
25:25 *Zimri.* Not to be confused with the Israelite king of that name, Zimri is perhaps the same as Zimran, whom Keturah bore to Abraham (see Gen 25:1–2). The region known as Zimri (location unknown) would then have been named after him. *Elam.* See 49:34–39; see also note on Gen 10:22. *Medes.* Later to join the Persians in conquering Babylon (see 51:11,28; see also note on Is 13:17).
25:26 *Sheshach.* A cryptogram for Babylon. The cryptogram is formed by substituting the first consonant of the Hebrew alphabet for the last, the second for the next-to-last, etc. Its purpose is not fully understood, though in some cases the cryptogram itself bears a suitable meaning (see note on 51:1). *shall drink after them.* The Lord's agents of judgment are not themselves exempt from His judgment (see 51:48–49).
25:27 *fall . . . because of the sword.* See note on v. 16.

28 And it shall be, if they refuse to take the
cup at thine hand to drink, then shalt thou say
unto them, Thus saith the LORD of hosts; Ye
shall certainly drink.
29 For lo, [a]I begin to bring evil on the city
[b][1]which is called by my name, and should ye
be utterly unpunished? Ye shall not be unpunished: for [c]I *will* call for a sword upon all the
inhabitants of the earth, saith the LORD of
hosts.
30 Therefore prophesy thou against them
all these words, and say unto them,

The LORD shall [a]roar from on high,
And utter his voice from [b]his holy
habitation;
He shall mightily roar upon [c]his
habitation;
He shall give [d]a shout, as they that
tread *the grapes,*
Against all the inhabitants of the earth.
31 A noise shall come *even* to the ends of
the earth;
For the LORD hath [a]a controversy with
the nations,
[b]He *will* plead with all flesh;
He will give them *that are* wicked to
the sword, saith the LORD.
32 Thus saith the LORD of hosts,
Behold, evil *shall* go forth from nation
to nation,
And [a]a great whirlwind shall be raised
up from the coasts of the earth.
33 [a]And the slain of the LORD shall be at
that day
From *one* end of the earth even unto
the *other* end of the earth:
They shall not be [b]lamented, [c]neither
gathered, nor buried;
They shall be dung upon the ground.
34 [a]Howl, ye shepherds, and cry;
And wallow yourselves *in the ashes,* ye
principal of the flock:
For [1]the days of your slaughter and of
your dispersions are accomplished.
And ye shall fall like [2]a pleasant vessel.
35 And [1]the shepherds shall have no way
to flee,
Nor the principal of the flock to escape.
36 A voice of the cry of the shepherds,
And a howling of the principal of the
flock, *shall be heard:*
For the LORD *hath* spoiled their pasture.
37 And the peaceable habitations are cut
down
Because of the fierce anger of the LORD.
38 He hath forsaken his covert, as the lion:
For their land is [1]desolate
Because of the fierceness of the
oppressor,
And because of his fierce anger.

Jeremiah arrested and released

26 In the beginning of the reign of Jehoiakim the son of Josiah king of Judah came this word from the LORD, saying,
2 Thus saith the LORD; Stand in [a]the court
of the LORD's house, and speak unto all the cities of Judah, which come to worship *in* the
LORD's house, [b]all the words that I command
thee to speak unto them; [c]diminish not a word:
3 [a]If so be they will hearken, and turn
every man from his evil way, that I may [b]re-
pent me of the evil, which I purpose to do
unto them because of the evil of their doings.
4 And thou shalt say unto them, Thus saith
the LORD; [a]If ye will not hearken to me, to
walk in my law, which I have set before you,
5 To hearken to the words of my servants
the prophets, [a]whom I sent unto you, both rising up early, and sending *them,* but ye have
not hearkened;
6 Then will I make this house like [a]Shiloh,
and will make this city [b]a curse to all the nations of the earth.

7 ¶ So the priests and the prophets and all
the people heard Jeremiah speaking these
words in the house of the LORD.
8 Now it came to pass, when Jeremiah had
made an end of speaking all that the LORD had

25:29 [1]Heb. *upon which my name is called* [a]Ezek. 9:6; Luke 23:31; 1 Pet. 4:17 [b]Dan. 9:18 [c]Ezek. 38:21
25:30 [a]Is. 42:13; Joel 3:16; Amos 1:2 [b]Ps. 11:4 [c]1 Ki. 9:3; Ps. 132:14 [d]Is. 16:9; ch. 48:33
25:31 [a]Hos. 4:1; Mic. 6:2 [b]Is. 66:16; Joel 3:2
25:32 [a]ch. 23:19; 30:23
25:33 [a]Is. 66:16 [b]ch. 16:4,6 [c]Ps. 79:3; ch. 8:2; Rev. 11:9
25:34 [1]Heb. *your days for slaughter* [2]Heb. *a vessel of desire* [a]ch. 4:8; 6:26
25:35 [1]Heb. *flight shall perish from the shepherds, and escaping from, etc.*
25:38 [1]Heb. *a desolation*
26:2 [a]ch. 19:14 [b]Ezek. 3:10; Mat. 28:20 [c]Acts 20:27
26:3 [a]ch. 36:3 [b]ch. 18:8; Jonah 3:8,9
26:4 [a]Lev. 26:14; Deut. 28:15
26:5 [a]ch. 7:13,25; 11:7; 25:3,4
26:6 [a]1 Sam. 4:10,11; Ps. 78:60; ch. 7:12,14 [b]Is. 65:15; ch. 24:9

25:29 *I begin.* See note on v. 18. *city . . . called by my name.* Jerusalem (see note on 7:10).
25:30 *The LORD shall roar . . . And utter his voice.* An echo of Joel 3:16; Amos 1:2 (see note there; see also Hos 11:10; Amos 3:8). *his habitation.* Judah. *shout, as they that tread the grapes.* See Is 9:3; 16:9–10; 63:3 and note; see also Is 16:10 and note.
25:31 *noise.* The sounds of war (see Amos 2:2). *controversy . . . plead.* See note on 2:9; see also 2:35; 12:1.
25:32 *great whirlwind . . . from the coasts of the earth.* The wrath of God (see 23:19), mediated through the coming invasion of the Babylonians (see note on Is 41:25).
25:33 *not be lamented . . . be dung upon the ground.* Repeated from 8:2 (see note there); 16:4.
25:34–36 *shepherds . . . principal of the flock.* See 10:21; 22:22.
25:34 *wallow . . . in the ashes.* See 6:26. *the days . . . are accomplished.* See Lam 4:18. *fall like a pleasant vessel.* Cf. the description of Jehoiachin (Coniah) in 22:28.
26:1–24 A summary (vv. 2–6)—and its results (vv. 7–24)—of one of Jeremiah's temple messages in ch. 7 (see note on 7:1–10:25).
26:1 *beginning of the reign.* See 27:1. The Babylonian equivalent of the Hebrew for this phrase implies that the first year of King Jehoiakim (609–608 B.C.) is probably meant.
26:2 *court of the LORD's house.* Perhaps near the new gate (see v. 10; see also note on 7:2). *which come to worship.* See 7:2 and note. *diminish not a word.* See Deut 4:2 and note.
26:3 See 7:3,5–7. *turn.* See vv. 13,19; see also notes on 4:28; 18:7–10.
26:4 *If ye will not hearken.* See v. 5; 7:13. *my law.* See 7:6,9 and notes.
‡**26:5** See 7:13,25–26. *my servants the prophets.* See note on 7:25. *rising . . . sending.* See note on 7:13.
26:6 *make this house like Shiloh.* See v. 9; see also note on 7:12. *this city.* Jerusalem. *a curse.* See 24:9; 25:18; see also note on Zech 8:13.
26:8 *Thou shalt surely die.* This same phrase occurs in Gen 2:17. A similar phrase describes the ultimate penalty for gross violations of the law of Moses (see, e.g., Ex 21:15–17; Lev 24:16–17, 21; Deut 18:20; cf. 1 Ki 21:13).

commanded *him* to speak unto all the people, that the priests and the prophets and all the people took him, saying, Thou shalt surely die.

9 Why hast thou prophesied in the name of the LORD, saying, This house shall be like Shiloh, and this city shall be desolate without an inhabitant? And all the people were gathered against Jeremiah in the house of the LORD.

10 When the princes of Judah heard these things, then they came up from the king's house *unto* the house of the LORD, and sat down [1]in the entry of the new gate of the LORD'S *house.*

11 Then spake the priests and the prophets unto the princes and to all the people, saying, [1]This man *is* worthy to die; [a]for he hath prophesied against this city, as ye have heard with your ears.

12 Then spake Jeremiah unto all the princes and to all the people, saying, The LORD sent me to prophesy against this house and against this city all the words that ye have heard.

13 Therefore now [a]amend your ways and your doings, and obey the voice of the LORD your God; and the LORD will [b]repent him of the evil that he hath pronounced against you.

14 As for me, behold, [a]I *am* in your hand: do with me [1]as seemeth good and meet unto you.

15 But know ye for certain, that if ye put me to death, ye shall surely bring innocent blood upon yourselves, and upon this city, and upon the inhabitants thereof: for of a truth the LORD hath sent me unto you to speak all these words in your ears.

16 ¶ Then said the princes and all the people unto the priests and to the prophets; This man *is* not worthy to die: for he hath spoken to us in the name of the LORD our God.

17 [a]Then rose up certain of the elders of the land, and spake to all the assembly of the people, saying,

18 [a]Micah the Morasthite prophesied in the days of Hezekiah king of Judah, and spake to all the people of Judah, saying, Thus saith the LORD of hosts;

[b]Zion shall be plowed *like* a field,
And Jerusalem shall become heaps,
And the mountain of the house as the high places of a forest.

19 ¶ Did Hezekiah king of Judah and all Judah put him at all to death? [a]did he not fear the LORD, and besought [1]the LORD, and the LORD [b]repented him of the evil which he had pronounced against them? [c]Thus *might* we procure great evil against our souls.

20 And there was also a man that prophesied in the name of the LORD, Urijah the son of Shemaiah of Kirjath-jearim, who prophesied against this city and against this land according to all the words of Jeremiah:

21 And when Jehoiakim the king, with all his mighty *men,* and all the princes, heard his words, the king sought to put him to death: but when Urijah heard *it,* he was afraid, and fled, and went *into* Egypt;

22 And Jehoiakim the king sent men *into* Egypt, *namely,* Elnathan the son of Achbor, and *certain* men with him into Egypt.

23 And they fet forth Urijah out of Egypt, and brought him unto Jehoiakim the king; who slew him with the sword, and cast his

26:10 [1]Or, *at the door*
26:11 [1]Heb. *The judgment of death* is *for this man* [a]ch. 38:4
26:13 [a]ch. 7:3 [b]ver. 3,19
26:14 [1]Heb. *as* it is *good and right in your eyes* [a]ch. 38:5
26:17 [a]See Acts 5:34
26:18 [a]Mic. 1:1 [b]Mic. 3:12
26:19 [1]Heb. *the face of the LORD* [a]2 Chr. 32:26 [b]Ex. 32:14; 2 Sam. 24:16 [c]Acts 5:39

26:9 *gathered against.* With hostile intent (see Num 16:3).

26:10 *princes of Judah.* Those responsible for making legal decisions concerning disputes taking place in the temple precincts. The priests and (false) prophets, who had a vested interest in Jerusalem and its temple, felt that Jeremiah should be sentenced to death because he was predicting the destruction of both the city and the Lord's house (see vv. 8–9,11). After hearing Jeremiah's defense (vv. 12–15), the officials decided in his favor (v. 16). The people, fickle and easily swayed, first opposed Jeremiah (vv. 8–9), then supported him (v. 16). *new gate.* See 36:10; possibly the same as the "upper Benjamin Gate" (see 20:2 and note).

26:11 Jeremiah's enemies judge him before he has a chance to defend himself (see Deut 19:6).

26:12 *The LORD sent me.* Contrast 23:21.

26:13 *amend your ways and your doings.* Repeated from 7:3 (see also 18:11; 35:15). *the LORD will repent him.* see notes on 4:28; 18:7–10.

26:15 *innocent blood.* See 7:6 and note; see also Mat 27:24–25; Acts 5:28.

26:16 Contrast v. 11; see note on v. 10.

26:17 *elders.* See 19:1; see also note on Ex 3:16.

26:18–19 The elders cite the precedent of Micah, who lived a century earlier and who (together with Isaiah) convinced King Hezekiah to pray for forgiveness on behalf of his people. The Lord answered the prayers of the king and the prophets, and in 701 B.C. Jerusalem and the temple were spared (see Is 37:33–37).

26:18 *Micah the Morasthite.* See Introduction to Micah: Author. *Zion shall be plowed . . . as the high places of a forest.* The Hebrew is quoted verbatim from Mic 3:12—the only place in the OT where one prophet quotes another and identifies his source.

‡26:19 *besought the LORD.* Cf. Ex 32:11; 1 Sam 13:12; 2 Ki 13:4; Ps 119:58. *the LORD repented.* See notes on 4:28; 18:7–10.

26:20–23 A parenthesis, cited as an example of the contrast between how a good king, Hezekiah, treated the Lord's prophets and how a wicked king, Jehoiakim, was known to have treated them.

26:20 *Urijah.* Not mentioned elsewhere in the OT, though it has been claimed (but not substantiated) that he appears in one of the Lachish letters (see note on 34:7; see also chart, p. xix).

26:21 *mighty men.* Perhaps the royal bodyguard. *Urijah . . . fled . . . into Egypt.* A fatal mistake, for now he could be accused of treason and sedition.

26:22 *Elnathan the son of Achbor.* One of King Jehoiakim's highest officials (see 36:12), he was impressed on another occasion by Jeremiah's prophecies (see 36:16), pleaded with the king not to burn Jeremiah's scroll (36:25), and warned the prophet to hide (see 36:19). An Elnathan (perhaps the same man) was Jehoiakim's father-in-law (see 2 Ki 24:6,8). An Achbor (perhaps the father of this Elnathan) was one of King Josiah's officials (see 2 Ki 22:12,14; see also note on v. 24).

26:23 *fet* [i.e."fetched"] *forth Urijah out of Egypt.* Mutual rights of extradition were a part of the treaty imposed on Judah by Egypt when Jehoiakim became the vassal of Pharaoh Neco II (see 2 Ki 23:34–35). *Jehoiakim . . . slew him.* Apart from divine

dead body into the graves of the [1]common people.

24 Nevertheless [a]the hand of Ahikam the son of Shaphan was with Jeremiah, that *they* should not give him into the hand of the people to put him to death.

Nebuchadnezzar's victory

27 In the beginning of the reign of Jehoiakim the son of Josiah [a]king of Judah came this word unto Jeremiah from the LORD, saying,

2 Thus [1]saith the LORD to me; Make thee bonds and yokes, [a]and put them upon thy neck,

3 And send them to the king of Edom, and to the king of Moab, and to the king of the Ammonites, and to the king of Tyrus, and to the king of Zidon, by the hand of the messengers which come *to* Jerusalem unto Zedekiah king of Judah;

4 And command them [1]to say unto their masters, Thus saith the LORD of hosts, the God of Israel; Thus shall ye say unto your masters;

5 [a]I have made the earth, the man and the beast that *are* upon the ground, by my great power and by my outstretched arm, and [b]have given it unto whom it seemed meet unto me.

6 [a]And now have I given all these lands into the hand of Nebuchadnezzar the king of Babylon, [b]my servant; and [c]the beasts of the field have I given him also to serve him.

7 [a]And all nations shall serve him, and his son, and his son's son, [b]until the very time of his land come: [c]and *then* many nations and great kings shall serve themselves of him.

8 And it shall come to pass, *that* the nation and kingdom which will not serve the same Nebuchadnezzar the king of Babylon, and that will not put their neck under the yoke of the king of Babylon, that nation will I punish, saith the LORD, with the sword, and with the famine, and with the pestilence, until I have consumed them by his hand.

9 Therefore hearken not ye to your prophets, nor to your diviners, nor to your [1]dreamers, nor to your enchanters, nor to your sorcerers, which speak unto you, saying, Ye shall not serve the king of Babylon:

10 [a]For they prophesy a lie unto you, to remove you far from your land; and *that* I should drive you out, and ye should perish.

11 But the nations that bring their neck under the yoke of the king of Babylon, and serve him, those will I let remain still in their own land, saith the LORD; and they shall till it, and dwell therein.

12 ¶ I spake also to [a]Zedekiah king of Judah according to all these words, saying, Bring your necks under the yoke of the king of Babylon, and serve him and his people, and live.

13 [a]Why will ye die, thou and thy people, by the sword, by the famine, and by the pestilence, as the LORD hath spoken against the nation that will not serve the king of Babylon?

26:23 [1]Heb. *sons of the people*
26:24 [a]2 Ki. 22:12,14; ch. 39:14
27:1 [a]See ver. 3,12,20; ch. 28:1
27:2 [1][Or, *hath the LORD said*] [a]ch. 28:10,12; Ezek. 4:1; 12:3; 24:3
27:4 [1]Or, *concerning their masters, saying*
27:5 [a]Ps. 115:15; 146:6; Is. 45:12 [b]Ps. 115:16; Dan. 4:17,25,32
27:6 [a]ch. 28:14 [b]ch. 25:9; 43:10; Ezek. 29:18,20 [c]ch. 28:14; Dan. 2:38
27:7 [a]2 Chr. 36:20
27:7 [b]ch. 25:12; 50:27; Dan. 5:26 [c]ch. 25:14
27:9 [1]Heb. *dreams*
27:10 [a]ver. 14
27:12 [a]ch. 28:1; 38:17
27:13 [a]Ezek. 18:31

intervention, Jeremiah probably would have fallen victim to the same fate (see 36:26). *graves of the common people.* See note on 17:19. Commoners were buried in the Kidron Valley east of Jerusalem (see 2 Ki 23:6).

26:24 *Ahikam the son of Shaphan.* One of King Josiah's officials (see 2 Ki 22:12,14), along with an Achbor who may have been the father of the Elnathan in v. 22 (see note there). Ahikam was also the father of Gedaliah, who would become governor of Judah after Jerusalem was destroyed in 586 B.C. (see 40:5) and who also befriended Jeremiah (see 39:14). *was with Jeremiah.* Ahikam's high position in Jehoiakim's court was doubtless instrumental in saving the prophet's life.

27:1–29:32 Further attempts by Jeremiah to counteract the teachings of false prophets, who were claiming that Babylon's doom was near and that rebellion against Nebuchadnezzar was therefore warranted and desirable.

27:1–22 Jeremiah tells the nations (see vv. 3–11), King Zedekiah (see vv. 12–15), and the priests and people of Judah (see vv. 16–22) to submit to the Babylonian yoke.

27:1 *In the beginning of the reign.* See note on 26:1. In this case, however, the phrase has been extended in meaning to include Zedekiah's fourth year (593 B.C.; see 28:1).

27:2 *yokes.* The kind worn by oxen. The yoke was a symbol of political submission (see vv. 8,11–12; Lev 26:13). That Jeremiah actually wore such a yoke for a time is clear from 28:10, 12.

27:3 *send them.* In his role as a "prophet to the nations" (1:5). *Edom . . . Moab . . . Ammonites.* Lands east and south of Judah (see 25:21 and note). *Tyrus . . . Zidon.* Tyre and Sidon, prominent cities in Phoenicia, north of Judah (see 25:22 and note). *messengers which come to . . . Zedekiah.* Perhaps to discuss rebellion against Babylonia. They may have counted on support from Egypt, where Psammetichus II had become pharaoh a year earlier (594 B.C.). Zedekiah went to Babylon in 593 (see 51:59), perhaps to be interrogated by Nebuchadnezzar. In any case, Zedekiah rebelled against him (see 52:3).

27:5 *great power and . . . outstretched arm.* See note on 21:5.

27:6 *Nebuchadnezzar . . . my servant.* See note on 25:9. *beasts of the field . . . given him . . . to serve him.* Nothing would be beyond the reach of Nebuchadnezzar's dominion (see 28:14; Dan 2:38).

27:7 *him . . . his son . . . his son's son.* Three generations of rulers, not necessarily in direct father-son relationships (cf. Deut 6:2). The words "son" and "father" are often used figuratively in the OT. "Son" may mean "descendants" or "successors" or "nations," while "father" may mean "ancestor" or "predecessor" or "founder." See notes on Gen 10:2,8; Dan 5:1. *time of his land come.* Babylonia will be judged (see note on 25:26). *many nations and great kings.* See note on 25:14.

27:8 *yoke.* See note on v. 2. *sword . . . famine . . . pestilence.* See note on 14:12. *until I have consumed.* See 9:16; 24:10.

‡27:9 See 29:8. *your prophets.* False prophets. *diviners . . . dreamers . . . sorcerers.* Forbidden in Israel (see Lev 19:26; Deut 18:10–11). The Hebrew for "dreamers" is a loanword from Akkadian (the language of Assyria and Babylonia). *dreamers.* Including prophets and diviners (see 23:25–28; 29:8).

27:10 *prophesy a lie.* See note on 5:31; cf. 2 Tim 4:3–4.

27:11 *yoke.* See note on v. 2. *serve . . . till.* The Hebrew underlying both words is the same ("work" is the common denominator in serving and tilling).

27:12 *your necks . . . serve . . . live.* The Hebrew for all these words is plural, since Jeremiah is speaking to the people of Judah as well as to Zedekiah (see v. 13). *yoke.* See note on v. 2.

27:13 See v. 8. *sword . . . famine . . . pestilence.* See note on 14:12.

14 Therefore hearken not unto the words
of the prophets that speak unto you, saying, Ye
shall not serve the king of Babylon: for they
prophesy [a]a lie unto you.
15 For I have not sent them, saith the
LORD, yet they prophesy [1]a lie in my name;
that I might drive you out, and that ye might
perish, ye, and the prophets that prophesy
unto you.
16 Also I spake to the priests and to all this
people, saying, Thus saith the LORD; Hearken
not to the words of your prophets that prophesy unto you, saying, Behold, [a]the vessels of the
LORD's house *shall* now shortly be brought
again from Babylon: for they prophesy a lie
unto you.
17 Hearken not unto them; serve the king
of Babylon, and live: wherefore should this
city be laid waste?
18 But if they *be* prophets, and if the word
of the LORD be with them, let them now make
intercession to the LORD of hosts, that the vessels which are left in the house of the LORD,
and *in* the house of the king of Judah, and at
Jerusalem, go not to Babylon.
19 For thus saith the LORD of hosts [a]con-
cerning the pillars, and concerning the sea,
and concerning the bases, and concerning the
residue of the vessels that remain in this city,
20 Which Nebuchadnezzar king of Babylon
took not, when he carried away [a]captive Jeconiah the son of Jehoiakim king of Judah from
Jerusalem to Babylon, and all the nobles of Judah and Jerusalem;
21 Yea, thus saith the LORD of hosts, the
God of Israel, concerning the vessels that remain *in* the house of the LORD, and *in* the
house of the king of Judah and of Jerusalem;
22 They shall be [a]carried to Babylon, and
there shall they be until the day that I [b]visit
them, saith the LORD; then [c]will I bring them
up, and restore them to this place.

27:14 [a]ch. 14:14; 23:21; 29:8,9
27:15 [1]Heb. *in a lie,* or, *lyingly*
27:16 [a]2 Chr. 36:7,10; ch. 28:3; Dan. 1:2
27:19 [a]2 Ki. 25:13; ch. 52:17,20,21
27:20 [a]2 Ki. 24:14,15; ch. 24:1
27:22 [a]2 Ki. 25:13; 2 Chr. 36:18 [b]2 Chr. 36:21; ch. 29:10; 32:5 [c]Ezra 1:7; 7:19

28:1 [a]ch. 27:1
28:2 [a]ch. 27:12
28:3 [1]Heb. *two years of days* [a]ch. 27:16
28:4 [1]Heb. *captivity*
28:6 [a]1 Ki. 1:36
28:9 [a]Deut. 18:22

Jeremiah exposes Hananiah

28 And [a]it came to pass the same year,
in the beginning of the reign of Zedekiah king of Judah, in the fourth year, *and* in
the fifth month, *that* Hananiah the son of Azur
the prophet, which *was* of Gibeon, spake unto
me in the house of the LORD, in the presence
of the priests and of all the people, saying,
2 Thus speaketh the LORD of hosts, the God
of Israel, saying, I have broken [a]the yoke of
the king of Babylon.
3 [a]Within [1]two full years *will* I bring again
into this place all the vessels of the LORD's
house, that Nebuchadnezzar king of Babylon
took away from this place, and carried them *to*
Babylon:
4 And I *will* bring again to this place Jeconiah the son of Jehoiakim king of Judah, with
all the [1]captives of Judah, that went into Babylon, saith the LORD: for I will break the yoke
of the king of Babylon.
5 Then the prophet Jeremiah said unto the
prophet Hananiah in the presence of the
priests, and in the presence of all the people
that stood in the house of the LORD,
6 Even the prophet Jeremiah said, [a]Amen:
the LORD do so: the LORD perform thy words
which thou hast prophesied, to bring again the
vessels of the LORD's house, and all that is carried away captive, from Babylon into this
place.
7 Nevertheless hear thou now this word
that I speak in thine ears, and in the ears of all
the people.
8 The prophets that have been before me
and before thee of old prophesied both against
many countries, and against great kingdoms,
of war, and of evil, and of pestilence.
9 [a]The prophet which prophesieth of
peace, when the word of the prophet shall
come to pass, *then* shall the prophet be
known, that the LORD hath truly sent him.

27:14 See v. 10.
27:15 See 14:14; 23:21 and note.
27:16 *prophets . . . saying . . . shortly.* As the prophet Hananiah was saying (see 28:1–3). *vessels of the LORD's house.* Some were carried off to Babylon by Nebuchadnezzar in 605 B.C. (see Dan 1:1–2), others in 597 (see 2 Ki 24:13). Still others would be carried off in 586 (see vv. 21–22; 52:17–23).
‡27:18 *if they be prophets . . . let them now make intercession.* If they are true prophets and in communion with the Lord, let them intercede for Judah, because the Lord has announced His intention to judge the nation. The adjective "false" is never used for a prophet in the OT Scriptures themselves.
27:19 *the pillars . . . the sea . . . the bases.* See 52:17; see also 1 Ki 7:15–37 and notes.
27:22 *they shall be carried to Babylon.* In 586 B.C. (see 52:17–23). *will I bring them up.* In 538 and shortly afterward (see Ezra 1:7–11).
28:1–17 The true prophet Jeremiah confronts the false prophet Hananiah.
28:1 *in the beginning of the reign.* See notes on 26:1; 27:1. *the reign of Zedekiah . . . the fourth year.* 593 B.C. *Hananiah.* Means "The LORD is gracious," an appropriate name for a prophet who believed strongly (though mistakenly) that the Lord would soon bring back the exiles of Judah and the temple articles (see vv. 3–4,11). *prophet.* The word is used for all prophets, whether true (vv. 5,10–12,15) or false (vv. 1,5,10,12,15,17). *Gibeon.* See 41:12,16; see also note on Josh 9:3.
28:2 *Thus speaketh the LORD.* See v. 11. Though a false prophet, Hananiah claims to have the same authority as Jeremiah (see vv. 13–14,16; see also 23:31). *yoke.* See note on 27:2.
28:3 Hananiah's prediction directly contradicts the words of Jeremiah (see 27:16–22 and notes). *two full years.* See v. 11. Contrast Jeremiah's 70 years (25:11–12; 29:10).
28:4 *bring again.* Contradicting Jeremiah's prophecy (see 22:24–27), which was fulfilled (see 52:34). *Jeconiah . . . went into Babylon.* In 597 B.C. *yoke.* See note on 27:2.
28:6 See 1 Ki 1:36. *Amen.* See 11:5 and note. *the LORD do so.* Fulfillment is one of the signs of a true prophecy (see v. 9).
28:7 *Nevertheless.* Though in sympathy with what Hananiah is predicting, Jeremiah reminds him that their true predecessors were basically prophets of doom (see v. 8).
28:8 *war . . . evil . . . pestilence.* An appropriate modification of Jeremiah's usual triad (see note on 14:12).
28:9 *peace.* Ordinarily the message of false prophets (see 6:14 and note).

10 Then Hananiah the prophet took the [a]yoke from off the prophet Jeremiah's neck, and brake it.

11 And Hananiah spake in the presence of all the people, saying, Thus saith the LORD; Even so will I break the yoke of Nebuchadnezzar king of Babylon [a]from the neck of all nations within the space of two full years. And the prophet Jeremiah went his way.

12 ¶ Then the word of the LORD came unto Jeremiah *the prophet,* after that Hananiah the prophet had broken the yoke from off the neck of the prophet Jeremiah, saying,

13 Go and tell Hananiah, saying, Thus saith the LORD; Thou hast broken the yokes of wood; but thou shalt make for them yokes of iron.

14 For thus saith the LORD of hosts, the God of Israel; [a]I have put a yoke of iron upon the neck of all these nations, that *they* may serve Nebuchadnezzar king of Babylon; and they shall serve him: and [b]I have given him the beasts of the field also.

15 Then said the prophet Jeremiah unto Hananiah the prophet, Hear now, Hananiah; The LORD hath not sent thee; but [a]thou makest this people to trust in a lie.

16 Therefore thus saith the LORD; Behold, I will cast thee from off the face of the earth: *this* year thou *shalt* die, because thou hast taught [a][1]rebellion against the LORD.

17 So Hananiah the prophet died the same year in the seventh month.

A letter to the captives

29 Now these *are* the words of the letter that Jeremiah the prophet sent from Jerusalem unto the residue of the elders which were carried away captives, and to the priests, and to the prophets, and to all the people whom Nebuchadnezzar had carried away captive from Jerusalem to Babylon;

2 (After that [a]Jeconiah the king, and the queen, and the [1]eunuchs, the princes of Judah and Jerusalem, and the carpenters, and the smiths, were departed from Jerusalem;)

3 By the hand of Elasah the son of Shaphan, and Gemariah the son of Hilkiah, whom Zedekiah king of Judah sent unto Babylon to Nebuchadnezzar king of Babylon, saying,

4 ¶ Thus saith the LORD of hosts, the God of Israel, unto all that are carried away captives, whom I have caused to be carried away from Jerusalem unto Babylon;

5 [a]Build ye houses, and dwell *in them;* and plant gardens, and eat the fruit of them;

6 Take ye wives, and beget sons and daughters; and take wives for your sons, and give your daughters to husbands, that they may bear sons and daughters; that ye may be increased there, and not diminished.

7 And seek the peace of the city whither I have caused you to be carried away captives, [a]and pray unto the LORD for it: for in the peace thereof shall ye have peace.

8 For thus saith the LORD of hosts, the God of Israel; Let not your prophets and your diviners, that *be* in the midst of you, [a]deceive you, neither hearken to your dreams which ye cause to be dreamed.

9 [a]For they prophesy [1]falsely unto you in my name: I have not sent them, saith the LORD.

10 For thus saith the LORD, That after [a]seventy years be accomplished at Babylon I will

28:10 [a]ch. 27:2
28:11 [a]ch. 27:7
28:14 [a]Deut. 28:48; ch. 27:7 [b]ch. 27:6
28:15 [a]ch. 29:31; Ezek. 13:22
28:16 [1]Heb. *revolt* [a]Deut. 13:5; ch. 29:32

29:2 [1]Or, *chamberlains* [a]2 Ki. 24:12; ch. 22:26; 28:4
29:5 [a]ver. 28
29:7 [a]Ezra 6:10; 1 Tim. 2:2
29:8 [a]ch. 14:14; 23:21; 27:14,15; Eph. 5:6
29:9 [1]Heb. *in a lie* [a]ver. 31
29:10 [a]2 Chr. 36:21,22; Ezra 1:1; ch. 25:12; 27:22; Dan. 9:2

28:10 *yoke from off the prophet Jeremiah's neck.* See note on 27:2. *brake it.* Perhaps symbolically to break the power of Jeremiah's earlier prophecies (see 25:11–12; 27:7), which contradicted his own.

28:11 *two full years.* See note on v. 3.

28:13 *yokes of iron.* The wooden yoke of submission (see note on 27:2) would be exchanged for the iron yoke of servitude (see v. 14; 38:17–23).

28:14 *all these nations . . . shall serve him.* See 27:7. *given him the beasts of the field.* See 27:6 and note.

28:15 *the LORD hath not sent thee.* A mark of the false prophet (see 23:21 and note).

28:16 *will cast.* The Hebrew root underlying this word is the same as that underlying "sent" in v. 15. The Lord had not "sent" Hananiah to prophesy, and therefore he would soon be "sent away" to his death. *taught rebellion.* Such activity on the part of false prophets was punishable by death (see Deut 13:5; see also Deut 18:20; cf. Ezek 11:13; Acts 5:1–11).

28:17 *Hananiah . . . died . . . in the seventh month.* He who had falsely prophesied restoration "within two years" (vv. 3,11) himself died within two months (see v. 1).

29:1–32 Jeremiah's letter to the exiles of 597 B.C. (vv. 4–23) is followed by God's message of judgment against the false prophet Shemaiah (vv. 24–32).

‡29:2 *queen.* His mother, Nehushta (2 Ki 24:8). *carpenters, and . . . smiths.* See 24:1 and note.

‡29:3 *by the hand of.* The letter was placed in the ancient equivalent of the diplomatic pouch to ensure its safe arrival. *Shaphan.* Perhaps the father also of Ahikam (see 26:24 and note) and/or Gemariah (see 36:10), both of whom were sympathetic to Jeremiah and his mission. *Hilkiah.* Perhaps the Hilkiah who was high priest under Josiah (see 2 Ki 22:12, where Hilkiah and one or more Shaphans are mentioned together). *Zedekiah . . . sent unto . . . Nebuchadnezzar.* Possibly at or about the same time (593 B.C.) that Zedekiah himself went to Babylon for a brief period (see 51:59). The purpose of the journey(s) is unknown.

29:4 *I.* The Lord (see v. 7). Since it is God who has exiled His people, they are to submit to their captors and not rebel against them.

29:5 *build . . . plant.* Reminiscent of Jeremiah's call (see 1:10), but here used in a literal sense. *dwell in them.* Ezekiel, e.g., lived in his own house in Babylonia (see Ezek 8:1).

29:6 *Take ye wives.* But among the exiles themselves, not among the women of Babylonia (cf. Deut 7:3–4; Ezra 9:1–2).

29:7 *seek the peace.* An unprecedented and unique concept in the ancient world: working toward and praying for the prosperity of one's captors. *peace . . . peace . . . peace.* The Hebrew word is *shalom* in all three cases. *city.* Every place in which the exiles settle down. *pray . . . for it.* See Ezra 6:10 and note; Mat 5:44; in the Apocrypha cf. 1 Maccabees 7:33.

29:8 *prophets . . . diviners . . . dreams.* See 27:9 and note. *in the midst of you.* The exiles in Babylon had their share of false prophets (see vv. 21,31), who had doubtless accompanied them when they were deported in 597 B.C.

29:9 See v. 31; see also notes on 23:16,21.

visit you, and perform my good word towards you, in causing you to return to this place.

11 For I know the thoughts that I think towards you, saith the LORD, thoughts of peace, and not of evil, to give you an [1]expected end.

12 Then shall ye [a]call upon me, and ye shall go and pray unto me, and I will hearken unto you.

13 And [a]ye shall seek me, and find *me,* when ye shall search for me [b]with all your heart.

14 And [a]I will be found of you, saith the LORD: and I will turn away your captivity, and [b]I will gather you from all the nations, and from all the places whither I have driven you, saith the LORD; and I will bring you again into the place whence I caused you to be carried away captive.

15 ¶ Because ye have said, The LORD hath raised us up prophets in Babylon;

16 *Know* that thus saith the LORD of the king that sitteth upon the throne of David, and of all the people that dwelleth in this city, *and of* your brethren that are not gone forth with you into captivity;

17 Thus saith the LORD of hosts; Behold, I will send upon them the sword, the famine, and the pestilence, and will make them like [a]vile figs, that cannot be eaten, they are so evil.

18 And I will persecute them with the sword, with the famine, and with the pestilence, and [a]will deliver them to be removed to all the kingdoms of the earth, [1]to be [b]a curse, and an astonishment, and a hissing, and a reproach, among all the nations whither I have driven them:

19 Because they have not hearkened to my words, saith the LORD, which [a]I sent unto them by my servants the prophets, rising up early and sending *them;* but ye would not hear, saith the LORD.

20 Hear ye therefore the word of the LORD, all *ye of* the captivity, whom I have sent from Jerusalem to Babylon:

21 Thus saith the LORD of hosts, the God of Israel, of Ahab the son of Kolaiah, and of Zedekiah, the son of Maaseiah, which prophesy a lie unto you in my name; Behold, I will deliver them into the hand of Nebuchadrezzar king of Babylon; and he shall slay them before your eyes;

22 [a]And of them shall be taken up a curse by all the captivity of Judah which *are* in Babylon, saying, The LORD make thee like Zedekiah and like Ahab, [b]whom the king of Babylon roasted in the fire;

23 Because [a]they have committed villany in Israel, and have committed adultery with their neighbours' wives, and have spoken lying words in my name, which I have not commanded them; even I know, and *am* a witness, saith the LORD.

A letter to Shemaiah

24 ¶ *Thus* shalt thou also speak to Shemaiah the [1]Nehelamite, saying,

25 Thus speaketh the LORD of hosts, the God of Israel, saying, Because thou hast sent letters in thy name unto all the people that *are* at Jerusalem, [a]and to Zephaniah the son of Maaseiah the priest, and to all the priests, saying,

26 The LORD hath made thee priest in the stead of Jehoiada the priest, that *ye* should be [a]officers in the house of the LORD, for every man *that is* [b]mad, and maketh himself a prophet, that thou shouldest [c]put him in prison, and in the stocks.

27 Now therefore why hast thou not reproved Jeremiah of Anathoth, which maketh himself a prophet to you?

28 For therefore he sent unto us *in* Babylon, saying, This *captivity is* long: [a]build ye

29:11 [1]Heb. *end and expectation*
29:12 [a]Dan. 9:3
29:13 [a]Lev. 26:39,40; Deut. 30:1 [b]ch. 24:7
29:14 [a]Deut. 4:7; Ps. 32:6; 46:1; Is. 55:6 [b]ch. 23:3,8; 30:3; 32:37
29:17 [a]ch. 24:8
29:18 [1]Heb. *for a curse* [a]Deut. 28:25; 2 Chr. 29:8; ch. 15:4; 24:9; 34:17 [b]ch. 26:6; 42:18
29:19 [a]ch. 25:4; 32:33
29:22 [a]See Gen. 48:20; Is. 65:15 [b]Dan. 3:6
29:23 [a]ch. 23:14
29:24 [1]Or, *dreamer*
29:25 [a]2 Ki. 25:18; ch. 21:1
29:26 [a]ch. 20:1 [b]2 Ki. 9:11; Acts 26:24 [c]ch. 20:2
29:28 [a]ver. 5

29:10 *seventy years.* See note on 25:11–12. *causing you to return.* See note on 27:22.

29:11 *I know.* See v. 23. Appearances to the contrary notwithstanding, the Lord has not forgotten His people. *peace.* See note on v. 7. *and not of evil.* God is the ultimate source of both prosperity and disaster (see Is 45:7).

29:12–13 Echoed from Deut 4:29–30. The Lord's gracious gift of prosperity is contingent on His people's willingness to repent.

‡29:14 A summary of Deut 30:3–5. *I will turn away your captivity.* See 30:3,18; 31:23; 32:44; 33:7,11,26; 48:47; 49:6,39; see also note on Ps 126:4. The Hebrew for "turn away" sounds very similar to that for "captivity."

29:15 *prophets in Babylon.* See note on v. 8.

29:16 *the king . . . upon the throne of David.* Zedekiah. *sitteth . . . dwelleth.* The Hebrew for both words is identical. King and people alike are guilty.

29:17 *sword . . . famine . . . pestilence.* See v. 18; see also note on 14:12. *vile figs, that cannot be eaten.* See 24:8.

29:18 See 24:9 and note.

‡29:19 *rising . . . sending.* See note on 7:13. *my servants the prophets.* See note on 7:25. *ye would not hear.* See Ezek 2:5,7; 3:7,11.

29:21 *Ahab . . . and . . . Zedekiah.* Not the well-known kings (of Israel and Judah respectively); rather, they were false prophets (see note on v. 8).

29:22 *curse . . . roasted.* The Hebrew underlying each of these words sounds like Kolaiah, the name of Ahab's father (v. 21). *fire.* Used in Babylonia as a method of execution (see Dan 3:6,24; this is also evident in the Code of Hammurapi, sections 25; 110; 157).

29:23 *they have committed villany in Israel.* See Gen 34:7 and note. *committed adultery . . . and . . . spoken lying words.* See note on 23:10. *I know, and am a witness.* See v. 11.

29:24 *Shemaiah.* A false prophet (see v. 31). *Nehelamite.* The Hebrew root underlying this word is the same as that for "dreams" in v. 8 (see 27:9 and note).

29:25 *Zephaniah.* Not the prophet of that name (see note on 21:1).

29:26 *Jehoiada.* Not the same as the priest during the days of King Joash (see 2 Ki 12:7). *officers in the house of the LORD.* See note on 20:1. *man that is mad.* Prophetic behavior sometimes appeared deranged to the casual observer (see 2 Ki 9:11). *stocks.* See note on 20:2.

29:27 *Anathoth.* See note on 1:1.

29:28 See v. 5 and note. *long.* Here 70 years (see 25:11–12 and note; see also 2 Sam 3:1).

houses, and dwell *in them;* and plant gardens,
and eat the fruit of them.
29 And Zephaniah the priest read this letter in the ears of Jeremiah the prophet.
30 Then came the word of the LORD unto
Jeremiah, saying,
31 Send to all them of the captivity, saying,
Thus saith the LORD concerning Shemaiah the
Nehelamite; Because that Shemaiah hath
prophesied unto you, [a]and I sent him not, and
he caused you to trust in a lie:
32 Therefore thus saith the LORD; Behold, I
will punish Shemaiah the Nehelamite, and his
seed: he shall not have a man to dwell among
this people; neither shall he behold the good
that I will do for my people, saith the LORD;
[a]because he hath taught [1]rebellion against the
LORD.

Restoration of Israel

30 The word that came to Jeremiah
from the LORD, saying,
2 Thus speaketh the LORD God of Israel,
saying, Write thee all the words that I have
spoken unto thee in a book.
3 For lo, the days come, saith the LORD,
that [a]I will bring again the captivity of my people Israel and Judah, saith the LORD: [b]and I will
cause them to return to the land that I gave to
their fathers, and they shall possess it.
4 And these *are* the words that the LORD
spake concerning Israel and concerning Judah.
5 For thus saith the LORD;
We have heard a voice of trembling,
[1]Of fear, and not of peace.

29:31 [a]ch. 28:15
29:32 [1]Heb. *revolt* [a]ch. 28:16
30:3 [a]ver. 18; ch. 32:44; Ezek. 39:25; Amos 9:14,15 [b]ch. 16:15
30:5 [1]Or, There is *fear, and not peace*

30:6 [1]Heb. *a male* [a]ch. 4:31; 6:24
30:7 [a]Joel 2:11,31; Amos 5:18; Zeph. 1:14 [b]Dan. 12:1
30:9 [a]Is. 55:3,4; Ezek. 34:23; 37:24; Hos. 3:5 [b]Luke 1:69; Acts 2:30; 13:23
30:10 [a]Is. 41:13; 43:5; 44:2; ch. 46:27,28 [b]ch. 3:18
30:11 [a]Amos 9:8 [b]ch. 4:27 [c]Ps. 6:1; Is. 27:8; ch. 10:24; 46:28

6 Ask ye now, and see whether [1]a man
doth travail with child?
Wherefore do I see every man *with* his
hands on his loins, [a]as a woman in
travail,
And all faces are turned into paleness?
7 [a]Alas! for that day *is* great, [b]so that
none *is* like it:
It *is* even the time of Jacob's trouble;
But he shall be saved out of it.
8 For it shall come to pass in that day,
saith the LORD of hosts,
That I will break his yoke from off thy
neck,
And will burst thy bonds,
And strangers shall no more serve
themselves of him:
9 But they shall serve the LORD their God,
And [a]David their king, whom I will
[b]raise up unto them.

10 Therefore [a]fear thou not, O my servant
Jacob, saith the LORD;
Neither be dismayed, O Israel:
For lo, I *will* save thee from afar,
And thy seed [b]from the land of their
captivity;
And Jacob shall return,
And shall be in rest, and be quiet,
And none shall make *him* afraid.
11 For I *am* with thee, saith the LORD, to
save thee:
[a]Though I make a full end of all nations
whither I have scattered thee,
[b]Yet will I not make a full end of thee:
But I will correct thee [c]in measure,

29:29 *Zephaniah ... read.* He was apparently sympathetic toward Jeremiah (see 21:1–2; 37:3).
29:31–32 The Lord's threat against Shemaiah is similar to that against Hananiah (see 28:15–16).
29:31 *caused you to trust in a lie.* See 28:15.
29:32 *taught rebellion against.* See 28:16 and note.
30:1–33:26 Often called Jeremiah's "book of consolation," the section depicts the ultimate restoration of both Israel (the northern kingdom) and Judah (the southern kingdom) and is the longest sustained passage in Jeremiah concerned with the future hope of the people of God (for other and briefer passages on restoration see 3:14–18; 16:14–15; 23:3–8; 24:4–7). The information in 32:1 may be used to date the entire section to 587 B.C., the year before Jerusalem was destroyed by Nebuchadnezzar and its people exiled to Babylon.
30:1–31:40 Written almost entirely in poetry, these two chapters are filled with optimism as the prophet looks forward to the time when God would redeem His people.
30:1 The heading for chs. 30–31 (and perhaps chs. 32–33 as well).
30:2 *Write.* In order to preserve for future generations the predictions of restoration. *book.* In scroll form (see, e.g., 36:2,4; 45:1; see also note on Ex 17:14). *all the words that I have spoken unto thee.* Concerning the future redemption of God's people. The phrase is less comprehensive here than in 36:2.
‡30:3 *I will bring again the captivity ... cause them to return.* See note on 29:14. *Israel and Judah.* The northern and southern kingdoms, the first of which was exiled in 721 B.C. and the second of which would be entering the final stage of its exile in about a year (see note on 30:1–33:26).
30:5 *voice of trembling.* The sound of battle and destruction.
30:6 *woman in travail.* A symbol of anguish and distress (see note on 4:19).
30:7 A description of the day of the Lord (see notes on Is 2:11,17,20; Amos 5:18; 8:9). Jeremiah's immediate reference is to the foreseeable future (see vv. 8,18), but a more remote time in the Messianic age is also in view. *great.* See Joel 2:11; Zeph 1:14; cf. Joel 1:15. *so that none is like it.* See Dan 12:1; Joel 2:2; Mat 24:21. *time of ... trouble.* See Dan 12:1; Mat 24:21 and note; Rev 16:18). *Jacob's.* Israel's (see v. 10).
30:8 *in that day.* See note on Is 2:11,17,20. *yoke.* See note on 27:2. *burst thy bonds.* The Hebrew underlying this phrase is translated "break their bands asunder" in Ps 2:3, where the nations plot to free themselves from the Lord and His anointed ruler. Here the Lord promises to free His people from enslavement to the nations. *strangers.* Including, but not limited to, Babylonia.
30:9 *David their king.* The Messiah (see note on 23:5). The Targum (ancient Aramaic paraphrase) here reads "Messiah, the son of David, their king." *raise up.* See note on 23:5.
30:10–11 Repeated almost verbatim in 46:27–28.
30:10 *my servant Jacob.* See Is 41:8–9 and note; 44:1–2,21; 45:4; 48:20. *And none shall make him afraid.* Contrast v. 5; see Lev 26:6; Job 11:19; Is 17:2; Ezek 34:28; 39:26; Mic 4:4 and note; Zeph 3:13.
30:11 *I am with thee ... to save thee.* Words spoken originally to Jeremiah alone (see 1:8,19; 15:20) are now spoken to all God's people. *scattered.* See 9:16 and note; 23:1–2. *not make a full*

And will not leave thee altogether
unpunished.
12 For thus saith the LORD,
[a]Thy bruise *is* incurable,
And thy wound *is* grievous.
13 *There is* none to plead thy cause, [1]that
thou mayest be bound up:
[a]Thou hast no healing medicines.
14 [a]All thy lovers have forgotten thee;
They seek thee not;
For I have wounded thee *with* the
wound [b]of an enemy, *with* the
chastisement [c]of a cruel one,
For the multitude of thine iniquity;
[d]*Because* thy sins were increased.
15 Why [a]criest thou for thine affliction?
Thy sorrow *is* incurable for the
multitude of thine iniquity:
Because thy sins were increased, I
have done these things unto thee.
16 Therefore all they that devour thee
[a]shall be devoured;
And all thine adversaries, every one of
them, shall go into captivity;
And they that spoil thee shall be a
spoil,
And all that prey upon thee will I give
for a prey.
17 [a]For I will restore health unto thee,
And I will heal thee of thy wounds,
saith the LORD;
Because they called thee an Outcast,
saying,
This *is* Zion, whom no man seeketh
after.

18 Thus saith the LORD:
Behold, [a]I *will* bring again the captivity
of Jacob's tents,
And [b]have mercy on his dwelling places;
And the city shall be builded upon her
own [1]heap,
And the palace shall remain after the
manner thereof.
19 And [a]out of them shall proceed
thanksgiving and the voice of them
that make merry:
[b]And I will multiply them, and they
shall not be few;
I will also glorify them, and they shall
not be small.
20 Their children also shall be [a]as
aforetime,
And their congregation shall be
established before me,
And I will punish all that oppress them.
21 And their nobles shall be of
themselves,
[a]And their governor shall proceed from
the midst of them;
And I will [b]cause him to draw near,
and he shall approach unto me:
For who *is* this that engaged his heart
to approach unto me? saith the LORD.
22 And ye shall be [a]my people, and I will
be your God.
23 Behold, the [a]whirlwind of the LORD
goeth forth *with* fury,
A [1]continuing whirlwind:
It shall [2]fall with pain upon the head of
the wicked.
24 The fierce anger of the LORD shall not
return, until he have done *it,*
And until he have performed the
intents of his heart:
[a]In the latter days ye shall consider it.

31

At [a]the same time, saith the LORD,
[b]Will I be the God of all the families
of Israel,

30:12 [a]2 Chr. 36:16; ch. 15:18
30:13 [1]Heb. *for binding up,* or, *pressing* [a]ch. 8:22
30:14 [a]Lam. 1:2 [b]Job 13:24; 16:9; 19:11 [c]Job 30:21 [d]ch. 5:6
30:15 [a]ch. 15:18
30:16 [a]Ex. 23:22; Is. 33:1; 41:11; ch. 10:25
30:17 [a]ch. 33:6
30:18 [a]ver. 3; ch. 33:7,11 [b]Ps. 102:13
30:18 [1]Or, *little hill*
30:19 [a]Is. 51:11 [b]Zech. 10:8
30:20 [a]Is. 1:26
30:21 [a]Gen. 49:10 [b]Num. 16:5
30:22 [a]ch. 31:1,33
30:23 [1]Heb. *cutting* [2]Or, *remain* [a]ch. 23:19; 25:32
30:24 [a]Gen. 49:1
31:1 [a]ch. 30:24 [b]ch. 30:22

end of thee. See 4:27 and note. *will not leave thee altogether unpunished.* See 25:29; 49:12.
30:12–13 See 8:22; Hos 5:13; 6:1; 7:1; 11:3.
30:12 *Thy.* Judah's. *bruise is incurable.* See 15:18 and note. *wound is grievous.* See 14:17.
30:13 *plead thy cause.* Against your enemies. *Thou hast no healing medicines.* See Hos 5:13.
30:14 *lovers.* See note on 22:20. Egypt, e.g., often supported Judah against the Babylonians (see 37:5–7). *Because thy sins were increased.* See 5:6; 13:22. The Hebrew for this clause is repeated verbatim in v. 15.
30:16 *all they that devour thee.* See 3:24; 5:17; 8:16; 10:25. *shall be devoured.* See note on 25:26; see also 51:48–49. *shall be a spoil.* See Is 17:14.
30:17 *restore health unto thee.* Contrast 8:22; see 33:6; Is 58:8.
30:18 *bring again the captivity.* See note on 29:14. *the city . . . the palace.* Lit. "a city . . . a palace," perhaps referring to Judah's cities and palaces in general (see Amos 9:14). It is possible, however, that only Jerusalem and its palace are intended (see 31:38). *heap.* The Hebrew for this word is *tel(l),* referring to a mound of ruins resulting from the accumulation of the debris of many years or centuries of occupation and on which successive series of towns were often built (see, e.g., Josh 11:13).
30:19 *thanksgiving.* See 33:11. *make merry.* See 31:4 and note; contrast 15:17. *multiply . . . not be few;* See 29:6; Ezek 36:37–38. *glorify . . . not be small* See Is 9:1.
‡30:20 *aforetime.* Probably the early days of the united kingdom, especially the reign of David. *congregation.* The political and religious governing body of the people. *shall be established before me.* See Ps 102:28; 2 Sam 7:24.
30:21 *nobles . . . governor.* Although the Targum renders "Messiah" here, the terms probably refer in the first place to the rulers of Judah immediately after the exile. But Jesus Christ ultimately fulfills the promise. *of themselves . . . from the midst of them.* Not foreigners (cf. Deut 18:15,18). *cause him to draw near . . . approach.* See Num 16:5; contrast Ex 24:2. Unauthorized approaches into God's presence were punishable by death (see Ex 19:21; Num 8:19).
30:22 See 31:1; see also note on 7:23.
30:23–24 Repeated almost verbatim from 23:19–20 (see notes there).
‡31:1–40 Continuing the theme of restoration begun in 30:1, Jeremiah records the words of the Lord to (1) all the people of God, v. 1; (2) the restored northern kingdom of Israel, vv. 2–22; (3) the restored southern kingdom of Judah, vv. 23–26; and (4) Israel and Judah together, vv. 27–40 (prologue, vv. 27–30; body, vv. 31–37; epilogue, vv. 38–40—each section beginning with the words " Behold, the days come,").

And they shall be my people.
2 Thus saith the LORD,
The people which were left of the sword found grace in the wilderness;
Even Israel when [a]*I* went to cause him to rest.
3 The LORD hath appeared [1]of old unto me, *saying,*
Yea, [a]I have loved thee *with* [b]an everlasting love;
Therefore [2]*with* lovingkindness have I [c]drawn thee.
4 Again [a]I will build thee, and thou shalt be built, O virgin of Israel:
Thou shalt again be adorned *with* thy [b1]tabrets,
And shalt go forth in the dances of them that make merry.
5 [a]Thou shalt yet plant vines upon the mountains of Samaria:
The planters shall plant, and shall [b1]eat *them* as common things.
6 For there shall be a day,
That the watchmen upon the mount Ephraim shall cry,
[a]Arise ye, and let us go up *to* Zion unto the LORD our God.
7 For thus saith the LORD;
[a]Sing with gladness for Jacob,
And shout among the chief of the nations:
Publish ye, praise ye, and say,
O LORD, save thy people, the remnant of Israel.
8 Behold, I *will* bring them [a]from the north country,
And [b]gather them from the coasts of the earth,
And with them the blind and the lame,
The woman with child and her that travaileth with child together:
A great company shall return thither.
9 [a]They shall come with weeping,
And with [b1]supplications will I lead them:
I will cause them to walk [c]by the rivers of waters
In a straight way, wherein they shall not stumble:
For I am a father to Israel,
And Ephraim *is* my [d]firstborn.
10 Hear the word of the LORD, O ye nations,
And declare *it* in the isles afar off, and say,
He that scattered Israel [a]will gather him,
And keep him as a shepherd *doth* his flock.
11 For [a]the LORD hath redeemed Jacob,
And ransomed him [b]from the hand of *him that was* stronger than he.

31:2 [a]Num. 10:33; Deut. 1:33; Ps. 95:11; Is. 63:14
31:3 [1]Heb. *from afar* [2]Or, *have I extended lovingkindness* unto *thee* [a]Mal. 1:2 [b]Rom. 11:28 [c]Hos. 11:4
31:4 [1]Or, *timbrels* [a]ch. 33:7 [b]Ex. 15:20; Judg. 11:34; Ps. 149:3
31:5 [1]Heb. *profane* them [a]Is. 65:21; Amos 9:14 [b]Deut. 20:6
31:6 [a]Is. 2:3; Mic. 4:2
31:7 [a]Is. 12:5,6
31:8 [a]ch. 3:12,18; 23:8 [b]Ezek. 20:34,41; 34:13
31:9 [1]Or, *favours* [a]ch. 50:4 [b]Zech. 12:10 [c]Is. 35:8; 43:19; 49:10,11 [d]Ex. 4:22
31:10 [a]Is. 40:11; Ezek. 34:12-14
31:11 [a]Is. 44:23; 48:20 [b]Is. 49:24

31:1 See 30:22; see also note on 7:23. *all the families of Israel.* All 12 tribes.

31:2 *people which were left of the sword.* The righteous remnant (see v. 7; see also note on 6:9), who will return from captivity. *wilderness.* The Arabian Desert, the antitype of the Sinai wilderness through which Israel's ancestors marched after the exodus. Return from exile is often pictured as or compared to release from Egyptian slavery at the time of the exodus (see 16:14–15 and note; see also Is 35:1–11 and notes; 40:3–4; 42:14–16; 43:18–21; 48:20–21; 51:9–11; cf. Hos 2:14–15). *Israel.* The northern kingdom (see also vv. 4,7,9–10,21). Other names for it are Samaria (v. 5), Ephraim (vv. 6,9,18,20), Jacob (vv. 7,11) and Rachel (v. 15). *rest.* See 6:16; contrast Deut 28:65. See notes on Deut 3:20; Josh 1:13.

31:3 *with lovingkindness . . . drawn.* The Hebrew underlying this phrase is translated "continue Thy lovingkindness" in Ps 36:10 (see note on Ps 6:4).

‡31:4 *build.* See 1:10 and note. *virgin of Israel.* See v. 21; 18:13; see also 14:17 and note. *tabrets.* That is, "tambourines," which were used on joyful occasions (see Ps 68:25), especially following a military victory (see Ex 15:20 and note; Judg 11:34)—in contrast to Judah's experience during the exile (see Ps 137:1–3). *dances.* See v. 13; often a religious activity in ancient times (see 2 Sam 6:14). *make merry.* See 30:19.

‡31:5 *plant.* See 1:10 and note. *Samaria.* Conquered in 722–721 B.C. (see 2 Ki 17:24), it would someday be resettled by God's people. *plant, and shall eat them as common things.* The idea is that they will enjoy eating them. See Deut 28:30; Is 62:8–9; 65:21–22. Since the law stipulated that the fruit of a tree could not be eaten until the fifth year after planting it (see Lev 19:23–25), a return to normalcy is envisioned here.

31:6 *watchmen upon the mount.* For example, in later times watchmen were stationed in appropriate locations to observe and give notice of the appearance of various phases of the moon to fix the times of the most important feasts (see Deut 16:16). *Ephraim . . . to Zion.* In the days of Jeroboam I, the people of the northern kingdom had been required to worship at northern shrines (see 1 Ki 12:26–30). In the future, however, they would worship the Lord only in Jerusalem (cf. John 4:20). *go up.* The verb is often used of journeys to Jerusalem (see, e.g., Ezra 1:3; 7:7; Is 2:3), whose elevation is above the surrounding countryside.

31:7 *chief of the nations.* See Deut 26:19; Amos 6:1. Israel was the greatest nation not because of intrinsic merit but because of divine grace and appointment (see Deut 7:6–8; 2 Sam 7:23–24). *save.* The Hebrew for this word is the basis of "Hosanna," the cry of the people of Jerusalem on Palm Sunday (see Mat 21:9 and note; see also Ps 20:9; 28:9; 86:2; and especially 118:25). *remnant.* See note on 6:9.

31:8 *the north country.* See 3:18 and note; 4:6 and note; 6:22; 16:15. *coasts of the earth.* See 6:22; 25:32. *blind . . . lame.* See Is 35:5–6 and notes; 42:16.

31:9 *with weeping.* Contrast Ps 126:5–6; Is 55:12. *will I lead them.* See Is 40:11; 48:21; contrast Is 20:4. *by the rivers of waters.* See Is 49:10; see also 41:18. *straight way.* See Is 40:3–4 and notes; 43:16,19. *I am a father to Israel.* See 3:4 and note; see also Deut 32:6; Is 63:16; 64:8. *firstborn.* Cf. v. 20; see Ex 4:22 and note; Hos 11:1–4.

31:10 *isles.* Remote areas to the west of Israel (see 2:10; 25:22 and note; 47:4; Ps 72:10; Is 41:1,5; 42:10,12; 49:1). *scattered Israel . . . keep him as a shepherd doth his flock.* See 23:1–3 and notes.

31:11 *redeemed.* See note on Ruth 2:20. As the Lord had redeemed His people from Egyptian slavery (see Ex 6:6; 15:13; Deut 7:8; 9:26), so now He would redeem their descendants from Babylonian exile (see Is 41:14 and note; 43:1 and note; 52:9). *from . . . him that was stronger than he.* See Ps 35:10.

12 Therefore they shall come and sing in
[a]the height of Zion,
And shall flow *together* to [b]the
goodness of the LORD,
For wheat, and for wine, and for oil,
And for the young of the flock and of
the herd:
And their soul shall be as a [c]watered
garden;
[d]And they shall not sorrow any more
at all.
13 Then shall the virgin rejoice in the
dance,
Both young men and old together:
For I will turn their mourning into joy,
And will comfort them, and make
them rejoice from their sorrow.
14 And I will satiate the soul of the priests
with fatness,
And my people shall be satisfied with
my goodness, saith the LORD.

15 Thus saith the LORD;
[a]A voice was heard in [b]Ramah,
Lamentation, *and* bitter weeping;
Rahel weeping for her children
Refused to be comforted for her
children, because [c]they *were* not.
16 Thus saith the LORD,
Refrain thy voice from weeping,
And thine eyes from tears:
For thy work shall be rewarded, saith
the LORD;
And [a]they shall come again from the
land of the enemy.
17 And there is hope in thine end, saith
the LORD,
That *thy* children shall come again to
their own border.

31:12 [a]Ezek. 17:23 [b]Hos. 3:5 [c]Is. 58:11 [d]Is. 35:10; 65:19; Rev. 21:4
31:15 [a]Mat. 2:17,18 [b]Josh. 18:25 [c]Gen. 42:13
31:16 [a]ver. 4,5; Ezra 1:5; Hos. 1:11
31:18 [a]Lam. 5:21
31:19 [a]Deut. 30:2
31:20 [1]Heb. *sound* [a]Deut. 32:36; Is. 63:15; Hos. 11:8 [b]Is. 57:18; Hos. 14:4
31:21 [a]ch. 50:5
31:22 [a]ch. 2:18,23,36 [b]ch. 3:6,8, 11, 12,14,22
31:23 [a]Ps. 122:5-8; Is. 1:26 [b]Zech. 8:3

18 I have surely heard Ephraim
bemoaning himself *thus;*
Thou hast chastised me, and I was
chastised,
As a bullock unaccustomed *to the yoke;*
[a]Turn thou me, and I shall be turned;
For thou *art* the LORD my God.
19 Surely [a]after that I was turned, I
repented;
And after that I was instructed, I smote
upon *my* thigh:
I was ashamed, yea, even confounded,
Because I did bear the reproach of my
youth.
20 *Is* Ephraim my dear son? *is he* a
pleasant child?
For since I spake against him, I do
earnestly remember him still:
[a]Therefore my bowels [1]are troubled
for him;
[b]I will surely have mercy upon him,
saith the LORD.
21 Set thee up waymarks, make thee high
heaps:
[a]Set thine heart toward the highway,
Even the way *which* thou wentest:
Turn again, O virgin of Israel,
Turn again to these thy cities.
22 How long wilt thou [a]go about, O thou
[b]backsliding daughter?
For the LORD hath created a new *thing*
in the earth,
A woman shall compass a man.
23 Thus saith the LORD of hosts, the God
of Israel;
As yet they shall use this speech in the
land of Judah and in the cities thereof,
When I shall bring again their captivity;
[a]The LORD bless thee, O habitation of
justice, *and* [b]mountain of holiness.

31:12 *height of Zion.* See note on 17:12. *goodness of the LORD.* Primarily material blessings (see v. 14; Hos 3:5). *wheat . . . wine . . . oil.* See note on Deut 7:13; see also Hos 2:8. *as a watered garden.* See Is 58:11 and note. *not sorrow any more.* See note on Is 25:8.
31:14 *fatness.* Either (1) a synonym for God's bounty (see Ps 36:8; 63:5; Is 55:2) or (2) a reference to the special portions of the sacrificial animal reserved for the priests (see Lev 7:31–36).
31:15 Quoted in Mat 2:18, where Herod's orders to kill all the male infants in Bethlehem and all its vicinity (Mat 2:16) are stated to be a fulfillment of this passage. *Ramah.* Located about five miles north of Jerusalem, it was one of the towns through which Jerusalem's people passed on their way to exile in Babylonia (see 40:1; cf. Is 10:29; Hos 5:8). *Rahel.* I.e. Rachel, Jacob's favorite wife (see Gen 29:30) and the grandmother of Ephraim and Manasseh (see Gen 30:22–24; 48:1–2), the two most prominent and powerful tribes in the northern kingdom. The name is used here to personify that kingdom (see note on v. 2).
31:16 *For thy work shall be rewarded.* Echoed in 2 Chr 15:7. Here the work is the bearing and raising of children.
31:17 *hope in thine end.* See 29:11. *children shall come again.* Cf. Hos 11:10–11.
31:18–19 *Turn thou me . . . I shall be turned . . . was turned.* The same Hebrew root underlies all three phrases (see 8:4–5 and notes).
31:18 *As a bullock unaccustomed to the yoke.* The same figure of speech is used in Hos 4:16; 10:11.
31:19 *smote upon my thigh.* A gesture of mourning and grief (see Ezek 21:12). Similar expressions are found in other ancient literature, such as the Babylonian *Descent of Ishtar,* verse 21; Homer, *Iliad,* 15.397–398; 16.125; *Odyssey,* 13.198–199. *ashamed . . . confounded.* See Is 45:16. *youth.* Early history (see 2:2; 3:24–25; 22:21; 32:30; Is 54:4; Ezek 16:22).
31:20 *pleasant child.* Cf. Is 5:7. *Therefore . . . I will surely have mercy upon him.* See Hos 11:1–4,8–9. *my bowels are troubled.* Or, "my heart yearns." See Is 16:11.
31:21 The departing exiles are advised to set up markers along their path to exile so that in due time they will be able to find their way back to Judah. *waymarks.* Tombstone-shaped markers (see 2 Ki 23:17; Ezek 39:15). *virgin of Israel.* See v. 4; see also 14:17 and note.
31:22 *backsliding daughter.* The people of Judah are apostate (see 3:14,22). *created a new thing.* See Is 42:9 and note. *compass.* Embrace with tender and unfailing love (see Ps 32:7,10; see also Ps 26:6). Judah would someday return to the Lord and love Him without reservation.
31:23 *bring again their captivity.* See note on 29:14. *The LORD bless thee.* See Ps 128:5; 134:3. *habitation of justice.* Jerusalem (cf. Is 1:21,26). *mountain of holiness.* The temple hill (see Ps 2:6; 48:1–2; Is 2:2–3; 11:9; 27:13; 66:20).

24 And there shall dwell in Judah itself,
And [a]*in* all the cities thereof together,
Husbandmen, and they *that* go forth
with flocks.
25 For I have satiated the weary soul,
And I have replenished every sorrowful
soul.
26 Upon this I awaked, and beheld;
And my sleep was sweet unto me.
27 Behold, the days come, saith the LORD,
That [a]I will sow the house of Israel and
the house of Judah
With the seed of man, and *with* the
seed of beast.
28 And it shall come to pass, *that* like as I
have [a]watched over them,
[b]To pluck up, and to break down, and
to throw down,
And to destroy, and to afflict;
So will I watch over them, [c]to build,
and to plant, saith the LORD.
29 [a]In those days they shall say no more,
The fathers have eaten a sour grape,
And the children's teeth are set on
edge.
30 [a]But every one shall die for his own
iniquity:
Every man that eateth the sour grape,
His teeth shall be set on edge.
31 Behold, the [a]days come, saith the LORD,
That I will make a new covenant
With the house of Israel, and with the
house of Judah:
32 Not according to the covenant that I
made with their fathers
In the day *that* [a]I took them by the
hand,
To bring them out of the land of Egypt;
Which my covenant they brake,
[1]Although I was a husband unto them,
saith the LORD:
33 [a]But this *shall be* the covenant that I
will make with the house of Israel;
After those days, saith the LORD,
[b]I will put my law in their inward
parts,
And write it in their hearts;
[c]And will be their God,
And they shall be my people.
34 And they shall teach no more every
man his neighbour, and every man
his brother, saying,
Know the LORD:
For [a]they shall all know me,
From the least of them unto the
greatest of them, saith the LORD:
For [b]I will forgive their iniquity,
And I will remember their sin no more.

35 Thus saith the LORD, [a]which giveth the
sun for a light by day,
And the ordinances of the moon and of
the stars for a light by night,

31:24 [a]ch. 33:12
31:27 [a]Ezek. 36:9-11
31:28 [a]ch. 44:27 [b]ch. 1:10; 18:7 [c]ch. 24:6
31:29 [a]Ezek. 18:2,3
31:30 [a]Gal. 6:5,7
31:31 [a]ch. 32:40; 33:14; Ezek. 37:26; Heb. 8:8-12; 10:16,17
31:32 [1]Or, *Should I have continued a husband unto them?* [a]Deut. 1:31
31:33 [a]ch. 32:40 [b]Ps. 40:8; Ezek. 11:19; 36:26,27 [c]ch. 24:7; 30:22; 32:38
31:34 [a]Is. 54:13; John 6:45; 1 Cor. 2:10; 1 John 2:20 [b]ch. 33:8; 50:20; Mic. 7:18; Acts 10:43; 13:39; Rom. 11:27
31:35 [a]Gen. 1:16; Ps. 72:5,17; 89:2,36; 119:91

31:26 *I awaked.* Jeremiah had evidently received the previous divine revelation (beginning in 30:3) in a dream (for similar examples see Dan 10:9; Zech 4:1). *sleep was sweet.* See Prov 3:24.
31:27 *sow . . . seed.* See Ezek 36:8–11. The same Hebrew root underlies both words. *Israel and . . . Judah.* North and south would again be united (see 3:18 and note.)
31:28 *watched . . . watch.* See note on 1:12. *pluck up . . . break down . . . throw down . . . , to destroy . . . build . . . plant.* See note on 1:10.
31:29 *The fathers . . . set on edge.* Repeated in Ezek 18:2. This was apparently a popular proverb that originated in a misunderstanding of such passages as Ex 20:5 and Num 14:18, which teach that a man's sins can have a negative effect on his descendants. In the time of Jeremiah and Ezekiel, many people felt that God's hand of judgment against them was due not to their own sins, but to the sins of their ancestors.
31:30 *every one shall die for his own iniquity.* See Deut 24:16; Ezek 18:3,20; 33:7–18. Although group or collective responsibility is an important concept, Jeremiah and Ezekiel emphasize individual responsibility as both preparation and explanation for the imminent destruction of Jerusalem, which the people might have been tempted to blame on the sins of their forefathers.
31:31–34 The high point of Jeremiah's prophecies, this passage is the longest sequence of OT verses to be quoted in its entirety in the NT (see note on Heb 8:8–12; see also Heb 10:16–17). Verse 31 contains the only OT use of the phrase "new covenant," which (together with its NT echoes) has come down to us (via Latin) as "new testament," the name that would later be applied to the distinctively Christian part of the Biblical canon.
31:31 *the days come.* See vv. 27,38. The phrase often refers to the Messianic era. *make.* Lit. "cut" (see notes on 34:18; Gen 15:18). *new covenant.* See note on vv. 31–34; see also 1 Cor 11:25; 2 Cor 3:6; Heb 9:15; 12:24; and note on Mark 14:24. As the old covenant was solemnized by the blood of sacrificial animals, so the new would be solemnized by the blood of Christ. *house of Israel . . . house of Judah.* The reunited people of God (see 3:18 and note).
31:32 *covenant that I made with their fathers.* See 7:23; 11:1–8; Ex 19:5; 20:22–23:19 and notes. The covenant at Sinai eventually became known as the "old covenant" (2 Cor 3:14) or "first covenant" (Heb 8:7; 9:15,18). *took them by the hand.* See Hos 11:3–4. *Which my covenant they brake.* See 11:10. The people, not God, were responsible for violating His covenant (see note on Is 24:5). *I was a husband.* See 3:14 and note.
31:33 *house of Israel.* Here includes both Israel and Judah (see v. 31 and note on 3:18). *put my law in their inward parts.* Internally (see Deut 6:6; 11:18; 30:14; Ezek 11:19; 18:31; 36:26–27), in contrast to setting it before them externally (see 9:13; Deut 4:8; 11:32). *write it in their hearts.* So that it effectively governs their lives, in contrast to the ineffectiveness of merely presenting it in writing, though inscribed on durable stone (see Ex 24:4; 31:18; 32:15–16; 34:28–29; Deut 4:13; 5:22; 9:9,11; 10:4). *their God . . . my people.* See note on 7:23. The "new" covenant does not abolish the "old" but supersedes it in the sense that through the new covenant the old is fulfilled and its purpose achieved.
31:34 *teach no more . . . his neighbour.* When the Lord has done His new work, there will no longer be among His people those who are ignorant of Him and His will for human lives. True knowledge of the Lord will be shared by all—young and old, the peasant and the powerful (see 5:4–5 and notes; see also 32:38–40; Is 54:13 and note; Ezek 11:19–20; 36:25–27; Eph 3:12; Heb 4:16; 10:19–22). *Know.* In the experiential, not the academic, sense (see Ex 6:3 and note). *I will forgive their inquity.* The glorious basis of the new covenant (see Heb 10:14–17).
31:35 *giveth the sun . . . moon . . . stars.* See Gen 1:16–18 and

Which divideth [b]the sea when the
waves thereof roar;
[c]The LORD of hosts *is* his name:
36 [a]If those ordinances depart from before
me, saith the LORD,
Then the seed of Israel also shall cease
From being a nation before me for ever.
37 Thus saith the LORD;
[a]If heaven above can be measured,
And the foundations of the earth
searched out beneath,
I will also cast off all the seed of Israel
For all that they have done, saith the
LORD.
38 Behold, the days come, saith the LORD,
That the city shall be built to the LORD
[a]From the tower of Hananeel unto the
gate of the corner.
39 And [a]the measuring line shall yet go
forth over against it
Upon the hill Gareb, and shall compass
about to Goath.
40 And the whole valley of the dead
bodies, and of the ashes,
And all the fields unto the brook of
Kidron,
[a]Unto the corner of the horse gate
towards the east,
[b]*Shall be* holy unto the LORD;
It shall not be plucked up, nor thrown
down any more for ever.

Jeremiah buys a field

32 The word that came to Jeremiah
from the LORD [a]in the tenth year of
Zedekiah king of Judah, which *was* the eighteenth year of Nebuchadrezzar.
2 For then the king of Babylon's army besieged Jerusalem: and Jeremiah the prophet
was shut up [a]in the court of the prison, which
was in the king of Judah's house.
3 For Zedekiah king of Judah had shut him
up, saying, Wherefore dost thou prophesy, and
say, Thus saith the LORD, [a]Behold, I *will* give
this city into the hand of the king of Babylon,
and he shall take it;
4 And Zedekiah king of Judah [a]shall not escape out of the hand of the Chaldeans, but shall
surely be delivered into the hand of the king of
Babylon, and shall speak with him mouth to
mouth, and his eyes shall behold his eyes;
5 And he shall lead Zedekiah *to* Babylon,
and there shall he be [a]until I visit him, saith
the LORD: [b]though ye fight with the Chaldeans, ye shall not prosper.

6 ¶ And Jeremiah said, The word of the
LORD came unto me, saying,
7 Behold, Hanameel the son of Shallum
thine uncle *shall* come unto thee, saying, Buy
thee my field that *is* in Anathoth: for the [a]right
of redemption *is* thine to buy *it.*
8 So Hanameel mine uncle's son came to
me in the court of the prison according to the
word of the LORD, and said unto me, Buy my
field, I pray thee, that *is* in Anathoth, which *is*
in the country of Benjamin: for the right of inheritance *is* thine, and the redemption *is*
thine; buy *it* for thyself. Then I knew that this
was the word of the LORD.
9 And I bought the field of Hanameel my
uncle's son, that *was* in Anathoth, and
[a]weighed him the money, *even* [1]seventeen
shekels of silver.
10 And I [1]subscribed the evidence, and
sealed *it,* and took witnesses, and weighed
him the money in the balances.
11 So I took the evidence of the purchase,

31:35 [b]Is. 51:15 [c]ch. 10:16
31:36 [a]Ps. 148:6; Is. 54:9,10; ch. 33:20
31:37 [a]ch. 33:22
31:38 [a]Neh. 3:1; Zech. 14:10
31:39 [a]Ezek. 40:8; Zech. 2:1
31:40 [a]2 Chr. 23:15; Neh. 3:28 [b]Joel 3:17
32:1 [a]2 Ki. 25:1; ch. 39:1
32:2 [a]Neh. 3:25; ch. 33:1; 37:21; 39:14
32:3 [a]ch. 34:2
32:4 [a]ch. 34:3; 38:18,23; 39:5; 52:9
32:5 [a]ch. 27:22 [b]ch. 21:4; 33:5
32:7 [a]Lev. 25:24,25,32; Ruth 4:4
32:9 [1]Or, *seven shekels and ten pieces of silver* [a]Gen. 23:16; Zech. 11:12
32:10 [1]Heb. *wrote in the book*

notes. *Which divideth the sea . . . is his name.* The same line is found in Is 51:15 (see Ps 46:3; Is 17:12).
31:36 See 33:20–21,25–26. Just as God's creation order is established and secure, so also Israel will always have descendants.
31:37 *cast off all.* Israel will continue to exist, even though a terrible judgment is about to sweep the kingdom of Judah away.
31:38–40 See Zech 14:10–11.
31:38 *the city.* Jerusalem. *tower of Hananeel . . . gate of the corner.* The eastern and western ends of the northern wall (see note on Zech 14:10).
31:39 *measuring line.* Mentioned in connection with restored Jerusalem also in Ezek 40:3; Zech 1:16; 2:1. *Gareb . . . Goath.* Exact locations unknown, but probably to the west of Jerusalem.
31:40 *valley.* Probably the Hinnom Valley (see 2:23 and note). *horse gate.* See note on Neh 3:28. *holy unto the LORD.* See Zech 14:20 and note. *plucked up, nor thrown down.* See note on 1:10.
32:1–44 Though with some reluctance (see v. 25), Jeremiah obeys the Lord's command to buy a field in Anathoth from his cousin (see vv. 8–9) even as the Babylonians are besieging Jerusalem (see vv. 2,24).
32:1 *tenth year of Zedekiah . . . eighteenth year of Nebuchadrezzar.* 587 B.C., the year before Jerusalem was destroyed by the Babylonians (see 52:12–13). The siege began in 588 (see 39:1; 52:4).
32:2 *shut up in the court of the prison.* See Neh 3:25 and note. Jeremiah was imprisoned by King Zedekiah (see 37:21) and remained in the courtyard of the guard until Jerusalem fell (see 38:13,28; 39:14).
32:3–5 See 21:3–7; 34:2–5; 37:17. The fulfillment is recorded in 52:7–14.
32:5 *until I visit him.* After his capture by the Babylonians, Zedekiah was taken to Babylon, where he eventually died (see 52:11). *ye shall not prosper.* See note on 29:4.
32:7 *Anathoth.* Jeremiah's hometown (see note on 1:1). *the right of redemption is thine.* In accordance with the ancient law of redemption (see Lev 25:23–25; see also notes on Ruth 2:20; 4:3).
‡32:8 *came to me in the court.* Though imprisoned, Jeremiah was allowed to have visitors.
32:9 *I bought.* In obedience to the Lord's command (see v. 7). *weighed him the money.* Coinage had not yet been invented. *seventeen shekels of silver.* About 7 ounces of silver. The size of the field is unknown, but the price was probably not exorbitant (contrast Gen 23:15; see note there).
32:10 *sealed.* Not to attest his signature (as, e.g., in Esth 3:12; see note on Gen 38:18) but to guarantee the contents of the deed and keep it from being tampered with (see Is 8:16; 29:11; Dan 12:4,9; Rev 15:1–5).
32:11 *that which was open.* For ready reference, the authenticity of which would then be guaranteed by the sealed copy if

both that which was sealed *according to* the
law and custom, and that which was open:
12 And I gave the evidence of the purchase
unto [a]Baruch the son of Neriah, the son of Maaseiah, in the sight of Hanameel mine uncle's
son, and in the presence of the [b]witnesses
that subscribed the book of the purchase, before all the Jews that sat in the court of the
prison.
13 And I charged Baruch before them, saying,
14 Thus saith the LORD of hosts, the God of
Israel; Take these evidences, this evidence of
the purchase, both which is sealed, and this
evidence which is open; and put them in an
earthen vessel, that they may continue many
days.
15 For thus saith the LORD of hosts, the
God of Israel; Houses and fields and vineyards
[a]shall be possessed again in this land.
16 ¶ Now when I had delivered the evidence of the purchase unto Baruch the son of
Neriah, I prayed unto the LORD, saying,
17 Ah Lord GOD! behold, [a]thou hast made
the heaven and the earth by thy great power
and stretched out arm, *and* [b]there is nothing
[1]too hard for thee:
18 Thou shewest [a]lovingkindness unto
thousands, and recompensest the iniquity of
the fathers into the bosom of their children after them: the Great, [b]the Mighty God, [c]the
LORD of hosts, *is* his name,
19 [a]Great in counsel, and mighty in
[1]work: for thine [b]eyes *are* open upon all the
ways of the sons of men: [c]to give every one according to his ways, and according to the fruit
of his doings:
20 Which hast set signs and wonders in
the land of Egypt, *even* unto this day, and in Israel, and amongst *other* men; and hast made
thee [a]a name, as *at* this day;
21 And [a]hast brought forth thy people Israel out of the land of Egypt with signs, and with
wonders, and with a strong hand, and with a
stretched out arm, and with great terror;
22 And hast given them this land, which
thou didst swear to their fathers to give them,
[a]a land flowing with milk and honey;
23 And they came in, and possessed it; but
[a]they obeyed not thy voice, neither walked in
thy law; they have done nothing of all that
thou commandedst them to do: therefore thou
hast caused all this evil to come upon them:
24 Behold the [a][1]mounts, they are come
unto the city to take it; and the city [b]is given
into the hand of the Chaldeans, that fight
against it, because of [c]the sword, and *of* the
famine, and *of* the pestilence: and what thou
hast spoken is come to pass; and behold, thou
seest *it.*
25 And thou hast said unto me, O Lord
GOD, Buy thee the field for money, and take
witnesses; [1]for [a]the city is given into the hand
of the Chaldeans.
26 ¶ Then came the word of the LORD unto
Jeremiah, saying,
27 Behold, I *am* the LORD, the [a]God of all
flesh: [b]is there any thing too hard for me?
28 Therefore thus saith the LORD; Behold,
[a]I *will* give this city into the hand of the
Chaldeans, and into the hand of Nebuchadrezzar king of Babylon, and he shall take it:
29 And the Chaldeans, that fight against
this city, shall come and [a]set fire on this city,
and burn it with the houses, [b]upon whose
roofs they have offered incense unto Baal, and
poured out drink offerings unto other gods, to
provoke me to anger.

32:12 [a]ch. 36:4 [b]See Is. 8:2
32:15 [a]ver. 37,43
32:17 [1]Or, *hid from thee* [a]2 Ki. 19:15 [b]ver. 27; Gen. 18:14; Luke 1:37
32:18 [a]Ex. 20:6; 34:7; Deut. 5:9,10 [b]Is. 9:6 [c]ch. 10:16
32:19 [1]Heb. *doing* [a]Is. 28:29 [b]Job 34:21; Ps. 33:13; Prov. 5:21; ch. 16:17 [c]ch. 17:10
32:20 [a]Ex. 9:16; 1 Chr. 17:21; Is. 63:12; Dan. 9:15
32:21 [a]Ex. 6:6; 2 Sam. 7:23; 1 Chr. 17:21; Ps. 136:11,12
32:22 [a]Ex. 3:8,17; ch. 11:5
32:23 [a]Neh. 9:26; ch. 11:8; Dan. 9:10-14
32:24 [1]Or, *engines of shot* [a]ch. 33:4 [b]ver. 25,36 [c]ch. 14:12
32:25 [1][Or, *though*] [a]ver. 24
32:27 [a]Num. 16:22 [b]ver. 17
32:28 [a]ver. 3
32:29 [a]ch. 21:10; 37:8,10; 52:13 [b]ch. 19:13

the unsealed deed should be lost, damaged or changed (deliberately or otherwise). Examples of tied and sealed papyrus documents of the fifth and subsequent centuries B.C. have been found at Elephantine in southern Egypt, in the desert of Judah west of the Dead Sea, and elsewhere (see chart, p. xix).

32:12 *Baruch.* Means "blessed (by the Lord)." He was Jeremiah's faithful secretary and friend (see Introduction: Author and Date).

32:14 *put them in an earthen vessel, that they may continue many days.* Documents found in clay jars at Elephantine (see note on v. 11) and Qumran (west of the Dead Sea) were preserved almost intact for more than 2,000 years (see essay, p. 1346).

32:15 Jeremiah's deed of purchase would enable him (or his heirs) to reclaim the field as soon as normal economic activity resumed after the exile.

32:17 See 27:5. *great power and stretched out arm.* See v. 21; see also note on 21:5. *nothing too hard for thee.* See note on Gen 18:14. The Lord's reply to Jeremiah echoes these words (see v. 27).

32:18 *shewest lovingkindess unto thousands . . . recompensest the iniquity of the fathers.* See Ex 20:5–6; 34:7; see also note on Ex 20:6. *recompensest . . . into the bosom.* A symbol of retribution (see Ps 79:12; Is 65:6–7; cf. Luke 6:38). *the Great, the Mighty God.* See Deut 10:17. *LORD of hosts, is his name.* See 31:35; Is 54:5; Amos 4:13.

32:19 *Great in counsel, and mighty in work.* See Ps 66:5; Is 9:6; 28:29. *to give to every one according to . . . his ways.* The Hebrew is repeated verbatim from 17:10 (see note there; see also 1 Cor 3:8; Eph 6:8).

32:20 *signs and wonders.* See v. 21; Ex 7:3; see also notes on Ex 3:12; 4:8. *at this day.* See 11:7.

32:21 Repeated almost verbatim from Deut 26:8 (see Deut 4:34). *strong hand . . . stretched out arm.* See v. 17 and note on 21:5. *great terror.* See Ex 15:14–16.

32:22 *land flowing with milk and honey.* See 11:5; see also note on Ex 3:8.

32:24 *the mounts.* See 6:6; 33:4; see also note on Is 37:33. *sword . . . famine . . . pestilence.* See note on 14:12.

32:25 Jeremiah expresses his doubts concerning what must seem to him to be an unwise investment. Nevertheless, he remains the obedient servant (see vv. 8–9).

32:27 *the LORD, the God of all flesh.* Echoes Num 16:22; 27:16, emphasizing God's universal dominion. *is there any thing too hard for me?* Responds to the description in Jeremiah's prayer (see v. 17 and note on Gen 18:14), stressing God's omnipotence. God is worthy of obedience because He is always faithful in fulfilling His promises.

32:29 *burn it.* See 21:10; 34:2; 37:8. *offered incense unto Baal.* See 1:16 and note. *upon whose roofs.* See note on 19:13. *drink offerings unto other gods.* See 7:18 and note; 19:13. *provoke me to anger.* See 7:18; Deut 31:29.

30 For the children of Israel and the children of Judah [a]have only done evil before me
from their youth: for the children of Israel
have only provoked me to anger with the work
of their hands, saith the LORD.
31 For this city hath been to me *as* [1]a
provocation of mine anger and of my fury from
the day that they built it even unto this day;
[a]that *I* should remove it from before my face,
32 Because of all the evil of the children of
Israel and of the children of Judah, which they
have done to provoke me to anger, [a]they, their
kings, their princes, their priests, and their
prophets, and the men of Judah, and the inhabitants of Jerusalem.
33 And they have turned unto me the
[a][1]back, and not the face: though *I* taught
them, [b]rising up early and teaching *them,* yet
they have not hearkened to receive instruction.
34 But they [a]set their abominations in the
house, which is called by my name, to defile
it.
35 And they built the high places of Baal,
which *are* in the valley of the son of Hinnom,
to [a]cause their sons and their daughters to
pass through *the fire* unto [b]Molech; [c]which I
commanded them not, neither came it into my
mind, that *they* should do this abomination, to
cause Judah to sin.
36 ¶ And now therefore thus saith the
LORD, the God of Israel, concerning this city,
whereof ye say, [a]It shall be delivered into the
hand of the king of Babylon by the sword, and
by the famine, and by the pestilence;
37 Behold, I *will* [a]gather them out of all
countries, whither I have driven them in mine
anger, and in my fury, and in great wrath; and
I will bring them again unto this place, and I
will cause them [b]to dwell safely:
38 And they shall be [a]my people, and I will
be their God:
39 And I will [a]give them one heart, and one
way, that *they* may fear me [1]for ever, for the
good of them, and of their children after them:
40 And [a]I will make an everlasting covenant with them, that I will not turn away
[1]from them, to do them good; but [b]I will put
my fear in their hearts, that *they* shall not depart from me.
41 Yea, [a]I will rejoice over them to do
them good, and [b]I will plant them in this land
[1]assuredly with my whole heart and with my
whole soul.
42 For thus saith the LORD; [a]Like as I have
brought all this great evil upon this people, so
will I bring upon them all the good that I have
promised them.
43 And [a]fields shall be bought in this land,
[b]whereof ye say, *It is* desolate without man or
beast; it is given into the hand of the
Chaldeans.
44 *Men* shall buy fields for money, and subscribe evidences, and seal *them,* and take witnesses in [a]the land of Benjamin, and in the
places about Jerusalem, and in the cities of Judah, and in the cities of the mountains, and in
the cities of the valley, and in the cities of the
south: for [b]I will cause their captivity to return, saith the LORD.

Promise of restoration

33 Moreover the word of the LORD came
unto Jeremiah the second time,
while he was yet [a]shut up in the court of the
prison, saying,
2 Thus saith the LORD the [a]maker thereof,
the LORD that formed it, to establish it; [b][1]the
LORD *is* his name;
3 [a]Call unto me, and I will answer thee,

32:30 [a]ch. 2:7; 3:25; 7:22-26; Ezek. 20:28
32:31 [1]Heb. *for my anger* [a]2 Ki. 24:3
32:32 [a]Is. 1:4,6; Dan. 9:8
32:33 [1]Heb. *neck* [a]ch. 2:27; 7:24 [b]ch. 7:13
32:34 [a]ch. 23:11; Ezek. 8:5,6
32:35 [a]ch. 7:31; 19:5 [b]Lev. 18:21; 1 Ki. 11:33 [c]ch. 7:31
32:36 [a]ver. 24
32:37 [a]Deut. 30:3; ch. 23:3; 29:14; Ezek. 37:21 [b]ch. 33:16
32:38 [a]ch. 24:7; 30:22; 31:33
32:39 [1]Heb. *all days* [a]ch. 24:7; Ezek. 11:19
32:40 [1]Heb. *from after them* [a]Is. 55:3; ch. 31:31 [b]ch. 31:33
32:41 [1]Heb. *in truth,* or, *stability* [a]Deut. 30:9; Zeph. 3:17 [b]ch. 24:6; 31:28; Amos 9:15
32:42 [a]ch. 31:28
32:43 [a]ver. 15 [b]ch. 33:10
32:44 [a]ch. 17:26 [b]ch. 33:7,11
33:1 [a]ch. 32:2,3
33:2 [1][Or, *JEHOVAH*] [a]Is. 37:26 [b]Ex. 15:3; Amos 5:8; 9:6
33:3 [a]Ps. 91:15; ch. 29:12

32:30 Echoes Deut 31:29. *youth.* See note on 31:19. *the work of their hands.* A reference to idols.
32:31 *remove it from before my face.* See 52:3; 2 Ki 24:3.
32:32 *kings . . . princes . . . priests . . . prophets.* See 1:18 and note.
32:33 *rising . . . teaching.* See note on 7:13. *not . . . receive instruction.* See 2:30; 5:3; 7:28; 17:23.
32:34–35 Repeated from 7:30–31 (see notes there).
32:35 *Molech.* The god of the Ammonites (see 49:1,3; see also note on Lev 18:21).
32:36 *now therefore.* After judgment on the wicked comes restoration for the righteous. *ye.* The pronoun is plural, referring to the people of Judah as a whole. *sword . . . famine . . . pestilence.* See note on 14:12.
32:37 See Deut 30:1–5. *mine anger . . . fury . . . great wrath.* See note on 21:5. *bring them again . . . dwell safely.* See Ezek 36:11,33; Hos 11:11. The Hebrew underlying the first phrase sounds like that underlying the second.
32:38 See 31:33; see also note on 7:23.
32:39 *one heart.* See 24:7; 31:32 and note; Ezek 11:19. *their children after them.* See Deut 4:9–10.
32:40 *everlasting covenant.* See Is 55:3 and note; Ezek 16:60; 37:26. Unlike the old covenant (see 31:32; Is 24:5), the new covenant would never be broken. *put my fear in their hearts.* See Deut 6:24; see also note on Gen 20:11. *shall not depart from me.* See 26:3; Is 53:6.
32:41 *rejoice . . . to do them good.* See Deut 30:9; Is 62:5; 65:19.
32:43–44 *fields shall be bought.* The field purchased by Jeremiah (see v. 9) is symbolic of the many fields that will be purchased in Judah after the Babylonian exile, when economic conditions return to normal (see note on v. 15).
32:43 *ye.* See note on v. 36. *desolate without man or beast.* See 4:23–26 and notes.
32:44 *land of Benjamin.* See 1:1. Here Benjamin is mentioned first because it was the region in which Jeremiah's hometown was located (see vv. 7–8 and notes). *mountains . . . valley.* See note on Deut 1:7. south. See note on Gen 12:9. *cause their captivity to return.* See note on 29:14.
33:1–26 Concluding Jeremiah's "book of consolation" (see note on 30:1–33:26), the section is divided into two roughly equal parts: (1) vv. 1–13, which continue and build on ch. 32, and (2) vv. 14–26, which summarize a wider range of earlier passages in Jeremiah and elsewhere—they are not found in the Septuagint (the Greek translation of the OT).
33:1 *the second time.* Ch. 32 comprises the first time. *yet shut up.* In 587 B.C. (see note on 32:1). *court of the prison.* See 32:2 and note.
33:2 See 10:12; 32:17; 51:15; see also 31:35 and note.
‡33:3 *call . . . and I will answer.* Man's prayer invites—and assures—God's response (see Ps 3:4; 4:3; 18:6; 27:7; 28:1–2; 30:8;

and shew thee great and [b] [1] mighty *things*, which thou knowest not.

4 For thus saith the LORD, the God of Israel, concerning the houses of this city, and concerning the houses of the kings of Judah, which are thrown down by [a] the mounts, and by the sword;

5 [a] They come to fight with the Chaldeans, but *it is* to fill them with the dead bodies of men, whom I have slain in mine anger and in my fury, and for all whose wickedness I have hid my face from this city.

6 Behold, [a] I *will* bring it health and cure, and I will cure them, and will reveal unto them the abundance of peace and truth.

7 And [a] I will cause the captivity of Judah and the captivity of Israel to return, and will build them, [b] as at the first.

8 And I will [a] cleanse them from all their iniquity, whereby they have sinned against me, and I will [b] pardon all their iniquities, whereby they have sinned, and whereby they have transgressed against me.

9 [a] And it shall be to me a name of joy, a praise and an honour before all the nations of the earth, which shall hear all the good that I do unto them: and they shall [b] fear and tremble for all the goodness and for all the prosperity that I procure unto it.

10 Thus saith the LORD; Again there shall be heard in this place, [a] which ye say *shall be* desolate without man and without beast, *even* in the cities of Judah, and in the streets of Jerusalem, that are desolate, without man, and without inhabitant, and without beast,

11 The [a] voice of joy, and the voice of gladness, the voice of the bridegroom, and the voice of the bride, the voice of them that shall say, [b] Praise the LORD of hosts: for the LORD *is* good; for his mercy *endureth* for ever: *and* of them that shall bring [c] the sacrifice of praise *into* the house of the LORD. For [d] I will cause to return the captivity of the land as at the first, saith the LORD.

12 Thus saith the LORD of hosts, [a] Again in this place, *which is* desolate without man and without beast, and in all the cities thereof, shall be a habitation of shepherds causing *their* flocks to lie down.

13 [a] In the cities of the mountains, in the cities of the vale, and in the cities of the south, and in the land of Benjamin, and in the places about Jerusalem, and in the cities of Judah, shall the flocks [b] pass again under the hands of him that telleth *them*, saith the LORD.

14 ¶ [a] Behold, the days come, saith the LORD, that [b] I will perform *that* good thing which I have promised unto the house of Israel and to the house of Judah.

15 In those days, and at that time, will I cause the [a] Branch of righteousness to grow up unto David; and he shall execute judgment and righteousness in the land.

16 In those days shall Judah be saved, and Jerusalem shall dwell safely: and this *is the name* wherewith she shall be called, [1] The LORD our righteousness.

17 For thus saith the LORD; [1] David shall never [a] want a man to sit upon the throne of the house of Israel;

18 Neither shall the priests the Levites want a man before me to [a] offer burnt offerings, and to kindle meat offerings, and to do sacrifice continually.

33:3 [1] Or, *hidden* [b] Is. 48:6
33:4 [a] ch. 32:24
33:5 [a] ch. 32:5
33:6 [a] ch. 30:17
33:7 [a] ch. 30:3; 32:44 [b] Is. 1:26; ch. 24:6; 30:20; 31:4,28; 42:10
33:8 [a] Ezek. 36:25; Zech. 13:1; Heb. 9:13,14 [b] ch. 31:34; Mic. 7:18
33:9 [a] Is. 62:7; ch. 13:11 [b] Is. 60:5
33:10 [a] ch. 32:43
33:11 [a] ch. 7:34; 16:9; 25:10; Rev. 18:23
33:11 [b] 1 Chr. 16:8; 2 Chr. 5:13; Ezra 3:11; Ps. 136:1; Is. 12:4 [c] Lev. 7:12; Ps. 107:22; 116:17 [d] ver. 7
33:12 [a] Is. 65:10; ch. 31:24; 50:19
33:13 [a] ch. 17:26; 32:44 [b] Lev. 27:32
33:14 [a] ch. 23:5; 31:27,31 [b] ch. 29:10
33:15 [a] Is. 4:2; 11:1; ch. 23:5
33:16 [1] Heb. *Jehovah-tsidkenu*
33:17 [1] Heb. *There shall not be cut off from David* [a] 2 Sam. 7:16; 1 Ki. 2:4; Ps. 89:29; Luke 1:32
33:18 [a] Rom. 12:1; 15:16; 1 Pet. 2:5,9; Rev. 1:6

55:17; Mat 7:7; contrast 11:14). *great and mighty.* The Hebrew for this phrase usually refers to the formidable cities of Canaan and is translated "great and walled up to heaven" (Deut 1:28; see Num 13:28; Deut 9:1; Josh 14:12). *mighty things, which thou knowest not.* The Hebrew (with the change of one letter) for this phrase echoes Is 48:6: "hidden things, and thou didst not know them." As the rest of ch. 33 demonstrates, the Lord will first judge His people (vv. 4–5) and then restore them in ways that will be nothing short of incredible (vv. 6–26).

33:4 Jerusalem's houses—including those of the king—were torn down so that their stones could be used to repair the city's battered walls (see Is 22:10 and note). *the mounts.* To help the invaders bring up battering rams and scale Jerusalem's walls (see 6:6).

33:5 *fight with the Chaldeans.* See 32:5. *dead bodies.* Of Jerusalem's defenders.

33:6 *health and cure.* See 30:17; contrast 8:22.

33:7 *I will cause the captivity . . . to return.* See vv. 11,26; see also note on 29:14. *Judah and . . . Israel.* See note on 3:18.

33:8 *pardon all their iniquities.* The basis of the institution of the new covenant (see 31:34 and note; see also 50:20; Ezek 36:25–26).

33:9 *tremble for all the goodness.* See Hos 3:5.

33:10 See 32:43 and note.

33:11 *voice of joy . . . voice of the bride.* The glorious reversal of the judgment proclaimed in 7:34; 16:9; 25:10. *that shall say, Praise the LORD.* See note on 17:26. *For I will cause to return the captivity.* See note on 29:14.

33:12 *shepherds causing their flocks to lie down.* See Ezek 20:37.

33:13 *the mountains . . . cities of Judah.* See 17:26 and note; 32:44.

33:15–16 Repeated from 23:5–6 (see notes there).

33:16 *she shall be called.* Because of Jerusalem's intimate relationship to the Messiah, it is given the same name by which He is called in 23:6 (for other examples see Judg 6:24; Ezek 48:35).

33:17–26 In the face of the impending judgment in which the nation will be swept away and the promised land reduced to a desolate wasteland, all God's past covenants with His people appear to be rendered of no effect—His covenants with Israel, with David and with Phinehas (see chart, p. 16). This series of oracles, however, gives reassurance that the ancient covenants are not being repudiated, that they are as secure as God's covenant concerning the creation order, and that in the future restoration they will all yet be fulfilled.

33:17 See 2 Sam 7:12–16; 1 Ki 2:4; 8:25; 9:5; 2 Chr 6:16; 7:18. This passage is fulfilled ultimately in Jesus (see Luke 1:32–33).

33:18 See Num 25:13. The priestly covenant with the Levites, like the royal covenant with David, was not a private grant to the priestly family involving only that family and the Lord. It was rather an integral part of the Lord's dealings with His people in which Israel was assured of the ministry of a priesthood that was acceptable to the Lord and through whose mediation they could enjoy communion with Him. That ministry was and is being fulfilled by Jesus, who administers a higher and better

19 ¶ And the word of the LORD came unto Jeremiah, saying,

20 Thus saith the LORD; [a]If you can break my covenant of the day, and my covenant of the night, and that there should not be day and night in their season;

21 *Then* may also [a]my covenant be broken with David my servant, that he should not have a son to reign upon his throne; and with the Levites the priests, my ministers.

22 As [a]the host of heaven cannot be numbered, neither the sand of the sea measured: so will I multiply the seed of David my servant, and the Levites that minister unto me.

23 ¶ Moreover the word of the LORD came to Jeremiah, saying,

24 Considerest thou not what this people have spoken, saying, [a]The two families which the LORD hath chosen, he hath even cast them off? thus they have despised my people, that *they* should be no more a nation before them.

25 Thus saith the LORD; If [a]my covenant *be* not with day and night, *and if* I have not [b]appointed the ordinances of heaven and earth;

26 [a]Then will I cast away the seed of Jacob, and David my servant, *so* that *I* will not take *any* of his seed *to be* rulers over the seed of Abraham, Isaac, and Jacob: for [b]I will cause their captivity to return, and have mercy on them.

Zedekiah's broken promise

34 The word which came unto Jeremiah from the LORD, [a]when Nebuchadnezzar king of Babylon, and all his army, and [b]all the kingdoms of the earth [1]of his dominion, and all the people, fought against Jerusalem, and against all the cities thereof, saying,

2 Thus saith the LORD, the God of Israel; Go and speak to Zedekiah king of Judah, and tell him, Thus saith the LORD; Behold, [a]I *will* give this city into the hand of the king of Babylon, and [b]he shall burn it with fire:

3 And [a]thou shalt not escape out of his hand, but shalt surely be taken, and delivered into his hand; and thine eyes shall behold the eyes of the king of Babylon, and [1]he shall speak with thee mouth to mouth, and thou shalt go *to* Babylon.

4 Yet hear the word of the LORD, O Zedekiah king of Judah; Thus saith the LORD of thee, Thou shalt not die by the sword:

5 *But* thou shalt die in peace: and with [a]the burnings of thy fathers, the former kings which were before thee, [b]so shall they burn *odours* for thee; and [c]they will lament thee, *saying,* Ah lord! for I have pronounced the word, saith the LORD.

6 Then Jeremiah the prophet spake all these words unto Zedekiah king of Judah in Jerusalem,

7 When the king of Babylon's army fought against Jerusalem, and against all the cities of Judah that were left, against Lachish, and against Azekah: for [a]these defenced cities remained of the cities of Judah.

8 ¶ *This is* the word that came unto Jeremi-

33:20 [a]ver. 25; Ps. 89:37; Is. 54:9; ch. 31:36
33:21 [a]Ps. 89:34
33:22 [a]Gen. 15:5
33:24 [a]ver. 21,22
33:25 [a]ver. 20; Gen. 8:22 [b]Ps. 74:16; 104:19; ch. 31:35,36
33:26 [a]ch. 31:37 [b]ver. 7,11; Ezra 2:1
34:1 [a]2 Ki. 25:1; ch. 39:1; 52:4

34:1 [1]Heb. *the dominion of his hand* [b]ch. 1:15
34:2 [a]ch. 21:10; 32:3,28 [b]ver. 22; ch. 32:29
34:3 [1]Heb. *his mouth shall speak to thy mouth* [a]ch. 32:4
34:5 [a]2 Chr. 16:14; 21:19 [b]Dan. 2:46 [c]See ch. 22:18
34:7 [a]2 Ki. 18:13; 19:8; 2 Chr. 11:5,9

priesthood (see Ps 110:4; Heb 5:6–10; 6:19–20; 7:11–25). *the priests the Levites.* See Deut 17:9,18.

33:20 *covenant of the day, and . . . the night.* See v. 25; 31:35–36. Although reference may be to God's sovereign establishment of the creation order in the beginning, more likely the covenant of Gen 9:8–17 (see Gen 8:22) is in view.

33:21 *covenant . . . with the Levites the priests.* See Mal 2:4.

33:22 In words that echo the covenant promises to the patriarchs (Abraham, Gen 22:17; Isaac, Gen 26:4; Jacob, Gen 32:12), the Lord assures the flourishing of the two mediatorial (royal and priestly) families and thus the continuation of this ministry in the spiritual commonwealth He has established with His people. This promise of a numerous progeny to both the royal and priestly families is no doubt fulfilled in that great throng who (will) reign with Christ (see Rom 5:17; 8:17; 1 Cor 6:3; 2 Tim 2:12; Rev 3:21; 5:10; 20:5–6; 22:5; see also Mat 19:28; Luke 22:30) and who in Christ have been consecrated to be priests (see 1 Pet 2:5,9; Rev 1:6; 5:10; 20:6; see also Is 66:21; Rom 6:13; 12:1; 15:16; Eph 5:2; Phil 4:18; Heb 13:15–16).

33:24 *two families.* Israel and Judah. But because of the use of the word "families" instead of "kingdoms," the reference may be to the two mediatorial (royal and priestly) families, or to the families of Jacob and David (see v. 26). *the LORD hath chosen.* See Amos 3:2 and note.

33:25–26 See v. 20 and note.

33:26 *I will cause their captivity to return, . . . have mercy.* Echoes Deut 30:3; see note on 29:14.

34:1–35:19 The first major division of the book (chs. 2–35) now draws to a close. Jeremiah's warnings and exhortations to Judah are concluded with a historical appendix (chs. 34–35), a technique used to conclude the third major division of the book (chs. 39–45) as well (see note on 45:1–5). Ch. 52, written by someone other than Jeremiah, serves as a fitting historical appendix to the entire book.

34:1–22 The chapter divides naturally into two parts (vv. 1–7 and 8–22), each of which dates to 588 B.C. (see notes on vv. 7, 21–22).

34:1–7 Jeremiah's warning to King Zedekiah parallels the prophet's similar admonition in 21:1–10 (see notes there).

34:1 *kingdoms . . . of his dominion, and all the people.* Nebuchadnezzar's empire was vast (see Ezek 26:7; Dan 3:2–4; 4:1; cf. the similar description of the Medes in 51:28). *fought against Jerusalem.* Subject nations were expected to supply troops to fight alongside those of their overlord (see 2 Ki 24:2). In a 14th-century B.C. treaty between the Hittite ruler Mursilis II and Duppi-tessub king of the Amorites, Mursilis says, "If you do not send your son or brother with your foot soldiers and charioteers to help the Hittite king, you act in disregard of the gods of the oath." *all the cities.* See 19:15 and note.

34:2–3 See 32:3–5 and note; see also 39:4–7; Ezek 12:12–13; 17:11–20.

34:4 *not die by the sword.* See 32:5; 38:17,20; 52:11; Ezek 17:16.

34:5 *the former kings . . . burn odours for thee.* Not cremation (see 2 Chr 16:14; 21:19; see also note on Amos 6:10). *Ah lord!* Words of mourning at the death of a king (see 22:18; cf. 1 Ki 13:30).

34:7 *Lachish, and against Azekah.* Solomon's son Rehoboam had fortified them (see 2 Chr 11:5,9), but Lachish was later besieged (701 B.C.) during Hezekiah's reign by the Assyrian king Sennacherib (see 2 Chr 32:9). A contemporary relief depicting Sennacherib's conquest states that he "sat on a throne and passed in review the plunder taken from Lachish." In 1935, 18 ostraca (broken pottery fragments used as writing material) were discovered at Lachish, nearly all of them in the ruins of

ah from the LORD, after that the king Zedekiah had made a covenant with all the people which *were* at Jerusalem, to proclaim [a]liberty unto them;

9 [a]That every man should let his manservant, and every man his maidservant, *being* a Hebrew or a Hebrewess, go free; [b]that none should serve himself of them, *to wit,* of a Jew his brother.

10 *Now* when all the princes, and all the people, which had entered into the covenant, heard that every one should let his manservant, and every one his maidservant, go free, that none should serve themselves of them any more, then they obeyed, and let *them* go.

11 But [a]afterwards they turned, and caused the servants and the handmaids, whom they had let go free, to return, and brought them into subjection for servants and for handmaids.

Jeremiah warns of punishment

12 ¶ Therefore the word of the LORD came to Jeremiah from the LORD, saying,

13 Thus saith the LORD, the God of Israel; I made a covenant with your fathers in the day that I brought them forth out of the land of Egypt, out of the house of bondmen, saying,

14 At the end of [a]seven years let ye go every man his brother a Hebrew, which [1]hath been sold unto thee; and when he hath served thee six years, thou shalt let him go free from thee: but your fathers hearkened not unto me, neither inclined their ear.

15 And ye were [1]now turned, and had done right in my sight, in proclaiming liberty every man to his neighbour; and ye had [a]made a covenant before me [b]in the house [2]which is called by my name.

16 But ye turned and [a]polluted my name, and caused every man his servant, and every man his handmaid, whom ye had set at liberty at their pleasure, to return, and brought them into subjection, to be unto you for servants and for handmaids.

17 Therefore thus saith the LORD; Ye have not hearkened unto me, in proclaiming liberty, every one to his brother, and every man to his neighbour: [a]behold, I proclaim a liberty for you, saith the LORD, [b]to the sword, to the pestilence, and to the famine; and I will make you [1]to be [c]removed into all the kingdoms of the earth.

18 And I will give the men that have transgressed my covenant, which have not performed the words of the covenant which they had made before me, when [a]they cut the calf in twain, and passed between the parts thereof,

19 The princes of Judah, and the princes of Jerusalem, the eunuchs, and the priests, and all the people of the land, which passed between the parts of the calf;

20 I will even give them into the hand of their enemies, and into the hand of them that seek their life: and their [a]dead bodies shall be for meat unto the fowls of the heaven, and to the beasts of the earth.

21 And Zedekiah king of Judah and his princes will I give into the hand of their enemies, and into the hand of them that seek their life, and into the hand of the king of Babylon's army, [a]which are gone up from you.

22 [a]Behold, I *will* command, saith the LORD, and cause them to return to this city; and they shall fight against it, [b]and take it, and burn it with fire: and [c]I will make the cities of Judah a desolation without an inhabitant.

The Rechabites

35 The word which came unto Jeremiah from the LORD in the days of Jehoiakim the son of Josiah king of Judah, saying,

34:8 [a]ver. 14; Ex. 21:2; Lev. 25:10
34:9 [a]Neh. 5:11 [b]Lev. 25:39-46
34:11 [a]See ver. 21; ch. 37:5
34:14 [1]Or, *hath sold himself* [a]Ex. 21:2; 23:10; Deut. 15:12
34:15 [1]Heb. *today* [2]Heb. *whereupon my name is called* [a]2 Ki. 23:3; Neh. 10:29 [b]ch. 7:10
34:16 [a]Ex. 20:7; Lev. 19:12
34:17 [1]Heb. *for a removing* [a]Mat. 7:2; Gal. 6:7; Jas. 2:13 [b]ch. 32:24,36 [c]Deut. 28:25,64; ch. 29:18
34:18 [a]See Gen. 15:10,17
34:20 [a]ch. 7:33; 16:4; 19:7
34:21 [a]See ch. 37:5,11
34:22 [a]ch. 37:8,10 [b]ch. 38:3; 39:1,2,8; 52:7,13 [c]ch. 9:11; 44:2,6

the latest occupation level (588 B.C.) of the Israelite gate-tower. Ostracon 4, written to the commander at Lachish shortly after the events described here, ends as follows: "We are watching for the fire-signals of Lachish ... for we cannot see Azekah." See note on 6:1.

34:8–22 Contemporary with the events of 37:4–12 (see note on vv. 21–22).

34:8 *proclaim liberty.* See Lev 25:10 and note. *liberty unto them.* In accordance with the general provisions of the law of Moses (see Ex 21:2–11 and notes; Lev 25:39–55; Deut 15:12–18).

34:9 *Hebrew.* See Ex 21:2; see also note on Gen 14:13. *none should serve . . . a Jew his brother.* See Lev 25:39,42.

34:10 *they . . . let them go.* To gain God's blessing, and/or in the hope that the freed slaves would be more willing to help defend Jerusalem.

34:11 *afterwards.* When the Babylonian siege was temporarily lifted due to Egyptian intervention (see vv. 21–22; 37:5,11). *caused the servants . . . to return.* In violation of Deut 15:12. *brought them into subjection.* Cf. 2 Chr 28:10.

34:13 *house of bondmen.* Lit. "house of slaves" (see Ex 13:3,14; 20:2; Deut 5:6; 6:12; 8:14; 13:5; Josh 24:17; Judg 6:8). The Israelites were to free their slaves because God had earlier freed the Israelites (see Deut 15:15).

34:14 *end of seven years . . . let him go.* A loose quotation of Deut 15:12.

34:15–16 *were now turned . . . ye turned.* The Hebrew for the two phrases is identical, providing an ironic play on words (see note on v. 18).

34:16 *ye . . . polluted my name.* By breaking the Lord's covenant. Zedekiah was a man whose word could not be trusted (see Ezek 17:15,18). *liberty at their pleasure.* See Deut 21:14.

‡34:17 *sword . . . pestilence . . . famine.* See note on 14:12.

34:18 *transgressed . . . passed.* The Hebrew root underlying both words is the same, again providing an ironic play on words (see note on vv. 15–16). *made . . . cut.* The Hebrew for the two words is identical. In ancient times, making a covenant involved a self-maledictory oath ("May thus and so be done to me if I do not keep this covenant"), which was often symbolized by cutting an animal in two and walking between the two halves (see Gen 15:18 and note). *between the parts thereof.* See note on Gen 15:17.

34:20 *meat unto the fowls . . . of the earth.* See 7:33 and note.

34:21–22 Because of the arrival of the Egyptians on the scene, the Babylonians in 588 B.C. temporarily lifted the siege of Jerusalem (see note on v. 11).

34:21 *gone up from you.* See the hope expressed in 21:2.

34:22 *I will . . . cause them to return.* See 37:8.

35:1–19 The family of the Rechabites, who obeyed their forefather's command, are an example and rebuke to the people of Judah, who have disobeyed the Lord (see v. 16). The mention of

2 Go unto the house of the [a]Rechabites,
and speak unto them, and bring them *into* the
house of the LORD, into one of [b]the chambers,
and give them wine to drink.
3 Then I took Jaazaniah the son of Jeremiah, the son of Habaziniah, and his brethren,
and all his sons, and the whole house of the
Rechabites;
4 And I brought them *into* the house of the
LORD, into the chamber of the sons of Hanan,
the son of Igdaliah, a man of God, which *was*
by the chamber of the princes, which *was*
above the chamber of Maaseiah the son of
Shallum, [a]the keeper of the [1]door:
5 And I set before the sons of the house of
the Rechabites pots full *of* wine, and cups, and
I said unto them, Drink ye wine.
6 But they said, We will drink no wine: for
[a]Jonadab the son of Rechab our father commanded us, saying, Ye shall drink no wine,
neither ye, nor your sons for ever:
7 Neither shall ye build house, nor sow
seed, nor plant vineyard, nor have *any:* but all
your days ye shall dwell in tents; [a]that ye may
live many days in the land where ye *be*
strangers.
8 Thus have we obeyed the voice of Jonadab the son of Rechab our father in all that he
hath charged us, to drink no wine all our days,
we, our wives, our sons, nor our daughters;
9 Nor to build houses for us to dwell in:
neither have we vineyard, nor field, nor seed:
10 But we have dwelt in tents, and have
obeyed, and done according to all that Jonadab
our father commanded us.
11 But it came to pass, when Nebuchadrezzar king of Babylon came up into the land,
that we said, Come, and let us go *to* Jerusalem
for fear of the army of the Chaldeans, and for
fear of the army of the Syrians: so we dwell at
Jerusalem.
12 ¶ Then came the word of the LORD unto
Jeremiah, saying,
13 Thus saith the LORD of hosts, the God of
Israel; Go and tell the men of Judah and the inhabitants of Jerusalem, Will ye not [a]receive instruction to hearken to my words? saith the
LORD.
14 The words of Jonadab the son of
Rechab, that he commanded his sons not to
drink wine, are performed; for unto this day
they drink none, but obey their father's commandment: [a]notwithstanding I have spoken
unto you, [b]rising early and speaking; but ye
hearkened not unto me.
15 I have sent also unto you all my servants
the prophets, rising up early and sending
them, saying, [a]Return ye now every man from
his evil way, and amend your doings, and go
not after other gods to serve them, and ye shall
dwell in the land which I have given to you
and to your fathers: but ye have not inclined
your ear, nor hearkened unto me.
16 Because the sons of Jonadab the son of
Rechab have performed the commandment of
their father, which he commanded them; but
this people hath not hearkened unto me:
17 Therefore thus saith the LORD God of
hosts, the God of Israel; Behold, I will bring
upon Judah and upon all the inhabitants of Jerusalem all the evil that I have pronounced
against them: [a]because I have spoken unto
them, but they have not heard; and I have
called unto them, but they have not answered.
18 ¶ And Jeremiah said unto the house of
the Rechabites, Thus saith the LORD of hosts,

35:2 [a]2 Ki. 10:15; 1 Chr. 2:55 [b]1 Ki. 6:5
35:4 [1]Heb. *threshold,* or, *vessel* [a]2 Ki. 12:9; 25:18; 1 Chr. 9:18,19
35:6 [a]2 Ki. 10:15
35:7 [a]Ex. 20:12; Eph. 6:2,3
35:13 [a]ch. 32:33
35:14 [a]2 Chr. 36:15 [b]ch. 7:13; 25:3
35:15 [a]ch. 18:11; 25:5,6
35:17 [a]Prov. 1:24; Is. 65:12; 66:4; ch. 7:13

"the army of the Chaldeans and . . . Syrians [Arameans]" (v. 11) dates the chapter to no earlier than the eighth year of King Jehoiakim, who began his reign in 609 B.C., whose capital city of Jerusalem was besieged in 605 (see Dan 1:1 and note) by Nebuchadnezzar, and who rebelled against Nebuchadnezzar three or four years later—an unwise act that led to raids on his territory by Babylonians, Syrians and others (see 2 Ki 24:1–2). (The raids are perhaps reflected in 12:7–13.)

35:1 *in the days of Jehoiakim.* Chs. 35–36 (see 36:1) are a flashback to the reign of Jehoiakim (609–598 B.C.; see Introduction: Outline).

35:2 *Rechabites.* A nomadic tribal group related to the Kenites (see 1 Chr 2:55), some of whom lived among or near the Israelites (see Judg 1:16; 4:11; 1 Sam 27:10) and were on friendly terms with them (see 1 Sam 15:6; 30:26,29). *the house of the LORD . . . the chambers.* Used for storage and/or as living quarters (see 1 Ki 6:5; 1 Chr 28:12; 2 Chr 31:11; Neh 13:4–5).

35:3 *Jaazaniah.* Means "The LORD hears." It was a common name in Jeremiah's time (see 40:8; Ezek 8:11; 11:1) and appears on a stamp seal (discovered at Tell en-Nasbeh north of Jerusalem and dating c. 600 B.C.) as well as on one of the Lachish ostraca (see note on 34:7). *Jeremiah.* Not the prophet.

35:4 *sons.* Perhaps here in the sense of "disciples" (see Amos 7:14 and note). *man of God.* A synonym for "prophet" (see 1 Ki 12:22; see also note on 1 Sam 9:9), emphasizing his relationship to the One who has called him. *Maaseiah.* Perhaps the man of the same name mentioned in 21:1; 29:25; 37:3. *keeper of the door.* One of three supervisors (see 52:24) over those who guarded the entrances to the temple (see 2 Ki 12:9).

35:5 *pots.* Large vessels, from which smaller cups would be filled.

35:6 *We will drink no wine.* A permanent vow taken by the Rechabites; cf. the Nazarites' temporary vow (see Num 6:2–3,20; Judg 13:4–7). Malchiah son of Rechab may have been a later renegade exception to the Rechabite vow, since he was "ruler of part of Beth-haccerem" (Neh 3:14), which means "house of the vineyard." *Jonadab.* Spelled "Jehonadab" in 2 Ki 10:15,23. Nearly 250 years before the days of Jeremiah, he helped King Jehu destroy Baal worship (at least temporarily) in the northern kingdom.

35:7 *shall dwell in tents.* Except during times of national emergency (see v. 11). *ye may live many days in the land.* An echo of Ex 20:12, where honoring one's parents is commanded.

35:8 *have we obeyed . . . Jonadab.* Contrast Judah's disobedience toward God (see v. 16).

35:11 See note on vv. 1–19.

‡35:13 *receive instruction.* The Hebrew (*muwcar,* "discipline") underlying this phrase is, in the negative, translated "received no correction" in 2:30; and again, in the affirmative, "receiveth correction" in 7:28 (see 5:3; 17:23 and note).

‡35:14–15 *rising . . . speaking.* See note on 7:13.

35:15 See 25:4–5 and notes.

35:17 See 11:11.

the God of Israel; Because ye have obeyed the commandment of Jonadab your father, and kept all his precepts, and done according unto all that he hath commanded you:

19 Therefore thus saith the LORD of hosts, the God of Israel; [1]Jonadab the son of Rechab shall not want a man to [a]stand before me for ever.

The reading of the roll

36 And it came to pass in the fourth year of Jehoiakim the son of Josiah king of Judah, *that* this word came unto Jeremiah from the LORD, saying,

2 Take thee a [a]roll of a book, and [b]write therein all the words that I have spoken unto thee against Israel, and against Judah, and against [c]all the nations, from the day I spake unto thee, from the days of [d]Josiah, even unto this day.

3 [a]It may be that the house of Judah will hear all the evil which I purpose to do unto them; that they may [b]return every man from his evil way; that I may forgive their iniquity and their sin.

4 Then Jeremiah [a]called Baruch the son of Neriah: and [b]Baruch wrote from the mouth of Jeremiah all the words of the LORD, which he had spoken unto him, upon a roll of a book.

5 And Jeremiah commanded Baruch, saying, I *am* shut up; I cannot go *into* the house of the LORD:

6 Therefore go thou, and read in the roll, which thou hast written from my mouth, the words of the LORD in the ears of the people *in* the LORD's house upon [a]the fasting day: and also thou shalt read them in the ears of all Judah that come out of their cities.

7 [a]It may be [1]they will present their supplication before the LORD, and will return every one from his evil way: for great *is* the anger and the fury that the LORD hath pronounced against this people.

8 And Baruch the son of Neriah did according to all that Jeremiah the prophet commanded him, reading in the book the words of the LORD *in* the LORD's house.

9 And it came to pass in the fifth year of Jehoiakim the son of Josiah king of Judah, in the ninth month, *that* they proclaimed a fast before the LORD *to* all the people in Jerusalem, and *to* all the people that came from the cities of Judah unto Jerusalem.

10 Then read Baruch in the book the words of Jeremiah *in* the house of the LORD, in the chamber of Gemariah the son of Shaphan the scribe, in the higher court *at* the [a1]entry of the new gate of the LORD's house, in the ears of all the people.

11 ¶ When Michaiah the son of Gemariah, the son of Shaphan, had heard out of the book all the words of the LORD,

12 Then he went down *into* the king's house, into the scribe's chamber: and lo, all the princes sat there, *even* Elishama the scribe, and Delaiah the son of Shemaiah, and Elnathan the son of Achbor, and Gemariah the son of Shaphan, and Zedekiah the son of Hananiah, and all the princes.

13 Then Michaiah declared unto them all the words that he had heard, when Baruch read the book in the ears of the people.

14 Therefore all the princes sent Jehudi the son of Nethaniah, the son of Shelemiah, the son of Cushi, unto Baruch, saying, Take in thine hand the roll wherein thou hast read in the ears of the people, and come. So Baruch the son of Neriah took the roll in his hand, and came unto them.

15 And they said unto him, Sit down now, and read it in our ears. So Baruch read *it* in their ears.

16 Now it came to pass when they had heard all the words, they were afraid both one and other, and said unto Baruch, We will surely tell the king of all these words.

17 And they asked Baruch, saying, Tell us now, How didst thou write all these words at his mouth?

18 Then Baruch answered them, He pro-

35:19 [1]Heb. *There shall not a man be cut off from [Jonadab the son of Rechab to stand]*, *etc.* [a]ch. 15:19
36:2 [a]Is. 8:1; Ezek. 2:9; Zech. 5:1 [b]ch. 30:2 [c]ch. 25:15 [d]ch. 25:3
36:3 [a]ver. 7; ch. 26:3 [b]ch. 18:8; Jonah 3:8
36:4 [a]ch. 32:12 [b]See ch. 45:1
36:6 [a]Lev. 16:29; 23:27-32; Acts 27:9
36:7 [1]Heb. *their supplication shall fall* [a]ver. 3
36:10 [1]Or, *door* [a]ch. 26:10

35:19 *not want a man to stand before me.* See 33:18. Various traditions in the Jewish Mishnah claim that the Rechabites were later given special duties to perform in connection with the Jerusalem temple built after the return from Babylonian exile.
36:1–38:28 Three chapters united by the common theme of Jeremiah's suffering and persecution.
36:1–32 An account of King Jehoiakim's attempt to destroy Jeremiah's written prophecies.
36:1 *fourth year of Jehoiakim.* 605 B.C.—a critical year in Judah's history (see notes on 25:1; 46:2).
36:2 *roll of a book.* See notes on 30:2; Ex 17:14. *write therein.* To preserve Jeremiah's messages for future generations. *all the words that I have spoken unto thee.* This "earliest edition" of Jeremiah's prophecies may have included all or most of chs. 1–26; 46–51. *from the day I spake unto thee, from the days of Josiah.* See note on 1:2.
36:3 *It may be . . . that.* If the people repent, the Lord will relent (see 18:7–10 and note; 26:3).
36:4 *Baruch.* See note on 32:12.
36:5 *I am shut up.* Perhaps because of his unpopular temple message(s) (see 7:2–15; 26:2–6), or perhaps because of the events recorded in 19:1–20:6.
36:6 *fasting day.* Proclaimed because of a national emergency (cf. Joel 2:15), perhaps in this case the Babylonian attack of 605 B.C. (see Dan 1:1 and note).
36:7 See v. 3 and note.
36:8 If the book were in chronological order, ch. 45 would appear after this verse (see Introduction: Outline).
36:9 *fifth year . . . in the ninth month.* December, 604 B.C., during a time of cold weather (see v. 22).
36:10 Cf. 2 Ki 23:2. *chamber.* See note on 35:2. *Gemariah.* A common name in Jeremiah's time (see 29:3), found on one of the Lachish ostraca (see note on 34:7) as well as in at least two of the Elephantine papyri (see note on 32:11) a century later. *Shaphan.* Secretary of state under King Josiah (see 2 Ki 22:3; see also notes on 26:24; 29:3). *entry of the new gate.* See 26:10 and note.
36:12 *Elnathan the son of Achbor.* See note on 26:22.
36:18 *ink.* Mentioned only here in the OT (but see also 2 Cor 3:3; 2 John 12; 3 John 13). In ancient times, ink was made from

nounced all these words unto me with his
mouth, and I wrote *them* with ink in the book.
19 Then said the princes unto Baruch, Go,
hide thee, thou and Jeremiah; and let no man
know where ye *be.*
20 ¶ And they went in to the king into the
court, but they laid up the roll in the chamber
of Elishama the scribe, and told all the words
in the ears of the king.
21 So the king sent Jehudi to fet the roll:
and he took it out of Elishama the scribe's
chamber. And Jehudi read it in the ears of the
king, and in the ears of all the princes which
stood beside the king.
22 Now the king sat *in* [a]the winterhouse
in the ninth month: and *there was a fire on*
the hearth burning before him.
23 And it came to pass, *that* when Jehudi
had read three or four leaves, he cut it with
the penknife, and cast *it* into the fire that *was*
on the hearth, until all the roll was consumed
in the fire that *was* on the hearth.
24 Yet they were not afraid, nor [a]rent their
garments, *neither* the king, nor any of his servants that heard all these words.
25 Nevertheless Elnathan and Delaiah and
Gemariah had made intercession to the king
that *he* would not burn the roll: but he would
not hear them.
26 But the king commanded Jerahmeel the
son [1]of Hammelech, and Seraiah the son of
Azriel, and Shelemiah the son of Abdeel, to
take Baruch the scribe and Jeremiah the
prophet: but the LORD hid them.
27 ¶ Then the word of the LORD came to
Jeremiah, after that the king had burnt the
roll, and the words which Baruch wrote at the
mouth of Jeremiah, saying,
28 Take thee again another roll, and write in
it all the former words that were in the first roll,
which Jehoiakim the king of Judah hath burnt.
29 And thou shalt say to Jehoiakim king of
Judah, Thus saith the LORD; Thou hast burnt
this roll, saying, Why hast thou written therein, saying, The king of Babylon shall certainly
come and destroy this land, and shall cause to
cease from thence man and beast?
30 Therefore thus saith the LORD of Jehoiakim king of Judah; [a]He shall have none to
sit upon the throne of David: and his dead
body shall be [b]cast out in the day to the heat,
and in the night to the frost.
31 And I will [a][1]punish him and his seed
and his servants for their iniquity; and I will
bring upon them, and upon the inhabitants of
Jerusalem, and upon the men of Judah, all the
evil that I have pronounced against them; but
they hearkened not.
32 Then took Jeremiah another roll, and
gave it to Baruch the scribe, the son of Neriah;
who wrote therein from the mouth of Jeremiah all the words of the book which Jehoiakim
king of Judah had burnt in the fire: and there
were added besides unto them many [1]like
words.

36:22 [a]See Amos 3:15
36:24 [a]2 Ki. 22:11; Is. 36:22; 37:1
36:26 [1]Or, *of the king*
36:30 [a]ch. 22:30 [b]ch. 22:19
36:31 [1]Heb. *visit upon* [a]ch. 23:34
36:32 [1]Heb. *as they*
37:1 [a]2 Ki. 24:17; 2 Chr. 36:10; ch. 22:24
37:2 [1]Heb. *by the hand of the prophet* [a]2 Chr. 36:12,14
37:3 [a]ch. 21:1,2; 29:25; 52:24
37:5 [a]See 2 Ki. 24:7; Ezek. 17:15 [b]ver. 11; ch. 34:21

Jeremiah's imprisonment

37 And king [a]Zedekiah the son of Josiah
reigned instead of Coniah the son of
Jehoiakim, whom Nebuchadrezzar king of
Babylon made king in the land of Judah.
2 [a]But neither he, nor his servants, nor the
people of the land, did hearken unto the words
of the LORD, which he spake [1]by the prophet
Jeremiah.
3 And Zedekiah the king sent Jehucal the
son of Shelemiah and [a]Zephaniah the son of
Maaseiah the priest to the prophet Jeremiah,
saying, Pray now unto the LORD our God for us.
4 Now Jeremiah came in and went out
among the people: for they had not put him
into prison.
5 Then [a]Pharaoh's army was come forth
out of Egypt: [b]and when the Chaldeans that

---

soot or lampblack mixed with gum arabic, oil, or a metallic substance (as in the case of the Lachish ostraca; see note on 34:7).

36:19 The officials were understandably concerned about the safety of Jeremiah and Baruch (cf. 26:20–23).

36:20 *they laid up the roll.* For safekeeping (see Is 10:28).

36:22 *winterhouse.* See Amos 3:15; here probably a large room in the king's palace. *ninth month.* See note on v. 9. *hearth.* A depression or container in the middle of the floor where coals were kept burning to warm the room.

36:23 Contrast King Josiah's desire to know the word of God and obey it (see 2 Ki 22:11–23:3; 23:21–24). *leaves.* Lit. "doors," so called because of their rectangular shape. *cut.* Lit. "tore." Instead of tearing his clothes (see note on v. 24), the king tore the prophet's scroll.

36:24 *they were not afraid.* See v. 31. Contrast the response of the "princes" (v. 12; see vv. 16,25). *nor rent their garments.* Contrast the response of Jehoiakim's father Josiah (see 2 Ki 22:11; cf. 1 Ki 21:27).

36:26 *Jerahmeel the son.* Since Jehoiakim was only about 30 years old (see 2 Ki 23:36), the phrase probably is not to be understood literally but means he was a member of the royal court (as also in 38:6; 1 Ki 22:26; Zeph 1:8).

36:30 *Jehoiakim . . . shall have none to sit upon the throne.* His son Jehoiachin (see 2 Ki 24:6) "ruled" only 3 months (see 2 Ki 24:8) and then was captured and carried off to exile in Babylonia (see 2 Ki 24:15), where he eventually died (see 52:33–34). *his dead body shall be cast out.* As punishment for the fact that he "cast" (v. 23) the prophet's scroll into the fire (see 22:18–19 and notes).

36:31 See 11:11; 19:15; 35:17. *servants.* See note on v. 24.

36:32 *another roll.* Cf. similarly Ex 34:1.

37:1–38:28 During the last two years of Zedekiah's reign (588–586 B.C.), Jeremiah is imprisoned by the authorities (see 20:2 and note).

37:1 See 2 Ki 24:15,17–18. *Zedekiah.* Means "The LORD is my righteousness." See Introduction: Background. *reigned instead of Coniah.* In 597 B.C. This fulfills the prophecy concerning Jehoiakim in 36:30.

37:3 *Zedekiah the king sent . . . to . . . Jeremiah.* See 21:1. *Jehucal the son of Shelemiah.* Later became Jeremiah's enemy (see 38:1,4). *Zephaniah the son of Maaseiah the priest.* "Priest" here refers to Zephaniah (see 21:1 and note). *Pray . . . for us.* See 21:2 and note; perhaps to ask the Lord to make the temporary withdrawal of the Babylonians in 588 B.C. (see note on 34:21–22) permanent.

37:5 *Pharaoh's army.* The troops of Pharaoh-hophra (see

besieged Jerusalem heard tidings of them, they
departed from Jerusalem.
6 ¶ Then came the word of the LORD unto
the prophet Jeremiah, saying,
7 Thus saith the LORD, the God of Israel;
Thus shall ye say to the king of Judah, [a]that
sent you unto me to inquire of me; Behold,
Pharaoh's army, which is come forth to help
you, shall return *to* Egypt into their own land.
8 [a]And the Chaldeans shall come again,
and fight against this city, and take it, and burn
it with fire.
9 Thus saith the LORD; Deceive not
your[1] selves, saying, The Chaldeans shall surely depart from us: for they shall not depart.
10 [a]For though ye had smitten the whole
army of the Chaldeans that fight against you,
and there remained *but* [1]wounded men
among them, *yet* should they rise up every
man in his tent, and burn this city with fire.
11 ¶ [a]And it came to pass, *that* when the
army of the Chaldeans was [1]broken up from
Jerusalem for fear of Pharaoh's army,
12 Then Jeremiah went forth out of Jerusalem to go *into* the land of Benjamin, [1]to separate himself thence in the midst of the people.
13 And when he was in the gate of Benjamin, a captain of the ward *was* there, whose
name *was* Irijah, the son of Shelemiah, the son
of Hananiah; and he took Jeremiah the prophet, saying, Thou fallest away to the Chaldeans.
14 Then said Jeremiah, *It is* [1]false; I fall not
away to the Chaldeans. But he hearkened not
to him: so Irijah took Jeremiah, and brought
him to the princes.
15 Wherefore the princes were wroth with
Jeremiah, and smote him, [a]and put him *in*
prison *in* the house of Jonathan the scribe: for
they had made that the prison.
16 ¶ When Jeremiah was entered into [a]the
dungeon, and into the [1]cabins, and Jeremiah
had remained there many days;
17 Then Zedekiah the king sent, and took
him *out:* and the king asked him secretly in his
house, and said, Is there *any* word from the
LORD? And Jeremiah said, There is: for, said
he, thou shalt be delivered into the hand of
the king of Babylon.
18 Moreover Jeremiah said unto king Zedekiah, What have I offended against thee, or
against thy servants, or against this people,
that ye have put me in prison?
19 Where *are* now your prophets which
prophesied unto you, saying, The king of Babylon shall not come against you, nor against
this land?
20 Therefore hear now, I pray thee, O my
lord the king: [1]let my supplication, I pray
thee, be accepted before thee, that thou cause
me not to return *to* the house of Jonathan the
scribe, lest I die there.
21 Then Zedekiah the king commanded
that they should commit Jeremiah [a]into the
court of the prison, and that *they* should give
him daily a piece of bread out of the bakers'
street, [b]until all the bread in the city were
spent. Thus Jeremiah remained in the court of
the prison.

The miry dungeon

38 Then Shephatiah the son of Mattan,
and Gedaliah the son of Pashur, and
[a]Jucal the son of Shelemiah, and [b]Pashur the
son of Malchiah, [c]heard the words that Jeremiah had spoken unto all the people, saying,
2 Thus saith the LORD, [a]He that remaineth
in this city shall die by the sword, by the
famine, and by the pestilence: but he that
goeth forth to the Chaldeans shall live; for he
shall have his life for a prey, and shall live.
3 Thus saith the LORD, [a]This city shall surely be given into the hand of the king of Babylon's army, which shall take it.
4 Therefore the princes said unto the king,
We beseech thee, [a]let this man be put to
death: for thus he weakeneth the hands of the

37:7 [a]ch. 21:2
37:8 [a]ch. 34:22
37:9 [1]Heb. *souls*
37:10 [1]Heb. *thrust through* [a]ch. 21:4,5
37:11 [1]Heb. *made to ascend* [a]ver. 5
37:12 [1]Or, *to slip away from thence in the midst of the people*
37:14 [1]Heb. *falsehood,* or, [a] *lie*
37:15 [a]ch. 38:26
37:16 [1]Or, *cells* [a]ch. 38:6
37:20 [1]Heb. *let my supplication fall*
37:21 [a]ch. 32:2; 38:13,28 [b]ch. 38:9; 52:6
38:1 [a]ch. 37:3 [b]ch. 21:1 [c]ch. 21:8
38:2 [a]ch. 21:9
38:3 [a]ch. 21:10; 32:3
38:4 [a]See ch. 26:11

44:30), called Apries by Greek historians. *come forth out of Egypt.* Probably to help Zedekiah at his request; Lachish ostracon 3 (see note on 34:7) mentions a visit to Egypt made by the commander of Judah's army. All such ploys by Zedekiah would fail, however (see Ezek 17:15,17). *Chaldeans . . . they departed.* To deal with the Egyptian threat (see 34:21 and note).

37:7 *Pharaoh's army . . . return to Egypt.* Pharaoh-hophra would soon be defeated by Nebuchadnezzar (see note on Ezek 30:21).

37:10 *wounded.* Lit. "pierced through," "mortally wounded." Though seriously handicapped, the Babylonians would still destroy Jerusalem.

‡37:12 *land of Benjamin.* Where Jeremiah's hometown, Anathoth, was located (see note on 1:1). *to separate himself.* Or, "to buy land." See 1 Sam 30:24. While there was a brief lull in the Babylonian invasion, Jeremiah wanted to settle matters of estate with the other members of his family.

37:13 *gate of Benjamin.* See 38:7; see also note on Zech 14:10. *Thou fallest away to the Chaldeans.* Irijah's fear was understandable, since Jeremiah recommended surrendering to the Babylonians (see 21:9; 38:2) and since many Judahites in fact defected (see 38:19; 39:9; 52:15).

37:14 *It is false.* See 2 Ki 9:12.

37:15 *smote him.* See 20:2 and note. *house of Jonathan.* Jeremiah would later look back on this prison as a place of great danger for him (see v. 20; 38:26).

37:16 *dungeon.* Lit. "house of the cistern," probably underground (see Ex 12:29).

37:17 *Zedekiah . . . asked him secretly.* Not wanting to do so in the presence of his officials, whom he apparently feared. *thou shalt be delivered into the hand of the king of Babylon.* See 32:4; 34:3.

37:19 *your prophets.* False prophets (see Deut l8:22).

37:20 *let my supplication . . . be accepted before thee.* See 36:7

38:1 *Pashur.* See note on 20:1. *Jucal the son of Shelemiah.* See note on 37:3. *Pashur the son of Malchiah.* See note on 21:1. *Jeremiah had spoken unto all the people.* Though he was confined in the courtyard of the guard (see 37:21), he was allowed to have visitors and to speak freely to them (see 32:8,12).

38:2 Echoes 21:9 (see note there).

38:3 Echoes 32:28 (see 34:2; 37:8).

‡38:4 *princes.* Those named in v. 1. *he weakeneth.* See Ezra 4:4; lit. "weakening the hands of," as in a similar situation in Lachish ostracon 6 (see note on 34:7): "The words of the officials are not good; they serve only to weaken our hands." Contrast

men of war that remain in this city, and the
hands of all the people, in speaking such
words unto them: for this man seeketh not the
[1]welfare of this people, but the hurt.
5 Then Zedekiah the king said, Behold, he
is in your hand: for the king *is* not *he that* can
do *any* thing against you.
6 [a]Then took they Jeremiah, and cast him
into the dungeon of Malchiah the son [1]of
Hammelech, that *was* in the court of the
prison: and they let down Jeremiah with
cords. And in the dungeon *there was* no water,
but mire: so Jeremiah sunk in the mire.
7 ¶ [a]Now when Ebed-melech the Ethiopian, one of the eunuchs which *was* in the king's
house, heard that they had put Jeremiah in the
dungeon; the king then sitting in the gate of
Benjamin;
8 Ebed-melech went forth out of the king's
house, and spake to the king, saying,
9 My lord the king, these men have done
evil in all that they have done to Jeremiah the
prophet, whom they have cast into the dungeon; and [1]he is like to die for hunger in the
place where he is: for *there is* no more bread
in the city.
10 Then the king commanded Ebed-melech the Ethiopian, saying, Take from hence
thirty men [1]with thee, and take up Jeremiah
the prophet out of the dungeon, before he die.
11 So Ebed-melech took the men with
him, and went *into* the house of the king under the treasury, and took thence old cast
clouts and old rotten rags, and let them down
by cords into the dungeon to Jeremiah.
12 And Ebed-melech the Ethiopian said
unto Jeremiah, Put now *these* old cast clouts
and rotten rags under thine armholes under
the cords. And Jeremiah did so.
13 [a]So they drew up Jeremiah with cords,
and took him up out of the dungeon: and Jeremiah remained [b]in the court of the prison.

38:4 [1]Heb. *peace*
38:6 [1]Or, *of the king* [a]ch. 37:21
38:7 [a]ch. 39:16
38:9 [1]Heb. *he will die*
38:10 [1]Heb. *in thine hand*
38:13 [a]ver. 6 [b]ch. 37:21
38:14 [1]Or, *principal*
38:16 [a]Is. 57:16
38:17 [a]2 Ki. 24:12 [b]ch. 39:3
38:18 [a]ver. 23; ch. 32:4; 34:3
38:19 [a]1 Sam. 31:4
38:22 [1]Heb. *Men of thy peace*

Jeremiah's advice to Zedekiah

14 ¶ Then Zedekiah the king sent, and took
Jeremiah the prophet unto him into the [1]third
entry that *is* in the house of the LORD: and the
king said unto Jeremiah, I *will* ask thee a thing;
hide nothing from me.
15 Then Jeremiah said unto Zedekiah, If I
declare *it* unto thee, wilt thou not surely put
me to death? and if I give thee counsel, wilt
thou not hearken unto me?
16 So Zedekiah the king sware secretly
unto Jeremiah, saying, *As* the LORD liveth,
[a]that made us this soul, I will not put thee to
death, neither will I give thee into the hand of
these men that seek thy life.
17 Then said Jeremiah unto Zedekiah,
Thus saith the LORD, the God of hosts, the God
of Israel; If thou wilt assuredly [a]go forth [b]unto
the king of Babylon's princes, then thy soul
shall live, and this city shall not be burnt with
fire; and thou shalt live, and thine house:
18 But if thou wilt not go forth to the king
of Babylon's princes, then shall this city be giv-
en into the hand of the Chaldeans, and they
shall burn it with fire, and [a]thou shalt not escape out of their hand.
19 And Zedekiah the king said unto Jeremiah, I am afraid of the Jews that are fallen to
the Chaldeans, lest they deliver me into their
hand, and they [a]mock me.
20 But Jeremiah said, They shall not deliver *thee.* Obey, I beseech thee, the voice of the
LORD, which I speak unto thee: so it shall be
well unto thee, and thy soul shall live.
21 But if thou refuse to go forth, this *is* the
word that the LORD hath shewed me:
22 And behold, all the women that are left
in the king of Judah's house *shall be* brought
forth to the king of Babylon's princes, and
those *women shall* say, [1]Thy friends have set
thee on, and have prevailed against thee: thy

Is 35:3. *seeketh . . . the welfare.* The Hebrew underlying this phrase is translated "seek the peace" in 29:7 (see note there). *welfare . . . hurt.* The Hebrew for these words is translated "peace . . . evil" in Is 45:7.

38:5 *the king is not he that can do any thing.* Not because of inability or lack of authority but through failure of nerve. He feared his own officials (see vv. 25–26; see also 37:17 and note).

‡38:6 *dungeon.* Shaped like a bell, with the narrow end at the top (see 37:16 and note). *Malchiah the son of Hammelech.* See KJV marg. See also note on 36:26. *in the dungeon there was no water.* Zedekiah's officials wanted to kill Jeremiah (see v. 4), but not by taking his life with their own hands (cf. Gen 37:20–24).

‡38:7 *Ebed-melech.* Means "king's servant." *king then sitting in the gate of Benjamin.* See 37:13; see also note on Zech 14:10. Since a city gateway was often used as a courtroom or town hall (see notes on Gen 19:1; Ruth 4:1), Zedekiah may have been settling various legal complaints on this occasion (see 2 Sam 15:2–4) and would therefore be in a position to help Ebed-melech who is described as an Ethiopian eunuch (see Acts 8:27).

38:9 *no more bread in the city.* See 37:21 and note.

38:10 *thirty men.* The large number was probably to keep the officials (see v. 4) and their friends from trying to prevent Jeremiah's rescue.

38:11 *under the treasury.* Perhaps a wardrobe storeroom (see 2 Ki 10:22).

38:12 *Put now these old cast clouts . . . under the cords.* Ebed-melech's kindnesses to Jeremiah were evidence that he trusted in the Lord, and the Lord rewarded him (see 39:15–18).

38:13 *remained in the court of the prison.* See note on 32:2.

38:14 *a thing . . . nothing.* Lit. "a word . . . a word," probably referring to a "word from the LORD" (37:17).

38:16 *As the LORD liveth.* See note on Gen 42:15. *these men that seek thy life.* Zedekiah's officials (see v. 4 and note).

38:17–18 See vv. 2–3; 21:9–10; 32:3–4; 34:2–5. *go forth to.* See 2 Ki 18:31; 24:12. *king of Babylon's princes.* Those in charge of the siege of Jerusalem (see 39:3,13).

38:19 *I am afraid.* See v. 5 and note. If Zedekiah had trusted in the Lord, he would not have had to fear either officials or deserters (see Prov 29:25). *fallen to the Chaldeans.* See 37:13 and note. *mock me.* See Judg 19:25; 1 Chr 10:4.

38:22 *women . . . in the king of Judah's house . . . brought forth to the king of Babylon's princes.* Women in a conquered king's harem became the property of the conquerors (cf. 2 Sam 16:21–22). *Thy friends have set thee on, and have prevailed against thee.* Repeated almost verbatim in Obad 7 (see 20:10 and note). Zedekiah's so-called friends were his officials (see

feet are sunk in the mire, *and* they are turned away back.

23 So they *shall* bring out all thy wives and [a]thy children to the Chaldeans: and thou shalt not escape out of their hand, but shalt be taken by the hand of the king of Babylon: and [1]thou shalt cause this city to be burnt with fire.

24 ¶ Then said Zedekiah unto Jeremiah, Let no man know of these words, and thou shalt not die.

25 But if the princes hear that I have talked with thee, and they come unto thee, and say unto thee, Declare unto us now what thou hast said unto the king, hide *it* not from us, and we will not put thee to death; also what the king said unto thee:

26 Then thou shalt say unto them, [a]I presented my supplication before the king, that *he* would not cause me to return [b]*to* Jonathan's house, to die there.

27 Then came all the princes unto Jeremiah, and asked him: and he told them according to all these words that the king had commanded. So [1]they left off speaking with him; for the matter was not perceived.

28 So [a]Jeremiah abode in the court of the prison until the day that Jerusalem was taken: and he was *there* when Jerusalem was taken.

The fall of Jerusalem

39 In the [a]ninth year of Zedekiah king of Judah, in the tenth month, came Nebuchadrezzar king of Babylon and all his army against Jerusalem, and they besieged it.

2 *And* in the eleventh year of Zedekiah, in the fourth month, the ninth *day* of the month, the city was broken up.

3 [a]And all the princes of the king of Babylon came in, and sat in the middle gate, *even* Nergal-sharezer, Samgar-nebo, Sarsechim, Rab-saris, Nergal-sharezer, Rab-mag, with all the residue of the princes of the king of Babylon.

4 [a]And it came to pass, *that* when Zedekiah the king of Judah saw them, and all the men of war, then they fled, and went forth out of the city by night, *by* the way of the king's garden, by the gate betwixt the two walls: and he went out the way of the plain.

5 But the Chaldeans' army pursued after them, and [a]overtook Zedekiah in the plains of Jericho: and when they had taken him, they brought him up to Nebuchadnezzar king of Babylon to [b]Riblah in the land of Hamath, where he [1]gave judgment upon him.

6 Then the king of Babylon slew the sons of Zedekiah in Riblah before his eyes: also the king of Babylon slew all the nobles of Judah.

7 Moreover [a]he put out Zedekiah's eyes, and bound him [1]with chains to carry him to Babylon.

8 ¶ [a]And the Chaldeans burnt the king's house, and the houses of the people, with fire, and brake down the walls of Jerusalem.

9 [a]Then Nebuzar-adan the [1][2]captain of the guard carried away captive *into* Babylon the remnant of the people that remained in the city, and those that fell away, that fell to him, with the rest of the people that remained.

10 But Nebuzar-adan the captain of the guard left of the poor of the people, which had nothing, in the land of Judah, and gave them vineyards and fields [1]at the same time.

11 ¶ Now Nebuchadrezzar king of Babylon gave charge concerning Jeremiah [1]to Nebuzar-adan the captain of the guard, saying,

12 Take him, and [1]look well to him, and do him no harm; but do unto him even as he shall say unto thee.

13 So Nebuzar-adan the captain of the guard sent, and Nebushasban, Rab-saris, and Nergal-sharezer, Rab-mag, and all the king of Babylon's princes;

14 Even they sent, [a]and took Jeremiah out of the court of the prison, and committed him

38:23 [1]Heb. *thou shalt burn, etc.* [a]ch. 39:6; 41:10
38:26 [a]ch. 37:20 [b]ch. 37:15
38:27 [1]Heb. *they were silent from him*
38:28 [a]ch. 37:21; 39:14
39:1 [a]2 Ki. 25:1-4
39:3 [a]ch. 38:17
39:4 [a]2 Ki. 25:4; ch. 52:7
39:5 [1]Heb. *spake with him judgments* [a]ch. 32:4; 38:18,23 [b]2 Ki. 23:33
39:7 [1]Heb. *with two brazen chains,* or, *fetters* [a]Ezek. 12:13, compared with ch. 32:4
39:8 [a]2 Ki. 25:9; ch. 38:18; 52:13
39:9 [1]Or, *chief marshal* [2]Heb. *chief of the executioners,* or, *slaughtermen:* and so ver. 10,11,13 [a]2 Ki. 25:11
39:10 [1]Heb. *in that day*
39:11 [1]Heb. *by the hand of*
39:12 [1]Heb. *set thine eyes upon him*
39:14 [a]ch. 38:28

v. 4) and false prophets (see 37:19). *feet are sunk in the mire.* Symbolic of great distress (see Ps 69:14).
38:26 See 37:20. *Jonathan's house.* See 37:15 and note.
38:27 *told them . . . all . . . that the king had commanded.* Jeremiah was not obliged to give the officials the other information, which had been shared in confidence.
38:28 *abode in the court of the prison.* See v. 13; see also note on 32:2.
39:1–45:5 The most detailed account in the OT of the Babylonian conquest of Jerusalem and its aftermath. The section concludes with a brief appendix (ch. 45).
39:1–10 A vivid summary of the siege and fall of Jerusalem and of the exile of its inhabitants (see 52:4–27).
39:1–2 Summarizes 52:4–7a.
39:1 *ninth year of Zedekiah . . . tenth month.* The final Babylonian siege of Jerusalem began on the tenth day of the month (see 52:4; 2 Ki 25:1; Ezek 24:1–2), or Jan. 15, 588 B.C.
39:2 *eleventh year . . . fourth month . . . ninth day.* July 18, 586 B.C. (see 52:5–6; 2 Ki 25:2–3). The siege lasted just over two and a half years.
39:3 *sat in the middle gate.* In fulfillment of 1:15. The middle gate may have been located in the wall separating the citadel of mount Zion from the lower city, therefore serving as a strategic vantage point for the invaders. *Nergal-sharezer.* Means "Nergal [a god; see 2 Ki 17:30], protect the king." One of the two men so named here (see v. 13) is probably Neriglissar, who later became a successor of Nebuchadnezzar as ruler of Babylonia (560–556 B.C.). *Rab-saris.* See v. 13; see also note on 2 Ki 18:17. *Rab-mag.* See v. 13. The Hebrew for this phrase is cognate to Babylonian *rab mu(n)gi,* a high military official who sometimes served as an envoy to foreign rulers.
39:4–7 See 52:7–11; see also 2 Ki 25:4–7 and notes.
39:8–10 See 52:12–16; see also 2 Ki 25:8–12 and notes.
39:12 *look well to him.* See note on 40:4.
39:13 *Nergal-sharezer.* See note on v. 3.
39:14 *took Jeremiah out.* Either (1) a summary statement of Jeremiah's release from prison, the specific details of which are given in 40:1–6; or (2) a brief description of the first of two releases, the second of which (made necessary because Jeremiah had been arrested again by mistake in the confusion surrounding the capture and transporting of thousands of exiles) is detailed in 40:1–6. *court of the prison.* See note on 32:2. *Gedaliah the son of Ahikam the son of Shaphan.* See note on 26:24. *home.* The governor's residence. An early sixth-century seal impression found at Lachish reads: "Belonging to Ged-

[b]unto Gedaliah the son of [c]Ahikam the son of Shaphan, that *he* should carry him home: so he dwelt among the people.

15 ¶ Now the word of the LORD came unto Jeremiah, while he was shut up in the court of the prison, saying,

16 Go and speak to [a]Ebed-melech the Ethiopian, saying, Thus saith the LORD of hosts, the God of Israel; Behold, [b]I *will* bring my words upon this city for evil, and not for good; and they shall be *accomplished* in that day before thee.

17 But I will deliver thee in that day, saith the LORD: and thou shalt not be given into the hand of the men of whom thou *art* afraid.

18 For I will surely deliver thee, and thou shalt not fall by the sword, but [a]thy life shall be for a prey unto thee: [b]because thou hast put thy trust in me, saith the LORD.

Jeremiah released

40 The word which came to Jeremiah from the LORD, [a]after that Nebuzaradan the captain of the guard had let him go from Ramah, when he had taken him being bound in [1]chains among all that were carried away captive of Jerusalem and Judah, which were carried away captive unto Babylon.

2 And the captain of the guard took Jeremiah, and [a]said unto him, The LORD thy God hath pronounced this evil upon this place.

3 Now the LORD hath brought *it,* and done according as he hath said: [a]because ye have sinned against the LORD, and have not obeyed his voice, therefore this thing is come upon you.

4 And now behold, I loose thee *this* day from the chains which [1]*were* upon thine hand. [a]If it seem good unto thee to come with me *into* Babylon, come; and [2]I will look well unto thee: but if it seem ill unto thee to come with me *into* Babylon, forbear: behold, [b]all the land *is* before thee: whither it seemeth good and convenient for thee to go, thither go.

5 Now while he was not yet gone back, *he said,* Go back also to Gedaliah the son of Ahikam the son of Shaphan, [a]whom the king of Babylon hath made governor over the cities of Judah, and dwell with him among the people: or go wheresoever it seemeth convenient unto thee to go. So the captain of the guard gave him victuals and a reward, and let him go.

6 [a]Then went Jeremiah unto Gedaliah the son of Ahikam to [b]Mizpah; and dwelt with him among the people that were left in the land.

Gedaliah slain by Ishmael

7 ¶ [a]*Now* when all the captains of the forces which *were* in the fields, *even* they and their men, heard that the king of Babylon had made Gedaliah the son of Ahikam governor in the land, and had committed unto him men, and women, and children, and of [b]the poor of the land, of *them* that were not carried away captive to Babylon;

8 Then they came to Gedaliah to Mizpah, [a]even Ishmael the son of Nethaniah, and Johanan and Jonathan the sons of Kareah, and Seraiah the son of Tanhumeth, and the sons of Ephai the Netophathite, and Jezaniah the son of a Maachathite, they and their men.

9 And Gedaliah the son of Ahikam the son of Shaphan sware unto them and to their men, saying, Fear not to serve the Chaldeans: dwell in the land and serve the king of Babylon, and it shall be well with you.

10 As for me, behold, I *will* dwell at Mizpah [1]to serve the Chaldeans, which will come unto us: but ye, gather ye wine, and summer fruits, and oil, and put *them* in your vessels, and dwell in your cities that ye have taken.

11 Likewise when all the Jews that *were* in Moab, and among the Ammonites, and in Edom, and that *were* in all the countries, heard that the king of Babylon had left a remnant of Judah, and that he had set over them Gedaliah the son of Ahikam the son of Shaphan;

12 Even all the Jews returned out of all places whither they were driven, and came *to* the land of Judah, to Gedaliah, unto Mizpah,

39:14 [b]ch. 40:5 [c]ch. 26:24
39:16 [a]ch. 38:7,12 [b]Dan. 9:12
39:18 [a]ch. 21:9; 45:5 [b]1 Chr. 5:20; Ps. 37:40
40:1 [1]Or, *manicles* [a]ch. 39:14
40:2 [a]ch. 50:7
40:3 [a]Deut. 29:24,25; Dan. 9:11
40:4 [1][Or, are *upon thine hand*] [2]Heb. *I will set mine eye upon thee* [a]ch. 39:12 [b]Gen. 20:15
40:5 [a]See ch. 41:10
40:6 [a]ch. 39:14 [b]Judg. 20:1
40:7 [a]2 Ki. 25:23 [b]ch. 39:10
40:8 [a]ch. 41:1
40:10 [1]Heb. *to stand before*

aliah [probably the man named in this verse], who is over the house."

39:15–18 See note on 38:12.

39:16 *Go and speak.* Though confined in prison, Jeremiah was permitted to have visitors (see note on 38:1). *I will bring my words upon this city.* See 19:15.

39:17 *the men . . . thou art afraid.* The court officials (see 38:1) who, in Ebed-melech's judgment, had "acted wickedly" (38:9).

39:18 *thy life shall be for a prey.* See note on 21:9. *thou hast put thy trust in me.* Ebed-melech had expressed his faith in God by securing Jeremiah's release from the cistern (see 38:7–13; see also note on 38:12).

40:1–44:30 A lively narrative of the aftermath of the fall of Jerusalem. Chronologically, the chapters are the latest in the book (although 52:31–34 is later, it is part of the appendix and not of the book proper).

40:1 *The word which came.* A heading introducing the prophecies of Jeremiah after the exile, just as "the word . . . came" (1:2) introduces his prophecies from the time of his call up to the exile (see 1:3). *Nebuzar-adan . . . let him go.* See note on 39:14. *Ramah.* See note on 31:15. *chains.* Manacles that were fastened to the wrists (see v. 4; see also Job 36:8; Is 45:14).

40:2–3 Nebuzaradan doubtless knew the basic content of Jeremiah's prophetic message against Jerusalem, and he here repeats it to the prophet in summary fashion.

40:4 *I will look well unto thee.* Nebuzaradan promises to carry out Nebuchadnezzar's wishes concerning Jeremiah (see 39:12). *all the land is before thee.* Cf. Abram's offer to Lot in Gen 13:9.

40:5–9 See 2 Ki 25:22–24 and notes.

‡40:5 *Gedaliah the son of Ahikam.* See note on 26:24. *victuals.* Or "provisions." The Hebrew for this word is translated "portion" in 52:34.

40:8 *Jezaniah.* See note on 2 Ki 25:23.

40:10 *gather ye wine, and summer fruits, and oil.* Nebuzaradan (see 39:9) had arrived in Jerusalem in August of 586 B.C. (see note, on 52:12). Grapes, figs and olives were harvested in the Holy Land during August and September.

and gathered wine and summer fruits very
much.
13 ¶ Moreover Johanan the son of Kareah,
and all the captains of the forces that *were* in
the fields, came to Gedaliah to Mizpah,
14 And said unto him, Dost thou certainly
know that [a]Baalis the king of the Ammonites
hath sent Ishmael the son of Nethaniah [1]to
slay thee? But Gedaliah the son of Ahikam believed them not.
15 Then Johanan the son of Kareah spake
to Gedaliah in Mizpah secretly, saying, Let me
go, I pray thee, and I will slay Ishmael the son
of Nethaniah, and no man shall know *it:*
wherefore should he slay thee, that all the
Jews which are gathered unto thee should be
scattered, and the remnant in Judah perish?
16 But Gedaliah the son of Ahikam said
unto Johanan the son of Kareah, Thou shalt
not do this thing: for thou speakest falsely of
Ishmael.

41 Now it came to pass in the seventh
month, [a]*that* Ishmael the son of
Nethaniah the son of Elishama, of the seed
royal, and the princes of the king, even ten
men with him, came unto Gedaliah the son of
Ahikam to Mizpah; and there they did eat
bread together in Mizpah.
2 Then arose Ishmael the son of Nethaniah, and the ten men that were with him, and
[a]smote Gedaliah the son of Ahikam the son of
Shaphan with the sword, and slew him, whom
the king of Babylon had made governor over
the land.
3 Ishmael also slew all the Jews that were
with him, *even* with Gedaliah at Mizpah, and
the Chaldeans that were found there, *and* the
men of war.
4 ¶ And it came to pass the second day after
he had slain Gedaliah, and no man knew *it,*
5 That there came certain from Shechem,
from Shiloh, and from Samaria, *even* fourscore
men, [a]having their beards shaven, and their
clothes rent, and having cut themselves, with
offerings and incense in their hand, to bring
them to [b]the house of the LORD.
6 And Ishmael the son of Nethaniah went
forth from Mizpah to meet them, [1]weeping all
along as he went: and it came to pass, as he
met them, he said unto them, Come to Gedaliah the son of Ahikam.
7 And it was *so,* when they came into the
midst of the city, that Ishmael the son of Nethaniah slew them, *and cast them* into the midst
of the pit, he, and the men that *were* with him.
8 But ten men were found among them
that said unto Ishmael, Slay us not: for we
have treasures in the field, *of* wheat, and *of*
barley, and *of* oil, and *of* honey. So he forbare,
and slew them not among their brethren.
9 Now the pit wherein Ishmael had cast all
the dead bodies of the men, whom he had
slain [1][2]because of Gedaliah, *was* it [a]which
Asa the king had made for fear of Baasha king
of Israel: *and* Ishmael the son of Nethaniah
filled it *with them that were* slain.
10 Then Ishmael carried away captive all
the residue of the people that *were* in Mizpah,
[a]*even* the king's daughters, and all the people
that remained in Mizpah, [b]whom Nebuzar-
adan the captain of the guard had committed to
Gedaliah the son of Ahikam: and Ishmael the
son of Nethaniah carried them away captive,
and departed to go over to [c]the Ammonites.
11 ¶ But when Johanan the son of Kareah,
and all [a]the captains of the forces that *were*
with him, heard of all the evil that Ishmael the
son of Nethaniah had done,
12 Then they took all the men, and went to
fight with Ishmael the son of Nethaniah, and
found him by [a]the great waters that *are* in Gibeon.

40:14 [1]Heb. *to strike thee in soul?* [a]See ch. 41:10
41:1 [a]2 Ki. 25:25; ch. 40:6,8
41:2 [a]2 Ki. 25:25
41:5 [a]Lev. 19:27,28; Deut. 14:1; Is. 15:2 [b]See 1 Sam. 1:7; 2 Ki. 25:9
41:6 [1]Heb. *in going and weeping*
41:9 [1]Or, *near Gedaliah* [2]Heb. *by the hand,* or, *by the side of Gedaliah* [a]1 Ki. 15:22; 2 Chr. 16:6
41:10 [a]ch. 43:6 [b]ch. 40:7 [c]ch. 40:14
41:11 [a]ch. 40:7,8,13
41:12 [a]2 Sam. 2:13

40:14 *Baalis.* Either (1) "King Ba'lay," as his name is written on an early sixth-century B.C. bottle discovered in Jordan, or (2) Ba'al-Yasha', an Ammonite king whose name appears on a stamp seal found at Tell el- 'Umeiri in Jordan in 1984. *Ammonites.* Ammon was among the nations that earlier had been allies against Babylonia (see 27:3 and note; see also Ezek 21:18–32).
40:15 *secretly.* See note on 38:16. *remnant.* See note on 6:9.
40:16 *speakest falsely.* See 37:14 and note. Gedaliah's naive faith in Ishmael's integrity would cost him his life.
41:1–3 See 2 Ki 25:25 and note.
41:1 *the princes of the king.* Ishmael's loyalty to Zedekiah might explain his assassination of Gedaliah, whom he considered to be a Babylonian puppet ruler. *there they did eat bread together.* Ancient custom with respect to hospitality probably made Gedaliah assume that his guests would not harm him, much less kill him (see note on Judg 4:21).
41:5 *came.* In the "seventh month" (v. 1) to celebrate the feast of tabernalces (see note on Ex 23:16). *Shechem . . . Shiloh . . . Samaria.* Formerly worship centers in the north (see notes on 7:12; Gen 12:6; see also Josh 24:25–26). After the northern kingdom was destroyed in 722–721 B.C., many Israelites made periodic pilgrimages to Jerusalem, especially during the reform movements of Hezekiah (see 2 Chr 30:11) and Josiah (see 2 Chr 34:9). *beards shaven . . . clothes rent . . . having cut themselves.* Signs of mourning (see 16:6 and note; see also note on Ezra 9:3), probably over the destruction of Jerusalem. *offerings and incense.* Bloodless offerings, since the altar of the Jerusalem temple had been destroyed. *house of the LORD.* Though the temple itself was in ruins, the site was still considered holy.
41:6 *weeping.* Pretending to share the sorrow of the mourners from the north.
41:7 *the city.* Mizpah. *pit.* A favorite place to dispose of victims, whether living or dead (see 37:16 and note; 38:6).
41:8 *wheat . . . barley . . . oil . . . honey.* Supplies that Ishmael perhaps would have taken with him when he fled to Ammon (see v. 15).
41:9 *the pit . . . which Asa the king had made.* Probably as part of the fortifications Asa had built at Mizpah (see 1 Ki 15:22), since cisterns were essential for storing water during times of siege. Archaeologists have discovered numerous cisterns in the ruins of ancient Mizpah (modern Tell en-Nasbeh, seven and a half miles north of Jerusalem).
41:10 *king's daughters.* Women who had been members of King Zedekiah's court, not necessarily daughters of the king himself (see note on 36:26). *Ammonites.* See 40:14 and note.
41:12 *great waters . . . in Gibeon.* Perhaps the same as the one mentioned in 2 Sam 2:13.

13 Now it came to pass, *that* when all the people which *were* with Ishmael saw Johanan the son of Kareah, and all the captains of the forces that *were* with him, then they were glad.

14 So all the people that Ishmael had carried away captive from Mizpah cast about and returned, and went unto Johanan the son of Kareah.

15 But Ishmael the son of Nethaniah escaped from Johanan with eight men, and went to the Ammonites.

16 Then took Johanan the son of Kareah, and all the captains of the forces that *were* with him, all the remnant of the people whom he had recovered from Ishmael the son of Nethaniah, from Mizpah, after *that* he had slain Gedaliah the son of Ahikam, *even* mighty men of war, and the women, and the children, and the eunuchs, whom he had brought again from Gibeon:

17 And they departed, and dwelt in the habitation of [a]Chimham, which *is* by Beth-lehem, to go to enter *into* Egypt,

18 Because of the Chaldeans: for they were afraid of them, because Ishmael the son of Nethaniah had slain Gedaliah the son of Ahikam, [a]whom the king of Babylon made governor in the land.

The flight to Egypt

42 Then all the captains of the forces, [a]and Johanan the son of Kareah, and Jezaniah the son of Hoshaiah, and all the people from the least even unto the greatest, came near,

2 And said unto Jeremiah the prophet, [1]Let, we beseech thee, our supplication be accepted before thee, and [a]pray for us unto the LORD thy God, *even* for all this remnant; (for we are left *but* [b]a few of many, as thine eyes do behold us:)

3 That the LORD thy God may shew us [a]the way wherein we may walk, and the thing that we may do.

4 Then Jeremiah the prophet said unto them, I have heard *you;* behold, I *will* pray unto the LORD your God according to your words; and it shall come to pass, *that* [a]whatsoever thing the LORD shall answer you, I will declare *it* unto you; I will [b]keep nothing back from you.

5 Then they said to Jeremiah, [a]The LORD be a true and faithful witness between us, if we do not even according to all things *for* the which the LORD thy God shall send thee to us.

6 Whether *it be* good, or whether *it be* evil, we will obey the voice of the LORD our God, to whom we send thee; [a]that it may be well with us, when we obey the voice of the LORD our God.

7 ¶ And it came to pass after ten days, that the word of the LORD came unto Jeremiah.

8 Then called he Johanan the son of Kareah, and all the captains of the forces which *were* with him, and all the people from the least even to the greatest,

9 And said unto them, Thus saith the LORD, the God of Israel, unto whom ye sent me to present your supplication before him:

10 If ye will still abide in this land, then [a]will I build you, and not pull *you* down, and I will plant you, and not pluck *you* up: for I [b]repent me of the evil that I have done unto you.

11 Be not afraid of the king of Babylon, of whom ye *are* afraid; be not afraid of him, saith the LORD: [a]for I *am* with you to save you, and to deliver you from his hand.

12 And [a]I will shew mercies unto you, that he may have mercy upon you, and cause you to return to your own land.

13 But if [a]ye say, We will not dwell in this land, neither obey the voice of the LORD your God,

14 Saying, No; but we will go *into* the land of Egypt, where we shall see no war, nor hear the sound of the trumpet, nor have hunger of bread; and there will we dwell:

15 And now therefore hear the word of the LORD, ye remnant of Judah; Thus saith the LORD of hosts, the God of Israel; If ye [a]wholly set [b]your faces to enter *into* Egypt, and go to sojourn there;

16 Then it shall come to pass, *that* the sword, which ye feared, shall overtake you there in the land of Egypt, and the famine, whereof ye were afraid, [1]shall follow close after you there *in* Egypt; and there ye shall die.

17 [1]So shall it be with all the men that set their faces to go *into* Egypt to sojourn there;

41:17 [a]2 Sam. 19:37,38 **41:18** [a]ch. 40:5 **42:1** [a]ch. 40:8,13; 41:11 **42:2** [1]Or, *Let our supplication fall before thee* [a]1 Sam. 7:8; 12:19; Is. 37:4; Jas. 5:16 [b]Lev. 26:22 **42:3** [a]Ezra 8:21 **42:4** [a]1 Ki. 22:14

42:4 [b]1 Sam. 3:18; Acts 20:20 **42:5** [a]Gen. 31:50 **42:6** [a]Deut. 6:3; ch. 7:23 **42:10** [a]ch. 24:6; 31:28; 33:7 [b]Deut. 32:36; ch. 18:8 **42:11** [a]Is. 43:5; Rom. 8:31 **42:12** [a]Ps. 106:45,46 **42:13** [a]ch. 44:16 **42:15** [a]Deut. 17:16; ch. 44:12-14 [b]Luke 9:51 **42:16** [1]Heb. *shall cleave after you* **42:17** [1]Heb. *So shall all the men be*

41:15 *escaped . . . with eight men.* Ishmael lost only two of his men (see v. 2) in the fight with Johanan.

41:17 *habitation of Chimham.* Location unknown; perhaps means "lodging place of Chimham," a friend of David who returned with him to Jerusalem after Absalom's death (see 2 Sam 19:37–40).

42:1 *Jezaniah the son of Hoshaiah.* Possibly the same as "Jezaniah the son of the Maacathite" (40:8). Apparently, Jezaniah was also known as Jaazaniah (2 Ki 25:23) and Azariah (as found in the Septuagint of this verse; see also 43:2), as was King Uzziah (see notes on 2 Ki 14:21; 2 Chr 26:1).

42:2 *Jeremiah.* Had probably been among the "remnant" from Mizpah (41:16). *Let . . . our supplication be accepted before thee.* See v. 9; 37:20.

42:3 The people may be asking the Lord to confirm what they sincerely believe to be their only option: flight to Egypt (see v. 17; 41:17).

42:6 *we will obey . . . the LORD our God.* Though they twice declare here their desire to do God's will, they soon demonstrate that they have already decided to follow their own inclinations (see 43:2).

42:7 *after ten days.* Jeremiah does not bring God's word to the people until he is sure of it himself (see 28:10–12).

42:10 *build you . . . pull you down . . . plant . . . pluck.* See 1:10 and note; see also 31:4,28; 33:7.

42:12 *that he may have mercy upon you.* For similar examples see Gen 43:14; 1 Ki 8:50.

42:16 *the sword, which ye feared, shall overtake you.* See 43:11 and note.

42:17–18 See 44:11–14.

they shall die [a]by the sword, by the famine,
and by the pestilence: and [b]none of them shall
remain or escape from the evil that I *will* bring
upon them.
18 For thus saith the LORD of hosts, the
God of Israel; As mine anger and my fury hath
been [a]poured forth upon the inhabitants of Jerusalem; so shall my fury be poured forth upon
you, when ye shall enter *into* Egypt: and [b]ye
shall be an execration, and an astonishment,
and a curse, and a reproach; and ye shall see
this place no more.
19 The LORD hath said concerning you, O ye
remnant of Judah; [a]Go ye not *into* Egypt: know
certainly that I have [1]admonished you *this* day.
20 For [1]ye dissembled in your hearts,
when ye sent me unto the LORD your God, saying, Pray for us unto the LORD our God; and according unto all that the LORD our God shall
say, so declare unto us, and we will do *it.*
21 And *now* I have *this* day declared *it* to
you; but ye have not obeyed the voice of the
LORD your God, nor any *thing* for the which he
hath sent me unto you.
22 Now therefore know certainly that [a]ye
shall die by the sword, by the famine, and by
the pestilence, in the place whither ye desire
[1]to go *and* to sojourn.
43 And it came to pass, *that* when Jeremiah had made an end of speaking
unto all the people all the words of the LORD
their God, *for* which the LORD their God had
sent him to them, *even* all these words;
2 [a]Then spake Azariah the son of Hoshaiah, and Johanan the son of Kareah, and all the
proud men, saying unto Jeremiah, Thou speakest falsely: the LORD our God hath not sent
thee to say, Go not *into* Egypt to sojourn there:
3 But Baruch the son of Neriah setteth thee
on against us, for to deliver us into the hand of
the Chaldeans, that *they* might put us to death,
and carry us away captives *into* Babylon.
4 So Johanan the son of Kareah, and all the
captains of the forces, and all the people,
obeyed not the voice of the LORD, to dwell in
the land of Judah.
5 But Johanan the son of Kareah, and all
the captains of the forces, took [a]all the remnant of Judah, that were returned from all nations, whither they had been driven, to dwell
in the land of Judah:
6 *Even* men, and women, and children,
[a]and the king's daughters, [b]and every person
that Nebuzar-adan the captain of the guard had
left with Gedaliah the son of Ahikam the son
of Shaphan, and Jeremiah the prophet, and
Baruch the son of Neriah.
7 So they came *into* the land of Egypt: for
they obeyed not the voice of the LORD: thus
came they *even* to [a][1]Tahpanhes.
8 ¶ Then came the word of the LORD unto
Jeremiah in Tahpanhes, saying,
9 Take great stones in thine hand, and hide
them in the clay in the brickkiln, which *is* at
the entry of Pharaoh's house in Tahpanhes, in
the sight of the men of Judah;
10 And say unto them, Thus saith the LORD
of hosts, the God of Israel; Behold, I *will* send
and take Nebuchadrezzar the king of Babylon,
[a]my servant, and will set his throne upon
these stones that I have hid; and he shall
spread his royal pavilion over them.
11 [a]And when he cometh, he shall smite
the land of Egypt, *and deliver* [b]such *as are* for
death to death; and such *as are* for captivity to
captivity; and such *as are* for the sword to the
sword.
12 And I will kindle a fire in the houses of
[a]the gods of Egypt; and he shall burn them,
and carry them away captives: and he shall array himself with the land of Egypt, as a shepherd putteth on his garment; and he shall go
forth from thence in peace.
13 He shall break also the [1]images of
[2]Beth-shemesh, that *is* in the land of Egypt;
and the houses of the gods of the Egyptians
shall he burn with fire.

The refugees rebuked

44 The word that came to Jeremiah concerning all the Jews which dwell in
the land of Egypt, which dwell at [a]Migdol, and

42:17 [a]ver. 22; ch. 24:10 [b]See ch. 44:14,28
42:18 [a]ch. 7:20 [b]ch. 18:16; 24:9; 26:6; 29:18,22; 44:12; Zech. 8:13
42:19 [1]Heb. *testified against you* [a]Deut. 17:16
42:20 [1]Or, *you have used deceit against your souls*
42:22 [1][Or, *to go to sojourn*] [a]ver. 17; Ezek. 6:11
43:2 [a]ch. 42:1
43:5 [a]ch. 40:11,12
43:6 [a]ch. 41:10 [b]ch. 39:10; 40:7
43:7 [1][Called *Hanes,* Is. 30:4] [a]ch. 2:16; 44:1
43:10 [a]ch. 25:9; 27:6; See Ezek. 29:18,20
43:11 [a]ch. 44:13; 46:13 [b]ch. 15:2; Zech. 11:9
43:12 [a]ch. 46:25
43:13 [1]Heb. *statues,* or, *standing images* [2]Or, *The house of the sun*
44:1 [a]Ex. 14:2; ch. 46:14

42:17 *sword . . . famine . . . pestilence.* See note on 14:12.

42:18 *mine anger and my fury hath been poured forth.* See 7:20; 44:6. *an execration . . . and an astonishment.* See notes on 24:9; 25:18; see also 29:18. *this place.* Jerusalem.

42:19 *I have admonished you.* See 11:7.

43:2 *Azariah.* See note on 42:1. *proud men.* They demonstrate themselves to be such by their words.

43:3 *Baruch.* See note on 32:12. Jeremiah's opponents decide to put the blame on someone they consider less spiritually formidable than the prophet himself.

43:6 *king's daughters.* See note on 41:10. *Jeremiah . . . and Baruch.* No doubt they went to Egypt unwillingly, in the light of 32:6–15; 40:1–6; 42:13–22.

43:7 *Tahpanhes.* See note on 2:16.

43:9 *Pharaoh's house.* Not necessarily his main residence. One of the Elephantine papyri, e.g., mentions the "king's house," apparently a more modest dwelling for Pharaoh's use when he visited Elephantine in southern Egypt.

43:10 *Nebuchadrezzar . . . my servant.* See note on 25:9. *his throne.* Symbolizing his authority.

43:11 See 15:2 and note. *he shall smite . . . Egypt.* A fragmentary text now owned by the British Museum in London states that Nebuchadnezzar carried out a punitive expedition against Egypt in his 37th year (568–567 B.C.) during the reign of Pharaoh Amasis (see Ezek 29:17–20 and notes).

43:12 *he shall array himself . . . as a shepherd putteth on his garment.* Routinely and confidently.

43:13 *images of Beth-shemesh . . . in the land of Egypt.* The qualifying phrase is used to distinguish the site from "Beth-shemesh, which belongeth to Judah" (2 Ki 14:11). The Egyptian city is probably to be identified with Heliopolis (Greek for "city of the sun"), called *On* in Hebrew (see note on Gen 41:45). *images.* Sacred pillars, for which ancient Heliopolis was famous.

44:1–30 The last of Jeremiah's recorded prophecies (see note on 40:1–44:30).

44:1 *Jews which dwell in . . . Egypt.* As a result of previous deportations (see, e.g., 2 Ki 23:34) and/or the Jews mentioned in

at [b]Tahpanhes, and at [c]Noph, and in the country of Pathros, saying,

2 Thus saith the LORD of hosts, the God of Israel; Ye have seen all the evil that I have brought upon Jerusalem, and upon all the cities of Judah; and behold, this day they *are* [a]a desolation, and no man dwelleth therein,

3 Because of their wickedness which they have committed to provoke me to anger, in that *they* went [a]to burn incense, *and* to [b]serve other gods, whom they knew not, *neither* they, you, nor your fathers.

4 Howbeit [a]I sent unto you all my servants the prophets, rising early and sending *them,* saying, Oh, do not this abominable thing that I hate.

5 But they hearkened not, nor inclined their ear to turn from their wickedness, to burn no incense unto other gods.

6 Wherefore my fury and mine anger was poured forth, and was kindled in the cities of Judah and in the streets of Jerusalem; and they are wasted *and* desolate, as *at* this day.

7 Therefore now thus saith the LORD, the God of hosts, the God of Israel; Wherefore commit ye *this* great evil [a]against your souls, to cut off from you man and woman, child and suckling, [1]out of Judah, to leave you none to remain;

8 In that *ye* [a]provoke me unto wrath with the works of your hands, burning incense unto other gods in the land of Egypt, whither ye be gone to dwell, that ye might cut yourselves off, and that *ye* might be [b]a curse and a reproach among all the nations of the earth?

9 Have ye forgotten the [1]wickedness of your fathers, and the wickedness of the kings of Judah, and the wickedness of their wives, and your own wickedness, and the wickedness of your wives, which they have committed in the land of Judah, and in the streets of Jerusalem?

10 They are not [1]humbled *even* unto this day, neither have they [a]feared, nor walked in my law, nor in my statutes, that I set before you and before your fathers.

11 ¶ Therefore thus saith the LORD of hosts, the God of Israel; Behold, [a]I will set my face against you for evil, and to cut off all Judah.

12 And I will take the remnant of Judah, that have set their faces to go *into* the land of Egypt to sojourn there, and [a]they shall all be consumed, *and* fall in the land of Egypt; they shall *even* be consumed by the sword, *and* by the famine: they shall die, from the least even unto the greatest, by the sword and by the famine: and [b]they shall be an execration, *and* an astonishment, and a curse, and a reproach.

13 [a]For I will punish them that dwell in the land of Egypt, as I have punished Jerusalem, by the sword, by the famine, and by the pestilence:

14 So that none of the remnant of Judah, which are gone into the land of Egypt to sojourn there, shall escape or remain, that *they* should return *into* the land of Judah, to the which they [1]have a desire to return to dwell there: for [a]none shall return but such as shall escape.

15 ¶ Then all the men which knew that their wives had burnt incense unto other gods, and all the women that stood *by,* a great multitude, even all the people that dwelt in the land of Egypt, in Pathros, answered Jeremiah, saying,

16 *As for* the word that thou hast spoken unto us in the name of the LORD, [a]we will not hearken unto thee.

17 But we will certainly do [a]whatsoever thing goeth forth out of our own mouth, to burn incense unto the [b1]queen of heaven, and to pour out drink offerings unto her, as we have done, we, and our fathers, our kings, and our princes, in the cities of Judah, and in the streets of Jerusalem: for *then* had we plenty of [2]victuals, and were well, and saw no evil.

18 But since we left off to burn incense to the queen of heaven, and to pour out drink offerings unto her, we have wanted all *things,* and have been consumed by the sword and by the famine.

19 [a]And when we burnt incense to the queen of heaven, and poured out drink offerings unto her, did we make her cakes to wor-

44:1 [b]ch. 43:7 [c]Is. 19:13
44:2 [a]ch. 9:11; 34:22
44:3 [a]ch. 19:4 [b]Deut. 13:6; 32:17
44:4 [a]2 Chr. 36:15; ch. 7:25; 25:4; 26:5; 29:19
44:7 [1]Heb. *out of the midst of Judah* [a]Num. 16:38; ch. 7:19
44:8 [a]ch. 25:6,7 [b]ver. 12; ch. 42:18
44:9 [1]Heb. *wickednesses,* or, *punishments, etc.*
44:10 [1]Heb. *contrite* [a]Prov. 28:14
44:11 [a]Lev. 17:10; 20:5,6; ch. 21:10; Amos 9:4
44:12 [a]ch. 42:15-17,22 [b]ch. 42:18
44:13 [a]ch. 43:11
44:14 [1]Heb. *lift up their soul* [a]ver. 28
44:16 [a]ch. 6:16
44:17 [1]Or, *frame of heaven* [2]Heb. *bread* [a]See ver. 25; Num. 30:12; Deut. 23:23; Judg. 11:36 [b]ch. 7:18
44:19 [a]ch. 7:18

43:5–7. In either case, some time must have elapsed between chs. 43 and 44 to bring about the gathering mentioned in v. 15. *land of Egypt . . . country of Pathros.* See note on Is 11:11. *Migdol.* Location uncertain; probably in northern Egypt (see 46:14). The name means "watchtower." *Tahpanhes, Noph.* See notes on 2:16; Is 19:13.

44:3 See note on 1:16; see also 11:17; 19:4; 32:32.

44:4 See note on 7:25. *do not this abominable thing.* See Judg 19:24.

44:6 *my fury and mine anger was poured forth.* See 7:20; 42:18.

44:7 *great evil against your souls.* See 26:19. *man and woman, child and suckling.* A stock phrase meaning "everyone" (see 1 Sam 15:3; 22:19).

44:8 *works of your hands.* Idols (see 1:16 and note). *a curse and a reproach.* See 42:18; see also notes on 24:9; 25:18.

44:9 *wickedness of . . . kings . . . their wives . . . your wives.* The women joined their husbands in worshiping the "queen of heaven" (v. 19; see v. 15).

44:10 *nor walked in my law.* See 9:13; 26:4; see also 7:9 and note.

44:11–14 See 42:17–18 and notes.

44:11 *set my face.* See 21:10.

44:15 *wives . . . women.* See v. 19; see also note on v. 9. *in the land of Egypt, in Pathros.* See v. 1; see also note on Is 11:11.

44:17 *queen of heaven.* See note on 7:18. *then had we plenty.* Judah had been relatively prosperous during King Manasseh's lengthy reign.

44:18 *since we left off.* As a result of King Josiah's reform movement, which began in 621 B.C. *we have wanted all things.* Beginning with Josiah's death in 609, a series of disasters, including invasion and exile, had struck Judah. The people understandably (though mistakenly) attributed their misfortune to their failure to worship the queen of heaven.

44:19 Since Ishtar (the "queen of heaven") was a Babylonian goddess of fertility, women played a major role in her worship. *we make her cakes to worship her.* See 7:18 and note. *without*

ship her, and pour out drink offerings unto her, without our [1]men?

20 ¶ Then Jeremiah said unto all the people, to the men, and to the women, and to all the people which had given him *that* answer, saying,

21 The incense that ye burnt in the cities of Judah, and in the streets of Jerusalem, ye, and your fathers, your kings, and your princes, and the people of the land, did not the LORD remember them, and came it *not* into his mind?

22 So that the LORD could no longer bear, because of the evil of your doings, *and* because of the abominations which ye have committed; therefore is your land [a]a desolation, and an astonishment, and a curse, without an inhabitant, [b]as *at* this day.

23 Because you have burnt incense, and because ye have sinned against the LORD, and have not obeyed the voice of the LORD, nor walked in his law, nor in his statutes, nor in his testimonies; [a]therefore this evil is happened unto you, as *at* this day.

24 ¶ Moreover Jeremiah said unto all the people, and to all the women, Hear the word of the LORD, all Judah [a]that *are* in the land of Egypt:

25 Thus saith the LORD of hosts, the God of Israel, saying; [a]Ye and your wives have both spoken with your mouths, and fulfilled with your hand, saying, We will surely perform our vows that we have vowed, to burn incense to the queen of heaven, and to pour out drink offerings unto her: ye will surely accomplish your vows, and surely perform your vows.

26 Therefore hear ye the word of the LORD, all Judah that dwell in the land of Egypt; Behold, [a]I have sworn by my great name, saith the LORD, that [b]my name shall no more be named in the mouth of any man of Judah in all the land of Egypt, saying, The Lord GOD liveth.

27 [a]Behold, I *will* watch over them for evil, and not for good: and all the men of Judah that *are* in the land of Egypt [b]shall be consumed by the sword and by the famine, until there be an end of them.

28 Yet [a]a small number that escape the sword shall return out of the land of Egypt *into* the land of Judah, and all the remnant of Judah, that are gone into the land of Egypt to sojourn there, shall know whose [b]words shall stand, [1]mine, or theirs.

29 And this *shall be* a sign unto you, saith the LORD, that I will punish you in this place, that ye may know that my words shall surely stand against you for evil:

30 Thus saith the LORD; Behold, [a]I *will* give Pharaoh-hophra king of Egypt into the hand of his enemies, and into the hand of them that seek his life; as I gave [b]Zedekiah king of Judah into the hand of Nebuchadrezzar king of Babylon, his enemy, and that sought his life.

44:19 [1]Or, *husbands?*
44:22 [a]ch. 25:11,18,38 [b]ver. 6
44:23 [a]Dan. 9:11,12
44:24 [a]ver. 15; ch. 43:7
44:25 [a]ver. 15
44:26 [a]Gen. 22:16 [b]Ezek. 20:39
44:27 [a]ch. 1:10; 31:28; Ezek. 7:6 [b]ver. 12
44:28 [1]Heb. *from me, or from them* [a]ver. 14; Is. 27:13 [b]ver. 17,25,26
44:30 [a]ch. 46:25,26; Ezek. 29:3; 30:21 [b]ch. 39:5
45:1 [a]ch. 36:1,4,32
45:4 [a]Is. 5:5
45:5 [a]ch. 25:26 [b]ch. 21:9; 38:2; 39:18
46:1 [a]ch. 25:15

Encouragement to Baruch

45 The [a]word that Jeremiah the prophet spake unto Baruch the son of Neriah, when he had written these words in a book at the mouth of Jeremiah, in the fourth year of Jehoiakim the son of Josiah king of Judah, saying,

2 Thus saith the LORD, the God of Israel, unto thee, O Baruch;

3 Thou didst say, Woe is me now! for the LORD hath added grief to my sorrow; I fainted in my sighing, and I find no rest.

4 Thus shalt thou say unto him, The LORD saith thus; Behold, [a]*that* which I have built *will* I break down, and *that* which I have planted I *will* pluck up, even this whole land.

5 And seekest thou great *things* for thyself? seek *them* not: for behold, [a]I *will* bring evil upon all flesh, saith the LORD: but thy life will I give unto thee [b]for a prey in all places whither thou goest.

The prophecy about Egypt

46 The word of the LORD which came to Jeremiah the prophet against [a]the Gentiles;

---

our men. To have validity, a religious vow made by a married woman (see v. 25) had to be confirmed by her husband (see Num 30:10–15).

44:22 *desolation.* See v. 6. *a curse.* See v. 12.

44:23 *testimonies.* Of the Lord's covenant with His people (see Deut 4:45; 6:17,20).

44:25 *ye will surely accomplish your vows.* Spoken in irony (see 7:21 and note).

44:26 *I have sworn by my great name.* See notes on 22:5; Gen 22:16. *The LORD God liveth.* See note on Gen 42:15.

44:27 *will watch.* See note on 1:12; see also 31:28.

44:28 *a small number.* See v. 14.

44:30 *Pharaoh-hophra.* Ruled Egypt 589–570 B.C. (see 37:5 and note). *his enemies . . . them that seek his life.* Pharaoh-hophra was killed by his Egyptian rivals during a power struggle. *I gave Zedekiah . . . into the hand of Nebuchadrezzar.* See 39:5–7.

45:1–5 A brief message of encouragement to Baruch, Jeremiah's faithful secretary (see note on 32:12). Though out of chronological order, the section provides a suitable historical appendix to chs. 39–44 as well as a smooth transition to chs. 46–51 (see notes on v. 1; 46:2).

45:1 *had written . . . in a book.* See 36:4; see also 36:2 and note. *fourth year of Jehoiakim.* 605 B.C. Ch. 45 fits chronologically between 36:8 and 36:9 (see note on 36:8).

45:3 To some extent Baruch shared Jeremiah's anguish, the result of Jeremiah's prophetic call and ministry (see, e.g., 8:18–9:2; 20:7–18). *fainted in my sighing.* See Ps 6:6. *I find no rest.* See Lam 5:5.

45:4 *built . . . break down . . . planted . . . pluck up.* See note on 1:10; see also 2:21; 31:4–5,28,40; 32:41; 33:7. *land.* Or "earth" (see "all flesh" in v. 5; see also 25:15,31; 46–51).

45:5 *great things . . . seek them not.* See Ps 131:1. Baruch's brother Seraiah would occupy an important position under King Zedekiah (see 32:12; 51:59), but Baruch himself was not to be ambitious or self-seeking. *thy life will I give unto thee for a prey.* See note on 21:9.

46:1–51:64 See notes on 25:1–38; 25:13; 25:19–26. Chs. 46–51 consist of a series of prophecies against the nations (see Is 13–23; Ezek 25–32; Amos 1–2; Zeph 2:4–15). They begin with Egypt (ch. 46) and end with Babylonia (chs. 50–51), the two

2 Against Egypt, [a]against the army of Pharaoh-necho king of Egypt, which was by the river Euphrates in Carchemish, which Nebuchadrezzar king of Babylon smote in the
fourth year of Jehoiakim the son of Josiah king
of Judah.

3 [a]Order ye the buckler and shield, and
draw near to battle.
4 Harness the horses; and get up, ye
horsemen,
And stand forth with *your* helmets;
Furbish the spears, *and* put on the
brigandines.
5 Wherefore have I seen them dismayed
and turned away back?
And their mighty ones are [1]beaten
down,
And are [2]fled apace, and look not back:
For [a]fear *was* round about, saith the
LORD.
6 Let not the swift flee away, nor the
mighty *man* escape;
They shall [a]stumble, and fall toward
the north by the river Euphrates.
7 Who *is* this *that* cometh up [a]as a flood,
Whose waters are moved as the rivers?
8 Egypt riseth up like a flood,
And *his* waters are moved like the
rivers;
And he saith, I will go up, *and* will
cover the earth;
I will destroy the city and the
inhabitants thereof.
9 Come up, ye horses; and rage, ye
chariots;
And let the mighty *men* come forth;
[1]The Ethiopians and [2]the Libyans, that
handle the shield;
And the Lydians, [a]that handle *and*
bend the bow.
10 For this *is* [a]the day of the Lord GOD of
hosts,
A day of vengeance, that *he* may
avenge him of his adversaries:
And [b]the sword shall devour, and it
shall be satiate and made drunk with
their blood:
For the Lord GOD of hosts [c]hath a
sacrifice
In the north country by the river
Euphrates.
11 [a]Go up *into* Gilead, and take balm,
[b]O virgin, the daughter of Egypt:
In vain shalt thou use many medicines;
For [c][1]thou shalt not be cured.
12 The nations have heard *of* thy shame,
And thy cry hath filled the land:
For the mighty *man* hath stumbled
against the mighty,
And they are fallen both together.

13 ¶ The word that the LORD spake to Jeremiah the prophet, how Nebuchadrezzar king
of Babylon should come and [a]smite the land of
Egypt.

14 Declare ye in Egypt, and publish in
Migdol,
And publish in Noph and in
Tahpanhes:
Say ye, [a]Stand fast, and prepare thee;
For [b]the sword shall devour round
about thee.
15 Why are thy valiant *men* swept away?

46:2 [a]2 Ki. 23:29; 2 Chr. 35:20; Fulfilled presently
46:3 [a]ch. 51:11,12; Nah. 2:1; 3:14
46:5 [1]Heb. *broken in pieces* [2]Heb. *fled a flight* [a]ch. 49:29
46:6 [a]Dan. 11:19
46:7 [a]Is. 8:7,8; ch. 47:2
46:9 [1]Heb. *Cush* [2]Heb. *Put* [a]Is. 66:19
46:10 [a]Is. 13:6; Joel 1:15 [b]Deut. 32:42; Is. 34:6 [c]Is. 34:6; Zeph. 1:7; See Ezek. 39:17
46:11 [1]Heb. *no cure shall be unto thee* [a]ch. 8:22 [b]Is. 47:1 [c]Ezek. 30:21
46:13 [a]Is. 19:1; Ezek. 29; 30; 32
46:14 [a]ver. 3,4 [b]ver. 10

powers that vied for control of Judah during Jeremiah's ministry. The arrangement of the prophecies is in a generally west-to-east direction.

46:1 *The word of the LORD . . . against.* See 14:1; 47:1; 49:34; 50:1. *Gentiles.* To whom Jeremiah was called to prophesy (see 1:5 and note).

46:2 *Against Egypt.* See Is 19–20; Ezek 29–32. *Pharaoh-necho.* Ruled Egypt 610–595 B.C. *Carchemish.* See 2 Chr 35:20; Is 10:9. The name means "fortress of Chemosh" (chief god of Moab; see 2 Ki 23:13), as clarified by the Ebla tablets (see Introduction to Genesis: Background; see also chart, p. xix). *which Nebuchadrezzar.* Egypt's defeat by Babylonia at Carchemish was one of the most decisive battles in the ancient world, ending Egypt's age-long claims and pretensions to power in Syro-Palestine. *fourth year of Jehoiakim.* 605 B.C., the first year of Nebuchadrezzar's reign (see 25:1).

46:3 *Order ye.* Spoken to the Egyptians in sarcasm (see, e.g., Nah 2:1; 3:14).

46:4 *horses.* Egypt was a prime source for the finest horses (see 1 Ki 10:28). *put on the brigandines.* See 51:3.

46:5 *fear was round about.* The phrase is used in 6:25 (see note there) with reference to the Babylonian army (see 6:22 and note).

46:7–8 *Whose waters are moved as the rivers?* In the northern Egyptian delta, where the Nile branches out into numerous streams.

46:8 *riseth up . . . and will cover the earth.* The same metaphor is used of Assyria in Is 8:7–8 (see note there). *city.* The Hebrew for this word is in the singular but should be interpreted as a generic plural ("city" is generic also in 8:16).

46:9 *Come up.* See note on v. 3; see also 8:6; Nah 3:3. *rage, ye chariots.* See Nah 2:4. *Libyans.* See note on Gen 10:6. *Lydians.* See note on Is 66:19. Men from Cush, Put and Lydia were mercenaries in the Egyptian army.

‡46:10 *day of vengeance.* See Is 34:8 and note. The Lord will avenge Egypt's cruelties toward Judah (see, e.g., 2 Ki 23:29,33–35). *sword shall devour.* See v. 14. *shall be satiate and made drunk with their blood . . . a sacrifice.* The imagery of "blood" and "sacrifice" found in the Israelite sacrificial ritual was often used to describe battles (see Is 34:5–7 and notes; Zeph 1:7–8).

46:11 *Gilead . . . balm.* See 8:22 and note. *virgin, the daughter of Egypt.* See v. 19; Is 23:12 and note; Is 47:1; see also 14:17 and note; 18:13; 31:4,21. *In vain . . . medicines . . . thou shalt not be cured.* The statement is ironic in the light of Egypt's reputation for expertise in the healing arts.

46:12 *stumbled . . . fallen.* See vv. 6,16.

46:13 *Nebuchadrezzar . . . smite . . . Egypt.* In 568–567 B.C. (see note on 43:11), long after the battle of Carchemish (see note on v. 2).

46:14 *Migdol.* See note on 44:1. *Noph and . . . Tahpanhes.* See 44:1; see also notes on 2:16; Is 19:13. *ye, Stand fast.* See v. 4. *sword shall devour.* See v. 10.

46:15 *valiant men.* The Hebrew for this phrase is not the same as that for "mighty men" (vv. 5,9) or "warrior" (v. 12). It often refers to powerful animals ("stallions" in 8:16; 47:3; 50:11;

They stood not, because the LORD did
drive them.
16 He [1]made many to fall,
Yea, [a]one fell upon another:
And they said, Arise, and let us go
again to our own people,
And to the land of our nativity,
From the oppressing sword.
17 They did cry there, Pharaoh king of
Egypt *is but* a noise;
He hath passed the time appointed.
18 *As* I live, saith the King,
[a]Whose name *is* the LORD of hosts,
Surely as Tabor *is* among the
mountains,
And as Carmel by the sea, *so* shall he
come.
19 O [a]thou daughter dwelling in Egypt,
[1]Furnish thyself [b]to go into captivity:
For Noph shall be waste
And desolate without an inhabitant.
20 Egypt *is like* a very fair [a]heifer,
But destruction cometh; it cometh [b]out
of the north.
21 Also her hired men *are* in the midst of
her like [1]fatted bullocks;
For they also are turned back, *and* are
fled away together; they did not
stand,
Because [a]the day of their calamity was
come upon them, *and* the time of
their visitation.
22 [a]The voice thereof shall go like a
serpent;
For they shall march with an army,
And come against her with axes, as
hewers of wood.
23 They shall [a]cut down her forest, saith
the LORD,
Though it cannot be searched;
Because they are more than the
[b]grasshoppers,
And *are* innumerable.
24 The daughter of Egypt shall be
confounded;
She shall be delivered into the hand of
[a]the people of the north.
25 The LORD of hosts, the God of Israel,
saith;
Behold, I will punish the [1 2]multitude
of [a]No,
And Pharaoh, and Egypt, [b]with their
gods, and their kings;
Even Pharaoh, and *all* them that trust
in him:
26 [a]And I will deliver them into the hand
of those that seek their lives,
And into the hand of Nebuchadrezzar
king of Babylon,
And into the hand of his servants:
And [b]afterwards it shall be inhabited,
As *in* the days of old, saith the LORD.
27 [a]But fear not thou, O my servant Jacob,
And be not dismayed, O Israel:
For behold, I *will* save thee from afar
off,
And thy seed from the land of their
captivity;
And Jacob shall return, and be in rest
and at ease,
And none shall make *him* afraid.
28 Fear thou not, O Jacob my servant,
Saith the LORD: for I *am* with thee;
For I will make a full end of all the
nations whither I have driven thee:
But I will not make [a]a full end of thee,
But correct thee in measure;
Yet will I [1]not leave thee wholly
unpunished.

46:16 [1]Heb. *multiplied the faller* [a]Lev. 26:37
46:18 [a]Is. 47:4; ch. 48:15
46:19 [1]Heb. *Make thee instruments of captivity* [a]ch. 48:18 [b]Is. 20:4
46:20 [a]Hos. 10:11 [b]ch. 1:14
46:21 [1]Heb. *bullocks of the stall* [a]Ps. 37:13; ch. 50:27
46:22 [a]Is. 29:4
46:23 [a]Is. 10:34
46:23 [b]Judg. 6:5
46:24 [a]ch. 1:15
46:25 [1]Or, *nourisher* [2]Heb. *Amon* [a]Ezek. 30:14 [b]ch. 43:12
46:26 [a]Ezek. 32:11 [b]Ezek. 29:11,13,14
46:27 [a]Is. 41:13
46:28 [1]Or, *not utterly cut thee off* [a]ch. 10:24

"steeds" in Judg 5:22). In Ps 22:12; 50:13; 68:30; Is 34:7 the Hebrew word is translated "bulls" (see note on Ps 68:30). *swept away.* The Hebrew for this phrase is translated "Apis has fled" in the Septuagint (the Greek translation of the OT). Apis was a bull-god worshiped in Egypt, especially at Noph (see v. 14). An alternative translation of v. 15 would then read as follows: "Why did Apis flee? Why did your bull [many manuscripts have the singular form] not stand? Because the LORD pushed him down."
46:16 *He made many to fall.* See vv. 6,12; lit. "He will make many stumble." *they said, . . . let us go.* The mercenaries in Pharaoh's army (see v. 9 and note) will decide to return to their homelands. *oppressing sword.* See 25:38; 50:16.
46:17 *a noise.* In Is 30:7, Egypt is called the one "who has been exterminated." *He hath passed the time appointed.* After the battle of Carchemish (see v. 2), Nebuchadnezzar returned to Babylonia on learning of his father's death. Egypt failed to press its advantage at that time.
46:18 *As I live.* See notes on Gen 22:16; 42:15. *King.* God is called "King" also in 8:19; 10:7,10; 48:15; 51:57. *he.* Nebuchadnezzar. *Tabor . . . Carmel.* Two prominent mountains in Israel (see notes on Judg 4:6; Sol 7:5; Is 33:9).
46:19 *daughter . . . Egypt.* See v. 11 and note. *Furnish thyself to go into captivity.* Echoed in Ezek 12:3. *desolate without an inhabitant.* Judah is so described in 2:15; 9:12.
‡**46:20** *heifer.* Perhaps an ironic reference to Egyptian bull-worship (see note on v. 15). *destruction.* Can be translated "horsefly" or "gadfly." Insects are often used to symbolize an attacking enemy (see note on Ex 23:28).
46:21 *hired men.* See note on v. 9. *bullocks.* See note on v. 20. *day of their calamity.* See 18:17. *time of their visitation.* See 11:23; 23:12; 50:27.
46:22 *serpent.* Often used by Egyptian pharaohs as a symbol of their sovereignty (see note on Ex 4:3). *with axes, as hewers of wood.* See 21:14; see also Is 10:18–19,33–34 and notes.
46:23 *more than the grasshoppers.* Here an invading army is compared to grasshoppers. In Joel 2:11,25 locusts are compared to an invading army.
46:24 *daughter of Egypt.* See note on v. 11.
‡**46:25** *multitude.* Hebrew *Amon.* Amon was the chief god of Egypt during much of its history. Wicked King Manasseh may have named his son after the Egyptian deity (see 2 Ki 21:18; 2 Chr 33:22). *No.* Hebrew for Thebes. The capital of Upper (southern) Egypt (see Ezek 30:14–16).
46:26 *it shall be inhabited, As in the days of old.* Cf. 48:47; 49:6,39. Egypt would be restored in the Messianic age (see Is 19:23–25).
46:27–28 Repeated almost verbatim from 30:10–11 (see notes there).

Prophecy about the Philistines

47 The word of the LORD that came to Jeremiah the prophet [a]against the Philistines, [b]before that Pharaoh smote [1]Gaza.

2 Thus saith the LORD;
Behold, [a]waters rise up [b]out of the north,
And shall be an overflowing flood,
And shall overflow the land, and [1]all that is therein;
The city, and them that dwell therein:
Then the men shall cry,
And all the inhabitants of the land shall howl.
3 At the [a]noise of the stamping of the hoofs of his strong *horses,*
At the rushing of his chariots,
And at the rumbling of his wheels,
The fathers shall not look back to *their* children
For feebleness of hands;
4 Because of the day that cometh to spoil all the Philistines,
And to cut off from [a]Tyrus and Zidon every helper that remaineth:
For the LORD *will* spoil the Philistines,
[b]The remnant of [1]the country of [c]Caphtor.
5 [a]Baldness is come upon Gaza;
[b]Ashkelon is cut off *with* the remnant of their valley:
How long wilt thou cut thyself?
6 O thou [a]sword of the LORD, how long *will it be* ere thou be quiet?
[1]Put up thyself into thy scabbard, rest, and be still.
7 [1]How can it be quiet, seeing the LORD hath [a]given it a charge
Against Ashkelon, and against the sea shore? there hath he [b]appointed it.

47:1 [1]Heb. *Azzah* [a]Zeph. 2:4 [b]Amos 1:6
47:2 [1]Heb. *the fulness thereof* [a]Is. 8:7 [b]ch. 1:14
47:3 [a]ch. 8:16
47:4 [1]Heb. *the isle* [a]ch. 25:22 [b]Ezek. 25:16 [c]Gen. 10:14
47:5 [a]Mic. 1:16 [b]ch. 25:20
47:6 [1]Heb. *Gather thyself* [a]Ezek. 21:3
47:7 [1]Heb. *How canst thou* [a]Ezek. 14:17 [b]Mic. 6:9
48:1 [1]Or, *The high place* [a]Is. 15; 16 [b]Is. 15:2 [c]Num. 32:37
48:2 [1]Or, *be brought to silence* [2]Heb. *go after thee* [a]Is. 16:14 [b]Is. 15:4
48:5 [1]Heb. *Weeping with weeping* [a]Is. 15:5
48:6 [1]Or, *a naked tree* [a]ch. 17:6
48:7 [a]Num. 21:29; Judg. 11:24; Is. 46:1,2

The prophecy against Moab

48 Against [a]Moab thus saith the LORD of hosts, the God of Israel;
Woe unto [b]Nebo! for it is spoiled:
[c]Kiriathaim is confounded *and* taken:
[1]Misgab is confounded and dismayed.
2 [a]*There shall be* no more praise of Moab:
In [b]Heshbon they have devised evil against it;
Come, and let us cut it off from *being* a nation.
Also thou shalt [1]be cut down, O Madmen;
The sword shall [2]pursue thee.
3 A voice of crying *shall be* from Horonaim,
Spoiling and great destruction.
4 Moab is destroyed;
Her little ones have caused a cry to be heard.
5 [a]For *in* the going up of Luhith
[1]Continual weeping shall go up;
For in the going down of Horonaim
The enemies have heard a cry of destruction.
6 Flee, save your lives,
And be like [1]the [a]heath in the wilderness.
7 For because thou hast trusted in thy works and in thy treasures,
Thou shalt also be taken:
And [a]Chemosh shall go forth into captivity

47:1 *against the Philistines.* See Is 14:28–32; Ezek 25:15–17; Amos 1:6–8; Zeph 2:4–7. *Pharaoh.* It is uncertain whether Neco II (see 46:2; see also note on 2 Ki 23:29) or Hophra (see notes on 37:5; 44:30) is intended. *Gaza.* See v. 5; 25:20; see also note on Judg 1:18.
47:2 *waters rise up* See notes on 46:7–8. *the north.* Babylonia, as in 1:13–14; 46:20. *the land . . . that dwell therein.* The Hebrew for this phrase is repeated verbatim from 8:16. *land.* Phoenicia and Philistia. *city.* A generic singular used as a plural (see note on 46:8); includes Tyre and Sidon (see v. 4) as well as Gaza, Ashkelon (see v. 5) and other Philistine cities.
47:3 *strong horses.* Lit. "strong ones" (see note on 46:15). *feebleness of hands.* Paralyzed by terror (see 6:24; Is 13:7).
47:4 *Tyrus and Zidon.* See notes on v. 2; 25:22; 27:3. *remnant.* See v. 5. *Caphtor.* Crete (the Kerethites of Zeph 2:5 and elsewhere were probably Cretans), one of many islands in the Mediterranean believed to be the original homeland of the Philistines (see Gen 10:14 and note; see also Deut 2:23).
47:5 *Baldness is come.* See note on 16:6; see also 48:37. *Gaza.* See v. 1; 25:20; see also note on Judg 1:18. *Ashkelon.* See v. 7; 25:20; see also note on Judg 1:18. *remnant.* See note on v. 4. *valley.* Roughly equivalent to the modern Gaza Strip, it lay west of the foothills that separated Philistia from Judah. *cut thyself.* See note on 16:6; see also 48:37.
47:6 *thou.* The Philistines.
47:7 *Against Ashkelon.* The immediate fulfillment took place under Nebuchadnezzar in 604 B.C. *sea shore.* See Ezek 25:16; the Philistine plain (see note on v. 5).
48:1 *Against Moab.* See Is 15–16; Ezek 25:8–11; Amos 2:1–3; Zeph 2:8–11. Josephus (*Antiquities,* 10.9.7) implies that Jeremiah's prophecy concerning the future destruction of Moab was fulfilled in the "twenty-third year of Nebuchadnezzar's reign" (582 B.C.; see 52:30). *Nebo.* See v. 22; a town originally allotted to the tribe of Reuben (see Num 32:3,37–38; see also Is 15:2 and note). *Kiriathaim.* See v. 23. An ancient town (see Gen 14:5), it too was allotted to Reuben (see Josh 13:19 and note). Nebo, Kiriathaim and several other towns referred to in this chapter are mentioned also in an important Moabite inscription written by Mesha king of Moab (see 2 Ki 3:4) and discovered in 1868 (see chart, p. xix).
48:2 *Heshbon.* See vv. 34,45; 49:3; Num 21:25. Originally allotted to Reuben (see Num 32:37; Josh 13:17), it was later reassigned to Gad as a Levitical town (see Josh 21:39). *have devised.* The Hebrew for this phrase is a pun on "Heshbon." *Madmen.* Location unknown; perhaps a longer spelling of "Dimon" (Is 15:9—but see note there). In Is 25:10, the feminine form of the Hebrew word *madmen* is translated "dunghill." *sword shall pursue thee.* See 9:16; 42:16.
48:3 *Horonaim.* See vv. 5,34; location unknown.
48:4 *destroyed.* Like an earthen vessel (see 19:11).
48:5 *Luhith.* Location unknown (see Is 15:5).
48:6 *Flee, save your lives.* See 51:6. *like the heath.* See note on 17:6.
48:7 *Chemosh.* See vv. 13,46; the national god of Moab (see

With his [b]priests and his princes
together.
8 And [a]the spoiler shall come upon
every city,
And no city shall escape:
The valley also shall perish,
And the plain shall be destroyed,
As the LORD hath spoken.
9 [a]Give wings unto Moab,
That it may flee and get away:
For the cities thereof shall be desolate,
Without any to dwell therein.
10 [a]Cursed *be* he that doeth the work of
the LORD [1]deceitfully,
And cursed *be* he that keepeth back
his sword from blood.

11 Moab hath been at ease from his
youth,
And he [a]*hath* settled on his lees,
And hath not been emptied from vessel
to vessel,
Neither hath he gone into captivity:
Therefore his taste [1]remained in him,
And his sent is not changed.
12 Therefore behold, the days come, saith
the LORD,
That I will send unto him wanderers,
that shall cause him to wander,
And shall empty his vessels, and break
their bottles.
13 And Moab shall be ashamed of
[a]Chemosh,
As the house of Israel [b]was ashamed of
[c]Beth-el their confidence.
14 How say ye, [a]We *are* mighty and
strong men for the war?

15 [a]Moab is spoiled, and gone up *out of*
her cities,
And [1]his chosen young men are [b]gone
down to the slaughter,
Saith [c]the King, whose name *is* the
LORD of hosts.
16 The calamity of Moab *is* near to come,
And his affliction hasteth fast.
17 All ye that are about him, bemoan him;
And all ye that know his name,
Say, [a]How is the strong staff broken,
And the beautiful rod!
18 [a]Thou daughter that dost inhabit
[b]Dibon,
Come down from *thy* glory, and sit in
thirst;
For [c]the spoiler of Moab shall come
upon thee,
And he shall destroy thy strong holds.
19 O [1]inhabitant of [a]Aroer,
[b]Stand by the way and espy;
Ask him that fleeth, and her that
escapeth,
And say, What is done?
20 Moab is confounded; for it is broken
down:
[a]Howl and cry;
Tell ye *it* in [b]Arnon, that Moab is
spoiled,
21 And judgment is come upon [a]the plain
country;
Upon Holon, and upon Jahazah, and
upon Mephaath,
22 And upon Dibon, and upon Nebo, and
upon Beth-diblathaim,
23 And upon Kiriathaim, and upon
Beth-gamul, and upon Beth-meon,

48:7 [b]ch. 49:3
48:8 [a]ch. 6:26
48:9 [a]Ps. 55:6
48:10 [1]Or, *negligently* [a]Judg. 5:23; 1 Sam. 15:3; 1 Ki. 20:42
48:11 [1]Heb. *stood* [a]Zeph. 1:12
48:13 [a]1 Ki. 11:7 [b]Hos. 10:6 [c]1 Ki. 12:29
48:14 [a]Is. 16:6
48:15 [1]Heb. *the choice of* [a]ver. 8,9,18 [b]ch. 50:27 [c]ch. 46:18
48:17 [a]Is. 9:4; 14:4,5
48:18 [a]Is. 47:1 [b]Num. 21:30; Is. 15:2 [c]ver. 8
48:19 [1]Heb. *inhabitress* [a]Deut. 2:36 [b]1 Sam. 4:13
48:20 [a]Is. 16:7 [b]Num. 21:13
48:21 [a]ver. 8

1 Ki 11:7,33; 2 Ki 23:13). The Hebrew text here implies the alternate spelling Chemish, as in "Carchemish" (see note on 46:2). *shall go forth into captivity . . . and his princes.* A stock phrase (see 49:3; Amos 1:15). Images of pagan deities were often carried about from place to place (see 43:12; Amos 5:26).

48:8 *spoiler.* See v. 32; probably Nebuchadnezzar. *valley . . . plain.* Much of western Moab overlooks the Jordan Valley.

48:9 See 17:6. *Give wings unto Moab.* Or "Put salt on Moab"—to make its farmland unproductive and barren (see note on Judg 9:45).

48:10 *deceitfully.* Those whom the Lord designates to destroy Moab are urged on in their appointed task.

‡48:11 A copy of the Hebrew text of this verse has been found inscribed on a large clay seal, dating to the early Christian era and apparently used for stamping the bitumen with which the mouths of wine jars were sealed. *from his youth.* From his early history. *he hath settled.* Or "like wine left," an apt figure, since Moab was noted for its vineyards (see vv. 32–33; Is 16:8–10). *on his lees.* In order to improve with age (see Is 25:6). *Neither hath he gone into captivity.* Unlike Israel.

‡48:12 *days come.* Moab will be destroyed (see note on v. 1). *wanderers.* Or "those who tip vessels," probably with the idea of "tipping" the drinking vessel gently, in order to leave the unwanted sediment in the bottom. But these men will be the agents of divine judgment and will "destroy" Moab (see v. 4 and note).

48:13 *Chemosh.* See note on v. 7. *house of Israel.* The northern kingdom, destroyed and exiled in 722–721 B.C. *Beth-el.* Either (1) the well-known town where one of Jeroboam's golden calves was placed (see 1 Ki 12:28–30) or, (2) in parallelism with Chemosh, the West Semitic deity known from contemporary Babylonian inscriptions as well as from the Elephantine papyri a century later.

48:14 *How say ye . . . ?* See 2:23; 8:8.

48:15 *gone down to the slaughter.* See 50:27; for war depicted as the slaughter of sacrificial animals see Is 34:6 and note. *King.* See note on 46:18. The true King is the Lord, not Chemosh.

48:16 See Deut 32:35.

48:17 *are about him . . . that know his name.* Nations near and far respectively. *strong.* At one time Moab had been powerful and feared (see 27:3; 2 Ki 1:1; 3:5; 24:2). *staff . . . rod.* Symbols of authority and dominion (see Gen 49:10; Ps 2:9; Ezek 19:11,14).

48:18 *daughter.* See note on Is 23:10. *Dibon.* See v. 22; Num 21:30; see also note on Is 15:2. *Come down . . . sit.* See Is 47:1 and note.

48:19 *Aroer.* See Num 32:34; Deut 2:36.

48:20 *Arnon.* Moab's most important river.

48:21 *plain.* See note on v. 8. *Holon.* Not the same as the town mentioned in Josh 15:51; 21:15. Its location is unknown. *Jahazah.* See 1 Chr 6:78; elsewhere called Jahaz (see v. 34; see also Is 15:4 and note).

48:22 *Dibon.* See v. 18. *Nebo.* See note on v. 1. *Beth-diblathaim.* Perhaps the same as, or near, Almon-diblathaim (see Num 33:46).

48:23 *Kiriathaim.* See note on v. 1. *Beth-gamul.* Modern Khirbet Jumeil, five miles east of Aroer. *Beth-meon.* The same as

24 And upon [a]Kerioth, and upon Bozrah,
And upon all the cities of the land of
Moab, far or near.
25 [a]The horn of Moab is cut off,
And his [b]arm is broken, saith the LORD.

26 [a]Make ye him drunken: for he
magnified *himself* against the LORD:
Moab also shall wallow in his vomit,
And he also shall be in derision.
27 For [a]was not Israel a derision unto
thee?
[b]Was he found among thieves?
For since thou spakest of him, thou
[1]skippedst for joy.
28 O ye that dwell in Moab, leave the
cities, and [a]dwell in the rock,
And be like [b]the dove *that* maketh her
nest in the sides of the hole's mouth.
29 We have heard the [a]pride of Moab; *he*
is exceeding proud:
His loftiness, and his arrogancy, and his
pride, and the haughtiness of his
heart.
30 I know his wrath, saith the LORD; but *it*
shall not *be* so;
[a][1]His lies shall not so effect *it.*
31 Therefore [a]will I howl for Moab,
And I will cry out for all Moab;
Mine heart shall mourn for the men of
Kir-heres.
32 [a]O vine of Sibmah, I will weep for thee
with the weeping of Jazer:
Thy plants are gone over the sea,
They reach *even* to the sea of Jazer:
The spoiler is fallen upon thy summer
fruits and upon thy vintage.
33 And [a]joy and gladness is taken from
the plentiful field, and from the land
of Moab;
And I have caused wine to fail from
the wine presses:
None shall tread *with* shouting;
Their shouting *shall be* no shouting.

48:24 [a]Amos 2:2
48:25 [a]Ps. 75:10 [b]Ezek. 30:21
48:26 [a]ch. 25:15
48:27 [1]Or, *movedst thyself* [a]Zeph. 2:8 [b]ch. 2:26
48:28 [a]Ps. 55:6,7 [b]Sol. 2:14
48:29 [a]Is. 16:6
48:30 [1]Or, *Those on whom he stayeth* (Heb. *his bars*) *do not right* [a]Is. 16:6; ch. 50:36
48:31 [a]Is. 15:5
48:32 [a]Is. 16:8,9
48:33 [a]Is. 16:10; Joel 1:12
48:34 [1]Heb. *desolations* [a]Is. 15:4-6 [b]Is. 15:5,6
48:35 [a]Is. 15:2; 16:12
48:36 [a]Is. 15:5; 16:11 [b]Is. 15:7
48:37 [1]Heb. *diminished* [a]Is. 15:2,3 [b]Gen. 37:34
48:38 [a]ch. 22:28
48:39 [1]Heb. *neck*
48:40 [a]Deut. 28:49; Hab. 1:8 [b]Is. 8:8
48:41 [1]Or, *The cities* [a]ver. 24 [b]Is. 13:8; 21:3; Mic. 4:9

34 [a]From the cry of Heshbon *even* unto
Elealeh,
And even unto Jahaz, have they uttered
their voice,
[b]From Zoar *even* unto Horonaim,
As a heifer of three years old:
For the waters also of Nimrim shall be
[1]desolate.
35 Moreover I will cause to cease in
Moab, saith the LORD, [a]him that
offereth *in* the high places,
And him that burneth incense to his
gods.
36 Therefore [a]mine heart shall sound for
Moab like pipes,
And mine heart shall sound like pipes
for the men of Kir-heres:
Because [b]the riches *that* he hath
gotten are perished.
37 For [a]every head *shall be* bald,
And every beard [1]clipt:
Upon all the hands *shall be* cuttings,
And [b]upon the loins sackcloth.
38 *There shall be* lamentation generally
upon all the housetops of Moab, and
in the streets thereof:
For I have broken Moab like [a]a vessel
wherein *is* no pleasure, saith the
LORD.
39 They shall howl, *saying,* How is it
broken down!
How hath Moab turned the [1]back with
shame!
So shall Moab be a derision and a
dismaying to all them about him.
40 For thus saith the LORD;
Behold, [a]he shall fly as an eagle,
And shall [b]spread his wings over
Moab.
41 [a][1]Kerioth is taken, and the strong
holds are surprised,
And [b]the mighty *men's* hearts in Moab
at that day shall be
As the heart of a woman in her pangs.

Baal-meon (see Num 32:38) and Beth-baal-meon (see Josh 13:17).

‡48:24 *Kerioth.* See note on Amos 2:2. The location of this Moabite city is unknown. *Bozrah.* Not the same as Bozrah in Edom (see 49:13,22), but another name for Bezer in Moab (see note on Deut 4:43).

48:26 The Lord speaks to the Babylonian invaders. *Make ye him drunken.* By drinking down the cup of God's wrath (see 13:13; 25:15–17,28). *wallow in his vomit.* See 25:27; Is 19:14. *he also shall be in derision.* As he had once ridiculed others (see v. 27; Zeph 2:8,10).

‡48:27 *thou skippedst for joy.* Or, "shake your head in scorn." See 18:16 and note; see also Ps 64:8.

48:28 *like the dove . . . the hole's mouth.* See Ps 55:6–8; Sol 2:14.

48:29–30 An expanded version of the description of Moab found in Is 16:6.

48:29 *pride of Moab.* It had long since become proverbial (see Is 25:10–11; Zeph 2:8–10).

48:31–33 See Is 16:7–10.

48:31–32 *I.* The prophet (as in Is 16:9; cf. Is 15:5).

48:31 *mourn.* Like a mourning dove (see Is 38:14; 59:11). *Kir-heres.* See Is 16:7,11; see also note on Is 15:1.

48:32 *vine.* See note on v. 11. *Jazer . . . Sibmah . . . sea.* See note on Is 16:8. *will weep . . . of Jazer.* See Is 16:9. *spoiler.* See v. 8; probably Nebuchadnezzar.

48:33 *tread.* See note on Is 16:10. *shall be no shouting* [of joy]. Instead, shouts of judgment (see 25:30; 51:14).

48:34 See Is 15:4–6 and notes.

48:36 See Is 16:11. *pipes.* Played by mourners at funerals (see Mat 9:23–24).

48:37 Signs of mourning (see Is 15:2–3 and notes). *cuttings.* See note on 16:6.

48:38 *broken . . . like a vessel wherein is no pleasure.* See v. 4 and note on v. 12; cf. the description of King Jehoiachin in 22:28 (see note there).

48:39 *derision.* See v. 26 and note.

48:40–41 Echoed in 49:22 with respect to Edom.

48:40 *eagle.* Nebuchadnezzar (as in Ezek 17:3); see Deut 28:49 and note.

48:41 *Kerioth.* Location uncertain (see v. 24; see also note on Amos 2:2).

42 And Moab shall be destroyed [a]from
being a people,
Because he hath magnified *himself*
against the LORD.
43 [a]Fear, and the pit, and the snare, *shall
be* upon thee,
O inhabitant of Moab, saith the LORD.
44 He that fleeth from the fear shall fall
into the pit;
And he that getteth up out of the pit
shall be taken in the snare:
For [a]I will bring upon it, *even* upon
Moab, the year of their visitation,
saith the LORD.
45 They that fled stood under the shadow
of Heshbon because of the force:
But [a]a fire shall come forth out of
Heshbon,
And a flame from the midst of Sihon,
And [b]shall devour the corner of Moab,
And the crown of the head of the
[1]tumultuous ones.
46 [a]Woe be unto thee, O Moab!
The people of Chemosh perisheth:
For thy sons are taken [1]captives,
And thy daughters captives.
47 Yet will I bring again the captivity of
Moab
[a]In the latter days, saith the LORD.
Thus far *is* the judgment of Moab.

The prophecy against Ammon

49 [1]Concerning [a]the Ammonites, thus
saith the LORD;
Hath Israel no sons? Hath he no heir?
Why *then* doth [2]their king inherit
[b]Gad,
And his people dwell in his cities?
2 Therefore behold, the days come, saith
the LORD,

48:42 [a]Ps. 83:4
48:43 [a]Is. 24:17
48:44 [a]ch. 11:23
48:45 [1]Heb. *children of noise* [a]Num. 21:28 [b]Num. 24:17
48:46 [1]Heb. *in captivity* [a]Num. 21:29
48:47 [a]ch. 49:6
49:1 [1]Or, *Against* [2]Or, *Melcom* [a]Ezek. 21:28; 25:2; Amos 1:13; Zeph. 2:8,9 [b]Amos 1:13
49:2 [a]Ezek. 25:5; Amos 1:14
49:3 [1]Or, *Melcom* [a]Is. 32:11 [b]ch. 48:7
49:4 [1]Or, *Thy valley floweth* [a]ch. 3:14 [b]ch. 21:13
49:6 [a]ver. 39; ch. 48:47
49:7 [a]Ezek. 25:12 [b]Obad. 8 [c]Is. 19:11
49:8 [1]Or, *they are turned back* [a]ver. 30 [b]ch. 25:23

That I will cause an alarm of war to be
heard in [a]Rabbah of the Ammonites;
And it shall be a desolate heap,
And her daughters shall be burnt with
fire:
Then shall Israel be heir unto them
that were his heirs, saith the LORD.
3 Howl, O Heshbon, for Ai is spoiled:
Cry, ye daughters of Rabbah, [a]gird ye
with sackcloth;
Lament, and run to and fro by the
hedges;
For [1]their king shall go into captivity,
And his [b]priests and his princes
together.
4 Wherefore gloriest thou in the valleys,
[1]Thy flowing valley, [a]O backsliding
daughter?
That trusted in her treasures, [b]*saying,*
Who shall come unto me?
5 Behold, I will bring a fear upon thee,
saith the Lord GOD of hosts,
From all those that be about thee;
And ye shall be driven out every man
right forth;
And none shall gather up him that
wandereth.
6 And [a]afterward I will bring again the
captivity of the children of Ammon,
saith the LORD.

The prophecy against Edom

7 [a]Concerning Edom, thus saith the LORD
of hosts;
[b]*Is* wisdom no more in Teman?
[c]Is counsel perished from the prudent?
Is their wisdom vanished?
8 [a]Flee ye, [1]turn back,
Dwell deep, O inhabitants of [b]Dedan;

48:43 *Fear . . . pit . . . and the snare.* The Hebrew original illustrates Jeremiah's fondness for the well-turned phrase (see Introduction: Literary Features)—though in this case Jeremiah was not its creator (see note on Is 24:17).
48:44 *He that fleeth . . . shall fall . . . getteth up out . . . shall be taken in the snare.* Divine judgment, once determined, is unavoidable (see Amos 5:19).
48:45–46 Echoed from Num 21:28–29; 24:17. Balaam's oracles against Moab are about to be fulfilled.
48:45 *Heshbon.* See note on v. 2. Apparently at this time it was controlled by the Ammonites (see 49:3). *Sihon.* Refers to the associates of Sihon king of the Amorites, whose chief city was Heshbon (see Num 21:27) during the time of the exodus. *tumultuous ones.* See note on v. 29.
48:46 *Chemosh.* See note on v. 7.
48:47 See 46:26. *bring again the captivity.* See note on 29:14. *In the latter days.* During the Messianic era. *Thus far.* A note by the final compiler of the book of Jeremiah (see 51:64).
‡49:1 *Concerning the Ammonites.* See Ezek 25:1–7; Amos 1:13–15; Zeph 2:8–11. Ammon was east of the Jordan and north of Moab (see note on Gen 19:36–38). "Their king" is probably Molech, the chief god of the Ammonites (see 1 Ki 11:5,7,33), also known as Milcom (see 1 Ki 11:5). Both titles are related to the West Semitic word for "king" (Hebrew *melek*). *their king inherit Gad.* Probably refers to the aftermath of Tiglath-pileser III's conquest of Transjordan in 734–732 B.C. The Ammonites later apparently recovered from their defeat and overran some of the territory owned by the Israelite tribe of Gad. *his.* Molech's.
49:2 *alarm of war.* See Amos 1:14. *Rabbah of the Ammonites.* See note on Deut 3:11. *heap.* See note on 30:18.
‡49:3 *Heshbon.* See note on 48:45; see also Judg 11:26–27. *Ai.* Not the Ai of Josh 8. Its location is unknown. *hedges.* The Hebrew for this word refers not to city walls but to walls separating vineyards from each other (see Num 21:24). *their king.* See note on v. 1. *shall go into captivity . . . and his princes.* See note on 48:7.
49:4 *backsliding daughter.* Applied to the people of Judah in 31:22. *That trusted in her treasures.* Spoken to Moab in 48:7. *Who shall come unto me?* According to Josephus (*Antiquities,* 10.9.7) Nebuchadnezzar destroyed Ammon in the 23rd year of his reign (582 B.C.).
49:6 See 48:47; see also note on 29:14.
49:7–22 Shares many memorable phrases and concepts with the book of Obadiah.
49:7 *Concerning Edom.* See Is 21:11–12; Ezek 25:12–14; Amos 1:11–12; Obad 1–16. *wisdom.* For which Edom was justly famed (see notes on Job 1:1; 2:11). *Teman.* An important Edomite town located south of the Dead Sea (see note on Job 2:11). In v. 20 it is used in parallelism with Edom itself.
49:8 *Flee ye, turn back.* See v. 24; 46:21. *Dedan.* See 25:23; see

For I will bring the calamity of Esau
upon him,
The time *that* I will visit him.
9 If [a]grapegatherers come to thee, would
they not leave *some* gleaning grapes?
If thieves by night, they will destroy
[1]till they have enough.
10 [a]But I have made Esau bare,
I have uncovered his secret places,
And he shall not be able to hide
himself:
His seed is spoiled, and his brethren,
and his neighbours, and [b]he *is* not.
11 Leave thy fatherless children, I will
preserve *them* alive;
And let thy widows trust in me.
12 For thus saith the LORD;
Behold, [a]they whose judgment *was* not
to drink of the cup have assuredly
drunken;
And *art* thou he *that* shall altogether go
unpunished?
Thou shalt not go unpunished, but
thou shalt surely drink *of it.*
13 For [a]I have sworn by myself, saith the
LORD,
That [b]Bozrah shall become a
desolation,
A reproach, a waste, and a curse;
And all the cities thereof shall be
perpetual wastes.
14 I have heard a [a]rumour from the LORD,
And an ambassador *is* sent unto the
heathen, *saying,*
Gather ye together,
And come against her, and rise up to
the battle.
15 For lo, I will make thee small among
the heathen,
And despised among men.
16 Thy terribleness hath deceived thee,
and the pride of thine heart,
O thou that dwellest in the clefts of the
rock,
That holdest the height of the hill:
[a]Though thou shouldest make thy
[b]nest as high as the eagle,
[c]I will bring thee down from thence,
saith the LORD.
17 Also Edom shall be a desolation:
[a]Every one that goeth by it shall be
astonished,
And shall hiss at all the plagues
thereof.
18 [a]As *in* the overthrow of Sodom and
Gomorrah
And the neighbour *cities* thereof, saith
the LORD,
No man shall abide there,
Neither shall a son of man dwell in it.
19 [a]Behold, he shall come up like a lion
from [b]the swelling of Jordan
Against the habitation of the strong:
But I will suddenly make him run away
from her:
And who *is* a chosen *man, that* I may
appoint over her?
For [c]who *is* like me? and who will
[1]appoint me the time?
And [d]who *is* that shepherd that will
stand before me?
20 [a]Therefore hear the counsel of the
LORD,
That he hath taken against Edom;
And his purposes, that he hath
purposed against the inhabitants of
Teman:
Surely the least of the flock shall draw
them out:
Surely he shall make their habitations
desolate with them.
21 [a]The earth is moved at the noise of
their fall,
At the cry, the noise thereof was heard
in the [1]Red sea.
22 Behold, [a]he shall come up and fly as
the eagle,
And spread his wings over Bozrah:

49:9 [1]Heb. *their sufficiency* [a]Obad. 5
49:10 [a]Mal. 1:3 [b]Is. 17:14
49:12 [a]ch. 25:29; Obad. 16
49:13 [a]Gen. 22:16; Is. 45:23; Amos 6:8 [b]Is. 34:6; 63:1
49:14 [a]Obad. 1-3
49:16 [a]Obad. 4 [b]Job 39:27 [c]Amos 9:2
49:17 [a]ch. 18:16; 50:13
49:18 [a]Gen. 19:25; Deut. 29:23; ch. 50:40
49:19 [1]Or, *convent me in judgment* [a]ch. 50:44 [b]ch. 12:5 [c]Ex. 15:11 [d]Job 41:10
49:20 [a]ch. 50:45
49:21 [1]Heb. *Weedy sea* [a]ch. 50:46
49:22 [a]ch. 48:40,41

also notes on Is 21:13; Ezek 25:13. *Esau.* The patriarch Jacob's brother, and another name for Edom (see Gen 25:29–30; 36:1), just as Israel was another name for Jacob (see Gen 32:28). The fact that Esau was Jacob's brother made Edom's enmity toward Israel all the more reprehensible (see Amos 1:11; Obad 10).
49:9–10 Paralleled in Obad 5–6.
49:9 *grapegatherers.* See note on v. 13. *leave some gleaning grapes.* For the poor to glean (see note on Ruth 2:2).
49:10 *have made Esau bare.* See note on 13:22. *is not.* See 31:15; Is 19:7.
49:12 Echoed from 25:28–29. *they whose judgment was not to drink . . . have assuredly drunken.* Though they are God's chosen ones, the people of Judah will be punished because of their sin (see Amos 3:2).
‡49:13 *sworn by myself.* See notes on Gen 22:16; Is 45:23; see also 22:5; 51:14. *Bozrah.* Not the Bozrah of 48:24 (see note there); the Edomite Bozrah was probably the capital of Edom in the days of Jeremiah (see v. 22; Gen 36:33; see also notes on Is 34:6; Amos 1:12). The Hebrew root underlying Bozrah is the same as that for "grapegatherers" in v. 9. *desolation . . . reproach.* See 25:18. *perpetual wastes.* See 25:9; Ps 74:3; Is 58:12 and note.
49:14–16 Paralleled in Obad 1–4.
49:16 *pride.* Edom's besetting sin (see v. 4; Obad 11–13; cf. 48:29–30). *rock.* Perhaps a reference to Petra (see note on 2 Ki 14:7), the most spectacular of the mountain strongholds for which Edom was noted.
49:17 Echoed from 19:8.
49:18 Repeated almost verbatim in 50:40, and echoed in part in v. 33. *overthrow of Sodom and Gomorrah.* See Gen 19:24–25. Later calamities were often compared with the one that befell Sodom and Gomorrah (see note on Amos 4:11). *neighbour.* Primarily Admah and Zeboiim (see Gen 14:2,8; Deut 29:23; Hos 11:8).
49:19–21 Repeated almost verbatim in the oracle against Babylon (see 50:44–46).
49:19 *swelling of Jordan.* See 12:5 and note. *shepherd.* Ruler (see note on 2:8).
49:20 *Teman.* See note on v. 7. *flock.* The people of Edom.
‡49:22 Echoed from 48:40–41. *eagle.* Represents Nebuchadnezzar in 48:40 (see note there), and probably here also. A more complete subjugation of the Edomites, however, was accomplished by Nabatean Arabs (perhaps the "dragons of the

And at that day shall the heart of the
mighty *men* of Edom
Be as the heart of a woman in her
pangs.

23 [a]Concerning Damascus.
Hamath is confounded, and Arpad:
For they have heard evil tidings: they
are [1]fainthearted;
[b]*There is* sorrow [2]on the sea; it cannot
be quiet.
24 Damascus is waxed feeble, *and* turneth
herself to flee,
And fear hath seized on *her:*
[a]Anguish and sorrows have taken her
as a woman in travail.
25 How is [a]the city of praise not left,
The city of my joy!
26 [a]Therefore her young men shall fall in
her streets,
And all the men of war shall be cut off
in that day,
Saith the LORD of hosts.
27 And I will kindle a [a]fire in the wall of
Damascus,
And it shall consume the palaces of
Ben-hadad.

The prophecy against Kedar

28 [a]Concerning Kedar, and concerning
the kingdoms of Hazor, which
Nebuchadrezzar king of Babylon shall
smite, thus saith the LORD;
Arise ye, go up to Kedar,
And spoil [b]the men of the east.
29 Their [a]tents and their flocks shall they
take *away:*
They shall take to themselves their
curtains,
And all their vessels, and their camels;
And they shall cry unto them, [b]Fear *is*
on every side.
30 [a]Flee, [1]get you far off, dwell deep,
O ye inhabitants of Hazor,
Saith the LORD;
For Nebuchadrezzar king of Babylon
hath taken counsel against you,
And hath conceived a purpose against
you.
31 Arise, get you up unto [a]the [1]wealthy
nation,
That dwelleth without care, saith the
LORD,
Which have neither gates nor bars,
which [b]dwell alone.
32 And their camels shall be a booty,
And the multitude of their cattle a spoil:
And I will scatter into all winds them
that are [1]in the utmost corners;
And I will bring their calamity from all
sides thereof, saith the LORD.
33 And Hazor [a]shall be a dwelling for
dragons,
And a desolation for ever:
[b]There shall no man abide there,
Nor *any* son of man dwell in it.

The prophecy against Elam

34 The word of the LORD that came to
Jeremiah the prophet against [a]Elam
in the beginning of the reign of
Zedekiah king of Judah, saying,
35 Thus saith the LORD of hosts;
Behold, I *will* break [a]the bow of Elam,
The chief of their might.
36 And upon Elam will I bring the four
winds
From the four quarters of heaven,
And [a]will scatter them towards all
those winds;
And there shall be no nation
Whither the outcasts of Elam shall not
come.
37 For I will cause Elam to be dismayed
before their enemies,
And before them that seek their life:
And I will bring evil upon them,
Even my fierce anger, saith the LORD;
[a]And I will send the sword after them,
Till I have consumed them:

49:23 [1]Heb. *melted* [2]Or, as *on the sea* [a]Is. 17:1; 37:13; Amos 1:3; Zech. 9:1,2 [b]Is. 57:20
49:24 [a]Is. 13:8; ch. 4:31; 6:24; 48:41
49:25 [a]ch. 33:9
49:26 [a]ch. 50:30
49:27 [a]Amos 1:4
49:28 [a]Is. 21:13 [b]Judg. 6:3; Job 1:3
49:29 [a]Ps. 120:5 [b]ch. 46:5
49:30 [1]Heb. *flit greatly* [a]ver. 8
49:31 [1]Or, *that is at ease* [a]Ezek. 38:11 [b]Num. 23:9; Deut. 33:28; Mic. 7:14
49:32 [1]Heb. *cut off into corners,* or, *that have the corners* of their *hair polled*
49:33 [a]ch. 9:11; 10:22; Mal. 1:3 [b]ver. 18
49:34 [a]ch. 25:25
49:35 [a]Is. 22:6
49:36 [a]ver. 32
49:37 [a]ch. 9:16

wilderness" of Mal 1:3) beginning c. 550 B.C. *Bozrah.* See note on v. 13.

49:23 *Concerning Damascus.* See Is 17; Amos 1:3–5 (see also note on Is 17:1). *Hamath.* An important city in the kingdom of Aram (see Is 10:9 and note). *Arpad.* See note on Is 10:9. *sorrow on the sea.* See Is 57:20.

49:24 *Anguish.* See note on 4:19.

49:26 Repeated almost verbatim in 50:30.

49:27 A conventional word of judgment (see note on Amos 1:4).

49:28 *Concerning Kedar.* See Is 21:13–17; see also 2:10 and note. *kingdoms of Hazor.* See vv. 30,33; not the Hazor north of the sea of Galilee (see Josh 11:1). These kingdoms may have included Dedan, Tema, Buz and other Arab regions (see 25:23–24 and notes), since the Hebrew root of the proper name Hazor often serves as a common noun meaning "settlement" (see especially Is 42:11; see also Gen 25:16). *Nebuchadrezzar . . . shall smite.* In 599–598 B.C. *men of the east.* See Job 1:3; Ezek 25:4. The Hebrew for this phrase is translated "children of the east" in Judg 6:3 (see note there).

49:29 *Fear is on every side.* See note on 6:25.

49:30 *dwell deep.* See v. 8.

49:31 *wealthy nation . . . without care.* Completely secure (see Job 21:23). *without care.* In safety, unsuspecting (see Judg 18:7; Ezek 38:11). *have neither gates nor bars.* Lives in unwalled villages (see Deut 3:5; cf. 1 Sam 23:7). *alone.* A condition that elsewhere characterizes Israel (see Num 23:9; Deut 33:28).

49:32 *scatter into all winds.* See Ezek 5:12; 12:4. *utmost corners.* See note on 9:26. *calamity from all sides.* Contrast the description of Solomon's realm in 1 Ki 5:4.

49:33 *dwelling for dragons.* See note on 9:11. *no man . . . dwell in it.* Repeated verbatim from v. 18.

49:34 *The word of the LORD . . . against.* See note on 46:1. *Elam.* See note on Is 11:11. *Zedekiah.* Ruled 597–586 B.C.

49:35 *bow.* The Elamites were skilled archers (see Is 22:6).

49:36 Contrast Is 11:12. *all those winds.* In every direction (see Ezek 37:9; Dan 7:2; 8:8; see also Zech 6:5, where "spirits" could be translated "winds," but cf. note on Zech 6:1).

49:37 *I will send . . . have consumed them.* The Hebrew for this sentence is repeated verbatim from 9:16.

38 And I will [a]set my throne in Elam,
And will destroy from thence the king
and the princes,
Saith the LORD.
39 But it shall come to pass [a]in the latter
days,
That I will bring again the captivity of
Elam,
Saith the LORD.

The prophecy against Babylon

50 The word that the LORD spake
[a]against Babylon *and* against the
land of the Chaldeans [1]by Jeremiah
the prophet.
2 Declare ye among the nations, and
publish, and [1]set up a standard;
Publish, *and* conceal not:
Say, Babylon is taken, [a]Bel is
confounded, Merodach is broken in
pieces;
[b]Her idols are confounded, her images
are broken in pieces.
3 [a]For out of the north there cometh up
[b]a nation against her,
Which shall make her land desolate,
And none shall dwell therein:
They shall remove, they shall depart,
both man and beast.
4 In those days, and in that time, saith
the LORD,
The children of Israel shall come,
[a]They and the children of Judah
together,
[b]Going and weeping: they shall go,
[c]And seek the LORD their God.
5 They shall ask the way *to* Zion with
their faces thitherward, *saying,*
Come, and let us join ourselves to the
LORD
In [a]a perpetual covenant *that* shall not
be forgotten.

49:38 [a]ch. 43:10
49:39 [a]ch. 48:47
50:1 [1]Heb. *by the hand of Jeremiah* [a]Is. 13:1; 47:1
50:2 [1]Heb. *lift up* [a]Is. 46:1; ch. 51:44 [b]See ch. 43:12,13
50:3 [a]ch. 51:48 [b]Is. 13:17,18,20
50:4 [a]Hos. 1:11 [b]Ezra 3:12; ch. 31:9; Zech. 12:10 [c]Hos. 3:5
50:5 [a]ch. 31:31

50:6 [1]Heb. *place to lie down in* [a]Is. 53:6; 1 Pet. 2:25 [b]ch. 2:20; 3:6,23
50:7 [a]Ps. 79:7 [b]ch. 40:2,3; Zech. 11:5 [c]See ch. 2:3; Dan. 9:16 [d]Ps. 90:1; 91:1 [e]Ps. 22:4
50:8 [a]Is. 48:20; ch. 51:6,45; Zech. 2:6,7; Rev. 18:4
50:9 [1]Or, *destroyer* [a]ch. 15:14; 51:27 [b]2 Sam. 1:22
50:10 [a]Rev. 17:16
50:11 [1]Heb. *big,* or, *corpulent* [2][Or, *neigh as steeds*] [a]Is. 47:6 [b]Hos. 10:11

6 My people hath been [a]lost sheep:
Their shepherds have caused them to
go astray, they have turned them
away *on* [b]the mountains:
They have gone from mountain to hill,
They have forgotten their [1]resting
place.
7 All that found them have [a]devoured
them:
And [b]their adversaries said, [c]We
offend not,
Because they have sinned against the
LORD, [d]the habitation of justice,
Even the LORD, [e]the hope of their
fathers.
8 [a]Remove out of the midst of Babylon,
And go forth out of the land of the
Chaldeans,
And be as the he goats before the
flocks.
9 [a]For lo, I *will* raise and cause to come
up against Babylon
An assembly of great nations from the
north country:
And they shall set *themselves* in array
against her;
From thence she shall be taken:
Their arrows *shall be* as of a mighty
[1]expert *man;*
[b]None shall return in vain.
10 And Chaldea shall be a spoil:
[a]All that spoil her shall be satisfied,
saith the LORD.
11 [a]Because ye were glad, because ye
rejoiced,
O ye destroyers of mine heritage,
Because ye are grown [1]fat [b]as the
heifer at grass,
And [2]bellow as bulls;
12 Your mother shall be sore confounded;
She that bare you shall be ashamed:

49:38 *set my throne in.* See 1:15 and note.
49:39 See note on 29:14.
50:1–51:64 See Is 13:1–14:23; 21:1–9. Jeremiah's prophecy concerning Babylon is by far the longest of his oracles against foreign nations (chs. 46–51) and expands on his earlier and briefer statements (see 25:12–14,26). Its date, in whole or in part, is 593 B.C. (see 51:59 and note). The two chapters divide into three main sections (50:2–28; 50:29–51:26; 51:27–58), each of which begins with a summons concerning war against Babylon, Judah's mortal enemy (see 50:2–3; 50:29–32; 51:27–32).
50:1 *word.* Or "message" (as in 46:13), comprising chs. 50–51. *by.* See 37:2. The message would eventually be sent by the prophet to Babylon itself (see 51:59–61).
50:2 *Declare . . . and publish.* See 4:5; 46:14. *set up a standard.* See 4:6; see also note on Is 5:26. *Babylon is taken.* Fulfilled in 539 B.C. *Bel.* See 51:44; Is 46:1 and note. *is confounded . . . broken in pieces.* The repetition of each of these phrases emphasizes that the chief god of Babylon and his images and idols are alike doomed. *Her . . . her.* Babylon's. *idols.* Lit. "little pellets of dung." Derogatory references concerning idols and idolatry are common in the OT (see, e.g., Is 44:9–20).
‡**50:3** *out of the north . . . nation.* In Jeremiah, the foe from the north is almost always Babylon (see, e.g., 1:14–15). Here, however, the reference is probably to Persia. Babylon's nemesis is expanded to "an assembly of great nations" in v. 9, specified by name in 51:27–28. *man and beast.* See 33:12.
50:4 *Israel . . . Judah together.* See note on 3:18. *weeping.* Tears of repentance (see 3:21–22; 31:9).
50:5 *perpetual covenant.* See 32:40 and note; see also 31:31–34; 33:20–21.
50:6 *lost sheep.* See Jesus' parable in Luke 15:3–7. *shepherds.* Rulers (see note on 2:8). *on the mountains.* Places where pagan gods were worshiped (see note on 2:20). *their resting place.* The Lord (see v. 7).
50:7 *hope of their fathers.* See 14:8,22; Acts 28:20.
50:8 *be as the he goats before the flocks.* Judah would be among the first of the captive peoples to be released from exile in Babylon.
50:9 *assembly of great nations.* See Is 13:4. They are named in 51:27–28 (see note on v. 3). *None shall return in vain.* See Is 55:11.
50:11 *ye.* Babylon. *mine heritage.* God's land and people (see 2:7; 12:7 and notes). *as the heifer at grass.* See Mal 4:2. *bulls.* See note on 8:16.
50:12 *mother.* Either (1) the city or, more likely, (2) the land (see Is 50:1; Hos 2:5). *hindermost.* Lit. "last." As Amalek, "first of

Behold, the hindermost of the nations
Shall be a wilderness, a dry land, and a
desert.
13 Because of the wrath of the LORD it
shall not be inhabited,
[a]But it shall be wholly desolate: [b]every
one that goeth by Babylon shall be
astonished,
And hiss at all her plagues.
14 [a]Put *yourselves* in array against
Babylon round about:
All ye [b]that bend the bow, shoot at her,
spare no arrows:
For she hath sinned against the LORD.
15 Shout against her round about:
She hath [a]given her hand:
Her foundations are fallen, [b]her walls
are thrown down:
For [c]it *is* the vengeance of the LORD:
take vengeance upon her;
As she hath done, do unto her.
16 Cut off the sower from Babylon,
And him that handleth the [1]sickle in
the time of harvest;
For fear of the oppressing sword
[a]They shall turn every one to his
people,
And they shall flee every one to his
own land.

17 Israel *is* [a]a scattered sheep;
[b]The lions have driven *him* away:
First [c]the king of Assyria hath
devoured him;
And last this [d]Nebuchadrezzar king of
Babylon hath broken his bones.
18 Therefore thus saith the LORD of hosts,
the God of Israel;
Behold, I *will* punish the king of
Babylon and his land,
As I have punished the king of Assyria.
19 [a]And I will bring Israel again to his
habitation,
And he shall feed on Carmel and
Bashan,
And his soul shall be satisfied upon
mount Ephraim and Gilead.
20 In those days, and in that time, saith
the LORD,
[a]The iniquity of Israel shall be sought
for, and *there shall be* none;
And the sins of Judah, and they shall
not be found:
For I will pardon them [b]whom I
reserve.

21 Go up against the land [1]of Merethaim,
even against it,
And against the inhabitants of
[a][2]Pekod:
Waste and utterly destroy after them,
saith the LORD,
And do [b]according to all that I have
commanded thee.
22 [a]A sound of battle *is* in the land,
And of great destruction.
23 How is [a]the hammer of the whole
earth cut asunder and broken!
How is Babylon become a desolation
among the nations!
24 I have laid a snare for thee, and thou
art also taken, O Babylon,
[a]And thou wast not aware:
Thou art found, and also caught,
Because thou hast striven against the
LORD.
25 The LORD hath opened his armoury,
And hath brought forth [a]the weapons
of his indignation:
For this *is* the work of the Lord GOD of
hosts
In the land of the Chaldeans.

50:13 [a]ch. 25:12 [b]ch. 49:17
50:14 [a]ch. 51:2 [b]ver. 29
50:15 [a]1 Chr. 29:24; 2 Chr. 30:8; Lam. 5:6; Ezek. 17:18 [b]ch. 51:58 [c]ch. 51:6,11
50:16 [1]Or, *sythe* [a]Is. 13:14
50:17 [a]ver. 6 [b]ch. 2:15 [c]2 Ki. 17:6 [d]2 Ki. 24:10,14
50:19 [a]Is. 65:10; ch. 33:12; Ezek. 34:13
50:20 [a]ch. 31:34 [b]Is. 1:9
50:21 [1]Or, *of the rebels* [2]Or, *Visitation* [a]Ezek. 23:23 [b]See 2 Sam. 16:11; 2 Ki. 18:25; 2 Chr. 36:23; Is. 10:6; 44:28; 48:14
50:22 [a]ch. 51:54
50:23 [a]Is. 14:6; ch. 51:20
50:24 [a]ch. 51:8,31; Dan. 5:30
50:25 [a]Is. 13:5

the nations" (Num 24:20) to attack Israel, was destroyed, so Babylon, the last to attack Israel (up to Jeremiah's time), would be destroyed.

50:13 *not be inhabited.* See Is 13:20 and note. *every one that goeth by . . . at all her plagues.* Said of Jerusalem in 19:8 and of Edom in 49:17.

50:14 *ye that bend the bow.* Including the Medes (see Is 13:17–18).

50:15 *Shout against her round about.* See Josh 6:16. *vengeance of the LORD.* See v. 28; 51:11. Though originating in His sovereign holiness, it was often carried out by His people (see Num 31:3).

50:16 *oppressing sword.* See 46:16. *They shall turn every one . . . to his own land.* The Hebrew for this passage has a parallel in Is 13:14. The captive peoples are warned to flee Babylon in order to avoid being cut down by her invaders.

50:17 *scattered sheep.* See Joel 3:2. *lions.* Symbolic of Assyria and Babylon (see 4:7; Is 15:9 and notes). *First the king of Assyria.* The Assyrians destroyed Israel (the northern kingdom) in 722–721 B.C. *last this Nebuchadrezzar.* The Babylonians destroyed Judah (the southern kingdom) in 586 B.C.

50:18 *I have punished the king of Assyria.* Nineveh, the proud Assyrian capital, fell in 612 B.C., and Assyria herself was conquered by a coalition of Medes and Babylonians in 609.

50:19 *Carmel.* See Is 33:9 and note. *Bashan.* See note on Is 2:13. *mount Ephraim.* The lush mountainsides of central Israel (see Ezek 34:13–14). *Gilead.* See Num 32:1; Mic 7:14.

50:20 See 33:8 and note; see also 36:3; Mic 7:18–19.

50:21 *Merethaim.* Means "double rebellion [against the Lord]," perhaps referring to vv. 24,29 (see Judg 3:8; Is 40:2 and notes). It is probably a pun on the Babylonian word *marratu,* which sometimes referred to a region in southern Babylonia that was characterized by briny waters. *Pekod.* See Ezek 23:23; means "punishment [from the Lord]," a pun on *Puqudu,* the Babylonian name for an Aramean tribe living on the eastern bank of the lower Tigris River. *utterly destroy.* See v. 26; 25:9 and note; 51:3; see also note on Deut 2:34.

50:22 *great destruction.* See 4:6; 6:1; cf. 48:3; 51:54.

50:23 *hammer of the whole earth.* See note on Is 10:5. *Babylon . . . a desolation among the nations!* The Hebrew for this sentence is repeated verbatim in 51:41.

50:24 *taken . . . not aware.* The Persian attack in 539 B.C. would catch the city of Babylon completely by surprise (see 51:8; Is 47:11).

50:25 *weapons of his indignation.* The nations (see 51:27–28) that the Lord would use to conquer Babylon (see Is 13:5 and note). *the work of the Lord.* See 48:10.

26 Come against her [1] from the utmost
border,
Open her storehouses:
[2] Cast her up as heaps, and destroy her
utterly:
Let nothing of her be left.
27 Slay all her [a] bullocks; let them go
down to the slaughter:
Woe unto them! for their day is come,
The time of [b] their visitation.
28 The voice of them that flee and escape
out of the land of Babylon,
[a] To declare in Zion the vengeance of
the LORD our God,
The vengeance of his temple.
29 Call together the archers against
Babylon:
[a] All ye that bend the bow, camp
against it round about;
Let none thereof escape:
[b] Recompense her according to her
work;
According to all that she hath done, do
unto her:
[c] For she hath been proud against the
LORD, against the Holy One of Israel.
30 [a] Therefore shall her young men fall in
the streets,
And all her men of war shall be cut off
in that day, saith the LORD.
31 Behold, I *am* against thee, *O thou*
[1] most proud,
Saith the Lord GOD of hosts:
For [a] thy day is come, the time *that* I
will visit thee.
32 And [1] the most proud shall stumble and
fall,
And none shall raise him up:
And [a] I will kindle a fire in his cities,
And it shall devour all round about him.

33 Thus saith the LORD of hosts;
The children of Israel and the children
of Judah *were* oppressed together:
And all that took them captives held
them fast;
They refused to let them go.
34 [a] Their redeemer *is* strong;
[b] The LORD of hosts *is* his name:
He shall throughly plead their cause,
That he may give rest to the land,
And disquiet the inhabitants of
Babylon.
35 A sword *is* upon the Chaldeans, saith
the LORD,
And upon the inhabitants of Babylon,
And [a] upon her princes, and upon [b] her
wise *men.*
36 A sword *is* [a] upon the [1] [2] liars; and they
shall dote:
A sword *is* upon her mighty *men;* and
they shall be dismayed.
37 A sword *is* upon their horses, and
upon their chariots,
And upon all [a] the mingled people that
are in the midst of her;
And [b] they shall become as women:
A sword *is* upon her treasures; and
they shall be robbed.
38 [a] A drought *is* upon her waters; and
they shall be dried up:
For it *is* the land of [b] graven images,
And they are mad upon *their* idols.
39 [a] Therefore the wild beasts of the
desert
With the wild beasts of the islands
shall dwell *there,*
And the owls shall dwell therein:
[b] And it shall be no more inhabited for
ever;
Neither shall it be dwelt in from
generation to generation.
40 [a] As God overthrew Sodom and
Gomorrah
And the neighbour *cities* thereof, saith
the LORD;
So shall no man abide there,
Neither shall any son of man dwell
therein.

41 [a] Behold, a people shall come from the
north,

50:26 [1] Heb. *from the end* [2] Or, *Tread her*
50:27 [a] Ps. 22:12; Is. 34:7; ch. 46:21 [b] ch. 48:44
50:28 [a] ch. 51:10
50:29 [a] ver. 14 [b] ver. 15; ch. 51:56; Rev. 18:6 [c] Is. 47:10
50:30 [a] ch. 49:26; 51:4
50:31 [1] Heb. *pride* [a] ver. 27
50:32 [1] Heb. *pride* [a] ch. 21:14
50:34 [a] Rev. 18:8 [b] Is. 47:4
50:35 [a] Dan. 5:30 [b] Is. 47:13
50:36 [1] Or, *chief stays* [2] Heb. *bars* [a] Is. 44:25; ch. 48:30
50:37 [a] ch. 25:20; Ezek. 30:5 [b] ch. 51:30; Nah. 3:13
50:38 [a] Is. 44:27; ch. 51:36; Rev. 16:12 [b] ver. 2
50:39 [a] Is. 13:21,22; 34:14; ch. 51:37; Rev. 18:2 [b] Is. 13:20; ch. 25:12
50:40 [a] Gen. 19:25; Is. 13:19; ch. 51:26
50:41 [a] ver. 9; ch. 6:22; 25:14; 51:27; Rev. 17:16

50:26 *heaps.* The Hebrew for this expression is used in Neh 4:2 to describe heaps of rubble that had been burned. *destroy her utterly.* By burning (see note on v. 21; see also Josh 11:11–13).
50:27 *bullocks.* The people of Babylon, including especially her fighting men (see Is 34:6–7 and notes). *go down to the slaughter.* See note on 48:15. *time of their visitation.* See 11:23; 23:12; 46:21.
50:28 *flee and escape.* Jewish exiles who had fled the destruction overtaking Babylon. *vengeance . . . vengeance of his temple.* See v. 15 and note; 46:10; 51:6. The conquest of Babylon was the Lord's response to Babylon's burning of the Jerusalem temple.
50:29 *Recompense her according to her work.* Echoed from 25:14 (see 51:24). *According to all that she hath done.* See v. 15. *Holy One of Israel.* A title of God found frequently in Isaiah (see note on Is 1:4), it occurs in Jeremiah only here and in 51:5.
50:30 Repeated almost verbatim from 49:26.
50:31–32 A distant echo of 21:13–14, spoken there to Jerusalem but here to Babylon.
50:33 *all that took them captives.* See Is 14:2. *refused to let them go.* Reminiscent of Pharaoh's repeated refusals before the exodus (see, e.g., Ex 7:14; 8:2,32; 9:2,7).
50:34 *redeemer.* See 31:11 and note. *plead their cause.* See 51:36. *give rest.* See 31:2 and note; see also Is 14:3,7 and notes on Deut 3:20; Josh 1:13.
50:35–38 Cf. Ezek 21.
‡50:36 *dote.* Or "become fools." The Hebrew words rendered "fools" in the OT usually denote persons who are morally deficient. See Is 44:25; see also Num 12:11.
50:37 *upon their horses, and . . . chariots.* See Is 43:17; see also Ps 20:7. *mingled people.* See 25:20,24; Neh 13:3. *become as women.* See Nah 3:13.
50:38 *are mad.* See 25:16 and note. *idols.* See 51:52; see also note on Is 21:9.
50:39 See Is 13:20–22 and notes.
50:40 Repeated almost verbatim from 49:18 (see note there).
50:41–43 Repeated almost verbatim from 6:22–24 (see notes

And a great nation, and many kings
Shall be raised up from the coasts of
the earth.
42 [a]They shall hold the bow and the lance:
[b]They *are* cruel, and will not shew
mercy:
[c]Their voice shall roar like the sea,
And they shall ride upon horses,
Every one put in array, like a man to
the battle,
Against thee, O daughter of Babylon.
43 The king of Babylon hath heard the
report of them,
And his hands waxed feeble:
Anguish took hold of him,
And pangs as of a woman in travail.

44 [a]Behold, he shall come up like a lion
from the swelling of Jordan
Unto the habitation of the strong:
But I will make them suddenly run
away from her:
And who *is* a chosen *man, that* I may
appoint over her?
For who *is* like me? and who will
[1]appoint me the time?
And [b]who *is* that shepherd that will
stand before me?
45 Therefore hear ye [a]the counsel of the
LORD,
That he hath taken against Babylon;
And his purposes, that he hath purposed
against the land of the Chaldeans:
Surely the least of the flock shall draw
them out:
Surely he shall make *their* habitation
desolate with them.
46 [a]At the noise of the taking of Babylon
the earth is moved,
And the cry is heard among the nations.

51 Thus saith the LORD;
Behold, I *will* raise up against
Babylon,
And against them that dwell in the
[1]midst of them that rise up against
me,
[a]A destroying wind;
2 And will send unto Babylon [a]fanners,
that shall fan her,
And shall empty her land:
[b]For in the day of trouble they shall be
against her round about.
3 Against *him that* bendeth [a]let the
archer bend his bow,
And against *him that* lifteth himself up
in his brigandine:
And spare ye not her young men;
[b]Destroy ye utterly all her host.
4 Thus the slain shall fall in the land of
the Chaldeans,
[a]And *they that are* thrust through in
her streets.
5 For Israel *hath* not *been* forsaken,
Nor Judah of his God, of the LORD of
hosts;
Though their land was filled *with* sin
Against the Holy One of Israel.
6 [a]Flee out of the midst of Babylon,
And deliver every man his soul:
Be not cut off in her iniquity;
For [b]this *is* the time of the LORD's
vengeance;
[c]He *will* render unto her a recompence.
7 [a]Babylon *hath been* a golden cup in the
LORD's hand,
That made all the earth drunken:
[b]The nations have drunken of her wine;
Therefore the nations [c]are mad.
8 Babylon is suddenly [a]fallen and
destroyed:
[b]Howl for her;
[c]Take balm for her pain,
If so be she may be healed.
9 We would have healed Babylon, but
she is not healed:
Forsake her, and [a]let us go every one
into his own country:
[b]For her judgment reacheth unto
heaven,
And is lifted up *even* to the skies.
10 The LORD hath [a]brought forth our
righteousness:
Come, and let us [b]declare in Zion

50:42 [a]ch. 6:23 [b]Is. 13:18 [c]Is. 5:30
50:44 [1]Or, *convent me to plead?* [a]ch. 49:19 [b]Job 41:10; ch. 49:19
50:45 [a]Is. 14:24; ch. 51:11
50:46 [a]Rev. 18:9
51:1 [1]Heb. *heart*
51:1 [a]2 Ki. 19:7; ch. 4:11
51:2 [a]ch. 15:7 [b]ch. 50:14
51:3 [a]ch. 50:14 [b]ch. 50:21
51:4 [a]ch. 49:26; 50:30,37
51:6 [a]ch. 50:8; Rev. 18:4 [b]ch. 50:15 [c]ch. 25:14
51:7 [a]Rev. 17:4 [b]Rev. 14:8 [c]ch. 25:16
51:8 [a]Is. 21:9; Rev. 14:8; 18:2 [b]ch. 48:20; Rev. 18:9,11,19 [c]ch. 46:11
51:9 [a]Is. 13:14; ch. 50:16 [b]Rev. 18:5
51:10 [a]Ps. 37:6 [b]ch. 50:28

there). The earlier oracle, referring to Jerusalem, is here applied to Babylon.

50:44–46 Repeated almost verbatim from 49:19–21 (see notes there). The oracle against Edom is here applied to Babylon.

51:1 *I will raise up . . . wind.* See 1 Chr 5:26; Hag 1:14. The Hebrew underlying this phrase is translated "stirred up . . . the spirit of" in 2 Chr 21:16. *midst of them . . . against me.* Hebrew *Leb-kamai,* a cryptogram for Chaldea (Babylon). See note on 25:26. *destroying.* See note on 4:7; here including the "kings of the Medes" (v. 11).

51:2 *fanners, that shall fan her.* The Hebrew for this phrase is an excellent example of alliteration and assonance (see Introduction: Literary Features).

51:3 *Destroy . . . her host.* See note on 25:9. See also note on Deut 2:34.

51:4 *fall . . . in her streets.* See 49:26; 50:30.

51:5 *forsaken.* Lit. "widowed"; contrast Is 54:4,6–7 and notes. *Holy One of Israel.* See note on 50:29.

‡51:6 *Flee . . . deliver every man his soul.* See v. 45; 48:6. This was spoken to the people of Judah (as in 50:8). In most, if not all cases, in the OT, "soul" means life or being. *the LORD's vengeance.* See note on 50:15. *render unto her a recompense.* See Is 59:18; 66:6.

51:7 See 25:15–16 and notes. *Babylon . . . a golden cup.* See note on Dan 2:32–43.

51:8 *Babylon is suddenly fallen.* See Is 21:9 and note. *balm.* See note on 8:22.

51:9 The speakers are the nations conquered by Babylon. *every one into his own country.* See 50:16 and note. *her judgment.* Her sin, deserving of judgment. *reacheth unto heaven . . . up even to the skies.* Poetic exaggeration (see Deut 1:28; Ps 57:10; 108:4).

51:10 Judah speaks (see 50:28). *The LORD hath brought . . . righteousness.* See Ps 37:6.

The work of the LORD our God.
11 [a]Make [1]bright the arrows: gather the shields:
[b]The LORD hath raised up the spirit of the kings of the Medes:
[c]For his device *is* against Babylon, to destroy it;
Because it *is* [d]the vengeance of the LORD,
The vengeance of his temple.
12 [a]Set up the standard upon the walls of Babylon,
Make the watch strong, set up the watchmen,
Prepare the [1]ambushes:
For the LORD hath both devised and done
That which he spake against the inhabitants of Babylon.
13 [a]O thou that dwellest upon many waters, abundant in treasures,
Thine end is come, *and* the measure of thy covetousness.
14 [a]The LORD of hosts hath sworn [1]by himself, *saying,*
Surely I will fill thee *with* men, [b]as *with* caterpillars;
And they shall [2]lift [c]up a shout against thee.

15 [a]He hath made the earth by his power,
He hath established the world by his wisdom,
And [b]hath stretched out the heaven by his understanding.
16 When he uttereth *his* voice, *there is* a [1]multitude of waters in the heavens;
And [a]he causeth the vapours to ascend from the ends of the earth:
He maketh lightnings with rain,
And bringeth forth the wind out of his treasures.
17 [a]Every man [1]is brutish by *his* knowledge;
Every founder is confounded by the graven image:
[b]For his molten image *is* falsehood, and *there is* no breath in them.
18 [a]They *are* vanity, the work of errors:

51:11 [1]Heb. *pure* [a]ch. 46:4 [b]ver. 28; Is. 13:17 [c]ch. 50:45 [d]ch. 50:28
51:12 [1]Heb. *liers in wait* [a]Nah. 2:1; 3:14
51:13 [a]Rev. 17:1,15
51:14 [1]Heb. *by his soul* [2]Heb. *utter* [a]ch. 49:13; Amos 6:8 [b]Nah. 3:15 [c]ch. 50:15
51:15 [a]Gen. 1:1,6; ch. 10:12 [b]Job 9:8; Ps. 104:2; Is. 40:22
51:16 [1]Or, *noise* [a]Ps. 135:7
51:17 [1]Or, *is more brutish than to know* [a]ch. 10:14 [b]ch. 50:2
51:18 [a]ch. 10:15
51:19 [a]ch. 10:16
51:20 [1]Or, *in thee, or, by thee* [a]Is. 10:5,15; ch. 50:23
51:22 [a]2 Chr. 36:17
51:24 [a]ch. 50:15
51:25 [a]Is. 13:2; Zech. 4:7 [b]Rev. 8:8
51:26 [1]Heb. *everlasting desolations* [a]ch. 50:40
51:27 [a]Is. 13:2

In the time of their visitation they shall perish.
19 [a]The portion of Jacob *is* not like them;
For he *is* the former of all *things:*
And *Israel is* the rod of his inheritance:
The LORD of hosts *is* his name.

20 [a]Thou *art* my battle axe *and* weapons of war:
For [1]with thee will I break in pieces the nations,
And with thee will I destroy kingdoms:
21 And with thee will I break in pieces the horse and his rider;
And with thee will I break in pieces the chariot and his rider;
22 With thee also will I break in pieces man and woman;
And with thee will I break in pieces [a]old and young;
And with thee will I break in pieces the young man and the maid;
23 I will also break in pieces with thee the shepherd and his flock;
And with thee will I break in pieces the husbandman and his yoke of oxen;
And with thee will I break in pieces captains and rulers.
24 [a]And I will render unto Babylon
And to all the inhabitants of Chaldea
All their evil that they have done in Zion
In your sight, saith the LORD.
25 Behold, I *am* against thee,
[a]O destroying mountain, saith the LORD,
Which destroyest all the earth:
And I will stretch out mine hand upon thee,
And roll thee down from the rocks,
[b]And will make thee a burnt mountain.
26 And they shall not take of thee a stone for a corner,
Nor a stone for foundations;
[a]But thou shalt be [1]desolate for ever, saith the LORD.
27 [a]Set ye up a standard in the land,
Blow the trumpet among the nations,

51:11 *raised up the spirit of.* See note on v. 1. *Medes.* See v. 28; Is 13:17 and note; Is 21:2; Dan 5:28,31; 6:8,12,15; 8:20. *vengeance . . . vengeance of his temple.* See note on 50:28.
51:12 *Prepare the ambushes.* To keep defenders from retreating to the safety of their fortifications (see Josh 8:14–22; Judg 20:29–39).
51:13 *many waters.* The "rivers of Babylon" (Ps 137:1), including the mighty Euphrates along with a magnificent system of irrigation canals, were proverbial.
51:14 *sworn by himself.* See note on Gen 22:16. *with caterpillars.* See 46:23. *shout against thee.* See note on 48:33.
51:15–19 Repeated almost verbatim from 10:12–16 (see notes there).
51:20–23 Illustrates Jeremiah's fondness for the effective use of repetition (see 4:23–26; see also Introduction: Literary Features).
51:20 *Thou art my battle axe.* Cf. Prov 25:18; either (1) Cyrus of Persia, soon to conquer Babylon, or, more likely, (2) Babylon, destroyer of nations (see 50:23; see also note on Is 10:5). *break in pieces.* See vv. 21–23. The Hebrew root for this verb is the same as that for "battle axe." See also Ex 15:6. The Hebrew verb is translated "dash (to pieces)" in Ps 137:9; Hos 10:14; 13:16.
51:24 *render unto Babylon . . . All their evil that they have done.* See v. 6; 50:15,29. *your.* Judah's.
51:25 *destroying mountain.* Symbolizes a powerful kingdom (see Dan 2:35,44–45), here Babylon. *burnt mountain.* After being judged by the Lord, Babylon will be like an extinct volcano.
51:26 *desolate for ever.* See 25:12; 50:12–13; see also note on Is 13:20.
51:27 See 50:29. *Set ye up a standard . . . Blow the trumpet.* See 4:5–6; 6:1 and notes. *prepare . . . against her.* See note on 6:4. *the kingdoms.* Allies of the Medes (see v. 11 and note). *Ararat.*

[b]Prepare the nations against her,
Call together against her [c]the kingdoms of Ararat, Minni, and Ashchenaz;
Appoint a captain against her;
Cause the horses to come up as the rough caterpillars.
28 Prepare against her the nations with [a]the kings of the Medes,
The captains thereof, and all the rulers thereof,
And all the land of his dominion.
29 And the land shall tremble and sorrow:
For every purpose of the LORD shall be performed against Babylon,
[a]To make the land of Babylon a desolation
Without an inhabitant.
30 The mighty *men* of Babylon have forborn to fight,
They have remained in *their* holds:
Their might hath failed; [a]they became as women:
They have burnt her dwelling places;
[b]Her bars are broken.
31 [a]One post shall run to meet another,
And one messenger to meet another,
To shew the king of Babylon
That his city is taken at *one* end,
32 And *that* [a]the passages are stopped,
And the reeds they have burnt with fire,
And the men of war are affrighted.
33 For thus saith the LORD of hosts, the God of Israel;
The daughter of Babylon *is* [a]like a threshingfloor,
[b][1]*It is* time to thresh her:
Yet a little while, [c]and the time of her harvest shall come.
34 Nebuchadrezzar the king of Babylon hath [a]devoured me, he hath crushed me,
He hath made me an empty vessel,
He hath swallowed me up like a dragon,
He hath filled his belly with my delicates,
He hath cast me out.
35 [1]The violence done to me and *to* my [2]flesh *be* upon Babylon,
Shall the [3]inhabitant of Zion say;
And my blood upon the inhabitants of Chaldea,
Shall Jerusalem say.
36 Therefore thus saith the LORD;
Behold, [a]I *will* plead thy cause,
And take vengeance for thee;
[b]And I will dry up her sea,
And make her springs dry.
37 [a]And Babylon shall become heaps,
A dwelling place for dragons,
[b]An astonishment, and a hissing,
Without an inhabitant.
38 They shall roar together like lions:
They shall [1]yell as lions' whelps,
39 In their heat I will make their feasts,
And [a]I will make them drunken, that they may rejoice,
And sleep a perpetual sleep,
And not wake, saith the LORD.
40 I will bring them down like lambs to the slaughter,
Like rams with he goats.
41 How is [a]Sheshach taken!
And *how* is [b]the praise of the whole earth surprised!
How is Babylon become an astonishment among the nations!
42 [a]The sea is come up upon Babylon:
She is covered with the multitude of the waves thereof.
43 [a]Her cities are a desolation,
A dry land, and a wilderness,
A land wherein no man dwelleth,
Neither doth *any* son of man pass thereby.
44 [a]And I will punish Bel in Babylon,

51:27 [b]ch. 25:14 [c]ch. 50:41
51:28 [a]ver. 11
51:29 [a]ver. 43; ch. 50:13
51:30 [a]Is. 19:16; ch. 48:41; 50:37 [b]Lam. 2:9; Amos 1:5; Nah. 3:13
51:31 [a]ch. 50:24
51:32 [a]ch. 50:38
51:33 [1]Or, In *the time that* he *thresheth her* [a]Is. 21:10; Amos 1:3; Mic. 4:13 [b]Is. 41:15; Hab. 3:12 [c]Is. 17:5; Hos. 6:11; Joel 3:13; Rev. 14:15
51:34 [a]ch. 50:17
51:35 [1]Heb. *My violence* [2]Or, *remainder* [3]Heb. *inhabitress*
51:36 [a]ch. 50:34 [b]ch. 50:38
51:37 [a]Is. 13:22; ch. 50:39; Rev. 18:2 [b]ch. 25:9,18
51:38 [1]Or, *shake themselves*
51:39 [a]ver. 57
51:41 [a]ch. 25:26 [b]Is. 13:19
51:42 [a]See Is. 8:7
51:43 [a]ver. 29; ch. 50:39
51:44 [a]Is. 46:1

See note on Gen 8:4. *Minni.* A region mentioned in Assyrian inscriptions, it was located somewhere in Armenia. *Ashchenaz.* See note on Gen 10:3. *captain.* The Hebrew for this word appears again in the OT only in Nah 3:17. It is a Babylonian loanword meaning lit. "scribe." *as the rough caterpillars.* See note on 46:23.

51:28 *Medes.* See note on v. 11. *land of his dominion.* See note on 34:1; see also 1 Ki 9:19.

51:29 *land shall tremble and sorrow.* At the fearful prospect of war.

51:30 *might hath failed; they became as women.* In the Hebrew there is a play on words. *became as women.* See 50:37; Nah 3:13.

51:31 *One post shall run to meet another.* They run to the palace from all parts of the city.

51:32 *passages.* River crossings and ferries (and perhaps bridges). *reeds they have burnt with fire.* To destroy the reeds and prevent fugitives from hiding among them.

51:33 *daughter of Babylon.* See 50:42; see also note on Is 47:1. *threshingfloor.* The destruction of a city or nation is often depicted as a harvest (see Is 27:12; Joel 3:13; Mic 4:12–13).

51:34 *dragon.* The Hebrew for this word is also translated "dragon" in Is 51:9, where it symbolizes Egypt (see note on Gen 1:21). *delicates.* See Gen 49:20.

51:35 *flesh.* See Mic 3:2–3.

‡51:36 *take vengeance for thee.* See vv. 6,11; see also note on 50:15. *sea . . . springs.* See note on v. 13. Babylonia is called the "desert of the sea" in Is 21:1 (see note there).

51:37 See 9:11; 18:16 and notes.

51:38 *roar . . . as lions' whelps.* See 2:15 and note.

51:39 *In their heat.* For a similar image see Hos 7:4–7. *drunken.* See v. 57; see also notes on 25:15–16,26.

51:40 *lambs . . . rams . . . goats.* Symbolic of the people (see Is 34:6; Ezek 39:18) of Babylon. *slaughter.* See Is 53:7 and note.

51:41 *Sheshach.* See note on 25:26.

51:42 *sea . . . multitude of the waves.* See Is 17:12 and note; here and in v. 55, Babylon's enemies (see 46:7 and note).

51:43 See 48:9; 49:18,33; 50:12–13.

51:44 *Bel.* See 50:2; Is 46:1 and note. *which he hath swallowed up.* Captive peoples (including Judah) and plundered goods (including vessels from the temple in Jerusalem; see Dan 5:2–3). *wall of Babylon.* A wall of double construction, the outer wall

And I will bring forth out of his mouth
that which he hath swallowed up:
And the nations shall not flow *together*
any more unto him:
Yea, [b]the wall of Babylon shall fall.
45 [a]My people, go ye out of the midst of
her,
And deliver ye every man his soul
From the fierce anger of the LORD.
46 And [1]lest your heart faint,
And ye fear [a]for the rumour that shall
be heard in the land;
A rumour shall both come *one* year,
And after that in *another* year *shall
come* a rumour,
And violence in the land, ruler against
ruler.
47 Therefore behold, the days come,
That [a]I will [1]do judgment upon the
graven images of Babylon:
And her whole land shall be
confounded,
And all her slain shall fall in the midst
of her.
48 Then [a]the heaven and the earth, and
all that *is* therein, shall sing for
Babylon:
[b]For the spoilers shall come unto her
from the north, saith the LORD.
49 [1]As Babylon *hath caused* the slain of
Israel to fall,
So at Babylon shall fall the slain of all
[2]the earth.
50 [a]Ye that have escaped the sword, go
away, stand not still:
Remember the LORD afar off,
And let Jerusalem come into your mind.
51 [a]We are confounded, because we have
heard reproach:
Shame hath covered our faces:
For strangers are come into the
sanctuaries of the LORD's house.
52 Wherefore behold, the days come,
saith the LORD,
[a]That I will do judgment upon her
graven images:
And through all her land the wounded
shall groan.
53 [a]Though Babylon should mount up *to*
heaven,
And though she should fortify the
height of her strength,
Yet from me shall spoilers come unto
her, saith the LORD.
54 [a]A sound of a cry *cometh* from Babylon,
And great destruction from the land of
the Chaldeans:
55 Because the LORD *hath* spoiled Babylon,
And destroyed out of her the great
voice;
When her waves do roar like great
waters,
A noise of their voice is uttered:
56 Because the spoiler is come upon her,
even upon Babylon,
And her mighty *men* are taken,
Every one of their bows is broken:
[a]For the LORD God of recompences
shall surely requite.
57 [a]And I will make drunk her princes,
and her wise *men,*
Her captains, and her rulers, and her
mighty *men:*
And they shall sleep a perpetual sleep,
and not wake,
Saith [b]the King, whose name *is* the
LORD of hosts.
58 Thus saith the LORD of hosts;
[a][1]The broad walls of Babylon shall be
utterly [2]broken,
And her high gates shall be burnt with
fire;
And [b]the people shall labour in vain,
And the folk in the fire, and they shall
be weary.

59 ¶ The word which Jeremiah the prophet
commanded Seraiah the son of Neriah, the son
of Maaseiah, when he went [1]with Zedekiah
the king of Judah *into* Babylon in the fourth
year of his reign. And *this* Seraiah *was* a [2]qui-
et prince.

51:44 [b]ver. 58
51:45 [a]ver. 6; ch. 50:8; Rev. 18:4
51:46 [1][Or, *let not*] [a]2 Ki. 19:7
51:47 [1]Heb. *visit upon* [a]ver. 52
51:48 [a]Is. 44:23 [b]ch. 50:3,41
51:49 [1]Or, *Both Babylon is to fall, O ye slain of Israel, and with Babylon, etc.* [2]Or, *the country*
51:50 [a]ch. 44:28
51:51 [a]Ps. 44:15; 79:4
51:52 [a]ver. 47
51:53 [a]ch. 49:16; Amos 9:2; Obad. 4
51:54 [a]ch. 50:22
51:56 [a]ver. 24; Ps. 94:1; ch. 50:29
51:57 [a]ver. 39 [b]ch. 46:18; 48:15
51:58 [1]Or, *The walls of broad Babylon* [2]Or, *made naked* [a]ver. 44 [b]Hab. 2:13
51:59 [1]Or, *on the behalf of* [2]Or, *prince of Menucha,* or, *chief chamberlain*

(12 feet thick) being separated from the inner wall (21 feet thick) by a dry moat 23 feet wide.
51:45 *deliver ye every man his soul.* See note on v. 6. *fierce anger.* See 4:8,26; Is 13:13; Nah 1:6.
51:46 *ye fear for the rumour . . . heard in the land.* While giving His Olivet discourse, Jesus may have had this passage in mind (see Mat 24:6; Mark 13:7; Luke 21:9).
51:47 *I will do judgment upon the graven images of Babylon.* See v. 52; see also note on 50:2.
51:48 *heaven and the earth . . . shall sing for Babylon.* See Is 44:23; Rev 18:20; 19:1–3. *from the north.* See note on 50:3.
51:49 See note on 25:26.
51:50 *stand not still.* See note on v. 6.
51:51 *strangers are come into the sanctuaries of the LORD's house.* Refers to Nebuchadnezzar's defiling the Jerusalem temple in 586 B.C. The same sacrilege would occur under Antiochus Epiphanes in 168 B.C. and under the Romans in A.D. 70.
51:52 *judgment upon her graven images.* See note on 50:2.
51:53 *mount up to heaven.* Cf. Job 20:6; see Gen 11:4 and note; see also Is 14:13–15. *spoilers.* See vv. 48,56.
51:54 See 50:46. *great destruction.* See note on 4:6.
51:55 *waves.* See note on v. 42. *like great waters.* See note on Ps 32:6.
51:56 *God of recompences.* See note on v. 24.
51:57 *drunk.* See v. 39; see also notes on 25:15–16,26. *princes, and . . . wise men.* See 50:35. *King.* See note on 46:18. The true King is the Lord, not Bel/Marduk (see 50:2 and note).
51:58 *broad walls.* See note on v. 44. *high gates.* The famous Ishtar Gate was almost 40 feet high. *the people . . . in the fire.* Very similar to Hab 2:13.
51:59–64 A prose conclusion to the book in general and to the oracle against Babylon in particular.
51:59 *Seraiah the son of Neriah.* An ancient seal has been found that bears the inscription "Belonging to Seraiah son of Neriah," and it no doubt refers to the man mentioned here. He was a brother of Jeremiah's secretary, Baruch (see 32:12). *he.* Seraiah. *Zedekiah . . . fourth year.* 593 B.C. Zedekiah may have been summoned to Babylon by Nebuchadnezzar to be interro-

60 So Jeremiah wrote in a book all the evil that should come upon Babylon, *even* all these words that are written against Babylon.

61 And Jeremiah said to Seraiah, When thou comest *to* Babylon, and shalt see, and shalt read all these words;

62 Then shalt thou say, O LORD, thou hast spoken against this place, to cut it off, that [a]none shall remain in it, neither man nor beast, but that it shall be [1]desolate for ever.

63 And it shall be, when thou hast made an end of reading this book, [a]*that* thou shalt bind a stone to it, and cast it into the midst of Euphrates:

64 And thou shalt say, Thus shall Babylon sink, and shall not rise from the evil that I *will* bring upon her: [a]and they shall be weary. Thus far *are* the words of Jeremiah.

Downfall of Jerusalem

52 Zedekiah *was* [a]one and twenty year old when he [1]*began* to reign, and he reigned eleven years in Jerusalem. And his mother's name *was* Hamutal the daughter of Jeremiah of Libnah.

2 And he did *that* which *was* evil in the eyes of the LORD, according to all that Jehoiakim had done.

3 For through the anger of the LORD it came to pass in Jerusalem and Judah, till he had cast them out from his presence, that Zedekiah rebelled against the king of Babylon.

4 And it came to pass in the [a]ninth year of his reign, in the tenth month, in the tenth *day* of the month, *that* Nebuchadrezzar king of Babylon came, he and all his army, against Jerusalem, and pitched against it, and built forts against it round about.

5 So the city was besieged unto the eleventh year of king Zedekiah.

6 And in the fourth month, in the ninth *day* of the month, the famine was sore in the city, so that there was no bread for the people of the land.

7 Then the city was broken up, and all the men of war fled, and went forth out of the city by night *by* the way of the gate between the two walls, which *was* by the king's garden; (now the Chaldeans *were* by the city round about:) and they went *by* the way of the plain.

8 But the army of the Chaldeans pursued after the king, and overtook Zedekiah in the plains of Jericho; and all his army was scattered from him.

9 [a]Then they took the king, and carried him up unto the king of Babylon to Riblah in the land of Hamath; where he gave judgment upon him.

10 [a]And the king of Babylon slew the sons of Zedekiah before his eyes: he slew also all the princes of Judah in Riblah.

11 Then he [1]put out the eyes of Zedekiah; and the king of Babylon bound him in [2]chains, and carried him to Babylon, and put him in [3]prison till the day of his death.

12 ¶ [a]Now in the fifth month, in the tenth *day* of the month, [b]which *was* the nineteenth year of Nebuchadrezzar king of Babylon, [c]came Nebuzar-adan, [1 2]captain of the guard, *which* [3]served the king of Babylon, into Jerusalem,

13 And burnt the house of the LORD, and the king's house; and all the houses of Jerusalem, and all the houses of the great *men,* burnt he with fire:

14 And all the army of the Chaldeans, that *were* with the captain of the guard, brake down all the walls of Jerusalem round about.

15 [a]Then Nebuzar-adan the captain of the guard carried away captive *certain* of the poor of the people, and the residue of the people that remained in the city, and those that fell away, that fell to the king of Babylon, and the rest of the multitude.

16 But Nebuzar-adan the captain of the guard left *certain* of the poor of the land for vinedressers and for husbandmen.

17 [a]Also the [b]pillars of brass that *were* in the house of the LORD, and the bases, and the brasen sea that *was* in the house of the LORD, the Chaldeans brake, and carried all the brass of them to Babylon.

18 [a]The caldrons also, and the [1]shovels, and the snuffers, and the [2]bowls, and the spoons, and all the vessels of brass wherewith they ministered, took they *away.*

19 And the basons, and the [1]firepans, and the bowls, and the caldrons, and the candlesticks, and the spoons, and the cups; *that* which *was of* gold *in* gold, and *that* which *was of* silver *in* silver, took the captain of the guard *away.*

20 The two pillars, one sea, and twelve brasen bulls that *were* under the bases, which

51:62 [1]Heb. *desolations* [a]ver. 29; ch. 50:3,39
51:63 [a]See Rev. 18:21
51:64 [a]ver. 58
52:1 [1]Heb. *reigned* [a]2 Ki. 24:18
52:4 [a]2 Ki. 25:1-27; ch. 39:1; Zech. 8:19
52:9 [a]ch. 32:4
52:10 [a]Ezek. 12:13
52:11 [1]Heb. *blinded* [2]Or, *fetters* [3]Heb. *house of the wards*
52:12 [1]Or, *chief marshal* [2]Heb. *chief of the executioners,* or, *slaughtermen.* And so ver. 14, etc. [3]Heb. *stood before* [a]Zech. 7:5; 8:19 [b]See ver. 29 [c]ch. 39:9
52:15 [a]ch. 39:9
52:17 [a]ch. 27:19 [b]See 1 Ki. 7:15,23,27,50
52:18 [1]Or, *instruments to remove the ashes* [2]Or, *basons* [a]Ex. 27:3; 2 Ki. 25:14-16
52:19 [1]Or, *censers*

gated by him (see note on 27:3). *quiet prince.* Lit."resting-place officer" (see Num 10:33), the official responsible for determining when and where his men on the march should stay overnight.

51:60 *book.* See note on Ex 17:14. *all . . . all these words that are written against Babylon.* Probably the oracle of 50:2–51:58 (see note on 50:1).

51:62 *thou hast spoken against.* See v. 26.

51:64 *Thus far are the words of Jeremiah.* A note by the final compiler of the book of Jeremiah (see 48:47).

52:1–27,31–34 Paralleled almost verbatim in 2 Ki 24:18–25:21,27–30 (see notes there). (52:4–27 is summarized in 39:1–10; see notes there.) The writer(s) of Kings and the writer of the appendix to Jeremiah (perhaps Baruch) doubtless had access to the same sources. It is unlikely that either of the two accounts copied from the other, since each has peculiarities characteristic of the larger work that it concludes. In a few passages, Jeremiah is fuller than Kings (compare especially vv. 10–11 with 2 Ki 25:7; v. 15 with 2 Ki 25:11; vv. 19–23 with 2 Ki 25:15–17; v. 31 with 2 Ki 25:27; v. 34 with 2 Ki 25:30).

52:1 *Jeremiah.* Not the prophet.

52:12 *tenth day.* The parallel in 2 Ki 25:8 reads "seventh day"; one of the numbers is a copyist's error, but we cannot tell which (see vv. 22,25,31).

52:18–19 See notes on 1 Ki 7:40,45,50.

52:20 *twelve brasen bulls.* See note on 2 Chr 4:4.

king Solomon had made in the house of the LORD: [a][1]the brass of all these vessels was without weight.

21 And *concerning* the [a]pillars, the height of one pillar *was* eighteen cubits; and a [1]fillet of twelve cubits did compass it; and the thickness thereof *was* four fingers: *it was* hollow.

22 And a chapiter of brass *was* upon it; and the height of one chapiter *was* five cubits, with network and pomegranates upon the chapiters round about, all *of* brass. The second pillar also and the pomegranates *were* like unto these.

23 And there were ninety and six pomegranates on a side; *and* [a]all the pomegranates upon the network *were* an hundred round about.

24 And [a]the captain of the guard took Seraiah the chief priest, [b]and Zephaniah the second priest, and the three keepers of the [1]door:

25 He took also out of the city an eunuch, which had the charge of the men of war; and seven men of them that [1]were near the king's person, which were found in the city; and the [2]principal scribe of the host, who mustered the people of the land; and threescore men of the people of the land, that were found in the midst of the city.

26 So Nebuzar-adan the captain of the guard took them, and brought them to the king of Babylon to Riblah.

27 And the king of Babylon smote them, and put them to death in Riblah in the land of Hamath. Thus Judah was carried away captive out of his own land.

28 ¶ [a]This *is* the people whom Nebuchadrezzar carried away captive: in the [b]seventh year [c]three thousand Jews and three and twenty:

29 [a]In the eighteenth year of Nebuchadrezzar he carried away captive from Jerusalem eight hundred thirty and two [1]persons:

30 In the three and twentieth year of Nebuchadrezzar Nebuzar-adan the captain of the guard carried away captive *of* the Jews seven hundred forty and five persons: all the persons *were* four thousand and six hundred.

The honour given Jehoiachin

31 ¶ [a]And it came to pass in the seven and thirtieth year of the captivity of Jehoiachin king of Judah, in the twelfth month, in the five and twentieth *day* of the month, *that* Evil-merodach king of Babylon in the *first* year of his reign [b]lifted up the head of Jehoiachin king of Judah, and brought him forth out of prison;

32 And spake [1]kindly unto him, and set his throne above the throne of the kings that *were* with him in Babylon,

33 And changed his prison garments: [a]and he did continually eat bread before him all the days of his life.

34 And *for* his diet, there was a continual diet given him of the king of Babylon, [1]every day a portion until the day of his death, all the days of his life.

52:20 [1]Heb. *their brass* [a]1 Ki. 7:47
52:21 [1]Heb. *thread* [a]1 Ki. 7:15; 2 Ki. 25:17; 2 Chr. 3:15
52:23 [a]See 1 Ki. 7:20
52:24 [1]Heb. *threshold* [a]2 Ki. 25:18 [b]ch. 21:1; 29:5
52:25 [1]Heb. *saw the face of the king* [2]Or, *scribe of the captain of the host*
52:28 [a]2 Ki. 24:2 [b]See 2 Ki. 24:12 [c]See 2 Ki. 24:14
52:29 [1]Heb. *souls* [a]See ver. 12; ch. 39:9
52:31 [a]2 Ki. 25:27-30 [b]Gen. 40:13,20
52:32 [1]Heb. *good things with him*
52:33 [a]2 Sam. 9:13
52:34 [1]Heb. *the matter of the day in his day*

52:21–23 See notes on 1 Ki 7:15–22.
52:22 *five cubits.* About 7 1/2 feet. The parallel in 2 Ki 25:17 reads "three cubits" (about 4 1/2 feet; see note there), probably a copyist's error.
52:25 *seven.* The parallel in 2 Ki 25:19 reads "five"; see note on v. 12.
52:28 *seventh year.* Of Nebuchadnezzar's reign (see vv. 29–30), which was 597 B.C. *three thousand Jews and three and twenty.* Probably includes only adult males, since the corresponding figure(s) in 2 Ki 24:14,16 are significantly higher.
52:29 *eighteenth year.* 586 B.C. In v. 12 the same year is called the "nineteenth year"; the difference is due to alternate ways of computing regnal years (for a similar case see note on Dan 1:1).
52:30 *three and twentieth year.* 581 B.C. *Nebuzar-adan . . . carried away captive.* Either (1) to quell further rebellion (see v. 3), or (2) in belated reprisal for Gedaliah's assassination (see 41:1–3).
52:31–34 Paralleled almost verbatim in 2 Ki 25:27–30 (see notes there). Jeremiah and Kings thus conclude with the same happy ending.
‡52:31 *five and twentieth.* The parallel in 2 Ki 25:27 reads "seven and twentieth"; see note on v. 12.
52:34 *until the day of his death.* See v. 11. Since the phrase does not appear in the parallel verses in 2 Kings in either case, its intention is probably to highlight the contrast between Zedekiah, who remained in prison till the day he died (see v. 11), and Jehoiachin, who was released from prison and treated well by the Babylonian kings till the day he died.

The Lamentations
of Jeremiah

INTRODUCTION

Title

The Hebrew title of the book is *'ekah* ("How . . . !"), the first word not only in 1:1 but also in 2:1; 4:1. Because of its subject matter, the book is also referred to in Jewish tradition as *qinot,* "Lamentations" (the title given to it in the Greek Septuagint and Latin Vulgate).

Author and Date

Although Lamentations is anonymous and we cannot be certain who wrote it, ancient Jewish and Christian tradition ascribes it to Jeremiah. This is partly on the basis of 2 Chr 35:25 (though the "Lamentations" are not to be identified with the OT book of Lamentations); partly on the basis of such texts as Jer 7:29; 8:21; 9:1,10,20; and partly because of the similarity of vocabulary and style between the books of Jeremiah and Lamentations. Also, since the prophet Jeremiah was an eyewitness to the divine judgment on Jerusalem in 586 B.C., it is reasonable to assume that he was the author of the book that so vividly portrays the event. Lamentations poignantly shares the overwhelming sense of loss that accompanied the destruction of the city, temple and ritual as well as the exile of Judah's inhabitants.

The earliest possible date for the book is 586 B.C., and the latest is 516 (when the rebuilt Jerusalem temple was dedicated). The graphic immediacy of Lamentations argues for an earlier date, probably before 575.

Literary Features

The entire book is poetic. Each of its five laments contains 22 verses (except the third, which has 66 verses—3 times 22), reflecting the number of letters in the Hebrew alphabet. Moreover, the first four are alphabetic acrostics (beginning in 1:1; 2:1; 3:1; 4:1). The first three laments are equal in length; in the first and second each verse (except 1:7) has three Hebrew lines, while in the third each of the 66 verses has one Hebrew line. The fourth is shorter (each of its 22 verses has two Hebrew lines), and the fifth is shorter still (each verse has one Hebrew line). Use of the alphabet as a formal structure indicates that, however passionate these laments, they were composed with studied care.

Themes and Theology

Lamentations is not the only OT book that contains individual or community laments. (A large number of the Psalms are lament poems, and every prophetic book except Haggai includes one or more examples of the lament genre.) However, it is the only book that consists solely of laments.

As a series of laments over the destruction of Jerusalem in 586 B.C., it stands in a tradition with such ancient non-Biblical writings as the Sumerian "Lamentation over the Destruction of Ur," "Lamentation over the Destruction of Sumer and Ur," and "Lamentation over the Destruction of Nippur." Orthodox Jews customarily read it aloud in its entirety on the ninth day of Ab, the traditional date of the destruction of Solomon's temple in 586 as well as the date of the destruction of Herod's temple in A.D. 70. Many also read it each week at the Western Wall (known also as the "Wailing Wall") in the Old City of Jerusalem. In addition the book is important in traditional Roman Catholic liturgy, where it is read during the last three days of Holy Week.

This latter tradition reminds us that the book of Lamentations describes Jerusalem's destruction not only for its own sake but also for the profound theological lessons to be learned from it. The horrors of 586 B.C. are not overlooked, of course:

1. Wholesale devastation and slaughter engulf kings (2:6,9; 4:20), princes (1:6; 2:2,9; 4:7–8; 5:12), elders (1:19; 2:10; 4:16; 5:12), priests (1:4,19; 2:6,20; 4:16), prophets (2:9,20) and commoners (2:10–12; 3:48; 4:6) alike.

2. Starving mothers are reduced to cannibalism (2:20; 4:10).
3. The flower of Judah's citizenry is dragged off into ignominious exile (1:3,18).
4. An elaborate system of ceremony and worship comes to an end (1:4,10).

But other matters, ultimately of far greater significance, are probed as well.

The author of Lamentations understands clearly that the Babylonians were merely the human agents of divine retribution and that God Himself has destroyed His city and temple (1:12–15; 2:1–8,17,22; 4:11). Nor was the Lord's action arbitrary; blatant, God-defying sin and covenant-breaking rebellion were the root causes of his people's woes (1:5,8–9; 4:13; 5:7,16). Although weeping (1:16; 2:11,18; 3:48–51) is to be expected and cries for redress against the enemy (1:22; 3:59–66) are understandable, the proper response in the wake of judgment is sincere, heartfelt contrition (3:40–42). The book that begins with lament (1:1–2) rightly ends in repentance (5:21–22).

In the middle of the book, the theology of Lamentations reaches its apex as it focuses on the goodness of God. He is the Lord of hope (3:21,24–25), of love (3:22), of faithfulness (3:23), of salvation (3:26). In spite of all evidence to the contrary, "His compassions fail not. They are new every morning; great is thy faithfulness" (3:22–23).

Outline

I. Jerusalem's Misery and Desolation (ch. 1)
II. The Lord's Anger against His People (ch. 2)
III. Judah's Complaint—and Basis for Consolation (ch. 3)
IV. The Contrast between Zion's Past and Present (ch. 4)
V. Judah's Appeal for God's Forgiveness (ch. 5)

Jerusalem's desolation

1 How doth the city sit solitary, *that was* full of people!
[a]*How* is she become as a widow! she *that was* great among the nations,
And princess among the provinces, *how* is she become tributary!
2 She [a]weepeth sore in the [b]night, and her tears *are* on her cheeks:
Among all her lovers she hath none to comfort *her:*
All her friends have dealt treacherously with her, they are become her enemies.
3 Judah is gone into captivity because of affliction, and [1]because of great servitude:
[a]She dwelleth among the heathen, she findeth no rest:
All her persecutors overtook her between the straits.
4 The ways of Zion do mourn, because none come to the solemn feasts:
All her gates are desolate: her priests sigh:
Her virgins *are* afflicted, and she *is* in bitterness.
5 Her adversaries [a]are the chief, her enemies prosper;
For the LORD hath afflicted her [b]for the multitude of her transgressions:
Her [c]children are gone *into* captivity before the enemy.
6 And from the daughter of Zion all her beauty is departed:
Her princes are become like harts *that* find no pasture,
And they are gone without strength before the pursuer.

1:1 [a]Is. 47:7,8
1:2 [a]Jer. 13:17 [b]Job 7:3
1:3 [1]Heb. *for the greatness of servitude* [a]ch. 2:9
1:5 [a]Deut. 28:43 [b]Jer. 30:14; Dan. 9:7 [c]Jer. 52:28
1:7 [1]Or, *desirable*
1:8 [1]Heb. *is become a removing,* or, *wandering* [a]1 Ki. 8:46 [b]Jer. 13:22; Ezek. 16:37; Hos. 2:10
1:9 [a]Deut. 32:29; Is. 47:7 [b]ver. 2,17,21
1:10 [1]Or, *desirable* [a]ver. 7 [b]Jer. 51:51 [c]Deut. 23:3; Neh. 13:1
1:11 [1]Or, *to make the soul to come again* [a]Jer. 38:9; 52:6
1:12 [1]Or, It is *nothing* [2]Heb. *pass by the way?* [a]Dan. 9:12

7 Jerusalem remembered in the days of her affliction and of her miseries
All her [1]pleasant things that she had in the days of old,
When her people fell into the hand of the enemy, and none did help her:
The adversaries saw her, *and* did mock at her sabbaths.
8 [a]Jerusalem hath grievously sinned; therefore she [1]is removed:
All that honoured her despise her, because [b]they have seen her nakedness:
Yea, she sigheth, and turneth backward.
9 Her filthiness *is* in her skirts; she [a]remembereth not her last end;
Therefore she came down wonderfully: [b]she had no comforter.
O LORD, behold my affliction: for the enemy hath magnified *himself.*
10 The adversary hath spread out his hand upon [a]all her [1]pleasant things:
For she hath seen *that* [b]the heathen entered into her sanctuary,
Whom thou didst command *that* [c]they should not enter into thy congregation.
11 All her people sigh, [a]they seek bread;
They have given their pleasant things for meat [1]to relieve the soul:
See, O LORD, and consider; for I am become vile.
12 [1]*Is it* nothing to you, all ye that [2]pass by? behold, and see
[a]If there be any sorrow like unto my sorrow, which is done unto me,
Wherewith the LORD hath afflicted *me* in the day of his fierce anger.
13 From above hath he sent fire into my bones, and it prevaileth against them:

1:1 *How . . . !* Expresses a mixture of shock and despair (see 2:1; 4:1–2; Is 1:21; Jer 48:17). *sit solitary.* The Hebrew underlying this phrase is translated "sat alone" in Jer 15:17. There the prophet sat alone; here his beloved city does the same. *city.* Jerusalem. *was full of people.* See Is 1:21. *full . . . great.* The Hebrew is the same for both words. *great among the nations.* Contrast Jer 49:15. *tributatry.* Or "slave." See Ex 1:11; 1 Ki 4:6.
1:2 *She weepeth sore.* As did Jeremiah, and for much the same reason (see Jer 13:17). *in the night.* See 2:18–19. *none to comfort her.* See vv. 9,16–17,21. *lovers . . . friends.* Political allies (see, e.g., Jer 2:36–37; 27:3). *All . . . have dealt treacherously with her.* See v. 19; like Edom (see 4:21–22; Ps 137:7) and Ammon (see Jer 40:14; Ezek 25:2–3,6). *become her enemies.* See v. 17.
1:3 *among the heathen . . . findeth no rest.* As Moses warned in Deut 28:65.
1:4 *mourn. . . . desolate.* (see Judg 5:6; Is 33:8 and notes). *solemn feasts.* See Ex 23:14–17 and notes; Lev 23:2. *virgins are afflicted.* A sign of utter defeat (contrast Ex 15:20 and note; Judg 21:19,21; Ps 68:25; Jer 31:13).
1:5 *chief.* Lit. "head"—in accordance with Deut 28:44 (contrast Deut 28:13). *prosper.* See Jer 12:1.
1:6 *daughter of Zion.* A personification of Jerusalem and its inhabitants. *Her princes are become like harts . . . before the pursuer.* See Jer 52:7–8.
1:7 *affliction and of her miseries.* See 3:19. *pleasant things.* See vv. 10–11. *days of old.* For example, the days of David and Solomon. *fell into the hand of the enemy.* See 2 Sam 24:14. *her sabbaths.* Lit. "cessation" (see Lev 26:34–35). Here the meaning is "ruin" or "destruction."
1:8 *she is removed.* Or "unclean." See v. 17 and note. It refers to the ceremonial uncleanness of a woman during her monthly period (see Lev 12:2,5; 15:19); Jerusalem is here personified as a woman (see v. 6).
1:9 *filthiness.* Ceremonial uncleanness (see note on Lev 4:12), here caused by willful sin. *she remembereth not her last end.* See Is 47:7. *O LORD, behold.* See vv. 11,20. *enemy hath magnified himself.* Or "triumphed." See v. 16.
1:10 *command that they should not enter into thy congregation.* See Ezek 44:7,9.
‡1:11 *seek bread.* Food shortages were an ever-present problem during and after the siege of Jerusalem. *relieve the soul.* Or "keep themselves alive"; see v. 19; 1 Sam 30:12. The word for "soul" can also be translated "life."
1:12 See v. 18. Up to this point, the author has been the main speaker. Now, at the halfway mark of ch. 1, the main speaker changes to Jerusalem personified. *fierce anger.* See 2:3,6; 4:11. The Hebrew for this expression is common in Jeremiah (see Jer 4:8,26; 12:13; 25:37–38; 44:6; 49:37; 51:45).
1:13 *From above hath he sent fire.* See 1 Ki 18:38; 2 Ki 1:10,12,

He hath [a]spread a net for my feet, he
hath turned me back;
He hath made me desolate *and* faint all
the day.
14 [a]The yoke of my transgressions is
bound by his hand:
They are wreathed, *and* come up upon
my neck: he hath made my strength
to fall,
The Lord hath delivered me into *their*
hands, *from whom* I am not able to
rise up.
15 The Lord hath trodden under foot all
my mighty *men* in the midst of me:
He hath called an assembly against me
to crush my young men:
[a]The Lord hath trodden [1]the virgin, the
daughter of Judah, *as in* a winepress.
16 For these *things* I weep; [a]mine eye,
mine eye runneth down *with* water,
Because [b]the comforter that *should*
[1]relieve my soul is far from me:
My children are desolate, because the
enemy prevailed.
17 [a]Zion spreadeth forth her hands, *and*
[b]*there is* none to comfort her:
The LORD hath commanded concerning
Jacob, *that* his adversaries *should be*
round about him:
Jerusalem is as a menstruous *woman*
among them.
18 The LORD *is* [a]righteous; for I have
[b]rebelled against his [1]commandment:
Hear, I pray you, all people, and behold
my sorrow:
My virgins and my young men are
gone into captivity.
19 I called for my lovers, *but* [a]they
deceived me:
My priests and mine elders gave up the
ghost in the city,
[b]While they sought their meat, to
relieve their souls.
20 Behold, O LORD; for I *am* in distress:
my [a]bowels are troubled;

1:13 [a]Ezek. 12:13
1:14 [a]Deut. 28:48
1:15 [1]Or, *the winepress of the virgin, etc.* [a]Is. 63:3; Rev. 14:19
1:16 [1]Heb. *bring back* [a]Jer. 13:17; ch. 2:18 [b]ver. 2,9
1:17 [a]Jer. 4:31 [b]ver. 2,9
1:18 [1]Heb. *mouth* [a]Neh. 9:33; Dan. 9:7,14 [b]1 Sam. 12:14
1:19 [a]ver. 2; Jer. 30:14 [b]ver. 11
1:20 [a]Job 30:27; Is. 16:11; Jer. 4:19; Hos. 11:8
1:20 [b]Deut. 32:25; Ezek. 7:15
1:21 [1]Or, *proclaimed* [a]ver. 2 [b]Is. 13; Jer. 46
1:22 [a]Ps. 109:15 [b]ch. 5:17
2:1 [a]Mat. 11:23 [b]2 Sam. 1:19 [c]1 Chr. 28:2; Ps. 99:5
2:2 [1]Heb. *made to touch* [a]Ps. 89:39
2:3 [a]Ps. 74:11 [b]Ps. 89:46
2:4 [a]Is. 63:10

Mine heart is turned within me; for I
have grievously rebelled:
[b]Abroad the sword bereaveth, at home
there is as death.
21 They have heard that I sigh; [a]*there is*
none to comfort me:
All mine enemies have heard of my
trouble; they are glad that thou hast
done *it:*
Thou wilt bring [b]the day *that* thou hast
[1]called, and they shall be like unto
me.
22 [a]Let all their wickedness come before
thee;
And do unto them, as thou hast done
unto me for all my transgressions:
For my sighs *are* many, and [b]my heart
is faint.

The judgment of the LORD

2 How hath the Lord covered the
daughter of Zion with a cloud in his
anger,
[a]*And* cast down from heaven *unto* the
earth [b]the beauty of Israel,
And remembered not [c]his footstool in
the day of his anger!
2 The Lord hath swallowed up all the
habitations of Jacob, and hath not
pitied:
He hath thrown down in his wrath the
strong holds of the daughter of Judah;
He hath [1]brought *them* down to the
ground: [a]he hath polluted the
kingdom and the princes thereof.
3 He hath cut off in *his* fierce anger all
the horn of Israel:
[a]He hath drawn back his right hand
from before the enemy,
[b]And he burned against Jacob like a
flaming fire, *which* devoureth round
about.
4 [a]He hath bent his bow like an enemy:
he stood *with* his right hand as an
adversary,

14; 2 Chr 7:1. *my bones.* The bones of Jerusalem (personified as a woman; see note on v. 8). In a strikingly similar image, the word of the Lord was like fire in the bones of the prophet (see Jer 20:9 and note). *spread a net for my feet.* See Ps 57:6; Prov 29:5. *desolate.* Like Absalom's sister Tamar (see 2 Sam 13:20).

1:15 *trodden . . . as in a winepress.* A common metaphor of divine judgment (see Is 63:2–3; Joel 3:13; Rev 14:19–20; 19:15). *virgin, the daughter of Judah.* See 2:13; see also notes on 2 Ki 19:21; Jer 14:17.

1:16 *mine eye runneth down with water.* See 3:48; Jer 9:18; 13:17; 14:17; see also Jer 9:1. *enemy prevailed.* See v. 9.

1:17 *his adversaries.* See v. 2. *menstrous woman.* See note on v. 8; for the same imagery elsewhere see Ezra 9:11; Is 30:22; 64:6; Ezek 7:19–20; 36:17.

1:18 *The LORD is righteous.* See Deut 32:4; 2 Chr 12:6; Ps 119:137; Jer 12:1; see also note on Ps 4:1. *rebelled against his commandment.* See Num 20:24. *Hear, I pray you, all people.* See 1 Ki 22:28; Ps 49:1; Mic 1:2.

1:19 *lovers . . . deceived me.* See v. 2 and note. *To relieve their souls.* See note on v. 11.

1:20 *my bowels are troubled.* Repeated in 2:11. *Abroad . . . at home.* See Jer 14:18. The Sumerian "Lamentation over the Destruction of Ur" contains a striking parallel: "Inside it we die of famine, outside we are killed by weapons" (lines 403–404).

1:21 *day that thou hast called.* Day of God's judgment on the nations (see Jer 25:15–38).

1:22 *wickedness . . . before thee.* See Ps 109:14–15. *my heart is faint.* The same expression is found in Jer 8:18; see Lam 5:17; Is 1:5.

2:1 *How . . . !* See note on 1:1. *daughter of Zion.* See 1:6 and note. *cast down from . . . the beauty of Israel.* The imagery is that of a falling star (as in Is 14:12). *footstool.* Either (1) the ark of the covenant (see 1 Chr 28:2) or, more likely, (2) mount Zion (see Ps 99:5,9).

2:2 *swallowed up . . . all the habitations.* See v. 5. *daughter of Judah.* See note on 1:15.

2:3 *flaming fire, which devoureth.* See Num 11:3; Job 1:16; Ps 106:18.

2:4 *bent his bow.* See Deut 32:42; Ps 7:12–13; Zech 9:13–14.

And slew [b] [1] all *that were* pleasant to
the eye,
In the tabernacle of the daughter of
Zion: he poured out his fury like fire.
5 [a] The Lord was as an enemy: he hath
swallowed up Israel,
[b] He hath swallowed up all her palaces:
he hath destroyed his strong holds,
And hath increased in the daughter of
Judah mourning and lamentation.
6 And he hath violently [a] taken away his
[1] tabernacle, [b] as *if it were of* a
garden: he hath destroyed his places
of the assembly:
[c] The LORD hath caused the solemn feasts
and sabbaths to be forgotten in Zion,
And hath despised in the indignation
of his anger the king and the priest.
7 The Lord hath cast off his altar, he hath
abhorred his sanctuary,
He hath [1] given up into the hand of the
enemy the walls of her palaces;
[a] They have made a noise in the house
of the LORD, as *in* the day of a solemn
feast.
8 The LORD hath purposed to destroy the
wall of the daughter of Zion:
[a] He hath stretched out a line, he hath
not withdrawn his hand from
[1] destroying:
Therefore he made the rampart and
the wall to lament; they languished
together.
9 Her gates are sunk into the ground; he
hath destroyed and [a] broken her bars:
[b] Her king and her princes *are* among
the Gentiles: [c] the law *is* no *more;*
Her [d] prophets also find no vision from
the LORD.

2:4 [1] Heb. *all the desirable of the eye* [b] Ezek. 24:25
2:5 [a] Jer. 30:14 [b] 2 Ki. 25:9; Jer. 52:13
2:6 [1] Or, *hedge* [a] Ps. 80:12; 89:40; Is. 5:5 [b] Is. 1:8 [c] ch. 1:4
2:7 [1] Heb. *shut up* [a] Ps. 74:4
2:8 [1] Heb. *swallowing up* [a] 2 Ki. 21:13; Is. 34:11
2:9 [a] Jer. 51:30 [b] Deut. 28:36; 2 Ki. 24:15 [c] 2 Chr. 15:3 [d] Ps. 74:9; Ezek. 7:26

10 The elders of the daughter of Zion [a] sit
upon the ground, *and* keep silence:
They have [b] cast up dust upon their
heads; they have [c] girded themselves
with sackcloth:
The virgins of Jerusalem hang down
their heads to the ground.
11 [a] Mine eyes do fail with tears, [b] my
bowels are troubled,
[c] My liver is poured upon the earth, for
the destruction of the daughter of my
people;
Because [d] the children and the
sucklings [1] swoon in the streets of
the city.
12 They say to their mothers, Where *is*
corn and wine?
When they swooned as the wounded
in the streets of the city,
When their soul was poured out into
their mothers' bosom.
13 What *thing* shall I take to witness for
thee? [a] what *thing* shall I liken to
thee, O daughter of Jerusalem?
What shall I equal to thee, that I may
comfort thee, O virgin daughter of
Zion?
For thy breach *is* great like the sea:
who can heal thee?
14 Thy [a] prophets have seen vain and
foolish things for thee:
And they have not [b] discovered thine
iniquity, to turn away thy captivity;
But have seen for thee false burdens
and causes of banishment.
15 All that pass [1] by [a] clap *their* hands at
thee;
They hiss [b] and wag their head at the
daughter of Jerusalem, *saying,*

2:10 [a] Job 2:13; Is. 3:26 [b] Job 2:12 [c] Is. 15:3
2:11 [1] Or, *faint* [a] ch. 3:48 [b] ch. 1:20 [c] Job 16:13; Ps. 22:14 [d] ch. 4:4
2:13 [a] ch. 1:12; Dan. 9:12
2:14 [a] Jer. 2:8; Ezek. 13:2 [b] Is. 58:1
2:15 [1] Heb. *by the way* [a] Ezek. 25:6 [b] 2 Ki. 19:21; Ps. 44:14

poured out his fury. See Ps 69:24; 79:6; Jer 6:11; 7:20; 10:25; 42:18; 44:6; Hos 5:10; Zeph 3:8.

2:5 *palaces . . . strong holds.* See Hos 8:14. *increased . . . mourning.* The Sumerian "Lamentation over the Destruction of Sumer and Ur" offers this parallel: "In the desolate city there was uttered nothing but laments and dirges" (lines 361–362, 486–487). *daughter of Judah.* See note on 1:15.

2:6 *his tabernacle.* The Hebrew word can refer to either the tabernacle or the temple (see Ps 27:4–5). *as if it were of a garden.* Cf. Is 5:5–6; Jer 5:10; 12:10. *his places of the assembly.* The tabernacle/temple, where God met with His people (see Ex 25:22; 29:42–43; Ps 74:4).

2:7 *cast off . . . abhorred.* These two verbs are found in Ps 89:38–39 in connection with the Lord's forsaking of the king from the dynasty of David. *made a noise in the house of the LORD.* See Ps 74:4. *the day of a solemn feast.* See Hos 12:9.

2:8 *purposed to destroy.* See Jer 32:31. *daughter of Zion.* A personification of Jerusalem and its inhabitants. *stretched out a line.* To destroy with the same standards of precision and propriety used in building (see Is 28:17 and note; Amos 7:7–8 and notes). *rampart . . . wall.* See Is 26:1. The ramparts were the outer fortifications (see 2 Sam 20:15).

‡2:9 *prophets also find no vision.* For a time the Lord was no longer communicating to His people through prophets (see Ps 74:9; Amos 8:11 and note; Mic 3:7).

2:10 *elders.* See note on Ex 3:16. *sit upon the ground . . . cast up dust upon their heads . . . girded themselves with sackcloth . . . hang down their heads.* Signs of mourning (see Job 2:12–13; Ps 35:13–14). *virgins of Jerusalem.* See 1:4 and note.

2:11 *Mine eyes do fail.* See note on Ps 6:7. *tears.* See note on 1:16. *my bowels are troubled.* Repeated from 1:20. *my people.* See 3:48; 4:10; see also note on Jer 14:17.

‡2:12 *their soul was poured out.* See Job 30:16; Ps 107:5; Jonah 2:7. For "soul" see note at 1:11.

2:13 *take to witness for thee.* See Job 29:11. *daughter of Jerusalem . . . virgin daughter of Zion.* See notes on 1:6; Jer 14:17.

‡2:14 *prophets . . . false.* Jeremiah often denounced false prophets but no genuine prophet of Yahweh, in the OT, was ever called "false." (see Jer 5:12–13; 6:13–15; 8:10–12; 14:13–15; 23:9–40; 27:9–28:17). *foolish.* Or "worthless"; see Ezek 13:10–16; 22:28. *banishment.* The unusual Hebrew word underlying this word comes from the same root as that underlying "drive you out" in Jer 27:10,15. The lies of false prophets mislead the people and thus are a cause of "banishment" by the Lord—so they are "banishing" in their effect.

‡2:15 *All that pass by.* See 1:12. *clap their hands.* See Job 27:23. *hiss.* See v. 16; see also note on Jer 19:8. *wag their head.* See note on Job 16:4; see also Ps 44:14; 109:25; Jer 18:16. *daughter of Jerusalem.* See notes on 1:6; Jer 14:17. *saying . . .*

Is this the city that *men* call [c]The
perfection of beauty, The joy of the
whole earth?
16 [a]All thine enemies have opened their
mouth against thee:
They hiss and gnash the teeth: they
say, [b]We have swallowed *her* up:
Certainly this *is* the day that we looked
for; we have found, [c]we have seen it.
17 The LORD hath done *that* which he had
[a]devised; he hath fulfilled his word
that he had commanded in the days
of old:
He hath thrown down, and hath not
pitied: and he hath caused *thine*
enemy to [b]rejoice over thee,
He hath set up the horn of thine
adversaries.
18 Their heart cried unto the Lord,
O wall of the daughter of Zion, [a]let tears
run down like a river day and night:
Give thyself no rest; let not the apple
of thine eye cease.
19 Arise, [a]cry out in the night: in the
beginning of the watches,
[b]Pour out thine heart like water before
the face of the Lord:
Lift up thy hands toward him for the
life of thy young children,
That faint for hunger [c]in the top of
every street.
20 Behold, O LORD, and consider to whom
thou hast done this.
[a]Shall the women eat their fruit, *and*
children [1]of a span long?
[b]Shall the priest and the prophet be
slain in the sanctuary of the Lord?
21 [a]The young and the old lie on the
ground in the streets:
My virgins and my young men are
fallen by the sword;
Thou hast slain *them* in the day of
thine anger; [b]thou hast killed, *and*
not pitied.
22 Thou hast called as *in* a solemn day
[a]my terrors round about,
So that in the day of the LORD's anger
none escaped nor remained:
[b]Those that I have swaddled and
brought up hath mine enemy
consumed.

2:15 [c]Ps. 48:2
2:16 [a]Job 16:9; ch. 3:46 [b]Ps. 56:2 [c]Ps. 35:21
2:17 [a]Lev. 26:16; Deut. 28:15 [b]Ps. 38:16
2:18 [a]Jer. 14:17
2:19 [a]Ps. 119:147 [b]Ps. 62:8 [c]Is. 51:20; Nah. 3:10
2:20 [1]Or, *swaddled with their hands?* [a]Lev. 26:29; Deut. 28:53; Jer. 19:9; ch. 4:10 [b]ch. 4:13,16
2:21 [a]2 Chr. 36:17
2:21 [b]ch. 3:43
2:22 [a]Ps. 31:13; Jer. 6:25; 46:5 [b]Hos. 9:12
3:4 [a]Job 16:8 [b]Ps. 51:8; Is. 38:13
3:6 [a]Ps. 88:5,6
3:7 [a]Hos. 2:6
3:8 [a]Job 30:20
3:10 [a]Is. 38:13; Hos. 5:14
3:11 [a]Hos. 6:1
3:12 [a]Job 7:20; Ps. 38:2

Lament and hope

3 I *am* the man *that* hath seen affliction
by the rod of his wrath.
2 He hath led me, and brought *me into*
darkness, but not *into* light.
3 Surely against me is he turned; he
turneth his hand *against me* all the
day.
4 [a]My flesh and my skin hath he made
old; he hath [b]broken my bones.
5 He hath builded against me, and
compassed *me* with gall and travail.
6 [a]He hath set me in dark places, as they
that be dead of old.
7 [a]He hath hedged me about, that I
cannot get out: he hath made my
chain heavy.
8 Also [a]when I cry and shout, he
shutteth out my prayer.
9 He hath inclosed my ways with hewn
stone, he hath made my paths
crooked.
10 [a]He *was* unto me *as* a bear lying in
wait, *and as* a lion in secret places.
11 He hath turned aside my ways, and
[a]pulled me in pieces: he hath made
me desolate.
12 He hath bent his bow, and [a]set me as a
mark for the arrow.

The joy of the whole earth. As in Ps 48:2 (see note there; cf. Jer 51:41). *The perfection of beauty.* As in Ps 50:2 (see note there).
2:16 *swallowed her up.* See vv. 2,5; Jer 51:34.
2:17 *hath fulfilled his word.* See Is 55:11 and note. *in the days of old.* The days of Moses (see, e.g. the threats of Lev 26:23–39; Deut 28:15–68). *set up the horn.* Increased the strength (see 1 Sam 2:1; Ps 75:4).
2:18 See Jer 14:17. *O wall.* A city gate is similarly addressed in Is 14:31. *daughter of Zion.* A personification of Jerusalem and its inhabitants.
2:19 *beginning of the watches.* See note on Judg 7:19; see also Ps 63:6. *Pour out thine heart.* In earnest prayer (see Ps 62:8). *like water.* A common simile with "pour out" (see Deut 12:16,24; 15:23; Ps 79:3; Hos 5:10). *lift up thy hands.* In prayer and praise (see Ps 28:2; 63:4; 1 Tim 2:8). *young children . . . faint for hunger.* See vv. 11–12.
2:20–22 The prayer called for in v. 19.
2:20 *women eat their fruit.* See note on Jer 19:9.
2:21 See Jer 6:11 and note.
2:22 *called . . . my.* See 1:15. *terrors round about.* See note on Jer 6:25. *day of the LORD's anger.* The chapter ends as it began (see v. 1). *none escaped nor remained.* See Jer 42:17; 44:14.
3:1–2 *I . . . me.* Whether the author is Jeremiah or an anonymous mourner, he speaks not only for himself but also for the suffering community of which he is a part (see "we" and "us" in vv. 40–47). The Hebrew text of v. 1 is at the exact center of the book.
3:1 *affliction.* See v. 19. *rod of his wrath.* See Job 9:34; 21:9. The reference is to Babylon (see Is 10:5 and note).
3:2 *darkness, but not into light.* See Job 12:25; characteristic of the "day of the LORD" (Amos 5:18).
3:4 *hath he made old.* See Job 13:28 ("consumeth"); Ps 49:14 ("consume"). *broken my bones.* See Is 38:13 and note.
3:5 *gall.* Lit. "poison" (see Jer 8:14 and note).
3:6 Reminiscent of Ps 143:3.
3:7 *hedged me about.* The Hebrew for this word is the same as that for "inclosed" in v. 9 (see Job 19:8; Hos 2:6). *cannot get out.* See Ps 88:8.
3:8 *shutteth out my prayer.* See v. 44; Ps 18:41; Prov 1:28; Jer 7:16 and note.
3:9 *hewn stone.* Of enormous size, like those used in the foundation of Solomon's temple (see 1 Ki 5:17). *made . . . crooked.* Or "distorted/destroyed" (as in Is 24:1); for the imagery see Job 30:13.
3:10 *as a bear . . . as a lion.* See Ps 10:9; 17:12; Jer 4:7; 5:6; 49:19; 50:44.
3:11 See 1:2.
3:12 *bent his bow.* See note on 2:4. *set me as a mark for the arrow.* See note on Job 6:4.

13 He hath caused [a]the [1]arrows of his quiver to enter into my reins.
14 I was a [a]derision to all my people; *and* [b]their song all the day.
15 [a]He hath filled me with [1]bitterness, he hath made me drunken *with* wormwood.
16 He hath also broken my teeth [a]with gravel stones, he hath [1]covered me with ashes.
17 And thou hast removed my soul far off from peace: I forgat [1]prosperity.
18 [a]And I said, My strength and my hope is perished from the LORD:
19 [1]Remembering mine affliction and my misery, [a]the wormwood and the gall.
20 My soul hath *them* still in remembrance, and is [1]humbled in me.
21 This I [1]recall to my mind, therefore have I hope.
22 [a]*It is of* the LORD's mercies that we are not consumed, because his compassions fail not.
23 *They are* new [a]every morning: great *is* thy faithfulness.
24 The LORD *is* my [a]portion, saith my soul; therefore will I hope in him.
25 The LORD *is* good unto them that [a]wait for him, to the soul *that* seeketh him.
26 *It is* good *that a man should* both hope [a]and quietly wait for the salvation of the LORD.
27 [a]*It is* good for a man that he bear the yoke in his youth.

3:13 [1]Heb. *sons* [a]Job 6:4
3:14 [a]Jer. 20:7 [b]Job 30:9; Ps. 69:12
3:15 [1]Heb. *bitternesses* [a]Jer. 9:15
3:16 [1]Or, *rolled me in the ashes* [a]Prov. 20:17
3:17 [1]Heb. *good*
3:18 [a]Ps. 31:22
3:19 [1]Or, *Remember* [a]Jer. 9:15
3:20 [1]Heb. *bowed*
3:21 [1]Heb. *make to return to my heart*
3:22 [a]Mal. 3:6
3:23 [a]Is. 33:2
3:24 [a]Ps. 16:5
3:25 [a]Is. 30:18; Mic. 7:7
3:26 [a]Ps. 37:7
3:27 [a]Ps. 94:12
3:28 [a]Jer. 15:17
3:29 [a]Job 42:6
3:30 [a]Is. 50:6; Mat. 5:39
3:31 [a]Ps. 94:14
3:33 [1]Heb. *from his heart* [a]Ezek. 33:11
3:35 [1]Or, *a superior*
3:36 [1]Or, *seeth not* [a]Hab. 1:13
3:37 [a]Ps. 33:9
3:38 [a]Job 2:10; Amos 3:6
3:39 [1]Or, *murmur* [a]Prov. 19:3 [b]Mic. 7:9
3:41 [a]Ps. 86:4
3:42 [a]Dan. 9:5

28 [a]He sitteth alone and keepeth silence, because he hath borne *it* upon him.
29 [a]He putteth his mouth in the dust; if so be there may be hope.
30 [a]He giveth *his* cheek to him that smiteth him: he is filled full with reproach.
31 [a]For the Lord will not cast off for ever:
32 But though he cause grief, yet will he have compassion according to the multitude of his mercies.
33 For [a]he doth not afflict [1]willingly nor grieve the children of men.
34 To crush under his feet all the prisoners of the earth,
35 To turn aside the right of a man before the face of [1]the most High,
36 To subvert a man in his cause, [a]the Lord [1]approveth not.
37 Who *is* he [a]*that* saith, and it cometh to pass, *when* the Lord commandeth *it* not?
38 Out of the mouth of the most High proceedeth not [a]evil and good.
39 [a]Wherefore doth a living man [1]complain, [b]a man for the punishment of his sins?
40 Let us search and try our ways, and turn again to the LORD.
41 [a]Let us lift up our heart with *our* hands unto God in the heavens.
42 [a]We have transgressed and have rebelled: thou hast not pardoned.

3:13 *my reins.* Or "heart," lit. "kidneys" (as in Job 16:13).
3:14 See Jeremiah's complaint in Jer 20:7. *their song.* See v. 63; Ps 69:12.
3:15 *filled me with bitterness.* Lit. "filled me with bitter herbs"; see note on Jer 9:15. For the significance of the bitter herbs eaten during the Passover meal see note on Ex 12:8.
3:18 *the LORD.* The first mention of God in ch. 3.
3:19 The poet remembers all these experiences and verbalizes them once again. *affliction and my misery.* See 1:7.
3:21–26 The theological high point of the book of Lamentations (see Introduction: Themes and Theology).
3:22 *mercies.* See v. 32; Ps 107:43. The Hebrew for this word denotes the Lord's loving faithfulness to His covenant promises (see Ps 89:1). See note on Ps 6:4.
3:23 *They.* The "mercies" and "compassions" (v. 22) of the Lord. *every morning.* See Is 33:2. *great is thy faithfulness.* It is beyond measure (see note on v. 32; see also Ps 36:5).
3:24 *The LORD is my portion.* See Ps 73:26; 142:5. He was the inheritance share of the priests and Levites (see Num 18:20; see also note on Gen 15:1). *therefore will I hope.* This phrase serves as a refrain (see v. 21).
3:25 *The LORD is good.* See Ps 34:8; 86:5. *that wait for him.* See Ps 25:3; 69:7.
3:26 See Is 26:3; 30:15.
3:27 *a man that he bear the yoke.* Echoes the thought of v. 1: "the man that hath seen affliction."
3:28 *sitteth alone.* See note on 1:1. *it.* The yoke (v. 27).
3:29 *if so be there may be hope.* See Job 11:18.
3:30 *giveth his cheek.* See Mat 5:39. *filled full with reproach.* See Ps 123:3–4.
3:31 See Jer 3:5 and note.
3:32 The same God who judges also restores (see Job 5:18; Ps 30:5; Is 54:8). *The multitude of his mercies.* See note on v. 22; see also "Great is Your faithfulness" (v. 23)—faithfulness and unfailing lovingkindness are often used together to sum up God's covenant mercies toward His people.
3:33 *doth not afflict willingly.* See Ezek 18:23,32; Hos 11:8; 2 Pet 3:9.
3:34 *crush under his feet.* As the Babylonians had done in 586 B.C.
‡3:35 *To turn aside the right of a man.* As the leaders of Judah had done, in direct violation of the law (see Ex 23:6). *Before the face of the most High.* In the presence of those whom the most High designates to dispense justice (see Ex 22:8–9); see also introduction to Ps 82). *most High.* See note on Gen 14:19.
3:36 *subvert. . . in his cause.* Men might act unjustly, but God never does (see Job 8:3; 34:12).
3:37 *saith. . . cometh to pass.* See note on Gen 1:3.
3:38 See Amos 3:6.
3:39 *complain.* As the Israelites did in the wilderness (see Num 11:1).
3:40 *us.* See note on vv. 1–2. *search . . . our ways.* See 1 Cor 11:28.
3:41 *lift up . . . hands.* See note on 2:19. *heavens.* Where God is enthroned (see Ps 2:4).
3:42 *We have transgressed and have rebelled.* For similar confessions see Ps 106:6; Dan 9:5.

43 Thou hast covered with anger, and
persecuted us: thou hast slain, thou
hast not pitied.
44 Thou hast covered thyself with a cloud,
[a]that *our* prayer should not pass
through.
45 Thou hast made us *as* the [a]offscouring
and refuse in the midst of the people.
46 [a]All our enemies have opened their
mouths against us.
47 [a]Fear and a snare is come upon us,
[b]desolation and destruction.
48 [a]Mine eye runneth down *with* rivers of
water for the destruction of the
daughter of my people.
49 [a]Mine eye trickleth down, and ceaseth
not, without any intermission,
50 Till the LORD [a]look down, and behold
from heaven.
51 Mine eye affecteth [1]mine heart
[2]because of all the daughters of my
city.
52 Mine enemies chased me sore, like a
bird, [a]without cause.
53 They have cut off my life [a]in the
dungeon, and [b]cast a stone upon me.
54 [a]Waters flowed over mine head; *then*
[b]I said, I am cut off.

55 [a]I called upon thy name, O LORD, out
of the low dungeon.
56 [a]Thou hast heard my voice: hide not
thine ear at my breathing, at my cry.
57 Thou [a]drewest near in the day *that* I
called upon thee: thou saidst, Fear
not.
58 O Lord, thou hast [a]pleaded the causes of
my soul; [b]thou hast redeemed my life.
59 O LORD, thou hast seen my wrong:
[a]judge thou my cause.
60 Thou hast seen all their vengeance *and*
all their [a]imaginations against me.
61 Thou hast heard their reproach,
O LORD, *and* all their imaginations
against me;
62 The lips of those that rose up against
me, and their device against me all
the day.
63 Behold their [a]sitting down, and their
rising up; I *am* their musick.
64 [a]Render unto them a recompence,
O LORD, according to the work of
their hands.
65 Give them [1]sorrow of heart, thy curse
unto them.
66 Persecute and destroy them in anger
[a]from under the [b]heavens of the
LORD.

The punishment of Zion

4 How is the gold become dim! *how* is
the most fine gold changed!
The stones of the sanctuary are poured
out [a]in the top of every street.
2 The precious sons of Zion, comparable
to fine gold,
How are they esteemed [a]as earthen
pitchers, the work of the hands of
the potter!
3 Even the [1]sea monsters draw out the
breast, they give suck to their young
ones:
The daughter of my people *is* become
cruel, [a]like the ostriches in the
wilderness.
4 [a]The tongue of the sucking child
cleaveth to the roof of his mouth for
thirst:
[b]The young children ask bread, *and* no
man breaketh *it* unto them.
5 They that did feed delicately are
desolate in the streets:
They that were brought up in scarlet
[a]embrace dunghills.
6 For the [1]punishment of the iniquity of
the daughter of my people is greater
than the punishment of the sin of
Sodom,
That was [a]overthrown as in a moment,
and no hands stayed on her.

3:44 [a]ver. 8
3:45 [a]1 Cor. 4:13
3:46 [a]ch. 2:16
3:47 [a]Is. 24:17 [b]Is. 51:19
3:48 [a]Jer. 4:19
3:49 [a]Ps. 77:2
3:50 [a]Is. 63:15
3:51 [1]Heb. *my soul* [2]Or, *more than all*
3:52 [a]Ps. 35:7
3:53 [a]Jer. 37:16 [b]Dan. 6:17
3:54 [a]Ps. 69:2 [b]Is. 38:10
3:55 [a]Ps. 130:1
3:56 [a]Ps. 3:4
3:57 [a]Jas. 4:8
3:58 [a]Ps. 35:1; Jer. 51:36 [b]Ps. 71:23
3:59 [a]Ps. 9:4
3:60 [a]Jer. 11:19
3:63 [a]Ps. 139:2
3:64 [a]Ps. 28:4; Jer. 11:20
3:65 [1]Or, *obstinacy of heart*
3:66 [a]Deut. 25:19; Jer. 10:11 [b]Ps. 8:3
4:1 [a]ch. 2:19
4:2 [a]Is. 30:14; Jer. 19:11
4:3 [1]Or, *sea calves* [a]Job 39:14
4:4 [a]Ps. 22:15 [b]See ch. 2:11,12
4:5 [a]Job 24:8
4:6 [1]Or, *iniquity* [a]Gen. 19:25

3:43 *with anger, and persecuted us.* See v. 66; Jer 29:18. *slain . . . not pitied.* See 2:21.
3:46 See note on 2:16.
3:48 *eye runneth down with . . . water.* See note on 1:16. *my people.* See note on 2:11.
3:51 *daughters of my city.* See 1:4,18; 2:20–21; 5:11.
3:52 *Mine enemies . . . without cause.* See note on Ps 35:19. *like a bird.* See Ps 11:1.
3:53 *cast a stone upon me.* See Lev 20:2,27; 1 Ki 12:18.
3:54 *Waters flowed over mine head.* See note on Ps 42:7. *cut off.* See Ps 31:22; Is 53:8.
3:55 *low dungeon.* See note on Ps 30:1.
3:56 *my cry.* See Job 32:20; Ps 118:5.
3:57 *near in the day that I called.* See Ps 145:18. *Fear not.* Reminiscent of Jeremiah's call to prophesy (see Jer 1:8 and note).
3:58 *redeemed my life.* See Ps 103:4; see also note on Ps 25:22.
3:63 *sitting down, and . . . rising.* Engaging in any kind of activity (see Deut 6:7; 11:19; Ps 139:2; Is 37:28). *I am their musick.* See note on v. 14.
3:64 Paralleled in Ps 28:4; see note on Ps 5:10.
3:65 *thy curse unto them.* Contrast Ps 3:8.
4:1 *How . . . !* See note on 1:1. *gold . . . stones of the sanctuary.* Symbolic of God's chosen people (see v. 2). For the imagery see Sol 5:11–12,14–15; Zech 9:16; see also "The Babylonian Theodicy": "O . . . my precious brother, . . . jewel of gold" (lines 56–57). *gold changed.* Contrast Mal 3:6. *in the top of every street.* See 2:19; Is 51:20.
4:2 *comparable to fine gold.* See Job 28:15–19. *earthen pitchers . . . hands of the potter.* See Is 45:9; 60:21 and notes.
4:3 *my people.* See vv. 6,10; see also note on 2:11.
‡4:5 *brought up in scarlet.* The Hebrew word is now understood to be "purple." See Gen 49:20. Purple was the color of royalty (see, e.g. Judg 8:26; see also note on Sol 7:5); cf. the expressions "born to the purple" and "royal blue." *desolate.* See note on 1:13.
4:6 *my people.* See note on 2:11. *Sodom.* See note on Jer 20:16. *overthrown as in a moment.* And therefore spared the suffering of a lengthy siege (like that of Jerusalem).

7 Her Nazarites were purer than snow,
they were whiter than milk,
They were more ruddy *in* body than
rubies, their polishing *was of*
sapphire:
8 Their visage is [a] [1] blacker than a coal;
they are not known in the streets:
[b] Their skin cleaveth to their bones; it
is withered, it is become like a stick.
9 *They that be* slain with the sword are
better than *they that be* slain with
hunger:
For these [1] pine away, stricken through
for *want of* the fruits of the field.
10 [a] The hands of the [b] pitiful women have
sodden their own children:
They were their [c] meat in the
destruction of the daughter of my
people.
11 The LORD hath accomplished his fury;
[a] he hath poured out his fierce anger,
And [b] hath kindled a fire in Zion, and it
hath devoured the foundations
thereof.
12 The kings of the earth, and all the
inhabitants of the world, would not
have believed
That the adversary and the enemy
should have entered into the gates of
Jerusalem.
13 [a] For the sins of her prophets, *and* the
iniquities of her priests,
[b] That *have* shed the blood of the just
in the midst of her,
14 They have wandered *as* blind *men* in
the streets, [a] they have polluted
themselves with blood,
[b] [1] So that *men* could not touch their
garments.
15 They cried unto them, Depart ye; [1] *it is*
[a] unclean; depart, depart, touch not,
when they fled away and wandered:
They said among the heathen, They
shall no more sojourn *there.*
16 The [1] anger of the LORD hath divided
them; he will no more regard them:
[a] They respected not the persons of the
priests, they favoured not the elders.
17 As for us, [a] our eyes as yet failed for our
vain help:
In our watching we have watched for a
nation *that* could not save *us.*
18 [a] They hunt our steps, that *we* cannot
go in our streets:
Our end is near, our days are fulfilled;
for [b] our end is come.
19 Our persecutors are [a] swifter than the
eagles of the heaven:
They pursued us upon the mountains,
they laid wait for us in the wilderness.
20 The [a] breath of our nostrils, the
anointed of the LORD, [b] was taken in
their pits,
Of whom we said, Under his shadow
we shall live among the heathen.
21 Rejoice and be glad, O daughter of
Edom, that dwellest in the land of Uz;
[a] The cup also shall pass through unto
thee: thou shalt be drunken, and
shalt make thyself naked.
22 [a] [1] The punishment of thine iniquity is
accomplished, O daughter of Zion; he
will no more carry thee away into
captivity:
[b] He will visit thine iniquity,
O daughter of Edom; he will
[2] discover thy sins.

A prayer for mercy

5 [a] Remember, O LORD, what is come
upon us:
Consider, and behold [b] our reproach.
2 [a] Our inheritance is turned to
strangers,
Our houses to aliens.
3 We are orphans and fatherless,
Our mothers *are* as widows.
4 We have drunken our water for money;
Our wood [1] is sold *unto us.*
5 [a] [1] Our necks *are* under persecution:
We labour, *and* have no rest.
6 [a] We have given the hand [b] *to* the
Egyptians,

4:8 [1] Heb. *darker than blackness* [a] ch. 5:10; Joel 2:6; Nah. 2:10 [b] Ps. 102:5
4:9 [1] Heb. *flow out*
4:10 [a] ch. 2:20 [b] Is. 49:15 [c] Deut. 28:57
4:11 [a] Jer. 7:20 [b] Deut. 32:22
4:13 [a] Jer. 6:13; Ezek. 22:26 [b] Mat. 23:31
4:14 [1] Or, *In that they could not but touch* [a] Jer. 2:34 [b] Num. 19:16
4:15 [1] Or, *ye polluted* [a] Lev. 13:45
4:16 [1] Or, *face*
4:16 [a] ch. 5:12
4:17 [a] 2 Ki. 24:7; Is. 20:5; Jer. 37:7
4:18 [a] 2 Ki. 25:4 [b] Ezek 7:2,3
4:19 [a] Deut. 28:49
4:20 [a] Gen. 2:7 [b] Jer. 52:9; Ezek. 12:13
4:21 [a] Jer. 25:15; Obad. 10
4:22 [1] Or, *Thine iniquity* [2] Or, *carry thee captive for thy sins* [a] Is. 40:2 [b] Ps. 137:7
5:1 [a] Ps. 89:50 [b] Ps. 79:4; ch. 2:15
5:2 [a] Ps. 79:1
5:4 [1] Heb. *cometh for price*
5:5 [1] Heb. *On our necks are we persecuted* [a] Jer. 28:14
5:6 [a] Gen. 24:2 [b] Hos. 12:1

4:7 *whiter . . . ruddy.* The Hebrew underlying these two words is also translated "white . . . ruddy" in Sol 5:10. *than rubies.* See Job 28:18. *sapphire.* See Sol 5:14 and note; Is 54:11 and note.
4:8 *skin cleaveth to their bones.* See Job 19:20.
4:10 See note on Jer 19:9. *my people.* See note on 2:11.
4:11 *fierce anger.* See note on 1:12. *kindled a fire . . . devoured.* See note on Jer 17:27.
4:13 *For the the sins of her prophets, and . . . priests.* See Jer 26:7–11,16; see also Jer 6:13–15; 23:11–12; Ezek 22:26,28.
4:14 *wandered as blind men in the streets.* See Deut 28:28–29; Is 29:9 and note; 59:10 and note; Zeph 1:17. *polluted themselves with blood.* See Is 59:3.
‡4:15 *unclean.* The cry of the person with a skin disease (see Lev 13:45). The language echoes Is 52:11. *They shall no more sojourn there.* Threatened in Deut 28:65–66.
4:16 *anger.* Threatened in Deut 28:49–50.
4:17 *our eyes as yet failed.* See Deut 28:28; Ps 69:3. *nation that could not save.* For example, Egypt (see Ezek 29:16).
4:19 *eagles.* See Jer 4:13; 48:40 and notes. *wilderness.* The "plains of Jericho" (Jer 39:5; 52:8).
4:20 *The breath of our nostrils.* A title used also of Pharaoh Rameses II in an inscription found at Abydos in Egypt. *anointed of the LORD.* King Zedekiah. *was taken.* See Jer 39:4–7; 52:7–11. *shadow.* Protection (see note on Judg 9:15).
4:21 *Edom.* See note on Jer 49:8. *land of Uz.* See Jer 25:20; see also note on Job 1:1. *cup.* See note on Jer 25:15. *make thyself naked.* See 1:8; see also Jer 49:10; Nah 3:5.
4:22 *daughter of Zion.* A personification of Jerusalem and its inhabitants. *Discover thy sins.* Contrast Ps 32:1; 85:2.
5:2 *Our inheritance.* The land of Judah (see Jer 2:7 and note; 3:18).
5:4 *We have drunken our water for money . . . wood.* Contrast Deut 29:11; Josh 9:21, 23, 27. *wood.* Firewood.
‡5:6 *have given the hand.* Or, "have submitted." See 1 Chr 29:24; 2 Chr 30:8; Jer 50:15; see also 2 Ki 10:15. *Assyrians.*

And to the Assyrians, to be satisfied
with bread.
7 [a]Our fathers have sinned, *and are* not;
And we have borne their iniquities.
8 Servants have ruled over us:
There is none that doth deliver *us* out
of their hand.
9 We gat our bread with *the peril of* our
lives
Because of the sword of the
wilderness.
10 Our skin was black like an oven
Because of the [1]terrible famine.
11 They ravished the women in Zion,
And the maids in the cities of Judah.
12 Princes are hanged up by their hand:
The faces of elders were not honoured.
13 They took the young men to grind,
And the children fell under the wood.
14 The elders have ceased from the gate,
The young men from their musick.
15 The joy of our heart is ceased;
Our dance is turned into mourning.
16 [a][1]The crown is fallen *from* our head:
Woe unto us, that we have sinned!
17 For this our heart is faint;
[a]For these *things* our eyes are dim.
18 Because of the mountain of Zion,
which is desolate,
The foxes walk upon it.

19 Thou, O LORD, [a]remainest for ever;
[b]Thy throne from generation to
generation.
20 [a]Wherefore dost thou forget us for
ever,
And forsake us [1]so long time?
21 Turn thou us unto thee, O LORD, and
we shall be turned;
Renew our days as of old.
22 [1]But thou hast utterly rejected us;
Thou art very wroth against us.

5:7 [a]Jer. 31:29
5:10 [1]Or, *terrors,* or, *storms*
5:16 [1]Heb. *The crown of our head is fallen* [a]Ps. 89:39
5:17 [a]Ps. 6:7
5:19 [a]Ps. 9:7 [b]Ps. 45:6
5:20 [1]Heb. *for length of days?* [a]Ps. 13:1
5:22 [1]Or, *For wilt thou utterly reject us?*

Either (1) Assyria literally (see Jer 2:18), or (2) territory formerly occupied by Assyrians (see note on Ezra 6:22).
5:7 *fathers.* Fathers and sons alike are responsible for the calamity that has befallen Jerusalem (see v. 16; Jer 16:11–12; 31:29–30; Ezek 18:2–4; cf. Is 65:7).
5:8 *Servants.* An ironic reference to the Babylonians, who now rule over Jerusalem (formerly "princess among the provinces," 1:1); see Prov 30:21–22.
5:9 *sword of the wilderness.* Marauding bandits.
5:12 *hanged up.* An added indignity following execution (see notes on Deut 21:22–23).
5:13 *young men to grind.* Humiliating work (see note on Judg 9:53; see also Is 47:2).
5:14 *gate.* The municipal court (see Josh 20:4), but also a gathering place for conversation and entertainment (cf. 1:4).
5:15 See Jer 7:34; 16:9; 25:10; contrast Ps 30:11; Jer 31:13.
5:16 *crown.* Symbolizes the glory and honor embodied in the city of Jerusalem (see 1:1; 2:15; cf. Is 28:1,3).
5:17 *heart is faint.* See note on 1:22. *eyes are dim.* See 2:11; see also note on Ps 6:7.
5:18 *foxes.* Can also be translated "jackals" (see note on Judg 15:4).
5:19 Paralleled in Ps 102:12 (see note there).
5:21 *Turn thou... we shall be turned.* See Jer 31:18; see also note on Jer 31:18–19.
‡5:22 *But.* See Jer 14:19. A similarly somber ending characterizes not only other laments (e.g. Ps 88) but also other OT books (e.g. Isaiah and Malachi).

The Book of the Prophet
Ezekiel

INTRODUCTION

Background

Ezekiel lived during a time of international upheaval. The Assyrian empire that had once conquered the Syro-Israelite area and destroyed the northern kingdom of Israel (which fell to the Assyrians in 722–721 B.C.) began to crumble under the blows of a resurgent Babylon. In 612 the great Assyrian city of Nineveh fell to a combined force of Babylonians and Medes. Three years later, Pharaoh Neco II of Egypt marched north to assist the Assyrians and to try to reassert Egypt's age-old influence over Palestine and Aram (Syria). At Megiddo, King Josiah of Judah, who may have been an ally of Babylon as King Hezekiah had been, attempted to intercept the Egyptian forces but was crushed, losing his life in the battle (see 2 Ki 23:29–30; 2 Chr 35:20–24).

Jehoahaz, a son of Josiah, ruled Judah for only three months, after which Neco installed Jehoiakim, another son of Josiah, as his royal vassal in Jerusalem (609 B.C.). In 605 the Babylonians overwhelmed the Egyptian army at Carchemish (see Jer 46:2), then pressed south as far as the Philistine plain. In the same year, Nebuchadnezzar was elevated to the Babylonian throne and Jehoiakim shifted allegiance to him. When a few years later the Egyptian and Babylonian forces met in a standoff battle in southwestern Palestine, Jehoiakim rebelled against his new overlord.

Nebuchadnezzar soon responded by sending a force against Jerusalem, subduing it in 597 B.C. Jehoiakim's son Jehoiachin and about 10,000 Jews (see 2 Ki 24:14), including Ezekiel, were exiled to Babylon, where they joined those who had been exiled in Jehoiakim's "third year" (see Dan 1:1 and note). Nebuchadnezzar placed Jehoiachin's uncle, Zedekiah, on the throne in Jerusalem, but within five or six years he too rebelled. The Babylonians laid siege to Jerusalem in 588, and in July, 586, the walls were breached and the city plundered. On Aug. 14, 586, the city and temple were burned.

Under Nebuchadnezzar and his successors, Babylon dominated the international scene until it was crushed by Cyrus the Persian in 539 B.C. Israel's monarchy was ended; the City of David and the Lord's temple no longer existed.

Author

What is known of Ezekiel is derived solely from the book that bears his name. He was among the Jews exiled to Babylon by Nebuchadnezzar in 597 B.C., and there among the exiles he received his call to become a prophet (see 1:1–3). He was married (see 24:15–18), lived in a house of his own (see 3:24; 8:1) and, along with his fellow exiles, had a relatively free existence.

He was of a priestly family (see note on 1:3) and therefore was eligible to serve as a priest. As a priest-prophet called to minister to the exiles (cut off from the temple of the Lord with its symbolism, sacrifices, priestly ministrations and worship rituals), his message had much to do with the temple (see especially chs. 8—11; 40—48) and its ceremonies.

Ezekiel was obviously a man of broad knowledge, not only of his own national traditions but also of international affairs and history. His acquaintance with general matters of culture, from shipbuilding to literature, is equally amazing. He was gifted with a powerful intellect and was capable of grasping large issues and of dealing with them in grand and compelling images. His style is often detached, but in places it is passionate and earthy (see chs. 16; 23).

More than any other prophet he was directed to involve himself personally in the divine word by acting it out in prophetic symbolism.

Occasion, Purpose and Summary of Contents

Though Ezekiel lived with his fellow exiles in Babylon, his divine call forced him to suppress any natural expectations he may have had of an early return to an undamaged Jerusalem. For the first seven years of his ministry (593–586 B.C.) he faithfully relayed to his fellow Jews the harsh, heart-rending, hope-crushing word of divine judgment: Jerusalem would fall (see chs. 1—24). Their being God's

covenant people and Jerusalem's being the city of His temple would not bring their early release from exile or prevent Jerusalem from being destroyed (see Jer 29—30). The only hope the prophet was authorized to extend to his hearers was that of living at peace with themselves and with God during their exile.

After being informed by the Lord that Jerusalem was under siege and would surely fall (24:1–14), Ezekiel was told that his beloved wife would soon die. The delight of his eyes would be taken from him just as the temple, the delight of Israel's eyes, would be taken from her. He was not to mourn openly for his wife, as a sign to his people not to mourn openly for Jerusalem (24:15–27). He was then directed to pronounce a series of judgments on the seven nations of Ammon, Moab, Edom, Philistia, Tyre, Sidon and Egypt (chs. 25—32). The day of God's wrath was soon to come, but not on Israel alone.

Once news was received that Jerusalem had fallen, Ezekiel's message turned to the Lord's consoling word of hope for His people—they would experience revival, restoration and a glorious future as the redeemed and perfected kingdom of God in the world (chs. 33—48).

Date

Since the book of Ezekiel contains more dates (see chart below) than any other OT prophetic book, its prophecies can be dated with considerable precision. In addition, modern scholarship, using archaeology (Babylonian annals on cuneiform tablets) and astronomy (accurate dating of eclipses referred to in ancient archives), provides precise modern calendar equivalents.

Twelve of the 13 dates specify times when Ezekiel received a divine message. The other is the date of the arrival of the messenger who reported the fall of Jerusalem (33:21).

Having received his call in July, 593 B.C., Ezekiel was active for 22 years, his last dated oracle being received in April, 571 (see 29:17). If the "thirtieth year" of 1:1 refers to Ezekiel's age at the time of his call, his prophetic career exceeded a normal priestly term of service by two years (see Num 4:3). His period of activity coincides with Jerusalem's darkest hour, preceding the 586 destruction by 7 years and following it by 15.

Themes

The OT in general and the prophets in particular presuppose and teach God's sovereignty over all creation, over people and nations and the course of history. And nowhere in the Bible are God's initiative and control expressed more clearly and pervasively than in the book of Ezekiel. From the first chapter, which graphically describes the overwhelming invasion of the divine presence into Ezekiel's world, to the last phrase of Ezekiel's vision ("The LORD is there") the book sounds and echoes God's sovereignty.

This sovereign God resolved that He would be known and acknowledged. No less than 65 occurrences of the clause (or variations) "Then they will know that I am the LORD" testify to that divine desire and intention (see note on 5:13). Chs. 1—24 teach that God will be revealed in the fall of Jerusalem and the destruction of the temple; chs. 25—32 teach that the nations likewise will know God through His judgments; and chs. 33—48 promise that God will be known through the restoration and spiritual renewal of Israel.

God's total sovereignty is also evident in His mobility. He is not limited to the temple in Jerusalem. He can respond to His people's sin by leaving His sanctuary in Israel, and He can graciously condescend to visit His exiled children in Babylon.

God is free to judge, and He is equally free to be gracious. His stern judgments on Israel ultimately reflect His grace. He allows the total dismemberment of Israel's political and religious life so that her renewed life and His presence with her will be clearly seen as a gift from the Lord of the universe.

Furthermore, as God's spokesman, Ezekiel's "son of man" status (see note on 2:1) testifies to the sovereign God he was commissioned to serve.

Literary Features

The three major prophets (Isaiah, Jeremiah, Ezekiel) and Zephaniah all have the same basic sequence of messages: (1) oracles against Israel, (2) oracles against the nations, (3) consolation for Israel. In no other book is this pattern as clear as in Ezekiel (see Outline).

Besides clarity of structure, the book of Ezekiel reveals symmetry. The vision of the desecrated temple fit for destruction (chs. 8—11) is balanced by the vision of the restored and purified temple

(chs. 40—48). The God presented in agitated wrath (ch. 1) is also shown to be a God of comfort ("The LORD is there," 48:35). Ezekiel's call to be a watchman of divine judgment (ch. 3) is balanced by his call to be a watchman of the new age (ch. 33). In one place (ch. 6) the mountains of Israel receive a prophetic rebuke, but in another (ch. 36) they are consoled.

Prophetic books are usually largely poetic, the prophets apparently having spoken in imaginative and rhythmic styles. Most of Ezekiel, however, is prose, perhaps due to his priestly background. His repetitions have an unforgettable hammering effect, and his priestly orientation is also reflected in a case-law type of sentence (compare 3:19, "If thou warn the wicked . . . ," with Ex 21:2, "If thou buy a Hebrew servant . . .").

The book contains four visions (chs. 1—3; 8—11; 37:1–14; 40—48) and 12 symbolic acts (3:22–26; 4:1–3; 4:4–8; 4:9–11; 4:12–14; 5:1–3; 12:1–16; 12:17–20; 21:6–7; 21:18–24; 24:15–24; 37:15–28). Five messages are in the form of parables (chs. 15; 16; 17; 19; 23).

Theological Significance

Other prophets deal largely with Israel's idolatry, with her moral corruption in public and private affairs, and with her international intrigues and alliances on which she relied instead of the Lord. They announce God's impending judgment on His rebellious nation but speak also of a future redemption: a new exodus, a new covenant, a restored Jerusalem, a revived Davidic dynasty, a worldwide recognition of the Lord and His Messiah and a paradise-like peace.

The contours and sweep of Ezekiel's message are similar, but he focuses uniquely on Israel as the holy people of the holy temple, the holy city and the holy land. By defiling her worship, Israel had rendered herself unclean and had defiled temple, city and land. From such defilement God could only withdraw and judge His people with national destruction.

But God's faithfulness to His covenant and His desire to save were so great that He would revive His people once more, shepherd them with compassion, cleanse them of all their defilement, reconstitute them as a perfect expression of His kingdom in the promised land under the hand of David, overwhelm all the forces and powers arrayed against them, display His glory among the nations and restore the glory of His presence to the holy city.

Dates in Ezekiel

REFERENCE	YEAR	MONTH	DAY	MODERN RECKONING	EVENT
1. 1:1	30	4	5	July 31, 593 B.C.	Inaugural vision
1:2	5	—	5		
3:16	"At the end of seven days"				
2. 8:1	6	6	5	Sept. 17, 592	Transport to Jerusalem
3. 20:1-2	7	5	10	Aug. 14, 591	Negative view of Israel's history
4. 24:1	9	10	10	Jan. 15, 588	Beginning of siege (see also 2 Ki 25:1)
5. 26:1	11	—	1	Apr. 23, 587 to Apr. 13, 586	Oracle against Tyre
6. 29:1	10	10	12	Jan. 7, 587	Oracle against Egypt
7. 29:17	27	1	1	Apr. 26, 571	Egypt in exchange for Tyre
8. 30:20	11	1	7	Apr. 29, 587	Oracle against Pharaoh
9. 31:1	11	3	1	June 21, 587	Oracle against Pharaoh
10. 32:1	12	12	1	Mar. 3, 585	Lament over Pharaoh
11. 32:17	12	—	15	Apr. 13, 586 to Apr. 1, 585	Egypt dead
12. 33:21	12	10	5	Jan. 8, 585	Arrival of first fugitive
13. 40:1	25	1	10	Apr. 28, 573	Vision of the future
40:1	"fourteenth year after that the the city was smitten"				

Ezekiel powerfully depicts the grandeur and glory of God's sovereign rule (see Themes) and His holiness, which He jealously safeguards. The book's theological center is the unfolding of God's saving purposes in the history of the world—from the time in which He must withdraw from the defilement of His covenant people to the culmination of His grand design of redemption. The message of Ezekiel, which is ultimately eschatological, anticipates—even demands—God's future works in history proclaimed by the NT.

Outline

I. Oracles of Judgment against Israel (chs. 1—24)
   A. Ezekiel's Inaugural Vision (chs. 1—3)
      1. The divine overwhelming (ch. 1)
      2. The equipping and commissioning (2:1—3:15)
      3. The watchman (3:16–21)
      4. Further stipulations (3:22–27)
   B. Symbolic Acts Portraying the Siege of Jerusalem (chs. 4—5)
      1. The city of Jerusalem on a tile (4:1–3)
      2. Prophetic immobility (4:4–8)
      3. Diet for the siege and exile (4:9–17)
      4. The divine razor and its consequences (ch. 5)
   C. Oracles Explaining Divine Judgment (chs. 6—7)
      1. Doom for the mountains of Israel (ch. 6)
      2. The end (ch. 7)
   D. Vision of the Corrupted Temple (chs. 8—11)
      1. Four abominations (ch. 8)
      2. Destruction of the city (ch. 9)
      3. God's glory leaves Jerusalem (ch. 10)
      4. Conclusion of the vision (ch. 11)
   E. Symbolic Acts Portraying Jerusalem's Exile (ch. 12)
      1. An exile's baggage (12:1–16)
      2. Anxious eating (12:17–20)
      3. The nearness of judgment (12:21–28)
   F. Oracles Explaining Divine Judgment (chs. 13—24)
      1. False prophets and magic charms (ch. 13)
      2. The penalty for idolatry (14:1–11)
      3. Noah, Daniel and Job (14:12–23)
      4. Jerusalem as a burnt vine branch (ch. 15)
      5. Jerusalem as a wayward foundling (16:1–43)
      6. Jerusalem compared to other cities (16:44–63)
      7. Jerusalem's kings allegorized (17:1–21)
      8. The new tree (17:22–24)
      9. The lesson of three generations (ch. 18)
      10. The twofold lament (ch. 19)
      11. Israel as a hardened repeater (ch. 20)
      12. The sword of the Lord (ch. 21)
      13. Jerusalem the city of blood (ch. 22)
      14. Oholah and Oholibah (ch. 23)
      15. The final fire: Jerusalem's end (24:1–14)
      16. The death of Ezekiel's wife and the destruction of the temple (24:15–27)

II. Oracles of Judgment against the Nations (chs. 25—32)
   A. Against Ammon (25:1–7)
   B. Against Moab (25:8–11)
   C. Against Edom (25:12–14)
   D. Against Philistia (25:15–17)
   E. Against Tyre (26:1—28:19)
      1. The end of the city (ch. 26)
      2. A lament for Tyre (ch. 27)
      3. Against the king of Tyre (28:1–19)

F. Against Sidon (28:20–24)
G. A Note of Promise for Israel (28:25–26)
H. Against Egypt (chs. 29—32)
   1. As a doomed dragon (29:1–16)
   2. As payment to Nebuchadnezzar (29:17–21)
   3. The approaching day (30:1–19)
   4. Pharaoh's arms are broken (30:20–26)
   5. As a felled cedar (ch. 31)
   6. A lament over Pharaoh (32:1–16)
   7. As consigned to the pit among the uncircumcised (32:17–32)

III. Oracles of Consolation for Israel (chs. 33—48)
A. The Watchman (33:1–20)
B. Jerusalem's Fall Reported and Explained (33:21–33)
C. The Lord as the Good Shepherd (ch. 34)
D. Oracles against Edom (ch. 35)
E. Consolations for the Mountains of Israel (36:1–15)
F. Summary of Ezekiel's Theology (36:16–38)
G. Vision of National Restoration (ch. 37)
   1. National resurrection (37:1–14)
   2. National reunification (37:15–28)
H. The Final Battle (chs. 38—39)
I. Vision of Renewed Worship (chs. 40—48)
   1. Wall around the temple (40:1–47)
   2. Temple exterior (40:48—41:26)
   3. Temple interior (ch. 42)
   4. The return of God's glory (ch. 43)
   5. The priesthood (ch. 44)
   6. Land allotment (ch. 45)
   7. The duties of the prince (ch. 46)
   8. Life-giving water (47:1–12)
   9. Land allotment (47:13—48:35)

The vision of the four creatures

1 Now it came to pass in the thirtieth year, in the fourth *month,* in the fifth *day* of the month, as I *was* among the [1] captives [a] by the river of Chebar, *that* [b] the heavens were opened, and I saw [c] visions of God.

2 In the fifth *day* of the month, which *was* the fifth year of [a] king Jehoiachin's captivity,

3 The word of the LORD came expressly unto [1] Ezekiel the priest, the son of Buzi, in the land of the Chaldeans by the river Chebar; and [a] the hand of the LORD was there upon him.

4 ¶ And I looked, and behold, [a] a whirlwind came [b] out of the north, a great cloud, and a fire [1] infolding itself, and a brightness *was* about it, and out of the midst thereof as the colour of amber, out of the midst of the fire.

5 [a] Also out of the midst thereof *came* the likeness of four living creatures. And [b] this *was* their appearance; they had [c] the likeness of a man.

6 And *every* one had four faces, and every one had four wings.

7 And their feet *were* [1] straight feet; and the sole of their feet *was* like the sole of a calf's foot: and they sparkled [a] like the colour of burnished brass.

8 [a] And *they had* the hands of a man under their wings on their four sides; and they four had their faces and their wings.

9 [a] Their wings *were* joined one to another; [b] they turned not when they went; they went every one straight forward.

10 As for [a] the likeness of their faces, they four [b] had the face of a man, [c] and the face of a lion, on the right side: [d] and they four had the face of an ox on the left side; [e] they four also had the face of an eagle.

11 Thus *were* their faces: and their wings *were* [1] stretched upward; two *wings* of every one *were* joined one to another, and [a] two covered their bodies.

12 And [a] they went every one straight forward: [b] whither the spirit was to go, they went; *and* they turned not when they went.

13 As for the likeness of the living creatures, their appearance *was* like burning coals of fire, [a] *and* like the appearance of lamps: it went up and down among the living creatures; and the fire was bright, and out of the fire went forth lightning.

14 And the living creatures ran and returned [a] as the appearance of a flash of lightning.

The vision of the four wheels

15 ¶ Now as I beheld the living creatures, behold [a] one wheel upon the earth by the living creatures, with his four faces.

16 [a] The appearance of the wheels and their work *was* [b] like unto the colour of a beryl: and they four had one likeness: and their appearance and their work *was* as it were a wheel in the middle of a wheel.

17 When they went, they went upon their four sides: [a] *and* they turned not when they went.

18 As for their rings, they were so high that they were dreadful; and their [1] rings *were* [a] full *of* eyes round about them four.

19 And [a] when the living creatures went, the wheels went by them: and when the living creatures were lift up from the earth, the wheels were lift up.

20 [a] Whithersoever the spirit was to go, they went, thither *was their* spirit to go; and the wheels were lifted up over against them: [b] for the spirit [1] of the living creature *was* in the wheels.

1:1 [1] Heb. *captivity* [a] ch. 3:15,23 [b] Mat. 3:16; Acts 7:56 [c] ch. 8:3
1:2 [a] 2 Ki. 24:12
1:3 [1] Heb. *Jehezkel* [a] 1 Ki. 18:46; ch. 3:14
1:4 [1] Heb. *catching itself* [a] Jer. 23:19; 25:32 [b] Jer. 1:14
1:5 [a] Rev. 4:6 [b] ch. 10:8 [c] ch. 10:14
1:7 [1] Heb. *a straight foot* [a] Dan. 10:6; Rev. 1:15
1:8 [a] ch. 10:8
1:9 [a] ver. 11 [b] ver. 12
1:10 [a] Rev. 4:7 [b] Num. 2:10 [c] Num. 2:3 [d] Num. 2:18 [e] Num. 2:25
1:11 [1] Or, *divided above* [a] Is. 6:2
1:12 [a] ch. 10:22 [b] ver. 20
1:13 [a] Rev. 4:5
1:14 [a] Mat. 24:27
1:15 [a] ch. 10:9
1:16 [a] ch. 10:9,10 [b] Dan. 10:6
1:17 [a] ver. 12
1:18 [1] Or, *strakes* [a] ch. 10:12; Zech. 4:10
1:19 [a] ch. 10:16,17
1:20 [1] Or, *of life* [a] ver. 12 [b] ch. 10:17

1:1 *the thirtieth year.* Or "my thirtieth year," probably Ezekiel's age. According to Num 4:3, a person entered the Levitical priesthood in his 30th year. Denied the priesthood in exile, Ezekiel received another commission—that of prophet. *river of Chebar.* A canal of the Euphrates near the city of Nippur, south of Babylon, and possibly a place of prayer for the exiles (see Ps 137:1; cf. Acts 16:13). *visions of God.* A special term, always in the plural and always with the word "God" (not with the more personal "LORD"). The expression precedes this and the two other major visions of the prophet (8:3; 40:2).

‡1:2 *fifth year of king Jehoiachin's captivity.* Verses 2–3, written in the third person (the only third-person narrative in the book), clarify the date in v. 1. Jehoiachin led an early group of exiles to Babylon in 597 B.C. (see Introduction: *curse.* Total destruction. If Israel does not repent, she will be dealt with as God had dealt with Edom (see Is 34:5; cf. Mal 1:3–4). (See Introduction: Background). Ezekiel was among them and received his prophetic call in 593.

1:3 *Ezekiel.* See 24:24. Means "God is strong" (cf. 3:14), "God strengthens" (cf. 30:25; 34:16) or "God makes hard" (cf. 3:8). Jehezkel (1 Chr 24:16) is the same name in Hebrew but does not refer to the same person. *priest.* Member of a priestly family (the text could be translated "Ezekiel the son of Buzi the priest"). *hand of the LORD.* A phrase repeated six times in the book (3:14,22; 8:1; 33:22; 37:1; 40:1), indicating an overpowering experience of divine revelation.

1:4 *I looked.* Introduces the first part of the vision: storm and living creatures (vv. 4–14). The "I looked" of v. 15 introduces the second part: wheels and the glory of the Lord. *whirlwind.* See Ps 18:10–12.

1:5 *four living creatures.* "Four," which stands for completeness (cf. the four directions in Gen 13:14 and the four quarters of the earth in Is 11:12), is used often in this chapter—and over 40 times in the book. The living creatures, called "cherubims" in ch. 10, are throne attendants, here (see v. 10) representing God's creation: "man," God's ordained ruler of creation (see Gen 1:26–28; Ps 8); "lion," the strongest of the wild beasts; "ox," the most powerful of the domesticated animals; "eagle," the mightiest of the birds. These four creatures appear again in Rev 4:7 and often are seen in the paintings and sculpture of the Middle Ages, where they represent the four Gospels.

1:7 *like the sole of a calf's foot.* Perhaps indicates agility (cf. Ps 29:6; Mal 4:2).

1:12 *the spirit.* See v. 20.

1:16 *beryl.* The precise identification of this stone is uncertain. See Ex 28:20, where the stone appears in the priestly breastplate. *as it were a wheel in the middle of a wheel.* Probably two wheels intersecting at right angles in order to move in all four directions (see v. 17). The imagery symbolizes the omnipresence of God.

1:18 *full of eyes.* Symbolizes God's all-seeing nature.

21 [a]When those went, *these* went; and when those stood, *these* stood; and when those were lifted up from the earth, the wheels were lifted up over against them: for the spirit [1]of the living creature *was* in the wheels.

22 [a]And the likeness of the firmament upon the heads of the living creature *was* as the colour of the terrible crystal, stretched forth over their heads above.

23 And under the firmament *were* their wings straight, the one toward the other: every one had two, which covered on this *side,* and every one had two, which covered on that *side,* their bodies.

24 [a]And when they went, I heard the noise of their wings, [b]like the noise of great waters, as [c]the voice of the Almighty, the voice of speech, as the noise of a host: when they stood, they let down their wings.

25 And there was a voice from the firmament that *was* over their heads, when they stood, *and* had let down their wings.

26 ¶ [a]And above the firmament that *was* over their heads *was* the likeness of a throne, [b]as the appearance of a sapphire stone: and upon the likeness of the throne *was* the likeness as the appearance of a man above upon it.

27 [a]And I saw as the colour of amber, as the appearance of fire round about within it, from the appearance of his loins even upward, and from the appearance of his loins even downward, I saw as it were the appearance of fire, and it had brightness round about.

28 [a]As the appearance of the bow that is in the cloud in the day of rain, so *was* the appearance of the brightness round about. [b]This *was* the appearance of the likeness of the glory of the LORD. And when I saw *it,* [c]I fell upon my face, and I heard a voice of one that spake.

Ezekiel's commission

2 And he said unto me, Son of man, [a]stand upon thy feet, and I will speak unto thee.

2 And [a]the spirit entered into me when he spake unto me, and set me upon my feet, that I heard him that spake unto me.

3 And he said unto me, Son of man, I send thee to the children of Israel, to a rebellious [1]nation that hath rebelled against me: [a]they and their fathers have transgressed against me, *even* unto this very day.

4 [a]For *they are* [1]impudent children and stiff hearted. I do send thee unto them; and thou shalt say unto them, Thus saith the Lord GOD.

5 [a]And they, whether they will hear, or whether they will forbear, (for they *are* a rebellious house,) yet [b]shall know that there hath been a prophet among them.

6 And thou, son of man, [a]be not afraid of them, neither be afraid of their words, though [b][1]briers and thorns *be* with thee, and thou dost dwell among scorpions: [c]be not afraid of their words, nor be dismayed at their looks, [d]though they *be* a rebellious house.

7 [a]And thou shalt speak my words unto them, [b]whether they will hear, or whether they will forbear: for they *are* [1]most rebellious.

8 But thou, son of man, hear what I say unto thee; Be not thou rebellious like *that* rebellious house: open thy mouth, and [a]eat that I give thee.

9 ¶ And when I looked, behold, [a]a hand *was* sent unto me; and lo, [b]a roll of a book *was* therein;

10 And he spread it before me; and it *was* written within and without: and *there was* written therein lamentations, and mourning, and woe.

3 Moreover he said unto me, Son of man, eat that thou findest; [a]eat this roll, and go speak unto the house of Israel.

2 So I opened my mouth, and he caused me to eat that roll.

3 And he said unto me, Son of man, cause thy belly to eat, and fill thy bowels with this

1:21 [1]Or, *of life* [a]ver. 19,20; ch. 10:17
1:22 [a]ch. 10:1
1:24 [a]ch. 10:5 [b]ch. 43:2; Dan. 10:6; Rev. 1:15 [c]Job 37:4,5; Ps. 29:3,4; 68:33
1:26 [a]ch. 10:1 [b]Ex. 24:10
1:27 [a]ch. 8:2
1:28 [a]Rev. 4:3; 10:1 [b]ch. 3:23; 8:4 [c]ch. 3:23; Dan. 8:17; Acts 9:4; Rev. 1:17
2:1 [a]Dan. 10:11
2:2 [a]ch. 3:24
2:3 [1]Heb. *nations* [a]Jer. 3:25; ch. 20:18,21,30
2:4 [1]Heb. *hard of face* [a]ch. 3:7
2:5 [a]ch. 3:11, 26,27 [b]ch. 33:33
2:6 [1]Or, *rebels* [a]Jer. 1:8,17; Luke 12:4 [b]Is. 9:18; Jer. 6:28; Mic. 7:4 [c]ch. 3:9; 1 Pet. 3:14 [d]ch. 3:9,26,27
2:7 [1]Heb. *rebellion* [a]Jer. 1:7,17 [b]ver. 5
2:8 [a]Rev. 10:9
2:9 [a]Jer. 1:9; ch. 8:3 [b]ch. 3:1
3:1 [a]ch. 2:8,9

1:22 *firmament.* The same word occurs in Gen 1:6–8, where its function is to separate the waters above from the waters below. Here it separates the creatures from the glory of the Lord.
1:26 *likeness . . . as the appearance of a man.* Ezekiel is reporting his vision of God, but he carefully avoids saying he saw God directly (see Gen 16:13; Ex 3:6; Judg 13:22).
1:28 *likeness.* See note on v. 26. *glory of the LORD.* When God's glory was symbolically revealed, it took the form of brilliant light (see Ex 40:34 and note; Is 6:3). What is remarkable about Ezekiel's experience is that God's glory had for centuries been associated with the temple in Jerusalem (see 1 Ki 8:11; Ps 26:8; 63:2; 96:6; 102:16). Now God had left His temple and was appearing to His exiled people in Babylon—a major theme in the first half of Ezekiel's message (see 10:4; 11:23). In his vision of the restored Jerusalem the prophet saw the glory of the Lord returning (43:2).
2:1 *Son of man.* A term used 93 times in Ezekiel, emphasizing the prophet's humanity as he was addressed by the transcendent God (see note on Ps 8:4). Dan 7:13 and 8:17 are the only other places where the phrase is used as a title in the OT. Jesus' frequent use of the phrase in referring to Himself showed that He was the eschatological figure spoken of in Dan 7:13 (see, e.g., Mark 8:31 and note).
2:2 *the spirit entered into me . . . and set me upon my feet.* The Spirit of God, who empowered the chariot wheels (1:12,19; 10:16–17) and the creatures (1:20), now entered Ezekiel—symbolizing the Lord's empowering of the prophet's entire ministry.
2:3 *rebellious nation.* A keynote of Ezekiel's preaching: The entire nation throughout its history had been rebellious against God.
2:6 *briers and thorns . . . scorpions.* Vivid images of those who would make life difficult for the prophet.
2:10 *written within and without.* Normally, ancient scrolls were written on one side only. The implication here is that the scroll was thoroughly saturated with words of divine judgment. See Zech 5:3 and Rev 5:1 for the same figure. *lamentations, and mourning, and woe.* Although Ezekiel was later commanded to preach hope (see note on 33:1–48:35), his initial commission (until the fall of Jerusalem) was to declare God's displeasure and the certainty of His judgment on Jerusalem and all of Judah.

roll that I give thee. Then did I [a]eat *it;* and it was in my mouth [b]as honey for sweetness.

4 ¶ And he said unto me, Son of man, go, get thee unto the house of Israel, and speak with my words unto them.

5 For thou *art* not sent to a people [1]of a strange speech and of a hard language, *but* to the house of Israel;

6 Not to many people [1]of a strange speech and of a hard language, whose words thou canst not understand. [2]Surely, [a]had I sent thee to them, they would have hearkened unto thee.

7 But the house of Israel will not hearken unto thee; [a]for they will not hearken unto me: [b]for all the house of Israel *are* [1]impudent and hardhearted.

8 Behold, I have made thy face strong against their faces, and thy forehead strong against their foreheads.

9 [a]As an adamant harder than flint have I made thy forehead: [b]fear them not, neither be dismayed at their looks, though they *be* a rebellious house.

10 Moreover he said unto me, Son of man, all my words that I shall speak unto thee receive in thine heart, and hear with thine ears.

11 And go, get thee to them of the captivity, unto the children of thy people, and speak unto them, and tell them, [a]Thus saith the Lord GOD; whether they will hear, or whether they will forbear.

12 Then [a]the spirit took me up, and I heard behind me a voice of a great rushing, *saying,* Blessed *be* the glory of the LORD from his place.

13 *I heard* also the noise of the wings of the living creatures that [1]touched one another, and the noise of the wheels over against them, and a noise of a great rushing.

14 So [a]the spirit lifted me up, and took me away, and I went [1]in bitterness, in the [2]heat of my spirit; but [b]the hand of the LORD was strong upon me.

Warning to Israel

15 ¶ Then I came to them of the captivity *at* Tel-abib, that dwelt by the river of Chebar, and [a]I sat where they sat, and remained there astonished among them seven days.

16 And it came to pass at the end of seven days, that the word of the LORD came unto me, saying,

17 [a]Son of man, I have made thee [b]a watchman unto the house of Israel: therefore hear the word at my mouth, and give them warning from me.

18 When I say unto the wicked, Thou shalt surely die; and thou givest him not warning, nor speakest to warn the wicked from his wicked way, to save his life; the same wicked *man* [a]shall die in his iniquity; but his blood will I require at thine hand.

19 Yet if thou warn the wicked, and he turn not from his wickedness, nor from his wicked way, he shall die in his iniquity; [a]but thou hast delivered thy soul.

20 Again, When a [a]righteous *man* doth turn from his righteousness, and commit iniquity, and I lay a stumblingblock before him, he shall die: because thou hast not given him warning, he shall die in his sin, and his [1]righteousness which he hath done shall not be remembered; but his blood will I require at thine hand.

21 Nevertheless if thou warn the righteous *man,* that the righteous sin not, and he doth not sin, he shall surely live, because he is warned; also thou hast delivered thy soul.

22 ¶ [a]And the hand of the LORD was there upon me; and he said unto me, Arise, go forth [b]into the plain, and I will there talk with thee.

23 Then I arose, and went forth into the plain: and behold, [a]the glory of the LORD stood there, as the glory which I [b]saw by the river of Chebar: [c]and I fell on my face.

24 Then [a]the spirit entered into me, and set me upon my feet, and spake with me, and said unto me, Go, shut thyself within thine house.

3:3 [a]Rev. 10:9; See Jer. 15:16 [b]Ps. 19:10; 119:103
3:5 [1]Heb. *deep of lip, and heavy of tongue;* and so ver. 6
3:6 [1]Heb. *deep of lip, and heavy [of] language* [2]Or, *If I had sent thee, etc., would they not have hearkened unto thee?* [a]Mat. 11:21
3:7 [1]Heb. *stiff of forehead, and hard of heart* [a]John 15:20 [b]ch. 2:4
3:9 [a]Is. 50:7; Jer. 1:18; Mic. 3:8 [b]Jer. 1:8,17; ch. 2:6
3:11 [a]ch. 2:5,7
3:12 [a]ch. 8:3; 1 Ki. 18:12; Acts 8:39
3:13 [1]Heb. *kissed*
3:14 [1]Heb. *bitter* [2]Heb. *hot anger* [a]ver. 12; ch. 8:3 [b]2 Ki. 3:15; ch. 1:3; 8:1
3:15 [a]Job 2:13; Ps. 137:1
3:17 [a]ch. 33:7-9 [b]Is. 52:8; 56:10; Jer. 6:17
3:18 [a]ch. 33:6; John 8:21
3:19 [a]Is. 49:4,5; Acts 20:26
3:20 [1]Heb. *righteousnesses* [a]ch. 18:24; 33:12,13
3:22 [a]ch. 1:3 [b]ch. 8:4
3:23 [a]ch. 1:28 [b]ch. 1:1 [c]ch. 1:28
3:24 [a]ch. 2:2

3:3 *in my mouth as honey.* What Jeremiah experienced emotionally (Jer 15:16) was experienced by Ezekiel in a more sensory way: Words from God are sweet to the taste (see Ps 19:10; 119:103)—even when their content is bitter (see Rev 10:9–10).

‡3:6 *they would have hearkened unto thee.* Jesus spoke similar words to Israel (see Mat 11:21).

3:9 *harder than flint have I made thy forehead.* Strength and courage were necessary equipment for a prophet, especially when preaching judgment. Jeremiah was similarly equipped (see Jer 1:18).

3:10 *receive in thine heart . . . hear with thine ears.* The prophet is to stand in marked contrast to the people, who do not listen.

3:11 *go . . . to them of the captivity . . . the children of thy people.* Ezekiel's ministry was to the exilic community, most of whom refused to believe that God would abandon Jerusalem and the temple. After the fall of Jerusalem, therefore, they were strongly inclined to despair.

3:14 *in bitterness, in the heat of my spirit.* The prophet, knowing the righteousness of God's anger, personally identified with the divine emotions. *hand of the LORD was strong upon me.* See note on 1:3.

3:15 *Tel-abib.* The only mention of the specific place where the exiles lived. In Babylonian the name meant "mound of the flood [i.e., destruction]," apparently referring to the ruined condition of the site. When used of the modern Israeli city, Tel Aviv, this name (Abib and Aviv are the same word in Hebrew) is understood to mean "hill of grain." *seven days.* Considering Ezekiel's priestly background (see note on 1:3), the seven-day period may have been a parallel to the time required for a priest's ordination (see Lev 8:1–33).

3:17 *I have made thee a watchman.* In ancient Israel, watchmen were stationed on the highest parts of the city wall to inform its inhabitants of the progress of a battle (1 Sam 14:16) or of approaching messengers (2 Sam 18:24–27; 2 Ki 9:17–20). The prophets were spiritual watchmen, relaying God's word to the people (see Jer 6:17; Hos 9:8; Hab 2:1). Ezekiel's function as a watchman was not so much to warn the exiles of the impending doom of Jerusalem as to teach that God holds each one responsible for his own behavior. This commission, repeated in 33:7–9, is spelled out in ch. 18.

3:22 *hand of the LORD.* See note on 1:3.

25 But thou, O son of man, behold, [a]they shall put bands upon thee, and shall bind thee with them, and thou shalt not go out among them:

26 And [a]I will make thy tongue cleave to the roof of thy mouth, that thou shalt be dumb, and shalt not be to them [1]a reprover: [b]for they *are* a rebellious house.

27 [a]But when I speak with thee, I will open thy mouth, and thou shalt say unto them, [b]Thus saith the Lord GOD; He that heareth, let him hear; and he that forbeareth, let him forbear: for they *are* a rebellious house.

Symbol of the siege and exile

4 Thou also, son of man, take thee a tile, and lay it before thee, and pourtray upon it *the* city, *even* Jerusalem:

2 And lay siege against it, and build a fort against it, and cast a mount against it; set the camp also against it, and set [1]*battering* rams against it round about.

3 Moreover take thou unto thee [1]an iron pan, and set it *for* a wall of iron between thee and the city: and set thy face against it, and it shall be besieged, and thou shalt lay siege against it. [a]This *shall be* a sign to the house of Israel.

4 ¶ Lie thou also upon thy left side, and lay the iniquity of the house of Israel upon it: *according to* the number of the days that thou shalt lie upon it thou shalt bear their iniquity.

5 For I have laid upon thee the years of their iniquity, according to the number of the days, three hundred and ninety days: [a]so shalt thou bear the iniquity of the house of Israel.

6 And when thou hast accomplished them, lie again on thy right side, and thou shalt bear the iniquity of the house of Judah forty days: I have appointed thee [1]each day for a year.

7 Therefore thou shalt set thy face toward the siege of Jerusalem, and thine arm *shall be* uncovered, and thou shalt prophesy against it.

8 [a]And behold, I will lay bands upon thee, and thou shalt not turn thee [1]from one side to another, till thou hast ended the days of thy siege.

9 ¶ Take thou also unto thee wheat, and barley, and beans, and lentiles, and millet, and [1]fitches, and put them in one vessel, and make thee bread thereof, *according to* the number of the days that thou shalt lie upon thy side, three hundred and ninety days shalt thou eat thereof.

10 And thy meat which thou shalt eat *shall be* by weight, twenty shekels a day: from time to time shalt thou eat it.

11 Thou shalt drink also water by measure, the sixth *part* of a hin: from time to time shalt thou drink.

12 And thou shalt eat it *as* barley cakes, and thou shalt bake it with dung that cometh out of man, in their sight.

13 And the LORD said, Even thus [a]shall the children of Israel eat their defiled bread among the Gentiles, whither I will drive them.

14 Then said I, [a]Ah Lord GOD, behold, my soul *hath* not *been* polluted: for from my youth up even till now have I not eaten *of* [b]that which dieth of itself, or is torn in pieces; neither came there [c]abominable flesh into my mouth.

15 Then he said unto me, Lo, I have given thee cow's dung for man's dung, and thou shalt prepare thy bread therewith.

16 Moreover he said unto me, Son of man, behold, I will break the [a]staff of bread in Jerusalem: and they shall [b]eat bread by weight, and with care; and they shall [c]drink water by measure, and with astonishment:

17 That they may want bread and water, and be astonied one with another, and [a]consume away for their iniquity.

5 And thou, son of man, take thee a sharp knife, take thee a barber's rasor, [a]and cause *it* to pass upon thine head and upon thy beard: then take thee balances to weigh, and divide *the hair.*

2 [a]Thou shalt burn with fire a third *part* in the midst of [b]the city, when [c]the days of the

3:25 [a]ch. 4:8
3:26 [1][Heb.] *a man reproving* [a]ch. 24:27; Luke 1:20 [b]ch. 2:5-7
3:27 [a]ch. 24:27; 33:22 [b]ver. 11
4:2 [1]Or, *chief leaders*
4:3 [1]Or, *a flat plate,* or, *slice* [a]ch. 12:6,11; 24:24,27
4:5 [a]Num. 14:34
4:6 [1]Heb. *a day for a year, a day for a year*
4:8 [1]Heb. *from thy side to thy side* [a]ch. 3:25
4:9 [1]Or, *spelt*
4:13 [a]Hos. 9:3
4:14 [a]Acts 10:14 [b]Ex. 22:31; Lev. 11:40; 17:15 [c]Deut. 14:3; Is. 65:4
4:16 [a]Lev. 26:26; Ps. 105:16; Is. 3:1; ch. 5:16; 14:13 [b]ver. 10; ch. 12:19 [c]ver. 11
4:17 [a]Lev. 26:39; ch. 24:23
5:1 [a]See Lev. 21:5; Is. 7:20; ch. 44:20
5:2 [a]ver. 12 [b]ch. 4:1 [c]ch. 4:8,9

3:26 *thy tongue cleave to the roof of thy mouth.* Verses 26–27 indicate that the prophet would be unable to speak except when he had a direct word from the Lord. His enforced silence underscored Israel's stubborn refusal to take God's word seriously. This condition was relieved only after the fall of Jerusalem (24:27; 33:22). From that time on, Ezekiel was given messages of hope, which he continually shared with his fellow exiles.

4:1 *take thee a tile.* The first of several symbolic acts to be performed by the prophet. After inscribing a likeness of the city of Jerusalem on a moist clay tablet, such as those commonly used in Babylonia, Ezekiel was to place around it models of siege works to represent the city under attack (v. 2). He was then to place an iron pan (perhaps a baking griddle) between himself and the symbolized city (v. 3) to indicate the unbreakable strength of the siege.

4:3 *besieged.* Ezekiel's own presence in the scene signified that the siege would actually be laid by the Lord Himself.

4:4 *thou shalt bear their iniquity.* A representative rather than a substitutionary bearing of sin. The prophet's action symbolized Israel's sins; it did not remove them.

‡4:5 *years . . . three hundred and ninety days.* The 390 years may represent the period from the time of Solomon's unfaithfulness to the fall of Jerusalem. Correspondingly, the 40 years of v. 6 may represent the long reign of wicked Manasseh before his repentance (see 2 Ki 21:11–15; 23:26–27; 24:3–4; 2 Chr 33:12–13).

4:6 *on thy right side.* Lying on his left side (see v. 5) placed Ezekiel to the north of the symbolic city; lying on his right side placed him to the south—signifying the northern and southern kingdoms respectively.

4:9 *Take . . . wheat, and barley, and beans, and lentiles, and millet, and fitches.* A scant, vegetarian diet representing the meager provisions of a besieged city.

4:15 *cow's dung.* Commonly used in the Near East as a fuel for baking, even today. Ezekiel again showed his sensitivity to things ceremonially unclean (see note on 1:3), and God graciously responded to the prophet's objection by allowing this substitute for human excrement.

5:1 *take thee a sharp knife.* What Isaiah had expressed in a metaphor (Is 7:20) Ezekiel acted out in prophetic symbolism.

siege are fulfilled: and thou shalt take a third *part, and* smite about it with a knife: and a third *part* thou shalt scatter in the wind; and I will draw out a sword after them.

3 [a]Thou shalt also take thereof a few in number, and bind them in thy [1]skirts.

4 Then take of them again, and [a]cast them into the midst of the fire, and burn them in the fire; *for* thereof shall a fire come forth into all the house of Israel.

5 ¶ Thus saith the Lord GOD; This *is* Jerusalem: I have set it in the midst of the nations and countries *that are* round about her.

6 And she hath changed my judgments into wickedness more than the nations, and my statutes more than the countries that *are* round about her: for they have refused my judgments, and my statutes, they have not walked in them.

7 Therefore thus saith the Lord GOD; Because ye multiplied more than the nations that *are* round about you, *and* have not walked in my statutes, neither have kept my judgments, [a]neither have done according to the judgments of the nations that *are* round about you;

8 Therefore thus saith the Lord GOD; Behold, I, even I, *am* against thee, and will execute judgments in the midst of thee in the sight of the nations.

9 [a]And I will do in thee that which I have not done, and whereunto I will not do any more the like, because of all thine abominations.

10 Therefore the fathers [a]shall eat the sons in the midst of thee, and the sons shall eat their fathers; and I will execute judgments in thee, and the whole remnant of thee will I [b]scatter into all the winds.

11 Wherefore, *as* I live, saith the Lord GOD; Surely, because thou hast [a]defiled my sanctuary with all thy [b]detestable things, and with all thine abominations, therefore will I also diminish *thee;* [c]neither shall mine eye spare, neither will I have any pity.

12 [a]A third *part* of thee shall die with the pestilence, and with famine shall they be consumed in the midst of thee: and a third *part* shall fall by the sword round about thee; and [b]I will scatter a third *part* into all the winds, and [c]I will draw out a sword after them.

5:3 [1]Heb. *wings* [a]Jer. 40:6; 52:16
5:4 [a]Jer. 41:1,2; 44:14
5:7 [a]Jer. 2:10,11; ch. 16:47
5:9 [a]Lam. 4:6; Dan. 9:12; Amos 3:2
5:10 [a]Lev. 26:29; Deut. 28:53; 2 Ki. 6:29; Jer. 19:9; Lam. 2:20; 4:10 [b]Lev. 26:33; Deut. 28:64; ch. 12:14; Zech. 2:6
5:11 [a]2 Chr. 36:14; ch. 7:20 [b]ch. 11:21 [c]ch. 7:4,9
5:12 [a]Jer. 15:2; 21:9; ch. 6:12 [b]Jer. 9:16 [c]ver. 2; Lev. 26:33; ch. 12:14
5:13 [a]Lam. 4:11; ch. 6:12; 7:8 [b]ch. 21:17 [c]Deut. 32:36; Is. 1:24 [d]ch. 36:6; 38:19
5:14 [a]Lev. 26:31; Neh. 2:17
5:15 [a]Deut. 28:37; 1 Ki. 9:7; Ps. 79:4; Jer. 24:9; Lam. 2:15 [b]ch. 25:17
5:16 [a]Deut. 32:23 [b]Lev. 26:26; ch. 4:16; 14:13
5:17 [a]Lev. 26:22; Deut. 32:24; ch. 14:21; 33:27; 34:25 [b]ch. 38:22
6:2 [a]ch. 20:46; 21:2; 25:2 [b]ch. 36:1
6:3 [a]Lev. 26:30
6:4 [1]Or, *sun images,* and so ver. 6 [a]Lev. 26:30
6:5 [1]Heb. *give*

13 Thus shall mine anger [a]be accomplished, and I will [b]cause my fury to rest upon them, [c]and I will be comforted: [d]and they shall know that I the LORD have spoken *it* in my zeal, when I have accomplished my fury in them.

14 Moreover [a]I will make thee waste, and a reproach among the nations that *are* round about thee, in the sight of all that pass by.

15 So it shall be a [a]reproach and a taunt, an instruction and an astonishment unto the nations that *are* round about thee, when I shall execute judgments in thee in anger and in fury and in [b]furious rebukes. I the LORD have spoken *it.*

16 When I shall [a]send upon them the evil arrows of famine, which shall be for *their* destruction, *and* which I will send to destroy you: and I *will* increase the famine upon you, and will break your [b]staff of bread:

17 So will I send upon you famine and [a]evil beasts, and they shall bereave thee; and [b]pestilence and blood shall pass through thee; and I will bring the sword upon thee. I the LORD have spoken *it.*

The high places to be destroyed

6 And the word of the LORD came unto me, saying,

2 Son of man, [a]set thy face towards the [b]mountains of Israel, and prophesy against them,

3 And say, Ye mountains of Israel, hear the word of the Lord GOD; Thus saith the Lord GOD to the mountains, and to the hills, to the rivers, and to the valleys; Behold, I, *even* I, *will* bring a sword upon you, and [a]I will destroy your high places.

4 And your altars shall be desolate, and your [1]images shall be broken: and [a]I will cast down your slain *men* before your idols.

5 And I will [1]lay the dead carcases of the children of Israel before their idols; and I will scatter your bones round about your altars.

6 In all your dwelling places the cities shall be laid waste, and the high places shall be desolate; that your altars may be laid waste and made desolate, and your idols may be broken and cease, and your images may be cut down, and your works may be abolished.

5:5 *This is Jerusalem.* After wordlessly acting out the symbols (beginning in 4:1), Ezekiel received and probably related the divine explanations. *In the midst of the nations.* A privileged position, which made Israel's responsibility and judgment all the more severe (see note on 38:12).

5:8 *I, even I, am against thee.* A short and effective phrase of judgment used often by Ezekiel (see 13:8; 21:3; 26:3; 28:22; 29:3,10; 30:22; 34:10; 35:3; 38:3; 39:1; see also Jer 23:30–32; 50:31; 51:25; Nah 2:13; 3:5).

5:10 *fathers shall eat the sons.* Cannibalism, the most gruesome extremity of life under siege, was threatened as a consequence of breaking the covenant (Deut 28:53; see Jer 19:9; Lam 2:20; Zech 11:9).

5:11 *as I live.* See note on 18:3.

5:13 *they shall know that I the LORD, have spoken.* The first of 65 occurrences in Ezekiel of this or similar declarations. God's acts of judgment and salvation reveal who He is. Since the people would not listen to God's words, they would be taught by His actions. *accomplished my fury in them.* An expression frequently used by the Lord in this book (see 6:12; 7:8; 13:15; 20:8,21).

5:15 *a reproach and a taunt, an instruction and an astonishment.* A fourfold list (see note on 1:5).

6:3 *high places.* Open-air sanctuaries of Canaanite origin, condemned throughout the OT. The high places, together with the "altars," "incense altars" and "idols" (v. 4), make up a list of four objects (see note on 1:5).

6:4 *altars.* Made of burnt clay, about two feet high, usually inscribed with animal figures and idols of Canaanite gods. *idols.* The Hebrew for this word is a derisive term (lit. "dung pellets"), used especially by Ezekiel (38 times, as opposed to only 9 times elsewhere in the OT).

7 And the slain shall fall in the midst of you, and [a]ye shall know that I *am* the LORD.

8 ¶ [a]Yet will I leave a remnant, that ye may have *some* that shall escape the sword among the nations, when ye shall be scattered through the countries.

9 And they that escape of you shall remember me among the nations whither they shall be carried captives, because [a]I am broken with their whorish heart, which hath departed from me, and [b]with their eyes, which go a whoring after their idols: and [c]they shall lothe themselves for the evils which they have committed in all their abominations.

10 And they shall know that I *am* the LORD, *and that* I have not said in vain that *I* would do this evil unto them.

11 ¶ Thus saith the Lord GOD; Smite [a]with thine hand, and stamp with thy foot, and say, Alas for all the evil abominations of the house of Israel: [b]for they shall fall by the sword, by the famine, and by the pestilence.

12 *He* that *is* far off shall die of the pestilence; and *he* that *is* near shall fall by the sword; and he that remaineth and is besieged shall die by the famine: [a]thus will I accomplish my fury upon them.

13 Then [a]shall ye know that I *am* the LORD, when their slain *men* shall be among their idols round about their altars, [b]upon every high hill, [c]in all the tops of the mountains, and [d]under every green tree, and under every thick oak, the place where they did offer sweet savour to all their idols.

14 So will I [a]stretch out mine hand upon them, and make the land desolate, yea, [1]more desolate than the wilderness toward [b]Diblath, in all their habitations: and they shall know that I *am* the LORD.

An end is come

7 Moreover the word of the LORD came unto me, saying,

2 Also, thou son of man, thus saith the Lord GOD unto the land of Israel; [a]An end, the end is come upon the four corners of the land.

3 Now *is* the end *come* upon thee, and I will send mine anger upon thee, and will judge thee according to thy ways, and will [1]recompense upon thee all thine abominations.

4 And [a]mine eye shall not spare thee, neither will I have pity: but I will recompense thy ways upon thee, and thine abominations shall be in the midst of thee: [b]and ye shall know that I *am* the LORD.

5 ¶ Thus saith the Lord GOD; An evil, an only evil, behold, is come.

6 An end is come, the end is come: it [1]watcheth for thee; behold, it is come.

7 [a]The morning is come unto thee, O thou that dwellest in the land: [b]the time is come, the day of trouble *is* near, and not the [1]sounding again of the mountains.

8 Now will I shortly [a]pour out my fury upon thee, and accomplish mine anger upon thee: and I will judge thee according to thy ways, and will recompense thee for all thine abominations.

9 And mine eye shall not spare, neither will I have pity: I will recompense [1]thee according to thy ways and thine abominations *that* are in the midst of thee; and ye shall know that I *am* the LORD that smiteth.

10 Behold the day, behold, it is come: [a]the morning is gone forth; the rod hath blossomed, pride hath budded.

11 [a]Violence is risen up into a rod of wickedness: none of them *shall remain,* nor of their multitude, nor of any of [1]theirs: [b]neither *shall there be* wailing for them.

12 The time is come, the day draweth near: let not the buyer rejoice, nor the seller mourn: for wrath *is* upon all the multitude thereof.

13 For the seller shall not return to that which is sold, [1]although they were yet alive: for the vision *is* touching the whole multitude thereof, *which* shall not return; neither shall any strengthen himself [2]in [3]the iniquity of his life.

14 ¶ They have blown the trumpet, even to make all ready; but none goeth to the battle: for my wrath *is* upon all the multitude thereof.

15 [a]The sword *is* without, and the pestilence and the famine within: he that *is* in the field shall die with the sword; and he that *is* in the city, famine and pestilence shall devour him.

16 But they that escape of them shall escape, and shall be on the mountains like doves of the valleys, all of them mourning, every one for his iniquity.

17 All [a]hands shall be feeble, and all knees shall [1]be weak *as* water.

18 They shall also [a]gird *themselves* with sackcloth, and horror shall cover them; and

6:7 [a]ver. 13; ch. 7:4,9
6:8 [a]Jer. 44:28; ch. 5:2,12; 12:16; 14:22
6:9 [a]Ps. 78:40; Is. 7:13; 43:24 [b]Num. 15:39; ch. 20:7,24 [c]Lev. 26:39; Job 42:6; ch. 20:43; 36:31
6:11 [a]ch. 21:14 [b]ch. 5:12
6:12 [a]ch. 5:13
6:13 [a]ver. 7 [b]Jer. 2:20 [c]Hos. 4:13 [d]Is. 57:5
6:14 [1]Or, *desolate from the wilderness* [a]Is. 5:25 [b]Num. 33:46; Jer. 48:22
7:2 [a]Amos 8:2; Mat. 24:6,13,14
7:3 [1]Heb. *give*
7:4 [a]ch. 5:11
7:4 [b]ch. 12:20
7:6 [1]Heb. *awaketh against thee*
7:7 [1]Or, *echo* [a]ver. 10 [b]Zeph. 1:14,15
7:8 [a]ch. 20:8,21
7:9 [1]Heb. *upon thee*
7:10 [a]ver. 7
7:11 [1]Or, *their tumultuous* persons. Heb. *tumult* [a]Jer. 6:7 [b]Jer. 16:5,6; ch. 24:16,22
7:13 [1]Heb. *though their life* were *yet among the living* [2]Or, *whose life* is *in his iniquity* [3]Heb. *his iniquity*
7:15 [a]Deut. 32:25; Lam. 1:20
7:17 [1]Heb. *go* into *water* [a]Is. 13:7; Jer. 6:24
7:18 [a]Is. 3:24; Amos 8:10

6:7 *know that I am the LORD.* See Introduction: Themes.

6:9 *they that escape . . . shall remember me.* The corrective outcome God intends from the severe judgment to come (see v. 10).

6:11 *Smite with thine hand.* A command to Ezekiel, calling for his personal involvement in the tragedy—though Israel's enemies were condemned for the same practice (see 25:6).

6:14 *will I stretch out my hand upon them.* A common expression in Ezekiel (see 14:9,13; 16:27; 25:7; 35:3). *Diblath.* Perhaps the Beth-diblathaim of Jer 48:22, a city in Moab; or Riblah, a city north of Damascus on the Orontes River (a few Hebrew manuscripts read "Riblah").

7:2 *four corners of the land.* The whole world would be affected by God's judgment on the land of Israel (see note on 1:5).

7:7 *the day.* The day of the Lord. Beginning with Amos (Amos 5:18–20), that day is seen by all the prophets as a day of great judgment—and often (though not here) as a judgment that sweeps away all the enemies that threaten God's people, thereby bringing peace. *trouble . . . not the sounding again of.* Cf. Amos 5:20 ("darkness instead of light").

7:8 *pour out my fury.* A common expression in Ezekiel (see 9:8; 14:19; 20:8,13,21; 22:31; 30:15; 36:18).

7:12 *let not the buyer rejoice.* End-time advice similar to that of Jesus (see Mat 24:17–18).

shame *shall be* upon all faces, and baldness
upon all their heads.
19 They shall cast their silver in the
streets, and their gold shall be [1]removed: their
[a]silver and their gold shall not be able to deliver them in the day of the wrath of the LORD:
they shall not satisfy their souls, neither fill
their bowels: [2]because it is the stumblingblock of their iniquity.
20 ¶ As for the beauty of his ornament, he set
it in majesty: [a]but they made the images of their
abominations *and* of their detestable things
therein: therefore have I [1]set it far from them.
21 And I will give it into the hands of the
strangers for a prey, and to the wicked of the
earth for a spoil; and they shall pollute it.
22 My face will I turn also from them, and
they shall pollute my secret *place:* for the
[1]robbers shall enter into it, and defile it.
23 Make a chain: for [a]the land is full *of*
bloody crimes, and the city is full *of* violence.
24 Wherefore I will bring the worst of the
heathen, and they shall possess their houses: I
will also make the pomp of the strong to cease;
and [1]their holy places shall be defiled.
25 [1]Destruction cometh; and they shall
seek peace, and *there shall be* none.
26 [a]Mischief shall come upon mischief,
and rumour shall be upon rumour; [b]then shall
they seek a vision of the prophet; but the law
shall perish from the priest, and counsel from
the ancients.
27 The king shall mourn, and the prince
shall be clothed with desolation, and the
hands of the people of the land shall be troubled: I will do unto them after their way, and
[1]according to their deserts will I judge them;
and they shall know that I *am* the LORD.

An end is come

8 And it came to pass in the sixth year, in
the sixth *month,* in the fifth *day* of the
month, as I sat in mine house, and [a]the elders
of Judah sat before me, that [b]the hand of the
Lord GOD fell there upon me.
2 [a]Then I beheld, and lo, a likeness as the
appearance of fire: from the appearance of his
loins even downward, fire; and from his loins
even upward, as the appearance of brightness,
[b]as the colour of amber.
3 And he [a]put forth the form of a hand, and
took me by a lock of mine head; and [b]the spirit
lift me up between the earth and the heaven,
and [c]brought me in the visions of God to Jerusalem, to the door of the inner gate that looketh
toward the north; [d]where *was* the seat of the
image of jealousy, which [e]provoketh to jealousy.
4 And behold, the glory of the God of Israel *was* there, according to the vision that I
[a]saw in the plain.
5 ¶ Then said he unto me, Son of man, lift
up thine eyes now the way towards the north.
So I lift up mine eyes the way toward the
north, and behold, northward at the gate of
the altar this image of jealousy in the entry.
6 He said furthermore unto me, Son of
man, seest thou what they do? *even* the great
abominations that the house of Israel committeth here, that *I* should go far off from my sanctuary? but turn thee yet again, *and* thou shalt
see greater abominations.
7 And he brought me to the door of the
court; and when I looked, behold a hole in the
wall.
8 Then said he unto me, Son of man, dig
now in the wall: and when I had digged in the
wall, behold a door.
9 And he said unto me, Go in, and behold
the wicked abominations that they do here.
10 So I went in and saw; and behold every
form of creeping things, and abominable
beasts, and all the idols of the house of Israel,
pourtrayed upon the wall round about.
11 And there stood before them seventy
men of the ancients of the house of Israel, and
in the midst of them stood Jaazaniah the son of

7:19 [1]Heb. *for a separation,* or, *uncleanness* [2]Or, *because their iniquity is* their *stumblingblock* [a]Prov. 11:4; Zeph. 1:18
7:20 [1]Or, *made it unto them an unclean thing* [a]Jer. 7:30
7:22 [1]Or, *burglers*
7:23 [a]2 Ki. 21:16
7:24 [1]Or, *they shall inherit their holy places*
7:25 [1]Heb. *Cutting off*
7:26 [a]Deut. 32:23; Jer. 4:20 [b]Ps. 74:9; ch. 20:1,3
7:27 [1]Heb. *with their judgments*
8:1 [a]ch. 14:1; 20:1; 33:31
8:1 [b]ch. 1:3; 3:22
8:2 [a]ch. 1:26,27 [b]ch. 1:4
8:3 [a]Dan. 5:5 [b]ch. 3:14 [c]ch. 11:1,24; 40:2 [d]Jer. 7:30; 32:34; ch. 5:11 [e]Deut. 32:16,21
8:4 [a]ch. 1:28; 3:22,23

7:19 *They shall cast their silver.* See Is 2:20.
7:20 *beauty of his ornament.* See Ex 32:2–4.
7:22 *my secret place.* The Jerusalem temple.
7:24 *pomp of the strong.* The Jerusalem temple, described similarly in 24:21; 33:28.
7:26 *prophet . . . priest . . . the ancients.* There would be no guidance from God and no direction from the elders (see 1 Sam 28:6; Amos 8:11–12; Mic 3:6–7).
7:27 *king . . . prince.* Here both nouns describe the same person. Ezekiel considered Jehoiachin to be the true king (1:2) and Zedekiah a mere prince (12:12). *people of the land.* Full citizens of Judah who owned land and served in the army (cf. 12:19; 45:16,22; 46:3).
8:1–11:25 The vision contained in these four chapters vividly depicts the departure of the divine glory from the corrupted temple (see 8:4; 9:3; 10:18–19; 11:23).
8:1 *in the sixth year, in the sixth month, in the fifth day of the month.* Sept. 17, 592 B.C.—the second of 13 dates in Ezekiel. This one, like those in 1:2 and 40:1, introduces a vision. *Sat in mine house.* The exiles were free to build houses (see Jer 29:5). *elders of Judah sat before me.* They also had freedom of movement, assembly and worship. A year and two months after his inaugural vision and preaching, the prophet commanded a hearing. Some have seen in such meetings the beginnings of the synagogue form of worship. *hand of the Lord GOD.* See note on 1:3.
8:2 *a likeness.* An angel, similar in appearance to God in 1:26–27. *the appearance of fire . . . as the colour of amber.* A way of describing the blinding brightness of the divine messenger (see Mat 28:3; cf. Acts 9:3).
8:3 *brought me . . . to Jerusalem.* Ezekiel had been directed to prophesy stern judgments on Jerusalem (chs. 1–7). Now he was transported to Jerusalem in visions of God (see 11:24) and shown the reason for the judgments. *image . . . which provoketh to jealousy.* Any idol in the temple provoked the Lord to jealousy, but this one seems to be a statue of Asherah, the Canaanite goddess of fertility, which Josiah had removed some 30 years previously (see 2 Ki 23:6).
8:5 *image of jealousy.* See note on v. 3.
‡8:10 *every form of creeping things, and abominable beasts.* Probably reflecting Egyptian influence (see 2 Ki 23:31–35). These idols are specifically identified with the northern kingdom of Israel.
8:11 *Jaazaniah.* Not the same person as in 11:1. Ironically, the

Shaphan, with every man his censer in his hand; and a thick cloud of incense went up.

12 Then said he unto me, Son of man, hast thou seen what the ancients of the house of Israel do in the dark, every man in the chambers of his imagery? for they say, [a]The LORD seeth us not; the LORD hath forsaken the earth.

13 He said also unto me, Turn thee yet again, *and* thou shalt see great*er* abominations that they do.

14 ¶ Then he brought me to the door of the gate of the LORD's house which *was* towards the north; and behold, there sat women weeping for Tammuz.

15 Then said he unto me, Hast thou seen *this,* O son of man? turn thee yet again, *and* thou shalt see greater abominations than these.

16 And he brought me into the inner court of the LORD's house, and behold, *at* the door of the temple of the LORD, [a]between the porch and the altar, [b]*were* about five and twenty men, [c]*with* their backs toward the temple of the LORD, and their faces towards the east; and they worshipped [d]the sun towards the east.

17 Then he said unto me, Hast thou seen *this,* O son of man? [1]Is it a light thing to the house of Judah that *they* commit the abominations which they commit here? for they have [a]filled the land *with* violence, and have returned to provoke me to anger: and lo, they put the branch to their nose.

18 [a]Therefore will I also deal in fury: mine [b]eye shall not spare, neither will I have pity: and though they [c]cry in mine ears *with* a loud voice, *yet* will I not hear them.

The slaughter of the idolaters

9 He cried also in mine ears *with* a loud voice, saying, Cause them that have charge over the city to draw near, even every man *with* his destroying weapon in his hand.

2 And behold, six men came from the way of the higher gate, [1]which lieth toward the north, and every man [2]a slaughter weapon in his hand; [a]and one man among them *was* clothed *with* linen, with a writer's inkhorn [3]by his side: and they went in, and stood beside the brasen altar.

3 And [a]the glory of the God of Israel was gone up from the cherub, whereupon he was, to the threshold of the house. And he called to the man clothed *with* linen, which *had* the writer's inkhorn by his side;

4 And the LORD said unto him, Go through the midst of the city through the midst of Jerusalem, and [1]set [a]a mark upon the foreheads of the men [b]that sigh and that cry for all the abominations that be done in the midst thereof.

5 And to the others he said in [1]mine hearing, Go ye after him through the city, and smite: [a]let not your eye spare, neither have ye pity:

6 [a]Slay [1]utterly old *and* young, both maids, and little children, and women: but [b]come not near any man upon whom *is* the mark; and [c]begin at my sanctuary. [d]Then they began at the ancient men which *were* before the house.

7 And he said unto them, Defile the house, and fill the courts *with* the slain: go ye forth. And they went forth, and slew in the city.

8 ¶ And it came to pass, while they were slaying them, and I *was* left, that I [a]fell upon my face, and cried, and said, [b]Ah Lord GOD, *wilt* thou destroy all the residue of Israel in thy pouring out of thy fury upon Jerusalem?

9 Then said he unto me, The iniquity of the house of Israel and Judah *is* exceeding great, and [a]the land is [1]full *of* blood, and the city full *of* [2]perverseness: for they say, [b]The LORD hath forsaken the earth, and [c]the LORD seeth not.

10 And *as for* me also, mine [a]eye shall not spare, neither will I have pity, *but* [b]I will recompense their way upon their head.

11 And behold, the man clothed with linen, which *had* the inkhorn by his side, [1]reported the matter, saying, I have done as thou hast commanded me.

The glory of the LORD

10 Then I looked, and behold, in the [a]firmament that *was* above the head

8:12 [a]ch. 9:9
8:16 [a]Joel 2:17 [b]ch. 11:1 [c]Jer. 2:27; 32:33 [d]Deut. 4:19; 2 Ki. 23:5,11; Job 31:26; Jer. 44:17
8:17 [1]Or, *Is there* any thing *lighter than to commit* [a]ch. 9:9
8:18 [a]ch. 5:13; 16:42; 24:13 [b]ch. 5:11; 7:4,9; 9:5,10 [c]Prov. 1:28; Is. 1:15; Jer. 11:11; 14:12; Mic. 3:4; Zech. 7:13
9:2 [1]Heb. *which is turned* [2]Heb. *a weapon of his breaking in pieces* [3]Heb. *upon his loins* [a]Lev. 16:4; ch. 10:2,6,7; Rev. 15:6
9:3 [a]See ch. 3:23; 8:4; 10:4,18; 11:22,23
9:4 [1]Heb. *mark a mark* [a]Ex. 12:7; Rev. 7:3; 9:4; 13:16,17; 20:4 [b]Ps. 119:53,136; Jer. 13:17; 2 Cor. 12:21; 2 Pet. 2:8
9:5 [1]Heb. *mine ears* [a]ver. 10; ch. 5:11
9:6 [1]Heb. *to destruction* [a]2 Chr. 36:17 [b]Rev. 9:4 [c]Jer. 25:29; 1 Pet. 4:17 [d]ch. 8:11,12,16
9:8 [a]Num. 14:5; 16:4,22,45; Josh. 7:6 [b]ch. 11:13
9:9 [1]Heb. *filled with* [2]Or, *wresting of judgment* [a]2 Ki. 21:16; ch. 8:17 [b]ch. 8:12 [c]Ps. 10:11; Is. 29:15
9:10 [a]ch. 5:11; 7:4; 8:18 [b]ch. 11:21
9:11 [1]Heb. *returned the word*
10:1 [a]ch. 1:2,26

name means "The LORD hears," and the irony is sharpened by the quotation in v. 12.

‡8:14 *Tammuz.* The only Biblical reference to this Babylonian fertility god. The women of Jerusalem were bewailing his dying, which they felt caused the annual wilting of vegetation. Weeping was done in an attempt to resurrect the cycle of nature. According to some interpreters, he is alluded to in Dan 11:37 ("the desire of women"—see note there).

‡8:16 *with their backs toward the temple.* Almost all ancient temples were oriented toward the east. Worshiping the sun as it rose required one to turn his back to the temple. Sun worship was particularly emphasized in Egypt.

8:17 *they put the branch to their nose.* A ceremonial gesture in nature worship, not documented elsewhere in the Bible.

‡9:1 *loud voice.* The thunderous voice of God (see Ex 19:19 and Ps 29).

9:2 *six men came from the way of the higher gate.* These six guardian angels of the city, plus the seventh clothed in linen (cf. the seven angels of the judgment in Rev 8:2,6), came from the place where the idol that provoked to jealousy stood (see 8:3 and note). *slaughter weapon.* Probably a war club or a battle axe.

‡9:3 *the glory . . . was gone up.* God began to vacate the temple, His glory moving to the door (see note on 8:1–11:25). Ezekiel pictures His departure in deliberate, but reluctant stages.

9:4 *mark.* A *taw,* the last letter of the Hebrew alphabet, which originally looked like an "x" (cf. Rev 7:2–4; 13:16; 14:9,11; 20:4; 22:4). *the men that sigh and that cry.* The remnant (see Ex 12:23; 1 Ki 19:18).

9:6 *begin at my sanctuary.* Judgment begins with God's people (see 1 Pet 4:17).

9:8 *wilt thou . . . upon Jerusalem?* One of the few times Ezekiel questioned the Lord (see 11:13).

10:1 *I looked.* Ch. 10 echoes ch. 1, underscoring the identity of what Ezekiel saw at the river Chebar with what he now sees in

of the cherubims there appeared over them as it were a sapphire stone, as the appearance of the likeness of a throne.

2 [a]And he spake unto the man clothed with linen, and said, Go in between the wheels, *even* under the cherub, and fill [1] thine hand *with* [b]coals of fire from between the cherubims, and [c]scatter *them* over the city. And he went in in my sight.

3 Now the cherubims stood on the right side of the house, when the man went in; and the cloud filled the inner court.

4 [a]Then the glory of the LORD [1]went up from the cherub, *and stood* over the threshold of the house; and [b]the house was filled with the cloud, and the court was full of the brightness of the LORD'S glory.

5 And the [a]sound of the cherubims' wings was heard *even* to the utter court, as [b]the voice of the Almighty God when he speaketh.

6 And it came to pass, *that* when he had commanded the man clothed with linen, saying, Take fire from between the wheels, from between the cherubims; then he went in, and stood beside the wheels.

7 And *one* cherub [1]stretched forth his hand from between the cherubims unto the fire that *was* between the cherubims, and took *thereof,* and put *it* into the hands of *him that was* clothed with linen: who took *it,* and went out.

8 ¶ [a]And there appeared in the cherubims the form of a man's hand under their wings.

9 [a]And when I looked, behold the four wheels by the cherubims, one wheel by one cherub, and another wheel by another cherub: and the appearance of the wheels *was* as the colour of a [b]beryl stone.

10 And *as for* their appearances, they four had one likeness, as if a wheel had been in the midst of a wheel.

11 [a]When they went, they went upon their four sides; they turned not as they went, but *to* the place whither the head looked they followed it; they turned not as they went.

12 And their whole [1]body, and their backs, and their hands, and their wings, and the wheels, *were* full *of* eyes round about, *even* the wheels that they four had.

13 As for the wheels, [1]it was cried unto them in my hearing, O wheel.

14 [a]And *every* one had four faces: the first face *was* the face of a cherub, and the second face *was* the face of a man, and the third the face of a lion, and the fourth the face of an eagle.

15 And the cherubims were lifted up. This *is* [a]the living creature that I saw by the river of Chebar.

16 [a]And when the cherubims went, the wheels went by them: and when the cherubims lift up their wings to mount up from the earth, the same wheels also turned not from beside them.

17 [a]When they stood, *these* stood; and when they were lifted up, *these* lift up themselves *also:* for the spirit [1]of the living creature *was* in them.

18 ¶ Then [a]the glory of the LORD [b]departed from off the threshold of the house, and stood over the cherubims.

19 And [a]the cherubims lift up their wings, and mounted up from the earth in my sight: when they went out, the wheels also *were* besides them, and *every one* stood *at* the door of the east gate of the LORD'S house; and the glory of the God of Israel *was* over them above.

20 [a]This *is* the living creature that I saw under the God of Israel [b]by the river of Chebar; and I knew that they *were the* cherubims.

21 [a]Every one had four faces apiece, and every one four wings; and the likeness of the hands of a man *was* under their wings.

22 And [a]the likeness of their faces *was* the same faces which I saw by the river of Chebar, their appearances and themselves: [b]they went every one straight forward.

Ungodly rulers to be punished

11 Moreover [a]the spirit lift me up, and brought me unto [b]the east gate of the LORD'S house, which looketh eastward: and behold [c]at the door of the gate five and twenty men; among whom I saw Jaazaniah the son of Azur, and Pelatiah the son of Benaiah, princes of the people.

2 Then said he unto me, Son of man, these *are* the men that devise mischief, and give wicked counsel in this city:

3 Which say, [1]*It is* not [a]near; *let us* build houses: [b]this *city is* the caldron, and we *be* the flesh.

10:2 [1] Heb. *the hollow of thine hand* [a] ch. 9:2,3 [b] ch. 1:13 [c] See Rev. 8:5
10:4 [1] Heb. *was lifted up* [a] See ver. 18; ch. 1:28; 9:3 [b] 1 Ki. 8:10; ch. 43:5
10:5 [a] ch. 1:24 [b] Ps. 29:3
10:7 [1] Heb. *sent forth*
10:8 [a] ver. 21
10:9 [a] ch. 1:15 [b] ch. 1:16
10:11 [a] ch. 1:17
10:12 [1] Heb. *flesh*
10:13 [1] Or, *they were called in my hearing, wheel,* or, *Galgal*
10:14 [a] ch. 1:6,10
10:15 [a] ch. 1:5
10:16 [a] ch. 1:19
10:17 [1] Or, *of life* [a] ch. 1:12,20,21
10:18 [a] ver. 4 [b] Hos. 9:12
10:19 [a] ch. 11:22
10:20 [a] ver. 15; ch. 1:22 [b] ch. 1:1
10:21 [a] ch. 1:6
10:22 [a] ch. 1:10 [b] ch. 1:12
11:1 [a] ver. 24; ch. 3:12,14 [b] ch. 10:19 [c] See ch. 8:16
11:3 [1] Or, It is not for us to build houses near [a] ch. 12:22,27; 2 Pet. 3:4 [b] See Jer. 1:13; ch. 24:3

---

his vision (see 8:4). The creatures in ch. 1 are here called cherubims (see note on 1:5).

10:2 *coals of fire.* While in 1:13 the living creatures looked like burning coals, here there are real coals. *scatter them over the city.* A judgment by fire (see Gen 19:24; Amos 7:4).

‡10:4 *over the threshold.* The glory of God begins to ascend above the holy of holies.

10:7 *one cherub stretched forth his hand.* Though the "man clothed with linen" was initially commanded to get the coals himself (v. 2), he received them from the hand of one of the creatures (see 1:8). *who took it, and went out.* No further report is given, but the destructive spreading of the coals over Jerusalem is assumed.

10:14 *the first face was the face of a cherub.* While the faces of the man, lion and eagle are identical with those in 1:10, the ox is here called a cherub (see note on Gen 3:24).

‡10:19 *of the east gate . . . and the glory of the God of Israel was over them.* Another movement of the glory, again in an easterly direction (see 9:3; 10:4; see also note on 8:1–11:25). He departs gradually and unnoticed.

11:1 *Jaazaniah.* See note on 8:11. *Pelatiah.* Means "The LORD delivers."

11:3 *let us build houses.* The residents of Jerusalem who were not exiled in 597 B.C. felt smugly secure, thinking that nothing worse would befall them. *caldron.* As in ch. 24, Jerusalem is compared to a cooking pot. Those left behind boasted that they were the "meat," the choice portions—the inference being that the exiles in Babylon were the discarded bones (see v. 15).

4 Therefore prophesy against them, prophesy, O son of man.

5 And [a]the Spirit of the LORD fell upon me, and said unto me, Speak; Thus saith the LORD; Thus have ye said, O house of Israel: for I know the things that come into your mind, *every one of* them.

6 [a]Ye have multiplied your slain in this city, and ye have filled the streets thereof *with* the slain.

7 Therefore thus saith the Lord GOD; [a]Your slain whom ye have laid in the midst of it, they *are* the flesh, and this *city is* the caldron: [b]but *I* will bring you forth out of the midst of it.

8 Ye have feared the sword; and I will bring a sword upon you, saith the Lord GOD.

9 And I will bring you out of the midst thereof, and deliver you into the hands of strangers, and [a]will execute judgments among you.

10 [a]Ye shall fall by the sword; I will judge you in [b]the border of Israel; [c]and ye shall know that I *am* the LORD.

11 [a]This *city* shall not be your caldron, neither shall ye be the flesh in the midst thereof; *but* I will judge you in the border of Israel:

12 And [a]ye shall know that I *am* the LORD: [1]for ye have not walked in my statutes, neither executed my judgments, but [b]have done after the manners of the heathen that *are* round about you.

Hope for the remnant of Israel

13 ¶ And it came to pass, when I prophesied, that [a]Pelatiah the son of Benaiah died. Then [b]fell I down upon my face, and cried *with* a loud voice, and said, Ah Lord GOD, *wilt* thou make a full end of the remnant of Israel?

14 Again the word of the LORD came unto me, saying,

15 Son of man, thy brethren, *even* thy brethren, the men of thy kindred, and all the house of Israel wholly, *are* they unto whom the inhabitants of Jerusalem have said, Get ye far from the LORD: unto us is this land given in possession.

16 Therefore say, Thus saith the Lord GOD; Although I have cast them far off among the heathen, and although I have scattered them among the countries, [a]yet will I be to them as a little sanctuary in the countries where they shall come.

11:5 [a]ch. 2:2; 3:24
11:6 [a]ch. 7:23
11:7 [a]ch. 24:3,6; Mic. 3:3 [b]ver. 9
11:9 [a]ch. 5:8
11:10 [a]2 Ki. 25:19-21; Jer. 39:6; 52:10 [b]1 Ki. 8:65; 2 Ki. 14:25 [c]Ps. 9:16; ch. 6:7; 13:9,14,21,23
11:11 [a]See ver. 3
11:12 [1]Or, *which have not walked* [a]ver. 10 [b]Lev. 18:3,24; Deut. 12:30,31; ch. 8:10,14,16
11:13 [a]Acts 5:5 [b]ch. 9:8
11:16 [a]Ps. 90:1; 91:9; Is. 8:14

11:17 [a]Jer. 24:5; ch. 38:25; 34:13
11:18 [a]ch. 37:23
11:19 [a]Jer. 32:39; ch. 36:26; See Zeph. 3:9 [b]Ps. 51:10; Jer. 31:33; ch. 18:31 [c]Zech. 7:12
11:20 [a]Ps. 105:45 [b]Jer. 24:7; ch. 14:11; 36:28; 37:27
11:21 [a]ch. 9:10; 22:31
11:22 [a]ch. 1:19; 10:19
11:23 [a]ch. 8:4; 9:3; 10:4,18; 43:4 [b]See Zech. 14:4 [c]ch. 43:2
11:24 [a]ch. 8:3
12:2 [a]ch. 2:3,6-8; 3:26,27 [b]Is. 6:9; 42:20; Jer. 5:21; Mat. 13:13,14 [c]ch. 2:5
12:3 [1]Or, *instruments*

17 Therefore say, Thus saith the Lord GOD; [a]I will even gather you from the people, and assemble you out of the countries where ye have been scattered, and I will give you the land of Israel.

18 And they shall come thither, and [a]they shall take away all the detestable things thereof and all the abominations thereof from thence.

19 And [a]I will give them one heart, and I will put [b]a new spirit within you; and I will take [c]the stony heart out of their flesh, and will give them a heart of flesh:

20 [a]That they may walk in my statutes, and keep mine ordinances, and do them: [b]and they shall be my people, and I will be their God.

21 But *as for them* whose heart walketh after the heart of their detestable things and their abominations, [a]I will recompense their way upon their own heads, saith the Lord GOD.

22 ¶ Then did the cherubims [a]lift up their wings, and the wheels besides them; and the glory of the God of Israel *was* over them above.

23 And [a]the glory of the LORD went up from the midst of the city, and stood [b]upon the mountain [c]which *is* on the east side of the city.

24 Afterwards [a]the spirit took me up, and brought me in vision by the Spirit of God into Chaldea, to them of the captivity. So the vision that I had seen went up from me.

25 Then I spake unto them of the captivity all the things that the LORD had shewed me.

Captivity symbolized

12 The word of the LORD also came unto me, saying,

2 Son of man, thou dwellest in the midst of [a]a rebellious house, which [b]have eyes to see, and see not; they have ears to hear, and hear not: [c]for they *are* a rebellious house.

3 Therefore thou son of man, prepare thee [1]stuff for removing, and remove by day in their sight; and thou shalt remove from thy place to another place in their sight: it may be they will consider, though they *be* a rebellious house.

4 Then shalt thou bring forth thy stuff by

11:7 *Your slain whom ye have laid . . . are the flesh.* The meat, redefined by the prophet, is not those in power in Jerusalem (who will be driven out) but the innocent people they killed.
11:11 *in the border of Israel.* At Riblah (see 2 Ki 25:20–21).
11:13 *wilt thou . . . end.* See note on 9:8.
11:16 *will I be to them as a little sanctuary.* A key verse in Ezekiel. Although the exiles had been driven from Jerusalem and its sanctuary (the symbol of God's presence among His people), God Himself became their sanctuary, i.e., He was present among them. Later Christ also became a substitute for the temple (see John 2:19–21).
11:19 *one heart . . . new spirit.* Inner spiritual and moral transformation that results in single-minded commitment to the Lord and to His will (see 36:26).
11:20 *they shall be my people, and I will be their God.* The heart of God's covenant promise (see Ex 6:7).
‡11:23 *the glory of the LORD went up.* The final eastward movement of the glory (as the Lord left His temple), which stopped above the mount of Olives (see 9:3; 10:4,19; see also note on 8:1–11:25). God's glory ascends back to heaven from the same place where Jesus would later ascend (Acts 1:9–11), leaving the temple void of His presence.
11:24 See note on 8:3.
12:2 *eyes to see, and see not.* The hardening about which the Lord had spoken to Isaiah (Is 6:9–10).
12:3 *prepare thee stuff for removing.* Another symbolic act, which, like those in chs. 4–5, follows a vision. *it may be they will consider.* Some hope remained that they would change.

day in their sight, as stuff for removing: and thou shalt go forth at even in their sight, [1]as they that go forth into captivity.

5 [1]Dig thou through the wall in their sight, and carry out thereby.

6 In their sight shalt thou bear *it* upon *thy* shoulders, *and* carry *it* forth in the twilight: thou shalt cover thy face, that thou see not the ground: [a]for I have set thee *for* a sign unto the house of Israel.

7 And I did so as I was commanded: I brought forth my stuff by day, as stuff for captivity, and in the even I [1]digged through the wall with mine hand; I brought *it* forth in the twilight, *and* I bare *it* upon *my* shoulder in their sight.

8 ¶ And in the morning came the word of the LORD unto me, saying,

9 Son of man, hath not the house of Israel, [a]the rebellious house, said unto thee, [b]What doest thou?

10 Say thou unto them, Thus saith the Lord GOD; This [a]burden *concerneth* the prince in Jerusalem, and all the house of Israel that *are* among them.

11 Say, [a]I *am* your sign: like as I have done, so shall it be done unto them: [b1]they shall remove *and* go into captivity.

12 And [a]the prince that *is* among them shall bear upon *his* shoulder in the twilight, and shall go forth: they shall dig through the wall to carry out thereby: he shall cover his face, that he see not the ground with *his* eyes.

13 My [a]net also will I spread upon him, and he shall be taken in my snare: and [b]I will bring him to Babylon *to* the land of the Chaldeans; yet shall he not see it, though he shall die there.

14 And [a]I will scatter toward every wind all that *are* about him to help him, and all his bands; and [b]I will draw out the sword after them.

15 [a]And they shall know that I *am* the LORD, when I shall scatter them among the nations, and disperse them in the countries.

16 [a]But I will leave [1]a few men of them from the sword, from the famine, and from the pestilence; that they may declare all their abominations among the heathen whither they come; and they shall know that I *am* the LORD.

17 ¶ Moreover the word of the LORD came to me, saying,

18 Son of man, [a]eat thy bread with quaking, and drink thy water with trembling and with carefulness;

19 And say unto the people of the land, Thus saith the Lord GOD, of the inhabitants of Jerusalem, *and* of the land of Israel; They shall eat their bread with carefulness, and drink their water with astonishment, that her land may [a]be desolate from [1]all that is therein, [b]because of the violence of all them that dwell therein.

20 And the cities that are inhabited shall be laid waste, and the land shall be desolate; and ye shall know that I *am* the LORD.

21 ¶ And the word of the LORD came unto me, saying,

22 Son of man, what *is* that proverb *that* ye have in the land of Israel, saying, [a]The days are prolonged, and every vision faileth?

23 Tell them therefore, Thus saith the Lord GOD; I will make this proverb to cease, and they shall no more use it as a proverb in Israel; but say unto them, [a]The days are at hand, and the effect of every vision.

24 For [a]there shall be no more any [b]vain vision nor flattering divination within the house of Israel.

25 For I *am* the LORD: I will speak, and [a]the word that I shall speak shall come to pass; it shall be no more prolonged: for in your days, O rebellious house, will I say the word, and will perform it, saith the Lord GOD.

26 ¶ Again the word of the LORD came to me, saying,

27 [a]Son of man, behold, *they of* the house of Israel say, The vision that he seeth *is* for many days *to come,* and he prophesieth of the times *that are* far off.

28 [a]Therefore say unto them, Thus saith the Lord GOD; There shall none of my words be prolonged any more, but the word which I have spoken shall be done, saith the Lord GOD.

Prophecy against false prophets

13 And the word of the LORD came unto me, saying,

12:4 [1]Heb. *as the goings forth of captivity*
12:5 [1]Heb. *Dig for thee*
12:6 [a]ver. 11; Is. 8:18; ch. 4:3; 24:24
12:7 [1]Heb. *digged for me*
12:9 [a]ch. 2:5 [b]ch. 17:12; 24:19
12:10 [a]Mal. 1:1
12:11 [1]Heb. *by removing go into captivity* [a]ver. 6 [b]2 Ki. 25:4,5,7
12:12 [a]Jer. 39:4
12:13 [a]Job 19:6; Jer. 52:9; Lam. 1:13; ch. 17:20 [b]2 Ki. 25:7; Jer. 52:11; ch. 17:16
12:14 [a]2 Ki. 25:4; ch. 5:10 [b]ch. 5:2,12
12:15 [a]ver. 16,20; Ps. 9:16; ch. 6:7,14; 11:10
12:16 [1]Heb. *men of number* [a]ch. 6:8-10
12:18 [a]ch. 4:16
12:19 [1]Heb. *the fulness thereof* [a]Zech. 7:14 [b]Ps. 107:34
12:22 [a]ver. 27; ch. 11:3; Amos 6:3; 2 Pet. 3:4
12:23 [a]Joel 2:1; Zeph. 1:14
12:24 [a]ch. 13:23 [b]Lam. 2:14
12:25 [a]ver. 28; Is. 55:11; Dan. 9:12; Luke 21:33
12:27 [a]ver. 22
12:28 [a]ver. 23,25

12:5 *Dig . . . through the wall.* Not the city wall, which was made of stone and was many feet thick, but the sun-dried brick wall of his house.

12:6 *sign.* Prophets were often instructed to perform symbolic acts (see, e.g., v. 11; 24:24,27).

12:8 *in the morning.* After Ezekiel "did . . . as . . . commanded" (v. 7). Again the divine explanation follows the prophet's unquestioning obedience (see note on 8:3).

12:9 *What doest thou?* The book's first indication of the people's response to the prophet's symbolic acts.

12:10 *prince in Jerusalem.* Zedekiah (see note on 7:27).

12:13 *yet shall he not see it.* Nebuchadnezzar's men would put out Zedekiah's eyes (see 2 Ki 25:7).

12:18 *eat . . . with quaking.* Another prophetic symbol. Ezekiel's trembling must have been particularly violent, because the Hebrew word for "quake" is used elsewhere to describe an earthquake (see 1 Ki 19:11; Amos 1:1).

12:19 *inhabitants . . . of the land.* See note on 7:27.

12:22 *proverb.* A mocking proverb (probably coined by false prophets; see ch. 13; Jer 23:9–40; 28), which had become a popular saying. *vision.* The Hebrew for this word is not the same as that used in 1:1 but is the one used in 7:26, referring to a message that could be written down (see Hab 2:2)—specifically Ezekiel's oracles of judgment.

12:23 *effect of every vision.* Divine affirmation of the true prophetic word (cf. Is 55:11).

12:27 *for many days to come.* Whereas the first proverb denies that Ezekiel's words would ever be fulfilled, this one allows that they might be fulfilled in the distant future, beyond the concern of the present generation.

2 Son of man, prophesy against the prophets of Israel that prophesy, and say thou unto [a][1]them that prophesy out of their own [b]hearts, Hear ye the word of the LORD;

3 Thus saith the Lord GOD; Woe unto the foolish prophets, that [1]follow their own spirit, [2]and have seen nothing!

4 O Israel, thy prophets are [a]like the foxes in the deserts.

5 Ye [a]have not gone up into the [1]gaps, neither [2]made up the hedge for the house of Israel to stand in the battle in the day of the LORD.

6 [a]They have seen vanity and lying divination, saying, The LORD saith: and the LORD hath not sent them: and they have made *others* to hope that *they* would confirm the word.

7 Have ye not seen a vain vision, and have ye not spoken a lying divination, whereas ye say, The LORD saith *it;* albeit I have not spoken?

8 Therefore thus saith the Lord GOD; Because ye have spoken vanity, and seen lies, therefore behold, I *am* against you, saith the Lord GOD.

9 And mine hand shall be upon the prophets that see vanity, and that divine lies: they shall not be in the [1]assembly of my people, [a]neither shall they be written in the writing of the house of Israel, [b]neither shall they enter into the land of Israel; [c]and ye shall know that I *am* the Lord GOD.

10 Because, even because they have seduced my people, saying, [a]Peace; and *there was* no peace; and one built up [1]a wall, and lo, others [b]daubed it *with* untempered *morter:*

11 Say unto them which daub *it with* untempered *morter,* that it shall fall: [a]there shall be an overflowing shower; and ye, O great hailstones, shall fall; and a stormy wind shall rent *it.*

12 Lo, when the wall is fallen, shall it not be said unto you, Where *is* the daubing where*with* ye have daubed *it?*

13 Therefore thus saith the Lord GOD; I will even rent *it with* a stormy wind in my fury; and there shall be an overflowing shower in mine anger, and great hailstones in *my* fury to consume *it.*

13:2 [1]Heb. *them that are prophets out of their own hearts* [a]ver. 17 [b]Jer. 14:14; 23:16,26
13:3 [1]Heb. *walk after* [2]Or, *and things which they have not seen*
13:4 [a]Sol. 2:15
13:5 [1]Or, *breaches* [2]Heb. *hedged the hedge* [a]Ps. 106:23,30; ch. 22:30
13:6 [a]ver. 23; ch. 12:24; 22:28
13:9 [1]Or, *secret,* or, *counsel* [a]Ezra 2:59,62; Neh. 7:5; Ps. 69:28 [b]ch. 20:38 [c]ch. 11:10,12
13:10 [1]Or, *a slight wall* [a]Jer. 6:14; 8:11 [b]ch. 22:28
13:11 [a]ch. 38:22
13:14 [a]ver. 9,21,23; ch. 14:8
13:16 [a]Jer. 6:14; 28:9
13:17 [a]ch. 20:46; 21:2 [b]ver. 2
13:18 [1]Or, *elbows* [a]2 Pet. 2:14
13:19 [a]See Prov. 28:21; Mic. 3:5
13:20 [1]Or, *into gardens*
13:21 [a]ver. 9
13:22 [1]Or, *that I should save his life* [2]Heb. *by quickening him* [a]Jer. 23:14
13:23 [a]ver. 6; ch. 12:24; Mic. 3:6

14 So will I break down the wall that ye have daubed *with* untempered *morter,* and bring it down to the ground, so that the foundation thereof shall be discovered, and it shall fall, and ye shall be consumed in the midst thereof: [a]and ye shall know that I *am* the LORD.

15 Thus will I accomplish my wrath upon the wall, and upon them that have daubed it *with* untempered *morter,* and will say unto you, The wall *is* no *more,* neither they that daubed it;

16 *To wit,* the prophets of Israel which prophesy concerning Jerusalem, and which [a]see visions of peace for her, and *there is* no peace, saith the Lord GOD.

17 ¶ Likewise thou son of man, [a]set thy face against the daughters of thy people, [b]which prophesy out of their own heart; and prophesy thou against them,

18 And say, Thus saith the Lord GOD; Woe to *the women* that sew pillows to all [1]armholes, and make kerchiefs upon the head of every stature to hunt souls! Will ye [a]hunt the souls of my people, and will ye save the souls alive *that come* unto you?

19 And will ye pollute me among my people [a]for handfuls of barley and for pieces of bread, to slay the souls that should not die, and to save the souls alive that should not live, by your lying to my people that hear *your* lies?

20 Wherefore thus saith the Lord GOD; Behold, I *am* against your pillows, where*with* ye there hunt the souls [1]to make *them* fly, and I will tear them from your arms, and will let the souls go, *even* the souls that ye hunt to make *them* fly.

21 Your kerchiefs also will I tear, and deliver my people out of your hand, and they shall be no more in your hand to be hunted; [a]and ye shall know that I *am* the LORD.

22 Because *with* lies *ye* have made the heart of the righteous sad, whom I have not made sad; and [a]strengthened the hands of the wicked, that *he* should not return from his wicked way, [1][2]by promising him life:

23 Therefore [a]ye shall see no more vanity, nor divine divinations: for I will deliver my

---

‡13:2 *out of their own hearts.* Cf. Jer 23:21–22.
13:3 *have seen nothing.* No revelation from God was received.
‡13:4 *foxes.* The Hebrew word may also be translates as "jackals." Both are animals that travel in packs and feed on dead flesh—a powerfully negative image (see Ps 63:10; Lam 5:18).
13:5 *Ye have not gone up.* The function of true prophets is described (cf. 22:30; Ps 106:23). *day of the LORD.* See note on 7:7.
13:6 *They have seen vanity.* Whether the false prophets had actual visions is unknown, but they claimed to have received revelations from God when in reality their messages only proclaimed what their hearers wanted to hear (see Is 30:10; Jer 23:9–17; 2 Tim 4:3).
13:8 *I am against you.* See 5:8 and note.
13:9 *they shall not be.* Part of a threefold punishment, resulting in total exclusion from the community.
13:10 *Peace; and there was no peace.* See v. 16; Jer 6:14; 8:11. *untempered morter.* The Hebrew for this word is used only by Ezekiel (see 22:28). A similar-sounding Hebrew word means "unsatisfying things," and Ezekiel may have chosen the word he did because of its similarity to the other one.
13:11 *shall be an overflowing shower.* The violent thunderstorm of God's judgment (imagery frequently used in the OT) was about to sweep them away (see, e.g., Ps 18:7–15; 77:17–18; 83:15; Is 28:17; 30:30; Jer 23:19; 30:23).
13:18 *women that sew pillows to all armholes.* Exactly what the women were doing is not known, but that it was some kind of black magic or voodoo is clear. The Bible consistently avoids explicit description of occult practices.
13:19 *for handfuls of barley.* Involvement in religious matters of any kind for mere gain is consistently condemned in the Bible (see, e.g., Jer 6:13; 8:10; Mic 3:5,11; Acts 8:9–24; Tit 1:11). For the proper attitude and motivation see 2 Cor 11:7; 2 Thes 3:8; 1 Tim 3:3. *to . . . slay.* The women had used their evil powers to unjust ends, involving even matters of life and death.

people out of your hand: and ye shall know that I *am* the LORD.

Call to turn from idols

14 Then [a]came certain of the elders of Israel unto me, and sat before me.

2 And the word of the LORD came unto me, saying,

3 Son of man, these men have set up their idols in their heart, and put [a]the stumblingblock of their iniquity before their face: [b]should I be inquired of at all by them?

4 Therefore speak unto them, and say unto them, Thus saith the Lord GOD; Every man of the house of Israel that setteth up his idols in his heart, and putteth the stumblingblock of his iniquity before his face, and cometh to the prophet; I the LORD will answer him that cometh according to the multitude of his idols;

5 That *I* may take the house of Israel in their own heart, because they are all estranged from me through their idols.

6 Therefore say unto the house of Israel, Thus saith the Lord GOD; Repent, and turn [1]*yourselves* from your idols; and turn away your faces from all your abominations.

7 For every one of the house of Israel, or of the stranger that sojourneth in Israel, which separateth himself from me, and setteth up his idols in his heart, and putteth the stumblingblock of his iniquity before his face, and cometh to a prophet to inquire of him concerning me; I the LORD will answer him by myself:

8 And [a]I will set my face against that man, and will make him a [b]sign and a proverb, and I will cut him off from the midst of my people; [c]and ye shall know that I *am* the LORD.

9 And if the prophet be deceived when he hath spoken a thing, I the LORD [a]have deceived that prophet, and I will stretch out my hand upon him, and will destroy him from the midst of my people Israel.

10 And they shall bear the punishment of their iniquity: the punishment of the prophet shall be even as the punishment of him that seeketh *unto him;*

11 That the house of Israel may [a]go no more astray from me, neither be polluted any more with all their transgressions; [b]but that they may be my people, and I may be their God, saith the Lord GOD.

Deliverance through righteousness

12 ¶ The word of the LORD came again to me, saying,

13 Son of man, when the land sinneth against me by trespassing grievously, then will I stretch out mine hand upon it, and will break the [a]staff of the bread thereof, and will send famine upon it, and will cut off man and beast from it:

14 [a]Though these three men, Noah, Daniel, and Job, were in it, they should deliver *but* their own souls [b]by their righteousness, saith the Lord GOD.

15 If I cause [a]noisome beasts to pass through the land, and they [1]spoil it, so that it be desolate, that no man may pass through because of the beasts:

16 [a]*Though* these three men *were* [1]in it, *as* I live, saith the Lord GOD, they shall deliver neither sons nor daughters; they only shall be delivered, but the land shall be desolate.

17 Or *if* [a]I bring a sword upon that land, and say, Sword, go through the land; so that I [b]cut off man and beast from it:

18 [a]Though these three men *were* in it, *as* I live, saith the Lord GOD, they shall deliver neither sons nor daughters, but they only shall be delivered themselves.

19 Or *if* I send [a]a pestilence into that land, and [b]pour out my fury upon it in blood, to cut off from it man and beast:

20 [a]Though Noah, Daniel, and Job, *were* in it, *as* I live, saith the Lord GOD, they shall deliver neither son nor daughter; they shall *but* deliver their own souls by their righteousness.

21 For thus saith the Lord GOD; [1]How much more when [a]I send my four sore judgments upon Jerusalem, the sword, and the famine, and the noisome beast, and the pestilence, to cut off from it man and beast?

22 [a]Yet behold, therein shall be left a remnant that shall be brought forth, *both* sons and daughters: behold, they *shall* come forth unto you, and [b]ye shall see their way and their doings: and ye shall be comforted concerning the evil that I have brought upon Jerusalem, *even* concerning all that I have brought upon it.

14:1 [a]ch. 8:1; 20:1; 33:31
14:3 [a]ver. 4,7; ch. 7:19 [b]2 Ki. 3:13
14:6 [1]Or, others
14:8 [a]Lev. 17:10; 20:3,5,6; Jer. 44:11; ch. 15:7 [b]Num. 26:10; Deut. 28:37; ch. 5:15 [c]ch. 6:7
14:9 [a]1 Ki. 22:23; Job 12:16; Jer. 4:10; 2 Thes. 2:11
14:11 [a]2 Pet. 2:15 [b]ch. 11:20; 37:27
14:13 [a]Lev. 26:26; Is. 3:1; ch. 4:16; 5:16
14:14 [a]ver. 16,18,20; Jer. 15:1; See Jer. 7:16; 11:14; 14:11 [b]Prov. 11:4
14:15 [1]Or, *bereave* [a]Lev. 26:22; ch. 5:17
14:16 [1]Heb. *in the midst of it* [a]ver. 14,18,20
14:17 [a]Lev. 26:25; ch. 5:12; 21:3,4; 29:8; 38:21 [b]ch. 25:13; Zeph. 1:3
14:18 [a]ver. 14
14:19 [a]2 Sam. 24:15; ch. 38:22 [b]ch. 7:8
14:20 [a]ver. 14
14:21 [1]Or, *Also when* [a]ch. 5:17; 33:27
14:22 [a]ch. 6:8 [b]ch. 20:43

14:1 *elders of Israel.* Apparently interchangeable with "elders of Judah" (see note on 8:1).

14:3 *idols.* See note on 6:4. *be inquired of.* A technical term for seeking an oracle from a prophet (see 2 Ki 1:16; 3:11; 8:8).

‡14:4 *I the LORD will answer him.* The punishment for idolatry was death (Deut 13:6–18).

14:6 *Repent.* First of three calls for repentance from Ezekiel, who elsewhere proclaims inescapable judgment (see 18:30; 33:11, "turn ye").

14:9 *be deceived.* Related to the divine hardening (3:20; cf. 1 Ki 22:19–23).

14:14,20 *Noah, Daniel, and Job.* Three ancient men of renown, selected because of their proverbial righteousness. Because the Hebrew here spells "Danel" instead of "Daniel," another Daniel may be referred to (Ugaritic literature speaks of an honored "Danel"; see chart, p. xix), since the Biblical Daniel's righteousness probably had not become proverbial so soon (Daniel and Ezekiel were contemporaries; see Dan 1:1). If the Biblical Daniel is meant, what he shared in common with Noah and Job was not only righteousness but also deliverance (part of Ezekiel's emphasis).

‡14:20 *neither son nor daughter.* When God comes in judgment against a nation or people, no one can count on another's righteousness—not even that of his parents—to deliver him.

14:21 *my four sore judgments.* See note on 1:5. *sword, and the famine, and the noisome beast, and the pestilence.* Cf. the "four horsemen of the Apocalypse" (see Rev 6:1–8, and especially Rev 6:8).

23 And they shall comfort you, when ye see their ways and their doings: and ye shall know that I have not done [a]without cause all that I have done in it, saith the Lord GOD.

The parable of the vine

15 And the word of the LORD came unto me, saying,

2 Son of man, What is the vine tree more than any tree, *or than* a branch which is among the trees of the forest?

3 Shall wood be taken thereof to do *any* work? or will *men* take a pin of it to hang any vessel thereon?

4 Behold, [a]it is cast into the fire for fuel; the fire devoureth both the ends of it, and the midst of it is burnt. [1]Is it meet for *any* work?

5 Behold, when it was whole, it was [1]meet for no work: how much less shall it be meet yet for *any* work, when the fire hath devoured it, and it is burned?

6 Therefore thus saith the Lord GOD; As the vine tree among the trees of the forest, which I have given to the fire for fuel, so will I give the inhabitants of Jerusalem.

7 And [a]I will set my face against them; [b]they shall go out from *one* fire, and *another* fire shall devour them; [c]and ye shall know that I *am* the LORD, when I set my face against them.

8 And I will make the land desolate, because they have [1]committed a trespass, saith the Lord GOD.

The judgment upon Israel

16 Again the word of the LORD came unto me, saying,

2 Son of man, [a]cause Jerusalem to know her abominations,

3 And say, Thus saith the Lord GOD unto Jerusalem; Thy [1]birth [a]and thy nativity *is* of the land of Canaan; [b]thy father *was* an Amorite, and thy mother a Hittite.

4 And *as for* thy nativity, [a]in the day thou wast born thy navel was not cut, neither wast thou washed in water [1]to supple *thee;* thou wast not salted at all, nor swaddled at all.

5 None eye pitied thee, to do any of these unto thee, to have compassion upon thee; but thou wast cast out in the open field, to the lothing of thy person, in the day that thou wast born.

6 ¶ And when I passed by thee, and saw thee [1]polluted in thine own blood, I said unto thee *when thou wast* in thy blood, Live; yea, I said unto thee *when thou wast* in thy blood, Live.

7 [a]I have [1]caused thee to multiply as the bud of the field, and thou hast increased and waxen great, and thou art come to [2]excellent ornaments: *thy* breasts are fashioned, and thine hair is grown, whereas thou *wast* naked and bare.

8 Now when I passed by thee, and looked upon thee, behold, thy time *was* the time of love; [a]and I spread my skirt over thee, and covered thy nakedness: yea, I sware unto thee, and entered into a covenant with thee, saith the Lord GOD, and [b]thou becamest mine.

9 Then washed I thee with water; yea, I throughly washed away thy [1]blood from thee, and I anointed thee with oil.

10 I clothed thee also with broidered work, and shod thee *with* badgers' *skin,* and I girded thee about with fine linen, and I covered thee *with* silk.

11 I decked thee also *with* ornaments, and I [a]put bracelets upon thine hands, [b]and a chain on thy neck.

14:23 [a]Jer. 22:8,9
15:4 [1]Heb. *Will it prosper?* [a]John 15:6
15:5 [1]Heb. *made* fit
15:7 [a]Lev. 17:10; ch. 14:8 [b]Is. 24:18 [c]ch. 7:4
15:8 [1]Heb. *trespassed a trespass*
16:2 [a]ch. 20:4; 22:2
16:3 [1]Heb. *cutting out,* or, *habitation* [a]ch. 21:30 [b]ver. 45
16:4 [1]Or, *when I looked* upon thee [a]Hos. 2:3
16:6 [1]Or, *trodden under foot*
16:7 [1]Heb. *made thee a million* [2]Heb. *ornament of ornaments* [a]Ex. 1:7
16:8 [a]Ruth 3:9 [b]Ex. 19:5; Jer. 2:2
16:9 [1]Heb. *bloods*
16:11 [a]Gen. 24:22 [b]Prov. 1:9

14:23 *shall comfort you.* When the exiles see the wickedness of those brought to Babylon from Jerusalem, they will know that God's judgment on the city was just. *you.* Plural; i.e., the exiles in Babylon.

15:2 *vine.* For Israel as a vine see Ps 80:8–13; Is 5:1–7; cf. Luke 20:9–19; John 15:1–17.

15:3 *will men take a pin . . . to hang any vessel thereon?* See Is 22:23–25.

15:4 *Is it meet for any work?* Whereas Isaiah (5:1–7) and Jeremiah (2:21) express divine disappointment over Israel's failure to produce good fruit, Ezekiel typically laments her total uselessness.

15:7 *they shall go out from one fire, and another.* A reference to the siege of Jerusalem in 597 B.C., which resulted in the exile of which Ezekiel was a part (see 1:2; 2 Ki 24:10–16). *fire shall devour them.* Prophecy threatening another and more devastating siege—Ezekiel's main message before 586 (see 5:2,4; 10:2,7).

16:3 Cf. Deut 26:5. *Thy birth and thy nativity.* Jerusalem had a centuries-old, pre-Israelite history (Gen 14:18), and the city long resisted Israelite conquest (Josh 15:63). It became fully Israelite only after David's conquest (2 Sam 5:6–9). *father . . . mother.* A reference to Jerusalem's non-Israelite origin generally, not to any specific individuals. *Amorite.* Cf. v. 45. Like the Canaanites, the Amorites were pre-Israelite, Semitic inhabitants of Canaan (Gen 48:22; Josh 5:1; 10:5; Judg 1:34–36). *Hittite.* The Hittites were non-Semitic residents of Canaan, who earlier had flourished in Asia Minor during the second millennium B.C. (see Gen 23:10–20; 26:34; 1 Sam 26:6; 2 Sam 11:2–27; 1 Ki 11:1).

16:4 *thou wast not salted at all.* This practice has been observed among Arab peasants in the Holy Land as late as A.D. 1918. *swaddled.* Cf. Luke 2:7.

‡16:5 *cast out in the open field.* Abandoned to die. Exposure of infants, common in ancient pagan societies, was abhorrent to Israel.

16:6 *blood.* Of childbirth. *Live.* God's basic desire for all people, summed up in one word (see 18:23,32; 1 Tim 2:4; 2 Pet 3:9).

16:7 *hair.* Pubic hair (see Is 7:20).

16:8 *spread my skirt.* Symbolic of entering a marriage relationship (see notes on Deut 22:30; Ruth 3:9). *covenant.* Since the maiden symbolizes Jerusalem, this does not refer to the Sinai covenant but to marriage as a covenant (see Mal 2:14).

16:9 *blood.* Menstrual blood, indicating sexual maturity.

16:10 *broidered work, and shod thee with badgers' skin . . . fine linen.* Representative of the very best garments. *broidered work.* See 27:16,24; colored, variegated material fit for a queen (see Ps 45:14). *badgers' skin.* The same kind of leather was used to cover the tabernacle (Ex 25:5; 26:14).

‡16:11 *bracelets upon thine hands.* See Gen 24:22.

16:12 *on thy forehead.* See KJV marg. The jewel did not pierce

12 And I put a jewel on thy [1]forehead, and
earrings in thine ears, and a beautiful crown
upon thine head.
13 Thus wast thou decked *with* gold and
silver; and thy raiment *was of* fine linen, and
silk, and broidered work; [a]thou didst eat fine
flour, and honey, and oil: and thou wast exceeding [b]beautiful, and thou didst prosper into
a kingdom.
14 And [a]thy renown went forth among the
heathen for thy beauty: for it *was* perfect
through my comeliness, which I had put upon
thee, saith the Lord GOD.
15 ¶ [a]But thou didst trust in thine own
beauty, [b]and playedst the harlot because of thy
renown, and pouredst out thy fornications on
every one that passed by; his it was.
16 [a]And of thy garments thou didst take,
and deckedst thy high places with divers
colours, and playedst the harlot thereupon: *the
like things shall* not come, neither shall it be *so.*
17 Thou hast also taken thy fair jewels of
my gold and of my silver, which I had given
thee, and madest to thyself images [1]of men,
and didst commit whoredom with them,
18 And tookest thy broidered garments,
and coveredst them: and thou hast set mine oil
and mine incense before them.
19 [a]My meat also which I gave thee, fine
flour, and oil, and honey, *wherewith* I fed thee,
thou hast even set it before them for [1]a sweet
savour: and *thus* it was, saith the Lord GOD.
20 [a]Moreover thou hast taken thy sons and
thy daughters, whom thou hast borne unto
me, and these hast thou sacrificed unto them
[1]to be devoured. *Is this* of thy whoredoms a
small matter,
21 That thou hast slain my children, and
delivered them to cause them to pass through
the fire for them?
22 And in all thine abominations and thy
whoredoms thou hast not remembered the
days of thy [a]youth, [b]when thou wast naked
and bare, *and* wast polluted in thy blood.
23 And it came to pass after all thy wickedness, (woe, woe unto thee! saith the Lord GOD;)
24 *That* [a]thou hast also built unto thee an
[1]eminent place, and [b]hast made thee a high
place in every street.
25 Thou hast built thy high place [a]at every
head of the way, and hast made thy beauty to
be abhorred, and hast opened thy feet to every
one that passed by, and multiplied thy whoredoms.
26 Thou hast also committed fornication
with [a]the Egyptians thy neighbours, great of
flesh; and hast increased thy whoredoms, to
provoke me to anger.
27 Behold therefore, I have stretched out
my hand over thee, and have diminished thine
ordinary *food,* and delivered thee unto the
will of them that hate thee, [a]the [1]daughters of
the Philistines, which are ashamed of thy lewd
way.
28 Thou hast played the whore also with
the Assyrians, because thou wast unsatiable;
yea, thou hast played the harlot with them,
and yet couldest not be satisfied.
29 Thou hast moreover multiplied thy fornication in the land of Canaan [a]unto Chaldea;
and yet thou wast not satisfied herewith.
30 How weak is thine heart, saith the Lord
GOD, seeing thou doest all these *things,* the
work of an imperious whorish woman;
31 [1]In that [a]thou buildest thine eminent
place in the head of every way, and makest
thine high place in every street; and hast not
been as a harlot, in that *thou* scornest hire;
32 *But as* a wife that committeth adultery,
which taketh strangers instead of her husband.
33 They give gifts to all whores: but [a]thou
givest thy gifts to all thy lovers, and [1]hirest
them, that *they* may come unto thee on every
side for thy whoredom.
34 And the contrary is in thee from *other*
women in thy whoredoms, whereas none followeth thee to commit whoredoms: and in
that thou givest a reward, and no reward is
given unto thee, therefore thou art contrary.
35 ¶ Wherefore, O harlot, hear the word of
the LORD:
36 Thus saith the Lord GOD; Because thy
filthiness was poured out, and thy nakedness
discovered through thy whoredoms with thy

16:12 [1][Heb. *nose:* See Is. 3:21] **16:13** [a]Deut. 32:13,14 [b]Ps. 48:2 **16:14** [a]Lam. 2:15 **16:15** [a]Deut. 32:15; Jer. 7:4; Mic. 3:11 [b]Is. 1:21; 57:8; Jer. 2:20; 3:2,6,20; ch. 23:3,8 **16:16** [a]2 Ki. 23:7; ch. 7:20; Hos. 2:8 **16:17** [1]Heb. *of a male* **16:19** [1]Heb. *a savour of rest* [a]Hos. 2:8 **16:20** [1]Heb. *to devour* [a]2 Ki. 16:3; Ps. 106:37; Is. 57:5; Jer. 7:31; ch. 20:26 **16:22** [a]ver. 43,60; Jer. 2:2; Hos. 11:1 [b]ver. 4,5,6 **16:24** [a]ver. 31

16:24 [1]Or, *brothel house* [b]Is. 57:5,7; Jer. 2:20; 3:2 **16:25** [a]Prov. 9:14 **16:26** [a]ch. 8:10,14 **16:27** [1]Or, *cities* [a]ver. 57; 2 Chr. 28:18 **16:29** [a]ch. 23:14 **16:31** [1]Or, *In thy daughters is thine, etc.* [a]ver. 24,39 **16:33** [1]Heb. *bribest* [a]Is. 30:6; Hos. 8:9

the nose but was worn on the outer portion of it (see Gen 28:47). *earrings.* Circular ear ornaments, worn by men (Num 31:50). The Hebrew for this word is not the same as that used in Gen 35:4; Ex 32:2–3. *crown.* The wedding crown (see Sol 3:11, where the groom wears it).

16:13 *gold and silver.* Cf. Hos 2:8. *fine flour.* Used in offerings, therefore of high quality (see v. 19; 46:14). *oil.* Cf. Hos 2:8. For the combination of honey and oil see Deut 32:13. *thou wast exceeding beautiful.* Cf. Eph 5:27.

16:14 *thy renown went forth.* Especially in the time of David and Solomon.

16:15 *harlot.* The accusation of prostitution referred both to spiritual turning away from the Lord and to physical involvement with the fertility rites of Canaanite paganism (cf. Jer 3:1–5; Hos 4:13–14; 9:1). *fornications.* Sexual favors. Verb and noun forms of the Hebrew for this word occur 23 times in this chapter. *every one that passsed by.* Cf. Gen 38:14–16.

16:16 *garments.* All of the Lord's previous gifts were used by Jerusalem in prostituting herself. Cloths of some kind were needed in the Asherah cult practices (see 2 Ki 23:7). They may have been used as curtains or as bedding (see Amos 2:7–8).

16:17 *images of men.* Phallic symbols or pictures of naked men (see 23:14).

16:20 *sons and thy daughters . . . sacrificed.* See 20:26,31; 23:37; 2 Ki 21:6; 23:10; Jer 7:31; 19:5; 32:35. Laws against child sacrifice are recorded in Lev 18:21; 20:2; Deut 12:31; 18:10.

16:24 *an eminent place . . . high place.* Cultic prostitution was moved from the high places (v. 15), which were outside the towns, into Jerusalem.

16:26 *neighbours.* Nowhere else in the OT are the Egyptians called "neighbors." *great of flesh.* The Hebrew is more graphic: "having oversized organs." The language reflects both God's and Ezekiel's disgust with Jerusalem's apostasy.

16:33 *thou givest thy gifts to all thy lovers.* Jerusalem's perversity is here pictured as worse than adultery and ordinary prostitution (see also v. 34).

lovers, and with all the idols of thy abominations, and by [a]the blood of thy children, which thou didst give unto them;

37 Behold therefore, [a]I will gather all thy lovers, with whom thou hast taken pleasure, and all *them* that thou hast loved, with all *them* that thou hast hated; I will even gather them round about against thee, and will discover thy nakedness unto them, that they may see all thy nakedness.

38 And I will judge thee, [1]as [a]*women* that break wedlock and [b]shed blood are judged; and I will give thee blood in fury and jealousy.

39 And I will also give thee into their hand, and they shall throw down [a]thine eminent place, and shall break down thy high places: [b]they shall strip thee also of thy clothes, and shall take [1]thy fair jewels, and leave thee naked and bare.

40 [a]They shall also bring up a company against thee, [b]and they shall stone thee with stones, and thrust thee through with their swords.

41 And they shall [a]burn thine houses with fire, and [b]execute judgments upon thee in the sight of many women: and I will cause thee to [c]cease from playing the harlot, and thou also shalt give no hire any more.

42 So [a]will I make my fury towards thee to rest, and my jealousy shall depart from thee, and I will be quiet, and will be no more angry.

43 Because [a]thou hast not remembered the days of thy youth, but hast fretted me in all these *things;* behold therefore, [b]I also will recompense thy way upon *thine* head, saith the Lord GOD: and thou shalt not commit *this* lewdness above all thine abominations.

44 ¶ Behold, every one that useth proverbs shall use *this* proverb against thee, saying, As *is* the mother, *so is* her daughter.

45 Thou *art* thy mother's daughter, that lotheth her husband and her children; and thou *art* the sister of thy sisters, which lothed their husbands and their children: [a]your mother *was* a Hittite, and your father an Amorite.

46 And thine elder sister *is* Samaria, she and her daughters that dwell at thy left hand: and [a][1]thy younger sister, that dwelleth at thy right hand, *is* Sodom and her daughters.

47 Yet hast thou not walked after their ways, nor done after their abominations: but, [1]as *if that were* a very little *thing,* [a]thou wast corrupted more than they in all thy ways.

48 *As* I live, saith the Lord GOD, [a]Sodom thy sister hath not done, she nor her daughters, as thou hast done, thou and thy daughters.

49 Behold, this was the iniquity of thy sister Sodom, pride, [a]fulness of bread, and abundance of idleness was in her and in her daughters, neither did she strengthen the hand of the poor and needy.

50 And they were haughty, and [a]committed abomination before me: therefore [b]I took them away as I saw *good.*

51 Neither hath Samaria committed half of thy sins; but thou hast multiplied thine abominations more than they, and [a]hast justified thy sisters in all thine abominations which thou hast done.

52 Thou also, which hast judged thy sisters, bear thine own shame for thy sins that thou hast committed more abominable than they: they are more righteous than thou: yea, be thou confounded also, and bear thy shame, in that thou hast justified thy sisters.

53 ¶ [a]When I shall bring again their captivity, [b]the captivity of Sodom and her daughters, and the captivity of Samaria and her daughters, then *will I bring again* the captivity of thy captives in the midst of them:

54 That thou mayest bear thine own shame, and mayest be confounded in all that thou hast done, in that thou art [a]a comfort unto them.

55 When thy sisters, Sodom and her daughters, shall return to their former estate, and Samaria and her daughters shall return to their former estate, then thou and thy daughters shall return to your former estate.

56 For thy sister Sodom was not [1]mentioned by thy mouth in the day of thy [2]pride,

57 Before thy wickedness was discovered, as *at* the time of *thy* [a]reproach of the daughters of [1]Syria, and all *that are* round about her, [b]the daughters of the Philistines, which [2]despise thee round about.

58 [a]Thou hast [1]borne thy lewdness and thine abominations, saith the LORD.

59 For thus saith the Lord GOD; I will even deal with thee as thou hast done, which hast [a]despised [b]the oath in breaking the covenant.

16:36 [a]ver. 20; Jer. 2:34
16:37 [a]Jer. 13:22,26; Lam. 1:8; ch. 23:9,10,22,29; Hos. 2:10; 8:10; Nah. 3:5
16:38 [1]Heb. with *judgments of* [a]Lev. 20:10; Deut. 22:22; ch. 23:45 [b]See ver. 20,36; Gen. 9:6; Ex. 21:12
16:39 [1]Heb. *instruments of thine ornament* [a]ver. 24,31 [b]ch. 23:26; Hos. 2:3
16:40 [a]ch. 23:46 [b]John 8:5,7
16:41 [a]Deut. 13:16; 2 Ki. 25:9; Jer. 39:8; 52:13 [b]ch. 5:8; 23:10,48 [c]ch. 23:27
16:42 [a]ch. 5:13
16:43 [a]ver. 22; Ps. 78:42 [b]ch. 9:10; 11:21; 22:31
16:45 [a]ver. 3
16:46 [1]Heb. *lesser than thou* [a]Deut. 32:32; Is. 1:10
16:47 [1]Or, *that was lothed as a small* thing [a]ver. 48,51; 2 Ki. 21:9; ch. 5:6,7
16:48 [a]Mat. 10:15; 11:24
16:49 [a]Gen. 13:10
16:50 [a]Gen. 13:13; 18:20; 19:5 [b]Gen. 19:24
16:51 [a]Jer. 3:11; Mat. 12:41
16:53 [a]See Is. 1:9; ver. 60 [b]Jer. 20:16
16:54 [a]ch. 14:22
16:56 [1]Heb. *for a report,* or, *hearing* [2]Heb. *prides,* or, *excellencies*
16:57 [1]Heb. *Aram* [2]Or, *spoil* [a]2 Ki. 16:5; 2 Chr. 28:18; Is. 7:1; 14:28 [b]ver. 27
16:58 [1]Heb. *borne them* [a]ch. 23:49
16:59 [a]ch. 17:13 [b]Deut. 29:12

16:37 *discover thy nakedness.* A reversal of the marriage covering (v. 8) and a return to the state described in v. 7.

16:38 *judge thee.* The punishment was death (see Lev 20:10; Deut 22:22) by stoning (see v. 40; Deut 22:21–24; John 8:5–7) or burning (Gen 38:24).

16:39 *thine eminent place . . . thy high places.* The cultic centers within the city (see v. 24).

16:40 *a company . . . shall stone thee.* Cf. 23:47.

16:41 *burn thine houses.* A common form of punishment (see Judg 12:1; 15:6). *shalt give no hire any more.* See v. 33.

16:44 *As is the mother, so is her daughter.* Referring to Jerusalem's continual and seemingly hereditary tendency toward evil (cf. vv. 3,45).

16:46 *daughters.* Suburbs or satellite cities.

‡16:47 *corrupted more than they.* The Bible frequently compares a city or people to Sodom (see v. 46) as the epitome of evil and degradation (see Deut 29:23; 32:32; Is 1:9–10; 3:9; Jer 23:14; Lam 4:6; Mat 10:15; 11:23–24; Jude 7).

16:49 *the iniquity of thy sister Sodom.* Here social injustice rather than sexual perversion (Gen 19) is highlighted.

16:56 *the day of thy pride.* Referring to a time long before Ezekiel, when Jerusalem (as an Israelite city) was still relatively uncorrupted—as in the days of David and the early years of Solomon.

‡16:57 *reproach of the daughters of Syria.* The OT frequently condemns Edom for this (see 25:12–14; 35; Is 63:1; Obadiah). The difference in Hebrew between "Edom" and "Aram" (Syria) is quite small. On occasion, the two are mistaken for one another. Most modern versions have chosen the reading "Edom."

16:59 *covenant.* See v. 8 and note.

60 Nevertheless I will [a]remember my covenant with thee in the days of thy youth, and I will establish unto thee [b]an everlasting covenant.

61 Then [a]thou shalt remember thy ways, and be ashamed, when thou shalt receive thy sisters, thine elder and thy younger: and I will give them unto thee for [b]daughters, [c]but not by thy covenant.

62 [a]And I will establish my covenant with thee; and thou shalt know that I *am* the LORD:

63 That thou mayest remember, and be confounded, [a]and never open thy mouth any more, because of thy shame, when I am pacified toward thee for all that thou hast done, saith the Lord GOD.

The eagles and the cedar

17 And the word of the LORD came unto me, saying,

2 Son of man, put forth a riddle, and speak a parable unto the house of Israel;

3 And say, Thus saith the Lord GOD; [a]A great eagle with great wings, longwinged, full *of* feathers, which had [1]divers colours, came unto Lebanon, and [b]took the highest branch of the cedar:

4 He cropt off the top of his young twigs, and carried it into a land of traffick; he set it in a city of merchants.

5 He took also of the seed of the land, and [1]planted it in [a]a fruitful field; he placed *it* by great waters, *and* set it [b]*as* a willow tree.

6 And it grew, and became a spreading vine [a]of low stature, whose branches turned toward him, and the roots thereof were under him: so it became a vine, and brought forth branches, and shot forth sprigs.

7 There was also another great eagle with great wings and many feathers: and behold, [a]this vine did bend her roots toward him, and shot forth her branches toward him, that *he* might water it by the furrows of her plantation.

8 It *was* planted in a good [1]soil by great waters, that *it* might bring forth branches, and that *it* might bear fruit, that *it* might be a goodly vine.

9 Say thou, Thus saith the Lord GOD; Shall it prosper? [a]shall he not pull up the roots thereof, and cut off the fruit thereof, that it wither? it shall wither *in* all the leaves of her spring, even without great power or many people to pluck it up by the roots thereof.

10 Yea behold, *being* planted, shall it prosper? [a]shall it not utterly wither, when the east wind toucheth it? it shall wither in the furrows where it grew.

11 ¶ Moreover the word of the LORD came unto me, saying,

12 Say now to [a]the rebellious house, Know ye not what these *things mean?* tell *them,* Behold, [b]the king of Babylon is come *to* Jerusalem, and hath taken the king thereof, and the princes thereof, and led them with him to Babylon;

13 [a]And hath taken of the king's seed, and made a covenant with him, [b]and hath [1]taken an oath of him: he hath also taken the mighty of the land:

14 That the kingdom might be [a]base, that *it* might not lift itself up, [1]*but* that by keeping of his covenant it might stand.

15 But [a]he rebelled against him in sending his ambassadors *into* Egypt, [b]that *they* might give him horses and much people. [c]Shall he prosper? shall he escape that doeth such *things?* or shall he break the covenant, and be delivered?

16 *As* I live, saith the Lord GOD, surely [a]in the place *where* the king *dwelleth* that made him king, whose oath he despised, and whose covenant he brake, *even* with him in the midst of Babylon he shall die.

17 [a]Neither shall Pharaoh with *his* mighty army and great company make for him in the war, [b]by casting up mounts, and building forts, to cut off many persons:

18 Seeing he despised the oath by breaking the covenant, when lo, he had [a]given his hand, and hath done all these *things,* he shall not escape.

19 Therefore thus saith the Lord GOD; *As* I live, surely mine oath that he hath despised, and my covenant that he hath broken, even it will I recompense upon his own head.

16:60 [a]Ps. 106:45 [b]Jer. 32:40; 50:5
16:61 [a]ch. 20:43; 36:31 [b]Is. 54:1; 60:4; Gal. 4:26 [c]Jer. 31:31
16:62 [a]Hos. 2:19
16:63 [a]Rom 3:19
17:3 [1]Heb. *embroidering* [a]See ver. 12 [b]2 Ki. 24:12
17:5 [1]Heb. *put it in a field of seed* [a]Deut. 8:7 [b]Is. 44:4
17:6 [a]ver. 14
17:7 [a]ver. 15
17:8 [1]Heb. *field*
17:9 [a]2 Ki. 25:7
17:10 [a]ch. 19:12; Hos. 13:15
17:12 [a]ch. 2:5; 12:9 [b]ver. 3; 2 Ki. 24:11-16
17:13 [1]Heb. *brought him to an oath* [a]2 Ki. 24:17 [b]2 Chr. 36:13
17:14 [1]Heb. *to keep his covenant, to stand to it* [a]ver. 6; ch. 29:14
17:15 [a]2 Ki. 24:20; 2 Chr. 36:13 [b]Deut. 17:16; Is. 31:1,3; 36:6,9 [c]ver. 9
17:16 [a]Jer. 32:5; 34:3; ch. 12:13
17:17 [a]Jer. 37:7 [b]Jer. 52:4
17:18 [a]1 Chr. 29:24; Lam. 5:6

16:60 *everlasting covenant.* See 37:26; Is 55:3; Jer 32:40.

17:2 *riddle . . . parable.* The riddle/parable is in vv. 3–10, the explanation in vv. 11–21.

17:3 *great eagle.* Nebuchadnezzar (see v. 12). *Lebanon.* Jerusalem (see v. 12). *cedar.* David's dynasty; his royal family.

17:4 *top of his young twigs.* Jehoiachin. *land of traffick.* The country of Babylonia (see v. 12; 16:29).. *city of merchants.* Babylon.

17:5 *seed.* Zedekiah son of Josiah; he was the brother of Jehoahaz and Jehoiakim and uncle of Jehoiachin (see 2 Ki 23–24). *planted it.* Made him king (2 Ki 24:17).

17:6 *spreading vine.* No longer a tall cedar, because thousands of Judah's leading citizens had been deported (see 2 Ki 24:15–16; see also Jer 52:28). But see note on 15:2.

17:7 *another great eagle.* An Egyptian pharaoh, either Psammetichus II (595–589 B.C.) or Pharaoh-hophra (589–570). Pharaoh-hophra, mentioned in Jer 44:30, is probably the pharaoh who offered help to Jerusalem in 586 (see Jer 37:5). If the fact that ch. 17 is located between ch. 8 (dated 592) and ch. 20 (dated 591) is chronologically meaningful, Psammetichus is meant. *bend her roots toward him.* Zedekiah appealed to Egypt for military aid (v. 15), an act of rebellion against Nebuchadnezzar (see 2 Ki 24:20).

17:10 *east wind.* The hot, dry wind known as the khamsin, which withers vegetation (see 19:12). Here it stands for Nebuchadnezzar and his Babylonian forces.

17:12 *the rebellious house.* See 2:3 and note.

17:15 *shall he escape that doeth such things?* The point of the chapter (see vv. 16,18).

17:16 *in the midst of Babylon he shall die.* See 2 Ki 25:7.

17:19 *mine oath . . . my covenant.* The king of Judah would have sworn faithfulness to the treaty in the name of the Lord. To swear such an oath and then violate it was to despise God.

20 And I will [a]spread my net upon him,
and he shall be taken in my snare, and I will
bring him to Babylon, and [b]will plead with
him there *for* his trespass that he hath trespassed against me.
21 And [a]all his fugitives with all his bands
shall fall by the sword, and they that remain
shall be scattered towards all winds: and ye
shall know that I the LORD have spoken *it.*
22 ¶ Thus saith the Lord GOD; I will also
take of the highest [a]branch of the high cedar,
and will set *it;* I will crop off from the top of
his young twigs [b]a tender one, and will [c]plant
it upon a high mountain and eminent:
23 [a]In the mountain of the height of Israel
will I plant it: and it shall bring forth boughs,
and bear fruit, and be a goodly cedar: and [b]un-
der it shall dwell all fowl of every wing; in the
shadow of the branches thereof shall they
dwell.
24 And all the trees of the field shall know
that I the LORD [a]have brought down the high
tree, have exalted the low tree, have dried up
the green tree, and have made the dry tree to
flourish: [b]I the LORD have spoken and have
done *it.*

The soul that sinneth shall die

18 And the word of the LORD came unto
me again, saying,
2 What mean ye, that ye use this proverb
concerning the land of Israel, saying, The [a]fa-
thers have eaten sour grapes, and the children's teeth are set on edge?
3 *As* I live, saith the Lord GOD, ye shall not
have *occasion* any more to use this proverb in
Israel.
4 Behold, all souls *are* mine; as the soul of
the father, so also the soul of the son *is* mine:
[a]the soul that sinneth, it shall die.
5 ¶ But if a man be just, and do [1]that which
is lawful and right,
6 [a]*And* hath not eaten upon the mountains, neither hath lift up his eyes to the idols
of the house of Israel, neither hath [b]defiled his
neighbour's wife, neither hath come near to [c]a
menstruous woman,
7 And hath not [a]oppressed any, *but* hath
restored *to* the debtor his [b]pledge, hath
spoiled none by violence, hath [c]given his
bread to the hungry, and hath covered the
naked with a garment;
8 He *that* hath not given forth upon [a]usury,
neither hath taken any increase, *that* hath
withdrawn his hand from iniquity, [b]hath executed true judgment between man and man,
9 Hath walked in my statutes, and hath
kept my judgments, to deal truly; he *is* just, he
shall surely [a]live, saith the Lord GOD.
10 ¶ If he beget a son *that is* a [1]robber, [a]a
shedder of blood, and [2]*that* doeth the like to
any one of these *things,*
11 And that doeth not any of those *duties,*
but even hath eaten upon the mountains, and
defiled his neighbour's wife,
12 Hath oppressed the poor and needy,
hath spoiled by violence, hath not restored the
pledge, and hath lift up his eyes to the idols,
hath [a]committed abomination,
13 Hath given forth upon usury, and hath
taken increase: shall he then live? he shall not

17:20 [a]ch. 12:13 [b]ch. 20:36 **17:21** [a]ch. 12:14 **17:22** [a]Is. 11:1; Jer. 23:5; Zech. 3:8 [b]Is. 53:2 [c]Ps. 2:6 **17:23** [a]Is. 2:2,3 [b]See ch. 31:6; Dan. 4:12 **17:24** [a]Luke 1:52 [b]ch. 22:14 **18:2** [a]Jer. 31:29; Lam. 5:7

18:4 [a]Rom. 6:23 **18:5** [1]Heb. *judgment and justice* **18:6** [a]ch. 22:9 [b]Lev. 18:20; 20:10 [c]Lev. 18:19; 20:18 **18:7** [a]Ex. 22:21; Lev. 19:15; 25:14 [b]Ex. 22:26; Deut. 24:12 [c]Deut. 15:7; Is. 58:7; Mat. 25:35 **18:8** [a]Ex. 22:25; Lev. 25:36; Deut. 23:19; Neh. 5:7; Ps. 15:5 [b]Deut. 1:16; Zech. 8:16 **18:9** [a]ch. 20:11; Amos 5:4 **18:10** [1]Or, *breaker up of a house* [2]Or, *that doeth to his brother besides any of these* [a]Gen. 9:6; Ex. 21:12; Num. 35:31 **18:12** [a]ch. 8:6,17

‡17:22 *I will.* A beautiful Messianic promise follows, using the previous imagery in a totally new and unexpected way. *highest branch.* A member of David's family (cf. Is 11:1; Zech 3:8; 6:12). *cedar.* See note on v. 3. *plant it.* Make him king (see v. 5). *high mountain and eminent.* Jerusalem.

17:23 *fowl . . . shall they dwell.* See Mark 4:32.

18:2 *this proverb.* Cf. Jer 31:29, which indicates that the proverb arose first in Jerusalem. Jeremiah predicted the cessation of the proverb, and Ezekiel said its end had come. *concerning the land of Israel.* And about the fate of those who have suffered loss. *The fathers . . . on edge.* The proverb, though it expresses self-pity, fatalism and despair, and though it mocks the justice of God, had its origin in Israelite belief in corporate solidarity (see Ex 20:5; 34:7 and Ezekiel's own words in chs. 16; 23). In Lam 5:7 the thought appears as a sincere confession. *set on edge.* The Hebrew for this phrase perhaps means "blunted" or "worn" (cf. Eccl 10:10), but it may refer to the sensation in the mouth when eating something bitter or sour.

18:3 *As I live.* A divine oath, revealing God's unalterable intention. It is used often in Ezekiel (5:11; 14:16,18,20; 16:48; 17:16,19; 20:3,31,33; 33:11,27; 34:8; 35:6,11).

18:4 *the soul that sinneth, it shall die.* Or "Only the soul . . ." Ezekiel spoke out against a false use the people were making of a doctrine of inherited guilt (perhaps based on a false understanding of Ex 20:5; 34:7). What follows is his description of three men, standing for three generations, who break the three/four-generation pattern. *soul.* "Life" or "person," not used here to distinguish spirit from body.

18:5 *if a man be just.* The first generation that keeps the law. The following 15 commandments are partly ceremonial but are mostly moral injunctions. See the ten commandments in Ex 20 and Deut 5; cf. Ps 15:2–5; 24:3–6; Is 33:15.

18:6 *eaten upon the mountains.* Eating meat sacrificed to idols on the high places (see 6:3; Hos 4:13). *lift up his eyes to.* Seek help from (see 23:27; 33:25; Ps 121:1). *idols.* See note on 6:4. *defiled.* Adultery (condemned in Ex 20:14; Deut 22:22; Lev 18:20; 20:10) is here associated with a menstrual prohibition (see Lev 15:19–24; 18:19; 20:18), which is absent from the two listings that follow (cf. vv. 11,15).

‡18:7 *oppressed.* The rich taking advantage of the poor. *restored to the debtor his pledge.* See Ex 22:26; Deut 24:12–13; Amos 2:8. *hath spoiled none by violence.* Committed robbery. See the commandment against stealing in Ex 20:15; Deut 5:19. This is violent ("armed") robbery rather than secret theft or burglary (see Lev 19:13). *bread to the hungry.* See Deut 15:7–11; Mat 25:31–46.

18:8 *given forth upon usury.* See 22:12; Ps 15:5; Prov 28:8. What is forbidden in Ex 22:25; Lev 25:35–37; Deut 23:19 is interest on loans to the needy. Deut 23:20 allows an Israelite to charge interest to a foreigner; Ezekiel condemns usury. (Interest on modern commercial loans is a different matter.)

‡18:9 *he is just, he shall surely live.* After the checklist of commandments has been gone over, the verdict is rendered (cf. Ps 15:5; 24:5). *live.* See note on 16:6. This is life as more than mere existence; it includes communion with God (see Ps 63:3; 73:27–28).

18:10 *a son that is a robber.* Evil, second generation. About half (eight) of the previous commandments follow, but in a

live: he hath done all these abominations; he
shall surely die; [a]his [1]blood shall be upon him.
14 ¶ Now lo, *if* he beget a son, that seeth all
his father's sins which he hath done, and considereth, and doeth not such like,
15 [a]*That* hath not eaten upon the mountains, neither hath lift up his eyes to the idols
of the house of Israel, hath not defiled his
neighbour's wife,
16 Neither hath oppressed any, [1]hath not
withholden the pledge, neither hath spoiled
by violence, *but* hath given his bread to the
hungry, and hath covered the naked with a
garment,
17 *That* hath taken off his hand from the
poor, *that* hath not received usury nor increase, hath executed my judgments, hath
walked in my statutes; he shall not die for the
iniquity of his father, he shall surely live.
18 *As for* his father, because he cruelly oppressed, spoiled *his* brother by violence, and
did *that* which *is* not good among his people,
lo, even [a]he shall die in his iniquity.
19 ¶ Yet say ye, Why? [a]doth not the son
bear the iniquity of the father? When the son
hath done that which is lawful and right, *and*
hath kept all my statutes, and hath done them,
he shall surely live.
20 [a]The soul that sinneth, it shall die. [b]The
son shall not bear the iniquity of the father,
neither shall the father bear the iniquity of the
son: [c]the righteousness of the righteous shall
be upon him, [d]and the wickedness of the
wicked shall be upon him.
21 But [a]if the wicked will turn from all his
sins that he hath committed, and keep all my
statutes, and do that which is lawful and right,
he shall surely live, he shall not die.
22 [a]All his transgressions that he hath
committed, they shall not be mentioned unto
him: in his righteousness that he hath done he
shall live.
23 [a]Have I any pleasure at all that the
wicked should die? saith the Lord GOD: *and*
not that he should return from his ways, and
live?

18:13 [1]Heb. *bloods* [a]Lev. 20:9,11-13, 16,27; ch. 3:18; Acts 18:6
18:15 [a]ver. 6
18:16 [1]Heb. *hath not pledged the pledge,* or, *taken to pledge*
18:18 [a]ch. 3:18
18:19 [a]Ex. 20:5; Deut. 5:9; 2 Ki. 23:26; 24:3,4
18:20 [a]ver. 4 [b]Deut. 24:16; 2 Ki. 14:6; 2 Chr. 25:4; Jer. 31:29,30 [c]Is. 3:10,11 [d]Rom. 2:9
18:21 [a]ver. 27; ch. 33:12,19
18:22 [a]ch. 33:16
18:23 [a]ver. 32; ch. 33:11; 1 Tim. 2:4; 2 Pet. 3:9
18:24 [a]ch. 3:20; 33:12,13,18 [b]2 Pet. 2:20
18:25 [a]ver. 29; ch. 33:17,20
18:26 [a]ver. 24
18:27 [a]ver. 21
18:28 [a]ver. 14
18:29 [a]ver. 25
18:30 [1]Or, others [a]ch. 7:3; 33:20 [b]Mat. 3:2; Rev. 2:5
18:31 [a]Eph. 4:22,23 [b]Jer. 32:39; ch. 11:19; 36:26
18:32 [1]Or, others [a]ver. 23; Lam. 3:33; ch. 33:11; 2 Pet. 3:9
19:1 [a]ch. 26:17; 27:2

24 ¶ But [a]when the righteous turneth away
from his righteousness, and committeth iniquity, *and* doeth according to all the abominations that the wicked *man* doeth, shall he live?
[b]All his righteousness that he hath done shall
not be mentioned: in his trespass that he hath
trespassed, and in his sin that he hath sinned,
in them shall he die.
25 Yet ye say, [a]The way of the Lord is not
equal. Hear now, O house of Israel; Is not my
way equal? are not your ways unequal?
26 [a]When a righteous *man* turneth away
from his righteousness, and committeth iniquity, and dieth in them; for his iniquity that he
hath done shall he die.
27 Again, [a]when the wicked *man* turneth
away from his wickedness that he hath committed, and doeth that which is lawful and
right, he shall save his soul alive.
28 Because he [a]considereth, and turneth
away from all his transgressions that he hath
committed, he shall surely live, he shall not die.
29 [a]Yet saith the house of Israel, The way
of the Lord is not equal. O house of Israel, are
not my ways equal? are not your ways unequal?
30 ¶ [a]Therefore I will judge you, O house
of Israel, every one according to his ways,
saith the Lord GOD. [b]Repent, and turn [1]*yourselves* from all your transgressions; so iniquity
shall not be your ruin.
31 [a]Cast away from you all your transgressions, whereby ye have transgressed; and
make you a [b]new heart and a new spirit: for
why will ye die, O house of Israel?
32 For [a]I have no pleasure in the death of
him that dieth, saith the Lord GOD: wherefore
turn [1]*yourselves,* and live ye.

Lament for Israel's princes

19 Moreover [a]take thou up a lamentation for the princes of Israel,
2 And say, What *is* thy mother? A lioness:
she lay down among lions, she nourished her
whelps among young lions.
3 And she brought up one of her whelps:

different order.

18:13 *his blood shall be upon him.* He is held responsible for his own sin (see Lev 20:9,11–12,16,27).

18:14 *a son.* Righteous, third generation. Twelve commandments follow.

18:21 *But if the wicked will turn . . . and keep . . . he shall surely live.* Verses 1–20 indicate that the chain of inherited guilt can be broken, and vv. 21–29 teach that the power of guilt accumulated within a person's life can be overcome.

‡18:24 *But when the righteous turneth away.* See Heb 2:3; 2 Pet 2:20–22 for warnings against those who knowingly and willfully turn from righteousness.

18:26 *When a righteous man.* Verses 26–29 repeat the argument developed in vv. 21–25.

18:30 *Therefore.* Concluding, summary oracle. *every one.* While the house of Israel as a whole was guilty, God's judgment would be just and individual. *Repent.* Second call to repentance (see 14:6).

18:31 *make . . . a new heart.* What had been promised unconditionally (11:19; 36:26) is here portrayed as attainable but not inevitable (cf. the same tension between Phil 2:12 and 2:13).

18:32 *I have no pleasure.* Verse 23 is echoed in this final, grand summary, called by some the most important message in the whole book of Ezekiel (see note on 16:6).

19:1 *lamentation.* A metered (three beats plus two beats) chant usually composed for funerals of fallen leaders (as in 2 Sam 1:17–27), but often used sarcastically by the OT prophets to lament or to ironically predict the death of a nation (see Is 14:4–21; Amos 5:1–3). See also 2:10. *princes.* Kings.

19:2 *lioness.* Although a lament, this chapter is an allegory like that in ch. 17 (to which it is related in content). Ch. 17 gives an interpretation, but this one does not. The lioness may be a personification of Israel (see v. 1), Judah (see 4:6; 8:1,17; 9:9) or Jerusalem (see 5:5), all of which may be considered to be mother to the kings (see vv. 10–14).

19:3 *one of her whelps.* Jehoahaz (see 2 Ki 23:31–34; Jer 22:10–12), who reigned only three months. *devoured men.* A reference to his oppressive policies (see Jer 22:13).

[a]it became a young lion, and it learned to catch the prey; it devoured men.

4 The nations also heard of him; he was taken in their pit, and they brought him with chains unto the land of [a]Egypt.

5 Now when she saw that she had waited, *and* her hope was lost, then she took [a]another of her whelps, *and* made him a young lion.

6 [a]And he went up and down among the lions, [b]he became a young lion, and learned to catch the prey, *and* devoured men.

7 And he knew [1]their desolate palaces, and he laid waste their cities; and the land was desolate, and the fulness thereof, by the noise of his roaring.

8 [a]Then the nations set against him on every side from the provinces, and spread their net over him: [b]he was taken in their pit.

9 [a]And they put him in ward [1]in chains, and brought him to the king of Babylon: they brought him into holds, that his voice should no more be heard upon [b]the mountains of Israel.

10 ¶ Thy mother *is* [a]like a vine [1]in thy blood, planted by the waters: she was [b]fruitful and full of branches by reason of many waters.

11 And she had strong rods for the sceptres of them that bare rule, and her [a]stature was exalted among the thick branches, and she appeared in her height with the multitude of her branches.

12 But she was plucked up in fury, she was cast down to the ground, and the [a]east wind dried up her fruit: her strong rods were broken and withered; the fire consumed them.

13 And now she *is* planted in the wilderness, in a dry and thirsty ground.

14 [a]And fire is gone out of a rod of her branches, *which* hath devoured her fruit, so that she hath no strong rod *to be* a sceptre to rule. [b]This *is* a lamentation, and shall be for a lamentation.

19:3 [a]ver. 6; 2 Ki. 23:31,32
19:4 [a]2 Ki. 23:33; 2 Chr. 36:4; Jer. 22:11,12
19:5 [a]2 Ki. 23:34
19:6 [a]Jer. 22:13-17 [b]ver. 3
19:7 [1]Or, *their widows*
19:8 [a]2 Ki. 24:2 [b]ver. 4
19:9 [1]Or, *in hooks* [a]2 Chr. 36:6; Jer. 22:18 [b]ch. 6:2
19:10 [1]Or, *in thy quietness*, or, *in thy likeness* [a]ch. 17:6 [b]Deut. 8:7-9
19:11 [a]ch. 31:3; Dan. 4:11
19:12 [a]ch. 17:10; Hos. 13:15
19:14 [a]Judg. 9:15; 2 Ki. 24:20; ch. 17:18 [b]Lam. 4:20

Israel's apostasy

20 And it came to pass in the seventh year, in the fifth *month*, the tenth *day* of the month, *that* [a]certain of the elders of Israel came to inquire of the LORD, and sat before me.

2 Then came the word of the LORD unto me, saying,

3 Son of man, speak unto the elders of Israel, and say unto them, Thus saith the Lord GOD; Are ye come to inquire of me? *As* I live, saith the Lord GOD, [a]I will not be inquired of by you.

4 Wilt thou [a][1]judge them, son of man, wilt thou judge *them?* [b]cause them to know the abominations of their fathers:

5 And say unto them, Thus saith the Lord GOD; In the day when [a]I chose Israel, and [1]lifted up mine hand unto the seed of the house of Jacob, and made myself [b]known unto them in the land of Egypt, when I lifted up mine hand unto them, saying, [c]I *am* the LORD your God;

6 In the day *that* I lifted up mine hand unto them, [a]to bring them forth of the land of Egypt into a land that I had espied for them, flowing with milk and honey, [b]which *is* the glory of all lands:

7 Then said I unto them, [a]Cast ye away every man [b]the abominations of his eyes, and defile not yourselves with [c]the idols of Egypt: I *am* the LORD your God.

8 But they rebelled against me, and would not hearken unto me: they did not every man cast away the abominations of their eyes, neither did they forsake the idols of Egypt: then I said, *I* will [a]pour out my fury upon them, to accomplish my anger against them in the midst of the land of Egypt.

9 [a]But I wrought for my name's sake, that *it* should not be polluted before the heathen, among whom they *were*, in whose sight I made myself known unto them, in bringing them forth out of the land of Egypt.

20:1 [a]ch. 8:1
20:3 [a]ch. 14:3
20:4 [1]Or, *plead for them* [a]ch. 22:2 [b]ch. 16:2
20:5 [1]Or, *sware:* and so ver. 6, etc. [a]Ex. 6:7; Deut. 7:6 [b]Ex. 3:8; 4:31; Deut. 4:34 [c]Ex. 20:2
20:6 [a]Ex. 3:8,17; Deut. 8:7-9; Jer. 32:22 [b]ver. 15; Ps. 48:2; Dan. 8:9; Zech. 7:14
20:7 [a]ch. 18:31 [b]2 Chr. 15:8 [c]Lev. 18:3; Deut. 29:16; Josh. 24:14
20:8 [a]ch. 7:8
20:9 [a]Num. 14:13; ch. 36:21,22

19:5 *another of her whelps.* Perhaps Jehoiachin (who reigned only three months, 2 Ki 24:8), but probably Zedekiah (of whom v. 7 appears a more likely description). Both were taken to Babylon (v. 9). If the reference is to Jehoiachin (2 Ki 24:15), this was a true lament; if to Zedekiah, it was a prediction (2 Ki 25:7).
19:10 *Thy mother is like a vine.* The one previously pictured as a lioness (v. 2) is here a vine (see 15:2 and note; 17:7).
19:12 *east wind.* Nebuchadnezzar and his army (see note on 17:10).
19:13 *wilderness.* Babylonia—which to Israel seemed like a wilderness (see 20:35).
19:14 *fire.* Rebellion (see 2 Ki 24:20). *her branches.* Zedekiah. *shall be for a lamentation.* Indicates repeated use (see Ps 137:1).
20:1 *seventh year . . . fifth month . . . tenth day of the month.* Aug. 14, 591 B.C., the third date (see 1:2; 8:1). Since Ezekiel had received many revelations before this (see opening verses of chs. 12–18), the date must emphasize the importance of this chapter. Like chs. 16 and 23, it presents a negative view of Israel's history; unlike them, it does not employ allegory. *elders of Israel.* See notes on 8:1; 14:1. *inquire.* See v. 3 and note on 14:3.
20:3 *As I live.* See note on 18:3. *be inquired of.* See note on 14:3.
20:5 *I chose.* The only occurrence of the word "choose" in Ezekiel. Verses 5–26 present Israel's history in three acts (vv. 5–9, Egypt; vv. 10–17, Wilderness, Part 1; vv. 18–26, Wilderness, Part 2); but see note on v. 28. Each act has four scenes: (1) revelation, (2) rebellion, (3) wrath, (4) reconsideration. *lifted up my hand.* See vv. 15,23,42. *I am the LORD your God.* See Ex 3:6, 14–15 and notes.
20:6 *land . . . flowing with milk and honey.* See note on Ex 3:8. *the glory of all lands.* Cf. Deut 8:7–10; Jer 3:19 for the land's natural beauty. Its real beauty lay in being selected as God's dwelling place (Deut 12:5,11).
20:7 *idols.* See note on 6:4.
20:8 *But they rebelled.* See vv. 13,21; see also Josh 24:14. *I will pour out my fury upon them.* An internal refrain (see vv. 13,21); see also note on 7:8. *accomplish my anger against.* See note on 5:13.
20:9 *for my name's sake.* See vv. 14,22,44. Name and person are closely connected in the Bible. God's name is His identity and reputation—that by which He is known. The phrase used here is equivalent to "for My own sake" (cf. Is 37:35; 43:25). God's acts of deliverance—past and future—identify Him, revealing His true nature (see 36:22; Ps 23:3; Is 48:9). *polluted.* By ridicule (see Num 14:15–16).

10 Wherefore I [a]caused them to go forth out of the land of Egypt, and brought them into the wilderness.

11 [a]And I gave them my statutes, and [1]shewed them my judgments, [b]which *if* a man do, he shall even live in them.

12 Moreover also I gave them my [a]sabbaths, to be a sign between me and them, that *they* might know that I *am* the LORD that sanctify them.

13 But the house of Israel [a]rebelled against me in the wilderness: they walked not in my statutes, and they [b]despised my judgments, which *if* a man do, he shall even live in them; and my sabbaths they greatly [c]polluted: then I said, *I* would pour out my fury upon them in the [d]wilderness, to consume them.

14 [a]But I wrought for my name's sake, that *it* should not be polluted before the heathen, in whose sight I brought them out.

15 Yet also [a]I lifted up my hand unto them in the wilderness, that *I* would not bring them into the land which I had given *them,* flowing with milk and honey, [b]which *is* the glory of all lands;

16 [a]Because they despised my judgments, and walked not in my statutes, but polluted my sabbaths: for [b]their heart went after their idols.

17 [a]Nevertheless mine eye spared them from destroying them, neither did I make an end of them in the wilderness.

18 But I said unto their children in the wilderness, Walk ye not in the statutes of your fathers, neither observe their judgments, nor defile yourselves with their idols:

19 I *am* the LORD your God; [a]walk in my statutes, and keep my judgments, and do them;

20 [a]And hallow my sabbaths; and they shall be a sign between me and you, that *ye* may know that I *am* the LORD your God.

21 Notwithstanding [a]the children rebelled against me: they walked not in my statutes, neither kept my judgments to do them, [b]which *if* a man do, he shall even live in them; they polluted my sabbaths: then I said, [c]*I* would pour out my fury upon them, to accomplish my anger against them in the wilderness.

22 [a]Nevertheless I withdrew mine hand, and [b]wrought for my name's sake, that *it* should not be polluted in the sight of the heathen, in whose sight I brought them forth.

23 I lifted up mine hand unto them also in the wilderness, that [a]*I* would scatter them among the heathen, and disperse them through the countries;

24 [a]Because they had not executed my judgments, but had despised my statutes, and had polluted my sabbaths, and [b]their eyes were after their fathers' idols.

25 Wherefore [a]I gave them also statutes *that were* not good, and judgments whereby they should not live;

26 And I polluted them in their own gifts, in that they caused to pass [a]through *the fire* all that openeth the womb, that I might make them desolate, to the end that they [b]might know that I *am* the LORD.

27 ¶ Therefore, son of man, speak unto the house of Israel, and say unto them, Thus saith the Lord GOD; Yet *in* this your fathers have [a]blasphemed me, in that they have [1]committed a trespass against me.

28 *For* when I had brought them into the land, *for* the which I lifted up mine hand to give it to them, then [a]they saw every high hill, and all the thick trees, and they offered there their sacrifices, and there they presented the provocation of their offering: there also they made their [b]sweet savour, and poured out there their drink offerings.

29 Then [1]I said unto them, What *is* the high place whereunto ye go? And the name thereof is called Bamah unto this day.

30 Wherefore say unto the house of Israel, Thus saith the Lord GOD; Are ye polluted after the manner of your fathers? and commit ye whoredom after their abominations?

31 For when *ye* offer [a]your gifts, when *ye* make your sons to pass through the fire, ye pollute yourselves with all your idols, *even* unto *this* day: and shall I be inquired of by you, O house of Israel? *As* I live, saith the Lord GOD, I will not be inquired of by you.

Israel purged and accepted

32 ¶ And that [a]which cometh into your mind shall not be at all, that ye say, We will be

20:10 [a]Ex. 13:18
20:11 [1]Heb. *made them to know* [a]Deut. 4:8; Neh. 9:13; Ps. 147:19 [b]Lev. 18:5; Rom. 10:5; Gal. 3:12
20:12 [a]Ex. 20:8; Deut. 5:12; Neh. 9:14
20:13 [a]Num. 14:22; Ps. 78:40; 95:8-10 [b]Prov. 1:25 [c]Ex. 16:27 [d]Num. 14:29; Ps. 106:23
20:14 [a]ver. 9,22
20:15 [a]Num. 14:28; Ps. 95:11; 106:26 [b]ver. 6
20:16 [a]ver. 13,24 [b]Num. 15:39; Ps. 78:37; Amos 5:25; Acts 7:42
20:17 [a]Ps. 78:38
20:19 [a]Deut. 5:32; chs. 6,7,8,10,11,12
20:20 [a]Jer. 17:22
20:21 [a]Num. 25:1; Deut. 9:23 [b]ver. 11,13 [c]ver. 8,13
20:22 [a]ver. 17
20:22 [b]ver. 9,14
20:23 [a]Lev. 26:33; Deut. 28:64; Ps. 106:27; Jer. 15:4
20:24 [a]ver. 13,16 [b]See ch. 6:9
20:25 [a]See Ps. 81:12; Rom. 1:24; 2 Thes. 2:11
20:26 [a]2 Ki. 17:17; 21:6; 2 Chr. 28:3; 33:6; Jer. 32:35; ch. 16:20 [b]ch. 6:7
20:27 [1]Heb. *trespassed a trespass* [a]Rom. 2:24
20:28 [a]Is. 57:5; ch. 6:13 [b]ch. 16:19
20:29 [1]Or, *I told them what the high place was,* or, *Bamah*
20:31 [a]ver. 26
20:32 [a]ch. 11:5

20:10 *wilderness.* Act Two (see note on v. 5).
20:11 *shall even live.* See vv. 13,21; contrast v. 25. See notes on 16:6; 18:9; see also Lev 18:5 and note.
20:12 *sabbaths, to be a sign.* Israel's observance of the sabbath was to serve as a sign that she was the Lord's holy people (see Ex 31:13–17). Ezekiel highlights the sabbath (see 22:8,26; 23:38; 44:24; 45:17; 46:3), as did Jeremiah (Jer 17:19–27; cf. Neh 13:17–18). Jewish legalism later corrupted the sabbath law (see Mat 12:1–14).
20:13 *greatly polluted.* By not observing the sabbath-rest (see Jer 17:21–23) or by not observing it in the manner and spirit God intended (see Amos 8:5).
20:18 *I said unto their children.* Act Three (see note on v. 5). God began anew with the second generation in the wilderness (see Num 14:26–35).
20:25–26 Cf. the principle of divine working in Rom 1:24–32.
20:26 *caused to pass through the fire all that openeth the womb.* See v. 31 and note on 16:20. *that they might know that I am the LORD.* God will go to any lengths to get His people to acknowledge Him (see Introduction: Themes; see also note on 5:13).
20:28 *when I had brought them into the land.* Apparently Act Four in Ezekiel's history (see note on v. 5), but it is not carried through with the same schematic consistency.
20:30 *Are ye . . . ?* The point of the chapter: "How will you act?"
20:31 *inquired of.* See note on 14:3.
20:32 *shall not be at all.* As happened to those who were exiled to Egypt (see Jer 44:15–19). *families of the countries.* The temptation to lose its uniqueness was always present for Israel (see 1 Sam 8:5).

as the heathen, as the families of the countries, to serve wood and stone.

33 *As* I live, saith the Lord GOD, surely with a mighty hand, and [a]with a stretched out arm, and with fury poured out, will I rule over you:

34 And I will bring you out from the people, and will gather you out of the countries wherein ye are scattered, with a mighty hand, and with a stretched out arm, and with fury poured out.

35 And I will bring you into the wilderness of the people, and there [a]will I plead with you face to face.

36 [a]Like as I pleaded with your fathers in the wilderness of the land of Egypt, so will I plead with you, saith the Lord GOD.

37 And I will cause you to [a]pass under the rod, and I will bring you into the [1]bond of the covenant:

38 And [a]I will purge out from among you the rebels, and them that transgress against me: I will bring them forth out of the country where they sojourn, and [b]they shall not enter into the land of Israel: and ye shall know that I *am* the LORD.

39 As for you, O house of Israel, thus saith the Lord GOD; [a]Go ye, serve ye every one his idols, and hereafter *also,* if ye will not hearken unto me: [b]but pollute ye my holy name no more with your gifts, and with your idols.

40 For [a]in mine holy mountain, in the mountain of the height of Israel, saith the Lord GOD, there shall all the house of Israel, all of them in the land, serve me: there [b]will I accept them, and there will I require your offerings, and the [1]firstfruits of your oblations, with all your holy *things.*

41 I will accept you with *your* [a][1]sweet savour, when I bring you out from the people, and gather you out of the countries wherein ye have been scattered; and I will be sanctified in you before the heathen.

42 [a]And ye shall know that I *am* the LORD, [b]when I shall bring you into the land of Israel, into the country *for* the which I lifted up mine hand to give it to your fathers.

43 And [a]there shall ye remember your ways, and all your doings, wherein ye have been defiled; and [b]ye shall lothe yourselves in your own sight for all your evils that ye have committed.

44 [a]And ye shall know that I *am* the LORD, when I have wrought with you [b]for my name's sake, not according to your wicked ways, nor according to your corrupt doings, O ye house of Israel, saith the Lord GOD.

The prophecy against the south

45 ¶ Moreover the word of the LORD came unto me, saying,

46 [a]Son of man, set thy face toward the south, and drop *thy word* toward the south, and prophesy against the forest of the south field;

47 And say to the forest of the south, Hear the word of the LORD; Thus saith the Lord GOD; Behold, [a]I *will* kindle a fire in thee, and it shall devour [b]every green tree in thee, and every dry tree: the flaming flame shall not be quenched, and all faces [c]from the south to the north shall be burnt therein.

48 And all flesh shall see that I the LORD have kindled it: it shall not be quenched.

49 Then said I, Ah Lord GOD, they say of me, Doth he not speak parables?

The LORD's sword

21 And the word of the LORD came unto me, saying,

2 [a]Son of man, set thy face toward Jerusa-

20:33 [a]Jer. 21:5
20:35 [a]Jer. 2:9,35; ch. 17:20
20:36 [a]Num. 14:21-23,28
20:37 [1]Or, *delivering* [a]Lev. 27:32; Jer. 33:13
20:38 [a]ch. 34:17; Mat. 25:32 [b]Jer. 44:14
20:39 [a]Judg. 10:14; Ps. 81:12; Amos 4:4 [b]Is. 1:13; ch. 23:38
20:40 [1]Or, *chief* [a]Is. 2:2,3; ch. 17:23; Mic. 4:1 [b]Is. 56:7; 60:7; Zech. 8:20; Mal. 3:4; Rom. 12:1
20:41 [1]Heb. *savour of rest* [a]Eph. 5:2; Phil. 4:18
20:42 [a]ver. 38,44; ch. 36:23; 38:23 [b]ch. 11:17; 34:13; 36:24
20:43 [a]ch. 16:61 [b]Lev. 26:39; ch. 6:9; Hos. 5:15
20:44 [a]ver. 38; ch. 24:24 [b]ch. 36:22
20:46 [a]ch. 21:2
20:47 [a]Jer. 21:14 [b]Luke 23:31 [c]ch. 21:4
21:2 [a]ch. 20:46

20:33 *mighty hand . . . stretched out arm.* Terminology of the exodus (cf. Deut 4:34; 5:15; 7:19; 11:2; 26:8).

20:35 *wilderness of the people.* Exile among the nations would be for Israel like a return to the wilderness through which she journeyed on the way to the promised land (see Hos 2:14).

20:37 *cause you to pass under the rod.* The way a shepherd counts or separates his flock (see Lev 27:32; Jer 33:13; Mat 25:32–33). *I will bring you into the bond of the covenant.* As He had in the Sinai wilderness (see 16:60,62).

20:38 *purge.* As in the first wilderness experience, many were not allowed to enter the land (see Num 14:26–35).

20:39 *Go ye, serve ye every one his idols.* Irony; the opposite is meant (cf. 1 Ki 22:15; Amos 4:4).

20:40 *mine holy mountain.* Mentioned only here in Ezekiel, it refers to Jerusalem or Zion (see Ps 2:6; 3:4; 15:1; see also Is 11:9; 56:7; 57:13; 65:11; Obad 16; Zeph 3:11). *all the house of Israel.* Includes the northern kingdom, which fell in 722–721 B.C. (see 11:15; 36:10). *will I require.* See Deut 23:21; Mic 6:8. *offerings.* Possibly refers to a prescribed contribution. The other 19 occurrences in Ezekiel of the Hebrew for this word are confined to chs. 44–48, where the reference is to the land set aside for the temple and priests (see 45:1; 48:8–10) or to the special gifts for the priests (see 44:30). *firstfruits of your oblations.* Voluntary contributions.

20:41 *with your sweet savour.* Or, "as a sweet savour," used either in a metaphorical sense (as in Eph 5:2) or in a literal sense (as in 6:13). *bring you out.* Cf. v. 34.

20:43 *shall ye remember . . . and . . . lothe yourselves.* A thorough repentance (see 6:9; 16:63; 36:31; Luke 15:17–19).

20:44 *for my name's sake.* Summarizes and concludes the oracle (see note on v. 9).

‡20:46 *set thy face.* A posture required eight times of Ezekiel (here; 13:17; 21:2; 25:2; 28:21; 29:2; 35:2; 38:2). *toward the south.* I.e. toward Judah and Jerusalem, the object of all of Ezekiel's prophesying in these chapters. Any Babylonian invasion would traverse the Holy Land from north to south (see 26:7). Some translations read "toward Teman"; the Hebrew may be translated as a place name (Teman) or as a point of the compass (south).

20:47 *kindle a fire.* Common figurative language for invading forces (see Is 10:16–19; Jer 15:14; 17:4,27; 21:14; see also note on 15:7). *green . . . dry tree.* All trees (cf. 17:24; Luke 23:31). *from the south to the north.* Expresses totality, not direction; equivalent to saying, "from the border on the right to that on the left."

20:49 *parables.* See note on 17:2; for other ridiculing of the prophet see 12:21–28; 33:32.

21:2 *set thy face.* See note on 20:46. *toward the holy places.* See 9:6 and note.

lem, and [b]drop *thy word* toward the holy
places, and prophesy against the land of Israel,
3 And say to the land of Israel, Thus saith
the LORD; Behold, I *am* against thee, and will
draw forth my sword out of his sheath, and will
cut off from thee [a]the righteous and the wicked.
4 Seeing then that I will cut off from thee
the righteous and the wicked, therefore shall
my sword go forth out of his sheath against all
flesh [a]from the south *to* the north:
5 That all flesh may know that I the LORD
have drawn forth my sword out of his sheath:
it [a]shall not return any more.
6 [a]Sigh therefore, thou son of man, with
the breaking of *thy* loins; and with bitterness
sigh before their eyes.
7 And it shall be, when they say unto thee,
Wherefore sighest thou? that thou shalt answer, For the tidings; because it cometh: and
every heart shall melt, and [a]all hands shall be
feeble, and every spirit shall faint, and all
knees [1]shall be weak *as* water: behold, it
cometh, and shall be brought to pass, saith the
Lord GOD.
8 ¶ Again the word of the LORD came unto
me, saying,
9 Son of man, prophesy, and say, Thus saith
the LORD; Say, [a]A sword, a sword is sharpened,
and also furbished:
10 It is sharpened to make a sore slaughter;
it is furbished that it may glitter: should we
then make mirth? [1]it contemneth the rod of
my son, *as* every tree.
11 And he hath given it to be furbished,
that *it* may be handled: this sword is sharpened, and it *is* furbished, to give it into the
hand of [a]the slayer.
12 Cry and howl, son of man: for it shall be
upon my people, it *shall be* upon all the
princes of Israel: [1]terrors by reason of the
sword shall be upon my people: [a]smite therefore upon *thy* thigh.
13 [1]Because *it is* [a]a trial, and what if *the
sword* contemn even the rod? [b]it shall be no
more, saith the Lord GOD.
14 Thou therefore, son of man, prophesy,
and [a]smite *thine* [1]hands together, and let the
sword be doubled the third time, the sword of
the slain: it *is* the sword of the great *men that
are* slain, which entereth into their [b]privy
chambers.
15 I have set the [1]point of the sword
against all their gates, that *their* heart may
faint, and *their* ruins be multiplied: ah, [a]*it is*
made bright, *it is* [2]wrapt up for the slaughter.
16 [a]Go thee one way or other, *either* on
the right hand, [1]*or* on the left, whithersoever
thy face *is* set.
17 I will also [a]smite mine hands together,
and [b]I will cause my fury to rest: I the LORD
have said *it.*
18 ¶ The word of the LORD came unto me
again, saying,
19 Also, thou son of man, appoint thee two
ways, that the sword of the king of Babylon
may come: both twain shall come forth out of
one land: and choose thou a place, choose *it,*
at the head of the way to the city.
20 Appoint a way, that the sword may
come to [a]Rabbath of the Ammonites, and to
Judah in Jerusalem the defenced.
21 For the king of Babylon stood at the
[1]parting of the way, at the head of the two
ways, to use divination: he made *his* [2]arrows
bright, he consulted with [3]images, he looked
in the liver.

21:2 [b]Amos 7:16
21:3 [a]Job 9:22
21:4 [a]ch. 20:47
21:5 [a]Is. 45:23; 55:11
21:6 [a]Is. 22:4
21:7 [1]Heb. *shall go into water* [a]ch. 7:17
21:9 [a]ver. 15,28; Deut. 32:41
21:10 [1]Or, it is *the rod of my son, it despiseth every tree*
21:11 [a]ver. 19
21:12 [1]Or, *they are thrust down to the sword with my people* [a]Jer. 31:19
21:13 [1]Or, *When the trial* hath been, *what then? shall they not also belong to the despising rod?* [a]Job 9:23; 2 Cor. 8:2 [b]ver. 27
21:14 [1]Heb. *hand to hand* [a]Num. 24:10 [b]1 Ki. 20:30
21:15 [1]Or, *glittering,* or, *fear* [2]Or, *sharpened* [a]ver. 10,28
21:16 [1]Heb. *set thyself, take the left hand* [a]ch. 14:17
21:17 [a]ver. 14; ch. 22:13 [b]ch. 5:13
21:20 [a]Jer. 49:2; Amos 1:14
21:21 [1]Heb. *mother of the way* [2]Or, *knives* [3]Heb. *teraphim*

21:3 *I am against thee.* See note on 5:8. *my sword.* For the sword of the Lord's judgment see Is 31:8; 34:6; 66:16. This is the first of five sword oracles (see vv. 8–17, 18–24, 25–27, 28–32). Here the sword refers to Babylon and Nebuchadnezzar (v. 19). *the righteous and the wicked.* Indicates the completeness of the judgment that is about to come on Israel. No one will escape its devastating effects, not even the righteous in the land. Contrast God's deliverance of Noah (Gen 6:7–8) and Lot (Gen 18:23; 19:12–13).
21:4 *from the south to the north.* See note on 20:47.
21:6 *Sigh therefore, . . . with bitterness sigh.* Ezekiel's display of intense grief is to serve as another prophetic sign and as an occasion for a new message of impending judgment.
21:7 *when they say unto thee.* Cf. 12:9 for the people's response to Ezekiel's behavior. This is Ezekiel's seventh symbolic act (see Introduction: Literary Features).
21:9 *A sword, a sword.* A sword song (see note on v. 3), possibly accompanied by dancing or symbolic actions. Such songs may have been sung by warriors about to go into battle (see note on 2 Sam 1:18).
21:10 To think that the Babylonians would conquer every other country except Judah was a false hope. *rod.* Represents rule, government or kingdom. *my son.* Corresponds to "my people" in v. 12 (see Gen 49:9).
21:11 *slayer.* Nebuchadnezzar (v. 19).
21:12 *Cry and howl . . . smite. . . thy thigh.* Eighth symbolic act (see Introduction: Literary Features).
21:13 *it is a trial.* Of Judah. *what if the sword contemn even the rod?* See note on v. 10. The question anticipates the final interruption of Davidic kingship, which came in 586 B.C. (see vv. 25–27).
21:14 *smite thine hands together.* See 6:11 and note. *let the sword be doubled.* Cf. 2 Ki 13:18–19.
21:17 *smite mine hands together.* In scorn and in harmony with God's command to Ezekiel in v. 14.
21:19 *king of Babylon.* Nebuchadnezzar. *one land.* Babylon, or possibly Aram (Syria)—Nebuchadnezzar headquartered at Riblah in northern Aram (see 2 Ki 25:6).
21:20 *Rabbath.* Capital of Ammon (Jer 49:2); modern Amman (capital of Jordan).
21:21 *to use divination . . . his arrows.* For the purpose of seeking good omens for the coming campaign—a practice not elsewhere mentioned in the Bible. Apparently arrows were labeled (e.g., "Rabbath," "Jerusalem"), placed into a quiver and drawn out, one with each hand. Right-hand selection was seen as a good omen (see v. 22). *images.* Miniature representations of the gods worshiped by the family or clan (see Gen 31:19). Consulting them is referred to in Hos 3:4; Zech 10:2. The household idols of Gen 31:19–35 were small enough to hide in a saddle, but others were life-size (1 Sam 19:13–16). *looked in the liver.* Looking at the color and configurations of sheep livers to foretell the future was common in ancient Babylonia and Rome, but the practice is not mentioned elsewhere in the Bible.

22 At his right hand was the divination for Jerusalem, to appoint [1][2]captains, to open the mouth in the slaughter, to [a]lift up the voice with shouting, [b]to appoint *battering* rams against the gates, to cast a mount, *and* to build a fort.

23 And it shall be unto them as a false divination in their sight, [1]to them that [a]have sworn oaths: but he will call to remembrance the iniquity, that *they* may be taken.

24 Therefore thus saith the Lord GOD; Because ye have made your iniquity to be remembered, in that your transgressions are discovered, so that in all your doings your sins do appear; because, *I say,* that ye are come to remembrance, ye shall be taken with the hand.

25 ¶ And thou, [a]profane wicked prince of Israel, [b]whose day is come, when iniquity *shall have* an end,

26 Thus saith the Lord GOD; Remove the diadem, and take off the crown: this *shall* not *be* the same: [a]exalt *him that is* low, and abase *him that is* high.

27 [1]I will overturn, overturn, overturn it: [a]and it shall be no *more,* until he come whose right it is; and I will give it *him.*

28 ¶ And thou, son of man, prophesy and say, Thus saith the Lord GOD [a]concerning the Ammonites, and concerning their reproach; even say thou, The sword, the sword *is* drawn: for the slaughter *it is* furbished, to consume because of the glittering:

29 Whiles *they* [a]see vanity unto thee, whiles *they* divine a lie unto thee, to bring thee upon the necks of *them that are* slain of the wicked, [b]whose day is come, when *their* iniquity *shall have* an end.

30 [a][1]Shall I cause *it* to return into his sheath? [b]I will judge thee in the place where thou wast created, [c]in the land of thy nativity.

31 And I will [a]pour out mine indignation upon thee, I will [b]blow against thee in the fire of my wrath, and deliver thee into the hand of [1]brutish men, *and* skilful to destroy.

32 Thou shalt be for fuel to the fire; thy blood shall be in the midst of the land; [a]thou shalt be no *more* remembered: for I the LORD have spoken *it.*

The indictment of Jerusalem

22 Moreover the word of the LORD came unto me, saying,

2 Now, thou son of man, [a]wilt thou [1]judge, wilt thou judge [b]the [2]bloody city? yea, thou shalt [3]shew her all her abominations.

3 Then say thou, Thus saith the Lord GOD, The city sheddeth blood in the midst of it, that her time may come, and maketh idols against herself to defile *herself.*

4 Thou art become guilty in thy blood that thou hast [a]shed; and hast defiled *thyself* in thine idols which thou hast made; and thou hast caused thy days to draw near, and art come *even* unto thy years: [b]therefore have I made thee a reproach unto the heathen, and a mocking to all countries.

5 *Those that be* near, and *those that be* far from thee, shall mock thee, *which art* [1]infamous *and* much vexed.

6 Behold, [a]the princes of Israel, every one were in thee to their [1]power to shed blood.

7 In thee have they [a]set light by father and mother: in the midst of thee have they [b]dealt by [1]oppression with the stranger: in thee have they vexed the fatherless and the widow.

8 Thou hast despised mine holy *things,* and hast [a]profaned my sabbaths.

9 In thee are [a][1]men that carry tales to shed blood: [b]and in thee they eat upon the mountains: in the midst of thee they commit lewdness.

10 In thee have they [a]discovered their father's nakedness: in thee have they humbled her that was [b]set apart for pollution.

11 And [1]one hath committed abomination [a]with his neighbour's wife; and [1]another [b]hath [2]lewdly defiled his daughter in law; and [1]another in thee hath humbled his [c]sister, his father's daughter.

21:22 [1]Or, battering *rams* [2]Heb. *rams* [a]Jer. 51:14 [b]ch. 4:2
21:23 [1]Or, *for the oaths made unto them* [a]ch. 17:13
21:25 [a]Jer. 52:2 [b]ver. 29
21:26 [a]Luke 1:52
21:27 [1]Heb. *Perverted, perverted, perverted, will I make it* [a]Gen. 49:10; Luke 1:32
21:28 [a]ch. 25:2,3
21:29 [a]ch. 12:24 [b]Job 18:20; Ps. 37:13
21:30 [1]Or, *Cause it to return* [a]Jer. 47:6,7 [b]Gen. 15:14 [c]ch. 16:3
21:31 [1]Or, *burning* [a]ch. 7:8 [b]ch. 22:20
21:32 [a]ch. 25:10
22:2 [1]Or, *plead for* [2]Heb. *city of bloods?* [3]Heb. *make her know* [a]ch. 20:4 [b]Nah. 3:1
22:4 [a]2 Ki. 21:16 [b]Deut. 28:37; Dan. 9:16
22:5 [1]Heb. *polluted of name, much in vexation*
22:6 [1]Heb. *arm* [a]Is. 1:23
22:7 [1]Or, *deceit* [a]Deut. 27:16 [b]Ex. 22:21
22:8 [a]Lev. 19:30
22:9 [1]Heb. *men of slanders* [a]Lev. 19:16 [b]ch. 18:6,11
22:10 [a]Lev. 18:7,8 [b]Lev. 18:19
22:11 [1]Or, *every one* [2]Or, *by lewdness* [a]Lev. 18:20 [b]Lev. 18:15 [c]Lev. 18:9

21:23 *false divination.* The leaders of Jerusalem, once submissive to Nebuchadnezzar but now in rebellion (2 Ki 24:20), hoped that the result of the omen-seeking (vv. 21–22) was misleading.
21:25 *prince of Israel.* Zedekiah (see note on 7:27).
21:26 *diadem.* Only here is it mentioned as royal headwear. Elsewhere it is worn by priests (Ex 28:4,37,39; 29:6; 39:28,31; Lev 8:9; 16:4), as a setting for the crown (Ex 28:36–37; 29:6; 39:31; Lev 8:9). It was made of fine linen (Ex 28:39; 39:28). *exalt . . . low . . . abase . . . high.* A common Biblical expression for the reversal of human conditions because of the intervention of the Lord (see 17:24; 1 Sam 2:7–8; Luke 1:52–53).
21:27 *overturn, overturn, overturn.* Threefold repetition for emphasis (see Is 6:3; Jer 7:4). *until he come whose right it is.* The Messiah; apparently an allusion to Gen 49:10 (see note there). Or possibly the reference is to Nebuchadnezzar, translating "whose right it is" as "whose is the judgment" (see 2 Ki 25:6).
21:28 *the Ammonites.* See v. 20. After judgment on Jerusalem, the foreigners would be dealt with (cf. Is 10:5). *their reproach.* See 25:3,6; also cf. 36:15. *The sword, the sword.* Nebuchadnezzar's (see vv. 9,19 and notes).
21:29 *see vanity . . . divine a lie.* Apparently Ammon also had false prophets of peace (see v. 10 and note; 13:10; Jer 6:14; 8:11–12). *to bring thee.* Nebuchadnezzar's sword.
21:30 *Shall I cause it . . . ?* Or, "Cause it," addressing Nebuchadnezzar.
21:31 *brutish men.* The people of the East, as in 25:4.
22:2 *wilt thou judge . . . ?* Cf. 20:4. *the bloody city.* Jerusalem, the usual focal point of Ezekiel's prophecy (see 5:5).
22:3 *sheddeth blood . . . maketh idols.* Two categories of sins are developed: social injustices and idol worship. *idols.* See note on 6:4.
22:6 *princes of Israel.* Leaders generally, not kings; contrast 21:12 with 19:1.
22:7 *vexed the fatherless and the widow.* Cf. Is 1:17.
22:8 *sabbaths.* A major concern in Ezekiel (see note on 20:12).
22:9 *eat upon the mountains . . . commit lewdness.* See notes on 6:3; 16:15; 18:6.
22:10 *humbled her that was set apart for pollution.* Cf. 18:6.
22:11 *abomination.* All the sins mentioned in this verse were specifically forbidden in the law (Lev 18:7–20; 20:10–21; Deut 22:22–23,30; 27:22).

12 In thee [a]have they taken gifts to shed
blood; [b]thou hast taken usury and increase,
and thou hast greedily gained of thy neighbours by extortion, and [c]hast forgotten me,
saith the Lord GOD.
13 Behold therefore, I have [a]smitten mine
hand at thy dishonest gain which thou hast
made, and at thy blood which hath been in the
midst of thee.
14 [a]Can thine heart endure, or can thine
hands be strong, in the days that I shall deal
with thee? [b]I the LORD have spoken *it,* and will
do *it.*
15 And [a]I will scatter thee among the heathen, and disperse thee in the countries, and
[b]will consume thy filthiness out of thee.
16 And thou [1]shalt take thine inheritance
in thyself in the sight of the heathen, and
[a]thou shalt know that I *am* the LORD.
17 ¶ And the word of the LORD came unto
me, saying,
18 Son of man, [a]the house of Israel is to
me become dross: all they *are* brass, and tin,
and iron, and lead, in the midst of the furnace;
they are *even the* [1]dross *of* silver.
19 Therefore thus saith the Lord GOD; Because ye are all become dross, behold therefore, I will gather you into the midst of Jerusalem.
20 [1]*As they* gather silver, and brass, and
iron, and lead, and tin, into the midst of the
furnace, to blow the fire upon it, to melt *it;* so
will I gather *you* in mine anger and in my fury,
and I will leave *you there,* and melt you.
21 Yea, I will gather you, and blow upon
you in the fire of my wrath, and ye shall be
melted in the midst thereof.
22 As silver is melted in the midst of the
furnace, so shall ye be melted in the midst
thereof; and ye shall know that I the LORD
have [a]poured out my fury upon you.
23 ¶ And the word of the LORD came unto
me, saying,
24 Son of man, say unto her, Thou *art* the
land that is not cleansed, nor rained upon in
the day of indignation.
25 [a]*There is* a conspiracy of her prophets
in the midst thereof, like a roaring lion ravening the prey; they [b]have devoured souls; [c]they
have taken the treasure and precious things;
they have made her many widows in the midst
thereof.
26 [a]Her priests have [1]violated my law, and
have [b]profaned mine holy *things:* they have
put no [c]difference between the holy and profane, neither have they shewed *difference* between the unclean and the clean, and have hid
their eyes from my sabbaths, and I am profaned among them.
27 Her [a]princes in the midst thereof *are*
like wolves ravening the prey, to shed blood,
and to destroy souls, to get dishonest gain.
28 And [a]her prophets have daubed them
with untempered *morter,* [b]seeing vanity, and
divining lies unto them, saying, Thus saith the
Lord GOD, when the LORD hath not spoken.
29 The people of the land have used [1]op-
pression, and exercised robbery, and have
vexed the poor and needy: yea, they have [a]op-
pressed the stranger [2]wrongfully.
30 [a]And I sought for a man among them,
that *should* [b]make up the hedge, and [c]stand in
the gap before me for the land, that *I* should
not destroy it: but I found none.
31 Therefore have I [a]poured out mine indignation upon them; I have consumed them
with the fire of my wrath: [b]their own way
have I recompensed upon their heads, saith
the Lord GOD.

Two adulterous sisters

23 The word of the LORD came again
unto me, saying,
2 Son of man, there were [a]two women, the
daughters of one mother:
3 And [a]they committed whoredoms in
Egypt; they committed whoredoms in [b]their
youth: there were their breasts pressed, and
there they bruised the teats of their virginity.
4 And the names of them *were* Aholah the
elder, and Aholibah her sister: and [a]they were
mine, and they bare sons and daughters. Thus
were their names; Samaria *is* [1]Aholah, and Jerusalem [2]Aholibah.
5 ¶ And Aholah played the harlot when she
was mine; and she doted on her lovers, on
[a]the Assyrians *her* neighbours,
6 *Which were* clothed with blue, captains

22:12 [a]Ex. 23:8; Deut. 16:19 [b]Ex. 22:25 [c]Jer. 3:21
22:13 [a]ch. 21:17
22:14 [a]ch. 21:7 [b]ch. 17:24
22:15 [a]Deut. 4:27 [b]ch. 23:27
22:16 [1]Or, *shalt be profaned* [a]Ps. 9:16
22:18 [1]Heb. *drosses* [a]Ps. 119:119; Is. 1:22; Jer. 6:28
22:20 [1]Heb. According to *the gathering*
22:22 [a]ch. 20:8,33
22:25 [a]Hos. 6:9 [b]Mat. 23:14 [c]Mic. 3:11
22:26 [1]Heb. *offered violence to* [a]Mal. 2:8 [b]1 Sam. 2:29 [c]Lev. 10:10
22:27 [a]Is. 1:23; ch. 22:6
22:28 [a]ch. 13:10 [b]ch. 13:6,7
22:29 [1]Or, *deceit* [2]Heb. *without right* [a]Ex. 23:9; Lev. 19:33
22:30 [a]Jer. 5:1 [b]ch. 13:5 [c]Ps. 106:23
22:31 [a]ver. 22 [b]ch. 9:10
23:2 [a]Jer. 3:7,8
23:3 [a]Lev. 17:7; Josh. 24:14 [b]ch. 16:22
23:4 [1][That is, *His tent,* or, *tabernacle*] [2][That is, *My tabernacle in her,* 1 Ki. 8:29] [a]ch. 16:8,20
23:5 [a]Hos. 8:9

22:12 *usury and increase.* See note on 18:8.
22:13 *smitten mine hand.* In anger (see 21:14,17).
22:18 *dross.* For references to Jerusalem as a furnace see Is 1:21–26; Jer 6:27–30. Typically, imagery used by others to represent purifying was used by Ezekiel to picture total destruction (see note on 15:4).
22:25 *prophets.* Ezekiel begins to speak plainly concerning the "dross" of vv. 18–22. All of Jerusalem's leaders and people were included: prophets (here and v. 28), priests (v. 26), princes (v. 27), people (v. 29). *like a roaring lion.* Cf. v. 27; 13:4; Zeph 3:3.
22:26 *they have put no difference between the holy and profane.* The main duty of priests (see 44:23). *sabbaths.* See note on v. 8.
22:28 *daubed them with untempered morter.* See 13:10 and note.
22:29 *people of the land.* See 7:27 and note.
22:30 *I sought for a man.* Cf. Is 51:18; 59:16; 63:5. *stand in the gap before me.* See note on 13:5. To intercede with God in behalf of the people was part of a prophet's task (Gen 20:7; 1 Sam 12:23; Jer 37:3; 42:2). Some interpret the task here as teaching, particularly calling the people to repentance. Cf. the task of the prophetic "watchman" (3:17–21; 33:1–6).
23:4 *Aholah.* Means "her tent." *Aholibah.* Means "My tent is in her." Cf. the two sisters of Jer 3:6–12. "Tent" could stand for Canaanite high places, for the Lord's tabernacle (except that Ezekiel never uses the word elsewhere for the legitimate shrine) or for Israel's tent-dwelling origin.
23:5 *played the harlot.* Here represents political alliances with pagan powers—not idolatry as in ch. 16 (see note on 16:15). The graphic language of the chapter underscores God's and Ezekiel's disgust with Israel for playing the worldly game of international politics rather than relying on the Lord for her

and rulers, all of them desirable young men, horsemen riding upon horses.

7 Thus she [1]committed her whoredoms with them, *with* all them *that were* [2]the chosen men of Assyria, and with all *on* whom she doted: with all their idols she defiled herself.

8 Neither left she her whoredoms *brought* [a]from Egypt: for in her youth they lay with her, and they bruised the breasts of her virginity, and poured their whoredom upon her.

9 Wherefore I have delivered her into the hand of her lovers, into the hand of the [a]Assyrians, upon whom she doted.

10 These discovered her nakedness: they took her sons and her daughters, and slew her with the sword: and she became [1]famous among women; for they had executed judgment upon her.

11 ¶ And [a]when her sister Aholibah saw *this,* [b1]she was more corrupt in her inordinate love than she, and in her whoredoms [2]more than her sister in *her* whoredoms.

12 She doted upon the [a]Assyrians *her* neighbours, [b]captains and rulers clothed most gorgeously, horsemen riding upon horses, all of them desirable young men.

13 Then I saw that she was defiled, *that* they took both one way,

14 And *that* she increased her whoredoms: for when she saw men pourtrayed upon the wall, the images of the Chaldeans pourtrayed with vermilion,

15 Girded with girdles upon their loins, exceeding in dyed attire upon their heads, all of them princes to look to, *after* the manner of the Babylonians of Chaldea, the land of their nativity:

16 [a]And [1]as soon as she saw them with her eyes, she doted upon them, and sent messengers unto them into Chaldea.

17 And the [1]Babylonians came to her into the bed of love, and they defiled her with their whoredom, and she was polluted with them, and [a]her mind was [2]alienated from them.

18 So she discovered her whoredoms, and discovered her nakedness: then [a]my mind was alienated from her, like as my mind was alienated from her sister.

19 Yet she multiplied her whoredoms, in calling to remembrance the days of her youth, [a]wherein she had played the harlot in the land of Egypt.

20 For she doted upon their paramours, whose flesh *is as* the flesh of asses, and whose issue *is like* the issue of horses.

21 Thus thou calledst to remembrance the lewdness of thy youth, in bruising thy teats by the Egyptians for the paps of thy youth.

22 ¶ Therefore, O Aholibah, thus saith the Lord GOD; [a]Behold, I will raise up thy lovers against thee, from whom thy mind is alienated, and I will bring them against thee on every side;

23 The Babylonians, and all the Chaldeans, [a]Pekod, and Shoa, and Koa, all the Assyrians with them: [b]all of them desirable young men, captains and rulers, great lords and renowned, all of them riding upon horses.

24 And they shall come against thee *with* chariots, wagons, and wheels, and with an assembly of people, *which* shall set against thee buckler and shield and helmet round about: and I will set judgment before them, and they shall judge thee according to their judgments.

25 And I will set my jealousy against thee, and they shall deal furiously with thee: they shall take away thy nose and thine ears; and thy remnant shall fall by the sword: they shall take thy sons and thy daughters; and thy residue shall be devoured by the fire.

26 [a]They shall also strip thee out of thy clothes, and take away thy [1]fair jewels.

27 Thus [a]will I make thy lewdness to cease from thee, and thy [b]whoredom *brought* from the land of Egypt: so that thou shalt not lift up thine eyes unto them, nor remember Egypt any more.

28 For thus saith the Lord GOD; Behold, I *will* deliver thee into the hand *of them* [a]whom thou hatest, into the hand *of them* [b]from whom thy mind is alienated:

29 And they shall deal with thee hatefully, and shall take *away* all thy labour, and [a]shall leave thee naked and bare: and the nakedness of thy whoredoms shall be discovered, both thy lewdness and thy whoredoms.

30 *I will* do these *things* unto thee, because thou hast [a]gone a whoring after the heathen, *and* because thou art polluted with their idols.

31 Thou hast walked in the way of thy sister; therefore will I give her [a]cup into thine hand.

23:7 [1]Heb. *bestowed her whoredoms upon them* [2]Heb. *the choice of the children of Asshur* 23:8 [a]ver. 3 23:9 [a]2 Ki. 17:3 23:10 [1]Heb. *a name* 23:11 [1]Heb. *she corrupted her inordinate love more than, etc.* [2]Heb. *more than the whoredoms of her sister* [a]Jer. 3:8 [b]Jer. 3:11 23:12 [a]2 Ki. 16:7 [b]ver. 6,23 23:16 [1]Heb. *at the sight of her eyes* [a]2 Ki. 24:1 23:17 [1]Heb. *children of Babel* [2]Heb. *loosed, or, disjointed* [a]ver. 22,28 23:18 [a]Jer. 6:8

23:19 [a]ver. 3 23:22 [a]ver. 28; ch. 16:37 23:23 [a]Jer. 50:21 [b]ver. 12 23:26 [1]Heb. *instruments of thy decking* [a]ch. 16:39 23:27 [a]ch. 16:41; 22:15 [b]ver. 3,19 23:28 [a]ch. 16:37 [b]ver. 17 23:29 [a]ver. 26; ch. 16:39 23:30 [a]ch. 6:9 23:31 [a]Jer. 25:15

security—as clear a case of religious prostitution as idolatry. *Assyrians.* See 2 Ki 15:19.

23:8 *from Egypt.* Cf. 20:5–8. Israel's entire history was marked by unfaithfulness. For her attachment to Egypt see Ex 17:3; Num 11:5,18,20; 14:2–4; 21:5.

23:10 *discovered her nakedness.* A reference to the fall of Samaria to the Assyrians in 722–721 B.C.

23:14 *men pourtrayed upon the wall.* Arousal through pictures was even more perverted (see 16:17 and note). *pourtrayed with vermilion.* Jeremiah, too, noted red interior decorations with disfavor (Jer 22:14).

23:15 *girdles.* Cf. Is 5:27 for similar Assyrian military equipment.

23:20 *flesh.* Probably referring to genitals (see note on 16:26).

23:23 *Babylonians . . . Chaldeans.* Often identified with one another (see 12:13), here distinguished (as in v. 15), probably because the Chaldeans were relative newcomers. *Pekod.* Aramaic people located east of Babylon. *Shoa, and Koa.* Babylonian allies of uncertain origin and location.

23:24 *their judgments.* Which were cruel and gruesome (see v. 25).

23:25 *fire.* See notes on 15:7; 20:47.

23:27 *of Egypt.* See note on v. 8.

23:31 *cup.* Filled with the anger of the Lord. To drink it was to die. For a development of the imagery cf. Ps 75:8; Is 51:17,22; Jer 25:15–29; 49:12; Lam 4:21; Obad 16; Hab 2:16; Mat 20:22; 26:39; Rev 14:10.

32 Thus saith the Lord GOD; Thou shalt drink *of* thy sister's cup deep and large: [a]thou shalt be laughed to scorn and had in derision; *it* containeth much.

33 Thou shalt be filled *with* drunkenness and sorrow, *with* the cup of astonishment and desolation, *with* the cup of thy sister Samaria.

34 Thou shalt [a]even drink it and suck *it* out, and thou shalt break the sheards thereof, and pluck off thine own breasts: for I have spoken *it*, saith the Lord GOD.

35 Therefore thus saith the Lord GOD; Because thou [a]hast forgotten me, and [b]cast me behind thy back, therefore bear thou also thy lewdness and thy whoredoms.

36 ¶ The LORD said moreover unto me; Son of man, wilt thou [a][1]judge Aholah and Aholibah? yea, [b]declare unto them their abominations;

37 That they have committed adultery, and [a]blood *is* in their hands, and with their idols have they committed adultery, and have also caused their sons, [b]whom they bare unto me, to pass for them through *the fire*, to devour *them*.

38 Moreover this they have done unto me: they have defiled my sanctuary in the same day, and [a]have profaned my sabbaths.

39 For when they had slain their children to their idols, then they came the same day into my sanctuary to profane it; and lo, [a]thus have they done in the midst of mine house.

40 And furthermore, that ye have sent for men [1]to come from far, [a]unto whom a messenger *was* sent; and lo, they came: for whom thou didst [b]wash *thyself*, [c]paintedst thy eyes, and deckedst thyself with ornaments,

41 And satest upon a [1]stately [a]bed, and a table prepared before it, [b]whereupon thou hast set mine incense and mine oil.

42 And a voice of a multitude being at ease *was* with her: and with the men [1]of the common sort *were* brought [2]Sabeans from the wilderness, which put bracelets upon their hands, and beautiful crowns upon their heads.

43 Then said I unto *her that was* old *in* adulteries, Will they now commit [1]whoredoms with her, and she *with them?*

44 Yet they went in unto her, as *they* go in unto a woman that playeth the harlot: so went they in unto Aholah and unto Aholibah, the lewd women.

45 ¶ And *the* righteous men, they shall [a]judge them after the manner of adulteresses, and after the manner of *women* that shed blood; because they *are* adulteresses, and [b]blood *is* in their hands.

46 For thus saith the Lord GOD; [a]*I will* bring up a company upon them, and *will* give them [1]to be removed and spoiled.

47 [a]And the company shall stone them with stones, and [1]dispatch them with their swords; [b]they shall slay their sons and their daughters, and burn up their houses with fire.

48 Thus [a]will I cause lewdness to cease out of the land, [b]that all women may be taught not to do after your lewdness.

49 And they shall recompense your lewdness upon you, and ye shall [a]bear the sins of your idols: [b]and ye shall know that I *am* the Lord GOD.

The parable of the boiling pot

24 Again in the ninth year, in the tenth month, in the tenth *day* of the month, the word of the LORD came unto me, saying,

2 Son of man, write thee the name of the day, *even* of this same day: the king of Babylon set himself against Jerusalem [a]this same day.

3 [a]And utter a parable unto the rebellious house, and say unto them, Thus saith the Lord GOD; [b]Set on a pot, set *it* on, and also pour water into it:

4 Gather the pieces thereof into it, *even* every good piece, the thigh, and the shoulder; fill *it with* the choice bones.

5 Take the choice of the flock, and [1]burn also the bones under it, *and* make it boil well, and let them seethe the bones of it therein.

6 ¶ Wherefore thus saith the Lord GOD; Woe to [a]the bloody city, to the pot whose scum *is* therein, and whose scum is not gone out of it! bring it out piece by piece; let no [b]lot fall upon it.

7 For her blood is in the midst of her; she set it upon the top of a rock; [a]she poured it not upon the ground, to cover it with dust;

8 That *it* might cause fury to come up to

23:32 [a]ch. 22:4,5 **23:34** [a]Ps. 75:8; Is. 51:17 **23:35** [a]Jer. 2:32; 3:21; 13:25; ch. 22:12 [b]1 Ki. 14:9; Neh. 9:26 **23:36** [1]Or, *plead for* [a]ch. 20:4; 22:2 [b]Is. 58:1 **23:37** [a]ver. 45; ch. 16:38 [b]ch. 16:20, 21,36,45; 20:26,31 **23:38** [a]ch. 22:8 **23:39** [a]2 Ki. 21:4 **23:40** [1]Heb. *coming* [a]Is. 57:9 [b]Ruth 3:3 [c]2 Ki. 9:30; Jer. 4:30 **23:41** [1]Heb. *honourable* [a]Esth. 1:6; Is. 57:7; Amos 2:8; 6:4 [b]Prov. 7:17; ch. 16:18,19; Hos. 2:8 **23:42** [1]Heb. *of the multitude of men* [2]Or, *drunkards* **23:43** [1]Heb. *her whoredoms*

23:45 [a]ch. 16:38 [b]ver. 37 **23:46** [1]Heb. *for a removing and spoil* [a]ch. 16:40 **23:47** [1]Or, *single them out* [a]ch. 16:40 [b]2 Chr. 36:17,19; ch. 24:21 **23:48** [a]ch. 22:15 [b]Deut. 13:11; 2 Pet. 2:6 **23:49** [a]ver. 35 [b]ch. 20:38,42, 44; 25:5 **24:2** [a]2 Ki. 25:1; Jer. 39:1; 52:4 **24:3** [a]ch. 17:12 [b]See Jer. 1:13; ch. 11:3 **24:5** [1]Or, *heap* **24:6** [a]ch. 22:3 [b]See 2 Sam. 8:2; Joel 3:3; Obad. 11; Nah. 3:10 **24:7** [a]Lev. 17:13; Deut. 12:16

23:37 *sons . . . to pass for them through the fire.* See note on 16:20.

23:38 *defiled my sanctuary.* See ch. 8. *sabbaths.* See note on 22:8.

‡23:40 *ye have sent for men.* Possibly a reference to the Jerusalem summit meeting in Zedekiah's time (Jer 27). *thou.* Jerusalem. *paintedst thy eyes.* By daubing them with kohl, a soot-like compound, to draw attention to the eyes.

23:41 *a stately bed, and a table prepared before it.* Ready for a banquet (see Is 21:5; also Prov 9:2).

24:1 *ninth year . . . tenth month . . . tenth day of the month.* Jan. 15, 588 B.C.; Ezekiel's fourth date (see 1:2; 8:1; 20:1).

24:2 *write . . . this same day: the king . . . this same day.* God revealed to Ezekiel what was happening in Jerusalem.

24:3 *parable.* Cf. 17:2; 20:49. *rebellious house.* The last occurrence of this condemning phrase in Ezekiel (see 2:5,6,8; 3:9,26–27; 12:2–3,9,25; 17:12). Jerusalem's rebellion would soon be crushed. *pot.* The image of 11:3–12, a discussion of the remnant, here pictures total destruction. The cooking pot is Jerusalem (cf. 11:3).

24:4 *every good piece.* The people of Jerusalem who thought they were spared the exile in 597 B.C. because of their goodness (see 11:3 and note).

24:6 *bloody city.* Cf. 22:3. *whose scum.* Representing Jerusalem's irredeemable situation. *let no lot fall upon it.* After the siege of Jerusalem in 597, perhaps the Babylonians had cast lots to see whom they would take away into exile. Now everyone would go.

24:7 *blood . . . upon the top of a rock.* Jerusalem had brazenly left on display the blood she unjustly shed (cf. Is 3:9). For uncovered blood see Gen 4:10; Job 16:18; Is 26:21.

24:8 *fury.* God's wrath. What Jerusalem had begun (v. 7), God

take vengeance; [a]I have set her blood upon
the top of a rock, that *it* should not be covered.
9 Therefore thus saith the Lord GOD; [a]Woe
to the bloody city! I will even make the pile for
fire great.
10 Heap on wood, kindle the fire, consume
the flesh, and spice it well, and let the bones
be burnt.
11 Then set it empty upon the coals thereof, that the brass of it may be hot, and may
burn, and *that* [a]the filthiness of it may be
molten in it, *that* the scum of it may be consumed.
12 She hath wearied *herself with* lies, and
her great scum went not forth out of her: her
scum *shall be* in the fire.
13 In thy filthiness *is* lewdness: because I
have purged thee, and thou wast not purged,
thou shalt not be purged from thy filthiness
any more, [a]till I have caused my fury to rest
upon thee.
14 [a]I the LORD have spoken *it:* it shall come
to pass, and I will do *it;* I will not go back,
[b]neither will I spare, neither will I repent; according to thy ways, and according to thy doings, shall they judge thee, saith the Lord GOD.

The death of Ezekiel's wife

15 ¶ Also the word of the LORD came unto
me, saying,
16 Son of man, behold, I take away from
thee the desire of thine eyes with a stroke: yet
neither shalt thou mourn nor weep, neither
shall thy tears [1]run down.
17 [1]Forbear to cry, [a]make no mourning *for*
the dead, [b]bind the tire of thine head upon
thee, and [c]put on thy shoes upon thy feet, and
[d]cover not *thy* [e][2]lips, and eat not the bread of
men.
18 So I spake unto the people in the morning: and at even my wife died; and I did in the
morning as I was commanded.
19 ¶ And the people said unto me, [a]Wilt

24:8 [a]Mat. 7:2
24:9 [a]ver. 6; Hab. 2:12
24:11 [a]ch. 22:15
24:13 [a]ch. 8:18
24:14 [a]1 Sam. 15:29 [b]ch. 5:11
24:16 [1]Heb. *go*
24:17 [1]Heb. *Be silent* [2]Heb. *upper lip* [a]Jer. 16:5 [b]See Lev. 10:6; 21:10 [c]2 Sam. 15:30 [d]Mic. 3:7 [e]ver. 22; Lev. 13:45
24:19 [a]ch. 12:9; 37:18
24:21 [1]Heb. *the pity of your soul* [a]Jer. 7:14; ch. 7:20 [b]ch. 23:47
24:22 [a]ver. 17; Jer. 16:6,7
24:23 [a]Job 27:15; Ps. 78:64 [b]Lev. 26:39
24:24 [a]Is. 20:3; ch. 4:3; 12:6,11 [b]Jer. 17:15; John 13:19; 14:29 [c]ch. 6:7; 25:5
24:25 [1]Heb. *the lifting up of [their] soul* [a]ver. 21
24:26 [a]ch. 33:21
24:27 [a]ch. 3:26
25:2 [a]ch. 35:2 [b]Jer. 49:1; ch. 21:28; Zeph. 2:9
25:3 [a]Prov. 17:5; ch. 26:2

thou not tell us what these *things are* to us,
that thou doest *so?*
20 Then I answered them, The word of the
LORD came unto me, saying,
21 Speak unto the house of Israel, Thus
saith the Lord GOD; Behold, [a]I *will* profane my
sanctuary, the excellency of your strength, the
desire of your eyes, and [1]that which your soul
pitieth; [b]and your sons and your daughters
whom ye have left shall fall by the sword.
22 And ye shall do as I have done: [a]ye shall
not cover *your* lips, nor eat the bread of men.
23 And your tires *shall be* upon your
heads, and your shoes upon your feet: [a]ye
shall not mourn nor weep; but [b]ye shall pine
away for your iniquities, and mourn one towards another.
24 Thus [a]Ezekiel is unto you a sign: according to all that he hath done shall ye do:
[b]and when this cometh, [c]ye shall know that I
am the Lord GOD.
25 ¶ Also, thou son of man, *shall it* not *be*
in the day when I take from them [a]their
strength, the joy of their glory, the desire of
their eyes, and [1]that whereupon they set their
minds, their sons and their daughters,
26 *That* [a]he that escapeth in that day shall
come unto thee, to cause *thee* to hear *it* with
thine ears?
27 [a]In that day shall thy mouth be opened
to him which is escaped, and thou shalt speak,
and be no more dumb: and thou shalt be a sign
unto them; and they shall know that I *am* the
LORD.

Prophecy against Ammon

25 The word of the LORD came again
unto me, saying,
2 Son of man, [a]set thy face [b]against the
Ammonites, and prophesy against them;
3 And say unto the Ammonites, Hear the
word of the Lord GOD; Thus saith the Lord
GOD; [a]Because thou saidst, Aha, against my

would complete through judgment. Compare Ex 8:32 with Ex 9:12.

24:11 *it empty.* Jerusalem, emptied of inhabitants, would be set to the torch, in a vain final effort at purification.

24:13 *lewdness.* See 16:27; 22:9.

‡24:16 *desire of thine eyes.* The object of loving attention (see vv. 21,25)—refers to the prophet's wife. *a stroke.* Some swiftly fatal disease, one that often reached plague proportions (see Ex 9:14; Num 14:37).

24:17 *bind the tire of thine head.* The mourner normally removed his turban and put dust on his head (see Josh 7:6; 1 Sam 4:12). *shoes upon thy feet.* To remove them showed grief (see 2 Sam 15:30). *cover not thy lips.* A gesture of shame (Mic 3:7) or uncleanness (Lev 13:45). *bread of men.* The funeral meal (see Jer 16:7).

24:19 *the people said unto me.* The third time that the people responded to Ezekiel's behavior (see 12:9; 21:7).

24:21 *profane.* By letting Nebuchadnezzar burn it down.

24:24 *Ezekiel.* The prophet speaks of himself in the third person. Elsewhere his name occurs only in 1:3 (see note there). *sign.* See note on 12:6.

24:26 *he that escapeth.* The first of the exiles of 586 B.C. *to cause thee to hear it.* About the siege—its beginning (verifying the accuracy of vv. 1–2) and its ending (see note on 33:21).

24:27 *be no more dumb.* Ezekiel's wife died the same day the temple was burned (Aug. 14, 586 B.C.; see 2 Ki 25:8–9). See notes on 3:26; 33:21. *sign.* See note on 12:6.

‡25:1–32:32 Oracles against the nations. Frequently in the prophets, God's word of judgment on Israel is accompanied by oracles of judgment on the nations. These make clear that, while judgment begins "at the house of God" (1 Pet 4:17), the pagan nations would not escape God's wrath. Often these judgments are implicit messages of salvation for Israel (see 28:25–26) since the Lord's victories over hostile powers remove an enemy of His people or punish them for their cruel attacks on His people. In the case of Ezekiel there are seven oracles (the seventh of which has seven parts, each introduced by the phrase "The word of the LORD came to me"; see Introduction: Outline).

25:2 *set thy face.* See note on 20:46. *Ammonites.* Ammon (part of modern Jordan) was immediately east of Israel (see 21:20; see also Jer 9:26; 49:1–6; Amos 1:13–15; Zeph 2:8–11). For hostile Ammonite action during this time and later see 2 Ki 24:2; Neh 4:7.

‡25:3 *Aha.* A cry of malicious joy (cf. 26:2; 36:2; Ps 35:21–25).

sanctuary, when it was profaned; and against the land of Israel, when it was desolate; and against the house of Judah, when they went into captivity;

4 Behold therefore, I *will* deliver thee to the [1]men of the east for a possession, and they shall set their palaces in thee, and make their dwellings in thee: they shall eat thy fruit, and they shall drink thy milk.

5 And I will make [a]Rabbah [b]a stable for camels, and the Ammonites a couching place for flocks: [c]and ye shall know that I *am* the LORD.

6 For thus saith the Lord GOD; Because thou [a]hast clapped *thine* [1]hands, and stamped with the [2]feet, and [b]rejoiced in [3]heart with all thy despite against the land of Israel;

7 Behold therefore, I will [a]stretch out mine hand upon thee, and will deliver thee for [1]a spoil to the heathen; and I will cut thee off from the people, and I will cause thee to perish out of the countries: I will destroy thee; and thou shalt know that I *am* the LORD.

Prophecy against Moab

8 ¶ Thus saith the Lord GOD; Because that [a]Moab and [b]Seir do say, Behold, the house of Judah *is* like unto all the heathen;

9 Therefore behold, I *will* open the [1]side of Moab from the cities, from his cities *which are* on his frontiers, the glory of the country, Beth-jeshimoth, Baal-meon, and Kiriathaim,

10 [a]Unto the men of the east [1]with the Ammonites, and will give them in possession, that the Ammonites [b]may not be remembered among the nations.

11 And I will execute judgments upon Moab; and they shall know that I *am* the LORD.

25:4 [1]Heb. *children*
25:5 [a]ch. 21:20 [b]Is. 17:2 [c]ch. 24:24
25:6 [1]Heb. *hand* [2]Heb. *foot* [3]Heb. *soul* [a]Job 27:23; Lam. 2:15; Zeph. 2:15 [b]ch. 36:5
25:7 [1]Or, *meat* [a]ch. 35:3
25:8 [a]Is. 15; 16; Jer. 48:1; Amos 2:1 [b]ch. 35:2,5
25:9 [1]Heb. *shoulder of Moab*
25:10 [1]Or, *against the children of Ammon* [a]ver. 4 [b]ch. 21:32

25:12 [1]Heb. *by revenging revengement* [a]2 Chr. 28:17; Ps. 137:7; Jer. 49:7,8; Amos 1:11; Obad. 10
25:13 [1]Or, *they shall fall by the sword unto Dedan*
25:14 [a]Is. 11:14
25:15 [1]Or, with *perpetual hatred* [a]Jer. 25:20; Amos 1:6 [b]2 Chr. 28:18
25:16 [1]Or, *haven of the sea* [a]Zeph. 2:4 [b]1 Sam. 30:14 [c]Jer. 47:4
25:17 [1]Heb. *vengeances* [a]ch. 5:15 [b]Ps. 9:16
26:2 [a]Is. 23; Jer. 25:22; Amos 1:9; Zech. 9:2 [b]ch. 25:3

Prophecy against Edom

12 ¶ Thus saith the Lord GOD; [a]Because that Edom hath dealt against the house of Judah [1]by taking vengeance, and hath greatly offended, and revenged himself upon them;

13 Therefore thus saith the Lord GOD; I will also stretch out mine hand upon Edom, and will cut off man and beast from it; and I will make it desolate from Teman; and [1]they of Dedan shall fall by the sword.

14 And [a]I will lay my vengeance upon Edom by the hand of my people Israel: and they shall do in Edom according to mine anger and according to my fury; and they shall know my vengeance, saith the Lord GOD.

Prophecy against Philistia

15 ¶ Thus saith the Lord GOD; [a]Because [b]the Philistines have dealt by revenge, and have taken vengeance with a despiteful heart, to destroy *it* [1]*for* the old hatred;

16 Therefore thus saith the Lord GOD; Behold, [a]I *will* stretch out mine hand upon the Philistines, and I will cut off the [b]Cherethims, [c]and destroy the remnant of the [1]sea coast.

17 And I will [a]execute great [1]vengeance upon them with furious rebukes, [b]and they shall know that I *am* the LORD, when I shall lay my vengeance upon them.

Prophecy against Tyrus

26 And it came to pass in the eleventh year, in the first *day* of the month, *that* the word of the LORD came unto me, saying,

2 Son of man, [a]because that Tyrus hath said against Jerusalem, [b]Aha, she is broken *that was* the gates of the people: she is turned unto me: I shall be replenished, *now* she is laid waste:

25:4 *men of the east.* Probably nomadic tribes of the desert east of Ammon, though this could be a reference to Nebuchadnezzar and his army (see 21:31).
25:5 *Rabbah.* See note on 21:20. *stable . . . couching place.* A common OT description for destroyed cities (see Is 34:13–15; Zeph 2:13–15). The sites were returned to the conditions they were in before the cities were built, representing the undoing of human efforts.
25:6 *clapped thine hands.* See 6:11 and note.
25:7 *I will stretch out mine hand upon.* See note on 6:14. *spoil to the heathen.* Cf. 26:5; 34:28. *cut thee off.* Cf. v. 16.
25:8 *Moab.* Immediately to the south of Ammon, east of the Dead Sea (see Is 15–16; Jer 48; Amos 2:1–3; Zeph 2:8–11). *Seir.* Edom, a country south of Moab and south of the Dead Sea (see ch. 35, especially v. 15; 36:5; Is 34:5–17; 63:1–6; Jer 49:7–11; Amos 1:11–12). *like unto all the heathen.* Israel wanted to be like the nations (see 20:32 and note), but when the nations saw Judah in her apparent vulnerability and lost their awe of her, they failed to take her God seriously (cf. Lam 4:12).
25:9 *side of Moab.* Lower hills rising from the Dead Sea, visible from Jerusalem. *Beth-jeshimoth.* A town in the plains of Moab. *Baal-meon.* A major Moabite town mentioned in an inscribed monument of Mesha, king of Moab (see chart, p. xix). *Kiriathaim.* A city also mentioned in the Mesha inscription (cf. 2 Ki 3:4–5).
25:12 *Edom.* See note on v. 8 ("Seir"). *taking vengeance.* By not harboring Judah's refugees after 586 B.C. (see Obad 11–14).
25:13 *Teman.* A district near Petra in central Edom (see Jer 49:7,20; Amos 1:12; Obad 9; Hab 3:3). *Dedan.* A tribe and territory in southern Edom (see 27:20; 38:13; Is 21:13; Jer 49:8).
25:15 *Philistines.* Inhabitants of the coastal plain along the Mediterranean west of Judah (1 Sam 6:17), who strove for control of Canaan until subdued by David. Their hostility to Israel continued, however (see Is 14:29–31; Jer 47; Amos 1:6–8; Zeph 2:4–7), until Nebuchadnezzar deported them.
25:16 *Cherethims,* Related to, if not identical with, the Philistines (see 1 Sam 30:14 and note; 2 Sam 8:18; 15:18; 20:7). *sea coast.* Of the Mediterranean.
26:1 *eleventh year . . . first day of the month.* The number of the month is missing. The entire year dates from Apr. 23, 587, to Apr. 13, 586 B.C. The oracle must date from the end of that year, in the 11th (Feb. 13, 586) or the 12th month (Mar. 15, 586). See note on 33:21. This is the fifth date in the book (see 1:2; 8:1; 20:1; 24:1).
‡26:2 *Tyrus.* Or "Tyre," the island capital of Phoenicia (present-day Lebanon). It was involved in an anti-Assyrian coalition in 594 B.C. (see Jer 27:3). Ezekiel, more than any other prophet, prophesied against Tyre (see chs. 27–28; but see Is 23; Jer 25:22; 47:4; Joel 3:4–5; Amos 1:9–10; Zech 9:2–4). *Aha.* See note on 25:3. *gates of the people.* Because of its geographical location, its political importance and the central role it played in international trade. The anti-Assyrian summit meeting was held there (see Jer 27).

3 Therefore thus saith the Lord GOD; Behold, I *am* against thee, O Tyrus, and will cause many nations to come up against thee, as the sea causeth his waves to come up.

4 And they shall destroy the walls of Tyrus, and break down her towers: I will also scrape her dust from her, and [a]make her like the top of a rock.

5 It shall be *a place for* the spreading of nets [a]in the midst of the sea: for I have spoken *it,* saith the Lord GOD: and it shall become a spoil to the nations.

6 And her daughters which *are* in the field shall be slain by the sword; [a]and they shall know that I *am* the LORD.

7 ¶ For thus saith the Lord GOD; Behold, I *will* bring upon Tyrus Nebuchadrezzar king of Babylon, [a]a king of kings, from the north, with horses, and with chariots, and with horsemen, and companies, and much people.

8 He shall slay with the sword thy daughters in the field: and he shall [a]make a fort against thee, and [1]cast a mount against thee, and lift up the buckler against thee.

9 And he shall set engines of war against thy walls, and with his axes he shall break down thy towers.

10 By reason of the abundance of his horses their dust shall cover thee: thy walls shall shake at the noise of the horsemen, and of the wheels, and of the chariots, when he shall enter into thy gates, [1]as men enter into a city wherein is made a breach.

11 With the hoofs of his horses shall he tread down all thy streets: he shall slay thy people by the sword, and thy strong garrisons shall go down to the ground.

12 And they shall make a spoil of thy riches, and make a prey of thy merchandise: and they shall break down thy walls, and destroy [1]thy pleasant houses: and they shall lay thy stones and thy timber and thy dust in the midst of the water.

13 [a]And I will cause the noise of [b]thy songs to cease; and the sound of thy harps shall be no more heard.

14 And [a]I will make thee like the top of a rock: thou shalt be *a place* to spread nets upon; thou shalt be built no more: for I the LORD have spoken *it,* saith the Lord GOD.

15 ¶ Thus saith the Lord GOD to Tyrus; Shall not the isles [a]shake at the sound of thy fall, when the wounded cry, when the slaughter is made in the midst of thee?

16 Then all the [a]princes of the sea shall [b]come down from their thrones, and lay away their robes, and put off their broidered garments: they shall clothe themselves with [1]trembling; [c]they shall sit upon the ground, and [d]shall tremble at every moment, and [e]be astonished at thee.

17 And they shall take up a [a]lamentation for thee, and say to thee, How art thou destroyed, *that wast* inhabited [1]of seafaring men, the renowned city, which wast [b]strong in the sea, she and her inhabitants, which cause their terror *to be* on all that haunt it.

18 Now shall [a]the isles tremble *in* the day of thy fall; yea, the isles that *are* in the sea shall be troubled at thy departure.

19 For thus saith the Lord GOD; When I shall make thee a desolate city, like the cities that are not inhabited; when *I* shall bring up the deep upon thee, and great waters shall cover thee;

20 When I shall bring thee down [a]with them that descend into the pit, with the people of old time, and shall set thee in the low parts of the earth, in places desolate of old, with them that go down to the pit, that thou be not inhabited; and I shall set glory [b]in the land of the living;

21 [a]I will make thee [1]a terror, and thou *shalt be* no *more:* [b]though thou be sought for, yet shalt thou never be found again, saith the Lord GOD.

The lament for Tyrus

27 The word of the LORD came again unto me, saying,

2 Now, thou son of man, [a]take up a lamentation for Tyrus;

3 And say unto Tyrus, [a]O thou that art situate at the entry of the sea, *which art* [b]a merchant of the people for many isles, Thus saith

26:4 [a]ver. 14
26:5 [a]ch. 27:32
26:6 [a]ch. 25:5
26:7 [a]Ezra 7:12; Dan. 2:37
26:8 [1]Or, *pour out the engine of shot* [a]ch. 21:22
26:10 [1]Heb. *according to the enterings of a city broken up*
26:12 [1]Heb. *houses of thy desire*
26:13 [a]Is. 14:11; 24:8; Jer. 7:34; 25:10 [b]Is. 23:16; ch. 28:13; Rev. 18:22
26:14 [a]ver. 4,5
26:15 [a]ver. 18; Jer. 49:21; ch. 27:28
26:16 [1]Heb. *tremblings* [a]Is. 23:8 [b]Jonah 3:6 [c]Job 2:13 [d]ch. 32:10 [e]ch. 27:35
26:17 [1]Heb. *of the seas* [a]ch. 27:32; Rev. 18:9 [b]Is. 23:4
26:18 [a]ver. 15
26:20 [a]ch. 32:18 [b]ch. 32:23
26:21 [1]Heb. *terrors* [a]ch. 28:19 [b]Ps. 37:36
27:2 [a]ch. 26:17
27:3 [a]ch. 28:2 [b]Is. 23:3

26:3 *I am against thee.* See note on 5:8. *as the sea causeth his waves to come up.* For invading armies likened to waves of the sea cf. Is 17:12–13. Since Tyre was an island, the metaphor is especially appropriate here.
26:5 *spoil to the nations.* Cf. 25:7; 34:28.
26:7 *Nebuchadrezzar.* The first of four references to him in Ezekiel (see 29:18–19; 30:10). He ruled from 605 to 562 B.C., and his name means "O (god) Nabu, protect my son" or "O (god) Nabu, protect my boundary." Jeremiah and Ezekiel both proclaimed that this pagan king would be used by God to do His work (see Jer 25:9; 27:6). *I will bring.* A clear indication of God's sovereignty over the nations (cf. 28:7; 29:8). *north.* The direction from which Nebuchadnezzar would descend on Tyre after first marching his army up the Euphrates River valley rather than across the Arabian Desert (cf. Jer 1:13).
26:8 *fort.* Nebuchadnezzar's 15-year siege of Tyre began shortly after the fall of Jerusalem. There is no record that Tyre fell at this time (see note on 29:18).
26:14 *be built no more.* Eventually fulfilled by Alexander's devastating siege in 332 B.C. (see note on Is 23:1).
26:16 *princes of the sea.* Called kings in 27:35, they were probably trading partners with Tyre. *lay away their robes.* Usually mourners tore their clothes (Job 2:12) and put on sackcloth, but cf. the king of Nineveh (Jonah 3:6). *clothe themselves with trembling.* Because of political shock waves from the fall of such a powerful city (cf. 7:27; Ps 35:26; 109:29).
26:17 *lamentation.* See note on 19:1.
26:19 *the deep.* The primeval, chaotic mass (as in Gen 1:2). Tyre's collapse into the sea is described in almost cosmic terms.
26:20 *pit.* The grave, "the earth below" (cf. Ps 69:15). *people of old.* Those long dead (Ps 143:3; Lam 3:6).
26:21 See 27:36; 28:19.
27:2 *lamentation.* See note on 19:1.
27:3 *I am of perfect beauty.* See 28:12; cf. 28:2 for a similar

the Lord GOD; O Tyrus, thou hast said, [c]I *am*
[1]of perfect beauty.
4 Thy borders *are* in the [1]midst of the seas,
thy builders have perfected thy beauty.
5 They have [1]made all thy *ship* boards of
fir trees of [a]Senir: they have taken cedars from
Lebanon to make masts for thee.
6 *Of* the oaks of Bashan have they made
thine oars; [1 2]the company of the Ashurites
have made thy benches *of* ivory, *brought* out of
[a]the isles of Chittim.
7 Fine linen with broidered work from
Egypt was that which thou spreadest forth to
be thy sail; [1]blue and purple from the isles of
Elishah was that which covered thee.
8 The inhabitants of Zidon and Arvad were
thy mariners: thy wise *men,* O Tyrus, *that*
were in thee, *were* thy pilots.
9 The ancients of [a]Gebal and the wise *men*
thereof were in thee thy [1 2]calkers: all the
ships of the sea with their mariners were in
thee to occupy thy merchandise.
10 They of Persia and of Lud and of Phut
were in thine army, thy men of war: they
hanged the shield and helmet in thee; they set
forth thy comeliness.
11 The men of Arvad with thine army *were*
upon thy walls round about, and the Gammadims were in thy towers: they hanged their
shields upon thy walls round about; they have
made [a]thy beauty perfect.
12 [a]Tarshish *was* thy merchant by reason
of the multitude of all *kind of* riches; with silver, iron, tin, and lead, they traded in thy fairs.
13 [a]Javan, Tubal, and Meshech, they *were*
thy merchants: they traded [b]the persons of
men and vessels of brass in thy [1]market.
14 They of the house of [a]Togarmah traded
in thy fairs with horses and horsemen and
mules.
15 The men of [a]Dedan *were* thy merchants; many isles *were* the merchandise of
thine hand: they brought thee *for* a present
horns of ivory and ebeny.
16 Syria *was* thy merchant by reason of the
multitude of [1]the wares of thy making: they
occupied in thy fairs with emeralds, purple,
and broidered work, and fine linen, and coral,
and [2]agate.
17 Judah, and the land of Israel, they *were*
thy merchants: they traded in thy market
wheat of [a]Minnith, and Pannag, and honey,
and oil, and [b 1]balm.
18 Damascus *was* thy merchant in the multitude of the wares of thy making, for the multitude of all riches; in the wine of Helbon, and
white wool.
19 Dan also and Javan [1]going to and fro occupied in thy fairs: bright iron, cassia, and calamus, were in thy market.
20 [a]Dedan *was* thy merchant in [1]precious
clothes for chariots.
21 Arabia, and all the princes of [a]Kedar,
[1]they occupied with thee in lambs, and rams,
and goats: in these *were they* thy merchants.
22 The merchants of [a]Sheba and Raamah,
they *were* thy merchants: they occupied in thy
fairs with chief of all spices, and with all precious stones, and gold.

27:3 [1]Heb. *perfect of beauty* [c]ch. 28:12
27:4 [1]Heb. *heart*
27:5 [1]Heb. *built* [a]Deut. 3:9
27:6 [1]Or, *they have made [thy] hatches of ivory well trodden* [2]Heb. *the daughter* [a]Jer. 2:10
27:7 [1]Or, *purple and scarlet*
27:9 [1]Or, *stoppers of chinks* [2]Heb. *strengtheners* [a]1 Ki. 5:18; Ps. 83:7
27:11 [a]ver. 3
27:12 [a]Gen. 10:4; 2 Chr. 20:36
27:13 [a]Gen. 10:2
27:13 [1]Or, *merchandise* [b]Rev. 18:13
27:14 [a]ch. 38:6
27:15 [a]Gen. 10:7
27:16 [1]Heb. *[thy] works* [2]Or, *chrysoprase*
27:17 [1]Or, *rosin* [a]Judg. 11:33 [b]Jer. 8:22
27:19 [1]Or, *Meuzal*
27:20 [1]Heb. *clothes of freedom* [a]Gen. 25:3
27:21 [1]Heb. *they* were *the merchants of thy hand* [a]Gen. 25:13; Is. 60:7
27:22 [a]Gen. 10:7; 1 Ki. 10:1,2; Ps. 72:10; Is. 60:6

prideful statement. Since Tyre is described as a stately ship in the following verses, some translate, "You are a ship, perfect in beauty."
27:4 *perfected thy beauty.* See v. 11.
27:5 *Senir.* Amorite name for Hermon, the Anti-Lebanon mountain (or range) famed for cedar.
27:6 *Bashan.* See note on 39:18. *Chittim.* Hebrew *Kittim,* which was originally the name of a town in southern Cyprus colonized by Phoenicia.
27:7 *Elishah.* A city on the east side of Cyprus; also the oldest name for Cyprus (but see note on Gen 10:4).
27:8 *Zidon.* Or "Sidon," a harbor city 25 miles north of Tyre, which sometimes rivaled her in political and commercial importance (see note on 28:21). *Arvad.* Another Phoenician island-city, off the Mediterranean coast and north of Sidon.
27:9 *Gebal.* Byblos, an important ancient city on the coast between Sidon and Arvad (see 1 Ki 5:18).
27:10 *Lud.* "Lydia," in Asia Minor. *Phut.* Libya, in North Africa, west of Egypt. *men of war.* The ship image is abandoned, and Tyre is now described literally—as a city (see "walls" and "towers" in v. 11), complete with a mercenary army gathered from the whole world.
27:11 *Arvad.* See note on v. 8. *Gammadims.* Men of Gammad, which was either (1) northern Asia Minor or (2) a coastal town near Arvad. It is not mentioned elsewhere in the Bible.
27:12 *Tarshish.* Traditionally located on the coast of southern Spain, but the island of Sardinia has also been suggested. Passages such as 1 Ki 10:22; Jonah 1:3 imply that it was a long distance from the Canaanite coast. The list of places in vv. 12–23 generally follows a west-to-east direction.
27:13 *Tubal, and Meshech.* Both in Asia Minor.
‡27:14 *house of Togarmah.* Or "Beth-Togarmah," located in eastern Asia Minor, present-day Armenia (see 38:6). *horses.* Asia Minor was known for its horses (see 1 Ki 10:28).
27:15 *Dedan.* See note on 25:13.
27:16. *Syria.* Since Damascus, the capital of Aram, (Syria) is mentioned in v. 18, perhaps Edom is meant here (some manuscripts read "Edom" instead of "Aram"; see also 25:12 and note).
27:17 *Israel . . . thy merchants.* In the past. Since 722–721 B.C. Israel had ceased to exist as a political state. *Minnith.* An Ammonite town, apparently famous for its wheat; "wheat of Minnith" possibly denoted a superior quality of wheat. *balm.* Gum or oil from one of several plants; a product of Gilead (see Gen 37:25; Jer 8:22; 46:11).
27:18 *Damascus.* Capital of Aram (see note on v. 16; see also Is 7:8). *Helbon.* A town north of Damascus, still in existence and still a wine-making center. The name occurs only here in the Bible.
‡27:19 *Dan also.* Can be read as a place name, "Vedan." Dan was a term that Homer used for Greeks. See Gen 10:27; 1 Chr 1:21; perhaps Yemen or the area between Haran and the Tigris. *cassia.* Similar to the cinnamon tree. *calamus.* An aromatic reed.
27:20 *Dedan.* See note on 25:13.
27:21 *Arabia, and . . . Kedar.* A general expression for the Bedouin tribes from Aram to the Arabian Desert. For Kedar see Is 42:11; 60:7; Jer 49:28.
27:22 *Sheba.* See note on 23:42. *Raamah.* A city in southern Arabia.

23 [a]Haran, and Canneh, and Eden, the merchants of [b]Sheba, Asshur, *and* Chilmad, *were* thy merchants.

24 These *were* thy merchants in [1]all sorts of things, in blue [2]clothes, and broidered work, and in chests of rich apparel, bound with cords, and made of cedar, among thy merchandise.

25 [a]The ships of Tarshish did sing of thee *in* thy market: and thou wast replenished, and made very glorious [b]in the midst of the seas.

26 Thy rowers have brought thee into great waters: [a]the east wind hath broken thee in the [1]midst of the seas.

27 Thy [a]riches, and thy fairs, thy merchandise, thy mariners, and thy pilots, thy calkers, and the occupiers of thy merchandise, and all thy men of war, that *are* in thee, [1]and in all thy company which *is* in the midst of thee, shall fall into the [2]midst of the seas in the day of thy ruin.

28 The [a] [1]suburbs shall shake at the sound of the cry of thy pilots.

29 And [a]all that handle the oar, the mariners, *and* all the pilots of the sea, shall come down from their ships, they shall stand upon the land;

30 And shall cause their voice to be heard against thee, and shall cry bitterly, and shall [a]cast up dust upon their heads, they [b]shall wallow themselves in the ashes:

31 And they shall [a]make themselves utterly bald for thee, and gird them with sackcloth, and they shall weep for thee with bitterness of heart *and* bitter wailing.

32 And in their wailing they shall [a]take up a lamentation for thee, and lament over thee, *saying,* [b]What *city is* like Tyrus, like the destroyed in the midst of the sea?

33 [a]When thy wares went forth out of the seas, thou filledst many people; thou didst enrich the kings of the earth with the multitude of thy riches and of thy merchandise.

34 *In* the time when [a]*thou shalt be* broken by the seas in the depths of the waters, [b]thy merchandise and all thy company in the midst of thee shall fall.

27:23 [a]Gen. 11:31; 2 Ki. 19:12 [b]Gen. 25:3
27:24 [1]Or, *excellent things* [2]Heb. *foldings*
27:25 [a]Ps. 48:7; Is. 2:16 [b]ver. 4
27:26 [1]Heb. *heart* [a]Ps. 48:7
27:27 [1]Or, *even with all* [2]Heb. *heart* [a]Prov. 11:4
27:28 [1]Or, *waves* [a]ch. 26:15
27:29 [a]Rev. 18:17
27:30 [a]Job 2:12; Rev. 18:19 [b]Esth. 4:1,3; Jer. 6:26
27:31 [a]Jer. 16:6
27:32 [a]ch. 26:17 [b]Rev. 18:18
27:33 [a]Rev. 18:19
27:34 [a]ch. 26:19 [b]ver. 27
27:35 [a]ch. 26:15
27:36 [1]Heb. *terrors* [2]Heb. shalt *not be for ever* [a]Jer. 18:16 [b]ch. 26:21
28:2 [1]Heb. *heart* [a]ver. 9 [b]ch. 27:3,4 [c]Is. 31:3
28:3 [a]Zech. 9:2
28:5 [1]Heb. *By the greatness of thy wisdom* [a]Ps. 62:10; Zech. 9:3
28:7 [a]ch. 30:11; 31:12; 32:12
28:9 [1]Or, *woundeth* [a]ver. 2
28:10 [a]ch. 31:18; 32:19,21, 25,27
28:12 [a]ch. 27:2

35 [a]All the inhabitants of the isles shall be astonished at thee, and their kings shall be sore afraid, they shall be troubled *in their* countenance.

36 The merchants among the people [a]shall hiss at thee; [b]thou shalt be [1]a terror, and [2]never *shalt be* any more.

Tyrus' pride and ruin

28 The word of the LORD came again unto me, saying,

2 Son of man, say unto the prince of Tyrus, Thus saith the Lord GOD; Because thine heart *is* lifted up, and [a]thou hast said, I *am* a God, I sit *in* the seat of God, [b]in the [1]midst of the seas; [c]yet thou *art* a man, and not God, though thou set thine heart as the heart of God:

3 Behold, [a]thou *art* wiser than Daniel; *there is* no secret *that* they can hide *from* thee:

4 With thy wisdom and with thine understanding thou hast gotten thee riches, and hast gotten gold and silver into thy treasures:

5 [a] [1]By thy great wisdom *and* by thy traffick hast thou increased thy riches, and thine heart is lifted up because of thy riches:

6 Therefore thus saith the Lord GOD; Because thou hast set thine heart as the heart of God;

7 Behold therefore, I *will* bring strangers upon thee, [a]the terrible of the nations: and they shall draw their swords against the beauty of thy wisdom, and they shall defile thy brightness.

8 They shall bring thee down to the pit, and thou shalt die the deaths of *them that are* slain in the midst of the seas.

9 Wilt thou yet [a]say before him that slayeth thee, I *am* God? but thou *shalt be* a man, and no God, in the hand of him that [1]slayeth thee.

10 Thou shalt die the deaths of [a]the uncircumcised by the hand of strangers: for I have spoken *it,* saith the Lord GOD.

11 ¶ Moreover the word of the LORD came unto me, saying,

12 Son of man, [a]take up a lamentation upon the king of Tyrus, and say unto him,

27:23 *Haran.* A city east of Carchemish, in present-day eastern Turkey. It was well-known in ancient times as a center both for trade and for the worship of the moon-god Sin. From here Abraham moved to Canaan (see Gen 11:31; 12:4). *Canneh.* Of uncertain location, presumably in Mesopotamia. It is often identified with Calneh (Is 10:9, "Calno"; Amos 6:2). *Eden.* A district south of Haran, mentioned in connection with Haran in 2 Ki 19:12. See Beth-eden in Amos 1:5. *Sheba.* See note on 23:42. *Asshur.* Can mean the city, the country (Assyria) or the people (Assyrians). Here it is probably the city south of Nineveh that gave its name to the country. *Chilmad.* If a town, it is yet unidentified; presumably in Mesopotamia. Some read "all Media."

27:25 *Tarshish.* See note on v. 12. The ship image is resumed (see notes on vv. 3,10).

27:26 *east wind.* Disastrous at sea (Ps 48:7) as well as on land (Jer 18:17). It possibly symbolizes Nebuchadnezzar (as in 17:10; 19:12).

27:30 *dust upon their heads.* See 26:16 for a similar scene. *wallow themselves in the ashes.* Cf. Mic 1:10.

27:31 *make themselves utterly bald.* Cf. 7:18; Is 15:2; 22:12.

28:2 *prince of Tyrus.* May refer to the city of Tyre as ruler, or to Ethbaal II, the king then ruling Tyre (see v. 12). His namesake Ethbaal I was the father of Jezebel (1 Ki 16:31). *lifted up.* In pride; cf. 27:3; Prov 16:18; Acts 12:21–23.

28:3 *Daniel.* See note on 14:14.

28:7 *strangers.* The Babylonians; see next phrase.

28:8 *pit.* Cf. Job 33:22,24; see note on 26:20.

28:10 *uncircumcised.* Used here in the sense of barbarian or uncouth. The Phoenicians, like the Israelites and the Egyptians, practiced circumcision (see 31:18; 32:19).

28:12 *lamentation.* See note on 19:1. *king of Tyrus.* Cf. v. 2, but see note on Is 14:12–15. *sealest up the sum.* See Hag 2:23, where Zerubbabel is called God's "signet" (ring) With cutting irony Ezekiel depicts the proud king of Tyre as the first man created, radiant with wisdom and beauty.

Thus saith the Lord GOD; [b]Thou sealest up the
sum, full *of* wisdom, and perfect in beauty.
13 Thou hast been in [a]Eden the garden of
God; every precious stone *was* thy covering,
the [1]sardius, topaz, and the diamond, the
[2]beryl, the onyx, and the jasper, the sapphire,
the [3]emerald, and the carbuncle, and gold: the
workmanship of [b]thy tabrets and of thy pipes
was prepared in thee in the day that thou wast
created.
14 Thou *art* the anointed [a]cherub that covereth; and I have set thee *so:* thou wast upon
[b]the holy mountain of God; thou hast walked
up and down in the midst of the stones of fire.
15 Thou *wast* perfect in thy ways from the
day that thou wast created, till iniquity was
found in thee.
16 By the multitude of thy merchandise
they have filled the midst of thee *with* violence, and thou hast sinned: therefore I will
cast thee as profane out of the mountain of
God: and I will destroy thee, [a]O covering cherub, from the midst of the stones of fire.
17 [a]Thine heart was lifted up because of
thy beauty, thou hast corrupted thy wisdom by
reason of thy brightness: I will cast thee to the
ground, I will lay thee before kings, that *they*
may behold thee.
18 Thou hast defiled thy sanctuaries by the
multitude of thine iniquities, by the iniquity of
thy traffick; therefore will I bring forth a fire
from the midst of thee, it shall devour thee,
and I will bring thee to ashes upon the earth in
the sight of all them that behold thee.
19 All they that know thee among the people shall be astonished at thee: [a]thou shalt be
[1]a terror, and never *shalt* thou *be* any more.

Zidon to perish

20 ¶ Again the word of the LORD came unto
me, saying,

28:12 [b]ver. 3; ch. 27:3
28:13 [1]Or, *ruby* [2]Or, *chrysolite* [3]Or, *chrysoprase* [a]ch. 31:8,9 [b]ch. 26:13
28:14 [a]ver. 16; See Ex. 25:20 [b]ch. 20:40
28:16 [a]ver. 14
28:17 [a]ver. 2,5
28:19 [1]Heb. *terrors* [a]ch. 26:21; 27:36
28:21 [a]ch. 6:2; 25:2; 29:2 [b]Is. 23:4,12; Jer. 25:22; 27:3; ch. 32:30
28:22 [a]Ex. 14:4,17; ch. 39:13 [b]Ps. 9:16 [c]ver. 25; ch. 20:41; 36:23
28:23 [a]ch. 38:22
28:24 [a]Num. 33:55; Josh. 23:13
28:25 [a]Is. 11:12; ch. 11:17; 20:41; 34:13; 37:21 [b]ver. 22
28:26 [1]Or, *with confidence* [2]Or, *spoil* [a]Jer. 23:6; ch. 36:28 [b]Is. 65:21; Amos 9:14 [c]Jer. 31:5
29:2 [a]ch. 28:21 [b]Is. 19:1; Jer. 25:19; 46:2,25
29:3 [a]ver. 10; Jer. 44:30; ch. 28:22 [b]Ps. 74:13,14; Is. 27:1; 51:9; ch. 32:2

21 Son of man, [a]set thy face [b]against Zidon, and prophesy against it,
22 And say, Thus saith the Lord GOD; [a]Be-
hold, I *am* against thee, O Zidon; and I will be
glorified in the midst of thee: and [b]they shall
know that I *am* the LORD, when I shall have
executed judgments in her, and shall be [c]sanc-
tified in her.
23 [a]For I will send into her pestilence, and
blood into her streets; and the wounded shall
be judged in the midst of her by the sword
upon her on every side; and they shall know
that I *am* the LORD.
24 And there shall be no more [a]a pricking
brier unto the house of Israel, nor *any* grieving
thorn of all *that are* round about them, that despised them; and they shall know that I *am* the
Lord GOD.
25 Thus saith the Lord GOD; When I shall
have [a]gathered the house of Israel from the
people among whom they are scattered, and
shall be [b]sanctified in them in the sight of the
heathen, then shall they dwell in their land
that I have given to my servant Jacob.
26 And they shall [a]dwell [1]safely therein,
and shall [b]build houses, and [c]plant vineyards;
yea, they shall dwell with confidence, when I
have executed judgments upon all those that
[2]despise them round about them; and they
shall know that I *am* the LORD their God.

Egypt's pride and desolation

29 In the tenth year, in the tenth *month,*
in the twelfth *day* of the month, the
word of the LORD came unto me, saying,
2 Son of man, [a]set thy face against Pharaoh
king of Egypt, and prophesy against him, and
[b]against all Egypt:
3 Speak, and say, Thus saith the Lord GOD;
[a]Behold, I *am* against thee, Pharaoh king of
Egypt, the great [b]dragon that lieth in the midst

28:13 *Thou hast been in Eden.* Like Adam (Gen 2:15). Ezekiel continues to use imagery of the creation and the fall to picture the career of the king of Tyre (see 31:9,16,18). *every precious stone.* Unlike Adam, who was naked (Gen 2:25), the king is pictured as a fully clothed priest, ordained (v. 14) to guard God's holy place. The 9 stones are among the 12 worn by the priest (Ex 28:17–20). (The Septuagint lists all 12.) *thy tabrets and of thy pipes.* For the precious stones. *in the day that thou wast created.* Cf. v. 15; Gen 5:2.
28:14 *cherub that covereth.* Cf. v. 16. The Genesis account has cherubim (plural) stationed at the border of the garden after the expulsion of Adam and Eve (Gen 3:24). *holy mountain of God.* Cf. v. 16. This does not reflect the Genesis story. See Is 14:13 for the figure of God dwelling on a mountain. *stones of fire.* The precious stones (v. 13; cf. Rev 4:1–6; 21:15–21).
28:15 *Thou wast perfect in thy ways . . . till.* The parallel to Gen 2–3 is clear (see Gen 6:9; 17:1).
‡28:16 *the multitude of thy merchandise . . . filled . . . thee with violence.* Tyre's major crime.
28:17 *I will cast thee to the ground.* Expulsion from the heavenly garden.
28:21 *set thy face.* See note on 20:46. *Zidon.* See 27:8 and note. This is the only time in the OT that Sidon is mentioned apart from Tyre (cf. Is 23:1–4; Jer 47:4; Joel 3:4; Zech 9:2).
28:22 *I am against thee.* Possibly because of Sidon's involvement in the Jerusalem summit conference (Jer 27:3; see note on 5:8). *I will be glorified in the midst of thee.* The Lord's glory would be recognized in Sidon's punishment.
28:24 *pricking brier.* For references to Israel's enemies as briers see Num 33:55; Josh 23:13.
28:25 *When I shall have gathered . . . Israel.* A frequent promise in Ezekiel and later (see 11:17; 20:34,41–42; 29:13; 34:13; 36:24; 37:21; 38:8; 39:27; Neh 1:9; Zech 10:8,10). *my servant Jacob.* Cf. 37:25. For the promise see Gen 28:13; 35:12; Ps 105:10–11.
28:26 *dwell safely therein.* A perennial ideal that had become an especially meaningful promise (cf. 34:28; 38:8,11,14; 39:26; Lev 25:18–19; Jer 23:6; 32:37; 33:16). *houses . . . vineyards.* Basic necessities of the good life (cf. Is 65:21; Jer 29:5,28; Amos 9:14).
29:1 *tenth year . . . tenth month . . . twelfth day of the month.* Jan. 7, 587 B.C.; the sixth date in Ezekiel (see 1:2; 8:1; 20:1; 24:1; 26:1). This is the first of seven oracles against Egypt, all of which are dated, except one (30:1). They represent divine and prophetic anger at Egypt's actions (or nonactions) at this time.
29:2 *set thy face.* See note on 20:46. *Pharaoh.* Pharaoh-hophra, 589–570 B.C. (see Jer 44:30).
29:3 *I am against thee.* See note on 5:8. *great dragon.* Or

of his rivers, [c]which hath said, My river *is*
mine own, and I have made *it for* myself.
4 But [a]I will put hooks in thy jaws, and I
will cause the fish of thy rivers to stick unto
thy scales, and I will bring thee up out of the
midst of thy rivers, and all the fish of thy rivers
shall stick unto thy scales.
5 And I will leave thee *thrown* into the
wilderness, thee and all the fish of thy rivers:
thou shalt fall upon the [1]open fields; [a]thou
shalt not be brought together, nor gathered: [b]I
have given thee for meat to the beasts of the
field and to the fowls of the heaven.
6 And all the inhabitants of Egypt shall
know that I *am* the LORD, because they have
been a [a]staff of reed to the house of Israel.
7 [a]When they took hold of thee by thy
hand, thou didst break, and rent all their
shoulder: and when they leaned upon thee,
thou brakest, and madest all their loins to be at
a stand.
8 Therefore thus saith the Lord GOD; Behold, I *will* bring [a]a sword upon thee, and cut
off man and beast out of thee.
9 And the land of Egypt shall be desolate
and waste; and they shall know that I *am* the
LORD: because he hath said, The river *is* mine,
and I have made *it.*
10 Behold therefore, I *am* against thee, and
against thy rivers, [a]and I will make the land of
Egypt [1]utterly waste *and* desolate, [b2]from the
tower of [3]Syene even unto the border of
Ethiopia.
11 [a]No foot of man shall pass through it,
nor foot of beast shall pass through it, neither
shall it be inhabited forty years.
12 [a]And I will make the land of Egypt desolate in the midst of the countries *that are* desolate, and her cities among the cities *that are*
laid waste shall be desolate forty years: and I
will scatter the Egyptians among the nations,
and will disperse them through the countries.
13 Yet thus saith the Lord GOD; At the [a]end
of forty years will I gather the Egyptians from
the people whither they were scattered:
14 And I will bring again the captivity of
Egypt, and will cause them to return *into* the
land of Pathros, into the land of their [1]habita-
tion; and they shall be there a [a2]base kingdom.
15 It shall be the basest of the kingdoms;
neither shall it exalt itself any more above the
nations: for I will diminish them, that *they*
shall no more rule over the nations.
16 And it shall be no more [a]the confidence
of the house of Israel, which bringeth *their* iniquity to remembrance, when they shall look
after them: but they shall know that I *am* the
Lord GOD.

17 ¶ And it came to pass in the seven and
twentieth year, in the first *month,* in the first
day of the month, the word of the LORD came
unto me, saying,
18 Son of man, [a]Nebuchadrezzar king of
Babylon caused his army to serve a great service against Tyrus: every head *was* made bald,
and every shoulder *was* peeled: yet had he no
wages, nor his army, for Tyrus, for the service
that he had served against it:
19 Therefore thus saith the Lord GOD; Behold, I *will* give the land of Egypt unto Nebuchadrezzar king of Babylon; and he shall take
her multitude, and [1]take her spoil, and take
her prey; and it shall be the wages for his army.
20 I have given him the land of Egypt [1]*for*
his labour wherewith he [a]served against it, because they wrought for me, saith the Lord
GOD.
21 In that day [a]will I cause the horn of the
house of Israel to bud forth, and I will give
thee [b]the opening of the mouth in the midst of
them; and they shall know that I *am* the LORD.

A lament for Egypt

30 The word of the LORD came again
unto me, saying,

29:3 [c]See ch. 28:2
29:4 [a]Is. 37:29; ch. 38:4
29:5 [1]Heb. *face of the field* [a]Jer. 8:2; 16:4; 25:33 [b]Jer. 7:33; 34:20
29:6 [a]2 Ki. 18:21; Is. 36:6
29:7 [a]Jer. 37:5,7,11; ch. 17:17
29:8 [a]ch. 14:17; 32:11-13
29:10 [1]Heb. *wastes of waste* [2][Or, *from Migdol* to *Syene*] [3]Heb. *Seveneh* [a]ch. 30:12 [b]ch. 30:6
29:11 [a]ch. 32:13
29:12 [a]ch. 30:7,26
29:13 [a]Is. 19:23; Jer. 46:26
29:14 [1]Or, *birth* [2]Heb. *low* [a]ch. 17:6,14
29:16 [a]Is. 30:2,3; 36:4,6
29:18 [a]Jer. 27:6; ch. 26:7,8
29:19 [1]Heb. *spoil her spoil, and prey her prey*
29:20 [1]Or, for *his hire* [a]Jer. 25:9
29:21 [a]Ps. 132:17 [b]ch. 24:27

"crocodile"; pictured as being in the Nile. See note on Ex 4:3; see also Job 41:1 and note; Is 27:1. *his rivers.* Nile delta and canals (cf. Is 7:18; 19:6; 37:25). *which hath said.* Boasts inscribed on Egyptian monuments (such as in Shelley's "Ozymandias") had become proverbial.

29:4 *hooks.* Cf. 19:4. *fish of thy rivers.* Egypt's conquered territories or mercenaries.

29:5 *meat to the beasts.* Particularly frustrating to the pharaoh's great hopes for an afterlife, as symbolized by the pyramids and expressed in the Egyptian "Book of the Dead."

29:6 *they have been a staff of reed.* A comparison made earlier (see Is 36:6 and note). Pharaoh-hophra briefly but unsuccessfully diverted the Babylonians from laying siege to Jerusalem (see Jer 37:1–10).

29:8 *sword.* Nebuchadnezzar's (see note on 21:3). For the entire expression, which is not found in other prophetic books, see 6:3; 11:8; 14:17; 33:2; see also Lev 26:25.

‡29:10 *tower.* Or "Migdol" (see KJV marg.), which probably refers to a fortified city on the northern border of Egypt (see Jer 44:1; 46:14). *Syene.* Or "Aswan," a town in southern Egypt. *from the tower of Syene.* See 30:6. "From Migdol to Syene" probably indicated all Egypt, just as "from Dan to Beersheba" meant all Israel (see, e.g., Judg 20:1; 1 Sam 3:20).

29:11 *forty years.* Sometimes used to signify a long and difficult period (cf. 4:6).

29:14 *Pathros.* Southern Egypt (see 30:14; Jer 44:1,15).

29:17 The second oracle against Egypt (see note on v. 1). *the seven and twentieth . . . first month . . . first day of the month.* Apr. 26, 571 B.C.; the seventh date in Ezekiel (see v. 1; 1:2; 8:1; 20:1; 24:1; 26:1) and the latest date given in the book. Since the remaining dated oracles are in more or less chronological order, the date is mentioned here probably because of the subject matter (Egypt).

29:18 *caused his army to serve a great service.* Nebuchadnezzar besieged Tyre for 15 years, from 586 to 571 B.C. (see 26:7–14). *every head was made bald.* Probably from the leather helmets.

29:19 *I will give.* God's sovereignty over the nations is again proclaimed.

29:21 *will I cause the horn . . . to bud forth.* Revive the strength of. The passage is not a Messianic prophecy. *the opening of the mouth.* Ezekiel's muteness (3:26; 24:27) would be removed, and this word anticipates that of 33:22.

30:1 The third oracle against Egypt (see note on 29:1). No date

2 Son of man, prophesy and say, Thus saith
the Lord GOD; [a]Howl ye, Woe worth the day!
3 For [a]the day *is* near, even the day of the
LORD *is* near, a cloudy day; it shall be the time
of the heathen.
4 And the sword shall come upon Egypt,
and great [1]pain shall be in Ethiopia, when the
slain shall fall in Egypt, and they [a]shall take
away her multitude, and [b]her foundations
shall be broken down.
5 Ethiopia, and [1]Libya, and Lydia, and [a]all
the mingled people, and Chub, and the [2]men
of the land that is in league, shall fall with
them by the sword.
6 Thus saith the LORD; They also that uphold Egypt shall fall; and the pride of her power shall come down: [a1]from the tower of
Syene shall they fall in it by the sword, saith
the Lord GOD.
7 [a]And they shall be desolate in the midst
of the countries *that are* desolate, and her cities shall be in the midst of the cities *that are*
wasted.
8 And they shall know that I *am* the LORD,
when I have set a fire in Egypt, and *when* all
her helpers shall be [1]destroyed.
9 In that day [a]shall messengers go forth
from me in ships to make the careless Ethiopians afraid, and great pain shall come upon
them, as *in* the day of Egypt: for lo, it cometh.
10 Thus saith the Lord GOD; [a]I will also
make the multitude of Egypt to cease by the
hand of Nebuchadrezzar king of Babylon.
11 He and his people with him, [a]the terrible of the nations, *shall be* brought to destroy
the land: and they shall draw their swords
against Egypt, and fill the land *with* the slain.
12 And [a]I will make the rivers [1]dry, and
[b]sell the land into the hand of the wicked: and
I will make the land waste, and [2]all that is
therein, by the hand of strangers: I the LORD
have spoken *it.*
13 Thus saith the Lord GOD; I will also [a]de-
stroy the idols, and I will cause *their* images to
cease out of Noph; [b]and there shall be no
more a prince of the land of Egypt: [c]and I will
put a fear in the land of Egypt.
14 And I will make [a]Pathros desolate, and
will set fire in [b1]Zoan, [c]and will execute judgments in No.
15 And I will pour my fury upon [1]Sin, the
strength of Egypt; and [a]I will cut off the multitude of No.
16 And I will [a]set fire in Egypt: Sin shall
have great pain, and No shall be rent asunder,
and Noph *shall have* distresses daily.
17 The young men of [1]Aven and of [2]Phi-
beseth shall fall by the sword: and these *cities*
shall go into captivity.
18 [a]At Tehaphnehes also the day shall be
[1]darkened, when I shall break there the yokes
of Egypt: and the pomp of her strength shall
cease in her: *as for* her, a cloud shall cover her,
and her daughters shall go into captivity.
19 Thus will I execute judgments in Egypt:
and they shall know that I *am* the LORD.

20 ¶ And it came to pass in the eleventh
year, in the first *month,* in the seventh *day* of
the month, *that* the word of the LORD came
unto me, saying,
21 Son of man, I have [a]broken the arm of
Pharaoh king of Egypt; and lo, [b]it shall not be
bound up to be healed, to put a roller to bind
it, to make it strong to hold the sword.
22 Therefore thus saith the Lord GOD; Behold, I *am* against Pharaoh king of Egypt, and
will [a]break his arms, the strong, and that
which was broken; and I will cause the sword
to fall out of his hand.

30:2 [a]Is. 13:6 30:3 [a]ch. 7:7,12; Joel 2:1; Zeph. 1:7 30:4 [1]Or, *fear* [a]ch. 29:19 [b]Jer. 50:15 30:5 [1]Heb. *Phut* [2]Heb. *children* [a]Jer. 25:20,24 30:6 [1][Or, *from Migdol* to *Syene*] [a]ch. 29:10 30:7 [a]ch. 29:12 30:8 [1]Heb. *broken* 30:9 [a]Is. 18:1,2 30:10 [a]ch. 29:19 30:11 [a]ch. 28:7 30:12 [1]Heb. *drought* [2]Heb. *the fulness thereof* [a]Is. 19:5,6 [b]Is. 19:4

30:13 [a]Is. 19:1; Jer. 43:12; 46:25; Zech. 13:2 [b]Zech. 10:11 [c]Is. 19:16 30:14 [1]Or, *Tanis* [a]ch. 29:14 [b]Ps. 78:12,43 [c]Nah. 3:8-10 30:15 [1]Or, *Pelusium* [a]Jer. 46:25 30:16 [a]ver. 8 30:17 [1]Or, *Heliopolis* [2]Or, *Pubastum* 30:18 [1]Or, *restrained* [a]Jer. 2:16 30:21 [a]Jer. 48:25 [b]Jer. 46:11 30:22 [a]Ps. 37:17

is given, but it was probably between January and April of 587 B.C. Compare 29:1 with 30:20. Jerusalem was under siege at this time.

30:2–3 *the day . . . the day of the LORD.* The day of God's coming in judgment (see 7:7 and note). Egypt's judgment is announced.

30:3 *the day of the Lord is near.* Cf. Is 13:6. *a cloudy day.* Cf. Joel 2:2; Zeph 1:15.

30:4 *sword.* Nebuchadnezzar's (see v. 10; see also note on 21:3).

‡30:5. *Ethiopia.* Cush. *Libya.* Phut, in North Africa (see note on 27:10). *Lydia.* "Lud," fourth listed son of Shem. Not in Asia Minor (see note on 27:10) but descendents of Shem somewhere in northern Africa. *Chub.* obscure, but probably from Northern Africa in league with others listed here. *men of the land.* Or, "covenant men," apparently Jews living in Egypt (see Jer 44).

30:6 *from the tower of Syene.* See note on 29:10.

30:8 *set a fire in.* Make war on.

‡30:9 *messengers . . . in ships.* See Is 18 for a similar oracle on Cush involving ships on the Nile.

30:11 *the terrible of the nations.* A common phrase for the Babylonians, who were known for their cruelty (see 2 Ki 25:7).

‡30:13 *images.* See note on 6:4. *Noph.* Another name for Memphis. Located 15 miles south of Cairo, Memphis was a former capital of Egypt and one of her largest cities. The list of towns reveals no discernible pattern but is a literary device used to underscore the scope of the destruction (cf. Is 10:9–11,27–32; Mic 1:10–15; Zeph 2:4). *prince.* King.

‡30:14 *Pathros.* See 29:14 and note. *Zoan.* A city in northeast Egypt in the delta region; also called Raamses (see Ex 1:11), Avaris and Tanis (see Is 19:11,13; 30:4). *No.* Thebes, the capital of Upper Egypt; present-day Luxor and Karnak.

‡30:15 *Sin.* A fortress in the eastern delta region of the Nile.

‡30:17 *Aven.* Heliopolis ("city of the sun"), the Greek name for On, located six miles northeast of Cairo. *Phi-beseth.* Bubastis, at one time the capital of Lower (northern) Egypt; located 40 miles northeast of Cairo.

30:18 *Tehaphnehes.* Tahpanhes, in extreme northeast Egypt. Johanan son of Kareah and his men fled there after the murder of Gedaliah (see Jer 43:4–7). *darkened.* A common Biblical metaphor describing ruin, destruction or death. *cloud shall cover her.* See v. 3 and note; 32:7.

30:20 The fourth oracle against Egypt (see note on 29:1). *eleventh year . . . first month . . . seventh day of the month.* Apr. 29, 587 B.C.; the eighth date in Ezekiel (see 1:2; 8:1; 20:1; 24:1; 26:1; 29:1,17).

30:21 *I have broken the arm of Pharaoh.* Refers to Pharaohhophra's defeat by Nebuchadnezzar the previous year (see notes on 29:6; Jer 37:10).

23 [a]And I will scatter the Egyptians among the nations, and will disperse them through the countries.

24 And I will strengthen the arms of the king of Babylon, and put my sword in his hand: but I will break Pharaoh's arms, and he shall groan before him *with* the groanings of a deadly wounded *man.*

25 But I will strengthen the arms of the king of Babylon, and the arms of Pharaoh shall fall down; and [a]they shall know that I *am* the LORD, when I shall put my sword into the hand of the king of Babylon, and he shall stretch it out upon the land of Egypt.

26 [a]And I will scatter the Egyptians among the nations, and disperse them among the countries; and they shall know that I *am* the LORD.

Parable of the cedar of Lebanon

31 And it came to pass in the eleventh year, in the third *month,* in the first *day* of the month, *that* the word of the LORD came unto me, saying,

2 Son of man, speak unto Pharaoh king of Egypt, and to his multitude; [a]Whom art thou like in thy greatness?

3 [a]Behold, the Assyrian *was* a cedar in Lebanon [1]with fair branches, and with a shadowing shrowd, and of a high stature; and his top was among the thick boughs.

4 [a]The waters [1]made him great, the deep [2]set him up on high with her rivers running round about his plants, and sent out her [3]little rivers unto all the trees of the field.

5 Therefore [a]his height was exalted above all the trees of the field, and his boughs were multiplied, and his branches became long because of the multitude of waters, [1]when he shot forth.

6 All the [a]fowls of heaven made their nests in his boughs, and under his branches did all the beasts of the field bring forth their young, and under his shadow dwelt all great nations.

7 Thus was he fair in his greatness, in the length of his branches: for his root was by great waters.

8 The cedars in the [a]garden of God could not hide him: the fir trees were not like his boughs, and the chesnut trees were not like his branches; nor any tree in the garden of God was like unto him in his beauty.

9 I have made him fair by the multitude of his branches: so that all the trees of Eden, that *were* in the garden of God, envied him.

10 ¶ Therefore thus saith the Lord GOD; Because thou hast lifted up thyself in height, and he hath shot up his top among the thick boughs, and [a]his heart is lifted up in his height;

11 I have therefore delivered him into the hand of the mighty one of the heathen; [1]he shall surely deal with him: I have driven him out for his wickedness.

12 And strangers, [a]the terrible of the nations, have cut him off, and have left him: [b]upon the mountains and in all the valleys his branches are fallen, and his boughs are broken by all the rivers of the land; and all the people of the earth are gone down from his shadow, and have left him.

13 [a]Upon his ruin shall all the fowls of the heaven remain, and all the beasts of the field shall be upon his branches:

14 To the end that none of all the trees by the waters exalt themselves for their height, neither shoot up their top among the thick boughs, neither [1]their trees stand up in their height, all that drink water: for [a]they are all delivered unto death, [b]to the nether parts of the earth, in the midst of the children of men, with them that go down to the pit.

15 ¶ Thus saith the Lord GOD; In the day when he went down to the grave I caused a mourning: I covered the deep for him, and I restrained the floods thereof, and the great waters were stayed: and I caused Lebanon [1]to mourn for him, and all the trees of the field fainted for him.

16 I made the nations to [a]shake at the sound of his fall, when I [b]cast him down to hell with them that descend into the pit: and [c]all the trees of Eden, the choice and best of Lebanon, all that drink water, [d]shall be comforted in the nether parts of the earth.

17 They also went down into hell with him unto *them that be* slain with the sword; and *they that were* his arm, *that* [a]dwelt under his shadow in the midst of the heathen.

18 [a]To whom art thou thus like in glory and

30:23 [a]ver. 26; ch. 29:12
30:25 [a]Ps. 9:16
30:26 [a]ver. 23; ch. 29:12
31:2 [a]ver. 18
31:3 [1]Heb. *fair of branches* [a]Dan. 4:10
31:4 [1]Or, *nourished* [2]Or, *brought him up* [3]Or, *conduits* [a]Jer. 51:36
31:5 [1]Or, *when it sent them forth* [a]Dan. 4:11
31:6 [a]ch. 17:23; Dan. 4:12
31:8 [a]Gen. 2:8; 13:10; ch. 28:13
31:10 [a]Dan. 5:20
31:11 [1]Heb. *in doing he shall do unto him*
31:12 [a]ch. 28:7 [b]ch. 32:5; 35:8
31:13 [a]Is. 18:6; ch. 32:4
31:14 [1]Or, *stand upon themselves for their height* [a]Ps. 82:7 [b]ch. 32:18
31:15 [1]Heb. *to be black*
31:16 [a]ch. 26:15 [b]Is. 14:15 [c]Is. 14:8 [d]ch. 32:31
31:17 [a]Lam. 4:20
31:18 [a]ver. 2; ch. 32:19

30:24 *put my sword in his hand.* See note on 21:3.

31:1 The fifth oracle against Egypt (see note on 29:1). *eleventh year . . . third month . . . first day of the month.* June 21, 587 B.C.; the ninth date in Ezekiel (see 1:2; 8:1; 20:1; 24:1; 26:1; 29:1, 17; 30:20).

‡31:3 *Behold, the Assyrian.* A great nation that had fallen. In 609 B.C. Pharaoh Neco went to Carchemish to help the Assyrian empire, which was reeling from Babylonian attacks. The effort failed and Assyria passed from history. *was a cedar.* The beginning of another allegory (see Ezekiel's allegorical use of the cedar in ch. 17). *Lebanon.* Known for its cedars (see vv. 15–18; Judg 9:15; 1 Ki 4:33; 5:6; 2 Ki 14:9; Ezra 3:7; Ps 29:5; 92:12; 104:16).

31:4 *waters.* The Tigris and Euphrates. *the deep.* See note on 26:19.

‡31:6 *fowls of heaven.* See 17:23 and note; see also Dan 4:12.

‡31:8 *garden of God.* The note of pride is introduced (see v. 10; cf. 28:13).

31:11 *mighty one of the heathen.* Probably Nabopolassar; or possibly Nebuchadnezzar. *his wickedness.* Pride (see v. 10; Gen 11:1–8).

31:12 *strangers, the terrible of the nations.* Babylon (see note on 30:11).

31:15 *the deep.* See note on 26:19.

31:16 *nations . . . shake.* As at Tyre's fall (see 27:35; 28:19). *shall be comforted.* Because the mightiest of trees had joined them in the grave (Sheol).

31:17 *them that be slain with the sword.* Those who met a premature death.

31:18 *thou.* The Egyptian pharaoh. *yet shalt thou.* It would happen to Pharaoh as it had happened to Assyria. *uncircumcised.* See note on 28:10.

in greatness among the trees of Eden? yet shalt
thou be brought down with the trees of Eden
unto the nether parts of the earth: [b]thou shalt
lie in the midst of the uncircumcised with *them*
that be slain with the sword. This *is* Pharaoh
and all his multitude, saith the Lord GOD.

The lament for Pharaoh

32 And it came to pass in the twelfth
year, in the twelfth month, in the
first *day* of the month, *that* the word of the
LORD came unto me, saying,
2 Son of man, [a]take up a lamentation for
Pharaoh king of Egypt, and say unto him,
[b]Thou art like a young lion of the nations, [c]and
thou *art* as a [1]whale in the seas: and thou
camest forth with thy rivers, and troubledst the
waters with thy feet, and [d]fouledst their rivers.
3 Thus saith the Lord GOD; I will therefore
[a]spread out my net over thee with a company
of many people; and they shall bring thee up
in my net.
4 Then [a]will I leave thee upon the land, I
will cast thee forth upon the open field, and
[b]will cause all the fowls of the heaven to remain upon thee, and I will fill the beasts of the
whole earth with thee.
5 And I will lay thy flesh [a]upon the mountains, and fill the valleys *with* thy height.
6 I will also water with thy blood [1]the land
wherein thou swimmest, *even* to the mountains; and the rivers shall be full of thee.
7 And when *I* shall [1]put thee out, [a]I will
cover the heaven, and make the stars thereof
dark; I will cover the sun with a cloud, and the
moon shall not give her light.
8 All the [1]bright lights of heaven will I
make [2]dark over thee, and set darkness upon
thy land, saith the Lord GOD.
9 I will also [1]vex the hearts of many people, when I shall bring thy destruction among
the nations, into the countries which thou
hast not known.
10 Yea, I will make many people amazed at
thee, and their kings shall be horribly afraid
for thee, when I shall brandish my sword before them; and [a]they shall tremble at every
moment, every man for his own life, in the
day of thy fall.
11 ¶ [a]For thus saith the Lord GOD; The
sword of the king of Babylon shall come *upon*
thee.
12 By the swords of the mighty will I cause
thy multitude to fall, [a]the terrible of the nations, all of them: and [b]they shall spoil the
pomp of Egypt, and all the multitude thereof
shall be destroyed.
13 I will destroy also all the beasts thereof
from besides the great waters; [a]neither shall
the foot of man trouble them any more, nor
the hoofs of beasts trouble them.
14 Then will I make their waters deep, and
cause their rivers to run like oil, saith the Lord
GOD.
15 When I shall make the land of Egypt
desolate, and the country shall be [1]destitute of
that whereof it was full, when I shall smite all
them that dwell therein, [a]then shall they
know that I *am* the LORD.
16 This *is* the [a]lamentation wherewith
they shall lament her: the daughters of the nations shall lament her: they shall lament for
her, *even* for Egypt, and for all her multitude,
saith the Lord GOD.
17 ¶ It came to pass also in the twelfth year,
in the fifteenth *day* of the month, *that* the
word of the LORD came unto me, saying,
18 Son of man, wail for the multitude of
Egypt, and [a]cast them down, *even* her, and the
daughters of the famous nations, unto the
nether parts of the earth, with them that go
down into the pit.
19 [a]Whom dost thou pass in beauty? [b]go
down, and be thou laid with the uncircumcised.
20 They shall fall in the midst of *them that*
are slain by the sword: [1]she is delivered *to* the
sword: draw her and all her multitudes.
21 [a]The strong among the mighty shall
speak to him out of the midst of hell with
them that help him: they are [b]gone down,
they lie uncircumcised, slain by the sword.

31:18 [b]ch. 28:10; 32:19,21,24
32:2 [1]Or, *dragon* [a]ver. 16; ch. 27:2 [b]ch. 19:3,6; 38:13 [c]ch. 29:3 [d]ch. 34:18
32:3 [a]ch. 12:13; 17:20; Hos. 7:12
32:4 [a]ch. 29:5 [b]ch. 31:13
32:5 [a]ch. 31:12
32:6 [1]Or, *the land of thy swimming*
32:7 [1]Or, *extinguish* [a]Is. 13:10; Joel 2:31; 3:15; Amos 8:9; Mat. 24:29; Rev. 6:12,13
32:8 [1]Heb. *lights of the light in heaven* [2]Heb. *them dark*
32:9 [1]Heb. *provoke to anger,* or, *grief*
32:10 [a]ch. 26:16
32:11 [a]Jer. 46:26; ch. 30:4
32:12 [a]ch. 28:7 [b]ch. 29:19
32:13 [a]ch. 29:11
32:15 [1]Heb. *desolate from the fulness thereof* [a]Ex. 7:5; 14:4,18; Ps. 9:16; ch. 6:7
32:16 [a]ver. 2; 2 Sam. 1:17; 2 Chr. 35:25; ch. 26:17
32:18 [a]ch. 26:20; 31:14
32:19 [a]ch. 31:2,18 [b]ver. 21,24; ch. 28:10
32:20 [1]Or, *the sword is laid*
32:21 [a]ver. 27; Is. 1:31; 14:9,10 [b]ver. 19,25

32:1 The sixth oracle against Egypt (see note on 29:1). *twelfth year . . . twelfth month . . . first day of the month.* Mar. 3, 585 B.C.; the tenth date in Ezekiel (see 1:2; 8:1; 20:1; 24:1; 26:1; 29:1,17; 30:20; 31:1). If the Septuagint and Syriac are followed ("eleventh year"), then the chronological order of the Egypt oracles is preserved (and the date would be Mar. 13, 586). Cf. 29:1; 30:20; 31:1; see v. 17 and note.

32:2 *lamentation.* See note on 19:1. *lion of the nations.* A figure for royalty and grandeur (see 19:1–9). *a whale.* Or "dragon" (see KJV marg.); see also 29:3 and note. *seas . . . rivers.* Canals of the Nile (see note on 29:3).

32:3 *spread out my net.* Earlier it was Zedekiah over whom God's net was thrown (see 12:13; 17:20; 19:8).

32:4 *will I leave.* God's actions here are very similar to those described in 29:3–5.

32:7 *I will cover the heaven.* The first of seven clauses threatening the darkness associated with the day of the Lord (see Joel 2:2,10,31; 3:15; Amos 5:18–20; Zeph 1:15).

32:9 *vex the hearts.* This and the next verse reflect the fear brought about whenever great world powers fall, reminding lesser nations that they are even more vulnerable. Cf. similar feelings aroused by Tyre's fall (26:16–18; 27:35; 28:19).

32:10 *my sword.* See note on 21:3.

32:11 *king of Babylon.* Nebuchadnezzar (cf. 21:19).

32:12 *the terrible of the nations.* Babylon (see note on 30:11).

32:14 *rivers to run like oil.* Their surface undisturbed by any form of life. This is the only place in the Bible where this eerie metaphor is used to describe desolation.

32:16 *daughters of the nations.* A world chorus of professional wailers (see Jer 9:17–18).

32:17 The seventh and last oracle against Egypt (see note on 29:1). *twelfth year . . . fifteenth day of the month.* No month is given (as in 26:1; 40:1). The whole year dates from Apr. 13, 586, to Apr. 1, 585 B.C. The Septuagint suggests the first month, the 15th day of which would be Apr. 27, 586.

32:18 *daughters of the famous nations.* See note on v. 16. *nether parts of the earth.* Same as "Sheol" (grave) in 31:15.

32:19 *uncircumcised.* See note on 28:10.

22 Asshur *is* there and all her company: his graves *are* about him: all of them slain, fallen by the sword:

23 [a]Whose graves are set in the sides of the pit, and her company is round about her grave: all of them slain, fallen by the sword, which [b]caused [1]terror in the land of the living.

24 There *is* [a]Elam and all her multitude round about her grave, all of them slain, fallen by the sword, which are [b]gone down uncircumcised into the nether parts of the earth, [c]which caused their terror in the land of the living; yet have they borne their shame with them that go down to the pit.

25 They have set her a bed in the midst of the slain with all her multitude: her graves *are* round about him: all of them uncircumcised, slain by the sword: though their terror was caused in the land of the living, yet have they borne their shame with them that go down to the pit: he is put in the midst of *them that be* slain.

26 There *is* [a]Meshech, Tubal, and all her multitude: her graves *are* round about him: all of them [b]uncircumcised, slain by the sword, though they caused their terror in the land of the living.

27 [a]And they shall not lie with the mighty *that are* fallen of the uncircumcised, which are gone down *to* hell [1]with their weapons of war: and they have laid their swords under their heads, but their iniquities shall be upon their bones, though *they were* the terror of the mighty in the land of the living.

28 Yea, thou shalt be broken in the midst of the uncircumcised, and shalt lie with *them that are* slain with the sword.

29 There *is* [a]Edom, her kings, and all her princes, which with their might are [1]laid by *them that were* slain by the sword: they shall lie with the uncircumcised, and with them that go down to the pit.

30 [a]There *be* the princes of the north, all of them, and all the [b]Zidonians, which are gone down with the slain; with their terror *they are* ashamed of their might; and they lie uncircumcised with *them that be* slain by the sword, and bear their shame with them that go down to the pit.

31 Pharaoh shall see them, and shall be [a]comforted over all his multitude, *even* Pharaoh and all his army slain by the sword, saith the Lord GOD.

32 For I have caused my terror in the land of the living: and he shall be laid in the midst of the uncircumcised with *them that are* slain with the sword, *even* Pharaoh and all his multitude, saith the Lord GOD.

32:23 [1]Or, *dismaying* [a]Is. 14:15 [b]ver. 24-27,32
32:24 [a]Jer. 49:34 [b]ver. 21 [c]ver. 23
32:26 [a]Gen. 10:2; ch. 27:13 [b]ver. 19,20
32:27 [1]Heb. *with weapons of their war* [a]ver. 21; Is. 14:18,19
32:29 [1]Heb. *given,* or, *put* [a]ch. 25:12
32:30 [a]ch. 38:6,15; 39:2 [b]ch. 28:21
32:31 [a]ch. 31:16

Ezekiel as Israel's watchman

33 Again the word of the LORD came unto me, saying,

2 Son of man, speak to [a]the children of thy people, and say unto them, [b][1]When I bring the sword upon a land, if the people of the land take a man of their coasts, and set him for their [c]watchman:

3 *If* when he seeth the sword come upon the land, he blow the trumpet, and warn the people;

4 Then [1]whosoever heareth the sound of the trumpet, and taketh not warning; if the sword come, and take him away, [a]his blood shall be upon his own head.

5 He heard the sound of the trumpet, and took not warning; his blood shall be upon him. But he that taketh warning shall deliver his soul.

6 But if the watchman see the sword come, and blow not the trumpet, and the people be not warned; if the sword come, and take *any* person from among them, [a]he is taken *away* in his iniquity; but his blood will I require at the watchman's hand.

7 [a]So thou, O son of man, I have set thee a watchman unto the house of Israel; therefore thou shalt hear the word at my mouth, and warn them from me.

8 When I say unto the wicked, O wicked *man,* thou shalt surely die; if thou dost not speak to warn the wicked from his way, that wicked *man* shall die in his iniquity; but his blood will I require at thine hand.

9 Nevertheless, if thou warn the wicked of his way to turn from it; if he do not turn from his way, he shall die in his iniquity; but thou hast delivered thy soul.

10 ¶ Therefore, O thou son of man, speak unto the house of Israel; Thus ye speak, saying, If our transgressions and our sins *be* upon us, and we [a]pine away in them, [b]how should we then live?

33:2 [1]Heb. *A land when I bring a sword upon her* [a]ch. 3:11 [b]ch. 14:17 [c]ver. 7; 2 Sam. 18:24,25; 2 Ki. 9:17; Hos. 9:8
33:4 [1]Heb. *he that hearing heareth* [a]ch. 18:13
33:6 [a]ver. 8
33:7 [a]ch. 3:17
33:10 [a]ch. 24:23 [b]Is. 49:14

32:24 *Elam.* A country east of Assyria; in present-day Iran.

32:26 *Meshech, Tubal.* Peoples and territories in Asia Minor.

32:30 *Zidonians.* Sidonians. See note on 28:21.

33:1–48:35 A section depicting consolation for Israel (see Introduction: Outline).

33:1–37:28 Sermons and oracles of comfort following the fall of Jerusalem. Interspersed are words of warning and judgment (e.g., 33:23–29; 34:1–19; 35; 36:1–7), some of which may have been intended to comfort a downtrodden people.

33:2 *children of thy people.* Fellow Israelites in exile with Ezekiel. *sword.* The invading army. *people of the land.* Full citizens who owned land and served in the army (see 7:27; 12:19; 45:16,22; 46:3). *watchman.* A figure introduced in ch. 3 and expanded in ch. 18 (see note on 3:17).

33:3 *trumpet.* An instrument made from a ram's horn (Josh 6:4,6,13), used to warn of approaching danger (Neh 4:18–20; Jer 4:19; Amos 3:6) and to announce the beginnings of religious periods (e.g., day of atonement, Lev 25:9; new moon festival, Ps 81:3).

33:4 *his blood shall be upon his own head.* See note on 18:13.

‡33:6 *his blood.* His life, blood being the life principle (see Gen 9:5; 42:22).

33:7 *house of Israel.* Both the nation and the individuals. Compare vv. 7–9 with 3:17–19.

33:10 *our transgressions and our sins.* The first time the exiles expressed consciousness of sin. Previously they had blamed their fathers (18:2) and even God (18:19,25).

11 Say unto them, *As* I live, saith the Lord GOD, [a]I have no pleasure in the death of the wicked; but that the wicked turn from his way and live: turn ye, turn ye from your evil ways; for [b]why will ye die, O house of Israel?

12 Therefore, thou son of man, say unto the children of thy people, The [a]righteousness of the righteous shall not deliver him in the day of his transgression: as for the wickedness of the wicked, [b]he shall not fall thereby in the day that he turneth from his wickedness; neither shall the righteous be able to live for his *righteousness* in the day that he sinneth.

13 When I shall say to the righteous, *that* he shall surely live; [a]if he trust to his own righteousness, and commit iniquity, all his righteousnesses shall not be remembered; but for his iniquity that he hath committed, he shall die for it.

14 Again, [a]when I say unto the wicked, Thou shalt surely die; if he turn from his sin, and do [1]that which is lawful and right;

15 *If* the wicked [a]restore the pledge, [b]give again that he had robbed, walk in [c]the statutes of life, without committing iniquity; he shall surely live, he shall not die.

16 [a]None of his sins that he hath committed shall be mentioned unto him: he hath done that which is lawful and right; he shall surely live.

17 [a]Yet the children of thy people say, The way of the Lord is not equal: but *as for* them, their way is not equal.

18 [a]When the righteous turneth from his righteousness, and committeth iniquity, he shall even die thereby.

19 But if the wicked turn from his wickedness, and do that which is lawful and right, he shall live thereby.

20 Yet ye say, [a]The way of the Lord is not equal. O ye house of Israel, I will judge you every one after his ways.

Jerusalem's fall

21 ¶ And it came to pass in the twelfth year [a]of our captivity, in the tenth *month,* in the fifth *day* of the month, [b]*that* one that had escaped out of Jerusalem came unto me, saying, [c]The city is smitten.

22 Now [a]the hand of the LORD was upon me in the evening, afore he that was escaped came; and had opened my mouth, until *he* came to me in the morning; [b]and my mouth was opened, and I was no more dumb.

23 Then the word of the LORD came unto me, saying,

24 Son of man, [a]they that inhabit those [b]wastes of the land of Israel speak, saying, [c]Abraham was one, and he inherited the land: [d]but we *are* many; the land is given us for inheritance.

25 Wherefore say unto them, Thus saith the Lord GOD; [a]Ye eat with the blood, and [b]lift up your eyes toward your idols, and [c]shed blood: and shall ye possess the land?

26 Ye stand upon your sword, ye work abomination, and ye [a]defile every one his neighbour's wife: and shall ye possess the land?

27 Say thou thus unto them, Thus saith the Lord GOD; *As* I live, surely [a]*they* that *are* in the wastes shall fall by the sword, and him that *is* in the open field [b]will I give to the beasts [1]to be devoured, and *they* that *be* in the forts and [c]in the caves shall die of the pestilence.

28 [a]For I will lay the land [1]most desolate, and the [b]pomp of her strength shall cease; and [c]the mountains of Israel shall be desolate, that none shall pass through.

29 Then shall they know that I *am* the LORD, when I have laid the land most desolate because of all their abominations which they have committed.

30 ¶ Also, thou son of man, the children of thy people still are talking [1]against thee by the walls and in the doors of the houses, and [a]speak one to another, every one to his brother, saying, Come, I pray you, and hear what *is* the word that cometh forth from the LORD.

31 And [a]they come unto thee [1]as the people cometh, and [2]they [b]sit before thee *as* my people, and they hear thy words, but they will not do them: [c]for with their mouth [3]they

33:11 [a]2 Sam. 14:14; 2 Pet. 3:9 [b]ch. 18:31
33:12 [a]ch. 3:20; 18:24,26 [b]2 Chr. 7:14
33:13 [a]ch. 3:20; 18:24
33:14 [1]Heb. *judgment and justice* [a]ch. 3:18,19; 18:27
33:15 [a]ch. 18:7 [b]Ex. 22:1,4; Lev. 6:2,4,5 [c]Lev. 18:5; ch. 20:11,13,21
33:16 [a]ch. 18:22
33:17 [a]ver. 20; ch. 18:25,29
33:18 [a]ch. 18:26
33:20 [a]ver. 17; ch. 18:25
33:21 [a]ch. 1:2
33:21 [b]ch. 24:26
33:21 [c]2 Ki. 25:4
33:22 [a]ch. 1:3 [b]ch. 24:27
33:24 [a]ch. 34:2 [b]ver. 27; ch. 36:4 [c]Is. 51:2; Acts 7:5 [d]Mic. 3:11; Mat. 3:9; John 8:39
33:25 [a]Gen. 9:4; Lev. 3:17; 7:26; 17:10; 19:26; Deut. 12:16 [b]ch. 18:6 [c]ch. 22:6,9
33:26 [a]ch. 18:6; 22:11
33:27 [1]Heb. *to devour him* [a]ver. 24 [b]ch. 39:4 [c]Judg. 6:2; 1 Sam. 13:6
33:28 [1]Heb. *desolation and desolation* [a]Jer. 44:2,6,22; ch. 36:34,35 [b]ch. 7:24; 24:21; 30:6,7 [c]ch. 6:2,3,6
33:30 [1][Or, *of thee*] [a]Is. 29:13
33:31 [1]Heb. *according to the coming of the people* [2]Or, *my people sit before thee* [3]Heb. *they make loves,* or, *jests* [a]ch. 14:1; 20:1 [b]ch. 8:1 [c]Ps. 78:36,37; Is. 29:13

33:11 *As I live.* See note on 18:3. *I have no pleasure.* The question of 18:23 is now a statement. God's basic intention for His creation is life, not death (see note on 16:6). *turn from his way.* The third call for repentance (see 14:6; 18:30).

33:12–20 Deals with the same subject as 18:21–29—namely, that the individual, whether righteous or wicked, has a choice to live righteously each day.

33:15 *restore the pledge, give again that he had robbed.* See note on 18:7. *statutes of life.* The purpose of God's law was to foster and protect life (cf. 20:13,21). *he shall surely live.* The entire section is Ezekiel's answer to the despairing question of v. 10.

33:17 *The way of the Lord is not equal.* Cf. 18:25,29.

33:21 *twelfth year ... tenth month ... fifth day of the month.* Jan. 8, 585 B.C., five months after the Jerusalem temple was burned. See date in 2 Ki 25:8, which in modern reckoning is Aug. 14, 586. The journey between Jerusalem and Babylon could be made in four months (Ezra 7:9). *one that had escaped out of Jerusalem.* The first of the exiles of 586 (see 24:26, "he that escapeth"). *The city is smitten.* With this statement all of Ezekiel's previous prophecies were fulfilled and vindicated. He was then sent with a new mission: pastoral comfort.

33:22 *no more dumb.* The muteness that had come upon him at the beginning of his ministry was lifted (see 3:26 and note).

33:24 *they that inhabit those wastes of the land.* The residents of Jerusalem not exiled in 586 B.C. *Abraham was one ... but we are many.* A boast by the unrepentant, similar to that of 11:15 (cf. Luke 3:8).

33:25 *eat with the blood.* Forbidden in Gen 9:4; Lev 7:26–27; 17:10; Deut 12:16,23. *lift up your eyes toward your idols.* See note on 18:6.

33:27 *As I live.* See note on 18:3. *sword ... beasts ... pestilence.* Cf. the threefold threat in 5:12; 7:15; 12:16 and the fourfold threat in 14:12–21.

33:30–33 Words of assurance meant for Ezekiel alone.

33:31 *sit before thee.* As the elders had (8:1; 14:1). *goeth after their covetousness.* The people were waiting for Ezekiel to

shew much love, *but* [d]their heart goeth after
their covetousness.
32 And lo, thou *art* unto them as [1]a very
lovely song *of* one that hath a pleasant voice,
and can play well on an instrument: for they
hear thy words, but they do them not.
33 [a]And when this cometh to pass, (lo, it
will come) then [b]shall they know that a prophet hath been among them.

Israel's shepherds

34 And the word of the LORD came unto
me, saying,
2 Son of man, prophesy against the shepherds of Israel, prophesy, and say unto them,
Thus saith the Lord GOD unto the shepherds;
[a]Woe *be* to the shepherds of Israel that do feed
themselves! should not the shepherds feed the
flocks?
3 [a]Ye eat the fat, and ye clothe you with
the wool, ye kill them that are fed: *but* ye feed
not the flock.
4 [a]The diseased have ye not strengthened,
neither have ye healed that which was sick,
neither have ye bound up that which was broken, neither have ye brought again that which
was driven away, neither have ye [b]sought that
which was lost; but with [c]force and with cruelty have ye ruled them.
5 [a]And they were [b]scattered, [c1]because
there is no shepherd: [d]and they became meat
to all the beasts of the field, when they were
scattered.
6 My sheep wandered through all the
mountains, and upon every high hill: yea, my
flock was scattered upon all the face of the
earth, and none did search or seek *after them.*

33:31 [d]Mat. 13:22
33:32 [1]Heb. *a song of loves*
33:33 [a]1 Sam. 3:20 [b]ch. 2:5
34:2 [a]Jer. 23:1; Zech. 11:17
34:3 [a]Is. 56:11; Zech. 11:16
34:4 [a]Zech. 11:16 [b]Luke 15:4 [c]1 Pet. 5:3
34:5 [1]Or, *without a shepherd:* and so ver. 8 [a]ch. 33:21 [b]1 Ki. 22:17; Mat. 9:36 [c]ver. 8 [d]Is. 56:9; Jer. 12:9
34:8 [a]ver. 5,6 [b]ver. 2,10
34:10 [a]ch. 3:18; Heb. 13:17 [b]ver. 2,8
34:12 [1]Heb. *According to the seeking* [a]ch. 30:3
34:13 [a]Is. 65:9,10; Jer. 23:3
34:14 [a]Ps. 23:2 [b]Jer. 33:12

7 ¶ Therefore, ye shepherds, hear the word
of the LORD;
8 *As* I live, saith the Lord GOD, surely because my flock became a prey, and my flock
[a]became meat to every beast of the field, because *there was* no shepherd, neither did my
shepherds search for my flock, [b]but the shepherds fed themselves, and fed not my flock;
9 Therefore, O ye shepherds, hear the
word of the LORD;
10 Thus saith the Lord GOD; Behold, I *am*
against the shepherds; and [a]I will require my
flock at their hand, and cause them to cease
from feeding the flock; neither shall the shepherds [b]feed themselves any more; for I will deliver my flock from their mouth, that they may
not be meat for them.

The Lord GOD is a shepherd

11 ¶ For thus saith the Lord GOD; Behold, I,
even I, will both search my sheep, and seek
them out.
12 [1]As a shepherd seeketh out his flock in
the day that he is among his sheep *that are*
scattered; so will I seek out my sheep, and will
deliver them out of all places where they have
been scattered in [a]the cloudy and dark day.
13 And [a]I will bring them out from the
people, and gather them from the countries,
and will bring them to their own land, and
feed them upon the mountains of Israel by the
rivers, and in all the inhabited places of the
country.
14 [a]I will feed them in a good pasture, and
upon the high mountains of Israel shall their
fold be: [b]there shall they lie in a good fold, and
in a fat pasture shall they feed upon the mountains of Israel.

---

tell them how they could personally profit from the situation rather than what God's larger designs were for them (cf. Mat 20:20–28).

33:32 *one that hath a pleasant voice.* May indicate that Ezekiel chanted his oracles (see 2 Ki 3:15; Is 5:1), but more likely the prophet was using a metaphor. *they hear . . . but they do them not.* See Is 29:13; Mat 21:28–32; cf. Jas 1:22–25.

34:2 *shepherds of Israel.* Those responsible for providing leadership, especially the kings and their officials (see 2 Sam 7:7; Jer 25:18–19), but also the prophets and priests (see Is 56:11; Jer 23:9–11). Ezekiel had earlier singled out the princes, priests and prophets for special rebuke (ch. 22). To call a king a shepherd was common throughout the ancient Near East. For David's rise from shepherd to shepherd-king see Ps 78:70–71. For condemnation of the shepherds cf. Jer 23:1–4.

34:3 *eat . . . clothe . . . kill.* Legitimate rewards for shepherds. Their crime was that they did not care for the flock.

34:4 *sought that which was lost.* Cf. Jer 50:6; Mat 18:12–14; Luke 15:4; 19:10.

‡34:5 *scattered.* Often used by Ezekiel to describe Israel's exile and dispersion (11:16–17; 12:15; 20:23,34,41; 22:15; 28:25). *there is no shepherd.* A picture used often in the Bible (e.g., Mark 6:34). It is likely that Jesus drew his language in John 10 from this chapter. His picture there is consistent with the kings of old who took the royal title "Shepherd." That title is used most often in the context in which the king provides for his flock and protects his flock from those who would harm it. Jesus, however, altered the royal language by laying down His life instead of killing the wolf.

‡34:8 *beast of the field.* Hostile foreign nations; but see v. 28, where they are contrasted.

34:10 *I am against the shepherds.* See note on 5:8.

‡34:11 *I, will . . . search my sheep.* Having dealt with the faithless shepherds (vv. 1–10), the Lord committed Himself to shepherd His flock (see Jer 23:3–4).

34:12 *out of all places.* Babylon was not the only place where the Israelites had gone (see Jer 43:1–7). *cloudy and dark day.* The day of the Lord that had come upon Israel when Jerusalem fell in August of 586 B.C. (see 7:7 and note).

34:13 *I will bring them out.* The promises of restoration—begun in 11:17 and repeated in 20:34,41–42; 28:25—find special emphasis in this part (chs. 33–39) of Ezekiel (see 36:24; 37:21; 38:8; 39:27). *mountains of Israel.* Compare the tone of 6:3–7 with judgment now past (see v. 12). The mountains perhaps represented the scene of salvation.

‡34:14 *I will feed them.* See Is 40:11; John 10:11. *in a good pasture.* These images for those who would lead a people appear often in the ancient Near East. Tukulti-Ninurta I (c 1245–1208 B.C.) in a royal inscription spoke of "the king" as one who shepherds his land in green pastures with his beneficent staff—the one who with his fierce valour subdued princes and all kings with his just sceptre. Note the twin activities of providing and protecting.

15 I will feed my flock, and I will cause
them to lie down, saith the Lord GOD.
16 [a]I will seek that which was lost, and
bring again that which was driven away, and
will bind up that which was broken, and will
strengthen that which was sick: but I will destroy [b]the fat and the strong; I will feed them
[c]with judgment.
17 And *as for* you, O my flock, thus saith
the Lord GOD; [a]Behold, I judge between [1]cat-
tle and cattle, between the rams and the [2]he
goats.
18 *Seemeth it* a small thing unto you to
have eaten up the good pasture, but ye must
tread down with your feet the residue of your
pastures? and to have drunk of the deep waters, but ye must foul the residue with your
feet?
19 And *as for* my flock, they eat that which
ye have trodden with your feet; and they drink
that which ye have fouled with your feet.
20 ¶ Therefore thus saith the Lord GOD
unto them; [a]Behold, I, *even* I, will judge between the fat cattle and between the lean cattle.
21 Because ye have thrust with side and
with shoulder, and pusht all the diseased with
your horns, till ye have scattered them abroad;
22 Therefore will I save my flock, and they
shall no more be a prey; and I will judge between cattle and cattle.
23 And I will set up one [a]shepherd over
them, and he shall feed them, [b]*even* my servant David; he shall feed them, and he shall be
their shepherd.
24 And [a]I the LORD will be their God, and
my servant David [b]a prince among them; I the
LORD have spoken *it.*
25 And [a]I will make with them a covenant
of peace, and [b]will cause the evil beasts to
cease out of the land: and they [c]shall dwell
safely in the wilderness, and sleep in the
woods.
26 And I will make them and the places
round about [a]my hill [b]a blessing; and I will
[c]cause the shower to come down in his season; there shall be [d]showers of blessing.
27 And [a]the tree of the field shall yield her
fruit, and the earth shall yield her increase,
and they shall be safe in their land, and shall
know that I *am* the LORD, when I have [b]broken
the bands of their yoke, and delivered them
out of the hand of those that [c]served themselves of them.
28 And they shall no more be a prey to the
heathen, neither shall the beast of the land devour them; but [a]they shall dwell safely, and
none shall make *them* afraid.
29 And I will raise up for them a [a]plant [1]of
renown, and they shall be no more [2]con-
sumed with hunger in the land, [b]neither bear
the shame of the heathen any more.
30 Thus shall they know that [a]I the LORD
their God *am* with them, and *that* they, *even*
the house of Israel, *are* my people, saith the
Lord GOD.
31 And ye my [a]flock, the flock of my pasture, *are* men, *and* I *am* your God, saith the
Lord GOD.

Prophecy against mount Seir

35 Moreover the word of the LORD came
unto me, saying,
2 Son of man, set thy face against [a]mount
Seir, and [b]prophesy against it,
3 And say unto it, Thus saith the Lord GOD;
Behold, O mount Seir, I *am* against thee, and
[a]I will stretch out mine hand against thee, and
I will make thee [1]most desolate.
4 I will lay thy cities waste, and thou shalt
be desolate, and thou shalt know that I *am* the
LORD.

34:16 [a]Is. 40:11; Mic. 4:6; Mat. 18:11; Luke 5:32 [b]Is. 10:16; Amos 4:1 [c]Jer. 10:24
34:17 [1]Heb. *small cattle of lambs and kids* [2]Heb. *great he goats* [a]ch. 20:37; Mat. 25:32
34:20 [a]ver. 17
34:23 [a]Is. 40:11; John 10:11; Heb. 13:20; 1 Pet. 2:25 [b]Jer. 30:9; Hos. 3:5
34:24 [a]Ex. 29:45 [b]ch. 37:22
34:25 [a]ch. 37:26 [b]Lev. 26:6; Is. 11:6-9; Hos. 2:18 [c]Jer. 23:6
34:26 [a]Is. 56:7 [b]Gen. 12:2; Is. 19:24; Zech. 8:13 [c]Lev. 26:4 [d]Ps. 68:9
34:27 [a]Lev. 26:4; Ps. 85:12; Is. 4:2 [b]Jer. 2:20 [c]Jer. 25:14
34:28 [a]Jer. 30:10
34:29 [1]Or, *for renown* [2]Heb. *taken away* [a]Is. 11:1 [b]ch. 36:3,6
34:30 [a]ver. 24
34:31 [a]Ps. 100:3; John 10:11
35:2 [a]Deut. 2:5 [b]Amos 1:11
35:3 [1]Heb. *desolation and desolation* [a]ch. 6:14

34:16 *the fat and the strong.* Those with power who had fattened themselves by oppressing the other "sheep" (see vv. 17–22).
34:17 *rams and . . . goats.* People of power and influence who were oppressing poorer Israelites. This prophetic word shows the same concern for social justice found elsewhere in the prophets (see Is 3:13–15; 5:8; Amos 5:12; 6:1–7; Mic 2:1–5). Cf. the treatment of slaves Jeremiah observed (Jer 34:8–11).
‡34:23 *my servant David.* A ruler like David and from his line (see Ps 89:4,20,29; Jer 23:5–6). In John 10:24, the people ask, "If thou be the Christ, tell us plainly," to which Jesus responds, in v. 25, "I told you." He was the Christ, the son of David.
34:24 *prince.* The Lord announced a theocracy, a kingdom where He would be King and the earthly king a "prince" (cf. 37:25; 44:3; 45:7,16–17,22; 46:2–18; 48:21–22).
‡34:25 *covenant of peace.* Cf. 37:26. All of God's covenants aim at peace (see Gen 26:28–31; Num 25:12; Is 54:10; Mal 2:5). This covenant (the "new covenant" spoken of by Jeremiah, 31:31–34) looks to the final peace, initiated by Christ (Phil 4:7) and still awaiting final fulfillment. "Peace" (Hebrew *shalom*) is more than absence of hostility; it is fullness of life enjoyed in complete security. *sleep in the woods.* Often dangerous (see Ps 104:20–21; Jer 5:6). The phrase "none shall make them afraid" is stock language for the shepherd sections of the OT: Is 17:2; Jer 30:9–10; Mic 4:4, and most importantly in the merger of shepherd language with covenant language in Lev 26:6.
34:26 *the shower . . . in his season.* Autumn rains, which signal the beginning of the rainy season, and spring rains, which come at the end (cf. Jer 5:24). *showers of blessing.* Blessing, the power of life promised to God's people through Abraham (Gen 12:1–3), is beautifully symbolized in the life-giving effects of rain.
34:27 *bands of their yoke.* The bands were bars that were wooden pegs inserted down through holes in the yoke and tied below the animal's neck with cords (Is 58:6) to form a collar (cf. 30:18; Lev 26:13; Jer 27:2; 28:10–13). The entire picture represents foreign domination.
34:29 *shame of the heathen.* See 22:4.
34:30 *I the LORD their God am with them . . . they . . . are my people.* Covenant language (cf. 11:20; Ex 6:7; Hos 1:9), though the exact wording of this verse has no parallel elsewhere in Ezekiel.
35:2 *set thy face against.* See note on 20:46. *mount Seir.* Edom (v. 15), Israel's relative (Jacob and Esau being twins, Gen 25:21–30) and constant enemy, from whom brotherhood was sought but seldom found (cf. Amos 1:11). Edom (Seir) had to be dealt with before Israel could find peace (cf. Gen 32–33). See 25:12 and note; Is 63:1–6.
35:3 *I am against thee.* See note on 5:8.

5 [a]Because thou hast had a [1]perpetual hatred, and hast [2]shed *the blood of* the children of Israel by the [3]force of the sword in the time of their calamity, [b]in the time *that their* iniquity *had* an end:

6 Therefore, *as* I live, saith the Lord GOD, I will prepare thee unto blood, and blood shall pursue thee: [a]sith thou hast not hated blood, even blood shall pursue thee.

7 Thus will I make mount Seir [1]most desolate, and cut off from it [a]him that passeth out and him that returneth.

8 And I will fill his mountains *with* his slain *men:* in thy hills, and in thy valleys, and in all thy rivers, shall they fall *that are* slain with the sword.

9 [a]I will make thee perpetual desolations, and thy cities shall not return: [b]and ye shall know that I *am* the LORD.

10 Because thou hast said, These two nations and these two countries shall be mine, and we will [a]possess it; [1]whereas [b]the LORD was there:

11 Therefore, *as* I live, saith the Lord GOD, I will even do [a]according to thine anger, and according to thine envy which thou hast used out of thy hatred against them; and I will make myself known amongst them, when I have judged thee.

12 [a]And thou shalt know that I *am* the LORD, *and that* I have heard all thy blasphemies which thou hast spoken against the mountains of Israel, saying, They are laid desolate, they are given us [1]to consume.

13 Thus [a]with your mouth ye have [1]boasted against me, and have multiplied your words against me: I have heard *them.*

14 Thus saith the Lord GOD; [a]When the whole earth rejoiceth, I will make thee desolate.

15 [a]As thou didst rejoice at the inheritance of the house of Israel, because it was desolate, so will I do unto thee: thou shalt be desolate, O mount Seir, and all Idumea, *even* all of it: and they shall know that I *am* the LORD.

35:5 [1]Or, *hatred of old* [2]Heb. *poured out the children* [3]Heb. *hands* [a]ch. 25:12 [b]Ps. 137:7; Dan. 9:24
35:6 [a]Ps. 109:17
35:7 [1]Heb. *desolation and desolation* [a]Judg. 5:6
35:9 [a]Jer. 49:17 [b]ch. 36:11
35:10 [1]Or, *though the LORD was there* [a]Ps. 83:4,12 [b]Ps. 48:1,3; ch. 48:35
35:11 [a]Mat. 7:2; Jas. 2:13
35:12 [1]Heb. *to devour* [a]Ps. 9:16
35:13 [1]Heb. *magnified* [a]1 Sam. 2:3
35:14 [a]Is. 65:13
35:15 [a]Obad. 12,15

A prophecy to Israel

36 Also, thou son of man, prophesy unto the [a]mountains of Israel, and say, Ye mountains of Israel, hear the word of the LORD:

2 Thus saith the Lord GOD; Because [a]the enemy hath said against you, Aha, [b]even the ancient high places [c]are ours in possession:

3 Therefore prophesy and say, Thus saith the Lord GOD; [1]Because *they* have made *you* desolate, and swallowed you up on every side, that ye might be a possession unto the residue of the heathen, [a]and [2]ye are taken up in the lips of talkers, and *are* an infamy of the people:

4 Therefore, ye mountains of Israel, hear the word of the Lord GOD; Thus saith the Lord GOD to the mountains, and to the hills, to the [1]rivers, and to the valleys, to the desolate wastes, and to the cities that are forsaken, which [a]became a prey and [b]derision to the residue of the heathen that *are* round about;

5 Therefore thus saith the Lord GOD; [a]Surely in the fire of my jealousy have I spoken against the residue of the heathen, and against all Idumea, [b]which have appointed my land into their possession with the joy of all *their* heart, with despiteful minds, to cast it out for a prey.

6 Prophesy therefore concerning the land of Israel, and say unto the mountains, and to the hills, to the rivers, and to the valleys, Thus saith the Lord GOD; Behold, I have spoken in my jealousy and in my fury, because ye have [a]borne the shame of the heathen:

7 Therefore thus saith the Lord GOD; I have [a]lifted up mine hand, Surely the heathen that *are* about you, they shall bear their shame.

8 ¶ But ye, O mountains of Israel, ye shall shoot forth your branches, and yield your fruit to my people of Israel; for they are at hand to come.

9 For behold, I *am* for you, and I will turn unto you, and ye shall be tilled and sown:

10 And I will multiply men upon you, all the house of Israel, *even* all of it: and the cities

36:1 [a]ch. 6:2,3
36:2 [a]ch. 25:3 [b]Deut. 32:13 [c]ch. 35:10
36:3 [1]Heb. *Because, for because* [2]Or, *ye are made to come up on the lip of the tongue* [a]Deut. 28:37
36:4 [1]Or, *bottoms,* or, *dales* [a]ch. 34:28 [b]Ps. 79:4
36:5 [a]Deut. 4:24; ch. 38:19 [b]ch. 35:10,12
36:6 [a]ver. 15; Ps. 123:3,4; ch. 34:29
36:7 [a]ch. 20:5

35:5 *perpetual hatred.* Beginning with Jacob's deception of Isaac for Esau's blessing (Gen 27; see especially v. 41) and continuing later (Num 20:14–21; 2 Sam 8:13–14; 1 Ki 9:26–28). *time of their calamity.* Edom looted Jerusalem in 586 B.C. (see Obad 11–14).
‡35:6 *as I live.* See note on 18:3. *blood shall pursue thee.* Retributive justice based on Gen 9:6.
35:9 *perpetual desolations.* To experience no restoration like Egypt's (see 29:13–16).
35:10 *These two nations.* Israel and Judah.
35:11 *as I live.* See note on 18:3.
35:13 *ye have boasted against me.* Cf. Obad 12; Zeph 2:8,10; also Ps 35:26; Jer 48:26,42.
36:1–15 The comforting counterpart to ch. 6. Verses 1–7 announce punishment for the nations, vv. 8–15 restoration for Israel.
36:2 *the enemy hath said against you.* See 25:3; 26:2. *Aha.* See note on 25:3. *ancient high places.* The promised land, of which the elevated region between the Jordan Valley and the Mediterranean coast was the central core.
36:3 *residue of the heathen.* All nations that in the past had conquered parts of Israel—until finally they took full possession.
36:4 *mountains . . . hills . . . rivers . . . valleys.* See 6:3 and note on 1:5.
‡36:5 *fire of my jealousy.* The Lord was personally offended by the ridicule of the nations because it was His special land they were mocking and plundering (see "my land" later in the verse). *Idumea.* Or Edom, singled out because of their long-standing hostility to Israel (see ch. 35, especially vv. 2,5 and notes). For Edom in the Day of the Lord, see Am 9:12; see also Obadiah, where Edom is used as a catch word to connect the two books and their theme of the coming day.
36:8 *branches, and . . . fruit.* Signs of productivity (see 17:8,23) and the Lord's restored favor (see Lev 26:3–5); to be contrasted with Edom's desolation in 35:3,7,15. *at hand.* As judgment neared (7:7; 12:23), a speedy return of the exiles was announced.
36:9 *I will turn unto you.* Cf. Lev 26:9 for the identical clause in a similar context.
36:10 *all the house of Israel.* In this chapter (as in 37:15–23) Ezekiel is speaking of the restoration of all Israel.

shall be inhabited, and [a]the wastes shall be
builded:
11 And [a]I will multiply upon you man and
beast; and they shall increase and bring fruit:
and I will settle you after your old estates, and
will do better *unto you* than at your beginnings: [b]and ye shall know that I *am* the LORD.
12 Yea, I will cause men to walk upon you,
even my people Israel; [a]and they shall possess
thee, and thou shalt be their inheritance, and
thou shalt no more henceforth [b]bereave them
of men.
13 Thus saith the Lord GOD; Because they
say unto you, [a]Thou *land* devourest up men,
and hast bereaved thy nations;
14 Therefore thou shalt devour men no
more, neither [1]bereave thy nations any more,
saith the Lord GOD.
15 [a]Neither will I cause *men* to hear in
thee the shame of the heathen any more, neither shalt thou bear the reproach of the people
any more, neither shalt thou cause thy nations
to fall any more, saith the Lord GOD.
16 ¶ Moreover the word of the LORD came
unto me, saying,
17 Son of man, when the house of Israel
dwelt in their own land, [a]they defiled it by
their own way and by their doings: their way
was before me as [b]the uncleanness of a removed woman.
18 Wherefore I poured my fury upon them
[a]for the blood that they had shed upon the
land, and for their idols *wherewith* they had
polluted it:
19 And I scattered them among the heathen, and they were dispersed through the
countries: [a]according to their way and according to their doings I judged them.
20 And when they entered unto the heathen, whither they went, they [a]profaned my
holy name, when *they* said to them, These *are*
the people of the LORD, and are gone forth out
of his land.
21 But I had pity [a]for mine holy name,
which the house of Israel had profaned among
the heathen, whither they went.
22 Therefore say unto the house of Israel,
Thus saith the Lord GOD; I do not *this* for your
sakes, O house of Israel, [a]but for mine holy
name's sake, which ye have profaned among
the heathen, whither ye went.
23 And I will sanctify my great name,
which was profaned among the heathen,
which ye have profaned in the midst of them;
and the heathen shall know that I *am* the
LORD, saith the Lord GOD, when I shall be
[a]sanctified in you before [1]their eyes.
24 For [a]I will take you from among the
heathen, and gather you out of all countries,
and will bring you into your own land.
25 ¶ [a]Then will I sprinkle clean water upon
you, and ye shall be clean: [b]from all your filthiness, and from all your idols, will I cleanse you.
26 A [a]new heart also will I give you, and a
new spirit will I put within you: and I will take
away the stony heart out of your flesh, and I
will give you a heart of flesh.
27 And I will put my [a]spirit within you,
and cause you to walk in my statutes, and ye
shall keep my judgments, and do *them.*
28 [a]And ye shall dwell in the land that I
gave to your fathers; [b]and ye shall be my people, and I will be your God.

36:10 [a]ver. 33; Is. 58:12; 61:4; Amos 9:14
36:11 [a]Jer. 31:27; 33:12 [b]ch. 35:9; 37:6,13
36:12 [a]Obad. 17 [b]See Jer. 15:7
36:13 [a]Num. 13:32
36:14 [1]Or, *cause to fall*
36:15 [a]ch. 34:29
36:17 [a]Lev. 18:25,27,28; Jer. 2:7 [b]Lev. 15:19
36:18 [a]ch. 16:36,38; 23:37
36:19 [a]ch. 7:3; 18:30; 39:24
36:20 [a]Is. 52:5; Rom. 2:24
36:21 [a]ch. 20:9,14
36:22 [a]Ps. 106:8
36:23 [1]Or, *your* [a]ch. 20:41; 28:22
36:24 [a]ch. 34:13; 37:21
36:25 [a]Is. 52:15; Heb. 10:22 [b]Jer. 33:8
36:26 [a]Jer. 32:39; ch. 11:19
36:27 [a]ch. 11:19; 37:14
36:28 [a]ch. 28:25; 37:25 [b]Jer. 30:22; ch. 11:20; 37:27

36:11 *increase and bring fruit.* Identical terminology to the divine blessing at creation (Gen 1:22,28; see Gen 8:17; 9:1,7) and the subsequent covenant blessing (see Gen 17:6; 35:11; 48:3–4; Ex 1:7). *ye shall know that I am the LORD.* These words of recognition, used throughout the book to express God's revelation through judgment, here point to God's self-disclosure in salvation (see note on 5:13; cf. 34:30).

36:12 *walk upon you.* The mountains of Israel are still being addressed. *bereave them of men.* The mountains are poetically pictured as having contributed to the depopulation brought by the exile. This may refer to the fact that Canaan contained the Canaanites and their religious centers ("high places"), which had led Israel astray and so brought God's wrath down on His people (see 6:3 and note).

36:16–38 Summarizes all that Ezekiel prophesied concerning Israel.

‡36:18 *blood . . . for their idols.* A summary reference to Israel's social injustices and idolatrous religious practices (see 22:3 and note). *idols.* See note on 6:4.

36:20 *they profaned my holy name.* Because Israel had been removed from her land, it seemed to the nations that her God was unable to protect and preserve His people (cf. Num 14:15–16; 2 Ki 18:32–35; 19:10–12).

36:22 *I do not this for your sakes.* Not because God did not care for Israel, but because they did not deserve what He was about to do (cf. Deut 9:4–6). Statements like these make Ezekiel a preacher of pure grace. *for mine holy name's sake.* The reason given in ch. 20 for the withholding of divine punishment (see 20:9,14,22) is here given as a reason for divine restoration.

36:23 *the heathen shall know that I am the LORD.* The ultimate purpose of God's plans with Israel is that the whole world may know the true God.

36:24–30 There are four stages of restoration in this central passage of Ezekiel: (1) return of the exiles (v. 24), (2) cleansing from sin (v. 25), (3) enablement by God's Spirit to live God's way (vv. 26–27), and (4) prosperity in the land (vv. 28–30).

‡36:25 *will I sprinkle clean water.* For sprinkling with water as a ritual act of cleansing see Ex 30:19–20; Lev 14:51; Num 19:18; cf. Zech 13:1; Heb 10:22. *idols.* See note on 6:4. *will I cleanse.* See v. 33; 37:23; Jer 33:8.

36:26–27 Contains "new covenant" terminology (see Jer 31:33–34).

36:26 *new heart.* See notes on 11:19; 18:31. *a new spirit will I put within you.* Transform your mind and heart. Here and in 11:19 God declared that He would bring about the change. In 18:31 (see note there) He called on His people to effect the change. What He requires of His people He always provides. *heart out of your flesh.* "Flesh" in the OT is often a symbol for weakness and frailty (Is 31:3); in the NT it often stands for the sinful nature as a God-opposing force (as in Rom 8:5–8). Here it stands (in opposition to stone) for a pliable, teachable heart.

36:27 *my spirit.* God bestows His Spirit to enable the human spirit to do His will. Verses 25–27 are closely paralleled in Ps 51:7–11.

36:28 *my people . . . your God.* Covenant language (see 11:20 and note).

29 I will also [a]save you from all your uncleannesses: and [b]I will call for the corn, and
will increase it, and [c]lay no famine upon
you.
30 [a]And I will multiply the fruit of the tree,
and the increase of the field, that ye shall receive no more reproach of famine among the
heathen.
31 Then [a]shall ye remember your own evil
ways, and your doings that *were* not good, and
[b]shall lothe yourselves in your own sight for
your iniquities and for your abominations.
32 [a]Not for your sakes do I *this,* saith the
Lord GOD, be it known unto you: be ashamed
and confounded for your own ways, O house
of Israel.
33 Thus saith the Lord GOD; In the day that
I shall have cleansed you from all your iniquities, I will also cause *you* to dwell in the cities,
[a]and the wastes shall be builded.
34 And the desolate land shall be tilled,
whereas it lay desolate in the sight of all that
passed by.
35 And they shall say, This land that was
desolate is become like the garden of [a]Eden;
and the waste and desolate and ruined cities
are become fenced, *and* are inhabited.
36 Then the heathen that are left round
about you shall know that I the LORD build
the ruined *places, and* plant that that was
desolate: [a]I the LORD have spoken *it,* and I
will do *it.*
37 Thus saith the Lord GOD; [a]I will yet *for*
this be inquired of by the house of Israel, to do
it for them; I will [b]increase them *with* men
like a flock.
38 As the [1]holy flock, as the flock of Jerusalem in her solemn feasts; so shall the waste cities be filled *with* flocks of men: and they shall
know that I *am* the LORD.

36:29 [a]Mat. 1:21; Rom. 11:26 [b]See Ps. 105:16 [c]ch. 34:29
36:30 [a]ch. 34:27
36:31 [a]ch. 16:61,63 [b]Lev. 26:39; ch. 6:9; 20:43
36:32 [a]ver. 22; Deut. 9:5
36:33 [a]ver. 10
36:35 [a]Is. 51:3; ch. 28:13; Joel 2:3
36:36 [a]ch. 17:24; 22:14; 37:14
36:37 [a]See ch. 14:3; 20:3,31 [b]ver. 10
36:38 [1]Heb. *flock of holy things*

37:1 [a]ch. 1:3 [b]ch. 3:14; 8:3; 11:24; Luke 4:1
37:2 [1]Or, *champaign*
37:3 [a]Deut. 32:39; 1 Sam. 2:6; John 5:21; Rom. 4:17; 2 Cor. 1:9
37:5 [a]ver. 9; Ps. 104:30
37:6 [a]ch. 6:7; 35:12; Joel 2:27; 3:17
37:9 [1]Or, *breath* [a]ver. 5; Ps. 104:30
37:10 [a]Rev. 11:11

Vision of dry bones in the valley

37 The [a]hand of the LORD was upon me,
and carried me out [b]in the spirit of
the LORD, and set me down in the midst of the
valley which *was* full *of* bones,
2 And caused me to pass by them round
about: and behold, *there were* very many in
the open [1]valley; and lo, *they were* very dry.
3 And he said unto me, Son of man, can
these bones live? And I answered, O Lord
GOD, [a]thou knowest.
4 Again he said unto me, Prophesy upon
these bones, and say unto them, O ye dry
bones, hear the word of the LORD.
5 Thus saith the Lord GOD unto these
bones; Behold, I *will* [a]cause breath to enter
into you, and ye shall live:
6 And I will lay sinews upon you, and will
bring up flesh upon you, and cover you with
skin, and put breath in you, and ye shall live;
[a]and ye shall know that I *am* the LORD.
7 So I prophesied as I was commanded:
and as I prophesied, there was a noise, and behold a shaking, and the bones came together,
bone to his bone.
8 And when I beheld, lo, the sinews and
the flesh came up upon them, and the skin
covered them above: but *there was* no breath
in them.
9 Then said he unto me, Prophesy unto the
[1]wind, prophesy, son of man, and say to the
wind, Thus saith the Lord GOD; [a]Come from
the four winds, O breath, and breathe upon
these slain, that they may live.
10 So I prophesied as he commanded me,
[a]and the breath came into them, and they
lived, and stood up upon their feet, an exceeding great army.
11 Then he said unto me, Son of man,
these bones *are* the whole house of Israel: be-

36:29 *from all your uncleannesses.* From cultic and moral defilement (see v. 25; 37:23). *I will call.* As at the beginning when God called creation into being (cf. Gen 1:5,8,10).
36:30 *reproach.* As in v. 15.
36:31 *Then shall ye remember.* God's undeserved grace leads to recollection and repentance (cf. 6:9; 16:63; 20:43; Ps 130:4).
36:32 *Not for your sakes.* See note on v. 22.
36:33 *In the day.* Connects the promise of cleansing (vv. 24–32) and the promise of repopulation (vv. 33–36).
36:35 *garden of Eden.* Primeval fertility is suggested (cf. 28:13; 31:9). *are become fenced.* In contrast to 38:11.
36:36 *heathen . . . shall know.* See note on v. 23.
36:37 *I will yet for this be inquired of by the house of Israel.* Allowing petitions to come to Him again, God reversed His earlier refusals to hear (cf. 14:3; 20:3,31).
36:38 *holy flock . . . in her solemn feasts.* See 1 Ki 8:63; 1 Chr 29:21; 2 Chr 35:7 for the appropriateness of the comparison.
37:1–28 One of Ezekiel's major visions. Surprisingly no date is given (as in 1:2; 8:1; 40:1), but the event must have occurred sometime after 586 B.C.
37:1 *hand of the LORD.* See note on 1:3. *spirit of the LORD.* Used elsewhere in Ezekiel only in 11:5; usually simply "the Spirit," as in 8:3; 11:1,24. *valley.* The Hebrew for this word is the same as that translated "plain" in 3:22–23; 8:4. Ezekiel now received a message of hope, where he had previously heard God's word of judgment. *bones.* Verse 11 interprets them as symbolizing Israel's apparently hopeless condition in exile.
37:2 *there were very many.* Symbolizing the whole community of exiles. *very dry.* Long dead, far beyond the reach of resuscitation (1 Ki 17:17–24; 2 Ki 4:18–37; but see 2 Ki 13:21).
37:4 *Prophesy upon these bones.* Ezekiel had previously prophesied to inanimate objects (mountains, 6:2; 36:1; forests, 20:47) and now prophesied to lifeless bones and the "wind" (v. 9).
37:6 *sinews . . . flesh . . . skin . . . breath.* Lists of four items are common in Ezekiel (see note on 1:5).
37:7 *a shaking.* Probably the sound of the bones coming together, but possibly recalling the sound accompanying God's presence, as in 3:12–13 ("noise of a great rushing").
‡37:8 *but there was no breath.* This visionary re-creation of God's people recalls the two-step creation of man in Gen 2:7, where man was first formed from the dust and then received the breath of life. Many also view this as a promise of physical regathering, followed by the spiritual rebirth of Israel.
‡37:9 *four.* See note on 1:5. *breath.* The Hebrew for this word can also mean "wind" or "spirit." *slain.* What Ezekiel saw was a battlefield strewn with the bones of the fallen (see v. 10).
37:11 *Our bones . . . cut off.* A sense of utter despair, to which the vision offers hope.

hold, they say, [a]Our bones are dried, and our
hope is lost: we are cut off for our parts.
12 Therefore prophesy and say unto them,
Thus saith the Lord GOD; Behold, [a]O my people, I *will* open your graves, and cause you to
come up out of your graves, and [b]bring you
into the land of Israel.
13 And ye shall know that I *am* the LORD,
when I have opened your graves, O my people, and brought you up out of your graves,
14 And [a]shall put my spirit in you, and ye
shall live, and I shall place you in your own
land: then shall ye know that I the LORD have
spoken *it,* and performed *it,* saith the LORD.

The parable of the two sticks

15 ¶ The word of the LORD came again unto
me, saying,
16 Moreover, thou son of man, [a]take thee
one stick, and write upon it, For Judah, and for
[b]the children of Israel his companions: then
take another stick, and write upon it, For Joseph, the stick of Ephraim, and *for* all the
house of Israel his companions:
17 And [a]join them one to another into one
stick; and they shall become one in thine
hand.
18 And when the children of thy people
shall speak unto thee, saying, [a]Wilt thou not
shew us what thou meanest by these?
19 [a]Say unto them, Thus saith the Lord
GOD; Behold, I *will* take [b]the stick of Joseph,
which *is* in the hand of Ephraim, and the
tribes of Israel his fellows, and will put them
with him, *even* with the stick of Judah, and
make them one stick, and they shall be one in
mine hand.
20 And the sticks whereon thou writest
shall be in thine hand [a]before their eyes.
21 And say unto them, Thus saith the Lord
GOD; Behold, [a]I *will* take the children of Israel

37:11 [a]Ps. 141:7; Is. 49:14
37:12 [a]Is. 26:19; Hos. 13:14 [b]ver. 25; ch. 36:24
37:14 [a]ch. 36:27
37:16 [a]See Num. 17:2 [b]2 Chr. 11:12,13,16; 15:9; 30:11,18
37:17 [a]See ver. 22,24
37:18 [a]ch. 12:9; 24:19
37:19 [a]Zech. 10:6 [b]ver. 16,17
37:20 [a]ch. 12:3
37:21 [a]ch. 36:24
37:22 [a]Is. 11:13; Jer. 3:18; Hos. 1:11 [b]ch. 34:23; John 10:16
37:23 [a]ch. 36:25 [b]ch. 36:28
37:24 [a]Is. 40:11; Jer. 23:5; Luke 1:32 [b]John 10:16 [c]ch. 36:27
37:25 [a]ch. 36:28 [b]Is. 60:21; Joel 3:20; Amos 9:15 [c]John 12:34
37:26 [a]Ps. 89:3; Is. 55:3; Jer. 32:40 [b]ch. 36:10 [c]2 Cor. 6:16
37:27 [a]Lev. 26:11; John 1:14 [b]ch. 11:20
37:28 [a]ch. 36:23 [b]ch. 20:12

from among the heathen, whither they be
gone, and will gather them on every side, and
bring them into their own land:
22 And [a]I will make them one nation in
the land upon the mountains of Israel; and
[b]one king shall be king to them all: and they
shall be no more two nations, neither shall
they be divided into two kingdoms any more
at all:
23 [a]Neither shall they defile themselves
any more with their idols, nor with their detestable things, nor with any of their transgressions: but [b]I will save them out of all their
dwelling places, wherein they have sinned,
and will cleanse them: so shall they be my
people, and I will be their God.
24 And [a]David my servant *shall be* king
over them; and [b]they all shall have one shepherd: [c]they shall also walk in my judgments,
and observe my statutes, and do them.
25 [a]And they shall dwell in the land that I
have given unto Jacob my servant, wherein
your fathers have dwelt; and they shall dwell
therein, *even* they, and their children, and
their children's children [b]for ever: and [c]my
servant David *shall be* their prince for ever.
26 Moreover I will make a [a]covenant of
peace with them; it shall be an everlasting covenant with them: and I will place them, and
[b]multiply them, and will set my [c]sanctuary in
the midst of them for evermore.
27 [a]My tabernacle also shall be with them:
yea, I will be [b]their God, and they shall be my
people.
28 [a]And the heathen shall know that I the
LORD do [b]sanctify Israel, when my sanctuary
shall be in the midst of them for evermore.

Prophecy against Gog

38 And the word of the LORD came unto
me, saying,

37:12 *graves.* The imagery shifts from a scattering of bones on a battlefield (see note on v. 9) to a cemetery with sealed graves.

37:14 *I shall place you in your own land.* These words make it clear that the Lord is not speaking here of a resurrection from the dead but of the national restoration of Israel.

37:16 *take . . . one stick.* Ezekiel's last symbolic act involving a material object (cf. 4:1,3,9; 5:1). *write upon it.* Zech 11:7 seems to be based on this passage in Ezekiel.

‡37:17 *join them . . . one to another.* The sticks may have been miraculously joined, or Ezekiel may have joined the sticks together in his hand to symbolize the future unification of Israel.

37:18 *Wilt thou not shew us . . . ?* The symbolic act successfully aroused the people's curiosity (see 12:9; 21:7; 24:19).

37:19 *they shall be one in mine hand.* God would duplicate Ezekiel's symbolic act by uniting the two kingdoms separated since Solomon's death (see 1 Ki 12). For similar prophecies of the reunion of Israel see 33:23,29; Jer 3:18; 23:5–6; Hos 1:11; Amos 9:11.

37:22 *mountains of Israel.* See 6:2–3; 34:13; 36:1. *one king.* Only here and in v. 24 is the word "king" used of the future ruler. Usually "prince" is used (see note on 34:24), as in v. 25. See 7:27 and note; see also 44:3; 45:7–9 and frequently in chs. 45–48, where the ruler in the ideal age is always referred to as "prince."

37:23 *idols.* The old and basic offense (see note on 6:4). *save them out of . . . dwelling places.* Or "save them from their backslidings"; see Jer 2:19; 3:22. *cleanse.* Cf. 36:25 for the same notion. *My people . . . their God.* See note on 11:20.

37:24 *David my servant.* As in 34:23 (see note there) the coming Messianic ruler is called David because He would be a descendant of David and would achieve for Israel what David had—except more fully. *king.* See note on v. 22. *shepherd.* As in 34:23 the coming ruler is likened to a shepherd who cares for his flock (cf. John 10, especially v. 16).

37:25 *Jacob my servant.* See 28:25 and note.

37:26 *covenant of peace.* See 34:25 and note. *everlasting covenant.* See 16:60 and note. The phrase occurs 16 times in the OT, referring at times to the Noahic covenant (Gen 9:16), the Abrahamic (Gen 17:7,13,19), the Davidic (2 Sam 23:5) and the "new" (Jer 32:40). Cf. the covenant with Phinehas (Num 25:12–13). *set my sanctuary in the midst of them.* As he had done before. This word is further developed in Ezekiel's vision of the future age, in which the rebuilt sanctuary would have central position (chs. 40–48). See vv. 27–28.

38:1 This statement, repeated often for receiving God's word, stands as an introduction to chs. 38–39, which are a unit. The future restoration of Israel under the reign of the house of

2 [a]Son of man, [b]set thy face against [c]Gog, the land of Magog, [1]the chief prince of [d]Meshech and Tubal, and prophesy against him,

3 And say, Thus saith the Lord GOD; Behold, I *am* against thee, O Gog, the chief prince of Meshech and Tubal:

4 And [a]I will turn thee back, and put hooks into thy jaws, and I will bring thee forth, and all thine army, horses and horsemen, [b]all of them clothed with all sorts *of armour, even* a great company *with* bucklers and shields, all of them handling swords:

5 Persia, Ethiopia, and [1]Libya with them; all of them *with* shield and helmet:

6 [a]Gomer, and all his bands; the house of [b]Togarmah *of* the north quarters, and all his bands: *and* many people with thee.

7 [a]Be thou prepared, and prepare for thyself, thou, and all thy company that are assembled unto thee, and be thou a guard unto them.

8 [a]After many days [b]thou shalt be visited: in the latter years thou shalt come into the land *that is* brought back from the sword, [c]*and is* gathered out of many people, against [d]the mountains of Israel, which have been always waste: but it is brought forth out of the nations, and they shall [e]dwell safely all of them.

9 Thou shalt ascend and come [a]like a storm, thou shalt be [b]like a cloud to cover the land, thou, and all thy bands, and many people with thee.

10 ¶ Thus saith the Lord GOD; It shall also come to pass, *that* at the same time shall things come into thy mind, and thou shalt [1]think an evil thought:

11 And thou shalt say, I will go up to the land of unwalled villages; I will [a]go *to* them that are at rest, [b]that dwell [1]safely, all of them dwelling without walls, and having neither bars nor gates,

12 [a][1]To take a spoil, and to take a prey; to turn thine hand upon the desolate places *that are now* inhabited, [b]and upon the people *that are* gathered out of the nations, which have gotten cattle and goods, that dwell in the [2]midst of the land.

13 [a]Sheba, and [b]Dedan, and the merchants [c]of Tarshish, with all [d]the young lions thereof, shall say unto thee, Art thou come to take a spoil? hast thou gathered thy company to take a prey? to carry away silver and gold, to take *away* cattle and goods, to take a great spoil?

14 Therefore, son of man, prophesy and say unto Gog, Thus saith the Lord GOD; [a]In that day when my people of Israel [b]dwelleth safely, shalt thou not know *it?*

15 [a]And thou shalt come from thy place out of the north parts, thou, [b]and many people with thee, all of them riding upon horses, a great company, and a mighty army:

38:2 [1]Or, *prince of the chief* [a]ch. 39:1 [b]ch. 35:2,3 [c]Rev. 20:8 [d]ch. 32:26
38:4 [a]2 Ki. 19:28; ch. 29:4 [b]ch. 23:12
38:5 [1]Or, *Phut*
38:6 [a]Gen. 10:2 [b]ch. 27:14
38:7 [a]Is. 8:9,10; Jer. 46:3,4
38:8 [a]ver. 16; Deut. 4:30 [b]Is. 29:6 [c]ch. 34:13 [d]ch. 36:1,4 [e]Jer. 23:6
38:9 [a]Is. 28:2 [b]Jer. 4:13
38:10 [1]Or, *conceive a mischievous purpose*
38:11 [1]Or, *confidently* [a]Jer. 49:31 [b]ver. 8
38:12 [1]Heb. *To spoil the spoil, and to prey the prey* [2]Heb. *navel* [a]ch. 29:19 [b]ver. 8
38:13 [a]ch. 27:22 [b]ch. 27:15 [c]ch. 27:12 [d]ch. 19:3,5
38:14 [a]Is. 4:1 [b]ver. 8
38:15 [a]ch. 39:2 [b]ver. 6

David (ch. 37) will bring about a massive coalition of world powers to destroy God's kingdom. But the vast host that comes against Jerusalem will end up as dead bodies strewn over the fields of the promised land. Israel will become the cemetery of the enemy hordes (cf. ch. 37).

‡38:2 *Son of man.* See note on 2:1. *set thy face.* See note on 20:46. *Gog.* Apparently a leader or king whose name appears only here and in Rev 20:8. Several identifications have been attempted, notably Gyges, king of Lydia (c. 660 B.C.). Possibly the name is purposely vague, standing for a mysterious, as yet undisclosed, enemy of God's people. *the land of Magog.* In Gen 10:2; 1 Chr 1:5 Magog is one of the sons of Japheth, thus the name of a people. In Ezek 39:6 it appears to refer to a people. But since the Hebrew prefix *ma-* can mean "place of," Magog may here simply mean "land of Gog." Israel had long experienced the hostility of the Hamites and other Semitic peoples; the future coalition here envisioned will include—and in fact be led by—peoples descended from Japheth (cf. Gen 10). *chief prince of.* Could refer to a military commander-in-chief. There is little grammatical evidence for translating this as "prince of Rosh." Of the 599 times this word apears, this would be the only case in which it is translated as a place name. *Meshech and Tubal.* These sons of Japheth (see Gen 10:2; 1 Chr 1:5) are probably located in eastern Asia Minor (cf. 27:13; 32:26). They are peoples and territories to the north of Israel (cf. vv. 6,15; 39:2). As in the days of the Assyrians and Babylonians, the major attack will come from the north.

38:3 *I am against thee.* See note on 5:8.

38:4 *I will turn thee back.* Emphasis is on the fact that God is completely in control of all that is to follow. *put hooks into thy jaws.* As with Pharaoh in 29:4, Gog is likened to a beast led around by God.

38:5 *Ethiopia.* Hebrew *Cush,* the upper (southern) Nile region. The invading forces from the north (see v. 2 and note) are joined by armies from the south. *Libya.* Africa.

‡38:6 *Gomer.* Another of Gog's northern allies (see note on v. 2), mentioned in Gen 10:3; 1 Chr 1:6 as one of the sons of Japheth. According to non-Biblical sources, these peoples originated north of the Black Sea. *house of Togarmah.* Or "Beth-togarmah." See note on 27:14. According to Gen 10:3 and 1 Chr 1:6, Togarmah is one of the children of Gomer.

‡38:8 *After many days . . . in the latter years.* After all the events of national restoration, the immigration and settlement in Israel as described in chs. 34–37 will be completed. Since no such invasion has yet occurred in Israel, many believe it will come in the future as part of the eschatological conflict of the last days.

38:9 *like a cloud.* Jeremiah similarly describes the invasion from the north in Jer 4:13.

38:10 *at the same time.* A phrase also common to other prophetic writings; here it refers to the day of Gog's invasion of Israel. *shall things come into thy mind.* The divine initiative (v. 4) is paralleled, as it often is in Scripture, by human action (cf. Deut 31:3; Is 10:6–7). *evil thought.* A raiding expedition (see v. 12).

38:11 *land of unwalled villages.* Speaks of a blissfully peaceful, ideal future time when walls no longer will be needed. See Zech 2:4–5, which assumes, as does this passage, that the Lord alone is sufficient protection (cf. 36:35–36).

38:12 *midst of the land.* The Hebrew for "midst" also means "navel," a graphic image for the belief that Israel was the vital link between God and the world (the idea occurs also in 5:5). The word occurs elsewhere in the Bible only in Judg 9:37. Since the Hebrew for "world" can also mean "land," theologically Jerusalem is both the center of the land of Israel and the center of the earth.

38:13 *Sheba.* Southwest corner of the Arabian peninsula (modern Yemen), known for trading (Job 6:19; see 23:42; 27:22; 1 Ki 10:1–2). *Dedan.* See note on 25:13. *Tarshish.* See note on 27:12.

16 [a]And thou shalt come up against my people of Israel, as a cloud to cover the land; [b]it shall be in the latter days, and I will bring thee against my land, that the heathen may know me, when I shall be sanctified in thee, O Gog, before their eyes.

17 ¶ Thus saith the Lord GOD; *Art* thou he of whom I have spoken in old time [1]by my servants the prophets of Israel, which prophesied in those days *many* years, that *I* would bring thee against them?

18 And it shall come to pass at the same time when Gog shall come against the land of Israel, saith the Lord GOD, *that* my fury shall come up in my face.

19 For [a]in my jealousy [b]*and* in the fire of my wrath have I spoken, [c]Surely in that day there shall be a great shaking in the land of Israel;

20 So that [a]the fishes of the sea, and the fowls of the heaven, and the beasts of the field, and all creeping things that creep upon the earth, and all the men that *are* upon the face of the earth, shall shake at my presence, [b]and the mountains shall be thrown down, and the [1]steep places shall fall, and every wall shall fall to the ground.

21 And I will [a]call *for* [b]a sword against him throughout all my mountains, saith the Lord GOD: [c]every man's sword shall be against his brother.

22 And I will [a]plead against him with [b]pestilence and with blood; and [c]I will rain upon him, and upon his bands, and upon the many people that *are* with him, an overflowing rain, and [d]great hailstones, fire, and brimstone.

23 Thus will I magnify myself, and [a]sanctify myself; [b]and I will be known in the eyes of many nations, and they shall know that I *am* the LORD.

39 Therefore [a]thou son of man, prophesy against Gog, and say, Thus saith the Lord GOD; Behold, I *am* against thee, O Gog, the chief prince of Meshech and Tubal:

2 And I will turn thee back, and [1]leave but the sixth part of thee, [a]and will cause thee to come up from [2]the north parts, and will bring thee upon the mountains of Israel:

3 And I will smite thy bow out of thy left hand, and will cause thine arrows to fall out of thy right hand.

4 [a]Thou shalt fall upon the mountains of Israel, thou, and all thy bands, and the people that *is* with thee: [b]I will give thee unto the ravenous birds of every [1]sort, and *to* the beasts of the field [2]to be devoured.

5 Thou shalt fall upon [1]the open field: for I have spoken *it,* saith the Lord GOD.

6 [a]And I will send a fire on Magog, and among them that dwell [1]carelessly in [b]the isles: and they shall know that I *am* the LORD.

7 [a]So will I make my holy name known in the midst of my people Israel; and I will not let *them* [b]pollute my holy name any more: [c]and the heathen shall know that I *am* the LORD, the Holy One in Israel.

8 ¶ [a]Behold, it is come, and it is done, saith the Lord GOD; this *is* the day [b]whereof I have spoken.

9 And they that dwell in the cities of Israel shall go forth, and shall set on fire and burn the weapons, both the shields and the bucklers, the bows and the arrows, and the [1]handstaves, and the spears, and they shall [2]burn them with fire seven years:

10 So that they shall take no wood out of the field, neither cut down *any* out of the forests; for they shall burn the weapons with fire: [a]and they shall spoil those that spoiled them, and rob those that robbed them, saith the Lord GOD.

11 And it shall come to pass in that day, *that* I will give unto Gog a place there of graves in Israel, the valley of the passengers *on* the east of the sea: and it *shall* stop the [1]*noses of the* passengers: and there shall they bury Gog and all his multitude: and they shall call *it* The valley of [2]Hamon-gog.

12 And seven months shall the house of Israel be burying of them, [a]that *they* may cleanse the land.

13 Yea, all the people of the land shall bury *them;* and it shall be to them a renown the day that [a]I shall be glorified, saith the Lord GOD.

38:16 [a]ver. 9 [b]ver. 8
38:17 [1]Heb. *by the hand [of]*
38:19 [a]ch. 36:5,6 [b]Ps. 89:46 [c]Hag. 2:6,7; Rev. 16:18
38:20 [1]Or, *towers,* or, *stairs* [a]Hos. 4:3 [b]Jer. 4:24
38:21 [a]Ps. 105:16 [b]ch. 14:17 [c]Judg. 7:22; 1 Sam. 14:20
38:22 [a]Is. 66:16; Jer. 25:31 [b]ch. 5:17 [c]Ps. 11:6; Is. 30:30 [d]Rev. 16:21
38:23 [a]ch. 36:23 [b]ch. 37:28
39:1 [a]ch. 38:2,3
39:2 [1]Or, *strike thee with six plagues;* or, *draw thee back with a hook of six teeth,* as ch. 38:4 [a]ch. 38:15
39:2 [2]Heb. *the sides of the north*
39:4 [1]Heb. *wing* [2]Heb. *to devour* [a]ch. 38:21 [b]ch. 33:27
39:5 [1]Heb. *the face of the field*
39:6 [1]Or, *confidently* [a]Amos 1:4 [b]Ps. 72:10
39:7 [a]ver. 22 [b]Lev. 18:21 [c]ch. 38:16
39:8 [a]Rev. 16:17; 21:6 [b]ch. 38:17
39:9 [1]Or, *javelins* [2]Or, *make a fire for them*
39:10 [a]Is. 14:2
39:11 [1]Or, mouths [2]That is, *The multitude of Gog*
39:12 [a]Deut. 21:23
39:13 [a]ch. 28:22

38:17 *Art thou he of whom I have spoken . . . ?* Probably a general reference to earlier prophecies of divine judgment on the nations arrayed against God and His people.
38:19 *great shaking.* Signaling the mighty presence of God, who comes to overwhelm the great army invading His land.
38:20 The fourfold listing of the animal world indicates the totality of nature (see note on 1:5; cf. Gen 9:2; 1 Ki 4:33; Job 12:7–8 for similar listings).
38:21 *I will call for a sword.* God's sword of judgment (Is 34:5–6; Jer 25:29). *every man's sword shall be against his brother.* The coalition of Israel's enemies will turn on itself, as did the armies that attacked Judah in the time of Jehoshaphat (2 Chr 20:22–23).
38:22 The list of divine weapons suggests that God will intervene directly without the benefit of an earthly army.
‡39:1 *Gog, the chief prince of Meshech.* see note on 38:2. While vv. 1–16 add new details, the same basic events as those in ch. 38 are described.
39:2 *from the north parts.* As in 38:6,15.
39:3 *bow.* Cf. Jer 6:23. The Lord will disarm Israel's enemies before they can shoot an arrow.
39:4 *give thee unto the ravenous birds.* A theme expanded in vv. 17–20.
39:6 *I will send a fire.* See 30:8 and note.
39:9 *burn them.* Cf. Ps 46:9, where God does the burning. *seven.* A symbolic number signifying the finality of this great battle against God's people, as well as indicating the size of the invading armies.
39:12 *seven.* As in v. 9, the number seven symbolizes totality, completeness and finality, and it also reveals the large number of invaders. *cleanse the land.* Ritual purity is a basic element in Ezekiel's theology (see 22:26; 24:13; 36:25,33; 37:23). Corpses were especially unclean (see Lev 5:2; 21:1,11; 22:4; Num 5:2; 6:6–12; 19:16; 31:19).
39:13 *people of the land.* See 7:27 and note, though here a special class may not be implied.

14 And they shall sever out [1]men of continual employment, passing through the land to bury with the passengers those that remain upon the face of the earth, [a]to cleanse it: after the end of seven months shall they search.

15 And the passengers *that* pass through the land, when *any* seeth a man's bone, then shall he [1]set up a sign by it, till the buriers have buried it in the valley of Hamon-gog.

16 And also the name of the city *shall be* [1]Hamonah. Thus shall they [a]cleanse the land.

17 ¶ And thou son of man, thus saith the Lord GOD; [a]Speak [1]unto every feathered fowl, and to every beast of the field, [b]Assemble yourselves, and come; gather yourselves on every side to my [2]sacrifice that I do sacrifice for you, *even* a great sacrifice [c]upon the mountains of Israel, that ye may eat flesh, and drink blood.

18 [a]Ye shall eat the flesh of the mighty, and drink the blood of the princes of the earth, of rams, of lambs, and of [1]goats, of bullocks, all of them [b]fatlings of Bashan.

19 And ye shall eat fat till *ye* be full, and drink blood till *ye* be drunken, of my sacrifice which I have sacrificed for you.

20 [a]Thus ye shall be filled at my table *with* horses and chariots, [b]with mighty *men*, and *with* all men of war, saith the Lord GOD.

21 [a]And I will set my glory among the heathen, and all the heathen shall see my judgment that I have executed, and [b]my hand that I have laid upon them.

22 [a]So the house of Israel shall know that I *am* the LORD their God from that day and forward.

39:14 [1]Heb. *men of continuance* [a]ver. 12
39:15 [1]Heb. *build*
39:16 [1]That is, *The multitude* [a]ver. 12
39:17 [1]Heb. *to the fowl of every wing* [2]Or, *slaughter* [a]Rev. 19:7 [b]Is. 18:6; Zeph. 1:7 [c]ver. 4
39:18 [1]Heb. *great goats* [a]Rev. 19:18 [b]Deut. 32:14; Ps. 22:12
39:20 [a]Ps. 76:6; ch. 38:4 [b]Rev. 19:18
39:21 [a]ch. 38:16,23 [b]Ex. 7:4
39:22 [a]ver. 7,28
39:23 [a]ch. 36:18-20,23 [b]Deut. 31:17; Is. 59:2 [c]Lev. 26:25
39:24 [a]ch. 36:19
39:25 [a]Jer. 30:3,18; ch. 34:13; 36:24 [b]ch. 20:40; Hos. 1:11
39:26 [a]Dan. 9:16 [b]Lev. 26:5,6
39:27 [a]ch. 28:25,26 [b]ch. 36:23,24; 38:16
39:28 [1]Heb. *by my causing of them, etc.* [a]ver. 22; ch. 34:30
39:29 [a]Is. 54:8 [b]Joel 2:28; Zech. 12:10; Acts 2:17
40:1 [a]ch. 33:21

23 [a]And the heathen shall know that the house of Israel went into captivity for their iniquity: because they trespassed against me, therefore [b]hid I my face from them, and [c]gave them into the hand of their enemies: so fell they all by the sword.

24 [a]According to their uncleanness and according to their transgressions have I done unto them, and hid my face from them.

25 ¶ Therefore thus saith the Lord GOD; [a]Now will I bring again the captivity of Jacob, and have mercy upon the [b]whole house of Israel, and will be jealous for my holy name;

26 [a]After that they have borne their shame, and all their trespasses whereby they have trespassed against me, when they [b]dwelt safely in their land, and none made *them* afraid.

27 [a]When I have brought them again from the people, and gathered them out of their enemies' lands, and [b]am sanctified in them in the sight of many nations;

28 [a]Then shall they know that I *am* the LORD their God, [1]which caused them to be led into captivity among the heathen: but I have gathered them unto their own land, and have left none of them any more there.

29 [a]Neither will I hide my face any more from them: for I have [b]poured out my spirit upon the house of Israel, saith the Lord GOD.

The new temple arrangements

40 In the five and twentieth year of our captivity, in the beginning of the year, in the tenth *day* of the month, in the fourteenth year after that [a]the city was smit-

39:14 *sever out men of continual employment.* After the seven-month burial period observed by all the people, special squads will be hired full time to ensure total cleansing of the land—by marking for burial any human bones that may have been missed. Total ritual purity is the aim.
39:15 *sign.* Probably of stone, either a large one or a heap of smaller ones.
39:17 *Speak unto every feathered fowl . . . gather . . . to my sacrifice.* Various interpretations are: 1. Since the enemies are all dead and buried, this section (vv. 17–20) is perhaps to be understood as poetic imagery. 2. However, if the passage reverts back to v. 4, a more literal interpretation is possible—the dead bodies were not all buried at once. 3. Verses 17–20 involve a restating of vv. 9–16, employing a different figure (see Is 34:6; Jer 46:10; Zeph 1:7). The metaphor of sacrifice suggests a consecration to the Lord in judgment, as with Jericho (see Josh 6:17 and note).
39:18 *Ye shall eat the flesh of the mighty.* A gory description of what birds of prey commonly do (see previous note and Rev 19:17–21). The bodies of the victims are compared to animals commonly used for sacrifices. *Bashan.* Rich pastureland east of the sea of Galilee, known for its sleek cattle (Deut 32:14; Ps 22:12; Amos 4:1) and its oak trees (27:6; Is 2:13).
39:19 *eat fat . . . drink blood.* Further indication that this is the Lord's sacrificial feast, in that fat and blood were normally reserved for God (see 44:15; Lev 3:17).
39:20 *my table.* Sacrificial altar. See 40:38–43 and 41:22 for description of the tables in the new temple.
39:21 *my glory.* God's visible presence in the world (see note on 1:28). Here that visibility is due to divine intervention in history.
39:22–23 *the house of Israel shall know . . . the heathen shall know.* As God had made Himself known to Israel and the nations through His saving acts in Israel's behalf (see Ex 6:7; 7:5,17; 10:2; 14:18; 16:6–7,12; Josh 3:10; 4:24; cf. Josh 2:9–11; 5:1), so now Israel and the nations will see Him again at work as He judges His people for their sin (see v. 27).
39:23 *hid I my face.* Expression of divine displeasure (see Ps 30:7; Is 54:8; 57:17).
39:24 *their uncleanness and . . . their transgressions.* Spelled out especially in ch. 22, but also throughout chs. 6–24.
39:25 *Jacob.* The nation of Israel, as in 20:5. The parallelism within the verse supports this identity. *my holy name.* See note on 20:9.
39:26 *After that they have borne their shame.* The remembrance of shame previously called for is here erased. (6:9; 20:43; 36:31)
39:27 *I . . . am sanctified in them.* God will reveal Himself anew in a restored, holy people (cf. 20:41; 28:25; 36:23).
39:28 *Then shall they know.* See note on v. 22.
39:29 *I have poured out my spirit.* The gift of God's enabling Spirit (see 11:19; 36:26–27; 37:14).
40:1 *five and twentieth year . . . beginning . . . tenth.* Apr. 28, 573 B.C. *of our captivity.* All the dates in the book of Ezekiel (see chart, p. 1148) are reckoned from the 597 exile, but only here and in 33:21 is the exile specifically mentioned (see 1:2). *the beginning of the year.* Hebrew *Rosh Hashanah,* the well-known Jewish New Year festival. It has long occurred in the fall (in ei-

ten, in the selfsame day [b]the hand of the LORD was upon me, and brought me thither.

2 [a]In the visions of God brought he me into the land of Israel, and [b]set me upon a very high mountain, [1]by which *was* as the frame of a city on the south.

3 And he brought me thither, and behold, *there was* a man, whose appearance *was* [a]like the appearance of brass, [b]with a line of flax in his hand, [c]and a measuring reed; and he stood in the gate.

4 And the man said unto me, [a]Son of man, behold with thine eyes, and hear with thine ears, and set thine heart upon all that I shall shew thee; for to the intent that *I* might shew *them* unto thee art thou brought hither: [b]declare all that thou seest to the house of Israel.

5 And behold [a]a wall on the outside of the house round about, and in the man's hand a measuring reed of six cubits *long* by the cubit and a hand breadth: so he measured the breadth of the building, one reed; and the height, one reed.

6 ¶ Then came he unto the gate [1]which looketh toward the east, and went up the stairs thereof, and measured the threshold of the gate, *which was* one reed broad; and the other threshold *of the gate, which was* one reed broad.

7 And *every* little chamber *was* one reed long, and one reed broad; and between the little chambers *were* five cubits; and the threshold of the gate by the porch of the gate within *was* one reed.

8 He measured also the porch of the gate within, one reed.

9 Then measured he the porch of the gate, eight cubits; and the posts thereof, two cubits; and the porch of the gate *was* inward.

10 And the little chambers of the gate eastward *were* three on this side, and three on that side; they three *were* of one measure: and the posts had one measure on this side and on that side.

11 And he measured the breadth of the entry of the gate, ten cubits; *and* the length of the gate, thirteen cubits.

12 The [1]space also before the little chambers *was* one cubit *on this side,* and the space *was* one cubit on that side: and the little chambers *were* six cubits on this side, and six cubits on that side.

13 He measured then the gate from the roof of *one* little chamber to the roof of another: the breadth *was* five and twenty cubits, door against door.

14 He made also posts *of* threescore cubits, even unto the post of the court round about the gate.

15 And from the face of the gate of the entrance unto the face of the porch of the inner gate *were* fifty cubits.

16 And *there were* [a][1]narrow windows to the little chambers, and to their posts within the gate round about, and likewise to the [2]arches: and windows *were* round about [3]inward: and upon *each* post *were* palm trees.

17 ¶ Then brought he me into [a]the outward court, and lo, *there were* [b]chambers, and a pavement made for the court round about: [c]thirty chambers *were* upon the pavement.

18 And the pavement by the side of the gates over against the length of the gates *was* the lower pavement.

19 Then he measured the breadth from the forefront of the lower gate unto the forefront of the inner court [1]without, an hundred cubits east*ward* and north*ward.*

Location and size of gates

20 ¶ And the gate of the outward court [1]that looked toward the north, he measured the length thereof, and the breadth thereof.

40:1 [b]ch. 1:3
40:2 [1]Or, *upon which* [a]ch. 8:3 [b]Rev. 21:10
40:3 [a]ch. 1:7; Dan. 10:6 [b]ch. 47:3 [c]Rev. 11:1; 21:15
40:4 [a]ch. 44:5 [b]ch. 43:10
40:5 [a]ch. 42:20
40:6 [1]Heb. *whose face* was *the way toward the east*
40:12 [1]Heb. *limit,* or, *bound*
40:16 [1]Heb. *closed* [2]Or, *galleries,* or, *porches* [3]Or, *within* [a]1 Ki. 6:4
40:17 [a]Rev. 11:2 [b]1 Ki. 6:5 [c]ch. 45:5
40:19 [1]Or, *from without*
40:20 [1]Heb. *whose face* was

ther September or October), but since throughout the book Ezekiel uses a different and older religious calendar, the spring date as given above is correct (see note on Lev 23:24). *hand of the LORD was upon me.* See note on 1:3.

40:2 *visions of God.* Introduces all three of Ezekiel's major visions (see 1:1; 8:3). *very high mountain.* mount Zion, also seen as extraordinarily high in other prophetic visions (17:22; Is 2:2; Mic 4:1; Zech 14:10). Height here signifies importance, as the earthly seat of God's reign. *on the south.* With the city located on its southern slopes, the mountain is to the north (cf. Ps 48; see Ps 48:2 and note).

40:3 *appearance of brass.* Indicates the man was other than human. *line of flax.* Used for longer measurements such as those in 47:3. *measuring reed.* Used for shorter measurements—about ten feet and four inches long. *in the gate.* Presumably of the outer court (see vv. 17–19).

40:5 *wall on the outside of the house round about.* Separating the sacred from the secular. *six cubits.* In using the long cubit (seven handbreadths, or about 21 inches), which was older than the shorter cubit (six handbreadths, or about 18 inches), Ezekiel was returning to more ancient standards for the new community (see 2 Chr 3:3).

40:6 *gate which looketh toward the east.* The gate of the outer court. The three gates (east, north, south) of the outer court were similar to the three in the inner court (v. 32), having six alcoves for the guards (three on each side) and a portico (vv. 8–9). Comparable gate plans have been discovered at Megiddo, Gezer and Hazor, all dating from the time of Solomon (see 1 Ki 9:15). The guards kept out anyone who might profane the temple area (see Ezra 2:62). *went up the stairs.* The first of three sets of stairs leading to the temple. This one had seven steps (v. 22); the next one (inner court), eight (v. 31); the last (temple), ten (v. 49; based on the Septuagint reading of this verse)— possibly indicating increasing degrees of "holiness" (sacredness).

40:9 *porch of the gate was inward.* The reverse position of the porticoes of the inner court gates, which faced away from the temple (v. 34).

40:10 *little chambers . . . were three.* The alcoves for the guards, mentioned in v. 7.

40:16 *palm trees.* As in Solomon's temple (see 1 Ki 6:29,32,35).

40:17 *thirty chambers.* The exact location of these rooms is not given. They were probably intended for the people's use (see Jer 35:2,4).

40:19 *hundred cubits.* Over 170 feet separated the outer wall from the inner wall and was the width of the outer court.

40:20 *gate . . . looked toward the north.* Both it and the south gate (v. 24) were identical to the east gate.

21 And the little chambers thereof *were* three on this side and three on that side; and the posts thereof and the [1]arches thereof were after the measure of the first gate: the length thereof *was* fifty cubits, and the breadth five and twenty cubits.

22 And their windows, and their arches, and their palm trees, *were* after the measure of the gate that looketh towards the east; and they went up unto it by seven steps; and the arches thereof *were* before them.

23 And the gate of the inner court *was* over against the gate toward the north, and toward the east; and he measured from gate to gate an hundred cubits.

24 ¶ After that he brought me toward the south, and behold a gate toward the south: and he measured the posts thereof and the arches thereof according to these measures.

25 And *there were* windows in it and in the arches thereof round about, like those windows: the length *was* fifty cubits, and the breadth five and twenty cubits.

26 And *there were* seven steps to go up to it, and the arches thereof *were* before them: and it had palm trees, one on this side, and another on that side, upon the posts thereof.

27 And *there was* a gate in the inner court toward the south: and he measured from gate to gate toward the south an hundred cubits.

28 ¶ And he brought me to the inner court by the south gate: and he measured the south gate according to these measures;

29 And the little chambers thereof, and the posts thereof, and the arches thereof, according to these measures: and *there were* windows in it and in the arches thereof round about: *it was* fifty cubits long, and five and twenty cubits broad.

30 And the arches round about *were* [a]five and twenty cubits long, and five cubits [1]broad.

31 And the arches thereof *were* toward the utter court; and palm trees *were* upon the posts thereof: and the going up to it *had* eight steps.

32 ¶ And he brought me into the inner court toward the east: and he measured the gate according to these measures.

33 And the little chambers thereof, and the posts thereof, and the arches thereof, *were* according to these measures: and *there were* windows therein and in the arches thereof round about: *it was* fifty cubits long, and five and twenty cubits broad.

34 And the arches thereof *were* toward the outward court; and palm trees *were* upon the posts thereof, on this side, and on that side: and the going up to it *had* eight steps.

35 ¶ And he brought me to the north gate, and measured *it* according to these measures;

36 The little chambers thereof, the posts thereof, and the arches thereof, and the windows to it round about: the length *was* fifty cubits, and the breadth five and twenty cubits.

37 And the posts thereof *were* toward the utter court; and palm trees *were* upon the posts thereof, on this side, and on that side: and the going up to it *had* eight steps.

38 And the chambers and the entries thereof *were* by the posts of the gates, where they washed the burnt offering.

The porch and its furnishings

39 ¶ And in the porch of the gate *were* two tables on this side, and two tables on that side, to slay thereon the burnt offering and [a]the sin offering and [b]the trespass offering.

40 And at the side without, [1]as one goeth up to the entry of the north gate, *were* two tables; and on the other side, which *was* at the porch of the gate, *were* two tables.

41 Four tables *were* on this side, and four tables on that side, by the side of the gate; eight tables, whereupon they slew *their sacrifices.*

42 And the four tables *were* of hewn stone for the burnt offering, of a cubit and a half long, and a cubit and a half broad, and one cubit high: whereupon also they laid the instruments wherewith they slew the burnt offering and the sacrifice.

43 And within *were* [1]hooks, a hand broad, fastened round about: and upon the tables *was* the flesh of the offering.

44 ¶ And without the inner gate *were* the chambers of [a]the singers in the inner court, which *was* at the side of the north gate; and their prospect *was* toward the south: one at the side of the east gate *having* the prospect toward the north.

45 And he said unto me, This chamber, whose prospect *is* toward the south, *is* for the priests, [a]the keepers of the [1]charge of the house.

46 And the chamber whose prospect *is* toward the north *is* for the priests, [a]the keepers of the charge of the altar: these *are* the sons of [b]Zadok among the sons of Levi, which come near to the LORD to minister unto him.

47 So he measured the court, an hundred cubits long, and an hundred cubits broad, foursquare; and the altar *that was* before the house.

40:21 [1]Or, *galleries,* or, *porches*
40:30 [1]Heb. *breadth* [a]See ver. 21,25,33,36
40:39 [a]Lev. 4:2,3 [b]Lev. 5:6; 6:6; 7:1
40:40 [1]Or, *at the step*
40:43 [1]Or, *andirons,* or, *the two hearth stones*
40:44 [a]1 Chr. 6:31
40:45 [1]Or, *ward,* or, *ordinance:* And so ver. 46 [a]Lev. 8:35; Num. 3:27,28,32,38; 18:5; 1 Chr. 9:23; 2 Chr. 13:11; Ps. 134:1
40:46 [a]Num. 18:5; ch. 44:15 [b]1 Ki. 2:35; ch. 43:19; 44:15,16

40:22 *seven steps.* See note on v. 6.
40:28 *south gate.* Of the inner wall, which is not described but must be assumed. *he measured . . . according to these measures.* In both the outer walls (see note on v. 6).
40:34 *eight steps.* See note on v. 6.
40:38 *by the posts of the gates.* The porticoes of the inner gateways were on the side of the outer court, facing away from the temple. *washed.* The inner parts and the legs were washed (Lev 1:9).
40:39 *burnt offering.* Probably one of the oldest kinds of sacrifice. The entire animal was burned in consecration to God (see Lev 1). *sin offering and the trespass offering.* Discussed in Lev 4–7. The peace offerings, which were more festive, are notable by their absence from this listing (see 43:27; 45:17; 46:2,12).
40:46 *sons of Zadok.* For the distinction between the sons of Zadok and the Levites see the fuller discussion in the notes on 44:15–31.
40:47 *altar.* Described in 43:13–17.

48 ¶ And he brought me to the porch of the house, and measured *each* post of the porch, five cubits on this side, and five cubits on that side: and the breadth of the gate *was* three cubits on this side, and three cubits on that side.

49 [a]The length of the porch *was* twenty cubits, and the breadth eleven cubits; and *he brought me* by the steps whereby they went up to it: and *there were* [b]pillars by the posts, one on this side, and another on that side.

The temple and its walls

41 Afterward he brought me to the temple, and measured the posts, six cubits broad on the one side, and six cubits broad on the other side, *which was* the breadth of the tabernacle.

2 And the breadth of the [1]door *was* ten cubits; and the sides of the door *were* five cubits on the one side, and five cubits on the other side: and he measured the length thereof, forty cubits: and the breadth, twenty cubits.

3 Then went he inward, and measured the post of the door, two cubits; and the door, six cubits; and the breadth of the door, seven cubits.

4 So [a]he measured the length thereof, twenty cubits; and the breadth, twenty cubits, before the temple: and he said unto me, This *is* the most holy *place.*

5 After he measured the wall of the house, six cubits; and the breadth of *every* side chamber, four cubits, round about the house on every side.

6 [a]And the side chambers *were* three, [1]one over another, and [2]thirty *in* order; and they entered into the wall which *was* of the house for the side chambers round about, that *they* might [3]have hold, but they had not hold in the wall of the house.

7 And [a][1]*there was* an enlarging, and a winding about still upward to the side chambers: for the winding about of the house *went* still upward round about the house: therefore the breadth of the house *was still* upward, and so increased *from* the lowest *chamber* to the highest by the midst.

8 I saw also the height of the house round about: the foundations of the side chambers *were* [a]a full reed of six great cubits.

9 The thickness of the wall, which *was* for the side chamber without, *was* five cubits: and *that* which *was* left *was* the place of the side chambers that *were* within.

10 And between the chambers *was* the wideness of twenty cubits round about the house on every side.

11 And the doors of the side chambers *were* toward *the place* that *was* left, one door toward the north, and another door toward the south: and the breadth of the place that was left *was* five cubits round about.

12 ¶ Now the building that *was* before the separate place *at* the end toward the west *was* seventy cubits broad; and the wall of the building *was* five cubits thick round about, and the length thereof ninety cubits.

13 So he measured the house, an hundred cubits long; and the separate place, and the building, with the walls thereof, an hundred cubits long;

14 Also the breadth of the face of the house, and of the separate place toward the east, an hundred cubits.

15 And he measured the length of the building over against the separate place which *was* behind it, and the [1]galleries thereof on the one side and on the other side, an hundred cubits, with the inner temple, and the porches of the court;

16 The door posts, and [a]the narrow windows, and the galleries round about on their three *stories,* over against the door, [1]cieled with wood round about, [2]and *from* the ground up to the windows, and the windows *were* covered;

17 To *that* above the door, even unto the inner house, and without, and by all the wall round about within and without, *by* [1]measure.

18 And *it was* made [a]*with* cherubims and palm trees, so that a palm tree *was* between a cherub and a cherub; and *every* cherub had two faces;

19 [a]So that the face of a man *was* toward the palm tree on the one side, and the face of a young lion toward the palm tree on the other side: *it was* made through all the house round about.

20 From the ground unto above the door *were* cherubims and palm trees made, and *on* the wall of the temple.

21 ¶ The [1]posts of the temple *were* squared, *and* the face of the sanctuary; the appearance *of the one* as the appearance *of the other.*

22 [a]The altar *of* wood *was* three cubits

40:49 [a]1 Ki. 6:3 [b]1 Ki. 7:21
41:2 [1]Or, *entrance*
41:4 [a]1 Ki. 6:20; 2 Chr. 3:8
41:6 [1]Heb. *side chamber over side chamber* [2]Or, *three and thirty times,* or, *foot* [3]Heb. *be holden* [a]1 Ki. 6:5,6
41:7 [1]Heb. *it was* made *broader, and went round* [a]1 Ki. 6:8
41:8 [a]ch. 40:5
41:15 [1]Or, *several walks,* or, *walks with pillars*
41:16 [1]Heb. *cieling of wood* [2]Or, *and the ground unto the windows* [a]ver. 26; ch. 40:16
41:17 [1]Heb. *measures*
41:18 [a]1 Ki. 6:29
41:19 [a]See ch. 1:10
41:21 [1]Heb. *post*
41:22 [a]Ex. 30:1

40:48 *porch.* Similar to the portico in Solomon's temple but slightly larger (see 1 Ki 6:3).
40:49 *pillars.* Called Jachin and Boaz in Solomon's temple (see 1 Ki 7:21).
‡41:1 *temple.* The nave was the largest of the three rooms comprising the temple. This outer sanctuary was identical in size to Solomon's (see 1 Ki 6:17).
‡41:3 *went he inward.* Only the angel, not Ezekiel, entered the most holy place. Lev 16 forbids any but the high priest to enter it, and then only once a year (see Heb 9:7). *six cubits.* Or "six cubits wide"; note the progressive narrowness of the door openings as one approaches the inner sanctuary (40:48, 14 cubits; 41:2, 10 cubits).
41:6 *thirty in order.* These 90 side rooms were probably storerooms for the priests, possibly for the tithes (see Mal 3:10).
41:13 *hundred.* The 100-cubit symmetry stood for perfection.
41:16 *cieled with wood round about.* As in Solomon's temple (1 Ki 6:15).
‡41:18 *cherubims.* Angelic beings who served as guards (cf. Gen 3:24). These, as opposed to those mentioned in ch. 10, have only two faces—a man's and a lion's (see 1 Ki 6:29,32,35).
41:22 *altar . . . of wood.* As the great altar stood outside the temple proper (43:13–17), so a smaller altar (3′5″ square by 5′ high) stood outside the most holy place. It served as a table, no

Ezekiel's Temple

- **A.** Wall (40:5,16-20)
- **B.** East gate (40:6-14,16)
- **C.** Portico (40:8)
- **D.** Outer court (40:17)
- **E.** Pavement (40:17)
- **F.** Inner court (40:19)
- **G.** North gate (40:20-22)
- **H.** Inner court (40:23)
- **I.** South gate (40:24-26)
- **J.** South inner court (40:27)
- **K.** Gateway (40:28-31)
- **L.** Gateway (40:32-34)
- **M.** Gateway (40:35-38)
- **N.** Priests' rooms (40:44-45)
- **O.** Court (40:47)
- **P.** Temple portico (40:48-49)
- **Q.** Outer sanctuary (41:1-2)
- **R.** Most holy place (41:3-4)
- **S.** Temple walls (41:5-7,9,11)
- **T.** Base (41:8)
- **U.** Open area (41:10)
- **V.** West building (41:12)
- **W.** Priests' rooms (42:1-10)
- **X.** Altar (43:13-17)
- **AA.** Rooms for preparing sacrifices (40:39-43)
- **BB.** Ovens (46:19-20)
- **CC.** Kitchens (46:21-24)

Ezekiel uses a long or "royal" cubit, 20.4 inches or 51.81 cm ("cubit and a handbreadth," Ezek 40:5) as opposed to the standard Hebrew cubit of 17.6 inches or 44.7 cm.

Scripture describes a floor plan, but provides few height dimensions. This artwork shows an upward projection of the temple over the floor plan. This temple existed only in a vision of Ezekiel (Eze 40:2), and has never actually been built as were the temples of Solomon, Zerubbabel and Herod.

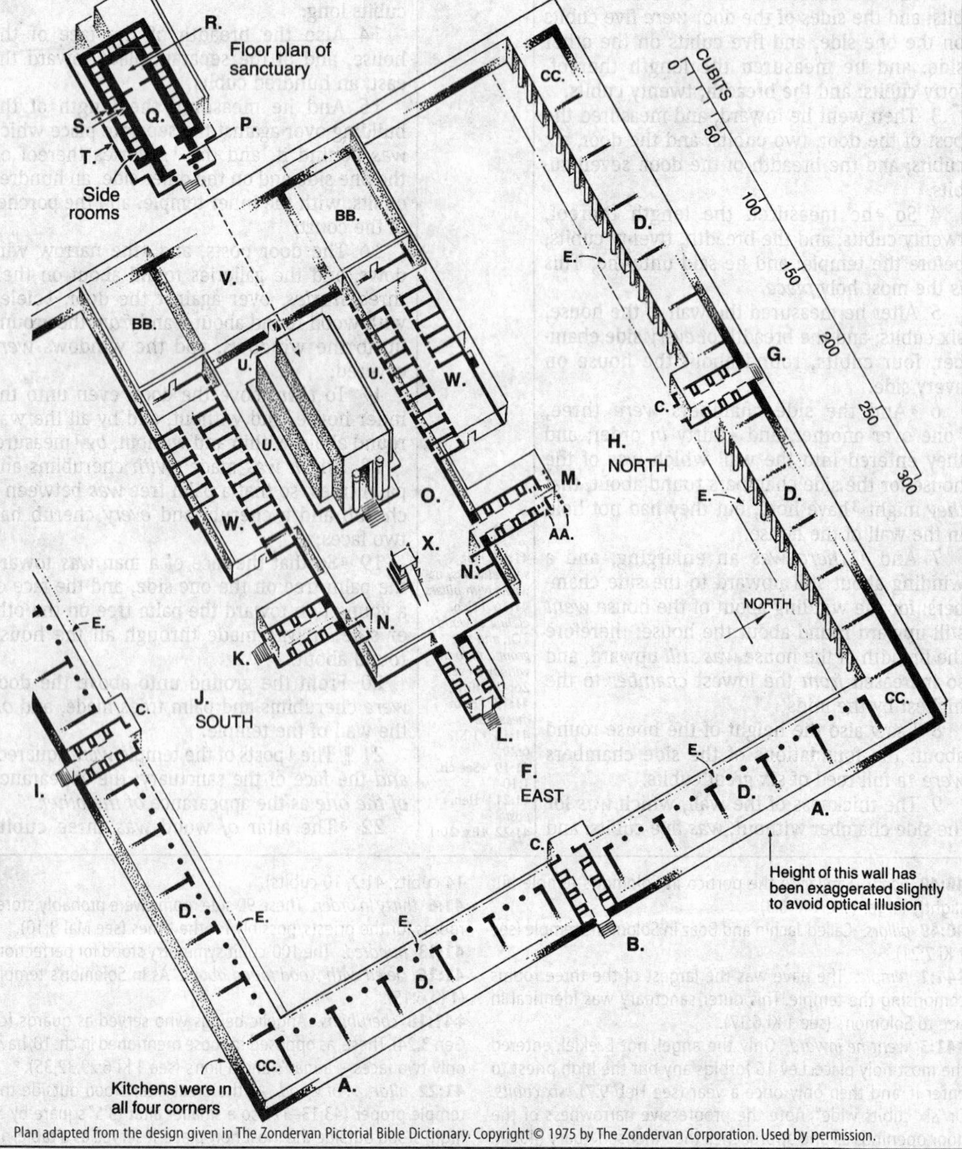

high, and the length thereof two cubits; and the corners thereof, and the length thereof, and the walls thereof, *were of* wood: and he said unto me, This *is* [b]the table that *is* [c]before the LORD.

23 [a]And the temple and the sanctuary had two doors.

24 And the doors had two leaves *apiece,* two turning leaves; two *leaves* for the one door, and two leaves for the other *door.*

25 And *there were* made on them, on the doors of the temple, cherubims and palm trees, like as *were* made upon the walls; and *there were* thick planks upon the face of the porch without.

26 And *there were* [a]narrow windows and palm trees on the one side and on the other side, on the sides of the porch, and *upon* the side chambers of the house, and thick planks.

The priests' chambers

42 Then he brought me forth into the utter court, the way toward the north: and he brought me into [a]the chamber that *was* over against the separate place, and which *was* before the building toward the north.

2 Before the length of an hundred cubits *was* the north door, and the breadth *was* fifty cubits.

3 Over against the twenty *cubits* which *were* for the inner court, and over against the pavement which *was* for the utter court, *was* [a]gallery against gallery in three *stories.*

4 And before the chambers *was* a walk of ten cubits breadth inward, a way of one cubit; and their doors toward the north.

5 Now the upper chambers *were* shorter: for the galleries [1]were higher than these, [2]than the lower, and than the middlemost of the building.

6 For they *were* in three *stories,* but had not pillars as the pillars of the courts: therefore *the building* was straitened more than the lowest and the middlemost from the ground.

7 And the wall that *was* without over against the chambers, towards the utter court on the forepart of the chambers, the length thereof *was* fifty cubits.

8 For the length of the chambers that *were* in the utter court *was* fifty cubits: and lo, before the temple *were* an hundred cubits.

9 And [1]from under these chambers *was* [2]the entry on the east side, [3]as one goeth into them from the utter court.

10 The chambers *were* in the thickness of the wall of the court toward the east, over against the separate place, and over against the building.

11 And [a]the way before them *was* like the appearance of the chambers which *were* toward the north, as long as they, *and* as broad as they: and all their goings out *were* both according to their fashions, and according to their doors.

12 And according to the doors of the chambers that *were* toward the south *was* a door in the head of the way, *even* the way directly before the wall toward the east, as *one* entereth into them.

13 ¶ Then said he unto me, The north chambers *and* the south chambers, which *are* before the separate place, they *be* holy chambers, where the priests that approach unto the LORD [a]shall eat the most holy *things:* there shall they lay the most holy *things,* and [b]the meat offering, and the sin offering, and the trespass offering; for the place *is* holy.

14 [a]When the priests enter *therein,* then shall they not go out of the holy *place* into the utter court, but there they shall lay their garments wherein they minister; for they *are* holy; and shall put on other garments, and shall approach to *those things* which *are* for the people.

15 ¶ Now when he had made an end of measuring the inner house, he brought me forth toward the gate whose prospect *is* toward the east, and measured it round about.

16 He measured the east [1]side with the measuring reed, five hundred reeds, with the measuring reed round about.

17 He measured the north side, five hundred reeds, with the measuring reed round about.

18 He measured the south side, five hundred reeds, with the measuring reed.

19 He turned about to the west side, *and* measured five hundred reeds with the measuring reed.

20 He measured it by the four sides: [a]it had a wall round about, [b]five hundred *reeds* long, and five hundred broad, to make a separation between the sanctuary and the profane *place.*

The LORD's glory fills the temple

43 Afterward he brought me to the gate, *even* the gate [a]that looketh toward the east:

2 [a]And behold, the glory of the God of Israel came from the way of the east: and [b]his

41:22 [b]ch. 44:16; Mal. 1:7,12 [c]Ex. 30:8
41:23 [a]1 Ki. 6:31-35
41:26 [a]ver. 16; ch. 40:16
42:1 [a]ch. 41:12,15
42:3 [a]ch. 41:16
42:5 [1]Or, *did eat of these* [2]Or, and *the building consisted of the lower and the middlemost*
42:9 [1]Or, *from the place* [2]Or, *he that brought* me [3]Or, *as he came*
42:11 [a]ver. 4
42:13 [a]Lev. 6:16,26; 24:9 [b]Lev. 2:3,10; 6:14,17,25,29
42:14 [a]ch. 44:19
42:16 [1]Heb. *wind*
42:20 [a]ch. 40:5 [b]ch. 45:2
43:1 [a]ch. 10:19; 46:1
43:2 [a]ch. 11:23 [b]ch. 1:24; Rev. 1:15; 14:2

doubt to hold the shewbread (Ex 25:30; Lev 24:5–9; see 1 Ki 7:48 and note). Ezekiel makes no mention of an altar of incense or of candlesticks, such as were found in Solomon's temple and in the tabernacle before it. Also not included are the "sea" (1 Ki 7:23) and the ark of the covenant.

41:23 *two doors.* Folding doors, so that the entry could be made still narrower.

42:1 *chamber . . . over against the separate place.* The chambers' function is described in vv. 13–14. They have no parallel in Solomon's temple as described in 1 Ki 6.

42:13 *priests that approach unto the LORD.* The sons of Zadok (see 40:6 and note on 44:15). *eat the most holy things.* The priests normally received partial maintenance by being allowed to eat certain sacrifices (see Lev 2:3; 5:13; 6:16,26,29; 7:6,10).

‡42:20 *measured it by the four sides.* Perfect symmetry in the ideal temple's total area.

43:2 *behold, the glory.* The high point of chs. 40–48. The temple had been prepared for this moment, and all that follows

voice *was* like a noise of many waters: [c]and the earth shined with his glory.

3 And *it was* [a]according to the appearance of the vision which I saw, *even* according to the vision that I saw [b1]when I came [c]to destroy the city: and the visions *were* like the vision that I saw [d]by the river Chebar; and I fell upon my face.

4 [a]And the glory of the LORD came into the house by the way of the gate whose prospect *is* toward the east.

5 [a]So the spirit took me up, and brought me into the inner court; and behold, [b]the glory of the LORD filled the house.

6 And I heard *him* speaking unto me out of the house; and [a]*the* man stood by me.

7 And he said unto me, Son of man, [a]the place of my throne, and [b]the place of the soles of my feet, [c]where I will dwell in the midst of the children of Israel for ever, and my holy name, shall the house of Israel [d]no more defile, *neither* they, nor their kings, by their whoredom, nor by [e]the carcases of their kings *in* their high places.

8 [a]In their setting of their threshold by my thresholds, and their post by my posts, [1]and the wall between me and them, they have even defiled my holy name by their abominations that they have committed: wherefore I have consumed them in mine anger.

9 Now let them put away their whoredom, and [a]the carcases of their kings, far from me, [b]and I will dwell in the midst of them for ever.

10 ¶ Thou son of man, [a]shew the house to the house of Israel, that they may be ashamed of their iniquities: and let them measure the [1]pattern.

11 And if they be ashamed of all that they have done, shew them the form of the house, and the fashion thereof, and the goings out thereof, and the comings in thereof, and all the forms thereof, and all the ordinances thereof, and all the forms thereof, and all the laws thereof: and write *it* in their sight, that they may keep the whole form thereof, and all the ordinances thereof, and do them.

12 This *is* the law of the house; Upon [a]the top of the mountain the whole limit thereof round about *shall be* most holy. Behold, this *is* the law of the house.

The size and use of the altar

13 ¶ And these *are* the measures of the altar after the cubits: [a]The cubit *is* a cubit and a hand breadth; even the [1]bottom *shall be* a cubit, and the breadth a cubit, and the border thereof by the [2]edge thereof round about *shall be* a span: and this *shall be* the higher place of the altar.

14 And from the bottom *upon* the ground *even* to the lower settle *shall be* two cubits, and the breadth one cubit; and from the lesser settle *even* to the greater settle *shall be* four cubits, and the breadth *one* cubit.

15 So [1]the altar *shall be* four cubits; and from [2]the altar and upward *shall be* four horns.

16 And [1]the altar *shall be* twelve *cubits* long, twelve broad, square in the four squares thereof.

17 And the settle *shall be* fourteen *cubits* long and fourteen broad in the four squares

43:2 [c]ch. 10:4; Rev. 18:1
43:3 [1]Or, *when I came* to prophesy *that the city should be destroyed:* See ch. 9:[1],2,5 [a]ch. 1:4,28 [b]See ch. 9:1 [c]Jer. 1:10 [d]ch. 3:23
43:4 [a]ch. 10:19
43:5 [a]ch. 3:12,14; 8:3 [b]1 Ki. 8:10,11
43:6 [a]ch. 40:3
43:7 [a]Ps. 99:1 [b]1 Chr. 28:2; Ps. 99:5 [c]Ex. 29:45; Ps. 68:16; 132:14; Joel 3:17; John 1:14; 2 Cor. 6:16 [d]ch. 39:7 [e]Lev. 26:30; Jer. 16:18
43:8 [1]Or, *for there was but a wall between me and them* [a]See 2 Ki. 16:14; 21:4,5,7; ch. 8:3; 23:39; 44:7
43:9 [a]ver. 7 [b]ver. 7
43:10 [a]ch. 40:4
43:10 [1]Or, *sum,* or, *number*
43:12 [a]ch. 40:2
43:13 [1]Heb. *bosom* [2]Heb. *lip* [a]ch. 41:8
43:15 [1]Heb. *Harel,* that is, *the mountain of God* [2]Heb. *Ariel,* that is, *the lion of God*
43:16 [1]Heb. *Ariel,* that is, *the lion of God*

flows from this appearance. *came from the . . . east.* The direction Ezekiel had seen God leave (see 11:23). In the book of Ezekiel God's glory is always active (see vv. 4–5; 3:23; 9:3; 10:4,18; 44:4). *like a noise of many waters.* Ezekiel experienced an audition as well as a vision. For the comparison see 1:24; Rev 1:15; 14:2; 19:6. *the earth shined with his glory.* God's visible glory is always described as being very bright (see 10:4; Luke 2:9; Rev 21:11,23).

43:3 *according to . . . the vision which I saw.* And yet it was different, for no creatures or wheels are mentioned here. *when I came to destroy the city.* See ch. 9. *by the river Chebar.* See ch. 1. *I fell upon my face.* See 1:28; 3:23; 9:8; 11:13; 44:4.

43:4 *by the . . . gate whose prospect is . . . east.* See note on v. 2.

43:5 *So the spirit took me up.* With God being nearer, the function of the guiding angel was taken over by the Spirit of God. Ezekiel was transported into the inner court but not into the temple (cf. 3:14; 8:3; 11:1,24). *filled the house.* As at the consecration of Solomon's temple (1 Ki 8:11; see Ex 40:34–35; Is 6:4).

43:6 *him.* God, but out of reverence not named here, preserving an air of awe and mystery.

‡43:7 *place of my throne.* See Is 6:1; Jer 3:17. *place of the soles of my feet.* See 1 Chr 28:2; Ps 99:5; 132:7; Is 60:13; Lam 2:1. *I will dwell in the midst of the children of Israel for ever.* Renewing the promise of 37:26–28 (see v. 9; 1 Ki 6:13; Zech 2:11). *whoredom.* The word can stand either for the sacred prostitution in the Canaanite religion (Baalism) or for spiritual apostasy from true worship of the Lord (see note on 16:15). *carcases.* The reference is either to idols or to monuments or graves of past kings. Fourteen kings of Judah were buried in Jerusalem, possibly near (too near for Ezekiel) the temple area (see 2 Ki 21:18,26; 23:30).

‡43:8 *their threshold by my thresholds.* Solomon's temple was surrounded by many of his own private structures (see 1 Ki 7:1–12). The distinction between God's holy temple and the rest of the world is a central idea in the book of Ezekiel (see v. 12; 44:23). *I have consumed them.* As elsewhere in Ezekiel, the unstable practices of the people and their kings brought about their destruction (see 5:11; 18:10–12; and especially 22:1–15).

43:12 *This is the law.* Refers to the contents of chs. 40–42.

43:13 *altar.* Alluded to in 40:47 and here described in detail. Although the material is not mentioned, dressed stones were probably to be used. Ex 20:24–26 allowed an altar to be made of earth, but use of dressed stones for those altars was strictly forbidden (see notes on Ex 20:24–25). Solomon's altar was bronze (1 Ki 8:64). Ezekiel's altar, much larger than Solomon's, was over 20 feet tall, made up of three slabs of decreasing size, like a pyramid or Babylonian ziggurat: the "lower settle" (v. 14), two cubits high; the "greater settle" (v. 14), four cubits high; and the "altar [hearth]" (v. 15), four cubits high.

43:15 *altar* [hearth]. The Hebrew for this term appears only here in the OT and may also mean "mountain of God" or "lion of God" (see KJV marg.); it is a variant of a form that appears in Is 29:1–2. *four horns.* Stone projections from each of the four corners of the altar hearth. On earlier altars they afforded a refuge of last resort for an accused person (see Ex 21:12–14; 1 Ki 1:50–51; 2:28–29).

thereof; and the border about it *shall be* half a cubit; and the bottom thereof *shall be* a cubit about; and [a]his stairs *shall* look toward the east.

18 ¶ And he said unto me, Son of man, thus saith the Lord GOD; These *are* the ordinances of the altar in the day when *they* shall make it, to offer burnt offerings thereon, and to [a]sprinkle blood thereon.

19 And thou shalt give to [a]the priests the Levites that *be* of the seed of Zadok, which approach unto me, to minister unto me, saith the Lord GOD, [b]a young bullock for a sin offering.

20 And thou shalt take of the blood thereof, and put *it* on the four horns of it, and on the four corners of the settle, and upon the border round about: thus shalt thou cleanse and purge it.

21 Thou shalt take the bullock also of the sin offering, and he [a]shall burn it in the appointed place of the house, [b]without the sanctuary.

22 And on the second day thou shalt offer a kid of the goats without blemish for a sin offering; and they shall cleanse the altar, as they did cleanse *it* with the bullock.

23 When thou hast made an end of cleansing *it,* thou shalt offer a young bullock without blemish, and a ram out of the flock without blemish.

24 And thou shalt offer them before the LORD, [a]and the priests shall cast salt upon them, and they shall offer them up *for* a burnt offering unto the LORD.

25 [a]Seven days shalt thou prepare every day a goat *for* a sin offering: they shall also prepare a young bullock, and a ram out of the flock, without blemish.

26 Seven days shall they purge the altar and purify it; and they shall [1]consecrate themselves.

27 [a]And when *these* days are expired, it shall be, *that* upon the eight day, and *so* forward, the priests shall make your burnt offerings upon the altar, and your [1]peace offerings; and I will [b]accept you, saith the Lord GOD.

43:17 [a]See Ex. 20:26
43:18 [a]Lev. 1:5
43:19 [a]ch. 44:15 [b]Ex. 29:10; Lev. 8:14; ch. 45:18
43:21 [a]Ex. 29:14 [b]Heb. 13:11
43:24 [a]Lev. 2:13
43:25 [a]Ex. 29:35; Lev. 8:33
43:26 [1]Heb. *fill their hands*
43:27 [1]Or, *thank offerings* [a]Lev. 9:1 [b]ch. 20:40,41; Rom. 12:1; 1 Pet. 2:5

44:1 [a]ch. 43:1
44:2 [a]ch. 43:4
44:3 [a]Gen. 31:54; 1 Cor. 10:18 [b]ch. 46:2,8
44:4 [a]ch. 3:23 [b]ch. 1:28
44:5 [1]Heb. *set thine heart* [a]ch. 40:4
44:6 [a]ch. 2:5 [b]ch. 45:9; 1 Pet. 4:3
44:7 [1]Heb. *children of a stranger* [a]ver. 9; ch. 43:8; Acts 21:28 [b]Lev. 22:25 [c]Lev. 26:41; Acts 7:51 [d]Lev. 21:17 [e]Lev. 3:16
44:8 [1]Or, *ward,* or, *ordinance:* And so ver. 14, [15], 16 [a]Lev. 22:2
44:9 [a]ver. 7
44:10 [a]2 Ki. 23:8; ch. 48:11

The use of the temple

44 Then he brought me back the way of the gate of the outward sanctuary [a]which looketh *toward* the east; and it *was* shut.

2 Then said the LORD unto me; This gate shall be shut, it shall not be opened, and no man shall enter in by it; [a]because the LORD, the God of Israel, hath entered in by it, therefore it shall be shut.

3 *It is* for the prince; the prince, he shall sit in it to [a]eat bread before the LORD; [b]he shall enter by the way of the porch of *that* gate, and shall go out by the way of the same.

4 ¶ Then brought he me the way of the north gate before the house: and I looked, and [a]behold, the glory of the LORD filled the house of the LORD: [b]and I fell upon my face.

5 And the LORD said unto me, [a]Son of man, [1]mark well, and behold with thine eyes, and hear with thine ears all that I say unto thee concerning all the ordinances of the house of the LORD, and all the laws thereof; and [1]mark well the entering in of the house, with every going forth of the sanctuary.

6 And thou shalt say to the [a]rebellious, *even* to the house of Israel, Thus saith the Lord GOD; O ye house of Israel, [b]let it suffice you of all your abominations,

7 [a]In that ye have brought *into my sanctuary* [b][1]strangers, [c]uncircumcised in heart, and uncircumcised in flesh, to be in my sanctuary, to pollute it, *even* my house, when ye offer [d]my bread, [e]the fat and the blood, and they have broken my covenant because of all your abominations.

8 And ye have not [a]kept the charge of mine holy *things:* but ye have set keepers of my [1]charge in my sanctuary for yourselves.

9 ¶ Thus saith the Lord GOD; [a]No stranger, uncircumcised in heart, nor uncircumcised in flesh, shall enter into my sanctuary, of any stranger that *is* among the children of Israel.

10 [a]And the Levites that are gone away far from me, when Israel went astray, which went

43:17 *his stairs.* Forbidden in Ex 20:26 but here required because of the size (see note on v. 13).
43:18 *burnt offerings.* See note on 40:39. *sprinkle blood.* See Ex 29:16; Lev 4:6; 5:9.
43:19 *of the seed of Zadok.* See note on 44:15. *sin offering.* To cleanse the altar from the pollution of human sin (see note on 40:39).
43:21 *without* [i.e."outside"] *the sanctuary.* As prescribed in Ex 29:14; Lev 4:12,21; 8:17; 9:11; 16:27. This action foreshadows one aspect of Christ's sacrifice (see Heb 13:11–13).
43:22 *cleanse.* By the sprinkling of the blood (see v. 20).
43:27 *peace offerings.* After the seven-day consecration by burnt offerings and sin offerings, the altar was ready for the celebration of the more festive peace offerings where the people partook of some of the meat (see Lev 3).
44:2 *gate shall be shut.* The reason given here is that God entered through the east gate (43:1–2), thus making it holy. Related reasons may be that God would never again leave as before (10:19; 11:23) and that sun worship would be made impossible (see 8:16). Today the east gate (called the Golden Gate) of the sacred Moslem area (*Haram esh-Sharif*) in Jerusalem is likewise sealed shut as a result of a later but possibly related tradition.
44:3 *prince.* The first mention of the prince in chs. 40–48 (see 34:24 and note). *to eat.* Probably his part of the peace offering (see Lev 7:15; Deut 12:7; see also Ezek 43:27 and note). While this honor is accorded the prince, it is significant that he is given no other part in the ceremonial functions, reserved now solely for the priests (see 2 Chr 26:16–20). *by the way of the porch.* From the inside of the outer court.
44:7 *uncircumcised in heart.* Spiritually unfit.
44:9 *No stranger, uncircumcised . . . shall enter into my sanctuary.* Nehemiah enforced this restriction when he dismissed Tobiah (Neh 13:8), an Ammonite (Neh 2:10; see Deut 23:3). Foreigners could, however, be a part of Israel (see 47:22).
44:10 *Levites.* Members of the tribe of Levi served as priests from the earliest days (see Deut 33:8–11; Judg 17:13). *when Israel went astray.* The reference is mainly to the period of the

astray away from me after their idols; they
shall even bear their iniquity.
11 Yet they shall be ministers in my sanctuary, [a]*having* charge at the gates of the house,
and ministering to the house: [b]they shall slay
the burnt offering and the sacrifice for the people, and [c]they shall stand before them to minister unto them.
12 Because they ministered unto them before their idols, and [a][1]caused the house of Israel to fall into iniquity; therefore have I [b]lift
up mine hand against them, saith the Lord
GOD, and they shall bear their iniquity.
13 [a]And they shall not come near unto me,
to do the office of a priest unto me, nor to
come near to any of my holy *things,* in the
most holy *place:* but they shall [b]bear their
shame, and their abominations which they
have committed.
14 But I will make them [a]keepers of the
charge of the house, for all the service thereof,
and for all that shall be done therein.
15 [a]But the priests the Levites, [b]the sons
of Zadok, that kept the charge of my sanctuary
[c]when the children of Israel went astray from
me, they shall come near to me to minister
unto me, and they [d]shall stand before me to
offer unto me [e]the fat and the blood, saith the
Lord GOD:
16 They shall enter into my sanctuary, and
they shall come near to [a]my table, to minister
unto me, and they shall keep my charge.
17 ¶ And it shall come to pass, *that* when
they enter in at the gates of the inner court,
[a]they shall be clothed with linen garments;
and no wool shall come upon them, whiles
they minister in the gates of the inner court,
and within.
18 [a]They shall have linen bonnets upon
their heads, and shall have linen breeches
upon their loins; they shall not gird *themselves*
[1][2]with any thing that causeth sweat.
19 And when they go forth into the utter
court, *even* into the utter court to the people,
[a]they shall put off their garments wherein
they ministered, and lay them in the holy
chambers, and they shall put on other garments; and they shall [b]not sanctify the people
with their garments.
20 [a]Neither shall they shave their heads,
nor suffer *their* locks to grow long; they shall
only poll their heads.
21 [a]Neither shall any priest drink wine,
when they enter into the inner court.
22 Neither shall they take for their wives a
[a]widow, nor her that is [1]put away: but they
shall take maidens of the seed of the house of
Israel, or a widow [2]that had a priest before.
23 And [a]they shall teach my people *the difference* between the holy and profane, and
cause them to discern between the unclean
and the clean.
24 And [a]in controversy they shall stand in
judgment; *and* they shall judge it according to
my judgments: and they shall keep my laws
and my statutes in all mine assemblies; [b]and
they shall hallow my sabbaths.
25 And they shall come at no dead person
to defile *themselves:* but for father, or for
mother, or for son, or for daughter, for brother,
or for sister that hath had no husband, they
may defile themselves.
26 And [a]after he is cleansed, they shall
reckon unto him seven days.
27 And in the day that he goeth into the
sanctuary, [a]unto the inner court, to minister in
the sanctuary, [b]he shall offer his sin offering,
saith the Lord GOD.
28 And it shall be unto them for an inheritance: I [a]*am* their inheritance: and ye shall
give them no possession in Israel: I *am* their
possession.
29 [a]They shall eat the meat offering, and
the sin offering, and the trespass offering; and
[b]every [1]dedicate thing in Israel shall be theirs.
30 And the [a][1]first of all the firstfruits of all

44:11 [a]1 Chr. 26:1 [b]2 Chr. 29:34 [c]Num. 16:9
44:12 [1]Heb. *were for a stumblingblock of iniquity unto, etc.* [a]Is. 9:16; Mal. 2:8 [b]Ps. 106:26
44:13 [a]Num. 18:3; 2 Ki. 23:9 [b]ch. 32:30
44:14 [a]Num. 18:4; 1 Chr. 23:28
44:15 [a]ch. 40:46 [b]1 Sam. 2:35 [c]ver. 10 [d]Deut. 10:8 [e]ver. 7
44:16 [a]ch. 41:22
44:17 [a]Ex. 28:39
44:18 [1]Or, *in sweating places* [2]Heb. *in,* or, *with sweat* [a]Ex. 28:40; 39:28
44:19 [a]ch. 42:14 [b]ch. 46:20; Ex. 30:29; Lev. 6:27; Mat. 23:17
44:20 [a]Lev. 21:5
44:21 [a]Lev. 10:9
44:22 [1]Heb. *thrust forth* [2]Heb. *from a priest* [a]Lev. 21:7
44:23 [a]ch. 22:26; Mal. 2:7
44:24 [a]Deut. 17:8; 2 Chr. 19:8 [b]See ch. 22:26
44:26 [a]Num. 6:10; 19:11
44:27 [a]ver. 17 [b]Lev. 4:3
44:28 [a]Num. 18:20; Deut. 10:9; 18:1,2; Josh. 13:14
44:29 [1]Or, *devoted* [a]Lev. 7:6 [b]Lev. 27:21,28, compared with Num. 18:14
44:30 [1]Or, *chief* [a]Ex. 13:2; 22:29; 23:19; Num. 3:13; 18:12

monarchy, especially to the last years, during which Ezekiel so often criticized the people's idolatry (see 6:3–6; 14:3–11; 16:18–21; 23:36–49; 36:17–18; 37:23).

44:11 *stand before them.* Cf. standing before the Lord (see v. 15); the Levites still had an honorable position.

44:15 *Zadok.* Traced his Levitical lineage to Aaron through Aaron's son Eleazar (1 Chr 6:50–53). He served as priest under David, along with Abiathar (see 2 Sam 8:17 and note; 15:24–29; 20:25). He supported Solomon (as opposed to Abiathar, who pledged himself to Adonijah) and thus secured for himself and his descendants the privilege of serving in the Jerusalem temple (see 1 Ki 1). Later the Zadokites were removed from office, but the Qumran (Dead Sea Scrolls) community remained loyal to them. *that kept the charge.* A distinction Ezekiel did not make in his oracles of judgment (see 7:26; 22:26 and the thrust of all of ch. 8). In chs. 40–48, however, the Zadokites received special consideration because of their faithfulness.

44:16 *They shall enter.* This elevation of the Zadokites and demotion of the Levites were part of the concern for ritual purity, a major theme of chs. 40–48. Only the fittest were to serve. *my table.* Either the table that held the bread (see 41:22 and note) or the large altar on which the Lord's food was presented (v. 7).

44:17 *linen.* Cooler than wool (see v. 18).

44:18 *linen bonnets.* Ezekiel wore one ("tire," 24:17).

44:19 *put off their garments.* In the interest of ritual purity.

44:20 *Neither shall they shave their heads.* Because it was a mourning ritual (7:18) that rendered the mourner unclean (see Lev 21:1–5). *nor suffer their locks to grow long.* Because it implied the taking of a vow that might prevent the priest from serving (see Num 6:5; Acts 21:23–26).

44:23 *difference between the holy and profane.* One of Ezekiel's central concerns. The important task of declaring God's will on matters of clean and unclean food, the fitness of sacrificial animals and ritual purity either had been done for pay (see Mic 3:11) or had been neglected altogether (see Jer 2:8; Ezek 22:26). See Hag 2:10–13 for a positive example.

44:24 *they shall stand in judgment.* One of their functions from earliest days (see 1 Sam 4:18 and note; see also 2 Chr 19:8–11).

44:25 *dead person.* Contact with the dead made a person ceremonially unclean (Lev 21:1–3; Hag 2:13).

44:28 *no possession.* The statement that priests were not to own land agrees with Num 18:20,23–24; Deut 10:9; Josh 13:14,33; 18:7.

things, and every oblation of all, of every *sort* of your oblations, shall be the priests': ye [b]shall also give unto the priest the first of your dough, [c]that he may cause the blessing to rest in thine house.

31 The priests shall not eat *of* any thing that is [a]dead of itself, or torn, whether it be fowl or beast.

Division of the land

45 Moreover, [1]when ye shall [a]divide *by lot* the land for inheritance, ye shall [b]offer an oblation unto the LORD, [2]a holy *portion* of the land: the length *shall be* the length *of* five and twenty thousand *reeds,* and the breadth *shall be* ten thousand. This *shall be* holy in all the borders thereof round about.

2 Of this there shall be for the sanctuary five hundred *in length,* with five hundred *in breadth,* square round about; and fifty cubits round about *for* the [1]suburbs thereof.

3 And of this measure shalt thou measure the length of five and twenty thousand, and the breadth of ten thousand: [a]and in it shall be the sanctuary *and* the most holy *place.*

4 [a]The holy *portion* of the land shall be for the priests the ministers of the sanctuary, which shall come near to minister unto the LORD: and it shall be a place for their houses, and a holy place for the sanctuary.

5 [a]And *the* five and twenty thousand of length, and *the* ten thousand of breadth, shall also the Levites, the ministers of the house, have for themselves, for a possession *for* [b]twenty chambers.

6 [a]And ye shall appoint the possession of the city five thousand broad, and five and twenty thousand long, over against the oblation of the holy *portion:* it shall be for the whole house of Israel.

7 [a]And *a portion shall be* for the prince on the one side and on the other side of the oblation of the holy *portion,* and of the possession of the city, before the oblation of the holy *portion,* and before the possession of the city, from the west side westward, and from the east side eastward: and the length *shall be* over against one of the portions, from the west border unto the east border.

8 In the land shall be his possession in Israel: and [a]my princes shall no more oppress my people; and *the rest of* the land shall they give to the house of Israel according to their tribes.

Laws about weights and offerings

9 ¶ Thus saith the Lord GOD; [a]Let it suffice you, O princes of Israel: [b]remove violence and spoil, and execute judgment and justice, take away your [1]exactions from my people, saith the Lord GOD.

10 Ye shall have just [a]balances, and a just ephah, and a just bath.

11 The ephah and the bath shall be of one measure, that the bath may contain the tenth part of a homer, and the ephah the tenth *part* of a homer: the measure thereof shall be after the homer.

12 And the [a]shekel *shall be* twenty gerahs: twenty shekels, five and twenty shekels, fifteen shekels, shall be your maneh.

13 This *is* the oblation that ye shall offer; the sixth *part* of an ephah of a homer of wheat, and ye shall give the sixth part of an ephah of a homer of barley:

14 Concerning the ordinance of oil, the bath *of* oil, *ye shall offer* the tenth part of a bath out of the cor, *which is* a homer of ten baths; for ten baths *are* a homer:

15 And one [1]lamb out of the flock, out of two hundred, out of the fat pastures of Israel; for a meat offering, and for a burnt offering, and for [2]peace offerings, [a]to make reconciliation for them, saith the Lord GOD.

16 All the people of the land [1]shall give this oblation [2]for the prince in Israel.

17 And it shall be the prince's part *to give* burnt offerings, and meat offerings, and drink offerings, in the feasts, and in the new moons,

44:30 [b]Num. 15:20; Neh. 10:37 [c]Prov. 3:9; Mal. 3:10
44:31 [a]Ex. 22:31; Lev. 22:8
45:1 [1]Heb. *when ye cause the land to fall* [2]Heb. *holiness* [a]ch. 47:22 [b]ch. 48:8
45:2 [1]Or, *void places*
45:3 [a]ch. 48:10
45:4 [a]ver. 1; ch. 48:10
45:5 [a]ch. 48:13 [b]See ch. 40:17
45:6 [a]ch. 48:15
45:7 [a]ch. 48:21
45:8 [a]See Jer. 22:17; ch. 22:27; 46:18
45:9 [1]Heb. *expulsions* [a]ch. 44:6 [b]Jer. 22:3
45:10 [a]Lev. 19:35,36; Prov. 11:1
45:12 [a]Ex. 30:13; Lev. 27:25; Num. 3:47
45:15 [1]Or, *kid* [2]Or, *thank offerings* [a]Lev. 1:4
45:16 [1]Heb. *shall be for* [2]Or, *with*

‡44:31 *is dead of itself.* That is, died a natural death, a restriction applied to all Israel according to Lev 7:24.

45:1 *when ye shall divide by lot the land.* Envisioned a new acquisition and redistribution of the land. *offer . . . unto the LORD.* The entire square area in the center of the land was to be set aside for the Lord. *five and twenty thousand reeds.* With the 5,000-cubit city area (v. 6) it was a perfect square. *holy in all the borders.* Set apart for the Lord and owned by no tribe.

‡45:2 *five hundred . . . square round about.* The temple area discussed in 42:16–20. *suburbs.* Unoccupied strips of land that served as buffers between the more holy and the less holy, though the whole area was holy (see 42:20).

45:3 *shalt thou measure.* The middle strip of the holy square was specifically for the temple.

45:4 *land . . . for the priests.* Not to own (see 44:28) but to live on.

45:5 *Levites . . . have for themselves.* A section of equal size just to the north was for the Levites to dwell on, even though it was in the holy area. The Levites, as opposed to the Zadokite priests, could hold land as a possession.

45:6 *city.* The former Jerusalem contained the temple area. The new holy city would not, but would be adjacent to the temple. *five thousand broad.* The southernmost section of the city completed the perfectly square area. *it shall be for the whole house of Israel.* Not to any one tribe or person as in former days.

45:7 *a portion shall be for the prince.* A considerable portion of territory. In view of the next verse (cf. 46:18) the generous allotment should have kept the prince from greed like that of Ahab (see 1 Ki 21). The prince was also responsible for sizable offerings (v. 17).

45:9 *O princes of Israel.* The language of this verse is reminiscent of the preaching Ezekiel did before 586 B.C. (see 22:6).

45:10 *Ye shall have just balances.* Israel was not to repeat the economic injustices of the past. The OT often warns against cheating in weights and measures (see Lev 19:35–36; Deut 25:13–16; Mic 6:10–12).

45:11 *shall be of one measure.* A little more than half a bushel. *homer.* About six bushels.

45:13 *oblation.* Given to the prince as distinct from the gifts given to the priests (44:30). The prince is to use these gifts in part for the offerings to the Lord (see v. 16).

45:17 *drink offerings.* Usually wine is meant (see Num 15:5;

and in the sabbaths in all solemnities of the
house of Israel: he shall prepare the sin offering, and the meat offering, and the burnt offering, and the [1]peace offerings, to make reconciliation for the house of Israel.
18 ¶ Thus saith the Lord GOD; In the first
month, in the first *day* of the month, thou
shalt take a young bullock without blemish,
and [a]cleanse the sanctuary:
19 [a]And the priest shall take of the blood
of the sin offering, and put *it* upon the posts of
the house, and upon the four corners of the
settle of the altar, and upon the posts of the
gate of the inner court.
20 And so thou shalt do the seventh *day* of
the month [a]for every one that erreth, and for
him that is simple: so shall ye reconcile the
house.
21 [a]In the first *month,* in the fourteenth
day of the month, ye shall have the passover, a
feast of seven days; unleavened bread shall be
eaten.
22 And upon that day shall the prince prepare for himself and for all the people of the
land [a]a bullock *for* a sin offering.
23 And [a]seven days of the feast he shall
prepare a burnt offering to the LORD, seven
bullocks and seven rams without blemish daily the seven days; [b]and a kid of the goats daily
for a sin offering.
24 [a]And he shall prepare a meat offering *of*
an ephah for a bullock, and an ephah for a
ram, and a hin of oil for an ephah.
25 In the seventh *month,* in the fifteenth
day of the month, shall he do the like in the
[a]feast *of* the seven days, according to the sin
offering, according to the burnt offering, and
according to the meat offering, and according
to the oil.
46 Thus saith the Lord GOD; The gate of
the inner court that looketh *toward*
the east shall be shut the six working days; but
on the sabbath it shall be opened, and in the
day of the new moon it shall be opened.
2 [a]And the prince shall enter by the way of
the porch of *that* gate without, and shall stand
by the post of the gate, and the priests shall
prepare his burnt offering and his peace offerings, and he shall worship at the threshold of
the gate: then he shall go forth; but the gate
shall not be shut until the evening.
3 Likewise the people of the land shall worship *at* the door of this gate before the LORD in
the sabbaths and in the new moons.
4 And the burnt offering that [a]the prince
shall offer unto the LORD in the sabbath day
shall be six lambs without blemish, and a ram
without blemish.
5 [a]And the meat offering *shall be* an ephah
for a ram, and the meat offering for the lambs
[b1]as he shall be able to give, and a hin of oil to
an ephah.
6 And in the day of the new moon *it shall*
be a young bullock without blemish, and six
lambs, and a ram: they shall be without blemish.
7 And he shall prepare a meat offering, an
ephah for a bullock, and an ephah for a ram,
and for the lambs according as his hand shall
attain unto, and a hin of oil to an ephah.
8 [a]And when the prince shall enter, he
shall go in *by* the way of the porch of *that* gate,
and he shall go forth by the way thereof.
9 ¶ But when the people of the land [a]shall
come before the LORD in the solemn feasts, he
that entereth in *by* the way of the north gate to
worship shall go out *by* the way of the south
gate; and he that entereth *by* the way of the
south gate shall go forth *by* the way of the
north gate: he shall not return *by* the way of
the gate whereby he came in, but shall go
forth over against it.
10 And the prince in the midst of them,
when they go in, shall go in; and when they go
forth, shall go forth.
11 And in the feasts and in the solemnities
[a]the meat offering shall be an ephah to a bullock, and an ephah to a ram, and to the lambs
as he is able to give, and a hin of oil to an
ephah.
12 Now when the prince shall prepare a
voluntary burnt offering or peace offerings voluntarily unto the LORD, [a]*one* shall then open
him the gate that looketh *toward* the east, and

45:17 [1]Or, *thank offerings*
45:18 [a]Lev. 16:16
45:19 [a]ch. 43:20
45:20 [a]Lev. 4:27
45:21 [a]Ex. 12:18; Lev. 23:5,6; Num. 9:2,3; 28:16,17; Deut. 16:1
45:22 [a]Lev. 4:14
45:23 [a]Lev. 23:8 [b]See Num. 28:15,22,30; 29:5,11,16,19
45:24 [a]ch. 46:5,7
45:25 [a]Lev. 23:34; Num. 29:12; Deut. 16:13
46:2 [a]ver. 8; ch. 44:3
46:4 [a]ch. 45:17
46:5 [1]Heb. *the gift of his hand* [a]ver. 7,11; ch. 45:24 [b]Deut. 16:17
46:8 [a]ver. 2
46:9 [a]Ex. 23:14-17; Deut. 16:16
46:11 [a]ver. 5
46:12 [a]ver. 2; ch. 44:3

Hos 9:4); but wine is not mentioned here, though oil is (vv. 14,24).

45:18–46:24 This entire section involves so many variations from Pentateuchal law that the rabbis spent a great deal of effort trying to reconcile them. For example, the provision in 45:18 for an annual purification of the temple does not seem to take into consideration the day of atonement ritual of Lev 16.

45:19 *priest.* High priest.

45:22 *sin offering.* See note on 40:39.

45:25 *seventh month . . . fifteenth day . . . in the feast.* In some respects the most important of the festivals—called the feast of ingathering (Ex 23:16; 34:22) and the feast of tabernacles (Deut 16:16).

46:1 *gate of the inner court.* While the east gate of the outer court was permanently closed (44:2), the east gate of the inner court could be opened on festival days.

46:2 *by the way of the porch of that gate.* The portico of the gate of the inner court faced the outer court. *stand by the post of the gate.* Which had been ritually cleansed (45:19). From there the prince could observe the sacrifices being performed on the great altar in the inner court, but he was not allowed into the inner court itself.

46:3 *at the door of this gate.* But in the outer court.

46:4 *six lambs . . . and a ram.* Another example of a difference from Pentateuchal laws (see note on 45:18–46:24). Num 28:9 calls for two lambs and no ram on the sabbath.

46:5 *ephah.* Contrast Num 28:9.

46:6 *day of the new moon.* The first day of the month. Contrast the requirement of Num 28:11.

46:7 *a meat offering, an ephah.* Contrast Num 28:12.

46:9 *he that entereth in . . . the north gate.* These appear to be crowd control measures. If so, the new era would see masses of people thronging the sanctuary on the festival day.

46:12 *voluntary burnt offering.* Above and beyond what was required of the prince.

he shall prepare his burnt offering and his peace offerings, as he did on the sabbath day: then he shall go forth; and after his going forth *one* shall shut the gate.

13 [a]Thou shalt daily prepare a burnt offering unto the LORD *of* a lamb [1]of the first year without blemish: thou shalt prepare it [2]every morning.

14 And thou shalt prepare a meat offering for it every morning, the sixth *part* of an ephah, and the third *part* of a hin of oil, to temper with the fine flour; a meat offering continually *by* a perpetual ordinance unto the LORD.

15 Thus shall they prepare the lamb, and the meat offering, and the oil, every morning *for* a continual burnt offering.

16 ¶ Thus saith the Lord GOD; If the prince give a gift unto any of his sons, the inheritance thereof shall be his sons'; it *shall be* their possession by inheritance.

17 But if he give a gift of his inheritance to one of his servants, then it shall be his to [a]the year of liberty; after, it shall return to the prince: but his inheritance shall be his sons' for them.

18 Moreover [a]the prince shall not take of the people's inheritance, by oppression to thrust them out of their possession; *but* he shall give his sons inheritance out of his own possession: that my people be not scattered every man from his possession.

19 ¶ After, he brought me through the entry, which *was* at the side of the gate, into the holy chambers of the priests, which looked toward the north: and behold, there *was* a place on the two sides westward.

20 Then said he unto me, This *is* the place where the priests shall [a]boil the trespass offering and the sin offering, where they shall [b]bake the meat offering; that *they* bear *them* not out into the utter court, [c]to sanctify the people.

21 Then he brought me forth into the utter court, and caused me to pass by the four corners of the court; and behold, [1]in every corner of the court *there was* a court.

22 In the four corners of the court *there were* courts [1]joined *of* forty *cubits* long and thirty broad: these four [2]corners *were* of one measure.

23 And *there was* a row *of building* round about in them, round about them four, and *it was* made *with* boiling places under the rows round about.

24 Then said he unto me, These *are* the places of them that boil, where the ministers of the house shall [a]boil the sacrifice of the people.

46:13 [1]Heb. [*a son*] *of his year* [2]Heb. *morning by morning* [a]Ex. 29:38; Num. 28:3
46:17 [a]Lev. 25:10
46:18 [a]ch. 45:8
46:20 [a]2 Chr. 35:13 [b]Lev. 2:4,5,7 [c]ch. 44:19
46:21 [1]Heb. *a court in a corner of a court, and a court in a corner of a court*
46:22 [1]Or, *made with chimneys*
46:22 [2]Heb. *cornered*
46:24 [a]See ver. 20
47:1 [a]Joel 3:18; Zech. 13:1; 14:8; Rev. 22:1
47:3 [1]Heb. *waters of the ankles* [a]ch. 40:3
47:5 [1]Heb. *waters of swimming*
47:7 [1]Heb. *lip* [a]ver. 12; Rev. 22:2
47:8 [1]Or, *plain*

The river from the temple

47 Afterward he brought me again unto the door of the house; and behold, [a]waters issued out from under the threshold of the house eastward: for the forefront of the house *stood toward* the east, and the waters came down from under from the right side of the house, at the south *side* of the altar.

2 Then brought he me out *of* the way of the gate northward, and led me about the way without unto the utter gate *by* the way that looketh east*ward;* and behold, there ran out waters on the right side.

3 And when [a]the man that had the line in his hand went forth east*ward,* he measured a thousand cubits, and he brought me through the waters; [1]the waters *were* to the ankles.

4 Again he measured a thousand, and brought me through the waters; the waters *were to* the knees. Again he measured a thousand, and brought me through; the waters *were* to the loins.

5 Afterward he measured a thousand; *and it was* a river that I could not pass over: for the waters were risen, [1]waters to swim in, a river that could not be passed over.

6 ¶ And he said unto me, Son of man, hast thou seen *this?* Then he brought me, and caused me to return to the brink of the river.

7 Now when I had returned, behold, at the [1]bank of the river *were* very many [a]trees on the one side and on the other.

8 Then said he unto me, These waters issue out toward the east country, and go down into the [1]desert, and go into the sea: *which being* brought forth into the sea, the waters shall be healed.

46:13 *every morning.* Contrast Num 28:3–8, where the daily sacrifice consists of one lamb in the morning and one in the evening (see 1 Chr 16:40; 2 Chr 13:11; 31:3). A different custom appears in 2 Ki 16:15, where a burnt offering was offered in the mornings, a grain offering in the evenings.
46:14 *sixth part of an ephah . . . third part of an hin.* Contrast Num 28:5.
46:16 *his sons.* Ezekiel pictured a hereditary rulership.
46:17 *to the year of liberty.* The year of jubilee—held, theoretically, every 50th year (see Lev 25:8–15, especially v. 13).
46:18 *the prince shall not take.* See note on 45:7.
46:19–24 Fits well after 42:13–14, where other rooms for priests are described. The provisions here are a fitting conclusion to the sacrifice laws. The priests' area (vv. 19–20) was to be kept separate from the cooking areas of the Levites (vv. 21–24).
47:1 *he.* The angelic guide (40:3), who here appears for the last time, concluded Ezekiel's visionary tour of the new temple. *door of the house.* Ezekiel was standing in the inner court. *waters.* The rest of this section (vv. 1–12) makes it clear that healing, life-nurturing water is meant (see Ps 36:8; 46:4 and notes; see also Joel 3:18; Zech 13:1; 14:8; Rev 22:1–2). In the larger background was the river flowing from the garden of Eden (Gen 2:10).
47:2 *brought he me out of the way of the gate northward.* Because the east gate was closed (44:2).
47:5 *measured a thousand.* For a total of four measurings (see note on 1:5). *river that I could not pass over.* Amazing, in that a stream fed by no tributaries does not increase as it flows.
47:7 *very many trees.* Reminiscent of Eden (Gen 2:9).
‡47:8 *toward the east country.* Contrast Zech 14:8. *the desert.* Arabah. Here the waterless region between Jerusalem and the Dead Sea (i.e., part of the Jordan Valley). *the sea.* Usually means the Mediterranean Sea, but here obviously the Dead Sea is intended. *shall be healed.* Figurative for "become fresh." That this

9 And it shall come to pass, *that* every thing that liveth, which moveth, whithersoever the [1]rivers shall come, shall live: and there shall be a very great multitude of fish, because these waters shall come thither: for they shall be healed; and every *thing* shall live whither the river cometh.

10 And it shall come to pass, *that* the fishers shall stand upon it from En-gedi even unto En-eglaim; they shall be a place to spread forth nets; their fish shall be according to their kinds, as the fish [a]of the great sea, exceeding many.

11 But the miry places thereof and the marishes thereof [1]shall not be healed; they shall be given to salt.

12 And [a]by the river upon the bank thereof, on this side and on that side, [1]shall grow all trees for meat, [b]whose leaf shall not fade, neither shall the fruit thereof be consumed: it shall bring forth [2]new fruit according to his months, because their waters they issued out of the sanctuary: and the fruit thereof shall be for meat, and the leaf thereof [3]for [c]medicine.

The borders of the land

13 ¶ Thus saith the Lord GOD; This *shall be* the border, whereby ye shall inherit the land according to the twelve tribes of Israel: [a]Joseph *shall have two* portions.

14 And ye shall inherit it, one as well as another: *concerning* the which I [a][1]lifted up mine hand to give it unto your fathers: and this land shall [b]fall unto you for inheritance.

15 And this *shall be* the border of the land toward the north side, from the great sea, [a]the way of Hethlon, as *men* go to [b]Zedad;

16 [a]Hamath, [b]Berothah, Sibraim, which *is* between the border of Damascus and the border of Hamath; [1]Hazar-hatticon, which *is* by the coast of Hauran.

17 And the border from the sea shall be [a]Hazar-enan, the border of Damascus, and the north northward, and the border of Hamath. And *this is* the north side.

18 And the east side ye shall measure [1]from Hauran, and [1]from Damascus, and [1]from Gilead, and [1]from the land of Israel *by* Jordan, from the border unto the east sea. And *this is* the east side.

19 And the south side southward, from Tamar *even* to [a]the waters of [1]strife *in* Kadesh, *the* [2]river to the great sea. And *this is* the south side [3]southward.

20 The west side also *shall be* the great sea from the border, till *a man* come over against Hamath. This *is* the west side.

21 So shall ye divide this land unto you according to the tribes of Israel.

22 ¶ And it shall come to pass, *that* ye shall divide it *by lot* for an inheritance unto you, [a]and to the strangers that sojourn among you, which shall beget children among you: [b]and they shall be unto you as born in the country among the children of Israel; they shall have inheritance with you among the tribes of Israel.

23 And it shall come to pass, *that* in what tribe the stranger sojourneth, there shall ye give *him* his inheritance, saith the Lord GOD.

47:9 [1]Heb. *two rivers* 47:10 [a]Num. 34:3; Josh. 23:4; ch. 48:28 47:11 [1]Or, *and that which shall not be healed* 47:12 [1]Heb. *shall come up* [2]Or, *principal* [3]Or, *for bruises and sores* [a]ver. 7 [b]Job 8:16; Ps. 1:3; Jer. 17:8 [c]Rev. 22:2 47:13 [a]Gen. 48:5; 1 Chr. 5:1; ch. 48:4,5 47:14 [1]Or, *swore* [a]Gen. 12:7; 13:15; 15:7; 17:8; 26:3; 28:13; ch. 20:5,6,28,42 [b]ch. 48:29

47:15 [a]ch. 48:1 [b]Num. 34:8 47:16 [1]Or, *the middle village* [a]Num. 34:8 [b]2 Sam. 8:8 47:17 [a]Num. 34:9; ch. 48:1 47:18 [1]Heb. *from between* 47:19 [1]Or, *Meribah* [2]Or, *valley* [3]Or, *toward Teman* [a]Num. 20:13; Deut. 32:51; Ps. 81:7; ch. 48:28 47:22 [a]See Eph. 3:6; Rev. 7:9,10 [b]Rom. 10:12; Gal. 3:28; Col. 3:11

lowest (1,300 feet below sea level) and saltiest (25 percent) body of water in the world should sustain such an abundance of life indicates the wonderful renewing power of this "river of water of life" (Rev 22:1).

47:9 *every thing . . . shall live.* Overtones of Gen 1:20–21 point to a new creation.

47:10 *En-gedi.* Means "spring of the goat"; a strong spring midway along the western side of the Dead Sea. *En-eglaim.* Means "spring of the two calves." It is possibly Ain Feshkha, at the northwestern corner of the Dead Sea, though some suggest a location on the east bank. *the great sea.* The Mediterranean.

47:11 *they shall be given to salt.* Perhaps to provide the salt needed in the sacrifices (43:24).

47:12 *new fruit . . . according to his months.* A marvelous extension of the promises in 34:27; 36:30 (see Amos 9:13).

47:13 *Joseph shall have two portions.* Since the tribe of Levi received none (44:28), Ephraim and Manasseh, Joseph's two sons adopted by Jacob (Gen 48:17–20), each received an allotment (see 48:4–5).

47:14 *which I lifted up my hand to give.* A reference to the covenant made with Abram (Gen 15:9–21; see Ezek 20:5; 36:28).

‡47:15 *this shall be the border.* Approximates Israel's borders at the time of David and Solomon, except that the region across the Jordan is not included (see v. 18)—which, in any event, was never within the boundaries of the promised land proper. The following specified boundaries closely resemble those in Num 34:1–12. *way of Hethlon.* Probably situated on the Mediterranean coast, somewhere in present-day Lebanon. *to Zedad.* Or "past Lebo Hamath to Zedad." Lebo probably does not mean "entrance," but should be identified with modern Lebweh, about 15 miles northeast of Baalbek and 20 miles southwest of Kadesh on the Orontes River, near Riblah. At one time Lebo must have served as a fortress guarding the southern route to Hamath. Perhaps the phrase should be translated "Lebo of Hamath." It is often referred to in Scripture as the northern limit of Israel (see v. 20; 48:1; Num 13:21; 34:8; Josh 13:5; 1 Ki 8:65; 2 Ki 14:25; Amos 6:14). Zedad is mentioned in Num 34:8 as one of the landmarks on the northern border of Israel as promised by Moses and restated here.

47:16 *Berothah.* Probably to be identified with the Berothai of 2 Sam 8:8, but otherwise unknown. *Sibraim.* Location unknown; probably the Sepharvaim of 2 Ki 17:24; 18:34. *Damascus.* Capital of Aram (Syria); according to v. 17 it was included in Israel. *Hamath.* A city about 120 miles north of Damascus on the Orontes River. *Hazer-hatticon.* Means "the middle enclosure." Its location is unknown, but it is possibly the same as Hazar-enan in v. 17.

47:18 *east sea.* The Dead Sea (see Joel 2:20; Zech 14:8).

‡47:19 *waters of strife in Kadesh.* Or "Meribath-kadesh," a district about 50 miles south of Beer-sheba, identified with Kadesh-barnea in Num 34:4. *the river.* The Wadi el-Arish, a deeply cut riverbed with seasonal flow that runs from the Sinai north-northwest until it enters the Mediterranean, 50 miles south of Gaza. It marked the southernmost extremity of Solomon's kingdom (1 Ki 8:65).

‡47:22 *they shall be unto you as born in the country.* A gracious inclusiveness that went beyond the provision of 14:7. It reflects the same universalism that is found in such prophecies as Is 56:3–8.

The division of the land

48 Now these *are* the names of the tribes. [a]From the north end to the coast of the way of Hethlon, as *one* goeth to Hamath, Hazar-enan, the border of Damascus northward, to the coast of Hamath; for these are his sides east *and* west; [1]a *portion for* Dan.

2 And by the border of Dan, from the east side unto the west side, a *portion for* Asher.

3 And by the border of Asher, from the east side even unto the west side, a *portion for* Naphtali.

4 And by the border of Naphtali, from the east side unto the west side, a *portion for* Manasseh.

5 And by the border of Manasseh, from the east side unto the west side, a *portion for* Ephraim.

6 And by the border of Ephraim, from the east side even unto the west side, a *portion for* Reuben.

7 And by the border of Reuben, from the east side unto the west side, a *portion for* Judah.

8 ¶ And by the border of Judah, from the east side unto the west side, shall be [a]the offering which ye shall offer *of* five and twenty thousand *reeds in* breadth, and *in* length as one of the *other* parts, from the east side unto the west side: and the sanctuary shall be in the midst of it.

9 The oblation that ye shall offer unto the LORD *shall be of* five and twenty thousand *in* length, and *of* ten thousand *in* breadth.

10 And for them, *even* for the priests, shall be *this* holy oblation; toward the north five and twenty thousand *in length,* and toward the west ten thousand *in* breadth, and toward the east ten thousand *in* breadth, and toward the south five and twenty thousand *in* length: and the sanctuary of the LORD shall be in the midst thereof.

11 [a][1]*It shall be* for the priests that are sanctified of the sons of Zadok; which have kept my [2]charge, which went not astray when the children of Israel went astray, [b]as the Levites went astray.

12 And *this* oblation of the land that is offered shall be unto them *a thing* most holy by the border of the Levites.

48:1 [1][Heb. *one* portion] [a]ch. 47:15
48:8 [a]ch. 45:1-6
48:11 [1]Or, *The sanctified* portion shall be *for the priests* [2]Or, *ward,* or, *ordinance* [a]ch. 44:15 [b]ch. 44:10

13 And over against the border of the priests, the Levites *shall have* five and twenty thousand *in* length, and ten thousand *in* breadth: all the length *shall be* five and twenty thousand, and the breadth ten thousand.

14 [a]And they shall not sell of it, neither exchange, nor alienate the firstfruits of the land: for *it is* holy unto the LORD.

15 ¶ [a]And the five thousand, that are left in the breadth over against the five and twenty thousand, *shall be* [b]a profane *place* for the city, for dwelling, and for suburbs: and the city shall be in the midst thereof.

16 And these *shall be* the measures thereof; the north side four thousand and five hundred, and the south side four thousand and five hundred, and on the east side four thousand and five hundred, and the west side four thousand and five hundred.

17 And the suburbs of the city shall be toward the north two hundred and fifty, and toward the south two hundred and fifty, and toward the east two hundred and fifty, and toward the west two hundred and fifty.

18 And the residue in length over against the oblation of the holy *portion shall be* ten thousand eastward, and ten thousand westward: and it shall be over against the oblation of the holy *portion;* and the increase thereof shall be for food unto them that serve the city.

19 [a]And they that serve the city shall serve it out of all the tribes of Israel.

20 All the oblation *shall be* five and twenty thousand by five and twenty thousand: ye shall offer the holy oblation foursquare, with the possession of the city.

21 [a]And the residue *shall be* for the prince, on the one side and on the other of the holy oblation, and of the possession of the city, over against the five and twenty thousand of the oblation toward the east border, and westward over against the five and twenty thousand toward the west border, over against the portions for the prince: and it shall be the holy oblation; [b]and the sanctuary of the house *shall be* in the midst thereof.

22 Moreover from the possession of the Levites, *and* from the possession of the city, *being* in the midst *of that* which is the prince's, between the border of Judah and the border of Benjamin, shall be for the prince.

48:14 [a]Ex. 22:29; Lev. 27:10,28,33
48:15 [a]ch. 45:6 [b]ch. 42:20
48:19 [a]ch. 45:6
48:21 [a]ch. 45:7 [b]ver. 8,10

48:1 *Hethlon . . . to the coast of Hamath.* See note on 47:15. *Hazar-enan.* See note on 47:16. *Dan.* Occupies its historical location as the northernmost tribe (see the phrase "from Dan to Beersheba," giving northern and southern boundaries—e.g., in Judg 20:1; 1 Sam 3:20). Dan was born to Rachel's maidservant Bilhah (Gen 35:25).

48:2 *Asher.* Born to Leah's maidservant Zilpah (Gen 35:26). The tribes descended from maidservants were placed farthest from the sanctuary (see Dan, v. 1; Naphtali, v. 3; Gad, v. 27).

48:3 *Naphtali.* Born to Rachel's maidservant Bilhah (see note on v. 2).

48:4 *Manasseh.* See note on 47:13.

48:5 *Ephraim.* See note on 47:13.

48:6 *Reuben.* Leah's firstborn (Gen 29:31).

48:7 *Judah.* Son of Leah (Gen 35:23). He had the most prestigious place, bordering the central holy portion (v. 8), because his tribe was given the Messianic promise (Gen 49:8–12).

48:8–22 An expansion of 45:1–8.

48:9 *ten thousand in breadth.* The width of the entire sacred district was 20,000 cubits (see 45:1). This must refer to the width of either the priests' or the Levites' area. The Septuagint reads "20,000."

48:11 *sons of Zadok; which have kept my charge.* See note on 44:15.

48:14 *not sell of it, neither exchange.* Since it was the Lord's, it was not to be an object of commerce.

48:19 *out of all the tribes of Israel.* The sacred district was national property, not the prince's private domain.

23 ¶ As for the rest of the tribes, from the east side unto the west side, Benjamin *shall have* [1]a *portion.*

24 And by the border of Benjamin, from the east side unto the west side, Simeon *shall have* a *portion.*

25 And by the border of Simeon, from the east side unto the west side, Issachar a *portion.*

26 And by the border of Issachar, from the east side unto the west side, Zebulun a *portion.*

27 And by the border of Zebulun, from the east side unto the west side, Gad a *portion.*

28 And by the border of Gad, at the south side southward, the border shall be even from Tamar *unto* [a]the waters of [1]strife *in* Kadesh, *and to the* river toward the great sea.

29 [a]This *is* the land which ye shall divide *by lot* unto the tribes of Israel for inheritance, and these *are* their portions, saith the Lord God.

48:23 [1]Heb. *one portion*
48:28 [1]Or, *Meribah-kadesh* [a]ch. 47:19
48:29 [a]ch. 47:14,21,22
48:31 [a]Rev. 21:12
48:35 [1]Heb. *Jehovah-shammah* [a]Jer. 33:16 [b]Jer. 3:17; Joel 3:21; Zech. 2:10; Rev. 21:3; 22:3

The name of the city

30 ¶ And these *are* the goings out of the city: on the north side, four thousand and five hundred measures.

31 [a]And the gates of the city *shall be* after the names of the tribes of Israel: three gates northward; one gate of Reuben, one gate of Judah, one gate of Levi.

32 And at the east side four thousand and five hundred: and three gates; and one gate of Joseph, one gate of Benjamin, one gate of Dan.

33 And *at* the south side four thousand and five hundred measures: and three gates; one gate of Simeon, one gate of Issachar, one gate of Zebulun.

34 *At* the west side four thousand and five hundred, *with* their three gates; one gate of Gad, one gate of Asher, one gate of Naphtali.

35 *It was* round about eighteen thousand *measures:* [a]and the name of the city from *that* day *shall be,* [b][1]The Lord *is* there.

48:23 *Benjamin.* Rachel's son (Gen 35:24).
48:24 *Simeon.* Leah's son (Gen 35:23).
48:25 *Issachar.* Leah's son (Gen 35:23).
48:26 *Zebulun.* Leah's son (Gen 35:23).
48:27 *Gad.* Son of Zilpah, Leah's maid (see note on v. 2).
48:28 *Tamar.* See note on 47:18. *strife in Kadesh.* See note on 47:19. *the river.* See note on 47:19.
48:31 *Reuben . . . Judah . . . Levi.* The three most influential tribes—Reuben, the firstborn; Judah, the Messianic tribe; Levi, the tribe of the priesthood—had gates together on the north side. Since Levi was included in this list, Joseph (v. 32) represented Ephraim and Manasseh (see note on 47:13) in order to keep the number at 12. For the gates cf. Rev 21:12–14.
48:35 *The Lord is there.* The great decisive word concerning the holy city; in Hebrew *Yahweh-Shammah,* a possible wordplay on *Yerushalayim,* the Hebrew pronunciation of Jerusalem. For other names of Jerusalem see 23:4; Is 1:26; 60:*14;* 62:2–4,12; Jer 3:17; 33:16; Zech 8:3.

The Book of
Daniel

INTRODUCTION

Author, Date and Authenticity

The book mentions Daniel as its author in several passages, such as 9:2 and 10:2. That Jesus concurred is clear from His reference to " 'the abomination of desolation,' spoken of by Daniel the prophet" (Mat 24:15), quoting 9:27; 11:31; 12:11. The book was probably completed c. 530 B.C., shortly after the capture of Babylon by Cyrus in 539.

The widely held view that the book of Daniel is largely fictional rests mainly on the modern philosophical assumption that long-range predictive prophecy is impossible. Therefore all fulfilled predictions in Daniel, it is claimed, had to have been composed no earlier than the Maccabean period (second century B.C.), after the fulfillments had taken place. But objective evidence excludes this hypothesis on several counts:

1. To avoid fulfillment of long-range predictive prophecy in the book, the adherents of the late-date view usually maintain that the four empires of chs. 2 and 7 are Babylon, Media, Persia and Greece. But in the mind of the author, "the Medes and Persians" (5:28) together constituted the second in the series of four kingdoms (2:36–43). Thus it becomes clear that the four empires are the Babylonian, Medo-Persian, Greek and Roman. See chart, p. 1226.

2. The language itself argues for a date earlier than the second century. Linguistic evidence from the Dead Sea Scrolls (which furnish authentic samples of Hebrew and Aramaic writing from the second century B.C.; see essay, p. 1344) demonstrates that the Hebrew and Aramaic chapters of Daniel must have been composed centuries earlier. Furthermore, as recently demonstrated, the Persian and Greek words in Daniel do not require a late date. Some of the technical terms appearing in ch. 3 were already so obsolete by the second century B.C. that translators of the Septuagint (the Greek translation of the OT) translated them incorrectly.

3. Several of the fulfillments of prophecies in Daniel could not have taken place by the second century anyway, so the prophetic element cannot be dismissed. The symbolism connected with the fourth kingdom makes it unmistakably predictive of the Roman empire (see 2:33; 7:7,19), which did not take control of Syro-Palestine until 63 B.C. Also, the prophecy concerning the coming of "the Messiah the Prince," 483 years after "the going forth of the commandment to restore and to build Jerusalem" (9:25), works out to the time of Jesus' ministry.

Objective evidence, therefore, appears to exclude the late-date hypothesis and indicates that there is insufficient reason to deny Daniel's authorship.

Theme

The theological theme of the book is God's sovereignty: "The most high God ruled in the kingdom of men" (5:21). Daniel's visions always show God as triumphant (7:11, 26–27; 8:25; 9:27; 11:45; 12:13). The climax of His sovereignty is described in Revelation: "The kingdoms of this world are become the kingdoms of our Lord, and of his Christ; and he shall reign for ever and ever" (Rev 11:15; cf. Dan 2:44; 7:27).

Literary Form

The book is made up primarily of historical narrative (found mainly in chs. 1—6) and apocalyptic (revelatory) material (found mainly in chs. 7—12). The latter may be defined as symbolic, visionary, prophetic literature, usually composed during oppressive conditions and being chiefly eschatological in theological content. Apocalyptic literature is primarily a literature of encouragement to the people of God (see Introduction to Zechariah: Literary Form; see also Introduction to Revelation: Literary Form). For the symbolic use of numbers in apocalyptic literature see Introduction to Revelation: Distinctive Feature.

Outline

- I. Prologue: The Setting (ch. 1; in Hebrew)
  - A. Historical Introduction (1:1–2)
  - B. Daniel and His Friends Are Taken Captive (1:3–7)
  - C. The Young Men Are Faithful (1:8–16)
  - D. The Young Men Are Elevated to High Positions (1:17–21)
- II. The Destinies of the Nations of the World (chs. 2—7; in Aramaic, beginning at 2:4b)
  - A. Nebuchadnezzar's Dream of a Great Image (ch. 2)
  - B. Nebuchadnezzar's Making of a Gold Image and His Decree That It Be Worshiped (ch. 3)
  - C. Nebuchadnezzar's Dream of an Enormous Tree (ch. 4)
  - D. Belshazzar's and Babylon's Downfall (ch. 5)
  - E. Daniel's Deliverance (ch. 6)
  - F. Daniel's Dream of Four Beasts (ch. 7)
- III. The Destiny of the Nation of Israel (chs. 8—12; in Hebrew)
  - A. Daniel's Vision of a Ram and a Goat (ch. 8)
  - B. Daniel's Prayer and His Vision of the 70 "Weeks" (ch. 9)
  - C. Daniel's Vision of Israel's Future (chs. 10—12)
    1. Revelation of things to come (10:1–3)
    2. Revelation from the angelic messenger (10:4—11:1)
    3. Prophecies concerning Persia and Greece (11:2–4)
    4. Prophecies concerning Egypt and Syria (11:5–35)
    5. Prophecies concerning the antichrist (11:36–45)
    6. Distress and deliverance (12:1)
    7. Two resurrections (12:2–3)
    8. Instruction to Daniel (12:4)
    9. Conclusion (12:5–13)

The test of Daniel and his friends

1 In the third year of the reign of Jehoiakim king of Judah [a]came Nebuchadnezzar king of Babylon *unto* Jerusalem, and besieged it.
2 And the Lord gave Jehoiakim king of Judah into his hand, with [a]part of the vessels of
the house of God: which he carried [b]*into* the
land of Shinar *to* the house of his god; [c]and he
brought the vessels *into* the treasure house of
his god.
3 ¶ And the king spake unto Ashpenaz the
master of his eunuchs, that *he* should bring
certain of the children of Israel, and of the
king's seed, and of the princes;
4 Children [a]in whom *was* no blemish, but
well favoured, and skilful in all wisdom, and
cunning in knowledge, and understanding science, and such as *had* ability in them to stand
in the king's palace, and [b]whom *they* might
teach the learning and the tongue of the
Chaldeans.
5 And the king appointed them a daily provision of the king's meat, and of [1]the wine
which he drank: so nourishing them three
years, that at the end thereof they might
[a]stand before the king.
6 Now among these were of the children of
Judah, Daniel, Hananiah, Mishael, and Azariah:
7 [a]Unto whom the prince of the eunuchs
gave names: [b]for he gave unto Daniel *the*
name of Belteshazzar; and to Hananiah, of
Shadrach; and to Mishael, of Meshach; and to
Azariah, of Abed-nego.
8 ¶ But Daniel purposed in his heart that he
would not defile himself [a]with the portion of
the king's meat, nor with the wine which he
drank: therefore he requested of the prince of
the eunuchs that he might not defile himself.
9 Now [a]God had brought Daniel into
favour and tender love with the prince of the
eunuchs.

1:1 [a]2 Ki. 24:1; 2 Chr. 36:6
1:2 [a]Jer. 27:19 [b]Gen. 10:10; Zech. 5:11 [c]2 Chr. 36:7
1:4 [a]See Lev. 24:19,20 [b]Acts 7:22
1:5 [1]Heb. *the wine of his drink* [a]ver. 19; Gen. 41:46; 1 Ki. 10:8
1:7 [a]Gen. 41:45; 2 Ki. 24:17 [b]ch. 4:8; 5:12
1:8 [a]Deut. 32:38; Ezek. 4:13; Hos. 9:3
1:9 [a]See Gen. 39:21; Ps. 106:46; Prov. 16:7
1:10 [1]Heb. *sadder* [2]Or, *term, or, continuance?*
1:11 [1]Or, *the steward*
1:12 [1]Heb. *of pulse* [2]Heb. *that we may eat, etc.*
1:17 [1]Or, *he made Daniel understand* [a]1 Ki. 3:12; Jas. 1:5,17 [b]Acts 7:22 [c]Num. 12:6; 2 Chr. 26:5; ch. 5:11,12,14; 10:1
1:19 [a]ver. 5; Gen. 41:46
1:20 [1]Heb. *wisdom of understanding* [a]1 Ki. 10:1

10 And the prince of the eunuchs said unto
Daniel, I fear my lord the king, who hath appointed your meat and your drink: for why
should he see your faces [1]worse liking than the
children which *are* of your [2]sort? then shall ye
make *me* endanger my head to the king.
11 Then said Daniel to [1]Melzar, whom the
prince of the eunuchs had set over Daniel,
Hananiah, Mishael, and Azariah,
12 Prove thy servants, I beseech thee, ten
days; and let them give us [1]pulse [2]to eat, and
water to drink.
13 Then let our countenances be looked
upon before thee, and the countenance of the
children that eat *of* the portion of the king's
meat: and as thou seest, deal with thy servants.
14 So he consented to them in this matter,
and proved them ten days.
15 And at the end of ten days their countenances appeared fairer and fatter in flesh than
all the children which did eat the portion of
the king's meat.
16 Thus Melzar took away the portion of
their meat, and the wine that they should
drink; and gave them pulse.
17 ¶ As for these four children, [a]God gave
them [b]knowledge and skill in all learning and
wisdom: and [1]Daniel had [c]understanding in
all visions and dreams.
18 Now at the end of the days that the king
had said *he* should bring them in, then the
prince of the eunuchs brought them in before
Nebuchadnezzar.
19 And the king communed with them;
and among them all was found none like Daniel, Hananiah, Mishael, and Azariah: therefore
[a]stood they before the king.
20 [a]And *in* all matters of [1]wisdom *and* understanding, that the king inquired of them,
he found them ten times better than all the
magicians *and* astrologers that *were* in all his
realm.

1:1 *third year.* According to the Babylonian system of computing the years of a king's reign, the third year of Jehoiakim would have been 605 B.C., since his first full year of kingship began on New Year's Day after his accession in 608. But according to the Judahite system, which counted the year of accession as the first year of reign, this was the fourth year of Jehoiakim (Jer 25:1; 46:2).

1:2 *carried into.* Judah was exiled to Babylonia because she disobeyed God's word regarding covenant-keeping, the sabbath years and idolatry (see Lev 25:1–7; 26:27–35; 2 Chr 36:14–21). The first deportation (605 B.C.) included Daniel, and the second (597) included Ezekiel. A third deportation took place in 586, when the Babylonians destroyed Jerusalem and the temple.

1:4 *learning and the tongue of the Chaldeans.* Including the classical literature in Sumerian and Akkadian cuneiform, a complicated syllabic writing system. But the language of normal communication in multiracial Babylon was Aramaic, written in an easily learned alphabetic script (see 2:4 and note).

1:6 *Daniel.* Means "God is (my) Judge." *Hananiah.* Means "The LORD shows grace." *Mishael.* Means "Who is what God is?" *Azariah.* Means "The LORD helps."

1:7 *Belteshazzar.* Probably means, in Babylonian, "Bel (i.e. Marduk), protect his life!" *Shadrach.* Probably means "command of Aku (Sumerian moon-god)." *Meshach.* Probably means "Who is what Aku is?" *Abed-nego.* Means "servant of Nego/Nebo (i.e. Nabu)."

1:8 *king's meat ... wine.* Israelites considered food from Nebuchadnezzar's table to be contaminated because the first portion of it was offered to idols. Likewise a portion of the wine was poured out on a pagan altar. Ceremonially unclean animals were used and were neither slaughtered nor prepared according to the regulations of the law. *he requested ... that he might not defile himself.* He demonstrated the courage of his convictions.

1:9 *God had brought Daniel into favour.* The careers of Joseph and Daniel were similar in many respects (see Gen 39–41).

1:12 *Prove thy servants.* Daniel used good judgment by offering an alternative instead of rebelling. *ten.* Often had the symbolic significance of completeness.

1:17 With God's help, Daniel and his friends mastered the Babylonian literature on astrology and divination by dreams. But in the crucial tests of interpretation and prediction (see 2:3–11; 4:7), all the pagan literature proved worthless. Only by God's special revelation (2:17–28) was Daniel able to interpret correctly.

1:20 *ten.* See note on v. 12. *magicians.* See note on Gen 41:8.

21 [a]And Daniel continued *even* unto the first year of king Cyrus.

Nebuchadnezzar's dream

2 And in the second year of the reign of Nebuchadnezzar, Nebuchadnezzar dreamed dreams, [a]wherewith his spirit was troubled, and [b]his sleep brake from him.

2 [a]Then the king commanded to call the magicians, and the astrologers, and the sorcerers, and the Chaldeans, for to shew the king his dreams. So they came and stood before the king.

3 And the king said unto them, I have dreamed a dream, and my spirit was troubled to know the dream.

4 Then spake the Chaldeans to the king in Syriack, [a]O king, live for ever: tell thy servants the dream, and we will shew the interpretation.

5 The king answered and said to the Chaldeans, The thing is gone from me: if ye will not make known unto me the dream, with the interpretation thereof, ye shall be [a][1]cut in pieces, and your houses shall be made a dunghill.

6 [a]But if ye shew the dream, and the interpretation thereof, ye shall receive of me gifts and [b][1]rewards and great honour: therefore shew me the dream, and the interpretation thereof.

7 They answered again and said, Let the king tell his servants the dream, and we will shew the interpretation of it.

8 The king answered and said, I know of certainty that ye would [1]gain the time, because ye see the thing is gone from me.

9 But if ye will not make known unto me the dream, *there is but* one decree for you: for ye have prepared lying and corrupt words to speak before me, till the time be changed: therefore tell me the dream, and I shall know that ye can shew me the interpretation thereof.

10 The Chaldeans answered before the king, and said, There is not a man upon the earth that can shew the king's matter: therefore *there is* no king, lord, nor ruler, *that* asked such things at any magician, or astrologer, or Chaldean.

11 And *it is* a rare thing that the king requireth, and there is none other that can shew it before the king, [a]except the gods, whose dwelling is not with flesh.

12 For this cause the king was angry and very furious, and commanded to destroy all the wise *men* of Babylon.

13 And the decree went forth that the wise *men* should be slain; and they sought Daniel and his fellows to be slain.

14 ¶ Then Daniel [1]answered with counsel and wisdom to Arioch the [2][3]captain of the king's guard, which was gone forth to slay the wise *men* of Babylon:

15 He answered and said to Arioch the king's captain, Why *is* the decree *so* hasty from the king? Then Arioch made the thing known to Daniel.

16 Then Daniel went in, and desired of the king that he would give him time, and that *he* would shew the king the interpretation.

17 Then Daniel went to his house, and made the thing known to Hananiah, Mishael, and Azariah, his companions:

18 [a]That *they* would desire mercies [1]of the God of heaven concerning this secret; [2]that Daniel and his fellows should not perish with the rest of the wise *men* of Babylon.

19 ¶ Then *was* the secret revealed unto Daniel [a]in a night vision. Then Daniel blessed the God of heaven.

20 Daniel answered and said,

[a]Blessed be the name of God for ever
and ever:
[b]For wisdom and might are his:

21 And he changeth [a]the times and the
seasons:
[b]He removeth kings, and setteth up
kings:
[c]He giveth wisdom unto the wise,
And knowledge to them that know
understanding:

22 [a]He revealeth the deep and secret
things:
[b]He knoweth what *is* in the darkness,
And [c]the light dwelleth with him.

23 I thank thee, and praise thee, O thou
God of my fathers,
Who hast given me wisdom and might,
And hast made known unto me now
what we [a]desired of thee:
For thou hast *now* made known unto
us the king's matter.

Daniel interprets the dream

24 ¶ Therefore Daniel went in unto Arioch, whom the king had ordained to destroy the

1:21 [a]ch. 6:28; 10:1
2:1 [a]Gen. 41:8; ch. 4:5 [b]Esth. 6:1; ch. 6:18
2:2 [a]Gen. 41:8; Ex. 7:11; ch. 5:7
2:4 [a]1 Ki. 1:31; ch. 3:9; 5:10; 6:6,21
2:5 [1]Chald. *made pieces* [a]2 Ki. 10:27; Ezra 6:11; ch. 3:29
2:6 [1]Or, *fee* [a]ch. 5:16 [b]ver. 48; ch. 5:17
2:8 [1]Chald. *buy*
2:11 [a]ch. 5:11
2:14 [1]Chald. *returned* [2]Or, *chief marshal* [3]Chald. *chief of the executioners,* or, *slaughtermen*
2:18 [1]Chald. *from before God* [2]Or, *that they should not destroy Daniel, etc.* [a]Mat. 18:19
2:19 [a]Num. 12:6; Job 33:15
2:20 [a]Ps. 113:2 [b]Jer. 32:19
2:21 [a]Esth. 1:13 [b]Job 12:18; Ps. 75:6,7; Jer. 27:5 [c]Jas. 1:5
2:22 [a]Job 12:22; Ps. 25:14 [b]Ps. 139:11; Heb. 4:13 [c]ch. 5:11,14
2:23 [a]ver. 18

1:21 *first year of king Cyrus.* Over Babylon (539 B.C.). Daniel was still living in the year 537 (10:1), so he saw the exiles return to Judah from Babylonian captivity.

2:1 *second year of . . . Nebuchadnezzar.* 604 B.C.

‡2:4 *Syriack.* Or "Aramaic." Since the astrologers were of various racial backgrounds, they communicated in Aramaic, the language everyone understood. From here to the end of ch. 7 the entire narrative is in Aramaic. These six chapters deal with matters of importance to the Gentile nations of the Near East and were written in a language understandable to all. But the last five chapters (8–12) revert to Hebrew, since they deal with special concerns of the chosen people.

2:11 *whose dwelling is not with flesh.* Who are not readily accessible.

2:14 *Arioch.* Meaning uncertain. It is also the name of a Mesopotamian king who lived centuries earlier (Gen 14:1,9).

2:18 *God of heaven.* See note on Ezra 1:2. *secret.* A key word in Daniel (2:19,27–30,47; 4:9). It also appears often in the writings (Dead Sea Scrolls) of the Qumran sect (see essay, p. 1344). The Greek equivalent is used in the NT to refer to the secret purposes of God that He reveals only to His chosen prophets and apostles (see note on Rom 11:25).

2:22 *light dwelleth with him.* See Ps 36:9.

wise *men* of Babylon: he went and said thus
unto him; Destroy not the wise *men* of Babylon: bring me in before the king, and I will
shew unto the king the interpretation.
25 Then Arioch brought in Daniel before
the king in haste, and said thus unto him, [1]I
have found a man of the [2]captives of Judah,
that will make known unto the king the interpretation.
26 The king answered and said to Daniel,
whose name *was* Belteshazzar, Art thou able
to make known unto me the dream which I
have seen, and the interpretation thereof?
27 Daniel answered in the presence of the
king, and said, The secret which the king hath
demanded cannot the wise *men,* the astrolo-
gians, the magicians, the soothsayers, shew
unto the king;
28 [a]But there is a God in heaven that revealeth secrets, and [1]maketh known to the
king Nebuchadnezzar [b]what shall be in the latter days. Thy dream, and the visions of thy
head upon thy bed, *are* these;
29 *As for* thee, O king, thy thoughts [1]came
into thy mind upon thy bed, what should come
to pass hereafter: [a]and he that revealeth secrets maketh known to thee what shall come
to pass.
30 [a]But *as for* me, this secret *is* not revealed to me for *any* wisdom that I have more
than any living, [1]but for *their* sakes that shall
make known the interpretation to the king,
[b]and *that* thou mightest know the thoughts of
thy heart.
31 ¶ Thou, O king, [1]sawest, and behold a
great image. This great image, whose brightness *was* excellent, stood before thee; and the
form thereof *was* terrible.
32 [a]This image's head *was* of fine gold, his
breast and his arms of silver, his belly and his
[1]thighs of brass,
33 His legs of iron, his feet part of iron and
part of clay.
34 Thou sawest till that a stone was cut out
[a][1]without hands, which smote the image
upon his feet *that were* of iron and clay, and
brake them in pieces.
35 Then was the iron, the clay, the brass,
the silver, and the gold, broken to pieces together, and became [a]like the chaff of the summer threshingfloors; and the wind carried
them away, that [b]no place was found for them:
and the stone that smote the image [c]became a
great mountain, [d]and filled the whole earth.
36 ¶ This *is* the dream; and we will tell the
interpretation thereof before the king.
37 [a]Thou, O king, *art* a king of kings: [b]for
the God of heaven hath given thee a kingdom,
power, and strength, and glory.
38 [a]And wheresoever the children of men
dwell, the beasts of the field and the fowls of
the heaven hath he given into thine hand, and
hath made thee ruler over them all. [b]Thou *art*
this head of gold.
39 And after thee shall arise [a]another kingdom [b]inferior to thee, and another third kingdom of brass, which shall bear rule over all the
earth.
40 And [a]the fourth kingdom shall be
strong as iron: forasmuch as iron breaketh in
pieces and subdueth all *things:* and as iron
that breaketh all these, shall it break in pieces
and bruise.
41 And whereas thou sawest the feet and
toes, part of potter's clay, and part of iron, the
kingdom shall be divided; but there shall be in
it of the strength of the iron, forasmuch as
thou sawest the iron mixed with miry clay.
42 And *as* the toes of the feet *were* part of
iron, and part of clay, *so* the kingdom shall be
partly strong, and partly [1]broken.
43 And whereas thou sawest iron mixt
with miry clay, they shall mingle themselves
with the seed of men: but they shall not cleave
[1]one to another, even as iron is not mixed
with clay.
44 And in [1]the days of these kings [a]shall
the God of heaven set up a kingdom, [b]which
shall never be destroyed: and the [2]kingdom
shall not be left to other people, [c]*but* it shall
break in pieces and consume all these kingdoms, and it shall stand for ever.
45 [a]Forasmuch as thou sawest that the
stone was cut out of the mountain [1]without
hands, and *that* it brake in pieces the iron, the
brass, the clay, the silver, and the gold; the
great God hath made known to the king what
shall come to pass [2]hereafter: and the dream *is*
certain, and the interpretation thereof sure.
46 ¶ [a]Then the king Nebuchadnezzar fell
upon his face, and worshipped Daniel, and
commanded that *they* should offer an oblation
[b]and sweet odours unto him.
47 The king answered unto Daniel, and
said, Of a truth *it is,* that your God *is* a God of
gods, and a Lord of kings, and a revealer of secrets, seeing thou couldest reveal this secret.
48 Then the king made Daniel a great man,

2:25 [1] Chald. *That I have found* [2] Chald. *children of the captivity of Judah*
2:28 [1] Chald. *hath made known* [a] Gen. 40:8; Amos 4:13 [b] Gen. 49:1
2:29 [1] Chald. *came up* [a] ver. 22,28
2:30 [1] [Or, *but for the intent that the interpretation may be made known to the king*] [a] Acts 3:12 [b] ver. 47
2:31 [1] Chald. *wast seeing*
2:32 [1] Or, *sides* [a] See ver. 38
2:34 [1] Or, *which* was *not in hands:* as ver. 45 [a] Zech. 4:6; 2 Cor. 5:1; Heb. 9:24
2:35 [a] Hos. 13:3 [b] Ps. 37:10,36 [c] Is. 2:2,3 [d] Ps. 80:9
2:37 [a] Ezra 7:12; Is. 47:5; Jer. 27:6,7; Ezek. 26:7; Hos. 8:10 [b] Ezra 1:2
2:38 [a] ch. 4:21,22; Jer. 27:6 [b] ver. 32
2:39 [a] ch. 5:28,31 [b] ver. 32
2:40 [a] ch. 7:7,23
2:42 [1] Or, *brittle*
2:43 [1] Chald. *this with this*
2:44 [1] Chald. *their days* [2] Chald. *kingdom thereof* [a] ver. 28 [b] ch. 4:3,34; 6:26; 7:14,27; Mic. 4:7; Luke 1:32,33 [c] Ps. 2:9; Is. 60:12; 1 Cor. 15:24
2:45 [1] Or, *which* was *not in hands* [2] Chald. *after this* [a] ver. 35; Is. 28:16
2:46 [a] See Acts 10:25; 14:13; 28:6 [b] Ezra 6:10

2:32–43 See map No. 7b and map No. 13 at the end of the study Bible. The gold head represents the Neo-Babylonian empire (v. 38; see Jer 51:7); the silver chest and arms, the Medo-Persian empire established by Cyrus in 539 B.C. (the date of the fall of Babylon); the bronze ("brass") belly and thighs, the Greek empire established by Alexander the Great c. 330; the iron legs and feet, the Roman empire. The toes (v. 41) are understood by some to represent a later confederation of states occupying the territory formerly controlled by the Roman empire. The diminishing value of the metals from gold to silver to bronze to iron represents the decreasing power and grandeur (v. 39) of the rulers of the successive empires, from the absolute despotism of Nebuchadnezzar to the democratic system of checks and balances that characterized the Roman senates and assemblies. The metals also symbolize a growing degree of toughness and endurance, with each successive empire lasting longer than the preceding one.

2:35 *broken to pieces.* See Mat 21:44.

‡2:44 The final kingdom is the eternal kingdom of God, built on the ruins of the sinful empires of man. Its authority will extend over "the whole earth" (v. 35) and ultimately over "a new heaven and a new earth" (Rev 21:1).

[a]and gave him many great gifts, and made him ruler over the whole province of Babylon, and [b]chief of the governors over all the wise *men* of Babylon.

49 Then Daniel requested of the king, [a]and he set Shadrach, Meshach, and Abed-nego, over the affairs of the province of Babylon: but Daniel [b]*sat* in the gate of the king.

The fiery furnace

3 Nebuchadnezzar the king made an image of gold, whose height *was* threescore cubits, *and* the breadth thereof six cubits: he set it up in the plain of Dura, in the province of Babylon.

2 Then Nebuchadnezzar the king sent to gather together the princes, the governors, and the captains, the judges, the treasurers, the counsellers, the sheriffs, and all the rulers of the provinces, to come to the dedication of the image which Nebuchadnezzar the king had set up.

3 Then the princes, the governors and captains, the judges, the treasurers, the counsellers, the sheriffs, and all the rulers of the provinces, were gathered together unto the dedication of the image that Nebuchadnezzar the king had set up; and they stood before the image that Nebuchadnezzar had set up.

4 Then a herald cried [1]aloud, To you [2]it is commanded, [a]O people, nations, and languages,

5 *That* at what time ye hear the sound of the cornet, flute, harp, sackbut, psaltery, [1][2]dulcimer, and all kinds of musick, ye fall down and worship the golden image that Nebuchadnezzar the king hath set up:

6 And whoso falleth not down and worshippeth shall the same hour [a]be cast into the midst of a burning fiery furnace.

7 Therefore at that time, when all the people heard the sound of the cornet, flute, harp, sackbut, psaltery, and all kinds of musick, all the people, the nations, and the languages, fell down *and* worshipped the golden image that Nebuchadnezzar the king had set up.

8 ¶ Wherefore at that time certain Chaldeans [a]came near, and accused the Jews.

9 They spake and said to the king Nebuchadnezzar, [a]O king, live for ever.

10 Thou, O king, hast made a decree, that every man that shall hear the sound of the cornet, flute, harp, sackbut, psaltery, and dulcimer, and all kinds of musick, shall fall down and worship the golden image:

11 And whoso falleth not down and worshippeth, *that* he should be cast into the midst of a burning fiery furnace.

12 [a]There are certain Jews whom thou hast set over the affairs of the province of Babylon, Shadrach, Meshach, and Abed-nego; these men, O king, [1]have not regarded thee: they serve not thy gods, nor worship the golden image which thou hast set up.

13 ¶ Then Nebuchadnezzar in *his* rage and fury commanded to bring Shadrach, Meshach, and Abed-nego. Then they brought these men before the king.

14 Nebuchadnezzar spake and said unto them, *Is it* [1]true, O Shadrach, Meshach, and Abed-nego, do not ye serve my gods, nor worship the golden image which I have set up?

15 Now if ye be ready that at what time ye hear the sound of the cornet, flute, harp, sackbut, psaltery, and dulcimer, and all kinds of musick, ye fall down and worship the image which I have made; [a]*well:* but if ye worship not, ye shall be cast the same hour into the midst of a burning fiery furnace; [b]and who *is* that God that shall deliver you out of my hands?

16 Shadrach, Meshach, and Abed-nego, answered and said to the king, O Nebuchadnezzar, [a]we *are* not careful to answer thee in this matter.

17 If it be *so,* our God whom we serve *is* able to deliver us from the burning fiery furnace, and he will deliver *us* out of thine hand, O king.

18 But if not, be it known unto thee, O king, that we will not serve thy gods, nor worship the golden image which thou hast set up.

19 ¶ Then was Nebuchadnezzar [1]full *of* fury, and the form of his visage was changed against Shadrach, Meshach, and Abed-nego: *therefore* he spake, and commanded that *they* should heat the furnace one seven *times* more than *it was* wont to be heat.

20 And he commanded the [1]most mighty men that *were* in his army to bind Shadrach, Meshach, and Abed-nego, *and* to cast *them* into the burning fiery furnace.

21 Then these men were bound in their

2:48 [a]ver. 6 [b]ch. 4:9; 5:11
2:49 [a]ch. 3:12 [b]Esth. 2:19,21; 3:2
3:4 [1]Chald. *with might* [2]Chald. *they command* [a]ch. 4:1; 6:25
3:5 [1]Or, *singing* [2]Chald. *symphony*
3:6 [a]Jer. 29:22; Rev. 13:15
3:8 [a]ch. 6:12
3:9 [a]ch. 2:4; 5:10; 6:6,21
3:12 [1]Chald. *have set no regard upon thee* [a]ch. 2:49
3:14 [1]Or, of *purpose,* as Ex. 21:13 (Heb.)
3:15 [a]As Ex. 32:32; Luke 13:9 [b]Ex. 5:2; 2 Ki. 18:35
3:16 [a]Mat. 10:19
3:19 [1]Chald. *filled*
3:20 [1]Chald. *mighty of strength*

2:48 Cf. the story of Joseph (Gen 41:41–43).

3:1 *image of gold.* Large statues of this kind were not made of solid gold but were plated with gold. *height was threescore cubits.* Ninety feet, including the lofty pedestal on which it no doubt stood. *Dura.* Either the name of a place now marked by a series of mounds (located a few miles south of Babylon) or a common noun meaning "walled enclosure."

3:2 The seven classifications of government officials were to pledge full allegiance to the newly established empire as they stood before the image. The image probably represented the god Nabu, whose name formed the first element in Nebuchadnezzar's name (in Akkadian *Nabu-kudurri-uṣur,* meaning "Nabu, protect my son!" or "Nabu, protect my boundary!").

‡3:5 The words for "harp," "psaltery" and "dulcimer" are the only Greek loanwords in Daniel. Greek musicians and instruments are mentioned in Assyrian inscriptions written before the time of Nebuchadnezzar.

3:12 *they serve not thy gods, nor worship the golden image.* They obeyed the word of God (Ex 20:3–5) above the word of the king.

3:17 See Heb 11:34.

3:18 *if not.* Whether God decides to rescue them (v. 17) or not, their faith is fully resigned to His will.

3:19 The temperature was controlled by the number of bellows forcing air into the fire chamber. Therefore sevenfold intensification was achieved by seven bellows pumping at the

[1]coats, their hosen, and their [2]hats, and their *other* garments, and were cast into the midst of the burning fiery furnace.

22 Therefore because the king's [1]commandment *was* urgent, and the furnace exceeding hot, the [2]flame of the fire slew those men that took up Shadrach, Meshach, and Abed-nego.

23 And these three men, Shadrach, Meshach, and Abed-nego, fell down bound into the midst of the burning fiery furnace.

24 ¶ Then Nebuchadnezzar the king was astonied, and rose up in haste, *and* spake, and said unto his [1]counsellers, Did not we cast three men bound into the midst of the fire? They answered and said unto the king, True, O king.

25 He answered and said, Lo, I see four men loose, [a]walking in the midst of the fire, and [1]they have no hurt; and the form of the fourth *is* like [b]the Son of God.

26 Then Nebuchadnezzar came near to the [1]mouth of the burning fiery furnace, *and* spake, and said, Shadrach, Meshach, and Abed-nego, ye servants of the most high God, come forth, and come *hither.* Then Shadrach, Meshach, and Abed-nego, came forth of the midst of the fire.

27 And the princes, governors, and captains, and the king's counsellers, being gathered together, saw these men, [a]upon whose bodies the fire had no power, nor was a hair of their head singed, neither were their coats changed, nor the smell of fire had passed on them.

28 *Then* Nebuchadnezzar spake, and said, Blessed *be* the God of Shadrach, Meshach, and Abed-nego, who hath sent his angel, and delivered his servants that [a]trusted in him, and have changed the king's word, and yielded their bodies, that they might not serve nor worship any god, except their own God.

29 [a]Therefore [1]I make a decree, That every people, nation, and language, which speak [2]any thing amiss against the God of Shadrach, Meshach, and Abed-nego, shall be [b][3]cut in pieces, and their houses shall be made a dunghill: [c]because there is no other God that can deliver after this sort.

30 Then the king [1]promoted Shadrach, Meshach, and Abed-nego, in the province of Babylon.

3:21 [1]Or, *mantles* [2]Or, *turbants*
3:22 [1]Chald. *word* [2]Or, *spark*
3:24 [1]Or, *governors*
3:25 [1]Chald. *there is no hurt in them* [a]Is. 43:2 [b]ver. 28; Job 1:6; 38:7; Ps. 34:7
3:26 [1]Chald. *door*
3:27 [a]Heb. 11:34
3:28 [a]Ps. 34:7,8; Jer. 17:7; ch. 6:22,23
3:29 [1]Chald. *a decree* is *made by me* [2]Chald. *error* [3]Chald. *made pieces* [a]ch. 6:26 [b]ch. 2:5 [c]ch. 6:27
3:30 [1]Chald. *made to prosper*

4:1 [a]ch. 3:4; 6:25
4:2 [1]Chald. *It was seemly before me* [a]ch. 3:26
4:3 [a]ch. 6:27 [b]ver. 34; ch. 2:44; 6:26
4:5 [a]ch. 2:28,29 [b]ch. 2:1
4:7 [a]ch. 2:2
4:8 [a]ch. 1:7 [b]ver. 18; Is. 63:11; ch. 2:11; 5:11,14
4:9 [a]ch. 2:48; 5:11
4:10 [1]Chald. *I was seeing* [a]ver. 20; Ezek. 31:3
4:12 [a]Ezek. 17:23; 31:6; See Lam. 4:20
4:13 [a]ver. 17,23 [b]Deut. 33:2; ch. 8:13; Zech. 14:5; Jude 14
4:14 [1]Chald. *with might* [a]Mat. 3:10 [b]Ezek. 31:12

The king's dream

4 Nebuchadnezzar the king, [a]unto all people, nations, and languages, that dwell in all the earth; Peace be multiplied unto you.

2 [1]I thought it good to shew the signs and wonders [a]that the high God hath wrought toward me.

3 [a]How great *are* his signs! and how mighty *are* his wonders! his kingdom *is* [b]an everlasting kingdom, and his dominion *is* from generation to generation.

4 ¶ I Nebuchadnezzar was at rest in mine house, and flourishing in my palace:

5 I saw a dream which made me afraid, [a]and the thoughts upon my bed and the visions of my head [b]troubled me.

6 Therefore made I a decree to bring in all the wise *men* of Babylon before me, that they might make known unto me the interpretation of the dream.

7 [a]Then came in the magicians, the astrologers, the Chaldeans, and the soothsayers: and I told the dream before them; but they *did* not make known unto me the interpretation thereof.

8 But at the last Daniel came in before me, [a]whose name *was* Belteshazzar, according to the name of my god, [b]and in whom *is* the spirit of the holy gods: and before him I told the dream, *saying,*

9 O Belteshazzar, [a]master of the magicians, because I know that the spirit of the holy gods *is* in thee, and no secret troubleth thee, tell *me* the visions of my dream that I have seen, and the interpretation thereof.

10 Thus *were* the visions of mine head in my bed; [1]I saw, and behold, [a]a tree in the midst of the earth, and the height thereof *was* great.

11 The tree grew, and was strong, and the height thereof reached unto heaven, and the sight thereof to the end of all the earth:

12 The leaves thereof *were* fair, and the fruit thereof much, and in it *was* meat for all: [a]the beasts of the field had shadow under it, and the fowls of the heaven dwelt in the boughs thereof, and all flesh was fed of it.

13 I saw in the visions of my head upon my bed, and behold, [a]a watcher and [b]a holy one came down from heaven;

14 He cried [1]aloud, and said thus, [a]Hew down the tree, and cut off his branches, shake off his leaves, and scatter his fruit: [b]let the beasts get away from under it, and the fowls from his branches:

same time. But the expression "seven times more than it was wont to be heat" may have been figurative for "as hot as possible" (seven signifies completeness).

3:25 See Ps 91:9–12. *the Son of God.* Nebuchadnezzar was speaking as a pagan polytheist and was content to conceive of the fourth figure as a lesser heavenly being (v. 28) sent by the all-powerful God of the Israelites.

3:29 See 2:5.

4:1–3 Nebuchadnezzar reached this conclusion after the experiences of vv. 4–37. The language of his confession may reflect Daniel's influence.

4:8 *according to the name of my god.* See note on 1:7. Bel ("lord") was a title for the god Marduk.

4:10 *tree.* Interpreted in v. 22.

4:11 *grew . . . strong.* In one of Nebuchadnezzar's building inscriptions, Babylon is compared to a spreading tree (cf. v. 22). *the height thereof reached unto heaven.* A phrase often used of Mesopotamian temple-towers (see note on Gen 11:4).

4:13 *watcher.* Or "messenger"; also in vv. 17,23.

15 Nevertheless leave the stump of his roots in the earth, even with a band of iron and brass, in the tender grass of the field; and let it be wet with the dew of heaven, and *let* his portion *be* with the beasts in the grass of the earth:

16 Let his heart be changed from man's, and let a beast's heart be given unto him; and let seven [a]times pass over him.

17 *This* matter *is* by the decree of the watchers, and the demand *by* the word of the holy ones: to the intent [a]that the living may know [b]that the most High ruleth in the kingdom of men, and giveth it to whomsoever he will, and setteth up over it the basest of men.

18 This dream I king Nebuchadnezzar have seen. Now thou, O Belteshazzar, declare the interpretation thereof, [a]forasmuch as all the wise *men* of my kingdom are not able to make known unto me the interpretation: but thou *art* able; [b]for the spirit of the holy gods *is* in thee.

The interpretation and warning

19 ¶ Then Daniel, [a]whose name *was* Belteshazzar, was astonied for one hour, and his thoughts troubled him. The king spake, and said, Belteshazzar, let not the dream, or the interpretation thereof, trouble thee. Belteshazzar answered and said, My lord, [b]the dream *be* to them that hate thee, and the interpretation thereof to thine enemies.

20 [a]The tree that thou sawest, which grew, and was strong, whose height reached unto the heaven, and the sight thereof to all the earth;

21 Whose leaves *were* fair, and the fruit thereof much, and in it *was* meat for all; under which the beasts of the field dwelt, and upon whose branches the fowls of the heaven had their habitation:

22 [a]It *is* thou, O king, that art grown and become strong: for thy greatness is grown, and reacheth unto heaven, [b]and thy dominion to the end of the earth.

23 [a]And whereas the king saw a watcher and a holy one coming down from heaven, and saying, Hew the tree down, and destroy it; yet leave the stump of the roots thereof in the earth, even with a band of iron and brass, in the tender grass of the field; and let it be wet with the dew of heaven, [b]and *let* his portion *be* with the beasts of the field, till seven times pass over him;

24 This *is* the interpretation, O king, and this *is* the decree of the most High, which is come upon my lord the king:

25 That they *shall* [a]drive thee from men, and thy dwelling shall be with the beasts of the field, and they shall make thee [b]to eat grass as oxen, and they *shall* wet thee with the dew of heaven, and seven times shall pass over thee, [c]till thou know that the most High ruleth in the kingdom of men, and [d]giveth it to whomsoever he will.

26 And whereas they commanded to leave the stump of the tree roots; thy kingdom *shall be* sure unto thee, after that thou shalt have known that the [a]heavens do rule.

27 Wherefore, O king, let my counsel be acceptable unto thee, and [a]break off thy sins by righteousness, and thine iniquities by shewing mercy to the poor; [b]if it may be [c][1]a lengthening of thy tranquillity.

The dream is fulfilled

28 ¶ All this came upon the king Nebuchadnezzar.

29 At the end of twelve months he walked [1]in the palace of the kingdom of Babylon.

30 The king [a]spake, and said, *Is* not this great Babylon, that I have built for the house of the kingdom by the might of my power, and for the honour of my majesty?

31 [a]While the word *was* in the king's mouth, there fell [b]a voice from heaven, *saying,* O king Nebuchadnezzar, to thee it is spoken; The kingdom is departed from thee.

32 And [a]they *shall* drive thee from men, and thy dwelling *shall be* with the beasts of the field: they shall make thee to eat grass as oxen, and seven times shall pass over thee, until thou know that the most High ruleth in the kingdom of men, and giveth it to whomsoever he will.

33 The same hour was the thing fulfilled upon Nebuchadnezzar: and he *was* driven from men, and did eat grass as oxen, and his body was wet with the dew of heaven, till his hairs were grown like eagles' *feathers,* and his nails like birds' *claws.*

34 And [a]at the end of the days I Nebuchadnezzar lift up mine eyes unto heaven, and mine understanding returned unto me, and I

4:16 [a]ch. 11:13; 12:7
4:17 [a]Ps. 9:16 [b]ver. 25,32; ch. 2:21; 5:21
4:18 [a]Gen. 41:8,15; ch. 5:8,15 [b]ver. 8
4:19 [a]ver. 8 [b]See 2 Sam. 18:32; Jer. 29:7
4:20 [a]ver. 10,11,12
4:22 [a]ch. 2:38 [b]Jer. 27:6-8
4:23 [a]ver. 13 [b]ch. 5:21
4:25 [a]ver. 32; ch. 5:21 [b]Ps. 106:20 [c]ver. 17,32; Ps. 83:18 [d]Jer. 27:5
4:26 [a]Mat. 21:25; Luke 15:18
4:27 [1]Or, *a healing of thine error* [a]1 Pet. 4:8 [b]Ps. 41:1 [c]1 Ki. 21:29
4:29 [1]Or, *upon*
4:30 [a]Prov. 16:18; ch. 5:20
4:31 [a]ch. 5:5; Luke 12:20 [b]ver. 24
4:32 [a]ver. 25
4:34 [a]ver. 26

4:15 *leave the stump.* Implies that the tree will be revived later (see v. 26).

4:16 *seven.* Signifies completeness. *times.* Or "years." The term referred to a given season of the year, and so to the year as a whole (see 7:25). For example, every recurrent spring meant that another full year had elapsed since the previous spring. Alternatively, the "times" can be indefinite.

4:17 *watchers.* The agents of God, who is the ultimate source (v. 24).

4:19 *Daniel . . . was astonied.* Possibly over how to state the interpretation in an appropriate way.

4:25 *till thou know that the most High ruleth in the kingdom of men.* He learned the lesson (compare v. 30 with v. 37).

4:26 *heavens.* A Jewish title for God, later reflected in the NT expression "kingdom of heaven" (compare Mat 5:3 with Luke 6:20).

4:28 *All this came upon.* But only because Nebuchadnezzar did not follow Daniel's advice.

4:30 *great Babylon.* Illustrated, e.g., in the city's ramparts, temples and hanging gardens (see note on Is 13:19).

4:31 *the word was in the king's mouth.* See Luke 12:19–20.

‡4:33 *was the thing fulfilled.* See Prov 16:18. *driven from men.* Possibly into the palace gardens. His counselors, perhaps led by Daniel (see 2:48–49), could have administered the kingdom efficiently.

blessed the most High, and I praised and honoured him [b]that liveth for ever, whose dominion *is* [c]an everlasting dominion, and his kingdom *is* from generation to generation:
35 And [a]all the inhabitants of the earth *are*
reputed as nothing: and [b]he doeth according
to his will in the army of heaven, and *among*
the inhabitants of the earth: and [c]none can
stay his hand, or say unto him, [d]What doest
thou?
36 At the same time my reason returned
unto me; [a]and for the glory of my kingdom,
mine honour and brightness returned unto me;
and my counsellers and my lords sought unto
me; and I was established in my kingdom, and
excellent majesty was [b]added unto me.
37 Now I Nebuchadnezzar praise and extol
and honour the King of heaven, [a]all whose
works *are* truth, and his ways judgment: [b]and
those that walk in pride he *is* able to abase.

4:34 [b]ch. 12:7; Rev. 4:10 [c]Ps. 10:16; ch. 2:44; Mic. 4:7; Luke 1:33
4:35 [a]Is. 40:15 [b]Ps. 115:3; 135:6 [c]Job 34:29 [d]Job 9:12; Is. 45:9; Rom. 9:20
4:36 [a]ver. 26 [b]Job 42:12; Prov. 22:4; Mat. 6:33
4:37 [a]Ps. 33:4; Rev. 15:3 [b]Ex. 18:11; ch. 5:20

5:1 [a]Esth. 1:3
5:2 [1][Or, *grandfather:* as Jer. 27:7; 2 Sam. 9:7; 2 Chr. 15:16; ver. 11,13] [2]Chald. *brought forth* [a]ch. 1:2; Jer. 52:19
5:4 [a]Rev. 9:20
5:5 [a]ch. 4:31

The handwriting on the wall

5 Belshazzar the king [a]made a great feast
to a thousand of his lords, and drank
wine before the thousand.
2 Belshazzar, whiles *he* tasted the wine,
commanded to bring the golden and silver vessels [a]which his [1]father Nebuchadnezzar had
[2]taken out of the temple which *was* in Jerusalem; that the king, and his princes, his wives,
and his concubines, might drink therein.
3 Then they brought the golden vessels
that were taken out of the temple of the house
of God which *was* at Jerusalem; and the king,
and his princes, his wives, and his concubines,
drank in them.
4 They drank wine, [a]and praised the gods
of gold, and of silver, of brass, of iron, of wood,
and of stone.
5 ¶ [a]In the same hour came forth fingers of
a man's hand, and wrote over against the can-

4:34 *whose dominion . . . from generation to generation.* See v. 3; 6:26; 7:14.
4:36 See Job 42:10,12.
4:37 *those that walk in pride he is able to abase.* See Prov 3:34; Jas 4:6,10; 1 Pet 5:5–6.
5:1–4 The orgy of revelry and blasphemy on such occasions is confirmed by the ancient Greek historians Herodotus and Xenophon.
5:1 *king.* Belshazzar (meaning "Bel, protect the king!") was the son and viceroy of Nabonidus. He is called the "son" of Nebuchadnezzar (v. 22), but the Aramaic term could also mean "grandson" or "descendant" or even "successor." Likewise, "father" could mean "ancestor" or "predecessor" (see vv. 2,11,13,18). See also note on v. 10.
5:5 *In the same hour.* See notes on 4:31; Prov 29:1; 1 Thes 5:3.

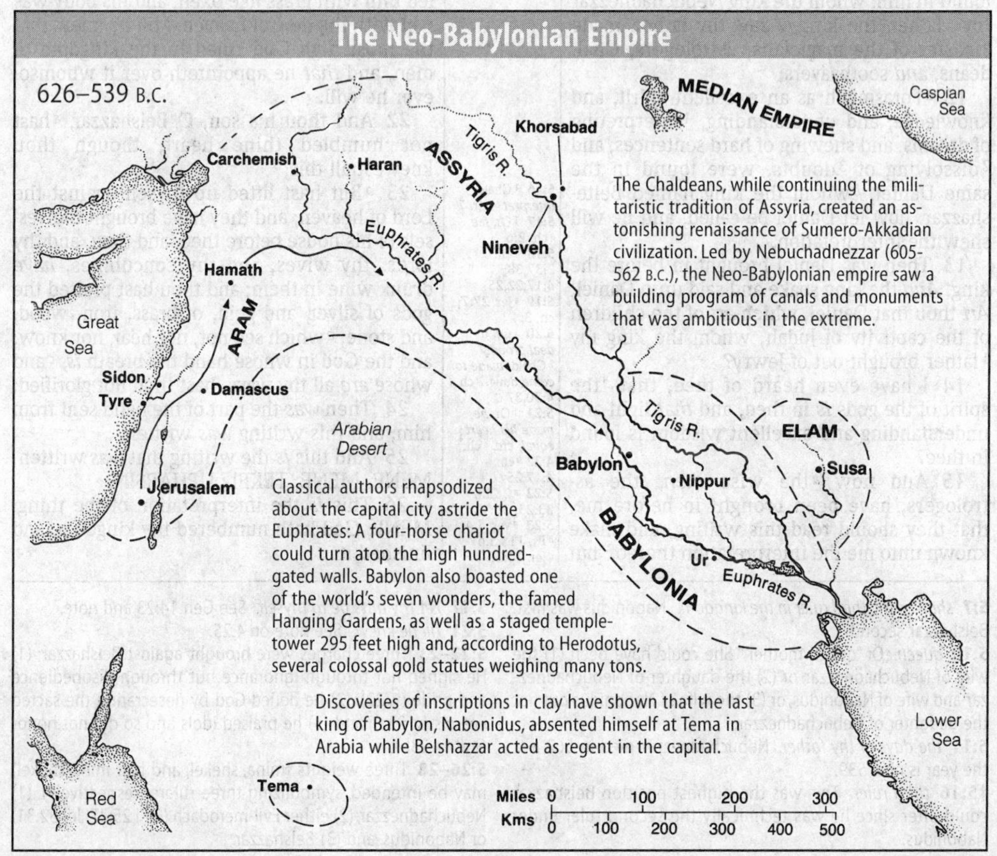

The Neo-Babylonian Empire
626–539 B.C.
MEDIAN EMPIRE
Caspian Sea
Khorsabad
Tigris R.
ASSYRIA
Carchemish
Haran
Euphrates R.
Nineveh
Hamath
ARAM
Great Sea
Sidon
Tyre
Damascus
Arabian Desert
Jerusalem
Tigris R.
ELAM
Babylon
Nippur
Susa
BABYLONIA
Ur
Euphrates R.
Tema
Red Sea
Lower Sea
Miles 0 100 200 300
Kms 0 100 200 300 400 500
The Chaldeans, while continuing the militaristic tradition of Assyria, created an astonishing renaissance of Sumero-Akkadian civilization. Led by Nebuchadnezzar (605-562 B.C.), the Neo-Babylonian empire saw a building program of canals and monuments that was ambitious in the extreme.
Classical authors rhapsodized about the capital city astride the Euphrates: A four-horse chariot could turn atop the high hundred-gated walls. Babylon also boasted one of the world's seven wonders, the famed Hanging Gardens, as well as a staged temple-tower 295 feet high and, according to Herodotus, several colossal gold statues weighing many tons.
Discoveries of inscriptions in clay have shown that the last king of Babylon, Nabonidus, absented himself at Tema in Arabia while Belshazzar acted as regent in the capital.

dlestick upon the plaister of the wall of the king's palace: and the king saw the part of the hand that wrote.

6 Then the king's [1]countenance [2]was changed, and his thoughts troubled him, so that the [a][3][4]joints of his loins were loosed, and his [b]knees smote one against another.

7 [a]The king cried [1]aloud to bring in [b]the astrologers, the Chaldeans, and the soothsayers. *And* the king spake, and said to the wise *men* of Babylon, Whosoever shall read this writing, and shew me the interpretation thereof, shall be clothed with [2]scarlet, and *have* a chain of gold about his neck, [c]and shall be the third ruler in the kingdom.

8 Then came in all the king's wise *men:* [a]but they could not read the writing, nor make known to the king the interpretation thereof.

9 Then *was* king Belshazzar greatly [a]troubled, and his [1]countenance *was* changed in him, and his lords *were* astonied.

10 ¶ *Now* the queen, by reason of the words of the king and his lords, came into the banquet house: *and* the queen spake and said, O king, live for ever: let not thy thoughts trouble thee, nor let thy countenance be changed.

11 [a]There is a man in thy kingdom, in whom *is* the spirit of the holy gods; and in the days of thy [1]father light and understanding and wisdom, like the wisdom of the gods, was found in him; whom the king Nebuchadnezzar thy [1]father, the king, *I say,* thy father, made [b]master of the magicians, astrologers, Chaldeans, *and* soothsayers;

12 [a]Forasmuch as an excellent spirit, and knowledge, and understanding, [1]interpreting of dreams, and shewing of hard sentences, and [2]dissolving of [3]doubts, were found in the same Daniel, [b]whom the king named Belteshazzar: now let Daniel be called, and he will shew the interpretation.

13 Then was Daniel brought in before the king. *And* the king spake and said unto Daniel, *Art* thou that Daniel, which *art* of the children of the captivity of Judah, whom the king my [1]father brought out of Jewry?

14 I have even heard of thee, that [a]the spirit of the gods *is* in thee, and *that* light and understanding and excellent wisdom is found in thee.

15 And now [a]the wise *men,* the astrologers, have been brought in before me, that they should read this writing, and make known unto me the interpretation thereof: but they could not shew the interpretation of the thing:

16 And I have heard of thee, that thou canst [1]make interpretations, and dissolve doubts: [a]now if thou canst read the writing, and make known to me the interpretation thereof, thou shalt be clothed with scarlet, and *have* a chain of gold about thy neck, and shalt be the third ruler in the kingdom.

17 Then Daniel answered and said before the king, Let thy gifts be to thyself, and give thy [a][1]rewards to another; yet I will read the writing unto the king, and make known to him the interpretation.

18 ¶ O thou king, [a]the most high God gave Nebuchadnezzar thy father a kingdom, and majesty, and glory, and honour:

19 And for the majesty that he gave him, [a]all people, nations, and languages, trembled and feared before him: whom he would he slew; and whom he would he kept alive; and whom he would he set up; and whom he would he put down.

20 [a]But when his heart was lifted up, and his mind hardened [1]in pride, he was [2]deposed from his kingly throne, and they took *his* glory from him:

21 And he *was* [a]driven from the sons of men; and [1]his heart was made like the beasts, and his dwelling *was* with the wild asses: they fed him with grass like oxen, and his body was wet with the dew of heaven; [b]till he knew that the most high God ruled in the kingdom of men, and *that* he appointeth over it whomsoever he will.

22 And thou his son, O Belshazzar, [a]hast not humbled thine heart, though thou knewest all this;

23 [a]But hast lifted up thyself against the Lord of heaven; and they have brought the vessels of his house before thee, and thou, and thy lords, thy wives, and thy concubines, *have* drunk wine in them; and thou hast praised the gods of silver, and gold, of brass, iron, wood, and stone, [b]which see not, nor hear, nor know: and the God in whose hand thy breath *is,* [c]and whose *are* all thy ways, hast thou not glorified:

24 Then *was* the part of the hand sent from him; and this writing *was* written.

25 And this *is* the writing that *was* written, MENE, MENE, TEKEL, UPHARSIN.

26 This *is* the interpretation of the thing: MENE; God hath numbered thy kingdom, and finished it.

5:6 [1]Chald. *brightnessess* [2]Chald. *changed it* [3]Or, *girdles* [4]Chald. *bindings,* or, *knots* [a]Is. 5:27 [b]Nah. 2:10
5:7 [1]Chald. *with might* [2]Or, *purple* [a]ch. 4:6 [b]Is. 47:13 [c]ch. 6:2
5:8 [a]ch. 2:27
5:9 [1]Chald. *brightnesses* [a]ch. 2:1
5:11 [1]Or, *grandfather* [a]ch. 2:48; 4:8,9,18 [b]ch. 4:9
5:12 [1]Or, of *an interpreter, etc.* [2]Or, of *a dissolver* [3]Chald. *knots* [a]ch. 6:3 [b]ch. 1:7
5:13 [1]Or, *grandfather*
5:14 [a]ver. 11,12
5:15 [a]ver. 7,8
5:16 [1]Chald. *interpret* [a]ver. 7
5:17 [1]Or, *fee* [a]ch. 2:6
5:18 [a]ch. 2:37,38; 4:17,22,25
5:19 [a]Jer. 27:7; ch. 3:4
5:20 [1]Or, *to deal proudly* [2]Chald. *made to come down* [a]ch. 4:30,37
5:21 [1]Or, *he made his heart equal, etc.* [a]ch. 4:32 [b]ch. 4:17,25
5:22 [a]2 Chr. 33:23; 36:12
5:23 [a]ver. 3,4 [b]Ps. 115:5,6 [c]Jer. 10:23

5:7 *shall be the third ruler in the kingdom.* Nabonidus was first, Belshazzar second.

5:10 *queen.* Or "queen mother." She could have been (1) the wife of Nebuchadnezzar, or (2) the daughter of Nebuchadnezzar and wife of Nabonidus, or (3) the wife of Nabonidus but not the daughter of Nebuchadnezzar.

5:11 *the days of thy father.* Nebuchadnezzar died in 562 B.C.; the year is now 539.

‡5:16 *third ruler.* This was the highest position Belshazzar could offer since he was technically the second ruler under Nabonidus.

5:17 *Let thy gifts be to thyself.* See Gen 14:23 and note.

5:21 *till he knew.* See note on 4:25.

5:22–23 Three charges were brought against Belshazzar: (1) He sinned not through ignorance but through disobedience and pride (v. 22); (2) he defied God by desecrating the sacred vessels (v. 23a); and (3) he praised idols and so did not honor God (v. 23b).

5:26–28 Three weights (mina, shekel, and half mina/shekel) may be intended, symbolizing three rulers (respectively): (1) Nebuchadnezzar, (2) either Evil-merodach (2 Ki 25:27; Jer 52:31) or Nabonidus, and (3) Belshazzar.

27 TEKEL; [a]Thou art weighed in the balances, and art found wanting.

28 PERES; Thy kingdom is divided, and given to the [a]Medes and [b]Persians.

29 ¶ Then commanded Belshazzar, and they clothed Daniel with scarlet, and *put* a chain of gold about his neck, and made a proclamation concerning him, [a]that *he* should be the third ruler in the kingdom.

30 [a]In that night *was* Belshazzar the king of the Chaldeans slain.

31 [a]And Darius the Median took the kingdom, [1]*being* [2]about threescore and two year old.

Daniel in the den of lions

6 It pleased Darius to set over the kingdom an hundred and twenty princes, which should be over the whole kingdom;

2 And over these three presidents; of whom Daniel *was* first: that the princes might give accounts unto them, and the king should have no damage.

3 Then this Daniel was preferred above the presidents and princes, [a]because an excellent spirit *was* in him; and the king thought to set him over the whole realm.

4 ¶ [a]Then the presidents and princes sought to find occasion against Daniel concerning the kingdom; but they could find none occasion nor fault; forasmuch as he *was* faithful, neither was there any error or fault found in him.

5 Then said these men, We shall not find any occasion against this Daniel, except we find *it* against him concerning the law of his God.

6 Then these presidents and princes [1]assembled *together* to the king, and said thus unto him, [a]King Darius, live for ever.

7 All the presidents of the kingdom, the governors, and the princes, the counsellers and the captains, have consulted together to establish a royal statute, and to make a firm [1]decree, that whosoever shall ask a petition of any God or man for thirty days, save of thee, O king, he shall be cast into the den of lions.

8 Now, O king, establish the decree, and sign the writing, that *it* be not changed, according to the [a]law of the Medes and Persians, which [1]altereth not.

9 Wherefore king Darius signed the writing and the decree.

10 ¶ Now when Daniel knew that the writing *was* signed, he went into his house; and his windows being open in his chamber [a]toward Jerusalem, he kneeled upon his knees [b]three times a day, and prayed, and gave thanks before his God, as he did aforetime.

11 Then these men assembled, and found Daniel praying and making supplication before his God.

12 [a]Then they came near, and spake before the king concerning the king's decree; Hast thou not signed a decree, that every man that shall ask *a petition* of any God or man within thirty days, save of thee, O king, shall be cast into the den of lions? The king answered and said, The thing *is* true, [b]according to the law of the Medes and Persians, which altereth not.

13 Then answered they and said before the king, *That* Daniel, [a]which *is* of the children of the captivity of Judah, [b]regardeth not thee, O king, nor the decree that thou hast signed, but maketh his petition three times a day.

14 Then the king, when he heard *these* words, [a]was sore displeased with himself, and set *his* heart on Daniel to deliver him: and he laboured till the going down of the sun to deliver him.

15 Then these men assembled unto the king, and said unto the king, Know, O king, that [a]the law of the Medes and Persians *is*, That no decree nor statute which the king establisheth may be changed.

16 Then the king commanded, and they brought Daniel, and cast *him* into the den of lions. *Now* the king spake and said unto Daniel, Thy God whom thou servest continually, he will deliver thee.

17 [a]And a stone was brought, and laid upon the mouth of the den; [b]and the king sealed it with his own signet, and with the signet of his lords; that the purpose might not be changed concerning Daniel.

18 ¶ Then the king went to his palace, and passed the night fasting: neither were [1]instruments of musick brought before him: [a]and his sleep went from him.

19 Then the king arose very early in the morning, and went in haste unto the den of lions.

20 And when he came to the den, he cried with a lamentable voice unto Daniel: *and* the king spake and said to Daniel, O Daniel, servant of the living God, [a]is thy God, whom thou servest continually, able to deliver thee from the lions?

5:27 [a]Job 31:6; Ps. 62:9; Jer. 6:30
5:28 [a]Foretold Is. 21:2; ver. 31; ch. 9:1 [b]ch. 6:28
5:29 [a]ver. 7
5:30 [a]Jer. 51:31,39,57
5:31 [1]Chald. he *as the son of, etc.* [2]Or, *now* [a]ch. 9:1
6:3 [a]ch. 5:12
6:4 [a]Eccl. 4:4
6:6 [1]Or, *came tumultuously* [a]ver. 21; Neh. 2:3; ch. 2:4
6:7 [1]Or, *interdict*
6:8 [1]Chald. *passeth not* [a]ver. 12,15; Esth. 1:19; 8:8
6:10 [a]1 Ki. 8:44,48; Ps. 5:7; Jonah 2:4 [b]Ps. 55:17; Acts 2:1,2,15; 3:1; 10:9
6:12 [a]ch. 3:8 [b]ver. 8
6:13 [a]ch. 1:6; 5:13 [b]ch. 3:12
6:14 [a]Mark 6:26
6:15 [a]ver. 8
6:17 [a]Lam. 3:53 [b]Mat. 27:66
6:18 [1]Or, *table* [a]ch. 2:1
6:20 [a]ch. 3:15

5:27 *weighed in the balances.* Measured in the light of God's standards (cf. Job 31:6; Ps 62:9; Prov 24:12).

5:28 *Medes and Persians.* The second kingdom of the series of four predicted in ch. 2 (see Introduction: Author, Date and Authenticity).

5:30 *In that night.* See Luke 12:20.

5:31 *Darius the Median.* Perhaps another name for Gubaru, referred to in Babylonian inscriptions as the governor that Cyrus put in charge of the newly conquered Babylonian territories. Or "Darius the Median" may have been Cyrus's throne name in Babylon (see 6:28, which can be read, "in the reign of Darius, that is, the reign of Cyrus the Persian"; see also 1 Chr 5:26 for a similar phenomenon). *took the kingdom.* The head of gold is now no more, as predicted in 2:39.

6:7 The conspirators lied in stating that "all" the royal administrators supported the proposed decree, since they knew that Daniel (totally unaware of the proposal) was the foremost of the three administrators.

6:8,12 *it be not changed.* See notes on Esth 1:19; 8:8.

6:10 *toward Jerusalem.* See 2 Chr 6:38–39. *three times a day.* See Ps 55:17.

6:16 *thou servest continually.* See 1 Cor 15:58.

21 Then said Daniel unto the king, [a]O king, live for ever.

22 [a]My God hath sent his angel, and hath [b]shut the lions' mouths, that they have not hurt me: forasmuch as before him innocency was found in me; and also before thee, O king, have I done no hurt.

23 Then was the king exceeding glad for him, and commanded that *they* should take Daniel up out of the den. So Daniel was taken up out of the den, and no manner of hurt was found upon him, [a]because he believed in his God.

24 And the king commanded, [a]and they brought those men which had accused Daniel, and they cast *them* into the den of lions, them, [b]their children, and their wives; and the lions had the mastery of them, and brake all their bones in pieces or ever they came at the bottom of the den.

25 ¶ [a]Then king Darius wrote unto all people, nations, and languages, that dwell in all the earth; Peace be multiplied unto you.

26 [a]I make a decree, That in every dominion of my kingdom *men* [b]tremble and fear before the God of Daniel: [c]for he *is* the living God, and stedfast for ever, and his kingdom *that* which shall not be [d]destroyed, and his dominion *shall be even* unto the end.

27 He delivereth and rescueth, [a]and he worketh signs and wonders in heaven and in earth, who hath delivered Daniel from the [1]power of the lions.

28 So this Daniel prospered in the reign of Darius, [a]and in the reign of [b]Cyrus the Persian.

Daniel's dream of four beasts

7 In the first year of Belshazzar king of Babylon [a]Daniel [1]had a dream and [b]visions of his head upon his bed: then he wrote the dream, *and* told the sum of the [2]matters.

2 Daniel spake and said, I saw in my vision by night, and behold, the four winds of the heaven strove upon the great sea.

3 And four great beasts [a]came up from the sea, diverse one from another.

4 The first *was* [a]like a lion, and had eagle's wings: I beheld till the wings thereof were pluckt, [1]and it was lifted up from the earth, and made stand upon the feet as a man, and a man's heart was given to it.

5 [a]And behold, another beast, a second, like to a bear, and [1]it raised up itself on one side, and *it had* three ribs in the mouth of it between the teeth of it: and they said thus unto it, Arise, devour much flesh.

6 After this I beheld, and lo another, like a leopard, which had upon the back of it four wings of a fowl; the beast had also [a]four heads; and dominion *was* given to it.

7 After this I saw in the night visions, and behold, [a]a fourth beast, dreadful and terrible, and strong exceedingly; and it had great iron teeth: it devoured and brake in pieces, and stamped the residue with the feet of it: and it *was* diverse from all the beasts that *were* before it; [b]and it had ten horns.

8 I considered the horns, and behold, [a]there came up among them another little horn, before whom there were three of the first horns pluckt up by the roots: and behold, in this horn *were* eyes like the eyes [b]of man, [c]and a mouth speaking great *things.*

9 ¶ [a]I beheld till the thrones were cast *down,* and [b]the Ancient of days did sit, [c]whose garment *was* white as snow, and the hair of his head like the pure wool: his throne *was like* the fiery flame, [d]*and* his wheels *as* burning fire.

10 [a]A fiery stream issued and came forth from before him: [b]thousand thousands ministered unto him, and ten thousand times ten thousand stood before him: [c]the judgment was set, and the books were opened.

11 I beheld then because of the voice of the great words which the horn spake: [a]I beheld *even* till the beast *was* slain, and his body destroyed, and given to the burning flame.

12 As concerning the rest of the beasts, they had their dominion taken away: yet [1]their lives were prolonged for a season and time.

13 I saw in the night visions, and behold,

6:21 [a]ch. 2:4
6:22 [a]ch. 3:28 [b]Heb. 11:33
6:23 [a]Heb. 11:33
6:24 [a]Deut. 19:19 [b]Esth. 9:10; See Deut. 24:16; 2 Ki. 14:6
6:25 [a]ch. 4:1
6:26 [a]ch. 3:29 [b]Ps. 99:1 [c]ch. 4:34 [d]ch. 2:44; 4:3,34; Luke 1:33
6:27 [1]Chald. *hand* [a]ch. 4:3
6:28 [a]ch. 1:21 [b]Ezra 1:1,2
7:1 [1]Chald. *saw* [2]Or, *words* [a]Num. 12:6; Amos 3:7 [b]ch. 2:28
7:3 [a]Rev. 13:1
7:4 [1]Or, *wherewith* [a]Deut. 28:49; 2 Sam. 1:23; Jer. 48:40; Ezek. 17:3; Hab. 1:8
7:5 [1]Or, *it raised up one dominion* [a]ch. 2:39
7:6 [a]ch. 8:8,22
7:7 [a]ch. 2:40 [b]ch. 2:41; Rev. 13:1
7:8 [a]ch. 8:9 [b]Rev. 9:7 [c]Ps. 12:3; Rev. 13:5
7:9 [a]Rev. 20:4 [b]Ps. 90:2 [c]Ps. 104:2; Rev. 1:14 [d]Ezek. 1:15
7:10 [a]Ps. 50:3; Is. 30:33; 66:15 [b]1 Ki. 22:19; Ps. 68:17; Rev. 5:11 [c]Rev. 20:4
7:11 [a]Rev. 19:20
7:12 [1]Chald. *a prolonging in life was given them*

6:23 *he . . . believed in his God.* That the lions were ravenously hungry (v. 24) was no obstacle to the Lord's rewarding Daniel's faith by saving his life.

6:24 *them, their children, and their wives.* In accordance with Persian custom.

7:1 *first year of Belshazzar.* Probably 553 B.C. The events of ch. 7 preceded those of ch. 5.

7:2 *the great sea.* The world of nations and peoples (see also vv. 3,17).

7:3 *beasts.* The insignia or symbols of many Gentile nations were beasts (or birds) of prey (see v. 17).

7:4–7 The lion with an eagle's wings is a cherub (see note on Gen 3:24), symbolizing the Neo-Babylonian empire. The rest of v. 4 perhaps reflects the humbling experience of Nebuchadnezzar, as recorded in ch. 4. The bear (v. 5), raised up on one of its sides, refers to the superior status of the Persians in the Medo-Persian federation. The three ribs may represent the three principal conquests: Lydia (546 B.C.), Babylon (539) and Egypt (525). The leopard with four wings (v. 6) represents the speedy conquests of Alexander the Great (334–330), and the four heads correspond to the four main divisions into which his empire fell after his untimely death in 323 (see 8:22): Macedon and Greece (under Antipater and Cassander), Thrace and Asia Minor (under Lysimachus), Syria (under Seleucus I), the Holy Land and Egypt (under Ptolemy I). The fourth, unnamed, beast (v. 7), with its irresistible power and surpassing all its predecessors, points to the Roman empire. Its ten horns correspond to the ten toes of 2:41–42.

7:7 *ten horns.* Indicative of the comprehensiveness of the beast's sphere of authority (see note on 1:12).

7:8 *another little horn.* The antichrist, or a world power sharing in the characteristics of the antichrist. *mouth speaking great things.* See 11:36; 2 Thes 2:4; Rev 13:5–6.

7:9 *Ancient of days.* God. *throne . . . wheels.* See Ezek 1:15–21, 26–27.

7:10 *thousands . . . ten thousand times ten thousand.* See 1 Sam 18:7 and note.

‡7:13 *like the Son of man.* See Rev 1:13. This is the first refer-

[a]*one* like the Son of man came with the clouds
of heaven, and came to the Ancient of days,
and they brought him near before him.
14 [a]And there *was* given him dominion,
and glory, and a kingdom, that all [b]people, nations, and languages, should serve him: his dominion *is* [c]an everlasting dominion, which
shall not pass away, and his kingdom *that*
which shall not be destroyed.

The dream explained

15 ¶ I Daniel was grieved in my spirit in
the midst of *my* [1]body, and the visions of my
head troubled me.
16 I came near unto one of them that stood
by, and asked him the truth of all this. So he
told me, and made me know the interpretation
of the things.
17 ¶ These great beasts, which *are* four, *are*
four kings, *which* shall arise out of the earth.
18 But [a]the saints of the [1]most High shall
take the kingdom, and possess the kingdom
for ever, even for ever and ever.
19 Then I would know the truth of the
fourth beast, which was diverse [1]from all the
others, exceeding dreadful, whose teeth *were*
of iron, and his nails *of* brass; *which* devoured,
brake in pieces, and stamped the residue with
his feet;
20 And of the ten horns that *were* in his
head, and *of* the other which came up, and before whom three fell; even *of* that horn that
had eyes, and a mouth that spake very great
things, whose look *was* more stout than his
fellows.
21 I beheld, [a]and the same horn made war
with the saints, and prevailed against them;
22 Until the Ancient of days came, [a]and
judgment *was* given to the saints of the most
High; and the time came that the saints possessed the kingdom.
23 Thus he said, The fourth beast shall be
[a]the fourth kingdom upon earth, which shall
be diverse from all kingdoms, and shall devour
the whole earth, and shall tread it down, and
break it in pieces.
24 [a]And the ten horns out of this kingdom
are ten kings *that* shall arise: and another shall
rise after them; and he shall be diverse from
the first, and he shall subdue three kings.
25 [a]And he shall speak *great* words against
the most High, and shall [b]wear out the saints
of the most High, and [c]think to change times
and laws: and [d]they shall be given into his
hand [e]until a time and times and the dividing
of time.
26 [a]But the judgment shall sit, and they
shall take away his dominion, to consume and
to destroy *it* unto the end.
27 And the [a]kingdom and dominion, and
the greatness of the kingdom under the whole
heaven, *shall be* given to the people of the
saints of the most High, [b]whose kingdom *is* an
everlasting kingdom, [c]and all [1]dominions
shall serve and obey him.
28 Hitherto *is* the end of the matter. *As for*
me Daniel, [a]my cogitations much troubled me,
and my countenance changed in me: but I
[b]kept the matter in my heart.

Vision of the ram, goat and horn

8 In the third year of the reign of king Belshazzar a vision appeared unto me, *even*
unto me Daniel, after that which appeared
unto me [a]at the first.
2 And I saw in a vision; and it came to pass,
when I saw, that I *was* at [a]Shushan *in* the
palace, which *is* in the province of Elam; and I
saw in a vision, and I was by the river of Ulai.
3 Then I lifted up mine eyes, and saw, and
behold, there stood before the river a ram
which had two horns: and the two horns *were*
high; but one *was* higher than [1]the other, and
the higher came up last.
4 I saw the ram pushing westward, and
northward, and southward; so that no beasts
might stand before him, neither *was there any*
that could deliver out of his hand; [a]but he did
according to his will, and became great.
5 And as I was considering, behold, a he
goat came from the west on the face of the
whole earth, and [1]touched not the ground:
and the goat *had* [2]a notable horn between his
eyes.
6 And he came to the ram that had two
horns, which I had seen standing before the
river, and ran unto him in the fury of his power.
7 And I saw him come close unto the ram,
and he was moved with choler against him,
and smote the ram, and brake his two horns:
and there was no power in the ram to stand
before him, but he cast him down to the

7:13 [a]Ezek. 1:26; Mat. 24:30; Rev. 1:7
7:14 [a]Ps. 2:6-8; Mat. 28:18; John 3:35; 1 Cor. 15:27; Eph. 1:22 [b]ch. 3:4 [c]Ps. 145:13; Mic. 4:7; Luke 1:33; John 12:34; Heb. 12:28
7:15 [1]Chald. *sheath*
7:18 [1]Chald. *high ones,* that is *things,* or, *places* [a]Is. 60:12; 2 Tim. 2:11; Rev. 2:26
7:19 [1]Chald. *from all those*
7:21 [a]Rev. 17:14
7:22 [a]Rev. 1:6
7:23 [a]ch. 2:40
7:24 [a]Rev. 17:12
7:25 [a]Is. 37:23
7:25 [b]Rev. 17:6 [c]ch. 2:21 [d]Rev. 13:7 [e]Rev. 12:14
7:26 [a]ver. 10,22
7:27 [1]Or, *rulers* [a]ver. 14,18 [b]Luke 1:33; John 12:34; Rev. 11:15 [c]Is. 60:12
7:28 [a]ch. 8:27 [b]Luke 2:19
8:1 [a]ch. 7:1
8:2 [a]Esth. 1:2
8:3 [1]Heb. *the second*
8:4 [a]ch. 5:19
8:5 [1]Or, *none touched him in the earth* [2]Heb. *a horn of sight*

ence to the Messiah as the Son of Man, a title that Jesus applied to Himself. He will be enthroned as ruler over the whole earth (previously misruled by the four kingdoms of men), and His kingdom "shall not be destroyed" (v. 14), whether on earth or in heaven. *came with the clouds of heaven.* See Mark 14:62; Rev 1:7.

7:16 *one of them . . . stood by.* An angel.

7:18 *saints.* Exalted privileges will be enjoyed by Christ's followers during the Messianic kingdom age (Mat 19:28–29; Luke 22:29–30). See also Rev 1:6; 20:4–6.

7:24 *ten kings.* All the political powers (see note on 1:12) that will arise out of the fourth kingdom—not necessarily simultaneously (but see 2:44). *three kings.* Some of the ten. Three often signified a small, indefinite number.

7:25 *he.* See note on v. 8. *a time and times and the dividing of time.* Or "a year, two years, and half a year."

7:27 *given to . . . the saints.* For their benefit. God and the Messiah will rule (see Rev 19–22).

8:1–12:13 These chapters are written in Hebrew (see note on 2:4).

8:1 *third year.* About 551 B.C. The events of ch. 8 preceded those of ch. 5.

8:3 *ram.* The ram represents the Medo-Persian empire (v. 20). The longer of his two horns reflects the predominant position of Persia.

8:5 *goat.* The rapidly charging goat is Greece, and the prominent horn is Alexander the Great, "the first king" (v. 21).

8:7 *brake his two horns.* Greece crushes Medo-Persia.

ground, and stamped upon him: and there was none that could deliver the ram out of his hand.

8 Therefore the he goat waxed very great: and when he was strong, the great horn was broken; and for it came up [a]four notable ones toward the four winds of heaven.

9 [a]And out of one of them came forth a little horn, which waxed exceeding great, [b]toward the south, and toward the east, and toward the [c]pleasant *land.*

10 [a]And it waxed great, *even* [1]to [b]the host of heaven; and [c]it cast down *some* of the host and of the stars to the ground, and stamped upon them.

11 Yea, [a]he magnified *himself even* [1]to [b]the prince of the host, [c]and [2]by him [d]the daily *sacrifice* was taken away, and the place of his sanctuary was cast down.

12 And [a] [1]a host was given *him* against the daily *sacrifice* by reason of transgression, and it cast down [b]the truth to the ground; and it [c]practised, and prospered.

13 Then I heard [a]one saint speaking, and another saint said unto [1][2]that certain *saint* which spake, How long *shall be* the vision *concerning* the daily *sacrifice,* and the transgression [b][3]of desolation, to give both the sanctuary and the host to be trodden under foot?

14 And he said unto me, Unto two thousand and three hundred [1]days; then shall the sanctuary be [2]cleansed.

8:8 [a]ver. 22
8:9 [a]ch. 11:21 [b]ch. 11:25 [c]Ps. 48:2
8:10 [1]Or, *against the host* [a]ch. 11:28 [b]Is. 14:13 [c]Rev. 12:4
8:11 [1]Or, *against* [2]Or, *from him* [a]ch. 11:36 [b]Josh. 5:14 [c]ch. 11:31 [d]Ex. 29:38
8:12 [1]Or, *the host was given over for the transgression against the daily* sacrifice [a]ch. 11:31 [b]Ps. 119:43; Is. 59:14 [c]ver. 4
8:13 [1][Or,] *the numberer of secrets,* or, *the wonderful numberer* [2]Heb. *Palmoni* [3]Or, *making desolate* [a]ch. 4:13; 1 Pet. 1:12 [b]ch. 11:31
8:14 [1]Heb. *evening morning* [2]Heb. *justified*

8:8 *the great horn was broken.* The death of Alexander the Great at the height of his power (323 B.C.). *four notable ones.* See note on 7:4–7 ("four heads").

‡8:9–12 *little horn.* Another horn emerges (v. 9) not from the ten horns belonging to the fourth kingdom (as in 7:8), but rather from one of the four horns belonging to the third kingdom. This "little horn" is Antiochus IV Epiphanes, who during the last few years of his reign (168–164 B.C.) made a determined effort to destroy the Jewish faith. He in turn served as a type of the even more ruthless beast of the last days, who is also referred to in 7:8 as "another little horn." Antiochus was to extend his power over Israel, "the pleasant land" (v. 9; see Jer 3:19), and defeat the godly believers there (referred to as "the host of heaven," v. 10; see also v. 12), many of whom died for their faith. Then he set himself up to be the equal of God ("the prince of the host," v. 11) and ordered the daily sacrifices to end. Eventually the army of Judas Maccabeus recaptured Jerusalem and rededicated the temple (v. 14) to the Lord (December, 165)—the origin of the Feast of Hanukkah (see John 10:22 and note), still celebrated by Jews today (in the Apocrypha see 1 Maccabees 1–4).

8:13 *one saint.* An angel.

8:14 There were two daily sacrifices for the continual burnt offering (9:21; Ex 29:38–42), representing the atonement required

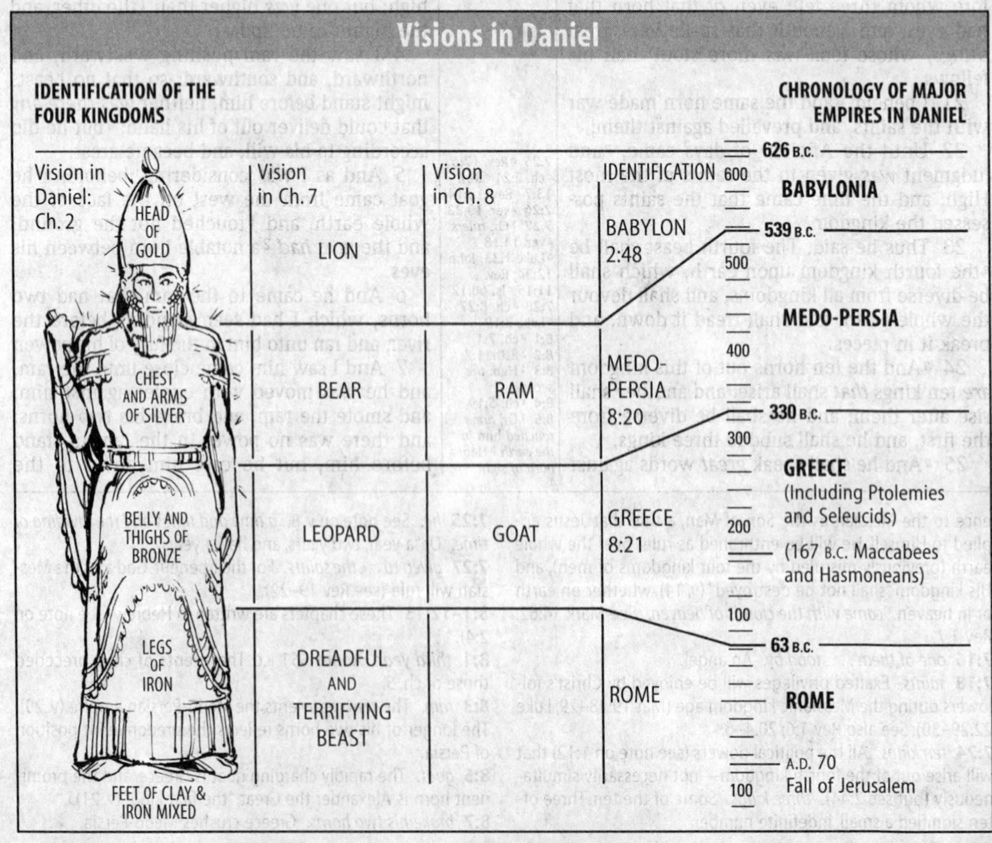

Gabriel explains the vision

15 ¶ And it came to pass, when I, *even* I Daniel, had seen the vision, and [a]sought for the meaning, then behold, there stood before me [b]as the appearance of a man.

16 And I heard a man's voice [a]between *the banks of* Ulai, which called, and said, [b]Gabriel, make this *man* to understand the vision.

17 So he came near where I stood: and when he came, I was afraid, and [a]fell upon my face: but he said unto me, Understand, O son of man: for at the time of the end *shall be* the vision.

18 [a]Now as he was speaking with me, I was in a deep sleep on my face toward the ground: [b]but he touched me, and [1]set me upright.

19 And he said, Behold, I *will* make thee know what shall be in the last end of the indignation: [a]for at the time appointed the end *shall be.*

20 The ram which thou sawest having two horns *are* the kings of Media and Persia.

21 And the rough goat *is* the king of Grecia: and the great horn that *is* between his eyes [a]*is* the first king.

22 [a]Now that being broken, whereas four stood up for it, four kingdoms shall stand up out of the nation, but not in his power.

23 And in the latter time of their kingdom, when the transgressors [1]are come to the full, a king [a]of fierce countenance, and understanding dark sentences, shall stand up.

24 And his power shall be mighty, [a]but not by his own power: and he shall destroy wonderfully, [b]and shall prosper, and practise, [c]and shall destroy the mighty and the [1]holy people.

25 And [a]through his policy also he shall cause craft to prosper in his hand; [b]and he shall magnify *himself* in his heart, and by [1]peace shall destroy many: [c]he shall also stand up against the Prince of princes; but he shall be [d]broken without hand.

26 And the vision of the evening and the morning which was told *is* true: [a]wherefore shut thou up the vision; for *it shall be* for many days.

27 [a]And I Daniel fainted, and was sick *certain* days; afterward I rose up, and did the king's business; and I was astonished at the vision, but none understood *it.*

Daniel's prayer for the people

9 In the first year [a]of Darius the son of Ahasuerus, of the seed of the Medes, [1]which was made king over the realm of the Chaldeans;

2 In the first year of his reign I Daniel understood by books the number of the years, where*of* the word of the LORD came to [a]Jeremiah the prophet, that *he* would accomplish seventy years in the desolations of Jerusalem.

3 [a]And I set my face unto the Lord God, to seek *by* prayer and supplications, with fasting, and sackcloth, and ashes:

4 And I prayed unto the LORD my God, and made my confession, and said,

¶ [a]O Lord, the great and dreadful God, keeping the covenant and mercy to them that love him, and to them that keep his commandments;

5 [a]We have sinned, and have committed iniquity, and have done wickedly, and have rebelled, even by departing from thy precepts and from thy judgments:

6 [a]Neither have we hearkened unto thy servants the prophets, which spake in thy name to our kings, our princes, and our fathers, and to all the people of the land.

7 O Lord, [a]righteousness [1]*belongeth* unto thee, but unto us confusion of faces, as *at* this day; to the men of Judah, and to the inhabitants of Jerusalem, and unto all Israel, *that are* near, and *that are* far off, through all the countries whither thou hast driven them, because of their trespass that they have trespassed against thee.

8 O Lord, to us *belongeth* confusion of face, to our kings, to our princes, and to our fathers, because we have sinned against thee.

9 [a]To the Lord our God *belong* mercies and forgivenesses, though we have rebelled against him;

10 Neither have we obeyed the voice of the LORD our God, to walk in his laws, which he set before us by his servants the prophets.

11 Yea, [a]all Israel have transgressed thy law, even by departing, that *they* might not obey thy voice; therefore the curse is poured upon us, and the oath that *is* written in the [b]law of Moses the servant of God, because we have sinned against him.

12 And he hath [a]confirmed his words, which he spake against us, and against our judges that judged us, by bringing upon us a great evil: [b]for under the whole heaven hath not been done as hath been done upon Jerusalem.

13 [a]As *it is* written in the law of Moses, all

8:15 [a]1 Pet. 1:10 [b]Ezek. 1:26
8:16 [a]ch. 12:6,7 [b]Luke 1:19
8:17 [a]Ezek. 1:28; Rev. 1:17
8:18 [1]Heb. *made me stand upon my standing* [a]Luke 9:32 [b]Ezek. 2:2
8:19 [a]Hab. 2:3
8:21 [a]ch. 11:3
8:22 [a]ch. 11:4
8:23 [1]Heb. *are accomplished* [a]Deut. 28:50
8:24 [1]Heb. *people of the holy ones* [a]Rev. 17:13 [b]ch. 11:36 [c]ch. 7:25
8:25 [1]Or, *prosperity* [a]ch. 11:21 [b]ch. 11:36 [c]ch. 11:36 [d]Job 34:20; Lam. 4:6
8:26 [a]Ezek. 12:27; Rev. 22:10
8:27 [a]ch. 7:28
9:1 [a]ch. 1:21

9:1 [1]Or, in *which he, etc.*
9:2 [a]2 Chr. 36:21; Jer. 25:11
9:3 [a]Neh. 1:4; Jer. 29:12; ch. 6:10
9:4 [a]Ex. 20:6; Deut. 7:9
9:5 [a]1 Ki. 8:47; Ps. 106:6; Jer. 14:7
9:6 [a]2 Chr. 36:15
9:7 [1]Or, *thou* hast, etc. [a]Neh. 9:33
9:9 [a]Ps. 130:4,7
9:11 [a]Is. 1:4-6 [b]Lev. 26:14; Deut. 27:15; Lam. 2:17
9:12 [a]Zech. 1:6 [b]Lam. 1:12; Ezek. 5:9; Amos 3:2
9:13 [a]Deut. 28:15; Lam. 2:17

---

for Israel as a whole. The 2,300 evenings and mornings probably refer to the number of sacrifices consecutively offered on 1,150 days, the interval between the desecration of the Lord's altar and its reconsecration by Judas Maccabeus on Kislev 25, 165 B.C. The pagan altar set up by Antiochus on Kislev 25, 168, was apparently installed almost two months after the Lord's altar was removed, accounting for the difference between 1,095 days (an exact three years) and the 1,150 specified here.

8:17 *son of man.* See note on Ezek 2:1.

8:23–25 A description of Antiochus IV and his rise to power by intrigue and deceit (he was not the rightful successor to the Seleucid throne).

8:25 *Prince of princes.* God. *broken without hand.* Antiochus died in 164 B.C. at Tabae in Persia through illness or accident; God "broke" him.

9:1 *first year.* 539–538 B.C. *Ahasuerus.* Or "Xerxes"; not the Ahasuerus (Xerxes) of the book of Esther.

9:2 *Jeremiah . . . seventy years.* See note on Jer 25:11–12.

9:3–19 Daniel's prayer contains humility (v. 3), worship (v. 4), confession (vv. 5–15) and petition (vv. 16–19).

9:3 *sackcloth, and ashes.* See note on Gen 37:34.

9:11 *curse . . . written in the law.* See Lev 26:33; Deut 28:63–67.

this evil is come upon us: [b]yet [1]made we not our prayer before the LORD our God, that *we* might turn from our iniquities, and understand thy truth.

14 Therefore hath the LORD [a]watched upon the evil, and brought it upon us: for [b]the LORD our God *is* righteous in all his works which he doeth: for we obeyed not his voice.

15 And now, O Lord our God, [a]that hast brought thy people forth out of the land of Egypt with a mighty hand, and hast [1]gotten thee [b]renown, as *at* this day; we have sinned, we have done wickedly.

16 O Lord, [a]according to all thy righteousness, I beseech thee, let thine anger and thy fury be turned away from thy city Jerusalem, [b]thy holy mountain: because for our sins, [c]and for the iniquities of our fathers, [d]Jerusalem and thy people [e]*are become* a reproach to all *that are* about us.

17 Now therefore, O our God, hear the prayer of thy servant, and his supplications, [a]and cause thy face to shine upon thy sanctuary [b]that is desolate, [c]for the Lord's sake.

18 [a]O my God, incline thine ear, and hear; open thine eyes, [b]and behold our desolations, and the city [c][1]which is called by thy name: for we do not [2]present our supplications before thee for our righteousnesses, but for thy great mercies.

19 O Lord, hear; O Lord, forgive; O Lord, hearken and do; defer not, for thine own sake, O my God: for thy city and thy people are called by thy name.

The meaning of the seventy weeks

20 ¶ And whiles I *was* speaking, and praying, and confessing my sin and the sin of my people Israel, and presenting my supplication before the LORD my God for the holy mountain of my God;

21 Yea, whiles I *was* speaking in prayer, even the man [a]Gabriel, whom I had seen in the vision at the beginning, being caused to fly [1]swiftly, touched me about the time of the evening oblation.

22 And he informed *me,* and talked with me, and said, O Daniel, I am now come forth [1]to give thee skill and understanding.

23 At the beginning of thy supplications the [1]commandment came forth, and I am come to shew *thee;* for thou *art* [2]greatly beloved: therefore [a]understand the matter, and consider the vision.

24 Seventy weeks are determined upon thy people and upon thy holy city, [1]to finish the transgression, and [2]to make an end of sins, [a]and to make reconciliation for iniquity, [b]and to bring in everlasting righteousness, and to seal up the vision and [3]prophecy, [c]and to anoint the most Holy.

25 Know therefore and understand, *that* from the going forth of the commandment [1]to restore and to build Jerusalem unto [a]the Messiah [b]the Prince *shall be* seven weeks, and threescore and two weeks: the street [2]shall be built again, and the [3]wall, even [4]in troublous times.

26 And after threescore and two weeks [a]shall Messiah be cut off, [b][1][2]but not for himself: [3]and [c]the people of the prince that *shall* come [d]shall destroy the city and the sanctuary; and the end thereof *shall be* with a flood, and unto the end of the war [4]desolations *are* determined.

27 And he shall confirm [a][1]the covenant with [b]many *for* one week: and *in* the midst of the week he shall cause the sacrifice and the oblation to cease, [2]and [3]for the overspreading of abominations he *shall* make *it* desolate, [c]even until the consummation, and that determined shall be poured [4]upon the desolate.

9:13 [1]Heb. *intreated [we not] the face [of the, etc.]* [b]Is. 9:13; Jer. 2:30; Hos. 7:7
9:14 [a]Jer. 31:28 [b]Neh. 9:33
9:15 [1]Heb. *made thee a name* [a]Ex. 32:11; 1 Ki. 8:51; Neh. 1:10 [b]Ex. 14:18; Neh. 9:10; Jer. 32:20
9:16 [a]1 Sam. 12:7; Ps. 31:1; Mic. 6:4,5 [b]Zech. 8:3 [c]Ex. 20:5 [d]Lam. 2:16 [e]Ps. 79:4
9:17 [a]Num. 6:25 [b]Lam. 5:18 [c]John 16:24
9:18 [1]Heb. *whereupon thy name is called* [2]Heb. *cause to fall* [a]Is. 37:17 [b]Ex. 3:7 [c]Jer. 25:29
9:21 [a]ch. 8:16
9:21 [1]Heb. *with weariness,* or, *flight*
9:22 [1]Heb. *to make thee skilful of understanding*
9:23 [1]Heb. *word* [2]Heb. a man of *desires* [a]Mat. 24:15
9:24 [1]Or, *to restrain* [2]Or, *to seal up* [3]Heb. *prophet* [a]Is. 53:10 [b]Rev. 14:6 [c]Ps. 45:7
9:25 [1][Or, *to build again Jerusalem:* as 2 Sam. 15:25; Ps. 71:20] [2]Heb. *shall return and be built* [3]Or, *breach,* or, *ditch* [4]Heb. *in strait of times* [a]John 1:41 [b]Is. 55:4
9:26 [1]Or, [*and*] *shall have nothing* [2][Or, *and* [*the Jews*] *they shall be no more his* people, ch. 11:17] [3][Or, *and the prince's* [*Messiah's,* ver. 25] *future people*] [4]Or, it shall be *cut off by desolations* [a]Is. 53:8 [b]1 Pet. 2:21 [c]Mat. 22:7 [d]Luke 19:44
9:27 [1][Or, *a*] [2][Or, *and upon the battlements* shall be *the idols of the desolator*] [3]Or, *with the abominable armies* [4][Or, *upon the desolator*] [a]Is. 42:6 [b]Mat. 26:28 [c]ch. 11:36

9:18 *but for thy great mercies.* God answers prayer because of His grace, not because of our works.

9:20 *whiles I was speaking.* See Is 65:24.

‡9:24 *weeks.* Probably seven-year periods of time, making a total of 490 years, but the numbers may be symbolic. Of the six purposes mentioned (all to be fulfilled through the Messiah), some believe that the last three were not achieved by the crucifixion and resurrection of Christ but await His further action: the establishment of everlasting righteousness (on earth), the complete fulfillment of vision and prophecy, and the anointing of the "most Holy" (either "most holy place" or "most holy One").

‡9:25–27 The time between the decree authorizing the rebuilding of Jerusalem (v. 25) and the coming of the Messiah ("the Anointed One") was to be 69 (7 plus 62) "weeks," or 483 years (see note on Ezra 7:11). The "seven weeks" may refer to the period of the complete restoration of Jerusalem (partially narrated in Ezra and Nehemiah) and the "threescore and two weeks" to the period between that restoration and the Messiah's coming to Israel. The final (70th) "week" is not mentioned specifically until v. 27, following the prophecy of the destruction of Jerusalem by "the people of the prince that shall come" (Titus in A.D. 70). Therefore, while many hold that the 70th "week" was fulfilled during Christ's earthly ministry and the years immediately following, others conclude that there is an indeterminate interval between the 69th and the 70th "week"—a period of "war" and "desolations" (v. 26; cf also 11:31, 32; 12:11; Mat 24:9–28). According to this latter opinion, in the 70th "week" the little horn or beast of the last days (referred to here as the one who "for the overspreading of abominations . . . shall make it desolate" and who is the antitype of the Roman Titus) will establish a covenant for seven years with the Jews (the "many") but will violate the covenant halfway through that period (but see also note on v. 27). The cutting off of the Messiah (v. 26) refers to the crucifixion of Christ.

‡9:27 *he shall confirm the covenant . . . shall cause the sacrifice . . . to cease.* According to some, a reference to the Messiah's (v. 26) instituting the new covenant and putting a stop to the OT sacrificial system; according to others, a reference to the antichrist's ("the [ultimate] prince that shall come," v. 26) making a treaty with the Jews in the future and then disrupting their system of worship. *abominations.* See note on 11:31.

Daniel's vision of an angel

10 In the third year of Cyrus king of Persia a thing was revealed unto Daniel,
whose name was called Belteshazzar; and the
thing *was* true, but the time appointed *was*
[1]long: and he understood the thing, and had
understanding of the vision.
2 In those days I Daniel was mourning
three [1]full weeks.
3 I ate no [1]pleasant bread, neither came
flesh nor wine in my mouth, neither did I
anoint myself at all, till three whole weeks
were fulfilled.
4 And in the four and twentieth day of the
first month, as I was by the side of the great
river, which *is* Hiddekel;
5 Then I lift up mine eyes, and looked, and
behold, [1]a certain man clothed *in* linen,
whose loins *were* [a]girded with fine gold of
Uphaz:
6 His body also *was* like the beryl, and his
face as the appearance of lightning, and his
eyes as lamps of fire, and his arms and his feet
like in colour to polished brass, [a]and the voice
of his words like the voice of a multitude.
7 And I Daniel alone saw the vision: for the
men that were with me saw not the vision;
but a great quaking fell upon them, so that
they fled to hide themselves.
8 Therefore I was left alone, and saw this
great vision, and there remained no strength
in me: for my [1]comeliness was turned in me
into corruption, and I retained no strength.
9 Yet heard I the voice of his words: and
when I heard the voice of his words, then was
I in a deep sleep on my face, and my face toward the ground.
10 [a]And behold, a hand touched me,
which [1]set me upon my knees and *upon* the
palms of my hands.
11 And he said unto me, O Daniel, [a][1]a
man greatly beloved, understand the words
that I speak unto thee, and [2]stand upright: for
unto thee am I now sent. And when he had
spoken this word unto me, I stood trembling.
12 Then said he unto me, [a]Fear not, Daniel: for from the first day that thou didst set
thine heart to understand, and to chasten thyself before thy God, [b]thy words were heard,
and I am come for thy words.
13 [a]But the prince of the kingdom of Persia
withstood me one and twenty days: but lo,
[b]Michael, one of [1]the chief princes, came to

10:1 [1]Heb. *great*
10:2 [1]Heb. *weeks of days*
10:3 [1]Heb. *bread of desires*
10:5 [1]Heb. *one man* [a]Rev. 1:13
10:6 [a]Rev. 1:15
10:8 [1]Or, *vigour*
10:10 [1]Heb. *moved* [a]ch. 9:21
10:11 [1]Heb. *a man of desires* [2]Heb. *stand upon thy standing* [a]ch. 9:23
10:12 [a]Rev. 1:17 [b]ch. 9:3,4,22,23; Acts 10:4
10:13 [1]Or, *the first* [a]ver. 20 [b]ver. 21; ch. 12:1; Jude 9; Rev. 12:7
10:14 [a]Gen. 49:1; ch. 2:28 [b]ver. 1; ch. 8:26; Hab. 2:3
10:15 [a]ver. 9; ch. 8:18
10:16 [a]ch. 8:15 [b]ver. 10; Jer. 1:9 [c]ver. 8
10:17 [1]Or, *this servant of my lord*
10:19 [a]ver. 11 [b]Judg. 6:23
10:20 [a]ver. 13
10:21 [1]Heb. *strengtheneth himself* [a]ver. 13; Jude 9; Rev. 12:7
11:1 [a]ch. 9:1 [b]ch. 5:31
11:3 [a]ch. 7:6; 8:5 [b]ver. 16,36; ch. 8:4
11:4 [a]ch. 8:8 [b]ch. 8:22

help me; and I remained there with the kings
of Persia.
14 Now I am come to make thee under-
stand what shall befall thy people [a]in the latter
days: [b]for yet the vision *is* for *many* days.
15 And when he had spoken such words
unto me, [a]I set my face toward the ground,
and I became dumb.
16 And behold, [a]*one* like the similitude of
the sons of men [b]touched my lips: then I
opened my mouth, and spake, and said unto
him that stood before me, O my lord, by the
vision [c]my sorrows are turned upon me, and I
have retained no strength.
17 For how can [1]the servant of this my
lord talk with this my lord? for as for me,
straightway there remained no strength in me,
neither is there breath left in me.
18 Then there came again and touched me
one like the appearance of a man, and he
strengthened me,
19 [a]And said, O man greatly beloved, [b]fear
not: peace *be* unto thee, be strong, yea, be
strong. And when he had spoken unto me, I
was strengthened, and said, Let my lord speak;
for thou hast strengthened me.
20 ¶ Then said he, Knowest thou wherefore I come unto thee? and now will I return to
fight [a]with the prince of Persia: and when I
am gone forth, lo, the prince of Grecia shall
come.
21 But I will shew thee that which is noted
in the scripture of truth: and *there is* none that
[1]holdeth with me in these *things,* [a]but Michael your prince.
11 Also I [a]in the first year of [b]Darius the
Mede, *even* I, stood to confirm and to
strengthen him.

Conflict between north and south

2 ¶ And now will I shew thee the truth. Behold, there *shall* stand up yet three kings in
Persia; and the fourth shall be far richer than
they all: and by his strength through his riches
he shall stir up all against the realm of Grecia.
3 And [a]a mighty king shall stand up, that
shall rule *with* great dominion, and [b]do according to his will.
4 And when he shall stand up, [a]his kingdom shall be broken, and shall be divided toward the four winds of heaven; and not to his
posterity, [b]nor according to his dominion
which he ruled: for his kingdom shall be
pluckt up, even for others besides those.

10:1 *third year of Cyrus.* The third year after his conquest of Babylonia in 539 B.C.
10:3 See 1:8–16.
10:5–6 See Rev 1:12–16.
10:7 Cf. Acts 9:7.
‡10:13 *prince of the kingdom of Persia.* Apparently a demon exercising influence over the Persian realm in the interests of Satan (see also v. 20). His resistance was finally overcome by the archangel Michael, "the great prince which standeth" over the people of God (12:1).
10:20 *prince of Grecia.* See note on v. 13. This spiritual power will also have to be opposed.
10:21 *scripture of truth.* See 12:1; perhaps a reference to the divine record of the destinies of all human beings (see note on Ex 32:32).
11:1 *Darius the Mede.* See note on 5:31.
11:2 *three kings.* Cambyses (530–522 B.C.), Pseudo-Smerdis or Gaumata (522) and Darius I (522–486). *fourth.* Xerxes I (486–465), who attempted to conquer Greece in 480 (see note on Esth 1:1).
11:3 *mighty king.* Alexander the Great (336–323).
11:4 *four winds.* See 7:2–3 and note on 7:4–7 (four heads).

5 ¶ And the king of the south shall be
strong, and *one* of his princes; and he shall be
strong above him, and have dominion; his dominion *shall be* a great dominion.
6 And in the end of years they [1]shall join
themselves together; for the king's daughter of
the south shall come to the king of the north to
make [2]an agreement: but she shall not retain
the power of the arm; neither shall he stand,
nor his arm: but she shall be given up, and they
that brought her, and [3]he that begat her, and
he that strengthened her in *these* times.
7 But out of a branch of her roots shall *one*
stand up [a][1]*in* his estate, which shall come
with an army, and shall enter into the fortress
of the king of the north, and shall deal against
them, and shall prevail:
8 And shall also carry captives *into* Egypt
their gods, with their princes, *and* with [1]their
precious vessels *of* silver and *of* gold; and he
shall continue *more* years than the king of the
north.
9 So the king of the south shall come into
his kingdom, and shall return into his own land.
10 But his sons [1]shall be stirred up, and
shall assemble a multitude of great forces: and
one shall certainly come, [a]and overflow, and
pass through: [2]then shall he return, and be
stirred up, [b]*even* to his fortress.
11 And the king of the south shall be
moved with choler, and shall come forth and
fight with him, *even* with the king of the
north: and he shall set forth a great multitude;
but the multitude shall be given into his hand.
12 *And* when he hath taken away the multitude, his heart shall be lifted up; and he shall
cast down *many* ten thousands: but he shall
not be strengthened *by it.*

11:6 [1]Heb. *shall associate themselves* [2]Heb. *rights* [3]Or, *whom she brought forth*
11:7 [1][Or, in *his place*, or, *office*] [a]ver. 20
11:8 [1]Heb. *vessels of their desire*
11:10 [1]Or, *shall war* [2][Or, *then shall he be stirred up again*] [a]Is. 8:8; ch. 9:26 [b]ver. 7

11:5 *king of the south.* Ptolemy I Soter (323–285 B.C.) of Egypt (see chart and map, below). *one of his princes.* Seleucus I Nicator (311–280). *his dominion.* Initially Babylonia, to which he then added extensive territories both east and west.
11:6 *king's daughter of the south.* Berenice, daughter of Ptolemy II Philadelphus (285–246 B.C.) of Egypt. *king of the north.* Antiochus II Theos (261–246) of Syria. *an agreement.* A treaty cemented by the marriage of Berenice to Antiochus. *she shall not retain the power . . . neither shall he stand.* Antiochus's former wife, Laodice, conspired to have Berenice and Antiochus put to death. *that begat her.* Berenice's father Ptolemy died at about the same time.
11:7 *one . . . her roots.* Berenice's brother, Ptolemy III Euergetes (246–221 B.C.) of Egypt, who did away with Laodice. *fortress.* Either (1) Seleucia (see Acts 13:4), which was the port of Antioch, or (2) Antioch itself. *king of the north.* Seleucus II Callinicus (246–226 B.C.) of Syria.
11:8 *their gods.* Images of Syrian deities, and also of Egyptian gods that the Persian Cambyses had carried off after conquering Egypt in 525 B.C.
‡11:10 *his sons.* Seleucus III Ceraunus (226–223 B.C.) and Antiochus III (the Great) (223–187), sons of Seleucus II. *his fortress.* Ptolemy's fortress at Raphia (southwest of Gaza).
11:11 *king of the south.* Ptolemy IV Philopator (221–203 B.C.) of Egypt. *king of the north.* Antiochus III. *given into his hand.* At Raphia in 217.
11:12 *cast down . . . many ten thousands.* The historian Polybius records that Antiochus lost nearly 10,000 infantrymen at Raphia.

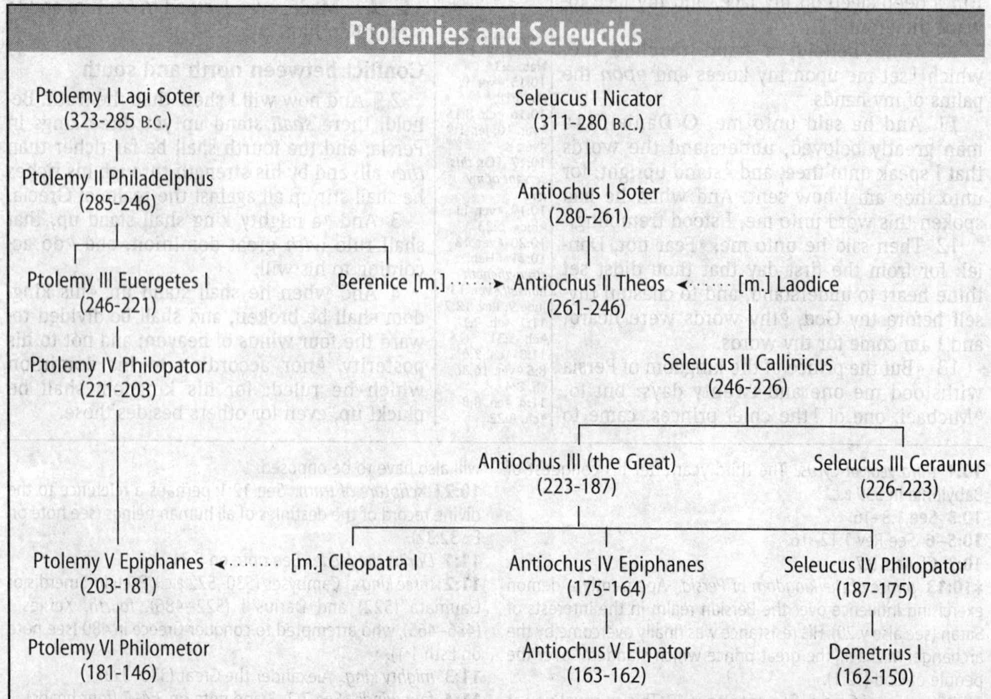

13 For the king of the north shall return, and shall set forth a multitude greater than the former, and shall certainly come [1]after certain years with a great army and with much riches.

14 And in those times there shall many stand up against the king of the south: also [1]the robbers of thy people shall exalt themselves to establish the vision; but they shall fall.

15 So the king of the north shall come, and cast up a mount, and take [1]the most fenced cities: and the arms of the south shall not withstand, neither [2]his chosen people, neither *shall there be any* strength to withstand.

16 But he that cometh against him [a]shall do according to his own will, and [b]none shall stand before him: and he shall stand in the [1][2]glorious land, which by his hand shall be consumed.

17 He shall also [a]set his face to enter with the strength of his whole kingdom, and [1]upright ones with him; thus shall he do: and he shall give him the daughter of women, [2]corrupting her: but she shall not stand *on his side,* [b]neither be for him.

18 After this shall he turn his face unto the isles, and shall take many: but a prince [1]for his own behalf shall cause [2]the reproach offered by him to cease; without his own reproach he shall cause *it* to turn upon him.

19 Then he shall turn his face towards the fort of his own land: but he shall stumble and fall, [a]and not be found.

20 Then shall stand up [1]in his estate [2]a raiser of taxes *in* the glory of the kingdom: but within few days he shall be destroyed, neither in [3]anger, nor in battle.

21 ¶ And [1]in his estate [a]shall stand up a vile person, to whom they shall not give the honour of the kingdom: but he shall come in peaceably, and obtain the kingdom by flatteries.

11:13 [1]Heb. *at the end of times, even years*
11:14 [1]Heb. *the children of robbers*
11:15 [1]Heb. the *city of munitions* [2]Heb. *the people of his choices*
11:16 [1]Or, *goodly land* [2]Heb. *the land of ornament* [a]ch. 8:4,7 [b]Josh. 1:5
11:17 [1]Or, *much uprightness:* or, *equal conditions* [a]2 Chr. 20:3 [b]ch. 9:26
11:17 [2]Heb. *to corrupt*
11:18 [1]Heb. *for him* [2]Heb. *his reproach*
11:19 [a]Ps. 37:36
11:20 [1][Or, *in his place*] [2]Heb. *one that causeth an exacter to pass over* [3]Heb. *angers*
11:21 [1][Or, *in his place*] [a]ch. 7:8

11:14 *king of the south.* Ptolemy V Epiphanes (203–181 B.C.) of Egypt. *robbers of thy people.* Jews who joined the forces of Antiochus. *they shall fall.* The Ptolemaic general Scopas crushed the rebellion in 200.
11:15 *most fenced cities.* The Mediterranean port of Sidon.
11:16 *he that cometh.* Antiochus, who was in control of the Holy Land by 197 B.C. *glorious land.* See note on 8:9–12.
11:17 *he shall give him the daughter of women.* Antiochus gave his daughter Cleopatra I in marriage to Ptolemy V in 194 B.C.
11:18 *he.* Antiochus. *isles.* Asia Minor and perhaps also mainland Greece. *prince.* The Roman consul Lucius Cornelius Scipio Asiaticus, who defeated Antiochus at Magnesia in Asia Minor in 190 B.C.
11:19 *stumble and fall.* Antiochus died in 187 B.C. while attempting to plunder a temple in the province of Elymais.
11:20 *in his estate.* Seleucus IV Philopator (187–175 B.C.), son and successor of Antiochus the Great. *raiser of taxes.* Seleucus's finance minister, Heliodorus. *he shall be destroyed.* Seleucus was the victim of a conspiracy engineered by Heliodorus.
11:21 *vile person.* Seleucus's younger brother, Antiochus IV Epiphanes (175–164 B.C.) *they shall not give the honour of the kingdom.* Antiochus seized power while the rightful heir to the throne, the son of Seleucus (later to become Demetrius I), was still very young. *kingdom.* Syro-Palestine.

Soon after the death of Alexander the Great in 323 B.C., his generals divided his empire into four parts, two of which—Egypt and Syria—were under the rule of the Ptolemies and Seleucids respectively. The Holy Land was controlled from Egypt by the Ptolemaic dynasty from 323 to 198, and was subsequently governed by the Seleucids of Syria from 198 to 142.

The Diadochi, as the successors of Alexander were called, struggled bitterly for power over his domain. At first Ptolemy I seized his own satrapy, Egypt and North Africa, which had splendid resources and natural defense capabilities. Seleucus gained Syria and Mesopotamia, and by 301 Lysimachus held Thrace and Asia Minor and Cassander ruled Macedon. The situation changed again by 277, when only three major Hellenistic kingdoms stabilized in Egypt, in Syria, and in Macedonia under the Antigonids (277-168). Each continued until the eventual triumph of Rome.

Dan 11 treats the "king of the south" and the "king of the north," describing their conflicts, wars and alliances. Their hostility toward the people of God culminated in the "abomination that maketh desolate" (Dan 11:31), identified historically with the reign of Antiochus IV Epiphanes (175-164). The Maccabean revolt followed, leading eventually to the founding of the Hasmonean dynasty.

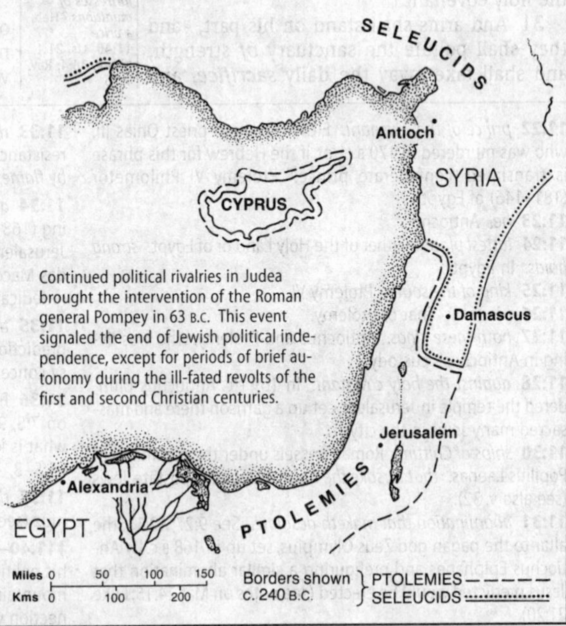

Continued political rivalries in Judea brought the intervention of the Roman general Pompey in 63 B.C. This event signaled the end of Jewish political independence, except for periods of brief autonomy during the ill-fated revolts of the first and second Christian centuries.

22 And *with* the arms of a flood shall they
be overflown from before him, and shall be
broken; [a]yea also, the prince of the covenant.
23 And after the league *made* with him [a]he
shall work deceitfully: for he shall come up,
and shall become strong with a small people.
24 He shall enter [1]peaceably even upon
the fattest places of the province; and he shall
do *that* which his fathers have not done, nor
his fathers' fathers; he shall scatter among
them the prey, and spoil, and riches: *yea,* and
he shall [2]forecast his devices against the
strong holds, even for a time.
25 And he shall stir up his power and his
courage against the king of the south with a
great army; and the king of the south shall be
stirred up to battle with a very great and
mighty army; but he shall not stand: for they
shall forecast devices against him.
26 Yea, they that feed of the portion of his
meat shall destroy him, and his army shall
overflow: and many shall fall down slain.
27 And both these kings' [1]hearts *shall be*
to do mischief, and they shall speak lies at one
table; but it shall not prosper: for yet the end
shall be at the time appointed.
28 Then shall he return *into* his land with
great riches; and his heart *shall be* against the
holy covenant; and he shall do *exploits,* and
return to his own land.
29 At the time appointed he shall return,
and come toward the south; but it shall not be
as the former, or as the latter.
30 [a]For *the* ships of Chittim shall come
against him: therefore he shall be grieved, and
return, and have indignation against the holy
covenant: so shall he do; he shall even return,
and have intelligence with them that forsake
the holy covenant.
31 And arms shall stand on his part, [a]and
they shall pollute the sanctuary *of* strength,
and shall take away the daily *sacrifice,* and
they shall place the abomination that [1]maketh
desolate.
32 And such as do wickedly against the
covenant shall he [1]corrupt by flatteries: but
the people that do know their God shall be
strong, and do *exploits.*
33 And they that understand among the
people shall instruct many: yet they shall fall
by the sword, and by flame, by captivity, and
by spoil, *many* days.
34 Now when they shall fall, they shall be
holpen *with* a little help: but many shall cleave
to them with flatteries.
35 And *some* of them of understanding
shall fall, [a]to try [1]them, and to purge, and to
make *them* white, *even* to the time of the end:
because *it is* yet for a time appointed.

The power of the northern king

36 ¶ And the king shall do according to his
will; and he shall [a]exalt himself, and magnify
himself above every god, and shall speak marvellous *things* against the God of gods, and
shall prosper till the indignation be accomplished: for that that is determined shall be
done.
37 Neither shall he regard the God of his
fathers, nor the desire of women, [a]nor regard
any god: for he shall magnify himself above all.
38 [1]But [2]in his estate shall he honour the
God of [3][4]forces: and a god whom his fathers
knew not shall he honour with gold, and silver, and with precious stones, and [5]pleasant
things.
39 Thus shall he do in the [1]most strong
holds with a strange god, whom he shall acknowledge *and* increase *with* glory: and he
shall cause them to rule over many, and shall
divide the land for [2]gain.
40 And at the time of the end shall the king
of the south push at him: and the king of the
north shall come against him [a]like a whirlwind, with chariots, [b]and with horsemen, and

11:22 [a]ch. 8:10,11
11:23 [a]ch. 8:25
11:24 [1]Or, *into the peaceable and fat, etc.* [2]Heb. *think [his] thoughts*
11:27 [1]Heb. *their hearts*
11:30 [a]Jer. 2:10
11:31 [a]ch. 8:11

11:31 [1]Or, *astonisheth*
11:32 [1]Or, *cause to dissemble*
11:35 [1]Or, *by them* [a]ch. 12:10
11:36 [a]ch. 7:8,25
11:37 [a]Is. 14:13
11:38 [1][Or, *But in his stead*] [2]Or, *as for the Almighty God, in his seat he shall honour, yea, he shall honour a god, whom, etc.* [3]Or, *munitions* [4]Heb. *Mauzzim,* [or, *God's protectors*] [5]Heb. things *desired*
11:39 [1]Heb. *fortresses of munitions* [2]Heb. *a price*
11:40 [a]Is. 21:1 [b]Ezek. 38:4; Rev. 9:16

11:22 *prince of the covenant.* Either the high priest Onias III, who was murdered in 170 B.C., or, if the Hebrew for this phrase is translated "confederate prince," Ptolemy VI Philometor (181–146) of Egypt.
11:23 *he.* Antiochus.
11:24 *fattest places.* Either of the Holy Land or of Egypt. *strong holds.* In Egypt.
11:25 *king of the south.* Ptolemy VI.
11:26 *his army.* That of Ptolemy.
11:27 *both these kings.* Antiochus and Ptolemy, who was living in Antiochus's custody.
11:28 *against the holy covenant.* In 169 B.C. Antiochus plundered the temple in Jerusalem, set up a garrison there and massacred many Jews in the city.
11:30 *ships of Chittim.* Roman vessels under the command of Popilius Laenas. *that forsake the holy covenant.* Apostate Jews (see also v. 32).
11:31 *abomination that maketh desolate.* See 9:27; 12:11; the altar to the pagan god Zeus Olympius, set up in 168 B.C. by Antiochus Epiphanes and prefiguring a similar abomination that Jesus predicted would be erected (see notes on Mat 24:15; Luke 21:20).
11:33 *they that understand.* The godly leaders of the Jewish resistance movement, also called the Hasidim. *fall by sword and by flame, by captivity, and by spoil.* See Heb 11:36–38.
11:34 *a little help.* The early successes of the guerrilla uprising (168 B.C.) that originated in Modein, 17 miles northwest of Jerusalem, under the leadership of Mattathias and his son Judas Maccabeus. In December, 165, the altar of the temple was rededicated.
11:35 *time of the end.* See v. 40; 12:4,9. Daniel concludes his predictions about Antiochus Epiphanes and begins to prophesy concerning the more distant future.
11:36 From here to the end of ch. 11 the antichrist (see notes on 7:8; 9:27) is in view. The details of this section do not fit what is known of Antiochus Epiphanes. See 2 Thes 2:4; cf. Rev 13:5–8.
11:37 *the desire of women.* Usually interpreted as either Tammuz (see note on Ezek 8:14) or the Messiah.
‡11:40–45 Conflicts to be waged between the antichrist and his political enemies. He will meet his end at the "glorious holy mountain" (v. 45), Jerusalem's temple mount, doubtless in connection with the battle of Armageddon (Rev 16:13–16).

with many ships; and he shall enter into the countries, and shall overflow and pass over.

41 He shall enter also into the [1,2]glorious land, and many *countries* shall be overthrown: but these shall escape out of his hand, [a]*even* Edom, and Moab, and the chief of the children of Ammon.

42 He shall [1]stretch forth his hand also upon the countries: and the land of Egypt shall not escape.

43 But he shall have power over the treasures of gold and of silver, and over all the precious *things* of Egypt: and the Libyans and the Ethiopians *shall be* [a]at his steps.

44 But tidings out of the east and out of the north shall trouble him: therefore he shall go forth with great fury to destroy, and utterly to make away many.

45 And he shall plant the tabernacles of his palace between the seas in [a]the [1,2]glorious holy mountain; [b]yet he shall come to his end, and none shall help him.

The time of great trouble

12 And at that time shall Michael stand up, the great prince which standeth for the children of thy people: [a]and there shall be a time of trouble, such as never was since there was a nation *even* to that same time: and at that time thy people [b]shall be delivered, every one that *shall* be found [c]written in the book.

2 And many of them that sleep in the dust of the earth shall awake, [a]some to everlasting life, and some to shame [b]*and* everlasting contempt.

3 And they that be [1]wise shall [a]shine as the brightness of the firmament; [b]and they that turn many to righteousness [c]as the stars for ever and ever.

4 But thou, O Daniel, [a]shut up the words, and seal the book, *even* to the time of the end: many shall run to and fro, and knowledge shall be increased.

5 ¶ Then I Daniel looked, and behold, there stood other two, the one on this side of the [1]bank of the river, and the other on that side of the [1]bank [a]of the river.

6 And *one* said to the man clothed in linen, which *was* [1]upon the waters of the river, [a]How long *shall it be to* the end of *these* wonders?

7 And I heard the man clothed in linen, which *was* upon the waters of the river, when he [a]held up his right hand and his left hand unto heaven, and sware by him [b]that liveth for ever [c]that *it shall be* for a time, times, and [1]a half; [d]and when *he* shall have accomplished to scatter the power of [e]the holy people, all these *things* shall be finished.

8 And I heard, but I understood not: then said I, O my lord, what *shall be* the end of these *things?*

9 And he said, Go thy way, Daniel: for the words *are* closed up and sealed till the time of the end.

10 [a]Many shall be purified, and made white, and tried; [b]but the wicked shall do wickedly: and none of the wicked shall understand; but [c]the wise shall understand.

11 And from the time *that* the daily *sacrifice* shall be taken away, and [1]the abomination that [2]maketh desolate set up, *there shall be* a thousand two hundred and ninety days.

12 Blessed *is* he that waiteth, and cometh to the thousand three hundred *and* five and thirty days.

13 But go thou thy way till the end *be:* [a,1]for thou shalt rest, [b]and stand in thy lot at the end of the days.

11:41 [1]Or, *goodly land* [2]Heb. *land of delight,* or, *ornament* [a]Is. 11:14
11:42 [1]Heb. *send forth*
11:43 [a]Ex. 11:8
11:45 [1]Or, *goodly* [2]Heb. *mountain of delight of holiness* [a]Ps. 48:2 [b]Rev. 19:20
12:1 [a]Is. 26:20; Jer. 30:7; Rev. 16:18 [b]Rom. 11:26 [c]Ex. 32:32; Ps. 56:8
12:2 [a]Mat. 25:46; John 5:28; Acts 24:15 [b]Is. 66:24; Rom. 9:21
12:3 [1]Or, *teachers* [a]Mat. 13:43 [b]Jas. 5:20 [c]1 Cor. 15:41
12:4 [a]Rev. 22:10
12:5 [1]Heb. *lip* [a]ch. 10:4
12:6 [1]Or, *from above* [a]ch. 8:13
12:7 [1]Or, *part* [a]Deut. 32:40 [b]ch. 4:34 [c]ch. 7:25 [d]Luke 21:24 [e]ch. 8:24
12:10 [a]Zech. 13:9 [b]Hos. 14:9 [c]John 8:47
12:11 [1]Heb. *to set up the abomination, etc.* [2]Or, *astonisheth*
12:13 [1]Or, *and thou, etc.* [a]Rev. 14:13 [b]Ps. 1:5

12:1 *Michael.* See note on 10:13. *time of trouble.* See Jer 30:7; Mat 24:21 and notes; cf. Rev 16:18. *book.* See 10:21; Ps 9:5; 51:1; 69:28 and notes.

12:2 The first clear reference to a resurrection of both the righteous and the wicked. Cf. John 5:24–30. *everlasting life.* The phrase occurs only here in the OT.

12:5 *other two.* Two was the minimum number of witnesses to an oath (see v. 7; Deut 19:15).

12:7 *time, times, and a half.* See note on 7:25.

12:11–12 Apparently representing either (1) further calculations relating to the persecutions of Antiochus Epiphanes (see 8:14; 11:28 and notes) or (2) further end-time calculations.

12:13 *rest.* Die (see Job 3:17).

The Book of the Twelve, or the Minor Prophets

In Ecclesiasticus (an Apocryphal book written c. 190 B.C.), Jesus ben Sira spoke of "the twelve prophets" (Ecclesiasticus 49:10) as a unit parallel to Isaiah, Jeremiah and Ezekiel. He thus indicated that these 12 prophecies were at that time thought of as a unit and were probably already written together on one scroll, as is the case in later times. Josephus (*Against Apion,* 1.8.3) also was aware of this grouping. Augustine (*The City of God,* 18.25) called them the "Minor Prophets," referring to the small size of these books by comparison with the major prophetic books and not at all suggesting that they are of minor importance.

In the traditional Jewish canon these works are arranged in what was thought to be their chronological order: (1) the books that came from the period of Assyrian power (Hosea, Joel, Amos, Obadiah, Jonah, Micah), (2) those written about the time of the decline of Assyria (Nahum, Habakkuk, Zephaniah) and (3) those dating from the postexilic era (Haggai, Zechariah, Malachi). On the other hand, their order in the Septuagint (the earliest Greek translation of the OT) is: Hosea, Amos, Micah, Joel, Obadiah, Jonah, Nahum, Habakkuk, Zephaniah, Haggai, Zechariah, Malachi (the order of the first six was probably determined by length, except for Jonah, which is placed last among them because of its different character).

In any event, it appears that within a century after the composition of Malachi the Jews had brought together the 12 shorter prophecies to form a book (scroll) of prophetic writings, which was received as canonical and paralleled the three major prophetic books of Isaiah, Jeremiah and Ezekiel. The great Greek manuscripts Alexandrinus and Vaticanus place the Twelve before the major prophets, but in the traditional Jewish canon and in all modern versions they appear after them.

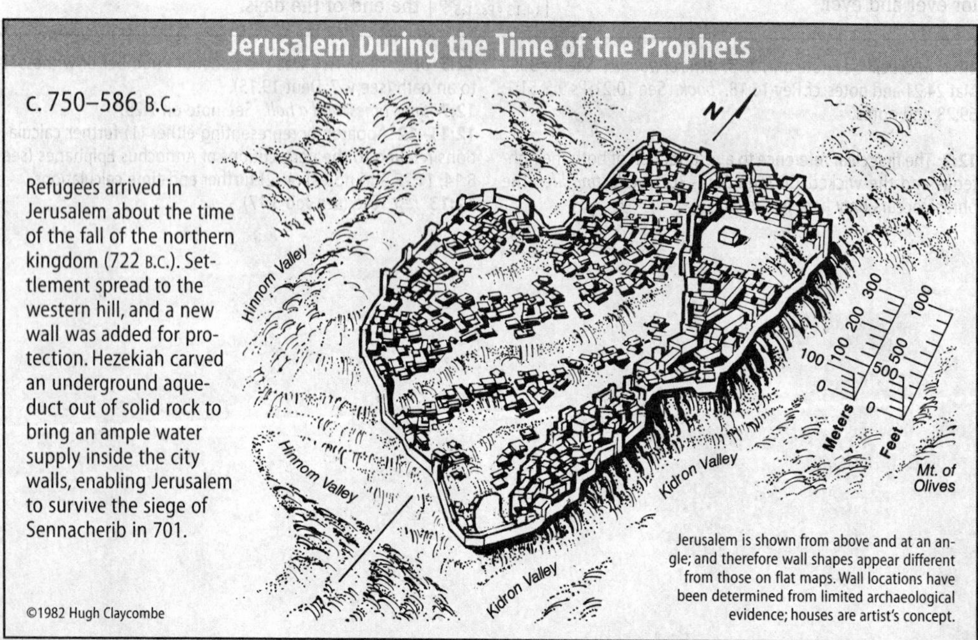

Jerusalem During the Time of the Prophets
c. 750–586 B.C.
Refugees arrived in Jerusalem about the time of the fall of the northern kingdom (722 B.C.). Settlement spread to the western hill, and a new wall was added for protection. Hezekiah carved an underground aqueduct out of solid rock to bring an ample water supply inside the city walls, enabling Jerusalem to survive the siege of Sennacherib in 701.
N
Hinnom Valley
Hinnom Valley
Kidron Valley
Kidron Valley
Mt. of Olives
Meters
Feet
0
100
200
300
0
500
1000
Jerusalem is shown from above and at an angle; and therefore wall shapes appear different from those on flat maps. Wall locations have been determined from limited archaeological evidence; houses are artist's concept.

Hosea

INTRODUCTION

Author and Date

Hosea son of Beeri prophesied about the middle of the eighth century B.C., his ministry beginning during or shortly after that of Amos. Amos threatened God's judgment on Israel at the hands of an unnamed enemy; Hosea identifies that enemy as Assyria (7:11; 8:9; 10:6; 11:11). Judging from the kings mentioned in 1:1, Hosea must have prophesied for at least 38 years, though almost nothing is known about him from sources outside his book. He was the only one of the writing prophets to come from the northern kingdom (Israel), and his prophecy is primarily directed to that kingdom. But since his prophetic activity is dated by reference to kings of Judah, the book was probably written in Judah after the fall of the northern capital, Samaria (722–721)—an idea suggested by references to Judah throughout the book (1:7,11; 4:15; 5:5,10,13; 6:4,11; 10:11; 11:12; 12:2). Whether Hosea himself authored the book that preserves his prophecies is not known. The book of Hosea stands first in the division of the Bible called the Book of the Twelve (in the Apocrypha; see Ecclesiasticus 49:10) or the Minor Prophets (a name referring to the brevity of these books as compared to Isaiah, Jeremiah and Ezekiel).

Background

Hosea lived in the tragic final days of the northern kingdom, during which six kings (following Jeroboam II) reigned within 25 years (2 Ki 15:8—17:41). Four (Zechariah, Shallum, Pekahiah, Pekah) were murdered by their successors while in office, and one (Hoshea) was captured in battle; only one (Menahem) was succeeded on the throne by his son. These kings, given to Israel by God "in . . . anger" and taken away "in . . . wrath" (13:11), floated away "as the foam upon the water" (10:7). "Blood" followed "blood" (4:2). Assyria was expanding westward, and Menahem accepted that world power as overlord and paid tribute (2 Ki 15:19–20). But shortly afterward, in 733 B.C., Israel was dismembered by Assyria because of the intrigue of Pekah (who had gained Israel's throne by killing Pekahiah, Menahem's son and successor). Only the territories of Ephraim and western Manasseh were left to the king of Israel. Then, because of the disloyalty of Hoshea (Pekah's successor), Samaria was captured and its people exiled in 722–721, bringing the northern kingdom to an end.

Theme and Message

The first part of the book (chs. 1—3) narrates the family life of Hosea as a symbol (similar to the symbolism in the lives of Isaiah, Jeremiah and Ezekiel) to convey the message the prophet had from the Lord for His people. God ordered Hosea to marry an adulterous wife, Gomer, and their three children were each given a symbolic name representing part of the ominous message. Ch. 2 alternates between Hosea's relation to Gomer and its symbolic representation of God's relation to Israel. The children are told to drive the unfaithful mother out of the house; but it was her reform, not her riddance, that was sought. The prophet was ordered to continue loving her, and he took her back and kept her in isolation for a while (ch. 3). The affair graphically represents the Lord's relation to the Israelites (cf. 2:4,9,18), who had been disloyal to Him by worshiping Canaanite deities as the source of their abundance. Israel was to go through a period of exile (cf. 7:16; 8:14; 9:3,6,17; 11:5). But the Lord still loved His covenant people and longed to take them back, as Hosea took back Gomer. This return is described with imagery recalling the exodus from Egypt and settlement in Canaan (cf. 1:11; 2:14–23; 3:5; 11:10–11; 14:4–7). Hosea saw Israel's past experiences with the Lord as the fundamental pattern, or type, of God's future dealings with His people.

The second part of the book (chs. 4—14) gives the details of Israel's involvement in Canaanite religion, but a systematic outline of the material is difficult. Like other prophetic books, Hosea carried a call to repentance. Israel's alternative to destruction was to forsake her idols and return to the Lord (chs. 6; 14). Information gleaned from materials discovered at Ugarit (dating from the 15th century

B.C.; see chart, p. xix) and from the writings of the early Christian historian Eusebius enables us to know more clearly the religious practices against which Hosea protested.

Hosea saw the failure to acknowledge God (4:6; 13:4) as Israel's basic problem. God's relation to Israel was that of love (2:19; 4:1; 6:6; 10:12; 12:6). The intimacy of the covenant relationship between God and Israel, illustrated in the first part of the book by the husband-wife relationship, is later amplified by the father-child relationship (11:1–4). Disloyalty to God was spiritual adultery (4:13–14; 5:4; 9:1; cf. Jer 3). Israel had turned to Baal worship and had sacrificed at the pagan high places, which included associating with the sacred prostitutes at the sanctuaries (4:14) and worshiping the calf image at Samaria (8:5; 10:5–6; 13:2). There was also international intrigue (5:13; 7:8–11) and materialism. Yet despite God's condemnation and the harshness of language with which the unavoidable judgment was announced, the major purpose of the book is to proclaim God's compassion and love that cannot—finally—let Israel go.

Special Problems

The book of Hosea has at least two perplexing problems. The first concerns the nature of the story told in chs. 1—3 and the character of Gomer. While some interpreters have thought the story to be merely an allegory of the relation between God and Israel, others claim, more plausibly, that the story is to be taken literally. Among the latter, some insist that Gomer was faithful at first and later became unfaithful, others that she was unfaithful even before the marriage.

The second problem of the book is the relation of ch. 3 to ch. 1. Despite the fact that no children are mentioned in ch. 3, some interpreters claim that the two chapters are different accounts of the same episode. The traditional interpretation, however, is more likely, namely, that ch. 3 is a sequel to ch. 1—i.e., after Gomer proved unfaithful, Hosea was instructed to take her back.

Outline

- I. Superscription (1:1)
- II. The Unfaithful Wife and the Faithful Husband (1:2—3:5)
  - A. The Children as Signs (1:2—2:1)
  - B. The Unfaithful Wife (2:2–23)
    - 1. The Lord's judgment of Israel (2:2–13)
    - 2. The Lord's restoration of Israel (2:14–23)
  - C. The Faithful Husband (ch. 3)
- III. The Unfaithful Nation and the Faithful God (chs. 4—14)
  - A. Israel's Unfaithfulness (4:1—6:3)
    - 1. The general charge (4:1–3)
    - 2. The cause declared and the results described (4:4–19)
    - 3. A special message to the people and leaders (ch. 5)
    - 4. A sorrowful plea (6:1–3)
  - B. Israel's Punishment (6:4—10:15)
    - 1. The case stated (6:4—7:16)
    - 2. The judgment pronounced (chs. 8—9)
    - 3. Summary and appeal (ch. 10)
  - C. The Lord's Faithful Love (chs. 11—14)
    - 1. The Lord's fatherly love (11:1–11)
    - 2. Israel's punishment for unfaithfulness (11:12—13:16)
    - 3. Israel's restoration after repentance (ch. 14)

Hosea's wife and children

1 The [a]word of the LORD that came unto
Hosea, the son of Beeri, in the days of
Uzziah, Jotham, Ahaz, *and* Hezekiah, kings of
Judah, and in the days of Jeroboam the son of
Joash, king of Israel.
2 The beginning of the word of the LORD by
Hosea. And the LORD said to Hosea, [a]Go, take
unto thee a wife of whoredoms and children of
whoredoms: for [b]the land hath committed
great whoredom, *departing* from the LORD.
3 So he went and took Gomer the daughter
of Diblaim; which conceived, and bare him a
son.
4 And the LORD said unto him, Call his
name Jezreel; for yet a little *while,* [a]and I will
[1]avenge the blood of Jezreel upon the house of
Jehu, [b]and will cause to cease the kingdom of
the house of Israel.
5 [a]And it shall come to pass at that day,
that I will break the bow of Israel in the valley
of Jezreel.
6 And she conceived again, and bare a
daughter. And *God* said unto him, Call her
name [1]Lo-ruhamah: [a]for [2]I will no more have
mercy upon the house of Israel; [3]but I will utterly take them away.
7 [a]But I will have mercy upon the house of
Judah, and will save them by the LORD their
God, and [b]will not save them by bow, nor by
sword, nor by battle, by horses, nor by horsemen.
8 Now when she had weaned Lo-ruhamah,
she conceived, and bare a son.
9 Then said *God,* Call his name [1]Lo-ammi:
for ye *are* not my people, and I will not be your
God.
10 Yet [a]the number of the children of Israel shall be as the sand of the sea, which cannot
be measured nor numbered; [b]and it shall
come to pass, *that* [1]in the place where it was
said unto them, Ye *are* not my people, *there* it
shall be said unto them, *Ye are* [c]the sons of the
living God.
11 [a]Then shall the children of Judah and
the children of Israel be gathered together, and
appoint themselves one head, and they shall
come up out of the land: for great *shall be* the
day of Jezreel.

2 Say ye unto your brethren, [1]Ammi;
And to your sisters, [2]Ruhamah.

Gomer punished and restored

2 Plead with your mother, plead:
For [a]she *is* not my wife, neither *am* I
her husband:
Let her therefore put away her
[b]whoredoms out of her sight,
And her adulteries from between her
breasts;
3 Lest [a]I strip her naked, and set her as
in the day that she was [b]born,
And make her as a wilderness, and set
her like a dry land,
And slay her with [c]thirst.
4 And I will not have mercy upon her
children;
For they *be the* [a]children of
whoredoms.
5 For their mother hath played the harlot:

1:1 [a]2 Pet. 1:21
1:2 [a]ch. 3:1
[b]Deut. 31:16; Ps. 73:27; Jer. 2:13; Ezek. 23:3
1:4 [1]Heb. *visit*
[a]2 Ki. 10:11
[b]2 Ki. 15:10
1:5 [a]2 Ki. 15:29
1:6 [1]That is, *Not having obtained mercy*
[2]Heb. *I will not add any more* to
[3]Or, *that I should altogether pardon them*
[a]2 Ki. 17:6
1:7 [a]2 Ki. 19:35
[b]Zech. 4:6
1:9 [1]That is, *Not my people*
1:10 [1]Or, *instead of that*
[a]Gen. 32:12
[b]1 Pet. 2:10
[c]John 1:12
1:11 [a]Is. 11:12
2:1 [1]That is, *My people* [2]That is, *Having obtained mercy*
2:2 [a]Is. 50:1
[b]Ezek. 16:25
2:3 [a]Jer. 13:22
[b]Ezek. 16:4
[c]Amos 8:11
2:4 [a]John 8:41

1:1 *word of the LORD.* A claim of authority paralleling that of Joel (1:1), Micah (1:1) and Zechariah (1:1,7). *Hosea.* Means "salvation." *Uzziah.* Reigned 792–740 B.C. *Jotham.* 750–732. *Ahaz.* 735–715. *Hezekiah.* 729–686. Some of the reigns overlapped, the co-regency of Ahaz and Hezekiah being the longest (see note on Is 36:1). *Jeroboam.* Jeroboam II, 793–753. Hosea was a contemporary of Isaiah, Amos and Micah (see the similar first verse in their prophecies).

1:2 *take . . . a wife of whoredoms.* See Introduction: Special Problems. *whoredoms.* Spiritual harlotry (unfaithfulness) is the one great sin of which the Lord (through Hosea) accuses Israel.

1:3 *Gomer.* Not mentioned outside this book. *him.* The omission of this word in vv. 6, 8 may indicate that Hosea was not the father of Gomer's next two children.

1:4 *Jezreel.* Means "God scatters," here used to reinforce the announcement of judgment on the reigning house (see notes on v. 11; 2:22). Jeroboam II was of the dynasty of Jehu (841–814 B.C.), which was established at Jezreel by the overthrow of Ahab's son Joram (2 Ki 9:14–37; cf. 1 Ki 19:16–17). Jehu's dynasty ended with the murder of Zechariah in 753 (2 Ki 15:8–10).

1:5 *the bow of Israel.* Israel's military power, broken in 724 B.C., though Samaria held out under siege for some two years longer (2 Ki 17:5–6).

‡1:6 *Lo-ruhamah.* Means "not loved" (see KJV marg.). The naming represents a reversal of the love (compassion) that God had earlier shown to Israel (Ex 33:19; Deut 7:6–8) but that later was promised again (2:23).

1:7 *Judah . . . save them.* They were saved from Assyria by the Lord in 722–721 B.C. and again in 701 (see 2 Ki 19:32–36).

‡1:9 *Lo-ammi.* Means "not my people" (see KJV marg.). The naming represents a break in the covenant relationship between the Lord and Israel (see Ex 6:7; Jer 7:23), which later, however, would be restored (v. 10; 2:1,23). The warnings became more severe in moving from the first to the third child.

‡1:10 Cited in Rom 9:26; 1 Pet 2:10 and applied to the mission to the Gentiles. *Yet.* The threatened punishment (vv. 4–9) would be for only a limited time, and a period of blessing would follow. *sand of the sea.* See the promise to Abraham and Jacob (Gen 22:17; 32:12; cf. Jer 33:22; Heb 11:12). *sons.* Contrasts with "children of whoredoms" (v. 2; 2:4). *living God.* Contrasts with idols—"who were not God" (Deut 32:17).

1:11 *gathered together.* Israel and Judah would become one nation again. *up out of the land.* Possibly the land of exile (cf. Ex 1:10). Another interpretation is that they would spring up from the ground as plants do. *Jezreel.* Here "God scatters" (see note on v. 4) refers to sowing or planting, indicating a reversal of the meaning of the first child's name (see 2:21–23).

‡2:1 *Ammi . . . Ruhamah.* The negatives associated with the names of Hosea's children (see notes on 1:6, 9) are dropped.

2:2 *not my wife.* The marriage was broken by unfaithfulness, but reconciliation, not divorce, was sought (cf. vv. 7–15).

2:3 *strip her.* The husband supplied the wife's clothing (see Ex 21:10; Ezek 16:10), and here her unfaithfulness was exposed (see Jer 13:26; Ezek 16:39). *set her . . . in the day that she was born.* As Israel was when the Lord found her in Egypt—in slavery and with nothing (cf. Ezek 16:4–8; Nah 3:5).

2:4 *children of whoredoms.* See 1:2. This contrasts with being "sons" of the Lord (1:10; 11:1).

She that conceived them hath done shamefully:
For she said, I will go after my lovers,
[a]That give *me* my bread and my water,
My wool and my flax, mine oil and my [1]drink.
6 Therefore behold, [a]I will hedge up thy way with thorns,
And [1]make a wall, that she shall not find her paths.
7 And she shall follow after her lovers, but she shall not overtake them;
And she shall seek them, but shall not find *them:*
Then shall she say, [a]I will go and return to my [b]first husband;
For then *was it* better with me than now.
8 For she did not [a]know that I gave her corn, and [1]wine, and oil,
And multiplied her silver and gold,
[2]*Which* they prepared for Baal.
9 Therefore will I return, and take *away* my corn in the time thereof,
And my wine in the season thereof,
And will [1]recover my wool and my flax *given* to cover her nakedness.
10 And now [a]will I discover her [1]lewdness in the sight of her lovers,
And none shall deliver her out of mine hand,
11 [a]I will also cause all her mirth to cease,
Her feast *days,* her new moons, and her sabbaths, and all her solemn feasts.
12 And I will [1]destroy her vines and her fig trees,
Where*of* she hath said, These *are* my rewards that my lovers have given me:
And I will make them a forest,
And the beasts of the field shall eat them.
13 And I will visit upon her the days of Baalim, where*in* she burnt incense to them,
And she decked herself with her earrings and her jewels,
And she went after her lovers, and forgat me, saith the LORD.
14 Therefore behold, I *will* allure her,
And bring her *into* the wilderness,
And speak [1][2]comfortably unto her.
15 And I will give her her vineyards from thence,
And [a]the valley of Achor for a door of hope:
And she shall sing there, as *in* [b]the days of her youth,
And [c]as *in* the day when she came up out of the land of Egypt.
16 And it shall be at that day, saith the LORD, *that* thou shalt call *me* [1]Ishi;
And shalt call me no more [2]Baali.
17 For [a]I will take away the names of Baalim out of her mouth,
And they shall no more be remembered by their name.
18 And in that day will I make a [a]covenant for them with the beasts of the field,

2:5 [1]Heb. *drinks* [a]ver. 8,12
2:6 [1]Heb. *wall a wall* [a]Lam. 3:7,9
2:7 [a]Luke 15:18 [b]Ezek. 16:8
2:8 [1]Heb. *new wine* [2]Or, Wherewith *they made Baal* [a]Is. 1:3
2:9 [1]Or, *take away*
2:10 [1]Heb. *folly,* or, *villany* [a]Ezek. 16:37
2:11 [a]Amos 8:10
2:12 [1]Heb. *make desolate*
2:14 [1]Or, *friendly* [2]Heb. *to her heart*
2:15 [a]Josh. 7:26 [b]Jer. 2:2; Ezek. 16:8 [c]Ex. 15:1
2:16 [1]That is, *My husband* [2]That is, *My lord*
2:17 [a]Ex. 23:13; Ps. 16:4
2:18 [a]Job 5:23

2:5 *go after.* The wife was chasing other men (see Jer 3:2; Ezek 16:33). *lovers.* See vv. 7,10. The reference is to Canaanite deities (such as Baal), whose worshipers hoped to gain agricultural fertility. *That give me my bread . . . my drink.* Ugaritic texts attribute crops to rain given by Baal. *wool . . . flax . . . oil . . . drink.* The agricultural staples of the Holy Land. Israel does not know the true source of her blessings.

2:6 *hedge up thy way.* Rather than punish Israel with death (cf. Deut 22:21; Ezek 16:39–40; Nah 3:5–7), the Lord would isolate her.

‡2:7 *follow after.* A cultic term in Hosea; elsewhere the Hebrew for this word is translated "pursue" in 8:3 and "follow" in 6:3 and 12:1. *seek.* See 5:6,15. *not find.* See 5:6. *return.* The Hebrew for this expression often means "repent." *my first husband.* The Lord.

2:8 *she did not know.* The Canaanites attributed grain, wine and oil to Baal. *silver and gold.* Used for making idols (see 8:4; 9:6; 13:2). *Baal.* The Canaanite god who was believed to control the weather and the fertility of crops, animals and man (see note on Judg 2:13).

2:9 *will I return.* By withholding the fruits of field and flock, the Lord made known the true source of those blessings.

2:10 *discover her lewdness.* The unfaithful wife was exposed to public shame (see Lam 1:8; Ezek 16:37; 23:29). *none shall deliver her.* Baal had no power.

2:11 *cause . . . mirth . . . cease.* In exile these joyous seasons would be only a memory. *feasts.* See Ex 23:14–17; Deut 16:16. See also chart, pp. 166–167. *new moons.* See 2 Ki 4:23; Is 1:13; Amos 8:5. *sabbaths.* See Ex 20:8–11.

2:12 *rewards . . . my lovers have given.* The harlot's pay (see 9:1; Deut 23:18; Ezek 16:33; Mic 1:7). Israel attributed her agricultural products to the false gods she worshiped, rather than to the Lord (see Deut 11:13–14). *forest.* See Is 5:5–6; 7:23; 32:13; Mic 3:12.

2:13 *days.* Festival days. *Baalim.* See v. 17; 11:2. Hosea used the plural here, suggesting the idols at the many local shrines (see Jer 2:23; 9:14). *went after.* See note on v. 5. *forgat.* The opposite of "know" in Hosea (cf. 13:4–6).

2:14 *into the wilderness.* For a second betrothal (see vv. 19–20). It refers back to the days of Israel's wilderness wandering, before she was tempted by the Baals in Canaan. *speak comfortably unto.* Reassure, encourage, comfort (cf. Gen 34:3; Ruth 2:13; Is 40:2). God continually shows love in the midst of judgment.

2:15 *valley of Achor.* Near Jericho (see Josh 7:1–26; 15:7; Is 65:10). As the prophet reversed the meaning of the names of his children, so also the meaning of Achor ("trouble")—where God first judged His people in the promised land—became a symbol of new opportunity.

‡2:16–17 *Ishi . . . Baali . . . Baalim.* See KJV marg. for the wordplay. Of the two Hebrew words for husband, one ("lord") is identical with the name of the god Baal. There will be such a vigorous reaction against Baal worship that this Hebrew word for "lord" will no longer be used of the Lord.

2:18 *make a covenant.* See 6:7; 8:1. Animals, the instruments of destruction in v. 12, as well as birds and insects, would no longer threaten life. Nature and history combine in a picture of peace (see Is 11:6–9; 65:25). *bow . . . sword.* See 1:5. War is terminated. *earth.* Israel (see 1:2; 4:1,3; 9:3; 10:1). *lie down safely.* See Jer 33:16; Ezek 34:24–28.

And with the fowls of heaven, and
with the creeping things of the
ground:
And [b]I will break the bow and the
sword and the battle out of the earth,
And will make them to [c]lie down
safely.
19 And I will betroth thee unto me for
ever;
Yea, I will betroth thee unto me in
righteousness, and in judgment,
And in lovingkindness, and in mercies.
20 I will even betroth thee unto me in
faithfulness:
And [a]thou shalt know the LORD.
21 And it shall come to pass in that day,
[a]I will hear, saith the LORD, I will hear
the heavens,
And they shall hear the earth;
22 And the earth shall hear the corn, and
the wine, and the oil;
And they shall hear Jezreel.
23 And [a]I will sow her unto me in the
earth;
[b]And I will have mercy upon her that
had not obtained mercy;
And I [c]will say to *them which were* not
my people, Thou *art* my people;
And they shall say, *Thou art* my God.

2:18 [b]Is. 2:4 [c]Lev. 26:5; Jer. 23:6
2:20 [a]Jer. 31:33; John 17:3
2:21 [a]Zech. 8:12
2:23 [a]Jer. 31:27 [b]ch. 1:6 [c]ch. 1:10

3:1 [1]Heb. *of grapes* [a]ch. 1:2 [b]Jer. 3:20
3:2 [1]Heb. *lethech*
3:3 [a]Deut. 21:13
3:4 [1]Heb. *a standing,* or, *statue,* [or, *pillar,* Is. 19:19] [a]ch. 10:3 [b]Ex. 28:6 [c]Judg. 17:5
3:5 [a]ch. 5:6 [b]Jer. 30:9; Ezek. 34:23,24 [c]Is. 2:2; Jer. 30:24; Ezek. 38:8
4:1 [a]Is. 1:18 [b]Jer. 4:22

Israel will return to God

3 Then said the LORD unto me, [a]Go yet, love a woman beloved of *her* [b]friend, yet an adulteress, according to the love of the LORD toward the children of Israel, who look to other gods, and love flagons [1]of wine.

2 So I bought her to me for fifteen *pieces* of silver, and *for* a homer of barley, and a [1]half homer of barley:

3 And I said unto her, Thou shalt [a]abide for me many days; thou shalt not play the harlot, and thou shalt not be for *another* man: so *will* I also *be* for thee.

4 For the children of Israel shall abide many days [a]without a king, and without a prince, and without a sacrifice, and without [1]an image, and without an [b]ephod, and *without* [c]teraphim:

5 Afterward shall the children of Israel return, and [a]seek the LORD their God, and [b]David their king; and shall fear the LORD and his goodness in the [c]latter days.

Israel's immorality

4 Hear the word of the LORD, ye children
of Israel:
For the LORD hath a [a]controversy with
the inhabitants of the land,
Because *there is* no truth, nor mercy,
nor [b]knowledge of God in the land.

2:19–20 Rather than money, these five traits necessary to the covenant relationship make up the bride-price (see Ex 22:16–17; Deut 22:23–29; 1 Sam 18:25; 2 Sam 3:14).
2:19 *righteousness.* See 10:12; Jer 23:6; Amos 6:12; Mic 6:5. *judgment.* See Amos 5:24. *lovingkindness.* See 4:1; 6:4; 10:12; 12:6. *mercies.* A reversal of God's threatened withdrawal of compassion (see 1:6 and note). "Lo-ruhamah" means lit. "not having obtained mercy" (cf. Ps 51:1; 103:3–14).
2:20 *faithfulness.* Dependability (see Deut 32:4; Ps 88:11). *know.* The Hebrew for this word can refer to intimate marital relations (Gen 19:8; Num 31:17–18,35), but it also refers to active acknowledgment of a covenant partner (see 4:1,6; 5:4; 6:3,6; 8:2; 11:3; 13:4).
‡2:21 *hear.* Or "respond." The woman (Israel) responded to the Lord's overtures; now God responded to her new behavior. The land also responded in becoming productive (vv. 21–22).
‡2:22 *Jezreel.* Here used in the sense "God sows" (see note on 1:11). The threats represented by the names of the children are turned into blessings (see 1:10). The terms of the covenant were: "I will take you to me for a people and I will be to you a God" (Ex 6:7; see note on Zech 8:8).
2:23 *Thou art my God.* The people respond to God's graciousness. This verse is quoted in part in Rom 9:25; 1 Pet 2:10 and applied to Gentiles coming into the church.
‡3:1 *said . . . unto me.* Ch. 3 is narrated in the first person, ch. 1 in the third person. *Go . . . love a woman.* Hosea's love for unfaithful Gomer illustrated God's love for unfaithful Israel. God's love for Israel (see 11:1; 14:4) is the basic theme of the book. *other gods.* See Ex 20:3; Deut 31:20. *flagons of wine.* Possibly "raisin cakes" (see KJV marg.) offered to Baal in thanksgiving for harvest.
3:2 Gomer had evidently become a slave, and Hosea bought her back. *fifteen pieces of silver.* Half the usual price of a slave (Ex 21:7,32) or of the redemption value of a woman's vow (Lev 27:4). *a homer . . . and half.* Probably about 10 bushels. Comparison with prices in 2 Ki 7:1,16,18 suggests that half was paid in money (silver) and half in produce (barley)—for a total value of 30 shekels.
3:3–5 A picture of exile and return.
3:3 *many days.* Not forever. There would be an "afterward" (v. 5), a future. *be for thee.* Or "wait for thee"; suggests a period of isolation (see 2:6 and note), comparable to Israel's exile.
3:4 *king.* See 1:4; 5:1; 8:4,10; 10:15; 13:10–11. *prince.* See 5:10; 7:3,5; 8:4; 13:10. *without a sacrifice.* See 6:6; 8:11,13. *image.* See 10:1–2; Deut 16:22; 1 Ki 14:23; 2 Ki 17:10; Mic 5:13. *ephod.* Here an image associated with idols (see Judg 8:27; 17:5). *teraphim.* See Gen 31:30; 1 Sam 19:13,16.
‡3:5 *return.* A basic word in Hosea's vocabulary (see 2:7; 5:4; 6:1; 7:10; 11:5; 12:6; 14:1–2). *seek.* Israel's repentance is envisioned (cf. 5:15)—the reverse of her present stubborn rebellion (7:10). *LORD their God.* See 12:9; 13:4; Jer 50:4. *David their king.* The Messianic king from the dynasty of David (see Jer 30:9; Ezek 34:24). After the death of Solomon, Israel (the northern kingdom) had abandoned the Davidic kings. *his goodness.* The vineyards and olive groves that had been taken away (see 2:12–13,21) and all of God's gifts (see Jer 31:12–14). *latter days.* The Hebrew for this phrase occurs 13 times in the OT, sometimes simply meaning the future ("the last days," Gen 49:1), but most of the time, as no doubt here, referring to the Messianic age ("afterward," Joel 2:28; cf. Acts 2:17; Heb 1:2).
4:1–14:9 Deals with Israel's involvement in Canaanite religion, her moral sins and her international intrigues.
‡4:1 *Hear the word.* See, e.g., Is 1:10; Jer 2:4; Ezek 6:3. *a controversy.* This is a technical term in Hebrew for a "lawsuit." As the Lord's spokesman, Hosea brought charges against unfaithful, covenant-breaking Israel (cf. v. 4; Is 3:13; Jer 2:9; Mic 6:2). *truth.* Loyalty to the covenant Lord (Josh 24:14) and right dealing with men (Prov 3:3). *mercy.* See 2:19; 10:12. *knowledge of God.* See 2:20 and note; 5:4; 6:6.

2 By swearing, and lying, and killing, and
stealing, and committing adultery,
they break out,
And [1]blood toucheth blood.
3 Therefore [a]shall the land mourn,
And [b]every one that dwelleth therein
shall languish,
With the beasts of the field, and with
the fowls of heaven;
Yea, the fishes of the sea also shall be
taken away.
4 Yet let no man strive, nor reprove
another:
For thy people *are* as they [a]that strive
with the priest.
5 Therefore shalt thou fall [a]*in* the day,
And the prophet also shall fall with
thee *in* the night,
And I will [1]destroy thy mother.
6 [a]My people are [1]destroyed for lack of
knowledge,
Because thou hast rejected knowledge,
I will also reject thee, that *thou* shalt
be no priest to me:
Seeing thou hast forgotten the law of
thy God,
I will also forget thy children.
7 As they were increased, so they sinned
against me:
[a]*Therefore* will I change their glory
into shame.
8 They eat *up* the sin of my people,
And they [1]set their heart on their
iniquity.
9 And there shall be, [a]like people, like
priest:
And I will [1]punish them for their ways,
And [2]reward them their doings.
10 For [a]they shall eat, and not have
enough:
They shall commit whoredom, and
shall not increase:
Because they have left off to take heed
to the LORD.
11 Whoredom and wine and new wine
[a]take *away* the heart.
12 My people ask *counsel* at their [a]stocks,
And their staff declareth unto them:
For [b]the spirit of whoredoms hath
caused *them* to err,
And they have gone a whoring from
under their God.
13 [a]They sacrifice upon the tops of the
mountains,
And burn incense upon the hills,
Under oaks and poplars and elms,
Because the shadow thereof *is* good:
[b]Therefore your daughters shall
commit whoredom,
And your spouses shall commit
adultery.
14 [1]I will not punish your daughters
when they commit whoredom,
Nor your spouses when they commit
adultery:
For themselves are separated with
whores,
And they sacrifice with harlots:
Therefore the people *that* doth not
understand shall [2]fall.

15 Though thou, Israel, play the harlot,
Yet let not Judah offend;
[a]And come not ye *unto* Gilgal,

4:2 [1]Heb. *bloods* 4:3 [a]Amos 5:16 [b]Zeph. 1:3 4:4 [a]Deut. 17:12 4:5 [1]Heb. *cut off* [a]Jer. 15:8 4:6 [1]Heb. *cut off* [a]Is. 5:13 4:7 [a]1 Sam. 2:30; Mal. 2:9 4:8 [1]Heb. *lift up their soul to their iniquity* 4:9 [1]Heb. *visit upon* [a]Is. 24:2; Jer. 5:31 4:9 [2]Heb. *cause to return* 4:10 [a]Lev. 26:26; Mic. 6:14 4:11 [a]Is. 28:7 4:12 [a]Jer. 2:27 [b]Is. 44:20 4:13 [a]Is. 1:29; Ezek. 6:13 [b]Amos 7:17; Rom. 1:28 4:14 [1]Or, *Shall I not, etc.* [2]Or, *be punished* 4:15 [a]ch. 9:15

4:2 *swearing . . . adultery.* The sins detailed (paralleled in Jer 7:9) transgress the ten commandments (see Ex 20:13–16; Deut 5:17–20). *blood toucheth blood.* Includes (1) murder (see 6:8–9), (2) the assassinations following the death of Jeroboam II when three kings reigned in one year (2 Ki 15:10–14) and (3) human sacrifice (Ps 106:38; Ezek 16:20–21; 23:37). Where God is not acknowledged (v. 1), moral uprightness disappears.
4:3 *land mourn.* God's judgment on man's sin affects all living things in man's world (see, e.g., Is 24:3–6; Jer 4:23–28). *languish.* See Is 19:8; Jer 14:2; 15:9; Joel 1:10.
4:4–9 An indictment against the priests, whose duty it was to be guardians of God's law and to furnish religious instruction (see Deut 31:9–13; 33:10; 2 Chr 17:8–9; Ezra 7:6,10; Jer 18:18). Hosea warned the priests not to lodge charges against the people for bringing God's judgment down on the nation, for they themselves were guilty, and the people could also bring charges against them—as Hosea proceeded to do (see v. 9; Is 28:7; Jer 2:26; 4:9; 23:11).
4:5 *fall.* See 5:5. *prophet.* See Mic 2:6,11; 3:5–7. *thy mother.* The nation (see 2:2,5; Is 50:1).
4:6 *My people.* Israel (see vv. 8,12; 2:1,23; 6:11; 11:7; Mic 6:3). *destroyed for lack of knowledge.* Partly because the priests had failed to teach God's word to the people. *rejected knowledge . . . reject thee.* Punishment in kind. *law of thy God.* Israel's source of life (see Deut 32:47), which the priests should have been faithfully promoting.
4:7 *their glory.* God (see Ps 106:20).
4:8 *eat up the sin.* Priests devoured the sacrifices (1 Sam 2:13–17), profiting from the continuation of the sin rather than helping to cure it (see 8:13).
4:9 *like people, like priest.* Without exception, all would be punished for their sins.
‡4:10 *eat, and not have enough.* The idea is that of a "futility curse." The punishment fit the sin. *commit whoredom.* See vv. 12,18; 2:4; 6:10; 9:1; Ps 106:39. Instead of giving themselves to the Lord, they chose the fertility rituals of Canaanite religion.
4:11 *wine.* See 7:5; 9:10; 14:7. *new wine.* See 2:8–9,22; 7:14; 9:2.
4:12 *their stocks.* An image of a god (see Jer 2:27; 10:8; Hab 2:19). *staff.* See Ezek 21:21 and note. *spirit of whoredoms.* See 5:4. Hebrew idioms often describe inner tendencies in terms of "spirit."
‡4:13 *They sacrifice.* See 8:13. *tops of the mountains.* Places commonly chosen for pagan altars (see 10:8; Deut 12:2; 1 Ki 14:23; 2 Ki 17:10; Jer 2:20; 3:6). Clay tablets from Ugarit (see chart, p. xix) tell of fertility rites carried out by the Canaanites at the high places. *elms.* Hebrew *terebinth,* trees noted for their shade. *commit whoredom.* Canaanite fertility rites involved sexual activity (v. 14) that led to general erosion of morals.
4:14 *not punish.* The men would punish their women for immorality, but God would have no part in their hypocrisy. *whores.* Common prostitutes (see Gen 34:31; Lev 21:14; Ezek 16:31). *harlots.* Women of the sanctuaries who served as partners for men in cultic sexual activity (cf. Gen 38:21–22; Deut 23:18). *doth not understand.* Contrast 14:9.
4:15 *Judah.* An aside warning (see Introduction: Author and

Neither go ye up *to* [b]Beth-aven,
[c]Nor swear, The LORD liveth.
16 For Israel [a]slideth back as a backsliding heifer:
Now the LORD will feed them as a lamb in a large place.
17 Ephraim *is* joined to idols:
[a]Let him alone.
18 Their drink [1]is sour; they have committed whoredom continually:
[a]Her [2]rulers *with* shame do love, Give ye.
19 [a]The wind hath bound her up in her wings,
And [b]they shall be ashamed because of their sacrifices.

God's severity toward Israel

5 Hear ye this, O priests;
And hearken, ye house of Israel;
And give ye ear, O house of the king;
For judgment *is* toward you,
Because [a]ye have been a snare on Mizpah,
And a net spread upon Tabor.
2 And the revolters are [a]profound to make slaughter,
[1]Though I *have been* [2]a rebuker of them all.

4:15 [b]1 Ki. 12:29 [c]Amos 8:14
4:16 [a]Jer. 3:6
4:17 [a]Mat. 15:14
4:18 [1]Heb. *is gone* [2]Heb. *shields* [a]Mic. 3:11
4:19 [a]Jer. 51:1 [b]Is. 1:29
5:1 [a]ch. 6:9
5:2 [1]Or, *And, etc.* [2]Heb. *a correction* [a]Is. 29:15
5:3 [a]Amos 3:2 [b]ch. 4:17
5:4 [1]Heb. *They will not give* [2]Or, *Their doings will not suffer* them [a]ch. 4:12
5:6 [a]Prov. 1:28
5:7 [a]Jer. 3:20
5:8 [a]Joel 2:1 [b]Is. 10:30 [c]Josh. 7:2

3 [a]I know Ephraim, and Israel is not hid from me:
For now, O Ephraim, [b]thou committest whoredom, *and* Israel is defiled.
4 [1][2]They will not frame their doings to turn unto their God:
For [a]the spirit of whoredoms *is* in the midst of them,
And they have not known the LORD.
5 And the pride of Israel doth testify to his face:
Therefore shall Israel and Ephraim fall in their iniquity;
Judah also shall fall with them.
6 [a]They shall go with their flocks and with their herds to seek the LORD;
But they shall not find *him;* he hath withdrawn himself from them.
7 They have [a]dealt treacherously against the LORD:
For they have begotten strange children:
Now shall a month devour them with their portions.
8 [a]Blow ye the cornet in Gibeah,
And the trumpet in Ramah:
[b]Cry aloud *at* [c]Beth-aven,
After thee, O Benjamin.

Date). *Gilgal.* A site near Jericho (see 9:15; 12:11; Josh 4:19–20; 1 Sam 11:13–15) where the Israelites had established a religious shrine. *offend.* See 10:2; 13:1; 14:1. *Neither go . . . Nor.* The nation as a whole was addressed. *Beth-aven.* A sarcastic substitute name for Beth-el (Beth-aven means "house of wickedness," while Beth-el means "house of God"; see also 5:8), site of one of the cult centers established by Jeroboam I (1 Ki 12:29). *The LORD liveth.* A form of solemn oath (see Judg 8:19; Ruth 3:13; 1 Sam 14:39; 26:10,16; Jer 4:2; 38:16). Though proper in itself—since it invoked the true God (see Deut 6:13; 10:20; Josh 23:7)—it was here forbidden because it was being used deceitfully, as though the Israelites were truly honoring the Lord (see Jer 5:2).

4:16 *slideth back.* See Neh 9:29; Zech 7:11. *backsliding heifer.* See 10:11; Jer 2:20; an apt figure for unruly Israel (see 11:4; Jer 31:18).

4:17 *Ephraim.* Israel, the northern kingdom. *idols.* The golden calf (8:5; 13:2; 1 Ki 12:28) and the cult of Baal (2:8,13). *Let him alone.* Nothing could be done to help (see 2 Sam 16:11; 2 Ki 23:18).

‡4:19 *The wind hath bound her up in her wings.* Probably a metaphor from the threshing floor (see 13:3; Ps 1:4) for the sudden violence that would bring the exile. Since the Hebrew for the words "wind" and "spirit" is the same, there is a possible play on words with the "spirit of whoredoms" (v. 12; 5:4). *ashamed.* By means of their sacrifices they hoped to flourish, but God's punishment for their idolatry would bring them into disgrace among the nations (see 10:6).

5:1 *priests . . . house of Israel . . . house of the king.* The three groups addressed were all responsible for maintaining justice, but it miscarried at their hands. *snare . . . net.* Devices for catching animals and birds, here used as metaphors for those who by economic and legal devices took cruel advantage of innocent people (see Job 18:8–10; Ps 140:5; Prov 29:5; Lam 1:13). *Mizpah.* Either (1) Mizpah in Gilead east of the Jordan (Gen 31:43–49) or (2) Mizpah in Benjamin (1 Sam 7:5–6; 10:17). *Tabor.* A mountain at the southeastern edge of the Jezreel Valley. Reference must have been to well-known events that illustrated Israel's corruption.

5:2 *rebuker.* A significant word in the prophets for God's corrective action against His people (see Is 26:16; Jer 2:30; 5:3; 7:28).

5:3 *Ephraim.* Israel, the northern kingdom. *committest whoredom.* See 1:2; 4:10,18.

5:4 *their doings.* See 4:9; 7:2; 9:15; 12:2. Persistent sin can make repentance impossible (see Jer 13:23; John 8:34; Rom 6:6,16). *spirit of whoredoms.* See 4:12. *have not known the LORD.* See 4:6; Is 1:2–4.

5:5 *pride.* Stubborn rebellion against the Lord (see Deut 1:43; 1 Sam 15:23; Neh 9:16; Job 35:12; Ps 10:2; Ezek 16:56–57). *testify.* In the case God presented against His people (see 4:1 and note). *fall.* Experience calamity (see 4:5). *Judah.* See Introduction: Author and Date.

5:6 *seek the LORD.* Go to Him with prayer and sacrifices (see 3:5; Amos 5:4–5). *not find him.* Offering sacrifices in their situation was useless (see 2:7; cf. Is 1:10–14; Amos 5:21–25; Mic 6:6–8). The Lord would be "found" by Israel only when she turned to Him with integrity of heart (see 3:5; 5:15; Deut 4:29–31; Jer 29:13).

5:7 *dealt treacherously.* See Jer 5:11. *strange children.* Children they had prayed to the Baals for and had credited to their fertility rites. *a month.* Or "new moon," usually a festive occasion (see, e.g., 2:11; 1 Sam 20:5,18; Amos 8:5; Col 2:16), but now a time of judgment. Or the meaning may be that one month would be sufficient to accomplish their punishment.

5:8 Some interpreters suggest that the Aramean (Syrian)-Ephraimite (Israelite) war (2 Ki 16:5–9; Is 7:1–9) forms the background of this oracle. *cornet.* Made of a ram's horn, which here sounds the alarm that an army is approaching (see 8:1). *Gibeah.* Two miles north of Jerusalem. *Ramah.* North of Gibeah. *Beth-aven.* See note on 4:15. *After thee, O Benjamin.* Thought to be the Benjamite war cry (see Judg 5:14).

9 Ephraim shall be desolate in the day of
rebuke:
Among the tribes of Israel have I made
known that which shall surely be.
10 The princes of Judah were like them
that [a]remove the bound:
Therefore I will pour out my wrath
upon them like water.
11 Ephraim *is* [a]oppressed *and* broken in
judgment,
Because he willingly walked after [b]the
commandment.
12 Therefore *will* I *be* unto Ephraim as a
moth,
And to the house of Judah [a]as
[1]rottenness.
13 When Ephraim saw his sickness,
And Judah *saw* his [a]wound,
Then went Ephraim [b]to the Assyrian,
And sent [1]to king Jareb:
Yet could he not heal you
Nor cure you of your wound.
14 For [a]I *will be* unto Ephraim as a lion,
And as a young lion to the house of
Judah:
[b]I, *even* I, will tear and go away;
I will take away, and none shall rescue
him.

15 I will go *and* return to my place,
[1]Till they acknowledge their offence,
and seek my face:
In their affliction they will seek me
early.

6 Come and let us return unto the LORD:
For [a]he hath torn, and [b]he will heal us;
He hath smitten, and he will bind us up.

5:10 [a]Deut. 19:14
5:11 [a]Deut. 28:33 [b]Mic. 6:16
5:12 [1]Or, *a worm* [a]Prov. 12:4
5:13 [1]Or, *to the king of Jareb:* or, *to the king* that *should plead* [a]Jer. 30:12 [b]2 Ki. 15:19
5:14 [a]Lam. 3:10 [b]Ps. 50:22
5:15 [1]Heb. *Till they be guilty*
6:1 [a]Deut. 32:39 [b]Jer. 30:17
6:2 [a]1 Cor. 15:4
6:3 [a]Is. 54:13 [b]2 Sam. 23:4 [c]Ps. 72:6 [d]Job 29:23
6:4 [1]Or, *mercy,* or, *kindness*
6:5 [1]Or, *That thy judgments might be, etc.* [a]Jer. 23:29
6:6 [a]Mat. 9:13 [b]Is. 1:11 [c]John 17:3
6:7 [1]Or, *like Adam*
6:8 [1]Or, *cunning for blood*
6:9 [1]Heb. *with one shoulder,* or, *to Shechem* [2]Or, *enormity*

2 [a]After two days will he revive us:
In the third day he will raise us up,
And we shall live in his sight.
3 [a]Then shall we know, *if* we follow on
to know the LORD:
His going forth *is* prepared [b]as the
morning;
And [c]he shall come unto us [d]as the rain,
As the latter *and* former rain *unto* the
earth.

Israel's unfaithfulness

4 O Ephraim, what shall I do unto thee?
O Judah, what shall I do unto thee?
For your [1]goodness *is* as a morning
cloud,
And as the early dew *it* goeth away.
5 Therefore have I hewed *them* by the
prophets;
I have slain them by [a]the words of my
mouth:
[1]And thy judgments *are as* the light
that goeth forth.
6 For I desired [a]mercy, and [b]not sacrifice;
And the [c]knowledge of God more than
burnt offerings.
7 But they [1]like men have transgressed
the covenant:
There have they dealt treacherously
against me.
8 Gilead *is* a city of them that work
iniquity,
And is [1]polluted with blood.
9 And as troops *of robbers* wait for a man,
So the company of priests murder *in*
the way [1]by consent:
For they commit [2]lewdness.

5:9 *desolate.* See Jer 25:11,38.
5:10 *remove the bound.* Or, "move boundary stones." Judah had seized Israelite territory (1 Ki 15:16–22; see Deut 19:14; 27:17; Prov 22:28; 23:10; Is 5:8; Mic 2:2). *my wrath.* See 13:11.
5:12 *moth . . . rottenness.* Both consume (see Job 13:28).
5:13 *sickness . . . wound.* Metaphors for the national wounds the two nations had suffered at the hands of their enemies (see Is 1:5–6; 17:4,11; Jer 30:12–13). *went . . . to the Assyrian.* Assyrian records tell of the tribute paid to Tiglath-pileser III by the Israelite kings Menahem and Hoshea (cf. 2 Ki 15:19–20; 17:3). *Could he not heal.* The alliances were worthless.
5:14 *lion.* See 13:7. The Lord might use human agents (Is 10:5–6), but He would be responsible for Israel's punishment, from which there was no escape (see Is 5:29; 42:22; Amos 9:1–4; Mic 5:8).
5:15 *return to my place.* God threatened to withdraw from Israel until, out of desperation, she truly repented. This idea sets the stage for the prophet's next theme.
6:1 *let us return.* A shallow (see v. 4) proposal of repentance (using phrases from 5:13–15), in which Israel acknowledged that God, not Assyria (cf. 5:13), was the true physician (cf. 7:1).
6:2 *two days . . . third day.* A brief time. Israel supposed that God's wrath would only be temporary.
6:3 *know the LORD.* A key concept in Hosea (see v. 6; 2:8,20; 4:1,6; 5:4). *As the latter and former rain.* Israel believed that, as surely as seasonal rains fell, reviving the earth, God's favor would return and restore her.
‡6:4 *Ephraim.* Israel, the northern kingdom. *what shall I do . . . ?* See Is 5:4. God saw through Israel's superficial repentance. *Judah.* See Introduction: Author and Date. *goodness.* Or "lovingkindness." See 2:19; see also note on v. 6. *morning cloud . . . dew.* Figurative for that which is temporary.
6:5 *the prophets.* God's spokesmen (see Jer 1:9; 15:19) had denounced the people's sin. *words of my mouth.* The judgments spoken by the Lord's faithful prophets. *the light that goeth forth.* See Deut 32:41.
6:6 *mercy.* See v. 4; Hebrew *ḥesed,* a word that can refer to right conduct toward one's fellowman or loyalty to the Lord or both—the sum of what God requires of His servants. Here it perhaps refers to both. *not sacrifice.* Sacrifice apart from faithfulness to the Lord's will is wholly unacceptable to Him (see 1 Sam 15:22–23; Is 1:11–20; Jer 7:21–22; Amos 5:21–24; Mic 6:6–8; Mat 9:13; 12:7).
‡6:7 *like men.* See KJV marg. The allusion is uncertain, since Scripture records no covenant with Adam. Two other possibilities exist. "Adam" could be a reference to the place named Adam (see Josh 3:16), as suggested by "There" in the verse. Or "Adam" could be a reference to mankind in general rather than the man Adam. *transgressed the covenant.* See 8:1; Josh 7:11.
6:8 *Gilead.* See 12:11; Judg 10:17; 12:7. *polluted with blood.* The allusion is unclear, but Hosea may have been referring to a more recent event than the bloodbath of Judg 12:1–6—such as Pekah's rebellion against Pekahiah (see 2 Ki 15:25).
6:9 *murder.* The specific event is unknown.

10 I have seen a horrible thing in the
house of Israel:
There *is* the whoredom of Ephraim,
Israel is defiled.
11 Also, O Judah, he hath set a harvest for
thee,
When I returned the captivity of my
people.

7 When I *would have* healed Israel,
Then the iniquity of Ephraim was
discovered, and the [1]wickedness of
Samaria:
For [a]they commit falsehood; and the
thief cometh in,
And the troop *of robbers* [2]spoileth
without.
2 And they [1]consider not in their hearts
That I [a]remember all their wickedness:
Now their own doings have beset them
about;
They are before my face.
3 They make the king glad with their
wickedness,
And the princes [a]with their lies.
4 [a]They *are* all adulterers, as an oven
heated by the baker,
[1]*Who* ceaseth [2]from raising after *he*
hath kneaded the dough, until it be
leavened.
5 *In* the day of our king the princes have
made *him* sick [1]*with* bottles of wine;
He stretched out his hand with scorners.
6 For they have [1]made ready their heart
like an oven, whiles they lie in wait:
Their baker sleepeth all the night;
In the morning it burneth as a flaming
fire.
7 They are all hot as an oven,
And have devoured their judges;
All their kings are fallen:
[a]*There is* none among them that
calleth unto me.
8 Ephraim, he [a]hath mixed himself
among the people;
Ephraim is a cake not turned.
9 [a]Strangers have devoured his strength,
and he knoweth *it* not:
Yea, gray hairs are [1]here and there
upon him, yet he knoweth not.
10 And the [a]pride of Israel testifieth to his
face:
And [b]they do not return to the LORD
their God, nor seek him for all this.

11 [a]Ephraim also is like a silly dove,
without heart:
[b]They call *to* Egypt, they go *to* Assyria.
12 When they shall go, I will spread my
net upon them;
I will bring them down as the fowls of
the heaven;
I will chastise them, [a]as their
congregation hath heard.
13 Woe unto them! for they have fled
from me:
[1]Destruction unto them! because they
have transgressed against me:
Though [a]I have redeemed them, yet
they have spoken lies against me.
14 [a]And they have not cried unto me with
their heart,
When they howled upon their beds:
They assemble themselves for corn and
wine,
And they rebel against me.
15 Though I [1]have bound *and*
strengthened their arms,

7:1 [1]Heb. *evils* [2]Heb. *strippeth* [a]ch. 5:1
7:2 [1]Heb. *say not to* [a]Jer. 17:1
7:3 [a]Rom. 1:32
7:4 [1]Or, *The raiser will cease* [2]Or, *from waking* [a]Jer. 9:2
7:5 [1]Or, with *heat through wine*
7:6 [1]Or, *applied*
7:7 [a]Is. 64:7
7:8 [a]Ps. 106:35
7:9 [1]Heb. *sprinkled* [a]ch. 8:7
7:10 [a]ch. 5:5 [b]Is. 9:13
7:11 [a]ch. 11:11 [b]ch. 5:13
7:12 [a]Lev. 26:14; Deut. 28:15; 2 Ki. 17:13
7:13 [1]Heb. *Spoil* [a]Mic. 6:4
7:14 [a]Job 35:9; Jer. 3:10; Zech. 7:5
7:15 [1]Or, *chastened*

6:10 *whoredom.* See chs. 2; 4.
6:11 *harvest.* A figure for God's judgments (see 8:7; 10:12–13; Jer 51:33; Joel 3:13; Mat 13:39; Rev 14:15). *returned the captivity.* Paralleling "heal" (7:1), the phrase refers to the restoration of the wounded national body (see Joel 3:1; Zeph 3:20).
7:1 *healed.* See 5:13; 6:1; 11:3; 14:4; Jer 51:8–9. *iniquity.* See 4:8; 5:5; 8:13. *Ephraim.* Israel, the northern kingdom. *discovered.* God sees them. *wickedness.* See v. 3. *Samaria.* Another name for the northern kingdom, of which Samaria was the royal city, selected by Omri to be capital of Israel (1 Ki 16:24). *Commit falsehood.* See Jer 6:13; 8:10; probably refers to both feigned repentance and treacherous foreign alliances. *thief.* See 4:2. *robbers.* See 6:9; Gen 49:19; Jer 18:22.
7:2 *I remember.* All is open before the Lord (see Ps 90:8), but the wicked believe God does not see (see Ps 10:6,11; 14:1; Ezek 8:12).
7:3 *make the king glad.* Probably in conjunction with one of the palace revolts (see 2 Ki 15:8–30). *king . . . princes.* Paired also in 3:4; 8:4; 13:10. *lies.* See 11:12; Ps 59:12; Nah 3:1.
7:4 *adulterers.* See 3:1; 4:2,13; Jer 9:2; Ezek 23:37. *baker.* Perhaps the leader of the conspiracy. *from raising.* From stirring the fire. Fire was a metaphor for political intrigue (see vv. 6–7). The fire was banked until ready to use; then it broke out.
7:5 *day of our king.* Probably a coronation or birthday that became a drunken party. King Elah died in drunkenness (1 Ki 16:9–10). *scorners.* See Prov 21:24. Isaiah (28:1–8,14) condemned Israel's drunkenness and her scoffers.
7:6 The intrigue was kept secret until a suitable time.
7:7 *judges . . . kings.* Four kings were assassinated in 20 years, Zechariah and Shallum in a seven-month period (2 Ki 15:10–15). *none . . . calleth unto me.* The reason for the shameful situation.
7:8 *cake not turned.* A metaphor describing unwise policies. Baked on hot stones (cf. 1 Ki 19:6), the cake was burned on the bottom and raw on the top.
7:9 *gray hairs.* He was old before his time, but ignored the danger signals. Tribute to Tiglath-pileser (2 Ki 15:19–20,29) and to Egypt had sapped the country economically.
7:10 *not return.* See 3:5; 5:4; Amos 4:6–11. *seek.* See 2:7; 5:6.
7:11 *dove.* See 11:11 and note, where a different image is intended. See also note on Ps 68:13. *without heart*. See Jer 5:21. Menahem turned to Assyria (2 Ki 15:19–20), and Pekah to Egypt. Hoshea alternated in allegiance to both (2 Ki 17:4).
7:12 *my net.* The Lord Himself was the hunter—not the nations—and Israel was certain to be caught.
7:13 *Woe.* Often used in conjunction with threats of judgment (see 9:12). *Destruction.* See 9:6; Is 13:6. *redeemed.* See 13:14; also used for deliverance from Egypt (see, e.g., Ex 6:6; Mic 6:4). *lies.* Possibly of ascribing prosperity and destiny to gods other than the Lord.
‡7:14 *howled.* See Joel 1:13. *corn and wine.* See 2:8,22; 9:1–2. *assemble themselves.* Or, "They slash themselves" (cf. Lev 19:28; 21:5).
7:15 *I have bound.* As children (or, perhaps, as troops).

Yet do they imagine mischief against
 me.
16 They return, *but* not *to* the most High:
[a]They are like a deceitful bow:
Their princes shall fall by the sword for
 the [b]rage of their tongue:
This *shall be* their derision [c]in the land
 of Egypt.

God's sentence

8 *Set* the trumpet to [1]thy mouth.
He shall come [a]as an eagle against the
 house of the LORD,
Because they have transgressed my
 covenant,
And trespassed against my law.
2 [a]Israel shall cry unto me, My God, [b]we
 know thee.
3 Israel hath cast off *the thing that is*
 good:
The enemy shall pursue him.
4 [a]They have set up kings, but not by me:
They have made princes, and I knew *it*
 not:
Of their silver and their gold have they
 made them idols,
That they may be cut off.
5 Thy calf, O Samaria, hath cast *thee* off;
Mine anger is kindled against them:
[a]How long *will it be* ere they attain to
 innocency?
6 For from Israel *was* it also:
The workman made it; therefore it *is*
 not God:
But the calf of Samaria shall be broken
 in pieces.
7 For [a]they have sown the wind, and
 they shall reap the whirlwind:
It hath no [1]stalk: the bud shall yield no
 meal:
If so be it yield, *the* strangers shall
 swallow it up.
8 [a]Israel is swallowed up:
Now shall they be among the Gentiles
 [b]as a vessel wherein *is* no pleasure.
9 For they are gone up *to* Assyria, [a]a
 wild ass alone by himself:
Ephraim [b]hath hired [1]lovers.
10 Yea, though they have hired among the
 nations, now [a]will I gather them,
And they shall [1]sorrow [2]a little for the
 burden of [b]the king of princes.
11 Because Ephraim hath made many
 altars to sin,
Altars shall be unto him to sin.
12 I have written to him [a]the great things
 of my law,
But they were counted as a strange
 thing.
13 [a][1]They sacrifice flesh *for* the sacrifices
 of mine offerings, and eat *it;*
[b]*But* the LORD accepteth them not;
Now will he remember their iniquity,
 and visit their sins:
They shall return *to* Egypt.
14 [a]For Israel hath forgotten [b]his Maker,
 and buildeth temples;
And Judah hath multiplied fenced
 cities:
But [c]I will send a fire upon his cities,
And it shall devour the palaces thereof.

Israel's punishment

9 Rejoice not, O Israel, for joy, as *other*
 people:

7:16 [a]Ps. 78:57 [b]Ps. 73:9 [c]ch. 9:3,6
8:1 [1]Heb. *the roof of thy mouth* [a]Deut. 28:49; Jer. 4:13
8:2 [a]Ps. 78:34 [b]Tit. 1:16
8:4 [a]2 Ki. 15:13,17,25, Shallum, Menahem, Pekahiah
8:5 [a]Jer. 13:27
8:7 [a]Prov. 22:8
8:7 [1]Or, *standing corn*
8:8 [a]2 Ki. 17:6 [b]Jer. 22:28
8:9 [1]Heb. *loves* [a]Jer. 2:24 [b]Ezek. 16:33,34
8:10 [1]Or, *begin* [2][Or, in *a little* while as Hag. 2:6] [a]Ezek. 16:37 [b]Is. 10:8; Ezek. 26:7; Dan. 2:37
8:12 [a]Deut. 4:6,8; Ps. 119:18
8:13 [1]Or, In *the sacrifices of mine offerings they, etc.* [a]Zech. 7:6 [b]Jer. 14:10
8:14 [a]Deut. 32:18 [b]Is. 29:23 [c]Jer. 17:27

strengthened their arms. See Ezek 30:24–25.

7:16 *deceitful bow.* See Ps 78:57. The arrow missed the mark; Israel missed her purpose for being. *derision.* Egypt would fail to assist Israel and then would belittle God's power (see Deut 9:28). *Egypt.* See 8:13; 9:6; 11:5. There is no record of a forced exile of large numbers to Egypt. Some captives were taken there (2 Ki 23:34; Jer 22:11–14), and some fugitives voluntarily went there (2 Ki 25:26; Jer 42–44). A return from Egypt is envisioned in 11:11; Is 11:11; 27:13; Zech 10:10.

8:1 *trumpet.* Of alarm (see 5:8; Joel 2:1; Amos 3:6). *thy.* The prophet's. *eagle.* Or "vulture," referring to Assyria. *house of the LORD.* The land of Israel, not just the temple (see 9:15 and note; cf. Ex 15:17). *covenant.* The demands of the covenant.

8:2 *we . . . know thee.* But their worship of the Lord was thoroughly corrupted by pagan notions and practices, as vv. 3–6 indicate (see Amos 2:4,7–8; 3:14; 5:26).

8:4 *set up kings.* After Jeroboam II, five kings ruled over Israel in 13 years (2 Ki 15:8–30), three of whom seized the throne by violence (see 7:7).

8:5 *calf.* Jeroboam I (930–909 B.C.) had set up golden calves in Beth-el and Dan, saying, "Behold your gods" (see 1 Ki 12:28–33 and note on 1 Ki 12:28).

‡8:6 *the workman made it.* For prophetic satire on idolatry see Is 40:20; 41:22–24; 44:9–20; see also Ps 115:4–8. Aaron (Ex 32:8) and Jeroboam I had said, "These be thy gods"; but Hosea said, "It is not God."

8:7 *sown . . . reap.* A familiar proverb about the results of doing evil (see 10:13; Job 4:8; Ps 126:5–6; Prov 11:18; 22:8; 2 Cor 9:6; Gal 6:7). Israel sowed the wind of idolatry and reaped the whirlwind of Assyria. *Hath no stalk . . . meal.* The prophet played on the similar sound of the Hebrew words. *strangers.* Assyria.

8:8 Israel was chosen to be God's own people (Ex 19:5; Amos 3:2), but since she had conformed to the other nations, she lost her special identity and so became worthless to God.

8:9 *Ephraim hath hired lovers.* For the "prostitute's fees" of Assyrian protection. Menahem (2 Ki 15:19) and Hoshea (2 Ki 17:3), kings of Israel, paid tribute to Assyria.

8:10 Even though Israel paid tribute to Assyria, that would not buy her security, for God would send judgment by the king of Assyria. Israel's real "enemy" was the Lord Himself (see 2:8–9,13; 7:12).

8:11 *made many altars.* To Baal.

8:13 *sacrifices of mine.* See v. 2 and note. *eat it.* Some of the sacrifices were partly eaten by the offerer and priests (see Lev 7:11–18; Deut 12:7; Jer 7:21). *accepteth them not.* See note on 6:6. *Egypt.* Israel, who had trusted in Egypt and Assyria, was to go back to "Egypt," i.e., into bondage in a foreign land, primarily Assyria (see 9:3). But see note on 7:16.

8:14 *Israel hath forgotten.* The cause of all their problems (cf. Judg 2:10). *buildeth temples . . . multiplied fenced cities* . Israel's trust was not in her Maker but in what she herself had accomplished. *Judah.* See Introduction: Author and Date. *fire.* See Amos 1:4,7,10,14; 2:5.

9:1 This verse begins a section that was probably spoken at a

For thou hast gone a whoring from thy God,
Thou hast loved a [a]reward [1]upon every cornfloor.
2 The floor and the [1]winepress shall not feed them,
And the new wine shall fail in her.
3 They shall not dwell in [a]the LORD's land;
[b]But Ephraim shall return *to* Egypt,
And [c]they shall eat unclean *things* in Assyria.
4 They shall not offer wine *offerings* to the LORD,
[a]Neither shall they be pleasing unto him:
Their sacrifices *shall be* unto them as the bread of mourners;
All that eat thereof shall be polluted:
For their bread for their soul shall not come *into* the house of the LORD.
5 What will ye do in the solemn day,
And in the day of the feast of the LORD?
6 For lo, they are gone because of [1]destruction:
Egypt shall gather them up, Memphis shall bury them:
[2 3]The pleasant *places* for their silver, nettles shall possess them:
Thorns *shall be* in their tabernacles.
7 The days of visitation are come,
The days of recompence are come;
Israel shall know *it:*
The prophet *is* a fool, [a]the [1]spiritual man *is* mad,
For the multitude of thine iniquity, and the great hatred.

9:1 [1]Or, *in, etc.* [a]Jer. 44:17
9:2 [1]Or, *winefat*
9:3 [a]Lev. 25:23; Jer. 2:7 [b]ch. 8:13 [c]Ezek. 4:13
9:4 [a]Jer. 6:20
9:6 [1]Heb. *spoil* [2]Or, *Their silver shall be desired, the nettle, etc.* [3]Heb. *The desire*
9:7 [1]Heb. *man of the spirit* [a]Mic. 2:11

8 The watchman of Ephraim *was* with my God:
But the prophet *is* a snare of a fowler in all his ways,
And hatred [1]in the house of his God.
9 [a]They have deeply corrupted *themselves,* as *in* the days of [b]Gibeah:
Therefore he will remember their iniquity, he will visit their sins.
10 I found Israel like grapes in the wilderness;
I saw your fathers as the firstripe in the fig tree at her first time:
But they went *to* [a]Baal-peor, and separated themselves unto *that* shame;
[b]And *their* abominations were according as they loved.
11 *As for* Ephraim, their glory shall fly away like a bird,
From the birth, and from the womb, and from the conception.
12 Though they bring up their children,
Yet will I bereave them, *that there shall* not *be* a man *left:*
Yea, [a]woe also to them when I depart from them!
13 Ephraim, [a]as I saw Tyrus, *is* planted in a pleasant place:
But Ephraim *shall* bring forth his children to the murderer.
14 Give them, O LORD: what wilt thou give?
Give them [a]a [1]miscarrying womb and dry breasts.

9:8 [1]Or, *against*
9:9 [a]ch. 10:9 [b]Judg. 19:22
9:10 [a]Num. 25:3; Ps. 106:28 [b]Ps. 81:12
9:12 [a]Deut. 31:17
9:13 [a]Ezek. 26; 27; 28
9:14 [1]Heb. *that casteth the fruit* [a]Luke 23:29

harvest festival, such as the feast of tabernacles (Lev 23:33–43; Deut 16:13–15). *gone a whoring.* See 1:2; 2:2–5. *reward.* See 2:5,12; not to be taken literally, but in the sense of spiritual adultery. *upon every cornfloor.* Since the threshing floor at threshing time was a man's world—the threshers stayed there all night to protect the grain and feasted at the end of the day's labors—prostitutes were not uncommon visitors (see Ruth 3:2–3 and notes).

9:3 *LORD's land.* The promised land, which the Lord claimed as His own (cf. Lev 25:23; Josh 22:19; Jer 2:7; Ezek 38:16; Joel 1:6). *Ephraim.* Israel, the northern kingdom. *Egypt . . . Assyria.* Israel was threatened with exile to the lands it depended on—where the temple sacrifice could not be offered (see 8:13 and note). *unclean.* A foreign country was ceremonially unclean (see Amos 7:17 and note). What grew there was likewise unclean, because it was the product of fertility credited to pagan gods (see Ezek 4:13).

9:4 *as the bread of mourners.* Unclean, like bread in a house where there had been a death (see Num 19:14; Deut 26:14; Jer 16:7). All who touched it became ceremonially unclean. *not come into the house of the LORD.* In exile Israel would have no place (not even those places established by Jeroboam I; 1 Ki 12:28–33) where she could bring sacrifices to the Lord or celebrate her religious festivals (v. 5).

9:6 *Egypt.* See 7:16 and note. *Memphis.* The capital of Lower (northern) Egypt. *nettles . . . Thorns.* Cf. a similar threat against Edom (Is 34:13).

9:7 *spiritual man.* See Mic 2:11; 3:8. *mad.* See 2 Ki 9:11; Jer 29:26; cf. 1 Sam 21:15.

9:8 *watchman.* See Is 56:10; Jer 6:17; Ezek 3:17; 33:2–8. *snare . . . hatred.* Israel showed only hostility toward the watchmen (the true prophets) whom God sent to warn His people of the great dangers that threatened (see Jer 1:19; 11:19; 15:10; Amos 7:10–12).

9:9 *corrupted themselves.* The word used of the Israelites who worshiped the golden calf (Ex 32:7; Deut 9:12; 32:5). *days of Gibeah.* A reference to the corrupt events of Judg 19–21. *he will remember.* Sins unrepented of are remembered, as well as the accumulated sins of generations (see 13:12).

9:10 The covenant relation is traced back to the wilderness (see 2:14–15; 13:5; Deut 32:10). *grapes . . . fig.* Refreshing delicacies (see Is 28:4; Mic 7:1). The images used here (grapes in the wilderness, early fruit of the fig tree) beautifully convey God's delight in Israel when she, out of all the nations, committed herself to Him in covenant at Sinai. *Baal-peor.* A shortened form of Beth-baal-peor. Peor was a mountain (Deut 3:29). Baal-peor refers to the god of Peor (Num 25:1–4) and was used interchangeably with Beth-peor, "the temple of Peor" (see Deut 3:29; 4:3,46; Josh 13:20). Hosea refers here to the incident in Num 25. *abominations.* See Is 5:2,4,7.

9:11 *Ephraim, their glory.* Their large population and prosperity. The punishment fit the sin. Prostitution produces no increase (see 4:10).

9:12 *to them.* To the children.

9:13 *Tyrus.* Tyre, noted for its wealth, pleasant environment and security (see Ezek 27:2–26).

9:14 Hosea did not pray out of hateful vengeance against Israel, but because he shared God's holy wrath against her sins.

15 All their wickedness *is* in Gilgal, for
there I hated them:
For the wickedness of their doings I
will drive them out of mine house,
I will love them no more:
[a]All their princes *are* revolters.
16 Ephraim is smitten, their root is dried
up, they shall bear no fruit:
Yea, though they bring forth, yet will I
slay *even* [a][1]the beloved *fruit* of their
womb.
17 My God will cast them away, because
they did not hearken unto him:
And they shall be wanderers among
the nations.

10 Israel *is* [a][1]an empty vine, he
bringeth forth fruit unto himself:
According to the multitude of his fruit
[b]he hath increased the altars;
According to the goodness of his land
they have made goodly [2]images.
2 [1]Their heart is [a]divided; now shall
they be found faulty:
He shall [2]break down their altars, he
shall spoil their [3]images.
3 For now they shall say, We have no king,
Because we feared not the LORD;
What then should a king do to us?
4 They have spoken words, swearing
falsely in making a covenant:
Thus judgment springeth up [a]as
hemlock in the furrows of the field.
5 The inhabitants of Samaria shall fear
because of the calves of Beth-aven:
For the people thereof shall mourn
over it,
And [a][1]the priests thereof *that* rejoiced
on it,
For the glory thereof, because it is
departed from it.
6 It shall be also carried unto Assyria *for*
a present to king Jareb:
Ephraim shall receive shame,
And Israel shall be ashamed of his own
counsel.
7 *As for* Samaria, her king is cut off
As the foam upon [1]the water.
8 The high places also of Aven, [a]the sin
of Israel, shall be destroyed:
The thorn and the thistle shall come
up on their altars;
[b]And they shall say to the mountains,
Cover us;
And to the hills, Fall on us.
9 O Israel, thou hast sinned from the
days of Gibeah: there they stood:
The battle in Gibeah against the
children of iniquity did not overtake
them.
10 *It is* in my desire that I should chastise
them;
And [a]*the* people shall be gathered
against them,
[1]When *they* shall bind themselves in
their two furrows.
11 And Ephraim *is as* [a]a heifer *that is*
taught, *and* loveth to tread out *the*
corn;
But I passed over upon [1]her fair neck:
I will make Ephraim to ride;
Judah shall plow,
And Jacob shall break his clods.
12 Sow to yourselves in righteousness,
Reap in mercy;
[a]Break up your fallow ground:
For *it is* time to seek the LORD,
Till he come and rain righteousness
upon you.
13 [a]Ye have plowed wickedness, ye have
reaped iniquity;
Ye have eaten the fruit of lies:
Because thou didst trust in thy way,
In the multitude of thy mighty *men*.

9:15 [a]Is. 1:23
9:16 [1]Heb. *the desires* [a]Ezek. 24:21
10:1 [1]Or, *a vine emptying the fruit* which *it giveth* [2]Heb. *statues,* or, *standing images* [a]Nah. 2:2 [b]ch. 8:11
10:2 [1]Or, *He hath divided their heart* [2]Heb. *behead* [3]Heb. *statues,* or, *standing images* [a]1 Ki. 18:21; Mat. 6:24
10:4 [a]Amos 5:7
10:5 [1][Or,] *Chemarim* [a]2 Ki. 23:5
10:7 [1]Heb. *the face of the water*
10:8 [a]Deut. 9:21 [b]Is. 2:19; Luke 23:30
10:10 [1]Or, *When* I *shall bind them for their two transgressions,* or, *in their two habitations* [a]Jer. 16:16
10:11 [1]Heb. *the beauty of her neck* [a]Mic. 4:13
10:12 [a]Jer. 4:3
10:13 [a]Prov. 22:8; Gal. 6:7,8

9:15 *Gilgal.* See note on 4:15. *drive them out of my house.* As the unfaithful wife was driven from the husband's house, so Israel was driven from God's "house"—i.e., His land (see 8:1 and note). *princes . . . revolters.* A wordplay in Hebrew.
9:17 *My God.* Hosea's words alone, for God was no longer Israel's God. *cast . . . away.* See 4:6; 2 Ki 17:20. *wanderers.* Like Cain (Gen 4:14–15).
10:1 *Israel.* The nation personified and called by the name of its ancestor. *vine.* A frequent metaphor for Israel (Deut 32:32; Ps 80:8–11; Is 5:1; Jer 2:21; cf. John 15:1). *the multitude.* The prosperity during the period of Jeroboam II (793–753 B.C.) was probably in view.
10:2 *Their heart is divided.* Israel formally called to God (8:2), but they dishonored Him by pagan worship.
10:3 *We have no king.* Such would soon be their condition when Assyria destroyed the nation.
10:4 *They have spoken words.* The last kings of Israel were notoriously corrupt and deceitful.
10:5 *Samaria.* The royal city of Israel (see note on 7:1). *calves of Beth-aven.* The idol that Jeroboam set up at Beth-el (Beth-aven means "house of wickedness," a derogatory name for Beth-el, which means "house of God"; see also 1 Ki 12:32–33).
10:6 *Ephraim.* Israel, the northern kingdom.
10:8 *high places.* See 4:13–14. *Aven.* Refers to Beth-aven ("house of wickedness"; see v. 5 and note). *Cover us . . . Fall on us.* Cries of utter despair; quoted by Jesus (Luke 23:30) and alluded to in Rev 6:16 (see Is 2:19).
10:9 *Gibeah.* See 9:9 and note. As war came on Gibeah, so war and captivity would come on Israel.
10:11 *heifer . . . taught.* Up to now Ephraim (Israel) had been as contented as a young cow that ate while threshing grain. But now God would cause Israel (here called both Ephraim and Jacob) and Judah to do the heavy work of plowing and harrowing under a yoke—a picture of going into the Assyrian and Babylonian captivities. *Judah.* See Introduction: Author and Date. *break his clods.* Be no longer unproductive, but repentant, making a radical new beginning and becoming productive and fruitful.
10:12 *Reap in mercy.* If Israel would only do what was right ("kindness" translates the Hebrew word *ḥesed;* see note on 6:6, "loyalty"), she would be blessed by God. *righteousness.* God's covenant blessings that in righteousness He would shower on His people if they in righteousness were loyal to Him, their covenant Lord.
10:13 *lies.* Israel had been living a lie—and by lies (see 7:3; 10:4; 12:1).

14 Therefore shall a tumult arise among
thy people,
And all thy fortresses shall be spoiled,
As Shalman spoiled Beth-arbel in the
day of battle:
The mother was dashed in pieces upon
her children.
15 So shall Beth-el do unto you because of
[1]your great wickedness;
In a morning shall the king of Israel
utterly be cut off.

God's compassion toward Israel

11 When Israel *was* a child, then I
loved him,
And [a]called my [b]son out of Egypt.
2 *As* they called them, so they went from
them:
They sacrificed unto Baalim, and
burned incense to graven images.
3 [a]I taught Ephraim also to go, taking
them by their arms;
But they knew not that [b]I healed them.
4 I drew them with cords of a man, with
bands of love:
And [a]I was to them as they that [1]take
off the yoke on their jaws,
And [b]I laid meat unto them.

5 He shall not return into the land of
Egypt,
But the Assyrian shall be his king,
Because they refused to return.
6 And the sword shall abide on his cities,
And shall consume his branches, and
devour *them*,
Because of their own counsels.
7 And my people are bent to [a]backsliding
from me:
Though they called them to the most
High,
[1]None at all would exalt *him*.
8 [a]How shall I give thee up, Ephraim?
How shall I deliver thee, Israel?
How shall I make thee as [b]Admah?
How shall I set thee as Zeboim?
Mine heart is turned within me,
My repentings are kindled together.
9 I will not execute the fierceness of
mine anger,
I will not return to destroy Ephraim:
[a]For I *am* God, and not man;
The Holy One in the midst of thee:
And I will not enter into the city.
10 They shall walk after the LORD: [a]he
shall roar like a lion:
When he shall roar, then the children
shall tremble from the west.
11 They shall tremble as a bird out of Egypt,
[a]And as a dove out of the land of
Assyria:
[b]And I will place them in their houses,
saith the LORD.

Israel's sin

12 Ephraim compasseth me about with lies,
and the house of Israel with deceit:
But Judah yet ruleth with God, and is
faithful [1]with the saints.

12 Ephraim feedeth on wind, and
followeth after the east wind:
He daily increaseth lies and desolation;
[a]And they do make a covenant with
the Assyrians,
And [b]oil is carried into Egypt.

10:15 [1]Heb. *the evil of your evil*
11:1 [a]Mat. 2:15 [b]Ex. 4:22
11:3 [a]Deut. 1:31 [b]Ex. 15:26
11:4 [1]Heb. *lift up* [a]Lev. 26:13 [b]Ps. 78:25
11:7 [1]Heb. *Together they exalted not* [a]Jer. 3:6
11:8 [a]Jer. 9:7 [b]Gen. 14:8
11:9 [a]Num. 23:19
11:10 [a]Joel 3:16
11:11 [a]Is. 60:8 [b]Ezek. 28:25,26
11:12 [1]Or, *with the most holy*
12:1 [a]2 Ki. 17:4 [b]Is. 30:6

10:14 *Shalman spoiled Beth-arbel.* The event is otherwise unknown, as are the names mentioned. Atrocities against civilians were common in ancient warfare (cf. 9:13; 13:16; 2 Ki 8:12–13; Ps 137:8–9; Is 13:16; Amos 1:13; Nah 3:10).

11:1 A third appeal to history (see 9:10; 10:9) traces God's choice of Israel back to Egypt, the exodus from that country (cf. 12:9; 13:4) having given birth to the nation. Israel's response to the Lord is now illustrated by the wayward son rather than by the unfaithful wife (chs. 1–3). For Israel as a son see Ex 4:22–23; Is 1:2–4; and for God as Father see Deut 32:6; Jer 2:14. Hosea saw God's love as the basis (cf. 3:1) for the election of Israel. Matthew found in the call of Israel from Egypt a typological picture of Jesus' coming from Egypt (see Mat 2:15 and note).

11:2 *graven images.* See Deut 7:25; 12:3.

11:3 *Ephraim.* Israel, the northern kingdom. *go.* This picture of a father teaching his child to walk is one of the most tender in the OT. *knew not.* See 2:5–8. *healed.* See 5:13; 6:1; 7:1.

11:4 The imagery is unclear, but the figure seems to change to a farmer tending his work animals. Another interpretation sees a continuation of the son image, with the father lifting the son to his cheek. *laid meat unto them.* God supplied miraculous food in the wilderness (see Ex 16; Deut 8:16).

11:5 *Egypt . . . Assyrian.* See 8:13 and note; 9:3. The tender tone (vv. 1–4) changes to threat of exile to the two countries between which Israel had vacillated. It is ironic that the people rescued from Egypt should be returned there because of their disloyalty to the One who had rescued them.

11:7 *called . . . to the most High.* See 7:16.

11:8 The stubborn son was subject to stoning (Deut 21:18–21), but the Lord's compassion overcame His wrath and He refused to destroy Ephraim (Israel). *Admah . . . Zeboim.* Cities of the plain (Gen 10:19; 14:2,8), overthrown when Sodom was destroyed (Gen 19:24–25; Deut 29:23; Jer 49:18) and symbolizing total destruction.

11:9 *God, and not man.* Although Israel has been as unreliable as man, God will not be untrue to the love He has shown toward Israel (see vv. 1–4; see also 1 Sam 15:29; Mal 3:6). Israel was to be punished, but not destroyed. *The Holy One in the midst of thee.* See notes on Is 1:4; 6:1; cf. Is 12:6. God's holiness is alluded to only here in Hosea.

11:10 The return from exile. *roar like a lion:* Rather than threatening destruction (cf. 5:14; 13:7), God's roar was now a clear signal to return from exile. *the west.* The islands of the sea (as well as coastlands).

11:11 *as a bird . . . as a dove.* Suggests swiftness of return (cf. Is 60:8) and is not derogatory, as was the earlier comparison to a silly dove (7:11). *out of Egypt . . . Assyria.* See 9:3. *saith the LORD.* See 2:13,16,21.

11:12 *lies . . . deceit.* See 7:3; 10:13 and note. *Judah.* See Introduction: Author and Date. *ruleth with God.* See Jer 2:31.

12:1 *wind.* See 8:7; Eccl 1:14. *east wind.* See 13:15; Job 15:2; 27:21; Is 27:8; Jer 18:17. Pursuing the wind symbolized Israel's futile foreign policy, which vacillated between Egypt (2 Ki 17:4; Is 30:6–7) and Assyria (cf. 5:13; 7:11; 8:9; 2 Ki 17:3).

2 [a]The LORD hath also a controversy with
Judah,
And *will* [1]punish Jacob according to his
ways;
According to his doings will he
recompense him.
3 He took his brother [a]by the heel in the
womb,
And by his strength he [b1]had power
with God:
4 Yea, he had power over *the* angel, and
prevailed:
He wept, and made supplication unto
him:
He found him *in* [a]Beth-el, and there he
spake with us;
5 Even the LORD God of hosts; the LORD
is his [a]memorial.
6 [a]Therefore turn thou to thy God:
Keep mercy and judgment,
And wait on thy God continually.
7 *He is* [1]a merchant, [a]the balances of
deceit *are* in his hand:
He loveth to [2]oppress.
8 And Ephraim said, [a]Yet I am become
rich, I have found me out substance:
[1]*In* all my labours they shall find none
iniquity in me [2]that *were* sin.
9 And I *that am* the LORD thy God from
the land of Egypt
[a]Will yet make thee to dwell in
tabernacles, as *in* the days of the
solemn feast.
10 [a]I have also spoken by the prophets,
and I have multiplied visions,
And used similitudes [1]by the ministry
of the prophets.
11 *Is there* iniquity *in* Gilead? surely they
are vanity:
They sacrifice bullocks in Gilgal;
Yea, their altars *are* as heaps in the
furrows of the fields.
12 And Jacob [a]fled *into* the country of Syria,
And Israel served for a wife, and for a
wife he kept *sheep*.
13 [a]And by a prophet the LORD brought
Israel out of Egypt,
And by a prophet was he preserved.
14 Ephraim provoked *him* to anger [1]most
bitterly:
Therefore shall he leave his [2]blood
upon him,
[a]And his reproach shall his Lord return
unto him.

12:2 [1]Heb. *visit upon* [a]Mic. 6:2
12:3 [1]Heb. *was a prince,* or, *behaved himself princely* [a]Gen. 25:26 [b]Gen. 32:28
12:4 [a]Gen. 28:12
12:5 [a]Ex. 3:15
12:6 [a]Mic. 6:8
12:7 [1]Or, *Canaan* [2]Or, *deceive* [a]Amos 8:5
12:8 [1]Or, *All my labours suffice me not:* he shall have *punishment of iniquity* in *whom* is *sin* [2]Heb. *which* [a]Rev. 3:17
12:9 [a]Lev. 23:42
12:10 [1]Heb. *by the hand* [a]2 Ki. 17:13
12:12 [a]Gen. 28:5
12:13 [a]Ex. 12:50
12:14 [1]Heb. with *bitternesses* [2]Heb. *bloods* [a]Dan. 11:18
13:2 [1]Heb. *they add to sin*

Ephraim's doom

13 When Ephraim spake trembling, he
exalted *himself* in Israel;
But when he offended in Baal, he died.
2 And now [1]they sin more and more,
And have made them molten images of
their silver,

12:2 *controversy.* See 4:1. *Judah.* See Introduction: Author and Date. *Jacob.* Israel (see 10:11). The Lord indicted both kingdoms—all the descendants of Father Jacob. In their deceitfulness, Israel and Judah were living up to the name of their forefather (Jacob means "he grasps the heel"; figuratively, "he deceives").
12:3 *took his brother by the heel.* See note on v. 2. God's covenant people here relived the experiences of Father Jacob and now had to return to God, just as Jacob was called back to Beth-el (Gen 35:1–15). *in the womb.* See Gen 25:26; 27:36.
12:4 *had power over the angel.* See Gen 32:22–28. The Hebrew for "Israel" means "he struggles with God." *Beth-el.* See Gen 28:12–19; 35:1–15. In Hosea's time, Beth-el was the most important royal sanctuary in the northern kingdom (cf. Amos 7:13).
12:5 *LORD God of hosts.* Paralleled in Amos 3:13; 6:14; 9:5.
12:6 *mercy.* Hebrew *ḥesed;* see 6:6 and note. *judgment.* See Amos 5:15,24; Mic 6:8.
12:7 *merchant.* As Hosea had played on the meaning of Jacob in v. 2, he here uses a wordplay on Canaan (the Hebrew for "merchant" sounds like Canaan) to charge that Israel was no better than a Canaanite.
12:8 *I am become rich.* Riches brought a sense of self-sufficiency (cf. 10:13; Deut 32:15–18). *they shall find none inquity in me.* Like a dishonest merchant, Ephraim (Israel) was confident that her deceitfulness (cf. 11:12) would not come to light.
12:9 *I that am the LORD thy God.* See 13:4; cf. Ex 20:2. *tabernacles.* As during the wilderness journey long ago (cf. 2:14–15). *solemn feast.* Probably the feast of tabernacles (Lev 23:42–44), which commemorated the wilderness journey.
12:10 *spoken by the prophets.* See 6:5; Amos 2:11; Heb 1:1. There had been ample warning. *visions.* Revelations (see Num 12:6–8; Amos 1:1). *similitudes.* Parables containing messages of warning from God (see 2 Sam 12:1–4; Ps 78:2; Is 5:1–7; Ezek 17:2; 24:3).
12:11 *iniquity in Gilead.* See 6:8–9 and notes. Gilead was overrun by Assyria in 734–732 B.C. (2 Ki 15:29). *Gilgal.* See 4:15; 9:15. The Hebrew contains a wordplay between "Gilgal" and "heaps" (Hebrew *gallim*). Rather than assuring safety, the altars themselves would be destroyed. *furrows of . . . fields.* Israelite farmers gathered into piles the stones turned up by their plows.
12:12 Jacob fled from Esau to Padan-aram (Gen 28:2,5), serving Laban seven years for each wife (Gen 29:20–28), and then continued as Laban's herdsman (Gen 30:31; 31:41).
12:13 *prophet.* Moses (cf. Num 12:6–8; Deut 18:15; 34:10). *was he preserved.* As Jacob had cared for Laban's flocks, so the Lord cared for Israel during her wilderness wandering. Earlier leadership by the prophet Moses stands in contrast with Israel's present disregard for prophets (cf. 4:5; 6:5; 9:7).
‡12:14 *Ephraim provoked.* Despite warnings. *his blood.* Cf. 1:4; 4:2; 5:2; 6:8. This may refer either to violence against the prophets or to human sacrifice (cf. 2 Ki 17:17). In legal passages (Lev 20:11–27), "their blood shall be upon them" describes guilt. The prophet drew a contrast between past divine preservation and present divine anger that would bring punishment. *return.* See Is 65:7.
13:1 *When Ephraim spake.* In accordance with Jacob's blessing (Gen 48:10–20), Ephraim became a powerful tribe (Judg 8:1–3; 12:1–7; 1 Sam 1:1–4), from which came such prominent leaders as Joshua (Josh 24:30) and Jeroboam I (1 Ki 11:26; 12:20). *Israel.* The 12 tribes. *died.* The wages of sin was death (cf. Rom 6:23), and the end of the nation was at hand.
13:2 *molten images.* See 4:12; 8:5–6; 11:2. *men . . . kiss the calves.* This phrase calls to mind the calves (and the sacrifices made to them) set up by Jeroboam to win the allegiance of the northern tribes in Israel (see 1 Ki 12:26–33). *kiss.* Show homage to (cf. 1 Ki 19:18).

And idols according to their own
understanding,
All of it the work of the craftsmen:
They say of them, Let [2]the men that
sacrifice kiss the calves.
3 Therefore they shall be as the morning
cloud,
And as the early dew that passeth
away,
[a]As the chaff *that* is driven with a
whirlwind out of the floor,
And as the smoke out of the chimney.
4 Yet [a]I *am* the LORD thy God from the
land of Egypt,
And thou shalt know no god but me:
For [b]*there is* no saviour beside me.
5 [a]I did know thee in the wilderness,
[b]In the land of [1]great drought.
6 [a]According to their pasture, so were
they filled;
They were filled, and their heart was
exalted;
Therefore have they forgotten me.
7 Therefore [a]I will be unto them as a
lion:
As [b]a leopard by the way will I observe
them:
8 I will meet them [a]as a bear *that is*
bereaved of her whelps,
And will rent the caul of their heart,
And there will I devour them like a
lion:
[1]The wild beast shall tear them.
9 O Israel, *thou* hast destroyed thyself;
but in me [1]*is* thine help.
10 [1]I will be thy king: [a]where *is any other*
that may save thee in all thy cities?
And thy judges *of* whom [b]thou saidst,
Give me a king and princes?

13:2 [2]Or, *the sacrificers of men*
13:3 [a]Dan. 2:35
13:4 [a]Is. 43:11 [b]Is. 43:11
13:5 [1]Heb. *droughts* [a]Deut. 2:7 [b]Deut. 8:15
13:6 [a]Deut. 8:12
13:7 [a]Lam. 3:10 [b]Jer. 5:6
13:8 [1]Heb. *The beast of the field* [a]2 Sam. 17:8
13:9 [1]Heb. *in thy help*
13:10 [1][Rather, *Where is thy king?* King Hoshea being then in prison, 2 Ki. 17:4] [a]Deut. 32:38 [b]1 Sam. 8:5
13:11 [a]1 Sam. 8:7
13:12 [a]Deut. 32:34
13:13 [1]Heb. *a time* [a]Is. 13:8
13:14 [1]Heb. *the hand* [a]1 Cor. 15:54 [b]Jer. 15:6
13:15 [1]Heb. *vessels of desire* [a]Jer. 4:11
13:16 [1][Fulfilled about B.C. 721] [a]2 Ki. 8:12
14:1 [a]Joel 2:13

11 [a]I gave thee a king in mine anger,
And took *him away* in my wrath.
12 [a]The iniquity of Ephraim *is* bound up;
his sin *is* hid.
13 [a]The sorrows of a travailing *woman*
shall come upon him:
He *is* an unwise son;
For he should not stay [1]long in *the
place of* the breaking forth of
children.
14 I will ransom them from [1]the power of
the grave;
I will redeem them from death:
[a]O death, I will be thy plagues;
O grave, I will be thy destruction:
[b]Repentance shall be hid from mine
eyes.
15 Though he be fruitful among *his*
brethren,
[a]An east wind shall come, the wind of
the LORD *shall* come up from the
wilderness,
And his spring shall become dry, and
his fountain shall be dried up:
He shall spoil the treasure of all
[1]pleasant vessels.
16 [1]Samaria shall become desolate;
For she hath rebelled against her God:
[a]They shall fall by the sword:
Their infants shall be dashed in pieces,
And their women with child shall be
ript up.

The call to repent

14 O Israel, [a]return unto the LORD thy
God;
For thou hast fallen by thine iniquity.
2 Take with you words, and turn to the
LORD:

13:3 "Cloud" and "dew" (see 6:4), "chaff" (see Ps 1:4; 35:5; Is 17:13; 29:5) and "smoke" (see Ps 37:20; 68:2; Is 51:6) are all figurative for Ephraim, who was soon to vanish as a nation.
13:4 *I am the LORD.* See 12:9; Ex 20:2–3; Deut 5:6. The contrast is with Jeroboam's declaration, "Behold your gods" (1 Ki 12:28). *know no god.* See 4:1; 6:3; 8:2.
13:5 *wilderness.* See 2:14; 9:10.
13:6 *filled.* See Deut 6:11–12; 8:10–14; 11:15–16. *forgotten me.* Cf. Deut 8:14; 31:20; 32:15,18.
13:7–8 The Lord, previously pictured as a shepherd (4:16), would attack like the wild beasts that often ravaged the flocks.
13:7 *lion.* See 5:14. *leopard.* See Jer 5:6; Rev 13:2.
13:8 *bear that is bereaved of her whelps.* See 2 Sam 17:8; 2 Ki 2:24; Prov 17:12.
13:9 *help.* See Ps 10:14; 30:10; 54:4.
13:10 *where is any other that may save thee . . . ?* Help is only from the Lord, not from kings. The prophet likely alludes to the royal assassinations of his day (see 3:4; 7:7; 8:4; 10:3). *Give me a king.* Though all Israel asked for a king in the days of Samuel (1 Sam 8:5,20), the reference here is only to the northern monarchy. They selected Jeroboam I (1 Ki 12:26) in preference to the Davidic kings.
13:11 The monarchy is here considered a rebellion (see 1 Sam 8:7).
13:12 *iniquity . . . bound up.* See 9:9 and note; Job 14:17. *Ephraim.* Israel, the northern kingdom. *sin is hid.* See 7:2; Deut 32:34–35.
13:13 *a travailing woman.* Their helpless situation was comparable to that of a woman in childbirth (see Is 13:8; 21:3; 26:17; Jer 4:31; 13:21; Mic 4:9–10; Mat 24:8) who cannot deliver the child (see 2 Ki 19:3; Is 37:3) and consequently dies.
‡13:14 *death.* The personified reference is to the death of the nation (see v. 1). Paul applies this passage to resurrection (1 Cor 15:55). *grave.* Hebrew *Sheol.* For a description of Sheol see Job 3:13–19; Ps 18:5; 116:3; Is 14:9–10; see also notes on Gen 37:35; Jonah 2:2.
13:15 *he be fruitful.* In Hebrew a wordplay on Ephraim (meaning "fruitful"). The drought-bringing east wind (cf. Job 1:19; Is 27:8; Jer 4:11; 13:24; 18:17) is here a figure for Assyria, an instrument of the Lord (Is 10:5,15). Assyria invaded the northern kingdom in 734 B.C., then crushed it and exiled its people in 722–721. *all pleasant vessels.* See Nah 2:9.
13:16 *Samaria.* See 7:1 and note; 8:5–6; 10:5,7; here, the northern kingdom. *rebelled against.* See Ps 5:10; Ezek 20:8,13,21. *infants . . . women.* For atrocities against women and children see 10:14; 2 Ki 8:12; 15:16; Ps 137:8–9; Is 13:16; Amos 1:13; Nah 3:10.
14:1 *return.* Another appeal for repentance (see 10:12; 12:6). Unlike that of ch. 6, this repentance would have to be sincere in order for the people to receive the gracious response from the Lord promised in vv. 4–8 (cf. Ps 130:7–8; Is 55:6–9).
14:2 *Take . . . words.* None could appear empty-handed (Ex 23:15; 34:20), but animal sacrifices would not be enough. Only

Say unto him, Take away all iniquity,
and [1] receive *us* graciously:
So will we render the [a] calves of our
lips.
3 Asshur shall not save us: [a] we will not
ride upon horses:
Neither will we say any more to the
work of our hands, *Ye are* our gods:
[b] For in thee the fatherless findeth
mercy.

4 I will heal their backsliding, I will love
them freely:
For mine anger is turned away from
him.
5 I will be as [a] the dew unto Israel:
He shall [1] grow as the lily,
And [2] cast forth his roots as
Lebanon.
6 His branches [1] shall spread,
And [a] his beauty shall be as the olive
tree,
And [b] his smell as Lebanon.
7 [a] They that dwell under his shadow
shall return;
They shall revive *as* the corn, and
[1] grow as the vine:
The [2] sent thereof *shall be* as the wine
of Lebanon.
8 Ephraim *shall say,* What have I to do
any more with idols?
I have heard *him,* and observed him:
I *am* like a green fir tree.
From me is thy fruit found.
9 Who *is* wise, and he shall understand
these *things?*
Prudent, and he shall know them?
For [a] the ways of the LORD *are* right,
And the just shall walk in them:
But the transgressors shall fall therein.

14:2 [1] Or, *give good* [a] Heb. 13:15
14:3 [a] Ps. 33:17 [b] Ps. 10:14
14:5 [1] Or, *blossom* [2] Heb. *strike* [a] Prov. 19:12
14:6 [1] Heb. *shall go*
14:6 [a] Ps. 52:8 [b] Gen. 27:27
14:7 [1] Or, *blossom* [2] Or, *memorial* [a] Ps. 91:1
14:9 [a] Prov. 10:29

words of true repentance would be sufficient. *calves of our lips.* As thank offerings to the Lord.
14:3 *fatherless.* Penitent Israel (see Ps 10:14; 68:5; Lam 5:3). *findeth mercy.* Cf. the name of the child Lo-ruhamah (see 1:6 and note; see also 2:1,23).
14:4 *heal.* See 11:3. *backsliding.* See 11:7. *love . . . freely.* See Is 54:6–8. *love.* See 3:1; 11:1,8–9. *anger . . . turned away.* Contrasts with the burning anger that brought destruction (see 8:5).
‡14:5 *dew.* Here not a symbol of transitoriness (cf. 6:4; 13:3) but of God's blessing (cf. Deut 33:13). *Lebanon.* See Ps 104:16; Is 35:2; 60:13. See also notes on Judg 9:15; 1 Ki 5:6; Is 9:10. "Lebanon" refers to the "cedars" of that region. See Ps 80:9–11.
14:7 *shadow.* Protection (cf. Judg 9:15; Sol 2:3; Lam 4:20; Ezek 31:6). *vine.* See 10:1; Ps 80; Is 5:1–7.
14:8 *Ephraim.* Israel, the northern kingdom. *green fir tree.* Only here in the OT is God compared to a tree. For the point of the imagery see Ezek 31:3–7; Dan 4:12. *fruit.* Ephraim ("fruitful"; cf. Gen 41:52) received his fruitfulness from the Lord (cf. 2:8).
14:9 *ways of the* LORD. See Ps 18:21. The prophet concludes by offering each reader the alternatives of walking or stumbling (cf. 4:5; 5:5)—of obedience or rebellion.

Joel

INTRODUCTION

Author

The prophet Joel cannot be identified with any of the 12 other figures in the OT who have the same name. He is not mentioned outside the books of Joel and Acts (Acts 2:16). The non-Biblical legends about him are unconvincing. His father, Pethuel (1:1), is also unknown. Judging from his concern with Judah and Jerusalem (see 2:32; 3:1,6,8,16–20), it seems likely that Joel lived in that area.

Date

The book contains no references to datable historical events, but a good case can be made for its being written in the ninth century B.C. Many interpreters, however, date the book as late as the postexilic period (sixth century), after Haggai and Zechariah. In either case, its message is not significantly affected by its dating.

The book of Joel has striking linguistic parallels to those of Amos, Micah, Zephaniah, Jeremiah and Ezekiel. The literary relationships of these books are determined by one's view of the date of Joel. If it was written early, the other prophets borrowed his phrases; if it was later, the reverse may have taken place. Some scholars maintain that all the prophets drew more or less from the religious literary traditions that they and their readers shared in common—liturgical and otherwise.

Message

Joel sees the massive locust plague and severe drought devastating Judah as a harbinger of the "great and the terrible day of the LORD" (2:31). (The locusts he mentions in 1:4; 2:25 are best understood as real, not as allegorical representations of the Babylonians, Medo-Persians, Greeks and Romans, as held by some interpreters.) Confronted with this crisis, he calls on everyone to repent: old and young (1:2–3), drunkards (1:5), farmers (1:11) and priests (1:13). He describes the locusts as the Lord's army and sees in their coming a reminder that the day of the Lord is near. He does not voice the popular notion that the day will be one of judgment on the nations but deliverance and blessing for Israel. Instead—with Isaiah (2:10–21), Jeremiah (4:6), Amos (5:18–20) and Zephaniah (1:7–18)—he describes the day as one of punishment for unfaithful Israel as well. Restoration and blessing will come only after judgment and repentance.

Outline

I. Title (1:1)
II. Judah Experiences a Foretaste of the Day of the Lord (1:2—2:17)
   A. A Call to Mourning and Prayer (1:2–14)
   B. The Announcement of the Day of the Lord (1:15—2:11)
   C. A Call to Repentance and Prayer (2:12–17)
III. Judah Is Assured of Salvation in the Day of the Lord (2:18—3:21)
   A. The Lord's Restoration of Judah (2:18–27)
   B. The Lord's Renewal of His People (2:28–32)
   C. The Coming of the Day of the Lord (ch. 3)
      1. The nations judged (3:1–16)
      2. God's people blessed (3:17–21)

1

The word of the LORD that came to Joel
the son of Pethuel.

The plague of insects

2 Hear this, ye old men,
And give ear, all ye inhabitants of the land.
[a]Hath this been in your days,
Or even in the days of your fathers?
3 [a]Tell ye your children of it,
And *let* your children *tell* their children,
And their children another generation.
4 [a] [1]That which the palmerworm hath left hath the locust eaten;
And that which the locust hath left hath the cankerworm eaten;
And that which the cankerworm hath left hath the caterpillar eaten.

5 Awake, ye drunkards, and weep;
And howl, all ye drinkers of wine,
Because of the new wine, [a]for it is cut off from your mouth.
6 For [a]a nation is come up upon my land,
Strong, and without number,
[b]Whose teeth *are* the teeth of a lion,
And he hath the cheek-teeth of a great lion.
7 He hath [a]laid my vine waste,
And [1]barked my fig tree:
He hath made it clean bare, and cast *it* away;
The branches thereof are made white.
8 [a]Lament like a virgin girded with sackcloth for [b]the husband of her youth.

1:2 [a]ch. 2:2
1:3 [a]Ps. 78:4
1:4 [1]Heb. *The residue of the palmerworm* [a]Deut. 28:38
1:5 [a]Is. 32:10
1:6 [a]Prov. 30:23 [b]Rev. 9:8
1:7 [1]Heb. laid *my fig tree for a barking* [a]Is. 5:6
1:8 [a]Is. 22:12 [b]Prov. 2:17; Jer. 3:4

1:9 [a]ch. 2:14
1:10 [1]Or, *ashamed* [a]Jer. 12:11 [b]Is. 24:7
1:11 [a]Jer. 14:3,4
1:12 [a]ver. 10 [b]Is. 24:11; Jer. 48:33
1:13 [a]Jer. 4:8
1:14 [1]Or, day of *restraint* [a]2 Chr. 20:3 [b]Lev. 23:36 [c]2 Chr. 20:13
1:15 [a]Jer. 30:7 [b]Is. 13:6,9

9 [a]The meat offering and the drink offering is cut off from the house of the LORD;
The priests, the LORD'S ministers, mourn.
10 The field is wasted, [a]the land mourneth;
For the corn is wasted, [b]the new wine is [1]dried up, the oil languisheth.
11 [a]Be ye ashamed, O ye husbandmen;
howl, O ye vinedressers,
For the wheat and for the barley;
Because the harvest of the field is perished.
12 [a]The vine is dried up, and the fig tree languisheth;
The pomegranate tree, the palm tree also, and the apple tree,
Even all the trees of the field, are withered:
Because [b]joy is withered away from the sons of men.
13 [a]Gird yourselves, and lament, ye priests:
Howl, ye ministers of the altar:
Come, lie all night in sackcloth, ye ministers of my God;
For the meat offering and the drink offering is withholden from the house of your God.
14 [a]Sanctify ye a fast, call [b]a [1]solemn assembly,
Gather the elders *and* [c]all the inhabitants of the land
Into the house of the LORD your God,
And cry unto the LORD,
15 [a]Alas for the day! for [b]the day of the LORD *is* at hand,

---

1:1 *The word of the LORD that came to Joel.* Joel's claim of prophetic authority is similar to that of several other prophets (see Jer 1:2; Ezek 1:3; Hos 1:1; Jonah 1:1,3; 3:1; Mic 1:1; Zeph 1:1; Hag 1:1; Zech 1:1; Mal 1:1). *Joel.* Means "The LORD is God"; cf. Elijah's name, which means "(My) God is the LORD."
1:2 *old men.* Either the older men of the community or the recognized officials (see v. 14; 2:16,28; see also note on Ex 3:16).
1:4 See 2:25.
1:5 *weep.* Various segments of the community (drunkards, here; general population, v. 8; farmers, v. 11; priests, v. 13) are called to mourn. The destruction of the vines by the locusts leaves the drunkards without a source of wine. *drinkers of wine.* Although Joel calls for repentance, drunkenness is the only specific sin mentioned in the book. It suggests a self-indulgent lifestyle (cf. Is 28:7–8; Amos 4:1) pursued by those who value material things more than spiritual.
1:6 The locusts are compared here to a nation; cf. the ants and conies in Prov 30:25–26. Elsewhere they are called the Lord's "army" (2:11,25). The reverse comparison—that of armies to locusts in regard to numbers—is as old as Ugaritic literature (15th century B.C.; see chart, p. xix) and is common in the OT (see Judg 6:5; 7:12; Jer 46:23; 51:14,27; Nah 3:15). *without number.* A phrase used to describe the locusts in the plague in Egypt (see Ps 105:34; see also Ex 10:4–6,12–15). *teeth.* Joel's comparison of the locusts' teeth to lions' teeth is reflected in Rev 9:8.
1:7 *my.* The personal pronouns here and elsewhere in Joel (vv. 6,13–14; 2:13–14,17–18,23,26–27; 3:2–5,17) offer a hint of hope, since they indicate that the people belong to the Lord (cf. Josh 22:19).
1:8 *virgin.* The community is addressed. In Israel, when a woman was pledged to be married to a man, he was called her husband and she his wife, though she was still a virgin (see Deut 22:23–24). This verse refers to such a husband who died before the marriage was consummated. *sackcloth.* See v. 13; Gen 37:34 and note.
1:9 *offering.* The locusts have left nothing that can be offered as sacrifice. The grain offering (Lev 2:1–2) and the drink offering, which was a libation of wine (Lev 23:13), were part of the daily offering (Ex 29:40; Num 28:5–8).
1:10 *mourneth.* The land is thrown into "mourning" because of the locusts' devastation. *corn . . . new wine . . . oil.* An important OT triad, related to the agriculture of that day (see 2:19). *is dried up.* See v. 12. The destruction caused by the locusts was intensified by drought.
1:13 *your God.* See note on v. 7. The phrase occurs eight times in Joel (here; v. 14; 2:13; 2:14; 2:23; 2:26; 2:27; 3:17).
1:14 *fast . . . assembly.* See 2:15. Fasting, required on the day of atonement (see note on Lev 16:29,31) and also practiced in times of calamity (see Judg 20:26; 2 Sam 12:16; Jer 14:12; Jonah 3:4–5; Zech 7:3), was a sign of penitence and humility. The Bible speaks against outward signs that do not reflect a corresponding inward belief or attitude (see Mat 6:1–8; 23:1–36).
1:15 *day of the LORD.* This phrase occurs five times in Joel and is the dominant theme (here; 2:1; 2:11; 2:31; 3:14). Six other

And as a destruction from the Almighty
shall it come.
16 Is not the meat cut off before our eyes,
Yea, [a]joy and gladness from the house
of our God?
17 The [1]seed is rotten under their clods,
The garners are laid desolate, the barns
are broken down;
For the corn is withered.
18 How do [a]the beasts groan!
The herds of cattle are perplexed,
Because they have no pasture;
Yea, the flocks of sheep are made
desolate.
19 O LORD, [a]to thee will I cry:
For [b]the fire hath devoured the
[1]pastures of the wilderness,
And the flame hath burnt all the trees
of the field.
20 The beasts of the field [a]cry also unto
thee:
For [b]the rivers of waters are dried up,
And the fire hath devoured the
pastures of the wilderness.

The coming day of the LORD

2 [a]Blow ye the [1]trumpet in Zion, and
[b]sound an alarm in my holy
mountain:
Let all the inhabitants of the land
tremble:
For [c]the day of the LORD cometh, for *it*
is nigh at hand;
2 [a]A day of darkness and of gloominess,
A day of clouds and of thick darkness,
As the morning spread upon the
mountains:
[b]A great people and a strong;
[c]There hath not been ever the like,
Neither shall be any more after it,
Even to the years [1]of many generations.
3 A fire devoureth before them;
And behind them a flame burneth:
The land *is* as [a]the garden of Eden
before them,
[b]And behind them a desolate
wilderness;
Yea, and nothing shall escape them.
4 [a]The appearance of them *is* as the
appearance of horses;
And as horsemen, so shall they run.
5 [a]Like the noise of chariots on the tops
of mountains shall they leap,
Like the noise of a flame of fire that
devoureth the stubble,
As a strong people set in battle array.
6 Before their face *the* people shall be
much pained:
[a]All faces shall gather [1]blackness.
7 They shall run like mighty *men;* they
shall climb the wall like men of war;
And they shall march every one on his
ways,
And they shall not break their ranks:
8 Neither shall one thrust another;
They shall walk every one in his path:
And *when* they fall upon the [1]sword,
they shall not be wounded.
9 They shall run to and fro in the city;
They shall run upon the wall,
They shall climb up upon the houses;

1:16 [a]See Deut. 12:6,7
1:17 [1]Heb. *grains*
1:18 [a]Hos. 4:3
1:19 [1]Or, *habitations* [a]Ps. 50:15 [b]Jer. 9:10
1:20 [a]Job 38:41; Ps. 104:21 [b]1 Ki. 17:7
2:1 [1]Or, *cornet* [a]Jer. 4:5 [b]Num. 10:5 [c]Obad. 15; Zeph. 1:14
2:2 [a]Amos 5:18
2:2 [1]Heb. *of generation and generation* [b]ch. 1:6 [c]Ex. 10:14
2:3 [a]Gen. 2:8; Is. 51:3 [b]Zech. 7:14
2:4 [a]Rev. 9:7
2:5 [a]Rev. 9:9
2:6 [1]Heb. *pot* [a]Jer. 8:21; Lam. 4:8; Nah. 2:10
2:8 [1]Or, *dart*

prophets also use it: Isaiah (13:6,9), Ezekiel (13:5; 30:3), Amos (5:18,20), Obadiah (15), Zephaniah (1:7,14) and Malachi (4:5); and an equivalent expression occurs in Zech 14:1. Sometimes abbreviated as "that day," the term often refers to the decisive intervention of God in history, such as through the invasion of locusts in Joel or at the battle of Carchemish, 605 B.C. (see Jer 46:2,10). It can also refer to Christ's coming to consummate history (see Mal 4:5; Mat 11:24; 1 Cor 5:5; 2 Cor 1:14; 1 Thes 5:2; 2 Pet 3:10). When the term is not used for divine judgments in the midst of history, it refers to the final day of the Lord, which generally has two aspects: (1) God's triumph over and punishment of His enemies and (2) His granting of rest (security) and blessing to His people. *destruction . . . Almighty.* The Hebrew for each of these two words is a pun on the other (as in Is 13:6).

1:18 Cf. the description of a drought in Jer 14:5–6. *groan.* The Hebrew for this word is used for the groaning of Israel in Egypt (Ex 2:23) and of others in distress (Prov 29:2; Is 24:7; Lam 1:4,8,11,21; Ezek 9:4; 21:12). *are perplexed.* The Hebrew for this verb is used to describe Israel's confused movements in the desert (Ex 14:3). *Yea . . . sheep.* Sheep are the last to suffer, because they can even grub the grass roots out of the soil.

1:19–20 *fire.* Although the destruction caused by the locusts is elsewhere compared to that of a fire (see 2:3), here the prophet likely is describing the effects of a drought. In both cases he evokes the fire of God's judgment (see, e.g., Jer 4:4; 15:14; 17:27; Ezek 5:4; 15:6–7; 20:47; 21:32; Hos 8:14; Amos 1:4,7,10,12,14; 2:2,5).

2:1 *trumpet.* See v. 15. Made of a ram's or bull's horn, it was used to signal approaching danger (Jer 4:5; 6:1; Ezek 33:3). Its sound brought trembling (from fear) to the people (see Amos 3:6). *Zion.* See v. 15; 3:17. Here, parallel to God's "holy mountain" (see note on Ps 2:6), it refers to Jerusalem as the capital of the nation.

2:2 *day of darkness.* Darkness is a common prophetic figure used of the day of the Lord (see Amos 5:18,20) and is generally a metaphor for distress and suffering (see Is 5:30; 8:22; 50:3; 59:9; Jer 2:6,31; 13:16; Lam 3:6; Ezek 34:12). *morning.* Usually suggests relief from sorrow or gloom, the end of darkness (cf. Is 8:20; 58:8). Here, however, it is used as bitter irony, describing the locust infestation that spreads across the land like the light of dawn, which first lights up the eastern horizon and then spreads across the whole countryside.

2:3–11 The staccato character of the poetry is appropriate for the imagery of war.

2:3 *before them.* Joel creates a special impact by using this phrase four times (twice in v. 3, once in v. 6 and once in v. 10) and "behind them" twice (v. 3). *Eden.* See Gen 2:8,15 (the garden before the fall); Gen 13:10 (the Jordan Valley before the destruction of Sodom); and Is 51:3; Ezek 28:13; 31:8–9,16,18; 36:35 (all of which describe a desert that has become like Eden).

2:4 *horses.* Whereas Job compared the horse to a locust (Job 39:20), Joel does the opposite.

2:5 *mountains.* Though barriers to ordinary horses and chariots, are no deterrent to locusts.

2:6 *much pained.* Because of the famine that the locusts will cause.

2:9 *climb up upon the houses.* As in the Egyptian plague of

They shall [a]enter in at the windows
[b]like a thief.
10 [a]The earth shall quake before them;
The heavens shall tremble:
[b]The sun and the moon shall be dark,
And the stars shall withdraw their
shining:
11 [a]And the LORD shall utter his voice
before his army:
For his camp *is* very great:
[b]For *he is* strong that executeth his
word:
For the [c]day of the LORD *is* great and
very terrible;
And [d]who can abide it?

The call to repentance

12 Therefore also now, saith the LORD,
[a]Turn ye *even* to me with all your heart,
And with fasting, and with weeping,
and with mourning:
13 And [a]rent your heart, and not [b]your
garments,
And turn unto the LORD your God:
For he *is* [c]gracious and merciful,
Slow to anger, and of great kindness,
And repenteth him of the evil.
14 [a]Who knoweth *if* he will return and
repent,
And leave [b]a blessing behind him;
Even [c]a meat offering and a drink
offering unto the LORD your God?

15 [a]Blow the trumpet in Zion,
[b]Sanctify a fast, call a solemn assembly:
16 Gather the people, [a]sanctify the
congregation, assemble the elders,
Gather the children, and those that
suck the breasts:
[b]Let the bridegroom go forth of his
chamber, and the bride out of her
closet.
17 Let the priests, the ministers of the
LORD, weep [a]between the porch and
the altar,
And let them say, [b]Spare thy people,
O LORD,
And give not thine heritage to
reproach,
That the heathen should [1]rule over
them:
[c]Wherefore should they say among the
people, Where *is* their God?

Deliverance to follow repentance

18 Then will the LORD [a]be jealous for his
land,
[b]And pity his people.
19 Yea, the LORD will answer and say unto
his people,
Behold, I *will* send you [a]corn, and
wine, and oil,
And ye shall be satisfied therewith:
And I will no more make you a
reproach among the heathen:
20 But [a]I will remove far off from you
[b]the northern *army,*
And will drive him into a land barren
and desolate,
With his face toward the east sea,
And his hinder part [c]towards the
utmost sea,
And his stink shall come up, and his ill
savour shall come up,
Because [1]he hath done great things.

21 Fear not, O land; be glad and rejoice:
For the LORD [1]will do great things.

2:9 [a]Jer. 9:21 [b]John 10:1 **2:10** [a]Ps. 18:7 [b]Is. 13:10; Mat. 24:29 **2:11** [a]Jer. 25:30 [b]Jer. 50:34; Rev. 18:8 [c]Jer. 30:7; Amos 5:18; Zeph. 1:15 [d]Mal. 3:2 **2:12** [a]Jer. 4:1; Hos. 12:6 **2:13** [a]Ps. 34:18 [b]Gen. 37:34; 2 Sam. 1:11; Job 1:20 [c]Ex. 34:6 **2:14** [a]Josh. 14:12; 2 Ki. 19:4 [b]Hag. 2:19 [c]ch. 1:9,13 **2:15** [a]Num. 10:3 [b]ch. 1:14 **2:16** [a]Ex. 19:10

2:16 [b]1 Cor. 7:5 **2:17** [1]Or, *use a byword against them* [a]Ezek. 8:16; Mat. 23:35 [b]Ex. 32:11,12 [c]Ps. 42:10 **2:18** [a]Zech. 1:14 [b]Is. 60:10 **2:19** [a]ch. 1:10; Mal. 3:10 **2:20** [1]Heb. *he hath magnified to do* [a]Ex. 10:19 [b]Jer. 1:14 [c]Deut. 11:24 **2:21** [1]Heb. *he hath magnified to do*

locusts (Ex 10:6). Latticed windows with no glass would not stop them.
2:10 *earth shall quake.* See Ps 68:8; 77:18; Is 24:18–20; Jer 4:23–24; Amos 8:8; Nah 1:5–6. *heavens shall tremble.* See 2 Sam 22:8; Is 13:13; Hag 2:21; Heb 12:26–28. *be dark.* Joel links God's judgment through the locusts to the cosmic phenomena of the day of the Lord.
2:11 Just as Isaiah saw the Assyrians (Is 10:5–7; 13:4) and Jeremiah the Babylonians (Jer 25:9; 43:10) as the Lord's instruments, so Joel sees the locusts as the Lord's army (cf. Josh 5:14; Ps 68:7,17; Hab 3:8–9)—the army of the Lord with which He will come against His enemies in the day of the Lord (see 3:9–11). This passage parallels Zeph 1:14 (cf. v. 31; 3:14; Mal 4:1,5). *utter his voice.* See 3:16. *great . . . very terrible.* Two ideas often associated in the OT (see Deut 7:21; 10:21; Ps 106:21–22). The terms are frequently used to describe the day of the Lord (see v. 31; Mal 4:5). *who can abide it?* See Nah 1:6; Mal 3:2; Rev 6:17. There is no escape except in turning to God.
2:13 *gracious . . . great kindness.* Recalls the great self-characterization of God in Ex 34:6–7, which runs like a golden thread through the OT (see note on Ex 34:6–7; see also Deut 4:31; Mic 7:18).
2:15 *trumpet.* Not an alarm as in v. 1, but a call to religious assembly (see Lev 23:24; 25:9; Num 10:10; Josh 6:4–5; 2 Chr 15:14; Ps 47:5; 81:3; 98:6; 150:3). *fast . . . assembly.* See note on 1:14.
2:16 As with the call to mourning in ch. 1, no segment of the community was exempt. *congregation.* The Hebrew for this word refers to the religious community (see Num 16:3; 2 Chr 30:2,4,13,23–25; Mic 2:5). *elders.* See note on 1:2. *chamber.* The place where the marriage was consummated.
‡2:17 *thine heritage.* Israel is God's special possession (see Ex 19:5 and note; see also Ex 15:17; 34:9). Judah is to plead, not her innocence, but that God's honor is at stake before the world (see Ex 32:12; Num 14:13; Deut 9:28; Josh 7:9). *reproach.* In the sense of "byword." See note on 1 Ki 9:7. *Where is their God?* A rhetorical question with sarcastic intent (see Ps 42:3,10; 79:10; 115:2; Mic 7:10).
2:18 Joel begins a new section by turning from the destruction caused by the locusts to the blessings God will give to a repentant people. *jealous.* See note on Ex 20:5. The Lord will respond to the prayer of v. 17 and arouse Himself to defend His honor and have pity on His people.
‡2:19 *corn . . . wine . . . and oil.* See note on 1:10.
2:20 *northern army.* Since enemies in ancient times did not invade from the sea or across the desert, Canaan's geographical location made her vulnerable only from the south (Egypt) and from the north (Assyria and Babylon). The hordes of locusts are pictured here as a vast army of Israel's most feared enemies. *stink.* Because the locusts are now dead.
2:21–23 As there was a threefold call to grief (1:5,8,13), so there is a threefold call to joy: The land (v. 21), the wild animals

22 Be not afraid, ye beasts of the field:
For [a]the pastures of the wilderness do spring,
For the tree beareth her fruit,
The fig tree and the vine do yield their strength.
23 Be glad then, ye children of Zion, and
[a]rejoice in the LORD your God:
For he hath given you [1]the former rain
[2]moderately,
And he [b]will cause to come down for you the rain,
The former rain, and the latter rain in the first *month.*
24 And the floors shall be full *of* wheat,
And the fats shall overflow *with* wine and oil.
25 And I will restore to you the years
[a]that the locust hath eaten,
The cankerworm, and the caterpillar, and the palmerworm,
My great army which I sent among you.
26 And ye shall [a]eat in plenty, and be satisfied,
And praise the name of the LORD your God,
That hath dealt wondrously with you:
And my people shall never be ashamed.
27 And ye shall know that I *am* [a]in the midst of Israel,
And *that* [b]I *am* the LORD your God, and none else:
And my people shall never be ashamed.

2:22 [a]ch. 1:19
2:23 [1]Or, a *teacher of righteousness* [2]Heb. *according to righteousness* [a]Is. 41:16; Hab. 3:18; Zech. 10:7 [b]Lev. 26:4; Deut. 11:14
2:25 [a]ch. 1:4
2:26 [a]Lev. 26:5
2:27 [a]Lev. 26:11 [b]Is. 45:5

Promised outpouring of the Spirit

28 [a]And it shall come to pass afterward,
That I [b]will pour out my spirit upon all flesh;
[c]And your sons and [d]your daughters shall prophesy,
Your old men shall dream dreams,
Your young men shall see visions:
29 And also upon [a]the servants and upon the handmaids
In those days will I pour out my spirit.
30 And [a]I will shew wonders in the heavens and in the earth,
Blood, and fire, and pillars of smoke.
31 [a]The sun shall be turned into darkness, and the moon into blood,
[b]Before the great and the terrible day of the LORD come.
32 And it shall come to pass, *that*
[a]whosoever shall call on the name of the LORD shall be delivered:
For [b]in mount Zion and in Jerusalem shall be deliverance,
As the LORD hath said,
And in [c]the remnant whom the LORD *shall* call.

Judgment of Judah's enemies

3 For behold, [a]in those days, and in that time,
When I shall bring again the captivity of Judah and Jerusalem,
2 [a]I will also gather all nations,
And will bring them down into the valley of Jehoshaphat,

2:28 [a]Ezek. 39:29 [b]Zech. 12:10 [c]Is. 54:13 [d]Acts 21:9
2:29 [a]Gal. 3:28
2:30 [a]Mat. 24:29; Mark 13:24; Luke 21:11
2:31 [a]Is. 13:9,10 [b]Mal. 4:5
2:32 [a]Rom. 10:13 [b]Is. 46:13; Rom. 11:26 [c]Is. 11:11; Jer. 31:7; Mic. 4:7; Rom. 9:27
3:1 [a]Jer. 30:3; Ezek. 38:14
3:2 [a]Zech. 14:2

(v. 22) and the people (v. 23) are called on to rejoice in the Lord's bounty.

2:22 The wild animals now find green open pastures (cf. 1:19–20). The same land, with its trees (see 1:7,12,19) that the locusts and drought had devastated, is now productive.

‡2:23 *former rain moderately.* "Moderately" may have the sense of "in righteousness" (see KJV marg.). The religious sect at Qumran (which produced most of the Dead Sea Scrolls; see essay, p. 1344) hailed their most revered teacher of the law, whom they called the "Teacher of Righteousness," as the fulfillment of this prophecy. However, the term may also suggest "vindication." This latter sense is supported by the context.

2:24 *floors.* See note on Ruth 1:22.

2:25 See 1:4.

2:26 *dealt wondrously.* God worked wonders for the people when they were in Egypt (see Ex 7:3), and now will work wonders in restoring the devastated land.

2:27 *Israel.* Probably refers to all God's people, with no distinction between the northern and southern kingdoms, as also in 3:2,16. *I am the LORD your God.* This clause recalls the covenant at Sinai (see Ex 20:2). *and none else.* See note on Deut 4:35.

2:28–32 Quoted by Peter at Pentecost (Acts 2:16–21), but with a few variations from both the Hebrew text and the Septuagint (the Greek translation of the OT).

‡2:28 *afterward.* In the Messianic period, beyond the restoration just spoken of. *pour out my spirit.* See v. 29; Is 32:15; 44:3; Jer 31:33–34; Ezek 36:26–27; 39:29; Zech 12:10–13:1. *all flesh.* All will participate without regard to sex, age or rank; and then Moses' wish (Num 11:29) will be realized (cf. Gal 3:28). Peter extends the "all" of this verse and the "whoever" of v. 32 to the Gentiles ("all that are afar off," Acts 2:39), who will not be excluded from the Spirit's outpouring or deliverance (cf. Rom 11:11–24). *prophesy . . . dream dreams . . . see visions.* See Num 12:6.

2:30–31 These cosmic events are often associated with the day of the Lord (see Is 13:9–10; 34:4; Mat 24:29; Rev 6:12; 8:8–9; 9:1–19; 14:14–20; 16:4,8–9).

2:30 *Blood.* From war. *fire . . . smoke.* Signs of God's presence (see Gen 15:17 and note; Ex 19:18).

2:31 *blood.* The moon will become blood-red.

2:32 *call on the name of the LORD.* Worship God (cf. Gen 4:26; 12:8) and pray to Him (see Ps 116:4). *delivered.* From the wrath of God's judgment (see Mat 24:13). *As the LORD hath said.* Perhaps Joel is recalling the Lord's covenant with David (see 2 Sam 7; Ps 132:13–18). *remnant.* See Zech 13:8–9; 14:2.

‡3:1 *in those days.* At the time of Israel's final redemption. *bring again the captivity.* Or "bring back from captivity" (see vv. 6–7; see also Jer 29:14 and note).

‡3:2 *valley of Jehoshaphat.* See v. 12. Called the "valley of decision" in v. 14, it seems to be a symbolic name for a valley near Jerusalem that is here depicted as the place of God's ultimate judgment on the nations gathered against Jerusalem. There King Jehoshaphat had witnessed one of the Lord's historic victories over the nations (see 2 Chr 20:1–30). *my heritage.* See note on 2:17. Seven times in four verses (vv. 2–5) God uses "my," emphasizing His covenant relationship with Israel. *Israel.* See note on 2:27.

And [b]will plead with them there for
my people and *for* my heritage Israel,
Whom they have scattered among the
nations, and parted my land.
3 And they have [a]cast lots for my people;
And have given a boy for a harlot,
And sold a girl for wine, that they
might drink.
4 Yea, and what have ye to do with me,
[a]O Tyre, and Zidon,
And all the coasts of Palestine?
Will ye render me a recompence?
And if ye recompense me,
Swiftly *and* speedily will I return your
recompence upon your own head;
5 Because ye have taken my silver and
my gold,
And have carried into your temples my
goodly [a][1]pleasant things:
6 The children also of Judah and the
children of Jerusalem have ye sold
unto [1]the Grecians,
That *ye* might remove them far from
their border.
7 Behold, [a]I *will* raise them out of the
place whither ye have sold them,
And will return your recompence upon
your own head:
8 And I will sell your sons and your
daughters
Into the hand of the children of Judah,
And they shall sell them to the
[a]Sabeans, to a people [b]far off:
For the LORD hath spoken *it.*
9 [a]Proclaim ye this among the Gentiles;
[1]Prepare war, wake up the mighty
men,
Let all the men of war draw near; let
them come up:
10 [a]Beat your plowshares into swords,
And your [1]pruninghooks into spears:
[b]Let the weak say, I *am* strong.
11 Assemble yourselves, and come, all ye
heathen,
And gather yourselves together round
about:
Thither [1]cause [a]thy mighty ones to
come down, O LORD.
12 Let the heathen be wakened, and come
up to the valley of Jehoshaphat:
For there will I sit to [a]judge all the
heathen round about.
13 [a]Put ye in the sickle, for [b]the harvest
is ripe:
Come, get you down; for the [c]press is
full, the fats overflow;
For their wickedness *is* great.
14 Multitudes, multitudes in the valley of
[1]decision:
For [a]the day of the LORD *is* near in the
valley of decision.
15 The sun and the moon shall be
darkened,
And the stars shall withdraw their
shining.
16 The LORD also shall roar out of Zion,
And utter his voice from Jerusalem;
And the heavens and the earth shall
shake:
[a]But the LORD *will be* the [1]hope of his
people,
And the strength of the children of
Israel.
17 So shall ye know that I *am* the LORD
your God

3:2 [b]Is. 66:16; Ezek. 38:22
3:3 [a]Obad. 11; Nah. 3:10
3:4 [a]Amos 1:6
3:5 [1]Heb. *desirable* [a]Dan. 11:38
3:6 [1]Heb. *the sons of the Grecians*
3:7 [a]Is. 43:5,6; Jer. 23:8
3:8 [a]Ezek. 23:42 [b]Jer. 6:20
3:9 [1]Heb. *Sanctify* [a]Ezek. 38:7
3:10 [1]Or, *sythes* [a]Is. 2:4; Mic. 4:3 [b]Zech. 12:8
3:11 [1]Or, *the LORD shall bring down* [a]Ps. 103:20; Is. 13:3
3:12 [a]Ps. 96:13; Is. 2:4
3:13 [a]Mat. 13:39; Rev. 14:15 [b]Jer. 51:33 [c]Is. 63:3; Rev. 14:19
3:14 [1]Or, *concision,* or, *threshing* [a]ch. 2:1
3:16 [1]Heb. *place of repair,* or, *harbour* [a]Is. 51:5,6

3:3 *cast lots for my people.* This happened to Judah at the time of the captivity (586 B.C.) and is mentioned in Obad 11. The Israelites were treated by their enemies as mere chattel, to be traded off for the pleasures of prostitution and wine.
3:4–8 A parenthetical interlude. In vv. 1–3,9–11 God announces judgment against the nations hostile to Israel, but here He addresses the nations directly.
‡3:4 *me.* The Lord. *Tyre . . . Zidon . . . Palestine.* Tyre had sold Israelites as slaves (see Amos 1:9), and Palestine (i.e. "Philistia") had often plundered Israel (see Judg 13:1; 1 Sam 5:1; 2 Chr 21:16–17; Ezek 25:15–17). God punished them by allowing Zidon (i.e. "Sidon") to be enslaved by Antiochus III in 345 B.C. and by allowing Tyre to be besieged by the Babylonians in 586 and to be captured by the Greeks (under Alexander the Great) in 332.
3:6 The Greeks were trading with the Phoenicians as early as 800 B.C.
3:8 *Sabeans.* From Sheba, whose queen visited Solomon (see 1 Ki 10:1–13). *far off.* It was located in the southern part of the Arabian peninsula (present-day Yemen).
3:9–21 In vv. 9–11 Joel is the speaker; in vv. 12–13 God speaks; in vv. 14–16, Joel; and in vv. 17–21, God. When Joel speaks, he does so as the spokesman of the Lord, who has commissioned him to be His prophet.
3:9–11 Joel commands that the nations be told to prepare for battle, for the Lord would come against them with His invincible heavenly army and bring them into judgment (cf. Ezek 38–39; Rev 19).
3:10 The first part of this verse is the reverse of Is 2:4 and Mic 4:3, where the peaceful effect of God's reign is portrayed. Here God's enemies are summoned to their last great confrontation with Him.
3:11 *Assemble yourselves.* In the valley of Jehoshaphat for judgment (vv. 2,12).
3:13 As a result of the Lord's great army that had marched against Judah (2:3–11), there had been no harvest (2:3). That harvest was to be restored (2:19,22,24,26). In the final great day of the Lord, there will also be a harvest—the harvest of God's judgment on the nations. Rev 14:14–20 draws heavily on this picture of judgment.
3:14 *valley of decision.* The valley of Jehoshaphat (judgment) of vv. 2,12. "Jehoshaphat" speaks of God's role as Judge (see note on v. 2). Here "decision" (from a different Hebrew word) refers to the heavenly Judge's decision or judicial decree. The valley is now viewed as the place where that decree will be executed.
3:15 See 2:10 and note.
3:16 *roar.* Like a lion, God will destroy the nations. The first two lines occur also in Amos 1:2 (see Jer 25:30). *utter his voice.* As God at the head of His army had thundered against Jerusalem (2:11), so He will then thunder against Jerusalem's enemies, and He will do so from His royal city, from which He rules His "heritage" (see v. 17; Amos 1:2).
3:17–21 God blesses His people in a dual way: negatively, by destroying their enemies; and positively, by giving them good things.

Dwelling in Zion, my holy mountain:
Then shall Jerusalem be [1]holy,
And there shall no strangers pass
through her any more.

Eternal blessing for God's people

18 And it shall come to pass in that day,
That the mountains shall drop down
new wine,
And the hills shall [1]flow *with* milk,
And all the rivers of Judah shall [1]flow
with waters,
And a fountain shall come forth of the
house of the LORD,
And shall water the valley of Shittim.
19 Egypt shall be a desolation,
And Edom shall be a desolate
wilderness,
For the violence against the children of
Judah,
Because they have shed innocent blood
in their land.
20 But Judah shall [1]dwell for ever,
And Jerusalem from generation to
generation.
21 For I will [a]cleanse their blood *that* I
have not cleansed:
[1]For the LORD dwelleth in Zion.

3:17 [1] Heb. *holiness*
3:18 [1] Heb. *go*
3:20 [1] Or, *abide*
3:21 [1] Or, *Even I the LORD that dwelleth in Zion*
[a] Is. 4:4

3:17 *I . . . Dwelling in Zion.* The Lord Himself will dwell with them (see v. 21). The same picture is found in 2:27; Ps 46:4 (cf. Rev 21:3). The final blessed state of the now unholy and vulnerable city will be God's abiding presence in her (see v. 21 and note; Rev 21). Then she will be holy and impregnable.

‡3:18 *in that day.* The same as "in those days" of v. 1. The Edenic lushness pictured in this verse is in great contrast to the drought in 1:10 (see Amos 9:13). *And a fountain shall come forth of the house of the LORD.* Flowing from God's presence, streams of blessing will refresh His people and make their place endlessly fruitful (cf. Ps 36:8; 46:4; 87:7; Ezek 47:1–12; Rev 22:1–2). *Shittim.* See notes on Num 25:1; Josh 2:1.

3:19 *Egypt . . . Edom.* As old enemies of Israel, they here represent all the nations hostile to God's people. *desolation . . . desolate wilderness.* Figures for the removal of all life-sustaining blessings, thus setting in sharp focus the contrasting destinies of God's people and the enemies of God's kingdom. This picture of desolation also recalls the earlier description of Judah's condition (2:3).

3:20 *shall dwell for ever.* When God's judgment and redemption are consummated, His kingdom will endure and flourish eternally.

3:21 This book of judgment ends on a promising and encouraging note: "*the LORD dwelleth in Zion,*" and therefore all is right with those who trust in God and live with Him.

Amos

INTRODUCTION

Author

Amos was from Tekoa (1:1), a small town about 6 miles south of Beth-lehem and 11 miles from Jerusalem. He was not a man of the court like Isaiah, or a priest like Jeremiah. He earned his living from the flock and the sycamore-fig grove (1:1; 7:14–15). Whether he owned the flocks and groves or only worked as a hired hand is not known. His skill with words and the strikingly broad range of his general knowledge of history and the world preclude his being an ignorant peasant. Though his home was in Judah, he was sent to announce God's judgment on the northern kingdom (Israel). He probably ministered for the most part at Beth-el (7:10–13; see note on Gen 12:8), Israel's main religious sanctuary, where the upper echelons of the northern kingdom worshiped.

The book brings his prophecies together in a carefully organized form intended to be read as a unit. It offers few, if any, clues as to the chronological order of his spoken messages—he may have repeated them on many occasions to reach everyone who came to worship. The book is addressed also to the southern kingdom (hence the references to Judah and Jerusalem).

Date and Historical Situation

According to the first verse, Amos prophesied during the reigns of Uzziah over Judah (792–740 B.C.) and Jeroboam II over the Israel (793–753). The main part of his ministry was probably carried out c. 760–750. Both kingdoms were enjoying great prosperity and had reached new political and military heights (cf. 2 Ki 14:23—15:7; 2 Chr 26). It was also a time of idolatry, extravagant indulgence in luxurious living, immorality, corruption of judicial procedures and oppression of the poor. As a consequence, God would soon bring about the Assyrian captivity of the northern kingdom (722–721).

Israel at the time was politicaly secure and spiritually smug. About 40 years earlier, at the end of his ministry, Elisha had prophesied the resurgence of Israel's power (2 Ki 13:17–19), and more recently Jonah had prophesied her restoration to a glory not known since the days of Solomon (2 Ki 14:25). The nation felt sure, therefore, that she was in God's good graces. But prosperity increased Israel's religious and moral corruption. God's past punishments for unfaithfulness were forgotten, and His patience was at an end—which He sent Amos to announce.

With Amos, the messages of the prophets began to be preserved in permanent form, being brought together in books that would accompany Israel through the coming debacle and beyond. (Since Amos was a contemporary of Hosea and Jonah, see Introductions to those books.)

Theme and Message

The dominant theme is clearly stated in 5:24, which calls for social justice as the indispensable expression of true piety. Amos was a vigorous spokesman for God's justice and righteousness, whereas Hosea emphasized God's love, grace, mercy and forgiveness. Amos declared that God was going to judge His unfaithful, disobedient, covenant-breaking people. Despite His special choice of Israel and His kindnesses to her during the exodus and conquest and in the days of David and Solomon, His people continually failed to honor and obey Him. The shrines at Beth-el and other places of worship were often paganized, and Israel had a worldly view of even the ritual that the Lord Himself had prescribed. They thought performance of the rites was all God required, and, with that done, they could do whatever they pleased—an essentially pagan notion. Without commitment to God's law, they had no basis for standards of conduct. Amos condemns all who make themselves powerful or rich at the expense of others. Those who had acquired two splendid houses (3:15), expensive furniture and richly furnished tables by cheating, perverting justice and crushing the poor would lose everything they had.

God's imminent judgment on Israel would not be a mere punitive blow to warn (as often before,

4:6–11), but an almost total destruction. The unthinkable was about to happen: Because they had not faithfully consecrated themselves to His lordship, God would uproot His chosen people by the hands of a pagan nation. Even so, if they would repent, there was hope that "the LORD God of hosts will be gracious unto the remnant" (5:15; see 5:4–6,14). In fact, the Lord had a glorious future for His people, beyond the impending judgment. The house of David would again rule over Israel—even extend its rule over many nations—and Israel would once more be secure in the promised land, feasting on wine and fruit (9:11–15). The God of Israel, the Lord of history, would not abandon His chosen people or His chosen program of redemption.

The God for whom Amos speaks is God of more than merely Israel. He also uses one against another to carry out His purposes (6:14). He is the Great King who rules the whole universe (4:13; 5:8; 9:5–6). Because He is all-sovereign, the God of Israel holds the history and destiny of all peoples and of the world in His hands. Israel must know not only that He is the Lord of her future, but also that He is Lord over all, and that He has purposes and concerns that reach far beyond her borders. For that reason, Amos is the only prophet to open his book with oracles against the nations. As the first prophet to introduce the day of the Lord, he is the first to introduce the truth that God is no respector of nations. Israel had a unique, but not an exclusive, claim on God. She needed to remember not only His covenant commitments to her but also her covenant obligations to Him. (See further the prophecy of Jonah.)

Outline

- I. Superscription (1:1)
- II. Introduction to Amos's Message (1:2)
- III. Judgments on the Nations (1:3—2:16)
  - A. Judgment on Aram (1:3–5)
  - B. Judgment on Philistia (1:6–8)
  - C. Judgment on Phoenicia (1:9–10)
  - D. Judgment on Edom (1:11–12)
  - E. Judgment on Ammon (1:13–15)
  - F. Judgment on Moab (2:1–3)
  - G. Judgment on Judah (2:4–5)
  - H. Judgment on Israel (2:6–16)
    1. Ruthless oppression of the poor (2:6–7a)
    2. Unbridled profanation of religion (2:7b-8)
    3. Contrasted position of the Israelites (2:9–12)
    4. The oppressive system will perish (2:13–16)
- IV. Oracles against Israel (3:1—5:17)
  - A. Judgment on the Chosen People (ch. 3)
    1. God's punishment announced (3:1–2)
    2. The announcement vindicated (3:3–8)
    3. The punishment vindicated (3:9–15)
  - B. Judgment on an Unrepentant People (ch. 4)
    1. Judgment on the socialites (4:1–3)
    2. Perversion of religious life (4:4–5)
    3. Past calamities brought no repentance (4:6–11)
    4. No hope for a hardened people (4:12–13)
  - C. Judgment on an Unjust People (5:1–17)
    1. The death dirge (5:1–3)
    2. Exhortation to life (5:4–6)
    3. Indictment of injustices (5:7–13)
    4. Exhortation to life (5:14–15)
    5. Prosperity will turn to grief (5:16–17)
- V. Announcements of Exile (5:18—6:14)
  - A. A Message of Woe against Israel's Perverted Religion (5:18–27)
  - B. A Message of Woe against Israel's Complacent Pride (6:1–7)
  - C. A Sworn Judgment on the Proud and Unjust Nation (6:8–14)
- VI. Visions of Divine Retribution (7:1—9:10)
  - A. Judgment Relented (7:1–6)

1. A swarm of grasshoppers (7:1–3)
2. A consuming fire (7:4–6)

B. Judgment Unrelented (7:7—9:10)

1. The plumbline (7:7–17)
   a. The vision (7:7–9)
   b. Challenged and vindicated (7:10–17)
2. The basket of summer fruit (ch. 8)
   a. The vision (8:1–3)
   b. The exposition (8:4–14)
3. The Lord by the altar (9:1–10)
   a. The vision (9:1–4)
   b. The exposition (9:5–10)

VII. Restored Israel's Blessed Future (9:11–15)

A. Revival of the House of David (9:11–12)

B. Restoration of Israel to an Edenic Promised Land (9:13–15)

1 The words of Amos, who was among the
herdmen of [a]Tekoa, which he saw concerning Israel in the days of Uzziah king of Judah, and in the days of [b]Jeroboam the son of
Joash king of Israel, two year before the
[c]earthquake.
2 And he said,
The LORD will [a]roar from Zion,
And utter his voice from Jerusalem;
And the habitations of the shepherds
shall mourn,
And the top of [b]Carmel shall wither.

Judgment on the nations

3 Thus saith the LORD;
For three transgressions of [a]Damascus,
[1]And for four, I will not [2]turn away *the punishment* thereof;
Because they have threshed Gilead
with threshing *instruments* of iron:
4 [a]But I will send a fire into the house of
Hazael,
Which shall devour the palaces of Ben-hadad.
5 I will break also the [a]bar of Damascus,
And cut off the inhabitant from [1]the
plain of Aven,
And him that holdeth the sceptre from
[2]the house of Eden:
And [3]the people of Syria shall go into
captivity unto Kir, saith the LORD.

6 Thus saith the LORD;
For three transgressions of [a]Gaza,
And for four, I will not turn away *the punishment* thereof;
Because they [1]carried away captive the
whole captivity,
To deliver *them* up to Edom:
7 [a]But I will send a fire on the wall of
Gaza,
Which shall devour the palaces thereof:
8 And I will cut off the inhabitant [a]from
Ashdod,
And him that holdeth the sceptre from
Ashkelon,
And I will [b]turn mine hand against
Ekron:
And [c]the remnant of the Philistines
shall perish, saith the Lord GOD.

1:1 [a]2 Sam. 14:2 [b]ch. 7:10 [c]Zech. 14:5
1:2 [a]Joel 3:16 [b]1 Sam. 25:2; Is. 33:9
1:3 [1]Or, *Yea, for four* [2]Or, *convert it*, or, *let it be quiet:* and so ver. 6, etc. [a]Is. 8:4
1:4 [a]Jer. 17:27
1:5 [a]Jer. 51:30
1:5 [1]Or, *Bikath-aven* [2]Or, *Beth-eden* [3][Fulfilled, 2 Ki. 16:9]
1:6 [1]Or, *carried them away with an entire captivity* [a]Jer. 47:4,5
1:7 [a]Jer. 47:1
1:8 [a]Zeph. 2:4 [b]Ps. 81:14 [c]Ezek. 25:16

‡1:1 *Amos.* Apparently a shortened form of a name like Amasiah (2 Chr 17:16), meaning "The LORD carries" or "The LORD upholds." *herdmen.* The Hebrew for this word occurs elsewhere in the OT only in reference to the king of Moab (2 Ki 3:4, where it is translated "sheepmaster"). Perhaps Amos was not a simple shepherd but was in charge of the royal flocks. Cf. 7:14, where a different Hebrew word is used. Amos was not a professional prophet who earned his living from his ministry; he stood outside religious institutions. *Tekoa.* See Introduction: Author. *saw.* Received by divine revelation. *Uzziah.* See Introduction: Date and Historical Situation; see also note on Is 6:1. *Jeroboam.* See Introduction: Date and Historical Situation. *earthquake.* Evidently a major shock, long remembered, and probably the one mentioned in Zech 14:5. Reference to the earthquake suggests that the author viewed it as a kind of divine reinforcement of the words of judgment. Amos uses the verb form in 9:1 (shake) to create an envelope effect between the past and coming quake.

‡1:2–2:16 A series of oracles against the nations. After pronouncing judgments on Israel's neighbors for various atrocities—judgments that Israel would naturally applaud—Amos announces God's condemnation of His own two kingdoms for despising God's laws. His listing of Israel's sins under the same form of indictment used against the other nations shockingly pictures Israel's sins alongside those of her pagan neighbors. It is significant to note that he is the only prophet to begin his book with oracles against the nations.

‡1:2 A thematic verse, ominously announcing the main thrust of Amos's message. *roar.* Amos, a shepherd, was sent to Israel to warn her that he had heard a lion roar and that the lion is none other than the Lord Himself, who has only wanted to be Israel's shepherd. (For the use of this imagery in other contexts see Jer 25:30; Joel 3:16.) The term suggests that it is "day of the Lord" language that is being used. "Roar" is also a "link" word connecting Joel and Amos. See Joel 3:16. *from Zion.* The Lord established His earthly throne in Jerusalem, among His special people, and from there He announces His judgments on them, as well as on the other nations. *habitations . . . top of Carmel.* See 9:3. From the driest portion of the land to the greenest, the Lord's judgment will be felt like a severe drought that devastates the whole land.

1:3 *For three transgressions . . . four.* For their many sins, especially the one named; see also vv. 6,9,11,13; 2:1,4,6. For similar numerical expressions see Prov 6:16; 30:15,18,21,29; Mic 5:5. *Damascus.* Capital of the Aramean state directly north of Israel and a constant enemy in that day. Her crime was brutality to the conquered people of Gilead, Israel's territory east of Galilee. *threshed . . . instruments of iron.* Heads of grain were threshed by driving a wooden sledge fitted with sharp teeth over the cut grain (cf. Job 41:30; Is 28:27; 41:15; see 2 Ki 13:7 and note on Ruth 1:22).

1:4 *send a fire . . . shall devour.* See vv. 7,10,12; 2:2,5; cf. v. 14; a common description of the threat of divine judgment, usually carried out by a devastating war that resulted in the burning of major cities and fortresses. See the judgments mentioned in Jer 17:27; 49:27; 50:32; Hos 8:14. *Hazael.* King of Damascus c. 842–796 B.C. and founder of a new line of kings (see 2 Ki 8:7–15). *palaces.* See vv. 7,10,12,14; 2:2,5; perhaps referring to the fortress-like palatial dwellings of the rich and powerful. *Ben-hadad.* Son of Hazael (2 Ki 13:24) and the second king with this name (cf. 2 Ki 8:14–15), ruling c. 796–775.

‡1:5 *inhabitant.* See v. 8; lit. "one who sits [enthroned]." *plain of Aven.* Possibly the Beqaa Valley between the Lebanon and Anti-Lebanon mountains, but may refer to the river valley in which Damascus is located, calling it the "valley of wickedness" ("Aven" means "wickedness"). *house of Eden.* Probably Damascus, the garden spot of that region. Beth Eden was also a powerful Aramean kingdom in upper Mesopotamia. *Syria.* See note on Gen 10:22. *Kir.* An unidentified place, possibly in the vicinity of Elam (2 Ki 16:9; Is 22:6), from which the Arameans of Damascus are said to have come (9:7).

‡1:6 *Gaza.* One of the five Philistine cities (see map, p. 313); it guarded the entry to Canaan from Egypt. *carried away . . . the whole* (people). See v. 9; not just warriors captured in battle. The reference may be to villages in south Judah on the trade route from Edom to Gaza. *to Edom.* See v. 9; trading the people like cattle to another country. Edom is singled out by Amos; he closes with the promise that Israel would "possess" Edom, and it serves as a link word for the following book, Obadiah, "the house of Jacob will possess . . ." (Edom).

1:8 *Ashdod . . . Ashkelon . . . Ekron.* Three more cities of the Philistine group (see note on v. 6). Gath, the fifth (cf. 6:2), may

9 Thus saith the LORD;
For three transgressions of [a]Tyrus,
And for four, I will not turn away *the punishment* thereof;
Because they delivered up the whole captivity to Edom,
And remembered not [b][1]the brotherly covenant:
10 But I will send a fire on the wall of Tyrus,
Which shall devour the palaces thereof.

11 Thus saith the LORD;
For three transgressions of [a]Edom,
And for four, I will not turn away *the punishment* thereof;
Because he did pursue his brother with the sword,
And [1]did cast off all pity,
And his anger did tear perpetually,
And he kept his wrath for ever:
12 But [a]I will send a fire upon the Teman,
Which shall devour the palaces of Bozrah.

13 Thus saith the LORD;
For three transgressions of [a]the children of Ammon,
And for four, I will not turn away *the punishment* thereof;
Because they have [1]ript up the women with child at Gilead,
That *they* might enlarge their border:
14 But I will kindle a fire in the wall of [a]Rabbah,
And it shall devour the palaces thereof,
[b]With shouting in the day of battle,
With a tempest in the day of the whirlwind:

1:9 [1]Heb. *the covenant of brethren* [a]Is. 23:1 [b]1 Ki. 5:1
1:11 [1]Heb. *corrupted his compassions* [a]Is. 21:11; Jer. 49:8
1:12 [a]Obad. 9,10
1:13 [1]Or, *divided the mountains* [a]Jer. 49:1; Ezek. 25:2
1:14 [a]Deut. 3:11 [b]ch. 2:2

15 And [a]their king shall go into captivity,
He and his princes together, saith the LORD.

2 Thus saith the LORD;
For three transgressions of Moab,
And for four, I will not turn away *the punishment* thereof;
Because he [a]burnt the bones of the king of Edom into lime:
2 But I will send a fire upon Moab,
And it shall devour the palaces of [a]Kerioth:
And Moab shall die with tumult,
With shouting, *and* with the sound of the trumpet:
3 And I will cut off [a]the judge from the midst thereof,
And will slay all the princes thereof with him, saith the LORD.

4 Thus saith the LORD;
For three transgressions of Judah,
And for four, I will not turn away *the punishment* thereof;
[a]Because they have despised the law of the LORD,
And have not kept his commandments,
And [b]their lies caused them to err,
[c]After the which their fathers have walked:
5 [a]But I will send a fire upon Judah,
And it shall devour the palaces of Jerusalem.

Prophecy against Israel

6 Thus saith the LORD;
For three transgressions of Israel,
And for four, I will not turn away *the punishment* thereof;

1:15 [a]Jer. 49:3
2:1 [a]2 Ki. 3:27
2:2 [a]Jer. 48:41
2:3 [a]Num. 24:17; Jer. 48:7
2:4 [a]Lev. 26:14 [b]Is. 28:15; Jer. 16:19 [c]Ezek. 20:13,16,18
2:5 [a]Jer. 17:27; Hos. 8:14

already have been subdued by Uzziah (see 2 Chr 26:6). *the remnant.* There would be no remnant. Philistia was finally destroyed by Nebuchadnezzar.

‡1:9 *Tyrus.* The senior Phoenician merchant city, allied to Israel by a "brotherly covenant" in the days of David (1 Ki 5:1), later in the time of Solomon (1 Ki 5:12) and later still during the reign of Ahab, whose father-in-law ruled Tyre (the more common spelling) and Sidon (1 Ki 16:30–31). *they delivered.* Their crime was like Philistia's (v. 6).

1:10 *wall.* Tyre had an almost impregnable island fortress, so she was boastful of her security (cf. Ezek 26:1–28:19).

1:11 *Edom.* The nation descended from Esau (Gen 36; cf. Gen 25:23–30; 27:39–40). *brother.* Israel (cf. Obad 8–10). Reference may be to treaty "brother" (see note on v. 9). Edom's crime was in violating this relationship by persistent hostility.

1:12 *Teman . . . Bozrah.* Major cities of Edom, the former thought to be near Petra, the latter now identified with Buseirah, 37 miles to the north. With their destruction, Edom would lose its capacity for continual warfare.

1:13 *Ammon.* Judgment centered on Rabbah (see note on Deut 3:11), modern Amman. Greed for land bred a brutal genocide that would be punished by a tumult of men and nature, leaving the state without leaders to continue such practices.

1:14 Fulfilled through the Assyrians.

‡1:15 *their king.* See Jer 49:1,3 and notes. *captivity.* Note how Amos uses this as an "envelope" word (9:14). It should be remembered that the Assyrians had not yet instituted the practice of wholesale deportation. It is small wonder then that Israel found Amos's message about impending captivity unbelievable.

2:1 *burnt the bones of the king of Edom.* Thus depriving the king's spirit of the rest that was widely believed to result from decent burial.

2:2 *Kerioth.* Perhaps a plural noun meaning "cities" (therefore "citadels of her cities") or the name of a major town (see Jer 48:24) and shrine of Chemosh, the national god of Moab (see 1 Ki 11:7,33).

2:4 *despised the law of the LORD.* Judah's sins differed in kind from those of the other nations. Those nations violated the generally recognized laws of humanity, but Judah disobeyed the revealed law of God. These sins may be included in the indictment against Israel that follows.

‡2:5 *fire . . . devour the palaces.* Judah's punishment is the same as Aram's (1:4), Gaza's (1:7), Tyre's (1:10), Edom's (1:12), Ammon's (1:14) and Moab's (2:2)—loss of the defenses and wealth in which they trusted. These eight oracles reveal Amos's incredible literary skill. Seven times "I will send fire" is followed by two triads, "on the wall" and "upon" (Teman), followed by seven times "it shall devour," followed by another triadic dual, "its palaces" and "the palaces of Jerusalem" and a final triad, "I will cut off." He was hardly a simple shepherd.

‡2:6 Israel's sins revealed the general moral deterioration of

Because [a]they sold the righteous for silver,
And the poor for a pair of shoes;
7 That pant after the dust of the earth on the head of the poor,
And [a]turn aside the way of the meek:
[b]And a man and his father will go in unto the *same* [1]maid,
[c]To profane my holy name:
8 And they lay *themselves* down upon clothes [a]laid to pledge [b]by every altar,
And they drink the wine of [1]the condemned *in* the house of their god.
9 Yet destroyed I the [a]Amorite before them,
Whose height *was* like the height of the cedars,
And he *was* strong as the oaks;
Yet I [b]destroyed his fruit from above,
And his roots from beneath.
10 Also [a]I brought you up from the land of Egypt,
And [b]led you forty years through the wilderness,
To possess the land of the Amorite.
11 And I raised up of your sons for prophets,
And of your young men for [a]Nazarites.
Is it not even thus, O ye children of Israel? saith the LORD.
12 But ye gave the Nazarites wine to drink;
And commanded the prophets, [a]saying, Prophesy not.
13 [a]Behold, [1]I am pressed under you,
As a cart is pressed *that is* full *of* sheaves.
14 [a]Therefore the flight shall perish from the swift,
And the strong shall not strengthen his force,
[b]Neither shall the mighty deliver [1]himself:
15 Neither shall he stand that handleth the bow;
And *he that is* swift of foot shall not deliver *himself:*
Neither shall he that rideth the horse deliver himself.
16 And he *that is* [1]courageous among the mighty
Shall flee away naked in that day, saith the LORD.

The relation of Israel to God

3 Hear this word that the LORD hath spoken against you, O children of Israel,
Against the whole family which I brought up from the land of Egypt, saying,
2 [a]You only have I known of all the families of the earth:
[b]Therefore I will [1]punish you for all your iniquities.

2:6 [a]Is. 29:21
2:7 [1]Or, *young woman* [a]ch. 5:12 [b]Ezek. 22:11 [c]Lev. 20:3
2:8 [1]Or, *such as have fined,* or, *mulcted* [a]Ex. 22:26 [b]1 Cor. 8:10
2:9 [a]Num. 21:24; Deut. 2:31 [b]Is. 5:24; Mal. 4:1
2:10 [a]Ex. 12:51 [b]Deut. 2:7
2:11 [a]Num. 6:2; Judg. 13:5
2:12 [a]Is. 30:10; Jer. 11:21; Mic. 2:6
2:13 [1]Or, *I will press your place, as a cart full of sheaves presseth* [a]Is. 1:14
2:14 [1]Heb. *his soul,* or, *life* [a]Jer. 9:23 [b]Ps. 33:16
2:16 [1]Heb. *strong of his heart*
3:2 [1]Heb. *visit upon* [a]Deut. 7:6; Ps. 147:19 [b]Mat. 11:22; Rom. 2:9

the nation. *the righteous.* Probably those who were not in debt and whom there was no lawful reason to sell (cf. Lev 25:39–43). *the poor.* God had commanded that they be helped (Deut 15:7–11), but they were instead sold for failure to repay a (perhaps paltry) debt, for which a pair of sandals had been given in pledge (see 8:6). For a similar practice see Joel 3:3.

2:7 *poor . . . meek.* To care for them and to protect them from injustice were clearly commanded by Israel's law (Ex 23:6–8); also, throughout the ancient Near East, kings were supposed to defend such people. *a man and his father will go in unto the same maid.* Whether the girl in question was a household servant (in which case father and son used her as a family prostitute) is not clear. In any case, the law required that if there were sexual relations with a girl, marriage was obligatory (Ex 22:16; Deut 22:28–29). For a father and son to have sexual relations with the same girl or woman was strictly forbidden (Lev 18:7–8,15; 20:11–12). *profane my holy name.* Cf. Lev 18:21; 19:12; 20:3; 21:6; 22:2,32; Jer 34:16; Ezek 20:9,14,22,39; 36:20–23; 39:7.

2:8 *clothes laid to pledge.* The law prohibited keeping a man's cloak overnight as a pledge (Ex 22:26–27; Deut 24:12–13), or taking a widow's cloak at all (Deut 24:17). *by every altar . . . in the house of their god.* Israelites who broke the laws protecting the powerless brazenly used their wrongly gotten gains even in places supposed to be holy. *wine of the condemned.* As restitution for damages suffered. Exorbitant claims or even false charges of damage seem to be suggested.

‡2:9 *Yet destroyed I.* Israel not only had known God's law but had been specially favored by His powerful help. *Amorite.* Here used for all the inhabitants of Canaan (see notes on Gen 10:16; 15:16; Judg 6:10; see also Deut 7:1 and note). *his fruit from above, And his roots from beneath.* That is, totally. See Mal 4:l.

‡2:10 *I brought you up.* See 3:1. God's great blessings to Israel in the past added to her guilt, and now they are recalled as a part of the Lord's indictment against His people.

‡2:11 *I raised up . . . prophets, And . . . Nazarites.* Prophets, as God's faithful spokesmen (Deut 18:15–19), and Nazarites, as those uniquely dedicated to Him (Num 6:1–21; Judg 13:5), are singled out as special gifts to His people. These persons who were outside the priesthood were used by God through word and example to call His people to faithfulness.

2:12 *But ye.* They showed utter disdain for God's faithful servants and thus betrayed their callous insensitivity to God's working among them (cf. 7:16).

2:13 *cart is pressed.* A loaded cart crushes anything that falls beneath its wheels.

2:14–16 No one who might be expected to stand his ground or escape would be able to save himself.

2:16 *that day.* The day God comes in judgment—as He did through the Assyrian invasion that swept the northern kingdom away

‡3:1–5:17 Oracles that underscore the certainty of God's judgment on Israel. It would seem that the rest of Amos's book is a continuation of his oracle against Israel.

3:1 *Hear this word.* See 4:1; 5:1. The Lord calls His people to account because of their sins. *I.* He now speaks more directly than in 1:2–2:16.

‡3:2 *You only.* Israel's present strength and prosperity gave rise to complacency about her privileged status as the Lord's chosen people. She is shockingly reminded of the long-forgotten responsibilities her privileges entailed. *known.* A covenant term with the idea "you only have I entered covenant with."

3 Can two walk together, except they be
agreed?
4 Will a lion roar in the forest, when he
hath no prey?
Will a young lion [1]cry out of his den, if
he have taken nothing?
5 Can a bird fall in a snare upon the
earth, where no gin *is* for him?
Shall *one* take up a snare from the
earth, and have taken nothing at all?
6 Shall a trumpet be blown in the city,
and the people [1]not be afraid?
[a]Shall there be evil in a city, [2]and the
LORD hath not done *it?*
7 Surely the Lord GOD will do nothing,
But [a]he revealeth his secret unto his
servants the prophets.
8 The lion hath roared, who will not fear?
The Lord GOD hath spoken, [a]who can
but prophesy?

9 Publish in the palaces at Ashdod,
And in the palaces in the land of Egypt,
And say, Assemble yourselves upon the
mountains of Samaria,
And behold the great tumults in the
midst thereof,
And the [1]oppressed in the midst
thereof.
10 For they [a]know not to do right, saith
the LORD,
Who store up violence and [1]robbery in
their palaces.
11 Therefore thus saith the Lord GOD;
An adversary *there shall be* even round
about the land;
And he shall bring down thy strength
from thee,
And thy palaces shall be spoiled.
12 Thus saith the LORD;
As the shepherd [1]taketh out of the
mouth of the lion two legs, or a piece
of an ear;
So shall the children of Israel be taken
out
That dwell in Samaria in the corner of
a bed, and [2]in Damascus *in* a couch.
13 Hear ye, and testify in the house of
Jacob,
Saith the Lord GOD, the God of hosts,
14 That in the day that I shall [1]visit the
transgressions of Israel upon him
I will also [1]visit the altars of Beth-el:
And the horns of the altar shall be cut
off,
And fall to the ground.
15 And I will smite [a]the winter house
with [b]the summer house;
And [c]the houses of ivory shall perish,
And the great houses shall have an
end, saith the LORD.

4 Hear this word, ye [a]kine of Bashan,
that *are* in the mountain of Samaria,
Which oppress the poor, which crush
the needy,
Which say to their masters, Bring, and
let us drink.
2 [a]The Lord GOD hath sworn by his
holiness,
That lo, the days shall come upon you,
That he will take you away [b]with hooks,
And your posterity with fishhooks.

3:4 [1]Heb. *give forth his voice*
3:6 [1]Or, *not run together?* [2]Or, *and shall not the LORD do somewhat?* [a]Is. 45:7
3:7 [a]Gen. 6:13; John 15:15
3:8 [a]Acts 4:20
3:9 [1]Or, *oppressions*
3:10 [1]Or, *spoil* [a]Jer. 4:22
3:12 [1]Heb. *delivereth* [2]Or, *on the bed's feet*
3:14 [1]Or, *punish Israel for*
3:15 [a]Jer. 36:22 [b]Judg. 3:20 [c]1 Ki. 22:39
4:1 [a]Ps. 22:12; Ezek. 39:18
4:2 [a]Ps. 89:35 [b]Jer. 16:16; Hab. 1:15

3:3–6 With these rhetorical questions (involving comparisons) Amos builds up to the statements of vv. 7–8, to explain why he is speaking such terrifying words. Each picture is of cause and effect, using figures drawn from daily life—and culminating in divine action (v. 6).
3:8 *The lion.* Echoes 1:2. *who can but prophesy?* Amos speaks because God has spoken.
3:9 The rich and powerful of Philistia and Egypt are summoned to witness the Lord's indictment against those who store up ill-gotten riches in the fortresses of Samaria (see v. 15). *palaces.* See note on 1:4. *mountains of Samaria.* Courtroom language as the pagans are on the surrounding mountains witnessing Israel's behaviour, scandalous even to pagans. *great tumults.* The result of a violent, selfish power structure that was heedless of the justice called for in God's law.
3:10 *Who store up.* Cf. 2:6–8. The prosperity of Israel's wealthy depended on oppression and robbery. The following verses announce God's judgment on such greed (cf. Hab 2:6–11).
3:11 *adversary.* Assyria. *palaces shall be spoiled.* Those that Samaria's wealthy had greedily filled with plunder.
‡3:12 *As the shepherd taketh out . . . two legs.* To prove to the owner that the sheep had been eaten by a wild animal, not stolen by the shepherd. *the children . . . That dwell in Samaria.* In idle luxury (cf. 6:4). Excavations have confirmed the opulent wealth of the capital city. *be taken out.* Only a mutilated remnant would survive. The nation as such would be more than wounded—it would be destroyed.
3:13 *Hear ye, and testify.* Addressed to those summoned in v. 9. The rich and powerful of Philistia and Egypt are called upon to hear the Lord's indictment of the rich and powerful in Samaria and to testify that His indictment is true and that His judgment is warranted. Even these pagans will agree with God's judgment.
3:14 *altars of Beth-el.* Israel's sins were rooted in the false shrine built by Jeroboam I at Beth-el (1 Ki 12:26–33). *horns of the altar.* Even the last refuge for a condemned man (cf. 1 Ki 1:50–53) will afford Israel no protection.
3:15 *winter house . . . summer house.* Cf. 6:11; further signs of opulence that would not benefit their owners on the day of God's judgment—nor would expensive imported decorations, carvings and inlays of ivory (cf. 6:4; 1 Ki 22:39). Many examples of such carvings have been found in ruined palaces in Samaria and other cities.
4:1 *Hear this word.* See note on 3:1. *kine of Bashan.* Upper-class women, directly addressed, are compared with the best breed of cattle in ancient Canaan, which were raised (and pampered) in the pastures of northern Transjordan (cf. Ps 22:12; Ezek 39:18). Whether the metaphor was intended as an insult or as ironic flattery is uncertain.
4:2 *The Lord GOD hath sworn.* Stresses the solemnity of the situation and the certainty of the events. *by his holiness.* Contrasts with Israel's sin, reminding them of what they could have been (Ex 19:6) if they had faithfully kept their side of the covenant—as God had His. *hooks.* According to Assyrian reliefs (pictures engraved on stone), prisoners of war were led away with a rope fastened to a hook that pierced the nose or lower lip (cf. 2 Ki 19:28; 2 Chr 33:11; Ezek 19:4,9; Hab 1:15). The Hebrew word here may, in fact, refer to ropes.

3 And [a]ye shall go out *at* the breaches,
every *cow at that which is* before her;
And [1]ye shall cast *them* into the
palace, saith the LORD.

Israel's failure to return to God

4 [a]Come *to* Beth-el, and transgress;
At [b]Gilgal multiply transgression;
And [c]bring your sacrifices *every*
morning,
[d]*And* your tithes after [1]three years:
5 [a]And [1]offer a sacrifice of thanksgiving
with leaven,
And proclaim *and* publish [b]the free
offerings:
For [2]this liketh you, O ye children of
Israel, saith the Lord GOD.
6 And I also have given you cleanness of
teeth in all your cities,
And want of bread in all your places:
[a]Yet have ye not returned unto me,
saith the LORD.
7 And also I have withholden the rain
from you,
When *there were* yet three months to
the harvest:
And I caused it to rain upon one city,
and caused it not to rain upon
another city:
One piece was rained upon, and the
piece whereupon it rained not
withered.
8 So two *or* three cities wandered unto
one city, to drink water;
But they were not satisfied:
Yet have ye not returned unto me,
saith the LORD.
9 [a]I have smitten you with blasting and
mildew:
[1]When your gardens and your
vineyards and your fig trees and your
olive trees increased,

4:3 [1] Or, *ye shall cast away the* things of *the palace* [a] Ezek. 12:5
4:4 [1] Heb. *three* years *of days* [a] Ezek. 20:39 [b] Hos. 4:15 [c] Num. 28:3 [d] Deut. 14:28
4:5 [1] Heb. *offer by burning* [2] Heb. *so ye love* [a] Lev. 7:13 [b] Lev. 22:18; Deut. 12:6
4:6 [a] Is. 26:11; Jer. 5:3; Hag. 2:17
4:9 [1] Or, *The multitude of your gardens, etc. did the palmerworm, etc.* [a] Deut. 28:22; Hag. 2:17

4:9 [b] Joel 1:4
4:10 [1] Or, *in the way* [2] Heb. *with the captivity of your horses* [a] Ex. 9:3,6; Deut. 28:27; Ps. 78:50 [b] 2 Ki. 13:7
4:11 [a] Gen. 19:24; Is. 13:19
4:12 [a] Ezek. 13:5
4:13 [1] Or, *spirit* [a] Ps. 139:2; Dan. 2:28 [b] Mic. 1:3 [c] Is. 47:4; Jer. 10:16
5:1 [a] Jer. 7:29

[b]The palmerworm devoured *them:*
Yet have ye not returned unto me,
saith the LORD.
10 I have sent among you the pestilence
[a] [1]after the manner of Egypt:
Your young men have I slain with the
sword, [b] [2]and have taken away your
horses;
And I have made the stink of your
camps to come up unto your nostrils:
Yet have ye not returned unto me,
saith the LORD.
11 I have overthrown *some* of you, as God
overthrew [a]Sodom and Gomorrah,
And ye were as a firebrand pluckt out
of the burning:
Yet have ye not returned unto me,
saith the LORD.
12 Therefore thus will I do unto thee,
O Israel:
And because I will do this unto thee,
[a]Prepare to meet thy God, O Israel.
13 For lo, he that formeth the mountains,
and createth the [1]wind,
[a]And declareth unto man what *is* his
thought,
That maketh the morning darkness,
[b]And treadeth upon the high places of
the earth,
[c]The LORD, The God of hosts, *is* his
name.

5 Hear ye this word which I [a]take up
against you,
Even a lamentation, O house of Israel.
2 The virgin of Israel is fallen; she shall
no more rise:
She is forsaken upon her land; *there is*
none to raise her up.
3 For thus saith the Lord GOD;
The city that went out *by* a thousand
shall leave an hundred,

‡4:3 *breaches.* See 2 Ki 17:5. *palace.* Hebrew *harmon;* some translate as a place-name ("Harmon"), though it is not otherwise known.
4:4–5 Spoken in irony.
4:4 *Beth-el* ... *Gilgal.* These towns had historical importance as places where God's help was commemorated (cf. Gen 35:1–15; Josh 4:20–24), and both were popular places of worship in Amos's day (5:5; cf. Hos 4:15; 9:15; 12:11). *sacrifices every morning.* See Ex 29:38–42. *tithes.* Apparently the special tithe that was to be brought every three years (cf. Deut 14:28; 26:12).
4:5 *with leaven.* The burning of leavened bread in the sacrifices was strictly forbidden (see Lev 6:17; 7:12). Either Amos rebukes the Israelites for willful transgression of the law, or he speaks of burning in a general way for offering inappropriate gifts to the Lord. Leavened bread could accompany a peace offering (see Lev 7:13). *For this liketh you.* They loved the forms and rituals of religion but did not love what God loves—goodness, mercy, kindness, justice (see 5:15; Is 5:7; 61:8; Hos 6:6; Mic 6:8).
4:6–11 In the past, God had used natural disasters to discipline and warn His people, but those lessons were soon forgotten (cf. Deut 28:22,39–40,42,48,56–57).
4:6 *I.* These were not simply natural disasters; they were direct acts of God (3:6). *Yet ... me.* See vv. 8–11.
4:7–8 Lack of rain three months before harvest would prevent full development of the grain.
4:9 *palmerworm.* Or "locust" (cf. 7:1; Joel 1:4).
4:10 *pestilence ... after ... Egypt.* See Ex 7:14–12:30.
4:11 *Sodom and Gomorrah.* Exemplified total destruction, God's judgment on those cities (see Gen 19:24–25) having already become proverbial (cf. Deut 29:23; Is 1:9; 13:19; Jer 49:18; 50:40; Zeph 2:9). *firebrand pluckt out of the burning.* Saved only by God's grace (cf. Zech 3:2).
4:12 *Prepare to meet thy God.* Devastated Israel, brought to her knees by the Assyrians, would meet the God she had covenanted with at Sinai and had now so grievously offended.
4:13 See note on 5:8–9. The God of such power and majesty is easily able to execute the judgment announced in v. 12.
5:1 *Hear ye this word.* See note on 3:1. *lamentation.* Amos sorrowfully fashioned a lament as if Israel were already dead.
5:2 *virgin of Israel.* See Jer 18:13; 31:4,21; see also notes on 2 Ki 19:21; Is 23:12. *is forsaken.* Left like a dead body on the open field (cf. Jer 9:22).
‡5:3 *city.* The Hebrew expression denotes communities of varying size, all of which would suffer.

And that which went forth *by* an
hundred shall leave ten,
To the house of Israel.

The call to repentance

4 For thus saith the LORD unto the house
of Israel,
[a]Seek ye me, [b]and ye shall live:
5 But seek not [a]Beth-el, nor enter *into*
Gilgal,
And pass not *to* [b]Beer-sheba:
For Gilgal shall surely go into captivity,
And [c]Beth-el shall come to nought.
6 Seek the LORD, and ye shall live;
Lest he break out like fire *in* the house
of Joseph,
And devour *it,* and *there be* none to
quench *it* in Beth-el.
7 *Ye* who [a]turn judgment to wormwood,
And leave off righteousness in the
earth,
8 *Seek him* that maketh the [a]seven stars
and Orion,
And turneth the shadow of death into
the morning,
[b]And maketh the day dark *with* night:
That [c]calleth for the waters of the sea,
And poureth them out upon the face of
the earth:
[d]The LORD *is* his name:
9 That strengtheneth the [1]spoiled against
the strong,
So that the [1]spoiled shall come against
the fortress.
10 [a]They hate him that rebuketh in the
gate,

5:4 [a]Jer. 29:13 [b]Is. 55:3
5:5 [a]ch. 4:4 [b]ch. 8:14 [c]Hos. 4:15
5:7 [a]ch. 6:12
5:8 [a]Job 9:9 [b]Ps. 104:20 [c]Job 38:34 [d]ch. 4:13
5:9 [1]Heb. *spoil*
5:10 [a]Is. 29:21

5:10 [b]1 Ki. 22:8
5:11 [1]Heb. *vineyards of desire* [a]Mic. 6:15
5:12 [1]Or, *a ransom* [a]ch. 2:6 [b]Is. 29:21
5:13 [a]ch. 6:10
5:14 [a]Mic. 3:11
5:15 [a]Rom. 12:9 [b]Joel 2:14
5:16 [a]Jer. 9:17

And they [b]abhor him that speaketh
uprightly.
11 Forasmuch therefore as your treading
is upon the poor,
And ye take from him burdens of wheat:
[a]Ye have built houses of hewn stone,
But ye shall not dwell in them;
Ye have planted [1]pleasant vineyards,
But ye shall not drink wine of them.
12 For I know your manifold
transgressions and your mighty sins:
[a]They afflict the just, they take [1]a bribe,
And they [b]turn aside the poor in the
gate *from their right.*
13 Therefore [a]the prudent shall keep
silence in that time;
For it *is* an evil time.
14 Seek good, and not evil, that ye may
live:
And so the LORD, the God of hosts,
shall be with you, [a]as ye have
spoken.
15 [a]Hate the evil, and love the good, and
establish judgment in the gate:
[b]It may be that the LORD God of hosts
will be gracious unto the remnant of
Joseph.
16 Therefore the LORD, the God of hosts,
the Lord, saith thus;
Wailing *shall be* in all streets;
And they shall say in all the highways,
Alas! alas!
And they shall call the husbandman to
mourning,
And [a]such as are skilful of lamentation
to wailing.

5:4 *Seek.* See vv. 6,14. *live.* If they would seek the Lord, they (or at least a remnant, v. 15) could yet escape the violent death anticipated in Amos's lament.

5:5 *Beth-el ... Gilgal.* See note on 4:4. *Beer-sheba.* Located in the south of Judah, it also had evidently become a place of pilgrimage and idolatry (cf. 8:14). All shrines where the worship of God was abused would be destroyed.

5:6 The places of idolatry were doomed; yet if Israel turned to God, there was hope for her as a nation. Otherwise the people, too, would be destroyed. *house of Joseph.* The northern kingdom of Israel, dominated by the tribe of Ephraim, descendants of Joseph (also in v. 15; 6:6). *Beth-el.* The main religious center of the northern kingdom (see 7:13; see also 3:14; 4:4; 7:10). The god the Israelites worshiped there would be powerless to save the place when the true God brought His judgment.

5:7 *Ye who turn judgment to wormwood.* They corrupted the procedures and institutions of justice (the courts), making them instruments of injustice ("wormwood" was a synonym for bitterness = injustice; see Prov 5:4; Lam 3:19). Turning God's order upside down is inevitable in a society that ignores His law and despises true religion (see 6:12).

5:8–9 As in 4:13, a brief hymn is inserted (see 9:5–6). Here Amos highlights the contrast between "those who turn" good into bad (v. 7) and the One "who ... changes" night into day and governs the order of the universe—and whose power can smash the walls His people hide behind.

‡5:8 *Orion.* A group of seven stars (part of the constellation Taurus); see note on Job 9:9. *death into the morning ... day dark with night.* The orderly sequence of day and night (cf. Jer 31:35). *waters of the sea.* The waters above the expanse (see 9:6; Gen 1:7; see also notes on Ps 36:8; 42:7; 104:3,13); alternatively, waters evaporated from the sea and condensed as rain.

5:10 Continues the sentence begun in v. 7. This poetic paragraph is continued and completed in vv. 12b–13, which (in the Hebrew) uses the third person, while the preceding passage (vv. 11–12a) uses the second person. The indictment of vv. 7,10,12b–13 is therefore more objective and descriptive, while that of vv. 11–12a is more direct and pointed. *rebuketh ... speaketh uprightly.* Those who are concerned that the courts uphold justice.

5:11 *Ye have built.* God would take away their prized possessions acquired through wrongful gain. Their prosperity would be turned to grief (cf. Deut 28:30,38–40).

5:13 *prudent.* He knows he cannot change the state of affairs, and therefore only awaits judgment.

5:14 *Seek good.* Cf. "Seek me" (v. 4); see Is 1:16–17 and note on Is 1:17. *that ye may live.* The purpose is more definitely expressed than in vv. 4,6, and the way to change is explicit. *with you.* As your security and source of blessing.

5:15 *It may be.* Emphasizes the danger of presuming on God's grace. Even a widespread change of attitude would need the test of time to prove its genuineness. *remnant.* Implies that a change now would benefit the individual survivors of the disaster, though the nation as a whole would perish.

‡5:16–17 A return to the theme of lament with which this section began (vv. 1–2). *streets ... highways ... husbandman ... vineyards.* All will be affected by God's punishment. Even farmers, usually too busy for such things, would join the professional

17 And in all vineyards *shall be* wailing:
For [a]I will pass through thee, saith the
LORD.

The day of the LORD

18 [a]Woe unto *you* that desire the day of
the LORD!
To what end *is* it for you?
[b]The day of the LORD *is* darkness, and
not light.
19 [a]As if a man did flee from a lion, and a
bear met him;
Or went *into* the house, and leaned his
hand on the wall, and a serpent bit
him.
20 *Shall* not the day of the LORD *be*
darkness, and not light?
Even very dark, and no brightness in it?
21 [a]I hate, I despise your feast *days,*
And [b]I will not [1]smell in your solemn
assemblies.
22 [a]Though ye offer me burnt offerings
and your meat offerings, I will not
accept *them:*
Neither will I regard the [1]peace
offerings of your fat beasts.
23 Take thou away from me the noise of
thy songs;
For I will not hear the melody of thy
viols.
24 [a]But let judgment [1]run down as waters,
And righteousness as a mighty stream.
25 [a]Have ye offered unto me sacrifices
and offerings in the wilderness forty
years, O house of Israel?

5:17 [a]Ex. 12:12
5:18 [a]Is. 5:19; Jer. 17:15 [b]Joel 2:2
5:19 [a]Jer. 48:44
5:21 [1]Or, *smell your holy days* [a]Is. 1:11-16 [b]Lev. 26:31
5:22 [1]Or, *thank offerings* [a]Is. 66:3; Mic. 6:6,7
5:24 [1]Heb. *roll* [a]Hos. 6:6; Mic. 6:8
5:25 [a]Deut. 32:17; Josh. 24:14; Is. 43:23
5:26 [1]Or, *Siccuth your king* [a]1 Ki. 11:33
5:27 [a]2 Ki. 17:6 [b]ch. 4:13
6:1 [1]Or, are *secure* [2]Or, *first fruits* [a]Luke 6:24 [b]Ex. 19:5
6:2 [a]Jer. 2:10 [b]Is. 10:9 [c]2 Ki. 18:34 [d]Nah. 3:8
6:3 [1]Or, *habitation* [a]Ezek. 12:27 [b]ch. 5:18 [c]ch. 5:12 [d]Ps. 94:20
6:4 [1]Or, *abound with superfluities*
6:5 [1]Or, *quaver* [a]Is. 5:12 [b]1 Chr. 23:5
6:6 [1]Or, *in bowls of wine*

26 But ye have borne [1]the tabernacle [a]of
your Moloch and Chiun your images,
The star of your god, which ye made to
yourselves.
27 Therefore will I cause you to go into
captivity [a]beyond Damascus,
Saith the LORD, [b]whose name *is* The
God of hosts.

Captivity inevitable

6 Woe [a]to them *that* [1]*are* at ease in Zion,
And trust in the mountain of Samaria,
Which are named [b2]chief of the
nations,
To whom the house of Israel came!
2 [a]Pass ye *unto* [b]Calneh, and see;
And from thence go ye *to* [c]Hamath the
great:
Then go down *to* Gath of the
Philistines:
[d]*Be they* better than these kingdoms?
Or their border greater than your
border?
3 Ye that [a]put far away the [b]evil day,
[c]And cause [d]the [1]seat of violence to
come near;
4 That lie upon beds of ivory,
And [1]stretch themselves upon their
couches,
And eat the lambs out of the flock,
And the calves out of the midst of the
stall;
5 [a]That [1]chant to the sound of the viol,
And invent to themselves instruments
of musick, [b]like David;
6 That drink [1]wine in bowls,

mourners in lament, and mourning would overflow from the cities to the vineyards. When the holy God "will pass through" (as He did in Egypt, Ex 12:12), punishment for the unholy and unjust will be inescapable (cf. Is 6:5).

‡5:18 *day of the LORD.* The time when God will show Himself the victor over the world, vindicating His claims to be the Lord over all the earth (see notes on 8:9; Is 2:11,17,20). Israel expected to be exalted as His people and longed for that day to come. Amos warned that the day would come, but not as Israel expected—it would be a day of "darkness, and not light" (v. 20) for her, because she had not been faithful to God. (Cf. "the day of our Lord Jesus Christ" and variations in 1 Cor 1:8; 3:12–15; 5:5; 2 Cor 1:14; Phil 1:6,10; 2:16.) Amos speaks primarily of an imminent and decisive judgment on Israel, not exclusively of the last day.

5:19–20 The two pictures (v. 19) emphasize vividly the inescapability of God's coming judgment.

5:21–27 Again God directly addresses Israel with the charge of unfaithfulness.

5:21–23 These three verses summarize and reject the current practice of religion in Israel. The institutions were not wrong in themselves; it was the worshipers and the ways they worshiped that were wrong. The people had no basis on which to come to God, because their conduct reflected disobedience to His law (see Is 1:11–15 and note).

5:21 *I despise.* Lit. "I do not inhale with delight."

5:24 *judgment . . . righteousness.* Prerequisites for acceptance by God; but these are what Israel had rejected and scorned (cf. vv. 7,10,12b). *as a mighty stream.* In contrast to stream beds that are dry much of the year. The simile is especially apt: As plant and animal life flourishes where there is water, so human life flourishes where there is justice and righteousness.

5:25 Israel's right relationship with the Lord was never established primarily by sacrifices. It was above all based on obedience (see 1 Sam 15:22–23; cf. Rom 1:5). *in the wilderness forty years.* See Num 14:32–35.

‡5:26 The obscure language of this verse speaks of Israelite idolatry, but whether it was in the wilderness long ago or more recently in the promised land, or both, is not clear. The proper names are derived from Akkadian and refer to idolatrous objects of worship. The Septuagint (the Greek translation of the OT) represents a somewhat different text, which is followed by Acts 7:42–43.

5:27 This punishment is the final one—exile from the God-given land to remote foreign places.

6:1 *in Zion . . . in the mountain of Samaria.* Although Amos spoke primarily to Israel, Judah (Zion) also deserved his rebuke (cf. 2:4–5), for Israel properly comprised all 12 tribes. *chief of the nations.* In Israel's self-complacent eyes in this time of her newly recovered power and prosperity.

6:2 Perhaps Calneh and Hamath had fallen in Jeroboam II's campaign (2 Ki 14:28), and the wall of Gath had been broken down by Uzziah (2 Chr 26:6). These words may have been spoken by the "house of Israel" (v. 1, i.e., people of Israel) who, when they came before their notables, flattered their vanity and thus reinforced their arrogant complacency.

6:4 *ivory.* See 3:15 and note.

6:5 *like David.* See 1 Sam 16:15–23; 2 Sam 23:1.

And anoint themselves *with* the chief
ointments:
[a]But they are not grieved for the
[2]affliction of Joseph.
7 Therefore now shall they go captive
with the first that go captive,
And the banquet of them that
stretched themselves shall be
removed.
8 [a]The Lord GOD hath sworn by himself,
saith the LORD the God of hosts,
I abhor [b]the excellency of Jacob, and
hate his palaces:
Therefore will I deliver up the city
with all [1]that is therein.

Oppression and desolation

9 And it shall come to pass, if there
remain ten men in one house, that
they shall die.
10 And a man's uncle shall take him up,
and he that burneth him,
To bring out the bones out of the
house,
And shall say unto *him* that *is* by the
sides of the house,
Is there yet *any* with thee? and he shall
say, No.
Then shall he say, [a]Hold thy tongue:
[b]For [1]*we may* not make mention of the
name of the LORD.
11 For behold, [a]the LORD commandeth,
[b]And he will smite the great house
with [1]breaches,
And the little house *with* clefts.

12 Shall horses run upon the rock?
Will *one* plow *there* with oxen?
For [a]ye have turned judgment into gall,

6:6 [2]Heb. *breach* [a]Gen. 37:25
6:8 [1]Heb. *the fulness thereof* [a]Jer. 51:14 [b]Ps. 47:4; Ezek. 24:21
6:10 [1]Or, they will *not*, or, have *not* [a]ch. 5:13 [b]ch. 8:3
6:11 [1]Or, *droppings* [a]Is. 55:11 [b]ch. 3:15
6:12 [a]Hos. 10:4
6:14 [1]Or, *valley* [a]Jer. 5:15 [b]1 Ki. 8:65
7:1 [1]Or, *green worms*
7:2 [1]Or, *Who of (or, for,) Jacob shall stand?* [a]Is. 51:19
7:3 [a]Deut. 32:36; Jonah 3:10; Jas. 5:16
7:5 [1]Or, *Who of (or, for,) Jacob shall stand?* [a]ver. 2,3

And the fruit of righteousness into
hemlock:
13 *Ye* which rejoice in a thing of nought,
Which say, Have we not taken to us
horns by our own strength?
14 But behold, [a]I *will* raise up against you
a nation, O house of Israel, saith the
LORD the God of hosts;
And they shall afflict you from the
[b]entering in of Hemath unto the
[1]river of the wilderness.

Two plagues

7 Thus hath the Lord GOD shewed unto
me; and behold, he formed [1]grasshop-
pers in the beginning of the shooting up of the
latter growth; and lo, *it was* the latter growth
after the king's mowings.
2 And it came to pass, *that* when they had
made an end of eating the grass of the land,
then I said,
O Lord GOD, forgive, I beseech thee:
[a][1]*By* whom shall Jacob arise? for he *is*
small.
3 [a]The LORD repented for this:
It shall not be, saith the LORD.

4 ¶ Thus hath the Lord GOD shewed unto
me: and behold, the Lord GOD called to contend by fire, and it devoured the great deep,
and did eat up a part.
5 Then said I,
O Lord GOD, cease, I beseech thee:
[a][1]*By* whom shall Jacob arise? for he *is*
small.
6 The LORD repented for this:
This also shall not be, saith the Lord
GOD.

The vision of the plumbline

7 ¶ Thus he shewed me: and behold, the

6:6 *Joseph.* See note on 5:6.
6:8 *sworn by himself.* See note on Gen 22:16; cf. Heb 6:13–14. By this oath God declares that the verdict is final.
6:10–11 A fearful scene: Apparently a survivor is cowering inside the house, the relative forbidding him even to pray because God's wrath had fallen on the city.
‡6:10 *he that burneth.* "The undertaker." Reference may be to burning a memorial fire in honor of the dead (see Jer 34:5). Cremation was not generally practiced, being reserved primarily for serious offenders (see Lev 20:14; 21:9; Josh 7:15,25; cf. 1 Sam 31:11–13).
6:11 *great house . . . little house.* Cf. perhaps the "summer house" and "winter house" of 3:15.
‡6:12 *plow there with oxen?* The Hebrew for this phrase is sometimes translated (with a slight textual change) "plow the sea with oxen." Israel's perversion of justice flies in the face of even common human wisdom about the right order of things.
‡6:13 *thing of nought.* Hebrew *Lodebar,* a place name. *taken to us horns.* Hebrew *Karnaim,* a place name. These two places may have been regained from Hazael by Jehoash (2 Ki 10:32–33; 13:25), then taken by the Assyrians ("a nation," v. 14) soon after Amos's day (2 Ki 15:29)—beginning the sequence of events that would lead to the loss of all territory conquered by Jeroboam II.
6:14 *from the entering in of Hemath unto the river of the wilderness.* From the Orontes River in north Lebanon to the Dead Sea—thus the whole land (cf. 2 Ki 14:25).
7:1 *shewed unto me.* Introduces reports of visions that convey God's message through things seen as well as heard (see vv. 4,7; 8:1; cf. 9:1). *grasshoppers.* Or "locusts." Cf. 4:9; Joel 1:4. *latter growth.* The growth that came up in the fields after the grains and early hay were harvested. On these the flocks and herds pastured until the summer drought stopped all growth (cf. 1 Ki 18:5). *king's mowings.* Apparently the earlier crop, from which the royal taxes were taken.
7:2 See v. 5. *By whom shall Jacob arise?* Mass starvation would afflict all the people. *Jacob.* Israel. *small.* Powerless to withstand the calamity. Amos makes no appeal to the Lord's covenant with Israel—perhaps because Israel's unfaithfulness had removed all right to such an appeal.
7:3 See v. 6. *The LORD repented.* In response to the prophetic intercession (cf. Gen 20:7)—but forgiveness is not offered.
7:4 *great deep.* Probably the Mediterranean Sea. *part.* Lit. "portion," probably referring to the promised land or, more precisely, to everything growing on the land (cf. Joel 1:19).
7:5 See note on v. 2.
7:6 See note on v. 3.

Lord stood upon a wall made by a plumbline,
with a plumbline in his hand.
8 And the LORD said unto me, Amos, what
seest thou? And I said, A plumbline. Then said
the Lord,

Behold, [a]I *will* set a plumbline in the
midst of my people Israel:
[b]I will not again pass by them any more:

9 And [1]the high places of Isaac shall be
desolate,
And the sanctuaries of Israel shall be
laid waste;
And [a]I will rise against the house of
Jeroboam with the sword.

10 ¶ Then Amaziah [a]*the* priest of Beth-el
sent to [b]Jeroboam king of Israel, saying, Amos
hath conspired against thee in the midst of the
house of Israel: the land is not able to bear all
his words.
11 For thus Amos saith, Jeroboam shall die
by the sword, and Israel shall surely be led
away captive out of their own land.
12 ¶ Also Amaziah said unto Amos, O thou
seer, go, flee thee away into the land of Judah,
and there eat bread, and prophesy there:
13 But [a]prophesy not again any more *at*
Beth-el: [b]for it *is* the king's [1]chapel, and it *is*
the [2]king's court.
14 Then answered Amos, and said to Ama-
ziah, I *was* no prophet, neither *was* I [a]a prophet's son; [b]but I *was* a herdman, and a gatherer
of [1]sycomore fruit:
15 And the LORD took me [1]as I followed
the flock, and the LORD said unto me, Go,
prophesy unto my people Israel.

7:8 [a]See 2 Ki. 21:13; Is. 28:17; Lam. 2:8 [b]Mic. 7:18
7:9 [1][Beer-sheba, Gen. 26:23; 46:1; ch. 5:5; 8:14] [a]Fulfilled 2 Ki. 15:10
7:10 [a]1 Ki. 12:32 [b]2 Ki. 14:23
7:13 [1]Or, *sanctuary* [2]Heb. *house of the kingdom* [a]ch. 2:12 [b]1 Ki. 12:32
7:14 [1]Or, *wild figs* [a]1 Ki. 20:35; 2 Ki. 2:5 [b]Zech. 13:5
7:15 [1]Heb. *from behind*
7:16 [a]Ezek. 21:2; Mic. 2:6
7:17 [a]Jer. 28:12; 29:21,32 [b]Is. 13:16; Lam. 5:11; Hos. 4:13; Zech. 14:2
8:2 [a]Ezek. 7:2 [b]ch. 7:8
8:3 [1]Heb. *shall howl* [2]Heb. *be silent* [a]ch. 5:23 [b]ch. 6:9,10
8:4 [a]Ps. 14:4; Prov. 30:14

16 Now therefore hear thou the word of
the LORD:
Thou sayest, Prophesy not against
Israel,
And [a]drop not *thy word* against the
house of Isaac.
17 [a]Therefore thus saith the LORD;
[b]Thy wife shall be a harlot in the city,
And thy sons and thy daughters shall
fall by the sword,
And thy land shall be divided by line;
And thou shalt die in a polluted land:
And Israel shall surely go into captivity
forth of his land.

The vision of Israel's ruin

8 Thus hath the Lord GOD shewed unto
me: and behold, a basket of summer
fruit.
2 And he said, Amos, what seest thou? And
I said, A basket of summer fruit. Then said the
LORD unto me,

[a]The end is come upon my people *of*
Israel;
[b]I will not again pass by them any
more.

3 And [a]the songs of the temple [1]shall be
howlings in that day, saith the Lord
GOD:
There shall be many dead bodies in
every place; [b]they shall cast *them*
forth [2]with silence.
4 Hear this, O ye that [a]swallow up the
needy,
Even to make the poor of the land to
fail,

7:7 Israel is compared to a wall built true to plumb—what she should have been, after all the Lord had done for her.
7:8–9 In vv. 1–6 God proposed wholesale punishments amounting to total destruction, but relented at Amos's prayer—though without promise of forgiveness. Now the Lord is no longer open to such intercession (cf. Jer 7:16; 11:14; 14:11; 15:1).
7:8 *plumbline.* God's people had been built according to God's standards (v. 7). They were expected to be true to those standards, but were completely out of plumb when tested (cf. 2 Ki 21:13). *my people.* Here, for the first time in the book of Amos, the Lord calls Israel "my people" (see v. 15; 8:2; 9:10,14). *I will not again pass by them any more.* See 8:2.
7:9 *high places . . . sanctuaries . . . house.* The centers of religious and political pretension and of self-righteous pride would be wiped out. *Isaac.* Israel's (Jacob's) father, a way of referring to Israel found only in Amos (see v. 16). *Jeroboam.* The oracles of chs. 1–6 were spoken to the leading people of Israel and Samaria as a whole; here Amos names one man, the king.
7:11 Amaziah's words summarize Amos's message (see note on v. 17). *Jeroboam.* That is, his "house" (v. 9), the king's name also representing his dynasty. *shall die.* Jeroboam died naturally (2 Ki 14:29), but his son and successor Zechariah (2 Ki 15:8) was assassinated (2 Ki 15:10).
7:12 *seer.* Amaziah dismissed Amos as a prophet for hire whom he need not take seriously.
7:13 *king's chapel.* Amaziah served the king in Samaria, not Israel's heavenly King; hence he would not allow a prophetic word to be spoken against Jeroboam or his realm at the royal chapel.
7:14 *no prophet, neither . . . a prophet's son.* Amos denied any previous connection with the prophets or their disciples (see note on 1 Ki 20:35). No one had hired him to come and announce judgment on Jeroboam and Israel. *herdman.* See note on 1:1, but the Hebrew uses a different word here—one not found elsewhere in the OT. The Hebrew for this word is, however, related to a word for "cattle," suggesting that Amos may also have tended cattle. *sycomore fruit.* A large tree, yielding fig-like fruit (see KJV marg.) as well as useful timber. To ensure good fruit, the gardener had to slit the top of each fig—which may be the procedure referred to by the obscure Hebrew word here rendered "took care of."
7:15 *followed.* See 2 Sam 7:8. The Hebrew stresses the location of the shepherd rather than his activity. *Go.* Amos was in Beth-el because God had sent him to prophesy there.
7:16 *Prophesy not.* Cf. 2:12.
7:17 Amos turned to condemn the priest personally. *harlot.* With the exile of Amaziah, the death of his children and the loss of the family estate, Amaziah's wife would be reduced to prostitution to survive. *thy land.* Amaziah's private estate would be divided up and given to others. *polluted land.* Where his ceremonial purity as a priest would be defiled. *Israel shall surely go . . . land.* Amos repeats—verbatim in the Hebrew—the last two lines of Amaziah's earlier summary of Amos's message (v. 11).
8:1 *shewed me.* See note on 7:1.
8:2 *summer fruit . . . The end is come.* A wordplay in Hebrew; Israel was ready to be plucked.
8:3 *that day.* See note on 5:18. *howlings . . . silence.* There would be no thanksgiving songs for this harvest (contrast Lev 23:39–41)—only the silence of despair.

5 Saying, When will the [1]new moon be
gone, that we may sell corn?
And [a]the sabbath, that we may [2]set
forth wheat,
[b]Making the ephah small, and the
shekel great,
And [3]falsifying the balances by deceit?
6 That *we* may buy the poor for [a]silver,
And the needy for a pair of shoes;
Yea, and sell the refuse of the wheat?
7 The LORD hath sworn by [a]the
excellency of Jacob,
Surely [b]I will never forget any of their
works.
8 [a]Shall not the land tremble for this,
And every one mourn that dwelleth
therein?
And it shall rise up wholly as a flood;
And it shall be cast out and drowned,
[b]as *by* the flood of Egypt.
9 And it shall come to pass [1]in that day,
saith the Lord GOD,
[a]That I will cause the sun to go down
at noon,
And I will darken the earth in the clear
day:
10 And I will turn your feasts into
mourning,
And all your songs into lamentation;
[a]And I will bring up sackcloth upon all
loins,
And baldness upon every head;
[b]And I will make it as the mourning of
an only *son,*
And the end thereof as a bitter day.

11 Behold, the days come, saith the Lord
GOD,
That I will send a famine in the land,
Not a famine of bread, nor a thirst for
water,
But [a]of hearing the words of the LORD:
12 And they shall wander from sea to sea,
and from the north even to the east,
They shall run to and fro to seek the
word of the LORD, and shall not find *it.*
13 In that day shall the fair virgins and
young men faint for thirst.
14 They that [a]swear by [b]the sin of
Samaria,
And say, Thy god, O Dan, liveth;
And, The [1]manner of [c]Beer-sheba
liveth;
Even they shall fall, and never rise up
again.

The destruction of the sanctuary

9 I saw the Lord standing upon the altar:
and he said,
Smite the [1]lintel of the door, that the
posts may shake:
And [a][2]cut them in the head, all of
them;
And I will slay the last of them with
the sword:
[b]He that fleeth of them shall not flee
away,
And he that escapeth of them shall not
be delivered.
2 [a]Though they dig into hell, thence
shall mine hand take them;
[b]Though they climb up *to* heaven,
thence will I bring them down:
3 And though they hide themselves in
the top of Carmel,
I will search and take them out thence;

8:5 [1]Or, *month* [2]Heb. *open* [3]Heb. *perverting the balances of deceit* [a]Neh. 13:15 [b]Mic. 6:10
8:6 [a]ch. 2:6
8:7 [a]ch. 6:8 [b]Hos. 8:13
8:8 [a]Hos. 4:3 [b]ch. 9:5
8:9 [1]B.C. 791. [or B.C. 784, or 771 or 770] [a]Job 5:14; Is. 13:10; 59:9,10; Jer. 15:9; Mic. 3:6
8:10 [a]Is. 15:2,3; Jer. 48:37; Ezek. 27:31 [b]Jer. 6:26; Zech. 12:10
8:11 [a]1 Sam. 3:1; Ps. 74:9; Ezek. 7:26
8:14 [1][Heb. *way:* See Acts 9:2; 18:25; 19:9,23; 24:14] [a]Hos. 4:15 [b]Deut. 9:21 [c]ch. 5:5
9:1 [1]Or, *chapiter,* or, *knop* [2]Or, *wound them* [a]Ps. 68:21; Hab. 3:13 [b]ch. 2:14
9:2 [a]Ps. 139:8 [b]Jer. 51:53

8:5 *new moon . . . sabbath.* The official religious festivals, when commerce ceased (cf. Num 28:9–15; 2 Ki 4:23). *ephah small . . . shekel great . . . falsifying the balances.* See Lev 19:35–36; Deut 25:13–16; Prov 11:1; 16:11; 20:10,23.
8:6 See note on 2:6.
8:7 *sworn by the excellency of Jacob.* Israel took pride in the fact that the Lord was her God.
‡8:8 *as by the flood of Egypt.* Because of the heavy seasonal rains in Ethiopia, the Nile in Egypt annually rose by as much as 25 feet, flooding the whole valley except for the towns and villages standing above it. Its waters carried a large amount of rich soil, which was deposited on the land—perhaps referred to by the words "cast out."
8:9 *that day.* See note on 5:18. *darken the earth* As elsewhere, the "day of the LORD" is described as one in which the cosmic (world) order is disrupted and light is turned to darkness (see Is 13:10; 24:23; 34:4; 50:3; Ezek 32:7–8; Joel 2:10,31; Mic 3:6), as if creation is being undone (see Jer 4:23).
‡8:10 *mourning.* Illustrated by King David (2 Sam 18:33). *bring up sackcloth . . . baldness upon every head.* Signs of mourning (see Gen 37:34; Jer 47:5). *only son.* On whose life the future of the family depended (cf. 2 Sam 18:18). *bitter day.* The opposite of a "good day" (Esth 9:22).
8:11 *days.* When God's judgment begins to take effect. *famine . . . of hearing the words of the LORD.* In times of great distress Israel turned to the Lord for a prophetic word of hope or guidance (see, e.g., 2 Ki 19:1–4,14; 22:13–14; Jer 21:2; Ezek 14:3,7), but in the coming judgment the Lord will answer all such appeals with silence—the awful silence of God (see 1 Sam 28:6; Ezek 7:26; 20:1–3; Mic 3:4,7).
8:12 *sea to sea . . . north . . . east.* Throughout the land of Israel, even to the land across the Jordan.
8:13 *thirst.* Both physical and spiritual. Their strength sapped, even the lovely girls and strong boys of the nation would faint and fall useless.
‡8:14 *They that swear.* By the gods of their various religious centers—the false gods in which they trusted rather than in the Lord.
‡9:1 *I saw the Lord.* See note on 7:1. God is now poised on earth. *standing upon the altar.* Lit. "beside the altar." God is about to initiate the destruction from the very place from which the people expect to hear a word of peace and blessing. *lintel.* God will shatter the temple completely, from the decorated "capitals" down to the heavy stone thresholds. The next lines depict the destruction. Whether the vision shows the Lord at Jerusalem or at Beth-el is unclear, but we know of no temple structure at Beth-el.
9:2–4 These verses emphasize the impossibility of escape from God's impending judgment. The imaginary extremes to which a person might go may be compared with those in Ps 139:7–12. God's domain includes every place, even the realm of the grave (v. 2).
9:3 *top of Carmel.* See note on 1:2. *serpent.* In pagan mythology, the fierce monster of the sea. If someone should seek to

And though they be hid from my sight
in the bottom of the sea,
Thence will I command the serpent,
and he shall bite them:
4 And though they go into captivity
before their enemies,
[a]Thence will I command the sword,
and it shall slay them:
And [b]I will set mine eyes upon them
for evil, and not for good.
5 And the Lord GOD of hosts *is* he that
toucheth the land, and it shall [a]melt,
[b]And all that dwell therein shall
mourn:
And it shall rise up wholly like a flood;
And shall be drowned, as *by* the flood
of Egypt.
6 *It is* he that buildeth his [a][1][2]stories in
the heaven,
And hath founded his [3]troop in the
earth;
He that [b]calleth for the waters of the
sea,
And poureth them out upon the face of
the earth:
[c]The LORD *is* his name.
7 *Are* ye not as children of the
Ethiopians unto me, O children of
Israel? saith the LORD.
Have not I brought up Israel out of the
land of Egypt?
And the [a]Philistines from [b]Caphtor,
and the Syrians from [c]Kir?
8 Behold, [a]the eyes of the Lord GOD *are*
upon the sinful kingdom,
And I [b]will destroy it from off the face
of the earth;

9:4 [a]Lev. 26:33 [b]Lev. 17:10
9:5 [a]Mic. 1:4 [b]ch. 8:8
9:6 [1]Or, *spheres* [2]Heb. *ascensions* [3]Or, *bundle* [a]Ps. 104:3 [b]ch. 5:8 [c]ch. 4:13
9:7 [a]Jer. 47:4 [b]Deut. 2:23; Jer. 47:4 [c]ch. 1:5
9:8 [a]ver. 4 [b]Jer. 30:11; Obad. 16,17
9:9 [1]Heb. *cause to move* [2]Heb. *stone*
9:10 [a]ch. 6:3
9:11 [1]Heb. *hedge,* or, *wall* [a]Acts 15:16
9:12 [1]Heb. *Upon whom my name is called* [a]Obad. 19 [b]Num. 24:18
9:13 [1]Heb. *draweth forth* [2]Or, *new wine* [a]Lev. 26:5 [b]Joel 3:18
9:14 [a]Jer. 30:3 [b]Is. 61:4

Saving that I will not utterly destroy
the house of Jacob, saith the LORD.
9 For lo, I will command, and I will [1]sift
the house of Israel among all nations,
Like as *corn* is sifted in a sieve, yet
shall not the least [2]grain fall *upon*
the earth.
10 All the sinners of my people shall die
by the sword,
[a]Which say, The evil shall not overtake
nor prevent us.

Israel's fortunes to be restored

11 [a]In that day will I raise up the
tabernacle of David that is fallen,
And [1]close up the breaches thereof;
And I will raise up his ruins,
And I will build it as *in* the days of old:
12 [a]That they may possess the remnant of
[b]Edom, and of all the heathen,
[1]Which are called by my name,
Saith the LORD that doeth this.
13 Behold, [a]the days come, saith the
LORD,
That the plowman shall overtake the
reaper,
And the treader of grapes him that
[1]soweth seed;
[b]And the mountains shall drop [2]sweet
wine,
And all the hills shall melt.
14 [a]And I will bring again the captivity of
my people of Israel,
And [b]they shall build the waste cities,
and inhabit *them;*
And they shall plant vineyards, and
drink the wine thereof;

escape by hiding in the depths, he could still not evade God, for even there all are subject to Him.

9:4 *go . . . before their enemies . . . will I command.* Even those dispersed among the nations will not escape God's judgment. *I will set mine eyes . . . for evil.* Contrast Ps 33:18; 34:15.

9:5 *The Lord . . . that.* Introduces a hymnic reminder that Israel's God is the Creator and Sustainer of the universe, thus underlining the pronouncements of the previous verses (cf. 4:13; 5:8–9). *land . . . melt.* See note on Ps 46:6. *flood of Egypt.* See 8:8 and note.

9:6 *his stories in the heaven.* Contrasts the scale of God with the scale of man, whose structures fall at the movement of the earth (v. 5). See Ps 104:3 and note. *sea.* See 5:8 and note.

9:7 *children of the Ethiopians.* A dark-skinned people who lived south of Egypt, probably in the upper Nile region. *Have not I brought up Israel . . . ?* See note on Ex 20:2. Israel could not rely on God's past blessings as an assurance of His future benevolence. Her stubborn rebelliousness robbed the exodus of all special meaning for her; her journey from Egypt is reduced to no more significance than the movements of other peoples. *Philistines from Caphtor.* See note on Jer 47:4. *Kir.* See note on 1:5.

9:8 *sinful kingdom.* Israel, the chosen, whose disobedience was far worse than the sins of other nations (cf. 1:3–2:16; 3:1–2).

9:9 *sieve.* Separates the wheat from small stones and other refuse gathered with it when scooped up from the ground.

9:10 *All the sinners . . . shall die.* For their persistent rebellion.

9:11 The verse is also regarded as Messianic in the Jewish Talmud. *will I raise up.* Raises a hope underlying Amos's words—one that runs through the whole OT from Gen 3:15 on: God will bring blessing after judgment and will not ultimately reject Israel. *tabernacle.* Lit. "hut" (or rough booth)—either the dynasty ("house") of David or the united kingdom of the 12 tribes (David's kingdom). The word "hut" may have been chosen to recall David's humble beginnings. *as in the days of old.* In the days of David and Solomon.

9:12 *remnant of Edom.* Whatever is left of Israel's bitter enemy (see note on 1:11) after her punishment. *all of the heathen, Which are called by my name.* Refers to the extent of the rule of the Lord's anointed future King, recalling that David had reigned over many nations surrounding Israel. It represents the fulfillment of the Abrahamic and Davidic covenants. The Messiah will reign even over former enemies, of whom Edom is symbolic (see notes on Is 34:5; Joel 3:19). *that doeth this.* God does what He says.

9:13–15 After all the forecasts of destruction, dearth and death (cf. 5:9,11,27), Amos's final words picture a glorious Edenic prosperity, when the seasons will run together so that sowing and reaping are without interval, and there will be a continuous supply of fresh produce (a reversal of the conditions portrayed in 4:6–11).

9:13 Note the similarity to Joel 3:18.

9:14–15 *I will bring again . . . they shall build . . . they shall plant . . . And I will plant them.* In the promised land, God will make His people productive, fruitful and secure.

9:14 *my people.* See note on 7:8; contrast Hos 1:9, but cf. Hos 2:23. *build the waste cities.* See Is 58:12 and note.

They shall also make gardens, and eat
the fruit of them.
15 And I will plant them upon their
land,
And [a]they shall no more be pulled up
out of their land which I have given
them,
Saith the LORD thy God.

9:15 [a]Ezek. 34:28

9:15 *no more.* When Israel is finally and fully restored, she will never again be destroyed. *thy God.* Contrast Hos 1:9, but cf. Hos 2:23.

Obadiah

INTRODUCTION

Author

The author's name is Obadiah, which means "servant (or worshiper) of the LORD." His was a common name (see 1 Ki 18:3–16; 1 Chr 3:21; 7:3; 8:38; 9:16; 12:9; 27:19; 2 Chr 17:7; 34:12; Ezra 8:9; Neh 10:5; 12:25). Neither his father's name nor the place of his birth is given.

Date and Place of Writing

The date and place of composition are disputed. Dating the prophecy is mainly a matter of relating vv. 11–14 to one of two specific events in Israel's history:

1. The invasion of Jerusalem by Philistines and Arabs during the reign of Jehoram (853–841 B.C.); see 2 Ki 8:20–22; 2 Chr 21:8–20. In this case, Obadiah would be a contemporary of Elisha.

2. The Babylonian attacks on Jerusalem (605–586). Obadiah would then be a contemporary of Jeremiah. This alternative seems more likely.

The parallels between Obad 1–9 and Jer 49:7–22 have caused many to suggest some kind of interdependence between Obadiah and Jeremiah, but it may be that both prophets were drawing on a common source not otherwise known to us.

Unity and Theme

There is no compelling reason to doubt the unity of this brief prophecy. Its theme is that Edom, proud over her own security, has gloated over Israel's devastation by foreign powers. However, Edom's participation in that disaster will bring on God's wrath. She herself will be destroyed, but mount Zion and Israel will be delivered, and God's kingdom will triumph.

Edom's hostile activities have spanned the centuries of Israel's existence. The following Biblical references are helpful in understanding the relation of Israel and Edom: Gen 27:41–45; 32:1–21; 33; 36; Ex 15:15; Num 20:14–21; Deut 2:1–6; 23:7; 1 Sam 22 with Ps 52; 2 Sam 8:13–14; 2 Ki 8:20–22; 14:7; Ps 83; Ezek 35; Joel 3:18–19; Amos 1:11–12; 9:12.

Since the Edomites are related to the Israelites (v. 10), their hostility is all the more reprehensible. Edom is fully responsible for her failure to assist Israel and for her open aggression. The fact that God rejected Esau (Gen 25:23; Mal 1:3; Rom 9:13) in no way exonerates the Edomites. Edom, smug in its mountain strongholds, will be dislodged and sacked. But Israel will prosper because God is with her. It would seem that Obadiah's oracle against Edom and day of the Lord theme (v. 15) would explain its positioning after Amos.

I. Title and Introduction (1)
II. Judgment on Edom (2–14)
  A. Edom's Destruction Announced (2–7)
    1. The humbling of her pride (2–4)
    2. The completeness of her destruction (5–7)
  B. Edom's Destruction Reaffirmed (8–14)
    1. Her shame and destruction (8–10)
    2. Her crimes against Israel (11–14)
III. The Day of the Lord (15–21)
  A. Judgment on the Nations but Deliverance for Zion (15–18)
  B. The Lord's Kingdom Established (19–21)

Edom's destruction

1 ¶ The vision of Obadiah.
Thus saith the Lord GOD [a]concerning
Edom;
We [b]have heard a rumour from the
LORD,
And an ambassador is sent among the
heathen,
Arise ye, and let us rise up against her
in battle.
2 Behold, I have made thee small among
the heathen:
Thou *art* greatly despised.
3 The pride of thine heart hath deceived
thee,
Thou that dwellest in the clefts of the
rock, whose habitation *is* high;
[a]That saith in his heart, Who shall
bring me down *to* the ground?
4 [a]Though thou exalt *thyself* as the
eagle,
And though *thou* [b]set thy nest among
the stars,
Thence will I bring thee down, saith
the LORD.
5 If [a]thieves came to thee, if robbers by
night, (how art thou cut off!)
Would they not have stolen till they
had enough?
If the grape-gatherers came to thee,
[b]Would they not leave [1]*some* grapes?
6 How are *the things of* Esau searched
out!
How are his hid things sought up!
7 All the men of thy confederacy have
brought thee *even* to the border:
[a][1]The men that were at peace with
thee have deceived thee, *and*
prevailed against thee;
[2]*They that eat* thy bread have laid a
wound under thee:
[b]*There is* none understanding [3]in him.
8 [a]Shall I not in that day, saith the LORD,
Even destroy the wise *men* out of
Edom,
And understanding out of the mount of
Esau?
9 And thy [a]mighty *men,* [b]O Teman, shall
be dismayed,
To the end that every one of the mount
of Esau may be cut off by slaughter.

10 For *thy* [a]violence against thy brother
Jacob shame shall cover thee,
And [b]thou shalt be cut off for ever.
11 In the day that thou stoodest on the
other side,
In the day that the strangers [1]carried
away captive his forces,
And foreigners entered *into* his gates,
And [a]cast lots upon Jerusalem,
Even thou *wast* as one of them.
12 But [1]thou shouldest not have [a]looked
on the day of thy brother in the day
that he became a stranger;
Neither shouldest thou have [b]rejoiced
over the children of Judah in the day
of their destruction;
Neither shouldest thou have [2]spoken
proudly in the day of distress.

1 [a]Is. 21:11; Ezek. 25:12; Joel 3:19; Mal. 1:3 [b]Jer. 49:14
3 [a]Is. 14:13-15; Rev. 18:7
4 [a]Job 20:6 [b]Hab. 2:9
5 [1]Or, *gleanings?* [a]Jer. 49:9 [b]Deut. 24:21
7 [1]Heb. *The men of thy peace* [2]Heb. The men *of thy bread* [3]Or, *of it* [a]Jer. 38:22 [b]Is. 19:11
8 [a]Job 5:12; Is. 29:14
9 [a]Ps. 76:5 [b]Jer. 49:7
10 [a]Gen. 27:41 [b]Ezek. 35:9
11 [1]Or, *carried away his substance* [a]Nah. 3:10
12 [1]Or, *do not behold, etc.* [2]Heb. *magnified thy mouth* [a]Mic. 4:11 [b]Prov. 17:5

‡1 *vision.* Commonly used in the OT to designate a revelation from God. *Obadiah.* See Introduction: Author. *We.* Either (1) the editorial "we," or (2) the prophet's association of Israel with himself, or (3) other prophets' pronouncements against Edom. In any case, the rest of the verse sets the stage for Obadiah's prophetic message, which begins with v. 2. *rumour.* An envoy had been sent to the nations, calling them to battle against Edom. Perhaps a conspiracy was under way between some of Edom's allies (v. 7). Although Edom feels secure (trusting in her mountain fortresses and her wise men, vv. 2–4,8–9), Obadiah announces God's judgment on her for her hostility to Israel. *Arise.* Note that this is the exact wording of Jonah 1:2 and serves to interlock Obadiah and Jonah. The twelve minor prophets were meant to be read as one book.

2 *I have made thee small.* Cf. the colloquial expression, "cut one down to size."

‡3 *rock.* Sela was the capital of Edom. Perhaps the later Petra (both Sela and Petra mean "rock" or "cliff"), this rugged site is located some 50 miles south of the southern end of the Dead Sea. See note on 2 Ki 14:7.

4 *eagle.* A proud and regal bird, noted for strength, keenness of vision and power of flight. *stars.* Hyperbole for high, inaccessible places in the mountains.

5 *If thieves . . . If the grape-gatherers.* For a similar oracle against Edom see Jer 49:9.

6 *hid things.* The ancient Greek historian Diodorus Siculus indicates that the Edomites put their wealth—accumulated from trade—in vaults in the rocks.

7 *eat thy bread.* Those whom a person "eats bread with" are "*com-panions*" (Latin *cum,* "with," and *panis,* "bread"). See note on Ps 41:9. *laid a wound under thee.* However the Hebrew for this expression is understood (its meaning is uncertain), it must indicate some act of treachery on the part of previously trusted close friends.

8 *in that day.* The day of Edom's destruction; but the words also have an eschatological ring. Since in OT prophecy Edom was often emblematic of all the world powers hostile to God and His kingdom, her judgment anticipates God's complete removal of all such opposition in that day. *wise men.* In whom Edom put so much confidence for her security (see Jer 49:7). Eliphaz, one of Job's three friends, was a Temanite (see note on v. 9). *Esau.* Another name for Edom (see Gen 36:1).

9 *Teman.* A reference to all Edom, as in Jer 49:7,20 (see also Amos 1:12). Teman means "south," and the name probably refers to Edom as the southland. Some, however, identify Teman with Tawilan, a site about three miles east of Petra.

10 *thy brother Jacob.* Edom's violent crimes are all the more reprehensible because they were committed against the brother nation. *shame shall cover thee.* A striking expression since shame is usually associated with nakedness.

11 See Introduction: Date and Place of Writing. *strangers . . . foreigners.* These terms put in relief the sin of Edom: He did not act like a brother (v. 12) but was like one of the strangers.

‡12–14 A rebuke of Edom's hostile actions. The eight rebukes in this section proceed from the general to the particular. See Ezek 35:13 and Ps 137 for examples of Edom's reactions to Judah's misfortunes. "The day" of Jacob's abuse by Edom is matched by "that day" (v 8) when Edom's judgment will come.

13 Thou shouldest not have entered into
the gate of my people in the day of
their calamity:
Yea, thou shouldest not have looked on
their affliction in the day of their
calamity,
Nor have laid *hands* on their
[1]substance in the day of their
calamity;
14 Neither shouldest thou have stood in
the crossway, to cut off those of his
that did escape;
Neither shouldest thou have [1]delivered
up those of his that did remain in the
day of distress.

Judgment upon the nations

15 [a]For the day of the LORD *is* near upon
all the heathen:
[b]As thou hast done, it shall be done
unto thee;
Thy reward shall return upon thine
own head.
16 [a]For as ye have drunk upon my holy
mountain,
So shall all the heathen drink
continually,
Yea, they shall drink, and they shall
[1]swallow down,
And they shall be as though they had
not been.

13 [1]Or, *forces*
14 [1]Or, *shut up*
15 [a]Ezek. 30:3
[b]Hab. 2:8
16 [1]Or, *sup up*
[a]Joel 3:17

17 [1]Or, *they that escape* [2]Or, *it shall be holy*
[a]Amos 9:8
18 [a]Zech. 12:6
19 [a]Zeph. 2:7
20 [1]Or, shall possess *that which* is in *Sepharad* [a]1 Ki. 17:9 [b]Jer. 32:44
21 [a]Jas. 5:20
[b]Rev. 11:15

Deliverance in Zion

17 But upon mount Zion [a]shall be
[1]deliverance, and [2]there shall be
holiness;
And the house of Jacob shall possess
their possessions.
18 And the house of Jacob [a]shall be a fire,
And the house of Joseph a flame,
And the house of Esau for stubble,
And they shall kindle in them, and
devour them;
And there shall not be *any* remaining
of the house of Esau;
For the LORD hath spoken *it.*
19 And *they of* the south shall possess the
mount of Esau;
[a]And *they of* the plain the Philistines:
And they shall possess the fields of
Ephraim, and the fields of Samaria:
And Benjamin *shall possess* Gilead.
20 And the captivity of this host of the
children of Israel *shall possess* that of
the Canaanites, *even* [a]unto
Zarephath;
And the captivity of Jerusalem, [1]which
is in Sepharad,
[b]Shall possess the cities of the south.
21 And [a]saviours shall come up on mount
Zion to judge the mount of Esau;
And the [b]kingdom shall be the LORD's.

15 *the day of the LORD is near upon all the heathen.* If there was an eschatological glimmering in "in that day" (v. 8), it here becomes a strong ray. The day of the Lord brings judgment for the nations (including, but not limited to, Edom) and salvation for the house of Jacob. *upon thine own head.* The situation will be reversed in retribution for Edom's hostility against God's people detailed in vv. 11–14. Ezekiel's denunciation of Edom (ch. 35) reflects a similar punishment-fits-the-crime principle.

‡16 *as ye have drunk.* As the Edomites profaned the holy mountain by carousing, so the nations will drink and drink. Their drinking, however, is that of the bitter potion of God's judgment—which they will be compelled to keep on drinking. For drinking as punishment see Jer 25:15–16; 49:12. Note the strong emphasis on this sin in Amos (2:8; 4:1; 5:11; 6:6). The reversal of fortunes in "that day" will result when the Israelites "drink the wine" (Amos 9:14).

‡17 *upon mount Zion shall be . . . deliverance.* Beginning with this verse the blessings on the house of Jacob are mentioned. Eschatological references are twofold: judgment on God's enemies, blessing on God's people. *possess.* This root appears five times in vss. 17–20 and interlocks Obadiah with Amos 9:12, "that they may possess the remnant of Edom."

18 *Jacob . . . Joseph.* Previously it was stated that the Lord would destroy Edom, using other nations (v. 7); now it is to be done by God's people. *not be any remaining.* The final word to Esau is that his house (or nation) will be totally destroyed; there will be no Edomite survivors. Yet compare Am 9:12 with Ac 15:17 and see note on Am 9:12.

19 *they . . . shall possess.* With Edom annihilated, others will occupy Edomite territory. Although not expressly identified, these are most likely the remnant of Israel referred to in the lines immediately following. *south.* See note on Gen 12:9. *Philistines.* See note on Gen 10:14. *Gilead.* See notes on Gen 31:21; Sol 4:1.

20 *Zarephath.* See note on 1 Ki 17:9. *Sepharad.* Usually taken to refer to Sardis in Asia Minor (present-day Turkey), though some think that Sparta (the city in Greece) might be meant.

‡21 *saviours.* Having developed the theme of possessing lands around Zion, the prophet now turns to the center. The "saviours" come from mount Zion and rule over the mountains of Esau. Mount Zion is exalted over the mountains of Esau. The Messiah, the Deliverer par excellence, may ultimately be in view. *the kingdom shall be the LORD's.* The conclusion of the prophecy—and the final outcome of history. The last book of the Bible echoes this theme (Rev 11:15). Positioned before Jonah, the phrase effectively reminds the readers that God's kingdom includes even the Gentiles.

Jonah

INTRODUCTION

Title

The book is named after its principal character, whose name means "dove"; see the simile used of Ephraim in Hos 7:11 to portray the northern kingdom as "without heart." See also Ps 68:13; 74:19 and notes.

Author

Though the book does not identify its author, tradition has ascribed it to the prophet himself, Jonah son of Amittai (1:1), from Gath-hepher (2 Ki 14:25) in Zebulun (Josh 19:10,13). In view of its many similarities with the narratives about Elijah and Elisha, however, it may come from the same prophetic circles that originally composed the accounts about those prophets, perhaps in the eighth century B.C. (see Introduction to 1 Kings: Author, Sources and Date).

Background

In the half-century during which the prophet Jonah ministered (800–750 B.C.), a significant event affected the northern kingdom of Israel: King Jeroboam II (793–753) restored her traditional borders, ending almost a century of sporadic seesaw conflict between Israel and Damascus.

Jeroboam, in God's good providence (2 Ki 14:26–27), capitalized on Assyria's defeat of Damascus (in the latter half of the ninth century), which temporarily crushed that center of Aramean power. Prior to that time, not only had Israel been considerably reduced in size, but the king of Damascus had even been able to control internal affairs in the northern kingdom (2 Ki 13:7). However, after the Assyrian campaign against Damascus in 797, Jehoash, king of Israel, had been able to recover the territory lost to the king of Damascus (2 Ki 13:25). Internal troubles in Assyria subsequently allowed Jeroboam II to complete the restoration of Israel's northern borders. Nevertheless, Assyria remained the real threat from the north at this time.

The prophets of the Lord were speaking to Israel regarding these events. About 797 B.C. Elisha spoke to the king of Israel concerning future victories over Damascus (2 Ki 13:14–19). A few years later Jonah prophesied the restoration that Jeroboam II accomplished (2 Ki 14:25). But soon after Israel had triumphed, she began to gloat over her new-found power. Because she was relieved of foreign pressures—relief that had come in accordance with encouraging words from Elisha and Jonah—she felt jealously complacent about her favored status with God (Amos 6:1). She focused her religion on expectations of the "day of the LORD" (Amos 5:18–20), when God's darkness would engulf the other nations, leaving Israel to bask in its light.

It was in such a time that the Lord sent Amos and Hosea to announce to His people Israel that he would "not again pass by them any more" (Amos 7:8; 8:2) but would send them into exile "beyond Damascus" (Amos 5:27), i.e., to Assyria (Hos 9:3; 10:6; 11:5). During this time the Lord also sent Jonah to Nineveh to warn it of the imminent danger of divine judgment.

Since Jonah was a contemporary of Amos, see Introduction to Amos: Date and Historical Situation for additional details.

Date of Writing

For a number of reasons, including the preaching to Gentiles, the book is often assigned a postexilic date. At least, it is said, the book must have been written after the destruction of Nineveh in 612 B.C. But these considerations are not decisive. The similarity of this narrative to the Elijah-Elisha accounts has already been noted. One may also question whether mention of the repentance of Nineveh and the consequent averted destruction of the city would have had so much significance to the author after Nineveh's overthrow. And to suppose that proclaiming God's word to Gentiles had no relevance in the eighth century is to overlook the fact that already in the previous century Elijah and Eli-

sha had extended their ministries to foreign lands (1 Ki 17:7–24; 2 Ki 8:7–17). Moreover, the prophet Amos (c. 760–750) set God's redemptive work in behalf of Israel in the context of His dealings with the nations (Amos 1:3—2:16; 9:7,12). Perhaps the third quarter of the eighth century is the most likely date for the book, after the public ministries of Amos and Hosea and before the fall of Samaria to Assyria in 722–721.

Interpretation

Many have questioned whether the book of Jonah is historical. The supposed legendary character of some of the events (e.g., the episode involving the great fish) has caused them to suggest alternatives to the traditional view that the book is historical, biographical narrative. Although their specific suggestions range from fictional short story to allegory to parable, they share the common assumption that the account sprang essentially from the author's imagination, despite its serious and gracious message.

Such interpretations, often based in part on doubt about the miraculous as such, too quickly dismiss (1) the similarities between the narrative of Jonah and other parts of the OT and (2) the pervasive concern of the OT writers, especially the prophets, for history. They also fail to realize that OT narrators had a keen ear for recognizing how certain past events in Israel's pilgrimage with God illumine (by way of analogy) later events. (For example, the events surrounding the birth of Moses illumine the exodus, those surrounding Samuel's birth illumine the series of events narrated in the books of Samuel, and the ministries of Moses and Joshua illumine those of Elijah and Elisha.) Similarly, the prophets recognized that the future events they announced could be illumined by reference to analogous events of the past. Overlooking these features in OT narrative and prophecy, many have supposed that a story that too neatly fits the author's purpose must therefore be fictional.

On the other hand, it must be acknowledged that Biblical narrators were more than historians. They interpretatively recounted the past with the unswerving purpose of bringing it to bear on the present and the future. In the portrayal of past events, they used their materials to achieve this purpose effectively. Nonetheless, the integrity with which they treated the past ought not to be questioned. The book of Jonah recounts real events in the life and ministry of the prophet himself. Further, Jesus certainly understood it as real history (Mat 12:39–41).

Literary Characteristics

Unlike most other prophetic parts of the OT, this book is a narrative account of a single prophetic mission. Its treatment of that mission is thus similar to the accounts of the ministries of Elijah and Elisha found in 1,2 Kings, and to certain narrative sections of Isaiah, Jeremiah and Ezekiel.

As is often the case in Biblical narratives, the author has compressed much into a small space; 40 verses tell the entire story (eight additional verses of poetry are devoted to Jonah's prayer of thanksgiving). In its scope (a single extended episode), compactness, vividness and character delineation, it is much like the book of Ruth.

Also as in Ruth, the author uses structural symmetry effectively. The story is developed in two parallel cycles that call attention to a series of comparisons and contrasts (see Outline). The story's climax is Jonah's grand prayer of confession, "Salvation is of the LORD"—the middle confession of three from his lips (1:9; 2:9; 4:2). The last sentence emphasizes that the Lord's word is final and decisive, while Jonah is left sitting in the hot, open country outside Nineveh.

The author uses the art of representative roles in a straightforward manner. In this story of God's loving concern for all people, Nineveh, the great menace to Israel, is representative of the Gentiles. Correspondingly, stubbornly reluctant Jonah represents Israel's jealousy of her favored relationship with God and her unwillingness to share the Lord's compassion with the nations.

The book depicts the larger scope of God's purpose for Israel: that she might rediscover the truth of His concern for the whole creation and that she might better understand her own role in carrying out that concern.

Outline

I. Jonah Flees His Mission (chs. 1—2)
   A. Jonah's Commission and Flight (1:1–3)
   B. The Endangered Sailors' Cry to Their Gods (1:4–6)
   C. Jonah's Disobedience Exposed (1:7–10)

D. Jonah's Punishment and Deliverance (1:11—2:1; 2:10)
E. His Prayer of Thanksgiving (2:2–9)

II. Jonah Reluctantly Fulfills His Mission (chs. 3—4)
A. Jonah's Renewed Commission and Obedience (3:1–4)
B. The Endangered Ninevites' Repentant Appeal to the Lord (3:5–9)
C. The Ninevites' Repentance Acknowledged (3:10—4:4)
D. Jonah's Deliverance and Rebuke (4:5–11)

Jonah flees to Tarshish

1 Now the word of the LORD came unto
[1]Jonah the son of Amittai, saying,
2 Arise, go to Nineveh, *that* [a]great city, and
cry against it; for [b]their wickedness is come up
before me.
3 But Jonah rose up to flee unto Tarshish
from the presence of the LORD, and went down
to [a]Joppa; and he found a ship going *to* Tarshish: so he paid the fare thereof, and went
down into it, to go with them unto Tarshish
[b]from the presence of the LORD.

4 ¶ But [a]the LORD [1]sent out a great wind
into the sea, and there was a mighty tempest
in the sea, so that the ship [2]was like to be broken.
5 Then the mariners were afraid, and cried
every man unto his god, and cast forth the
wares that *were* in the ship into the sea, to
lighten *it* of them. But Jonah was gone down
[a]into the sides of the ship; and he lay, and was
fast asleep.
6 So the shipmaster came to him, and said
unto him, What meanest thou, O sleeper?
arise, [a]call upon thy God, [b]if so be that God
will think upon us, that we perish not.
7 ¶ And they said every one to his fellow,
Come, and let us [a]cast lots, that we may know
for whose cause this evil *is* upon us. So they
cast lots, and the lot fell upon Jonah.

1:1 [1]Called, Mat. 12:39, *Jonas*
1:2 [a]Gen. 10:11 [b]Gen. 18:20
1:3 [a]Josh. 19:46 [b]Gen. 4:16
1:4 [1]Heb. *cast forth* [a]Ps. 107:25
1:4 [2]Heb. *thought to be broken*
1:5 [a]1 Sam. 24:3
1:6 [a]Ps. 107:28 [b]Joel 2:14
1:7 [a]Josh. 7:14; 1 Sam. 14:41

1:1 *the word of the LORD came.* See 3:1; a common phrase used to indicate the divine source of the prophet's revelation (see, e.g., 1 Ki 17:8; Jer 1:2,4; Hos 1:1; Joel 1:1; Hag 1:1,3; Zech 1:1,7). *Jonah.* See Introduction: Title; Author.

‡1:2 *Arise, go.* See note on Obad 1. *great city.* See 3:2; 4:11; see also note on 3:3. The expression is used as a marker to divide the book into two sections (3:2). According to Gen 10:11–12, it was first built by Nimrod (perhaps along with Rehoboth Ir, Calah and Resen) and was traditionally known as the "great city." About 700 B.C. Sennacherib made it the capital of Assyria, which it remained until its fall in 612 (see Introduction to Nahum: Background). Nineveh is over 500 miles from Gath-hepher, Jonah's hometown. *cry against.* A strategic word reappearing in 1:6,14; 2:2; 3:2,4,5,8. *their wickedness is come up.* Cf. Sodom and Gomorrah (Gen 18:20–21). Except for the violence (3:8) of Nineveh, her "evil way" (3:8,10) is not described in Jonah. Nahum later states that Nineveh's sins included plotting evil against the Lord (Nah 1:11), cruelty and plundering in war (Nah 2:12–13; 3:1,19), prostitution and witchcraft (Nah 3:4) and commercial exploitation (Nah 3:16).

‡1:3 *rose up to flee.* The reason is found in 4:2. The futility of trying to run away from the Lord is acknowledged in Ps 139:7,9–10. *Tarshish.* Perhaps the city of Tartessus in southwest Spain, a Phoenician mining colony near Gibraltar. By heading in the opposite direction from Nineveh, to what seemed like the end of the world, Jonah intended to escape his divinely appointed task. The drama is enhanced by repeating the exact word of the call "arise" with "But Jonah rose up."

1:4–5 Although Jonah's mission was to bring God's warning of impending judgment to the pagan world, his refusal to go to Nineveh brings these pagan sailors into peril.

1:4 *the LORD sent out a great wind.* God's sovereign working in Jonah's mission is evident at several other points also: the fish (v. 17), the release of Jonah (2:10), the plant (4:6), the worm (4:7) and the wind (4:8).

1:5 *his god.* Apparently the sailors, who may have come from various ports, worshiped several pagan gods.

1:6 *the shipmaster came to him.* The pagan captain's concern for everyone on board contrasts with the believing prophet's refusal to carry God's warning to Nineveh.

‡1:7 *let us cast lots.* The casting of lots was a custom widely practiced in the ancient Near East. The precise method is unclear, though it appears that, for the most part, sticks or marked pebbles were drawn from a receptacle into which they had

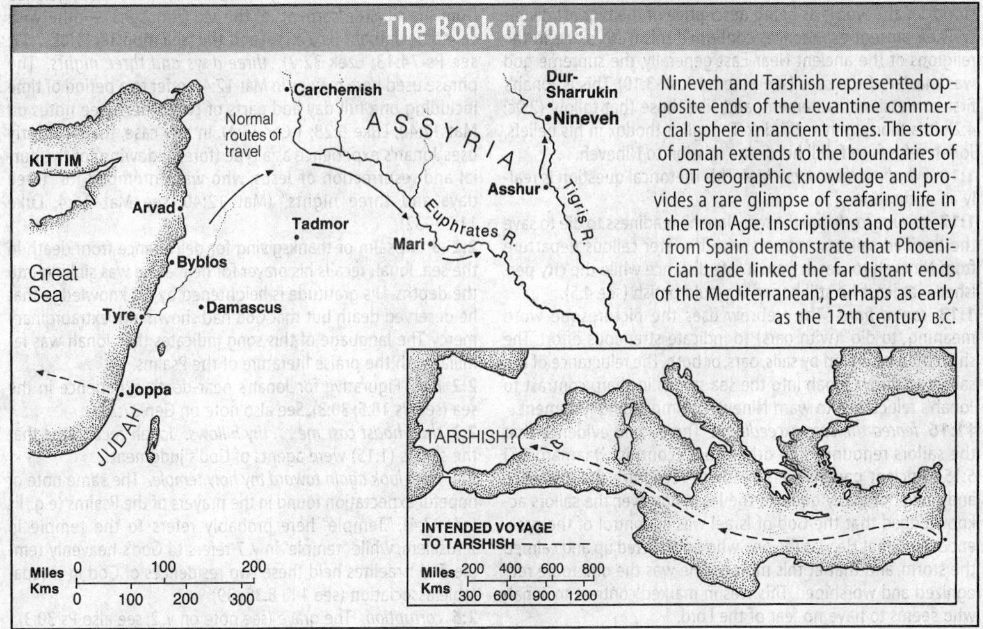

Nineveh and Tarshish represented opposite ends of the Levantine commercial sphere in ancient times. The story of Jonah extends to the boundaries of OT geographic knowledge and provides a rare glimpse of seafaring life in the Iron Age. Inscriptions and pottery from Spain demonstrate that Phoenician trade linked the far distant ends of the Mediterranean, perhaps as early as the 12th century B.C.

8 Then said they unto him, [a]Tell us, we
pray thee, for whose cause this evil *is* upon us;
What *is* thine occupation? and whence comest
thou? what *is* thy country? and of what people
art thou?
9 And he said unto them, I *am* a Hebrew;
and I fear [1]the LORD, the God of heaven,
[a]which hath made the sea and the dry *land.*
10 Then were the men [1]exceedingly afraid,
and said unto him, Why hast thou done this?
For the men knew that he fled from the presence of the LORD, because he had told them.
11 Then said they unto him, What shall we
do unto thee, that the sea [1]may be calm unto
us? for the sea [2][3]wrought, and was tempestuous.
12 And he said unto them, [a]Take me up,
and cast me forth into the sea; so shall the sea
be calm unto you: for I know that for my sake
this great tempest *is* upon you.
13 Nevertheless the men [1]rowed hard to
bring *it* to the land; [a]but they could not: for
the sea [2][3]wrought, and was tempestuous
against them.
14 Wherefore they cried unto the LORD,
and said, We beseech thee, O LORD, we beseech thee, let us not perish for this man's life,
and [a]lay not upon us innocent blood: for thou,
O LORD, [b]hast done as it pleased thee.
15 So they took up Jonah, and cast him
forth into the sea: [a]and the sea [1]ceased from
her raging.
16 Then the men [a]feared the LORD exceedingly, and [1]offered a sacrifice unto the LORD,
and made vows.

Prayer and deliverance of Jonah

17 ¶ Now the LORD had prepared a great fish
to swallow up Jonah. And [a]Jonah was in the
[1]belly of the fish three days and three nights.

2 Then Jonah prayed unto the LORD his
God out of the fish's belly,
2 And said,
I [a]cried [1]by reason of mine affliction
unto the LORD, [b]and he heard me;
Out of the belly of [c][2]hell cried I, *and*
thou heardest my voice.
3 [a]For thou hadst cast me *into* the deep,
in the [1]midst of the seas;
And the floods compassed me about:
[b]All thy billows and thy waves passed
over me.
4 [a]Then I said, I am cast out of thy sight;
Yet I will look again [b]toward thy holy
temple.
5 The [a]waters compassed me about, *even*
to the soul:
The depth closed me round about,
The weeds *were* wrapt about my head.
6 I went down to the [1]bottoms of the
mountains;
The earth *with* her bars *was* about me
for ever:
Yet hast thou brought up my life [a]from
[2]corruption, O LORD my God.

1:8 [a]Josh. 7:19
1:9 [1][Or, *JEHOVAH*] [a]Ps. 146:6; Acts 17:24
1:10 [1]Heb. with *great fear*
1:11 [1]Heb. *may be silent from us* [2]Or, *grew more and more tempestuous* [3]Heb. *went*
1:12 [a]John 11:50
1:13 [1]Heb. *digged* [2]Or, *grew more and more tempestuous* [3]Heb. *went* [a]Prov. 21:30
1:14 [a]Deut. 21:8 [b]Ps. 115:3
1:15 [1]Heb. *stood* [a]Ps. 89:9; Luke 8:24
1:16 [1]Heb. *sacrificed a sacrifice [unto the LORD], and vowed vows* [a]Mark 4:41; Acts 5:11
1:17 [1]Heb. *bowels* [a]Mat. 12:40; Luke 11:30
2:2 [1]Or, *out of mine affliction* [2]Or, *the grave* [a]Ps. 120:1; Lam. 3:55 [b]Ps. 65:2 [c]Is. 14:9
2:3 [1]Heb. *heart* [a]Ps. 88:6 [b]Ps. 42:7
2:4 [a]Ps. 31:22 [b]1 Ki. 8:38
2:5 [a]Ps. 69:1; Lam. 3:54
2:6 [1]Heb. *cuttings off* [2]Or, *the pit* [a]Ps. 16:10

been "cast." *evil.* Here meaning "calamity." *lot fell upon Jonah.* By the lot of judgment the Lord exposed the guilty one (cf. Josh 7:14–26; 1 Sam 14:38–44; Prov 16:33).

1:9 *Hebrew.* See note on Gen 14:13. *God of heaven, which hath made the sea and the dry land.* The sailors would have understood Jonah's words as being descriptive of the highest divinity. Their present experiences confirmed this truth, since, in the religions of the ancient Near East generally, the supreme god was master of the seas (see note on Josh 3:10). This is Jonah's first confessional statement, and, like those that follow (2:9c; 4:2), it is thoroughly orthodox. Though orthodox in his beliefs, Jonah refuses to fulfill his divine mission to Nineveh.

1:10 *Why hast thou done this?* This rhetorical question is really an accusation.

1:12 *cast me forth into the sea.* Jonah's readiness to die to save the terrified sailors contrasts with his later callous departure from Nineveh to watch from a safe distance while the city perishes—at least he still hoped it would perish (see 4:5).

1:13 *rowed hard.* The Hebrew uses the picturesque word meaning "to dig" (with oars) to indicate strenuous effort. The ship could be driven by sails, oars, or both. The reluctance of the sailors to throw Jonah into the sea stands in sharp contrast to Jonah's reluctance to warn Nineveh of impending judgment.

‡1:16 *feared the LORD exceedingly.* There is no evidence that the sailors renounced all other gods (contrast Naaman, 2 Ki 5:15). Ancient pagans were ready to recognize the existence and power of many gods. At the least, however, the sailors acknowledged that the God of Israel was in control of the present events, that He was the one who both stirred up and calmed the storm, and that at this moment He was the one to be recognized and worshiped. This was in marked contrast to Jonah who seems to have no fear of the Lord.

‡1:17 *the LORD had prepared.* This characteristic phrase occurs also in 4:6–8 and reflects the book's strong emphasis on the sovereignty of God. *great fish.* The Hebrew here and the Greek of Mat 12:40 are both general terms for a large fish, not necessarily a whale. This great fish is carefully distinguished from the sinister "serpent" of the sea (Amos 9:3)—otherwise called "leviathan" (Is 27:1)—and the "sea monster" (Job 7:12; see Ps 74:13; Ezek 32:2). *three days and three nights.* The phrase used here may, as in Mat 12:40, refer to a period of time including one full day and parts of two others (see notes on Mat 12:40; Luke 9:28; 1 Cor 15:4). In any case, the NT clearly uses Jonah's experience as a type (foreshadowing) of the burial and resurrection of Jesus, who was entombed for "three days and three nights" (Mat 12:40; see Mat 16:4; Luke 11:29–32).

2:2–9 A psalm of thanksgiving for deliverance from death in the sea. Jonah recalls his prayer for help as he was sinking into the depths. His gratitude is heightened by his knowledge that he deserved death but that God had shown him extraordinary mercy. The language of this song indicates that Jonah was familiar with the praise literature of the Psalms.

2:2 *hell.* Figurative for Jonah's near-death experience in the sea (see Ps 18:5; 30:3). See also note on Gen 37:35.

2:3 *thou hadst cast me . . . thy billows.* Jonah recognizes that the sailors (1:15) were agents of God's judgment.

2:4 *I will look again toward thy holy temple.* The same note of hopeful expectation found in the prayers of the Psalms (e.g., Ps 5:7; 27:4). "Temple" here probably refers to the temple in Jerusalem, while "temple" in v. 7 refers to God's heavenly temple. The Israelites held these two residences of God in inseparable association (see 1 Ki 8:38–39).

2:6 *corruption.* The grave (see note on v. 2; see also Ps 30:3).

7 When my soul fainted within me I
remembered the LORD:
[a]And my prayer came in unto thee,
into thine holy temple.
8 They that observe [a]lying vanities
forsake their own mercy.
9 But I will [a]sacrifice unto thee with the
voice of thanksgiving;
I will pay *that* that I have vowed.
[b]Salvation *is* of the LORD.
10 ¶ And the LORD spake unto the fish, and
it vomited out Jonah upon the dry *land.*

Jonah preaches at Nineveh

3 And the word of the LORD came unto Jonah the second time, saying,
2 Arise, go unto Nineveh, *that* great city,
and preach unto it the preaching that I bid thee.
3 So Jonah arose, and went unto Nineveh,
according to the word of the LORD. Now Nineveh was an [1]exceeding great city of three
days' journey.
4 And Jonah began to enter into the city a
day's journey, and [a]he cried, and said, Yet forty
days, and Nineveh *shall be* overthrown.
5 So the people of Nineveh [a]believed God,
and proclaimed a fast, and put on sackcloth,
from the greatest of them even to the least of
them.
6 For word came unto the king of Nineveh,
and he arose from his throne, and he laid his
robe from him, and covered *him* with sackcloth, [a]and sat in ashes.
7 [a]And he caused *it* to be proclaimed and
[1]published through Nineveh by the decree of

2:7 [a]Ps. 18:6
2:8 [a]2 Ki. 17:15; Jer. 10:8
2:9 [a]Ps. 50:14; Hos. 14:2 [b]Ps. 3:8
3:3 [1]Heb. *of God*
3:4 [a]Deut. 18:22
3:5 [a]Mat. 12:41; Luke 11:32
3:6 [a]Job 2:8
3:7 [1]Heb. *said* [a]2 Chr. 20:3; Joel 2:15
3:7 [2]Heb. *great men*
3:8 [a]Is. 58:6 [b]Is. 59:6
3:9 [a]2 Sam. 12:22; Joel 2:14
3:10 [a]Jer. 18:8; Amos 7:3,6
4:2 [a]ch. 1:3 [b]Ex. 34:6; Ps. 86:5; Joel 2:13
4:3 [a]1 Ki. 19:4 [b]ver. 8
4:4 [1]Or, *Art thou greatly angry?*
4:6 [1]Or, *palmcrist* [2]Heb. *Kikajon*

the king and his [2]nobles, saying, Let neither
man nor beast, herd nor flock, taste any thing:
let them not feed, nor drink water:
8 But let man and beast be covered with
sackcloth, and cry mightily unto God: yea, [a]let
them turn every one from his evil way, and
from [b]the violence that *is* in their hands.
9 [a]Who can tell *if* God will turn and repent, and turn away from his fierce anger, that
we perish not?
10 [a]And God saw their works, that they
turned from their evil way; and God repented
of the evil, that he had said that he would do
unto them; and he did *it* not.

Sparing of the city angers Jonah

4 But it displeased Jonah exceedingly, and
he was very angry.
2 And he prayed unto the LORD, and said, I
pray thee, O LORD, *was* not this my saying,
when I was yet in my country? Therefore I
[a]fled before unto Tarshish: for I knew that
thou *art* a [b]gracious God, and merciful, slow to
anger, and of great kindness, and repentest
thee of the evil.
3 [a]Therefore now, O LORD, take, I beseech
thee, my life from me; for [b]*it is* better for me
to die than to live.
4 Then said the LORD, [1]Doest thou well to
be angry?
5 So Jonah went out of the city, and sat on
the east side of the city, and there made him a
booth, and sat under it in the shadow, till he
might see what would become of the city.
6 And the LORD God prepared a [1][2]gourd,

2:9 *that I have vowed.* In the book of Psalms, prayers were commonly accompanied by vows, usually involving thank offerings (e.g., Ps 50:14; 56:12; 61:8; 65:1; 66:13–14; 116:12–19). *Salvation is of the LORD.* The climax of Jonah's thanksgiving prayer. It is Jonah's second confessional statement (see note on 1:9) and stands at the literary midpoint of the book.

‡3:2 *preach unto it the preaching that I bid thee.* "Preach" ("cry against" in 1:2). The words presage that of the Great Commission itself. A prophet was the bearer of a message from God, not primarily a foreteller of coming events.

‡3:3 *arose, and went.* But reluctantly, still wanting the Ninevites to be destroyed (4:1–5). *exceeding great city.* See 4:11, which says the city had more than 120,000 inhabitants. Archaeological excavations indicate that the later imperial city of Nineveh was about eight miles around. The fact, however, that the city was a "three days' walk" may suggest a larger area, such as the four-city complex of Nineveh, Rehoboth Ir, Calah and Resen mentioned in Gen 10:11–12. Greater Nineveh covered an area of some 60 miles in circumference. On the other hand, "three days" represented, in the ancient Near Eastern idiom, a long journey (see Gen 30:36; Ex 3:18; Josh 9:16–17). Another alternative is that it may refer to the length of his ministry there at Nineveh.

3:5–6 *fast . . . sackcloth . . . ashes.* Customary signs of humbling oneself in repentance (see 1 Ki 21:27; Neh 9:1).

3:5 *believed God.* This may mean that the Ninevites genuinely turned to the Lord (cf. Mat 12:41). On the other hand, their belief in God may have gone no deeper than had the sailors' fear of God (see note on 1:16). At least they took the prophet's warning seriously and acted accordingly.

‡3:6 *king of Nineveh.* Probably the king of Assyria, though this could refer to a governor or important city official.

‡3:8 *man and beast.* Inclusion of the domestic animals was unusual and expressed the urgency with which the Ninevites sought mercy (see also 4:11).

‡3:9 *Who can tell . . . ?* God often responds in mercy to man's repentance by canceling threatened punishment (v. 10). See note on Jer 18:7–10. In Hebrew, this expression implies that God's compassion overcomes His anger; cf. Joel 2:14.

‡4:1 *angry.* Jonah was angry that God would have compassion on an enemy of Israel. He wanted God's goodness to be shown only to Israelites, not to the hated Assyrians.

‡4:2 *gracious . . . merciful.* See Ex 34:6–7 and note. Jonah again uses a fixed, confessional formula (see note on 1:9). It may be that Jonah understood that the Lord's compassion was not the result of the covenant at mount Sinai but the cause of it. Just as God showed compassion to the willfully disobedient idolators in Ex 33, now he will show compassion because it is His very nature. *slow to anger.* In contrast, Jonah became angry quickly (vv. 1,9).

4:3 *take . . . my life.* Cf. 1 Ki 19:4 (Elijah). To Jonah, God's mercy to the Ninevites meant an end to Israel's favored standing with Him. Jonah shortly before had rejoiced in his deliverance from death, but now that Nineveh lives, he prefers to die.

4:5 *booth.* Apparently this shelter did not provide enough shade since the next verse indicates that God provided a plant to give more shade. *till he might see.* Jonah still hoped that Nineveh would be destroyed.

‡4:6 *LORD God prepared.* This characteristic phrase occurs also in vv. 7–8; 1:17. This is the first use of the compound divine

and made *it* to come up over Jonah, that *it*
might be a shadow over his head, to deliver
him from his grief. So Jonah [3]was exceeding
glad of the gourd.
7 But God prepared a worm when the
morning rose the next day, and it smote the
gourd, that it withered.
8 And it came to pass, when the sun did
arise, that God prepared a [1]vehement east
wind; and the sun beat upon the head of Jonah,
that he fainted, and wished in himself to die,
and said, [a]*It is* better for me to die than to live.

4:6 [3]Heb. *rejoiced* with *great joy*
4:8 [1]Or, *silent* [a]ver. 3
4:9 [1]Or, *Art thou greatly angry?* [2]Or, *I am greatly angry*
4:10 [1]Or, *spared* [2]Heb. *was the son of* the *night*
4:11 [a]ch. 1:2; 3:2,3 [b]Deut. 1:39 [c]Ps. 36:6; 145:9

9 And God said to Jonah, [1]Doest thou well
to be angry for the gourd? And he said, [2]I do
well to be angry, *even* unto death.
10 Then said the LORD, Thou hast [1]had pity
on the gourd, for the which thou hast not
laboured, neither madest it grow; which
[2]came up in a night, and perished in a night:
11 And should not I spare Nineveh, [a]*that*
great city, wherein are more than sixscore
thousand persons [b]that cannot discern between their right hand and their left hand; and
also much [c]cattle?

---

name. The author had reserved "God" for the Ninevites and "LORD" (Hebrew "Yahweh," which is His covenant name in Ex 6:3) for Jonah. Following 4:6, he consistently uses the word "God." This would suggest that Jonah and Nineveh were united. Both needed to repent and both needed God's covenant love (mercy). The irony, however, is that Jonah refuses in his anger to repent, while Nineveh gladly does. This approach draws proper attention to the God who extends grace to all people. *gourd.* Probably a castor oil plant, a shrub growing over 12 feet high with large, shady leaves. God graciously increased the comfort of His stubbornly defiant prophet.

4:8 *It is better for me to die.* See note on v. 3.

‡4:10 *came up in a night, and perished in a night.* Jonah shows a willful preoccupation with mortal issues in contrast to the great issues bound up with "The LORD prepared."

4:11 *should not I spare . . . ?* God had the first word (1:1), and He also has the last. The commission He gave Jonah displayed His mercy and compassion to the Ninevites, and His last word to Jonah emphatically proclaimed that concern for every creature, both man and animal. The Lord not only "preservest man and beast" (Ps 36:6; see Neh 9:6; Ps 145:16), but He takes "no pleasure in the death of the wicked, but [desires] that the wicked turn from his way and live" (Ezek 33:11; see Ezek 18:21–23). Jonah and his countrymen traditionally rejoiced in God's special mercies to Israel but wished only His wrath on their enemies. God here rebukes such hardness and proclaims His own gracious benevolence. *cannot discern . . . their right hand and their left hand.* Like small children (cf. Deut 1:39; Is 7:15–16), the Ninevites needed God's fatherly compassion. *and also much cattle.* God's concern extended even to domestic animals.

Micah

INTRODUCTION

Author

Little is known about the prophet Micah beyond what can be learned from the book itself and Jer 26:18. Micah was from the town of Moresheth (1:1), probably Moresheth-gath (1:14) in southern Judah. The prophecy attests to Micah's deep sensitivity to the social ills of his day, especially as they affected the small towns and villages of his homeland.

Date

Micah prophesied sometime between 750 and 686 B.C. during the reigns of Jotham, Ahaz and Hezekiah, kings of Judah (1:1; Jer 26:18). He was therefore a contemporary of Isaiah (see Is 1:1) and Hosea (see Hos 1:1). Micah predicted the fall of Samaria (1:6), which took place in 722–721. This would place his early ministry in the reigns of Jotham (750–732) and Ahaz (735–715). (The reigns of Jotham and Ahaz overlapped.) Micah's message reflects social conditions prior to the religious reforms under Hezekiah (715–686). (The reigns of Ahaz and Hezekiah seem to have overlapped from c. 729 to 715; see 2 Ki 18:9 and note on Is 36:1.)

Background

The background of the book is the same as that found in the earlier portions of Isaiah, though Micah does not exhibit the same knowledge of Jerusalem's political life as Isaiah does. Perhaps this is because he, like Amos, was from a Judahite village.

Israel was in an apostate condition. Micah predicted the fall of her capital, Samaria (1:5–7), and also foretold the inevitable desolation of Judah (1:9–16).

Three significant historical events occurred during this period:

1. In 734–732 B.C. Tiglath-pileser III of Assyria led a military campaign against Aram (Syria), Philistia and parts of Israel and Judah. Ashkelon and Gaza were defeated. Judah, Ammon, Edom and Moab paid tribute to the Assyrian king, but Israel did not fare as well. According to 2 Ki 15:29 the northern kingdom lost most of its territory, including all of Gilead and much of Galilee. Damascus fell in 732 and was annexed to the Assyrian empire. Significantly, he was the first Assyrian king to institute the policy of wholesale deportation. Thus, not only was Israel defeated in battle, but it was taken into exile.

2. In 722–721 Samaria fell, and the northern kingdom of Israel was conquered by Assyria.

3. In 701 Judah joined a revolt against Assyria and was overrun by King Sennacherib and his army, though Jerusalem was spared.

Literary Characteristics

Micah's style is similar to that of Isaiah. Both prophets use vigorous language and many figures of speech; both show great tenderness in threatening punishment and in promising justice. Micah makes frequent use of plays on words, 1:10–16 being the classic example.

Theme and Message

As the Outline shows, Micah's message alternates between oracles of doom and oracles of hope. The theme is judgment and deliverance by God. Micah also stresses that God hates idolatry, injustice, rebellion and empty ritualism, but He delights in pardoning the penitent. Finally, the prophet declares that Zion will have greater glory in the future than ever before. The Davidic kingdom, though it will seem to come to an end, will reach greater heights through the coming Messianic deliverer.

Outline

- I. Superscription (1:1)
- II. Judgment against Israel and Judah (1:2—3:12)
  - A. Introduction (1:2)
  - B. The Predicted Destruction (1:3–7)
  - C. Lamentation for the Destruction (1:8–16)
  - D. Corruption in Micah's Society (2:1–11)
  - E. Hope in the Midst of Gloom (2:12–13)
  - F. The Leaders Condemned (ch. 3)
- III. Hope for Israel and Judah (chs. 4—5)
  - A. The Coming Kingdom (ch. 4)
  - B. The Coming King (5:1–5a)
  - C. Victory for the People of God (5:5b-15)
- IV. The Lord's Case against Israel (ch. 6)
  - A. The Lord's Accusation (6:1–8)
  - B. The Coming Judgment (6:9–16)
- V. Gloom Turns to Triumph (ch. 7)
  - A. Micah Laments the Corruption of His Society (7:1–6)
  - B. Micah's Assurance of Hope (7:7)
  - C. A Bright Future for God's People (7:8–13)
  - D. Victory for God's Kingdom (7:14–20)

1 The word of the LORD that came to [a]Micah the Morasthite in the days of Jotham, Ahaz, *and* Hezekiah, kings of Judah, which he saw concerning Samaria and Jerusalem.

Samaria and Judah

2 [1]Hear, all ye people;
Hearken, O earth, and [2]all that therein is:
And let the Lord GOD be witness against you,
The Lord from [a]his holy temple.
3 For behold, the LORD cometh forth out of his place,
And will come down and tread upon the high places of the earth.
4 And [a]the mountains shall be molten under him,
And the valleys shall be cleft,
As wax before the fire,
And as the waters *that are* poured down [1]a steep place.
5 For the transgression of Jacob *is* all this,
And for the sins of the house of Israel.
What *is* the transgression of Jacob? *is it* not Samaria?
And what *are* the high places of Judah? *are they* not Jerusalem?
6 Therefore I will make Samaria [a]as a heap of the field,
And as plantings of a vineyard:
And I will pour down the stones thereof into the valley,
And I will [b]discover the foundations thereof.
7 And all the graven images thereof shall be beaten to pieces,
And all the [a]hires thereof shall be burnt with the fire,
And all the idols thereof will I lay desolate:
For she gathered *it* of the hire of a harlot,
And they shall return to the hire of a harlot.

The lament of the prophet

8 Therefore I will wail and howl,
I will go stript and naked:
[a]I will make a wailing like the dragons,
And mourning as the [1]owls.
9 For [1]her wound *is* incurable;
For [a]it is come unto Judah;
He is come unto the gate of my people, *even* to Jerusalem.

10 [a]Declare ye *it* not at Gath, weep ye not at all:
In the house of [1]Aphrah roll thyself *in* the dust.
11 Pass ye away, [1]thou [2]inhabitant of Saphir, having *thy* shame naked:
The [2]inhabitant of [3]Zaanan came not forth *in* the mourning of [4]Beth-ezel;
He shall receive of you his standing.

1:1 [a]Jer. 26:18
1:2 [1]Heb. *Hear, ye people, all of them* [2]Heb. *the fulness thereof* [a]Ps. 11:4
1:4 [1]Heb. *a descent* [a]Amos 9:5
1:6 [a]2 Ki. 19:25
1:6 [b]Ezek. 13:14
1:7 [a]Hos. 2:5
1:8 [1]Heb. *daughters of the owl* [a]Ps. 102:6
1:9 [1]Or, she is *grievously sick of her wounds* [a]2 Ki. 18:13
1:10 [1]That is, *Dust* [a]2 Sam. 1:20
1:11 [1]Or, *thou that dwellest fairly* [2]Heb. *inhabitress* [3]Or, *The country of flocks* [4]Or, *A place near*

‡**1:1** *Micah.* Means "Who is like the LORD?" *Morasthite.* Means "of Moresheth." See Introduction: Author. *Jotham, Ahaz, and Hezekiah.* See Introduction: Date. For background on these kings and the book of Micah see 2 Ki 15:32–16:20; 18–20. Isaiah, Hosea and Micah prophesied at roughly the same time (see Is 1:1; Hos 1:1). *which he saw.* In a prophetic vision (see Is 1:1 and note). *Samaria and Jerusalem.* The capitals of Israel and Judah respectively. The judgment predicted by Micah involved these nations and not just their capital cities.
‡**1:2** *Hear.* The Hebrew for this word introduces prophetic addresses also in 3:1 and 6:1 (see also 3:9; 6:2). *people . . . earth.* All nations—an announcement that the day of the Lord is at hand, when God will call the nations to account. In view of that day Micah speaks in his prophecy of the impending judgments on Israel and Judah. In the OT tradition there were many "days of the Lord." The fall of Samaria in 722 would have been one fulfillment of "day of the Lord" statements. There is yet a great day of the Lord which is graphically described throughout the book of Revelation. *holy temple.* Heaven (see v. 3), as in Ps 11:4; Jonah 2:7; Hab 2:20.
1:3 *the LORD cometh forth.* An OT expression describing the Lord's intervention in history (see Ps 18:9; 96:13; 144:5; Is 26:21; 31:4; 64:1–3). *high places.* May refer to mountains as well as to pagan shrines, since both are cited here (vv. 4–5). Cf. Amos 4:13.
‡**1:4** *mountains shall be molten.* See Ps 97:5; Nah 1:5; Amos 9:5
1:5 *Jacob.* Jacob was an alternate name for Israel (see Gen 32:28 and note; 35:10). *Israel.* Here (and in v. 13) specifically the northern kingdom, but Micah uses the name also for the southern kingdom (see 3:1,8–9; 5:1,3) or for the whole covenant people (see vv. 14–15; 2:12; 5:2; 6:2). *high places.* Pagan centers of idolatry (see 2 Chr 28:25).
1:6–7 God is the speaker. This prophecy was fulfilled during Micah's lifetime when Assyria destroyed Samaria in 722–721 B.C. (2 Ki 17:6).
1:6 *into the valley.* Samaria was built on a hill (1 Ki 16:24).
1:7 *harlot.* Prostitution is often an OT symbol for idolatry or spiritual unfaithfulness (Ex 34:15–16; Judg 2:17; Ezek 23:29–30). *hire.* The wealth that Samaria had gained from her idolatry will be taken by the Assyrians and placed in their own temples to be used again in the worship of idols.
1:8 *Therefore.* Because of the coming destruction of Samaria. *stript.* A sign of mourning (2 Sam 15:30). It is possible that Micah actually walked stripped and barefoot through Jerusalem (cf. Is 20:2). *naked.* Clothed only in a loincloth.
1:9 *wound.* The judgment about to overtake Samaria. *incurable.* See Is 17:11 and note; Jer 30:12. *gate.* The Assyrian destruction of the northern kingdom will spread like a malignant disease to the gate of Jerusalem (v. 12). The gate was where the process of town government was carried on (see Gen 19:1 and note; Ruth 4:1–4).
‡**1:10–15** Micah employs several plays on words; e.g., "Gath" sounds like the Hebrew for "declare." The towns mentioned lie in the Shephelah, i.e., the foothills (500–1,500 feet high) between the Mediterranean coastal plain and the mountains of Judah.
‡**1:10** *Declare ye it not at Gath.* These words introduce a funeral lament over Judah. Micah did not want the pagan people in Gath to gloat over the downfall of God's people. Cf. 2 Sam 1:20. *Aphrah roll thyself in the dust.* For the wordplay, see KJV marg. Rolling in the dust was a sign of grief over the coming catastrophe. See Is 47:1 and note.
‡**1:11** *thy shame naked . . . inhabitant.* The rhyme here is with "shame" and "inhabitant." A reference to their future condition as prisoners (see Is 20:4). *came not forth.* Because of the invasion, the people will not dare to go outside their houses.

12 For the [1]inhabitant of Maroth [2]waited
carefully for good:
But [a]evil came down from the LORD
unto the gate of Jerusalem.
13 O thou [1]inhabitant of [a]Lachish, bind
the chariot to the swift beast:
She *is* the beginning of the sin to the
daughter of Zion:
For the transgressions of Israel were
found in thee.
14 Therefore shalt thou [a]give presents [1]to
Moresheth-gath:
The houses of [b2]Achzib *shall be* a lie
to the kings of Israel.
15 Yet will I bring an heir unto thee,
O [1]inhabitant of [a]Mareshah:
[2]He shall come unto [b]Adullam the
glory of Israel.
16 Make thee [a]bald, and poll thee for thy
[b]delicate children;
Enlarge thy baldness as the eagle;
For they are gone into captivity from
thee.

Wicked deeds of the rich

2 Woe to them that devise iniquity, and
work evil upon their beds!
When the morning is light, they
practise it,
Because it is in the power of their hand.
2 And they covet fields, and take *them*
by violence;
And houses, and take *them* away:
So they [1]oppress a man and his house,
Even a man and his heritage.
3 Therefore thus saith the LORD;
Behold, against this family do I devise
an evil,
From which ye shall not remove your
necks;
Neither shall ye go haughtily:
For this time *is* evil.

4 In that day shall *one* take up a parable
against you,
And [a]lament [1]with a doleful
lamentation,
And say, We be utterly spoiled:
He hath changed the portion of my
people:
How hath he removed *it* from me!
[2]Turning away he hath divided our
fields.
5 Therefore thou shalt have none that
shall cast a cord by lot
In the congregation of the LORD.
6 [1 2]Prophesy ye not, *say they to them
that* prophesy:
They shall not prophesy to them, *that*
they shall not take shame.
7 O *thou that art* named the house of
Jacob,
Is the spirit of the LORD [1]straitened?
Are these his doings?
Do not my words do good to him that
walketh [2]uprightly?
8 Even [1]of late my people is risen up as
an enemy:

1:12 [1]Heb. *inhabitress* [2]Or, *was grieved* [a]Amos 3:6 **1:13** [1]Heb. *inhabitress* [a]2 Ki. 18:14 **1:14** [1]Or, *for* [2]That is, *A lie* [a]2 Sam. 8:2; 2 Ki. 18:14 [b]Josh. 15:44 **1:15** [1]Heb. *inhabitress* [2]Or, *The glory of Israel shall come, etc.* [a]Josh. 15:44 [b]2 Chr. 11:7 **1:16** [a]Job 1:20; Is. 15:2; Jer. 7:29 [b]Lam. 4:5 **2:2** [1]Or, *defraud* **2:4** [1]Heb. *with a lamentation of lamentations* [2]Or, *Instead of restoring* [a]2 Sam. 1:17 **2:6** [1]Or, *Prophesy not as they prophesy* [2]Heb. *Drop, etc.* **2:7** [1]Or, *shortened?* [2]Heb. *upright?* **2:8** [1]Heb. *yesterday*

1:12 *came down.* Micah foresees the future so clearly that to him it seems as though it has already come.

‡1:13 *Lachish . . . swift beast.* "Lachish" sounds like the Hebrew for "team" (i.e. of horses), another wordplay. Lachish was one of the largest towns in Judah (see Is 36:2 and note). Later, Sennacherib was so proud of capturing it that he decorated his palace at Nineveh with a relief picturing his exploits. *bind the chariot.* In order to escape. *daughter of Zion.* A personification of Jerusalem and its inhabitants.

‡1:14-15 *presents.* Or, "parting gifts." Jerusalem must give up Moresheth-gath, as a father gives a "dowry" to his daughter when she marries. *Achzib . . . lie.* See KJV marg. for the wordplay. Achzib and "lie" rhyme in the original. The word "liar" in Jer 15:18 is compared with a brook that has dried up in summer. Like such a brook, the city of Achzib will cease to exist. *Israel.* See note on 1:5.

1:15 Micah again represents God as speaking, as in vv. 6–7. *come unto Adullam.* In judgment (if reference is to God), or in flight (if reference is to Israel's leaders). *glory of Israel.* Either God Himself (see 1 Sam 15:29) or Israel's leaders (more likely in this context).

‡1:16 Israel was taken into exile by the Assyrians in 722–721 B.C., and Judah by the Babylonians in 586. Like Amos (ch 7), Micah predicted exile before deportation actually occurred by the Assyrians. This, no doubt, made his message more difficult to believe.

2:1–5 Directed primarily against wealthy landowners who oppressed the poor.

2:1 *power of their hand.* The rich, oppressing classes continued to get rich at the expense of the poor because they controlled the power structures of their society.

2:2 *they covet.* In violation of the tenth commandment (see Ex 20:17 and note; Deut 5:21). *heritage.* Land that was to be the permanent possession of a particular family. See Lev 25:10,13 (year of jubile); Num 27:1–11; 36:1–12 (Zelophehad's daughters); 1 Ki 21:1–19 (Naboth's vineyard).

‡2:3 *Therefore.* Because of the sins of Israel's influential classes, calamity will strike. *evil.* The impending exile. *shall ye go haughtily.* See 6:8 where they are told to "walk humbly."

‡2:4 *We . . . me!* The rich landowners, on whom God's judgment will fall. There is bitter irony in the human condition; they had felt no qualms for the poor whose land they confiscated. *he.* God.

2:5 *thou.* The oppressing classes—the rich landowners. *none that shall cast a cord by lot.* They will be cut off from all the promises of the covenant people.

‡2:6 *they.* The false prophets whose words were addressed to Micah. Micah is employing the "disputation" genre also seen in Malachi. In this genre the prophet is in ongoing dispute with his opponents, whether false prophets, corrupt priests or the wealthy.

‡2:7 Verses 6–7a are spoken by Micah; vv. 7b–13 are spoken by God. One of the beliefs of that day was that no harm could come to those in covenant with God. It is possible that the false prophets are quoting the Lord out of context . . . the God who would do only good. See especially 3:11: "they . . . say, 'Is not the LORD among us? None evil can come upon us.'"

‡2:8–9 The extreme plight of the poor and atrocities of the rich are a telling indictment on the failure of the kings whose sacred task was to establish justice. Even pagan nations had a higher view of societal justice.

Ye pull off the robe [2]with the garment
From them that pass by securely *as men* averse from war.
9 The [1]women of my people have ye cast out from their pleasant houses;
From their children have ye taken *away* my glory for ever.
10 Arise ye, and depart; for this *is* not *your* [a]rest:
Because it is [b]polluted, it shall destroy *you,* even *with* a sore destruction.
11 If a man [1]walking *in* the spirit and falsehood do lie, *saying,*
I will prophesy unto thee of wine and of strong drink;
He shall even be the prophet of this people.

The remnant regathered

12 [a]I will surely assemble, O Jacob, all of thee;
I will surely gather the remnant of Israel;
I will put them together [b]as the sheep of Bozrah,
As the flock in the midst of their fold:
[c]They shall make great noise by reason of *the multitude of* men.
13 The breaker is come up before them:
They have broken up, and have passed through the gate, and are gone out by it:
And [a]their king shall pass before them,
[b]And the LORD on the head of them.

Israel's sins denounced

3 And I said, Hear, I pray you, O heads of Jacob,
And ye princes of the house of Israel;
[a]*Is it* not for you to know judgment?
2 Who hate the good, and love the evil;
Who pluck off their skin from off them,
And their flesh from off their bones;
3 Who also [a]eat the flesh of my people,
And flay their skin from off them;
And they break their bones,
And chop *them* in pieces, as for the pot,
And [b]as flesh within the caldron.
4 Then [a]shall they cry unto the LORD, but he will not hear them:
He will even hide his face from them at that time,
As they have behaved themselves ill in their doings.
5 Thus saith the LORD [a]concerning the prophets that make my people err,
That [b]bite with their teeth, and cry, Peace;
And [c]he that putteth not into their mouths,
They even prepare war against him.
6 [a]Therefore night *shall be* unto you,
[1]that *ye* shall not have a vision;
And it shall be dark unto you, [2]that *ye* shall not divine;
[b]And the sun shall go down over the prophets,
And the day shall be dark over them.
7 Then shall the seers be ashamed, and the diviners confounded:
Yea, they shall all cover their [1]lips;
[a]For *there is* no answer of God.
8 But truly I am full *of* power by the spirit of the LORD,
And *of* judgment, and *of* might,
[a]To declare unto Jacob his transgression,
And to Israel his sin.

Destruction of Jerusalem foretold

9 Hear this, I pray you, ye heads of the house of Jacob,
And princes of the house of Israel,
That abhor judgment, and pervert all equity.
10 [a]They build up Zion with [b1]blood,
And Jerusalem with iniquity.
11 [a]The heads thereof judge for reward,
And [b]the priests thereof teach for hire,
And the prophets thereof divine for money:

2:8 [2]Heb. *over against a garment* 2:9 [1]Or, *wives* 2:10 [a]Deut. 12:9 [b]Lev. 18:25; Jer. 3:2 2:11 [1]Or, *walk with the wind, and lie falsely* 2:12 [a]ch. 4:6,7 [b]Jer. 31:10 [c]Ezek. 36:37 2:13 [a]Hos. 3:5 [b]Is. 52:12 3:1 [a]Jer. 5:4,5 3:3 [a]Ps. 14:4

3:3 [b]Ezek. 11:3 3:4 [a]Ps. 18:41; Prov. 1:28; Is. 1:15 3:5 [a]Is. 56:10,11; Ezek. 13:10 [b]Mat. 7:15 [c]Ezek. 13:18 3:6 [1]Heb. *from a vision* [2]Heb. *from divining* [a]Is. 8:20; Ezek. 13:23 [b]Amos 8:9 3:7 [1]Heb. *upper lip* [a]Amos 8:11 3:8 [a]Is. 58:1 3:10 [1]Heb. *bloods* [a]Jer. 22:13 [b]Ezek. 22:27; Zeph. 3:3 3:11 [a]Is. 1:23; Ezek. 22:12 [b]Jer. 6:13

2:10 *your rest.* A place that could be regarded as one's own possession, where a people could settle in security (cf. Josh 1:13–15; 21:43–44; 22:4).
‡2:11 *prophesy . . . of strong drink.* The place of alcohol in the world of the rich is a common prophetic subject.
‡2:12–13 *I will surely.* It is typical of Micah to juxtapose the Word of God with words from the false prophets, often with no warning. It should be remembered that Micah has collected oracles he has preached elsewhere and inserted them in this new context (see note on Is 1:9).
2:12 *Jacob . . . Israel.* Here perhaps the entire nation, north and south. Contrast 1:5; 3:1,9–10.
3:1–12 Verses 1–4 deal with the sins of the leaders of Israel, vv. 5–7 with the false prophets and vv. 9–12 with the leaders, priests and prophets.
3:1 *Jacob . . . Israel.* Both names refer to Judah here (see vv. 9–10).
3:2 *hate the good, and love the evil.* Contrast Amos 5:15; Rom 12:9.
‡3:2–3 *pluck off their skin . . . as flesh within the caldron.* A series of figures of speech describing the cruel way the leaders treat the people. This is some of the harshest language in the whole prophetic corpus.
3:4 *they.* The leaders. *he will not hear them.* See v. 7. *hide his face.* See Deut 31:17; Is 1:15 and note. Disobedience leads to separation from God.
‡3:5 *cry, Peace.* The false prophets predicted peace for Judah while Micah predicted destruction and captivity (see v. 12; 4:10). See also Jer 6:13–14; 8:10–11. Perhaps the best example of this is Jer 26 where the true prophets, Jeremiah and Urijah, are persecuted for not preaching peace.
3:7 *seers.* An older term for "prophets" (see note on 1 Sam 9:9).
‡3:8 One of the chief purposes of Micah was to declare to Judah its sin. *full of power by the spirit.* The prophets were Spirit-filled messengers (see Is 48:16) in contrast with "a man walking in the spirit and falsehood" (2:11; here "spirit" suggests "breath"). The false prophets were full of hot air.
‡3:11 *for money.* Or, "for a bribe." See Is 1:23; 5:23.

[c]Yet will they lean upon the LORD,
[1]and say,
Is not the LORD among us?
None evil can come upon us.
12 Therefore shall Zion for your sake be
[a]plowed *as* a field,
[b]And Jerusalem shall become heaps,
And [c]the mountain of the house as the
high places of the forest.

The coming of law and peace

4 But [a]in the last days it shall come to
pass,
That the mountain of the house of the
LORD shall be established in the top
of the mountains,
And *it shall be* exalted above the hills;
And people shall flow unto it.
2 And many nations shall come, and say,
Come, and let us go up to the
mountain of the LORD,
And to the house of the God of Jacob;
And he will teach us of his ways,
And we will walk in his paths:
For the law shall go forth of Zion,
And the word of the LORD from
Jerusalem.
3 And he shall judge among many
people,
And rebuke strong nations afar off;
And they shall beat their swords into
[a]plowshares,
And their spears into [1]pruninghooks:
Nation shall not lift up a sword against
nation,
[b]Neither shall they learn war any
more.
4 [a]But they shall sit every man under his
vine and under his fig tree;
And none shall make *them* afraid:
For the mouth of the LORD of hosts
hath spoken *it*.
5 For all people will walk every one in
the name of his god,
And [a]we will walk in the name of the
LORD our God for ever and ever.

3:11 [1]Heb. *saying* [c]Is. 48:2; Jer. 7:4
3:12 [a]Jer. 26:18 [b]Ps. 79:1 [c]ch. 4:2
4:1 [a]Ezek. 17:22
4:3 [1]Or, *sythes* [a]Is. 2:4; Joel 3:10 [b]Ps. 72:7
4:4 [a]1 Ki. 4:25; Zech. 3:10
4:5 [a]Zech. 10:12
4:6 [a]Ezek. 34:16 [b]Ps. 147:2; Ezek. 34:13
4:7 [a]ch. 2:12 [b]Is. 9:6; Dan. 7:14; Luke 1:33; Rev. 11:15
4:8 [1][Or, *Edar*: Gen. 35:21]
4:9 [a]Jer. 8:19 [b]Is. 13:8; Jer. 30:6
4:11 [a]Lam. 2:16 [b]Obad. 12
4:12 [a]Is. 55:8 [b]Is. 21:10
4:13 [a]Jer. 51:33

The LORD reigns in Zion

6 In that day, saith the LORD, [a]will I
assemble her that halteth,
[b]And I will gather her that is driven out,
And *her* that I have afflicted;
7 And I will make her that halted a
[a]remnant,
And her that was cast far off a strong
nation:
And the LORD [b]shall reign over them in
mount Zion
From henceforth, even for ever.
8 And thou, O tower of [1]the flock,
The strong hold of the daughter of
Zion,
Unto thee shall it come, even the first
dominion;
The kingdom shall come to the
daughter of Jerusalem.
9 Now why dost thou cry out aloud?
[a]*Is there* no king in thee?
Is thy counseller perished?
For [b]pangs have taken thee as a
woman in travail.
10 Be in pain, and labour to bring forth,
O daughter of Zion, like a woman in
travail:
For now shalt thou go forth out of the
city, and thou shalt dwell in the field,
And thou shalt go *even* to Babylon;
there shalt thou be delivered;
There the LORD shall redeem thee from
the hand of thine enemies.
11 [a]Now also many nations are gathered
against thee,
That say, Let her be defiled, and let our
eye [b]look upon Zion.
12 But they know not [a]the thoughts of the
LORD,
Neither understand they his counsel:
For he shall gather them [b]as the
sheaves into the floor.
13 [a]Arise and thresh, O daughter of Zion:
For I will make thine horn iron, and I
will make thy hoofs brass:

3:12 The destruction of Jerusalem occurred in 586 B.C. This verse was quoted a century later in Jer 26:18. Jer 26:19 indicates that Micah's preaching may have been instrumental in the revival under King Hezekiah (see 2 Ki 18:1–6; 2 Chr 29–31).
‡4:1–4 See notes on Is 2:2–4, a passage that is almost the same as these verses. These verses need to be understood as a perfect counterpart to 3:9–12: Zion is both plowed as a field (3:12) and exalted above the hills (4:1). She is built in violence and bloodshed (3:10) and yet is the place from which the Lord's word and teaching go forth and nations are judged (4:2). Only God can effect such radical transformation.
‡4:4 *vine and . . . fig tree.* A reference to the peaceful security of the kingdom of God. See 1 Ki 4:25; Zech 3:10. *none shall make them afraid.* See Zeph 3:13. Fear will be a thing of the past. See Lev 26:6; Jer 30:10; 46:27, which may echo Mic 2:12 where the sheep bleat nervously in the presence of men.
4:5 *walk in the name of the LORD.* Confess, love, obey and rely on the Lord. Cf. Zech 10:12.
4:6 *In that day.* The Messianic period (see v. 1; see also note on Is 2:11,17,20).
4:7 *remnant.* The people of God (see 2:12; see also note on Is 1:9).
‡4:8 *tower of the flock.* The capital city of David, the shepherd-king. Micah commonly uses shepherd language. See especially 5:4–6 where the twin activities of shepherd kings, to provide and to protect, are in force. See note at Ezek 34. *first dominion.* The kingdom of David will be restored under the Messiah.
‡4:9–13 In vv. 9–10 Micah foresees the collapse of the monarchy and the impending exile in 586 B.C. as well as the restoration beginning in 538. Verses 11–13 are a prophecy of judgment against the gloating enemies of Jerusalem. If this oracle was delivered after 701 when God saved Jerusalem from Sennacherib, then Micah's language could be understood in light of the prayer of King Hezekiah. No doubt, that event (2 Ki 19:1–19) led many to conclude that God would always "deliver" Jerusalem. The phrase "taken thee" in v. 9 is from the same root as Hezekiah's name. Relying on a new Hezekiah is futile.

And thou shalt [b]beat in pieces many
people:
[c]And I will consecrate their gain unto
the LORD,
And their substance unto [d]the Lord of
the whole earth.

The coming ruler and his reign

5 Now gather thyself in troops,
O daughter of troops:
He hath laid siege against us:
They shall [a]smite the judge of Israel
with a rod upon the cheek.
2 But thou, [a]Beth-lehem Ephratah,
Though thou be little [b]among the
[c]thousands of Judah,
Yet out of thee shall he come forth
unto me *that is* to be [d]ruler in Israel;
[e]Whose goings forth *have been* from of
old, from [1]everlasting.
3 Therefore will he give them up,
Until the time *that* [a]she which
travaileth hath brought forth:
Then [b]the remnant of his brethren shall
return unto the children of Israel.
4 And he shall stand and [a][1]feed in the
strength of the LORD,
In the majesty of the name of the LORD
his God;
And they shall abide:
For now [b]shall he be great unto the
ends of the earth.
5 And this *man* [a]shall be *the* peace,
When the Assyrian shall come into our
land:
And when he shall tread in our
palaces,
Then shall we raise against him seven
shepherds,
And eight [1]principal men.
6 And they shall [1]waste the land of
Assyria with the sword,
And the land of [a]Nimrod [2]in the
entrances thereof:
Thus shall he [b]deliver *us* from the
Assyrian,
When he cometh into our land,
And when he treadeth within our
borders.
7 And [a]the remnant of Jacob shall be in
the midst of many people
[b]As a dew from the LORD,
As the showers upon the grass,
That tarrieth not for man,
Nor waiteth for the sons of men.
8 And the remnant of Jacob shall be
among the Gentiles in the midst of
many people
As a lion among the beasts of the forest,
As a young lion among the flocks of
[1]sheep:
Who, if he go through, both treadeth
down, and teareth in pieces,
And none can deliver.
9 Thine hand shall be lift up upon thine
adversaries,
And all thine enemies shall be cut off.

Idols and weapons destroyed

10 [a]And it shall come to pass in that day,
saith the LORD,
That I will cut off thy horses out of the
midst of thee,
And I will destroy thy chariots:
11 And I will cut off the cities of thy land,
And throw down all thy strong holds:
12 And I will cut off witchcrafts out of
thine hand;
And thou shalt have no *more*
[a]soothsayers:
13 [a]Thy graven images also will I cut off,
And thy [1]standing images out of the
midst of thee;
And thou shalt [b]no more worship the
work of thine hands.
14 And I will pluck up thy groves out of
the midst of thee:
So will I destroy thy [1]cities.

4:13 [b]Dan. 2:44 [c]Is. 18:7 [d]Zech. 4:14
5:1 [a]Lam. 3:30
5:2 [1]Heb. *the days of eternity* [a]Mat. 2:6; John 7:42 [b]1 Sam. 23:23 [c]Ex. 18:25 [d]Gen. 49:10; Is. 9:6 [e]Ps. 90:2; John 1:1
5:3 [a]ch. 4:10 [b]ch. 4:7
5:4 [1]Or, *rule* [a]Is. 40:11; Ezek. 34:23 [b]Ps. 72:8; Is. 52:13; Zech. 9:10
5:5 [1]Heb. *princes of men* [a]Ps. 72:7; Is. 9:6
5:6 [1]Heb. *eat up* [2]Or, *with her own naked swords* [a]Gen. 10:8
5:6 [b]Luke 1:71
5:7 [a]ver. 3 [b]Deut. 32:2; Ps. 72:6
5:8 [1]Or, *goats*
5:10 [a]Zech. 9:10
5:12 [a]Is. 2:6
5:13 [1]Or, *statues* [a]Zech. 13:2 [b]Is. 2:8
5:14 [1]Or, *enemies*

‡4:13 *thou shalt beat in pieces many people.* When Micah promised that "the kingdom shall come to the daughter of Jerusalem" in v. 8, he preached here that the kingdom would come by force (a common prophetic emphasis).

‡5:1 Jerusalem will be besieged, and her kings will be seized and taken to Babylon (the last king, Zedekiah, was blinded; see 2 Ki 25:7). These following verses are clearly Messianic, but less obvious is the relationship to the failed kingship of Micah's era. Mighty Jerusalem bows to the village of Beth-lehem, whose coming ruler finds his strength not in military power but "in the strength of the LORD" (v. 4).

5:2 In contrast to the dire prediction of v. 1, Micah shifts to a positive note. *Ephratah.* The region in which Beth-lehem was located (see Ruth 1:2; 4:11; 1 Sam 17:12). *ruler.* Ultimately Christ, who will rule (see note on 4:8) for God the Father. *goings forth . . . from of old.* His beginnings were much earlier than His human birth (see John 8:58). *from everlasting.* Within history (cf. 2 Sam 7:12–16; Is 9:6–7; Amos 9:11), and even from eternity.

5:3 *will he give them up.* Until the Messiah is born and begins His rule. *Israel.* See note on 1:5.

‡5:4 *strength . . . majesty.* The Messiah will shepherd and rule in the strength and majesty of God the Father. See John 10 and especially vv. 24–25.

‡5:5 *the peace.* Jesus is "our peace" (Eph 2:14). In addition to freedom from war, the Hebrew word for "peace" also connotes prosperity in the OT. See notes on Is 9:6 ("Prince of Peace"); Luke 2:14. Contrast with those proclaiming false peace in 3:5. *Assyrian.* Symbolic of all the enemies of God's people in every age. See Is 11:11; Zech 10:10–11. *we.* The people of God. *seven . . . eight.* A figurative way of saying "many" (see note on Job 5:19).

5:6 *land of Nimrod.* Assyria. See Gen 10:8–11. *he.* The ruler of v. 2.

5:8 *lion.* Like the previous simile (v. 7) this pictures the inevitable progress of the people of God toward triumph over their enemies (v. 9).

‡5:10–14 In the Messianic era the people of God will not depend on weapons of war or pagan idols. The successes of His people are always achieved by dependence on Him. Much of Micah's language in this unit can be replicated in the curse section of Lev 26:21 ff. He has singled out militarism and heathenism in this unit for special condemnation.

15 And I will [a]execute vengeance in anger
and fury upon the heathen,
Such as they have not heard.

God's complaint

6 Hear ye now what the LORD saith;
Arise, contend thou [1]before the
mountains,
And let the hills hear thy voice.
2 [a]Hear ye, O mountains, [b]the LORD'S
controversy,
And ye strong foundations of the earth:
For [c]the LORD hath a controversy with
his people,
And he will plead with Israel.
3 O my people, [a]what have I done unto
thee?
And wherein have I wearied thee?
Testify against me.
4 [a]For I brought thee up out of the land
of Egypt,
And redeemed thee out of the house of
servants;
And I sent before thee Moses, Aaron,
and Miriam.
5 O my people, remember now what
[a]Balak king of Moab consulted,
And what Balaam the son of Beor
answered him;
From [b]Shittim unto Gilgal;
That *ye* may know [c]the righteousness
of the LORD.
6 Wherewith shall I come before the
LORD,
And bow myself before the high God?
Shall I come before him with burnt
offerings,
With calves [1]of a year old?
7 [a]Will the LORD be pleased with
thousands of rams,
Or with ten thousands of [b]rivers of oil?
[c]Shall I give my firstborn *for* my
transgression,
The fruit of my [1]body *for* the sin of my
soul?
8 He hath [a]shewed thee, O man, what *is*
good;
And what doth the LORD require of
thee,
But [b]to do justly, and to love mercy,
And to [1]walk humbly with thy God?

The corruption of Israel

9 The LORD'S voice crieth unto the city,
And [1]*the man of* wisdom shall see thy
name:
Hear ye the rod, and who hath
appointed it.
10 [1]Are there yet the treasures of
wickedness *in* the house of the
wicked,
And the [a][2]scant measure *that is*
abominable?
11 [1]Shall I count *them* pure with [a]the
wicked balances,
And with the bag of deceitful weights?
12 For the rich *men* thereof are full *of*
violence,
And the inhabitants thereof have
spoken lies,
And [a]their tongue *is* deceitful in their
mouth.
13 Therefore also will I [a]make *thee* sick in
smiting thee,
In making *thee* desolate because of thy
sins.
14 [a]Thou shalt eat, but not be satisfied;
And thy casting down *shall be* in the
midst of thee;
And thou shalt take hold, but shalt not
deliver;
And *that* which thou deliverest will I
give up to the sword.
15 Thou shalt [a]sow, but thou shalt not
reap;

5:15 [a]2 Thes. 1:8
6:1 [1]Or, *with*
6:2 [a]Ps. 50:1,4 [b]Hos. 12:2 [c]Is. 1:18
6:3 [a]Jer. 2:5,31
6:4 [a]Deut. 4:20
6:5 [a]Num. 22:5; Josh. 24:9 [b]Num. 25:1 [c]Judg. 5:11
6:6 [1]Heb. *sons of a year?*
6:7 [a]Ps. 50:9; Is. 1:11 [b]Job 29:6 [c]2 Ki. 16:3; Ezek. 23:37
6:7 [1]Heb. *belly*
6:8 [1]Heb. *humble* thyself *to walk* [a]Deut. 10:12; 1 Sam. 15:22 [b]Gen. 18:19; Is. 1:17
6:9 [1]Or, *thy name shall see that which is*
6:10 [1]Or, Is there *yet* unto *every man a house of the wicked, etc.* [2]Heb. *measure of leanness* [a]Amos 8:5
6:11 [1]Or, *Shall I be pure with, etc.* [a]Hos. 12:7
6:12 [a]Jer. 9:3,5
6:13 [a]Lev. 26:16; Ps. 107:17
6:14 [a]Lev. 26:26
6:15 [a]Amos 5:11

6:1–16 This chapter depicts a courtroom scene in which the Lord lodges a legal complaint against Israel. In vv. 1–2 the Lord summons the people to listen to His accusation and to prepare their defense against the charges that follow in vv. 9–16. The Lord speaks in vv. 3–5, poignantly reminding the people of His gracious acts in their behalf. In vv. 6–7 Israel is speaking, and in v. 8 Micah responds directly to the nation, answering the questions of vv. 6–7. God charges the people with specific wrongs in vv. 9–16.
6:1–2 *mountains . . . foundations of the earth.* Inanimate objects were called on as third-party witnesses because of their enduring nature and because they were witnesses to His covenant (see Deut 32:1; Josh 24:27; Is 1:2 and note).
‡6:2 *plead with.* This is legal language with the idea of disputing with Israel rather than compassionate begging. *Israel.* Primarily Judah here.
‡6:3 *my people.* Indicative of a tender rebuke (see also v. 5). *wearied . . . Testify against me.* The Lord is frequently wearied with his people (Is 1:14), but they have no reason to be wearied with him.
6:5 *Balak . . . Balaam.* See Num 22–24; see also note on Num 22:8. *Shittim unto Gilgal.* See Josh 3:1; 4:19.
6:6 The same thought is expressed in 1 Sam 15:22; Ps 51:16; Hos 6:6; Is 1:11–15 (see note there). Micah does not deny the desirability of sacrifices but shows that it does no good to offer them without obedience.
‡6:8 *O man.* The use of the singular makes the accusation personal, though Micah is speaking to all Israel (see also Deut 10:12–13). *do justly, and to love mercy.* The kind of obedience God expects from His covenant people. It is important to recognize 6:1–8 as a disputation or court conflict. The speaker in vv. 6–7 is not asking sincerely how to come to the Lord. All of his questions imply that he can, through human effort, satisfy his accuser in court. Micah's threefold response is as much condemnatory as it is invitational. Throughout his book his opponents have been characterized by various forms of arrogance or pride.
‡6:9 *city.* Jerusalem. *rod.* Indeed, calamity will come against them precisely because the Lord is just.
6:10 *measure.* About half a bushel.
‡6:11 See Prov 11:1; 20:23; Hos 12:7; See the note at Amos 8:5.
‡6:12 *inhabitants.* Of Jerusalem.
6:13 *Therefore.* See note on 2:3.

Thou shalt tread the olives, but thou shalt not anoint *thee with* oil;
And sweet wine, but shalt not drink wine.
16 For [1]the statutes of [a]Omri are [b]kept,
And all the works of the house of Ahab,
And ye walk in their counsels;
That I should make thee a [2]desolation,
And the inhabitants thereof a hissing:
Therefore ye shall bear the [c]reproach of my people.

The counsel of despair

7 Woe is me! for I am as [1]when they have gathered the summer fruits,
As [a]the grapegleanings of the vintage:
There is no cluster to eat:
[b]My soul desired the firstripe fruit.
2 The [a1]good *man* is perished out of the earth:
And *there is* none upright among men:
They all lie in wait for blood;
[b]They hunt every man his brother *with* a net.
3 That *they* may do evil with both hands earnestly,
The prince asketh, and the judge *asketh* for a reward;
And the great *man,* he uttereth [1]his mischievous desire:
So they wrap it up.
4 The best of them [a]*is* as a brier:
The *most* upright *is sharper* than a thorn hedge:
The day of thy watchmen *and* thy visitation cometh;
Now shall be their perplexity.
5 Trust ye not in a friend,
Put ye not confidence in a guide:
Keep the doors of thy mouth from her that lieth in thy bosom.
6 For [a]the son dishonoureth the father,
The daughter riseth up against her mother,
The daughter in law against her mother in law;
A man's enemies *are* the men of his own house.

6:16 [1]Or, *he doth much keep the, etc.* [2]Or, *astonishment* [a]1 Ki. 16:25 [b]Hos. 5:11 [c]Is. 25:8
7:1 [1]Heb. *the gatherings of summer* [a]Is. 17:6 [b]Is. 28:4
7:2 [1]Or, *godly,* or, *merciful* [a]Ps. 12:1; Is. 57:1 [b]Hab. 1:15
7:3 [1]Heb. *the mischief of his soul*
7:4 [a]Ezek. 2:6; Is. 55:13
7:6 [a]Mat. 10:21
7:8 [a]Prov. 24:17 [b]Ps. 37:24; Prov. 24:16
7:9 [a]Lam. 3:39
7:10 [1]Or, *And thou wilt see her* that is *mine enemy, and cover her* with *shame* [2]Heb. *she shall be for a treading down* [a]Ps. 35:26 [b]Ps. 42:3
7:12 [1]Or, *even to* [a]Is. 11:16
7:13 [1]Or, *After that it hath been* [a]Jer. 21:14
7:14 [1]Or, *Rule* [a]Ps. 28:9 [b]Is. 37:24
7:15 [a]Ps. 68:22

Trust in God's salvation

7 Therefore I will look unto the LORD;
I will wait for the God of my salvation:
My God will hear me.
8 [a]Rejoice not against me, O mine enemy:
[b]When I fall, I shall arise;
When I sit in darkness, the LORD *shall be* a light unto me.
9 [a]I will bear the indignation of the LORD, because I have sinned against him,
Until he plead my cause, and execute judgment for me:
He will bring me forth to the light, *and* I shall behold his righteousness.
10 [1]Then she *that is* mine enemy shall see *it,* and [a]shame shall cover her
Which said unto me, [b]Where is the LORD thy God?
Mine eyes shall behold her:
Now [2]shall she be trodden down as the mire of the streets.
11 *In* the day that thy walls are *to be* built,
In that day shall the decree be far removed.
12 *In* that day *also* [a]he shall come even to thee
From Assyria, [1]and *from* the fortified cities,
And from the fortress even to the river,
And from sea *to* sea, and *from* mountain *to* mountain.
13 [1]Notwithstanding the land shall be desolate because of them that dwell therein,
[a]For the fruit of their doings.
14 [a1]Feed thy people with thy rod, the flock of thine heritage,
Which dwell solitarily *in* [b]the wood, in the midst of Carmel:
Let them feed *in* Bashan and Gilead, as *in* the days of old.

God's pardon and love

15 [a]According to the days of thy coming out of the land of Egypt
Will I shew unto him marvellous *things.*

---

‡6:16 *Omri . . . Ahab.* 1 Ki 16:25,30 says that they did more evil than all the kings who preceded them. Omri emphasized militarism, internationalism, materialism and heathenism. See the important passage in Dt 17:14–20.

7:1–20 The speakers in this chapter are Micah (vv. 1–7), Zion (vv. 8–10), Micah (vv. 11–13), perhaps Zion (v. 14), God (v. 15), Micah (vv. 16–20). The chapter begins on a note of gloom but ends with a statement of hope.

‡7:1–2 Looking for the godly is like looking for summer fruit when the harvest has ended (see also Jer 8:20). *soul.* Not the immaterial part of man but his living body.

‡7:3 *That they may do evil with both hands earnestly.* Precisely the reason why God will send "evil" upon them. The punishment fits the crime.

7:4 *day . . . thy watchmen.* The day of judgment that the prophets warned about (see Jer 6:17; Ezek 3:17–21).

‡7:6 The family unit was disintegrating. Poverty is harmful to any society, but poverty because of oppressive leadership or rich land barons is such that society itself will degenerate into anarchy.

‡7:8 *me.* Zion. *mine enemy.* Other nations. *When I fall.* Micah foresees the destruction of Zion in 586 B.C. *light.* The age-old metaphor of God that was personified in "the Light of the World" (John 8:12).

7:14 *heritage.* Israel (see also v. 18; Ps 94:14).

7:15–17 It is possible that these verses constitute a prayer that God will show His wonders again as in the exodus, that the nations will see and be ashamed, and that they will turn to the Lord in fear.

16 The nations [a]shall see and be
confounded at all their might:
[b]They shall lay *their* hand upon *their*
mouth, their ears shall be deaf.
17 They shall lick the [a]dust like a serpent,
[b]They shall move out of their holes
like [1]worms of the earth:
They shall be afraid of the LORD our
God,
And shall fear because of thee.

18 [a]Who *is* a God like unto thee, that
[b]pardoneth iniquity,
And passeth by the transgression of
[c]the remnant of his heritage?
[d]He retaineth not his anger for ever,
Because he delighteth in mercy.
19 He will turn again, he will have
compassion upon us;
He will subdue our iniquities;
And thou wilt cast all their sins into
the depths of the sea.
20 [a]Thou wilt perform the truth to Jacob,
and the mercy to Abraham,
[b]Which thou hast sworn unto our
fathers from the days of old.

7:16 [a]Is. 26:11 [b]Job 21:5
7:17 [1]Or, *creeping things* [a]Ps. 72:9; Is. 49:23 [b]Ps. 18:45
7:18 [a]Ex. 15:11 [b]Ex. 34:6; Jer. 50:20
7:18 [c]ch. 4:7 [d]Ps. 103:9; Is. 57:16
7:20 [a]Luke 1:72 [b]Ps. 105:9

7:16 When the nations see God's power at the Messiah's coming, they will be amazed.
7:17 *lick the dust like a serpent.* A picture of defeat.
7:18–20 The conclusion to the whole book, not just to ch. 7.
‡7:18 *Who is a God like unto thee . . . ?* Perhaps a pun on Micah's name (see note on 1:1). Cf. Ex 15:11; Ps 89:6. The phrase also creates an "envelope" effect emphasizing the importance of God.
‡7:19 *cast all their sins into the depths of the sea.* See note on Is 38:17. God's grace is as strong as His justice. God's justice in Amos 9:3 ("though they be hid from my sight in the bottom of the sea . . . I will command the serpent") is matched with his grace in this verse.
‡7:20 *Jacob . . . Abraham.* God had sworn to Abraham (Gen 22:17) and Jacob (Gen 28:14) that their descendants would be as numerous as the dust of the earth and the sand on the seashore, and He had promised Abraham that he would be the father of many nations (Gen 17:5; cf. Luke 1:54–55). All believers are ultimately included in this promise (Rom 4; Gal 3:6–29; Heb 11:12). The transgression of Jacob (1:5) is the reason for the beginning of his book, but the faithfulness of God to his covenant is the answer to the question, "Who is a God like unto thee . . . ?" (v. 18).

Nahum

INTRODUCTION

Author

The book contains the "vision of Nahum" (1:1), whose name means "comfort" and is related to the name Nehemiah, meaning "The LORD comforts" or "comfort of the LORD." (Nineveh's fall, which is Nahum's theme, would bring comfort to Judah.) Nothing is known about him except his hometown (Elkosh), and even its general location is uncertain.

Date

In 3:8–10 the author speaks of the fall of Thebes, which happened in 663 B.C., as already past. In all three chapters Nahum prophesied Nineveh's fall, which was fulfilled in 612. Nahum therefore uttered this oracle between 663 and 612, perhaps near the end of this period since he represents the fall of Nineveh as imminent (2:1; 3:14,19). This would place him during the reign of Josiah and make him a contemporary of Zephaniah and the young Jeremiah.

Background

Assyria (represented by Nineveh, 1:1) had already destroyed Samaria (722–721 B.C.), resulting in the captivity of the northern kingdom of Israel, and posed a present threat to Judah. The Assyrians were brutally cruel, their kings often being depicted as gloating over the gruesome punishments inflicted on conquered peoples. They conducted their wars with shocking ferocity, uprooted whole populations as state policy and deported them to other parts of their empire. The leaders of conquered cities were tortured and horribly mutilated before being executed (see note on 3:3). No wonder the dread of Assyria fell on all her neighbors!

About 700 B.C. King Sennacherib made Nineveh the capital of the Assyrian empire, and it remained the capital until it was destroyed in 612. Jonah had announced its destruction earlier (Jonah 3:4), but the people repented and the destruction was temporarily averted. Not long after that, however, Nineveh reverted to its extreme wickedness, brutality and pride. The brutality reached its peak under Ashurbanipal (669–627), the last great ruler of the Assyrian empire. After his death, Assyria's influence and power waned rapidly until 612, when Nineveh was overthrown (see notes on 1:14; 2:1). (Further historical information is given in notes throughout the book.)

Recipients

Some words are addressed to Judah (see 1:12–13,15), but most are addressed to Nineveh (see 1:11,14; 2:1,13; 3:5–17,19) or its king (3:18). The book, however, was meant for Judahite readers.

Literary Style

The contents are primarily judicial (judgment oracles), with appropriate descriptions and vocabulary, as well as intense moods, sights and sounds. The language is poetic, with frequent use of metaphors and similes, vivid word pictures, repetition and many short—often staccato—phrases (see, e.g., 3:2–3). Rhetorical questions punctuate the flow of thought, which has a marked stress on moral indignation toward injustice.

Theological Themes

The focal point of the entire book is the Lord's judgment on Nineveh for her oppression, cruelty, idolatry and wickedness. The book ends with the destruction of the city.

According to Rom 11:22, God is not only kind but also stern. In Nahum, God is not only "slow to anger" (1:3) and "a strong hold . . . and he knoweth them that trust in him" (1:7), but also one who

"will not at all acquit the wicked" (1:3). God's righteous and just kingdom will ultimately triumph, for kingdoms built on wickedness and tyranny must eventually fall, as Assyria did.

In addition, Nahum declares the universal sovereignty of God. God is Lord of history and of all nations; as such He controls their destinies.

Outline

I. Title (1:1)
II. Nineveh's Judge (1:2–15)
  A. The Lord's Kindness and Sternness (1:2–8)
  B. Nineveh's Overthrow and Judah's Joy (1:9–15)
III. Nineveh's Judgment (ch. 2)
  A. Nineveh Besieged (2:1–10)
  B. Nineveh's Desolation Contrasted with Her Former Glory (2:11–13)
IV. Nineveh's Total Destruction (ch. 3)
  A. Nineveh's Sins (3:1–4)
  B. Nineveh's Doom (3:5–19)

God's vengeance and goodness

1 The burden [a]of Nineveh. The book of the vision of Nahum the Elkoshite.
2 [1]God *is* [a]jealous, and the LORD revengeth;
The LORD revengeth, and [2]*is* furious;
The LORD will take vengeance on his adversaries,
And he reserveth *wrath* for his enemies.
3 The LORD *is* [a]slow to anger, and [b]great in power,
And will not at all acquit *the wicked:*
[c]The LORD *hath* his way in the whirlwind and in the storm,
And the clouds *are* the dust of his feet.
4 [a]He rebuketh the sea, and maketh it dry,
And drieth up all the rivers:
[b]Bashan languisheth, and Carmel,
And the flower of Lebanon languisheth.
5 The mountains quake at him, and the hills melt,
And the earth is burnt at his presence,
Yea, the world, and all that dwell therein.
6 Who can stand before his indignation?
And [a]who can [1]abide in the fierceness of his anger?
His fury is poured out like fire,
And the rocks are thrown down by him.
7 [a]The LORD *is* good, a [1]strong hold in the day of trouble;
And he knoweth them that trust in him.
8 But with an overrunning flood he will make an utter end of the place thereof,
And darkness shall pursue his enemies.
9 [a]What do ye imagine against the LORD?
[b]He *will* make an utter end:
Affliction shall not rise up the second time.
10 For while *they be* folden together [a]*as* thorns,
[b]And while they be drunken *as* drunkards,
[c]They shall be devoured as stubble fully dry.
11 There is *one* come out of thee, that imagineth evil against the LORD,
[1]A wicked counseller.
12 Thus saith the LORD;
[1]Though *they be* quiet, and likewise many,
Yet thus shall they be [2]cut down, when he shall pass through.
Though I have afflicted thee, I will afflict thee no more.
13 For now will I break his yoke from off thee,
And will burst thy bonds in sunder.
14 And the LORD hath given a commandment concerning thee,
That no more of thy name be sown:
Out of the house of thy gods will I cut off the graven image and the molten image:
I will make thy grave; for thou art vile.

1:1 [a]Zeph. 2:13
1:2 [1]Or, *The* LORD is *a jealous God, and a revenger, etc.* [2]Heb. *that hath fury* [a]Ex. 20:5; Deut. 4:24; Josh. 24:19
1:3 [a]Ex. 34:6,7; Neh. 9:17 [b]Job 9:4 [c]Ps. 18:7
1:4 [a]Mat. 8:26 [b]Is. 33:9
1:6 [1]Heb. *stand up* [a]Mal. 3:2
1:7 [1]Or, *strength* [a]Jer. 33:11
1:9 [a]Ps. 2:1 [b]1 Sam. 3:12
1:10 [a]2 Sam. 23:6 [b]ch. 3:11 [c]Mal. 4:1
1:11 [1]Heb. *a counseller of Belial*
1:12 [1]Or, *If* they would have been *at peace, so* should they have been *many, and so should they have been shorn, and he should have passed away* [2]Heb. *shorn*

1:1 The title of the book. *burden.* See note on Is 13:1. *Nineveh.* See Introduction: Background; see also notes on Jonah 1:2; 3:3. Here the capital city stands for the entire Assyrian empire. *vision.* See note on Is 1:1. *Nahum the Elkoshite.* See Introduction: Author.
1:2–3 The covenant name Yahweh ("the LORD") is emphasized.
1:2 *jealous.* See note on Ex 20:5. *revengeth . . revengeth . . . . vengeance.* God acts justly in judgment toward all who oppose Him and His kingdom. The repetition is for emphasis.
‡1:3 *the wicked.* Such as Nineveh. This idea is the necessary counterpart to Mic 7:18–20. God's compassion tempers His judgment of sin but not in such as way as to leave Assyria's gross sin unpunished. *whirlwind . . . storm . . . clouds.* See notes on Ps 18:7–15; 68:4; 77:16–19; 104:3–4.
1:4 *rebuketh the sea, and maketh it dry.* As at the crossing of the Red sea (Ex 14). *drieth up all the rivers.* As at the crossing of the Jordan (Josh 3). *Bashan . . . Carmel . . . Lebanon.* See notes on Sol 7:5; Is 2:13; 33:9; 35:2; Amos 4:1. These three places were noted for their fertility, vineyards and trees, but at the Lord's word they wither.
‡1:5 *mountains . . . hills . . . earth . . . world.* Emblems of stability and permanence. *hills melt.* The great day of the Lord. See Amos 9:13; Mic 1:4.
1:6 *Who can stand . . . ? who can abide . . . ?* Rhetorical questions. If mountains quake before the Lord (v. 5), what human being can think that he is not vulnerable? Cf. Rom 2:3–5.
1:7 *them that trust in him.* Such as Judah.
1:8 *overruning flood.* Symbolic of an invading army (see Is 8:7–8). *end . . . darkness.* In 612 B.C. that end came for Nineveh, and the darkness enveloped her. Through the ministry of Jonah, Nineveh had formerly experienced the light of God. But she later rejected it, and the result was the darkness of judgment.
‡1:9 *ye imagine.* See note on v. 11. *Affliction shall not rise up the second time.* This statement only means that Assyria will not do exactly to Judah what it did to Samaria in 722 B.C. In fact, in 701, Sennacherib succeeded in destroying 46 walled cities and carried over 200,000 Judahites into captivity. God, however, chose to spare Judah complete captivity due to the blasphemy of the Rab-shakeh; see 2 Ki 18:13–19:37; Is 36–37).
1:10 *drunken as drunkards.* See 3:11 and note.
‡1:11 *that imagineth evil.* Possibly the Assyrian king Ashurbanipal (669–627 B.C.), the last great Assyrian king, whose western expeditions succeeded in subduing Egypt and to whom King Manasseh had to submit as a vassal (see 2 Chr 33:11–13). For the same verb, see Mic 2:1. *counseller.* See Mic 4:9.
1:12 *they.* The Assyrians. *I have afflicted thee.* God had used Assyria as the rod of His anger against His covenant-breaking people in the days of Ahaz (Is 10:5) and again in the time of Manasseh.
1:13 *will I break his yoke.* Judah was Assyria's vassal; that yoke would be broken.
1:14 *I will make thy grave.* God used the Babylonians, the Medes and the Scythians to dig Nineveh's grave in 612 B.C. For the fulfillment of this prophecy see Ezek 32:22–23.

15 Behold upon the mountains the feet of
him that bringeth good tidings, that
publisheth peace.
O Judah, [1]keep thy solemn feasts,
perform thy vows:
For [2]the wicked shall no more pass
through thee;
He is utterly cut off.

The siege of Nineveh

2 [1]He that dasheth in pieces is come up
before thy face:
Keep the munition, watch the way,
make *thy* loins strong, fortify *thy*
power mightily.
2 For the LORD hath turned *away* [1]the
excellency of Jacob,
As the excellency of Israel:
For the emptiers have emptied them
out,
And marred their vine branches.
3 The shield of his mighty *men is* made
red,
The valiant men *are* [1]in scarlet:
The chariots *shall be* with [2]flaming
torches in the day of his preparation,
And the fir trees shall be terribly
shaken.
4 The chariots shall rage in the streets,
They shall justle one against another in
the broad ways:
[1]They shall seem like torches,
They shall run like the lightnings.
5 He shall recount his [1]worthies:
They shall stumble in their walk;
They shall make haste *to* the wall
thereof,
And the [2]defence shall be prepared.
6 The gates of the rivers shall be opened,
And the palace shall be [1]dissolved.
7 And [1]Huzzab shall be [2]led away
captive, she shall be brought up,
And her maids *shall* lead *her* as *with*
the voice of doves,
Tabring upon their breasts.
8 But Nineveh *is* [1]of old like a pool of
water:
Yet they *shall* flee away.
Stand, stand, *shall they cry;* but none
shall [2]look back.
9 Take ye the spoil of silver, take the
spoil of gold:
[1]For *there is* none end of the store *and*
glory out of all the [2]pleasant
furniture.
10 She *is* empty, and void, and waste:
And the heart melteth, and the knees
smite together,
And much pain *is* in all loins,
And the faces of them all gather
blackness.
11 Where *is* the dwelling of the lions,
And the feeding place of the young
lions,
Where the lion, *even* the old lion,
walked,

1:15 [1]Heb. *feast* [2]Heb. *Belial*
2:1 [1]Or, *The disperser,* or, *hammer*
2:2 [1]Or, *the pride of Jacob as the pride of Israel*
2:3 [1]Or, *dyed scarlet* [2]Or, *fiery torches*
2:4 [1]Heb. *Their show*
2:5 [1]Or, *gallants* [2]Heb. *covering,* or, *coverer*
2:6 [1]Or, *molten*
2:7 [1]Or, *that which was established,* or, *there was a stand made* [2]Or, *discovered*
2:8 [1]Or, *from the days* that *she* hath been [2]Or, *cause them to turn*
2:9 [1]Or, *And their infinite store, etc.* [2]Heb. *vessels of desire*

1:15 *mountains.* Of Jerusalem and Judah. *feet of him that bringeth good tidings.* This verse sets forth a principle that is applicable in several contexts of deliverance. Here the reference is to the good news of deliverance from the Assyrian threat; in Is 52:7, deliverance from Babylonian exile; in Rom 10:15, deliverance from sin through the gospel ("good news") of Christ. *keep thy solemn feasts.* In the joy of your deliverance. *perform thy vows.* Those you uttered in the time of distress (see note on Ps 7:17). *For the wicked shall no more pass through thee.* The Assyrian invasion in the days of Manasseh was the last. *wicked.* See note on Deut 13:13. *utterly cut off.* Fulfilled in 612 when Nineveh fell (see note on v. 14).

2:1 *He that dasheth.* Refers to the alliance of the Babylonians, the Medes and the Scythians—particularly the Medes under Cyaxares and the Babylonians under Nabopolassar. *Keep the munition . . . fortify thy power mightily*. Probably irony, touched with sarcasm. *way.* By which the enemies will come.

2:2 *LORD hath turned away the excellency of Jacob . . . Israel.* The whole nation will be restored and united again.

‡2:3 *his mighty men.* Those of the attacker (v. 1), or perhaps those of Nineveh itself. *red.* Either (1) the color of the shields, or (2) a reference to blood on them, or (3) the result of the reflection of the sun shining on them. *shall be terribly shaken.* The probable idea is that the branches are ready to be used as weapons such as spears.

2:4 *chariots . . . justle.* Refers to either (1) the Assyrian war chariots and their unprecedented speed as the Assyrians take frantic but vain steps to defend themselves, or (2) the chariots of Nineveh's invaders.

2:5 *He.* Perhaps the king of Assyria, though Nabopolassar is equally possible (see note on v. 1). *wall.* A moat 150 feet wide had to be filled in before reaching Nineveh's wall, which was almost 8 miles long with 15 gates. Then battering rams were moved up. *the defence.* A defensive framework covered with hides to deflect stones and arrows.

2:6 *gates of the rivers.* Perhaps the dams on the Khoser River, which ran through the city to the Tigris River. They were either already in place, or quickly built, to back up the river water, then suddenly released so the flood would damage the walls. *palace shall be dissolved.* One ancient historian (the author of the *Babylonian Chronicles*) speaks of a flood that washed away some of the wall, making it easier for the invaders to enter the city.

2:7 *her maids.* Possibly temple prostitutes, whose places of business and idols were being destroyed.

2:8 *like a pool . . . flee away.* Some think that this refers to the Tigris and the smaller rivers encircling and running through parts of the city, and to a system of dams to make the city more impenetrable. Others take the language less literally as a reference to Nineveh's people fleeing, like water draining from a pool.

2:9 The cry of the invaders.

2:10 *She is empty . . . void, and waste.* The Hebrew for all three words is similar. The *Babylonian Chronicles* confirms the fact that a great quantity of plunder was carried off by the invaders. *the heart melteth.* The powerful, insolent Ninevites become helpless with fear.

2:11–13 Nahum ironically contrasts the devastated and desolate city of Nineveh with its former glory and power, expressed in figurative terms.

‡2:11 *the lion . . . the old lion.* Nahum references "lions" 10 times in vv. 11–13 using 4 differing Hebrew words. Cf. Is 5:29; Jer 4:7; Hos 5:14; Mic 5:8. The lion is an appropriate image to apply to Assyria because of the rapacious ways of the Assyrian monarchs and because Nineveh contained numerous lion sculptures.

And the lion's whelp, and none made
them afraid?
12 The lion did tear in pieces enough for
his whelps,
And strangled for his lionesses,
And filled his holes *with* prey,
And his dens *with* ravin.
13 Behold, I *am* against thee, saith the
LORD of hosts,
And I will burn her chariots in the
smoke,
And the sword shall devour thy young
lions:
And I will cut off thy prey from the
earth,
And the voice of thy messengers shall
no more be heard.

The sure destruction

3 Woe to the [1]bloody city!
It *is* all full *of* lies *and* robbery;
The prey departeth not;
2 The noise of a whip, and the noise of
the rattling of the wheels,
And of the pransing horses, and of the
jumping chariots.
3 The horseman lifteth up both [1]the
bright sword and the glittering spear:
And *there is* a multitude of slain, and a
great number of carcases;
And *there is* none end of *their* corpses;
they stumble upon their corpses:
4 Because of the multitude of the
whoredoms of the wellfavoured
harlot,
[a]The mistress of witchcrafts,
That selleth nations through her
whoredoms,
And families through her witchcrafts.
5 [a]Behold, I *am* against thee, saith the
LORD of hosts;
And [b]I will discover thy skirts upon thy
face,
And I will shew the nations thy
nakedness,
And the kingdoms thy shame.
6 And I will cast abominable filth upon
thee, and make thee vile,
And will set thee as [a]a gazing-stock.
7 And it shall come to pass, *that* all they
that look upon thee [a]shall flee from
thee, and say,
Nineveh is laid waste: [b]who will
bemoan her?
Whence shall I seek comforters for
thee?
8 [a]Art thou better than [1 2]populous [b]No,
That was situate among the rivers, *that*
had the waters round about it,
Whose rampart *was* the sea, *and* her
wall *was* from the sea?
9 Ethiopia and Egypt *were* her strength,
and *it was* infinite;
Put and Lubim were [1]thy helpers.
10 Yet *was* she carried away, she went
into captivity:
[a]Her young children also were dashed
in pieces [b]at the top of all the
streets:
And they [c]cast lots for her honourable
men,
And all her great *men* were bound in
chains.
11 Thou also shalt be [a]drunken: thou shalt
be hid,
Thou also shalt seek strength because
of the enemy.
12 All thy strong holds *shall be like* [a]fig
trees with the firstripe figs:
If they be shaken, they shall even fall
into the mouth of the eater.
13 Behold, [a]thy people in the midst of
thee *are* women:
The gates of thy land shall be set wide
open unto thine enemies:
The fire shall devour thy [b]bars.

3:1 [1]Heb. *city of bloods*
3:3 [1]Heb. *the flame of the sword, and the lightning of the spear*
3:4 [a]Is. 47:9,12
3:5 [a]ch. 2:13 [b]Is. 47:2,3
3:6 [a]Heb. 10:33
3:7 [a]Rev. 18:10 [b]Jer. 15:5
3:8 [1]Or, *nourishing* [2]Heb. *No Amon* [a]Amos 6:2 [b]Jer. 46:25
3:9 [1]Heb. *in thy help*
3:10 [a]Ps. 137:9; Is. 13:16; Hos. 13:16 [b]Lam. 2:19 [c]Joel 3:3; Obad. 11
3:11 [a]Jer. 25:17; ch. 1:10
3:12 [a]Rev. 6:13
3:13 [a]Jer. 50:37 [b]Ps. 147:13; Jer. 51:30

2:12 *filled his holes with prey.* Nineveh was filled with the spoils of war from many conquered nations.

2:13 *I will burn.* Nineveh's fall will not be caused by merely natural forces or the superior power of her attackers; it will be an act of God. Nineveh had been put on trial, found guilty and sentenced to destruction. *voice of thy messengers . . . no more be heard.* History has confirmed this prediction.

‡3:1 *bloody city!* Nineveh's bloody massacres of her conquered rivals were well known. *prey departeth not.* The Assyrians were noted for their ruthlessness, brutality and terrible atrocities. Many of their victims were beheaded, impaled, burned or skinned alive.

3:3 *great number of carcases.* The Assyrian king Shalmaneser III boasted of erecting a pyramid of chopped-off heads in front of an enemy's city. Other Assyrian kings stacked corpses like cordwood by the gates of defeated cities. Nahum's description of the cruel Assyrians is apropos.

3:4 *harlot.* Probably a reference to the chief love goddess of Nineveh and, by extension, to the city as a whole. The lure of luxury and wealth brought multitudes to Nineveh. *witchcrafts . . . witchcrafts.* See Deut 18:10.

3:5 *I will discover thy skirts upon thy face.* The punishment of prostitutes and adulteresses.

3:6 Nineveh will be humiliated.

3:7 *who . . . ? Whence. . . ?* Rhetorical questions. Nineveh will receive no sympathy.

‡3:8 *No.* Hebrew name for Thebes. See KJV marg. *No-amon* is the more common spelling and means "city of (the god) Amon." Thebes was the great capital of Upper Egypt. Its site is occupied today by the towns of Luxor and Karnak. It was destroyed by the Assyrians in 663 B.C.

3:9 *Put.* A neighbor of Egypt, but its location is uncertain.

3:10 *her great men were bound in chains.* Assyrian kings often did this; e.g., King Ashurbanipal gave this description of his treatment of a captured leader: "I . . . put a dog chain on him and made him occupy a kennel at the eastern gate of Nineveh."

3:11 *shalt be drunken.* Probably from the cup of God's wrath.

3:12 *fig trees with the firstripe figs.* A metaphor for the eagerness with which the victors gather the rich loot of Nineveh. *they shall even fall into the mouth of the eater.* Nineveh's fortresses will finally fall just as easily.

3:13 *thy people . . . are women.* They are weak and unable to stand against the invading armies.

14 Draw thee waters for the siege, [a]fortify
thy strong holds:
Go into clay, and tread the morter,
make strong the brickkiln.
15 There shall the fire devour thee;
The sword shall cut thee off,
It shall eat thee up like [a]the
cankerworm:
Make thyself many as the cankerworm,
Make thyself many as the locusts.
16 Thou hast multiplied thy merchants
above the stars of heaven:
The cankerworm [1]spoileth, and flieth
away.
17 [a]Thy crowned *are* as the locusts, and
thy captains as the great
grasshoppers,
Which camp in the hedges in the cold
day,
But when the sun ariseth they flee away,
And their place is not known where
they *are*.
18 [a]Thy shepherds slumber, [b]O king of
Assyria: thy [1]nobles shall dwell *in
the dust:*
Thy people is [c]scattered upon the
mountains, and no man gathereth
them.
19 *There is* no [1]healing of thy bruise; [a]thy
wound *is* grievous:
[b]All that hear the bruit of thee shall
clap the hands over thee:
For upon whom hath not thy
wickedness passed continually?

3:14 [a]ch. 2:1
3:15 [a]Joel 1:4
3:16 [1]Or, *spreadeth himself*
3:17 [a]Rev. 9:7
3:18 [1]Or, *valiant ones* [a]Ex. 15:16; Ps. 76:6 [b]Jer. 50:18; Ezek. 31:3 [c]1 Ki. 22:17
3:19 [1]Heb. *wrinkling* [a]Mic. 1:9 [b]Lam. 2:15; Zeph. 2:15

3:14 *Draw . . . waters.* A normal preparation for siege. *fortify thy strong holds.* Irony, the point being that it will do no good (see note on 2:1).

3:15 *There.* Inside your strong fortifications. *fire devour thee.* Confirmed by history and archaeology. Assyria's king died in the flames of his palace.

3:16 *thy merchants above the stars of heaven.* Speaks of Assyria's vast trading and commercial enterprises. *cankerworm spoileth.* In the time of Nineveh's adversity the merchants stripped the land of its treasures, and the trade network was destroyed.

3:17 *locusts.* Feared by the farmers of the ancient Near East, because they came in huge swarms and devoured everything in their path. Their activity provided an apt simile for the exploitative actions of Nineveh's officials during her destruction. *place is not known.* Thus will Nineveh's officials disappear, without a trace. Interestingly, for centuries no one knew where Nineveh itself lay buried; in 1845 it was finally uncovered by archaeologists.

‡3:18 *shepherds.* Leaders. *slumber.* Die. *O king.* The reigning king at the time of Nineveh's fall was Sin-shar-ishkun; so these words are prophetically addressed to him. *people is scattered.* "Scattered" is an unusual word appearing only here, but the idea of sheep scattered on the mountains without a shepherd is ancient, common and enduring into the New Testament (see Mt 26:31; Mk 14:27). The age-old scene of refugees fleeing a place of destruction is repeated at Nineveh.

‡3:19 *Your wound is grievous* ("incurable"). See Mic 1:9. Micah and Nahum share the major theme of the day of the Lord, but for Micah it was Judah while for Nahum it would be Assyria. Nineveh was so totally destroyed that it was never rebuilt, and within a few centuries it was covered with windblown sand. So that "great city" (Jonah 1:2; cf. 3:2) fell in 612 B.C., never to rise again—all in fulfillment of God's word through His prophet Nahum. It is significant that the last phrase in Nahum is "thy wickness . . ." God will by no means leave such behavior unpunished.

Habakkuk

INTRODUCTION

Author

Little is known about Habakkuk except that he was a contemporary of Jeremiah and a man of vigorous faith rooted deeply in the religious traditions of Israel. The account of his ministering to the needs of Daniel in the lions' den in the Apocryphal book *Bel and the Dragon* is legendary rather than historical.

Date

The prediction of the coming Babylonian invasion (1:6) indicates that Habakkuk lived in Judah toward the end of Josiah's reign (640–609 B.C.) or at the beginning of Jehoiakim's (609–598). The prophecy is generally dated a little before or after the battle of Carchemish (605), when Egyptian forces, who had earlier gone to the aid of the last Assyrian king, were routed by the Babylonians under Nabopolassar and Nebuchadnezzar and were pursued as far as the Egyptian border (Jer 46). Habakkuk, like Jeremiah, probably lived to see the initial fulfillment of his prophecy when Jerusalem was attacked by the Babylonians in 597.

Message

Among the prophetic writings, Habakkuk is somewhat unique in that it includes no oracle addressed to Israel. It contains, rather, a dialogue between the prophet and God (see Outline). (The book of Jonah, while narrative, presents an account of conflict between the Lord and one of his prophets.) In the first two chapters, Habakkuk argues with God over His ways that appear to Him unfathomable, if not unjust. Having received replies, he responds with a beautiful confession of faith (ch. 3).

This account of wrestling with God is, however, not just a fragment from a private journal that has somehow entered the public domain. It was composed for Israel. No doubt it represented the voice of the godly in Judah, struggling to comprehend the ways of God. God's answers therefore spoke to all who shared Habakkuk's troubled doubts. And Habakkuk's confession became a public expression—as indicated by its liturgical notations (see note on 3:1).

Habakkuk was perplexed that wickedness, strife and oppression were rampant in Judah but God seemingly did nothing. When told that the Lord was preparing to do something about it through the fierce Babylonians (1:6), his perplexity only intensified: How could God, who is "of purer eyes than to behold evil [with approval]" (1:13), "establish them for correction" (1:12) "when the wicked devoureth the man that is more righteous than he" (1:13)?

God makes it clear, however, that eventually the corrupt destroyer will itself be destroyed. In the end, Habakkuk learns to rest in God's appointments and await his working in a spirit of worship.

Literary Features

The author wrote clearly and with great feeling, and penned many memorable phrases (2:2,4,14,20; 3:2,17–19). The book was popular during the intertestamental period; a complete commentary on its first two chapters has been found among the Dead Sea Scrolls (see essay, p. 1344–1346).

Outline

I. Title (1:1)
II. Habakkuk's First Complaint: Why does the evil in Judah go unpunished? (1:2–4)
III. God's Answer: The Babylonians will punish Judah (1:5–11)
IV. Habakkuk's Second Complaint: How can a just God use wicked Babylon to punish a people more righteous than themselves? (1:12—2:1)
V. God's Answer: Babylon will be punished, and faith will be rewarded (2:2–20)
VI. Habakkuk's Prayer: After asking for manifestations of God's wrath and mercy (as he has seen in the past), he closes with a confession of trust and joy in God (ch. 3)

Wrong judgment prevails

1 The burden which Habakkuk the prophet did see.

2 O LORD, how long shall I cry, [a]and thou
wilt not hear?
Even cry out unto thee *of* violence, and
thou wilt not save?
3 Why dost thou shew me iniquity, and
cause *me* to behold grievance?
For spoiling and violence *are* before
me:
And there are *that* raise up strife and
contention.
4 Therefore the law is slacked, and
judgment doth never go forth:
For the [a]wicked doth compass about
the righteous;
Therefore [1]wrong judgment
proceedeth.

Punishment by the Chaldeans

5 [a]Behold ye among the heathen, and
regard, and wonder marvellously:
For *I will* work a work in your days,
Which ye will not believe, though it be
told *you.*
6 For lo, [1]I raise up the Chaldeans, *that*
bitter and hasty nation,
Which *shall* march through the
[2]breadth of the land,
To possess the dwelling places *that are*
not theirs.
7 They *are* terrible and dreadful:
[1]Their judgment and their dignity shall
proceed of themselves.
8 Their horses also are swifter than the
leopards,
And are more [1]fierce than the evening
wolves:
And their horsemen shall spread
themselves,
And their horsemen shall come from far;
They shall fly as the eagle *that* hasteth
to eat.
9 They shall come all for violence:
[1 2]Their faces shall sup up *as* the east
wind,
And they shall gather the captivity as
the sand.
10 And they shall scoff at the kings,
And the princes *shall be* a scorn unto
them:
They shall deride every strong hold;
For they shall heap dust, and take it.
11 Then shall *his* mind change, and he
shall pass over, and offend,
[a]*Imputing* this his power unto his god.

The wicked destroy the righteous

12 *Art* thou not from everlasting,
O LORD my God, mine Holy One? we
shall not die.
O LORD, [a]thou hast ordained them for
judgment;
And, O [1]mighty God, thou hast
[2]established them for correction.
13 *Thou art* of purer eyes than to behold
evil,
And canst not look on [1]iniquity:
Wherefore lookest thou upon them
that deal treacherously,
And holdest thy tongue when the
wicked devoureth *the man that is*
more righteous than he?

1:2 [a]Lam. 3:8
1:4 [1]Or, *wrested* [a]Jer. 12:1
1:5 [a]Is. 29:14
1:6 [1][Fulfilled, 2 Chr. 36:6] [2]Heb. *breadths*
1:7 [1]Or, *From them shall proceed the judgment of these, and the captivity of these*
1:8 [1]Heb. *sharp*
1:9 [1]Or, *The supping up of their faces, etc.* Or, *Their faces shall look toward the east* [2]Heb. *The opposition of their faces toward the east*
1:11 [a]Dan. 5:4
1:12 [1]Heb. *rock* [2]Heb. *founded* [a]Is. 10:5-7
1:13 [1]Or, *grievance*

‡1:1 *burden.* Or "oracle," such as the two found here (vv. 5–11; 2:2–20). Oracles were frequently received in visions. The Hebrew word for "burden" or "pronouncement" often refers to revelations containing warnings of impending doom (cf. Is 15:1; 19:1; 22:1, and especially Nah 1:1), but in Zech 9:1; 12:1; Mal 1:1 it refers to messages that also contain hope. *Habakkuk.* The name is probably Babylonian and refers to a kind of garden plant. *prophet.* Habakkuk is called a prophet also in 3:1, tying ch. 3 closely to chs. 1–2. See note on Ex 7:1–2.

1:2–2:20 A dialogue between the prophet and God. The basic theme is age-old: Why does evil seem to go unpunished? Why does God not respond to prayer?

‡1:2 *violence.* Vv. 2–4 virtually groan with painful words like this one. At this time Judah was probably under King Jehoiakim, who was ambitious, cruel and corrupt. Habakkuk describes the social corruption and spiritual apostasy of Judah in the late seventh century B.C.

1:3 *cause me to behold grievance.* See v. 13. The prophet was amazed that God seemed to condone cruelty and violence.

1:4 *law is slacked . . . judgment doth never go forth.* Because wealthy landowners controlled the courts through bribery.

‡1:5 *will not believe.* To the people of Judah it was incredible that God would give them over to the arrogant Babylonians. The phrase identifies the human condition: willful disbelief that God will do anything. See Mic 3:11; Zeph 1:12.

1:6 The apostate nation of Judah is to be punished by an invasion of the Babylonians, a powerful people who regained their independence from Assyria in 626 B.C., destroyed Assyrian power completely in 612–605, and flourished until 539. In this context, the Chaldeans are synonymous with the newly resurgent Babylonians. *possess the dwelling places.* See 2:6–8.

1:7 *Their judgment and their dignity shall proceed of themselves.* A mark of arrogance.

‡1:8 The speed with which Babylon conquered her enemies had become proverbial. Habakkuk's vocabulary and ingenuity in using analogy is these verses is energetic, vivid and effective. He establishes his own identity within the prophetic community with his unique, descriptive words.

‡1:9 *gather the captivity as the sand.* Only Habakkuk uses this analogy. Like their Assyrian predecessors, the Babylonians deported conquered peoples as a matter of deliberate national policy (see 2:5).

1:10 *shall heap dust.* Or, "build earthen ramps," a siege method.

1:11 *Imputing this his power unto his god.* The Babylonians were so proud and confident of their military might that it had virtually become their god (see v. 16).

1:12 Habakkuk cannot see the justice in Judah's being punished by an even more wicked nation, and thinks that the Babylonians surely would not be allowed to conquer Judah completely. *from everlasting.* See Ps 90:2. *thou hast ordained them.* The prophet recognizes Babylon as God's agent of judgment (cf. Is 7:18–20; 44:28–45:1).

1:13 A classic statement of the problem of evil within the context of Israel's faith: Why does evil appear to flourish unchecked by a just and holy God? *treacherously . . . wicked.* The Babylonians. *the man that is more righteous than he.* Judah.

14 And makest men as the fishes of the sea,
As the [1]creeping things, *that have* no ruler over them?
15 They take up all of them with the angle,
They catch them in their net, and gather them in their [1]drag:
Therefore they rejoice and are glad.
16 Therefore [a]they sacrifice unto their net, and burn incense unto their drag;
Because by them their portion *is* fat, and their meat [1][2]plenteous.
17 Shall they therefore empty their net,
And not spare continually to slay the nations?

Life to the just

2 I will [a]stand upon my watch, and set me upon the [1]tower,
And will watch to see what he will say [2]unto me,
And what I shall answer [3][4]when I am reproved.

2 And the LORD answered me, and said,
[a]Write the vision, and make *it* plain upon tables,
That he may run that readeth it.
3 For [a]the vision *is* yet for an appointed time,
But at the end it shall speak, and not lie:
Though it tarry, wait for it;
Because it will [b]surely come, it will not tarry.

1:14 [1]Or, *moving*
1:15 [1]Or, *flue net*
1:16 [1]Or, *dainty* [2]Heb. *fat* [a]Deut. 8:17
2:1 [1]Heb. *fenced place* [2]Or, *in me* [3]Or, *when I am argued with* [4]Heb. *upon my reproof,* or, *arguing* [a]Is. 21:8,11
2:2 [a]Is. 8:1
2:3 [a]Dan. 10:14 [b]Heb. 10:37
2:4 [a]John 3:36
2:5 [1]Or, *How much more*
2:6 [1]Or, *Ho, he*
2:8 [1]Heb. *bloods* [a]Is. 33:1

4 Behold, his soul *which* is lifted up is not upright in him:
But the [a]just shall live by his faith.
5 [1]Yea also, because he transgresseth *by* wine,
He is a proud man, neither keepeth at home,
Who enlargeth his desire as hell,
And *is* as death, and cannot be satisfied,
But gathereth unto him all nations,
And heapeth unto him all people:

Woe to the unrighteous

6 Shall not all these take up a parable against him,
And a taunting proverb against him, and say,

[1]Woe to him that increaseth *that which is* not his! how long?
And to him that ladeth himself with thick clay!
7 Shall they not rise up suddenly that *shall* bite thee,
And awake that *shall* vex thee,
And thou shalt be for booties unto them?
8 [a]Because thou hast spoiled many nations,
All the remnant of the people shall spoil thee;
Because of men's [1]blood, and *for* the violence of the land,
Of the city, and *of* all that dwell therein.

---

‡**1:15** *angle.* A fish hook. See note on Amos 4:2. *they catch them in their net.* Babylon's victims are as powerless as fish swimming into a net. Mesopotamian reliefs portray, in symbolic fashion, conquering rulers capturing the enemy in fishnets. Just as a net captures many kinds of fish, so Babylon would conquer many nations. The repetition of "net" reflects Habakkuk's agitated state.

‡**1:16** See note on v. 11. Their violent behavior is bad enough, but their pagan faith simply defies understanding to the believing Habakkuk. Honesty is the measure of any true relationship, and Habakkuk has been honest with his Lord. His words are not words of *un*belief; rather, they are words of *dis*belief. He cannot understand why God would use the cruel Babylonians.

‡**2:1** *I will stand upon my watch.* The figure of a guard looking out from a tower and expecting a response to his challenge. Any reproof would be for questioning God's justice. *tower.* The walls of Jerusalem. Having vented his frustration, he affirms his personal belief in God. This kind of affirmation in the OT often springs forth from lament.

2:2–3 *vision.* See 1 Chr 17:15; Prov 29:18. The Hebrew for this word refers specifically to a prophet's vision (see, e.g., Is 1:1).

2:2 *That he may run that readeth it.* So that a messenger may run to deliver the message and read it to those to whom he has been sent.

2:3 *wait for it.* The following message deals with the fall of Babylon in 539 B.C., about 66 years after Habakkuk's prophecy. The Lord tells Habakkuk (and Judah) that fulfillment of the prophecy may "tarry," but that he and the people are to expect it (see 3:16).

‡**2:4** *lifted up.* Collective for the Babylonians, but with special reference to their king. *But.* In contrast to the Babylonians, whose desires are not upright. *the just shall live by his faith.* See Is 26, especially vv. 1–6. In light of God's revelation about how (and when) He is working, His people are to wait patiently and live by faith—trusting in their sovereign God. The clause is quoted frequently in the NT to support the teaching that people are saved by grace through faith (Rom 1:17; Gal 3:11; cf. Eph 2:8) and should live by faith (Heb 10:38–39). It became the rallying cry of the Protestant Reformation in the 16th century. The same principle that was applicable in the realm of national deliverance is applicable in the area of spiritual deliverance (salvation).

‡**2:5** *enlargeth his desire as hell.* The Hebrew for "hell" here is *Sheol*, meaning "grave." The grave never says, "Enough" (Prov 30:15–16; see note on Ps 49:14).

2:6–20 This taunt falls into two halves of ten (Hebrew) lines each (vv. 6–14 and vv. 15–20), each half concluding with a significant theological statement (vv. 14,20). Together these two statements set the five "woes" pronounced against Babylon (vv. 6,9,12,15,19; cf. Is 5:8–23; Mat 23:13–32; Luke 6:24–26; Rev 9:12; 11:14) in a larger frame of reference.

2:6 *all these . . . against him.* The threatened victims of the Babylonian onslaught, especially Judah, will taunt ruthless Babylon. *Woe.* The Babylonians' greed for conquest is condemned.

‡**2:8** *men's blood.* See v. 17. Therefore Babylon's blood would be shed (see note on Gen 9:6). See Ob 15.

9 Woe to him that [1]coveteth an evil
covetousness to his house,
That *he* may [a]set his nest on high, that
he may be delivered from the
[2]power of evil!
10 Thou hast consulted shame to thy
house
By cutting off many people,
And *hast* sinned *against* thy soul.
11 For the stone shall cry out of the wall,
And the [1]beam out of the timber shall
[2]answer it.

12 Woe to him that buildeth a town with
[1]blood,
And stablisheth a city by iniquity!
13 Behold, *is it* not of the LORD of hosts
That the people shall labour in the very
fire,
And the people shall weary themselves
[1]for very vanity?
14 For the earth shall be filled [1]with the
knowledge of the glory of the LORD,
As the waters cover the sea.

15 Woe unto him that giveth his
neighbour drink,
That puttest thy [a]bottle to *him,* and
makest *him* drunken also,
That thou mayest look on their
nakedness!
16 Thou art filled [1]*with* shame for glory:
Drink thou also, and let thy foreskin be
uncovered:
The cup of the LORD's right hand shall
be turned unto thee,
And shameful spuing *shall be* on thy
glory.

2:9 [1]Or, *gaineth an evil gain* [2]Heb. *palm of the hand* [a]Obad. 4
2:11 [1]Or, *piece,* or, *fastening* [2]Or, *witness against it*
2:12 [1]Heb. *bloods*
2:13 [1]Or, *in vain?*
2:14 [1]Or, *by knowing the glory of the LORD*
2:15 [a]Hos. 7:5
2:16 [1]Or, *more with shame than with glory*

17 For the violence of Lebanon shall cover
thee,
And the spoil of beasts, *which* made
them afraid,
Because of men's blood, and *for* the
violence of the land,
Of the city, and *of* all that dwell
therein.
18 What profiteth the graven image that
the maker thereof hath graven it;
The molten image, and a teacher of
lies,
That [1]the maker of his work trusteth
therein, to make dumb idols?
19 Woe unto him that saith to the wood,
Awake; to the dumb stone, Arise, it
shall teach!
Behold, it *is* laid over *with* gold and
silver,
And *there is* no breath at all in the
midst of it.
20 But the LORD *is* in his holy temple:
[1]Let all the earth keep silence before
him.

Habakkuk's prayer

3 A prayer of Habakkuk the prophet
[1]upon Shigionoth.
2 O LORD, I have heard [1]thy speech, *and*
was afraid:
O LORD, [2]revive thy work in the midst
of the years,
In the midst of the years make known;
In wrath remember mercy.

3 God came from [1]Teman,
And the Holy One from mount Paran.
Selah.

2:18 [1]Heb. *the fashioner of his fashion*
2:20 [1]Heb. *Be silent all the earth before him*
3:1 [1]Or, *according to variable songs,* or, *tunes,* called in Hebrew, *Shigionoth*
3:2 [1]Heb. *thy report,* or, *thy hearing* [2]Or, *preserve alive*
3:3 [1]Or, *the south*

‡2:9 *Woe.* The Babylonians' pride in building is condemned. *nest on high.* Like the eagle building an inaccessible nest, the Babylonians thought their empire to be unconquerable (see Obad 3–4; cf. Is 14:4,13–15). Arrogant independence of the living God is one of the OT's most heinous sins.
2:11 *the stone shall cry out . . . And the beam.* The stones and beams in Babylonian houses were purchased with plunder, and thus testified against the occupants.
2:12 *Woe.* Babylonian injustice is condemned.
2:13 *labour in the very fire.* The cities built by the labor of the Babylonians (v. 12) will be burned.
2:14 The Lord's future destruction of proud Babylon and all her worldly glory will cause His greater glory to be known throughout the world (see Ex 14:4,17–18; Is 11:9; Rev 17:1–19:4).
‡2:15 Cf. Gen 9:20–22. *Woe.* Babylonian violence is condemned. Her rapacious treatment of her neighbors, which stripped them of all their wealth (cf. what she later did to Jerusalem, 2 Ki 25:8–21), is compared to one who makes his neighbor drunk so he can take lewd pleasure from the man's nakedness. Habakkuk has a greater ratio per verse of words for "violence" than any other OT writer.
2:16 *Thou art filled with shame . . . let thy foreskin be uncovered.* The Lord will do to Babylon what she has done to others. *cup of the LORD's right hand.* A symbol of divine retribution (see Is 51:17,22; Jer 25:15–17; Lam 4:21; Rev 14:10; 16:19).
2:17 *violence of Lebanon.* The Babylonians apparently had ravaged the cedar forests of Lebanon to adorn their temples and palaces (cf. Is 14:8). *spoil of beasts.* Assyrian inscriptions record hunting expeditions in the Lebanon range, and such sport may have been indulged in by the invading Babylonians as well. Babylonian violence was destructive of all forms of life, not only of lands and cities.
2:18 *graven image.* The Hebrew for this word means "godlet" or "nonentity" (cf. Is 41:29; 44:9; Jer 10:15 and the condemnation of idolatry in Ex 20:4–5; Ps 115:4–8).
2:19 *Woe.* Babylonian idolatry is condemned.
‡2:20 *But.* The stone and wood idols of the nations (v. 19) are silent before people, but the people of the world are to be silent before the true God, who is about to judge (cf. Is 41:1; Zeph 1:7; Zech 2:13). *holy temple.* Heaven. See Zeph 1:7; Zech 2:13.
3:1 In the strict sense, petition is found in this prayer only in v. 2 but, as with many of the psalms, it is set in a larger context of recollection (vv. 3–15) and expression of confidence and trust (vv. 16–19). In fact, Habakkuk's prayer appears to have been used as a psalm; note the psalm-like heading (v. 1) and the musical and/or literary notations (vv. 1,3,9,13,19).
3:2 *I have heard thy speech.* In vv. 3–15 Habakkuk recalls a poetic celebration of God's mighty saving acts of old—perhaps one he had heard at the temple (see v. 16).
3:3 *God came.* When celebrating the exodus, the OT poets (and poet-prophets) combined recollections of the mighty acts of God with conventional images of a fearsome manifestation of

His glory covered the heavens,
And the earth was full *of* his praise.
4 And *his* brightness was as the light;
He had [1]horns *coming* out of his hand:
And there *was* the hiding of his power.
5 Before him went the pestilence,
And [1]burning coals went forth at his feet.
6 He stood, and measured the earth:
He beheld, and drove asunder the nations;
[a]And the everlasting mountains were scattered,
The perpetual hills did bow:
His ways *are* everlasting.
7 I saw the tents of [1]Cushan [2]in affliction:
And the curtains of the land of Midian did tremble.
8 Was the LORD displeased against the rivers?
Was thine anger against the rivers?
Was thy wrath against the sea,
That thou didst ride upon thine horses *and* [1]thy chariots of salvation?
9 Thy bow was made quite naked,
According to the oaths of the tribes, *even thy* word. Selah.
[1]Thou didst cleave the earth *with* rivers.
10 The mountains saw thee, *and* they trembled:
The overflowing of the water passed by:
The deep uttered his voice,
And [a]lift up his hands on high.
11 The sun *and* moon stood still in *their* habitation:

3:4 [1]Or, *bright beams out of his side*
3:5 [1]Or, *burning diseases*
3:6 [a]Nah. 1:5
3:7 [1]Or, *Ethiopia* [2]Or, *under affliction,* or, *vanity*
3:8 [1]Or, *thy chariots* were *salvation?*
3:9 [1]Or, *Thou didst cleave the rivers of the earth*
3:10 [a]Ex. 14:22
3:11 [1]Or, *Thine arrows walked in the light, etc.*
3:13 [1]Heb. *making naked*
3:14 [1]Heb. *were tempestuous*
3:15 [1]Or, *mud* [a]Ps. 77:19
3:16 [1]Or, *cut them in pieces* [a]Ps. 119:120
3:17 [1]Heb. *lie*

[1]At the light of thine arrows they went,
And at the shining of thy glittering spear.
12 Thou didst march through the land in indignation,
Thou didst thresh the heathen in anger.
13 Thou wentest forth for the salvation of thy people,
Even for salvation with thine anointed;
Thou woundedst the head out of the house of the wicked,
By [1]discovering the foundation unto the neck. Selah.
14 Thou didst strike through with his staves the head of his villages:
They [1]came out as a whirlwind to scatter me:
Their rejoicing *was* as to devour the poor secretly.
15 [a]Thou didst walk through the sea *with* thine horses,
Through the [1]heap of great waters.
16 When I heard, [a]my belly trembled;
My lips quivered at the voice:
Rottenness entered into my bones, and I trembled in myself,
That I might rest in the day of trouble:
When *he* cometh up unto the people, he will [1]invade them with his troops.

17 Although the fig tree shall not blossom,
Neither *shall* fruit *be* in the vines;
The labour of the olive shall [1]fail,
And the fields shall yield no meat;
The flock shall be cut off from the fold,
And *there shall be* no herd in the stalls:

---

the Lord. He came down with His heavenly host and rode on the mighty thunderstorm as His chariot, with His arrows flying in all directions, a cloudburst of rain descending on the earth and the mountains quaking before Him (see Deut 33:2; Judg 5:4–5; Ps 18:7–15; 68:4–10,32–35; 77:16–19; Mic 1:3–4). Such figures characterize many of the references in the following verses. *Teman.* Means "southland." God is pictured as coming from the area south of Judah during the exodus. *mount Paran.* See Deut 33:2; probably northwest of the Gulf of Aqaba and south of Kadesh-barnea, between Edom and Sinai. *earth was full.* See note on 2:14.

3:5 *pestilence . . . burning coals.* Means of divine punishment (cf. Ex 7:14–12:30; Lev 26:25; Ps 91:3,6).

3:6 God's presence was frequently marked by earthquakes (see Ex 19:18; Ps 18:7; Jer 4:24–26; 10:10). Landslides may also be alluded to here.

3:7 *Cushan . . . Midian.* Arab tribes living near Edom. *affliction . . . did tremble.* When Israel was delivered from Egypt under Moses, neighboring peoples were filled with fear (see Ex 15:14–16; Josh 2:9–10).

3:8 Poetic allusions to the plague on the Nile (Ex 7:20–24) and/or the stopping of the Jordan (Josh 3:15–17), and to the parting of the Red sea (Ex 14:15–31). But see note on v. 3.

3:9 *Thy bow was.* Probably thunderbolts unleashed by the heavenly archer. *didst cleave the earth with rivers.* Caused by the accompanying thunderstorms.

‡3:11 *sun and moon stood still in their habitation.* Probably an allusion to the victory at Gibeon (Josh 10:12–13), indicating that God's triumph over His enemies would be just as complete as on that occasion. These two stars are theologically sensitive to the Hebrews because of their prominence in all the ancient religious systems. Often, therefore, in theophanic language, they are shown in submission to the God of the universe.

3:12 *march through.* The Hebrew can also be translated "thresh." See note on Amos 1:3.

3:13 *salvation of thy people.* God fought against the nations of Canaan (v. 12) but delivered His people. *salvation of.* Giving of victory to. *anointed.* The covenant nation ("thy people"), the "kingdom of priests" (Ex 19:6), which God came to deliver. He destroyed the enemy, and in this great act of wrath (v. 12) remembered mercy (v. 2). *head out of the house of the wicked.* Pharaoh (see Ex 14:5–9).

3:14–15 Another reference to the destruction of the Egyptians in the Red sea. God will likewise vanquish present foes.

3:15 *horses.* See v. 8 and note.

‡3:16 Hearing the hymnic recollection of God's mighty deeds of old in Israel's behalf (vv. 3–15) fills the prophet with an awe so profound that he feels physically weak. Alternatively, it is possible that the message from the Lord that Babylon would be sent against Judah (1:5–11) had so devastated him that he felt ill—until he heard the Lord's further word. *rest.* See note on 2:3 and Zeph 3:8. *people . . . he will invade them.* Babylonia.

3:17 Probably anticipates the awful results of the imminent Babylonian invasion and devastation.

18 Yet I will rejoice in the LORD,
I will joy in the God of my salvation.
19 The Lord GOD *is* my strength,
And he will make my feet like [a]hinds' *feet,*
And he will make me to [b]walk upon mine high places.

To the chief singer on my [1]stringed instruments.

3:19 [a]2 Sam. 22:34

3:19 [1]Heb. *Neginoth* [b]Deut. 32:13

‡3:18–19 Habakkuk has learned the lesson of faith (2:4)—to trust in God's providence regardless of circumstances. He declares that even if God should send suffering and loss, he would still rejoice in his Savior-God—one of the strongest affirmations of faith in all Scripture. His book reflects the spiritual odyssey of every true believer—consternation with the injustices of life, consideration of God as sovereign and conclusion that God can and must be trusted.

3:19 *make my feet like hinds' feet.* Given me sure-footed confidence. *chief singer.* Probably the conductor of the temple musicians. This chapter may have formed part of the temple prayers that were chanted with the accompaniment of instruments (see 1 Chr 16:4–7). *stringed instruments.* Including harp and lyre (Ps 33:2; 92:3; 144:9).

Zephaniah

INTRODUCTION

Author

The prophet Zephaniah was evidently a person of considerable social standing in Judah and was probably related to the royal line. The prophecy opens with a statement of the author's ancestry (1:1), which in itself is an unusual feature of the Hebrew prophetic tradition. Zephaniah was the fourth-generation descendant of Hezekiah, a notable king of Judah from 715 to 686 B.C. Apart from this statement, nothing more is said about his background. Whereas the prophet Micah dealt carefully and sympathetically with the problems of the common people of Judah, Zephaniah's utterances show a much greater familiarity with court circles and current political issues. Zephaniah was probably familiar with the writings of such prominent eighth-century prophets as Isaiah and Amos, whose utterances he reflects, and he may also have been aware of the ministry of the young Jeremiah.

Date

According to 1:1, Zephaniah prophesied during the reign of King Josiah (640–609 B.C.), making him a contemporary of Jeremiah, Nahum and perhaps Habakkuk. His prophecy is probably to be dated relatively early in Josiah's reign, before that king's attempt at reform (and while conditions brought about by the reigns of Manasseh and Amon still prevailed) and before the Assyrian king Ashurbanipal's death in 627 (while Assyria was still powerful, though threatened).

Background

See Introductions to Jeremiah and Nahum: Background; see also 2 Ki 22:1–23:30; 2 Chr 34–35 and notes.

Purpose and Theme

The intent of the author was to announce to Judah God's approaching judgment. A Scythian incursion into Canaan may have provided the immediate occasion. This fierce, horse-mounted people originated in what is now southern Russia, but by the seventh century B.C. had migrated across the Caucasus and settled in and along the northern territories of the Assyrian empire. Alternately the enemies and allies of Assyria, they seem to have thrust south along the Mediterranean sometime in the 620s, destroying Ashkelon and Ashdod and halting at the Egyptian border only because of a payoff by Pharaoh Psamtik (Psammetichus). Ultimately, however, the destruction prophesied by Zephaniah came at the hands of the Babylonians after they had overpowered Assyria and brought that ancient power to its end.

Zephaniah's main theme is the coming of the day of the Lord (see notes on Is 2:11,17,20; Joel 1:15; 2:2; Amos 5:18; 8:9), when God will severely punish the nations, including apostate Judah. He portrays the stark horror of that ordeal with the same graphic imagery found elsewhere in the prophets. But he also makes it clear that God will yet be merciful toward His people; like many other prophets, he ends his pronouncements of doom on the positive note of Judah's restoration by the Lord, "the king of Israel" (3:15; see note there).

Outline

- I. Introduction (1:1–3)
  - A. Title: The Prophet Identified (1:1)
  - B. Prologue: Double Announcement of Total Judgment (1:2–3)
- II. The Day of the Lord Coming on Judah and the Nations (1:4–18)
  - A. Judgment on the Idolaters in Judah (1:4–9)
  - B. Wailing throughout Jerusalem (1:10–13)
  - C. The Inescapable Day of the Lord's Wrath (1:14–18)

- III. God's Judgment on the Nations (2:1—3:8)
  - A. Call to Repentance (2:1–3)
  - B. Judgment on Philistia (2:4–7)
  - C. Judgment on Moab and Ammon (2:8–11)
  - D. Judgment on Cush (Ethiopia) (2:12)
  - E. Judgment on Assyria (2:13–15)
  - F. Judgment on Jerusalem (3:1–5)
  - G. Jerusalem's Refusal to Repent (3:6–8)
- IV. Redemption of the Remnant (3:9–20)
  - A. The Nations Purified, the Remnant Restored, Jerusalem Purged (3:9–13)
  - B. Rejoicing in the City (3:14–17)
  - C. The Nation Restored (3:18–20)

1 The word of the LORD which came unto
Zephaniah the son of Cushi, the son of
Gedaliah, the son of Amariah, the son of Hizkiah, in the days of Josiah the son of Amon,
king of Judah.

Judgment upon Jerusalem

2 [1]I will utterly consume all *things* from
off [2]the land, saith the LORD.
3 [a]I will consume man and beast;
I will consume the fowls of the heaven,
and the fishes of the sea,
And the [1]stumblingblocks with the
wicked;
And I will cut off man from off the
land, saith the LORD.
4 I will also stretch out mine hand upon
Judah,
And upon all the inhabitants of
Jerusalem;
And I will cut off the remnant of Baal
from this place,
And the name of [a]the Chemarims with
the priests;
5 And them [a]that worship the host of
heaven upon the housetops;
And them that worship *and* that swear
[1]by the LORD,
And that swear [b]by Malcham;
6 And [a]them that are turned back from
the LORD;
And *those* that [b]have not sought the
LORD, nor inquired for him.

1:2 [1]Heb. *By taking away I will make an end* [2]Heb. *the face of the land*
1:3 [1]Or, *idols* [a]Hos. 4:3
1:4 [a]Hos. 10:5
1:5 [1]Or, *to the* LORD [a]2 Ki. 23:12 [b]Josh. 23:7
1:6 [a]Is. 1:4; Jer. 2:13 [b]Hos. 7:7
1:7 [1]Heb. *sanctified,* or, *prepared* [a]Hab. 2:20; Zech. 2:13 [b]Is. 13:6 [c]Is. 34:6; Jer. 46:10
1:8 [1]Heb. *visit upon* [a]Jer. 39:6
1:10 [a]2 Chr. 33:14
1:11 [a]Jas. 5:1
1:12 [1]Heb. *curded,* or, *thickened* [a]Jer. 48:11 [b]Ps. 94:7

7 [a]Hold thy peace at the presence of the
Lord GOD:
[b]For the day of the LORD *is* at hand:
For [c]the LORD hath prepared a sacrifice,
He hath [1]bid his guests.
8 And it shall come to pass in the day of
the LORD's sacrifice,
That I will [1]punish [a]the princes, and
the king's children,
And all such as are clothed with
strange apparel.
9 In the same day also will I punish all
those that leap on the threshold,
Which fill their masters' houses *with*
violence and deceit.
10 And it shall come to pass in that day,
saith the LORD,
That there shall be the noise of a cry
from [a]the fish gate,
And a howling from the second,
And a great crashing from the hills.
11 [a]Howl, ye inhabitants of Maktesh,
For all the merchant people are cut
down;
All they that bear silver are cut off.
12 And it shall come to pass at that time,
That I will search Jerusalem with
candles,
And punish the men that are [a][1]settled
on their lees:
[b]That say in their heart, The LORD will
not do good, neither will he do evil.
13 Therefore their goods shall become a
booty, and their houses a desolation:

---

‡1:1 *The word of the* LORD. A common introductory phrase in the prophets (see, e.g., Jer 1:4; Hos 1:1; Mic 1:1). *Zephaniah.* Means "The LORD hides" or "The LORD protects," perhaps referring to God's protection of Zephaniah during the infamous reigns of Manasseh and Amon, the predecessors of good King Josiah. *son of Hizkiah.* Archaic spelling for king Hezekiah. From the author's pedigree, scholars suggest that he was in his early 20s when he began to prophesy. He is more closely identified with the ruling class than was Isaiah, although Isaiah also moved regularly in court circles and was perhaps of noble birth.
1:2 *utterly consume.* See v. 3. Zephaniah speaks of the coming catastrophe in language reminiscent of God's utterances prior to the flood (Gen 6:7). But this time it will be by God's fire (v. 18; 3:8).
‡1:3 *stumblingblocks.* Alternatively, the sense may be that God will place formidable obstacles in the paths of the wicked and destroy them completely.
1:4–6 Seems to indicate that Zephaniah's main ministry took place before 621 B.C., since the practices condemned here were abolished in Josiah's reforms (2 Ki 23:4–16). Perhaps Zephaniah's message was partly instrumental in motivating King Josiah and the people to undertake the reforms (cf. 2 Chr 34:1–7).
1:4 Judah is censured for its unrepentant participation in the gross idolatry of Baal worship. *Baal.* See note on Judg 2:13. *this place.* Jerusalem, where Zephaniah probably lived.
‡1:5 *worship . . . the host of heaven.* See Deut 4:15–19; 2 Ki 17:16; 21:3; Is 47:13. *upon the housetops.* See 2 Ki 23:12; Jer 19:13. *swear by the* LORD *. . . by Malcham.* Syncretism (worship of one's own god along with other gods). Malcham was worshiped by the Ammonites, and his rituals sometimes involved child sacrifice. Molech worship (Malcham and Molech were variant names referring to the same god) was forbidden to the Israelites (Lev 18:21; 20:1–5). Despite this, Solomon set up an altar to Molech on the mount of Olives (1 Ki 11:7). Manasseh established the rituals in the valley of Ben-hinnom (2 Chr 33:6; Jer 7:31; 32:35).
‡1:7 *Hold thy peace at the presence of the Lord* GOD. See Hab 2:20; Am 6:10. *day of the* LORD. Zephaniah's main theme (see Introduction: Purpose and Theme); not of deliverance for Judah, but of divine vengeance on the idolatrous covenant nation. Zephaniah is more vague than the other prophets and does not identify Babylon as the oppressor nation. *sacrifice.* The victim is Judah. *bid.* Since the coming slaughter of judgment is called a sacrifice, God "sanctifies" (see KJV marg.) His guests in preparation for their feasting on the plunder. *his guests.* The pagan conquerors (mainly Babylon).
1:9 *leap on the threshold.* Or "leap over," perhaps referring to a pagan custom that began in the time of Samuel (1 Sam 5:5).
1:10–13 Wailing throughout the city (contrast 3:14–17).
1:10 Merchants who had grown rich through corrupt business practices would be destroyed. *fish gate.* See note on Neh 3:3. *second.* See note on Neh 11:9.
‡1:11 *Maktesh.* May have been an area in the Tyropoeon Valley, just south of mount Moriah, where some foreign merchants lived (see 1 Ki 20:34 and note).
1:12 *search Jerusalem with candles.* The Babylonians later dragged people from houses, streets, sewers and tombs, where they had hidden. *The* LORD *will not do.* A typical depiction of the arrogance of the wicked (see note on Ps 10:11; see also Mic 3:11 and 2 Pet 3:4).
1:13 The assets of those who have become wealthy through dishonesty will be exposed and plundered (see Deut 28:30).

They shall also build houses, but [a]not
inhabit *them;*
And they shall plant vineyards, but
[b]not drink the wine thereof.

The day of wrath

14 [a]The great day of the LORD *is* near,
It is near, and hasteth greatly,
Even the voice of the day of the LORD:
The mighty *man* shall cry there bitterly.
15 [a]That day *is* a day of wrath,
A day of trouble and distress,
A day of wasteness and desolation,
A day of darkness and gloominess,
A day of clouds and thick darkness,
16 A day of [a]the trumpet and alarm
Against the fenced cities, and against
the high towers.
17 And I will bring distress upon men,
that they shall [a]walk like blind *men,*
Because they have sinned against the
LORD:
And [b]their blood shall be poured out as
dust, and their flesh [c]as the dung.
18 [a]Neither their silver nor their gold
shall be able to deliver them
In the day of the LORD's wrath;
But the whole land shall be [b]devoured
by the fire of his jealousy:
For [c]he shall make even a speedy
riddance of all them that dwell in the
land.

The call to repentance

2 [a]Gather yourselves together, yea, gather
together, O nation [1]not desired;
2 Before the decree bring forth, *before*
the day pass [a]as the chaff,
Before [b]the fierce anger of the LORD
come upon you,
Before the day of the LORD's anger
come upon you.

1:13 [a]Amos 5:11 [b]Mic. 6:15
1:14 [a]Joel 2:1,11
1:15 [a]Is. 22:5; Jer. 30:7
1:16 [a]Jer. 4:19
1:17 [a]Deut. 28:29 [b]Ps. 79:3 [c]Jer. 9:22
1:18 [a]Ezek. 7:19 [b]ch. 3:8 [c]ver. 2,3
2:1 [1]Or, *not desirous* [a]Joel 2:16
2:2 [a]Job 21:18; Is. 17:13 [b]2 Ki. 23:26
2:3 [a]Amos 5:6 [b]Ps. 76:9 [c]Amos 5:15
2:4 [a]Zech. 9:5,6 [b]Jer. 6:4
2:5 [a]Ezek. 25:16 [b]Josh. 13:3
2:6 [a]Is. 17:2
2:7 [1]Or, *When, etc.* [a]Mic. 5:7,8 [b]Luke 1:68 [c]Jer. 29:14
2:8 [a]Jer. 48:27 [b]Ezek. 25:3 [c]Jer. 49:1
2:9 [a]Is. 15 [b]Amos 1:13

3 [a]Seek ye the LORD, [b]all ye meek of the
earth,
Which have wrought his judgment;
Seek righteousness, seek meekness:
[c]It may be ye shall be hid in the day of
the LORD's anger.

The woe upon the nations

4 For [a]Gaza shall be forsaken, and
Ashkelon a desolation:
They shall drive out Ashdod [b]at the
noon day, and Ekron shall be rooted
up.
5 Woe unto the inhabitants of [a]the sea
coast, the nation of the Cherethites!
The word of the LORD *is* against you;
[b]O Canaan, the land of the Philistines,
I will even destroy thee, that there
shall be no inhabitant.
6 And the sea coast shall be dwellings
and cottages for shepherds, [a]and
folds for flocks.
7 And the coast shall be for [a]the remnant
of the house of Judah;
They shall feed thereupon:
In the houses of Ashkelon shall they lie
down in the evening:
[1]For the LORD their God shall [b]visit
them, and [c]turn away their captivity.
8 [a]I have heard the reproach of Moab,
And [b]the revilings of the children of
Ammon,
Whereby they have reproached my
people,
And [c]magnified *themselves* against
their border.
9 Therefore *as* I live, saith the LORD of
hosts, the God of Israel,
Surely [a]Moab shall be as Sodom, and
[b]the children of Ammon as
Gomorrah,

1:14–18 In a dramatic passage of great lyrical power, the Lord describes the destruction that will sweep the earth in the day of God's wrath.
1:15 *darkness . . . thick darkness.* See Amos 5:18–20.
1:17 *like blind men.* See Deut 28:28–29.
‡1:18 *Neither . . . silver nor . . . gold shall be able to deliver them.* In the day of God's judgment, material wealth cannot buy deliverance from punishment. *the whole land.* I.e. "completely." In 1:2 God said that he would "utterly [completely] consume," and now the chapter closes with another word of completeness. "Whole land" is actually "he will completely" in Hebrew. Though the two words are different in Hebrew, they envelope the chapter and ensure the thoroughness of the Day's destruction.
2:1–3 The prophet's exhortation to repent. This call to repentance and the later indictment of Jerusalem for refusal to repent (see 3:6–8 and note) frame the series of judgments that illustratively detail God's acts in the coming day of the Lord (2:4–3:5).
2:2 *as the chaff.* See note on Ps 1:4.
2:3 *Seek ye the LORD.* Even though destruction is imminent, there is still time to be sheltered from the calamity if only the nation will repent. *meekness.* Those who abandon the arrogance of their idolatry and wickedness and humble themselves in repentance before God.
2:4–3:8 God's coming judgment on the nations—including Jerusalem (cf. Amos 1–2).
‡2:4 *Gaza . . . Ashkelon . . . Ashdod . . . Ekron.* See notes on Josh 13:3; Judg 3:3; Amos 1:6,8; see also map, p. 313. Of the minor prophets, only Amos and Zephaniah have oracles against these nations.
2:5 *Cherethites.* See note on 1 Sam 30:14. *Canaan.* See note on Gen 10:6. *I . . . no inhabitant.* The Lord's announced purpose.
2:6 The once-populous Philistine cities will revert to pastureland.
2:7 The faithful remnant of Judah will occupy this land and graze their flocks on it. *turn away their captivity.* Or "bring back their captives." Here and in vv. 9,11 the prophet anticipates the ultimate outcome of the day of the Lord, which he spells out more fully in 3:9–20.
2:8 *Moab . . . children of Ammon.* See notes on Gen 19:36–38; Amos 1:13. For the hostility of Ammon and Moab toward Israel see Amos 1:13–15; 2:1–3. They had often threatened to occupy Israelite territory (see Judg 11:12–13; Ezek 25:3–6).
2:9 *Sodom . . . Gomorrah.* See Gen 19. They were used in the

[c]*Even* the breeding of nettles, and saltpits, and a perpetual desolation:
[d]The residue of my people shall spoil them,
And the remnant of my people shall possess them.
10 This shall they have [a]for their pride,
Because they have reproached and magnified *themselves* against the people of the LORD of hosts.
11 The LORD *will be* terrible unto them:
For he will [1]famish all the gods of the earth;
[a]And *men* shall worship him, every one from his place,
Even all [b]the isles of the heathen.

12 [a]Ye Ethiopians also, ye *shall be* slain by [b]my sword.
13 And he will stretch out his hand against the north, and [a]destroy Assyria;
And will make Nineveh a desolation, *and* dry like a wilderness.
14 And [a]flocks shall lie down in the midst of her, all [b]the beasts of the nations:
Both the [c1]cormorant and the bittern shall lodge in the [2]upper lintels of it;
Their voice shall sing in the windows;
desolation *shall be* in the thresholds:
[3]For he shall uncover the [d]cedar work.
15 This *is* the rejoicing city [a]that dwelt carelessly,
[b]That said in her heart, I *am,* and *there is* none beside me:
How is she become a desolation, a place for beasts to lie down in!
Every one that passeth by her [c]shall hiss, *and* [d]wag his hand.

2:9 [c]Deut. 29:33 [d]ver. 7
2:10 [a]Is. 16:6; Jer. 48:29
2:11 [1]Heb. *make lean* [a]Mal. 1:11; John 4:21 [b]Gen. 10:5
2:12 [a]Is. 18:1; Jer. 46:9 [b]Ps. 17:13
2:13 [a]Is. 10:12; Nah. 1:1
2:14 [1]Or, *pelican* [2]Or, *knops,* or, *chapiters* [3]Or, *When he hath uncovered* [a]ver. 6 [b]Is. 13:21 [c]Is. 34:11 [d]Jer. 22:14
2:15 [a]Is. 47:8 [b]Rev. 18:7 [c]Lam. 2:15 [d]Nah. 3:19

3:1 [1]Or, *gluttonous* [2]Heb. *craw*
3:2 [1]Or, *instruction* [a]Jer. 22:21 [b]Jer. 5:3
3:3 [a]Ezek. 22:27; Mic. 3:9 [b]Hab. 1:8
3:4 [a]Hos. 9:7 [b]Ezek. 22:26
3:5 [1]Heb. *Morning by morning* [a]Deut. 32:4 [b]Mic. 3:11 [c]Jer. 3:3
3:6 [1]Or, *corners*
3:7 [a]Jer. 8:6 [b]Gen. 6:12
3:8 [a]Prov. 20:22

The future of Jerusalem

3 Woe to [12]her that is filthy and polluted, to the oppressing city!
2 She [a]obeyed not the voice; she [b]received not [1]correction;
She trusted not in the LORD; she drew not near to her God.
3 [a]Her princes within her *are* roaring lions;
Her judges *are* [b]evening wolves;
They gnaw not the bones till the morrow.
4 Her [a]prophets *are* light *and* treacherous persons:
Her priests have polluted the sanctuary, they have done [b]violence to the law.
5 [a]The just LORD [b]*is* in the midst thereof; he will not do iniquity:
[1]Every morning doth he bring his judgment to light, he faileth not;
But [c]the unjust knoweth no shame.
6 I have cut off *the* nations: their [1]towers are desolate;
I made their streets waste, that none passeth by:
Their cities are destroyed, so that there is no man, that there is none inhabitant.
7 [a]I said, Surely thou wilt fear me, thou wilt receive instruction;
So their dwelling should not be cut off, howsoever I punished them:
But they rose early, *and* [b]corrupted all their doings.

8 Therefore [a]wait ye upon me, saith the LORD,

OT to typify complete destruction at the hands of God (see Deut 29:23; Is 13:19; Jer 49:18), and their mention added ominous overtones to the prophet's description of the day of the Lord. *nettles.* Or "weeds," a symbol of depopulation (see Is 7:23–25). *remnant . . . shall possess them.* See note on v. 7.

2:10 *This shall they have for their pride . . . reproached . . . magnified themselves.* In reprisal, the faithful remnant will occupy Ammonite and Moabite territory.

2:11 *men shall worship him.* See 3:9 and note.

2:12 *Ye.* Without elaboration, the prophet simply announces God's purpose against Egypt (see v. 5 and note). *Ethiopians.* Lit. "Cushites," people from the upper (southern) Nile region. Egypt was ruled from 715 to 663 B.C. by a Cushite dynasty. *my sword.* Probably Babylon.

2:13 *north.* Although Nineveh was east of Judah, Assyrian armies normally invaded Canaan from the north, having first marched west along the Euphrates. *Nineveh.* See the books of Jonah and Nahum. Since Nineveh was destroyed in 612 B.C., Zephaniah's ministry had to be before that date. *desolation.* Even the site of Nineveh was later forgotten—until discovered through modern excavations.

2:15 *I am . . . none beside me.* See Is 47:10. Assyria's boast belongs properly to God alone (see Is 45:5–6,18,21). *is she become.* Anticipating Nineveh's impending destruction.

3:1 *oppressing.* See Jer 22:3. *city.* Apostate Jerusalem is condemned for its sins.

3:3–4 *princes . . . judges . . . prophets . . . priests.* All classes of Judah's leaders are castigated for indulging in conduct completely opposed to their vocations and covenant mandated responsibilities (see Jer 1:18 and note).

3:3 *roaring lions . . . evening wolves.* Those in power are rapacious.

3:4 *are light and treacherous persons.* Claiming to be prophets of the Lord, they proclaimed only lies (see Jer 5:31; 14:14; 23:16,32). *priests . . . have done violence to the law.* When they should have been teachers of the law (see Deut 31:9–13; 2 Chr 17:8–9; 19:8; Ezra 7:6; Jer 2:8; 18:18; Mal 2:7).

‡3:5 *no shame.* "Shame" is a prophetic by-word. The wicked don't have any; but in judgment, God will give it to them in full measure. "Shame" appears only 3 times in the historical books but 19 times in the prophetic literature. See Hos 9:10; Mic 1:11; Hab 2:10; Zeph 3:19 (Hebrew *bosheth*). The KJV also translates 6 other Hebrew words as "shame" (cf. e.g. Ex 32:25; Judg 18:6; 2 Sam 13:13; Ps 4:2; 44:7; 71:24).

3:6–8 Jerusalem's refusal to repent (see 2:1–3 and note).

3:6 *I have cut off the nations.* The destruction of other nations was meant to serve as a warning to wanton Judah, but to no avail (see v. 7).

3:7 *corrupted all their doings.* See, e.g., Jer 7:13,25–26.

3:8 *wait.* A sarcastic statement to Judah to wait for the threatened catastrophe. *I rise up to the prey.* That is, to lodge accusations (see Ps 50:7)—and then proceed to execute judgments. *my determination .* The Lord concludes His announcement of judgment with a general declaration of His intent.

Until the day that I rise up to the
prey:
For my determination *is* to [b]gather the
nations,
That I may assemble the kingdoms,
To pour upon them mine indignation,
even all my fierce anger:
For all the earth [c]shall be devoured
with the fire of my jealousy.
9 For then will I turn to the people [a]a
pure [1]language,
That they may all call upon the name
of the LORD,
To serve him *with* one [2]consent.
10 [a]From beyond the rivers of Ethiopia
My suppliants, *even* the daughter of
my dispersed, shall bring mine
offering.
11 In that day shalt thou not be ashamed
for all thy doings,
Wherein thou hast transgressed against
me:
For then I will take away out of the
midst of thee them that [a]rejoice in
thy pride,
And thou shalt no more be haughty
[1]because of my holy mountain.
12 I will also leave in the midst of thee
[a]an afflicted and poor people,
And they shall trust in the name of the
LORD.
13 [a]The remnant of Israel [b]shall not do
iniquity, [c]nor speak lies;
Neither shall a deceitful tongue be
found in their mouth:
For [d]they shall feed and lie down, and
none shall make *them* afraid.

3:8 [b]Joel 3:2 [c]ch. 1:18
3:9 [1]Heb. *lip* [2]Heb. *shoulder* [a]Is. 19:18
3:10 [a]Ps. 68:31; Acts 8:27
3:11 [1]Heb. *in my holy* [a]Mat. 3:9
3:12 [a]Is. 14:32
3:13 [a]Mic. 4:7 [b]Is. 60:21 [c]Rev. 14:5 [d]Ezek. 34:28
3:14 [a]Is. 12:6
3:15 [a]John 1:49 [b]Ezek. 48:35; Rev. 7:15
3:16 [1]Or, *faint* [a]Is. 35:3,4 [b]Heb. 12:12
3:17 [1]Heb. *He will be silent* [a]ver. 15 [b]Is. 62:5; Jer. 32:41
3:18 [1]Heb. *the burden upon it was reproach* [a]Lam. 2:6
3:19 [1]Heb. *I will set them for a praise* [2]Heb. *of their shame* [a]Ezek. 34:16; Mic. 4:6,7
3:20 [a]Is. 11:12; Ezek. 28:25

14 [a]Sing, O daughter of Zion; shout,
O Israel;
Be glad and rejoice with all the heart,
O daughter of Jerusalem.
15 The LORD hath taken away thy
judgments, he hath cast out thine
enemy:
[a]The king of Israel, *even* the LORD, [b]*is*
in the midst of thee:
Thou shalt not see evil any more.
16 In that day [a]it shall be said to
Jerusalem, Fear thou not:
And to Zion, [b]Let not thine hands be
[1]slack.
17 The LORD thy God [a]in the midst of thee
is mighty;
He will save, [b]he will rejoice over thee
with joy;
[1]He will rest in his love, he will joy
over thee with singing.
18 I will gather *them that* [a]*are* sorrowful for
the solemn assembly, *who* are of thee,
To whom [1]the reproach of it *was* a
burden.
19 Behold, at that time I *will* undo all that
afflict thee:
And I will save her that [a]halteth,
And gather her that was driven out;
And [1]I will get them praise and fame
In every land [2]where they have been
put to shame.
20 At that time [a]will I bring you *again,*
even in the time that I gather you:
For I will make you a name and a
praise among all people of the earth,
When I turn back your captivity before
your eyes, saith the LORD.

3:9–20 A three-part oracle (vv. 9–13, 14–17, 18–20) announcing redemption that will follow God's judgment.
3:9–13 The Lord gives assurance that the nations will be purified, the scattered remnant restored and Jerusalem purged.
‡3:9 *call upon the name of the LORD.* See Joel 2:32. God's fearful judgment of the nations will effect (or be followed by) their purification so that they will call on His name and serve Him. Israel's God will be acknowledged by the nations, and God's people will be held in honor by them (cf. vv. 19–20).
3:10 *Ethiopia.* The most distant area imaginable (see note on 2:12). The most widely dispersed will be restored. *bring mine offering.* Rather than Baal's and Molech's (cf. 1:4–5).
3:11 *For then.* This line begins the same as the first line of v. 9. Thus vv. 9–11a constitute a three-line unit (in Hebrew) and vv. 11b,c–12 a three-line unit. The latter speaks of a purified Jerusalem. Verse 13 is a summary conclusion. *my holy mountain.* Mount Zion (see Ps 2:6).
‡3:12 *afflicted and poor.* Not to be understood as a negative. The idea, rather, is that they won't suffer from the pride and arrogance that plague the "haughty" in v. 11.
‡3:13 *none shall make them afraid.* See Mic 4:4 and the note. The present language has the Lord as the Shepherd and the people as His sheep.
3:14–17 Joy in the restored city (in two parts: vv. 14–15 and vv. 16–17)—the prophet's reassurance (contrast 1:10–13).
3:14 *daughter of Zion ... Jerusalem.* Personification of Jerusalem and its inhabitants.
‡3:15 *thine enemy.* All those arrayed against Israel. *The king of Israel, even the LORD.* See Is 44:6. There is a discernible shift away from the line of David toward the end of the OT. Earthly kingship has failed and the kingship of God is highlighted. The elevation of the Lord's kingship is highlighted in both Isaiah and Zechariah. This kingship is fulfilled, of course, in Christ. The prophet Zechariah wrote that "the LORD shall be king over all the earth" (14:9) and "all the nations ... shall ... go ... to worship the King, the LORD of hosts ..." (14:16). See also the Introduction to Psalms: Theology.
3:16 *Let not thine hands be slack.* Do not be discouraged.
3:18–20 Summary announcement of restoration—the Lord's final assurance.
3:18 *solemn assembly.* See Lev 23.
‡3:19 *at that time.* The "now" of vv. 15–16 ("the king ... is in the midst of thee") and the "not yet" ("at that time") is the tension that every mature believer embraces. Christ is with us now and will be with us at His coming.
3:20 *will make you a name.* See Gen 12:2–3.

Haggai

INTRODUCTION

Author

Haggai (1:1) was a prophet who, along with Zechariah, encouraged the returned exiles to rebuild the temple (see Ezra 5:1–2; 6:14). Haggai means "festal," which may indicate that the prophet was born during one of the three pilgrimage feasts (unleavened bread, Pentecost or weeks, and tabernacles; cf. Deut 16:16). Based on 2:3 (see note there) Haggai may have witnessed the destruction of Solomon's temple. If so, he must have been in his early 70s during his ministry.

Background

In 538 B.C. the conqueror of Babylon, Cyrus king of Persia, issued a decree allowing the Jews to return to Jerusalem and rebuild the temple (see Ezra 1:2–4; 6:3–5). Led by Zerubbabel (but see note on Ezra 1:8, "Sheshbazzar"), about 50,000 Jews journeyed home and began work on the temple. About two years later (536) they completed the foundation amid great rejoicing (Ezra 3:8–10). Their success aroused the Samaritans and other neighbors who feared the political and religious implications of a rebuilt temple in a thriving Jewish state. They therefore opposed the project vigorously and managed to halt work until Darius the Great became king of Persia in 522 B.C. (Ezra 4:1–5,24).

Darius was interested in the religions of his empire, and Haggai and Zechariah began to preach in his second year, 520 B.C. (see 1:1; Zech 1:1). The Jews were more to blame for their inactivity than their opponents, and Haggai tried to arouse them from their lethargy. When the governor of Trans-Euphrates and other officials tried to interfere with the rebuilding efforts, Darius fully supported the Jews (Ezra 5:3–6; 6:6–12). In 516 B.C. the temple was finished and dedicated (Ezra 6:15–18).

Date

The messages of Haggai were given during a four-month period in 520 B.C., the second year of King Darius. The first message was delivered on the first day of the sixth month (Aug. 29), the last on the 24th day of the ninth month (Dec. 18). See notes on 1:1; 2:1,10; see also Introduction to Zechariah: Dates.

Themes and Teaching

Next to Obadiah, Haggai is the shortest book in the OT, but its teachings are none the less significant. Haggai clearly shows the consequences of disobedience (1:6,11; 2:16–17) and obedience (2:7–9,19). When the people give priority to God and His house, they are blessed rather than cursed (cf. Luke 12:31 and note). Obedience brings the encouragement and strength of the Spirit of God (2:4–5).

Ch. 2 speaks of the coming of the Messiah, called "the desire of all nations" in v. 7. His coming would fill the rebuilt temple with glory (see 2:9 and note). The Lord made Zerubbabel his "signet (ring)" as a guarantee that the Messiah would come (see 2:23 and note). These passages are linked with the judgment of the nations at Christ's second coming, when the nations will be shaken and kingdoms overthrown (see 2:6–7,21–22 and notes; cf. Heb 12:25–29 and notes).

Literary Features

Like Malachi, Haggai uses a number of questions to highlight key issues (see 1:4,9; 2:3,19). He also makes effective use of repetition: "Consider your ways" occurs in 1:5,7; 2:15,18, and "I am with you" in 1:13; 2:4. "I will shake the heavens and the earth" is found in 2:6,21. The major sections of the book are marked off by the date on which the word of the Lord came "to" (or "by," or "through" or "unto") Haggai (1:1; 2:1,10,20).

Several times the prophet appears to echo other Scriptures (compare 1:6 with Deut 28:38–39 and 2:17 with Deut 28:22). The threefold use of "be strong" in 2:4 (see note there) reflects the encouragement given in Josh 1:6–7,9,18.

Outline

- I. First Message: The Call to Rebuild the Temple (1:1–11)
  - A. The People's Lame Excuse (1:1–4)
  - B. The Poverty of the People (1:5–6)
  - C. The Reason God Has Cursed Them (1:7–11)
- II. The Response of Zerubbabel and the People (1:12–15)
  - A. The Leaders and Remnant Obey (1:12)
  - B. The Lord Strengthens the Workers (1:13–15)
- III. Second Message: The Temple to Be Filled with Glory (2:1–9)
  - A. The People Encouraged (2:1–5)
  - B. The Promise of Glory and Peace (2:6–9)
- IV. Third Message: A Defiled People Purified and Blessed (2:10–19)
  - A. The Rapid Spread of Sin (2:10–14)
  - B. Poor Harvests because of Disobedience (2:15–17)
  - C. Blessing to Come as the Temple Is Rebuilt (2:18–19)
- V. Fourth Message: The Promise to Zerubbabel (2:20–23)
  - A. The Judgment of the Nations (2:20–22)
  - B. The Significance of Zerubbabel (2:23)

The call to rebuild the temple

1 In [a]the second year of Darius the king, in
the sixth month, in the first day of the
month, came the word of the LORD [1]by Haggai
the prophet unto [b]Zerubbabel the son of
Shealtiel, [2]governor of Judah, and to [c]Joshua
the son of [d]Josedech the high priest, saying,
2 Thus speaketh the LORD of hosts, saying,
This people say, The time is not come, the
time that the LORD's house should be built.
3 Then came the word of the LORD [a]by
Haggai the prophet, saying,

4 [a]*Is it* time for you, O ye, to dwell in
your cieled houses,
And this house *lie* waste?
5 Now therefore thus saith the LORD of
hosts; [a][1]Consider your ways.
6 Ye have [a]sown much, and bring in little;
Ye eat, but ye have not enough;
Ye drink, but ye are not filled with
drink;
Ye clothe you, but there is none warm;
And [b]he that earneth wages earneth
wages *to put it* into a bag [1]with holes.
7 Thus saith the LORD of hosts; Consider
your ways.
8 Go up *to* the mountain, and bring
wood, and build the house;
And I will take pleasure in it, and I will
be glorified, saith the LORD.

1:1 [1]Heb. *by the hand of Haggai* [2]Or, *captain* [a]Ezra 4:24 [b]1 Chr. 3:17 [c]Ezra 5:2 [d]1 Chr. 6:15
1:3 [a]Ezra 5:1
1:4 [a]2 Sam. 7:2
1:5 [1]Heb. *Set your heart on your ways* [a]Lam. 3:40
1:6 [1]Heb. *pierced through* [a]Deut. 28:38 [b]Zech. 8:10

1:9 [1]Or, *blow it away* [a]ch. 2:16 [b]ch. 2:17
1:10 [a]Lev. 26:19; Deut. 28:23; 1 Ki. 8:35
1:11 [a]1 Ki. 17:1; 2 Ki. 8:1 [b]ch. 2:17
1:12 [a]Ezra 5:2
1:13 [a]Mat. 28:20; Rom. 8:31
1:14 [a]2 Chr. 36:22; Ezra 1:1

9 [a]*Ye* looked for much, and lo, *it came* to
little;
And when ye brought *it* home, [b]I did
[1]blow upon it.
Why? saith the LORD of hosts.
Because of mine house that *is* waste,
And ye run every man unto his own
house.
10 Therefore [a]the heaven over you is
stayed from dew,
And the earth is stayed *from* her fruit.
11 And I [a]called *for* a drought upon the
land, and upon the mountains,
And upon the corn, and upon the new
wine, and upon the oil,
And upon *that* which the ground
bringeth forth,
And upon men, and upon cattle, and
[b]upon all the labour of the hands.

12 ¶ [a]Then Zerubbabel the son of Shealtiel,
and Joshua the son of Josedech the high priest,
with all the remnant of the people, obeyed the
voice of the LORD their God, and the words of
Haggai the prophet, as the LORD their God had
sent him, and the people did fear before the
LORD.
13 Then spake Haggai the LORD's messenger in the LORD's message unto the people,
saying, [a]I *am* with you, saith the LORD.
14 And [a]the LORD stirred up the spirit of

1:1 *second year . . . sixth month . . . first day.* Aug. 29, 520 B.C. *Darius the king.* Darius Hystaspis (or Hystaspes) ruled Persia from 522 to 486 B.C. It was he who prepared the trilingual inscription on the Behistun (Bisitun) cliff wall (located in modern Iran), through which cuneiform languages were deciphered. *first day.* The new moon was the day on which prophets were sometimes consulted (see 2 Ki 4:22–23 and note on Is 1:14). *Zerubbabel.* See note on Ezra 1:8,"Sheshbazzar." *Shealtiel.* According to 1 Chr 3:17–19 he was Zerubbabel's grandfather (in Hebrew "son" sometimes means "grandson"). *Joshua.* Mentioned with Zerubbabel also in vv. 12,14; 2:2,4. *Josedech.* Had been taken captive by Nebuchadnezzar (1 Chr 6:15).

‡1:2 *LORD of hosts.* Used more than 90 times in Haggai, Zechariah and Malachi. See notes on 1 Sam 1:3; Is 13:4. *This people.* See 2:14. Because of their sin, the nation is not called "my people" (see Is 6:9; 8:6,11–12; Jer 14:10–11; see also note on Hos 1:9). *time is not come.* After the foundation of the temple had been laid in 536 B.C. (see Ezra 3:8–10), opposition hindered and then halted the work until 520 (see Ezra 4:1–5,24). "Time is not yet come" is strategic for Haggai's message. It interlocks with Zephaniah's "at that time" (3:19–20), which is the object of faith for his readers; that is, "wait" (3:8) for that time when the Lord would come to institute the great day of the Lord. Haggai uses it in a deeply ironic fashion, as the pious claim they are simply "waiting" for that time—the specific task of the faithful. See further comments on v. 4. Another possible interlock word is Zeph 3:18, "solemn assembly" which is the exact root of Haggai's name. The 12 minor prophets were edited in antiquity to be read as one book.

‡1:4 *cieled houses.* Or "paneled houses," usually connected with royal dwellings, which had cedar paneling (1 Ki 7:3,7; Jer 22:14). This unusual word appears only six times, and its meaning is obscure. It may have had the meaning of "beam," as in houses built with beams (a luxury, as the normal house was built with mud brick). Haggai's main message appears centered on the responsibility of the faithful as stewards of time. One response is to "wait" for the day of the Lord. Haggai is challenging them that until that day comes, they are to use "time" as an opportunity to work for God in the same way they have worked for themselves.

1:6 *sown much, and bring in little.* A curse for disobedience (see Deut 28:38–39). Lev 26:20 also describes the unfruitfulness of a land judged by God. *drink . . . not filled with drink.* Cf. Is 55:1–2. The people experience futility in all their activities, legitimate or illegitimate (cf. Hos 4:10–11; Mic 6:13–15). *a bag with holes.* Famine causes prices to rise sharply.

‡1:8 *mountain . . . wood.* Perhaps wood from the hills around Jerusalem was to supplement the cedar wood already purchased from Lebanon (see Ezra 3:7). *I will take pleasure in it.* And with the sacrifices offered there (contrast Is 1:11). *be glorified.* An obedient nation would bring praise and honor to God (see Jer 13:11). Haggai's message seems to be that obedience brings success. Israel's God of the heavens is using the king of Persia to effect his will via the faithful obedience of God's people.

1:10 *dew.* Normally abundant, and often as valuable as rain (see 2 Sam 1:21; 1 Ki 17:1).

‡1:11 *mountains.* The hills were cultivated, especially through terracing (see Ps 104:13–15; Is 7:25; Joel 3:18). *the corn . . . the new wine . . . the oil.* The three basic crops of the land, often mentioned in a context of blessing or cursing (see Deut 7:13; 11:14; 28:51; Hos 2:8,22). Corn actually referred to wheat and barley. Olive oil was used as food, ointment or medicine. *men, and upon cattle.* The drought affected men and cattle and so could be said to be "upon" them too.

‡1:12 *remnant.* See note on Is 1:9. *did fear before the LORD.* Showed respect and obedience (see Deut 31:12–13; Mal 1:6; 3:5,16). This is a remarkable response since most prophets were rejected. It reinforces the interpretation that their main problem was misunderstanding their responsibility to "time."

‡1:13 *messenger.* A title for prophets (see 2 Chr 36:15; Is

Zerubbabel the son of Shealtiel, [b]governor of
Judah, and the spirit of Joshua the son of
Josedech the high priest, and the spirit of all
the remnant of the people; [c]and they came
and did work in the house of the LORD of hosts,
their God,
15 In the four and twentieth day of the sixth
month, in the second year of Darius the king.

1:14 [b]ch. 2:21 [c]Ezra 5:2,8
2:1 [1]Heb. *by the hand of*
2:3 [a]Ezra 3:12 [b]Zech. 4:10
2:4 [a]Zech. 8:9

Comfort and hope from God

2 In the seventh *month,* in the one and
twentieth *day* of the month, came the
word of the LORD [1]by the prophet Haggai, saying,
2 Speak now to Zerubbabel the son of
Shealtiel, governor of Judah, and to Joshua the
son of Josedech the high priest and to the
residue of the people, saying,

3 [a]Who *is* left among you that saw this
house in her first glory?
And how do ye see it now?
[b]*Is it* not in your eyes in comparison of
it as nothing?
4 Yet now [a]be strong, O Zerubbabel,
saith the LORD;
And be strong, O Joshua, son of
Josedech, the high priest;
And be strong, all ye people of the
land, saith the LORD, and work:
For I *am* with you, saith the LORD of
hosts:
5 [a]*According to* the word that I
covenanted with you when ye came
out of Egypt,
So [b]my spirit remaineth among you:
fear ye not.
6 For thus saith the LORD of hosts; [a]Yet
once, it *is* a little while,
And [b]I *will* shake the heavens, and the
earth, and the sea, and the dry *land;*
7 And I will shake all nations, [a]and the
desire of all nations shall come:
And I will fill this house *with* glory,
saith the LORD of hosts.
8 The silver *is* mine, and the gold *is*
mine, saith the LORD of hosts.
9 [a]The glory of this latter house shall be
greater than of the former, saith the
LORD of hosts:
And in this place will I give [b]peace,
saith the LORD of hosts.

2:5 [a]Ex. 29:45,46 [b]Neh. 9:20; Is. 63:11
2:6 [a]ver. 21; Heb. 12:26 [b]Joel 3:16
2:7 [a]Gen. 49:10; Mal. 3:1
2:9 [a]John 1:14 [b]Ps. 85:8,9; Luke 2:14; Eph. 2:14

Holiness and uncleanness

10 ¶ In the four and twentieth *day* of the
ninth *month,* in the second year of Darius,
came the word of the LORD by Haggai the
prophet, saying,

42:19 and note) or priests (see Mal 2:7). *I am with you.* A sure indication of success (see 2:4; Num 14:9; Gen 26:3 and note). God had, in the past, been "absent" for long periods of time (400 years in Egypt) and had seemed to be so for these two generations in exile. This formula would have reminded every Jew of Ex 3:12–15. Both the curse they were experiencing and this timely reminder of God's presence assured them that His covenant was still in effect. Every New Covenant believer has this same promise from Christ: "I am with you alway" (Mat 28:20).

1:14 *stirred up the spirit.* See Ezra 1:5, where God stirred up many of these same people to return home and rebuild the temple.

1:15 *four and twentieth day of the sixth month.* Sept. 21, 520 B.C.

2:1 *In the seventh month, in the one and twentieth day.* Oct. 17, 520 B.C., the last day of the feast of tabernacles. It was a time to celebrate the summer harvest (see Lev 23:34–43), though the crops were meager (see 1:11; cf. John 7:37). Solomon had dedicated the temple during this feast (1 Ki 8:2).

2:3 *is left.* Some of the older exiles (perhaps including Haggai himself) had seen Solomon's magnificent temple, destroyed by the Babylonians 66 years earlier. *this house in her first glory.* See vv. 7,9. Zerubbabel's temple was considered a continuation of Solomon's. *in your eyes . . . as nothing.* Cf. the reaction when the foundation of the temple was finished (Ezra 3:12).

‡2:4 *be strong . . . work.* David used these words in 1 Chr 28:20 when he encouraged Solomon to build the temple. Joshua son of Nun had been exhorted with similar words (Josh 1:6–7,9,18). *I am with you.* See 1:13 and note; 1 Chr 28:20. I am the same God who performed the great wonders of the exodus. The same God who helped Solomon will empower Zerubbabel and the people.

‡2:5 *Egypt.* Proof that Haggai had Ex 3 in mind for his "I am with you" saying. *my spirit.* The Holy Spirit had rested on Moses and the 70 elders as they had led the people out of Egypt and through the wilderness (see Num 11:16–17,25; Is 63:11). See also Zech 4:6 and note. *fear ye not.* See notes on v. 4; Josh 1:18; Is 41:10.

2:6 An announcement of the coming day of God's judgment on the nations—which the fall of Persia to Alexander the Great (333–330 B.C.) would foreshadow. Heb 12:26–27 relates this verse to the judgment of the nations at the second coming of Christ. The background for the shaking of the nations here and in vv. 21–22 is the judgment on Egypt at the Red sea. Cf. also Is 14:16–17.

‡2:7 *desire of all nations shall come.* Can refer to individuals, as in 1 Sam 9:20; Dan 9:23 (where the same Hebrew verb is translated "greatly beloved"); 11:37. Thus it may have Messianic significance (cf. Mal 3:1). The same Hebrew word (See note on 1:8 for comments on the interplay of these two accounts) can also refer to articles of value, however (see 2 Chr 20:25; 32:27)—such as the contribution of King Darius to the temple (Ezra 6:8). If that is the intent here, the bringing of the "wealth of the nations" to Zion in Is 60:5 is a close parallel (see note there). *fill . . . with glory.* "Glory" can refer to material splendor (see Is 60:7,13 and notes) or to the presence of God (Ex 40:34–35; 1 Ki 8:10–11). Given Haggai's message, it would seem that he has the latter in mind; just as God filled the tabernacle, so He will fill this new temple. The latter references connect the glory of the Lord with the cloud that filled the sanctuary. When Christ came to the earthly temple, God's presence was evident as never before (see Luke 2:27,32). See especially John 1:14: "we beheld his glory . . ." and "dwelt among us . . ."). The latter verb is literally "tabernacled among us." Jesus is the glory of the temple incarnate.

2:8 *silver . . . gold.* God provided for Solomon's temple (1 Chr 29:2,7) and for Zerubbabel's (Ezra 6:5).

2:9 *glory . . . greater.* Ultimately because the Messiah would be present there (see v. 7 and note). *this place.* Probably Jerusalem (see Is 60:17 and note). *will I give peace.* Probably an allusion to the priestly benediction (see Num 6:26).

2:10 *four and twentieth. . . ninth month.* Dec. 18, 520 B.C.—when winter crops were planted.

11 Thus saith the LORD of hosts; [a]Ask now
the priests *concerning* the law, saying,
12 If one bear holy flesh in the skirt of his
garment, and with his skirt do touch bread, or
pottage, or wine, or oil, or any meat, shall it be
holy? And the priests answered and said, No.
13 Then said Haggai, If *one that is* [a]unclean
by a dead body touch any of these, shall
it be unclean? And the priests answered and
said, It shall be unclean.
14 Then answered Haggai, and said,
[a]So *is* this people, and so *is* this nation
before me, saith the LORD;
And so *is* every work of their hands;
And *that* which they offer there *is*
unclean.
15 And now, I pray you, [a]consider from
this day and upward,
From before a stone was laid upon a
stone in the temple of the LORD:
16 Since those *days* were, [a]when *one*
came to a heap of twenty *measures,*
there were *but* ten:
When *one* came to the pressfat for to
draw out fifty *vessels out of* the
press, there were *but* twenty.
17 [a]I smote you with blasting and with
mildew and with hail
[b]*In* all the labours of your hands;
[c]Yet ye *turned* not to me, saith the LORD.
18 Consider now from this day and
upward,
From the four and twentieth day of the
ninth *month,*

2:11 [a]Lev. 10:10,11; Deut. 33:10; Mal. 2:7
2:13 [a]Num. 19:11
2:14 [a]Tit. 1:15
2:15 [a]ch. 1:5
2:16 [a]ch. 1:6,9; Zech. 8:10
2:17 [a]Deut. 28:22; 1 Ki. 8:37; Amos 4:9; ch. 1:9 [b]ch. 1:11 [c]Jer. 5:3; Amos 4:6,8-11
2:18 [a]Zech. 8:9
2:19 [a]Zech. 8:12
2:21 [a]ch. 1:14 [b]ver. 6,7
2:22 [a]Dan. 2:44 [b]Mic. 5:10; Zech. 9:10
2:23 [a]Sol. 8:6; Jer. 22:24 [b]Is. 42:1; 43:10

Even from [a]the day that the foundation
of the LORD's temple was laid,
consider *it.*
19 [a]*Is* the seed yet in the barn?
Yea, as yet the vine, and the fig tree,
and the pomegranate, and the olive
tree, hath not brought forth:
From this day will I bless *you.*

Zerubbabel chosen by the LORD

20 ¶ And again the word of the LORD came
unto Haggai in the four and twentieth *day* of
the month, saying,
21 Speak to Zerubbabel, [a]governor of Judah,
saying,
[b]I *will* shake the heavens and the
earth;
22 And [a]I will overthrow the throne of
kingdoms,
And I will destroy the strength of the
kingdoms of the heathen;
And [b]I will overthrow the chariots, and
those that ride in them;
And the horses and their riders shall
come down,
Every one by the sword of his brother.
23 In that day, saith the LORD of hosts,
Will I take thee, O Zerubbabel, my
servant, the son of Shealtiel, saith
the LORD,
[a]And will make thee as a signet:
For [b]I have chosen thee, saith the LORD
of hosts.

2:11 *priests.* They were consulted about the precise meaning of the law (see Jer 18:18; Mal 2:7–9).
2:12 *holy flesh.* Meat from an animal set apart for a sacrifice. *shall it be holy?* A question about transmitting holiness. Consecrated meat made the garment "holy" because it was in direct contact with that garment (see Lev 6:27), but the garment could not pass on that holiness to a third object. Cf. Ezek 46:20.
2:13 *shall it be unclean?* Ceremonial uncleanness is transmitted much more easily than holiness. Anything touched by an unclean person becomes unclean (see Num 19:11–13,22).
2:14 *this people.* See 1:2 and note. *every work . . . is unclean.* Even though the people were back in the Holy Land, that holiness did not make them pure. They needed to obey the Lord, particularly with regard to rebuilding the temple. See notes on vv. 12–13.
2:15 *before a stone was laid.* Before the 24th day of the sixth month (1:15).
2:16 *heap.* See Jer 50:26. *ten . . . twenty.* The poor harvests were related to the sin of the people. See 1:11; Is 5:10 and note. *pressfat.* Or "wine vat," a trough into which grape juice flowed. See note on Is 16:10.
2:17 *blasting and with mildew.* A scorching east wind resulted in blight on plant life (see Gen 41:6 and note). Blight and mildew are mentioned as a curse for disobedience in Deut 28:22. See also 1 Ki 8:37; Amos 4:9. *hail.* Sent to destroy the fields and livestock of Egypt (see Ex 9:25; Ps 78:47–48). *Yet ye turned not to me.* See Amos 4:9.
‡2:18 *the LORD's temple was laid.* The same potential for blessing existed at the time when the foundation of the temple was laid in 536 B.C. (Ezra 3:11). This is a warning not to fail again and an encouragement that they were still in covenant with God.
‡2:19 *vine . . . fig tree . . . pomegranate . . . olive tree.* Grapes, figs and pomegranates ripened in August and September, and olives from September to November. These harvests, like the earlier grain crops, had produced little. See 1:11 and note. *will I bless you.* Because of their response to Haggai's message, future abundance is assured. Cf. Mal 3:10. See also Ex 20:24, "An altar of earth thou shalt make unto me . . . and I will bless thee." See Ex 23:25.
2:20 See note on v. 10.
2:21 *shake . . . the earth.* See v. 6 and note.
2:22 *overthrow . . . overthrow.* The Hebrew for these words is used with reference to Sodom and Gomorrah (see Gen 19:25; Amos 4:11). *chariots . . . horses . . . riders.* Cf. the destruction of Pharaoh's army at the Red sea (Ex 15:1,4,19,21). *Every one . . . of his brother.* The plight of the armies of Midian (Judg 7:22), Gog (Ezek 38:21) and the nations fighting against Jerusalem in the last days (Zech 14:13).
‡2:23 *In that day.* The day of the Lord. See Is 2:11,17,20; 10:20,27; Zech 2:11 and notes. *my servant.* A term applied to the forefathers, Abraham (Deut 9:27) and Moses (Deut 34:5); to prophets (see Is 20:3 and note), political leaders (Is 22:20) and the Messiah (see Is 41:8–9; 42:1 and notes). *signet.* A kind of seal that functioned as a signature (see Esth 8:8) and was worn on one's finger (Esth 3:10). Like other seals (cf. Gen 38:18) it could be used as a pledge or guarantee of full payment. Its mention here probably reverses the curse placed on King Jehoiachin in Jer 22:24 (cf. Judg 17:2). Zerubbabel would then be a guarantee that someday the Messiah descended from David will come (cf. Mat 1:1,12). In 2 Cor 1:22 the Holy Spirit is the seal guaranteeing the believer's future inheritance (cf. Eph 1:13–14). *chosen thee.* See Is 41:8–9; 42:1 and notes.

Zechariah

INTRODUCTION

Background

Zechariah's prophetic ministry took place in the postexilic period, the time of the Jewish restoration from Babylonian captivity. For historical details see Introduction to Haggai: Background.

Author and Unity

Like Jeremiah (1:1) and Ezekiel (1:3), Zechariah was not only a prophet (1:1) but also a priest. He was born in Babylonia and was among those who returned to Judah in 538 B.C. under the leadership of Zerubbabel and Joshua (his grandfather Iddo is named among the returnees in Neh 12:4). At a later time, when Joiakim was high priest, Zechariah apparently succeeded Iddo (1:1,7) as head of that priestly family (Neh 12:10–16). Since the grandson succeeded the grandfather, it has been suggested that the father (Berechiah, 1:1,7) died at an early age.

Zechariah was a contemporary of Haggai (Ezra 5:1; 6:14) but continued his ministry long after him (compare 1:1 and 7:1 with Hag 1:1; see also Neh 12:1–16). His young age (see 2:4) in the early period of his ministry makes it possible that he ministered even into the reign of Artaxerxes I (465–424 B.C.).

Most likely Zechariah wrote the entire book that bears his name. Some have questioned his authorship of chs. 9 to 14—citing differences in style and other compositional features, and giving historical and chronological references that allegedly require a different date and author from those of chs. 1 to 8. All these objections, however, can be explained in other satisfactory ways, so there is no compelling reason to question the unity of the book.

Dates

The dates of Zechariah's recorded messages are best correlated with those of Haggai and with other historical events as follows:

1.	Haggai's first message (Hag 1:1–11; Ezra 5:1)	Aug. 29, 520 B.C.
2.	Resumption of the building of the temple (Hag 1:12–15; Ezra 5:2) (The rebuilding seems to have been hindered from 536 to c. 530 [Ezra 4:1–5], and the work ceased altogether from c. 530 to 520 [Ezra 4:24].)	Sept. 21, 520
3.	Haggai's second message (Hag 2:1–9)	Oct. 17, 520
4.	Beginning of Zechariah's preaching (1:1–6)	Oct./Nov., 520
5.	Haggai's third message (Hag 2:10–19)	Dec. 18, 520
6.	Haggai's fourth message (Hag 2:20–23)	Dec. 18, 520
7.	Tatnai's letter to Darius concerning the rebuilding of the temple (Ezra 5:3—6:14) (There must have been a lapse of time between the resumption of the building and Tatnai's appearance.)	519–518
8.	Zechariah's eight night visions (1:7—6:8)	Feb. 15, 519
9.	Joshua crowned (6:9–15)	Feb. 16 (?), 519
10.	Repentance urged, blessings promised (chs. 7—8)	Dec. 7, 518
11.	Dedication of the temple (Ezra 6:15–18)	Mar. 12, 516
12.	Zechariah's final prophecy (chs. 9—14)	After 480 (?)

Occasion and Purpose

The occasion is the same as that of the book of Haggai (see Background; Dates). The chief purpose of Zechariah (and Haggai) was to rebuke the people of Judah and to encourage and motivate them to complete the rebuilding of the temple (Zech 4:8–10; Hag 1—2), though both prophets were clearly

interested in spiritual renewal as well. In addition, the purpose of the eight night visions (1:7—6:8) is explained in 1:3,5–6: The Lord said that if Judah would return to Him, He would return to them. Furthermore, His word would continue to be fulfilled.

Theological Teaching

The theological teaching of the book is related to its Messianic as well as its apocalyptic and eschatological motifs. Regarding the Messianic emphasis, Zechariah foretold Christ's coming in lowliness (6:12), His humanity (6:12; 13:7), His rejection and betrayal for 30 pieces of silver (11:12–13), His crucifixion (struck by the "sword" of the Lord; 13:7), His priesthood (6:13), His kingship (6:13; 9:9; 14:9,16), His coming in glory (14:4), His building of the Lord's temple (6:12–13), His reign (9:10; 14) and His establishment of enduring peace and prosperity (3:10; 9:9–10). These Messianic passages give added significance to Jesus' words in Luke 24:25–27,44.

Concerning the apocalyptic and eschatological emphasis, Zechariah foretold the siege of Jerusalem (12:1–3; 14:1–2), the initial victory of Judah's enemies (14:2), the Lord's defense of Jerusalem (14:3–4), the judgment on the nations (12:9; 14:3), the topographical changes in Judah (14:4–5), the celebration of the feast of tabernacles in the Messianic kingdom age (14:16–19) and the ultimate holiness of Jerusalem and her people (14:20–21).

There is also theological significance in the prophet's name, which means "The LORD (Yahweh) remembers." "The LORD" is the personal, covenant name of God and is a perpetual testimony to His faithfulness to His promises (see note on Ex 3:14). He "remembers" His covenant promises and takes action to fulfill them. In the book of Zechariah God's promised deliverance from Babylonian exile, including a restored kingdom community and a functioning temple (the earthly throne of the divine King), leads into even grander pictures of the salvation and restoration to come through the Messiah.

Finally, the book as a whole teaches the sovereignty of God in history, over people and nations—past, present and future.

Literary Form and Themes

The book is primarily a mixture of exhortation (call to repentance, 1:2–6), prophetic visions (1:7—6:8) and judgment and salvation oracles (chs. 9—14). The prophetic visions of 1:7—6:8 are called apocalyptic (revelatory) literature, which is essentially a literature of encouragement to God's people. When the apocalyptic section is read along with the salvation (or deliverance) oracles in chs. 9—14, it becomes obvious that the dominant emphasis of the book is encouragement because of the glorious future that awaits the people of God.

In fact, encouragement is the book's central theme—primarily encouragement to complete the rebuilding of the temple. Various means are used to accomplish this end, and these function as subthemes. For example, great stress is laid on the coming of the Messiah and the overthrow of all antikingdom forces by Him so that God's rule can be finally and fully established on earth. The then-current local scene thus becomes the basis for contemplating the universal, eschatological picture.

Outline

Part I (chs. 1—8)

- I. Introduction (1:1–6)
  - A. The Date and the Author's Name (1:1)
  - B. A Call to Repentance (1:2–6)
- II. A Series of Eight Night Visions (1:7—6:8)
  - A. The Horseman among the Myrtle Trees (1:7–17)
  - B. The Four Horns and the Four Carpenters (1:18–21)
  - C. A Man with a Measuring Line (ch. 2)
  - D. Clean Garments for the High Priest (ch. 3)
  - E. The Golden Candlesticks and the Two Olive Trees (ch. 4)
  - F. The Flying Roll (5:1–4)
  - G. The Woman in the Ephah (5:5–11)
  - H. The Four Chariots (6:1–8)
- III. The Symbolic Crowning of Joshua the High Priest (6:9–15)
- IV. The Problem of Fasting and the Promise of the Future (chs. 7—8)

- A. The Question by the Delegation from Beth-el (7:1–3)
- B. The Rebuke by the Lord (7:4–7)
- C. The Command to Repent (7:8–14)
- D. The Restoration of Israel to God's Favor (8:1–17)
- E. Kingdom Joy and Jewish Favor (8:18–23)

Part II (chs. 9—14)

- V. Two Prophetic Oracles: The Great Messianic Future and the Full Realization of God's Kingdom (chs. 9—14)
  - A. The First Oracle: The Advent and Rejection of the Messiah (chs. 9—11)
    1. The advent of the Messianic King (chs. 9—10)
    2. The rejection of the Messianic Shepherd-King (ch. 11)
  - B. The Second Oracle: The Advent and Reception of the Messiah (chs. 12—14)
    1. The deliverance and conversion of Israel (chs. 12—13)
    2. The Messiah's coming and His kingdom (ch. 14)

Call for national repentance

1 In the eighth month, [a]in the second year
of Darius, came the word of the LORD
[b]unto Zechariah, the son of Berechiah, the son
of Iddo the prophet, saying,
2 The LORD hath been [1]sore displeased
with your fathers.
3 Therefore say thou unto them, Thus
saith the LORD of hosts;
Turn [a]ye unto me, saith the LORD of
hosts,
And I will turn unto you, saith the
LORD of hosts.
4 Be ye not as your fathers, [a]unto whom
the former prophets have cried,
saying,
Thus saith the LORD of hosts; [b]Turn ye
now from your evil ways, and *from*
your evil doings:
But they did not hear, nor hearken
unto me, saith the LORD.
5 Your fathers, where *are* they?
And the prophets, do they live for
ever?
6 But [a]my words and my statutes, which
I commanded my servants the
prophets,
Did they not [1]take hold of your
fathers?
And they returned and said, [b]Like as
the LORD of hosts thought to do
unto us,
According to our ways, and according
to our doings, so hath he dealt
with us.

1:1 [a]Ezra 4:24; Hag. 1:1 [b]Ezra 5:1; Mat. 23:35
1:2 [1]Heb. with *displeasure*
1:3 [a]Jer. 25:5; 35:15; Mic. 7:19; Mal. 3:7; Luke 15:20; Jas. 4:8
1:4 [a]2 Chr. 36:15,16 [b]Is. 31:6; Jer 3:12; 18:11; Ezek. 18:30; Hos. 14:1
1:6 [1]Or, *overtake* [a]Is. 55:1 [b]Lam. 1:18; 2:17

The horsemen among the myrtles

7 ¶ Upon the four and twentieth day of the
eleventh month, which *is* the month Sebat, in
the second year of Darius, came the word of
the LORD unto Zechariah, the son of Berechiah, the son of Iddo the prophet, saying,
8 I saw by night, and behold [a]a man riding
upon a red horse, and he stood among the
myrtle trees that *were* in the bottom; and behind him *were there* [b]red horses, [1]speckled,
and white.
9 Then said I, O my lord, what *are* these?
And the angel that talked with me said unto
me, I will shew thee what these *be*.
10 And the man that stood among the myrtle trees answered and said, [a]These *are they*
whom the LORD hath sent to walk to and fro
through the earth.
11 [a]And they answered the angel of the
LORD that stood among the myrtle trees, and
said, We have walked to and fro through the
earth, and behold, all the earth sitteth still,
and is at rest.
12 Then the angel of the LORD answered
and said, O LORD of hosts, how long wilt thou
not have mercy on Jerusalem and on the cities
of Judah, *against* which thou hast had indignation [a]these threescore and ten years?
13 And the LORD answered the angel that
talked with me *with* [a]good words *and* comfortable words.
14 So the angel that communed with me
said unto me, Cry thou, saying,
Thus saith the LORD of hosts;
I am [a]jealous for Jerusalem and for
Zion *with* a great jealousy.

1:8 [1]Or, *bay* [a]Josh. 5:13; Rev. 6:4 [b]ch. 6:2-7
1:10 [a]Heb. 1:14
1:11 [a]Ps. 103:20,21
1:12 [a]Jer. 25:11,12; Dan. 9:2; ch. 7:5
1:13 [a]Jer. 29:10
1:14 [a]Joel 2:18; ch. 8:2

1:1 *eighth month . . . the second year.* October-November, 520 B.C. Haggai also began his prophetic ministry in Darius's second year, on the first day of the sixth month, i.e., on Aug. 29, 520 (Hag 1:1). *the word of the LORD.* A technical phrase for the prophetic word of revelation (see 9:1; 12:1; Jer 1:2; Ezek 1:3; Hos 1:1; Joel 1:1; Jonah 1:1; 3:1; Mic 1:1; Zeph 1:1; Hag 1:1; Mal 1:1). See also note on 6:9. *Iddo.* See v. 7; Ezra 5:1; 6:14; Neh 12:4,16; see also Introduction: Author. *prophet.* One called by God to be His spokesman (see note on Ex 7:1–2).

1:2 *sore displeased with your fathers.* The Lord was angry because of the covenant-breaking sins of the Jews' preexilic forefathers, resulting in the destruction of Jerusalem and the temple in 586 B.C., followed by exile to Babylonia. God's anger should not be explained away, for to deny that God has genuine emotions is to deprive Him of one of the clear marks of personality.

1:3 *Turn ye unto me . . . I will turn unto you.* Cf. 7:13. If the people of Zechariah's day would change their course and go in the opposite direction from that of their forefathers (v. 4), the Lord would return to them with blessing instead of with a curse (see v. 16; see also Jer 18:7–10).

1:4 *former prophets.* Such as Isaiah (see Is 45:22), Jeremiah (see Jer 18:11) and Ezekiel (see Ezek 33:11). See also 7:7,12; Jer 25:4–5; 35:15.

1:5 *do they live for ever?* No, but God's words through them live on to be fulfilled (see v. 6).

‡1:6 *my servants the prophets.* See 2 Ki 9:7; 17:13,23; 21:10; 24:2; Ezra 9:11; Jer 7:25 and note; 25:4; Ezek 38:17; Dan 9:6,10; Amos 3:7. *Did they not take hold of your fathers?* Cf. Is 40:6–8; 55:10–11. For the imagery see Deut 28:2,15,45. *they returned.* Apparently a reference to what happened to some of the preexilic forefathers and/or their offspring during the exile and immediately afterward (cf. Ezra 9; 10:1–17; Dan 9:1–19).

1:7–17 The first vision. Although God's covenant people are troubled while the oppressing nations are at ease, God is jealous (see note on Ex 20:5) for His people and will restore them and their towns and the temple. The imagery of the first vision is reflected in that of the eighth and final vision (6:1–8).

1:7 *four and twentieth day of . . . Sebat.* Feb. 15, 519 B.C., about three months after the date of v. 1.

1:8 *I saw.* Not in a dream (see 4:1) but in a vision. The visions were given to Zechariah while he was fully awake. *night.* Zechariah had all eight visions (1:7–6:8) in one night. *a man riding.* The angel of the Lord (v. 11). He must not be confused with the interpreting angel, who is mentioned in vv. 9,13–14,19; 2:3; 4:1,4–5; 5:5,10; 6:4–5. *horses.* Perhaps angelic messengers (v. 10).

1:11 *angel of the LORD.* See note on Gen 16:7. *sitteth still.* Cf. 6:8. While the Persian empire as a whole was secure and at ease by this time (v. 15), the Jews in Judah were oppressed and still under foreign domination (v. 12).

1:12 *threescore and ten years.* Seventy years. See 7:5 and note; Jer 25:11–12 and note; 29:10; cf. 2 Chr 36:21; Ezra 1:1; Dan 9:2.

1:13 *comfortable words.* Those of vv. 14–17.

1:14 *jealous.* See 8:2. Through the use of such language the Lord's love for Judah is shown (see note on Ex 20:5; cf. Jas 4:4). The key idea is that of God vindicating Judah for the violations against her (v. 15).

15 And I am very sore displeased with the
heathen *that are* at ease:
For [a]I was *but* a little displeased, and
they helped forward the affliction.
16 Therefore thus saith the LORD; [a]I am
returned to Jerusalem with mercies:
My house shall be built in it, saith the
LORD of hosts,
And [b]a line shall be stretched forth
upon Jerusalem.
17 Cry yet, saying, Thus saith the LORD of
hosts;
My cities through [1]prosperity shall yet
be spread abroad;
[a]And the LORD shall yet comfort Zion,
And [b]shall yet choose Jerusalem.

Four horns and four carpenters

18 ¶ Then lift I up mine eyes, and saw, and
behold four horns.
19 And I said unto the angel that talked
with me, What *be* these? And he answered
me, [a]These *are* the horns which have scattered Judah, Israel, and Jerusalem.
20 And the LORD shewed me four carpenters.
21 Then said I, What come these to do?
And he spake, saying, These *are* the horns
which have scattered Judah, so that no man
did lift up his head: but these are come to fray
them, to cast out the horns of the Gentiles,
which [a]lift up *their* horn over the land of Judah to scatter it.

The measuring line of Jerusalem

2 I lift up mine eyes again, and looked, and
behold, [a]a man with a measuring line in
his hand.
2 Then said I, Whither goest thou? And he
said unto me, [a]To measure Jerusalem, to see
what *is* the breadth thereof, and what *is* the
length thereof.
3 And behold, the angel that talked with
me went forth, and another angel went out to
meet him,
4 And said unto him, Run, speak to this
young man, saying,
[a]Jerusalem shall be inhabited *as* towns
without walls
For the multitude of men and cattle
therein:
5 For I, saith the LORD, will be unto her
[a]a wall of fire round about,
[b]And will be the glory in the midst of
her.
6 Ho, ho, *come forth,* and flee [a]from the
land of the north, saith the LORD:
For I have [b]spread you abroad as the
four winds of the heaven, saith the
LORD.
7 [a]Deliver thyself, O Zion, that dwellest
with the daughter of Babylon.
8 For thus saith the LORD of hosts;
After the glory hath he sent me unto
the nations which spoiled you:
For he that [a]toucheth you toucheth the
apple of his eye.
9 For behold, I *will* [a]shake mine hand
upon them,
And they shall be a spoil to their
servants:
And [b]ye shall know that the LORD of
hosts hath sent me.

10 [a]Sing and rejoice, O daughter of Zion:
For lo, I come, and I [b]will dwell in the
midst of thee, saith the LORD.
11 [a]And many nations shall be joined to
the LORD [b]in that day,
And shall be [c]my people:
And I will dwell in the midst of thee,
And [d]thou shalt know that the LORD of
hosts hath sent me unto thee.
12 And the LORD shall [a]inherit Judah his
portion in the holy land,

1:15 [a]Is. 47:6
1:16 [a]Is. 12:1; 54:8; ch. 2:10; 8:3 [b]ch. 2:1,2
1:17 [1]Heb. *good* [a]Is. 51:3 [b]Is. 14:1; ch. 2:12; 3:2
1:19 [a]Ezra 4:1,4,7; 5:3
1:21 [a]Ps. 75:4,5
2:1 [a]Ezek. 40:3
2:2 [a]Rev. 11:1
2:4 [a]Jer. 31:27; Ezek. 36:10
2:5 [a]Is. 26:1 [b]Is. 60:19
2:6 [a]Is. 48:20 [b]Deut. 28:64; Ezek. 17:21
2:7 [a]Rev. 18:4
2:8 [a]Deut. 32:10
2:9 [a]Is. 19:16 [b]ch. 4:9
2:10 [a]Is. 12:6 [b]Lev. 26:12
2:11 [a]Is. 2:2,3 [b]ch. 3:10 [c]Ex. 12:49 [d]Ezek. 33:33
2:12 [a]Deut. 32:9

1:15 *helped forward the affliction.* God was angry with Israel and used the Assyrians (Is 10:5) and Babylonians (Is 47:6; Jer 25:9) to punish her, but they went too far by trying to destroy the Jews as a people.
1:16 *I am returned.* See note on v. 3. *My house shall be built.* See Ezra 6:14–16. *a line shall be stretched.* A symbol of restoration (cf. Jer 31:38–40).
1:17 *choose Jerusalem.* See 2:12; 3:2.
1:18–21 The second vision. The nations that devastated Israel (v. 19) will in turn be destroyed by other nations.
1:18 *four.* If the number is to be taken literally, the reference is probably to Assyria, Egypt, Babylonia and Medo-Persia. *horns.* Symbolic of strength in general (Ps 18:2), or the strength of a country, i.e., its king (Ps 89:17; Dan 7:7–8; 8:20–21; Rev 17:12), or, as here (see v. 21), the power of a nation in general.
1:20 *four carpenters.* If the number is to be understood literally, probably the reference is to Egypt, Babylonia, Persia and Greece. What is clear is that all Judah's enemies will ultimately be defeated (v. 21).
2:1–13 The third vision. There will be full restoration and blessing for the covenant people, temple and city.
2:1 *measuring line.* See note on 1:16.
2:4 *young man.* Evidently Zechariah. *without walls.* The city's population will overflow to the point that it will be as though it had no walls (see 10:8,10; see also note on Is 49:19–20).
2:5 *wall of fire.* Here symbolic of divine protection (see Ex 13:21 and note; Is 4:5–6 and note). *glory.* See Ex 40:34.
2:6 *land of the north.* Babylon (v. 7) invaded Judah from the north (Jer 1:14; 4:6; 6:1,22; 10:22). *as the four winds.* In all directions. The exiles would return from north, south, east and west (Is 43:5–6; 49:12).
2:7 *Deliver thyself.* Cf. Rev 18:4–8. *Zion.* Jerusalem's exiles in Babylon.
2:8 *apple of his eye.* See note on Deut 32:10.
2:9 *hand.* Power.
2:10 See 9:9. *I will dwell in the midst of thee.* See v. 11; 8:3; Lev 26:11–12; Ezek 37:27; John 1:14; 2 Cor 6:16; Rev 21:3.
2:11 *many nations.* In fulfillment of the promise to Abraham (Gen 12:3; cf. Zec. 8:20–23; Gen 18:18; 22:18; Is 2:2–4; 60:3). *that day.* The day of the Lord (see 3:10; see also note on Is 2:11, 17,20).
2:12 *holy land.* The Hebrew for this designation occurs only here in Scripture. The land was rendered holy chiefly because it was the site of the earthly throne and sanctuary of the holy

And [b]shall choose Jerusalem again.
13 [a]Be silent, O all flesh, before the LORD:
For he is raised up [b]out of [1]his holy
habitation.

Joshua cleansed and reclothed

3 And he shewed me [a]Joshua the high
priest standing before the angel of the
LORD, and [b 1]Satan standing at his right hand
[2]to resist him.
2 And the LORD said unto Satan,
[a]The LORD rebuke thee, O Satan;
Even the LORD that [b]hath chosen
Jerusalem rebuke thee:
[c]*Is* not this a brand pluckt out of the
fire?
3 ¶ Now Joshua was clothed with [a]filthy
garments, and stood before the angel.
4 And he answered and spake unto those
that stood before him, saying, Take away the
filthy garments from him. And unto him he
said, Behold, I have caused thine iniquity to
pass from thee, [a]and *I will* clothe thee with
change of raiment.
5 And I said, Let them set a fair [a]mitre
upon his head. So they set a fair mitre upon
his head, and clothed him with garments. And
the angel of the LORD stood *by.*
6 And the angel of the LORD protested unto
Joshua, saying,
7 Thus saith the LORD of hosts;

2:12 [b]ch. 1:17
2:13 [1]Heb. *the habitation of his holiness* [a]Hab. 2:20 [b]Ps. 68:5; Is. 57:15
3:1 [1]That is, *an adversary* [2]Heb. *to be his adversary* [a]Hag. 1:1 [b]Ps. 109:6
3:2 [a]Jude 9 [b]Rom. 8:33 [c]Amos 4:11; Rom. 11:5
3:3 [a]Is. 64:6
3:4 [a]Is. 61:10; Luke 15:22
3:5 [a]Ex. 29:6
3:7 [1]Or, *ordinance* [2]Heb. *walks* [a]Lev. 8:35; Ezek. 44:16 [b]Deut. 17:9 [c]ch. 4:14
3:8 [1]Heb. *men of wonder* [or, *sign*, as Ezek. 12:11; 24:24] [a]Ps. 71:7; Is. 8:18 [b]Is. 42:1; Ezek. 34:23 [c]Is. 11:1; ch. 6:12
3:9 [a]Ps. 118:22; Is. 28:16 [b]Rev. 5:6 [c]Jer. 31:34; Mic. 7:18
3:10 [a]ch. 2:11 [b]Is. 36:16; Mic. 4:4
4:1 [a]ch. 2:3 [b]Dan. 8:18

If thou wilt walk in my ways, and if
thou wilt [a]keep my [1]charge,
Then thou shalt also [b]judge my house,
and shalt also keep my courts,
And I will give thee [2]places to walk
among these that [c]stand *by.*
8 Hear now, O Joshua the high priest,
thou,
And thy fellows that sit before thee:
For they *are* [a 1]men wondered at:
For behold, I *will* bring forth [b]my
servant the [c]BRANCH.
9 For behold the stone that I have laid
before Joshua;
[a]Upon one stone *shall be* [b]seven eyes:
Behold, I *will* engrave the graving
thereof, saith the LORD of hosts,
And [c]I will remove the iniquity of that
land in one day.
10 [a]In that day, saith the LORD of hosts,
Shall ye call every man his neighbour,
[b]Under the vine and under the fig tree.

The candlestick and two olive trees

4 And [a]the angel that talked with me came
again, and waked me, [b]as a man that is
wakened out of his sleep,
2 And said unto me, What seest thou? And
I said, I have looked, and behold, [a]a candlestick all of gold, [1]with a bowl upon the top of

4:2 [1]Heb. *with her bowl* [a]Rev. 1:12

King, who dwelt there among His covenant people. See note on Ex 3:5. *choose Jerusalem.* See 1:17; 3:2.

2:13 *Be silent . . . before the LORD.* See Hab 2:20; Zeph 1:7. *he is raised up.* To judge (cf. v. 9).

3:1–10 The fourth vision. Israel will be cleansed and restored as a priestly nation (see Ex 19:6 and note).

‡3:1 *Joshua.* A variant of Jeshua, here and elsewhere in Zechariah and in Haggai. In Ezra 2:2 and Neh 7:7 he is referred to as Jeshua. Here he represents the sinful nation of Israel (see vv. 8–9). The names "Joshua" and "Jeshua" were common in ancient times. The Greek equivalent is spelled "Jesus" in English, and all three forms of the name mean "The LORD saves" (see note on Mat 1:21). *standing before.* Ministering before—as priest (see Deut 10:8; 2 Chr 29:11; Ezek 44:15). *angel of the LORD.* See 1:11; see also note on Gen 16:7. *Satan.* Cf. Job 1:6–12; 2:1–7; Rev 12:10. *right hand.* See Ps 109:6. *resist.* The Hebrew for this word has the same root as the Hebrew for "Satan."

3:2 *rebuke . . . rebuke.* Repeated for emphasis (see 4:7; see also note on Is 40:1). *chosen Jerusalem.* See 1:17; 2:12. *brand pluckt out of the fire.* The Jews were retrieved from the fire of Babylonian exile to carry out God's future purpose for them (see Amos 4:11; see also Zech 13:8–9; Deut 4:20 and note; 7:7–8; 1 Ki 8:51; Is 48:10; Jer 11:4; 30:7; Rev 12:13–16).

3:4 *those that stood before him.* Probably angels (see also v. 7). *Take away the filthy garments.* Thus depriving him of his priestly office. The act is here symbolic also of the removal of sin (see note on v. 9).

‡3:5 *set a fair mitre upon his head.* Or, "put a clean turban on his head," thus reinstating him into his high-priestly function so that Israel once again has a divinely authorized priestly mediator. On the front of the turban were the words: "HOLINESS TO THE LORD" (Ex 28:36; 39:30; cf. 14:20).

3:7 If Joshua and his priestly associates are faithful, they will be co-workers with the angels in the carrying out of God's purposes for Zion and Israel. *these . . . stand by.* See note on v. 4.

3:8 *fellows.* Fellow priests. *my servant.* See notes on Ex 14:31; Ps 18 title; Is 41:8–9; 42:1–4; 42:1; Hag 2:23; Rom 1:1. *BRANCH.* A Messianic title (see 6:12; Is 4:2 and note; 11:1; Jer 23:5; 33:15).

3:9 *stone.* Probably another figure of the Messiah (cf. Ps 118:22–23; Is 8:13–15; 28:16 and note; Dan 2:35,45; Mat 21:42; Eph 2:19–22; 1 Pet 2:6–8). *seven eyes.* Perhaps symbolic of infinite intelligence (omniscience). See note on 4:10. *I will remove the iniquity of that land.* The symbolic act of v. 4 is now explained. "Land" stands for the people of Israel. For the cleansing spoken of here see also 12:10–13:1. *in one day.* Ultimately Good Friday, though some believe that the reference also includes Christ's second coming.

‡3:10 *that day.* The day of the Lord (see 2:11; see also note on Is 2:11,17,20). *Under the vine and under the fig tree.* A proverbial picture of peace, security and contentment (see 2 Ki 18:31; Mic 4:4 and note).

4:1–14 The fifth vision. The Jews are encouraged to rebuild the temple by being reminded of their divine resources. The light from the candlestick in the tabernacle/temple represents the reflection of God's glory in the consecration and the holy service of God's people (see note on Ex 25:31)—made possible only by the power of God's Spirit (see v. 6; the oil, v. 12). This enabling power will equip and sustain Zerubbabel in the rebuilding of the temple (vv. 6–10). And in the performance of their offices, Zerubbabel and Joshua (as representatives of the royal and priestly mediatorial offices) will channel the Spirit's enablement to God's people (vv. 11–14).

4:1 *waked me.* On the same night (see note on 1:8).

4:2 *What seest thou?* See 5:2; see also Jer 1:11 and note. The vision here was probably of seven lamps arranged around a large bowl that served as a bountiful reservoir of oil. Each lamp had seven "spouts" or "lips" that held the wicks of the oil lamps, making a total of 49 flames. Another possibility is that the

it, [b]and his seven lamps thereon, and [2]seven pipes to the seven lamps, which *were* upon the top thereof:

3 [a]And two olive trees by it, one upon the right *side* of the bowl, and the other upon the left *side* thereof.

4 So I answered and spake to the angel that talked with me, saying, What *are* these, my lord?

5 Then the angel that talked with me answered and said unto me, Knowest thou not what these *be?* And I said, No, my lord.

6 Then he answered and spake unto me, saying, This *is* the word of the LORD unto Zerubbabel, saying,

[a]Not by [1]might, nor by power, but by
my spirit,
Saith the LORD of hosts.
7 Who *art* thou, [a]O great mountain?
before Zerubbabel *thou shalt* become
a plain:
And he shall bring forth [b]the
headstone *thereof* [c]*with* shoutings,
crying, Grace, grace unto it.
8 Moreover the word of the LORD came
unto me, saying,
9 The hands of Zerubbabel [a]have laid the
foundation of this house;
His hands [b]shall also finish *it;*
And [c]thou shalt know that the [d]LORD
of hosts hath sent me unto you.
10 For who hath despised the day of
[a]small *things?*

4:2 [2]Or, *seven several pipes to the lamps, etc.* [b]Rev. 4:5
4:3 [a]Rev. 11:4
4:6 [1]Or, *army* [a]Hos. 1:7
4:7 [a]Jer. 51:25; Mat. 21:21 [b]Ps. 118:22 [c]Ezra 3:11,13
4:9 [a]Ezra 3:10 [b]Ezra 6:15 [c]ch. 2:9,11; 6:15 [d]Is. 48:16; ch. 2:8
4:10 [a]Hag. 2:3
4:10 [1]Or, *Sith the seven eyes of the LORD shall rejoice* [2]Heb. *stone of tin* [b]2 Chr. 16:9; Prov. 15:3; ch. 3:9
4:11 [a]ver. 3
4:12 [1]Heb. *by the hand [of]* [2]Or, *empty out of themselves* oil into *the gold* [3]Heb. *the gold*
4:14 [1]Heb. *sons of oil* [a]Rev. 11:4 [b]ch. 3:7 [c]See Josh. 3:11,13; ch. 6:5
5:1 [a]Ezek. 2:9
5:3 [1]Or, *every one of this* people *that stealeth holdeth* himself *guiltless, as it* doth [a]Mal. 4:6

[1]For they shall rejoice, and shall see
the [2]plummet in the hand of
Zerubbabel *with* those seven;
[b]They *are* the eyes of the LORD, which
run to and fro through the whole
earth.

11 ¶ Then answered I, and said unto him, What *are* these [a]two olive trees upon the right *side* of the candlestick and upon the left *side* thereof?

12 And I answered again, and said unto him, What *be these* two olive branches which [1]through the two golden pipes [2]empty [3]the golden *oil* out of themselves?

13 And he answered me and said, Knowest thou not what these *be?* And I said, No, my lord.

14 Then said he, [a]These *are* the two [1]anointed ones, [b]that stand by [c]the Lord of the whole earth.

The flying roll

5 Then I turned, and lift up mine eyes, and looked, and behold, a flying [a]roll.

2 And he said unto me, What seest thou? And I answered, I see a flying roll; the length thereof *is* twenty cubits, and the breadth thereof ten cubits.

3 Then said he unto me,
This *is* the [a]curse that goeth forth over
the face of the whole earth:
For [1]every one that stealeth shall be
cut off *as* on this *side* according to it;

"spouts" were "channels" conveying the oil from the bowl to the lamps. In any event, the bowl represents an abundant supply of oil, symbolizing the fullness of God's power through His Spirit, and the "seven . . . seven" represents the abundant light shining from the lamps (seven being the number of fullness or completeness).

4:3 *two olive trees.* Cf. Rev 11:4. The two olive trees stand for the priestly and royal offices and symbolize a continuing supply of oil. The two olive branches (v. 12) stand for Joshua the priest (ch. 3) and Zerubbabel from the royal house of David (ch. 4; cf. v. 14). These two leaders were to do God's work (e.g., on the temple and in the lives of the people) in the power of His Spirit (v. 6). The combination of the priestly and royal lines and their functions points ultimately to the Messianic King-Priest and His offices and functions (cf. 6:13).

4:4 *these.* The two olive trees of v. 3, as v. 11 makes clear. The answer to the question is postponed until v. 14.

4:6 *Not by might, nor by power.* Even though Zerubbabel does not possess the royal might and power that David and Solomon had enjoyed. *by my spirit.* Interprets the symbolism of the oil (v. 12). The angel encouraged Zerubbabel to complete the rebuilding of the temple (vv. 7–10) and assured him of the Spirit's enablement.

4:7 *mountain . . . plain.* Faith in the power of God's Spirit can overcome mountainous obstacles. The figurative mountain probably included opposition (Ezra 4:1–5,24) and the people's unwillingness to persevere (Hag 1:14; 2:1–5). Cf. the same or similar imagery in Is 40:4; 41:15; 49:11; Mat 17:20; 21:21; Mark 11:23; 1 Cor 13:2; 2 Cor 10:4. *headstone.* The final stone to be put in place (see Ps 118:22), marking the completion of the restoration temple by Zerubbabel (see v. 9). *Grace, grace unto it.* Repeated for emphasis (see 3:2; see also note on Is 40:1).

4:8 See note on 6:9.

4:9 *laid the foundation.* In 537–536 B.C. (Ezra 3:8–11; 5:16). *finish it.* In 516 (Ezra 6:14–16).

4:10 *day of small things.* Some thought the work on the temple was insignificant (Ezra 3:12; Hag 2:3), but God was in the rebuilding program and, by His Spirit (v. 6), would enable Zerubbabel to finish it. *plummet.* Or "plumbline." The meaning of the Hebrew for this phrase is uncertain. If "plummet" is correct, the text states that the people would rejoice when they saw this implement in Zerubbabel's hand to complete the task. But the Hebrew for these words may also be rendered "separated (i.e., chosen) stone," referring to the top stone of v. 7. *They . . . eyes.* See note on 3:9. God oversees the whole earth and is therefore in control of the situation in Judah.

4:14 The meaning of the vision is now explained. *two anointed ones.* Zerubbabel from the royal line of David and Joshua the priest. The oil (v. 12) used in anointing symbolizes the Holy Spirit (v. 6). The combination of ruler and priest points ultimately to the Messianic King-Priest (cf. 6:13; Ps 110; Heb 7). *Lord of the whole earth.* The master of the circumstances in which Zerubbabel and the people found themselves.

5:1–4 The sixth vision. Lawbreakers are condemned by the law they have broken; sinners will be purged from the land.

5:1 *flying.* Unrolled and waving like a banner, for all to read. *roll.* Scroll. See note on Ex 17:14.

5:2 *What seest thou?* See 4:2; see also Jer 1:11 and note. *twenty cubits . . . ten cubits.* Thirty feet long and 15 feet wide; unusually large (especially in its width), for all to see. Such a bold, clear message of judgment against sin should spur the people on to repentance and righteousness.

5:3 *curse.* See Deut 27:26 and note. *every one that stealeth.* Breaking the eighth commandment (Ex 20:15). *on this side . . .*

And every one that sweareth shall be
cut off *as* on that *side* according to it.
4 I will bring it forth, saith the LORD of
hosts,
And it shall enter into the house of the
thief,
And into the house of [a]him that
sweareth falsely by my name:
And it shall remain in the midst of his
house,
And [b]shall consume it with the timber
thereof and the stones thereof.

The ephah of iniquity

5 ¶ Then the angel that talked with me went forth, and said unto me, Lift up now thine eyes, and see what *is* this that goeth forth.

6 And I said, What *is* it? And he said, This *is* an ephah that goeth forth. He said moreover, This *is* their resemblance through all the earth.

7 And behold, there *was* lift up a [1]talent of lead: and this *is* a woman that sitteth in the midst of the ephah.

8 And he said, This *is* wickedness. And he cast it into the midst of the ephah; and he cast the weight of lead upon the mouth thereof.

9 Then lift I up mine eyes, and looked, and behold, there came out two women, and the wind *was* in their wings; for they had wings like the wings of a stork: and they lift up the ephah between the earth and the heaven.

10 Then said I to the angel that talked with me, Whither do these bear the ephah?

5:4 [a]Lev. 19:12; ch. 8:17; Mal. 3:5 [b]See Lev. 14:45
5:7 [1]Or, *weighty piece*
5:11 [a]Jer. 29:5,28 [b]Gen. 10:10
6:2 [a]ch. 1:8 [b]Rev. 6:5
6:3 [1]Or, *strong*
6:4 [a]ch. 5:10
6:5 [1]Or, *winds* [a]Ps. 104:4; Heb. 1:7,14 [b]1 Ki. 22:19; Dan. 7:10; ch. 4:14; Luke 1:19
6:6 [a]Jer. 1:14
6:7 [a]Gen. 13:17; ch. 1:10
6:8 [a]Eccl. 10:4

11 And he said unto me, To [a]build it a house in [b]the land of Shinar: and it shall be established, and set there upon her own base.

Four chariots of divine judgment

6 And I turned, and lift up mine eyes, and looked, and behold, there came four chariots out from between two mountains; and the mountains *were* mountains of brass.

2 In the first chariot *were* [a]red horses; and in the second chariot [b]black horses;

3 And in the third chariot white horses; and in the fourth chariot grisled *and* [1]bay horses.

4 Then I answered [a]and said unto the angel that talked with me, What *are* these, my lord?

5 And the angel answered and said unto me, [a]These *are* the four [1]spirits of the heavens, *which* go forth from [b]standing before the Lord of all the earth.

6 The black horses which *are* therein go forth into [a]the north country; and the white go forth after them; and the grisled go forth toward the south country.

7 And the bay went forth, and sought to go that *they* might [a]walk to and fro through the earth: and he said, Get ye *hence,* walk to and fro through the earth. So they walked to and fro through the earth.

8 Then cried he upon me, and spake unto me, saying, Behold, these that go toward the north country have quieted my [a]spirit in the north country.

The crowning of Joshua

9 ¶ And the word of the LORD came unto me, saying,

---

on that side. Like the two tablets of the law (Ex 32:15), the scroll is inscribed on both sides (cf. Ezek 2:9–10; Rev 5:1). *every one that sweareth.* See 8:17. Such a person violates the third commandment (compare v. 4 with Ex 20:7). Although theft and perjury may have been the most common forms of lawbreaking at the time, they are probably intended as representative sins. The people of Judah had been guilty of infractions against the whole law (cf. Jas 2:10).

5:4 *it shall enter . . . shall consume.* "It" refers to the curse (v. 3). God's word, whether promise (ch. 4) or warning (as here), always accomplishes its purpose (cf. Ps 147:15; Is 55:10–11; Heb 4:12–13).

5:5–11 The seventh vision. Not only must flagrant, persistent sinners be removed from the land (vv. 1–4), but the whole sinful system will be removed—apparently to a more fitting place (Babylonia).

‡5:6 *ephah.* A measuring basket. A normal ephah-sized container would not be large enough to hold a person. This one was undoubtedly enlarged (like the flying roll of vv. 1–2) for the purpose of the vision. *resemblance.* Some ancient versions read "iniquity." See v. 8 ("wickedness").

5:7 *woman.* Perhaps the reason the people's wickedness was personified as a woman (cf. also Rev 17:3–6) is that the Hebrew word for "wickedness" (v. 8) is feminine in gender.

5:8 *wickedness.* A general word denoting moral, religious and civil evil—frequently used as an antonym of righteousness (e.g., Prov 13:6; Ezek 33:12). The whole evil system was to be destroyed (cf. 2 Thes 2:6–8).

5:9 *two women.* Divinely chosen agents. *wind.* Also an instrument of God (Ps 104:3–4). The removal of wickedness would be the work of God alone.

5:11 *Shinar.* Babylonia (see Gen 10:10; 11:2; Rev 17–18). Babylonia, a land of idolatry, was an appropriate locale for wickedness—but not Israel, where God chose to dwell with His people. Only after purging it of its evil would the promised land truly be the "holy land" (2:12).

6:1–8 The eighth and last vision. It corresponds to the first (1:7–17), though there are differences in details, such as in the order and colors of the horses. As in the first vision, the Lord is depicted as the one who controls the events of history. He will conquer the nations that oppress Israel.

6:1 *four chariots.* Angelic spirits as agents of divine judgment (v. 5). *two mountains.* Possibly mount Zion and the mount of Olives, with the Kidron Valley between them. *brass.* Bronze, perhaps symbolic of judgment (cf. Num 21:9).

6:2–3 *red . . . black . . . white . . . grisled and bay.* The horses may signify various divine judgments on the earth (see note on v. 8). See also Rev 6:1–8 and note on Rev 6:2.

6:4 *these.* The chariots, with the horses harnessed to them.

6:5 *four spirits.* See note on v. 1. *Lord of all the earth.* See note on 4:14.

6:8 *the north country.* Primarily Babylonia, but also the direction from which most of Israel's foes invaded their nation (see note on 2:6). *have quieted my spirit.* The angelic beings dispatched to the north have triumphed and thus have pacified or appeased God's Spirit (i.e., His anger). See 1:15, where God's displeasure was aroused against oppressive nations. Another view reads "have given my Spirit rest." In either case, since conquest was announced in the north, victory was assured over all enemies.

6:9–15 The fourth and fifth visions were concerned with the

10 Take of *them of* the captivity, *even* of
Heldai, of Tobijah, and of Jedaiah, which are
come from Babylon, and come thou the same
day, and go *into* the house of Josiah the son of
Zephaniah;
11 Then take silver and gold, and make
[a]crowns, and set *them* upon the head of Joshua the son of Josedech the high priest;
12 And speak unto him, saying, Thus
speaketh the LORD of hosts, saying,

Behold [a]the man whose name *is* The
[b]BRANCH;
And he shall [1]grow up out of his place,
[c]And he shall build the temple of the
LORD:
13 Even he shall build the temple of the
LORD;
And he [a]shall bear the glory,
And shall sit and rule upon his throne:
And [b]he shall be a priest upon his
throne:
And the counsel of peace shall be
between them both.

14 ¶ And the crowns shall be to Helem, and
to Tobijah, and to Jedaiah, and to Hen the son
of Zephaniah, [a]for a memorial in the temple of
the LORD.
15 And [a]*they that are* far off shall come and
build in the temple of the LORD, and ye shall
know that the LORD of hosts hath sent me unto
you. And *this* shall come to pass, if ye will diligently obey the voice of the LORD your God.

Hearts of stone

7 And it came to pass in the fourth year of
king Darius, *that* the word of the LORD
came unto Zechariah in the fourth *day* of the
ninth month, *even* in Chisleu;
2 When they had sent *unto* the house of
God Sherezer and Regemmelech, and their
men, [a][1]to pray before the LORD,
3 *And* to [a]speak unto the priests which
were in the house of the LORD of hosts, and to
the prophets, saying, Should I weep in [b]the
fifth month, separating myself, as I have done
these so many years?
4 ¶ Then came the word of the LORD of
hosts unto me, saying,
5 Speak unto all the people of the land, and
to the priests, saying, When ye [a]fasted and
mourned in the fifth [b]and seventh *month,*
[c]even those seventy years, did ye at all fast
[d]*unto* me, *even to* me?
6 And when ye did eat, and when ye did
drink, [1]did not ye eat *for yourselves,* and drink
for yourselves?
7 [1]*Should ye* not *hear* the words which the
LORD hath cried [2]by the former prophets,
when Jerusalem was inhabited and in prosperity, and the cities thereof round about her,
when *men* inhabited [a]the south and the plain?
8 ¶ And the word of the LORD came unto
Zechariah, saying,

9 Thus speaketh the LORD of hosts,
saying,
[a][1]Execute true judgment,
And shew mercy and compassions
every man to his brother:
10 And [a]oppress not the widow, nor the
fatherless, the stranger, nor the poor;
[b]And let none of you imagine evil
against his brother in your heart.

6:11 [a]Ex. 29:6
6:12 [1]Or, *branch up from under him* [a]Luke 1:78; John 1:45 [b]ch. 3:8 [c]Mat. 16:18; Eph. 2:20; Heb. 3:3
6:13 [a]Is. 22:24 [b]Ps. 110:4; Heb. 3:1
6:14 [a]Ex. 12:14; Mark 14:9
6:15 [a]Is. 57:19; Eph. 2:13
7:2 [1]Heb. *to intreat the face of the LORD* [a]1 Sam. 13:12
7:3 [a]Deut. 17:9; Mal. 2:7 [b]ch. 8:19
7:5 [a]Is. 58:5 [b]Jer. 41:1 [c]ch. 1:12 [d]Rom. 14:6
7:6 [1]Or, *be not ye they that, etc.*
7:7 [1]Or, *Are not these the words* [2]Heb. *by the hand of, etc.* [a]Jer. 17:26
7:9 [1]Heb. *Judge judgment of truth* [a]Is. 58:6,7; Jer. 7:23
7:10 [a]Ex. 22:21; Is. 1:17; Jer. 5:28 [b]Ps. 36:4; Mic. 2:1

high priest and the civil governor (in the Davidic line). Zechariah now relates the message of those two visions to the Messianic King-Priest.

6:9 Introduces a prophetic oracle (see 4:8; 7:4,8; 8:1,18; see also note on 1:1).

6:10 *Take.* Gifts (including "silver and gold," v. 11) for the temple (cf. Ezra 6:5; Hag 2:8).

‡6:11 *crowns.* The Hebrew for this word is *keren,* from which the English "crown" is derived. It is not the same as that used for the high priest's turban, but one referring to an ornate crown with many diadems (cf. Rev 19:12). The royal crowning of the high priest foreshadows the goal and consummation of prophecy—the crowning and reign of the Messianic King-Priest (see vv. 12–13; cf. Ps 110:4; Heb 7:1–3).

‡6:12 *Behold the man.* Cf. Pilate's introduction of Jesus in John 19:5. *BRANCH.* See note on 3:8. According to the Aramaic Targum (a paraphrase), the Jerusalem Talmud (a collection of religious instruction) and the Midrash (practical exposition), Jews early regarded this verse as Messianic. *grow.* The Hebrew means "to build," "have children." *up out.* The Hebrew means "to bud forth," a wordplay depicting restoration. *temple.* Cf. Is 2:2–3; Ezek 40–43; Hag 2:6–9.

6:13 *his throne.* See 2 Sam 7:16; Is 9:7 and note; Luke 1:32. *priest upon his throne.* The coming Davidic King will also be a priest. *both.* Probably the royal and priestly offices. Such a combination was not normally possible in Israel. For this reason, the sect of Qumran (see essay, p. 1344) expected two Messianic figures—a high-priest Messiah and a Davidic one. But the two offices and functions would in fact be united in the one person of the Messiah (cf. Ps 110; Heb 7).

6:14 *Hen.* Means "gracious one" perhaps another name for Josiah—to honor him for his hospitality (v. 10).

6:15 *they that are far off shall come and build.* Cf. Is 60:4–7.

7:1 *fourth year . . . fourth day . . . ninth month.* Dec. 7, 518 B.C.—not quite two years after the eight night visions (see note on 1:7).

‡7:2 *they . . . unto the house of God.* Or "the people of Beth-el."

‡7:3 *prophets.* Including Zechariah. *I.* The people (of Beth-el) collectively. *weep in the fifth month.* See note on 8:19. *so many years.* "Those seventy years" (v. 5).

7:4–7 A rebuke for selfish and insincere fasting on the part of the people and the priests.

7:4,8 See note on 6:9.

7:5 *fasted . . . fifth and seventh.* See note on 8:19. *seventy years.* See 1:12 and note. Since these fasts commemorated events related to the destruction of Jerusalem and the temple (see note on 8:19), the 70 years here are to be reckoned from 586 B.C. Strictly speaking, 68 years had transpired; 70 is thus a round number.

7:6 *for yourselves.* Cf. Is 1:11–17; 58:1–7,13–14.

7:7,12 *former prophets.* See note on 1:4.

7:7 *south.* See note on Gen 12:9. *plain.* Sloping toward the Mediterranean.

7:9–10 Four tests of faithful covenant living, consisting of a series of social, moral and ethical commands.

7:9 *judgment.* The proper ordering of all society (cf. 8:16; see Is 42:1,4; Mic 6:8). *mercy.* Cf. Hos 10:12; 12:6. *compassions.* See note on 1:16.

7:10 *oppress.* Oppression is denounced frequently in the OT

11 But they refused to hearken, and
[a][1] pulled away the shoulder,
And [b][2] stopped their ears, that *they*
should not hear.
12 Yea, they made their [a] hearts *as* an
adamant stone, [b] lest *they* should
hear the law,
And the words which the LORD of hosts
hath sent in his spirit [1] by the former
prophets:
[c] Therefore came a great wrath from
the LORD of hosts.
13 Therefore it is come to pass, *that* as he
cried, and they would not hear;
So [a] they cried, and I would not hear,
saith the LORD of hosts:
14 But [a] I scattered them with a whirlwind
among all the nations whom they
knew not:
Thus the land was desolate after them,
that no man passed through nor
returned:
For they laid the [1] pleasant land
desolate.

God's intent to restore Jerusalem

8 Again the word of the LORD of hosts
came *to me,* saying,
2 Thus saith the LORD of hosts;
[a] I was jealous for Zion *with* great
jealousy,
And I was jealous for her *with* great
fury.
3 Thus saith the LORD; I am returned
unto Zion,
And will dwell in the midst of
Jerusalem:
And Jerusalem [a] shall be called a city of
truth;
And [b] the mountain of the LORD of
hosts [c] the holy mountain.
4 Thus saith the LORD of hosts;
[a] There shall yet old men and old
women dwell in the streets of
Jerusalem,
And every man with his staff in his
hand [1] for very age.
5 And the streets of the city shall be full
of boys and girls
Playing in the streets thereof.
6 Thus saith the LORD of hosts;
If it be [1] marvellous in the eyes of the
remnant of this people in these days,
[a] Should it also be [1] marvellous in my
eyes? saith the LORD of hosts.
7 Thus saith the LORD of hosts;
Behold, [a] I *will* save my people from
the east country,
And from [b][1] the west country;
8 And I will bring them, and they shall
dwell in the midst of Jerusalem:
[a] And they shall be my people, and I
will be their God,
[b] In truth and in righteousness.
9 ¶ Thus saith the LORD of hosts; [a] Let your
hands be strong, ye that hear in these days
these words by the mouth of [b] the prophets,
which *were* in [c] the day *that* the foundation of
the house of the LORD of hosts was laid, that
the temple might be built.
10 For before these days [1] there was no
[a] hire for man, nor any hire for beast; neither
was there any peace to him that went out or
came in because of the affliction: for I set all
men every one against his neighbour.
11 But now I *will* not *be* unto the residue
of this people as *in* the former days, saith the
LORD of hosts.

7:11 [1] Heb. *they gave a backsliding shoulder* [2] Heb. *made heavy* [a] Neh. 9:29 [b] Acts 7:57
7:12 [1] Heb. *by the hand of* [a] Ezek. 11:19 [b] Neh. 9:29 [c] 2 Chr. 36:16; Dan. 9:11
7:13 [a] Prov. 1:24; Is. 1:15; Mic. 3:4
7:14 [1] Heb. *land of desire* [a] Deut. 28:64
8:2 [a] Nah. 1:2
8:3 [a] Is. 1:21 [b] Is. 2:2,3 [c] Jer. 31:23
8:4 [1] Heb. *for multitude of days* [a] 1 Sam. 2:31; Is. 65:20
8:6 [1] Or, *hard,* or, *difficult* [a] Gen. 18:14; Luke 1:37
8:7 [1] Heb. *the country of the going down of the sun* [a] Is. 11:11; Ezek. 37:21 [b] See Ps. 50:1
8:8 [a] Jer. 31:1,33 [b] Jer. 4:2
8:9 [a] Hag. 2:4 [b] Ezra 5:1,2 [c] Hag. 2:18
8:10 [1] Or, *the hire of man became nothing, etc.* [a] Hag. 1:6,9

(e.g., Amos 2:6–8; 4:1; 5:11–12,21–24; 8:4–6). *widow . . . fatherless . . . stranger . . . poor.* For the Biblical concern for such people see, e.g., Deut 10:18; Is 1:17 and note; Jer 5:28; Jas 1:27; 1 John 3:16–18. In the ancient Near East, the ideal king was expected to protect the oppressed and needy members of society. *imagine evil against his brother.* See 8:17.

7:11 *they.* The preexilic forefathers, as the reference to the "former prophets" in v. 12 shows. *pulled away the shoulder.* See Deut 9:6,13,27. *stopped their ears, that they should not hear.* See Ps 58:4; Is 6:10 and note; cf. Is 33:15.

7:12 *adamant stone.* See Ezek 3:8–9. *words . . . sent in his spirit.* The words of the prophets were inspired by God's Spirit (cf. Neh 9:30; 2 Pet 1:21). *great wrath.* See 1:2,15.

7:13 See note on 1:3.

7:14 *scattered them.* One of the curses for covenant disobedience (Deut 28:36–37,64–68; see note on Deut 28:64). *whirlwind.* See Prov 1:27; Is 40:24; Hos 4:19. *land . . . desolate.* See Deut 28:41–42,45–52. *For they laid . . . desolate.* By their sins. *pleasant land.* Cf. Ps 106:24; Jer 3:19.

8:1–23 Ten promises of blessing, each beginning with "Thus saith the LORD [of hosts]" (vv. 2,3,4,6,7,9,14,19,20,23).

8:1,18 See note on 6:9.

8:2 *jealous.* See 1:14; see also note on Ex 20:5.

8:3 *I am returned.* See 1:3 and note; 1:16. *dwell.* See note on 2:10. *a city of truth.* Cf. v. 16; see Is 1:26 and note. *the holy mountain.* Cf. 14:20–21.

8:4–5 See Is 11:6–9 and note; 65:20–25.

8:6,11–12 *remnant.* See notes on Is 1:9; 10:20–22.

‡8:6 *Should it also be marvellous in my eyes?* "Marvellous" can be translated "wonderful" in both instances in this verse (see Gen 18:14 and note; Jer 32:17,27).

8:7 *save my people.* Deliver them from exile, bondage and dispersion (cf. Is 11:11–12; 43:5–7; Jer 30:7–11; 31:7–8). *from the east country. . . the west.* Lit. "from the land of the sunrise and from the land of the going in of the sun," i.e., from everywhere—wherever the people are (cf. Ps 50:1; 113:3; Mal 1:11).

8:8 *they shall be my people, and I will be their God.* Covenant terminology, pertaining to intimate fellowship in a covenant relationship (see 13:9; Gen 17:7 and note; Ex 6:7; 29:45–46; Lev 11:45; 22:33; 25:38; 26:12 and note; 26:45; Num 15:41; Deut 29:13; Jer 24:7; 31:33; 32:38; Ezek 34:30–31; 36:28; 37:27; Hos 1:9–10; 2:23; 2 Cor 6:16; Heb 8:10; Rev 21:3). *truth and in righteousness.* Judah's restoration to covenant favor and blessing rests on the faithfulness (truthfulness, dependability) and righteousness of God.

8:9 *hands be strong.* See v. 13. *prophets.* Including Haggai (1:1) and Zechariah (1:1; cf. Ezra 5:1–2).

8:10 *before these days.* Before the temple foundation was laid (see v. 9). *nor any hire.* See Hag 1:6–11; 2:15–19. *against his neighbour.* For example, the Samaritans (Ezra 4:1–5).

8:11 *But now.* The reasons for discouragement have passed; God will now provide the grounds for encouragement.

12 [a]For the seed *shall be* [1]prosperous; the
vine shall give her fruit, and [b]the ground shall
give her increase, and [c]the heavens shall give
their dew; and I will cause the remnant of this
people to possess all these *things.*
13 And it shall come to pass, *that* as ye
were [a]a curse among the heathen, O house of
Judah, and house of Israel; so will I save you,
and [b]ye shall be a blessing: fear not, *but* let
your hands be strong.
14 For thus saith the LORD of hosts; [a]As I
thought to punish you, when your fathers provoked me to wrath, saith the LORD of hosts,
[b]and I repented not:
15 So again have I thought in these days to
do well unto Jerusalem and to the house of Judah: fear ye not.
16 These *are* the things that ye shall do;
[a]Speak ye every man the truth to his neighbour; [1]execute the judgment of truth and
peace in your gates:
17 [a]And let none of you imagine evil in
your hearts against his neighbour; and love no
false oath: for all these *are things* that I hate,
saith the LORD.
18 ¶ And the word of the LORD of hosts
came unto me, saying,
19 Thus saith the LORD of hosts; [a]The fast
of the fourth *month,* [b]and the fast of the fifth,
[c]and the fast of the seventh, [d]and the fast of
the tenth, shall be to the house of Judah [e]joy
and gladness, and cheerful [1]feasts; [f]therefore
love the truth and peace.
20 Thus saith the LORD of hosts;

8:12 [1]Heb. *of peace* [a]Joel 2:22 [b]Ps. 67:6 [c]Hag. 1:10
8:13 [a]Jer. 42:18 [b]Gen. 12:2; Ruth 4:11
8:14 [a]Jer. 31:28 [b]2 Chr. 36:16
8:16 [1]Heb. *judge truth, and the judgment of peace* [a]Eph. 4:25
8:17 [a]Prov. 3:29
8:19 [1]Or, *solemn,* or, *set times* [a]Jer. 52:6 [b]Jer. 52:12 [c]2 Ki. 25:25; Jer. 41:1,2 [d]Jer. 52:4 [e]Esth. 8:17 [f]ver. 16
8:21 [1]Or, *continually* [2]Heb. *going* [3]Heb. *to intreat the face [of the LORD]* [a]Is. 2:3; Mic. 4:1,2
8:22 [1]Heb. *to intreat the face [of the LORD]* [a]Is. 60:3
8:23 [a]Is. 3:6 [b]1 Cor. 14:25
9:1 [a]Jer. 23:33 [b]Amos 1:3 [c]2 Chr. 20:12; Ps. 145:15
9:2 [a]Jer. 49:23 [b]Is. 23; Ezek. 26 [c]1 Ki. 17:9 [d]Ezek. 28:3

It shall yet *come to pass,* that there
shall come people,
And the inhabitants of many cities:
21 And the inhabitants of one *city* shall go
to another, saying,
[a]Let us go [1 2]speedily [3]to pray before
the LORD,
And to seek the LORD of hosts: I will go
also.
22 Yea, [a]many people and strong nations
shall come
To seek the LORD of hosts in Jerusalem,
And [1]to pray before the LORD.
23 Thus saith the LORD of hosts;
In those days *it shall come to pass,* that
ten men shall [a]take hold out of all
languages of the nations,
Even shall take hold of the skirt of him
that is a Jew, saying,
We will go with you: for we have
heard [b]*that* God *is* with you.

The coming of the king

9 The [a]burden of the word of the LORD
in the land of Hadrach,
And [b]Damascus *shall be* the rest thereof:
When [c]the eyes of man, as of all the
tribes of Israel, *shall be* toward the
LORD.
2 And [a]Hamath also shall border thereby;
[b]Tyrus, and [c]Zidon, though it be very
[d]wise.
3 And Tyrus did build herself a strong
hold,

8:12 Contrast with Hag 1:10–11. In Hag 2:19 God had predicted just such a reversal as is depicted here. Fertility and bounty are part of the covenant blessings for obedience promised in Lev 26:3–10; Deut 28:11–12; cf. Ezek 34:25–27.
8:13 *curse among the heathen.* Part of the covenant curses for disobedience threatened in Deut 28:15–68 (see Deut 28:37); cf. Jer 24:9; 25:18. *Judah, and . . . Israel.* The whole nation will experience this deliverance and blessing (cf. Jer 31:1–31; Ezek 37:15–28). *blessing.* See vv. 20–23; cf. Gen 12:2. *hands be strong.* See note on v. 9.
8:14–17 Verses 14–15 specify God's part in the people's restoration to favor and blessing; vv. 16–17 delineate their part.
8:14 *your fathers provoked me to wrath.* See note on 1:2.
8:15 *do well.* See vv. 12–13.
8:16–17 See 7:9–10. Such moral and ethical behavior sums up the character of those who are in covenant relationship with the Lord.
8:16 *gates.* See Gen 19:1 and note; 2 Sam 18:24.
‡8:17 *false oath.* See note on 5:3. *all these . . . I hate.* Prov 6:16–19 lists seven things the Lord hates, three of which relate directly to vv. 16–17 here: "a lying tongue," "a heart that devises wicked imaginations" and "a false witness, that speaketh lies."
8:19 See 7:2–6. *fourth.* The fast that lamented the breaching of the walls of Jerusalem by Nebuchadnezzar (2 Ki 25:3–4; Jer 39:2; 52:6–7). *fifth.* Commemorated the burning of the temple and the other important buildings (2 Ki 25:8–10; Jer 52:12–14). *seventh.* Marked the anniversary of Gedaliah's assassination (2 Ki 25:22–25; Jer 41:1–3). *tenth.* Mourned the beginning of Nebuchadnezzar's siege of Jerusalem (2 Ki 25:1; Jer 39:1; 52:4; Ezek 24:1–2). *cheerful feasts.* Cf. Is 65:18–19; Jer 31:10–14.
8:20–23 For similar predictions about Gentiles seeking the Lord see 2:11 and note; Is 2:2–4; Mic 4:1–5.
8:22 *strong nations.* Anticipates a fulfillment of the promise of Gentile blessing in the Abrahamic covenant (Gen 12:3; Gal 3:8,26–29; see also Is 55:5; 56:6–7; cf. Mark 11:17).
8:23 *ten.* One way of indicating a large or complete number in Hebrew (see Gen 31:7 and note; Lev 26:26; Num 14:22; 1 Sam 1:8; Neh 4:12). *Jew.* The word, used of the people of the kingdom of Judah after the exile, occurs first in Jer 32:12. *we have heard that God is with you.* True godliness attracts others to the Lord (see Gen 26:28; 30:27; see also notes on Gen 39:2–6; 1 Cor 14:24).
9:1–8 Probably a prophetic description of the Lord's march south to Jerusalem, destroying—as Divine Warrior—the traditional enemies of Israel. As history shows, the agent of His judgment was Alexander the Great (333 B.C.).
9:1 *The burden of the word of the LORD.* The Hebrew for this phrase occurs only two other times in the OT (12:1; Mal 1:1), making it likely that Zech 9–14 and Malachi were written during the same general period (see Introduction: Date). *Hadrach.* Hatarikka, north of Hamath on the Orontes River (see v. 2). *Damascus.* The leading city-state of the Arameans. *eyes . . . toward the LORD.* The thought may be that the eyes of men, especially all the tribes of Israel, are turned toward the Lord (for deliverance).
9:2 *And Hamath also.* Judgment will rest upon Hamath, just as upon Hadrach and Damascus. Hamath is modern Hama. See Amos 6:2. *it.* Damascus. *Tyrus, and Zidon.* Tyre and Sidon, Phoenician (modern Lebanese) coastal cities. Their judgment (vv. 3–4) is also foretold in Is 23; Ezek 26:3–14; 28:20–24; Amos 1:9–10.
‡9:3 *strong hold.* The Hebrew for this word is a pun on the He-

And heaped up silver as the dust,
And fine gold as the mire of the streets.
4 Behold, [a]the Lord will cast her out,
And he will smite [b]her power in the sea;
And she shall be devoured with fire.
5 Ashkelon shall see *it,* and fear;
Gaza also *shall see it,* and be very sorrowful,
And Ekron; for her expectation shall be ashamed;
And the king shall perish from Gaza,
And Ashkelon shall not be inhabited.
6 And a bastard shall dwell [a]in Ashdod,
And I will cut off the pride of the Philistines.
7 And I will take away his [1]blood out of his mouth,
And his abominations from between his teeth:
But he that remaineth, even he, *shall be* for our God,
And he shall be as a governor in Judah,
And Ekron as a Jebusite.
8 And [a]I will encamp about mine house because of the army,
Because of him that passeth by, and because of him that returneth:
And no oppressor shall pass through them any more:
For now have I seen with mine eyes.

9 [a]Rejoice greatly, O daughter of Zion;
Shout, O daughter of Jerusalem:
Behold, [b]thy King cometh unto thee:
He *is* just, and [1]having salvation;
Lowly, and riding upon an ass,
And upon a colt the foal of an ass.
10 And I [a]will cut off the chariot from Ephraim,
And the horse from Jerusalem,
And the battle bow shall be cut off:
And he shall speak peace unto the heathen:
And his dominion *shall be* from sea *even* to sea,
And from the river *even* to the ends of the earth.
11 *As for* thee also, [a][1]by the blood of thy covenant
I have sent forth thy [b]prisoners out of the pit wherein *is* no water.
12 Turn ye to the strong hold, [a]ye prisoners of hope:
Even to day do I declare *that* I will render double unto thee;
13 When I have bent Judah for me, filled the bow *with* Ephraim,
And raised up thy sons, O Zion, against thy sons, O Greece,
And made thee as the sword of a mighty *man.*
14 And the LORD shall be seen over them,
And [a]his arrow shall go forth as the lightning:

9:4 [a]Is. 23:1 [b]Ezek. 26:17
9:6 [a]Amos 1:8
9:7 [1]Heb. *bloods*
9:8 [a]Ps. 34:7
9:9 [1]Or, *saving himself* [a]ch. 2:10 [b]Jer. 23:5; Luke 19:38
9:10 [a]Hos. 1:7; Mic. 5:10
9:11 [1]Or, *whose covenant is by blood* [a]Ex. 24:8 [b]Is. 42:7
9:12 [a]Is. 49:9
9:14 [a]Ps. 18:14

brew for "Tyrus" (meaning "rock" but also "seige enclosure"). The stronghold was Tyre's island fortress (Is 23:4; Ezek 26:5), which became a "rampart" for invading forces. It fell (v. 4) to Alexander in 332 B.C. *silver as the dust . . . gold as the mire.* Cf. 1 Ki 10:21,27. Tyre was a center of trade and commerce, and her wealth was proverbial (see Is 23:2–3,8,18; Ezek 26:12; 27:3–27,33; 28:4–5,7,12–14, 16–18).

9:5–7 The Philistine cities were greatly alarmed at Alexander's steady advance.

9:5 *her expectation shall be ashamed.* As the northernmost city of Philistia, Ekron would be the first to suffer. Her hope that Tyre would stem the tide would meet with disappointment.

9:6 *bastard.* People of mixed nationality; they characterized the postexilic period (Neh 13:23–24). *I.* God. *Philistines.* See note on Gen 10:14. At one time their control of Canaan was so extensive that the land was eventually named after them ("Palestine").

9:7 *blood.* Of idolatrous sacrifices. *abominations.* Ceremonially unclean food. *Jebusite.* These ancient inhabitants of Jerusalem (see note on Gen 10:16) were absorbed into Judah (e.g., Araunah in 2 Sam 24:16–24; 1 Chr 21:18–26). So would it be with a remnant of the Philistines.

9:8 *encamp about mine house.* See 2:5. Alexander spared the temple and the city of Jerusalem. *oppressor.* The Hebrew for this word is translated "taskmaster(s)" in Ex 3:7; 5:6,10 and elsewhere; thus it echoes the Egyptian bondage motif. *have I seen with mine eyes.* See Ex 3:7; Ps 32:8; 121.

‡9:9 Quoted in the NT as Messianic and as referring ultimately to the Triumphal Entry of Jesus into Jerusalem (Mat 21:5; John 12:15). *daughter of Zion.* A personification of Jerusalem and its inhabitants. *thy King.* The Davidic ("your") Messianic King. *just.* Conforming to the divine standard of morality and ethics, particularly as revealed in the Mosaic legislation; a characteristic of the ideal king (see 2 Sam 23:3–4; Ps 72:1–3; Is 9:7; 11:4–5; 53:11; Jer 23:5–6; 33:15–16). *Lowly.* Or "humble" (cf. Is 53:2-3, 7; Mat 11:29. *riding upon an ass.* A suitable choice, since the donkey was a lowly animal of peace (contrast the warhorse of v. 10) as well as a princely mount (Judg 10:4; 12:14; 2 Sam 16:2) before the horse came into common use. The royal mount used by David and his sons was the mule (2 Sam 18:9; 1 Ki 1:33). See Mat 11:29 and, of course, the triumphal entry of Christ into Jerusalem.

‡9:10 *cut off the chariot . . . horse . . . battle bow.* A similar era of disarmament is foreseen in Is 2:4; 9:5–7; 11:1–10; Mic 5:10–11. *Ephraim.* See note on v. 13. *peace unto the heathen.* In sharp contrast to Alexander's empire, which was founded on bloodshed, the Messianic King will establish a universal kingdom of peace as the ultimate fulfillment of the Abrahamic covenant (cf. 14:16; see Gen 12:3; 18:18; 22:18). Nonetheless, Revelation describes the great day of battle yet to come as the Divine Warrior comes riding upon his war steed. *his dominion shall be from . . . to.* It will be universal (see Ps 22:27–28; 72:8–11; Is 45:22; 52:10; 66:18).

9:11 *blood of thy covenant.* Probably the Mosaic covenant (Ex 24:3–8). *prisoners.* Perhaps those still in Babylonia, the land of exile. *pit . . . no water.* Cf. Gen 37:24; Jer 38:6.

9:12 *strong hold.* Either (1) Jerusalem (Zion) and environs or (2) God Himself (cf. 2:5). *hope.* In the future delivering King (vv. 9–10). *double.* Full or complete restoration (cf. Is 61:7).

9:13 See note on 10:4. The Lord compares Himself to a warrior who uses Judah as His bow and Ephraim (the northern kingdom) as His arrow. *thy sons, O Zion.* The Maccabees (see note on Dan 11:34). *thy sons, O Greece.* The Seleucids of Syria (after the breakup of Alexander's empire).

And the Lord GOD shall blow the
trumpet,
And shall go [b]with whirlwinds of the
south.
15 The LORD of hosts shall defend them;
and they shall devour,
And [1]subdue *with* sling stones;
And they shall drink, *and* make a noise
as *through* wine;
And they [2]shall be filled like bowls,
and as the corners of the altar.
16 And the LORD their God shall save
them in that day as the flock of his
people:
For [a]*they shall be as* the stones of a
crown, [b]lifted up as an ensign upon
his land.
17 For [a]how great *is* his goodness, and
how great *is* his beauty!
[b]Corn shall make the young men
[1]cheerful, and new wine the maids.

The redemption of God's people

10 Ask ye [a]of the LORD [b]rain [c]in the
time of the latter rain;
So the LORD *shall* make [1]bright clouds,
And give them showers of rain,
To every one grass in the field.
2 For the [a][1]idols have spoken vanity,
And the diviners have seen a lie,
And have told false dreams;
They [b]comfort in vain:
Therefore they went their way as a
flock,
They [2]were troubled, [c]because *there
was* no shepherd.
3 Mine anger was kindled against the
shepherds,
[a]And I [1]punished the goats:

9:14 [b]Is. 21:1
9:15 [1]Or, *subdue the stones of the sling* [2]Or, *shall fill both the bowls, etc.*
9:16 [a]Is. 62:3; Mal. 3:17 [b]Is. 11:12
9:17 [1]Or, *grow, or, speak* [a]Ps. 31:19 [b]Joel 3:18
10:1 [1]Or, *lightnings* [a]Jer. 14:22 [b]Deut. 11:14 [c]Joel 2:23
10:2 [1]Heb. *teraphims* [2]Or, *answered that, etc.* [a]Jer. 10:8; Hab. 2:18 [b]Job 13:4 [c]Ezek. 34:5
10:3 [1]Heb. *visited upon* [a]Ezek. 34:17
10:3 [b]Luke 1:68 [c]Sol. 1:9
10:4 [a]Is. 28:16 [b]Is. 22:23
10:5 [1]Or, *they shall make the riders on horses ashamed* [a]Ps. 18:42
10:6 [a]Jer. 3:18; Ezek. 37:21 [b]Hos. 1:7 [c]ch. 13:9
10:7 [a]Ps. 104:15
10:8 [a]Is. 5:26 [b]Is. 49:19; Ezek. 36:37
10:9 [a]Hos. 2:23 [b]Deut. 30:1

For the LORD of hosts [b]hath visited his
flock the house of Judah,
And [c]hath made them as his goodly
horse in the battle.
4 Out of him came forth [a]the corner, out
of him [b]the nail,
Out of him the battle bow, out of him
every oppressor together.
5 And they shall be as mighty *men*,
which [a]tread down *their enemies*
In the mire of the streets in the battle:
And they shall fight, because the LORD
is with them,
And [1]the riders on horses shall be
confounded.
6 And I will strengthen the house of
Judah,
And I will save the house of Joseph,
And [a]I will bring them *again* to place
them; for I [b]have mercy upon them:
And they shall be as though I had not
cast them off:
For I *am* the LORD their God, and [c]will
hear them.
7 And *they of* Ephraim shall be like a
mighty *man*,
And their [a]heart shall rejoice as
through wine:
Yea, their children shall see *it*, and be
glad;
Their heart shall rejoice in the LORD.
8 I will [a]hiss for them, and gather them;
for I have redeemed them:
[b]And they shall increase as they have
increased.
9 And [a]I will sow them among the
people:
And they shall [b]remember me in far
countries;

9:14 See Ps 18:7–15; Hab 3:3–15. *trumpet.* Probably a reference to thunder (cf. Ex 19:16–19). *south.* In the region of mount Sinai, where the Mosaic covenant was given (see v. 11) and where the Lord's dwelling was (see Judg 5:4–5; Ps 68:8; Hab 3:3).
9:15 The Apocryphal book 1 Maccabees (3:16–24; 4:6–16; 7:40–50) records a partial fulfillment of this verse. *sling stones.* Hurled at defenders on the city wall and onto the inhabitants inside. *like bowls.* See Ex 27:1–3; Lev 4:6–7.
9:16 *that day.* See note on 2:11.
10:1 *the LORD . . . give them showers . . . grass.* The Lord, not the Canaanite god, Baal, is the one who controls the weather and the rain, giving life and fertility to the land (see Jer 14:22; Amos 5:8). Therefore God's people are to pray to and trust in Him. See further Is 55:10–12; Hos 2:8; 6:3; Joel 2:21–27; Mat 5:45.
‡10:2 *idols.* Hebrew *teraphim,* household gods (see Gen 31:19 and note). They were used for divination during the period of the judges (Judg 17:5; 18:14–20). *diviners.* Included among false prophets, they were the occult counterpart to true prophets. Cf. Jer 23:30–32; 27:9–10. Resorting to such sources for information and guidance is expressly forbidden in Deut 18:9–14 because God provided true prophets (and ultimately the Messianic Prophet) for that purpose (Deut 13:1–5; 18:15–22; see John 4:25; 6:14; Acts 3:22–23,26; see also note on Gen 30:27). *they went their way as a flock.* See Is 53:6 and note. *there was no shepherd.* Spiritual leadership is missing (cf. Mark 6:34). "Shepherd" is primarily a royal motif, whether referring to human kings (2 Sam 5:2; Is 44:28; Jer 23:2–4) or to God as King (Ps 23:1; 100:3; Ezek 34:11–16) or to the Messianic, Davidic King (Ezek 34:23–24; John 10:11–16; Heb 13:20; 1 Pet 5:4).
10:3 *Mine anger . . . against the shepherds.* Cf. Ezek 34:1–10. *as his goodly horse.* Triumphant.
10:4 Probably Messianic (indicated by the Aramaic Targum). *Out of him.* Out of Judah. See Gen 49:10; Jer 30:21; Mic 5:2. *the corner.* See note on 3:9; see especially Is 28:16; Eph 2:20. *nail.* The ruler as the support of the state (see note on Is 22:23; see also Is 22:24). *battle bow.* Part of the Divine Warrior terminology (cf. 9:13; Ps 7:12; 45:5; Lam 2:4; 3:12; Hab 3:9).
10:5 *they.* Judah (v. 4), i.e., its people. *the LORD is with them.* See Josh 1:5; Jer 1:8,19; 15:20. *shall be confounded.* Partly fulfilled in the Maccabean victories (during the period between the OT and the NT).
10:6 *Judah . . . Joseph.* The people of the southern and northern kingdoms will be reunited (see note on 8:13).
10:7 *Ephraim.* See note on 9:13. *rejoice as through wine.* Cf. Ps 104:15.
‡10:8 *hiss.* Lit. "whistle" or "signal," a continuation of the shepherd metaphor (see Judg 5:16). Zechariah uses the shepherd image more than any other book does. *redeemed.* The Hebrew for this word is often used of ransoming from slavery or captivity (see Is 35:10; Mic 6:4; cf. 1 Pet 1:18–19). *shall increase as they have increased.* See Ex 1:6–20.
10:9 *they shall remember me.* According to the meaning of

And they shall live with their children,
and turn again.
10 [a]I will bring them again also out of the
land of Egypt,
And gather them out of Assyria;
And I will bring them into the land of
Gilead and Lebanon;
And [b]*place* shall not be found for them.
11 [a]And he shall pass through the sea
with affliction,
And shall smite the waves in the sea,
And all the deeps of the river shall dry
up:
And [b]the pride of Assyria shall be
brought down,
And [c]the sceptre of Egypt shall depart
away.
12 And I will strengthen them in the
LORD;
And [a]they shall walk up and down in
his name, saith the LORD.

The rejection of the king

11 Open [a]thy doors, O Lebanon, that
the fire may devour thy cedars.
2 Howl, fir tree; for the cedar is fallen;
because the [1]mighty are spoiled:
Howl, O ye oaks of Bashan; [a]for [2]the
forest of the vintage is come down.
3 *There is* a voice of the howling of the
shepherds; for their glory is spoiled:
A voice of the roaring of young lions;
for the pride of Jordan is spoiled.
4 Thus saith the LORD my God; Feed the
flock of the slaughter;
5 Whose possessors slay them, and [a]hold
themselves not guilty:
And they that sell them [b]say, Blessed
be the LORD; for I am rich:
And their own shepherds pity them not.
6 For I will no more pity the inhabitants
of the land, saith the LORD:
But lo, I *will* [1]deliver the men
Every one into his neighbour's hand,
and into the hand of his king:
And they shall smite the land, and out
of their hand I will not deliver *them.*
7 And I will feed the flock of slaughter,
[1]*even* you, [a]O poor of the flock.

¶ And I took unto me two staves; the one I
called Beauty, and the other I called [2]Bands;
and I fed the flock.
8 Three shepherds also I cut off [a]in one
month; and my soul [1]lothed them, and their
soul also abhorred me.
9 Then said I, I will not feed you: [a]that that
dieth, let it die; and that that is to be cut off,
let it be cut off; and let the rest eat every one
the flesh [1]of another.
10 And I took my staff, *even* Beauty, and
cut it asunder, that *I* might break my covenant
which I had made with all the people.

10:10 [a]Is. 11:11; Hos. 11:11 [b]Is. 49:20
10:11 [a]Is. 11:15 [b]Is. 14:25 [c]Ezek. 30:13
10:12 [a]Mic. 4:5
11:1 [a]ch. 10:10
11:2 [1]Or, *gallants* [2]Or, *the defenced forest* [a]Is. 32:19
11:5 [a]Jer. 2:3; 50:7 [b]Deut. 29:19; Hos. 12:8
11:6 [1]Heb. *make to be found*
11:7 [1]Or, *verily the poor* [2]Or, *Binders* [a]Zeph. 3:12; Mat. 11:5
11:8 [1]Heb. *was straitened for them* [a]Hos. 5:7
11:9 [1]Heb. *of his fellow,* or, *neighbour* [a]Jer. 15:2

Zechariah's name, "the LORD remembers" (His covenant people and promises). Now they will remember Him.

10:10 *Egypt . . . Assyria.* See v. 11. Probably representing all the countries where the Israelites are dispersed, these two evoke memories of slavery and exile. *bring them.* See Is 11:11–16; Ezek 39:27–29. *Gilead.* See note on Gen 31:21; see also Sol 6:5; Jer 50:19; Mic 7:14. *Lebanon.* See 2 Ki 19:23; Is 33:9 and note; 35:2 and note; Jer 22:6. *place shall not be found for them.* See v. 8; 2:4; see also note on Is 49:19–20.

10:11 *pass through the sea with affliction.* As at the Red sea (see Ex 14:22 and note).

11:1–3 Some interpret this brief poem as a taunt song related to the lament that will be sung over the destruction of the nations' power and arrogance (ch. 10), represented by the cedar, the pine and the oak (vv. 1–2). Their kings are represented by the shepherds and the lions (v. 3). Understood in this way, vv. 1–3 would provide the conclusion to the preceding section. Other interpreters, however, without denying the presence of figurative language, see the piece more literally as a description of the devastation of Syro-Palestine due to the rejection of the Messianic Good Shepherd (vv. 4–14). Verses 1–3 would then furnish the introduction to the next section. The geography of the text—Lebanon, Bashan and Jordan—would seem to favor this interpretation. Part of the fulfillment would be the destruction and further subjugation of the area by the Romans, including the fall of Jerusalem in A.D. 70 and of Masada in 73. Understood in this way, the passage is in sharp contrast with ch. 10 and its prediction of Israel's full deliverance and restoration to the covenant land. Now the scene is one of desolation for the land (vv. 1–3), followed by the threat of judgment and disaster for both land and people (vv. 4–6).

11:1 *Lebanon.* See 10:10 and note.

11:2 *Bashan.* See note on Is 2:13. The Israelites took this region from the Amorite king, Og, at the time of the conquest of Canaan (Num 21:33–35). It was allotted to the half-tribe of Manasseh (Josh 13:29–30; 17:5). *forest of the vintage is come down.* Of Lebanon.

11:3 If the language is figurative, the shepherds and lions represent the rulers or leaders of the Jews (see v. 5; 10:3; cf. Jer 25:34–36). *pride of Jordan.* Where the lions had their lairs.

11:4–14 The reason for the judgment on Israel in vv. 1–3 is now given, namely, the people's rejection of the Messianic Shepherd-King. Just as the Servant in the "servant songs" (see note on Is 42:1–4) is rejected, so here the Good Shepherd (a royal figure) is rejected. The same Messianic King is in view in both instances.

11:4 *saith.* To Zechariah. *flock.* Israel.

11:5 *Whose possessors.* The sheep (the Jews) are bought as slaves by outsiders. Part of the fulfillment came in A.D. 70 and the following years. *that sell them.* "Their own shepherds (rulers or leaders)."

11:6 *land.* The Holy Land. *king.* Perhaps the Roman emperor (cf. John 19:15). *they.* Includes the Romans prophetically.

11:7 *I.* Zechariah, as a type (foreshadowing) of the Messianic Shepherd-King. *one I called Beauty.* To ensure divine favor on the flock. *Bands.* Or "Union." See Ezek 37:15–28. Such unity would be the result of the gracious leadership of the Good Shepherd. (For the significance of the subsequent breaking of the two staffs see vv. 10,14.)

11:8 *Three shepherds also I cut off.* Although the three cannot be specifically identified, the Good Shepherd will dispose of all such unfit leaders. *my soul lothed them.* Cf. Is 1:13–14.

11:9 *that dieth, let it die.* The Good Shepherd terminates His providential care of the sheep. *eat every one the flesh of another.* According to Josephus, this actually happened during the Roman siege of Jerusalem in A.D. 70 (cf. also Lam 4:10).

11:10 *covenant.* Apparently a covenant of security and restraint, by which the Shepherd had been holding back the na-

11 And it was broken in that day: and [1]so [a]the poor of the flock that waited upon me knew that it *was* the word of the LORD.

12 And I said unto them, [1]If ye think good, give *me* my price; and if not, forbear. So they [a]weighed *for* my price thirty *pieces* of silver.

13 And the LORD said unto me, Cast it unto the [a]potter: a goodly price that I was prised at of them. And I took the thirty *pieces* of silver, and cast them to the potter *in* the house of the LORD.

14 Then I cut asunder mine other staff, *even* [1]Bands, that I might break the brotherhood between Judah and Israel.

The false shepherd described

15 ¶ And the LORD said unto me, [a]Take unto thee yet the instruments of a foolish shepherd.

16 ¶ For lo, I *will* raise up a shepherd in the land,
Which shall not visit those that be [1]cut off,
Neither shall seek the young one,
Nor heal that that is broken,
Nor [2]feed that that standeth still:
But he shall eat the flesh of the fat,
And tear their claws in pieces.
17 [a]Woe to the idol shepherd that leaveth the flock!
The sword *shall be* upon his arm, and upon his right eye:
His arm shall be clean dried up,
And his right eye shall be utterly darkened.

11:11 [1]Or, *the poor of the flock, etc. certainly knew* [a]Zeph. 3:12
11:12 [1]Heb. *If it be good in your eyes* [a]Mat. 26:15; Ex. 21:32
11:13 [a]Mat. 27:9
11:14 [1]Or, *Binders*
11:15 [a]Ezek. 34:2
11:16 [1]Or, *hidden* [2]Or, *bear*
11:17 [a]Jer. 23:1; Ezek. 34:2; John 10:12

12:1 [a]Is. 42:5; 44:24 [b]Num. 16:22; Eccl. 12:7; Is. 57:16
12:2 [1]Or, *slumber,* or, *poison* [2]Or, *And also against Judah shall he be* which shall be *in siege against Jerusalem* [a]Is. 51:17
12:3 [a]ver. 4,6,8; ch. 13:1 [b]Mat. 21:44
12:4 [a]Ps. 76:6; Ezek. 38:4

12

The burden of the word of the LORD for Israel, saith the LORD,
[a]Which stretcheth forth the heavens, and layeth the foundation of the earth,
And [b]formeth the spirit of man within him.
2 Behold, I *will* make Jerusalem [a]a cup of [1]trembling unto all the people round about,
[2]When they shall be in the siege both against Judah *and* against Jerusalem.
3 [a]And in that day will I make Jerusalem [b]a burdensome stone for all people:
All that burden themselves with it shall be cut in pieces,
Though all the people of the earth be gathered together against it.
4 In that day, saith the LORD,
[a]I will smite every horse with astonishment, and his rider with madness:
And I will open mine eyes upon the house of Judah,
And will smite every horse of the people with blindness.
5 And the governors of Judah shall say in their heart,

tions from His people (cf. Ezek 34:25; Hos 2:18). Now, however, the nations (e.g., the Romans) will be permitted to overrun them.

‡11:11 *the poor of the flock.* Probably the faithful few, who recognize the authoritative word of the Lord (see also v. 7). "Poor" translates the same word for "lowly" in 9:9 and suggests that the flock of the Good Shepherd share in his piety and sufferings. *it.* Probably Israel's affliction by the nations. *word of the LORD.* The faithful discern that what happens (e.g., the judgment on Jerusalem and the temple in A.D. 70) is a fulfillment of God's prophetic word—as a result of such actions as those denounced in Mat 23, which led to the rejection of the Good Shepherd.

11:12 *give me my price.* Refers to the severance of the relationship. *if not, forbear.* A more emphatic way of ending the relationship. *thirty pieces of silver.* The price of a slave among the Israelites in ancient times (see note on Ex 21:32); also, a way of indicating a trifling amount.

11:13 *goodly price.* Irony and sarcasm. *cast them to the potter in the house of the LORD.* For the NT use of vv. 12–13 see Mat 26:14–15; 27:3–10; see also note on Mat 27:9.

11:14 *cut asunder mine other staff, even Bands.* Signifying the dissolution of the covenant nation, particularly of the unity between the south and the north. The breaking up of the nation into parties hostile to each other was characteristic of later Jewish history; it greatly hindered the popular cause in the war against Rome (cf. John 11:48).

11:15 *yet.* Or "again." See v. 7. *foolish shepherd.* With the Shepherd of the Lord's choice removed from the scene, a foolish and worthless (v. 17) shepherd replaces Him. A selfish, greedy, corrupt leader will arise and afflict the flock (the people of Israel).

11:16 *visit those that be cut off.* Cf. Gen 33:13; Is 40:11. *tear their claws in pieces.* Apparently in a greedy search for the last edible piece.

11:17 *idol shepherd.* See note on v. 15. This counterfeit shepherd may have found a partial historical fulfillment in such leaders as Simeon bar Kosiba or Kokhba (who led the Jewish revolt against the Romans in A.D. 132–135 and who was hailed as the Messiah by Rabbi Akiba). But it would seem that the final stage of the progressive fulfillment of the complete prophecy awaits the rise of the final antichrist (cf. Ezek 34:2–4; Dan 11:36–39; John 5:43; 2 Thes 2:3–10; Rev 13:1–8). *leaveth the flock.* Contrast the Good Shepherd of John 10:11–16. *His arm shall be clean dried up.* His power will be paralyzed. *his right eye shall be utterly darkened.* His intelligence will be nullified. Thus this leader will be powerless to fight.

12:1–14:21 This second oracle in Part II of the book revolves around two scenes: the final siege of Jerusalem, and the Messiah's return to defeat Israel's enemies and establish His kingdom.

12:1 *burden.* See note on 9:1. *Israel.* The whole nation, not just the northern kingdom. Judah and Jerusalem, however, are the main focus of attention. *the LORD, Which stretcheth . . . layeth . . . formeth.* This description of the Lord's creative power shows that He is able to perform what He predicts; it also strengthens the royal and sovereign authority of the message.

12:2 *cup of trembling.* See note on Is 51:17.

12:3 *that day.* See note on 2:11. The phrase is used often in chs. 12–14 (12:4,6,8–9,11; 13:1–2,4; 14:4,6,8–9,13,20–21). *all the people of the earth . . . gathered together against it.* See 14:2,12; Joel 3:9–16; cf. Rev 16:16–21.

12:4 *astonishment . . . madness . . . blindness.* Listed in Deut 28:28 among Israel's curses for disobeying the stipulations of the covenant. Now these curses are turned against Israel's enemies. *will open my eyes upon the house of Judah* See Ps 32:8; 33:18; 121.

[1]The inhabitants of Jerusalem *shall be* my strength
In the LORD of hosts their God.
6 In that day will I make the governors of Judah [a]like a hearth of fire among the wood,
And like a torch of fire in a sheaf;
And they shall devour all the people round about, on the right hand and on the left:
And Jerusalem shall be inhabited again in her own place, *even* in Jerusalem.
7 The LORD also shall save the tents of Judah first,
That the glory of the house of David
And the glory of the inhabitants of Jerusalem
Do not magnify *themselves* against Judah.
8 In that day shall the LORD defend the inhabitants of Jerusalem;
And he that is [1 2]feeble among them at that day shall be as David;
And the house of David *shall be* as God,
As the angel of the LORD before them.
9 And it shall come to pass in that day,
That I will seek to [a]destroy all the nations
That come against Jerusalem.

The compassion of Jerusalem

10 [a]And I will pour upon the house of David, and upon the inhabitants of Jerusalem,
The spirit of grace and of supplications:
And they shall [b]look upon me whom they have pierced,
And they shall mourn for him, [c]as one mourneth for *his* only *son*,
And shall be in bitterness for him, as one that is in bitterness for *his* firstborn.
11 In that day shall there be a great [a]mourning in Jerusalem,
[b]As the mourning of Hadadrimmon in the valley of Megiddon.
12 [a]And the land shall mourn, [1]every family apart;
The family of the house of David apart, and their wives apart;
The family of the house of [b]Nathan apart, and their wives apart;
13 The family of the house of Levi apart, and their wives apart;
The family [1]of Shimei apart, and their wives apart;
14 All the families that remain,
Every family apart, and their wives apart.

13 In that day there shall be [a]a fountain opened
To the house of David and to the inhabitants of Jerusalem
For sin and for [1]uncleanness.
2 And it shall come to pass in that day, saith the LORD of hosts,
That I will [a]cut off the names of the idols out of the land,
And they shall no more be remembered:
And also I will cause [b]the prophets and the unclean spirit to pass out of the land.
3 And it shall come to pass, *that* when any shall yet prophesy,
Then his father and his mother that begat him shall say unto him, Thou shalt not live;
For thou speakest lies in the name of the LORD:
And his father and his mother that begat him [a]shall thrust him through when he prophesieth.
4 And it shall come to pass in that day,
That [a]the prophets shall be ashamed every one of his vision, when he hath prophesied;
Neither shall they wear [b 1]a rough garment [2]to deceive:

12:5 [1]Or, There is *strength to me* and *to the inhabitants, etc.* 12:6 [a]Obad. 18 12:8 [1]Or, *abject* [2]Heb. *fallen* 12:9 [a]Hag. 2:22 12:10 [a]Jer. 31:9; 50:4; Ezek. 39:29; Joel 2:28 [b]John 19:34; Rev. 1:7 [c]Jer. 6:26; Amos 8:10 12:11 [a]Acts 2:37

12:11 [b]2 Ki. 23:29 12:12 [1]Heb. *families, families* [a]Rev. 1:7 [b]Luke 3:31 12:13 [1][Or, *of Simeon,* as LXX] 13:1 [1]Heb. *separation for uncleanness* [a]Heb. 9:14 13:2 [a]Ex. 23:13 [b]2 Pet. 2:1 13:3 [a]Deut. 18:20 13:4 [1]Heb. *a garment of hair* [2]Heb. *to lie* [a]Mic. 3:6,7 [b]2 Ki. 1:8

12:6 Like a fire destroying wood and sheaves of grain, Judah's discerning leaders (see v. 5) will consume their enemies (cf. Judg 15:3–5; see note on Is 1:31).

12:8 *as David.* Like a great warrior. *as God.* Cf. Ex 4:16; 7:1. *As the angel of the LORD.* See Gen 48:16 and note; Ex 14:19; 23:20; 32:34; 33:2,14–15,22; Hos 12:3–4; see also Gen 16:7 and note.

12:10 *The spirit.* See Is 32:15 and note; 44:3; 59:20–21; Jer 31:31,33; Ezek 36:26–27; 39:29; Joel 2:28–29. *look upon.* Or "look to." The emphasis seems to be on looking "to" the Messiah in faith (cf. Num 21:9; Is 45:22; John 3:14–15). *pierced.* Cf. Ps 22:16; Is 53:5; John 19:34; partly fulfilled in John 19:37. *mourneth for his only son.* Cf. Jer 6:26 and note. *in bitterness for his firstborn.* Cf. Ex 11:5–6.

12:11 *Hadadrimmon.* The name of either (1) a place near Megiddo, where the people mourned the death of King Josiah (2 Chr 35:20–27; see v. 22 there for the plain of Megiddo and vv. 24–25 for the mourning), or (2) a Semitic storm god (see 2 Ki 5:18), whose name means "Hadad the thunderer" in Babylonian (as in the *Epic of Gilgamesh,* 11:98; see also Ezek 8:14 for an example of the practice of weeping for a Babylonian deity).

12:12 *Nathan.* David's son (2 Sam 5:14; cf. Luke 3:31).

12:13 *family of Shimei.* Shimei was the son of Gershon, the son of Levi (Num 3:17–18,21). The repentance and mourning are led, then, by the civil (royal) and religious leaders.

13:1 *For sin and for uncleanness.* See 3:4–9; cleansing from sin is one of the provisions of the new covenant (Jer 31:34; Ezek 36:25).

13:2 *names of the idols.* The influence and fame, and even the very existence, of the idols. *prophets.* False prophecy was still a problem in the postexilic period (see Neh 6:12–14) and would again be a problem in the future (see Mat 24:4–5,11,23–24; 2 Thes 2:2–4).

‡13:3 *speaketh lies.* False prophecies. *father and his mother . . . shall thrust him through.* In obedience to Deut 13:6–9. The Hebrew for "thrust" is the same as the verb for "pierced" in 12:10, perhaps indicating that the feelings and actions exhibited in piercing the Messiah will now be directed toward the false prophets.

‡13:4–6 Because of the stern measures just mentioned, a false prophet will be reluctant to identify himself as such and will be

5 [a]But he shall say, I *am* no prophet, I
am a husbandman;
For man taught me *to keep cattle* from
my youth.
6 And *one* shall say unto him, What *are*
these wounds in thine hands?
Then he shall answer, *Those with*
which I was wounded *in* the house
of my friends.

Israel chastened

7 Awake, O sword, against [a]my
shepherd, and against the man [b]*that*
is my fellow,
Saith the LORD of hosts:
[c]Smite the shepherd, and the sheep
shall be scattered:
And I will turn mine hand upon [d]the
little ones.
8 And it shall come to pass, *that* in all
the land, saith the LORD,
Two parts therein shall be cut off *and*
die;
[a]But the third shall be left therein.
9 And I will bring the third *part*
[a]through the fire,
And will [b]refine them as silver is
refined,
And will try them as gold is tried:
[c]They shall call on my name, and I will
hear them:
[d]I will say, It *is* my people:
And they shall say, The LORD *is* my
God.

Judah's king supreme

14 Behold, [a]the day of the LORD
cometh,
And thy spoil shall be divided in the
midst of thee.

13:5 [a]Amos 7:14
13:7 [a]Is. 40:11 [b]John 10:30 [c]Mat. 26:31 [d]Luke 12:32
13:8 [a]Rom. 11:5
13:9 [a]Is. 48:10 [b]1 Pet. 1:6 [c]Ps. 50:15 [d]Jer. 30:22
14:1 [a]Is. 13:9

2 For [a]I will gather all nations against
Jerusalem to battle;
And the city shall be taken, and the
houses rifled, and the women
ravished;
And half of the city shall go forth into
captivity,
And the residue of the people shall not
be cut off from the city.
3 Then shall the LORD go forth, and fight
against those nations,
As when he fought in the day of battle.
4 And his feet shall stand in that day
[a]upon the mount of Olives,
Which *is* before Jerusalem on the east,
And the mount of Olives shall cleave in
the midst thereof toward the east
and toward the west,
[b]*And there shall be* a very great valley;
And half of the mountain shall remove
toward the north,
And half of it toward the south.
5 And ye shall flee *to* the valley of [1]the
mountains;
[2]For the valley of the mountains shall
reach unto Azal:
Yea, ye shall flee, like as ye fled from
before the [a]earthquake
In the days of Uzziah king of Judah:
[b]And the LORD my God shall come,
And [c]all the saints with thee.
6 And it shall come to pass in that day,
[1]*That* the light shall not be [2]clear, *nor*
[3]dark:
7 But [1]it shall be one day [a]which shall
be known to the LORD,
Not day, nor night:
But it shall come to pass, *that* at
[b]evening time it shall be light.
8 And it shall be in that day,

14:2 [a]Joel 3:2
14:4 [a]Ezek. 11:23 [b]Joel 3:12
14:5 [1]Or, *my mountains* [2]Or, *When he shall touch the valley of the mountains to* the place *he separated* [a]Amos 1:1 [b]Mat. 24:30 [c]Joel 3:11
14:6 [1]*i.e.* it shall not be clear in some places, and dark in other places of the world [2]Heb. *precious* [3]Heb. *thickness*
14:7 [1]Or, *the day shall be one* [a]Mat. 24:36 [b]Is. 30:26

evasive in his responses to interrogation. To help conceal his true identity, he will not wear a "rough garment" (v. 4), such as Elijah wore (2 Ki 1:8; see also Mat 3:4). Instead, to avoid the death penalty (v. 3), he will deny being a prophet and will claim to have been a farmer since his youth (v. 5). And if a suspicious person notices marks on his body and inquires about them (v. 6), he will claim he received them in a scuffle with friends (or perhaps as discipline from his parents during childhood). Apparently the accuser suspects that the false prophet's wounds were self-inflicted to arouse his prophetic ecstasy in idolatrous rites (as in 1 Ki 18:28; cf. also Lev 19:28; 21:5 and note; Deut 14:1; Jer 16:6; 41:5; 48:37).

13:6 Some take this verse as Messianic, but the interpretation given above seems preferable from the context (e.g., v. 5).

13:7 *my shepherd.* The royal (Messianic) Good Shepherd (cf. the true Shepherd of 11:4–14; contrast the foolish and worthless shepherd of 11:15–17). *Smite the shepherd.* In 11:17 it was the worthless shepherd who was to be struck; now it is the Good Shepherd (cf. also 12:10). *sheep shall be scattered.* In fulfillment of the curses for covenant disobedience (Deut 28:64; 29:24–25). This part of the verse is quoted by Jesus not long before His arrest (Mat 26:31; Mark 14:27) and applied to the scattering of the apostles (Mat 26:56; Mark 14:49–50), who in turn are probably typological of the dispersion of the Jews in A.D. 70 and the subsequent years.

13:8–9 These verses depict a refining process for Israel (see note on Is 48:10).

13:8 *the third.* A remnant, thus revealing God's mercy in the midst of judgment.

13:9 *It is my people . . . The LORD is my God.* See note on 8:8. They will be restored to proper covenant relationship with the Lord (see also Ezek 20:30–44).

14:1 *thy . . . thee.* Jerusalem (v. 2) is the object of the plunder.

14:2 *all nations . . . to battle.* See v. 12; see also note on 12:3.

14:3 *day of battle.* Any occasion when the Lord supernaturally intervenes to deliver His people, such as at the Red sea (see note on Ex 14:14).

14:4 *mount of Olives.* Called by this name elsewhere in the OT only in 2 Sam 15:30. This prophecy is probably referred to in Acts 1:11–12. *east.* Thus it faced the temple mount and, being about 2,700 feet high, rose about 200 feet above it. Cf. Ezek 11:23; 43:1–2.

14:5 *Azal.* The name of a place east of Jerusalem, marking the eastern end of the newly formed valley. The location is unknown. *saints.* May include both believers and angels. They will accompany our Lord when He comes (cf. Mat 25:31; 1 Thes 3:13; Jude 14; Rev 19:14).

14:7 *day which shall be known to the LORD.* Due to the topographical, cosmic and cataclysmic changes. See also Is 60:19–20 and notes; cf. Rev 21:23–25; 22:5.

That living [a]waters shall go out from
Jerusalem:
Half of them toward the [1]former sea,
And half of them toward the hinder
sea:
In summer and in winter shall it be.
9 And the LORD shall be [a]king over all
the earth:
In that day shall there be [b]one LORD,
and his name one.
10 All the land shall be [1]turned as a plain
from Geba to Rimmon south of
Jerusalem:
And it shall be lifted up, and
[a2]inhabited in her place,
From Benjamin's gate unto the place of
the first gate, unto the corner gate,
[b]And *from* the tower of Hananeel unto
the king's winepresses.
11 And *men* shall dwell in it, and there
shall be [a]no more utter destruction;
[b]But Jerusalem [1]shall be safely
inhabited.

12 And this shall be the plague where*with*
the LORD will smite all the people
That have fought against Jerusalem;
Their flesh *shall* consume away while
they stand upon their feet,
And their eyes shall consume away in
their holes,
And their tongue shall consume away
in their mouth.
13 And it shall come to pass in that day,
That [a]a great tumult from the LORD
shall be among them;
And they shall lay hold every one on
the hand of his neighbour,
And [b]his hand shall rise up against the
hand of his neighbour.

14:8 [1]Or, *eastern* [a]Ezek. 47:1
14:9 [a]Rev. 11:15 [b]Eph. 4:5,6
14:10 [1]Or, *compassed* [2]Or, *shall abide* [a]ch. 12:6 [b]Neh. 3:1
14:11 [1]Or, *shall abide* [a]Jer. 31:40 [b]Jer. 23:6
14:13 [a]1 Sam. 14:15,20 [b]Judg. 7:22; 2 Chr. 20:23; Ezek. 38:21

14:14 [1]Or, *thou also, O Judah, shalt* [2]Or, *against* [a]Ezek. 39:10,17
14:15 [a]ver. 12
14:16 [a]Is. 60:6; 66:23 [b]Lev. 23:34; Neh. 8:14; Hos. 12:9; John 7:2
14:17 [a]Is. 60:12
14:18 [1]Heb. *upon whom there is not* [a]Deut. 11:10
14:19 [1]Or, *sin*
14:20 [1]Or, *bridles* [a]Is. 23:18

14 And [1]Judah also shall fight [2]at
Jerusalem;
[a]And the wealth of all the heathen
round about shall be gathered
together,
Gold, and silver, and apparel, in great
abundance.
15 And [a]so shall be the plague of the
horse,
Of the mule, of the camel, and of the
ass,
And of all the beasts that shall be in
these tents, as this plague.
16 And it shall come to pass, *that* every
one that is left of all the nations
Which came against Jerusalem
Shall even [a]go up from year to year
To worship the King, the LORD of hosts,
And to keep [b]the feast of tabernacles.
17 [a]And it shall be, *that* whoso will not
come up
Of *all* the families of the earth unto
Jerusalem
To worship the King, the LORD of hosts,
Even upon them shall be no rain.
18 And if the family of Egypt go not up,
and come not, [a1]that *have* no *rain;*
There shall be the plague, where*with*
the LORD will smite the heathen
That come not up to keep the feast of
tabernacles.
19 This shall be the [1]punishment of
Egypt,
And the punishment of all nations
That come not up to keep the feast of
tabernacles.
20 In that day shall there be upon the
[1]bells of the horses,
[a]HOLINESS UNTO THE LORD;

14:8 *living waters shall go.* Perhaps both literal and symbolic (cf. Ps 46:4; 65:9; Is 8:6; Jer 2:13; Ezek 47:1–12; Joel 3:18; John 4:10–14; 7:38; Rev 22:1–2).
14:9 *the LORD shall be king over all the earth.* A pervasive theological theme in Scripture. *shall there be . . . one LORD.* See Deut 6:4; Is 43:11 and notes.
14:10 *plain.* Hebrew *Arabah* (see note on Deut 1:1). All the land around Jerusalem is to be leveled. *Geba.* About six miles north-northeast of Jerusalem at the northern boundary of Judah (2 Ki 23:8). *Rimmon.* Also called En Rimmon (Neh 11:29; cf. Josh 15:32), it was about 35 miles south-southwest of Jerusalem, where the hill country of Judah slopes away into the Negev. *it shall be lifted up.* See note on Is 2:2–4. The elevation may be both physical and in prominence. *Benjamin's gate . . . first gate . . . tower of Hananeel.* All were probably at the northeastern part of the city wall (cf. Jer 31:38; 37:12–13; 38:7). *corner gate.* At the northwest corner (cf. Jer 31:38). *king's winepresses.* Just south of the city. Thus the whole city is included.
14:11 *dwell in it.* See 2:4. *no more utter destruction.* As at the time of the exile to Babylonia (see Is 43:28 and note). *Jerusalem shall be safely inhabited.* See Jer 31:40.
14:12 *plague.* See Is 37:36 and note. *people . . . against Jerusalem.* See v. 2; see also note on 12:3.
14:13 *great tumult . . . hand of . . . against . . . his neighbour.* See note on Judg 7:22.
14:14 *Gold, and silver, and apparel.* The plunder of battle, thus reversing the situation in v. 1.
14:15 A similar plague will strike the beasts of burden, preventing the people from using them to escape.
14:16 See Is 2:2–4 and note. *feast of tabernacles.* See notes on Ex 23:16; Ps 81:3. Of the three great pilgrimage festivals (see Ex 23:14–17), perhaps tabernacles was selected as the one for representatives of the various Gentile nations because it was the last and greatest festival of the Hebrew calendar, gathering up into itself the year's worship. (See note on Ezek 45:25.) It was to be a time of grateful rejoicing (Lev 23:40; Deut 16:13–15; Neh 8:17). Beginning with the period of Ezra and Nehemiah, the reading and teaching of "the book of the law of God" became an integral part of the festivities (Neh 8:18; cf. Is 2:3). The festival seems to speak of the final, joyful regathering and restoration of Israel, as well as of the ingathering of the nations. See chart, pp. 166–167.
14:17 *no rain.* One of the curses for covenant disobedience (Deut 28:22–24; cf. Zech 9:11–10:1).
14:18 *family of Egypt . . . that have no rain.* The withholding of rain will affect the Egyptians, for drought (v. 17) would cause even the Nile inundation to fail.
14:20 *HOLINESS UNTO THE LORD.* Engraved on the gold plate worn on the high priest's turban (Ex 28:36–38) as a reminder of his consecration to the Lord's service. See note on 3:5. God's

And the pots in the LORD'S house shall
be like the bowls before the altar.
21 Yea, every pot in Jerusalem and in
Judah shall be holiness unto the LORD
of hosts:
And all they that sacrifice shall come
and take of them, and seethe therein:
And in that day there shall be no more
the [a]Canaanite in [b]the house of the
LORD of hosts.

14:21 [a]Is. 35:8; Joel 3:17; Rev. 21:27; 22:15 [b]Eph. 2:19-22

original purpose for Israel (see Ex 19:6 and note) will be realized. **14:21** *every pot in Jerusalem . . . holiness.* See Joel 3:17. Even common things become holy when they are used for God's service. *Canaanite.* Represents anyone who is morally or spiritually unclean—anyone who is not included among the chosen people of God (cf. Is 35:8; Ezek 43:7; 44:9; Rev 21:27).

Malachi

INTRODUCTION

Author

The book is ascribed to Malachi, whose name means "My messenger." Since the term occurs in 3:1, and since both prophets and priests were called messengers of the Lord (see 2:7; Hag 1:13), some have thought "Malachi" to be only a title that tradition has given the author. The view has been supported by appeal to the early Greek translation (the Septuagint), which translates the term in 1:1 "His messenger" rather than as a proper noun. The matter, however, remains uncertain, and it is still very likely that Malachi was in fact the author's name.

Background

Spurred on by the prophetic activity of Haggai and Zechariah, the returned exiles under the leadership of their governor Zerubbabel finished the temple in 516 B.C. In 458 the community was strengthened by the coming of Ezra the priest and several thousand more Jews. King Artaxerxes of Persia encouraged Ezra to develop the temple worship (Ezra 7:17) and to make sure the law of Moses was being obeyed (Ezra 7:25–26).

Thirteen years later (445) the same Persian king permitted his cupbearer Nehemiah to return to Jerusalem and rebuild the walls (Neh 6:15). As newly appointed governor, Nehemiah also spearheaded reforms to help the poor (Neh 5:2–13), and he convinced the people to shun mixed marriages, to keep the sabbath (Neh 10:30–31) and to bring their tithes and offerings faithfully (Neh 10:37–39).

In 433 B.C. Nehemiah returned to the service of the Persian king, and during his absence the Jews fell into sin once more. Later, however, Nehemiah came back to Jerusalem to discover that the tithes were ignored, the sabbath was broken, the people had intermarried with foreigners, and the priests had become corrupt (Neh 13:7–31). Several of these sins are condemned by Malachi (see 1:6–14; 2:14–16; 3:8–11).

Date

The similarity between the sins denounced in Nehemiah and those denounced in Malachi suggest that the two leaders were contemporaries. Malachi may have been written after Nehemiah returned to Persia in 433 B.C. or during his second period as governor. Since the governor mentioned in 1:8 (see note there) probably was not Nehemiah, the first alternative may be more likely. Malachi was most likely the last prophet of the OT era (though some place Joel later).

Themes and Theology

Although the Jews had been allowed to return from exile and rebuild the temple, several discouraging factors brought about a general religious malaise: (1) Their land remained but a small province in the backwaters of the Persian empire, (2) the glorious future announced by the prophets (including the other post-exilic prophets, Haggai and Zechariah) had not (yet) been realized, and (3) their God had not (yet) come to His temple (3:1) with majesty and power (as celebrated in Ps 68) to exalt His kingdom in the sight of the nations. Doubting God's covenant love (1:2) and no longer trusting His justice (2:17; 3:14–15), the Jews of the restored community began to lose hope. So their worship degenerated into a listless perpetuation of mere forms, and they no longer took the law seriously.

Malachi rebukes their doubt of God's love (1:2–5) and the faithlessness of both priests (1:6—2:9) and people (2:10–16). To their charge that God is unjust ("Where is the God of judgment?" 2:17) because He has failed to come in judgment to exalt His people, Malachi answers with an announcement and a warning. The Lord they seek will come—but He will come "like a refiner's fire" (3:1–4). He will come to judge—but He will judge His people first (3:5).

Because the Lord does not change in His commitments and purpose, Israel has not been com-

pletely destroyed for her persistent unfaithfulness (3:6). But only through repentance and reformation will she again experience God's blessing (3:6–12). Those who honor the Lord will be spared when He comes to judge (3:16–18).

In conclusion, Malachi once more reassures and warns his readers that "the day ['the great and dreadful day of the LORD,' 4:5] cometh" and that it will burn "as an oven" (4:1). In that day the righteous will rejoice, and "ye shall tread down the wicked" (4:1–3). So "remember the law of Moses my servant" (4:4). To prepare His people for that day the Lord will send "Elijah the prophet" to call them back to the godly ways of their forefathers (4:5–6).

Literary Features

Malachi is called a "burden" (see 1:1 and note), i.e. an "oracle," and is written in what might be called lofty prose. The text features a series of questions asked by both God and the people. Along with Micah it reflects the "disputation" technique in which the author and/or God disputes with his opponents, often in courtroom settings. Frequently the Lord's statements are followed by sarcastic questions introduced by "yet ye say" (1:2,6–7; 2:14,17; 3:7–8,13; cf. 1:13). In each case the Lord's response is given.

Repetition is a key element in the book. The name "LORD of hosts" occurs 20 times. The book begins with a description of the wasteland of Edom (1:3–4) and ends with a warning of Israel's destruction (4:6).

Several vivid figures are employed within the book of Malachi. The priests sniff contemptuously at the altar of the Lord (1:13), and the Lord spreads on their faces the offal from their sacrifices (2:3). As Judge, "He is like a refiner's fire and like fullers' sope" (3:2), but for the righteous "shall the Sun of righteousness arise with healing in his wings" (4:2).

Outline

I. Title (1:1)
II. Introduction: God's Covenant Love for Israel Affirmed (1:2–5)
III. Israel's Unfaithfulness Rebuked (1:6—2:16)
   A. The Unfaithfulness of the Priests (1:6—2:9)
      1. They dishonor God in their sacrifices (1:6–14)
      2. They do not faithfully teach the law (2:1–9)
   B. The Unfaithfulness of the People (2:10–16)
IV. The Lord's Coming Announced (2:17—4:6)
   A. The Lord Will Come to Purify the Priests and Judge the People (2:17—3:5)
   B. A Call to Repentance in View of the Lord's Coming (3:6–18)
      1. An exhortation to faithful giving (3:6–12)
      2. An exhortation to faithful service (3:13–18)
   C. The Day of the Lord Announced (ch. 4)

Fall of Edom shows God's love

1 The burden of the word of the LORD to Israel [1] by Malachi.
2 [a] I have loved you, saith the LORD.
Yet ye say, Wherein hast thou loved us?
Was not Esau Jacob's brother? saith the LORD:
Yet [b] I loved Jacob,
3 And I hated Esau,
And [a] laid his mountains and his heritage waste for the dragons of the wilderness.
4 Whereas Edom saith, We are impoverished,
But we will return and build the desolate places;
Thus saith the LORD of hosts,
They shall build, but I will throw down;
And they shall call them, The border of wickedness,
And, The people *against* whom the LORD hath indignation for ever.
5 And your eyes shall see, and ye shall say,
[a] The LORD will be magnified [1 2] from the border of Israel.

The sins of the priesthood

6 A son [a] honoureth *his* father, and a servant his master:
[b] If then I *be* a father, where *is* mine honour?
And if I *be* a master, where *is* my fear?
Saith the LORD of hosts unto you,
O priests, that despise my name.
[c] And ye say, Wherein have we despised thy name?
7 *Ye* [1] offer [a] polluted bread upon mine altar;
And ye say, Wherein have we polluted thee?
In that ye say, [b] The table of the LORD *is* contemptible.
8 And [a] if ye offer the blind [1] for sacrifice, *is it* not evil?
And if ye offer the lame and sick, *is it* not evil?
Offer it now unto thy governor;
Will he be pleased with thee, or [b] accept thy person? saith the LORD of hosts.
9 And now, I pray you, beseech [1] God that he will be gracious unto us:
[a] This hath been [2] by your means:
Will he regard your persons? saith the LORD of hosts.
10 Who *is there* even among you that would shut the doors *for nought?*
[a] Neither do ye kindle *fire on* mine altar for nought.
I have no pleasure in you, saith the LORD of hosts,
[b] Neither will I accept an offering at your hand.
11 For [a] from the rising of the sun even unto the going down of the same
My name *shall be* great [b] among the Gentiles;
[c] And in every place [d] incense *shall be* offered unto my name, and a pure offering:
[e] For my name *shall be* great among the heathen, saith the LORD of hosts.
12 But ye *have* profaned it, in that ye say,
[a] The table of the LORD *is* polluted;

1:1 [1] Heb. *by the hand of Malachi*
1:2 [a] Deut. 7:8; 10:15 [b] Rom. 9:13
1:3 [a] Jer. 49:18; Ezek. 35:3; Obad. 10
1:5 [1] Or, *upon* [2] Heb. *from upon* [a] Ps. 35:27
1:6 [a] Ex. 20:12 [b] Luke 6:46 [c] ch. 2:14
1:7 [1] Or, *bring unto, etc.* [a] Deut. 15:21 [b] Ezek. 41:22
1:8 [1] Heb. *to sacrifice* [a] Lev. 22:22 [b] Job 42:8
1:9 [1] Heb. *the face of God* [2] Heb. *from your hand* [a] Hos. 13:9
1:10 [a] 1 Cor. 9:13 [b] Is. 1:11
1:11 [a] Is. 59:19 [b] Is. 60:3,5 [c] 1 Tim. 2:8 [d] Rev. 8:3 [e] Is. 66:19
1:12 [a] ver. 7

1:1 *burden.* Or "oracle." See Zech 9:1 and note; 12:1; see also Hab 1:1 and note.
1:2 *loved you.* The Lord's reassuring word to His disheartened people.
‡1:3 *I hated Esau.* If Israel doubts God's covenant love, she should consider the contrast between God's ways with her and His ways with Jacob's brother Esau (Edom). Paul explains God's love for Jacob and hatred for Esau on the basis of election (Rom 9:10–13). God chose Jacob but not Esau. "Love" and "hate" are covenant words throughout the ancient Near East. Clearly then, the idea is that God made a covenant with Jacob but refused to make one with Esau. For other possible meanings of "love" and "hate", cf. how Leah was "hated" in that Jacob loved Rachel more (Gen 29:31,33; cf. Deut 21:16–17). Likewise, believers are to "hate" their parents (Luke 14:26) in the sense that they love Christ even more (Mat 10:37). *waste.* Malachi's words about Edom echo those of the earlier prophets (see Is 34:5–15; Jer 49:7–22; Ezek 25:12–14; 35:1–15; Obadiah). Between c. 550 and 400 B.C. the Nabatean Arabs gradually forced the Edomites from their homeland resulting in the formation of Idumea in NT times.
1:4 *Whereas Edom saith.* Her proud self-reliance has not assured her security and will not secure her future (cf. Jer 49:16).
1:5 *The LORD . . . Israel.* When she sees the ultimate fate of Edom, doubting Israel will acknowledge that the Lord is the great Ruler over all the nations.
1:6–2:9 The Lord rebukes the priests.
1:6 *son honoureth his father.* Cf. Is 1:2–3. *priests, that despise my name.* Contrast 2:5; cf. Is 1:4.
1:7 *bread.* The offerings (see v. 12; Lev 21:8,21). *Wherein have we polluted thee?* By offering defiled sacrifices they defile the Lord Himself. *The table of the LORD.* The altar (see v. 12; Ezek 44:16). Since the priests ate from the sacrifices, the altar was also the table from which they got their food. *contemptible.* As the priests despised the Lord's altar and its sacrifices, so the Lord would cause the priests to be despised by the people (see 2:9 and note).
1:8 *blind . . . lame.* Animals with defects or serious flaws were unacceptable as sacrifices (see Deut 15:21). *governor.* Probably the Persian governor.
1:10 *shut the doors.* Better no sacrifices than sacrifices offered with contempt (cf. Is 1:11–15).
‡1:11 *rising of the sun.* Malachi brackets his book with this metaphor. See 4:2. It is a common OT phrase. See Ps 50:1; 113:3; Is 41:25; 45:6. Usually it is used to celebrate God's universal rule. See also Ps 84:11, "For the LORD God is a sun and shield." *incense. . . a pure offering.* Cf. the acceptable offerings presented by foreigners in Is 56:6–7; 60:7. Some interpreters understand "incense" to mean "prayer" (cf. Rev 5:8) and "offering" to mean "praise" (cf. Heb 13:15). *great among the heathen.* Cf. v. 14. God's judgment on Edom (v. 5) and other nations demonstrates His superiority over their gods, and it ultimately will evoke their recognition of Him (see Zeph 2:11).
‡1:12 *profaned . . . polluted.* See v. 7. In a world where religion was central to life, their behavior was scandalous to pagans who

And the fruit thereof, *even* his meat, *is*
contemptible.
13 Ye said also, Behold, what a weariness
is it!
[1] And ye have snuffed at it, saith the
LORD of hosts;
And ye brought *that which was* torn,
and the lame, and the sick;
Thus ye brought an offering:
[a] Should I accept this of your hand?
saith the LORD.
14 But cursed *be* [a] the deceiver, [1] which
hath in his flock a male,
And voweth, and sacrificeth unto the
Lord a corrupt *thing:*
For [b] I *am* a great King, saith the LORD
of hosts,
And my name *is* dreadful among the
heathen.

The warning to the priesthood

2 And now, O ye priests, this
commandment *is* for you.
2 [a] If ye will not hear, and if ye will not
lay *it* to heart,
To give glory unto my name, saith the
LORD of hosts,
I will even send a curse upon you, and
will curse your blessings:
Yea, I have cursed them already,
because ye do not lay *it* to heart.
3 Behold, I *will* [1] corrupt your seed,
And [2] spread dung upon your faces,
even the dung of your solemn feasts;
And [3] *one* shall [a] take you away with it.
4 And ye shall know that I have sent this
commandment unto you,
That my covenant might be with Levi,
saith the LORD of hosts.
5 [a] My covenant was with him of life and
peace;

1:13 [1] Or, *Whereas you might have blown it away* [a] Lev. 22:20
1:14 [1] Heb. *in whose flock is* [a] ver. 8 [b] Ps. 47:2; 1 Tim. 6:15
2:2 [a] Deut. 28:15
2:3 [1] Or, *reprove* [2] Heb. *scatter* [3] Or, *it shall take you away to it* [a] 1 Ki. 14:10
2:5 [a] Num. 25:12; Ezek. 34:25

2:5 [b] Deut. 33:9
2:6 [a] Deut. 33:10 [b] Jer. 23:22; Jas. 5:20
2:7 [a] Deut. 17:9 [b] Gal. 4:14
2:8 [1] Or, *fall in the law* [a] Jer. 18:15 [b] Neh. 13:29
2:9 [1] Or, *lifted up the face against* [2] Heb. *accepted faces* [a] 1 Sam. 2:30
2:10 [a] 1 Cor. 8:6 [b] Job 31:15
2:11 [1] Or, *ought to love* [a] Ezra 9:1; Neh. 13:23

And I gave them to him [b] *for* the fear
wherewith he feared me,
And was afraid before my name.
6 [a] The law of truth was in his mouth,
And iniquity was not found in his lips:
He walked with me in peace and
equity,
And did [b] turn many away from
iniquity.
7 [a] For the priest's lips should keep
knowledge,
And they should seek the law at his
mouth:
[b] For he *is* the messenger of the LORD
of hosts.
8 But ye are departed out of the way;
Ye [a] have caused many to [1] stumble at
the law;
[b] Ye have corrupted the covenant of
Levi, saith the LORD of hosts.
9 Therefore [a] have I also made you
contemptible and base before all the
people,
According as ye have not kept my
ways,
But [1] [2] have been partial in the law.

The warning to the unfaithful

10 [a] Have we not all one father?
[b] Hath not one God created us?
Why do we deal treacherously every
man against his brother,
By profaning the covenant of our
fathers?
11 Judah hath dealt treacherously,
And an abomination is committed in
Israel and in Jerusalem;
For Judah hath profaned the holiness of
the LORD which he [1] loved,
[a] And hath married the daughter of a
strange god.

would have carefully avoided wrongs like this.
1:13 *snuffed at it.* Sniffed contemptuously. Cf. the behavior of Eli's sons in 1 Sam 2:15–17. *was torn . . . and . . . sick.* See v. 8 and note.
1:14 *voweth . . . a corrupt thing.* An animal sacrificed in fulfillment of a vow had to be a male without defect or blemish (see Lev 22:18–23). *great King.* See Zech 14:9. *my name is dreadful.* More than the governor of v. 8 (see v. 11 and note).
2:2 *curse your blessings.* It was the function of the priests to pronounce God's blessing on the people (see Num 6:23–27), but their blessings will become curses so that their uniquely priestly function will be worse than useless.
‡2:3 *spread dung upon your faces.* To disgrace you (see Nah 3:6). *dung of . . . feasts.* The entrails of an animal that were taken "outside the camp" and burned along with its hide and flesh (see Ex 29:14; Lev 8:17; 16:27). As gruesome as this is to a modern reader, it is simply a case of doing to them as they had done to the Lord. It is the ancient legal concept of "an eye for an eye."
2:4 *Levi.* The priests were chosen from the tribe of Levi (see Num 3:12–13; Neh 13:29).
2:5 *covenant . . . of life and peace.* An allusion to the covenant with Phinehas, Aaron's grandson, in Num 25:10–13. Phinehas defended God's honor by killing two offenders involved in the idolatry and immorality connected with Baal-peor (Num 25:1–3). *he feared me.* Phinehas showed this by his zeal for God (see Num 25:13).
2:6–7 *The law.* Priests were responsible to teach the law of Moses (see Lev 10:11; see also notes on Zeph 3:4; Hag 2:11).
2:6 *peace and equity.* Linked together also in Ps 37:37, but here "walked with me in peace and equity" probably refers to covenant loyalty.
2:7 *messenger.* As teacher of the law and as one through whom people could inquire of God (see notes on 3:1; Hag 1:13).
2:8 *corrupted the covenant.* By unfaithful teaching, but also, it seems, by intermarriage with foreigners (see Ezra 9:1; 10:18–22; Neh 13:27–29). *of Levi.* See v. 4 and note on v. 5.
2:9 *contemptible.* See 1:7,12 and note on 1:7. *partial in the law.* Forbidden in Lev 19:15. The priests were to be like God in this respect (see Deut 10:17).
‡2:10–16 Malachi rebukes the people—in a passage framed by references to "deal treacherously." Two examples of their sin are specifically mentioned: marrying pagan women and divorce.
2:10 *one father.* See Is 63:16. *created us.* As His special people (see Is 43:1 and note). *deal treacherously.* One could not even trust his own fellow Israelites or the national leaders—like the priests. *covenant of our fathers?* The covenant God made with their forefathers at mount Sinai.
2:11 *daughter of a strange god.* A pagan woman. Such mar-

12 The LORD will cut off the man that doth
this, [1]the master and the scholar,
Out of the tabernacles of Jacob,
[a]And him that offereth an offering unto
the LORD of hosts.
13 And this have ye done again,
Covering the altar of the LORD *with* tears,
with weeping, and *with* crying out,
Insomuch that *he* regardeth not the
offering any more,
Or receiveth *it with* good will at your
hand.
14 Yet ye say, Wherefore?
Because the LORD hath been witness
between thee and [a]the wife of thy
youth,
Against whom thou hast dealt
treacherously:
[b]Yet *is* she thy companion, and the
wife of thy covenant.
15 And [a]did not he make one? Yet had he
the [1]residue of the spirit.
And wherefore one? That he might
seek [b2]a godly seed.
Therefore take heed to your spirit,
And let none deal [3]treacherously
against the wife of his youth.
16 *For* [a]the LORD, the God of Israel, saith
[1]that he hateth [2]putting away:
For *one* covereth violence with his
garment, saith the LORD of hosts:
Therefore take heed to your spirit, that
ye deal not treacherously.

2:12 [1]Or, *him that waketh, and him that answereth* [a]Neh. 13:29
2:14 [a]Prov. 5:18 [b]Prov. 2:17
2:15 [1]Or, *excellency* [2]Heb. *a seed of God* [3]Or, *unfaithfully* [a]Mat. 19:4 [b]Ezra 9:2; 1 Cor. 7:14
2:16 [1]Or, *if he hate* her, *put* her *away* [2]Heb. *to put away* [a]Deut. 24:1; Mat. 5:32

The sending of the Messiah

17 [a]Ye have wearied the LORD with your
words.
Yet ye say, Wherein have we wearied
him?
When ye say, Every one that doeth evil
is good in the sight of the LORD,
And he delighteth in them;
Or, Where *is* the God of judgment?

3 Behold, [a]I *will* send my messenger, and
he shall [b]prepare the way before me:
And the LORD, whom ye seek, shall
suddenly come to his temple,
[c]Even the messenger of the covenant,
whom ye delight in:
Behold, [d]he *shall* come, saith the LORD
of hosts.
2 But who *may* abide [a]the day of his
coming?
And [b]who *shall* stand when he
appeareth?
For [c]he *is* like a refiner's fire, and like
fullers' sope:
3 And [a]he shall sit *as* a refiner and
purifier of silver:
And he shall purify the sons of Levi,
and purge them as gold and silver,
That they may [b]offer unto the LORD an
offering in righteousness.
4 Then [a]shall the offering of Judah and
Jerusalem be pleasant unto the LORD,
As *in* the days of old, and as *in* [1]former
years.

2:17 [a]Is. 43:24
3:1 [a]Mat. 11:10; Luke 1:76 [b]Is. 40:3 [c]Is. 63:9 [d]Hag. 2:7
3:2 [a]ch. 4:1 [b]Rev. 6:17 [c]Is. 4:4; Mat. 3:10
3:3 [a]Is. 1:25 [b]1 Pet. 2:5
3:4 [1]Or, *ancient* [a]ch. 1:11

riages were strictly forbidden in the covenant law because they would lead to apostasy (see Ex 34:15–16; Deut 7:3–4; 1 Ki 11:1–6; cf. Josh 23:12–13). Ezra and Nehemiah both wrestled with this problem (Ezra 9:1–2; Neh 13:23–29).

‡2:12 An alternative reading of the Hebrew text offers another possibility: If anyone "gives testimony" (instead of "the master and the scholar") in behalf of one marrying a foreign woman, the one giving testimony is to be cut off. The verb for "gives testimony" is found in this sense in Gen 30:33; Deut 5:20; Ruth 1:21; 1 Sam 12:3; 2 Sam 1:16; Is 3:9; Jer 14:7. On this reading, then, the one to be cut off is the one who speaks in defense of the wrongdoer. *tabernacles of Jacob.* A figurative expression for the community (see Jer 30:18).

2:13 *weeping, and . . . crying out.* Because the Lord does not respond to their sacrifices with blessing, they add wailing to their prayers.

2:14 *witness . . . wife of thy covenant.* Marriage was a covenant (see Prov 2:17; Ezek 16:8), and covenants were affirmed before witnesses (see notes on Deut 30:19; 1 Sam 20:23; Is 8:1–2).

2:15 Although the verse is difficult, it may refer to Abraham, who "married" the foreigner Hagar in order to have a son (Gen 16:1–4). But Abraham did not divorce Sarah, who had suggested the union with Hagar in the first place.

2:16 *he hateth putting away.* Or, "he hates divorce." See Is 50:1 and note. *violence.* See 3:5.

2:17–4:6 The second half of Malachi's prophecy speaks of God's coming to His people. They had given up on God (see 2:17, which introduces this section) and had grown religiously cynical and morally corrupt. So God's coming will mean judgment and purification as well as redemption.

‡2:17 *wearied the LORD with your words.* In Is 43:24 Israel's sins had wearied God. See Mic 6:3. *Every one that doeth evil is good.* Such was the depth of their cynicism. *Where is . . . judgment?* Or "justice." This word is translated 239 times as "judgment," but 29 different English words in the KJV are used to translate it throughout the OT. Judgment is favored by the Psalms (65 times), Isaiah (40 times), Deuteronomy and Ezekiel (37 times) and Jeremiah (31 times). The idea here is probably "justice". Cf. the sarcastic taunts of Is 5:19.

3:1 *my messenger.* The Hebrew for these words is *mal'aki;* it is normally used of a priest or prophet (see Hag 1:13 and note). This is fulfilled in John the Baptist (see Mat 11:10; Mark 1:2; Luke 1:76). *he shall prepare the way.* When the Lord comes, it will be to purify (v. 3) and judge (v. 5), but He will mercifully send one before Him to prepare His people (see 4:5–6 and notes; see also Is 40:3 and note). *the LORD, whom ye seek . . . whom ye delight in . . . shall come.* See Hag 2:7 and note. *messenger of the covenant.* The Messiah, who as the Lord's representative will confirm and establish the covenant (see note on Is 42:6).

3:2 *day of his coming.* The day of the Lord (see 4:1; see also note on Is 2:11,17,20). Malachi announces the Lord's coming to complete God's work in history, especially the work he outlines in the rest of his book. His word is fulfilled in the accomplishments of the Messiah. *who shall stand . . . ?* Those who desire the Lord's coming must know that clean hands and a pure heart are required (cf. Ps 24:3–4; Is 33:14–15). *refiner's fire.* See Is 1:25; Zech 13:8–9 and notes. *fullers' sope.* Or "launderer's soap." See Is 7:3 and note. White clothes signified purity (cf. Mark 9:3; Rev 3:5).

3:3 *purify the sons of Levi.* Those who are supposed to be "messengers" of the Lord and who serve at the altar will be purged of their sins and unfaithfulness—such as the Lord has rebuked in 1:6–2:9.

3:4 *be pleasant.* Or "acceptabale." See 1:8 and note. *days of old.* Probably the time of Moses and Phinehas (see note on 2:5).

5 And I will come near to you to
judgment;
And I will be a swift witness
Against the sorcerers, and against the
adulterers, [a]and against false swearers,
And against those that [1]oppress the
hireling in *his* wages,
The widow, and the fatherless,
And that turn aside the stranger *from
his right,* and fear not me,
Saith the LORD of hosts.
6 For I *am* the LORD, [a]I change not;
[b]Therefore ye sons of Jacob are not
consumed.

The sins of the people

7 Even from the days of [a]your fathers ye
are gone away from mine ordinances,
and have not kept *them.*
[b]Return unto me, and I will return
unto you, saith the LORD of hosts.
[c]But ye said, Wherein shall we return?
8 Will a man rob God? Yet ye *have*
robbed me.
But ye say, Wherein have we robbed
thee?
[a]*In* tithes and offerings.
9 Ye *are* cursed with a curse: for ye *have*
robbed me,
Even this whole nation.
10 [a]Bring ye all the tithes into [b]the
storehouse,
That there may be meat in mine
house,
And prove me now herewith, saith the
LORD of hosts,
If I will not open you the [c]windows of
heaven,
And [d1]pour you out a blessing, that
there shall not *be room* enough *to
receive it.*
11 And I will rebuke [a]the devourer for
your sakes,

3:5 [1]Or, *defraud* [a]Zech. 5:4; Jas. 5:4
3:6 [a]Num. 23:19; Rom. 11:29; Jas. 1:17 [b]Lam. 3:22
3:7 [a]Acts 7:51 [b]Zech. 1:3 [c]ch. 1:6
3:8 [a]Neh. 13:10
3:10 [1]Heb. *empty out* [a]Prov.
3:9 [b]1 Chr. 26:20; 2 Chr. 31:11; Neh. 10:38 [c]Gen. 7:11; 2 Ki. 7:2 [d]2 Chr. 31:10
3:11 [a]Amos 4:9
3:11 [1]Heb. *corrupt*
3:12 [a]Dan. 8:9
3:13 [a]ch. 2:17
3:14 [1]Heb. *his observation* [2]Heb. *in black* [a]Job 21:14
3:15 [1]Heb. *are built* [a]Ps. 73:12 [b]Ps. 95:9
3:16 [a]Ps. 66:16 [b]Heb. 3:13 [c]Ps. 56:8; Is. 65:6; Rev. 20:12
3:17 [1]Or, *special treasure* [a]Ex. 19:5; Deut. 7:6; Ps. 135:4 [b]Is. 62:3 [c]Ps. 103:13
3:18 [a]Ps. 58:11

And he shall not [1]destroy the fruits of
your ground;
Neither shall your vine cast her fruit
before the time in the field, saith the
LORD of hosts.
12 And all nations shall call you blessed:
For ye shall be [a]a delightsome land,
saith the LORD of hosts.
13 [a]Your words have been stout against
me, saith the LORD.
Yet ye say, What have we spoken so
much against thee?
14 [a]Ye have said, It *is* vain to serve God:
And what profit *is it* that we have kept
[1]his ordinance,
And that we have walked [2]mournfully
before the LORD of hosts?
15 And now [a]we call the proud happy;
Yea, they that work wickedness [1]are
set up;
Yea, *they that* [b]tempt God are even
delivered.

16 Then they [a]that feared the LORD [b]spake
often one to another:
And the LORD hearkened, and heard *it,*
And [c]a book of remembrance was
written before him
For them that feared the LORD, and that
thought upon his name.
17 And [a]they shall be mine, saith the
LORD of hosts,
In that day when I make *up my*
[b1]jewels;
And [c]I will spare them, as a man
spareth his own son that serveth
him.
18 [a]Then shall ye return, and discern
between the righteous and the
wicked,
Between him that serveth God and
him that serveth him not.

3:5 When He comes, the Lord will both purify the Levites (vv. 3–4) and judge the people. *sorcerers.* Common in the ancient Near East (see Ex 7:11; Deut 18:10).
3:6 *I change not.* See Jas 1:17. Contrary to what many in Malachi's day were thinking, God remains faithful to His covenant. *not consumed.* In contrast to Edom (1:3–5) and in spite of Israel's history of unfaithfulness.
3:7 *Return . . . and I will return.* If the Lord is to come for Israel's redemption, she must repent.
3:9 *cursed.* See 2:2 and note.
‡3:10 *storehouse.* The treasury rooms of the sanctuary (see 1 Ki 7:51; 2 Chr 31:11–12; Neh 13:12). In the ancient world, there were no banks. Temples were places where wealth was stored. *windows of heaven.* Elsewhere the idiom refers to abundant provision of food (see 2 Ki 7:2,19; Ps 78:23–24). *pour you out a blessing.* The promised covenant blessing (see Deut 28:12; cf. Is 44:3).
3:11 *devourer . . . vine cast her fruit.* Examples of the threatened covenant curses (see Deut 28:39–40).
3:12 *call you blessed.* In fulfillment of the promise to Abraham (see Gen 12:2–3; see also Is 61:9 and note).
3:14 *It is vain to serve God.* Because the redemption they longed for had not yet been realized. *walked mournfully.* In sackcloth and ashes.
3:15 *proud.* Evildoers—those who challenge God (see note on Ps 10:11). *happy.* Or "blessed." In their unbelief, the Jews call blessed those whom the godly know to be cursed (see Ps 119:21)—but it is they who will be called blessed if they repent (v. 12). *they that work wickedness are set up . . . delivered.* Note the psalmist's struggle with the prosperity of the wicked in Ps 73:3, 9–12.
3:16 *they that feared the LORD.* Those who had not given way to doubts and cynicism. *spake often one to another.* In the face of the widespread complaining against God (vv. 14–15), they sought mutual encouragement in fellowship. *book of remembrance.* Analogous to the records of notable deeds kept by earthly rulers (see Esth 6:1–3; Is 4:3; Dan 7:10; 12:1). *that thought upon his name.* Contrast the priests (1:12) and many among the people (vv. 14–15; 2:17).
3:17 *my jewels.* See note on Ex 19:5. *spare them.* In the day of judgment (see 4:1–2). *that serveth him.* Cf. 1:6.
3:18 *Then shall ye return, and discern.* As they apparently do not now; hence their cynicism. *the righteous and the wicked.* See 2:17 and note.

The coming day of the LORD

4 For behold, [a]the day cometh, that *shall* burn as an oven;
And all [b]the proud, yea, and all that do wickedly, shall be [c]stubble:
And the day that cometh shall burn them up, saith the LORD of hosts,
That it shall [d]leave them neither root nor branch.
2 But unto you that [a]fear my name shall the [b]Sun of righteousness arise
With healing in his wings;
And ye shall go forth, and grow up as calves of the stall.
3 [a]And ye shall tread down the wicked;
For they shall be ashes under the soles of your feet
In the day that I *shall* do *this,* saith the LORD of hosts.

4 Remember ye the [a]law of Moses my servant,
Which I commanded unto him [b]in Horeb for all Israel,
With [c]the statutes and judgments.

5 Behold, I *will* send you [a]Elijah the prophet
[b]Before the coming of the great and dreadful day of the LORD:
6 And he shall turn the heart of the fathers to the children,
And the heart of the children to their fathers,
Lest I come and [a]smite the earth *with* [b]a curse.

4:1 [a]Joel 2:31; 2 Pet. 3:7 [b]ch. 3:18 [c]Obad. 18 [d]Amos 2:9
4:2 [a]ch. 3:16 [b]Luke 1:78; Eph. 5:14; Rev. 2:28
4:3 [a]Mic. 7:10
4:4 [a]Ex. 20:3 [b]Deut. 4:10 [c]Ps. 147:19
4:5 [a]Mat. 11:14; Luke 1:17 [b]Joel 2:31
4:6 [a]Zech. 14:12 [b]Zech. 5:3

‡4:1 *the day.* The day of the Lord (see v. 5; 3:2 and note). *burn as an oven.* See 3:2–3; Is 1:31; 66:15–16 and notes. *proud.* The Hebrew has an extensive vocabulary for pride or arrogance. It is an issue of much greater proportional importance in the Bible than in contemporary culture. See 3:15 and note. *stubble.* See Is 47:14 and John the Baptist's prophecy about the work of Christ in Mat 3:12. *burn them up.* Nothing of them will be left (see Ezek 17:8–9). *neither root nor branch.* See Am 2:9. An idiom for complete destruction.

‡4:2 *Sun of righteousness* See note at 1:11. God and His glory are compared with the sun in Is 60:1,19 (see notes there). Christ is the "Sunrise" from heaven (see Luke 1:78–79; see also Is 9:2 and note). The metaphor of a king rising like the sun is ancient. *righteousness.* There are few conventions more common in the ancient world than that of the "just king." *healing.* Salvation and renewal are intended (see Is 45:8; 46:13; 53:5; Jer 30:17 and notes). *his wings.* A strikingly beautiful idea found only here. Jer 14:19; 33:6 had spoken of a time of healing. Malachi seems to be saying that the coming Messiah will establish peace and end militarism. Jesus used his healings as proof of his Messianic identity. When the Baptist's disciples asked Him if He were really the Messiah, He answered by pointing out that "the blind receive their sight, and the lame walk, the lepers are cleansed, and the deaf hear, the dead are raised up" (Mat 11:5). *as calves of the stall.* Frisky young calves often frolic about when released from confinement.

4:3 *tread down the wicked.* As one treads the winepress (see Is 63:2–3 and notes).

‡4:4 *Remember ye the law.* A final exhortation to those who impatiently wait for the Lord's coming. Many of the strong emphases of Judaism, such as law, ritual and the temple, are established in these last books of the prophets. *my servant.* See Ex 14:31; Deut 34:5; Judg 2:8; Ps 18 title; Is 20:3; 41:8–9; 42:1 and notes. *Horeb.* Mount Sinai (cf. Ex 3:1).

‡4:5 See 3:1 and note. *Elijah.* As Elijah came before Elisha (whose ministry was one of judgment and redemption), so "Elijah" will be sent to prepare God's people for the Lord's coming. John the Baptist ministered "in the spirit and power of Elias" (Luke 1:17; see Mat 11:13–14; 17:12–13; Mark 9:11–13). And some feel that Elijah may also be one of the two witnesses in Rev 11:3. *great and dreadful day.* See v. 1; 3:2 and note; Joel 2:11,31.

‡4:6 *he shall turn the heart.* Cf. Gen 18:19; Deut 7:9–11. According to Luke 1:17 John the Baptist sought to accomplish this. *curse.* Total destruction. If Israel does not repent, she will be dealt with as God had dealt with Edom (see Is 34:5; cf. Mal 1:3–4). The OT is largely a book of promise. Malachi ends his book with a reminder that God will fulfill His promises in that great day of the Lord. In the meantime the reader is left waiting for the coming of the Messiah to fulfill these promises.

From Malachi to Christ

THE PERSIAN PERIOD
450-330 B.C.

For about 200 years after Nehemiah's time the Persians controlled Judah, but the Jews were allowed to carry on their religious observances and were not interfered with. During this time Judah was ruled by high priests who were responsible to the Jewish government.

Rule of Alexander the Great

THE HELLENISTIC PERIOD
330-166 B.C.

In 333 B.C. the Persian armies stationed in Macedonia were defeated by Alexander the Great. He was convinced that Greek culture was the one force that could unify the world. Alexander permitted the Jews to observe their laws and even granted them exemption from tribute or tax during their sabbath years. When he built Alexandria in Egypt, he encouraged Jews to live there and gave them some of the same privileges he gave his Greek subjects. The Greek conquest prepared the way for the translation of the OT into Greek (Septuagint version) c. 250 B.C.

Rule of the Ptolemies of Egypt

Rule of the Seleucids of Syria

THE HASMONEAN PERIOD
166-63 B.C.

When this historical period began, the Jews were being greatly oppressed. The Ptolemies had been tolerant of the Jews and their religious practices, but the Seleucid rulers were determined to force Hellenism on them. Copies of the Scriptures were ordered destroyed and laws were enforced with extreme cruelty. The oppressed Jews revolted, led by Judas the Maccabee.

Hasmonean Dynasty

THE ROMAN PERIOD
63 B.C. . . .

In the year 63 B.C. Pompey, the Roman general, captured Jerusalem, and the provinces of the Holy Land became subject to Rome. The local government was entrusted part of the time to princes and the rest of the time to procurators who were appointed by the emperors. Herod the Great was ruler of all the Holy Land at the time of Christ's birth.

Herod the Great rules as king; subject to Rome

410	Malachi c. 430 B.C.
400 B.C.	
390	
380	
370	
360	
350	
340	
330	334-323 Alexander the Great conquers the East
320	330-328 Alexander's years of power 320 Ptolemy (I) Soter conquers Jerusalem
310	311 Seleucus conquers Babylon;
300	Seleucid dynasty begins
290	
280	
270	
260	
250	
240	
230	
220	226 Antiochus III (the Great) of Syria overpowers the Holy Land
210	223-187 Antiochus becomes Seleucid ruler of Syria
200	
190	198 Antiochus defeats Egypt and gains control of the Holy Land
180	
170	175-164 Antiochus (IV) Epiphanes rules Syria; Judaism is prohibited
160	167 Mattathias and his sons rebel against Antiochus; Maccabean revolt begins
150	166-160 Judas Maccabeus's leadership
140	160-143 Jonathan is high priest 142 Tower of Jerusalem cleansed
130	142-134 Simon becomes high priest; establishes
120	Hasmonean dynasty
110	134-104 John Hyrcanus enlarges the independent Jewish state
100	103 Aristobulus's rule
90	102-76 Alexander Janneus's rule
80	75-67 Rule of Salome Alexandra with Hyrcanus II as high priest
70	
60	66-63 Battle between Aristobulus II and Hyrcanus II
50	63 Pompey invades the Holy Land; Roman rule begins 63-40 Hyrcanus II rules but is subject to Rome
40	40-37 Parthians conquer Jerusalem
30	
20	37 Jerusalem besieged for six months 32 Herod defeated
10	19 Herod's temple begun 16 Herod visits Agrippa 4 Herod dies; Archelaus succeeds
10	
20	
A.D. 30	

The Time Between the Testaments

The time between the Testaments was one of ferment and change—a time of the realignment of traditional power blocs and the passing of a Near Eastern cultural tradition that had been dominant for almost 3,000 years.

In Biblical history, the approximately 400 years that separate the time of Nehemiah from the birth of Christ are known as the intertestamental period (c. 432–5 B.C.). Sometimes called the "silent" years, they were anything but silent. The events, literature and social forces of these years would shape the world of the NT.

History

With the Babylonian captivity, Israel ceased to be an independent nation and became a minor territory in a succession of larger empires. Very little is known about the latter years of Persian domination because the Jewish historian Josephus, our primary source for the intertestamental period, all but ignores them.

With Alexander the Great's acquisition of the Holy Land (332 B.C.), a new and more insidious threat to Israel emerged. Alexander was committed to the creation of a world united by Greek language and culture, a policy followed by his successors. This policy, called Hellenization, had a dramatic impact on the Jews.

At Alexander's death (323 B.C.) the empire he won was divided among his generals. Two of them founded dynasties—the Ptolemies in Egypt and the Seleucids in Syria and Mesopotamia—that would contend for control of the Holy Land for over a century.

The rule of the Ptolemies was considerate of Jewish religious sensitivities, but in 198 B.C. the Seleucids took control and paved the way for one of the most heroic periods in Jewish history.

The early Seleucid years were largely a continuation of the tolerant rule of the Ptolemies, but Antiochus IV Epiphanes (whose title means "God made manifest" and who ruled 175–164 B.C.) changed that when he attempted to consolidate his fading empire through a policy of radical Hellenization. While a segment of the Jewish aristocracy had already adopted Greek ways, the majority of Jews were outraged.

Antiochus's atrocities were aimed at the eradication of Jewish religion. He prohibited some of the central elements of Jewish practice, attempted to destroy all copies of the Torah (the Pentateuch) and required offerings to the Greek god Zeus. His crowning outrage was the erection of a statue of Zeus and the sacrificing of a pig in the Jerusalem temple itself.

Opposition to Antiochus was led by Mattathias, an elderly villager from a priestly family, and his five sons: Judas (Maccabeus), Jonathan, Simon, John and Eleazar. Mattathias destroyed a Greek altar established in his village, Modein, and killed Antiochus's emissary. This triggered the Maccabean revolt, a 24-year war (166–142 B.C.) that resulted in the independence of Judah until the Romans took control in 63 B.C.

The victory of Mattathias's family was Pyrrhic, however. With the death of his last son, Simon, the Hasmonean dynasty that they founded soon evolved into an aristocratic, Hellenistic regime sometimes hard to distinguish from that of the Seleucids. During the reign of Simon's son, John Hyrcanus, the orthodox Jews who had supported the Maccabees fell out of favor. With only a few exceptions, the rest of the Hasmoneans supported the Jewish Hellenizers. The Pharisees were actually persecuted by Alexander Janneus (102–76 B.C.).

The Hasmonean dynasty ended when, in 63 B.C., an expanding Roman empire intervened in a dynastic clash between the two sons of Janneus, Aristobulus II and Hyrcanus II. Pompey, the general who subdued the East for Rome, took Jerusalem after a three-month siege of the temple area, massacring priests in the performance of their duties and entering the most holy place. This sacrilege began Roman rule in a way that Jews could neither forgive nor forget.

Literature

During these unhappy years of oppression and internal strife, the Jewish people produced a sizable body of literature that both recorded and addressed their era. Three of the more significant works are the Septuagint, the Apocrypha and the Dead Sea Scrolls.

Septuagint. Jewish legend says that 72 scholars, under the sponsorship of Ptolemy Philadelphus (c. 250 B.C.), were brought together on the island of Pharos, near Alexandria, where they produced a Greek translation of the OT in 72 days. From this tradition the Latin word for 70, "Septuagint," became the name attached to the translation. The Roman numeral for 70, LXX, is used as an abbreviation for it.

Behind the legend lies the probability that at least the Torah (the five books of Moses) was translated into Greek c. 250 B.C. for the use of the Greek-speaking Jews of Alexandria. The rest of the OT and some noncanonical books were also included in the LXX before the dawning of the Christian era, though it is difficult to be certain when.

The Septuagint quickly became the Bible of the Jews outside the Holy Land who, like the Alexandrians, no longer spoke Hebrew. It would be difficult to overestimate its influence. It made the Scriptures available both to the Jews who no longer spoke their ancestral language and to the entire Greek-speaking world. It later became the Bible of the early church. Also, its widespread popularity and use contributed to the retention of the Apocrypha by some branches of Christendom.

Apocrypha. Derived from a Greek word that means "hidden," Apocrypha has acquired the meaning "false," but in a technical sense it describes a specific body of writings. This collection consists of a variety of books and additions to canonical books that, with the exception of 2 Esdras (c. A.D. 90), were written during the intertestamental period. Their recognition as authoritative in Roman and Eastern Christianity is the result of a complex historical process.

The canon of the OT accepted by Protestants today was very likely established by the dawn of the second century A.D., though after the fall of Jerusalem and the destruction of the temple in 70. The precise scope of the OT was discussed among the Jews until the Council of Jamnia (c. 90). This Hebrew canon was not accepted by the early church, which used the Septuagint. In spite of disagreements among some of the church fathers as to which books were canonical and which were not, the Apocryphal books continued in common use by most Christians until the Reformation. During this period most Protestants decided to follow the original Hebrew canon while Rome, at the Council of Trent (1546) and more recently at the First Vatican Council (1869–70), affirmed the larger "Alexandrian" canon that includes the Apocrypha.

The Apocryphal books have retained their place primarily through the weight of ecclesiastical authority, without which they would not commend themselves as canonical literature. There is no clear evidence that Jesus or the apostles ever quoted any Apocryphal works as Scripture. The Jewish community that produced them repudiated them, and the historical surveys in the apostolic sermons recorded in Acts completely ignore the period they cover. Even the sober, historical account of 1 Maccabees is tarnished by numerous errors and anachronisms.

There is nothing of theological value in the Apocryphal books that cannot be duplicated in canonical Scripture, and they contain much that runs counter to its teachings. Nonetheless, this body of literature does provide a valuable source of information for the study of the intertestamental period.

Dead Sea Scrolls. In the spring of 1947 an Arab shepherd chanced upon a cave in the hills overlooking the southwestern shore of the Dead Sea that contained what has been called "the greatest manuscript discovery of modern times." The documents and fragments of documents found in those caves, dubbed the "Dead Sea Scrolls," included OT books, a few books of the Apocrypha, apocalyptic works, pseudepigrapha (books that purport to be the work of ancient heroes of the faith), and a number of books peculiar to the sect that produced them.

Approximately a third of the documents are Biblical, with Psalms, Deuteronomy and Isaiah—the books quoted most often in the NT—occurring most frequently. One of the most remarkable finds was a complete 24-foot-long scroll of Isaiah.

The Scrolls have made a significant contribution to the quest for a form of the OT texts most accurately reflecting the original manuscripts; they provide copies 1,000 years closer to the originals than were previously known. The understanding of Biblical Hebrew and Aramaic and knowledge of the development of Judaism between the Testaments have been increased significantly. Of great importance to readers of the Bible is the demonstration of the care with which OT texts were copied, thus providing objective evidence for the general reliability of those texts.

Social Developments

The Judaism of Jesus' day is, to a large extent, the result of changes that came about in response to the pressures of the intertestamental period.

Diaspora. The Diaspora (dispersion) of Israel begun in the exile accelerated during these years until a writer of the day could say that Jews filled "every land and sea."

Jews outside the Holy Land, cut off from the temple, concentrated their religious life in the study of the Torah and the life of the synagogue (see below). The missionaries of the early church began their Gentile ministries among the Diaspora, using their Greek translation of the OT.

Sadducees. In the Holy Land, the Greek world made its greatest impact through the party of the Sadducees. Made up of aristocrats, it became the temple party. Because of their position, the Sadducees had a vested interest in the status quo.

Relatively few in number, they wielded disproportionate political power and controlled the high priesthood. They rejected all religious writings except the Torah, as well as any doctrine (such as the resurrection) not found in those five books.

Synagogue. During the exile, Israel was cut off from the temple, divested of nationhood and surrounded by pagan religious practices. Her faith was threatened with extinction. Under these circumstances, the exiles turned their religious focus from what they had lost to what they retained—the Torah and the belief that they were God's people. They concentrated on the law rather than nationhood, on personal piety rather than sacramental rectitude, and on prayer as an acceptable replacement for the sacrifices denied to them.

When they returned from the exile, they brought with them this new form of religious expression, as well as the synagogue (its center), and Judaism became a faith that could be practiced wherever the Torah could be carried. The emphases on personal piety and a relationship with God, which characterized synagogue worship, not only helped preserve Judaism but also prepared the way for the Christian gospel.

Pharisees. As the party of the synagogue, the Pharisees strove to reinterpret the law. They built a "hedge" around it to enable Jews to live righteously before God in a world that had changed drastically since the days of Moses. Although they were comparatively few in number, the Pharisees enjoyed the support of the people and influenced popular opinion if not national policy. They were the only party to survive the destruction of the temple in A.D. 70 and were the spiritual progenitors of modern Judaism.

Essenes. An almost forgotten Jewish sect until the discovery of the Dead Sea Scrolls, the Essenes were a small, separatist group that grew out of the conflicts of the Maccabean age. Like the Pharisees, they stressed strict legal observance, but they considered the temple priesthood corrupt and rejected much of the temple ritual and sacrificial system. Mentioned by several ancient writers, the precise nature of the Essenes is still not certain, though it is generally agreed that the Qumran community that produced the Dead Sea Scrolls was an Essene group.

Because they were convinced that they were the true remnant, these Qumran Essenes had separated themselves from Judaism at large and devoted themselves to personal purity and preparation for the final war between the "Sons of Light and the Sons of Darkness." They practiced an apocalyptic faith, looking back to the contributions of their "Teacher of Righteousness" and forward to the coming of two, and possibly three, Messiahs. The destruction of the temple in A.D. 70, however, seems to have delivered a death blow to their apocalyptic expectations.

Attempts have been made to equate aspects of the beliefs of the Qumran community with the origins of Christianity. Some have seen a prototype of Jesus in their "Teacher of Righteousness," and both John the Baptist and Jesus have been assigned membership in the sect. There is, however, only a superficial, speculative basis for these conjectures.

THE NEW TESTAMENT

The Synoptic Gospels

A careful comparison of the four Gospels reveals that Matthew, Mark and Luke are noticeably similar, while John is quite different. The first three Gospels agree extensively in language, in the material they include, and in the order in which events and sayings from the life of Christ are recorded. (Chronological order does not appear to have been rigidly followed in any of the Gospels, however.) Because of this agreement, these three books are called the Synoptic Gospels (*syn,* "together with"; *optic,* "seeing"; thus "seeing together"). For an example of agreement in content see Mat 9:2–8; Mark 2:3–12; Luke 5:18–26. An instance of verbatim agreement is found in Mat 10:22a; Mark 13:13a; Luke 21:17. A mathematical comparison shows that 91 percent of Mark's Gospel is contained in Matthew, while 53 percent of Mark is found in Luke. Such agreement raises questions as to the origin of the Synoptic Gospels. Did the authors rely on a common source? Were they interdependent? Questions such as these constitute what is known as the Synoptic Problem. Several suggested solutions have been advanced:

1. *The use of oral tradition.* Some have thought that tradition had become so stereotyped that it provided a common source from which all the Gospel writers drew.

2. *The use of an early Gospel.* Some have postulated that the Synoptic authors all had access to an earlier Gospel, now lost.

3. *The use of written fragments.* Some have assumed that written fragments had been composed concerning various events from the life of Christ and that these were used by the Synoptic authors.

4. *Mutual dependence.* Some have suggested that the Synoptic writers drew from each other with the result that what they wrote was often very similar.

5. *The use of two major sources.* The most common view currently is that the Gospel of Mark and a hypothetical document, called *Quelle* (German for "source") or *Q,* were used by Matthew and Luke as sources for most of the materials included in their Gospels.

6. *The priority and use of Matthew.* Another view suggests that the other two Synoptics drew from Matthew as their main source.

7. *A combination of most of the above.* This theory assumes that the authors of the Synoptic Gospels made use of oral tradition, written fragments, mutual dependence on other Synoptic writers or on their Gospels, and the testimony of eyewitnesses.

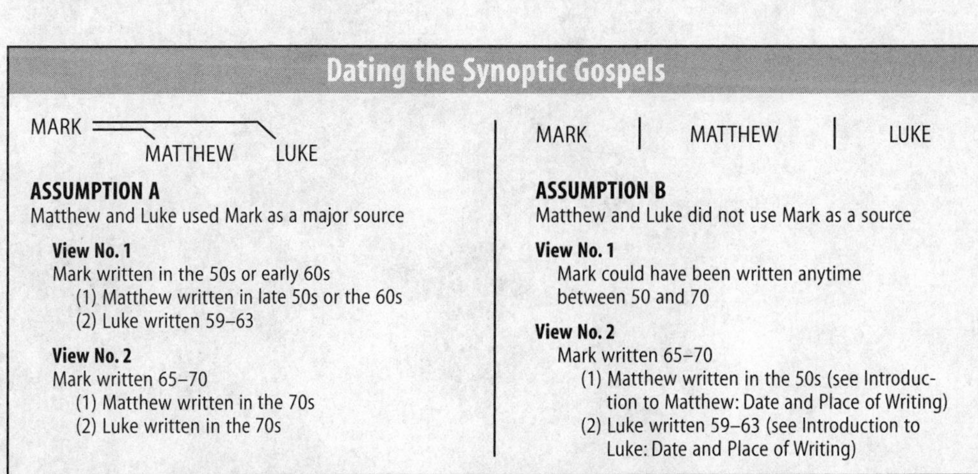

Dating the Synoptic Gospels

MARK → MATTHEW, LUKE

ASSUMPTION A

Matthew and Luke used Mark as a major source

View No. 1

Mark written in the 50s or early 60s

(1) Matthew written in late 50s or the 60s

(2) Luke written 59–63

View No. 2

Mark written 65–70

(1) Matthew written in the 70s

(2) Luke written in the 70s

MARK | MATTHEW | LUKE

ASSUMPTION B

Matthew and Luke did not use Mark as a source

View No. 1

Mark could have been written anytime between 50 and 70

View No. 2

Mark written 65–70

(1) Matthew written in the 50s (see Introduction to Matthew: Date and Place of Writing)

(2) Luke written 59–63 (see Introduction to Luke: Date and Place of Writing)

The Gospel According to
S. Matthew

INTRODUCTION

See "The Synoptic Gospels," p. 1349.

Author

The early church fathers were unanimous in holding that Matthew, one of the 12 apostles, was the author of this Gospel. However, the results of modern critical studies—in particular those that stress Matthew's alleged dependence on Mark for a substantial part of his Gospel—have caused some Biblical scholars to abandon Matthean authorship. Why, they ask, would Matthew, an eyewitness to the events of our Lord's life, depend so heavily on Mark's account? The best answer seems to be that he agreed with it and wanted to show that the apostolic testimony to Christ was not divided.

Matthew, whose name means "gift of the LORD," was a tax collector who left his work to follow Jesus (9:9–13). In Mark and Luke he is called by his other name, Levi, and Mark also mentions that he was the "son of Alpheus" (2:14). As a tax official he had to be intelligent and literate, and thus capable of precisely recording events in the life of our Lord. Matthew frequently mentions money and has an interest in large figures (18:24; 25:15).

Date and Place of Writing

The Jewish nature of Matthew's Gospel may suggest that it was written in the Holy Land, though many think it may have originated in Syrian Antioch. Some have argued on the basis of its Jewish characteristics that it was written in the early church period, possibly the early part of A.D. 50, when the church was largely Jewish and the gospel was preached to Jews only (Ac 11:19). However, those who have concluded that both Matthew and Luke drew extensively from Mark's Gospel date it later—after the Gospel of Mark had been in circulation for a period of time. See chart, p. 1349. Accordingly, some feel that Matthew would have been written in the late 50s or in the 60s. Others, who assume that Mark was written between 65 and 70, place Matthew in the 70s or even later.

Recipients

Since his Gospel was written in Greek, Matthew's readers were obviously Greek-speaking. They also seem to have been Jews. Many elements point to Jewish readership: Matthew's concern with fulfillment of the OT (he has more quotations from and allusions to the OT than any other Gospel writer); his tracing of Jesus' descent from Abraham (1:1–17); his lack of explanation of Jewish customs (especially in contrast to Mark); his use of Jewish terminology (e.g., "kingdom of heaven" and "Father in heaven," where "heaven" reveals the Jewish reverential reluctance to use the name of God); his emphasis on Jesus' role as "Son of David" (1:1; 9:27; 12:23; 15:22; 20:30–31; 21:9,15; 22:41–45). This does not mean, however, that Matthew restricts his Gospel to Jews. He records the coming of the wise men (non-Jews) to worship the infant Jesus (2:1–12), as well as Jesus' statement that the "field is the world" (13:38). He also gives a full statement of the Great Commission (28:18–20). These passages show that, although Matthew's Gospel is Jewish, it has a universal outlook.

Purpose

Matthew's main purpose is to prove to his Jewish readers that Jesus is their Messiah. He does this primarily by showing how Jesus in His life and ministry fulfilled the OT Scriptures. Although all the Gospel writers quote the OT, Matthew includes nine additional proof texts (1:22–23; 2:15; 2:17–18; 2:23; 4:14–16; 8:17; 12:17–21; 13:35; 27:9–10) to drive home his basic theme: Jesus is the fulfillment of the OT predictions of the Messiah. Matthew even finds the history of God's people in the OT recapitulated in some aspects of Jesus' life (see, e.g., his quotation of Hos 11:1 in 2:15). To accomplish his purpose Matthew also emphasizes Jesus' Davidic lineage (see Recipients above).

Structure

The way the material is arranged reveals an artistic touch. The whole Gospel is woven around six great discourses: (1) chs. 5—7; (2) ch. 10; (3) ch. 13; (4) ch. 18; (5) ch. 23; (6) chs. 24—25. That this is deliberate is clear from the refrain that concludes each discourse: "When Jesus had finished these words," or similar phrases (7:28; 11:1; 13:53; 19:1; 26:1). The narrative sections, in each case, appropriately lead up to the discourses. The Gospel has a fitting prologue (chs. 1—2) and a challenging epilogue (28:16–20).

Matthew begins as "The book of the generation of Jesus Christ," much as Genesis begins each of its ten main sections with "the generations of . . ." (see note on Gen 2:4). Jewish readers notice the similarity immediately. Matthew gives Jesus' royal lineage and supernatural birth (1–2), followed by his qualifications through baptism and the temptation (3–4). Then he gives Jesus' basic message (5–7), followed by a grouping of miracles (8–10). After Christ's rejection as seen in ch. 11–12, Matthew records Jesus' parables showing a different direction from the immediate kingdom he had been announcing for the Jews. The climax of Matthew is found in the passion story which makes up so much of the rest of the book.

Outline

I. The Birth and Early Years of Jesus (chs. 1—2)
  A. His Genealogy (1:1–17)
  B. His Birth (1:18—2:12)
  C. His Sojourn in Egypt (2:13–23)
II. The Beginnings of Jesus' Ministry (3:1—4:11)
  A. His Forerunner (3:1–12)
  B. His Baptism (3:13–17)
  C. His Temptation (4:1–11)
III. Jesus' Ministry in Galilee (4:12—14:12)
  A. The Beginning of the Galilean Campaign (4:12–25)
  B. The Sermon on the Mount (chs. 5—7)
  C. A Collection of Miracles (chs. 8—9)
  D. The Commissioning of the 12 Apostles (ch. 10)
  E. Ministry throughout Galilee (chs. 11—12)
  F. The Parables of the Kingdom (ch. 13)
  G. Herod's Reaction to Jesus' Ministry (14:1–12)
IV. Jesus' Withdrawals from Galilee (14:13—17:20)
  A. To the Eastern Shore of the Sea of Galilee (14:13—15:20)
  B. To Phoenicia (15:21–28)
  C. To the Decapolis (15:29—16:12)
  D. To Caesarea Philippi (16:13—17:20)
V. Jesus' Last Ministry in Galilee (17:22—18:35)
  A. Prediction of Jesus' Death (17:22–23)
  B. Temple Tax (17:24–27)
  C. Discourse on Life in the Kingdom (ch. 18)
VI. Jesus' Ministry in Judea and Perea (chs. 19—20)
  A. Teaching concerning Divorce (19:1–12)
  B. Teaching concerning Little Children (19:13–15)
  C. The Rich Young Man (19:16–30)
  D. The Parable of the Laborers in the Vineyard (20:1–16)
  E. Prediction of Jesus' Death (20:17–19)
  F. A Mother's Request (20:20–28)
  G. Restoration of Sight at Jericho (20:29–34)
VII. Passion Week (chs. 21—27)
  A. The Triumphal Entry (21:1–11)
  B. The Cleansing of the Temple (21:12–17)
  C. The Last Controversies with the Jewish Leaders (21:18—22:46)
  D. The Denunciation of the Scribes and Pharisees (23)
  E. The Olivet Discourse concerning the End of the Age (chs. 24—25)
  F. The Anointing of Jesus' Feet (26:1–13)
  G. The Arrest, Trials and Death of Jesus (26:14—27:66)
VIII. The Resurrection (ch. 28)

The genealogy of Jesus

1 The book of the [a]generation of Jesus
Christ, [b]the son of David, [c]the son of
Abraham.
2 [a]Abraham begat Isaac; and [b]Isaac begat
Jacob; and [c]Jacob begat Judas and his brethren;
3 And [a]Judas begat Phares and Zara of
Thamar; and [b]Phares begat Esrom; and Esrom
begat Aram;
4 And Aram begat Aminadab; and Aminadab begat Naasson; and Naasson begat Salmon;
5 And Salmon begat Booz of Rachab; and
Booz begat Obed of Ruth; and Obed begat Jesse;
6 And [a]Jesse begat David the king; and
[b]David the king begat Solomon of *her that had
been* the *wife* of Urias;
7 And [a]Solomon begat Roboam; and
Roboam begat Abia; and Abia begat Asa;
8 And Asa begat Josaphat; and Josaphat begat Joram; and Joram begat Ozias;
9 And Ozias begat Joatham; and Joatham
begat Achaz; and Achaz begat Ezekias;
10 And [a]Ezekias begat Manasses; and Manasses begat Amon; and Amon begat Josias;
11 And [a][1]Josias begat Jechonias and his
brethren, about the time they were [b]carried
away to Babylon:
12 And after they were brought to Babylon,
[a]Jechonias begat Salathiel; and Salathiel begat
[b]Zorobabel;
13 And Zorobabel begat Abiud; and Abiud
begat Eliakim; and Eliakim begat Azor;
14 And Azor begat Sadoc; and Sadoc begat
Achim; and Achim begat Eliud;
15 And Eliud begat Eleazar; and Eleazar begat Matthan; and Matthan begat Jacob;
16 And Jacob begat Joseph the husband of
Mary, of whom was born Jesus, who is called
Christ.
17 So all the generations from Abraham to
David *are* fourteen generations; and from David until the carrying away into Babylon *are*
fourteen generations; and from the carrying
away into Babylon unto Christ *are* fourteen
generations.

The birth of Jesus

18 ¶ Now the [a]birth of Jesus Christ was
on this wise: When as his mother Mary was
espoused to Joseph, before they came together, she was found with child [b]of the Holy
Ghost.
19 Then Joseph her husband, being a just
man, and not willing [a]to make her a publick
example, was minded to put her away privily.
20 But while he thought on these *things,*
behold, *the* angel of the Lord appeared unto
him in a dream, saying, Joseph, *thou* son of
David, fear not to take unto *thee* Mary thy
wife: [a]for that which is [1]conceived in her is of
the Holy Ghost.

1:1 [a]Luke 3:23 [b]Ps. 132:11; Is. 11:1; Jer. 23:5; ch. 22:42; John 7:42; Acts 2:30; Rom. 1:3 [c]Gen. 12:3
1:2 [a]Gen. 21:2 [b]Gen. 25:26 [c]Gen. 29:35
1:3 [a]Gen. 38:27 [b]Ruth 4:18; 1 Chr. 2:5
1:6 [a]1 Sam. 16:1; 17:12 [b]2 Sam. 12:24
1:7 [a]1 Chr. 3:10
1:10 [a]2 Ki. 20:21; 1 Chr. 3:13
1:11 [1]Some read, *Josias begat Jakim, and Jakim begat Jechonias* [a]See 1 Chr. 3:15,16 [b]2 Ki. 24:14-16; 25:11; 2 Chr. 36:10; Jer. 27:20; 52:11,15; Dan. 1:2
1:12 [a]1 Chr. 3:17 [b]Ezra 3:2; Neh. 12:1; Hag. 1:1
1:18 [a]Luke 1:27 [b]Luke 1:35
1:19 [a]Deut. 24:1
1:20 [1][Gr. *begotten*] [a]Luke 1:35

‡1:1–16 Matthew's Gospel begins by connecting Jesus to the promised Messianic line in the Old Testament. For a comparison of Matthew's genealogy with Luke's see note on Luke 3:23–38. The types of people mentioned in this genealogy reveal the broad scope of those who make up the people of God as well as the genealogy of Jesus.
1:1 *the son of David.* A Messianic title (see note on 9:27) found several times in this Gospel (in 1:20 it is not a Messianic title). *the son of Abraham.* Because Matthew was writing to Jews, it was important to identify Jesus in this way.
1:3 *Thamar.* In Matthew's genealogy four women are named: Thamar (here), Rachab (v. 5), Ruth (v. 5) and Bathsheba (v. 6). At least three of these women were Gentiles (Tamar, Rahab and Ruth). Bathsheba was probably an Israelite (1 Chr 3:5) but was closely associated with the Hittites because of Uriah, her Hittite husband. By including these women (contrary to custom) in his genealogy, Matthew may be indicating at the very outset of his Gospel that God's activity is not limited to men or the people of Israel.
1:4 *Aminadab.* Father-in-law of Aaron (Ex 6:23).
1:5 *Rachab.* See Josh 2. Since quite a long time had elapsed between Rahab and David and because of Matthew's desire for systematic organization (see note on v. 17), many of the generations between these two ancestors were assumed, but not listed, by Matthew.
1:8 *Joram begat.* Matthew calls Joram the father of Ozias, but from 2 Chr 21:4–26:23 it is clear that, again, several generations were assumed (Ahaziah, Joash and Amaziah) and that "begat" is used in the sense of "became the forefather of."
‡1:11 *Josias begat.* Similarly (see note on v. 8), Josias is called the father of Jechonias (i.e., Jehoiachin), whereas he was actually the father of Jehoiakim and the grandfather of Jehoiachin (2 Chr 36:1–9).
1:12 *Salathiel begat.* See note on 1 Chr 3:19.
‡1:16 Matthew does not say that Joseph was the father of Jesus but only that he was the husband of Mary and that Jesus was born of her. In this genealogy Matthew shows that, although Jesus is not the physical son of Joseph, He is the legal son and therefore a descendant of David. By not being Joseph's son, Jesus avoided the curse on Jechonias's descendants (Jer 22:30).
1:17 *fourteen generations . . . fourteen . . . fourteen.* These divisions reflect two characteristics of Matthew's Gospel: (1) an apparent fondness for numbers and (2) concern for systematic arrangement. The number 14 may have been chosen because it is twice seven (the number of completeness) and/or because it is the numerical value of the name David (see note on Rev 13:17). For the practice of telescoping genealogies to achieve the desired number of names see Introduction to 1 Chronicles: Genealogies.
‡1:18 *was espoused.* There were no sexual relations during a Jewish betrothal period, but it was a much more binding relationship than a modern engagement and could be broken only by divorce (see v. 19). In Deut 22:24 a betrothed woman is called a "wife," though the preceding verse speaks of her as being "betrothed unto a husband." Matthew uses the terms "husband" (v. 19) and "wife" (v. 24) of Joseph and Mary before their betrothal was consummated.
1:19 *just.* To Jews this meant being zealous in keeping the law. *put her away privily.* He would sign the necessary legal papers for a divorce but not have her judged publicly and stoned (see Deut 22:23–24).
1:20 *in a dream.* The phrase occurs five times in the first two chapters of Matthew (here; 2:12–13,19,22) and indicates the means the Lord used for speaking to Joseph. *son of David.* Perhaps a hint that the message of the angel related to the expected Messiah. *Take unto thee Mary thy wife.* They were legally bound to each other, but not yet living together as husband

21 [a]And she shall bring forth a son, and thou shalt call his name [1]JESUS: for [b]he shall save his people from their sins.

22 Now all this was done, that it might be fulfilled which was spoken of the Lord by the prophet, saying,

23 [a]Behold, a virgin shall be with child, and shall bring forth a son, and [1]they shall call his name Emmanuel, which being interpreted is, God with us.

24 Then Joseph being raised from sleep did as the angel of the Lord had bidden him, and took unto *him* his wife:

25 And knew her not till she had brought forth [a]her firstborn son: and *he* called his name JESUS.

The coming of the wise men

2 Now when [a]Jesus was born in Bethlehem of Judea in the days of Herod the king, behold, there came wise men [b]from the east to Jerusalem,

2 Saying, [a]Where is he that is born King of the Jews? for we have seen [b]his star in the east, and are come to worship him.

3 When Herod the king had heard *these things,* he was troubled, and all Jerusalem with him.

4 And when he had gathered all [a]the chief priests and [b]scribes of the people together, [c]he demanded of them where Christ should be born.

5 And they said unto him, In Bethlehem of Judea: for thus it is written by the prophet,

6 [a]And thou Bethlehem, *in* the land of Juda, art not the least among the princes of Juda: for out of thee shall come a Governor, [b]that shall [1]rule my people Israel.

7 Then Herod, when he had privily called the wise men, inquired of them diligently what time the star appeared.

8 And he sent them to Bethlehem, and said, Go and search diligently for the young child; and when ye have found *him,* bring me word again, that I may come and worship him also.

9 When they had heard the king, they departed; and lo, the star, which they saw in the east, went before them, till it came and stood over where the young child was.

10 When they saw the star, they rejoiced *with* exceeding great joy.

11 And when they were come into the house, they saw the young child with Mary his mother, and fell down, and worshipped him: and when they had opened their treasures, [a]they [1]presented unto him gifts; gold, and frankincense, and myrrh.

1:21 [1][That is, *Saviour,* Heb.] [a]Luke 1:31 [b]Acts 4:12; 5:31; 13:23,38
1:23 [1]Or, *his name shall be called* [a]Is. 7:14
1:25 [a]Ex:13:2; Luke 2:7,21
2:1 [a]Luke 2:4,6 [b]Gen. 25:6; 1 Ki. 4:30
2:2 [a]Luke 2:11 [b]Num. 24:17; Is. 60:3
2:4 [a]2 Chr. 36:14
2:4 [b]2 Chr. 34:13 [c]Mal. 2:7
2:6 [1]Or, *feed* [a]John 7:42 [b]Rev. 2:27
2:11 [1]Or, *offered* [a]Ps. 72:10; Is. 60:6

and wife. *that which is conceived in her is of the Holy Ghost.* This agrees perfectly with the announcement to Mary (Luke 1:35), except that the latter is more specific (see note on Luke 1:26–35).

1:21 *JESUS... shall save.* Jesus is the Greek form of Joshua, which means "The LORD saves."

‡1:22 *that it might be fulfilled.* 16 times (here; 2:15,17,23; 3:15; 4:14; 5:18; 8:17; 12:17; 13:14,35; 21:4; 24:34; 26:56; 27:9,35) Matthew speaks of the OT being fulfilled, i.e., of events in NT times that were prophesied in the OT—a powerful testimony to the divine origin of Scripture and its accuracy even in small details. In the fulfillments we also see the writer's concern for linking the gospel with the OT. Matthew, writing especially for the Jews, demonstrates how Jesus fulfilled numerous prophecies.

1:23 See note on Is 7:14. This is the first of at least 47 quotations, most of them Messianic, that Matthew takes from the OT (see marg. refs. throughout Matthew). *a virgin.* Refers to Mary, the mother of Jesus. Quoting Isaiah 7:14, Matthew uses the Greek *parthenos* to translate the Hebrew *'almah* precisely as a "virgin" in the technical sense. His usage of "fulfill" clearly indicates that he believed the Isaiah passage was predicting the virginal conception of Jesus. *Emmanuel.* Means "God with us" and is used as a title of Jesus' divinity.

1:25 *and knew her not till.* Both Matthew and Luke (1:26–35) make it clear that Jesus was born of a virgin. Although this doctrine is often ridiculed, it is an important part of the evangelical faith.

‡2:1 *Bethlehem of Judea.* A village about five miles south of Jerusalem. Matthew says nothing of the events in Nazareth (cf. Luke 1:26–56). Possibly wanting to emphasize Jesus' Davidic background, he begins with the events that happened in David's city. It is called "Bethlehem of Judea," not to distinguish it from the town of the same name about seven miles northwest of Nazareth, but to emphasize that Jesus came from the tribe and territory that produced the line of Davidic kings. That Jews expected the Messiah to be born in Bethlehem and to be from David's family is clear from John 7:42. *Herod the king.* Herod the Great (37–4 B.C.), to be distinguished from the other Herods in the Bible (see chart, p. 1355). Herod was a non-Jew, an Idumean, who was appointed king of Judea by the Roman Senate in 40 B.C. and gained control only by military conquest by 37 B.C. Like many other rulers of the day, he was ruthless. Herod murdered one of his wives, three of his sons, a mother-in-law, brother-in-law, uncle and many others—not to mention the babies in Bethlehem (v. 16). His reign was also noted for splendor, as seen in the many theaters, amphitheaters, monuments, pagan altars, fortresses and other buildings he erected or refurbished—including the greatest work of all, the rebuilding of the temple in Jerusalem, begun in 19 B.C. and finished 68 years after his death. *wise men.* Perhaps they were from Persia or southern Arabia, both of which are east of the Holy Land. *Jerusalem.* Since they were looking for the "King of the Jews" (v. 2), they naturally came to the Jewish capital city (see map No. 8 at the end of the study Bible).

‡2:2 *King of the Jews.* Indicates the wise men were Gentiles. Matthew shows that people of all nations acknowledged Jesus as "King of the Jews" and came to worship Him as Lord. *star.* Probably not an ordinary star, planet or comet, though some scholars have identified it with the conjunction of Jupiter and Saturn. It must have been a supernatural object that looked like a star, but which could actually move along and lead the wise men. It eventually led them to the proper house (v. 9).

2:4 *chief priests.* Sadducees (see note on 3:7) who were in charge of worship at the temple in Jerusalem. *scribes.* The Jewish scholars of the day, professionally trained in the development, teaching and application of OT law. Their authority was strictly human and traditional.

2:6 This prophecy from Mic 5:2 had been given seven centuries earlier.

‡2:11 *house.* Contrary to tradition, the wise men did not visit Jesus at the manger on the night of His birth as did the shepherds. They came some months later and visited Him as a "child" in His "house." *the young child with Mary his mother.* Every time the child Jesus and His mother are mentioned together, He is

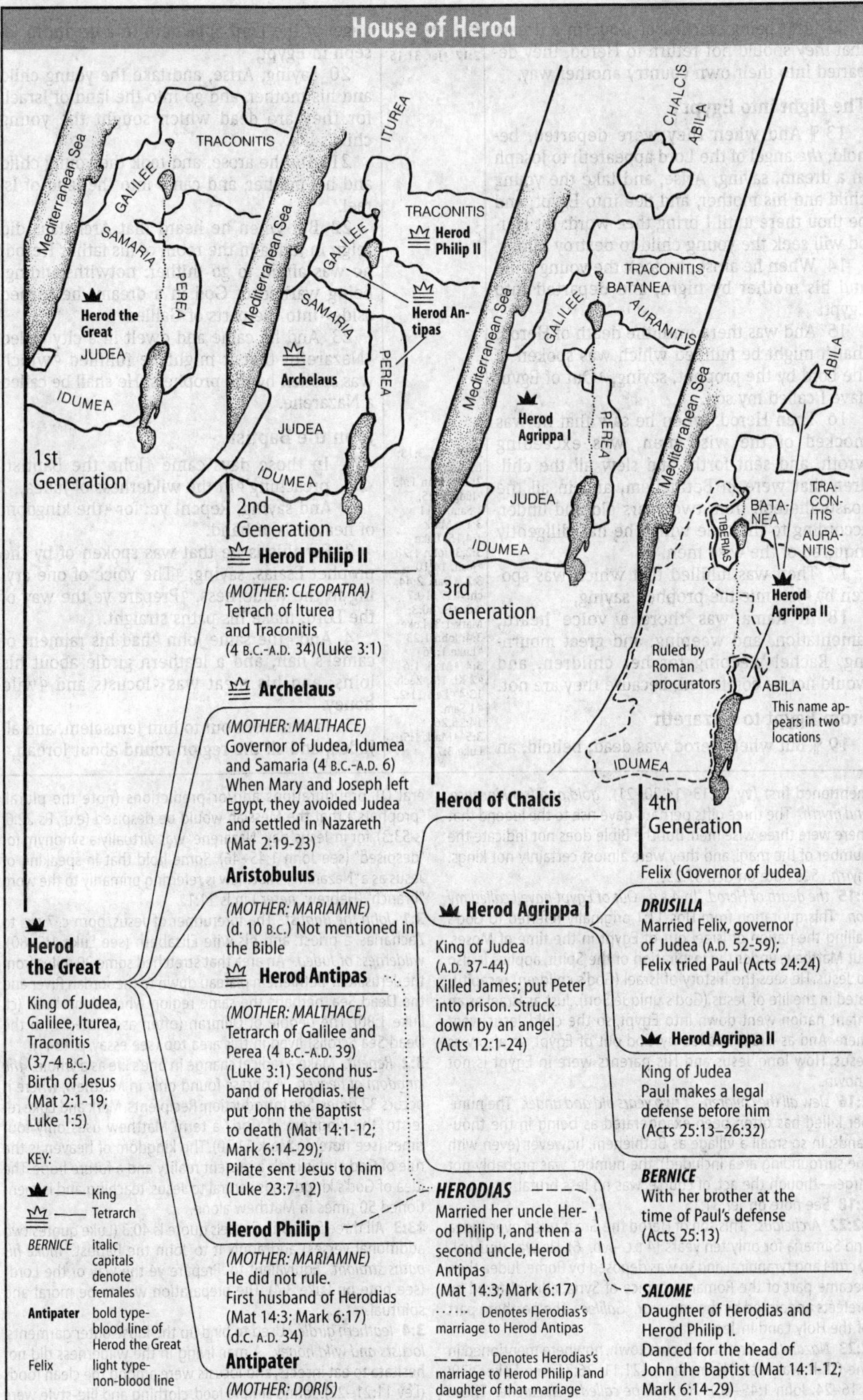

House of Herod
Mediterranean Sea
TRACONITIS
GALILEE
SAMARIA
PEREA
Herod the Great
JUDEA
IDUMEA
1st Generation
ITUREA
Mediterranean Sea
TRACONITIS
Herod Philip II
GALILEE
SAMARIA
Herod Antipas
PEREA
Archelaus
JUDEA
IDUMEA
2nd Generation
CHALCIS
ABILA
TRACONITIS
BATANEA
AURANITIS
GALILEE
Mediterranean Sea
Herod Agrippa I
PEREA
JUDEA
IDUMEA
3rd Generation
ABILA
Mediterranean Sea
TRA-CON-ITIS
BATA-NEA
AURA-NITIS
TIBERIAS
Herod Agrippa II
Ruled by Roman procurators
ABILA
This name appears in two locations
IDUMEA
4th Generation
Herod the Great
King of Judea, Galilee, Iturea, Traconitis (37-4 B.C.)
Birth of Jesus (Mat 2:1-19; Luke 1:5)
KEY:
— King
—— Tetrarch
BERNICE italic capitals denote females
Antipater bold type-blood line of Herod the Great
Felix light type-non-blood line
Herod Philip II
(MOTHER: CLEOPATRA)
Tetrach of Iturea and Traconitis (4 B.C.-A.D. 34)(Luke 3:1)
Archelaus
(MOTHER: MALTHACE)
Governor of Judea, Idumea and Samaria (4 B.C.-A.D. 6)
When Mary and Joseph left Egypt, they avoided Judea and settled in Nazareth (Mat 2:19-23)
Aristobulus
(MOTHER: MARIAMNE)
(d. 10 B.C.) Not mentioned in the Bible
Herod Antipas
(MOTHER: MALTHACE)
Tetrarch of Galilee and Perea (4 B.C.-A.D. 39) (Luke 3:1) Second husband of Herodias. He put John the Baptist to death (Mat 14:1-12; Mark 6:14-29);
Pilate sent Jesus to him (Luke 23:7-12)
Herod Philip I
(MOTHER: MARIAMNE)
He did not rule.
First husband of Herodias (Mat 14:3; Mark 6:17)
(d.c. A.D. 34)
Antipater
(MOTHER: DORIS)
Herod of Chalcis
Herod Agrippa I
King of Judea (A.D. 37-44)
Killed James; put Peter into prison. Struck down by an angel (Acts 12:1-24)
HERODIAS
Married her uncle Herod Philip I, and then a second uncle, Herod Antipas (Mat 14:3; Mark 6:17)
...... Denotes Herodias's marriage to Herod Antipas
—— Denotes Herodias's marriage to Herod Philip I and daughter of that marriage
Felix (Governor of Judea)
DRUSILLA
Married Felix, governor of Judea (A.D. 52-59);
Felix tried Paul (Acts 24:24)
Herod Agrippa II
King of Judea
Paul makes a legal defense before him (Acts 25:13–26:32)
BERNICE
With her brother at the time of Paul's defense (Acts 25:13)
SALOME
Daughter of Herodias and Herod Philip I.
Danced for the head of John the Baptist (Mat 14:1-12; Mark 6:14-29)

12 And being warned of God [a]in a dream
that *they* should not return to Herod, they departed into their own country another way.

The flight into Egypt

13 ¶ And when they were departed, behold, *the* angel of the Lord appeareth to Joseph
in a dream, saying, Arise, and take the young
child and his mother, and flee into Egypt, and
be thou there until I bring thee word: for Herod will seek the young child to destroy him.
14 When he arose, he took the young child
and his mother by night, and departed into
Egypt:
15 And was there until the death of Herod:
that it might be fulfilled which was spoken of
the Lord by the prophet, saying, [a]Out of Egypt
have I called my son.
16 Then Herod, when he saw that he was
mocked of the wise men, was exceeding
wroth, and sent forth, and slew all the children that were in Bethlehem, and in all the
coasts thereof, from two years old and under,
according to the time which he had diligently
inquired of the wise men.
17 Then was fulfilled that which was spoken by [a]Jeremie the prophet, saying,
18 In Rama was there a voice heard,
lamentation, and weeping, and great mourning, Rachel weeping for her children, and
would not be comforted, because they are not.

From Egypt to Nazareth

19 ¶ But when Herod was dead, behold, an
angel of the Lord appeareth in a dream to Joseph in Egypt,
20 Saying, Arise, and take the young child
and his mother, and go into the land of Israel:
for they are dead which sought the young
child's life.
21 And he arose, and took the young child
and his mother, and came into the land of Israel.
22 But when he heard that Archelaus did
reign in Judea in the room of his father Herod,
he was afraid to go thither: notwithstanding,
being warned of God in a dream, he turned
aside [a]into the parts of Galilee:
23 And he came and dwelt in a city called
[a]Nazareth: that it might be fulfilled [b]which
was spoken by the prophets, He shall be called
a Nazarene.

John the Baptist

3 In those days came [a]John the Baptist,
preaching [b]in the wilderness of Judea,
2 And saying, Repent ye: for [a]the kingdom
of heaven is at hand.
3 For this is he that was spoken of by the
prophet Esaias, saying, [a]The voice of one crying in the wilderness, [b]Prepare ye the way of
the Lord, make his paths straight.
4 And [a]the same John [b]had his raiment of
camel's hair, and a leathern girdle about his
loins; and his meat was [c]locusts and [d]wild
honey.
5 [a]Then went out to him Jerusalem, and all
Judea, and all the region round about Jordan,

2:12 [a]ch. 1:20
2:15 [a]Hos. 11:1
2:17 [a]Jer. 31:15
2:22 [a]ch. 3:13; Luke 2:39
2:23 [a]John 1:45 [b]Judg. 13:5; 1 Sam. 1:11
3:1 [a]Mark 1:4,15; Luke 3:2,3; John 1:28 [b]Josh. 14:10
3:2 [a]Dan. 2:44; ch. 4:17; 10:7
3:3 [a]Is. 40:3; Mark 1:3; Luke 3:4; John 1:23 [b]Luke 1:76
3:4 [a]Mark 1:6 [b]2 Ki. 1:8; Zech. 13:4 [c]Lev. 11:22 [d]1 Sam. 14:25,26
3:5 [a]Mark 1:5; Luke 3:7

mentioned first (vv. 11,13–14,20–21). *gold,and frankincense, and myrrh.* The three gifts perhaps gave rise to the legend that there were three wise men. But the Bible does not indicate the number of the magi, and they were almost certainly not kings. *myrrh.* See note on Gen 37:25.

2:15 *the death of Herod.* In 4 B.C. *Out of Egypt have I called my son.* This quotation from Hos 11:1 originally referred to God's calling the nation of Israel out of Egypt in the time of Moses. But Matthew, under the inspiration of the Spirit, applies it also to Jesus. He sees the history of Israel (God's children) recapitulated in the life of Jesus (God's unique Son). Just as Israel as an infant nation went down into Egypt, so the child Jesus went there. And as Israel was led by God out of Egypt, so also was Jesus. How long Jesus and His parents were in Egypt is not known.

2:16 *slew all the children . . . two years old and under.* The number killed has often been exaggerated as being in the thousands. In so small a village as Bethlehem, however (even with the surrounding area included), the number was probably not large—though the act, of course, was no less brutal.

2:18 See note on Jer 31:15.

‡2:22 *Archelaus.* This son of Herod the Great ruled over Judea and Samaria for only ten years (4 B.C.–A.D. 6). He was unusually cruel and tyrannical and so was deposed by Rome. Judea then became part of the Roman province of Syria, administered by prefects appointed by the emperor. *Galilee.* The northern part of the Holy Land in Jesus' day.

2:23 *Nazareth.* A rather obscure town, nowhere mentioned in the OT. It was Jesus' hometown (21:11; 26:71; see Luke 2:39; 4:16–24; John 1:45–46). *He shall be called a Nazarene.* These exact words are not found in the OT and probably refer to several OT prefigurations and/or predictions (note the plural, "prophets") that the Messiah would be despised (e.g., Ps 22:6; Is 53:3), for in Jesus' day "Nazarene" was virtually a synonym for "despised" (see John 1:45–46). Some hold that in speaking of Jesus as a "Nazarene," Matthew is referring primarily to the word "branch" (Hebrew *neser*) in Is 11:1.

3:1 *John the Baptist.* The forerunner of Jesus, born c. 7 B.C. to Zacharias, a priest, and his wife Elisabeth (see Luke 1:5–80). *wilderness of Judea.* An area that stretched some 20 miles from the Jerusalem-Bethlehem plateau down to the Jordan River and the Dead Sea, perhaps the same region where John lived (cf. Luke 1:80). The people of Qumran (often associated with the Dead Sea Scrolls) lived in this area too (see essay, p. 1344).

3:2 *Repent.* Make a radical change in one's life as a whole. *the kingdom of heaven.* A phrase found only in Matthew, where it occurs 32 times. See Introduction: Recipients. Mark and Luke refer to "the kingdom of God," a term Matthew uses only four times (see note on Mark 11:30). The kingdom of heaven is the rule of God and is both a present reality and a future hope. The idea of God's kingdom is central to Jesus' teaching and is mentioned 50 times in Matthew alone.

‡3:3 All three Synoptic Gospels quote Is 40:3 (Luke quotes two additional verses) and apply it to John the Baptist. *make his paths straight.* Equivalent to "Prepare ye the way of the Lord" (see note on Luke 3:4). The preparation was to be moral and spiritual.

3:4 *leathern girdle.* Used to bind up the loose outer garments. *locusts and wild honey.* A man living in the wilderness did not hesitate to eat insects, and locusts were among the clean foods (Lev 11:21–22). John's simple food, clothing and life-style were a visual protest against self-indulgence.

6 [a]And were baptized of him in Jordan,
confessing their sins.
7 But when he saw many of the Pharisees
and Sadducees come to his baptism, he said
unto them, [a]O generation of vipers, who hath
warned you to flee from [b]the wrath to come?
8 Bring forth therefore fruits [1]meet for repentance:
9 And think not to say within yourselves,
[a]We have Abraham to *our* father: for I say unto
you, that God is able of these stones to raise up
children unto Abraham.
10 And now also the axe is laid unto the
root of the trees: [a]therefore every tree which
bringeth not forth good fruit is hewn down,
and cast into the fire.
11 [a]I indeed baptize you with water unto
repentance: but he that cometh after me is
mightier than I, whose shoes I am not worthy
to bear: [b]he shall baptize you with the Holy
Ghost, and *with* fire:
12 [a]Whose fan *is* in his hand, and he will
throughly purge his floor, and gather his wheat

3:6 [a]Acts 19:4,18
3:7 [a]ch. 12:34; 23:33; Luke 3:7-9 [b]Rom. 5:9; 1 Thes. 1:10
3:8 [1]Or, *answerable to amendment of life*
3:9 [a]John 8:33,39; Acts 13:26; Rom. 4:1,11,16
3:10 [a]ch. 7:19; Luke 13:7,9; John 15:6
3:11 [a]Mark 1:8; Luke 3:16; John 1:15,26,33; Acts 1:5; 11:16; 19:4 [b]Is 4:4; 44:3; Mal. 3:2; Acts 2:3,4; 1 Cor. 12:13
3:12 [a]Mal. 3:3

3:6 *Jordan.* See note on Mark 1:5.
3:7 *Pharisees and Sadducees.* The Pharisees (see notes on Mark 2:16; Luke 5:17) were a legalistic and separatistic group who strictly, but often hypocritically, kept the law of Moses and the unwritten "tradition of the elders" (15:2). The Sadducees (see notes on Mark 12:18; Luke 20:27; Acts 4:1) were more worldly and politically minded, and were theologically unorthodox—among other things denying the resurrection, angels and spirits (Acts 23:8). *baptism.* See note on Mark 1:4. *the wrath to come.* The arrival of the Messiah will bring repentance or judgment.
3:9 *We have Abraham to our father.* See John 8:39. Salvation does not come as a birthright (even for the Jews) but through faith in Christ (Rom 2:28–29; Gal 3:7,9,29). *these stones.* John may have pointed to the stones in the Jordan River. *children unto Abraham.* The true people of God are not limited to the physical descendants of Abraham (cf. Rom 9:6)
3:10 *The axe is laid unto the root of the trees.* Judgment is near.
‡3:11 *with water unto repentance.* John's baptism presupposed repentance, and he would not baptize the Pharisees and Sadducees because they failed to give any evidence of repentance (vv. 7–8). *with the Holy Ghost and . . . fire.* Demonstrated in a dramatic way at Pentecost (Acts 1:5,8; 2:1–13; 11:16), though here "fire" may refer to judgment to come (see v. 12). The outpouring of the Holy Spirit on all God's people was promised in Joel 2:28–29.
3:12 *fan.* Or "winnowing fork." For the process of winnowing see note on Ruth 1:22. Here it is figurative for the day of

Journey to Bethlehem, Flight to Egypt and Return to Nazareth

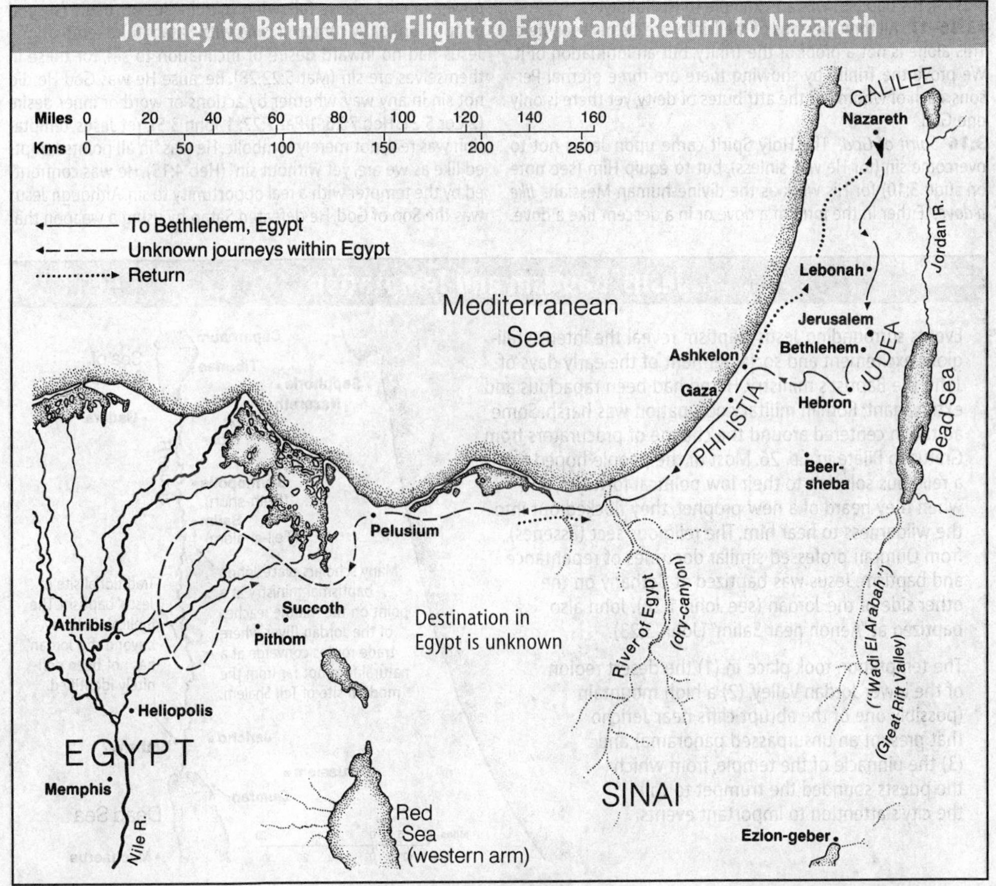

into the garner; but will [b]burn up the chaff with unquenchable fire.

The baptism of Jesus

13 ¶ [a]Then cometh Jesus [b]from Galilee to Jordan unto John, to be baptized of him.
14 But John forbad him, saying, I have need to be baptized of thee, and comest thou to me?
15 And Jesus answering said unto him, Suffer *it to be so* now: for thus it becometh us to fulfil all righteousness. Then he suffered him.
16 [a]And Jesus, when he was baptized, went up straightway out of the water: and lo, the heavens were opened unto him, and he saw [b]the Spirit of God descending like a dove, and lighting upon him:
17 [a]And lo a voice from heaven, saying, [b]This is my beloved Son, in whom I am well pleased.

3:12 [b]Mal. 4:1; ch. 13:30
3:13 [a]Mark 1:9; Luke 3:21 [b]ch. 2:22
3:16 [a]Mark 1:10
3:16 [b]Is. 11:2; 42:1; Luke 3:22; John 1:32
3:17 [a]John 12:28 [b]Ps. 2:7; Is. 42:1; ch. 17:5; Mark 1:11; Luke 9:35; Eph. 1:6; Col. 1:13; 2 Pet. 1:17

The temptation in the wilderness

4 Then was [a]Jesus led up of [b]the Spirit into the wilderness to be tempted of the devil.

4:1 [a]Mark 1:12; Luke 4:1 [b]See 1 Ki. 18:12; Ezek. 3:14; 8:3; 11:1,24; 40:2; 43:5; Acts 8:39

judgment at Christ's second coming. The OT prophets and NT writers sometimes compress the first and second comings of Christ so that they seem to be one event.

3:15 This occasion marked the beginning of Christ's Messianic ministry. There were several reasons for His baptism: 1. The first, mentioned here, was "to fulfil all righteousness." The baptism indicated that He was consecrated to God and officially approved by Him, as especially shown in the descent of the Holy Spirit (v. 16) and the words of the Father (v. 17; cf. Ps 2:7; Is 42:1). All God's righteous requirements for the Messiah were fully met in Jesus. 2. At Jesus' baptism John publicly announced the arrival of the Messiah and the inception of His ministry (John 1:31–34). 3. By His baptism Jesus completely identified Himself with man's sin and failure (though He Himself needed no repentance or cleansing from sin), becoming our substitute (2 Cor 5:21). 4. His baptism was an example to His followers.

‡3:16–17 All three persons of the Trinity are clearly seen here. This alone is not a proof of the Trinity, but an intimation of it. We prove the Trinity by showing there are three eternal Persons, each of whom has the attributes of deity, yet there is only one God.

3:16 *Spirit of God.* The Holy Spirit came upon Jesus not to overcome sin (for He was sinless), but to equip Him (see note on Judg 3:10) for His work as the divine-human Messiah. *like a dove.* Either in the form of a dove or in a descent like a dove. See also note on Mark 1:10.

‡3:17 *a voice from heaven.* The voice (1) authenticated Jesus' unique Sonship and echoes Ps 2:7 ("Thou art my Son"), (2) identified Jesus with the suffering servant of Is 42:1 ("whom I uphold"), and (3) offered the Father's support of Jesus in His mission ("In whom I am well pleased"). This word from the Father must have tremendously encouraged Jesus at the very outset of His earthly ministry. *I am well pleased.* The tense of the Greek verb used here is timeless. God has always been and always will be pleased with His Son.

‡4:1–11 The significance of Jesus' temptations, especially because they occurred at the outset of His public ministry, seems best understood in terms of the kind of Messiah He was to be. He would not accomplish His mission by using His supernatural power for His own needs (first temptation), by using His power to win a large following by miracles or magic (second temptation) or by compromising with Satan (third temptation). Jesus had no inward desire or inclination to sin, for these in themselves are sin (Mat 5:22,28). Because He was God He did not sin in any way, whether by actions or word or inner desire (2 Cor 5:21; Heb 7:26; 1 Pet 2:22; 1 John 3:5). Yet Jesus' temptation was real, not merely symbolic. He was "in all points tempted like as we are, yet without sin" (Heb 4:15). He was confronted by the tempter with a real opportunity to sin. Although Jesus was the Son of God, He defeated Satan by using a weapon that

Jesus' Baptism and Temptation

Events surrounding Jesus' baptism reveal the intense religious excitement and social ferment of the early days of John the Baptist's ministry. Herod had been rapacious and extravagant; Roman military occupation was harsh. Some agitation centered around the change of procurators from Gratus to Pilate in A.D. 26. Most of the people hoped for a religious solution to their low political fortunes, and when they heard of a new prophet, they flocked out into the wilderness to hear him. The religious sect (Essenes) from Qumran professed similar doctrines of repentance and baptism. Jesus was baptized at Bethany on the other side of the Jordan (see John 1:28). John also baptized at "Aenon near Salim" (John 3:23).

The temptation took place in (1) the desert region of the lower Jordan Valley, (2) a high mountain (possibly one of the abrupt cliffs near Jericho that present an unsurpassed panorama) and (3) the pinnacle of the temple, from which the priests sounded the trumpet to call the city's attention to important events.

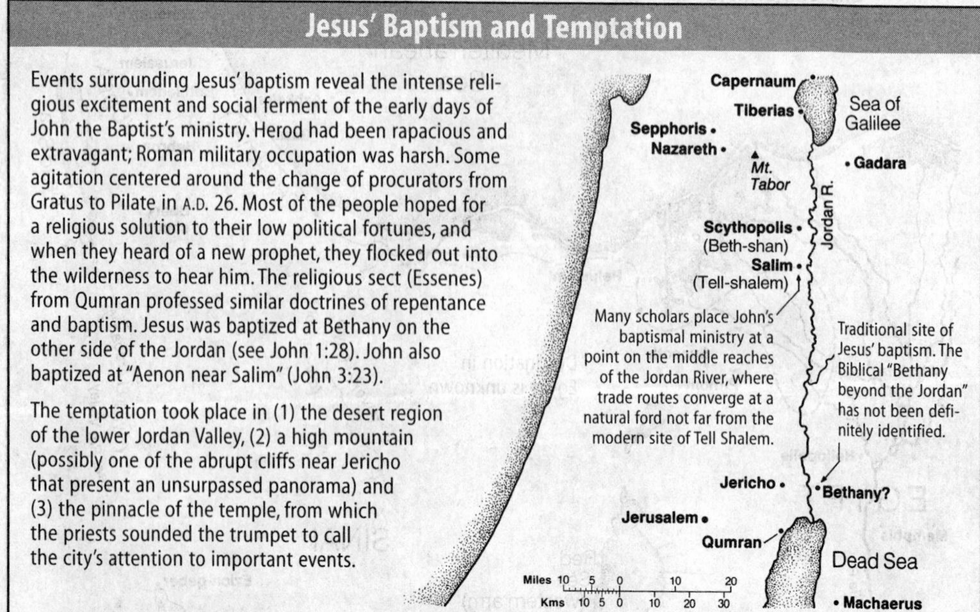
Capernaum
Tiberias
Sea of Galilee
Sepphoris
Nazareth
Mt. Tabor
Gadara
Jordan R.
Scythopolis (Beth-shan)
Salim (Tell-shalem)
Many scholars place John's baptismal ministry at a point on the middle reaches of the Jordan River, where trade routes converge at a natural ford not far from the modern site of Tell Shalem.
Traditional site of Jesus' baptism. The Biblical "Bethany beyond the Jordan" has not been definitely identified.
Jericho
Bethany?
Jerusalem
Qumran
Dead Sea
Machaerus
Miles 10 5 0 10 20
Kms 10 5 0 10 20 30

2 And when he had fasted forty days and
forty nights, he was afterward a hungred.
3 And when the tempter came to him, he
said, If thou be the Son of God, command that
these stones be made bread.
4 But he answered and said, It is written,
[a]Man shall not live by bread alone, but by
every word that proceedeth out of the mouth
of God.
5 Then the devil taketh him *up* [a]into the
holy city, and setteth him on a pinnacle of the
temple,
6 And saith unto him, If thou be the Son of
God, cast thyself down: for it is written, [a]He
shall give his angels charge concerning thee:
and in *their* hands they shall bear thee up, lest
at any time thou dash thy foot against a stone.
7 Jesus said unto him, It is written again,
[a]Thou shalt not tempt the Lord thy God.
8 Again, the devil taketh him *up* into an
exceeding high mountain, and sheweth him
all the kingdoms of the world, and the glory of
them;
9 And saith unto him, All these *things* will
I give thee, if thou wilt fall down and worship
me.
10 Then saith Jesus unto him, Get thee
hence, Satan: for it is written, [a]Thou shalt
worship the Lord thy God, and him only shalt
thou serve.
11 Then the devil leaveth him, and behold,
[a]angels came and ministered unto him.

4:4 [a]Deut. 8:3
4:5 [a]Neh. 11:1; Is. 48:2; 52:1; ch. 27:53; Rev. 11:2
4:6 [a]Ps. 91:11,12
4:7 [a]Deut. 6:16
4:10 [a]Deut. 6:13; 10:20; Josh. 24:14; 1 Sam. 7:3
4:11 [a]Heb. 1:14
4:12 [1]Or, *delivered up* [a]Mark 1:14; Luke 3:20; 4:14,31; John 4:43
4:15 [a]Is. 9:1,2
4:16 [a]Is. 42:7; Luke 2:32
4:17 [a]Mark 1:14 [b]ch. 3:2; 10:7

The beginning of Jesus' ministry

12 ¶ [a]Now when Jesus had heard that John
was [1]cast into prison, he departed into Galilee;
13 And leaving Nazareth, he came and
dwelt in Capernaum, which is upon the sea
coast, in the borders of Zabulon and Nephthalim:
14 That it might be fulfilled which was spoken by Esaias the prophet, saying,
15 [a]The land of Zabulon, and the land of
Nephthalim, *by* the way of the sea, beyond Jordan, Galilee of the Gentiles;
16 [a]The people which sat in darkness saw
great light; and to them which sat in the region and shadow of death light is sprung up.

Jesus calls four disciples

17 ¶ [a]From that time Jesus began to
preach, and to say, [b]Repent: for the kingdom
of heaven is at hand.

everyone has at his or her disposal: the sword of the Spirit, which is the Word of God (Eph 6:17). He met all three temptations with Scriptural truth (vv. 4,7,10) from Deuteronomy. Jesus was able to withstand temptation because he knew and relied upon God's Word.

‡4:1 *led up of the Spirit . . . to be tempted.* This testing of Jesus (the Greek verb translated "tempted" can also be rendered "tested"), which was divinely intended, has as its primary background Deut 8:1–5, from which Jesus also quotes in His first reply to the devil (see v. 4 and cross reference). There Moses recalls how the Lord led the Israelites in the wilderness 40 years "to humble thee, and to prove thee, to know what was in thine heart, whether thou wouldest keep his commandments, or no." Here at the beginning of His ministry Jesus is subjected to a similar test and shows himself to be the true Israelite who lives "by every word that proceedeth out of the mouth of the Lord." And whereas Adam failed the great test and plunged the whole race into sin (Gen 3), Jesus was faithful and thus demonstrated His qualification to become the Savior of all who receive Him. It was, moreover, important that Jesus be tested/tempted as Israel and we are, so that He could become our "merciful and faithful high priest" (Heb 2:17) and thus be "able to succour them that are tempted" (Heb 2:18; see Heb 4:15–16). Finally, as the one who remained faithful in temptation He became the model for all believers when they are tempted. *tempted of the devil.* God surely tests His people, but it is the devil who tempts to evil (see note on Gen 22:1; see also 1 John 3:8; Rev 2:9–10 and notes; Rev 12:9–10). Like the Hebrew for "Satan," the Greek for "devil" means "accuser" or "slanderer." The devil is a personal being, not a mere force or influence. He is the great archenemy of God and the leader of the hosts of darkness.

4:2 *forty days and forty nights.* The number recalls the experiences of Moses (Ex 24:18; 34:28) and Elijah (1 Ki 19:8), as well as the 40 years of Israel's temptation (testing) in the wilderness (Deut 8:2–3).

4:3 *If thou be the Son of God.* Meaning "Since You are." The devil is not casting doubt on Jesus' divine sonship, but is tempting Him to use His supernatural powers as the Son of God for His own ends.

4:4 Just as God gave the Israelites manna in a supernatural way (Deut 8:3), so also man must rely on God for spiritual feeding. Jesus relied on His Father, not His own miracle power, for provision of food.

‡4:5 See note on Luke 4:2. *pinnacle of the temple.* See note on Luke 4:9. *temple.* The temple, including the entire temple area, had been rebuilt by Herod the Great (see note on 2:1; see also John 2:20). The courtyard had been greatly enlarged, to about 330 by 500 yards. To accomplish this a huge platform had been erected to compensate for the sharp falling off of the land to the southeast. An enormous retaining wall made of massive stones was built to support the platform. Today the drop from the pinnacle area is large. It was even more pronounced in Jesus' day. On the platform stood the temple building, porches and courtyards flanked by beautiful colonnades.

4:10 *Satan.* See note on v. 1.

4:12 See map No. 9 at the end of the study Bible. *John was cast into prison.* See Mark 1:14 and note on Luke 3:20. The reason for John's imprisonment is given in 14:3–4.

‡4:13 *Capernaum.* Although not mentioned in the OT, it was evidently a sizable town in Jesus' day. Peter's house there became Jesus' base of operations during His extended ministry in Galilee (see Mark 2:1; 9:33). A fifth-century basilica now stands over the supposed site of Peter's house, and a fourth-century synagogue is located just several hundred feet from it.

4:15–16 Another Messianic prophecy from Isaiah. Jesus spent most of His public ministry "in the land of Zabulon and Nephtalim" (v. 13), which is north and west of the sea of Galilee.

‡4:17 *From that time.* These words indicate an important turning point in the life of Jesus and occur three times in Matthew's Gospel (see also 16:21; 26:16). Some think these words mark the three main sections of the book. *Repent.* Jesus began His public ministry with the same message as that of John the Baptist (3:2). The people must repent because God's reign was drawing near in the person and ministry of Jesus Christ. Repentance is more than a change of mind or feeling sorry for one's sins. It is a radical and deliberate change that affects one's intellect, emotions and will. *kingdom of heaven.* See note on 3:2.

18 [a]And Jesus, walking by the sea of Galilee, saw two brethren, Simon [b]called Peter, and Andrew his brother, casting a net into the sea: for they were fishers.
19 And he saith unto them, Follow me, and [a]I will make you fishers of men.
20 [a]And they straightway left *their* nets, and followed him.
21 [a]And going on from thence, he saw other two brethren, James the *son* of Zebedee, and John his brother, in a ship with Zebedee their father, mending their nets; and he called them.
22 And they immediately left the ship and their father, and followed him.

4:18 [a]Mark 1:16-18; Luke 5:2 [b]John 1:42
4:19 [a]Luke 5:10
4:20 [a]Mark 10:28; Luke 18:28
4:21 [a]Mark 1:19; Luke 5:10

4:23 [a]ch. 9:35; Mark 1:21,39; Luke 4:15,44 [b]ch. 24:14; Mark 1:14 [c]Mark 1:34
4:25 [a]Mark 3:7

23 ¶ And Jesus went about all Galilee, [a]teaching in their synagogues and preaching [b]the gospel of the kingdom, [c]and healing all *manner of* sickness and all *manner of* disease among the people.
24 And his fame went throughout all Syria: and they brought unto him all sick people that were taken with divers diseases and torments, and those which were possessed with devils, and those which were lunatick, and those that had the palsy; and he healed them.
25 [a]And there followed him great multitudes *of people* from Galilee, and *from* De-

4:18 *sea of Galilee.* See note on Mark 1:16. *net.* A circular casting net used either from a boat or while standing in shallow water.
4:19 *fishers of men.* Evangelism was at the heart of Jesus' call to His disciples.
4:20 See note on Mark 1:17.
4:21 *mending their nets.* Washing, mending and hanging the nets up to dry in preparation for the next day's work.
4:23 *teaching . . . preaching . . . healing.* Jesus' threefold ministry. The synagogues (see note on Mark 1:21) provided a place for Him to teach on the sabbath. During the week He preached to larger crowds in the open air. *gospel.* See note on Mark 1:1.
‡4:24 *Syria.* The area north of Galilee and between Damascus and the Mediterranean Sea. *lunatick.* The Greek word for this expression originally meant "moonstruck" and reflects the ancient superstition that seizures were caused by changes of the moon. *palsy.* A transliteration of the Greek, paralytic, has come directly into English. Greek physicians were among the best in ancient times, and many of our medical terms come from their language.
4:25 *Decapolis.* A league of free cities (Decapolis means "the Ten Cities") characterized by high Greek culture. All but one,

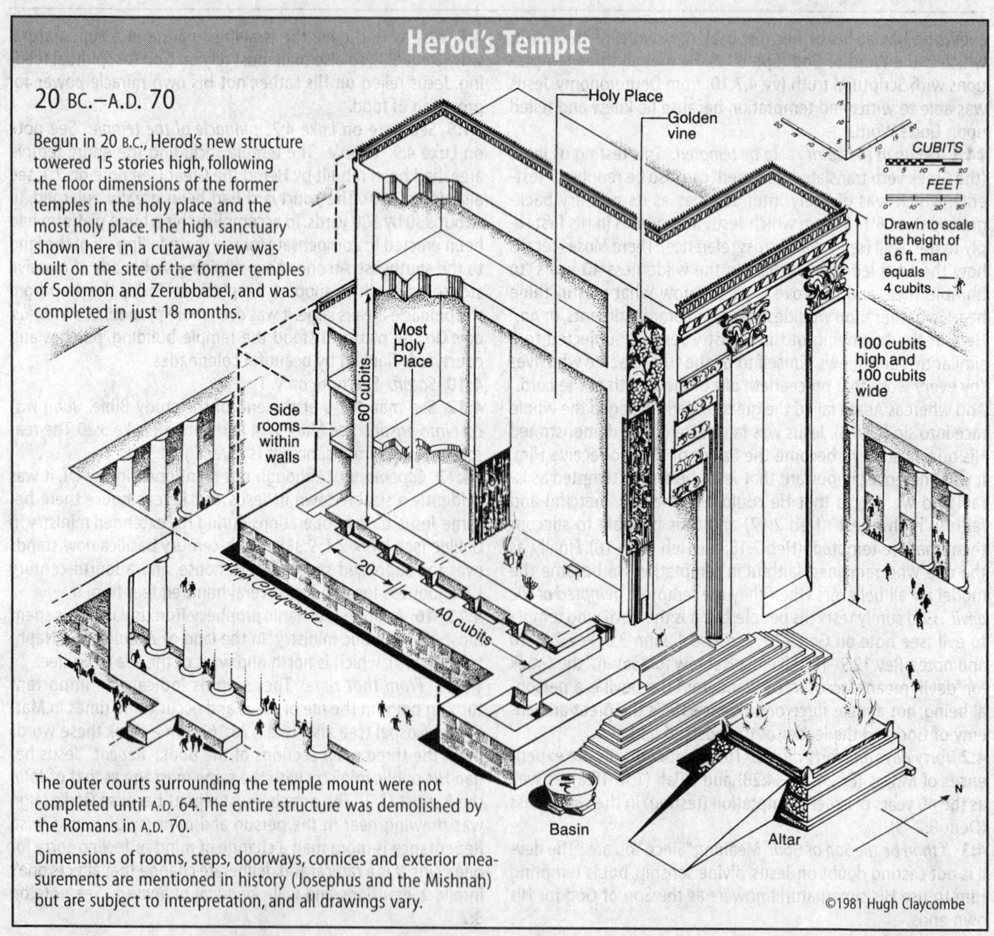

Herod's Temple

20 BC.–A.D. 70

Begun in 20 B.C., Herod's new structure towered 15 stories high, following the floor dimensions of the former temples in the holy place and the most holy place. The high sanctuary shown here in a cutaway view was built on the site of the former temples of Solomon and Zerubbabel, and was completed in just 18 months.

The outer courts surrounding the temple mount were not completed until A.D. 64. The entire structure was demolished by the Romans in A.D. 70.

Dimensions of rooms, steps, doorways, cornices and exterior measurements are mentioned in history (Josephus and the Mishnah) but are subject to interpretation, and all drawings vary.

capolis, and *from* Jerusalem, and *from* Judea,
and *from* beyond Jordan.

The Beatitudes

5 And seeing the multitudes, [a]he went up
into a mountain: and when he was set,
his disciples came unto him:

2 And he opened his mouth, and taught
them, saying,

3 [a]Blessed *are* the poor in spirit: for
theirs is the kingdom of heaven.

4 [a]Blessed *are* they that mourn: for they
shall be comforted.

5 [a]Blessed *are* the meek: for [b]they shall
inherit the earth.

6 Blessed *are* they which do hunger and
thirst after righteousness: [a]for they
shall be filled.

7 Blessed *are* the merciful: [a]for they shall
obtain mercy.

8 [a]Blessed *are* the pure in heart: for
[b]they shall see God.

9 Blessed *are* the peacemakers: for they
shall be called the children of God.

10 [a]Blessed *are* they which are persecuted
for righteousness' sake: for theirs is
the kingdom of heaven.

5:1 [a]Mark 3:13
5:3 [a]Luke 6:20; See Ps. 51:17; Prov. 16:19; 29:23; Is. 57:15; 66:2
5:4 [a]Is. 61:2,3; Luke 6:21; John 16:20; 2 Cor. 1:7; Rev. 21:4
5:5 [a]Ps. 37:11 [b]Rom. 4:13
5:6 [a]Is. 55:1; 65:13
5:7 [a]Ps. 41:1; Mark 11:25
5:8 [a]Ps. 15:2; Heb. 12:14 [b]1 Cor. 13:12
5:10 [a]2 Cor. 4:17; 1 Pet. 3:14

5:11 [1]Gr. *lying* [a]Luke 6:22 [b]1 Pet. 4:14
5:12 [a]Luke 6:23; Acts 5:41; 1 Pet. 4:13 [b]Neh. 9:26; Acts 7:52
5:13 [a]Mark 9:50; Luke 14:34
5:14 [a]Prov. 4:18; Phil. 2:15
5:15 [1]*The word in the original signifieth a measure containing about a pint less than a peck* [a]Mark 4:21; Luke 8:16

11 [a]Blessed are ye, when *men* shall revile
you, and persecute *you*, and shall say
all manner of [b]evil against you
[1]falsely, for my sake.

12 [a]Rejoice, and be exceeding glad: for
great *is* your reward in heaven: for
[b]so persecuted they the prophets
which were before you.

Teaching about salt and light

13 ¶ Ye are the salt of the earth: [a]but if the
salt have lost his savour, wherewith shall it be
salted? it is thenceforth good for nothing, but to
be cast out, and to be trodden under foot of men.

14 [a]Ye are the light of the world. A city
that is set on a hill cannot be hid.

15 Neither do men [a]light a candle, and put
it under [1]a bushel, but on a candlestick; and it
giveth light unto all that are in the house.

16 Let your light so shine before men,
[a]that they may see your good works, and [b]glo-
rify your Father which is in heaven.

The higher righteousness

17 ¶ [a]Think not that I am come to destroy
the law, or the prophets: I am not come to destroy, but to fulfil.

5:16 [a]1 Pet. 2:12 [b]John 15:8; 1 Cor. 14:25 5:17 [a]Rom. 10:4

Scythopolis (Beth Shan), were east of the sea of Galilee and the Jordan River. The league stretched from a point northeast of the sea of Galilee southward to Philadelphia (modern Amman).

‡5:1–7:29 The Sermon on the Mount is the first of six great discourses in Matthew (chs. 5–7; 10; 13; 18; 23; 24–25). It contains three types of material: (1) beatitudes, i.e., declarations of blessedness (5:1–12), (2) ethical admonitions (5:13–20; 6:1–7:23) and (3) contrasts between Jesus' ethical teaching and Jewish legalistic traditions (5:21–48). The Sermon ends with a short parable stressing the importance of practicing what has just been taught (7:24–27) and an expression of amazement by the crowds at the authority with which Jesus spoke (7:28–29).

Opinion differs as to whether the Sermon is a summary of what Jesus taught on one occasion or a compilation of teachings presented on numerous occasions. Matthew possibly took a single sermon and expanded it with other relevant teachings of Jesus. Thirty-four of the verses in Matthew's Sermon occur in different contexts in Luke than the apparently parallel Sermon on the Plain (Luke 6:17–49).

The Sermon on the Mount's call to moral and ethical living is so high that some have dismissed it as being completely unrealistic or have projected its fulfillment to the future kingdom. There is no doubt, however, that Jesus (and Matthew) gave the Sermon as a standard for all Christians, realizing that its demands cannot be met in our own power. It is also true that Jesus occasionally used hyperbole to make His point (see, e.g., note on 5:29–30).

5:1 *mountain.* The exact location is uncertain. It may have been the gently sloping hillside at the northwest corner of the sea of Galilee, not far from Capernaum (see note on Luke 6:20–49). The new law, like the old (Ex 19:3), was given from a mountain. *when he was set.* It was the custom for Jewish rabbis to be seated while teaching (see Mark 4:1; 9:35; Luke 4:20; 5:3; John 8:2). *disciples.* Lit. "learners." Since at the end of the Sermon the "crowds" expressed amazement at Jesus' teaching (7:28), "disciples" may here be used in a broader sense than the twelve. Or perhaps the Sermon is addressed to the twelve with the crowds also listening.

5:3 *Blessed.* The word means more than "happy," because happiness is an emotion often dependent on outward circumstances. "Blessed" here refers to the ultimate well-being and distinctive spiritual joy of those who share in the salvation of the kingdom of God. See notes on Ps 1:1; Rev 1:3. *poor in spirit.* In contrast to the spiritually proud and self-sufficient. *theirs is the kingdom of heaven.* The kingdom is not something earned. It is more a gift than a recompense.

5:5 *meek.* This beatitude is taken from Ps 37:11 and refers not so much to an attitude toward people as to a disposition before God, namely, humility. *the earth.* The new promised land (cf. Rev 21:1).

5:8 *heart.* The center of one's being, including mind, will and emotions (see note on Ps 4:7).

5:9 *peacemakers.* Those who promote peace, as far as it depends on them (Rom 12:18). In so doing, they reflect the character of their heavenly Father and so are called "sons of God."

5:10 *theirs is the kingdom of heaven.* A present reality as well as a future hope.

5:13 *salt.* Used for flavoring and preserving. *lost his savour.* Most of the salt used in Israel came from the Dead Sea and was full of impurities. This caused it to lose some of its flavor.

5:15 *candle.* In Jesus' day people used small clay lamps that burned olive oil drawn up by a wick (see note on Ex 25:37). *bushel.* A basket that held about 8 quarts of ground meal or flour.

5:16 *Father which is in heaven.* Matthew uses the term "Father which is in heaven" or "heavenly Father" 19 times, Mark twice, Luke once, and John not at all.

5:17 *the law.* The first five books of the Jewish Scriptures (our OT). *the prophets.* Not only the Latter Prophets—Isaiah, Jeremiah and Ezekiel, which we call Major Prophets, and the 12 Minor Prophets (lumped together by the Jews as "the Book of the Twelve")—but also the so-called Former Prophets (Joshua, Judges, Samuel and Kings). Taken together, "the Law" and "the Prophets" designated the entire OT, including the Writings, the

18 For verily I say unto you, [a]Till heaven and earth pass, one jot or one tittle shall in no wise pass from the law, till all be fulfilled.

19 [a]Whosoever therefore shall break one of these least commandments, and shall teach men so, he shall be called the least in the kingdom of heaven: but whosoever shall do and teach *them,* the same shall be called great in the kingdom of heaven.

20 For I say unto you, That except your righteousness shall exceed [a]*the righteousness* of the scribes and Pharisees, ye shall in no case enter into the kingdom of heaven.

Anger and reconciliation; adultery and divorce

21 ¶ Ye have heard that it was said [1]by them of old time, [a]Thou shalt not kill; and whosoever shall kill shall be in danger of the judgment:

22 But I say unto you, That [a]whosoever is angry with his brother without a cause shall be in danger of the judgment: and whosoever shall say to his brother, [b][1]Raca, shall be in danger of the council: but whosoever shall say, *Thou* fool, shall be in danger of hell fire.

23 Therefore [a]if thou bring thy gift to the altar, and there rememberest that thy brother hath ought against thee;

24 [a]Leave there thy gift before the altar, and go thy way; first be reconciled to thy brother, and then come and offer thy gift.

25 [a]Agree with thine adversary quickly, [b]whiles thou art in the way with him; lest at any time the adversary deliver thee to the judge, and the judge deliver thee to the officer, and thou be cast into prison.

26 Verily I say unto thee, Thou shalt by no means come out thence, till thou hast paid the uttermost farthing.

27 Ye have heard that it was said by them of old time, [a]Thou shalt not commit adultery:

28 But I say unto you, That whosoever [a]looketh on a woman to lust after her hath committed adultery with her already in his heart.

29 [a]And if thy right eye [1]offend thee, [b]pluck it out, and cast *it* from thee: for it is profitable for thee that one of thy members should perish, and not *that* thy whole body should be cast into hell.

30 And if thy right hand offend thee, cut it off, and cast *it* from thee: for it is profitable for thee that one of thy members should perish, and not *that* thy whole body should be cast into hell.

31 It hath been said, [a]Whosoever shall put away his wife, let him give her a writing of divorcement:

32 But I say unto you, That [a]whosoever shall put away his wife, saving for the cause of fornication, causeth her to commit adultery: and whosoever shall marry her that is divorced committeth adultery.

Oaths and retaliation

33 ¶ Again, ye have heard that [a]it hath been said by them of old time, [b]Thou shalt not forswear thyself, but [c]shalt perform unto the Lord thine oaths:

34 But I say unto you, [a]Swear not at all; neither by heaven; for it is [b]God's throne:

35 Nor by the earth; for it is his footstool: neither by Jerusalem; for it is [a]the city of the great King.

5:18 [a]Luke 16:17
5:19 [a]Jas. 2:10
5:20 [a]Rom. 10:3
5:21 [1]Or, *to them* [a]Ex. 20:13
5:22 [1][That is, *Vain fellow,* 2 Sam. 6:20] [a]1 John 3:15 [b]Jas. 2:20
5:23 [a]ch. 8:4
5:24 [a]Job 42:8; 1 Tim. 2:8; 1 Pet. 3:7
5:25 [a]Prov. 25:8; Luke 12:58 [b]Ps. 32:6; Is. 55:6
5:27 [a]Ex. 20:14; Deut. 5:18
5:28 [a]Job 31:1; Prov. 6:25
5:29 [1]Or, *do cause thee to offend* [a]Mark 9:43 [b]Col. 3:5
5:31 [a]Deut. 24:1; Jer. 3:1; Mark 10:2
5:32 [a]Luke 16:18; Rom. 7:3
5:33 [a]ch. 23:16 [b]Ex. 20:7; Lev. 19:12 [c]Deut. 23:23
5:34 [a]ch. 23:16; Jas. 5:12 [b]Is. 66:1
5:35 [a]Ps. 48:2

third section of the Hebrew Bible. See 13:35, where Matthew introduces a quotation from the Writings (Ps 78:2) with "which was spoken by the prophet." *fulfil.* Jesus fulfilled the Law in the sense that He gave it its full meaning. He emphasized its deep, underlying principles and total commitment to it rather than mere external acknowledgment and obedience.

5:18–20 Jesus is not speaking against observing all the requirements of the Law, but against hypocritical, Pharisaical legalism. Such legalism was not the keeping of all details of the Law but the hollow sham of keeping laws externally, to gain merit before God, while breaking them inwardly. It was following the letter of the Law while ignoring its spirit. Jesus repudiates the Pharisees' interpretation of the Law and their view of righteousness by works. He preaches a righteousness that comes only through faith in Him and His work. In the verses that follow, He gives six examples of Pharisaical externalism.

5:18 *jot.* One word in Greek (*iota*), which we use when we say, "It doesn't make one iota of difference." It is the nearest Greek equivalent to the Hebrew *yodh,* the smallest letter of the Hebrew alphabet (see Ps 119:73 title). *tittle.* The Greek word means "horn" and was used to designate the slight embellishment or extension of certain letters of the Hebrew alphabet (somewhat like the bottom of a "j").

‡5:21 *Ye have heard that it was said.* The contrast that Jesus sets up (vv. 21,27,31,33,38,43) is not between the OT and His teaching (He has just established the validity of the OT Law). Rather, it is between externalistic interpretation of the rabbinic tradition on the one hand, and Jesus' correct interpretation of the Law on the other. *kill.* This word, as that used in Ex 20:13 specifically means "murder."

‡5:22 *Raca.* This word may be related to the Aramaic word for "empty" and mean "Empty-head!" *council.* See note on Mark 14:55. *hell.* The Greek word is *ge(h)enna,* which derives its name from a deep ravine south of Jerusalem, the "Valley of (the Sons of) Hinnom" (Hebrew *ge hinnom*). During the reigns of the wicked Ahaz and Manasseh, human sacrifices to the Ammonite god Molech were offered there. Josiah desecrated the valley because of the pagan worship there (2 Ki 23:10; see Jer 7:31–32; 19:6). It became a sort of perpetually burning city dump and later a figure for the place of final punishment.

5:23–26 Two illustrations of dealing with anger by means of reconciliation.

5:26 *farthing.* The smallest Roman copper coin.

5:28 *looketh on a woman to lust after her.* Not a passing glance but a willful, calculated stare that arouses sexual desire. According to Jesus this is a form of adultery even if it is only "in his heart."

5:29–30 Jesus is not teaching self-mutilation, for even a blind man can lust. The point is that we should deal as drastically with sin as necessary.

5:30 *hell.* See note on v. 22.

5:32 *saving for the cause of fornication.* See note on 19:3. Neither Mark 10:11–12 nor Luke 16:18 mentions this exception.

5:33–37 The OT allowed oaths except those that profaned the name of God. Jesus would do away with all oaths, in favor of always speaking the truth.

36 Neither shalt thou swear by thy head, because thou canst not make one hair white or black.

37 [a]But let your communication be, Yea, yea; Nay, nay: for whatsoever is more than these cometh of evil.

38 ¶ Ye have heard that it hath been said, [a]An eye for an eye, and a tooth for a tooth:

39 But I say unto you, [a]That *ye* resist not evil: but [b]whosoever shall smite thee on thy right cheek, turn to him the other also.

40 And if any man will sue thee at the law, and take *away* thy coat, let him have *thy* cloke also.

41 And whosoever [a]shall compel thee to go a mile, go with him twain.

42 Give to him that asketh thee, and [a]from him that would borrow of thee turn not thou away.

Neighbours and enemies

43 ¶ Ye have heard that it hath been said, [a]Thou shalt love thy neighbour, [b]and hate thine enemy.

44 But I say unto you, [a]Love your enemies, bless them that curse you, do good to them that hate you, and pray [b]for them which despitefully use you, and persecute you;

45 That ye may be the children of your Father which is in heaven: for [a]he maketh his sun to rise on the evil and *on* the good, and sendeth rain on the just and *on* the unjust.

46 [a]For if ye love them which love you, what reward have ye? do not even the publicans the same?

47 And if ye salute your brethren only, what do ye more *than others?* do not even the publicans so?

48 [a]Be ye therefore perfect, even [b]as your Father which is in heaven is perfect.

Piety and almsgiving

6 Take heed that *ye* do not your [1]alms before men, to be seen of them: otherwise ye have no reward [2]of your Father which is in heaven.

2 Therefore [a]when thou doest *thine* alms, [1]do not sound a trumpet before thee, as the hypocrites do in the synagogues and in the streets, that they may have glory of men. Verily I say unto you, They have their reward.

3 But when thou doest alms, let not thy left hand know what thy right hand doeth:

4 That thine alms may be in secret: and thy Father which seeth in secret himself [a]shall reward thee openly.

Prayer and fasting

5 ¶ And when thou prayest, thou shalt not be as the hypocrites *are:* for they love to pray standing in the synagogues and in the corners of the streets, that they may be seen of men. Verily I say unto you, They have their reward.

6 But thou, when thou prayest, [a]enter into thy closet, and when thou hast shut thy door, pray to thy Father which is in secret; and thy Father which seeth in secret shall reward thee openly.

7 But when ye pray, [a]use not vain repetitions, as the heathen *do:* [b]for they think that they shall be heard for their much speaking.

8 Be not ye therefore like unto them: for

5:37 [a]Col. 4:6; Jas. 5:12
5:38 [a]Ex. 21:24; Lev. 24:20; Deut. 19:21
5:39 [a]Prov. 20:22; Luke 6:29; Rom. 12:17; 1 Cor. 6:7; 1 Pet. 3:9 [b]Is. 50:6; Lam. 3:30
5:41 [a]ch. 27:32
5:42 [a]Deut. 15:8; Luke 6:30
5:43 [a]Lev. 19:18 [b]Deut. 23:6; Ps. 41:10
5:44 [a]Luke 6:27; Rom. 12:14 [b]Luke 23:34; Acts 7:60; 1 Cor. 4:12; 1 Pet. 2:23
5:45 [a]Job 25:3
5:46 [a]Luke 6:32
5:48 [a]Gen. 17:1; Lev. 11:44; 19:2; Luke 6:36; Col. 1:28; 4:12; Jas. 1:4; 1 Pet. 1:15 [b]Eph. 5:1
6:1 [1][Or, *righteousness.* Deut. 24:13; Ps. 112:9; Dan. 4:27; 2 Cor. 9:9,10] [2]Or, *with*
6:2 [1]Or, *cause not a trumpet to be sounded* [a]Rom. 12:8
6:4 [a]Luke 14:14
6:6 [a]2 Ki. 4:33
6:7 [a]Eccl. 5:2 [b]1 Ki. 18:26

5:38 See notes on Ex 21:23–25; Lev 24:20.

5:39 *resist.* Here it probably means in a court of law. *smite.* The Greek verb used here means "slaps you with the back of the hand." It was more of an insult than an act of violence. The point is that it is better to be insulted even twice than to take the matter to court.

5:40 *coat . . . cloke.* The first was an undergarment, the second a loose outer one.

5:41 *compel.* The Greek verb comes from a Persian word meaning "press into service" and is used in 27:32, where the Roman soldiers pressed Simon into service to carry Jesus' cross.

5:42 Probably not a general requirement to give to everyone who asks, but a reference to the poor (cf. Deut 15:7–11; Ps 112:5,9).

5:43 *hate thine enemy.* Words not found anywhere in the OT. However, hatred for one's enemies was an accepted part of the Jewish ethic at that time. See note on Lev 19:18.

5:44 *pray.* Prayer is one of the practical ways love expresses itself (cf. Job 42:8–10).

5:45 *That ye may be the children of your Father which is in heaven.* Loving one's enemy does not make one a son of the heavenly Father. But it does make one known as a son. *on the just and on the unjust.* God shows His love to people without distinction.

5:46 *publicans.* Or "tax collectors," local men employed by Roman tax contractors to collect taxes for them. Because they worked for Rome and often demanded unreasonable payments, the tax collectors gained a bad reputation and were generally hated and considered traitors.

5:48 *Be ye therefore perfect.* Christ sets up the high ideal of perfect love (see vv. 43–47)—not that we can fully attain it in this life. That, however, is God's high standard for us.

6:1 *alms.* Or "righteousness." This verse introduces the discussion of three acts of righteousness: (1) giving (vv. 2–4), (2) praying (vv. 5–15) and (3) fasting (vv. 16–18). *reward of your Father.* Spiritual growth and maturity or perhaps a heavenly reward of some kind.

6:2 *sound a trumpet before thee.* Perhaps a reference to the noise made by coins as they were thrown into the temple treasury. Or the phrase may be used figuratively to mean "make a big show of it." *hypocrites.* The Greek word means "play-actor." Matthew uses the word 13 times (Mark, twice; Luke, three times). Here it refers to those who fake being pious. *They have their reward.* The honor they receive from people is all the reward they get.

6:3 *let not thy left hand know what thy right hand doeth.* Not to be taken literally but as a way of emphasizing that one should not call attention to one's giving. Self-glorification is always a present danger.

6:6 *closet.* The Greek word means "storeroom." Unlike most of the rooms in the house, it had a door that could be shut.

6:7 *use not vain repetitions, as the heathen do.* They used long lists of the names of their gods in their prayers, hoping that by constantly repeating them they would call on the name of the god that could help them. Jesus is not necessarily condemning all long prayers, but meaningless verbiage in praying.

your Father knoweth what *things* ye have need of, before ye ask him.

9 After this manner therefore pray ye:

¶ [a]Our Father which art in heaven, Hallowed be thy name.

10 Thy kingdom come. [a]Thy will be done in earth, [b]as *it is* in heaven.

11 Give us this day our [a]daily bread.

12 And [a]forgive us our debts, as we forgive our debtors.

13 [a]And lead us not into temptation, but [b]deliver us from evil: [c]For thine is the kingdom, and the power, and the glory, for ever. Amen.

14 ¶ [a]For if ye forgive men their trespasses, your heavenly Father will also forgive you:

15 But [a]if ye forgive not men their trespasses, neither will your Father forgive your trespasses.

16 ¶ Moreover [a]when ye fast, be not as the hypocrites, of a sad countenance: for they disfigure their faces, that they may appear unto men to fast. Verily I say unto you, They have their reward.

17 But thou, when thou fastest, [a]anoint thine head, and wash thy face;

18 That thou appear not unto men to fast, but unto thy Father which is in secret: and thy Father, which seeth in secret, shall reward thee openly.

Possessions and masters

19 ¶ [a]Lay not up for yourselves treasures upon earth, where moth and rust doth corrupt, and where thieves break through and steal:

20 [a]But lay up for yourselves treasures in heaven, where neither moth nor rust doth corrupt, and where thieves do not break through nor steal:

21 For where your treasure is, there will your heart be also.

22 [a]The light of the body is the eye: if therefore thine eye be single, thy whole body shall be full of light.

23 But if thine eye be evil, thy whole body shall be full of darkness. If therefore the light that is in thee be darkness, how great *is* that darkness?

6:9 [a]Luke 11:2
6:10 [a]ch. 26:39; Acts 21:14 [b]Ps. 103:20
6:11 [a]See Job 23:12; Prov. 30:8
6:12 [a]ch. 18:21
6:13 [a]ch. 26:41; 1 Cor. 10:13; 2 Pet. 2:9; Rev. 3:10 [b]John 17:15 [c]1 Chr. 29:11
6:14 [a]Mark 11:25; Eph. 4:32; Col 3:13
6:15 [a]ch. 18:35; Jas. 2:13
6:16 [a]Is. 58:5
6:17 [a]Ruth 3:3; Dan. 10:3
6:19 [a]Prov. 23:4; 1 Tim. 6:17; Heb. 13:5; Jas. 5:1
6:20 [a]ch. 19:21; Luke 12:33; 18:22; 1 Tim. 6:19; 1 Pet. 1:4
6:22 [a]Luke 11:34

6:24 [a]Luke 16:13 [b]Gal. 1:10; 1 Tim. 6:17; Jas. 4:4; 1 John 2:15
6:25 [a]Ps. 55:22; Luke 12:22; Phil. 4:6; 1 Pet. 5:7
6:26 [a]Job 38:41; Ps. 147:9; Luke 12:24
6:33 [a]See 1 Ki. 3:13; Ps. 37:25; Mark 10:30; Luke 12:31; 1 Tim. 4:8
7:1 [a]Luke 6:37; Rom. 14:3; 1 Cor. 4:3; Jas. 4:11
7:2 [a]Mark 4:24; Luke 6:38
7:3 [a]Luke 6:41

Anxiety and God's kingdom

24 ¶ [a]No *man* can serve two masters: for either he will hate the one, and love the other; or else he will hold to the one, and despise the other. [b]Ye cannot serve God and mammon.

25 Therefore I say unto you, [a]Take no thought for your life, what ye shall eat, or what ye shall drink; nor yet for your body, what ye shall put on. Is not the life more than meat, and the body than raiment?

26 [a]Behold the fowls of the air: for they sow not, neither do they reap, nor gather into barns; yet your heavenly Father feedeth them. Are ye not much better than they?

27 Which of you by taking thought can add one cubit unto his stature?

28 And why take ye thought for raiment? Consider the lilies of the field, how they grow; they toil not, neither do they spin:

29 And yet I say unto you, That even Solomon in all his glory was not arrayed like one of these.

30 Wherefore, if God so clothe the grass of the field, which to day is, and to morrow is cast into the oven, *shall he* not much more *clothe* you, O ye of little faith?

31 Therefore take no thought, saying, What shall we eat? or, What shall we drink? or, Wherewithal shall we be clothed?

32 (For after all these *things* do the Gentiles seek): for your heavenly Father knoweth that ye have need of all these *things.*

33 But [a]seek ye first the kingdom of God, and his righteousness; and all these *things* shall be added unto you.

34 Take therefore no thought for the morrow: for the morrow shall take thought for the *things* of itself. Sufficient unto the day *is* the evil thereof.

Judging and hypocrisy

7 [a]Judge not, that ye be not judged.

2 For with what judgment ye judge, ye shall be judged: [a]and with what measure ye mete, it shall be measured to you again.

3 [a]And why beholdest thou the mote that is in thy brother's eye, but considerest not the beam that is in thine own eye?

6:12 *debts.* Moral debts, i.e., sins (see note on Luke 11:4).
6:16 *fast.* See notes on Mark 2:18 and Luke 18:12.
6:17 *anoint thine head, and wash thy face.* Jews put ashes on their heads when fasting. But Jesus told them to maintain their regular appearance. Fasting should not be done in an ostentatious way.
6:19–21 The dangers of riches are often mentioned in the NT (e.g., v. 24; 13:22; 19:22; Mark 10:17–30; Luke 12:16–21; 1 Tim 6:9–10,17–19; Heb 13:5), but nowhere are they condemned in and of themselves. What Jesus condemns here is greed and hoarding of money.
6:19 *moth and rust.* Representative of all agents and processes that destroy worldly possessions. *break through and steal.* Houses in the Holy Land had walls made of mud bricks and could be broken into easily.
6:20 *treasures in heaven.* Anything done in this life that has eternal value. The phrase is the equivalent of being "rich toward God" (Luke 12:21). In this context it probably more specifically refers to using one's material wealth for good causes.
6:28 *lilies.* Here represents flowers generally.
6:30 *cast into the oven.* Grass was commonly used to heat the clay ovens of the Holy Land.
‡7:1 The Christian is not to judge hypocritically or self-righteously, as can be seen from the context (v. 5). The same thought is expressed in 23:13–39 (cf. Rom 2:1). To obey Christ's commands in this chapter, we must first evaluate a person's character—whether he is a "dog" (v. 6) or a false prophet (v. 15), or whether his life shows fruit (v. 16). Scripture repeatedly exhorts believers to evaluate carefully and choose between good and bad people and things (sexually immoral, 1 Cor 5:9; those who masquerade as angels of light, 2 Cor 11:14; dogs, Phil 3:2; false prophets, 1 John 4:1). The Christian is to "prove all things." (1 Thes 5:21).
7:3 *mote . . . beam.* An example of hyperbole in the teachings

4 Or how wilt thou say to thy brother, Let me pull out the mote out of thine eye; and behold, a beam *is* in thine own eye?

5 *Thou* hypocrite, first cast out the beam out of thine own eye; and then shalt thou see clearly to cast out the mote out of thy brother's eye.

6 ¶ [a]Give not that which is holy unto the dogs, neither cast ye your pearls before swine, lest they trample them under their feet, and turn *again* and rent you.

Prayer and the Golden Rule

7 ¶ [a]Ask, and it shall be given you; seek, and ye shall find; knock, and it shall be opened unto you:

8 For [a]every one that asketh receiveth; and he that seeketh findeth: and to him that knocketh it shall be opened.

9 [a]Or what man is there of you, whom if his son ask bread, will he give him a stone?

10 Or if he ask a fish, will he give him a serpent?

11 If ye then, [a]being evil, know how to give good gifts unto your children, how much more shall your Father which is in heaven give good *things* to them that ask him?

12 Therefore all *things* [a]whatsoever ye would that men should do to you, do ye even so to them: for [b]this is the law and the prophets.

The strait and wide gates

13 ¶ [a]Enter ye in at the strait gate: for wide *is* the gate, and broad *is* the way, that leadeth to destruction, and many there be which go in thereat:

14 [1]Because strait *is* the gate, and narrow *is* the way, which leadeth unto life, and few there be that find it.

The test of false prophets

15 ¶ [a]Beware of false prophets, [b]which come to you in sheep's clothing, but inwardly they are [c]ravening wolves.

16 [a]Ye shall know them by their fruits. [b]Do *men* gather grapes of thorns, or figs of thistles?

17 *Even* so [a]every good tree bringeth forth good fruit; but a corrupt tree bringeth forth evil fruit.

7:6 [a]Prov. 9:7,8; 23:9; Acts 13:45 **7:7** [a]ch. 21:22; Mark 11:24; Luke 11:9; 18:1; John 14:13; 15:7; 16:23,24; Jas. 1:5,6; 1 John 3:22; 5:14,15 **7:8** [a]Prov. 8:17; Jer. 29:12 **7:9** [a]Luke 11:11 **7:11** [a]Gen. 6:5; 8:21 **7:12** [a]Luke 6:31 [b]Lev. 19:18; ch. 22:40; Rom. 13:8; Gal. 5:14; 1 Tim. 1:5 **7:13** [a]Luke 13:24 **7:14** [1]Or, *How* **7:15** [a]Deut. 13:3; Jer. 23:16; ch. 24:4,5; Mark 13:22; Rom. 16:17; Eph. 5:6; Col. 2:8; 2 Pet. 2:1; 1 John 4:1 [b]Mic. 3:5; 2 Tim. 3:5 [c]Acts 20:29 **7:16** [a]ver. 20 [b]Luke 6:43 **7:17** [a]Jer. 11:19; ch. 12:33

7:19 [a]ch. 3:10; Luke 3:9; John 15:2 **7:21** [a]Hos. 8:2; ch. 25:11; Luke 6:46; 13:25; Acts 19:13; Rom. 2:13; Jas. 1:22 **7:22** [a]Num. 24:4; John 11:51; 1 Cor. 13:2 **7:23** [a]ch. 25:12; Luke 13:25; 2 Tim. 2:19 [b]Ps. 5:5; 6:8; ch. 25:41 **7:24** [a]Luke 6:47 **7:28** [a]ch. 13:54; Mark 1:22; 6:2; Luke 4:32 **7:29** [a]John 7:46 **8:2** [a]Mark 1:40; Luke 5:12

18 A good tree cannot bring forth evil fruit, neither *can* a corrupt tree bring forth good fruit.

19 [a]Every tree that bringeth not forth good fruit is hewn down, and cast into the fire.

20 Wherefore by their fruits ye shall know them.

21 ¶ Not every one that saith unto me, [a]Lord, Lord, shall enter into the kingdom of heaven; but he that doeth the will of my Father which is in heaven.

22 Many will say to me in that day, Lord, Lord, have we [a]not prophesied in thy name? and in thy name have cast out devils? and in thy name done many wonderful works?

23 And [a]then will I profess unto them, I never knew you: [b]depart from me, ye that work iniquity.

The wise and foolish builders

24 ¶ Therefore [a]whosoever heareth these sayings of mine, and doeth them, I will liken him unto a wise man, which built his house upon a rock:

25 And the rain descended, and the floods came, and the winds blew, and beat upon that house; and it fell not: for it was founded upon a rock.

26 And every one that heareth these sayings of mine, and doeth them not, shall be likened unto a foolish man, which built his house upon the sand:

27 And the rain descended, and the floods came, and the winds blew, and beat upon that house; and it fell: and great was the fall of it.

28 And it came to pass, when Jesus had ended these sayings, [a]the people were astonished at his doctrine:

29 [a]For he taught them as *one* having authority, and not as the scribes.

The leper cleansed

8 When he was come down from the mountain, great multitudes followed him.

2 [a]And behold, there came a leper and worshipped him, saying, Lord, if thou wilt, thou canst make me clean.

---

of Jesus (cf. 19:24, where Jesus speaks of a camel going through the eye of a needle). Its purpose is to drive home a point.

7:6 Teaching should be given in accordance with the spiritual capacity of the learners. *dogs.* The unclean dogs of the street were held in low esteem.

7:8 *asketh . . . seeketh . . . knocketh.* Greek present imperatives are used here, indicating constant asking, seeking and knocking. Persistent prayer is being emphasized.

7:12 The so-called Golden Rule is found in negative form in rabbinic Judaism and also in Hinduism, Buddhism and Confucianism. It occurred in various forms in Greek and Roman ethical teaching. Jesus stated it in positive form. *the law and the prophets.* See note on 5:17.

7:13 *strait gate.* The gate that leads into the kingdom of heaven. It is synonymous with "life" (v. 14). *destruction.* Separation from God in hell.

7:15 *false prophets.* People who have not been sent by God but who claim that they have (see 24:24; Jer 23:16 and note).

7:21 *Lord.* A title that sometimes means only "sir" or "master" but here seems to mean more than that in view of the fact that Jesus is the One who makes the final decision about a person's eternal destiny. *kingdom of heaven.* See note on 3:2.

7:22 *that day.* The day of judgment (cf. Mal 3:17–18). *prophesied.* In the NT this verb primarily means to give a message from God, not necessarily to predict. *devils.* Or "demons." See note on Mark 1:23.

7:29 *authority.* The teachers of the law quoted other rabbis to support their own teaching (see note on 2:4), but Jesus spoke with divine authority.

8:2 *leper.* The Greek word was used for various diseases affecting the skin—not necessarily leprosy (see Lev 13–14 and note on Lev 13:2). *Lord.* See note on 7:21. *make me clean.* Leprosy made a person ceremonially unclean as well as physically afflicted (see note on Luke 5:12–16).

3 And Jesus put forth *his* hand, and touched him, saying, I will; be thou clean. And immediately his leprosy was cleansed.

4 And Jesus saith unto him, [a]See thou tell no *man;* but go thy way, shew thyself to the priest, and offer the gift that [b]Moses commanded for a testimony unto them.

The centurion's servant healed

5 ¶ [a]And when Jesus was entered into Capernaum, there came unto him a centurion, beseeching him,

6 And saying, Lord, my servant lieth at home sick of the palsy, grievously tormented.

7 And Jesus saith unto him, I will come and heal him.

8 The centurion answered and said, Lord, [a]I am not worthy that thou shouldest come under my roof: but [b]speak the word only, and my servant shall be healed.

9 For I am a man under authority, having soldiers under me: and I say to this *man,* Go, and he goeth; and to another, Come, and he cometh; and to my servant, Do this, and he doeth *it.*

10 When Jesus heard *it,* he marvelled, and said to them that followed, Verily I say unto you, I have not found so great faith, no not in Israel.

11 And I say unto you, That [a]many shall come from the east and west, and shall sit down with Abraham, and Isaac, and Jacob, in the kingdom of heaven.

12 But [a]the children of the kingdom [b]shall be cast out into outer darkness: there shall be weeping and gnashing of teeth.

13 And Jesus said unto the centurion, Go thy way; and as thou hast believed, *so* be it done unto thee. And his servant was healed in the selfsame hour.

Peter's mother-in-law healed

14 ¶ [a]And when Jesus was come into Peter's house, he saw [b]his wife's mother laid, and sick of a fever.

15 And he touched her hand, and the fever left her: and she arose, and ministered unto them.

16 [a]When the even was come, they brought unto him many *that were* possessed with devils: and he cast out the spirits with *his* word, and healed all that were sick:

17 That it might be fulfilled which was spoken by Esaias the prophet, saying [a]Himself took our infirmities, and bare our sicknesses.

Teaching about discipleship

18 ¶ Now when Jesus saw great multitudes about him, he gave commandment to depart unto the other side.

19 [a]And a certain scribe came, and said unto him, Master, I will follow thee whithersoever thou goest.

20 And Jesus saith unto him, The foxes have holes, and the birds of the air *have* nests; but the Son of man hath not where to lay *his* head.

21 [a]And another of his disciples said unto him, Lord, [b]suffer me first to go and bury my father.

22 But Jesus said unto him, Follow me; and let the dead bury their dead.

The storm stilled

23 ¶ And when he was entered into a ship, his disciples followed him.

24 [a]And behold, there arose a great tempest in the sea, insomuch that the ship was covered with the waves: but he was asleep.

25 And his disciples came to *him,* and awoke him, saying, Lord, save us: we perish.

26 And he saith unto them, Why are ye fearful, O ye of little faith? Then [a]he arose, and rebuked the winds and the sea; and there was a great calm.

27 But the men marvelled, saying, What

8:4 [a]ch. 9:30; Mark 5:43 [b]Lev. 14:3,4,10; Luke 5:14
8:5 [a]Luke 7:1
8:8 [a]Luke 15:19,21 [b]Ps. 107:20
8:11 [a]Gen. 12:3; Is. 2:2,3; 11:10; Mal. 1:11; Luke 13:29; Acts 10:45; 11:18; 14:27; Rom. 15:9; Eph. 3:6
8:12 [a]ch. 21:43 [b]ch. 13:42,50; 22:13; 24:51; 25:30; Luke 13:28; 2 Pet. 2:17; Jude 13
8:14 [a]Mark 1:29-31; Luke 4:38,39
8:14 [b]1 Cor. 9:5
8:16 [a]Mark 1:32; Luke 4:40,41
8:17 [a]Is. 53:4; 1 Pet. 2:24
8:19 [a]Luke 9:57,58
8:21 [a]Luke 9:59,60 [b]See 1 Ki. 19:20
8:24 [a]Mark 4:37; Luke 8:23
8:26 [a]Ps. 65:7; 89:9; 107:29

8:4 *tell no man.* Perhaps for several reasons: (1) Jesus did not want to be considered just a miracle worker, (2) He did not want His teaching ministry hindered by too much publicity being given to His healing miracles, and (3) He did not want His death to come prematurely, i.e., before He had finished His ministry. See 9:30; 12:16; Mark 1:44; 5:43; 7:36; Luke 8:56. *shew thyself to the priest.* See note on Luke 5:14. *them.* The priests.

8:5–13 Although the incident in John 4:43–54 is similar, it probably is a separate episode in the life of Jesus.

8:5 *Capernaum.* See note on 4:13. *centurion.* A Roman military officer in charge of 100 soldiers. In Luke's account (Luke 7:1–5) Jewish elders and friends of the centurion came to Jesus on his behalf, but Matthew does not mention these intermediaries. A parallel situation was the flogging of Jesus by Pilate, in which the act was obviously not carried out by Pilate himself but by the Roman soldiers at Pilate's command (27:26, lit. "he flogged Jesus").

‡8:8 *I am not worthy that thou shouldest come under my roof.* In Greek the words "I am not worthy" are the same as those used by John the Baptist in 3:11 ("I am not worthy"). The entire statement reveals how highly the centurion regarded Jesus. Or perhaps his response reflects his own sense of moral guilt in the presence of Jesus.

8:11 The universality of the gospel is one of Matthew's themes (see Introduction: Recipients). *sit down with . . . in the kingdom of heaven.* The eschatological Messianic banquet that symbolizes the blessings of an intimate relationship with God (see Is 25:6–9).

8:12 *children of the kingdom.* Jews who thought their Judaism was an inherited passport for entrance into the kingdom (see 3:9–10 and note on 3:9).

8:14 *his wife's mother.* See notes on Mark 1:30 and Luke 4:38.

‡8:18 *the other side.* The east side. The sea of Galilee is about 12 miles long and 8 miles wide.

8:19 *scribe.* See note on 2:4.

8:20 *Son of man.* See note on Mark 8:31.

8:22 *let the dead bury their dead.* Let the spiritually dead bury the physically dead. The time of Jesus' ministry was short and demanded full attention and commitment. This statement stresses the radical demands of Jesus' discipleship, since Jews placed great importance on the duty of children to bury their parents.

8:24 *great tempest.* See note on Mark 4:37. *but he was asleep.* See note on Mark 4:38.

manner of man is this, that even the winds
and the sea obey him?

Devils cast out

28 ¶ [a]And when he was come to the other
side into the country of the Gergesenes, there
met him two possessed with devils, coming
out of the tombs, exceeding fierce, so that no
man might pass by that way.
29 And behold, they cried out, saying,
What have we to do with thee, Jesus, *thou* Son
of God? art thou come hither to torment us before the time?
30 And there was a good way off from
them a herd of many swine feeding.
31 So the devils besought him, saying, If
thou cast us out, suffer us to go away into the
herd of swine.
32 And he said unto them, Go. And when
they were come out, they went into the herd
of swine: and behold, the whole herd of swine
ran violently down a steep place into the sea,
and perished in the waters.
33 And they that kept *them* fled, and went
their ways into the city, and told every *thing,*
and what was befallen to the possessed of the
devils.
34 And behold, the whole city came out to
meet Jesus: and when they saw him, [a]they besought *him* that he would depart out of their
coasts.

A man with palsy healed

9 And he entered into a ship, and passed
over, [a]and came into his own city.
2 [a]And behold, they brought to him a man
sick of the palsy, lying on a bed: [b]and Jesus seeing their faith said unto the sick of the palsy;
Son, be of good cheer; thy sins be forgiven thee.
3 And behold, certain of the scribes said
within themselves, This *man* blasphemeth.
4 And Jesus [a]knowing their thoughts said,
Wherefore think ye evil in your hearts?
5 For whether is easier, to say, *Thy* sins be
forgiven thee; or to say, Arise, and walk?
6 But that ye may know that the Son of
man hath power on earth to forgive sins, (then
saith he to the sick of the palsy,) Arise, take up
thy bed, and go unto thine house.
7 And he arose, and departed to his house.
8 But when the multitudes saw *it,* they
marvelled, and glorified God, which had given
such power unto men.

Matthew called

9 ¶ [a]And as Jesus passed forth from thence,
he saw a man, named Matthew, sitting at the
receipt of custom: and he saith unto him, Follow me. And he arose, and followed him.
10 [a]And it came to pass, as Jesus sat at
meat in the house, behold, many publicans
and sinners came and sat down with him and
his disciples.
11 And when the Pharisees saw *it,* they
said unto his disciples, Why eateth your Master with [a]publicans and [b]sinners?
12 But when Jesus heard *that,* he said unto
them, They that be whole need not a physician, but they that are sick.
13 But go ye and learn what *that* meaneth,
[a]I will have mercy, and not sacrifice: for I am
not come to call *the* righteous, [b]but sinners to
repentance.

The question about fasting

14 ¶ Then came to him the disciples of
John, saying, [a]Why do we and the Pharisees
fast oft, but thy disciples fast not?
15 And Jesus said unto them, Can [a]the
children of the bridechamber mourn, as long
as the bridegroom is with them? but the days
will come, when the bridegroom shall be tak-
en from them, and [b]then shall they fast.
16 No *man* putteth a piece of [1]new cloth
unto an old garment; for that which is put in to
fill it up taketh from the garment, and the rent
is made worse.
17 Neither do *men* put new wine into old
bottles: else the bottles break, and the wine
runneth out, and the bottles perish: but they
put new wine into new bottles, and both are
preserved.

8:28 [a]Mark 5:1; Luke 8:26
8:34 [a]See Deut. 5:25; 1 Ki. 17:18; Luke 5:8; Acts 16:39
9:1 [a]ch. 4:13
9:2 [a]Mark 2:3; Luke 5:18 [b]ch. 8:10
9:4 [a]Ps. 139:2; ch. 12:25; Mark 12:15; Luke 5:22; 6:8; 9:47; 11:17
9:9 [a]Mark 2:14; Luke 5:27
9:10 [a]Mark 2:15; Luke 5:29
9:11 [a]ch. 11:19; Luke 5:30; 15:2 [b]Gal. 2:15
9:13 [a]Hos. 6:6; Mic. 6:6-8; ch. 12:7 [b]1 Tim. 1:15
9:14 [a]Mark 2:18; Luke 5;33; 18:12
9:15 [a]John 3:29 [b]Acts 13:2,3; 14:23; 1 Cor. 7:5
9:16 [1]Or, *raw,* or, *unwrought cloth*

‡8:28 *country of the Gergesenes.* The region around the city of Gergesa, in the hills to the east of the sea of Galilee. Mark and Luke identify the region by the city of Gadara, located about six miles southeast of the sea. *two.* Mark (5:2) and Luke (8:27; see note there) mention only one Gadarene/Gergesene demoniac.
8:29 *time.* The time of their judgment (see notes on Mark 5:10 and Luke 8:31).
8:30 *herd of many swine.* Large numbers of Gentiles lived in Galilee. Normally Jews did not raise pigs, since they were considered the most "unclean" of all animals.
8:32 Though Jesus seemingly consented to the demons' request, the pigs carried the demons into the depths of the sea—perhaps symbolic of the Abyss (see Luke 8:31 and note).
8:34 *besought him that he would depart.* They were probably more concerned about their financial loss than about the deliverance of the miserable demon-possessed man.
9:1 *passed over.* The northern end of the sea of Galilee. *his own city.* Capernaum (see note on 4:13).
9:2 *their faith.* The faith of the men who carried him as well as the faith of the paralytic.
9:3 *blasphemeth.* Here the term includes usurping God's prerogative to forgive sins (see note on Mark 2:7).
9:5–6 See notes on Mark 2:9–10; 14:64.
9:6 *Son of man.* See note on Mark 8:31.
9:9 *Matthew.* Mark and Luke call this disciple Levi in the parallel accounts (but see also Mark 3:18; Luke 6:15; Acts 1:13). *receipt of custom.* See note on Mark 2:14. *arose, and followed him.* See note on Luke 5:28.
9:10 *publicans.* See notes on 5:46 and Mark 2:16. *sinners.* See note on Mark 2:15.
9:11 *Pharisees.* See note on Mark 2:16.
9:13 *I am not come to call the righteous, but sinners.* See note on Mark 2:17.
9:14 *the disciples of John.* See notes on Mark 2:18 and Luke 5:33. *fast.* See notes on Mark 2:18 and Luke 5:33.
9:15 See notes on Mark 2:19–20.
9:17 *new bottles.* Or "new wineskins." In ancient times goatskins were used to hold wine. As the fresh grape juice fer-

A ruler's daughter raised

18 ¶ [a]While he spake these *things* unto
them, behold, there came a *certain* ruler, and
worshipped him, saying, My daughter is even
now dead: but come and lay thy hand upon
her, and she shall live.
19 And Jesus arose, and followed him, and
so did his disciples.
20 ([a]And behold, a woman, which was diseased with an issue of blood twelve years,
came behind *him,* and touched the hem of his
garment:
21 For she said within herself, If I may but
touch his garment, I shall be whole.
22 But Jesus turned him about, and when
he saw her, he said, Daughter, be of good comfort; [a]thy faith hath made thee whole. And the
woman was made whole from that hour.)
23 [a]And when Jesus came into the ruler's
house, and saw [b]the minstrels and the people
making a noise,
24 He said unto them, [a]Give place: for the
maid is not dead, but sleepeth. And they
laughed him to scorn.
25 But when the people were put forth, he
went in, and took her by the hand, and the
maid arose.
26 And [1]the fame hereof went abroad into
all that land.
27 ¶ And when Jesus departed thence, two
blind men followed him, crying, and saying,
[a]*Thou* Son of David, have mercy on us.
28 And when he was come into the house,
the blind men came to him: and Jesus saith
unto them, Believe ye that I am able to do
this? They said unto him, Yea, Lord.
29 Then touched he their eyes, saying, According to your faith be it unto you.
30 And their eyes were opened; and Jesus
straitly charged them, saying, [a]See *that* no
man know *it.*
31 [a]But they, when they were departed,
spread abroad his fame in all that country.

The need for labourers

32 ¶ [a]As they went out, behold, they
brought to him a dumb man possessed with a
devil.
33 And when the devil was cast out, the
dumb spake: and the multitudes marvelled,
saying, It was never so seen in Israel.
34 But the Pharisees said, [a]He casteth out
the devils through the prince of the devils.
35 And Jesus went about all the cities and
villages, [a]teaching in their synagogues, and
preaching the gospel of the kingdom, and healing every sickness and every disease among
the people.
36 [a]But when he saw the multitudes, he
was moved with compassion on them, because
they [1]fainted, and were scattered abroad, [b]as
sheep having no shepherd.
37 Then saith he unto his disciples, [a]The
harvest truly is plenteous, but the labourers
are few;
38 [a]Pray ye therefore the Lord of the harvest, that he will send forth labourers into his
harvest.

The mission of the twelve

10 And [a]when he had called unto *him*
his twelve disciples, he gave them
power [1]against unclean spirits, to cast them
out, and to heal all *manner of* sickness and all
manner of disease.
2 Now the names of the twelve apostles
are these; The first, Simon, [a]who is called Peter, and Andrew his brother; James, the *son* of
Zebedee, and John his brother;
3 Philip, and Bartholomew; Thomas, and
Matthew the publican; James the *son* of
Alpheus, and Lebbeus, whose surname was
Thaddeus;
4 [a]Simon the Canaanite, and Judas [b]Iscari-
ot, who also betrayed him.
5 These twelve Jesus sent forth, and commanded them, saying, [a]Go not into the way of
the Gentiles, and into *any* city of [b]the Samaritans enter ye not:
6 [a]But go rather to the [b]lost sheep of the
house of Israel.
7 [a]And as ye go, preach, saying, [b]The kingdom of heaven is at hand.

9:18 [a]Mark 5:22; Luke 8:41 9:20 [a]Mark 5:25; Luke 8:43 9:22 [a]Luke 7:50; 8:48; 17:19; 18:42 9:23 [a]Mark 5:38; Luke 8:51 [b]See 2 Chr. 35:25 9:24 [a]Acts 20:10 9:26 [1]Or, *this fame* 9:27 [a]ch. 15:22; Mark 10:47; Luke 18:38 9:30 [a]ch. 8:4; Luke 5:14 9:31 [a]Mark 7:36 9:32 [a]ch. 12:22; Luke 11:14

9:34 [a]ch. 12:24; Luke 11:15 9:35 [a]ch. 4:23 9:36 [1]Or, *were tired and lay down* [a]Mark 6:34 [b]Num. 27:17; 1 Ki. 22:17 9:37 [a]Luke 10:2; John 4:35 9:38 [a]2 Thes. 3:1 10:1 [1]Or, *over* [a]Mark 3:13; Luke 6:13 10:2 [a]John 1:42 10:4 [a]Luke 6:15; Acts 1:13 [b]John 13:26 10:5 [a]ch. 4:15 [b]2 Ki. 17:24; John 4:9 10:6 [a]ch. 15:24; Acts 13:46 [b]Is. 53:6; Jer. 50:6; Ezek. 34:5; 1 Pet. 2:25 10:7 [a]Luke 9:2 [b]ch. 3:2; Luke 10:9

mented, the wine would expand, and the new wineskin would stretch. But a used skin, already stretched, would break. Jesus brings a newness that cannot be confined within the old forms.

9:18 *certain ruler.* From Mark and Luke we know that the official was Jairus (see note on Mark 5:22).

9:20 *an issue of blood twelve years.* See notes on Lev 15:25; Mark 5:25.

9:21 See note on Mark 5:28.

9:22 *Daughter.* See notes on Luke 8:4–8. *made thee whole.* See note on Mark 5:34.

9:23 *minstrels.* Musicians hired to play in mourning ceremonies. *people making a noise.* Mourners hired to wail and lament.

9:24 *not dead, but sleepeth.* See note on Luke 8:52.

9:27 *blind men.* Isaiah predicted the healing of the blind in the Messianic age (Is 35:5). *Son of David.* A popular Jewish title for the coming Messiah (e.g., 12:23; 20:30; 21:9; 22:41–45; see note on 1:1).

9:30 See notes on 8:4 and 16:20.

9:32 *dumb man.* Isaiah also predicted that the mute would talk in the Messianic age (Is 35:6).

9:34 *prince of the devils.* See note on 10:25.

9:35 *synagogues.* See note on Mark 1:21. *gospel.* See note on Mark 1:1.

10:2–4 See notes on Luke 6:14–16.

10:2 *apostles.* The only occurrence of this word in Matthew's Gospel. See note on Mark 6:30.

10:5 *Go not.* The good news about the kingdom was to be proclaimed first to Jews only. After His death and resurrection, Jesus commanded the message to be taken to all nations (28:19; cf. 21:43). *Samaritans.* A mixed-blood race resulting from the intermarriage of Israelites left behind when the people of the northern kingdom were exiled and Gentiles brought into the land by the Assyrians (2 Ki 17:24). Bitter hostility existed between Jews and Samaritans in Jesus' day (see John 4:9).

10:7 *kingdom of heaven.* See note on 3:2.

8 Heal the sick, cleanse the lepers, raise the dead, cast out devils: [a]freely ye have received, freely give.

9 [a][1]Provide neither gold, nor silver, nor [b]brass in your purses;

10 Nor scrip for *your* journey, neither two coats, neither shoes, nor yet [1]staves: [a]for the workman is worthy of his meat.

11 [a]And into whatsoever city or town ye shall enter, inquire who in it is worthy; and there abide till ye go thence.

12 And when ye come into a house salute it.

13 [a]And if the house be worthy, let your peace come upon it: [b]but if it be not worthy, let your peace return to you.

14 [a]And whosoever shall not receive you, nor hear your words, when ye depart out of that house or city, [b]shake off the dust of your feet.

15 Verily I say unto you, [a]It shall be more tolerable for the land of Sodom and Gomorrha in the day of judgment, than for that city.

16 ¶ [a]Behold, I send you forth as sheep in the midst of wolves: [b]be ye therefore wise as serpents, and [c][1]harmless as doves.

17 But beware of men: for [a]they will deliver you up to the councils, and [b]they will scourge you in their synagogues;

18 And [a]ye shall be brought before governors and kings for my sake, for a testimony against them and the Gentiles.

19 [a]But when they deliver you up, take no thought how or what ye shall speak: for [b]it shall be given you in that *same* hour what ye shall speak.

20 [a]For it is not ye that speak, but the Spirit of your Father which speaketh in you.

21 [a]And the brother shall deliver up the brother to death, and the father the child: and the children shall rise up against *their* parents, and cause them to be put to death.

22 And [a]ye shall be hated of all *men* for my name's sake: [b]but he that endureth to the end shall be saved.

10:8 [a]Acts 8:18
10:9 [1]Or, *Get* [a]1 Sam. 9:7; Mark 6:8; Luke 9:3; 10:4 [b]Mark 6:8
10:10 [1][Gr. *a staff*] [a]Luke 10:7; 1 Cor. 9:7; 1 Tim. 5:18
10:11 [a]Luke 10:8
10:13 [a]Luke 10:5 [b]Ps. 35:13
10:14 [a]Mark 6:11; Luke 9:5; 10:10,11 [b]Neh. 5:13; Acts 13:51
10:15 [a]ch. 11:22
10:16 [1]Or, *simple* [a]Luke 10:3 [b]Rom. 16:19; Eph. 5:15 [c]Phil. 2:15
10:17 [a]Mark 13:9; Luke 12:11 [b]Acts 5:40
10:18 [a]Acts 12:1; 25:7,23; 2 Tim. 4:16
10:19 [a]Luke 21:14 [b]Ex. 4:12; Jer. 1:7
10:20 [a]2 Sam. 23:2; 2 Tim. 4:17
10:21 [a]Mic. 7:6; Luke 21:16
10:22 [a]Luke 21:17 [b]Dan. 12:12; Mark 13:13
10:23 [1]Or, *end*, or, *finish* [a]ch. 2:13; Acts 8:1 [b]ch. 16:28
10:24 [a]Luke 6:40; John 15:20
10:25 [1][Gr. *Beelzebul*] [a]Mark 3:22; John 8:48
10:26 [a]Mark 4:22; Luke 8:17; 12:2,3
10:28 [a]Is. 8:12,13; Luke 12:4; 1 Pet. 3:14
10:29 [1]*It is in value halfpenny farthing in the original, as being the tenth part of the Roman penny*

23 But [a]when they persecute you in this city, flee ye into another: for verily I say unto you, Ye shall not [1]have gone over the cities of Israel, [b]till the Son of man be come.

24 [a]The disciple is not above *his* master, nor the servant above his lord.

25 *It is* enough for the disciple that he be as his master, and the servant as his lord. If [a]they have called the master of the house [1]Beelzebub, how much more *shall they call* them of his household?

26 Fear them not therefore: [a]for there is nothing covered, that shall not be revealed; and hid, that shall not be known.

27 What I tell you in darkness, *that* speak ye in light: and what ye hear in the ear, *that* preach ye upon the housetops.

28 [a]And fear not them which kill the body, but are not able to kill the soul: but rather fear him which is able to destroy both soul and body in hell.

29 Are not two sparrows sold for a [1]farthing? and one of them shall not fall on the ground without your Father.

30 [a]But the very hairs of your head are all numbered.

31 Fear ye not therefore, ye are of more value than many sparrows.

32 [a]Whosoever therefore shall confess me before men, [b]him will I confess also before my Father which is in heaven.

33 [a]But whosoever shall deny me before men, him will I also deny before my Father which is in heaven.

34 ¶ [a]Think not that I am come to send peace on earth: I came not to send peace, but a sword.

35 For I am come to set a man at variance [a]against his father, and the daughter against her mother, and the daughter in law against her mother in law.

10:30 [a]1 Sam. 14:45; Luke 21:18; Acts 27:34 10:32 [a]Luke 12:8; Rom. 10:9 [b]Rev. 3:5 10:33 [a]Luke 9:26; 2 Tim. 2:12 10:34 [a]Luke 12:49 10:35 [a]Mic. 7:6

10:8 *lepers.* The Greek word for leprosy was used for various diseases affecting the skin—not necessarily leprosy. See note on Lev 13:2.

10:9–10 See notes on Mark 6:8–9.

‡10:12 *salute it.* The Jews' greeting then, even as now, was *shalom*, "peace."

10:14 *shake off the dust of your feet.* A symbolic act practiced by the Pharisees when they left an "unclean" Gentile area. Here it represented an act of solemn warning to those who rejected God's message (see notes on Luke 9:5; Acts 13:51; cf. Acts 18:6).

10:15 *Sodom and Gomorrha.* See Gen 19:23–29.

10:16 Cf. Paul's statement in Rom 16:19: "I would have you wise unto that which is good, and simple concerning evil."

10:17 *councils.* The lower courts, connected with local synagogues, that tried less serious cases and flogged those found guilty. *synagogues.* See notes on Mark 1:21 and Luke 21:12.

10:19 *take no thought how or what you shall speak.* Not to be used by preachers as an excuse for lack of sermon preparation! See Luke 21:14–15.

10:22 *he that endureth to the end shall be saved.* See note on Mark 13:13.

10:23 Jesus' saying here is probably best understood as referring to His coming in judgment on the Jews when Jerusalem and the temple were destroyed in A.D. 70.

‡10:25 *Beelzebub.* Satan, the ruler of demons (12:24); the Hebrew epithet Baal-Zebub ("lord of flies") is a parody on and mockery of the Hebrew name Baal-Zebul ("Exalted Baal" or "Prince Baal"). See Judg 10:6.

10:28 *soul.* The true self. Body and soul are closely related in this life but are separated at death and then reunited at the resurrection (cf. 2 Cor 5:1–10; Phil 1:23–24). *fear him.* God. He alone determines the final destiny of us all. *hell.* See note on 5:22.

10:34 At first glance this saying sounds like a contradiction of Is 9:6 ("Prince of Peace"), Luke 2:14 ("on earth peace among men") and John 14:27 ("Peace I leave with you"). It is true that Christ came to bring peace—peace between the believer and God, and peace among men. Yet the inevitable result of Christ's coming is conflict—between Christ and the antichrist, between light and darkness, between Christ's children and the devil's children. This conflict can occur even between members of the same family (vv. 35–36).

36 And [a]a man's foes *shall be* they of his own household.

37 [a]He that loveth father or mother more than me is not worthy of me: and he that loveth son or daughter more than me is not worthy of me.

38 [a]And he that taketh not his cross, and followeth after me, is not worthy of me.

39 [a]He that findeth his life shall lose it: and he that loseth his life for my sake shall find it.

40 ¶ [a]He that receiveth you receiveth me, and he that receiveth me receiveth him that sent me.

41 [a]He that receiveth a prophet in the name of a prophet shall receive a prophet's reward; and he that receiveth a righteous *man* in the name of a righteous *man* shall receive a righteous *man's* reward.

42 [a]And whosoever shall give to drink unto one of these little ones a cup of cold *water* only in the name of a disciple, verily I say unto you, he shall in no wise lose his reward.

Tribute to John the Baptist

11 And it came to pass, when Jesus had made an end of commanding his twelve disciples, he departed thence to teach and to preach in their cities.

2 [a]Now when John had heard [b]in the prison the works of Christ, he sent two of his disciples,

3 And said unto him, Art thou [a]he that should come, or do we look for another?

4 Jesus answered and said unto them, Go and shew John again *those things* which ye do hear and see:

5 [a]The blind receive their sight, and the lame walk, the lepers are cleansed, and the deaf hear, the dead are raised up, and [b]the poor have the gospel preached to them.

6 And blessed is *he,* whosoever shall not [a]be offended in me.

7 ¶ [a]And as they departed, Jesus began to say unto the multitudes concerning John, What went ye out into the wilderness to see? [b]A reed shaken with the wind?

8 But what went ye out for to see? A man clothed in soft raiment? behold, they that wear soft *clothing* are in kings' houses.

9 But what went ye out for to see? A prophet? yea, I say unto you, [a]and more than a prophet.

10 For this is *he,* of whom it is written, [a]Behold, I send my messenger before thy face, which shall prepare thy way before thee.

11 Verily I say unto you, Among *them that are* born of women there hath not risen a greater than John the Baptist: notwithstanding he that is least in the kingdom of heaven is greater than he.

12 [a]And from the days of John the Baptist until now the kingdom of heaven [1]suffereth violence, and the violent take it by force.

13 [a]For all the prophets and the law prophesied until John.

14 And if ye will receive *it,* this is [a]Elias, which was for to come.

15 [a]He that hath ears to hear, let him hear.

16 ¶ [a]But whereunto shall I liken this generation? It is like unto children sitting in the markets, and calling unto their fellows,

17 And saying, We have piped unto you, and ye have not danced; we have mourned unto you, and ye have not lamented.

18 For John came neither eating nor drinking, and they say, He hath a devil.

19 The Son of man came eating and drinking, and they say, Behold a man gluttonous, and a winebibber, [a]a friend of publicans and sinners. [b]But wisdom is justified of her children.

10:36 [a]Ps. 41:9; 55:13; John 13:18
10:37 [a]Luke 14:26
10:38 [a]Mark 8:34
10:39 [a]Luke 17:33; John 12:25
10:40 [a]Luke 9:48; John 12:44; Gal. 4:14
10:41 [a]1 Ki. 17:10; 2 Ki. 4:8
10:42 [a]ch. 25:40; Mark 9:41; Heb. 6:10
11:2 [a]Luke 7:18 [b]ch. 14:3
11:3 [a]Gen. 49:10; Num. 24:17; Dan. 9:24; John 6:14
11:5 [a]Is. 29:18; 35:4-6; John 2:23 [b]Ps. 22:26; Is. 61:1; Luke 4:18; Jas. 2:5
11:6 [a]Is. 8:14,15; Rom. 9:32; 1 Pet. 2:8
11:7 [a]Luke 7:24 [b]Eph. 4:14
11:9 [a]Luke 1:76
11:10 [a]Mal. 3:1; Mark 1:2; Luke 1:76
11:12 [1]Or, *is gotten by force, and they that thrust men* [a]Luke 16:16
11:13 [a]Mal. 4:6
11:14 [a]Mal. 4:5; Luke 1:17
11:15 [a]ch. 13:9; Luke 8:8; Rev. 2:7,11,17,29; 3:6,13
11:16 [a]Luke 7:31
11:19 [a]ch. 9:10 [b]Luke 7:35

10:38 *his cross.* The first mention of the cross in Matthew's Gospel. The cross was an instrument of death and here symbolizes the necessity of total commitment—even unto death—on the part of Jesus' disciples (see note on Mark 8:34).

10:40–42 During times of persecution, hospitality was especially important and could be dangerous. So Jesus indicates that those who provide it and show kindness to God's people will receive a reward.

11:1 While the 12 apostles were carrying out their first mission, Jesus continued His ministry in Galilee.

11:3 *he that should come.* The Messiah. *look for another.* See note on Luke 7:19.

11:4 *shew John again those things.* See note on Luke 7:22.

11:5 *lepers.* See notes on 8:2; Lev 13:2. *the poor have the gospel preached to them.* See note on Luke 7:22.

11:6 *whosoever shall not be offended.* See note on Luke 7:23.

11:11 *greater than he.* John belonged to the age of the old covenant, which was preparatory to Christ. The least NT saint has a higher privilege in Christ as a part of His bride (the church, Eph 5:25–27,32) than John the Baptist, who was only a friend of the bridegroom (John 3:29). Another view, however, stresses the expression "he that is least," holding that the key to its meaning is found in 18:4—"whosoever . . . shall humble himself as this little child." Such a person, though "least," is regarded by God as even greater than John the Baptist.

11:12 *suffereth violence.* The Greek here is taken in a passive sense. In this context its passive meaning is, "suffers violent attacks." The verse emphasizes the ongoing persecution of the people of the kingdom.

11:13 *prophets and the law.* The entire OT prophesied the coming of the kingdom. John represented the end of the old economy.

11:14 *this is Elias.* A reference to Mal 4:5, which prophesied the reappearance of Elijah before the day of the Lord. Some of the people remembered the prophecy and asked John the Baptist, "Art thou Elias?" He answered, "I am not" (John 1:21). John was not literally the reincarnation of Elijah, but he did fulfill the function and role of the prophet (see Mat 17:10–13 and note on Luke 1:17).

11:16 *like unto children sitting in the markets.* See note on Luke 7:32.

‡11:17 *piped.* As providing music at a wedding. *mourned.* As at a funeral. The latter symbolized the ministry of John, the former that of Jesus. The people of Jesus' "generation" (v. 16) were like children who refused to respond on either occasion.

11:19 *Son of man.* See note on Mark 8:31. *wisdom is justified of her children.* Apparently means that God (wisdom) had sent both John and Jesus in specific roles, and that this would be vindicated by the lasting works of both Jesus and John (see note on Luke 7:35).

The judgment of the unrepentant

20 ¶ [a]Then began he to upbraid the cities wherein most of his mighty works were done, because they repented not.

21 Woe unto thee, Chorazin, woe unto thee, Bethsaida: for if the mighty works which were done in you, had been done in Tyre and Sidon they would have repented long ago [a]in sackcloth and ashes.

22 But I say unto you, [a]It shall be more tolerable for Tyre and Sidon at the day of judgment, than for you.

23 And thou, Capernaum, [a]which art exalted unto heaven, shalt be brought down to hell: for if the mighty works, which have been done in thee, had been done in Sodom, it would have remained until this day.

24 But I say unto you, [a]that it shall be more tolerable for the land of Sodom in the day of judgment, than for thee.

Jesus reveals the Father

25 ¶ [a]At that time Jesus answered and said, I thank thee, O Father, Lord of heaven and earth, because [b]thou hast hid these *things* from the wise and prudent, [c]and hast revealed them unto babes.

26 Even so, Father: for so it seemed good in thy sight.

27 [a]All *things* are delivered unto me of my Father: and no *man* knoweth the Son, but the Father; [b]neither knoweth any *man* the Father, save the Son, and *he* to whomsoever the Son will reveal *him.*

28 ¶ Come unto me, all *ye* that labour and are heavy laden, and I will give you rest.

29 Take my yoke upon you, [a]and learn of me; for I am meek and [b]lowly in heart: [c]and ye shall find rest unto your souls.

30 [a]For my yoke *is* easy, and my burden is light.

Jesus the Lord of the sabbath

12 At that time [a]Jesus went on the sabbath day through the corn; and his disciples were a hungred, and began to pluck the ears of corn, and to eat.

2 But when the Pharisees saw *it,* they said unto him, Behold, thy disciples do *that* which is not lawful to do upon the sabbath day.

3 But he said unto them, Have ye not read [a]what David did, when he was a hungred, and they that were with him;

4 How he entered into the house of God, and did eat [a]the shewbread, which was not lawful for him to eat, neither for them which were with him, [b]but only for the priests?

5 Or have ye not read in the [a]law, how that on the sabbath days the priests in the temple profane the sabbath, and are blameless?

6 But I say unto you, That in this place is [a]*one* greater than the temple.

7 But if ye had known what *this* meaneth, [a]I will have mercy, and not sacrifice, ye would not have condemned the guiltless.

8 For the Son of man is Lord even of the sabbath day.

9 ¶ [a]And when he was departed thence, he went into their synagogue:

10 And behold, there was a man which had *his* hand withered. And they asked him, saying, [a]Is it lawful to heal on the sabbath days? that they might accuse him.

11 And he said unto them, What man shall there be among you, that shall have one sheep, and if [a]it fall into a pit on the sabbath day, will he not lay hold on it, and lift *it* out?

12 How much then is a man better than a sheep? Wherefore it is lawful to do well on the sabbath days.

13 Then saith he to the man, Stretch forth thine hand. And he stretched *it* forth; and it was restored whole, *like* as the other.

Jesus heals many

14 ¶ Then [a]the Pharisees went out, and [1]held a council against him, how they might destroy him.

15 But when Jesus knew *it,* [a]he withdrew himself from thence: [b]and great multitudes followed him, and he healed them all,

16 And [a]charged them that they should not make him known:

11:20 [a]Luke 10:13
11:21 [a]Jonah 3:7
11:22 [a]ver. 24; ch. 10:15
11:23 [a]See Is. 14:13; Lam. 2:1
11:24 [a]ch. 10:15
11:25 [a]Luke 10:21 [b]Ps. 8:2; 1 Cor. 1:19; 2:8; 2 Cor. 3:14 [c]ch. 16:17
11:27 [a]ch. 28:18; Luke 10:22; John 3:35; 13:3; 17:2; 1 Cor. 15:27 [b]John 1:18; 6:46; 10:15
11:29 [a]John 13:15; Phil. 2:5; 1 Pet. 2:21; 1 John 2:6 [b]Zech. 9:9; Phil. 2:7,8 [c]Jer. 6:16
11:30 [a]1 John 5:3
12:1 [a]Deut. 23:25; Mark 2:23; Luke 6:1
12:3 [a]1 Sam. 21:6
12:4 [a]Ex. 25:30; Lev. 24:5 [b]Ex. 29:32; Lev. 8:31; 24:9
12:5 [a]Num. 28:9; John 7:22
12:6 [a]2 Chr. 6:18; Mal. 3:1
12:7 [a]Hos. 6:6; Mic. 6:6-8; ch. 9:13
12:9 [a]Mark 3:1; Luke 6:6
12:10 [a]Luke 13:14; 14:3; John 9:16
12:11 [a]See Ex. 23:4,5; Deut. 22:4
12:14 [1]Or, *took counsel* [a]ch. 27:1; Mark 3:6; Luke 6:11; John 5:18; 10:39; 11:53
12:15 [a]See ch. 10:23; Mark 3:7 [b]ch. 19:2
12:16 [a]ch. 9:30

11:21 *Chorazin.* Mentioned in the Bible only twice (here and in Luke 10:13), it was near the sea of Galilee, probably about two miles north of Capernaum. *Bethsaida.* On the northeast shore of the sea of Galilee. Philip the tetrarch rebuilt Bethsaida and named it "Julias," after Julia, daughter of Caesar Augustus. *Tyre and Sidon.* Cities on the Phoenician coast north of the Holy Land. *sackcloth.* Here a sign of repentance (see note on Gen 37:34). Cf. Rev 6:12. *ashes.* Also a sign of repentance.
11:23 *Capernaum.* See note on Luke 10:15.
11:25 *these things.* The "things" probably include an understanding of Jesus' mission. *the wise and prudent.* The teachers of the law and the Pharisees. *babes.* The humble followers of Jesus.
‡12:1 *the corn.* Fields of wheat or barley, the latter eaten by poorer people. *pluck the ears of corn.* They pulled off some of the wheat. See note on Mark 2.23.
12:2 *Pharisees.* See note on Mark 2:16. *that which is not lawful to do upon the sabbath.* See note on Mark 2:24.
12:3 *what David did.* See note on Mark 2:25.
‡12:4 *shewbread.* Each sabbath, 12 fresh loaves of bread were to be set on a table in the holy place (Ex 25:30; Lev 24:5–9). The old loaves were eaten by the priests. The "hot bread" replaced the old every sabbath day (1 Sam 21:6).
12:5 *profane the sabbath.* By doing work associated with the sacrifices.
12:8 *the Son of man is Lord even of the sabbath day.* See note on Luke 6:5.
12:9 *synagogue.* See note on Mark 1:21.
12:10 *heal on the sabbath.* The rabbis prohibited healing on the sabbath, unless it was feared the victim would die before the next day. Obviously the man with the withered hand was in no danger of this.
‡12:13 *Stretch forth thine hand. And he stretched it forth.* The fact that the man did what Jesus asked shows a connection between faith and Jesus' healing power. He did not say, "I can't, I'm paralyzed." He stretched out his hand by faith and was healed.
12:16 *not make him known.* See note on 8:4.

17 That it might be fulfilled which was spoken by Esaias the prophet, saying,

18 [a]Behold my servant, whom I have chosen; my beloved, [b]in whom my soul is well pleased: I will put my spirit upon him, and he shall shew judgment to the Gentiles.

19 He shall not strive, nor cry; neither shall any *man* hear his voice in the streets.

20 A bruised reed shall he not break, and smoking flax shall he not quench, till he send forth judgment unto victory.

21 And in his name shall the Gentiles trust.

The Pharisees' slander

22 ¶ [a]Then was brought unto him one possessed with a devil, blind, and dumb: and he healed him, insomuch that the blind and dumb both spake and saw.

23 And all the people were amazed, and said, Is this the son of David?

24 [a]But when the Pharisees heard *it,* they said, This *fellow* doth not cast out devils, but by [1]Beelzebub the prince of the devils.

25 And Jesus [a]knew their thoughts, and said unto them, Every kingdom divided against itself is brought to desolation; and every city or house divided against itself shall not stand:

26 And if Satan cast out Satan, he is divided against himself; how shall then his kingdom stand?

27 And if I by Beelzebub cast out devils, by whom do your children cast *them* out? therefore they shall be your judges.

28 But if I cast out devils by the Spirit of God, then [a]the kingdom of God is come unto you.

29 [a]Or else how can one enter into a strong *man's* house, and spoil his goods, except he first bind the strong *man?* and then he will spoil his house.

30 He that is not with me is against me; and he that gathereth not with me scattereth abroad.

31 Wherefore I say unto you, [a]All *manner of* sin and blasphemy shall be forgiven unto men: [b]but the blasphemy against the *Holy* Ghost shall not be forgiven unto men.

12:18 [a]Is. 42:1 [b]ch. 3:17; 17:5
12:22 [a]See ch. 9:32; Mark 3:11; Luke 11:14
12:24 [1][Gr. *Beelzebul:* and so ver. 27] [a]ch. 9:34; Mark 3:22; Luke 11:15
12:25 [a]ch. 9:4; John 2:25; Rev. 2:23
12:28 [a]Dan. 2:44; 7:14; Luke 1:33; 11:20; 17:20,21
12:29 [a]Is. 49:24; Luke 11:21-23
12:31 [a]Mark 3:28; Luke 12:10; Heb. 6:4; 10:26,29; 1 John 5:16 [b]Acts 7:51
12:32 [a]ch. 11:19; 13:55; John 7:12,52 [b]1 Tim. 1:13
12:33 [a]ch. 7:17; Luke 6:43
12:34 [a]ch. 3:7; 23:33 [b]Luke 6:45
12:38 [a]ch. 16:1; Mark 8:11; Luke 11:16; John 2:18; 1 Cor. 1:22
12:39 [a]Is. 57:3; ch. 16:4; Mark 8:38; John 4:48
12:40 [a]Jonah 1:17
12:41 [a]Luke 11:32 [b]See Jer. 3:11; Ezek. 16:51; Rom. 2:27 [c]Jonah 3:5
12:42 [a]1 Ki. 10:1; 2 Chr. 9:1; Luke 11:31
12:43 [a]Luke 11:24 [b]Job 1:7; 1 Pet. 5:8

32 And whosoever [a]speaketh a word against the Son of man, [b]it shall be forgiven him: but whosoever speaketh against the Holy Ghost, it shall not be forgiven him, neither in this world, neither in the *world* to come.

33 Either make the tree good, and [a]his fruit good; or else make the tree corrupt, and his fruit corrupt: for the tree is known by *his* fruit.

34 O [a]generation of vipers, how can ye, being evil, speak good *things?* [b]for out of the abundance of the heart the mouth speaketh.

35 A good man out of the good treasure of the heart bringeth forth good *things:* and an evil man out of the evil treasure bringeth forth evil *things.*

36 But I say unto you, That every idle word that men shall speak, they shall give account thereof in the day of judgment.

37 For by thy words thou shalt be justified, and by thy words thou shalt be condemned.

Warning against seeking signs

38 ¶ [a]Then certain of the scribes and of the Pharisees answered, saying, Master, we would see a sign from thee.

39 But he answered and said to them, An evil and [a]adulterous generation seeketh after a sign; and there shall no sign be given to it, but the sign of the prophet Jonas:

40 [a]For as Jonas was three days and three nights in the whale's belly; so shall the Son of man be three days and three nights in the heart of the earth.

41 [a]*The* men of Nineveh shall rise in judgment with this generation, and [b]shall condemn it: [c]because they repented at the preaching of Jonas; and behold, a greater than Jonas *is* here.

42 [a]*The* queen of the south shall rise up in the judgment with this generation, and shall condemn it: for she came from the uttermost parts of the earth to hear the wisdom of Solomon; and behold, a greater than Solomon *is* here.

43 ¶ [a]When the unclean spirit is gone out of a man, [b]he walketh through dry places, seeking rest, and findeth none.

12:18–21 Another fulfillment passage (see note on 1:22). This one is from Isaiah's first servant song (42:1–4) and is the longest OT quotation in Matthew's Gospel. It summarizes the quiet ministry of the Lord's servant, who will bring justice and hope to the nations.
12:18 *my servant.* Jesus is called God's servant only here and in Acts 3:13 (see note there), 26; 4:27,30. *my beloved, in whom my soul is well pleased.* See note on 3:17.
12:20 Jesus mends broken lives (see v. 15; John 4:4–42; 8:3–11).
12:23 *the son of David.* See note on 9:27.
12:24 *Beelzebub.* See note on 10:25.
12:28 *kingdom of God.* See note on 3:2.
12:31 *blasphemy against the Holy Ghost shall not be forgiven.* The context (vv. 24,28,32) suggests that the "unpardonable sin" was attributing to Satan Christ's authenticating miracles done in the power of the Holy Spirit (see note on Mark 3:29).
12:38 *sign.* The Pharisees wanted to see a spectacular miracle, preferably in the sky (see Luke 11:16), as the sign that Jesus was the Messiah. Instead, He cites them a "sign" from history. See note on Luke 11:29.
12:39 *adulterous.* Referring to spiritual, not physical, adultery, in the sense that their generation had become unfaithful to its spiritual husband (God).
12:40 *three days and three nights.* Including at least part of the first day and part of the third day, a common Jewish reckoning of time. See note on Luke 24:46. *whale's belly.* The Greek word means "sea creature," i.e., a huge fish or marine mammal (see note on Jon 1:17).
12:41–42 *a greater than Jonas . . . a greater than Solomon.* See note on Luke 11:31–32.
12:42 *queen of the south.* In 1 Ki 10:1 she is called the queen of Sheba, a country in southwest Arabia, now called Yemen.
12:43–45 See note on Luke 11:24.

44 Then he saith, I will return into my house from whence I came out; and when he is come, he findeth *it* empty, swept, and garnished.

45 Then goeth he, and taketh with himself seven other spirits more wicked than himself, and they enter in and dwell there: [a]and the last *state* of that man is worse than the first. *Even* so shall it be also unto this wicked generation.

Jesus' true family

46 ¶ While he yet talked to the people, [a]behold, *his* mother and [b]his brethren stood without, desiring to speak with him.

47 Then one said unto him, Behold, thy mother and thy brethren stand without, desiring to speak with thee.

48 But he answered and said unto him that told him, Who is my mother? and who are my brethren?

49 And he stretched forth his hand toward his disciples, and said, Behold my mother and my brethren.

50 For [a]whosoever shall do the will of my Father which is in heaven, the same is my brother, and sister, and mother.

The parable of the sower

13 The same day went Jesus out of the house, [a]and sat by the sea side.

2 [a]And great multitudes were gathered together unto him, so that [b]he went into a ship, and sat; and the whole multitude stood on the shore.

3 And he spake many *things* unto them in parables, saying, [a]Behold, a sower went forth to sow;

4 And when he sowed, some *seeds* fell by the way side, and the fowls came and devoured them up:

5 Some fell upon stony *places,* where they had not much earth: and forthwith they sprung up, because *they* had no deepness of earth:

6 And when the sun was up, they were scorched; and because *they* had not root, they withered away.

7 And some fell among thorns; and the thorns sprung up, and choked them:

8 But other fell into good ground, and brought forth fruit, some [a]an hundred*fold,* some sixty*fold,* some thirty*fold.*

9 [a]Who hath ears to hear, let him hear.

10 ¶ And the disciples came, and said unto him, Why speakest thou unto them in parables?

11 He answered and said unto them, Because [a]it is given unto you to know the mysteries of the kingdom of heaven, but to them it is not given.

12 [a]For whosoever hath, to him shall be given, and he shall have *more* abundance: but whosoever hath not, from him shall be taken away even that he hath.

13 Therefore speak I to them in parables: because they seeing see not; and hearing they hear not, neither do they understand.

14 And in them is fulfilled the prophecy of Esaias, which saith, [a]By hearing ye shall hear, and shall not understand; and seeing ye shall see, and shall not perceive:

15 For this people's heart is waxed gross, and *their* ears [a]are dull of hearing, and their eyes they have closed; lest at any time they should see with *their* eyes, and hear with *their* ears, and should understand with *their* heart, and should be converted, and I should heal them.

16 But [a]blessed *are* your eyes, for they see: and your ears, for they hear.

17 For verily I say unto you, [a]That many prophets and righteous *men* have desired to see *those things* which ye see, and have not seen *them;* and to hear *those things* which ye hear, and have not heard *them.*

18 [a]Hear ye therefore the parable of the sower.

19 When any one heareth the word [a]of the kingdom, and understandeth *it* not, then cometh the wicked one, and catcheth away that which was sown in his heart. This is he which received seed by the way side.

20 But he that received the seed into stony *places,* the same is he that heareth the word, and anon [a]with joy receiveth it;

21 Yet hath he not root in himself, but dureth for a while: for when tribulation or persecution ariseth because of the word, by and by [a]he is offended.

22 [a]He also that received seed [b]among the thorns is he that heareth the word; and the care

12:45 [a]Heb. 6:4; 10:26; 2 Pet. 2:20-22
12:46 [a]Mark 3:31; Luke 8:19-21 [b]ch. 13:55; Mark 6:3; John 2:12; 7:3,5; Acts 1:14; 1 Cor. 9:5; Gal. 1:19
12:50 [a]See John 15:14; Gal. 5:6; 6:15; Col. 3:11; Heb. 2:11
13:1 [a]Mark 4:1
13:2 [a]Luke 8:4 [b]Luke 5:3
13:3 [a]Luke 8:5
13:8 [a]Gen. 26:12
13:9 [a]ch. 11:15; Mark 4:9
13:11 [a]ch. 11:25; 16:17; Mark 4:11; 1 Cor. 2:10; 1 John 2:27
13:12 [a]ch. 25:29; Mark 4:25; Luke 8:18; 19:26
13:14 [a]Is. 6:9; Ezek. 12:2; Mark 4:12; Luke 8:10; John 12:40; Acts 28:26,27; Rom. 11:8; 2 Cor. 3:14,15
13:15 [a]Heb. 5:11
13:16 [a]ch. 16:17; Luke 10:23,24; John 20:29
13:17 [a]Heb. 11:13; 1 Pet. 1:10,11
13:18 [a]Mark 4:14; Luke 8:11
13:19 [a]ch. 4:23
13:20 [a]Is. 58:2; Ezek. 33:31,32; John 5:35
13:21 [a]ch. 11:6; 2 Tim. 1:15
13:22 [a]ch. 19:23; Mark 10:23; Luke 18:24; 1 Tim. 6:9; 2 Tim. 4:10 [b]Jer. 4:3

12:46 *mother and his brethren.* See note on Luke 8:19.
12:50 *whosoever shall do the will of my Father.* See note on Mark 3:35.
13:2 *sat.* See note on Mark 4:1.
13:3–9 See vv. 18–23 for the interpretation of this first parable.
13:3 *parables.* Our word "parable" comes from the Greek *parabole,* which means "a placing beside"—and thus a comparison or an illustration. Its most common use in the NT is for the illustrative stories that Jesus drew from nature and human life. The Synoptic Gospels contain about 30 of these stories. John's Gospel contains no parables but uses other figures of speech (see notes on Mark 4:2; Luke 8:4). *to sow.* See note on Luke 8:5.
13:4–6 See note on Mark 4:3–8.
13:5 *stony places.* Not ground covered with small stones, but shallow soil on top of solid rock. See note on Luke 8:6.
13:8 *an hundredfold.* See note on Luke 8:8.
13:10 See note on Luke 8:9.
13:11 *mysteries of the kingdom of heaven.* See notes on Mark 4:11 and Luke 8:10.
13:13–14 Jesus speaks in parables because of the spiritual dullness of the people (see note on Luke 8:4).
13:13 *they seeing see not.* See notes on Mark 4:12 and Luke 8:10.
13:18 *Hear ye therefore the parable of the sower.* Jesus seldom interpreted His parables, but here He does.
13:19 *the wicked one.* The devil.

of this world, and the deceitfulness of riches, choke the word, and he becometh unfruitful.

23 But he that received seed into the good ground is he that heareth the word, and understandeth *it;* which also beareth fruit, and bringeth forth, some an hundred*fold,* some sixty, some thirty.

Parables about the kingdom

24 ¶ Another parable put he forth unto them, saying, The kingdom of heaven is likened unto a man which sowed good seed in his field:

25 But while men slept, his enemy came and sowed tares among the wheat, and went his way.

26 But when the blade was sprung up, and brought forth fruit, then appeared the tares also.

27 So the servants of the householder came and said unto him, Sir, didst not thou sow good seed in thy field? from whence then hath it tares?

28 He said unto them, An enemy hath done this. The servants said unto him, Wilt thou then *that* we go and gather them up?

29 But he said, Nay; lest while ye gather up the tares, ye root up also the wheat with them.

30 Let both grow together until the harvest: and in the time of harvest I will say to the reapers, Gather ye together first the tares, and bind them in bundles to burn them: but [a]gather the wheat into my barn.

31 ¶ Another parable put he forth unto them, saying, [a]The kingdom of heaven is like unto a grain of mustard seed, which a man took, and sowed in his field:

32 Which indeed is the least of all seeds: but when it is grown, it is the greatest among herbs, and becometh a tree, so that the birds of the air come and lodge in the branches thereof.

33 ¶ [a]Another parable spake he unto them; The kingdom of heaven is like unto leaven, which a woman took, and hid in three [1]measures of meal, till the whole was leavened.

34 [a]All these *things* spake Jesus unto the multitude in parables; and without a parable spake he not unto them:

35 That it might be fulfilled which was spoken by the prophet, saying, [a]I will open my mouth in parables; [b]I will utter *things which have been* kept secret from the foundation of the world.

Parable of the tares explained

36 ¶ Then Jesus sent the multitude away, and went into the house: and his disciples came unto him, saying, Declare unto us the parable of the tares of the field.

37 He answered and said unto them, He that soweth the good seed is the Son of man;

38 [a]The field is the world; the good seed are the children of the kingdom; but the tares are [b]the children of the wicked one;

39 The enemy that sowed them is the devil; [a]the harvest is the end of the world; and the reapers are *the* angels.

40 As therefore the tares are gathered and burnt in the fire; so shall it be in the end of this world.

41 The Son of man shall send forth his angels, [a]and they shall gather out of his kingdom all [1]things that offend, and them which do iniquity;

42 [a]And shall cast them into a furnace of fire: [b]there shall be wailing and gnashing of teeth.

43 [a]Then shall the righteous shine forth as the sun in the kingdom of their Father. [b]Who hath ears to hear, let him hear.

Further parables of the kingdom

44 ¶ Again, the kingdom of heaven is like unto treasure hid in a field; the which when a

13:30 [a]ch. 3:12
13:31 [a]Is. 2:2,3; Mic. 4:1; Mark 4:30; Luke 13:18
13:33 [a]Luke 13:20

13:33 [1]*The word in the Greek is a measure containing about a peck and a half, wanting a little more than a pint*
13:34 [a]Mark 4:33
13:35 [a]Ps. 78:2 [b]Rom. 16:25,26; 1 Cor. 2:7; Eph. 3:9; Col. 1:26
13:38 [a]ch. 24:14; 28:19; Mark 16:15; Luke 24:47; Rom. 10:18; Col. 1:6 [b]Gen. 3:15; John 8:44; Acts 13:10; 1 John 3:8
13:39 [a]Joel 3:13; Rev. 14:15
13:41 [1]Or, *scandals* [a]ch. 18:7; 2 Pet. 2:1,2
13:42 [a]ch. 3:12; Rev. 19:20; 20:10 [b]ver. 50; ch. 8:12
13:43 [a]Dan. 12:3; 1 Cor. 15:42,43,58 [b]ver. 9

13:24–30 See vv. 36–43 for the interpretation.
13:24 *The kingdom of heaven is likened unto.* This phrase introduces six of the seven parables in this chapter (all but the parable of the sower).
13:25 *tares.* Probably darnel, which looks very much like wheat while it is young, but can later be distinguished. This parable does not refer to unbelievers in the professing church. The field is the world (v. 38). Thus the people of the kingdom live side by side with the people of the evil one.
13:31–32 Although the kingdom will seem to have an insignificant beginning, it will eventually spread throughout the world.
‡13:32 *least of all seeds . . . greatest among herbs.* The mustard seed is not the smallest seed known today, but it was the smallest seed used by farmers and gardeners in the Holy Land, and under favorable conditions the plant could reach some ten feet in height. *a tree . . . the branches thereof.* This could be an allusion to Dan 4:21, suggesting that the kingdom of heaven will expand to world dominion and that people from all nations will find rest in it (cf. Dan 2:35,44–45; 7:27; Rev 11:15), or it could picture evil coming into the kingdom, since the birds in v. 4 are interpreted as "the wicked one" in v. 19.
‡13:33 In the Bible, leaven usually symbolizes that which is evil or unclean (see note on Mark 8:15). Here it could picture evil, or possibly be a is a symbol of growth. As leaven permeates a batch of dough, so the kingdom of heaven spreads through a person's life. Or it may signify the growth of the kingdom by the inner working of the Holy Spirit (using God's word).
13:35 *spoken by the prophet.* The quotation is from Ps 78, a psalm ascribed to Asaph, who according to 2 Chr 29:30 was a "seer" (prophet).
13:37 *Son of man.* See note on Mark 8:31.
‡13:42 *furnace of fire.* Often mentioned in connection with the final judgment in apocalyptic literature (see Rev 19:20; 20:14). Notice that the fire of the parable is clearly said to be fire in Christ's interpretation. *wailing and gnashing of teeth.* Occurs six times in Matthew's Gospel (8:12; here; 13:50; 22:13; 24:51; 25:30) and nowhere else in the NT.
13:44–46 These two parables teach the same truth: The kingdom is of such great value that one should be willing to give up all he has in order to gain it. Jesus did not imply that one can purchase the kingdom with money or good deeds.
‡13:44 *treasure hid in a field.* In ancient times it was common to hide treasure in the ground since there was no widespread equivalent of modern bank vaults for the safekeeping of funds—though there were "exchangers" (see Mat 25:27 and

man hath found, he hideth, and for joy thereof goeth and [a]selleth all that he hath, and [b]buyeth that field.

45 ¶ Again, the kingdom of heaven is like unto a merchant man, seeking goodly pearls:

46 Who, when he had found [a]one pearl of great price, went and sold all that he had, and bought it.

47 ¶ Again, the kingdom of heaven is like unto a net, *that was* cast into the sea, and [a]gathered of every kind:

48 Which, when it was full, they drew to shore, and sat down, and gathered the good into vessels, but cast the bad away.

49 So shall it be at the end of the world: the angels shall come forth, and [a]sever the wicked from among the just,

50 And shall cast them into the furnace of fire: there shall be wailing and gnashing of teeth.

51 ¶ Jesus saith unto them, Have ye understood all these *things?* They say unto him, Yea, Lord.

52 Then said he unto them, Therefore every scribe *which is* instructed unto the kingdom of heaven is like unto a man *that is* a householder, which bringeth forth out of his treasure [a]*things* new and old.

Jesus rejected at Nazareth

53 ¶ And it came to pass, *that* when Jesus had finished these parables, he departed thence.

54 [a]And when he was come into his own country, he taught them in their synagogue, insomuch that they were astonished, and said, Whence hath this *man* this wisdom, and *these* mighty works?

55 [a]Is not this the carpenter's son? is not his mother called Mary? and [b]his brethren, [c]James, and Joses, and Simon, and Judas?

56 And his sisters, are they not all with us? Whence then hath this *man* all these *things?*

57 And they [a]were offended in him. But Jesus said unto them, [b]A prophet is not without honour, save in his own country, and in his own house.

58 And [a]he did not many mighty works there, because of their unbelief.

Death of John the Baptist

14 At that time [a]Herod the tetrarch heard of the fame of Jesus,

2 And said unto his servants, This is John the Baptist; he is risen from the dead; and therefore mighty works [1]do shew forth themselves in him.

3 [a]For Herod had laid hold on John, and bound him, and put *him* in prison for Herodias' sake, his brother Philip's wife.

4 For John said unto him, [a]It is not lawful for thee to have her.

5 And when he would have put him to death, he feared the multitude, [a]because they counted him as a prophet.

6 But when Herod's birthday was kept, the daughter of Herodias danced [1]before them, and pleased Herod.

7 Whereupon he promised with an oath to give her whatsoever she would ask.

8 And she, being before instructed of her mother, said, Give me here John Baptist's head in a charger.

9 And the king was sorry: nevertheless for the oaths' sake, and them which sat with him at meat, he commanded *it* to be given *her.*

10 And he sent, and beheaded John in the prison.

11 And his head was brought in a charger, and given to the damsel: and she brought *it* to her mother.

12 And his disciples came, and took up the body, and buried it, and went and told Jesus.

13:44 [a]Phil. 3:7,8 [b]Is. 55:1; Rev. 3:18
13:46 [a]Prov. 2:4; 3:14,15; 8:10,19
13:47 [a]ch. 22:10
13:49 [a]ch. 25:32
13:52 [a]Sol. 7:13
13:54 [a]ch. 2:23; Mark 6:1; Luke 4:16
13:55 [a]Is. 49:7; Mark 6:3; Luke 3:23; John 6:42 [b]ch. 12:46 [c]Mark 15:40
13:57 [a]ch. 11:6; Mark 6:3,4 [b]Luke 4:24; John 4:44
13:58 [a]Mark 6:5,6
14:1 [a]Mark 6:14; Luke 9:7
14:2 [1]Or, *are wrought by him*
14:3 [a]Mark 6:17; Luke 3:19,20
14:4 [a]Lev. 18:16; 20:21
14:5 [a]ch. 21:26; Luke 20:6
14:6 [1][Gr. *in the midst*]

note). Sometimes one unexpectedly stumbles across the gospel message, without searching for it, as with finding this treasure.

‡13:45 *seeking goodly pearls.* The pearl was found after a diligent search, in contrast to the treasure.

13:47–51 The parable of the net teaches the same general lesson as the parable of the tares: There will be a final separation of the righteous and the wicked. The parable of the tares also emphasizes that we are not to try to make such a separation now and that this is entirely the Lord's business (vv. 28–30, 41–42).

13:53 Concludes a teaching section and introduces a narrative section (cf. 7:28–29).

13:54 *his own country.* Nazareth (see note on 2:23). *he taught them in their synagogue.* See note on Mark 1:21.

‡13:55 *carpenter's son.* The word translated "carpenter" could mean "stonemason." See note on Mark 6:3. Joseph may or may not have been living at the time of this incident. *brethren.* Sons born to Joseph and Mary after the virgin birth of Jesus (see note on Luke 8:19).

13:58 *unbelief.* The close relationship between faith and miracles is stressed in Matthew's Gospel (cf. 8:10,13; 9:2,22,28–29).

14:1 *tetrarch.* The ruler of a fourth part of a region. Herod the tetrarch (Herod Antipas) was one of several sons of Herod the Great. When Herod the Great died, his kingdom was divided among three of his sons (see pp. 1355, 1451). Herod Antipas ruled over Galilee and Perea (4 B.C.–A.D. 39). Matthew correctly refers to him as tetrarch here, as Luke regularly does (Luke 3:19; 9:7; Acts 13:1). But in v. 9 Matthew calls him "king"—as Mark also does (Mark 6:14)—because that was his popular title among the Galileans, as well as in Rome.

14:2 *John . . . risen from the dead.* See note on Mark 6:16.

14:3 *Herodias.* A granddaughter of Herod the Great. First she married her uncle, Herod Philip (Herod the Great also had another son named Philip), who lived in Rome. While a guest in their home, Herod Antipas persuaded Herodias to leave her husband for him. Marriage to one's brother's wife, while the brother was still living, was forbidden by the Mosaic law (Lev 18:16). *Philip.* The son of Herod the Great and Mariamne, the daughter of Simon the high priest, and thus a half-brother of Herod Antipas, born to Malthace (see chart, p. 1355).

14:6 *the daughter of Herodias.* Salome, according to Josephus. She later married her granduncle, the other Philip (son of Herod the Great), who ruled the northern territories (Luke 3:1). At this time Salome was a young woman of marriageable age. Her dance was undoubtedly lascivious, and the performance pleased both Herod and his guests.

14:8 *charger.* A flat wooden dish on which meat was served.

The five thousand fed

13 ¶ [a]When Jesus heard *of it,* he departed thence by ship into a desert place apart: and when the people had heard *thereof,* they followed him on foot out of the cities.

14 And Jesus went forth, and saw a great multitude, and [a]was moved with compassion toward them, and he healed their sick.

15 [a]And when it was evening, his disciples came to him, saying, *This* is a desert place, and the time is now past; send the multitude away, that they may go into the villages, and buy themselves victuals.

16 But Jesus said unto them, They need not depart; give ye them to eat.

17 And they say unto him, We have here but five loaves, and two fishes.

18 He said, Bring them hither to me.

19 And he commanded the multitude to sit down on the grass, and took the five loaves, and the two fishes, and looking up to heaven, [a]he blessed, and brake, and gave the loaves to *his* disciples, and the disciples to the multitude.

20 And they did all eat, and were filled: and they took up of the fragments that remained twelve baskets full.

21 And they that had eaten were about five thousand men, beside women and children.

Jesus walks on the sea

22 ¶ And straightway Jesus constrained his disciples to get into a ship, and to go before him unto the other side, while he sent the multitudes away.

23 [a]And when he had sent the multitudes away, he went up into a mountain apart to pray: [b]and when the evening was come, he was there alone.

24 But the ship was now in the midst of the sea, tossed with waves: for the wind was contrary.

25 And in the fourth watch of the night Jesus went unto them, walking on the sea.

26 And when the disciples saw him [a]walking on the sea, they were troubled, saying, It is a spirit; and they cried out for fear.

14:13 [a]ch. 10:23; 12:15; Mark 6:32; Luke 9:10; John 6:1,2
14:14 [a]ch. 9:36; Mark 6:34
14:15 [a]Mark 6:35; Luke 9:12; John 6:5
14:19 [a]ch. 15:36
14:23 [a]Mark 6:46 [b]John 6:16
14:26 [a]Job 9:8

14:30 [1]Or, *strong*
14:33 [a]Ps. 2:7; ch. 16:16; 26:63; Mark 1:1; Luke 4:41; John 1:49; 6:69; 11:27; Acts 8:37; Rom. 1:4
14:34 [a]Mark 6:53
14:36 [a]ch. 9:20; Mark 3:10; Luke 6:19; Acts 19:12
15:1 [a]Mark 7:1
15:2 [a]Mark 7:5
15:4 [a]Ex. 20:12; Lev. 19:3; Deut. 5:16; Prov. 23:22; Eph. 6:2 [b]Ex. 21:17; Lev. 20:9; Deut. 27:16; Prov. 20:20; 30:17
15:5 [a]Mark 7:11,12

27 But straightway Jesus spake unto them, saying, Be of good cheer; it is I, be not afraid.

28 And Peter answered him and said, Lord, if it be thou, bid me come unto thee on the water.

29 And he said, Come. And when Peter was come down out of the ship, he walked on the water, to go to Jesus.

30 But when he saw the wind [1]boysterous, he was afraid; and beginning to sink, he cried, saying, Lord, save me.

31 And immediately Jesus stretched forth *his* hand, and caught him, and said unto him, O thou of little faith, wherefore didst thou doubt?

32 And when they were come into the ship, the wind ceased.

33 Then they that were in the ship came and worshipped him, saying, Of a truth [a]thou art the Son of God.

34 ¶ [a]And when they were gone over, they came into the land of Gennesaret.

35 And when the men of that place had knowledge of him, they sent out into all that country round about, and brought unto him all that were diseased;

36 And besought him that they might only touch the hem of his garment: and [a]as many as touched were made perfectly whole.

What defiles a man

15 Then [a]came to Jesus scribes and Pharisees, which were of Jerusalem, saying,

2 [a]Why do thy disciples transgress the tradition of the elders? for they wash not their hands when they eat bread.

3 But he answered and said unto them, Why do you also transgress the commandment of God by your tradition?

4 For God commanded, saying, [a]Honour thy father and mother: and, [b]He that curseth father or mother, let him die the death.

5 But ye say, Whosoever shall say to *his* father or *his* mother, [a]*It is* a gift, *by* whatsoever thou mightest be profited by me;

14:13–21 See Mark 6:32–44; Luke 9:10–17; John 6:1–13 and notes.

14:21 *beside women and children.* Matthew alone notes this. He was writing to the Jews, who did not permit women and children to eat with men in public. So they were in a place by themselves.

‡14:22 *constrained.* The Greek word used here is strong. It means "to compel" and suggests a crisis. John records that after the miracle of the loaves and fish the crowds "would come and take him by force, to make him a king" (6:15). This involved a complete misunderstanding of the mission of Jesus. The disciples may have been caught up in the enthusiasm and needed to be removed from the area quickly (cf. 16:5–12).

‡14:23 *to pray.* Matthew speaks of Jesus praying fewer times than does Luke, who emphasizes Jesus' humanity. Besides here in Gethsemane (cf. 26:36–46), and on the cross (27:46), Jesus thanked the Father for the provision both for the 5,000 (14:19) and the 4,000 (15:36).

14:25 *fourth watch.* 3:00–6:00 A.M. According to Roman reckoning the night was divided into four watches: (1) 6:00–9:00 P.M., (2) 9:00–midnight, (3) midnight–3:00 A.M. and (4) 3:00–6:00 A.M. (see note on Mark 13:35). The Jews had only three watches during the night: (1) sunset–10:00 P.M., (2) 10:00 P.M.–2:00 A.M. and (3) 2:00 A.M.–sunrise (see Judg 7:19; 1 Sam 11:11). *walking on the sea.* See note on Mark 6:48.

14:34 *Gennesaret.* Either the narrow plain, about four miles long and less than two miles wide, on the west side of the sea of Galilee near the north end (north of Magdala), or a town in the plain. The plain was considered a garden spot of the Holy Land, fertile and well watered.

14:36 *touch the hem of his garment.* See note on Mark 5:28.

15:2 *the tradition of the elders.* After the Babylonian captivity, the Jewish rabbis began to make meticulous rules and regulations governing the daily life of the people. These were interpretations and applications of the law of Moses, handed down from generation to generation. In Jesus' day this "tradition of the elders" was in oral form. It was not until C. A.D. 200 that it was put into writing in the Mishnah. *wash.* See Mark 7:1–4.

6 And honour not his father or his mother,
he shall be free. Thus have ye made the commandment of God of none effect by your tradition.
7 *Ye* [a]hypocrites, well did Esaias prophesy
of you, saying,
8 [a]This people draweth nigh unto me with
their mouth, and honoureth me with *their*
lips; but their heart is far from me.
9 But in vain they do worship me, [a]teach-
ing for doctrines the commandments of men.
10 ¶ [a]And he called the multitude, and said
unto them, Hear, and understand:
11 [a]Not that which goeth into the mouth
defileth a man; but that which cometh out of
the mouth, this defileth a man.
12 Then came his disciples, and said unto
him, Knowest thou that the Pharisees were offended, after they heard *this* saying?
13 But he answered and said, [a]Every plant,
which my heavenly Father hath not planted,
shall be rooted up.
14 Let them alone: [a]they be blind leaders
of the blind. And if the blind lead the blind,
both shall fall into the ditch.
15 [a]Then answered Peter and said unto
him, Declare unto us this parable.
16 And Jesus said, [a]Are ye also yet without
understanding?
17 Do not ye yet understand, that [a]whatso-
ever entereth in at the mouth goeth into the
belly, and is cast out into the draught?
18 But [a]those *things* which proceed out of
the mouth come forth from the heart; and they
defile the man.
19 [a]For out of the heart proceed evil
thoughts, murders, adulteries, fornications,
thefts, false witness, blasphemies:
20 These are *the things* which defile a
man: but to eat with unwashen hands defileth
not a man.

The faith of a Canaanite woman

21 ¶ [a]Then Jesus went thence, and departed into the coasts of Tyre and Sidon.
22 And behold, a woman of Canaan came
out of the same coasts, and cried unto him,
saying, Have mercy on me, O Lord, *thou* Son
of David; my daughter is grievously vexed
with a devil.
23 But he answered her not a word. And
his disciples came and besought him, saying,
Send her away; for she crieth after us.

15:7 [a]Mark 7:6
15:8 [a]Is. 29:13; Ezek. 33:31
15:9 [a]Is. 29:13; Col. 2:18-22; Tit. 1:14
15:10 [a]Mark 7:14
15:11 [a]Acts 10:15; Rom. 14:14,17,20; 1 Tim. 4:4; Tit. 1:15
15:13 [a]John 15:2; 1 Cor. 3:12
15:14 [a]Is 9:16; Mal. 2:8; ch. 23:16; Luke 6:39
15:15 [a]Mark 7:17
15:16 [a]ch. 16:9; Mark 7:18
15:17 [a]1 Cor. 6:13
15:18 [a]Jas. 3:6
15:19 [a]Gen. 6:5; 8:21; Prov. 6:14; Jer. 17:9; Mark 7:21
15:21 [a]Mark 7:24
15:24 [a]ch. 10:5,6
15:26 [a]ch. 7:6; Phil. 3:2
15:29 [a]Mark 7:31 [b]ch. 4:18
15:30 [a]Is. 35:5,6; ch. 11:5; Luke 7:22
15:32 [a]Mark 8:1
15:33 [a]2 Ki. 4:43
15:36 [a]ch. 14:19 [b]1 Sam. 9:13; Luke 22:19
15:39 [a]Mark 8:10

24 But he answered and said, [a]I am not sent
but unto the lost sheep of the house of Israel.
25 Then came she and worshipped him,
saying, Lord, help me.
26 But he answered and said, It is not meet
to take the children's bread, and to cast *it* to
[a]dogs.
27 And she said, Truth, Lord: yet the dogs
eat of the crumbs which fall from their masters' table.
28 Then Jesus answered and said unto her,
O woman, great *is* thy faith: be it unto thee
even as thou wilt. And her daughter was made
whole from that *very* hour.
29 [a]And Jesus departed from thence, and
came nigh [b]unto the sea of Galilee; and went
up into a mountain, and sat down there.
30 [a]And great multitudes came unto him,
having with them *those that were* lame, blind,
dumb, maimed, and many others, and cast
them *down* at Jesus' feet; and he healed them:
31 Insomuch that the multitude wondered,
when they saw the dumb to speak, the maimed
to be whole, the lame to walk, and the blind to
see: and they glorified the God of Israel.

The four thousand fed

32 ¶ [a]Then Jesus called his disciples unto
him, and said, I have compassion on the multitude, because they continue with me now
three days, and have nothing to eat: and I will
not send them away fasting, lest they faint in
the way.
33 [a]And his disciples say unto him,
Whence should we have so much bread in the
wilderness, as to fill so great a multitude?
34 And Jesus saith unto them, How many
loaves have ye? And they said, Seven, and a
few little fishes.
35 And he commanded the multitude to sit
down on the ground.
36 And [a]he took the seven loaves and the
fishes, and [b]gave thanks, and brake *them,* and
gave to his disciples, and the disciples to the
multitude.
37 And they did all eat, and were filled:
and they took up of the broken *meat* that was
left seven baskets full.
38 And they that did eat were four thousand men, beside women and children.
39 ¶ [a]And he sent away the multitude, and
took ship, and came into the coasts of Magdala.

15:5–6 See notes on Mark 7:11,13.

15:7–20 See Mark 7:6–23 and notes.

15:21 *Tyre.* See note on Mark 7:24. *Sidon.* About 25 miles north of Tyre.

‡15:22 *a woman of Canaan.* A term found many times in the OT but only here in the NT. In NT times there was no country known as Canaan. Some think this was the Semitic manner of referring to the people of Phoenicia at this time. Mark says the woman was "a Greek, a Syrophenician" (7:26).

15:26 *children's.* "The lost sheep of the house of Israel" (v. 24). *dogs.* The Greek says "little dogs," meaning a pet dog in the home, and Jesus' point was that the gospel was to be given first to Jews. The woman understood Jesus' implication and was willing to settle for "crumbs." Jesus rewarded her faith (v. 28).

15:27 *Truth, Lord.* See note on Mark 7:28.

15:29–39 See Mark 7:31–8:10 and notes.

‡15:37 The feeding of the 5,000 is recorded in all four Gospels, but the feeding of the 4,000 is only in Matthew and Mark. The 12 baskets mentioned in the feeding of the 5,000 were possibly for the 12 apostles. Some think Jesus gave the extra food to the little boy. The seven baskets mentioned here were possibly larger.

‡15:39 *Magdala.* The home of Mary Magdalene. Mark (8:10) has "Dalmanutha."

Pharisees ask for a sign

16 The [a]Pharisees also with the Sadducees came, and tempting desired
him that *he* would shew them a sign from
heaven.
2 He answered and said unto them, When
it is evening, ye say, *It will be* fair weather: for
the sky is red.
3 And in the morning, *It will be* foul weather to day: for the sky is red and lowring. O *ye*
hypocrites, ye can discern the face of the sky;
but can ye not *discern* the signs of the times?
4 [a]A wicked and adulterous generation
seeketh after a sign; and there shall no sign be
given unto it, but the sign of the prophet
Jonas. And he left them, and departed.
5 ¶ And [a]when his disciples were come to
the other side, they had forgotten to take
bread.
6 Then Jesus said unto them, [a]Take heed
and beware of the leaven of the Pharisees and
of the Sadducees.
7 And they reasoned among themselves,
saying, *It is* because we have taken no bread.
8 *Which* when Jesus perceived, he said
unto them, O ye of little faith, why reason ye
among yourselves, because ye have brought no
bread?
9 [a]Do ye not yet understand, neither remember the five loaves of the five thousand,
and how many baskets ye took up?
10 [a]Neither the seven loaves of the four
thousand, and how many baskets ye took up?
11 How *is it that* ye do not understand that
I spake *it* not to you concerning bread, that *ye*
should beware of the leaven of the Pharisees
and *of the* Sadducees?
12 Then understood they how that he bade
them not beware of the leaven of bread, but of
the doctrine of the Pharisees and *of the* Sadducees.

Peter's confession of faith

13 ¶ When Jesus came into the coasts of
Cesarea Philippi, he asked his disciples, saying,
[a]Whom do men say that I the Son of man am?
14 And they said, [a]Some *say that thou art*
John the Baptist: some, Elias; and others, Jere-
mias, or one of the prophets.
15 He saith unto them, But whom say ye
that I am?
16 And Simon Peter answered and said,
[a]Thou art the Christ, the Son of the living
God.
17 And Jesus answered and said unto him,
Blessed art thou, Simon Bar-jona: [a]for flesh
and blood hath not revealed *it* unto thee, but
[b]my Father which is in heaven.
18 And I say also unto thee, That [a]thou art
Peter, and [b]upon this rock I will build my
church; and [c]the gates of hell shall not prevail
against it.
19 [a]And I will give unto thee the keys of
the kingdom of heaven: and whatsoever thou
shalt bind on earth shall be bound in heaven:
and whatsoever thou shalt loose on earth shall
be loosed in heaven.
20 [a]Then charged he his disciples that they
should tell no *man* that he was Jesus the
Christ.

16:1 [a]ch. 12:38; Mark 8:11; Luke 11:16; 12:54-56; 1 Cor. 1:22
16:4 [a]ch. 12:39
16:5 [a]Mark 8:14
16:6 [a]Luke 12:1
16:9 [a]ch. 14:17; John 6:9
16:10 [a]ch. 15:34
16:13 [a]Mark 8:27; Luke 9:18
16:14 [a]ch. 14:2; Luke 9:7-9
16:16 [a]ch. 14:33; Mark 8:29; Luke 9:20; John 6:69; 11:27; Acts 8:37; 9:20; Heb. 1:2,5; 1 John 4:15
16:17 [a]Eph. 2:8 [b]1 Cor. 2:10; Gal. 1:16
16:18 [a]John 1:42 [b]Eph. 2:20; Rev. 21:14 [c]Job 38:17; Ps. 9:13; 107:18; Is. 38:10
16:19 [a]ch. 18:18; John 20:23
16:20 [a]ch. 17:9; Luke 9:21

16:1 *sign from heaven.* See note on Mark 8:11.

16:4 *the sign of the prophet Jonas.* See 12:39–40 and note on Luke 11:30.

16:6 *leaven of the Pharisees and of the Sadducees.* See v. 12. Also see notes on 3:7; Mark 2:16; 8:15; 12:18.

16:12 Matthew often explains the meaning of Jesus' words (cf. 17:13).

‡16:13 *Cesarea Philippi.* To be distinguished from the magnificent city of Caesarea, which Herod the Great had built on the coast of the Mediterranean. Caesarea Philippi, rebuilt by Herod's son Philip (who named it after Tiberius Caesar and himself), was 25 miles north of the sea of Galilee, near the slopes of mount Hermon. Originally it was called Paneas (the ancient name survives today as Banias) in honor of the Greek god Pan, whose shrine was located there. The region was especially pagan. *Son of man.* See note on Mark 8:31.

‡16:16 *Christ.* Or *Messiah;* also in v. 20. Both mean "the Anointed One." The OT equivalent (*Messiah*) is used of anyone who was anointed with the holy oil, such as the priests and kings of Israel (e.g., Ex 29:7,21; 1 Sam 10;1,6; 16:13; 2 Sam 1:14,16). The word carries the idea of being chosen by God, consecrated to His service, and endued with His power to accomplish the assigned task. Toward the end of the OT period the word assumed a special meaning. It denoted the ideal king anointed and empowered by God to rescue His people from their enemies and establish His righteous kingdom (Dan 9:25–26). The ideas that clustered around the title *Messiah* tended to be political and national in nature. Probably for that reason Jesus seldom used the term. Jesus did, however, on occasion acknowledge Himself as Messiah (cf. Mark 8:27–30; 14:61–63; John 4:25–26).

16:18 *Peter . . . rock . . . church.* In the Greek "Peter" is *petros* ("detached stone") and "rock" is *petra* ("bedrock"). Several interpretations have been given to these words. The "bedrock" on which the church is built is (1) Christ; (2) Peter's confession of faith in Jesus as the Messiah (v. 16); (3) Christ's teachings—one of the great emphases of Matthew's Gospel; (4) Peter himself, understood in terms of his role on the day of Pentecost (Acts 2), the Cornelius incident (Acts 10) and his leadership among the apostles. Eph 2:20 indicates that the church is "built on the foundation of the apostles and prophets." *church.* In the Gospels this word is used only by Matthew (here and twice in 18:17). In the Septuagint it is used for the congregation of Israel. In Greek circles of Jesus' day it indicated the assembly of free, voting citizens in a city (cf. Acts 19:32,39,41). *hell.* The Greek name for the place of departed spirits, generally equivalent to the Hebrew *Sheol* (see note on Gen 37:35). The "gates of hell" may mean the "powers of death," i.e., all forces opposed to Christ and His kingdom (but see note on Job 17:16).

16:19 *keys.* Perhaps Peter used these keys on the day of Pentecost (Acts 2) when he announced that the door of the kingdom was unlocked to Jews and proselytes and later when he acknowledged that it was also opened to Gentiles (Acts 10). *bind . . . loose.* Not authority to determine, but to announce, guilt or innocence (see 18:18 and the context there; cf. Acts 5:3,9).

16:20 *that they should tell no man.* Because of the false concepts of the Jews, who looked for an exclusively national and political Messiah, Jesus told His disciples not to publicize Peter's confession, lest it precipitate a revolution against Rome (see note on 8:4).

Future events foretold

21 ¶ From that time forth began Jesus [a]to shew unto his disciples, how that he must go unto Jerusalem, and suffer many *things* of the elders and chief priests and scribes, and be killed, and be raised *again* the third day.

22 Then Peter took him, and began to rebuke him, saying, [1]Be it far from thee, Lord: this shall not be unto thee.

23 But he turned, and said unto Peter, Get thee behind me, [a]Satan: [b]thou art an offence unto me: for thou savourest not the *things* that be of God, but *those* that be of men.

24 [a]Then said Jesus unto his disciples, If any *man* will come after me, let him deny himself, and take up his cross, and follow me.

25 For [a]whosoever will save his life shall lose it: and whosoever will lose his life for my sake shall find it.

26 For what is a man profited, if he shall gain the whole world, and lose his own soul? or [a]what shall a man give in exchange for his soul?

27 For [a]the Son of man shall come in the glory of his Father [b]with his angels: [c]and then he shall reward every man according to his works.

28 Verily I say unto you, [a]There be some standing here, which shall not taste of death, till they see the Son of man coming in his kingdom.

The transfiguration

17 And [a]after six days Jesus taketh Peter, James, and John his brother, and bringeth them up into a high mountain apart,

2 And was transfigured before them: and his face did shine as the sun, and his raiment was white as the light.

3 And behold, there appeared unto them Moses and Elias talking with him.

4 Then answered Peter, and said unto Jesus, Lord, it is good for us to be here: if thou wilt, let us make here three tabernacles: one for thee, and one for Moses, and one for Elias.

5 [a]While he yet spake, behold, a bright cloud overshadowed them: and behold a voice out of the cloud, which said, [b]This is my beloved Son, [c]in whom I am well pleased; [d]hear ye him.

6 [a]And when the disciples heard *it,* they fell on their face, and were sore afraid.

7 And Jesus came and [a]touched them, and said, Arise, and be not afraid.

8 And when they had lift up their eyes, they saw no *man,* save Jesus only.

9 ¶ And as they came down from the mountain, [a]Jesus charged them, saying, Tell the vision to no *man,* until the Son of man be risen again from the dead.

10 And his disciples asked him, saying, [a]Why then say the scribes that Elias must first come?

11 And Jesus answered and said unto them, Elias truly shall first come, and [a]restore all *things.*

12 [a]But I say unto you, That Elias is come already, and they knew him not, but [b]have done unto him whatsoever they listed. Likewise [c]shall also the Son of man suffer of them.

13 [a]Then the disciples understood that he spake unto them of John the Baptist.

16:21 [a]ch. 20:17; Mark 8:31; 9:31; 10:33; Luke 9:22; 18:31; 24:6,7
16:22 [1][Gr. *Pity thyself*]
16:23 [a]See 2 Sam. 19:22 [b]Rom. 8:7
16:24 [a]Mark 8:34; Luke 9:23; 14:27; Acts 14:22; 1 Thes. 3:3; 2 Tim. 3:12
16:25 [a]Luke 17:33; John 12:25
16:26 [a]Ps. 49:7,8
16:27 [a]ch. 26:64; Mark 8:38; Luke 9:26 [b]Dan. 7:10; Zech. 14:5; ch. 25:31; Jude 14 [c]Job 34:11; Ps. 62:12; Prov. 24:12; Jer. 17:10; 32:19; Rom. 2:6; 1 Cor. 3:8; 2 Cor. 5:10; 1 Pet. 1:17; Rev. 2:23; 22:12
16:28 [a]Mark 9:1; Luke 9:27
17:1 [a]Mark 9:2; Luke 9:28
17:5 [a]2 Pet. 1:17 [b]ch. 3:17; Mark 1:11; Luke 3:22 [c]Is. 42:1 [d]Deut. 18:15,19; Acts 3:22,23
17:6 [a]2 Pet. 1:18
17:7 [a]Dan. 8:18; 9:21; 10:10,18
17:9 [a]ch. 16:20; Mark 8:30; 9:9
17:10 [a]Mal. 4:5; ch. 11:14; Mark 9:11
17:11 [a]Mal. 4:6; Luke 1:16,17; Acts 3:21
17:12 [a]ch. 11:14; Mark 9:12,13 [b]ch. 14:3,10 [c]ch. 16:21
17:13 [a]ch. 11:14

16:21 *began.* The beginning of a new emphasis in Jesus' ministry. Instead of teaching the crowds in parables, He concentrated on preparing the disciples for His coming suffering and death.

16:23 *Satan.* A loanword from Hebrew, meaning "adversary" or "accuser" (see note on Rev 2:9).

16:24 *take up his cross.* See notes on 10:38; Mark 8:34.

16:27 *Son of man.* See note on Mark 8:31. *shall come.* The *parousia,* the eschatological coming of Christ.

16:28 There are two main interpretations of this verse: 1. It is a prediction of the transfiguration, which happened a week later (17:1) and which demonstrated that Jesus will return in His Father's glory (16:27). 2. It refers to the Son of man's authority and kingly reign in His post-resurrection church. Some of His disciples will witness—even participate in—this as described in the book of Acts. The context seems to favor the first view. See note on 2 Pet 1:16.

17:1–9 The transfiguration was: (1) a revelation of the glory of the Son of God, a glory hidden now but to be fully revealed when He returns; (2) a confirmation of the difficult teaching given to the disciples at Caesarea Philippi (16:13–20); and (3) a beneficial experience for the disciples, who were discouraged after having been reminded so recently of Jesus' impending suffering and death (16:21). See notes on Mark 9:2–7; Luke 9:28–35.

17:1 *six days.* Mark also says "six days" (Mark 9:2), counting just the days between Peter's confession and the transfiguration, whereas Luke, counting all the days involved, says, "about an eight days" (Luke 9:28). *Peter, James, and John.* These three disciples had an especially close relationship to Jesus (see 26:37; Mark 5:37). *high mountain.* Its identity is unknown. However, the reference to Caesarea Philippi (16:13) may suggest that it was mount Hermon, which was just northeast of Caesarea Philippi (see note on Luke 9:28). *apart.* Luke adds "to pray" (Luke 9:28).

17:2 *was transfigured.* His appearance changed. The three disciples saw Jesus in His glorified state (see John 17:5; 2 Pet 1:17).

17:3 *Moses and Elias* [i.e. "Elijah"]. Moses appears as the representative of the old covenant and the promise of salvation, which was soon to be fulfilled in the death of Jesus. Elijah appears as the appointed restorer of all things (Mal 4:5–6; Mark 9:11–13). Luke 9:31 says that they talked about Christ's death. See note on Luke 9:30.

17:4 *three tabernacles.* See notes on Mark 9:5; Luke 9:33.

17:5 *them.* Jesus, Moses and Elijah. *This is my beloved Son, in whom I am well pleased.* The same words spoken from heaven at Jesus' baptism (3:17). No mere man, but the very Son of God, was transfigured.

17:6 *sore afraid.* Primarily with a sense of awe at the presence and majesty of God.

17:10 The traditional eschatology of the teachers of the law, based on Mal 4:5–6, held that Elijah must appear before the coming of the Messiah. The disciples reasoned that if Jesus really was the Messiah, as the transfiguration proved Him to be, why had not Elijah appeared?

‡17:12 *Likewise.* As John the Baptist was not recognized, but was killed, so Jesus would be rejected and killed.

17:13 See note on 16:12.

A demoniac boy healed

14 ¶ [a]And when they were come to the multitude, there came to him a *certain* man, kneeling down to him, and saying,

15 Lord, have mercy on my son: for he is lunatick, and sore vexed: for ofttimes he falleth into the fire, and oft into the water.

16 And I brought him to thy disciples, and they could not cure him.

17 Then Jesus answered and said, O faithless and perverse generation, how long shall I be with you? how long shall I suffer you? bring him hither to me.

18 And Jesus rebuked the devil; and he departed out of him: and the child was cured from that *very* hour.

19 Then came the disciples to Jesus apart, and said, Why could not we cast him out?

20 And Jesus said unto them, Because of your unbelief: for verily I say unto you, [a]If ye have faith as a grain of mustard seed, ye shall say unto this mountain, Remove hence to yonder place; and it shall remove; and nothing shall be unpossible unto you.

21 Howbeit this kind goeth not out but by prayer and fasting.

22 ¶ [a]And while they abode in Galilee, Jesus said unto them, The Son of man shall be betrayed into the hands of men:

23 And they shall kill him, and the third day he shall be raised *again*. And they were exceeding sorry.

The money in the fish's mouth

24 ¶ And [a]when they were come to Capernaum, they that received [b][1]tribute money came to Peter, and said, Doth not your master pay [1]tribute?

25 He saith, Yes. And when he was come into the house, Jesus prevented him, saying, What thinkest thou, Simon? of whom do the kings of the earth take custom or tribute? of their own children, or of strangers?

26 Peter saith unto him, Of strangers. Jesus saith unto him, Then are the children free.

27 Notwithstanding, lest we should offend them, go thou to the sea, and cast a hook, and take up the fish that first cometh up; and when thou hast opened his mouth, thou shalt find [1]a piece of money: that take, and give unto them for me and thee.

The greatest in the kingdom

18 At [a]the same time came the disciples unto Jesus, saying, Who is the greatest in the kingdom of heaven?

2 And Jesus called a little child unto *him*, and set him in the midst of them.

3 And said, Verily I say unto you, [a]Except ye be converted, and become as little children, ye shall not enter into the kingdom of heaven.

4 [a]Whosoever therefore shall humble himself as this little child, the same is greatest in the kingdom of heaven.

5 And [a]whoso shall receive one such little child in my name receiveth me.

6 [a]But whoso shall offend one of these little ones which believe in me, it were better for him that a millstone were hanged about his neck, and *that* he were drowned in the depth of the sea.

7 Woe unto the world because of offences: for [a]it must needs be that offences come; but [b]woe to that man by whom the offence cometh.

8 [a]Wherefore if thy hand or thy foot offend thee, cut them off, and cast *them* from thee: it is better for thee to enter into life halt or maimed, rather than having two hands or two feet to be cast into everlasting fire.

9 And if thine eye offend thee, pluck it out, and cast *it* from thee: it is better for thee to enter into life with one eye, rather than having two eyes to be cast into hell fire.

The parable of the lost sheep

10 ¶ Take heed that ye despise not one of these little ones; for I say unto you, That in heaven [a]their angels do always [b]behold the face of my Father which is in heaven.

11 [a]For the Son of man is come to save that which was lost.

12 [a]How think ye? if a man have an hundred sheep, and one of them be gone astray, doth he not leave the ninety and nine, and goeth into the mountains, and seeketh that which is gone astray?

13 And if so be that he find it, verily I say unto you, he rejoiceth more of that *sheep*, than of the ninety and nine which went not astray.

17:14 [a]Mark 9:14; Luke 9:37
17:20 [a]ch. 21:21; Mark 11:23; Luke 17:6; 1 Cor. 12:9; 13:2
17:22 [a]ch. 16:21; 20:17; Mark 8:31; 9:30,31; 10:33; Luke 9:22,44; 18:31; 24:6,7
17:24 [1]*Called in the original, didrachma, being in value fifteen pence* [a]Mark 9:33 [b]Ex. 30:13; 38:26
17:27 [1]*Or, a stater. It is half an ounce of silver, in value two shillings and six pence, after five shillings the ounce*
18:1 [a]Mark 9:33; Luke 9:46; 22:24
18:3 [a]Ps. 131:2; ch. 19:14; Mark 10:14; Luke 18:16; 1 Cor. 14:20; 1 Pet. 2:2
18:4 [a]ch. 20:27; 23:11
18:5 [a]ch. 10:42; Luke 9:48
18:6 [a]Mark 9:42; Luke 17:1,2
18:7 [a]Luke 17:1; 1 Cor. 11:19 [b]ch. 26:24
18:8 [a]ch. 5:29,30; Mark 9:43,45
18:10 [a]Ps. 34:7; Zech. 13:7; Heb. 1:14 [b]Esth. 1:14; Luke 1:19
18:11 [a]Luke 9:56; 19:10; John 3:17; 12:47
18:12 [a]Luke 15:4

17:18 Not all cases of lunacy were the result of demon possession, but this one was.
‡17:20 *mustard seed.* See 13:31–32 and notes. *say unto this mountain, Remove hence to yonder place.* A proverbial statement meaning to remove great difficulties (cf. Is 54:10; 1 Cor 13:2).
17:22 The second prediction of Christ's death, the first being in 16:21.
‡17:24 *tribute money.* The annual temple tax required of every male 20 years of age and older (Ex 30:13; 2 Chr 24:9; Neh 10:32). It was literally a double drachma, worth approximately two days' wages, and was used for the upkeep of the temple.
17:26 *Then are the children free.* The implication is that Peter and the rest of the disciples belonged to God's royal household, but unbelieving Jews did not (see 21:43).
18:1 *Who is the greatest . . . ?* See note on Luke 9:46.
18:3 *as little children.* Trusting and unpretentious.
18:6 *millstone.* Lit. "a millstone of a donkey," i.e., a millstone turned by a donkey—far larger and heavier than the small millstones (24:41) used by women each morning in their homes.
18:8–9 See note on 5:29–30.
‡18:10 *their angels.* Guardian angels not exclusively for children, but for God's people in general (Ps 34:7; 91:11; Heb 1:14). *do always behold.* Have constant access to God.
18:12–14 The parable of the lost sheep is also found in Luke 15:3–7. There it applies to unbelievers, here to believers. Jesus used the same parable to teach different truths in different situations.
18:12 *sheep.* See note on Luke 15:4.

14 *Even* so it is not the will of your Father which is in heaven, that one of these little ones should perish.

Sin and forgiveness

15 ¶ Moreover [a]if thy brother shall trespass against thee, go and tell him his fault between thee and him alone: if he shall hear thee, [b]thou hast gained thy brother.

16 But if he will not hear *thee, then* take with thee one or two more, that in [a]the mouth of two or three witnesses every word may be established.

17 And if he shall neglect to hear them, tell *it* unto the church: but if he neglect to hear the church, let him be unto thee as a [a]heathen *man* and a publican.

18 Verily I say unto you, [a]Whatsoever ye shall bind on earth shall be bound in heaven: and whatsoever ye shall loose on earth shall be loosed in heaven.

19 [a]Again I say unto you, That if two of you shall agree on earth as touching any thing that they shall ask, [b]it shall be done for them of my Father which is in heaven.

20 For where two or three are gathered together in my name, there am I in the midst of them.

Parable of the unforgiving servant

21 ¶ Then came Peter to him, and said, Lord, how oft shall my brother sin against me, and I forgive him? [a]till seven times?

22 Jesus saith unto him, I say not unto thee, Until seven times: [a]but, Until seventy times seven.

23 Therefore is the kingdom of heaven likened unto a certain king, which would take account of his servants.

24 And when he had begun to reckon, one was brought unto him, which ought him ten thousand [1]talents.

25 But forasmuch as he had not to pay, his lord commanded him [a]to be sold, and his wife, and children, and all that he had, and payment to be made.

26 The servant therefore fell down, and [1]worshipped him, saying, Lord, have patience with me, and I will pay thee all.

27 Then the lord of that servant was moved with compassion, and loosed him, and forgave him the debt.

28 But the same servant went out, and found one of his fellowservants, which ought him an hundred [1]pence: and he laid hands on him, and took *him* by the throat, saying, Pay me that thou owest.

29 And his fellowservant fell down at his feet, and besought him, saying, Have patience with me, and I will pay thee all.

30 And he would not: but went and cast him into prison, till he should pay the debt.

31 So when his fellowservants saw what was done, they were very sorry, and came and told unto their lord all that was done.

32 Then his lord, after that he had called him, said unto him, O *thou* wicked servant, I forgave thee all that debt, because thou desiredst me:

33 Shouldest not thou also have had compassion on thy fellowservant, even as I had pity on thee?

34 And his lord was wroth, and delivered him to the tormentors, till he should pay all that was due unto him.

35 [a]So likewise shall my heavenly Father do *also* unto you, if ye from your hearts forgive not every one his brother their trespasses.

Marriage and divorce

19 And it came to pass, [a]*that* when Jesus had finished these sayings, he departed from Galilee, and came into the coasts of Judea beyond Jordan;

2 [a]And great multitudes followed him; and he healed them there.

3 The Pharisees also came unto him, tempting him, and saying unto him, Is it lawful for a man to put away his wife for every cause?

4 And he answered and said unto them, Have ye not read, [a]that he which made *them* at the beginning made them male and female,

5 And said, [a]For this cause shall a man leave father and mother, and shall cleave to his wife: and [b]they twain shall be one flesh?

6 Wherefore they are no more twain, but

18:15 [a]Lev. 19:17; Luke 17:3 [b]Jas. 5:20; 1 Pet. 3:1
18:16 [a]Deut. 17:6; 19:15; John 8:17; 2 Cor. 13:1; Heb. 10:28
18:17 [a]Rom. 16:17; 1 Cor. 5:9; 2 Thes. 3:6,14; 2 John 10
18:18 [a]ch. 16:19; John 20:23; 1 Cor. 5:4
18:19 [a]ch. 5:24 [b]1 John 3:22; 5:14
18:21 [a]Luke 17:4
18:22 [a]ch. 6:14; Mark 11:25; Col. 3:13
18:24 [1]*A talent is 750 ounces of silver, which after five shillings the ounce is 187l. 10s.*
18:25 [a]2 Ki. 4:1; Neh. 5:8
18:26 [1]Or, *besought him*
18:28 [1]*The Roman penny is the eighth part of an ounce, which after five shillings the ounce is seven pence halfpenny*
18:35 [a]Prov. 21:13; ch. 6:12; Mark 11:26; Jas. 2:13
19:1 [a]Mark 10:1; John 10:40
19:2 [a]ch. 12:15
19:4 [a]Gen. 1:27; 5:2; Mal. 2:15
19:5 [a]Gen. 2:24; Mark 10:5-9; Eph. 5:31 [b]1 Cor. 6:16; 7:2

18:15 *brother.* A fellow believer.

‡18:17 *church.* The local congregation. Here and 16:18 are the only two places where the Gospels speak of the "church." The future tense of the verb indicates a future church. *heathen.* For the Jews this meant any non-Jewish person. *publican.* See note on 5:46. This verse establishes one basis for excommunication.

18:18 See note on 16:19.

18:22 *seventy times seven.* Or "seventy-seven times." In either case the sense is "times without number" or "as many times as necessary."

18:23 *kingdom of heaven.* See note on 3:2.

18:25 For this practice of selling into slavery see Ex 21:2; Lev 25:39; 2 Ki 4:1; Neh 5:5; Is 50:1.

18:35 *forgive.* The one main teaching of the parable.

19:1 *beyond Jordan.* The east side, known later as Transjordan or Perea and today simply as Jordan. Jesus now began ministering there (see note on Luke 13:22).

19:3 *Pharisees.* See note on Mark 2:16. *for every cause.* This last part of the question is not in the parallel passage in Mark (10:2). Matthew possibly included it because he was writing to the Jews, who were aware of the dispute between the schools of Shammai and Hillel over the interpretation of Deut 24:1–4. Shammai held that "some indecency" (Deut 24:1) meant "immorality" (Mat 19:9)—the only allowable cause for divorce. Hillel (c. 60 B.C.–A.D. 20) emphasized the preceding clause, "she finds no favor in his eyes." He would allow a man to divorce his wife if she did anything he disliked—even if she burned his food while cooking it. Jesus clearly took the side of Shammai (see v. 9), but only after first pointing back to God's original ideal for marriage in Gen 1:27; 2:24.

one flesh. What therefore God hath joined together, let not man put asunder.

7 They say unto him, [a]Why did Moses then command to give a writing of divorcement, and to put her away?

8 He saith unto them, Moses because of the hardness of your hearts suffered you to put away your wives: but from the beginning it was not so.

9 [a]And I say unto you, Whosoever shall put away his wife, except *it be* for fornication, and shall marry another, committeth adultery: and whoso marrieth her *which is* put away doth commit adultery.

10 His disciples say unto him, [a]If the case of the man be so with *his* wife, it is not good to marry.

11 But he said unto them, [a]All *men* cannot receive this saying, save *they* to whom it is given.

12 For there are *some* eunuchs, which were so born from *their* mother's womb: and there are *some* eunuchs, which were made eunuchs of men: and [a]there be eunuchs, which have made themselves eunuchs for the kingdom of heaven's sake. He that is able to receive *it,* let him receive *it.*

Jesus blesses the little children

13 ¶ [a]Then were there brought unto him little children, that he should put *his* hands on them, and pray: and the disciples rebuked them.

14 But Jesus said, Suffer little children, and forbid them not, to come unto me: for [a]of such is the kingdom of heaven.

15 And he laid *his* hands on them, and departed thence.

The rich young ruler

16 ¶ [a]And behold, one came and said unto him, [b]Good Master, what good *thing* shall I do, that I may have eternal life?

17 And he said unto him, Why callest thou me good? *there is* none good but one, *that is,* God: but if thou wilt enter into life, keep the commandments.

18 He saith unto him, Which? Jesus said, [a]Thou shalt do no murder, Thou shalt not commit adultery, Thou shalt not steal, Thou shalt not bear false witness,

19 [a]Honour thy father and *thy* mother: and, [b]Thou shalt love thy neighbour as thyself.

20 The young man saith unto him, All these *things* have I kept from my youth up: what lack I yet?

21 Jesus said unto him, If thou wilt be perfect, [a]go *and* sell that thou hast, and give to the poor, and thou shalt have treasure in heaven: and come *and* follow me.

22 But when the young man heard *that* saying, he went away sorrowful: for he had great possessions.

23 ¶ Then said Jesus unto his disciples, Verily I say unto you, That [a]a rich *man* shall hardly enter into the kingdom of heaven.

24 And again I say unto you, It is easier for a camel to go through the eye of a needle, than for a rich *man* to enter into the kingdom of God.

25 When his disciples heard *it,* they were exceedingly amazed, saying, Who then can be saved?

26 But Jesus beheld *them,* and said unto them, With men this is impossible; but [a]with God all *things* are possible.

The worker in the vineyard

27 ¶ Then answered Peter and said unto him, Behold, [a]we have forsaken all, and followed thee; what shall we have therefore?

28 And Jesus said unto them, Verily I say

19:7 [a]Deut. 24:1; ch. 5:31
19:9 [a]ch. 5:32; Mark 10:11; Luke 16:18; 1 Cor. 7:10
19:10 [a]Prov. 21:19
19:11 [a]1 Cor. 7:2,7,9,17
19:12 [a]1 Cor. 7:32; 9:5,15
19:13 [a]Mark 10:13; Luke 18:15
19:14 [a]ch. 18:3
19:16 [a]Mark 10:17; Luke 18:18
19:16 [b]Luke 10:25
19:18 [a]Ex. 20:13; Deut. 5:17
19:19 [a]ch. 15:4 [b]Lev. 19:18; ch. 22:39; Rom. 13:9; Gal. 5:14; Jas. 2:8
19:21 [a]ch. 6:20; Luke 12:33; 16:9; Acts 2:45; 4:34,35; 1 Tim. 6:18,19
19:23 [a]ch. 13:22; Mark 10:24; 1 Cor. 1:26; 1 Tim. 6:9
19:26 [a]Gen. 18:14; Job 42:2; Jer. 32:17; Zech. 8:6; Luke 1:37; 18:27
19:27 [a]Deut. 33:9; ch. 4:20; Luke 5:11

19:10–12 See 1 Cor 7:7–8,26,32–35.

19:11 *this saying.* The disciples' conclusion in v. 10: "it is not good to marry." Not everyone can accept this teaching because it is not meant for everyone. Jesus then gives three examples of persons for whom it is meant in v. 12.

19:12 *made themselves eunuchs for the kingdom of heaven's sake.* Those who have voluntarily adopted a celibate life-style in order to give themselves more completely to God's work. Under certain circumstances celibacy is recommended in Scripture (cf. 1 Cor 7:25–38), but it is never presented as superior to marriage.

19:14 *kingdom of heaven.* See note on 3:2. *of such is.* See note on Mark 10:14.

19:16 *one came.* See note on Mark 10:17. *what good thing shall I do . . . ?* The rich man was thinking in terms of righteousness by works. Jesus had to correct this misunderstanding first before answering the question more fully. *eternal life.* The first use of this term in Matthew's Gospel (see v. 29; 25:46). In John it occurs much more frequently, often taking the place of the term "kingdom of God (or heaven)" used in the Synoptics, which treat the following three expressions as synonymous: (1) eternal life (v. 16; Mark 10:17; Luke 18:18), (2) entering the kingdom of heaven (v. 23; cf. Mark 10:24; Luke 18:24) and (3) being saved (vv. 25–26; Mark 10:26–27; Luke 18:26–27).

19:17 *there is none good but one.* The good is not something to be done as meritorious in itself. God alone is good, and all other goodness derives from him—even the keeping of the commandments, which Jesus proceeded to enumerate (vv. 18–20). *if thou wilt enter into life, keep the commandments.* "To enter into life" is the same as "have eternal life" (v. 16). The requirement to "keep the commandments" is not to establish one's merit before God but is to be an expression of true faith. The Bible always teaches that salvation is a gift of God's grace received through faith (see Eph 2:8).

19:20 *All these things have I kept.* See note on Mark 10:20.

19:21 *perfect.* Greek *teleios,* "goal, end." His goal was eternal life, but wealth and lack of commitment stood in his way. *go and sell that thou hast.* In His listing of the commandments, Jesus omitted "Do not covet." This was the rich man's main problem and was preventing him from entering life (see note on Mark 10:21).

19:22 *he went away sorrowful.* See note on Mark 10:22.

19:23 *kingdom of heaven.* See note on 3:2.

19:24 *camel to go through the eye of a needle.* See note on Mark 10:25.

19:26 See note on Mark 10:27.

19:28 *Verily I say unto you.* See note on Mark 10:29. *Son of man.* See note on Mark 8:31. *judging.* Governing or ruling. The

unto you, That ye which have followed me, in the regeneration, when the Son of man shall sit in the throne of his glory, [a]ye also shall sit upon twelve thrones, judging the twelve tribes of Israel.

29 [a]And every one that hath forsaken houses, or brethren, or sisters, or father, or mother, or wife, or children, or lands, for my name's sake, shall receive an hundredfold, and shall inherit everlasting life.

30 [a]But many *that are* first shall be last; and *the* last *shall be* first.

20 For the kingdom of heaven is like unto a man *that is* a householder, which went out early in the morning to hire labourers into his vineyard.

2 And when he had agreed with the labourers for a [1]penny a day, he sent them into his vineyard.

3 And he went out about the third hour, and saw others standing idle in the marketplace,

4 And said unto them; Go ye also into the vineyard, and whatsoever is right I will give you. And they went their way.

5 Again he went out about the sixth and ninth hour, and did likewise.

6 And about the eleventh hour he went out, and found others standing idle, and saith unto them, Why stand ye here all the day idle?

7 They say unto him, Because no *man* hath hired us. He saith unto them, Go ye also into the vineyard; and whatsoever is right, *that* shall ye receive.

8 So when even was come, the lord of the vineyard saith unto his steward, Call the labourers, and give them *their* hire, beginning from the last unto the first.

9 And when they came that *were hired* about the eleventh hour, they received every man a penny.

10 But when the first came, they supposed that they should have received more; and they likewise received every man a penny.

11 And when they had received *it,* they murmured against the goodman of the house,

12 Saying, These last [1]have wrought *but* one hour, and thou hast made them equal unto us, which have borne the burden and heat of the day.

13 But he answered one of them, and said, Friend, I do thee no wrong: didst not thou agree with me for a penny?

14 Take *that* thine *is,* and go thy way: I will give unto this last, even as unto thee.

15 [a]Is it not lawful for me to do what I will with mine own? [b]Is thine eye evil, because I am good?

16 [a]So the last shall be first, and the first last: [b]for many be called, but few chosen.

Jesus foretells his death

17 ¶ [a]And Jesus going up to Jerusalem took the twelve disciples apart in the way, and said unto them,

18 [a]Behold, we go up to Jerusalem; and the Son of man shall be betrayed unto the chief priests and *unto the* scribes, and they shall condemn him to death,

19 [a]And shall deliver him to the Gentiles to mock, and to scourge, and to crucify *him:* and the third day he shall rise again.

The ambition of James and John

20 ¶ [a]Then came to him the mother of [b]Zebedee's children with her sons, worshipping *him,* and desiring a certain *thing* of him.

21 And he said unto her, What wilt thou? She saith unto him, Grant that these my two sons [a]may sit, the one on thy right hand, and the other on the left, in thy kingdom.

22 But Jesus answered and said, Ye know not what ye ask. Are ye able to drink *of* [a]the cup that I shall drink *of,* and to be baptized *with* [b]the baptism that I am baptized *with?* They say unto him, We are able.

23 And he saith unto them, [a]Ye shall drink indeed *of* my cup, and be baptized *with* the baptism that I am baptized *with:* but to sit on

19:28 [a]ch. 10:21; Luke 22:28-30; 1 Cor. 6:2; Rev. 2:26
19:29 [a]Mark 10:29,30; Luke 18:29,30
19:30 [a]ch. 20:16; 21:31,32; Mark 10:31; Luke 13:30
20:2 [1]*The Roman penny is the eighth part of an ounce, which after five shillings the ounce is seven pence halfpenny*
20:12 [1]Or, *have continued one hour* only
20:15 [a]Rom. 9:21 [b]Deut. 15:9; Prov. 23:6; ch. 6:23
20:16 [a]ch. 19:30 [b]ch. 22:14
20:17 [a]Mark 10:32; Luke 18:31; John 12:12
20:18 [a]ch. 16:21
20:19 [a]ch. 27:2; Mark 15:1,16; Luke 23:1; John 18:28; Acts 3:13
20:20 [a]Mark 10:35 [b]ch. 4:21
20:21 [a]ch. 19:28
20:22 [a]ch. 26:39,42; Mark 14:36; Luke 22:42; John 18:11 [b]Luke 12:50
20:23 [a]Acts 12:2; Rom. 8:17; 2 Cor. 1:7; Rev. 1:9

12 disciples will someday rule with Christ in his literal millennial kingdom on this earth (cf. Acts 1:6; cf. the OT "judge"; see Introduction to Judges: Title).

19:29 *shall receive an hundredfold.* Mark adds, "along with persecutions" (see note on Mark 10:30).

‡20:1–16 This parable is unique to Matthew. It may emphasize the sovereign graciousness and generosity of God extended to "latecomers" (the poor and the outcasts of society) into God's kingdom. It also is in answer to Peter's question in 19:27. Just serve and leave the rewards to God.

‡20:2 *a penny.* This coin, the denarius, was the usual daily wage of a common laborer. A Roman soldier also received one denarius a day.

20:3 *third hour.* 9:00 A.M.

20:5 *sixth and ninth hour.* Noon and 3:00 P.M. respectively.

20:6 *eleventh hour.* 5:00 P.M.

20:8 *when even was come.* Because farm workers were poor, the law of Moses required that they be paid at the end of each day (cf. Lev 19:13; Deut 24:14–15).

‡20:15 *Is thine eye evil.* Apparently the evil eye was associated with jealousy and envy (cf. 1 Sam 18:9).

20:17–19 See Mark 10:32–34; Luke 18:31–33 and notes.

20:19 *And shall deliver him to the Gentiles to mock, and to scourge, and to crucify him.* An additional statement in this third prediction of the passion. Jesus would not be killed by the Jews, which would have been by stoning, but would be crucified by the Romans. All three predictions include His resurrection on the third day (16:21; 17:23).

20:20 *mother of Zebedee's children.* Mark has "James and John, the two sons of Zebedee," asking the question (Mark 10:35–37), yet there is no contradiction. The three joined in making the petition.

20:21 *What wilt thou?* See note on Mark 10:35–36. *sit, the one on thy right hand, and the other on the left.* See note on Mark 10:37.

20:22 *drink of the cup.* A figure of speech meaning to "undergo" or "experience." Here the reference is to suffering (cf. 26:39). The same figure of speech is used in Jer 25:15; Ezek 23:32; Hab 2:16; Rev 14:10; 16:19; 18:6 for divine wrath or judgment. See note on Mark 10:38.

my right hand, and on my left, is not mine to [b]give, but *it shall be given to them* for whom it is prepared of my Father.

24 [a]And when the ten heard *it,* they were moved with indignation against the two brethren.

25 But Jesus called them unto *him,* and said, Ye know that the princes of the Gentiles exercise dominion over them, and they *that are* great exercise authority upon them.

26 But [a]it shall not be so among you: but [b]whosoever will be great among you, let him be your minister;

27 [a]And whosoever will be chief among you, let him be your servant:

28 [a]Even as the [b]Son of man came not to be ministered unto, [c]but to minister, and [d]to give his life a ransom [e]for many.

Healing of two blind men

29 ¶ [a]And as they departed from Jericho, a great multitude followed him.

30 And behold, [a]two blind men sitting by the way side, when they heard that Jesus passed by, cried out, saying, Have mercy on us, O Lord, *thou* Son of David.

31 And the multitude rebuked them, because they should hold their peace: but they cried the more, saying, Have mercy on us, O Lord, *thou* Son of David.

32 And Jesus stood still, and called them, and said, What will ye *that* I shall do unto you?

33 They say unto him, Lord, that our eyes may be opened.

34 So Jesus had compassion *on them,* and touched their eyes: and immediately their eyes received sight, and they followed him.

20:23 [b]ch. 25:34
20:24 [a]Mark 10:41; Luke 22:24,25
20:26 [a]1 Pet. 5:3 [b]ch. 23:11; Mark 9:35; 10:43
20:27 [a]ch. 18:4
20:28 [a]John 13:4 [b]Phil. 2:7 [c]Luke 22:27; John 13:14 [d]Is. 53:10,11; Dan. 9:24,26; John 11:51,52; 1 Tim. 2:6; Tit. 2:14; 1 Pet. 1:19 [e]ch. 26:28; Rom. 5:15,19; Heb. 9:28
20:29 [a]Mark 10:46; Luke 18:35
20:30 [a]ch. 9:27
21:1 [a]Mark 11:1; Luke 19:29 [b]Zech. 14:4
21:5 [a]Is. 62:11; Zech. 9:9; John 12:15
21:6 [a]Mark 11:4
21:7 [a]2 Ki. 9:13
21:8 [a]See Lev. 23:40; John 12:13
21:9 [a]Ps. 118:25 [b]Ps. 118:26; ch. 23:39
21:10 [a]Mark 11:15; Luke 19:45; John 2:13,15
21:11 [a]ch. 2:23; Luke 7:16; John 6:14; 7:40; 9:17
21:12 [a]Mark 11:11; Luke 19:45; John 2:15

The triumphal entry

21 And [a]when they drew nigh unto Jerusalem, and were come to Bethphage, unto [b]the mount of Olives, then sent Jesus two disciples,

2 Saying unto them, Go into the village over against you, and straightway ye shall find an ass tied, and a colt with her: loose *them,* and bring *them* unto me.

3 And if any *man* say ought unto you, ye shall say, The Lord hath need of them; and straightway he will send them.

4 All this was done, that it might be fulfilled which was spoken by the prophet, saying,

5 [a]Tell ye the daughter of Sion, Behold, thy King cometh unto thee, meek, and sitting upon an ass, and a colt the foal of an ass.

6 [a]And the disciples went, and did as Jesus commanded them,

7 And brought the ass, and the colt, and [a]put on them their clothes, and they set *him* thereon.

8 And a very great multitude spread their garments in the way; [a]others cut down branches from the trees, and strawed *them* in the way.

9 And the multitudes that went before, and that followed, cried, saying, [a]Hosanna to the Son of David: [b]Blessed *is* he that cometh in the name of the Lord; Hosanna in the highest.

10 [a]And when he was come into Jerusalem, all the city was moved, saying, Who is this?

11 And the multitude said, This is Jesus [a]the prophet of Nazareth of Galilee.

Cleansing of the temple

12 ¶ [a]And Jesus went into the temple of God, and cast out all them that sold and

20:23 *is not mine to give.* See note on Mark 10:40.

20:24 See note on Mark 10:41.

20:26 *it shall not be so among you.* See note on Mark 10:43.

‡20:28 *ransom.* This word was often used for the price paid to redeem a slave. Similarly, Christ paid the ransom price of His own life to free us from the slavery of sin. *for.* This preposition emphasizes the substitutionary nature of Christ's death. *many.* Christ "gave himself a ransom for all" (1 Tim 2:6). Salvation is offered to "all," but only the "many," those who receive Christ, obtain it. See note on Mark 10:45.

20:29 *Jericho.* See note on Mark 10:46.

20:30 *two blind men.* The other Synoptics mention only one (see note on Luke 18:35). *Son of David.* A Messianic title (see note on 9:27).

21:1 *Jerusalem.* See map No. 8 at the end of the study Bible. *Bethphage.* The name means "house of figs." It is not mentioned in the OT, and in the NT only in connection with the Triumphal Entry. In the Talmud it is spoken of as being near Jerusalem. *mount of Olives.* See note on Mark 11:1.

‡21:2 *an ass.* The donkey was symbolic of humility, peace and Davidic royalty (see notes on Zech 9:9; Luke 19:30). See also note on Mark 11:2. *colt.* See notes on Mark 11:2 and Luke 19:30.

21:3 *Lord.* See note on Luke 19:31.

21:7 *brought the ass, and the colt.* We know from Mark (11:2) and Luke (19:30) that He rode the colt. Typically, a mother donkey followed her offspring closely. Matthew mentions two animals, while the other Gospels have only one (see note on Luke 19:30).

21:8 *spread their garments in the way.* An act of royal homage (see 2 Ki 9:13). *branches.* See note on Mark 11:8.

21:9 These are three separate quotations, not necessarily spoken at the same time. *Hosanna.* See note on Jer 31:7; both prayer and praise. *Son of David.* See note on 9:27. *in the highest.* That is, may those in heaven sing "Hosanna" (see Ps 148:1–2; Luke 2:14).

21:12–17 In the Synoptics the cleansing of the temple occurs during the last week of Jesus' ministry; in John it takes place during the first few months (John 2:12–16). Two explanations are possible: 1. There were two cleansings, one at the beginning and the other at the end of Jesus' public ministry. 2. There was only one cleansing, which took place during Passion Week but which John placed at the beginning of his account for theological reasons—to show that God's judgment was operative through the Messiah from the outset of His ministry. However, different details are present in the two accounts (the selling of cattle and sheep in John 2:14, the whip in John 2:15, and the statements of Jesus in Mat 21:13; John 2:16). From Matthew's and Luke's accounts we might assume that the cleansing of the temple took place on Sunday, following the so-called Triumphal Entry (21:1–11). But Mark (11:15–19) clearly indicates that it was on Monday. Matthew often compressed narratives.

21:12 *temple.* The buying and selling took place in the large

bought in the temple, and overthrew the tables of the [b]moneychangers, and the seats of
them that sold doves,
13 And said unto them, It is written, [a]My
house shall be called the house of prayer; [b]but
ye have made it a den of thieves.
14 And *the* blind and *the* lame came to him
in the temple; and he healed them.
15 And when the chief priests and scribes
saw the wonderful *things* that he did, and the
children crying in the temple, and saying, Hosanna to the Son of David; they were sore displeased,
16 And said unto him, Hearest thou what
these say? And Jesus saith unto them, Yea;
have ye never read, [a]Out of the mouth of
babes and sucklings thou hast perfected
praise?
17 And he left them, and went out of the
city into [a]Bethany; and he lodged there.

The barren fig tree

18 ¶ [a]Now in the morning as he returned
into the city, he hungered.
19 [a]And when he saw [1]a fig tree in the
way, he came to it, and found nothing thereon,
but leaves only, and said unto it, Let no fruit
grow on thee henceforward for ever. And
presently the fig tree withered away.
20 [a]And when the disciples saw *it,* they
marvelled, saying, How soon is the fig tree
withered away!
21 Jesus answered and said unto them,
Verily I say unto you, [a]If ye have faith, and
[b]doubt not, ye shall not only do this which is
done to the fig tree, [c]but also if ye shall say
unto this mountain, Be thou removed, and be
thou cast into the sea; it shall be done.
22 And [a]all *things,* whatsoever ye shall ask
in prayer, believing, ye shall receive.

Jesus' authority challenged

23 ¶ [a]And when he was come into the temple, the chief priests and the elders of the people came unto him as he was teaching, and
[b]said, By what authority doest thou these
things? and who gave thee this authority?
24 And Jesus answered and said unto
them, I also will ask you one thing, which if ye
tell me, I in like wise will tell you by what authority I do these *things.*

21:12 [b]Deut. 14:25
21:13 [a]Is. 56:7 [b]Jer. 7:11; Mark 11:17; Luke 19:46
21:16 [a]Ps. 8:2
21:17 [a]Mark 11:11; John 11:18
21:18 [a]Mark 11:12
21:19 [1][Gr. *one fig tree*] [a]Mark 11:13
21:20 [a]Mark 11:20
21:21 [a]ch. 17:20 [b]Jas. 1:6 [c]1 Cor. 13:2
21:22 [a]ch. 7:7; Mark 11:24; Luke 11:9; Jas. 5:16; 1 John 3:22; 5:14
21:23 [a]Mark 11:27; Luke 20:1 [b]Ex. 2:14; Acts 4:7; 7:27
21:26 [a]ch. 14:5; Mark 6:20; Luke 20:6
21:31 [a]Luke 7:29,50
21:32 [a]ch. 3:1 [b]Luke 3:12,13
21:33 [a]Ps. 80:9; Sol. 8:11; Is. 5:1; Jer. 2:21; Mark 12:1; Luke 20:9 [b]ch. 25:14
21:34 [a]Sol. 8:11,12
21:35 [a]2 Chr. 24:21; 36:16; Neh. 9:26; ch. 5:12; 23:34,37; Acts 7:52; 1 Thes. 2:15; Heb. 11:36,37
21:38 [a]Ps. 2:8; Heb. 1:2 [b]Ps. 2:2; ch. 26:3; 27:1; John 11:53; Acts 4:27
21:39 [a]ch. 26:50; Mark 14:46; Luke 22:54; John 18:12; Acts 2:23

25 The baptism of John, whence was it?
from heaven, or of men? And they reasoned
with themselves, saying, If we shall say, From
heaven; he will say unto us, Why did ye not
then believe him?
26 But if we shall say, Of men; we fear the
people; [a]for all hold John as a prophet.
27 And they answered Jesus, and said, We
cannot tell. And he said unto them, Neither
tell I you by what authority I do these *things.*
28 But what think you? A *certain* man had
two sons; and he came to the first, and said,
Son, go work to day in my vineyard.
29 He answered and said, I will not: but afterward he repented, and went.
30 And he came to the second, and said
likewise. And he answered and said, I *go,* sir:
and went not.
31 Whether of *them* twain did the will of
his father? They say unto him, The first. Jesus
saith unto them, [a]Verily I say unto you, That
the publicans and the harlots go into the kingdom of God before you.
32 For [a]John came unto you in the way of
righteousness, and ye believed him not: [b]but
the publicans and the harlots believed him:
and ye, when ye had seen *it,* repented not afterward, that *ye* might believe him.

The parable of the husbandmen

33 ¶ Hear another parable: There was a certain householder, [a]which planted a vineyard,
and hedged it round about, and digged a winepress in it, and built a tower, and let it out to
husbandmen, and [b]went into a far country:
34 And when the time of the fruit drew
near, he sent his servants to the husbandmen,
[a]that *they* might receive the fruits of it.
35 [a]And the husbandmen took his servants, and beat one, and killed another, and
stoned another.
36 Again, he sent other servants moe than
the first: and they did unto them likewise.
37 But last *of all* he sent unto them his son,
saying, They will reverence my son.
38 But when the husbandmen saw the son,
they said among themselves, [a]This is the heir;
[b]come, let us kill him, and let us seize on his
inheritance.
39 [a]And they caught him, and cast *him* out
of the vineyard, and slew *him.*

outer court of the Gentiles, which covered several acres (see notes on Mark 11:15 and Luke 19:45).

21:13 *house of prayer.* See note on Mark 11:17.

21:17 *Bethany.* A village on the eastern slope of the mount of Olives, about two miles from Jerusalem and the final station on the road from Jericho to Jerusalem.

21:18–22 See note on vv. 12–17; another example of compressing narratives. Mark (11:12–14,20–25) places the cursing of the fig tree on Monday morning and the disciples' finding it withered on Tuesday morning. In Matthew's account the tree withered as soon as Jesus cursed it, emphasizing the immediacy of judgment. For the theological meaning of this event see note on Mark 11:14.

21:18 *city.* Jerusalem.

21:21 *say unto this mountain, Be thou removed.* See note on 17:20.

21:23 *chief priests.* See notes on 2:4; Mark 8:31; Luke 19:47. *By what authority . . . ?* See notes on Mark 11:28 and Luke 20:2.

21:25 *from heaven or of men?* See notes on Mark 11:30; Luke 20:4.

21:33–46 See notes on Mark 12:1–12 and Luke 20:9–19.

21:33 *tower.* For guarding the vineyard, especially when the grapes ripened, and for shelter. The rabbis specified that it was to be a raised wooden platform, 15 feet high and 6 feet square.

‡21:35–37 The husbandmen are the Jews, or their leaders. The servants represent the OT prophets, many of whom were killed. The son represents Christ, who was condemned to death by the religious leaders. *They will reverence my son.* The own-

40 When the lord therefore of the vineyard cometh, what will he do unto those husbandmen?

41 [a]They say unto him, [b]He will miserably destroy those wicked *men,* [c]and will let out *his* vineyard unto other husbandmen, which shall render him the fruits in their seasons.

42 Jesus saith unto them, [a]Did ye never read in the scriptures, The stone which the builders rejected, the same is become the head of the corner: this is the Lord's doing, and it is marvellous in our eyes?

43 Therefore say I unto you, [a]The kingdom of God shall be taken from you, and given to a nation bringing forth the fruits thereof.

44 And whosoever [a]shall fall on this stone shall be broken: but on whomsoever it shall fall, [b]it will grind him to powder.

45 And when the chief priests and Pharisees had heard his parables, they perceived that he spake of them.

46 But when they sought to lay hands on him, they feared the multitude, because [a]they took him for a prophet.

The marriage dinner

22 And Jesus answered [a]and spake unto them again by parables, and said,

2 The kingdom of heaven is like unto a certain king, which made a marriage for his son,

3 And sent forth his servants to call them that were bidden to the wedding: and they would not come.

4 Again, he sent forth other servants, saying, Tell them which are bidden, Behold, I have prepared my dinner: [a]my oxen and *my* fatlings *are* killed, and all *things are* ready: come unto the marriage.

5 But they made light of *it,* and went their ways, one to his farm, another to his merchandise:

6 And the remnant took his servants, and entreated *them* spitefully, and slew *them.*

21:41 [a]Luke 20:16 [b]Luke 21:24; Heb. 2:3 [c]Acts 13:46; 15:7; 18:6; 28:28; Rom. 9; 10; 11
21:42 [a]Ps. 118:22; Is. 28:16; Mark 12:10; Luke 20:17; Acts 4:11; Eph. 2:20; 1 Pet. 2:6,7
21:43 [a]ch. 8:12
21:44 [a]Is. 8:14,15; Zech. 12:3; Luke 20:18; Rom. 9:33; 1 Pet. 2:8 [b]Is. 60:12; Dan. 2:44
21:46 [a]ver. 11; Luke 7:16; John 7:40
22:1 [a]Luke 14:16; Rev. 19:7,9
22:4 [a]Prov. 9:2
22:7 [a]Dan. 9:26; Luke 19:27
22:8 [a]ch. 10:11; Acts 13:46
22:10 [a]ch. 13:38
22:11 [a]2 Cor. 5:3; Eph. 4:24; Col. 3:10,12; Rev. 3:4; 16:15; 19:8
22:13 [a]ch. 8:12
22:14 [a]ch. 20:16
22:15 [a]Mark 12:13; Luke 20:20
22:19 [1]*In value seven pence halfpenny:* ch. 18:28; 20:2
22:20 [1]Or, *inscription?*

7 But when the king heard *thereof,* he was wroth: and he sent forth [a]his armies, and destroyed those murderers, and burnt up their city.

8 Then saith he to his servants, The wedding is ready, but they which were bidden were not [a]worthy.

9 Go ye therefore into the highways, and as many as ye shall find, bid to the marriage.

10 So those servants went out into the *high*ways, and [a]gathered together all as many as they found, both bad and good: and the wedding was furnished with guests.

11 And when the king came in to see the guests, he saw there a man [a]which had not on a wedding garment:

12 And he saith unto him, Friend, how camest thou in hither not having a wedding garment? And he was speechless.

13 Then said the king to the servants, Bind him hand and foot, and take him away, and cast *him* [a]into outer darkness; there shall be weeping and gnashing of teeth.

14 [a]For many are called, but few *are* chosen.

Tribute money to Cesar

15 ¶ [a]Then went the Pharisees, and took counsel how they might entangle him in *his* talk.

16 And they sent out unto him their disciples with the Herodians, saying, Master, we know that thou art true, and teachest the way of God in truth, neither carest thou for any *man:* for thou regardest not the person of men.

17 Tell us therefore, What thinkest thou? Is it lawful to give tribute unto Cesar, or not?

18 But Jesus perceived their wickedness, and said, Why tempt ye me, *ye* hypocrites?

19 Shew me the tribute money. And they brought unto him a [1]penny.

20 And he saith unto them, Whose *is* this image and [1]superscription?

---

er stands for God, even though He knew what they would do to His son.

21:41 *other husbandmen.* Gentiles, to whom Paul turned when the Jews, for the most part, rejected the gospel (Acts 13:46; 18:6). By the second century the church was composed almost entirely of Gentiles.

21:44 *shall be broken.* See note on Luke 20:18.

21:45 *chief priests.* See notes on 2:4; Mark 8:31; Luke 19:47. *Pharisees.* See notes on 3:7, Mark 2:16; Luke 5:17. *parables.* See notes on 13:3; Mark 4:2; Luke 8:4.

‡22:7 *burnt up their city.* A common military practice; here possibly an allusion to the coming destruction of Jerusalem in A.D. 70.

22:11 *had not on a wedding garment.* It has been conjectured that it may have been the custom for the host to provide the guests with wedding garments. This would have been necessary for the guests at this feast in particular, for they were brought in directly from the streets (vv. 9–10). The failure of the man in question to avail himself of a wedding garment was therefore an insult to the host, who had made the garments available.

22:13 *gnashing of teeth.* See note on 13:42.

22:14 A proverbial summary of the meaning of the parable. God invites "many" (perhaps "all" in view of the Semitic usage of "many") to be part of His kingdom, but only a "few" are chosen by Him. This does not mean that God chooses arbitrarily. The invitation must be accepted, followed by appropriate conduct. Proper behavior is evidence of being chosen.

‡22:15–17 The Pharisees were ardent nationalists, opposed to Roman rule, while the Herodians, as their name indicates, supported the Roman rule of the Herods. Now, however, the Pharisees enlisted the help of the Herodians to trap Jesus in His words. After trying to put Him off guard with flattery, they sprang their question: "Is it lawful to give tribute unto Cesar, or not?" (v. 17). If He said "No," the Herodians would report Him to the Roman governor and He would be executed for treason. If He said "Yes," the Pharisees would denounce Him to the people as disloyal to His nation.

‡22:19 *penny.* The *denarius,* the common Roman coin of that day (see note on 20:2). On one side was the portrait of Emperor Tiberius and on the other the inscription in Latin: "Tiberius Caesar Augustus, son of the divine Augustus." The coin was issued by Tiberius and was used for paying tax to him.

21 They say unto him, Cesar's. Then saith
he unto them, [a]Render therefore unto Cesar
the *things* which are Cesar's; and unto God
the *things* that are God's.
22 When they had heard *these words,* they
marvelled, and left him, and went their way.

Sadducees and the resurrection

23 ¶ [a]The same day came to him *the* Sadducees, [b]which say that there is no resurrection, and asked him,
24 Saying, Master, [a]Moses said, If a man
die, having no children, his brother shall marry his wife, and raise up seed unto his brother.
25 Now there were with us seven brethren: and the first, when he had married *a wife,*
deceased, and, having no issue, left his wife
unto his brother:
26 Likewise the second also, and the third,
unto the [1]seventh.
27 And last of all the woman died also.
28 Therefore in the resurrection whose
wife shall she be of the seven? for they all had
her.
29 Jesus answered and said unto them, Ye
do err, [a]not knowing the scriptures, nor the
power of God.
30 For in the resurrection they neither
marry, nor are given in marriage, but [a]are as
the angels of God in heaven.
31 But as touching the resurrection of the
dead, have ye not read that which was spoken
unto you by God, saying,
32 [a]I am the God of Abraham, and the God
of Isaac, and the God of Jacob? God is not the
God of the dead, but of the living.
33 And when the multitude heard *this,*
[a]they were astonished at his doctrine.

The great commandment

34 ¶ [a]But when the Pharisees had heard
that he had put the Sadducees to silence, they
were gathered together.
35 Then one of them, *which was* [a]a lawyer,
asked *him a question,* tempting him, and saying,
36 Master, which *is* the great commandment in the law?
37 Jesus said unto him, [a]Thou shalt love

22:21 [a]ch. 17:25; Rom. 13:7
22:23 [a]Mark 12:18; Luke 20:27 [b]Acts 23:8
22:24 [a]Deut. 25:5
22:26 [1][Gr. *seven*]
22:29 [a]John 20:9
22:30 [a]1 John 3:2
22:32 [a]Ex. 3:6,16; Mark 12:26; Luke 20:37; Acts 7:32; Heb. 11:16
22:33 [a]ch. 7:28
22:34 [a]Mark 12:28
22:35 [a]Luke 10:25
22:37 [a]Deut. 6:5; 10:12; 30:6; Luke 10:27
22:39 [a]Lev. 19:18; ch. 19:19; Mark 12:31; Luke 10:27; Rom. 13:9; Gal. 5:14; Jas. 2:8
22:40 [a]ch. 7:12; 1 Tim. 1:5
22:41 [a]Mark 12:35; Luke 20:41
22:44 [a]Ps. 110:1; Acts 2:34; 1 Cor. 15:25; Heb. 1:13; 10:12,13
22:46 [a]Luke 14:6 [b]Mark 12:34; Luke 20:40
23:2 [a]Neh. 8:4,8; Mal. 2:7; Mark 12:38; Luke 20:45
23:3 [a]Rom. 2:19
23:4 [a]Luke 11:46; Acts 15:10; Gal. 6:13
23:5 [a]ch. 6:1,2,5,16 [b]Num. 15:38; Deut. 6:8; 22:12; Prov. 3:3
23:6 [a]Mark 12:38,39; Luke 11:43; 20:46; 3 John 9
23:8 [a]Jas. 3:1; See 2 Cor. 1:24; 1 Pet. 5:3

the Lord thy God with all thy heart, and with
all thy soul, and with all thy mind.
38 This is the first and great commandment.
39 And the second *is* like unto it, [a]Thou
shalt love thy neighbour as thyself.
40 [a]On these two commandments hang all
the law and the prophets.

The question about David's son

41 ¶ [a]While the Pharisees were gathered
together, Jesus asked them,
42 Saying, What think ye of Christ? whose
son is he? They say unto him, *The Son* of David.
43 He saith unto them, How then doth David in spirit call him Lord, saying,
44 [a]The LORD said unto my Lord, Sit thou
on my right hand, till I make thine enemies
thy footstool?
45 If David then call him Lord, how is he
his son?
46 [a]And no *man* was able to answer him a
word, [b]neither durst any *man* from that day
forth ask him any moe *questions.*

The woes upon the Pharisees

23 Then spake Jesus to the multitude,
and to his disciples,
2 Saying, [a]The scribes and the Pharisees sit
in Moses' seat:
3 All therefore whatsoever they bid you observe, *that* observe and do; but do not ye after
their works: for [a]they say, and do not.
4 [a]For they bind heavy burdens and grievous to be borne, and lay *them* on men's shoulders; but they *themselves* will not move them
with *one of* their fingers.
5 But [a]all their works they do for to be
seen of men: [b]they make broad their phylacteries, and enlarge the borders of their garments,
6 [a]And love the uppermost rooms at feasts,
and the chief seats in the synagogues,
7 And greetings in the markets, and to be
called of men, Rabbi, Rabbi.
8 [a]But be not ye called Rabbi: for one is
your Master, *even* Christ; and all ye are brethren.

22:21 *unto God the things that are God's.* In distinguishing clearly between Caesar and God, Jesus also protested against the false and idolatrous claims made on the coins (see previous note and note on Mark 12:17).

22:23 *Sadducess.* See notes on 3:7; Mark 12:18; Luke 20:27; Acts 4:1.

22:24 *Moses said.* Jesus quoted from the Pentateuch when arguing with the Sadducees, since those books had special authority for them (see note on Mark 12:18). The reference (Deut 25:5–6) is to the levirate law (from Latin *levir,* "brother-in-law"), which was given to protect the widow and guarantee continuance of the family line.

22:25–40 See Mark 12:18–31; Luke 20:27–40 and notes.

22:37,39 *love.* The Greek verb is not *phileo,* which expresses friendly affection, but *agapao,* the commitment of devotion that is directed by the will and can be commanded as a duty.

22:37 *with all thy heart . . . soul . . . mind.* With your whole being. The Hebrew of Deut 6:5 has "heart . . . soul . . . might," but some manuscripts of the Septuagint (the Greek translation of the OT) add "mind." Jesus combined all four terms in Mark 12:30.

22:40 *all the law and the prophets.* The entire OT (see note on 5:17).

22:41–46 See notes on Mark 12:35–40; Luke 20:44–47.

23:2 *sit in Moses' seat.* The authorized successors of Moses as teachers of the law.

23:5 *phylacteries.* These small boxes, worn on forehead and arm, contained four passages (Ex 13:1–10; 13:11–16; Deut 6:4–9; 11:13–21).

23:6 *chief seats in the synagogues.* See note on Mark 12:39.

23:8–10 The warning is against seeking titles of honor to foster pride. Obviously, we should avoid unreasonable literalism in applying such commands.

9 And call no *man* your father upon the earth: [a]for one is your Father, which is in heaven.

10 Neither be ye called masters: for one is your Master, *even* Christ.

11 But [a]he that is greatest among you shall be your servant.

12 [a]And whosoever shall exalt himself shall be abased; and he that shall humble himself shall be exalted.

13 ¶ But [a]woe unto you, scribes and Pharisees, hypocrites! for ye shut up the kingdom of heaven against men: for ye neither go in yourselves, neither suffer ye them that are entering to go in.

14 ¶ Woe unto you, scribes and Pharisees, hypocrites! [a]for ye devour widows' houses, and for a pretence make long prayer: therefore ye shall receive the greater damnation.

15 ¶ Woe unto you, scribes and Pharisees, hypocrites! for ye compass sea and land to make one proselyte, and when he is made, ye make him twofold more *the* child of hell than yourselves.

16 ¶ Woe unto you, [a]*ye* blind guides, which say, [b]Whosoever shall swear by the temple, it is nothing; but whosoever shall swear by the gold of the temple, he is a debtor.

17 *Ye* fools and blind: for whether is greater, the gold, [a]or the temple that sanctifieth the gold?

18 And, Whosoever shall swear by the altar, it is nothing; but whosoever sweareth by the gift that is upon it, he is [1]guilty.

19 *Ye* fools and blind: for whether *is* greater, the gift, or [a]the altar that sanctifieth the gift?

20 Whoso therefore shall swear by the altar, sweareth by it, and by all *things* thereon.

21 And whoso shall swear by the temple, sweareth by it, and by [a]him that dwelleth therein.

22 And he that shall swear by heaven, sweareth by [a]the throne of God, and by him that sitteth thereon.

23:9 [a]Mal. 1:6
23:11 [a]ch. 20:26,27
23:12 [a]Job 22:29; Prov. 15:33; 29:23; Luke 14:11; 18:14; Jas. 4:6; 1 Pet. 5:5
23:13 [a]Luke 11:52
23:14 [a]Mark 12:40; Luke 20:47; 2 Tim. 3:6; Tit. 1:11
23:16 [a]ver. 24; ch. 15:14 [b]ch. 5:33,34
23:17 [a]Ex. 30:29
23:18 [1]Or, *debtor,* or, *bound*
23:19 [a]Ex. 29:37
23:21 [a]1 Ki. 8:13; 2 Chr. 6:2; Ps. 26:8; 132:14
23:22 [a]Ps. 11:4; ch. 5:34; Acts 7:49

‡23:15 Jesus does not criticize the Pharisees for their evangelistic zeal. He objects to its results. The converts wound up "out-Phariseeing" the Pharisees, and that meant they became even more children of hell (i.e., bound for hell) than their teachers. *hell.* See notes on 5:22 and Luke 12:5.
‡23:23 Jesus does not criticize the observance of the min-

Jewish Sects

PHARISEES

Their roots can be traced to the second century B.C.—to the Hasidim.

1. Along with the Torah, they accepted as equally inspired and authoritative all material contained within the oral tradition.
2. On free will and determination, they held to a mediating view that made it impossible for either free will or the sovereignty of God to cancel out the other.
3. They accepted a rather developed hierarchy of angels and demons.
4. They taught that there was a future for the dead.
5. They believed in the immortality of the soul and in reward and retribution after death.
6. They were champions of human equality.
7. The emphasis of their teaching was ethical rather than theological.

SADDUCEES

They probably had their beginning during the Hasmonean period (166-63 B.C.). Their demise occurred c. A.D. 70 with the fall of Jerusalem.

1. They denied that the oral law was authoritative and binding.
2. They interpreted Mosaic law more literally than did the Pharisees.
3. They were very exacting in Levitical purity.
4. They attributed all to free will.
5. They argued there is neither resurrection of the dead nor a future life.
6. They rejected a belief in angels and demons.
7. They rejected the idea of a spiritual world.
8. Only the books of Moses were canonical Scripture.

ESSENES

They probably originated among the Hasidim, along with the Pharisees, from whom they later separated (I Maccabees 2:42; 7:13). They were a group of very strict and zealous Jews who took part with the Maccabeans in a revolt against the Syrians, c. 165-155 B.C.

1. They followed a strict observance of the purity laws of the Torah.
2. They were notable for their communal ownership of property.
3. They had a strong sense of mutual responsibility.
4. Daily worship was an important feature along with a daily study of their sacred scriptures.
5. Solemn oaths of piety and obedience had to be taken.
6. Sacrifices were offered on holy days and during sacred seasons.
7. Marriage was not condemned in principle but was avoided.
8. They attributed all that happened to fate.

ZEALOTS

They originated during the reign of Herod the Great c. 6 B.C. and ceased to exist in A.D. 73 at Masada.

1. They opposed payment of tribute for taxes to a pagan emperor, saying that allegiance was due only to God.
2. They held a fierce loyalty to the Jewish traditions.
3. They were opposed to the use of the Greek language in the Holy Land.
4. They prophesied the coming of the time of salvation.

23 ¶ Woe unto you, scribes and Pharisees, hypocrites! [a]for ye pay tithe of mint and [1]anise and cummin, and [b]have omitted the weightier *matters* of the law, judgment, mercy, and faith: these ought *ye* to have done, and not to leave the other undone.

24 *Ye* blind guides, which strain out a gnat, and swallow a camel.

25 ¶ Woe unto you, scribes and Pharisees, hypocrites! [a]for ye make clean the outside of the cup and of the platter, but within they are full of extortion and excess.

26 *Thou* blind Pharisee, cleanse first that *which is* within the cup and platter, that the outside of them may be clean also.

27 ¶ Woe unto you, scribes and Pharisees, hypocrites! [a]for ye are like unto whited sepulchres, which indeed appear beautiful outward, but are within full of dead *men's* bones, and of all uncleanness.

28 *Even* so ye also outwardly appear righteous unto men, but within ye are full of hypocrisy and iniquity.

29 ¶ [a]Woe unto you, scribes and Pharisees, hypocrites! because ye build the tombs of the prophets, and garnish the sepulchres of the righteous,

30 And say, If we had been in the days of our fathers, we would not have been partakers with them in the blood of the prophets.

31 Wherefore ye be witnesses unto yourselves, that [a]ye are the children of them which killed the prophets.

32 [a]Fill ye up then the measure of your fathers.

33 *Ye* serpents, *ye* [a]generation of vipers, how can ye escape the damnation of hell?

34 ¶ [a]Wherefore behold, I send unto you prophets, and wise *men*, and scribes: and [b]*some* of them ye shall kill and crucify; and [c]*some* of them shall ye scourge in your synagogues, and persecute *them* from city to city:

35 [a]That upon you may come all the righteous blood shed upon the earth, [b]from the blood of righteous Abel unto [c]the blood of Zacharias son of Barachias, whom ye slew between the temple and the altar.

36 Verily I say unto you, All these *things* shall come upon this generation.

37 ¶ [a]O Jerusalem, Jerusalem, *thou* that killest the prophets, [b]and stonest them which are sent unto thee, how often would [c]I have gathered thy children together, even as a hen gathereth her chickens [d]under *her* wings, and ye would not?

38 Behold, your house is left unto you desolate.

39 For I say unto you, Ye shall not see me henceforth, till ye shall say, [a]Blessed is he that cometh in the name of the Lord.

Signs of the end of this age

24 And [a]Jesus went out, and departed from the temple: and his disciples came to *him* for to shew him the buildings of the temple.

2 And Jesus said unto them, See ye not all these *things?* verily I say unto you, [a]There shall not be left here one stone upon another, that shall not be thrown down.

3 And as he sat upon the mount of Olives, [a]the disciples came unto him privately, saying, [b]Tell us, when shall these *things* be? and what *shall be* the sign of thy coming, and of the end of the world?

4 And Jesus answered and said unto them, [a]Take heed that no *man* deceive you.

5 For [a]many shall come in my name, saying, I am Christ; [b]and shall deceive many.

6 And ye shall hear of wars and rumours of wars: see that ye be not troubled: for all *these things* must come to pass, but the end is not yet.

7 For [a]nation shall rise against nation, and kingdom against kingdom: and there shall be famines, and pestilences, and earthquakes in divers places.

8 All these *are* the beginning of sorrows.

23:23 [1][Gr. ἄνηθον, *dill*] [a]Luke 11:42 [b]1 Sam. 15:22; Hos. 6:6; Mic. 6:8; ch. 9:13; 12:7
23:25 [a]Mark 7:4; Luke 11:39
23:27 [a]Luke 11:44; Acts 23:3
23:29 [a]Luke 11:47
23:31 [a]Acts 7:51,52; 1 Thes. 2:15
23:32 [a]Gen. 15:16; 1 Thes. 2:16
23:33 [a]ch. 3:7; 12:34
23:34 [a]ch. 21:34,35; Luke 11:49 [b]Acts 5:40; 7:58,59; 22:19 [c]ch. 10:17; 2 Cor. 11:24,25
23:35 [a]Rev. 18:24 [b]Gen. 4:8; 1 John 3:12
23:35 [c]2 Chr. 24:20,21
23:37 [a]Luke 13:34 [b]2 Chr. 24:21 [c]Deut. 32:11,12 [d]Ps. 17:8; 91:4
23:39 [a]Ps. 118:26; ch. 21:9
24:1 [a]Mark 13:1; Luke 21:5
24:2 [a]1 Ki. 9:7; Jer. 26:18; Mic. 3:12; Luke 19:44
24:3 [a]Mark 13:3 [b]1 Thes. 5:1
24:4 [a]Eph. 5:6; Col. 2:8,18; 2 Thes. 2:3; 1 John 4:1
24:5 [a]ver. 24; Jer. 14:14; 23:21,25; John 5:43 [b]ver. 11
24:7 [a]2 Chr. 15:6; Is. 19:2; Hag. 2:22; Zech. 14:13

utiae of the law (He says, "these ought ye to have done," but He does criticize the hypocrisy often involved (see note on 5:18–20).

23:24 *strain out.* The strict Pharisee would carefully strain his drinking water through a cloth to be sure he did not swallow a gnat, the smallest of unclean animals. But, figuratively, he would swallow a camel—one of the largest.

23:27 *whited sepulchres.* A person who stepped on a grave became ceremonially unclean (see Num 19:16), so graves were whitewashed to make them easily visible, especially at night. They appeared clean and beautiful on the outside, but they were dirty and rotten on the inside.

23:33 *hell.* See notes on 5:22 and Luke 12:5.

‡23:35 *Abel unto . . . Zacharias* [i.e. Zechariah]. The murder of Abel is recorded in Gen 4:8 and that of Zechariah, son (probably grandson) of Jehoiada, in 2 Chr 24:20–22 (Chronicles is placed at the end of the OT in the Hebrew arrangement of the books). The expression was somewhat like our "from Genesis to Revelation." Jesus was summing up the history of martyrdom in the OT.

23:37–39 See notes on Luke 13:34–35.

‡24:1–25:46 The Olivet discourse, the sixth and last of the great discourses in Matthew's Gospel (see notes on 5:1–7:29; Mark 13:1–37).

24:2 *There shall not be left here one stone upon another.* Fulfilled literally in A.D. 70, when the Romans under Titus completely destroyed Jerusalem and the temple buildings. Stones were even pried apart to collect the gold leaf that melted from the roof when the temple was set on fire. *stone.* See note on Mark 13:1. *thrown down.* Excavations in 1968 uncovered large numbers of these stones, toppled from the walls by the invaders.

24:3 *mount of Olives.* A ridge a little more than a mile long, beyond the Kidron Valley east of Jerusalem and rising about 200 feet above the city (see note on Mark 11:1). *when shall these things be? and what shall be the sign of thy coming, and of the end of the world?* Jesus deals with these questions but does not distinguish them sharply. However, it appears that the description of the end of the age is discussed in vv. 4–14, the destruction of Jerusalem in vv. 15–22 (see Luke 21:20) and Christ's coming in vv. 23–31.

24:5 *Christ.* See note on 16:16.

‡24:8 *sorrows.* The rabbis, as well as the prophets, spoke of "birth pangs," i.e., sufferings, that would precede the coming of

9 ¶ [a]Then shall they deliver you up to be afflicted, and shall kill you: and ye shall be hated of all nations for my name's sake.

10 And then shall many [a]be offended, and shall betray one another, and shall hate one another.

11 And [a]many false prophets shall rise, and [b]shall deceive many.

12 And because iniquity shall abound, the love of many shall wax cold.

13 [a]But he that shall endure unto the end, the same shall be saved.

14 And this [a]gospel of the kingdom [b]shall be preached in all the world for a witness unto all nations; and then shall the end come.

15 ¶ [a]When ye therefore shall see the abomination of desolation, spoken of by [b]Daniel the prophet, stand in the holy place, ([c]whoso readeth, let him understand:)

16 Then let them which be in Judea flee into the mountains:

17 Let him which is on the housetop not come down to take any *thing* out of his house:

18 Neither let him which is in the field return back to take his clothes.

19 And [a]woe unto them that are with child, and to them that give suck in those days.

20 But pray ye that your flight be not in the winter, neither on the sabbath day:

21 For [a]then shall be great tribulation, such as was not since the beginning of the world to this time, no, nor ever shall be.

22 And except those days should be shortened, there should no flesh be saved: [a]but for the elect's sake those days shall be shortened.

23 [a]Then if any *man* shall say unto you, Lo, here *is* Christ, or there; believe *it* not.

24 For [a]there shall arise false Christs, and false prophets, and shall shew great signs and wonders; insomuch that, [b]if *it were* possible, *they shall* deceive the very elect.

25 Behold, I have told you before.

26 Wherefore if they shall say unto you, Behold, he is in the desert; go not forth: behold, *he is* in the secret chambers; believe *it* not.

27 [a]For as the lightning cometh out of the east, and shineth *even* unto the west; so shall also the coming of the Son of man be.

28 [a]For wheresoever the carcase is, there will the eagles be gathered together.

29 ¶ [a]Immediately after the tribulation of those days [b]shall the sun be darkened, and the moon shall not give her light, and the stars shall fall from heaven, and the powers of the heavens shall be shaken:

30 [a]And then shall appear the sign of the Son of man in heaven: [b]and then shall all the tribes of the earth mourn, [c]and they shall see the Son of man coming in the clouds of heaven with power and great glory.

31 [a]And he shall send his angels [1]with a great sound of a trumpet, and they shall gather together his elect from the four winds, from one end of heaven to the other.

32 Now learn [a]a parable of the fig tree; When his branch is yet tender, and putteth forth leaves, ye know that summer *is* nigh:

33 So likewise ye, when ye shall see all these *things*, know [a]that [1]it is near, *even* at the doors.

34 Verily I say unto you, [a]This generation shall not pass, till all these *things* be fulfilled.

35 [a]Heaven and earth shall pass away, but my words shall not pass away.

36 ¶ [a]But of that day and hour knoweth no *man*, no, not the angels of heaven, [b]but my Father only.

37 But as the days of Noe *were*, so shall also the coming of the Son of man be.

38 [a]For as in the days that were before the flood they were eating and drinking, marrying and giving in marriage, until the day that Noe entered into the ark,

24:9 [a]ch. 10:17; Luke 21:12; John 16:2; Acts 4:2,3 **24:10** [a]2 Tim. 1:15; 4:10,16 **24:11** [a]Acts 20:29; 2 Pet. 2:1 [b]1 Tim. 4:1 **24:13** [a]ch. 10:22; Mark 13:13; Rev. 2:10 **24:14** [a]ch. 4:23 [b]Rom. 10:18; Col. 1:6,23 **24:15** [a]Mark 13:14; Luke 21:20 [b]Dan. 9:27; 12:11 [c]Dan. 9:23 **24:19** [a]Luke 23:29 **24:21** [a]Dan. 9:26; Joel 2:2 **24:22** [a]Is. 65:8,9; Zech. 14:2 **24:23** [a]Mark 13:21; Luke 17:23; 21:8 **24:24** [a]Deut. 13:1; 2 Thes. 2:9; Rev. 13:13 [b]John 6:37; 10:28,29; Rom. 8:28; 2 Tim. 2:19

24:27 [a]Luke 17:24 **24:28** [a]Job 39:30; Luke 17:37 **24:29** [a]Dan. 7:11 [b]Ezek. 32:7; Joel 2:10; Amos 8:9; Mark 13:24; Acts 2:20 **24:30** [a]Dan. 7:13 [b]Zech. 12:12 [c]Mark 13:26; Rev. 1:7 **24:31** [1]Or, *with a trumpet, and a great voice* [a]1 Cor. 15:52; 1 Thes. 4:16 **24:32** [a]Luke 21:29 **24:33** [1][Or, *he*] ver. 30 [a]Jas. 5:9 **24:34** [a]ch. 16:28; Mark 13:30; Luke 21:32

24:35 [a]Ps. 102:26; Is. 51:6; Jer. 31:35; Mark 13:31; Luke 21:33
24:36 [a]Mark 13:32; Acts 1:7; 1 Thes. 5:2; 2 Pet. 3:10 [b]Zech. 14:7
24:38 [a]Gen. 6:3-5; Luke 17:26; 1 Pet. 3:20

the Messiah. They will lead into "the time of Jacob's trouble," (Jer 30:7).

‡24:15 *the abomination of desolation.* The detestable thing causing the desolation of the holy place. The primary reference in Daniel (9:27; 11:31; 12:11) was to 168 B.C., when Antiochus Epiphanes erected a pagan altar to Zeus on the sacred altar in the temple of Jerusalem. There are two more stages in the progressive fulfillment of the predictions in Daniel and Matthew: (1) the Roman destruction of the temple in A.D. 70 and (2) the setting up of an image of the antichrist in Jerusalem (see 2 Thes 2:4; Rev 13:14–15; see also notes on Dan 9:25–27; 11:31).

‡24:16 *the mountains.* The Transjordan mountains, where Pella was located. Christians in Jerusalem fled to that area during the Roman siege shortly before A.D. 70. A similar fleeing will occur during the future great tribulation period (identified with Daniel's 70th "week," Dan 9:27). See note on Rev 12:6,14.

24:19 See note on Mark 13:17.

24:20 *in the winter.* See note on Mark 13:18. *neither on the sabbath.* Matthew alone includes this because he was writing to Jews, who were forbidden to travel more than about half a mile on the sabbath.

‡24:21 *great tribulation.* Josephus, the Jewish historian who was there, describes the destruction of Jerusalem in almost identical language. Many believe the reference is also to a future period of great tribulation (see Dan 12:1).

‡24:22 *days should be shortened.* Some hold that this statement means that the tribulation will be of such intensity that, if allowed to continue, it would destroy everyone. Others believe that Christ is referring to the cutting short of a previously determined time period (such as the 70th "seven" of Dan 9:27 or the 42 months of Rev 11:2; 13:5). *the elect's sake.* The people of God, during the tribulation, including some Jews and Gentiles.

24:28 *there will the eagles be gathered together.* The coming of Christ will be as obvious as the gathering of vultures around a carcass (see note on Luke 17:37, where the saying is used in a slightly different sense).

24:29 See note on Mark 13:25.

24:30 *Son of man.* See note on Mark 8:31.

24:34 *Verily I say unto you.* See note on Mark 3:28. *This generation.* See notes on Mark 13:30; Luke 21:32.

24:35 Jesus' words are more certain than the existence of the universe.

24:36 *knoweth no man.* See note on Mark 13:32.

39 And knew not until the flood came, and took *them* all away; so shall also the coming of the Son of man be.

40 [a]Then shall two be in the field; the one shall be taken, and the other left.

41 Two *women shall be* grinding at the mill; *the* one shall be taken, and *the* other left.

42 [a]Watch therefore: for ye know not what hour your Lord doth come.

Faithful and unfaithful servants

43 ¶ [a]But know this, that if the goodman of the house had known in what watch the thief would come, he would have watched, and would not have suffered his house to be broken up.

44 [a]Therefore be ye also ready: for in such an hour as you think not the Son of man cometh.

45 [a]Who then is a faithful and wise servant, whom his lord hath made ruler over his household, to give them meat in due season?

46 [a]Blessed *is* that servant, whom his lord when he cometh shall find so doing.

47 Verily I say unto you, That [a]he shall make him ruler over all his goods.

48 But *and* if that evil servant shall say in his heart, My lord delayeth his coming;

49 And shall begin to smite *his* fellowservants, and to eat and drink with the drunken;

50 The lord of that servant shall come in a day when he looketh not for *him,* and in an hour that he is not ware of,

51 And shall [1]cut him asunder, and appoint *him* his portion with the hypocrites: [a]there shall be weeping and gnashing of teeth.

The parable of the ten virgins

25 Then shall the kingdom of heaven be likened unto ten virgins, which took their lamps, and went forth to meet [a]the bridegroom.

2 [a]And five of them were wise, and five *were* foolish.

3 They that *were* foolish took their lamps, and took no oil with them:

4 But the wise took oil in their vessels with their lamps.

5 While the bridegroom tarried, [a]they all slumbered and slept.

6 And at midnight [a]there was a cry made, Behold, the bridegroom cometh; go ye out to meet him.

7 Then all those virgins arose, and [a]trimmed their lamps.

24:40 [a]Luke 17:34
24:42 [a]ch. 25:13; Luke 21:36
24:43 [a]Luke 12:39; 1 Thes. 5:2; Rev. 3:3
24:44 [a]1 Thes. 5:6
24:45 [a]Luke 12:42; Acts 20:28
24:46 [a]Rev. 16:15
24:47 [a]ch. 25:21,23; Luke 22:29
24:51 [1]Or, *cut him off* [a]ch. 8:12; 25:30
25:1 [a]Eph. 5:29,30; Rev. 19:7; 21:2,9
25:2 [a]ch. 13:47; 22:10
25:5 [a]1 Thes. 5:6
25:6 [a]ch. 24:31; 1 Thes. 4:16
25:7 [a]Luke 12:35
25:8 [1]Or, *going out*
25:10 [a]Luke 13:25
25:11 [a]ch. 7:21-23
25:12 [a]Ps. 5:5; Hab. 1:13; John 9:31
25:13 [a]ch. 24:42,44; Mark 13:33,35; Luke 21:36
25:14 [a]Luke 19:12 [b]ch. 21:33
25:15 [1]*A talent is 187l. 10s.* [a]Rom. 12:6; 1 Cor. 12:7,11, 29; Eph. 4:11
25:21 [a]ver. 34,46; ch. 24:47; Luke 12:44; 22:29,30 [b]2 Tim. 2:12; Heb. 12:2; 1 Pet. 1:8
25:23 [a]ver. 21

8 And the foolish said unto the wise, Give us of your oil; for our lamps are [1]gone out.

9 But the wise answered, saying, *Not so;* lest there be not enough for us and you: but go ye rather to them that sell, and buy for yourselves.

10 And while they went to buy, the bridegroom came; and they *that were* ready went in with him to the marriage: and [a]the door was shut.

11 Afterward came also the other virgins, saying, [a]Lord, Lord, open to us.

12 But he answered and said, Verily I say unto you, [a]I know you not.

13 [a]Watch therefore, for ye know neither the day nor the hour wherein the Son of man cometh.

The parable of the talents

14 ¶ [a]For *the kingdom of heaven is* [b]as a man travelling into a far country, *who* called his own servants, and delivered unto them his goods.

15 And unto one he gave five [1]talents, to another two, and to another one; [a]to every man according to his several ability; and straightway took his journey.

16 Then he that had received the five talents went and traded with the same, and made *them* other five talents.

17 And likewise he that *had received* two, he also gained other two.

18 But he that had received one went and digged in the earth, and hid his lord's money.

19 After a long time the lord of those servants cometh, and reckoneth with them.

20 And *so* he that had received five talents came and brought other five talents, saying, Lord, thou deliveredst unto me five talents: behold, I have gained besides them five talents moe.

21 His lord said unto him, Well *done, thou* good and faithful servant: thou hast been faithful over a few *things,* [a]I will make thee ruler over many *things:* enter thou into [b]the joy of thy lord.

22 He also that had received two talents came and said, Lord, thou deliveredst unto me two talents: behold, I have gained two other talents besides them.

23 His lord said unto him, [a]Well *done,* good and faithful servant; thou hast been faithful over a few *things,* I will make thee ruler over many *things:* enter thou into the joy of thy lord.

24:51 *weeping and gnashing of teeth.* See note on 13:42.

25:1 *ten virgins.* The bridesmaids, who were responsible for preparing the bride to meet the bridegroom. *lamps.* Torches that consisted of a long pole with oil-drenched rags at the top. (Small clay lamps would have been of little use in an outdoor procession.)

25:3 *oil.* Olive oil.

25:7 *trimmed.* The charred ends of the rags were cut off and oil was added.

25:9 *there be not enough.* Torches required large amounts of oil in order to keep burning, and the oil had to be replenished about every 15 minutes.

‡25:13 *Watch.* The main point of the parable. *the day nor the hour.* Christ's coming is always imminent, therefore, be ready.

25:15 *talents.* The term was first used for a unit of weight (about 75 pounds), then for a unit of coinage. The present-day use of "talent" to indicate an ability or gift is derived from this parable since they received 5, 2, or just 1 talent, "to every man according to his several ability" (see note on Luke 19:13).

24 Then he which had received the one talent came and said, Lord, I knew thee that thou art a hard man, reaping where thou hast not sown, and gathering where thou hast not strawed:

25 And I was afraid, and went and hid thy talent in the earth: lo, *there* thou hast *that is* thine.

26 His lord answered and said unto him, *Thou* wicked and slothful servant, thou knewest that I reap where I sowed not, and gather where I have not strawed:

27 Thou oughtest therefore to have put my money to the exchangers, and *then* at my coming I should have received mine own with usury.

28 Take therefore the talent from him, and give *it* unto him which hath ten talents.

29 [a]For unto every one that hath shall be given, and he shall have abundance: but from him that hath not shall be taken away even *that* which he hath.

30 And cast ye the unprofitable servant [a]into outer darkness: there shall be weeping and gnashing of teeth.

The judgment

31 ¶ [a]When the Son of man shall come in his glory, and all the holy angels with him, then shall he sit upon the throne of his glory:

32 And [a]before him shall be gathered all nations: and [b]he shall separate them one from another, as a shepherd divideth *his* sheep from the goats:

33 And he shall set the sheep on his right hand, but the goats on the left.

34 ¶ Then shall the King say unto them on his right hand, Come, ye blessed of my Father, [a]inherit the kingdom [b]prepared for you from the foundation of the world:

35 [a]For I was a hungred, and ye gave me meat: I was thirsty, and ye gave me drink: [b]I was a stranger, and ye took me in:

36 [a]Naked, and ye clothed me: I was sick, and ye visited me: [b]I was in prison, and ye came unto me.

25:29 [a]ch. 13:12; Mark 4:25; Luke 8:18; 19:26; John 15:2
25:30 [a]ch. 8:12; 24:51
25:31 [a]Zech. 14:5; ch. 16:27; 19:28; Mark 8:38; Acts 1:11; 1 Thes. 4:16; 2 Thes. 1:7; Jude 14; Rev. 1:7
25:32 [a]Rom. 14:10; 2 Cor. 5:10; Rev. 20:12 [b]Ezek. 20:38
25:34 [a]Rom. 8:17; 1 Pet. 1:4,9; 3:9; Rev. 21:7 [b]ch. 20:23; Mark 10:40; 1 Cor. 2:9; Heb. 11:16
25:35 [a]Is. 58:7; Ezek. 18:7; Jas. 1:27 [b]Heb. 13:2; 3 John 5
25:36 [a]Jas. 2:15,16 [b]2 Tim. 1:16

37 Then shall the righteous answer him, saying, Lord, when saw we thee a hungred, and fed *thee?* or thirsty, and gave *thee* drink?

38 When saw we thee a stranger, and took *thee* in? or naked, and clothed *thee?*

39 Or when saw we thee sick, or in prison, and came unto thee?

40 And the King shall answer and say unto them, Verily I say unto you, [a]Inasmuch as ye have done *it* unto one of the least of these my brethren, ye have done *it* unto me.

41 ¶ Then shall he say also unto them on the left hand, [a]Depart from me, ye cursed, [b]into everlasting fire, prepared for [c]the devil and his angels:

42 For I was a hungred, and ye gave me no meat: I was thirsty, and ye gave me no drink:

43 I was a stranger, and ye took me not in: naked, and ye clothed me not: sick, and in prison, and ye visited me not.

44 Then shall they also answer him, saying, Lord, when saw we thee a hungred, or athirst, or a stranger, or naked, or sick, or in prison, and did not minister unto thee?

45 Then shall he answer them, saying, Verily I say unto you, [a]Inasmuch as ye did *it* not to one of the least of these, ye did *it* not to me.

46 And [a]these shall go away into everlasting punishment: but the righteous into life eternal.

The plot to kill Jesus

26 And it came to pass, when Jesus had finished all these sayings, he said unto his disciples,

2 [a]Ye know that after two days is *the feast of* the passover, and the Son of man is betrayed to be crucified.

3 [a]Then assembled together the chief priests, and the scribes, and the elders of the people, unto the palace of the high priest, who was called Caiaphas,

4 And consulted that they might take Jesus by subtilty, and kill *him.*

5 But they said, Not on the feast *day,* lest there be an uproar among the people.

25:40 [a]Prov. 14:31; 19:17; ch. 10:42; Mark 9:41; Heb. 6:10
25:41 [a]Ps. 6:8; ch. 7:23; Luke 13:27 [b]ch. 13:40,42 [c]2 Pet. 2:4; Jude 6
25:45 [a]Prov. 14:31; 17:5; Zech. 2:8; Acts 9:5
25:46 [a]Dan 12:2; John 5:29; Rom. 2:7
26:2 [a]Mark 14:1; Luke 22:1; John 13:1
26:3 [a]Ps. 2:2; John 11:47; Acts 4:25

25:27 *the exchangers.* The Greek for this word comes from *trapeza* ("table"), a word seen on the front of banks in Greece today. Bankers sat at small tables and changed money (cf. 21:12). *usury.* The Greek for this word was first used in the sense of offspring, interest being the "offspring" of invested money.

25:29 The main point of the parable. Being ready for Christ's coming involves more than playing it safe and doing little or nothing. It demands the kind of service that produces results.

25:31–46 The two most widely accepted interpretations of this judgment are: 1. It will occur at the beginning of an earthly millennial kingdom (vv. 31,34). Its purpose will be to determine who will be allowed to enter the kingdom (v. 34). The criterion for judgment will be the kind of treatment shown to the Jewish people ("these brothers of mine," v. 40) during the preceding great tribulation period (vv. 35–40,42–45). Ultimately, how a person treats the Jewish people will reveal whether or not he is saved (vv. 41,46). 2. The judgment referred to occurs at the great white throne at the end of the age (Rev 20:11–15). Its purpose will be to determine who will be allowed to enter the eternal kingdom of the saved and who will be consigned to eternal punishment in hell (vv. 34,46). The basis for judgment will be whether love is shown to God's people (see 1 John 3:14–15).

25:32 *before him shall be gathered all nations.* The word *ethnoi,* nations, properly means here ethnic groups. All people will be judged as individuals. No one enters God's kingdom because of his relationship with a certain country, but rather because of his relationship with Jesus Christ.

25:34–40 Rewards in the kingdom of heaven are given to those who serve without thought of reward. There is no hint of merit here, for God gives out of grace, not debt.

26:2 *passover.* See note on Mark 14:1. *Son of man.* See note on Mark 8:31.

26:3 *chief priests, and the scribes, and the elders of the people.* The clerical and lay leadership of the Sanhedrin (see note on 2:4). *Caiaphas.* High priest A.D. 18–36 and the son-in-law of Annas (John 18:13), a former high priest, who served A.D. 6–15.

26:5 *an uproar among the people.* Hundreds of thousands of Jewish pilgrims came to Jerusalem for passover, and riots were

Anointing of Jesus at Bethany

6 ¶ [a]Now when Jesus was in [b]Bethany, in the house of Simon the leper,

7 There came unto him a woman having an alabaster box of very precious ointment, and poured *it* on his head, as he sat at meat.

8 [a]But when his disciples saw *it,* they had indignation, saying, To what purpose *is* this waste?

9 For this ointment might have been sold for much, and given to the poor.

10 When Jesus understood *it,* he said unto them, Why trouble ye the woman? for she hath wrought a good work upon me.

11 [a]For ye have the poor always with you; but [b]me ye have not always.

12 For in that she hath poured this ointment on my body, she did *it* for my burial.

13 Verily I say unto you, Wheresoever this gospel shall be preached in the whole world, *there* shall also *this,* that this *woman* hath done, be told for a memorial of her.

The bargain of Judas Iscariot

14 ¶ [a]Then one of the twelve, called [b]Judas Iscariot, went unto the chief priests,

15 And said *unto them,* [a]What will ye give me, and I will deliver him unto you? And they covenanted with him for thirty pieces of silver.

16 And from that time he sought opportunity to betray him.

The last supper

17 ¶ [a]Now the first *day* of the *feast of* unleavened bread the disciples came to Jesus, saying unto him, Where wilt thou *that* we prepare for thee to eat the passover?

18 And he said, Go into the city to such a man, and say unto him, The Master saith, My time is at hand; I will keep the passover at thy house with my disciples.

26:6 [a]Mark 14:3; John 11:1,2; 12:3 [b]ch. 21:17
26:8 [a]John 12:4
26:11 [a]Deut. 15:11; John 12:8 [b]See ch. 18:20; 28:20; John 13:33; 14:19; 16:5,28; 17:11
26:14 [a]Mark 14:10; Luke 22:3; John 13:2,30 [b]ch. 10:4
26:15 [a]Zech. 11:12; ch. 27:3
26:17 [a]Ex. 12:6,18; Mark 14:12; Luke 22:7
26:20 [a]Mark 14:17-21; Luke 22:14; John 13:21
26:23 [a]Ps. 41:9; Luke 22:21; John 13:18
26:24 [a]Ps. 22; Is. 53; Dan. 9:26; Mark 9:12; Luke 24:25,26,46; Acts 17:2,3; 26:22,23; 1 Cor. 15:3 [b]John 17:12
26:26 [1]Many Greek copies have, *gave thanks* [a]Mark 14:22; Luke 22:19 [b]1 Cor. 11:23 [c]1 Cor. 10:16
26:27 [a]Mark 14:23
26:28 [a]See Ex. 24:8; Lev. 17:11 [b]Jer. 31:31 [c]ch. 20:28; Rom. 5:15; Heb. 9:22
26:29 [a]Mark 14:25; Luke 22:18 [b]Acts 10:41
26:30 [1]Or, *psalm* [a]Mark 14:26
26:31 [a]Mark 14:27; John 16:32 [b]ch. 11:6 [c]Zech. 13:7

19 And the disciples did as Jesus had appointed them; and they made ready the passover.

20 ¶ [a]Now when the even was come, he sat down with the twelve.

21 And as they did eat, he said, Verily I say unto you, that one of you shall betray me.

22 And they were exceeding sorrowful, and began every one of them to say unto him, Lord, is it I?

23 And he answered and said, [a]He that dippeth *his* hand with me in the dish, the same shall betray me.

24 The Son of man goeth [a]as it is written of him: but [b]woe unto that man by whom the Son of man is betrayed: it had been good for that man if he had not been born.

25 Then Judas, which betrayed him, answered and said, Master, is it I? He said unto him, Thou hast said.

26 ¶ [a]And as they were eating, [b]Jesus took bread, and [1]blessed *it,* and brake *it,* and gave *it* to the disciples, and said, Take, eat; [c]this is my body.

27 And he took the cup, and gave thanks, and gave *it* to them, saying, [a]Drink ye all of it;

28 For [a]this is my blood [b]of the new testament, which is shed [c]for many for the remission of sins.

29 But [a]I say unto you, I will not drink henceforth of this fruit of the vine, [b]until that day when I drink it new with you in my Father's kingdom.

30 ¶ [a]And when they had sung a [1]hymn, they went out into the mount of Olives.

31 Then saith Jesus unto them, [a]All ye shall [b]be offended because of me this night: for it is written, [c]I will smite the shepherd, and the sheep of the flock shall be scattered abroad.

not unknown. The religious leaders (v. 3) knew that many people admired Jesus.

26:6–13 See note on John 12:1–11.

26:6 *Bethany.* See note on 21:17. *Simon the leper.* Mentioned elsewhere only in Mark 14:3, though Simon was a common Jewish name in the first century. He was probably a well-known victim of leprosy who had been healed by Jesus.

26:7 *alabaster box.* Most "alabaster" of ancient times was actually marble (see note on Mark 14:3).

26:10 *good.* The Greek word has an aesthetic as well as an ethical meaning.

26:14 *Iscariot.* See note on Mark 3:19.

26:15 *thirty pieces of silver.* Equivalent to 120 denarii. Laborers customarily received one denarius for a day's work (see 20:1–16).

26:17 *the first day of the feast of unleavened bread.* The 14th of Nisan (March-April), it was also called the preparation of the passover. The passover meal was eaten the evening of the 14th after sunset—and therefore technically on the 15th, since the Jewish day ended at sunset. The feast of unleavened bread lasted seven days, from the 15th to the 21st of Nisan (see Lev 23:5–6), but in the time of Christ the entire period, Nisan 14–21, was referred to under that name (see note on Mark 14:12).

26:18–30 These verses clearly indicate that Jesus ate the passover meal with His disciples the night before His crucifixion. For more information on the Lord's Supper see notes on Mark 14:22,24.

26:18 *My time.* A reference to Jesus' crucifixion.

26:19 *made ready the passover.* See note on Mark 14:15.

26:20 *sat down.* See note on Mark 14:18.

26:21 *Verily I say unto you.* See note on Mark 3:28.

26:23 *dippeth his hand with me in the dish.* It was the custom—still practiced by some in the Middle East—to take a piece of bread, or a piece of meat wrapped in bread, and dip it into a bowl of sauce (made of stewed fruit) on the table. *shall betray me.* In that culture, as among Arabs today, to eat with a person was tantamount to saying, "I am your friend and will not hurt you." This fact made Judas's deed all the more despicable (cf. Ps 41:9).

26:24 *as it is written of him.* See note on Mark 14:21. *Son of man.* See note on Mark 8:31.

26:26–28 See notes on Mark 14:22–24.

26:30 *hymn.* The passover fellowship was concluded with the second half of the Hallel Psalms (Ps 115–118).

26:31 *All ye shall be offended.* Not Peter only, but all the eleven (Judas had previously withdrawn, John 13:30). The meaning of the words "be offended" is seen in Peter's denial (vv. 69–75) and in the terrified flight of the other disciples (v. 56). *I will smite the shepherd.* See note on Zech 13:7.

32 But after I am risen *again,* [a]I will go before you into Galilee.

33 Peter answered and said unto him, Though all *men* shall be offended because of thee, *yet* will I never be offended.

34 Jesus said unto him, [a]Verily I say unto thee, That this night, before *the* cock crow, thou shalt deny me thrice.

35 Peter said unto him, Though I should die with thee, *yet* will I not deny thee. Likewise also said all the disciples.

Jesus' agony in Gethsemane

36 ¶ [a]Then cometh Jesus with them unto a place called Gethsemane, and saith unto the disciples, Sit ye here, while I go and pray yonder.

37 And he took with *him* Peter and [a]the two sons of Zebedee, and began to be sorrowful and very heavy.

38 Then saith he unto them, [a]My soul is exceeding sorrowful, *even* unto death: tarry ye here, and watch with me.

39 And he went a little further, and fell on his face, and [a]prayed, saying, [b]O my Father, if it be possible, [c]let this cup pass from me: nevertheless [d]not as I will, but as thou *wilt.*

40 And he cometh unto the disciples, and findeth them asleep, and saith unto Peter, What, could ye not watch with me one hour?

41 [a]Watch and pray, that ye enter not into temptation: the spirit indeed *is* willing, but the flesh *is* weak.

42 He went away again the second time, and prayed, saying, O my Father, if this cup may not pass away from me, except I drink it, thy will be done.

43 And he came and found them asleep again: for their eyes were heavy.

44 And he left them, and went away again, and prayed the third time, saying the same words.

45 Then cometh he to his disciples, and saith unto them, Sleep on now, and take your rest: behold, the hour is at hand, and the Son of man is betrayed into the hands of sinners.

46 Rise, let us be going: behold, he is at hand that doth betray me.

Jesus' betrayal and arrest

47 ¶ And [a]while he yet spake, lo, Judas, one of the twelve, came, and with him a great multitude with swords and staves, from the chief priests and elders of the people.

48 Now he that betrayed him gave them a sign, saying, Whomsoever I shall kiss, that *same* is he: hold him fast.

49 And forthwith he came to Jesus, and said, Hail, master; [a]and kissed him.

50 And Jesus said unto him, [a]Friend, wherefore art thou come? Then came they, and laid hands on Jesus, and took him.

51 And behold, [a]one of them which were with Jesus stretched out *his* hand, and drew his sword, and stroke a servant of the high priest's, and smote off his ear.

52 Then said Jesus unto him, Put up again thy sword into his place: [a]for all they that take the sword shall perish with the sword.

53 Thinkest thou that I cannot now pray to my Father, and he shall presently give me [a]more than twelve legions of angels?

54 *But* how then shall the scriptures be fulfilled, [a]that thus it must be?

55 In that *same* hour said Jesus to the multitudes, Are ye come out as against a thief with swords and staves for to take me? I sat daily with you teaching in the temple, and ye laid no hold on me.

56 But all this was done, that the [a]scriptures of the prophets might be fulfilled. Then [b]all the disciples forsook him, and fled.

Jesus before Caiaphas

57 ¶ [a]And they that had laid hold on Jesus led *him* away to Caiaphas the high priest, where the scribes and the elders were assembled.

58 But Peter followed him afar off unto the high priest's palace, and went in, and sat with the servants, to see the end.

59 Now the chief priests, and elders, and

26:32 [a]ch. 28:7,10; Mark 14:28; 16:7
26:34 [a]Mark 14:30; Luke 22:34; John 13:38
26:36 [a]Mark 14:32-35; Luke 22:39; John 18:1
26:37 [a]ch. 4:21
26:38 [a]John 12:27
26:39 [a]Mark 14:36; Luke 22:42; Heb. 5:7 [b]John 12:27 [c]ch. 20:22 [d]John 5:30; 6:38; Phil. 2:8
26:41 [a]Mark 13:33; 14:38; Luke 22:40,46; Eph. 6:18
26:47 [a]Mark 14:43; Luke 22:47; John 18:3; Acts 1:16
26:49 [a]2 Sam. 20:9
26:50 [a]Ps. 41:9; 55:13
26:51 [a]John 18:10
26:52 [a]Gen. 9:6; Rev. 13:10
26:53 [a]2 Ki. 6:17; Dan. 7:10
26:54 [a]ver. 24; Is. 53:7; Luke 24:25,44,46
26:56 [a]Lam. 4:20 [b]See John 18:15
26:57 [a]Mark 14:53; Luke 22:54; John 18:12,13,24

26:32 *into Galilee.* Cf. 28:10,16–20; Mark 16:7; John 21:1–23.
26:34 *before the cock crow.* The reference may be to the third of the Roman watches into which the night was divided (see note on 14:25; see also Mark 13:35). Or it may simply refer to early morning when the rooster crows.
26:36 *Gethsemane.* The name means "oil press," a place for squeezing the oil from olives (see note on Mark 14:32).
‡26:37 *Peter and the two sons of Zebedee.* The latter were James and John. These three disciples seem to have been especially close to Jesus (see note on Mark 5:37). They were the only disciples to accompany Jesus into Jairus's house and to the mount of transfiguration.
26:38–39 Jesus did not die serenely as many martyrs have. He was no mere martyr; He was the Lamb of God bearing the penalty of the sins of the entire human race. The wrath of God was turned loose on Him. Only this can adequately explain what took place at Gethsemane.
26:39 *cup.* A symbol of deep sorrow and suffering. Here it refers to His Father's face being turned away from Him when He who had no sin was made sin (i.e., a sin offering) for us (see 27:46; 2 Cor 5:21).
26:41 See note on Mark 14:38.
26:45 *Son of man.* See note on Mark 8:31.
26:47 *a great multitude with swords and staves.* See note on Mark 14:43. *chief priests and elders.* See notes on v. 3 and 2:4.
26:48 *Whomsoever I shall kiss.* See note on Luke 22:47.
‡26:49 *master.* Hebrew word for "(my) teacher." *kissed him.* The same word is used of the father's kissing of the prodigal son, indicating affection. *he* [Judas]. See notes on Mark 14:45 and Luke 22:47.
26:51 *one of them which were with Jesus.* Peter (see John 18:10). *a servant of the high priest's.* Malchus (see John 18:10).
26:53 *legions.* A Roman legion had 6,000 soldiers.
26:54 *scriptures be fulfilled.* In view of v. 56 probably a reference to Zech 13:7.
26:57—27:26 For a summary of the two stages (religious and civil) of the trial of Jesus see note on Mark 14:53–15:15.

all the council, sought false witness against
Jesus, to put him to death;
60 But found none: yea, though [a]many
false witnesses came, *yet* found they none. At
the last came [b]two false witnesses,
61 And said, This *fellow* said, [a]I am able to
destroy the temple of God, and to build it in
three days.
62 [a]And the high priest arose, and said
unto him, Answerest thou nothing? what *is it*
which these witness against thee?
63 But [a]Jesus held his peace. And the high
priest answered and said unto him, [b]I adjure
thee by the living God, that thou tell us
whether thou be the Christ, the Son of God.
64 Jesus saith unto him, Thou hast said:
nevertheless I say unto you, [a]Hereafter shall
ye see the Son of man [b]sitting on the right
hand of power, and coming in the clouds of
heaven.
65 [a]Then the high priest rent his clothes,
saying, He hath spoken blasphemy; what further need have we of witnesses? behold, now
ye have heard his blasphemy.
66 What think ye? They answered and
said, [a]He is guilty of death.
67 [a]Then did they spit in his face, and buffeted him; and [b]others smote *him* with [1]the
palms of their hands,
68 Saying, [a]Prophesy unto us, *thou* Christ,
Who is he that smote thee?

Peter's denial of Jesus

69 ¶ [a]Now Peter sat without in the palace:
and a damsel came unto him, saying, Thou
also wast with Jesus of Galilee.
70 But he denied before *them* all, saying, I
know not what thou sayest.
71 And when he was gone out into the
porch, another *maid* saw him, and said unto
them that were there, This *fellow* was also
with Jesus of Nazareth.
72 And again he denied with an oath, I do
not know the man.
73 And after a while came unto *him* they
that stood *by,* and said to Peter, Surely thou
also art *one* of them; for thy [a]speech bewrayeth thee.

26:60 [a]Ps. 27:12; 35:11; Mark 14:55; Acts 6:13 [b]Deut. 19:15
26:61 [a]ch. 27:40; John 2:19
26:62 [a]Mark 14:60
26:63 [a]Is. 53:7; ch. 27:12 [b]Lev. 5:1; 1 Sam. 14:24,26
26:64 [a]Dan. 7:13; ch. 16:27; 24:30; 25:31; Luke 21:27; John 1:51; Rom. 14:10; 1 Thes. 4:16; Rev. 1:7 [b]Ps. 110:1; Acts 7:55
26:65 [a]2 Ki. 18:37
26:66 [a]Lev. 24:16; John 19:7
26:67 [1]Or, *rods,* as in John 18:22 marg. [a]Is. 50:6; 53:3; ch. 27:30 [b]Luke 22:63
26:68 [a]Mark 14:65; Luke 22:64
26:69 [a]Mark 14:66; Luke 22:55; John 18:16,17,25
26:73 [a]Luke 22:59
26:74 [a]Mark 14:71
26:75 [a]ver. 34; Luke 22:61; John 13:38
27:1 [a]Ps. 2:2; Mark 15:1; Luke 22:66; 23:1; John 18:28
27:2 [a]ch. 20:19; Acts 3:13
27:3 [a]ch. 26:14
27:5 [a]2 Sam. 17:23; Acts 1:18
27:8 [a]Acts 1:19
27:9 [1]Or, *whom they bought of the children of Israel* [a]Zech. 11:12
27:11 [a]Mark 15:2; Luke 23:3; John 18:33 [b]John 18:37; 1 Tim. 6:13

74 Then [a]began he to curse and to swear,
saying, I know not the man. And immediately
the cock crew.
75 And Peter remembered the word of
Jesus, which said unto him, [a]Before *the* cock
crow, thou shalt deny me thrice. And he went
out, and wept bitterly.

The death of Judas Iscariot

27 When the morning was come, [a]all
the chief priests and elders of the
people took counsel against Jesus to put him to
death:
2 And when they had bound him, they led
him away, and [a]delivered him to Pontius Pilate
the governor.
3 ¶ [a]Then Judas, which had betrayed him,
when he saw that he was condemned, repented himself, and brought again the thirty pieces
of silver to the chief priests and elders,
4 Saying, I have sinned in that I have betrayed *the* innocent blood. And they said,
What *is that* to us? see thou *to that.*
5 And he cast down the pieces of silver in
the temple, [a]and departed, and went and
hanged himself.
6 And the chief priests took the silver
pieces, and said, It is not lawful for to put
them into the treasury, because it is the price
of blood.
7 And they took counsel, and bought with
them the potter's field, to bury strangers in.
8 Wherefore that field was called, [a]The
field of blood, unto this day.
9 Then was fulfilled that which was spoken
by Jeremie the prophet, saying, [a]And they
took the thirty pieces of silver, the price of him
that was valued, [1]whom they of the children
of Israel did value;
10 And gave them for the potter's field, as
the Lord appointed me.

Jesus before Pontius Pilate

11 ¶ And Jesus stood before the governor:
[a]and the governor asked him, saying, Art thou
the King of the Jews? And Jesus said unto him,
[b]Thou sayest.

26:59 *council.* See note on Mark 14:55.

26:61 *I am able to destroy the temple of God.* Evidently an intentional distortion of Jesus' words (John 2:19).

26:63 *I adjure thee.* Jesus refused to answer the question of v. 62 (see v. 63a). But when the high priest used this form, He was legally obliged to reply. *Christ.* See note on 16:16.

26:65 *rent his clothes.* Ordinarily the high priest was forbidden by law to do this (Lev 10:6; 21:10), but this was considered a highly unusual circumstance. The high priest interpreted Jesus' answer in v. 64 as blasphemy (see note on Mark 14:64).

26:67–68 Mark reports that they blindfolded Jesus (Mark 14:65), which explains the mocking command: "Prophesy . . . Who smote thee?"

26:73 *thy speech bewrayeth thee.* Peter had a decidedly Galilean accent that was conspicuous in Jerusalem.

27:1 *When the morning was come.* The Sanhedrin could not have a legal session at night, so at daybreak a special meeting was held to make the death sentence (see 26:66) official. See note on Mark 15:1.

27:2 *delivered him to Pontius Pilate.* The Sanhedrin had been deprived by the Roman government of the right to carry out capital punishment, except in the case of a foreigner who invaded the sacred precincts of the temple. So Jesus had to be handed over to Pilate for execution. For additional information about Pilate see note on Mark 15:1.

27:3–10 See Acts 1:16–19.

27:5 *hanged himself.* See note on Acts 1:18.

27:8 *The field of blood.* Cf. "the valley of slaughter" in Jer 19:6.

27:9 *Jeremie.* The quotation that follows seems to be a combining of Zech 11:12–13 and Jer 19:1–13 (or perhaps Jer 18:2–12 or Jer 32:6–9). But Matthew attributes it to the major prophet Jeremiah, just as Mark (1:2-3) quotes Mal 3:1 and Is 40:3 but attributes them to the major prophet Isaiah.

The Life of Christ

CHILDHOOD

Birth of Jesus, BETHLEHEM, c. 6/5 B.C., Mat 1:18-25; Luke 2:1-7

Visit by shepherds, BETHLEHEM, Luke 2:8-20

Presentation in the temple, JERUSALEM, Luke 2:21-40

Visit by the Magi, BETHLEHEM, Mat 2:1-12

Escape to Egypt, NILE DELTA, Mat 2:13-18

Return to Nazareth, LOWER GALILEE, Mat 2:19-23

Visit to temple as a boy, JERUSALEM, c A.D. 7/8, Luke 2:41-52

YEAR OF INAUGURATION

YEAR OF POPULARITY

YEAR OF OPPOSITION

Begin less than full year of ministry

10 | 5 | B.C. A.D. | 5 | 10 | 15 | 20 | 25 | 30 | 35

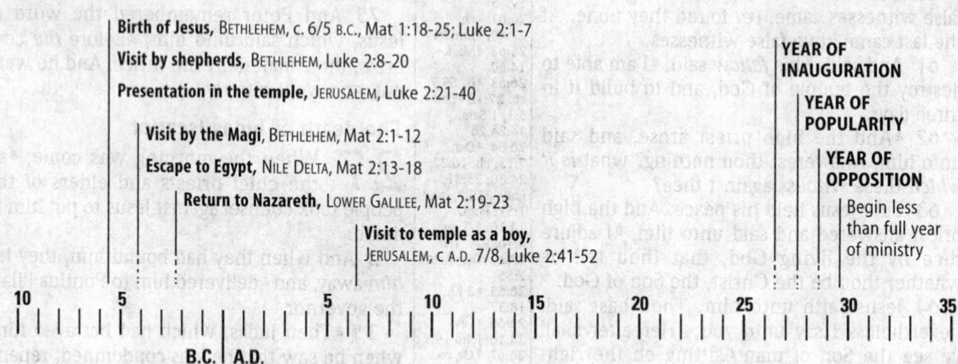

Jesus baptized
JORDAN RIVER
c. A.D. 26
Mat 3:13-17; Mark 1:9-11; Luke 3:21-23; John 1:29-39

Jesus tempted by Satan
WILDERNESS
Mat 4:1-11; Mark 1:12-13; Luke 4:1-13

Jesus' first miracle
CANA
John 2:1-11

4 fishermen become Jesus' followers
SEA OF GALILEE AT CAPERNAUM
A.D. 27
Mat 4:18-22; Mark 1:16-20; Luke 5:1-11

Jesus heals Peter's mother-in-law
CAPERNAUM
Mat 8:14-17; Mark 1:29-34; Luke 4:38-41

YEAR OF INAUGURATION — YEAR OF POPULARITY

FALL | A.D. **27** WINTER | SPRING | SUMMER | FALL | **28** WINTER

Jesus' cleansing of the temple
A.D. 27
John 2:14-22

Jesus and Nicodemus
JERUSALEM
A.D. 27
John 3:1-21

Jesus talks to the Samaritan woman
SAMARIA
John 4:5-42

Jesus heals a nobleman's son
CANA
John 4:46-54

The people of Jesus' hometown try to kill Him
NAZARETH
Luke 4:16-31

Jesus begins His first preaching trip through Galilee
Mat 4:23-25; Mark 1:35-39; Luke 4:42-44

Matthew decides to follow Jesus
CAPERNAUM
Mat 9:9-13; Mark 2:13-17; Luke 5:27-32

Jesus chooses the 12 disciples
A.D. 28
Mark 3:13-19; Luke 6:12-15

Jesus preaches the "Sermon on the Mount"
Mat 5:1–7:29; Luke 6:20-49

Jesus feeds 5,000 people
NEAR BETHSAIDA
Spring, A.D. 29
Mat 14:13-21; Mark 6:30-44; Luke 9:10-17; John 6:1-14

Jesus walks on water
Mat 14:22-33; Mark 6:45-52; John 6:16-21

Jesus withdraws to Tyre and Sidon
Mat 15:21-28; Mark 7:24-30

Jesus feeds 4,000 people
Mat 15:32-39; Mark 8:1-9

A sinful woman anoints Jesus
CAPERNAUM
Luke 7:36-50

Peter says that Jesus is the Son of God
Mat 16:13-20; Mark 8:27-30; Luke 9:18-21

Jesus travels again through Galilee
Luke 8:1-3

Jesus tells His disciples He is going to die soon
CAESAREA PHILIPPI
Mat 16:21-26; Mark 8:31-37; Luke 9:22-25

Jesus tells parables about the kingdom
Mat 13:1-52; Mark 4:1-34; Luke 8:4-18

Jesus is transfigured
Mat 17:1-13; Mark 9:2-13; Luke 9:28-36

Jesus calms the storm
SEA OF GALILEE
Mat 8:23-27; Mark 4:35-41; Luke 8:22-25

Jesus pays His temple taxes
CAPERNAUM
Later in that year
Mat 17:24-27

YEAR OF OPPOSITION

SPRING | **SUMMER** | **FALL** *Oct. 29* | **29** **WINTER** | **SPRING** | **SUMMER** | **FALL**

Jesus attends the Feast of Tabernacles
JERUSALEM
October, A.D. 29
John 7:11-52

Jairus's daughter is brought back to life by Jesus
CAPERNAUM
Mat 9:18-26; Mark 5:21-43; Luke 8:40-56

Jesus heals a man who was born blind
JERUSALEM
John 9:1-41

Jesus sends His 12 followers out to preach and heal
Mat 9:35–11:1; Mark 6:6-13; Luke 9:1-6

Jesus visits Mary and Martha
BETHANY
Luke 10:38-42

John the Baptist is killed by Herod
MACHAERUS
A.D. 28
Mat 14:1-12; Mark 6:14-29; Luke 9:7-9

Jesus raises Lazarus from the dead
BETHANY
Winter, A.D. 29
John 11:1-44

The Life of Christ –continued

Jesus begins His last trip to Jerusalem
A.D. 30
Luke 17:11

Jesus blesses the little children
ACROSS THE JORDAN
Mat 19:13-15; Mark 10:13-16; Luke 18:15-17

Jesus talks to the rich young man
ACROSS THE JORDAN
Mat 19:16-30; Mark 10:17-31; Luke 18:18-30

Jesus again tells about His death and resurrection
NEAR THE JORDAN
Mat 20:17-19; Mark 10:32-34; Luke 18:31-34

Jesus heals blind Bartimeus
JERICHO
Mat 20:29-34; Mark 10:46-52; Luke 18:35-43

Jesus talks to Zaccheus
JERICHO
Luke 19:1-10

Jesus returns to Bethany to visit Mary and Martha
BETHANY
John 11:55-12:1

THE LAST WEEK

The Triumphal Entry, JERUSALEM, Sunday
Mat 21:1-11; Mark 11:1-10; Luke 19:29-44; John 12:12-19

Jesus curses the fig tree, Monday
Mat 21:18-19; Mark 11:12-14

Jesus cleanses the temple, Monday
Mat 21:12-13; Mark 11:15-18

The authority of Jesus questioned, Tuesday
Mat 21:23-27; Mark 11:27-33; Luke 20:1-8

Jesus teaches in the temple, Tuesday
Mat 21:28–23:39; Mark 12:1-44; Luke 20:9–21:4

Jesus anointed, BETHANY, Tuesday
Mat 26:6-13; Mark 14:3-9; John 12:2-11

The plot against Jesus, Wednesday
Mat 26:14-16; Mark 14:10-11; Luke 22:3-6

The Last Supper, Thursday
Mat 26:17-29; Mark 14:12-25; Luke 22:7-20; John 13:1-38

Jesus comforts the disciples, Thursday
John 14:1–16:33

Gethsemane, Thursday
Mat 26:36-46; Mark 14:32-42; Luke 22:40-46

Jesus' arrest and trial, Thursday night and Friday
Mat 26:47–27:26; Mark 14:43–15:15; Luke 22:47–23:25; John 18:2–19:16

Jesus' crucifixion and death, GOLGOTHA, Friday
Mat 27:27-56; Mark 15:16-41; Luke 23:26-49; John 19:17-30

The burial of Jesus, JOSEPH'S TOMB, Friday
Mat 27:57-66; Mark 15:42-47; Luke 23:50-56; John 19:31-42

30 WINTER | SPRING | SUMMER | FALL | **A.D. 31** WINTER | SPRING | SUMMER

AFTER THE RESURRECTION

The empty tomb, JERUSALEM, Sunday
Mat 28:1-10; Mark 16:1-8; Luke 24:1-12; John 20:1-10

Mary Magdalene sees Jesus in the garden
JERUSALEM, Sunday
Mat 16:9-11; John 20:11-18

Jesus appears to the two going to Emmaus
Sunday
Mark 16:12-13; Luke 24:13-35

Jesus appears to 10 disciples
JERUSALEM, Sunday
Mark 16:14; Luke 24:36-43; John 20:19-25

Jesus appears to the 11 disciples
JERUSALEM, One week later
John 20:26-31

Jesus talks with some of His disciples
SEA OF GALILEE, One week later
John 21:1-25

Jesus ascends to His Father in Heaven
MOUNT OF OLIVES, 40 days later
Mat 28:16-20; Mark 16:19-20; Luke 24:44-53

Dotted lines leading to the timeline are meant to define sequence of events only. Exact dates, even year dates, are generally unknown.

12 And when he was accused of the chief priests and elders, [a]he answered nothing.

13 Then said Pilate unto him, [a]Hearest thou not how many *things* they witness against thee?

14 And he answered him to never a word; insomuch that the governor marvelled greatly.

15 ¶ [a]Now at *that* feast the governor was wont to release unto the people a prisoner, whom they would.

16 And they had then a notable prisoner, called Barabbas.

17 Therefore when they were gathered together, Pilate said unto them, Whom will ye *that* I release unto you? Barabbas, or Jesus which is called Christ?

18 For he knew that for envy they had delivered him.

19 When he was set down on the judgment seat, his wife sent unto him, saying, Have thou nothing to do with that just *man:* for I have suffered many *things* this day in a dream because of him.

20 [a]But the chief priests and elders persuaded the multitude that they should ask Barabbas, and destroy Jesus.

21 The governor answered and said unto them, Whether of the twain will ye *that* I release unto you? They said, Barabbas.

22 Pilate saith unto them, What shall I do then with Jesus which is called Christ? *They* all say unto him, Let him be crucified.

23 And the governor said, Why, what evil hath he done? But they cried out the more, saying, Let him be crucified.

24 When Pilate saw that he could prevail nothing, but *that* rather a tumult was made, he [a]took water, and washed *his* hands before the multitude, saying, I am innocent of the blood of this just *person:* see ye *to it.*

25 Then answered all the people, and said, [a]His blood *be* on us, and on our children.

26 Then released he Barabbas unto them: and when [a]he had scourged Jesus, he delivered *him* to be crucified.

Jesus crowned with thorns

27 ¶ [a]Then the soldiers of the governor took Jesus into the [1]common hall, and gathered unto him the whole band *of soldiers.*

28 And they stripped him, and [a]put on him a scarlet robe.

29 [a]And when they had platted a crown of thorns, they put *it* upon his head, and a reed in his right hand: and they bowed the knee before him, and mocked him, saying, Hail, King of the Jews!

30 And [a]they spit upon him, and took the reed, and smote him on the head.

31 And after that they had mocked him, they took the robe off from him, and put his own raiment on him, [a]and led him away to crucify *him.*

32 [a]And as they came out, [b]they found a man of Cyrene, Simon by name: him they compelled to bear his cross.

Jesus crucified

33 ¶ [a]And when they were come unto a place called Golgotha, that is to say, a place of a skull,

34 [a]They gave him vinegar to drink mingled with gall: and when he had tasted *thereof,* he would not drink.

35 [a]And they crucified him, and parted his garments, casting lots: that it might be fulfilled which was spoken by the prophet, [b]They parted my garments among them, and upon my vesture did they cast lots.

36 [a]And sitting down they watched him there;

37 And [a]set up over his head his accusation written, THIS IS JESUS THE KING OF THE JEWS.

38 [a]Then were there two thieves crucified with him, one on the right hand, and another on the left.

39 ¶ And [a]they that passed by, reviled him, wagging their heads,

40 And saying, [a]*Thou* that destroyest the temple, and buildest *it* in three days, save thyself. [b]If thou be the Son of God, come down from the cross.

41 Likewise also the chief priests mocking *him,* with the scribes and elders, said,

42 He saved others; himself he cannot save. If he be the King of Israel, let him now

27:12 [a]ch. 26:63; John 19:9
27:13 [a]ch. 26:62; John 19:10
27:15 [a]Mark 15:6; Luke 23:17; John 18:39
27:20 [a]Mark 15:11; Luke 23:18; John 18:40; Acts 3:14
27:24 [a]Deut. 21:6
27:25 [a]Deut. 19:10; Josh. 2:19; 2 Sam. 1:16; 1 Ki. 2:32; Acts 5:28
27:26 [a]Is. 53:5; Mark 15:15; Luke 23:16,24, 25; John 19:1,16
27:27 [a]Mark 15:16; John 19:2
27:27 [1]Or, *governor's house*
27:28 [a]Luke 23:11
27:29 [a]Ps. 69:19; Is. 53:3
27:30 [a]Is. 50:6; ch. 26:67
27:31 [a]Is. 53:7
27:32 [a]Num. 15:35; 1 Ki. 21:13; Acts 7:58; Heb. 13:12 [b]Mark 15:21; Luke 23:26
27:33 [a]Mark 15:22; Luke 23:33; John 19:17
27:34 [a]See ver. 48; Ps. 69:21
27:35 [a]Mark 15:24; Luke 23:34; John 19:24 [b]Ps. 22:18
27:36 [a]ver. 54
27:37 [a]Mark 15:26; Luke 23:38; John 19:19
27:38 [a]Is. 53:12; Mark 15:27; Luke 23:32,33; John 19:18
27:39 [a]Ps. 22:7; 109:25; Mark 15:29; Luke 23:35
27:40 [a]ch. 26:61; John 2:19 [b]ch. 26:63

27:15 *the governor was wont.* A custom of which nothing is known outside the Gospels.

‡27:16 *notable prisoner.* Barabbas had taken part in a rebellion (Luke 23:19; John 18:40), presumably against the Romans. So he would have been a folk hero among the Jews.

27:19 This incident is found only in Matthew's Gospel.

27:25 A chilling response by a bloodthirsty crowd. It has often been used to justify the persecution of the Jewish people. It should be noted, however, that it was not God but the people themselves who uttered these words. There is no evidence here that God granted their request. If there was a fulfillment, it was most likely seen in the destruction of Jerusalem in A.D. 70.

27:26 *scourged.* Roman floggings were so brutal that sometimes the victim died before crucifixion. See note on Mark 15:15.

‡27:27 *the common hall.* The *praetorium* was the governor's official residence in Jerusalem (see note on Mark 15:16).

27:28 *scarlet robe.* The outer cloak of a Roman soldier.

27:29 *crown of thorns.* See note on Mark 15:17. *reed.* A mock scepter.

‡27:32 *Cyrene.* A city in North Africa on the Mediterranean Sea about 700 miles west of Jerusalem. *Simon . . . to bear his cross.* See note on Mark 15:21.

27:33 *Golgotha.* See note on Mark 15:22.

27:34 *mingled with gall.* Tradition says that the women of Jerusalem customarily furnished this pain-killing narcotic to prisoners who were crucified. Jesus refused to drink it because He wanted to be fully conscious until His death (v. 50).

27:35 *crucified.* See note on Mark 15:24. *casting lots.* Explained more precisely in John 19:23–24.

27:37 See note on Mark 15:26.

27:38 *two thieves.* See note on Mark 15:27.

come down from the cross, and we will believe him.

43 [a]He trusted in God; let him deliver him now, if he will have him: for he said, I am the Son of God.

44 [a]The thieves also, which were crucified with him, cast the same in his teeth.

45 ¶ [a]Now from the sixth hour there was darkness over all the land unto the ninth hour.

46 And about the ninth hour [a]Jesus cried with a loud voice, saying, ELI, ELI, LAMA SABACHTHANI? that is to say, [b]My God, my God, why hast thou forsaken me?

47 Some of them that stood there, when they heard *that,* said, This *man* calleth for Elias.

48 And straightway one of them ran, and took a spunge, [a]and filled *it* with vinegar, and put *it* on a reed, and gave him to drink.

49 The rest said, Let be, let us see whether Elias will come to save him.

The death of Jesus

50 ¶ [a]Jesus, when he had cried again with a loud voice, yielded up the ghost.

51 ¶ And behold, the [a]vail of the temple was rent in twain from the top to the bottom; and the earth did quake, and the rocks rent;

52 And the graves were opened; and many bodies of saints which slept arose,

53 And came out of the graves after his resurrection, and went into the holy city, and appeared unto many.

54 [a]Now when the centurion, and they that were with him, watching Jesus, saw the earthquake, and *those things* that were done, they feared greatly, saying, Truly this was the Son of God.

55 And many women were there beholding afar off, [a]which followed Jesus from Galilee, ministering unto him:

56 [a]Among which was Mary Magdalene, and Mary the mother of James and Joses, and the mother of Zebedee's children.

Jesus laid in the sepulchre

57 ¶ [a]When the even was come, there came a rich man of Arimathea, named Joseph, who also himself was Jesus' disciple:

58 He went to Pilate, and begged the body of Jesus. Then Pilate commanded the body to be delivered.

59 And when Joseph had taken the body, he wrapped it in a clean linen cloth,

60 And [a]laid it in his own new tomb, which he had hewn out in the rock: and he rolled a great stone to the door of the sepulchre, and departed.

61 And there was Mary Magdalene, and the other Mary, sitting over against the sepulchre.

The sepulchre guarded

62 ¶ Now the next day, that followed the *day of the* preparation, the chief priests and Pharisees came together unto Pilate,

63 Saying, Sir, we remember that that deceiver said, while he was yet alive, [a]After three days I will rise *again.*

64 Command therefore that the sepulchre be made sure until the third day, lest his disciples come by night, and steal him *away,* and say unto the people, He is risen from the dead: so the last error shall be worse than the first.

65 Pilate said unto them, Ye have a watch: go your way, make *it* as sure as you can.

66 So they went, and made the sepulchre sure, [a]sealing the stone, and setting a watch.

The resurrection of Jesus

28 In the [a]end of the sabbath, as it began to dawn towards the first *day* of the week, came Mary Magdalene [b]and the other Mary to see the sepulchre.

2 And behold, there [1]was a great earthquake: for [a]*the* angel of the Lord descended from heaven, and came and rolled back the stone from the door, and sat upon it.

3 [a]His countenance was like lightning, and his raiment white as snow:

27:43 [a]Ps. 22:8
27:44 [a]Mark 15:32; Luke 23:39
27:45 [a]Amos 8:9; Mark 15:33; Luke 23:44
27:46 [a]Heb. 5:7 [b]Ps. 22:1
27:48 [a]Ps. 69:21; Mark 15:36; Luke 23:36; John 19:29
27:50 [a]Mark 15:37; Luke 23:46
27:51 [a]Ex. 26:31; 2 Chr. 3:14; Mark 15:38; Luke 23:45
27:54 [a]ver. 36; Mark 15:39; Luke 23:47
27:55 [a]Luke 8:2,3
27:56 [a]Mark 15:40
27:57 [a]Mark 15:42; Luke 23:50; John 19:38
27:60 [a]Is. 53:9
27:63 [a]ch. 16:21; 17:23; 20:19; 26:61; Mark 8:31; 10:34; Luke 9:22; 18:33; 24:6,7; John 2:19
27:66 [a]Dan. 6:17
28:1 [a]Mark 16:1; Luke 24:1; John 20:1 [b]ch. 27:56
28:2 [1]Or, *had been* [a]See Mark 16:5; Luke 24:4; John 20:12
28:3 [a]Dan. 10:6

27:45 *from the sixth hour . . . unto the ninth hour.* From noon until 3:00 P.M.

27:46 *ELI, ELI, LAMA SABACHTHANI?* A mixture of Aramaic and Hebrew, translated by Matthew for his readers (see note on Mark 15:34).

27:49 See note on Mark 15:35.

27:51 *vail.* The inner curtain that separated the holy place from the most holy place. The tearing of the curtain signified Christ's making it possible for believers to go directly into God's presence (see Heb 9:1–14; 10:14–22).

‡27:52–53 An incident found only in Matthew's Gospel. These rose after Christ did. Jesus was "the firstfruits of them that slept" (1 Cor 15:20). They were a witness to Christ's victory over death.

27:54 *centurion.* See note on 8:5. *Son of God.* It cannot be determined whether the centurion made a fully Christian confession, or was only acknowledging that, since the gods had so obviously acted to vindicate this judicial victim, Jesus must be one especially favored by them (the Greek can also be translated "a son"). But in view of the ridicule voiced by "those passing by" (vv. 39–40), it seems probable that Matthew intended the former. See note on Luke 23:47.

27:56 See note on Mark 15:40.

27:57 *Arimathea.* A village in the hill country of Ephraim, about 20 miles northwest of Jerusalem.

27:58 *begged the body of Jesus.* See note on Luke 23:52.

27:59–60 See note on Mark 15:46.

27:62 *the next day, that followed the day of the preparation.* Saturday, the sabbath. Friday was the preparation day for the sabbath (sunset Friday to sunset Saturday).

27:64 *the last error shall be worse than the first.* The first would be that Jesus was the Messiah, the second that He had risen as the Son of God.

27:65 *Ye have a watch.* Of Roman soldiers (28:4,11–12).

28:1 *first day of the week.* See note on Luke 24:1. *the other Mary.* The wife of Clopas (see 27:56; John 19:25).

‡28:2 *a great earthquake.* Only Matthew mentions this earthquake and the one at Jesus' death (27:51,54). It is also clear from the parallel accounts (Mark 16:2–6; Luke 24:1–7; John 20:1) that the events of vv. 2–4 occurred before the women actually arrived at the tomb.

4 And for fear of him the keepers did
shake, and became as dead *men.*
5 And the angel answered and said unto
the women, Fear not ye: for I know that ye
seek Jesus, which was crucified.
6 He is not here: for he is risen, [a]as he
said. Come, see the place where the Lord lay.
7 And go quickly, and tell his disciples that
he is risen from the dead; and behold, [a]he
goeth before you into Galilee; there shall ye
see him: lo, I have told you.
8 And they departed quickly from the
sepulchre with fear and great joy; and did run
to bring his disciples word.
9 And as they went to tell his disciples, behold, [a]Jesus met them, saying, *All* hail. And
they came and held him by the feet, and worshipped him.
10 Then said Jesus unto them, Be not
afraid: go tell [a]my brethren that they go into
Galilee, and there shall they see me.

The bribing of the soldiers

11 ¶ Now when they were going, behold,
some of the watch came into the city, and
shewed unto the chief priests all the *things*
that were done.

28:6 [a]ch. 12:40; 16:21; 17:23; 20:19
28:7 [a]ch. 26:32; Mark 16:7
28:9 [a]See Mark 16:9; John 20:14
28:10 [a]See John 20:17; Rom. 8:29; Heb. 2:11
28:16 [a]ver. 7; ch. 26:32
28:18 [a]Dan. 7:13,14; ch. 11:27; 16:28; Luke 1:32; 10:22; John 3:35; 5:22; 13:3; 17:2; Acts 2:36; Rom. 14:9; 1 Cor. 15:27; Eph. 1:10,21; Phil. 2:9,10; Heb. 1:2; 2:8; 1 Pet. 3:22; Rev. 17:14
28:19 [1][Or, *make disciples,* or, *Christians of all nations*] [a]Mark 16:15 [b]Is. 52:10; Luke 24:47; Acts 2:38,39; Rom. 10:18; Col. 1:23
28:20 [a]Acts 2:42

12 And when they were assembled with
the elders, and had taken counsel, they gave
large money unto the soldiers,
13 Saying, Say ye, His disciples came by
night, and stole him *away* while we slept.
14 And if this come to the governor's ears,
we will persuade him, and secure you.
15 So they took the money, and did as they
were taught: and this saying is commonly reported among the Jews until this day.

The Great Commission

16 ¶ Then the eleven disciples went *away*
into Galilee, into a mountain [a]where Jesus had
appointed them.
17 And when they saw him, they worshipped him: but some doubted.
18 And Jesus came and spake unto them,
saying, [a]All power is given unto me in heaven
and in earth.
19 [a]Go ye therefore, and [b 1]teach all nations, baptizing them in the name of the Father, and of the Son, and of the Holy Ghost:
20 [a]Teaching them to observe all *things*
whatsoever I have commanded you: and lo, I
am with you alway, *even* unto the end of the
world. Amen.

28:11–15 Only Matthew tells of the posting of the guard (27:62–66), and he follows up by telling of their report.

28:16 *eleven.* Judas had committed suicide (27:5). *had appointed.* See v. 10.

‡28:19 *all nations.* Contrast 10:5–6. *baptizing them.* As a sign of their union with and commitment to Christ (see notes on Acts 2:38; Rom 6:3–4). Christ is associated with the other persons of deity in the Trinity. Christ's Great Commission, though spoken to the eleven, was meant for the entire church, in all ages until He returns.

28:20 *with you.* Matthew ends with the reassuring and empowering words of Him who came to earth to be "God with us" (1:23).

The Gospel According to
S. Mark

INTRODUCTION

See "The Synoptic Gospels," p. 1349.

Author

Although there is no direct internal evidence of authorship, it was the unanimous testimony of the early church that this Gospel was written by John Mark. The most important evidence comes from Papias (c. A.D. 140), who quotes an even earlier source as saying: (1) Mark was a close associate of Peter, from whom he received the tradition of the things said and done by the Lord; (2) this tradition did not come to Mark as a finished, sequential account of the life of our Lord, but as the preaching of Peter—preaching directed to the needs of the early Christian communities; (3) Mark accurately preserved this material. The conclusion drawn from this tradition is that the Gospel of Mark largely consists of the preaching of Peter arranged and shaped by John Mark (see note on Acts 10:37).

John Mark in the NT

It is generally agreed that the Mark who is associated with Peter in the early non-Biblical tradition is also the John Mark of the NT. The first mention of him is in connection with his mother, who had a house in Jerusalem that served as a meeting place for believers (Acts 12:12). This house was also thought to be the upper room (Mark 14:12–15). When Paul and Barnabas returned to Antioch from Jerusalem after the famine visit, Mark accompanied them (Acts 12:25). Mark next appears as a "helper" to Paul and Barnabas on their first missionary journey (Acts 13:5), but he deserted them at Perga, in Pamphylia, to return to Jerusalem (Acts 13:13). Paul must have been deeply disappointed with Mark's actions on this occasion, because when Barnabas proposed taking Mark on the second journey, Paul flatly refused, a refusal that broke up their working relationship (Acts 15:36–39). Barnabas took Mark, who was his cousin, and departed for Cyprus. No further mention is made of either of them in the book of Acts. Mark reappears in Paul's letter to the Colossians written from Rome. Paul sends a greeting from Mark and adds: "touching whom ye received commandments; if he come unto you, receive him" (Col 4:10; see Philem 24, written about the same time). At this point Mark was apparently beginning to win his way back into Paul's confidence. By the end of Paul's life, Mark had fully regained Paul's favor (see 2 Tim 4:11). It is also thought that the one Peter mentions as "Marcus my son" (1 Pet 5:13) is this same Mark. He was Peter's son in the faith.

Date of Composition

Some, who hold that Matthew and Luke used Mark as a major source, have suggested that Mark may have been composed in the 50s or early 60s. Others have felt that the content of the Gospel and statements made about Mark by the early church fathers indicate that the book was written shortly before the destruction of Jerusalem in A.D. 70. See chart, p. 1349.

Place of Origin

According to early church tradition, Mark was written "in the regions of Italy" (Anti-Marcionite Prologue) or, more specifically, in Rome (Irenaeus and Clement of Alexandria). These same authors closely associate Mark's writing of the Gospel with the apostle Peter. The above evidence is consistent with (1) the historical probability that Peter was in Rome during the last days of his life and was martyred there, and (2) the Biblical evidence that Mark also was in Rome about the same time and was closely associated with Peter (see 2 Tim 4:11; 1 Pet 5:13, where the word "Babylon" is possibly a cryptogram for Rome).

Recipients

The evidence points to the church at Rome or at least to Gentile readers. Mark explains Jewish

customs (7:2–4; 15:42), translates Aramaic words (3:17; 5:41; 7:11,34; 15:22) and seems to have a special interest in persecution and martyrdom (8:34–38; 13:9–13)—subjects of special concern to Roman believers. A Roman destination would explain the almost immediate acceptance of this Gospel and its rapid dissemination.

Occasion and Purpose

Since Mark's Gospel is traditionally associated with Rome, it may have been occasioned by the persecutions of the Roman church in the period c. A.D. 64–67. The famous fire of Rome in 64—probably set by Nero himself but blamed on Christians—resulted in widespread persecution. Even martyrdom was not unknown among Roman believers. Mark may be writing to prepare his readers for this suffering by placing before them the life of our Lord. There are many references, both explicit and veiled, to suffering and discipleship throughout his Gospel (see 1:12–13; 3:22,30; 8:34–38; 10:30,33–34,45; 13:8,11–13).

Emphases

1. *The cross.* Both the human cause (12:12; 14:1–2; 15:10) and the divine necessity (8:31; 9:31; 10:33) of the cross are emphasized by Mark.

2. *Discipleship.* Special attention should be paid to the passages on discipleship that arise from Jesus' predictions of His passion (8:34—9:1; 9:35—10:31; 10:42–45).

3. *The teachings of Jesus.* Although Mark records far fewer actual teachings of Jesus than the other Gospel writers, there is a remarkable emphasis on Jesus as teacher. The words "teacher," "teach" or "teaching," and "Master" are applied to Jesus in Mark nearly 40 times.

4. *The Messianic secret.* On several occasions Jesus warns His disciples or the person for whom He has worked a miracle to keep silent about who He is or what He has done (1:34,44; 3:12; 5:43; 7:36–37; 8:26,30; 9:9).

5. *Son of God.* Although Mark emphasizes the humanity of Jesus (see 3:5; 6:6,31,34; 7:34; 8:12,33; 10:14; 11:12), he does not neglect His deity (see 1:1,11; 3:11; 5:7; 9:7; 12:1–11; 13:32; 15:39).

Special Characteristics

Mark's Gospel is a simple, succinct, unadorned, yet vivid account of Jesus' ministry, emphasizing more what Jesus did than what He said. Mark moves quickly from one episode in Jesus' life and ministry to another, often using the adverb translated "immediately" (see note on 1:12). The book as a whole is characterized as "The beginning of the gospel" (1:1). The life, death and resurrection of Christ comprise the "beginning," of which the apostolic preaching in Acts is the continuation.

Outline

- I. The Beginnings of Jesus' Ministry (1:1–13)
  - A. His Forerunner (1:1–8)
  - B. His Baptism (1:9–11)
  - C. His Temptation (1:12–13)
- II. Jesus' Ministry in Galilee (1:14—6:29)
  - A. Early Galilean Ministry (1:14—3:12)
    1. Call of the first disciples (1:14–20)
    2. Miracles in Capernaum (1:21–34)
    3. A tour of Galilee (1:35–45)
    4. Ministry in Capernaum (2:1–22)
    5. Sabbath controversy (2:23—3:12)
  - B. Later Galilean Ministry (3:13—6:29)
    1. Selection of the 12 apostles (3:13–19)
    2. Teachings in Capernaum (3:20–35)
    3. Parables of the kingdom (4:1–34)
    4. Trip across the sea of Galilee (4:35—5:20)
    5. More Galilean miracles (5:21–43)
    6. Unbelief in Jesus' hometown (6:1–6)
    7. Six apostolic teams tour Galilee (6:7–13)
    8. King Herod's reaction to Jesus' ministry (6:14–29)

- III. Withdrawals from Galilee (6:30—9:32)
  - A. To the Eastern Shore of the Sea of Galilee (6:30–52)
  - B. To the Western Shore of the Sea of Galilee (6:53—7:23)
  - C. To Phoenicia (7:24–30)
  - D. To the Region of the Decapolis (7:31—8:10)
  - E. To the Vicinity of Caesarea Philippi (8:11—9:32)
- IV. Final Ministry in Galilee (9:33–50)
- V. Jesus' Ministry in Judea and Perea (ch. 10)
  - A. Teaching concerning Divorce (10:1–12)
  - B. Teaching concerning Children (10:13–16)
  - C. The Rich Young Ruler (10:17–31)
  - D. Prediction of Jesus' Death (10:32–34)
  - E. A Request of Two Brothers (10:35–45)
  - F. Restoration of Bartimeus's Sight (10:46–52)
- VI. The Passion of Jesus (chs. 11—15)
  - A. The Triumphal Entry (11:1–11)
  - B. The Cleansing of the Temple (11:12–19)
  - C. Concluding Controversies with Jewish Leaders (11:20—12:44)
  - D. The Olivet Discourse concerning the End of the Age (ch. 13)
  - E. The Anointing of Jesus (14:1–11)
  - F. The Arrest, Trial and Death of Jesus (14:12—15:47)
- VII. The Resurrection of Jesus (ch. 16)

John the Baptist

1 The beginning of the gospel of Jesus
Christ, [a]the Son of God;
2 As it is written in the prophets, [a]Behold,
I send my messenger before thy face, which
shall prepare thy way before thee.
3 [a]The voice of one crying in the wilderness, Prepare ye the way of the Lord, make his
paths straight.
4 [a]John did baptize in the wilderness, and
preach the baptism of repentance [1]for the remission of sins.
5 [a]And there went out unto him all the
land of Judea, and they of Jerusalem, and were
all baptized of him in the river *of* Jordan, confessing their sins.
6 And John was [a]clothed with camel's hair,
and with a girdle of a skin about his loins; and
he did eat locusts and wild honey;
7 And preached, saying, [a]There cometh
one mightier than I after me, the latchet of
whose shoes I am not worthy to stoop down
and unloose.
8 [a]I indeed have baptized you with water:
but he shall baptize you [b]with the Holy Ghost.

1:1 [a]Mat. 14:33; Luke 1:35; John 1:34
1:2 [a]Mal. 3:1; Mat. 11:10; Luke 7:27
1:3 [a]Is. 40:3; Mat. 3:3; Luke 3:4; John 1:15,23
1:4 [1]Or, *unto*
[a]Mat. 3:1; Luke 3:3; John 3:23
1:5 [a]Mat. 3:5
1:6 [a]Mat. 3:4
1:7 [a]Mat. 3:11; John 1:27; Acts 13:25
1:8 [a]Acts 1:5; 11:16; 19:4 [b]Is. 44:3; Joel 2:28; Acts 2:4; 10:45; 11:15,16; 1 Cor. 12:13
1:9 [a]Mat. 3:13; Luke 3:21
1:10 [1]Or, *cloven*, or, *rent* [a]Mat. 3:16; John 1:32
1:11 [a]Ps. 2:7; Mat. 3:17; ch. 9:7
1:12 [a]Mat. 4:1; Luke 4:1
1:13 [a]Mat. 4:11
1:14 [a]Mat. 4:12 [b]Mat. 4:23
1:15 [a]Dan. 9:25; Gal. 4:4; Eph. 1:10 [b]Mat. 3:2; 4:17

Baptism and temptation of Jesus

9 ¶ [a]And it came to pass in those days, *that*
Jesus came from Nazareth of Galilee, and was
baptized of John in Jordan.
10 [a]And straightway coming up out of the
water, he saw the heavens [1]opened, and the
Spirit like a dove descending upon him:
11 And there came a voice from heaven,
saying, [a]Thou art my beloved Son, in whom I
am well pleased.
12 ¶ [a]And immediately the Spirit driveth
him into the wilderness.
13 And he was there in the wilderness forty
days, tempted of Satan; and was with the wild
beasts; [a]and the angels ministered unto him.
14 ¶ [a]Now after that John was put in
prison, Jesus came into Galilee, [b]preaching
the gospel of the kingdom of God,
15 And saying, [a]The time is fulfilled, and
[b]the kingdom of God is at hand: repent ye, and
believe the gospel.

Jesus calls four disciples

16 ¶ [a]Now as he walked by the sea of Galilee, he saw Simon and Andrew his brother

1:16 [a]Mat. 4:18; Luke 5:4

1:1 *The beginning.* See Introduction: Special Characteristics; suggests the opening verse of Genesis (see John 1:1). *gospel.* From the Old English *godspel,* "good story" or "good news," which accurately translates the Greek. The good news is that God has provided salvation through the life, death and resurrection of Jesus Christ

‡1:2 *in the prophets.* The quotation that immediately follows comes from Mal 3:1 and is followed by one from Is 40:3. Understanding the ministry of Jesus must begin with the OT. What these two prophets say about God applies to Jesus, His Son (v. 1). The passages cited speak of the messenger, the wilderness and the Lord, each of which is stressed in vv. 4–8.

1:4 *John.* Mark, like John, has no nativity narrative, but begins with the ministry of John the Baptist. The name John means "The LORD is gracious." *did baptize.* John's practice of baptizing those who came to him in repentance was so characteristic of his ministry that he became known as "the Baptist" or "the Baptizer." *the wilderness.* The arid region west of the Dead Sea, whose inhabitants included those who wrote and preserved the Dead Sea Scrolls. *baptism.* John was preaching repentance-baptism, i.e., baptism that was preceded or accompanied by repentance. Baptism was not new to John's audience. They knew of baptism for Gentile converts, but had not heard that the descendants of Abraham (Jews) needed to repent and be baptized. *repentance.* Involves deliberate turning from sin to righteousness, and John's emphasis on repentance recalls the preaching of the prophets (e.g., Hos 3:4–5). God always grants forgiveness when there is repentance.

‡1:5 *all . . . all.* Obvious hyperbole, indicating the high interest created by John's preaching. For centuries Israel had had no prophet. *river of Jordan.* Even though the Jordan is the principal river in the Holy Land, it is located in the rift valley away from the population centers. It begins from the snows of mount Hermon and ends at the Dead Sea. Its closest point to Jerusalem is about 20 miles.

1:6 *camel's hair . . . a girdle of a skin.* Worn by Elijah and other prophets (2 Ki 1:8; cf. Zech 13:4). *locusts and wild honey.* See note on Mat 3:4.

1:7 *preached.* Mark's account of John's preaching is brief (cf. Mat 3:7–12; Luke 3:7–17) and focuses on the coming of the mighty One.

1:8 *baptize you with the Holy Ghost.* See note on Mat 3:11.

1:9 *in those days.* Jesus probably began His public ministry c. A.D. 27, when He was approximately 30 years old (Luke 3:23). As far as we know, He had spent most of His previous life in Nazareth. *Nazareth.* See note on Mat 2:23. *baptized of John.* For the significance of Jesus' baptism see Mat 3:15 and note.

1:10–11 All three persons of the Trinity are involved: (1) the Father speaks, (2) the Son is baptized, and (3) the Holy Spirit descends on the Son.

1:10 *the Spirit . . . descending upon him.* Jesus' anointing for ministry—an anointing He claimed in the synagogue at Nazareth (Luke 4:18). *like a dove.* Symbolizing the gentleness, purity and guilelessness of the Holy Spirit (see Mat 10:16).

1:11 An allusion to Ps 2:7 and Is 42:1. *a voice.* God sometimes spoke directly from heaven (see 9:7; John 12:28–29). *Thou art my beloved Son.* In v. 1 Mark proclaims Jesus as the Son of God; here God the Father Himself proclaims Jesus as His Son.

1:12 *immediately.* A distinctive characteristic of Mark's style is his use (some 47 times) of this Greek word that is also translated as "just then" (v. 23).

1:13 *forty.* See note on Mat 4:2. *tempted.* See notes on Mat 4:1–11. *Satan.* See notes on Gen 3:1; Zech 3:1; Rev 2:9–10; 12:9–10. *wild beasts.* In Jesus' day there were many more wild animals—including lions—in Israel than today. Only Mark reports their presence in this connection; he emphasizes that God kept Jesus safe in the wilderness. *angels ministered unto him.* As they had attended Israel in the wilderness (see Ex 23:20,23; 32:34).

‡1:14 *after that John was put in prison.* See Mat 4:12, and note on John 3:24 and note on Luke 3:20. *the gospel of the kingdom of God.* The good news from God, as well as about the kingdom of God.

1:15 *the kingdom of God.* See note on Mat 3:2. *is at hand.* The coming of Christ (the King) brings the kingdom near to the people.

1:16 *sea of Galilee.* A beautiful lake, almost 700 feet below sea level, 14 miles long and 6 miles wide, fed by the waters of the

casting a net into the sea: for they were fishers.

17 And Jesus said unto them, Come ye after me, and I will make you to become fishers of men.

18 And straightway [a]they forsook their nets, and followed him.

19 [a]And when he had gone a little further thence, he saw James the *son* of Zebedee, and John his brother, who also *were* in the ship mending *their* nets.

20 And straightway he called them: and they left their father Zebedee in the ship with the hired servants, and went after him.

The unclean spirit cast out

21 ¶ [a]And they went into Capernaum; and straightway on the sabbath day he entered into the synagogue, and taught.

22 [a]And they were astonished at his doctrine: for he taught them as *one* that had authority, and not as the scribes.

23 And there was in their synagogue a man with an unclean spirit; and he cried out,

24 Saying, Let *us* alone; [a]what have we to do with thee, *thou* Jesus of Nazareth? art thou come to destroy us? I know thee who thou art, the Holy One of God.

25 And Jesus [a]rebuked him, saying, Hold thy peace, and come out of him.

26 And when the unclean spirit [a]had torn him, and cried with a loud voice, he came out of him.

27 And they were all amazed, insomuch that *they* questioned among themselves, saying, What *thing* is this? what new doctrine *is* this? for with authority commandeth he even the unclean spirits, and they do obey him.

28 And immediately his fame spread abroad throughout all the region round about Galilee.

The sick healed; devils cast out

29 ¶ [a]And forthwith, when they were come out of the synagogue, they entered into the house of Simon and Andrew, with James and John.

30 But Simon's wife's mother lay sick of a fever, and anon they tell him of her.

31 And he came and took her by the hand, and lift her up; and immediately the fever left her, and she ministered unto them.

32 [a]And at even, when the sun did set, they brought unto him all that were diseased, and them that were possessed with devils.

33 And all the city was gathered together at the door.

34 And he healed many *that were* sick of divers diseases, and cast out many devils; and [a]suffered not the devils [1]to speak, because they knew him.

Jesus preaches in Galilee

35 ¶ And [a]in the morning, rising up a great while before day, he went out, and departed into a solitary place, and there prayed.

36 And Simon and they that were with him followed after him.

1:18 [a]Mat. 19:27; Luke 5:11
1:19 [a]Mat. 4:21
1:21 [a]Mat. 4:13; Luke 4:31
1:22 [a]Mat. 7:28
1:24 [a]Mat. 8:29
1:25 [a]ver. 34
1:26 [a]ch. 9:20
1:29 [a]Mat. 8:14; Luke 4:38
1:32 [a]Mat. 8:16; Luke 4:40
1:34 [1]Or, *to say that they knew him* [a]ch. 3:12; Luke 4:41; See Acts 16:17,18
1:35 [a]Luke 4:42

upper Jordan River. It was also called the lake of Gennesaret (Luke 5:1) and the sea of Tiberias (John 6:1; 21:1). In OT times it was known as the sea of Chinnereth (e.g., Num 34:11). *Simon.* Probably a contraction of the OT name Simeon. Jesus gave Simon the name Peter (3:16; Mat 16:18; John 1:42). *net.* See note on Mat 4:18.

‡1:17 *Come ye after me.* The call to discipleship is definite and demands a response of total commitment. This was not Jesus' first encounter with Simon and Andrew (see John 1:35–42). John 2–3 record these disciples being with Jesus at the wedding at Cana and at the passover in Jerusalem where they encountered Nicodemus. They had been with Jesus on a part-time basis; now Jesus called them to follow Him full-time. *fishers of men.* Evangelists (see Luke 5:10).

1:21 *Capernaum.* See note on Mat 4:13. *synagogue.* A very important religious institution among the Jews of that day. Originating during the exile, it provided a place where Jews could study the Scriptures and worship God. A synagogue could be established in any town where there were at least ten married Jewish men. *taught.* Jesus, like Paul (see Acts 13:15; 14:1; 17:2; 18:4), took advantage of the custom that allowed visiting teachers to participate in the worship service by invitation of the synagogue leaders.

1:22 *astonished.* Mark frequently reported the amazement that Jesus' teaching and actions produced (see 2:12; 5:20,42; 6:2,51; 7:37; 10:26; 11:18; see also 15:5). In these instances it was Christ's inherent authority that amazed. He did not quote human authorities, as did the teachers of the law, because his authority was directly from God. *scribes.* See note on Mat 2:4.

1:23 *a man... cried out.* It was actually the demon who cried out. *with an unclean spirit.* Demonic possession intended to torment and destroy those who are created in God's image, but the demon recognized that Jesus was a powerful adversary, capable of destroying the forces of Satan.

1:24 *the Holy One of God.* Apart from the parallel in Luke 4:34, the title is used elsewhere only in John 6:69 and points to Christ's divine origin rather than His Messiahship (see Luke 1:35). The name was perhaps used by the demons in accordance with the occult belief that the precise use of a person's name gave certain control over him. The man was possessed by more than one demon (see 5:9), but only one spoke.

1:25 *Hold thy peace.* Lit. "Be muzzled!" Jesus' superior power silences the shrieks of the demon-possessed man.

1:27 *with authority.* Jesus' authority in how He taught (v. 22) and in what He did (here) impressed the people.

1:29 *into the house of Simon and Andrew.* Jesus and the disciples probably went there for a meal, since the main sabbath meal was served immediately following the synagogue service.

1:30 *Simon's wife's mother.* 1 Cor 9:5 speaks of Peter's being married.

1:32 *they brought unto him.* They waited until the sabbath was over (after sunset) before carrying anything (see Jer 17:21–22).

‡1:34 *because they knew him.* Luke says, "for they knew that he was Christ" (Luke 4:41). Jesus probably wanted first to show by word and deed the kind of Messiah He was (in contrast to popular notions) before He clearly declared Himself, and He would not let the demons frustrate this intent.

‡1:35 *a great while before day . . . a solitary place . . . prayed.* Jesus' prayer life was effective because it was planned, private and prolonged. He got up early enough, went far enough away, and stayed long enough to commune with the Father. The verb for "prayed" indicates continued action.

1:36 *Simon and they that were with him.* Andrew, James, John and perhaps Philip and Nathanael (cf. John 1:43–45).

37 And when they had found him, they said unto him, All *men* seek for thee.

38 And he said unto them, [a]Let us go into the next towns, that I may preach there also: for [b]therefore came I forth.

39 [a]And he preached in their synagogues throughout all Galilee, and cast out devils.

The leper cleansed

40 ¶ [a]And there came a leper to him, beseeching him, and kneeling down to him, and saying unto him, If thou wilt, thou canst make me clean.

41 And Jesus, moved with compassion, put forth *his* hand, and touched him, and saith unto him, I will; be thou clean.

42 And as soon as he had spoken, immediately the leprosy departed from him, and he was cleansed.

43 And he straitly charged him, and forthwith sent him away;

44 And saith unto him, See thou say nothing to any *man:* but go thy way, shew thyself to the priest, and offer for thy cleansing *those things* [a]which Moses commanded, for a testimony unto them.

45 [a]But he went out, and began to publish *it* much, and to blaze abroad the matter, insomuch that *Jesus* could no more openly enter into the city, but was without in desert places: [b]and they came to him from every quarter.

A man with palsy healed

2 And again [a]he entered into Capernaum after *some* days; and it was noised that he was in the house.

2 And straightway many were gathered together, insomuch that there was no room to receive *them,* no, not so much as about the door: and he preached the word unto them.

3 And they come unto him, bringing one sick of the palsy, *which was* borne of four.

4 And when they could not come nigh unto him for the press, they uncovered the roof where he was: and when they had broken *it* up, they let down the bed wherein the sick of the palsy lay.

5 When Jesus saw their faith, he said unto the sick of the palsy, Son, thy sins be forgiven thee.

6 But there were certain of the scribes sitting there, and reasoning in their hearts,

7 Why doth this *man* thus speak blasphemies? [a]who can forgive sins but God only?

8 And immediately, when Jesus perceived in his spirit that they so reasoned within themselves, he said unto them, Why reason ye these *things* in your hearts?

9 [a]Whether is it easier to say to the sick of the palsy, *Thy* sins be forgiven thee; or to say, Arise, and take up thy bed, and walk?

10 But that ye may know that the Son of man hath power on earth to forgive sins, (he saith to the sick of the palsy,)

11 I say unto thee, Arise, and take up thy bed, and go thy way into thine house.

12 And immediately he arose, took up the bed, and went forth before *them* all; insomuch that *they* were all amazed, and glorified God, saying, We never saw *it* on this fashion.

Matthew called

13 ¶ [a]And he went forth again by the sea side; and all the multitude resorted unto him, and he taught them.

14 [a]And as he passed by, he saw Levi the

1:38 [a]Luke 4:43 [b]Is. 61:1; John 16:28; 17:4
1:39 [a]Mat. 4:23; Luke 4:44
1:40 [a]Mat. 8:2; Luke 5:12
1:44 [a]Lev. 14:3,4,10
1:45 [a]Luke 5:15 [b]ch. 2:13
2:1 [a]Mat. 9:1
2:7 [a]Job 14:4; Is. 43:25
2:9 [a]Mat. 9:5
2:13 [a]Mat. 9:9
2:14 [a]Mat. 9:9; Luke 5:27

1:39 *throughout all Galilee.* The first of what seem to be three tours of Galilee (second tour, Luke 8:1; third tour, Mark 6:6 and Mat 11:1).

1:40 *leper.* See Lev 13–14 and note on Lev 13:2.

1:41 *touched him.* An act that, according to Mosaic law, brought defilement (see Lev 13, especially vv. 45–46; cf. Lev 5:2). Jesus' compassion for the man superseded ceremonial considerations.

1:44 *See thou say nothing to any man.* See notes on Mat 8:4; 16:20. *Go thy way, shew thyself to the priest.* See note on Luke 5:14. *a testimony unto them.* The sacrifices were to be evidence to the priests and the people that the cure was real and that Jesus respected the law. The healing was also a testimony to Jesus' divine power, since Jews believed that only God could cure leprosy (see 2 Ki 5:1–14).

1:45 *no more openly enter into the city.* Jesus' growing popularity with the people (see 1:28; 3:7–8; Luke 7:17) and the increasing opposition from Jewish leaders (see 2:6–7,16,23–24; 3:2,6,22) finally made it necessary for Him to withdraw from Galilee into surrounding territories.

2:1 *in the house.* When in Capernaum, Jesus probably made His home at Peter's house (see 1:21,29).

2:2 *many were gathered together.* The same enthusiasm that greeted Jesus earlier (1:32–33,37) was evident at His return.

2:3 *one sick of the palsy.* Nothing definite can be said about the nature of the man's affliction beyond the fact that he could not walk. The determination of the four men to reach Jesus suggests that his condition was desperate.

2:4 *they uncovered the roof.* A typical Palestinian house had a flat roof accessible by means of an outside staircase. The roof was often made of a thick layer of clay (packed with a stone roller), supported by mats of branches across wood beams.

2:5 *When Jesus saw their faith.* Jesus recognized that the bold action of the paralyzed man and his friends gave evidence of faith. *Son, thy sins be forgiven thee.* Jesus first met the man's deepest need: forgiveness.

2:7 *Why doth this thus man speak blasphemies? who can forgive sins but God only?* In Jewish theology even the Messiah could not forgive sins, and Jesus' forgiveness of sin was a claim to deity—which they considered to be blasphemous (see note on 14:64).

2:9 *Whether is it easier . . . ?* Jesus' point probably was that neither forgiving sins nor healing was easier. Both are equally impossible to men and equally easy to God.

‡2:10 *But that ye may know.* Probably spoken to the teachers of the law. The words "he saith to the sick of the palsy" are parenthetical to explain a change in the persons addressed. For a discussion of the title "Son of man" see note on 8:31. It is clear that one purpose of miracles was to give evidence of Jesus' deity. See the use of miraculous signs in John's Gospel (2:11; 20:30–31).

2:12 *they were all amazed.* See note on 1:22.

2:14 *Levi the son of Alpheus.* Matthew (see Mat 9:9; 10:3). His given name was probably Levi, and Matthew ("gift of the LORD")

son of Alpheus sitting [1]at the receipt of custom, and said unto him, Follow me. And he
arose and followed him.
15 [a]And it came to pass, that as *Jesus* sat at
meat in his house, many publicans and sinners
sat also together with Jesus and his disciples:
for there were many, and they followed him.
16 And when the scribes and Pharisees
saw him eat with publicans and sinners, they
said unto his disciples, How *is it* that he eateth
and drinketh with publicans and sinners?
17 When Jesus heard *it,* he saith unto
them, [a]They that are whole have no need of
the physician, but they that are sick: I came
not to call *the* righteous, but sinners to repentance.

The question about fasting

18 ¶ [a]And the disciples of John and of the
Pharisees used to fast: and they come and say
unto him, Why do the disciples of John and of
the Pharisees fast, but thy disciples fast not?
19 And Jesus said unto them, Can the children of the bridechamber fast, while the bridegroom is with them? as long as they have the
bridegroom with them, they cannot fast.
20 But the days will come, when the bridegroom shall be taken away from them, and
then shall they fast in those days.

2:14 [1]Or, *at the place where the custom was received*
2:15 [a]Mat. 9:10
2:17 [a]Mat. 9:12,13; 18:11; Luke 5:31,32; 19:10; 1 Tim. 1:15
2:18 [a]Mat. 9:14; Luke 5:33

2:21 [1]Or, *raw, or, unwrought*
2:23 [a]Mat. 12:1; Luke 6:1 [b]Deut. 23:25
2:25 [a]1 Sam. 21:6
2:26 [a]Ex. 29:32,33; Lev. 24:9

21 No *man* also seweth a piece of [1]new
cloth on an old garment: else the new piece
that filled it up taketh away *from* the old, and
the rent is made worse.
22 And no *man* putteth new wine into old
bottles: else the new wine doth burst the bottles, and the wine is spilled, and the bottles
will be marred: but new wine must be put into
new bottles.

Jesus the Lord of the sabbath

23 ¶ [a]And it came to pass, that he went
through the corn fields on the sabbath day;
and his disciples began, as they went, [b]to
pluck the ears of corn.
24 And the Pharisees said unto him, Behold, why do they on the sabbath day *that*
which is not lawful?
25 And he said unto them, Have ye never
read [a]what David did, when he had need, and
was a hungred, he, and they *that were* with
him?
26 How he went into the house of God in
the days of Abiathar the high priest, and did
eat the shewbread, [a]which is not lawful to eat
but for the priests, and gave also to them
which were with him?
27 And he said unto them, The sabbath was
made for man, *and* not man for the sabbath:

his apostolic name. *the receipt of custom.* Levi was a tax collector (see note on Luke 3:12) under Herod Antipas, tetrarch of Galilee. The tax collector's booth where Jesus found Levi was probably a toll booth on the major international road that went from Damascus through Capernaum to the Mediterranean coast and to Egypt (see Is 9:1 and note). *he arose and followed him.* See note on Luke 5:28.

2:15 *sat at meat.* To eat with a person was a sign of friendship. *sinners.* Notoriously evil people as well as those who refused to follow the Mosaic law as interpreted by the scribes. The term was commonly used of tax collectors, adulterers, robbers and the like.

2:16 *scribes and Pharisees.* Not all scribes were Pharisees—successors of the Hasidim, pious Jews who joined forces with the Maccabees during the struggle for freedom from Syrian oppression (166–142 B.C.). They first appear under the name Pharisees during the reign of John Hyrcanus (135–105). Although some, no doubt, were godly, most of those who came into conflict with Jesus were hypocritical, envious, rigid and formalistic. According to Pharisaism, God's grace extended only to those who kept his law. See notes on Mat 3:7; Luke 5:17. *publicans.* Jewish tax collectors were regarded as outcasts. They could not serve as witnesses or as judges and were expelled from the synagogue. In the eyes of the Jewish community their disgrace extended to their families. See note on Mat 5:46.

2:17 *I came not to call the righteous, but sinners to repentance.* A self-righteous man does not realize his need for salvation, but an admitted sinner does.

2:18 *the disciples of John.* John the Baptist's disciples may have been fasting because he was in prison (see 1:14), or this may have been a practice among them as an expression of repentance, intended to hasten the coming of redemption announced by John. *fasting.* In the Mosaic law only the fast of the day of atonement was required (Lev 16:29,31; 23:27–32; Num 29:7). After the Babylonian exile four other yearly fasts were observed by the Jews (see Zech 7:5; 8:19 and notes). In Jesus' time the Pharisees fasted twice a week (see Luke 18:12). *and of the Pharisees.* Pharisees as such were not teachers, but some were also "scribes" (teachers of the law), who often had disciples. Or perhaps the phrase is used in a nontechnical way to refer to people influenced by the Pharisees.

2:19 *Can the children of the bridechamber fast, while the bridegroom is with them?* Jesus compared his disciples with the guests of a bridegroom. A Jewish wedding was a particularly joyous occasion, and the celebration associated with it often lasted a week. It was unthinkable to fast during such festivities, because fasting was associated with sorrow.

2:20 *when the bridegroom shall be taken away from them.* Jesus is the bridegroom, who would be taken from them by death, and then fasting would be in order.

2:22 *new bottles.* See note on Mat 9:17.

2:23 *to pluck the ears of corn.* There was nothing wrong in the action itself, which comes under the provision of Deut 23:25.

2:24 *on the sabbath day that which is not lawful.* According to Jewish tradition (in the Mishnah), harvesting (which is what Jesus' disciples technically were doing) was forbidden on the sabbath. See Ex 34:21.

2:25 *what David did.* See 1 Sam 21:1–6. The relationship between the OT incident and the apparent infringement of the sabbath by the disciples lies in the fact that on both occasions godly men did something forbidden. Since, however, it is always "lawful" to do good and to save life (even on the sabbath), both David and the disciples were within the spirit of the law (see Is 58:6–7; Luke 6:6–11; 13:10–17; 14:1–6).

2:26 *in the days of Abiathar the high priest.* According to 1 Sam 21:1, Ahimelech, Abiathar's father, was then high priest (see note on 2 Sam 8:17). *shewbread.* See note on Mat 12:4.

2:27 *The sabbath was made for man, and not man for the sabbath.* Jewish tradition had so multiplied the requirements and restrictions for keeping the sabbath that the burden had become intolerable. Jesus cut across these traditions and emphasized the God-given purpose of the sabbath—a day intended for man (for spiritual, mental and physical restoration; see Ex 20:8–11).

28 Therefore [a]the Son of man is Lord also of the sabbath.

3 And [a]he entered again into the synagogue; and there was a man there which had a withered hand.

2 And they watched him, whether he would heal him on the sabbath day; that they might accuse him.

3 And he saith unto the man which had the withered hand, [1]Stand forth.

4 And he saith unto them, Is it lawful to do good on the sabbath days, or to do evil? to save life, or to kill? But they held their peace.

5 And when he had looked round about on them with anger, being grieved for the [1]hardness of their hearts, he saith unto the man, Stretch forth thine hand. And he stretched *it* out: and his hand was restored whole as the other.

6 [a]And the Pharisees went forth, and straightway took counsel with [b]the Herodians against him, how they might destroy him.

Jesus heals many by the sea

7 ¶ But Jesus withdrew himself with his disciples to the sea: and a great multitude from Galilee followed him, [a]and from Judea,

8 And from Jerusalem, and from Idumea, and *from* beyond Jordan; and they about Tyre and Sidon, a great multitude, when they had heard what great *things* he did, came unto him.

9 And he spake to his disciples, that a small ship should wait on him because of the multitude, lest they should throng him.

10 For he had healed many; insomuch that *they* [1]pressed upon him for to touch him, as many as had plagues.

11 [a]And unclean spirits, when they saw him, fell down before him, and cried, saying, [b]Thou art the Son of God.

12 And [a]he straitly charged them that they should not make him known.

13 [a]And he goeth up into a mountain, and calleth unto *him* whom he would: and they came unto him.

14 And he ordained twelve, that they should be with him, and that he might send them forth to preach,

15 And to have power to heal sicknesses, and to cast out devils:

16 And Simon [a]he surnamed Peter;

17 And James the *son* of Zebedee, and John the brother of James; (and he surnamed them Boanerges, which is, The sons of thunder:)

18 And Andrew, and Philip, and Bartholomew, and Matthew, and Thomas, and James the *son* of Alpheus, and Thaddeus, and Simon the Canaanite,

19 And Judas Iscariot, which also betrayed him.

¶ And they went [1]into a house.

20 And *the* multitude cometh together again, [a]so that they could not so much as eat bread.

21 And when his [1]friends heard *of it*, they

2:28 [a]Mat. 12:8
3:1 [a]Mat. 12:9; Luke 6:6
3:3 [1][Gr. *Arise,* stand forth *in the midst*]
3:5 [1]Or, *blindness*
3:6 [a]Mat. 12:14 [b]Mat. 22:16
3:7 [a]Luke 6:17
3:10 [1]Or, *rushed*
3:11 [a]ch. 1:23,24; Luke 4:41 [b]Mat. 14:33; ch. 1:1
3:12 [a]Mat. 12:16; ch. 1:25,34
3:13 [a]Mat. 10:1; Luke 6:12; 9:1
3:16 [a]John 1:42
3:19 [1]Or, *home*
3:20 [a]ch. 6:31
3:21 [1]Or, *kinsmen*

2:28 See note on Luke 6:5.
3:1–6 A demonstration that Jesus is Lord of the sabbath (see 2:28).
3:2 *they.* The Pharisees (v. 6; cf. Luke 6:7). *whether he would heal him on the sabbath day.* An indication that the Pharisees believed in Jesus' power to perform miracles. The question was not "Could he?" but "Would he?" Jewish tradition prescribed that aid could be given the sick on the sabbath only when the person's life was threatened, which obviously was not the case here. See notes on 2:25; Luke 13:14. *might accuse him.* Jesus' presence demanded a decision about His preaching, His acts and His person. The hostility, first seen in 2:6–7, continues to spread. See note on v. 6.
3:4 *to do good on the sabbath days, or to do evil? to save life, or to kill?* Jesus asks: Which is better, to preserve life by healing or to destroy life by refusing to heal? The question is ironic since, whereas Jesus was ready to heal, the Pharisees were plotting to put Him to death. It is obvious who was guilty of breaking the sabbath. *they held their peace.* See 12:34.
3:6 *the Pharisees . . . took counsel.* The decision to seek Jesus' death was not the result of this incident alone, but was the response to a series of incidents (see 2:6–7,16–17,24). The plotting of the Pharisees and the Herodians is seen again on Tuesday of Passion Week (12:13). *Herodians.* Evidently influential Jews who favored the Herodian dynasty, meaning they were supporters of Rome, from which the Herods received their authority. They joined the Pharisees in opposing Jesus because they feared He might have an unsettling political influence on the people. See note on Mat 22:15–17.
3:8 Here we see impressive evidence of Jesus' rapidly growing popularity among the people. This geographical list indicates that the crowds came not only from the areas in the vicinity of Capernaum but also from considerable distances. The regions mentioned included virtually all of Israel and its surrounding neighbors. Mark tells of Jesus' work in all these regions except Idumea (see 1:14, Galilee; 5:1 and 10:1, the region across the Jordan; 7:24,31, Tyre and Sidon; 10:1, Judea; 11:11, Jerusalem). *Idumea.* The Greek form of the Hebrew "Edom," but here referring to an area south of Judea, not to earlier Edomite territory. (See map, p. 1451.)
3:11 *unclean spirits.* See note on 1:23. *Thou art the Son of God.* The evil spirits recognized who Jesus was, but they did not believe in Him (see note on 1:24).
3:12 *should not make him known.* The time for revealing Jesus' identity had not yet come (see 1:34 and note; see also notes on Mat 8:4; 16:20), and demons were hardly the proper channel for such disclosure.
3:14 *that they should be with him.* The training of the twelve included not only instruction and practice in various forms of ministry but also continuous association and intimate fellowship with Jesus Himself.
3:16–19 See notes on Luke 6:14–16.
3:17 *sons of thunder.* Probably descriptive of their dispositions (see notes on 10:37; Luke 9:54–55).
‡3:18 *Thaddeus.* Apparently the same as "Judas the brother of James" (see Luke 6:16; Acts 1:13). *the Canaanite.* See note on Mat 10:4.
‡3:19 *Iscariot.* Probably means "the man from Kerioth," the town Kerioth-hezron (Josh 15:25), 12 miles south of Hebron (Jer 48:24). For Judas's betrayal of Jesus see 14:10–11,43–46. *house.* Probably the home of Peter and Andrew (see 1:29; 2:1).
3:21 *his friends . . . went out to lay hold on him.* No doubt they

went out to lay hold on him: [a]for they said, He
is beside himself.
22 And the scribes which came down from
Jerusalem said, [a]He hath Beelzebub, and by
the prince of the devils casteth he out devils.
23 [a]And he called them unto *him,* and said
unto them in parables, How can Satan cast out
Satan?
24 And if a kingdom be divided against itself, that kingdom cannot stand.
25 And if a house be divided against itself,
that house cannot stand.
26 And if Satan rise up against himself, and
be divided, he cannot stand, but hath an end.
27 [a]No *man* can enter into a strong *man's*
house, and spoil his goods, except he will first
bind the strong *man;* and then he will spoil his
house.
28 [a]Verily I say unto you, All sins shall be
forgiven unto the sons of men, and blasphemies wherewith soever they shall blaspheme:
29 But he that shall blaspheme against the
Holy Ghost hath never forgiveness, but is in
danger of eternal damnation.
30 Because they said, He hath an unclean
spirit.

Jesus' true family

31 ¶ [a]There came then *his* brethren and
his mother, and, standing without, sent unto
him, calling him.
32 And *the* multitude sat about him, and
they said unto him, Behold, thy mother and
thy brethren without seek for thee.
33 And he answered them, saying, Who is
my mother, or my brethren?
34 And he looked round about on them
which sat about him, and said, Behold my
mother and my brethren.
35 For whosoever shall do the will of God,
the same is my brother, and my sister, and
mother.

3:21 [a]John 7:5; 10:20
3:22 [a]Mat. 9:34; 10:25; Luke 11:15; John 7:20; 8:48,52; 10:20
3:23 [a]Mat. 12:25
3:27 [a]Is. 49:24; Mat. 12:29
3:28 [a]Mat. 12:31; Luke 12:10; 1 John 5:16
3:31 [a]Mat. 12:46; Luke 8:19

4:1 [a]Mat. 13:1; Luke 8:4
4:2 [a]ch. 12:38
4:8 [a]John 15:5; Col. 1:6
4:10 [a]Mat. 13:10; Luke 8:9
4:11 [a]1 Cor. 5:12; Col. 4:5; 1 Thes. 4:12; 1 Tim. 3:7
4:12 [a]Is. 6:9; Mat. 13:14; Luke 8:10; John 12:40; Acts 28:26; Rom. 11:8

The parable of the sower

4 And [a]he began again to teach by the sea
side: and there was gathered unto him a
great multitude, so that he entered into a ship,
and sat in the sea; and the whole multitude
was by the sea on the land.
2 And he taught them many *things* by parables, [a]and said unto them in his doctrine,
3 Hearken; Behold, there went out a sower
to sow:
4 And it came to pass, as *he* sowed, some
fell by the way side, and the fowls of the air
came and devoured it up.
5 And some fell on stony ground, where it
had not much earth; and immediately it sprang
up, because *it* had no depth of earth:
6 But when the sun was up, it was
scorched; and because *it* had no root, it withered away.
7 And some fell among thorns, and the
thorns grew up, and choked it, and it yielded
no fruit.
8 And other fell on good ground, [a]and did
yield fruit that sprang up and increased; and
brought forth, some thirty, and some sixty, and
some an hundred.
9 And he said unto them, He that hath ears
to hear, let him hear.
10 ¶ [a]And when he was alone, they that
were about him with the twelve asked of him
the parable.
11 And he said unto them, Unto you it is
given to know the mystery of the kingdom of
God: but unto [a]them that are without, all
these things are done in parables:
12 [a]That seeing they may see, and not perceive; and hearing they may hear, and not understand; lest at any time they should be converted, and *their* sins should be forgiven them.
13 And he said unto them, Know ye not
this parable? and how *then* will ye know all
parables?

---

had come to Capernaum from Nazareth, some 30 miles away (see v. 31).

3:22 *Beelzebub.* See note on Mat 10:25.

3:23 *parables.* In this context the word is used in the general sense of comparisons (see note on 4:2).

3:27 *enter into a strong man's house, and spoil his goods.* Jesus was doing this very thing when He freed people from Satan's control.

3:28 *Verily I say unto you.* A solemn affirmation used by Jesus to strengthen His assertions (see 8:12; 9:1,41; 10:15,29; 11:23; 12:43; 13:30; 14:9,18,25,30).

3:29 *he that shall blaspheme against the Holy Ghost hath never forgiveness.* Jesus identifies this sin in v. 30 (cf. v. 22)—the teachers of the law attributed Jesus' healing to Satan's power rather than to the Holy Spirit (see note on Mat 12:31).

3:31 *his brethren and his mother.* See note on Luke 8:19.

3:35 *whosoever shall do the will of God.* Membership in God's spiritual family, evidenced by obedience to Him, is more important than membership in our human families (see note on 10:30).

4:1 *and sat.* Sitting was the usual position for Jewish teachers (see Mat 5:1; Luke 5:3; John 8:2).

4:2 *parables.* Usually stories out of ordinary life used to illustrate spiritual or moral truth, sometimes in the form of brief similes, comparisons (see note on 3:23), analogies or proverbial sayings. Ordinarily they had a single main point, and not every detail was meant to have significance. See notes on Mat 13:3; Luke 8:4.

4:3–8 In that day seed was broadcast by hand—which, by its nature, scattered some seed on unproductive ground (see note on Luke 8:5).

4:8 *did yield . . . an hundred.* A hundredfold yield was an unusually productive harvest (see Gen 26:12). Harvest was a common figure for the consummation of God's kingdom (see Joel 3:13; Rev 14:14–20).

4:11 *mystery of the kingdom of God.* In the NT "mystery" refers to something God has revealed to His people. The mystery (that which was previously unknown) is proclaimed to all, but only those who have faith understand. In this context the mystery seems to be that the kingdom of God had drawn near in the coming of Jesus Christ.

4:12 *that.* Jesus likens His preaching in parables to the ministry of Isaiah, which, while it gained some disciples (Is 8:16), was also to expose the hardhearted resistance of the many to God's warning and appeal.

Jerusalem during the Ministry of Jesus

Herod the Great (reigned 37–4 B.C.) rebuilt the temple and its surrounding walls, built a palace, a fortress, a theater and a hippodrome (stadium) for horse and chariot races. He brought the city to the zenith of its architectural beauty and Roman cultural expression. This became Jerusalem in the time of Jesus.

The **"THIRD WALL"** *(shown with dotted line)* was begun by Herod Agrippa I between A.D. 41 and 44 to enclose the growing northern suburbs, but the work was apparently stopped. Its construction was resumed, in haste, only after the First Jewish Revolt broke out in A.D. 66.

The **"SECOND WALL"** was built by Herod I or by earlier Hasmonean kings. Precise location is difficult to determine. This wall was put up around a market area in a valley, protecting it from raiding and looting, but was of questionable military value. At its eastern end, however, Herod built a military barracks (Antonia Fortress).

The **"FIRST WALL,"** so named by Josephus, encircled the city during the Hasmonean period, 167 B.C. After the revolt led by Judas Maccabeus in 167, Jerusalem expanded steadily in a period of independence under its own Jewish kings.

Hippodrome**

Psephinus Tower*

NORTH

Tyropoeon Street

Present Damascus Gate***

"Garden Tomb" (alternate crucifixion site) †††

Maximum city growth within walls by A.D. 70

Bridge over valley ("Wilson's Arch")***

Xystus (Greek exercise hall)*

Antonia Fortress*** (later Praetorium?)

Hasmonean Palace*

BEZETHA ("New City")

Traditional Crucifixion Site †††

Pool of Bethesda***

Herod's Towers

Herod's Royal Palace*

TEMPLE

MT. ZION ("Upper City")

Gentiles Court

HINNOM VALLEY

FIRST WALL

Meters 0 100 200 300

Feet 0 500 1,000

Essene Gate

Huldah Gates and Stairways***

Traditional Upper Room?

FIRST WALL

Archaeological excavations have revealed a monumental stairway and the continuation of Tyropoeon Street,*** that lies along the valley called "Way of the Cheesemongers" by Josephus.

Gihon Spring***

HINNOM VALLEY

SOUTH

MOUNT OF OLIVES

House of Caiphas the high priest,* identified here with today's Church of St. Peter in Gallicantu.

Ashpot Gate/ Tekoa Gate

KIDRON VALLEY

CITY OF DAVID "Lower City"

The Siloam Aqueduct-Tunnel*** was cut 1,749 ft. through solid bedrock, was 5′11″ high (average) and followed an "S" shaped course made necessary by engineering difficulties. It was carved by Hezekiah and provided water during the siege (2 Chr 32:30). Water flows through it to this day.

Pool of Siloam***

Theater**

Hugh Claycombe

Buildings, streets and roads shown here are artist's concept only unless otherwise named and located. Wall heights remain generally unknown, except for those surrounding the Temple Mount.

Deep valleys on the east, south and west permitted urban expansion only to the north.

* Location generally known, but style of architecture is unknown; artist's concept only, and Roman architecture is assumed.

** Location and architecture unknown, but referred to in written history; shown here for illustrative purposes.

*** Ancient feature has remained, or appearance has been determined from evidence.

14 [a]The sower soweth the word.
15 And these are they by the way side,
where the word is sown; but when they have
heard, Satan cometh immediately, and taketh
away the word that was sown in their hearts.
16 And these are they likewise which are
sown on stony ground; who, when they have
heard the word, immediately receive it with
gladness;
17 And have no root in themselves, and so
endure but for a time; afterward, when affliction or persecution ariseth for the word's sake,
immediately they are offended.
18 And these are they which are sown
among thorns; such as hear the word,
19 And the cares of this world, [a]and the
deceitfulness of riches, and the lusts of other
things entering in, choke the word, and it becometh unfruitful.
20 And these are they which are sown on
good ground; such as hear the word, and receive *it,* and bring forth fruit, some thirty*fold,*
some sixty, and some an hundred.

Parables about the kingdom

21 ¶ [a]And he said unto them, Is a candle
brought to be put under a [1]bushel, or under a
bed? *and* not to be set on a candlestick?
22 [a]For there is nothing hid, which shall
not be manifested; neither was *any thing* kept
secret, but that it should come abroad.
23 [a]If any *man* have ears to hear, let him
hear.
24 And he said unto them, Take heed what
you hear: [a]with what measure ye mete, it shall
be measured to you: and unto you that hear
shall more be given.
25 [a]For he that hath, to him shall be given:
and he that hath not, from him shall be taken
even *that* which he hath.
26 ¶ And he said, [a]So is the kingdom of
God, as if a man should cast seed into the
ground,
27 And should sleep, and rise night and
day, and the seed should spring and grow up,
he knoweth not how.
28 For the earth bringeth forth fruit of herself; first the blade, then the ear, after that the
full corn in the ear.
29 But when the fruit is [1]brought forth,
immediately [a]he putteth in the sickle, because
the harvest is come.
30 ¶ And he said, [a]Whereunto shall we
liken the kingdom of God? or with what comparison shall we compare it?
31 *It is* like a grain of mustard seed, which,
when it is sown in the earth, is less than all
the seeds that be in the earth:
32 But when it is sown, it groweth up, and
becometh greater than all herbs, and shooteth
out great branches; so that the fowls of the air
may lodge under the shadow of it.
33 [a]And with many such parables spake
he the word unto them, as they were able to
hear *it.*
34 But without a parable spake he not unto
them: and *when they were* alone, he expounded all *things* to his disciples.

The storm stilled

35 ¶ [a]And the same day, when the even
was come, he saith unto them, Let us pass
over unto the other side.
36 And when they had sent away the multitude, they took him *even* as he was in the
ship. And there were also with him other little
ships.
37 And there arose a great storm of wind,
and the waves beat into the ship, so that it was
now full.
38 And he was in the hinder part of the
ship, asleep on a pillow: and they awake him,

4:14 [a]Mat. 13:19
4:19 [a]1 Tim. 6:9,17
4:21 [1]*The word in the original signifieth a less measure, as* Mat. 5:15 [a]Mat. 5:15; Luke 8:16; 11:33
4:22 [a]Mat. 10:26
4:23 [a]ver. 9; Mat. 11:15
4:24 [a]Mat. 7:2; Luke 6:38
4:25 [a]Mat. 13:12; 25:29; Luke 8:18; 19:26
4:26 [a]Mat. 13:24
4:29 [1]Or, *ripe* [a]Rev. 14:15
4:30 [a]Mat. 13:31; Luke 13:18; Acts 2:41; 4:4; 5:14; 19:20
4:33 [a]Mat. 13:34; John 16:12
4:35 [a]Mat. 8:18,23; Luke 8:22

4:14 *the word.* The interpretation calls attention to the response to the word of God that Jesus has been preaching. In spite of many obstacles, God's word will accomplish His purpose.
4:17 *affliction or persecution.* See 8:34–38; 10:30; 13:9–13.
4:19 *deceitfulness of riches.* Prosperity tends to give a false sense of self-sufficiency, security and well-being (10:17–25; see Deut 8:17–18; 32:15; Eccl 2:4–11; Jas 5:1–6).
4:21 *Is a candle brought . . . ?* As a lamp is placed to give, not hide, light, so Jesus, the light of the world (John 8:12), is destined to be revealed. *candle.* See note on Mat 5:15.
4:25 *he that hath, to him shall be given.* The more we appropriate truth now, the more we will receive in the future; and if we do not respond to what little truth we may know already, we will not profit even from that.
4:26–29 Only Mark records this parable. Whereas the parable of the sower stresses the importance of proper soil for the growth of seed and the success of the harvest, here the mysterious power of the seed itself is emphasized. The gospel message contains its own power.
4:29 *immediately he putteth in the sickle, because the harvest is come.* A possible allusion to Joel 3:13, where harvest is a figure for the consummation of God's kingdom.
4:30–34 The main point of this parable is that the kingdom of God seemingly had insignificant beginnings. It was introduced by the despised and rejected Jesus and His 12 unimpressive disciples. But a day will come when its true greatness and power will be seen by all the world.
4:31 See notes on Mat 13:31–32.
4:34 *without a parable spake he not unto them.* Jesus used parables to illustrate truths, stimulate thinking and awaken spiritual perception. The people in general were not ready for the full truth of the gospel. When alone with His disciples Jesus taught more specifically, but even they usually needed to have things explained.
4:35–41 Although miracles are hard for modern man to accept, the NT makes it clear that Jesus is Lord not only over His church but also over all creation.
‡4:35 *unto the other side.* Jesus left the territory of Galilee to go to the region of the Gadarenes (5:1).
‡4:37 *there arose a great storm of wind.* Situated in a basin surrounded by mountains, the sea of Galilee is particularly susceptible to sudden, violent storms. Cool air from the mountains, including nearby mount Hermon, the highest point in all the Middle East, descends rapidly and clashes with the hot, humid air lying over the lake, which is 700 feet below sea level.
4:38 *asleep on a pillow.* The picture of Jesus, exhausted and asleep on the cushion customarily kept under the coxswain's seat, is characteristic of Mark's human touch.

and say unto him, Master, carest thou not that
we perish?
39 And he arose, and rebuked the wind,
and said unto the sea, Peace, be still. And the
wind ceased, and there was a great calm.
40 And he said unto them, Why are ye so
fearful? how *is it that* you have no faith?
41 And they feared exceedingly, and said
one to another, What *manner of* man is this,
that even the wind and the sea obey him?

Devils cast out

5 And [a]they came over unto the other side
of the sea, into the country of the Gadarenes.
2 And when he was come out of the ship,
immediately there met him out of the tombs a
man with an unclean spirit,
3 Who had *his* dwelling among the tombs;
and no *man* could bind him, no, not with
chains:
4 Because that he had been often bound
with fetters and chains, and the chains had
been plucked asunder by him, and the fetters
broken in pieces: neither could any *man* tame
him.
5 And always, night and day, he was in the
mountains, and in the tombs, crying, and cutting himself with stones.
6 But when he saw Jesus afar off, he ran
and worshipped him,
7 And cried with a loud voice, and said,
What have I to do with thee, Jesus, *thou* Son of
the most high God? I adjure thee by God, that
thou torment me not.

5:1 [a]Mat. 8:28; Luke 8:26

5:12 [a]Lev. 11:7; Deut. 14:8; Is. 65:4; Luke 15:15
5:17 [a]Mat. 8:34; Acts 16:39
5:18 [a]Luke 8:38

8 For he said unto him, Come out of the
man, *thou* unclean spirit.
9 And he asked him, What *is* thy name?
And he answered, saying, My name *is* Legion:
for we are many.
10 And he besought him much that he
would not send them away out of the country.
11 Now there was there nigh unto the
mountains a great herd of swine feeding.
12 And all the devils besought him, saying,
Send us into the [a]swine, that we may enter
into them.
13 And forthwith Jesus gave them leave.
And the unclean spirits went out, and entered
into the swine: and the herd ran violently down
a steep place into the sea, (they were about two
thousand,) and were choked in the sea.
14 And they that fed the swine fled, and
told *it* in the city, and in the country. And they
went out to see what it was that was done.
15 And they come to Jesus, and see him
that was possessed with the devil, and had the
legion, sitting, and clothed, and in his right
mind: and they were afraid.
16 And they that saw *it* told them how it
befell to him that was possessed with the devil, and *also* concerning the swine.
17 And [a]they began to pray him to depart
out of their coasts.
18 And when he was come into the ship,
[a]he that had been possessed with the devil
prayed him that he might be with him.
19 Howbeit Jesus suffered him not, but
saith unto him, Go home to thy *friends*, and
tell them how great *things* the Lord hath done
for thee, and hath had compassion on thee.

4:41 *What manner of man is this . . . ?* In view of what Jesus had just done, the only answer to this rhetorical question was: He is the very Son of God! God's presence, as well as His power, was demonstrated (see Ps 65:7; 107:25–30; Prov 30:4). Mark indicates his answer to this question in the opening line of his Gospel (1:1). By such miracles Jesus sought to establish and increase the disciples' faith in His deity.

‡5:1 *unto the other side of the sea.* The east side of the lake, a territory largely inhabited by Gentiles, as indicated by the presence of the large herd of pigs—animals Jews considered "unclean" and therefore unfit to eat. *country of the Gadarenes.* Gadara, located about six miles southeast of the sea of Galilee. Matthew (8:28) identifies the region by the city of Gergesa in the hills overlooking the eastern shore of the sea.

5:3 *had his dwelling among the tombs.* It was not unusual for the same cave to provide burial for the dead and shelter for the living. Very poor people often lived in such caves.

5:4 *he had been often bound with fetters and chains.* Though the villagers no doubt chained him partly for their own protection, this harsh treatment added to his humiliation.

5:5 *crying and cutting himself with stones.* Every word in the story emphasizes the man's pathetic condition as well as the purpose of demonic possession—to torment and destroy the divine likeness with which man was created.

5:7 *What have I to do with thee . . . ?* A way of saying, "What do we have in common?" Similar expressions are found in the OT (e.g., 2 Sam 16:10; 19:22), where they mean, "Mind your own business!" The demon was speaking, using the voice of the possessed man. *Son of the most high God.* See note on 1:24. *I adjure thee by God, that thou torment me not.* The demon sensed that he was to be punished and used the strongest basis for an oath that he knew, though his appeal to God was strangely ironic.

5:9 *My name is Legion: for we are many.* A Roman legion was made up of 6,000 men. Here the term suggests that the man was possessed by numerous demons and perhaps also represents the many powers opposed to Jesus, who embodies the power of God.

5:10 *not send them away out of the country.* The demons were fearful of being sent into eternal punishment, i.e., "into the deep" (Luke 8:31).

5:13 *Jesus gave them leave.* See note on Mat 8:32.

5:16 *and also concerning the swine.* In addition to the remarkable change in the demon-possessed man, the drowning of the pigs seemed to be a major concern, no doubt because it was so dramatic and brought considerable financial loss to the owners.

5:17 *pray him to depart out of their coasts.* Fear of further loss may have motivated this response, but also the fact that a powerful force was at work in their midst that they could not comprehend.

5:19 *tell them how great things the Lord hath done for thee.* This is in marked contrast to Jesus' exhortation to silence in the case of the man cleansed of leprosy (1:44; see 1:34; 3:12; see also note on Mat 8:4), perhaps because the healing of the demoniac was in Gentile territory, where there was little danger that Messianic ideas about Jesus might be circulated.

20 And he departed, and began to publish
in Decapolis how great *things* Jesus had done
for him: and all *men* did marvel.

Jairus' daughter raised

21 ¶ [a]And when Jesus was passed over again
by ship unto the other side, much people gathered unto him: and he was nigh unto the sea.

22 [a]And behold, there cometh one of the
rulers of the synagogue, Jairus by name; and
when he saw him, he fell at his feet,

23 And besought him greatly, saying, My
little daughter lieth at the point of death: *I
pray thee,* come and lay *thy* hands on her, that
she may be healed; and she shall live.

5:21 [a]Mat. 9:1; Luke 8:40
5:22 [a]Mat. 9:18; Luke 8:41
5:25 [a]Lev. 15:25; Mat. 9:20

24 And *Jesus* went with him; and much
people followed him, and thronged him.

25 And a certain woman, [a]which had an issue of blood twelve years,

26 And had suffered many *things* of many
physicians, and had spent all that she had, and
was nothing bettered, but rather grew worse,

27 When she had heard of Jesus, came in
the press behind, and touched his garment.

28 For she said, If I may touch but his
clothes, I shall be whole.

29 And straightway the fountain of her
blood was dried up; and she felt in *her* body
that she was healed of *that* plague.

30 And Jesus immediately knowing in him-

5:20 *Decapolis.* See note on Mat 4:25.
5:21 *the other side.* Jesus returned to the west side of the lake, perhaps to Capernaum.
5:22 *rulers of the synagogue.* A ruler of the synagogue was a layman whose responsibilities were administrative and included such things as looking after the building and supervising the worship. Though there were exceptions (see Acts 13:15), most synagogues had only one ruler. Sometimes the title was honorary, with no administrative responsibilities assigned.
5:25 *had an issue of blood twelve years.* The precise nature of the woman's problem is not known. Her existence was wretched because people shunned her generally, since anyone having contact with her was made ceremonially unclean (Lev 15:25–33).
5:26 *had suffered many things of many physicians.* The Jewish Talmud preserves a record of medicines and treatments prescribed for illnesses of this sort.
5:28 *If I may touch but his clothes.* Although it needed to be bolstered by physical contact, her faith was rewarded (v. 34; cf. Acts 19:12).

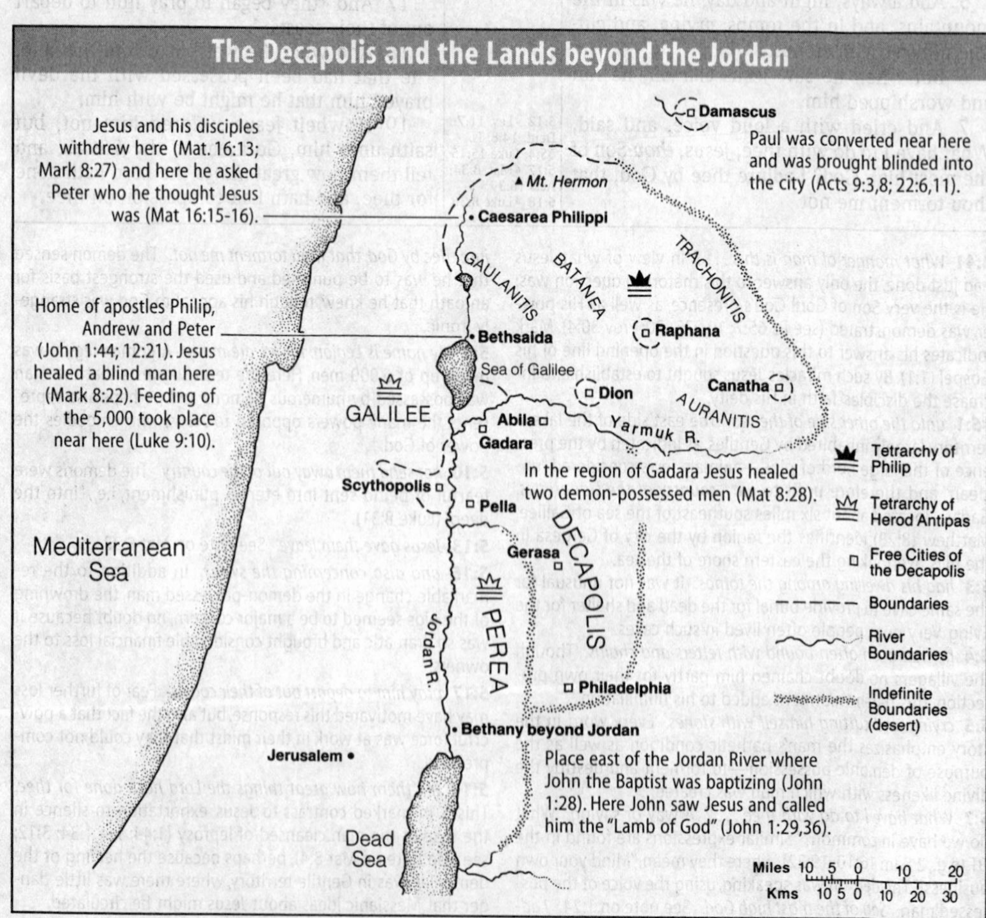
The Decapolis and the Lands beyond the Jordan
Jesus and his disciples withdrew here (Mat. 16:13; Mark 8:27) and here he asked Peter who he thought Jesus was (Mat 16:15-16).
Damascus
Paul was converted near here and was brought blinded into the city (Acts 9:3,8; 22:6,11).
Mt. Hermon
Caesarea Philippi
GAULANITIS
BATANEA
TRACHONITIS
Home of apostles Philip, Andrew and Peter (John 1:44; 12:21). Jesus healed a blind man here (Mark 8:22). Feeding of the 5,000 took place near here (Luke 9:10).
Bethsaida
Raphana
Sea of Galilee
Canatha
Dion
AURANITIS
GALILEE
Abila
Yarmuk R.
Gadara
Tetrarchy of Philip
In the region of Gadara Jesus healed two demon-possessed men (Mat 8:28).
Scythopolis
Pella
Tetrarchy of Herod Antipas
Mediterranean Sea
Gerasa
DECAPOLIS
Free Cities of the Decapolis
Boundaries
PEREA
Jordan R.
River Boundaries
Philadelphia
Indefinite Boundaries (desert)
Bethany beyond Jordan
Jerusalem
Place east of the Jordan River where John the Baptist was baptizing (John 1:28). Here John saw Jesus and called him the "Lamb of God" (John 1:29,36).
Dead Sea
Miles 10 5 0 10 20
Kms 10 5 0 10 20 30

self that [a]virtue had gone out of him, turned him about in the press, and said, Who touched my clothes?

31 And his disciples said unto him, Thou seest the multitude thronging thee, and sayest thou, Who touched me?

32 And he looked round about to see her that had done this *thing.*

33 But the woman fearing and trembling, knowing what was done in her, came and fell down before him, and told him all the truth.

34 And he said unto her, Daughter, [a]thy faith hath made thee whole; go in peace, and be whole of thy plague.

35 [a]While he yet spake, there came from the ruler of the synagogue's *house certain* which said, Thy daughter is dead: why troublest thou the Master any further?

36 As soon as Jesus heard the word *that was* spoken, he saith unto the ruler of the synagogue, Be not afraid, only believe.

37 And he suffered no *man* to follow him, save Peter, and James, and John the brother of James.

38 And he cometh to the house of the ruler of the synagogue, and seeth *the* tumult, and them that wept and wailed greatly.

39 And when he was come in, he saith unto them, Why make ye *this* ado, and weep? the damsel is not dead, but [a]sleepeth.

40 And they laughed him to scorn. [a]But when he had put *them* all out, he taketh the father and the mother of the damsel, and them that were with him, and entereth in where the damsel was lying.

41 And he took the damsel by the hand, and said unto her, TALITHA CUMI; which is, being interpreted, Damsel (I say unto thee) arise.

5:30 [a]Luke 6:19; 8:46
5:34 [a]Mat. 9:22; ch. 10:52; Acts 14:9
5:35 [a]Luke 8:49
5:39 [a]John 11:11
5:40 [a]Acts 9:40

5:43 [a]Mat. 8:4; 9:30; 12:16; 17:19; ch. 3:12; Luke 5:14
6:1 [a]Mat. 13:54; Luke 4:16
6:2 [a]John 6:42
6:3 [a]See Mat. 12:46; Gal. 1:19 [b]Mat. 11:6
6:4 [a]Mat. 13:57; John 4:44
6:5 [a]See Gen. 19:22; 32:25; Mat. 13:58; ch. 9:23
6:6 [a]Is. 59:16 [b]Mat. 9:35; Luke 13:22
6:7 [a]Mat. 10:1; ch. 3:13,14; Luke 9:1

42 And straightway the damsel arose, and walked; for she was *of the age* of twelve years. And they were astonished with a great astonishment.

43 And [a]he charged them straitly that no *man* should know it; and commanded that *something* should be given her to eat.

Jesus rejected at Nazareth

6 And [a]he went out from thence, and came into his own country; and his disciples follow him.

2 And when the sabbath day was come, he began to teach in the synagogue: and many hearing *him* were astonished, saying, [a]From whence hath this *man* these *things?* and what wisdom *is this* which is given unto him, that even such mighty works are wrought by his hands?

3 Is not this the carpenter, the son of Mary, [a]the brother of James, and Joses, and of Juda, and Simon? and are not his sisters here with us? And they [b]were offended at him.

4 But Jesus said unto them, [a]A prophet is not without honour, but in his own country, and among his own kin, and in his own house.

5 [a]And he could there do no mighty work, save that he laid *his* hands upon a few sick *folk,* and healed *them.*

6 And [a]he marvelled because of their unbelief. [b]And he went round about the villages, teaching.

The mission of the twelve

7 ¶ [a]And he calleth unto *him* the twelve, and began to send them forth by two and two; and gave them power over unclean spirits;

8 And commanded them that they should

5:30 *virtue had gone out of him.* The woman was healed because God graciously determined to heal her through the power then active in Jesus.

5:32 *looked round about to see her that had done this thing.* Jesus would not allow the woman to recede into the crowd without publicly commending her faith and assuring her that she was permanently healed.

‡5:34 *made thee whole.* The Greek for "made thee whole" actually means "saved you." Here both physical healing ("be whole of thy plague") and spiritual salvation ("go in peace") are meant. The two are often seen together in Mark's Gospel (see 2:1–12; 3:1–6).

5:37 *Peter, and James, and John.* These three disciples had an especially close relationship to Jesus (see note on Acts 3:1).

5:38 *them that wept and wailed greatly.* It was customary for professional mourners to be brought in at the time of death. In this case, however, it is not certain that enough time had elapsed for professional mourners to have been secured.

5:39 *not dead, but sleepeth.* See note on Luke 8:52.

‡5:41 *TALITHA CUMI.* Mark is the only Gospel writer who here preserves the original Aramaic—one of the languages of the Holy Land in the first century A.D. and probably the language Jesus and His disciples ordinarily spoke (though they probably also spoke Hebrew and Greek).

‡5:43 *that no man should know it.* In the vicinity of Galilee Jesus often cautioned people whom He healed not to spread the story of the miracle. His great popularity with the people, coupled with the growing opposition from the religious leaders, could have precipitated a crisis before Jesus' ministry was completed (see 1:44; 5:19; 7:36; 8:26). John's Gospel will express the concept that "his hour was not yet come" (see note on John 2:4).

6:1 *his own country.* Though Mark does not specifically mention Nazareth, it is obviously meant (see note on 1:9).

6:2 *teach in the synagogue.* See note on 1:21. *were astonished.* See note on 1:22.

6:3 *carpenter.* Matthew reports that Jesus was called "the carpenter's son" (Mat 13:55); only in Mark is Jesus Himself referred to as a carpenter. The Greek word can also apply to a mason or smith or builder in general. The question is derogatory, meaning, "Is He not a common worker with His hands like the rest of us?" *brother of James, and Joses, and of Juda, and Simon.* See note on Luke 8:19. *they were offended at him.* They saw no reason to believe that He was different from them, much less that He was specially anointed by God.

6:5 *he could there do no mighty work.* It was not that Jesus did not have power to perform miracles at Nazareth, but that He chose not to in such a climate of unbelief (v. 6).

6:6 *he marvelled.* See note on Luke 7:9.

6:7 *by two and two.* The purpose of going in pairs may have been to bolster credibility by having the testimony of more than one witness (cf. Deut 17:6), as well as to provide mutual support during their training period.

take nothing for *their* journey, save a staff only; no scrip, no bread, no [1]money in *their* purse:

9 But [a]*be* shod with sandals; and not put on two coats.

10 [a]And he said unto them, In what place soever ye enter into a house, there abide till ye depart from that place.

11 [a]And whosoever shall not receive you, nor hear you, when ye depart thence, [b]shake off the dust under your feet for a testimony against them. Verily I say unto you, It shall be more tolerable for Sodom [1]and Gomorrha in the day of judgment, than for that city.

12 And they went out, and preached that *men* should repent.

13 And they cast out many devils, [a]and anointed with oil many *that were* sick, and healed *them.*

Death of John the Baptist

14 ¶ [a]And king Herod heard *of him;* (for his name was spread abroad:) and he said, That John the Baptist was risen from the dead, and therefore mighty works do shew forth themselves in him.

15 [a]Others said, That it is Elias. And others said, That it is a prophet, or as one of the prophets.

16 [a]But when Herod heard *thereof,* he said, It is John, whom I beheaded: he is risen from the dead.

17 For Herod himself had sent forth and laid hold upon John, and bound him in prison for Herodias' sake, his brother Philip's wife: for he had married her.

18 For John had said unto Herod, [a]It is not lawful for thee to have thy brother's wife.

19 Therefore Herodias had [1]a quarrel against him, and would have killed him; but she could not:

20 For Herod [a]feared John, knowing that he *was* a just man and a holy, and [1]observed him; and when he heard him, he did many *things,* and heard him gladly.

21 [a]And when a convenient day was come, that Herod [b]on his birthday made a supper to his lords, high captains, and chief *estates* of Galilee;

22 And when the daughter of the said Herodias came in, and danced, and pleased Herod and them that sat with *him,* the king said unto the damsel, Ask of me whatsoever thou wilt, and I will give *it* thee.

23 And he sware unto her, [a]Whatsoever thou shalt ask of me, I will give *it* thee, unto the half of my kingdom.

24 And she went forth, and said unto her mother, What shall I ask? And she said, The head of John the Baptist.

25 And she came in straightway with haste unto the king, and asked, saying, I will that thou give me by and by in a charger the head of John the Baptist.

26 [a]And the king was exceeding sorry; *yet* for his oaths' sake, and for their sakes which sat with *him,* he would not reject her.

27 And immediately the king sent [1]an executioner, and commanded his head to be brought: and he went and beheaded him in the prison,

28 And brought his head in a charger, and gave it to the damsel: and the damsel gave it to her mother.

29 And when his disciples heard *of it,* they came and took up his corpse, and laid it in a tomb.

The five thousand fed

30 ¶ [a]And the apostles gathered themselves together unto Jesus, and told him all *things,* both what they had done, and what they had taught.

31 [a]And he said unto them, Come ye yourselves apart into a desert place, and rest a

6:8 [1]*The word signifieth a piece of brass money, in value somewhat less than a farthing,* Mat. 10:9: *but here it is taken in general for money*
6:9 [a]Acts 12:8
6:10 [a]Mat. 10:11; Luke 9:4; 10:7,8
6:11 [1][Gr. *or*] [a]Mat. 10:14; Luke 10:10 [b]Acts 13:51; 18:6
6:13 [a]Jas. 5:14
6:14 [a]Mat. 14:1; Luke 9:7
6:15 [a]Mat. 16:14; ch. 8:28
6:16 [a]Mat. 14:2; Luke 3:19
6:18 [a]Lev. 18:16; 20:21
6:19 [1]Or, *an inward grudge*
6:20 [1]Or, *kept him,* or, *saved him* [a]Mat. 14:5; 21:26
6:21 [a]Mat. 14:6 [b]Gen. 40:20
6:23 [a]Esth. 5:3,6; 7:2
6:26 [a]Mat. 14:9
6:27 [1]Or, *one of his guard*
6:30 [a]Luke 9:10
6:31 [a]Mat. 14:13

‡6:8 *no scrip, no bread, no money in their purse.* They were to depend entirely on the hospitality of those to whom they testified (see v. 10). A scrip was a small bag. We might call it a knapsack.

6:9 *not put on two coats.* At night an extra tunic was helpful as a covering to protect from the cold night air, and the implication here is that the disciples were to trust in God to provide lodging each night.

6:11 *shake off the dust under your feet.* See note on Mat 10:14.

6:12–13 *preached . . . cast out many devils.* This mission marks the beginning of the disciples' own ministry in Jesus' name (see 3:14–15), and their message was precisely the same as his (1:15).

6:12 *repent.* See note on 1:4.

6:13 *anointed with oil many that were sick.* In the ancient world olive oil was widely used as a medicine (see Is 1:6; Luke 10:34; Jas 5:14).

‡6:14 *king Herod.* See note on Mat 14:1. Mark may here have used the title "king" with a bit of sarcasm (since Herod was actually a tetrarch), or perhaps he simply used Herod's popular title.

6:15 *it is Elias.* See Mal 4:5.

6:16 *John . . . risen from the dead.* Herod, disturbed by an uneasy conscience and disposed to superstition, feared that John had come back to haunt him.

6:17 *laid hold upon John, and bound him in prison.* See 1:14; Luke 3:19–20. Josephus says that John was imprisoned at Machaerus, the fortress in Perea on the eastern side of the Dead Sea. *Herodias.* See note on Mat 14:3. *Philip.* See note on Mat 14:3.

6:22 *the daughter of the said Herodias.* See note on Mat 14:6.

6:23 *unto the half of my kingdom.* A proverbial reference to generosity, not to be taken literally (see Esth 5:3,6). Generosity suited the occasion and would win the approval of the guests.

‡6:30 *apostles.* In Mark's Gospel the word occurs only here and in 3:14 (in some manuscripts). The apostles were Jesus' authorized agents or representatives (see note on Heb 3:1). In the NT the word is sometimes used quite generally (see John 13:16, where the Greek *apostolos* is translated "one who is sent"). In the technical sense it is used (1) of the twelve—in which sense it is also applied to Paul (Rom 1:1)—and (2) of a larger group including Barnabas (Acts 14:14), possibly James the Lord's brother (Gal 1:19), and less probably Andronicus and Junias (Rom 16:7). *told him all things, both what they had done, and what they had taught.* Because He had commissioned them as His representatives. They were returning from a third preaching tour in Galilee (see note on 1:39).

while: for [b]there were many coming and going, and they had no leisure so much as to eat.

32 ¶ [a]And they departed into a desert place by ship privately.

33 And the people saw them departing, and many knew him, and ran afoot thither out of all cities, and outwent them, and came together unto him.

34 [a]And Jesus, when he came out, saw much people, and was moved with compassion toward them, because they were as sheep not having a shepherd: and [b]he began to teach them many *things.*

35 [a]And when the day was now far spent, his disciples came unto him, and said, *This* is a desert place, and now the time *is* far passed:

36 Send them away, that they may go into the country round about, and *into* the villages, and buy themselves bread: for they have nothing to eat.

37 He answered and said unto them, Give ye them to eat. And they say unto him, [a]Shall we go and buy two hundred [1]pennyworth of bread, and give them to eat?

38 He saith unto them, How many loaves have ye? go and see. And when they knew, they say, [a]Five, and two fishes.

39 And he commanded them to make all sit down by companies upon the green grass.

40 And they sat down in ranks, by hundreds, and by fifties.

41 And when he had taken the five loaves and the two fishes, he looked up to heaven, [a]and blessed, and brake the loaves, and gave *them* to his disciples to set before them; and the two fishes divided he among *them* all.

6:31 [b]ch. 3:20
6:32 [a]Mat. 14:13
6:34 [a]Mat. 9:36; 14:14 [b]Luke 9:11
6:35 [a]Mat. 14:15; Luke 9:12
6:37 [1]*The Roman penny is seven pence halfpenny; as* Mat. 18:28 [a]Num. 11:13,22; 2 Ki. 4:43
6:38 [a]Mat. 14:17; Luke 9:13; John 6:9; See Mat. 15:34; ch:8:5
6:41 [a]1 Sam. 9:13; Mat. 26:26

6:45 [1]Or, *over against Bethsaida* [a]Mat. 14:22; John 6:17
6:47 [a]Mat. 14:23; John 6:16,17
6:48 [a]See Luke 24:28
6:52 [a]ch. 8:17,18 [b]ch. 3:5; 16:14
6:53 [a]Mat. 14:34

42 And they did all eat, and were filled.

43 And they took up twelve baskets full of the fragments, and of the fishes.

44 And they that did eat *of* the loaves were about five thousand men.

Jesus walks on the sea

45 ¶ [a]And straightway he constrained his disciples to get into the ship, and to go to the other side before [1]unto Bethsaida, while he sent away the people.

46 And when he had sent them away, he departed into a mountain to pray.

47 [a]And when even was come, the ship was in the midst of the sea, and he alone on the land.

48 And he saw them toiling in rowing; for the wind was contrary unto them: and about the fourth watch of the night he cometh unto them, walking upon the sea, and [a]would have passed by them.

49 But when they saw him walking upon the sea, they supposed *it* had been a spirit, and cried out:

50 For they all saw him, and were troubled. And immediately he talked with them, and saith unto them, Be of good cheer: it is I; be not afraid.

51 And he went up unto them into the ship; and the wind ceased: and they were sore amazed in themselves beyond measure, and wondered.

52 For [a]they considered not *the miracle* of the loaves: for their [b]heart was hardened.

53 ¶ [a]And when they had passed over, they

6:32 *they departed into a desert place by ship privately.* John reports that they went to the other side of the sea of Galilee (John 6:1). Luke, more specifically, says they went to Bethsaida (Luke 9:10), which locates the feeding of the 5,000 on the northeast shore (see note on 7:24).

6:33 *ran afoot thither . . . and outwent them.* Perhaps a strong headwind slowed down the boat so that the people had time to go on foot around the lake and arrive before the boat.

‡6:37 *two hundred pennyworth.* The usual pay for a day's work was one penny or denarius (see Mat 20:2), meaning that about 200 denarii would take about eight months to earn.

6:39 *green grass.* Grass is green around the sea of Galilee after the late winter or early spring rains.

‡6:40 *in ranks, by hundreds, and by fifties.* Recalls the order of the Mosaic camp in the wilderness (e.g., Ex 18:21). The word translated "ranks" means "garden plots," a picturesque figure (v. 39).

6:42 *did all eat, and were filled.* Attempts to explain away this miracle (e.g., by suggesting that Jesus and His disciples shared their lunch and the crowd followed their good example) are inadequate. If Jesus was, as He claimed to be, God incarnate, the miracle presents no difficulties. God had promised that when the true Shepherd came the wilderness would become rich pasture where the sheep would be gathered and fed (Ezek 34:23–31), and here the Messiah feasts with followers in the desert (cf. Is 25:6–9). Jesus is the Shepherd who provides for all our needs so that we lack nothing (cf. Ps 23:1).

‡6:43 *twelve baskets full of the fragments, and of the fishes.* Bread was regarded by Jews as a gift of God, and it was required that scraps that fell on the ground during a meal be picked up. The fragments were collected in small wicker baskets that were carried as a part of daily attire. Each of the disciples may have returned with his basket full, or perhaps Jesus rewarded the little boy for his generosity (see 8:8; John 6:9; see also note on Mat 15:37).

‡6:44 *five thousand men.* The size of the crowd is amazing in light of the fact that the neighboring towns of Capernaum and Bethsaida probably had a population of only 2,000–3,000 each. *men.* Lit. "males," as in all four Gospels. Matthew further emphasizes the point by adding "beside women and children" (Mat 14:21).

‡6:45 *go to the other side before.* John indicates that the people were ready to take Jesus by force and make Him king (John 6:14–15), and Jesus therefore sent His disciples ahead of Himself ("before") across the lake while He slipped away into the hills to pray.

6:48 *fourth watch.* 3:00–6:00 A.M. See 13:35; see also note on Mat 14:25. *walking upon the sea.* A special display of the majestic presence and power of the transcendent Lord, who rules over the sea (see Ps 89:9; Is 51:10,15; Jer 31:35).

6:49 *a spirit.* Popular Jewish superstition held that the appearance of spirits during the night brought disaster. The disciples' terror was prompted by what they may have thought was a water spirit.

6:52 *they considered not the miracle of the loaves.* If they had understood the feeding of the 5,000, they would not have been amazed at Jesus' walking on the water or His calming the waves. *their heart was hardened.* They were showing themselves to be

came into the land of Genesaret, and drew to the shore.

54 And when they were come out of the ship, straightway they knew him,

55 And ran through that whole region round about, and began to carry about in beds those that were sick, where they heard he was.

56 And whithersoever he entered, into villages, or cities, or country, they laid the sick in the streets, and besought him that [a]they might touch if it were but the border of his garment: and as many as touched [1]him were made whole.

What defiles a man

7 Then [a]came together unto him the Pharisees, and certain of the scribes, which came from Jerusalem.

2 And when they saw some of his disciples eat bread with [1]defiled, that is to say, with unwashen, hands, they found fault.

3 For the Pharisees, and all the Jews, except they wash *their* hands [1]oft, eat not, holding the tradition of the elders.

4 And *when they come* from the market, except they wash, they eat not. And many other *things* there be, which they have received to hold, *as* the washing of cups, and [1]pots, brasen vessels, and of [2]tables.

5 [a]Then the Pharisees and scribes asked him, Why walk not thy disciples according to the tradition of the elders, but eat bread with unwashen hands?

6 He answered and said unto them, Well hath Esaias prophesied of you hypocrites, as it is written, [a]This people honoureth me with *their* lips, but their heart is far from me.

7 Howbeit in vain do they worship me, teaching for doctrines the commandments of men.

6:56 [1]Or, *it* [a]Mat. 9:20; ch. 5:27,28; Acts 19:12
7:1 [a]Mat. 15:1
7:2 [1]Or, *common*
7:3 [1]Or, *diligently:* in the original, *with the fist:* Theophylact, *up to the elbow*
7:4 [1]*Sextarius is about a pint and a half* [2]Or, *beds*
7:5 [a]Mat. 15:2
7:6 [a]Is. 29:13
7:9 [1]Or, *frustrate*
7:10 [a]Ex. 20:12; Deut. 5:16; Mat. 15:4 [b]Ex. 21:17; Lev. 20:9; Prov. 20:20
7:11 [a]Mat. 15:5; 23:18
7:14 [a]Mat. 15:10
7:16 [a]Mat. 11:15
7:17 [a]Mat. 15:15

8 For laying aside the commandment of God, ye hold the tradition of men, *as* the washing of pots and cups: and many other such like *things* ye do.

9 And he said unto them, Full well ye [1]reject the commandment of God, that ye may keep your own tradition.

10 For Moses said, [a]Honour thy father and thy mother; and, [b]Whoso curseth father or mother, let him die the death.

11 But ye say, If a man shall say to *his* father or mother, *It is* [a]Corban, that is to say, a gift, *by* whatsoever thou mightest be profited by me; *he shall be free.*

12 And ye suffer him no more to do ought for his father or his mother;

13 Making the word of God of none effect through your tradition, which ye have delivered: and many such like *things* do ye.

14 ¶ [a]And when he had called all the people unto *him,* he said unto them, Hearken unto me every one of you, and understand:

15 There is nothing from without a man, that entering into him can defile him: but the *things* which come out of him, those are they that defile the man.

16 [a]If any *man* have ears to hear, let him hear.

17 [a]And when he was entered into *the* house from the people, his disciples asked him concerning the parable.

18 And he saith unto them, Are ye so without understanding also? Do ye not perceive, that whatsoever *thing* from without entereth into the man, *it* cannot defile him;

19 Because it entereth not into his heart, but into the belly, and goeth out into the draught, purging all meats?

20 And he said, That which cometh out of the man, that defileth the man.

similar to Jesus' opponents, who also exhibited hardness of heart (3:5). See 8:17–21; see also note on Ex 4:21.

6:53 *Genesaret.* See note on Mat 14:34.

6:56 *touch if it were but the border of his garment.* See note on 5:28.

7:1 *the Pharisees . . . which came from Jerusalem.* Another delegation of fact-finding religious leaders from Jerusalem (see 3:22) sent to investigate the Galilean activities of Jesus. See notes on 2:16; Mat 2:4.

7:3 *wash their hands oft.* See note on John 2:6. *the tradition of the elders.* Considered to be binding (see v. 5 and note on Mat 15:2).

7:4 *market.* Where Jews would come into contact with Gentiles, or with Jews who did not observe the ceremonial law, and thus become ceremonially unclean.

‡7:6 *Esaias prophesied.* Isaiah roundly denounced the religious leaders of his day (Is 29:13), and Jesus uses a quotation from this prophet to describe the tradition of the elders as "the commandments of men" (v. 7).

7:8 *the commandment of God . . . the tradition of men.* Jesus clearly contrasts the two. God's commands are found in Scripture and are binding; the traditions of the elders (v. 3) are not Biblical and therefore not authoritative or binding.

7:10 The fifth commandment is cited in both its positive and negative forms.

7:11 *Corban.* The transliteration of a Hebrew word meaning "offering." By using this word in a religious vow an irresponsible Jewish son could formally dedicate to God (i.e., to the temple) his earnings that otherwise would have gone for the support of his parents. The money, however, did not necessarily have to go for religious purposes. The Corban formula was simply a means of circumventing the clear responsibility of children toward their parents as prescribed in the law. The teachers of the law held that the Corban oath was binding, even when uttered rashly. The practice was one of many traditions that adhered to the letter of the law while ignoring its spirit. *that is to say, a gift.* By explaining this Hebrew word, Mark reveals that he is addressing Gentile readers, probably Romans primarily.

7:13 *making the word of God of none effect through your tradition.* The teachers of the law appealed to Num 30:1–2 in support of the Corban vow, but Jesus categorically rejects the practice of using one Biblical teaching to nullify another. The scribal interpretation of Num 30:1–2 satisfied the letter of the passage but missed the meaning of the law as a whole. God never intended obedience to one command to nullify another.

7:19 *purging all meats.* Or, "declaring all foods clean." Mark adds this parenthetical comment to help his readers see the significance of Jesus' pronouncement for them (see Acts 10:9–16).

7:20 *defileth.* Jesus replaced the normal Jewish understand-

21 [a]For from within, out of the heart of men, proceed evil thoughts, adulteries, fornications, murders,

22 Thefts, [1]covetousness, wickedness, deceit, lasciviousness, an evil eye, blasphemy, pride, foolishness:

23 All these evil *things* come from within, and defile the man.

A Greek woman's faith

24 ¶ [a]And from thence he arose, and went into the borders of Tyre and Sidon, and entered into a house, and would have no *man* know *it:* but he could not be hid.

25 For a *certain* woman, whose young daughter had an unclean spirit, heard of him, and came and fell at his feet:

26 The woman was a [1]Greek, a Syrophenician by nation; and she besought him that he would cast forth the devil out of her daughter.

27 But Jesus said unto her, Let the children first be filled: for it is not meet to take the children's bread, and to cast *it* unto the dogs.

28 And she answered and said unto him, Yes, Lord: yet the dogs under the table eat of the children's crumbs.

29 And he said unto her, For this saying go thy way; the devil is gone out of thy daughter.

30 And when she was come to her house, she found the devil gone out, and *her* daughter laid upon the bed.

A deaf mute healed

31 ¶ [a]And again, departing from the coasts of Tyre and Sidon, he came unto the sea of Gal-

7:21 [a]Gen. 6:5; 8:21; Mat. 15:19
7:22 [1][Gr. *covetousnesses, wickednesses*]
7:24 [a]Mat. 15:21
7:26 [1]Or, *Gentile*
7:31 [a]Mat. 15:29

ings of defilement with the truth that defilement comes from an impure heart, not the violation of external rules. Fellowship with God is not interrupted by unclean hands or food, but by sin (see vv. 21–23).

7:24 *Tyre.* A Gentile city located in Phoenicia (modern Lebanon), which bordered Galilee to the northwest. A journey of about 30 miles from Capernaum would have brought Jesus to the vicinity of Tyre. *would have no man know it.* Ever since the feeding of the 5,000 (6:30–44) Jesus and His disciples had been, for the most part, skirting the region of Galilee. His purpose was to avoid the opposition in Galilee and to secure opportunity to teach His disciples privately (9:30–31). The regions to which He withdrew were: (1) the northeastern shore of the sea of Galilee (6:30–53), (2) Phoenicia (7:24–30), (3) the Decapolis (7:31–8:10) and (4) Caesarea Philippi (8:27–9:32).

7:26 *Syrophenician.* At that time Phoenicia belonged administratively to Syria. Mark possibly used the term to distinguish this woman from the Libyan-Phoenicians of North Africa.

7:27 *the children's bread, and to cast it unto the dogs.* See note on Mat 15:26.

‡7:28 *Yes, Lord.* The only time in this Gospel that Jesus is addressed as "Lord." It is astounding to behold the great reserve the Gospel writers used in not referring to Jesus as "Lord." At the time Mark was written, Paul and others had already spoken of Christ (in their "epistles" or "letters") as "the Lord" Jesus Christ. But Mark is recalling the history of the developing awareness of this truth, during which time it was still not generally known that Jesus was God.

7:31 *departing from the coasts of Tyre and Sidon, he came unto the sea of Galilee.* Apparently Jesus went north from Tyre to Sidon (about 25 miles) and then southeast through the territory of Herod Philip to the east side of the sea of Galilee. The route was circuitous possibly to avoid entering Galilee, where Herod Antipas was in power (see 6:17–29) and where many people wanted to take Jesus by force and make Him king (John 6:14–15). Herod had intimated a hostile interest in Jesus (6:14–16). *Decapolis.* See notes on v. 24; Mat 4:25.

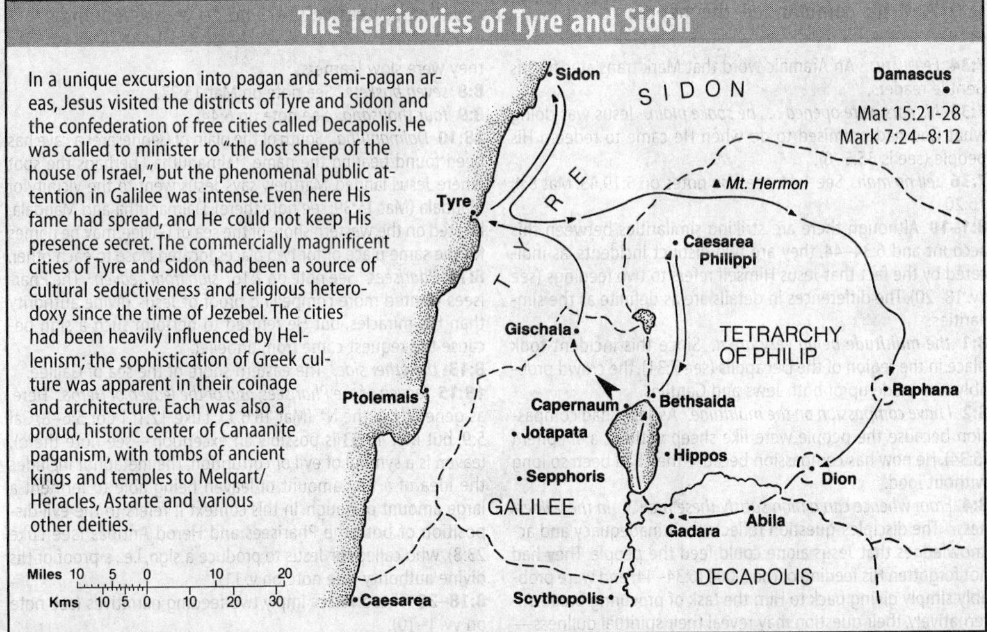
The Territories of Tyre and Sidon
In a unique excursion into pagan and semi-pagan areas, Jesus visited the districts of Tyre and Sidon and the confederation of free cities called Decapolis. He was called to minister to "the lost sheep of the house of Israel," but the phenomenal public attention in Galilee was intense. Even here His fame had spread, and He could not keep His presence secret. The commercially magnificent cities of Tyre and Sidon had been a source of cultural seductiveness and religious heterodoxy since the time of Jezebel. The cities had been heavily influenced by Hellenism; the sophistication of Greek culture was apparent in their coinage and architecture. Each was also a proud, historic center of Canaanite paganism, with tombs of ancient kings and temples to Melqart/Heracles, Astarte and various other deities.
Sidon
SIDON
Damascus
Mat 15:21-28
Mark 7:24-8:12
TYRE
Mt. Hermon
Tyre
Caesarea Philippi
Gischala
TETRARCHY OF PHILIP
Raphana
Ptolemais
Capernaum
Bethsaida
Jotapata
Hippos
Sepphoris
Dion
GALILEE
Abila
Gadara
DECAPOLIS
Miles 10 5 0 10 20
Kms 10 5 0 10 20 30
Caesarea
Scythopolis

ilee, through the midst of the coasts of Decapolis.

32 And [a]they bring unto him one *that was* deaf, and had an impediment in his speech; and they beseech him to put *his* hand upon him.

33 And he took him aside from the multitude, and put his fingers into his ears, and [a]he spit, and touched his tongue;

34 And [a]looking up to heaven, [b]he sighed, and saith unto him, EPHPHATHA, that is, Be opened.

35 [a]And straightway his ears were opened, and the string of his tongue was loosed, and he spake plain.

36 And [a]he charged them that they should tell no *man:* but the more he charged them, *so* much the more a great deal they published *it;*

37 And were beyond measure astonished, saying, He hath done all *things* well: he maketh both the deaf to hear, and the dumb to speak.

The four thousand fed

8 In those days [a]the multitude being very great, and having nothing to eat, Jesus called his disciples unto *him,* and saith unto them,

2 I have compassion on the multitude, because they have now been with me three days, and have nothing to eat:

3 And if I send them away fasting to their own houses, they will faint by the way: for divers of them came from far.

4 And his disciples answered him, From whence can a man satisfy these *men* with bread here in the wilderness?

5 [a]And he asked them, How many loaves have ye? And they said, Seven.

6 And he commanded the people to sit down on the ground: and he took the seven loaves, and gave thanks, and brake, and gave to his disciples to set before *them;* and they did set *them* before the people.

7 And they had a few small fishes: and [a]he blessed, and commanded to set them also before *them.*

8 So they did eat, and were filled: and they took up of the broken *meat* that was left seven baskets.

9 And they that had eaten were about four thousand: and he sent them away.

Pharisees ask for a sign

10 ¶ And [a]straightway he entered into a ship with his disciples, and came into the parts of Dalmanutha.

11 [a]And the Pharisees came forth, and began to question with him, seeking of him a sign from heaven, tempting him.

12 And he sighed deeply in his spirit, and saith, Why doth this generation seek after a sign? verily I say unto you, There shall no sign be given unto this generation.

13 And he left them, and entering into the ship again departed to the other side.

14 ¶ [a]Now *the disciples* had forgotten to take bread, neither had they in the ship with them more than one loaf.

15 [a]And he charged them, saying, Take heed, beware of the leaven of the Pharisees, and *of* the leaven of Herod.

16 And they reasoned among themselves, saying, *It is* because we have no bread.

17 And when Jesus knew *it,* he saith unto them, Why reason ye, because ye have no bread? [a]perceive ye not yet, neither understand? have ye your heart yet hardened?

18 Having eyes, see ye not? and having ears, hear ye not? and do ye not remember?

7:32 [a]Mat. 9:32; Luke 11:14
7:33 [a]ch. 8:23; John 9:6
7:34 [a]ch. 6:41; John 11:41; 17:1 [b]John 11:33,38
7:35 [a]Is. 35:5,6
7:36 [a]ch. 5:43
8:1 [a]Mat. 15:32
8:5 [a]Mat. 15:34; See ch. 6:38
8:7 [a]Mat. 14:19; ch. 6:41
8:10 [a]Mat. 15:39
8:11 [a]Mat. 12:38; 16:1; John 6:30
8:14 [a]Mat. 16:5
8:15 [a]Mat. 16:6; Luke 12:1
8:17 [a]ch. 6:52

7:34 *EPHPHATHA.* An Aramaic word that Mark translates for his Gentile readers.
7:35 *his ears were opened . . . he spake plain.* Jesus was doing what God had promised to do when He came to redeem His people (see Is 35:5–6).
7:36 *tell no man.* See 1:44; see also notes on 5:19,43; Mat 8:4; 16:20.
8:1–10 Although there are striking similarities between this account and 6:34–44, they are two distinct incidents, as indicated by the fact that Jesus Himself refers to two feedings (see vv. 18–20). The differences in details are as definite as the similarities.
8:1 *the multitude being very great.* Since this incident took place in the region of the Decapolis (see 7:31), the crowd probably was made up of both Jews and Gentiles.
8:2 *I have compassion on the multitude.* As Jesus had compassion because the people were like sheep without a shepherd (6:34), He now has compassion because they had been so long without food.
8:4 *From whence can a man satisfy these men . . . in the wilderness?* The disciples' question reflects their inadequacy and acknowledges that Jesus alone could feed the people. They had not forgotten His feeding of the 5,000 (6:34–44) and were probably simply giving back to Him the task of procuring bread. Alternatively, their question may reveal their spiritual dullness—they were slow learners.
8:8 *seven baskets.* See note on Mat 15:37.
8:9 *four thousand.* See note on 6:44.
‡8:10 *Dalmanutha.* South of the plain of Gennesaret a cave has been found bearing the name "Talmanutha," perhaps the spot where Jesus landed. Matthew says Jesus went to the vicinity of Magdala (Mat 15:39; see note there). Dalmanutha and Magdala, located on the western shore of the sea of Galilee, may be names for the same place or for two places located close to each other.
8:11 *Pharisees.* See note on 2:16. *sign from heaven.* The Pharisees wanted more compelling proof of Jesus' divine authority than His miracles, but He refused to perform such a sign because the request came from unbelief.
8:13 *the other side.* The eastern shore of the sea of Galilee.
‡8:15 *leaven of the Pharisees, and of the leaven of Herod.* Here, as generally in the NT (Mat 16:6,11; Luke 12:1; 1 Cor 5:6–8; Gal 5:9; but Mat 13:33 is possibly an exception—see note there), leaven is a symbol of evil or corruption. The metaphor includes the idea of a tiny amount of leaven being able to ferment a large amount of dough. In this context it refers to the evil disposition of both the Pharisees and Herod Antipas (see Luke 23:8), who called for Jesus to produce a sign, i.e., a proof of His divine authority (see note on v. 11).
8:18–20 These verses imply two feeding narratives (see note on vv. 1–10).

19 [a]When I brake the five loaves among
five thousand, how many baskets full of fragments took ye up? They say unto him, Twelve.
20 And [a]when the seven among four thousand, how many baskets full of fragments took
ye up? And they said, Seven.
21 And he said unto them, How *is it that*
[a]ye do not understand?

A blind man healed

22 ¶ And he cometh to Bethsaida; and they
bring a blind man unto him, and besought him
to touch him.
23 And he took the blind man by the hand,
and led him out of the town; and when [a]he
had spit on his eyes, and put *his* hands upon
him, he asked him if he saw ought.
24 And he looked up, and said, I see men
as trees, walking.
25 After that he put *his* hands again upon
his eyes, and made him look up: and he was
restored, and saw every *man* clearly.
26 And he sent him away to his house, saying, Neither go into the town, [a]nor tell *it* to
any in the town.

Peter's confession of faith

27 ¶ [a]And Jesus went out, and his disciples,
into the towns of Cesarea Philippi: and by the
way he asked his disciples, saying unto them,
Whom do men say that I am?
28 And they answered, [a]John the Baptist:
but some *say,* Elias; and others, One of the
prophets.
29 And he saith unto them, But whom say
ye that I am? And Peter answereth and saith
unto him, [a]Thou art the Christ.
30 [a]And he charged them that they should
tell no *man* of him.
31 And [a]he began to teach them, that the
Son of man must suffer many *things,* and be
rejected of the elders, and *of* the chief priests,
and scribes, and be killed, and after three days
rise again.
32 And he spake *that* saying openly. And
Peter took him, and began to rebuke him.
33 But when he had turned about and
looked on his disciples, he rebuked Peter, saying, Get thee behind me, Satan: for thou
savourest not the *things* that be of God, but
the *things* that be of men.
34 And when he had called the people
unto *him* with his disciples also, he said unto
them, [a]Whosoever will come after me, let him
deny himself, and take up his cross, and follow
me.
35 For [a]whosoever will save his life shall
lose it; but whosoever shall lose his life for my
sake and the gospel's, the same shall save it.
36 For what shall it profit a man, if he shall
gain the whole world, and lose his own soul?
37 Or what shall a man give in exchange
for his soul?
38 [a]Whosoever therefore [b]shall be

8:19 [a]Mat. 14:20; ch. 6:43; Luke 9:17; John 6:13
8:20 [a]ver. 8; Mat. 15:37
8:21 [a]ver. 17; ch. 6:52
8:23 [a]ch. 7:33
8:26 [a]Mat. 8:4; ch. 5:43
8:27 [a]Mat. 16:13; Luke 9:18
8:28 [a]Mat. 14:2
8:29 [a]Mat. 16:16; John 6:69; 11:27
8:30 [a]Mat. 16:20
8:31 [a]Mat. 16:21; 17:22; Luke 9:22
8:34 [a]Mat. 10:38; 16:24; Luke 9:23; 14:27
8:35 [a]John 12:25
8:38 [a]Mat. 10:33; Luke 9:26; 12:9 [b]See Rom. 1:16; 2 Tim. 1:8; 2:12

8:22 *Bethsaida.* See note on Mat 11:21.

8:24 *as trees, walking.* The man had no doubt bumped into trees in his blindness; now he dimly sees something like tree trunks moving about.

‡8:25 *he put his hands again upon his eyes.* This second laying on of hands is unique in Jesus' healing ministry, but as in God's original creation over six days, He can choose to do things in stages. *saw every man clearly.* Giving sight to the blind was another indication that Jesus was doing what God had promised to do when He came to bring salvation (Is 35:5).

8:26 *Neither go into the town.* So as not to broadcast what Jesus had done for him and precipitate a crisis before Jesus had completed His ministry. See 1:44; see also notes on 5:19,43; Mat 8:4; 16:20.

8:27 *Cesarea Philippi.* See notes on 7:24; Mat 16:13.

‡8:29 *Christ.* Because popular Jewish ideas associated with the term "Christ" were largely political and national, Jesus seldom used it. Of its seven occurrences in Mark, only three appear in the sayings of Jesus (9:41; 12:35; 13:21), and in none of these does He use the title of Himself (with the possible exception of 9:41). Mark identifies Jesus as the Christ in 1:1.

8:30 *tell no man of him.* See 1:44; see also notes on 5:19,43; Mat 8:4; 16:20.

8:31–10:52 A new section begins in 8:31 and centers on three predictions of Jesus' death (8:31; 9:31; 10:33–34). It indicates a geographical shift from Galilee, where most of Jesus' public ministry reported by Mark took place, to Jerusalem and the closing days of Jesus' life on earth. In this section Jesus defines the true meaning of "Christ" as the title applies to Him.

‡8:31 *Son of man.* Jesus' most common title for Himself, used 84 times in the Gospels and never used by anyone but Jesus. In Dan 7:13–14 the Son of man is pictured as a heavenly figure who in the end times is entrusted by God with absolute authority, divine glory and sovereign power. That Jesus used "Son of man" as a Messianic title is evident by His use of it (v. 31) in juxtaposition to Peter's use of "Christ" (v. 29). When Jesus referred to Himself as the "Son of man" before the Sanhedrin, they called it blasphemy, understanding it to be a claim of deity (Mark 14:62–64). See note on Dan 7:13. *must suffer.* As predicted in the Suffering Servant passage in Is 52:13–53:12 (see Mark 9:9,12,31; 10:33–34; 14:21,41). *elders.* The lay members of the Sanhedrin, the high court of the Jews. *chief priests.* See note on Mat 2:4. These included the ruling high priest, Caiaphas; the former high priest, Annas; and the high priestly families. *scribes.* See note on Mat 2:4. Representatives of the three groups mentioned here constituted the Sanhedrin.

8:32 *Peter . . . began to rebuke him.* Suffering and rejection had no place in Peter's conception of the Messiah, and he rebuked Jesus for teaching what to him seemed not only inconceivable but terribly wrong.

8:33 *Satan.* Peter's attempt to dissuade Jesus from going to the cross held the same temptation Satan gave at the outset of Jesus' ministry (see Mat 4:8–10), so Jesus severely rebuked him.

8:34 *deny himself.* Cease to make self the object of his life and actions. *take up his cross.* The picture is of a man, already condemned, required to carry the beam of his own cross to the place of execution (see John 19:17). Cross-bearing is a willingness to suffer and die for the Lord's sake. *and follow me.* Implying that His own death would be by crucifixion.

‡8:35 *save his life.* Physical life may be saved by denying Jesus, but eternal life will be lost. Conversely, discipleship may result in the loss of physical life, but that loss is insignificant when compared with gaining eternal life. This is a divine paradox and thus impossible for the natural man to grasp.

8:36 *the whole world.* All the things that could possibly be

ashamed of me and of my words in this adulterous and sinful generation; of him also shall the Son of man be ashamed, when he cometh in the glory of his Father with the holy angels.

9 And he said unto them, [a]Verily I say unto you, That there be some of them that stand here, which shall not taste of death, till they have seen [b]the kingdom of God come with power.

The transfiguration

2 ¶ [a]And after six days Jesus taketh with *him* Peter, and James, and John, and leadeth them up into a high mountain apart by themselves: and he was transfigured before them.

3 And his raiment became shining, exceeding [a]white as snow; so as no fuller on earth can white *them.*

4 And there appeared unto them Elias with Moses: and they were talking with Jesus.

5 And Peter answered and said to Jesus, Master, it is good for us to be here: and let us make three tabernacles; one for thee, and one for Moses, and one for Elias.

6 For he wist not what to say; for they were sore afraid.

7 And there was a cloud that overshadowed them: and a voice came out of the cloud, saying, This is my beloved Son: hear him.

8 And suddenly, when they had looked round about, they saw no *man* any more, save Jesus only with themselves.

9 ¶ [a]And as they came down from the mountain, he charged them that they should tell no *man* what *things* they had seen, till the Son of man were risen from the dead.

10 And they kept *that* saying with themselves, questioning *one* with *another* what the rising from the dead should mean.

11 And they asked him, saying, Why say the scribes [a]that Elias must first come?

12 And he answered and told them, Elias verily cometh first, and restoreth all *things;* and [a]how it is written of the Son of man, that he must suffer many *things,* and [b]be set at nought.

13 But I say unto you, That [a]Elias is indeed come, and they have done unto him whatsoever they listed, as it is written of him.

The demoniac boy cured

14 ¶ [a]And when he came to *his* disciples, he saw a great multitude about them, and *the* scribes questioning with them.

15 And straightway all the people, when they beheld him, were greatly amazed, and running to *him* saluted him.

16 And he asked the scribes, What question ye [1]with them?

17 And [a]one of the multitude answered and said, Master, I have brought unto thee my son, which hath a dumb spirit:

18 And wheresoever he taketh him, he [1]teareth him: and he foameth, and gnasheth with his teeth, and pineth away: and I spake to thy disciples that they should cast him out; and they could not.

19 He answereth him, and saith, O faithless

9:1 [a]Mat. 16:28; Luke 9:27 [b]Mat. 24:30
9:2 [a]Mat. 17:1; Luke 9:28
9:3 [a]Dan. 7:9
9:9 [a]Mat. 17:9
9:11 [a]Mal. 4:5; Mat. 17:10
9:12 [a]Ps. 22:6; Is. 53:2; Dan. 9:26 [b]Luke 23:11; Phil. 2:7
9:13 [a]Mat. 11:14; 17:12; Luke 1:17
9:14 [a]Mat. 17:14; Luke 9:37
9:16 [1]Or, *among yourselves?*
9:17 [a]Mat. 17:14; Luke 9:38
9:18 [1]Or, *dasheth him*

achieved or acquired in this life. *soul.* That is, eternal life (also in v. 37).

8:38 *ashamed of me and of my words.* Contrast Rom 1:16. A person who is more concerned about fitting into and pleasing his own "adulterous and sinful generation" than about following and pleasing Christ will have no part in God's kingdom. *Son of man.* See note on v. 31. *when he cometh in the glory of his Father.* See 2 Thes 1:6–10. The situation in which Jesus is rejected, humiliated and put to death will be reversed when He returns in glory as the Judge of all people.

9:1 *Verily I say unto you.* See note on 3:28. *not taste of death, till they have seen the kingdom of God come with power.* See note on Mat 16:28. *kingdom of God.* See note on Mat 3:2.

9:2 *after six days.* See note on Mat 17:1. *Peter, and James, and John.* See note on 5:37. *a high mountain.* See note on Luke 9:28. *transfigured.* See note on Mat 17:2.

9:4 *Elias with Moses.* See notes on Mat 17:3; Luke 9:30.

9:5 *Master.* Hebrew word for "(my) teacher." *three tabernacles.* Peter may have desired to erect new tabernacles where God could again communicate with his people (see Ex 29:42). Or he may have been thinking of the booths used at the feast of tabernacles (Lev 23:42). In any case, he seemed eager to find fulfillment of the promised glory then, prior to the sufferings that Jesus had announced as necessary.

9:7 *a voice came out of the cloud.* The cloud is frequently a symbol of God's presence to protect and guide (e.g., Ex 16:10; 19:9; 24:15–18; 33:9–10). *hear him* The full sense includes obeying Him. When God is involved, the only true hearing is obedient hearing (see Jas 1:22–25).

9:9 *tell no man . . . till.* After Jesus' resurrection the disciples were to tell everyone what they had experienced, for Jesus' finished work would have demonstrated His true and full character as the Messiah. *Son of man.* See note on 8:31.

9:10 *what the rising from the dead should mean.* As Jews they were familiar with the doctrine of the resurrection; it was the resurrection of the Son of Man that baffled them, because their theology had no place for a suffering and dying Messiah.

9:11 *Elias must first come.* See note on Mat 17:10.

9:12 *Elias verily cometh first, and restoreth all things.* A reference to the coming of Elijah, or one like him, in preparation for the coming of the Messiah (see note on Mat 17:10). *Son of man.* See note on 8:31. *must suffer many things, and be set at naught.* Just as "Elijah" (John the Baptist; see note on v. 13) has been rejected (see note on Mat 17:12).

9:13 *Elias is indeed come.* A reference to John the Baptist (see Mat 17:13). *they.* Herod and Herodias (see 6:17–29). John, like Elijah, was opposed by a weak ruler and his wicked consort. *as it is written of him.* What Scripture says about Elijah in his relationship to Ahab and Jezebel (1 Ki 19:1–10). There is no prediction of suffering associated with Elijah's ministry in the end times. However, what happened to Elijah under the threats of Jezebel foreshadowed what would happen to John the Baptist. The order of events suggested in vv. 11–13 is as follows: (1) Elijah ministered in the days of wicked Jezebel; (2) Elijah was a type of John the Baptist, who in turn suffered at the hands of Herodias; (3) the Son of man suffered and was rejected a short time after John was beheaded.

9:14 *his disciples.* The nine besides Peter, James and John (see v. 2).

9:18 Demonic possession was responsible for the boy's condition (see vv. 20,25–26).

generation, how long shall I be with you? how
long shall I suffer you? bring him unto me.
20 And they brought him unto him: and
[a]when he saw him, straightway the spirit tare
him; and he fell on the ground, and wallowed
foaming.
21 And he asked his father, How long is it
ago since this came unto him? And he said, Of
a child.
22 And ofttimes it hath cast him into the
fire, and into the waters, to destroy him: but if
thou canst do any *thing,* have compassion on
us, and help us.
23 Jesus said unto him, [a]If thou canst believe, all *things are* possible to him that believeth.
24 And straightway the father of the child
cried out, and said with tears, Lord, I believe;
help thou mine unbelief.
25 When Jesus saw that the people came
running together, he rebuked the foul spirit,
saying unto him, *Thou* dumb and deaf spirit, I
charge thee, come out of him, and enter no
more into him.
26 And *the spirit* cried, and rent him sore,
and came out of *him:* and he was as one dead;
insomuch that many said, He is dead.
27 But Jesus took him by the hand, and lifted him up; and he arose.
28 [a]And when he was come into *the*
house, his disciples asked him privately, Why
could not we cast him out?
29 And he said unto them, This kind can
come forth by nothing, but by prayer and fasting.
30 ¶ And they departed thence, and passed
through Galilee; and he would not that any
man should know *it.*
31 [a]For he taught his disciples, and said
unto them, The Son of man is delivered into
the hands of men, and they shall kill him; and
after that he is killed, he shall rise the third day.
32 But they understood not *that* saying,
and were afraid to ask him.

True discipleship

33 ¶ [a]And he came to Capernaum: and being in the house he asked them, What *was it*
that ye disputed among yourselves by the way?
34 But they held their peace: for by the
way they had disputed among themselves,
who *should be* the greatest.
35 And he sat down, and called the twelve,
and saith unto them, [a]If any *man* desire to be
first, *the same* shall be last of all, and servant
of all.
36 And [a]he took a child, and set him in the
midst of them: and when he had taken him in
his arms, he said unto them,
37 Whosoever shall receive one of such
children in my name, receiveth me: and
[a]whosoever shall receive me, receiveth not
me, but him that sent me.
38 ¶ [a]And John answered him, saying,
Master, we saw one casting out devils in thy
name, and he followeth not us: and we forbad
him, because he followeth not us.
39 But Jesus said, Forbid him not: [a]for
there is no *man* which shall do a miracle in my
name, that can lightly speak evil of me.
40 For [a]he that is not against us is on our
part.
41 [a]For whosoever shall give you a cup of
water to drink in my name, because ye belong
to Christ, verily I say unto you, he shall not
lose his reward.
42 [a]And whosoever shall [1]offend one of
these little ones that believe in me, it is better

9:20 [a]ch. 1:26; Luke 9:42
9:23 [a]Mat. 17:20; ch. 11:23; Luke 17:6; John 11:40
9:28 [a]Mat. 17:19
9:31 [a]Mat. 17:22; Luke 9:44
9:33 [a]Mat. 18:1; Luke 9:46; 22:24
9:35 [a]Mat. 20:26,27; ch. 10:43
9:36 [a]Mat. 18:2; ch. 10:16
9:37 [a]Mat. 10:40; Luke 9:48
9:38 [a]Num. 11:28; Luke 9:49
9:39 [a]1 Cor. 12:3
9:40 [a]See Mat. 12:30
9:41 [a]Mat. 10:42
9:42 [1]Or, *cause thee to offend:* and so ver. 45,47 [a]Mat. 18:6; Luke 17:1

9:22 *to destroy him.* See notes on 5:5,13.

9:23 *If thou canst believe, all things are possible to him that believeth.* The question was not whether Jesus had the power to heal the boy but whether the father had faith to believe it. A person who truly believes will set no limits on what God can do.

9:24 *I believe; help thou mine unbelief.* Since faith is never perfect, belief and unbelief are often mixed.

9:25 *When Jesus saw that the people came running together, he rebuked the foul spirit.* As much as possible, Jesus wanted to avoid further publicity.

‡9:29 *This kind.* Seems to suggest that there are different kinds of demons. *can come forth by nothing, but by prayer and fasting.* The disciples apparently had taken for granted the power given to them or had come to believe that it was inherent in them. Lack of prayer indicated they had forgotten that their power over the demonic spirits was from Jesus. Sometimes fasting is also required. It demonstrates to God our determination and perseverance, our willingness to sacrifice to see God's will accomplished (see 3:15; 6:7,13).

9:30 *passed through Galilee.* Jesus' public ministry in and around Galilee was completed (see note on 7:24), and He was now on His way to Jerusalem to suffer and die (see 10:32–34). As He had been doing for several months, Jesus continued to focus His teaching ministry on the twelve (v. 31).

9:31 *Son of man.* See note on 8:31.

9:32 *they understood not.* See v. 10; 8:32–33.

9:33 *Capernaum.* See notes on 1:21; Mat 4:13. *the house.* Probably the one belonging to Peter and Andrew (see 1:29).

9:34 *they held their peace.* No doubt due to embarrassment. *who should be the greatest.* Questions of rank and status are normal and played an important role in the life of Jewish groups at this time, but they had no place in Jesus' value system (see v. 35; 10:42–45).

9:35 *he sat down.* See note on 4:1.

9:38 *followeth not us.* The man apparently was a believer, but he was not one of the exclusive company of the twelve. Nevertheless he acted in Jesus' name and had done what the disciples, on at least one occasion, had not been able to do (see vv. 14–18,28).

‡9:39 *Forbid him not.* Jesus' view of discipleship was far more inclusive than the narrow view held by the twelve. Doctrinal differences are important, but we must remember that all true believers are still one in Christ.

9:41 *give you a cup of water.* God remembers even small acts of kindness extended to believers because they are believers. *verily I say unto you.* See note on 3:28. *his reward.* Including God's approval.

‡9:42 *one of these little ones that believe.* Perhaps the little children mentioned in vv. 36–37, or the man mentioned in v. 38. Jesus' point is clear: To cause even those whom we might consider to be the least of believers to sin will bring serious judg-

for him that a millstone were hanged about his neck, and he were cast into the sea.

43 [a]And if thy hand [1]offend thee, cut it off: it is better for thee to enter into life maimed, than having two hands to go into hell, into the fire that never shall be quenched:

44 [a]Where their worm dieth not, and the fire is not quenched.

45 And if thy foot [1]offend thee, cut it off: it is better for thee to enter halt into life, than having two feet to be cast into hell, into the fire that never shall be quenched:

46 Where their worm dieth not, and the fire is not quenched.

47 And if thine eye [1]offend thee, pluck it out: it is better for thee to enter into the kingdom of God with one eye, than having two eyes to be cast into hell fire:

48 Where their worm dieth not, and the fire is not quenched.

49 For every one shall be salted with fire, [a]and every sacrifice shall be salted with salt.

50 [a]Salt *is* good: but if the salt have lost his saltness, wherewith will you season it? [b]Have salt in yourselves, and [c]have peace one with another.

9:43 [1]Or, *cause thee to offend* [a]Deut. 13:6; Mat. 5:29; 18:8
9:44 [a]Is. 66:24
9:45 [1]Or, *cause thee to offend*
9:47 [1]Or, *cause thee to offend*
9:49 [a]Lev. 2:13; Ezek. 43:24
9:50 [a]Mat. 5:13; Luke 14:34 [b]Eph. 4:29; Col. 4:6 [c]Rom. 12:18; 14:19; 2 Cor. 13:11; Heb. 12:14

10:1 [a]Mat. 19:1; John 10:40; 11:7
10:2 [a]Mat. 19:3
10:4 [a]Deut. 24:1; Mat. 5:31; 19:7
10:6 [a]Gen. 1:27; 5:2
10:7 [a]Gen. 2:24; 1 Cor. 6:16; Eph. 5:31
10:11 [a]Mat. 5:32; 19:9; Luke 16:18; Rom. 7:3; 1 Cor. 7:10,11

Marriage and divorce

10 And [a]he rose from thence, and cometh into the coasts of Judea by the farther side of Jordan: and the people resort unto him again; and, as he was wont, he taught them again.

2 [a]And the Pharisees came to *him,* and asked him, Is it lawful for a man to put away *his* wife? tempting him.

3 And he answered and said unto them, What did Moses command you?

4 And they said, [a]Moses suffered to write a bill of divorcement, and to put *her* away.

5 And Jesus answered and said unto them, For the hardness of your heart he wrote you this precept.

6 But from the beginning of the creation [a]God made them male and female.

7 [a]For this cause shall a man leave his father and mother, and cleave to his wife;

8 And they twain shall be one flesh: so then they are no more twain, but one flesh.

9 What therefore God hath joined together, let not man put asunder.

10 And in the house his disciples asked him again of the same *matter.*

11 And he saith unto them, [a]Whosoever

ment. *millstone.* A heavy circular stone slab laid on its side and turned by a donkey in grinding grain.

9:43 *cut it off.* Hyperbole, a figure of speech that exaggerates to make its point, is used here to emphasize the need for drastic action. Often sin can be conquered only by radical "spiritual surgery." *life.* Eternal life in the presence of God. *hell.* See note on Mat 5:22.

‡9:44,46 Textual critics often point out that verses 44 and 46 are not found in some early manuscripts of the NT, and that they are identical with v. 48. However, these verses are not only in the majority of all manuscripts, but are also included by several early church fathers. It is not unusual for Jesus to repeat things He wants to emphasize. See for example Mat 19:30 and 20:16, and the oft repeated "Let him who hath ears to hear" statement in Rev 2–3.

9:47 *kingdom of God.* See note on Mat 3:2.

‡9:48 Is 66:24 speaks of the punishment for rebellion against God. As the final word of Isaiah's message, the passage became familiar as a picture of endless destruction. *worm dieth not.* Worms were always present in the rubbish dump (see note on Mat 5:22). *the fire is not quenched.* The fire in hell is real. That is clearly taught here; in Jesus' explanation of the burning of the tares in Mat 13:41–42; and in His plain statements in Mat 25:41 and 46.

9:49 The saying may mean that everyone who enters hell will suffer its fire, or (if only loosely connected with the preceding) it may mean that every Christian in this life can expect to undergo the fire of suffering and purification.

9:50 *Salt is good.* The distinctive mark of discipleship typified by salt is allegiance to Jesus and the gospel (see 8:35,38; see also note on Mat 5:13). *have peace one with another.* Strife is resolved and peace restored when we recognize in one another a common commitment to Jesus and the gospel.

10:1 *coasts of Judea.* The Greek and Roman equivalent to the OT land of Judah, essentially the southern part of the Holy Land (now exclusive of Idumea), which formerly had been the southern kingdom. For Jesus' ministry in Judea see note on Luke 9:51. *Jordan.* See note on 1:5. Jesus' journey took Him south from Capernaum, over the mountains of Samaria into Judea and then east across the Jordan into Perea, where He was in the territory of Herod Antipas (see note on Mat 14:1). For Jesus' ministry in Perea see note on Luke 13:22.

10:2 *Pharisees.* See note on 2:16. *came to him, and asked him.* The question of the Pharisees was hostile. It was for unlawful divorce and remarriage that John the Baptist denounced Herod Antipas and Herodias (see 6:17–18), and this rebuke cost him first imprisonment and then his life. Jesus was now within Herod's jurisdiction, and the Pharisees may have hoped that Jesus' reply would cause the tetrarch to seize Him as he had John. *Is it lawful . . . to put away his wife?* Jews of that day generally agreed that divorce was lawful, the only debated issue being the proper grounds for it (see note on Mat 19:3).

10:5 *For the hardness of your heart.* Divorce was an accommodation to human weakness and was used to bring order in a society that had disregarded God's will, but it was not the standard God had originally intended, as vv. 6–9 clearly indicate. The purpose of Deut 24:1 was not to make divorce acceptable, but to reduce the hardship of its consequences.

10:6 *from the beginning of the creation.* Jesus goes back to the time before human sin to show God's original intention. God instituted marriage as a great unifying blessing, bonding the male and female in His creation.

10:8 *no more twain, but one flesh.* The deduction drawn by Jesus affirms the ideal of the permanence of marriage.

10:9 *What therefore God hath joined together.* Jesus grounds the sanctity of marriage in the authority of God Himself, and His "No" to divorce safeguards against human selfishness, which always threatens to destroy marriage.

10:11 *Whosoever shall put away his wife.* In Jewish practice divorce was effected by the husband himself, not by a judicial authority or court. *committeth adultery against her.* A simple declaration of divorce on the part of a husband could not release him from the divine law of marriage and its moral obligations—this enduring force of the marriage bond was unrecognized in rabbinic courts. But see note on Mat 19:3; see also Mat 19:9,

Bartimeus receives his sight

46 ¶ [a]And they came to Jericho: and as he
went out of Jericho with his disciples and a
great number of people, blind Bartimeus, the
son of Timeus, sat by the *high*way side begging.
47 And when he heard that it was Jesus of
Nazareth, he began to cry out, and say, Jesus,
thou Son of David, have mercy on me.
48 And many charged him that he should
hold his peace: but he cried the more a great
deal, *Thou* Son of David, have mercy on me.
49 And Jesus stood still, and commanded
him to be called. And they call the blind man,
saying unto him, Be of good comfort, rise; he
calleth thee.
50 And he, casting away his garment, rose,
and came to Jesus.
51 And Jesus answered and said unto him,
What wilt thou *that* I should do unto thee?
The blind man said unto him, Lord, that I
might receive my sight.
52 And Jesus said unto him, Go thy way;
[a]thy faith hath [1]made thee whole. And immediately he received his sight, and followed
Jesus in the way.

The triumphal entry

11 And [a]when they came nigh to Jerusalem, unto Bethphage and Bethany, at
the mount of Olives, he sendeth forth two of
his disciples,

10:46 [a]Mat. 20:29; Luke 18:35
10:52 [1]Or, *saved thee* [a]Mat. 9:22; ch. 5:34
11:1 [a]Mat. 21:1; Luke 19:29; John 12:14
11:8 [a]Mat. 21:8
11:9 [a]Ps. 118:26
11:10 [a]Ps. 148:1
11:11 [a]Mat. 21:12

2 And saith unto them, Go your way into
the village over against you: and as soon as ye
be entered into it, ye shall find a colt tied,
whereon never man sat; loose him, and bring
him.
3 And if any *man* say unto you, Why do ye
this? say ye that the Lord hath need of him;
and straightway he will send him hither.
4 And they went their way, and found the
colt tied by the door without in a place where
two ways met; and they loose him.
5 And certain of them that stood there said
unto them, What do ye, loosing the colt?
6 And they said unto them even as Jesus
had commanded: and they let them go.
7 And they brought the colt to Jesus, and
cast their garments on him; and he sat upon
him.
8 [a]And many spread their garments in the
way: and others cut down branches off the
trees, and strawed *them* in the way.
9 And they that went before, and they that
followed, cried, saying, [a]Hosanna; Blessed *is*
he that cometh in the name of the Lord:
10 Blessed *be* the kingdom of our father
David, that cometh in the name of the Lord:
[a]Hosanna in the highest.
11 [a]And Jesus entered into Jerusalem, and
into the temple: and when he had looked
round about upon all *things*, and now the
eventide was come, he went out unto Bethany
with the twelve.

for our redemption, as Isaiah clearly predicted (Is 52:13–53:12). *Son of man.* See note on 8:31. *ransom.* Means "the price paid for release (from bondage)." Jesus gave His life to release us from bondage to sin and death. *for.* That is, "in place of," pointing to Christ's substitutionary death. See note on Mat 20:28. *many.* In contrast to the one life given for our ransom.

‡10:46 *Jericho.* A very ancient city located five miles west of the Jordan and about 15 miles northeast of Jerusalem, but down a decline of 3,700 feet to more than 1,000 below sea level. In Jesus' time OT Jericho was largely abandoned, but a new city, south of the old one, had been built by Herod the Great. *as he went out of Jericho.* Luke says Jesus "was come nigh unto Jericho" (Luke 18:35). He may have been referring to the new Jericho, while Matthew (20:29) and Mark may have meant the old city. *blind Bartimeus.* The presence of a blind beggar just outside the city gates, on a road pilgrims followed on the way to Jerusalem, was a common sight in that day and is not unknown in Israel today.

10:47 *Jesus of Nazareth.* See note on Mat 2:23. *Son of David.* A Messianic title (see Is 11:1–3; Jer 23:5–6; Ezek 34:23–24; and notes on Mat 1:1; 9:27). Verses 47–48 are the only places in Mark where it is used to address Jesus. Its only other occurrence in Mark is in 12:35.

‡10:51 *Lord.* This translates the Hebrew word *Rabboni*, which means literally "(my) teacher."

11:1–11 At this point a new section in the Gospel of Mark begins. Jesus arrives in Jerusalem, and the rest of his ministry takes place within the confines of the Holy City. The Triumphal Entry, which inaugurates Passion Week, is a deliberate Messianic action, and the clue to its understanding is found in Zech 9:9 (quoted in Mat 21:5; John 12:15). Jesus purposefully offers Himself as the Messiah, knowing that this will provoke Jewish leaders to take action against him.

‡11:1 *Bethphage.* See note on Mat 21:1. *Bethany.* See note on Mat 21:17. *mount of Olives.* Directly east of Jerusalem, it rises to a height of about 2,700 feet, some 200 feet higher than mount Zion. Its summit commands a magnificent view of the city and especially of the temple. Olive trees still grow on this mount, and the Garden of Gethsemane, with its ancient olive trees, is at the base of its western slope.

11:2 *the village over against you.* Probably Bethphage. *colt.* The Greek word can mean the young of any animal, but here it means the colt of a donkey (see Mat 21:2; John 12:15). *whereon never man sat.* Unused animals were regarded as especially suitable for religious purposes (see Num 19:2; Deut 21:3; 1 Sam 6:7).

11:3 *if any man say unto you.* The message concerning the colt is not directed specifically to the owner but to anyone who might question the disciples' action. *Lord.* See note on Luke 19:31.

11:8 *branches off the trees.* These were readily available in nearby fields. John identifies the branches as palm branches (John 12:13), which apparently came from Jericho, since they are not native to Jerusalem.

11:9 *Hosanna.* The English rendering of a Greek version of the Hebrew for "Save now!" as found in invocations such as Ps 118:25. *Blessed is he that cometh in the name of the Lord.* A quotation of Ps 118:26, one of the Hallel ("Praise") Psalms sung at passover and especially fitting for this occasion.

11:10 *the kingdom of our father David.* The Messianic kingdom promised to David's son (2 Sam 7:11–14).

11:11 *temple.* See note on Mat 4:5. *went out unto Bethany.* Apparently Jesus spent each night through Thursday of Passion Week in Bethany at the home of His friends Mary, Martha and Lazarus (see 11:19; 14:13; Mat 21:17; John 12:1–3). *the twelve.* See 3:16–19 and notes on Luke 6:14–16.

The cleansing of the temple

12 ¶ [a]And on the morrow, when they were come from Bethany, he was hungry:

13 [a]And seeing a fig tree afar off having leaves, he came, if haply he might find any *thing* thereon: and when he came to it, he found nothing but leaves; for the time of figs was not *yet.*

14 And Jesus answered and said unto it, No *man* eat fruit of thee hereafter for ever. And his disciples heard *it.*

15 ¶ [a]And they come to Jerusalem: and Jesus went into the temple, and began to cast out them that sold and bought in the temple, and overthrew the tables of the money-changers, and the seats of them that sold doves;

16 And would not suffer that any *man* should carry *any* vessel through the temple.

17 And he taught, saying unto them, Is it not written, [a]My house shall be called [1]of all nations the house of prayer? but [b]ye have made it a den of thieves.

18 And [a]the scribes and chief priests heard *it,* and sought how they might destroy him: for they feared him, because [b]all the people was astonished at his doctrine.

19 And when even was come, he went out of the city.

The power of faith

20 ¶ [a]And in the morning, as they passed by, they saw the fig tree dried up from the roots.

21 And Peter calling to remembrance saith unto him, Master, behold, the fig tree which thou cursedst is withered away.

22 And Jesus answering saith unto them, [1]Have faith in God.

23 For [a]verily I say unto you, That whosoever shall say unto this mountain, Be thou removed, and be thou cast into the sea; and shall not doubt in his heart, but shall believe that *those things* which he saith shall come to pass; he shall have whatsoever he saith.

24 Therefore I say unto you, [a]What *things* soever ye desire, when ye pray, believe that ye receive *them,* and ye shall have *them.*

25 And when ye stand praying, [a]forgive, if ye have ought against any: that your Father also which is in heaven may forgive you your trespasses.

26 But [a]if ye do not forgive, neither will your Father which is in heaven forgive your trespasses.

Jesus' authority challenged

27 ¶ And they come again to Jerusalem: [a]and as he was walking in the temple, there come to him the chief priests, and the scribes, and the elders,

28 And say unto him, By what authority

11:12 [a]Mat. 21:18
11:13 [a]Mat. 21:19
11:15 [a]Mat. 21:12; Luke 19:45; John 2:14
11:17 [1][Or, *a house of prayer for all nations?*] [a]Is. 56:7 [b]Jer. 7:11
11:18 [a]Mat. 21:45,46; Luke 19:47 [b]Mat. 7:28; ch. 1,22; Luke 4:32
11:20 [a]Mat. 21:19
11:22 [1]Or, *Have the faith of God*
11:23 [a]Mat. 17:20; 21:21; Luke 17:6
11:24 [a]Mat. 7:7; Luke 11:9; John 14:13; 15:7; 16:24; Jas. 1:5,6
11:25 [a]Mat. 6:14; Col. 3:13
11:26 [a]Mat. 18:35
11:27 [a]Mat. 21:23; Luke 20:1

11:12 *on the morrow.* Monday of Passion Week. *Bethany.* See note on Mat 21:17.

11:13 *the time of figs was not yet.* Fig trees around Jerusalem normally begin to get leaves in March or April but do not produce figs until their leaves are all out in June. This tree was an exception in that it was already, at passover time, full of leaves.

11:14 *No man eat fruit of thee hereafter for ever.* Perhaps the incident was a parable of judgment, with the fig tree representing Israel (see Hos 9:10; Nah 3:12). A tree full of leaves normally should have fruit, but this one was cursed because it had none. The fact that the cleansing of the temple (vv. 15–19) is sandwiched between the two parts of the account of the fig tree (vv. 12–14 and vv. 20–25) may underscore the theme of judgment (see note on v. 21). The only application Jesus makes, however, is as an illustration of believing prayer (vv. 21–25).

‡11:15–19 All three Synoptic writers mention a cleansing of the temple at the end of Jesus' ministry. John, who writes after the others, mentions an additional cleansing at the beginning. See notes on Mat 21:12–17; John 2:14–17.

11:15 *the temple.* This refers to the court of the Gentiles, the only part of the temple in which Gentiles could worship God and gather for prayer (see v. 17). *sold and bought.* Pilgrims coming to the passover feast needed animals that met the ritual requirements for sacrifice, and the vendors set up their animal pens and money tables in the court of the Gentiles. *the tables of the money-changers.* Pilgrims needed their money changed into the local currency because the annual temple tax had to be paid in that currency. Also, the Mishnah (see note on Mat 15:2) required Tyrian currency for some offerings. *them that sold doves.* Doves were required for the purification of women (Lev 12:6; Luke 2:22–24), the cleansing of those with certain skin diseases (Lev 14:22), and other purposes (Lev 15:14,29). They were also the usual offering of the poor (Lev 5:7).

11:16 *should carry any vessel through the temple.* A detail found only in Mark. Apparently the temple area was being used as a shortcut between the city and the mount of Olives. See note on v. 27.

11:17 *of all nations the house of prayer.* Is 56:7 assured godly non-Jews that they would be allowed to worship God in the temple. By allowing the court of the Gentiles to become a noisy, smelly marketplace, the Jewish religious leaders were interfering with God's provision. *den of thieves.* Not only because they took financial advantage of the people but because they robbed the temple of its sanctity.

11:18 *scribes and chief priests.* See note on Mat 2:4. *sought how they might destroy him.* See note on 3:6. They regarded Jesus as a danger ous threat to their whole way of life.

11:19 *he went out of the city.* To Bethany (see note on v. 11).

11:20 *in the morning.* Tuesday morning of Passion Week. *dried up from the roots.* This detail indicates that the destruction was total (see Job 18:16) and that no one in the future would eat fruit from the tree. It served as a vivid warning of the judgment to come in A.D. 70 (see 13:2 and note on Mat 24:2).

‡11:21 *Master.* A translation of the Hebrew word for "(my) teacher." *fig tree which thou cursedst.* See note on v. 14. *is withered away.* Perhaps prophetic of the fate of the Jewish authorities who were now about to reject their Messiah.

11:23 *verily I say unto you.* See note on 3:28. *this mountain . . . into the sea.* The mount of Olives, from which the Dead Sea is visible.

11:27 *temple.* Several courts surrounded the main temple buildings, including the court of the women, the court of the men (Israelite), and the court of the Gentiles (see v. 16). *the chief priests, and the scribes, and the elders.* See note on 8:31.

11:28 *authority.* The Sanhedrin was asking why Jesus performed what appeared to be an official act if He possessed no official status (see note on Luke 20:2).

doest thou these *things?* and who gave thee this authority to do these *things?*

29 And Jesus answered and said unto them, I will also ask of you one [1] question, and answer me, and I will tell you by what authority I do these *things.*

30 The baptism of John, was *it* from heaven, or of men? answer me.

31 And they reasoned with themselves, saying, If we shall say, From heaven; he will say, Why then did ye not believe him?

32 But if we shall say, Of men; they feared the people: for [a] all *men* counted John, that he was a prophet indeed.

33 And they answered and said unto Jesus, We cannot tell. And Jesus answering saith unto them, Neither do I tell you by what authority I do these *things.*

The parable of the husbandmen

12 And [a] he began to speak unto them by parables. A *certain* man planted a vineyard, and set a hedge about *it,* and digged *a place for* the winefat, and built a tower, and let it out to husbandmen, and went into a far country.

2 And at the season he sent to the husbandmen a servant, that he might receive from the husbandmen of the fruit of the vineyard.

3 And they caught him, and beat *him,* and sent *him* away empty.

4 And again he sent unto them another servant; and at him they cast stones, and wounded *him* in the head, and sent *him* away shamefully handled.

5 And again he sent another; and him they killed, and many others; beating some, and killing some.

6 Having yet therefore one son, his wellbeloved, he sent him also last unto them, saying, They will reverence my son.

7 But those husbandmen said amongst themselves, This is the heir; come, let us kill him, and the inheritance shall be ours.

8 And they took him, and killed *him,* and cast *him* out of the vineyard.

9 What shall therefore the lord of the vineyard do? he will come and destroy the husbandmen, and will give the vineyard unto others.

10 And have ye not read this scripture; [a] The stone which the builders rejected is become the head of the corner:

11 This was the Lord's doing, and it is marvellous in our eyes?

12 [a] And they sought to lay hold on him, but feared the people: for they knew that he had spoken the parable against them: and they left him, and went their way.

Tribute to Cesar

13 ¶ [a] And they send unto him certain of the Pharisees and of the Herodians, to catch him in *his* words.

14 And when they were come, they say unto him, Master, we know that thou art true, and carest for no *man:* for thou regardest not the person of men, but teachest the way of God in truth: Is it lawful to give tribute to Cesar, or not?

15 Shall we give, or shall we not give? But he, knowing their hypocrisy, said unto them, Why tempt ye me? bring me a [1] penny, that I may see *it.*

16 And they brought *it.* And he saith unto them, Whose *is* this image and superscription? And they said unto him, Cesar's.

17 And Jesus answering said unto them, Render to Cesar the *things* that are Cesar's, and to God the *things* that are God's. And they marvelled at him.

Sadducees and the resurrection

18 ¶ [a] Then come unto him *the* Sadducees,

11:29 [1] Or, *thing*
11:32 [a] Mat. 3:5; 14:5; ch. 6:20
12:1 [a] Mat. 21:33; Luke 20:9
12:10 [a] Ps. 118:22
12:12 [a] Mat. 21:45,46; ch. 11:18; John 7:25,30,44
12:13 [a] Mat. 22:15; Luke 20:20
12:15 [1] *Valuing of our money seven pence halfpenny, as* Mat. 18:28; 20:2; 22:19; ch. 6:37; 14:5
12:18 [a] Mat. 22:23; Luke 20:27

11:30 *from heaven, or of men?* "Heaven" was a common Jewish term for God, often substituted for the divine name to avoid a possible misuse of it (see Ex 20:7). Jesus' question implied that His authority, like that of John's baptism, came from God.

12:1–12 Most of Jesus' parables make one main point. This one is rather complex, and the details fit the social situation in Jewish Galilee in the first century. Large estates, owned by absentee landlords, were put in the hands of local peasants who cultivated the land as tenant farmers. The parable exposed the planned attempt on Jesus' life, and God's judgment on the planners. See notes on Mat 21:35–37,41.

12:1 *parables.* See note on 4:2. *A certain man planted a vineyard.* The description reflects the language of Is 5:1–2 where the vineyard clearly symbolizes Israel. *tower.* See note on Mat 21:33.

12:7 *the inheritance shall be ours.* Jewish law provided that a piece of property unclaimed by an heir would be declared "ownerless," and could be claimed by anyone. The husbandmen assumed that the son came as heir to claim his property, and that if he were slain, they could claim the land.

12:9 *others.* See note on Mat 21:41.

12:10 *the head of the corner.* See note on Ps 118:22.

12:12 *against them.* The representatives of the Sanhedrin mentioned in 11:27.

12:13–17 This incident probably took place on Tuesday of Passion Week in one of the temple courts (see chart, pp. 1432–1433).

12:13 *Pharisees.* See note on 2:16. *Herodians.* See note on 3:6. The plan to destroy Jesus, which had originated early in His Galilean ministry, had now matured and was gaining momentum in Jerusalem.

12:14 *give tribute to Cesar.* Jews in Judea were required to pay tribute money to the emperor. The tax was highly unpopular, and some Jews flatly refused to pay it, believing that payment was an admission of Roman right to rule. See note on Mat 22:15–17.

12:15 *penny.* See notes on 6:37; Mat 22:19.

‡12:17 *Render to Cesar the things that are Cesar's.* See note on Mat 22:21. There are obligations to the state that do not infringe on our obligations to God (see Rom 13:1–7; 1 Tim 2:1–6; Tit 3:1–2; 1 Pet 2:13–17). However, see Acts 4:29 and Dan 3:16–18, where for religious reasons one must be ready to respectfully obey God rather than men, if the occasion clearly warrants it.

12:18 *Sadducees.* A Jewish party that represented the wealthy

[b]which say there is no resurrection; and they
asked him, saying,
19 Master, [a]Moses wrote unto us, If a
man's brother die, and leave *his* wife *behind*
him, and leave no children, that his brother
should take his wife, and raise up seed unto
his brother.
20 Now there were seven brethren: and
the first took a wife, and dying left no seed.
21 And the second took her, and died, neither left he *any* seed: and the third likewise.
22 And the seven had her, and left no seed:
last of all the woman died also.
23 In the resurrection therefore, when
they shall rise, whose wife shall she be of
them? for the seven had her to wife.
24 And Jesus answering said unto them,
Do ye not therefore err, because ye know not
the scriptures, neither the power of God?
25 For when they shall rise from the dead,
they neither marry, nor are given in marriage;
but [a]are as *the* angels which are in heaven.
26 And as touching the dead, that they
rise: have ye not read in the book of Moses,
how in the bush God spake unto him, saying,
[a]I *am* the God of Abraham, and the God of
Isaac, and the God of Jacob?
27 He is not the God of the dead, but the
God of the living: ye therefore do greatly err.

The great commandment

28 ¶ [a]And one of the scribes came, and
having heard them reasoning together, and
perceiving that he had answered them well,
asked him, Which is the first commandment
of all?
29 And Jesus answered him, The first of all
the commandments *is,* [a]Hear, O Israel; The
Lord our God is one Lord:
30 And thou shalt love the Lord thy God
with all thy heart, and with all thy soul, and
with all thy mind, and with all thy strength:
this *is* the first commandment.
31 And the second *is* like, *namely* this,
[a]Thou shalt love thy neighbour as thyself.
There is none other commandment greater
than these.
32 And the scribe said unto him, Well,
Master, thou hast said the truth: for there is
one God; [a]and there is none other but he:
33 And to love him with all the heart, and
with all the understanding, and with all the
soul, and with all the strength, and to love *his*
neighbour as himself, [a]is more than all whole
burnt offerings and sacrifices.
34 And when Jesus saw that he answered
discreetly, he said unto him, Thou art not far
from the kingdom of God. [a]And no *man* after
that durst ask him *any question.*

The question about David's son

35 ¶ [a]And Jesus answered and said, while
he taught in the temple, How say the scribes
that Christ is the Son of David?
36 For David himself said [a]by the Holy
Ghost, [b]The LORD said to my Lord, Sit thou on
my right hand, till I make thine enemies thy
footstool.
37 David therefore himself calleth him
Lord; and whence is he *then* his son? And the
common people heard him gladly.
38 ¶ And [a]he said unto them in his doctrine, [b]Beware of the scribes, which love to go
in long clothing, and [c]*love* salutations in the
marketplaces,
39 And the chief seats in the synagogues,
and the uppermost rooms at feasts:
40 [a]Which devour widows' houses, and for
a pretence make long prayers: these shall receive greater damnation.

The widow's mite

41 ¶ [a]And Jesus sat over against the trea-

12:18 [b]Acts 23:8
12:19 [a]Deut. 25:5
12:25 [a]1 Cor. 15:42,49,52
12:26 [a]Ex. 3:6
12:28 [a]Mat. 22:35
12:29 [a]Deut. 6:4; Luke 10:27
12:31 [a]Lev. 19:18; Mat. 22:39; Rom. 13:9; Gal. 5:14; Jas. 2:8
12:32 [a]Deut. 4:39; Is. 45:6,14; 46:9
12:33 [a]1 Sam. 15:22; Hos. 6:6; Mic. 6:6-8
12:34 [a]Mat. 22:46
12:35 [a]Mat. 22:41; Luke 20:41
12:36 [a]2 Sam. 23:2 [b]Ps. 110:1
12:38 [a]ch. 4:2 [b]Mat. 23:1; Luke 20:46 [c]Luke 11:43
12:40 [a]Mat. 23:14
12:41 [a]Luke 21:1

and sophisticated classes. They were located largely in Jerusalem and made the temple and its administration their primary interest. Though they were small in number, in Jesus' time they exerted powerful political and religious influence. See notes on Mat 3:7; Luke 20:27; Acts 4:1. *which say there is no resurrection.* They denied the resurrection, accepted only the five books of Moses as authoritative and flatly rejected the oral tradition (see note on Mat 15:2). These beliefs set them against the Pharisees and common Jewish piety.

12:19 See note on Mat 22:24.

‡12:26 *book of Moses.* The Pentateuch, the first five books of the OT. *in the bush.* A common way of referring to Ex 3:1–6 (see Rom 11:2, where "of Elias" refers to 1 Ki 19:1–10).

12:28 *Which is the first commandment of all?* Jewish rabbis counted 613 individual statutes in the law, and attempted to differentiate between "heavy" (or "great") and "light" (or "little") commands.

12:29 The first quotation came to be known as the Shema, named after the first word of Deut 6:4 in Hebrew, which means "hear." The Shema became the Jewish confession of faith, which was recited by pious Jews every morning and evening. To this day it begins every synagogue service.

12:31 To the Shema Jesus joined the commandment from Lev 19:18 to show that love for neighbor is a natural and logical outgrowth of love for God. *neighbour.* See Luke 10:25–37.

12:33 *all whole burnt offerings and sacrifices.* The comparison was undoubtedly suggested by the fact that the discussion took place in the temple courtyard (see 11:27).

12:34 *kingdom of God.* See note on Mat 3:2.

12:35 *temple.* See note on 11:27. *Son of David.* See note on 10:47. Most of the people knew that the Messiah was to be from the family of David.

12:36 *The LORD said to my Lord.* God said to David's Lord, i.e., David's superior—ultimately the Messiah (see note on Ps 110:1). The purpose of the quotation was to show that the Messiah was more than a descendant of David—he was David's Lord.

12:38 *long clothing.* The scribes wore long, white linen robes that were fringed and almost reached to the ground.

12:39 *chief seats in the synagogues.* A reference to the bench in front of the "ark" that contained the sacred scrolls. Those who sat there could be seen by all the worshipers in the synagogue.

12:40 *devour widows' houses.* Since the scribes were not paid a regular salary, they were dependent on the generosity of patrons for their livelihood. Such a system was open to abuses, and widows were especially vulnerable to exploitation.

sury, and beheld how the people cast [1]money [b]into the treasury: and many *that were* rich cast in much.

42 And there came a certain poor widow, and she threw in two [1]mites, which make a farthing.

43 And he called unto *him* his disciples, and saith unto them, Verily I say unto you, That [a]this poor widow hath cast more in, than all they which have cast into the treasury:

44 For all *they* did cast in of their abundance; but she of her want did cast in all that she had, [a]*even* all her living.

Signs of the end of this age

13 And [a]as he went out of the temple, one of his disciples saith unto him, Master, see what manner of stones and what buildings *are here.*

2 And Jesus answering said unto him, Seest thou these great buildings? [a]there shall not be left one stone upon another, that shall not be thrown down.

3 And as he sat upon the mount of Olives over against the temple, Peter and James and John and Andrew asked him privately,

4 [a]Tell us, when shall these *things* be? and what *shall be* the sign when all these *things* shall be fulfilled?

5 And Jesus answering them began to say, [a]Take heed lest any *man* deceive you:

6 For many shall come in my name, saying, I am *Christ;* and shall deceive many.

7 And when ye shall hear of wars and rumours of wars, be ye not troubled: for *such things* must needs be; but the end *shall* not *be* yet.

12:41 [1]*A piece of brass money, see* Mat. 10:9 [b]2 Ki. 12:9
12:42 [1]*It is the seventh part of one piece of that brass money*
12:43 [a]2 Cor. 8:12
12:44 [a]Deut. 24:6; 1 John 3:17
13:1 [a]Mat. 24:1; Luke 21:5
13:2 [a]Luke 19:44
13:4 [a]Mat. 24:3; Luke 21:7
13:5 [a]Jer. 29:8; Eph. 5:6; 1 Thes. 2:3
13:8 [1]*The word in the original importeth the pains of a woman in travail* [a]Mat. 24:8
13:9 [a]Mat. 10:17,18; 24:9; Rev. 2:10
13:10 [a]Mat. 24:14
13:11 [a]Mat. 10:19; Luke 12:11; 21:14 [b]Acts 2:4; 4:8,31
13:12 [a]Mic. 7:6; Mat. 10:21; 24:10; Luke 21:16
13:13 [a]Mat. 24:9; Luke 21:17 [b]Dan. 12:12; Mat. 10:22; 24:13; Rev. 2:10
13:14 [a]Mat. 24:15 [b]Dan. 9:27 [c]Luke 21:21
13:17 [a]Luke 21:23

8 For nation shall rise against nation, and kingdom against kingdom: and there shall be earthquakes in divers places, and there shall be famines and troubles: [a]these *are* the beginnings of [1]sorrows.

9 ¶ But [a]take heed to yourselves: for they shall deliver you up to councils; and in the synagogues ye shall be beaten: and ye shall be brought before rulers and kings for my sake, for a testimony against them.

10 And [a]the gospel must first be published among all nations.

11 [a]But when they shall lead *you,* and deliver you up, take no thought beforehand what ye shall speak, neither do ye premeditate: but whatsoever shall be given you in that hour, that speak ye: for it is not ye that speak, [b]but the Holy Ghost.

12 Now [a]the brother shall betray the brother to death, and the father the son; and children shall rise up against *their* parents, and shall cause them to be put to death.

13 [a]And ye shall be hated of all *men* for my name's sake: but [b]he that shall endure unto the end, the same shall be saved.

14 ¶ [a]But when ye shall see the abomination of desolation, [b]spoken of by Daniel the prophet, standing where it ought not, (let him that readeth understand,) then [c]let them that be in Judea flee to the mountains:

15 And let him that is on the housetop not go down into the house, neither enter *therein,* to take any *thing* out of his house:

16 And let him that is in the field not turn back again for to take up his garment.

17 [a]But woe to them that are with child, and to them that give suck in those days.

12:41 *the treasury.* Located in the court of the women. Both men and women were allowed in this court, but women could go no farther into the temple buildings. It contained 13 trumpet-shaped receptacles for contributions brought by worshipers.

‡12:42 *two mites.* The smallest coins then in circulation in the Holy Land. Though her offering was meager, the widow brought "all her living" (v. 44; see note on 2 Cor 8:12). The widow could give all to God, because she had learned that God would supply all of her need.

12:43 *Verily I say unto you.* See note on 3:28.

13:1–37 The Olivet discourse, as this chapter of Mark is commonly called, falls into five sections: (1) Jesus' prophecy of the destruction of the temple and the questions of the disciples (vv. 1–4); (2) warnings against deceivers and false signs of the end (vv. 5–23); (3) the coming of the Son of man (vv. 24–27); (4) the lesson of the fig tree (vv. 28–31); (5) exhortation to watchfulness (vv. 32–37).

13:1 *what manner of stones.* According to Josephus (*Antiquities,* 15.11.3), they were white, and some of them were 37 feet long, 12 feet high and 18 feet wide.

13:2 See note on Mat 24:2.

13:3 *mount of Olives.* See note on 11:1. *Peter and James and John and Andrew.* See 1:16–20.

13:4 The disciples thought that the destruction of the temple would be one of the events that ushered in the end times (see Mat 24:3). *the sign.* The way by which the disciples might know that the destruction of the temple was about to take place and that the end of the age was approaching.

‡13:5 *Take heed.* It is clear from such words as "Take heed," both here and in v. 9, "But take ye heed" (v. 23), "Take ye heed, watch and pray" (v. 33), "Watch ye therefore" (v. 35) and "Watch" (v. 37) that one of the main purposes of the Olivet discourse was to alert the disciples to the danger of deception.

‡13:6 *I am Christ.* That is, many would come claiming to be the Messiah.

13:7 *the end.* Not the destruction of Jerusalem but the end of the age (see Mat 24:3).

13:8 *sorrows.* See note on Mat 24:8.

13:9 *to councils.* The religious courts made up of the synagogue elders. *beaten.* Infraction of Jewish regulations was punishable by flogging, the maximum penalty being 39 strokes with the whip (see 2 Cor 11:23–24).

13:10 *first.* Before the end of the age (see Mat 24:14).

13:13 *endure unto the end.* Such perseverance is a sure indication of salvation (cf. Heb 3:14; 6:11–12; 10:36).

13:14 *the abomination of desolation.* See notes on Dan 9:25–27; Mat 24:15. *standing where it ought not.* See 2 Thes 2:4. *let them that be in Judea flee to the mountains.* See note on Mat 24:16.

13:15 *the housetop.* See notes on 2:4; Luke 17:31.

13:16 *garment.* See note on Mat 5:40.

‡13:17 *them that are with child, and to them that give suck.* Representative of anyone forced to flee under especially difficult circumstances. A nursing baby and its mother might perish under such conditions.

Passion Week

Bethany, the Mount of Olives and Jerusalem

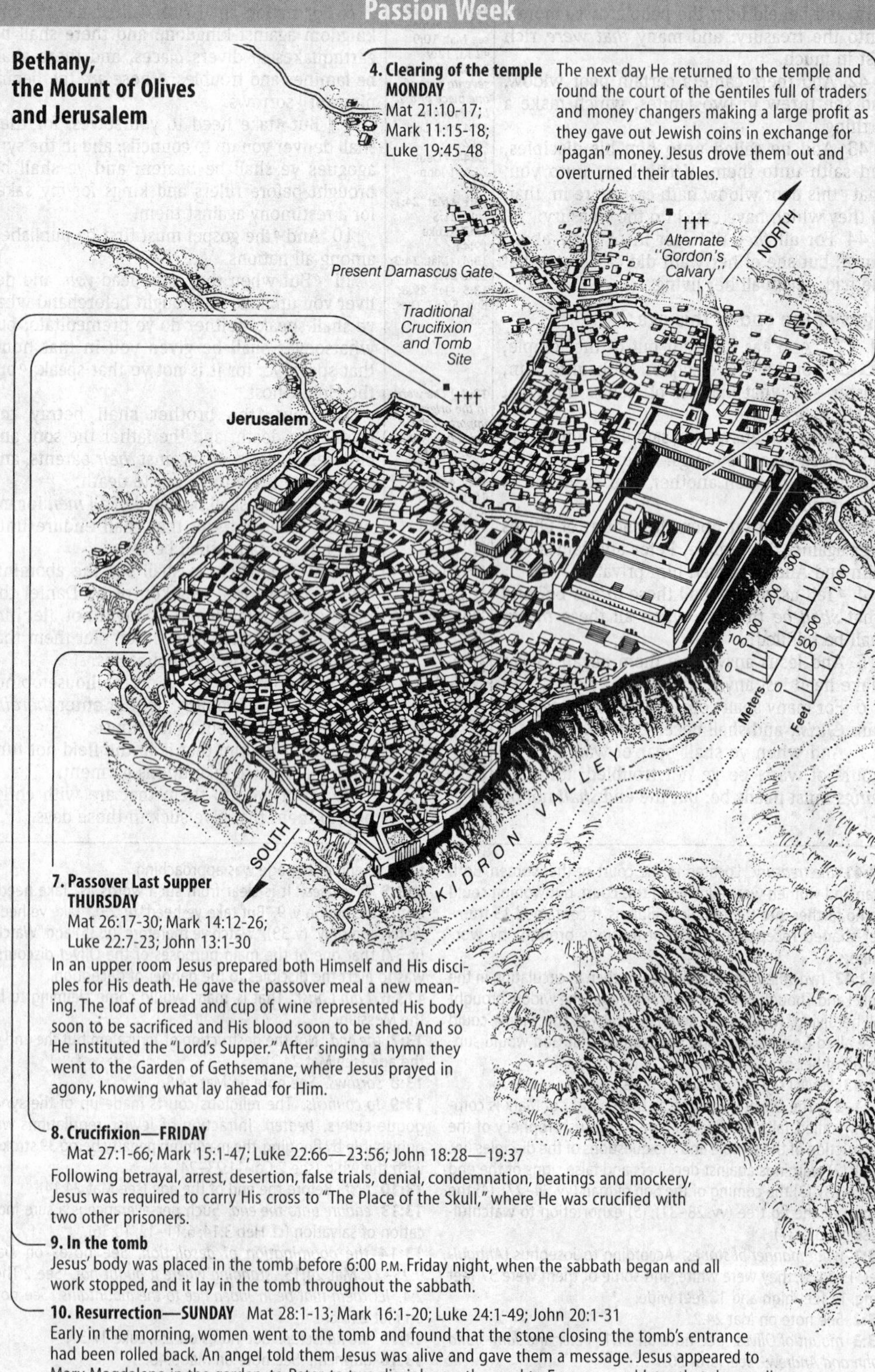

4. Clearing of the temple
MONDAY
Mat 21:10-17; Mark 11:15-18; Luke 19:45-48

The next day He returned to the temple and found the court of the Gentiles full of traders and money changers making a large profit as they gave out Jewish coins in exchange for "pagan" money. Jesus drove them out and overturned their tables.

7. Passover Last Supper
THURSDAY
Mat 26:17-30; Mark 14:12-26; Luke 22:7-23; John 13:1-30

In an upper room Jesus prepared both Himself and His disciples for His death. He gave the passover meal a new meaning. The loaf of bread and cup of wine represented His body soon to be sacrificed and His blood soon to be shed. And so He instituted the "Lord's Supper." After singing a hymn they went to the Garden of Gethsemane, where Jesus prayed in agony, knowing what lay ahead for Him.

8. Crucifixion—FRIDAY
Mat 27:1-66; Mark 15:1-47; Luke 22:66—23:56; John 18:28—19:37

Following betrayal, arrest, desertion, false trials, denial, condemnation, beatings and mockery, Jesus was required to carry His cross to "The Place of the Skull," where He was crucified with two other prisoners.

9. In the tomb
Jesus' body was placed in the tomb before 6:00 P.M. Friday night, when the sabbath began and all work stopped, and it lay in the tomb throughout the sabbath.

10. Resurrection—SUNDAY Mat 28:1-13; Mark 16:1-20; Luke 24:1-49; John 20:1-31

Early in the morning, women went to the tomb and found that the stone closing the tomb's entrance had been rolled back. An angel told them Jesus was alive and gave them a message. Jesus appeared to Mary Magdalene in the garden, to Peter, to two disciples on the road to Emmaus, and later that day to all the disciples but Thomas. His resurrection was established as a fact.

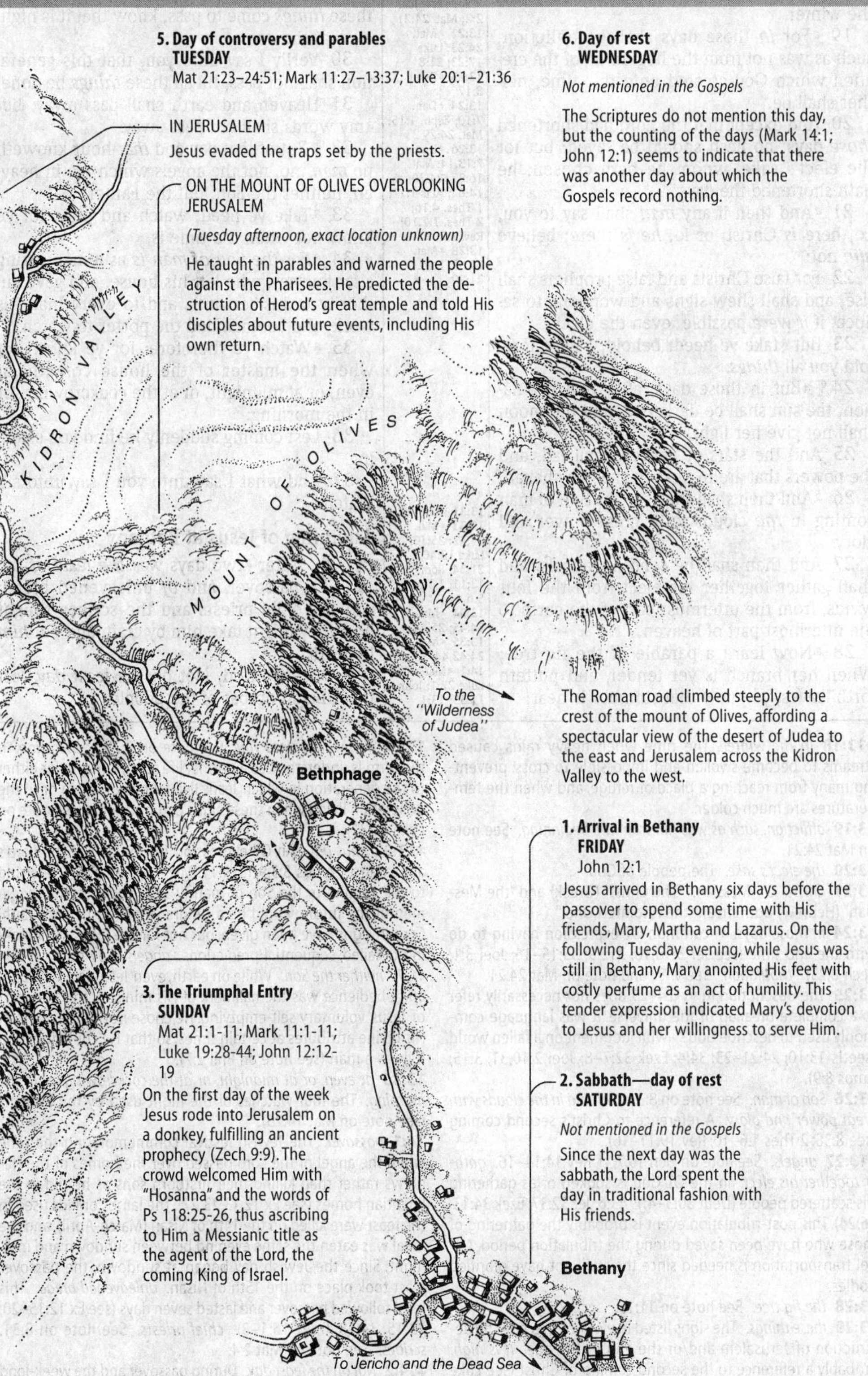
5. Day of controversy and parables
TUESDAY
Mat 21:23–24:51; Mark 11:27–13:37; Luke 20:1–21:36
IN JERUSALEM
Jesus evaded the traps set by the priests.
ON THE MOUNT OF OLIVES OVERLOOKING JERUSALEM
(Tuesday afternoon, exact location unknown)
He taught in parables and warned the people against the Pharisees. He predicted the destruction of Herod's great temple and told His disciples about future events, including His own return.
6. Day of rest
WEDNESDAY
Not mentioned in the Gospels
The Scriptures do not mention this day, but the counting of the days (Mark 14:1; John 12:1) seems to indicate that there was another day about which the Gospels record nothing.
KIDRON VALLEY
MOUNT OF OLIVES
To the "Wilderness of Judea"
The Roman road climbed steeply to the crest of the mount of Olives, affording a spectacular view of the desert of Judea to the east and Jerusalem across the Kidron Valley to the west.
Bethphage
1. Arrival in Bethany
FRIDAY
John 12:1
Jesus arrived in Bethany six days before the passover to spend some time with His friends, Mary, Martha and Lazarus. On the following Tuesday evening, while Jesus was still in Bethany, Mary anointed His feet with costly perfume as an act of humility. This tender expression indicated Mary's devotion to Jesus and her willingness to serve Him.
3. The Triumphal Entry
SUNDAY
Mat 21:1-11; Mark 11:1-11; Luke 19:28-44; John 12:12-19
On the first day of the week Jesus rode into Jerusalem on a donkey, fulfilling an ancient prophecy (Zech 9:9). The crowd welcomed Him with "Hosanna" and the words of Ps 118:25-26, thus ascribing to Him a Messianic title as the agent of the Lord, the coming King of Israel.
2. Sabbath—day of rest
SATURDAY
Not mentioned in the Gospels
Since the next day was the sabbath, the Lord spent the day in traditional fashion with His friends.
Bethany
To Jericho and the Dead Sea

18 And pray ye that your flight be not in the winter.

19 [a]For *in* those days shall be affliction, such as was not from the beginning of the creation which God created unto this time, neither shall be.

20 And except that the Lord had shortened *those* days, no flesh should be saved: but for the elect's sake, whom he hath chosen, he hath shortened the days.

21 [a]And then if any *man* shall say to you, Lo, here *is* Christ; or lo, *he is* there; believe *him* not:

22 For false Christs and false prophets shall rise, and shall shew signs and wonders, to seduce, if *it were* possible, even the elect.

23 But [a]take ye heed: behold, I have foretold you all *things.*

24 ¶ [a]But in those days, after that tribulation, the sun shall be darkened, and the moon shall not give her light,

25 And the stars of heaven shall fall, and the powers that are in heaven shall be shaken.

26 [a]And then shall they see the Son of man coming in *the* clouds with great power and glory.

27 And then shall he send his angels, and shall gather together his elect from the four winds, from the uttermost part of the earth to the uttermost part of heaven.

28 [a]Now learn a parable of the fig tree; When her branch is yet tender, and putteth forth leaves, ye know that summer is near:

29 So ye in like manner, when ye shall see these *things* come to pass, know that it is nigh, *even* at the doors.

30 Verily I say unto you, that this generation shall not pass, till all these *things* be done.

31 Heaven and earth shall pass away: but [a]my words shall not pass away.

32 ¶ But of that day and *that* hour knoweth no *man,* no, not the angels which are in heaven, neither the Son, but the Father.

33 [a]Take ye heed, watch and pray: for ye know not when the time is.

34 [a]*For the Son of man is* as a man taking a far journey, who left his house, and gave authority to his servants, and to every man his work, and commanded the porter to watch.

35 [a]Watch ye therefore: for ye know not when the master of the house cometh, at even, or at midnight, or at the cockcrowing, or in the morning:

36 Lest coming suddenly he find you sleeping.

37 And what I say unto you I say unto all, Watch.

Anointing of Jesus at Bethany

14 After [a]two days was *the feast of* the passover, and *of* unleavened bread: and the chief priests and the scribes sought how they might take him by craft, and put *him* to death.

2 But they said, Not on the feast *day,* lest there be an uproar of the people.

13:19 [a]Dan. 9:26; 12:1; Joel 2:2; Mat. 24:21
13:21 [a]Mat. 24:23; Luke 17:23; 21:8
13:23 [a]2 Pet. 3:17
13:24 [a]Dan. 7:10; Zeph. 1:15; Mat. 24:29
13:26 [a]Dan. 7:13,14; Mat. 16:27; 24:30; ch. 14:62; Acts 1:11; 1 Thes. 4:16; 2 Thes. 1:7,10; Rev. 1:7
13:28 [a]Mat. 24:32; Luke 21:29
13:31 [a]Is. 40:8
13:33 [a]Mat. 24:42; 25:13; Luke 12:40; 21:34; Rom. 13:11; 1 Thes. 5:6
13:34 [a]Mat. 24:45; 25:14
13:35 [a]Mat. 24:42,44
14:1 [a]Mat. 26:2; Luke 22:1; John 11:55; 13:1

‡13:18 *in the winter.* The time when heavy rains caused streams to become swollen and impossible to cross, preventing many from reaching a place of refuge, and when the temperatures are much colder.

13:19 *affliction, such as was not from the beginning.* See note on Mat 24:21.

13:20 *the elect's sake.* The people of God.

13:21 *Christ.* Or "Messiah." "The Christ" (Greek) and "the Messiah" (Hebrew) both mean "the Anointed One."

13:24 *in those days.* A common OT expression having to do with the end time (see Jer 3:16,18; 31:29; 33:15–16; Joel 3:1; Zech 8:23). *tribulation.* See v. 19 and note on Mat 24:21.

13:25 The description in vv. 24–25 does not necessarily refer to a complete breakup of the universe. It was language commonly used to describe God's awful judgment on a fallen world (see Is 13:10; 24:21–23; 34:4; Ezek 32:7–8; Joel 2:10,31; 3:15; Amos 8:9).

13:26 *Son of man.* See note on 8:31. *coming in the clouds with great power and glory.* A reference to Christ's second coming (see 8:38; 2 Thes 1:6–10; Rev 19:11–16).

‡13:27 *angels.* See note on Gen 16:7; cf. Rev 14:14–16. *gather together his elect.* In the OT God is spoken of as gathering His scattered people (Deut 30:3–4; Is 43:6; Jer 32:37; Ezek 34:13; 36:24). This post-tribulation event is probably the gathering of those who have been saved during the tribulation period. Angel transportation is needed since they will not have glorified bodies.

13:28 *the fig tree.* See note on 11:13.

13:29 *these things.* The signs listed in vv. 5–23 precede the destruction of Jerusalem and/or the end of the age. *it is nigh.* Probably a reference to the second coming of Christ (see Luke 21:31).

13:30 *Verily I say unto you.* See note on 3:28. *generation.* If the term is understood as a normal life span, it may refer either to the generation in which Jesus lived while on earth or to the generation living when these signs begin to occur (see note on Luke 21:32).

‡13:32 *that day.* An OT expression for the day of the Lord's appearance (Amos 8:3,9,13; 9:11; Mic 4:6; 5:10; 7:11), referring to the coming of the Son of man (v. 26). *knoweth no man.* A map of the future would be a hindrance, not a help, to faith. Certain signs have been given, but not for the purpose of making detailed, sequential predictions. *angels.* See note on Gen 16:7. *neither the Son.* While on earth, even Jesus lived by faith, and obedience was the hallmark of His ministry. This was part of Jesus' voluntary self-emptying. He chose not to use some of His divine attributes at certain times, so that He could function fully as a man (see note on Phil 2:7).

13:35 *at even, or at midnight, or at the cockcrowing, or in the morning.* The four watches of the night used by the Romans (see note on Mat 14:25).

14:1 *passover.* The Jewish festival commemorating the time when the angel of the Lord passed over the homes of the Hebrews rather than killing their firstborn sons as he did in the Egyptian homes (see Ex 12:13,23,27). The lambs or kids used in the feast were killed on the 14th of Nisan (March-April), and the meal was eaten the same evening between sundown and midnight. Since the Jewish day began at sundown, the passover feast took place on the 15th of Nisan. *unleavened bread.* This feast followed passover and lasted seven days (see Ex 12:15–20; 23:15; 34:18; Deut 16:1–8). *chief priests.* See note on 8:31. *scribes.* See note on Mat 2:4.

‡14:2 *Not on the feast day.* During passover and the week-long feast of unleavened bread the population of Jerusalem in-

3 ¶ [a]And being in Bethany in the house of Simon the leper, as he sat at meat, there came a woman having an alabaster box of ointment of [1]spikenard very precious; and she brake the box, and poured *it* on his head.

4 And there were some that had indignation within themselves, and said, Why was this waste of the ointment made?

5 For it might have been sold for more than three hundred [1]pence, and have been given to the poor. And they murmured against her.

6 And Jesus said, Let her alone; why trouble you her? she hath wrought a good work on me.

7 For ye have the poor with you always, and whensoever ye will ye may do them good: but me ye have not always.

8 She hath done what she could: she is come aforehand to anoint my body to the burying.

9 Verily I say unto you, Wheresoever this gospel shall be preached throughout the whole world, *this* also that she hath done shall be spoken of for a memorial of her.

10 ¶ [a]And Judas Iscariot, one of the twelve, went unto the chief priests, to betray him unto them.

11 And when they heard *it,* they were glad, and promised to give him money. And he sought how he might conveniently betray him.

The last supper

12 ¶ [a]And the first day of unleavened bread, when they [1]killed the passover, his disciples said unto him, Where wilt thou *that* we go and prepare that thou mayest eat the passover?

13 And he sendeth forth two of his disciples, and saith unto them, Go ye into the city, and there shall meet you a man bearing a pitcher of water: follow him.

14 And wheresoever he shall go in, say ye to the goodman of the house, The Master saith, Where is the guestchamber, where I shall eat the passover with my disciples?

15 And he will shew you a large upper room furnished *and* prepared: there make ready for us.

16 And his disciples went forth, and came into the city, and found as he had said unto them: and they made ready the passover.

17 ¶ [a]And in the evening he cometh with the twelve.

18 And as they sat and did eat, Jesus said, Verily I say unto you, One of you which eateth with me shall betray me.

19 And they began to be sorrowful, and to say unto him one by one, *Is* it I? and another *said, Is* it I?

20 And he answered and said unto them, *It is* one of the twelve, that dippeth with me in the dish.

21 [a]The Son of man indeed goeth, as it is written of him: but woe to that man by whom the Son of man is betrayed: good were it for that man if he had never been born.

14:3 [1] Or, *pure nard,* or, *liquid nard* [a] Mat. 26:6; John 12:1,3; See Luke 7:37
14:5 [1] See Mat. 18:28; ch. 12:15
14:10 [a] Mat. 26:14; Luke 22:3,4
14:12 [a] Mat. 26:17; Luke 22:7
14:12 [1] Or, *sacrificed*
14:17 [a] Mat. 26:20
14:21 [a] Mat. 26:24; Luke 22:22

creased from about 50,000 to several hundred thousand. It was thought to be too risky to apprehend Jesus with so large and excitable a crowd present.

14:3–9 In John's Gospel this incident occurred before Passion Week began (see John 12:1). Matthew and Mark may place it here to contrast the hatred of the religious leaders and the betrayal by Judas with the love and devotion of the woman who anointed Jesus.

‡14:3 *Bethany.* See note on Mat 21:17. *Simon the leper.* See note on Mat 26:6. *sat at meat.* The usual posture for eating a banquet meal was to recline. *a woman.* We know from John's Gospel (12:3) that she was Mary, the sister of Martha and Lazarus. *alabaster box.* A sealed flask with a long neck that was broken off when the contents were used. *spikenard.* A perfume made from the aromatic oil extracted from the root of a plant grown chiefly in India. *poured it on his head.* Anointing was a common custom at feasts (see Ps 23:5; Luke 7:46). Mary's action expressed her deep devotion to Jesus.

14:4 *some.* Matthew (26:8) identifies them as the disciples, while John (12:4–5) singles out Judas Iscariot.

‡14:5 *three hundred pence.* Practically an entire year's wages. This was no small sacrifice on Mary's part. *given to the poor.* It was a Jewish custom to give gifts to the poor on the evening of passover (see John 13:29).

14:7 *ye have the poor with you always.* This did not express lack of concern for the poor, for their needs lay close to Jesus' heart (see Mat 6:2–4; Luke 4:18; 6:20; 14:13,21; 18:22; John 13:29).

14:8 *to the burying.* It was a normal Jewish custom to anoint a body with aromatic oils in preparing it for burial (see 16:1). Jesus seems to anticipate suffering a criminal's death, for only in that circumstance was there no anointing of the body.

14:9 *Verily I say unto you.* See note on 3:28. *gospel.* See note on 1:1.

14:10 *Judas Iscariot.* See note on 3:19. *chief priests.* See note on 8:31. This was an unexpected opportunity that they seized, even though they had intended not to apprehend Jesus during the Feast (see v. 2).

14:11 *money.* Thirty silver coins (Mat 26:15).

14:12 *the first day of unleavened bread.* Ordinarily this would mean the 15th of Nisan, the day after passover (see note on v. 1). However, the added phrase, "when the passover lamb was being sacrificed," makes it clear that the 14th of Nisan is meant because passover lambs were killed on that day (Ex 12:6). The entire eight-day celebration was sometimes referred to as the feast of unleavened bread, and there is evidence that the 14th of Nisan may have been loosely referred to as the "first day of unleavened bread."

14:13 *two of his disciples.* Peter and John (Luke 22:8). *man bearing a pitcher.* He would easily have been identified because customarily only women carried water jars.

14:14 *Where is the guestchamber . . . ?* It was a Jewish custom that anyone in Jerusalem who had a room available would give it upon request to a pilgrim to celebrate the passover. It appears that Jesus had made previous arrangements with the owner of the house.

14:15 *make ready.* These would include food for the meal: unleavened bread, wine, bitter herbs, sauce and the lamb.

14:17 *in the evening.* Thursday of Passion Week.

14:18 *they sat and did eat.* Originally the passover meal was eaten standing (Ex 12:11), but in Jesus' time it was customary to eat it while reclining. *Verily I say unto you.* See note on 3:28.

14:20 *dippeth with me in the dish.* See note on Mat 26:23.

14:21 *Son of man.* See note on 8:31. *as it is written of him.*

22 ¶ [a]And as they did eat, Jesus took bread, and blessed, and brake *it,* and gave to them, and said, Take, eat: this is my body.

23 And he took the cup, and when he had given thanks, he gave *it* to them: and they all drank of it.

24 And he said unto them, This is my blood of the new testament, which is shed for many.

25 Verily I say unto you, I will drink no more of the fruit of the vine, until that day that I drink it new in the kingdom of God.

Peter's denial foretold

26 ¶ [a]And when they had sung a [1]hymn, they went out into the mount of Olives.

27 [a]And Jesus saith unto them, All ye shall be offended because of me this night: for it is written, [b]I will smite the shepherd, and the sheep shall be scattered.

28 But [a]after that I am risen, I will go before you into Galilee.

29 [a]But Peter said unto him, Although all shall be offended, yet *will* not I.

30 And Jesus saith unto him, Verily I say unto thee, That this day, *even* in this night, before *the* cock crow twice, thou shalt deny me thrice.

31 But he spake the more vehemently, If I should die with thee, I will not deny thee in any wise. Likewise also said they all.

Jesus' agony in Gethsemane

32 ¶ [a]And they came to a place which was named Gethsemane: and he saith to his disciples, Sit ye here, while I shall pray.

33 And he taketh with him Peter and James and John, and began to be sore amazed, and to be very heavy;

14:22 [a]Mat. 26:26; Luke 22:19; 1 Cor. 11:23
14:26 [1]Or, *psalm* [a]Mat. 26:30
14:27 [a]Mat. 26:31 [b]Zech. 13:7
14:28 [a]ch. 16:7
14:29 [a]Mat. 26:33,34; Luke 22:33,34; John 13:37,38
14:32 [a]Mat. 26:36; Luke 22:39; John 18:1
14:34 [a]John 12:27
14:36 [a]Rom. 8:15; Gal. 4:6 [b]Heb. 5:7 [c]John 5:30; 6:38
14:38 [a]Rom. 7:23; Gal. 5:17
14:41 [a]John 13:1
14:42 [a]Mat. 26:46; John 18:1,2
14:43 [a]Mat. 26:47; Luke 22:47; John 18:3

34 And saith unto them, [a]My soul is exceeding sorrowful unto death: tarry ye here, and watch.

35 And he went forward a little, and fell on the ground, and prayed that, if it were possible, the hour might pass from him.

36 And he said, [a]Abba, Father, [b]all *things are* possible unto thee; take away this cup from me: [c]nevertheless not that I will, but what thou *wilt.*

37 And he cometh, and findeth them sleeping, and saith unto Peter, Simon, sleepest thou? couldest not thou watch one hour?

38 Watch ye and pray, lest ye enter into temptation. [a]The spirit truly *is* ready, but the flesh *is* weak.

39 And again he went away, and prayed, and spake the same words.

40 And when he returned, he found them asleep again, (for their eyes were heavy,) neither wist they what to answer him.

41 And he cometh the third time, and saith unto them, Sleep on now, and take your rest: it is enough, [a]the hour is come; behold, the Son of man is betrayed into the hands of sinners.

42 [a]Rise up, let us go; lo, he that betrayeth me is at hand.

Jesus' betrayal and arrest

43 ¶ [a]And immediately, while he yet spake, cometh Judas, one of the twelve, and with him a great multitude with swords and staves, from the chief priests and the scribes and the elders.

44 And he that betrayed him had given them a token, saying, Whomsoever I shall kiss, *that* same is he; take him, and lead *him* away safely.

Jesus no doubt had the "suffering servant" passage of Is 53 in mind.

‡14:22 The NT gives four accounts of the Lord's Supper (Mat 26:26–28; Mark 14:22–24; Luke 22:19–20; 1 Cor 11:23–25). Matthew's account is very much like Mark's, while Luke's and Paul's have similarities. All the accounts include the taking of the bread; the thanksgiving or blessing; the breaking of the bread; the saying, "this is my body"; the taking of the cup; and the explanation of the relation of blood to the covenant. Only Paul and Luke record Jesus' command to continue to celebrate the Supper. *this is my body.* The bread represented His body, given for them (see Luke 22:19; 1 Cor 11:24).

14:23 *given thanks.* The word "Eucharist" is derived from the Greek term used here.

14:24 *my blood of the new testament.* The cup represents the blood of Jesus, which, in turn, represents His poured-out life (i.e., His death). God's commitments to His people in the new covenant are possible only through Christ's atoning death (see Jer 31:31–34; Heb 8:8–12; see also notes on Luke 22:20; Ex 24:6,8). *for many.* See note on Rom 5:15.

14:25 *Verily I say unto you.* See note on 3:28. *kingdom of God.* See note on Mat 3:2.

14:26 *a hymn.* See note on Mat 26:30. *mount of Olives.* See note on 11:1.

‡14:30 *Verily I say unto thee.* See note on 3:28.

14:32 *Gethsemane.* A garden or orchard on the lower slopes of the mount of Olives, one of Jesus' favorite places (see Luke 22:39; John 18:2). The name is Hebrew and means "oil press," i.e., a place for squeezing the oil from olives.

14:33 *Peter and James and John.* See note on 5:37.

14:36 *Abba, Father.* Expressive of an especially close relationship to God. *this cup.* The chalice of death and of God's wrath that Jesus took from the Father's hand in fulfillment of His mission. What Jesus dreaded was not death as such, but the manner of His death as the One who was taking the sin of mankind upon Himself. See note on 10:38.

14:37 *Simon.* See note on 1:16. Perhaps Simon is singled out because of his bold assertion that he would not fail Jesus (see vv. 29–31).

14:38 *enter into temptation.* Be attacked by temptation. Here the temptation is to be unfaithful in face of the threatening circumstances confronting them. *The spirit truly is ready.* When that part of man that is spirit is under God's control, it strives against human weakness. The expression is taken from Ps 51:12.

14:41 *Son of man.* See note on 8:31.

14:43 *Judas.* See note on 3:19. *a great multitude with swords and staves.* Auxiliary police or servants of the court assigned to the task of maintaining public order beyond the precincts of the temple. John (18:3) indicates that at least some of the Roman cohort of soldiers were in the arresting group, along with officers of the temple guard. The fact that some carried clubs suggests that they were conscripted at the last moment. *chief priests . . . scribes . . . elders.* See notes on 8:31; Mat 2:4. The warrant for Jesus' arrest had been issued by the Sanhedrin.

45 And as soon as he was come, he goeth
straightway to him, and saith, Master, master;
and kissed him.
46 And they laid their hands on him, and
took him.
47 And one of them that stood by drew a
sword, and smote a servant of the high priest,
and cut off his ear.
48 [a]And Jesus answered and said unto
them, Are ye come out, as against a thief, with
swords and *with* staves to take me?
49 I was daily with you in the temple
teaching, and ye took me not: but [a]the scriptures must be fulfilled.
50 [a]And they all forsook him, and fled.
51 And there followed him a certain young
man, having a linen cloth cast about *his* naked
body; and the young men laid hold on him:
52 And he left the linen cloth, and fled
from them naked.

Jesus before Caiaphas

53 ¶ [a]And they led Jesus away to the high
priest: and with him were assembled all the
chief priests and the elders and the scribes.
54 And Peter followed him afar off, even
into the palace of the high priest: and he sat
with the servants, and warmed himself at the
fire.
55 [a]And the chief priests and all the council sought for witness against Jesus to put him
to death; and found none.
56 For many bare false witness against
him, but *their* witness agreed not together.
57 And there arose certain, and bare false
witness against him, saying,
58 We heard him say, [a]I will destroy this
temple that is made with hands, and within
three days I will build another made without
hands.
59 But neither so did their witness agree
together.
60 [a]And the high priest stood up in the
midst, and asked Jesus, saying, Answerest
thou nothing? what *is it which* these witness
against thee?
61 But [a]he held his peace, and answered
nothing. [b]Again the high priest asked him,
and said unto him, Art thou the Christ, the
Son of the Blessed?
62 And Jesus said, I am: [a]and ye shall see
the Son of man sitting on the right hand of
power, and coming in the clouds of heaven.
63 Then the high priest rent his clothes,
and saith, What need we any further witnesses?
64 Ye have heard the blasphemy: what
think ye? And they all condemned him to be
guilty of death.

14:48 [a]Mat. 26:55; Luke 22:52
14:49 [a]Ps. 22:6; Is. 53:7; Luke 22:37; 24:44
14:50 [a]ver. 27; Ps. 88:8
14:53 [a]Mat. 26:57; Luke 22:54; John 18:13
14:55 [a]Mat. 26:59
14:58 [a]ch. 15:29; John 2:19
14:60 [a]Mat. 26:62
14:61 [a]Is. 53:7 [b]Mat. 26:63
14:62 [a]Mat. 24:30; 26:64; Luke 22:69

14:45 *Master.* Hebrew word for "(my) teacher." *kissed him.* A token of respect with which disciples customarily greeted their teacher. See note on Luke 22:47.

‡14:47 *one of them that stood by.* We know from John that it was Peter, and the servant he struck was named Malchus (John 18:10). John, an eye-witness, also tells us that it was Malchus's right ear. Malchus may have leaned his head over to avoid having his entire head severed.

14:49 *temple.* See note on 11:27. *the scriptures must be fulfilled.* Perhaps a reference to Is 53, or more particularly to Zech 13:7, quoted by Jesus in v. 27 and fulfilled (at least in part) at this time.

14:50 *they all forsook him.* In fulfillment of vv. 27–31.

‡14:51 *a certain young man.* Not specifically identified, but his anonymity may suggest that this was John Mark, writer of this Gospel. If the upper room were indeed at his mother's house, he may have followed Jesus and the others to the garden after the supper. *a linen cloth.* Ordinarily the outer garment was made of wool. The fine linen garment left behind in the hand of a guard indicates that the youth was from a wealthy family.

‡14:52 *fled from them naked.* The absence of an undergarment suggests that he had dressed hastily to follow Jesus. This was an embarrassing fact. Who would have known of this incident, since all of Jesus' disciples had fled; and why place this in the Gospel, unless to indicate that the author was there also?

14:53–15:15 Jesus' trial took place in two stages: a Jewish trial and a Roman trial, each of which had three episodes. For the Jewish trial these were: (1) the preliminary hearing before Annas, the former high priest (reported only in John 18:12–14, 19–23); (2) the trial before Caiaphas, the ruling high priest, and the Sanhedrin (14:53–65); and (3) the final action of the council, which terminated its all-night session (15:1). The three episodes of the Roman trial were: (1) the trial before Pilate (15:2–5); (2) the trial before Herod Antipas (only in Luke 23:6–12); and (3) the trial before Pilate continued and concluded (15:6–15). Since Mark gives no account of Jesus before Herod Antipas, the trial before Pilate forms a continuous and uninterrupted narrative in this Gospel (15:2–15).

14:53 *high priest.* Caiaphas, son-in-law of Annas, the former high priest. *all the chief priests and the elders and the scribes.* The entire Sanhedrin.

14:54 *palace of the high priest.* The Sanhedrin may have met at Caiaphas's house to ensure secrecy.

‡14:55 *council.* The Sanhedrin, the high court of the Jews. In NT times it was made up of three kinds of members: chief priests, elders, and scribes. Its total membership numbered 71, including the high priest, who was presiding officer. Under Roman jurisdiction this council was given a great deal of authority, but they could not impose capital punishment (see John 18:31 and note on Mat 27:2).

14:56 *many bare false witness against him.* In Jewish judicial procedure, witnesses functioned as the prosecution. *their witness agreed not together.* According to Deut 19:15 a person could not be convicted unless two or more witnesses gave testimony, which assumes that their testimonies had to agree.

14:58 There is no statement by Jesus precisely like this in the Gospels. It is probably an allusion to what is reported in John 2:19.

14:61 *Christ.* Or "Messiah." *Son of the Blessed.* "The Blessed" was a way of referring to God without pronouncing His name (see note on 11:30). The title was therefore equivalent to "Son of God," though in this context it would seem not to refer to deity but to royal Messiahship, since in popular Jewish belief the Messiah was to be a man, not God.

14:62 *Son of man.* See note on 8:31. This Son of man saying brings together Dan 7:13 and Ps 110:1.

14:63 *rent his clothes.* A sign of great grief or shock (see Gen 37:29; 2 Ki 18:37; 19:1). In the case of the high priest it was a form of judicial act expressing the fact that he regarded Jesus' answer as blasphemous (see note on Mat 26:65).

14:64 *blasphemy.* The sin of blasphemy not only involved reviling the name of God (see Lev 24:10–16) but also included

65 And some began to spit on him, and to
cover his face, and to buffet him, and to say
unto him, Prophesy: and the servants did
strike him with the palms of their hands.

Peter's denial of Jesus

66 ¶ [a]And as Peter was beneath in the
palace, there cometh one of the maids of the
high priest:
67 And when she saw Peter warming himself, she looked upon him, and said, *And* thou
also wast with Jesus of Nazareth.
68 But he denied, saying, I know not, neither understand I what thou sayest. And he
went out into the porch; and *the* cock crew.
69 [a]And a maid saw him again, and began
to say to them that stood by, This is *one* of
them.
70 And he denied *it* again. [a]And a little after, they that stood by said again to Peter, Surely thou art *one* of them: [b]for thou art a Galilean, and thy speech agreeth *thereto.*
71 But he began to curse and to swear, *saying,* I know not this man of whom ye speak.
72 [a]And the second time *the* cock crew.
And Peter called to mind the word that Jesus
said unto him, Before *the* cock crow twice,
thou shalt deny me thrice. And [1]when he
thought thereon, he wept.

Jesus before Pontius Pilate

15 And [a]straightway in the morning the
chief priests held a consultation with
the elders and scribes and the whole council,
and bound Jesus, and carried *him* away, and
delivered *him* to Pilate.
2 [a]And Pilate asked him, Art thou the King
of the Jews? And he answering said unto him,
Thou sayest *it.*
3 And the chief priests accused him of
many *things:* but he answered nothing.
4 [a]And Pilate asked him again, saying, Answerest thou nothing? behold how many
things they witness against thee.
5 [a]But Jesus yet answered nothing; so that
Pilate marvelled.
6 ¶ Now [a]at *that* feast he released unto
them one prisoner, whomsoever they desired.
7 And there was *one* named Barabbas,
which lay bound with them that had made insurrection with *him,* who had committed murder in the insurrection.
8 And the multitude crying aloud began to
desire *him to do* as he had ever done unto
them.
9 But Pilate answered them, saying, Will ye
that I release unto you the King of the Jews?
10 For he knew that the chief priests had
delivered him for envy.
11 But [a]the chief priests moved the people,
that he should rather release Barabbas unto
them.
12 And Pilate answered and said again
unto them, What will ye then *that* I shall do
unto him whom ye call the King of the Jews?
13 And they cried out again, Crucify him.
14 Then Pilate said unto them, Why, what
evil hath he done? And they cried out the
more exceedingly, Crucify him.
15 [a]And *so* Pilate, willing to content the
people, released Barabbas unto them, and delivered Jesus, when he had scourged *him,* to
be crucified.

14:66 [a]Mat. 26:58,69; Luke 22:55; John 18:16
14:69 [a]Mat. 26:71; Luke 22:58; John 18:25
14:70 [a]Mat. 26:73; Luke 22:59; John 18:26 [b]Acts 2:7
14:72 [1]Or, *he wept abundantly,* or, *he began to weep* [a]Mat. 26:75
15:1 [a]Ps. 2:2; Mat. 27:1; Luke 22:66; 23:1; John 18:28; Acts 3:13; 4:26
15:2 [a]Mat. 27:11
15:4 [a]Mat. 27:13
15:5 [a]Is. 53:7; John 19:9
15:6 [a]Mat. 27:15; Luke 23:17; John 18:39
15:11 [a]Mat. 27:20; Acts 3:14
15:15 [a]Mat. 27:26; John 19:1,16

any affront to His majesty or authority (see Mark 2:7; 3:28–29; John 5:18; 10:33). Jesus' claim to be the Messiah and, in fact, to have majesty and authority belonging only to God was therefore regarded by Caiaphas as blasphemy, for which the Mosaic law prescribed death by stoning (Lev 24:16).

14:65 *began to spit on him . . . buffet him.* Conventional gestures of rejection and condemnation (Num 12:14; Deut 25:9; Job 30:10; Is 50:6). *cover his face.* An old interpretation of Is 11:2–4 held that the Messiah could judge by smell without the aid of sight. *Prophesy.* Say who it was who struck you.

14:66 *beneath.* While Jesus was being beaten in an upstairs room of Caiaphas's house, Peter was below in the courtyard. *one of the maids.* The doorkeeper (John 18:16).

14:67 *of Nazareth.* See note on Mat 2:23.

14:68 *I know not, neither understand I what thou sayest.* Common in Jewish law for a formal, legal denial.

14:70 *Galilean.* Galileans were easily identified by their dialect. Peter's speech showed him to be a Galilean, and his presence among the Judeans in the courtyard suggested he was a follower of Jesus.

‡15:1 *straightway in the morning.* The working day of a Roman official began at daylight. *morning.* Friday of Passion Week. *held a consultation.* Apparently to accuse Jesus before the civil authority for treason rather than blasphemy (see Luke 23:1–14 and note on Luke 23:2). *council.* See note on 14:55. *Pilate.* The Roman governor of Judea from A.D. 26 to 36, whose official residence was in Caesarea, on the Mediterranean coast. (In 1961 archaeologists working at Caesarea unearthed a stone contemporary with Pilate and inscribed with his name.) When he came to Jerusalem, he stayed in the magnificent palace built by Herod the Great, located west and a little south of the temple area. Mark uses the Latin word "Pretorium" to indicate this palace in v. 16, and it was here that the Roman trial of Jesus took place.

15:2 *Pilate asked him.* Judgment in a Roman court was the sole responsibility of the imperial magistrate.

‡15:3 *of many things.* See note on Luke 23:2. Multiple charges were common in criminal cases.

15:4 *Answerest thou nothing?* If Jesus made no defense, according to Roman law Pilate would have to pronounce against Him.

15:6 *he released unto them.* See note on John 18:39.

‡15:7 *Barabbas.* Probably a member of the Zealots, a revolutionary Jewish group. *insurrection.* Nothing from other sources is known about this insurrection, or uprising, though Mark speaks of it as if it were well known. Under the Roman prefects such revolts were common (see Luke 13:1).

15:13 *Crucify.* See note on v. 24.

15:15 *scourged.* The Romans used a whip made of several strips of leather into which were embedded (near the ends) pieces of bone and lead. The Jews limited the number of stripes to a maximum of 40 (in practice to 39 in case of a miscount), but no such limitation was recognized by the Romans, and victims of Roman floggings often did not survive.

Jesus crowned with thorns

16 ¶ [a]And the soldiers led him away into the hall, called Pretorium; and they call together the whole band.

17 And they clothed him with purple, and platted a crown of thorns, and put *it* about his *head,*

18 And began to salute him, Hail, King of the Jews.

19 And they smote him on the head with a reed, and did spit upon him, and bowing *their* knees worshipped him.

20 And when they had mocked him, they took off the purple from him, and put his own clothes on him, and led him out to crucify him.

21 [a]And they compel one Simon a Cyrenian, who passed by, coming out of the country, the father of Alexander and Rufus, to bear his cross.

Jesus crucified

22 ¶ [a]And they bring him unto the place Golgotha, which is, being interpreted, The place of a skull.

23 [a]And they gave him to drink wine mingled with myrrh: but he received *it* not.

24 And when they had crucified him, [a]they parted his garments, casting lots upon them, what every *man* should take.

25 And [a]it was the third hour, and they crucified him.

26 And [a]the superscription of his accusation was written over, THE KING OF THE JEWS.

27 And [a]with him they crucify two thieves; the one on *his* right hand, and the other on his left.

28 And the scripture was fulfilled, which saith, [a]And he was numbered with the transgressors.

29 ¶ And [a]they that passed by railed on him, wagging their heads, and saying, Ah, [b]*thou* that destroyest the temple, and buildest *it* in three days,

30 Save thyself, and come down from the cross.

31 Likewise also the chief priests mocking said among themselves with the scribes, He saved others; himself he cannot save.

32 Let Christ the King of Israel descend now from the cross, that we may see and believe. And [a]they that were crucified with him reviled him.

The death of Jesus

33 ¶ And [a]when the sixth hour was come, there was darkness over the whole land until the ninth hour.

34 And at the ninth hour Jesus cried with a loud voice, saying, [a]ELOI, ELOI, LAMA SABACH-

15:16 [a]Mat. 27:27
15:21 [a]Mat. 27:32; Luke 23:26
15:22 [a]Mat. 27:33; Luke 23:33; John 19:17
15:23 [a]Mat. 27:34
15:24 [a]Ps. 22:18; Luke 23:34; John 19:23
15:25 [a]See Mat. 27:45; Luke 23:44; John 19:14
15:26 [a]Mat. 27:37; John 19:19
15:27 [a]Mat. 27:38
15:28 [a]Is. 53:12; Luke 22:37
15:29 [a]Ps. 22:7 [b]ch. 14:58; John 2:19
15:32 [a]Mat. 27:44; Luke 23:39
15:33 [a]Mat. 27:45; Luke 23:44
15:34 [a]Ps. 22:1; Mat. 27:46

15:16 *Pretorium.* The word was used originally of a general's tent, or of the headquarters in a military camp (see note on v. 1). *the whole band.* The soldiers quartered in the Pretorium were recruited from non-Jewish inhabitants of the Holy Land and assigned to the military governor.

15:17 *purple.* Probably an old military cloak, whose color suggested royalty (see Mat 27:28). *crown of thorns.* Made of a prickly plant (the Greek word means simply "briers"), of which there are many in the Holy Land. Both robe and crown were parts of the mock royal attire placed on Jesus.

15:18 *Hail, King of the Jews.* A mocking salutation that corresponded to "Hail, Caesar!"

15:19 *spit upon him.* Probably a parody on the kiss of homage that was customary in the Near East when in the presence of royalty.

‡15:21 *Simon.* Probably a Jew who was in Jerusalem to celebrate the passover (cf. "Cyrenians" in Acts 6:9). *a Cyrenian.* Cyrene was an important city of Libya in North Africa that had a large Jewish population. *Alexander and Rufus.* Only mentioned by Mark, but referred to in such a way as to suggest that they were known by those to whom Mark wrote. Rufus may be the same person spoken of in Rom 16:13. Otherwise, who would care to know the names of this man's children? *bear his cross.* Men condemned to death were usually forced to carry a beam of the cross, often weighing 30 or 40 pounds, to the place of crucifixion. Jesus started out by carrying His (see John 19:17), but He had been so weakened by flogging that Simon was pressed into service.

15:22 *place of a skull.* It may have been a small hill (though the Gospels say nothing of a hill) that looked like a skull, or it may have been so named because of the many executions that took place there.

15:23 *wine mingled with myrrh.* The Talmud gives evidence that incense was mixed with wine to deaden pain (see Prov 31:6). Myrrh is a spice derived from plants native to the Arabian deserts and parts of Africa (see note on Gen 37:25).

15:24 *crucified.* A Roman means of execution in which the victim was nailed to a cross. Heavy, wrought-iron nails were driven through the wrists and the heel bones. If the life of the victim lingered too long, death was hastened by breaking his legs (see John 19:33). Archaeologists have discovered the bones of a crucified man, near Jerusalem, dating between A.D. 7 and 66, which shed light on the position of the victim when nailed to the cross. Only slaves, the basest of criminals, and offenders who were not Roman citizens were executed in this manner. First-century authors vividly describe the agony and disgrace of being crucified. *parted his garments.* It was the accepted right of the executioner's squad to claim the minor possessions of the victim. Jesus' clothing probably consisted of an under and an outer garment, a belt, sandals and possibly a head covering.

15:25 *third hour.* See notes on Luke 23:44; John 19:14.

15:26 *his accusation.* It was customary to write the charge on a wooden board that was carried before the victim as he walked to the place of execution, and then the board was affixed to the cross above his head. *THE KING OF THE JEWS.* The wording of the charge differs slightly in the Gospels, but all agree that Jesus was crucified for claiming to be the king of the Jews.

15:27 *two thieves.* According to Roman law, robbery was not a capital offense. Mark's term must signify men guilty of insurrection, crucified for high treason.

‡15:28 Mark does not include many OT quotations, writing as he is for a non-Jewish audience, but these words are from Is 53:12.

15:29 See note on 14:58.

15:32 *Christ.* See note on 13:21. *they that were crucified with him.* One of the criminals later repented and asked to be included in Jesus' kingdom (Luke 23:39–43).

15:33 *sixth hour.* 12:00 noon. *ninth hour.* 3:00 P.M.

THANI? which is, being interpreted, My God,
my God, why hast thou forsaken me?
35 And some of them that stood by, when
they heard *it,* said, Behold, he calleth Elias.
36 And [a]one ran and filled a spunge *full* of
vinegar, and put *it* on a reed, and [b]gave him to
drink, saying, Let alone; let us see whether
Elias will come to take him down.
37 ¶ [a]And Jesus cried with a loud voice,
and gave up the ghost.
38 And [a]the vail of the temple was rent in
twain from the top to the bottom.
39 And [a]when the centurion, which stood
over against him, saw that he so cried out, and
gave up the ghost, he said, Truly this man was
the Son of God.
40 [a]There were also women looking on
[b]afar off: among whom was Mary Magdalene,
and Mary the mother of James the less and of
Joses, and Salome;
41 (Who also, when he was in Galilee, [a]fol-
lowed him, and ministered unto him;) and
many other *women* which came up with him
unto Jerusalem.

Jesus laid in the tomb

42 ¶ [a]And now when the even was come,
because it was the preparation, that is, the day
before the sabbath,
43 Joseph of Arimathea, an honourable
counseller, which also [a]waited for the kingdom of God, came, and went in boldly unto Pilate, and craved the body of Jesus.
44 And Pilate marvelled if he were already
dead: and calling unto *him* the centurion, he
asked him whether he had been any while
dead.
45 And when he knew *it* of the centurion,
he gave the body to Joseph.
46 [a]And he bought fine linen, and took
him down, and wrapped *him* in the linen, and
laid him in a sepulchre which was hewn out of
a rock, and rolled a stone unto the door of the
sepulchre.
47 And Mary Magdalene and Mary *the
mother* of Joses beheld where he was laid.

The resurrection of Jesus

16 And [a]when the sabbath was past,
Mary Magdalene, and Mary the
mother of James, and Salome, [b]had bought
sweet spices, that they might come and anoint
him.
2 [a]And very early in the morning the first
day of the week, they came unto the sepulchre
at the rising of the sun.
3 And they said among themselves, Who
shall roll us away the stone from the door of
the sepulchre?

15:36 [a]Mat. 27:48; John 19:29 [b]Ps. 69:21
15:37 [a]Mat. 27:50; Luke 23:46; John 19:30
15:38 [a]Mat. 27:51; Luke 23:45
15:39 [a]Mat. 27:54; Luke 23:47
15:40 [a]Mat. 27:55; Luke 23:49 [b]Ps. 38:11
15:41 [a]Luke 8:2,3
15:42 [a]Mat. 27:57; Luke 23:50; John 19:38
15:43 [a]Luke 2:25,38
15:46 [a]Mat. 27:59,60; Luke 23:53; John 19:40
16:1 [a]Mat. 28:1; Luke 24:1; John 20:1 [b]Luke 23:56
16:2 [a]Luke 24:1; John 20:1

‡15:34 The words were spoken in Aramaic (but with some Hebrew characteristics), one of the languages commonly spoken in the Holy Land in Jesus' day. They reveal how deeply Jesus felt His abandonment by God as He bore the sins of mankind (but see introduction to Ps 22 and note on Ps 22:1). For Jesus to quote the initial verse of this psalm was to declare its fulfillment in His own life.

15:35 *Elias.* The bystanders mistook the first words of Jesus' cry ("Eloi, Eloi") to be a cry for Elijah. It was commonly believed that Elijah would come in times of critical need to protect the innocent and rescue the righteous (v. 36).

‡15:36 *vinegar.* A type of wine used by laborers and soldiers. It may have quenched Jesus' thirst, but it did not deaden His pain.

15:37 *a loud voice.* The strength of the cry indicates that Jesus did not die the ordinary death of those crucified, who normally suffered long periods of complete agony, exhaustion and then unconsciousness before dying.

15:38 *vail of the temple.* The curtain that separated the holy place from the most holy place (Ex 26:31–33). The tearing of the curtain indicated that Christ had entered heaven itself for us so that we too may now enter God's very presence (Heb 9:8–10,12; 10:19–20).

15:39 *centurion.* A commander of 100 men in the Roman army. *saw that he so cried out, and gave up the ghost.* See note on v. 37. *the Son of God.* See notes on Mat 27:54; Luke 23:47.

15:40 *Mary Magdalene.* From 16:9 and Luke 8:2 we learn that Jesus had driven seven demons from her. *Mary the mother of James the less and of Joses.* See v. 47; 16:1. *Salome.* Probably the wife of Zebedee and the mother of James and John (see Mat 27:56).

15:42 *the preparation.* Friday. Since it was now late in the afternoon, there was an urgency to get Jesus' body down from the cross before sundown, when the sabbath began.

‡15:43 *Arimathea.* See note on Mat 27:57. *an honourable counseller.* Joseph was a member of the Sanhedrin (see note on 14:55). *kingdom of God.* See note on Mat 3:2. *Pilate.* See note on v. 1. *craved the body of Jesus.* He wanted to give Jesus a decent burial. Many criminals did not receive such. See note on Luke 23:52.

15:44 *marvelled.* Crucified men often lived two or three days before dying, and the early death of Jesus was therefore extraordinary.

15:45 *he gave the body to Joseph.* The release of the body of one condemned for high treason, and especially to one who was not an immediate relative, was quite unusual.

15:46 *sepulchre which was hewn out of a rock.* Matthew tells us that the tomb belonged to Joseph and that it was new, i.e., it had not been used before (Mat 27:60). The location of the tomb was in a garden very near the site of the crucifixion (see John 19:41). There is archaeological evidence that the traditional site of the burial of Jesus (the Church of the Holy Sepulchre in Jerusalem) was a cemetery during the first century A.D. However, there is also good evidence that the "Garden Tomb" was also used in the first century and that an early church was once constructed over that site as well. *stone.* A disc-shaped stone that rolled in a sloped channel. The stone, even though large, was probably not higher than one's waist, since the disciples had to stoop down to enter (see John 20:5).

16:1 *sabbath was past.* About 6:00 P.M. Saturday evening. No purchases were possible on the sabbath. *Mary Magdalene, and Mary the mother of James, and Salome.* See note on 15:40. *spices.* Embalming was not practiced by the Jews. These spices were brought as an act of devotion and love. *that they might come and anoint him.* The women had no expectation of Jesus' resurrection.

‡16:3 *Who shall roll us away the stone . . . ?* Setting the large stone in place was a relatively easy task, but once it had slipped into the groove cut in bedrock in front of the entrance it was very difficult to remove, as it probably weighed several hundred pounds.

4 And when they looked, they saw that the stone was rolled away: for it was very great.

5 [a]And entering into the sepulchre, they saw a young man sitting on the right side, clothed in a long white garment; and they were affrighted.

6 [a]And he saith unto them, Be not affrighted: Ye seek Jesus of Nazareth, which was crucified: he is risen; he is not here: behold the place where they laid him.

7 But go your way, tell his disciples and Peter that he goeth before you into Galilee: there shall ye see him, [a]as he said unto you.

8 And they went out quickly, and fled from the sepulchre; for they trembled and were amazed: [a]neither said they any *thing* to any *man;* for they were afraid.

9 ¶ Now when *Jesus* was risen early the first *day* of the week, he appeared first to Mary Magdalene, [a]out of whom he had cast seven devils.

10 [a]*And* she went and told them that had been with him, as they mourned and wept.

11 [a]And they, when they had heard that he was alive, and had been seen of her, believed not.

12 ¶ After that he appeared in another form [a]unto two of them, as they walked, and went into the country.

13 And they went and told *it* unto the residue: neither believed they them.

14 ¶ [a]Afterward he appeared unto the eleven as they sat [1]at meat, and upbraided them with their unbelief and hardness of heart, because they believed not them which had seen him after he was risen.

15 [a]And he said unto them, Go ye into all the world, [b]and preach the gospel to every creature.

16 [a]He that believeth and is baptized shall be saved; [b]but he that believeth not shall be damned.

17 And these signs shall follow them that believe; [a]In my name shall they cast out devils; [b]they shall speak with new tongues;

18 [a]They shall take up serpents; and if they drink any deadly *thing,* it shall not hurt them; [b]they shall lay hands on the sick, and they shall recover.

19 ¶ So then [a]after the Lord had spoken unto them, he was [b]received up into heaven, and [c]sat on the right hand of God.

20 And they went forth, and preached every where, the Lord working with *them,* [a]and confirming the word with signs following. Amen.

16:5 [a]Luke 24:3; John 20:11
16:6 [a]Mat. 28:5
16:7 [a]Mat. 26:32; ch. 14:28
16:8 [a]Mat. 28:8; Luke 24:9
16:9 [a]Luke 8:2
16:10 [a]Luke 24:10; John 20:18
16:11 [a]Luke 24:11
16:12 [a]Luke 24:13
16:14 [1]Or, *together* [a]Luke 24:36; John 20:19; 1 Cor. 15:5
16:15 [a]Mat. 28:19; John 15:16 [b]Col. 1:23
16:16 [a]John 3:18; Acts 2:38; 16:30-32; Rom. 10:9; 1 Pet. 3:21 [b]John 12:48
16:17 [a]Luke 10:17; Acts 5:16 [b]Acts 2:4; 1 Cor. 12:10
16:18 [a]Luke 10:19; Acts 28:5 [b]Acts 5:15; Jas. 5:14
16:19 [a]Acts 1:2,3 [b]Luke 24:51 [c]Ps. 110:1; Acts 7:55
16:20 [a]Acts 5:12; 1 Cor. 2:4,5; Heb. 2:4

16:5 *entering into the sepulchre.* Inside the large opening of the facade of the tomb was a forechamber, at the back of which a low rectangular opening led to the burial chamber. *young man . . . clothed in a long white garment.* Identified by Matthew (28:2) as an angel. See note on Luke 24:4.
16:6 *crucified.* See note on 15:24. *he is risen.* The climax of Mark's Gospel is the resurrection, without which Jesus' death, though noble, would be indescribably tragic. But in the resurrection He is declared to be the Son of God with power (Rom 1:4).
16:7 *and Peter.* Jesus showed special concern for Peter, in view of his confident boasting and subsequent denials (14:29–31, 66–72). *as he said unto you.* See 14:28.
‡16:9–20 Some textual critics, even conservative scholars, have serious doubts as to whether these verses belong to the Gospel of Mark. They point out that Mark 16:9–20 are absent from important early manuscripts and display certain peculiarities of vocabulary, style and theological content that are unlike the rest of Mark, noting that his Gospel probably ended at 16:8, or that its original ending has been lost. However, only a small handful of manuscripts omit these verses, and the arguments for seeing them as original are equally compelling.
16:9 *Mary Magdalene.* See note on 15:40.
16:12–13 A shortened account of the two going to Emmaus (see Luke 24:13–35).
16:14 *the eleven.* Judas Iscariot had committed suicide (see Mat 27:5).
‡16:15 *Go ye into all the world, and preach the gospel to every creature.* The Great Commission is found here, in the other three Gospels (Mat 28:19–20; Luke 24:47–48; John 20:21), and in Acts 1:8. Jesus' final words are our "marching orders." They are important, because apart from believing the gospel of Christ, no one shall enter heaven (see John 3:36; Rom 1:18).
‡16:16 *baptized.* Baptism does not save, nor is it required for salvation. Notice that in order to be "damned" one has only not to "believe." Nothing is said about not being baptized. All the believers in the book of Acts are referred to as being baptized. See notes on 1:4; Rom 6:3–4.
16:18 *drink any deadly thing.* No occurrence of drinking deadly poison without harm is found in the NT.
16:19 *right hand of God.* A position of authority second only to God's (see 14:62; Ps 110:1).

The Gospel According to
S. Luke

INTRODUCTION

See "The Synoptic Gospels," p. 1349.

Author

The author's name does not appear in the book, but much unmistakable evidence points to Luke. This Gospel is a companion volume to the book of Acts, and the language and structure of these two books indicate that both were written by the same person. They are addressed to the same individual, Theophilus, and the second volume refers to the first (Acts 1:1). Certain sections in Acts use the pronoun "we" (Acts 16:10–17; 20:5–15; 21:1–18; 27:1—28:16), indicating that the author was with Paul when the events described in these passages took place. By process of elimination, "Luke, the beloved physician" (Col 4:14), and Paul's "fellow labourer" (Philem 24) becomes the most likely candidate. His authorship is supported by the uniform testimony of early Christian writings (e.g., the Muratorian Canon, A.D. 170, and the works of Irenaeus, c. 180).

Luke was probably a Gentile by birth, well educated in Greek culture, a physician by profession, a companion of Paul at various times from his second missionary journey to his first imprisonment in Rome, and a loyal friend who remained with the apostle after others had deserted him (2 Tim 4:11). Antioch (of Syria) and Philippi are among the places suggested as his hometown.

Recipient and Purpose

The Gospel is specifically directed to Theophilus (1:3), whose name means "one who loves God" and almost certainly refers to a particular person rather than to lovers of God in general. The use of "most excellent" with the name further indicates an individual, and supports the idea that he was a Roman official or at least of high position and wealth. He was possibly Luke's patron, responsible for seeing that the writings were copied and distributed. Such a dedication to the publisher was common at that time.

Theophilus, however, was more than a publisher. The message of this Gospel was intended for his own instruction (1:4) as well as the instruction of those among whom the book would be circulated. The fact that the Gospel was initially directed to Theophilus does not narrow or limit its purpose. It was written to strengthen the faith of all believers and to answer the attacks of unbelievers. It was presented to displace disconnected and ill-founded reports about Jesus. Luke wanted to show that the place of the Gentile Christian in God's kingdom is based on the teaching of Jesus. He wanted to commend the preaching of the gospel to the whole world.

Date and Place of Writing

The two most commonly suggested periods for dating the Gospel of Luke are: (1) A.D. 59–63, and (2) the 70s or the 80s (see chart, p. 1349). Luke's Gospel was written before the Acts of the Apostles, and is referred to as Luke's "former treatise" (Acts 1:1). Since the Book of Acts closes with Paul in Rome awaiting trial, about A.D. 62, some assume that Luke was written while Paul was imprisoned in Caesarea awaiting the appeal of his trial to the Roman emperor. That would date the Gospel's publication at about A.D. 60.

The place of writing was probably Rome, though Achaia, Ephesus and Caesarea also have been suggested. The place to which it was sent would, of course, depend on the residence of Theophilus. By its detailed designations of places in the Holy Land, the Gospel seems to be intended for readers who were unfamiliar with that land. Antioch, Achaia and Ephesus are possible destinations.

Style

Luke had outstanding command of the Greek language. His vocabulary is extensive and rich, and his style at times approaches that of classical Greek (as in the preface, 1:1–4), while at other times it

is quite Semitic (1:5—2:52)—often like the Septuagint Greek translation of the OT. His vocabulary seems to reveal geographical and cultural sensitivity, in that it varies with the particular land or people being described. When Luke refers to Peter in a Jewish setting, he uses more Semitic language than when he refers to Paul in a Hellenistic setting.

Characteristics

The third Gospel presents the works and teachings of Jesus that are especially important for understanding the way of salvation. Its scope is complete from the birth of Christ to His ascension, its arrangement is orderly, and it appeals to both Jews and Gentiles. The writing is characterized by literary excellence, historical detail and warm, sensitive understanding of Jesus and those around him.

Since the Synoptic Gospels (Matthew, Mark and Luke) report many of the same episodes in Jesus' life, one would expect much similarity in their accounts. The dissimilarities reveal the distinctive emphases of the separate writers. Luke's characteristic themes include: (1) universality, recognition of Gentiles as well as Jews in God's plan; (2) emphasis on prayer, especially Jesus' praying before important occasions (see note on 3:21); (3) joy at the announcement of the gospel or "good news" (see note on 1:14); (4) special concern for the role of women; (5) special interest in the poor (some of the rich were included among Jesus' followers, but He seemed closest to the poor); (6) concern for sinners (Jesus was a friend to those deep in sin); (7) stress on the family circle (Jesus' activity included men, women and children, with the setting frequently in the home); (8) repeated use of the title "Son of man" (e.g., 19:10); (9) emphasis on the Holy Spirit (see note on 4:1).

Sources

Although Luke acknowledges that many others had written of Jesus' life (1:1), he does not indicate that he relied on these reports for his own writing. He used personal investigation and arrangement, based on testimony from "eyewitnesses and ministers of the word" (1:2)—including the preaching and oral accounts of the apostles. His language differences from the other Synoptics and his blocks of distinctive material (e.g., 10:1—18:14; 19:1–28) indicate independent work, though he obviously used some of the same sources. While Paul was imprisoned at Caesarea, Luke would have had ample time to research Jesus' life and to talk with many eyewitnesses then living in Israel.

Plan

Luke's account of Jesus' ministry can be divided into three major parts: (1) the events that occurred in and around Galilee (4:14—9:50), (2) those that took place in Judea and Perea (9:51—19:27), and (3) those of the final week in Jerusalem (19:28—24:53). Luke's uniqueness is especially seen in the amount of material devoted to Jesus' closing ministry in Judea and Perea. This material is predominantly made up of accounts of Jesus' discourses. Sixteen of the 23 parables that occur in Luke are found here (9:51—18:14; 19:1–28). Of the 20 miracles recorded in Luke, only 4 appear in these sections. Already in the ninth chapter (see note on 9:51), Jesus is seen anticipating His final appearance in Jerusalem and His crucifixion (see note on 13:22).

The main theme of the Gospel is the nature of Jesus' Messiahship and mission, and a key verse is 19:10.

Outline

- I. The Preface (1:1–4)
- II. The Coming of Jesus (1:5—2:52)
  - A. The Annunciations (1:5–56)
  - B. The Birth of John the Baptist (1:57–80)
  - C. The Birth and Childhood of Jesus (ch. 2)
- III. The Preparation of Jesus for His Public Ministry (3:1—4:13)
  - A. His Forerunner (3:1–20)
  - B. His Baptism (3:21–22)
  - C. His Genealogy (3:23–38)
  - D. His Temptation (4:1–13)
- IV. His Ministry in Galilee (4:14—9:9)
  - A. The Beginning of the Ministry in Galilee (4:14–41)
  - B. The First Tour of Galilee (4:42—5:39)
  - C. A Sabbath Controversy (6:1–11)

D. The Choice of the 12 Disciples (6:12–16)
E. The Sermon on the Plain (6:17–49)
F. Miracles in Capernaum and Nain (7:1–18)
G. The Inquiry of John the Baptist (7:19–29)
H. Jesus and the Pharisees (7:30–50)
I. The Second Tour of Galilee (8:1–3)
J. The Parables of the Kingdom (8:4–21)
K. The Trip across the Sea of Galilee (8:22–39)
L. The Third Tour of Galilee (8:40—9:9)

V. His Withdrawal to Regions around Galilee (9:10–50)
A. To the Eastern Shore of the Sea of Galilee (9:10–17)
B. To Caesarea Philippi (9:18–50)

VI. His Ministry in Judea (9:51—13:21)
A. Journey through Samaria to Judea (9:51–62)
B. The Mission of the 70 (10:1–24)
C. The Lawyer and the Parable of the Good Samaritan (10:25–37)
D. Jesus at Bethany with Mary and Martha (10:38–42)
E. Teachings in Judea (11:1—13:21)

VII. His Ministry in and around Perea (13:22—19:27)
A. The Narrow Gate (13:22–30)
B. Warning concerning Herod (13:31–35)
C. At a Pharisee's House (14:1–23)
D. The Cost of Discipleship (14:24–35)
E. The Parables of the Lost Sheep, the Lost Piece of Silver and the Lost Son (ch. 15)
F. The Parable of the Unrighteous Steward (16:1–18)
G. The Rich Man and Lazarus (16:19–31)
H. Miscellaneous Teachings (17:1–10)
I. Ten Healed of Leprosy (17:11–19)
J. The Coming of the Kingdom (17:20–37)
K. The Persistent Widow (18:1–8)
L. The Pharisee and the Publican (18:9–14)
M. Jesus and the Children (18:15–17)
N. The Rich Young Ruler (18:18–30)
O. Christ Foretells His Death (18:31–34)
P. A Blind Beggar Given His Sight (18:35–43)
Q. Jesus and Zaccheus (19:1–10)
R. The Parable of the Ten Pounds (19:11–27)

VIII. His Last Days: Sacrifice and Triumph (19:28—24:53)
A. The Triumphal Entry (19:28–44)
B. The Cleansing of the Temple (19:45–48)
C. The Last Controversies with the Jewish Leaders (ch. 20)
D. The Olivet Discourse (ch. 21)
E. The Last Supper (22:1–38)
F. Jesus Praying in Gethsemane (22:39–46)
G. Jesus' Arrest (22:47–65)
H. Jesus on Trial (22:66—23:25)
I. The Crucifixion (23:26–56)
J. The Resurrection (24:1–12)
K. The Post-Resurrection Ministry (24:13–49)
L. The Ascension (24:50–53)

Preface

1 Forasmuch as many have taken in hand
to set forth in order a declaration of
those things which are most surely believed
among us,
2 [a]Even as they delivered *them* unto us,
which [b]from the beginning were eyewitnesses, and ministers of the word;
3 [a]It seemed good to me also, having had
perfect understanding of all *things* from the
very first, to write unto thee [b]in order, [c]most
excellent Theophilus,
4 [a]That thou mightest know the certainty
of *those* things, wherein thou hast been instructed.

Birth of John foretold

5 ¶ There was [a]in the days of Herod, the
king of Judea, a certain priest named
Zacharias, [b]of the course of Abia: and his wife
was of the daughters of Aaron, and her name
was Elisabeth.
6 And they were both [a]righteous before
God, walking in all the commandments and
ordinances of the Lord blameless.
7 And they had no child, because that Elisabeth was barren, and they both were *now*
well stricken in years.
8 And it came to pass, *that* while he executed the priest's office before God [a]in the order of his course,

1:2 [a]Heb. 2:3; 1 Pet. 5:1; 2 Pet. 1:16 [b]Mark 1:1; John 15:27
1:3 [a]Acts 15:19; 1 Cor. 7:40 [b]Acts 11:4 [c]Acts 1:1
1:4 [a]John 20:31
1:5 [a]Mat. 2:1 [b]1 Chr. 24:10; Neh. 12:4
1:6 [a]Gen. 7:1; 1 Ki. 9:4; 2 Ki. 20:3
1:8 [a]1 Chr. 24:19; 2 Chr. 8:14
1:9 [a]Ex. 30:7,8; 1 Chr. 23:13; 2 Chr. 29:11
1:10 [a]Lev. 16:17
1:11 [a]Ex. 30:1
1:12 [a]Judg. 6:22; 13:22; Dan. 10:8; ch. 2:9; Acts 10:4; Rev. 1:17
1:13 [a]ver. 60,63
1:14 [a]ver. 58
1:15 [a]Num. 6:3; Judg. 13:4; ch. 7:33 [b]Jer. 1:5; Gal. 1:15
1:16 [a]Mal. 4:5,6
1:17 [1]Or, *by* [a]Mal. 4:5; Mat. 11:14; Mark 9:12
1:18 [a]Gen. 17:17

9 According to the custom of the priest's office, his lot was [a]to burn incense when he
went into the temple of the Lord.
10 [a]And the whole multitude of the people
were praying without at the time of incense.
11 And there appeared unto him an angel
of the Lord standing on the right side of [a]the
altar of incense.
12 And when Zacharias saw *him*, [a]he was
troubled, and fear fell upon him.
13 But the angel said unto him, Fear not,
Zacharias: for thy prayer is heard; and thy wife
Elisabeth shall bear thee a son, and [a]thou shalt
call his name John.
14 And thou shalt have joy and gladness;
and [a]many shall rejoice at his birth.
15 For he shall be great in the sight of the
Lord, and [a]shall drink neither wine nor strong
drink; and he shall be filled with the Holy
Ghost, [b]even from his mother's womb.
16 [a]And many of the children of Israel
shall he turn to the Lord their God.
17 [a]And he shall go before him in the spirit and power of Elias, to turn the hearts of the
fathers to the children, and the disobedient
[1]to the wisdom of the just; to make ready a
people prepared for the Lord.
18 And Zacharias said unto the angel,
[a]Whereby shall I know this? for I am an old
man, and my wife well stricken in years.
19 And the angel answering said unto him,

1:1–4 Using language similar to classical Greek, Luke begins with a formal preface, common to historical works of that time, in which he states his purpose for writing and identifies the recipient. He acknowledges other reports on the subject, shows the need for this new work and states his method of approach and sources of information.

1:1 *things which are most surely believed among us.* Things prophesied in the OT and now fully accomplished.

1:2 *delivered them unto us.* A technical term for passing on information as authoritative tradition. *eyewitnesses, and ministers of the word.* Luke, though not an eyewitness himself, received testimony from those who were eyewitnesses and were dedicated to spreading the gospel. Apostolic preaching and interviews with other individuals associated with Jesus' ministry were available to him.

1:3 *having had perfect understanding of all things.* Luke's account was exact in historical detail, having been checked in every way. Inspiration by the Holy Spirit did not rule out human effort. The account is complete, extending back to the very beginning of Jesus' earthly life. It has an orderly, meaningful arrangement that is generally chronological. *most excellent.* Paul used this respectful term for governors Felix (Acts 24:3) and Festus (Acts 26:25). *Theophilus.* See Introduction: Recipient and Purpose.

1:4 *That thou mightest know.* Cf. John's purpose for writing (John 20:31).

‡1:5 *Herod, the king of Judea.* Herod the Great reigned 37–4 B.C., and his kingdom included Samaria, Galilee, much of Perea and Coele-Syria (see note on Mat 2:1). The time referred to here is probably c. 7–6 B.C. *Zacharias . . . Elisabeth.* Both were of priestly descent from the line of Aaron. *course of Abia.* From the time of David the priests were organized into 24 divisions, and Abia (Abijah) was one of the "priests, the chief of the fathers" (Neh 12:12, 17; see 1 Chr 24:10).

1:6 *righteous . . . blameless.* They were not sinless, but were faithful and sincere in keeping God's commandments. Simeon (2:25) and Joseph (Mat 1:19) are given similar praise.

1:7 *no child.* See note on v. 25.

1:9 It was one of the priest's duties to keep the incense burning on the altar in front of the most holy place. He supplied it with fresh incense before the morning sacrifice and again after the evening sacrifice (Ex 30:6–8). Ordinarily a priest would have this privilege very infrequently, and sometimes never, since duty assignments were determined by lot. *his lot was.* See notes on Neh 11:1; Prov 16:33; Jonah 1:7; Acts 1:26.

1:11 *an angel of the Lord.* See v. 19. *right side of the altar.* The south side, since the altar faced east.

1:12 *fear.* A common reaction, as with Gideon (Judg 6:22–23) and Manoah (Judg 13:22).

1:13 *Fear not.* This word of reassurance is given many times in both OT and NT (see, e.g., v. 30; 2:10 and note; 5:10; 8:50; 12:7,32; Gen 15:1; 21:17; 26:24; Deut 1:21; Josh 8:1). *John.* The name (derived from Hebrew) means "The Lord is gracious."

1:14 *joy.* A keynote of these opening chapters (vv. 14,44,47,58; 2:10).

1:15 *wine nor strong drink.* It appears likely that John was to be subject to the Nazarite vow of abstinence from alcoholic drinks (Num 6:1–4). If so, he was a lifelong Nazarite, as were Samson (Judg 13:4–7) and Samuel (1 Sam 1:11).

‡1:17 *Elias.* John was not Elijah returning in the flesh (John 1:21), but he functioned like that OT preacher of repentance and was therefore a contingent fulfillment of Mal 4:5–6 (see Mat 11:14; 17:10–13). *to turn the hearts of the fathers to the children.* See note on Mal 4:6. *people prepared for the Lord.* John helped fulfill Isaiah's prophecy (Is 40:3–5), as Luke shows in 3:4–6.

1:18 *Whereby shall I know this?* Like Abraham (Gen 15:8), Gideon (Judg 6:17) and Hezekiah (2 Ki 20:8), Zacharias asked for a sign (cf. 1 Cor 1:22).

I am [a]Gabriel, that stand in the presence of God; and am sent to speak unto thee, and to shew thee these glad tidings.

20 And behold, [a]thou shalt be dumb, and not able to speak, until the day that these *things* shall be performed, because thou believest not my words, which shall be fulfilled in their season.

21 And the people waited for Zacharias, and marvelled that he tarried *so* long in the temple.

22 And when he came out, he could not speak unto them: and they perceived that he had seen a vision in the temple: for he beckoned unto them, and remained speechless.

23 And it came to pass *that,* as soon as [a]the days of his ministration were accomplished, he departed to his own house.

24 And after those days his wife Elisabeth conceived, and hid herself five months, saying,

25 Thus hath the Lord dealt with me in the days wherein he looked on *me,* to [a]take away my reproach among men.

The birth of Jesus foretold

26 ¶ And in the sixth month the angel Gabriel was sent from God unto a city of Galilee, named Nazareth,

27 To a virgin [a]espoused to a man whose name was Joseph, of the house of David; and the virgin's name *was* Mary.

28 And the angel came in unto her, and said, [a]Hail, *thou that art* [1]highly favoured, [b]the Lord *is* with thee: blessed *art* thou among women.

29 And when she saw *him,* [a]she was troubled at his saying, and cast in her mind what manner of salutation this should be.

30 And the angel said unto her, Fear not, Mary: for thou hast found favour with God.

31 [a]And behold, thou shalt conceive in *thy* womb, and bring forth a son, and [b]shalt call his name JESUS.

32 He shall be great, [a]and shall be called the Son of the Highest: and [b]the Lord God shall give unto him the throne of his father David:

33 [a]And he shall reign over the house of Jacob for ever; and of his kingdom there shall be no end.

34 Then said Mary unto the angel, How shall this be, seeing I know not a man?

35 And the angel answered and said unto her, [a]The Holy Ghost shall come upon thee, and the power of the Highest shall overshadow thee: therefore also *that* holy thing which shall be born of thee shall be called [b]the Son of God.

36 And behold, thy cousin Elisabeth, she hath also conceived a son in her old age: and this is the sixth month with her, who was called barren.

37 For [a]with God nothing shall be unpossible.

38 And Mary said, Behold the handmaid of the Lord; be it unto me according to thy word. And the angel departed from her.

1:19 [a]Dan. 8:16; 9:21-23; Mat. 18:10; Heb. 1:14
1:20 [a]Ezek. 3:26; 24:27
1:23 [a]2 Ki. 11:5; 1 Chr. 9:25
1:25 [a]Gen. 30:23; Is. 4:1; 54:1,4
1:27 [a]Mat. 1:18; ch. 2:4,5
1:28 [1]Or, *graciously accepted,* or, *much graced:* See ver. 30 [a]Dan. 9:23; 10:19
1:28 [b]Judg. 6:12
1:29 [a]ver. 12
1:31 [a]Is. 7:14; Mat. 1:21 [b]ch. 2:21
1:32 [a]Mark 5:7 [b]2 Sam. 7:11; Ps. 132:11; Is. 9:6,7; 16:5; Jer. 23:5; Rev. 3:7
1:33 [a]Dan. 2:44; 7:14,27; Obad. 21; Mic. 4:7; John 12:34; Heb. 1:8
1:35 [a]Mat. 1:20 [b]Mat. 14:33; 26:63,64; Mark 1:1; John 1:34; 20:31; Acts 8:37; Rom. 1:4
1:37 [a]Gen. 18:14; Jer. 32:17; Zech. 8:6; Mat. 19:26; Mark 10:27; ch. 18:27; Rom. 4:21

1:19 *Gabriel.* The name can mean "God is my hero" or "mighty man of God." Only two angels are identified by name in Scripture: Gabriel (Dan 8:16; 9:21) and Michael (Dan 10:13,21; Jude 9; Rev 12:7).

1:21 *And the people waited for Zacharias.* They were waiting for him to come out of the holy place and pronounce the Aaronic blessing (Num 6:24–26).

‡1:22 *he could not speak.* Luke begins with a priest who cannot speak to bless the people, and ends with Christ our high priest being lifted up into heaven as he dispenses a final blessing.

1:23 *the days of his ministration.* Each priest was responsible for a week's service at the temple once every six months. *his own house.* See v. 39.

1:24 *hid herself.* In joy, devotion and gratitude that the Lord had taken away her childlessness.

1:25 *the Lord . . . looked on me, to take away my reproach.* Not only did lack of children deprive the parents of personal happiness, but it was generally considered to indicate divine disfavor and often brought social reproach (see Gen 16:2, Sarai; 25:21, Rebekah; 30:23, Rachel; 1 Sam 1:1–18, Hannah; see also Lev 20:20–21; Ps 128:3; Jer 22:30).

1:26–35 This section speaks clearly of the virginal conception of Jesus (vv. 27,34–35; see Mat 1:18–25). The conception was the work of the Holy Spirit; the eternal Second Person of the Trinity, while remaining God, also "was made flesh" (John 1:14). From conception He was fully God and fully man.

1:26 *in the sixth month.* That is, from the time of John's conception. *Nazareth.* See note on Mat 2:23.

1:27 *espoused.* See note on Mat 1:18.

1:28 *Hail. Ave* in the Latin Vulgate (from which comes "Ave Maria").

1:31 *JESUS.* See note on Mat 1:21 for the meaning of this name.

‡1:32 *the Son of the Highest.* This title has two senses: (1) the divine Son of God and (2) the Messiah born in time. His Messiahship is clearly referred to in the following context (vv. 32b–33). *Highest.* A title frequently used of God in both the OT and NT (see vv. 35,76; 6:35; 8:28; Gen 14:19 and note; 2 Sam 22:14). *throne.* Promised in the OT to the Messiah descended from David (2 Sam 7:13,16; Ps 2:6–7; 89:26–27; Is 9:6–7). Jesus also promised his disciples that they would sit upon 12 thrones ruling over the 12 tribes of Israel, in conjunction with His own reign (Mat 19:28). *his father David.* Mary was a descendant of David, as was Joseph (see Mat 1:16); so Jesus could rightly be called a "son" of David.

1:33 *for ever.* See Ps 45:6; Rev 11:15. *of his kingdom there shall be no end.* Although Christ's role as mediator will one day be finished (see 1 Cor 15:24–28), the kingdom of the Father and Son, as one, will never end.

1:34 *How shall this be . . . ?* Mary did not ask in disbelief, as Zacharias did (v. 20). See v. 45.

‡1:35 *holy thing.* Jesus never sinned (2 Cor 5:21; Heb 4:15; 7:26; 1 Pet 2:22; 1 John 3:5). Jesus was born sinless because the supernatural overshadowing of the Holy Spirit prevented sin from being passed to Him from His mother. There are three prominent reasons why the virgin birth (conception) was necessary: (1) to fulfill prophecy (Is 7:14); (2) to be a "sign"; (3) to avoid the curse on Coniah (Jer 22:30).

‡1:36 *thy cousin Elisabeth.* It is not known whether she was a cousin, aunt or other relation. The Greek word has a breadth of meaning, suggesting simply a "relative."

Mary visits Elisabeth

39 ¶ And Mary arose in those days, and went into the hill country with haste, [a]into a city of Juda;

40 And entered into the house of Zacharias, and saluted Elisabeth.

41 And it came to pass *that,* when Elisabeth heard the salutation of Mary, the babe leaped in her womb; and Elisabeth was filled with the Holy Ghost:

42 And she spake out with a loud voice, and said, [a]Blessed *art* thou among women, and blessed *is* the fruit of thy womb.

43 And whence *is* this to me, that the mother of my Lord should come to me?

44 For lo, as soon as the voice of thy salutation sounded in mine ears, the babe leaped in my womb for joy.

45 And blessed *is* she [1]that believed: for there shall be a performance of those *things* which were told her from the Lord.

The song of Mary

46 And Mary said,
[a]My soul doth magnify the Lord,
47 And my spirit hath rejoiced in God my Saviour.
48 For [a]he hath regarded the low estate of his handmaiden:
For behold, from henceforth [b]all generations shall call me blessed.
49 For he *that is* mighty [a]hath done to me great things;
And [b]holy *is* his name.
50 And [a]his mercy *is* on them that fear him
From generation to generation.
51 [a]He hath shewed strength with his arm;
[b]He hath scattered the proud in the imagination of their hearts.
52 [a]He hath put down the mighty from *their* seats,
And exalted them of low degree.
53 [a]He hath filled the hungry with good *things;*
And the rich he hath sent empty away.
54 He hath holpen his servant Israel,
[a]In remembrance of *his* mercy,
55 ([a]As he spake to our fathers),
To Abraham, and to his seed for ever.

56 And Mary abode with her about three months, and returned to her own house.

The birth of John the Baptist

57 ¶ Now Elisabeth's full time came that she should be delivered; and she brought forth a son.

58 And *her* neighbours and her cousins heard how the Lord had shewed great mercy upon her; and they rejoiced with her.

59 And it came to pass, *that* [a]on the eighth day they came to circumcise the child; and they called him Zacharias, after the name of his father.

60 And his mother answered and said, [a]Not *so;* but he shall be called John.

61 And they said unto her, There is none of thy kindred that is called by this name.

62 And they made signs to his father, how he would have him called.

63 And he asked for a writing table, and wrote, saying, His name is John. And they marvelled all.

64 And his mouth was opened immediately, and his tongue *loosed,* and he spake, and praised God.

65 And fear came on all that dwelt round about them: and all these [1]sayings were noised abroad throughout all the hill country of Judea.

66 And all they that heard *them* [a]laid *them* up in their hearts, saying, What *manner of* child shall this be! And [b]the hand of the Lord was with him.

67 And his father Zacharias [a]was filled with the Holy Ghost, and prophesied, saying,

The song of Zacharias

68 [a]Blessed *be* the Lord God of Israel;
For [b]he hath visited and redeemed his people,
69 [a]And hath raised up a horn of salvation for us

1:39 [a]Josh. 21:9
1:42 [a]Judg. 5:24
1:45 [1]Or, *which believed, that there*
1:46 [a]1 Sam. 2:1; Ps. 34:2,3; Hab. 3:18
1:48 [a]1 Sam. 1:11; Ps. 138:6 [b]ch. 11:27
1:49 [a]Ps. 71:19; 126:2,3 [b]Ps. 111:9
1:50 [a]Gen. 17:7; Ex. 20:6; Ps. 103:17
1:51 [a]Ps. 98:1; 118:15; Is. 40:10 [b]Ps. 33:10; 1 Pet. 5:5
1:52 [a]1 Sam. 2:6; Job 5:11; Ps. 113:6
1:53 [a]1 Sam. 2:5; Ps. 34:10
1:54 [a]Ps. 98:3; Jer. 31:3
1:55 [a]Gen. 17:19; Ps. 132:11; Gal. 3:16
1:59 [a]Gen. 17:12; Lev. 12:3
1:60 [a]ver. 13
1:65 [1]Or, *things*
1:66 [a]ch. 2:19 [b]Gen. 39:2; Ps. 80:17; Acts 11:21
1:67 [a]Joel 2:28
1:68 [a]1 Ki. 1:48; Ps. 41:13 [b]Ex. 3:16; Ps. 111:9; ch. 7:16
1:69 [a]Ps. 132:17

1:44 *for joy.* In some mysterious way the Holy Spirit produced this remarkable response in the unborn baby.

1:46–55 One of four hymns preserved in Luke 1–2 (see vv. 68–79; 2:14; 2:29–32 and notes). This hymn of praise is known as the Magnificat because in the Latin Vulgate translation the opening word is *Magnificat,* which means "exalts." This song is like a psalm, and should also be compared with the song of Hannah (1 Sam 2:1–10; see note on 1 Sam 2:1).

1:50 *them that fear him.* Those who revere God and live in harmony with His will.

1:51 *his arm.* A figurative description of God's powerful acts. God does not have a body; He is spirit (John 4:24).

1:53 *hungry.* Both physically and spiritually (Mat 5:6; John 6:35). The coming of God's kingdom will bring changes affecting every area of life.

1:54 *In remembrance of his mercy.* The song ends with an assurance that God will be true to His promises to His people (see Gen 22:16–18).

1:56 *three months.* Mary evidently remained with Elisabeth until John's birth and then returned to her home in Nazareth.

1:59 *called him . . . after the name of his father.* An accepted practice in that day, as seen in Josephus (*Life,* 1).

1:62 *they made signs to his father.* Apparently assuming that since he was mute he was also deaf.

1:63 *a writing table.* Probably a small wooden board covered with wax.

‡1:67 *filled with the Holy Ghost . . . prophesied.* Prophecy not only predicts but also proclaims God's word. Both Zacharias and Elisabeth (vv. 41–45) were enabled by the Holy Spirit to express what otherwise they could not have formulated.

1:68–79 This hymn is called Benedictus ("Blessed be") because the opening word in the Latin Vulgate translation is *Benedictus.* Whereas the Magnificat (see note on 1:46–55) is similar to a psalm, the Benedictus is more like a prophecy.

1:68 *visited and redeemed his people.* Not limited to national security (v. 71), but including moral and spiritual salvation (vv. 75,77).

1:69 *horn.* Here symbolizes strength, as in the horn of an

In the house of his servant David;
70 ([a]As he spake by the mouth of his holy
prophets,
Which have been since the world
began:)
71 That *we* should be saved from our
enemies,
And from the hand of all that hate us;
72 [a]To perform the mercy *promised* to our
fathers,
And to remember his holy covenant;
73 [a]The oath which he sware to our
father Abraham,
74 That *he* would grant unto us, that *we*
being delivered out of the hand of
our enemies
Might [a]serve him without fear,
75 [a]In holiness and righteousness before
him,
All the days of our life.
76 And thou, child, shalt be called the
prophet of the Highest:
For [a]thou shalt go before the face of
the Lord
To prepare his ways;
77 To give knowledge of salvation unto his
people
[a][1]By the remission of their sins,
78 Through the [1]tender mercy of our
God;
Whereby the [2]dayspring from on high
hath visited us,
79 [a]To give light to them that sit in
darkness and *in* the shadow of death,

1:70 [a]Jer. 23:5; Dan. 9:24
1:72 [a]Lev. 26:42; Ezek. 16:60
1:73 [a]Gen. 12:3; Heb. 6:13
1:74 [a]Rom. 6:18; Heb. 9:14
1:75 [a]Jer. 32:39; Eph. 4:24; 2 Thes. 2:13
1:76 [a]Is. 40:3; Mal. 3:1; Mat. 11:10
1:77 [1]Or, *For* [a]Mark 1:4
1:78 [1]Or, *bowels of the mercy* [2]Or, *sunrising,* Mal. 4:2. or, *branch,* Num. 24:17? Is. 11:1
1:79 [a]Is. 9:2; Mat. 4:16
1:80 [a]ch. 2:40 [b]Mat. 3:1
2:1 [1]Or, *enrolled*
2:2 [a]Acts 5:37
2:3 [1]Or, *enrolled*
2:4 [a]1 Sam. 16:1; John 7:42 [b]Mat. 1:16
2:5 [1]Or, *enrolled* [a]Mat. 1:18
2:7 [a]Mat. 1:25
2:8 [1]Or, the *night watches*
2:9 [a]ch. 1:12

To guide our feet into the way of
peace.
80 And [a]the child grew, and waxed strong
in spirit, and [b]was in the deserts till the day of
his shewing unto Israel.

The birth of Jesus

2 And it came to pass in those days, *that*
there went out a decree from Cesar Augustus, that all the world should be [1]taxed.
2 ([a]*And* this taxing was first made when
Cyrenius was governor of Syria.)
3 And all went to be [1]taxed, every one into
his own city.
4 And Joseph also went up from Galilee,
out of the city of Nazareth, into Judea, unto
[a]the city of David, which is called Bethlehem;
([b]because he was of the house and lineage of
David:)
5 To be [1]taxed with Mary [a]his espoused
wife, being great with child.
6 And so it was *that,* while they were
there, the days were accomplished that she
should be delivered.
7 And [a]she brought forth her firstborn son,
and wrapped him in swaddling clothes, and
laid him in a manger; because there was no
room for them in the inn.
8 And there were in the same country
shepherds abiding in the field, keeping [1]watch
over their flock by night.
9 And lo, *the* angel of the Lord came upon
them, and the glory of the Lord shone round
about them: [a]and they were sore afraid.

---

animal (Deut 33:17; Ps 22:21; Mic 4:13). Jesus, the Messiah from the house of David, has the power to save.

1:74 *we being delivered.* No doubt including liberation from all kinds of oppression and bondage as well as deliverance from sin.

‡1:76 *called the prophet of the Highest.* Whereas Jesus will be called "the Son of the Highest" (see v. 32 and note). *prepare his ways.* See note on 3:4.

‡1:78 *the dayspring.* A reference to the coming of the Messiah (see also similar figures in Num 24:17; Is 9:2; 60:1; Mal 4:2). Zacharias not only praised his own son, the "prophet of the Highest" (vv. 76–77), but also gave honor to the coming Messiah (vv. 78–79).

1:79 *them that sit in darkness.* The lost, separated from God (Is 9:1–2; Mat 4:16). *peace.* See note on 2:14.

1:80 *was in the deserts.* John's parents, old at his birth, probably died while he was young, and he apparently grew up in the desert of Judea, which lies between Jerusalem and the Dead Sea. *till . . . his shewing unto Israel.* John's preaching and announcing the coming of the Messiah marked his public appearance. He was about 30 years old when he began his ministry (see note on 3:23).

‡2:1 Luke is the only Gospel writer who relates his narrative to dates of world history. *Cesar Augustus.* The first and (according to many) greatest Roman emperor (31 B.C.–A.D. 14). Having replaced the republic with an imperial form of government, he expanded the empire to include the entire Mediterranean world, established the famed *Pax Romana* ("Roman Peace") and ushered in the golden age of Roman literature and architecture. Augustus (which means "exalted") was a title voted to him by the Roman senate in 27 B.C. *the world.* The Roman world. See map No. 13 at the end of the study Bible. *taxed.* This was a type of census or enrollment used for military service and taxation. Jews, however, were exempt from Roman military service. God used the decree of a pagan emperor to fulfill the prophecy of Mic 5:2.

2:2 *Cyrenius.* This official was possibly in office for two terms, first 6–4 B.C. and then A.D. 6–9. A census is associated with each term. This is the first; Acts 5:37 refers to the second.

2:3 *own city.* Probably the city of their ancestral origin.

2:4 *Nazareth . . . Bethlehem.* Bethlehem, the town where David was born (1 Sam 17:12; 20:6), was at least a three-day trip from Nazareth. *Judea.* The Greco-Roman designation for the southern part of the Holy Land, earlier included in the kingdom of Judah.

2:5 *with Mary.* Mary too was of the house of David and probably was required to enroll. In Syria, the Roman province in which the Holy Land was located, women 12 years of age and older were required to pay a poll tax and therefore to register. *espoused.* See note on Mat 1:18.

2:7 *swaddling clothes.* Strips of cloth were regularly used to wrap a newborn infant. *manger.* The feeding trough of the animals. This is the only indication that Christ was born in a stable. Very early tradition suggests that it was a cave, perhaps used as a stable.

2:8 *abiding in the field.* Does not necessarily mean it was summer, the dry season. The flocks reserved for temple sacrifice were kept in the fields near Bethlehem throughout the year. *keeping watch.* Against thieves and predatory animals.

2:9 *the angel of the Lord.* A designation used throughout the birth narratives (see 1:11; Mat 1:20,24; 2:13,19). The angel in 1:11 is identified as Gabriel (1:19; see 1:26).

10 And the angel said unto them, Fear not: for behold, I bring you good tidings of great joy, [a]which shall be to all people.

11 [a]For unto you is born this day in the city of David [b]a Saviour, [c]which is Christ the Lord.

12 And this *shall be* a sign unto you; Ye shall find *the* babe wrapped in swaddling clothes, lying in a manger.

13 [a]And suddenly there was with the angel a multitude of the heavenly host praising God, and saying,

14 [a]Glory to God in the highest,
And on earth [b]peace,
[c]Good will towards men.

15 ¶ And it came to pass, as the angels were gone away from them into heaven, [1]the shepherds said one to another, Let us now go *even* unto Bethlehem, and see this thing which is come to pass, which the Lord hath made known unto us.

16 And they came with haste, and found Mary, and Joseph, and the babe lying in a manger.

17 And when they had seen *it,* they made known abroad the saying which was told them concerning this child.

18 And all they that heard *it* wondered at those *things* which were told them by the shepherds.

19 [a]But Mary kept all these things, and pondered *them* in her heart.

20 And the shepherds returned, glorifying and praising God for all *the things* that they had heard and seen, as it was told unto them.

Jesus presented in the temple

21 ¶ [a]And when eight days were accomplished for the circumcising of the child, his name was called [b]JESUS, which was *so* named of the angel before he was conceived in the womb.

22 ¶ And when [a]the days of her purification according to the law of Moses were accomplished, they brought him to Jerusalem, to present *him* to the Lord;

23 (As it is written in the law of the Lord, [a]Every male that openeth the womb shall be called holy to the Lord;)

24 And to offer a sacrifice according to [a]that which is said in the law of the Lord, A pair of turtledoves, or two young pigeons.

25 ¶ And behold, there was a man in Jerusalem, whose name *was* Simeon; and the same man *was* just and devout, [a]waiting for the consolation of Israel: and the Holy Ghost was upon him.

26 And it was revealed unto him by the Holy Ghost, that *he* should not [a]see death, before he had seen the Lord's Christ.

27 And he came [a]by the Spirit into the temple: and when the parents brought in the child Jesus, to do for him after the custom of the law,

28 Then took he him *up* in his arms, and blessed God, and said,

29 Lord, [a]now lettest thou thy servant depart
In peace, according to thy word:
30 For mine eyes [a]have seen thy salvation,
31 Which thou hast prepared before the face of all people;
32 [a]A light to lighten the Gentiles, and the glory of thy people Israel.

2:10 [a]Gen. 12:3; Mat. 28:19; Mark 1:15; Col. 1:23
2:11 [a]Is. 9:6 [b]Mat. 1:21 [c]Mat. 1:16; 16:16; Acts 2:36; Phil. 2:11
2:13 [a]Gen. 28:12; Ps. 103:20; 148:2; Dan. 7:10; Heb. 1:14; Rev. 5:11
2:14 [a]ch. 19:38; Eph. 1:6 [b]Is. 57:19; Rom. 5:1; Eph. 2:17; Col. 1:20 [c]John 3:16; Eph. 2:4,7; 2 Thes. 2:16; 1 John 4:9
2:15 [1][Gr. *the men the shepherds*]
2:19 [a]Gen. 37:11; ch. 1:66
2:21 [a]Gen. 17:12; Lev. 12:3; ch. 1:59
2:21 [b]Mat. 1:21,25; ch. 1:31
2:22 [a]Lev. 12:2
2:23 [a]Ex. 13:2; 22:29; Num. 3:13
2:24 [a]Lev. 12:2
2:25 [a]ver. 38; Is. 40:1; Mark 15:43
2:26 [a]Ps. 89:48; Heb. 11:5
2:27 [a]Mat. 4:1
2:29 [a]Gen. 46:30; Phil. 1:23
2:30 [a]Is. 52:10
2:32 [a]Is. 9:2; 42:6; 49:6; 60:1-3; Mat. 4:16; Acts 13:47; 28:28

2:10 *Fear not.* Fear was the common reaction to angelic appearances (see note on 1:13), and encouragement was needed.
2:11 *city of David.* Bethlehem. *Saviour.* Many Jews were looking for a political leader to deliver them from Roman rule, while others were hoping for a savior to deliver them from sickness and physical hardship. But this announcement concerns the Savior who would deliver from sin and death (see Mat 1:21; John 4:42). *Christ.* Or "Messiah." "The Christ" (Greek) and "the Messiah" (Hebrew) both mean "the Anointed One." *the Lord.* A designation originally reserved for God but later applied to the Messiah as well (see Acts 2:36; Phil 2:11).
‡2:14 See note on 1:46–55. This brief hymn is called the Gloria in Excelsis Deo, from the first words of the Latin Vulgate translation (meaning "Glory to God in the Highest"). The angels recognized the glory and majesty of God by giving praise to Him. *in the highest.* A reference to heaven, where God dwells (cf. Mat 6:9). *peace, Good will.* Peace is not assured to all, but only to those pleasing to God—the objects of His good pleasure (see Luke's use of the words "well pleased," "good," and "good pleasure" elsewhere: 3:22; 10:21; 12:32). The Roman world was experiencing the *Pax Romana* ("Roman Peace"), marked by external tranquillity. But the angels proclaimed a deeper, more lasting peace than that—a peace of mind and soul made possible by the Savior (v. 11). Peace with God is received by faith in Christ (Rom 5:1), and it is believers "with whom He is pleased." The Davidic Messiah was called "Prince of Peace" (Is 9:6), and Christ promised peace to His disciples (John 14:27). But Christ also brought conflict (the "sword"; see Mat 10:34–36; cf. Luke 12:49), for peace with God involves opposition to Satan and his work (Jas 4:4).
2:20 *praising God.* Terms of praise and giving glory to God often used by Luke (1:64; 2:13,28; 5:25–26; 7:16; 13:13; 17:15,18; 18:43; 19:37; 23:47; 24:53).
2:22 *her purification.* Following the birth of a son, the mother had to wait 40 days before going to the temple to offer sacrifice for her purification. If she could not afford a lamb and a pigeon (or dove), then two pigeons (or doves) would be acceptable (Lev 12:2–8; cf. Lev 5:11). *to Jerusalem.* The distance from Bethlehem to Jerusalem was only about six miles. *present him to the Lord.* The firstborn of both man and animal were to be dedicated to the Lord (see v. 23; Ex 13:12–13). The animals were sacrificed, but the human beings were to serve God throughout their lives. The Levites actually served in the place of all the firstborn males in Israel (see Num 3:11–13; 8:17–18).
2:25 *the consolation of Israel.* The comfort the Messiah would bring to His people at His coming (see vv. 26,38; 23:51; 24:21; Is 40:1–2; Mat 5:4). *the Holy Ghost was upon him.* Not in the way common to all believers after Pentecost. Simeon was given a special insight by the Spirit so that he would recognize the "Christ."
2:29–32 See note on 1:46–55. This hymn of Simeon has been called the Nunc Dimittis, from the first words of the Latin Vulgate translation, meaning "Now . . . You are releasing."
2:31 *all people.* As a Gentile himself, Luke was careful to emphasize the truth that salvation was offered to the Gentiles (v. 32) as well as to Jews.

33 ¶ And Joseph and his mother marvelled
at those *things* which were spoken of him.
34 And Simeon blessed them, and said
unto Mary his mother, Behold, this *child* is set
for the [a]fall and rising again of many in Israel;
and for [b]a sign which shall be spoken against;
35 (Yea, [a]a sword shall pierce through thy
own soul also,) that the thoughts of many
hearts may be revealed.
36 ¶ And there was *one* Anna, a prophetess, the daughter of Phanuel, of the tribe of
Aser: she was of a great age, and had lived
with a husband seven years from her virginity;
37 And she *was* a widow of about fourscore and four years, which departed not from
the temple, but served *God* with fastings and
prayers [a]night and day.
38 And she coming in that instant gave
thanks *likewise* unto the Lord, and spake of
him to all them that [a]looked for redemption in
[1]Jerusalem.
39 And when they had performed all
things according to the law of the Lord, they
returned into Galilee, to their own city Nazareth.
40 [a]And the child grew, and waxed strong
in spirit, filled with wisdom: and the grace of
God was upon him.

The boy Jesus in the temple

41 ¶ Now his parents went to Jerusalem
[a]every year at the feast of the passover.
42 And when he was twelve years old,
they went up to Jerusalem after the custom of
the feast.
43 And when they had fulfilled the days, as
they returned, the child Jesus tarried behind
in Jerusalem; and Joseph and his mother knew
not *of it.*
44 But they, supposing him to have been in
the company, went a day's journey; and they
sought him among *their* kinsfolk and acquaintance.
45 And when they found him not, they
turned back again to Jerusalem, seeking him.
46 And it came to pass, *that* after three
days they found him in the temple, sitting in
the midst of the doctors, both hearing them,
and asking them *questions.*
47 And [a]all that heard him were astonished at his understanding and answers.
48 And when they saw him, they were
amazed: and his mother said unto him, Son,
why hast thou thus dealt with us? behold, thy
father and I have sought thee sorrowing.
49 And he said unto them, How *is it* that
ye sought me? wist ye not that I must be about
[a]my Father's *business?*
50 And [a]they understood not the saying
which he spake unto them.
51 And he went down with them, and
came to Nazareth, and was subject unto them:
but his mother [a]kept all these sayings in her
heart.
52 And Jesus [a]increased in wisdom and
[1]stature, and in favour with God and man.

John the Baptist

3 Now in the fifteenth year of the reign of
Tiberius Cesar, Pontius Pilate being governor of Judea, and Herod being tetrarch of
Galilee, and his brother Philip tetrarch of Iturea and of the region of Trachonitis, and Lysanias the tetrarch of Abilene,

2:34 [a]Is. 8:14; Hos. 14:9; Mat. 21:44; Rom. 9:32; 1 Cor. 1:23; 2 Cor. 2:16; 1 Pet. 2:7,8 [b]Acts 28:22
2:35 [a]Ps. 42:10; John 19:25
2:37 [a]Acts 26:7; 1 Tim. 5:5
2:38 [1]Or, *Israel* [a]ver. 25; Mark 15:43; ch. 24:21
2:40 [a]ver. 52; ch. 1:80
2:41 [a]Ex. 23:15,17; 34:23; Deut. 16:1,16
2:47 [a]Mat. 7:28; Mark 1:22; ch. 4:22,32; John 7:15,46
2:49 [a]John 2:16
2:50 [a]ch. 9:45; 18:34
2:51 [a]ver. 19; Dan. 7:28
2:52 [1]Or, *age* [a]ver. 40; 1 Sam. 2:26

‡2:33 *Joseph.* Luke, aware of the virgin birth of Jesus (1:26–35), does not refer to Joseph as Jesus' human father. Naturally, he was Jesus' legal father.
2:34 *fall and rising again of many in Israel.* Christ raises up those who believe in Him, but is a stumbling block for those who disbelieve (see 20:17–18; 1 Cor 1:23; 1 Pet 2:6–8). *sign which shall be spoken against.* Christ points to the Father and His love for sinners, and those who oppose Him also oppose the Father.
‡2:35 *sword shall pierce through thy own soul also.* The word "also" indicates that Mary, as well as Jesus, would suffer deep anguish—the first reference in this Gospel to Christ's suffering and death.
2:36 *Anna.* Same name as OT Hannah (1 Sam 1:2), which means "gracious." Anna praised God for the child Jesus as Hannah had praised God for the child Samuel (1 Sam 2:1–10). *prophetess.* Other prophetesses were Miriam (Ex 15:20), Deborah (Judg 4:4), Huldah (2 Ki 22:14) and the daughters of Philip (Acts 21:9).
2:37 *departed not from the temple.* Herod's temple was quite large and included rooms for various uses, and Anna may have been allowed to live in one of them. This statement, however, probably means that she spent her waking hours attending and worshiping in the temple.
2:38 *Jerusalem.* The holy city of God's chosen people (Is 40:2; 52:9); here it stands for Israel as a whole.
2:39 *they returned into Galilee.* Luke does not mention the coming of the wise men, the danger from Herod, or the flight to and return from Egypt (cf. Mat 2:1–23).
2:41 *feast of the passover.* Annual attendance at three feasts by all adult males (normally accompanied by their families) was commanded in the law: passover, Pentecost and tabernacles (see notes on Ex 23:14–17; Deut 16:16). Distance prevented many from attending all three, but most Jews tried to be at passover.
2:42 *twelve.* At age 12 boys began preparing to take their places in the religious community the following year.
2:46 *three days.* One day traveling away from Jerusalem, a second traveling back and a third looking for Him. *the doctors.* The rabbis, experts in Judaism.
‡2:49 *about my Father's business.* Jesus pointed to His personal duty to His Father in heaven. He contrasted His "my Father" with Mary's "thy father" (v. 48). At 12 years of age He was aware of His unique relationship to God. But He was also obedient to His earthly parents (v. 51).
‡2:52 Luke appears to have borrowed the words of 1 Sam 2:26. *And Jesus increased.* Although Jesus was God, there is no indication that He had all knowledge and wisdom from birth. He seems to have matured like any other boy as to the regular elements of His human nature.
3:1–2 Historians frequently dated an event by giving the year of the ruler's reign in which the event happened.
3:1 *fifteenth year.* Several possible dates could be indicated by this description, but the date A.D. 25–26 (Tiberius had authority in the provinces beginning in A.D. 11) best fits the chronology of the life of Christ. The other rulers named do not help pinpoint the beginning of John's ministry, but only serve to indicate the general historical period. *Pontius Pilate.* The Roman prefect

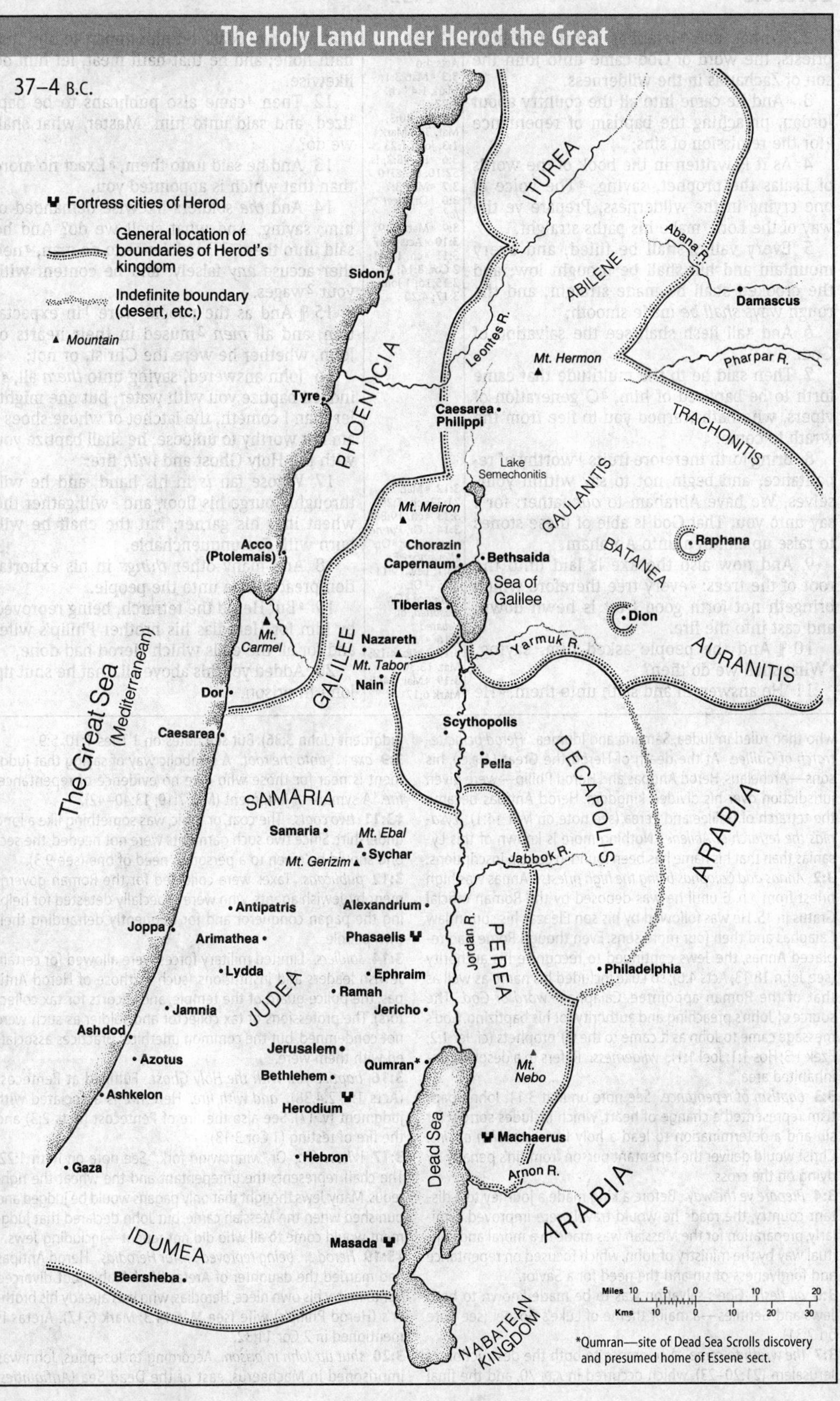

The Holy Land under Herod the Great
37–4 B.C.
Fortress cities of Herod
General location of boundaries of Herod's kingdom
Indefinite boundary (desert, etc.)
Mountain
The Great Sea (Mediterranean)
PHOENICIA
ITUREA
ABILENE
Abana R.
Damascus
Sidon
Leontes R.
Mt. Hermon
Pharpar R.
TRACHONITIS
Tyre
Caesarea Philippi
Lake Semechonitis
GAULANITIS
Mt. Meiron
BATANEA
Raphana
Acco (Ptolemais)
Chorazin
Capernaum
Bethsaida
Sea of Galilee
Tiberias
Dion
Mt. Carmel
Nazareth
Mt. Tabor
Nain
Yarmuk R.
AURANITIS
GALILEE
Dor
Scythopolis
Caesarea
Pella
DECAPOLIS
SAMARIA
ARABIA
Samaria
Mt. Ebal
Mt. Gerizim
Sychar
Jabbok R.
Antipatris
Alexandrium
Joppa
Arimathea
Phasaelis
Jordan R.
PEREA
Lydda
Ephraim
Philadelphia
Ramah
JUDEA
Jamnia
Jericho
Ashdod
Jerusalem
Azotus
Qumran*
Mt. Nebo
Bethlehem
Ashkelon
Herodium
Machaerus
Dead Sea
Hebron
Gaza
Arnon R.
ARABIA
IDUMEA
Masada
Beersheba
Miles 10 5 0 10 20
Kms 10 0 10 20 30
NABATEAN KINGDOM
*Qumran—site of Dead Sea Scrolls discovery and presumed home of Essene sect.

2 [a]Annas and Caiaphas being the high priests, the word of God came unto John the son of Zacharias in the wilderness.

3 [a]And he came into all the country about Jordan, preaching the baptism of repentance [b]for the remission of sins;

4 As it is written in the book of the words of Esaias the prophet, saying, [a]The voice of one crying in the wilderness, Prepare ye the way of the Lord, make his paths straight.

5 Every valley shall be filled, and every mountain and hill shall be brought low; and the crooked shall be made straight, and the rough ways *shall be* made smooth;

6 And [a]all flesh shall see the salvation of God.

7 Then said he to the multitude that came forth to be baptized of him, [a]O generation of vipers, who hath warned you to flee from the wrath to come?

8 Bring forth therefore fruits [1]worthy of repentance, and begin not to say within yourselves, We have Abraham to *our* father: for I say unto you, That God is able of these stones to raise up children unto Abraham.

9 And now also the axe is laid unto the root of the trees: [a]every tree therefore which bringeth not forth good fruit is hewn down, and cast into the fire.

10 ¶ And the people asked him, saying, [a]What shall we do then?

11 He answereth and saith unto them, [a]He that hath two coats, let him impart to him that hath none; and he that hath meat, let him do likewise.

12 Then [a]came also publicans to be baptized, and said unto him, Master, what shall we do?

13 And he said unto them, [a]Exact no more than that which is appointed you.

14 And *the* soldiers likewise demanded of him, saying, And what shall we do? And he said unto them, [1]Do violence to no man, [a]neither accuse *any* falsely; and be content with your [2]wages.

15 ¶ And as the people were [1]in expectation, and all *men* [2]mused in their hearts of John, whether he were the Christ, or not;

16 John answered, saying unto *them* all, [a]I indeed baptize you with water; but one mightier than I cometh, the latchet of whose shoes I am not worthy to unloose: he shall baptize you with the Holy Ghost and *with* fire:

17 Whose fan *is* in his hand, and he will throughly purge his floor, and [a]will gather the wheat into his garner; but the chaff he will burn with fire unquenchable.

18 And many other *things* in his exhortation preached he unto the people.

19 [a]But Herod the tetrarch, being reproved by him for Herodias his brother Philip's wife, and for all the evils which Herod had done,

20 Added yet this above all, that he shut up John in prison.

3:2 [a]John 11:49,51; 18:13; Acts 4:6
3:3 [a]Mat. 3:1; Mark 1:4 [b]ch. 1:77
3:4 [a]Is. 40:3; Mat. 3:3; Mark 1:3; John 1:23
3:6 [a]Ps. 98:2; Is. 52:10; ch. 2:10
3:7 [a]Mat. 3:7
3:8 [1]Or, *meet for*
3:9 [a]Mat. 7:19
3:10 [a]Acts 2:37
3:11 [a]ch. 11:41; 2 Cor. 8:14; Jas. 2:15,16; 1 John 3:17; 4:20
3:12 [a]Mat. 21:32; ch. 7:29
3:13 [a]ch. 19:8
3:14 [1]Or, *Put no man in fear* [2]Or, *allowance* [a]Ex. 23:1; Lev. 19:11
3:15 [1]Or, *in suspense* [2]Or, *reasoned,* or, *debated*
3:16 [a]Mat. 3:11
3:17 [a]Mic. 4:12; Mat. 13:30
3:19 [a]Mat. 14:3; Mark 6:17

who then ruled in Judea, Samaria and Idumea. *Herod being tetrarch of Galilee.* At the death of Herod the Great (4 B.C.), his sons—Archelaus, Herod Antipas and Herod Philip—were given jurisdiction over his divided kingdom. Herod Antipas became the tetrarch of Galilee and Perea (see note on Mat 14:1). *Lysanias the tetrarch of Abilene.* Nothing more is known of this Lysanias than that his name has been found in certain inscriptions.

3:2 *Annas and Caiaphas being the high priests.* Annas was high priest from A.D. 6 until he was deposed by the Roman official Gratus in 15. He was followed by his son Eleazar, his son-in-law Caiaphas and then four more sons. Even though Rome had replaced Annas, the Jews continued to recognize his authority (see John 18:13; Acts 4:6); so Luke included his name as well as that of the Roman appointee, Caiaphas. *word of God.* The source of John's preaching and authority for his baptizing. God's message came to John as it came to the OT prophets (cf. Jer 1:2; Ezek 1:3; Hos 1:1; Joel 1:1). *wilderness.* Refers to a desolate, uninhabited area.

3:3 *baptism of repentance.* See note on Mat 3:11. John's baptism represented a change of heart, which includes sorrow for sin and a determination to lead a holy life. *remission of sins.* Christ would deliver the repentant person from sin's penalty by dying on the cross.

3:4 *Prepare ye the way.* Before a king made a journey to a distant country, the roads he would travel were improved. Similarly, preparation for the Messiah was made in a moral and spiritual way by the ministry of John, which focused on repentance and forgiveness of sin and the need for a Savior.

3:6 *all flesh.* God's salvation was to be made known to both Jews and Gentiles—a major theme of Luke's Gospel (see note on 2:31).

3:7 *the wrath to come.* A reference to both the destruction of Jerusalem (21:20–23), which occurred in A.D. 70, and the final judgment (John 3:36). But see notes on 1 Thes 1:10; 5:9.

3:9 *axe . . . unto the root.* A symbolic way of saying that judgment is near for those who give no evidence of repentance. *fire.* A symbol of judgment (Mat 7:19; 13:40–42).

‡3:11 *two coats.* The coat, or tunic, was something like a long undershirt. Since two such garments were not needed, the second should be given to a person in need of one (see 9:3).

3:12 *publicans.* Taxes were collected for the Roman government by Jewish agents, who were especially detested for helping the pagan conqueror and for frequently defrauding their own people.

3:14 *soldiers.* Limited military forces were allowed for certain Jewish leaders and institutions (such as those of Herod Antipas, the police guard of the temple, and escorts for tax collectors). The professions of tax collector and soldier as such were not condemned, but the common unethical practices associated with them were.

3:16 *baptize you with the Holy Ghost.* Fulfilled at Pentecost (Acts 1:5; 2:4,38). *and with fire.* Here fire is associated with judgment (v. 17). See also the fire of Pentecost (Acts 2:3) and the fire of testing (1 Cor 3:13).

3:17 *Whose fan.* Or "winnowing fork." See note on Ruth 1:22. The chaff represents the unrepentant and the wheat the righteous. Many Jews thought that only pagans would be judged and punished when the Messiah came, but John declared that judgment would come to all who did not repent—including Jews.

‡3:19 *Herod . . . being reproved . . . for Herodias.* Herod Antipas had married the daughter of Aretas IV of Arabia, but divorced her to marry his own niece, Herodias, who was already his brother's (Herod Philip's) wife (see Mat 14:3; Mark 6:17). Aretas is mentioned in 2 Cor 11:32.

3:20 *shut up John in prison.* According to Josephus, John was imprisoned in Machaerus, east of the Dead Sea (*Antiquities,*

The baptism of Jesus

21 ¶ Now when all the people were baptized, [a]it came to pass, that *Jesus also being
baptized, and praying, the heaven was opened,
22 And the Holy Ghost descended in a bodily shape like a dove upon him, and a voice
came from heaven, which said, Thou art my
beloved Son; in thee I am well pleased.

The genealogy of Jesus

23 ¶ And Jesus himself began *to be* [a]about
thirty years of age, being (as was supposed)
[b]the son of Joseph, which was *the son* of Heli,
24 Which was *the son* of Matthat, which
was *the son* of Levi, which was *the son* of
Melchi, which was *the son* of Janna, which
was *the son* of Joseph,
25 Which was *the son* of Mattathias,
which was *the son* of Amos, which was *the
son* of Naum, which was *the son* of Esli, which
was *the son* of Nagge,
26 Which was *the son* of Maath, which
was *the son* of Mattathias, which was *the son*
of Semei, which was *the son* of Joseph, which
was *the son* of Juda,
27 Which was *the son* of Joanna, which
was *the son* of Rhesa, which was *the son* of
Zorobabel, which was *the son* of Salathiel,
which was *the son* of Neri,
28 Which was *the son* of Melchi, which
was *the son* of Addi, which was *the son* of Co-
sam, which was *the son* of Elmodam, which
was *the son* of Er,
29 Which was *the son* of Jose, which was
the son of Eliezer, which was *the son* of Jorim,
which was *the son* of Matthat, which was *the
son* of Levi,
30 Which was *the son* of Simeon, which
was *the son* of Juda, which was *the son* of Joseph, which was *the son* of Jonan, which was
the son of Eliakim,
31 Which was *the son* of Melea, which
was *the son* of Menan, which was *the son* of
Mattatha, which was *the son* of [a]Nathan,
[b]which was *the son* of David,
32 [a]Which was *the son* of Jesse, which was
the son of Obed, which was *the son* of Booz,
which was *the son* of Salmon, which was *the
son* of Naasson,
33 Which was *the son* of Aminadab, which
was *the son* of Aram, which was *the son* of Esrom, which was *the son* of Phares, which was
the son of Juda,
34 Which was *the son* of Jacob, which was
the son of Isaac, which was *the son* of Abraham, [a]which was *the son* of Thara, which was
the son of Nachor,
35 Which was *the son* of Saruch, which
was *the son* of Ragau, which was *the son* of
Phalec, which was *the son* of Heber, which
was *the son* of Sala,
36 [a]Which was *the son* of Cainan, which
was *the son* of Arphaxad, [b]which was *the son*
of Sem, which was *the son* of Noe, which was
the son of Lamech,
37 Which was *the son* of Mathusala, which
was *the son* of Enoch, which was *the son* of Jared, which was *the son* of Maleleel, which was
the son of Cainan,
38 Which was *the son* of Enos, which was
the son of Seth, which was *the son* of Adam,
[a]which was *the son* of God.

The temptation in the wilderness

4 And [a]Jesus being full of the Holy Ghost
returned from Jordan, and [b]was led by
the Spirit into the wilderness,
2 Being forty days tempted of the devil.

3:21 [a]Mat. 3:13; John 1:32
3:23 [a]See Num. 4:3,35,39,43,47 [b]Mat. 13:55; John 6:42
3:31 [a]Zech. 12:12 [b]2 Sam. 5:14; 1 Chr. 3:5
3:32 [a]Ruth 4:18; 1 Chr. 2:10
3:34 [a]Gen. 11:24,26
3:36 [a]See Gen. 11:12 [b]Gen. 5:6; 11:10
3:38 [a]Gen. 5:12
4:1 [a]Mat. 4:1; Mark 1:12 [b]ver. 14; ch. 2:27

18.5.2). This did not occur until sometime after the beginning of Jesus' ministry (see John 3:22–24), but Luke mentions it here in order to conclude his section on John's ministry before beginning his account of the beginning of Jesus' ministry (see also Mat 4:12; Mark 1:14). He later briefly alludes to John's death (9:7–9).

3:21 *being baptized.* See note on Mat 3:15. *and praying.* Only Luke notes Jesus' praying at the time of His baptism. Jesus in prayer is one of the special themes of Luke (see 5:16; 6:12; 9:18,28–29; 11:1; 22:32,41; 23:34,46).

3:22 *Holy Ghost descended.* Luke specifies "in a bodily shape." To John, it was a sign (see John 1:32–34; see also note on Mark 1:10). *Thou art my beloved Son.* See Ps 2:7; Is 42:1; Heb 1:5. Two other times the Gospel writers record the declarations of a voice from heaven addressing Jesus: (1) on the mount of Transfiguration (9:35), and (2) in the temple area during Jesus' final week (John 12:28).

‡3:23–38 There are several differences between Luke's genealogy and Matthew's (1:2–16). Matthew begins with Abraham (the father of the Jewish people), while Luke traces the line in the reverse order and goes all the way back to Adam, showing Jesus' relationship to the whole human race (see note on 2:31). From Abraham to David, the genealogies of Matthew and Luke are almost the same, but from David on they are different. Some scholars suggest that this is because Matthew traces the legal descent of the house of David using only heirs to the throne, while Luke traces the complete line of Joseph to David. A more likely explanation, however, is that Matthew follows the line of Joseph (Jesus' legal father), while Luke emphasizes that of Mary (Jesus' blood relative). Although tracing a genealogy through the mother's side was unusual, so was the virgin birth. Luke's explanation here that Jesus was the son of Joseph, "as was supposed" (v. 23), brings to mind his explicit virgin birth statement (1:34–35) and suggests the importance of the role of Mary in Jesus' genealogy.

3:23 *about thirty years of age.* Luke, a historian, relates the beginning of Jesus' public ministry both to world history (see vv. 1–2) and to the rest of Jesus' life. Thirty was the age when a Levite undertook his service (Num 4:47) and when a man was considered mature. *as was supposed.* Luke had already affirmed the virgin birth (1:34–35), and here makes clear again that Joseph was not Jesus' physical father.

‡3:36 *Cainan.* The mention of Cainan here, and not in Gen 10:24, demonstrates that the earlier genealogy was not meant to be complete. Thus, not too much should be made of adding up all the years given in the earlier genealogies.

‡4:1 *full of the Holy Ghost.* Luke emphasizes the Holy Spirit not only in his Gospel (1:35,41,67; 2:25–27; 3:16,22; 4:14,18; 10:21; 11:13; 12:10,12) but also in Acts, where the Holy Spirit is mentioned 55 times. *into the wilderness.* The desert of Judea (see Mat 3:1; see also note on 1:80).

4:2 *Being forty days tempted.* See notes on Mat 4:1–11; Heb

And [a]in those days he did eat nothing: and
when they were ended, he afterward hungered.
3 And the devil said unto him, If thou be
the Son of God, command this stone that it be
made bread.
4 And Jesus answered him, saying, [a]It is
written, That man shall not live by bread
alone, but by every word of God.
5 And the devil, taking him up into a high
mountain, shewed unto him all the kingdoms
of the world in a moment of time.
6 And the devil said unto him, All this
power will I give thee, and the glory of them:
for [a]*that* is delivered unto me; and to whomsoever I will I give it.
7 If thou therefore wilt [1]worship me, all
shall be thine.
8 And Jesus answered and said unto him,
Get thee behind me, Satan: for [a]it is written,
Thou shalt worship the Lord thy God, and him
only shalt thou serve.
9 [a]And he brought him to Jerusalem, and
set him on a pinnacle of the temple, and said
unto him, If thou be the Son of God, cast thyself down from hence:
10 For [a]it is written, He shall give his angels charge over thee, to keep thee:
11 And in *their* hands they shall bear thee
up, lest at any time thou dash thy foot against
a stone.
12 And Jesus answering said unto him, [a]It
is said, Thou shalt not tempt the Lord thy God.

4:2 [a]Ex. 34:28; 1 Ki. 19:8
4:4 [a]Deut. 8:3
4:6 [a]John 12:31; 14:30; Rev. 13:2,7
4:7 [1]Or, *fall down before me*
4:8 [a]Deut. 6:13; 10:20
4:9 [a]Mat. 4:5
4:10 [a]Ps. 91:11
4:12 [a]Deut. 6:16
4:13 [a]John 14:30; Heb. 4:15
4:14 [a]Mat. 4:12; John 4:43 [b]ver. 1 [c]Acts 10:37
4:16 [a]Mat. 2:23; 13:54; Mark 6:1 [b]Acts 13:14; 17:2
4:18 [a]Is. 61:1

13 And when the devil had ended all the
temptation, he departed from him [a]for a season.

Jesus rejected at Nazareth

14 ¶ [a]And Jesus returned [b]in the power of
the Spirit into [c]Galilee: and there went out a
fame of him through all the region round
about.
15 And he taught in their synagogues, being glorified of all.
16 And he came to [a]Nazareth, where he
had been brought up: and, as his custom was,
[b]he went into the synagogue on the sabbath
day, and stood up for to read.
17 And there was delivered unto him the
book of the prophet Esaias. And when he had
opened the book, he found the place where it
was written,
18 [a]The Spirit of the Lord *is* upon me, because he hath anointed me to preach the
gospel to the poor; he hath sent me to heal the
broken-hearted, to preach deliverance to the
captives, and recovering of sight to the blind,
to set at liberty *them that are* bruised,
19 To preach the acceptable year of the
Lord.
20 And he closed the book, and he gave *it*
again to the minister, and sat down. And the
eyes of all *them that were* in the synagogue
were fastened on him.
21 And he began to say unto them, This
day is this scripture fulfilled in your ears.

2:18; 4:15. Luke states that Jesus was tempted for the 40 days He was fasting, and the three specific temptations recounted in Matthew and Luke seem to have occurred at the close of this period—when Jesus' hunger was greatest and His resistance lowest. The sequence of the second and third temptations differs in Matthew and Luke. Matthew probably followed the chronological order, since at the end of the mountain temptation (Matthew's third) Jesus told Satan to leave (Mat 4:10). To emphasize a certain point the Gospel writers often bring various events together, not intending to give chronological sequence. Perhaps Luke's focus here is geographical, as he concludes with Jesus in Jerusalem.

4:3 *If thou be.* See note on Mat 4:3. *command this stone that it be made bread.* The devil always makes his temptations seem attractive.

‡4:4 *It is written.* Three times Jesus meets Satan's temptations with Scripture. Only God's Word can provide the strength needed to overcome Satan's wiles. All of Jesus' quotes were from Deuteronomy.

4:7 *worship me.* The devil was tempting Jesus to avoid the sufferings of the cross, which He came specifically to endure (Mark 10:45). The temptation offered an easy shortcut to world dominion.

4:9 *a pinnacle of the temple.* Either the southeast corner of the temple colonnade, from which there was a drop of some 100 feet to the Kidron Valley below, or the pinnacle of the temple proper. *If thou be.* See note on Mat 4:3. *cast thyself down.* Satan was tempting Jesus to test God's faithfulness and to attract public attention dramatically.

4:10 *For it is written.* This time Satan also quoted Scripture, though he misused Ps 91:11–12.

4:12 Jesus answered with Scripture from Deuteronomy (6:16) as He did on the first (Deut 8:3) and second (Deut 6:13) temptations.

4:13 *he departed from him for a season.* Satan continued his testing throughout Jesus' ministry (see Mark 8:33), culminating in the supreme test at Gethsemane.

4:14 *in the power of the Spirit.* See note on v. 1.

4:15 *he taught in their synagogues.* See note on Mark 1:21.

4:16 *he came to Nazareth.* Not at the start of His ministry but perhaps almost a year later (v. 23 presupposes that Jesus had already been ministering). Probably all the events of John 1:19–4:42 occurred between Luke 4:13 and 4:14. *as his custom was.* Jesus' custom of regular worship sets an example for all His followers. *to read.* Jesus probably read from Isaiah in Hebrew, and then He or someone else paraphrased it in Aramaic, one of the other common languages of the day.

4:17 *the book of the prophet Esaias.* The books of the OT were written on scrolls, kept in a special place in the synagogue and handed to the reader by a special attendant. The passage Jesus read about the Messiah (Is 61:1–2) may have been one He chose to read, or it may have been the assigned passage for the day.

4:18 This verse tells of the Messiah's ministry of preaching and healing—to meet every human need. *he hath anointed me.* Not with literal oil (see Ex 30:22–31), but with the Holy Spirit.

4:19 *the acceptable year of the Lord.* Not a calendar year, but the period when salvation would be proclaimed—the Messianic age. This quotation from Is 61:1–2 alludes to the year of jubile (Lev 25:8–55), when once every 50 years slaves were freed, debts were canceled and ancestral property was returned to the original family. Isaiah predicted primarily the liberation of Israel from the future Babylonian captivity, but Jesus proclaimed liberation from sin and all its consequences.

4:20 *sat down.* It was customary to stand while reading Scrip-

22 And all bare him witness, and [a]wondered at the gracious words which proceeded out of his mouth. And they said, [b]Is not this Joseph's son?

23 And he said unto them, Ye will surely say unto me this proverb, Physician, heal thyself: whatsoever we have heard done in [a]Capernaum, do also here in [b]thy country.

24 And he said, Verily I say unto you, No [a]prophet is accepted in his own country.

25 But I tell you of a truth, [a]many widows were in Israel in the days of Elias, when the heaven was shut up three years and six months, when great famine was throughout all the land;

26 But unto none of them was Elias sent, save unto Sarepta, *a city* of Sidon, unto a woman *that was* a widow.

27 [a]And many lepers were in Israel in the time of Eliseus the prophet; and none of them was cleansed, saving Naaman the Syrian.

28 And all *they* in the synagogue, when they heard these *things,* were filled with wrath,

29 And rose up, and thrust him out of the city, and led him unto the [1]brow of the hill whereon their city was built, that *they* might cast him down headlong.

30 But he [a]passing through the midst of them went *his way,*

4:22 [a]Ps. 45:2; Mat. 13:54; Mark 6:2; ch. 2:47 [b]John 6:42
4:23 [a]Mat. 4:13; 11:23 [b]Mat. 13:54; Mark 6:1
4:24 [a]Mat. 13:57; Mark 6:4; John 4:44
4:25 [a]1 Ki. 17:9; 18:1; Jas. 5:17
4:27 [a]2 Ki. 5:14
4:29 [1]Or, *edge*
4:30 [a]John 8:59; 10:39

ture (v. 16) but to sit while teaching (see Mat 5:1; 26:55; John 8:2; Acts 16:13).

4:23 *Capernaum.* See note on Mat 4:13. *thy country.* Nazareth. Although Jesus was born in Bethlehem, He was brought up in Nazareth, in Galilee (1:26; 2:39,51; Mat 2:23).

4:26–27 Mention of Jesus' reference to God's helping two non-Israelites (1 Ki 17:1–15; 2 Ki 5:1–14) reflects Luke's special concern for the Gentiles. Jesus' point was that when Israel rejected God's messenger of redemption, God sent him to the Gentiles—and so it will be again if they refuse to accept Jesus (see 10:13–15; Rom 9–11).

4:26 *Sidon.* One of the oldest Phoenician cities, 20 miles north of Tyre. Jesus later healed a Gentile woman's daughter in this region (Mat 15:21–28).

4:28 *filled with wrath.* Because of Jesus' inclusion of Gentiles as recipients of God's blessings.

4:30 *passing through the midst of them.* Luke does not explain whether the escape was miraculous or simply the result of

Capernaum Synagogue

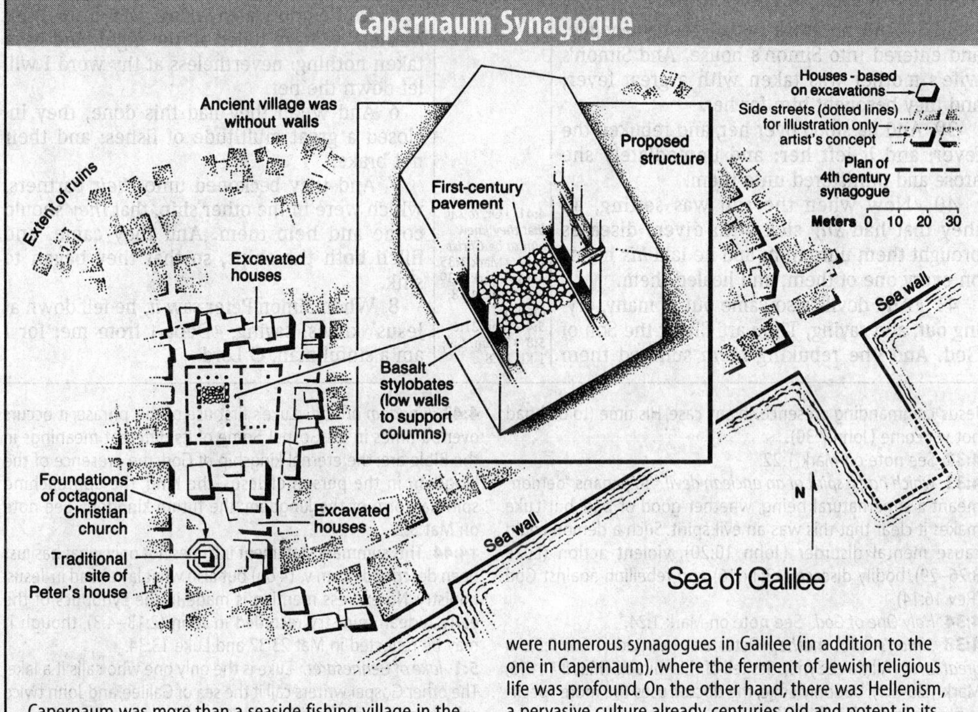

Capernaum was more than a seaside fishing village in the days of Jesus. It was the place that Christ chose to be the center of His ministry to the entire region of Galilee, and it possessed ideal characteristics as a point of dissemination for the gospel.

There were good reasons for this. The town itself was named *Kephar Nahum,* "village of (perhaps the prophet) Nahum," and was the centerpiece of a densely populated region having a bicultural flavor. On the one hand, there were numerous synagogues in Galilee (in addition to the one in Capernaum), where the ferment of Jewish religious life was profound. On the other hand, there was Hellenism, a pervasive culture already centuries old and potent in its paganism—a life-style that influenced manners, dress, architecture and political institutions as well.

Recent archaeological work at Capernaum has revealed a section of the pavement of a first-century synagogue below the still-existing ruins of the fourth-century one on the site. A private house later made into a church and a place of pilgrimage has yielded some evidence that may link it to the site of Simon Peter's house (Luke 4:38).

31 And [a]came down to Capernaum, a city of Galilee, and taught them on the sabbath days.

32 And they were astonished at his doctrine: [a]for his word was with power.

The unclean spirit cast out

33 ¶ [a]And in the synagogue there was a man, which had a spirit of an unclean devil, and cried out with a loud voice,

34 Saying, [1]Let *us* alone; what have we to do with thee, *thou* Jesus of Nazareth? art thou come to destroy us? [a]I know thee who thou art, [b]the Holy One of God.

35 And Jesus rebuked him, saying, Hold thy peace, and come out of him. And when the devil had thrown him in the midst, he came out of him, and hurt him not.

36 And they were all amazed, and spake among themselves, saying, What a word *is* this! for with authority and power he commandeth the unclean spirits, and they come out.

37 And the fame of him went out into every place of the country round about.

The sick healed; devils cast out

38 ¶ [a]And he arose out of the synagogue, and entered into Simon's house. And Simon's wife's mother was taken with a great fever; and they besought him for her.

39 And he stood over her, and rebuked the fever; and it left her: and immediately she arose and ministered unto them.

40 [a]Now when the sun was setting, all they that had *any* sick with divers diseases brought them unto him; and he laid *his* hands on every one of them, and healed them.

41 [a]And devils also came out of many, crying out, and saying, Thou art Christ the Son of God. And [b]he rebuking *them* suffered them not [1]to speak: for they knew that he was Christ.

42 ¶ [a]And when it was day, he departed and went into a desert place: and the people sought him, and came unto him, and stayed him, that *he* should not depart from them.

43 And he said unto them, I must preach the kingdom of God to other cities also: for therefore am I sent.

44 [a]And he preached in the synagogues of Galilee.

The call of the first disciples

5 And [a]it came to pass, that, as the people pressed upon him to hear the word of God, he stood by the lake of Gennesaret,

2 And saw two ships standing by the lake: but the fishermen were gone out of them, and were washing *their* nets.

3 And he entered into one of the ships, which was Simon's, and prayed him that *he* would thrust out a little from the land. And he sat down, and taught the people out of the ship.

4 Now when he had left speaking, he said unto Simon, [a]Launch out into the deep, and let down your nets for a draught.

5 And Simon answering said unto him, Master, we have toiled all the night, and have taken nothing: nevertheless at thy word I will let down the net.

6 And when they had this done, they inclosed a great multitude of fishes: and their net brake.

7 And they beckoned unto *their* partners, which were in the other ship, that *they* should come and help them. And they came, and filled both the ships, so that they began to sink.

8 When Simon Peter saw *it,* he fell down at Jesus' knees, saying, [a]Depart from me; for I am a sinful man, O Lord.

4:31 [a]Mat. 4:13; Mark 1:21
4:32 [a]Mat. 7:28,29
4:33 [a]Mark 1:23
4:34 [1]Or, *Away* [a]ver. 41 [b]Ps. 16:10; Dan. 9:24; ch. 1:35
4:38 [a]Mat. 8:14; Mark 1:29
4:40 [a]Mat. 8:16; Mark 1:32
4:41 [a]Mark 1:34; 3:11 [b]ver. 34,35; Mark 1:25,34
4:41 [1]Or, *to say that they knew him to be Christ*
4:42 [a]Mark 1:35
4:44 [a]Mark 1:39
5:1 [a]Mat. 4:18; Mark 1:16
5:4 [a]John 21:6
5:8 [a]2 Sam. 6:9; 1 Ki. 17:8

Jesus' commanding presence. In any case, His time (to die) had not yet come (John 7:30).

4:32 See note on Mark 1:22.

4:33 *which had a spirit of an unclean devil.* To pagans, "demon" meant a supernatural being, whether good or bad, but Luke makes it clear that this was an evil spirit. Such a demon could cause mental disorder (John 10:20), violent action (Luke 8:26–29), bodily disease (13:11,16) and rebellion against God (Rev 16:14).

4:34 *Holy One of God.* See note on Mark 1:24.

4:38 *Simon's wife's mother.* Peter was married (1 Cor 9:5). *a great fever.* All three Synoptics tell of this miracle (Mat 8:14–15; Mark 1:29–31), but only Luke, the doctor, uses the more specific phrase "great [i.e. "high"] fever."

4:40 *when the sun was setting.* The sabbath (v. 31) was over at sundown (about 6:00 P.M.). Until then, according to the tradition of the elders, Jews could not travel more than about two-thirds of a mile or carry a burden. Only after sundown could they carry the sick to Jesus, and their eagerness is seen in the fact that they set out while the sun was still setting.

4:41 *for they knew that he was Christ.* See note on Mark 1:34.

‡4:42 *desert place.* Mark includes the words "and there prayed" (Mark 1:35).

4:43 *kingdom of God.* Luke's first use of this phrase; it occurs over 30 times in his Gospel. Some of its different meanings in the Bible are: the eternal kingship of God; the presence of the kingdom in the person of Jesus, the King; the approaching spiritual form of the kingdom; the future kingdom. See note on Mat 3:2.

‡4:44 This summary statement includes not only what has just been described (from v. 14 on) but also what lay ahead in Jesus' ministry. No express mention is made in the Synoptics of the early Judean ministry recorded in John (2:13–4:3), though it may be reflected in Mat 23:37 and Luke 13:34.

5:1 *lake of Gennesaret.* Luke is the only one who calls it a lake. The other Gospel writers call it the sea of Galilee, and John twice calls it the sea of Tiberias (John 6:1; 21:1).

5:2 *washing their nets.* After each period of fishing, the nets were washed, stretched and prepared for use again.

5:3 *sat down.* The usual position for teaching (see note on 4:20). The boat provided an ideal arrangement, removed from the press of the crowd but near enough to be seen and heard.

5:7 *their partners.* See v. 10.

5:8 *Depart from me.* The nearer one comes to God, the more he feels his own sinfulness and unworthiness—as did Abraham (Gen 18:27), Job (42:6) and Isaiah (6:5).

9 For he was astonished, and all that were with him, at the draught of the fishes which they had taken:

10 And so *was* also James, and John, *the* sons of Zebedee, which were partners with Simon. And Jesus said unto Simon, Fear not; [a]from henceforth thou shalt catch men.

11 And when they had brought *their* ships to land, [a]they forsook all, and followed him.

The leper cleansed

12 ¶ [a]And it came to pass, when he was in a certain city, behold a man full of leprosy: who seeing Jesus fell on *his* face, and besought him, saying, Lord, if thou wilt, thou canst make me clean.

13 And he put forth *his* hand, and touched him, saying, I will: be thou clean. And immediately the leprosy departed from him.

14 [a]And he charged him to tell no *man:* but go, and shew thyself to the priest, and offer for thy cleansing, [b]according as Moses commanded, for a testimony unto them.

15 But *so much* the more went there a fame abroad of him: [a]and great multitudes came together to hear, and to be healed by him of their infirmities.

16 [a]And he withdrew himself into the wilderness, and prayed.

A man with palsy healed

17 ¶ And it came to pass on a certain day, as he was teaching, that there were Pharisees and doctors of the law sitting *by,* which were come out of every town of Galilee, and Judea, and Jerusalem: and the power of the Lord was *present* to heal them.

18 [a]And behold, men brought in a bed a man which was taken with a palsy: and they sought *means* to bring him in, and to lay *him* before him.

19 And when they could not find by what *way* they might bring him in because of the multitude, they went upon the housetop, and let him down through the tiling with *his* couch into the midst before Jesus.

20 And when he saw their faith, he said unto him, Man, thy sins are forgiven thee.

21 [a]And the scribes and the Pharisees began to reason, saying, Who is this which speaketh blasphemies? [b]Who can forgive sins, but God alone?

22 But when Jesus perceived their thoughts, he answering said unto them, What reason ye in your hearts?

23 Whether is easier, to say, Thy sins be forgiven thee; or to say, Rise up and walk?

24 But that ye may know that the Son of man hath power upon earth to forgive sins, (he said unto the sick of the palsy,) I say unto thee, Arise, and take up thy couch, and go into thine house.

25 And immediately he rose up before them, and took up *that* whereon he lay, and departed to his own house, glorifying God.

26 And they were all amazed, and they glorified God, and were filled with fear, saying, We have seen strange *things* to day.

The call of Levi

27 ¶ [a]And after these *things* he went forth, and saw a publican, named Levi, sitting at the receipt of custom: and he said unto him, Follow me.

28 And he left all, rose up, and followed him.

29 [a]And Levi made him a great feast in his own house: and [b]there was a great company of

5:10 [a]Mat. 4:19; Mark 1:17
5:11 [a]Mat. 4:20; 19:27; Mark 1:18; ch. 18:28
5:12 [a]Mat. 8:2; Mark 1:40
5:14 [a]Mat. 8:4 [b]Lev. 14:4,10, 21,22
5:15 [a]Mat. 4:25; Mark 3:7; John 6:2
5:16 [a]Mat. 14:23; Mark 6:46
5:18 [a]Mat. 9:2; Mark 2:3
5:21 [a]Mat. 9:3; Mark 2:6,7 [b]Ps. 32:5; Is. 43:25
5:27 [a]Mat. 9:9; Mark 2:13,14
5:29 [a]Mat. 9:10; Mark 2:15 [b]ch. 15:1

5:11 *forsook all, and followed him.* This was not the first time these men had been with Jesus (see John 1:40–42; 2:1–2). Their periodic and loose association now became a closely knit fellowship as they followed the Master. The scene is the same as Mat 4:18–22 and Mark 1:16–20, but the accounts relate events from different hours of the morning.
5:12–16 The healing of the man with leprosy is described in all three of the Synoptic Gospels, but the setting is different in each. In Matthew (8:1–4) it is part of a collection of miracles; in Mark (1:40–45) and Luke it is probably one incident that occurred on the first tour of Galilee.
5:12 *full of leprosy.* Luke alone notes the extent of his disease. The Greek term for "leprosy" could refer to other skin diseases as well as leprosy, and was not used for leprosy in medical literature. See note on Lev 13:2
5:14 *tell no man.* See notes on Mat 8:4; 16:20. *but go, and shew thyself to the priest.* By this command Jesus urged the man to keep the law, to provide further proof for the actual healing, to testify to the authorities concerning His ministry and to supply ritual certification of cleansing so the man could be reinstated into society. *a testimony unto them.* See note on Mark 1:44.
5:17 *Pharisees and doctors of the law.* See notes on Mat 2:4; 3:7; Mark 2:16. Opposition was rising in Galilee from these religious leaders. *Pharisees.* Mentioned here for the first time in Luke. Their name meaning "separated ones," they numbered about 6,000 and were spread over the whole of the Holy Land. They were teachers in the synagogues, religious examples in the eyes of the people and self-appointed guardians of the law and its proper observance. They considered the interpretations and regulations handed down by tradition to be virtually as authoritative as Scripture (Mark 7:8–13). Already Jesus had run counter to the Jewish leaders in Jerusalem (John 5:16–18). Now they came to a home in Capernaum (Mark 2:1–6) to hear and watch Him. *doctors of the law.* "Scribes," who studied, interpreted and taught the law (both written and oral). The majority of these teachers belonged to the party of the Pharisees.
5:19 *housetop.* See note on Mark 2:4. *tiling.* Probably ceiling tiles.
5:21 *Who is this which speaketh blasphemies?* See note on Mark 2:7. The Pharisees considered blasphemy to be the most serious sin a man could commit (see note on Mark 14:64).
5:23 *Whether is easier, to say . . . ?* See notes on Mark 2:9–10.
5:24 *that ye may know.* Jesus' power to heal was a visible affirmation of His power to forgive sins.
5:27 *a publican.* See note on 3:12. *receipt of custom.* The place where customs were collected (see note on Mark 2:14).
5:28 *left all, rose up, and followed him.* Since Jesus had been ministering in Capernaum for some time, Levi probably had known Him previously (see note on v. 11).
5:29 *a great feast.* When Levi began to follow Jesus, he did not do it secretly.

publicans and of others that sat down with
them.
30 But their scribes and Pharisees murmured against his disciples, saying, Why do ye
eat and drink with publicans and sinners?
31 And Jesus answering said unto them,
They that are whole need not a physician; but
they that are sick.
32 [a]I came not to call *the* righteous, but
sinners to repentance.

The question about fasting

33 ¶ And they said unto him, [a]Why do the
disciples of John fast often, and make prayers,
and likewise the *disciples* of the Pharisees; but
thine eat and drink?
34 And he said unto them, Can ye make
the children of the bridechamber fast, while
the bridegroom is with them?
35 But the days will come, when the bridegroom shall be taken away from them, and
then shall they fast in those days.
36 [a]And he spake also a parable unto
them; No *man* putteth a piece of a new garment upon an old; if otherwise, *then* both the
new maketh a rent, and the piece that was *tak-*
en out of the new agreeth not with the old.
37 And no *man* putteth new wine into old
bottles; else the new wine will burst the bottles, and be spilled, and the bottles shall perish.
38 But new wine must be put into new
bottles; and both are preserved.
39 No *man* also having drunk old *wine*
straightway desireth new: for he saith, The old
is better.

Jesus the Lord of the sabbath

6 And [a]it came to pass on the second sabbath after the first, that he went through
the corn fields; and his disciples plucked the
ears of corn, and did eat, rubbing *them* in *their*
hands.

5:32 [a]Mat. 9:13; 1 Tim. 1:15
5:33 [a]Mat. 9:14; Mark 2:18
5:36 [a]Mat. 9:16,17; Mark 2:21,22
6:1 [a]Mat. 12:1; Mark 2:23
6:2 [a]Ex. 20:10
6:3 [a]1 Sam. 21:6
6:4 [a]Lev. 24:9
6:6 [a]Mat. 12:9; Mark 3:1; See ch. 13:14; 14:3; John 9:16

2 And certain of the Pharisees said unto
them, Why do ye *that* [a]which is not lawful to
do on the sabbath days?
3 And Jesus answering them said, Have ye
not read so much as this, [a]what David did,
when himself was a hungred, and they which
were with him;
4 How he went into the house of God, and
did take and eat the shewbread, and gave also
to them that were with him; [a]which it is not
lawful to eat but for the priests alone?
5 And he said unto them, That the Son of
man is Lord also of the sabbath.
6 ¶ [a]And it came to pass also on another
sabbath, that he entered into the synagogue
and taught: and there was a man whose right
hand was withered.
7 And the scribes and Pharisees watched
him, whether he would heal on the sabbath
day; that they might find an accusation against
him.
8 But he knew their thoughts, and said to
the man which had the withered hand, Rise
up, and stand *forth* in the midst. And he arose
and stood *forth*.
9 Then said Jesus unto them, I will ask you
one *thing;* Is it lawful on the sabbath days to
do good, or to do evil? to save life, or to destroy *it?*
10 And looking round about upon them all,
he said unto the man, Stretch forth thy hand.
And he did so: and his hand was restored
whole as the other.
11 And they were filled with madness; and
communed one with another what they might
do to Jesus.

The choosing of the twelve

12 ¶ And it came to pass in those days, *that*
he went out into a mountain to pray, and continued all night in prayer to God.
13 And when it was day, he called unto

5:30 *Pharisees murmured.* They probably stood outside and registered their complaints from a distance. *eat with and drink with publicans and sinners.* See note on Mark 2:15.

5:31 *They that are whole need not a physician; but they that are sick.* Not to imply that the Pharisees were "they that are whole," but that a person must recognize himself as a sinner before he can be spiritually healed (see note on Mark 2:17).

5:33 *disciples of John fast often, and make prayers.* John the Baptist had grown up in the wilderness and learned to subsist on a meager, austere diet of locusts and wild honey. His ministry was characterized by a sober message and a strenuous schedule. For a contrast between Jesus' ministry and John the Baptist's see 7:24–28; Mat 11:1–19. The Pharisees also had rigorous life-styles (see note on 18:12). But Jesus went to banquets, and His disciples enjoyed a freedom not known by the Pharisees. *fast.* See note on Mark 2:18. While Jesus rejected fasting legalistically for display (cf. Is 58:3–11), He Himself fasted privately and permitted its voluntary use for spiritual benefit (Mat 4:2; 6:16–18).

5:35 See notes on Mark 2:19–20.

5:36 *parable.* See notes on Mat 13:3; Mark 4:2.

5:37 *old bottles.* See note on Mat 9:17.

5:39 *The old is better.* Jesus was indicating the reluctance of some people to change from their traditional religious ways and try the gospel.

6:1 *went through the corn fields.* See note on Mark 2:23.

6:3 *what David did.* See note on Mark 2:25.

6:4 *shewbread.* See note on Mat 12:4.

6:5 *Son of man.* See note on Mark 8:31. *Lord also of the sabbath.* Jesus has the authority to overrule laws concerning the sabbath, particularly as interpreted by the Pharisees (see Mat 12:8; Mark 2:27).

6:8 *stand forth.* So there would be no question about the healing.

6:9 *Is it lawful . . . to do good . . . ?* Jesus had been enduring questions and attacks from the Pharisees and now took the initiative by putting the questions to everyone in the synagogue (see note on Mark 3:4).

6:10 *looking round about upon them all.* Jesus wanted to see whether anyone objected to His question or the implied answer, but no one was bold enough to do so.

6:11 *they were filled with madness.* Because they could not withstand Jesus' reasoning. Already they were plotting to take His life (John 5:18). See note on Mark 3:6.

6:12 Characteristically, Jesus spent the night in prayer before the important work of selecting His 12 apostles.

him his disciples: [a]and of them he chose twelve, whom also he named apostles;

14 Simon, ([a]whom he also named Peter,) and Andrew his brother, James and John, Philip and Bartholomew,

15 Matthew and Thomas, James the *son* of Alpheus, and Simon called Zelotes,

16 *And* Judas [a]*the brother* of James, and Judas Iscariot, which also was the traitor.

Beatitudes and woes

17 ¶ And he came down with them, and stood in the plain, and the company of his disciples, [a]and a great multitude of people out of all Judea and Jerusalem, and *from* the sea coast of Tyre and Sidon, which came to hear him, and to be healed of their diseases;

18 And they that were vexed with unclean spirits: and they were healed.

19 And the whole multitude [a]sought to touch him: for [b]there went virtue out of him, and healed *them* all.

20 ¶ And he lifted up his eyes on his disciples, and said,

¶ [a]Blessed *be ye* poor: for yours is the kingdom of God.

21 ¶ [a]Blessed *are ye* that hunger now: for ye shall be filled.

¶ [b]Blessed *are ye* that weep now: for ye shall laugh.

22 ¶ [a]Blessed are ye, when men shall hate you, and when they [b]shall separate you *from their company,* and shall reproach *you,* and cast out your name as evil, for the Son of man's sake.

23 [a]Rejoice ye in that day, and leap *for joy:* for behold, your reward *is* great in heaven: for [b]in the like manner did their fathers unto the prophets.

24 ¶ [a]But woe unto you [b]that are rich: for [c]ye have received your consolation.

6:13 [a]Mat. 10:1
6:14 [a]John 1:42
6:16 [a]Jude 1
6:17 [a]Mat. 4:25; Mark 3:7
6:19 [a]Mat. 14:36 [b]Mark 5:30; ch. 8:46
6:20 [a]Mat. 5:3; 11:5; Jas. 2:5
6:21 [a]Is. 55:1; 65:13; Mat. 5:6 [b]Is. 61:3; Mat. 5:4
6:22 [a]Mat. 5:11; 1 Pet. 2:19; 3:14; 4:14 [b]John 16:2
6:23 [a]Mat. 5:12; Acts 5:41; Col. 1:24; Jas. 1:2 [b]Acts 7:51
6:24 [a]Amos 6:1; Jas. 5:1 [b]ch. 12:21 [c]Mat. 6:2,5,16; ch. 16:25
6:25 [a]Is. 65:13 [b]Prov. 14:13
6:26 [a]John 15:19; 1 John 4:5
6:27 [a]ver. 35; Ex. 23:4; Prov. 25:21; Mat. 5:44; Rom. 12:20
6:28 [a]ch. 23:34; Acts 7:60
6:29 [a]Mat. 5:39 [b]1 Cor. 6:7
6:30 [a]Deut. 15:7,8,10; Prov. 21:26; Mat. 5:42
6:31 [a]Mat. 7:12
6:32 [a]Mat. 5:46
6:34 [a]Mat. 5:42
6:35 [a]ver. 27 [b]ver. 30; Ps. 37:26 [c]Mat. 5:45
6:36 [a]Mat. 5:48
6:37 [a]Mat. 7:1

25 ¶ [a]Woe unto you that are full: for ye shall hunger.

¶ [b]Woe unto you that laugh now: for ye shall mourn and weep.

26 ¶ [a]Woe unto you, when all men shall speak well of you: for so did their fathers to the false prophets.

The law of love

27 ¶ [a]But I say unto you which hear, Love your enemies, do good to them which hate you,

28 Bless them that curse you, and [a]pray for them which despitefully use you.

29 [a]*And* unto him that smiteth thee on the *one* cheek offer also the other; [b]and him that taketh away thy cloke forbid not *to take thy* coat also.

30 [a]Give to every man that asketh of thee; and of him that taketh away thy *goods* ask *them* not again.

31 [a]And as ye would that men should do to you, do ye also to them likewise.

32 [a]For if ye love them which love you, what thank have ye? for sinners also love those that love them.

33 And if ye do good to them which do good to you, what thank have ye? for sinners also do *even* the same.

34 [a]And if ye lend *to them* of whom ye hope to receive, what thank have ye? for sinners also lend to sinners, to receive as much again.

35 But [a]love ye your enemies, and do good, and [b]lend, hoping for nothing again; and your reward shall be great, and [c]ye shall be the children of the Highest: for he is kind unto the unthankful and *to the* evil.

36 [a]Be ye therefore merciful, as your Father also is merciful.

37 [a]Judge not, and ye shall not be judged:

6:13 *he called unto him his disciples.* Among those who came to hear Jesus was a group who regularly followed Him and were committed to His teachings. At least 70 men were included, since this many disciples were sent out on an evangelistic campaign (10:1,17). Later, 120 believers waited and worshiped in Jerusalem following the ascension (Acts 1:15). From such disciples Jesus at this time chose 12 to be His apostles, meaning "ones sent with a special commission" (see notes on Mark 6:30; 1 Cor 1:1; Heb 3:1).

‡6:14–16 Lists of the apostles appear also in Mat 10:2–4; Mark 3:16–19; Acts 1:13. Although the order of the names varies, Peter is always first and Judas Iscariot last. The same disciples are always listed in each of the same three groupings of four each.

6:14 *Bartholomew.* Seems to be (in the Synoptics) the same as Nathanael (in John). Nathanael is associated with Philip in John 1:45.

6:15 *Matthew.* Another name for Levi. *James the son of Alpheus.* Probably the same as James the Less (Mark 15:40). *Simon called Zelotes.* See note on Mat 10:4.

6:16 *Judas the brother of James.* Another name for Thaddeus (Mat 10:3; Mark 3:18). *Judas Iscariot.* Probably the only one from Judea, the rest coming from Galilee (see note on Mark 3:19).

6:17 *stood in the plain.* Perhaps a plateau, which would satisfy both this context and that in Mat 5:1.

6:20–49 Luke's Sermon on the Plain, apparently parallel to Matthew's Sermon on the Mount (Mat 5–7). Although this sermon is much shorter than the one in Matthew, they both begin with the Beatitudes and end with the lesson of the builders. Some of Matthew's Sermon is found in other portions of Luke (e.g., 11:2–4; 12:22–31,33–34), suggesting that the material may have been given on various occasions in Jesus' preaching.

6:20–23 See Mat 5:3–12. The Beatitudes go deeper than material poverty (v. 20) and physical hunger (v. 21). Matthew's account indicates that Jesus spoke of poverty "in spirit" (Mat 5:3) and hunger "for righteousness" (Mat 5:6).

6:24–26 This section is a point-by-point negative counterpart of vv. 20–22.

6:27 *Love your enemies.* The heart of Jesus' teaching is love. While the Golden Rule (v. 31) is sometimes expressed in negative form outside the Bible, Jesus not only forbids treating others spitefully but also commands that we love everyone—even our enemies.

6:29 *offer also the other.* We are not to have a retaliatory attitude.

6:36 *as your Father also is merciful.* God's perfection should be our example and goal (see Mat 5:48).

6:37 *Judge not.* Jesus did not relieve His followers of the need

condemn not, and ye shall not be condemned:
forgive, and ye shall be forgiven:
38 [a]Give, and it shall be given unto you;
good measure, pressed down, and shaken *together,* and running over, shall *men* give into
your [b]bosom. For [c]with the same measure
that ye mete withal it shall be measured to you
again.
39 ¶ And he spake a parable unto them,
[a]Can the blind lead the blind? shall they not
both fall into the ditch?
40 [a]The disciple is not above his master:
but every one [1]*that is* perfect shall be as his
master.
41 [a]And why beholdest thou the mote that
is in thy brother's eye, but perceivest not the
beam that is in thine own eye?
42 Either how canst thou say to thy brother, Brother, let me pull out the mote that is in
thine eye, when thou thyself beholdest not the
beam that is in thine own eye? *Thou* hypocrite, cast out first the beam out of thine own
eye, and then shalt thou see clearly to pull out
the mote that is in thy brother's eye.
43 [a]For a good tree bringeth not forth corrupt fruit; neither doth a corrupt tree bring
forth good fruit.
44 For [a]every tree is known by his own
fruit. For of thorns *men* do not gather figs, nor
of a bramble bush gather they [1]grapes.
45 [a]A good man out of the good treasure of
his heart bringeth forth that which is good;
and an evil man out of the evil treasure of his
heart bringeth forth that which is evil: for [b]of
the abundance of the heart his mouth
speaketh.

The wise and foolish builders

46 ¶ [a]And why call ye me, Lord, Lord, and
do not *the things* which I say?
47 [a]Whosoever cometh to me, and heareth
my sayings, and doeth them, I will shew you
to whom he is like:
48 He is like a man which built a house,
and digged deep, and laid the foundation on a
rock: and when the flood arose, the stream
beat vehemently upon that house, and could
not shake it: for it was founded upon a rock.
49 But he that heareth, and doeth not, is
like a man that without a foundation built a
house upon the earth; against which the
stream did beat vehemently, and immediately
it fell; and the ruin of that house was great.

The centurion's servant healed

7 Now when he had ended all his sayings
in the audience of the people, [a]he entered into Capernaum.
2 And a certain centurion's servant, who
was dear unto him, was sick, and ready to die.
3 And when he heard of Jesus, he sent
unto him *the* elders of the Jews, beseeching
him that he would come and heal his servant.
4 And when they came to Jesus, they besought him instantly, saying, That he was worthy for whom he should do this:
5 For he loveth our nation, and he hath
built us a synagogue.
6 Then Jesus went with them. And when
he was now not far from the house, the centurion sent friends to him, saying unto him,
Lord, trouble not thyself: for I am not worthy
that thou shouldest enter under my roof:
7 Wherefore neither thought I myself worthy to come unto thee: but say in a word, and
my servant shall be healed.
8 For I also am a man set under authority,
having under me soldiers, and I say unto [1]one,
Go, and he goeth; and to another, Come, and
he cometh; and to my servant, Do this, and he
doeth *it.*
9 When Jesus heard these *things,* he marvelled at him, and turned him *about,* and said
unto the people that followed him, I say unto
you, I have not found so great faith, no, not in
Israel.
10 And they that were sent, returning to
the house, found the servant whole that had
been sick.

The raising of the widow's son

11 ¶ And it came to pass the *day* after, *that*
he went into a city called Nain; and many of
his disciples went with him, and much people.
12 Now when he came nigh to the gate of
the city, behold, there was a dead man carried
out, the only son of his mother, and she was a
widow: and much people of the city was with
her.
13 And when the Lord saw her, he had

6:38 [a]Prov. 19:17 [b]Ps. 79:12 [c]Mat. 7:2; Mark 4:24; Jas. 2:13
6:39 [a]Mat. 15:14
6:40 [1]Or, *shall be perfected as his master* [a]Mat. 10:24; John 13:16; 15:20
6:41 [a]Mat. 7:3
6:43 [a]Mat. 7:16,17
6:44 [1][Gr. *a grape*] [a]Mat. 12:33
6:45 [a]Mat. 12:35 [b]Mat. 12:34
6:46 [a]Mal. 1:6; Mat. 7:21; 25:11; ch. 13:25
6:47 [a]Mat. 7:24
7:1 [a]Mat. 8:5
7:8 [1][Gr. *this man*]

for discerning right and wrong (cf. vv. 43–45), but He condemned unjust and hypocritical judging of others.

‡6:38 *give into your bosom.* Probably refers to the way the outer garment was worn, leaving a fold over the belt that could be used as a large pocket to hold a measure of wheat. The promise is that you cannot outgive God.

6:41 *mote . . . beam.* Jesus used hyperbole (a figure of speech that overstates for emphasis) to sharpen the contrast and to emphasize how foolish and hypocritical it is for us to criticize someone for a fault while remaining blind to our own considerable faults.

7:2 *centurion's servant.* The centurion was probably a member of Herod Antipas's forces, which were organized in Roman fashion, ordinarily in companies of 100 men. Roman centurions referred to in the NT showed characteristics to be admired (e.g., Acts 10:2; 23:17–18; 27:43). This centurion showed genuine concern for his slave, and he was admired by the Jews, who spoke favorably of him even though he was a Gentile (see vv. 5,9).

7:3 *elders of the Jews.* Highly respected Jews of the community, though not necessarily rulers of the synagogue. They were willing to come and plead for the centurion. In Matthew's account (Mat 8:5–13) the centurion speaks with Jesus Himself, while in Luke's account he speaks with Jesus through his friends (see note on Mat 8:5).

7:6 *I am not worthy that thou shouldest enter under my roof.* See note on Mat 8:8.

7:9 *he marvelled.* The Greek word for "marvel" is used of Jesus only twice. Here He "marveled" at faith while in Mark 6:6 He "wondered" (same Greek word) at a lack of faith.

compassion on her, and said unto her, Weep not.

14 And he came and touched the [1]bier: and they that bare *him* stood still. And he said, Young man, I say unto thee, [a]Arise.

15 And he that was dead sat up, and began to speak. And he delivered him to his mother.

16 [a]And there came a fear on all: and they glorified God, saying, [b]That a great prophet is risen up among us; and, [c]That God hath visited his people.

17 And this rumour of him went forth throughout all Judea, and throughout all the region round about.

Tribute to John the Baptist

18 ¶ [a]And the disciples of John shewed him of all these *things.*

19 And John calling unto *him* two of his disciples sent *them* to Jesus, saying, Art thou he that should come? or look we for another?

20 When the men were come unto him, they said, John Baptist hath sent us unto thee, saying, Art thou he that should come? or look we for another?

21 And in that *same* hour he cured many of *their* infirmities and plagues, and of evil spirits; and unto many *that were* blind he gave sight.

22 [a]Then Jesus answering said unto them, Go *your way,* and tell John what *things* ye have seen and heard; [b]how that the blind see, the lame walk, the lepers are cleansed, the deaf hear, the dead are raised, [c]to the poor the gospel is preached.

23 And blessed is *he,* whosoever shall not be offended in me.

24 [a]And when the messengers of John were departed, he began to speak unto the people concerning John, What went ye out into the wilderness for to see? A reed shaken with the wind?

25 But what went ye out for to see? A man clothed in soft raiment? Behold, they which are gorgeously apparelled, and live delicately, are in kings' courts.

26 But what went ye out for to see? A prophet? Yea, I say unto you, and much more than a prophet.

27 This is *he,* of whom it is written, [a]Behold, I send my messenger before thy face, which shall prepare thy way before thee.

28 For I say unto you, Among *those that are* born of women there is not a greater prophet than John the Baptist: but he that is least in the kingdom of God is greater than he.

29 And all the people that heard *him,* and the publicans, justified God, [a]being baptized *with* the baptism of John.

30 But the Pharisees and lawyers [1]rejected [a]the counsel of God [2]against themselves, being not baptized of him.

31 ¶ And the Lord said, [a]Whereunto then shall I liken the men of this generation? and to what are they like?

32 They are like unto children sitting in the marketplace, and calling one to another, and saying, We have piped unto you, and ye have not danced; we have mourned to you, and ye have not wept.

33 For [a]John the Baptist came neither eating bread nor drinking wine; and ye say, He hath a devil.

34 The Son of man is come eating and drinking; and ye say, Behold a gluttonous man, and a winebibber, a friend of publicans and sinners.

35 But [a]wisdom is justified of all her children.

7:14 [1]Or, *coffin* [a]ch. 8:54; John 11:43; Acts 9:40; Rom. 4:17
7:16 [a]ch. 1:65 [b]ch. 24:19; John 4:19; 6:14; 9:17 [c]ch. 1:68
7:18 [a]Mat. 11:2
7:22 [a]Mat. 11:4 [b]Is. 35:5 [c]ch. 4:18
7:24 [a]Mat. 11:7
7:27 [a]Mal. 3:1
7:29 [a]Mat. 3:5; ch. 3:12
7:30 [1]Or, *frustrated* [2]Or, *within themselves* [a]Acts 20:27
7:31 [a]Mat. 11:16
7:33 [a]Mat. 3:4; Mark 1:6; ch. 1:15
7:35 [a]Mat. 11:19

7:14 *bier.* The man was probably carried in an open coffin, suggested by Jewish custom and the fact that he sat up in response to Jesus' command. This is the first of three instances of Jesus' raising someone from the dead, the others being Jairus's daughter (8:40–56) and Lazarus (John 11:38–44).

7:18 *disciples of John.* Despite John the Baptist's imprisonment, his disciples kept in contact with him and continued his ministry.

7:19 *look we for another?* John had announced the coming of the Christ, but now he himself had been languishing in prison for months, and the work of Jesus had not brought the results John apparently expected. His disappointment was natural. He wanted reassurance—and perhaps also wanted to urge Jesus to further action.

7:22 *tell John what things ye have seen and heard.* In answer, Jesus pointed to His healing and life-restoring miracles. He did not give promises but clearly observable evidence—evidence that reflected the predicted ministry of the Messiah. *to the poor the gospel is preached.* In Jesus' review of His works, He used an ascending scale of impressive deeds, ending with the dead raised and the gospel preached to the poor. In this way, Jesus reminded John that these were the things predicted of the Messiah in the Scriptures (see Is 29:18–21; 35:5–6; 61:1; see also Luke 4:18).

7:23 *whosoever shall not be offended in me.* Jesus did not want discouragement and doubt to ensnare John.

7:24 *What went ye out . . . to see?* John was not a weak messenger, swayed by the pressures of human opinion. On the contrary, he was a true prophet.

7:26 *much more than a prophet.* John was the unique prophet sent to prepare the way for the Messiah.

7:28 *he that is least in the kingdom of God.* See note on Mat 11:11.

7:30 *lawyers.* A designation used by Luke (see 10:25; 11:45–46,52; 14:3; see also Mat 22:35) for the "scribes" (the teachers of the law), most of whom were Pharisees (see note on 5:17). *rejected the counsel of God.* Tax collectors had shown their willingness to repent by accepting John's baptism, whereas the Pharisees showed their rejection of God's message by refusing to be baptized.

7:32 *like unto children sitting in the marketplace.* People had rejected both John and Jesus, but for different reasons—like children who refuse to play either a joyful game or a mournful one. They would not associate with John when he followed the strictest of rules or with Jesus when He freely associated with all kinds of people.

7:34 *a friend of publicans and sinners.* Jesus ate and talked with people who were religious and social outcasts. He even called a publican to be an apostle (5:27–32).

7:35 *wisdom is justified of all her children.* In contrast to the rejection by foolish critics, spiritually wise persons could see that

Jesus forgives a sinful woman

36 ¶ [a]And one of the Pharisees desired him
that he would eat with him. And he went into
the Pharisee's house, and sat down to meat.
37 And behold, a woman in the city, which
was a sinner, when she knew that *Jesus* sat at
meat in the Pharisee's house, brought an alabaster box of ointment,
38 And stood at his feet behind *him* weeping, and began to wash his feet with tears, and
did wipe *them* with the hairs of her head, and
kissed his feet, and anointed *them* with the
ointment.
39 Now when the Pharisee which had bidden him saw *it,* he spake within himself, saying, [a]This *man,* if he were a prophet, would
have known who and what manner of woman
this is that toucheth him: for she is a sinner.
40 And Jesus answering said unto him, Simon, I have somewhat to say unto thee. And
he saith, Master, say *on.*
41 There was a certain creditor which had
two debtors: the one ought five hundred
[1]pence, and the other fifty.
42 And when they had nothing to pay, he
frankly forgave *them* both. Tell me therefore,
which of them will love him most?
43 Simon answered and said, I suppose
that *he,* to whom he forgave most. And he said
unto him, Thou hast rightly judged.
44 And he turned to the woman, and said
unto Simon, Seest thou this woman? I entered
into thine house, thou gavest me no water for
my feet: but she hath washed my feet with
tears, and wiped *them* with the hairs of her
head.
45 Thou gavest me no kiss: but this *woman*
since the time I came in hath not ceased to
kiss my feet.
46 [a]Mine head with oil thou didst not
anoint: but this *woman* hath anointed my feet
with ointment.
47 [a]Wherefore I say unto thee, Her sins,
which are many, are forgiven; for she loved
much: but to whom little is forgiven, *the same*
loveth little.
48 And he said unto her, [a]Thy sins are forgiven.
49 And they that sat at meat with *him* began to say within themselves, [a]Who is this
that forgiveth sins also?
50 And he said to the woman, [a]Thy faith
hath saved thee; go in peace.

The parable of the sower

8 And it came to pass afterward, that he
went throughout every city and village,
preaching and shewing the glad tidings of the
kingdom of God: and the twelve *were* with
him,
2 And [a]certain women, which had been
healed of evil spirits and infirmities, Mary called
Magdalene, [b]out of whom went seven devils,
3 And Joanna the wife of Chuza Herod's
steward, and Susanna, and many others,
which ministered unto him of their substance.
4 ¶ [a]And when much people were gathered
together, and were come to him out of every
city, he spake by a parable:
5 A sower went out to sow his seed: and as
he sowed, some fell by the way side; and it
was trodden down, and the fowls of the air devoured it.
6 And some fell upon a rock; and as soon as

7:36 [a]Mat. 26:6; Mark 14:3; John 11:2
7:39 [a]ch. 15:2
7:41 [1]See Mat. 18:28; Mark 12:15
7:46 [a]Ps. 23:5
7:47 [a]1 Tim. 1:14
7:48 [a]Mat. 9:2; Mark 2:5
7:49 [a]Mat. 9:3; Mark 2:7
7:50 [a]Mat. 9:22; Mark 5:34; 10:52; ch. 8:48; 18:42
8:2 [a]Mat. 27:55,56 [b]Mark 16:9
8:4 [a]Mat. 13:2; Mark 4:1

the ministries of both John and Jesus were godly, despite their differences. See note on Mat 11:19.

7:36 *one of the Pharisees.* See note on 5:17. His motive may have been to entrap Jesus rather than to learn from Him.

7:37 *a woman . . . which was a sinner.* A prostitute. She must have heard Jesus preach, and in repentance she determined to lead a new life. She came out of love and gratitude, in the understanding that she could be forgiven. *alabaster box.* A long-necked, globular bottle. *ointment.* A perfumed ointment.

‡7:38 *stood at his feet behind him.* Jesus reclined on a couch with His feet extended away from the table, which made it possible for the woman to wipe His feet with her hair and still not disturb His eating. *anointed them with the ointment.* The anointing, perhaps originally intended for Jesus' head, was instead applied to His feet. A similar act was performed by Mary of Bethany the week before the crucifixion (John 12:3).

‡7:41 *five hundred pence.* Pence is the plural of penny, the denarius, a coin worth about a day's wages.

7:44 *water for my feet.* The minimal gesture of hospitality.

7:47 *for she loved much.* Her love was evidence of her forgiveness, but not the basis for it. Verse 50 clearly states that she was saved by faith. See Eph 1:7.

7:50 *Thy faith hath saved thee.* Her sins were forgiven and she could experience God's peace (see 1:79 and note on 2:14).

8:1 *he went throughout.* Jesus' ministry had been centered in Capernaum, and much of His preaching was in synagogues, but now He traveled again from town to town on a second tour of the Galilean countryside. For the first tour see 4:43–44; Mat 4:23–25; Mark 1:38–39. For the third tour see note on 9:1–6. *kingdom of God.* See note on 4:43.

8:2 *Mary called Magdalene.* Her hometown was Magdala. She is not to be confused with the sinful woman of ch. 7 or Mary of Bethany (John 11:1).

8:3 *Susanna.* Nothing more is known of her. *ministered unto him of their substance.* Jesus and His disciples did not provide for themselves by miracles, but were supported by the service and means of such grateful people as these women.

8:4 *parable.* From this point on Jesus used parables (see notes on Mat 13:3; Mark 4:2) more extensively as a means of teaching. They were particularly effective and easy to remember because He used familiar scenes. Although parables clarified Jesus' teaching, they also included hidden meanings needing further explanation. These hidden meanings challenged the sincerely interested to further inquiry, and taught truths that Jesus wanted to conceal from unbelievers (see v. 10). From parables Jesus' enemies could find no direct statements to use against Him. The parable of the sower is one of three parables recorded in each of the Synoptic Gospels (Mat 13:1–23; Mark 4:1–20). The others are those of the mustard seed (13:19; Mat 13:31–32; Mark 4:30–32) and of the vineyard (20:9–19; Mat 21:33–46; Mark 12:1–12).

8:5 *to sow his seed.* In Eastern practice the seed was sometimes sown first and the field plowed afterward. Roads and pathways went directly through many fields, and the traffic made much of the surface too hard for seed to take root in.

8:6 *upon a rock.* On a thin layer of soil that covered solid rock.

it was sprung up, it withered away, because *it* lacked moisture.

7 And some fell among thorns; and the thorns sprang up with *it,* and choked it.

8 And other fell on good ground, and sprang up, and bare fruit an hundredfold. **And when he said these *things,* he cried,** He that hath ears to hear, let him hear.

9 ¶ [a]**And his disciples asked him, saying, What might this parable be?**

10 **And he said,** Unto you it is given to know the mysteries of the kingdom of God: but to others in parables; [a]that seeing they might not see, and hearing they might not understand.

11 [a]Now the parable is this: The seed is the word of God.

12 Those by the way side are they that hear; then cometh the devil, and taketh away the word out of their hearts, lest they should believe and be saved.

13 They on the rock *are they,* which, when they hear, receive the word with joy; and these have no root, which for a while believe, and in time of temptation fall away.

14 And that which fell among thorns are they, which, when they have heard, go *forth,* and are choked with cares and riches and pleasures of *this* life, and bring no fruit to perfection.

15 But that on the good ground are they, which in an honest and good heart, having heard the word, keep *it,* and bring forth fruit with patience.

16 ¶ [a]No *man,* when he hath lighted a candle, covereth it with a vessel, or putteth *it* under a bed; but setteth *it* on a candlestick, that they which enter in may see the light.

8:9 [a]Mat. 13:10; Mark 4:10
8:10 [a]Is. 6:9; Mark 4:12
8:11 [a]Mat. 13:18; Mark 4:14
8:16 [a]Mat. 5:15; Mark 4:21; ch. 11:33
8:17 [a]Mat. 10:26; ch. 12:2
8:18 [1]Or, *thinketh that he hath* [a]Mat. 13:12; 25:29; ch. 19:26
8:19 [a]Mat. 12:46; Mark 3:31
8:22 [a]Mat. 8:23; Mark 4:35

17 [a]For nothing is secret, that shall not be made manifest; neither *any thing* hid, that shall not be known and come abroad.

18 Take heed therefore how ye hear: [a]for whosoever hath, to him shall be given; and whosoever hath not, from him shall be taken even *that* which he [1]seemeth to have.

Jesus' true family

19 ¶ [a]**Then came to him *his* mother and his brethren, and could not come at him for the press.**

20 **And it was told him *by certain* which said, Thy mother and thy brethren stand without, desiring to see thee.**

21 **And he answered and said unto them,** My mother and my brethren are these which hear the word of God, and do it.

The storm stilled

22 ¶ [a]**Now it came to pass on a certain day, that he went into a ship with his disciples: and he said unto them,** Let us go over unto the other side of the lake. **And they launched forth.**

23 **But as they sailed he fell asleep: and there came down a storm of wind on the lake; and they were filled *with water,* and were in jeopardy.**

24 **And they came to *him,* and awoke him, saying, Master, master, we perish. Then he rose, and rebuked the wind and the raging of the water: and they ceased, and there was a calm.**

25 **And he said unto them,** Where is your faith? **And they being afraid wondered, saying one to another, What *manner of man* is this? for he commandeth even the winds and water, and they obey him.**

Any moisture that fell there soon evaporated, and the germinating seed withered and died (see Mat 13:5–6).

8:8 *an hundredfold.* Luke's version is more abbreviated than Matthew's (13:8) and Mark's (4:8), but the point is the same: The quantity of increase depends on the quality of soil. *let him hear.* A challenge for listeners to understand the message and appropriate it for themselves.

8:9 *his disciples.* They included "his followers, along with the twelve" (Mark 4:10).

8:10 *mysteries of the kingdom of God.* Truths that can be known only by revelation from God (cf. Eph 3:2–5; 1 Pet 1:10–12). See note on Mark 4:11. *that seeing they might not see.* This quotation from Isaiah (6:9) does not express a desire that some would not understand, but simply states the sad truth that those who are not willing to receive Jesus' message will find the truth hidden from them. Their ultimate fate is implied in the fuller quotation in Mat 13:14–15 (see note on Mark 4:12).

8:11 *the word of God.* The message that comes from God.

8:12 *lest they should believe.* The devil's purpose is that people will not hear with understanding and therefore will not appropriate the message and be saved.

8:13 *for a while believe.* This kind of belief is superficial and does not save. It is similar to what James calls "dead" faith (Jas 2:17,20,26).

8:16 *lighted a candle.* Although Jesus couched much of His message in parables, He intended that the disciples make the truths known as widely as possible (see note on 11:33). *setteth it on a candlestick.* See note on Mat 5:15.

8:17 This verse explains v. 16. It is the destiny of the truth to be made known (cf. 12:2). The disciples were to begin a proclamation that would become universal.

8:18 *Take heed therefore how ye hear.* The disciples heard not only for themselves but also for those to whom they would minister (see Mark 4:24; cf. Jas 1:19–22). Truth that is not understood and appropriated will be lost (19:26), but truth that is used will be multiplied.

‡8:19 *Then came to him his mother and his brethren.* See note on Mark 3:21. More is known about their motive from Mark 3:21,31–32. The family, thinking "He is beside himself" (Mark 3:21), probably wanted to get Him away from His heavy schedule. *brethren.* Did not believe in Jesus at this time (John 7:5). Various interpretations concerning their relationship to Jesus arose in the early church: They were sons of Joseph by a previous marriage (according to Epiphanius) or were cousins (said Jerome). The most natural conclusion (suggested by Helvidius) is that they were the sons of Joseph and Mary, younger half brothers of Jesus. Four of these brothers are named in Mark 6:3, where it also says that Jesus had sisters. Since Joseph is not mentioned here, it is possible that he had died, or perhaps was home taking care of the carpenter's shop.

8:21 Jesus' reply was not meant to reject His natural family but to emphasize the higher priority of His spiritual relationship to those who believed in Him.

8:23 *a storm of wind.* See note on Mark 4:37.

Devils cast out

26 ¶ [a]And they arrived at the country of the Gadarenes, which is over against Galilee.

27 And when he went forth to land, there met him out of the city a certain man, which had devils long time, and ware no clothes, neither abode in *any* house, but in the tombs.

28 When he saw Jesus, he cried out, and fell down before him, and with a loud voice said, What have I to do with thee, Jesus, *thou* Son of God most high? I beseech thee, torment me not.

29 (For he had commanded the unclean spirit to come out of the man. For oftentimes it had caught him: and he was kept bound with chains and in fetters; and he brake the bands, and was driven of the devil into the wilderness.)

30 And Jesus asked him, saying, What is thy name? And he said, Legion: because many devils were entered into him.

31 And they besought him that he would not command them to go out [a]into the deep.

32 And there was there a herd of many swine feeding on the mountain: and they besought him that he would suffer them to enter into them. And [a]he suffered them.

33 Then went the devils out of the man, and entered into the swine: and the herd ran violently down a steep place into the lake, and were choked.

34 When they that fed *them* saw what was done, they fled, and went and told *it* in the city and in the country.

35 Then they went out to see what was done; and came to Jesus, and found the man, out of whom the devils were departed, sitting at the feet of Jesus, clothed, and in his right mind: and they were afraid.

36 They also which saw *it* told them by what means he that was possessed of the devils was healed.

37 [a]Then the whole multitude of the country of the Gadarenes round about [b]besought him to depart from them; for they were taken with great fear: and he went *up* into the ship, and returned *back again.*

38 Now [a]the man out of whom the devils were departed besought him that *he* might be with him: but Jesus sent him away, saying,

39 Return to thine own house, and shew how great *things* God hath done unto thee. And he went his way, and published throughout the whole city how great *things* Jesus had done unto him.

8:26 [a]Mat. 8:28; Mark 5:1
8:31 [a]Rev. 20:3
8:32 [a]Job 1:12; 12:16; Rev. 20:7
8:37 [a]Mat. 8:34 [b]Acts 16:39

A ruler's daughter raised

40 ¶ And it came to pass that, when Jesus was returned, the people gladly received him: for they were all waiting for him.

41 [a]And behold, there came a man named Jairus, and he was a ruler of the synagogue: and he fell down at Jesus' feet, and besought him that *he* would come into his house:

42 For he had one only daughter, about twelve years of age, and she lay a dying. (But as he went the people thronged him.

43 [a]And a woman having an issue of blood twelve years, which had spent all *her* living upon physicians, neither could be healed of any,

44 Came behind *him,* and touched the border of his garment: and immediately her issue of blood stanched.

45 And Jesus said, Who touched me? When all denied, Peter and they that were with him said, Master, the multitude throng thee and press *thee,* and sayest thou, Who touched me?

46 And Jesus said, Somebody hath touched me: for I perceive that [a]virtue is gone out of me.

47 And when the woman saw that she was not hid, she came trembling, and falling down before him, she declared unto him before all the people for what cause she had touched him, and how she was healed immediately.

48 And he said unto her, Daughter, be of good comfort: thy faith hath made thee whole; go in peace.)

8:38 [a]Mark 5:18
8:41 [a]Mat. 9:18; Mark 5:22
8:43 [a]Mat. 9:20
8:46 [a]Mark 5:30; ch. 6:19

‡8:26 *country of the Gadarenes.* The Gospels describe the location of this event in two ways: (1) the region of the Gergesenes (see note on Mat 8:28); (2) the region of the Gadarenes (see note on Mark 5:1). Some manuscripts of Mark and Luke read "Gergesenes," but this spelling may have been introduced in an attempt to resolve the differences with Matthew.
8:27 *man, which had devils.* See note on 4:33. Matthew (8:28) refers to two demon-possessed men, but Mark (5:2) and Luke probably mention only the one who was prominent and did the talking. *tombs.* An isolated burial ground avoided by most people (but see note on Mark 5:3).
‡8:28 *Son of God most high.* Cf. 1:32; 4:34. The title "God most high" was commonly used by Gentiles (see Gen 14:19 and note; Acts 16:17); its use here perhaps indicates that this man was not a Jew (but see note on Mark 1:24).
8:30 *What is thy name?* Jesus asked the man his name, but it was the demons who replied, thus showing they were in control. *Legion.* See note on Mark 5:9.
8:31 *the deep.* Or "the Abyss," a place of confinement for evil spirits and for Satan (see note on Rev 9:1).
8:32 *swine.* Pigs were unclean to Jews, and eating them was forbidden (Lev 11:7–8), but this was the Decapolis, a predominantly Gentile territory. *he suffered them.* See note on Mat 8:32.
8:39 *Return to thine own house, and shew how great things God hath done unto thee.* Although the man wanted to follow Jesus, he was directed to make the miracle known in his own native territory. There was no danger here of interference with Jesus' ministry (see note on Mark 5:19).
8:41 *a ruler of the synagogue.* The ruler was responsible for conducting services, selecting participants and maintaining order (see note on Mark 5:22).
8:43 *issue of blood.* The hemorrhage had made her ceremonially unclean for 12 years (see Lev 15:19–30). *neither could be healed of any.* Comparison with Mark 5:26 shows the restraint of Luke the physician in describing the failure of doctors to help her.
‡8:45 *Who touched me?* Jesus was not asking for information but insisted, for the woman's good and for a testimony to the crowd, that the miracle be made known.
8:46 *virtue is gone out of me.* See note on Mark 5:30.
8:48 *Daughter.* This woman is the only individual Jesus addressed with this tender term (cf. 23:28). *go in peace.* Cf. 7:50.

49 [a]While he yet spake, there cometh one from the ruler of the synagogue's *house,* saying to him, Thy daughter is dead; trouble not the Master.

50 But when Jesus heard *it,* he answered him, saying, Fear not: believe only, and she shall be made whole.

51 And when he came into the house, he suffered no *man* to go in, save Peter, and James, and John, and the father and the mother of the maiden.

52 And all wept, and bewailed her: but he said, Weep not; she is not dead, [a]but sleepeth.

53 And they laughed him to scorn, knowing that she was dead.

54 And he put *them* all out, and took her by the hand, and called, saying, Maid, [a]arise.

55 And her spirit came again, and she arose straightway: and he commanded to give her meat.

56 And her parents were astonished: but [a]he charged them that they should tell no *man* what was done.

The mission of the twelve

9 Then [a]he called his twelve disciples together, and gave them power and authority over all devils, and to cure diseases.

2 And [a]he sent them to preach the kingdom of God, and to heal the sick.

3 [a]And he said unto them, Take nothing for *your* journey, neither staves, nor scrip, neither bread, neither money; neither have two coats apiece.

4 [a]And whatsoever house ye enter into, there abide, and thence depart.

5 [a]And whosoever will not receive you, when ye go out of that city, [b]shake off the very dust from your feet for a testimony against them.

6 [a]And they departed, and went through the towns, preaching the gospel, and healing every where.

7 ¶ [a]Now Herod the tetrarch heard of all that was done by him: and he was perplexed, because that it was said of some, that John was risen from the dead;

8 And of some, that Elias had appeared; and *of* others, that one of the old prophets was risen again.

9 And Herod said, John have I beheaded: but who is this, of whom I hear such *things?* [a]And he desired to see him.

The five thousand fed

10 ¶ [a]And the apostles, when they were returned, told him all that they had done. [b]And he took them, and went aside privately into a desert place belonging to the city called Bethsaida.

11 And the people, when they knew *it,* followed him: and he received them, and spake unto them of the kingdom of God, and healed them that had need of healing.

12 [a]And *when* the day began to wear away, then came the twelve, and said unto him, Send the multitude away, that they may go into the towns and country round about, and lodge, and get victuals: for we are here in a desert place.

13 But he said unto them, Give ye them to eat. And they said, We have no more but five loaves and two fishes; except we should go and buy meat for all this people.

14 For they were about five thousand men. And he said to his disciples, Make them sit down by fifties in a company.

15 And they did so, and made *them* all sit down.

16 Then he took the five loaves and the two fishes, and looking up to heaven, he blessed them, and brake, and gave to the disciples to set before the multitude.

8:49 [a]Mark 5:35
8:52 [a]John 11:11,13
8:54 [a]ch. 7:14; John 11:43
8:56 [a]Mat. 8:4; 9:30; Mark 5:43
9:1 [a]Mat. 10:1; Mark 3:13; 6:7
9:2 [a]Mat. 10:7,8; Mark 6:12; ch. 10:1,9
9:3 [a]Mat. 10:9; Mark 6:8; ch. 10:4; 22:35
9:4 [a]Mat. 10:11; Mark 6:10
9:5 [a]Mat. 10:14 [b]Acts 13:51
9:6 [a]Mark 6:12
9:7 [a]Mark 14:1; Mark 6:14
9:9 [a]ch. 23:8
9:10 [a]Mark 6:30 [b]Mat. 14:13
9:12 [a]Mat. 14:15; Mark 6:35; John 6:1,5

8:50 *shall be made whole.* See note on Mark 5:34.

8:52 *wept, and bewailed.* See note on Mark 5:38. *not dead, but sleepeth.* Jesus meant that she was not permanently dead (see John 11:11–14 for a similar statement about Lazarus).

8:56 *charged them that they should tell no man.* See notes on Mat 8:4; Mark 5:43. Further publicity at this time concerning a raising from the dead would have been counterproductive to Jesus' ministry.

9:1–6 A new phase of Jesus' ministry began when He sent out the apostles to do the type of preaching, teaching and healing that they had observed Him doing (Mat 9:35). This was the third tour of Galilee by Jesus and His disciples (see note on 8:1). On the first tour Jesus traveled with the four fishermen; on the second all 12 were with Him; on the third Jesus traveled alone after sending out the twelve two by two.

9:1 *his twelve.* The apostles (see 6:13). *power and authority.* Special power to heal (see 5:17; 8:46) and authority in teaching and control over evil spirits. *devils.* Evil spirits (see note on 4:33).

9:3 *Take nothing.* No excess baggage that would encumber travel, not even the usual provisions. They were to be entirely dependent on the people with whom they were staying (see note on Mark 6:8).

9:4 *there abide.* They were not to move from house to house, seeking better lodging, but use only one home as headquarters while preaching in a community.

9:5 *shake off the very dust from your feet.* A sign of repudiation for their rejection of God's message and a gesture showing separation from everything associated with the place (see 10:11; see also notes on Mat 10:14; Acts 13:51).

9:7 *Herod the tetrarch.* See note on Mat 14:1. *John was risen from the dead.* See note on Mark 6:16. Luke does not give details about John's death (see Mat 14:1–12; Mark 6:17–29), which occurred about this time, but simply notes that it had taken place (v. 9).

9:8 *Elias had appeared.* See notes on 1:17; Mark 9:12.

9:9 *he desired to see him.* Herod's desire to see Jesus was not fulfilled until Jesus' trial (23:8–12).

9:10–17 The feeding of the 5,000 is the only miracle besides Jesus' resurrection that is reported in all four Gospels (see notes on Mark 6:30–44; John 6:1–14).

9:10 *Bethsaida.* See note on Mat 11:21. Jesus must have retired to a remote area near the town (v. 12).

9:12 *the day began to wear away.* After the preaching and healing, the question was raised about food and lodging because they were in an isolated place. Jesus may have introduced the question (see John 6:5), but the Synoptics indicate that the disciples were also concerned.

9:14 *sit down by fifties in a company.* See note on Mark 6:40.

17 And they did eat, and were all filled: and there was taken up of fragments that remained to them twelve baskets.

Peter's confession of faith

18 ¶ [a]And it came to pass, as he was alone praying, *his* disciples were with him: and he asked them, saying, Whom say the people that I am?

19 They answering said, [a]John the Baptist; but some *say,* Elias; and others *say,* that one of the old prophets is risen again.

20 He said unto them, But whom say ye that I am? [a]Peter answering said, The Christ of God.

21 [a]And he straitly charged them, and commanded *them* to tell no *man* that *thing;*

22 Saying, [a]The Son of man must suffer many *things,* and be rejected of the elders and chief priests and scribes, and be slain, and be raised the third day.

23 [a]And he said to *them* all, If any *man* will come after me, let him deny himself, and take up his cross daily, and follow me.

24 For whosoever will save his life shall lose it: but whosoever will lose his life for my sake, the same shall save it.

25 [a]For what is a man advantaged, if he gain the whole world, and lose himself, or be cast away?

26 [a]For whosoever shall be ashamed of me and of my words, of him shall the Son of man be ashamed, when he shall come in his own glory, and *in his* Father's, and of the holy angels.

27 [a]But I tell you of a truth, there be some standing here, which shall not taste of death, till they see the kingdom of God.

The transfiguration

28 ¶ [a]And it came to pass about an eight days after these [1]sayings, he took Peter and John and James, and went up into a mountain to pray.

29 And as he prayed, the fashion of his countenance was altered, and his raiment *was* white *and* glistering.

30 And behold, there talked with him two men, which were Moses and Elias:

31 Who appeared in glory, and spake of his decease which he should accomplish at Jerusalem.

32 But Peter and they that were with him [a]were heavy with sleep: and when they were awake, they saw his glory, and the two men that stood with him.

33 And it came to pass, as they departed from him, Peter said unto Jesus, Master, it is good for us to be here: and let us make three tabernacles; one for thee, and one for Moses, and one for Elias: not knowing what he said.

34 While he thus spake, there came a cloud, and overshadowed them: and they feared as they entered into the cloud.

35 And there came a voice out of the

9:18 [a]Mat. 16:13; Mark 8:27
9:19 [a]ver. 7,8; Mat. 14:2
9:20 [a]Mat. 16:16; John 6:69
9:21 [a]Mat. 16:20
9:22 [a]Mat. 16:21; 17:22
9:23 [a]Mat. 10:38; 16:24; Mark 8:34; ch. 14:27
9:25 [a]Mat. 16:26; Mark 8:36
9:26 [a]Mat. 10:33; Mark 8:38; 2 Tim. 2:12
9:27 [a]Mat. 16:28; Mark 9:1
9:28 [1]Or, *things* [a]Mat. 17:1; Mark 9:2
9:32 [a]Dan. 8:18; 10:9

9:17 *fragments . . . twelve baskets.* This act served as an example of avoiding wastefulness and as a demonstration that everyone had been adequately fed (see note on Mark 6:43).

9:18 *Whom say the people that I am?* The report brought by the disciples was the same as the one that reached Herod (see vv. 7–8). This event occurred to the north, outside Herod's territory, in the vicinity of Caesarea Philippi (see Mat 16:13 and note; see also note on Mark 7:24).

9:20 *Peter answering said.* He was the spokesman for the disciples. *The Christ of God.* See note on 2:11. This predicted Deliverer (the Messiah) had been awaited for centuries (see John 4:25; see also notes on Mat 16:18; Mark 8:29).

9:21 *straitly charged them . . . to tell no man.* The people had false notions about the Messiah and needed to be taught further before Jesus identified Himself explicitly to the public. He had a crucial schedule to keep and could not be interrupted by premature reactions (see notes on Mat 8:4; 16:20; Mark 1:34).

9:22 *Son of man.* See note on Mark 8:31. *must suffer.* Jesus' first explicit prediction of His death (for later references see v. 44; 12:50; 17:25; 18:31–33; cf. 24:7,25–27).

9:23 *take up his cross daily.* To follow Jesus requires self-denial, complete dedication and willing obedience. Luke emphasizes continued action, and "daily" is not mentioned explicitly in the parallel accounts (Mat 16:24–26; Mark 8:34). Disciples from Galilee knew what the cross meant, for hundreds of men had been executed by this means in their region.

9:24 *whosoever will lose his life for my sake.* A saying of Jesus found in all four Gospels and in two Gospels more than once (Mat 10:38–39; 16:24–25; Mark 8:34–35; Luke 14:26–27; 17:33; and, in slightly different form, John 12:25). No other saying of Jesus is given such emphasis.

9:26 *whosoever shall be ashamed.* See 12:9; see also note on Mark 8:38.

9:27 See note on Mat 16:28. *kingdom of God.* See note on Mat 3:2.

9:28 *an eight days.* Frequently used to indicate a week (cf. John 20:26; see note on Mat 17:1). *Peter and John and James.* These three were also with Jesus at the healing of Jairus's daughter (8:51) and in His last visit to Gethsemane (Mark 14:33). *into a mountain.* Although mount Tabor is the traditional site of the mount of transfiguration, its distance from Caesarea Philippi (the vicinity of the last scene), its height (about 1,800 feet) and its occupation by a fortress make it unlikely. Mount Hermon fits the context much better by being both closer and higher (over 9,000 feet; see Mark 9:2). *pray.* Again Luke points out the place of prayer in an important event.

9:30 *Moses and Elias.* Moses, the great OT deliverer and lawgiver, and Elijah, the representative of the prophets. Moses' work had been finished by Joshua, Elijah's by Elisha (another form of the name Joshua). They now spoke with Jesus (whose Hebrew name was Joshua) about the "exodus" He was about to accomplish, by which He would deliver His people from the bondage of sin and bring to fulfillment the work of both Moses and Elijah (see note on 1 Ki 19:16).

9:31 *decease.* Greek *exodos,* a euphemism for Jesus' approaching death. It may also link Jesus' saving death and resurrection with God's saving of His people out of Egypt.

9:32 *heavy with sleep.* Perhaps the event was at night. *saw his glory.* See note on Ex 33:18.

9:33 *three tabernacles.* Temporary structures to prolong the visit of the three important persons: lawgiver, prophet and Messiah. The idea was not appropriate, however, because Jesus had a work to finish in His few remaining days on earth (see note on Mark 9:5).

cloud, saying, [a]This is my beloved Son: [b]hear him.

36 And when the voice was past, Jesus was found alone. [a]And they kept *it* close, and told no *man* in those days any of *those things* which they had seen.

A demoniac boy healed

37 ¶ [a]And it came to pass, *that* on the next day, when they were come down from the hill, much people met him.

38 And behold, a man of the company cried out, saying, Master, I beseech thee, look upon my son: for he is mine only child.

39 And lo, a spirit taketh him, and he suddenly crieth out; and it teareth him that he foameth again, and bruising him hardly departeth from him.

40 And I besought thy disciples to cast him out; and they could not.

41 And Jesus answering said, O faithless and perverse generation, how long shall I be with you, and suffer you? Bring thy son hither.

42 And as he was yet a coming, the devil threw him down, and tare *him.* And Jesus rebuked the unclean spirit, and healed the child, and delivered him again to his father.

43 ¶ And they were all amazed at the mighty power of God. But while they wondered every one at all *things* which Jesus did, he said unto his disciples,

44 [a]Let these sayings sink down into your ears: for the Son of man shall be delivered into the hands of men.

45 [a]But they understood not this saying, and it was hid from them, that they perceived it not: and they feared to ask him of that saying.

True discipleship

46 ¶ [a]Then there arose a reasoning among them, which of them should be greatest.

47 And Jesus, perceiving the thought of their heart, took a child, and set him by him,

9:35 [a]Mat. 3:17 [b]Acts 3:22
9:36 [a]Mat. 17:9
9:37 [a]Mat. 17:14; Mark 9:14,17
9:44 [a]Mat. 17:22
9:45 [a]Mark 9:32; ch. 2:50; 18:34
9:46 [a]Mat. 18:1; Mark 9:34
9:48 [a]Mat. 10:40; 18:5; Mark 9:37; John 12:44; 13:20 [b]Mat. 23:11,12
9:49 [a]Mark 9:38; See Num. 11:28
9:50 [a]See Mat. 12:30; ch. 11:23
9:51 [a]Mark 16:19; Acts 1:2
9:53 [a]John 4:4,9
9:54 [a]2 Ki. 1:10,12
9:56 [a]John 3:17; 12:47
9:57 [a]Mat. 8:19
9:59 [a]Mat. 8:21

48 And said unto them, [a]Whosoever shall receive this child in my name receiveth me: and whosoever shall receive me receiveth him that sent me: [b]for he that is least among you all, the same shall be great.

49 ¶ [a]And John answered and said, Master, we saw one casting out devils in thy name; and we forbad him, because he followeth not with us.

50 And Jesus said unto him, Forbid *him* not: for [a]he that is not against us is for us.

James and John rebuked

51 ¶ And it came to pass, when the time was come that [a]he should be received up, he stedfastly set his face to go to Jerusalem,

52 And sent messengers before his face: and they went, and entered into a village of the Samaritans, to make ready for him.

53 And [a]they did not receive him, because his face was *as though he* would go to Jerusalem.

54 And when his disciples James and John saw *this,* they said, Lord, wilt thou *that* we command fire to come down from heaven, and consume them, even as [a]Elias did?

55 But he turned, and rebuked them, and said, Ye know not what manner of spirit ye are of.

56 For [a]the Son of man is not come to destroy men's lives, but to save *them.* And they went to another village.

The teaching about discipleship

57 ¶ [a]And it came to pass *that,* as they went in the way, a certain *man* said unto him, Lord, I will follow thee whithersoever thou goest.

58 And Jesus said unto him, Foxes have holes, and birds of the air *have* nests; but the Son of man hath not where to lay *his* head.

59 [a]And he said unto another, Follow me. But he said, Lord, suffer me first to go and bury my father.

9:35 *my beloved Son.* Or "my Chosen One," related to a Jewish title found in Dead Sea Scrolls literature, and possibly echoing Is 42:1. See 23:35. "Chosen" parallels "beloved" in Mat 17:5 (see 2 Pet 1:17).

9:39 *a spirit taketh him.* This evil spirit was causing seizures (Mat 17:15) and a speechless condition (Mark 9:17). Evil spirits were responsible for many kinds of affliction (see note on 4:33).

9:44 Another prediction of Jesus' coming death (see note on v. 22), an indication of how it will be brought about (see 22:21).

9:46 *which . . . should be greatest.* A subject that arose on a number of occasions (see 22:24; see also Mark 10:35–45).

9:48 *he that is least . . . be great.* A person will become great as he sincerely and unpretentiously looks away from self to revere God.

‡9:49 *followeth not with us.* See note on Mark 9:38.

9:50 *he that is not against us is for us.* Spoken in the context of opposition to the disciples' work (cf. 11:23, set in a different context).

‡9:51 *stedfastly set his face to go to Jerusalem.* (cf. Is 50:7). Luke emphasizes Jesus' determination to complete His mission (see note on 13:22). This journey to Jerusalem, however, is not the one that led to His crucifixion but marks the beginning of a period of ministry in Judea, of which Jerusalem was the central city. Mark 10:1 notes this departure for Judea, which John more specifically describes as a journey to Jerusalem during the time of the feast of tabernacles (John 7:1–10). The Judean ministry (see Introduction: Outline) is recounted in 9:51–13:21 and John 7:10–10:39.

9:52 *a village of the Samaritans.* Samaritans were particularly hostile to Jews who were on their way to observe religious festivals in Jerusalem. It was at least a three-day journey from Galilee to Jerusalem through Samaria, and Samaritans refused overnight shelter for the pilgrims. Because of this antipathy, Jews traveling between Galilee and Jerusalem frequently went on the east side of the Jordan River.

‡9:54 *command fire to come down from heaven.* As Elijah had (2 Ki 1:9–16). James and John were known as "sons of thunder" (Mark 3:17).

9:55 *rebuked them.* See note on 2 Ki 1:10.

9:57 *as they went in the way.* Continuing their journey through Samaria to Jerusalem.

9:59 *bury my father.* If his father had already died, the man would have been occupied with the burial then. But evidently he wanted to wait until after his father's death, which might have been years away. Jesus told him that the spiritually dead

60 Jesus said unto him, Let the dead bury their dead: but go thou and preach the kingdom of God.

61 And another also said, Lord, [a]I will follow thee; but let me first go bid them farewell, which are *at home* in my house.

62 And Jesus said unto him, No *man* having put his hand to the plough, and looking back, is fit for the kingdom of God.

The mission of the seventy

10 After these *things* the Lord appointed other seventy also, and [a]sent them two and two before his face into every city and place, whither he himself would come.

2 Therefore said he unto them, [a]The harvest truly *is* great, but the labourers *are* few: [b]pray ye therefore the Lord of the harvest, that he would send forth labourers into his harvest.

3 Go your ways: [a]behold, I send you forth as lambs among wolves.

4 [a]Carry neither purse, nor scrip, nor shoes: and [b]salute no *man* by the way.

5 [a]And into whatsoever house ye enter, first say, Peace *be* to this house.

6 And if the son of peace be there, your peace shall rest upon it: if not, it shall turn to you again.

7 [a]And in the same house remain, [b]eating and drinking such *things* as they give: for [c]the labourer is worthy of his hire. Go not from house to house.

8 And into whatsoever city ye enter, and they receive you, eat such *things* as are set before you:

9 [a]And heal the sick that are therein, and say unto them, [b]The kingdom of God is come nigh unto you.

10 But into whatsoever city ye enter, and they receive you not, go *your ways* out into the streets of the same, and say,

11 [a]Even the *very* dust of your city, which cleaveth on us, we do wipe off against you: notwithstanding be ye sure of this, that the kingdom of God is come nigh unto you.

12 But I say unto you, that [a]it shall be more tolerable in that day for Sodom, than for that city.

13 ¶ [a]Woe unto thee, Chorazin, woe unto thee, Bethsaida: [b]for if the mighty works had been done in Tyre and Sidon, which have been done in you, they had a great while ago repented, sitting in sackcloth and ashes.

14 But it shall be more tolerable for Tyre and Sidon at the judgment, than for you.

15 [a]And thou, Capernaum, which art [b]exalted to heaven, [c]shalt be thrust down to hell.

16 [a]He that heareth you heareth me; and [b]he that despiseth you despiseth me; [c]and he that despiseth me despiseth him that sent me.

17 ¶ And [a]the seventy returned *again* with joy, saying, Lord, even the devils are subject unto us through thy name.

18 And he said unto them, [a]I beheld Satan as lightning fall from heaven.

19 Behold, [a]I give unto you power to tread on serpents and scorpions, and over all the power of the enemy: and nothing shall by any means hurt you.

20 Notwithstanding in this rejoice not, that the spirits are subject unto you; but rather rejoice, because [a]your names are written in heaven.

21 ¶ [a]In that hour Jesus rejoiced in spirit, and said, I thank thee, O Father, Lord of heaven and earth, that thou hast hid these *things* from the wise and prudent, and hast revealed them unto babes: even so, Father; for so it seemed good in thy sight.

22 [a][1]All *things* are delivered to me of my Father: and [b]no *man* knoweth who the Son is, but the Father; and who the Father is, but the Son, and *he* to whom the Son will reveal *him.*

23 And he turned him unto *his* disciples,

9:61 [a]See 1 Ki. 19:20
10:1 [a]Mat. 10:1; Mark 6:7
10:2 [a]Mat. 9:37; John 4:35 [b]2 Thes. 3:1
10:3 [a]Mat. 10:16
10:4 [a]Mat. 10:9; Mark 6:8; ch. 9:3 [b]2 Ki. 4:29
10:5 [a]Mat. 10:12
10:7 [a]Mat. 10:11 [b]1 Cor. 10:27 [c]Mat. 10:10; 1 Cor. 9:4; 1 Tim. 5:18
10:9 [a]ch. 9:2 [b]ver. 11; Mat. 3:2; 4:17; 10:7
10:11 [a]Mat. 10:14; ch. 9:5; Acts 13:51; 18:6
10:12 [a]Mat. 10:15; Mark 6:11
10:13 [a]Mat. 11:21 [b]Ezek. 3:6
10:15 [a]Mat. 11:23 [b]See Gen. 11:4; Deut. 1:28; Is. 14:13; Jer. 51:53 [c]See Ezek. 26:20; 32:18
10:16 [a]Mat. 10:40; Mark 9:37; John 13:20 [b]1 Thes. 4:8 [c]John 5:23
10:17 [a]ver. 1
10:18 [a]John 12:31; 16:11; Rev. 9:1; 12:8,9
10:19 [a]Mark 16:18; Acts 28:5
10:20 [a]Ex. 32:32; Ps. 69:28; Is. 4:3; Dan. 12:1; Phil. 4:3; Heb. 12:23; Rev. 13:8; 20:12
10:21 [a]Mat. 11:25
10:22 [1]Many ancient copies add these words, *And turning to his disciples, he said* [a]Mat. 28:18; John 3:35; 5:27; 17:2 [b]John 1:18; 6:44,46

could bury the physically dead, and that the spiritually alive should be busy proclaiming the kingdom of God.

‡10:1 *appointed other seventy.* Recorded only in Luke, though similar instructions were given to the twelve (Mat 9:37–38; 10:7–16; Mark 6:7–11; cf. Luke 9:3–5). Jesus covered Judea with His message (see note on 9:51) as thoroughly as He had Galilee. *two and two.* During His ministry in Galilee, Jesus had also sent out the twelve in pairs (see 9:1–6; Mark 6:7 and notes), a practice continued in the early church (Acts 13:2; 15:27,39–40; 17:14; 19:22).

10:4 *Carry neither purse, nor scrip, nor shoes.* They were to travel light, without moneybag, luggage or extra sandals. *salute no man by the way.* They were not to stop along the way to visit and exchange customary lengthy greetings. The mission was urgent.

10:7 *Go not from house to house.* See note on 9:4.

10:9 *The kingdom of God is come nigh.* The heart of Jesus' message (see notes on 4:43; Mat 3:2).

10:11 *dust . . . we do wipe off.* See note on 9:5.

‡10:12 *more tolerable in that day for Sodom.* Although Sodom was so sinful that God destroyed it (Gen 19:24–28; Jude 7), the people who heard the message of Jesus and His disciples were even more accountable, because they had the gospel of the kingdom preached to them. This passage clearly teaches degrees of punishment. Some sins are worse than others and bring more judgment. *that day.* Judgment day.

10:13 *Chorazin . . . Bethsaida.* See note on Mat 11:21.

10:14 *Tyre and Sidon.* Gentile cities in Phoenicia, north of Galilee, which had not had opportunity to witness Jesus' miracles and hear His preaching as the people had in most of Galilee (see note on v. 12).

10:15 *Capernaum.* Jesus' headquarters on the north shore of Galilee (see Mat 4:13 and note), whose inhabitants had many opportunities to see and hear Jesus. Therefore the condemnation for their rejection was the greater.

‡10:18 *Satan as lightning fall from heaven.* Even the demons were driven out by the disciples (v. 17), which meant that Satan was suffering defeat. This could refer to Satan's original fall from glory (See 2 Pet 2:4; Jude 6; Rev 12:9).

10:19 *serpents and scorpions . . . power of the enemy.* The snakes and scorpions may represent evil spirits; the enemy is Satan himself.

10:20 Man's salvation is more important than power to overcome the evil one or escape his harm. *your names are written.* Salvation is recorded in heaven (see Ps 69:28; Dan 12:1; Phil 4:3; Heb 12:23; Rev 3:5).

and said privately, [a]Blessed *are* the eyes which
see *the things* that ye see:
24 For I tell you, [a]that many prophets and
kings have desired to see *those things* which
ye see, and have not seen *them;* and to hear
those things which ye hear, and have not
heard *them.*

The good Samaritan

25 ¶ And behold, a certain lawyer stood up,
and tempted him, saying, [a]Master, what shall I
do to inherit eternal life?
26 He said unto him, What is written in
the law? how readest thou?
27 And he answering said, [a]Thou shalt love
the Lord thy God with all thy heart, and with
all thy soul, and with all thy strength, and with
all thy mind; and [b]thy neighbour as thyself.
28 And he said unto him, Thou hast answered right: this do, and [a]thou shalt live.
29 But he, willing to [a]justify himself, said
unto Jesus, And who is my neighbour?
30 And Jesus answering said, A certain
man went down from Jerusalem to Jericho,
and fell among thieves, which stripped him of
his raiment, and wounded *him,* and departed,
leaving *him* half dead.
31 And by chance there came down a certain priest that way: and when he saw him,
[a]he passed by on the other side.
32 And likewise a Levite, when he was at
the place, came and looked *on him,* and
passed by on the other side.
33 But a certain [a]Samaritan, as he journeyed, came where he was: and when he saw
him, he had compassion *on him,*
34 And went to *him,* and bound up his
wounds, pouring in oil and wine, and set him
on his own beast, and brought him to an inn,
and took care of him.
35 And on the morrow when he departed,
he took out two [1]pence, and gave *them* to the
host, and said unto him, Take care of him; and
whatsoever thou spendest more, when I come
again, I will repay thee.
36 Which now of these three, thinkest
thou, was neighbour unto him that fell among
the thieves?
37 And he said, He that shewed mercy on
him. Then said Jesus unto him, Go, and do
thou likewise.

Jesus visits Mary and Martha

38 ¶ Now it came to pass, as they went,
that he entered into a certain village: and a
certain woman named [a]Martha received him
into her house.
39 And she had a sister called Mary,
[a]which also [b]sat at Jesus' feet, and heard his
word.
40 But Martha was cumbered about much
serving, and came to *him,* and said, Lord, dost
thou not care that my sister hath left me to
serve alone? bid her therefore that she help me.
41 And Jesus answered and said unto her,
Martha, Martha, thou art careful and troubled
about many *things:*
42 But [a]one *thing* is needful: and Mary
hath chosen *that* good part, which shall not be
taken away from her.

Jesus' teaching on prayer

11 And it came to pass *that,* as he was
praying in a certain place, when he
ceased, one of his disciples said unto him,
Lord, teach us to pray, as John also taught his
disciples.
2 And he said unto them, When ye pray,
say,
¶ [a]Our Father which art in heaven, Hallowed be thy name. Thy kingdom come. Thy
will be done, as in heaven, so in earth.
3 Give us [1]day by day our daily bread.
4 And forgive us our sins; for we also for-

10:23 [a]Mat. 13:16
10:24 [a]1 Pet. 1:10
10:25 [a]Mat. 19:16; 22:35
10:27 [a]Deut. 6:5 [b]Lev. 19:18
10:28 [a]Lev. 18:5; Neh. 9:29; Ezek. 20:11,13, 21; Rom. 10:5
10:29 [a]ch. 16:15
10:31 [a]Ps. 38:11
10:33 [a]John 4:9
10:35 [1]See Mat. 20:2; Mark 12:15
10:38 [a]John 11:1; 12:2,3
10:39 [a]1 Cor. 7:32 [b]ch. 8:35; Acts 22:3
10:42 [a]Ps. 27:4
11:2 [a]Mat. 6:9
11:3 [1]Or, *for the day*

10:25 *lawyer.* A scholar well versed in Scripture asked a common question (18:18; cf. Mat 22:35), either to take issue with Jesus or simply to see what kind of teacher He was. See note on 7:30.

10:27 *love . . . God . . . thy neighbour.* Elsewhere Jesus uses these words in reply to another question (Mat 22:35–40; Mark 12:28–32), putting the same two Scriptures together (Deut 6:5; Lev 19:18). Whether a fourfold love (heart, soul, strength and mind, as here and in Mark 12:30) or threefold (Deut 6:5; Mat 22:37; Mark 12:33), the significance is that total devotion is demanded.

10:29 *to justify himself.* The answer to his first question was obviously one he knew, so to gain credibility he asked for an interpretation. In effect he said, "But the real question is: Who is my neighbor?"

‡10:30 *Jerusalem to Jericho.* A distance of 17 miles and a descent from about 2,500 feet above sea level to about 800 feet below sea level. The road ran through rocky, completely desolate country, which provided places for robbers to waylay defenseless travelers.

‡10:31–33 *priest . . . Levite . . . Samaritan.* It is significant, and a completely shocking reversal, that the person Jesus commended was neither the religious leader nor the lay associate, but a hated foreigner. Jews viewed Samaritans as half-breeds, both physically (see note on Mat 10:5) and spiritually (see notes on John 4:20,22). Samaritans and Jews practiced open hostility (see note on 9:52), but Jesus asserted that love knows no national boundaries.

10:35 *two pence.* Two days' wages, which would keep a man up to two months in an inn.

10:36 *Which . . . was neighbour unto him . . . ?* The question now became: Who proves he is the good neighbor by his actions?

10:38 *a certain village.* Bethany, about two miles from Jerusalem, was the home of Mary and Martha (John 12:1–3).

11:1 *he was praying.* Not only on special occasions (e.g., baptism, 3:21; choosing the twelve, 6:12; Gethsemane, 22:41) but also as a regular practice (5:16; Mat 14:23; Mark 1:35). *teach us to pray.* The Lord's model prayer was given here in answer to a request, and is similar to Mat 6:9–13, where it is a part of the Sermon on the Mount. Six petitions are included in the prayer as given in the Sermon on the Mount by Matthew (combining the last two petitions into one), whereas five appear in the prayer in Luke.

11:4 *forgive us our sins.* Mat 6:12 has "debts," but the meaning is the same as "sins." Jesus taught this truth on other occa-

give every one *that is* indebted to us. And lead
us not into temptation; but deliver us from evil.
5 ¶ And he said unto them, Which of you
shall have a friend, and shall go unto him at
midnight, and say unto him, Friend, lend me
three loaves;
6 For a friend of mine [1]in *his* journey is
come to me, and I have nothing to set before
him:
7 And he from within shall answer and say,
Trouble me not: the door is now shut, and my
children are with me in bed; I cannot rise and
give thee?
8 I say unto you, [a]Though he will not rise
and give him, because *he* is his friend, yet because of his importunity he will rise and give
him as many as he needeth.
9 [a]And I say unto you, Ask, and it shall be
given you; seek, and ye shall find; knock, and
it shall be opened unto you.
10 For every one that asketh receiveth; and
he that seeketh findeth; and to him that
knocketh it shall be opened.
11 [a]*If* a son shall ask bread of any of you
that is a father, will he give him a stone? or if
he ask a fish, will he for a fish give him a serpent?
12 Or if he shall ask an egg, will he [1]offer
him a scorpion?
13 If ye then, being evil, know how to give
good gifts unto your children: how much more
shall *your* heavenly Father give the Holy Spirit
to them that ask him?

The Pharisees' slander

14 ¶ [a]And he was casting out a devil, and it
was dumb. And it came to pass, when the devil was gone out, the dumb spake; and the people wondered.

11:6 [1]Or, *out of his way*
11:8 [a]ch. 18:1
11:9 [a]Mat. 7:7; 21:22; Mark 11:24; John 15:7; Jas. 1:6; 1 John 3:22
11:11 [a]Mat. 7:9
11:12 [1][Gr. *give*]
11:14 [a]Mat. 9:32; 12:22
11:15 [1][Gr. *Beelzebul*, and so ver. 18,19] [a]Mat. 9:34; 12:24
11:16 [a]Mat. 12:38; 16:1
11:17 [a]Mat. 12:25; Mark 3:24 [b]John 2:25
11:20 [a]Ex. 8:19
11:21 [a]Mat. 12:29; Mark 3:27
11:22 [a]Is. 53:12; Col. 2:15
11:23 [a]Mat. 12:30
11:24 [a]Mat. 12:43
11:26 [a]John 5:14; Heb. 6:4; 10:26; 2 Pet. 2:20
11:27 [a]ch. 1:28,48

15 But some of them said, [a]He casteth out
devils through [1]Beelzebub the chief of the
devils.
16 And other, tempting *him,* [a]sought of
him a sign from heaven.
17 [a]But [b]he, knowing their thoughts, said
unto them, Every kingdom divided against itself is brought to desolation; and a house *divided* against a house falleth.
18 If Satan also be divided against himself,
how shall his kingdom stand? because ye say
that I cast out devils through Beelzebub.
19 And if I by Beelzebub cast out devils, by
whom do your sons cast *them* out? therefore
shall they be your judges.
20 But if I [a]with the finger of God cast out
devils, no doubt the kingdom of God is come
upon you.
21 [a]When a strong *man* armed keepeth his
palace, his goods are in peace:
22 But [a]when a stronger than he shall
come upon *him,* and overcome him, he taketh
from him all his armour wherein he trusted,
and divideth his spoils.
23 [a]He that is not with me is against me:
and he that gathereth not with me scattereth.
24 [a]When the unclean spirit is gone out of
a man, he walketh through dry places, seeking
rest; and finding none, he saith, I will return
unto my house whence I came out.
25 And when he cometh, he findeth *it*
swept and garnished.
26 Then goeth he, and taketh to *him* seven
other spirits more wicked than himself; and
they enter in, and dwell there: and [a]the last
state of that man is worse than the first.
27 ¶ And it came to pass, as he spake these
things, a certain woman of the company lift up
her voice, and said unto him, [a]Blessed *is* the

sions as well (Mat 18:35; Mark 11:25). The prayer is a pattern for believers, who have already been forgiven for their sins. Jesus speaks here of daily forgiveness, which is necessary to restore broken communion with God.

‡11:5–13 Jesus now urged persistence in prayer (vv. 5–8) and gave assurance that God answers prayer (vv. 9–13). The argument is from the lesser to the greater (see v. 13). If some humans will grant one's petitions, "how much more" will God help His dear children.

‡11:13 *give the Holy Spirit.* Mat 7:11 has "give good gifts," probably referring to spiritual gifts. Luke emphasizes the work of the Spirit, the greatest of God's gifts.

11:14 *devil, and it was dumb.* See note on 4:33. This evil spirit caused muteness. The probable parallel passage in Matthew (12:22–30; see also Mark 3:20–27) indicates that the man was also blind.

11:15 *Beelzebub the chief of the devils.* Satan (v. 18). See note on Mat 10:25.

11:16 *a sign from heaven.* Jesus had just healed a mute. Here was their sign, and they would not recognize it.

11:17 *kingdom divided against itself.* If Satan gave power to Jesus, who opposed Him in every way, Satan would be supporting an attack upon himself.

11:19 *by whom do your sons . . . ?* Jesus did not say whether the followers of the Pharisees (see Mat 12:24) actually drove out demons (see note on v. 24); but they claimed to drive them out by the power of God, and Jesus claimed the same. So to accuse Jesus of using Satanic power was implicitly to condemn their own followers as well. *your judges.* They will condemn you for your accusation against them.

11:20 *the kingdom of God is come.* In the sense that the King was present in the person of Jesus (see note on 4:43) and that the powers of evil were being overthrown.

11:22 *a stronger than he . . . overcome.* Jesus was stronger than Beelzebub, and by His exorcism of demons He demonstrated that He had overpowered Satan and disarmed him. It was therefore foolish to suggest that Jesus had cast out demons by Satan's power.

11:23 The one who does not intentionally support Jesus opposes Him, making neutrality impossible. Even the worker in 9:50, whom the disciples said "followeth not with us" (9:49), was apparently a believer, acting in Jesus' name (see note on Mark 9:38), and Jesus did not condemn him.

11:24 *unclean spirit is gone out.* Jesus is perhaps referring to the work of Jewish exorcists, who claimed to cast out demons (cf. v. 19) but who rejected the kingdom of God and whose exorcisms were therefore ineffective. See Mat 12:43–45, where Jesus makes a similar comment about the Jewish nation of that day.

11:25 *findeth it swept.* The place had been cleaned up but left unoccupied. A life reformed but lacking God's presence is open to reoccupancy by evil.

womb that bare thee, and the paps which thou hast sucked.

28 But he said, Yea [a]rather, blessed *are* they that hear the word of God, and keep it.

Warning against seeking signs

29 ¶ [a]And when the people were gathered thick together, he began to say, This is an evil generation: they seek a sign; and there shall no sign be given it, but the sign of Jonas the prophet.

30 For as [a]Jonas was a sign unto the Ninevites, so shall also the Son of man be to this generation.

31 [a]*The* queen of the south shall rise up in the judgment with the men of this generation, and condemn them: for she came from the utmost parts of the earth to hear the wisdom of Solomon; and behold, a greater than Solomon *is* here.

32 *The* men of Nineveh shall rise up in the judgment with this generation, and shall condemn it: for [a]they repented at the preaching of Jonas; and behold, a greater than Jonas *is* here.

The parable of the lighted candle

33 ¶ [a]No *man,* when he hath lighted a candle, putteth *it* in a secret place, neither under a [1]bushel, but on a candlestick, that they which come in may see the light.

34 [a]The light of the body is the eye: therefore when thine eye is single, thy whole body also is full of light; but when *thine eye* is evil, thy body also *is* full of darkness.

35 Take heed therefore that the light which is in thee be not darkness.

36 If thy whole body therefore *be* full of light, having no part dark, the whole shall be full of light, as when [1]the bright shining of a candle doth give thee light.

11:28 [a]Mat. 7:21; ch. 8:21; Jas. 1:25
11:29 [a]Mat. 12:38,39
11:30 [a]Jonah 1:17; 2:10
11:31 [a]1 Ki. 10:1
11:32 [a]Jonah 3:5
11:33 [1]See Mat. 5:15 [a]Mat. 5:15; Mark 4:21; ch. 8:16
11:34 [a]Mat. 6:22
11:36 [1][Gr. *a candle by* its *bright shining*]
11:38 [a]Mark 7:3
11:39 [a]Mat. 23:25 [b]Tit. 1:15
11:41 [1]Or, *as you are able* [a]Is. 58:7; Dan. 4:27; ch. 12:33
11:42 [a]Mat. 23:23
11:43 [a]Mat. 23:6; Mark 12:38,39
11:44 [a]Mat. 23:27 [b]Ps. 5:9
11:46 [a]Mat. 23:4
11:47 [a]Mat. 23:29

The warning against Pharisaism

37 ¶ And as *he* spake, a certain Pharisee besought him to dine with him: and he went in, and sat down to meat.

38 And [a]when the Pharisee saw *it,* he marvelled that he had not first washed before dinner.

39 [a]And the Lord said unto him, Now do ye Pharisees make clean the outside of the cup and the platter; but [b]your inward part is full of ravening and wickedness.

40 *Ye* fools, did not he that made that *which is* without make that *which is* within also?

41 [a]But rather give alms [1]*of* such *things* as *you* have; and behold, all *things* are clean unto you.

42 [a]But woe unto you, Pharisees! for ye tithe the mint and rue and all *manner of* herbs, and pass over judgment and the love of God: these ought *ye* to have done, and not to leave the other undone.

43 ¶ [a]Woe unto you, Pharisees! for ye love the uppermost seats in the synagogues, and greetings in the markets.

44 ¶ [a]Woe unto you, scribes and Pharisees, hypocrites! [b]for ye are as graves which appear not, and the men that walk over *them* are not aware *of them.*

45 ¶ Then answered one of the lawyers, and said unto him, Master, thus saying thou reproachest us also.

46 And he said,

¶ Woe unto you also, *ye* lawyers! [a]for ye lade men *with* burdens grievous to be borne, and ye yourselves touch not the burdens with one of your fingers.

47 ¶ [a]Woe unto you! for ye build the sepulchres of the prophets, and your fathers killed them.

48 Truly ye bear witness that ye allow the

11:29 *seek a sign.* On several occasions Jews asked for miraculous signs (v. 16; Mat 12:38; Mark 8:11), but Jesus rejected their requests because they had wrong motives.

11:30 *as Jonas was a sign.* Jonah spent three days (see note on Mat 12:40) "buried" in the huge fish, just as Jesus would be buried for three days before His resurrection.

‡11:31–32 *a greater than Solomon . . . a greater than Jonas.* Jesus argued from the lesser to the greater. If the queen of Sheba responded positively to the wisdom of Solomon, and the men of Nineveh to the preaching of Jonas, how much more should the people of Jesus' day have responded to the ministry of Jesus, who is infinitely greater than Solomon or Jonas!

11:31 *The queen of the south.* The queen of Sheba (see 1 Ki 10:1–10 and notes).

11:33 *a bushel.* A container holding about one peck. *may see the light.* A lamp is meant to give light to those who are near it (see v. 36). Jesus had publicly exhibited the light of the gospel for all to see, but "an evil generation" (v. 29) requested more spectacular signs. The problem was not with any failure on Jesus' part in giving light; it was with the faulty vision of his audience.

11:34 *thine eye is single.* Those asking for a sign do not need more light; they need clear eyes to allow the light to enter.

11:38 *he had not first washed before dinner.* Not commanded in the law but added in the tradition of the Pharisees (Mark 7:3; cf. Mat 15:9).

11:39 *clean the outside.* Engage in ceremonial washings of the body. *ravening and wickedness.* These Pharisees were more concerned about keeping ceremonies than about being moral (cf. Mark 7:20–23).

11:40 *make that which is within also.* The inside of man (the "heart" and inner righteousness) is more important than the outside (ceremonial cleansing).

11:41 *all things are clean.* Giving from the heart makes everything else right. If one gives to the poor, his heart is no longer in the grip of "ravening and wickedness" (v. 39).

11:44 *graves which appear not.* The Jews whitewashed their tombs so that no one would accidentally touch them and be defiled (cf. Num 19:16; Mat 23:27). Just as touching a grave resulted in ceremonial uncleanness, being influenced by these corrupt religious leaders could lead to moral uncleanness.

11:45 *lawyers.* See note on 7:30.

11:46 *lade men with burdens.* By adding rules and regulations to the authentic law of Moses (see note on Mat 15:2) and doing nothing to help others keep them (Mat 23:4), while inventing ways for themselves to circumvent them.

11:47 *sepulchres of the prophets.* Outwardly these "lawyers" (v. 46) appeared to honor the prophets in building or rebuilding

deeds of your fathers: for they indeed killed them, and ye build their sepulchres.

49 Therefore also said the wisdom of God, [a]I will send them prophets and apostles, and *some* of them they shall slay and persecute:

50 That the blood of all the prophets, which was shed from the foundation of the world, may be required of this generation;

51 [a]From the blood of Abel unto [b]the blood of Zacharias, which perished between the altar and the temple: verily I say unto you, It shall be required of this generation.

52 ¶ [a]Woe unto you, lawyers! for ye have taken away the key of knowledge: ye entered not in yourselves, and them that were entering in ye [1]hindered.

53 ¶ And as he said these *things* unto them, the scribes and the Pharisees began to urge *him* vehemently, and to provoke him to speak of many *things:*

54 Laying wait for him, and [a]seeking to catch something out of his mouth, that they might accuse him.

The value of life

12 In [a]the mean time, when there were gathered together an innumerable multitude of people, insomuch that *they* trode one upon another, he began to say unto his disciples first *of all,* [b]Beware ye of the leaven of the Pharisees, which is hypocrisy.

2 [a]For there is nothing covered, that shall not be revealed; neither hid, that shall not be known.

3 Therefore whatsoever ye have spoken in darkness shall be heard in the light; and *that* which ye have spoken in the ear in closets shall be proclaimed upon the housetops.

4 [a]And I say unto you [b]my friends, Be not afraid of them that kill the body, and after that have no more that *they* can do.

5 But I will *fore*warn you whom you shall fear: Fear him, which after *he* hath killed hath power to cast into hell; yea, I say unto you, Fear him.

6 Are not five sparrows sold for two [1]farthings, and not one of them is forgotten before God?

7 But even the *very* hairs of your head are all numbered. Fear not therefore: ye are of more value than many sparrows.

8 [a]Also I say unto you, Whosoever shall confess me before men, him shall the Son of man also confess before the angels of God:

9 But he that denieth me before men shall be denied before the angels of God.

10 And [a]whosoever shall speak a word against the Son of man, it shall be forgiven him: but unto him that blasphemeth against the Holy Ghost it shall not be forgiven.

11 [a]And when they bring you unto the synagogues, and *unto* magistrates, and powers, take ye no thought how or what *thing* ye shall answer, or what ye shall say:

12 For the Holy Ghost shall teach you in the same hour what ye ought to say.

The parable of the rich fool

13 ¶ And one of the company said unto him, Master, speak to my brother, that *he* divide the inheritance with me.

14 And he said unto him, [a]Man, who made me a judge or a divider over you?

11:49 [a]Mat. 23:34
11:51 [a]Gen. 4:8 [b]2 Chr. 24:20,21
11:52 [1]Or, *forbad* [a]Mat. 23:13
11:54 [a]Mark 12:13
12:1 [a]Mat 16:6; Mark 8:15 [b]Mat. 16:12
12:2 [a]Mat. 10:26; Mark 4:22; ch. 8:17
12:4 [a]Is. 51:7,8,12,13; Jer. 1:8; Mat. 10:28 [b]John 15:14,15
12:6 [1]See Mat. 10:29
12:8 [a]Mat. 10:32; Mark 8:38; 2 Tim. 2:12; 1 John 2:23
12:10 [a]Mat. 12:31,32; Mark 3:28; 1 John 5:16
12:11 [a]Mat. 10:19; Mark 13:11
12:14 [a]John 18:36

memorials, but inwardly they rejected the Christ the prophets announced. They lived in opposition to the teachings of the prophets, just as their forefathers had done.

11:49 *said the wisdom of God.* Not a quotation from the OT or any other known book. It may refer to God speaking through Jesus, or it may be referring in quotation form to God's decision to send prophets and apostles even though He knew they would be rejected.

11:51 *blood of Abel . . . Zacharias.* See note on Mat 23:35.

11:52 *the key of knowledge.* The very persons who should have opened the people's minds concerning the law obscured their understanding by faulty interpretation and an erroneous system of theology. They kept themselves and the people in ignorance of the way of salvation, or, as Matthew's account puts it, they "shut up the kingdom of heaven against men" (Mat 23:13).

11:54 *Laying wait . . . to catch something.* The determination of the religious leaders to trap Jesus is evident throughout Luke (6:11; 19:47–48; 20:19–20; 22:2).

12:1 *leaven of the Pharisees.* See note on Mark 8:15.

12:2 *nothing covered, that shall not be revealed.* In this context the meaning is that nothing hidden through hypocrisy will fail to be made known.

12:3 *in closets.* Storerooms were surrounded by other rooms so that no one could dig in from outside.

12:4 *after that have no more that they can do.* Encouragement in the face of persecution (see Mat 10:28).

12:5 *hath power to cast into hell.* God alone has this power. The Greek word for "hell" is *ge(h)enna* (see note on Mat 5:22), not to be confused with Hades, the general name for the place of the dead. In the NT *ge(h)enna* is used only in Matthew, Mark, Jas 3:6 and here. *Fear him.* Respect His authority, stand in awe of His majesty and trust in Him. Verses 6–7 give the basis for trust.

‡12:6 *five sparrows sold for two farthings.* God even cares for little birds, sold cheaply for food. Three Greek words used for Roman coins are *denarius* (Mat 18:28), *assarion* (Mat 10:29) and *kodrantes* (Mat 5:26), very loosely related to each other as are a 50-cent piece, nickel and penny. The coins here are *assaria,* so the transaction would be something like five birds for two nickels.

12:8 *confess me.* When a person acknowledges that Jesus is the Messiah, the Son of God (Mat 16:16; 1 John 2:22), Jesus acknowledges that the individual is His loyal follower (cf. Mat 7:21).

12:9 *shall be denied.* See 9:26; 2 Tim 2:12; cf. Mat 7:21; 25:41–46. The same word is used in Peter's denial (22:34, 61).

12:10 *blasphemeth against the Holy Ghost.* See note on Mat 12:31; cf. Mark 3:28–29.

12:13 *divide the inheritance.* Deut 21:17 gave the general rule that an elder son received double a younger one's portion. Disputes over such matters were normally settled by rabbis. This man's request of Jesus was selfish and materialistic. There is no indication that the man had been listening seriously to what Jesus had been saying (cf. vv. 1–11). Jesus replied with a parable about the consequences of greed.

15 And he said unto them, [a]Take heed, and beware of covetousness: for a man's life consisteth not in the abundance of the *things* which he possesseth.

16 And he spake a parable unto them, saying, The ground of a certain rich man brought forth plentifully:

17 And he thought within himself, saying, What shall I do, because I have no room where to bestow my fruits?

18 And he said, This will I do: I will pull down my barns, and build greater; and there will I bestow all my fruits and my goods.

19 And I will say to my soul, [a]Soul, thou hast much goods laid up for many years; take thine ease, eat, drink, *and* be merry.

20 But God said unto him, *Thou* fool, this night [a][1]thy soul shall be required of thee: [b]then whose shall *those things* be, which thou hast provided?

21 So *is* he that layeth up treasure for himself, [a]and is not rich towards God.

The teaching about anxiety

22 ¶ And he said unto his disciples, Therefore I say unto you, [a]Take no thought for your life, what ye shall eat; neither for the body, what ye shall put on.

23 The life is more than meat, and the body *is more* than raiment.

24 Consider the ravens: for they neither sow nor reap; which neither have storehouse nor barn; and [a]God feedeth them: how much more are ye better than the fowls?

25 And which of you with taking thought can add to his stature one cubit?

26 If ye then be not able *to do that thing which is* least, why take ye thought for the rest?

27 Consider the lilies how they grow: they toil not, they spin not; and yet I say unto you, *that* Solomon in all his glory was not arrayed like one of these.

28 If then God so clothe the grass, which is to day in the field, and to morrow is cast into the oven; how much more *will he clothe* you, O ye of little faith?

29 And seek not ye what ye shall eat, or what ye shall drink, [1]neither be ye of doubtful mind.

30 For all these *things* do the nations of the world seek after: and your Father knoweth that ye have need of these *things.*

31 [a]But rather seek ye the kingdom of God; and all these *things* shall be added unto you.

32 Fear not, little flock; for [a]it is your Father's good pleasure to give you the kingdom.

33 [a]Sell that ye have, and give alms; [b]provide yourselves bags which wax not old, a treasure in the heavens that faileth not, where no thief approacheth, neither moth corrupteth.

34 For where your treasure is, there will your heart be also.

Parable of the watching servants

35 ¶ [a]Let your loins be girded about, and [b]*your* lights burning;

36 And ye yourselves like unto men that wait for their lord, when he will return from the wedding; that when *he* cometh and knocketh, they may open unto him immediately.

37 [a]Blessed *are* those servants, whom the lord when he cometh shall find watching: verily I say unto you, that he shall gird himself, and make them to sit down to meat, and will come forth and serve them.

38 And if he shall come in the second watch, or come in the third watch, and find *them* so, blessed are those servants.

39 [a]And this know, that if the goodman of the house had known what hour the thief would come, he would have watched, and not have suffered his house to be broken through.

40 [a]Be ye therefore ready also: for the Son of man cometh at an hour when ye think not.

41 ¶ Then Peter said unto him, Lord, speakest thou this parable unto us, or even to all?

42 And the Lord said,

¶ [a]Who then is *that* faithful and wise steward, whom *his* lord shall make ruler over his household, to give *them their* portion of meat in due season?

43 Blessed *is* that servant, whom his lord when he cometh shall find so doing.

44 [a]Of a truth I say unto you, that he will make him ruler over all that he hath.

45 [a]But and if that servant say in his heart, My lord delayeth his coming; and shall begin to beat the menservants and maidens, and to eat and drink, and to be drunken;

46 The lord of that servant will come in a day when he looketh not for *him,* and at an

12:15 [a]1 Tim. 6:7
12:19 [a]Eccl. 11:9; 1 Cor. 15:32; Jas. 5:5
12:20 [1]Gr. *do they require thy soul* [a]Job 20:22; 27:8; Ps. 52:7; Jas. 4:14 [b]Ps. 39:6; Jer. 17:11
12:21 [a]ver. 33; Mat. 6:20; 1 Tim. 6:18,19; Jas. 2:5
12:22 [a]Mat. 6:25
12:24 [a]Job 38:41; Ps. 147:9
12:29 [1]Or, *live not in careful suspense*
12:31 [a]Mat. 6:33
12:32 [a]Mat. 11:25,26
12:33 [a]Mat. 19:21; Acts 2:45; 4:34 [b]Mat. 6:20; ch. 16:9; 1 Tim. 6:19
12:35 [a]Eph. 6:14; 1 Pet. 1:13 [b]Mat. 25:1
12:37 [a]Mat. 24:46
12:39 [a]Mat. 24:43; 1 Thes. 5:2; 2 Pet. 3:10; Rev. 3:3; 16:15
12:40 [a]Mat. 24:44; 25:13; Mark 13:33; ch. 21:34,36; 1 Thes. 5:6; 2 Pet. 3:12
12:42 [a]Mat. 24:45; 25:21; 1 Cor. 42
12:44 [a]Mat. 24:47
12:45 [a]Mat. 24:48

12:16 *parable.* See note on 8:4.
12:20 *fool.* A strong word (11:40; Eph 5:17).
12:31 *seek ye the kingdom.* Since v. 32 suggests that Jesus is speaking to believers, who already possess the kingdom, this command probably means that Christians should seek the spiritual benefits of the kingdom rather than the material goods of the world (cf. Mat 6:33).
12:33 *give alms.* The danger of riches and the need for giving are characteristic themes in Luke (3:11; 6:30; 11:41; 14:13–14; 16:9; 18:22; 19:8).
12:37 *shall gird himself.* The master reverses the normal roles and serves the slaves (cf. 22:27; Mark 10:45; John 13:4–5, 12–16).
12:38 *second watch, or come in the third.* Night was divided into four watches by the Romans (Mark 13:35) and three by the Jews (Judg 7:19); see note on Mat 14:25. These were probably the last two of the Jewish watches. The feast would have begun in the first watch.
12:40 Christ's return is certain, but the time is not known (cf. Mat 24:36).
12:41 Jesus taught the people in parables but used a more direct approach with the disciples. However, He did not intend these warnings of watchfulness just for the disciples (see Mark 13:37). In the following verses He emphasizes the duty to fulfill responsibilities.
12:42 *wise steward.* An outstanding slave (v. 43) was sometimes left in charge of an estate (see 16:1).

hour when he is not ware, and will [1]cut him in sunder, and will appoint *him* his portion with the unbelievers.

47 And [a]that servant, which knew his lord's will, and prepared not *himself,* neither did according to his will, shall be beaten with many *stripes.*

48 [a]But he that knew not, and did commit *things* worthy of stripes, shall be beaten with few *stripes.* For unto whomsoever much is given, of him shall be much required: and to whom *men* have committed much, of him they will ask the more.

Jesus the divider

49 ¶ [a]I am come to send fire on the earth; and what will I, if it be already kindled?

50 But [a]I have a baptism to be baptized *with;* and how am I [1]straitened till it be accomplished!

51 [a]Suppose ye that I am come to give peace on earth? I tell you, Nay; [b]but rather division:

52 [a]For from henceforth there shall be five in one house divided, three against two, and two against three.

53 The father shall be divided against the son, and the son against the father; the mother against the daughter, and the daughter against the mother; the mother in law against her daughter in law, and the daughter in law against her mother in law.

Interpreting the present time

54 ¶ And he said also to the people, [a]When ye see a cloud rise out of the west, straightway ye say, There cometh a shower; and so it is.

55 And when *ye see* the south wind blow, ye say, There will be heat; and it cometh to pass.

56 *Ye* hypocrites, ye can discern the face of the sky and of the earth; but how *is it that* ye do not discern this time?

57 *Yea,* and why even of yourselves judge ye not what *is* right?

58 [a]When thou goest with thine adversary to the magistrate, [b]*as thou art* in the way, give diligence that *thou* mayest be delivered from him; lest he hale thee to the judge, and the judge deliver thee to the officer, and the officer cast thee into prison.

59 I tell thee, thou shalt not depart thence, till thou hast paid the very last [1]mite.

Jesus' call to repentance

13 There were present at that season some that told him of the Galileans, whose blood Pilate had mingled with their sacrifices.

2 And Jesus answering said unto them, Suppose ye that these Galileans were sinners above all the Galileans, because they suffered such *things?*

3 I tell you, Nay: but, except ye repent, ye shall all likewise perish.

4 Or those eighteen, upon whom the tower in Siloam fell, and slew them, think ye that they were [1]sinners above all men that dwelt in Jerusalem?

5 I tell you, Nay: but except ye repent, ye shall all likewise perish.

6 He spake also this parable; [a]A certain *man* had a fig tree planted in his vineyard; and he came and sought fruit thereon, and found none.

7 Then said he unto the dresser of his vineyard, Behold, *these* three years I come seeking fruit on this fig tree, and find none: cut it down; why cumbereth it the ground?

8 And he answering said unto him, Lord, let it alone this year also, till I shall dig about it, and dung *it:*

12:46 [1]Or, *cut him off*
12:47 [a]Num. 15:30; Deut. 25:2; John 9:41; 15:22; Acts 17:30; Jas. 4:17
12:48 [a]Lev. 5:17; 1 Tim. 1:13
12:49 [a]ver. 51
12:50 [1]Or, *pained* [a]Mat. 20:22; Mark 10:38
12:51 [a]ver. 49; Mat. 10:34 [b]Mic. 7:6; John 7:43; 9:16; 10:19
12:52 [a]Mat. 10:35
12:54 [a]Mat. 16:2
12:58 [a]Prov. 25:8; Mat. 5:25 [b]See Ps. 32:6; Is. 55:6
12:59 [1]See Mark 12:42
13:4 [1]Or, *debtors*
13:6 [a]Is. 5:2; Mat. 21:19

12:46–48 *cut him in sunder . . . beaten with many stripes . . . shall be beaten with few.* Three grades of punishment that the judge will mete out in proportion to both the privileges each person has enjoyed and his response to those privileges (see Rom 2:12–16).

12:49 *fire.* Applied figuratively in different ways in the NT (see note on 3:16). Here it is associated with judgment (v. 49) and division (v. 51). Judgment falls on the wicked, who are separated from the righteous.

12:50 *baptism.* The suffering that Jesus was to endure on the cross (see note on Mark 10:38). *till it be accomplished.* The words from the cross would pronounce the completion (John 19:28,30). Jesus wished that the hour of suffering were already past.

12:51 *division.* See note on Mat 10:34.

12:54–56 Wind from the west was from the Mediterranean Sea; from the south it was from the desert. Although people could use such indicators to forecast the weather, they could not recognize the signs of spiritual crisis, the coming of the Messiah, the threat of His death, the coming confrontation with Rome, and the eternal consequences these events would have for their own lives.

12:57 *of yourselves judge.* Despite the insistence of the Pharisees, despite the Roman system, and even despite the pressure of family, a person must accept God on His terms. The signs of the times called for immediate decision—before judgment came on the Jewish nation.

12:58 *give diligence that thou mayest be delivered from him.* Settle accounts before it is too late.

12:59 *last mite.* Greek *lepton.* If a *kodrantes* is compared to a penny (see note on v. 6), this coin corresponds to half a penny.

13:1 *the Galileans.* The incident is otherwise unknown, but having people killed while offering sacrifices in the temple fits the reputation of Pilate. These Galileans may have broken an important Roman regulation, which led to their bloody punishment.

13:2,4 *sinners above . . . suffered such things.* In ancient times it was often assumed that a calamity would befall only those who were extremely sinful (see John 9:1–2; see also Job 4:7; 22:5, where Eliphaz falsely accused Job). But Jesus pointed out that all are sinners who must repent or face a fearful end.

13:4 *those eighteen.* Another unknown incident. *the tower in Siloam.* Built inside the southeast section of Jerusalem's wall.

13:6 *fig tree.* Probably refers to the Jewish nation (see note on Mark 11:14), but it may also apply to the individual soul.

13:7 *these three years.* A period of ample opportunity.

9 And if it bear fruit, *well:* and if not, *then* after that thou shalt cut it down.

A woman healed on the sabbath

10 ¶ And he was teaching in one of the synagogues on the sabbath.

11 And behold, there was a woman which had a spirit of infirmity eighteen years, and was bowed together, and could in no wise lift up *herself.*

12 And when Jesus saw her, he called *her* to *him,* and said unto her, Woman, thou art loosed from thy infirmity.

13 [a]And he laid *his* hands on her: and immediately she was made straight, and glorified God.

14 And the ruler of the synagogue answered with indignation, because that Jesus had healed on the sabbath day, and said unto the people, [a]There are six days in which *men* ought to work: in them therefore come and be healed, and [b]not on the sabbath day.

15 The Lord then answered him, and said, *Thou* hypocrite, [a]doth not each one of you on the sabbath loose his ox or *his* ass from the stall, and lead *him* away to watering?

16 And ought not this *woman,* [a]being a daughter of Abraham, whom Satan hath bound, lo *these* eighteen years, be loosed from this bond on the sabbath day?

17 And when he had said these *things,* all his adversaries were ashamed: and all the people rejoiced for all the glorious *things* that were done by him.

Parables about the kingdom

18 ¶ [a]Then said he, Unto what is the kingdom of God like? and whereunto shall I resemble it?

19 It is like a grain of mustard seed, which a man took, and cast into his garden; and it grew, and waxed a great tree; and the fowls of the air lodged in the branches of it.

20 And again he said, Whereunto shall I liken the kingdom of God?

21 It is like leaven, which a woman took and hid in three [1]measures of meal, till the whole was leavened.

The strait gate

22 ¶ [a]And he went through the cities and villages, teaching, and journeying towards Jerusalem.

23 Then said one unto him, Lord, are there few that be saved? And he said unto them,

24 [a]Strive to enter in at the strait gate: for [b]many, I say unto you, will seek to enter in, and shall not be able.

25 [a]When once the master of the house is risen up, and [b]hath shut to the door, and ye begin to stand without, and to knock at the door, saying, [c]Lord, Lord, open unto us; and he shall answer and say unto you, [d]I know you not whence you are:

26 Then shall ye begin to say, We have eaten and drunk in thy presence, and thou hast taught in our streets.

27 [a]But he shall say, I tell you, I know you not whence you are; [b]depart from me, all *ye* workers of iniquity.

28 [a]There shall be weeping and gnashing of teeth, [b]when ye shall see Abraham, and Isaac, and Jacob, and all the prophets, in the kingdom of God, and you yourselves thrust out.

29 And they shall come from the east, and *from* the west, and from the north, and *from* the south, and shall sit down in the kingdom of God.

30 [a]And behold, there are last which shall be first, and there are first which shall be last.

13:13 [a]Mark 16:18; Acts 9:17 **13:14** [a]Ex. 20:9 [b]Mat. 12:10; Mark 3:2; ch. 6:7; 14:3 **13:15** [a]ch. 14:5 **13:16** [a]ch. 19:9 **13:18** [a]Mat. 13:31; Mark 4:30

13:21 [1]See Mat. 13:33 **13:22** [a]Mat. 9:35; Mark 6:6 **13:24** [a]Mat. 7:13 [b]See John 7:34; 8:21; 13:33; Rom. 9:31 **13:25** [a]Ps. 32:6; Is. 55:6 [b]Mat. 25:10 [c]ch. 6:46 [d]Mat. 7:23; 25:12 **13:27** [a]ver. 25; Mat. 7:23; 25:41 [b]Ps. 6:8; Mat. 25:41 **13:28** [a]Mat. 8:12; 13:42; 24:51 [b]Mat. 8:11 **13:30** [a]Mat. 19:30; 20:16; Mark 10:31

13:11 *a spirit of infirmity.* Various disorders were caused by evil spirits (see note on 4:33). The description of this woman's infirmity suggests that the bones of her spine were rigidly fused together.

13:12 *loosed.* The spirit had been cast out, and the woman was freed from the bond of Satan and from her physical handicap.

13:14 *ruler of the synagogue.* See note on 8:41. *healed on the sabbath.* A focal point of attack against Jesus was His conduct on the sabbath (see 6:6–11; 14:1–6; Mat 12:1–8,11–12; John 5:1–18; see also Ex 20:9–10).

13:15 *loose his ox.* They had more regard for the needs of an animal than for the far greater need of a person. Jesus called His critics "hypocrites" because they pretended zeal for the law, but their motive was to attack Him and His healing.

13:19 *mustard seed.* See notes on Mat 13:31–32; Mark 4:31. Trees in Scripture are sometimes symbols of nations (see Ezek 17:23; 31:6; Dan 4:12,21).

‡13:21 *leaven.* See note on Mat 13:33. Its permeating quality is emphasized here as it works from the inside to affect all the dough. This parable could speak of the powerful influence of God's kingdom to change things, or it could represent how evil can pervade and grow even in God's institutions. *three measures.* About one-half bushel or 20 quarts (22 liters); same amount as used by Sarah in Gen 18:6.

13:22 *through the cities and villages.* See chart, pp. 1396–1398. Somewhere between the events of 11:1 and 13:21 Jesus left Judea and began His work in and around Perea, which is recorded in 13:22–19:27; Mat 19:1–20:28; Mark 10; John 10:40–42. During the last part of the Perean ministry, it appears that He went north to Galilee and then traveled south again through Perea to Jericho and to Jerusalem. Some of Jesus' sayings that Luke attributes to the period of ministry in Perea are found in different settings in Matthew (7:13–14,22–23). Perhaps He repeated various sayings on different occasions. *journeying towards Jerusalem.* Where He would die. Although Jesus was ministering throughout Perea, His eyes were constantly set on the Holy City and His ultimate destiny.

13:23 *are there few that be saved?* Perhaps the questioner had observed that in spite of the very large crowds that came to hear Jesus' preaching and be healed, there were only a few followers who were loyal. Jesus did not answer directly, but warned that many would try to enter after it was too late.

13:27 *I know you not whence you are.* See Mat 7:23; 25:12.

13:29 *they . . . from the east, and from the west, and from the north, and from the south.* From the four corners of the world (Ps 107:3) and from among all people, including Gentiles.

The lament over Jerusalem

31 ¶ The same day there came certain *of the* Pharisees, saying unto him, Get *thee* out, and depart hence: for Herod will kill thee.

32 And he said unto them, Go ye, and tell that fox, Behold, I cast out devils, and I do cures to day and to morrow, and the third *day* [a]I shall be perfected.

33 Nevertheless I must walk to day, and to morrow, and the *day* following: for it cannot be that a prophet perish out of Jerusalem.

34 [a]O Jerusalem, Jerusalem, which killest the prophets, and stonest them that are sent unto thee; how often would I have gathered thy children together, as a hen *doth gather* her brood under *her* wings, and ye would not?

35 Behold, [a]your house is left unto you desolate: and verily I say unto you, Ye shall not see me, until *the time* come when ye shall say, [b]Blessed *is* he that cometh in the name of the Lord.

Jesus heals on the sabbath

14 And it came to pass, as he went into the house of one of the chief Pharisees to eat bread on the sabbath day, that they watched him.

2 And behold, there was a certain man before him, which had the dropsy.

3 And Jesus answering spake unto the lawyers and Pharisees, saying, [a]Is it lawful to heal on the sabbath day?

4 And they held their peace. And he took *him*, and healed him, and let *him* go;

5 And answered them, saying, [a]Which of you shall have an ass or an ox fallen into a pit, and will not straightway pull him out on the sabbath day?

13:32 [a]Heb. 2:10
13:34 [a]Mat. 23:37
13:35 [a]Lev. 26:31,32; Ps. 69:25; Is. 1:7; Dan. 9:27; Mic. 3:12 [b]Ps. 118:26; Mat. 21:9; Mark 11:10; ch. 19:38; John 12:13
14:3 [a]Mat. 12:10
14:5 [a]Ex. 23:5; Deut. 22:4; ch. 13:15
14:10 [a]Prov. 25:6,7
14:11 [a]Job 22:29; Ps. 18:27; Prov. 29:23; Mat. 23:12; ch. 18:14; Jas. 4:6; 1 Pet. 5:5
14:13 [a]Neh. 8:10,12

6 And they could not answer him again to these *things*.

The honoured place

7 ¶ And he put forth a parable to those which were bidden, when he marked how they chose out the chief rooms; saying unto them,

8 When thou art bidden of any *man* to a wedding, sit not down in the highest room; lest a more honourable *man* than thou be bidden of him;

9 And he that bade thee and him come and say to thee, Give this *man* place; and thou begin with shame to take the lowest room.

10 [a]But when thou art bidden, go and sit down in the lowest room; that when he that bade thee cometh, he may say unto thee, Friend, go up higher: then shalt thou have worship in the presence of them that sit at meat with thee.

11 [a]For whosoever exalteth himself shall be abased; and he that humbleth himself shall be exalted.

12 ¶ Then said he also to him that bade him, When thou makest a dinner or a supper, call not thy friends, nor thy brethren, neither thy kinsmen, nor *thy* rich neighbours; lest they also bid thee again, and a recompence be made thee.

13 But when thou makest a feast, call [a]the poor, the maimed, the lame, the blind:

14 And thou shalt be blessed; for they cannot recompense thee: for thou shalt be recompensed at the resurrection of the just.

The parable of the great supper

15 ¶ And when one of them that sat at meat with *him* heard these *things*, he said

13:31 *Herod will kill thee.* See note on Mat 14:1. Jesus was probably in Perea, which was under Herod's jurisdiction (see note on 3:1). The Pharisees wanted to frighten Jesus into leaving this area and going to Judea.
13:32 *fox.* A crafty animal. *to day and to morrow.* In Semitic usage this phrase could refer to an indefinite but limited period of time. *be perfected.* Jesus' life had a predetermined plan that would be carried out, and no harm could come to Him until His purpose was accomplished (cf. 4:43; 9:22).
13:33 *out of Jerusalem.* Jesus' hour had not yet come (see 2:38; John 7:30; 8:20; cf. John 8:59; 10:39; 11:54). He would die in Jerusalem as had numerous prophets before Him.
13:34 *how often . . . ?* This lament over Jerusalem may suggest that Jesus was in Jerusalem more often than the Synoptics indicate (cf. John 2:13; 4:45; 5:1; 7:10; 10:22). However, the statement in vv. 34–35 may have been uttered some distance from Jerusalem, i.e., in Perea. According to Mat 23:37–38, the same utterance was spoken on Tuesday of Passion Week. Jesus repeated many of His teachings and sayings.
13:35 *house is left unto you desolate.* God will abandon His temple and His city (see 21:20,24; Jer 12:7; 22:5). *not see me, until.* See Zech 12:10; Rev 1:7; cf. Is 45:23; Rom 14:11; Phil 2:10–11.
14:1 *on the sabbath.* Of seven recorded miracles on the sabbath, Luke includes five (4:31,38; 6:6; 13:14; 14:1); the other two are John 5:10; 9:14. Concerning the vigil of the Pharisees see note on 13:14. Sabbath meals were prepared the day before.
14:2 *dropsy.* An accumulation of fluid that would indicate illness affecting other parts of the body. The Greek for this word is a medical term, *hydropikos,* found only here in the NT (see Introduction: Author).
14:3 *lawyers.* See notes on 5:17; 7:30. By questioning them before the miracle, Jesus made it difficult for them to protest afterward.
‡14:5 *have an ass or an ox.* In Deut 5:14 the law said that even animals were not to work on the sabbath, but it was never wrong to help an animal that was in need. Jesus' action was "unlawful" only according to rabbinic interpretations, not according to the Mosaic law itself.
14:7 *chief rooms.* Maneuvering for better seats may also have caused trouble at the Last Supper (22:24).
14:11 *humbleth himself shall be exalted.* A basic principle repeated often in the Bible (see 11:43; 18:14; 20:46; 2 Chr 7:14–15; Prov 3:34; 25:6- 7; Mat 18:4; 23:12; Jas 4:10; 1 Pet 5:6).
‡14:14 *resurrection of the just.* All will be resurrected (Dan 12:2; John 5:28–29; Acts 24:15). The resurrection of the righteous (1 Cor 15:23; 1 Thes 4:16; Rev 20:4–6) is distinct from the resurrection of the unrighteous. There is no "general resurrection" (1 Cor 15:12,21; Heb 6:2; Rev 20:11–15). *the just.* Those who have been pronounced so by God on the basis of Christ's atonement and who have evidenced their faith by their actions (cf. Mat 25:34–40).

unto him, [a]Blessed *is he* that shall eat bread in
the kingdom of God.
16 [a]Then said he unto him, A certain man
made a great supper, and bade many:
17 And [a]sent his servant at supper time to
say to them that were bidden, Come; for all
things are now ready.
18 And they all with one *consent* began to
make excuse. The first said unto him, I have
bought a piece of ground, and I must needs go
and see it: I pray thee have me excused.
19 And another said, I have bought five
yoke of oxen, and I go to prove them: I pray
thee have me excused.
20 And another said, I have married a wife,
and therefore I cannot come.
21 So that servant came, and shewed his
lord these *things*. Then the master of the
house being angry said to his servant, Go out
quickly into the streets and lanes of the city,
and bring in hither the poor, and the maimed,
and the halt, and the blind.
22 And the servant said, Lord, it is done as
thou hast commanded, and yet there is room.
23 And the lord said unto the servant, Go
out into the *high*ways and hedges, and compel
them to come in, that my house may be filled.
24 For I say unto you, [a]That none of those
men which were bidden shall taste of my supper.

The cost of discipleship

25 ¶ And there went great multitudes with
him: and he turned, and said unto them,
26 [a]If any *man* come to me, [b]and hate not
his father, and mother, and wife, and children,
and brethren, and sisters, [c]yea, and his own
life also, he cannot be my disciple.
27 And [a]whosoever doth not bear his
cross, and come after me, cannot be my disciple.
28 For [a]which of you, intending to build a
tower, sitteth not down first, and counteth the
cost, whether he have sufficient to finish it?
29 Lest haply, after he hath laid the foundation, and is not able to finish *it*, all that behold *it* begin to mock him,
30 Saying, This man began to build, and
was not able to finish.
31 Or what king, going to make war
against another king, sitteth not down first,
and consulteth whether he be able with ten
thousand to meet him that cometh against him
with twenty thousand?
32 Or else, while the other is yet a great
way off, he sendeth an ambassage, and desireth conditions of peace.
33 So likewise, whosoever *he be* of you
that forsaketh not all that he hath, he cannot
be my disciple.
34 [a]Salt *is* good: but if the salt have lost his
savour, wherewith shall it be seasoned?
35 It is neither fit for the land, nor yet for
the dunghill; *but men* cast it out. He that hath
ears to hear, let him hear.

The parable of the lost sheep

15 Then [a]drew near unto him all the
publicans and sinners for to hear
him.
2 And the Pharisees and scribes murmured, saying, This *man* receiveth sinners,
[a]and eateth with them.
3 And he spake this parable unto them,
saying,
4 [a]What man of you, having an hundred
sheep, if he lose one of them, doth not leave
the ninety and nine in the wilderness, and go
after that which is lost, until he find it?
5 And when he hath found *it*, he layeth *it*
on his shoulders, rejoicing.
6 And when he cometh home, he calleth
together *his* friends and neighbours, saying
unto them, Rejoice with me; for I have found
my sheep [a]which was lost.

14:15 [a]Rev. 19:9
14:16 [a]Mat. 22:2
14:17 [a]Prov. 9:2,5
14:24 [a]Mat. 21:43; 22:8; Acts 13:46
14:26 [a]Deut. 13:6; 33:9; Mat. 10:37 [b]Rom. 9:13 [c]Rev. 12:11
14:27 [a]Mat. 16:24; Mark 8:34; ch. 9:23; 2 Tim. 3:12
14:28 [a]Prov. 24:27
14:34 [a]Mat. 5:13; Mark 9:50
15:1 [a]Mat. 9:10
15:2 [a]Acts 11:3; Gal. 2:12
15:4 [a]Mat. 18:12
15:6 [a]1 Pet. 2:10,25

14:15 *eat bread in the kingdom.* The great Messianic banquet to come. Association of the future kingdom with a feast was common (13:29; Is 25:6; Mat 8:11; 25:1–10; 26:29; Rev 19:9).

14:16 *Then said he unto him.* Jesus used the man's remark as the occasion for a parable warning that not everyone would enter the kingdom.

14:18 *bought a piece of ground.* The initial invitation must have been accepted, but when the final invitation came (by Jewish custom the announcement that came when the dinner was ready), other interests took priority. None of the "reasons" given was genuine. For example, one did not buy a field without first seeing it, nor oxen without first trying them out (v. 19).

14:24 *those men which were bidden.* Without explicitly mentioning them, Jesus warned "the lawyers and Pharisees" (v. 3) that those who refused the invitation to his Messianic banquet would not get one taste of it, but others would (see 20:9–19; see also note on Mat 21:41).

14:26 *hate not his father.* A vivid hyperbole, meaning that one must love Jesus even more than his immediate family (see Mal 1:2–3 for another use of the figure). See Mat 10:37.

14:27 *bear his cross.* See 9:23; Mat 10:38 and notes.

14:28 *counteth the cost.* Jesus did not want a blind, naive commitment that expected only blessings. As a builder estimates costs or a king evaluates military strength (v. 31), so a person must consider what Jesus expects of His followers.

14:33 *forsaketh not all that he hath.* The cost, Jesus warned, is complete surrender to Him.

14:34 *Salt is good.* See note on Mark 9:50.

15:1 *publicans and sinners.* See notes on 3:12; Mark 2:15.

15:2 *murmured.* Complained among themselves, but not openly. *eateth with them.* More than simple association, eating with a person indicated acceptance and recognition (cf. Acts 11:3; 1 Cor 5:11; Gal 2:12).

‡15:3 *this parable.* Jesus responded with a story that contrasted the love of God with the exclusiveness of the Pharisees. The word "parable" appears only in v. 3. This parable has three parts—lost sheep, lost coin and lost son. The point of each part is that something was lost and then found and that there was rejoicing. The lost sheep (far from home) corresponds to the lost son who in turn pictures "the sinners" (v. 2). The lost coin (lost in the house) corresponds to the older son who in turn pictures the "Pharisees and scribes" (v. 2).

15:4 *that which is lost.* The shepherd theme was familiar from Ps 23; Is 40:11; Ezek 34:11–16.

7 I say unto you, that likewise joy shall be in heaven over one sinner that repenteth, [a]*more* than over ninety and nine just *persons* which need no repentance.

The lost piece of silver

8 ¶ Either what woman having ten [1]pieces of silver, if she lose one [1]piece, doth not light a candle, and sweep the house, and seek diligently till she find *it?*

9 And when she hath found *it,* she calleth *her* friends and *her* neighbours together, saying, Rejoice with me; for I have found the [1]piece which I had lost.

10 Likewise, I say unto you, there is joy in the presence of the angels of God over one sinner that repenteth.

The parable of the lost son

11 ¶ And he said, A certain man had two sons:

12 And the younger of them said to *his* father, Father, give me the portion of goods that falleth to *me.* And he divided unto them [a]*his* living.

13 And not many days after the younger son gathered all together, and took his journey into a far country, and there wasted his substance with riotous living.

14 And when he had spent all, there arose a mighty famine in that land; and he began to be in want.

15 And he went and joined himself to a citizen of that country; and he sent him into his fields to feed swine.

16 And he would fain have filled his belly with the husks that the swine did eat: and no *man* gave unto him.

17 And when he came to himself, he said, How many hired *servants* of my father's have bread enough and to spare, and I perish with hunger?

15:7 [a]ch. 5:32
15:8 [1]*Drachma, here translated a piece of silver, is the eighth part of an ounce, which cometh to seven pence halfpenny, and is equal to the Roman penny,* Mat. 18:28
15:9 [1]*Drachma, here translated a piece of silver, is the eighth part of an ounce, which cometh to seven pence halfpenny, and is equal to the Roman penny,* Mat. 18:28
15:12 [a]Mark 12:44
15:20 [a]Acts 2:39; Eph. 2:13,17
15:21 [a]Ps. 51:4
15:24 [a]ver. 32

18 I will arise and go to my father, and will say unto him, Father, I have sinned against heaven, and before thee,

19 And am no more worthy to be called thy son: make me as one of thy hired *servants.*

20 And he arose, and came to his father. But [a]when he was yet a great way off, his father saw him, and had compassion, and ran, and fell on his neck, and kissed him.

21 And the son said unto him, Father, I have sinned against heaven, [a]and in thy sight, and am no more worthy to be called thy son.

22 But the father said to his servants, Bring forth the best robe, and put *it* on him; and put a ring on his hand, and shoes on *his* feet:

23 And bring hither the fatted calf, and kill *it;* and let us eat, and be merry:

24 [a]For this my son was dead, and is alive again; he was lost, and is found. And they began to be merry.

25 Now his elder son was in the field: and as he came and drew nigh to the house, he heard musick and dancing.

26 And he called one of the servants, and asked what these *things* meant.

27 And he said unto him, Thy brother is come; and thy father hath killed the fatted calf, because he hath received him *safe and* sound.

28 And he was angry, and would not go in: therefore came his father out and intreated him.

29 And he answering said to *his* father, Lo, these many years do I serve thee, neither transgressed I at any time thy commandment: and yet thou never gavest me a kid, that I might make merry with my friends:

30 But as soon as this thy son was come, which hath devoured thy living with harlots, thou hast killed for him the fatted calf.

31 And he said unto him, Son, thou art ever with me, and all that I have is thine.

32 It was meet that *we* should make merry,

15:7 *joy shall be in heaven.* God's concern and joy at the sinner's repentance are set in stark contrast to the attitude of the Pharisees and the scribes (v. 2). *Just persons which need no repentance.* Probably irony: those who think they are righteous (such as the Pharisees and the scribes) and feel no need to repent.

15:8 *ten pieces of silver.* Ten *drachmas.* A *drachma* was a Greek coin approximately equivalent to the Roman denarius, worth about an average day's wages (Mat 20:2). *seek diligently.* Near Eastern houses frequently had no windows and only earthen floors, making the search for a single coin difficult.

‡15:12 *portion of goods.* The father might divide the inheritance (double to the older son; see Deut 21:17 and note on Luke 12:13) but retain the income from it until his death. But to give a younger son his portion of the inheritance upon request was highly unusual. *he divided unto them.* It was strange enough for the son to ask, but even more startling for the father to meet this request.

15:13 *gathered all together.* The son's motive becomes apparent when he departs, taking with him all his possessions and leaving nothing behind to come back to. He wants to be free of parental restraint and to spend his share of the family wealth as he pleases. *riotous living.* More specific in v. 30, though the older brother may have exaggerated because of his bitter attitude.

15:15 *to feed swine.* The ultimate indignity for a Jew; not only was the work distasteful but pigs were "unclean" animals (Lev 11:7).

15:16 *husks.* Or "pods," seeds of the carob tree.

15:22–23 *best robe . . . ring . . . shoes . . . fatted calf.* Each was a sign of position and acceptance (cf. Gen 41:42; Zech 3:4): a long robe of distinction, a signet ring of authority, sandals like a son (slaves went barefoot), and the fattened calf for a special occasion.

15:28 *he.* The older brother's resentment is like the attitude of the Pharisees and teachers of the law who opposed Jesus, whereas the forgiving love of the father symbolizes the divine mercy of God.

15:29 *a kid.* Cheaper food than a fattened calf.

15:30 *this thy son.* The older brother would not even recognize him as his brother, so bitter was his hatred.

15:31 *all that I have is thine.* The father's love included both brothers. The parable might better be called the parable of "The Father's Love" rather than "The Prodigal Son." It shows a contrast between the self-centered exclusiveness of the Pharisees, who failed to understand God's love, and the concern and joy of God at the repentance of sinners.

Parables of Jesus

PARABLE	MATTHEW	MARK	LUKE
Candle under a bushel	5:14-15	4:21-22	8:16; 11:33
Wise and foolish builders	7:24-27		6:47-49
New cloth on an old garment	9:16	2:21	5:36
New wine in old bottles	9:17	2:22	5:37-38
Sower and the soils	13:3-8,18-23	4:3-8,14-20	8:5-8,11-15
Tares	13:24-30,36-43		
Mustard seed	13:31-32	4:30-32	13:18-19
Leaven	13:33		13:20-21
Hidden treasure	13:44		
Valuable pearl	13:45-46		
Net	13:47-50		
Head of a household	13:52		
Lost sheep	18:12-14		15:4-7
Unmerciful servant	18:23-34		
Laborers in the vineyard	20:1-16		
Two sons	21:28-32		
Husbandmen	21:33-44	12:1-11	20:9-18
Marriage dinner	22:2-14		
Fig tree	24:32-35	13:28-29	21:29-31
Faithful and wise servant	24:45-51		12:42-48
Ten virgins	25:1-13		
Talents (minas)	25:14-30		19:12-27
Sheep and goats	25:31-46		
Growing seed		4:26-29	
Watchful servants		13:35-37	12:35-40
Creditor			7:41-43
Good Samaritan			10:30-37
Friend in need			11:5-8
Rich fool			12:16-21
Unfruitful fig tree			13:6-9
Lowest room at the feast			14:7-14
Great supper			14:16-24
Cost of discipleship			14:28-33
Lost piece of silver			15:8-10
Lost (prodigal) son			15:11-32
Unjust steward			16:1-8
Rich man and Lazarus			16:19-31
Master and his servant			17:7-10
Persistent widow			18:2-8
Pharisee and publican			18:10-14

and be glad: [a]for this thy brother was dead,
and is alive again; and was lost, and is found.

The unrighteous steward

16 And he said also unto his disciples,
There was a certain rich man, which
had a steward; and the same was accused unto
him that he had wasted his goods.
2 And he called him, and said unto him,
How *is* it *that* I hear this of thee? give an [a]ac-
count of thy stewardship; for thou mayest be
no longer steward.
3 Then the steward said within himself,
What shall I do? for my lord taketh away from
me the stewardship: I cannot dig; to beg I am
ashamed.
4 I am resolved what to do, that, when I
am put out of the stewardship, they may receive me into their houses.
5 So he called every one of his lord's
debtors unto *him,* and said unto the first, How
much owest thou unto my lord?
6 And he said, An hundred [1]measures of
oil. And he said unto him, Take thy bill, and sit
down quickly, and write fifty.
7 Then said he to another, And how much
owest thou? And he said, An hundred [1]mea-
sures of wheat. And he said unto him, Take
thy bill, and write fourscore.
8 And the lord commended the unjust
steward, because he had done wisely: for the
children of this world are in their generation
wiser than [a]the children of light.
9 And I say unto you, [a]Make to yourselves
friends of the [1]mammon of unrighteousness;
that, when ye fail, they may receive you into
everlasting habitations.
10 [a]He that is faithful in *that which is* least
is faithful also in much: and he that is unjust in
the least is unjust also in much.
11 If therefore ye have not been faithful in
the unrighteous [1]mammon, who will commit
to your trust the true *riches?*
12 And if ye have not been faithful in that
which is another *man's,* who shall give you
that which is your own?
13 [a]No servant can serve two masters: for
either he will hate the one, and love the other;
or else he will hold to the one, and despise the
other. Ye cannot serve God and mammon.
14 ¶ And the Pharisees also, [a]who were
covetous, heard all these *things:* and they derided him.
15 And he said unto them, Ye are they
which [a]justify yourselves before men; but
[b]God knoweth your hearts: for [c]that which is
highly esteemed amongst men is abomination
in the sight of God.
16 [a]The law and the prophets *were* until
John: since that time the kingdom of God is
preached, and every *man* presseth into it.
17 [a]And it is easier for heaven and earth to
pass, than one tittle of the law to fail.
18 [a]Whosoever putteth away his wife, and
marrieth another, committeth adultery: and

15:32 [a]ver. 24
16:2 [a]Eccl. 11:9,10; Rom. 14:12; 2 Cor. 5:10; 1 Pet. 4:5
16:6 [1]*The word Batus in the original containeth nine gallons three quarts*
16:7 [1]*The word here interpreted a measure in the original containeth about fourteen bushels and a pottle*
16:8 [a]John 12:36; Eph. 5:8; 1 Thes. 5:5
16:9 [1]Or, *riches* [a]Dan. 4:27; Mat. 6:19; 19:21; ch. 11:41; 1 Tim. 6:17-19
16:10 [a]Mat. 25:21; ch. 19:17
16:11 [1]Or, *riches*
16:13 [a]Mat. 6:24
16:14 [a]Mat. 23:14
16:15 [a]ch. 10:29 [b]Ps. 7:9 [c]1 Sam. 16:7
16:16 [a]Mat. 4:17; 11:12,13; ch. 7:29
16:17 [a]Ps. 102:26,27; Is. 40:8; 51:6; Mat. 5:18; 1 Pet. 1:25
16:18 [a]Mat. 5:32; 19:9; Mark 10:11; 1 Cor. 7:10,11

15:32 *was dead, and is alive again.* A beautiful picture of the return of the younger son, which also pictures Christian conversion (see Rom 6:13; Eph 2:1,5). The words "lost and is found" are often used to mean "perished and saved" (19:10; Mat 10:6; 18:10–14).

‡16:1 *disciples.* Perhaps more than just the twelve (see 6:13; 10:1). *steward.* A steward was one who handled all the business affairs of the owner. *wasted.* He had squandered his master's possessions, just as the prodigal ("wasteful") son (15:13).

‡16:3 *What shall I do?* The unjust steward (v. 8) had no scruples against using his position for his own benefit, even if it meant cheating his master. Knowing he would lose his job, the steward planned for his future by discounting the debts owed to his master in order to obligate the debtors to himself. Interpreters disagree as to whether his procedure of discounting was in itself dishonest. Was he giving away what really belonged to his master, or was he forgoing interest payments his master did not have a right to charge? Originally the steward may have overcharged the debtors, a common way of circumventing the Mosaic law that prohibited taking interest from fellow Jews (Deut 23:19). So, to reduce the debts, he may have returned the figures to their initial amounts, which would both satisfy the steward and gain the good favor of the debtors. In any event, the point remains the same: He was shrewd enough to use the means at his disposal to plan for his future well-being. A sinner must take extraordinary measures also if he would plan for the future time when God will cast him out. He must obtain salvation.

16:6 *hundred measures of oil.* The yield of about 450 olive trees.

16:7 *hundred measures of wheat.* The approximate yield of about 100 acres.

16:8 *children of light.* God's people (John 12:36; Eph 5:8; 1 Thes 5:5).

16:9 *Make to yourselves friends.* By helping those in need, who in the future will show their gratitude when they welcome their benefactors into heaven ("everlasting habitations"). In this way worldly wealth may be wisely used to gain eternal benefit. *the mammon of unrighteousness.* Or "worldly wealth." God's people should be alert to make use of what God has given them.

16:10 *faithful also in much.* Cf. 19:17; Mat 25:21. Faithfulness is not determined by the amount entrusted but by the character of the person who uses it.

16:11 *true riches.* The things of highest value, ultimately those of the spirit, the eternal.

16:13 *two masters.* See Mat 6:24; cf. Jas 4:4.

16:16 *until John.* The ministry of John the Baptist, which prepared the way for Jesus the Messiah, was the dividing line between the OT (the "Law and the Prophets") and the NT (see notes on Jer 31:31–34; Heb 8:6–12). *presseth into it.* The meaning is disputed, but it probably speaks of the fierce earnestness with which people were responding to the gospel of the kingdom. Multitudes were coming to hear Jesus and to receive His message.

16:17 The ministry of Jesus (introducing the new covenant era) was a fulfillment of the law (defining the old covenant era) in the most minute detail (cf. 21:33). *one tittle.* See notes on Mat 5:17–18.

16:18 *putteth away his wife.* See Mat 5:31–32; 19:9; Mark 10:11–12; 1 Cor 7:10–11. Jesus affirms the continuing authority of the law: For example, adultery was still adultery, still unlawful and still sinful. Matthew's treatment is fuller in that (1) it shows that the law was given because of man's hardened heart in regard to divorce, and (2) it includes one exception as

whosoever marrieth her that is put away from *her* husband committeth adultery.

The rich man and Lazarus

19 ¶ There was a certain rich man, which was clothed in purple and fine linen, and fared sumptuously every day:

20 And there was a certain beggar named Lazarus, which was laid at his gate, full of sores,

21 And desiring to be fed with the crumbs which fell from the rich *man's* table: moreover the dogs came and licked his sores.

22 And it came to pass, that the beggar died, and was carried by the angels into Abraham's bosom: the rich *man* also died, and was buried;

23 And in hell he lift up his eyes, being in torments, and seeth Abraham afar off, and Lazarus in his bosom.

24 And he cried and said, Father Abraham, have mercy on me, and send Lazarus, that he may dip the tip of his finger in water, and [a]cool my tongue; for I [b]am tormented in this flame.

25 But Abraham said, Son, [a]remember that thou in thy lifetime receivedst thy good *things,* and likewise Lazarus evil *things:* but now he is comforted, and thou art tormented.

26 And besides all this, between us and you there is a great gulf fixed: so that they which would pass from hence to you cannot; neither can they pass to us, that *would come* from thence.

27 Then he said, I pray thee therefore, father, that thou wouldest send him to my father's house:

28 For I have five brethren; that he may testify unto them, lest they also come into this place of torment.

29 Abraham saith unto him, [a]They have Moses and the prophets; let them hear them.

30 And he said, Nay, father Abraham: but if one went unto them from the dead, they will repent.

31 And he said unto him, If they hear not Moses and the prophets, [a]neither will they be persuaded, though one rose from the dead.

Faith and forgiveness

17 Then said he unto the disciples, [a]It is impossible but that offences will come: but woe *unto him,* through whom they come.

2 It were better for him that a millstone were hanged about his neck, and he cast into the sea, than that he should offend one of these little ones.

3 Take heed to yourselves: [a]If thy brother trespass against thee, [b]rebuke him; and if he repent, forgive him.

4 And if he trespass against thee seven times in a day, and seven times in a day turn again to thee, saying, I repent; thou shalt forgive him.

5 ¶ And the apostles said unto the Lord, Increase our faith.

6 [a]And the Lord said, If ye had faith as a grain of mustard seed, ye might say unto this sycamine tree, Be thou plucked up by the root, and be thou planted in the sea; and it should obey you.

7 But which of you, having a servant plowing or feeding cattle, will say *unto him* by and by, when he is come from the field, Go and sit down to meat?

8 And will not *rather* say unto him, Make ready wherewith I may sup, and gird thyself, [a]and serve me, till I have eaten and drunken; and afterward thou shalt eat and drink?

16:24 [a]Zech. 14:12 [b]Is. 66:24; Mark 9:44
16:25 [a]Job 21:13; ch. 6:24
16:29 [a]Is. 8:20; 34:16; John 5:39,45; Acts 15:21; 17:11
16:31 [a]John 12:10,11
17:1 [a]Mat. 18:6,7; Mark 9:42; 1 Cor. 11:19
17:3 [a]Mat. 18:15,21 [b]Lev. 19:17; Prov. 17:10; Jas. 5:19
17:6 [a]Mat. 17:20; 21:21; Mark 9:23; 11:23
17:8 [a]ch. 12:37

permissible grounds for divorce—marital unfaithfulness (Mat 19:9).

16:19 *a certain rich man.* Sometimes given the name Dives (from the Latin for "rich man"). *purple and fine linen.* Characteristic of costly garments.

‡16:20 *Lazarus.* Not the Lazarus Jesus raised from the dead (John 11:43–44). This story begins exactly as that in v. 1. It appears to be the real history of two individuals, yet like a parable it has one basic lesson—once death comes, one cannot change his eternal destiny. *full of sores.* The Greek for this phrase is a common medical term found only here in the NT (see Introduction: Author).

‡16:22 *Abraham's bosom.* The Talmud mentions both paradise (see 23:43) and Abraham's bosom as the home of the righteous. Abraham's bosom refers to the place of blessedness to which the righteous dead go to await future vindication. Its bliss is the quality of blessedness reserved for people like Abraham. Simply put, it is being with Abraham.

‡16:23 *hell.* The place to which the wicked dead go to await the final judgment. That torment begins in Hades is evident from the plight of the rich man. The location of Abraham's bosom is not specified, but it is separated from Hades by an impassable chasm. It could be the distance that separates heaven from hell. Hades includes the torment that characterizes hell (fire, Rev 20:10; agony, Rev 14:11; separation, Mat 8:12). Some understand Jesus' description of Abraham's side and Hades in a less literal way.

16:28 *I have five brethren.* For the first time the rich man showed concern for others.

16:29 *Moses and the prophets.* A way of designating the whole OT. The rich man had failed to pay attention to Scripture and its teaching, and feared his brothers would do the same.

16:30 *one went unto them from the dead.* The story may suggest that Lazarus was intended, but Luke's account seems to imply that Jesus was speaking also of His own resurrection (cf. v. 31; 9:22). If a person's mind is closed and Scripture is rejected, no evidence—not even a resurrection—will change him.

17:2 *millstone.* A heavy stone for grinding grain. *one of these little ones.* Either young in the faith or young in age (cf. 10:21; Mat 18:6; Mark 10:24).

17:3 *thy brother.* See Mat 18:15–17; cf. Mat 12:50.

17:4 *seven times.* That is, forgiveness is to be unlimited (cf. Ps 119:164; Mat 18:21–22).

17:5 *Increase our faith.* They felt incapable of measuring up to the standards set forth in vv. 1–4. They wanted greater faith to lay hold of the power to live up to Jesus' standards.

17:6 See Mat 17:20; Mark 11:23; see also notes on Mat 13:31–32; Mark 4:31.

17:7 *a servant.* A slave is used to illustrate performance of duty (cf. 12:37).

9 Doth he thank that servant because he did the *things* that were commanded him? I trow not.

10 So likewise ye, when ye shall have done all those *things* which are commanded you, say, We are [a]unprofitable servants: we have done *that* which was our duty to do.

The healing of the ten lepers

11 ¶ And it came to pass, [a]as he went to Jerusalem, that he passed through the midst of Samaria and Galilee.

12 And as he entered into a certain village, there met him ten men *that were* lepers, [a]which stood afar off:

13 And they lifted up *their* voices, and said, Jesus, Master, have mercy on us.

14 And when he saw *them,* he said unto them, [a]Go shew yourselves unto the priests. And it came to pass *that,* as they went, they were cleansed.

15 And one of them, when he saw that he was healed, turned back, and with a loud voice glorified God,

16 And fell down on *his* face at his feet, giving him thanks: and he was a Samaritan.

17 And Jesus answering said, Were there not ten cleansed? but where *are* the nine?

18 There are not found that returned to give glory to God, save this stranger.

19 [a]And he said unto him, Arise, go *thy way:* thy faith hath made thee whole.

The coming of the kingdom

20 ¶ And when he was demanded of the Pharisees, when the kingdom of God should come, he answered them and said, The kingdom of God cometh not [1]with observation:

21 [a]Neither shall they say, Lo here: or, lo there: for behold, [b]the kingdom of God is [1]within you.

22 And he said unto the disciples, [a]The days will come, when ye shall desire to see one of the days of the Son of man, and ye shall not see *it.*

23 [a]And they shall say to you, See here; or, see there: go not after *them,* nor follow *them.*

24 [a]For as the lightning, that lighteneth out of the one *part* under heaven, shineth unto the other *part* under heaven; so shall also the Son of man be in his day.

25 [a]But first must he suffer many *things,* and be rejected of this generation.

26 [a]And as it was in the days of Noe, so shall it be also in the days of the Son of man.

27 They did eat, they drank, they married *wives,* they were given in marriage, until the day that Noe entered into the ark, and the flood came, and destroyed *them* all.

28 [a]Likewise also as it was in the days of Lot; they did eat, they drank, they bought, they sold, they planted, they builded;

29 But [a]the *same* day that Lot went out of Sodom it rained fire and brimstone from heaven, and destroyed *them* all.

30 Even thus shall it be in the day when the Son of man [a]is revealed.

31 In that day, he [a]which shall be upon the housetop, and his stuff in the house, let him not come down to take it away: and he that is in the field, let him likewise not return back.

32 [a]Remember Lot's wife.

33 [a]Whosoever shall seek to save his life shall lose it; and whosoever shall lose *his life* shall preserve it.

34 [a]I tell you, in that night there shall be two *men* in one bed; the one shall be taken, and the other shall be left.

35 Two *women* shall be grinding together; the one shall be taken, and the other left.

17:10 [a]Job 22:3; 35:7; Ps. 16:2; Mat. 25:30; Rom. 3:12; 11:35; 1 Cor. 9:16,17; Philem. 11
17:11 [a]ch. 9:51,52; John 4:4
17:12 [a]Lev. 13:46
17:14 [a]Lev. 13:2; 14:2; Mat. 8:4; ch. 5:14
17:19 [a]Mat. 9:22; Mark 5:34; 10:52; ch. 7:50; 8:48; 18:42
17:20 [1]Or, *with outward shew*
17:21 [a]ver. 23
17:21 [1]Or, *among you* [b]Rom. 14:17
17:22 [a]See Mat. 9:15; John 17:12
17:23 [a]Mat. 24:23; Mark 13:21; ch. 21:8
17:24 [a]Mat. 24:27
17:25 [a]Mark 8:31; 9:31; 10:33; ch. 9:22
17:26 [a]Gen. 7; Mat. 24:37
17:28 [a]Gen. 19
17:29 [a]Gen. 19:16,24
17:30 [a]2 Thes. 1:7
17:31 [a]Mat. 24:17; Mark 13:15
17:32 [a]Gen. 19:26
17:33 [a]Mat. 10:39; 16:25; Mark 8:35; ch. 9:24; John 12:25
17:34 [a]Mat. 24:40,41; 1 Thes. 4:17

17:11 *through the midst of Samaria and Galilee.* From this point Jesus seems to have journeyed to Perea, where He ministered on His way south to Jerusalem (see notes on 9:51; 13:22).

17:14 *shew yourselves unto the priests.* Normal procedure after a cure (see Lev 13:2–3; 14:2–32).

17:16 *Samaritan.* See note on 10:31–33. Normally Jews did not associate with Samaritans (John 4:9), but leprosy broke down social barriers while erecting others (see notes on Lev 13:2,4,45–46).

‡17:19 *thy faith hath made thee whole.* See Mat 9:22. The phrase may also be rendered "thy faith hath saved thee" (7:50). The fact that the Samaritan returned to thank Jesus may indicate that he had received salvation in addition to the physical healing all ten had received (cf. 7:50; 8:48,50).

‡17:21 *the kingdom of God is within you.* Probably indicating that the kingdom is present in the person of its King, Jesus (cf. 19:11; 21:7; Acts 1:6; see also note on 4:43). "Within you" could mean that the kingdom is spiritual and internal (Mat 23:26), rather than physical and external (cf. John 18:36). If this is the correct view, the pronoun "you" in the phrase "within you" is to be taken in a general sense rather than as referring to the unbelieving Pharisees personally. The kingdom certainly was not within them. If "you" is specific rather than general, it argues for the "in your midst" interpretation.

17:22 *desire to see.* In time of trouble, believers will desire to experience the day when Jesus returns in His glory and delivers His people from their distress.

‡17:23 *go not after them, nor follow them.* Do not leave your work in order to pursue predictions of Christ's second advent. Many in history, and even in our own day, would be spared a lot of trouble by heeding this admonition.

17:24 *as the lightning.* His coming will be sudden, unexpected and public (cf. 12:40).

17:25 *must he suffer.* Jesus repeatedly foretold His coming death (5:35; 9:22,43–45; 12:50; 13:32–33; 18:32; 24:7; see Mat 16:21), which had to occur before His glorious return.

17:28 *in the days of Lot.* See Gen 18:16–19:28.

17:30 *Son of man is revealed.* At Jesus' second coming He will be plainly visible to all (1 Cor 1:7; 2 Thes 1:7; 1 Pet 1:7,13; 4:13).

17:31 *upon the housetop.* It was customary to relax on the flat rooftop. When the final hour comes, however, the individual there should not be thinking of going into the house to retrieve some material objects. Matthew and Mark refer similarly to flight at the fall of Jerusalem, and indirectly to the end time (Mat 24:17–18; Mark 13:15), but here the reference is explicitly to Jesus' return (see v. 30; cf. 21:21).

17:33 *whosoever shall lose his life shall preserve it.* See note on 9:24 (cf. Mat 10:39).

‡17:35 *taken.* Could refer to being "taken to/from destruction" or "taken into the kingdom." What is clear is that no matter how

36 [1]Two *men* shall be in the field; the one shall be taken, and the other left.

37 **And they answered and said unto him,** [a]Where, Lord? **And he said unto them,** Wheresoever the body *is,* thither will the eagles be gathered together.

The widow and the judge

18 **And he spake a parable unto them** *to this end,* **that** *men* **ought** [a]**always to pray, and not to faint;**

2 **Saying,** There was [1]in a city a judge, which feared not God, neither regarded man:

3 And there was a widow in that city; and she came unto him, saying, Avenge me of mine adversary.

4 And he would not for a while: but afterward he said within himself, Though I fear not God, nor regard man;

5 [a]Yet because this widow troubleth me, I will avenge her, lest by her continual coming she weary me.

6 **And the Lord said,** Hear what the unjust judge saith.

7 And [a]shall not God avenge his own elect, which cry day and night unto him, though he bear long with them?

8 I tell you [a]that he will avenge them speedily. Nevertheless when the Son of man cometh, shall he find faith on the earth?

The Pharisee and the publican

9 ¶ **And he spake this parable unto certain** [a]**which trusted in themselves** [1]**that they were righteous, and despised other:**

10 Two men went up into the temple to pray; the one a Pharisee, and the other a publican.

11 The Pharisee [a]stood and prayed thus with himself, [b]God, I thank thee, that I am not as other men *are,* extortioners, unjust, adulterers, or even as this publican.

12 I fast twice in the week, I give tithes of all that I possess.

13 And the publican, standing afar off, would not lift up so much as *his* eyes unto heaven, but smote upon his breast, saying, God be merciful to me a sinner.

14 I tell you, this man went down to his house justified *rather* than the other: [a]for every one that exalteth himself shall be abased; and he that humbleth himself shall be exalted.

Jesus and the little children

15 ¶ [a]**And they brought unto him also infants, that he would touch them: but when** *his* **disciples saw** *it,* **they rebuked them.**

16 **But Jesus called them unto** *him,* **and said,** Suffer little children to come unto me, and forbid them not: for [a]of such is the kingdom of God.

17 [a]Verily I say unto you, Whosoever shall not receive the kingdom of God as a little child shall in no wise enter therein.

The rich young ruler

18 ¶ [a]**And a certain ruler asked him, saying, Good Master, what shall I do to inherit eternal life?**

19 **And Jesus said unto him,** Why callest thou me good? none *is* good, save one, *that is,* God.

20 Thou knowest the commandments, [a]Do not commit adultery, Do not kill, Do not steal, Do not bear false witness, [b]Honour thy father and thy mother.

17:36 [1]*This 36th verse is wanting in most of the Greek copies*
17:37 [a]Job 39:30; Mat. 24:28
18:1 [a]ch. 11:5; 21:36; Rom. 12:12; Eph. 6:18; Col. 4:2; 1 Thes. 5:17
18:2 [1][Gr. *in a certain city*]
18:5 [a]ch. 11:8
18:7 [a]Rev. 6:10
18:8 [a]Heb. 10:37; 2 Pet. 3:8,9
18:9 [1]Or, *as being righteous* [a]ch. 10:29; 16:15
18:11 [a]Ps. 135:2
18:11 [b]Is. 1:15; 58:2; Rev. 3:17
18:14 [a]Job 22:29; Mat. 23:12; ch. 14:11; Jas. 4:6; 1 Pet. 5:5
18:15 [a]Mat. 19:13; Mark 10:13
18:16 [a]1 Cor. 14:20; 1 Pet. 2:2
18:17 [a]Mark 10:15
18:18 [a]Mat. 19:16; Mark 10:17
18:20 [a]Ex. 20:12,16; Deut. 5:16-20; Rom. 13:9 [b]Eph. 6:2; Col. 3:20

close two people may be in life, they have no guarantee of the same eternal destiny. One may go to judgment and condemnation, the other to salvation, reward and blessing. However, the reference here seems to be about judgment. The context talks about the people in the flood and in Sodom being swept away to destruction. Likewise, at Christ's return, a similar separation will occur.

‡17:36 *one shall be taken, and the other left.* This is probably not the rapture, but a taking away to judgment as the next verse seems to indicate.

‡17:37 *Where . . . thither will the eagles be gathered together.* A proverb. See note on Mat 24:28. Those taken away will become a feast for eagles and other birds of prey. (See Rev 19:17–18)

18:2 *neither regarded man.* Unconcerned about the needs of others or about their opinion of him.

18:3 *a widow.* Particularly helpless and vulnerable because she had no family to uphold her cause. Only justice and her own persistence were in her favor.

18:7 *shall not God avenge his own elect . . . ?* If an unworthy judge who feels no constraint of right or wrong is compelled by persistence to deal justly with a helpless individual, how much more will God answer prayer! *bear long with them.* God will not delay His support of the chosen ones when they are right. He is not like the unjust judge, who had to be badgered until he wearied and gave in.

18:8 *shall he find faith on the earth?* Particularly faith that perseveres in prayer and loyalty (see Mat 24:12–13). Christ makes a second application that looks forward to the time of His second coming. A period of spiritual decline and persecution is assumed—a time that will require perseverance such as the widow demonstrated.

18:10 *to pray.* Periods for prayer were scheduled daily in connection with the morning and evening sacrifices. People could also go to the temple at any time for private prayer.

18:12 *fast twice in the week.* Fasting was not commanded in the Mosaic law except for the fast on the day of atonement. However, the Pharisees also fasted on Mondays and Thursdays (see 5:33; Mat 6:16; 9:14; Mark 2:18; Acts 27:9). *tithes of all that I possess.* As a typical first-century Pharisee, he tithed all that he acquired, not merely what he earned.

18:13 *be merciful to me.* The verb used here means "to be propitiated" (see note on 1 John 2:2). The tax collector does not plead his good works but the mercy of God in forgiving his sin.

18:14 *justified.* God reckoned him to be righteous, i.e., his sins were forgiven and he was credited with righteousness—not his own (v. 9) but that which comes from God.

18:17 *as a little child.* With total dependence, full trust, frank openness and complete sincerity (see Mat 18:3; 19:14; Mark 10:15; cf. 1 Pet 2:2). See note on Mark 10:15.

18:18–27 For this event see notes on Mark 10:17–27.

18:18 *eternal life.* See note on Mat 19:16.

21 And he said, All these have I kept from
my youth up.
22 Now when Jesus heard these *things,* he
said unto him, Yet lackest thou one *thing:* [a]sell
all that thou hast, and distribute unto the poor,
and thou shalt have treasure in heaven: and
come, follow me.
23 And when he heard this, he was very
sorrowful: for he was very rich.
24 And when Jesus saw that he was very
sorrowful, he said, [a]How hardly shall they that
have riches enter into the kingdom of God!
25 For it is easier for a camel to go through
a needle's eye, than for a rich *man* to enter
into the kingdom of God.
26 And they that heard *it* said, Who then
can be saved?
27 And he said, [a]The *things which are* impossible with men are possible with God.
28 ¶ [a]Then Peter said, Lo, we have left all,
and followed thee.
29 And he said unto them, Verily I say unto
you, [a]There is no *man* that hath left house, or
parents, or brethren, or wife, or children, for
the kingdom of God's sake,
30 [a]Who shall not receive manifold more
in this *present* time, and in the world to come
life everlasting.

Jesus again foretells his death

31 ¶ [a]Then he took unto *him* the twelve,
and said unto them, Behold, we go up to Jerusalem, and all *things* [b]that are written by the
prophets concerning the Son of man shall be
accomplished.
32 For [a]he shall be delivered unto the Gentiles, and shall be mocked, and spitefully entreated, and spitted on:
33 And they shall scourge *him,* and put
him to death: and the third day he shall rise
again.
34 [a]And they understood none of these
things: and this saying was hid from them, neither knew they the *things* which were spoken.

A blind man healed

35 ¶ [a]And it came to pass, *that* as he was
come nigh unto Jericho, a certain blind man
sat by the way side begging:

18:22 [a]Mat. 6:19,20; 19:21; 1 Tim. 6:19
18:24 [a]Prov. 11:28; Mat. 19:23; Mark 10:23
18:27 [a]Jer. 32:17; Zech. 8:6; Mat. 19:26; ch. 1:37
18:28 [a]Mat. 19:27
18:29 [a]Deut. 33:9
18:30 [a]Job 42:10
18:31 [a]Mat. 16:21; 17:22; 20:17; Mark 10:32 [b]Ps. 22; Is. 53
18:32 [a]Mat. 27:2; ch. 23:1; John 18:28; Acts 3:13
18:34 [a]Mark 9:32; ch. 2:50; 9:45; John 10:6; 12:16
18:35 [a]Mat. 20:29; Mark 10:46
18:42 [a]ch. 17:19
18:43 [a]ch. 5:26; Acts 4:21; 11:18
19:7 [a]Mat. 9:11; ch. 5:30
19:8 [a]ch. 3:14 [b]Ex. 22:1; 1 Sam. 12:3; 2 Sam. 12:6

36 And hearing the multitude pass by, he
asked what it meant.
37 And they told him, that Jesus of Nazareth passeth by.
38 And he cried, saying, Jesus, *thou* Son of
David, have mercy on me.
39 And they which went before rebuked
him, that he should hold his peace: but he
cried *so* much the more, *Thou* Son of David,
have mercy on me.
40 And Jesus stood, and commanded him
to be brought unto him: and when he was
come near, he asked him,
41 Saying, What wilt thou *that* I shall do
unto thee? And he said, Lord, that I may receive my sight.
42 And Jesus said unto him, Receive thy
sight: [a]thy faith hath saved thee.
43 And immediately he received his sight,
and followed him, [a]glorifying God: and all the
people, when they saw *it,* gave praise unto
God.

The conversion of Zaccheus

19 And *Jesus* entered and passed
through Jericho.
2 And behold, *there was* a man named Zaccheus, which was *the* chief among the publicans, and he was rich.
3 And he sought to see Jesus who he was;
and could not for the press, because he was little of stature.
4 And he ran before, and climbed up into a
sycomore tree to see him: for he was to pass
that *way.*
5 And when Jesus came to the place, he
looked up, and saw him, and said unto him,
Zaccheus, make haste, and come down; for to
day I must abide at thy house.
6 And he made haste, and came down, and
received him joyfully.
7 And when they saw *it,* they all murmured, saying, [a]That he was gone to be guest
with a man *that is* a sinner.
8 And Zaccheus stood, and said unto the
Lord; Behold, Lord, the half of my goods I give
to the poor; and if I have taken any *thing* from
any *man* by [a]false accusation, [b]I restore *him*
fourfold.

18:30 *in this present time, and in the world to come.* The present age of sin and misery and the future age to be inaugurated by the return of the Messiah.
18:31 *all things that are written by the prophets.* Sometimes referred to as the third prediction of Jesus' death, though the total number is more than three (see note on 17:25). The first distinct prediction is in 9:22 and the second in 9:43–45. The Messiah's death had been predicted and/or prefigured centuries before (e.g., Ps 22; Is 53; Zech 13:7; see Luke 24:27; Mat 26:24,31,54). *Son of man.* See note on Mark 8:31.
18:35 *was come nigh unto Jericho.* See note on Mark 10:46. *a certain blind man.* Bartimeus (Mark 10:46). Matthew reports that two blind men were healed (see note on Mat 20:30). Probably since one was the spokesman and more outstanding, Mark and Luke did not record the presence of the other.
18:38–39 *Son of David.* A Messianic title (see Mat 22:41–45; Mark 12:35; John 7:42; see also 2 Sam 7:12–13; Ps 89:3–4; Amos 9:11; Mat 12:23; 21:15–16).
18:42 *thy faith.* See note on 17:19.
19:1 *entered and passed through Jericho.* See note on Mark 10:46.
19:2 *chief among the publicans.* A position referred to only here in the Bible, probably designating one in charge of a district, with other tax collectors under him. The region was prosperous at this time, so it is no wonder that Zaccheus had grown rich. See notes on 3:12; Mark 2:14–15.
19:4 *a sycomore tree.* A sturdy tree from 30 to 40 feet high, with a short trunk and spreading branches, capable of holding a grown man. (See note on Amos 7:14.)
19:5 *I must abide at thy house.* Implies a divine necessity.
19:8 *fourfold.* Almost the extreme repayment required under the law in case of theft (Ex 22:1; 2 Sam 12:6; cf. Prov 6:31).

9 And Jesus said unto him, This day is salvation come to this house, forsomuch as [a]he also is [b]a son of Abraham.

10 [a]For the Son of man is come to seek and to save that which was lost.

The parable of the pounds

11 ¶ And as they heard these *things,* he added and spake a parable, because he was nigh to Jerusalem, and *because* [a]they thought that the kingdom of God should immediately appear.

12 [a]He said therefore, A certain nobleman went into a far country to receive for himself a kingdom, and to return.

13 And he called his ten servants, and delivered them ten [1]pounds, and said unto them, Occupy till I come.

14 [a]But his citizens hated him, and sent a message after him, saying, We will not have this *man* to reign over us.

15 And it came to pass, that when he was returned, having received the kingdom, then he commanded these servants to be called unto him, to whom he had given the [1]money, that he might know how much every *man* had gained by trading.

16 Then came the first, saying, Lord, thy pound hath gained ten pounds.

17 And he said unto him, Well, *thou* good servant: because thou hast been [a]faithful in a very little, have thou authority over ten cities.

18 And the second came, saying, Lord, thy pound hath gained five pounds.

19 And he said likewise to him, Be thou also over five cities.

20 And another came, saying, Lord, behold, *here is* thy pound, which I have kept laid up in a napkin:

21 [a]For I feared thee, because thou art an austere man: thou takest up that thou layedst not down, and reapest that thou didst not sow.

22 And he saith unto him, [a]Out of thine own mouth will I judge thee, *thou* wicked servant. [b]Thou knewest that I was an austere man, taking up that I laid not down, and reaping that I did not sow:

23 Wherefore then gavest not thou my money into the bank, that at my coming I might have required *mine own* with usury?

24 And he said unto them that stood by, Take from him the pound, and give *it* to him that hath ten pounds.

25 (And they said unto him, Lord, he hath ten pounds.)

26 For I say unto you, [a]That unto every one which hath shall be given; and from him that hath not, even that he hath shall be taken away from him.

27 But those mine enemies, which would not that I should reign over them, bring hither, and slay *them* before me.

The triumphal entry

28 ¶ And when he had thus spoken, [a]he went before, ascending up to Jerusalem.

29 [a]And it came to pass, when he was come nigh to Bethphage and Bethany, at the mount called *the mount* of Olives, he sent two of his disciples,

30 Saying, Go ye into the village over

19:9 [a]Rom. 4:11,12,16; Gal. 3:7 [b]ch. 13:16
19:10 [a]Mat. 18:11; See Mat. 10:6; 15:24
19:11 [a]Acts 1:6
19:12 [a]Mat. 25:14; Mark 13:34
19:13 [1]*Mina, here translated a pound, is twelve ounces and a half; which according to five shillings the ounce is three pounds two shillings six pence*
19:14 [a]John 1:11
19:15 [1][Gr. *silver,* and so ver. 23]
19:17 [a]Mat. 25:21; ch. 16:10
19:21 [a]Mat. 25:24
19:22 [a]2 Sam. 1:16; Job 15:6; Mat. 12:37 [b]Mat. 25:26
19:26 [a]Mat. 13:12; 25:29; Mark 4:25; ch. 8:18
19:28 [a]Mark 10:32
19:29 [a]Mat. 21:1; Mark 11:1

19:9 *son of Abraham.* A true Jew—not only of the lineage of Abraham but one who also walks "in the steps" of Abraham's faith (Rom 4:12). Jesus recognized the tax collector as such, though Jewish society excluded him.

‡19:10 The key verse in Luke's Gospel. *Son of man.* A Messianic title (Dan 7:13) used only by Jesus in the four Gospels, by Stephen (Acts 7:56) and in John's vision (Rev 1:13). See Introduction: Plan; see also note on Mark 8:31. *to seek and to save.* An important summary of Jesus' purpose—to bring salvation, meaning eternal life (18:18), and the kingdom of God (18:25). See note on 15:32.

19:11 *kingdom of God should immediately appear.* They expected the Messiah to appear in power and glory and to set up His earthly kingdom, defeating all their political and military enemies.

19:12 *to receive for himself a kingdom.* A rather unusual procedure, but the Herods did just that when they went to Rome to be appointed rulers over the Jews. Similarly, Jesus was soon to depart and in the future is to return as King. During His absence, His servants are entrusted with their Master's affairs (for a similar parable see Mat 25:14–30).

‡19:13 *ten pounds.* Each pound, or *mina,* was about three months' wages. One talent equaled 60 minas (see Mat 25:15) and a mina equaled 100 drachmas, each drachma being worth about a day's wages (see note on 15:8). Thus the total amount was valued at between two and three years' average wages, and a tenth would be about three months' wages. This was small, however, compared with the amounts mentioned in the parable recorded in Matthew. Here all ten are given the same amount, showing equal responsibility to use what they were given.

‡19:14 *sent a message.* Such an incident had occurred over 30 years earlier in the case of Archelaus (Josephus, *Wars,* 2.6.1; *Antiquities,* 17.9.3), when the Jews complained to Rome of his cruelty, as well as in a number of other instances. This aspect of the story may have been included to warn the Jews against rejecting Jesus as King.

19:22 *Thou knewest that I was an austere man . . . ?* The master did not admit to the statement of the servant, but repeated it in a question. If this was the opinion of the servant, he should have acted accordingly.

19:26 *shall be given . . . shall be taken away.* See 8:18; 17:33; Mat 13:12. Those who seek spiritual gain in the gospel, for themselves and others, will become richer, and those who neglect or squander what is given them will become impoverished, losing even what they have.

19:27 *those mine enemies . . . slay them.* Perhaps a reference to Jerusalem's destruction in A.D. 70. The punishment of those who rebelled and actively opposed the king (v. 14) was much more severe than that of the negligent servant.

19:28–44 The Triumphal Entry occurred on Sunday of Passion Week. See charts, pp. 1396, 1432.

19:29 *Bethphage.* A village near the road going from Jericho to Jerusalem. *Bethany.* Another village about two miles southeast of Jerusalem (John 11:18), and the home of Mary, Martha and Lazarus. *mount called the mount of Olives.* A ridge a little more than a mile long, separated from Jerusalem by the Kidron Valley—to the east of the city (see notes on Zech 14:4; Mark 11:1). *two of his disciples.* Not named here or in the parallel passages (Mat 21:1; Mark 11:1; cf. John 12:14).

19:30 *village.* Probably Bethphage. *colt.* In other accounts a

against *you;* in the which at your entering ye
shall find a colt tied, whereon yet never man
sat: loose him, and bring *him hither.*
31 And if any *man* ask you, Why do ye
loose *him?* thus shall ye say unto him, Because
the Lord hath need of him.
32 And they that were sent went their
way, and found even as he had said unto them.
33 And as they were loosing the colt, the
owners thereof said unto them, Why loose ye
the colt?
34 And they said, The Lord hath need of
him.
35 And they brought him to Jesus: [a]and
they cast their garments upon the colt, and
they set Jesus thereon.
36 And as he went, they spread their
clothes in the way.
37 And when he was come nigh, *even* now
at the descent of the mount of Olives, the
whole multitude of the disciples began to rejoice and praise God with a loud voice for all
the mighty works that they had seen;
38 Saying, [a]Blessed *be* the King that
cometh in the name of the Lord: [b]peace in
heaven, and glory in the highest.
39 And some of the Pharisees from among
the multitude said unto him, Master, rebuke
thy disciples.
40 And he answered and said unto them, I
tell you that, if these should hold their peace,
[a]the stones would immediately cry out.
41 ¶ And when he was come near, he beheld the city, and [a]wept over it,
42 Saying, If thou hadst known, even thou,
at least in this thy day, the *things* which belong unto thy peace! but now they are hid
from thine eyes.

19:35 [a]2 Ki. 9:13; Mat. 21:7; Mark 11:7; John 12:14
19:38 [a]Ps. 118:26; ch. 13:35 [b]ch. 2:14; Eph. 2:14
19:40 [a]Hab. 2:11
19:41 [a]John 11:35
19:43 [a]Is. 29:3,4; Jer. 6:3,6; ch. 21:20
19:44 [a]1 Ki. 9:7,8; Mic. 3:12 [b]Mat. 24:2; Mark 13:2; ch. 21:6 [c]Dan. 9:24; ch. 1:68,78; 1 Pet. 2:12
19:45 [a]Mat. 21:12; Mark 11:11,15; John 2:14,15
19:46 [a]Is. 56:7 [b]Jer. 7:11
19:47 [a]Mark 11:18; John 7:19; 8:37
19:48 [1]Or, *hanged on him*
20:1 [a]Mat. 21:23
20:2 [a]Acts 4:7; 7:27

43 For the days shall come upon thee, that
thine enemies shall [a]cast a trench about thee,
and compass thee round, and keep thee in on
every side,
44 And [a]shall lay thee even with the
ground, and thy children within thee: and
[b]they shall not leave in thee one stone upon
another; [c]because thou knewest not the time
of thy visitation.

The cleansing of the temple

45 ¶ [a]And he went into the temple, and began to cast out them that sold therein, and
them that bought;
46 Saying unto them, [a]It is written, My
house is the house of prayer: but [b]ye have
made it a den of thieves.
47 And he taught daily in the temple. But
[a]the chief priests and the scribes and the chief
of the people sought to destroy him,
48 And could not find what they might do:
for all the people [1]were very attentive to hear
him.

Jesus' authority challenged

20 And [a]it came to pass, *that* on one of
those days, as he taught the people in
the temple, and preached the gospel, the chief
priests and the scribes came upon *him* with
the elders,
2 And spake unto him, saying, Tell us, [a]by
what authority doest thou these *things?* or
who is he that gave thee this authority?
3 And he answered and said unto them, I
will also ask you one thing; and answer me:
4 The baptism of John, was it from heaven,
or of men?
5 And they reasoned with themselves, say-

donkey colt (John 12:15) is specified and the mother of the colt (Mat 21:7) with him. Luke uses a Greek word that the Septuagint frequently employed to translate the Hebrew word for "donkey." Jesus chooses to enter Jerusalem this time mounted on a donkey to claim publicly that He was the chosen Son of David to sit on David's throne (1 Ki 1:33,44), the one of whom the prophets had spoken (Zech 9:9). *whereon yet never man sat.* One that had not been put to secular use (Num 19:2; 1 Sam 6:7).

19:31 *the Lord.* Either God or, more likely, Jesus Himself, here claiming His own unique status as Israel's Lord.

19:37 *all the mighty works.* The raising of Lazarus and the healing of blind Bartimeus were recent examples, but included also would be the works recorded in John on various occasions in Jerusalem, as well as the whole of His ministry in Galilee (cf. Mat 21:14; John 12:17).

19:43 *thine enemies shall cast a trench.* See 21:20; fulfilled when the Romans took Jerusalem in A.D. 70, using an embankment to besiege the city. The description is reminiscent of OT predictions (Is 29:3; 37:33; Ezek 4:1–3).

19:44 *the time of thy visitation.* God came to the Jews in the person of Jesus the Messiah, but they failed to recognize Him and rejected Him (see John 1:10–11; cf. Luke 20:13–16).

19:45 Mark (11:11–17) makes clear that this cleansing occurred the day after the Triumphal Entry, i.e., on Monday of Passion Week. *the temple.* The outer court (of the Gentiles), where animals for sacrifice were sold at unfair prices. John records a cleansing of the temple at the beginning of Jesus' ministry (John 2:13–25), but the Synoptics (see Mat 21:12–13; Mark 11:15–17) speak only of a cleansing at the close of Jesus' ministry (see notes on Mat 21:12–17; John 2:14–17).

19:47 *chief priests.* See 3:2; 22:52; 23:4; 24:20. They were part of the Sanhedrin, the ruling Jewish council (see note on Mark 14:55). *sought to destroy him.* See 20:19–20 (cf. John 7:1; 11:53–57).

20:1 The events of 20:1–21:36 all occurred on Tuesday of Passion Week—a long day of controversy. *one of those days.* Not specified, but Mark's parallel accounts (Mark 11:19–20,27–33) indicate that this day (Tuesday) followed the cleansing of the temple (Monday), which followed the Triumphal Entry (Sunday). *chief priests.* See 19:47 and note on Mat 2:4. *scribes.* See 5:30 and notes on 5:17; Mat 2:4. *elders.* See note on Mat 15:2. Each of these groups was represented in the Jewish council, the Sanhedrin (see 22:66).

20:2 *who . . . gave thee this authority?* They had asked this of John the Baptist (John 1:19–25) and of Jesus early in His ministry (John 2:18–22). Here the reference is to the cleansing of the temple, which not only defied the authority of the Jewish leaders but also hurt their monetary profits. The leaders may also have been looking for a way to discredit Jesus in the eyes of the people or raise suspicion of Him as a threat to the authority of Rome.

20:4 *The baptism of John, was it from heaven, or of men?* By replying with a question, Jesus put the burden on His opponents—indicating only two alternatives: The work of John was

ing, If we shall say, From heaven; he will say,
Why then believed ye him not?
6 But *and* if we say, Of men; all the people
will stone us: [a]for they be persuaded that John
was a prophet.
7 And they answered, that *they* could not
tell whence *it was.*
8 And Jesus said unto them, Neither tell I
you by what authority I do these *things.*

The parable of the husbandmen

9 ¶ Then began he to speak to the people
this parable; [a]A certain man planted a vineyard, and let it forth to husbandmen, and went
into a far country for a long time.
10 And at the season he sent a servant to
the husbandmen, that they should give him of
the fruit of the vineyard: but the husbandmen
beat him, and sent *him* away empty.
11 And again he sent another servant: and
they beat him also, and entreated *him* shamefully, and sent *him* away empty.
12 And again he sent a third: and they
wounded him also, and cast *him* out.
13 Then said the lord of the vineyard,
What shall I do? I will send my beloved son: it
may be they will reverence *him* when they see
him.
14 But when the husbandmen saw him,
they reasoned among themselves, saying, This
is the heir: come, let us kill him, that the inheritance may be ours.
15 So they cast him out of the vineyard,
and killed *him.* What therefore shall the lord
of the vineyard do unto them?
16 He shall come and destroy these husbandmen, and shall give the vineyard to others. And when they heard *it,* they said, God
forbid.
17 And he beheld them, and said, What is
this then that is written, [a]The stone which the
builders rejected, the same is become the
head of the corner?

20:6 [a]Mat. 14:5; 21:26; ch. 7:29
20:9 [a]Mat. 21:33; Mark 12:1
20:17 [a]Ps. 118:22; Mat. 21:42
20:18 [a]Dan. 2:34,35; Mat. 21:44
20:20 [a]Mat. 22:15
20:21 [1]Or, *of a truth* [a]Mat. 22:16; Mark 12:14
20:24 [1]See Mat. 18:28; Mark 12:15
20:27 [a]Mat. 22:23; Mark 12:18 [b]Acts 23:6,8

18 Whosoever shall fall upon that stone
shall be broken; but [a]on whomsoever it shall
fall, it will grind him to powder.
19 And the chief priests and the scribes the
same hour sought to lay hands on him; and
they feared the people: for they perceived that
he had spoken this parable against them.

Tribute to Cesar

20 ¶ [a]And they watched *him,* and sent
forth spies, which *should* feign themselves
just *men,* that they might take hold of his
words, that *so they* might deliver him unto the
power and authority of the governor.
21 And they asked him, saying, [a]Master,
we know that thou sayest and teachest rightly,
neither acceptest thou the person *of any,* but
teachest the way of God [1]truly:
22 Is it lawful for us to give tribute unto
Cesar, or no?
23 But he perceived their craftiness, and
said unto them, Why tempt ye me?
24 Shew me a [1]penny. Whose image and
superscription hath it? They answered and
said, Cesar's.
25 And he said unto them, Render therefore unto Cesar the *things* which be Cesar's,
and unto God the *things* which be God's.
26 And they could not take hold of his
words before the people: and they marvelled
at his answer, and held their peace.

Sadducees and the resurrection

27 ¶ [a]Then came to *him* certain of the Sadducees, [b]which deny that there is any resurrection; and they asked him,
28 Saying, Master, Moses wrote unto us, If
any *man's* brother die, having a wife, and he die
without children, that his brother should take
his wife, and raise up seed unto his brother.
29 There were therefore seven brethren:
and the first took a wife, and died without children.

either God-inspired or man-devised. By refusing to answer, they placed themselves in an awkward position. *from heaven.* See note on Mark 11:30.

20:10 *he sent a servant.* This parable (v. 9) is reminiscent of Is 5:1–7. The slaves who were sent to the husbandmen represent the prophets God sent in former times who were rejected (see Neh 9:26; Jer 7:25–26; 25:4–7; Mat 23:34; Acts 7:52; Heb 11:36–38). *give him of the fruit.* In accordance with a kind of sharecropping agreement, a fixed amount was due the landowner. At the proper time he would expect to receive his share.

20:13 *my beloved son.* The specific reference to the beloved son makes clearer the intended application of the son in the parable to the Son, Jesus Christ (see 3:22; Mat 17:5).

20:14 *inheritance may be ours.* See note on Mark 12:7.

20:16 *give the vineyard to others.* See note on Mat 21:41.

20:17 *the head of the corner.* See note on Ps 118:22.

20:18 *will grind him to powder.* As a pot dashed against a stone is broken, and as one lying beneath a falling stone is crushed, so those who reject Jesus the Messiah will be doomed (see Is 8:14; cf. Dan 2:34–35,44; Luke 2:34).

20:19 *scribes.* For their opposition to Jesus see 5:30; 9:22; 19:47; 22:2; 23:10.

20:20 *authority of the governor.* Fearing to take action themselves, the Jewish religious leaders hoped to draw from Jesus some statement that would bring action from the Roman officials and remove Him from His contact with the people.

20:22 *tribute unto Cesar.* To agree to the taxes demanded by Caesar would disappoint the people, but to advise no payment would disturb the Roman officials. The questioners hoped to trap Jesus with this dilemma.

‡20:24 *a penny.* The *denarius, a* Roman coin, was worth about a day's wages (see note on Mat 22:19).

20:25 *unto God the things which be God's.* See note on Mat 22:21.

20:27 *Saddducees.* An aristocratic, politically minded group, willing to compromise with secular and pagan leaders. They controlled the high priesthood at this time and held the majority of the seats in the Sanhedrin. They did not believe in the resurrection or an afterlife, and they rejected the oral tradition taught by the Pharisees (Josephus, *Antiquities,* 13.10.6.). See notes on Mat 2:4; 3:7; Mark 12:18; Acts 4:1.

20:28 *his brother should take his wife.* The levirate law (see note on Mat 22:24; cf. Gen 38:8).

30 And the second took her to wife, and he died childless.

31 And the third took her; and in like manner the seven also: and they left no children, and died.

32 Last of all the woman died also.

33 Therefore in the resurrection whose wife of them is she? for seven had her to wife.

34 And Jesus answering said unto them, The children of this world marry, and are given in marriage:

35 But they which shall be accounted worthy to obtain that world, and the resurrection from the dead, neither marry, nor are given in marriage:

36 Neither can they die any more: for [a]they are equal unto *the* angels; and are the children of God, [b]being the children of the resurrection.

37 Now that the dead are raised, [a]even Moses shewed at the bush, when he calleth the Lord the God of Abraham, and the God of Isaac, and the God of Jacob.

38 For he is not a God of the dead, but of the living: for [a]all live unto him.

The question about David's son

39 ¶ Then certain of the scribes answering said, Master, thou hast well said.

40 And after that they durst not ask him any *question at all.*

41 And he said unto them, [a]How say they that Christ is David's son?

42 And David himself saith in the book of Psalms, [a]The LORD said to my Lord, Sit thou on my right hand,

43 Till I make thine enemies thy footstool.

44 David therefore calleth him Lord, how is he then his son?

45 ¶ [a]Then in the audience of all the people he said unto his disciples,

46 [a]Beware of the scribes, which desire to walk in long robes, and [b]love greetings in the markets, and the highest seats in the synagogues, and the chief rooms at feasts;

47 [a]Which devour widows' houses, and for a shew make long prayers: the same shall receive greater damnation.

The widow's offering

21 And he looked up, [a]and saw the rich *men* casting their gifts into the treasury.

2 And he saw also a certain poor widow casting in thither two [1]mites.

3 And he said, Of a truth I say unto you, [a]that this poor widow hath cast in more than *they* all:

4 For all these have of their abundance cast in unto the offerings of God: but she of her penury hath cast in all the living that she had.

Signs of the end of this age

5 ¶ [a]And as some spake of the temple, how it was adorned with goodly stones and gifts, he said,

6 *As for* these *things* which ye behold, the days will come, in the which [a]there shall not be left one stone upon another, that shall not be thrown down.

7 And they asked him, saying, Master, but when shall these *things* be? and what sign *will there be* when these *things* shall come to pass?

8 ¶ And he said, [a]Take heed that ye be not deceived: for many shall come in my name, saying, I am *Christ;* [1]and the time draweth near: go ye not therefore after them.

9 But when ye shall hear of wars and commotions, be not terrified: for these *things* must first come to pass; but the end *is* not by and by.

20:36 [a]1 Cor. 15:42,49,52; 1 John 3:2 [b]Rom. 8:23
20:37 [a]Ex. 3:6
20:38 [a]Rom. 6:10,11
20:41 [a]Mat. 22:42; Mark 12:35
20:42 [a]Ps. 110:1; Acts 2:34
20:45 [a]Mat. 23:1; Mark 12:38
20:46 [a]Mat. 23:5 [b]ch. 11:43
20:47 [a]Mat. 23:14
21:1 [a]Mark 12:41
21:2 [1]See Mark 12:42
21:3 [a]2 Cor. 8:12
21:5 [a]Mat. 24:1; Mark 13:1
21:6 [a]ch. 19:44
21:8 [1][Or, *and, The time,* Mat. 3:2; 4:17] [a]Mat. 24:4; Mark 13:5; Eph. 5:6; 2 Thes. 2:3

20:34–35 *this world . . . that world.* See note on 18:30.
20:36 *equal unto the angels.* The resurrection order cannot be assumed to follow present earthly lines. In the new age there will be no marriage, no procreation and no death. *children of the resurrection.* Those who are to take part in the resurrection of the righteous (cf. Mat 22:23–33; Mark 12:18–27; Acts 4:1–2; 23:6–10).
20:37 *Moses shewed at the bush.* Since Scripture chapters and verses were not used at the time of Christ, the passage was identified in this way, referring to Moses' experience with the burning bush (Ex 3:2).
20:39 *Master, thou hast well said.* Even though there was great animosity against Jesus, the scribes (who were Pharisees) sided with Jesus against the Sadducees on the matter of resurrection.
20:44 *David therefore calleth him Lord.* If the Messiah was a descendant of David, how could this honored king refer to his offspring as Lord? Unless Jesus' opponents were ready to admit that the Messiah was also the divine Son of God, they could not answer His question. See also note on Ps 110:1.
20:46 *long robes . . . chief rooms.* See notes on Mark 12:38–39.
20:47 *devour widows' houses.* They take advantage of this defenseless group by fraud and schemes for selfish gain. *receive greater damnation.* Cf. 12:47–48. The higher the esteem of men, the more severe the demands of true justice; and the more hypocrisy (Mat 23:1–36), the greater the condemnation.
21:1 *the treasury.* In the court of women 13 boxes, shaped like inverted megaphones, were positioned to receive the donations of the worshipers.
21:2 *two mites.* Jewish coins worth very little.
‡21:3–4 See notes on 2 Cor 8:12; Mark 12:44.
21:5–36 See note on Mark 13:1–37.
21:5 *temple . . . was adorned.* One stone at the southwest corner was some 36 feet long. "Whatever was not overlaid with gold was purest white" (Josephus, *Jewish Wars,* 5.5.6.). Herod gave a golden vine for one of its decorations. Its grape clusters were as tall as a man. The full magnificence of the temple as elaborated and adorned by Herod has only recently come to light through archaeological investigations on the temple hill.
21:6 *not be left one stone.* Fulfilled in A.D. 70 when the Romans took Jerusalem and burned the temple (see note on Mat 24:2).
21:7 *when . . . ?* Mark reports that this question was asked by four disciples: Peter, James, John and Andrew (Mark 13:3). Matthew gives the question in a fuller form, including an inquiry for the sign of Jesus' coming and the end of the age (Mat 24:3). *what sign will there be . . . ?* What would be the indication that these things are about to happen?
21:8 *I am Christ.* I am Jesus the Messiah (having come a second time). *the time.* The end time.
21:9 *the end is not by and by.* Refers to the end of the age

10 ¶ [a]Then said he unto them, Nation shall
rise against nation, and kingdom against kingdom:
11 And great earthquakes shall be in divers
places, and famines, and pestilences; and fearful sights and great signs shall there be from
heaven.
12 [a]But before all these, they shall lay their
hands on you, and persecute *you,* delivering
you up to *the* synagogues, and [b]into prisons,
[c]being brought before kings and rulers [d]for my
name's sake.
13 And [a]it shall turn to you for a testimony.
14 [a]Settle *it* therefore in your hearts, not to
meditate before *what ye* shall answer:
15 For I will give you a mouth and wisdom,
[a]which all your adversaries shall not be able to
gainsay nor resist.
16 [a]And ye shall be betrayed both by parents, and brethren, and kinsfolks, and friends;
and [b]*some* of you shall they cause to be put to
death.
17 And [a]ye shall be hated of all *men* for my
name's sake.
18 [a]But there shall not a hair of your head
perish.
19 In your patience possess ye your souls.
20 ¶ [a]And when ye shall see Jerusalem
compassed with armies, then know that the
desolation thereof is nigh.
21 Then let them which are in Judea flee to
the mountains; and let them which are in the
midst of it depart out; and let not them that
are in the countries enter thereinto.
22 For these be *the* days of vengeance, that
[a]all *things* which are written may be fulfilled.

21:10 [a]Mat. 24:7
21:12 [a]Mark 13:9; Rev. 2:10 [b]Acts 4:3; 5:18; 12:4; 16:24 [c]Acts 25:23 [d]1 Pet. 2:13
21:13 [a]Phil. 1:28; 2 Thes. 1:5
21:14 [a]Mat. 10:19; Mark 13:11; ch. 12:11
21:15 [a]Acts 6:10
21:16 [a]Mic. 7:6; Mark 13:12 [b]Acts 7:59; 12:2
21:17 [a]Mat. 10:22
21:18 [a]Mat. 10:30
21:20 [a]Mat. 24:15; Mark 13:14
21:22 [a]Dan. 9:26,27; Zech. 11:1
21:23 [a]Mat. 24:19
21:24 [a]Dan. 9:27; 12:7; Rom. 11:25
21:25 [a]Mat. 24:29; Mark 13:24; 2 Pet. 3:10,12
21:26 [a]Mat. 24:29
21:27 [a]Mat. 24:30; Rev. 1:7; 14:14
21:28 [a]Rom. 8:19,23
21:29 [a]Mat. 24:32; Mark 13:28
21:33 [a]Mat. 24:35
21:34 [a]Rom. 13:13; 1 Thes. 5:6; 1 Pet. 4:7

23 [a]But woe unto them that are with child,
and to them that give suck, in those days, for
there shall be great distress in the land, and
wrath upon this people.
24 And they shall fall by the edge of the
sword, and shall be led away captive into all
nations: and Jerusalem shall be trodden down
of the Gentiles, [a]until the times of the Gentiles be fulfilled.
25 [a]And there shall be signs in the sun,
and in the moon, and in the stars; and upon
the earth distress of nations, with perplexity;
the sea and the waves roaring;
26 Men's hearts failing them for fear, and
for looking after those *things* which are coming on the earth: [a]for the powers of heaven
shall be shaken.
27 And then shall they see the Son of man
[a]coming in a cloud with power and great glory.
28 And when these *things* begin to come
to pass, *then* look up, and lift up your heads;
for [a]your redemption draweth nigh.
29 ¶ [a]And he spake to them a parable; Behold the fig tree, and all the trees;
30 When they now shoot forth, ye see and
know of your own selves that summer is now
nigh at hand.
31 So likewise ye, when ye see these
things come to pass, know ye that the kingdom of God is nigh at hand.
32 Verily I say unto you, This generation
shall not pass away, till all be fulfilled.
33 [a]Heaven and earth shall pass away: but
my words shall not pass away.
34 ¶ And [a]take heed to yourselves, lest at
any time your hearts be overcharged with sur-

(see Mat 24:3,6). All the events listed in vv. 8–18 are characteristic of the entire present age, not just signs of the end of the age.

21:11 *signs shall there be from heaven.* See v. 25. For prophetic descriptions of celestial signs accompanying the day of the Lord see note on Mark 13:25.

21:12 *delivering you up to the synagogues.* Synagogues were used not only for worship and school, but also for community administration and confinement while awaiting trial.

21:15 *your adversaries shall not be able to gainsay nor resist.* See Acts 6:9–10.

21:18 Although persecution and death may come, God is in control, and the ultimate outcome will be eternal victory. *Shall not a hair of your head perish.* In view of v. 16 this cannot refer to physical safety. The figure indicates that there will be no real, i.e., spiritual, loss.

21:19 See note on Mark 13:13.

21:20 *compassed with armies.* See 19:43. The sign that the end was near (cf. v. 7) would be the surrounding of Jerusalem with armies. Associated with this event would be the "abomination of desolation" (Mat 24:15).

21:21 *flee to the mountains.* When an army surrounds a city, it is natural to seek protection inside the walls, but Jesus directs His followers to seek the safety of the mountains because the city was doomed to destruction (see note on Mat 24:16).

21:22 *days of vengeance.* God's retributive justice as the consequence of faithlessness (cf. Is 63:4; Jer 5:29; Hos 9:7).

‡21:24 *Jerusalem shall be trodden down of the Gentiles.* Except for brief revolts in A.D. 66–70 and A.D. 132, Jerusalem remained under Gentile rule until June, 1967. Since that time the Jews have retaken their city, signaling that God's time clock with the Jews in now set in motion once again. *times of the Gentiles.* The Gentiles would have both spiritual opportunities (Mark 13:10; cf. Luke 20:16; Rom 11:25) and domination of Jerusalem.

21:27 *Then . . . Son of man.* The time of Christ's second coming (see Dan 7:13). Often the predictions in this discourse refer ultimately to the end times, while at the same time describing the more imminent destruction of Jerusalem in A.D. 70.

21:28 *lift up your heads.* Do not be downcast at the appearance of these signs, but look up in joy, hope and trust. *redemption.* Final, completed redemption.

21:29 *Behold the fig tree.* The coming of spring is announced by the greening of the trees (cf. Mat 24:32–35; Mark 13:28–31). In a similar way, one can anticipate the coming of the kingdom when its signs are seen. But "kingdom" is used in different ways (see note on 4:43). The reference in v. 31 is to the future kingdom.

21:32 *This generation.* If the reference is to the destruction of Jerusalem, which occurred about 40 years after Jesus spoke these words, "generation" is used in its ordinary sense of a normal life span. All these things were fulfilled in a preliminary sense in the A.D. 70 destruction of Jerusalem. If the reference is to the second coming of Christ, "generation" might indicate the Jewish people as a nation, who were promised existence to the very end. Or it might refer to the future generation alive at the beginning of these things. It does not mean that Jesus had a mistaken notion He was going to return immediately.

feiting, and drunkenness, and cares of *this* life,
and *so* that day come upon you unawares.
35 For [a]as a snare shall it come on all them
that dwell on the face of the whole earth.
36 [a]Watch ye therefore, and [b]pray always,
that ye may be accounted worthy to escape all
these *things* that shall come to pass, and [c]to
stand before the Son of man.
37 ¶ [a]And in the day time he was teaching
in the temple; and [b]at night he went out, and
abode in the mount that is called *the mount* of
Olives.
38 And all the people came early in the
morning to him in the temple, for to hear him.

The plot to kill Jesus

22 Now [a]the feast of unleavened bread
drew nigh, which is called the
Passover.
2 And [a]the chief priests and scribes sought
how they might kill him; for they feared the
people.
3 ¶ [a]Then entered Satan into Judas surnamed Iscariot, being of the number of the
twelve.
4 And he went his way, and communed
with the chief priests and captains, how he
might betray him unto them.
5 And they were glad, and [a]covenanted to
give him money.
6 And he promised, and sought opportunity to betray him unto them [1]in the absence of
the multitude.

The last supper

7 ¶ [a]Then came the day of unleavened
bread, when the passover must be killed.
8 And he sent Peter and John, saying, Go
and prepare us the passover, that we may eat.
9 And they said unto him, Where wilt thou
that we prepare?
10 And he said unto them, Behold, when
ye are entered into the city, there shall a man
meet you, bearing a pitcher of water; follow
him into the house where he entereth in.
11 And ye shall say unto the goodman of
the house, The Master saith unto thee, Where
is the guestchamber, where I shall eat the
passover with my disciples?
12 And he shall shew you a large upper
room furnished: there make ready.
13 And they went, and found as he had
said unto them: and they made ready the passover.
14 ¶ [a]And when the hour was come, he sat
down, and the twelve apostles with him.
15 And he said unto them, [1]With desire I
have desired to eat this passover with you before I suffer:
16 For I say unto you, I will not any more
eat thereof, [a]until it be fulfilled in the kingdom
of God.
17 And he took *the* cup, and gave thanks,

21:35 [a]1 Thes. 5:2; 2 Pet. 3:10; Rev. 3:3; 16:15
21:36 [a]Mat. 24:42; 25:13; Mark 13:33 [b]ch. 18:1 [c]Ps. 1:5; Eph. 6:13
21:37 [a]John 8:1,2 [b]ch. 22:39
22:1 [a]Mat. 26:2; Mark 14:1
22:2 [a]Ps. 2:2; John 11:47; Acts 4:27
22:3 [a]Mat. 26:14; Mark 14:10; John 13:2,27
22:5 [a]Zech. 11:12
22:6 [1]Or, *without tumult*
22:7 [a]Mat. 26:17; Mark 14:12
22:14 [a]Mat. 26:20; Mark 14:17
22:15 [1]Or, *I have heartily desired*
22:16 [a]ch. 14:15; Acts 10:41; Rev. 19:9

21:34 *that day.* When Christ returns and the future aspect of God's kingdom is inaugurated (cf. v. 31). *come upon you unawares.* Does not mean that Christ's second coming will be completely unannounced, since there will be introductory signs (vv. 28,31).

21:35 *the whole earth.* The second coming of Christ will involve the whole of mankind, whereas the fall of Jerusalem did not.

21:37 *in the day time.* Each day during the final week of His life, from His Triumphal Entry to the time of the passover (Sunday-Thursday). *mount that is called the mount of Olives.* See notes on 19:29; Mat 21:17.

22:1 *feast of unleavened bread . . . Passover.* "Passover" was used in two different ways: (1) a specific meal begun at twilight on the 14th of Nisan (Lev 23:4–5), and (2) the week following the passover meal (Ezek 45:21), otherwise known as the feast of unleavened bread, a week in which no leaven was allowed (Ex 12:15–20; 13:3–7). By NT times the two names for the week-long festival were virtually interchangeable.

22:2 *the chief priests and scribes.* See 20:1 and note.

22:3 *Then entered Satan into Judas.* In the Gospels this expression is used on two separate occasions: (1) before Judas went to the chief priests and offered to betray Jesus (here), and (2) during the Last Supper (John 13:27). Thus the Gospel writers depict Satan's control over Judas, who had never displayed a high motive of service or commitment to Jesus.

22:4 *captains.* All of these were Jews selected mostly from the Levites.

22:7 *passover must be killed.* The passover lamb had to be sacrificed on the 14th of Nisan between 2:30 and 5:30 P.M. in the court of the priests—Thursday of Passion Week.

22:10 *a man . . . bearing a pitcher.* It was extraordinary to see a man carrying a pitcher of water, since this was normally women's work.

22:11 *The Master saith.* This form of address may have been chosen because the owner was a follower already known to Jesus.

22:13 *as he had said unto them.* It may be that Jesus had made previous arrangements with the man in order to make sure that the passover meal would not be interrupted. Since Jesus did not identify ahead of time just where He would observe passover, Judas was unable to inform the enemy, who might have interrupted this important occasion.

22:14–30 It appears that Luke does not attempt to be strictly chronological in his account of the Last Supper. He records the most important part of the occasion first—the sharing of the bread and the cup. Then he tells of Jesus' comments about His betrayer and about the argument over who would be greatest, though both of these subjects seem to have been introduced earlier. John's Gospel (13:26–30), e.g., indicates that Judas had already left the room before the bread and cup of the Lord's Supper were shared, but Luke does not tell when he left.

22:14 *he sat down.* See note on Mark 14:3.

22:16 *until it be fulfilled.* Jesus yearned to keep this passover with His disciples because it was the last occasion before He Himself was to be slain as the perfect passover lamb (1 Cor 5:7) and thus fulfill this sacrifice for all time. Jesus would eat no more passover meals until the coming of the future kingdom. After this He will renew fellowship with those who through the ages have commemorated the Lord's Supper. Finally the fellowship will be consummated in the great Messianic "marriage supper" to come (Rev 19:9).

22:17 *he took the cup.* Either the first of the four cups shared during regular observance of the passover meal, or the third cup.

and said, Take this, and divide *it* among yourselves:
18 For [a]I say unto you, I will not drink of
the fruit of the vine, until the kingdom of God
shall come.
19 ¶ [a]And he took bread, and gave thanks,
and brake *it,* and gave unto them, saying, This
is my body which is given for you: [b]this do in
remembrance of me.
20 Likewise also the cup after supper, say-
ing, [a]This cup *is* the new testament in my
blood, which is shed for you.
21 ¶ [a]But behold, the hand of him that betrayeth me *is* with me on the table.
22 [a]And truly the Son of man goeth, [b]as it
was determined: but woe unto that man by
whom he is betrayed.
23 [a]And they began to inquire among
themselves, which of them it was that should
do this *thing.*
24 ¶ [a]And there was also a strife among
them, which of them should be accounted the
greatest.
25 [a]And he said unto them, The kings of
the Gentiles exercise lordship over them; and
they that exercise authority upon them are
called benefactors.
26 [a]But ye *shall* not *be* so: [b]but he that is
greatest among you, let him be as the younger;
and he that is chief, as he that doth serve.
27 [a]For whether *is* greater, he that sitteth at
meat, or he that serveth? *is* not he that sitteth at
meat? but [b]I am among you as he that serveth.
28 Ye are they which have continued with
me in [a]my temptations.
29 And [a]I appoint unto you a kingdom, as
my Father hath appointed unto me;

22:18 [a]Mat. 26:29; Mark 14:25
22:19 [a]Mat. 26:26; Mark 14:22 [b]1 Cor. 11:24
22:20 [a]1 Cor. 10:16
22:21 [a]Ps. 41:9; Mat. 26:21,23; Mark 14:18; John 13:21,26
22:22 [a]Mat. 26:24 [b]Acts 2:23; 4:28
22:23 [a]Mat. 26:22; John 13:22,25
22:24 [a]Mark 9:34; ch. 9:46
22:25 [a]Mat. 20:25; Mark 10:42
22:26 [a]Mat. 20:26; 1 Pet. 5:3 [b]ch. 9:48
22:27 [a]ch. 12:37 [b]Mat. 20:28; John 13:13,14; Phil. 2:7
22:28 [a]Heb. 4:15
22:29 [a]Mat. 24:47; ch. 12:32
22:30 [a]Mat. 8:11; ch. 14:15; Rev. 19:9 [b]Ps. 49:14; Mat. 19:28; 1 Cor. 6:2; Rev. 3:21
22:31 [a]1 Pet. 5:8 [b]Amos 9:9
22:32 [a]John 17:9,11,15
22:34 [a]Mat. 26:34; Mark 14:30; John 13:38
22:35 [a]Mat. 10:9; ch. 9:3; 10:4
22:37 [a]Is. 53:12; Mark 15:28

30 That [a]ye may eat and drink at my table
in my kingdom, [b]and sit on thrones judging
the twelve tribes of Israel.
31 ¶ And the Lord said, Simon, Simon, behold, [a]Satan hath desired *to have* you, that *he*
may [b]sift *you* as wheat:
32 But [a]I have prayed for thee, that thy
faith fail not: and when thou art converted,
strengthen thy brethren.
33 And he said unto him, Lord, I am ready
to go with thee, both into prison, and to death.
34 [a]And he said, I tell thee, Peter, *the* cock
shall not crow this day, before that thou shalt
thrice deny that *thou* knowest me.
35 [a]And he said unto them, When I sent
you without purse, and scrip, and shoes,
lacked ye any *thing?* **And they said, Nothing.**
36 Then said he unto them, But now, he
that hath a purse, let him take *it,* and likewise
his scrip: and he that hath no sword, let him
sell his garment, and buy one.
37 For I say unto you, that this that is written must yet be accomplished in me, [a]And he
was reckoned among the transgressors: for the
things concerning me have an end.
38 And they said, Lord, behold, here *are* two
swords. And he said unto them, It is enough.

Jesus' agony in Gethsemane

39 ¶ [a]And he came out, and [b]went, as he
was wont, to the mount of Olives; and his dis-
ciples also followed him.
40 [a]And when he was at the place, he said
unto them, Pray that *ye* enter not into temptation.

22:39 [a]Mat. 26:36; Mark 14:32; John 18:1 [b]ch. 21:37
22:40 [a]ver. 46; Mat. 6:13; 26:41; Mark 14:38

22:18 *until the kingdom of God shall come.* See notes on v. 16; 4:43.

22:19 *is.* Represents or signifies. *given for you.* Anticipating His substitutionary sacrifice on the cross. *in remembrance of me.* Just as the passover was a constant reminder and proclamation of God's redemption of Israel from bondage in Egypt, so the keeping of Christ's command would be a remembering and proclaiming of the deliverance of believers from the bondage of sin through Christ's atoning work on the cross.

‡22:20 *also the cup.* See note on Mark 14:24. *after supper.* Mentioned only here and in 1 Cor 11:25; see note on 1 Cor 11:23–26. *new testament.* Promised through the prophet Jeremiah (31:31–34)—the fuller administration of God's saving grace, founded on and sealed by the death of Jesus ("in my blood"). See note on 1 Cor 11:25. The New Covenant is for the Jew, but the Christian enters into the salvation aspects of that covenant, because Jesus would shed his blood once and for all—for the Jew, and for all peoples.

22:25 *benefactors.* A title assumed by or voted for rulers in Egypt, Syria and Rome as a display of honor, but frequently not representing actual service rendered.

22:26 *as he that doth serve.* Jesus urges and exemplifies servant leadership—a trait that was as uncommon then as it is now.

22:28 *in my temptations.* Including temptations (cf. 4:13), hardships (9:58) and rejection (John 1:11).

22:29 *I appoint unto you a kingdom.* The following context (v. 30) indicates that this kingdom is the future form of the kingdom (see notes on 4:43; Mat 3:2).

22:30 *sit on thrones.* As they shared in Jesus' trials, so they will share in His rule (2 Tim 2:12). *judging.* Leading or ruling. *the twelve tribes of Israel.* See Mat 19:28.

22:31 *sift you.* The Greek for "you" is plural. Satan wanted to test the disciples, hoping to bring them to spiritual ruin.

‡22:36 *purse . . . scrip.* Cf. previous instructions (9:3; 10:4). Until now they had been dependent on generous hospitality, but future opposition would require them to be prepared to pay their own way. *buy one.* An extreme figure of speech used to warn them of the perilous times about to come. They would need defense and protection, as Paul did when he appealed to Caesar (Acts 25:11) as the one who "beareth not the sword in vain" (Rom 13:4).

22:37 *reckoned among the transgressors.* Jesus was soon to be arrested as a criminal, in fulfillment of prophetic Scripture, and His disciples would also be in danger for being His followers.

22:38 *two swords . . . It is enough.* Sensing that the disciples had taken Him too literally, Jesus ironically closes the discussion with a curt "That's plenty!" Not long after this, Peter was rebuked for using a sword (v. 50).

22:39 *mount of Olives.* See 21:37; John 18:2. Matthew specifies Gethsemane (Mat 26:36), and John, an olive grove (John 18:1). The place apparently was located on the lower slopes of the mount of Olives.

22:40 *temptation.* Here refers to severe trial of the kind referred to in vv. 28–38, which might lead to a faltering of their faith.

41 [a]And he was withdrawn from them about a stone's cast, and kneeled down, and prayed,

42 Saying, Father, if thou be [1]willing, remove this cup from me: nevertheless [a]not my will, but thine, be done.

43 And there appeared [a]an angel unto him from heaven, strengthening him.

44 [a]And being in an agony he prayed more earnestly: and his sweat was as it were great drops of blood falling down to the ground.

45 And when he rose up from prayer, and was come to his disciples, he found them sleeping for sorrow,

46 And said unto them, Why sleep ye? rise and [a]pray, lest ye enter into temptation.

Jesus' betrayal and arrest

47 ¶ And while he yet spake, [a]behold a multitude, and he that was called Judas, one of the twelve, went before them, and drew near unto Jesus to kiss him.

48 But Jesus said unto him, Judas, betrayest thou the Son of man with a kiss?

49 When they which were about him saw what would follow, they said unto him, Lord, shall we smite with the sword?

50 And [a]one of them smote the servant of the high priest, and cut off his right ear.

51 And Jesus answered and said, Suffer ye thus far. And he touched his ear, and healed him.

52 [a]Then Jesus said unto the chief priests, and captains of the temple, and the elders, which were come to him, Be ye come out, as against a thief, with swords and staves?

53 When I was daily with you in the temple, ye stretched forth no hands against me: [a]but this is your hour, and the power of darkness.

Peter's denial of Jesus

54 ¶ [a]Then took they him, and led *him*, and brought him into the high priest's house. [b]And Peter followed afar off.

55 [a]And when they had kindled a fire in

22:41 [a]Mat. 26:39; Mark 14:35
22:42 [1][Gr. *willing to remove*] [a]John 5:30; 6:38
22:43 [a]Mat. 4:11
22:44 [a]John 12:27; Heb. 5:7
22:46 [a]ver. 40
22:47 [a]Mat. 26:47; Mark 14:43; John 18:3
22:50 [a]Mat. 26:51; Mark 14:47
22:52 [a]Mat. 26:55; Mark 14:48
22:53 [a]John 12:27
22:54 [a]Mat. 26:57 [b]Mat. 26:58; John 18:15
22:55 [a]Mat. 26:69; Mark 14:66; John 18:17,18
22:58 [a]Mat. 26:71; Mark 14:69; John 18:25
22:59 [a]Mat. 26:73; Mark 14:70; John 18:26
22:61 [a]Mat. 26:75; Mark 14:72 [b]Mat. 26:34,75; John 13:38
22:63 [a]Mat. 26:67,68; Mark 14:65
22:66 [a]Mat. 27:1 [b]Acts 4:26; See Acts 22:5
22:67 [a]Mat. 26:63; Mark 14:61
22:69 [a]Mat 26:64; Mark 14:62; Heb. 1:3; 8:1
22:70 [a]Mat. 26:64; Mark 14:62
22:71 [a]Mat. 26:65; Mark 14:63

the midst of the hall, and were set down together, Peter sat down among them.

56 But a certain maid beheld him as he sat by the fire, and earnestly looked upon him, and said, This *man* was also with him.

57 And he denied him, saying, Woman, I know him not.

58 And [a]after a little while another saw him, and said, Thou art also of them. And Peter said, Man, I am not.

59 [a]And about the space of one hour after another confidently affirmed, saying, Of a truth this *fellow* also was with him: for he is a Galilean.

60 And Peter said, Man, I know not what thou sayest. And immediately, while he yet spake, the cock crew.

61 And the Lord turned, and looked upon Peter. [a]And Peter remembered the word of the Lord, how he had said unto him, [b]Before *the* cock crow, thou shalt deny me thrice.

62 And Peter went out, and wept bitterly.

63 ¶ [a]And the men that held Jesus mocked him, and smote *him*.

64 And when they had blindfolded him, they struck him on the face, and asked him, saying, Prophesy, who is it that smote thee?

65 And many other *things* blasphemously spake they against him.

66 [a]And as soon as it was day, [b]the elders of the people and the chief priests and the scribes came together, and led him into their council, saying,

67 [a]Art thou the Christ? tell us. And he said unto them, If I tell you, ye will not believe:

68 And if I also ask *you*, ye will not answer me, nor let *me* go.

69 [a]Hereafter shall the Son of man sit on the right hand of the power of God.

70 Then said they all, Art thou then the Son of God? And he said unto them, [a]Ye say that I am.

71 [a]And they said, What need we any further witness? for we ourselves have heard of his own mouth.

22:42 *this cup.* The cup of suffering (Mat 20:22–23; cf. Is 51:17; Ezek 23:33). See note on Mark 14:36.

22:43 *an angel.* Matthew and Mark tell of angels ministering to Jesus at the close of His fasting and temptations (Mat 4:11; Mark 1:13), but Luke does not. Here Luke tells of the strengthening presence of an angel, but the other Gospels do not.

‡22:44 *drops of blood.* Probably hematidrosis, the actual mingling of blood and sweat as in cases of extreme anguish, strain or sensitivity.

22:47 *a multitude.* They were sent by the chief priests, elders (Mat 26:47) and teachers of the law (Mark 14:43), and they carried swords and clubs. Included was a detachment of soldiers with officials of the Jews (v. 52; John 18:3). *to kiss him.* This signal had been prearranged to identify Jesus to the authorities (Mat 26:48). It was unnecessary because Jesus identified Himself (John 18:5), but Judas acted out his plan anyway.

22:50 *the servant of the high priest.* Malchus by name; Simon Peter struck the blow (John 18:10).

22:51 *healed him.* Jesus rectified the wrong done by His follower. No faith on the part of Malchus was involved, but to allow such action would have been contrary to the teaching of Jesus.

22:53 *this is your hour.* It was the time appointed for Jesus' enemies to apprehend Him, the time when the forces of darkness (the powers of evil) would do their worst to defeat God's plan.

22:54 *the high priest's house.* See notes on 3:2; Mark 14:53.

22:59 *he is a Galilean.* Recognized by his speech (Mat 26:73) and identified by a relative of Malchus, the high priest's slave (John 18:26).

22:61 *the Lord . . . looked upon Peter.* Peter was outside in the enclosed courtyard, and perhaps Jesus was being taken from the trial by Caiaphas to the Sanhedrin when Jesus caught Peter's eye. *Peter remembered.* The words spoken by Jesus (v. 34).

22:66 *as soon as it was day.* Only after daylight could a legal trial take place for the whole council (Sanhedrin) to pass the death sentence.

‡22:67 *Art thou the Christ?* This demand is related to a question asked later: "Art thou then the Son of God?" (v. 70).

22:71 *we ourselves have heard.* The reaction to Jesus' reply

Jesus before Pontius Pilate

23 And [a]the whole multitude of them
arose, and led him unto Pilate.
2 And they began to accuse him, saying,
We found this *fellow* [a]perverting the nation,
and [b]forbidding to give tribute to Cesar, saying
[c]that he himself is Christ a King.
3 [a]And Pilate asked him, saying, Art thou
the King of the Jews? And he answered him
and said, Thou sayest *it.*
4 Then said Pilate to the chief priests and
to the people, [a]I find no fault in this man.
5 And they were the more fierce, saying,
He stirreth up the people, teaching throughout
all Jewry, beginning from Galilee to this place.
6 When Pilate heard of Galilee, he asked
whether the man were a Galilean.
7 And as soon as he knew that he belonged
unto [a]Herod's jurisdiction, he sent him to Herod, who himself also was at Jerusalem at that
time.
8 And when Herod saw Jesus, he was exceeding glad: for [a]he was desirous to see him
of a long *season,* because [b]*he* had heard many
things of him; and he hoped to have seen
some miracle done by him.
9 Then he questioned *with* him in many
words; but he answered him nothing.
10 And the chief priests and scribes stood
and vehemently accused him.
11 [a]And Herod with his men of war set him
at nought, and mocked *him,* and arrayed him in
a gorgeous robe, and sent him again to Pilate.
12 And the same day [a]Pilate and Herod
were made friends together: for before they
were at enmity between themselves.
13 ¶ [a]And Pilate, when he had called together the chief priests and the rulers and the
people,
14 Said unto them, [a]Ye have brought this
man unto me, as one that perverteth the people: and behold, [b]I, having examined *him* before you, have found no fault in this man
touching those things whereof ye accuse him:
15 No, nor yet Herod: for I sent you to him;
and lo, nothing worthy of death is done unto
him.
16 [a]I will therefore chastise him, and release *him.*
17 ([a]For of necessity he must release one
unto them at the feast.)
18 And [a]they cried out all at once, saying,
Away with this *man,* and release unto us Barabbas:
19 (Who for a certain sedition made in the
city, and *for* murder, was cast into prison.)
20 Pilate therefore, willing to release Jesus,
spake again to *them.*
21 But they cried, saying, Crucify *him,* crucify him.
22 And he said unto them the third time,
Why, what evil hath he done? I have found no
cause of death in him: I will therefore chastise
him, and let *him* go.
23 And they were instant with loud voices,
requiring that he might be crucified. And the
voices of them and of the chief priests prevailed.
24 And [a]Pilate [b][1]gave sentence that it
should be as they required.
25 And he released unto them him that for
sedition and murder was cast into prison,
whom they had desired; but he delivered Jesus
to their will.

Jesus crucified

26 ¶ [a]And as they led him away, they laid
hold upon one Simon, a Cyrenian, coming out

23:1 [a]Mat. 27:2; Mark 15:1; John 18:28
23:2 [a]Acts 17:7 [b]See Mat. 17:27; 22:21; Mark 12:17 [c]John 19:12
23:3 [a]Mat. 27:11; 1 Tim. 6:13
23:4 [a]1 Pet. 2:22
23:7 [a]ch. 3:1
23:8 [a]ch. 9:9 [b]Mat. 14:1; Mark 6:14
23:11 [a]Is 53:3
23:12 [a]Acts 4:27
23:13 [a]Mat. 27:23; Mark 15:14; John 18:38; 19:4
23:14 [a]ver. 1,2 [b]ver. 4
23:16 [a]Mat. 27:26; John 19:1
23:17 [a]Mat. 27:15; Mark 15:6; John 18:39
23:18 [a]Acts 3:14
23:24 [1]Or, *assented* [a]Mat. 27:26; Mark 15:15; John 19:16 [b]Ex. 23:2
23:26 [a]Mat. 27:32; Mark 15:21; See John 19:17

makes clear that His answer was a strong affirmative. Mark has simply, "I am" (Mark 14:62). It was blasphemy to claim to be the Messiah and the Son of God—unless, of course, the claim was true (see note on Mark 14:64).

‡23:1 *the whole multitude of them.* The multitude of the Sanhedrin (Mat 26:59; 27:1) who had met at the earliest hint of dawn (22:66). *led him unto Pilate.* See note on Mat 27:2. *Pilate.* See note on Mark 15:1. The Roman governor had his main headquarters in Caesarea, but he was in Jerusalem during passover to prevent trouble from the large number of Jews assembled for the occasion.

23:2 *perverting the nation.* Large crowds followed Jesus, but He was not misleading them or turning them against Rome. *forbidding to give tribute to Cesar.* Another untrue charge (see 20:25). *saying that he himself is Christ a King.* Jesus claimed to be the Messiah, but not a political or military king, the kind Rome would be anxious to eliminate.

23:3 *Thou sayest it.* Jesus affirms that He is a king, but then explains that His kingdom is not the kind that characterizes this world (John 18:33–38).

23:5 *throughout all Jewry.* May here refer to the whole of the land of the Jews (including Galilee) or to the southern section only, where the region of Judea proper was governed by Pilate (see note on 4:44).

23:7 *Herod's jurisdiction.* See note on 3:1. Although Pilate and Herod were rivals, Pilate did not want to handle this case; so he sent Jesus to Herod (cf. v. 12). *at Jerusalem.* Herod's main headquarters was in Tiberias on the sea of Galilee; but, like Pilate, he had come to Jerusalem because of the crowds at passover.

23:8 *was desirous to see him.* Herod was worried about Jesus' identity (9:7–9) and had desired to kill Him (13:31), though the two had never met. There is no record that Jesus ever preached in Tiberias, where Herod's residence was located.

23:11 *gorgeous robe.* See note on Mark 15:17.

23:16 *I will therefore chastise him.* Although Pilate found Jesus "not guilty" as charged, he was willing to have Him illegally beaten in order to satisfy the chief priests and the people and to warn against any possible trouble in the future. Scourging, though not intended to kill, was sometimes fatal (see note on Mark 15:15).

23:18 *Barabbas.* Means "son of Abba." Pilate offered a choice between Jesus and an obviously evil, dangerous criminal (see Mat 27:15–20; Mark 15:6–11; John 18:39–40).

23:19 *sedition . . . murder.* This particular uprising is otherwise unknown but, coupled with murder, it shows the gravity of his deeds (see John 18:40).

23:22 *third time.* See vv. 4,14.

23:25 *delivered Jesus.* Luke's account is abbreviated. Pilate had already handed Jesus over to the soldiers for scourging before He was convicted (John 19:1–5). He now handed Him over for crucifixion.

23:26 *Simon.* His sons, Rufus and Alexander (Mark 15:21), must

of the country, and on him they laid the cross, that *he* might bear *it* after Jesus.

27 And there followed him a great company of people, and of women, which also bewailed and lamented him.

28 But Jesus turning unto them, said, Daughters of Jerusalem, weep not for me, but weep for yourselves, and for your children.

29 [a]For behold, the days are coming, in the which they shall say, Blessed *are* the barren, and the wombs that never bare, and the paps which never gave suck.

30 [a]Then shall they begin to say to the mountains, Fall on us; and to the hills, Cover us.

31 [a]For if they do these *things* in a green tree, what shall be done in the dry?

32 [a]And there were also two other, malefactors, led with him to be put to death.

33 ¶ And [a]when they were come to the place, which is called [1]Calvary, there they crucified him, and the malefactors, one on the right hand, and the other on the left.

34 Then said Jesus, Father, [a]forgive them; for [b]they know not what they do. And [c]they parted his raiment, and cast lots.

35 And [a]the people stood beholding. And the [b]rulers also with them derided *him,* saying, He saved others; let him save himself, if he be Christ, the chosen of God.

36 And the soldiers also mocked him, coming to *him,* and offering him vinegar,

23:29 [a]Mat. 24:19; ch. 21:23
23:30 [a]Is. 2:19; Hos. 10:8; Rev. 6:16; 9:6
23:31 [a]Prov. 11:31; Jer. 25:29; Ezek. 20:47; 21:3,4; 1 Pet. 4:17
23:32 [a]Is. 53:12; Mat. 27:38
23:33 [1]Or, The place of a *skull* [a]Mat. 27:33; Mark 15:22; John 19:17,18
23:34 [a]Mat. 5:44; Acts 7:60; 1 Cor. 4:12 [b]Acts 3:17 [c]Mat. 27:35; Mark 15:24; John 19:23
23:35 [a]Ps. 22:17; Zech. 12:10 [b]Mat. 27:39; Mark 15:29
23:38 [a]Mat. 27:37; Mark 15:26; John 19:19
23:39 [a]Mat. 27:44; Mark 15:32
23:44 [1]Or, *land* [a]Mat. 27:45; Mark 15:33
23:45 [a]Mat. 27:51; Mark 15:38
23:46 [a]Ps. 31:5; 1 Pet. 2:23 [b]Mat. 27:50; Mark 15:37; John 19:30

37 And saying, If thou be the King of the Jews, save thyself.

38 [a]And a superscription also was written over him in letters of Greek, and Latin, and Hebrew, THIS IS THE KING OF THE JEWS.

39 ¶ [a]And one of the malefactors which were hanged railed on him, saying, If thou be Christ, save thyself and us.

40 But the other answering rebuked him, saying, Dost not thou fear God, seeing thou art in the same condemnation?

41 And we indeed justly; for we receive the due reward of our deeds: but this *man* hath done nothing amiss.

42 And he said unto Jesus, Lord, remember me when thou comest into thy kingdom.

43 And Jesus said unto him, Verily I say unto thee, To day shalt thou be with me in paradise.

The death of Jesus

44 ¶ [a]And it was about the sixth hour, and there was a darkness over all the [1]earth until the ninth hour.

45 And the sun was darkened, and [a]the vail of the temple was rent in the midst.

46 And when Jesus had cried with a loud voice, he said, [a]Father, into thy hands I commend my spirit: [b]and having said thus, he gave up the ghost.

47 ¶ [a]Now when the centurion saw what was done, he glorified God, saying, Certainly this was a righteous man.

23:47 [a]Mat. 27:54; Mark 15:39

have been known in Christian circles at a later time, and perhaps were associated with the church at Rome (Rom 16:13). *Cyrenian.* Cyrene was a leading city of Libya, west of Egypt. *on him they laid the cross.* See note on Mark 15:21.

23:28 *weep for yourselves, and for your children.* Because of the terrible suffering to befall Jerusalem some 40 years later when the Romans would besiege the city and utterly destroy the temple.

23:29 *Blessed are the barren.* It would be better not to have children than to have them experience such suffering. Cf. Jer 16:1–4; 1 Cor 7:25–35.

23:30 *Fall on us.* People would seek escape through destruction in death rather than endure continuing suffering and judgment (cf. Hos 10:8; Rev 6:16).

23:31 *green tree . . . dry.* If they treat the Messiah this way when the "tree" is well-watered and green, what will their plight be when He is withdrawn from them and they suffer for their rejection in the dry period?

23:32 *malefactors.* See note on v. 18.

‡23:33 *Calvary.* The Latin word for skull is *Calvaria,* hence the name "Calvary" (see note on Mark 15:22). *crucified.* See note on Mark 15:24.

23:34 *parted his raiment.* Any possessions an executed person had with him were taken by the executioners. Unwittingly the soldiers (cf. John 19:23–24) were fulfilling the words of Ps 22:18 (but see introduction to Ps 22 and notes on Ps 22:17,20–21).

23:35 *the chosen of God.* See note on 9:35.

23:36 *vinegar.* Or wine vinegar, a sour drink carried by the soldiers for the day. Jesus refused a sedative drink (Mat 27:34; Mark 15:23) but later was given the vinegar drink when He cried out in thirst (John 19:28–30). Luke shows that it was offered in mockery.

23:38 *superscription.* Indicated the crime for which a person was dying. This was Pilate's way of mocking the Jewish leaders as well as announcing what Jesus had been accused of. *THIS IS THE KING OF THE JEWS.* See note on Mark 15:26.

23:39 *one of the malefactors.* See note on Mark 15:32.

‡23:43 *paradise.* In the Septuagint (the Greek translation of the OT) the word designated a garden (Gen 2:8–10) or forest (Neh 2:8), but in the NT (used only here and in 2 Cor 12:4; Rev 2:7) it refers to the place of bliss and rest between death and resurrection (cf. Luke 16:22; 2 Cor 12:2), which is apparently in the very presence of God..

23:44 *about the sixth hour . . . the ninth hour.* From noon to three in the afternoon, by the Jewish method of designating time. Jesus had been put on the cross at the third hour (9:00 A.M., Mark 15:25). The "sixth hour" of John (John 19:14) may be Roman time (6:00 A.M.), when Pilate gave his decision (but see note on John 19:14).

23:45 *vail of the temple.* The curtain between the holy place and the most holy place. Its tearing symbolized Christ's opening the way directly to God (Heb 9:3,8; 10:19–22).

‡23:47 *glorified God.* Either for having seen God publicly vindicate Jesus by mighty signs from heaven, or out of fear (see Mat 27:54) to appease the heavenly Judge and thus ward off a divine penalty for having carried out an unjust judgment. *this was a righteous man.* He realized that Jesus was completely innocent. Matthew and Mark report the centurion's words as "Truly this was the Son (or son) of God." "The Righteous One" and "the Son of God" would have been essentially equivalent terms. Similarly, "the son of God" and "a righteous man" would have been virtual equivalents. Which one the centurion intended is difficult to determine (see note on Mat 27:54). It seems clear, however, that the Gospel writers saw in his declaration a vin-

48 And all the people that came together to that sight, beholding the *things* which were done, smote their breasts, and returned.

49 [a]And all his acquaintance, and the women that followed him from Galilee, stood afar off, beholding these *things.*

Jesus laid in the sepulchre

50 ¶ [a]And behold, *there was* a man named Joseph, a counseller; *and he was* a good man, and a just:

51 (The same had not consented to the counsel and deed of them;) *he was* of Arimathea, a city of the Jews: [a]who also himself waited for the kingdom of God.

52 This *man* went unto Pilate, and begged the body of Jesus.

53 [a]And he took it down, and wrapped it in linen, and laid it in a sepulchre *that was* hewn in stone, wherein never man before was laid.

54 And *that* day was [a]the preparation, and the sabbath drew on.

The resurrection of Jesus

55 ¶ And the women also, [a]which came with him from Galilee, followed after, and [b]beheld the sepulchre, and how his body was laid.

56 And they returned, and [a]prepared spices and ointments; and rested the sabbath day [b]according to the commandment.

23:49 [a]Ps. 38:11; Mat. 27:55; Mark 15:40; See John 19:25
23:50 [a]Mat. 27:57; Mark 15:42; John 19:38
23:51 [a]Mark 15:43; ch. 2:25,38
23:53 [a]Mat. 27:59; Mark 15:46
23:54 [a]Mat. 27:62
23:55 [a]ch. 8:2 [b]Mark 15:47
23:56 [a]Mark 16:1 [b]Ex. 20:10

24:1 [a]Mat. 28:1; Mark 16:1; John 20:1 [b]ch. 23:56
24:2 [a]Mat. 28:2; Mark 16:4
24:3 [a]ver. 23; Mark 16:5
24:4 [a]John 20:12; Acts 1:10
24:5 [1]Or, *him that liveth*
24:6 [a]Mat. 16:21; 17:23; Mark 8:31; 9:31; ch. 9:22
24:8 [a]John 2:22
24:9 [a]Mat. 28:8; Mark 16:10
24:10 [a]ch. 8:3

24 Now [a]upon the first *day* of the week, very early in the morning, they came unto the sepulchre, [b]bringing the spices which they had prepared, and certain *others* with them.

2 [a]And they found the stone rolled away from the sepulchre.

3 [a]And they entered in, and found not the body of the Lord Jesus.

4 And it came to pass, as they were *much* perplexed thereabout, [a]behold, two men stood by them in shining garments:

5 And as they were afraid, and bowed down *their* faces to the earth, they said unto them, Why seek ye [1]the living among the dead?

6 He is not here, but is risen: [a]remember how he spake unto you when he was yet in Galilee,

7 Saying, The Son of man must be delivered into the hands of sinful men, and be crucified, and the third day rise again.

8 And [a]they remembered his words,

9 [a]And returned from the sepulchre, and told all these *things* unto the eleven, and *to* all the rest.

10 It was Mary Magdalene, and [a]Joanna, and Mary *the mother* of James, and other *women that were* with them, which told these *things* unto the apostles.

dication of Jesus, and since the centurion was the Roman official in charge of the crucifixion, his testimony was viewed as significant (see also the declarations of Pilate: vv. 4,14–15,22; Mat 27:23–24).

23:48 *smote their breasts.* A sign of anguish, grief or contrition (cf. 18:13).

23:49 *the women ... from Galilee.* See Mat 27:55–56; Mark 15:40–41; John 19:25; cf. Luke 24:10.

23:50 *Joseph, a counseller.* Either Joseph was not present at the meeting of the Sanhedrin (22:66), or he did not support the vote to have Jesus killed (see v. 51). Mark 14:64 suggests he was not present, for the decision was supported by "all."

23:51 *Arimathea.* See note on Mat 27:57. *waited for the kingdom of God.* See 2:25.

23:52 The remains of an executed criminal often were left unburied or at best put in a dishonored place in a pauper's field. A near relative, such as a mother, might ask for the body, but it was a courageous gesture for Joseph, a member of the Sanhedrin, to ask for Jesus' body.

23:53 *wherein never man before was laid.* Rock-hewn tombs were usually made to accommodate several bodies. This one, though finished, had not yet been used. See notes on 19:30; Mark 15:46.

23:54 *the preparation.* Friday, the day before the sabbath, when preparation was made for keeping the sabbath. It could be used for passover preparation, but since in this instance it is followed by the sabbath, it indicates Friday.

23:55 *the women.* See v. 49; 24:10; cf. 8:2–3. They saw where Jesus was buried and would not mistake the location when they returned.

‡23:56 *spices and ointments.* Yards of cloth and large quantities of spices were used in preparing a body for burial. "About a hundred pounds" of myrrh and aloes were already used on that first evening (John 19:39). More was purchased for the return of the women after the sabbath. *according to the commandment.* It is clear by this phrase that the sabbath in question was Saturday, the day the fourth commandment enjoins to be kept holy. That Christ died on Friday seems beyond question.

24:1 *first day of the week.* Sunday began by Jewish time at sundown on Saturday. Spices could then be bought (Mark 16:1), and they were ready to set out early the next day. When the women started out, it was dark (John 20:1), and by the time they arrived at the tomb, it was still early dawn (see Mat 28:1; Mark 16:2).

24:2 *the stone rolled away.* A tomb's entrance was ordinarily closed to keep vandals and animals from disturbing the bodies. This stone, however, had been sealed by Roman authority for a different reason (see Mat 27:62–66).

‡24:4 *two men.* They looked like men, but their clothes were remarkable (see 9:29; Acts 1:10; 10:30). Other reports referring to them call them angels (v. 23; see also John 20:12). Although Matthew speaks of one angel (not two, Mat 28:2) and Mark of a young man in white (Mark 16:5), this is not strange because frequently only the spokesman is noted and an accompanying figure is not mentioned. Words and posture (seated, John 20:12; standing, Luke 24:4) often change in the course of events, so these variations are not necessarily contradictory. They are merely evidence of independent accounts. Angels are connected with Christ's birth and temptation, as well as his agony, resurrection and ascension.

24:6 *when he was yet in Galilee.* Jesus had predicted His death and resurrection on a number of occasions (9:22), but the disciples failed to comprehend or accept what He was saying.

24:9 *unto the eleven, and to all the rest.* "Eleven" is sometimes used to refer to the group of apostles (Acts 1:26; 2:14) after the betrayal by Judas. Judas was dead at the time the apostles first met the risen Christ, but the group was still called the twelve (John 20:24). The "rest" included disciples who, for the most part, came from Galilee.

24:10 *Mary Magdalene.* See note on 8:2. She is named first in

11 [a]And their words seemed to them as idle tales, and they believed them not.

12 [a]Then arose Peter, and ran unto the sepulchre; and stooping down, he beheld the linen clothes laid by themselves, and departed, wondering in himself at that which was come to pass.

The walk to Emmaus

13 ¶ [a]And behold, two of them went *that* same day to a village called Emmaus, which was from Jerusalem *about* threescore furlongs.

14 And they talked together of all these *things* which had happened.

15 And it came to pass, that while they communed *together* and reasoned, [a]Jesus himself drew near, and went with them.

16 But [a]their eyes were holden that *they* should not know him.

17 And he said unto them, What *manner of* communications *are* these that ye have one to another, as ye walk, and are sad?

18 And the one *of them,* [a]whose name *was* Cleopas, answering said unto him, Art thou only a stranger in Jerusalem, and hast not known the *things* which are come to pass there in these days?

19 And he said unto them, What *things?* And they said unto him, Concerning Jesus of Nazareth, [a]which was a prophet [b]mighty in deed and word before God and all the people:

20 [a]And how the chief priests and our rulers delivered him to be condemned to death, and have crucified him.

21 But we trusted [a]that it had been he which should have redeemed Israel: and beside all this, to day is the third day since these *things* were done.

22 Yea, and [a]certain women *also* of our company made us astonished, which were early at the sepulchre;

23 And when they found not his body, they came, saying, that *they* had also seen a vision of angels, which said that he was alive.

24 And [a]certain of them which were with us went to the sepulchre, and found *it* even so as the women had said: but him they saw not.

25 Then he said unto them, O fools, and slow of heart to believe all that the prophets have spoken:

26 [a]Ought not Christ to have suffered these *things,* and to enter into his glory?

27 [a]And beginning at [b]Moses and [c]all the prophets, he expounded unto them in all the scriptures the *things* concerning himself.

28 And they drew nigh unto the village, whither they went: and [a]he made as though *he* would have gone further.

29 But [a]they constrained him, saying, Abide with us: for it is towards evening, and the day is far spent. And he went in to tarry with them.

30 And it came to pass, as he sat at meat with them, [a]he took bread, and blessed *it,* and brake, and gave to them.

31 And their eyes were opened, and they knew him; and he [1]vanished out of their sight.

32 And they said one to another, Did not our heart burn within us, while he talked with us by the way, and while he opened to us the scriptures?

33 And they rose up the same hour, and returned to Jerusalem, and found the eleven gathered together, and them that were with them,

34 Saying, The Lord is risen indeed, and [a]hath appeared to Simon.

35 And they told what *things were done* in the way, and how he was known of them in breaking of bread.

Jesus appears to the ten

36 ¶ [a]And as they thus spake, Jesus himself stood in the midst of them, and saith unto them, Peace *be* unto you.

24:11 [a]ver. 25 **24:12** [a]John 20:3 **24:13** [a]Mark 16:12 **24:15** [a]Mat. 18:20 **24:16** [a]John 20:14; 21:4 **24:18** [a]John 19:25 **24:19** [a]Mat. 21:11; ch. 7:16; John 3:2; 4:19; 6:14; Acts 2:22 [b]Acts 7:22 **24:20** [a]ch. 23:1; Acts 13:27 **24:21** [a]ch. 1:68; 2:38; Acts 1:6 **24:22** [a]ver. 9,10; Mat. 28:8; Mark 16:10; John 20:18

24:24 [a]ver. 12 **24:26** [a]Acts 17:3; 1 Pet. 1:11 **24:27** [a]ver. 45 [b]Gen. 3:15; 22:18; 26:4; 49:10; Num. 21:9; Deut. 18:15 [c]Ps. 16:9,10; 22; 132:11; Is. 7:14; 9:6; 40:10,11; 50:6; Jer. 23:5; 33:14,15; Ezek. 34:23; 37:25; Dan. 9:24; Mic. 7:20; Mal. 3:1; 4:2; See John 1:45 **24:28** [a]Gen. 32:26; 42:7; Mark 6:48 **24:29** [a]Gen. 19:3; Acts 16:15 **24:30** [a]Mat. 14:19 **24:31** [1]Or, *ceased to be seen of them* **24:34** [a]1 Cor. 15:5 **24:36** [a]Mark 16:14; John 20:19; 1 Cor. 15:5

most of the lists of women (Mat 27:56; Mark 15:40; but cf. John 19:25) and was the first to see the risen Christ (John 20:13–18). *Joanna.* See 8:3. She is named by only Luke at this point (Mark is the only one who adds Salome at this time, Mark 16:1). *Mary the mother of James.* See Mark 16:1. She is the "other Mary" of Mat 28:1. The absence of the mother of Jesus is significant. She was probably with John (cf. John 19:27).

24:12 *Peter . . . ran.* John's Gospel (20:3–9) includes another disciple, John himself.

‡24:13 *two of them.* One was named Cleopas (v. 18.) Many have surmised that the other was Cleopas's wife.

‡24:16 *their eyes were holden.* By special divine intervention, they cannot recognize Jesus.

24:19 *a prophet.* They had respect for Jesus as a man of God, but after His death they apparently were reluctant to call Him the Messiah.

‡24:21 *we trusted.* The verb tense indicates that they used to be trusting. However, their hopes had been dashed. *have redeemed Israel.* To set the Jewish nation free from bondage to Rome and usher in the kingdom of God (1:68; 2:38; 21:28,31; cf. Tit 2:14; 1 Pet 1:18). *the third day.* A reference either to the Jewish belief that after the third day the soul left the body or to Jesus' remark that He would be resurrected on the third day (9:22). In any event, this time reference points to a Friday crucifixion, since Jews counted the day on which the event occurred as day one. They would have said it was the fifth day, for example, if Christ had been crucified on Wednesday.

24:23 *vision of angels.* See note on v. 4.

24:24 *certain of them . . . with us.* See v. 12 and note.

24:27 *Moses and all the prophets.* A way of designating the whole of the OT Scriptures.

24:28 *as though he would have gone further.* If they had not invited Him in, He apparently would have continued on by Himself.

‡24:31 *their eyes were opened.* Cf. v. 16;. Perhaps as they took the bread from His hands they saw the nail marks. But in any event it was more than a matter of simple recognition

24:33 *the eleven gathered together, and them that were with them.* See note on v. 9.

24:36 *Jesus himself stood in the midst of them.* Behind locked doors (John 20:19), indicating that His body was of a different order. It was the glorified body of the resurrection (cf. Mark 16:12).

‡24:39 *my hands and my feet.* Indicating that Jesus' feet as

37 But they were terrified and affrighted,
and supposed that *they* had seen [a]a spirit.
38 And he said unto them, Why are ye
troubled? and why do thoughts arise in your
hearts?
39 Behold my hands and my feet, that it is
I myself: [a]handle me, and see; for a spirit hath
not flesh and bones, as ye see me have.
40 And when he had thus spoken, he
shewed them *his* hands and *his* feet.
41 And while they yet believed not [a]for
joy, and wondered, he said unto them, [b]Have
ye here any meat?
42 And they gave him a piece of a broiled
fish, and of a honeycomb.
43 [a]And he took *it,* and did eat before
them.

24:37 [a]Mark 6:49
24:39 [a]John 20:20
24:41 [a]Gen. 45:26 [b]John 21:5
24:43 [a]Acts 10:41
24:44 [a]ver. 6; Mat. 16:21; 17:22; 20:18; Mark 8:31; ch. 9:22; 18:31
24:45 [a]Acts 16:14
24:46 [a]Ps. 22; Acts 17:3
24:47 [a]Dan. 9:24; Acts 13:38 [b]Ps. 22:27; Jer. 31:34; Mic. 4:2
24:48 [a]Acts 1:8
24:49 [a]Is. 44:3; Joel 2:28

44 And he said unto them, [a]These *are* the
words which I spake unto you, while I was yet
with you, that all *things* must be fulfilled,
which were written in the law of Moses, and
in the prophets, and *in* the psalms, concerning
me.
45 Then [a]opened he their understanding,
that *they* might understand the scriptures,
46 And said unto them, [a]Thus it is written,
and thus it behoved Christ to suffer, and to rise
from the dead the third day:
47 And that repentance and [a]remission of
sins should be preached in his name [b]among
all nations, beginning at Jerusalem.
48 And [a]ye are witnesses of these *things.*
49 [a]And behold, I send the promise of my
Father upon you: but tarry ye in the city of Je-

well as His hands were nailed to the cross (see note on Mark 15:24; cf. John 20:20,27). *flesh and bones.* Jesus retains His physical body, yet it has other powers as well.

24:42 *a piece of a broiled fish.* Demonstrating that He had a physical body that could consume food.

24:44 *law of Moses, and in the prophets, and in the psalms.* The three parts of the Hebrew OT (Psalms was the first book of the third section, called the Writings), indicating that Christ (the Messiah) was foretold in the whole OT.

24:45 *opened he their understanding.* By explaining the OT Scriptures (cf. v. 27).

24:46 *suffer . . . rise from the dead . . . third day.* The OT depicts the Messiah as one who would suffer (Ps 22; Is 53) and rise from the dead on the third day (Ps 16:9–11; Is 53:10–11; compare Jonah 1:17 with Mat 12:40).

24:47 *repentance and remission of sins.* See Acts 5:31; 10:43; 13:38; 26:18. The prediction of Christ's death and resurrection (v. 46) is joined with the essence of man's response (repentance) and the resulting benefit (forgiveness; cf. Is 49:6; Acts 13:47; 26:22–23). *beginning at Jerusalem.* Cf. Acts 1:8.

24:49 *the promise of my Father.* Cf. Joel 2:28–29. The reference is to the coming power of the Spirit, fulfilled in Acts 2:4.

Resurrection Appearances

EVENT	PLACE	DAY OF THE WEEK	MATTHEW	MARK	LUKE	JOHN	ACTS	1 COR
The empty tomb	Jerusalem	Resurrection Sunday	28:1-10	16:1-8	24:1-12	20:1-9		
To Mary Magdalene in the garden	Jerusalem	Resurrection Sunday		16:9-11		20:11-18		
To other women	Jerusalem	Resurrection Sunday	28:9-10					
To two people going to Emmaus	Road to Emmaus	Resurrection Sunday		16:12-13	24:13-32			
To Peter	Jerusalem	Resurrection Sunday			24:34			15:5
To the ten disciples in the upper room	Jerusalem	Resurrection Sunday			24:36-43	20:19-25		
To the eleven disciples in the upper room	Jerusalem	Following Sunday		16:14		20:26-31		15:5
To seven disciples fishing	Sea of Galilee	Some time later				21:1-23		
To the eleven disciples on a mountain	Galilee	Some time later	28:16-20	16:15-18				
To more than five hundred	Unknown	Some time later						15:6
To James	Unknown	Some time later						15:7
To His disciples at His ascension	Mount of Olives	Forty days after Jesus' resurrection			24:44-49		1:3-8	
To Paul	Damascus	Several years later					9:1-19 22:3-16 26:9-18	9:1

rusalem, until ye be endued with power from
on high.

Jesus' ascension

50 ¶ And he led them out [a] as far as to Bethany, and he lift up his hands, and blessed
them.

51 [a] And it came to pass, while he blessed
them, he was parted from them, and carried
up into heaven.
52 [a] And they worshipped him, and returned to Jerusalem with great joy:
53 And were continually [a] in the temple,
praising and blessing God. Amen.

24:50 [a] Acts 1:12
24:51 [a] Mark 16:19
24:52 [a] Mat. 28:9
24:53 [a] Acts 2:46

24:50 *Bethany.* A village on the mount of Olives (see notes on 19:29; Mat 21:17).

‡24:51 *while he blessed them.* This book begins with a priest who has no blessing to impart (Zacharias) and ends with our great high priest giving a blessing as he is departing from them. *carried up into heaven.* Different from His previous disappearances (4:30; 24:3; John 8:59). They saw Him ascend into a cloud (Acts 1:9).

24:53 *in the temple.* During the period of time immediately following Christ's ascension the believers met continually in the temple (Acts 2:46; 3:1; 5:21,42), where many rooms were available for meetings (see note on 2:37).

The Gospel According to
S. John

INTRODUCTION

See "The Synoptic Gospels," p. 1349.

Author

The author is the apostle John, the disciple "whom Jesus loved" (13:23; 19:26; 20:2; 21:7,20,24). He was prominent in the early church but is not mentioned by name in this Gospel—which would be natural if he wrote it, but hard to explain otherwise. The author knew Jewish life well, as seen from references to popular Messianic speculations (e.g., 1:20–21; 7:40–42), to the hostility between Jews and Samaritans (4:9), and to Jewish customs, such as the duty of circumcision on the eighth day taking precedence over the prohibition of working on the sabbath (see note on 7:22). He knew the geography of the Holy Land, locating Bethany about 15 furlongs (about two miles) from Jerusalem (11:18); that Jacob's well was deep (4:11); and mentioning Cana, a village not referred to in any earlier writing known to us (2:1; 21:2). The Gospel of John has many touches that were obviously based on the recollections of an eyewitness—such as the house at Bethany being filled with the fragrance of the broken perfume jar (12:3). Early writers such as Irenaeus and Tertullian say that John wrote this Gospel, and all other evidence agrees (see Introduction to 1 John: Author). The earliest manuscripts have as their title, "The Gospel According to John."

Date

In general, two views of the dating of this Gospel have been advocated:

1. The traditional view places it toward the end of the first century, c. A.D. 85 or later (see Introduction to 1 John: Date).

2. More recently, some scholars have suggested an earlier date, perhaps as early as the 50s and no later than 70.

The first view may be supported by reference to the statement of Clement of Alexandria that John wrote to supplement the accounts found in the other Gospels (Eusebius, *Ecclesiastical History,* 6.14.7), and thus his Gospel is later than the first three. It has also been argued that the seemingly more developed theology of the fourth Gospel indicates that it originated later.

The second view has found favor because it has been felt more recently that John wrote independently of the other Gospels. This does not contradict the statement of Clement referred to above. Also, those who hold this view point out that developed theology does not necessarily argue for a late origin. The theology of Romans (written c. 57) is every bit as developed as that in John. Further, the statement in 5:2 that there "is" (rather than "was") a pool "by the sheep market" may suggest a time before 70, when Jerusalem was destroyed. Others, however, observe that John elsewhere sometimes used the present tense when speaking of the past.

Purpose and Emphases

Some interpreters have felt that John's aim was to set forth a version of the Christian message that would appeal to Greek thinkers. Others have seen a desire to supplement (or correct) the Synoptic Gospels, to combat some form of heresy, to oppose the continuing followers of John the Baptist or to achieve a similar goal. But the writer himself states his main purpose clearly: "But these are written, that ye might believe that Jesus is the Christ, the Son of God; and that believing ye might have life through his name" (20:31). He may have had Greek readers mainly in mind, some of whom were being exposed to heretical influence, but his primary intention was evangelistic. It is possible to understand "might believe" in the sense of "may continue to believe"—in which case the purpose would be to build up believers as well as to win new converts.

John is the only Gospel writer to mention more than one passover. In fact, he lists three (2:13; 6:4; 13:1) and hints at a fourth (5:1). It is this enumeration which allows us to reconstruct a full

three-year ministry for Christ on earth. This also helps to demonstrate that John was familiar with the other three Gosepls and consciously supplemented as necessary. Fully 92 percent of John's Gospel is unique, that is, not contained in any of the other accounts. For the main emphases of the book see notes on 1:4,7,9,14,19,49; 2:4,11; 3:27; 4:34; 6:35; 13:1—17:26; 13:31; 17:1–2,5; 20:31.

Outline

I. Prologue (1:1–18)
II. Beginnings of Jesus' Ministry (1:19–51)
  A. The Ministry of His Forerunner (1:19–34)
  B. Jesus' Introduction to Some Future Disciples (1:35–51)
III. Jesus' Public Ministry: Signs and Discourses (chs. 2—11)
  A. Changing Water into Wine (2:1–11)
  B. Cleansing the Temple (2:12–25)
  C. Interview with Nicodemus (3:1–21)
  D. Parallel Ministry with John the Baptist (3:22—4:3)
  E. Journey through Samaria: The Woman at the Well (4:4–42)
  F. Healing of the Nobleman's Son (4:43–54)
  G. Trip to Jerusalem for an Annual Feast (ch. 5)
  H. The Feeding of the 5,000 and the Sermon on the Bread of Life (ch. 6)
  I. Jesus at the Feast of Tabernacles (chs. 7—8)
  J. Healing of the Man Born Blind (ch. 9)
  K. Parable of the Good Shepherd (10:1–21)
  L. Debating at the Feast of Dedication (10:22–39)
  M. Ministry in Perea (10:40–42)
  N. The Raising of Lazarus (ch. 11)
IV. The Passion Week (chs. 12—19)
  A. The Anointing of Jesus' Feet (12:1–11)
  B. The Triumphal Entry (12:12–19)
  C. The Coming of the Greeks (12:20–36)
  D. Continued Jewish Unbelief (12:37–50)
  E. Farewell Discourses (chs. 13—17)
    1. Discourse at the Last Supper (chs. 13—14)
    2. Discourse on the way to Gethsemane (chs. 15—16)
    3. Jesus' prayer of intercession (ch. 17)
  F. Jesus' Betrayal and Arrest (18:1–12)
  G. The Trials of Jesus (18:13—19:15)
  H. The Crucifixion and Burial (19:16—42)
V. The Resurrection (20:1–29)
VI. The Statement of Purpose (20:30–31)
VII. Epilogue (ch. 21)

The Word became flesh

1 In the beginning [a]was the Word, and the Word was [b]with God, [c]and the Word was God.

2 [a]The same was in the beginning with God.

3 [a]All *things* were made by him; and without him was not any *thing* made that was made.

4 [a]In him was life; and [b]the life was the light of men.

5 And [a]the light shineth in darkness; and the darkness comprehended it not.

6 ¶ [a]There was a man sent from God, whose name *was* John.

7 [a]The same came for a witness, to bear witness of the Light, that all *men* through him might believe.

8 He was not *that* Light, but *was sent* to bear witness of *that* Light.

9 [a]*That* was the true Light, which lighteth every man *that* cometh into the world.

10 He was in the world, and [a]the world was made by him, and the world knew him not.

11 [a]He came unto his own, and his own received him not.

12 But [a]as many as received him, to them gave he [1]power to become the sons of God, *even* to them that believe on his name:

13 [a]Which were born, not of blood, nor of the will of the flesh, nor of the will of man, but of God.

14 [a]And the Word [b]was made [c]flesh, and dwelt among us, (and [d]we beheld his glory, the glory as of the only begotten of the Father,) [e]full of grace and truth.

15 [a]John bare witness of him, and cried, saying, This was he of whom I spake, [b]He that cometh after me is preferred before me: [c]for he was before me.

16 And of his [a]fulness have all we received, and grace for grace.

17 For [a]the law was given by Moses, *but* [b]grace and [c]truth came by Jesus Christ.

18 [a]No *man* hath seen God at any time; [b]the only begotten Son, which is in the bosom of the Father, he hath declared *him*.

1:1 [a]Prov. 8:22; 1 John 1:1 [b]Prov. 8:30; ch. 17:5 [c]1 John 5:7
1:2 [a]Gen. 1:1
1:3 [a]Ps. 33:6; Eph. 3:9; Col. 1:16
1:4 [a]1 John 5:11 [b]ch. 8:12
1:5 [a]ch. 3:19
1:6 [a]Mal. 3:1; Mat. 3:1; Luke 3:2
1:7 [a]Acts 19:4
1:9 [a]Is. 49:6
1:10 [a]Heb. 1:2
1:11 [a]Luke 19:14
1:12 [1]Or, *the right,* or, *privilege* [a]Gal. 3:26
1:13 [a]1 Pet. 1:23
1:14 [a]Mat. 1:16; Luke 1:31 [b]Gal. 4:4 [c]Heb. 2:11 [d]Is. 40:5 [e]Col. 1:19
1:15 [a]ch. 3:32 [b]Mat. 3:11; Mark 1:7; Luke 3:16 [c]Col. 1:17
1:16 [a]Col. 1:19
1:17 [a]Ex. 20:1 [b]Rom. 5:21 [c]ch. 8:32
1:18 [a]Ex. 33:20; Mat. 11:27; 1 Tim. 6:16 [b]1 John 4:9

1:1 *In the beginning.* See Gen 1:1. *Word.* Greeks used this term not only of the spoken word but also of the unspoken word, the word still in the mind—the reason. When they applied it to the universe, they meant the rational principle that governs all things. Jews, on the other hand, used it as a way of referring to God. Thus John used a term that was meaningful to both Jews and Gentiles. *with God.* The Word was distinct from the Father. *was God.* Jesus was God in the fullest sense (see note on Rom 9:5). The prologue (vv. 1–18) begins and ends with a ringing affirmation of His deity (see note on v. 18).

1:3 *All things were made by him.* Jesus is the agent of creation. See also Col 1:16–18.

1:4 *life.* One of the great concepts of this Gospel. The Greek word for "life" (*zoe*) is found 36 times in John, while no other NT book uses it more than 17 times. Life is Christ's gift (10:28), and He, in fact, is "the life" (14:6). *light of men.* This Gospel also links light with Christ, from whom comes all spiritual illumination. He is the "light of the world," who holds out wonderful hope for man (8:12). For an OT link between life and light see Ps 36:9.

1:5 *darkness.* The stark contrast between light and darkness is a striking theme in this Gospel (see, e.g., 12:35).

1:6 *John.* In this Gospel the name John always refers to John the Baptist.

1:7 *for a witness, to bear witness.* John the Baptist's singular ministry was to testify to Jesus (10:41). "Witness" is another important concept in this Gospel. The Greek noun for "witness" or "testimony" is used 14 times (in Matthew not at all, in Mark three times, in Luke once) and the verb ("testify") 33 times (found once each in Matthew and Luke, not at all in Mark)—in both cases more often than anywhere else in the NT. John (the author) thereby emphasizes that the facts about Jesus are amply attested. *that all men through him might believe.* People were not to believe "in" John the Baptist but "through" him. Similarly, the writer's purpose was to draw them to belief in Christ (20:31); he uses the Greek verb *pisteuo* ("believe") 98 times.

‡1:9 John is referring to the incarnation of Christ. *lighteth every man.* Christ enlightens every human being so that none are without excuse. *world.* Another common word in John's writings, the Greek *kosmos* is found 78 times in this Gospel and 24 times in his letters (only 47 times in all of Paul's writings). It can mean the universe, the earth, the people on earth, most people, people opposed to God, or the human system opposed to God's purposes. John emphasizes the word by repetition, and moves without explanation from one meaning to another (see, e.g., 17:5,14–15 and notes).

1:12 *gave he power.* Membership in God's family is by grace alone—the gift of God (see Eph 2:8–9). It is never a human achievement, as v. 13 emphasizes; yet the imparting of the gift is dependent on man's reception of it, as the words "received" and "believe" make clear.

1:14 *was made flesh.* Indicates transition; the Word existed before He became man. *flesh.* A strong, almost crude, word that stresses the reality of Christ's manhood. *dwelt among us, (and we beheld his glory.* The Greek for "dwelt" is connected with the word for "tent/tabernacle"; the verse would have reminded John's Jewish readers of the tabernacle, which was filled by the glory of God (Ex 40:34–35). Christ revealed His glory to His disciples by the miracles He performed (see 2:11) and by His death and resurrection. *grace and truth.* The corresponding Hebrew terms are often translated "(unfailing) love and faithfulness" (see notes on Ps 26:3; Prov 16:6). *grace.* A significant Christian concept (see notes on Jonah 4:2; Gal 1:3; Eph 1:2), though John never uses the word after the prologue (vv. 1–18). *truth.* John uses this word, the Greek *aletheia,* 25 times and links it closely with Jesus, who is the truth (14:6).

1:15 *cried, saying.* Here the Greek is in the present tense, even though when John wrote it the action was in the past. The present tense in the original suggests the author John's sense that John the Baptist's message still sounded in people's ears beyond his death. John characteristically uses present tense verbs in his writing. *he was before me.* In ancient times the older person was given respect and regarded as greater than the younger. People would normally have ranked Jesus lower in respect than John, who was older. John the Baptist explains that this is only apparent, since Jesus, as the Word, existed before he was born on earth.

‡1:18 *the only begotten Son.* An explicit declaration of Christ's uniqueness (see vv. 1,14 and notes; 3:16). *hath declared him.* Sometimes in the OT people are said to have seen God (e.g., Ex 24:9–11). But we are also told that no one can see God and live (Ex 33:20). Therefore, since no human being can see God as He

John's witness to himself

19 ¶ And this is [a]the record of John, when
the Jews sent priests and Levites from Jerusalem to ask him, Who art thou?
20 And [a]he confessed, and denied not; but
confessed, I am not the Christ.
21 And they asked him, What then? Art
thou [a]Elias? And he saith, I am not. Art thou
[b][1]*that* prophet? And he answered, No.
22 Then said they unto him, Who art thou?
that we may give an answer to them that sent
us. What sayest thou of thyself?
23 [a]He said, I *am* the voice of one crying in
the wilderness, Make straight the way of the
Lord, as [b]said the prophet Esaias.
24 And they which were sent were of the
Pharisees.
25 And they asked him, and said unto him,
Why baptizest thou then, if thou be not *that*
Christ, nor Elias, neither *that* prophet?
26 John answered them, saying, [a]I baptize
with water: [b]but there standeth one among
you, whom ye know not;
27 [a]He it is, who coming after me is preferred before me, whose shoe's latchet I am
not worthy to unloose.

1:19 [a]ch. 5:33
1:20 [a]Luke 3:15; Acts 13:25
1:21 [1]Or, a *prophet?* [a]Mal. 4:5 [b]Deut. 18:15
1:23 [a]Mat. 3:3
1:23 [b]Is. 40:3
1:26 [a]Mat. 3:11 [b]Mal. 3:1
1:27 [a]Acts 19:4

really is, those who saw God saw Him in a form He took on Himself temporarily for the occasion. Those events are termed "Christophanies" or OT appearances of Christ in human form. Now, however, Christ has made Him known.

1:19 *the Jews.* The phrase occurs about 70 times in this Gospel. It is used in a favorable sense (e.g., 4:22) and in a neutral sense (e.g., 2:6). But generally John used it of the Jewish leaders who were hostile to Jesus (e.g., 8:48). Here it refers to the delegation sent by the Sanhedrin to look into the activities of an unauthorized teacher. *Levites.* Descendants of the tribe of Levi, who were assigned to specific duties in connection with the tabernacle and temple (Num 3:17–37). They also had teaching responsibilities (2 Chr 35:3; Neh 8:7–9), and it was probably in this role that they were sent with the priests to John the Baptist.

1:20 *I.* Emphatic, contrasting John the Baptist (or Baptizer) with someone else. Throughout the following verses this emphatic "I" occurs frequently, and almost invariably there is an implied contrast with Jesus, who is always given the higher place.

1:21 *Art thou Elias? . . . I am not.* The Jews remembered that Elijah had not died (2 Ki 2:11) and believed that the same prophet would come back to earth to announce the end time. In this sense, John properly denied that he was Elijah. When Jesus later said the Baptist was Elijah (Mat 11:14; 17:10–13), He meant it in the sense that John was a fulfillment of the prophecy of Mal 4:5 (cf. Luke 1:17). *that prophet.* The prophet of Deut 18:15,18. The Jewish people expected a variety of persons to be associated with the coming of the Messiah. John the Baptist emphatically denies being "that prophet." He had come to testify about Jesus, yet they kept asking him about himself. His answers became progressively more terse.

1:23 The Baptist applied the prophecy of Is 40:3 to his own ministry of calling people to repent in preparation for the coming of the Messiah. The men of Qumran (the community that produced the Dead Sea Scrolls; see essay, p. 1344) applied the same words to themselves, but they prepared for the Lord's coming by isolating themselves from the world to secure their own salvation. John concentrated on helping people come to the Messiah (the Christ).

1:24 *Pharisees.* The conservative religious party, who probed deeper than the rest of the delegation (v. 19). See notes on Mat 3:7; Mark 2:16; Luke 5:17.

1:25 *that Christ.* "Christ" (Greek) and "Messiah" (Hebrew) both mean "Anointed One." In OT times anointing signified being set apart for service, particularly as king (cf. 1 Sam 16:1,13; 26:11) or priest (Ex 40:13–15; Lev 4:3). But people were looking for not just *an* anointed one but *the* Anointed One, the Messiah.

‡1:27 *whose shoe's latchet I am not worthy to unloose.* A menial task, fit for a slave. Disciples would perform all sorts of service for their rabbis (teachers), but loosing sandal thongs was expressly excluded.

Sevens in John

John's focus is on showing that Jesus is the Son of God. John describes Jesus as the eternal Word who was with God from the beginning and who, in fact, is God (John 1:1). John was also careful to write down some of the many times Jesus referred to himself by the divine name "I am." Jesus said, "I am the bread of life (6:35–51), the light of the world (8:12—9:5), the door for the Father's sheep (10:7–9), the good shepherd (10:11–14), the resurrection and life (11:25), the way and the truth (14:6), and the true vine of God (15:1–5). John also arranges many things in his account in groups of seven, which was a sacred number to God's people. In this Gospel there are seven of Jesus' discourses, seven of his miracles and seven "I am" statements.

SEVEN DISCOURSES	SEVEN MIRACLES	SEVEN "I AM" STATEMENTS
1. New Birth (3:1–36)	**1.** Water into Wine (2:1–11)	**1.** Bread of Life (6:35–51)
2. Water of Life (4:1–42)	**2.** Healing the Nobleman's Son (4:43–54)	**2.** Light of the World (8:12—9:5)
3. Son of Man (5:19–47)	**3.** Healing the Lame Man (5:1–16)	**3.** Door of the Sheep (10:7–9)
4. Bread of Life (6:22–66)	**4.** Feeding the 5,000 (6:1–14)	**4.** Good Shepherd (10:11–14)
5. Rivers of Living Water (7:1–52)	**5.** Walking on Water (6:16–21)	**5.** Resurrection and Life (11:35)
6. Light of the World (8:12–59)	**6.** Healing the Blind Man (9:1–12)	**6.** Way, Truth and Life (14:6)
7. Good Shepherd (10:1–42)	**7.** Raising Lazarus from Dead (11:1–46)	**7.** True Vine (15:1–5)

28 These *things* were done [a]in Bethabara beyond Jordan, where John was baptizing.

John's witness to Jesus

29 ¶ The next day John seeth Jesus coming unto him, and saith, Behold [a]the Lamb of God, [b]which [1]taketh away the sin of the world.

30 [a]This is he of whom I said, After me cometh a man which is preferred before me: for he was before me.

31 And I knew him not: but that he should be made manifest to Israel, [a]therefore am I come baptizing with water.

32 [a]And John bare record, saying, I saw the Spirit descending from heaven like a dove, and it abode upon him.

33 And I knew him not: but he that sent me to baptize with water, the same said unto me, Upon whom thou shalt see the Spirit descending, and remaining on him, [a]the same is he which baptizeth with the Holy Ghost.

34 And I saw, and bare record that this is the Son of God.

Andrew and Peter follow Jesus

35 ¶ Again the next day *after* John stood, and two of his disciples;

36 And looking upon Jesus as he walked, he saith, [a]Behold the Lamb of God.

37 And the two disciples heard him speak, and they followed Jesus.

38 Then Jesus turned, and saw them following, and saith unto them, What seek ye? They said unto him, Rabbi, (which is to say, being interpreted, Master,) where [1]dwellest thou?

39 He saith unto them, Come and see. They came and saw where he dwelt, and abode with him that day: for it was [1]about the tenth hour.

1:28 [a]Judg. 7:24; ch. 10:40
1:29 [1]Or, *beareth* [a]Ex. 12:3; Is. 53:7; Acts 8:32; 1 Pet. 1:19; Rev. 5:6 [b]Is. 53:11; 1 Cor. 15:3; Gal. 1:4; Heb. 1:3; 2:17; 9:28; 1 Pet. 2:24; 3:18; 1 John 2:2; 3:5; Rev. 1:5
1:30 [a]ver. 15,27
1:31 [a]Mal. 3:1; Mat. 3:6; Luke 1:17,76,77; 3:3,4
1:32 [a]Mat. 3:16; Mark 1:10; ch. 5:32
1:33 [a]Mat. 3:11; Acts 2:4; 10:44
1:36 [a]ver. 29
1:38 [1]Or, *abidest*
1:39 [1]*that was two hours before night*
1:41 [1]Or, *the Anointed*
1:42 [1]Or, *Peter* [a]Mat. 16:18
1:44 [a]ch. 12:21
1:45 [a]ch. 21:2 [b]Gen. 3:15; 49:10; Deut. 18:18; See Luke 24:27 [c]Is. 4:2; 7:14; 9:6; Mic. 5:2; Zech. 6:12; See more on Luke 24:27 [d]Mat. 2:23; Luke 2:4
1:46 [a]ch. 7:41,42
1:47 [a]Ps. 32:2; 73:1; ch. 8:39; Rom. 2:28; 9:6
1:49 [a]Mat. 14:33 [b]Mat. 21:5; ch. 18:37

40 One of the two which heard John speak, and followed him, was Andrew, Simon Peter's brother.

41 He first findeth his own brother Simon, and saith unto him, We have found the Messias, which is, being interpreted, [1]the Christ.

42 And he brought him to Jesus. And when Jesus beheld him, he said, Thou art Simon the son of Jona: [a]thou shalt be called Cephas, which is by interpretation, [1]A stone.

Philip and Nathanael follow Jesus

43 ¶ The day following Jesus would go forth into Galilee, and findeth Philip, and saith unto him, Follow me.

44 Now [a]Philip was of Bethsaida, the city of Andrew and Peter.

45 Philip findeth [a]Nathanael, and saith unto him, We have found him, of whom [b]Moses in the law, and the [c]prophets, did write, Jesus [d]of Nazareth, the son of Joseph.

46 And Nathanael said unto him, [a]Can there any good *thing* come out of Nazareth? Philip saith unto him, Come and see.

47 Jesus saw Nathanael coming to him, and saith of him, Behold [a]an Israelite indeed, in whom is no guile.

48 Nathanael saith unto him, Whence knowest thou me? Jesus answered and said unto him, Before that Philip called thee, when thou wast under the fig tree, I saw thee.

49 Nathanael answered and saith unto him, Rabbi, [a]thou art the Son of God; thou art [b]the King of Israel.

50 Jesus answered and said unto him, Because I said unto thee, I saw thee under the fig tree, believest thou? thou shalt see greater *things* than these.

51 And he saith unto him, Verily, verily, I

1:28 *Bethabara.* The site of Bethabara is not known, except that it was located on the east side of the Jordan.

‡1:29 *Lamb of God.* An expression found in the Bible only here and in v. 36. Many suggestions have been made as to its precise meaning (e.g., the lamb offered at passover, or the lamb of Is 53:7, of Jer 11:19 or of Gen 22:8). But the expression seems to be a general reference to sacrifice, not the name for a particular offering. John was saying that Jesus would be the sacrifice that would atone for the sin of the world. There was first a sacrifice for the individual (Gen 4); then for a family at passover (Ex 12); and then for the nation on the day of atonement (Lev 16); now it is broadened so that Christ is a sacrifice for the entire world.

1:31 *I knew him not.* John the Baptist, who lived "in the deserts till the day of his shewing unto Israel" (Luke 1:80), may not have known Jesus at all. But the words probably mean only that he did not know that Jesus was the Messiah until he saw the sign mentioned in vv. 32–33.

1:32 See note on Mat 3:15 for Jesus' baptism.

1:33 *he which baptizeth with the Holy Ghost.* John baptized with water, but Jesus would baptize with the Spirit. If a specific event is intended by these words, the fulfillment was the sending of the Holy Spirit on the day of Pentecost (Acts 2).

1:34 *Son of God.* See vv. 14,18; 3:16; 20:31.

1:35 *two.* One was Andrew (v. 40). The other is not named, but from early times it has been thought that he was John, the author of this Gospel. *his disciples.* In the sense that they had been baptized by John and looked to him as their religious teacher.

1:36 *Lamb of God.* See note on v. 29.

1:39 *tenth hour.* 4:00 P.M.

1:41 *the Messias.* See note on v. 25.

1:42 *Cephas.* Both Cephas (Aramaic) and Peter (Greek) mean "rock." In the Gospels, Peter was anything but a rock; he was impulsive and unstable. In Acts, he was a pillar of the early church. Jesus named him not for what he was but for what, by God's grace, he would become.

1:44 *Bethsaida.* See note on Mat 11:21.

1:45 *son of Joseph.* Not a denial of the virgin birth of Christ (Mat 1:18,20,23,25; Luke 1:35). Joseph was Jesus' legal, though not His natural, father.

1:46 *Nazareth.* See 7:52; see also note on Mat 2:23.

1:47 *an Israelite indeed.* See 2:24–25.

1:48 *fig tree.* Its shade was a favorite place for study and prayer in hot weather.

1:49 *Son of God.* See vv. 14,18,34; 3:16; 20:31. At the beginning of Jesus' ministry Nathanael acknowledged Jesus with this meaningful title; later it was used in mockery (Mat 27:40; cf. John 19:7). *King of Israel.* See 12:13. In Mark 15:32 "Christ" and "King of Israel" are equated.

‡1:51 *Verily, verily.* Only John used the double "verily," and these words appear exactly 25 times throughout the book. They

say unto you, [a]Hereafter ye shall see heaven open, and the angels of God ascending and descending upon the Son of man.

Water made into wine

2 And the third day there was a marriage in [a]Cana of Galilee; and the mother of Jesus was there:

2 And both Jesus was called, and his disciples, to the marriage.

3 And when they wanted wine, the mother of Jesus saith unto him, They have no wine.

4 Jesus saith unto her, [a]Woman, [b]what have I to do with thee? [c]mine hour is not yet come.

5 His mother saith unto the servants, Whatsoever he saith unto you, do *it.*

6 And there were set there six waterpots of stone, [a]after the manner of the purifying of the Jews, containing two or three firkins apiece.

7 Jesus saith unto them, Fill the waterpots with water. And they filled them up to the brim.

8 And he saith unto them, Draw out now, and bear unto the governor of the feast. And they bare *it.*

9 When the ruler of the feast had tasted [a]the water *that was* made wine, and knew not whence it was: (but the servants which drew the water knew;) the governor of the feast called the bridegroom,

10 And saith unto him, Every man at the beginning doth set forth good wine; and when *men* have well drunk, then that which is worse: *but* thou hast kept the good wine until now.

11 This beginning of miracles did Jesus in Cana of Galilee, [a]and manifested forth his glory; and his disciples believed on him.

The cleansing of the temple

12 ¶ After this he went down to Capernaum, he, and his mother, and [a]his brethren, and his disciples: and they continued there not many days.

13 [a]And the Jews' passover was at hand, and Jesus went up to Jerusalem,

14 [a]And found in the temple those that sold oxen and sheep and doves, and the changers of money sitting:

15 And when he had made a scourge of small cords, he drove *them* all out of the temple, and the sheep and the oxen; and poured out the changers' money, and overthrew the tables;

16 And said unto them that sold doves, Take these *things* hence; make not [a]my Father's house a house of merchandise.

17 And his disciples remembered that it was written, [a]The zeal of thine house hath eaten me up.

18 ¶ Then answered the Jews and said unto him, [a]What sign shewest thou unto us, seeing that thou doest these *things?*

19 Jesus answered and said unto them, [a]Destroy this temple, and in three days I will raise it up.

1:51 [a]Gen. 28:12; Mat. 4:11; Luke 2:9,13; 22:43; Acts 1:10
2:1 [a]See Josh. 19:28
2:4 [a]ch. 19:26 [b]2 Sam. 16:10 [c]ch. 7:6
2:6 [a]Mark 7:3
2:9 [a]ch. 4:46
2:11 [a]ch. 1:14
2:12 [a]Mat. 12:46
2:13 [a]Ex. 12:14; Deut. 16:1; ch. 5:1
2:14 [a]Mat. 21:12; Mark 11:15; Luke 19:45
2:16 [a]Luke 2:49
2:17 [a]Ps. 69:9
2:18 [a]Mat. 12:38; ch. 6:30
2:19 [a]Mat. 26:61; 27:40; Mark 14:58; 15:29

signify important sayings. *heaven open.* In Jesus' ministry the disciples will see heaven's (God's) testimony to Jesus as plainly as if they heard an announcement from heaven concerning Him. *the angels of God ascending and descending.* As in Jacob's dream (see Gen 28:12 and note), thus marking Jesus as God's elect one through whom redemption comes to the world—perhaps identifying Jesus as *the* true Israelite (see v. 47). *Son of man.* Jesus' favorite self-designation (see notes on Mark 8:31; Luke 6:5; 19:10).

2:1 *a marriage.* Little is known of how a wedding was performed in the Holy Land in the first century, but clearly the feast was very important and might go on for a week. To fail in proper hospitality was a serious offense. *Cana.* Mentioned only in John's Gospel (2:11; 4:46; 21:2). It was west of the sea of Galilee, but the exact location is unknown.

2:3 *when they wanted wine.* More than a minor social embarrassment, since the family had an obligation to provide a feast of the socially required standard. There was no great variety in beverages, and people normally drank water or wine.

2:4 *mine hour is not yet come.* Several similar expressions scattered through this Gospel (7:6,8,30; 8:20) picture Jesus moving inevitably toward the destiny for which He had come: the time of His sacrificial death on the cross. At the crucifixion and resurrection Jesus' time had truly come (12:23,27; 13:1; 16:32; 17:1).

‡2:6 *manner of the purifying.* Jews became ceremonially defiled during the normal circumstances of daily life, and were cleansed by pouring water over the hands. For a lengthy feast with many guests a large amount of water was required for this purpose. *containing.* Refers to capacity, not actual content. *two or three firkins.* About 20 to 30 gallons.

‡2:10 *when men have well drunk.* This is not an indication of drunkenness, but simply of having consumed a lot of the particular beverage that was served.

‡2:11 *miracles.* John always uses the Greek word for "signs" to refer to Jesus' miracles, emphasizing the significance of the action rather than the marvel (see, e.g., 4:54; 6:14; 9:16; 11:47). They revealed Jesus' glory (see 1:14; cf. Is 35:1–2; Joel 3:18; Amos 9:13).

‡2:12 *went down.* Situated on the shore of the lake, Capernaum was at a lower level than Cana, which was in the hill country to the west. *brethren.* See note on Luke 8:19.

2:13 *passover.* See Ex 12 and notes on Ex 12:11–23; see also notes on Mat 26:17,18–30; Mark 14:1,12; Luke 22:1; and chart, pp. 166–167. Passover was one of the annual feasts that all Jewish men were required to celebrate in Jerusalem (Deut 16:16). See note on 5:1.

‡2:14–17 Matthew, Mark and Luke record a cleansing of the temple toward the end of Jesus' ministry (see note on Mat 21:12–17). Jesus also began his ministry with such a cleansing.

2:14 *oxen and sheep and doves.* Required for sacrifices. Jews who came great distances had to be able to buy sacrificial animals near the temple. The merchants, however, were selling them in the outer court of the temple itself, the one place where Gentiles could come to pray. *changers of money.* Many coins had to be changed into currency acceptable to the temple authorities, which made money changers necessary (see note on Mark 11:15). They should not, however, have been working in the temple itself.

2:19 The Jews thought Jesus was referring to the literal temple, but John tells us that He was not (v. 21). Just a few years later Jesus was accused of saying that He would destroy the temple and raise it again (Mat 26:60–61; Mark 14:57–59), and mockers repeated the charge as He hung on the cross (Mat 27:40; Mark 15:29). The same misunderstanding may have been behind the charge against Stephen (Acts 6:14).

Miracles of Jesus

HEALING MIRACLES	**MATTHEW**	**MARK**	**LUKE**	**JOHN**
Man with leprosy	8:2-4	1:40-42	5:12-13	
Roman centurion's servant	8:5-13		7:1-10	
Peter's mother-in-law	8:14-15	1:30-31	4:38-35	
Two men from Gadara	8:28-34	5:1-15	8:27-35	
Paralyzed man	9:2-7	2:3-12	5:18-25	
Woman with bleeding	9:20-22	5:25-29	8:43-48	
Two blind men	9:27-31			
Mute, demon-possessed man	9:32-33			
Man with a withered hand	12:10-13	3:1-5	6:6-10	
Blind, mute, demon-possessed man	12:22		11:14	
Canaanite woman's daughter	15:21-28	7:24-30		
Boy with a demon	17:14-18	9:17-29	9:38-43	
Two blind men (including Bartimeus)	20:29-34	10:46-52	18:35-43	
Deaf mute		7:31-37		
Possessed man in synagogue		1:23-26	4:33-35	
Blind man at Bethsaida		8:22-26		
Crippled woman			13:11-13	
Man with dropsy			14:1-4	
Ten men with leprosy			17:11-19	
The high priest's servant			22:50-51	
Nobleman's son at Capernaum				4:46-54
Sick man at pool of Bethesda				5:1-9
Man born blind				9:1-7
MIRACLES SHOWING POWER OVER NATURE				
Calming the storm	8:23-27	4:37-41	8:22-25	
Walking on water	14:25	6:48-51		6:19-21
Feeding of the 5,000	14:15-21	6:35-44	9:12-17	6:6-13
Feeding of the 4,000	15:32-38	8:1-9		
Coin in fish	17:24-27			
Fig tree withered	21:18-22	11:12-14,20-25		
Large catch of fish			5:4-11	
Water turned into wine				2:1-11
Another large catch of fish				21:1-11
MIRACLES OF RAISING THE DEAD				
Jairus's daughter	9:18-19,23-25	5:22-24,38-42	8:41-42,49-56	
Widow's son at Nain			7:11-15	
Lazarus				11:1-44

20 Then said the Jews, Forty and six years
was this temple in building, and wilt thou rear
it up in three days?
21 But he spake [a]of the temple of his body.
22 When therefore he was risen from the
dead, [a]his disciples remembered that he had
said this unto them; and they believed the
scripture, and the word which Jesus had said.
23 Now when he was in Jerusalem at the
passover, in the feast *day,* many believed in his
name, when they saw the miracles which he
did.
24 But Jesus did not commit himself unto
them, because he knew all *men,*
25 And needed not that any should testify
of man: for [a]he knew what was in man.

Nicodemus visits Jesus

3 There was a man of the Pharisees,
named Nicodemus, a ruler of the Jews:
2 [a]The same came to Jesus by night, and
said unto him, Rabbi, we know that thou art a
teacher come from God: for [b]no *man* can do
these miracles that thou doest, except [c]God be
with him.
3 Jesus answered and said unto him, Verily,
verily, I say unto thee, [a]Except a man be born
[1]again, he cannot see the kingdom of God.
4 Nicodemus saith unto him, How can a
man be born when he is old? can he enter the
second time into his mother's womb, and be
born?
5 Jesus answered, Verily, verily, I say unto
thee, [a]Except a man be born of water and *of*
the Spirit, he cannot enter into the kingdom of
God.
6 That which is born of the flesh is flesh;
and that which is born of the Spirit is spirit.
7 Marvel not that I said unto thee, Ye must
be born [1]again.
8 [a]The wind bloweth where it listeth, and
thou hearest the sound thereof, but canst not
tell whence it cometh, and whither it goeth:
so is every one that is born of the Spirit.
9 Nicodemus answered and said unto him,
[a]How can these *things* be?
10 Jesus answered and said unto him, Art
thou a master of Israel, and knowest not these
things?
11 [a]Verily, verily, I say unto thee, We speak
that we do know, and testify that we have
seen; and [b]ye receive not our witness.
12 If I have told you earthly *things,* and ye
believe not, how shall ye believe, if I tell you
of heavenly *things?*
13 And [a]no *man* hath ascended up to heav-
en, but he that came down from heaven, *even*
the Son of man which is in heaven.
14 [a]And as Moses lifted up the serpent in
the wilderness, *even* so [b]must the Son of man
be lifted up:
15 That whosoever believeth in him
should not perish, but [a]have eternal life.
16 [a]For God so loved the world, that he
gave his only begotten Son, that whosoever
believeth in him should not perish, but have
everlasting life.
17 [a]For God sent not his Son into the
world to condemn the world; but that the
world through him might be saved.
18 [a]He that believeth on him is not condemned: but he that believeth not is condemned already, because he hath not believed
in the name of the only begotten Son of God.
19 And this is the condemnation, [a]that
light is come into the world, and men loved
darkness rather than light, because their deeds
were evil.
20 For [a]every one that doeth evil hateth
the light, neither cometh to the light, lest his
deeds should be [1]reproved.
21 But he that doeth truth cometh to the

2:21 [a]Col. 2:9; Heb. 8:2; 1 Cor. 3:16; 6:19; 2 Cor. 6:16
2:22 [a]Luke 24:8
2:25 [a]1 Sam. 16:7; 1 Chr. 28:9; Mat. 9:4; Mark 2:8; ch. 6:64; 16:30; Acts 1:24; Rev. 2:23
3:2 [a]ch. 7:50; 19:39 [b]ch. 9:16,33; Acts 2:22 [c]Acts 10:38
3:3 [1]Or, *from above* [a]ch. 1:13; Gal. 6:15; Tit. 3:5; Jas. 1:18; 1 Pet. 1:23; 1 John 3:9
3:5 [a]Mark 16:16; Acts 2:38
3:7 [1]Or, *from above*
3:8 [a]Eccl. 11:5; 1 Cor. 2:11
3:9 [a]ch. 6:52,60
3:11 [a]Mat. 11:27; ch. 1:18; 7:16; 8:28 [b]ver. 32
3:13 [a]Prov. 30:4; ch. 6:33,38; Acts 2:34; 1 Cor. 15:47; Eph. 4:9
3:14 [a]Num. 21:9 [b]ch. 8:28; 12:32
3:15 [a]ver. 36; ch. 6:47
3:16 [a]Rom. 5:8; 1 John 4:9
3:17 [a]Luke 9:56; ch. 5:45; 8:15; 12:47; 1 John 4:14
3:18 [a]ch. 5:24; 6:40,47; 20:31
3:19 [a]ch. 1:4, 9-11; 8:12
3:20 [1]Or, *discovered* [a]Job 24:13; Eph. 5:13

2:20 *Forty and six years.* The temple was not finally completed until A.D. 64. The meaning is that work had been going on for 46 years. Since it had begun in 20 B.C., the year of the event recorded here is A.D. 26/27.
2:22 *remembered.* See 14:26.
2:23 *the passover.* See note on v. 13. *name.* In ancient times an individual's "name" summed up his whole person.
3:1 *a man of the Pharisees.* See notes on Mat 3:7; Mark 2:16; Luke 5:17.
‡3:2 *by night.* Perhaps Nicodemus was afraid to come by day. Or he may have wanted a long talk, which would have been difficult in the daytime with the crowds around Jesus. Each time Nicodemus is introduced by John, he mentions his night visit.
‡3:3 *born again.* The Greek here and in v. 7 may mean "born from above." Both meanings are consistent with Jesus' redeeming work. It is the new birth, a true salvation experience, equal with being saved.
‡3:5 *born of water.* A phrase understood in various ways: 1. It means much the same as "born of the Spirit" (v. 8; cf. Tit 3:5). 2. Water here refers to purification. 3. Water refers to baptism—that of John (1:31) or that of Jesus and His disciples (v. 22; 4:1–2). 4. Water refers to the natural birth. Even as one is born of water, he must experience a second, a spiritual new birth. *kingdom of God.* See note on Mat 3:2.
3:7 *Ye.* This assertion applies to everyone, not just Nicodemus (the Greek for "ye" is plural here). *must.* There are no exceptions. *born again.* See note on v. 3.
3:8 The Holy Spirit is sovereign. He works as He pleases in His renewal of the human heart.
3:11 *We.* The plural associates others, perhaps the disciples, with Jesus. The words are true of Christians as well as of Christ. *witness.* See note on 1:7.
‡3:13 *the Son of man.* Jesus' favorite self-designation (see notes on Mark 8:31; Luke 6:5; 19:10). *which is in heaven.* This could be a reference to Jesus' omnipresence while here on earth, similar to Mat 18:20.
3:14 *must the Son of man be lifted up.* See notes on 12:31–32.
3:15 *believeth.* See note on 1:7. *eternal life.* An infinitely high quality of life in living fellowship with God—both now and forever.
3:16 *God so loved the world.* The great truth that motivated God's plan of salvation (cf. 1 John 4:9–10). *world.* All people on earth—or perhaps all creation (see note on 1:9). *that he gave.* See Is 9:6. *only begotten Son.* See 1:14,18; cf. Gen 22:2,16; Rom 8:32. Although believers are also called "sons of God" (2 Cor 6:18; Rev 21:7), Jesus is God's Son in a unique sense.
3:18 *believeth ... believeth not.* John is not speaking of momentary beliefs and doubts but of continuing, settled attitudes.

light, that his deeds may be made manifest, that they are wrought in God.

John's testimony to Jesus

22 ¶ After these *things* came Jesus and his disciples into the land of Judea; and there he tarried with them, [a]and baptized.

23 And John also was baptizing in Aenon near to [a]Salim, because there was much water there: [b]and they came, and were baptized.

24 For [a]John was not yet cast into prison.

25 Then there arose a question between *some* of John's disciples and the Jews about purifying.

26 And they came unto John, and said unto him, Rabbi, *he* that was with thee beyond Jordan, [a]to whom thou barest witness, behold, the same baptizeth, and all *men* come to him.

27 John answered and said, [a]A man can [1]receive nothing, except it be given him from heaven.

28 Ye yourselves bear me witness, that I said, [a]I am not the Christ, but [b]that I am sent before him.

29 [a]He that hath the bride is the bridegroom: but [b]the friend of the bridegroom, which standeth and heareth him, rejoiceth greatly because of the bridegroom's voice: this my joy therefore is fulfilled.

30 He must increase, but I *must* decrease.

31 [a]He that cometh from above [b]is above all: [c]he that is of the earth is earthly, and speaketh of the earth: [d]he that cometh from heaven is above all.

32 And [a]what he hath seen and heard, that he testifieth; and no *man* receiveth his testimony.

33 He that hath received his testimony [a]hath set to *his* seal that God is true.

34 [a]For he whom God hath sent speaketh the words of God: for God giveth not the Spirit [b]by measure *unto him.*

35 [a]The Father loveth the Son, and hath given all *things* into his hand.

36 [a]He that believeth on the Son hath everlasting life: and he that believeth not the Son shall not see life; but the wrath of God abideth on him.

The woman of Samaria

4 When therefore the Lord knew how the Pharisees had heard that Jesus made and [a]baptized moe disciples than John,

2 (Though Jesus himself baptized not, but his disciples,)

3 He left Judea, and departed again into Galilee.

4 And he must needs go through Samaria.

5 Then cometh he to a city of Samaria, which is called Sychar, near to the parcel of ground [a]that Jacob gave to his son Joseph.

6 Now Jacob's well was there. Jesus therefore, being wearied with *his* journey, sat thus on the well: *and* it was about the sixth hour.

7 There cometh a woman of Samaria to draw water: Jesus saith unto her, Give me to drink.

3:22 [a]ch. 4:2
3:23 [a]1 Sam. 9:4 [b]Mat. 3:5,6
3:24 [a]Mat. 14:3
3:26 [a]ch. 1:7,15,27,34
3:27 [1]Or, *take unto himself* [a]1 Cor. 4:7; Heb. 5:4; Jas. 1:17
3:28 [a]ch. 1:20,27 [b]Mal. 3:1; Mark 1:2; Luke 1:17
3:29 [a]Mat. 22:2; 2 Cor. 11:2; Eph. 5:25,27; Rev. 21:9 [b]Sol. 5:1
3:31 [a]ver. 13; ch. 8:23 [b]Mat. 28:18; ch. 1:15,27; Rom. 9:5 [c]1 Cor. 15:47 [d]ch. 6:33; 1 Cor. 15:47; Eph. 1:21; Phil. 2:9
3:32 [a]ver. 11; ch. 8:26; 15:15
3:33 [a]Rom. 3:4; 1 John 5:10
3:34 [a]ch. 7:16 [b]ch. 1:16
3:35 [a]Mat. 11:27; 28:18; Luke 10:22; ch. 5:20,22; 13:3; 17:2; Heb. 2:8
3:36 [a]ver. 15,16; ch. 1:12; 6:47; Rom. 1:17; 1 John 5:10
4:1 [a]ch. 3:22,26
4:5 [a]Gen. 33:19; 48:22; Josh. 24:32

3:22 *baptized.* According to 4:2 only the disciples actually baptized.
3:23 *Aenon.* Possibly about eight miles south of Scythopolis (Beth-shean), west of the Jordan.
3:25 *question . . . about purifying.* The Dead Sea (Qumran) Scrolls (see essay, p. 1344) show that some Jews were deeply interested in the right way to achieve ceremonial purification.
3:26 *barest witness.* See note on 1:7. John's disciples knew that he had testified about Jesus, but they loved their master and were envious of Jesus' success.
3:27 The words are true of both Jesus and John (and of everyone). Both had what God had given them, so there was no place for envy. *given.* The Greek for "to give" is used frequently in this Gospel (75 times), especially of the things the Father gives the Son.
3:29 *the bridegroom.* The most important man at a wedding, referring here to Jesus. The friend (best man) is there only to help the bridegroom, which describes the role of John the Baptist. *rejoiceth greatly.* Not because he was on center stage, but because the bridegroom was there. John's joy was to hear of Jesus' success.
3:30 John the Baptist had been sent to prepare the way for the Messiah and here reaffirms his subordinate position.
3:31 *he that is of the earth.* A general expression that could apply to anyone, but here it particularly refers to John the Baptist. *he that cometh from heaven.* Jesus, whose heavenly origin (cf. 1 Cor 15:47) meant much to John.
3:32 *what he hath seen and heard.* Jesus taught from divine experience. *no man.* Does not mean that no person accepted what He said (see v. 33) but that people in general refused His teaching.
3:33 *set to his seal.* Or "certified." When anyone accepts Christ's testimony, he accepts the truth that Jesus came from heaven and that God was acting in Him for the world's salvation. He thereby certifies that God is truthful.
‡3:34 *he whom God hath sent.* Jesus. *giveth not the Spirit by measure.* It is to Jesus that the Spirit is given without limit.
3:36 *hath.* Eternal life is a present possession, not something the believer will only obtain later (see note on v. 15). *wrath of God.* A strong expression, meaning that God is actively opposed to everything evil. The word "wrath" occurs only here in John's Gospel (see note on Rom 1:18). *abideth.* A sinner cannot expect God's wrath eventually to fade away. God's opposition to evil is both total and permanent.
4:1 *Pharisees.* The religious leaders took a close interest in John the Baptist (see note on 1:24) and then also in Jesus.
4:2 The disciples did not baptize without Jesus' approval (3:22).
4:3 *left Judea.* Success (which aroused opposition; see 7:1), not failure, led Jesus to leave Judea.
4:4 *must needs go through.* The necessity lay in Jesus' mission, not in geography. *Samaria.* Here the whole region, not simply the city. Jews often avoided Samaria by crossing the Jordan and traveling on the east side (see notes on Mat 10:5; Luke 9:52).
4:5 *Sychar.* A small village near Shechem. Jacob bought some land in the vicinity of Shechem (Gen 33:18–19), and it was apparently this land that he gave to Joseph (Gen 48:21–22). See map, p. 1509.
4:6 *Jacob's well.* Mentioned nowhere else in Scripture. *about the sixth hour.* About 12:00 noon.
4:7 *to draw water.* People normally drew water at the end of the day rather than in the heat of midday (see Gen 24:11 and note). But the practice is attested by Josephus, who says that

8 (For his disciples were gone away unto the city to buy meat.)

9 Then saith the woman of Samaria unto him, How *is it that* thou, being a Jew, askest drink of me, which am a woman of Samaria? For [a]the Jews have no dealings with the Samaritans.

10 Jesus answered and said unto her, If thou knewest the gift of God, and who it is that saith to thee, Give me to drink; thou wouldest have asked of him, and he would have given thee [a]living water.

11 The woman saith unto him, Sir, thou hast nothing to draw with, and the well is deep: from whence then hast thou *that* living water?

12 Art thou greater than our father Jacob, which gave us the well, and drank thereof himself, and his children, and his cattle?

13 Jesus answered and said unto her, Whosoever drinketh of this water shall thirst again:

14 But [a]whosoever drinketh of the water that I shall give him shall never thirst; but the water that I shall give him [b]shall be in him a well of water springing up into everlasting life.

15 [a]The woman saith unto him, Sir, give me this water, that I thirst not, neither come hither to draw.

16 Jesus saith unto her, Go, call thy husband, and come hither.

17 The woman answered and said, I have no husband. Jesus said unto her, Thou hast well said, I have no husband:

18 For thou hast had five husbands; and he whom thou now hast is not thy husband: *in* that saidst thou truly.

19 The woman saith unto him, Sir, [a]I perceive that thou art a prophet.

20 Our fathers worshipped in [a]this mountain; and ye say, that in [b]Jerusalem is the place where *men* ought to worship.

21 Jesus saith unto her, Woman, believe me, the hour cometh, [a]when ye shall neither in this mountain, nor *yet* at Jerusalem, worship the Father.

22 Ye worship [a]ye know not what: we know what we worship: for [b]salvation is of the Jews.

23 But the hour cometh, and now is, when the true worshippers shall worship the Father in [a]spirit [b]and *in* truth: for the Father seeketh such to worship him.

24 [a]God *is* a Spirit: and they that worship him must worship *him* in spirit and *in* truth.

25 The woman saith unto him, I know that Messias cometh, which is called Christ: when he is come, [a]he will tell us all *things.*

26 Jesus saith unto her, [a]I that speak unto thee am *he.*

27 ¶ And upon this came his disciples, and marvelled that he talked with *the* woman: yet no *man* said, What seekest thou? or, Why talkest thou with her?

4:9 [a]2 Ki. 17:24; Luke 9:52,53; Acts 10:28
4:10 [a]Is. 12:3; 44:3; Jer. 2:13; Zech. 13:1; 14:8
4:14 [a]ch. 6:35,58 [b]ch. 7:38
4:15 [a]ch. 6:34; 17:2,3; Rom. 6:23; 1 John 5:20
4:19 [a]Luke 7:16; 24:19; ch. 6:14
4:20 [a]Judg. 9:7 [b]Deut. 12:5,11; 1 Ki. 9:3; 2 Chr. 7:12
4:21 [a]Mal. 1:11; 1 Tim. 2:8
4:22 [a]2 Ki. 17:29 [b]Is. 2:3; Luke 24:47; Rom. 9:4,5
4:23 [a]Phil. 3:3 [b]ch. 1:17
4:24 [a]2 Cor. 3:17
4:25 [a]ver. 29,39
4:26 [a]Mat. 26:63,64; Mark 14:61,62

---

the young ladies whom Moses helped (Ex 2:15–17) came to draw water at noon.

4:9 *have no dealings with.* The Greek implies the meaning, "do not use dishes Samaritans have used." A Jew would become ceremonially unclean if he used a drinking vessel handled by a Samaritan, since the Jews held that all Samaritans were "unclean."

4:10 *gift.* The Greek for this word is used only here in this Gospel and emphasizes God's grace through Christ. Jesus gave life and gave it freely. *living water.* In 7:38–39 the term is explained as meaning the Holy Spirit, but here it refers to eternal life (see v. 14).

‡4:11 *deep.* Christian pilgrim sources as early as the fourth century mention a well in this area that was about 100 feet deep. When the well was cleaned out in 1935, it was found to be 138 feet deep.

4:12 *our father Jacob.* Respect for the past prevented her from seeing the great opportunity of the present.

4:14 *springing up.* The expression is a vigorous one, with a meaning like "leaping up." Jesus was speaking of vigorous, abundant life (cf. 10:10).

4:15 Cf. the misunderstanding of Nicodemus (3:4). In both cases the way was opened for further instruction.

‡4:18 *five husbands.* The Jews held that a woman might be divorced twice or at the most three times. If the Samaritans had the same standard, the woman's life had certainly been a difficult one. Apparently she had not married her present partner.

4:19 *a prophet.* Because of His special insight.

4:20 *this mountain.* Perhaps the woman did not like the way the conversation was going and so began to argue. The proper place of worship had long been a source of debate between Jews and Samaritans. Samaritans held that "this mountain" (mount Gerizim) was especially sacred. Abraham and Jacob had built altars in the general vicinity (Gen 12:7; 33:20), and the people had been blessed from this mountain (Deut 11:29; 27:12). In the Samaritan Scriptures, mount Gerizim (rather than mount Ebal) was the mountain on which Moses had commanded an altar to be built (Deut 27:4–6). The Samaritans had built a temple on mount Gerizim c. 400 B.C., which the Jews destroyed c. 128. Both actions, of course, increased hostility between the two groups. See map, p. 1509.

4:22 *worship ye know not what.* The Samaritan Bible contained only the Pentateuch. They worshiped the true God, but their failure to accept much of His revelation meant that they knew little of Him. *salvation is of the Jews.* The Messiah would be a Jew.

4:24 *God is a Spirit . . . worship him in spirit and in truth.* The place of worship is irrelevant, because true worship must be in keeping with God's nature, which is spirit. In John's Gospel truth is associated with Christ (14:6; see note on 1:14), a fact that has great importance for the proper understanding of Christian worship.

4:25 *Messias . . . will tell us all things.* The woman's last attempt to evade the issue. The matter was too important, she reasoned, for people like Jesus and herself to work out. Understanding would have to await the coming of the Messiah (see note on 1:25). The Samaritans expected a Messiah, but their rejection of all the inspired writings after the Pentateuch meant that they knew little about Him. They thought of Him mainly as a teacher.

‡4:26 *I . . . am he.* The only occasion before His trial on which Jesus specifically said that He was the Messiah (but see Mark 9:41). The term did not have the political overtones in Samaria that it had in Judea, which may be part of the reason Jesus used the designation here, but He also spoke to the woman privately.

4:27 *marvelled.* Jewish religious teachers rarely spoke with women in public.

Jesus in Judea and Samaria

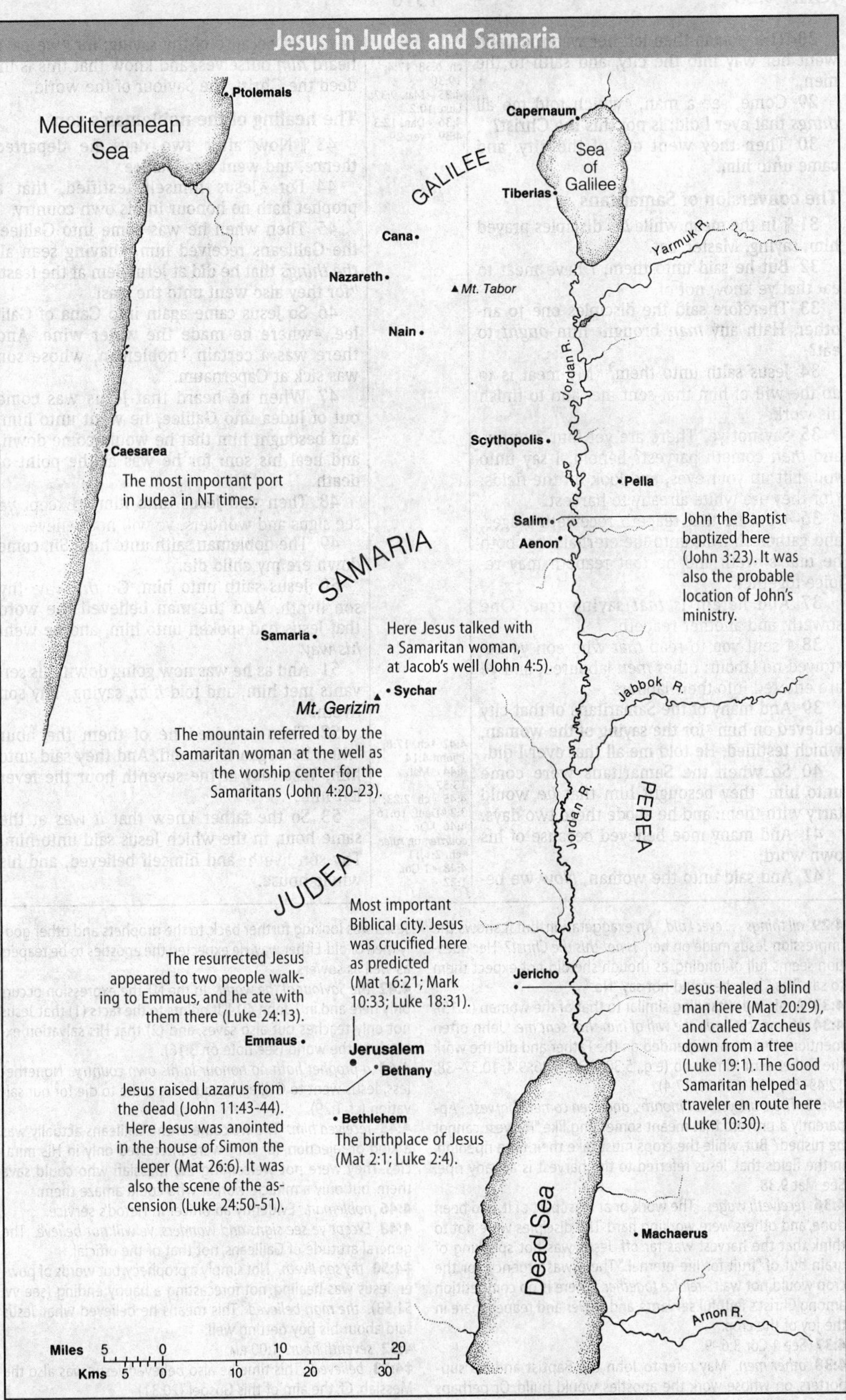

Ptolemais
Mediterranean Sea
Capernaum
Sea of Galilee
GALILEE
Tiberias
Yarmuk R.
Cana
Nazareth
Mt. Tabor
Nain
Jordan R.
Scythopolis
Caesarea
The most important port in Judea in NT times.
Pella
Salim
Aenon
John the Baptist baptized here (John 3:23). It was also the probable location of John's ministry.
SAMARIA
Samaria
Here Jesus talked with a Samaritan woman, at Jacob's well (John 4:5).
Sychar
Mt. Gerizim
Jabbok R.
The mountain referred to by the Samaritan woman at the well as the worship center for the Samaritans (John 4:20-23).
PEREA
JUDEA
Most important Biblical city. Jesus was crucified here as predicted (Mat 16:21; Mark 10:33; Luke 18:31).
The resurrected Jesus appeared to two people walking to Emmaus, and he ate with them there (Luke 24:13).
Jericho
Jesus healed a blind man here (Mat 20:29), and called Zaccheus down from a tree (Luke 19:1). The Good Samaritan helped a traveler en route here (Luke 10:30).
Emmaus
Jerusalem
Bethany
Jesus raised Lazarus from the dead (John 11:43-44). Here Jesus was anointed in the house of Simon the leper (Mat 26:6). It was also the scene of the ascension (Luke 24:50-51).
Bethlehem
The birthplace of Jesus (Mat 2:1; Luke 2:4).
Dead Sea
Machaerus
Arnon R.
Miles 5 0 10 20
Kms 5 0 10 20 30

28 The woman then left her waterpot, and
went her way into the city, and saith to the
men,
29 Come, see a man, [a]which told me all
things that ever I did: is not this the Christ?
30 Then they went out of the city, and
came unto him.

The conversion of Samaritans

31 ¶ In the mean while *his* disciples prayed
him, saying, Master, eat.
32 But he said unto them, I have meat to
eat that ye know not of.
33 Therefore said the disciples one to another, Hath any *man* brought him *ought* to
eat?
34 Jesus saith unto them, [a]My meat is to
do the will of him that sent me, and to finish
his work.
35 Say not ye, There are yet four months,
and *then* cometh harvest? behold, I say unto
you, Lift up your eyes, and look on the fields;
[a]for they are white already to harvest.
36 [a]And he that reapeth receiveth wages,
and gathereth fruit unto life eternal: that both
he that soweth and he that reapeth may rejoice together.
37 And herein is *that* saying true, One
soweth, and another reapeth.
38 I sent you to reap *that* whereon ye bestowed no labour: other *men* laboured, and ye
are entered into their labours.
39 And many of the Samaritans of that city
believed on him [a]for the saying of the woman,
which testified, He told me all that ever I did.
40 So when the Samaritans were come
unto him, they besought him that *he* would
tarry with them: and he abode there two days.
41 And many moe believed because of his
own word;
42 And said unto the woman, *Now* we believe, not because of thy saying: for [a]we have
heard *him* ourselves, and know that this is indeed the Christ, the Saviour of the world.

The healing of the nobleman's son

43 ¶ Now after two days he departed
thence, and went into Galilee.
44 For [a]Jesus himself testified, that a
prophet hath no honour in his own country.
45 Then when he was come into Galilee,
the Galileans received him, [a]having seen all
the things that he did at Jerusalem at the feast:
[b]for they also went unto the feast.
46 So Jesus came again into Cana of Galilee, [a]where he made the water wine. And
there was a certain [1]nobleman, whose son
was sick at Capernaum.
47 When he heard that Jesus was come
out of Judea into Galilee, he went unto him,
and besought him that he would come down,
and heal his son: for he was at the point of
death.
48 Then said Jesus unto him, [a]Except ye
see signs and wonders, ye will not believe.
49 The nobleman saith unto him, Sir, come
down ere my child die.
50 Jesus saith unto him, Go *thy way;* thy
son liveth. And the man believed the word
that Jesus had spoken unto him, and he went
his way.
51 And as he was now going down, his servants met him, and told *him,* saying, Thy son
liveth.
52 Then inquired he of them the hour
when he began to amend. And they said unto
him, Yesterday at the seventh hour the fever
left him.
53 So the father knew that *it was* at the
same hour, in the which Jesus said unto him,
Thy son liveth: and himself believed, and his
whole house.

4:29 [a]ver. 25
4:34 [a]Job 23:12; ch. 6:38; 17:4; 19:30
4:35 [a]Mat. 9:37; Luke 10:2
4:36 [a]Dan. 12:3
4:39 [a]ver. 29
4:42 [a]ch. 17:8; 1 John 4:14
4:44 [a]Mat. 13:57
4:45 [a]ch. 2:23; 3:2 [b]Deut. 16:16
4:46 [1]Or, *courtier,* or, *ruler* [a]ch. 2:1,11
4:48 [a]1 Cor. 1:22

4:29 *all things . . . ever I did.* An exaggeration, but it shows the impression Jesus made on her. *is not this the Christ?* Her question seems full of longing, as though she did not expect them to say "Yes," but she could not say "No."
4:33 A misunderstanding similar to that of the woman (v. 15).
4:34 *My meat is to do the will of him that sent me.* John often mentions that Jesus depended on the Father and did the work the Father sent Him to do (e.g., 5:30; 6:38; 8:26; 9:4; 10:37–38; 12:49–50; 14:31; 15:10; 17:4).
‡4:35 *There are yet four months, and then cometh harvest.* Apparently a proverb that meant something like "Harvest cannot be rushed." But, while the crops must take their time ripening, in the fields that Jesus referred to the harvest is already ripe. See Mat 9:38.
4:36 *receiveth wages.* The work, or at least part of it, had been done, and others were working hard. The disciples were not to think that the harvest was far off. Jesus was not speaking of grain but of "fruit for life eternal." There was urgency, for the crop would not wait. *rejoice together.* There is no competition among Christ's faithful servants, and sower and reaper share in the joy of the crop.
4:37 See 1 Cor 3:6–9.
4:38 *other men.* May refer to John the Baptist and his supporters, on whose work the apostles would build. Or perhaps Jesus was looking further back, to the prophets and other godly men of old. Either way, He expected the apostles to be reapers as well as sowers.
4:42 *the Saviour of the world.* In the NT the expression occurs only here and in 1 John 4:14. It points to the facts (1) that Jesus not only teaches but also saves, and (2) that His salvation extends to the world (see note on 3:16).
4:44 *a prophet hath no honour in his own country.* Nonetheless, Jesus went to Galilee, because He came to die for our salvation (cf. 1:29).
4:45 *received him.* The welcome of the Galileans actually was a kind of rejection, for they were interested only in His miracles. They were not welcoming the Messiah who could save them, but only a miracle worker who could amaze them.
4:46 *nobleman.* Evidently an officer in Herod's service.
4:48 *Except ye see signs and wonders, ye will not believe.* The general attitude of Galileans, not that of the official.
‡4:50 *thy son liveth.* Not simply a prophecy, but words of power. Jesus was healing, not forecasting a happy ending (see vv. 51,53). *the man believed.* This means he believed what Jesus said about his boy getting well.
4:52 *seventh hour.* 1:00 P.M.
‡4:53 *believed.* This time he also believed Jesus was also the Messiah. Cf. the aim of this Gospel (20:31).

54 This *is* again the second miracle *that* Jesus did, when he was come out of Judea into Galilee.

Jesus heals on the sabbath

5 After [a]this there was a feast of the Jews; and Jesus went up to Jerusalem.

2 Now there is at Jerusalem [a]by the sheep [1]*market* a pool, which is called in the Hebrew tongue Bethesda, having five porches.

3 In these lay a great multitude of impotent *folk,* of blind, halt, withered, waiting for the moving of the water.

4 For an angel went down at a *certain* season into the pool, and troubled the water: whosoever then first after the troubling of the water stepped in, was made whole of whatsoever disease he had.

5 And a certain man was there, which had an infirmity thirty *and* eight years.

6 When Jesus saw him lie, and knew that he had been now a long time *in that case,* he saith unto him, Wilt thou be made whole?

7 The impotent *man* answered him, Sir, I have no man, when the water is troubled, to put me into the pool: but while I am coming, another steppeth down before me.

8 Jesus saith unto him, [a]Rise, take up thy bed, and walk.

9 And immediately the man was made whole, and took up his bed, and walked: and [a]on the same day was the sabbath.

10 The Jews therefore said unto him that was cured, It is the sabbath day: [a]it is not lawful for thee to carry *thy* bed.

11 He answered them, He that made me whole, the same said unto me, Take up thy bed, and walk.

12 Then asked they him, What man is that which said unto thee, Take up thy bed, and walk?

13 And he that was healed wist not who it was: for Jesus had conveyed himself away, [1]a multitude being in *that* place.

14 Afterward Jesus findeth him in the temple, and said unto him, Behold, thou art made whole: [a]sin no more, lest a worse *thing* come unto thee.

15 The man departed, and told the Jews that it was Jesus, which had made him whole.

The Son's witness to the Father

16 ¶ And therefore did the Jews persecute Jesus, and sought to slay him, because he had done these *things* on the sabbath day.

17 But Jesus answered them, [a]My Father worketh hitherto, and I work.

18 Therefore the Jews [a]sought the more to kill him, because he not only had broken the sabbath, but said also that God was his Father, [b]making himself equal with God.

5:1 [a]Lev. 23:2; Deut. 16:1; ch. 2:13
5:2 [1]Or, gate [a]Neh. 3:1; 12:39
5:8 [a]Mat. 9:6; Mark 2:11; Luke 5:24
5:9 [a]ch. 9:14
5:10 [a]Ex. 20:10; Neh. 13:19; Jer. 17:21; Mat. 12:2; Mark 2:24; Luke 6:2
5:13 [1]Or, from *the multitude* that *was*
5:14 [a]Mat. 12:45; ch. 8:11
5:17 [a]ch. 9:4; 14:10
5:18 [a]ch. 7:19 [b]ch. 10:30; Phil. 2:6

4:54 *the second miracle.* There had, of course, already been many such miracles (2:23; 3:2), but this was the second time Jesus performed a miracle after coming from Judea to Galilee.
5:1 *After this.* An indefinite expression (cf. 6:1; 7:1). *a feast of the Jews.* Probably one of the three pilgrimage feasts to which all Jewish males were expected to go—passover, Pentecost or tabernacles. The identity of this feast is significant for the attempt to ascertain the number of passovers included in Jesus' ministry, and thus the number of years His ministry lasted. John explicitly mentions at least three different passovers: the first in 2:13,23 (see note on 2:13), the second in 6:4 and the third several times (e.g., in 11:55; 12:1). If three passovers are accepted, the length of Jesus' ministry was between two and three years. However, if the feast of 5:1 was a fourth passover or assumes that a fourth passover had come and gone, Jesus' ministry would have lasted between three and four years.
5:2 *there is.* Not "was." This may mean that the pool was still in existence at the time this was being written, i.e., that John wrote before the destruction of Jerusalem. However, this falls short of proving the time of writing (see Introduction: Date). *Bethesda.* The manuscripts have a variety of names (e.g., Bethzatha and Bethsaida), but one of the Dead Sea Scrolls seems to show that Bethesda is the right name. The site is generally identified with the twin pools near the present-day Saint Anne's Church. There would have been a colonnade on each of the four sides and another between the two pools.
‡5:3–4 Some manuscripts do not have vv. 3b–4. But these verses apparently explain why people waited by the pool in large numbers.
5:5 *had an infirmity.* John does not say what the trouble was, but it was a form of paralysis or at least lameness.
5:6 *Wilt thou be made whole?* The question was important. The man had not asked Jesus for help, and a beggar of that day could lose a sometimes profitable (and easy) income if he were cured. Or perhaps he had simply lost the will to be cured.
5:7 *when the water is troubled.* The man did not see Jesus as a potential healer, and his mind was set on the supposed curative powers of the water.
5:9 *the man was made whole.* Ordinarily, faith in Jesus was essential to the cure (e.g., Mark 5:34), but here the man did not even know who Jesus was (v. 13). So while Jesus usually healed in response to faith, He was not limited by a person's lack of it.
5:10 *it is not lawful for thee to carry thy bed.* It was not the law of Moses but their traditional interpretation of it that prohibited carrying loads of any kind on the sabbath. The Jews had very strict regulations on keeping the sabbath, but also had many curious loopholes that their lawyers made full use of (cf. Mat 23:4).
5:12 *What man.* The Jews were contrasting the authority of the law of God, which in their view prohibited the action, and that of a mere man (as they considered Jesus to be) who permitted it.
‡5:14 *worse thing.* The eternal consequences of sin are more serious than any physical ailment, or he could receive an even worse physical ailment as well.
5:16 *persecute.* John does not tell us what form the persecution took. *he had done.* The continuous action of the Greek verb points to more than one incident, and the Jews apparently discerned a pattern.
5:17 *My Father worketh hitherto.* Jesus' justification for His action was His close relation to His Father. The Jews did not refer to God as "My Father," regarding the term as too intimate—though they might have used "Our Father" or, in prayer, "My Father in heaven." Jesus also exemplified the way the sabbath should be observed. God does not stop His deeds of compassion on that day and neither did Jesus.
‡5:18 *his Father.* Referring to a special relationship, that with His own Father in a unique sense. The Jews did not object to the idea that God is the Father of all, but they strongly object-

19 Then answered Jesus and said unto them, Verily, verily, I say unto you, [a]The Son can do nothing of himself, but what he seeth the Father do: for what *things* soever he doeth, these also doeth the Son likewise.

20 For [a]the Father loveth the Son, and sheweth him all *things* that himself doeth: and he will shew him greater works than these, that ye may marvel.

21 For as the Father raiseth up the dead, and quickeneth *them;* [a]even so the Son quickeneth whom he will.

22 For the Father judgeth no *man,* but [a]hath committed all judgment unto the Son:

23 That all *men* should honour the Son, even as they honour the Father. [a]He that honoureth not the Son honoureth not the Father which hath sent him.

24 Verily, verily, I say unto you, [a]He that heareth my word, and believeth on him that sent me, hath everlasting life, and shall not come into condemnation; [b]but is passed from death unto life.

25 Verily, verily, I say unto you, The hour is coming, and now is, when [a]the dead shall hear the voice of the Son of God: and they that hear shall live.

26 For as the Father hath life in himself; so hath he given to the Son to have life in himself;

27 And [a]hath given him authority to execute judgment also, [b]because he is the Son of man.

28 Marvel not at this: for the hour is coming, in the which all that are in the graves shall hear his voice,

29 [a]And shall come forth; [b]they that have done good, unto the resurrection of life; and they that have done evil, unto the resurrection of damnation.

The Father's witness to the Son

30 [a]I can of mine own self do nothing: as I hear, I judge: and my judgment is just; because [b]I seek not mine own will, but the will of the Father which hath sent me.

31 [a]If I bear witness of myself, my witness is not true.

32 [a]There is another that beareth witness of me; and I know that the witness which he witnesseth of me is true.

33 Ye sent unto John, [a]and he bare witness unto the truth.

34 But I receive not testimony from man: but these *things* I say, that ye might be saved.

35 He was a burning and [a]a shining light: and [b]ye were willing for a season to rejoice in his light.

36 But [a]I have greater witness than *that of* John: for [b]the works which the Father hath given me to finish, the same works that I do, bear witness of me, that the Father hath sent me.

37 And the Father himself, which hath sent me, [a]hath borne witness of me. Ye have

5:19 [a]ver. 30; ch. 8:28; 9:4
5:20 [a]Mat. 3:17; ch. 3:35
5:21 [a]Luke 7:14; 8:54; ch. 11:25
5:22 [a]Mat. 11:27; 28:18; ch. 3:35; 17:2; Acts 17:31; 1 Pet. 4:5
5:23 [a]1 John 2:23
5:24 [a]ch. 3:16,18; 6:40,47; 8:51 [b]1 John 3:14
5:25 [a]Eph. 2:1,5; 5:14; Col 2:13
5:27 [a]Acts 10:42; 17:31 [b]Dan. 7:13
5:29 [a]Is. 26:19; 1 Cor. 15:52 [b]Dan. 12:2; Mat. 25:32,33,46
5:30 [a]ver. 19 [b]Mat. 26:39; ch. 4:34; 6:38
5:31 [a]ch. 8:14; Rev. 3:14
5:32 [a]Mat. 3:17; 17:5; ch. 8:18; 1 John 5:6
5:33 [a]ch. 1:15,19,27,32
5:35 [a]2 Pet. 1:19 [b]Mat. 13:20; Mark 6:20
5:36 [a]1 John 5:9 [b]ch. 3:2; 10:25; 15:24
5:37 [a]Mat. 3:17; 17:5; ch. 6:27; 8:18

---

ed to Jesus' claim that He stood in a special relationship to the Father—a relationship so close as to make Himself equal with God.

5:19 *can.* Because of who and what He was, it was not possible for Jesus to act except in dependence on the Father.

5:20 *the Father loveth the Son.* Therefore the Father revealed to the Son His plans and purposes, and the Son obediently carried them out. *greater works.* The Son's activities in raising the dead and judging (see following verses).

5:21 *the Father raiseth up the dead.* A firm belief among the Jews. They also held that He did not give this privilege to anyone else. Jesus claimed a prerogative that, according to His opponents, belonged only to God. *the Son quickeneth.* Probably refers to Christ's gift of abundant life here and now, though possibly also to the future resurrection (see 11:25–26).

5:22 *committed all judgment unto the Son.* The Jews believed that the Father is Judge of the world, so this teaching seemed heretical to them.

‡5:24 *believeth on him ... hath everlasting life.* Faith and life are connected (cf. 20:31). *hath everlasting life.* A present possession (see note on 3:15). *is passed.* The decisive action has taken place, and the believer no longer belongs to death. There is no undoing of this action.

5:25 *is coming, and now is.* A reference not only to the future resurrection but also to the fact that Christ gives life now. The spiritually dead who hear Him receive life from Him.

5:26 *hath life in himself.* Must be understood against the background of the OT, where life is spoken of as belonging to God and as being His gift (Deut 30:20; Job 10:12; 33:4; Ps 16:11; 27:1; 36:9; etc.). The Son has been given the same kind of life that the Father possesses (cf. also 1 John 5:11 for the benefit to man).

5:27 *authority to execute judgment.* Granted to the Son by the Father. *Son of man.* See note on 1:51.

5:28–29 A reference to the future raising of the dead.

5:29 *have done good ... life ... have done evil .... damnation.* As always in Scripture, judgment is on the basis of works, though salvation, of course, is a gift from God in response to faith (cf. v. 24).

5:30 *I can of mine own self do nothing.* Jesus stresses His dependence on the Father (see note on v. 19). He judges only as He hears from the Father, which makes His judgment fair.

5:31–47 This section stresses the testimonies (see note on 1:7) of John the Baptist (v. 33), of the works of Jesus (v. 36), of God the Father (v. 37), of the Scriptures (v. 39) and of Moses (v. 46).

5:31 Jesus' testimony about Himself required the support of all God's revelation. Otherwise, it would have been unacceptable.

5:32 *another.* The Father testifies concerning the Son. The Jews might not accept this testimony, but it was the testimony that mattered most.

5:33 *Ye sent unto John.* A reference to the delegation from the Jewish leaders to John the Baptist (see 1:19). *he bare witness.* The testimony of John was important, though not, of course, equal to the testimony of the Father. But had the Jews believed John, they would have believed Christ and would have been saved.

5:35 *He was.* The past tense may indicate that John was dead or at least imprisoned. In any case, his work was done. *was a burning and a shining.* John's giving light was costly to him. *for a season.* The Jewish leaders never came to grips with John's message, and their responses to him were always at best tentative and superficial.

5:36 *works.* The miracles of Jesus, which testified to what He is and to His divine mission (see 10:25).

5:37 *the Father ... hath borne witness ... his voice.* Probably a reference to God's voice in the Scriptures (see vv. 38–39). God

neither heard his voice at any time, [b]nor seen
his shape.
38 And ye have not his word abiding in you:
for whom he hath sent, him ye believe not.
39 [a]Search the Scriptures; for in them ye
think ye have eternal life: and [b]they are they
which testify of me.
40 [a]And ye will not come to me, that ye
might have life.
41 [a]I receive not honour from men.
42 But I know you, that ye have not the
love of God in you.
43 I am come in my Father's name, and ye
receive me not: if another shall come in his
own name, him ye will receive.
44 [a]How can ye believe, which receive
honour one of another, and seek not [b]the honour that *cometh* from God only?
45 Do not think that I will accuse you to
the Father: [a]there is *one* that accuseth you,
even Moses, in whom ye trust.
46 For had ye believed Moses, ye would
have believed me: [a]for he wrote of me.
47 But if ye believe not his writings, how
shall ye believe my words?

The five thousand fed

6 After [a]these *things* Jesus went over the
sea of Galilee, *which is* the *sea* of Tiberias.
2 And a great multitude followed him, because they saw his miracles which he did on
them that were diseased.
3 And Jesus went up into a mountain, and
there he sat with his disciples.
4 [a]And the passover, a feast of the Jews,
was nigh.

5:37 [b]Deut. 4:12; ch. 1:18; 1 Tim. 1:17; 1 John 4:12
5:39 [a]ver. 46; Is. 8:20; 34:16; Luke 16:29; Acts 17:11 [b]Deut. 18:15,18; Luke 24:27
5:40 [a]ch. 1:11; 3:19
5:41 [a]ver. 34; 1 Thes. 2:6
5:44 [a]ch. 12:43 [b]Rom. 2:29
5:45 [a]Rom. 2:12
5:46 [a]Gen. 3:15; 12:3; 18:18; 22:18; 49:10; Deut. 18:15,18; ch. 1:45; Acts 26:22
6:1 [a]Mat. 14:15; Mark 6:35; Luke 9:10,12
6:4 [a]Lev. 23:5,7; Deut. 16:1; ch. 2:13; 5:1
6:5 [a]Mat. 14:14; Mark 6:35; Luke 9:12
6:7 [a]See Num. 11:21,22
6:9 [a]2 Ki. 4:43
6:14 [a]Gen. 49:10; Deut. 18:15,18; Mat. 11:3; ch. 1:21; 4:19,25; 7:40

5 [a]When Jesus then lift up *his* eyes, and
saw a great company come unto him, he saith
unto Philip, Whence shall we buy bread, that
these may eat?
6 And this he said to prove him: for he
himself knew what he would do.
7 Philip answered him, [a]Two hundred pennyworth of bread is not sufficient for them,
that every one of them may take a little.
8 One of his disciples, Andrew, Simon Peter's brother, saith unto him,
9 There is a lad here, which hath five barley loaves, and two small fishes: [a]but what are
they among so many?
10 And Jesus said, Make the men sit down.
Now there was much grass in the place. So the
men sat down, *in* number about five thousand.
11 And Jesus took the loaves; and when he
had given thanks, he distributed to the disciples, and the disciples to them that were set
down; and likewise of the fishes as much as
they would.
12 When they were filled, he said unto his
disciples, Gather up the fragments that remain, that nothing be lost.
13 Therefore they gathered *them* together,
and filled twelve baskets with the fragments of
the five barley loaves, which remained over
and above unto them that had eaten.
14 Then *those* men, when they had seen
the miracle that Jesus did, said, This is of a truth
[a]*that* prophet that should come into the world.

Jesus walks on the sea

15 ¶ When Jesus therefore perceived that
they would come and take him by force, to

had also given His voice of approval at Jesus' baptism (see Mat 3:17). *nor seen his shape.* Probably refers to their lack of spiritual perception of who Jesus really is.

5:38 *ye believe not.* The Jews did not recognize what God was saying, as their failure to believe Jesus shows.

5:39 *Search the Scriptures.* The Jewish leaders studied Scripture in minute detail. Despite their reverence for the very letter of Scripture (see notes on Mat 5:18–21), they did not recognize the One to whom Scripture bears supreme testimony.

5:41 *honour from men.* Jesus did not accept human praise any more than human testimony (v. 34).

5:42 *love of God.* May mean God's love for them or theirs for God. Probably it is the latter, but people's love for God is in response to His prior love for them (1 John 4:19).

5:43–44 The Jews of v. 18 had their attention firmly fixed on people. Their emphasis on self-seeking and on human praise showed that they did not accept the One who came from God, and therefore they missed the praise that comes from God.

5:45 *one that accuseth you, even Moses.* Jesus' listeners prided themselves on their attachment to Moses, their great lawgiver. So it was an unexpected thrust for Jesus to say that Moses himself would accuse them before God.

5:46 *he wrote of me.* All the NT writers stressed, or assumed, that the OT, rightly read, points to Christ (cf. Luke 24:25–27,44). Jesus applied this truth specifically to the writings of Moses (see, e.g., notes on Gen 49:10; Ex 12:21; Lev 16:5; Num 24:17; Deut 18:15).

‡6:1–15 The feeding of the 5,000 is the one miracle, apart from the resurrection, found in all four Gospels. It shows Jesus as the supplier of human need, and sets the stage for His testimony that He is the bread of life (v. 35). This was perhaps Jesus' greatest miracle, witnessed by the largest number of people.

6:1 *After these things.* See 5:1 and note. *Tiberias.* Probably the official Roman name, while sea of Galilee was the popular name. The name came from the town of Tiberias (named after the emperor), founded c. A.D. 20, and probably was not much in use during Jesus' ministry.

6:2 *miracles.* See note on 2:11.

6:4 *passover.* See note on 2:13.

6:5 *Philip.* Since he came from nearby Bethsaida (1:44), it was appropriate to ask him.

6:9 *barley loaves.* Cheap bread, the food of the poor.

‡6:10 *much grass.* It was spring time. *about five thousand.* The number of men; women and children were not included (Mat 14:21).

6:12 *Gather up the fragments that remain.* See note on Mark 6:43.

6:13 *twelve baskets . . . which remained.* There was abundant supply.

6:14 *miracle.* It pointed people to the Son of man and the food for eternal life that He gives (v. 27), but they thought only of the prophet, i.e., the prophet of Deut 18:15 who would be like Moses (see 1:21 and note). Through Moses, God had provided food and water for the people in the wilderness, and they expected the prophet to do no more than this.

6:15 *take him by force, to make him a king.* Jesus rejected the world's version of kingship as a temptation of the devil (Mat 4:8–10; see note on John 18:36).

make him a king, he departed again into a
mountain himself alone.

16 [a]And when even was *now* come, his
disciples went down unto the sea,

17 And entered into a ship, and went over
the sea towards Capernaum. And it was now
dark, and Jesus was not come to them.

18 And the sea arose by reason of a great
wind that blew.

19 So when they had rowed about five and
twenty or thirty furlongs, they see Jesus walking on the sea, and drawing nigh unto the
ship: and they were afraid.

20 But he saith unto them, It is I; be not
afraid.

21 Then they willingly received him into
the ship: and immediately the ship was at the
land whither they went.

Jesus the bread of life

22 ¶ The day following, when the people
which stood on the other side of the sea saw
that there was none other boat there, save that
one whereinto his disciples were entered, and
that Jesus went not with his disciples into the
boat, but *that* his disciples were gone away
alone;

23 (Howbeit there came other boats from
Tiberias nigh unto the place where they did
eat bread, after that the Lord had given
thanks:)

24 When the people therefore saw that
Jesus was not there, neither his disciples, they
also took shipping, and came to Capernaum,
seeking for Jesus.

25 And when they had found him on the
other side of the sea, they said unto him, Rabbi, when camest thou hither?

26 Jesus answered them and said, Verily,
verily, I say unto you, Ye seek me, not because
ye saw *the* miracles, but because ye did eat of
the loaves, and were filled.

6:16 [a]Mat. 14:23; Mark 6:47

‡6:19 *five and twenty or thirty furlongs.* This would have been about three or four miles. Mark says they were "in the midst of the sea" (Mark 6:47). *afraid.* They thought they were seeing a ghost (Mat 14:26).

6:21 *immediately the ship was at the land.* Some think that this was another miracle. In any event, the boat's safe arrival is implicitly credited to Jesus.

6:22–24 The crowd could not figure out what had happened to Jesus. But they wanted to see Him again, so they looked for Him in the most likely place, Capernaum.

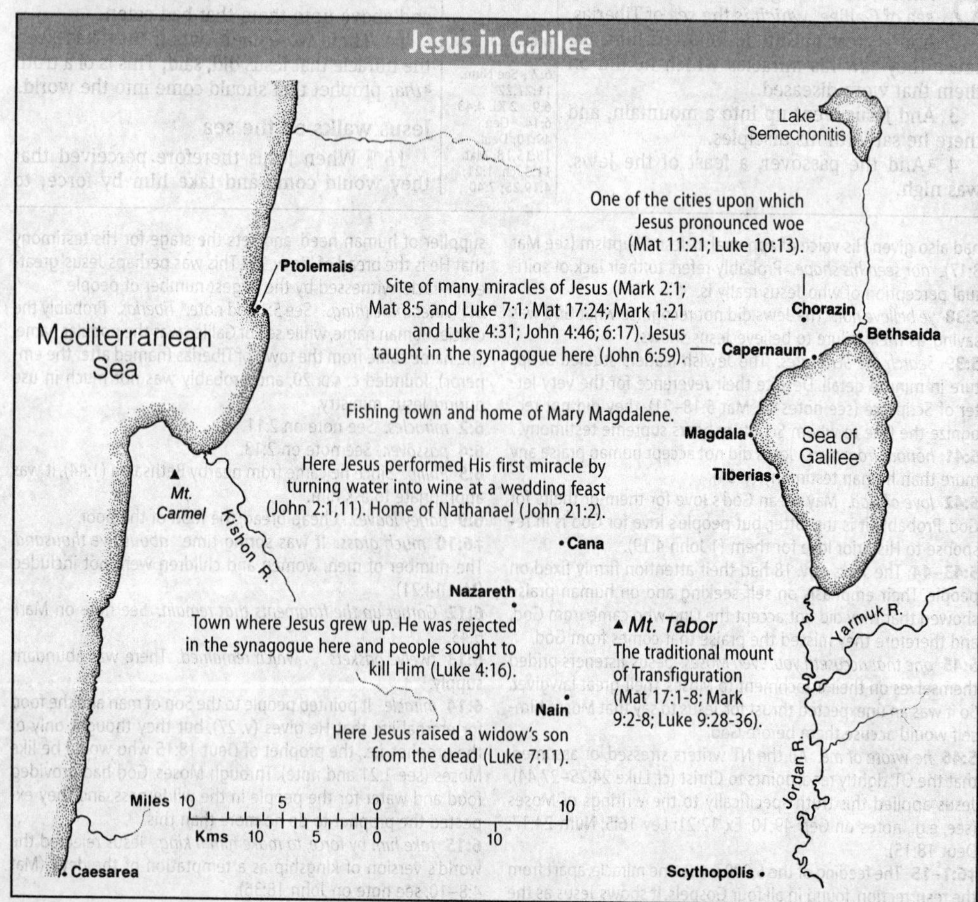
Jesus in Galilee
Lake Semechonitis
One of the cities upon which Jesus pronounced woe (Mat 11:21; Luke 10:13).
Ptolemais
Site of many miracles of Jesus (Mark 2:1; Mat 8:5 and Luke 7:1; Mat 17:24; Mark 1:21 and Luke 4:31; John 4:46; 6:17). Jesus taught in the synagogue here (John 6:59).
Chorazin
Bethsaida
Capernaum
Mediterranean Sea
Fishing town and home of Mary Magdalene.
Magdala
Sea of Galilee
Tiberias
Here Jesus performed His first miracle by turning water into wine at a wedding feast (John 2:1,11). Home of Nathanael (John 21:2).
Mt. Carmel
Kishon R.
Cana
Nazareth
Yarmuk R.
Town where Jesus grew up. He was rejected in the synagogue here and people sought to kill Him (Luke 4:16).
Mt. Tabor
The traditional mount of Transfiguration (Mat 17:1-8; Mark 9:2-8; Luke 9:28-36).
Nain
Here Jesus raised a widow's son from the dead (Luke 7:11).
Jordan R.
Miles 10 5 0 10
Kms 10 5 0 10
Caesarea
Scythopolis

27 [1]Labour not for the meat which perisheth, but [a]for *that* meat which endureth unto everlasting life, which the Son of man shall give unto you: [b]for him hath God the Father sealed.

28 Then said they unto him, What shall we do, that we might work the works of God?

29 Jesus answered and said unto them, [a]This is the work of God, that ye believe on *him* whom he hath sent.

30 They said therefore unto him, [a]What sign shewest thou then, that we may see, and believe thee? what dost thou work?

31 [a]Our fathers did eat manna in the desert; as it is written, [b]He gave them bread from heaven to eat.

32 Then Jesus said unto them, Verily, verily, I say unto you, Moses gave you not *that* bread from heaven; but my Father giveth you the true bread from heaven.

33 For the bread of God is he which cometh down from heaven, and giveth life unto the world.

34 [a]Then said they unto him, Lord, evermore give us this bread.

35 And Jesus said unto them, [a]I am the bread of life: [b]he that cometh to me shall never hunger; and he that believeth on me shall never thirst.

36 [a]But I said unto you, That ye also have seen me, and believe not.

37 [a]All that the Father giveth me shall come to me; and [b]him that cometh to me I will in no wise cast out.

38 For I came down from heaven, [a]not to do mine own will, [b]but the will of him that sent me.

6:27 [1]Or, *Work not* [a]ch. 4:14 [b]Mat. 3:17; 17:5; Mark 1:11; 9:7; Luke 3:22; 9:35; ch. 5:37; Acts 2:22; 2 Pet. 1:17
6:29 [a]1 John 3:23
6:30 [a]Mat. 12:38; 16:1; Mark 8:11; 1 Cor. 1:22
6:31 [a]Ex. 16:15; Num. 11:7; Neh. 9:15; 1 Cor. 10:3 [b]Ps. 78:24
6:34 [a]See ch. 4:15
6:35 [a]ver. 48,58 [b]ch. 4:14; 7:37
6:36 [a]ver. 26,64
6:37 [a]ver. 45 [b]Mat. 24:24; ch. 10:28,29; 2 Tim. 2:19; 1 John 2:19
6:38 [a]Mat. 26:39; ch. 5:30 [b]ch. 4:34
6:39 [a]ch. 10:28; 17:12; 18:9
6:40 [a]ver. 27,47,54; ch. 3:15,16; 4:14
6:42 [a]Mat. 13:55; Mark 6:3; Luke 4:22
6:44 [a]ver. 65; Sol. 1:4
6:45 [a]Is. 54:13; Jer. 31:34; Mic. 4:2; Heb. 8:10 [b]ver. 37
6:46 [a]ch. 1:18 [b]Mat. 11:27; Luke 10:22; ch. 7:29
6:47 [a]ch. 3:16,18
6:48 [a]ver. 33,35
6:49 [a]ver. 31
6:50 [a]ver. 51,58
6:51 [a]ch. 3:13

39 And this is the Father's will which hath sent me, [a]that of all which he hath given me I should lose nothing, but should raise it up *again* at the last day.

40 And this is the will of him that sent me, [a]that every one which seeth the Son, and believeth on him, may have everlasting life: and I will raise him up *at* the last day.

41 ¶ The Jews then murmured at him, because he said, I am the bread which came down from heaven.

42 And they said, [a]Is not this Jesus, the son of Joseph, whose father and mother we know? how *is it* then *that* he saith, I came down from heaven?

43 Jesus therefore answered and said unto them, Murmur not among yourselves.

44 [a]No *man* can come to me, except the Father which hath sent me draw him: and I will raise him up *at* the last day.

45 [a]It is written in the prophets, And they shall be all taught of God. [b]Every *man* therefore that hath heard, and hath learned of the Father, cometh unto me.

46 [a]Not that any *man* hath seen the Father, [b]save he which is of God, he hath seen the Father.

47 Verily, verily, I say unto you, [a]He that believeth on me hath everlasting life.

48 [a]I am *that* bread of life.

49 [a]Your fathers did eat manna in the wilderness, and are dead.

50 [a]This is the bread which cometh down from heaven, that a man may eat thereof, and not die.

51 I am the living bread [a]which came down from heaven: if any *man* eat of this

6:27 *everlasting life.* Not something to be achieved but to be received by faith in Christ (see vv. 28–29; see also note on 3:15). *Son of man.* See note on Mark 8:31. Submission of the Son to the Father is one of John's major themes (see note on 4:34).

6:28 *What shall we do . . . ?* They missed the point that eternal life is Christ's gift and were thinking in terms of achieving it by pious works.

6:29 *work of God.* Believing in Jesus Christ is the indispensable "work" God calls for—the one that leads to eternal life.

6:30 *What sign shewest thou . . . ?* They seek from Jesus a sign greater than the gift of manna that had accompanied Moses' ministry.

‡6:31 *manna.* A popular Jewish expectation was that when the Messiah came he would renew the sending of manna. The crowd probably reasoned that Jesus had done little compared to Moses. He had fed 5,000; Moses had fed a nation. He did it once; Moses did it for 40 years. He gave ordinary bread; Moses gave "bread from heaven."

6:32 Jesus corrected them, pointing out that the manna in the wilderness did not come from Moses but from God, and that the Father still "gives" (the present tense is important) the true bread from heaven (life through the Son).

6:33 *the bread of God.* Jesus moved the discussion to something (and Someone) much more important than manna.

6:34 *this bread.* Probably another misunderstanding, like that by the woman at the well (4:15; cf. also Nicodemus, 3:4). Their minds ran along materialistic lines.

6:35 *I am.* The first of seven self-descriptions of Jesus introduced by "I am" (see 8:12; 9:5; 10:7,9; 10:11,14; 11:25; 14:6; 15:1,5). In the Greek the words are solemnly emphatic and echo Ex 3:14. *the bread of life.* May mean "the bread that is living" and/or "the bread that gives life." What is implied in v. 33 is now made explicit and repeated with minor variations in vv. 41,48,51.

6:36 Contrast 20:29.

6:37 God's action (see v. 44; 10:29; 17:6; 18:9), not man's (v. 28), is primary in salvation, and Christ's mercy is unfailing (see vv. 31–40; 10:28; 17:9,12,15,19; 18:9).

6:38 *I came down from heaven.* Repeated six times in this context (vv. 33,38,41,50–51,58), emphasizing Jesus' divine origin. *to do . . . the will of him that sent me.* See note on 4:34.

6:39 *I should lose nothing.* The true believer will persevere because of Christ's firm hold on him (see Phil 1:6). *the last day.* An expression found only in John in the NT (see vv. 40,44,54).

6:40 *everlasting life.* See note on 3:15. *raise him up at the last day.* Death cannot destroy the life that Christ gives.

6:41 *The Jews.* See note on 1:19.

6:44 *draw.* People do not come to Christ strictly on their own initiative; the Father draws them.

6:45 *the prophets.* The section of the OT from which the quotation is taken. *Every man . . . learned of the Father, cometh.* Only those who learn from God come to salvation, and all who learn from Him are saved.

6:49 *are dead.* Jesus' opponents had set their hearts (cf. v. 31) on that which could neither give nor sustain spiritual life.

6:50 *eat . . . and not die.* Jesus' gift is in contrast; the life He gives is eternal.

bread, he shall live for ever: and [b]the bread that I will give is my flesh, which I will give for the life of the world.

52 The Jews therefore [a]strove amongst themselves, saying, How can this *man* give us *his* flesh to eat?

53 Then Jesus said unto them, Verily, verily, I say unto you, Except [a]ye eat the flesh of the Son of man, and drink his blood, ye have no life in you.

54 [a]Whoso eateth my flesh, and drinketh my blood, hath eternal life; and I will raise him up *at* the last day.

55 For my flesh is meat indeed, and my blood is drink indeed.

56 He that eateth my flesh, and drinketh my blood, [a]dwelleth in me, and I in him.

57 As the living Father hath sent me, and I live by the Father: so he that eateth me, even he shall live by me.

58 [a]This is *that* bread which came down from heaven: not as your fathers did eat manna, and are dead: he that eateth *of* this bread shall live for ever.

59 These *things* said he in the synagogue, as he taught in Capernaum.

The questioning disciples

60 ¶ [a]Many therefore of his disciples, when they had heard *this,* said, This is a hard saying; who can hear it?

61 When Jesus knew in himself that his disciples murmured at it, he said unto them, Doth this offend you?

62 [a]*What* and if ye shall see the Son of man ascend up where he was before?

63 [a]It is the spirit that quickeneth; the flesh profiteth nothing: the words that I speak unto you, *they* are spirit, and *they* are life.

64 But [a]there are some of you that believe not. For [b]Jesus knew from the beginning who they were that believed not, and who should betray him.

65 And he said, Therefore [a]said I unto you, that no *man* can come unto me, except it were given unto him of my Father.

66 ¶ [a]From that *time* many of his disciples went back, and walked no more with him.

67 Then said Jesus unto the twelve, Will ye also go away?

68 Then Simon Peter answered him, Lord, to whom shall we go? thou hast [a]the words of eternal life.

69 [a]And we believe and are sure that thou art *that* Christ, the Son of the living God.

70 Jesus answered them, [a]Have not I chosen you twelve, [b]and one of you is a devil?

71 He spake of Judas Iscariot *the son* of Simon: for he *it was that* should betray him, being one of the twelve.

Jesus at the feast of tabernacles

7 After these *things* Jesus walked in Galilee: for he would not walk in Jewry, [a]because the Jews sought to kill him.

2 [a]Now the Jews' feast of tabernacles was at hand.

6:51 [b]Heb. 10:5
6:52 [a]ch. 7:43; 9:16; 10:19
6:53 [a]Mat. 26:16
6:54 [a]ver. 27,40; ch. 4:14
6:56 [a]1 John 3:24; 4:15,16
6:58 [a]ver. 49-51
6:60 [a]ver. 66; Mat. 11:6
6:62 [a]Mark 16:19; ch. 3:13; Acts 1:9; Eph. 4:8
6:63 [a]2 Cor. 3:6
6:64 [a]ver. 36 [b]ch. 2:24,25; 13:11
6:65 [a]ver. 44,45
6:66 [a]ver. 60
6:68 [a]Acts 5:20
6:69 [a]Mat. 16:16; Mark 8:29; Luke 9:20; ch. 1:49; 11:27
6:70 [a]Luke 6:13 [b]ch. 13:27
7:1 [a]ch. 5:16,18
7:2 [a]Lev. 23:34

6:51 *eat of this bread.* Appropriates Jesus as the sustenance of one's life. *that I will give is my flesh.* Looking forward to Calvary. Providing eternal life would be costly to the Giver. *world.* See note on 4:42.

6:53–58 Jesus' absolute statement that "except ye eat the flesh of the Son of man and drink his blood, ye have no life in you" (v. 53) precludes a direct reference to the Lord's Supper. He clearly does not teach that receiving that sacrament is the one requirement for eternal life or that it is the only ordinance through which Christ and His saving benefits are received. In this very discourse He emphasizes faith in response to testimony (see vv. 35,40,47,51). Flesh and blood here point to Christ as the crucified One and the source of life. Jesus speaks of faith's appropriation of Himself as God's appointed sacrifice, not—at least not directly—of any ritual requirement.

6:54 *the last day.* See note on v. 39.

6:58 *that bread which came down from heaven.* As in v. 49, the value of the manna is limited and is contrasted with the heavenly food Christ gives. For the tenth time in this chapter reference is made to Jesus' coming down from heaven or to the bread from heaven.

6:60 *hard.* Hard to accept, not hard to understand. The thought of eating the flesh of the Son of Man and drinking His blood was doubtless shocking to most of Jesus' Jewish hearers (see note on vv. 53–58).

6:62 *Son of man.* See notes on Mark 8:31; Luke 6:5; 19:10. *ascend up.* Probably refers to the series of events that began with the cross, where Jesus was glorified (see note on 7:39). *where he was before.* Referring to Jesus' heavenly preexistence.

6:63 Cf. 3:5–6,8. *are spirit, and . . . life.* Are the Spirit at work producing life.

6:65 Coming to Christ for salvation is never a merely human achievement (see vv. 37,39,44–45).

‡6:66 *many . . . went back.* Jesus had already made clear what discipleship meant, and many were not ready to receive life in the way He taught.

6:68 As in the Synoptic Gospels, Peter acts as spokesman. *words of eternal life.* The expression is general. Peter was not speaking of a formula but of the thrust of Jesus' teaching. He perceived the truth of v. 63.

‡6:69 *we believe and are sure.* Since the Greek verbs are in the perfect tense, they mean, "We have entered a state of belief and knowledge that has continued until the present time."

6:70 *a devil.* Judas (v. 71) would oppose Christ in the spirit of Satan.

6:71 *Iscariot.* Means "a man from Kerioth" (in Judea; see Josh 15:25) and would apply equally to the father and the son (cf. 12:4). Judas seems to have been the only non-Galilean among the twelve. *one of the twelve.* And therefore one of the last persons likely to betray Jesus.

7:1–8:59 In chs. 7–8 John records strong opposition to Jesus, including repeated references to threats on His life (7:1,13,19,25, 30,32,44; 8:37,40,59). The apostle seems to have gathered the major arguments against the Messiahship of Jesus and here answers them.

7:1 *After these things.* As in 5:1 and 6:1 the time is indefinite. However, 6:4 refers to the passover feast and 7:2 to the feast of tabernacles, making the interval about six months.

7:2 *feast of tabernacles.* The great feast in the Jewish year, celebrating the completion of harvest and commemorating God's goodness to the people during the wilderness wanderings (see Lev 23:33–43; Deut 16:13–15; cf. Zech 14:16–19). The name came from the leafy shelters in which people lived throughout the seven days of the feast.

3 [a]His brethren therefore said unto him, Depart hence, and go into Judea, that thy disciples also may see the works that thou doest.

4 For *there is* no *man that* doeth any *thing* in secret, and he himself seeketh to be known openly. If thou do these *things,* shew thyself to the world.

5 For [a]neither did his brethren believe in him.

6 Then Jesus said unto them, [a]My time is not yet come: but your time is alway ready.

7 [a]The world cannot hate you; but me it hateth, [b]because I testify of it, that the works thereof are evil.

8 Go ye up unto this feast: I go not up yet unto this feast; [a]for my time is not yet full come.

9 When he had said these *words* unto them, he abode *still* in Galilee.

10 ¶ But when his brethren were gone up, then went he also up unto the feast, not openly, but as it were in secret.

11 Then [a]the Jews sought him at the feast, and said, Where is he?

12 And [a]there was much murmuring among the people concerning him: *for* [b]some said, He is a good *man:* others said, Nay; but he deceiveth the people.

13 Howbeit no *man* spake openly of him [a]for fear of the Jews.

7:3 [a]Mat. 12:46; Mark 3:31; Acts 1:14
7:5 [a]Mark 3:21
7:6 [a]ch. 2:4; 8:20
7:7 [a]ch. 15:19 [b]ch. 3:19
7:8 [a]ch. 8:20
7:11 [a]ch. 11:56
7:12 [a]ch. 9:16; 10:19 [b]ver. 40; Mat. 21:46; Luke 7:16; ch. 6:14
7:13 [a]ch. 9:22; 12:42; 19:38
7:15 [1]Or, *learning* [a]Mat. 13:54; Mark 6:2; Luke 4:22; Acts 2:7
7:16 [a]ch. 3:11; 8:28; 12:49; 14:10,24
7:17 [a]ch. 8:43
7:18 [a]ch. 5:41; 8:50
7:19 [a]Ex. 24:3; Deut. 33:4; ch. 1:17; Acts 7:38 [b]Mat. 12:14; Mark 3:6; ch. 5:16,18; 10:31,39; 11:53
7:20 [a]ch. 8:48,52; 10:20
7:22 [a]Lev. 12:3 [b]Gen. 17:10
7:23 [1]Or, *without breaking the law of Moses* [a]ch. 5:8,9,16

Jesus teaches in the temple

14 ¶ Now about the midst of the feast Jesus went up into the temple, and taught.

15 [a]And the Jews marvelled, saying, How knoweth this *man* [1]letters, having never learned?

16 Jesus answered them, and said, [a]My doctrine is not mine, but his that sent me.

17 [a]If any *man* will do his will, he shall know of the doctrine, whether it be of God, or *whether* I speak of myself.

18 [a]He that speaketh of himself seeketh his own glory: but he that seeketh his glory that sent him, the same is true, and no unrighteousness is in him.

19 [a]Did not Moses give you the law, and *yet* none of you keepeth the law? [b]Why go ye about to kill me?

20 The people answered and said, [a]Thou hast a devil: who goeth about to kill thee?

21 Jesus answered and said unto them, I have done one work, and ye all marvel.

22 [a]Moses therefore gave unto you circumcision, not because it is of Moses, [b]but of the fathers; and ye on the sabbath day circumcise a man.

23 If a man on the sabbath day receive circumcision, [1]that the law of Moses should not be broken; are ye angry at me, because [a]I have made a man every whit whole on the sabbath day?

7:3 *brethren.* See note on Luke 8:19.

7:4 It is not clear whether the brothers claimed some knowledge of Jesus' miracles that other people did not have or were suggesting that any claim to Messiahship must be decided in Jerusalem. Their advice was not given sincerely, for they did not yet believe in Jesus (v. 5).

7:6 *My time.* Jesus moved in accordance with the will of God (see note on 2:4).

7:7 *The world.* Either (1) people opposed to God or (2) the human system opposed to God's purposes (see note on 1:9). The brothers belonged to the world and therefore could not be the objects of its hatred. Jesus, however, rebuked the world and was hated accordingly.

7:8 *go not up yet.* Jesus was not refusing to go to the feast, but refusing to go in the way the brothers suggested—as a pilgrim. When He went, it would be to deliver a prophetic message from God, for which He awaited "His time" (see v. 6).

7:10 *not openly.* Rejecting the brothers' suggestion to show Himself (v. 4).

7:12 *murmuring.* Because there was significant disagreement about who He was (cf. v. 13).

7:14 *the midst of the feast.* When the crowds would be at their maximum. Teaching in the temple courts at such a time would reach many.

7:15 *the Jews.* Distinct from "the crowds" (v. 12), who were also Jews (see note on 1:19). *having never learned.* Under a rabbi. Jesus had never been the disciple of a recognized Jewish teacher.

7:16 *not mine.* The Father, from whom He came, had been His "rabbi" (see note on 4:34).

7:17 *will do his will.* Reflecting a whole attitude of life. A person sincerely set on doing God's will welcomes Jesus' teaching and believes in Him (cf. 6:29). *he shall know.* Augustine commented, "Understanding is the reward of faith . . . What is 'If any man be willing to do his will'? It is the same thing as to believe."

7:18 *the same is true.* They should recognize that Jesus was not self-seeking. In this Gospel, no one is spoken of as being "true" except God the Father (3:33; 8:26) and Jesus (here). Once more John ranks Jesus with God.

7:19 *the law.* The Jews congratulated themselves on being the chosen recipients of the law (cf. Rom 2:17), but Jesus told them that they all broke the law of which they were so proud.

7:20 *The people.* Probably the pilgrims who had come up to Jerusalem for the feast—different from "the Jews" who were trying to kill Jesus (v. 1) and the Jerusalem mob that knew of the plot (v. 25). *Thou hast a devil.* The accusation of demon possession is made elsewhere in John (e.g., 8:48–52; 10:20–21; cf. Mat 12:24–32; Mark 3:22–30).

7:21 *one work.* Evidently that of healing the lame man (5:1–9), as the discussion about the sabbath shows.

7:22 *circumcision.* The requirement of circumcision was included in the law Moses gave (Ex 12:44,48; Lev 12:3), yet it did not originate with Moses but went back to Abraham (Gen 17:9–14). The Jews took such regulations as that in Lev 12:3 to mean that circumcision must be performed on the eighth day even if it was the sabbath, a day on which no work should be done. This exception is of critical importance in understanding the controversy (v. 23). Jesus was not saying that the sabbath should not be observed or that the Jewish regulations were too harsh. He was saying that His opponents did not understand what the sabbath meant. The command to circumcise showed that sometimes work not only might be done on the sabbath but must be done then. Deeds of mercy were in this category.

24 [a]Judge not according to the appearance, but judge righteous judgment.

25 Then said some of them of Jerusalem, Is not this he, whom they seek to kill?

26 But lo, he speaketh boldly, and they say nothing unto him. [a]Do the rulers know indeed that this is the very Christ?

27 [a]Howbeit we know this *man* whence he is: but when Christ cometh, no *man* knoweth whence he is.

28 Then cried Jesus in the temple as he taught, saying, [a]Ye both know me, and ye know whence I am: and [b]I am not come of myself, but he that sent me [c]is true, [d]whom ye know not.

29 But [a]I know him: for I am from him, and he hath sent me.

30 Then [a]they sought to take him: but [b]no *man* laid hands on him, because his hour was not yet come.

31 And [a]many of the people believed on him, and said, When Christ cometh, will he do moe miracles than these which this *man* hath done?

32 The Pharisees heard that the people murmured such *things* concerning him; and the Pharisees and the chief priests sent officers to take him.

33 Then said Jesus unto them, [a]Yet a little while am I with you, and *then* I go unto him that sent me.

34 Ye [a]shall seek me, and shall not find *me:* and where I am, *thither* ye cannot come.

35 Then said the Jews among themselves, Whither will he go, that we shall not find him? will he go unto [a]the dispersed among the [1]Gentiles, and teach the [1]Gentiles?

36 What *manner of* saying is this that he said, Ye shall seek me, and shall not find *me:* and where I am, *thither* ye cannot come?

The last day of the feast

37 ¶ [a]In the last day, *that* great *day* of the feast, Jesus stood and cried, saying, [b]If any *man* thirst, let him come unto me, and drink.

38 [a]He that believeth on me, as the scripture hath said, [b]out of his belly shall flow rivers of living water.

39 ([a]But this spake he of the Spirit, which they that believe on him should receive: for the Holy Ghost was not yet *given;* because that Jesus was not yet [b]glorified.)

40 Many of the people therefore, when they heard *this* saying, said, Of a truth this is [a]the Prophet.

41 Others said, [a]This is the Christ. But some said, Shall Christ come [b]out of Galilee?

42 [a]Hath not the scripture said, That Christ cometh of the seed of David, and out of the town of Bethlehem, [b]where David was?

43 So [a]there was a division among the people because of him.

44 And [a]some of them would have taken him; but no *man* laid hands on him.

45 ¶ Then came the officers to the chief priests and Pharisees; and they said unto them, Why have ye not brought him?

46 The officers answered, Never man spake like this man.

47 Then answered them the Pharisees, Are ye also deceived?

48 [a]Have any of the rulers or of the Pharisees believed on him?

7:24 [a]Deut. 1:16; Prov. 24:23; ch. 8:15; Jas. 2:1 **7:26** [a]ver. 48 **7:27** [a]Mat. 13:55; Mark 6:3; Luke 4:22 **7:28** [a]ch. 8:14 [b]ch. 5:43; 8:42 [c]ch. 5:32; 8:26; Rom. 3:4 [d]ch. 1:18; 8:55 **7:29** [a]Mat. 11:27; ch. 10:15 **7:30** [a]Mark 11:18; Luke 19:47; 20:19; ch. 8:37 [b]ver. 44 **7:31** [a]Mat. 12:23; ch. 3:2; 8:30 **7:33** [a]ch. 13:33; 16:16 **7:34** [a]Hos. 5:6; ch. 8:21; 13:33 **7:35** [1]Or, *Greeks* [a]Is. 11:12; Jas. 1:1; 1 Pet. 1:1 **7:37** [a]Lev. 23:36 [b]Is. 55:1; ch. 6:35; Rev. 22:17 **7:38** [a]Deut. 18:15 [b]Prov. 18:4; Is. 12:3; 44:3; ch. 4:14 **7:39** [a]Is. 44:3; Joel 2:28; ch. 16:7; Acts 2:17,33,38 [b]ch. 12:16; 16:7 **7:40** [a]Deut. 18:15; ch. 1:21; 6:14 **7:41** [a]ch. 4:42; 6:69 [b]ver. 52; ch. 1:46 **7:42** [a]Ps. 132:11; Jer. 23:5; Mic. 5:2; Mat. 2:5; Luke 2:4 [b]1 Sam. 16:1,4 **7:43** [a]ver. 12; ch. 9:16; 10:19 **7:44** [a]ver. 30 **7:48** [a]ch. 12:42; Acts 6:7; 1 Cor. 1:20,26; 2:8

7:25 *them of Jerusalem.* An expression found only here and in Mark 1:5 in the NT, probably referring to the Jerusalem mob (see note on v. 20). They did not originate the plot against Jesus, but they knew of it.
7:26 *Do the rulers know indeed . . . Christ?* In Greek, the question is in a form that expects a negative answer. *the very Christ.* See note on 1:25.
7:27 *no man knoweth whence he is.* Some Jews held that the OT gave the origin of the Messiah (cf. v. 42; Mat 2:4–6), but others believed that it did not.
7:28 *Ye both know me, and.* Irony, because in a sense they knew Jesus and that He came from Nazareth, but in a deeper sense they did not know Jesus or the Father (8:19). Jesus mentioned again His dependence on the Father (cf. 4:34) and went on to declare that He had real knowledge of God and that they did not. Both His origin and mission were from God.
7:30 *they sought to take him.* Jesus' enemies were powerless against Him until His time came (see note on 2:4).
7:31 *many of the people.* Of pilgrims (see note on v. 20). Many of them believed on the basis of the miraculous signs (cf. 6:26).
7:32 *The Pharisees.* See notes on Mat 3:7; Mark 2:16; Luke 5:17. *the chief priests.* There was only one ruling chief priest, but the Romans had deposed a number of chief priests, and these retained the title by courtesy.
7:33 *then I go.* Jesus changed the topic from His miracles to His death, to which He referred enigmatically (v. 34).
7:35 *the dispersed among the Gentiles.* Or "Greeks." From the time of the exile, many Jews lived outside the Holy Land and were found in most cities throughout the Roman empire.
7:37 *the last . . . day of the feast.* Either the seventh or the eighth day: The feast of tabernacles lasted seven days (Lev 23:34; Deut 16:13,15) but had a "holy convocation" on the eighth day (Lev 23:36). See note on Mark 14:12. *stood and cried, saying.* Teachers usually sat, so Jesus drew special attention to His message.
7:38 *living water.* See note on 4:10.
7:39 *the Spirit.* Explaining the "living water" (v. 38). *was not yet given.* In the manner in which He would be given at Pentecost (see Acts 2). *glorified.* Here probably refers to Jesus' crucifixion, resurrection and exaltation (see note on 13:31). The fullness of the Spirit's work depends on Jesus' prior work of salvation.
7:40 *people.* The "crowd" of v. 20 (see note there).
7:42 *Bethlehem.* There were different ideas about the Messiah's place of origin (cf. v. 27).
7:46 *The officers.* They knew they would be in trouble for failing to make the arrest, but did not mention the hostility of part of the crowd, which would have given them something of an excuse before the Pharisees. They were favorably impressed by the teaching of Jesus and were not inclined to cause Him trouble.
7:47 *Then answered them the Pharisees.* They must have been greatly irritated. Ordinarily the chief priests would have rebuked the temple guards.

49 But this people who knoweth not the
law are cursed.
50 Nicodemus saith unto them, ([a]he that
came [1]to *Jesus* by night, being one of them,)
51 [a]Doth our law judge any man, before it
hear him, and know what he doeth?
52 They answered and said unto him, Art
thou also of Galilee? Search, and look: for [a]out
of Galilee ariseth no prophet.

The woman caught in adultery

53 ¶ And every man went unto his own
house.

8 Jesus went unto the mount of Olives.
2 And early in the morning he came
again into the temple, and all the people came
unto him; and he sat down, and taught them.
3 And the scribes and Pharisees brought
unto him a woman taken in adultery; and
when they had set her in the midst,
4 They say unto him, Master, this woman
was taken in adultery, in the very act.
5 [a]Now Moses in the law commanded us,
that such should be stoned: but what sayest
thou?
6 This they said, tempting him, that they
might have to accuse him. But Jesus stooped
down, and with *his* finger wrote on the
ground, *as though he heard them not.*
7 So when they continued asking him, he
lift up *himself,* and said unto them, [a]He that is
without sin among you, let him first cast a
stone at her.
8 And again he stooped down, and wrote
on the ground.
9 And they which heard *it,* [a]being convicted by *their own* conscience, went out one by
one, beginning at the eldest, *even* unto the
last: and Jesus was left alone, and the woman
standing in the midst.
10 When Jesus had lift up *himself,* and saw
none but the woman, he said unto her,
Woman, where are those thine accusers? hath
no *man* condemned thee?
11 She said, No *man,* Lord. And Jesus said
unto her, [a]Neither do I condemn thee: go, and
[b]sin no more.

Jesus the light of the world

12 ¶ Then spake Jesus again unto them,
saying, [a]I am the light of the world: he that followeth me shall not walk in darkness, but shall
have the light of life.
13 The Pharisees therefore said unto him,
[a]Thou bearest record of thyself; thy record is
not true.
14 Jesus answered and said unto them,
Though I bear record of myself, *yet* my record
is true: for I know whence I came, and whither I go; but [a]ye cannot tell whence I come, and
whither I go.

7:50 [1] [Gr. *to him*] [a]ch. 3:2
7:51 [a]Deut. 1:17; 17:8; 19:15
7:52 [a]ver. 41; Is. 9:1,2; Mat. 4:15; ch. 1:46
8:5 [a]Lev. 20:10; Deut. 22:22
8:7 [a]Deut. 17:7; Rom. 2:1
8:9 [a]Rom. 2:22
8:11 [a]Luke 9:56; 12:14; ch. 3:17 [b]ch. 5:14
8:12 [a]ch. 1:4,5,9; 3:19; 9:5; 12:35,36,46
8:13 [a]ch. 5:31
8:14 [a]ch. 7:28; 9:29

7:49 *this people.* The pilgrim crowd again (see note on v. 20). *knoweth not.* The Pharisees exaggerated the people's ignorance of Scripture (cf. v. 42). But the average Jew paid little attention to the minutiae that mattered so much to the Pharisees. The "traditions of the elders" were too great a burden for people who earned their living by hard physical work, and consequently these regulations were widely disregarded.

7:50–51 There is irony here. The Pharisees implied that no leader believed in Jesus, yet Nicodemus, "a ruler of the Jews" (3:1), spoke up. They called for people to observe the law, but Nicodemus pointed to their own disregard for the law in this instance.

7:52 *out of Galilee ariseth no prophet.* See 1:46. They were angry—and wrong. Jonah came from Galilee, and perhaps other prophets as well. Moreover, the Pharisees overlooked the right of God to raise up prophets from wherever He chooses.

‡7:53–8:11 This story is absent from some early manuscripts, and some that have it sometimes place it elsewhere (e.g., after Luke 21:38). However, this passage is contained in more than 1,700 NT Greek manuscripts. The story may well be authentic.

8:1 *mount of Olives.* See note on Mark 11:1.

8:3 *scribes.* See notes on Mat 2:4; Luke 5:17. *a woman taken in adultery.* This sin cannot be committed alone, so the question arises as to why only one offender was brought. The incident was staged to trap Jesus (v. 6), and provision had been made for the man to escape. The woman's accusers must have been especially eager to humiliate her, since they could have kept her in private custody while they spoke to Jesus.

8:4 *taken . . . in the very act.* Compromising circumstances were not sufficient evidence, as Jewish law required witnesses who had seen the act.

8:5 *such should be stoned.* They altered the law a little. The manner of execution was not prescribed unless the woman was a betrothed virgin (Deut 22:23–24). And the law required the execution of both parties (Lev 20:10; Deut 22:22), not just the woman.

8:6 *This they said, tempting him.* The Romans did not allow the Jews to carry out death sentences (18:31), so if Jesus had said to stone her, He could have been in conflict with the Romans. If He had said not to stone her, He could have been accused of being unsupportive of the law. *wrote.* We can only guess what Jesus wrote on the ground.

8:7 *without sin.* The phrase is quite general and means "without any sin," not "without this sin." *let him first.* Jesus' answer disarmed them. Since He spoke of throwing a stone, He could not be accused of failure to uphold the law. But the qualification for throwing it prevented anyone from acting.

8:9 *went out.* Because they were not "without sin" (v. 7). *the eldest.* They were the first to realize what was involved. But all the men were either conscience-stricken or afraid, and in the end only Jesus and the woman remained.

8:10 *Woman.* Not a harsh form of address (cf. its use in 19:26).

8:11 *go, and sin no more.* Jesus did not condone what the woman had done.

8:12 *I am.* See note on 6:35. *the light.* See 1:4 and note; 9:5; 12:46. It is also true that "God is light" (1 John 1:5). And as Jesus' followers reflect the light that comes from Him, they too are "the light of the world" (Mat 5:14; cf. Phil 2:15). *darkness.* Both the darkness of this world and that of Satan. *the light of life.* "God is light" (1 John 1:5); but Jesus is also the light from God that lights the way for life—as the pillar of fire lighted the way for the Israelites (see Ex 13:21; Neh 9:12).

8:13 *Pharisees.* See notes on Mat 3:7; Mark 2:16; Luke 5:17.

8:14 Jesus made two points in reply. First, He was qualified to bear testimony, whereas the Pharisees were not; and He knew both His origin and His destination, whereas they knew neither. (See note on vv. 16–18 for the second point.)

15 [a]Ye judge after the flesh; [b]I judge no *man.*

16 And yet if I judge, my judgment is true: for [a]I am not alone, but I and the Father that sent me.

17 [a]It is also written in your law, that the testimony of two men is true.

18 I am *one* that bear witness of myself, and [a]the Father that sent me beareth witness of me.

19 Then said they unto him, Where is thy Father? Jesus answered, [a]Ye neither know me, nor my Father: [b]if ye had known me, ye should have known my Father also.

20 These words spake Jesus in [a]the treasury, as he taught in the temple: and [b]no *man* laid hands on him; for [c]his hour was not yet come.

Jesus warns against unbelief

21 ¶ Then said Jesus again unto them, I go my way, and [a]ye shall seek me, and [b]shall die in your sins: whither I go, ye cannot come.

22 Then said the Jews, Will he kill himself? because he saith, Whither I go, ye cannot come.

23 And he said unto them, [a]Ye are from beneath; I am from above: [b]ye are of this world; I am not of this world.

24 [a]I said therefore unto you, that ye shall die in your sins: [b]for if ye believe not that I am *he,* ye shall die in your sins.

25 Then said they unto him, Who art thou? And Jesus saith unto them, Even the same that I said unto you *from* the beginning.

26 I have many *things* to say and to judge of you: but [a]he that sent me is true; and [b]I speak to the world those *things* which I have heard of him.

27 They understood not that he spake to them of the Father.

28 Then said Jesus unto them, When ye have [a]lift up the Son of man, [b]then shall ye know that I am *he,* and [c]*that* I do nothing of myself; but [d]as my Father hath taught me, I speak these *things.*

29 And [a]he that sent me is with me: [b]the Father hath not left me alone; [c]for I do always those *things* that please him.

30 As he spake these *words,* [a]many believed on him.

The true children of Abraham

31 ¶ Then said Jesus to those Jews which believed on him, If ye continue in my word, *then* are ye my disciples indeed;

32 And ye shall know the truth, and [a]the truth shall make you free.

33 They answered him, [a]We be Abraham's seed, and were never in bondage to any *man:* how sayest thou, Ye shall be made free?

34 Jesus answered them, Verily, verily, I say unto you, [a]Whosoever committeth sin is the servant of sin.

35 And [a]the servant abideth not in the house for ever: *but* the son abideth ever.

36 [a]If the Son therefore shall make you free, ye shall be free indeed.

37 I know that ye are Abraham's seed; but [a]ye seek to kill me, because my word hath no place in you.

38 [a]I speak *that* which I have seen with my Father: and ye do *that* which ye have seen with your father.

39 They answered and said unto him, [a]Abraham is our father. Jesus saith unto them, [b]If ye were Abraham's children, ye would do the works of Abraham.

40 [a]But now ye seek to kill me, a man that hath told you the truth, [b]which I have heard of God: this did not Abraham.

41 Ye do the deeds of your father. Then said they to him, We be not born of fornication; [a]we have one Father, *even* God.

42 Jesus said unto them, [a]If God were your Father, ye would love me: [b]for I proceeded

8:15 [a]ch. 7:24 [b]ch. 3:17; 12:47; 18:36
8:16 [a]ch. 16:32
8:17 [a]Deut. 17:6; 19:15; Mat. 18:16; 2 Cor. 13:1; Heb. 10:28
8:18 [a]ch. 5:37
8:19 [a]ch. 16:3 [b]ch. 14:7
8:20 [a]Mark 12:41 [b]ch. 7:30 [c]ch. 7:8
8:21 [a]ch. 7:34; 13:33 [b]ver. 24
8:23 [a]ch. 3:31 [b]ch. 15:19; 17:16; 1 John 4:5
8:24 [a]ver. 21 [b]Mark 16:16
8:26 [a]ch. 7:28 [b]ch. 3:32; 15:15
8:28 [a]ch. 3:14; 12:32 [b]Rom. 1:4
8:28 [c]ch. 5:19,30 [d]ch. 3:11
8:29 [a]ch. 14:10 [b]ver. 16 [c]ch. 4:34; 5:30; 6:38
8:30 [a]ch. 7:31; 10:42; 11:45
8:32 [a]Rom. 6:14,18,22; Jas. 1:25; 2:12
8:33 [a]Lev. 25:42; Mat. 3:9
8:34 [a]Rom 6:16; 2 Pet. 2:19
8:35 [a]Gal. 4:30
8:36 [a]Rom. 8:2; Gal. 5:1
8:37 [a]ch. 7:19
8:38 [a]ch. 3:32; 5:19,30; 14:10,24
8:39 [a]Mat. 3:9 [b]Rom. 2:28; 9:7; Gal. 3:7,29
8:40 [a]ver. 37 [b]ver. 26
8:41 [a]Is. 63:16; 64:8; Mal. 1:6
8:42 [a]1 John 5:1 [b]ch. 16:27; 17:8,25

8:15 The judgment of the Pharisees was limited and worldly. In the sense they meant, Jesus made it clear that He did not judge at all. In the proper sense, of course, He did judge (v. 26).

8:16–18 Jesus' second point was that His testimony was not unsupported. The Father was with Him, so He and the Father were the two witnesses required by the law (Deut 17:6; 19:15).

8:16 *the Father that sent me.* Jesus was always aware of His mission (see note on 4:34).

8:19 *if ye had known me.* John makes it clear that the Word (Jesus) was with God and was God (1:1) and reveals God (1:18). Jesus here stresses that the Father is known through the Son and that to know the one is to know the other.

8:20 *his hour.* See note on 2:4.

8:23 Things other than death divide people (cf., e.g., v. 47; 3:31; 15:19; 1 John 3:10 etc.). *of.* Here denotes origin. Jesus was certainly in the world, but He was not of the world. They belonged to "this world"—Satan's domain (1 John 5:19).

8:24 *believe.* See note on 1:7. *I am.* Jesus echoes God's great affirmation about Himself (see v. 58; see also notes on 6:35; Ex 3:14).

‡8:28 *lift up.* Normally used in the NT in the sense of "exalt," but John uses it of the crucifixion (see 3:14; 12:32–33). *Son of man.* See note on Mark 8:31. *I am.* See notes on vv. 24,58.

8:30 *believed.* Cf. 20:31.

‡8:31 *believed.* Here seems to mean "made a formal profession of faith." Their words show that these people were not true believers (see vv. 33,37). They were professors, but not possessors.

8:32 *the truth.* Closely connected with Jesus (v. 36; 14:6), it is not philosophical truth but the truth that leads to salvation. *free.* Freedom from sin, not from ignorance (see v. 36).

8:33 *were never in bondage to any man.* An amazing disregard of their Roman overlords.

8:34 *the servant of sin.* Because the sinner cannot break free by his own strength.

8:37 *ye seek to kill me.* See note on 7:1–8:59.

8:38 Note the contrasts: "I . . . ye"; "My Father . . . your father." Not until later (v. 44) did Jesus say who their father was, but it is clear even at this point that it was neither God nor Abraham as they claimed.

8:39–41 Their deeds revealed their parentage.

‡8:41 *born of fornication.* May have been a slander aimed at the circumstances surrounding Jesus' birth.

forth and came from God; [c]neither came I of myself, but he sent me.

43 [a]Why do ye not understand my speech? *even* because ye cannot hear my word.

44 [a]Ye are of *your* father the devil, and the lusts of your father ye will do. He was a murderer from the beginning, and [b]abode not in the truth, because there is no truth in him. When he speaketh a lie, he speaketh of his own: for he is a liar, and the father of it.

45 And because I tell *you* the truth, ye believe me not.

46 Which of you convinceth me of sin? And if I say the truth, why do ye not believe me?

47 [a]He that is of God heareth God's words: ye therefore hear *them* not, because ye are not of God.

Controversy with the Jews

48 Then answered the Jews, and said unto him, Say we not well that thou art a Samaritan, and [a]hast a devil?

49 Jesus answered, I have not a devil; but I honour my Father, and ye do dishonour me.

50 And [a]I seek not mine own glory: there is *one* that seeketh and judgeth.

51 Verily, verily, I say unto you, [a]If a man keep my saying, he shall never see death.

52 Then said the Jews unto him, Now we know that thou hast a devil. [a]Abraham is dead, and the prophets; and thou sayest, If a man keep my saying, he shall never taste of death.

53 Art thou greater than our father Abraham, which is dead? and the prophets are dead: whom makest thou thyself?

54 Jesus answered, If I honour myself, my honour is nothing: [a]it is my Father that honoureth me; of whom ye say, that he is your God:

55 Yet [a]ye have not known him; but I know him: and if I should say, I know him not, I shall be a liar like unto you: but I know him, and keep his saying.

56 Your father Abraham [a]rejoiced to see my day: [b]and he saw *it,* and was glad.

57 Then said the Jews unto him, Thou art not yet fifty years old, and hast thou seen Abraham?

58 Jesus said unto them, Verily, verily, I say unto you, Before Abraham was, [a]I am.

59 Then [a]took they up stones to cast at him: but Jesus hid himself, and went out of the temple, [b]going through the midst of them, and so passed by.

Jesus heals the man born blind

9 And as *Jesus* passed by, he saw a man *which was* blind from *his* birth.

2 And his disciples asked him, saying, Master, [a]who did sin, this *man,* or his parents, that he was born blind?

3 Jesus answered, Neither hath this *man* sinned, nor his parents: [a]but that the works of God should be made manifest in him.

4 [a]I must work the works of him that sent me, while it is day: the night cometh, when no *man* can work.

5 As long as I am in the world, [a]I am the light of the world.

6 When he had thus spoken, [a]he spat on the ground, and made clay of the spittle, and he [1]anointed the eyes of the blind man with the clay,

8:42 [c]ch. 5:43; 7:28,29
8:43 [a]ch. 7:17
8:44 [a]Mat. 13:38; 1 John 3:8 [b]Jude 6
8:47 [a]ch. 10:26; 1 John 4:6
8:48 [a]ver. 52; ch. 7:20; 10:20
8:50 [a]ch. 5:41; 7:18
8:51 [a]ch. 5:24; 11:26
8:52 [a]Zech. 1:5; Heb. 11:13
8:54 [a]ch. 5:41; 16:14; 17:1; Acts 3:13
8:55 [a]ch. 7:28,29
8:56 [a]Luke 10:24 [b]Heb. 11:13
8:58 [a]Ex. 3:14; Is. 43:13; ch. 17:5,24; Col. 1:17; Rev. 1:8
8:59 [a]ch. 10:31,39; 11:8 [b]Luke 4:30
9:2 [a]ver. 34
9:3 [a]ch. 11:4
9:4 [a]ch. 4:34; 5:19,36; 11:9; 12:35; 17:4
9:5 [a]ch. 1:5,9; 3:19; 8:12; 12:35,46
9:6 [1]Or, *spread the clay upon the eyes of the blind man* [a]Mark 7:33; 8:23

8:43 *my speech.* The form of expression—the actual words. *my word.* The content. These descendants of Abraham (v. 33) were so convinced of their own preconceptions that they did not really hear what Jesus was saying (cf. v. 47).
8:44 *your father the devil.* These Jews' relationship to Satan was now stated explicitly. Jesus clearly excluded the idea of the universal fatherhood of God. *ye will do.* Points to determination of will. Their problem was basically spiritual, not intellectual. Being oriented toward Satan, they were bent on murder (v. 37) and eventually would succeed (v. 28). *truth.* Foreign to Satan and those who are his (see 14:6).
8:46 *Which of you convinceth me of sin?* The asking of the question was more significant than the Jews' failure to answer, in that it showed Jesus had a perfectly clear conscience.
8:47 *heareth God's words.* See 10:3–4; 1 John 4:6.
8:48 *the Jews.* See note on 1:19. *a Samaritan.* Probably to suggest that He was lax in Jewish observances—"No better than a Samaritan." Or it may be a reflection on the birth of Jesus—perhaps claiming that His father was a Samaritan. *hast a devil.* See 10:20 and note on 7:20.
8:51 *my saying.* The whole of Jesus' message, which when accepted brings deliverance from death.
8:53 *Art thou greater . . . ?* The question was framed to expect the answer "No." This is ironic, since Jesus was indeed far greater than Abraham, even as He was greater than Moses (see 6:30–35 and notes).
8:56 *my day.* All that was involved in the incarnation. Jesus probably was not referring to any one occasion but to Abraham's general joy in the fulfilling of the purposes of God in Christ, by which all nations on earth would receive blessing (Gen 18:18). *he saw it.* In faith, from afar.
8:57 *not yet fifty years old.* A generous allowance for Jesus' maximum possible age. Jesus was "about" 30 when He began His ministry (Luke 3:23).
8:58 *I am.* A solemnly emphatic declaration echoing God's great affirmation in Ex 3:14 (see vv. 24,28; see also note on 6:35). Jesus did not say "I was" but "I am," expressing the eternity of His being and His oneness with the Father (see 1:1). With this climactic statement Jesus concludes His speech that began with the related claim, "I am the light of the world" (v. 12).
8:59 *stones to cast at him.* The Jews could not interpret Jesus' claim as other than blasphemy, for which stoning was the proper penalty (Lev 24:16).
9:1–12 Jesus performed more miracles of this kind than of any other. Giving sight to the blind was predicted as a Messianic activity (Is 29:18; 35:5; 42:7). Thus these miracles were additional evidence that Jesus was the Messiah (20:31).
9:2 *who did sin . . . ?* The rabbis had developed the principle that "There is no death without sin, and there is no suffering without iniquity." They were even capable of thinking that a child could sin in the womb or that its soul might have sinned in a preexistent state. They also held that terrible punishments came on certain people because of the sin of their parents. As the next verse shows, Jesus plainly contradicted these beliefs.
9:5 *the light of the world.* See note on 8:12.
9:6 Jesus used variety in His cures.

7 And said unto him, Go, wash [a]in the pool of Siloam, (which is by interpretation, Sent.) [b]He went his way therefore, and washed, and came seeing.

8 ¶ The neighbours therefore, and they which before had seen him that he was blind, said, Is not this he that sat and begged?

9 Some said, This is he: others *said,* He is like him: *but* he said, I am *he.*

10 Therefore said they unto him, How were thine eyes opened?

11 He answered and said, [a]A man *that is* called Jesus made clay, and anointed mine eyes, and said unto me, Go to the pool of Siloam, and wash: and I went and washed, and I received sight.

12 Then said they unto him, Where is he? He said, I know not.

Pharisees question the healed man

13 ¶ They brought to the Pharisees him that aforetime was blind.

14 And it was the sabbath day when Jesus made the clay, and opened his eyes.

15 Then again the Pharisees also asked him how he had received his sight. He said unto them, He put clay upon mine eyes, and I washed, and do see.

16 Therefore said some of the Pharisees, This man is not of God, because he keepeth not the sabbath day. Others said, [a]How can a man *that is* a sinner do such miracles? And [b]there was a division among them.

17 They say unto the blind man again, What sayest thou of him, that he hath opened thine eyes? He said, [a]He is a prophet.

18 But the Jews did not believe concerning him, that he had been blind, and received his sight, until they called the parents of him that had received his sight.

19 And they asked them, saying, Is this your son, who ye say was born blind? how then doth he now see?

20 His parents answered them and said, We know that this is our son, and that he was born blind:

21 But by what means he now seeth, we know not; or who hath opened his eyes, we know not: he is of age; ask him: he shall speak for himself.

22 These *words* spake his parents, because [a]they feared the Jews: for the Jews had agreed already, that if any *man* did confess that he *was* Christ, he [b]should be put out of the synagogue.

23 Therefore said his parents, He is of age; ask him.

24 Then again called they the man that was blind, and said unto him, [a]Give God the praise: [b]we know that this man is a sinner.

25 He answered and said, Whether he be a sinner *or no,* I know not: one *thing* I know, that, whereas I was blind, now I see.

26 Then said they to him again, What did he to thee? how opened he thine eyes?

27 He answered them, I have told you already, and ye did not hear: wherefore would you hear *it* again? will ye also be his disciples?

28 Then they reviled him, and said, Thou art his disciple; but we are Moses' disciples.

29 We know that God spake unto Moses: *as for* this *fellow,* [a]we know not from whence he is.

30 The man answered and said unto them, [a]Why herein is a marvellous *thing,* that ye know not from whence he is, and *yet* he hath opened mine eyes.

31 Now we know that [a]God heareth not sinners: but if any *man* be a worshipper of God, and doeth his will, him he heareth.

32 Since the world began was it not heard that any *man* opened the eyes of one that was born blind.

33 [a]If this *man* were not of God, he could do nothing.

34 They answered and said unto him, [a]Thou wast altogether born in sins, and dost thou teach us? And they [1]cast him out.

9:7 [a]Neh. 3:15 [b]See 2 Ki. 5:14
9:11 [a]ver. 6,7
9:16 [a]ver. 33; ch. 3:2 [b]ch. 7:12,43; 10:19
9:17 [a]ch. 4:19; 6:14
9:22 [a]ch. 7:13; 12:42; 19:38; Acts 5:13 [b]ver. 34; ch. 16:2
9:24 [a]Josh. 7:19; 1 Sam. 6:5 [b]ver. 16
9:29 [a]ch. 8:14
9:30 [a]ch. 3:10
9:31 [a]Job 27:9; 35:12; Ps. 18:41; 34:15; 66:18; Prov. 1:28; 15:29; 28:9; Is. 1:15; Jer. 11:11; 14:12; Ezek. 8:18; Mic. 3:4; Zech. 7:13
9:33 [a]ver. 16
9:34 [1]Or, *excommunicated him* [a]ver. 2

9:7 *Siloam.* Already an ancient name (see notes on 2 Ki 20:20; Neh 2:14; Job 28:10; Is 8:6). A rock-cut pool on the southern end of the main ridge on which Jerusalem was built, it served as part of the major water system developed by King Hezekiah. *Sent.* Or "one who has been sent."

9:8 *begged.* Not mentioned previously, but it was about the only way a blind person of that day could support himself.

9:13 *Pharisees.* See notes on Mat 3:7; Mark 2:16; Luke 5:17.

9:14 *sabbath.* Cf. 5:16 and the discussion that follows.

9:16 *some . . . Others.* The first group started from their entrenched position and ruled out the possibility of Jesus' being from God. The second started from the fact of the miraculous signs and ruled out the possibility of His being a sinner (cf. vv. 31–33).

9:17 *What sayest thou of him . . . ?* It is curious that they put such a question to such a person; their doing so reflected their perplexity. *a prophet.* Probably the highest designation of which the man could think. He progressed in his thinking about Jesus: from a man (v. 11), to a prophet (v. 17) who might be followed by disciples (v. 27), to one "from God" (v. 33), to one who was properly to be worshiped (v. 38).

9:18 *the Jews.* See note on 1:19. In their prejudice they did not learn from the sign but tried to discredit the miracle.

9:21 *he is of age.* There was much to which the parents could not testify, but their emphasis on the son's responsibility showed their fear of getting involved.

9:22 *put out of the synagogue.* Excommunication is reported as early as the time of Ezra (10:8), but there is practically no information about the way it was practiced in NT times. The synagogue was the center of Jewish community life, so excommunication cut a person off from many social relationships (though, in some of its forms, at least in later times, not from worship).

9:24 *we.* Emphatic in the Greek.

9:27 *will ye also be his disciples?* The man already counted himself a disciple.

9:30–33 Good reasoning from an unschooled man.

9:31 *God heareth not sinners.* Cf. the remark of some of the Pharisees in v. 16.

‡9:34 *cast him out.* May mean "expelled him physically from their assembly" or, more probably, "excommunicated him" (see note on v. 22).

Jesus talks to the healed man

35 Jesus heard that they had cast him out; and when he had found him, he said unto him, Dost thou believe on [a]the Son of God?

36 He answered and said, Who is he, Lord, that I might believe on him?

37 And Jesus said unto him, Thou hast both seen him, and [a]it is he that talketh with thee.

38 And he said, Lord, I believe. And he worshipped him.

39 ¶ And Jesus said, [a]For judgment I am come into this world, [b]that they which see not might see; and that they which see might be made blind.

40 And *some* of the Pharisees which were with him heard these *words,* [a]and said unto him, Are we blind also?

41 Jesus said unto them, [a]If ye were blind, ye should have no sin: but now ye say, We see; therefore your sin remaineth.

Jesus the good shepherd

10 Verily, verily, I say unto you, He that entereth not by the door into the sheepfold, but climbeth up some other way, the same is a thief and a robber.

2 But he that entereth in by the door is the shepherd of the sheep.

3 To him the porter openeth; and the sheep hear his voice: and he calleth his own sheep by name, and leadeth them out.

4 And when he putteth forth his own sheep, he goeth before them, and the sheep follow him: for they know his voice.

9:35 [a]Mat. 14:33; 16:16; Mark 1:1; ch. 10:36; 1 John 5:13
9:37 [a]ch. 4:26
9:39 [a]ch. 5:22,27; See ch. 3:17; 12:47 [b]Mat. 13:13
9:40 [a]Rom. 2:19
9:41 [a]ch. 15:22,24

10:9 [a]ch. 14:6; Eph. 2:18
10:11 [a]Is. 40:11; Ezek. 34:12,23; 37:24; Heb. 13:20; 1 Pet. 2:25; 5:4
10:12 [a]Zech. 11:16,17
10:14 [a]2 Tim. 2:19
10:15 [a]Mat. 11:27 [b]ch. 15:13
10:16 [a]Is. 56:8

5 And a stranger will they not follow, but will flee from him: for they know not the voice of strangers.

6 This parable spake Jesus unto them: but they understood not what *things* they were which he spake unto them.

7 ¶ Then said Jesus unto them again, Verily, verily, I say unto you, I am the door of the sheep.

8 All that ever came before me are thieves and robbers: but the sheep did not hear them.

9 [a]I am the door: by me if any *man* enter in, he shall be saved, and shall go in and out, and find pasture.

10 The thief cometh not, but for to steal, and to kill, and to destroy: I am come that they might have life, and that they might have *it more* abundantly.

11 [a]I am the good shepherd: the good shepherd giveth his life for the sheep.

12 But *he that is* a hireling, and not the shepherd, whose own the sheep are not, seeth the wolf coming, and [a]leaveth the sheep, and fleeth: and the wolf catcheth them, and scattereth the sheep.

13 The hireling fleeth, because he is a hireling, and careth not for the sheep.

14 I am the good shepherd, and [a]know my *sheep,* and am known of mine.

15 [a]As the Father knoweth me, *even* so know I the Father: [b]and I lay down my life for the sheep.

16 And [a]other sheep I have, which are not of this fold: them also I must bring, and they

9:35 *found him.* Jesus obviously had been looking for the man.

9:36 The man was ready to follow any suggestion from his benefactor.

9:38 *Lord . . . he worshipped him.* The man was giving Jesus the reverence due to God. *I believe.* See 20:31 and note on 1:7.

9:39 It is unlikely that the conversation of vv. 35–38 took place in the presence of the Pharisees. The incident of vv. 39–41, therefore, probably occurred a little later. *For judgment.* In a sense Jesus did not come for judgment (3:17; 12:47), but His coming divides people, and this always brings a type of judgment. Those who reject His gift end up "blind."

9:40 *Pharisees.* They found it incredible that anyone would consider them spiritually blind.

9:41 The Pharisees' claim to sight showed their complete unawareness of their spiritual blindness and need. And, though they claimed to have sight, their actions were evidence of their blindness.

10:1–30 Should be understood in light of the OT (and ancient Near Eastern) concept of "shepherd," symbolizing a royal caretaker of God's people. God Himself was called the "Shepherd of Israel" (Ps 80:1; cf. Ps 23:1; Is 40:10–11; Ezek 34:11–16), and He had given great responsibility to the leaders ("shepherds") of Israel, which they failed to respect. God denounced these false shepherds (see Is 56:9–12; Ezek 34) and promised to provide the true Shepherd, the Messiah, to care for the sheep (Ezek 34:23).

‡10:1 *sheepfold.* A court surrounded by walls but open to the sky, and with only one entrance. The walls kept the sheep from wandering and no doubt protected them from certain wild animals.

10:3 *the porter.* Apparently in charge of a large fold, where several flocks were kept. *his voice.* The sheep recognized the voice of their own shepherd and responded only to him. *his own sheep.* The shepherd did not call sheep randomly, but only those that belonged to him.

10:4 *he goeth before them.* The Palestinian shepherd led his sheep (he did not drive them), and the sheep followed because they knew his voice.

10:7 *I am.* See note on 6:35.

10:8 *All . . . before me.* "False shepherds" like the Pharisees and the chief priests, not the true OT prophets (see note on vv. 1–30).

10:9 *the door.* The one way into salvation. Inside there is safety, and one is able to go out and find pasture, i.e., the supply of all needs.

10:10 *thief.* His interest is in himself. Christ's interest is in His sheep, whom He enables to have life to the full (see note on 1:4).

10:11 *I am.* See note on 6:35. *giveth his life.* A shepherd might risk danger for his sheep (see Gen 31:39; 1 Sam 17:34–37), but he expected to come through alive. Jesus said that the good shepherd will die for his sheep.

10:12 *hireling.* He is interested in wages, not sheep. In time of danger he runs away because of what he is (v. 13) and abandons the flock to predators.

10:14 *know . . . am known of mine.* A deep mutual knowledge, like that of the Father and the Son.

10:15 *I lay down my life.* See v. 11; the fact of central importance.

10:16 *other sheep.* These already belonged to Christ, though they had not yet been brought to Him. *not of this fold.* Those

shall hear my voice; [b]and there shall be one
fold, *and* one shepherd.
17 Therefore doth *my* Father love me, [a]be-
cause I lay down my life, that I might take it
again.
18 No *man* taketh it from me, but I lay it
down of myself. I have power to lay it down,
and I [a]have power to take it again. [b]This commandment have I received of my Father.
19 [a]There was a division therefore again
among the Jews for these sayings.
20 And many of them said, [a]He hath a devil, and is mad; why hear ye him?
21 Others said, These are not the words of
him that hath a devil. [a]Can a devil [b]open the
eyes of the blind?

The Jews try to arrest Jesus

22 ¶ And it was at Jerusalem *the feast of*
the dedication, and it was winter.
23 And Jesus walked in the temple [a]in Solomon's porch.
24 Then came the Jews round about him,
and said unto him, How long dost thou [1]make
us to doubt? If thou be the Christ, tell us
plainly.
25 Jesus answered them, I told you, and ye
believe not: [a]the works that I do in my Father's name, they bear witness of me.

10:16 [b]Ezek. 37:22; Eph. 2:14; 1 Pet. 2:25
10:17 [a]Is. 53:7,8,12; Heb. 2:9
10:18 [a]ch. 2:19 [b]ch. 6:38; 15:10; Acts 2:24,32
10:19 [a]ch. 7:43; 9:16
10:20 [a]ch. 7:20; 8:48,52
10:21 [a]Ex. 4:11; Ps. 94:9; 146:8 [b]ch. 9:6,7,32,33
10:23 [a]Acts 3:11; 5:12
10:24 [1]Or, *hold us in suspense?*
10:25 [a]ver. 38; ch. 3:2; 5:36

10:26 [a]ch. 8:47
10:27 [a]ver. 4,14
10:29 [a]ch. 14:28 [b]ch. 17:2,6
10:30 [a]ch. 17:11,22
10:31 [a]ch. 8:59
10:33 [a]ch. 5:18
10:34 [a]Ps. 82:6
10:35 [a]Rom. 13:1
10:36 [a]ch. 6:27 [b]ch. 3:17; 5:36,37; 8:42 [c]ver. 30; ch. 5:17,18 [d]Luke 1:35; ch. 9:35,37

26 But [a]ye believe not, because ye are not
of my sheep, as I said unto you.
27 [a]My sheep hear my voice, and I know
them, and they follow me:
28 And I give unto them eternal life; and
they shall never perish, neither shall any *man*
pluck them out of my hand.
29 [a]My Father, [b]which gave *them* me, is
greater than all; and no *man* is able to pluck
them out of my Father's hand.
30 [a]I and *my* Father are one.
31 Then [a]the Jews took up stones again to
stone him.
32 Jesus answered them, Many good works
have I shewed you from my Father; for which
of those works do ye stone me?
33 The Jews answered him, saying, For a
good work we stone thee not; but for blasphemy; and because that thou, being a man,
[a]makest thyself God.
34 Jesus answered them, [a]Is it not written
in your law, I said, Ye are gods?
35 If he called them gods, [a]unto whom the
word of God came, and the scripture cannot
be broken;
36 Say ye *of him,* [a]whom the Father hath
sanctified, and [b]sent into the world, Thou
blasphemest; [c]because I said, I am [d]the Son of
God?

outside Judaism. Here is a glimpse of the future worldwide scope of the church. *one fold.* All God's people have the same Shepherd (see 17:20–23).

‡10:17–18 That Christ would die for His people runs through this section of John's Gospel. Both the love and the plan of the Father are involved, as well as the authority He gave to the Son. Christ obediently chose to die; otherwise, no one would have had the power to kill him. *I have power to take it again.* Jesus effected his own resurrection. However, the Father and the Holy Spirit were also involved. See Rom 8:11 and 1 Pet 3:18.

10:19 *division.* See 7:43; 9:16.

10:20 *hath a devil.* See note on 7:20.

10:21 Cf. 9:16.

‡10:22 *feast of the dedication.* The commemoration of the dedication of the temple by Judas Maccabeus in December, 165 B.C., after it had been profaned by Antiochus Epiphanes (see notes on Ezra 6:16; Dan 8:9–12). This was the last great deliverance the Jews had experienced. This is what modern Jews celebrate at Hannukah. Its origination antedates Christmas. *it was winter.* A description for those unfamiliar with the Jewish calendar.

10:23 *Solomon's porch.* See Acts 3:11; 5:12. It was a roofed structure—somewhat similar to a Greek stoa—commonly but erroneously thought to date back to Solomon's time.

10:24 *the Christ.* See note on 1:25 and cf. 20:31. This was the critical question, but it was not easy to answer because of the different ideas of Messiahship then in vogue.

10:25 *I told you.* Jesus had not specifically affirmed His Messiahship except to the Samaritan woman (4:26). He may have meant here that the general thrust of His teaching made His claim clear or that such statements as that in 8:58 were sufficient. Or He may have been referring to the evidence of His whole manner of life (including the miracles)—all He had done in the Father's name (for the name see note on 2:23).

10:26 *not of my sheep.* Their failure to believe arose from what they were.

10:27 *voice.* Cf. vv. 3–5. *I know them.* Cf. v. 14. *they follow.* Cf. vv. 4–5.

10:28 *eternal life.* Christ's gift (see note on 3:15). *never perish.* The Greek construction here is a strong denial that the sheep will ever perish. The sheep's security is in the power of the shepherd, who will let no one take them from him.

10:29 *My Father.* See note on 5:17. *is able.* The Father's power ("hand") is greater than that of any enemy, making the sheep completely secure.

10:30 *one.* The Greek is neuter—"one thing," not "one person." The two are one in essence or nature, but they are not identical persons. This great truth is what warrants Jesus' "I am" declarations (see 8:24,28,58 and note on 6:35; see also 17:21–22).

10:31 *the Jews.* See note on 1:19. *to stone him.* They took Jesus' words as blasphemy, and therefore prepared to carry out the law (Lev 24:16), though without due process.

10:32 *good works.* As, e.g., in Mat 5:16; 1 Tim 5:10,25; 6:18. Although the reference here includes Jesus' miracles, the underlying Greek words refer to works in general that are fine and noble in character first of all (see note on v. 38).

‡10:33 *blasphemy.* The Jewish leaders correctly understood the thrust of Jesus' words, but their preconceptions and unbelief prevented them from accepting His claim as true. *makest thyself God.* The Jews clearly understood Jesus to claim that He was God.

10:34 *your law.* In its strictest sense the term meant the Pentateuch, but was often used, as here, of the whole OT. *Ye are gods.* The words Jesus quotes from Ps 82:6 refer to the judges (or other leaders or rulers), whose tasks were divinely appointed (see Ex 22:28 and note; Deut 1:17; 16:18; 2 Chr 19:6).

10:35 *scripture cannot be broken.* Jesus testified to the complete authority and reliability of the OT.

10:36 If there is any sense in which men can be spoken of as "gods" (as Ps 82:6 speaks of human rulers or judges), how much more may the term be used of Him whom the Father set apart and sent!

37 [a]If I do not the works of my Father, believe me not.

38 But if I do, though ye believe not me, [a]believe the works: that ye may know, and believe, [b]that the Father *is* in me, and I in him.

39 [a]Therefore they sought again to take him: but he escaped out of their hand,

40 And went away again beyond Jordan into the place [a]where John at first baptized; and there he abode.

41 And many resorted unto him, and said, John did no miracle: [a]but all *things* that John spake of this *man* were true.

42 [a]And many believed on him there.

Jesus hears of Lazarus's death

11 Now a certain *man* was sick, *named* Lazarus, of Bethany, the town of [a]Mary and her sister Martha.

2 ([a]It was *that* Mary which anointed the Lord with ointment, and wiped his feet with her hair, whose brother Lazarus was sick.)

3 Therefore *his* sisters sent unto him, saying, Lord, behold, he whom thou lovest is sick.

4 When Jesus heard *that,* he said, This sickness is not unto death, [a]but for the glory of God, that the Son of God might be glorified thereby.

5 Now Jesus loved Martha, and her sister, and Lazarus.

6 When he had heard therefore that he was sick, [a]he abode two days *still* in the *same* place where he was.

7 Then after that saith he to *his* disciples, Let us go into Judea again.

8 *His* disciples say unto him, Master, [a]the Jews of late sought to stone thee; and goest thou thither again?

10:37 [a]ch. 15:24
10:38 [a]ch. 5:36; 14:10,11 [b]ch. 14:10,11; 17:21
10:39 [a]ch. 7:30,44; 8:59
10:40 [a]ch. 1:28
10:41 [a]ch. 3:30
10:42 [a]ch. 8:30; 11:45
11:1 [a]Luke 10:38,39
11:2 [a]Mat. 26:7; Mark 14:3; ch. 12:3
11:4 [a]ver. 40; ch. 9:3
11:6 [a]ch. 10:40
11:8 [a]ch. 10:31

11:9 [a]ch. 9:4
11:10 [a]ch. 12:35
11:11 [a]Deut. 31:16; Dan. 12:2; Mat. 9:24; Acts 7:60; 1 Cor. 15:18,51
11:18 [1]That is, *about two mile*

9 Jesus answered, Are there not twelve hours in the day? [a]If any *man* walk in the day, he stumbleth not, because he seeth the light of this world.

10 But [a]if a man walk in the night, he stumbleth, because there is no light in him.

11 These *things* said he: and after that he saith unto them, Our friend Lazarus [a]sleepeth; but I go, that I may awake him out of sleep.

12 Then said his disciples, Lord, if he sleep, he shall do well.

13 Howbeit Jesus spake of his death: but they thought that he had spoken of taking of rest in sleep.

14 Then said Jesus unto them plainly, Lazarus is dead.

15 And I am glad for your sakes that I was not there, to the intent ye may believe; nevertheless let us go unto him.

16 Then said Thomas, which is called Didymus, unto *his* fellow-disciples, Let us also go, that we may die with him.

Jesus the resurrection and the life

17 ¶ Then when Jesus came, he found that he had *lien* in the grave four days already.

18 Now Bethany was nigh unto Jerusalem, [1]about fifteen furlongs off:

19 And many of the Jews came to Martha and Mary, to comfort them concerning their brother.

20 Then Martha, as soon as she heard that Jesus was coming, went and met him: but Mary sat *still* in the house.

21 Then said Martha unto Jesus, Lord, if thou hadst been here, my brother had not died.

10:37 *the works of my Father.* The kind of works of compassion that the Father Himself does.

10:38 *works.* The miracles were a part of Jesus' works. It was Jesus' quality of life, not people's inability to explain His marvels, that He primarily spoke of here (see note on v. 32).

10:39 *they sought again to take him.* It is not clear if this was to arrest Him for trial or to take Him out for stoning. *he escaped.* John does not say why they failed, but he often makes it clear that Jesus could not be killed before the appointed time (see note on 2:4; see also Luke 4:30).

10:41 *all things that John spake.* For John the Baptist as a witness see 1:7 and note.

11:1 *Lazarus.* Mentioned only in chs. 11–12 of John's Gospel (the name is found also in the parable of Luke 16:19–31). The sisters are mentioned in Luke 10:38–42.

11:2 *anointed . . . with ointment.* See 12:3.

11:3 *he whom thou lovest.* The relationship must have been exceptionally close.

11:4 Cf. 9:3. *This sickness is not unto death.* Thus predicting the raising of Lazarus (v. 44), since Jesus already knew of his death (v. 14). In fact, Lazarus must have died shortly after the messengers left Bethany, accounting for the "four days" of vv. 17,39: one day for the journey of the messengers, the two days when Jesus remained where He was (v. 6; see 10:40), and a day for Jesus' journey to Bethany. But see note on v. 17. *glory.* See notes on 7:39; 12:41; 13:31. Here God's Son would be glorified through what happened to Lazarus, partly because the miracle displays the glory of God (who alone can raise the dead; see 5:21) in Jesus (v. 40) and partly because it would help initiate events leading to the cross (vv. 46–53).

11:6 *he abode . . . where he was.* Jesus moved as the Father directed, not as people (here Mary and Martha) wished (cf. 2:3–4).

11:8 *the Jews.* See note on 1:19. *sought to stone thee.* See note on 10:31. There was clear danger in going into Judea.

11:9 *twelve hours.* Enough time for what must be done, but no time for waste.

11:11 *sleepeth.* A euphemism for death, used by the unbelieving world as well as by Christians.

11:15 *believe.* Cf. 20:31.

‡11:16 *Thomas . . . Didymus.* The Hebrew word from which we get "Thomas" and the Greek word *Didymus* both mean "twin." We usually remember Thomas for his doubting, but he was also capable of devotion and courage, as perhaps here.

11:17 *four days.* See note on v. 4. Many Jews believed that the soul remained near the body for three days after death in the hope of returning to it. If this idea was in the minds of these people, they obviously thought all hope was gone—Lazarus was irrevocably dead.

11:19 *to comfort them.* Jewish custom provided for three days of very heavy mourning, then four of heavy mourning, followed by lighter mourning for the remainder of 30 days. It was usual for friends to visit the family to comfort them.

11:20 *she . . . went and met him.* Perhaps because as the elder she was hostess.

11:21 Repeated by Mary in v. 32. Perhaps the sisters had said this to one another often as they awaited Jesus' arrival.

22 But I know, that even now, [a]whatsoever thou wilt ask of God, God will give *it* thee.

23 Jesus saith unto her, Thy brother shall rise again.

24 Martha saith unto him, [a]I know that he shall rise again in the resurrection at the last day.

25 Jesus said unto her, I am [a]the resurrection, and the life: [b]he that believeth in me, though he were dead, *yet* shall he live:

26 And whosoever liveth and believeth in me shall never die. Believest thou this?

27 She saith unto him, Yea, Lord: [a]I believe that thou art the Christ, the Son of God, which should come into the world.

28 And when she had so said, she went her way, and called Mary her sister secretly, saying, The Master is come, and calleth for thee.

29 As soon as she heard *that,* she arose quickly, and came unto him.

30 Now Jesus was not yet come into the town, but was in *that* place where Martha met him.

31 [a]The Jews then which were with her in the house, and comforted her, when they saw Mary, that she rose up hastily and went out, followed her, saying, She goeth unto the grave to weep there.

32 Then when Mary was come where Jesus was, and saw him, she fell down at his feet, saying unto him, [a]Lord, if thou hadst been here, my brother had not died.

33 When Jesus therefore saw her weeping, and the Jews also weeping which came with her, he groaned in the spirit, and [1]was troubled,

34 And said, Where have ye laid him? They say unto him, Lord, come and see.

35 [a]Jesus wept.

36 Then said the Jews, Behold, how he loved him.

11:22 [a]ch. 9:31
11:24 [a]Luke 14:14; ch. 5:29
11:25 [a]ch. 5:21; 6:39,40,44 [b]ch. 3:36; 1 John 5:10
11:27 [a]Mat. 16:16; ch. 4:42; 6:14,69
11:31 [a]ver. 19
11:32 [a]ver. 21
11:33 [1]Gr. *he troubled himself*
11:35 [a]Luke 19:41

11:37 [a]ch. 9:6
11:40 [a]ver. 4,23
11:42 [a]ch. 12:30
11:44 [a]ch. 20:7
11:45 [a]ch. 2:23; 10:42; 12:11,18
11:47 [a]Ps. 2:2; Mat. 26:3; Mark 14:1; Luke 22:2 [b]ch. 12:19; Acts 4:16

37 And some of them said, Could not this *man,* [a]which opened the eyes of the blind, have caused that even this *man* should not have died?

Jesus raises Lazarus

38 Jesus therefore again groaning in himself cometh to the grave. It was a cave, and a stone lay upon it.

39 Jesus said, Take ye away the stone. Martha, the sister of him that was dead, saith unto him, Lord, by this time he stinketh: for he hath been *dead* four days.

40 Jesus saith unto her, Said I not unto thee, that, if thou wouldest believe, thou shouldest [a]see the glory of God?

41 Then they took away the stone *from the place* where the dead was laid. And Jesus lift up *his* eyes, and said, Father, I thank thee that thou hast heard me.

42 And I knew that thou hearest me always: but [a]because of the people which stand by I said *it,* that they may believe that thou hast sent me.

43 And when he thus had spoken, he cried with a loud voice, Lazarus, come forth.

44 And he that was dead came forth, bound hand and foot with graveclothes: and [a]his face was bound about with a napkin. Jesus saith unto them, Loose him, and let *him* go.

Pharisees plot to kill Jesus

45 ¶ Then many of the Jews which came to Mary, [a]and had seen *the things* which Jesus did, believed on him.

46 But some of them went their ways to the Pharisees, and told them what *things* Jesus had done.

47 [a]Then gathered the chief priests and the Pharisees a council, and said, [b]What do we? for this man doeth many miracles.

11:22 *whatsoever thou wilt ask.* This comment seems to mean that Martha hoped for an immediate resurrection in spite of the fact that Lazarus's body had already begun to decay. Nothing is too difficult for God to do.

11:25 *I am.* See note on 6:35. *life.* See note on 1:4. Jesus was saying more than that He gives resurrection and life. In some way these are identified with Him, and His nature is such that final death is impossible for Him. He is life (cf. 14:6; Acts 3:15; Heb 7:16). *he that believeth . . . shall he live.* See note on 1:7. Jesus not only is life but conveys life to the believer so that death will never triumph over him (cf. 1 Cor 15:54–57).

11:27 *I believe.* Martha is often remembered for her shortcoming recorded in Luke 10:40–41. But she was a woman of faith, as this magnificent declaration shows.

11:28 *The Master.* Or "the Teacher," a significant description to be given by a woman. The rabbis would not teach women (cf. 4:27), but Jesus taught them frequently.

11:31 *to weep there.* Wailing at a tomb was common, and the Jews immediately thought this was in Mary's mind. Because they followed her, Jesus got maximum publicity.

11:32 Cf. v. 21.

11:33 *weeping.* Both times the word denotes a loud expression of grief, i.e., "wailing." *troubled.* See note on 12:27; cf. 13:21.

11:35 *wept.* The Greek for this word is not the one for loud grief, as in v. 33, but one that denotes quiet weeping, i.e., "shed tears."

11:36 Cf. v. 5.

11:37 Their position was like that of Martha (v. 21) and Mary (v. 32), but they based it on Jesus' ability to give sight to the blind (cf. ch. 9).

11:39 *four days.* See notes on vv. 4,17.

11:40 *glory.* See note on v. 4.

11:44 *graveclothes.* Narrow strips, like bandages. Sometimes a shroud was used (see note on 19:40). *a napkin.* A separate item.

11:45 *many of the Jews . . . believed on him.* Perhaps some who had been opposed to Jesus now came to believe (see note on 1:19; cf. 20:31).

11:46 *Pharisees.* See notes on Mat 3:7; Mark 2:16; Luke 5:17.

11:47 *the chief priests and the Pharisees.* In all four Gospels the Pharisees appear as Jesus' principal opponents throughout His public ministry. But they lacked political power, and it is the chief priests who were prominent in the events that led to Jesus' crucifixion. Here both groups are associated in a meeting of the Sanhedrin (see note on Mark 14:55). They did not deny the reality of the miraculous signs (see note on 2:11), but they did not understand their meaning, for they failed to believe.

48 If we let him thus alone, all *men* will believe on him: and the Romans shall come and
take away both our place and nation.
49 And one of them, *named* [a]Caiaphas, being the high priest that *same* year, said unto
them, Ye know nothing at all,
50 [a]Nor consider that it is expedient for
us, that one man should die for the people,
and *that* the whole nation perish not.
51 And this spake he not of himself: but
being high priest that year, he prophesied that
Jesus should die for *that* nation;
52 And [a]not for *that* nation only, [b]but that
also he should gather together in one the children of God that were scattered abroad.
53 Then from that day forth they took
counsel together for to put him to death.
54 Jesus [a]therefore walked no more openly
among the Jews; but went thence unto a country
near to the wilderness, into a city called [b]Ephra-
im, and there continued with his disciples.
55 [a]And the Jews' passover was nigh at
hand: and many went out of the country up to
Jerusalem before the passover, to purify themselves.
56 [a]Then sought they for Jesus, and spake
among themselves, as they stood in the temple, What think ye, that he will not come to
the feast?
57 Now both the chief priests and the
Pharisees had given a commandment, that, if
any *man* knew where he were, he should
shew *it,* that they might take him.

11:49 [a]Luke 3:2; ch. 18:14; Acts 4:6
11:50 [a]ch. 18:14
11:52 [a]Is. 49:6; 1 John 2:2 [b]ch. 10:16; Eph. 2:14-17
11:54 [a]ch. 4:1,3; 7:1 [b]See 2 Chr. 13:19
11:55 [a]ch. 2:13; 5:1; 6:4
11:56 [a]ch. 7:11

12:1 [a]ch. 11:1,43
12:2 [a]Mat. 26:6; Mark 14:3
12:3 [a]Luke 10:38,39; ch. 11:2
12:6 [a]ch. 13:29
12:8 [a]Mat. 26:11; Mark 14:7
12:9 [a]ch. 11:43,44
12:10 [a]Luke 16:31
12:11 [a]ver. 18; ch. 11:45

Jesus anointed at Bethany

12 Then Jesus six days before the
passover came to Bethany, [a]where
Lazarus was which had been dead, whom he
raised from the dead.
2 [a]There they made him a supper; and
Martha served: but Lazarus was one of them
that sat at the table with him.
3 Then took [a]Mary a pound of ointment of
spikenard, very costly, and anointed the feet of
Jesus, and wiped his feet with her hair: and
the house was filled with the odour of the ointment.
4 Then saith one of his disciples, Judas Iscariot, Simon's *son,* which should betray him,
5 Why was not this ointment sold for three
hundred pence, and given to the poor?
6 This he said, not that he cared for the
poor; but because he was a thief, and [a]had the
bag, and bare what was put *therein.*
7 Then said Jesus, Let her alone: against
the day of my burying hath she kept this.
8 For [a]the poor always ye have with you;
but me ye have not always.
9 ¶ Much people of the Jews therefore
knew that he was there: and they came not for
Jesus' sake only, but that they might see Lazarus also, [a]whom he had raised from the dead.
10 [a]But the chief priests consulted that
they might put Lazarus also to death;
11 [a]Because that by reason of him many of
the Jews went away, and believed on Jesus.

11:48 *place.* Probably the temple (see Acts 6:13–14; 21:28), though sometimes the Jews used the expression to denote Jerusalem.

11:49 *Caiaphas.* High priest C. A.D. 18–36. He was the son-in-law of Annas (18:13), who had been deposed from the high priesthood by the Romans in A.D. 15. *high priest that same year.* Means "high priest at that time." The high priesthood was not an annual office but one supposed to be held for life. *Ye know nothing at all.* A remark typical of Sadducean rudeness (Caiaphas, as high priest, was a Sadducee). Josephus says that Sadducees "in their intercourse with their peers are as rude as to aliens." For Sadducees see notes on Mat 2:4; 3:7; Mark 12:18; Luke 20:27; Acts 4:1.

11:50 *expedient.* Caiaphas was concerned with political expediency, not with guilt and innocence. He believed that one man, no matter how innocent, should perish rather than that the nation be put in jeopardy. Ironically, the Jews went ahead with their execution of Jesus, and in A.D. 70 the nation still perished.

11:51 *being high priest.* Caiaphas was not a private citizen but was God's high priest, and God overruled in what he said. *that year.* See note on v. 49. *prophesied.* His words were true in a way he could not imagine. Prophecy in Scripture is the impartation of divinely revealed truth. In reality Caiaphas's words meant that Jesus' death would be for the nation, not by way of removing political trouble, but by taking away the sins of those who believed in Him.

11:52 *the children of God . . . scattered abroad.* Jesus' death would have effects far beyond the nation (cf. 1:29; 3:16; 4:42; 10:16; etc.).

11:54 *went thence.* Jesus was not to die before His "time" (see note on 2:4), but He would not act imprudently. Knowing the attitude of His opponents, He withdrew. He would die for others, but in His own time, not that of His enemies. *Ephraim.* If it was the city known as Ophrah, it was about 15 miles north of Jerusalem.

11:55 *passover.* See notes on 2:13; 5:1. *to purify themselves.* Especially important at a time like passover, because without it, it would not be possible to keep the feast (cf. 18:28; see note on 2:6).

12:1–11 All four Gospels have an account of a woman anointing Jesus. John's account seems to tell of the same incident recorded in Mat 26:6–13 and Mark 14:3–9, while that in Luke 7:36–50 is different.

12:1 *Bethany.* See note on Mat 21:17.

12:3 *spikenard.* The name of both a plant and the fragrant oil it yielded. Since it was very expensive, Mary's act of devotion was costly. It was also an unusual act, both because she poured the oil on Jesus' feet (normally it was poured on the head) and because she used her hair to wipe them (a respectable woman did not unbind her hair in public). Further, it showed her humility, for it was a servant's work to attend to the feet (see notes on 1:27; 13:5).

12:4 *Judas Iscariot.* See note on 6:71.

12:6 *a thief.* The one passage from which we learn that Judas was dishonest. Yet he must have been thought to be a man of some reliability, for he was keeper of the money bag.

12:7 *kept.* Probably the meaning is "save for this purpose." Perfume was normally associated with festivity, but it was also used in burials (see 19:39–40), and Jesus links it with His burial, which Mary's act unwittingly anticipates.

12:9 *Jews.* See note on 1:19.

12:10 The Jewish leaders previously had spoken of the death of one man (11:50), but now they wanted another death. Sin grows.

The triumphal entry

12 ¶ [a]On the next day much people that
were come to the feast, when they heard that
Jesus was coming to Jerusalem,
13 Took branches of palm trees, and went
forth to meet him, and cried, [a]Hosanna:
Blessed *is* the King of Israel that cometh in the
name of the Lord.
14 [a]And Jesus, when he had found a young
ass, sat thereon; as it is written,
15 [a]Fear not, daughter of Sion: behold, thy
King cometh, sitting on an ass's colt.
16 These *things* [a]understood not his disciples at the first: [b]but when Jesus was glorified,
[c]then remembered they that these *things*
were written of him, and *that* they had done
these *things* unto him.
17 The people therefore that was with him
when he called Lazarus out of *his* grave, and
raised him from the dead, bare record.
18 [a]For this cause the people also met him,
for that they heard that he had done this miracle.
19 The Pharisees therefore said among
themselves, [a]Perceive ye how ye prevail nothing? behold, the world is gone after him.

Jesus sought by the Gentiles

20 ¶ And there [a]were certain Greeks
among them [b]that came up to worship at the
feast:
21 The same came therefore to Philip,
[a]which was of Bethsaida of Galilee, and desired him, saying, Sir, we would see Jesus.

12:12 [a]Mat. 21:8; Mark 11:8; Luke 19:35,36
12:13 [a]Ps. 118:25,26
12:14 [a]Mat. 21:7
12:15 [a]Zech. 9:9
12:16 [a]Luke 18:34 [b]ch. 7:39 [c]ch. 14:26
12:18 [a]ver. 11
12:19 [a]ch. 11:47,48
12:20 [a]Acts 17:4 [b]1 Ki. 8:41,42; Acts 8:27
12:21 [a]ch. 1:44
12:23 [a]ch. 13:32; 17:1
12:24 [a]1 Cor. 15:36
12:25 [a]Mat. 10:39; 16:25; Mark 8:35; Luke 9:24; 17:33
12:26 [a]ch. 14:3; 17:24; 1 Thes. 4:17
12:27 [a]Mat. 26:38,39; Luke 12:50; ch. 13:21 [b]Luke 22:53; ch. 18:37
12:28 [a]Mat. 3:17
12:30 [a]ch. 11:42
12:31 [a]Mat. 12:29; Luke 10:18; ch. 14:30; 16:11; Acts 26:18; 2 Cor. 4:4; Eph. 2:2; 6:12
12:32 [a]ch. 3:14; 8:28 [b]Rom. 5:18; Heb. 2:9
12:33 [a]ch. 18:32
12:34 [a]Ps. 89:36,37; 110:4; Is. 9:7; 53:8; Ezek. 37:25; Dan. 2:44; 7:14,27; Mic. 4:7

22 Philip cometh and telleth Andrew: and
again Andrew and Philip tell Jesus.
23 And Jesus answered them, saying, [a]The
hour is come, that the Son of man should be
glorified.
24 Verily, verily, I say unto you, [a]Except a
corn of wheat fall into the ground and die, it
abideth alone: but if it die, it bringeth forth
much fruit.
25 [a]He that loveth his life shall lose it; and
he that hateth his life in this world shall keep
it unto life eternal.
26 If any *man* serve me, let him follow me;
and [a]where I am, there shall also my servant
be: if any *man* serve me, him will *my* Father
honour.
27 [a]Now is my soul troubled; and what
shall I say? Father, save me from this hour:
[b]but for this cause came I unto this hour.
28 Father, glorify thy name. [a]Then came
there a voice from heaven, *saying,* I have both
glorified *it,* and will glorify *it* again.
29 The people therefore, that stood *by,* and
heard *it,* said that it thundered: others said, An
angel spake to him.
30 Jesus answered and said, [a]This voice
came not because of me, but for your sakes.
31 Now is the judgment of this world: now
shall [a]the prince of this world be cast out.
32 And I, [a]if I be lifted up from the earth,
will draw [b]all *men* unto me.
33 [a]This he said, signifying what death he
should die.
34 The people answered him, [a]We have

12:12 *much people.* Pilgrims who had come up from the country for the passover feast. Many of the pilgrims had doubtless seen and heard Jesus in Galilee, and they welcomed the opportunity to proclaim Him as Messiah.

12:13 *branches of palm trees.* Used in celebration of victory. John saw a multitude with palm branches in heaven (Rev 7:9). *Hosanna.* A Hebrew expression meaning "Save!" that became an exclamation of praise (see note on Jer 31:7). *the King of Israel.* The people's addition to the words of the psalm (see Ps 118:25,26), which John alone records. It reflects his special interest in Jesus' royalty, which he brings out throughout the passion narrative. *the name.* See note on 2:23.

12:14 *young ass.* See notes on Zech 9:9; Mat 21:2,7; Mark 11:2; Luke 19:30.

12:16 An example of the meaning of 16:13. *glorified.* See notes on v. 41; 11:4; 13:31. Only after the crucifixion and the coming of the Holy Spirit did the disciples appreciate the meaning of the prophecy and its fulfillment.

12:19 *Pharisees.* See notes on Mat 3:7; Mark 2:16; Luke 5:17.

12:20 *Greeks.* Probably "God-fearers," people attracted to Judaism by its monotheism and morality, but repelled by its nationalism and requirements such as circumcision. They worshiped in the synagogues but did not become proselytes.

12:21 *Philip.* A Greek name, which may be why they came to this disciple (though he was not the only one of the Twelve to have a Greek name). *see.* Means "have an interview with." After v. 22 John records no more about these Greeks (yet see note on v. 32). He regarded their coming as important but not their conversation with Jesus. Jesus came to die for the world, and the coming of these Gentiles indicates the scope of the effectiveness of His approaching crucifixion.

12:23 *The hour is come.* The hour to which everything else led (see note on 2:4). *glorified.* Jesus was speaking about His death on the cross and His subsequent resurrection and exaltation (see notes on v. 41; 11:4; 13:31).

12:24 *if it die, it bringeth forth.* The principle of life through death is seen in the plant world. The kernel must perish as a kernel if there is to be a plant.

12:25 *he that hateth his life . . . shall keep it.* To love one's life here and now—to concentrate on one's own success—is to lose what matters (cf. Mat 16:24–25; Mark 8:34–35; Luke 9:23–24). Supremely, of course, the principle is seen in the cross of Jesus. *hateth.* Love for God must be such that all other loves are, by comparison, hatred. *life eternal.* See note on 3:15.

12:27 *troubled.* John's equivalent to the agony in Gethsemane described in the other Gospels. *this hour.* Jesus faced the prospect of becoming sin (or a sin offering) for sinful people (2 Cor 5:21). He considered praying for God to save Him from this death, but refused to pray it, because the very reason He had come was to die.

12:28 *Father, glorify thy name.* His prayer was not for deliverance but for the Father to be glorified. The voice from heaven gave the answer. *name.* See note on 2:23.

12:31 *of this world.* The cross was God's judgment on the world. *the prince of this world.* Satan (cf. 16:11). The cross would seem to be his triumph; in fact, it was his defeat. Out of it would flow the greatest good ever to come to the world.

12:32 *lifted up.* See note on 3:14. The cross was the supreme exaltation of Jesus (see notes on v. 41; 13:31). *all men.* Christ will draw people to Himself without regard for nationality, ethnic affiliation or status. It is significant that Greek Gentiles were present on this occasion (v. 20).

heard out of the law that Christ abideth for
ever: and how sayest thou, The Son of man
must be lift up? who is this Son of man?
35 Then Jesus said unto them, Yet a little
while [a]is the light with you. [b]Walk while ye
have the light, lest darkness come upon you:
for [c]he that walketh in darkness knoweth not
whither he goeth.
36 While ye have light, believe in the light,
that ye may be [a]the children of light. These
things spake Jesus, and departed, and [b]did
hide himself from them.

The cause of unbelief

37 ¶ But though he had done so many miracles before them, *yet* they believed not on him:
38 That the saying of Esaias the prophet
might be fulfilled, which he spake, [a]Lord, who
hath believed our report? and to whom hath
the arm of the Lord been revealed?
39 Therefore they could not believe, because that Esaias said again,
40 [a]He hath blinded their eyes, and hardened their heart; that they should not see with
their eyes, nor understand with *their* heart,
and be converted, and I should heal them.
41 [a]These *things* said Esaias, when he saw
his glory, and spake of him.
42 Nevertheless among the *chief* rulers
also many believed on him; but [a]because of
the Pharisees they did not confess *him*, lest
they should be put out of the synagogue:
43 [a]For they loved the praise of men more
than the praise of God.

A summary of Jesus' claims

44 ¶ Jesus cried and said, [a]He that believeth on me, believeth not on me, but on
him that sent me.
45 And [a]he that seeth me seeth him that
sent me.
46 [a]I am come a light into the world, that
whosoever believeth on me should not abide
in darkness.
47 And if any *man* hear my words, and believe not, [a]I judge him not: for [b]I came not to
judge the world, but to save the world.
48 [a]He that rejecteth me, and receiveth
not my words, hath *one* that judgeth him: [b]the
word that I have spoken, the same shall judge
him in the last day.
49 For [a]I have not spoken of myself; but
the Father which sent me, he gave me a commandment, [b]what I should say, and what I
should speak.
50 And I know that his commandment is
life everlasting: whatsoever I speak therefore,
even as the Father said unto me, so I speak.

Washing the disciples' feet

13 Now [a]before the feast of the passover, when Jesus knew that [b]his
hour was come that he should depart out of
this world unto the Father, having loved his

12:35 [a]ch. 1:9; 8:12; 9:5 [b]Jer. 13:16; Eph. 5:8 [c]ch. 11:10; 1 John 2:11
12:36 [a]Luke 16:8; Eph. 5:8; 1 Thes. 5:5; 1 John 2:9-11 [b]ch. 8:59; 11:54
12:38 [a]Is. 53:1; Rom. 10:16
12:40 [a]Is. 6:9,10; Mat. 13:14
12:41 [a]Is. 6:1
12:42 [a]ch. 7:13; 9:22
12:43 [a]ch. 5:44
12:44 [a]Mark 9:37; 1 Pet. 1:21
12:45 [a]ch. 14:9
12:46 [a]ver. 35,36; ch. 3:19; 9:5,39
12:47 [a]ch. 5:45; 8:15,26 [b]ch. 3:17
12:48 [a]Luke 10:16 [b]Deut. 18:19; Mark 16:16
12:49 [a]ch. 8:38; 14:10 [b]Deut. 18:18
13:1 [a]Mat. 26:2 [b]ch. 12:23; 17:1,11

12:34 *the law.* Here seems to mean OT Scripture in general (see note on 10:34), the reference being to passages such as Ps 89:36; 110:4; Is 9:7; Dan 7:14. *Christ.* See note on 1:25. *Son of man.* The only place in the Gospels where anyone other than Jesus used the expression, and even here Jesus is being quoted (see note on Mark 8:31).

12:35–36 *the light.* Light is closely identified with Jesus, as seen from the call to believe in the light (see notes on 1:4; 8:12).

12:37 *they believed not on him.* God's ancient people should have responded when God sent His Messiah. They should have seen the significance of the signs He did.

12:39 *could not believe.* Does not mean that the people in question had no choice. They purposely rejected God and chose evil, and v. 40 explains that God in turn brought on them a judicial blinding of eyes and hardening of hearts. Yet many Jewish leaders did believe in Jesus as the Messiah (v. 42).

12:40 These words from Is 6:10 are quoted by Jesus (Mat 13:14–15; Mark 4:12; Luke 8:10) and by Paul (Acts 28:26–27).

12:41 *saw his glory.* Isaiah spoke primarily of the glory of God (Is 6:3). John spoke of the glory of Jesus and made no basic distinction between the two, attesting Jesus' oneness with God. The thought of glory here is complex. There is the idea of majesty, and there is also the idea (which meant so much to John) that Jesus' death on the cross and His subsequent resurrection and exaltation show His real glory. Isaiah foresaw the rejection of Christ, as the passages quoted (Is 53:1; 6:10) show. He spoke of the Messiah both in the words about blind eyes and hard hearts, on the one hand, and about healing, on the other. This is the cross and this is glory, for the cross and resurrection and exaltation portray both suffering and healing, rejection and triumph, humiliation and glory.

12:42 *among the chief rulers . . . believed.* John does not give a picture of unrelieved gloom. Many Jewish leaders believed (see note on 1:7), though they remained secret believers for fear of excommunication (see note on 9:22).

12:44 *cried.* The words are given special emphasis by being spoken in a loud voice. *believeth not on me.* John ends his story of the public ministry of Jesus with an appeal for belief. He does not say when Jesus spoke these words (they may have been uttered earlier), but they are a fitting close to this part of his account. *him that sent me.* Jesus' mission, as well as the inseparability of the Father and the Son, are stressed throughout this Gospel.

12:46 *I am come . . . into the world.* Points to both Jesus' preexistence and His mission. *light.* See notes on 1:4; 8:12.

12:47 *to judge.* Not the purpose of Jesus' coming, but judgment is the other side of salvation. It is not the purpose of the sun's shining to cast shadows, but when the sun shines, shadows are inevitable.

12:49 *the Father . . . gave me a commandment, what I should say.* Jesus' hearers have a great responsibility. His "word" (v. 48) is that which the Father commanded Him to say. To reject it, therefore, is to reject God.

12:50 *life everlasting.* See note on 3:15. *therefore.* Jesus said what He did in order to fulfill the will of the Father—a wonderful note on which to end the account of Jesus' public ministry.

13:1–17:26 John has by far the longest account of the upper room, though curiously he says nothing about the institution of the Lord's Supper. Still we owe to him most of our information about what our Lord said to His disciples on that night. One feature of the discourse is Jesus' emphasis on love. The Greek noun *agape* ("love") and the verb *agapao* ("love") occur only eight times in chs. 1–12 but 31 times in chs. 13–17.

13:1 *feast of the passover.* See notes on 2:13; 5:1. *his hour.* See note on 2:4.

own which were in the world, he loved them unto the end.

2 And supper being ended, [a]the devil having now put into the heart of Judas Iscariot, Simon's *son,* to betray him;

3 Jesus knowing [a]that the Father had given all *things* into his hands, and that he was come from God, and went to God;

4 [a]He riseth from supper, and laid aside *his* garments; and took a towel, and girded himself.

5 After that, he poureth water into a bason, and began to wash the disciples' feet, and to wipe *them* with the towel wherewith he was girded.

6 Then cometh he to Simon Peter: and [1]*Peter* saith unto him, Lord, [a]dost thou wash my feet?

7 Jesus answered and said unto him, What I do thou knowest not now; [a]but thou shalt know hereafter.

8 Peter saith unto him, Thou shalt never wash my feet. Jesus answered him, [a]If I wash thee not, thou hast no part with me.

9 Simon Peter saith unto him, Lord, not my feet only, but also *my* hands and *my* head.

10 Jesus saith to him, He that is washed needeth not save to wash *his* feet, but is clean every whit: and [a]ye are clean, but not all.

11 For [a]he knew who should betray him; therefore said he, Ye are not all clean.

12 ¶ So after he had washed their feet, and had taken his garments, and was set down again, he said unto them, Know ye what I have done to you?

13 [a]Ye call me Master and Lord: and ye say well; for *so* I am.

14 [a]If I then, *your* Lord and Master, have washed your feet; [b]ye also ought to wash one another's feet.

15 For [a]I have given you an example, that ye should do as I have done to you.

16 [a]Verily, verily, I say unto you, The servant is not greater than his lord; neither he that is sent greater than he that sent him.

17 [a]If ye know these *things,* happy are ye if ye do them.

18 I speak not of you all: I know whom I have chosen: but that the scripture may be fulfilled, [a]He that eateth bread with me hath lift up his heel against me.

19 [a][1]Now I tell you before it come, that, when it is come to pass, ye may believe that I am *he.*

20 [a]Verily, verily, I say unto you, He that receiveth whomsoever I send receiveth me; and he that receiveth me receiveth him that sent me.

Jesus dismisses Judas

21 ¶ [a]When Jesus had thus said, [b]he was troubled in spirit, and testified, and said, Verily, verily, I say unto you, that [c]one of you shall betray me.

22 Then the disciples looked one on another, doubting of whom he spake.

13:2 [a]Luke 22:3
13:3 [a]Mat. 11:27; 28:18; ch. 3:35; 17:2; Acts 2:36; 1 Cor. 15:27; Heb. 2:8
13:4 [a]Luke 22:27; Phil. 2:7,8
13:6 [1][Gr. *he*] [a]Mat. 3:14
13:7 [a]ver. 12
13:8 [a]ch. 3:5; 1 Cor. 6:11; Eph. 5:26; Tit. 3:5; Heb. 10:22
13:10 [a]ch. 15:3
13:11 [a]ch. 6:64
13:13 [a]Mat. 23:8; Luke 6:46; 1 Cor. 8:6; 12:3; Phil. 2:11
13:14 [a]Luke 22:27 [b]Rom. 12:10; Gal. 6:1,2; 1 Pet. 5:5
13:15 [a]Mat. 11:29; Phil. 2:5; 1 Pet. 2:21; 1 John 2:6
13:16 [a]Mat. 10:24; Luke 6:40; ch. 15:20
13:17 [a]Jas. 1:25
13:18 [a]ver. 21; Ps. 41:9; Mat. 26:23
13:19 [1]Or, *From henceforth* [a]ch. 14:29; 16:4
13:20 [a]Mat. 10:40; 25:40; Luke 10:16
13:21 [a]Mat. 26:21; Mark 14:18; Luke 22:21 [b]ch. 12:27 [c]Acts 1:17; 1 John 2:19

13:2 *supper.* Some believe that this feast was a fellowship meal eaten sometime before the passover feast. This would mean that the Last Supper could not have been the passover meal as the Synoptic Gospels clearly indicate. However, this meal may have been the passover feast itself, in which case the accounts of the Synoptics and John would agree. *the devil.* See v. 27. *Judas Iscariot.* See note on 6:71.

13:3 *the Father had given all things into his hands.* John again emphasizes the fulfillment of God's plan and Jesus' control of the situation.

‡13:5 *began to wash the disciples' feet.* A menial task (see note on 1:27), normally performed by a servant. On this occasion there was no servant and no one else volunteered. Jesus' action was during the meal, not upon arrival, done deliberately to emphasize a point. It was a lesson in humility, but it also set forth the principle of selfless service that was so soon to be exemplified in the cross. John alone tells of this incident, but Luke says that in rebuking the disciples over a quarrel concerning who would be the greatest, Jesus said, "I am among you as he that serveth" (Luke 22:27). Jesus' life of service would culminate on the cross (see Phil 2:5–8 and notes).

13:8 *never.* Characteristically, Peter objected, though apparently no one else did. He was a mixture of humility (he did not want Jesus to perform this lowly service for him) and pride (he tried to dictate to Jesus). *If I wash thee not.* Jesus' reply looks beyond the incident to what it symbolizes: Peter needed a spiritual cleansing. The external washing was a picture of cleansing from sin, which Christians also sometimes need (see note on 1 John 1:9).

13:9 *my hands and my head.* Peter's response was wholehearted, but he was still dictating to Jesus.

13:10 *save to wash his feet.* A man would bathe himself before going to a feast. When he arrived, he only needed to wash his feet to be entirely clean again.

13:11 *he knew.* Again John emphasizes Jesus' command of the situation.

‡13:13 *Master . . . Lord.* An instructor would normally be called master, or teacher, but "Lord" referred to one occupying the supreme place. Jesus accepted both titles.

13:14–15 Some Christians believe that Christ intended to institute a foot-washing ordinance to be practiced regularly. Most Christians, however, interpret Christ's action here as providing an example of humble service.

13:14 *wash one another's feet.* Christians should be willing to perform the most menial services for one another.

13:16 With minor variations this saying, which Jesus used often, is found in 15:20; Mat 10:24; Luke 6:40 (cf. Luke 22:27).

13:18 *I speak not of you all.* Jesus was leading up to His prediction of the betrayal (v. 21). *eateth bread with me.* To eat bread together was a mark of close fellowship (see note on Ps 41:9). *hath lift up his heel against me.* May be derived from a horse's preparing to kick, or perhaps something like shaking off the dust from one's feet (Luke 9:5; 10:11).

13:19 *that, when . . . ye may believe.* See 20:31. Jesus' concern was for the disciples, not Himself. *I am he.* An emphatic form of speech, such as that in 8:58 (see note there).

13:20 *whomsoever I send . . . him that sent me.* Jesus' mission is a common theme in this Gospel, and now the mission of His followers is linked with it (cf. 20:21).

13:21 *troubled.* See 11:33. Though He knew of it long before it happened, Jesus was grieved by the betrayal of a friend.

13:22 *doubting of whom he spake.* The disciples' astonishment shows that Judas had concealed his contacts with the high priests. No one suspected him (see v. 28), but all seem to have

23 Now [a]there was leaning on Jesus' bosom one of his disciples, whom Jesus loved.

24 Simon Peter therefore beckoned to him, that *he* should ask who it should be of whom he spake.

25 He then lying on Jesus' breast saith unto him, Lord, who is it?

26 Jesus answered, He it is, to whom I shall give a [1]sop, when I have dipped *it.* And when he had dipped the sop, he gave *it* to Judas Iscariot, *the son* of Simon.

27 [a]And after the sop Satan entered into him. Then said Jesus unto him, That thou doest, do quickly.

28 Now no *man* at the table knew for what intent he spake this unto him.

29 For some *of them* thought, because [a]Judas had the bag, that Jesus had said unto him, Buy *those things* that we have need of against the feast; or that he should give something to the poor.

30 He then having received the sop went immediately out: and it was night.

31 ¶ Therefore, when he was gone out, Jesus said, [a]Now is the Son of man glorified, and [b]God is glorified in him.

32 If God be glorified in him, God shall also glorify him in himself, and [a]shall straightway glorify him.

33 Little children, yet a little while I am with you. Ye shall seek me: [a]and as I said unto the Jews, Whither I go, ye cannot come; so now I say to you.

34 [a]A new commandment I give unto you, That ye love one another; as I have loved you, that ye also love one another.

35 [a]By this shall all *men* know that ye are my disciples, if ye have love one to another.

13:23 [a]ch. 19:26; 20:2; 21:7,20
13:26 [1]Or, *morsel*
13:27 [a]Luke 22:3; ch. 6:70
13:29 [a]ch. 12:6
13:31 [a]ch. 12:23 [b]ch. 14:13; 1 Pet. 4:11
13:32 [a]ch. 12:23
13:33 [a]ch. 8:21
13:34 [a]Lev. 19:18; ch. 15:12,17; Eph. 5:2; 1 Thes. 4:9; Jas. 2:8; 1 Pet. 1:22; 1 John 2:7; 3:11,23
13:35 [a]1 John 2:5; 4:20
13:36 [a]ch. 21:18; 2 Pet. 1:14
13:37 [a]Mat. 26:33; Mark 14:29; Luke 22:33
14:1 [a]ver. 27
14:2 [a]ch. 13:33
14:3 [a]Acts 1:11 [b]ch. 12:26; 17:24; 1 Thes. 4:17
14:6 [a]Heb. 9:8 [b]ch. 8:32 [c]ch. 11:25 [d]ch. 10:9

Peter's denial foretold

36 ¶ Simon Peter said unto him, Lord, whither goest thou? Jesus answered him, Whither I go, thou canst not follow me now; but [a]thou shalt follow me afterwards.

37 Peter said unto him, Lord, why cannot I follow thee now? I will [a]lay down my life for thy sake.

38 Jesus answered him, Wilt thou lay down thy life for my sake? Verily, verily, I say unto thee, *The* cock shall not crow, till thou hast denied me thrice.

The way, the truth, and the life

14 Let [a]not your heart be troubled: ye believe in God, believe also in me.

2 In my Father's house are many mansions: if *it were* not *so,* I would have told you. [a]I go to prepare a place for you.

3 And if I go and prepare a place for you, [a]I will come again, and receive you unto myself; that [b]where I am, *there* ye may be also.

4 And whither I go ye know, and the way ye know.

5 Thomas saith unto him, Lord, we know not whither thou goest; and how can we know the way?

6 Jesus saith unto him, I am [a]the way, [b]the truth, and [c]the life: [d]no *man* cometh unto the Father, but by me.

---

thought that the betrayal would be involuntary (see Mark 14:19).

13:23 *was leaning.* At a dinner, guests reclined on couches, leaning on the left elbow with the head toward the table. *one of his disciples, whom Jesus loved.* Usually thought to be John, the author of this Gospel (see 19:26; 20:2; 21:7,20). The expression does not, of course, mean that Jesus did not love the others, but that there was a special bond with this man.

13:26 *He it is, to whom I shall give a sop, when I have dipped it.* Evidently Judas was near Jesus, possibly in the seat of honor. John used Judas's full name (see note on 6:71) in recording this solemn moment.

13:27 *after the sop.* Evidently the critical moment. If the giving of the bread to Judas was a mark of honor, it also seems to have been a final appeal—which Judas did not accept. *Satan.* The name is used only here in John (cf. v. 2). *do quickly.* Jesus' words once more indicate His control. He would die as He directed, not as His opponents determined.

13:29 *the feast.* See v. 1 and note on v. 2. *the poor.* See 12:5.

13:30 *night.* In light of John's emphasis on the conflict between light and darkness, this may have been more than a time note—picturing also the darkness of Judas's soul.

13:31 *Son of man.* See note on Mark 8:31. *glorified.* See v. 32 and note on 7:39. Here the idea of glory includes a reference to Jesus' sacrificial death on the cross and the glorious salvation that would result. *God is glorified in him.* The glory of the Father is closely bound to that of the Son.

13:34 *A new commandment.* In a sense it was an old one (see Lev 19:18), but for Christ's disciples it was new, because it was the mark of their brotherhood, created by Christ's great love for them (cf. Mat 22:37–39; Mark 12:30–31; Luke 10:27). *as I have loved you.* Our standard is Christ's love for us.

13:35 *love.* The distinguishing mark of Christ's followers (cf. 1 John 3:23; 4:7–8,11–12,19–21).

13:36 *whither goest thou?* Peter seems to have ignored Jesus' words about love and was more concerned about his Master's departure. In Jesus' reply "thou" is singular and thus personal to Peter, whereas in v. 33 the word "ye" is plural.

13:37 *I will lay down my life.* Words similar to those of the good shepherd in 10:11. Peter was characteristically sure of himself, when in fact he would not at this time lay down his life for Jesus. Exactly the opposite would be true.

13:38 *denied me thrice.* Peter's denial is prophesied in all four Gospels (Mat 26:33–35; Mark 14:29–31; Luke 22:31–34).

14:1 *Let not . . . be troubled.* "Your" is plural. The apostles had just received disturbing news (13:33,36). *believe.* The antidote for a troubled heart.

14:2 *my Father's house.* Heaven. *mansions.* Implies permanence.

14:3 *I will come again.* Jesus comes in many ways, but the primary reference here is to His second advent.

14:4 *way.* See v. 6.

14:5 *Thomas.* He was honest, and plainly told the Lord he did not understand (see note on 11:16).

14:6 *I am.* See note on 6:35. *the way.* To God. Jesus is not one way among many, but the way (cf. Acts 4:12; Heb 10:19–20). In the early church, Christianity was sometimes called "the Way" (e.g., Acts 9:2; 19:9,23). *the truth.* A key emphasis in this Gospel (see note on 1:14). *the life.* See note on 1:4. Very likely the statement means "I am the way (to the Father) in that I am the truth and the life."

7 [a]If ye had known me, ye should have known my Father also: and from henceforth ye know him, and have seen him.

8 Philip saith unto him, Lord, shew us the Father, and it sufficeth us.

9 Jesus saith unto him, Have I been so long time with you, and *yet* hast thou not known me, Philip? [a]he that hath seen me hath seen the Father; and how sayest thou *then,* Shew us the Father?

10 Believest thou not that [a]I am in the Father, and the Father in me? the words that I speak unto you, [b]I speak not of myself: but the Father that dwelleth in me, he doeth the works.

11 Believe me that I *am* in the Father, and the Father in me: [a]or else believe me for the very works' sake.

12 [a]Verily, verily, I say unto you, He that believeth on me, the works that I do shall he do also; and greater *works* than these shall he do; because I go unto my Father.

13 [a]And whatsoever ye shall ask in my name, that will I do, that the Father may be glorified in the Son.

14 If ye shall ask any *thing* in my name, I will do *it.*

The promise of the Spirit

15 ¶ [a]If ye love me, keep my commandments.

16 And I will pray the Father, and [a]he shall give you another Comforter, that he may abide with you for ever;

17 *Even* [a]the Spirit of truth; [b]whom the world cannot receive, because it seeth him not, neither knoweth him: but ye know him; for he dwelleth with you, [c]and shall be in you.

18 [a]I will not leave you [1]comfortless: [b]I will come to you.

19 Yet a little while, and the world seeth me no more; but [a]ye see me: [b]because I live, ye shall live also.

20 At that day ye shall know that [a]I *am* in my Father, and you in me, and I in you.

21 [a]He that hath my commandments, and keepeth them, he it is that loveth me: and he that loveth me shall be loved of my Father, and I will love him, and will manifest myself to him.

22 [a]Judas saith unto him, not Iscariot, Lord, how is it that thou wilt manifest thyself unto us, and not unto the world?

23 Jesus answered and said unto him, If a man love me, he will keep my words: and my Father will love him, [a]and we will come unto him, and make *our* abode with him.

24 He that loveth me not keepeth not my sayings: and [a]the word which you hear is not mine, but the Father's which sent me.

25 ¶ These *things* have I spoken unto you, being *yet* present with you.

26 But [a]the Comforter, *which is* the Holy Ghost, whom the Father will send in my name, [b]he shall teach you all *things,* and bring all *things* to your remembrance, what*soever* I have said unto you.

14:7 [a]ch. 8:19
14:9 [a]ch. 12:45; Col. 1:15; Heb. 1:3
14:10 [a]ch. 10:38; 17:21,23 [b]ch. 5:19; 8:28
14:11 [a]ch. 10:38
14:12 [a]Mat. 21:21; Mark 16:17; Luke 10:17
14:13 [a]Mat. 7:7; 21:22; Mark 11:24; Luke 11:9; ch. 15:7,16; 16:23,24; Jas. 1:5; 1 John 3:22; 5:14
14:15 [a]ver. 21,23; ch. 15:10; 1 John 5:3
14:16 [a]ch. 15:26; 16:7; Rom. 8:15
14:17 [a]ch. 15:26; 16:13; 1 John 4:6 [b]1 Cor. 2:14 [c]1 John 2:27
14:18 [1]Or, *orphans* [a]Mat. 28:20 [b]ver. 3,28
14:19 [a]ch. 16:16 [b]1 Cor. 15:20
14:20 [a]ch. 10:38
14:21 [a]1 John 2:5; 5:3
14:22 [a]Luke 6:16
14:23 [a]1 John 2:24; Rev. 3:20
14:24 [a]ch. 5:19
14:26 [a]Luke 24:49; ch. 15:26 [b]ch. 2:22; 12:16; 1 John 2:20

14:7 *me . . . my Father.* Once more Jesus stresses the intimate connection between the Father and Himself. Jesus brought a full revelation of the Father (cf. 1:18), so that the apostles had real knowledge of Him.

14:10 *of myself.* Jesus' teaching was not of human origin, and there was an inseparable connection between His words and His work.

14:11 *Believe . . . that I am in the Father, and the Father in me.* Saving faith is trust in a person, but it must also have factual content. Faith includes believing that Jesus is one with the Father.

14:12 *greater works.* Miracles (see v. 11). These depended on Jesus' going to the Father, because they are works done in the strength of the Holy Spirit, whom Jesus would send from the Father (15:26; cf. 14:16–17).

14:13 *in my name.* Not simply prayer that mentions Jesus' name but prayer in accordance with all that the person who bears the name is (see note on 2:23). It is prayer aimed at carrying forward the work Jesus did—prayer that He Himself will answer (see also v. 14).

14:15 *love . . . keep.* Love, like faith (Jas 2:14–26), cannot be separated from obedience.

14:16 *the Father . . . shall give you.* The first of a series of important passages about the Holy Spirit (v. 26; 15:26; 16:7–15), the gift of the Father. *another.* Besides Jesus. *Comforter.* Or "Counselor." It is a legal term, but with a broader meaning than "counsel for the defense" (see 1 John 2:1). It referred to any person who helped someone in trouble with the law. The Spirit will always stand by Christ's people.

14:17 *the Spirit of truth.* In essence and in action the Spirit is characterized by truth. He brings people to the truth of God. All three persons of the Trinity are linked with truth. See also the Father (4:23–24; cf. Ps 31:5; Is 65:16) and the Son (14:6). *the world.* Which takes no notice of the Spirit of God (cf. 1 Cor 2:14). But the Spirit was "with" Jesus' disciples and would be "in" them. Some believe the latter relationship (indwelling) specifically anticipates the coming of the Holy Spirit on the day of Pentecost (Acts 2; cf. Rom 8:9).

14:18 *I will come to you.* The words relate to the coming of the Spirit, but Jesus also speaks of His own appearances after the resurrection and at His second coming (see vv. 3, 19, 28; 16:22).

14:19 *the world . . . but ye.* The cross separated the world (who would not see Jesus thereafter) from the disciples (who would). *because I live, ye shall live also.* The life of the Christian always depends on the life of Christ (cf. 1:4; 3:15).

14:20 *At that day ye shall know.* The resurrection would radically change their thinking.

14:21 *keepeth . . . loveth.* Love for Christ and keeping His commands cannot be separated (see note on v. 15). *loved of my Father . . . I will love him.* The love of the Father cannot be separated from that of the Son.

14:22 *how is it . . . ?* Judas (and, for that matter, the others) probably looked for Jesus to fulfill popular Messianic expectations. It was not easy, therefore, to understand how that would mean showing Himself to the disciples but not to the world.

14:23 *love . . . keep . . . love.* Again love and obedience are linked (cf. vv. 15,21).

14:24 Once more the close relationship between Jesus' words and the Father's is stressed (see v. 10; 7:16).

14:26 *Comforter.* See note on v. 16. *Holy Ghost.* His normal title in the NT (though only here and at 1:33; 20:22 in this Gospel)—emphasizing His holiness, rather than His power or greatness. *whom the Father will send.* Both the Father and the Son are involved in the sending (see 15:26). *name.* See notes

27 [a]Peace I leave with you, my peace I give unto you: not as the world giveth, give I unto you. Let not your heart be troubled, neither let it be afraid.

28 Ye have heard how [a]I said unto you, I go away, and come *again* unto you. If ye loved me, ye would rejoice, because I said, [b]I go unto the Father: for [c]my Father is greater than I.

29 And [a]now I have told you before it come to pass, that, when it is come to pass, ye might believe.

30 Hereafter I will not talk much with you: [a]for the prince of this world cometh, and hath nothing in me.

31 But that the world may know that I love the Father; and [a]as the Father gave me commandment, *even* so I do. Arise, let us go hence.

Jesus the true vine

15 I am the true vine, and my Father is the husbandman.

2 [a]Every branch in me that beareth not fruit he taketh away: and every *branch* that beareth fruit, he purgeth it, that it may bring forth more fruit.

3 [a]Now ye are clean through the word which I have spoken unto you.

4 [a]Abide in me, and I in you. As the branch cannot bear fruit of itself, except it abide in the vine; no more can ye, except ye abide in me.

5 I am the vine, ye *are* the branches: He that abideth in me, and I in him, the same bringeth forth much [a]fruit: for [1]without me ye can do nothing.

6 If a man abide not in me, [a]he is cast forth as a branch, and is withered; and *men* gather them, and cast *them* into the fire, and they are burned.

7 If ye abide in me, and my words abide in you, [a]ye shall ask what ye will, and it shall be done unto you.

8 [a]Herein is my Father glorified, that ye bear much fruit; [b]so shall ye be my disciples.

9 As the Father hath loved me, so have I loved you: continue ye in my love.

10 [a]If ye keep my commandments, ye shall abide in my love; even as I have kept my Father's commandments, and abide in his love.

The hatred of the world

11 ¶ These *things* have I spoken unto you, that my joy might remain in you, and [a]*that* your joy might be full.

12 [a]This is my commandment, That ye love one another, as I have loved you.

13 [a]Greater love hath no *man* than this, that a man lay down his life for his friends.

14 [a]Ye are my friends, if ye do whatsoever I command you.

15 Henceforth I call you not servants; for the servant knoweth not what his lord doeth: but I have called you friends; [a]for all *things*

14:27 [a]Phil. 4:7; Col. 3:15
14:28 [a]ver. 3,18 [b]ch. 16:16; 20:17 [c]ch. 5:18; 10:30; Phil. 2:6
14:29 [a]ch. 13:19; 16:4
14:30 [a]ch. 12:31; 16:11
14:31 [a]ch. 10:18; Phil. 2:8; Heb. 5:8
15:2 [a]Mat. 15:13
15:3 [a]ch. 13:10; Eph. 5:26; 1 Pet. 1:22
15:4 [a]Col. 1:23; 1 John 2:6
15:5 [1]Or, *severed from me* [a]Hos. 14:8; Phil. 1:11; 4:13
15:6 [a]Mat. 3:10; 7:19
15:7 [a]ch. 16:23
15:8 [a]Mat. 5:16; Phil. 1:11 [b]ch. 8:31
15:10 [a]ch. 14:15
15:11 [a]ch. 16:24; 17:13; 1 John 1:4
15:12 [a]ch. 13:34; 1 Thes. 4:9; 1 Pet. 4:8; 1 John 3:11
15:13 [a]ch. 10:11; Rom. 5:7,8; Eph. 5:2; 1 John 3:16
15:14 [a]Mat. 12:50; ch. 14:15
15:15 [a]Gen. 18:17; ch. 17:26

on v. 13; 2:23. *bring all things to your remembrance, whatsoever I have said unto you.* Crucial for the life of the church—and for the writing of the NT.

14:27 *Peace . . . my peace.* A common Hebrew greeting (20:19,21,26), which Jesus uses here in an unusual way. The term speaks, in effect, of the salvation that Christ's redemptive work will achieve for His disciples—total well-being and inner rest of spirit, in fellowship with God. All true peace is His gift, which the repetition emphasizes. *not as the world giveth, give I unto you.* In its greetings of peace the world can only express a longing or wish. But Jesus' peace is real and present. *troubled.* See note on v. 1.

14:28 *heard how I said.* Cf. v. 3. *my Father is greater than I.* Revealing the subordinate role Jesus accepted as a necessary part of the incarnation. The statement must be understood in the light of the unity between the Father and the Son (10:30).

14:30 *prince of this world.* See note on 12:31. *hath nothing in me.* Satan has a hold on people because of their fallen state. Since Christ was sinless, Satan could have no hold on Him.

14:31 *as the Father gave me commandment, even so I do.* Jesus had stressed the importance of His followers being obedient (vv. 15,21,23), and He set the example. With these words He goes to fulfill His mission (chs. 18–19).

15:1 *I am.* See note on 6:35. *the true vine.* The vine is frequently used in the OT as a symbol of Israel (e.g., Ps 80:8–16; Is 5:1–7; Jer 2:21). When this imagery is used, Israel is often shown as lacking in some way. Jesus, however, is "the true vine."

15:2 *taketh away.* A reference to judgment (see note on v. 6). *purgeth.* Pruning produces fruitfulness. In the NT the figure of good fruit represents the product of a godly life (see Mat 3:8; 7:16–20) or virtues of character (see Gal 5:22–23; Eph 5:9; Phil 1:11).

‡15:3 *clean.* The Greek for "clean" is the same root word as "purgeth" (v. 2). *the word.* Sums up the message of Jesus. Christ wants to use the Word to cleanse us, but He has other more severe measures if we will not allow the Word to do its work in us.

15:4 *Abide in me.* The believer has no fruitfulness apart from his union and fellowship with Christ. A branch out of contact with the vine is lifeless.

15:5 *I am the vine.* See note on v. 1. The repetition gives emphasis. *abideth in me, and I in him.* A living union with Christ is absolutely necessary; without it there is nothing.

15:6 *cast them into the fire, and they are burned.* Judged (see note on v. 2). In light of such passages as 6:39; 10:27–28, these branches probably do not represent true believers. Genuine salvation is evidenced by a life of fruitfulness (see v. 10 and notes on vv. 2,4; see also Heb 6:9, "things that accompany salvation"; cf. Mat 7:19–23).

15:7 *my words abide in you.* It is impossible to pray correctly apart from knowing and believing the teachings of Christ. *ask what ye will.* See 14:13 and note.

15:8 *my Father glorified.* The Father is glorified in the work of the Son (13:31–32), and He is also glorified in the fruit-bearing of disciples (see Mat 7:20; Luke 6:43–45).

15:10 *keep . . . as I have kept.* Again the importance of obedience (cf. 14:15,21,23), and again the example of Christ (cf. 14:31). *my love . . . his love.* See vv. 12,14. Obedience and love go together (see 1 John 2:5; 5:2–3).

15:11 *joy.* Mentioned previously in this Gospel only in 3:29, but one of the characteristic notes of the upper room discourse (16:20–22,24; 17:13). The Christian way is never dreary, for Jesus desires His disciples' joy to be complete.

15:13 Christ's love was not only in words but also in His sacrificial death.

15:15 *servants . . . friends.* A servant is simply an agent, doing what his master commands and often not understanding his master's purpose. But Jesus takes His friends into His confidence.

that I have heard of my Father I have made known unto you.

16 [a]Ye have not chosen me, but I have chosen you, and [b]ordained you, that you should go and bring forth fruit, and *that* your fruit should remain: that [c]whatsoever ye shall ask of the Father in my name, he may give it you.

17 These *things* I command you, that ye love one another.

18 [a]If the world hate you, ye know that it hated me before *it hated* you.

19 [a]If ye were of the world, the world would love his own: but [b]because ye are not of the world, but I have chosen you out of the world, therefore the world hateth you.

20 Remember the word that I said unto you, [a]The servant is not greater than his lord. If they have persecuted me, they will also persecute you; [b]if they have kept my saying, they will keep yours also.

21 But [a]all these *things* will they do unto you for my name's sake, because they know not him that sent me.

22 [a]If I had not come and spoken unto them, they had not had sin: [b]but now they have no [1]cloke for their sin.

23 [a]He that hateth me hateth my Father also.

24 If I had not done among them [a]the works which none other *man* did, they had not had sin: but now have they both seen and hated both me and my Father.

25 But *this cometh to pass,* that the word might be fulfilled that is written in their law, [a]They hated me without a cause.

26 [a]But when the Comforter is come, whom I will send unto you from the Father, *even* the Spirit of truth, which proceedeth from the Father, [b]he shall testify of me:

27 And [a]ye also shall bear witness, because [b]ye have been with me from the beginning.

The coming of the Spirit

16 These *things* have I spoken unto you, that ye [a]should not be offended.

2 [a]They shall put you out of the synagogues: yea, the time cometh, [b]that whosoever killeth you will think that he doeth God service.

3 And [a]these *things* will they do unto you, because they have not known the Father, nor me.

4 But [a]these *things* have I told you, that when the time shall come, ye may remember that I told you of them. And these *things* I said not unto you at the beginning, because I was with you.

5 But now [a]I go my way to him that sent me; and none of you asketh me, Whither goest thou?

6 But because I have said these *things* unto you, sorrow hath filled your heart.

7 Nevertheless I tell you the truth; It is expedient for you that I go away: for if I go not

15:16 [a]ch. 6:70; 13:18; 1 John 4:10 [b]Mat. 28:19; Mark 16:15; Col. 1:6 [c]ver. 7
15:18 [a]1 John 3:13
15:19 [a]1 John 4:5 [b]ch. 17:14
15:20 [a]Mat. 10:24; Luke 6:40 [b]Ezek. 3:7
15:21 [a]Mat. 10:22; 24:9
15:22 [1]Or, *excuse* [a]ch. 9:41 [b]Rom. 1:20; Jas. 4:17
15:23 [a]1 John 2:23
15:24 [a]ch. 3:2
15:25 [a]Ps. 35:19; 69:4
15:26 [a]Luke 24:49; ch. 14:17; Acts 2:33 [b]1 John 5:6
15:27 [a]Luke 24:48; Acts 1:21; 2:32; 3:15; 4:20,33; 5:32; 10:39; 13:31; 1 Pet. 5:1; 2 Pet. 1:16 [b]Luke 1:2; 1 John 1:1
16:1 [a]Mat. 11:6; 24:10; 26:31
16:2 [a]ch. 9:22 [b]Acts 8:1; 9:1; 26:9,10
16:3 [a]ch. 15:21; Rom. 10:2; 1 Cor. 2:8; 1 Tim. 1:13
16:4 [a]ch. 13:19; 14:29
16:5 [a]ch. 7:33; 14:28

all things . . . I have made known to you. From 16:12 we learn that though Jesus had let His disciples know as much as they were able to absorb of the Father's plan, the revelation was not yet complete. The Spirit would make other things known in due course.

‡15:16 *I have chosen you . . . bring forth fruit . . . ask.* Disciples normally chose the particular rabbi to whom they wanted to be attached, but it was not so with Jesus' disciples. He chose them, and for a purpose—the bearing of fruit. We usually desire a strong prayer life in order that we may be fruitful, but here it is the other way around. Jesus enables us to bear fruit, and then the Father will hear our prayers. *name.* See notes on 2:23; 14:13. Normally prayer is addressed to the Father, in the name of Christ, meaning on the basis of his access, and with the help of the Holy Spirit.

15:18–19 *world.* Here refers to the human system that opposes God's purpose (see note on 1:9).

15:19 *ye are not of.* The believer's essential being, his new life, comes specially from God, and therefore he is not the same as those who oppose God.

15:21 *all these things will they do unto you.* Because Christians do not belong to the world, persecution from the world is inevitable. The basic reason is the world's ignorance and rejection of the Father (cf. 16:3). *name's sake.* See note on 2:23.

15:22 *no cloke.* See KJV. marg. Privilege and responsibility go together. The Jews had had the great privilege of having the Son of God among them—in addition to having received God's special revelation in the OT. Their rejection of Jesus left them totally guilty and without excuse. Had He not come to them they would still have been sinners, but they would not have been guilty of rejecting Him directly (see v. 24).

15:25 *that the word might be fulfilled that is written.* In the end God's purpose is always accomplished, despite the belief of sinful men that they have successfully opposed it. *law.* See notes on 10:34; 12:34.

15:26 *Comforter.* See note on 14:16. *I will send.* See notes on 14:16,26. *Spirit of truth.* See note on 14:17. *proceedeth from the Father.* Probably refers to the Spirit's being sent to do the Father's work on earth rather than to His eternal relationship with the Father. *testify.* See note on 1:7.

15:27 *ye also . . . witness.* Emphatic. Believers bear their testimony to Christ in the power of the Spirit. But it is their testimony, and they are responsible for bearing it. *from the beginning.* The apostles bore the definitive testimony, for they were uniquely chosen and taught by Christ and were eyewitnesses of His glory (see Luke 24:48; Acts 10:39,41).

16:2 *put you out of the synagogues.* See note on 9:22. *doeth God service.* Religious people have often persecuted others in the strong conviction that this was right (see Acts 26:9–11; Gal 1:13–14).

16:3 *the Father.* See note on 5:17. *nor me.* Again the Father and the Son are linked. Not to know Christ is to be ignorant of the Father.

16:5 *none of you asketh me, Whither goest thou?* Peter had asked such a question (13:36), but quickly turned his attention to another subject. His concern had been with what would happen to himself and the others and not for where Jesus was going.

16:6 *sorrow hath filled your heart.* Because of His announced departure.

16:7 *if I go not away.* Jesus did not say why the Spirit would not come until He went away, but clearly taught that His saving work on the cross was necessary before the sending of the Spirit. *Comforter.* See note on 14:16. *I will send him.* See note on 14:26.

away, [a]the Comforter will not come unto you; but [b]if I depart, I will send him unto you.

8 And when he is come, he will [1]reprove the world of sin, and of righteousness, and of judgment:

9 [a]Of sin, because they believe not on me;

10 [a]Of righteousness, [b]because I go to my Father, and ye see me no more;

11 [a]Of judgment, because [b]the prince of this world is judged.

12 ¶ I have yet many *things* to say unto you, [a]but ye cannot bear *them* now.

13 Howbeit when he, [a]the Spirit of truth, is come, [b]he will guide you into all truth: for he shall not speak of himself; but whatsoever he shall hear, *that* shall he speak: and he will shew you *things* to come.

14 He shall glorify me: for he shall receive of mine, and shall shew *it* unto you.

15 [a]All *things* that the Father hath are mine: therefore said I, that he shall take of mine, and shall shew *it* unto you.

16 A little while, and ye shall not see me: and again, a little while, and ye shall see me, [a]because I go to the Father.

Jesus' farewell to his disciples

17 ¶ Then said *some* of his disciples among themselves, What is this that he saith unto us, A little while, and ye shall not see me: and again, a little while, and ye shall see me: and, Because I go to the Father?

18 They said therefore, What is this that he saith, A little while? we cannot tell what he saith.

19 Now Jesus knew that they were desirous to ask him, and said unto them, Do ye inquire among yourselves of that I said, A little while, and ye shall not see me: and again, a little while, and ye shall see me?

20 Verily, verily, I say unto you, That ye shall weep and lament, but the world shall rejoice: and ye shall be sorrowful, but your sorrow shall be turned into joy.

21 [a]A woman when she is in travail hath sorrow, because her hour is come: but as soon as she is delivered of the child, she remembereth no more the anguish, for joy that a man is born into the world.

22 And ye now therefore have sorrow: but I will see you again, and [a]your heart shall rejoice, and your joy no *man* taketh from you.

23 And in that day ye shall ask me nothing. [a]Verily, verily, I say unto you, Whatsoever ye shall ask the Father in my name, he will give *it* you.

24 Hitherto have ye asked nothing in my name: ask, and ye shall receive, [a]that your joy may be full.

25 These *things* have I spoken unto you in [1]proverbs: but the time cometh, when I shall no more speak unto you in [1]proverbs, but I shall shew you plainly of the Father.

16:7 [a]ch. 7:39; 14:16,26; 15:26 [b]Acts 2:33; Eph. 4:8
16:8 [1]Or, *convince*
16:9 [a]Acts 2:22
16:10 [a]Acts 2:32 [b]ch. 5:32
16:11 [a]Acts 26:18 [b]Luke 10:18; Eph. 2:2; Col. 2:15; Heb. 2:14
16:12 [a]Mark 4:33; 1 Cor. 3:2; Heb. 5:12
16:13 [a]ch. 14:17 [b]ch. 14:26; 1 John 2:20
16:15 [a]Mat. 11:27; ch. 3:35
16:16 [a]ch. 13:3
16:21 [a]Is. 26:17
16:22 [a]Luke 24:41; ch. 14:1,27; 20:20; Acts 2:46; 13:52; 1 Pet. 1:8
16:23 [a]Mat. 7:7; ch. 14:13; 15:16
16:24 [a]ch. 15:11
16:25 [1]Or, *parables*

16:8 *He . . . will reprove the world.* The work the Spirit does in the world. The NT normally speaks of His work in believers. *reprove.* Or "expose the guilt of."

16:9 *Of sin.* Apart from the Spirit's convicting work, people can never see themselves as sinners. *because they believe not.* May mean that their sin is their failure to believe, or that their unbelief is a classic example of sin. Typically, John may have had both of these in mind.

16:10 *Of righteousness.* The righteousness brought about by Christ's sacrificial death (cf. Rom 1:17; 3:21–22). No one but the Holy Spirit can reveal to a person that a righteous status before God does not depend on good works but on Christ's death on the cross. *because I go to to my Father.* The ascension, which as part of Christ's exaltation placed God's seal of approval on Christ's redemptive act.

16:11 *Of judgment.* Jesus was speaking of the defeat of Satan, which was a form of judgment, not simply a victory. More than power is in question. God acts with justice. *prince of this world.* See note on 12:31.

16:12 *ye cannot bear them now.* This may mean "more than you can understand now," or "more than you can perform without the Spirit's help" (to live out Christ's teaching requires the enabling presence of the Spirit).

16:13 *Spirit of truth.* See note on 14:17. *whatsoever he shall hear.* We are not told whether He hears from the Father or the Son, but it obviously does not matter, for the verse stresses the close relationship among the three. *things to come.* Probably means the whole Christian way or revelation (presented and preserved in the apostolic writings), still future at the time Jesus spoke.

16:14 *glorify me.* See note on 1:14. The Spirit draws no attention to Himself but promotes the glory of Christ.

16:15 *All things that the Father hath are mine.* Cf. 17:10. The three Persons are closely related.

16:16 *A little while . . . a little while.* Few doubt that the first phrase refers to the interval before the crucifixion. But interpretations differ as to whether the second refers to the interval preceding the resurrection or the coming of the Spirit or the second coming of Christ. It seems that the language here best fits the resurrection.

16:17 *go to the Father.* See v. 10. Jesus had not linked this with "a little while," but the apostles saw them as connected.

16:20 *weep.* The same verb for loud wailing as in 11:33, which carries the idea of deep sorrow and its outward expression.

16:21 *A woman when she is in travail.* Giving birth usually causes both pain and joy (cf. Is 26:17–19; 66:7–14; Hos 13:13–14).

16:22 *I will see you again.* As in v. 16, probably a reference to Jesus' appearances after His resurrection. *your joy no man taketh from you.* The resurrection would change things permanently, bringing a joy that cannot be removed by the world's assaults.

16:23 *ye shall ask me nothing.* Seems to mean asking for information (rather than asking in prayer), which would not be necessary after the resurrection. Jesus then moved on to the subject of prayer. However, Jesus may have been saying that His disciples previously had been praying to Christ, but after His death and resurrection they were to go directly to the Father and pray in Christ's name (see vv. 24,26–27 and notes). *name.* See notes on 2:23; 14:13.

16:24 *Hitherto.* Previously they had asked the Father or Christ, but they had not asked the Father in Christ's name. *your joy.* See note on 15:11.

16:25 *have I spoken unto you in proverbs.* Throughout the discourse, not just in the immediately preceding words. *the time cometh.* After the resurrection.

26 At that day ye shall ask in my name: and I say not unto you, that I will pray the Father for you:

27 [a]For the Father himself loveth you, because ye have loved me, and [b]have believed that I came out from God.

28 [a]I came forth from the Father, and am come into the world: again, I leave the world, and go to the Father.

29 ¶ His disciples said unto him, Lo, now speakest thou plainly, and speakest no [1]proverb.

30 Now are we sure that [a]thou knowest all *things,* and needest not that any *man* should ask thee: by this [b]we believe that thou camest forth from God.

31 Jesus answered them, Do ye now believe?

32 [a]Behold, the hour cometh, yea, is now come, that ye shall be scattered, [b]every man to [1]his own, and shall leave me alone: and [c]*yet* I am not alone, because the Father is with me.

33 These *things* I have spoken unto you, that [a]in me ye might have peace. [b]In the world ye shall have tribulation: but be of good cheer; [c]I have overcome the world.

The prayer to be glorified

17 These *words* spake Jesus, and lift up his eyes to heaven, and said, Father, [a]the hour is come; glorify thy Son, that thy Son also may glorify thee:

2 [a]As thou hast given him power over all flesh, that he should give eternal life to as many [b]as thou hast given him.

3 And [a]this is life eternal, that they might know thee [b]the only true God, and Jesus Christ, [c]whom thou hast sent.

4 [a]I have glorified thee on the earth: [b]I have finished the work [c]which thou gavest me to do.

5 And now, O Father, glorify thou me with thine own self with the glory [a]which I had with thee before the world was.

The prayer for the disciples

6 ¶ [a]I have manifested thy name unto the men [b]which thou gavest me out of the world: thine they were, and thou gavest them me; and they have kept thy word.

7 Now they have known that all *things* whatsoever thou hast given me are of thee.

8 For I have given unto them the words [a]which thou gavest me; and they have received *them,* [b]and have known surely that I came out from thee, and they have believed that thou didst send me.

9 I pray for them: [a]I pray not for the world, but for *them* which thou hast given me; for they are thine.

10 And all mine are thine, and [a]thine are mine; and I am glorified in them.

11 [a]And *now* I am no more in the world, but these are in the world, and I come to thee. Holy Father, [b]keep through thine own name those whom thou hast given me, that they may be one, [c]as we *are.*

16:27 [a]ch. 14:21 [b]ch. 3:13
16:28 [a]ch. 13:3
16:29 [1]Or, *parable*
16:30 [a]ch. 21:17 [b]ch. 17:8
16:32 [1]Or, *his own* home [a]Mat. 26:31; Mark 14:27 [b]ch. 20:10 [c]ch. 8:29
16:33 [a]Is. 9:6; Rom. 5:1; Eph. 2:14 [b]2 Tim. 3:12 [c]Rom. 8:37; 1 John 4:4
17:1 [a]ch. 12:23
17:2 [a]Dan. 7:14; Mat. 11:27; ch. 3:35; Phil. 2:10; Heb. 2:8
17:2 [b]ver. 6,9,24; ch. 6:37
17:3 [a]Is. 53:11; Jer. 9:24 [b]1 Cor. 8:4; 1 Thes. 1:9 [c]ch. 3:34
17:4 [a]ch. 13:31 [b]ch. 4:34 [c]ch. 14:31
17:5 [a]Phil. 2:6; Col. 1:15; Heb. 1:3
17:6 [a]Ps. 22:22 [b]ch. 6:37
17:8 [a]ch. 8:28 [b]ch. 16:27
17:9 [a]1 John 5:19
17:10 [a]ch. 16:15
17:11 [a]ch. 13:1 [b]1 Pet. 1:5; Jude 1 [c]ch. 10:30

16:26 *in my name.* See notes on 2:23; 14:13. *I say not unto you, that I will pray the Father for you.* Not a contradiction of Rom 8:34; Heb 7:25; 1 John 2:1. Those passages mean that Christ's presence in heaven as the crucified and risen Lord is itself an intercession. Here the teaching is that there will be no need for Him to make petitions in our behalf.

16:27 *the Father himself loveth you.* Christ is explaining why the disciples can come directly to the Father in prayer. It is because the disciples have loved and trusted in Jesus, and in love God will hear their requests in Jesus' name.

16:29 *no proverb.* See v. 25 and note.

16:30 *believe that thou camest forth from God.* Two recurring themes of this Gospel: believing (see note on 1:7) and Jesus' coming from God (see notes on 4:34; 17:3,8).

16:32 *ye shall be scattered.* The disciples had faith, but not enough to stand firm in face of disaster. Jesus knew they would fail; however, His church is not built on people's strength but on God's ability to use people even after they have failed.

16:33 Notice the contrasts: between "in me" and "in the world" (see note on 1:9) and between "peace" and "tribulation." *I have overcome.* Just before His death Jesus affirms His final victory.

17:1–26 Jesus' longest recorded prayer.

17:1 *lift up his eyes to heaven.* The customary attitude in prayer (11:41; Ps 123:1; Mark 7:34), though sometimes the person prostrated himself (see Mat 26:39). *Father.* Used of God in John's Gospel 116 times. *the hour.* See note on 2:4. *glorify . . . glorify.* See notes on 1:14; 7:39; 13:31. The glory of the Father and that of the Son are closely connected, and the death by which Jesus would glorify God would lead to eternal life for believers (v. 2).

17:2 *hast given.* The thought of giving is stressed in this chapter (vv. 4,6–9,11–12,14,22,24); see note on 3:27. *he should give eternal life.* See note on 3:15. *as many as thou hast given him.* Again God's initiative in salvation is stressed.

17:3 *sent.* Again the mission of Jesus is mentioned.

17:4 *I have glorified thee.* Christ's mission was not self-centered. *the work which thou gavest me to do.* Jesus emphasized the supreme place of the Father.

17:5 *glorify me . . . with the glory which I had with thee.* Jesus asks the Father to return Him to His previous position of glory, to exchange humiliation for glorification. This occurred at Christ's resurrection and exaltation to God's right hand. *world.* The universe (see notes on v. 14; 1:9). The Greek for "world" occurs 18 times in this prayer.

17:6 *I have manifested thy name.* See notes on 2:23; 14:13; cf. 1:18. *the men which thou gavest me.* Again the divine initiative (cf. 6:44).

17:7 *all things . . . are of thee.* Only as people see the Father at work in Jesus do they have a proper concept of God. The disciples had at last reached this understanding.

17:8 Three things about the disciples are mentioned: 1. They accepted the teaching (unlike the Pharisees and others who heard it but did not receive it). 2. They knew with certainty Jesus' divine origin. Acceptance of the revelation led them further into truth. 3. They believed (see note on 1:7; cf. 1:12; 20:31).

17:9 *I pray not for the world.* The only prayer Jesus could pray for the world was that it cease to be worldly (i.e., opposed to God), and this He did pray (vv. 21,23).

17:11 *Holy Father.* A form of address found only here in the NT (but cf. 1 Pet 1:15–16; Rev 4:8; 6:10). The name suggests both remoteness and nearness; God is both awe-inspiring and loving. *that they may be one.* The latter part of the prayer strong-

12 While I was with them in the world, [a]I kept them in thy name: *those* that thou gavest me I have kept, and [b]none of them is lost, [c]but the son of perdition; [d]that the scripture might be fulfilled.

13 And now come I to thee; and these *things* I speak in the world, that they might have my joy fulfilled in themselves.

14 I have given them thy word; [a]and the world hath hated them, because they are not of the world, [b]even as I am not of the world.

15 I pray not that thou shouldest take them out of the world, but [a]that thou shouldest keep them from the evil.

16 They are not of the world, even as I am not of the world.

17 [a]Sanctify them through thy truth: [b]thy word is truth.

18 [a]As thou hast sent me into the world, even *so* have I also sent them into the world.

19 And [a]for their sakes I sanctify myself, that they also might be [1]sanctified through the truth.

The prayer for the church

20 Neither pray I for these alone, but for them also which shall believe on me through their word;

21 [a]That they all may be one; as [b]thou, Father, *art* in me, and I in thee, that they also may be one in us: that the world may believe that thou hast sent me.

22 And the glory which thou gavest me I have given them; [a]that they may be one, even as we are one:

23 I in them, and thou in me, [a]that they may be made perfect in one; and that the world may know that thou hast sent me, and hast loved them, as thou hast loved me.

24 [a]Father, I will that they also, whom thou hast given me, be with me where I am; that they may behold my glory, which thou hast given me: [b]for thou lovedst me before the foundation of the world.

25 O righteous Father, [a]the world hath not known thee: but [b]I have known thee, and [c]these have known that thou hast sent me.

26 [a]And I have declared unto them thy name, and will declare *it:* that the love [b]where*with* thou hast loved me may be in them, and I in them.

17:12 [a]Heb. 2:13 [b]1 John 2:19 [c]ch. 6:70 [d]Ps. 109:8; Acts 1:20 **17:14** [a]1 John 3:13 [b]ch. 8:23 **17:15** [a]Mat. 6:13; Gal. 1:4; 1 John 5:18 **17:17** [a]Acts 15:9; Eph. 5:26; 1 Pet. 1:22 [b]Ps. 119:142,151 **17:18** [a]ch. 20:21 **17:19** [1]Or, *truly sanctified* [a]1 Cor. 1:2; 1 Thes. 4:7; Heb. 10:10 **17:21** [a]ch. 10:16; Rom. 12:5; Gal. 3:28 [b]ch. 10:38 **17:22** [a]ch. 14:20; 1 John 1:3 **17:23** [a]Col. 3:14 **17:24** [a]ch. 12:26; 1 Thes. 4:17 [b]ver. 5 **17:25** [a]ch. 15:21; 16:3 [b]ch. 7:29; 8:55; 10:15 [c]ver. 8; ch. 16:27 **17:26** [a]ver. 6; ch. 15:15 [b]ch. 15:9

Jesus' betrayal and arrest

18 When Jesus had spoken these *words,* [a]he went forth with his disciples over [b]the brook Cedron, where was a garden, into the which he entered, and his disciples.

18:1 [a]Mat. 26:36; Mark 14:32; Luke 22:39 [b]2 Sam. 15:23

ly emphasizes unity. Here the unity is already given, not something to be achieved. The meaning is "that they continually be one" rather than "that they become one." The unity is to be like that between the Father and the Son. It is much more than unity of organization, but the church's present divisions are the result of the failures of Christians.

17:12 *I have kept.* Christ's power is adequate for every need. *the son of perdition.* Or "the son of destruction," i.e., one belonging to the sphere of damnation and destined for destruction (but predestination is not here in view). Reference is to Judas Iscariot.

17:13 *my joy.* See note on 15:11.

17:14 *the world.* The world that is hostile to God and God's people (see notes on v. 5; 1:9). *not of the world.* They do not have the mind-set of the world, i.e., hostility to God, for they have been "born of the Spirit" (3:8) and are "sons of God" (1:12).

‡17:15 *not . . . take them out of the world.* The world is where Jesus' disciples are to do their work; Jesus does not wish them to be taken from it until that work is done (see v. 18). *the evil.* Satan, who is especially active in the world (1 John 5:19), making God's protection indispensable.

17:17 *Sanctify.* Means "to set apart for sacred use" or "to make holy"; also in v. 19. *thy truth: thy word.* Sanctification and revelation (as recorded in God's word) go together. For the connection of Christ's teaching with truth cf. 8:31–32.

17:18 *As thou hast sent me . . . even so have I also sent them.* Jesus' mission is one of the dominant themes of this Gospel and is given as the pattern for His followers. *into the world.* We may long for heaven, but it is on earth that our work is done.

17:19 *I sanctify myself.* This statement appears to be unparalleled. In the Septuagint (the Greek translation of the OT) the verb is used of consecrating priests (Ex 28:41) and sacrifices (Ex 28:38; Num 18:9). Jesus solemnly "sets himself apart to do God's will," which at this point meant His death. *that they also might be sanctified.* Jesus died on the cross not only to save us but also to consecrate us to God's service (see note on v. 17).

17:20 *them also which shall believe on me.* Jesus had just spoken of the mission and the sanctification of His followers (vv. 18–19). He was confident that they would spread the gospel, and He prayed for those who would believe as a result. All future believers are included in this prayer.

17:21 *That they also may be one.* See note on v. 11. *Father.* See note on v. 1. *that the world may believe.* The unity of believers should have an effect on outsiders, to convince them of the mission of Christ. Jesus' prayer is a rebuke of the groundless and often bitter divisions among believers.

17:22 *the glory.* See note on v. l. Believers are to be characterized by humility and service, just as Christ was, and it is on them that God's glory rests. *they may be one, even as we are one.* Again the Lord emphasized the importance of unity among His followers, and again the standard is the unity of the Father and the Son.

17:23 *I in them, and thou in me.* There are two indwellings here: that of the Son in believers, and that of the Father in the Son. It is because the latter is a reality that the former can take place. *made perfect in one.* Again the emphasis on unity has an evangelistic aim. This time it is connected not only with the mission of Jesus but also with God's love for people and for Christ.

‡17:24 *Father.* See note on v. 1. *I will.* Jesus said, "I will"—His last will and testament for His followers. Where He Himself was concerned, He prayed, "not that I will, but what thou wilt" (Mark 14:36). *be with me.* The Christian's greatest blessing. *my glory.* Perhaps used here to refer to Jesus' eternal splendor (see 1 John 3:2). Or Jesus' prayer may have been that in the life to come they might fully appreciate the glory of His lowly service (cf. Eph 2:7).

17:25 *righteous Father.* A form of address found only here in the NT (cf. "Holy Father," v. 11). *these have known.* They did not know God directly and personally, but they knew God had sent Christ. To recognize God in Christ's mission is a great advance over anything the world can know.

18:1 *the brook Cedron.* East of Jerusalem and dry except during the rainy season.

2 And Judas also, which betrayed him,
knew the place: [a]for Jesus ofttimes resorted
thither with his disciples.
3 [a]Judas then, having received a band *of*
men, and officers from the chief priests and
Pharisees, cometh thither with lanterns and
torches and weapons.
4 Jesus therefore, knowing all *things* that
should come upon him, went forth, and said
unto them, Whom seek ye?
5 They answered him, Jesus of Nazareth.
Jesus saith unto them, I am *he.* And Judas also,
which betrayed him, stood with them.
6 As soon then as he had said unto them, I
am *he,* they went backward, and fell to the
ground.
7 Then asked he them again, Whom seek
ye? And they said, Jesus of Nazareth.
8 Jesus answered, I have told you that I am
he: if therefore ye seek me, let these go their
way:
9 That the saying might be fulfilled, which
he spake, [a]Of them which thou gavest me
have I lost none.
10 [a]Then Simon Peter having a sword
drew it, and smote the high priest's servant,
and cut off his right ear. The servant's name
was Malchus.
11 Then said Jesus unto Peter, Put up thy
sword into the sheath: [a]the cup which my Father hath given me, shall I not drink it?

18:2 [a]Luke 21:37; 22:39
18:3 [a]Mat. 26:47; Mark 14:43; Luke 22:47; Acts 1:16
18:9 [a]ch. 17:12
18:10 [a]Mat. 26:51; Mark 14:47; Luke 22:49,50
18:11 [a]Mat. 20:22; 26:39,42

18:13 [1]*And Annas sent Christ bound unto Caiaphas the high priest,* ver. 24 [a]See Mat. 26:57 [b]Luke 3:2
18:14 [a]ch. 11:50
18:15 [a]Mat. 26:58; Mark 14:54; Luke 22:54
18:16 [a]Mat. 26:69; Mark 14:66; Luke 22:54
18:20 [a]Mat. 26:55; Luke 4:15; ch. 7:14,26,28; 8:2

Jesus before Jewish authorities

12 ¶ Then the band and the captain and officers of the Jews took Jesus, and bound him,
13 And [a]led him away to [b]Annas first; for
he was father in law to Caiaphas, which was
the high priest that *same* year.[1]
14 [a]Now Caiaphas was he, which gave
counsel to the Jews, that it was expedient that
one man should die for the people.
15 ¶ [a]And Simon Peter followed Jesus, and
so did another disciple: that disciple was
known unto the high priest, and went in with
Jesus into the palace of the high priest.
16 [a]But Peter stood at the door without.
Then went out *that* other disciple, which was
known unto the high priest, and spake unto
her that kept the door, and brought in Peter.
17 Then saith the damsel that kept the
door unto Peter, Art not thou also *one* of this
man's disciples? He saith, I am not.
18 And the servants and officers stood
there, who had made a fire of coals; for it was
cold: and they warmed themselves: and Peter
stood with them, and warmed himself.
19 ¶ The high priest then asked Jesus of his
disciples, and of his doctrine.
20 Jesus answered him, [a]I spake openly to
the world; I ever taught in the synagogue, and
in the temple, whither the Jews always resort;
and in secret have I said nothing.
21 Why askest thou me? ask them which

18:3 *Judas.* See note on 6:71. *officers from the chief priests and Pharisees.* Equivalent to the temple guard sent by the Sanhedrin. *lanterns.* Terra-cotta holders into which household lamps could be inserted. *torches.* Resinous pieces of wood fastened together.

18:4 *knowing all things that should come upon him.* Jesus was not taken by surprise.

18:5 *I am.* See 6:35; 8:58 and notes. *with them.* John does not let us forget where Judas belonged.

18:6 *fell to the ground.* They came to arrest a meek peasant and instead were met in the dim light by a majestic person.

18:8 *I am.* The threefold repetition (vv. 5,6,8) emphasizes the solemn words. *let these go their way.* Jesus cared for the disciples even as He was going to His death. Twice He had made the arresting party say plainly that He was the one they wanted (vv. 4–5,7).

18:9 *That the saying might be fulfilled.* Words normally used in quoting Scripture, and Jesus' words are on the same level. See 6:39; 17:12.

18:10 *Simon Peter.* It is to John that we owe the information that the man with the sword (the Greek for this word refers to a short sword) was Peter, and that the man he wounded was named Malchus.

18:11 *the cup.* Often points to suffering (Ps 75:8; Ezek 23:31–34) and the wrath of God (Is 51:17,22; Jer 25:15; Rev 14:10; 16:19). *my Father hath given Me.* The Synoptic Gospels also speak of the cup at the time of Jesus' prayer at Gethsemane (Mat 26:39; Mark 14:36; Luke 22:42), and John says it came from the Father. God was in control.

18:12 *bound him.* The reason for the bonds is not clear. Perhaps their use was standard procedure, much like the modern use of handcuffs.

18:13 *Annas.* Had been deposed from the high priesthood by the Romans in A.D. 15 but was probably still regarded by many as the true high priest. In Jewish law a man could not be sentenced on the day his trial was held. The two examinations—this one (mentioned only by John) and that before Caiaphas—may have been conducted to give some form of legitimacy to what was done. *high priest that same year.* See note on 11:49.

18:14 *Caiaphas . . . gave counsel to the Jews.* A reference to 11:49–50. For John it was this unconscious prophecy that mattered most about Caiaphas. John may also have been hinting that a fair trial could not be expected from a man who had already said that putting Jesus to death was expedient.

18:15 *another disciple.* Perhaps John himself. *known unto the high priest.* Refers to more than casual acquaintance; he had entrée into the high priest's house and could bring Peter in.

18:17 *damsel that kept the door.* All four Gospels tell us that Peter's first challenge came from a slave girl, the most unimportant person imaginable. The form of the girl's question implied a negative answer, and Peter capitalized on her expectation by saying, "I am not." The other Gospels seem to indicate that the other denials followed immediately, but it is likely that there were intervals during which other things happened (see Luke 22:58–59).

18:18 *Peter stood with them.* On a cold night he would have been conspicuous if he had stayed away from the fire.

18:19 *asked Jesus.* Not legal questioning, since witnesses were supposed to be brought in first to establish guilt. The accused was not required to prove his innocence. Perhaps Annas regarded this as a preliminary inquiry, not a trial.

18:20 *I spake openly.* It should not have been difficult to find witnesses (v. 21). *in secret have I said nothing.* Not a denial that He taught the disciples privately, but a denial that He had secretly taught them subversive teaching different from His public message.

heard *me,* what I have said unto them: behold,
they know what I said.
22 And when he had thus spoken, one of
the officers which stood by [a]stroke Jesus [1]with
the palm of his hand, saying, Answerest thou
the high priest so?
23 Jesus answered him, If I have spoken
evil, bear witness of the evil: but if well, why
smitest thou me?
24 [a]Now Annas had sent him bound unto
Caiaphas the high priest.
25 ¶ And Simon Peter stood and warmed
himself. [a]They said therefore unto him, Art
not thou also *one* of his disciples? He denied
it, and said, I am not.
26 One of the servants of the high priest,
being *his* kinsman whose ear Peter cut off,
saith, Did not I see thee in the garden with
him?
27 Peter then denied again: and [a]immedi-
ately *the* cock crew.

Jesus before Pontius Pilate

28 ¶ [a]Then led they Jesus from Caiaphas
unto [b][1]the hall of judgment: and it was early;
[c]and they themselves went not into the judgment hall, lest they should be defiled; but that
they might eat the passover.
29 Pilate then went out unto them, and
said, What accusation bring you against this
man?

18:22 [1] Or, *with a rod* [a] Jer. 20:2; Acts 23:2
18:24 [a] Mat. 26:57
18:25 [a] Mat. 26:69,71; Mark 14:69; Luke 22:58
18:27 [a] Mat. 26:74; Mark 14:72; Luke 22:60; ch. 13:38
18:28 [1] Or, *Pilate's house,* ver. 33 [a] Mat. 27:2; Mark 15:1; Luke 23:1; Acts 3:13 [b] Mat. 27:27 [c] Acts 10:28; 11:3
18:32 [a] Mat. 20:19; ch. 12:32,33
18:33 [a] Mat. 27:11
18:36 [a] 1 Tim. 6:13 [b] Dan. 2:44; 7:14; Luke 12:14; ch. 6:15; 8:15
18:37 [a] ch. 8:47; 1 John 3:19; 4:6

30 They answered and said unto him, If he
were not a malefactor, we would not have delivered him up unto thee.
31 Then said Pilate unto them, Take ye
him, and judge him according to your law. The
Jews therefore said unto him, It is not lawful
for us to put any *man* to death:
32 [a]That the saying of Jesus might be fulfilled, which he spake, signifying what death
he should die.
33 [a]Then Pilate entered into the judgment
hall again, and called Jesus, and said unto him,
Art thou the King of the Jews?
34 Jesus answered him, Sayest thou this
thing of thyself, or did others tell *it* thee of me?
35 Pilate answered, Am I a Jew? Thine
own nation and the chief priests have delivered thee unto me: what hast thou done?
36 [a]Jesus answered, [b]My kingdom is not of
this world: if my kingdom were of this world,
then would my servants fight, that I should not
be delivered to the Jews: but now is my kingdom not from hence.
37 Pilate therefore said unto him, Art thou
a king then? Jesus answered, Thou sayest that
I am a king. To this end was I born, and for
this cause came I into the world, that I should
bear witness unto the truth. Every one that [a]is
of the truth heareth my voice.
38 Pilate saith unto him, What is truth?
And when he had said this, he went out again

18:22 *stroke.* Another illegality. The word apparently means a blow with the open hand—a slap.
18:23 *bear witness.* A legal term, indicating an invitation to act in proper legal form. John stresses the importance of testimony throughout his Gospel (see note on 1:7).
18:25 *They said therefore unto him.* Some find a difficulty in that Mat 26:71 says another girl asked this question, whereas Mark 14:69 says it was the same girl, and Luke 22:58 that it was a man. But with a group of servants talking around a fire, several would doubtless take up and repeat such a question, which could be the meaning of John's "they." As on the first occasion (v. 17) the question anticipated the answer "No." The servants probably did not really expect to find a follower of Jesus in the high priest's courtyard, but the question seemed worth asking.
18:26 *being his kinsman.* Another piece of information we owe to John. A relative would have a deeper interest in the swordsman than other people had. But the light in the garden would have been dim, as in the courtyard (a charcoal fire glows, but does not have flames). *Did not I see thee . . . ?* Expected the answer "Yes."
18:27 *the cock crew.* The fulfillment of the prophecy in 13:38.
18:28 *the hall of judgment.* The palace of the Roman governor, Pilate. John says little about the Jewish phase of Jesus' trial but much about the Roman trial (see note on Mark 14:53–15:15). It is possible that John was in the Praetorium, the governor's official residence, for this trial. *early.* The chief priests evidently held a second session of the Sanhedrin after daybreak to give some appearance of legality to what they did (Mark 15:1). This occasion would have been immediately after that, perhaps between 6:00 A.M. and 7:00 A.M. *defiled.* A result of entering a Gentile residence. *eat the passover.* Does not mean that the time of the passover meal had not yet come, for this would contradict the Synoptic Gospels, which have Jesus eating the passover meal the night before. The term "passover" was used to refer to the whole festival of passover and unleavened bread, which lasted seven days and included a number of meals.
18:29 *Pilate.* The Roman governor (see note on Mark 15:1). He showed himself tolerant of Jewish ways. *What accusation . . . ?* A normal question at the beginning of a trial, but it was difficult to answer, because the Jews had no charge that would stand up in a Roman court of law.
18:31 *Take ye him.* In other words, no Roman charge, no Roman trial. *not lawful for us to put any man to death.* They were looking for an execution, not a fair trial. The restriction was important, for otherwise Rome's supporters could be quietly removed by local legal executions. Sometimes the Romans seem to have condoned local executions (e.g., of Stephen, Acts 7), but normally they retained the right to inflict the death penalty.
18:32 *what death he should die.* Cf. 12:32–33 and "must" in 12:34. Jewish execution was by stoning, but Jesus' death was to be by crucifixion, whereby He would bear the curse (Deut 21:22–23). The Romans, not the Jews, had to put Jesus to death. God was overruling in the whole process.
18:33 *Art thou the King of the Jews?* Pilate's first words to Jesus, identical in all four Gospels. One glance was enough to show him that a dangerous rebel existed only in the imaginations of Jesus' enemies.
18:34 *Sayest thou this thing of thyself . . . ?* If so, Pilate's question (v. 33) had meant, "Are you a rebel?" If the question had originated with the Jews, it meant, "Are you the Messianic King?"
18:36 *My kingdom.* Jesus agrees that He has a kingdom, but asserts that it is not the kind of kingdom that has soldiers to fight for it. It was not built, nor is it maintained, by military might.
18:37 *bear witness unto the truth.* Two of this Gospel's important ideas (see 1:7; 1:14; 14:6 and notes).
18:38 *What is truth?* Pilate may have been jesting, and meant, "What does truth matter?" Or he may have been serious, and

unto the Jews, and saith unto them, [a]I find in
him no fault *at all.*
39 [a]But ye have a custom, that I should release unto you one at the passover: will ye
therefore *that* I release unto you the King of
the Jews?
40 [a]Then cried they all again, saying, Not
this *man,* but Barabbas. [b]Now Barabbas was a
robber.

Jesus crowned with thorns

19 Then [a]Pilate therefore took Jesus,
and scourged *him.*
2 And the soldiers platted a crown of
thorns, and put *it* on his head, and they put on
him a purple robe,
3 And said, Hail, King of the Jews: and they
smote him with their hands.
4 Pilate therefore went forth again, and saith
unto them, Behold, I bring him forth to you,
[a]that ye may know that I find no fault in him.
5 Then came Jesus forth, wearing the
crown of thorns, and the purple robe. And *Pilate* saith unto them, Behold the man.
6 [a]When the chief priests therefore and officers saw him, they cried out, saying, Crucify
him, crucify *him.* Pilate saith unto them, Take
ye him, and crucify *him:* for I find no fault in
him.
7 The Jews answered him, [a]We have a law,
and by our law he ought to die, because [b]he
made himself the Son of God.
8 ¶ When Pilate therefore heard that saying, he was the more afraid;

18:38 [a]Mat. 27:24; Luke 23:4; ch. 19:4,6
18:39 [a]Mat. 27:15; Mark 15:6; Luke 23:17
18:40 [a]Acts 3:14 [b]Luke 23:19
19:1 [a]Mat. 20:19; 27:26; Mark 15:15; Luke 18:33
19:4 [a]ver. 6; ch. 18:38
19:6 [a]Acts 3:13
19:7 [a]Lev. 24:16 [b]Mat. 26:65; ch. 5:18; 10:33

19:9 [a]Is. 53:7; Mat. 27:12,14
19:11 [a]Luke 22:53; ch. 7:30
19:12 [a]Luke 23:2 [b]Acts 17:7
19:14 [a]Mat. 27:62
19:15 [a]Gen. 49:10
19:16 [a]Mat. 27:26,31; Mark 15:15; Luke 23:24
19:17 [a]Mat. 27:31,33; Mark 15:21,22; Luke 23:26,33 [b]Num. 15:36; Heb. 13:12

9 And went again into the judgment hall,
and saith unto Jesus, Whence art thou? [a]But
Jesus gave him no answer.
10 Then saith Pilate unto him, Speakest
thou not unto me? knowest thou not that I
have power to crucify thee, and have power to
release thee?
11 Jesus answered, [a]Thou couldest have
no power *at all* against me, except it were giv-
en thee from above: therefore he that delivered me unto thee hath the greater sin.
12 *And* from thenceforth Pilate sought to
release him: but the Jews cried out, saying, [a]If
thou let this *man* go, thou art not Cesar's
friend: [b]whosoever maketh himself a king
speaketh against Cesar.
13 When Pilate therefore heard that saying, he brought Jesus forth, and sat down in
the judgment seat in a place *that is* called the
Pavement, but in the Hebrew, Gabbatha.
14 And [a]it was the preparation of the
passover, and about the sixth hour: and he
saith unto the Jews, Behold your King.
15 But they cried out, Away with *him,*
away with *him,* crucify him. Pilate saith unto
them, Shall I crucify your King? The chief
priests answered, [a]We have no king but Cesar.
16 [a]Then delivered he him therefore unto
them to be crucified.
¶ And they took Jesus, and led *him* away.

Jesus crucified

17 [a]And he bearing his cross [b]went forth

meant, "It is not easy to find truth. What is it?" Either way, it was clear to him that Jesus was no rebel. *find in him no fault at all.* Teaching the truth was not a criminal offense.

18:39 *ye have a custom.* Prisoners are known to have been released on special occasions in other places. *the King of the Jews.* John keeps his emphasis on the note of royalty. Pilate may have hoped that the use of the title would influence the people toward the way he wanted them to decide.

18:40 *Barabbas.* A rebel and a murderer (Luke 23:19). The name is Aramaic and means "son of Abba," i.e., "son of the father"; in place of this man, the "Son of the Father" died.

19:1 Pilate hoped a flogging would satisfy the Jews and enable him to release Jesus (see note on Mark 15:15).

19:2 *thorns.* A general term relating to any thorny plant. *purple.* A color used by royalty.

19:6 *Take ye him, and crucify him.* The petulant utterance of an exasperated man, for the Jews could not carry out this form of execution. *I find no fault.* For the third time Pilate proclaimed Jesus' innocence (see 18:38; 19:4). Luke also records this threefold proclamation (Luke 23:4,14,22).

19:7 *he ought to die.* Apparently referring to the penalty for blasphemy (Lev 24:16).

19:8 *the more afraid.* Pilate was evidently superstitious, and this charge frightened him.

19:9 *Jesus gave him no answer.* The reason is not clear since Jesus had answered other questions readily. Perhaps Pilate would not have understood the answer or would not have believed it.

19:10 *I have power.* Pilate was incredulous and very conscious of his authority. His second question indicates his personal responsibility for crucifying Jesus.

19:11 Jesus' last words to Pilate. *from above.* All earthly authority comes ultimately from God. *the greater sin.* That of Caiaphas (not Judas, who was only a means). But "greater" implies that there was a lesser sin, so Pilate's sin was also real.

19:12 *not Cesar's friend.* Some people had official status as "Friends of Caesar," but the term seems to be used here in the general sense. There was an implied threat that if he released Jesus, Pilate would be accused before Caesar. His record was such that he could not face such a prospect without concern.

19:13 *The Pavement.* Not a translation of *Gabbatha,* which seems to mean "the hill of the house," but a different name for the same place.

19:14 *the preparation.* Normally Friday was the day people prepared for the sabbath. Here the meaning is Friday of passover week. *about the sixth hour.* About noon. Mark 15:25 says that Jesus was crucified at "the third hour." It is possible that Mark's Gospel contains a copyist's error, for the Greek numerals for three and six could be confused. Or it may be that John was using Roman time, in which case the appearance before Pilate would have been at 6:00 A.M. and the crucifixion at 9:00 A.M. (the third hour according to Jewish reckoning; see Mark 15:33). For other time references see Mat 27:45–46; Mark 15:33–34; Luke 23:44. *the Jews.* See note on 1:19. *Behold your King.* John does not let us forget the sovereignty of Jesus. Pilate did not mean the expression seriously, but John did.

19:15 *We have no king but Cesar.* More irony. They rejected any suggestion that they were rebels against Rome, but expressed the truth of their spiritual condition.

19:17 *bearing his cross.* A cross might be shaped like a *T,* an *X,* a *Y,* or an *I,* as well as like the traditional form. A condemned man would normally carry a beam of it to the place of execu-

into a place called *the place* of a skull, which is called in the Hebrew Golgotha:

18 Where they crucified him, and two other with him, on either side one, and Jesus in the midst.

19 [a]And Pilate wrote a title, and put *it* on the cross. And the writing was, JESUS OF NAZARETH THE KING OF THE JEWS.

20 This title then read many of the Jews: for the place where Jesus was crucified was nigh to the city: and it was written in Hebrew, *and* Greek, *and* Latin.

21 Then said the chief priests of the Jews to Pilate, Write not, The King of the Jews; but that he said, I am King of the Jews.

22 Pilate answered, What I have written I have written.

23 [a]Then the soldiers, when they had crucified Jesus, took his garments, and made four parts, to every soldier a part; and *also his* coat: now the coat was without seam, [1]woven from the top throughout.

24 They said therefore among themselves, Let us not rent it, but cast lots for it, whose it shall be: that the scripture might be fulfilled, which saith, [a]They parted my raiment among them, and for my vesture they did cast lots. These *things* therefore the soldiers did.

25 ¶ [a]Now there stood by the cross of Jesus his mother, and his mother's sister, Mary the *wife* of [b][1]Cleophas, and Mary Magdalene.

26 When Jesus therefore saw *his* mother, and [a]the disciple standing by, whom he loved, he saith unto his mother, [b]Woman, behold thy son.

27 Then saith he to the disciple, Behold thy mother. And from that hour *that* disciple took her [a]unto his own *home.*

The death of Jesus

28 ¶ After this, Jesus knowing that all *things* were now accomplished, [a]that the scripture might be fulfilled, saith, I thirst.

29 Now there was set a vessel full of vinegar: and [a]they filled a spunge with vinegar, and put *it* upon hyssop, and put *it* to his mouth.

30 When Jesus therefore had received the vinegar, he said, [a]It is finished: and he bowed *his* head, and gave up the ghost.

31 ¶ The Jews therefore, [a]because it was the preparation, [b]that the bodies should not remain upon the cross on the sabbath day, (for that sabbath day was a high day,) besought Pilate that their legs might be broken, and *that* they might be taken away.

32 Then came the soldiers, and brake the legs of the first, and of the other which was crucified with him.

33 But when they came to Jesus, and saw that he was dead already, they brake not his legs:

34 But one of the soldiers with a spear pierced his side, and forthwith [a]came there out blood and water.

35 And he that saw *it* bare record, and his record is true: and he knoweth that he saith true, that ye might believe.

19:19 [a]Mat. 27:37; Mark 15:26; Luke 23:38
19:23 [1]Or, *wrought* [a]Mat. 27:35; Mark 15:24; Luke 23:34
19:24 [a]Ps. 22:18
19:25 [1]Or, *Clopas* [a]Mat. 27:55; Mark 15:40; Luke 23:49 [b]Luke 24:18
19:26 [a]ch. 13:23; 20:2; 21:7,20,24
19:26 [b]ch. 2:4
19:27 [a]ch. 1:11; 16:32
19:28 [a]Ps. 69:21
19:29 [a]Mat. 27:48
19:30 [a]ch. 17:4
19:31 [a]ver. 42; Mark 15:42 [b]Deut. 21:23
19:34 [a]1 John 5:6,8

tion. Somewhere along the way Simon of Cyrene took Jesus' cross (Mark 15:21), probably because Jesus was weakened by the flogging. *Golgotha.* Aramaic for "the skull." The name of the site is given in both Greek and Aramaic ("Calvary" is from the Latin with the same meaning). See note on Mark 15:22.

19:18 *they crucified him.* See note on Mark 15:24. As with the scourging, John describes this horror with one Greek word. None of the Gospel writers dwells on the physical sufferings of Jesus. *on either side one.* Perhaps meant as a final insult, but it brings out the important truth that in His death Jesus was identified with sinners.

19:19 *a title.* A placard stating the crime for which a man was executed was often fastened to his cross. *JESUS OF NAZARETH THE KING OF THE JEWS.* Again the royalty theme.

19:20 *Hebrew.* One of the languages of the Jewish people at that time (along with Aramaic). *Greek.* The common language of communication throughout the empire. *Latin.* The official language of Rome. The threefold inscription may account for the slight differences in wording in the four Gospels.

19:22 Pilate must have a sufficient reason for the execution, and he was not above mocking the Jews, but for John his insistence may also have served to underscore that Jesus' kingship is final and unalterable.

19:23 *coat.* A type of shirt, reaching from the neck to the knees or ankles. *without seam.* Therefore too valuable to be cut up.

19:24 See introduction to Ps 22 and notes on Ps 22:17,20–21.

19:25 *Cleophas.* Mentioned only here in the NT. *Mary Magdalene.* Appears in the crucifixion and resurrection story in all four Gospels, but apart from that we read of her only in Luke 8:2–3.

19:26 *disciple standing by, whom he loved.* John (see note on 13:23).

19:27 *took her unto his own home.* And so took responsibility for her. It may be that Jesus' brothers still did not believe in Him (see 7:5).

19:28 *I thirst.* May refer to Ps 69:21 (cf. Ps 22:15).

19:29 *vinegar.* Equivalent to cheap wine, the drink of ordinary people. *a spunge.* A useful way of giving drink to one on a cross, and may indicate forethought and compassion on someone's part. *hyssop.* The name given to a number of plants. See also note on Ex 12:22.

19:30 *It is finished.* Apparently the loud cry of Mat 27:50; Mark 15:37. Jesus died as a victor and had completed what He came to do. *gave up the ghost.* An unusual way of describing death, perhaps suggesting an act of will.

19:31 *The Jews.* See note on 1:19. *preparation.* See note on v. 14. *a high day.* The sabbath that fell at passover time. The passover meal had been eaten on Thursday evening, the day of preparation was Friday, and the sabbath came on Saturday. *legs might be broken.* To hasten death, because the victim then could not put any weight on his legs and breathing would be difficult.

19:34 *pierced his side.* Probably to make doubly sure that Jesus was dead, but perhaps simply an act of brutality (see v. 37; Is 53:5; Zech 12:10; cf. Ps 22:16). *blood and water.* The result of the spear piercing the pericardium (the sac that surrounds the heart) and the heart itself.

19:35 *he that saw it.* Either John himself or someone he regarded as reliable. Obviously he considered the incident important, and comments that it was well attested. *knoweth . . . believe.* See note on 1:7.

36 For these *things* were done, [a]that the
scripture should be fulfilled, A bone of him
shall not be broken.
37 And again another scripture saith,
[a]They shall look on *him* whom they pierced.

Jesus laid in the sepulchre

38 ¶ [a]And after this Joseph of Arimathea,
being a disciple of Jesus, but secretly [b]for fear
of the Jews, besought Pilate that he might take
away the body of Jesus: and Pilate gave *him*
leave. He came therefore, and took the body of
Jesus.
39 And there came also [a]Nicodemus,
which at the first came to Jesus by night, and
brought a mixture of myrrh and aloes, about
an hundred pound *weight.*
40 Then took they the body of Jesus, and
[a]wound it in linen clothes with the spices, as
the manner of the Jews is to bury.
41 Now in the place where he was crucified
there was a garden; and in the garden a new
sepulchre, wherein was never man yet laid.
42 [a]There laid they Jesus therefore [b]be-
cause of the Jews' preparation *day;* for the
sepulchre was nigh at hand.

The resurrection of Jesus

20 The [a]first *day* of the week cometh
Mary Magdalene early, when it was
yet dark, unto the sepulchre, and seeth the
stone taken away from the sepulchre.
2 Then she runneth, and cometh to Simon
Peter, and to the [a]other disciple, whom Jesus
loved, and saith unto them, They have taken
away the Lord out of the sepulchre, and we
know not where they have laid him.
3 [a]Peter therefore went forth, and *that* other disciple, and came to the sepulchre.
4 So they ran both together: and the other
disciple did outrun Peter, and came first to the
sepulchre.
5 And he stooping down, and looking in,
saw [a]the linen clothes lying; yet went he not in.
6 Then cometh Simon Peter following him,
and went into the sepulchre, and seeth the
linen clothes lie,
7 And [a]the napkin, that was about his
head, not lying with the linen clothes, but
wrapped together in a place by itself.
8 Then went in also *that* other disciple,
which came first to the sepulchre, and he saw,
and believed.
9 For as yet they knew not the [a]scripture,
that he must rise again from the dead.
10 Then the disciples went away again
unto their own home.

Jesus appears to the disciples

11 ¶ [a]But Mary stood without at the sepulchre weeping: and as she wept, she stooped
down, and looked into the sepulchre,
12 And seeth two angels in white sitting,
the one at the head, and the other at the feet,
where the body of Jesus had lain.
13 And they say unto her, Woman, why
weepest thou? She saith unto them, Because
they have taken away my Lord, and I know not
where they have laid him.
14 [a]And when she had thus said, she
turned herself back, and saw Jesus standing,
and [b]knew not that it was Jesus.
15 Jesus saith unto her, Woman, why
weepest thou? whom seekest thou? She, supposing him to be the gardener, saith unto him,
Sir, if thou have borne him *hence,* tell me
where thou hast laid him, and I will take him
away.

19:36 [a]Ex. 12:46; Num. 9:12; Ps. 34:20
19:37 [a]Ps. 22:16,17; Zech. 12:10; Rev. 1:7
19:38 [a]Mat. 27:57; Mark 15:42; Luke 23:50 [b]ch. 9:22; 12:42
19:39 [a]ch. 3:1,2; 7:50
19:40 [a]Acts 5:6
19:42 [a]Is. 53:9 [b]ver. 31
20:1 [a]Mat. 28:1; Mark 16:1; Luke 24:1
20:2 [a]ch. 13:23; 19:26; 21:7,20, 24
20:3 [a]Luke 24:12
20:5 [a]ch. 19:40
20:7 [a]ch. 11:44
20:9 [a]Ps. 16:10; Acts 2:25-31; 13:34,35
20:11 [a]Mark 16:5
20:14 [a]Mat. 28:9; Mark 16:9 [b]Luke 24:16,31; ch. 21:4

19:36–37 *scripture.* Again John observes God's overruling in the fulfillment of Scripture. It was extraordinary that Jesus was the only one of the three whose legs were not broken and that He suffered an unusual spear thrust that did not break a bone.
19:38 *Joseph.* A rich disciple (Mat 27:57), and a member of the Sanhedrin who had not agreed to Jesus' condemnation (Luke 23:51). *Arimathea.* See note on Mat 27:57. *secretly.* It would have been hard for a member of the Sanhedrin to support Jesus' cause openly. Jesus' closest followers all ran away (Mark 14:50), and it was left to Joseph and Nicodemus to provide for His burial. *Pilate gave him leave.* Otherwise people could take away their crucified friends before they died and revive them.
19:39 *Nicodemus.* John alone tells us that he joined Joseph in the burial. *an hundred pound weight.* A very large amount, such as was used in royal burials (cf. 2 Chr 16:14).
19:40 *linen clothes.* Thin strips like bandages. There was also a shroud, a large sheet (Mat 27:59; Mark 15:46; Luke 23:53).
19:41 *a new sepulchre.* Joseph's own tomb (Mat 27:60).
19:42 *preparation.* See note on v. 14. *nigh at hand.* Haste was necessary, since it was near sunset, when the sabbath would start and no work could be done.
20:1 *Mary Magdalene.* See note on 19:25; cf. Mark 16:9. *when it was yet dark.* Mark says it was "at the rising of the sun" (Mark 16:2). Perhaps the women came in groups, with Mary Magdalene coming very early. Or John may refer to the time of leaving home, Mark to that of arrival at the tomb.
20:2 *to Simon Peter.* Despite his denials, Peter was still the leading figure among the disciples. *disciple, whom Jesus loved.* John (see note on 13:23). *we.* Indicates that there were others with Mary (see Mat 28:1; Mark 16:1; Luke 24:10), though John does not identify them. *have laid him.* Mary had no thought of resurrection.
20:7 *wrapped together.* An orderly arrangement, not in disarray, as would have resulted from a grave robbery.
20:8 *he saw, and believed.* Cf. v. 29. John did not say what he believed, but it must have been that Jesus was resurrected.
20:9 *scripture.* First they came to know of the resurrection through what they saw in the tomb; only later did they see it in Scripture. It is obvious they did not make up a story of resurrection to fit a preconceived understanding of Scriptural prophecy. *must rise.* It was in Scripture and thus the will of God.
20:11 *Mary.* Perhaps Jesus appeared first to Mary because she needed Him most at that time. *weeping.* As in 11:33, it means "wailing," a loud expression of grief.
20:12 *two angels.* Matthew has one angel (Mat 28:2), Mark a young man (Mark 16:5) and Luke two men who were angels (Luke 24:4,23). See note on Luke 24:4.
20:14 *knew not that it was Jesus.* A number of times the risen Jesus was not recognized (21:4; Mat 28:17; Luke 24:16,37). He may have looked different, or He may intentionally have prevented recognition.

16 Jesus saith unto her, Mary. She turned
herself, and saith unto him, Rabboni; which is
to say, Master.
17 Jesus saith unto her, Touch me not; for I
am not yet ascended to my Father: but go to
[a]my brethren, and say unto them, [b]I ascend
unto my Father, and your Father; and *to* [c]my
God, and your God.
18 [a]Mary Magdalene came and told the
disciples that she had seen the Lord, and *that*
he had spoken these *things* unto her.
19 ¶ [a]Then the same day at evening, being
the first *day* of the week, when the doors were
shut where the disciples were assembled for
fear of the Jews, came Jesus and stood in the
midst, and saith unto them, Peace *be* unto
you.
20 And when he had so said, he shewed
unto them *his* hands and his side. [a]Then were
the disciples glad, when they saw the Lord.
21 Then said Jesus to them again, Peace *be*
unto you: [a]as *my* Father hath sent me, even *so*
send I you.
22 And when he had said this, he breathed
on *them,* and saith unto them, Receive ye the
Holy Ghost:
23 [a]Whose soever sins ye remit, they are
remitted unto them; *and* whose soever *sins* ye
retain, they are retained.

Thomas' doubt and belief

24 ¶ But Thomas, one of the twelve, [a]called
Didymus, was not with them when Jesus came.
25 The other disciples therefore said unto
him, We have seen the Lord. But he said unto
them, Except I shall see in his hands the print
of the nails, and put my finger into the print of
the nails, and thrust my hand into his side, I
will not believe.
26 And after eight days again his disciples
were within, and Thomas with them: *then*
came Jesus, the doors being shut, and stood in
the midst, and said, Peace *be* unto you.
27 Then saith he to Thomas, Reach hither
thy finger, and behold my hands; and [a]reach
hither thy hand, and thrust *it* into my side: and
be not faithless, but believing.
28 And Thomas answered and said unto
him, My Lord and my God.
29 Jesus saith unto him, Thomas, because
thou hast seen me, thou hast believed:
[a]blessed *are* they that have not seen, and *yet*
have believed.
30 ¶ [a]And many other signs truly did Jesus
in the presence of his disciples, which are not
written in this book:
31 [a]But these are written, that ye might
believe that Jesus is the Christ, the Son of
God; [b]and that believing ye might have life
through his name.

The appearance beside the sea

21 After these *things* Jesus shewed himself again to the disciples at the sea of
Tiberias; and on this wise shewed he *himself.*
2 There were together Simon Peter, and

20:17 [a]Ps. 22:22; Mat. 28:10; Rom. 8:29; Heb. 2:11 [b]ch. 16:28 [c]Eph. 1:17
20:18 [a]Mat. 28:10; Luke 24:10
20:19 [a]Mark 16:14; Luke 24:36; 1 Cor. 15:5
20:20 [a]ch. 16:22
20:21 [a]Mat. 28:18; ch. 17:18,19; 2 Tim. 2:2; Heb. 3:1
20:23 [a]Mat. 16:10; 18:18
20:24 [a]ch. 11:16
20:27 [a]1 John 1:1
20:29 [a]2 Cor. 5:7; 1 Pet 1:8
20:30 [a]ch. 21:25
20:31 [a]Luke 1:4 [b]ch. 3:15,16; 5:24; 1 Pet. 1:8,9

20:16 *Mary.* Cf. 10:3–4. *Rabboni.* A strengthened form of *Rabbi,* and in the NT found elsewhere only in Mark 10:51 (in the Greek). Although the word means "(my) teacher," there are few if any examples of its use in ancient Judaism as a form of address other than in calling on God in prayer. However, John's explanation casts doubt on any thought that Mary intended to address Jesus as God here.
20:17 *for I am not yet ascended.* The meaning appears to be that the ascension was still some time off. Mary would have opportunity to see Jesus again, so she need not cling to Him. Alternatively, Jesus may be reminding Mary that after His crucifixion she cannot have Him with her except through the Holy Spirit (see 16:5–16). *my brethren.* Probably the disciples (cf. v. 18; Mat 12:50). The members of His family did not believe in Him (7:5), though they became disciples not long after this (Acts 1:14). *my Father, and your Father.* God is Father both of Christ and of believers, but in different senses (see 1:12,14,18,34).
20:19 *disciples.* Probably includes others besides the apostles, "the twelve" (v. 24). *the Jews.* See note on 1:19. *Peace be unto you.* The normal Hebrew greeting (cf. Dan 10:19). Because of their behavior the previous Friday, they may have expected rebuke and censure; but Jesus calmed their fears (see note on 14:27).
20:20 *his hands and his side.* Where the wounds were (John does not refer to the wounds in the feet). According to Luke 24:37 they thought they were seeing a ghost. Jesus was clearly identifying Himself.
20:21 *Peace be unto you.* See note on v. 19. *even so send I you.* See note on 17:18.
20:22 *Receive ye the Holy Ghost.* Thus anticipating what happened 50 days later on the day of Pentecost (Acts 2). The disciples needed God's help to carry out the commission they had just been given.
20:23 Lit. "Those whose sins you forgive have already been forgiven; those whose sins you do not forgive have not been forgiven." God does not forgive people's sins because we do so, nor does He withhold forgiveness because we do. Rather, those who proclaim the gospel are in effect forgiving or not forgiving sins, depending on whether the hearers accept or reject Jesus Christ.
20:24 *Thomas.* See note on 11:16.
20:25 *Except I shall see . . . and put . . . I will not believe.* Hard-headed skepticism can scarcely go further than this.
20:26 *Peace.* See vv. 19,21 and note on 14:27.
20:28 *My Lord and my God.* To acknowledge Jesus as one's Lord and God is the high point of faith (see note on 1:1).
20:29 *they that have not seen, and yet have believed.* Would have been very few at this time. All whom John mentions had seen in some sense. The words, of course, apply to future believers as well.
20:30 *signs.* See note on 2:11. John had selected from among many. *in the presence of his disciples.* Those who could testify to what He had done. John again stresses testimony (see note on 1:7).
20:31 *that ye might believe.* Expresses John's evangelistic purpose. *believe.* See note on 1:7. *Jesus is the Christ, the Son of God.* Faith has content. *the Christ.* See note on 1:25. This whole Gospel is written to show the truth of Jesus' Messiahship and to present Him as the Son of God, so that the readers may believe in Him. *that believing ye might have life.* Another expression of purpose—to bring about faith that leads to life (see notes on 1:4; 3:15). *name.* Represents all that He is and stands for (see note on 2:23).
21:1 *sea of Tiberias.* See note on 6:1.

Thomas called Didymus, and [a]Nathanael of Cana in Galilee, and [b]the *sons* of Zebedee, and two other of his disciples.

3 Simon Peter saith unto them, I go a fishing. They say unto him, We also go with thee. They went forth, and entered into a ship immediately; and that night they caught nothing.

4 But when the morning was now come, Jesus stood on the shore: but the disciples [a]knew not that it was Jesus.

5 Then [a]Jesus saith unto them, [1]Children, have ye any meat? They answered him, No.

6 And he said unto them, [a]Cast the net on the right side of the ship, and ye shall find. They cast therefore, and now they were not able to draw it for the multitude of fishes.

7 Therefore [a]that disciple whom Jesus loved saith unto Peter, It is the Lord. Now when Simon Peter heard that it was the Lord, he girt *his* fisher's coat unto him, (for he was naked,) and did cast himself into the sea.

8 And the other disciples came in a little ship; (for they were not far from land, but as it were two hundred cubits,) dragging the net with fishes.

9 As soon then as they were come to land, they saw a fire of coals there, and fish laid thereon, and bread.

10 Jesus saith unto them, Bring of the fish which ye have now caught.

11 Simon Peter went up, and drew the net to land full of great fishes, an hundred and fifty *and* three: and for all there were so many, *yet* was not the net broken.

12 Jesus saith unto them, [a]Come *and* dine. And none of the disciples durst ask him, Who art thou? knowing that it was the Lord.

13 Jesus then cometh, and taketh bread, and giveth them, and fish likewise.

14 This *is* now [a]the third time *that* Jesus shewed himself to his disciples, after that he was risen from the dead.

Jesus questions Peter

15 ¶ So when they had dined, Jesus saith to Simon Peter, Simon, *son* of Jonas, lovest thou me more than these? He saith unto him, Yea, Lord; thou knowest that I love thee. He saith unto him, Feed my lambs.

16 He saith to him again the second time, Simon, *son* of Jonas, lovest thou me? He saith unto him, Yea, Lord; thou knowest that I love thee. [a]He saith unto him, Feed my sheep.

17 He saith unto him the third time, Simon, *son* of Jonas, lovest thou me? Peter was grieved because he said unto him the third time, Lovest thou me? And he said unto him, Lord, [a]thou knowest all *things;* thou knowest that I love thee. Jesus saith unto him, Feed my sheep.

18 [a]Verily, verily, I say unto thee, When thou wast young, thou girdedst thyself, and walkedst whither thou wouldest: but when thou shalt be old, thou shalt stretch forth thy hands, and another shall gird thee, and carry *thee* whither thou wouldest not.

19 This spake he, signifying [a]by what death he should glorify God. And when he had spoken this, he saith unto him, Follow me.

20 Then Peter, turning about, seeth the disciple [a]whom Jesus loved following; which

21:2 [a]ch. 1:45 [b]Mat. 4:21
21:4 [a]ch. 20:14
21:5 [1]Or, *Sirs* [a]Luke 24:41
21:6 [a]Luke 5:4,6,7
21:7 [a]ch. 13:23; 20:2
21:12 [a]Acts 10:41
21:14 [a]See ch. 20:19,26
21:16 [a]Acts 20:28; Heb. 13:20; 1 Pet. 2:25; 5:2,4
21:17 [a]ch. 2:24,25; 16:30
21:18 [a]ch. 13:36; Acts 12:3,4
21:19 [a]2 Pet. 1:14
21:20 [a]ch. 13:23,25; 20:2

21:2 *Simon Peter.* See note on Mark 1:16. *Thomas.* See note on 11:16. *sons of Zebedee.* Not named in this Gospel (see Mat 4:21).

21:3 *that night.* Nighttime was favored by fishermen in ancient times (as Aristotle, e.g., informs us).

21:4 *knew not that it was Jesus.* Cf. Mary Magdalene (see note on 20:14).

21:7 *disciple whom Jesus loved.* See note on 13:23. *his fisher's coat.* It is curious that he put on this garment (the word appears only here in the NT) preparatory to jumping into the water. But Jews regarded a greeting as a religious act that could be done only when one was clothed. Peter may have been preparing himself to greet the Lord.

21:11 *Peter . . . drew the net to land.* Appears to mean that Peter headed up the effort, for the whole group had not been able previously to haul the net into the boat (v. 6). *was not the net broken.* In contrast to the nets mentioned in Luke 5:6.

21:14 *the third time.* The third appearance to a group of disciples (20:19–23,24–29), though there had been other appearances to individuals.

‡21:15–17 *love.* The Greek word for "love" in Jesus' first two questions is different from the word for "love" in His third question, which is the same word Peter uses in all three answers. It is uncertain whether a distinction in meaning is intended since John often made slight word variations, apparently for stylistic reasons. Also, no distinction is made between these two words elsewhere in this Gospel. In this passage, however, they occur together, and the variations seem too deliberate to be explained on stylistic grounds. The "love" in Jesus' first two questions (*agapao*) refers to a love in which the entire personality, including the will, is involved. The "love" in Jesus' third question and in Peter's answers (*phileo*) refers to spontaneous natural affection or fondness in which emotion plays a more prominent role than will. Whatever interpretation is adopted, the important thing is that in so serious a matter as the reinstatement of Peter, the great question was whether he loved Jesus. Peter had been restored privately and personally (Luke 24:34; 1 Cor 15:5), but now it is to be a public matter. His had disowned Christ in public three times. Now he must own Christ three times in front of the other disciples.

21:15 *more than these.* May mean "more than you love these men" or "more than these men love Me" or "more than you love these things" (i.e., the fishing gear). Perhaps the second is best, for Peter had claimed a devotion above that of the others (cf. 13:37; Mat 26:33; Mark 14:29). Peter did not take up the comparison, and Jesus did not explain it.

21:17 *Thou knowest all things.* Peter's replies stress Christ's knowledge, not his own grasp of the situation.

21:18 *stretch forth thy hands.* The early church understood this as a prophecy of crucifixion.

21:19 *by what death.* Peter would be a martyr. Tradition indicates that he was crucified upside down.

21:20 *disciple whom Jesus loved.* See note on 13:23. *following.* He was doing what Peter was twice told to do (vv. 19,22). *at supper.* See 13:23–25.

also leaned on his breast at supper, and said,
Lord, which is he that betrayeth thee?
21 Peter seeing him saith to Jesus, Lord,
and what *shall* this *man do?*
22 Jesus saith unto him, If I will that he tarry [a]till I come, what *is that* to thee? follow
thou me.
23 Then went this saying abroad among
the brethren, that that disciple should not die:
yet Jesus said not unto him, He shall not die;
but, If I will that he tarry till I come, what *is*
that to thee?
24 ¶ This is the disciple which testifieth of
these *things,* and wrote these *things:* and [a]we
know that his testimony is true.
25 [a]And there are also many other *things*
which Jesus did, the which, if they should be
written every one, [b]I suppose that even the
world itself could not contain the books that
should be written. Amen.

21:22 [a]Mat. 16:27,28; 25:31; 1 Cor. 4:5; 11:26; Rev. 2:25; 3:11; 22:7,20
21:24 [a]ch. 19:35; 3 John 12
21:25 [a]ch. 20:30 [b]Amos 7:10

21:22 *till I come.* A clear declaration of the second coming.

‡21:24 *disciple which testifieth.* Testimony is important throughout this Gospel (see note on 1:7). We now learn that it was the beloved disciple who was the witness behind the account. *these things.* Must refer to the whole book. *and wrote these things.* The beloved disciple was not only the witness but also the actual author. *we know.* Evidently John here includes some of his contemporaries in a position to know the truth.

‡21:25 *many other things.* As in 20:30 we are assured that the author has been selective. *even the world itself could not contain.* Probably a hyperbole, but our historical knowledge of Jesus is at best partial. Nevertheless, we have been given all we need to know.

The Harmony of the Gospels

	MATTHEW	MARK	LUKE	JOHN
A PREVIEW OF WHO JESUS IS				
Luke's purpose in writing a gospel			1:1-4	
John's prologue: Jesus Christ, the preexistent Word incarnate				1:1-18
Jesus' legal lineage through Joseph and natural lineage through Mary	1:1-17		3:23b-38	
THE EARLY YEARS OF JOHN THE BAPTIST				
John's birth foretold to Zacharias			1:5-25	
Jesus' birth foretold to Mary			1:26-38	
Mary's visit to Elisabeth and Elisabeth's song			1:39-45	
Mary's song of joy			1:46-56	
John's birth			1:57-66	
Zacharias's prophetic song			1:67-79	
John's growth and early life			1:80	
THE EARLY YEARS OF JESUS CHRIST				
Circumstances of Jesus' birth explained to Joseph	1:18-25			
Birth of Jesus			2:1-7	
Praise of the angels and witness of the shepherds			2:8-20	
Circumcision of Jesus			2:21	
Jesus presented in the temple with the homage of Simeon and Anna			2:22-38	
Visit of the wise men	2:1-12			
Escape into Egypt and murder of boys in Bethlehem	2:13-18			
Return to Nazareth	2:19-23		2:39	
Growth and early life of Jesus			2:40	
Jesus' first passover in Jerusalem			2:41-50	
Jesus' growth to adulthood			2:51-52	
THE PUBLIC MINISTRY OF JOHN THE BAPTIST				
His ministry launched		1:1	3:1-2	
His person, proclamation, and baptism	3:1-6	1:2-6	3:3-6	
His messages to the Pharisees, Sadducees, crowds, publicans, and soldiers	3:7-10		3:7-14	
His description of Christ	3:11-12	1:7-8	3:15-18	
THE END OF JOHN'S MINISTRY AND THE BEGINNING OF CHRIST'S PUBLIC MINISTRY				
Jesus' baptism by John	3:13-17	1:9-11	3:21-23a	
Jesus' temptation in the wilderness	4:1-11	1:12-13	4:1-13	
John's testimony about himself to the priests and Levites				1:19-28
John's testimony to Jesus as the Son of God				1:29-34
Jesus' first followers				1:35-51
Jesus' first miracle: water becomes wine				2:1-11
Jesus' first stay in Capernaum with His relatives and early disciples				2:12
First cleansing of the temple at the passover				2:13-22
Early response to Jesus' miracles				2:23-25
Nicodemus's interview with Jesus				3:1-21
John superseded by Jesus				3:22-36
Jesus' departure from Judea	4:12	1:14a	3:19-20; 4:14a	4:1-4
Discussion with a Samaritan woman				4:5-26
Challenge of a spiritual harvest				4:27-38
Evangelization of Sychar				4:39-42
Arrival in Galilee				4:43-45
THE MINISTRY OF CHRIST IN GALILEE				
Opposition at Home and a New Headquarters				
Nature of the Galilean ministry	4:17	1:14b-15	4:14b-15	
Child at Capernaum healed by Jesus while at Cana				4:46-54
Ministry and rejection at Nazareth			4:16-31a	
Move to Capernaum	4:13-16			

	MATTHEW	MARK	LUKE	JOHN
Disciples Called and Ministry Throughout Galilee				
Call of the four	4:18-22	1:16-20	5:1-11	
Teaching in the synagogue of Capernaum authenticated by healing a demoniac		1:21-28	4:31b-37	
Peter's mother-in-law and others healed	8:14-17	1:29-34	4:38-41	
Tour of Galilee with Simon and others	4:23-25	1:35-39	4:42-44	
Cleansing of a man with leprosy, followed by much publicity	8:2-4	1:40-45	5:12-16	
Forgiving and healing of a paralytic	9:1-8	2:1-12	5:17-26	
Call of Matthew	9:9	2:13-14	5:27-28	
Banquet at Matthew's house	9:10-13	2:15-17	5:29-32	
Jesus defends His disciples for feasting instead of fasting with three parables	9:14-17	2:18-22	5:33-39	
Sabbath Controversies and Withdrawals				
Jesus heals an invalid on the sabbath				5:1-9
Effort to kill Jesus for breaking the sabbath and saying He was equal with God				5:10-18
Discourse demonstrating the Son's equality with the Father				5:19-47
Controversy over disciples' picking grain on the sabbath	12:1-8	2:23-28	6:1-5	
Healing of a man's withered hand on the sabbath	12:9-14	3:1-6	6:6-11	
Withdrawal to the sea of Galilee with large crowds from many places	12:15-21	3:7-12		
Appointment of the twelve and Sermon on the Mount				
Twelve apostles chosen		3:13-19	6:12-16	
Setting of the Sermon	5:1-2		6:17-19	
Blessings of those who inherit the kingdom and woes to those who do not	5:3-12		6:20-26	
Responsibility while awaiting the kingdom	5:13-16			
Law, righteousness, and the kingdom	5:17-20			
Six contrasts in interpreting the law	5:21-48		6:27-30, 32-36	
Three hypocritical "acts of righteousness" to be avoided	6:1-18			
Three prohibitions against avarice, harsh judgment, and unwise exposure of sacred things	6:19-7:6		6:37-42	
Application and conclusion	7:7-27		6:31, 43-49	
Reaction of the crowds	7:28-8:1			
Growing Fame and Emphasis on Repentance				
A centurion's faith and the healing of his servant	8:5-13		7:1-10	
A widow's son raised at Nain			7:11-17	
John the Baptist's relationship to the kingdom	11:2-19		7:18-35	
Woes upon Chorazin and Bethsaida for failure to repent	11:20-30			
Christ's feet anointed by a sinful but contrite woman			7:36-50	
First Public Rejection by Jewish Leaders				
A tour with the twelve and other followers			8:1-3	
Blasphemous accusation by the scribes and Pharisees	12:22-37	3:20-30		
Request for a sign refused	12:38-45			
Announcement of new spiritual kinship	12:46-50	3:31-35	8:19-21	
Secrets About the Kingdom Given in Parables				
TO THE CROWDS BY THE SEA				
The setting of the parables	13:1-3a	4:1-2	8:4	
The parable of the soils	13:3b-23	4:3-25	8:5-18	
The parable of the seed's spontaneous growth		4:26-29		
The parable of the tares	13:24-30			
The parable of the mustard tree	13:31-32	4:30-32		
The parable of the leavened loaf	13:33-35	4:33-34		
TO THE DISCIPLES IN THE HOUSE				
The parable of the tares explained	13:36-43			
The parable of the hidden treasure	13:44			

The Harmony of the Gospels –continued

	MATTHEW	MARK	LUKE	JOHN
The parable of the valuable pearl	13:45-46			
The parable of the net	13:47-50			
The parable of the head of a household	13:51-53			
Continuing Opposition				
Crossing the lake and calming the storm	8:18, 23-27	4:35-41	8:22-25	
Healing the Gerasene demoniacs and resultant opposition	8:28-34	5:1-20	8:26-39	
Return to Galilee, healing of a woman who touched Jesus' garment, and raising of Jairus's daughter	9:18-26	5:21-43	8:40-56	
Three miracles of healing and another blasphemous accusation	9:27-34			
Final visit to unbelieving Nazareth	13:54-58	6:1-6a		
Final Galilean Campaign				
Shortage of workers	9:35-38	6:6b		
Commissioning of the twelve	10:1-42	6:7-11	9:1-5	
Workers sent out	11:1	6:12-13	9:6	
Antipas's mistaken identification of Jesus	14:1-2	6:14-16	9:7-9	
Earlier imprisonment and beheading of John the Baptist	14:3-12	6:17-29		
THE MINISTRY OF CHRIST AROUND GALILEE				
Lesson on the Bread of Life				
Return of the workers		6:30	9:10a	
Withdrawal from Galilee	14:13-14	6:31-34	9:10b-11	6:1-3
Feeding the five thousand	14:15-21	6:35-44	9:12-17	6:4-13
A premature attempt to make Jesus king blocked	14:22-23	6:45-46		6:14-15
Walking on the water during a storm on the lake	14:24-33	6:47-52		6:16-21
Healings at Gennesaret	14:34-36	6:53-56		
Discourse on the true bread of life				6:22-59
Defection among the disciples				6:60-71
Lesson on the Leaven of the Pharisees, Sadducees, and Herodians				
Conflict over the tradition of ceremonial uncleanness	15:1-3a, 7-9b, 3b-6, 10-20	7:1-23		7:1
Ministry to a believing Greek woman in Tyre and Sidon	15:21-28	7:24-30		
Healings in Decapolis	15:29-31	7:31-37		
Feeding the four thousand in Decapolis	15:32-38	8:1-9a		
Return to Galilee and encounter with the Pharisees and Sadducees	15:39-16:4	8:9b-12		
Warning about the error of the Pharisees, Sadducees, and Herodians	16:5-12	8:13-21		
Healing a blind man at Bethsaida		8:22-26		
Lesson of Messiahship Learned and Confirmed				
Peter's identification of Jesus as the Christ and first prophecy of the church	16:13-20	8:27-30	9:18-21	
First direct prediction of the rejection, crucifixion, and resurrection	16:21-26	8:31-37	9:22-25	
Coming of the Son of man and judgment	16:27-28	8:38-9:1	9:26-27	
Transfiguration of Jesus	17:1-8	9:2-8	9:28-36a	
Discussion of resurrection, Elijah, and John the Baptist	17:9-13	9:9-13	9:36b	
Lessons on Responsibility to Others				
Healing of demoniac boy and unbelief rebuked	17:14-20	9:14-29	9:37-43a	
Second prediction of Jesus' death and resurrection	17:22-23	9:30-32	9:43b-45	
Payment of temple tax	17:24-27			
Rivalry over greatness in the kingdom	18:1-5	9:33-37	9:46-48	
Warning against causing believers to sin	18:6-14	9:38-50	9:49-50	
Treatment and forgiveness of a sinning brother	18:15-35			
Journey to Jerusalem for the Feast of Tabernacles				
Complete commitment required of followers	8:19-22		9:57-62	
Ridicule by Jesus' half-brothers				7:2-9
Journey through Samaria			9:51-56	7:10

	MATTHEW	MARK	LUKE	JOHN
THE LATER JUDEAN MINISTRY OF CHRIST				
Ministry Beginning at the Feast of Tabernacles				
Mixed reaction to Jesus' teaching and miracles				7:11-31
Frustrated attempt to arrest Jesus				7:32-52
Jesus' forgiveness of a woman caught in adultery				[7:53-8:11]
Conflict over Jesus' claim to be the light of the world				8:12-20
Jesus' relationship to God the Father				8:21-30
Jesus' relationship to Abraham, and attempted stoning				8:31-59
Healing of a man born blind				9:1-7
Response of the blind man's neighbors				9:8-12
Examination and excommunication of the blind man by the Pharisees				9:13-34
Jesus' identification of Himself to the blind man				9:35-38
Spiritual blindness of the Pharisees				9:39-41
Allegory of the good shepherd and the thief				10:1-18
Further division among the Jews				10:19-21
Private Lessons on Loving Service and Prayer				
Commissioning of the seventy			10:1-16	
Return of the seventy			10:17-24	
Story of the good Samaritan			10:25-37	
Jesus' visit with Mary and Martha			10:38-42	
Lesson on how to pray and parable of the bold friend			11:1-13	
Second Debate with the Scribes and the Pharisees				
A third blasphemous accusation and a second debate			11:14-36	
Woes to the Pharisees and the scribes while eating with a Pharisee			11:37-54	
Warning the disciples about hypocrisy			12:1-12	
Warning about greed and trust in wealth			12:13-34	
Warning against being unprepared for the Son of man's coming			12:35-48	
Warning about the coming division			12:49-53	
Warning against failing to discern the present time			12:54-59	
Two alternatives: repent or perish			13:1-9	
Opposition from a synagogue ruler for healing a woman on the sabbath			13:10-21	
Another attempt to stone or arrest Jesus for blasphemy at the feast of dedication				10:22-39
THE MINISTRY OF CHRIST IN AND AROUND PEREA				
Principles of Discipleship				
From Jerusalem to Perea				10:40-42
Question about salvation and entering the kingdom			13:22-30	
Anticipation of Jesus' coming death and His sorrow over Jerusalem			13:31-35	
Healing of a man with dropsy while eating with a prominent Pharisee on the sabbath, and three parables suggested by the occasion			14:1-24	
Cost of discipleship			14:25-35	
Parables in defense of association with sinners			15:1-32	
Parable to teach the proper use of money			16:1-13	
Story to teach the danger of wealth			16:14-31	
Four lessons on discipleship			17:1-10	
Sickness and death of Lazarus				11:1-16
Lazarus raised from the dead				11:17-44
Decision of the Sanhedrin to put Jesus to death				11:45-54
Teaching While on Final Journey to Jerusalem				
Healing of ten lepers while passing through Samaria and Galilee			17:11-21	
Instructions regarding the Son of man's coming			17:22-37	
Two parables on prayer: the persistent widow, and the Pharisee and the publican			18:1-14	
Conflict with Pharisaic teaching on divorce	19:1-12	10:1-12		

The Harmony of the Gospels –continued

	MATTHEW	MARK	LUKE	JOHN
Example of little children in relation to the kingdom	19:13-15	10:13-16	18:15-17	
Riches and the kingdom	19:16-30	10:17-31	18:18-30	
Parable of the landowner's sovereignty	20:1-16			
Third prediction of Jesus' death and resurrection	20:17-19	10:32-34	18:31-34	
Warning against ambitious pride	20:20-28	10:35-45		
Healing of blind Bartimeus and his companion	20:29-34	10:46-52	18:35-43	
Salvation of Zaccheus			19:1-10	
Parable to teach responsibility while the kingdom is delayed			19:11-28	
THE FORMAL PRESENTATION OF CHRIST TO ISRAEL AND THE RESULTING CONFLICT				
Triumphal Entry and the Fig Tree				
Arrival at Bethany				11:55-12:1, 9-11
Triumphal entry into Jerusalem	21:1-3, 6-7, 4-5, 8-11, 14-17	11:1-11	19:29-44	12:12-19
Cursing of the fig tree having leaves but no figs	21:18-19a	11:12-14		
Second cleansing of the temple	21:12-13	11:15-18	19:45-48	
Request of some Greeks to see Jesus and necessity of the Son of man's being lifted up				12:20-36a
Different responses to Jesus and Jesus' response to the crowds				12:36b-50
Withered fig tree and the lesson on faith	21:19b-22	11:19-25	21:37-38	
Official Challenge to Christ's Authority				
Questioning of Jesus' authority by the chief priests, teachers of the law, and elders	21:23-27	11:27-33	20:1-8	
Jesus' response with His own question and three parables	21:28-22:14	12:1-12	20:9-19	
Attempts by Pharisees and Herodians to trap Jesus with a question about paying taxes to Caesar	22:15-22	12:13-17	20:20-26	
Sadducees' puzzling question about the resurrection	22:23-33	12:18-27	20:27-40	
A Pharisee's legal question	22:34-40	12:28-34		
Christ's Response to His Enemies' Challenges				
Christ's relationship to David as son and Lord	22:41-46	12:35-37	20:41-44	
Seven woes against the scribes and Pharisees	23:1-36	12:38-40	20:45-47	
Jesus' sorrow over Jerusalem	23:37-39			
A poor widow's gift of all she had		12:41-44	21:1-4	
PROPHECIES IN PREPARATION FOR THE DEATH OF CHRIST				
The Olivet Discourse: Jesus Speaks Prophetically About the Temple and His Own Second Coming				
Setting of the discourse	24:1-3	13:1-4	21:5-7	
Beginning of birth pains	24:4-14	13:5-13	21:8-19	
Abomination of desolation and subsequent distress	24:15-28	13:14-23	21:20-24	
Coming of the Son of man	24:29-31	13:24-27	21:25-27	
Signs of nearness but unknown time	24:32-41	13:28-32	21:28-33	
Five parables to teach watchfulness and faithfulness	24:42-25:30	13:33-37	21:34-36	
Judgment at the Son of man's coming	25:31-46			
Arrangements for Betrayal				
Plot by the Sanhedrin to arrest and kill Jesus	26:1-5	14:1-2	22:1-2	
Mary's anointing of Jesus for burial	26:6-13	14:3-9		12:2-8
Judas's agreement to betray Jesus	26:14-16	14:10-11	22:3-6	
The Last Supper				
Preparation for the passover meal	26:17-19	14:12-16	22:7-13	
Beginning of the passover meal and dissension among the disciples over greatness	26:20	14:17	22:14-16, 24-30	
Washing the disciples' feet				13:1-20
Identification of the betrayer	26:21-25	14:18-21	22:21-23	13:21-30

	MATTHEW	MARK	LUKE	JOHN
Prediction of Peter's denial	26:31-35	14:27-31	22:31-38	13:31-38
Conclusion of the meal and the Lord's Supper instituted (1 Cor 11:23-26)	26:26-29	14:22-25	22:17-20	
Discourse and Prayers from the Upper Room to Gethsemane				
Questions about His destination, the Father, and the Holy Spirit answered				14:1-31
The vine and the branches				15:1-17
Opposition from the world				15:18-16:4
Coming and ministry of the Spirit				16:5-15
Prediction of joy over His resurrection				16:16-22
Promise of answered prayer and peace				16:23-33
Jesus' prayer for His disciples and all who believe				17:1-26
Jesus' three agonizing prayers in Gethsemane	26:30, 36-46	14:26, 32-42	22:39-46	18:1
THE DEATH OF CHRIST				
Betrayal and Arrest				
Jesus betrayed, arrested, and forsaken	26:47-56	14:43-52	22:47-53	18:2-12
Trial				
First Jewish phase, before Annas				18:13-14, 19-23
Second Jewish phase, before Caiaphas and the Sanhedrin	26:57, 59-68	14:53, 55-65	22:54a, 63-65	18:24
Peter's denials	26:58, 69-75	14:54, 66-72	22:54b-62	18:15-18, 25-27
Third Jewish phase, before the Sanhedrin	27:1	15:1a	22:66-71	
Remorse and suicide of Judas Iscariot (Acts 1:18-19)	27:3-10			
First Roman phase, before Pilate	27:2, 11-14	15:1b-5	23:1-5	18:28-38
Second Roman phase, before Herod Antipas			23:6-12	
Third Roman phase, before Pilate	27:15-26	15:6-15	23:13-25	18:39-19:16a
Crucifixion				
Mockery by the Roman soldiers	27:27-30	15:16-19		
Journey to Golgotha	27:31-34	15:20-23	23:26-33a	19:16b-17
First three hours of crucifixion	27:35-44	15:24-32	23:33b-43	19:18, 23-24, 19-22, 25-27
Last three hours of crucifixion	27:45-50	15:33-37	23:44-45a, 46	19:28-30
Witness of Jesus' death	27:51-56	15:38-41	23:45b, 47-49	
Burial				
Certification of Jesus' death and procurement of His body	27:57-58	15:42-45	23:50-52	19:31-38
Jesus' body placed in a tomb	27:59-60	15:46	23:53-54	19:39-42
The tomb watched by the women and guarded by the soldiers	27:61-66	15:47	23:55-56	
THE RESURRECTION AND ASCENSION OF CHRIST				
The Empty Tomb				
The tomb visited by the women	28:1	16:1		
The stone rolled away	28:2-4			
The tomb found to be empty by the women	28:5-8	16:2-8	24:1-8	20:1
The tomb found to be empty by Peter and John			24:9-12	20:2-10
The Post Resurrection Appearances				
Appearance to Mary Magdalene		[16:9-11]		20:11-18
Appearance to the other women	28:9-10			
Report of the soldiers to the Jewish authorities	28:11-15			
Appearance to the two disciples traveling to Emmaus		[16:12-13]	24:13-32	
Report of the two disciples to the rest (1 Cor. 15:5a)			24:33-35	
Appearance to the ten assembled disciples		[16:14]	24:36-43	20:19-25
Appearance to the eleven assembled disciples (1 Cor. 15:5b)				20:26-31
Appearance to the seven disciples while fishing				21:1-25
Appearance to the eleven in Galilee (1 Cor. 15:6)	28:16-20	[16:15-18]		
Appearance to James, Jesus' brother (1 Cor. 15:7)				
Appearance to the disciples in Jerusalem (Acts 1:3-8)			24:44-49	
The Ascension				
Christ's parting blessing and departure (Acts 1:9-12)		[16:19-20]	24:50-53	

Major Archaeological Finds Relating to the NT

SITE OR ARTIFACT	LOCATION	RELATING SCRIPTURE
	ISRAEL	
Herod's temple	Jerusalem	Luke 1:9
Herod's winter palace	Jericho	Mat 2:4
The Herodium (possible site of Herod's tomb)	Near Bethlehem	Mat 2:19
Masada	Southwest of Dead Sea	Cf. Luke 21:20
Early synagogue	Capernaum	Mark 1:21
Pool of Siloam	Jerusalem	John 9:7
Pool of Bethesda	Jerusalem	John 5:2
Pilate inscription	Caesarea	Luke 3:1
Inscription: Gentile entrance of temple sanctuary	Jerusalem	Acts 21:27-29
Skeletal remains of crucified man	Jerusalem	Luke 23:33
Peter's house	Capernaum	Mat 8:14
Jacob's well	Nablus	John 4:5-6
	ASIA MINOR	
Derbe inscription	Kerti Hüyük	Acts 14:20
Sergius Paulus inscription	Antioch in Pisidia	Acts 13:6-7
Zeus altar (Satan's throne?)	Pergamum	Rev 2:13
Fourth-century B.C. walls	Assos	Acts 20:13-14
Artemis temple and altar	Ephesus	Acts 19:27-28
Ephesian theater	Ephesus	Acts 19:29
Silversmith shops	Ephesus	Acts 19:24
Artemis statues	Ephesus	Acts 19:35
	GREECE	
Erastus inscription	Corinth	Rom 16:23
Synagogue inscription	Corinth	Acts 18:4
Meat market inscription	Corinth	1 Cor 10:25
Cult dining rooms (in Asklepius and Demeter temples)	Corinth	1 Cor 8:10
Court (bema)	Corinth	Acts 18:12
Marketplace (bema)	Philippi	Acts 16:19
Starting gate for races	Isthmia	1 Cor 9:24,26
Gallio inscription	Delphi	Acts 18:12
Egnatian Way	Kavalla (Neapolis), Philippi, Apollonia, Thessalonica	Cf. Acts 16:11-12; 17:1
Politarch inscription	Thessalonica	Acts 17:6
	ITALY	
Tomb of Augustus	Rome	Luke 2:1
Mamertine Prison	Rome	2 Tim 1:16-17; 2:9; 4:6-8
Appian Way	Puteoli to Rome	Acts 28:13-16
Golden House of Nero	Rome	Cf. Acts 25:10; 1 Pet 2:13
Arch of Titus	Rome	Cf. Luke 19:43-44; 21:6,20

The Acts of the Apostles

INTRODUCTION

Author

Although the author does not name himself, evidence outside the Scriptures and inferences from the book itself lead to the conclusion that the author was Luke.

The earliest of the external testimonies appears in the Muratorian Canon (c. A.D. 170), where the explicit statement is made that Luke was the author of both the third Gospel and the "Acts of All the Apostles." Eusebius (c. 325) lists information from numerous sources to identify the author of these books as Luke (*Ecclesiastical History,* 3.4).

Within the writing itself are some clues as to who the author was:

1. *Luke, the companion of Paul.* In the description of the happenings in Acts, certain passages make use of the pronoun "we." At these points the author includes himself as a companion of Paul in his travels (16:10–17; 20:5—21:18; 27:1—28:16). A historian as careful with details as this author proves to be would have good reason for choosing to use "we" in some places and "they" elsewhere. The author was therefore probably present with Paul at the particular events described in the "we" sections.

These "we" passages include the period of Paul's two-year imprisonment at Rome (ch. 28). During this time Paul wrote, among other letters, Philemon and Colossians. In them he sends greetings from his companions, and Luke is included among them (Philem 23–24; Col 4:10–17). In fact, after eliminating those who, for one reason or another, would not fit the requirements for the author of Acts, Luke is left as the most likely candidate.

2. *Luke, the physician.* Although it cannot be proved that the author of Acts was a physician simply from his vocabulary, the words he uses and the traits and education reflected in his writings fit well his role as a physician (see, e.g., note on 28:6). It is true that the doctor of the first century did not have as specialized a vocabulary as that of doctors today, but there are some usages in Luke-Acts that seem to suggest that a medical man was the author of these books. And it should be remembered that Paul uses the term "physician" in describing Luke (Col 4:14).

Date

Two dates are possible for the writing of this book: (1) c. A.D. 63, soon after the last event recorded in the book, and (2) c. 70 or even later.

The earlier date is supported by:

1. *Silence about later events.* While arguments from silence are not conclusive, it is perhaps significant that the book contains no allusion to events that happened after the close of Paul's two-year imprisonment in Rome: e.g., the burning of Rome and the persecution of the Christians there (A.D. 64), the martyrdom of Peter and Paul (possibly 67) and the destruction of Jerusalem (70).

2. *No outcome of Paul's trial.* If Luke knew the outcome of the trial Paul was waiting for (28:30), why did he not record it at the close of Acts? Perhaps it was because he had brought the history up to date.

Those who prefer the later date hold that 1:8 reveals one of the purposes Luke had in writing his history, and that this purpose influenced the way the book ended. Luke wanted to show how the church penetrated the world of his day in ever-widening circles (Jerusalem, Judea, Samaria, the ends of the earth) until it reached Rome, the world's political and cultural center. On this understanding, mention of the martyrdom of Paul (c. A.D. 67) and of the destruction of Jerusalem (70) was not pertinent. This would allow for the writing of Acts c. 70 or even later.

Recipient

The recipient of the book, Theophilus, is the same person addressed in the first volume, the Gospel of Luke (see Introduction to Luke: Recipient and Purpose).

Importance

The book of Acts provides a bridge for the writings of the NT. As a second volume to Luke's Gospel, it joins what Jesus "began both to do and teach" (1:1) as told in the Gospels with what He continued to do and teach through the apostles' preaching and the establishment of the church. Besides linking the Gospel narratives on the one hand and the apostolic letters on the other, it supplies an account of the life of Paul from which we can learn the setting for his letters. Geographically its story spans the lands between Jerusalem, where the church began, and Rome, the political center of the empire. Historically it recounts the first 30 years of the church. It is also a bridge that ties the church in its beginning with each succeeding age. This book may be studied to gain an understanding of the principles that ought to govern the church of any age.

Theme and Purpose

The theme of the work is best summarized in 1:8. It was ordinary procedure for a historian at this time to begin a second volume by summarizing the first volume and indicating the contents anticipated in his second volume. Luke summarized his first volume in 1:1–3; the theme of his second volume is presented in the words of Jesus: "Ye shall be witnesses unto me both in Jerusalem, and in all Judea, and in Samaria, and unto the uttermost part of the earth." This is, in effect, an outline of the book of Acts (see Plan and Outline).

The main purposes of the book appear to be:

1. *To present a history.* The significance of Acts as a historical account of Christian origins cannot be overestimated. It tells of the founding of the church, the spread of the gospel, the beginnings of congregations, and evangelistic efforts in the apostolic pattern. One of the unique aspects of Christianity is its firm historical foundation. The life and teachings of Jesus Christ are established in the four Gospel narratives, and the book of Acts provides a coordinated account of the beginnings of the church.

2. *To give a defense.* One finds embedded in Acts a record of Christian defenses made to both Jews (e.g., 4:8–12) and Gentiles (e.g., 25:8–11), with the underlying purpose of conversion. It shows how the early church coped with pagan and Jewish thought, the Roman government and Hellenistic society.

Luke probably wrote this work as Paul awaited trial in Rome. If his case came to court, what better court brief could Paul have had than a life of Jesus, a history of the beginnings of the church (including the activity of Paul) and an early collection of Paul's letters?

3. *To provide a guide.* Luke had no way of knowing how long the church would continue on this earth, but as long as it pursues its course, the book of Acts will be one of its major guides. In Acts we see basic principles being applied to specific situations in the context of problems and persecutions. These same principles continue to be applicable until Christ returns.

4. *To depict the triumph of Christianity in the face of bitter persecution.* The success of the church in carrying the gospel from Jerusalem to Rome and in planting local churches across the Roman empire demonstrated that Christianity was not a mere work of man. God was in it (see 5:35–39).

Characteristics

1. *Accurate historical detail.* Every page of Acts abounds with sharp, precise details, to the delight of the historian. The account covers a period of about 30 years and reaches across the lands from Jerusalem to Rome. Luke's description of these times and places is filled with all kinds of people and cultures, a variety of governmental administrations, court scenes in Cesarea, and dramatic events involving such centers as Antioch, Ephesus, Athens, Corinth and Rome. Barbarian country districts and Jewish centers are included as well. Yet in each instance archaeological findings reveal that Luke uses the proper terms for the time and place being described. Hostile criticism has not succeeded in disproving the detailed accuracy of Luke's political and geographical designations.

2. *Literary excellence.* Not only does Luke have a large vocabulary compared with other NT writers, but he also uses these words in literary styles that fit the cultural settings of the events he is recording. At times he employs good, classical Greek; at other times the Palestinian Aramaic of the first century shows through his expressions. This is an indication of Luke's careful practice of using language appropriate to the time and place being described. Aramaisms are used when Luke is describing happenings that took place in the Holy Land (chs. 1—12). When, however, Paul departs for Hellenistic lands beyond the territories where Aramaic-speaking people live, Aramaisms cease.

3. *Dramatic description.* Luke's skillful use of speeches contributes to the drama of his narrative. Not only are they carefully spaced and well balanced between Peter and Paul, but the speeches of a

number of other individuals add variety and vividness to the account. Luke's use of details brings the action to life. Nowhere in ancient literature is there an account of a shipwreck superior to Luke's with its nautical details (ch. 27). The book is vivid and fast-moving throughout.

4. *Objective account.* Luke's careful arrangement of material need not detract from the accuracy of his record. He demonstrates the objectivity of his account by recording the failures as well as the successes, the bad as well as the good, in the early church. Not only is the discontent between the Grecian Jews and the Hebraic Jews recorded (6:1) but also the discord between Paul and Barnabas (15:39). Divisions and differences are recognized (15:2; 21:20–21).

Plan and Outline

Luke weaves together different interests and emphases as he relates the beginnings and expansion of the church. The design of his book revolves around (1) key persons: Peter and Paul; (2) important topics and events: the role of the Holy Spirit, pioneer missionary outreach to new fields, conversions, the growth of the church, and life in the Christian community; (3) significant problems: conflict between Jews and Gentiles, persecution of the church by some Jewish elements, trials before Jews and Romans, confrontations with Gentiles, and other hardships in the ministry; (4) geographical advances: five significant stages (see the quotations in the outline; see also map, p. 1582).

I. Peter and the Beginnings of the Church in Palestine (chs. 1—12)
- A. "Throughout all Judea and Galilee and Samaria" (1:1—9:31; see 9:31)
  - 1. Introduction (1:1–2)
  - 2. Christ's postresurrection ministry (1:3–11)
  - 3. The period of waiting for the Holy Spirit (1:12–26)
  - 4. The filling with the Spirit (ch. 2)
  - 5. The healing of the lame beggar and the resultant arrest of Peter and John (3:1—4:31)
  - 6. The community of goods (4:32—5:11)
  - 7. The arrest of the 12 apostles (5:12–42)
  - 8. The choice of the seven (6:1–7)
  - 9. Stephen's arrest and martyrdom (6:8—7:60)
  - 10. The scattering of the Jerusalem believers (8:1–4)
  - 11. Philip's ministry (8:5–40)
    - a. In Samaria (8:5–25)
    - b. To the Ethiopian eunuch (8:26–40)
  - 12. Saul's conversion (9:1–31)
- B. "To Phenice and Cyprus and Antioch" (9:32—12:25; see 11:19)
  - 1. Peter's ministry on the Mediterranean coast (9:32—11:18)
    - a. To Aeneas and Dorcas (9:32–43)
    - b. To Cornelius (10:1—11:18)
  - 2. The new Gentile church in Antioch (11:19–30)
  - 3. Herod's persecution of the church and his subsequent death (ch. 12)

II. Paul and the Expansion of the Church from Antioch to Rome (chs. 13—28)
- A. "Through Phrygia and the region of Galatia" (13:1—15:35; see 16:6)
  - 1. Paul's first missionary journey (chs. 13—14)
  - 2. The Jerusalem council (15:1–35)
- B. "Over into Macedonia" (15:36—21:16; see 16:9)
  - 1. Paul's second missionary journey (15:36—18:22)
  - 2. Paul's third missionary journey (18:23—21:16)
- C. "To Rome" (21:17—28:31; see 28:14)
  - 1. Paul's imprisonment in Jerusalem (21:17—23:35)
    - a. Arrest (21:17—22:29)
    - b. Trial before the Sanhedrin (22:30—23:11)
    - c. Transfer to Cesarea (23:12–35)
  - 2. Paul's imprisonment in Cesarea (chs. 24—26)
    - a. Trial before Felix (ch. 24)
    - b. Trial before Festus (25:1–12)
    - c. Hearing before Festus and Agrippa (25:13—26:32)
  - 3. Voyage to Rome (27:1—28:15)
  - 4. Two years under house arrest in Rome (28:16–31)

The ascension

1 The former treatise have I made,
[a]O Theophilus, of all that Jesus began
both to do and teach,
2 [a]Until the day *in* which he was taken up,
after that he through the Holy Ghost [b]had giv-
en commandments unto the Apostles whom
he had chosen:
3 [a]To whom also he shewed himself alive
after his passion by many infallible proofs, being seen of them forty days, and speaking of
the *things* pertaining to the kingdom of God:
4 [a]And, [1]being assembled together with
them, commanded them that *they* should not
depart from Jerusalem, but wait for the promise of the Father, [b]which, *saith he,* ye have
heard of me.
5 [a]For John truly baptized with water; [b]but
ye shall be baptized with the Holy Ghost not
many days hence.
6 When they therefore were come together, they asked of him, saying, [a]Lord, wilt thou
at this time [b]restore again the kingdom to Israel?
7 And he said unto them, [a]It is not for you
to know *the* times or *the* seasons, which the
Father hath put in his own power.
8 [a]But ye shall receive [1]power, [b]after that
the Holy Ghost is come upon you: and [c]ye
shall be witnesses unto me both in Jerusalem,
and in all Judea, and in Samaria, and unto the
uttermost part of the earth.
9 [a]And when he had spoken these *things,*
while they beheld, [b]he was taken up; and a
cloud received him out of their sight.
10 And while they looked stedfastly toward
heaven as he went *up,* behold, two men stood
by them [a]in white apparel;
11 Which also said, [a]Ye men of Galilee,
why stand ye gazing up into heaven? this *same*
Jesus, which is taken up from you into heaven,
[b]shall so come *in* like manner as ye have seen
him go into heaven.
12 [a]Then returned they unto Jerusalem
from the mount called Olivet, which is from
Jerusalem a sabbath day's journey.
13 And when they were come in, they
went up [a]into an upper room, where abode
both [b]Peter, and James, and John, and Andrew, Philip, and Thomas, Bartholomew, and
Matthew, James *the son* of Alpheus, and [c]Si-
mon Zelotes, and [d]Judas *the brother* of James.
14 [a]These all continued with one accord in
prayer and supplication, with [b]the women,
and Mary the mother of Jesus, and with [c]his
brethren.

Matthias chosen to replace Judas

15 ¶ And in those days Peter stood up in

1:1 [a]Luke 1:3
1:2 [a]Mark 16:19; 1 Tim. 3:16 [b]Mat. 28:19; John 20:21
1:3 [a]Mark 16:14
1:4 [1]Or, *eating together with them* [a]Luke 24:43 [b]Luke 24:49; John 14:16
1:5 [a]Mat. 3:11 [b]Joel 3:18
1:6 [a]Mat. 24:3 [b]Is. 1:26
1:7 [a]1 Thes. 5:1
1:8 [1]Or, *the power of the Holy Ghost coming upon you* [a]ch. 2:1,4 [b]Luke 24:49 [c]Luke 24:48
1:9 [a]Luke 24:51 [b]ver. 2
1:10 [a]Mat. 28:3; Mark 16:5; Luke 24:4; John 20:12; ch. 10:3,30
1:11 [a]ch. 2:7; 13:31 [b]Dan. 7:13; Mat. 24:30; Mark 13:26; Luke 21:27; John 14:3; 1 Thes. 1:10; 4:16; 2 Thes. 1:10; Rev. 1:7
1:12 [a]Luke 24:52
1:13 [a]ch. 9:37,39; 20:8 [b]Mat. 10:2-4 [c]Luke 6:15 [d]Jude 1
1:14 [a]ch. 2:1,46 [b]Luke 23:49,55 [c]Mat. 13:55

1:1 *The former treatise.* The Gospel of Luke. Acts was addressed to the same patron, Theophilus (see Introduction to Luke: Recipient and Purpose). *began both to do and teach.* An apt summation of Luke's Gospel, implying that Jesus' work continues in Acts through His own personal interventions and the ministry of the Holy Spirit.
1:2 *taken up.* The last scene of Luke's Gospel (24:50–52) and the opening scene of this second volume (vv. 6–11). The ascension occurred 40 days after the resurrection (v. 3). *through the Holy Ghost.* Jesus' postresurrection instruction of His apostles was carried on through the Holy Spirit, and succeeding statements make it clear that what the apostles were to accomplish was likewise to be done through the Spirit (vv. 4–5,8; see Luke 24:49; John 20:22; see also Introduction to Judges: Theme and Theology). Luke characteristically stresses the Holy Spirit's work and enabling power (e.g., v. 8; 2:4,17; 4:8,31; 5:3; 6:3,5; 7:55; 8:16; 9:17,31; 10:44; 13:2,4; 15:28; 16:6; 19:2,6; see note on Luke 4:1).
1:3 *many infallible proofs.* See the resurrection appearances (Mat 28:1–20; Luke 24:1–53; John 20:1–29; 1 Cor 15:3–8). *kingdom of God.* The heart of Jesus' preaching (see notes on Mat 3:2; Luke 4:43).
1:4 *the promise of the Father.* The Holy Spirit (see John 14:26; 15:26–27; 16:12–13).
1:5 *John truly baptized with water.* See Luke 3:16. *not many days hence.* The day of Pentecost came ten days later, when the baptism with the Holy Spirit occurred (2:1–4).
1:6 *restore again the kingdom to Israel.* Like their fellow countrymen, they were looking for the deliverance of the people of Israel from foreign domination and for the establishment of an earthly kingdom. The reference to the coming of the Spirit had caused them to wonder if the new age was about to dawn.
1:7 *the times or the seasons.* The elapsing time or the character of coming events (see 1 Thes 5:1).
1:8 A virtual outline of Acts: The apostles were to be witnesses in Jerusalem (chs. 1–7), Judea and Samaria (chs. 8–9) and the ends of the earth—including Cesarea, Antioch, Asia Minor, Greece and Rome (chs. 10–28). However, they were not to begin this staggering task until they had been equipped with the power of the Spirit (vv. 4–5). *ye shall be witnesses unto me.* An important theme throughout Acts (2:32; 3:15; 5:32; 10:39; 13:31; 22:15). *Judea.* The region in which Jerusalem was located. *Samaria.* The adjoining region to the north.
1:10 *two men . . . in white apparel;* A common description of angels.
1:11 *men of Galilee.* All the twelve were from Galilee except Judas, and he was no longer present. *in like manner.* In the same resurrection body and in clouds and "great glory" (Mat 24:30).
1:12 *mount called Olivet.* The ascension occurred on the eastern slope of the mount between Jerusalem and Bethany (Luke 19:28–29,37; see notes on Zech 14:4; Mark 11:1; Luke 19:29). *sabbath day's journey.* About 3/4 mile (1,100 meters). This distance was drawn from rabbinical reasoning based on several OT passages (Ex 16:29; Num 35:5; Josh 3:4). A faithful Jew was to travel no farther on the sabbath.
‡1:13 *room.* Probably a room on the upper floor of a large house, such as the one where the Last Supper was held (Mark 14:15) or that of Mary, mother of Mark (see note on 12:12). *Bartholomew.* Apparently John calls him Nathanael (see John 1:45–49; 21:2). *James the son of Alpheus.* The same as James the younger (Mark 15:40). *Simon Zelotes.* See note on Mat 10:4. *Judas the brother of James.* Not Judas Iscariot, but the same as Thaddeus (Mat 10:3; Mark 3:18).
1:14 *with the women.* Possibly wives of the apostles (cf. 1 Cor 9:5) and those listed as ministering to Jesus (Mat 27:55; Luke 8:2–3; 24:22). *Mary the mother of Jesus.* Last mentioned here in Scripture. *brethren.* See note on Luke 8:19. These brothers would include James, who later became important in the church (12:17; 15:13; Gal 2:9).

the midst of the disciples, and said, (the number [a]of names together were about an hundred *and* twenty,)

16 Men *and* brethren, this scripture must needs have been fulfilled, [a]which the Holy Ghost by the mouth of David spake before concerning Judas, [b]which was guide to them that took Jesus.

17 For [a]he was numbered with us, and had obtained part of [b]this ministry.

18 [a]Now this *man* purchased a field with [b]the reward of iniquity; and falling headlong, he burst asunder in the midst, and all his bowels gushed out.

19 And it was known unto all the dwellers at Jerusalem; insomuch as that field is called in their proper tongue, Aceldama, that is to say, The field of blood.

20 For it is written in the book of Psalms, [a]Let his habitation be desolate, and let no man dwell therein: and [b]his [1]bishoprick let another take.

21 Wherefore of these men which have companied with us all the time that the Lord Jesus went in and out among us,

22 Beginning from the baptism of John, unto *that same* day that [a]he was taken up from us, must one be ordained [b]*to be* a witness with us of his resurrection.

23 And they appointed two, Joseph called [a]Barsabas, who was surnamed Justus, and Matthias.

24 And they prayed, and said, Thou, Lord, [a]which knowest the hearts of all *men,* shew whether of these two thou hast chosen,

25 [a]That *he* may take part of this ministry and apostleship, from which Judas by transgression fell, that *he* might go to his own place.

26 And they gave forth their lots; and the lot fell upon Matthias; and he was numbered with the eleven apostles.

1:15 [a]Rev. 3:4
1:16 [a]Ps. 41:9; John 13:18 [b]Luke 22:47; John 18:3
1:17 [a]Mat. 10:4; Luke 6:16 [b]ver. 25; ch. 12:25; 20:24; 21:19
1:18 [a]Mat. 27:5,7,8 [b]Mat. 26:15; 2 Pet. 2:15
1:20 [1]Or, *office,* or, *charge* [a]Ps. 69:25 [b]Ps. 109:8
1:22 [a]ver. 9 [b]ver. 8; John 15:27; ch. 4:33
1:23 [a]ch. 15:22
1:24 [a]1 Sam. 16:7; 1 Chr. 28:9; 29:17; Jer. 11:20; 17:10; ch. 15:8; Rev. 2:23
1:25 [a]ver. 17
2:1 [a]Lev. 23:15; Deut. 16:9; ch. 20:16 [b]ch. 1:14
2:2 [a]ch. 4:31
2:4 [a]ch. 1:5 [b]Mark 16:17; ch. 10:46; 19:6; 1 Cor. 12:10,28, 30; 13:1; 14:2

The gift of the Holy Spirit

2 And when [a]the day of Pentecost was fully come, [b]they were all with one accord in one place.

2 And suddenly there came a sound from heaven as of a rushing mighty wind, and [a]it filled all the house where they were sitting.

3 And there appeared unto them cloven tongues like as of fire, and it sat upon each of them.

4 And [a]they were all filled with the Holy Ghost, and began [b]to speak with other tongues, as the Spirit gave them utterance.

1:16 *this scripture must needs have been fulfilled.* The Scriptures referred to were Ps 69:25; 109:8 (see v. 20). Both before and after Christ came, numerous psalms were viewed as Messianic. What happened in the psalmist's experience was typical of the experiences of the Messiah. No doubt Jesus' instruction in Luke 24:27,45–47 included these Scriptures.

1:18 *this man purchased a field.* Judas bought the field indirectly: The money he returned to the priests (Mat 27:3) was used to purchase the potter's field (Mat 27:7). *falling headlong.* Mat 27:5 reports that Judas hanged himself. It appears that when the body finally fell, either because of decay or because someone cut it down, it was in a decomposed condition and so broke open in the middle. Another possibility is that "hanged" in Mat 27:5 means "impaled" (the Hebrew of Esth 2:23 can be translated "impaled"; see note there) and that the gruesome results of Judas's suicide are described here.

1:19 *Aceldama.* An Aramaic term, no doubt adopted by people who knew the circumstances, for the field was purchased with Judas's blood money (Mat 27:3–8).

1:20 *it is written.* Two passages of Scripture (Ps 69:25; 109:8; see v. 16) were put together to suggest that Judas had left a vacancy that had to be filled.

1:21 *went in and out among us.* Ministered publicly.

1:22 *a witness with us of his resurrection.* Apparently several met this requirement. On this occasion, however, the believers were selecting someone to become an official witness to the resurrection—thus, a 12th apostle (v. 25).

1:23 *Barsabas.* Means "son of (the) sabbath." This patronymic was used for two early Jewish Christians, possibly brothers. One was Joseph (here); the other was Judas, a prophet in Jerusalem who was sent to Antioch with Silas (15:22,32). *Justus.* Joseph's Hellenistic name. Nothing more is known of him.

1:26 *gave forth their lots.* See Prov 16:33. By casting lots they were able to allow God the right of choice. The use of rocks or sticks to designate the choice was common (see 1 Chr 26:13–16; see also notes on Neh 11:1; Jonah 1:7). This is the Bible's last mention of casting lots.

2:1 *day of Pentecost.* The 50th day after the sabbath of passover week (Lev 23:15–16), thus the first day of the week. Pentecost is also called the feast of weeks (Deut 16:10), the feast of harvest (Ex 23:16) and the day of the firstfruits (Num 28:26). *they were all with one accord.* The nearest antecedent of "they" is the 11 apostles (plus Matthias), but the reference is probably to all those mentioned in 1:13–15. *in one place.* Evidently not the upstairs room where they were staying (1:13) but perhaps some place in the temple precincts, for the apostles were "continually in the temple" when it was open (Luke 24:53; see note there).

2:2 *rushing mighty wind.* Breath or wind is a symbol of the Spirit of God (see Ezek 37:9,14; John 3:8). The coming of the Spirit is marked by audible (wind) and visible (fire) signs. *house.* May refer to the temple (cf. 7:47).

2:3 *tongues.* A descriptive metaphor appropriate to the context, in which several languages are about to be spoken. *fire.* A symbol of the divine presence (see Ex 3:2 and note), it was also associated with judgment (see Mat 3:12).

2:4 *all.* Could refer either to the apostles or to the 120. Those holding that the 120 are meant point to the fulfillment of Joel's prophecy (vv. 17–18) as involving more than the 12 apostles. The nearest reference, however, is to the apostles (see note on v. 1), and the narrative continues with Peter and the 11 standing to address the crowd (v. 14). *filled with the Holy Ghost.* A fulfillment of 1:5,8; see also Jesus' promise in Luke 24:49. Their spirits were completely under the control of the Spirit; their words were His words. *with other tongues.* The Spirit enabled them to speak in languages they had not previously learned (the Greek can mean "tongues" or "languages"; also in v. 11). Two other examples of speaking in tongues are found in Acts (10:46; 19:6). One extended NT passage deals with this spiritual gift (1 Cor 12–14). Not all agree, however, that these other passages refer to speaking in known languages. The gift had particular relevance here, where people of different nationalities and languages were gathered.

5 And there were dwelling at Jerusalem
Jews, devout men, out of every nation under
heaven.
6 Now [1]when this was noised abroad, the
multitude came together, and were [2]con-
founded, because that every man heard them
speak in his own language.
7 And they were all amazed and marvelled,
saying one to another, Behold, are not all these
which speak [a]Galileans?
8 And how hear we every man in our own
tongue, wherein we were born?
9 Parthians, and Medes, and Elamites, and
the dwellers in Mesopotamia, and in Judea,
and Cappadocia, in Pontus, and Asia,
10 Phrygia, and Pamphylia, in Egypt, and
in the parts of Libya about Cyrene, and
strangers of Rome, Jews and proselytes,
11 Cretes and Arabians, we do hear them
speak in our tongues the wonderful works of
God.
12 And they were all amazed, and were in
doubt, saying one to another, What meaneth
this?
13 Others mocking said, *These men* are
full of new wine.

2:6 [1] Gr. *when this voice was made* [2] Or, *troubled in mind*
2:7 [a] ch. 1:11

2:5 *Jews, devout men.* Devout Jews from different parts of the world but assembled now in Jerusalem either as visitors or as current residents (cf. Luke 2:25).
2:6 *speak in his own language.* Jews from different parts of the world would understand the Aramaic of their homeland. Also the Greek language was common to all parts of the world. But more than this was occurring; they heard the apostles speak in languages native to the different places represented.
2:9 *Parthians.* Inhabitants of the territory from the Tigris to India. *Medes.* Media lay east of Mesopotamia, northwest of Persia and south-southwest of the Caspian Sea. *Elamites.* Elam was north of the Persian Gulf, bounded on the west by the Tigris. *Mesopotamia.* Between the Euphrates and Tigris rivers. *Judea.* The homeland of the Jews, perhaps used here in the OT sense "from the river of Egypt unto the . . . Euphrates" (Gen 15:18), including Galilee. *Cappadocia, in Pontus, and Asia.* Districts in Asia Minor.
2:10 *Phrygia, and Pamphylia.* Districts in Asia Minor. *Egypt.* Contained a great number of Jews. Two out of the five districts of Alexandria were Jewish. *Libya.* A region west of Egypt. *Cyrene.* The capital of a district of Libya called Cyrenaica. *Rome.* Thousands of Jews lived in Rome. *proselytes.* Gentiles who undertook the full observance of the Mosaic law were received into full fellowship with the Jews.
2:11 *Cretes.* Represented an island lying south-southeast of Greece. *Arabians.* From a region to the east. The kingdom of the Nabatean Arabs lay between the Red sea and the Euphrates, with Petra as its capital. *we do hear them speak.* Not a miracle of hearing but of speaking. The believers were declaring God's wonders in the native languages of the various visiting Jews.

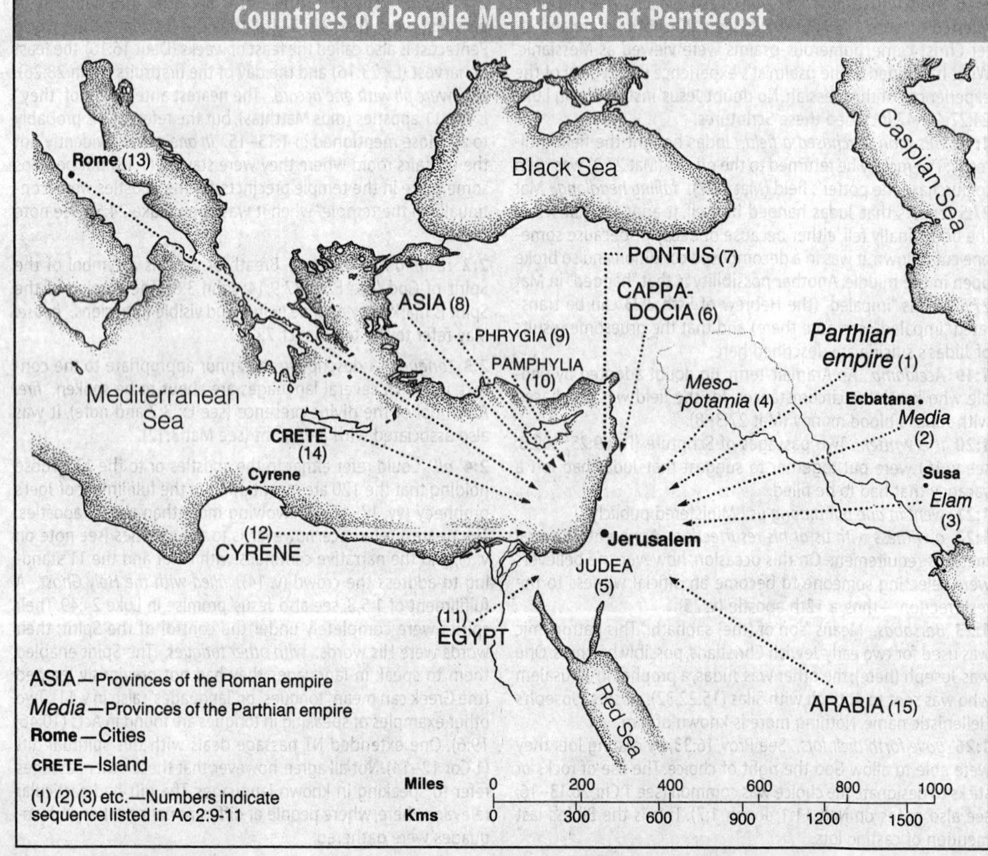

Peter's Pentecostal sermon

14 ¶ But Peter, standing up with the eleven, lift up his voice, and said unto them, Ye men of Judea, and all *ye* that dwell at Jerusalem, be this known unto you, and hearken to my words:

15 For these are not drunken, as ye suppose, [a]seeing it is *but* the third hour of the day.

16 But this is that which was spoken by the prophet Joel;

17 [a]And it shall come to pass in the last days, saith God, [b]I will pour out of my Spirit upon all flesh: and your sons and [c]your daughters shall prophesy, and your young men shall see visions, and your old men shall dream dreams:

18 And on my servants and on my handmaidens I will pour out in those days of my Spirit; [a]and they shall prophesy:

19 [a]And I will shew wonders in heaven above, and signs in the earth beneath; blood, and fire, and vapour of smoke:

20 [a]The sun shall be turned into darkness, and the moon into blood, before *that* great and notable day of the Lord come:

21 And it shall come to pass, *that* [a]whosoever shall call on the name of the Lord shall be saved.

22 Ye men of Israel, hear these words; Jesus of Nazareth, a man approved of God among you [a]by miracles and wonders and signs, which God did by him in the midst of you, as ye yourselves also know:

23 Him, [a]being delivered by the determinate counsel and foreknowledge of God, [b]ye have taken, and by wicked hands have crucified and slain:

24 [a]Whom God hath raised up, having loosed the pains of death: because it was not possible that he should be holden of it.

2:15 [a]1 Thes. 5:7
2:17 [a]Is. 44:3; Ezek. 11:19; Joel 2:28; Zech. 12:10; John 7:38 [b]ch. 10:45 [c]ch. 21:9
2:18 [a]ch. 21:4,9; 1 Cor. 12:10; 14:1
2:19 [a]Joel 2:30
2:20 [a]Mat. 24:29; Mark 13:24; Luke 21:25
2:21 [a]Rom. 10:13
2:22 [a]John 3:2; 14:10,11; ch. 10:38; Heb. 2:4
2:23 [a]Mat. 26:24; Luke 22:22; ch. 3:18 [b]ch. 5:30
2:24 [a]Rom. 8:11; 1 Cor. 6:14; 2 Cor. 4:14; Eph. 1:20; Col. 2:12; 1 Thes. 1:10; Heb. 13:20
2:25 [a]Ps. 16:8
2:29 [1]Or, I *may* [a]ch. 13:36
2:30 [a]2 Sam. 7:12; Ps. 132:11; Luke 1:32; Rom. 1:3; 2 Tim. 2:8
2:31 [a]Ps. 16:10
2:32 [a]ver. 24 [b]ch. 1:8
2:33 [a]Phil. 2:9; Heb. 10:12 [b]John 14:26; 16:7,13 [c]ch. 10:45; Eph. 4:8
2:34 [a]Ps. 110:1; Mat. 22:44; 1 Cor. 15:25; Eph. 1:20; Heb. 1:13

25 For David speaketh concerning him, [a]I foresaw the Lord always before my face, for he is on my right hand, that I should not be moved:

26 Therefore did my heart rejoice, and my tongue was glad; moreover also my flesh shall rest in hope:

27 Because thou wilt not leave my soul in hell, neither wilt thou suffer thine Holy One to see corruption.

28 Thou hast made known to me the ways of life; thou shalt make me full of joy with thy countenance.

29 Men *and* brethren, [1]let *me* freely speak unto you [a]of the patriarch David, that he is both dead and buried, and his sepulchre is with us unto this day.

30 Therefore being a prophet, [a]and knowing that God had sworn with an oath to him, that of the fruit of his loins, according to the flesh, *he* would raise up Christ to sit on his throne;

31 He seeing *this* before, spake of the resurrection of Christ, [a]that his soul was not left in hell, neither his flesh did see corruption.

32 [a]This Jesus hath God raised up, [b]whereof we all are witnesses.

33 Therefore [a]being by the right hand of God exalted, and [b]having received of the Father the promise of the Holy Ghost, he [c]hath shed forth this, which ye now see and hear.

34 For David is not ascended into the heavens: but he saith himself, [a]The LORD said unto my Lord, Sit thou on my right hand,

35 Until I make thy foes thy footstool.

36 Therefore let all the house of Israel know assuredly, that God hath made that same Jesus, whom ye have crucified, both Lord and Christ.

2:14–40 The pattern and themes of the message that follows became common in the early church: (1) an explanation of events (vv. 14–21); (2) the gospel of Jesus Christ—His death, resurrection and exaltation (vv. 22–36); (3) an exhortation to repentance and baptism (vv. 37–40). The outline of this sermon is similar to those in chs. 3; 10; 13.

2:14 *with the eleven.* The apostles had been baptized with the Holy Spirit and had spoken in other languages to various groups. Now they stood with Peter, who served as their spokesman.

2:15 *the third hour of the day.* On a festival day such as Pentecost, the Jew would not break his fast until at least 10:00 A.M. So it was extremely unlikely that a group of men would be drunk at such an early hour.

‡2:17–18 *all flesh . . . sons . . . daughters . . . young men . . . old men . . . servants . . . handmaidens.* The Spirit is bestowed on all, irrespective of sex, age and rank. (cf. Gal 3:26—4:7)

2:17 *last days.* See Is 2:2; Hos 3:5; Mic 4:1; Heb 1:2; see also notes on 1 Tim 4:1; 2 Tim 3:1; 1 Pet 1:20; 1 John 2:18. In the passage quoted from Joel the Hebrew has "after this" and the Septuagint "after these things." Peter interprets the passage as referring specifically to the latter days of the new covenant (see Jer 31:33–34; Ezek 36:26–27; 39:29) in contrast to the former days of the old covenant. The age of Messianic fulfillment has arrived. *my Spirit.* See note on 1:2.

2:21 *whosoever shall call.* Cf. v. 39; includes faith and response rather than merely using words (Mat 7:21).

2:22 *approved . . . by miracles and wonders and signs.* The mighty works done by Jesus were signs that the Messiah had come.

2:23 *wicked.* The Greek has "those not having the law," i.e., Gentiles. The reference is to the Romans involved in the trial and crucifixion of Christ. Here, however, the Gentiles were acting in an evil ("wicked") way.

‡2:27 *not leave my soul in hell.* David referred ultimately to the Messiah (v. 31). God would not allow His physical body to decompose in the grave (Hades).

‡2:29 *his sepulchre is with us.* The sepulchre of David could be seen in Jerusalem. It still contained the remains of David's body. The words of Ps 16:8–11 did not fully apply to him.

2:33 *promise of the Holy Ghost.* See note on 1:4. *hath shed forth.* See v. 17; Joel 2:28.

2:34 *The LORD said unto my Lord.* The Lord (God) said to my Lord (the Son of David, the Messiah). According to Peter, David addressed his descendant with uncommon respect because he, through the inspiration of the Spirit, recognized how great and divine He would be (Mat 22:41–45). Not only was He to be resurrected (vv. 31–32) but He was to be exalted to God's right hand (vv. 33–35). And His presence there was now being demonstrated by the sending of the Holy Spirit (v. 33; John 16:7). See also note on Ps 110:1.

The community of the believers

37 ¶ Now when they heard *this,* [a]they were pricked in *their* heart, and said unto Peter and *to* the rest of the apostles, Men *and* brethren, what shall we do?

38 Then Peter said unto them, [a]Repent, and be baptized every one of you in the name of Jesus Christ for the remission of sins, and ye shall receive the gift of the Holy Ghost.

39 For the promise is unto you, and [a]to your children, and [b]to all that are afar off, *even* as many as the Lord our God shall call.

40 And with many other words did he testify and exhort, saying, Save yourselves from this untoward generation.

41 ¶ Then they that gladly received his word were baptized: and the same day there were added *unto them* about three thousand souls.

42 [a]And they continued stedfastly in the apostles' doctrine and fellowship, and in breaking of bread, and in prayers.

43 And fear came upon every soul: and [a]many wonders and signs were done by the apostles.

44 And all that believed were together, and [a]had all *things* common;

45 And sold their possessions and goods, and [a]parted them to all *men,* as every *man* had need.

46 [a]And they, continuing daily with one accord [b]in the temple, and [c]breaking bread [1]from house to house, did eat *their* meat with gladness and singleness of heart,

47 Praising God, and [a]having favour with all the people. And [b]the Lord added to the church daily such as should be saved.

The healing of the lame man

3 Now Peter and John went up together [a]into the temple at the hour of prayer, [b]*being* the ninth *hour.*

2 And [a]a certain man lame from his mother's womb was carried, whom they laid daily at the gate of the temple which is called Beautiful, [b]to ask alms of them that entered into the temple;

3 Who seeing Peter and John about to go into the temple, asked an alms.

4 And Peter, fastening his eyes upon him with John, said, Look on us.

5 And he gave heed unto them, expecting to receive something of them.

6 Then Peter said, Silver and gold have I none; but such as I have give I thee: [a]In the name of Jesus Christ of Nazareth rise up and walk.

7 And he took him by the right hand, and lift *him* up: and immediately his feet and ankle bones received strength,

8 And he [a]leaping up stood, and walked, and entered with them into the temple, walking, and leaping, and praising God.

9 [a]And all the people saw him walking and praising God:

10 And they knew that it was he which [a]sat for alms at the Beautiful gate of the tem-

2:37 [a]Zech. 12:10; Luke 3:10; ch. 9:6
2:38 [a]Luke 24:47; ch. 3:19
2:39 [a]Joel 2:28; ch. 3:25 [b]ch. 11:15,18; Eph. 2:13
2:42 [a]ch. 1:14; Rom. 12:12; Eph. 6:18; Col. 4:2; Heb. 10:25
2:43 [a]Mark 16:17; ch. 5:12
2:44 [a]ch. 4:32,34
2:45 [a]Is. 58:7
2:46 [1]Or, *at home* [a]ch. 1:14 [b]Luke 24:53 [c]ch. 20:7
2:47 [a]ch. 4:33; Rom. 14:18 [b]ch. 5:14
3:1 [a]ch. 2:46 [b]Ps. 55:17
3:2 [a]ch. 14:8 [b]John 9:8
3:6 [a]ch. 4:10
3:8 [a]Is. 35:6
3:9 [a]ch. 4:16,21
3:10 [a]Like John 9:8

2:37 *pricked in their heart.* Reflects both belief in Jesus and regret over former rejection.

‡2:38 *Repent, and be baptized.* Repentance was important in the message of the forerunner, John the Baptist (Mark 1:4; Luke 3:3), in the preaching of Jesus (Mark 1:15; Luke 13:3) and in the directions Jesus left just before His ascension (Luke 24:47). So also baptism was important to John the Baptizer (Mark 1:4), in the instructions of Jesus (Mat 28:18–19) and in the preaching recorded in Acts—where it was associated with belief (8:12; 18:8), acceptance of the word (v. 41) and repentance (here). *in the name of Jesus Christ.* Not a contradiction to the fuller formula given in Mat 28:19. In Acts the abbreviated form emphasizes the distinctive quality of this baptism, for Jesus is now included in a way that He was not in John's baptism (19:4–5). *for the remission of sins.* Not that baptism effects remission (forgiveness). Rather, forgiveness comes through that which is symbolized by baptism (see Rom 6:3–4 and note). *Holy Ghost.* Two gifts are now given: the forgiveness of sins (see also 22:16) and the Holy Spirit. The promise of the indwelling gift of the Holy Spirit is given to all Christians (cf. Rom 8:9–11; 1 Cor 12:13).

2:41 *there were added.* Added to the number of believers.

2:42 *apostles' doctrine.* Included all that Jesus Himself taught (Mat 28:20), especially the gospel, which was centered in His death, burial and resurrection (see vv. 23–24; 3:15; 4:10; 1 Cor 15:1–4). It was a unique teaching in that it came from God and was clothed with the authority conferred on the apostles (2 Cor 13:10; 1 Thes 4:2). Today it is available in the books of the NT. *fellowship.* The corporate fellowship of believers in worship. *breaking of bread.* Although this phrase is used of an ordinary meal in v. 46 (see Luke 24:30,35), the Lord's supper seems to be indicated here (see note on 20:7; cf. 1 Cor 10:16; 11:20). *prayers.* Acts emphasizes the importance of prayer in the Christian life—private as well as public (1:14; 3:1; 6:4; 10:4,31; 12:5; 16:13,16).

2:44 *all that believed were together.* The unity of the early church. *all things common.* See 4:34–35. This was a voluntary sharing to provide for those who did not have enough for the essentials of living (see good and bad examples of sharing, 4:36–5:9).

2:46 *breaking bread from house to house.* Here the daily life of Christians is described, distinguishing their activity in the temple from that in their homes, where they ate their meals—not the Lord's supper (see note on v. 42)—with gladness and generosity. *gladness and singleness of heart.* The fellowship, oneness and sharing enjoyed in the early church are fruits of the Spirit. Joy is to be the mood of the believer (see note on 16:34).

3:1 *Peter and John.* Among the foremost apostles (Gal 2:9). Along with John's brother, James, they had been especially close to Jesus (Mark 9:2; 13:3; 14:33; Luke 22:8). Arrested together (4:3), they were also together in Samaria (8:14). *the hour of prayer.* The three stated times of prayer for later Judaism were midmorning (the third hour, 9:00 A.M.), the time of the evening sacrifice (the ninth hour, 3:00 P.M.) and sunset.

3:2 *gate . . . called Beautiful.* The favorite entrance to the temple court, it was probably the bronze-sheathed gate that led from the court of the Gentiles to the court of women, on the east wall of the temple proper.

3:6 *In the name of Jesus Christ.* Not by power of their own, but by the authority of the Messiah.

3:7 *and lift him up.* But he had faith to be healed (v. 16).

3:8 *entered . . . the temple.* From the outer court (for Gentiles also) into the court of women, containing the treasury (Mark 12:41–44), and then into the court of Israel (see map No. 8 at the end of the Study Bible). From the outer court, nine gates led into the inner courts.

ple: and they were filled with wonder and
amazement at that which had happened unto
him.

Peter's sermon

11 ¶ And as the lame *man* which was
healed held Peter and John, all the people ran
together unto them in the porch [a]that is called
Solomon's, greatly wondering.
12 And when Peter saw *it,* he answered
unto the people, Ye men of Israel, why marvel
ye at this? or why look ye *so* earnestly on us,
as though by our own power or holiness we
had made this *man* to walk?
13 [a]The God of Abraham, and of Isaac, and
of Jacob, the God of our fathers, [b]hath glorified
his Son Jesus; whom ye [c]delivered up, and
[d]denied him in the presence of Pilate, when
he was determined to let *him* go.
14 But ye denied [a]the Holy One [b]and the
Just, and desired a murderer to be granted
unto you;
15 And killed the [a][1]Prince of life, [b]whom
God hath raised from the dead; [c]whereof we
are witnesses.
16 [a]And his name through faith in his
name hath made this *man* strong, whom ye
see and know: yea, the faith which is by him
hath given him this perfect soundness in the
presence of you all.
17 And now, brethren, I wot that [a]through
ignorance ye did *it,* as *did* also your rulers.
18 But [a]*those things,* which God before
had shewed [b]by the mouth of all his prophets,
that Christ should suffer, he hath so fulfilled.
19 [a]Repent ye therefore, and be converted,
that your sins may be blotted out, when *the*

3:11 [a]John 10:23; ch. 5:12
3:13 [a]ch. 5:30 [b]John 7:39; 12:16; 17:1 [c]Mat. 27:2 [d]Mat 27:20; Mark 15:11; Luke 23:18; John 18:40; 19:15; ch. 13:28
3:14 [a]Ps. 16:10; Mark 1:24; Luke 1:35; ch. 2:27; 4:27 [b]ch. 7:52; 22:14
3:15 [1]Or, *Author* [a]1 John 5:11 [b]ch. 2:24 [c]ch. 2:32
3:16 [a]Mat. 9:22; ch. 4:10; 14:9
3:17 [a]Luke 23:34; John 16:3; ch. 13:27; 1 Cor. 2:8; 1 Tim. 1:13
3:18 [a]Luke 24:44; ch. 26:22 [b]Ps. 22; Is. 50:6; 53:5; Dan. 9:26; 1 Pet. 1:10
3:19 [a]ch. 2:38
3:21 [a]ch. 1:11 [b]Mat. 17:11 [c]Luke 1:70
3:22 [a]Deut. 18:15,18,19; ch. 7:37
3:25 [a]ch. 2:39; Rom. 9:4,8; 15:8; Gal. 3:26 [b]Gen. 12:3; 18:18; 22:18; 26:4; 28:14; Gal. 3:8
3:26 [a]Mat. 10:5; 15:24; Luke 24:47; ch. 13:32,33,46 [b]ver. 22 [c]Mat. 1:21
4:1 [1]Or, *ruler* [a]Luke 22:4; ch. 5:24

times of refreshing shall come from the presence of the Lord;
20 And he shall send Jesus Christ, which
before was preached unto you:
21 [a]Whom the heaven must receive until
the times of [b]restitution of all *things,* [c]which
God hath spoken by the mouth of all his holy
prophets since the world began.
22 For Moses truly said unto the fathers,
[a]A prophet shall the Lord your God raise up
unto you of your brethren, like unto me; him
shall ye hear in all *things* whatsoever he shall
say unto you.
23 And it shall come to pass, *that* every
soul, which will not hear that prophet, shall be
destroyed from among the people.
24 Yea, and all the prophets from Samuel
and those that follow after, as many as have
spoken, have likewise foretold of these days.
25 [a]Ye are the children of the prophets,
and of the covenant which God made with our
fathers, saying unto Abraham, [b]And in thy
seed shall all the kindreds of the earth be
blessed.
26 [a]Unto you first God, having raised up
his Son Jesus, [b]sent him to bless you, [c]in turning away every one of you from *his* iniquities.

Peter and John arrested

4 And as they spake unto the people, the
priests, and the [a][1]captain of the temple,
and the Saducees, came upon them,
2 Being grieved that they taught the people, and preached through Jesus the resurrection from the dead.
3 And they laid hands on them, and put

3:11 *porch that is called Solomon's.* A porch along the inner side of the wall enclosing the outer court, with rows of 27-foot-high stone columns and a roof of cedar (see note on John 10:23).
3:12–26 See note on 2:14–40.
3:13 *his Son Jesus.* Or "his servant." A reminder of the suffering servant prophesied in Is 52:13–53:12 (see Mat 12:18; Acts 4:27,30). *whom ye . . . denied.* Voted against Jesus, spurned Him, denied Him and refused to acknowledge Him as the true Messiah. *Pilate . . . was determined to let him go.* See John 19:12.
3:14 *Holy One and the Just.* Blameless in relation to God and man.
3:15 *killed . . . God hath raised . . . we are witnesses.* A recurring theme in the speeches of Acts (see 2:23–24; 4:10; 5:30–32; 10:39–41; 13:28–29; cf. 1 Cor 15:1–4).
3:18 *before had shewed by . . . all his prophets.* Echoes what Jesus had said (Luke 24:26–27). The suffering was prophesied (compare Is 53:7–8 with Acts 8:32–33; Ps 2:1–2 with Acts 4:25–26; Ps 22:1 with Mat 27:46; see also 1 Pet 1:11).
‡3:19 *Repent.* Repentance is a change of mind and will arising from sorrow for sin and leading to transformation of life (see note on 2:38). *be converted.* Subsequent to repentance and not completely identical with it. See 11:21 ("believed, and turned") and 26:20 ("repent and turn"; see also 9:35; 14:15; 15:19; 26:18; 28:27). In the strictest sense, repentance is turning from sin, and faith is turning to God. However, the word "turn" is not always used with such precision. *your sins . . . blotted out.* Your sins will be forgiven as a result of repentance. *when.* This Greek word normally means "so that"
‡3:20–21 *until the times of restitution.* This refers to the time after the return of Jesus Christ from heaven.
3:22–26 *raise up . . . raised up.* Christ is the fulfillment of prophecies made relative to Moses, David and Abraham. He was to be a prophet like Moses (vv. 22–23), He was foretold in Samuel's declarations concerning David (v. 24; see note there), and He was to bring blessing to all people as promised to Abraham (vv. 25–26).
3:24 *prophets from Samuel and those that follow after.* Samuel anointed David to be king and spoke of the establishment of his kingdom (1 Sam 16:13; cf. 13:14; 15:28; 28:17). Nathan's prophecy (2 Sam 7:12–16) was ultimately Messianic (see Acts 13:22–23, 34; Heb 1:5).
3:25 *seed.* The word is singular, ultimately signifying Christ (see Gal 3:16).
4:1 *priests.* Those who were serving that week in the temple precincts (see note on Luke 1:23). *captain of the temple.* A member of one of the leading priestly families; next in rank to the high priest (see 5:24,26; Luke 22:4,52). *Sadducees.* A Jewish sect whose members came from the priestly line and controlled the temple. They did not believe in the resurrection or a personal Messiah, but held that the Messianic age—an ideal time—was then present and must be preserved. The high priest, one of their number, presided over the Sanhedrin (see 5:17; 23:6–8; Mat 22:23–33). See also notes on Mat 3:7; Mark 12:18; Luke 20:27.

them in hold unto the next day: for it was now eventide.

4 Howbeit many of them which heard the word believed; and the number of the men was about five thousand.

5 And it came to pass on the morrow, that their rulers, and elders, and scribes,

6 And [a]Annas the high priest, and Caiaphas, and John, and Alexander, and as many as were of the kindred of the high priest, were gathered together at Jerusalem.

7 And when they had set them in the midst, they asked, [a]By what power, or by what name, have ye done this?

8 [a]Then Peter, filled with the Holy Ghost, said unto them, Ye rulers of the people, and elders of Israel,

9 If we this day be examined of the good deed done to the impotent man, by what *means* he is made whole;

10 Be it known unto you all, and to all the people of Israel, [a]that by the name of Jesus Christ of Nazareth, whom ye crucified, [b]whom God raised from the dead, *even* by him doth this *man* stand here before you whole.

11 [a]This is the stone which was set at nought of you builders, which is become the head of the corner.

12 [a]Neither is there salvation in any other: for there is none other name under heaven given among men, whereby we must be saved.

13 ¶ Now when they saw the boldness of Peter and John, [a]and perceived that they were unlearned and ignorant men, they marvelled; and they took knowledge of them, that they had been with Jesus.

14 And beholding the man which was healed [a]standing with them, they could say nothing against *it.*

15 But when they had commanded them to go aside out of the council, they conferred among themselves,

16 Saying, [a]What shall we do to these men? for that indeed a notable miracle hath been done by them *is* [b]manifest to all them that dwell in Jerusalem; and we cannot deny *it.*

17 But that it spread no further among the people, let us straitly threaten them, that *they* speak henceforth to no man in this name.

18 [a]And they called them, and commanded them not to speak at all nor teach in the name of Jesus.

19 But Peter and John answered and said unto them, [a]Whether it be right in the sight of God to hearken unto you more than unto God, judge ye.

20 [a]For we cannot but speak *the things* which [b]we have seen and heard.

21 So when they had further threatened *them,* they let them go, finding nothing how they might punish them, [a]because of the people: for all *men* glorified God for [b]that which was done.

22 For the man was above forty years old, on whom this miracle of healing was shewed.

The report to the believers

23 ¶ And being let go, [a]they went to their own *company,* and reported all that the chief priests and elders had said unto them.

24 And when they heard *that,* they lift up their voice to God with one accord, and said, Lord, [a]thou *art* God, which hast made heaven, and earth, and the sea, and all that in them is:

25 Who by the mouth of thy servant David hast said, [a]Why did the heathen rage, and the people imagine vain *things?*

26 The kings of the earth stood up, and the rulers were gathered together against the Lord, and against his Christ.

27 For [a]of a truth against [b]thy holy child Jesus, [c]whom thou hast anointed, both Herod, and Pontius Pilate, with the Gentiles, and the people of Israel, were gathered together,

28 [a]For to do whatsoever thy hand and thy counsel determined before to be done.

29 And now, Lord, behold their threatenings: and grant unto thy servants, [a]that with all boldness *they* may speak thy word,

4:6 [a]Luke 3:2; John 11:49; 18:13
4:7 [a]Ex. 2:14; Mat. 21:23; ch. 7:27
4:8 [a]Luke 12:11,12
4:10 [a]ch. 3:6,16 [b]ch. 2:24
4:11 [a]Ps. 118:22; Is. 28:16; Mat. 21:42
4:12 [a]Mat. 1:21; ch. 10:43; 1 Tim. 2:5,6
4:13 [a]Mat. 11:25; 1 Cor. 1:27
4:14 [a]ch. 3:11
4:16 [a]John 11:47 [b]ch. 3:9,10
4:18 [a]Again, ch. 5:40
4:19 [a]ch. 5:29
4:20 [a]ch. 1:8; 2:32 [b]ch. 22:15; 1 John 1:1,3
4:21 [a]Mat. 21:26; Luke 20:6,19; 22:2; ch. 5:26 [b]ch. 3:7,8
4:23 [a]ch. 12:12
4:24 [a]2 Ki. 19:15
4:25 [a]Ps. 2:1
4:27 [a]Mat. 26:3; Luke 22:2; 23:1,8 [b]Luke 1:35 [c]Luke 4:18; John 10:36
4:28 [a]ch. 2:23; 3:18
4:29 [a]ver. 13,31; ch. 9:27; 13:46; 14:3; 19:8; 26:26; Eph. 6:19

4:3 *eventide.* The evening sacrifices ended about 4:00 P.M., and the temple gates would be closed at that time. Any judgments involving life and death must be begun and concluded in daylight hours.

4:4 *men.* Lit."males." *five thousand.* A growth from the 3,000 at Pentecost (2:41); see later growth (5:14; 6:7).

4:5 *rulers, and elders, and scribes.* The three groups making up the Sanhedrin, Israel's supreme court (see Luke 22:66; see also notes on Mat 2:4; 15:2; Mark 14:55; Luke 5:17).

4:6 *Annas.* High priest A.D. 6–15, but deposed by the Romans and succeeded by his son, Eleazar, then by his son-in-law, Caiaphas (18–36), who was also called Joseph. However, Annas was still recognized by the Jews as high priest (Luke 3:2; cf. John 18:13, 24). *John.* May be Jonathan son of Annas, who was appointed high priest in A.D. 36. Others suggest it was Johanan ben Zaccai, who became the president of the Great Synagogue after the fall of Jerusalem. *Alexander.* Not further identified.

4:8 *filled with the Holy Ghost.* See note on 2:4.

4:11 *the stone . . . set at nought.* Fulfillment of prophecy was an important element in early Christian sermons and defenses. Jesus had also used Ps 118:22 (Mat 21:42; see 1 Pet 2:7 and cf. Rom 9:33; Is 28:16).

4:12 *none other name.* See 10:43; John 14:6; 1 Tim 2:5; see also note on Mat 1:21.

‡4:13 *boldness.* A certain boldness characterized by the assurance, authority and forthrightness of the apostles (2:29; 4:29; 28:31), and shared by the believers (4:31). *unlearned and ignorant men.* Meaning only that Peter and John had not been trained in the rabbinic schools, nor did they hold official positions in recognized religious circles.

‡4:20 *cannot but speak.* See 5:29 and Jer 20:9.

4:23 *went.* Probably to the same upper room where the apostles had met before (1:13) and where the congregation may have continued to meet (12:12).

4:27 *Herod.* Herod Antipas, tetrarch of Galilee and Perea (Luke 23:7–15). *Pontius Pilate.* Roman procurator of Judea (Luke 23:1–24).

4:28 *determined.* Not that God had compelled them to act as they did, but He willed to use them and their freely chosen acts to accomplish His saving purpose.

30 By stretching forth thine hand to heal; [a]and that signs and wonders may be done [b]by the name of [c]thy holy child Jesus.

31 And when they had prayed, [a]the place was shaken where they were assembled together; and they were all filled with the Holy Ghost, [b]and they spake the word of God with boldness.

The community of possessions

32 ¶ And the multitude of them that believed [a]were of one heart and of one soul: [b]neither said any *of them* that ought of the *things* which he possessed was his own; but they had all *things* common.

33 And with [a]great power gave the apostles [b]witness of the resurrection of the Lord Jesus: and [c]great grace was upon them all.

34 Neither was there any among them that lacked: [a]for as many as were possessors of lands or houses sold them, and brought the prices of the *things* that were sold,

35 [a]And laid *them down* at the apostles' feet: [b]and distribution was made unto every man according as he had need.

36 And Joses, who by the apostles was surnamed Barnabas, (which is, being interpreted, The son of consolation,) a Levite, *and* of the country of Cyprus,

37 [a]Having land, sold *it,* and brought the money, and laid *it* at the apostles' feet.

Ananias and Sapphira punished

5 But a certain man named Ananias, with Sapphira his wife, sold a possession,

2 And kept back *part* of the price, his wife also being privy *to it,* and brought a certain part, and laid *it* at the apostles' feet.

3 [a]But Peter said, Ananias, why hath [b]Satan filled thine heart [1]to lie to the Holy Ghost, and to keep back *part* of the price of the land?

4 Whiles it remained, was it not thine own? and after it was sold, was it not in thine own power? why hast thou conceived this thing in thine heart? thou hast not lied unto men, but unto God.

5 And Ananias hearing these words [a]fell down, and gave up the ghost: and great fear came on all them that heard these *things.*

6 And the young men arose, [a]wound him up, and carried *him* out, and buried *him.*

7 And it was about the space of three hours after, when his wife, not knowing what was done, came in.

8 And Peter answered unto her, Tell me whether ye sold the land for so much? And she said, Yea, for so much.

9 Then Peter said unto her, How *is it* that ye have agreed together [a]to tempt the Spirit of the Lord? behold, the feet of them which have buried thy husband *are* at the door, and shall carry thee out.

10 [a]Then fell she down straightway at his feet, and yielded up the ghost: and the young men came in, and found her dead, and, carrying *her* forth, buried *her* by her husband.

11 [a]And great fear came upon all the church, and upon as many as heard these *things.*

12 ¶ And [a]by the hands of the apostles were many signs and wonders wrought among the people; ([b]and they were all with one accord in Solomon's porch.

4:30 [a]ch. 2:43; 5:12 [b]ch. 3:6,16 [c]ver. 27
4:31 [a]ch. 2:2,4; 16:26 [b]ver. 29
4:32 [a]ch. 5:12; Rom. 15:5,6; 2 Cor. 13:11; Phil. 1:27; 2:2; 1 Pet. 3:8 [b]ch. 2:44
4:33 [a]ch. 1:8 [b]ch. 1:22 [c]ch. 2:45
4:34 [a]ch. 2:45
4:35 [a]ver. 37; ch. 5:2 [b]ch. 2:45; 6:1
4:37 [a]ver. 34,35; ch. 5:1,2
5:3 [1]Or, *to deceive* [a]Num. 30:2; Deut. 23:21; Eccl. 5:4 [b]Luke 22:3
5:5 [a]ver. 10,11
5:6 [a]John 19:40
5:9 [a]ver. 3; Mat. 4:7
5:10 [a]ver. 5
5:11 [a]ver. 5; ch. 2:43; 19:17
5:12 [a]ch. 2:43; 14:3; 19:11; Rom. 15:19; 2 Cor. 12:12; Heb. 2:4 [b]ch. 3:11; 4:32

4:30 *holy child.* Or "holy servant." See note on 3:13.
4:31 *was shaken.* An immediate sign that the prayers had been heard (see 16:26). *filled with the Holy Ghost.* See note on 2:4. *spake the word of God.* They continued preaching the gospel despite the warnings of the council (see note on v. 13).
4:32 *of one heart and of one soul.* In complete accord, extending to their attitude toward personal possessions (see 2:44).
4:33 *witness of the resurrection.* As significant as the death of Christ was, the most compelling event was the resurrection—an event about which the disciples could not keep silent.
4:34 *as many as were possessors of lands or houses sold them.* See note on 2:44.
4:36 *Barnabas.* Used here as a good example of giving. In this way Luke introduces the one who will become an important companion of Paul (see 13:1–4). For other significant contributions of this greathearted leader to the life and ministry of the early church see 9:27; 11:22,25; 15:37–39. *Levite.* Although Levites owned no inherited land in the Holy Land, these regulations may not have applied to the Levites in other countries (Cyprus). So perhaps Barnabas sold land he owned in Cyprus and brought the proceeds to the apostles (v. 37). Or he may have been married, and the land sold may have been from his wife's property. It is also possible that the prohibition against Levite ownership of land in the Holy Land was no longer observed. *of the country of Cyprus.* Cyprus was an island in the eastern part of the Mediterranean Sea. Jews had settled there from Maccabean times.
5:1 *Ananias . . . Sapphira.* Given as bad examples of sharing (Barnabas was the good example; see note on 4:36). Love of praise for (pretended) generosity and love for money led to the first recorded sin in the life of the church. It is a warning to the readers that "God is not mocked" (Gal 6:7). Compare this divine judgment at the beginning of the church era with God's judgments on Nadab and Abihu (Lev 10:2), on Achan (Josh 7:25) and on Uzzah (2 Sam 6:7).
5:2 *kept back part.* They had a right to keep back whatever they chose, but to make it appear that they had given all when they had not was sinful.
5:3 *Satan filled thine heart.* The continuing activity of Satan is noted (see Luke 22:3; John 13:2,27; 1 Pet 5:8). *lie to the Holy Ghost.* A comparison with v. 4 shows that the Holy Spirit is regarded as God Himself present with His people.
5:9 *to tempt the Spirit of the Lord.* If no dire consequences had followed this act of sin, the results among the believers would have been serious when the deceit became known. Not only would dishonesty appear profitable, but the conclusion that the Spirit could be deceived would follow. It was important to set the course properly at the outset in order to leave no doubt that God will not tolerate such hypocrisy and deceit.
5:11 *church.* The first use of the term in Acts. It can denote either the local congregation (8:1; 11:22; 13:1) or the universal church (see 20:28). The Greek word for "church" (*ekklesia*) was already being used for political and other assemblies (see 19:32,40) and, in the Septuagint (the Greek translation of the OT), for Israel when gathered in religious assembly.
5:12 *Solomon's porch.* See note on 3:11.

13 And [a]of the rest durst no *man* join himself to them: [b]but the people magnified them.

14 And believers were the more added to the Lord, multitudes both of men and women.)

15 Insomuch that *they* brought forth the sick [1]into the streets, and laid *them* on beds and couches, [a]that at the least the shadow of Peter passing by might overshadow some of them.

16 There came also a multitude *out* of the cities round about unto Jerusalem, bringing [a]sick *folks,* and *them which were* vexed with unclean spirits: and they were healed every one.

The apostles imprisoned

17 ¶ [a]Then the high priest rose up, and all they that were with him, (which is the sect of the Sadducees,) and were filled with [1]indignation,

18 [a]And laid their hands on the apostles, and put them in the common prison.

19 But [a]*the* angel of the Lord by night opened the prison doors, and brought them forth, and said,

20 Go, stand and speak in the temple to the people [a]all the words of this life.

21 And when they heard *that,* they entered into the temple early in the morning, and taught. [a]But the high priest came, and they that were with him, and called the council together, and all the senate of the children of Israel, and sent to the prison to have them brought.

22 But when the officers came, and found them not in the prison, they returned, and told,

23 Saying, The prison truly found we shut with all safety, and the keepers standing without before the doors: but when we had opened, we found no *man* within.

24 Now when the *high* priest and [a]the captain of the temple and the chief priests heard these things, they doubted of them whereunto this would grow.

25 Then came one and told them, saying, Behold, the men whom ye put in prison are standing in the temple, and teaching the people.

26 Then went the captain with the officers, and brought them without violence: [a]for they feared the people, lest they should have been stoned.

27 And when they had brought them, they set *them* before the council: and the high priest asked them,

28 Saying, [a]Did not we straitly command you that *you* should not teach in this name? and behold, ye have filled Jerusalem with your doctrine, [b]and intend to bring this man's [c]blood upon us.

29 Then Peter and the *other* apostles answered and said, [a]We ought to obey God rather than men.

30 [a]The God of our fathers raised up Jesus, whom ye slew and [b]hanged on a tree.

31 [a]Him hath God exalted with his right hand *to be* [b]a Prince and [c]a Saviour, [d]for to give repentance to Israel, and forgiveness of sins.

32 And [a]we are his witnesses of these things; and *so is* also the Holy Ghost, [b]whom God hath given to them that obey him.

The counsel of Gamaliel

33 ¶ [a]When they heard *that,* they were cut *to the heart,* and took counsel to slay them.

34 Then stood there up one in the council, a Pharisee, named [a]Gamaliel, a doctor of law, had in reputation among all the people, and commanded to put the apostles forth a little space;

5:13 [a]John 9:22; 12:42; 19:38 [b]ch. 2:47; 4:21
5:15 [1]Or, *in every street* [a]Mat. 9:21; 14:36; ch. 19:12
5:16 [a]Mark 16:17,18; John 14:12
5:17 [1]Or, *envy* [a]ch. 4:1,2,6
5:18 [a]Luke 21:12
5:19 [a]ch. 12:7; 16:26
5:20 [a]John 6:68; 17:3; 1 John 5:11
5:21 [a]ch. 4:5,6
5:24 [a]Luke 22:4; ch. 4:1
5:26 [a]Mat. 21:26
5:28 [a]ch. 4:18 [b]ch. 2:23,36; 3:15; 7:52 [c]Mat. 23:35; 27:25
5:29 [a]ch. 4:19
5:30 [a]ch. 3:13,15; 22:14 [b]ch. 10:39; 13:29; Gal. 3:13; 1 Pet. 2:24
5:31 [a]ch. 2:33,36; Phil. 2:9; Heb. 2:10; 12:2 [b]ch. 3:15 [c]Mat. 1:21 [d]Luke 24:47; ch. 3:26; 13:38; Eph. 1:7; Col. 1:14
5:32 [a]John 15:26,27 [b]ch. 2:4; 10:44
5:33 [a]ch. 2:37; 7:54
5:34 [a]ch. 22:3

5:13 *of the rest durst no man join himself to them.* Because of the fate of Ananias and his wife, no pretenders or halfhearted followers risked identification with the believers. Luke cannot mean that no one joined the Christian community, since v. 14 indicates that many were coming to Christ.

5:14 *added . . . multitudes both of men and women.* See 4:4. This is the first specific mention of women believing (cf. 8:3,12; 9:2; 13:50; 16:1,13–14; 17:4,12,34; 18:2; 21:5; but cf. also 1:14).

5:15 *the shadow of Peter.* Parallels such items as Paul's handkerchiefs (19:12) and the edge of Jesus' cloak (Mat 9:20)—not that any of these material objects had magical qualities, but the least article or shadow represented a direct means of contact with Jesus or His apostles.

5:17 *high priest.* The official high priest recognized by Rome was Caiaphas, but the Jews considered Annas, Caiaphas's father-in-law, to be the actual high priest since the high priesthood was to be held for life (see note on 4:6). *all they that were with him.* His family members. *sect of the Sadducees.* See note on 4:1.

5:18 *in the common prison.* To await trial the next day.

5:19 *angel of the Lord.* This phrase is used four other times in Acts: (1) Stephen speaks of him (7:30–38); (2) he guides Philip (8:26); (3) he liberates Peter (12:7–10); (4) he strikes down Herod (12:23). See also Mat 1:20–24; 2:13,19; 28:2; Luke 1:11–38; 2:9 and notes on Gen 16:7; 2 Ki 1:3; Zech 1:8.

5:21 *council.* The supreme Jewish court, consisting of 70 to 100 men (71 being the proper number). They sat in a semicircle, backed by three rows of disciples of the "learned men," with the clerks of the court standing in front.

5:24 *captain of the temple.* See note on 4:1.

5:28 *bring this man's blood upon us.* Probably a reference to the apostles' repeated declaration that some of the Jews and some of their leaders had killed Jesus (2:23; 3:13–15; 4:10–11; cf. Mat 27:25).

‡5:30 *tree.* Used to describe the cross (1 Pet 2:24; see Deut 21:22–23). Like its Hebrew counterpart, the Greek for this word could refer to a tree, a pole, a wooden beam or some similar object.

5:32 *so is also the Holy Ghost . . . given to those that obey him.* See John 15:26–27. The disciples' testimony was directed and confirmed by the Holy Spirit, who convicts the world through the word (John 16:8–11) and is given to those who respond to God with "obedience to the faith" (Rom 1:5; see note on 6:7).

5:34 *a Pharisee, named Gamaliel.* The most famous Jewish teacher of his time and traditionally listed among the "heads of the schools." Possibly he was the grandson of Hillel. Like Hillel (see note on Mat 19:3), he was moderate in his views, a characteristic that is apparent in his cautious recommendation on this occasion. Saul (Paul) was one of his students (22:3).

35 And said unto them, Ye men of Israel, take heed to yourselves what ye intend to do as touching these men.

36 For before these days rose up Theudas, boasting himself to be somebody; to whom a number of men, about four hundred, joined themselves: who was slain; and all, as many as [1]obeyed him, were scattered, and brought to nought.

37 After this *man* rose up Judas of Galilee in the days of the taxing, and drew away much people after him: he also perished; and all, *even* as many as [1]obeyed him, were dispersed.

38 And now I say unto you, Refrain from these men, and let them alone: [a]for if this counsel or this work be of men, it will come to nought:

39 [a]But if it be of God, ye cannot overthrow it; lest haply ye be found even [b]to fight against God.

40 And to him they agreed: and when they had [a]called the apostles, [b]and beaten *them,* they commanded that *they* should not speak in the name of Jesus, and let them go.

41 And they departed from the presence of the council, [a]rejoicing that they were counted worthy to suffer shame for his name.

42 And daily [a]in the temple, and in every house, [b]they ceased not to teach and preach Jesus Christ.

The appointment of the seven

6 And in those days, [a]when the number of the disciples was multiplied, there arose a murmuring of the [b]Grecians against the Hebrews, because their widows were neglected [c]in the daily ministration.

2 Then the twelve called the multitude of the disciples unto *them,* and said, [a]It is not reason that we should leave the word of God, and serve tables.

3 Wherefore, brethren, [a]look ye out among you seven men of honest report, full of the Holy Ghost and wisdom, whom we may appoint over this business.

4 But we [a]will give ourselves continually to prayer, and to the ministry of the word.

5 And the saying pleased the whole multitude: and they chose Stephen, [a]a man full of faith and of the Holy Ghost, and [b]Philip, and Prochorus, and Nicanor, and Timon, and Parmenas, and [c]Nicolas a proselyte of Antioch:

6 Whom they set before the apostles: and [a]when they had prayed, [b]they laid *their* hands on them.

7 And [a]the word of God increased; and the number of the disciples multiplied in Jerusalem greatly; and a great company [b]of the priests were obedient to the faith.

5:36 [1]Or, *believed*
5:37 [1]Or, *believed*
5:38 [a]Prov. 21:30; Is. 8:10; Mat. 15:13
5:39 [a]Luke 21:15; 1 Cor. 1:25 [b]ch. 7:51; 9:5; 23:9
5:40 [a]ch. 4:18 [b]Mat. 10:17; 23:34; Mark 13:9
5:41 [a]Mat. 5:12; Rom. 5:3; 2 Cor. 12:10; Phil. 1:29; Heb. 10:34; Jas. 1:2; 1 Pet. 4:13,16
5:42 [a]ch. 2:46 [b]ch. 4:20,29

6:1 [a]ch. 2:41; 4:4; 5:14; ver. 7 [b]ch. 9:29; 11:20 [c]ch. 4:35
6:2 [a]Ex. 18:17
6:3 [a]Deut. 1:13; ch. 1:21; 16:2; 1 Tim. 3:7
6:4 [a]ch. 2:42
6:5 [a]ch. 11:24 [b]ch. 8:5,26; 21:8 [c]Rev. 2:6,15
6:6 [a]ch. 1:24 [b]ch. 8:17; 9:17; 13:3; 1 Tim. 4:14; 5:22; 2 Tim. 1:6
6:7 [a]ch. 12:24; 19:20; Col. 1:6 [b]John 12:42

5:36 *Theudas.* We know of him from no other historical source.

‡5:37 *Judas of Galilee.* The Jewish historian Josephus refers to him as a man from Gamala in Gaulanitis who refused to give tribute to Caesar. His revolt was crushed, but a movement, started in his time, may have lived on in the party of the Zealots (see 1:13 and note on Mat 10:4). *days of the taxing.* Referring to a census for the purpose of taxing. Not the first census of Cyrenius, noted by Luke in his Gospel (2:2), but the one in A.D. 6.

‡5:40 *beaten.* Flogged with the Jewish penalty of "thirty-nine lashes" (2 Cor 11:24).

‡6:1 *the number of the disciples was multiplied.* A considerable length of time may have transpired since the end of ch. 5. The church continued to grow (see 5:14), but this gave rise to inevitable problems, both from within (6:1–7) and from without (6:8–7:60). At this stage of its development, the church was entirely Jewish in its composition. However, there were two groups of Jews within the fellowship: 1. *Grecians.* Hellenists—those born in lands other than the Holy Land who spoke the Greek language and were more Grecian than Hebraic in their attitudes and outlook. 2. *Hebrews.* Native Hebrews who spoke the Aramaic and/or Hebrew language(s) of the Holy Land and preserved Jewish culture and customs. *the daily ministration.* Daily funds were given to widows who had no one to care for them and so became the church's responsibility (cf. 4:35; 11:28–29; see also 1 Tim 5:3–16).

6:2 *the twelve.* At this early stage, the apostles were responsible for church life in general, including the ministry of the word of God and the care of the needy. *tables.* The early church was concerned about a spiritual ministry ("word of God" and "prayer"; see v. 4) and a material ministry ("serve tables").

6:3 *look ye out . . . seven men.* The church elected them (v. 5), and the apostles ordained them (v. 6). In this way they were appointed to their work. *full of the Holy Ghost.* See note on 2:4.

6:5 *they chose Stephen . . . Nicolas.* It is significant that all seven of the men chosen had Greek names. The murmuring had come from the Greek-speaking segment of the church; so those elected to care for the work came from their number so as to represent their interests fairly. Only Stephen and Philip of the seven receive further notice (Stephen, 6:8–7:60; Philip, 8:5–40; 21:8–9). *a proselyte of Antioch.* It is significant that a proselyte was included in the number and that Luke points out his place of origin as Antioch, the city to which the gospel was soon to be taken and which was to become the "headquarters" for the forthcoming Gentile missionary effort.

6:6 *they laid their hands on them.* Laying on of hands was used in the OT period to confer blessing (Gen 48:13–20), to transfer guilt from sinner to sacrifice (Lev 1:4) and to commission a person for a new responsibility (Num 27:23). In the NT period, laying on of hands was observed in healing (28:8; Mark 1:41), blessing (Mark 10:16), ordaining or commissioning (Acts 6:6; 13:3; 1 Tim 5:22) and imparting of spiritual gifts (Acts 8:17; 19:6; 1 Tim 4:14; 2 Tim 1:6). These seven men were appointed to responsibilities turned over to them by the twelve apostles. The Greek word used to describe their responsibility ("serve," v. 2) is the verb from which the noun "deacon" comes. Later one reads of deacons in Phil 1:1; 1 Tim 3:8–13. The Greek noun for "deacon" can also be translated "minister" or "servant." The men appointed on this occasion were simply called "the seven" (21:8), just as the apostles were called "the twelve." It is disputed whether these seven were the first deacons or were later replaced by deacons (see note on 1 Tim 3:8).

6:7 *the number of the disciples multiplied.* One of a series of progress reports given periodically throughout the book of Acts (1:15; 2:41; 4:4; 5:14; 6:7; 9:31; 12:24; 16:5; 19:20; 28:31). *a great company of the priests.* Though involved by lineage and life service in the priestly observances of the old covenant, they accepted the preaching of the apostles, which proclaimed a sacrifice that made the old sacrifices unnecessary (Heb 8:13; 10:1–4, 11–14). *were obedient to the faith.* Responded to the commands of the gospel. To believe is to obey God. Faith itself is obedience, but faith also produces obedience (Rom 1:5; Eph 2:8–10; Jas 2:14–26).

The arrest of Stephen

8 ¶ And Stephen, full of faith and power, did great wonders and miracles among the people.

9 Then there arose certain of the synagogue, which is called *the synagogue* of the Libertines, and Cyrenians, and Alexandrians, and of them of Cilicia and of Asia, disputing with Stephen.

10 And [a]they were not able to resist the wisdom and the spirit by which he spake.

11 [a]Then they suborned men, which said, We have heard him speak blasphemous words against Moses, and *against* God.

12 And they stirred up the people, and the elders, and the scribes, and came upon *him,* and caught him, and brought *him* to the council,

13 And set up false witnesses, which said, This man ceaseth not to speak blasphemous words against this holy place, and the law:

14 [a]For we have heard him say, that this Jesus of Nazareth shall [b]destroy this place, and shall change the [1]customs which Moses delivered us.

15 And all that sat in the council, looking stedfastly on him, saw his face as it had been the face of an angel.

The defence of Stephen

7 Then said the high priest, Are these *things* so?

2 And he said,

¶ [a]Men, brethren, and fathers, hearken; The God of glory appeared unto our father Abraham, when he was in Mesopotamia, before he dwelt in Charran,

3 And said unto him, [a]Get thee out of thy country, and from thy kindred, and come into the land which I shall shew thee.

4 Then [a]came he out of the land of the Chaldeans, and dwelt in Charran: and from thence, when his father was dead, he removed him into this land, wherein ye now dwell.

5 And he gave him none inheritance in it, no, not so much as to set his foot on: [a]yet he promised that *he* would give it to him for a possession, and to his seed after him, when *as yet* he had no child.

6 And God spake on this wise, [a]That his seed should sojourn in a strange land; and that they should bring them into bondage, and entreat *them* evil [b]four hundred years.

7 And the nation to whom they shall be in bondage will I judge, said God: and after that shall they come forth, and [a]serve me in this place.

8 [a]And he gave him the covenant of circumcision: [b]and so *Abraham* begat Isaac, and circumcised him the eighth day; [c]and Isaac *begat* Jacob; and [d]Jacob *begat* the twelve patriarchs.

9 [a]And the patriarchs, moved with envy,

6:10 [a]Luke 21:15; ch. 5:39; See Ex. 4:12; Is. 54:17
6:11 [a]1 Ki. 21:10,13; Mat. 26:59,60
6:14 [1]Or, *rites* [a]ch. 25:8 [b]Dan. 9:26

7:2 [a]ch. 22:1
7:3 [a]Gen. 12:1
7:4 [a]Gen. 11:31; 12:4,5
7:5 [a]Gen. 12:7; 13:15; 15:3,18; 17:8; 26:3
7:6 [a]Gen. 15:13,16 [b]Ex. 12:40; Gal. 3:17
7:7 [a]Ex. 3:12
7:8 [a]Gen. 17:9-11 [b]Gen. 21:2-4 [c]Gen. 25:26 [d]Gen. 29:31; 30:5; 35:18,23
7:9 [a]Gen. 37:4,11,28; Ps. 105:17

6:8 *great wonders and miracles.* Until now, Acts told of only the apostles working miracles (2:43; 3:4–8; 5:12). But now, after the laying on of the apostles' hands, Stephen too is reported as working miraculous signs. Philip also will soon do the same (8:6).

‡6:9 *there arose certain . . . Libertines.* Persons who had been freed from slavery. They came from different Hellenistic areas. *Cyrenians.* Cyrene was the chief city in Libya and north Africa (see note on 2:10), halfway between Alexandria and Carthage. One of its population groups was Jewish (see 11:19–21). *Alexandrians.* Alexandria was the capital of Egypt and second only to Rome in the empire. Two out of five districts in Alexandria were Jewish. *Cilicia.* A Roman province in the southeast corner of Asia Minor adjoining Syria. Tarsus, the birthplace of Paul, was one of its principal towns. *Asia.* A Roman province in the western part of Asia Minor. Ephesus, where Paul later ministered for a few years, was its major city. *disputing with Stephen.* Since Saul was from Tarsus, this may have been the synagogue he attended, and he may have been among those who argued with Stephen. He was present when Stephen was stoned (7:58).

6:11 *blasphemous words against Moses, and against God.* Since Stephen declared that the worship of God was no longer to be restricted to the temple (7:48–49), his opponents twisted these words to trump up an accusation that Stephen was attacking the temple, the law, Moses and, ultimately, God.

6:12 *the elders, and the scribes.* See notes on Mat 2:4; 15:2; Luke 5:17. *council.* See note on Mark 14:55.

6:13 *against this holy place, and the law.* Similar to the charges brought against Christ (see Mat 26:61). Stephen may have referred to Jesus' words as recorded in John 2:19, and the words may have been misunderstood or purposely misinterpreted (v. 14), as at the trial of Jesus.

7:1 *high priest.* Probably Caiaphas (see Mat 26:57–66), but see note on 4:6; cf. John 18:19, 24. *Are these things so?* See notes on 6:11,13.

‡7:2 *Abraham . . . in Mesopotamia, before he dwelt in Charran.* "Charran" the Greek spelling for "Haran." Abraham's call came in Ur, not Haran (cf. Gen 15:7; Neh 9:7). Or perhaps he was called first in Ur, and then later his call was renewed in Haran (see note on Jer 15:19–21).

7:4 *land of the Chaldeans.* A district in southern Babylonia, the name was later applied to a region that included all Babylonia. *when his father was dead.* Gen 11:26 does not mean that all three sons—Abraham, Nahor and Haran—were born to Terah in the same year when he was 70 years old. See Gen 11:26–12:1. It may be that Haran was Terah's firstborn and that Abraham was born 60 years later. Thus the death of Terah at 205 years of age could have occurred just before Abraham, at 75, left Haran.

7:6 *four hundred years.* A round number for the length of Israel's stay in Egypt (Ex 12:40–41 has 430 years). That four generations would represent considerably less than 400 years is not a necessary conclusion (see note on Gen 15:16). Ex 6:16–20 makes Moses the great-grandson of Levi, son of Jacob and brother of Joseph. This would make four generations from Levi to Moses. But in 1 Chr 7:22–27 a list of ten names represents the generations between Ephraim, the son of Joseph, and Joshua. The ten generations at 40 years each would equal 400 years, the same period of time noted as four generations. But one list is abbreviated and the other gives a full genealogy.

7:8 *covenant of circumcision.* See notes on Gen 17:10–11. The essential conditions for the religion of Israel were already fulfilled long before the temple was built and their present religious customs began. *twelve patriarchs.* See Gen 35:23–26.

7:9 *patriarchs . . . sold Joseph.* Israel consistently rejected God's favored individuals. Stephen builds his case about Jesus' rejec-

sold Joseph into Egypt: [b]but God was with him,

10 And delivered him out of all his afflictions, [a]and gave him favour and wisdom in the sight of Pharaoh king of Egypt; and he made him governor over Egypt and all his house.

11 [a]Now there came a dearth over all the land of Egypt and Canaan, and great affliction: and our fathers found no sustenance.

12 [a]But when Jacob heard that there was corn in Egypt, he sent out our fathers first.

13 [a]And at the second time Joseph was made known to his brethren; and Joseph's kindred was made known unto Pharaoh.

14 [a]Then sent Joseph, and called his father Jacob to *him,* and [b]all his kindred, threescore and fifteen souls.

15 [a]So Jacob went down into Egypt, [b]and died, he, and our fathers,

16 And [a]were carried over into Sychem, and laid in [b]the sepulchre that Abraham bought for a sum of money of the sons of Emmor the *father* of Sychem.

17 But when [a]the time of the promise drew nigh, which God had sworn to Abraham, [b]the people grew and multiplied in Egypt,

18 Till another king arose, which knew not Joseph.

19 The same dealt subtilly with our kindred, and evil entreated our fathers, [a]so that *they* cast out their young children, to the end *they* might not live.

20 [a]In which time Moses was born, and [b]was [1]exceeding fair, and nourished up in his father's house three months:

21 And [a]when he was cast out, Pharaoh's daughter took him up, and nourished him for her own son.

22 And Moses was learned in all the wisdom of the Egyptians, and was [a]mighty in words and in deeds.

23 [a]And when he was full forty years old, it came into his heart to visit his brethren the children of Israel.

24 And seeing one *of them* suffer wrong, he defended *him,* and avenged him that was oppressed, and smote the Egyptian:

25 [1]For he supposed his brethren would have understood how that God by his hand would deliver them: but they understood not.

26 And the next day he shewed himself unto them as they strove, and would have set them at one *again,* saying, Sirs, ye are brethren; why do ye wrong one to another?

27 But he that did his neighbour wrong thrust him away, saying, [a]Who made thee a ruler and a judge over us?

28 Wilt thou kill me, as thou didst the Egyptian yesterday?

29 [a]Then fled Moses at this saying, and was a stranger in the land of Madian, where he begat two sons.

30 [a]And when forty years were expired, there appeared to him in the wilderness of mount Sina an angel of the Lord in a flame of fire in a bush.

31 When Moses saw *it,* he wondered at the sight: and as he drew near to behold *it,* the voice of the Lord came unto him,

32 *Saying,* [a]I *am* the God of thy fathers, the God of Abraham, and the God of Isaac, and the God of Jacob. Then Moses trembled, and durst not behold.

33 [a]Then said the Lord to him, Put off *thy* shoes from thy feet: for the place where thou standest is holy ground.

34 [a]I have seen, I have seen the affliction of my people which is in Egypt, and I have heard their groaning, and am come down to deliver them. And now come, I will send thee into Egypt.

35 This Moses whom they refused, saying, Who made thee a ruler and a judge? the same did God send *to be* a ruler and a deliverer [a]by the hand of the angel which appeared to him in the bush.

36 [a]He brought them out, after that he had [b]shewed wonders and signs in the land of Egypt, [c]and in the Red sea, [d]and in the wilderness forty years.

7:9 [b]Gen. 39:2,21,23
7:10 [a]Gen. 41:37; 42:6
7:11 [a]Gen. 41:54
7:12 [a]Gen. 42:1
7:13 [a]Gen. 45:4,16
7:14 [a]Gen. 45:9,27 [b]Gen. 46:27; Deut. 10:22
7:15 [a]Gen. 46:5 [b]Gen. 49:33; Ex. 1:6
7:16 [a]Ex. 13:19; Josh. 24:32 [b]Gen. 23:16; 33:19
7:17 [a]ver. 6; Gen. 15:13 [b]Ex. 1:7-9; Ps. 105:24,25
7:19 [a]Ex. 1:22
7:20 [1]Or, *fair to God* [a]Ex. 2:2 [b]Heb. 11:23
7:21 [a]Ex. 2:3-10
7:22 [a]Luke 24:19
7:23 [a]Ex. 2:11,12
7:25 [1][Or, *Now*]
7:27 [a]See Luke 12:14; ch. 4:7
7:29 [a]Ex. 2:15,22; 4:20; 18:3,4
7:30 [a]Ex. 3:2
7:32 [a]Mat. 22:32; Heb. 11:16
7:33 [a]Ex. 3:5; Josh. 5:15
7:34 [a]Ex. 3:7
7:35 [a]Ex. 14:19; Num. 20:16
7:36 [a]Ex. 12:41; 33:1 [b]Ex. 7; 8; 9; 10; Ps. 105:27 [c]Ex. 14:21 [d]Ex. 16:1

tion by noting Joseph's rejection by his brothers (Gen 37:12–36).

7:13 *second time.* See Gen 43.

‡7:14 *Jacob . . . all his kindred, threescore and fifteen souls.* Seventy-five people. Although the Hebrew Bible uses the number 70 (Gen 46:27; Ex 1:5; Deut 10:22), the Greek translation of the OT (the Septuagint) adds at Gen 46:20 the names of one son of Manasseh, two of Ephraim, and one grandson of each. This makes the number 75 and is the number that Stephen uses.

7:16 Stephen greatly compresses OT accounts of two land purchases (by Abraham and Jacob) and two burial places (at Hebron and Shechem). According to the OT, Abraham purchased land at Hebron (Gen 23:17–18), where he (Gen 25:9–11), Isaac (Gen 35:29) and Jacob (Gen 50:13) were buried. Jacob bought land at Shechem (Gen 33:19), where Joseph was later buried (Josh 24:32). Josephus preserves a tradition that Joseph's brothers were buried at Hebron. Stephen's rhetorical device (by which he recalls that Jacob and the 12 patriarchs were not buried in Egypt but in Canaan) is strange to modern ears but would have been well understood by his hearers.

7:18 *another king . . . which knew not Joseph.* See note on Ex 1:8.

7:22 *Moses was learned in all the wisdom of the Egyptians.* Not explicitly stated in the OT but to be expected if he grew up in the household of Pharaoh's daughter. Both Philo and Josephus speak of Moses' great learning.

7:23 *when he was . . . forty.* Moses was 80 years old when sent to speak before Pharaoh (Ex 7:7) and 120 years old when he died (Deut 34:7). Stephen's words agree with a tradition that at Moses' first departure from Egypt he was 40 years of age.

‡7:29 *Madian.* Commonly known as Midian. Rejected by his own people, Moses feared that they would inform the Egyptians, and this led to his flight to Midian (Ex 2:15), the land flanking the Gulf of Aqaba on both sides. *begat two sons.* Gershom and Eliezer (Ex 2:22; 18:3–4; 1 Chr 23:15).

‡7:30 *when forty years were expired.* Plus the 40 years of v. 23, making the 80 years of Ex 7:7. *mount Sina* [i.e. Sinai]. Mount Sinai is called mount Horeb in Ex 3:1 (see note there).

7:35 *This Moses . . . a ruler and a judge.* Israel rejected Moses, their deliverer, just as the Jews of Stephen's day were rejecting

37 This is *that* Moses, which said unto the
children of Israel, [a]A prophet shall the Lord
your God raise up unto you of your brethren,
[1]like unto me; [b]him shall ye hear.
38 [a]This is he, that was in the church in the
wilderness with [b]the angel which spake to him
in the mount Sina, and *with* our fathers: [c]who
received *the* lively [d]oracles to give unto us:
39 To whom our fathers would not obey,
but thrust *him* from *them,* and in their hearts
turned *back again* into Egypt,
40 [a]Saying unto Aaron, Make us gods to go
before us: for *as for* this Moses, which brought
us out of the land of Egypt, we wot not what is
become of him.
41 [a]And they made a calf in those days,
and offered sacrifice unto the idol, and rejoiced in the works of their own hands.
42 Then [a]God turned, and gave them up to
worship [b]the host of heaven; as it is written in
the book of the prophets, [c]O *ye* house of Israel, have ye offered to me slain beasts and sacrifices *by the space of* forty years in the wilderness?
43 Yea, ye took up the tabernacle of
Moloch, and the star of your god Remphan, figures which ye made to worship them: and I
will carry you away beyond Babylon.
44 Our fathers had the tabernacle of Witness in the wilderness, as he had appointed,
[1]speaking unto Moses, [a]that *he* should make it
according to the fashion that he had seen.
45 [a]Which also our fathers [1]that came after brought in with Jesus into the possession of
the Gentiles, [b]whom God drave out before the
face of our fathers, unto the days of David;
46 [a]Who found favour before God, and
[b]desired to find a tabernacle for the God of Jacob.
47 [a]But Solomon built him a house.
48 Howbeit [a]the most High dwelleth not
in temples made with hands; as saith the
prophet,
49 [a]Heaven *is* my throne, and earth *is* my
footstool: what house will ye build me? saith
the Lord: or what *is* the place of my rest?
50 Hath not my hand made all these
things?
51 ¶ Ye [a]stiffnecked and [b]uncircumcised in
heart and ears, ye do always resist the Holy
Ghost: as your fathers *did,* so *do* ye.
52 [a]Which of the prophets have not your
fathers persecuted? and they have slain them
which shewed before of the coming of [b]the
Just One; of whom ye have been now the be-
trayers and murderers:
53 [a]Who have received the law by the disposition of angels, and have not kept *it.*

The stoning of Stephen

54 ¶ [a]When they heard these *things,* they
were cut to the heart, and they gnashed on
him *with their* teeth.
55 But he, [a]being full of the Holy Ghost,
looked up stedfastly into heaven, and saw the
glory of God, and Jesus standing on the right
hand of God,
56 And said, Behold, [a]I see the heavens
opened, and the [b]Son of man standing on the
right hand of God.
57 Then they cried out with a loud voice,
and stopped their ears, and ran upon him with
one accord,
58 And [a]cast *him* out of the city, [b]and
stoned *him:* and [c]the witnesses laid down
their clothes at a young man's feet, whose
name was Saul.
59 And they stoned Stephen, [a]calling
upon *God,* and saying, Lord Jesus, [b]receive
my spirit.

7:37 [1]Or, *as myself* [a]Deut. 18:15 [b]Mat. 17:5
7:38 [a]Ex. 19:3 [b]Is. 63:9; Gal. 3:19; Heb. 2:2 [c]Ex. 21:1; Deut. 5:27; John 1:17 [d]Rom. 3:2
7:40 [a]Ex. 32:1
7:41 [a]Deut. 9:16; Ps. 106:19
7:42 [a]Ps. 81:12; 2 Thes. 2:11 [b]Deut. 4:19; 2 Ki. 21:3 [c]Amos 5:25
7:44 [1][Or, *who spake*] [a]Ex. 25:40; Heb. 8:5
7:45 [1][Or, *having received*] [a]Josh. 3:14 [b]Neh. 9:24; Ps. 44:2
7:46 [a]2 Sam. 7:1; Ps. 89:19 [b]1 Chr. 22:7
7:47 [a]1 Ki. 8:20
7:48 [a]1 Ki. 8:27; 2 Chr. 2:6
7:49 [a]Is. 66:1,2; Mat. 5:34
7:51 [a]Ex. 32:9 [b]Lev. 26:41; Deut. 10:16; Jer. 4:4
7:52 [a]2 Chr. 36:16; Mat. 21:35; 1 Thes. 2:15 [b]ch. 3:14
7:53 [a]Ex. 20:1; Gal. 3:19
7:54 [a]ch. 5:33
7:55 [a]ch. 6:5
7:56 [a]Mat. 3:16 [b]Dan. 7:13
7:58 [a]Luke 4:29; Heb. 13:12 [b]Lev. 24:16 [c]Deut. 13:9
7:59 [a]ch. 9:14 [b]Ps. 31:5; Luke 23:46

Jesus, their deliverer. Yet both were sent by God. *angel which appeared to him in the bush.* See Ex 3:2.

7:37 *prophet . . . like unto me.* See 3:22–23; see also note on Deut 18:15.

‡7:38 *the church in the wilderness.* The Greek word *ekklesia* takes on a technical, theological sense in the New Testament. Its more common sense of assembly is used here. See note on 5:11. *angel which spoke to him.* According to Jewish interpretation at that time, the law was given to Moses by angel mediation—after the manner of the original call of Moses (see Ex 3:2; see also v. 53; Gal 3:19; Heb 2:2). *who received the lively oracles to give unto us.* Moses was the mediator between God and man on mount Sinai.

7:39 *would not obey.* Another rejection of God's representative and His commands.

7:40 *Make us gods.* While Moses was on Sinai receiving the law, the people made the golden calf, rejecting God and His representative (Ex 32:1). The people had not traveled far from the idolatry of Egypt.

7:42 *God . . . gave them up.* See note on Rom 1:24.

7:43 Stephen quotes Amos 5:25–27 as translated in the Septuagint, except that he replaces Damascus with Babylon in view of the fact that the final exile of Israel from the promised land was carried out by the Babylonians (Amos was speaking first of the Assyrian exile of the northern kingdom).

7:44–50 Because he had been accused of speaking against the "holy place" (6:13), Stephen concludes his recital with a word about the sanctuary. Presumably, he had been preaching that the risen Christ had now replaced the temple as the mediation of God's saving presence among His people and as the one (the "place") through whom they (and "all nations," Mark 11:17) could come to God in prayer (see note on 6:13).

7:44 *tabernacle of Witness.* Or "tabernacle of the Testimony," so called by Stephen because the primary contents of the wilderness tabernacle were the ark of the covenant and the two covenant tablets it contained, which were called "the Testimony" (see Ex 25:16,21 and notes).

7:49 Isaiah reminded Israel that all creation is the temple that God Himself had made. Stephen recalls that word to remind his hearers that ultimately God builds His own temple.

7:51 *uncircumcised in heart and ears.* Though physically circumcised, they were acting like the uncircumcised pagan nations around them. They were not truly consecrated to the Lord.

7:53 *law by the disposition of angels.* See note on v. 38.

7:55 *full of the Holy Ghost.* See note on 2:4; see also 6:5.

‡7:56 *Son of man.* See note on Mark 8:31. Jesus used this title of Himself (see Mark 2:10) to emphasize His relationship to Messianic prediction (Mat 25:31; Dan 7:13–14). It is unusual for someone other than Jesus to apply this term to Jesus Christ (see also Rev 1:13).

60 And he [a]kneeled down, and cried with a loud voice, [b]Lord, lay not this sin to their charge. And when he had said this, he fell asleep.

The persecution of the church

8 And [a]Saul was consenting unto his death.

¶ And at that time there was a great persecution against the church which was at Jerusalem; and [b]they were all scattered abroad throughout the regions of Judea and Samaria, except the apostles.

2 And devout men carried Stephen *to his burial,* and [a]made great lamentation over him.

3 As for Saul, [a]he made havock of the church, entering into every house, and haling men and women committed *them* to prison.

4 Therefore [a]they that were scattered abroad went every where preaching the word.

Philip at Samaria

5 ¶ Then [a]Philip went down to the city of Samaria, and preached Christ unto them.

6 And the people with one accord gave heed unto those *things* which Philip spake, hearing and seeing the miracles which he did.

7 For [a]unclean spirits, crying with loud voice, came out of many that were possessed *with them:* and many taken with palsies, and *that were* lame, were healed.

8 And there was great joy in that city.

Conversion of Simon the sorcerer

9 But there was a certain man, called Simon, which beforetime in the *same* city [a]used sorcery, and bewitched the people of Samaria, [b]giving out that himself was some great one:

10 To whom they all gave heed, from the least to the greatest, saying, This *man* is the great power of God.

11 And to him they had regard, because that of long time *he* had bewitched them with sorceries.

12 But when they believed Philip preaching the *things* [a]concerning the kingdom of God, and the name of Jesus Christ, they were baptized, both men and women.

13 Then Simon himself believed also: and when he was baptized, he continued with Philip, and wondered, beholding *the* [1]miracles and signs *which were* done.

14 ¶ Now when the apostles which were at Jerusalem heard that Samaria had received the word of God, they sent unto them Peter and John:

15 Who, when they were come down, prayed for them, [a]that they might receive the Holy Ghost:

16 (For [a]as yet he was fallen upon none of them: only [b]they were baptized in [c]the name of the Lord Jesus.)

17 Then [a]laid they *their* hands on them, and they received the Holy Ghost.

18 And when Simon saw that through laying on of the apostles' hands the Holy Ghost was given, he offered them money,

19 Saying, Give me also this power, that on whomsoever I lay hands, he may receive the Holy Ghost.

20 But Peter said unto him, Thy money perish with thee, because [a]thou hast thought that [b]the gift of God may be purchased with money.

21 Thou hast neither part nor lot in this matter: for thy heart is not right in the sight of God.

22 Repent therefore of this thy wickedness, and pray God, [a]if perhaps the thought of thine heart may be forgiven thee.

23 For I perceive that thou art in [a]the gall of bitterness, and *in* the bond of iniquity.

7:60 [a]ch. 9:40 [b]Mat. 5:44; Luke 6:28
8:1 [a]ch. 7:58 [b]ch. 11:19
8:2 [a]Gen. 23:2; 50:10; 2 Sam. 3:31
8:3 [a]ch. 7:58; 1 Cor. 15:9; Gal. 1:13; Phil. 3:6; 1 Tim. 1:13
8:4 [a]Mat. 10:23
8:5 [a]ch. 6:5
8:7 [a]Mark 16:17
8:9 [a]ch. 13:6 [b]ch. 5:36
8:12 [a]ch. 1:3
8:13 [1][Gr. *signs and great miracles*]
8:15 [a]ch. 2:38
8:16 [a]ch. 19:2 [b]Mat. 28:19; ch. 2:38 [c]ch. 10:48; 19:5
8:17 [a]ch. 6:6; 19:6; Heb. 6:2
8:20 [a]Mat. 10:8; See 2 Ki. 5:16 [b]ch. 2:38; 10:45; 11:17
8:22 [a]Dan. 4:27; 2 Tim. 2:25
8:23 [a]Heb. 12:15

7:58 *laid down their clothes at a young man's feet . . . Saul.* Some have thought that this marked Saul as being in charge of the execution. In any case, it is Luke's way of introducing the main character of the second section of the book.

7:60 *lay not this sin to their charge.* Compare with Jesus' words (Luke 23:34).

8:1 *was consenting.* See 22:20. *scattered abroad throughout . . . Judea and Samaria.* The beginning of the fulfillment of the commission in 1:8—not by the church's plan, but by events beyond the believers' control. See map, p. 1582. *except the apostles.* For the apostles to stay in Jerusalem would be an encouragement to those in prison and a center of appeal to those scattered. The church now went underground.

8:3 *made havock.* See 22:4. The Greek underlying this phrase sometimes describes the ravages of wild animals.

8:4 *preaching the word.* Many witnesses to the gospel went everywhere proclaiming the good news. The number of witnesses multiplied, and the territory covered was expanded greatly (cf. 11:19–20).

8:5 *Philip.* One of the seven in the Jerusalem church (6:3,5; see note on 6:6), who now becomes an evangelist, proclaiming the Christ (Messiah); see also 21:8. Philip is an example of one of those who were scattered. *the city of Samaria.* A reference to the old capital Samaria, renamed Sebaste or Neapolis (modern Nablus).

‡8:9 *Simon.* In early Christian literature the "sorcerer" (Simon Magus) is described as the arch-heretic of the church and the "father" of Gnostic teaching. See The Introduction to 1 John.

8:10 *the great power of God.* Simon claimed to be either God Himself or, more likely, His chief representative.

8:13 *Simon himself believed . . . baptized.* It is difficult to know whether Simon's faith was genuine. Even though Luke says Simon believed, Peter's statement that Simon had no part in the apostles' ministry because his heart was not "right in the sight of God" (v. 21) casts some doubt.

8:14 *had received the word of God.* Were obedient to the gospel proclaimed by Philip. *sent unto them Peter and John.* The Jerusalem church assumed the responsibility of inspecting new evangelistic efforts and the communities of believers they produced (see 11:22).

8:16 *was fallen upon none of them.* Since the day of Pentecost, those who belong to Christ (see Rom 8:9) also have the Holy Spirit. But the Spirit had not yet been made manifest to the Christians in Samaria by the usual signs. This deficiency was now graciously supplied (v. 17).

8:17 *laid . . . their hands on them.* See v. 18; 19:1–7; cf. 2 Tim 1:6; see also note on 6:6.

8:18 *he offered them money.* Simon had boasted of having great powers before (see v. 10 and note), and now he tried to buy this magical power he believed the apostles possessed.

8:23 *in the gall of bitterness.* See Deut 29:18.

24 Then answered Simon, and said, [a]Pray ye to the Lord for me, that none of *these things* which ye have spoken come upon me.

25 And they, when they had testified and preached the word of the Lord, returned to Jerusalem, and preached the gospel in many villages of the Samaritans.

Conversion of the Ethiopian

26 ¶ And *the* angel of the Lord spake unto Philip, saying, Arise, and go toward the south unto the way that goeth down from Jerusalem unto Gaza, which is desert.

27 And he arose and went: and behold, [a]a man of Ethiopia, an eunuch of great authority under Candace queen of the Ethiopians, who had the charge of all her treasure, and [b]had come to Jerusalem for to worship,

8:24 [a]Gen. 20:7,17; Ex. 8:8; Num. 21:7; 1 Ki. 13:6; Job 42:8; Jas. 5:16
8:27 [a]Zeph. 3:10 [b]John 12:20
8:32 [a]Is. 53:7,8

28 Was returning, and sitting in his chariot read Esaias the prophet.

29 Then the Spirit said unto Philip, Go near, and join thyself to this chariot.

30 And Philip ran *thither* to *him,* and heard him read the prophet Esaias, and said, Understandest thou what thou readest?

31 And he said, How can I, except some *man* should guide me? And he desired Philip that *he* would come up and sit with him.

32 The place of the scripture which he read was this, [a]He was led as a sheep to the slaughter; and like a lamb dumb before his shearer, so opened he not his mouth:

33 In his humiliation his judgment was taken away: and who shall declare his generation? for his life is taken from the earth.

34 And the eunuch answered Philip, and said, I pray thee, of whom speaketh the

8:26 *angel of the Lord.* Cf. v. 29; see note on 5:19. *from Jerusalem unto Gaza.* A distance of about 50 miles.
8:27 *a man of Ethopia.* Ethiopia corresponded in this period to Nubia, from the upper Nile region at the first cataract (Aswan) to Khartoum. *Candace.* The traditional title of the queen mother, responsible for performing the secular duties of the reigning king—who was thought to be too sacred for such activities. *come to Jerusalem for to worship.* If not a full-fledged proselyte (Deut 23:1), the Ethiopian was a Gentile God-fearer.
8:30 *heard him read.* It was customary practice to read aloud.
8:34 *of whom speaketh the prophet this?* Beginning with Is 53 (see v. 35), Philip may have identified the suffering servant with the Davidic Messiah of Is 11 or with the Son of man (Dan 7:13).

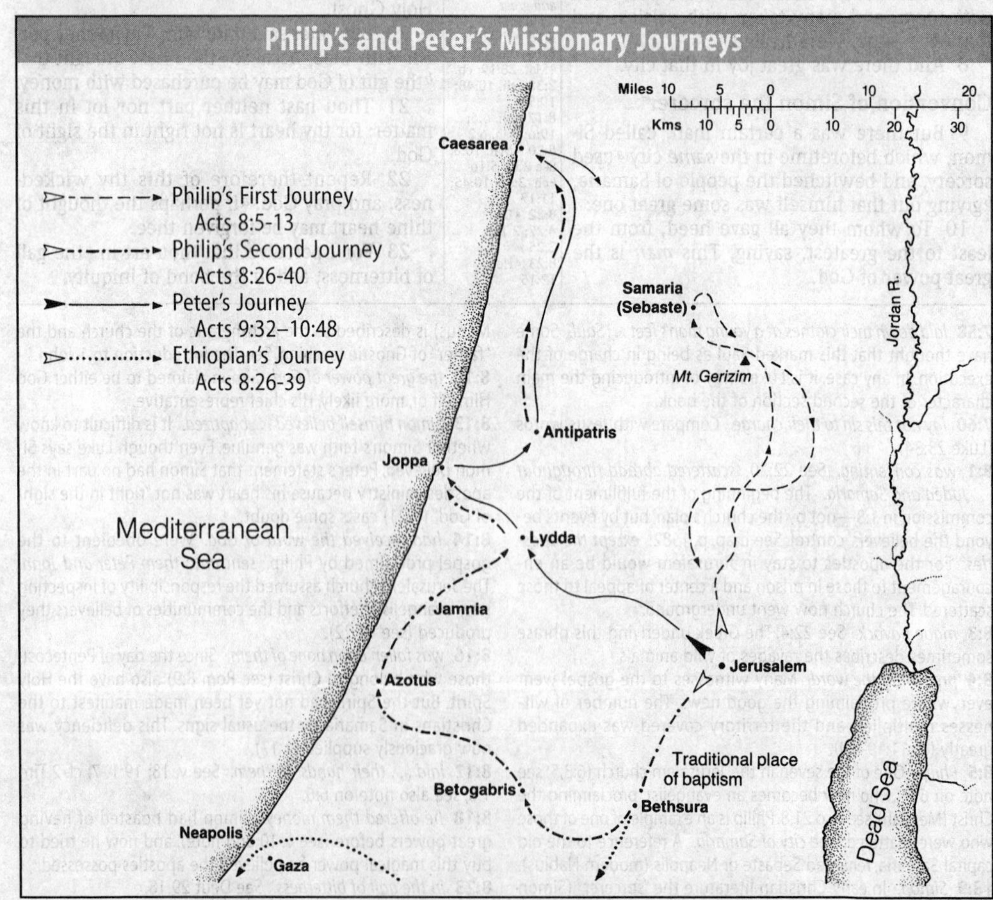

prophet this? of himself, or of some other *man?*

35 Then Philip opened his mouth, [a]and began at the same scripture, and preached unto him Jesus.

36 And as they went on *their* way, they came unto a certain water: and the eunuch said, See, *here is* water; [a]what doth hinder me to be baptized?

37 And Philip said, [a]If thou believest with all *thine* heart, *thou* mayest. And he answered and said, [b]I believe that Jesus Christ is the Son of God.

38 And he commanded the chariot to stand still: and they went down both into the water, both Philip and the eunuch; and he baptized him.

39 And when they were come up out of the water, [a]the Spirit of the Lord caught away Philip, that the eunuch saw him no more: and he went *on* his way rejoicing.

40 But Philip was found at Azotus: and passing through he preached in all the cities, till he came to Cesarea.

Conversion of Saul

9 And [a]Saul, yet breathing out threatenings and slaughter against the disciples of the Lord, went unto the high priest,

2 And desired of him letters to Damascus to the synagogues, that if he found any [a][1]of *this* way, whether they were men or women, he might bring *them* bound unto Jerusalem.

3 And [a]as *he* journeyed, he came near Damascus: and suddenly there shined round about him a light from heaven:

4 And he fell to the earth, and heard a voice saying unto him, Saul, Saul, [a]why persecutest thou me?

5 And he said, Who art thou, Lord? And the Lord said, I am Jesus whom thou persecutest: *it is* hard for thee to kick against the pricks.

6 And he trembling and astonished said, Lord, [a]what wilt thou have me to do? And the Lord *said* unto him, Arise, and go into the city, and it shall be told thee what thou must do.

7 And [a]the men which journeyed with him stood speechless, hearing a voice, but seeing no *man.*

8 And Saul arose from the earth; and when his eyes were opened, he saw no *man:* but they led him by the hand, and brought *him* into Damascus.

9 And he was three days without sight, and neither did eat nor drink.

10 ¶ And there was a certain disciple at Damascus, [a]named Ananias; and to him said the Lord in a vision, Ananias. And he said, Behold, I *am here,* Lord.

11 And the Lord *said* unto him, Arise, and go into the street which is called Straight, and inquire in the house of Judas for *one* called Saul, [a]of Tarsus: for behold, he prayeth,

12 And hath seen in a vision a man named Ananias coming in, and putting *his* hand on him, that he might receive his sight.

13 Then Ananias answered, Lord, I have heard by many of this man, [a]how much evil he hath done to thy saints at Jerusalem:

14 And here he hath authority from the chief priests to bind all [a]that call on thy name.

15 But the Lord said unto him, Go *thy way:* for [a]he is a chosen vessel unto me, to bear my

8:35 [a]Luke 24:27; ch. 18:28
8:36 [a]ch. 10:47
8:37 [a]Mat. 28:19; Mark 16:16 [b]Mat. 16:16; John 6:69; 9:35,38; 11:27; ch. 9:20; 1 John 4:15; 5:5,13
8:39 [a]1 Ki. 18:12; 2 Ki. 2:16; Ezek. 3:12,14
9:1 [a]ch. 8:3; Gal. 1:13; 1 Tim. 1:13
9:2 [1][Gr. *of the way:* So ch. 19:9,23] [a]ch. 19:9,23
9:3 [a]ch. 22:6; 26:12; 1 Cor. 15:8
9:4 [a]Mat. 25:40
9:6 [a]Luke 3:10; ch 2:37; 16:30
9:7 [a]Dan. 10:7; See ch. 22:9; 26:13
9:10 [a]ch. 22:12
9:11 [a]ch. 21:39; 22:3
9:13 [a]ver. 1
9:14 [a]ver. 21; ch. 7:59; 1 Cor. 1:2; 2 Tim. 2:22
9:15 [a]ch. 13:2; 22:21; Rom. 1:1; 1 Cor. 15:10; Gal. 1:15; Eph. 3:7,8; 1 Tim. 2:7; 2 Tim. 1:11

8:35 *preached unto him Jesus.* Proclaimed the way of salvation through Jesus Christ.

8:36 *they came unto a certain water.* There were several possibilities: a brook in the valley of Elah (which David crossed to meet Goliath, 1 Sam 17:40); the Wadi el-Hasi just north of Gaza; water from a spring or one of the many pools in the area.

8:39 *rejoicing.* Joy is associated with salvation in Acts (see note on 16:34).

8:40 *Azotus.* OT Ashdod (see 1 Sam 5:1), one of the five Philistine cities. It was about 19 miles from Gaza and 60 miles from Cesarea. *Cesarea.* Rebuilt by Herod and with an excellent harbor, it served as the headquarters of the Roman procurators. The account leaves Philip in Cesarea at this time; his next appearance is 20 years later, and he is still located in the same place (21:8).

9:1 *Saul.* Introduced at the stoning of Stephen (7:58), he was born in Tarsus and trained under Gamaliel (22:3). See note on Phil 3:4–14. *threatenings and slaughter.* We do not know that Saul was directly involved in the death of anyone other than Stephen (8:1), but there appear to have been similar cases (22:4; 26:10). *high priest.* Probably Caiaphas (see note on 4:6) and the members of the Sanhedrin, who had authority over Jews both in Judea and elsewhere.

‡9:2 *Damascus.* Located in the Roman province of Syria, it was the nearest important city outside the Holy Land. It also had a large Jewish population. The distance from Jerusalem to Damascus was about 150 miles, four to six days' travel. *of this way.* "The way" was an early name for Christianity which occurs a number of times in Acts (16:17; 18:25–26; 19:9,23; 22:4; 24:14,22; see 2 Pet 2:2). Jesus called himself "the way" (John 14:6). *bound unto Jerusalem.* Where the full authority of the council could be exercised in trial for either acquittal or death.

9:3 *a light from heaven.* "At midday" (26:13).

9:4 *why persecutest thou me?* To persecute the church is to persecute Christ, for the church is His body (see 1 Cor 12:27; Eph 1:22–23).

9:5 *Who art thou, Lord?* In rabbinic tradition such a voice from heaven would have been understood as the voice of God Himself. The solemn repetition of Saul's name and the bright light suggested to him that he was in the presence of deity.

9:7 *hearing a voice.* "Heard not" in 22:9 perhaps means that those with Saul did not understand what it was saying (cf. Dan 10:7).

9:10 *Ananias.* This Ananias is mentioned elsewhere only in 22:12. His was a common name (5:1; 23:2). The Greek form is derived from the Hebrew name Hananiah, meaning "The LORD is gracious/shows grace" (see Dan 1:6 and note).

9:11 *street which is called Straight.* Probably followed the same route of the long, straight street that today runs through the city from east to west. It is a decided contrast to the numerous crooked streets of the city (see map, p. 1572). *Tarsus.* See note on 22:3. *prayeth.* Prayer is often associated with visions in Luke and Acts (see 10:9–11; Luke 1:10; 3:21; 9:28).

9:13,32 *saints.* See notes on Rom 1:7; Phil 1:1.

name before [b]the Gentiles, and [c]kings, and
the children of Israel:
16 For [a]I will shew him how great *things*
he must suffer for my name's sake.
17 [a]And Ananias went his way, and entered
into the house; and [b]putting his hands on him
said, Brother Saul, the Lord, *even* Jesus, that
appeared unto thee in the way as thou camest,
hath sent me, that thou mightest receive thy
sight, and [c]be filled with the Holy Ghost.
18 And immediately there fell from his
eyes as it had been scales: and he received
sight forthwith, and arose, and was baptized,
19 And when he had received meat, he was
strengthened. [a]Then was Saul certain days
with the disciples which were at Damascus.

9:15 [b]Rom. 1:5; 11:13; Gal. 2:7,8 [c]ch. 25:22,23; 26:1
9:16 [a]ch. 20:23; 21:11; 2 Cor. 11:23
9:17 [a]ch. 22:12,13 [b]ch. 8:17 [c]ch. 2:4; 4:31; 8:17; 13:52
9:19 [a]ch. 26:20
9:21 [a]ver. 1; ch. 8:3; Gal. 1:13,23
9:22 [a]ch. 18:28
9:23 [a]ch. 23:12; 2 Cor. 11:26
9:24 [a]2 Cor. 11:32

Paul preaches at Damascus

20 And straightway he preached Christ in
the synagogues, that he is the Son of God.
21 But all that heard *him* were amazed,
and said; [a]Is not this he that destroyed them
which called on this name in Jerusalem, and
came hither for that *intent,* that he might
bring them bound unto the chief priests?
22 But Saul increased the more in strength,
[a]and confounded the Jews which dwelt at Damascus, proving that this is *very* Christ.

Paul escapes to Jerusalem

23 ¶ And after that many days were fulfilled, [a]the Jews took counsel to kill him:
24 [a]But their laying await was known of

9:15 *before the Gentiles.* See Rom 1:13–14. *kings.* Agrippa (26:1) and Caesar at Rome (25:11–12; 28:19).
9:17 *Jesus, that appeared unto thee.* The Damascus road experience was not merely a vision. The resurrected Christ actually appeared to Saul, and on this fact Saul based his qualification to be an apostle (1 Cor 9:1; 15:8).
9:20 *straightway.* Following his baptism. *synagogues.* It became Saul's regular practice to preach at every opportunity in the synagogues (13:5; 14:1; 17:1–2,10; 18:4,19; 19:8). *he is the Son of God.* Saul's message was a declaration of what he himself had become convinced of on the Damascus road: Christ's deity and Messiahship (see v. 22 and note on Luke 2:11).
9:23 *after that many days were fulfilled.* Three years (Gal 1:17–18). It is probable that the major part of this period was spent in Arabia, away from Damascus, though the borders of Arabia extended to the environs of Damascus. *the Jews took counsel to kill him.* Upon his return to Damascus, the governor under Aretas gave orders for his arrest (2 Cor 11:32). The absence of Roman coins struck in Damascus between A.D. 34 and 62 may indicate that Aretas was in control during that period.

Roman Damascus

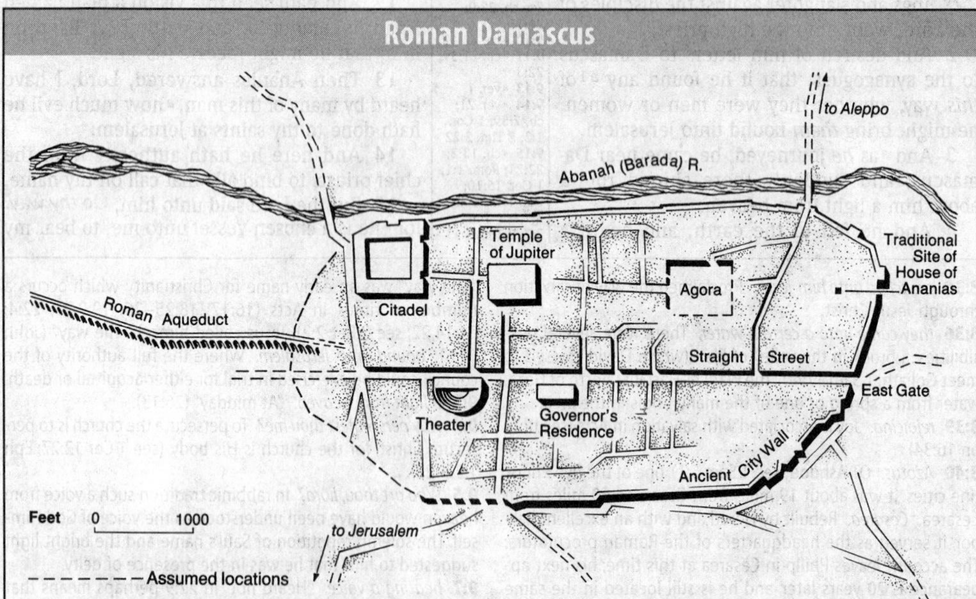

Damascus represented much more to Saul, the strict Pharisee, than any other stop on his campaign of repression. It was the hub of a vast commercial network with far-flung lines of caravan trade reaching into north Syria, Mesopotamia, Anatolia, Persia and Arabia. If the new "way" of Christianity flourished in Damascus, it would quickly reach all these places. From the viewpoint of the Sanhedrin and of Saul, the arch-persecutor, it had to be stopped in Damascus.

The city itself was a veritable oasis, situated in a plain watered by the Biblical rivers Abanah and Pharpar. Roman architecture overlaid the Hellenistic town plan with a great temple to Jupiter and a mile-long colonnaded street, the "street which is called Straight" of Acts 9:11. The city gates and a section of the town wall may still be seen today, as well as the lengthy bazaar that runs along the line of the ancient street.

The dominant political figure at the time of Paul's escape from Damascus (2 Cor 11:32-33) was Aretas IV, king of the Nabateans (9 B.C.–A.D. 40), though normally the Decapolis cities were attached to the province of Syria and were thus under the influence of Rome.

Saul. And they watched the gates day and night to kill him.

25 Then the disciples took him by night, and [a]let *him* down by the wall in a basket.

26 And [a]when Saul was come to Jerusalem, he assayed to join himself to the disciples: but they were all afraid of him, and believed not that he was a disciple.

27 [a]But Barnabas took him, and brought *him* to the apostles, and declared unto them how he had seen the Lord in the way, and that he had spoken to him, [b]and how he had preached boldly at Damascus in the name of Jesus.

28 And [a]he was with them coming in and going out at Jerusalem.

29 And he spake boldly in the name of the Lord Jesus, and disputed against the [a]Grecians: [b]but they went about to slay him.

30 Which when the brethren knew, they brought him down to Cesarea, and sent him forth to Tarsus.

31 [a]Then had the churches rest throughout all Judea and Galilee and Samaria, and were edified; and walking in the fear of the Lord, and in the comfort of the Holy Ghost, were multiplied.

Aeneas and Tabitha

32 ¶ And it came to pass, as Peter passed [a]throughout all *quarters,* he came down also to the saints which dwelt at Lydda.

33 And there he found a certain man named Aeneas, which had kept his bed eight years, and was sick of the palsy.

34 And Peter said unto him, Aeneas, [a]Jesus Christ maketh thee whole: arise, and make thy bed. And he arose immediately.

35 And all that dwelt at Lydda and [a]Saron saw him, and [b]turned to the Lord.

36 ¶ Now there was at Joppa a certain disciple named Tabitha, which by interpretation is called [1]Dorcas: this *woman* was full [a]of good works and almsdeeds which she did.

37 And it came to pass in those days, that she was sick, and died: whom when they had washed, they laid *her* in [a]an upper chamber.

38 And forasmuch as Lydda was nigh to Joppa, and the disciples had heard that Peter was there, they sent unto him two men, desiring *him* that *he* would not [1]delay to come to them.

39 Then Peter arose and went with them. When he was come, they brought him into the upper chamber: and all the widows stood by him weeping, and shewing the coats and garments which Dorcas made, while she was with them.

40 But Peter [a]put *them* all forth, and [b]kneeled down, and prayed; and turning *him* to the body [c]said, Tabitha, arise. And she opened her eyes: and when she saw Peter, she sat up.

41 And he gave her *his* hand, and lift her up, and when he had called the saints and widows, presented her alive.

42 And it was known throughout all Joppa; [a]and many believed in the Lord.

43 And it came to pass, that he tarried many days in Joppa with one [a]Simon a tanner.

Cornelius' vision

10 There was a certain man in Cesarea called Cornelius, a centurion of the band called the Italian *band,*

9:25 [a]Josh. 2:15; 1 Sam. 19:12
9:26 [a]ch. 22:17; Gal. 1:17,18
9:27 [a]ch. 4:36; 13:2 [b]ver. 20,22
9:28 [a]Gal. 1:18
9:29 [a]ch. 6:1; 11:20 [b]ver. 23; 2 Cor. 11:26
9:31 [a]See ch. 8:1
9:32 [a]ch. 8:14
9:34 [a]ch. 3:6,16; 4:10
9:35 [a]1 Chr. 5:16 [b]ch. 11:21
9:36 [1][Or, *Doe,* or, *Roe*] [a]1 Tim. 2:10; Tit. 3:8
9:37 [a]ch. 1:13
9:38 [1]Or, *be grieved*
9:40 [a]Mat. 9:25 [b]ch. 7:60 [c]Mark 5:41,42; John 11:43
9:42 [a]John 11:45
9:43 [a]ch. 10:6

9:25 *let him down by the wall in a basket.* See 2 Cor 11:33 (cf. Josh 2:15; 1 Sam 19:12).

9:26 *was come to Jerusalem.* From Gal 1:19 we learn that all the apostles were away except Peter and James, the Lord's brother. James was not one of the twelve, but he held a position in Jerusalem comparable to that of an apostle.

9:27 *Barnabas.* See note on 4:36.

9:29 *spake boldly.* Formerly Saul was arguing against Christ; now he is forcefully presenting Jesus as the Messiah.

9:30 *Cesarea.* See note on 8:40. *Tarsus.* Saul's birthplace (see note on 22:3).

9:31 *the churches.* The whole Christian body, including Christians in the districts of Judea, Galilee and Samaria. *walking . . . in the comfort of the Holy Ghost.* The work of the Spirit is particularly noted throughout the book of Acts (see 13:2 and note on 1:2). This is why the book is sometimes called the Acts of the Holy Spirit.

9:32 *Lydda.* A town two or three miles north of the road connecting Joppa and Jerusalem. Lydda is about 12 miles from Joppa.

9:33 *Aeneas.* Since Peter was there to visit the believers, Aeneas was probably one of the Christians.

‡9:35 *Saron.* The Greek spelling of "Sharon." The fertile plain of Sharon runs about 50 miles along the Mediterranean coast, roughly from Joppa to Cesarea. The reference here, however, may be to a village in the neighborhood of Lydda instead of to a district (an Egyptian papyrus refers to a town by that name in the Holy Land).

9:36 *Joppa.* About 38 miles from Jerusalem, the main seaport of Judea. Today it is known as Jaffa and is a suburb of Tel Aviv.

9:37 *washed.* In preparation for burial, a custom common to both Jews (Purification of the Dead) and Greeks. *upper chamber.* If burial was delayed, it was customary to lay the body in an upper room. In Jerusalem the body had to be buried the day the person died, but outside Jerusalem up to three days might be allowed for burial.

9:38 *nigh to Joppa.* See note on v. 32. *would not delay to come.* Whether for consolation or for a miracle, Peter was urged to hurry in order to arrive before the burial.

9:40 *put them all forth.* Cf. 1 Ki 17:23; 2 Ki 4:33. Peter had been present on all three occasions recorded in Scripture when Jesus raised individuals from the dead (Mat 9:25; Luke 7:11–17; John 11:1–44). As when Jesus raised Jairus's daughter, the crowd in the room was told to leave. Unlike Jesus, however, Peter knelt and prayed.

9:42 *many believed.* Cf. John 12:11.

9:43 *a tanner.* Occupations were frequently used with personal names to identify individuals further (see 16:14; 18:3; 19:24; 2 Tim 4:14), but in this case it is especially significant. A tanner was involved in treating the skins of dead animals, thus contacting the unclean according to Jewish law; so he was despised by many. Peter's decision to stay with him shows already a willingness to reject Jewish prejudice and prepares the way for his coming vision and the mission to the Gentiles.

10:1 *Cesarea.* Located 30 miles north of Joppa and named in honor of Augustus Caesar, it was the headquarters for the

2 [a]A devout *man,* and one that [b]feared God
with all his house, which gave much alms to
the people, and prayed to God alway.
3 [a]He saw in a vision evidently, about the
ninth hour of the day, an angel of God coming
in to him, and saying unto him, Cornelius.
4 And when he looked on him, he was
afraid, and said, What is it, Lord? And he said
unto him, Thy prayers and thine alms are
come up for a memorial before God.
5 And now send men to Joppa, and call for
one Simon, whose surname is Peter:
6 He lodgeth with one [a]Simon a tanner,
whose house is by the sea side: [b]he shall tell
thee what thou oughtest to do.
7 And when the angel which spake unto
Cornelius was departed, he called two of his
household servants, and a devout soldier of
them that waited on him continually;
8 And when he had declared all *these
things* unto them, he sent them to Joppa.

10:2 [a]ver. 22; ch. 8:2; 22:12 [b]ver. 35
10:3 [a]ver. 30; ch. 11:13
10:6 [a]ch. 9:43 [b]ch. 11:14
10:9 [a]ch. 11:5

Peter's vision

9 ¶ On the morrow, as they went on their
journey, and drew nigh unto the city, [a]Peter

Roman forces of occupation (see also note on 8:40). *Cornelius.* A Latin name made popular when Cornelius Sulla liberated some 10,000 slaves over 100 years earlier. These had all taken his family name, Cornelius. *centurion.* Commanded a military unit that normally numbered at least 100 men (see note on Luke 7:2). The Roman legion (about 6,000 men) was divided into ten regiments, each of which had a designation. This was the "Italian" (another was the "Imperial," or "Augustan," 27:1). A centurion commanded about a sixth of a regiment. Centurions were carefully selected; all of them mentioned in the NT appear to have had noble qualities (e.g., Luke 7:5). The Roman centurions provided necessary stability to the entire Roman system.
10:2 *devout.* In spite of all his good deeds, Cornelius needed to hear the way of salvation from a human messenger. The role of the angel (v. 3) was to bring Cornelius and Peter together (cf. 8:26; 9:10). *feared God.* The term used of one who was not a full Jewish proselyte but who believed in one God and respected the moral and ethical teachings of the Jews.
10:3 *a vision.* Not a dream or trance but a revelation through an angel to Cornelius while at prayer (see v. 30; see also note on 9:11). *about the ninth hour.* About 3:00 P.M. This is another indication that Cornelius followed Jewish religious practices, because three in the afternoon was a Jewish hour of prayer (see 3:1)—the hour of the evening incense.
10:4 *memorial.* A portion of the grain offering burned on the altar was called a "memorial" (Lev 2:2).
10:5–6 *Joppa . . . Simon a tanner.* See notes on 9:36,43.
10:9 *upon the house.* It was customary for eastern houses to

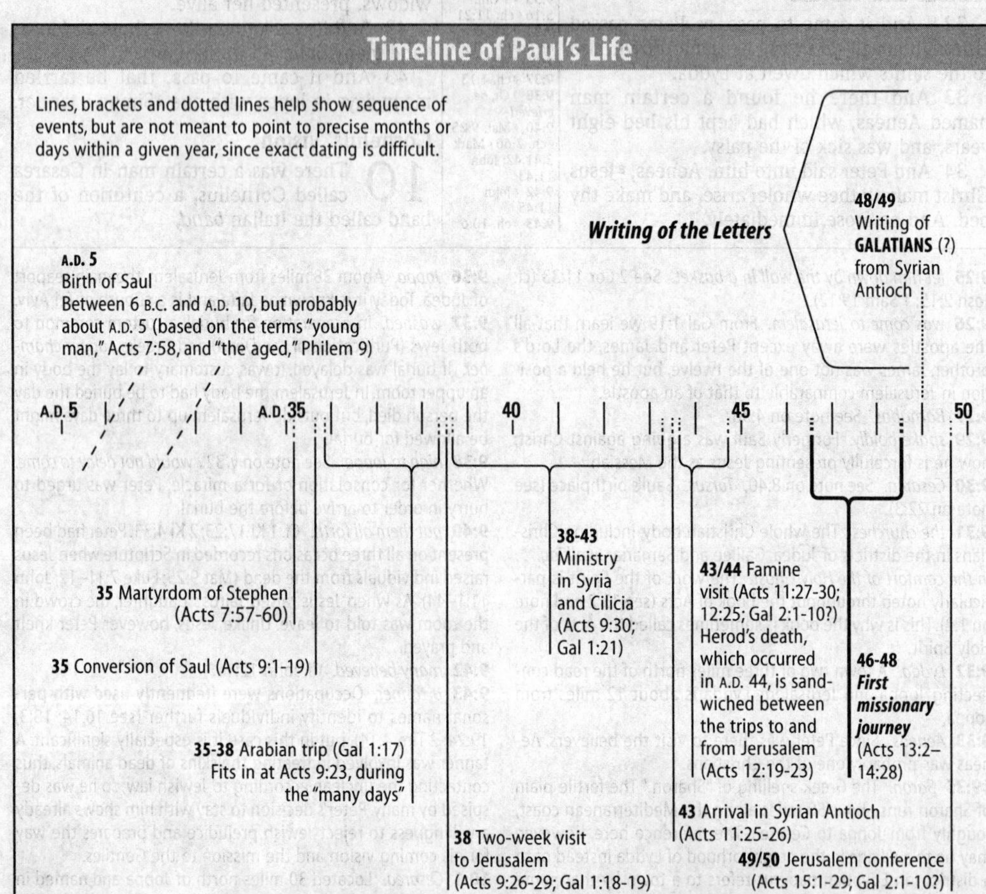
Timeline of Paul's Life
Lines, brackets and dotted lines help show sequence of events, but are not meant to point to precise months or days within a given year, since exact dating is difficult.
A.D. 5
Birth of Saul
Between 6 B.C. and A.D. 10, but probably about A.D. 5 (based on the terms "young man," Acts 7:58, and "the aged," Philem 9)
A.D. 5
A.D. 35
40
45
50
Writing of the Letters
48/49 Writing of GALATIANS (?) from Syrian Antioch
35 Martyrdom of Stephen (Acts 7:57-60)
35 Conversion of Saul (Acts 9:1-19)
35-38 Arabian trip (Gal 1:17) Fits in at Acts 9:23, during the "many days"
38 Two-week visit to Jerusalem (Acts 9:26-29; Gal 1:18-19)
38-43 Ministry in Syria and Cilicia (Acts 9:30; Gal 1:21)
43/44 Famine visit (Acts 11:27-30; 12:25; Gal 2:1-10?) Herod's death, which occurred in A.D. 44, is sandwiched between the trips to and from Jerusalem (Acts 12:19-23)
43 Arrival in Syrian Antioch (Acts 11:25-26)
46-48 First missionary journey (Acts 13:2–14:28)
49/50 Jerusalem conference (Acts 15:1-29; Gal 2:1-10?)

went up upon the house to pray about the
sixth hour:
10 And he became very hungry, and would
have eaten: but while they made ready, he fell
into a trance,
11 And [a]saw heaven opened, and a certain
vessel descending unto him, as *it had been* a
great sheet knit at the four corners, and let
down to the earth:
12 Wherein were all *manner of* fourfooted
beasts of the earth, and wild beasts, and creeping things, and fowls of the air.
13 And there came a voice to him, Rise,
Peter; kill, and eat.
14 But Peter said, Not so, Lord; [a]for I have
never eaten any *thing that is* common or unclean.
15 And *the* voice *spake* unto him again the
second time, [a]What God hath cleansed, *that*
call not thou common.
16 This was done thrice: and the vessel
was received up again into heaven.

Peter's visit to Cornelius

17 ¶ Now while Peter doubted in himself
what *this* vision which he had seen should
mean, behold, the men which were sent from
Cornelius had made inquiry for Simon's
house, and stood before the gate,
18 And called, and asked whether Simon,
which was surnamed Peter, were lodged
there.
19 While Peter thought on the vision, [a]the
Spirit said unto him, Behold, three men seek
thee:
20 [a]Arise therefore, and get *thee* down,

10:11 [a]ch. 7:56; Rev. 19:11
10:14 [a]Lev. 11:4; 20:25; Deut. 14:3,7; Ezek. 4:14
10:15 [a]ver. 28; Mat. 15:11; Rom. 14:14,17,20; 1 Cor. 10:25; 1 Tim. 4:4; Tit. 1:15
10:19 [a]ch. 11:12
10:20 [a]ch. 15:7

have flat roofs with outside stairways. The roof was used as a convenient place for relaxation and privacy.
10:10 *fell into a trance.* A state of mind God produced and used to communicate with Peter. It was not merely imagination or a dream. Peter's consciousness was heightened to receive the vision from God.
10:12 *all manner of fourfooted beasts.* Including animals both clean and unclean according to Lev 11.
10:14 *Not so, Lord.* So deeply ingrained was the observance of the laws of clean and unclean that Peter refused to obey immediately. *common or unclean.* Anything common (impure) was forbidden by the law to be eaten.
10:15 *God hath cleansed.* Jesus had already laid the groundwork for setting aside the laws of clean and unclean food (Mat 15:11; see 1 Tim 4:3–5).
10:16 *thrice.* To make a due impression on Peter.

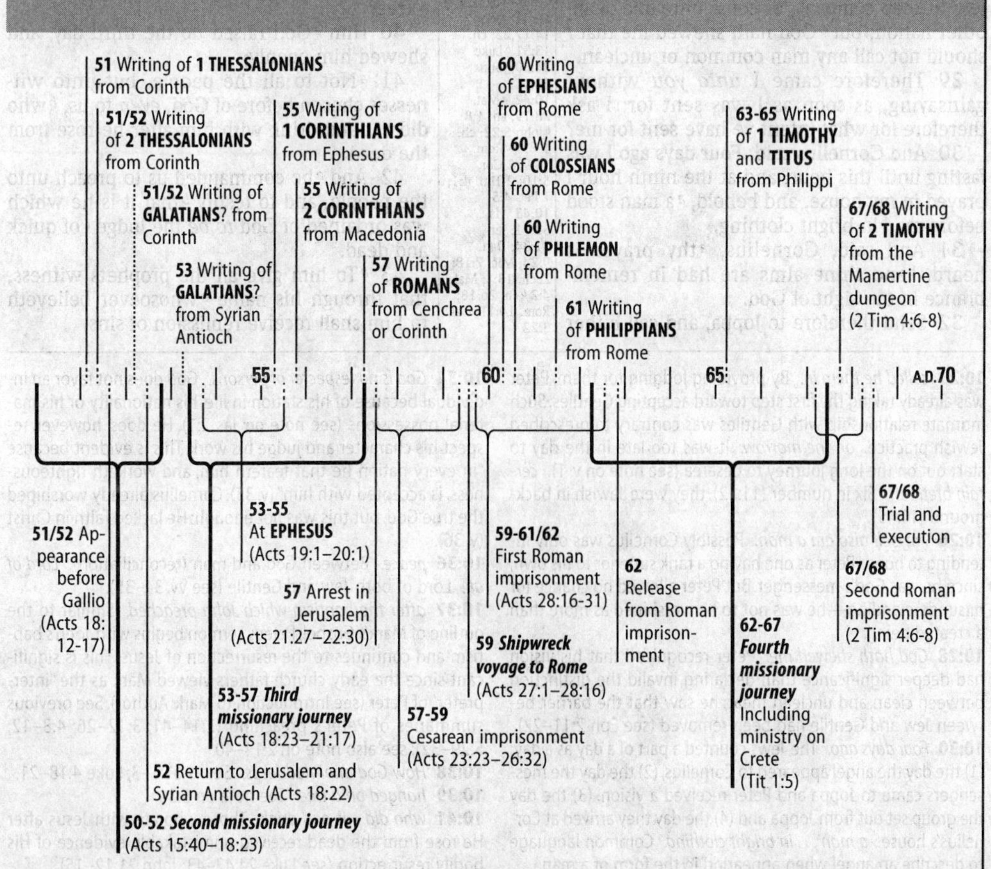

and go with them, doubting nothing: for I have
sent them.
21 Then Peter went down to the men
which were sent unto him from Cornelius;
and said, Behold, I am he whom ye seek: what
is the cause wherefore ye are come?
22 And they said, Cornelius the centurion,
a just man, and one that feareth God, and [a]of
good report among all the nation of the Jews,
was warned from God by a holy angel to send
for thee into his house, and to hear words of
thee.
23 Then called he them in, and lodged
them. And on the morrow Peter went away
with them, [a]and certain brethren from Joppa
accompanied him.
24 And the morrow *after* they entered into
Cesarea. And Cornelius waited for them, and
had called together his kinsmen and near
friends.
25 ¶ And as Peter was coming in, Cornelius
met him, and fell down at *his* feet, and worshipped *him.*
26 But Peter took him up, saying, [a]Stand
up; I myself also am a man.
27 And as he talked with him, he went in,
and found many *that were* come together.
28 And he said unto them, Ye know how
[a]that it is an unlawful *thing* for a man *that is* a
Jew to keep company, or come unto one of another nation; but [b]God hath shewed me that *I*
should not call any man common or unclean.
29 Therefore came I *unto you* without
gainsaying, as soon as I was sent for: I ask
therefore for what intent ye have sent for me?
30 And Cornelius said, Four days ago I was
fasting until this hour; and at the ninth hour I
prayed in my house, and behold, [a]a man stood
before me [b]in bright clothing,
31 And said, Cornelius, [a]thy prayer is
heard, [b]and thine alms are had in remembrance in the sight of God.
32 Send therefore to Joppa, and call hither

10:22 [a]ch. 22:12
10:23 [a]ch. 11:12
10:26 [a]ch. 14:14
10:28 [a]John 4:9; 18:28; ch. 11:3; Gal. 2:12 [b]ch. 15:8,9; Eph. 3:6
10:30 [a]ch. 1:10 [b]Mat. 28:3; Mark 16:5; Luke 24:4
10:31 [a]Dan. 10:12 [b]Heb. 6:10
10:34 [a]Deut. 10:17; 2 Chr. 19:7; Job 34:19; Rom. 2:11; Gal. 2:6; Eph. 6:9; Col. 3:25; 1 Pet. 1:17
10:35 [a]ch. 15:9; Rom. 2:13; 3:22; 10:12,13; 1 Cor. 12:13; Gal. 3:28; Eph. 2:13
10:36 [a]Is. 57:19; Eph. 2:14; Col. 1:20 [b]Mat. 28:18; Rom. 10:12; 1 Cor. 15:27; Eph. 1:20; 1 Pet. 3:22; Rev. 17:14
10:37 [a]Luke 4:14
10:38 [a]Luke 4:18; Heb. 1:9 [b]John 3:2
10:39 [a]ch. 2:32 [b]ch. 5:30
10:40 [a]ch. 2:24
10:41 [a]John 14:17,22; ch. 13:31 [b]Luke 24:30; John 21:13
10:42 [a]Mat. 28:19; ch. 1:8 [b]John 5:22; ch. 17:31 [c]Rom. 14:9; 2 Cor. 5:10; 2 Tim. 4:1; 1 Pet. 4:5
10:43 [a]Is. 53:11; Jer. 31:34; Dan. 9:24; Mic. 7:18; Zech. 13:1; Mal. 4:2 [b]ch. 26:18; Rom. 10:11; Gal. 3:22

Simon, whose surname is Peter; he is lodged
in the house of *one* Simon a tanner by the sea
side: who, when he cometh, shall speak unto
thee.
33 Immediately therefore I sent to thee;
and thou hast well done that thou art come.
Now therefore are we all here present before
God, to hear all *things* that are commanded
thee of God.
34 ¶ Then Peter opened *his* mouth, and
said, [a]Of a truth I perceive that God is no respecter of persons:
35 But [a]in every nation he that feareth
him, and worketh righteousness, is accepted
with him.
36 The word which *God* sent unto the children of Israel, [a]preaching peace by Jesus
Christ: ([b]he is Lord of all:)
37 *That* word, *I say,* you know, which was
published throughout all Judea, and [a]began
from Galilee, after the baptism which John
preached;
38 How [a]God anointed Jesus of Nazareth
with the Holy Ghost and with power: who went
about doing good, and healing all that were oppressed of the devil; [b]for God was with him.
39 And [a]we are witnesses of all *things*
which he did both in the land of the Jews, and
in Jerusalem; [b]whom they slew and hanged on
a tree:
40 Him [a]God raised up the third day, and
shewed him openly;
41 [a]Not to all the people, but unto witnesses chosen before of God, *even* to us, [b]who
did eat and drink with him after he rose from
the dead.
42 And [a]he commanded us to preach unto
the people, and to testify [b]that it is he which
was ordained of God *to be* the Judge [c]of quick
and dead.
43 [a]To him give all the prophets witness,
that through his name [b]whosoever believeth
in him shall receive remission of sins.

10:23 *called he them in.* By providing lodging for them, Peter was already taking the first step toward accepting Gentiles. Such intimate relationship with Gentiles was contrary to prescribed Jewish practice. *on the morrow.* It was too late in the day to start out on the long journey to Cesarea (see note on v. 1). *certain brethren.* Six in number (11:12), they were Jewish in background (10:45).

10:26 *I myself also am a man.* Possibly Cornelius was only intending to honor Peter as one having a rank superior to his own, since he was God's messenger. But Peter allowed no chance for misunderstanding—he was not to be worshiped as more than a created being.

10:28 *God hath shewed me.* Peter recognized that his vision had deeper significance than declaring invalid the distinction between clean and unclean meat; he saw that the barrier between Jew and Gentile had been removed (see Eph 2:11–22).

10:30 *Four days ago.* The Jews counted a part of a day as a day: (1) the day the angel appeared to Cornelius, (2) the day the messengers came to Joppa and Peter received a vision, (3) the day the group set out from Joppa and (4) the day they arrived at Cornelius's house. *a man . . . in bright clothing.* Common language to describe an angel when appearing in the form of a man.

10:34 *God is no respecter of persons.* God does not favor an individual because of his station in life, his nationality or his material possessions (see note on Jas 2:1). He does, however, respect his character and judge his work. This is evident because "in every nation he that feareth him, and worketh righteousness, is accepted with him" (v. 35). Cornelius already worshiped the true God, but this was not enough: He lacked faith in Christ (v. 36).

10:36 *peace.* Between God and man (reconciliation). *Lord of all.* Lord of both Jew and Gentile (see vv. 34–35).

10:37 *after the baptism which John preached.* Similar to the outline of Mark's Gospel, Peter's sermon begins with John's baptism and continues to the resurrection of Jesus. This is significant since the early church fathers viewed Mark as the "interpreter" of Peter (see Introduction to Mark: Author). See previous summaries of Peter's preaching (2:14–41; 3:12–26; 4:8–12; 5:29–32); see also note on 2:14–40.

10:38 *How God anointed Jesus.* See Is 61:1–3; Luke 4:18–21.

10:39 *hanged on a tree.* See note on 5:30.

10:41 *who did eat and drink.* Those who ate with Jesus after He rose from the dead received unmistakable evidence of His bodily resurrection (see Luke 24:42–43; John 21:12–15).

Gentiles receive the Holy Ghost

44 ¶ While Peter yet spake these words, [a]the Holy Ghost fell on all them which heard the word.

45 [a]And they of the circumcision which believed were astonished, as many as came with Peter, [b]because that on the Gentiles also was poured out the gift of the Holy Ghost.

46 For they heard them speak with tongues, and magnify God. Then answered Peter,

47 Can any *man* forbid water, that these should not be baptized, which have received the Holy Ghost [a]as well as we?

48 [a]And he commanded them to be baptized [b]in the name of the Lord. Then prayed they him to tarry certain days.

11 And the apostles and brethren that were in Judea heard that the Gentiles had also received the word of God.

2 And when Peter was come up to Jerusalem, [a]they that were of the circumcision contended with him,

3 Saying, [a]Thou wentest in to men uncircumcised, [b]and didst eat with them.

4 But Peter *rehearsed the matter* from the beginning, *and* expounded *it* [a]by order unto them, saying,

5 [a]I was in the city of Joppa praying: and in a trance I saw a vision, A certain vessel descend, as *it had been* a great sheet, let down from heaven by four corners; and it came *even* to me:

6 Upon the which when I had fastened mine eyes, I considered, and saw fourfooted beasts of the earth, and wild beasts, and creeping things, and fowls of the air.

7 And I heard a voice saying unto me, Arise, Peter; slay and eat.

8 But I said, Not so, Lord: for nothing common or unclean hath at any time entered into my mouth.

9 But *the* voice answered me again from heaven, What God hath cleansed, *that* call not thou common.

10 And this was done three times: and all were drawn up again into heaven.

11 And behold, immediately there were three men already come unto the house where I was, sent from Cesarea unto me.

12 And [a]the Spirit bade me go with them, nothing doubting. Moreover [b]these six brethren accompanied me, and we entered into the man's house:

13 [a]And he shewed us how he had seen an angel in his house, which stood and said unto him, Send men to Joppa, and call for Simon, whose surname is Peter;

14 Who shall tell thee words, whereby thou and all thy house shall be saved.

15 And as I began to speak, the Holy Ghost fell on them, [a]as on us at the beginning.

16 Then remembered I the word of the Lord, how that he said, [a]John indeed baptized with water; but [b]ye shall be baptized with the Holy Ghost.

17 [a]Forasmuch then as God gave them the like gift as *he did* unto us, who believed on the Lord Jesus Christ; [b]what was I, that I could withstand God?

18 When they heard these *things,* they held their peace, and glorified God, saying, [a]Then hath God also to the Gentiles granted repentance unto life.

The church at Antioch

19 ¶ [a]Now they which were scattered abroad upon the persecution that arose about Stephen travelled as far as Phenice, and Cyprus, and Antioch, preaching the word to none but unto *the* Jews only.

10:44 [a]ch. 4:31
10:45 [a]ver. 23 [b]ch. 11:18; Gal. 3:14
10:47 [a]ch. 11:17
10:48 [a]1 Cor. 1:17 [b]ch. 2:38; 8:16
11:2 [a]ch. 10:45
11:3 [a]ch. 10:28 [b]Gal. 2:12
11:4 [a]Luke 1:3
11:5 [a]ch. 10:9
11:12 [a]John 16:13; ch. 10:19; 15:7 [b]ch. 10:23
11:13 [a]ch. 10:30
11:15 [a]ch. 2:4
11:16 [a]Mat. 3:11; John 1:26,33; ch. 1:5; 19:4 [b]Is. 44:3; Joel 2:28; 3:18
11:17 [a]ch. 15:8,9 [b]ch. 10:47
11:18 [a]Rom. 10:12,13; 15:9,16
11:19 [a]ch. 8:1

10:44 *the Holy Ghost fell on all them.* See 8:16 and note.

10:45 *astonished . . . on the Gentiles also.* Apparently the early Jewish Christians failed to understand that the gospel was for the Gentiles as well as for the Jews, and that they would share alike in the benefits of redemption. Gentile proselytes to Judaism, however, were accepted (see 6:5).

10:47 *Can any man forbid water, that these should not be baptized?* The Gentiles had received the same gift (11:17) as the Jewish believers; they spoke in tongues as did the Jewish Christians on the day of Pentecost. This was unavoidable evidence that the invitation to the kingdom was open to Gentiles as well as to Jews.

11:1 *the apostles and brethren.* At times "brethren" is used to refer to those of common Jewish lineage (2:29; 7:2), but in Christian contexts it denotes those united in Christ (6:3; 10:23). In matters of deep concern, the apostles did not act alone. The divine will gave guidance, and the apostles interpreted and exhorted, but the consent of the whole church was sought ("the whole multitude," 6:5; "apostles and brethren," 11:1; "the church," 11:22; "the church . . . the apostles and elders," 15:4; cf. 15:22).

11:2 *they . . . of the circumcision.* Jewish Christians.

11:3 *men uncircumcised.* The Gentiles who would not observe the laws of clean and unclean food and would violate Jewish regulations concerning food preparation.

11:4–17 See notes on 10:1–23,28–33.

11:14 *thou and all thy house.* Not only the family but also slaves and employed individuals under Cornelius's authority (see note on Gen 6:18).

11:17 *withstand God.* Peter could not deny the Gentiles the invitation to be baptized (10:47) and to enjoy full fellowship in Christ with all believers. The Jewish believers were compelled to recognize that God was going to save Gentiles on equal terms with Jews. By divine action rather than by human choice, the door was being opened to Gentiles.

11:18 *repentance unto life.* A change of one's attitude toward sin, which leads to a turning from sin to God and results in eternal life (see note on 2:38).

‡11:19 *Phenice.* Commonly called Phoenicia, a country about 15 miles wide and 120 miles long stretching along the northeastern Mediterranean coast (modern Lebanon). Its important cities were Tyre and Sidon. *Cyprus.* An island in the northeastern Mediterranean; the home of Barnabas (4:36). *Antioch.* The third city of the Roman empire (after Rome and Alexandria). It was 15 miles inland from the northeast corner of the Mediterranean. The first largely Gentile local church was located here, and it was from this church that Paul's three missionary journeys were launched (13:1–4; 15:40; 18:23).

20 And some of them were men of Cyprus and Cyrene, which, when they were come to Antioch, spake unto [a]the Grecians, preaching the Lord Jesus.

21 And [a]the hand of the Lord was with them: and a great number believed, and [b]turned unto the Lord.

22 Then tidings of these *things* came unto the ears of the church which was in Jerusalem: and they sent forth [a]Barnabas, that *he* should go as far as Antioch.

23 Who, when he came, and had seen the grace of God, was glad, and [a]exhorted *them* all, that with purpose of heart *they* would cleave unto the Lord.

24 For he was a good man, and [a]full of the Holy Ghost and of faith: [b]and much people was added unto the Lord.

25 Then departed Barnabas to [a]Tarsus, for to seek Saul:

26 And when he had found him, he brought him unto Antioch. And it came to pass, that a whole year they assembled themselves [1]with the church, and taught much people, and the disciples were called Christians first in Antioch.

27 ¶ And in these days came [a]prophets from Jerusalem unto Antioch.

28 And there stood up one of them named [a]Agabus, and signified by the Spirit that there should be great dearth throughout all the world: which came to pass in the days of Claudius Cesar.

29 Then the disciples, every man according to his ability, determined to send [a]relief unto the brethren which dwelt in Judea:

30 [a]Which also they did, and sent it to the elders by the hands of Barnabas and Saul.

Peter delivered from prison

12 Now about that time Herod the king [1]stretched forth *his* hands to vex certain of the church.

2 And he killed James [a]the brother of John with the sword.

3 And because he saw it pleased the Jews, he proceeded further to take Peter also. (Then were [a]the days of unleavened bread.)

4 And [a]when he had apprehended him, he put *him* in prison, and delivered *him* to four quaternions of soldiers to keep him; intending after Easter to bring him forth to the people.

5 Peter therefore was kept in prison: but [a] [1]prayer was made without ceasing of the church unto God for him.

6 And when Herod would have brought him forth, the same night Peter was sleeping between two soldiers, bound with two chains: and *the* keepers before the door kept the prison.

7 And behold, [a]*the* angel of the Lord came upon *him,* and a light shined in the prison: and he smote Peter on the side, and raised him up, saying, Arise up quickly. And his chains fell off from *his* hands.

8 And the angel said unto him, Gird thyself, and bind on thy sandals. And so he did. And he saith unto him, Cast thy garment about thee, and follow me.

9 And he went out, and followed him; and

11:20 [a]ch. 6:1; 9:29
11:21 [a]Luke 1:66; ch. 2:47 [b]ch. 9:35
11:22 [a]ch. 9:27
11:23 [a]ch. 13:43; 14:22
11:24 [a]ch. 6:5 [b]ver. 21; ch. 5:14
11:25 [a]ch. 9:30
11:26 [1]Or, *in the church*
11:27 [a]ch. 2:17; 13:1; 15:32; 21:9; 1 Cor. 12:28; Eph. 4:11
11:28 [a]ch. 21:10
11:29 [a]Rom. 15:26; 1 Cor. 16:1; 2 Cor. 9:1
11:30 [a]ch. 12:25
12:1 [1]Or, *began*
12:2 [a]Mat. 4:21; 20:23
12:3 [a]Ex. 12:14,15; 23:15
12:4 [a]John 21:18
12:5 [1]Or, *instant and earnest prayer was made* [a]2 Cor. 1:11; Eph. 6:18; 1 Thes. 5:17
12:7 [a]ch. 5:19

11:20 *Cyrene.* See note on 2:10. *Grecians.* Not Greek-speaking Jews, but Gentiles.

11:21 *hand of the Lord.* Cf. 4:30; 13:11; cf. also Luke 1:66. It indicates divine approval and blessing, sometimes evidenced by signs and wonders (see Ex 8:19).

11:22 *Barnabas.* See notes on 4:36; 9:27. *Antioch.* See note on v. 19. The sending of Barnabas was apparently in keeping with the Jerusalem church's policy of sending leaders to check on new ministries that came to their attention (see 8:14).

11:24 *full of the Holy Ghost and of faith.* See the description of Stephen (6:5).

11:25 *Tarsus.* See 9:11,30 and note on 22:3.

11:26 *a whole year.* Luke notes definite periods of time (18:11; 19:8,10; 24:27;8:30). *Christians.* Whether adopted by believers or invented by enemies as a term of reproach, it is an apt title for those "belonging to Christ" (the meaning of the term).

11:27 *prophets.* The first mention of the gift of prophecy in Acts. Prophets preach, exhort, explain or, as in this case, foretell (see 13:1; 15:32; 19:6; 21:9–10; Rom 12:6; 1 Cor 12:10; 13:2,8; 14:3,6,29–37; see also notes on Jonah 3:2; Zech 1:1; Eph 4:11).

11:28 *Agabus.* Later foretells Paul's imprisonment (21:10). In Acts, prophets are engaged in foretelling (v. 27; 21:9–10) at least as often as in "forthtelling" (15:32).

11:30 *elders.* First reference to them in Acts (see notes on 1 Tim 3:1; 5:17). Since the apostles are not mentioned, they may have been absent from Jerusalem at this time.

12:1 *about that time.* Some hold that the events recorded in ch. 12 group together matters concerning Herod and may not be in strict chronological order. For example, the arrival of Barnabas and Saul in Jerusalem (11:30) may have followed Herod's persecution and Peter's release from prison. Since the date of Herod's death was A.D. 44, these events would probably have occurred in 43. According to this view, the famine of 11:28 occurred c. 46, following Herod's death (v. 23). Others hold that such juggling of events is not necessary. Thus the relief gift of 11:30 came before Herod's death in 44, and the return of Barnabas and Saul (v. 25) followed Herod's death. According to the former view, the Jerusalem visit of Gal 2:1–10 was the famine visit of v. 25; 11:30. According to the latter view, the Gal 2:1 visit was the Jerusalem council visit of 15:1–29. *Herod the king.* Agrippa I, grandson of Herod the Great (see notes on Mat 2:1; 14:1) and son of Aristobulus. He was a nephew of Herod Antipas, who had beheaded John the Baptist (Mat 14:3–12) and had tried Jesus (Luke 23:8–12). When Antipas was exiled, Agrippa received his tetrarchy as well as those of Philip and Lysanias (see Luke 3:1). In A.D. 41 Judea and Samaria were added to his realm.

12:2 *killed . . . with the sword.* Beheaded, like John the Baptist. *James.* Brother of John the apostle and son of Zebedee (Mat 4:21). This event took place about ten years after Jesus' death and resurrection. Jesus had warned of their coming suffering (Mat 20:23).

12:3 *days of unleavened bread.* See note on Luke 22:1.

‡12:4 *four quaternions.* One company of four soldiers for each of the four watches of the night. *Easter.* The New Testament word is "passover." It is another way of referring to the whole week of the festival (see note on Luke 22:1).

12:7 *a light shined.* The glory of the Lord (see Luke 2:9).

12:9 *he went out.* Out of the prison, probably the tower of Antonia, located at the northwest corner of the temple—the "barracks" where Paul was later held (see 21:34).

[a]wist not that it was true which was done by
the angel; but thought [b]he saw a vision.
10 When they were past the first and the
second ward, they came unto the iron gate
that leadeth unto the city; [a]which opened to
them of his own accord: and they went out,
and passed on through one street; and forthwith the angel departed from him.
11 And when Peter was come to himself,
he said, Now I know of a surety, that [a]the Lord
hath sent his angel, and [b]hath delivered me
out of the hand of Herod, and *from* all the expectation of the people of the Jews.
12 And when he had considered *the thing,*
[a]he came to the house of Mary the mother of
[b]John, whose surname was Mark; where
many were gathered together [c]praying.
13 ¶ And as Peter knocked at the door of
the gate, a damsel came [1]to hearken, named
Rhoda.
14 And when she knew Peter's voice, she
opened not the gate for gladness, but ran in,
and told how Peter stood before the gate.
15 And they said unto her, Thou art mad.
But she constantly affirmed that it was *even*
so. Then said they, [a]It is his angel.
16 But Peter continued knocking: and
when they had opened *the door,* and saw him,
they were astonished.
17 But he, [a]beckoning unto them with the
hand to hold their peace, declared unto them
how the Lord had brought him out of the
prison. And he said, *Go* shew these *things*
unto James, and to the brethren. And he departed, and went into another place.
18 Now as soon as it was day, there was no
small stir among the soldiers, what was become of Peter.
19 And when Herod had sought for him,
and found *him* not, he examined the keepers,
and commanded that *they* should be put to
death. And he went down from Judea to Cesarea, and *there* abode.

The death of Herod

20 ¶ And Herod [1]was highly displeased
with them of Tyre and Sidon: but they came
with one accord to him, and, having made
Blastus [2]the king's chamberlain their friend,
desired peace; because [a]their country was
nourished by the king's *country.*
21 And upon a set day Herod, arrayed in
royal apparel, sat upon his throne, and made
an oration unto them.
22 And the people gave a shout, *saying, It*
is the voice of a god, and not of a man.
23 And immediately *the* angel of the Lord
[a]smote him, because [b]he gave not God the
glory: and he was eaten of worms, and gave up
the ghost.
24 But [a]the word of God grew and multiplied.
25 And Barnabas and Saul returned from
Jerusalem, when they had fulfilled *their* [1]min-
istry, and [a]took with *them* [b]John, whose surname was Mark.

Paul and Barnabas on Cyprus

13 Now there were [a]in the church that
was at Antioch certain prophets and
teachers; as [b]Barnabas, and Simeon that was
called Niger, and [c]Lucius of Cyrene, and Man-

12:9 [a]Ps. 126:1 [b]ch. 10:3,17; 11:5
12:10 [a]ch. 16:26
12:11 [a]Ps. 34:7; Dan. 3:28; 6:22; Heb. 1:14 [b]Job 5:19; Ps. 33:18,19; 34:22; 41:2; 97:10; 2 Cor. 1:10; 2 Pet. 2:9
12:12 [a]ch. 4:23 [b]ch. 15:37 [c]ver. 5
12:13 [1]Or, *to ask who was there*
12:15 [a]Gen. 48:16; Mat. 18:10
12:17 [a]ch. 13:16; 19:33; 21:40
12:20 [1]Or, *bare a hostile mind, intending war* [2]Gr. *that was over the king's bedchamber* [a]1 Ki. 5:9,11; Ezek. 27:17
12:23 [a]1 Sam. 25:38; 2 Sam. 24:17 [b]Ps. 115:1
12:24 [a]Is. 55:11; ch. 6:7; 19:20; Col. 1:6
12:25 [1]Or, *charge* [a]ch. 13:5,13; 15:37 [b]ver. 12
13:1 [a]ch. 14:26 [b]ch. 11:22 [c]Rom. 16:21

12:12 *Mary.* The aunt of Barnabas (see Col 4:10). Apparently her home was a gathering place for Christians. It may have been the location of the upper room where the Last Supper was held (see Mark 14:13–15; see also Acts 1:13) and the place of prayer in 4:31. *John . . . Mark.* See note on v. 25.

12:13 *Rhoda.* A hired servant, but in sympathy with the family and the church.

12:15 *his angel.* Reflects the belief that everyone has a personal angel who ministers to him (cf. Mat 18:10; Heb 1:14), adding the idea that such an angel occasionally showed himself and that his appearance resembled the person under his care.

12:16 *they were astonished.* Though "prayer was made without ceasing of the church unto God for him" (v. 5).

12:17 *James.* The Lord's brother, a leader in the Jerusalem church (Gal 1:19). James, the brother of John, had been killed (see v. 2).

12:19 *Cesarea.* Not only a headquarters for Roman procurators, but Agrippa used it as his capital when no procurators were assigned to Judea (see notes on 8:40; 10:1).

12:20 *Tyre and Sidon.* The leading cities of Phoenicia (Lebanon today). They were dependent on the grainfields of Galilee for their food. *Blastus.* The treasurer; not otherwise known.

12:21 *upon a set day.* A festival Herod was celebrating in honor of Claudius Caesar (Josephus, *Antiquities,* 19.8.2). *royal apparel.* The historian Josephus describes a silver robe, dazzling bright, that Herod wore that day. When people acclaimed him a god, he did not deny it. He was seized with violent pains, was carried out and died five days later (Josephus, *Antiquities,* 19.8.2).

12:23 *angel of the Lord.* See note on v. 7. *eaten of worms.* A miserable death associated with Herod's acceptance of acclaim to be divine, but may also be seen as divine retribution for his persecution of the church.

12:24 *the word of God grew and multiplied.* Third summary report of progress (see 6:7; 9:31). Three more follow (16:5; 19:20; 28:31).

12:25 *John . . . Mark.* See v. 12. He was perhaps the young man who fled on the night of Jesus' arrest (Mark 14:51–52). He wrote the second Gospel (see Introduction to Mark: Author; John Mark in the NT) and accompanied Barnabas and Saul on the first part of their first missionary journey (see notes on 15:38–39).

13:1 *prophets.* See note on 11:27. The special gift of inspiration experienced by OT prophets (Deut 18:18–20; 2 Pet 1:21) was known in the NT as well (2:17–18; 1 Cor 14:29–32; Eph 3:5). The prophets are second to the apostles in Paul's lists (1 Cor 12:28–29; Eph 2:20; 4:11; but cf. Luke 11:49; Rom 12:6; 1 Cor 12:10). *teachers.* See 11:26; 15:35; 18:11; 20:20; 28:31; 1 Cor 12:28–29; Eph 4:11. *Barnabas . . . Saul.* The church leaders at Antioch, perhaps listed in the order of their importance. *Barnabas.* See note on 4:36. He was sent originally to Antioch by the church in Jerusalem (11:22), had recently returned from taking alms to Jerusalem (12:25) and was a recognized leader in the church at Antioch. *Simeon that was called Niger.* "Simeon" suggests Jewish background; in that case, Niger (Latin for "black") may indicate his dark complexion. *Lucius of Cyrene.*

aen, [1]which had been brought up with Herod the tetrarch, and Saul.

2 As they ministered to the Lord, and fasted, the Holy Ghost said, [a]Separate me Barnabas and Saul for the work [b]whereunto I have called them.

3 And [a]when they had fasted and prayed, and laid *their* hands on them, they sent *them* away.

4 So they, being sent forth by the Holy Ghost, departed unto Seleucia; and from thence they sailed to [a]Cyprus.

5 And when they were at Salamis, [a]they preached the word of God in the synagogues of the Jews: and they had also [b]John to *their* minister.

6 And when they had gone through the isle unto Paphos, they found [a]a certain sorcerer, a false prophet, a Jew, whose name *was* Barjesus:

7 Which was with the deputy *of the country,* Sergius Paulus, a prudent man; who called for Barnabas and Saul, and desired to hear the word of God.

8 But [a]Elymas the sorcerer (for so is his name by interpretation) withstood them, seeking to turn away the deputy from the faith.

9 Then Saul, (who also *is called* Paul,) [a]filled with the Holy Ghost, set his eyes on him,

10 And said, O full of all subtilty and all mischief, [a]*thou* child of the devil, *thou* enemy of all righteousness, wilt thou not cease to pervert the right ways of the Lord?

11 And now behold, [a]the hand of the Lord *is* upon thee, and thou shalt be blind, not seeing the sun for a season. And immediately there fell on him a mist and a darkness; and he went about seeking *some* to lead him by the hand.

12 Then the deputy, when he saw what was done, believed, being astonished at the doctrine of the Lord.

Preaching in Perga and Antioch

13 ¶ Now when Paul and his company loosed from Paphos, they came to Perga in Pamphylia: and [a]John departing from them returned to Jerusalem.

14 But when they departed from Perga, they came to Antioch in Pisidia, and [a]went into the synagogue on the sabbath day, and sat down.

15 And [a]after the reading of the law and the prophets the rulers of the synagogue sent unto them, saying, *Ye* men *and* brethren, if ye have [b]*any* word of exhortation for the people, say *on.*

13:1 [1]Or, *Herod's fosterbrother*
13:2 [a]Num. 8:14; ch. 9:15; 22:21; Rom. 1:1; Gal. 1:15; 2:9 [b]Mat. 9:38; ch. 14:26; Rom. 10:15; Eph. 3:7,8; 1 Tim. 2:7; 2 Tim. 1:11; Heb. 5:4
13:3 [a]ch. 6:6
13:4 [a]ch. 4:36
13:5 [a]ver. 46 [b]ch. 12:25; 15:37
13:6 [a]ch. 8:9
13:8 [a]Ex. 7:11; 2 Tim. 3:8
13:9 [a]ch. 4:8
13:10 [a]Mat. 13:38; 1 John 3:8
13:11 [a]1 Sam. 5:6
13:13 [a]ch. 15:38
13:14 [a]ch. 16:13
13:15 [a]Luke 4:16 [b]Heb. 13:22

Lucius is a Latin name. In the second group of preachers coming to Antioch, some were from Cyrene (11:20), capital of Libya (see 6:9 and note). *Manaen.* In Hebrew, Menahem. Since he was the foster brother of Herod Antipas, he would be able to tell of the thoughts and actions of Herod (see Luke 9:7–9).

13:2 *ministered to the Lord, and fasted.* Paul's first missionary journey did not result from a planning session but from the Spirit's initiative as the leaders worshiped (see v. 4). The communication from the Holy Spirit may have come through the prophets.

13:3 *laid their hands on them.* For the purpose of separating the two for the designated work (see 14:26 for the completion of the mission). Fasting and prayer accompany this appointment (see 14:23; cf. Luke 2:37).

13:4 See map No. 11 at the end of the study Bible. *Seleucia.* The seaport of Antioch (16 miles to the west, and 5 miles upstream from the mouth of the Orontes River). *Cyprus.* Many Jews lived there, and the gospel had already been preached there (11:19–20; see note on 11:19).

13:5 *Salamis.* A town on the east coast of the central plain of Cyprus, near modern Famagusta. *John.* John Mark, a cousin of Barnabas (see Col 4:10); see also note on 12:25.

13:6 *Paphos.* At the western end of Cyprus, nearly 100 miles from Salamis. It was the headquarters for Roman rule. *Bar-jesus.* "Bar" is Aramaic for "son of"; "Jesus" is derived from the Greek for "Joshua" (see note on Mat 1:21).

13:7 *deputy.* Since Cyprus was a Roman senatorial province, a proconsul was assigned to it.

13:8 *Elymas.* A Semitic name meaning "sorcerer" or "magician" or "wise man" (probably a self-assumed designation).

13:9 *Saul, (who also is called Paul,).* The names mean "asked [of God]" and "little" respectively. It was customary to have a given name, in this case Saul (Hebrew, Jewish background), and a later name, in this case Paul (Roman, Hellenistic background). From now on Saul is called Paul in Acts. This may be due to Saul's success in preaching to Paulus or to the fact that he is now entering the Gentile phase of his ministry. The order in which they are mentioned now changes from "Barnabas and Saul" to "Paul and Barnabas." Upon their return to the Jerusalem church, however, the order reverts to "Barnabas and Paul" (15:12).

‡13:12 *deputy . . . believed.* He was convinced by the miracle and the message. Also see note on verse 7.

13:13 *Perga in Pamphylia.* Perga was the capital of Pamphylia, a coastal province of Asia Minor between the provinces of Lycia and Cilicia, and was 5 miles inland and 12 miles east of the important seaport Attalia. *John departing from them.* Homesickness to get back to Jerusalem, an illness of Paul necessitating a change in plans and a trip to Galatia, and a change in leadership from Barnabas to Paul have all been suggested as reasons for John Mark's return. Paul's dissatisfaction with his departure is noted later (15:37–39).

13:14 *Antioch.* Named after Antiochus, king of Syria after the death of Alexander the Great. It was 110 miles from Perga and was at the hub of good roads and trade. The city had a large Jewish population. It was a Roman colony, which meant that a contingent of retired military men was settled there. They were given free land and were made citizens of the city of Rome, with all the accompanying privileges. *Pisidia.* See note on 14:24. *synagogue.* Paul's regular practice was to begin his preaching in the synagogue as long as the Jews would allow it (see v. 5; 14:1; 17:1,10,17; 18:4,19; 19:8). His reason for doing so was grounded in his understanding of God's redemptive plan (see v. 46; Rom 1:16; 2:9–10; see also Rom 9–11). He was not neglecting his Gentile mission, for the God-fearers (Gentiles committed to worshiping the one true God) were part of the audience. Moreover, the synagogue provided a ready-made preaching situation with a building, regularly scheduled meetings and a people who knew the OT Scriptures. It was customary to invite visitors, and especially visiting rabbis (such as Paul), to address the gathering.

13:15 *the law and the prophets.* Sections from the OT were read, followed by exposition and exhortation. *rulers of the synagogue.* Those who were responsible for calling readers and preachers, arranging the service and maintaining order.

16 Then Paul stood up, and beckoning with *his* hand said,

¶ Men of Israel, and [a]*ye* that fear God, give audience.

17 The God of this people of Israel [a]chose our fathers, and exalted the people [b]when *they* dwelt as strangers in the land of Egypt, and with a high arm brought he them out of it.

18 And [a]about the time of forty years [1]suffered he their manners in the wilderness.

19 And when he had destroyed seven nations in the land of Canaan, [a]he divided their land to them by lot.

20 And after that [a]he gave *unto them* judges about *the space of* four hundred and fifty years, [b]until Samuel the prophet.

21 [a]And afterward they desired a king: and God gave unto them Saul the son of Cis, a man of the tribe of Benjamin, *by the space of* forty years.

22 And [a]when he had removed him, [b]he raised up unto them David to be their king; to whom also he gave testimony, and said, [c]I have found David the *son* of Jesse, [d]a man after mine own heart, which shall fulfil all my will.

23 [a]Of this *man's* seed hath God according [b]to *his* promise raised unto Israel [c]a Saviour, Jesus:

24 [a]When John had first preached before his coming the baptism of repentance to all the people of Israel.

25 And as John fulfilled *his* course, he said, [a]Whom think ye that I am? I am not *he.* But behold, there cometh *one* after me, whose shoes of *his* feet I am not worthy to loose.

26 Men *and* brethren, children of the stock of Abraham, and whosoever among you feareth God, [a]to you is the word of this salvation sent.

27 For they that dwell at Jerusalem, and their rulers, [a]because they knew him not, nor *yet* the voices of the prophets which are read every sabbath day, they have fulfilled *them* in condemning *him.*

28 [a]And though they found no cause of death *in him, yet* desired they Pilate that he should be slain.

29 [a]And when they had fulfilled all that was written of him, [b]they took *him* down from the tree, and laid *him* in a sepulchre.

30 [a]But God raised him from the dead:

31 And [a]he was seen many days of them which came up with him from Galilee to Jerusalem, who are his witnesses unto the people.

32 And we declare unto you glad tidings, how that [a]the promise which was made unto the fathers,

33 God hath fulfilled the same unto us their children, in that he hath raised up Jesus again; as it is also written in the second psalm, [a]Thou art my Son, this day have I begotten thee.

34 And as concerning that he raised him up from the dead, *now* no more to return to corruption, he said on this wise, [a]I will give you the sure [1]mercies of David.

35 Wherefore he saith also in another *psalm,* [a]Thou shalt not suffer thine Holy One to see corruption.

36 For David, [1]after he had served his own generation by the will of God, [a]fell on sleep, and was laid unto his fathers, and saw corruption:

37 But he, whom God raised *again,* saw no corruption.

38 Be it known unto you therefore, men *and* brethren, that [a]through this *man* is preached unto you the forgiveness of sins:

39 And [a]by him all that believe are justified from all *things, from* which ye could not be justified by the law of Moses.

40 Beware therefore, lest that come upon you, which is spoken of in [a]the prophets;

41 Behold *ye* despisers, and wonder, and perish: for I work a work in your days, a work which you shall in no wise believe, though a man declare it unto you.

42 ¶ And when the Jews were gone out of the synagogue, the Gentiles besought that these words might be preached to them [1]the next sabbath.

43 Now when the congregation was broken up, many of the Jews and religious proselytes followed Paul and Barnabas: who, speaking to them, [a]persuaded them to continue in [b]the grace of God.

44 And the next sabbath day came almost the whole city together to hear the word of God.

45 But when the Jews saw the multitudes, they were filled with envy, and [a]spake against those *things* which were spoken by Paul, contradicting and blaspheming.

46 Then Paul and Barnabas waxed bold, and said, [a]It was necessary that the word of God should first have been spoken to you: but

13:16 [a]ch. 10:35 **13:17** [a]Deut. 7:6,7 [b]ch. 7:17 **13:18** [1]Gr. ἐτροποφόρησεν, perhaps for ἐτροφοφόρησεν, [*bore,* or, *fed them*] *as a nurse beareth, or feedeth her child,* Deut. 1:31, 2 Macc. 7:27. *according to the Sept. and so Chrysostom* [a]Ex. 16:35 **13:19** [a]Josh. 14:1 **13:20** [a]Judg. 2:16 [b]1 Sam. 3:20 **13:21** [a]1 Sam. 8:5 **13:22** [a]1 Sam. 15:23 [b]1 Sam. 16:13 [c]Ps. 89:20 [d]1 Sam. 13:14 **13:23** [a]Is. 11:1 [b]Ps. 132:11 [c]Mat. 1:21 **13:24** [a]Mat. 3:1; Luke 3:3 **13:25** [a]Mark 1:7 **13:26** [a]Mat. 10:6 **13:27** [a]Luke 23:34 **13:28** [a]Mat. 27:22 **13:29** [a]Luke 18:31 [b]Mat. 27:59 **13:30** [a]Mat. 28:6 **13:31** [a]Mat. 28:16

13:32 [a]Gen. 3:15 **13:33** [a]Heb. 1:5 **13:34** [1]Gr. τὰ ὅσια, *holy,* or, *just* things: *which word the Sept. both in the place of Is. 55:3, and in many others, use for that which is in the Hebrew, mercies* [Deut. 33:8; Ps. 12:1; 16:10; 30:4] [a]Is. 55:3 **13:35** [a]Ps. 16:10 **13:36** [1]Or, *after he had in his own age served the will of God* [a]ch. 2:29 **13:38** [a]Jer. 31:34 **13:39** [a]Is. 53:11 **13:40** [a]Hab. 1:5 **13:42** [1]Gr. *in the week between,* or, *in the sabbath between*

13:43 [a]ch. 11:23; 14:22 [b]Tit. 2:11; Heb. 12:15; 1 Pet. 5:12
13:45 [a]ch. 18:6; 1 Pet. 4:4; Jude 10 **13:46** [a]ver. 26; Mat. 10:6; ch. 3:26; Rom. 1:16

13:16 *ye that fear God.* See note on 10:2.

‡13:19-20 *about the space of four hundred and fifty years.* The Greek manuscripts create some uncertainty as to whether this phrase identifies the time of the events in verse 19 or 20. If verse 19, then it refers to the 400 years of the stay "in the land of Egypt" (v. 17; see note on 7:6) plus the 40 years in the wilderness and the time between the crossing of the Jordan and the distribution of the land (see Josh 14–19).

13:23 *according to his promise.* See, e.g., Is 11:1–16.

13:29–31 *tree . . . sepulchre . . . God raised . . . witnesses.* See note on 3:14.

13:31 *many days.* Forty days (see 1:3).

13:33 *this day have I begotten thee.* Here refers to the resurrection of Jesus (see note on Ps 2:7–9; cf. Rom 1:4).

13:35 *not suffer thine Holy One to see corruption.* Quoted also in Peter's sermon at Pentecost (see note on 2:27).

13:39 *justified from all things.* Justification combines two aspects: (1) the forgiveness of sins (here); (2) the gift of righteousness (Rom 3:21–22).

13:46 *It was necessary . . . first . . . spoken to you.* Since the

The Spread of the Gospel

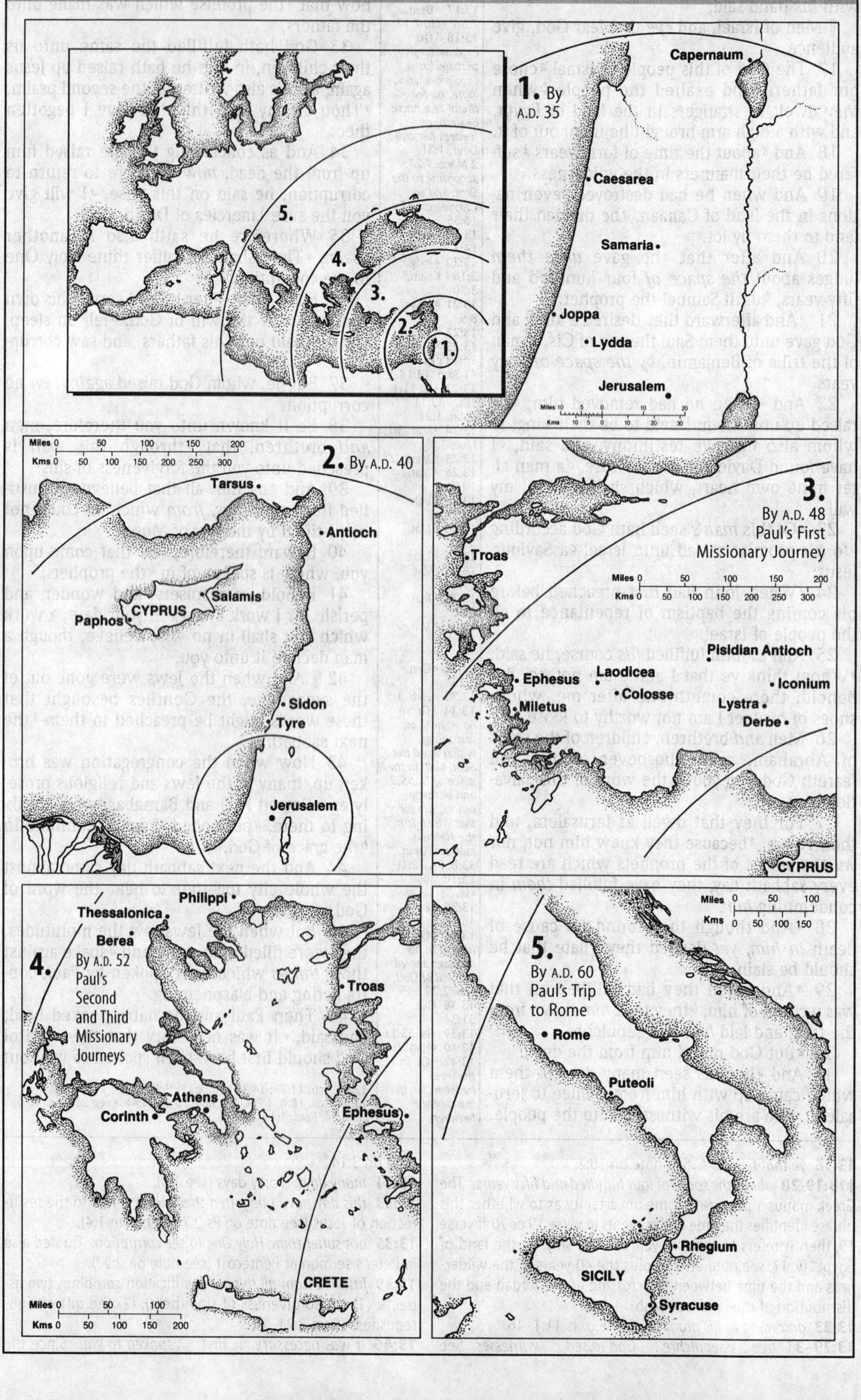

1. By A.D. 35
2.
3.
4.
5.
1.

Capernaum
Caesarea
Samaria
Joppa
Lydda
Jerusalem
Miles 10 5 0 10 20
Kms 10 5 0 10 20 30

2. By A.D. 40
Miles 0 50 100 150 200
Kms 0 50 100 150 200 250 300
Tarsus
Antioch
Salamis
CYPRUS
Paphos
Sidon
Tyre
Jerusalem

3. By A.D. 48
Paul's First Missionary Journey
Troas
Miles 0 50 100 150 200
Kms 0 50 100 150 200 250 300
Pisidian Antioch
Laodicea
Ephesus
Colosse
Iconium
Miletus
Lystra
Derbe
CYPRUS

4. By A.D. 52
Paul's Second and Third Missionary Journeys
Philippi
Thessalonica
Berea
Troas
Athens
Corinth
Ephesus
CRETE
Miles 0 50 100 150
Kms 0 50 100 150 200

5. By A.D. 60
Paul's Trip to Rome
Miles 0 50 100
Kms 0 50 100 150
Rome
Puteoli
Rhegium
SICILY
Syracuse

[b]seeing ye put it from *you,* and judge yourselves unworthy of everlasting life, lo, [c]we turn to the Gentiles.

47 For so hath the Lord commanded us, *saying,* [a]I have set thee to be a light of the Gentiles, that thou shouldest be for salvation unto the ends of the earth.

48 And when the Gentiles heard *this,* they were glad, and glorified the word of the Lord: [a]and as many as were ordained to eternal life believed.

49 And the word of the Lord was published throughout all the region.

50 But the Jews stirred up the devout and honourable women, and the chief *men* of the city, and [a]raised persecution against Paul and Barnabas, and expelled them out of their coasts.

51 [a]But they shook off the dust of their feet against them, and came unto Iconium.

52 And the disciples [a]were filled with joy, and with the Holy Ghost.

13:46 [b]Ex. 32:10; Deut. 32:21; Is. 55:5; Mat. 21:43; Rom. 10:19 [c]ch. 18:6; 28:28
13:47 [a]Is. 42:6; 49:6; Luke 2:32
13:48 [a]ch. 2:47
13:50 [a]2 Tim. 3:11
13:51 [a]Mat. 10:14; Mark 6:11; Luke 9:5; ch. 18:6
13:52 [a]Mat. 5:12; John 16:22; ch. 2:46
14:3 [a]Mark 16:20; Heb. 2:4
14:4 [a]ch. 13:2,3
14:5 [a]2 Tim. 3:11
14:6 [a]Mat. 10:23

Preaching at Iconium

14 And it came to pass in Iconium, that they went *both* together into the synagogue of the Jews, and so spake, that a great multitude both of the Jews and *also* of the Greeks believed.

2 But the unbelieving Jews stirred up the Gentiles, and made their minds evil affected against the brethren.

3 Long time therefore abode they speaking boldly in the Lord, [a]which gave testimony unto the word of his grace, and granted signs and wonders to be done by their hands.

4 But the multitude of the city was divided: and part held with the Jews, and part with the [a]apostles.

5 And when there was an assault made both of the Gentiles, and *also* of the Jews with their rulers, [a]to use *them* despitefully, and to stone them,

6 They were ware of *it,* and [a]fled unto Lystra and Derbe, cities of Lycaonia, and *unto* the region that lieth round about:

gospel came from and was for the Jews first and since Paul was himself a Jew with great compassion for his people (Rom 9:1–5; 10:1–3). See note on v. 14.

13:48 *as many as were ordained to eternal life believed.* Possession of eternal life involves both human faith and divine appointment.

13:51 *shook off the dust.* To show the severance of responsibility and the repudiation of those who had rejected their message and had brought suffering to the servants of the Lord (see note on Luke 9:5). *Iconium.* Modern Konya; it was an important crossroads and agricultural center in the central plain of the province of Galatia.

13:52 *filled . . . with the Holy Ghost.* See note on 2:4.

14:1 *great multitude.* At first there was good success, then bitter opposition from the Jews (v. 2). But these evidently failed in their initial attempt, for Paul and Barnabas remained there a considerable time (v. 3). A second wave of persecution was planned, involving violence (v. 5).

14:3 *gave testimony . . . and granted signs and wonders.* A major purpose of miracles was to confirm the truth of the words and the approval of God.

14:4 *apostles.* Both Paul and Barnabas are called apostles (see v. 14; see also note on Mark 6:30). The term is used here not of the twelve but in the broader sense to refer to persons sent on a mission, i.e., missionaries (see 13:2–3).

14:5 *stone them.* A Jewish mode of execution for blasphemy. Probably mob action was planned here.

14:6 *Lystra.* A Roman colony (see note on 13:14) and proba-

Paul's First Missionary Journey

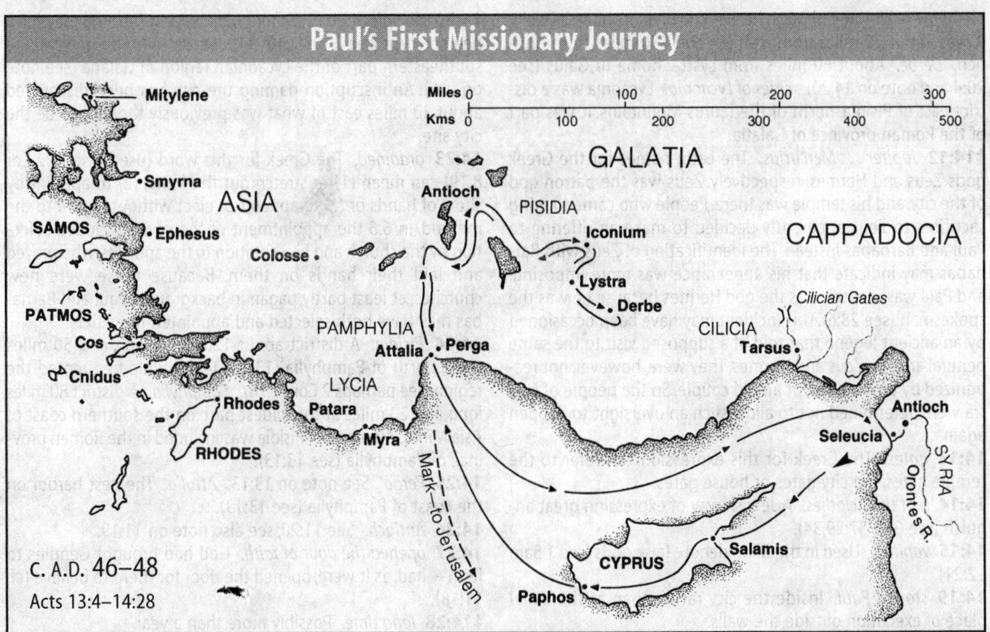

7 And there they preached the gospel.

Preaching at Lystra

8 ¶ [a]And there sat a certain man at Lystra,
impotent in *his* feet, being a cripple from his
mother's womb, who never had walked:
9 The same heard Paul speak: who stedfastly beholding him, and perceiving that he
had faith to be healed,
10 Said with a loud voice, [a]Stand upright
on thy feet. And he leaped and walked.
11 And when the people saw what Paul
had done, they lift up their voices, saying in
the speech of Lycaonia, [a]The gods are come
down to us in the likeness of men.
12 And they called Barnabas, Jupiter; and
Paul, Mercurius, because he was the chief
speaker.
13 Then the priest of Jupiter, which was
before their city, brought oxen and garlands
unto the gates, [a]and would have done sacrifice
with the people.
14 *Which* when the apostles, Barnabas and
Paul, heard *of,* [a]they rent their clothes, and
ran in among the people, crying out,
15 And saying, Sirs, [a]why do ye these
things? [b]We also are men of like passions with
you, and preach unto you that *ye* should turn
from [c]these vanities [d]unto the living God,
[e]which made heaven, and earth, and the sea,
and all *things* that are therein:
16 [a]Who in times past suffered all nations
to walk in their own ways.
17 [a]Nevertheless he left not himself without witness, in that he did good, and [b]gave us
rain from heaven, and fruitful seasons, filling
our hearts with food and gladness.
18 And with these sayings scarce restrained they the people, that *they* had not
done sacrifice unto them.

The return to Antioch

19 ¶ [a]And there came thither *certain* Jews
from Antioch and Iconium, who persuaded the
people, [b]and, having stoned Paul, drew *him*
out of the city, supposing he had been dead.
20 Howbeit, as the disciples stood round
about him, he rose up, and came into the city:
and the next day he departed with Barnabas to
Derbe.
21 And when they had preached the gospel
to that city, [a]and [1]had taught many, they returned *again* to Lystra, and *to* Iconium, and
Antioch,
22 Confirming the souls of the disciples,
and [a]exhorting *them* to continue in the faith,
and that [b]we must through much tribulation
enter into the kingdom of God.
23 And when they had [a]ordained them
elders in every church, and had prayed with
fasting, they commended them to the Lord, on
whom they believed.
24 And after they had passed throughout
Pisidia, they came to Pamphylia.
25 And when they had preached the word
in Perga, they went down into Attalia:
26 And thence sailed to Antioch, [a]from
whence they had been [b]recommended to the
grace of God for the work which they fulfilled.
27 And when they were come, and had
gathered the church together, [a]they rehearsed
all that God had done with them, and how he
had [b]opened *the* door of faith unto the Gentiles.
28 And there they abode long time with
the disciples.

14:8 [a]ch. 3:2
14:10 [a]Is. 35:6
14:11 [a]ch. 8:10; 28:6
14:13 [a]Dan. 2:46
14:14 [a]Mat. 26:65
14:15 [a]ch. 10:26 [b]Jas. 5:17; Rev. 19:10 [c]1 Sam. 12:21; 1 Ki. 16:13; Jer. 14:22; Amos 2:4; 1 Cor. 8:4 [d]1 Thes. 1:9 [e]Gen. 1:1; Ps. 33:6; 146:6; Rev. 14:7
14:16 [a]Ps. 81:12; ch. 17:30; 1 Pet. 4:3
14:17 [a]ch. 17:27; Rom. 1:20 [b]Lev. 26:4; Deut. 11:14; 28:12; Job 5:10; Ps. 65:10; 68:9; 147:8; Jer. 14:22; Mat. 5:45
14:19 [a]ch. 13:45 [b]2 Cor. 11:25; 2 Tim. 3:11
14:21 [1][Gr. *had made many disciples*] [a]Mat. 28:19
14:22 [a]ch. 11:23; 13:43 [b]Mat. 10:38; 16:24; Luke 22:28; Rom. 8:17; 2 Tim. 2:12; 3:12
14:23 [a]Tit. 1:5
14:26 [a]ch. 13:1,3 [b]ch. 15:40
14:27 [a]ch. 15:4,12; 21:19 [b]1 Cor. 16:9; 2 Cor. 2:12; Col. 4:3; Rev. 3:8

ble home of Timothy (though he was known in Iconium as well), it was about 20 miles from Iconium and 130 miles from Antioch. *Derbe.* About 60 miles from Lystra; home of Gaius (see 20:4 and note on 14:20). *cities of Lycaonia.* Lycaonia was a district east of Pisidia, north of the Taurus Mountains. It was part of the Roman province of Galatia.

‡14:12 *Jupiter . . . Mercurius.* The Latin names for the Greek gods Zeus and Hermes, respectively. Zeus was the patron god of the city, and his temple was there. People who came to bring sacrifices to Zeus apparently decided to make an offering to Paul and Barnabas instead. The identification of Zeus with Barnabas may indicate that his appearance was more imposing, and Paul was identified as the god Hermes because he was the spokesman (see 28:6). This incident may have been occasioned by an ancient legend that told of a supposed visit to the same general area by Zeus and Hermes. They were, however, not recognized by anyone except an old couple. So the people of Lystra were determined not to allow such an oversight to happen again.

14:13 *gates.* The Greek for this expression can refer to the temple gates, the city gates or house gates.

14:14 *rent their clothes.* A Jewish way of expressing great anguish (see Gen 37:29,34).

14:15 *vanities.* Used in the OT to denote false gods (see 1 Sam 12:21).

14:19 *stoned Paul.* Inside the city rather than at the usual place of execution outside the walls.

14:20 *disciples stood . . . about him.* Young Timothy may have been present (see 2 Tim 3:10–11). *Derbe.* A border town in the southeastern part of the Lycaonian region of Galatia (see note on v. 6). An inscription naming the city has been discovered about 30 miles east of what was previously thought to be the city site.

14:23 *ordained.* The Greek for this word (used also in 2 Cor 8:19) can mean (1) to stretch out the hand, (2) to appoint by show of hands or (3) to appoint or elect without regard to the method. In 6:6 the appointment of the seven included selection by the church and presentation to the apostles, who prayed and laid their hands on them. Because these were new churches, at least partly pagan in background, Paul and Barnabas may have both selected and appointed the elders.

14:24 *Pisidia.* A district about 120 miles long and 50 miles wide, north of Pamphylia (13:13–14). Bandits frequented the region (see perhaps 2 Cor 11:26). *Pamphylia.* A district 80 miles long and 20 miles at the widest part, on the southern coast of Asia Minor. After A.D. 74 Pisidia was included in the Roman province of Pamphylia (see 13:13).

14:25 *Perga.* See note on 13:13. *Attalia.* The best harbor on the coast of Pamphylia (see 13:13).

14:26 *Antioch.* See 11:20; see also note on 11:19.

14:27 *opened the door of faith.* God had brought Gentiles to faith—had, as it were, opened the door for them to believe (cf. 11:18).

‡14:28 *long time.* Possibly more than a year.

The council at Jerusalem

15 And [a]certain *men* which came down
from Judea taught the brethren, *and*
said, [b]Except ye be circumcised [c]after the
manner of Moses, ye cannot be saved.
2 When therefore Paul and Barnabas had
no small dissension and disputation with
them, they determined that [a]Paul and Barnabas, and certain other of them, should go up to
Jerusalem unto the apostles and elders about
this question.
3 And [a]being brought on their way by the
church, they passed through Phenice and
Samaria, [b]declaring the conversion of the Gentiles: and they caused great joy unto all the
brethren.
4 And when they were come to Jerusalem,
they were received of the church, and *of* the
apostles and elders, and [a]they declared all
things that God had done with them.
5 But there [1]rose up certain of the sect of
the Pharisees which believed, saying, [a]That it
was needful to circumcise them, and to command *them* to keep the law of Moses.
6 ¶ And the apostles and elders came together for to consider of this matter.
7 And when there had been much disputing, Peter rose up, and said unto them, [a]Men
and brethren, ye know how that a good while
ago God made choice among us, that the Gentiles by my mouth should hear the word of the
gospel, and believe.
8 And God, [a]which knoweth the hearts,
bare them witness, [b]giving them the Holy
Ghost, even as *he did* unto us;
9 [a]And put no difference between us and
them, [b]purifying their hearts by faith.
10 Now therefore why tempt ye God, [a]to
put a yoke upon the neck of the disciples,
which neither our fathers nor we were able to
bear?
11 But [a]we believe that through the grace
of the Lord Jesus Christ *we* shall be saved,
even as they.
12 Then all the multitude kept silence, and
gave audience to Barnabas and Paul, declaring
what miracles and wonders God had [a]wrought
among the Gentiles by them.
13 ¶ And after they had held their peace,
[a]James answered, saying, Men *and* brethren,
hearken unto me:
14 [a]Simeon hath declared how God at the
first did visit the Gentiles, to take out of them
a people for his name.
15 And to this agree the words of the
prophets; as it is written,
16 [a]After this I will return, and will build
again the tabernacle of David, which is fallen
down; and I will build again the ruins thereof,
and I will set it up:
17 That the residue of men might seek after the Lord, and all the Gentiles, upon whom
my name is called, saith the Lord, who doeth
all these *things.*
18 Known unto God are all his works from
the beginning of the world.
19 Wherefore [a]my sentence is, that *we*

15:1 [a]Gal. 2:12 [b]ver. 5; John 7:22; Gal. 5:2; Phil. 3:2; Col. 2:8,11,16 [c]Gen. 17:10; Lev. 12:3
15:2 [a]Gal. 2:1
15:3 [a]Rom. 15:24; 1 Cor. 16:6,11 [b]ch. 14:27
15:4 [a]ver. 12; ch. 14:27
15:5 [1][Or, *rose up,* said they, *certain*] [a]ver. 1
15:7 [a]ch. 10:20; 11:12
15:8 [a]1 Chr. 28:9; ch. 1:24
15:8 [b]ch. 10:44
15:9 [a]Rom. 10:12 [b]ch. 10:15,28; 1 Cor. 1:2; 1 Pet. 1:22
15:10 [a]Mat. 23:4; Gal. 5:1
15:11 [a]Rom. 3:24; Eph. 2:8; Tit. 2:11; 3:4,5
15:12 [a]ch. 14:27
15:13 [a]ch. 12:17
15:14 [a]ver. 7
15:16 [a]Amos 9:11
15:19 [a]See ver. 23

15:1 *certain men.* Probably from "the sect of the Pharisees" (v. 5). These were believers who insisted that before a person could become a true Christian he must keep the law of Moses, and the test of such compliance was circumcision. *from Judea.* Meant that these Judaizers (or legalists) were given a hearing, not that they correctly represented the apostles and elders of Jerusalem (cf. v. 24).

‡15:2 *go up to Jerusalem.* See notes on 12:1; Gal 2:1. Those who hold that Gal 2:1–10 refers to the famine visit of 11:27–30; 12:25 argue that since Gal 2:2 says that the visit mentioned there was occasioned by a revelation, it must refer to Agabus's prediction of the coming famine (11:27–28). Those who believe that Gal 2:1–10 refers to the Jerusalem council visit of 15:1–22 assert that the famine visit occurred at the time of Herod Agrippa's death in A.D. 44 (11:27–30; 12:25).

15:4–22 The sequence of meetings described in vv. 4–22 is: (1) a general meeting of welcome and report (vv. 4–5); (2) a meeting of the leaders (perhaps to one side) while the church was still assembled (vv. 6–11); (3) a meeting of the apostles, the elders and the whole assembly (vv. 12–22).

15:4 The first meeting was a report, cordially received, about the work done among the Gentiles.

15:5 *certain of the sect of the Pharisees which believed.* Some Pharisees became Christians and brought their Judaic beliefs with them. They believed that Gentiles must first become converts to Judaism and be circumcised (see v. 1), and then they would be eligible to be saved by faith. Perhaps some of them had gone to Antioch and now returned to present their case.

15:7 *Peter rose up.* After a period of considerable discussion by the apostles and elders, Peter addressed them. *Gentiles by my mouth should hear.* Peter's argument was his own experience: God had sent him to preach to the Gentiles (10:28–29).

15:8 *giving them the Holy Ghost.* The irrefutable proof of God's acceptance (see 10:44,47; 11:17–18).

15:9 *purifying their hearts by faith.* Peter's way of saying what Paul affirmed (Rom 5:1; cf. Gal 2:15–16).

15:10 *a yoke.* The law (see Gal 5:1; cf. Mat 11:28–29).

15:11 *through the grace of the Lord.* No circumcision was required. *we shall be saved, even as they.* See Rom 3:9.

15:12 *multitude kept silence.* See note on vv. 4–22. Apparently the people had remained in place while the apostles and elders met. The assembly had not remained quiet during that time, but now they became silent to listen to the leaders. *Barnabas and Paul.* The order here puts Barnabas first (perhaps reflecting his importance in Jerusalem), whereas in the account of the missionary journey the order was "Paul and Barnabas" after the events on the island of Cyprus (13:7,9,13,42,46). *miracles and wonders.* See 8:19–20; 14:3.

15:13 *James.* The brother of the Lord. His argument added proof from Scripture.

15:14 *Simeon.* Peter (see v. 7). James uses Peter's Hebrew name in its Hebrew form (Simeon is a variant of Simon). *a people for his name.* A new community largely made up of Gentiles but including Jews as well (John 10:16; cf. 1 Pet 2:9–10).

15:15 *prophets.* Specifically Amos 9:11–12.

‡15:16 *After this I will return.* This quotation from Amos may set forth a sequence of the end times, including (1) the church age (taking out "a people for his name," v. 14), (2) the restoration of Israel as a nation (v. 16) and (3) the inclusion of the Gentiles (vv. 17–18).

trouble not them, which from among the Gentiles [b]are turned to God:
20 But that *we* write unto them, that *they*
abstain [a]from pollutions of idols, and [b]*from*
fornication, and *from* things strangled, [c]and
from blood.
21 For Moses of old time hath in every city
them that preach him, [a]being read in the synagogues every sabbath day.

Letters sent to the Gentiles

22 ¶ Then pleased it the apostles and elders, with the whole church, to send chosen
men of their own company to Antioch with
Paul and Barnabas; *namely,* Judas surnamed
[a]Barsabas, and Silas, chief *men* among the
brethren:
23 And they wrote *letters* by them after
this manner; The apostles and elders and
brethren *send* greeting unto the brethren
which are of the Gentiles in Antioch and Syria
and Cilicia:
24 Forasmuch as we have heard, that [a]cer-
tain which went out from us have troubled
you with words, subverting your souls, saying,
Ye must be circumcised, and keep the law: to
whom we gave no *such* commandment:
25 It seemed good unto us, being assembled with one accord, to send chosen men
unto you with our beloved Barnabas and Paul,
26 [a]Men that have hazarded their lives for
the name of our Lord Jesus Christ.
27 We have sent therefore Judas and Silas,
who shall also tell *you* the same *things* by
[1]mouth.
28 For it seemed good to the Holy Ghost,
and to us, to lay upon you no greater burden
than these necessary *things;*
29 [a]That *ye* abstain from meats offered to
idols, and [b]from blood, and from things strangled, and from fornication: from which if ye
keep yourselves, ye shall do well. Fare ye well.
30 ¶ So when they were dismissed, they
came to Antioch: and when they had gathered
the multitude together, they delivered the
epistle:
31 *Which* when they had read, they rejoiced for the [1]consolation.
32 And Judas and Silas, being prophets also
themselves, [a]exhorted the brethren with
many words, and confirmed *them.*
33 And after they had tarried *there* a space,
they were let [a]go in peace from the brethren
unto the apostles.
34 Notwithstanding it pleased Silas to
abide there *still.*
35 [a]Paul also and Barnabas continued in
Antioch, teaching and preaching the word of
the Lord, with many others also.

Separation of Paul and Barnabas

36 ¶ And some days after Paul said unto
Barnabas, Let us go again and visit our brethren [a]in every city where we have preached
the word of the Lord, *and see* how they do.
37 And Barnabas determined to take with
them [a]John, whose surname was Mark.
38 But Paul thought not good to take him
with *them,* [a]who departed from them from
Pamphylia, and went not with them to the
work.
39 And the contention was so sharp *be-*
tween them, that they departed asunder one
from the other: and *so* Barnabas took Mark,
and sailed unto Cyprus;
40 And Paul chose Silas, and departed, [a]be-
ing recommended by the brethren unto the
grace of God.
41 And he went through Syria and Cilicia,
[a]confirming the churches.

15:19 [b]1 Thes. 1:9
15:20 [a]Gen. 35:2; Ex. 20:3,23; Ezek. 20:30; 1 Cor. 8:1; 10:20,28; Rev. 2:14 [b]1 Cor. 6:9; Gal. 5:19; Eph. 5:3; Col. 3:5; 1 Thes. 4:3; 1 Pet. 4:3 [c]Gen. 9:4; Lev. 3:17; Deut. 12:16
15:21 [a]ch. 13:15,27
15:22 [a]ch. 1:23
15:24 [a]ver. 1; Gal. 2:4; 5:12; Tit. 1:10,11
15:26 [a]ch. 13:50
15:27 [1][Gr. *word*]
15:29 [a]ver. 20; ch. 21:25; Rev. 2:14,20 [b]Lev. 17:14
15:31 [1]Or, *exhortation*
15:32 [a]ch. 14:22; 18:23
15:33 [a]1 Cor. 16:11; Heb. 11:31
15:35 [a]ch. 13:1
15:36 [a]ch. 13:4,13,14,51; 14:1,6,24,25
15:37 [a]ch. 12:12,25; 13:5; Col. 4:10; 2 Tim. 4:11; Philem. 24
15:38 [a]ch. 13:13
15:40 [a]ch. 14:26
15:41 [a]ch. 16:5

15:19 *trouble not them.* Circumcision was not required, but four stipulations were laid down (see note on v. 20). These were in areas where the Gentiles had particular weaknesses and where the Jews were particularly repulsed by Gentile violations. It would help both the individual and the relationship between Gentile and Jew if these requirements were observed. They involved divine directives that the Jews believed were given before the Mosaic laws.

15:20 *abstain from pollutions of idols.* See v. 29; 1 Cor 8:7–13; Rev 2:14,20. *fornication.* A sin taken too lightly by the Greeks and also associated with certain pagan religious festivals. *things strangled.* Thus retaining the blood that was forbidden to be eaten (see Gen 9:4). *blood.* Expressly forbidden in Jewish law (see Lev 17:10–12). Reference here may be to consuming blood apart from meat.

‡15:22 *apostles and elders, with the whole church.* Apparently there was unanimous agreement with the choice of messengers and with the contents of the letter (vv. 23–29). *Judas surnamed Barsabas.* The same surname as that of Joseph Barsabas (see 1:23 and note). The two may have been brothers. *Silas.* A leader in the Jerusalem church, a prophet (v. 32) and a Roman citizen (16:37).

15:23 *in Antioch and Syria and Cilicia.* Antioch was the leading city of the combined provinces of Syria and Cilicia.

15:28 *seemed good to the Holy Ghost, and to us.* Prior authority is given to the Spirit (whose working in the assembly is thus claimed), but there was also agreement among the apostles, elders and brothers (vv. 22–23).

15:29 *abstain from . . . fornication.* See note on v. 20.

15:32 *prophets.* One of the primary functions of prophets in the early church was, as here indicated, to encourage and strengthen the brothers.

15:36 *every city where we have preached the word.* Towns of the first missionary journey (see 13:4–14:26).

15:38 *who departed from them.* Mark had turned back at Perga and did not go to Antioch, Iconium, Lystra and Derbe (see note on 13:13).

15:39 *they departed asunder.* Barnabas and Mark do not appear again in Acts. However, in 1 Cor 9:6 Paul names Barnabas as setting a noble example in working to support himself. Also in Gal 2:11–13 another scene is described in Antioch that includes Barnabas. Mark evidently returned from his work with Barnabas and became associated with Peter (see 1 Pet 5:13). During Paul's first imprisonment, Mark was included in Paul's group (see Col 4:10; Philem 24). By the end of Paul's life he came to admire Mark so much that he requested him to come to be with him during his final days (2 Tim 4:11; see Introduction to Mark: John Mark in the NT). *Cyprus.* The island of Barnabas's birthplace (cf. 4:36).

The selection of Timothy

16 Then came he to [a]Derbe and Lystra:
and behold, a certain disciple was
there, [b]named Timotheus, [c]the son of a certain woman, *which was* a Jewess, and believed; but his father *was* a Greek:
2 Which [a]was well reported of by the
brethren that were at Lystra and Iconium.
3 Him would Paul have to go forth with
him; and [a]took and circumcised him because
of the Jews which were in those quarters: for
they knew all that his father was a Greek.
4 And as they went through the cities, they
delivered them the decrees for to keep, [a]that
were ordained of the apostles and elders
which were at Jerusalem.
5 And [a]so were the churches established in
the faith, and increased in number daily.

The Macedonian call

6 Now when they had gone throughout
Phrygia and the region of Galatia, and were
forbidden of the Holy Ghost to preach the
word in Asia,
7 After they were come to Mysia, they assayed to go into Bithynia: but the Spirit suffered them not.

16:1 [a]ch. 14:6 [b]ch. 19:22; Rom. 16:21; 1 Cor. 4:17; Phil. 2:19; 1 Thes. 3:2; 1 Tim. 1:2; 2 Tim. 1:2 [c]2 Tim. 1:5
16:2 [a]ch. 6:3
16:3 [a]1 Cor. 9:20; Gal. 2:3; See Gal. 5:2
16:4 [a]ch. 15:28,29
16:5 [a]ch. 15:41
16:8 [a]2 Cor. 2:12; 2 Tim. 4:13
16:9 [a]ch. 10:30
16:10 [a]2 Cor. 2:13
16:12 [1]Or, *the first* [a]Phil. 1:1
16:13 [1]Gr. *sabbath day*
16:14 [a]Luke 24:45

8 And they passing by Mysia [a]came down
to Troas.
9 And a vision appeared to Paul in the
night; There stood a [a]man of Macedonia, and
prayed him, saying, Come over into Macedonia, and help us.
10 And after he had seen the vision, immediately we endeavoured to go [a]into Macedonia, assuredly gathering that the Lord had
called us for to preach the gospel unto them.
11 Therefore loosing from Troas, we came
with a straight course to Samothracia, and the
next *day* to Neapolis;
12 And from thence to [a]Philippi, which is
[1]the chief city of *that* part of Macedonia, *and* a
colony: and we were in that city abiding certain days.

The conversion of Lydia

13 ¶ And on the [1]sabbath we went out of
the city by a river side, where prayer was wont
to be made; and we sat down, and spake unto
the women which resorted *thither.*
14 And a certain woman named Lydia, a
seller of purple, of the city of Thyatira, which
worshipped God, heard *us:* whose [a]heart the
Lord opened, that *she* attended unto the
things which were spoken of Paul.
15 And when she was baptized, and her

16:1 See map No. 11 at the end of the study Bible; see also map, p. 1588. *Derbe.* See notes on 14:6,20. Paul had approached Derbe on the first trip from the opposite direction, so the order of towns is reversed here. *Lystra.* See note on 14:6. *Timotheus.* Since Paul addressed him as a young man some 15 years later (see 1 Tim 4:12), he must have been in his teens at this time. *father was a Greek.* Statements concerning his mother's faith (here and in 2 Tim 1:5) and silence concerning any faith on his father's part suggest that the father was neither a convert to Judaism nor a believer in Christ.

‡16:3 *circumcised him.* As a matter of expediency so that his work among the Jews might be more effective. This was different from Titus's case (see Gal 2:3), where circumcision was refused because some were demanding it as necessary for salvation.

16:6 *they.* Paul, Silas and Timothy. *Phrygia.* The district was formerly the Hellenistic territory of Phrygia, but it had more recently been divided between the Roman provinces of Asia and Galatia. Iconium and Antioch were in Galatian Phrygia. *region of Galatia.* The name had been used to denote the Hellenistic kingdom, but in 25 B.C. it had been expanded considerably to become the Roman province of that name. *Asia.* This, too, had been a smaller area formerly but now was a Roman province including the Hellenistic districts of Mysia, Lydia, Caria and parts of Phrygia.

16:7 *Mysia.* In the northwest part of the province of Asia. Luke uses these old Hellenistic names, but Paul preferred the provincial (Roman) names. *Bithynia.* A senatorial province formed after 74 B.C., it was east of Mysia. *suffered them not.* The Spirit may have led in any of a number of ways: vision, circumstances, good sense or use of the prophetic gift.

16:8 *Troas.* Located ten miles from ancient Troy. Alexandria Troas (its full name) was a Roman colony and an important seaport for connections between Macedonia and Greece on the one hand and Asia Minor on the other. Paul returned to Troas following his work in Ephesus on his third journey (see 2 Cor 2:12). At some time—on Paul's second journey or on his third—a church was started there, for Paul ministered to believers in Troas when he returned from his third journey on his way to Jerusalem (20:5–12).

16:9 *vision.* One of the ways God gave direction (cf. 10:3). *man of Macedonia.* Macedonia had become a Roman province in 148 B.C. There is no indication that the man of the vision is Luke, as some have suggested, but he does join the group at this point.

16:10 *we endeavoured to go.* This is where the "we" passages of Acts begin (see Introduction: Author). The conclusion is that Luke is informing the reader that he had joined the party at Troas.

16:11 *Samothracia.* An island in the northeastern Aegean Sea. It was a convenient place for boats to anchor rather than risk sailing at night. *Neapolis.* The seaport for Philippi, ten miles away; modern Kavalla.

16:12 *Philippi.* A city in eastern Macedonia named after Philip II, father of Alexander the Great (see map, p. 1705). Since it was a Roman colony, it was independent of provincial administration and had a governmental organization modeled after that of Rome (see note on 13:14). Many retired legionnaires from the Roman army settled there, but few Jews. See Introduction to Philippians: Recipients. *chief city.* Thessalonica was the capital of Macedonia. But Macedonia had four districts, and Philippi was in the first of these.

16:13 *where prayer was wont to be made.* There were so few Jews in Philippi that there was no synagogue, so the Jews who were there met for prayer along the banks of the Gangites River (see map, p. 1705). It was customary for such places of prayer to be located outdoors near running water.

16:14 *Lydia.* A businesswoman. Her name may be associated with her place of origin, the Hellenistic district of Lydia. *Thyatira.* In the Roman province of Asia, 20 miles southeast of Pergamum (in the Hellenistic kingdom of Lydia). It was famous for its dyeing works, especially royal purple (crimson). See Rev 1:11 and note on Rev 2:18. *worshipped God.* Lydia was a Gentile who, like Cornelius (see 10:2), believed in the true God and followed the moral teachings of Scripture. She had not, however, become a full convert to Judaism. *whose heart the Lord opened.*

household, she besought *us,* saying, If ye have
judged me to be faithful to the Lord, come into
my house, and abide *there.* And [a]she constrained us.

Paul and Silas imprisoned

16 And it came to pass, as we went to
prayer, a certain damsel [a]possessed with a
spirit [1]of divination met us, which brought
her masters [b]much gain by soothsaying:
17 The same followed Paul and us, and
cried, saying, These men are the servants of
the most high God, which shew unto us the
way of salvation.
18 And this did she many days. But Paul,
[a]being grieved, turned and said to the spirit, I
command thee in the name of Jesus Christ to
come out of her. [b]And he came out the same
hour.
19 And [a]when her masters saw that the
hope of their gains was gone, they caught Paul
and Silas, and [b]drew *them* into the [1]market-
place unto the rulers,
20 And brought them to the magistrates,
saying, These men, being Jews, [a]do exceedingly trouble our city,
21 And teach customs, which are not lawful for us to receive, neither to observe, being
Romans.
22 And the multitude rose up together

16:15 [a]Gen. 19:3; 33:11; Judg. 19:21; Luke 24:29; Heb. 13:2
16:16 [1]Or, *of Python* [a]1 Sam. 28:7 [b]ch. 19:24
16:18 [a]See Mark 1:25,34 [b]Mark 16:17
16:19 [1]Or, *court* [a]ch. 19:25,26 [b]Mat. 10:18
16:20 [a]1 Ki. 18:17; ch. 17:6

After the resurrection the minds of the disciples were opened to understand the Scriptures (Luke 24:45); similarly, Lydia's heart was opened to respond to the gospel message of Paul.

16:16 *a spirit of divination.* A "python" spirit, a demonic spirit. The python was a mythical snake worshiped at Delphi and associated with the Delphic oracle. The term "python" came to be used of the persons through whom the python spirit supposedly spoke. Since such persons spoke involuntarily, the term "ventriloquist" was used to describe them. To what extent she actually predicted the future is not known.

16:17 *us.* The "we" section (see note on v. 10) ends here and begins again in 20:5. *most high God.* A title used by the man possessed by an evil spirit (Mark 5:7). It was a common title among both Jews (see Num 24:16; Is 14:14; Dan 3:26) and Greeks (found in inscriptions). But the title is not used of God in the NT by Christians or Jews (cf. Acts 7:48).

16:20 *magistrates.* The Greek term *strategos* (Latin *praetor*), not the usual word but a term of courtesy used in some Roman colonies, such as Philippi.

16:21 *customs . . . not lawful.* If a religion failed to receive Roman approval, it was considered *religio illicita.* Judaism had legal recognition, but Christianity did not.

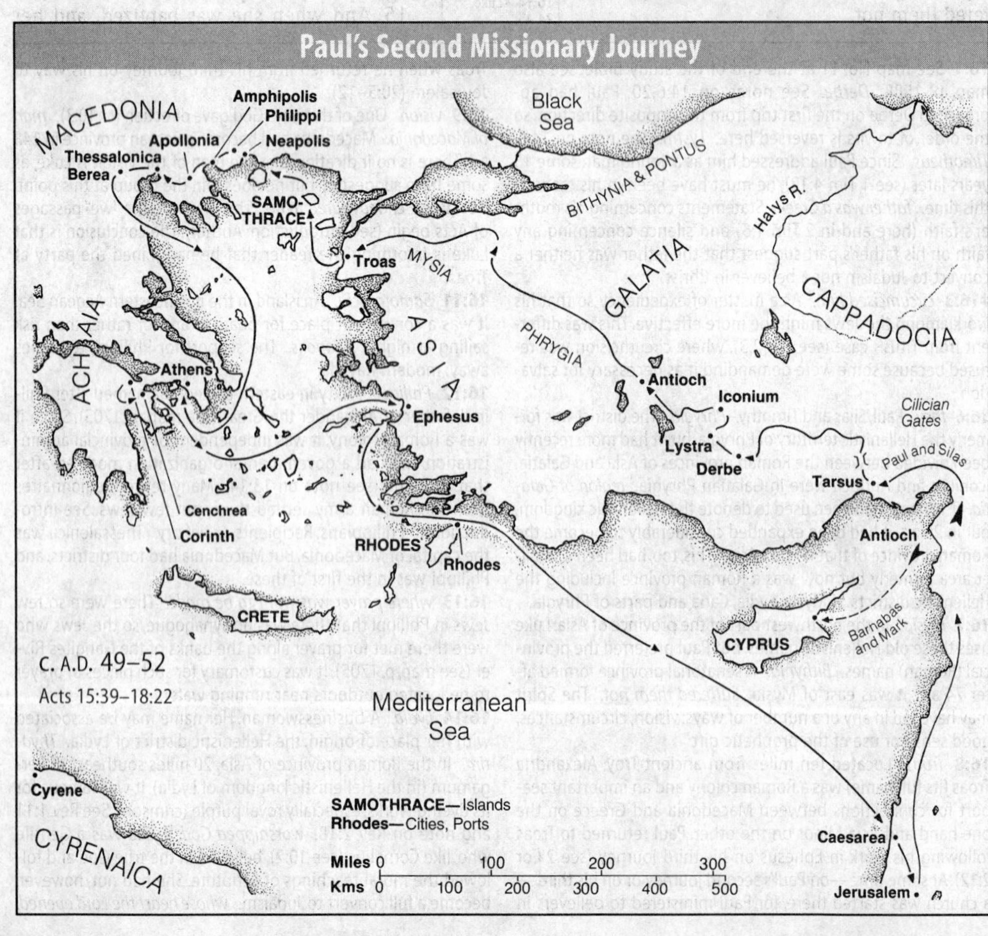

against them: and the magistrates rent off their clothes, [a]and commanded to beat *them.*

23 And when they had laid many stripes upon them, they cast *them* into prison, charging the jailor to keep them safely:

24 Who, having received such a charge, thrust them into the inner prison, and made their feet fast in the stocks.

25 ¶ And at midnight Paul and Silas prayed, and sang praises unto God: and the prisoners heard them.

26 [a]And suddenly there was a great earthquake, so that the foundations of the prison were shaken: and immediately [b]all the doors were opened, and every one's bands were loosed.

27 And the keeper of the prison awaking out of his sleep, and seeing the prison doors open, he drew out his sword, and would have killed himself, supposing that the prisoners had been fled.

28 But Paul cried with a loud voice, saying, Do thyself no harm: for we are all here.

29 Then he called for a light, and sprang in, and came trembling, and fell down before Paul and Silas,

30 And brought them out, and said, [a]Sirs, what must I do to be saved?

31 And they said, [a]Believe on the Lord Jesus Christ, and thou shalt be saved, and thy house.

32 And they spake unto him the word of the Lord, and to all that were in his house.

33 And he took them the same hour of the night, and washed *their* stripes; and was baptized, he and all his, straightway.

34 And when he had brought them into his house, [a]he set meat before *them,* and rejoiced, believing in God with all his house.

35 ¶ And when it was day, the magistrates sent the sergeants, saying, Let those men go.

36 And the keeper of the prison told this saying to Paul, The magistrates have sent to let you go: now therefore depart, and go in peace.

37 But Paul said unto them, They have beaten us openly uncondemned, [a]being Romans, and have cast *us* into prison; and now do they thrust us out privily? nay verily; but let them come themselves and fetch us out.

38 And the sergeants told these words unto the magistrates: and they feared, when they heard that they were Romans,

39 And they came and besought them, and brought *them* out, and [a]desired *them* to depart out of the city.

40 And they went out of the prison, [a]and entered into *the house of* Lydia: and when they had seen the brethren, they comforted them, and departed.

Paul at Thessalonica

17 Now when they had passed through Amphipolis and Apollonia, they came to Thessalonica, where was a synagogue of the Jews:

2 And Paul, as his manner was, [a]went in unto them, and three sabbath days reasoned with them out of the scriptures,

3 Opening and alleging, [a]that Christ must needs have suffered, and risen again from the dead; and that this Jesus, [1]whom I preach unto you, is Christ.

4 [a]And some of them believed, and consorted with Paul and [b]Silas; and of the devout Greeks a great multitude, and of the chief women not a few.

5 But the Jews which believed not, moved with envy, took unto *them* certain lewd fellows of the baser sort, and gathered a company, and set all the city on an uproar, and as-

16:22 [a]2 Cor. 6:5; 11:23,25; 1 Thes. 2:2
16:26 [a]ch. 4:31 [b]ch. 5:19; 12:7,10
16:30 [a]Luke 3:10; ch. 2:37; 9:6
16:31 [a]John 3:16,36; 6:47; 1 John 5:10
16:34 [a]Luke 5:29; 19:6
16:37 [a]ch. 22:25
16:39 [a]Mat. 8:34
16:40 [a]ver. 14
17:2 [a]Luke 4:16; ch. 9:20; 13:5,14; 14:1; 16:13; 19:8
17:3 [1][Or, *whom, said he, I preach*] [a]Luke 24:26,46; ch. 18:28; Gal. 3:1
17:4 [a]ch. 28:24 [b]ch. 15:22,27, 32,40

16:22 *beat them.* With rods.
16:24 *inner prison . . . stocks.* Used not only for extra security but also for torture.
16:27 *would have killed himself.* If a prisoner escaped, the life of the guard was demanded in his place (see 12:19). To take his own life would shorten the shame and distress.
16:30 *what must I do to be saved?* The jailer had heard that these were preachers of a way of salvation (v. 17). Now with the earthquake and his own impending death, he wanted to know about the way.
16:31 *Believe on the Lord Jesus Christ.* A concise statement of the way of salvation (see 10:43).
16:32 *word of the Lord.* See 10:36. Paul and Silas explained the gospel more thoroughly to the jailer and to all the other members of his household, and they all believed in Christ and were saved (v. 34).
16:34 *rejoiced.* The consistent consequence of conversion, regardless of circumstances (see note on 8:39).
16:35 *magistrates.* See note on v. 20.
16:37 *uncondemned.* Public beating for a Roman citizen (see v. 38) would have been illegal, let alone beating without a trial. *let them come themselves.* Paul and Silas were not asking for an escort to salve their injured pride as much as they were establishing their innocence for the sake of the church in Philippi and its future.
17:1 *Amphipolis . . . Thessalonica.* The Egnatian Way crossed the whole of present-day northern Greece east-west and included Philippi, Amphipolis, Apollonia and Thessalonica on its route. At several locations, such as Kavalla (Neapolis), Philippi and Apollonia, the road is still visible today. If a person traveled about 30 miles a day, each city could be reached after one day's journey. *Thessalonica.* About 100 miles from Philippi. It was the capital of the province of Macedonia and had a population of more than 200,000, including a colony of Jews (and a synagogue). All these contributed to Paul's decision to preach there. See Introduction to 1 Thessalonians: The City and the Church.
17:2 *went in unto them.* To the synagogue (v. 1; see note on 13:14). *three sabbath days.* These two weeks represent the time spent in the synagogue reasoning with the Jews, not Paul's total time in Thessalonica. An analysis of the Thessalonian letters reveals that Paul had taught them much more doctrine than would have been possible in two or three weeks.
17:4 *devout Greeks.* See notes on 10:2; 16:14. *chief women.* Perhaps the wives of the leading men of the city, but women who deserve notice and position in their own right (see also v. 12).
17:5 *moved with envy.* Because of the large number of people (including some Jews, many God-fearing Gentiles and many prominent women) who responded to Paul's ministry (cf. 13:45). *house of Jason.* Paul had probably been staying there.

saulted the house of [a]Jason, and sought to
bring them out to the people.
6 And when they found them not, they
drew Jason and certain brethren unto the
rulers of the city, crying, [a]These that have
turned the world upside down are come hither also;
7 Whom Jason hath received: and these all
do contrary to the decrees of Cesar, [a]saying
that there is another king, *one* Jesus.
8 And they troubled the people and the
rulers of the city, when they heard these
things.
9 And when they had taken security of Jason, and *of* the other, they let them go.

Paul at Berea

10 ¶ And [a]the brethren immediately sent
away Paul and Silas by night unto Berea: who
coming *thither* went into the synagogue of the
Jews.
11 These were more noble than those in
Thessalonica, in that they received the word
with all readiness of mind, and [a]searched the
scriptures daily, whether those *things* were so.
12 Therefore many of them believed; also
of honourable women which were Greeks,
and of men, not a few.
13 But when the Jews of Thessalonica had
knowledge that the word of God was preached
of Paul at Berea, they came thither also, and
stirred up the people.
14 [a]And then immediately the brethren
sent away Paul to go as *it were* to the sea: but
Silas and Timotheus abode there still.
15 And they that conducted Paul brought
him unto Athens: and [a]receiving a commandment unto Silas and Timotheus for to come to
him with all speed, they departed.

Paul at Athens

16 ¶ Now while Paul waited for them at
Athens, [a]his spirit was stirred in him, when
he saw the city [1]wholly given to idolatry.
17 Therefore disputed he in the synagogue
with the Jews, and with the devout *persons,*
and in the market daily with them that met
with *him.*
18 Then certain philosophers of the Epicureans, and of the Stoicks, encountered him.
And some said, What will this [1]babbler say?
other *some,* He seemeth to be a setter forth of
strange gods: because he preached unto them
Jesus, and the resurrection.
19 And they took him, and brought him
unto [1]Areopagus, saying, May we know what
this new doctrine, whereof thou speakest, *is?*
20 For thou bringest certain strange *things*
to our ears: we would know therefore what
these *things* mean.
21 (For all the Athenians and strangers
which were there spent their time in nothing
else, but *either* to tell, or to hear some new
thing.)
22 Then Paul stood in the midst of [1]Mars'
hill, and said,
¶ *Ye* men of Athens, I perceive that in all
things ye are too superstitious.
23 For as I passed by, and beheld your [1]de-
votions, I found an altar with this inscription,

17:5 [a]Rom. 16:21
17:6 [a]ch. 16:20
17:7 [a]Luke 23:2; John 19:12; 1 Pet. 2:13
17:10 [a]ver. 14; ch. 9:25
17:11 [a]Is. 34:16; Luke 16:29; John 5:39
17:14 [a]Mat. 10:23
17:15 [a]ch. 18:5
17:16 [1]Or, *full of idols* [a]2 Pet. 2:8
17:18 [1]Or, *base fellow*
17:19 [1]Or, *Mars' hill.* It was the highest court in Athens
17:22 [1]Or, *[the] court of the Areopagites*
17:23 [1]Or, *gods that ye worship*

17:6 *rulers of the city.* The Greek term *politarch* (lit. "city ruler"), used here and in v. 8, is found nowhere else in Greek literature, but it was discovered in 1835 in a Greek inscription on an arch that had spanned the Egnatian Way on the west side of Thessalonica. (The arch was destroyed in 1867, but the block with the inscription was rescued and is now in the British Museum in London.) The term has since been found in 16 other inscriptions in surrounding towns of Macedonia, and elsewhere.
17:7 *do contrary to the decrees of Cesar.* Blasphemy was the gravest accusation for a Jew, but treason—to support a rival king above Caesar—was the worst accusation for a Roman.
17:9 *taken security of.* Jason was forced to guarantee a peaceful, quiet community, or he would face the confiscation of his properties and perhaps even death.
17:10 *Paul and Silas.* It has been suggested that Timothy was left at Philippi and rejoined Paul and Silas at Berea (compare v. 10 with v. 14). *Berea.* Modern Verria, located 50 miles from Thessalonica in another district of Macedonia. *synagogue.* See note on 13:14.
17:14 *to go as it were to the sea.* One might conclude that Paul went by boat to Athens. But the road to Athens is also a coast road, and Paul may have walked the distance after having been escorted to the coast (some 20 miles). In any event, Christian companions stayed with him until reaching Athens.
17:15 *Athens.* Five centuries before Paul, Athens had been at the height of its glory in art, philosophy and literature. She had retained her reputation in philosophy through the years and still maintained a leading university in Paul's day.
17:17 *synagogue.* See note on 13:14. *devout persons.* God-fearing Gentiles. See note on 10:2.
17:18 *philosophers of the Epicureans.* Originally they taught that the supreme good is happiness—but not mere momentary pleasure or temporary gratification. By Paul's time, however, this philosophy had degenerated into a more sensual system of thought. *Stoicks.* They taught that people should live in accord with nature, recognize their own self-sufficiency and independence, and suppress their desires. At its best, Stoicism had some admirable qualities, but, like Epicureanism, by Paul's time it had degenerated into a system of pride. *babbler.* The Greek word meant "seed picker," a bird picking up seeds here and there. Then it came to refer to the loafer in the marketplace who picked up whatever scraps of learning he could find and paraded them without digesting them himself.
17:19 *Areopagus.* Means "hill of Ares." Ares was the Greek god of thunder and war (the Roman equivalent was Mars). The Areopagus was located just west of the acropolis and south of the Agora and had once been the site of the meeting of the Court or Council of the Areopagus. Earlier the Council governed a Greek city-state, but by NT times the Areopagus retained authority only in the areas of religion and morals and met in the Royal Portico at the northwest corner of the Agora. They considered themselves the custodians of teachings that introduced new religions and foreign gods.
17:22 *too superstitious.* The Greek for this word could be used to congratulate a person or to criticize him, depending on whether the person using it included himself in the circle of individuals he was describing. The Athenians would not know which meaning to take until Paul continued. In this context it is clear that Paul wanted to be complimentary in order to gain a hearing.

TO *THE* UNKNOWN GOD. Whom therefore ye ignorantly worship, him declare I unto you.

24 [a]God that made the world and all *things* therein, seeing that he is [b]Lord of heaven and earth, [c]dwelleth not in temples made with hands;

25 Neither is worshipped with men's hands, [a]as though he needed any *thing,* seeing [b]he giveth to all life, and breath, and all *things;*

26 And hath made of one blood all nations of men for to dwell on all the face of the earth, and hath determined the times before appointed, and [a]the bounds of their habitation;

27 [a]That *they* should seek the Lord, if haply they might feel after him, and find *him,* [b]though he be not far from every one of us:

28 For [a]in him we live, and move, and have our being; [b]as certain also of your own poets have said, For we are also his offspring.

29 Forasmuch then as we are the offspring of God, [a]we ought not to think that the Godhead is like unto gold, or silver, or stone, graven by art and man's device.

30 And [a]the times of *this* ignorance God winked at; but [b]now commandeth all men every where to repent:

31 Because he hath appointed a day, in the which [a]he will judge the world in righteousness by *that* man whom he hath ordained; *whereof* he [1]hath given assurance unto all *men,* in that [b]he hath raised him from the dead.

32 ¶ And when they heard of the resurrection of the dead, some mocked: and others said, We will hear thee again of this *matter.*

33 So Paul departed from among them.

34 Howbeit certain men clave unto him, and believed: among the which *was* Dionysius the Areopagite, and a woman named Damaris, and others with them.

Paul at Corinth

18 After these *things* Paul departed from Athens, and came to Corinth;

2 And found a certain Jew named [a]Aquila, born in Pontus, lately come from Italy, with his wife Priscilla; (because that Claudius had commanded all Jews to depart from Rome:) and came unto them.

3 And because *he* was of the same craft, he abode with them, [a]and wrought: for *by* their occupation they were tentmakers.

4 [a]And he reasoned in the synagogue every sabbath, and persuaded *the* Jews and *the* Greeks.

5 And [a]when Silas and Timotheus were come from Macedonia, Paul was [b]pressed in spirit, and testified to the Jews *that* Jesus [1]*was* Christ.

6 And [a]when they opposed themselves, and blasphemed, [b]he shook *his* raiment, and said unto them, [c]Your blood *be* upon your own heads; [d]I *am* clean: [e]from henceforth I will go unto the Gentiles.

7 And he departed thence, and entered into a certain *man's* house, named Justus, one

17:24 [a]ch. 14:15 [b]Mat. 11:25 [c]ch. 7:48
17:25 [a]Ps. 50:8 [b]Gen. 2:7; Num. 16:22; Job 12:10; 27:3; 33:4; Is. 42:5; 57:16; Zech. 12:1
17:26 [a]Deut. 32:8
17:27 [a]Rom. 1:20 [b]ch. 14:17
17:28 [a]Col. 1:17; Heb. 1:3 [b]Tit. 1:12
17:29 [a]Is. 40:18
17:30 [a]ch. 14:16; Rom. 3:25 [b]Luke 24:47; Tit. 2:11,12; 1 Pet. 1:14; 4:3
17:31 [1]Or, *offered faith* [a]ch. 10:42; Rom. 2:16; 14:10 [b]ch. 2:24
18:2 [a]Rom. 16:3; 1 Cor. 16:19; 2 Tim. 4:19
18:3 [a]ch. 20:34; 1 Cor. 4:12; 1 Thes. 2:9; 2 Thes. 3:8
18:4 [a]ch. 17:2
18:5 [1][Or, is *the Christ*] [a]ch. 17:14,15 [b]ver. 28; Job 32:18; ch. 17:3
18:6 [a]ch. 13:45 [b]Neh. 5:13; Mat. 10:14; ch. 13:51 [c]Lev. 20:9,11,12; 2 Sam. 1:16; Ezek. 18:13; 33:4 [d]Ezek. 3:18,19; 33:9; ch. 20:26 [e]ch. 13:46; 28:28

17:23 *TO THE UNKNOWN GOD.* The Greeks were fearful of offending any god by failing to give him attention; so they felt they could cover any omissions by the label "unknown god." Other Greek writers confirm that such altars could be seen in Athens—a striking point of contact for Paul.

17:24 *God that made the world.* Thus a personal Creator, in contrast with the views of pantheistic Stoicism.

17:26 *hath made of one blood all nations.* All people are of one family (whether Athenians or Romans, Greeks or barbarians, Jews or Gentiles). *determined the times before appointed.* He planned the exact times when nations should emerge and decline. *bounds of their habitation.* He also planned the specific area to be occupied by each nation. He is God, the Designer (things were not left to Chance, as the Epicureans thought).

17:28 *certain also of your own poets.* There are two quotations here: (1) "In Him we live and move and exist," from the Cretan poet Epimenides (c. 600 B.C.) in his *Cretica,* and (2) "For we also are His children," from the Cilician poet Aratus (c. 315–240) in his *Phaenomena,* as well as from Cleanthes (331–233) in his *Hymn to Zeus.* Paul quotes Greek poets elsewhere as well (see 1 Cor 15:33; Tit 1:12 and notes).

17:30 *times of this ignorance God winked at.* God had not judged them for worshiping false gods in their ignorance (see v. 31).

17:31 *man whom he hath ordained.* Jesus, the Son of man (see Dan 7:13; cf. Mat 25:31–46; Acts 10:42).

17:32 *resurrection of the dead.* Immortality of the soul was accepted by the Greeks, but not resurrection of a dead body.

17:34 *Dionysius.* Later tradition states, though it cannot be proved, that he became bishop of Athens. *Damaris.* Some have suggested that she must have been a foreign, educated woman to have been present at a public meeting such as the Areopagus. It is also possible that she was a God-fearing Gentile who had heard Paul at the synagogue (v. 17).

18:1 *came to Corinth.* Either by land along the isthmus (a distance of about 50 miles) or by sea from Piraeus, the port of Athens, to Cenchrea, on the eastern shore of the isthmus of Corinth. See Introduction to 1 Corinthians: The City of Corinth; see also map, p. 1641.

18:2 *Pontus.* In the northeastern region of Asia Minor, a province lying along the Black Sea between Bithynia and Armenia (see 2:9). *Priscilla.* The diminutive form of Prisca. Since no mention is made of a conversion and since a partnership is established in work (see v. 3), it is likely that they were already Christians. They may have been converted in Rome by those returning from Pentecost or by others at a later time. *Claudius.* Emperor of Rome (A.D. 41–54). *commanded all Jews to depart from Rome.* Recorded in Suetonius (*Claudius,* 25). The expulsion order was given, Suetonius writes, because of "their [the Jews'] continual tumults instigated by Chrestus" (a common misspelling of "Christ"). If "Chrestus" refers to Christ, the riots obviously were "about" Him rather than led "by" Him.

18:3 *tentmakers.* Paul would have been taught this trade as a youth. It was the Jewish custom to provide manual training for sons, whether rich or poor.

18:4 *synagogue.* See note on 13:14.

18:5 *when Silas and Timotheus were come from Macedonia.* Paul instructed these two to come to him at Athens (17:15). Evidently they did (1 Thes 3:1), but they may have been sent back to Macedonia almost immediately to check on the churches—perhaps Silas to Philippi and Timothy to Thessalonica.

that worshipped God, whose house joined hard to the synagogue.

8 [a]And Crispus, the *chief* ruler of the synagogue, believed on the Lord with all his house; and many of the Corinthians hearing believed, and were baptized.

9 Then [a]spake the Lord to Paul in the night by a vision, Be not afraid, but speak, and hold not thy peace:

10 [a]For I am with thee, and no *man* shall set on thee to hurt thee: for I have much people in this city.

11 And he [1]continued *there* a year and six months, teaching the word of God among them.

12 ¶ And when Gallio was the deputy of Achaia, the Jews made insurrection with one accord against Paul, and brought him to the judgment seat,

13 Saying, This *fellow* persuadeth men to worship God contrary to the law.

14 And when Paul was *now* about to open *his* mouth, Gallio said unto the Jews, [a]If it were a matter of wrong or wicked lewdness, O *ye* Jews, reason would that I should bear with you:

15 But if it be a question of words and names, and *of* your law, look ye *to it;* for I will be no judge of such *matters.*

16 And he drave them from the judgment seat.

17 Then all the Greeks took [a]Sosthenes, the *chief* ruler of the synagogue, and beat *him* before the judgment seat. And Gallio cared for none of those *things.*

Paul returns to Antioch

18 ¶ And Paul *after this* tarried *there* yet a good while, and then took his leave of the brethren, and sailed thence into Syria, and with him Priscilla and Aquila: having [a]shorn *his* head in [b]Cenchrea: for he had a vow.

19 And he came to Ephesus, and left them there: but he himself entered into the synagogue, and reasoned with the Jews.

20 When they desired *him* to tarry longer time with them, he consented not;

21 But bade them farewell, saying, [a]I must by all means keep *this* feast that cometh in Jerusalem: but I will return again unto you, [b]if God will. And he sailed from Ephesus.

22 And when he had landed at Cesarea, and gone up, and saluted the church, he went down to Antioch.

23 And after he had spent some time *there,* he departed, and went over *all* the country of [a]Galatia and Phrygia in order, [b]strengthening all the disciples.

Apollos' preaching at Ephesus

24 ¶ [a]And a certain Jew named Apollos, born at Alexandria, an eloquent man, *and* mighty in the scriptures, came to Ephesus.

25 This *man* was instructed in the way of the Lord; and being [a]fervent in the spirit, he spake and taught diligently the *things* of the Lord, [b]knowing only the baptism of John.

26 And he began to speak boldly in the synagogue: whom when Aquila and Priscilla had heard, they took him unto *them,* and ex-

18:8 [a]1 Cor. 1:14
18:9 [a]ch. 23:11
18:10 [a]Jer. 1:18,19
18:11 [1]Gr. *sat* there
18:14 [a]ch. 23:29; 25:11,19
18:17 [a]1 Cor. 1:1
18:18 [a]Num. 6:18; ch. 21:24 [b]Rom. 16:1
18:21 [a]ch. 19:21; 20:16 [b]1 Cor. 4:19; Heb. 6:3; Jas. 4:15
18:23 [a]Gal. 1:2; 4:14 [b]ch. 14:22; 15:32,41
18:24 [a]1 Cor. 1:12; 3:5,6; 4:6; Tit. 3:13
18:25 [a]Rom. 12:11 [b]ch. 19:3

18:8 *Crispus.* Paul baptized him (1 Cor 1:14). *ruler of the synagogue.* See note on 13:15. *believed, and were baptized.* The response to the gospel, a process going on daily, as the tense of the Greek verbs indicates.

18:9 *by a vision.* Paul had seen the Lord in a resurrection body at his conversion (9:4–6; 1 Cor 15:8) and in the temple at Jerusalem in a trance (22:17–18). Now he sees Him in a vision (see 23:11).

18:11 *a year and six months.* During this time he may also have taken the gospel to the neighboring districts of Achaia (2 Cor 1:1).

18:12 *Gallio.* The brother of Seneca, the philosopher, who was the tutor of Nero. Gallio was admired as a man of exceptional fairness and calmness. From an inscription found at Delphi, it is known that Gallio was proconsul of Achaia in A.D. 51–52. This information enables us to date Paul's visit to Corinth on his second journey as well as his writing of the Thessalonian letters.

18:13 *contrary to the law.* The Jews were claiming that Paul was advocating a religion not recognized by Roman law as Judaism was. If he had been given the opportunity to speak, he could have argued that the gospel he was preaching was the faith of his fathers (see 24:14–15; 26:6–7) and thus authorized by Roman law.

18:17 *took Sosthenes . . . and beat him.* It is not clear whether the Greeks beat Sosthenes, seeing the occasion as an opportunity to vent their feelings against the Jews, or the Jews beat their own synagogue ruler because he was unsuccessful in presenting their case—probably the former. A Sosthenes is included with Paul in the writing of 1 Corinthians (1:1). Perhaps he was the second ruler of the synagogue at Corinth to become a Christian in response to Paul's preaching (see v. 8).

18:18 *Priscilla and Aquila.* The order of the names used here (but cf. v. 2) may indicate the prominent role of Priscilla or her higher social position (see Rom 16:3; 2 Tim 4:19). *had a vow.* Grammatically this could refer to Aquila, but the emphasis on Paul and his activity makes Paul more probable. It was probably a temporary Nazarite vow (see Num 6:1–21). Different vows were frequently taken to express thanks for deliverance from grave dangers. Shaving the head marked the end of a vow.

18:19 *Ephesus.* Leading commercial city of Asia Minor, the capital of provincial Asia and the warden of the temple of Artemis (Diana). See Introduction to Ephesians: The City of Ephesus; see also map, p. 1694. *left them there.* Priscilla and Aquila would give valuable aid upon Paul's return, providing advice as to where and how the work there could be started. *synagogue.* See note on 13:14.

18:22 *saluted the church.* Could refer to a congregation in Cesarea, but the explanation that "he went up" makes it more likely that it was the church in Jerusalem, some 2,500 feet above sea level.

18:23 See map No. 11 at the end of the study Bible. *country of Galatia and Phrygia.* The same route he had taken when starting on his second missionary journey, but in the reverse order (16:6). The use of the phrase may indicate the southern part of Galatia in the Phrygian area (see note on 16:6).

18:24 *Alexandria.* Alexandria, in Egypt, was the second most important city in the Roman empire and had a large Jewish population.

18:25 *baptism of John.* It was not in the name of Jesus (see also 19:2–4). Apollos knew something about Jesus, but basically he, like John, was still looking forward to the coming of the Messiah. His baptism was based on repentance rather than

pounded unto him the way of God more perfectly.

27 And when he was disposed to pass into Achaia, the brethren wrote, exhorting the disciples to receive him: who, when he was come, [a]helped them much which had believed through grace:

28 For he mightily convinced the Jews, *and that* publickly, [a]shewing by the scriptures that Jesus [1]was Christ.

Paul's work in Ephesus

19 And it came to pass that, while [a]Apollos was at Corinth, Paul having passed through the upper coasts came to Ephesus: and finding certain disciples,

2 He said unto them, Have ye received the Holy Ghost since ye believed? And they said unto him, [a]We have not so much as heard whether there be *any* Holy Ghost.

3 And he said unto them, Unto what then were ye baptized? And they said, [a]Unto John's baptism.

4 Then said Paul, [a]John verily baptized *with* the baptism of repentance, saying unto the people, that they should believe on him which should come after him, that is, on Christ Jesus.

18:27 [a]1 Cor. 3:6
18:28 [1][Or, *is the Christ*] [a]ver. 5; ch. 9:22; 17:3
19:1 [a]1 Cor. 1:12; 3:5,6
19:2 [a]ch. 8:16; See 1 Sam. 3:7
19:3 [a]ch. 18:25
19:4 [a]Mat. 3:11; John 1:15,27,30; ch. 1:5; 11:16; 13:24,25

on faith in the finished work of Christ.

18:27 *Achaia.* The Roman province with Corinth as its capital.

19:1 *Apollos was at Corinth.* Apollos was introduced at Ephesus (18:24) in the absence of Paul; he moved to Corinth before Paul returned to Ephesus. But later Apollos came back to Ephesus during Paul's ministry there (see 1 Cor 16:12). *through the upper coasts.* Not the lower direct route down the Lycus and Meander valleys but the upper Phrygian route approaching Ephesus from a more northerly direction. If Paul got to northern Galatia, which is unlikely, it must have been on one of these trips through the interior (see 16:6; 18:23). *Ephesus.* See note on 18:19. *certain disciples.* These 12 (v. 7) seem to have been followers of Jesus, but indirectly through John the Baptist or some of his followers. Or perhaps they had received their teaching from Apollos himself in his earlier state of partial understanding (see 18:26). Like Apollos, they had a limited understanding of the gospel (see note on 18:25).

‡19:2 *Have ye received the Holy Ghost . . . ?* The response of these men to Paul's question is that they have not even heard of the Holy Spirit. Since they knew the OT and John's preaching, they probably did know of the Holy Spirit. What they apparently did not know was the fulfillment of John's preaching that occurred on the day of Pentecost with the coming and baptism of the Holy Spirit. The fact that these people were rebaptized clearly indicates the uniqueness of Christian baptism.

19:4 *John verily baptized.* See notes on Mat 3:11,15. *baptism*

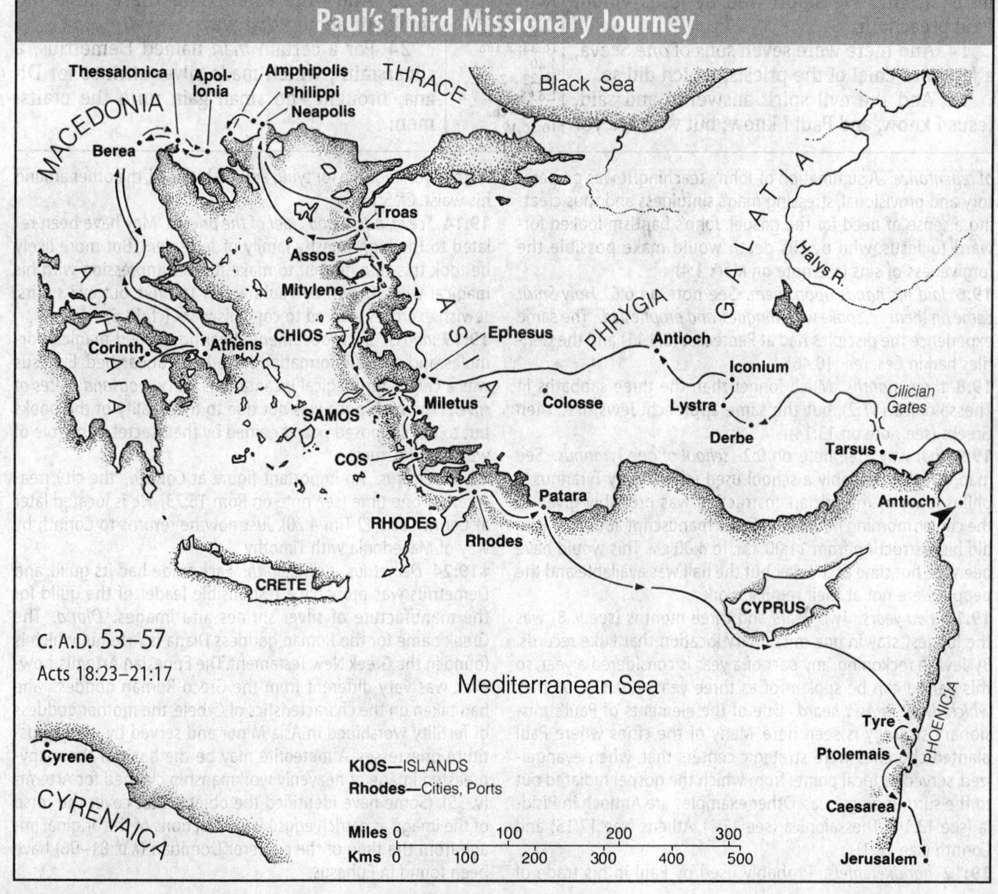

5 When they heard *this,* they were baptized [a]in the name of the Lord Jesus.
6 And when Paul had [a]laid *his* hands upon
them, the Holy Ghost came on them; and
[b]they spake with tongues, and prophesied.
7 And all the men were about twelve.
8 [a]And he went into the synagogue, and
spake boldly for the space of three months,
disputing and persuading the *things* [b]concern-
ing the kingdom of God.
9 But [a]when divers were hardened, and
believed not, but spake evil [b]of *that* way before the multitude, he departed from them,
and separated the disciples, disputing daily in
the school of one Tyrannus.
10 And [a]this continued by the space of two
years; so that all they which dwelt in Asia
heard the word of the Lord Jesus, both Jews
and Greeks.
11 And [a]God wrought special miracles by
the hands of Paul:
12 [a]So that from his body were brought
unto the sick handkerchiefs or aprons, and the
diseases departed from them, and the evil spirits went out of them.
13 ¶ [a]Then certain of the vagabond Jews,
exorcists, [b]took upon them to call over them
which had evil spirits the name of the Lord
Jesus, saying, We adjure you by Jesus whom
Paul preacheth.
14 And there were seven sons of *one* Sceva,
a Jew, *and* chief of the priests, which did so.
15 And the evil spirit answered and said,
Jesus I know, and Paul I know; but who are ye?

19:5 [a]ch. 8:16 **19:6** [a]ch. 6:6; 8:17 [b]ch. 2:4; 10:46 **19:8** [a]ch. 17:2; 18:4 [b]ch. 1:3; 28:23 **19:9** [a]2 Tim. 1:15; 2 Pet. 2:2; Jude 10 [b]ver. 23; See ch. 9:2; 22:4; 24:14 **19:10** [a]See ch. 20:31 **19:11** [a]Mark 16:20; ch. 14:3 **19:12** [a]See 2 Ki. 4:29; ch. 5:15 **19:13** [a]Mat. 12:27 [b]See Mark 9:38; Luke 9:49

19:17 [a]Luke 1:65; 7:16; ch. 2:43; 5:5,11 **19:18** [a]Mat. 3:6 **19:20** [a]ch. 6:7; 12:24 **19:21** [a]Rom. 15:25; Gal. 2:1 [b]ch. 20:22 [c]ch. 18:21; 23:11; Rom. 15:24-28 **19:22** [a]Rom. 16:23; 2 Tim. 4:20 **19:23** [a]2 Cor. 1:8 [b]See ch. 9:2 **19:24** [a]ch. 16:16,19

16 And the man in whom the evil spirit
was leapt on them, and overcame them, and
prevailed against them, so that *they* fled out of
that house naked and wounded.
17 And this was known to all the Jews and
Greeks also dwelling at Ephesus; and [a]fear fell
on them all, and the name of the Lord Jesus
was magnified.
18 And many that believed came, and
[a]confessed, and shewed their deeds.
19 Many also of them which used curious
arts brought their books together, and burned
them before all *men:* and they counted the
price of them, and found *it* fifty thousand
pieces of silver.
20 [a]So mightily grew the word of God and
prevailed.

The riot at Ephesus

21 ¶ [a]After these *things* were ended, Paul
[b]purposed in the spirit, when he had passed
through Macedonia and Achaia, to go to Jerusalem, saying, After I have been there, [c]I must
also see Rome.
22 So he sent into Macedonia two of them
that ministered unto him, Timotheus and
[a]Erastus; but he himself stayed in Asia for a
season.
23 And [a]the same time there arose no
small stir about [b]*that* way.
24 For a certain *man* named Demetrius, a
silversmith, which made silver shrines for Diana, brought [a]no small gain unto the craftsmen;

---

of repentance. A summation of John's teaching. It was preparatory and provisional, stressing man's sinfulness and thus creating a sense of need for the gospel. John's baptism looked forward to Jesus, who by His death would make possible the forgiveness of sins (see note on Mark 1:4).

19:6 *laid his hands upon them.* See note on 6:6. *Holy Spirit came on them . . . spake with tongues, and prophesied.* The same experience the disciples had at Pentecost (2:4,11) and the Gentiles had in Cesarea (10:46).

19:8 *three months.* Much longer than the three sabbaths in Thessalonica (17:2), but the same approach: Jews first, then Greeks (see note on 13:14).

19:9 *that way.* See note on 9:2. *school of one Tyrannus.* See map, p. 1694; probably a school used regularly by Tyrannus, a philosopher or rhetorician. Instruction was probably given in the cooler, morning hours. One Greek manuscript adds that Paul did his instructing from 11:00 A.M. to 4:00 P.M. This would have been the hot time of the day, but the hall was available and the people were not at their regular work.

19:10 *two years.* Two years and three months (see v. 8) was the longest stay in one missionary location that Luke records. By Jewish reckoning, any part of a year is considered a year; so this period can be spoken of as three years (20:31). *all they which dwelt in Asia heard.* One of the elements of Paul's missionary strategy is seen here. Many of the cities where Paul planted churches were strategic centers that, when evangelized, served as focal points from which the gospel radiated out to the surrounding areas. Other examples are Antioch in Pisidia (see 13:14), Thessalonica (see 17:1), Athens (see 17:15) and Corinth (see 18:1).

19:12 *handkerchiefs.* Probably used by Paul in his trade of leatherworking: one for tying around his head, the other around his waist. Cf. 5:15.

19:14 *Sceva, a Jew, and chief of the priests.* May have been related to the high priestly family of Jerusalem. But more likely he took this title himself to make further impression with his magical wiles. Drawn by Paul's ability to drive out evil spirits, Jewish exorcists wanted to copy his work (cf. 13:6).

19:19 *books.* Such documents bearing alleged magical formulas and secret information have been unearthed. Ephesus was a center for magical incantations. *fifty thousand pieces of silver.* The high price was not due to the quality of the books but to the supposed power gained by their secret rigmarole of words and names.

19:22 *Erastus.* An important figure at Corinth, "the city treasurer" at one time (see note on Rom 16:23). He is located later at Corinth also (2 Tim 4:20). Just now he returns to Corinth by way of Macedonia with Timothy.

‡19:24 *Demetrius, a silversmith.* Each trade had its guild, and Demetrius was probably a responsible leader of the guild for the manufacture of silver shrines and images. *Diana.* The Greek name for the Roman goddess Diana is Artemis, which is found in the Greek New Testament. The Ephesian Artemis, however, was very different from the Greco-Roman goddess. She had taken on the characteristics of Cybele, the mother goddess of fertility worshiped in Asia Minor and served by many prostitute priestesses. A meteorite may be the basis of the many-breasted image of heavenly workmanship claimed for Artemis (v. 35). (Some have identified the objects that cover the torso of the image as ostrich eggs.) Reproductions of the original image from the time of the emperor Domitian (A.D. 81–96) have been found in Ephesus.

25 Whom he called together with the workmen of like occupation, and said, Sirs, ye know that by this craft we have our wealth.

26 Moreover ye see and hear, that not alone at Ephesus, but almost throughout all Asia, this Paul hath persuaded and turned away much people, saying that [a]they be no gods, which are made with hands:

27 So *that* not only this our craft is in danger to be set at nought; but also that the temple of the great goddess Diana should be despised, and her magnificence should be destroyed, whom all Asia and the world worshippeth.

28 And when they heard *these sayings,* they were full of wrath, and cried out, saying, Great *is* Diana of the Ephesians.

29 And the whole city was filled with confusion: and having caught [a]Gaius and [b]Aristarchus, men of Macedonia, Paul's companions in travel, they rushed with one accord into the theatre.

30 And when Paul would have entered in unto the people, the disciples suffered him not.

31 And certain of the chief of Asia, which were his friends, sent unto him, desiring *him* that *he* would not adventure himself into the theatre.

32 Some therefore cried one *thing,* and some another: for the assembly was confused; and the more part knew not wherefore they were come together.

33 And they drew Alexander out of the multitude, the Jews putting him forward. And [a]Alexander [b]beckoned with the hand, and would have made *his* defence unto the people.

34 But when *they* knew that he was a Jew, all with one voice about the space of two hours cried out, Great *is* Diana of the Ephesians.

19:26 [a]Ps. 115:4; Is. 44:10-20; Jer. 10:3
19:29 [a]Rom. 16:23; 1 Cor. 1:14 [b]ch. 20:4; 27:2; Col. 4:10; Philem. 24
19:33 [a]1 Tim. 1:20; 2 Tim. 4:14 [b]ch. 12:17

19:35 [1]Gr. the *temple keeper*
19:38 [1]Or, *the court days are kept*
19:39 [1]Or, *ordinary*
20:1 [a]1 Cor. 16:5; 1 Tim. 1:3
20:3 [a]ch. 9:23; 23:12; 25:3; 2 Cor. 11:26
20:4 [a]ch. 19:29; 27:2; Col. 4:10 [b]ch. 19:29

35 And when the townclerk had appeased the people, he said, *Ye* men of Ephesus, what man is there that knoweth not how that the city of the Ephesians is [1]a worshipper of the great goddess Diana, and of the *image* which fell down from Jupiter?

36 Seeing then that these *things* cannot be spoken against, ye ought to be quiet, and to do nothing rashly.

37 For ye have brought *hither* these men, *which are* neither robbers of churches, nor yet blasphemers of your goddess.

38 Wherefore if Demetrius, and the craftsmen which are with him, have a matter against any *man,* [1]the law is open, and there are deputies: let them implead one another.

39 But if ye inquire any *thing* concerning other *matters,* it shall be determined in a [1]lawful assembly.

40 For we are in danger to be called in question for this day's uproar, there being no cause whereby we may give an account of this concourse.

41 And when he had thus spoken, he dismissed the assembly.

Macedonia and Greece

20 And after the uproar was ceased, Paul called unto *him* the disciples, and embraced *them,* and [a]departed for to go into Macedonia.

2 And when he had gone over those parts, and had given them much exhortation, he came into Greece,

3 And *there* abode three months: and [a]when the Jews laid wait for him, as he was about to sail into Syria, he purposed to return through Macedonia.

4 And there accompanied him into Asia Sopater of Berea; and of the Thessalonians, [a]Aristarchus and Secundus; and [b]Gaius of

19:25 *wealth.* Since the temple of Diana (Artemis) was one of the seven wonders of the ancient world, people came from far and wide to view it. Their purchase of silver shrines and images produced a lucrative business for the craftsmen.

19:27 *temple of the great goddess.* See map, p. 1694; the glory of Ephesus: 425 feet long and 220 feet wide, having 127 white marble columns 62 feet high and less than 4 feet apart. In the inner sanctuary was the many-breasted image supposedly dropped from heaven.

19:29 *Aristarchus.* Traveled later with Paul from Corinth to Jerusalem (20:3–4), and also accompanied Paul on the voyage from Jerusalem to Rome (27:1–2; Col 4:10).

19:31 *chief of Asia.* Greek *Asiarchon,* members of a council of men of wealth and influence elected to promote the worship of the emperor. Paul had friends in this highest circle.

‡19:33 *Alexander.* Pushed forward by the Jews either to make clear the disassociation of the Jews from the Christians and/or to accuse the Christians further of an offense against the Greeks. The crowd recognized that the Jews were not worshipers of Diana any more than the Christians.

19:35 *townclerk.* The secretary of the city who published the decisions of the civic assembly. He was the most important local official and the chief executive officer of the assembly, acting as go-between for Ephesus and the Roman authorities.

19:39 *lawful assembly.* The regular civil meeting ordinarily held three times a month.

20:1 *departed . . . into Macedonia.* Paul wanted to: (1) leave Ephesus, (2) preach in Troas on his way to Macedonia, (3) meet Titus at Troas with a report from Corinth (see 2 Cor 2:12–13) and (4) continue collecting the offering for Judea (see 1 Cor 16:1–4; 2 Cor 8:1–9:15; Rom 15:25–28).

20:2 *he had gone over those parts.* May cover a considerable period. He may have gone to Illyricum (see Rom 15:19) at this time.

20:3 *three months.* Probably a reference to the stay in Corinth, the capital of Achaia. These would be the winter months when ships did not sail regularly. Paul probably wrote Romans at this time (see Introduction to Romans: Occasion). *Jews laid wait for him.* The Jews were determined to take Paul's life; also, at this time he was carrying the offering for the Christians in Judea, so there would have been a temptation for theft as well. The port at Cenchrea would have provided a convenient place for Paul's enemies to detect him as he entered a ship to embark for Syria.

20:4 These men seem to be the delegates appointed to accompany Paul and the money given for the needy in Judea (see note on 2 Cor 8:23). Three were from Macedonia, two from Galatia and two from Asia. Luke may have joined them at Phi-

Derbe, and [c]Timotheus; and of Asia, [d]Tychicus
and [e]Trophimus.

From Philippi to Miletus

5 These going before tarried for us at Troas.
6 And we sailed away from Philippi after
[a]the days of unleavened bread, and came unto
them [b]to Troas in five days; where we abode
seven days.
7 And upon [a]the first *day* of the week,
when the disciples came together [b]to break
bread, Paul preached unto them, ready to depart on the morrow; and continued *his* speech
until midnight.
8 And there were many lights [a]in the upper
chamber, where they were gathered together.
9 And there sat in a window a certain
young man named Eutychus, being fallen into
a deep sleep: and as Paul was long preaching,
he sunk down with sleep, and fell down from
the third loft, and was taken up dead.
10 And Paul went down, and [a]fell on him,
and embracing *him* said, [b]Trouble not yourselves; for his life is in him.
11 When he therefore was come up *again,*
and had broken bread, and eaten, and talked a
long while, *even* till break of day, so he departed.

20:4 [c]ch. 16:1 [d]Eph. 6:21; Col. 4:7; 2 Tim. 4:12; Tit. 3:12 [e]ch. 21:29; 2 Tim. 4:20
20:6 [a]Ex. 12:14,15; 23:15 [b]ch. 16:8; 2 Cor. 2:12; 2 Tim. 4:13
20:7 [a]1 Cor. 16:2; Rev. 1:10 [b]ch. 2:42,46; 1 Cor. 10:16; 11:20
20:8 [a]ch. 1:13
20:10 [a]1 Ki. 17:21; 2 Ki. 4:34 [b]Mat. 9:24
20:16 [a]ch. 18:21; 19:21; 21:4,12 [b]ch. 24:17 [c]ch. 2:1; 1 Cor. 16:8
20:18 [a]ch. 18:19; 19:1,10

12 And they brought the young man alive,
and were not a little comforted.
13 ¶ And we went before to ship, and
sailed unto Assos, there intending to take in
Paul: for so had he appointed, minding himself
to go afoot.
14 And when he met with us at Assos, we
took him in, and came to Mitylene.
15 And we sailed thence, and came the
next *day* over against Chios; and the next *day*
we arrived at Samos, and tarried at Trogyllium;
and the next *day* we came to Miletus.
16 For Paul had determined to sail by Ephesus, because he would not spend the time in
Asia: for [a]he hasted, if it were possible for
him, [b]to be at Jerusalem [c]the day of Pentecost.

Paul and the Ephesian elders

17 And from Miletus he sent to Ephesus,
and called the elders of the church.
18 And when they were come to him, he
said unto them,
¶ Ye know, [a]from the first day that I came
into Asia, after what manner I have been with
you at all seasons,
19 Serving the Lord with all humility of
mind, and *with* many tears, and temptations,

lippi ("we sailed," v. 6; see note on 16:10). *Sopater.* May be the same as Sosipater (Rom 16:21). *Aristarchus.* See note on 19:29. *Secundus.* Not mentioned elsewhere. His name means "second," as Tertius (see Rom 16:22) means "third" and Quartus (see Rom 16:23) means "fourth." *Gaius of Derbe.* A Gaius from Macedonia was associated with Aristarchus (see 19:29), but the grouping of the names in pairs (after the reference to Sopater) indicates that this Gaius was associated with Roman Galatia and is different from the Macedonian Gaius. *Timotheus.* May have represented more than one particular church. He was from Lystra but had been responsible for working in other churches (1 Cor 16:10–11; Phil 2:19–23). He had been sent to Macedonia before Paul left Ephesus (19:22). *Tychicus.* A constant help to Paul, especially in association with the churches of Asia (Eph 6:21–22; Col 4:7–9; 2 Tim 4:12; Tit 3:12). *Trophimus.* Appears again in 21:29 (see 2 Tim 4:20). He was an Ephesian, and it is implied that he was a Gentile.

20:5 *Troas.* Was to be the rendezvous for Paul and those who went on ahead by sea from Neapolis, the seaport of Philippi (16:11). Paul and his immediate companions stayed in Philippi before sailing a week later.

20:6 *from Philippi.* From the seaport, Neapolis, about ten miles away. *days of unleavened bread.* Began with passover and lasted a week. Paul spent the period in Philippi. Formerly he had hoped to reach Jerusalem sooner (see 19:21), but now he hoped to arrive there for Pentecost (see 20:16). *in five days.* The voyage from Neapolis to Troas took five days. It had taken about two days the other direction (16:11). *seven days.* Although Paul was in a hurry to arrive at Jerusalem by Pentecost, he remained seven days at Troas. This might have been because of a ship schedule, but more likely the delay was in order to meet with the believers on the first day of the week to break bread.

20:7 *first day of the week.* Sunday. Although some maintain that they met on Saturday evening since the Jewish day began at six o'clock the previous evening, there is no indication that Luke is using the Jewish method of reporting time to tell of happenings in this Hellenistic city. *to break bread.* Here indicates the Lord's supper, since breaking bread was the expressed purpose for this formal gathering. The Lord's supper had been commanded (Luke 22:19), and it was observed regularly (see 2:42).

20:9 *Eutychus.* A name common among the freedman class (see note on 6:9).

20:10 *his life is in him.* As Peter had raised Tabitha (9:40), so Paul raised Eutychus.

20:13 *Assos.* On the opposite side of the peninsula from Troas—about 20 miles away by land. The coastline, however, was about 40 miles. Thus Paul was not far behind the ship that sailed around the peninsula.

20:14 *Mitylene.* After the first day of sailing, they put into this harbor on the southeast shore of the island of Lesbos.

20:15 *Chios.* The second night they spent off the shore of this larger island, which lay along the west coast of Asia Minor. *Samos.* Crossing the mouth of the bay that leads to Ephesus, they came on the third day to Samos, one of the most important islands in the Aegean. *Miletus.* Thirty miles south of Ephesus, the destination of the ship Paul was on. He would have had to change ships to put into Ephesus, which would have lost time (see v. 16). If he had come to Ephesus, he would have had to visit a number of families, which would have taken more time. If trouble should arise, such as the riot of a year ago (19:23–41), even more time would be lost. It could not be risked.

20:16 *the day of Pentecost.* Fifty days from passover. Five days plus seven days (v. 6) plus four days (vv. 13–15) had already gone by, leaving only about two-thirds of the time for the remainder of the trip.

20:17 *elders of the church.* The importance of the leadership of elders has been evident throughout Paul's ministry. He had delivered the famine gift from the church at Antioch to the elders of the Jerusalem church (11:30). He had appointed elders on his first missionary journey (see 14:23) and had addressed the holders of this office later in Philippi (Phil 1:1, "bishops"). He requested the Ephesian elders to meet with him on this solemn occasion (see v. 28). Some years later he wrote down instruction about the elders' qualifications (1 Tim 3; Tit 1).

20:19 *with many tears.* See v. 31. Paul's ministry at Ephesus was conducted with emotional fervency and a sense of urgency.

which befell me [a]by the lying in wait of the
Jews:
20 *And* how [a]I kept back nothing that was
profitable *unto you,* but have shewed you, and
have taught you publickly, and from house to
house,
21 [a]Testifying both to the Jews, and *also* to
the Greeks, [b]repentance toward God, and
faith toward our Lord Jesus Christ.
22 And now behold, [a]I go bound in the
spirit unto Jerusalem, not knowing the *things*
that shall befall me there:
23 Save that [a]the Holy Ghost witnesseth in
every city, saying that bonds and afflictions
[1]abide me.
24 But [a]none of these *things* move me,
neither count I my life dear unto myself, [b]so
that *I* might finish my course with joy, [c]and
the ministry, [d]which I have received of the
Lord Jesus, to testify the gospel of the grace of
God.
25 And now behold, [a]I know that ye all,
among whom I have gone preaching the kingdom of God, shall see my face no more.
26 Wherefore I take you to record this day,
that I *am* [a]pure from the blood of all *men.*
27 For [a]I have not shunned to declare unto
you all [b]the counsel of God.
28 [a]Take heed therefore unto yourselves,
and to all the flock, over the which the Holy
Ghost [b]hath made you overseers, to feed the
church of God, [c]which he hath purchased
[d]with his own blood.
29 For I know this, that after my departing
[a]shall grievous wolves enter in among you, not
sparing the flock.
30 Also [a]of your own selves shall men
arise, speaking perverse *things,* to draw away
disciples after them.
31 Therefore watch, and remember, that
[a]*by the space of* three years I ceased not to
warn every one night and day with tears.
32 And now, brethren, I commend you to

20:19 [a]ver. 3
20:20 [a]ver. 27
20:21 [a]ch. 18:5 [b]Mark 1:15; Luke 24:27; ch. 2:38
20:22 [a]ch. 19:21
20:23 [1]Or, *wait for me* [a]ch. 21:4,11; 1 Thes. 3:3
20:24 [a]ch. 21:13; Rom. 8:35; 2 Cor. 4:16 [b]2 Tim. 4:7 [c]ch. 1:17; 2 Cor. 4:1 [d]Gal. 1:1; Tit. 1:3
20:25 [a]ver. 38; Rom. 15:23
20:26 [a]ch. 18:6; 2 Cor. 7:2
20:27 [a]ver. 20 [b]Luke 7:30; John 15:15; Eph. 1:11
20:28 [a]1 Tim. 4:16; 1 Pet. 5:2 [b]1 Cor. 12:28 [c]Eph. 1:7,14; Col. 1:14; Heb. 9:12; 1 Pet. 1:19; Rev. 5:9 [d]See Heb. 9:14
20:29 [a]Mat. 7:15; 2 Pet. 2:1
20:30 [a]1 Tim. 1:20; 1 John 2:19
20:31 [a]ch. 19:10
20:32 [a]Heb. 13:9 [b]ch. 9:31 [c]ch. 26:18; Eph. 1:18; Col. 1:12; 3:24; Heb. 9:15; 1 Pet. 1:4
20:33 [a]1 Sam. 12:3; 1 Cor. 9:12; 2 Cor. 7:2; 11:9; 12:17
20:34 [a]ch. 18:3; 1 Cor. 4:12; 1 Thes. 2:9; 2 Thes. 3:8
20:35 [a]Rom. 15:1; 1 Cor. 9:12; 2 Cor. 11:9,12; 12:13; Eph. 4:28; 1 Thes. 4:11; 5:14; 2 Thes. 3:8
20:36 [a]ch. 7:60; 21:5

God, and [a]to the word of his grace, which is
able [b]to build *you* up, and to give you [c]an inheritance among all them which are sanctified.
33 [a]I have coveted no *man's* silver, or gold,
or apparel.
34 Yea, ye yourselves know, [a]that these
hands have ministered unto my necessities,
and to them that were with me.
35 I have shewed you all *things,* [a]how that
so labouring *ye* ought to support the weak, and
to remember the words of the Lord Jesus, how
he said, It is more blessed to give than to receive.
36 ¶ And when he had thus spoken, he
[a]kneeled down, and prayed with them all.
37 And *they* all wept sore, and [a]fell on
Paul's neck, and kissed him,
38 Sorrowing most *of all* for the words
[a]which he spake, that they should see his face
no more. And they accompanied him unto the
ship.

Paul travels to Cesarea

21 And it came to pass, that after we
were gotten from them, and had
launched, we came with a straight course unto
Cos, and the *day* following unto Rhodes, and
from thence unto Patara:
2 And finding a ship sailing over unto
Phenicia, we went aboard, and set forth.
3 Now when we had discovered Cyprus,
we left it on the left hand, and sailed into Syria, and landed at Tyre: for there the ship was
to unlade *her* burden.
4 And finding disciples, we tarried there
seven days: [a]who said to Paul through the
Spirit, that *he* should not go up to Jerusalem.
5 And when we had accomplished *those*
days, we departed and went *our way;* and *they*
all brought us on our way, with wives and chil-

20:37 [a]Gen. 45:14; 46:29 **20:38** [a]ver. 25 **21:4** [a]ver. 12; ch. 20:23

20:22 *bound in the spirit.* Paul did not go to Jerusalem against the direction of the Spirit, as some have suggested, but because of the guidance of the Spirit. People pleaded with him not to go (21:4,12), not because the Spirit prohibited his going but because the Spirit revealed the capture that awaited him there (21:11–12).

20:25 *shall see my face no more.* Not a message from God but what Paul anticipated. He had been mistaken before in his plans: He had intended to stay in Ephesus until Pentecost, but he had to leave earlier (see v. 1; 1 Cor 16:8–9). His prophetic power was not used to foresee his own future, just as his healing power was not used to heal his own disease (see 2 Cor 12:7–9). As it turned out, it seems that Paul did revisit Ephesus (see 1 Tim 1:3).

‡20:28 *overseers.* The "elders" (v. 17) were called "overseers" and told to pastor ("shepherd") the flock—demonstrating that the same men could be called "elders," "overseers" or "pastors." *his own blood.* Lit. "the blood of his own one," a term of endearment (such as "his own dear one," referring to His own Son).

20:31 *three years.* See note on 19:10.

20:32 *are sanctified.* Positional sanctification (see 26:18; see also note on 1 Cor 1:2).

20:34 *ministered unto my necessities.* Paul had worked in Thessalonica (1 Thes 2:9) and Corinth (Acts 18:3).

20:35 *remember the words of the Lord Jesus.* A formula regularly used in the early church to introduce a quotation from Jesus (1 Clement 46:7). This is a rare instance of a saying of Jesus not found in the canonical Gospels.

‡21:1 *a straight course unto Cos.* Favorable winds took them to a stopping place for the night at this island. *Rhodes.* The leading city on the island of Rhodes, once noted for its harbor colossus, one of the seven wonders of the ancient world (but demolished over two centuries before Paul arrived there). It took them a day to get to Rhodes. *Patara.* On the southern coast of Lycia. Paul changed ships from a vessel that hugged the shore of Asia Minor to one going directly to Tyre and Phoenicia.

21:3 *Cyprus.* See 13:4. *Tyre.* Paul had passed through this Phoenician area at least once before (15:3; cf. Mark 7:24).

‡21:4 *seven days.* These, added to the 29 days since the passover in Philippi, would leave only two weeks until Pentecost. *said to Paul . . . that he should not go up to Jerusalem.* The Spirit warned of the coming trials in store for Paul at Jerusalem. Because of these warnings, Paul's brothers urged him not to go on, knowing that trials lay ahead. But Paul felt "bound in the spirit" to go (20:22).

dren, till *we were* out of the city: and [a]we
kneeled down on the shore, and prayed.
6 And when we had taken our leave one of
another, we took ship; and they returned
[a]home *again.*
7 And when we had finished *our* course
from Tyre, we came to Ptolemais, and saluted the brethren, and abode with them one
day.
8 And the next day we that were of Paul's
company departed, and came unto Cesarea:
and we entered into the house of Philip [a]the
evangelist, [b]which was *one* of the seven; and
abode with him.
9 And the same *man* had four daughters,
virgins, [a]which did prophesy.
10 And as we tarried *there* many days,
there came down from Judea a certain prophet, named [a]Agabus.
11 And when he was come unto us, he
took Paul's girdle, and bound his *own* hands
and feet, and said, Thus saith the Holy Ghost,
[a]So shall the Jews at Jerusalem bind the man
that oweth this girdle, and shall deliver *him*
into the hands of the Gentiles.
12 And when we heard these *things,* both
we, and they of that place, besought him not
to go up to Jerusalem.
13 Then Paul answered, [a]What mean ye to
weep and to break mine heart? for I am ready
not to be bound only, but also to die at Jerusalem for the name of the Lord Jesus.
14 And when he would not be persuaded,
we ceased, saying, [a]The will of the Lord be
done.
15 And after those days we took up our carriages, and went up to Jerusalem.
16 There went with us also *certain* of the
disciples of Cesarea, and brought *with them*
one Mnason of Cyprus, an old disciple, with
whom we should lodge.

21:5 [a]ch. 20:36
21:6 [a]John 1:11
21:8 [a]Eph. 4:11; 2 Tim. 4:5 [b]ch. 6:5; 8:26,40
21:9 [a]Joel 2:28; ch. 2:17
21:10 [a]ch. 11:28
21:11 [a]ver. 33; ch. 20:23
21:13 [a]ch. 20:24
21:14 [a]Mat. 6:10; 26:42; Luke 11:2; 22:42
21:17 [a]ch. 15:4
21:18 [a]ch. 15:13; Gal. 1:19; 2:9
21:19 [a]ch. 15:4,12; Rom. 15:18,19 [b]ch. 1:17; 20:24
21:20 [a]ch. 22:3; Rom. 10:2; Gal. 1:14
21:24 [a]Num. 6:2,13,18; ch. 18:18
21:25 [a]ch. 15:20,29
21:26 [a]ch. 24:18 [b]Num. 6:13

Paul in Jerusalem

17 ¶ [a]And when we were come to Jerusalem, the brethren received us gladly.
18 And the *day* following Paul went in
with us unto [a]James; and all the elders were
present.
19 And when he had saluted them, [a]he declared particularly what *things* God had
wrought among the Gentiles [b]by his ministry.
20 And when they heard *it,* they glorified
the Lord, and said unto him, Thou seest,
brother, how many thousands of Jews there
are which believe; and they are all [a]zealous of
the law:
21 And they are informed of thee, that
thou teachest all the Jews which are among
the Gentiles to forsake Moses, saying that they
ought not to circumcise *their* children, neither
to walk after the customs.
22 What is it therefore? the multitude
must needs come together: for they will hear
that thou art come.
23 Do therefore this that we say to thee:
We have four men which have a vow on them;
24 Them take, and purify thyself with
them, and be at charges with them, that they
may [a]shave *their* heads: and all may know that
those things, whereof they were informed
concerning thee, are nothing; but *that* thou
thyself also walkest orderly, and keepest the
law.
25 As touching the Gentiles which believe,
[a]we have written and concluded that they observe no such *thing,* save only that they keep
themselves from things offered to idols, and
from blood, and from strangled, and from fornication.
26 Then Paul took the men, and the next
day purifying himself with them [a]entered into
the temple, [b]to signify the accomplishment of

21:7 *Ptolemais.* The modern city of Acco, north of and across the bay from mount Carmel. It was one day's journey from Tyre on the north and another 35 miles to Cesarea on the south.

21:8 *Cesarea.* A Gentile city, the capital of Roman Judea (see note on 10:1). *Philip the evangelist.* Philip's evangelistic work may have focused on Cesarea for almost 25 years (see note on 8:40). "Evangelist" is a title used only here and in Eph 4:11; 2 Tim 4:5.

21:9 *four daughters, virgins.* They may have been dedicated in a special way to serving the Lord. *which did prophesy*. See 1 Cor 11:5; 12:8–10; cf. Luke 2:36. For OT prophetesses see Ex 15:20; Judg 4:4; 2 Ki 22:14; Neh 6:14.

21:10 *prophet, named Agabus.* Evidently he held the office of prophet, as Philip held the office of evangelist (v. 8). This is the same prophet who had been in Antioch prophesying the coming famine in Jerusalem some 15 years earlier (11:27–29).

21:12 *we, and they of that place.* Now Luke, in the company of travelers with Paul, joins in urging Paul not to go to Jerusalem.

21:14 *will of the Lord be done.* May mean that they finally recognized that it was the Lord's will for Paul to go to Jerusalem.

21:16 *Mnason.* Must have been a disciple of some means to be able to accommodate Paul and a group of about nine men traveling with him.

21:17 *we were come to Jerusalem.* No more than a day or two before Pentecost. *the brethren received us gladly.* May indicate the grateful reception of the offering as well.

21:18 *James.* The brother of the Lord, author of the letter of James and leader of the church in Jerusalem (see Gal 1:19; 2:9). He is called an apostle but was not one of the twelve.

‡21:23 *a vow.* They were evidently under the temporary Nazarite vow and became unclean before the completion time of the vow (perhaps from contact with a dead body); cf. Num 6:2–12.

21:24 *purify thyself.* In some instances the purification rites included the offering of sacrifices. Such rites were observed by choice by some Jewish Christians but were not required of Christians, whether Jew or Gentile. *be at charges with them.* Paul's part in sponsoring these men would include (1) paying part or all of the expenses of the sacrificial victims (in this case eight pigeons and four lambs, Num 6:9–12) and (2) going to the temple to notify the priest when their days of purification would be fulfilled so the priests would be prepared to sacrifice their offerings (v. 26). *keepest the law.* Paul had earlier taken a vow himself (18:18), he had been a Jew to the Jews (see 1 Cor 9:20–21), and Timothy had been circumcised (16:3). However, Paul was very careful not to sacrifice Christian principle in any act of obedience to the law (he would not have Titus circumcised, Gal 2:3).

the days of purification, until that an offering
should be offered for every one of them.

Paul's arrest

27 And when the seven days were almost
ended, [a]the Jews which were of Asia, when
they saw him in the temple, stirred up all the
people, and [b]laid hands on him,
28 Crying out, Men of Israel, help: This is
the man, [a]that teacheth all *men* every where
against the people, and the law, and this place:
and further brought Greeks also into the temple, and hath polluted this holy place.
29 (For they had seen before with him in
the city [a]Trophimus an Ephesian, whom they
supposed that Paul had brought into the temple.)
30 And [a]all the city was moved, and the
people ran together: and they took Paul, and
drew him out of the temple: and forthwith the
doors were shut.
31 And as *they* went about to kill him, tidings came unto the chief captain of the band,
that all Jerusalem was in an uproar.
32 [a]Who immediately took soldiers and
centurions, and ran down unto them: and
when they saw the chief captain and the soldiers, they left beating of Paul.
33 Then the chief captain came near, and
took him, and [a]commanded *him* to be bound
with two chains; and demanded who he was,
and what he had done.
34 And some cried one *thing,* some another, among the multitude: and when he could
not know the certainty for the tumult, he commanded him to be carried into the castle.
35 And when he came upon the stairs, so it
was, that he was borne of the soldiers for the
violence of the people.
36 For the multitude of the people followed *after,* crying, [a]Away with him.

Paul's defence

37 ¶ And as Paul was to be led into the castle, he said unto the chief captain, May I speak
unto thee? Who said, Canst thou speak Greek?
38 [a]Art not thou *that* Egyptian, which before these days madest an uproar, and leddest
out into the wilderness four thousand men
that were murderers?
39 But Paul said, [a]I am a man *which am* a
Jew of Tarsus, *a city* in Cilicia, a citizen of no
mean city: and, I beseech thee, suffer me to
speak unto the people.
40 And when he had given *him* licence,
Paul stood on the stairs, and [a]beckoned with
the hand unto the people. And when there
was made a great silence, he spake unto *them*
in the Hebrew tongue, saying,

22 Men, [a]brethren, and fathers, hear
ye my defence *which I make* now
unto you.
2 (And when they heard that he spake in
the Hebrew tongue to them, they kept the
more silence: and he saith,)
3 [a]I am verily a man *which am* a Jew, born
in Tarsus, *a city* in Cilicia, yet brought up in
this city [b]at the feet of [c]Gamaliel, *and* taught
[d]according to the perfect manner of the law of
the fathers, and [e]was zealous towards God, [f]as
ye all are this day.
4 [a]And I persecuted this way unto the

21:27 [a]ch. 24:18 [b]ch. 26:21
21:28 [a]ch. 24:5,6
21:29 [a]ch. 20:4
21:30 [a]ch. 26:21
21:32 [a]ch. 23:27; 24:7
21:33 [a]ver. 11; ch. 20:23
21:36 [a]Luke 23:18; John 19:15; ch. 22:22
21:38 [a]See ch. 5:36
21:39 [a]ch. 9:11; 22:3
21:40 [a]ch. 12:17
22:1 [a]ch. 7:2
22:3 [a]ch. 21:39; 2 Cor. 11:22; Phil. 3:5 [b]Deut. 33:3 [c]ch. 5:34 [d]ch. 26:5 [e]ch. 21:20; Gal. 1:14 [f]Rom. 10:2
22:4 [a]ch. 8:3; 26:9-11; Phil. 3:6; 1 Tim. 1:13

21:27 *seven days.* Cf. Num 6:9. These were the days required for purification, shaving their heads at the altar, the sacrifice of a sin offering and burnt offering for each, and announcing the completion to the priests. *Jews which were of Asia.* Paul had suffered already from the hands of Asian Jews (20:19).

21:28 *brought Greeks also into the temple.* Explicitly forbidden according to inscribed stone markers (still in existence). Any Gentiles found within the bounds of the court of Israel would be killed. But there is no evidence that Paul had brought anyone other than Jews into the area.

‡21:29 *Trophimus.* Paul probably would not have taken him into the forbidden area. If he had, they should have attacked Trophimus rather than Paul.

21:30 *doors were shut.* By order of the temple officer to prevent further trouble inside the sacred precincts.

21:31 *chief captain.* Greek *chiliarch,* a commander of 1,000 (a regiment), Claudius Lysias by name (23:26), who was stationed at the Fortress of Antonia (see note on v. 37).

21:32 *centurions.* Since the plural is used, it is likely that at least two centurions and 200 soldiers were involved.

21:33 *two chains.* Probably his hands were chained to a soldier on either side.

21:37 *castle.* The Fortress of Antonia was connected to the northern end of the temple area by two flights of steps. The tower overlooked the temple area.

21:38 *that Egyptian, which . . . madest an uproar.* Josephus tells of an Egyptian false prophet who some years earlier had led 4,000 (Josephus, through a misreading of a Greek capital letter, says 30,000) out to the mount of Olives. Roman soldiers killed hundreds, but the leader escaped. *men that were murderers.* The Greek here is a loanword from Latin *sicarii,* meaning "dagger-men," who were violent assassins.

‡21:39 *no mean city.* The Greek means that Tarsus was not an obscure or insignificant city. See note on 22:3.

21:40 *the Hebrew tongue.* More likely Aramaic than Hebrew, since Aramaic was the most commonly used language among Palestinian Jews.

22:1 *brethren.* See note on 11:1.

22:2 *the Hebrew tongue.* See note on 21:40. Actually, if he had spoken in Hebrew, they would have become quieter in order not to miss a single word, because it would have been more difficult for them to understand.

22:3 *born in Tarsus.* Paul had citizenship in Tarsus (21:39) as well as being a Roman citizen. "No mean city" (21:39) was used by Euripides to describe Athens. Tarsus was 10 miles inland on the Cydnus River and 30 miles from the mountains, which were cut by a deep, narrow gorge called the Cilician Gates. It was an important commercial center, university city and crossroads of travel. *brought up in this city.* Paul must have come to Jerusalem at an early age. Another translation ("brought up in this city at the feet of Gamaliel, being thoroughly trained according to the law of our fathers") would suggest that Paul came to Jerusalem when he was old enough to begin training under Gamaliel. *Gamaliel.* The most honored rabbi of the first century. Possibly he was the grandson of Hillel (see also 5:34–40).

22:4 *I persecuted this way.* See 9:1–4.

death, binding and delivering into prisons both men and women.

5 As also the high priest doth bear me witness, and [a]all the estate of the elders: [b]from whom also I received letters unto the brethren, and went to Damascus, to bring them which were there, bound unto Jerusalem, for to be punished.

6 And [a]it came to pass that, as I made my journey, and was come nigh unto Damascus about noon, suddenly there shone from heaven a great light round about me.

7 And I fell unto the ground, and heard a voice saying unto me, Saul, Saul, why persecutest thou me?

8 And I answered, Who art thou, Lord? And he said unto me, I am Jesus of Nazareth, whom thou persecutest.

9 And [a]they that were with me saw indeed the light, and were afraid; but they heard not the voice of him that spake to me.

10 And I said, What shall I do, Lord? And the Lord said unto me, Arise, and go into Damascus; and there it shall be told thee of all *things* which are appointed for thee to do.

11 And when I could not see for the glory of that light, being led by the hand of them that were with me, I came into Damascus.

12 And [a]one Ananias, a devout man according to the law, [b]having a good report of all the [c]Jews which dwelt *there,*

13 Came unto me, and stood, and said unto me, Brother Saul, receive thy sight. And the same hour I looked up upon him.

14 And he said, [a]The God of our fathers [b]hath chosen thee, that *thou* shouldest know his will, and [c]see [d]*that* Just One, and [e]shouldest hear the voice of his mouth.

15 [a]For thou shalt be his witness unto all men of [b]what thou hast seen and heard.

16 And now why tarriest thou? arise, and be baptized, [a]and wash away thy sins, [b]calling on the name of the Lord.

17 And [a]it came to pass that, when I was come again to Jerusalem, even while I prayed in the temple, I was in a trance;

18 And [a]saw him saying unto me, [b]Make haste, and get *thee* quickly out of Jerusalem: for they will not receive thy testimony concerning me.

19 And I said, Lord, [a]they know that I imprisoned and [b]beat in every synagogue them that believed on thee:

20 [a]And when the blood of thy martyr Stephen was shed, I also was standing by, and [b]consenting unto his death, and kept the raiment of them that slew him.

21 And he said unto me, Depart: [a]for I will send thee far hence unto the Gentiles.

22 ¶ And they gave him audience unto this word, and *then* lift up their voices, and said, [a]Away with such *a fellow* from the earth: for it is not fit that [b]he should live.

23 And as they cried out, and cast *off their* clothes, and threw dust into the air,

24 The chief captain commanded him to be brought into the castle, and bade that he should be examined by scourging; that he might know wherefore they cried so against him.

25 And as they bound him with thongs, Paul said unto the centurion that stood *by,* [a]Is it lawful for you to scourge a man *that is* a Roman, and uncondemned?

26 When the centurion heard *that,* he went and told the chief captain, saying, Take heed what thou doest: for this man is a Roman.

27 Then the chief captain came, and said unto him, Tell me, art thou a Roman? He said, Yea.

28 And the chief captain answered, With a great sum obtained I this freedom. And Paul said, But I was *free* born.

22:5 [a]Luke 22:66; ch. 4:5 [b]ch. 9:2; 26:10,12
22:6 [a]ch. 9:3; 26:12,13
22:9 [a]Dan. 10:7; ch. 9:7
22:12 [a]ch. 9:17 [b]ch. 10:22 [c]1 Tim. 3:7
22:14 [a]ch. 3:13; 5:30 [b]ch. 9:15; 26:16 [c]1 Cor. 9:1; 15:8 [d]ch. 3:14; 7:52 [e]1 Cor. 11:23; Gal. 1:12
22:15 [a]ch. 23:11 [b]ch. 4:20; 26:16
22:16 [a]ch. 2:38; Heb. 10:22 [b]ch. 9:14; Rom. 10:13
22:17 [a]ch. 9:26; 2 Cor. 12:2
22:18 [a]ver. 14 [b]Mat. 10:14
22:19 [a]ver. 4; ch. 8:3 [b]Mat. 10:17
22:20 [a]ch. 7:58 [b]Luke 11:48; ch. 8:1; Rom. 1:32
22:21 [a]ch. 9:15; 13:2,46,47; 18:6; 26:17; Rom. 1:5; 11:13; 15:16; Gal. 1:15,16; 2:7,8; Eph. 3:7,8; 1 Tim. 2:7; 2 Tim. 1:11
22:22 [a]ch. 21:36 [b]ch. 25:24
22:25 [a]ch. 16:37

22:5 *high priest.* Caiaphas, the high priest over 20 years earlier, was now dead, and Ananias was high priest (see 23:2); but the records of the high priest would show Paul's testimony to be true.
22:6 *about noon.* A detail not included in the earlier account (9:1–22).
22:8 *Who art thou, Lord?* See note on 9:5. *persecutest.* See note on 9:4.
22:9 *they heard not the voice.* They heard the sound (9:7) but did not understand what was said.
22:12 *Ananias, a devout man according to the law.* Important to this audience (see note on Luke 1:6).
22:14 *see that Just One.* Cf. 3:14. To see the resurrected Jesus was all-important to Paul (see 26:16; 1 Cor 9:1; 15:8). It was that experience that had convinced him of the truth of the gospel and that became the foundation of his theology.
22:16 *wash away thy sins.* Baptism is the outward sign of an inward work of grace. The reality and the symbol are closely associated in the NT (see 2:38; Tit 3:5; 1 Pet 3:21). The outward rite, however, does not produce the inward grace (cf. Rom 2:28–29; Eph 2:8–9; Phil 3:4–9). See note on Rom 6:3–4.
22:17 *when I was come again to Jerusalem.* Refers to the visit described in 9:26; Gal 1:17–18. *in the temple, I was in a trance.* See Peter's trance (10:10; 11:5; cf. 2 Cor 12:3). Paul was not a blasphemer of the temple but continued to hold it in high honor.
22:20 *standing by, and consenting.* Does not necessarily mean that Paul had to be a member of the Sanhedrin, though some have thought so (see note on 26:10). He could show his approval by allowing them to put their cloaks at his feet.
22:24 *chief captain.* See note on 21:31. *castle.* See note on 21:37. *scourging.* Not with the rod, as at Philippi (16:22–24), but with the scourge, a merciless instrument of torture. It was legal to use it to force a confession from a slave or alien but never from a Roman citizen. The scourge consisted of a whip of leather thongs with pieces of bone or metal attached to the ends.
22:25 *bound him with thongs.* The Greek word used for tying a person to a post for whipping. *centurion.* See note on 10:1. *Roman.* According to Roman law, all Roman citizens were assured exclusion from all degrading forms of punishment: beating with rods, scourging, crucifixion.
22:28 *With a great sum obtained.* There were three ways to obtain Roman citizenship: (1) receive it as a reward for some outstanding service to Rome; (2) buy it at a considerable price; (3) be born into a family of Roman citizens. How Paul's father or an earlier ancestor had gained citizenship, no one knows. By

29 Then straightway they departed from him which should have [1]examined him: and the chief captain also was afraid, after he knew that he was a Roman, and because he had bound him.

Before the Sanhedrin

30 ¶ On the morrow, because he would have known the certainty wherefore he was accused of the Jews, he loosed him from *his* bands, and commanded the chief priests and all their council to appear, and brought Paul down, and set *him* before them.

23 And Paul, earnestly beholding the council, said, Men *and* brethren, [a]I have lived in all good conscience before God until this day.

2 And the high priest Ananias commanded them that stood by him [a]to smite him on the mouth.

3 Then said Paul unto him, God shall smite thee, *thou* whited wall: for sittest thou to judge me after the law, and [a]commandest me to be smitten contrary to the law?

4 And they that stood by said, Revilest thou God's high priest?

5 Then said Paul, [a]I wist not, brethren, that he was the high priest: for it is written, [b]Thou shalt not speak evil of the ruler of thy people.

6 But when Paul perceived that the one part were Sadducees, and the other Pharisees, he cried out in the council, Men *and* brethren, [a]I am a Pharisee, the son of a Pharisee: [b]of the hope and resurrection of the dead I am called in question.

7 And when he had so said, there arose a dissension between the Pharisees and the Sadducees: and the multitude was divided.

8 [a]For the Sadducees say that there is no resurrection, neither angel nor spirit: but the Pharisees confess both.

9 And there arose a great cry: and the scribes *that were* of the Pharisees' part arose, and strove, saying, [a]We find no evil in this man: but [b]if a spirit or an angel hath spoken to him, [c]let us not fight against God.

10 And when there arose a great dissension, the chief captain, fearing lest Paul should have been pulled in pieces of them, commanded the soldiers to go down, and to take him by force from among them, and to bring *him* into the castle.

The plot to kill Paul

11 ¶ And [a]the night following the Lord stood by him, and said, Be of good cheer, Paul: for as thou hast testified of me in Jerusalem, so must thou bear witness also at Rome.

12 And when it was day, [a]certain of the Jews banded together, and bound themselves [1]under a curse, saying that *they* would neither eat nor drink till they had killed Paul.

13 And they were more *than* forty which had made this conspiracy.

14 And they came to the chief priests and elders, and said, We have bound ourselves under a great curse, that *we* will eat nothing until we have slain Paul.

15 Now therefore ye with the council signify to the chief captain that he bring him down unto you to morrow, as though ye would inquire something more perfectly concerning him: and we, or ever he come near, are ready to kill him.

16 And when Paul's sister's son heard of *their* lying in wait, he went and entered into the castle, and told Paul.

17 Then Paul called one of the centurions unto *him,* and said, Bring this young man unto the chief captain: for he hath a certain *thing* to tell him.

18 So he took him, and brought *him* to the chief captain, and said, Paul the prisoner called me unto *him,* and prayed *me* to bring this young man unto thee, who hath something to say unto thee.

22:29 [1]Or, *tortured him*
23:1 [a]ch. 24:16; 1 Cor. 4:4; 2 Cor. 1:12; 4:2; 2 Tim. 1:3; Heb. 13:18
23:2 [a]1 Ki. 22:24; Jer. 20:2; John 18:22
23:3 [a]Lev. 19:35; Deut. 25:1,2; John 7:51
23:5 [a]ch. 24:17 [b]Ex. 22:28; Eccl. 10:20; 2 Pet. 2:10; Jude 8
23:6 [a]ch. 26:5; Phil. 3:5 [b]ch. 24:15,21; 26:6; 28:20
23:8 [a]Mat. 22:23; Mark 12:18; Luke 20:27
23:9 [a]ch. 25:25; 26:31 [b]ch. 22:7,17,18 [c]ch. 5:39
23:11 [a]ch. 18:9; 27:23,24
23:12 [1]Or, *with an oath of execration* [a]ver. 21,30; ch. 25:3

171 B.C. a large number of Jews were citizens of Tarsus, and in the time of Pompey (106–48) some of these could have received Roman citizenship as well. Cf. 16:37.

22:30 *he loosed him.* Paul was no longer bound, and presumably he would have been free completely if the council had not wished to detain him. *chief priests.* Those of the high priestly line of descent (mainly Sadducees), but the council now included a considerable number of Pharisees. These men constituted the ruling body of the Jews. The Jewish court was respected by the Roman governor, whose approval had to be obtained before sentencing to capital punishment.

23:1 *council.* See note on 5:21. *brethren.* Fellow Jews (see note on 11:1). *good conscience.* A consistent claim of Paul.

23:2 *Ananias.* High priest A.D. 47–59, son of Nebedaeus. He is not to be confused with the high priest Annas (A.D. 6–15; see note on Luke 3:2). Ananias was noted for cruelty and violence. When the revolt against Rome broke out, he was assassinated by his own people.

‡23:3 *whited wall.* Whitewashed, having an attractive exterior but filled with unclean contents, such as tombs holding dead bodies (see Mat 23:27); or walls that look substantial but fall before the winds (see Ezek 13:10–12). It is a metaphor for a hypocrite.

‡23:5 *I wist not, brethren, that he was the high priest.* Paul's unawareness is explained in different ways: 1. Paul had poor eyesight (suggested by such passages as Gal 4:15; 6:11) and failed to see that the one who presided was the high priest. 2. He failed to discern that the one who presided was the high priest because on some occasions others had sat in his place. 3. He was using pure irony: A true high priest would not give such an order. 4. He refused to acknowledge that Ananias was the high priest under these circumstances.

23:6 *Sadducees.* See notes on 4:1; Mat 3:7; Mark 12:18; Luke 20:27. They denied the resurrection and angels and spirits (v. 8). *Pharisees.* See notes on Mat 3:7; Mark 2:16; Luke 5:17.

23:10 *chief captain.* See note on 21:31. *castle.* See note on 21:37.

23:11 *the Lord stood by him.* In times of crisis and need for strength, Paul was given help (see 18:9; 22:18; 27:23).

‡23:12 *bound themselves under a curse.* Under an oath. Probably these were from the Zealots or the "terrorists" (see note on 21:38) later responsible for revolt against Rome.

23:17 *centurions.* See note on 10:1. *chief captain.* See note on 21:31.

19 Then the chief captain took him by the hand, and went *with him* aside privately, and asked *him,* What is that thou hast to tell me?

20 And he said, [a]The Jews have agreed to desire thee that thou wouldest bring down Paul to morrow into the council, as though they would inquire somewhat of him more perfectly.

21 But do not thou yield unto them: for there lie in wait for him of them moe *than* forty men, which have bound themselves with an oath, that *they* will neither eat nor drink till they have killed him: and now are they ready, looking for a promise from thee.

22 So the chief captain then let the young man depart, and charged *him, See thou* tell no *man* that thou hast shewed these *things* to me.

23 And he called unto *him* two centurions, saying, Make ready two hundred soldiers to go to Cesarea, and horsemen threescore *and* ten, and spearmen two hundred, at the third hour of the night;

24 And provide *them* beasts, that they may set Paul on, and bring *him* safe unto Felix the governor.

25 And he wrote a letter after this manner:

26 ¶ Claudius Lysias unto the most excellent governor Felix *sendeth* greeting.

27 [a]This man was taken of the Jews, and should have been killed of them: then came I with an army, and rescued him, having understood that he was a Roman.

28 [a]And when I would have known the cause wherefore they accused him, I brought him forth into their council:

29 Whom I perceived to be accused [a]of questions of their law, [b]but to have nothing laid to his charge worthy of death or of bonds.

30 And [a]when it was told me how that the Jews laid wait for the man, I sent straightway to thee, and [b]gave commandment to *his* accusers also to say before thee what *they had* against him. Farewell.

23:20 [a]ver. 12; ch. 20:3
23:27 [a]ch. 21:33; 24:7
23:28 [a]ch. 22:30
23:29 [a]ch. 18:15; 25:19
23:29 [b]ch. 26:31
23:30 [a]ver. 20 [b]ch. 24:8; 25:6
23:34 [a]ch. 21:39
23:35 [a]ch. 24:1,10; 25:16 [b]Mat. 27:27
24:1 [a]ch. 21:27 [b]ch. 23:2,30,35; 25:2

Paul taken to Cesarea

31 ¶ Then the soldiers, as it was commanded them, took Paul, and brought *him* by night to Antipatris.

32 On the morrow they left the horsemen to go with him, and returned to the castle:

33 Who, when they came to Cesarea, and delivered the epistle to the governor, presented Paul also before him.

34 And when the governor had read *the letter,* he asked of what province he was: and when he understood that *he was* of [a]Cilicia;

35 [a]I will hear thee, said he, when thine accusers are also come. And he commanded him to be kept in [b]Herod's judgment hall.

Paul tried before Felix

24 And after [a]five days [b]Ananias the high priest descended with the elders, and *with* a certain orator *named* Tertullus, who informed the governor against Paul.

2 And when he was called *forth,* Tertullus began to accuse *him,* saying,

¶ Seeing that by thee we enjoy great quietness, and that very worthy deeds are done unto this nation by thy providence,

3 We accept *it* always, and in all places, most noble Felix, with all thankfulness.

4 Notwithstanding, that I be not further te-

23:22 *tell no man.* For the boy's own safety and because of the commander's plans to transfer Paul under cover of night (see v. 23).

23:23 *soldiers . . . horsemen . . . spearmen.* Heavily armed infantry, cavalry and lightly armed soldiers. The commander assigned 470 men to protect Paul, the Roman citizen (cf. 22:25–29)—but the Greek for "spearmen" is an obscure word and could perhaps be translated "additional mounts and pack animals."

23:27 *having understood that he was a Roman.* Inserted to gain the commander's favor with Rome, but not a true statement, because the commander did not learn of Paul's citizenship until he was about to scourge him to gain information.

23:31 *Antipatris.* Rebuilt by Herod the Great and named for his father. It was a military post between Samaria and Judea—30 miles from Jerusalem.

23:33 *Cesarea.* The headquarters of Roman rule for Samaria and Judea—28 miles from Antipatris.

23:34 *he.* Antonius Felix. The emperor Claudius had appointed him governor of Judea C. A.D. 52, a time when Felix's brother was the emperor's favorite minister. The brothers had formerly been slaves, then freedmen, then high officials in government. The historian Tacitus said of Felix, "He held the power of a tyrant with the disposition of a slave." He married three queens in succession, one of whom was Drusilla (see note on 24:24). *of Cilicia.* If Paul had come from a province nearby, Felix might have turned him over for trial under another's jurisdiction.

23:35 *Herod's judgment hall.* Erected as a royal residence by Herod the Great but now used as a Roman government center (praetorium)—the place for the official business of the emperor and/or to house personnel directly responsible to the emperor. Praetoria were located in Rome (Phil 1:13), Ephesus, Jerusalem (John 18:28), Cesarea and other parts of the empire.

24:1 *after five days.* After the departure from Jerusalem. This would allow just enough time for a messenger to go from Cesarea to Jerusalem, the council to appoint their representatives, and the appointees to make the return journey to Cesarea. *Ananias.* See note on 23:2. The high priest himself made the 60-mile journey to supervise the case personally. *elders.* The council was made up of 71 elders. The designation was used of both the religious and the political councils. See notes on Ex 3:16; 2 Sam 3:17; Joel 1:2; Mat 15:2. *orator.* In a court trial one trained in forensic rhetoric would serve as an attorney at law. *Tertullus.* A common variant of the name Tertius. Possibly he was a Roman but more likely a Hellenistic Jew familiar with the procedures of the Roman court.

24:2–3 *great quietness . . . with all thankfulness.* The expected eulogy with which to introduce a speech before a judge. In his six years in office Felix had eliminated bands of robbers, thwarted organized assassins and crushed a movement led by an Egyptian (see note on 21:38). But in general his record was not good. He was recalled by Rome two years later because of misrule. His reforms and improvements are hard to identify historically.

dious unto thee, I pray *thee* that thou wouldest hear us of thy clemency a few words.

5 [a]For we have found this man a pestilent *fellow,* and a mover of sedition among all the Jews throughout the world, and a ringleader of the sect of the Nazarenes:

6 [a]Who also hath gone about to profane the temple: whom we took, and would [b]have judged according to our law.

7 [a]But the chief captain Lysias came *upon us,* and with great violence took *him* away out of our hands,

8 [a]Commanding his accusers to come unto thee: by examining of whom thyself mayest take knowledge of all these *things,* whereof we accuse him.

9 And the Jews also assented, saying that these *things* were so.

10 ¶ Then Paul, after that the governor had beckoned unto him to speak, answered, Forasmuch as I know that thou hast been of many years a judge unto this nation, I do the more cheerfully answer for myself:

11 Because that thou mayest understand, that there are *yet* but twelve days since I went up to Jerusalem [a]for to worship.

12 [a]And they neither found me in the temple disputing with any *man,* neither raising up the people, neither in the synagogues, nor in the city:

13 Neither can they prove *the things* whereof they now accuse me.

14 But this I confess unto thee, that after [a]the way which they call heresy, so worship I the [b]God of my fathers, believing all *things* which are written in [c]the law and the prophets:

15 And [a]have hope towards God, which they themselves also allow, [b]that there shall be a resurrection of the dead, both of the just and unjust.

16 And [a]herein do I exercise myself, to have always a conscience void of offence toward God, and *toward* men.

17 Now after many years [a]I came to bring alms to my nation, and offerings.

18 [a]Whereupon certain Jews from Asia found me purified in the temple, neither with multitude, nor with tumult.

19 [a]Who ought to have been here before thee, and object, if they had ought against me.

20 Or else let these same *here* say, if they have found any evil doing in me, while I stood before the council,

21 Except *it be* for this one voice, that I cried standing among them, [a]Touching the resurrection of the dead I am called in question by you this day.

22 ¶ And when Felix heard these *things,* having more perfect knowledge of *that* way, he deferred them, and said, When [a]Lysias the chief captain shall come down, I will know the uttermost of your matter.

23 And he commanded a centurion to keep Paul, and to let *him* have liberty, and [a]that *he* should forbid none of his acquaintance to minister or come unto him.

24 And after certain days, when Felix came with his wife Drusilla, which was a Jewess, he sent for Paul, and heard him concerning the faith in Christ.

25 And as he reasoned of righteousness, temperance, and judgment to come, Felix trembled, and answered, Go *thy way* for *this* time; when I have a convenient season, I will call for thee.

26 He hoped also that [a]money should have been given him of Paul, that he might loose

24:5 [a]Luke 23:2; ch. 6:13; 16:20; 17:6; 21:28; 1 Pet. 2:12,15
24:6 [a]ch. 21:28 [b]John 18:31
24:7 [a]ch. 21:33
24:8 [a]ch. 23:30
24:11 [a]ver. 17; ch. 21:26
24:12 [a]ch. 25:8; 28:17
24:14 [a]See Amos 8:14; ch. 9:2 [b]2 Tim. 1:3 [c]ch. 26:22; 28:23
24:15 [a]ch. 23:6; 26:6,7; 28:20 [b]Dan. 12:2; John 5:28,29
24:16 [a]ch. 23:1
24:17 [a]ch. 11:29,30; 20:16; Rom. 15:25; 2 Cor. 8:4; Gal. 2:10
24:18 [a]ch. 21:26,27; 26:21
24:19 [a]ch. 23:30; 25:16
24:21 [a]ch. 23:6; 28:20
24:22 [a]ver. 7
24:23 [a]ch. 27:3; 28:16
24:26 [a]Ex. 23:8

‡24:5 *pestilent fellow . . . ringleader of the sect of the Nazarenes.* Troublemaker. To excite dissension in the empire was treason against Caesar. To be a leader of a religious sect without Roman approval was contrary to law. *the sect of the Nazarenes.* Christianity.

24:6 *hath gone about to profane the temple.* The charge is now qualified by "an attempt," rather than the former claim (see note on 21:28).

24:10 Paul's reserved introduction lacks the flattery employed by Tertullus (vv. 2–4).

24:11 *yet but twelve days.* Paul answers each accusation. He was not a troublemaker, and he had not been involved in disturbances. He had but recently arrived in Jerusalem. He had spent five days in Cesarea and nearly seven in Jerusalem.

24:14 *after the way . . . so worship I . . . God.* Paul admits to his part in the way, but he still believes the law and the prophets. He shares the same hope as the Jews—resurrection and judgment (v. 15).

24:16 *conscience void of offence.* See note on 23:1.

24:17 *to bring alms to my nation.* The only explicit reference in Acts to the collection that was so important to Paul (see note on 20:4). *offerings.* May refer to Paul's help in sponsoring those who were fulfilling their vows (see 21:24). He also may have intended to present offerings for himself.

24:18 *Jews from Asia.* See 21:27–29. The absence of these Asian Jews would seem to suggest that they could not substantiate their accusations.

24:21 *Touching the resurrection.* Paul again introduces the point of contention between the Pharisees and Sadducees.

24:22 *having more perfect knowledge of that way.* Felix could not have governed Judea and Samaria for six years without becoming familiar with the place and activities of the Christians.

24:23 *let him have liberty.* Perhaps Paul was under house arrest similar to what he experienced while waiting trial in Rome (28:30–31)—in recognition of the fact that he was a Roman citizen who had not been found guilty of any crime.

24:24 *Drusilla.* Felix's third wife, daughter of Herod Agrippa I. At age 15 she married Azizus, king of Emesa, but deserted him for Felix a year later. Her son, also named Agrippa, died in the eruption of Vesuvius (A.D. 79).

24:25 *Felix trembled.* Hearing of righteousness, self-control and the judgment, Felix looked at his past life and was filled with fear. He had a spark of sincerity and concern. *when I have a convenient season.* Lust, pride, greed and selfish ambition made it continually inconvenient to change.

24:26 *money should have been given him.* Felix supposed that Paul had access to considerable funds. He had heard of his bringing an offering to the Jewish Christians in Jerusalem (see v. 17). So he wanted Paul to give him money in order to secure his release. Paul no longer had the money, nor would he offer a bribe if he had it.

him: wherefore he sent for him the oftener, and communed with him.

27 But after two years Porcius Festus came into Felix' room: and Felix, [a]willing to shew the Jews a pleasure, left Paul bound.

Paul tried before Festus

25 Now when Festus was come into the province, after three days he ascended from Cesarea to Jerusalem.

2 [a]Then the high priest and the chief of the Jews informed him against Paul, and besought him,

3 And desired favour against him, that he would send for him to Jerusalem, [a]laying wait in the way to kill him.

4 But Festus answered, that Paul should be kept at Cesarea, and that he himself would depart shortly *thither.*

5 Let them therefore, said he, which among you are able, go down with *me,* and accuse this man, [a]if there be any *wickedness* in him.

6 And when he had tarried among them [1]more than ten days, he went down unto Cesarea; and the next day sitting in the judgment seat, commanded Paul to be brought.

7 And when he was come, the Jews which came down from Jerusalem stood round about, [a]and laid many and grievous complaints against Paul, which they could not prove.

24:27 [a]Ex. 23:2; ch. 12:3; 25:9,14
25:2 [a]ver. 15; ch. 24:1
25:3 [a]ch. 23:12,15
25:5 [a]ver. 18; ch. 18:14
25:6 [1]Or, as some copies read, *no more than eight or ten days*
25:7 [a]Mark 15:3; Luke 23:2,10; ch. 24:5,13

25:8 [a]ch. 6:13; 24:12; 28:17
25:9 [a]ch. 24:27 [b]ver. 20
25:11 [a]ver. 25; ch. 18:14; 23:29; 26:31 [b]ch. 26:32; 28:19
25:14 [a]ch. 24:27
25:15 [a]ver. 2,3

8 While he answered for himself, [a]Neither against the law of the Jews, neither against the temple, nor *yet* against Cesar, have I offended any *thing at all.*

9 But Festus, [a]willing to do the Jews a pleasure, answered Paul, and said, [b]Wilt thou go up to Jerusalem, and there be judged of these *things* before me?

10 Then said Paul, I stand at Cesar's judgment seat, where I ought to be judged: to the Jews have I done no wrong, as thou very well knowest.

11 [a]For if I be an offender, or have committed any *thing* worthy of death, I refuse not to die: but if there be none *of these things* whereof these accuse me, no *man* may deliver me unto them. [b]I appeal unto Cesar.

12 Then Festus, when he had conferred with the council, answered, Hast thou appealed unto Cesar? unto Cesar shalt thou go.

Paul's case discussed

13 ¶ And after certain days king Agrippa and Bernice came unto Cesarea to salute Festus.

14 And when they had been there many days, Festus declared Paul's cause unto the king, saying, [a]There is a certain man left in bonds by Felix:

15 [a]About whom, when I was at Jerusalem, the chief priests and the elders of the

---

‡24:27 *Festus came into Felix' room.* Festus succeeded him. Felix was recalled to Rome in A.D. 59/60 to answer for disturbances and irregularities in his rule, such as his handling of riots between Jewish and Syrian inhabitants. Festus is not mentioned in existing historical records before his arrival in Judea. He died in office after two years, but his record for that time shows wisdom and honesty superior to both his predecessor, Felix, and his successor, Albinus. *willing to shew the Jews a pleasure.* To do them a favor. Felix did not want to incite more anger among the Jews, whom he would be facing in Roman court shortly. To release Paul from prison would do just that.

25:1 *from Cesarea to Jerusalem.* Sixty miles, a two-day trip. Festus was anxious to go immediately to the center of Jewish rule and worship.

25:2 *high priest and the chief of the Jews.* The council (see note on Mark 14:55).

‡25:3 *laying wait.* To ambush Paul. Probably the same group that had earlier made a vow to take Paul's life (see note on 23:12).

25:6 *sitting in the judgment seat.* To make his decision binding as a formal ruling.

25:7 *which they could not prove.* Again, as in the first hearing, Paul's adversaries produced no witnesses or evidence of any kind.

25:8 *Neither against the law . . . have I offended.* Paul had respect for the law (see Rom 7:12; 8:3–4; 1 Cor 9:20). *against the temple.* See notes on 21:28–29. Paul had not defied its customs by taking Trophimus into forbidden areas (21:29). Jesus had prophesied its destruction, but He was not responsible for its plight (Luke 21:5–6). *against Cesar.* Paul proclaimed the kingdom of God but not as a political rival of Rome (cf. 17:6–7). He advocated respect for law and order (see Rom 13:1–7) and prayer for civil rulers (see 1 Tim 2:2).

25:9 *Wilt thou go up to Jerusalem . . . ?* Obviously not. Festus had said that the trial would be before him; so Paul insisted that he was then standing in the Roman civil court (v. 10). He wanted to keep his trial there rather than suffer at the hands of a Jewish religious court. As a Roman citizen, he could refuse to go to a local provincial court; instead he looked to a higher Roman court.

25:11 *I appeal unto Cesar.* Nero had become the emperor by this time. It was the right of every Roman citizen to have his case heard before Caesar himself (or his representative) in Rome. This was the highest court of appeal, and winning such a case could have led to more than just Paul's acquittal. It could have resulted in official recognition of Christianity as distinct from Judaism.

25:12 *council.* The officials and legal experts who made up the advisory council for the Roman governor.

‡25:13 *king Agrippa.* Herod Agrippa II. He was 17 years old at the death of his father in A.D. 44 (12:23). Being too young to succeed his father, he was replaced by Roman procurators. Eight years later, however, a gradual extension of territorial authority began. Ultimately he ruled over territory north and northeast of the sea of Galilee, over several Galilean cities and over some cities in Perea. At the Jewish revolt, when Jerusalem fell, he was on the side of the Romans. He died C. A.D. 100—the last of the Herods. *Bernice.* The oldest daughter of Agrippa I, she was 16 years old at his death. When only 13, she married her uncle, Herod of Chalcis, and had two sons. When Herod died, she lived with her brother, Agrippa II. To silence rumors that she was living in incest with her brother, she married Polemon, king of Cilicia, but left him soon to return to Agrippa. She became the mistress of the emperor Vespasian's son Titus but was later ignored by him. *salute Festus.* Pay their respects. It was customary for rulers to pay a complimentary visit to a new ruler at the time of his assignment. It was advantageous to each that they get along (cf. Herod Antipas and Pilate, Luke 23:6–12).

Jews informed *me,* desiring *to have* judgment against him.

16 [a]To whom I answered, It is not the manner of the Romans to deliver any man to die, before that he which is accused have the accusers face to face, and have licence to answer for himself concerning the crime laid *against him.*

17 Therefore, when they were come hither, [a]without any delay, on the morrow I sat on the judgment seat, and commanded the man to be brought *forth.*

18 Against whom when the accusers stood *up,* they brought none accusation of *such things* as I supposed:

19 [a]But had certain questions against him of their own superstition, and of one Jesus, *which was* dead, whom Paul affirmed to be alive.

20 And because [1]I doubted of such *manner of* questions, I asked *him* whether he would go to Jerusalem, and there be judged of these *matters.*

21 But when Paul had appealed to be reserved unto the [1]hearing of Augustus, I commanded him to be kept till I might send him to Cesar.

22 Then [a]Agrippa said unto Festus, I would also hear the man myself. To morrow, said he, thou shalt hear him.

23 ¶ And on the morrow, when Agrippa was come, and Bernice, with great pomp, and were entered into the place of hearing, with the chief captains, and principal men of the city, at Festus' commandment Paul was brought *forth.*

24 And Festus said, King Agrippa, and all men which are here present with us, ye see this *man,* about whom [a]all the multitude of the Jews have dealt with me, both at Jerusalem, and *also* here, crying that he ought [b]not to live any longer.

25 But when I found that [a]he had committed nothing worthy of death, [b]and *that* he himself hath appealed to Augustus, I have determined to send him.

25:16 [a]ver. 4,5
25:17 [a]ver. 6
25:19 [a]ch. 18:15; 23:29
25:20 [1]Or, *I was doubtful how to inquire hereof*
25:21 [1]Or, *judgment*
25:22 [a]See ch. 9:15
25:24 [a]ver. 2,3,7 [b]ch. 22:22
25:25 [a]ch. 23:9,29; 26:31 [b]ver. 11,12

26:5 [a]ch. 22:3; 23:6; 24:15,21; Phil. 3:5
26:6 [a]ch. 23:6 [b]Gen. 3:15; 22:18; 26:4; 49:10; Deut. 18:15; 2 Sam. 7:12; Ps. 132:11; Is. 4:2; 7:14; 9:6; 40:10; Jer. 23:5; 33:14-16; Ezek. 34:23; 37:24; Dan. 9:24; ch. 13:32; Rom. 15:8; Tit. 2:13
26:7 [1][Gr. *night and day*] [a]Jas. 1:1 [b]Luke 2:37; 1 Thes. 3:10; 1 Tim. 5:5 [c]Phil. 3:11
26:9 [a]John 16:2; 1 Tim. 1:13
26:10 [a]ch. 8:3; Gal. 1:13 [b]ch. 9:14,21; 22:5

26 Of whom I have no certain *thing* to write unto *my* lord. Wherefore I have brought him forth before you, and specially before thee, O king Agrippa, that, after examination had, I might have somewhat to write.

27 For it seemeth to me unreasonable to send a prisoner, and not withal to signify the crimes *laid* against him.

26 Then Agrippa said unto Paul, Thou art permitted to speak for thyself. Then Paul stretched forth the hand, and answered for himself:

Paul tried before Agrippa

2 ¶ I think myself happy, king Agrippa, because I shall answer for myself this day before thee touching all *the things* whereof I am accused of the Jews:

3 Especially *because I know* thee to be expert in all customs and questions which are among the Jews: wherefore I beseech thee to hear me patiently.

4 My manner of life from *my* youth, which was at the first among mine own nation at Jerusalem, know all the Jews;

5 Which knew me from the beginning, if they would testify, that after [a]the most straitest sect of our religion I lived a Pharisee.

6 [a]And now I stand and am judged for the hope of [b]the promise made of God unto *our* fathers:

7 Unto which *promise* [a]our twelve tribes, instantly serving *God* [b][1]day and night, [c]hope to come. For which hope's sake, king Agrippa, I am accused of the Jews.

8 Why should it be thought *a thing* incredible with you, that God should raise the dead?

9 [a]I verily thought with myself, that *I* ought to do many *things* contrary to the name of Jesus of Nazareth.

10 [a]Which *thing* I also did in Jerusalem: and many of the saints did I shut up in prison, having received authority [b]from the chief priests; and when they were put to death, I gave my voice against *them.*

‡25:19 *superstition.* Or "religion," the same word used by Paul in 17:22 (see note there).

25:22 *I would also hear.* Agrippa had been wishing to hear Paul (cf. Antipas wanting to see Jesus, Luke 9:9; 23:8).

25:23 *place of hearing.* Not the judgment hall, for this was not a court trial. It was in an auditorium appropriate for the pomp of the occasion, with a king, his sister, the Roman governor and the outstanding leaders of both the Jews and the Roman government present. *chief captains.* Five regiments were stationed at Cesarea, so their five commanders would be in attendance (see note on 21:31).

25:26 *I have no certain thing.* Festus was required to send Caesar an explicit report on the case when an appeal was made. He hoped for some help from Agrippa in this matter. This was not an official trial but a special hearing to satisfy the curiosity of Agrippa and provide an assessment for Festus. *specially before thee, O king Agrippa.* He would be sensitive to differences between Pharisees and Sadducees, expectations of the Messiah, differences between Jews and Christians, and Jewish customs pertinent to these problems.

26:1 *permitted to speak.* Agrippa gave the permission because Festus allowed him to have charge of the hearing.

26:3 *expert in all customs and questions . . . among the Jews.* Agrippa as king controlled the temple treasury and the investments of the high priest, and could appoint the high priest. He was consulted by the Romans on religious matters. This is one of the reasons Festus wanted him to assess Paul.

‡26:5 *I lived a Pharisee.* Cf. Gal 1:14.

26:6 *the hope of the promise made of God.* Including God's kingdom, the Messiah and the resurrection (see v. 8).

‡26:8 Paul had been speaking to Agrippa but at this point must have addressed others as well, such as Festus and the chief captains (see note on 21:31), who did not believe in the resurrection. Agrippa was also allied with the Sadducees, whom he appointed high priests, and was likely to reject both the resurrection of Christ and resurrection in general.

‡26:10 *I gave my voice against them.* Meaning "I cast my vote against them," since the Greek word translated "voice" literally means a pebble which would be used to vote. Does not necessarily mean that Paul was a member of the council (see note

11 [a]And I punished them oft in every synagogue, and compelled *them* to blaspheme;
and being exceedingly mad against them, I
persecuted *them* even unto strange cities.
12 [a]Whereupon as I went to Damascus
with authority and commission from the chief
priests,
13 At midday, O king, I saw in the way a
light from heaven, above the brightness of the
sun, shining round about me and them which
journeyed with me.
14 And when we were all fallen to the
earth, I heard a voice speaking unto me, and
saying in the Hebrew tongue, Saul, Saul, why
persecutest thou me? *it is* hard for thee to kick
against the pricks.
15 And I said, Who art thou, Lord? And he
said, I am Jesus whom thou persecutest.
16 But rise, and stand upon thy feet: for I
have appeared unto thee for this *purpose,* [a]to
make thee a minister and a witness both of
these things which thou hast seen, and *of those*
things in the which I will appear unto thee;
17 Delivering thee from the people, and
from the Gentiles, [a]unto whom now I send
thee,
18 [a]To open their eyes, *and* [b]to turn *them*
from darkness to light, and *from* the power of
Satan unto God, [c]that they may receive forgiveness of sins, and [d]inheritance among them
which are [e]sanctified by faith that is in me.
19 Whereupon, O king Agrippa, I was not
disobedient unto the heavenly vision:
20 But [a]shewed first unto them of Damascus, and at Jerusalem, and throughout all the
coasts of Judea, and *then* to the Gentiles, that
they should repent and turn to God, and do
[b]works meet for repentance.
21 For these causes [a]the Jews caught me in
the temple, and went about to kill *me.*
22 Having therefore obtained help of God,
I continue unto this day, witnessing both to

26:11 [a]ch. 22:19
26:12 [a]ch. 9:3; 22:6
26:16 [a]ch. 22:15
26:17 [a]ch. 22:21
26:18 [a]Is. 35:5; 42:7; Luke 1:79; John 8:12; 2 Cor. 4:4; Eph. 1:18; 1 Thes. 5:5 [b]2 Cor. 6:14; Eph. 4:18; 5:8; Col. 1:13; 1 Pet. 2:9 [c]Luke 1:77 [d]Eph. 1:11; Col. 1:12 [e]ch. 20:32
26:20 [a]ch. 9:20,22; 11:26; chs. 13,14; 16-21 [b]Mat. 3:8
26:21 [a]ch. 21:30
26:22 [a]Luke 24:27; ch. 24:14; 28:23; Rom. 3:21 [b]John 5:46
26:23 [a]Luke 24:26 [b]1 Cor. 15:20; Col. 1:18; Rev. 1:5 [c]Luke 2:32
26:24 [a]2 Ki. 9:11; John 10:20; 1 Cor. 1:23; 2:13,14; 4:10
26:29 [a]1 Cor. 7:7
26:31 [a]ch. 23:9,29; 25:25
26:32 [a]ch. 25:11
27:1 [a]ch. 25:12,25

small and great, saying none other *things* than
those [a]which the prophets and [b]Moses did say
should come:
23 [a]That Christ should suffer, *and* [b]that he
should be the first *that* should rise from the
dead, and [c]should shew light unto the people,
and to the Gentiles.
24 ¶ And as he thus spake for himself, Festus said with a loud voice, Paul, [a]thou art beside thyself; much learning doth make thee
mad.
25 But he said, I am not mad, most noble
Festus; but speak forth *the* words of truth and
soberness.
26 For the king knoweth of these *things,*
before whom also I speak freely: for I am persuaded that none of these *things* are hidden
from him; for this *thing* was not done in a corner.
27 King Agrippa, believest thou the prophets? I know that thou believest.
28 Then Agrippa said unto Paul, Almost
thou persuadest me to be a Christian.
29 And Paul said, [a]I would to God, that not
only thou, but also all that hear me this day,
were both almost, and altogether such as I am,
except these bonds.
30 And when he had thus spoken, the king
rose up, and the governor, and Bernice, and
they that sat with them:
31 And when they were gone aside, they
talked between themselves, saying, [a]This man
doeth nothing worthy of death or of bonds.
32 Then said Agrippa unto Festus, This
man might have been set at liberty, [a]if he had
not appealed unto Cesar.

Paul sent to Rome

27 And when [a]it was determined that
we should sail into Italy, they delivered Paul and certain other prisoners unto *one*
named Julius, a centurion of Augustus' band.

on 22:20). He may have been appointed to a commission to carry out the prosecution (see v. 12), where his vote was given.

26:11 *compelled them to blaspheme.* He tried to force them either to curse Jesus or to confess publicly that Jesus is the Son of God, in which case they could be condemned for blasphemy, a sufficient cause for death (see Mat 26:63–66).

26:12 *as I went to Damascus.* Again Paul gives an account of his conversion (see 9:1–19; 22:4–21 and notes).

‡26:14 *I heard a voice.* See notes on 9:7; 22:9. *to kick against the pricks.* A Greek proverb for useless resistance—the ox succeeds only in hurting itself in kicking the pricks on the goad.

26:17 *unto whom now I send thee.* Not only to the Jews but also to the Gentiles (see 22:21; Gal 1:15–16). His mission was from God (Gal 1:1).

26:18 *from darkness to light.* A figure especially characteristic of Paul (see Rom 13:12; 2 Cor 4:6; Eph 5:8–14; Col 1:13; 1 Thes 5:5). *are sanctified.* Positional sanctification (see notes on 20:32; 1 Cor 1:2).

26:22 *the prophets and Moses.* The OT Scriptures (Luke 24:27, 44).

26:23 *the Gentiles.* Cf. Isa 49:6.

‡26:24 *thou art beside thyself.* You are out of your mind! See John 10:20; 1 Cor 14:23. The governor felt that Paul's education and reading of the sacred Scriptures had led him to a mania about prophecy and resurrection.

26:26 *was not done in a corner.* This gospel is based on actual events, lived out in historical times and places. The king must himself attest to the truth of what Paul has affirmed.

26:27 *believest thou the prophets.* King Agrippa was faced with a dilemma. If he said "Yes," Paul would press him to recognize their fulfillment in Jesus; if he said "No," he would be in trouble with the devout Jews, who accepted the message of the prophets as the very word of God.

‡26:28 *Almost thou persuadest me to be a Christian.* The Greek phrase has the sense of either "by few words" or "in a short time" you will persuade me to become a Christian. His answer is an evasion of Paul's question and an answer to what he anticipates Paul's next question to be. His point is that he will not be persuaded by such a brief statement.

26:29 *these bonds.* Paul was still bound as a prisoner.

‡27:1 See map No. 11 at the end of the study Bible. *we should sail.* The "we" narrative (see note on 16:10) begins again (the last such reference appeared in 21:18). Probably Luke has spent the two years of Paul's Cesarean imprisonment nearby, and now he joins those ready to sail. *Julius, a centurion.* Otherwise unknown. Perhaps he was given the specific duties of an imperial

2 And entering into a ship of Adramyttium,
we launched, meaning to sail by the coasts of
Asia; *one* [a] Aristarchus, a Macedonian of Thessalonica, being with us.
3 And the next *day* we touched at Sidon.
And Julius [a] courteously entreated Paul, and
gave *him* liberty to go unto *his* friends to refresh himself.
4 And when we had launched from thence,
we sailed under Cyprus, because the winds
were contrary.
5 And when we had sailed over the sea of
Cilicia and Pamphylia, we came to Myra, *a city*
of Lycia.
6 And there the centurion found a ship of
Alexandria sailing into Italy; and he put us
therein.
7 And when we had sailed slowly many
days, and scarce were come over against Cnidus, the wind not suffering us, we sailed under [1] Crete, over against Salmone;
8 And hardly passing it, came unto a place
which is called The fair havens; nigh whereunto was the city *of* Lasea.
9 Now when much time was spent, and
when sailing was now dangerous, [a] because
the fast was now already past, Paul admonished *them,*
10 And said unto them, Sirs, I perceive
that *this* voyage will be with [1] hurt and much
damage, not only of the lading and ship, but
also of our lives.
11 Nevertheless the centurion believed the
master and the owner of the ship, more than
those *things* which were spoken by Paul.
12 And because the haven was not com-
modious to winter in, the more part advised to
depart thence also, if by any means they might
attain to Phenice, *and there* to winter; *which
is* a haven of Crete, and lieth toward the south
west and north west.

The storm at sea

13 And when the south wind blew softly,
supposing that *they* had obtained *their* purpose, loosing *thence,* they sailed close by
Crete.
14 But not long after there [1] arose against it
a tempestuous wind, called Euroclydon.
15 And when the ship was caught, and
could not bear up into the wind, we let *her*
drive.
16 And running under a certain island
which is called Clauda, we had much work to
come by the boat:
17 Which when they had taken up, they
used helps, undergirding the ship; and fearing
lest they should fall into the quicksands, strake
sail, and so were driven.

27:2 [a] ch. 19:29
27:3 [a] ch. 24:23; 28:16
27:7 [1] Or, *Candy*
27:9 [a] The fast was on the tenth day of the seventh month; Lev. 23:27,29
27:10 [1] Or, *injury*
27:14 [1] Or, *beat*

courier, which included delivering prisoners for trial. *Augustus' band.* A Roman band or cohort was a military unit composed of 300–600 men. The Roman legions were designated by number, and each of the regiments also had designations. The identification "Augustan," or "Imperial" (belonging to the empire), was common (see note on 10:1).

27:2 *Adramyttium.* A harbor on the west coast of the province of Asia, southeast of Troas, east of Assos. *by the coasts.* At one of these stops, Julius would plan to transfer to a ship going to Rome. *Aristarchus.* See 19:29; 20:4; see also Philem 24 and Col 4:10, indicating he was in Rome with Paul later.

27:3 *Sidon.* About 70 miles north of Cesarea.

27:4 *sailed under Cyprus.* They sought the protecting shelter of the island by sailing north on the eastern side of the island, then west along the northern side. *the winds were contrary.* Prevailing winds in summer were westerly.

27:5 *Cilicia and Pamphylia.* Adjoining provinces on the southern shore of Asia Minor. From Sidon to Myra along this coast would normally be a voyage of 10 to 15 days. *Myra . . . of Lycia.* The growing importance of the city of Myra was associated with the development of navigation. Instead of hugging the coast from point to point, more ships were daring to run directly from Alexandria in Egypt to harbors like Myra on the southern coast of Asia Minor. It was considerably out of the way on the trip to Rome from Egypt, but the prevailing westerly wind would not allow a direct voyage toward the west. Myra became an important grain-storage city as well.

27:6 *ship of Alexandria.* A ship from Egypt (with grain cargo, v. 38) bound for Rome. Paul and the others could have remained on the first ship and continued up the coast to Macedonia, then taken the land route over the Egnatian Way across Greece and on to Rome, entering Italy at the port of Brundisium. But Julius chose to change ships here, accepting the opportunity of a voyage direct to Rome. Some suggest that Aristarchus from Macedonia stayed with the first ship and went to his home area to tell of Paul's coming imprisonment in Rome. If so, he later joined Paul in Rome (see note on v. 2).

27:7 *Cnidus.* From Myra to Cnidus at the southwest point of Asia Minor was about 170 miles. The trip probably took another 10 to 15 days. *Crete.* An island 160 miles long. Rather than cross the open sea to Greece, the ship was forced to bear south, seeking to sail west with the protection of the island of Crete on the north ("under the shelter of Crete"). *Salmone.* A promontory on the northeast point of Crete.

27:8 *fair havens; . . . Lasea.* The former was a port about midway on the southern coast of Crete, and the latter was a city about five miles away.

27:9 *the fast.* The Jewish day of atonement fell in the latter part of September or in October. The usual sailing season by Jewish calculation lasted from Pentecost (May-June) to tabernacles, which was five days after the fast. The Romans considered sailing after Sept. 15 doubtful and after Nov. 11 suicidal.

‡27:12 *Phenice.* Also known as Phoenix, a major city that served as a wintering place, having a harbor with protection against the storms.

27:14 *Euroclydon.* A typhoon-like, east-northeast wind (a "northeaster"), which drove the ship away from their destination.

‡27:16 *Clauda.* An island about 23 miles from Crete. This provided enough shelter to make preparation against the storm. *to come by the boat.* A small boat was being towed behind the ship. It was interfering with the progress of the ship and with the steering. It may also have been in danger of being crushed against the ship in the wind and the waves. It had to be taken aboard (v. 17).

‡27:17 *used helps, undergirding the ship.* Used cables, probably placed crosswise, in order to keep the ship from being broken apart by the storm. *fall into the quicksands.* A long stretch of desolate banks of quicksand (called Syrtis) along northern Africa off the coast of Tunis and Tripoli—still far away, but in such a storm the ship could be driven a great distance.

18 And we being exceedingly tossed with a
tempest, the next *day* they lightened the ship;
19 And the third *day* [a]we cast *out* with our
own hands the tackling of the ship.
20 And when neither sun nor stars in
many days appeared, and no small tempest lay
on *us,* all hope that we should be saved was
then taken away.
21 But after long abstinence Paul stood
forth in the midst of them, and said, Sirs, *ye*
should have hearkened unto me, and not have
loosed from Crete, and to have gained this
harm and loss.
22 And now I exhort you to be of good
cheer: for there shall be no loss of *any man's*
life among you, but of the ship.
23 [a]For there stood by me this night *the*
angel of God, whose I am, and [b]whom I serve,
24 Saying, Fear not, Paul; thou must be
brought before Cesar: and lo, God hath given
thee all them that sail with thee.
25 Wherefore, sirs, be of good cheer: [a]for I
believe God, that it shall be even as it was told
me.

27:19 [a]Jonah 1:5
27:23 [a]ch. 23:11 [b]Dan. 6:16; Rom. 1:9; 2 Tim. 1:3
27:25 [a]Luke 1:45; Rom. 4:20,21; 2 Tim. 1:12
27:26 [a]ch. 28:1

26 Howbeit [a]we must be cast upon a certain island.

The shipwreck

27 ¶ But when the fourteenth night was
come, as we were driven up and down in
Adria, about midnight the shipmen deemed
that they drew near to some country;
28 And sounded, and found *it* twenty fath-
oms: and when they had gone a little further,
they sounded again, and found *it* fifteen fath-
oms.
29 Then fearing lest we should have fallen
upon rocks, they cast four anchors out of the
stern, and wished for the day.
30 And as the shipmen were about to flee
out of the ship, when they had let down the
boat into the sea, under colour as though they
would have cast anchors out of the foreship,
31 Paul said to the centurion and to the soldiers, Except these abide in the ship, ye cannot be saved.
32 Then the soldiers cut off the ropes of
the boat, and let her fall off.

‡27:18 *lightened the ship.* By dumping the cargo. They kept some bags of grain, however (see v. 38).

27:19 *tackling of the ship.* Spars, planks and perhaps the yardarm with the mainsail attached. At times these were dragged behind, serving as a brake.

27:21 *should have hearkened unto me.* Although they had not done so, Paul had good news for everyone (vv. 22–26).

‡27:27 *fourteenth night.* After leaving the fair havens. *In Adria.* That is, in the Adriatic Sea which lies between Italy, Malta, Crete and Greece. In ancient times the Adriatic Sea extended as far south as Sicily and Crete. (Some think this sea included all the area between Greece, Italy and Africa and that it was known as the Adrian, not the Adriatic, Sea.) Its extent now has been considerably reduced. *deemed that they drew near.* By the sound of breakers.

27:28 *sounded.* Measured the depth of the sea by letting down a weighted line.

27:30 *were about to flee out of the ship.* Without a port for the ship, the sailors felt their chance for survival was better in the single lifeboat, unencumbered by the many passengers.

27:31 *Except these abide.* If the sailors had been allowed to desert the ship in seeking to save themselves, the passengers would have been unable to beach the ship the following day.

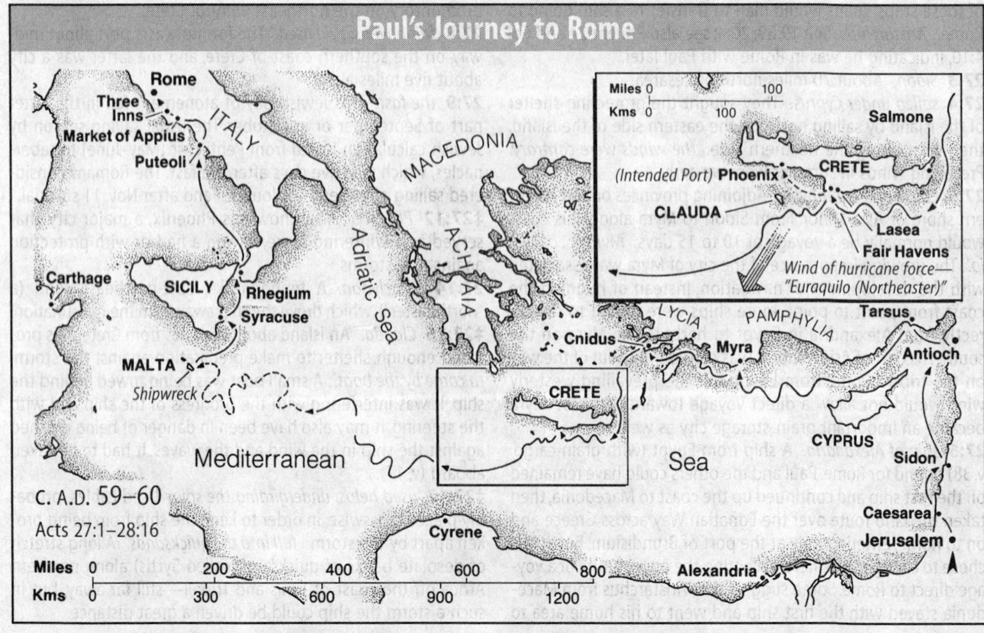

Paul's Journey to Rome

33 And while the day was coming on, Paul besought *them* all to take meat, saying, This day is the fourteenth day that ye have tarried and continued fasting, having taken nothing.

34 Wherefore I pray you to take *some* meat: for this is for your health: for [a]there shall not a hair fall from the head of any of you.

35 And when he had thus spoken, he took bread, and [a]gave thanks to God in presence of *them* all: and when he had broken *it,* he began to eat.

36 Then were they all of good cheer, and they also took *some* meat.

37 And we were in all in the ship two hundred threescore *and* sixteen [a]souls.

38 And when they had eaten enough, they lightened the ship, and cast out the wheat into the sea.

39 And when it was day, they knew not the land: but they discovered a certain creek with a shore, into the which they were minded, if it were possible, to thrust in the ship.

40 And when they had [1]taken up the anchors, they committed *themselves* unto the sea, and loosed the rudder bands, and hoised up the mainsail to the wind, and made toward shore.

41 And falling into a place where two seas met, [a]they ran the ship aground; and the forepart stuck fast, and remained unmoveable, but the hinder part was broken with the violence of the waves.

42 And the soldiers' counsel was to kill the prisoners, lest any *of them* should swim out, and escape.

43 But the centurion, willing to save Paul, kept them from *their* purpose; and commanded that they which could swim should cast *themselves* first into *the sea,* and get to land:

44 And the rest, some on boards, and some on broken pieces of the ship. And so it came to pass, [a]that *they* escaped all safe to land.

27:34 [a]1 Ki. 1:52; Mat. 10:30; Luke 12:7; 21:18
27:35 [a]1 Sam. 9:13; Mat. 15:36; Mark 8:6; John 6:11; 1 Tim. 4:3,4
27:37 [a]ch. 2:41; 7:14; Rom. 13:1; 1 Pet. 3:20
27:40 [1]Or, *cut the anchors, they left* them *in the sea, etc.*
27:41 [a]2 Cor. 11:25
27:44 [a]ver. 22
28:1 [a]ch. 27:26
28:2 [a]Rom. 1:14; 1 Cor. 14:11; Col. 3:11
28:5 [a]Mark 16:18; Luke 10:19
28:6 [a]ch. 14:11
28:8 [a]Jas. 5:14,15 [b]Mark 6:5; 7:32; 16:18; Luke 4:40; ch. 19:11,12; 1 Cor. 12:9,28
28:10 [a]Mat. 15:6; 1 Tim. 5:17

The stopover at Melita

28 And when they were escaped, then they knew that [a]the island was called Melita.

2 And the [a]barbarous people shewed us no little kindness: for they kindled a fire, and received us every one, because of the present rain, and because of the cold.

3 And when Paul had gathered a bundle of sticks, and laid *them* on the fire, there came a viper out of the heat, and fastened on his hand.

4 And when the barbarians saw the *venomous* beast hang on his hand, they said among themselves, No doubt this man is a murderer, whom, though he hath escaped the sea, yet Vengeance suffereth not to live.

5 And he shook off the beast into the fire, and [a]felt no harm.

6 Howbeit they looked when he should have swollen, or fallen down dead suddenly: but after they had looked a great while, and saw no harm come to him, they changed *their minds,* and [a]said that he was a god.

7 In the same quarters were possessions of the chief *man* of the island, whose name was Publius; who received us, and lodged *us* three days courteously.

8 And it came to pass, that the father of Publius lay sick of a fever and of a bloody flixe: to whom Paul entered in, and [a]prayed, and [b]laid *his* hands on him, and healed him.

9 So when this was done, others also, which had diseases in the island, came, and were healed:

10 Who also honoured us with many [a]honours; and when we departed, they laded *us* with such *things* as were necessary.

11 ¶ And after three months we departed

27:33 *having taken nothing.* No provisions had been distributed nor regular meals eaten since the storm began.

27:35 *took bread, and gave thanks.* Paul gave two good examples: He ate food for physical nourishment and gave thanks to God. To give thanks before a meal was common practice among God's people (see Luke 9:16; 24:30; 1 Tim 4:4–5).

27:37 *two hundred threescore and sixteen souls.* To note the number on board may have been necessary in preparation for the distribution of food or perhaps for the coming attempt to get ashore. The number is not extraordinary for the time. Josephus refers to a ship that had 600 aboard (*Life,* 15).

27:38 *lightened the ship.* They threw overboard the remaining bags of wheat (see v. 18), which had probably been kept for food supply. The lighter the ship, the farther it could sail in to shore.

‡27:40 *loosed the rudder bands.* They loosed the ropes of the rudder in order to lower the stern rudders into place so the ship could be steered toward the sandy shore. Ancient ships had a steering oar on either side of the stern.

27:42 *soldiers' counsel was to kill the prisoners.* If a prisoner escaped, the life of his guard was taken in his place. The soldiers did not want to risk having a prisoner escape.

27:43 Once more the centurion is to be admired for stopping this plan and trusting the prisoners.

‡28:1 *Melita.* Also known as Malta. It was included in the province of Sicily and is located 58 miles south of that large island.

‡28:2 *barbarous people.* All non-Greek-speaking people were called this by Greeks. Far from being uncivilized tribesmen, they were Phoenician in ancestry and used a Phoenician dialect but were thoroughly Romanized. *rain, and . . . cold.* It was the end of October or the beginning of November.

28:3 *a viper.* Must have been known to the islanders to be poisonous.

28:6 *should have swollen.* The usual medical term for inflammation; it is used only by Luke in the NT (see Introduction to Luke: Author). *said that he was a god.* Parallel to the Lystrans' attempt to worship Paul and Barnabas (14:11–18).

‡28:7 *chief.* The "first man" of Melita, a technical term for the top authority. Luke's designation is accurate here, as elsewhere, even though the Greek term used is not a common one. Cf. also "proconsul" (Greek *anthypatos,* 13:7), "magistrates" (Greek *strategoi,* 16:20), "city authorities" (Greek *politarchas,* 17:6), "Asiarchs" (Greek *Asiarchon,* 19:31). *Publius.* A Roman name, but the first name and not the family name. It must have been what the islanders called him.

28:11 *after three months.* They had to remain here until the sailing season opened in late February or early March. *Castor*

in a ship of Alexandria, which had wintered in
the isle, *whose* sign *was* Castor and Pollux.
12 And landing at Syracuse, we tarried
there three days.
13 And from thence we fet a compass, and
came to Rhegium: and after one day the south
wind blew, and we came the next day to Puteoli:
14 Where we found brethren, and were
desired to tarry with them seven days: and so
we went toward Rome.
15 And from thence, when the brethren
heard of us, they came to meet us as far as Appii forum, and The three taverns: whom when
Paul saw, he thanked God, and took courage.
16 And when we came to Rome, the centurion delivered the prisoners to the captain of
the guard: but [a]Paul was suffered to dwell by
himself with a soldier that kept him.

The arrival at Rome

17 ¶ And it came to pass, that after three
days Paul called the chief of the Jews together:
and when they were come together, he said
unto them, Men *and* brethren, [a]though I have
committed nothing against the people, or customs of our fathers, *yet* [b]was I delivered prisoner from Jerusalem into the hands of the Romans.
18 Who, [a]when they had examined me,
would have let *me* go, because there was no
cause of death in me.
19 But when the Jews spake against *it,* [a]I
was constrained to appeal unto Cesar; not that
I had ought to accuse my nation of.
20 For this cause therefore have I called for
you, to see *you,* and to speak with *you:* because that [a]for the hope of Israel I am bound
with [b]this chain.
21 And they said unto him, We neither received letters out of Judea concerning thee,
neither any of the brethren that came shewed
or spake any harm of thee.
22 But we desire to hear of thee what thou
thinkest: for as concerning this sect, we know
that every where [a]it is spoken against.
23 And when they had appointed him a
day, there came many to him into *his* lodging;
[a]to whom he expounded and testified the
kingdom of God, persuading them concerning
Jesus, [b]both out of the law of Moses, and *out
of* the prophets, from morning till evening.
24 And [a]some believed the *things* which
were spoken, and some believed not.
25 And when they agreed not among
themselves, they departed, after that Paul had
spoken one word, Well spake the Holy Ghost
by Esaias the prophet unto our fathers,
26 Saying, [a]Go unto this people, and say,
Hearing ye shall hear, and shall not understand;
and seeing ye shall see, and not perceive:
27 For the heart of this people is waxed
gross, and *their* ears are dull of hearing, and
their eyes have they closed; lest they should
see with *their* eyes, and hear with *their* ears,
and understand with *their* heart, and should
be converted, and I should heal them.
28 Be it known therefore unto you, that
the salvation of God is sent [a]unto the Gentiles,
and *that* they will hear it.
29 And when he had said these *words,* the
Jews departed, and had great reasoning among
themselves.
30 ¶ And Paul dwelt two whole years in his

28:16 [a]ch. 24:25; 27:3
28:17 [a]ch. 24:12,13 [b]ch. 21:33
28:18 [a]ch. 22:24; 24:10; 25:8
28:19 [a]ch. 25:11
28:20 [a]ch. 26:6,7 [b]ch. 26:29; Eph. 3:1; 4:1; 6:20; 2 Tim. 1:16; Philem. 10,13
28:22 [a]Luke 2:34; ch. 24:5,14; 1 Pet. 2:12; 4:14
28:23 [a]Luke 24:27; ch. 17:3; 19:8 [b]See ch. 26:6,22
28:24 [a]ch. 14:4; 19:9
28:26 [a]Is. 6:9; Jer. 5:21; Ezek. 12:2; Mat. 13:14; Mark 4:12; Luke 8:10; John 12:40; Rom. 11:8
28:28 [a]Mat. 21:41; ch. 13:46; 18:6; 26:17,18; Rom. 11:11

and Pollux. The two "sons of Zeus" (Greek *Dioscuroi*), the guardian deities of sailors.

28:12 *Syracuse.* The leading city on the island of Sicily, situated on the east coast.

28:13 *Rhegium.* A town on the coast of Italy, near the southwestern tip and close to the narrowest point of the strait separating that country from Sicily, opposite Messina. Around the promontory north of the town was the whirlpool of Charybdis and the rock of Scylla. Coming from his triumph in Judea, the general Titus landed here on his way to Rome. *Puteoli.* Modern Pozzuoli, almost 200 miles from Rhegium. It was situated in the northern part of the Bay of Naples and was the chief port of Rome, though 75 miles away. The population included Jews as well as Christians.

28:14 *tarry with them seven days.* As at Troas (20:6) and Tyre (21:4), Paul was with them for one or perhaps two Sundays to observe the keeping of the Lord's supper and to teach and preach. Either the centurion had business to care for or he was free to delay the journey at Paul's request (see 27:42–43; see also 27:3). *Rome.* See map, p. 1612.

‡28:15 *Appii forum.* Or the market of Appius which was a small town 43 miles from Rome, noted for its wickedness. Some Roman Christians came this far to meet Paul. Beyond this they would not be certain of the way he would come. *The three taverns.* Or Three Inns, a town 33 miles from Rome. Other Roman believers met Paul here. The term "inn" was used to designate any kind of shop.

28:16 *to dwell by himself.* "In his own hired house" (v. 30). He had committed no flagrant crime and was not a politically dangerous rival. So he was allowed to have his own living quarters, but a guard was with him at all times, perhaps chained to him (Eph 6:20; Phil 1:13–14,17; Col 4:3,18; Philem 10,13).

28:17 *chief of the Jews.* The decree of the emperor Claudius (see 18:2) had been allowed to lapse, and Jews had returned to Rome with their leaders. *brethren.* An epithet that recognized the common Jewish blood he shared with them. Cf. the usage in v. 15, referring to brothers in Christ.

28:20 *the hope of Israel.* See note on 26:6.

28:22 *we desire to hear . . . what thou thinkest.* The Jews in Rome were well aware of the dispute over whether Jesus was the Messiah. They wanted to hear Paul's presentation, and he was eager to present it before the arrival of adverse opinions from the Jewish leaders of Jerusalem.

28:23 *law of Moses . . . prophets.* The OT Scriptures (see Luke 24:27,44).

28:28 *salvation of God is sent unto the Gentiles.* The main thought of the book of Acts. The gospel is meant for all. And Paul was a chosen vessel to carry the message to Gentiles as well as to Jews.

28:30 *two whole years.* Paul served the Lord (v. 31) during the full period of waiting for his accusers to press the trial in Rome. There are a number of indications that he was released from this imprisonment: 1. Acts stops abruptly at this time. 2. Paul wrote to churches expecting to visit them soon; so he must have anticipated a release (see Phil 2:24; Philem 22). 3. A number of the details in the Pastoral Letters do not fit into the

own hired house, and received all that came in
unto him,
31 [a]Preaching the kingdom of God, and
teaching those *things* which concern the Lord
Jesus Christ, with all confidence, no man forbidding him.

28:31 [a]ch. 4:31; Eph. 6:19

historical setting given in the book of Acts. Following the close of the book, these details indicate a return to Asia Minor, Crete and Greece. 4. Tradition indicates that Paul went to Spain. Even if he did not go, the very fact that a tradition arose suggests a time when he could have taken that journey. See map, pp. 1738–1739.

Rome in the Time of Paul

The Neronian persecution in A.D. 64 was a transparent attempt by the emperor to blame Christians for the great fire that destroyed large parts of the city. The populace, however, blamed Nero and felt sorry for those unjustly tortured in the arena (cf. Tacitus, *Annals*, 15.44).

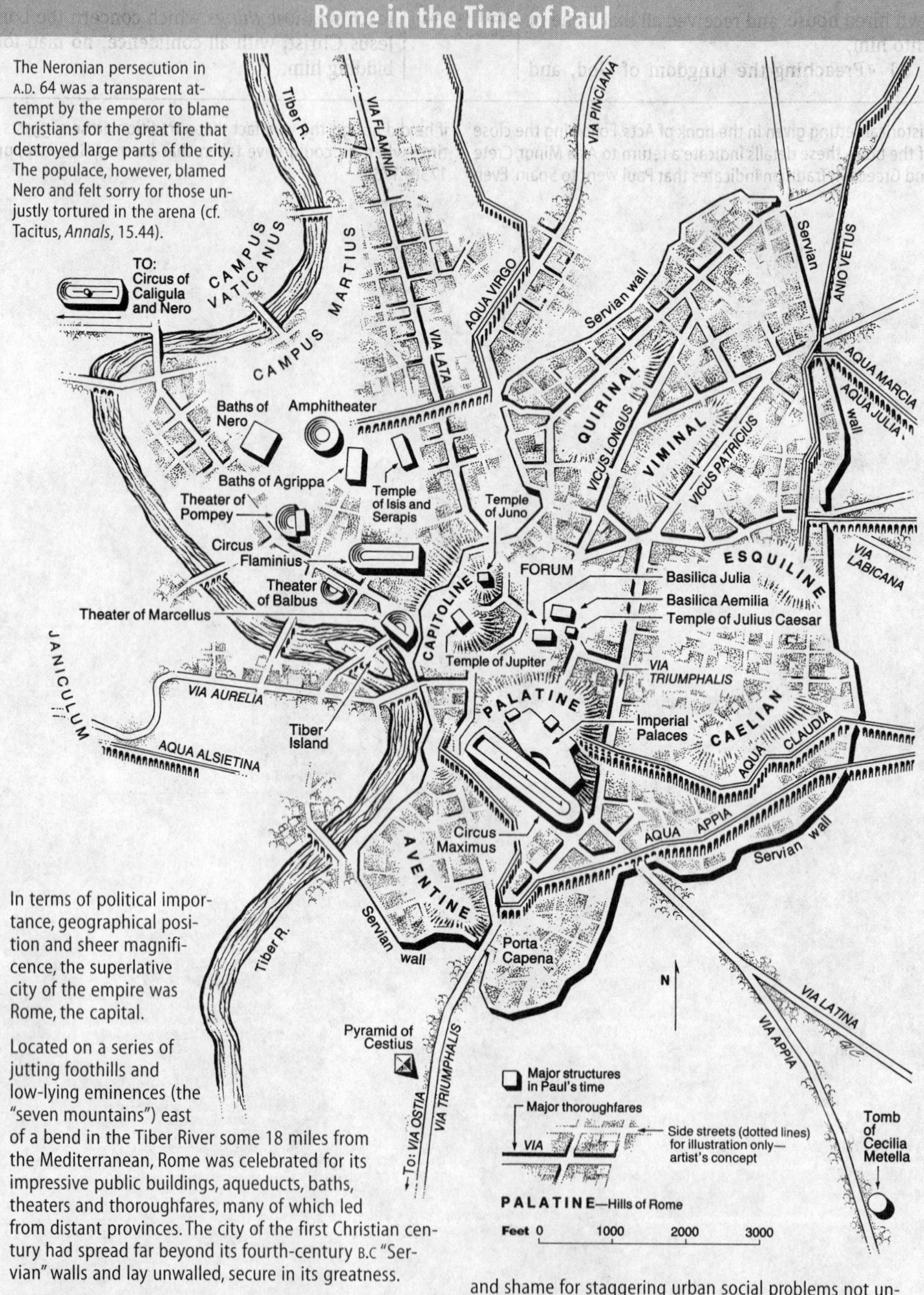

In terms of political importance, geographical position and sheer magnificence, the superlative city of the empire was Rome, the capital.

Located on a series of jutting foothills and low-lying eminences (the "seven mountains") east of a bend in the Tiber River some 18 miles from the Mediterranean, Rome was celebrated for its impressive public buildings, aqueducts, baths, theaters and thoroughfares, many of which led from distant provinces. The city of the first Christian century had spread far beyond its fourth-century B.C "Servian" walls and lay unwalled, secure in its greatness.

The most prominent features were the Capitoline hill, with temples to Jupiter and Juno, and the nearby Palatine, adorned with imperial palaces, including Nero's "Golden House." Both hills overlooked the Roman Forum, the hub of the entire empire.

Alternatively described as the glorious crowning achievement of mankind and as the sewer of the universe where all the scum from every corner of the empire gathered, Rome had reasons for both civic pride in its architecture and shame for staggering urban social problems not unlike those of cities today.

The apostle Paul entered the city from the south on the Via Appia. He first lived under house arrest and then, after a period of freedom, as a condemned prisoner in the Mamertine dungeon near the Forum. Remarkably, Paul was able to proclaim the gospel among all classes of people, from the palace to the prison. According to tradition, he was executed at a spot on the Ostian Way outside Rome in A.D. 68.

The Epistle of Paul the Apostle to the Romans

INTRODUCTION

Author

The writer of this letter was the apostle Paul (see 1:1). No voice from the early church was ever raised against his authorship. The letter contains a number of historical references that agree with known facts of Paul's life. The doctrinal content of the book is typical of Paul, which is evident from a comparison with other letters he wrote.

Date and Place of Writing

The book was probably written in the early spring of A.D. 57. Very likely Paul was on his third missionary journey, ready to return to Jerusalem with the offering from the mission churches for poverty-stricken believers in Jerusalem (see 15:25–27). In 15:26 it is suggested that Paul had already received contributions from the churches of Macedonia and Achaia, so he either was at Corinth or had already been there. Since he had not yet been at Corinth (on his third missionary journey) when he wrote 1 Corinthians (cf. 1 Cor 16:1–4) and the collection issue had still not been resolved when he wrote 2 Corinthians (2 Cor 8—9), the writing of Romans must follow that of 1,2 Corinthians (dated c. 55).

The most likely place of writing is either Corinth or Cenchrea (about six miles away) because of references to Phebe of Cenchrea (16:1) and to Gaius, Paul's host (16:23), who was probably a Corinthian (see 1 Cor 1:14). Erastus (16:23) may also have been a Corinthian (see 2 Tim 4:20).

Recipients

The original recipients of the letter were the people of the church at Rome (1:7), who were predominantly Gentile. Jews, however, must have constituted a substantial minority of the congregation (see 4:1; chs. 9—11; see also note on 1:13). Perhaps Paul originally sent the entire letter to the Roman church, after which he or someone else used a shorter form (chs. 1—14 or 1—15) for more general distribution. See note on 2 Pet 3:15.

Major Theme

Paul's primary theme in Romans is the basic gospel, God's plan of salvation and righteousness for all mankind, Jew and Gentile alike (1:16–17). Although justification by faith has been suggested by some as the theme, it would seem that a broader theme states the message of the book more adequately. "Righteousness of God" (1:17) includes justification by faith, but it also embraces such related ideas as guilt, sanctification and security.

Purpose

Paul's purposes for writing this letter were varied:

1. He wrote to prepare the way for his coming visit to Rome and his proposed mission to Spain (1:10–15; 15:22–29).

2. He wrote to present the basic system of salvation to a church that had not received the teaching of an apostle before.

3. He sought to explain the relationship between Jew and Gentile in God's overall plan of redemption. The Jewish Christians were being rejected by the larger Gentile group in the church (14:1) because the Jewish believers still felt constrained to observe dietary laws and sacred days (14:2–6).

Occasion

When Paul wrote this letter, he was probably at Corinth (Acts 20:2–3) on his third missionary journey. His work in the eastern Mediterranean was almost finished (see 15:18–23), and he greatly desired to visit the Roman church (see 1:11–12; 15:23–24). At this time, however, he could not go

to Rome because he felt he must personally deliver the collection taken among the Gentile churches for the poverty-stricken Christians of Jerusalem (see 15:25–28). So instead of going to Rome, he sent a letter to prepare the Christians there for his intended visit in connection with a mission to Spain (see 15:23–24). For many years Paul had wanted to visit Rome to minister there (see 1:13–15), and this letter served as a careful and systematic theological introduction to that hoped-for personal ministry. Since he was not acquainted directly with the Roman church, he says little about its problems (but see 14:1—15:13; cf. also 13:1–7; 16:17–18).

Content

Paul begins by surveying the spiritual condition of all mankind. He finds Jews and Gentiles alike to be sinners and in need of salvation. That salvation has been provided by God through Jesus Christ and His redemptive work on the cross. It is a provision, however, that must be received by faith—a principle by which God has always dealt with mankind, as the example of Abraham shows. Since salvation is only the beginning of Christian experience, Paul moves on to show how the believer is freed from sin, law and death—a provision made possible by his union with Christ in both death and resurrection and by the indwelling presence and power of the Holy Spirit. Paul then shows that Israel too, though presently in a state of unbelief, has a place in God's sovereign redemptive plan. Now she consists of only a remnant, allowing for the conversion of the Gentiles, but the time will come when "all Israel shall be saved" (11:26). The letter concludes with an appeal to the readers to work out their Christian faith in practical ways, both in the church and in the world. None of Paul's other letters states so profoundly the content of the gospel and its implications for both the present and the future.

Special Characteristics

1. *The most systematic of Paul's letters.* It reads more like an elaborate theological essay than a letter.
2. *Emphasis on Christian doctrine.* The number and importance of the theological themes touched upon are impressive: sin, salvation, grace, faith, righteousness, justification, sanctification, redemption, death, resurrection and glorification.
3. *Widespread use of OT quotations.* Although Paul regularly quotes from the OT in his letters, in Romans the argument is sometimes carried along by such quotations (see especially chs. 9—11).
4. *Deep concern for Israel.* Paul writes about her present status, her relationship to the Gentiles and her final salvation.

Outline

- I. Introduction (1:1–15)
- II. Theme: Righteousness of God (1:16–17)
- III. The Unrighteousness of All Mankind (1:18—3:20)
  - A. Gentiles (1:18–32)
  - B. Jews (2:1—3:8)
  - C. Summary: All People (3:9–20)
- IV. Righteousness Imputed: Justification (3:21—5:21)
  - A. Through Christ (3:21–26)
  - B. Received by Faith (3:27—4:25)
    - 1. The principle established (3:27–31)
    - 2. The principle illustrated (ch. 4)
  - C. The Fruits of Righteousness (5:1–11)
  - D. Summary: Man's Unrighteousness Contrasted with God's Gift of Righteousness (5:12–21)
- V. Righteousness Imparted: Sanctification (chs. 6—8)
  - A. Freedom from Sin's Tyranny (ch. 6)
  - B. Freedom from the Law's Condemnation (ch. 7)
  - C. Life in the Power of the Holy Spirit (ch. 8)
- VI. God's Righteousness Vindicated: The Problem of the Apparent Rejection of Israel (chs. 9—11)
  - A. The Justice of the Rejection (9:1–29)
  - B. The Cause of the Rejection (9:30—10:21)

- C. Facts That Lessen the Difficulty (ch. 11)
  1. The rejection is not total (11:1–10)
  2. The rejection is not final (11:11–24)
  3. God's ultimate purpose is mercy (11:25–36)
- VII. Righteousness Practiced (12:1—15:13)
  - A. In the Body—the Church (ch. 12)
  - B. In the World (ch. 13)
  - C. Among Weak and Strong Christians (14:1—15:13)
- VIII. Conclusion (15:14–33)
- IX. Commendation and Greetings (ch. 16)

1 Paul, a servant of Jesus Christ, [a]called *to*
be an apostle, [b]separated unto the gospel
of God,
2 ([a]Which he had promised afore [b]by his
prophets in the holy scriptures,)
3 Concerning his Son Jesus Christ our
Lord, which was [a]made of the seed of David
according to the flesh;
4 *And* [a][1]declared *to be* the Son of God
with power, according [b]to the Spirit of holiness, by the resurrection from the dead:
5 By whom [a]we have received grace and
apostleship, [1]for [b]obedience to the faith
among all nations, [c]for his name:
6 Among whom are ye also *the* called of
Jesus Christ:
7 To all that be in Rome, beloved of God,
[a]called *to be* saints: [b]Grace to you and peace
from God our Father, and the Lord Jesus
Christ.

Thanksgiving and prayers

8 ¶ First, [a]I thank my God through Jesus
Christ for you all, that [b]your faith is spoken of
throughout the whole world.
9 For [a]God is my witness, [b]whom I serve
[1]with my spirit in the gospel of his Son, that
[c]without ceasing I make mention of you, always in my prayers,
10 Making request, if by any means now at
length I might have a prosperous journey by
the will of God to come unto you.
11 For I long to see you, that [a]I may impart
unto you some spiritual gift, to the end you
may be established;
12 That is, that *I* may be comforted together [1]with you by [a]the mutual faith both of you
and me.
13 Now I would not have you ignorant,
brethren, that oftentimes I purposed to come
unto you, (but [a]was let hitherto,) that I might
have some [b]fruit [1]among you also, even as
among other Gentiles.
14 I am debtor both to the Greeks, and to
the barbarians; both to the wise, and to the
unwise.
15 So, as much as in me is, I am ready to
preach the gospel to you that are at Rome also.
16 For [a]I am not ashamed of the gospel of
Christ: for [b]it is the power of God unto salvation to every one that believeth; [c]to the Jew
first, and *also* to the Greek.
17 For [a]therein is the righteousness of God
revealed from faith to faith: as it is written,
[b]The just shall live by faith.

The Gentiles: guilty before God

18 ¶ [a]For the wrath of God is revealed from
heaven against all ungodliness and unrighteousness of men, who hold the truth in unrighteousness;

1:1 [a]1 Tim. 1:11 [b]Acts 9:15
1:2 [a]Acts 26:6 [b]Gal. 3:8
1:3 [a]Gal. 4:4
1:4 [1]Gr. *determined* [a]Acts 13:33 [b]Heb. 9:14
1:5 [1]Or, *to the obedience of faith* [a]Eph. 3:8 [b]Acts 6:7 [c]Acts 9:15
1:7 [a]1 Cor. 1:2 [b]1 Cor. 1:3
1:8 [a]1 Cor. 1:4 [b]ch. 16:19
1:9 [1]Or, *in my spirit* [a]ch. 9:1 [b]Acts 27:23 [c]1 Thes. 3:10
1:11 [a]ch. 15:29
1:12 [1]Or, *in you* [a]Tit. 1:4
1:13 [1]Or, *in you* [a]1 Thes. 2:18 [b]Phil. 4:17
1:16 [a]Ps. 40:9,10; Mark 8:38 [b]1 Cor. 1:18 [c]Luke 2:30; Acts 13:26
1:17 [a]ch. 3:21 [b]Hab. 2:4; John 3:36; Gal. 3:11
1:18 [a]Acts 17:30; Eph. 5:6

‡1:1 *Paul.* In ancient times writers put their names at the beginning of letters. For more information on Paul see notes on Acts 9:1; Phil 3:4–14. *servant.* The Greek for this word means (1) a "slave," who completely belongs to his owner and has no freedom to leave, and (2) a "servant," who willingly chooses to serve his master. See notes on Ex 14:31; Ps 18 title; Is 41:8–9; 42:1. *apostle.* One specially commissioned by Christ (see notes on Mark 6:30; 1 Cor 1:1; Heb 3:1). *gospel.* See note on Mark 1:1.

1:2 *prophets.* Not just the writers of the prophetic books, for the whole OT prophesied about Jesus (see Luke 24:27,44). *holy scriptures.* The OT.

1:7 *saints.* The basic idea of the Greek for this word is "holiness." All Christians are saints in that they are positionally "set apart" to God and are experientially being made increasingly "holy" by the Holy Spirit (see note on 1 Cor 1:2). *Grace.* See notes on Jonah 4:2; Gal 1:3; Eph 1:2. *peace.* See notes on John 14:27; 20:19; Gal 1:3; Eph 1:2.

1:8 *thank.* Paul often began his letters with thanks (see 1 Cor 1:4; Eph 1:16; Phil 1:3; Col 1:3; 1 Thes 1:2; 2 Thes 1:3; 2 Tim 1:3; Philem 4). *through Jesus Christ.* The Christian must go through Christ not only for requests to God (see John 15:16) but also to give thanks. *throughout the whole world.* Every place where the gospel has been preached.

1:9 *gospel of his Son.* The same as the "gospel of God" (v. 1).

1:12 *together.* Paul's genuine humility is seen in his desire to be ministered to by the believers at Rome as well as to minister to them.

1:13 *fruit.* New converts as well as spiritual growth by those already converted. *among you . . . among other Gentiles.* Suggests that the church at Rome was predominantly Gentile.

‡1:14 *Greeks.* Those Gentiles who spoke Greek or followed the Greek way of life, even though they may have been Latin-speaking citizens of the Roman empire. *barbarians.* A word that probably imitated the unintelligible sound of their languages to Greek ears. They were the other Gentiles to whom Paul ministered.

1:16–17 The theme of the entire book.

1:16 *not ashamed.* Not even in the capital city of the Roman empire (see v. 15). *gospel.* See note on Mark 1:1. *first.* Not only in time but also in privilege. "Salvation is of the Jews" (John 4:22), and the Messiah was a Jew. The "oracles of God" (3:2), the covenants, law, temple worship, revelation of the divine glory, and Messianic prophecies came to them (9:3–5). These privileges, however, were not extended to the Jews because of their superior merit or because of God's partiality toward them. It was necessary that the invasion of this world by the gospel begin at a particular point with a particular people, who in turn were responsible to carry that gospel to the other nations.

1:17 *righteousness.* The state of being "in the right" in relation to God (see notes on 2:13; 3:21,24).

1:18–3:20 In developing the theme of righteousness from God (1:17; 3:21–5:21), Paul sets the stage by showing that all have sinned and therefore need the righteousness that only God can provide. He shows the sin of the Gentiles (1:18–32) and the sin of the Jews (2:1–3:8) and then summarizes the sin of all—Gentile and Jew alike (3:9–20).

1:18–20 No one—not even one who has not heard of the Bible or of Christ—has an excuse for not honoring God, because the whole created world reveals Him.

1:18 *wrath of God.* Not a petulant, irrational burst of anger, such as humans often exhibit, but a holy, just revulsion against what is contrary to and opposes His holy nature and will. *is revealed.* God's wrath is not limited to the end-time judgment of the wicked (1 Thes 1:10; Rev 19:15; 20:11–15). Here the wrath of God is His abandonment of the wicked to their sins (vv. 24–32). *the truth.* The truth about God revealed in the creation order.

19 Because [a]that which may be known of God is manifest [1]in them; for [b]God hath shewed *it* unto them.

20 For [a]the invisible *things* of him from the creation of the world are clearly seen, being understood by the things that are made, *even* his eternal power and Godhead; [1]so that they are without excuse:

21 Because that, when they knew God, they glorified *him* not as God, neither were thankful; but [a]became vain in their imaginations, and their foolish heart was darkened.

22 [a]Professing *themselves* to be wise, they became fools,

23 And changed the glory of the uncorruptible [a]God into an image made like to corruptible man, and to birds, and fourfooted beasts, and creeping things.

24 [a]Wherefore God also gave them up to uncleanness through the lusts of their own hearts, [b]to dishonour their own bodies [c]between themselves:

25 Who changed [a]the truth of God [b]into a lie, and worshipped and served the creature [1]more than the Creator, who is blessed for ever. Amen.

26 ¶ For this cause God gave them up unto [a]vile affections: for even their women did change the natural use into that which is against nature:

27 And likewise also the men, leaving the natural use of the woman, burned in their lust one towards another; men with men working that which is unseemly, and receiving in themselves *that* recompence of their error which was meet.

28 And even as they did not like [1]to retain God in *their* knowledge, God gave them over to [2]a reprobate mind, to do those *things* [a]which are not convenient;

29 Being filled with all unrighteousness, fornication, wickedness, covetousness, maliciousness; full of envy, murder, debate, deceit, malignity; whisperers,

30 Backbiters, haters of God, despiteful, proud, boasters, inventors of evil *things*, disobedient to parents,

31 Without understanding, covenantbreakers, [1]without natural affection, implacable, unmerciful:

32 Who [a]knowing the judgment of God, that they which commit such *things* [b]are worthy of death, not only do the same, but [c][1]have pleasure in them that do *them*.

God's principles of judgment

2 Therefore thou art [a]inexcusable, O man, whosoever thou art that judgest: [b]for wherein thou judgest another, thou condemnest thyself; for thou that judgest doest the same *things*.

2 But we are sure that the judgment of God is according to truth against them which commit such *things*.

3 And thinkest thou this, O man, that judgest them which do such *things*, and doest the same, that thou shalt escape the judgment of God?

4 Or despisest thou [a]the riches of his goodness and [b]forbearance and [c]longsuffering; [d]not knowing that the goodness of God leadeth thee to repentance?

5 But after thy hardness and impenitent heart [a]treasurest up unto thyself wrath against the day of wrath and revelation of the righteous judgment of God;

6 [a]Who will render to every *man* according to his deeds:

7 To them who by patient continuance in well doing seek for glory and honour and immortality, eternal life:

8 But unto them that are contentious, and

1:19 [1]Or, *to them* [a]Acts 14:17 [b]John 1:9
1:20 [1]Or, *that they may be* [a]Ps. 19:1; Acts 14:17
1:21 [a]2 Ki. 17:15; Jer. 2:5; Eph. 4:17
1:22 [a]Jer. 10:14
1:23 [a]Deut. 4:16; Ps. 106:20; Is. 40:18
1:24 [a]Ps. 81:12; Acts 7:42; Eph. 4:18 [b]1 Cor. 6:18; 1 Thes. 4:4 [c]Lev. 18:22
1:25 [1][Or, *rather*] [a]1 Thes. 1:9; 1 John 5:20 [b]Is. 44:20; Jer. 10:14
1:26 [a]Lev. 18:22; Eph. 5:12
1:28 [1]Or, *to acknowledge* [2]Or, *a mind void of judgment* [a]Eph. 5:4
1:31 [1]Or, *unsociable*
1:32 [1]Or, *consent with them* [a]ch. 2:2 [b]ch. 6:21 [c]Ps. 50:18; Hos. 7:3
2:1 [a]ch. 1:20 [b]2 Sam. 12:5; Mat. 7:1,2; John 8:9
2:4 [a]Eph. 1:7 [b]ch. 3:25 [c]Ex. 34:6 [d]Is. 30:18; 2 Pet. 3:9
2:5 [a]Deut. 32:34; Jas. 5:3
2:6 [a]Job 34:11; Ps. 62:12; Prov. 24:12; Jer. 17:10; 2 Cor. 5:10

1:21 *knew God.* From seeing His revelation in creation (vv. 19–20). The fact that these people were idolaters (v. 23) and knew God only through the creation order indicates that they were Gentiles. *thankful.* For earthly blessings, such as sun, rain and crops (see Mat 5:45; Acts 14:17).

1:23 *glory.* God's unique majesty (see Is 48:11), which fallen mankind has lost sight of and for which they have substituted deities of their own devising, patterned after various creatures.

1:24,26,28 *God . . . gave them up.* Or "God gave them over." God allowed sin to run its course as an act of judgment.

1:25 *Amen.* Can mean either "Yes indeed, it is so" or "So be it" (see 9:5; 11:36; 15:33; 16:27; see also note on Deut 27:15; cf. 1 Ki 1:36).

1:26 *their women.* Not necessarily their wives.

1:27 Homosexual practice is sinful in God's eyes. The OT also condemns the practice (see Lev 18:22).

1:28 *retain God in their knowledge.* See vv. 19,21. *a reprobate mind.* The intent precedes the act (see v. 21; Mark 7:20–23).

1:32 *knowing.* Their outrageous conduct was not due to total ignorance of what God required but to self-will and rebellion. *have pleasure in them that do them.* The extreme of sin is applauding, rather than regretting, the sins of others.

2:1–16 In this section Paul sets forth principles that govern God's judgment. God judges (1) according to truth (v. 2), (2) according to deeds (vv. 6–11) and (3) according to the light a person has (vv. 12–15). These principles lay the groundwork for Paul's discussion of the guilt of the Jews (vv. 17–29).

2:1 *inexcusable.* Paul's teaching about judging agrees with that of Jesus (see note on Mat 7:1), who did not condemn judging as such, but hypocritical judging. *whosoever . . . that judgest.* A warning that had special relevance for Jews, who were inclined to look down on Gentiles because of their ignorance of God's revelation in the OT and because of their immoral lives.

2:2 *we are sure.* An expression Paul frequently used that assumed the persons addressed agreed with the statement that followed (see 3:19; 7:14; 8:22,28; 1 Cor 8:1,4; 2 Cor 5:1; 1 Tim 1:8).

2:3 Jesus also condemned this attitude (Mat 7:3; cf. Luke 18:9).

2:4 The purpose of God's kindness is to give opportunity for repentance (2 Pet 3:9). The Jews had misconstrued His patience to be a lack of intent to judge.

2:5 *day of wrath.* Judgment at the end of time in contrast to the judgment discussed in 1:18–32.

‡2:6–8 Paul is not contradicting his continual emphasis in all his writings, including Romans, that a person is saved not by what he does but by faith in what Christ does for him. Rather, he is discussing the principle of judgment according to deeds (see note on vv. 1–16). If anyone persists in doing good deeds

[a]do not obey the truth, but obey unrighteousness, indignation and wrath,

9 Tribulation and anguish, upon every soul of man that doeth evil, of the Jew [a]first, and *also* of the [1]Gentile;

10 [a]But glory, honour, and peace, to every *man* that worketh good, to the Jew first, and *also* to the [1]Gentile:

11 For [a]there is no respect of persons with God.

12 For as many as have sinned without law shall also perish without law: and as many as have sinned in the law shall be judged by the law;

13 (For [a]not the hearers of the law *are* just before God, but the doers of the law shall be justified.

14 For when *the* Gentiles, which have not the law, do by nature the *things* contained in the law, these, having not the law, are a law unto themselves:

15 Which shew the work of the law written in their hearts, [1]their conscience also bearing witness, and *their* thoughts [2]the mean while accusing or else excusing one another;)

16 [a]In the day when God shall judge the secrets of men [b]by Jesus Christ [c]according to my gospel.

The Jews: guilty before God

17 ¶ Behold, [a]thou art called a Jew, and [b]restest in the law, [c]and makest thy boast of God,

18 And [a]knowest *his* will, and [b1]approvest the *things* that are more excellent, being instructed out of the law;

19 And [a]art confident that thou thyself art a guide of the blind, a light of them which are in darkness,

20 An instructor of the foolish, a teacher of babes, [a]which hast the form of knowledge and of the truth in the law.

21 [a]Thou therefore which teachest another, teachest thou not thyself? thou that preachest *a man* should not steal, dost thou steal?

22 Thou that sayest *a man* should not commit adultery, dost thou commit adultery? thou that abhorrest idols, [a]dost thou commit sacrilege?

23 Thou that [a]makest thy boast of the law, through breaking the law dishonourest thou God?

24 For the name of God is blasphemed among the Gentiles through you, as it is [a]written.

25 [a]For circumcision verily profiteth, if thou keep the law: but if thou be a breaker of the law, thy circumcision is made uncircumcision.

26 Therefore [a]if the uncircumcision keep the righteousness of the law, shall not his uncircumcision be counted for circumcision?

27 And shall not uncircumcision which is by nature, if it fulfil the law, [a]judge thee, who by the letter and circumcision dost transgress the law?

28 For [a]he is not a Jew, which is one outwardly; neither *is that* circumcision, which is outward in the flesh:

29 But he *is* a Jew, [a]which is one inwardly; and [b]circumcision *is that* of the heart, [c]in the spirit, *and* not *in* the letter; [d]whose praise *is* not of men, but of God.

3 What advantage then hath the Jew? or what profit *is there* of circumcision?

2 Much every way: chiefly, because that [a]unto them were committed the oracles of God.

3 For what if [a]some did not believe? [b]shall

2:8 [a]Job 24:13; 2 Thes. 1:8
2:9 [1]Gr. *Greek* [a]Amos 3:2; Luke 12:47; 1 Pet. 4:17
2:10 [1]Gr. *Greek* [a]1 Pet. 1:7
2:11 [a]Deut. 10:17; Job 34:19; Acts 10:34; Eph. 6:9
2:13 [a]Jas. 1:22; 1 John 3:7
2:15 [1]Or, *the conscience witnessing with them* [2]Or, *between themselves*
2:16 [a]Eccl. 12:14; Mat. 25:31; Rev. 20:12 [b]John 5:22; Acts 10:42 [c]1 Tim. 1:11
2:17 [a]Mat. 3:9; John 8:33 [b]Mic. 3:11 [c]Is. 48:2
2:18 [1]Or, *triest the things that differ* [a]Deut. 4:8 [b]Phil. 1:10
2:19 [a]Mat. 15:14; John 9:34
2:20 [a]2 Tim. 3:5
2:21 [a]Ps. 50:16; Mat. 23:3
2:22 [a]Mal. 3:8
2:23 [a]ver. 17
2:24 [a]2 Sam. 12:14; Is. 52:5; Ezek. 36:20
2:25 [a]Gal. 5:3
2:26 [a]Acts 10:34
2:27 [a]Mat. 12:41
2:28 [a]Mat. 3:9; John 8:39; Gal. 6:15
2:29 [a]1 Pet. 3:4 [b]Phil. 3:3 [c]ch. 7:6 [d]1 Cor. 4:5; 2 Cor. 10:18; 1 Thes. 2:4
3:2 [a]Deut. 4:7; Ps. 147:19
3:3 [a]Heb. 4:2 [b]Num. 23:19; 2 Tim. 2:13

(i.e., lives a perfect life), he will receive eternal life. No one can do this, (cf. 3:10–12), but if anyone could, God would give him life, since God judges according to what a person does.

2:9 *of the Jew first.* With spiritual privilege comes spiritual responsibility (see Amos 3:2; Luke 12:48).

2:11 A basic teaching of both the OT and the NT.

2:12 *law.* The Mosaic law. "For as many as have sinned without law" refers to Gentiles. God judges according to the light available to people. Gentiles will not be condemned for not obeying a law they did not possess. Their judgment will be on other grounds (see 1:18–20; 2:15; cf. Amos 1:3–2:3).

2:13 *shall be justified.* At God's pronouncement of acquittal on judgment day (see note on 3:24).

2:14 *by nature.* By natural impulse without the external constraint of the Mosaic law. *things contained in the law.* Does not mean that pagans fulfilled the requirements of the Mosaic law but refers to practices in pagan society that agreed with the law, such as caring for the sick and elderly, honoring parents and condemning adultery. *law unto themselves.* The moral nature of pagans, enlightened by conscience (v. 15), functioned for them as the Mosaic law did for the Jews.

‡2:16 This verse picks up Paul's thought from v. 12, vv. 13–15 being parenthetical in Paul's argument.

2:17–24 The presentation takes the form of a dialogue. Paul knew how a self-righteous Jew thought, for he had been one himself. He cites one advantage after another that Jews considered to be unqualified assets. But those assets became liabilities when there was no correspondence between profession and practice. Paul applied to the Jew the principles of judgment set forth in vv. 1–16 (see note on those verses).

2:19–20 *the blind . . . babes.* Gentiles, to whom Jews regarded themselves as vastly superior because they (the Jews) possessed the Mosaic law.

‡2:22 *dost thou commit sacrilege?* Lit. "rob temples." See Acts 19:37. Large amounts of wealth were often stored in pagan temples.

2:25 *circumcision.* A sign of the covenant that God made with Israel (see Lev 12:3) and a pledge of the covenant blessing (see Gen 17 and notes on Gen 17:10–11). The Jews had come to regard circumcision as a guarantee of God's favor.

2:27 If a Gentile's deeds excelled those of a Jew in righteousness, that very fact condemned the Jew, who had an immeasurably better set of standards in the law of Moses.

2:29 *in the spirit.* The true sign of belonging to God is not an outward mark on the physical body, but the regenerating power of the Holy Spirit within—what Paul meant by "circumcision . . . of the heart" (see Deut 30:6).

3:2 *chiefly.* Paul does not discuss the other advantages of being a Jew until 9:4–5. *committed.* The advantage of having the very words of God involves a duty.

their unbelief make the faith of God without
effect?
4 [a]God forbid: yea, let [b]God be true, but
[c]every man a liar; as it is written, [d]That thou
mightest be justified in thy sayings, and mightest overcome when thou art judged.
5 But if our unrighteousness commend the
righteousness of God, what shall we say? *Is*
God unrighteous who taketh vengeance? ([a]I
speak as a man)
6 God forbid: for then [a]how shall God
judge the world?
7 For if the truth of God hath *more* abounded through my lie unto his glory; why yet am I
also judged as a sinner?
8 And not *rather,* (as we be slanderously reported, and as some affirm that we say,) [a]Let
us do evil, that good may come? whose damnation is just.

The world: guilty before God

9 ¶ What then? are we better *than they?* No,
in no wise: for we have before [1]proved both
Jews and Gentiles, that [a]*they* are all under sin;
10 As it is written, [a]There is none righteous, no, not one:
11 There is none that understandeth, there
is none that seeketh after God.
12 They are all gone out of the way, they
are together become unprofitable; there is
none that doeth good, no, not one.
13 [a]Their throat *is* an open sepulchre; with
their tongues they have used deceit; [b]the poison of asps *is* under their lips:
14 [a]Whose mouth is full of cursing and bitterness:
15 [a]Their feet *are* swift to shed blood:
16 Destruction and misery *are* in their
ways:
17 And the way of peace have they not
known:
18 [a]There is no fear of God before their
eyes.
19 Now we know that what *things* soever
[a]the law saith, it saith to them who are under
the law: that [b]every mouth may be stopped,
and [c]all the world may become [1]guilty before
God.
20 Therefore [a]by the deeds of the law
there shall no flesh be justified in his sight: for
[b]by the law *is* the knowledge of sin.

Faith: the means of salvation

21 ¶ But now [a]the righteousness of God
without the law is manifested, [b]being witnessed by the law [c]and the prophets;
22 Even the righteousness of God *which is*
[a]by faith of Jesus Christ unto all and upon all
them that believe: for [b]there is no difference:
23 For [a]all have sinned, and come short of
the glory of God;
24 Being justified freely [a]by his grace
[b]through the redemption that is in Christ
Jesus:

3:4 [a]Job 40:8 [b]John 3:33 [c]Ps. 62:9 [d]Ps. 51:4
3:5 [a]Gal. 3:15
3:6 [a]Gen. 18:25
3:8 [a]ch. 5:20
3:9 [1]Gr. *charged* [a]Gal. 3:22
3:10 [a]Ps. 14:1-3
3:13 [a]Ps. 5:9; Jer. 5:16
3:13 [b]Ps. 140:3
3:14 [a]Ps. 10:7
3:15 [a]Prov. 1:16; Is. 59:7,8
3:18 [a]Ps. 36:1
3:19 [1]Or, *subject to the judgment of God* [a]John 10:34 [b]Job 5:16; Ps. 107:42 [c]ch. 2:2
3:20 [a]Ps. 143:2; Acts 13:39; Gal. 2:16 [b]ch. 7:7
3:21 [a]Acts 15:11; ch. 1:17 [b]John 5:46 [c]1 Pet. 1:10
3:22 [a]ch. 4 [b]ch. 10:12; Gal. 3:28; Col. 3:11
3:23 [a]ch. 11:32; Gal. 3:22
3:24 [a]ch. 4:16; Eph. 2:8; Tit. 3:5,7 [b]Mat. 20:28; Eph. 1:7; Col. 1:14; 1 Tim. 2:6; Heb. 9:12; 1 Pet. 1:18

‡**3:3** *faith of God.* The Greek word means either "faith" or "faithfulness." Here it means "faithfulness." God is faithful to His promises and would punish Israel for its unbelief (v. 5; see 2 Tim 2:13).
3:4 God's punishment of sin exhibits His faithfulness to His righteous character.
3:5 *commend the righteousness of God.* By contrast, in showing it up against the dark background of man's sin. *I speak as a man.* Or "I am using a human argument," in the sense of its weakness and absurdity.
3:6 *judge.* On judgment day. *the world.* All moral creatures (also in v. 19)—a more limited reference than in 1:20.
3:9 *are we better than they?* Are Jews better than Gentiles in the sight of God? *all.* Nine times in four verses (vv. 9–12) Paul mentions the universality of sin ("all," two times; "none," four times; "not even one," two times; "together," once). *under sin.* Under its power and condemnation.
3:10–18 A collection of OT quotations that underscores Paul's charge that both Jews and Gentiles are under the power of sin. Several factors explain why the citations are not always verbatim: 1. NT quotations sometimes gave the general sense and were not meant to be word-for-word. 2. Quotation marks were not used in Greek. 3. The quotations were often taken from the Greek translation (the Septuagint) of the Hebrew OT, because Greek readers were not familiar with the Hebrew Bible. 4. Sometimes the NT writer, in order to drive home his point, would purposely (under the inspiration of the Holy Spirit) adapt an OT passage or combine two or more passages.
3:11 *understandeth.* About God and what is right.
3:13 *open sepulchre.* Expressing the corruption of the heart.
3:18 *fear of God.* Awesome reverence for God; the source of all godliness (see note on Gen 20:11).
3:19 *we know.* See note on 2:2. *law.* The OT (as in John 10:34; 15:25; 1 Cor 14:21). *them who are under the law.* Jews. *every mouth . . . all the world.* Jews as well as Gentiles are guilty.
3:20 *justified.* See notes on v. 24; 2:13.
3:21–5:21 Having shown that all (both Gentiles and Jews) are unrighteous (1:18–3:20), Paul now shows that God has provided a righteousness for mankind.
3:21 *But now.* There are two possible meanings: (1) temporal—all of time is divided into two periods, and in the "now" period the righteousness from God has been made known; (2) logical—the contrast is between the righteousness gained by observing the law (which is impossible, v. 20) and the righteousness provided by God. *witnessed by the law and the prophets.* See Gen 15:6; Ps 32:1–2; Hab 2:4.
‡**3:22–23** *for there is no difference . . . glory of God.* A parenthetical thought: "All them that believe" (v. 22) are "justified freely" (v. 24), not "all have sinned" (v. 23) are "justified freely" (v. 24). Thus "justified" goes with "believe," not with "sinned."
3:22 *no difference.* Between Jews and Gentiles (see 10:12).
3:23 *glory of God.* What God intended man to be. The glory that man had before the fall (see Gen 1:26–28; Ps 8:5–6; cf. Eph 4:24; Col 3:10) the believer will again have through Christ (see Heb 2:5–9).
‡**3:24** *justified.* Paul uses the Greek verb for "justified" 27 times, mostly in Romans and Galatians. The term describes what happens when someone believes in Christ as his Savior: From the negative viewpoint, God declares the person to be not guilty; from the positive viewpoint, He declares him to be righteous. He cancels the guilt of the person's sin and credits righteousness to him. Paul emphasizes two points in this regard: 1. No one lives a perfectly good, holy, righteous life. On the contrary, "there is none righteous" (v. 10), and "all have sinned, and come short of the glory of God" (v. 23). "By the deeds of the law there shall no flesh be justified in his sight" (v. 20). 2. But even though all are sinners and not sons, God will declare everyone who puts

25 Whom God hath [1]set forth [a]*to be* a propitiation through faith [b]in his blood, to declare his righteousness for the [2]remission of [c]sins that are past, through the forbearance of God;

26 To declare, *I say,* at this time his righteousness: that he might be just, and the justifier of him which believeth in Jesus.

27 [a]Where *is* boasting then? It is excluded. By what law? of works? Nay: but by the law of faith.

28 Therefore we conclude [a]that a man is justified by faith without the deeds of the law.

29 *Is he* the God of the Jews only? *is he* not also of the Gentiles? Yes, of the Gentiles also:

30 Seeing [a]*it is* one God, which shall justify the circumcision by faith, and uncircumcision through faith.

31 Do we then make void the law through faith? God forbid: yea, we establish the law.

Abraham saved by faith

4 What shall we say then that [a]Abraham our father, as pertaining to the flesh, hath found?

2 For if Abraham were [a]justified by works, he hath whereof to glory; but not before God.

3 For what saith the scripture? [a]Abraham believed God, and it was counted unto him for righteousness.

4 Now [a]to him that worketh is the reward not reckoned of grace, but of debt.

5 But to him that worketh not, but believeth on him that justifieth [a]the ungodly, his faith is counted for righteousness.

6 Even as David also describeth the blessedness of the man, unto whom God imputeth righteousness without works,

7 *Saying,* [a]Blessed *are they* whose iniquities are forgiven, and whose sins are covered.

8 Blessed *is* the man to whom the Lord will not impute sin.

9 *Cometh* this blessedness then upon the circumcision *only,* or upon the uncircumcision also? for we say that faith was reckoned to Abraham for righteousness.

10 How was it then reckoned? when he was in circumcision, or in uncircumcision? Not in circumcision, but in uncircumcision.

11 And [a]he received the sign of circumcision, a seal of the righteousness of the faith which he had *yet* being uncircumcised: that [b]he might be the father of all them that believe, though they be not circumcised; that righteousness might be imputed unto them also:

12 And the father of circumcision to them who are not of the circumcision only, but who also walk in the steps of *that* faith of our father Abraham, which he had being *yet* uncircumcised.

13 For the promise, that he should be the [a]heir of the world, *was* not to Abraham, or to his seed, through the law, but through the righteousness of faith.

3:25 [1]Or, *foreordained* [2]Or, *passing over* [a]Lev. 16:15; 1 John 2:2; 4:10 [b]Col. 1:20 [c]Acts 17:30; Heb. 9:15
3:27 [a]ch. 2:17,23; 1 Cor. 1:29; Eph. 2:9
3:28 [a]ver. 20-22; Gal. 2:16
3:30 [a]ch. 10:12; Gal. 3:8,20
4:1 [a]Is. 51:2; Mat. 3:9; John 8:33; 2 Cor. 11:22
4:2 [a]ch. 3:20,27
4:3 [a]Gen. 15:6; Gal. 3:6; Jas. 2:23
4:4 [a]ch. 11:6
4:5 [a]Josh. 24:2
4:7 [a]Ps. 32:1,2
4:11 [a]Gen. 17:10 [b]ver. 12,16; Luke 19:9; Gal. 3:7
4:13 [a]Gen. 17:4; Gal. 3:29

---

his trust in Jesus not guilty but righteous. This legal declaration is valid because Christ died to pay the penalty for our sin and lived a life of perfect righteousness that can in turn be imputed to us. This is the central theme of Romans and is stated in the theme verse, 1:17 ("the righteousness of God"). Christ's righteousness (His obedience to God's law and His sacrificial death) will be credited to believers as their own. Paul uses one Greek word meaning "reckoned, imputed, or counted" 11 times in ch. 4 alone. *freely by his grace.* The central thought in justification is that, although man clearly and totally deserves to be declared guilty (vv. 9–19), because of his trust in Christ God declares him righteous. This is stated in several ways here: (1) "freely" (for nothing), (2) "by his grace," (3) "through the redemption that is in Christ Jesus" and (4) "through faith" (v. 25). *redemption.* A word taken from the slave market—the basic idea is that of obtaining release by payment of a ransom. Paul uses this word to refer to release from guilt, with its liability for judgment, and to deliverance from slavery to sin, because Christ in His death paid the ransom for us.

‡3:25 *to be a propitiation.* Or, "as the One who would turn aside God's wrath, taking away sin." The Greek for this phrase speaks of a sacrifice that satisfies the righteous wrath of God: Without this appeasement all people are justly destined for eternal punishment. See also note on 1 John 2:2. *through faith in his blood.* Saving faith looks to Jesus Christ in His sacrificial death for us.

3:25b–26 The sins of God's people, punished symbolically in the animal sacrifices of the OT period, would be totally punished in the once-for-all sacrifice of Christ on the cross.

3:28 *by faith.* When Luther translated this passage, he added the word "alone," which, though not in the Greek, accurately reflects the meaning (see note on Jas 2:14–26).

‡3:30 *Seeing it is one God.* By appealing to the first article of Jewish faith ("the LORD our God is one!" Deut 6:4), Paul argues that there is only one way of salvation for both Jew and Gentile, namely, faith in Christ.

‡3:31 Paul anticipated being charged with antinomianism (against law): If justification comes by faith alone, then is not the law rejected? He gives a more complete answer in chs. 6–7 and reasserts the validity of the law in 13:8–10. cf. also 1 Tim 1:8–10.

4:1 *Abraham our father.* The great patriarch of the Jewish nation, the true example of a justified person (see Jas 2:21–23). The Jews of Jesus' time used Abraham as an example of justification by works, but Paul holds him up as a shining example of righteousness by faith (see Gal 3:6–9).

4:3 The reference is to Gen 15:6, where nothing is mentioned about works. *counted unto him.* Abraham had kept no law, rendered no service and performed no ritual that earned credit to his account before God. His belief in God, who had made promises to him, was credited to him as righteousness.

‡4:6–8 God does not continue to impute unrighteousness to the sinner who repents, but forgives him when he confesses (see Ps 32:3–5; Ezek 18:23,27–28,32; 33:14–16).

4:9 *circumcision.* Jews. *uncircumcision.* Gentiles.

4:10 *Not in circumcision . . . uncircumcision.* Abraham was declared righteous (Gen 15) some 14 years before he was circumcised (Gen 17). See Gal 3:17 for a similar statement.

‡4:11 *sign.* Circumcision was, among other things, the outward sign of the righteousness that God had credited to Abraham for his faith. *that . . . father.* Abraham is the "father" of believing Gentiles (the uncircumcised), because he believed and was justified before the rite of circumcision (the mark of Jews) was instituted.

4:12 *father of circumcision.* Abraham is also the father of believing Jews. Thus his story shows that for Jew and Gentile alike there is only one way of justification—the way of faith.

‡4:13 *heir of the world.* "World" here refers to the creation, as

14 For [a]if they which are of the law *be*
heirs, faith is made void, and the promise
made of none effect:
15 Because [a]the law worketh wrath: for
where no law is, *there is* no transgression.
16 Therefore *it is* of faith, that *it might be*
[a]by grace; [b]to the end the promise might be
sure to all the seed; not to that only which is of
the law, but to that also which is of the faith of
Abraham; [c]who is the father of us all,
17 (As it is written, [a]I have made thee a father of many nations,) [1]before *him* whom he
believed, *even* God, [b]who quickeneth the
dead, and calleth those [c]*things* which be not
as though they were.
18 Who against hope believed in hope,
that he might become the father of many nations; according to that which was spoken, [a]So
shall thy seed be.
19 And being not weak in faith, [a]he considered not his own body now dead, when he
was about an hundred year old, neither *yet* the
deadness of Sara's womb:
20 He staggered not at the promise of God
through unbelief; but was strong in faith, giving glory to God;
21 And being fully persuaded that, what he
had promised, [a]he was able also to perform.
22 And therefore it was imputed to him for
righteousness.
23 Now [a]it was not written for his sake
alone, that it was imputed to him;
24 But for us also, to whom it shall be imputed, if we believe [a]on him that raised up
Jesus our Lord from the dead;
25 [a]Who was delivered for our offences,
and [b]was raised *again* for our justification.

Results of justification by faith

5 Therefore [a]being justified by faith, we
have [b]peace with God through our Lord
Jesus Christ:
2 [a]By whom also we have access by faith
into this grace [b]wherein we stand, and [c]re-
joice in hope of the glory of God.
3 And not only *so,* but [a]we glory in tribulations also: [b]knowing that tribulation worketh
patience;
4 [a]And patience, experience; and experience, hope:
5 [a]And hope maketh not ashamed; [b]because

4:14 [a]Gal. 3:18 **4:15** [a]ch. 3:20; 7:8,10,11; 1 Cor. 15:56; 2 Cor. 3:7,9; Gal. 3:10; 1 John 3:4 **4:16** [a]ch. 3:24 [b]Gal. 3:22 [c]Is. 51:2; ch. 9:8 **4:17** [1]Or, *like unto him* [a]Gen. 17:5 [b]ch. 8:11; Eph. 2:1,5 [c]ch. 9:26; 1 Cor. 1:28; 1 Pet. 2:10 **4:18** [a]Gen. 15:5 **4:19** [a]Gen. 17:17; 18:11; Heb. 11:11 **4:21** [a]Ps. 115:3; Luke 1:37; Heb. 11:19 **4:23** [a]ch. 15:4; 1 Cor. 10:6 **4:24** [a]Acts 2:24 **4:25** [a]Is. 53:5,6; ch. 3:25; Gal. 1:4; Heb. 9:28 [b]1 Cor. 15:17; 1 Pet. 1:21 **5:1** [a]Is. 32:17; John 16:33 [b]Eph. 2:14 **5:2** [a]John 10:9; Eph. 2:18 [b]1 Cor. 15:1 [c]Heb. 3:6

5:3 [a]Mat. 5:11; Acts 5:41; 2 Cor. 12:10; Phil. 2:17; Jas. 1:2 [b]Jas. 1:3 **5:4** [a]Jas. 1:12 **5:5** [a]Phil. 1:20 [b]2 Cor. 1:22; Eph. 1:13

in 1:20. No express mention of this heirship is made in the Genesis account of Abraham. He is promised "seed as the dust of the earth" (Gen 13:16) and possession of the land of Canaan (Gen 12:7; 13:14–15; 15:7,18–21; 17:8), and that all the peoples on earth will be blessed through him (Gen 12:3; 18:18) or his offspring (Gen 22:18). But since, as Genesis already makes clear, God purposed through Abraham and his offspring to work out the destiny of the whole world, it was implicit in the promises to Abraham that he and his offspring would "inherit the earth" (see Ps 37:9,11,22,29,34; Mat 5:5). The full realization of this awaits the consummation of the Messianic kingdom at Christ's return. *not . . . through the law.* Not on the condition that the promise be merited by works of the law. *his seed.* All those of whom Abraham is said to be father (vv. 11–12).

4:14 *they which are of the law.* Those whose claim to the inheritance is based on the fulfillment of the law. *promise.* See note on v. 13.

‡4:15 *law worketh wrath.* The law, because it reveals sin and even stimulates it (see 7:7–11), produces wrath, not promise. *transgression.* Overstepping a clearly defined line. Where there is no law there is still sin, but it does not have the character of transgression or violation.

4:16 A summary of the thought of vv. 11–12. For the close correlation between faith and grace see 3:24–25; Eph 2:8. *which is of the law.* Jewish Christians. *which is of the faith of Abraham.* Gentile Christians who share Abraham's faith but who, like Abraham, do not possess the law.

4:17 *before him.* God considers Abraham the father of Jews and believing Gentiles alike, no matter how others (especially the Jews) may see him. *God, who quickeneth the dead.* The main reference is to the birth of Isaac through Abraham and Sarah, both of whom were far past the age of childbearing (see Gen 18:11). Secondarily Paul alludes also to the resurrection of Christ (see vv. 24–25). *calleth . . . as though they were.* God has the ability to create out of nothing, as He demonstrated in the birth of Isaac.

4:18 *against hope believed in hope.* When all hope, as a human possibility, failed, Abraham placed his hope in God.

4:19 *being not weak in faith.* Abraham had some anxious moments (see Gen 17:17–18), but God did not count these against him. *considered not.* Faith does not refuse to face reality but looks beyond all difficulties to God and His promises. *deadness of Sara's womb.* Sarah was ten years younger than Abraham (see Gen 17:17) but well past the age of bearing children.

4:20 *giving glory to God.* Because Abraham had faith to believe that God would do what He promised. Whereas works are man's attempt to establish a claim on God, faith brings glory to Him.

‡4:22 *therefore.* Abraham's faith was "reckoned to him for righteousness" because it was true faith, i.e., complete confidence in God's promise.

4:23 *not written for his sake alone.* Abraham's experience was not private or individual but had broad implications. If justification by faith was true for him, it is universally true.

‡4:24 *But for us also.* As Abraham was justified because he believed in a God who brought life from the dead, so we will be justified by believing "on him that raised up Jesus our Lord from the dead."

5:1 *peace with God.* Not merely a subjective feeling (peace of mind) but primarily an objective status, a new relationship with God: Once we were His enemies, but now we are His friends (see v. 10; Eph 2:16; Col 1:21–22).

5:2 *have access.* Jesus ushers us into the presence of God. The heavy curtain (of the temple) that separated man from God and God from man has been removed (see note on Mat 27:51). *hope of the glory of God.* The Christian's confidence that the purpose for which God created him will be ultimately realized (see note on 3:23).

5:3 *glory in tribulations.* Not "because of" but "in." Paul does not advocate a morbid view of life but a joyous and triumphant one.

5:4 A Christian can rejoice in suffering because he knows that it is not meaningless. Part of God's purpose is to produce character in His children.

5:5 *hope maketh not ashamed.* The believer's hope is not to be equated with unfounded optimism. On the contrary, it is the blessed assurance of our future destiny and is based on God's love, which is revealed to us by the Holy Spirit and objectively

the love of God is shed abroad in our hearts by
the Holy Ghost which is given unto us.
6 For when we were yet without strength,
[1]in due time [a]Christ died for the ungodly.
7 For scarcely for a righteous *man* will one
die: yet peradventure for a good *man* some
would even dare to die.
8 But [a]God commendeth his love toward
us, in that, while we were yet sinners, Christ
died for us.
9 Much more then, being now justified [a]by
his blood, we shall be saved [b]from wrath
through him.
10 For [a]if, when we were enemies, [b]we
were reconciled to God by the death of his
Son, much more, being reconciled, we shall be
saved [c]by his life.
11 And not only *so,* but we also [a]joy in
God through our Lord Jesus Christ, by whom
we have now received the [1]atonement.

Christ the basis of our salvation

12 ¶ Wherefore, as [a]by one man sin entered into the world, and [b]death by sin; and so
death passed upon all men, [1]for that all have
sinned:
13 For until the law sin was in the world:
but [a]sin is not imputed when there is no law.
14 Nevertheless death reigned from Adam
to Moses, even over them that had not sinned
after the similitude of Adam's transgression,
[a]who is the figure of *him* that was to come.
15 But not as the offence, so also *is* the free
gift. For if through the offence of one many be
dead, much more the grace of God, and the
gift by grace, which is by one man, Jesus
Christ, hath abounded [a]unto many.
16 And not as *it was* by one that sinned, *so*
is the gift: for the judgment *was* by one to
condemnation, but the free gift *is* of many offences unto justification.
17 For if [1]by one man's offence death
reigned by one; much more they which receive
abundance of grace and of the gift of righteousness shall reign in life by one, Jesus Christ.
18 Therefore as [1]by the offence of one
judgment came upon all men to condemnation; even so [2]by the righteousness of one *the*
free gift came [a]upon all men unto justification
of life.
19 For as by one man's disobedience many
were made sinners, so by the obedience of one
shall many be made righteous.
20 Moreover [a]the law entered, that the offence might abound. But where sin abounded,
grace did much [b]more abound:

5:6 [1]Or, *according to the time* [a]ch. 4:25
5:8 [a]John 15:13
5:9 [a]Eph. 2:13; 1 John 1:7 [b]1 Thes. 1:10
5:10 [a]ch. 8:32 [b]2 Cor. 5:18; Eph. 2:16 [c]John 14:19
5:11 [1][Or, *reconciliation*] [a]Gal. 4:9
5:12 [1]Or, *in whom* [a]Gen. 3:6; 1 Cor. 15:21 [b]Gen. 2:17
5:13 [a]1 John 3:4
5:14 [a]1 Cor. 15:21
5:15 [a]Is. 53:11
5:17 [1]Or, *by one offence*
5:18 [1]Or, *by one offence* [2]Or, *by one righteousness* [a]John 12:32; Heb. 2:9
5:20 [a]John 15:22; Gal. 3:19 [b]Luke 7:47

demonstrated to us in the death of Christ. Paul has moved from faith (v. 1) to hope (vv. 2,4–5) to love (v. 5; see 1 Cor 13:13; see also note on 1 Thes 1:3). *is shed abroad.* The verb indicates a present status resulting from a past action. When we first believed in Christ, the Holy Spirit poured out His love in our hearts, and His love for us continues to dwell in us.

5:6 *in due time.* The appointed moment in God's redemptive plan (Mark 1:15; Gal 4:4). *Christ died for the ungodly.* Christ's love is grounded in God's free grace and is not the result of any inherent worthiness found in its objects (mankind). In fact, it is lavished on us in spite of our undesirable character.

5:7 *righteous man . . . good man.* We were neither righteous nor good, but sinners, when Christ died for us (see v. 8; 3:10–12).

‡5:9 *by his blood.* By laying down His life as a sacrifice—a reference to Christ's death for our sins (see 3:25). *wrath.* The final judgment, as the verb "shall be saved" makes clear (cf. 1 Thes 1:9–10).

‡5:10 *enemies.* Man is the enemy of God, not the reverse. Thus the hostility must be removed from man if reconciliation is to be accomplished. God took the initiative in bringing this about through the death of His Son (see v. 11; Col 1:21–22). *reconciled.* To reconcile is "to put an end to hostility," and is closely related to the term "justify," as the parallelism in vv. 9–10 indicates:

v. 9	v. 10
justified	reconciled
by his blood	by the death of his Son
we shall be saved	we shall be saved

saved by his life. A reference to the unending life and ministry of the resurrected Christ for His people (see Heb 7:25). Since we were reconciled when we were God's enemies, we will be saved because Christ lives to keep us.

‡5:11 *atonement.* This is the noun form of the verb used twice in v. 10: "reconciled." This noun is translated with the sense of reconciliation elsewhere in the N.T. See 2 Cor 5:18,19. Reconciliation, like justification (v. 1), is a present reality for Christians and is something to rejoice about.

5:12–21 A contrast between Adam and Christ. Adam introduced sin and death into the world; Christ brought righteousness and life. The comparison begun in v. 12 is completed in v. 18; these two verses summarize the whole passage. These two men also sum up the message of the book up to this point. Adam stands for man's condemnation (1:18–3:20); Christ stands for the believer's justification (3:21–5:11).

5:12 *death.* Physical death is the penalty for sin. It is also the symbol of spiritual death, man's ultimate separation from God. *for that all have sinned.* Not a repetition of 3:23. The context shows that Adam's sin involved the rest of mankind in condemnation (vv. 18–19) and death (v. 15). We do not start life with even the possibility of living it sinlessly; we begin it with a sinful nature (see Gen 8:21; Ps 51:5; 58:3; Eph 2:3).

5:13 *sin is not imputed.* In the period when there was no (Mosaic) law, sin was not charged against man (see 4:15). Death, however, continued to occur (v. 14). Since death is the penalty for sin, people between Adam and Moses were involved in the sin of someone else, namely, Adam (see note on v. 12).

5:14 *figure.* Adam by his sin brought universal ruin on the human race. In this act he is the prototype of Christ, who through one righteous act (v. 18) brought universal blessing. The analogy is one of contrast.

‡5:15 *many.* The same as "all men" in v. 12 (see Is 53:11; Mark 10:45). *much more.* A theme that runs through this section. God's grace is infinitely greater for good than is Adam's sin for evil.

5:16 *gift.* Salvation. *many offences.* The sins of the succeeding generations.

5:17 *shall reign in life.* The future reign of believers with Jesus Christ (2 Tim 2:12; Rev 22:5).

5:18 *free gift came upon all men.* Does not mean that everyone eventually will be saved, but that salvation is available to all. To be effective, God's gracious gift must be received (see v. 17).

5:19 *made righteous.* A reference to a standing (status) before God (see 2 Cor 5:21), not to a change in character. The latter (the doctrine of sanctification) is developed in chs. 6–8.

5:20 *law entered.* Not to bring about redemption but to point

21 That as sin hath reigned unto death,
even so might grace reign through righteousness unto eternal life by Jesus Christ our Lord.

Believers dead to sin

6 What shall we say then? [a]Shall we continue in sin, that grace may abound?
2 God forbid. How shall we, that are [a]dead
to sin, live any longer therein?
3 Know ye not, that [a]so many of us as
[1]were baptized into Jesus Christ [b][1]were baptized into his death?
4 Therefore we are [a]buried with him by
baptism into death: that [b]like as Christ was
raised up from the dead by [c]the glory of the
Father, [d]*even* so we also should walk in newness of life.
5 [a]For if we have been planted together in
the likeness of his death, we shall be also *in
the likeness* of *his* resurrection:
6 Knowing this, that [a]our old man is crucified with *him,* that [b]the body of sin might be
destroyed, that henceforth we should not
serve sin.
7 For [a]he that is dead is [1]freed from sin.

6:1 [a]ch. 3:8
6:2 [a]Gal. 2:19; Col. 3:3
6:3 [1]Or, *are* [a]Gal. 3:27 [b]1 Cor. 15:29
6:4 [a]Col. 2:12 [b]ch. 8:11; 1 Cor. 6:14 [c]John 2:11 [d]Gal. 6:15
6:5 [a]Phil. 3:10
6:6 [a]Gal. 2:20 [b]Col. 2:11
6:7 [1]Gr. *justified* [a]1 Pet. 4:1
6:8 [a]2 Tim. 2:11
6:9 [a]Rev. 1:18
6:10 [a]Heb. 9:27 [b]Luke 20:38
6:11 [a]ver. 2 [b]Gal. 2:19
6:12 [a]Ps. 19:13
6:13 [1]Gr. *arms,* or, *weapons* [a]ch. 7:5; Col. 3:5; Jas. 4:1 [b]ch. 12:1; 1 Pet. 2:24; 4:2
6:14 [a]ch. 7:4,6; 8:2; Gal. 5:18
6:15 [a]1 Cor. 9:21

8 Now [a]if we be dead with Christ, we believe that we shall also live with him:
9 Knowing that [a]Christ being raised from
the dead dieth no more; death hath no more
dominion over him.
10 For in that he died, [a]he died unto sin
once: but in that he liveth, [b]he liveth unto God.
11 Likewise reckon ye also yourselves to
be [a]dead indeed unto sin, but [b]alive unto God
through Jesus Christ our Lord.
12 [a]Let not sin therefore reign in your
mortal body, that *ye* should obey it in the lusts
thereof.
13 Neither yield ye your [a]members *as* [1]in-
struments of unrighteousness unto sin: but
[b]yield yourselves unto God, as *those that are*
alive from the dead, and your members *as* [1]in-
struments of righteousness unto God.
14 For [a]sin shall not have dominion over
you: for ye are not under the law, but under
grace.

Slaves to righteousness

15 ¶ What then? shall we sin, [a]because we
are not under the law, but under grace? God
forbid.

up the need for it. The law made sin even more sinful by revealing what sin is in stark contrast to God's holiness.

6:1–8:39 In 3:21–5:21 Paul explains how God has provided for our redemption and justification. He next explains the doctrine of sanctification—the process by which believers grow to maturity in Christ. He treats this subject in three parts: (1) freedom from sin's tyranny (ch. 6), (2) freedom from the law's condemnation (ch. 7) and (3) life in the power of the Holy Spirit (ch. 8).

6:1 *Shall we continue in sin, that grace may abound?* This question arose out of what Paul had just said in 5:20: "Where sin abounded, grace did much more abound." Such a question expresses an antinomian (against law) viewpoint. Apparently some objected to Paul's teaching of justification by faith alone because they thought it would lead to moral irresponsibility.

6:2 *dead to sin.* The reference is to an event in the past and is explained in v. 3.

6:3–4 The when and how of the Christian's death to sin. In NT times baptism so closely followed conversion that the two were considered part of one event (see Acts 2:38 and note). So although baptism is not a means by which we enter into a vital faith relationship with Jesus Christ, it is closely associated with faith. Baptism depicts graphically what happens as a result of the Christian's union with Christ, which comes with faith—through faith we are united with Christ, just as through our natural birth we are united with Adam. As we fell into sin and became subject to death in father Adam, so we now have died and been raised again with Christ—which baptism symbolizes.

6:4 *buried with him by baptism into death.* Amplified in vv. 5–7. *by the glory of the Father.* By the power of God. God's glory is His divine excellence, His perfection. Any one of His attributes is a manifestation of His excellence. Thus His power is a manifestation of His glory, as is His righteousness (see 3:23). Glory and power are often closely related in the Bible (see Ps 145:11; Col 1:11; 1 Pet 4:11; Rev 1:6; 4:11; 5:12–13; 7:12; 19:1). *walk in newness of life.* Amplified in vv. 8–10.

6:6 *our old man.* Our unregenerate self; what we once were. *body of sin.* The self in its pre-Christian state, dominated by sin. This is a figurative expression in which the old self is personified. It is a "body" that can be put to death. For the believer, this old self has been rendered powerless so that it can no longer enslave us to sin—whatever lingering vitality it may yet exert in its death throes.

6:7 *is dead.* The believer's death with Christ to sin's ruling power. *freed from sin.* Set free from its shackles and power.

6:8 As resurrection followed death in the experience of Christ, so the believer who dies with Christ is raised to a new quality of moral life here and now. Resurrection in the sense of a new birth is already a fact, and it increasingly exerts itself in the believer's life.

‡6:10 *he died unto sin once.* In His death Christ (for the sake of sinners) submitted to the "reign" of sin (5:21); but His death broke the judicial link between sin and death, and He passed forever from the sphere of sin's "reign." Having been raised from the dead, He now lives forever to glorify God. *unto God.* For the glory of God.

‡6:11 *reckon . . . yourselves.* The first step toward victory over sin in the believer's life (for the succeeding steps see note on vv. 12–13). He is dead to sin and alive to God, and by faith he is to live in the light of this truth.

6:12–13 A call for the Christian to become in experience what he already is in position—dead to sin (see vv. 5–7) and alive to God (see vv. 8–10). The second step toward the Christian's victory over sin is refusal to let sin reign in his life (v. 12). The third step is to offer himself to God (v. 13).

‡6:13 *yield.* Putting yourselves in the service of, perhaps also echoing the language of sacrifice. *your members.* All the separate capacities of your being (also in v. 19).

6:14 *sin shall not have dominion over you.* Paul conceived of sin as a power that enslaves, and so personified it. *not under the law.* The meaning is not that the Christian has been freed from all moral authority. He has, however, been freed from the law in the manner in which God's people were under law in the OT era. law provides no enablement to resist the power of sin; it only condemns the sinner. But grace enables. *under grace.* For the disciplinary aspect of grace see Tit 2:11–12.

6:15–23 The question raised here seems to come from those who are afraid that the doctrine of justification by faith alone will remove all moral restraint. Paul rejects such a suggestion and shows that a Christian does not throw morality to the

16 Know ye not, that [a]to whom ye yield
yourselves servants to obey, *his* servants ye are
to whom ye obey; whether of sin unto death,
or of obedience unto righteousness?
17 But God be thanked, that ye were the
servants of sin, but ye have obeyed from the
heart [a]*that* form of doctrine [1]which was delivered you.
18 Being then [a]made free from sin, ye became the servants of righteousness.
19 I speak after the manner of men because of the infirmity of your flesh: for as ye
have yielded your members servants to uncleanness and to iniquity unto iniquity; *even*
so now yield your members servants to righteousness unto holiness.
20 For when ye were [a]the servants of sin,
ye were free [1]from righteousness.
21 [a]What fruit had ye then *in those things*
whereof ye are now ashamed? for [b]the end of
those *things is* death.
22 But now [a]being made free from sin, and
become servants to God, ye have your fruit
unto holiness, and the end everlasting life.
23 For [a]the wages of sin *is* death; but [b]the
gift of God *is* eternal life through Jesus Christ
our Lord.

Married to Christ

7 Know ye not, brethren, (for I speak to
them that know the law,) how that the
law hath dominion over a man, as long as he
liveth?
2 For [a]the woman which hath a husband is
bound by the law to *her* husband so long as he
liveth; but if the husband be dead, she is
loosed from the law of the husband.
3 So then [a]if, while *her* husband liveth, she
be married to another man, she shall be called
an adulteress: but if *her* husband be dead, she
is free from *that* law; so that she is no adulteress, though she be married to another man.
4 Wherefore, my brethren, ye also are become [a]dead to the law by the body of Christ;
that ye should be married to another, *even* to
him who is raised from the dead, that we
should [b]bring forth fruit unto God.
5 For when we were in the flesh, the [1]mo-
tions of sins, which were by the law, [a]did
work in our members [b]to bring forth fruit unto
death.
6 But now we are delivered from the law,
[1]*that* being dead wherein we were held; that
we should serve [a]in newness of spirit, and not
in the oldness of the letter.

The Christian struggle

7 ¶ What shall we say then? *Is* the law sin?
God forbid. Nay, [a]I had not known sin, but by
the law: for I had not known [1]lust, except the
law had said, [b]Thou shalt not covet.
8 But [a]sin, taking occasion by the commandment, wrought in me all *manner of* concupiscence. For [b]without the law sin *was*
dead.
9 For I was alive without the law once: but
when the commandment came, sin revived,
and I died.

6:16 [a]Mat. 6:24; John 8:34; 2 Pet. 2:19
6:17 [1]Gr. *whereto ye were delivered* [a]2 Tim. 1:13
6:18 [a]John 8:32; 1 Cor. 7:22; Gal. 5:1; 1 Pet. 2:16
6:20 [1]Gr. *to righteousness* [a]John 8:34
6:21 [a]ch. 7:5 [b]ch. 1:32
6:22 [a]John 8:32
6:23 [a]Gen. 2:17; ch. 5:12; Jas. 1:15 [b]ch. 2:7; 1 Pet. 1:4
7:2 [a]1 Cor. 7:39
7:3 [a]Mat. 5:32
7:4 [a]Gal. 2:19; 5:18; Col. 2:14 [b]Gal. 5:22
7:5 [1]Gr. *passions* [a]ch. 6:13 [b]ch. 6:21; Gal. 5:19; Jas. 1:15
7:6 [1]Or, *being dead* to that [a]ch. 2:29; 2 Cor. 3:6
7:7 [1]Or, *concupiscence* [a]ch. 3:20 [b]Ex. 20:17; Deut. 5:21; Acts 20:33
7:8 [a]ch. 4:15 [b]1 Cor. 15:56

winds. To the contrary, he exchanges sin for righteousness as his master.

6:16 The contrast between sin and obedience suggests that sin is by nature disobedience to God.

6:17 *obeyed from the heart.* Christian obedience is not forced or legalistic, but willing. *form of doctrine.* May refer to a summary of the moral and ethical teachings of Christ that was given to new converts in the early church.

6:18 *servants of righteousness.* A Christian has changed masters. Whereas he was formerly a slave to sin, now he becomes a slave (a willing servant) to righteousness.

6:19 *I speak after the manner of men.* An apology for using an imperfect analogy. The word "servant" when applied to Christians, who are free in Christ, naturally presents problems.

‡6:22 *made free from sin.* See note on v. 6. *holiness.* Slavery to God produces holiness, (or sanctification) and the end of the process is eternal life (viewed not in its present sense but in its final, future sense). There is no eternal life without holiness (see Heb 12:14). Anyone who has been justified will surely give evidence of that fact by the presence of holiness in his life. For other uses of various forms of the word "sanctification" see v. 19; 1 Cor 1:30; 1 Thes 4:3–4,7; 2 Thes 2:13; 1 Tim 2:15; Heb 12:14; 1 Pet 1:2.

6:23 Two kinds of servitude are contrasted here. One brings death as its wages; the other results in eternal life, not as wages earned or merited, but as a gift of God. For the contrast between wages and gift see 4:4.

7:1 *law.* Perhaps Paul has in mind the Mosaic law, but his concern here is with the fundamental character of law as such.

7:2–3 These verses illustrate the principle set down in v. 1. Death decisively changes a person's relationship to the law.

7:4 *Wherefore.* Paul now draws the conclusion from the principle stated in v. 1 and illustrated in vv. 2–3. *dead to the law.* The law's power to condemn no longer threatens the Christian, whose death here is to be understood in terms of 6:2–7. There, however, he dies to sin; here he dies to the law. The result is that the law has no more hold on him. *by the body of Christ.* His physical body (self) crucified. *married to another.* The resurrected Christ (see 6:5). The purpose of this union is to produce the fruit of holiness.

‡7:5 *in the flesh.* A condition, so far as Christians are concerned, that belongs to the past—the unregenerate state. *by the law.* The law not only reveals sin; it also stimulates it. The natural tendency in man is to desire the forbidden thing. *death.* Physical death and, beyond that, spiritual death—final separation from God—were the fruit of our "union" with the law.

‡7:6 *delivered from the law.* In the sense of its condemnation (see note on v.4). *wherein we were held.* The law; see vv. 4,6. *newness of spirit.* See note on 8:4. *oldness of the letter.* Life under the OT law.

7:7 *Is the law sin?* This question was occasioned by the remarks about the law in vv. 4–6. *I.* Paul seems to be using the first person pronoun of himself, but also as representative of mankind in general (vv. 7–12) and of Christians in particular (vv. 13–25). *I had not known sin.* The law fulfilled the important function of revealing the presence and fact of sin.

7:8 *occasion by the commandment.* See note on v. 5. *sin was dead.* Not nonexistent but not fully perceived.

7:9 *I was alive . . . once.* Paul reviews his own experience from the vantage point of his present understanding. Before he realized that the law condemned him to death, he was alive. Reference is to the time either before his *bar mitzvah* (see below)

10 And the commandment, [a]which was *ordained* to life, I found *to be* unto death.
11 For sin, taking occasion by the commandment, deceived me, and by it slew *me.*
12 Wherefore [a]the law *is* holy, and the commandment holy, and just, and good.
13 Was then that which is good made death unto me? God forbid. But sin, that it might appear sin, working death in me by that which is good; that sin by the commandment might become exceeding sinful.
14 ¶ For we know that the law is spiritual: but I am carnal, [a]sold under sin.
15 For *that* which I do I [1]allow not: for [a]what I would, that do I not; but what I hate, that do I.
16 If then I do that which I would not, I consent unto the law that *it is* good.
17 Now then it is no more I that do it, but sin that dwelleth in me.
18 For I know that [a]in me (that is, in my flesh,) dwelleth no good *thing:* for to will is present with me; but *how* to perform that which is good I find not.
19 For the good that I would I do not: but the evil which I would not, that I do.
20 Now if I do that I would not, it is no more I that do it, but sin that dwelleth in me.
21 I find then a law, that, when I would do good, evil is present with me.
22 For I [a]delight in the law of God after [b]the inward man:
23 But [a]I see another law in [b]my members, warring against the law of my mind, and bringing me into captivity to the law of sin which is in my members.
24 O wretched man that I am! who shall deliver me from [1]the body of this death?
25 [a]I thank God through Jesus Christ our Lord. So then with the mind I myself serve the law of God; but with the flesh the law of sin.

Life in the Spirit

8 *There is* therefore now no condemnation to them *which are* in Christ Jesus who [a]walk not after the flesh, but after the Spirit.
2 For [a]the law of [b]the Spirit of life in Christ Jesus hath made me free from [c]the law of sin and death.
3 For [a]what the law could not do, in that it

7:10 [a]Lev. 18:5; Ezek. 20:11,13, 21; 2 Cor. 3:7
7:12 [a]Ps. 19:8; 119:38; 1 Tim. 1:8
7:14 [a]2 Ki. 17:17
7:15 [1]Gr. *know* [a]Gal. 5:17
7:18 [a]Gen. 6:5; 8:21
7:22 [a]Ps. 1:2 [b]2 Cor. 4:16; Eph. 3:16; Col. 3:9,10
7:23 [a]Gal. 5:17 [b]ch. 6:13,19
7:24 [1]Or, *this body of death*
7:25 [a]1 Cor. 15:57
8:1 [a]Gal. 5:16
8:2 [a]ch. 6:18,22 [b]1 Cor. 15:45 [c]ch. 7:24,25
8:3 [a]Acts 13:39; Heb. 7:18

or before his conversion, when the true rigor of the law became clear to him (see Luke 18:20–21; Phil 3:6). *when the commandment came.* When Paul came to the realization that he stood guilty before the law—a reference either to his *bar mitzvah,* when he, at age 13, assumed full responsibility for the law, or to the time when he became aware of the full force of the law (at his conversion). *I died.* Paul came to realize he was condemned to death, because law reveals sin, and sin's wages is death (6:23).

7:10 *ordained to life.* See Lev 18:5. As it worked out, law became the avenue through which sin entered—both in Paul's experience and in that of mankind. Instead of giving life, the law brought condemnation; instead of producing holiness, it stimulated sin.

7:12 *the law is holy.* Despite the despicable use that sin made of the law, the law was not to blame. The law is God's and as such is holy, righteous and good.

‡7:13–25 Whether Paul is describing a Christian or non-Christian experience has been hotly debated through the centuries. That he is speaking of the non-Christian life is suggested by: (1) the use of phrases such as "sold under sin" (v. 14), "I know that in me . . . dwelleth no good thing" (v. 18) and "wretched man that I am!" (v. 24)—which do not seem to describe Christian experience; (2) the contrast between ch. 7 and ch. 8, making it difficult for the other view to be credible; (3) the problem of the value of conversion if one ends up in spiritual misery. In favor of the view that Paul is describing Christian experience are: (1) the use of the present tense throughout the passage; (2) Paul's humble opinion of himself (v. 18); (3) his high regard for God's law (vv. 14,16); (4) the location of this passage in the section of Romans where Paul is dealing with sanctification—the growth of the Christian in holiness.

7:13 Sin used a holy thing (law) for an unholy end (death). By this fact the contemptible nature of sin is revealed.

7:14 *spiritual.* The law had its origin in God. *I am.* The personal pronoun and the verb, taken together, suggest that Paul is describing his present (Christian) experience. *carnal.* Even a believer has the seeds of rebellion in his heart. *sold under sin.* A phrase so strong that many refuse to accept it as descriptive of a Christian. However, it may graphically point out the failure even of Christians to meet the radical ethical and moral demands of the gospel. It also points up the persistent nature of sin.

‡7:15 *I allow not.* I do not understand. The struggle within creates tension, ambivalence and confusion.

7:16 *I consent unto the law that it is good.* Even when Paul is rebellious and disobedient, the Holy Spirit reveals to him the essential goodness of the law.

7:17 *no more I that do it.* Not an attempt to escape moral responsibility but a statement of the great control sin can have over a Christian's life.

7:18 *in me . . . dwelleth no good thing.* A reference to man's fallen nature, as the last phrase of the sentence indicates. Paul is not saying that no goodness at all exists in Christians.

7:20 *sin . . . in me.* See note on v. 17.

7:22 *I delight in the law of God.* The Mosaic law or God's law generally. It is difficult to see how a non-Christian could say this.

7:23 *another law.* A principle or force at work in Paul preventing him from giving obedience to God's law. *law of my mind.* His desire to obey God's law. *law of sin.* Essentially the same as "another law," mentioned above.

7:24 *body of this death.* Figurative for the body of sin (6:6) that hung on him like a corpse and from which he could not gain freedom.

7:25 The first half of this verse is the answer to the question stated in v. 24—deliverance comes, not through legalistic effort, but through Christ. The last half is a summary of vv. 13–24. *I myself.* The real self—the inner being that delights in God's law (v. 22).

8:1 *condemnation.* The law brings condemnation because it points out, stimulates and condemns sin. But the Christian is no longer "under the law" (6:14). *in Christ Jesus.* United with him, as explained in 6:1–10 (see note on 6:11).

‡8:2 *the law of the Spirit of life.* The controlling power of the Holy Spirit, who is life-giving. Paul uses the word "law" in several different ways in Romans—to mean, e.g., a controlling power (here); God's law (2:17–20; 9:31; 10:3–5); the Pentateuch (3:21b); the OT as a whole (3:19); a principle (3:27). *law of sin and death.* The controlling power of sin, which ultimately produces death.

8:3 *could not do.* The law was not able to overcome sin. It could

was weak through the flesh, [b]God sending his own Son in the likeness of sinful flesh, and [1]for sin, condemned sin in the flesh:

4 That the righteousness of the law might be fulfilled in us, [a]who walk not after the flesh, but after the Spirit.

5 For [a]they that are after the flesh do mind the *things* of the flesh; but they *that are* after the Spirit [b]the *things* of the Spirit.

6 For [a] [1]to be carnally minded *is* death; but [2]to be spiritually minded *is* life and peace.

7 Because [a] [1]the carnal mind *is* enmity against God: for it is not subject to the law of God, [b]neither indeed can be.

8 So then they that are in the flesh cannot please God.

9 But ye are not in the flesh, but in the Spirit, if so be that the Spirit of God dwell in you. Now if any *man* have not [a]the Spirit of Christ, he is none of his.

10 And if Christ *be* in you, the body *is* dead because of sin; but the Spirit *is* life because of righteousness.

11 But if the Spirit of [a]him that raised up Jesus from the dead dwell in you, [b]he that raised up Christ from the dead shall also quicken your mortal bodies [1]by his Spirit that dwelleth in you.

12 ¶ [a]Therefore, brethren, we are debtors, not to the flesh, to live after the flesh.

13 For [a]if ye live after the flesh, ye shall die: but if ye through the Spirit do [b]mortify the deeds of the body, ye shall live.

14 For [a]as many as are led by the Spirit of God, they are the sons of God.

15 For [a]ye have not received the spirit of bondage again [b]to fear; but ye have received the [c]Spirit of adoption, whereby we cry, [d]Abba, Father.

16 [a]The Spirit itself beareth witness with our spirit, that we are the children of God:

17 And if children, then heirs; [a]heirs of God, and joint-heirs with Christ; [b]if so be that we suffer with *him,* that we may be also glorified together.

The future glory

18 For I reckon that [a]the sufferings of *this* present time *are* not worthy to be compared with the glory which shall be revealed in us.

19 For [a]the earnest expectation of the creature waiteth for the manifestation of the sons of God.

20 For [a]the creature was made subject to vanity, not willingly, but by reason of him who hath subjected *the same,* in hope,

21 Because the creature itself also shall be

8:3 [1]Or, by a sacrifice *for sin* [b]2 Cor. 5:21; Gal. 3:13
8:4 [a]ver. 1
8:5 [a]John 3:6 [b]Gal. 5:22
8:6 [1]Gr. *the minding of the flesh* [2]Gr. *the minding of the Spirit* [a]Gal. 6:8
8:7 [1]Gr. *the minding of the flesh* [a]Jas. 4:4 [b]1 Cor. 2:14
8:9 [a]John 3:34; Gal. 4:6
8:11 [1]Or, *because of his Spirit* [a]Acts 2:24 [b]1 Cor. 6:14; 2 Cor. 4:14
8:12 [a]ch. 6:7,14
8:13 [a]Gal. 6:8 [b]Eph. 4:22
8:14 [a]Gal. 5:18
8:15 [a]1 Cor. 2:12; Heb. 2:15 [b]2 Tim. 1:7; 1 John 4:18 [c]Is. 56:5 [d]Mark 14:36
8:16 [a]Eph. 1:13
8:17 [a]Acts 26:18 [b]Phil. 1:29
8:18 [a]2 Cor. 4:17; 1 Pet. 1:6
8:19 [a]2 Pet. 3:13
8:20 [a]Gen. 3:19

point out, condemn and even stimulate sin, but it could not remove it. *in the likeness of sinful flesh.* Christ in His incarnation became truly a man, but, unlike all other men, was sinless. *in the flesh.* "Flesh" may refer either to man's flesh or to Christ's. If the latter, it states where God condemned sin, namely, in Christ's human (but not sinful) nature—the interpretation that seems more consistent with Paul's teaching.

8:4 *righteousness of the law.* The law still plays a role in the life of a believer—not, however, as a means of salvation but as a moral and ethical guide, obeyed out of love for God and by the power that the Spirit provides. This is the fulfillment of Jer 31:33–34 (a prophecy of the new covenant). *fulfilled.* God's aim in sending His Son was that believers might be enabled to embody the true and full intentions of the law. *after the Spirit.* How the law's righteous requirements can be fully met—by no longer letting the sinful nature hold sway but by yielding to the directing and empowering ministry of the Holy Spirit.

8:5–8 Two mind-sets are described here: that of the sinful nature and that of the Spirit. The former leads to death, the latter to life and peace. The sinful nature is bound up with death (v. 6), hostility to God (v. 7), insubordination (v. 7) and unacceptability to God (v. 8).

‡8:9 *he is none of his.* If a person does not possess the indwelling Holy Spirit, he does not possess Christ either. The Christian is indwelt by the Spirit as a result of his justification.

‡8:10 *the body is dead because of sin.* Even a Christian's body is subject to physical death, the consequence of sin. *Spirit is life.* And "body" is understood as in 7:24. *because of righteousness.* Because the spirit of the Christian has been justified, it is not subject to death as is his body.

8:11 For the close connection between the resurrection of Christ and that of believers see 1 Cor 6:14; 15:20,23; 2 Cor 4:14; Phil 3:21; 1 Thes 4:14. *quicken your mortal bodies.* The resurrection of our bodies, guaranteed to believers by the indwelling presence of the Holy Spirit—whose presence is evidenced by a Spirit-controlled life (vv. 4–9), which in turn provides assurance that our resurrection is certain even now.

8:14 *sons of God.* God is the Father of all in the sense that He created all and His love and providential care are extended to all (see Mat 5:45). But not all are His children. Jesus said to the unbelieving Jews of His day, "Ye are of your father the devil" (John 8:44). People become children of God through faith in God's unique Son (see John 1:12–13), and being led by God's Spirit is the hallmark of this relationship.

8:15 *adoption.* The underlying Greek term for "adoption" occurs four other times in the NT (v. 23; 9:4; Gal 4:5 [see note there]; Eph 1:5). Adoption was common among the Greeks and Romans, who granted the adopted son all the privileges of a natural son, including inheritance rights. Christians are adopted sons by grace; Christ, however, is God's Son by nature. *Abba, Father.* Abba (Aramaic for "Father") is expressive of an especially close relationship to God.

8:16 *beareth witness with our spirit.* The inner testimony of the Holy Spirit to our relationship to Christ. *children of God.* The same as "sons of God," terms that in the NT are synonymous.

8:17 *heirs.* Those who have already entered, at least partially, into the possession of their inheritance. *joint-heirs with Christ.* Everything really belongs to Christ, but by grace we share in what is His. *if so be that we suffer with him.* The Greek construction used here does not set forth a condition but states a fact. The meaning, then, is not that there is some doubt about sharing Christ's glory. Rather, despite the fact that Christians presently suffer, they are assured a future entrance into their inheritance.

‡8:19 *the creature.* Both animate and inanimate, but exclusive of human beings (see vv. 22–23, where "whole creation" and "ourselves" are contrasted). *the manifestation of the sons of God.* Christians are already sons of God, but the full manifestation of all that this means will not come until the end (see 1 John 3:1–2).

8:20 *was made subject to vanity.* A reference to Gen 3:17–19. *in hope.* A possible allusion to the promise of Gen 3:15.

delivered from the bondage of corruption into
the glorious liberty of the children of God.
22 For we know that [1]the whole creation
[a]groaneth and travaileth in pain together until
now.
23 And not only *they,* but ourselves also,
which have [a]the firstfruits of the Spirit, [b]even
we ourselves groan within ourselves, [c]waiting
for the adoption, *to wit,* the [d]redemption of
our body.
24 For we are saved by hope: but [a]hope
that is seen is not hope: for what a man seeth,
why doth he yet hope for?
25 But if we hope for that we see not, *then*
do we with patience wait for *it.*
26 Likewise the Spirit also helpeth our infirmities: for [a]we know not what we should
pray for as we ought: but [b]the Spirit itself
maketh intercession for us with groanings
which cannot be uttered.
27 And [a]he that searcheth the hearts
knoweth what *is* the mind of the Spirit, [1]be-
cause he maketh intercession for the saints
[b]according to *the will of* God.
28 And we know that all *things* work together for good to them that love God, to them
[a]who are *the* called according to *his* purpose.
29 For whom [a]he did foreknow, [b]he also
did predestinate [c]*to be* conformed to the image of his Son, [d]that he might be the firstborn
amongst many brethren.
30 Moreover whom he did predestinate,
them he also [a]called: and whom he called,
them he also [b]justified: and whom he justified,
them he also [c]glorified.
31 What shall we then say to these *things?*
[a]If God *be* for us, who *can be* against us?
32 [a]He that spared not his own Son, but
[b]delivered him up for us all, how shall he not
with him also freely give us all *things?*
33 Who shall lay any thing to the charge of
God's elect? [a]*It is* God that justifieth:
34 [a]Who *is* he that condemneth? *It is*
Christ that died, yea rather, that is risen *again,*
[b]who is even at the right hand of God, [c]who
also maketh intercession for us.
35 Who shall separate us from the love of
Christ? *shall* tribulation, or distress, or persecution, or famine, or nakedness, or peril, or
sword?
36 As it is written, [a]For thy sake we are
killed all the day long; we are accounted as
sheep for the slaughter.
37 [a]Nay, in all these *things* we are more
than conquerors through him that loved us.
38 For I am persuaded, that neither death,
nor life, nor angels, nor [a]principalities, nor
powers, nor *things* present, nor *things* to
come,

8:22 [1]Or, *every creature* [a]Jer. 12:11
8:23 [a]2 Cor. 5:5; Eph. 1:14 [b]2 Cor. 5:2 [c]Luke 20:36 [d]Luke 21:28; Eph. 4:30
8:24 [a]2 Cor. 5:7; Heb. 11:1
8:26 [a]Mat. 20:22; Jas. 4:3 [b]Eph. 6:18
8:27 [1]Or, *that* [a]1 Chr. 28:9; Acts 1:24 [b]1 John 5:14
8:28 [a]2 Tim. 1:9
8:29 [a]2 Tim. 2:19 [b]Eph. 1:5 [c]2 Cor. 3:18; 1 John 3:2 [d]Col. 1:15; Heb. 1:6
8:30 [a]1 Pet. 2:9 [b]1 Cor. 6:11 [c]John 17:22; Eph. 2:6
8:31 [a]Num. 14:9; Ps. 118:6
8:32 [a]ch. 5:6,10 [b]ch. 4:25
8:33 [a]Is. 50:8,9; Rev. 12:10
8:34 [a]Job 34:29 [b]Mark 16:19; Col. 3:1; Heb. 1:3 [c]Heb. 7:25; 9:24; 1 John 2:1
8:36 [a]Ps. 44:22; 2 Cor. 4:11
8:37 [a]1 Cor. 15:57; 1 John 4:4
8:38 [a]Eph. 1:21

8:21 *shall be delivered from the bondage of corruption.* The physical universe is not destined for destruction (annihilation) but for renewal (see 2 Pet 3:13; Rev 21:1). And living things will no longer be subject to death and decay, as they are today.

8:22 *groaneth.* Creation is personified as a woman in labor waiting for the birth of her child.

‡8:23 *firstfruits of the Spirit.* The Christian's possession of the Holy Spirit is not only evidence of his present salvation (vv. 14,16) but is also a pledge of his future inheritance—and not only a pledge but also the down payment on that inheritance (see 2 Cor 1:22; 5:5; Eph 1:14). *adoption.* See note on v. 15. Christians are already God's children, but this is a reference to the full realization of our inheritance in Christ. *redemption of our body.* The resurrection, as the final stage of our adoption. The first stage was God's predestination of our adoption (see Eph 1:5); the second is our present inclusion as children of God (see v. 14; Gal 3:26).

8:24 *by hope.* We are saved by faith (see Eph 2:8), not hope; but hope accompanies salvation.

8:26 *Likewise.* As hope sustains the believer in suffering, so the Holy Spirit helps him in prayer. *with groanings which cannot be uttered.* In v. 23 it is the believer who groans; here it is the Holy Spirit. Whether Paul means words that are unspoken or words that cannot be expressed in human language is not clear—probably the former, though v. 27 seems to suggest the latter.

8:27 The relationship between the Holy Spirit and God the Father is so close that the Holy Spirit's prayers need not be audible. God knows His every thought.

8:28 *good.* That which conforms us "to the image of His Son" (v. 29). *called.* Effectual calling: the call of God to which there is invariably a positive response.

8:29 *did foreknow.* Some insist that the knowledge here is not abstract but is couched in love and mixed with purpose. They hold that God not only knew us before we had any knowledge of Him but that He also knew us, in the sense of choosing us by His grace, before the foundation of the world (see Eph 1:4; 2 Tim 1:9 and notes). Others believe that Paul here refers to the fact that in eternity past God knew those who by faith would become His people. *predestinate.* Predestination here is to moral conformity to the likeness of His Son. *that he might be the firstborn amongst many brethren.* The reason God foreknew, predestined and conformed believers to Christ's likeness is that the Son might hold the position of highest honor in the great family of God.

8:30 *predestinate . . . glorified.* The sequence by which God carries out His predestination. *glorified.* Since this final stage is firmly grounded in God's set purpose, it is as certain as if it had already happened.

8:31 *If God be for us.* The form of the condition makes it clear that there is no doubt about it.

8:32 The argument (from the greater to the lesser) here is similar to that in 5:9–10. If God gave the supreme gift of His Son to save us, He will certainly also give whatever is necessary to bring to fulfillment the work begun at the cross. See note on Gen 22:16.

8:33–34 A court of law is in mind. No charge can be brought against the Christian because God has already pronounced a verdict of not guilty.

8:34 Three reasons are given as to why no one can condemn God's elect: (1) Christ died for us; (2) He is alive and seated at the right hand of God, the position of power; (3) He is interceding for us.

8:35–39 Paul wanted to show his readers that suffering does not separate believers from Christ but actually carries them along toward their ultimate goal.

8:36 Ps 44:22 is quoted to show that suffering has always been part of the experience of God's people.

8:37 *that loved us.* Referring especially to Christ's death on the cross.

39 Nor height, nor depth, nor any other creature, shall be able to separate us from the love of God, which is in Christ Jesus our Lord.

God's righteousness and mercy

9 [a]I say the truth in Christ, I lie not, my conscience also bearing me witness in the Holy Ghost,

2 [a]That I have great heaviness and continual sorrow in my heart.

3 For [a]I could wish that myself were [1]accursed from Christ for my brethren, my kinsmen according to the flesh:

4 Who are Israelites; [a]to whom pertaineth the adoption, and [b]the glory, and [c]the [1]covenants, and [d]the giving of the law, and [e]the service *of God,* and [f]the promises;

5 [a]Whose *are* the fathers, and [b]of whom as concerning the flesh Christ *came,* [c]who is over all, God blessed for ever. Amen.

6 [a]Not as though the word of God hath taken none effect. For [b]they *are* not all Israel, which are of Israel:

7 [a]Neither, because they are the seed of Abraham, *are they* all children: but, In [b]Isaac shall thy seed be called.

8 That is, *They which are* the children of the flesh, these *are* not the children of God: but [a]the children of the promise are counted for the seed.

9 For this *is* the word of promise, [a]At this time will I come, and Sara shall have a son.

10 And not only *this;* but when [a]Rebecca also had conceived by one, *even* by our father Isaac;

11 (For *the children* being not yet born, neither having done any good or evil, that the purpose of God according to election might stand, not of works, but of [a]him that calleth;)

12 It was said unto her, [a]The [1]elder shall serve the [2]younger.

13 As it is written, [a]Jacob have I loved, but Esau have I hated.

14 ¶ What shall we say then? [a]*Is there* unrighteousness with God? God forbid.

15 For he saith to Moses, [a]I will have mercy on whom I will have mercy, and I will have compassion on whom I will have compassion.

16 So then *it is* not of him that willeth, nor of him that runneth, but of God that sheweth mercy.

17 For [a]the scripture saith unto Pharaoh, [b]Even for this same *purpose* have I raised thee up, that I might shew my power in thee, and that my name might be declared throughout all the earth.

9:1 [a]2 Cor. 1:23; Gal. 1:20; 1 Tim. 2:7
9:2 [a]ch. 10:1
9:3 [1]Or, *separated* [a]Ex. 32:32
9:4 [1]Or, *testaments* [a]Ex. 4:22; Deut. 14:1 [b]1 Sam. 4:21; 1 Ki. 8:11 [c]Acts 3:25 [d]Ps. 147:19 [e]Heb. 9:1 [f]Acts 13:32; Eph. 2:12
9:5 [a]Deut. 10:15 [b]Luke 3:23 [c]Jer. 23:6; Heb. 1:8
9:6 [a]Num. 23:19 [b]John 8:39; Gal. 6:16
9:7 [a]Gal. 4:23 [b]Gen. 21:12
9:8 [a]Gal. 4:28
9:9 [a]Gen. 18:10
9:10 [a]Gen. 25:21
9:11 [a]ch. 4:17
9:12 [1]Or, *greater* [2]Or, *lesser* [a]Gen. 25:23
9:13 [a]Mal. 1:2,3; Mat. 10:37
9:14 [a]Deut. 32:4; Job 8:3
9:15 [a]Ex. 33:19
9:17 [a]Gal. 3:8 [b]Ex. 9:16

8:39 *Nor height, nor depth.* It is impossible to get beyond God's loving reach. *nor any other creature.* Includes all created things. Only God is not included, and He is the one who has justified us (v. 33).

9:1 *in the Holy Ghost.* Conscience is a reliable guide only when enlightened by the Holy Spirit.

9:3 *accursed.* The Greek for this word is *anathema,* and it means delivered over to the wrath of God for eternal destruction (see 1 Cor 12:3; 16:22; Gal 1:8–9). Such was Paul's great love for his fellow Jews. For a similar expression of love see Ex 32:32.

9:4 *Israelites.* The descendants of Jacob (who was renamed Israel by God; see Gen 32:28). The name was used of the entire nation (see Judg 5:7), then of the northern kingdom after the nation was divided (see 1 Ki 12), the southern kingdom being called Judah. During the intertestamental period and later in NT times, Palestinian Jews used the title to indicate that they were the chosen people of God. Its use here is especially relevant because Paul is about to show that, despite Israel's unbelief and disobedience, God's promises to her are still valid. *adoption.* Israel had been accepted as God's son (see Ex 4:22–23; Jer 31:9; Hos 11:1). *glory.* The evidence of the presence of God among His people (see Ex 16:7,10; Lev 9:6,23; Num 16:19). *covenants.* For example, the Abrahamic (Gen 15:17–21; 17:1–8); the Mosaic (Ex 19:5; 24:1–4), renewed on the plains of Moab (Deut 29:1–15), at mounts Ebal and Gerizim (Josh 8:30–35) and at Shechem (Josh 24); the Levitical (Num 25:12–13; Jer 33:21; Mal 2:4–5); the Davidic (2 Sam 7; 23:5; Ps 89:3–4,28–29; 132:11–12); and the new (prophesied in Jer 31:31–40). *promises.* Especially those made to Abraham (Gen 12:7; 13:14–17; 17:4–8; 22:16–18) but also including the many OT Messianic promises (e.g., 2 Sam 7:12,16; Is 9:6–7; Jer 23:5; 31:31–34; Ezek 34:23–24; 37:24–28).

9:5 *fathers.* Abraham, Isaac, Jacob and his sons. *Christ . . . who is over all, God.* One of the clearest statements of the deity of Jesus Christ found in the entire NT, assuming that "God" refers to "Christ." See also 1:4; Mat 1:23; 28:19; Luke 1:35; 5:20–21; John 1:1,3,10,14,18; 5:18; 20:28; 2 Cor 13:14; Phil 2:6; Col 1:15–20; 2:9; Tit 2:13; Heb 1:3,8; 2 Pet 1:1; Rev 1:13–18; 22:13.

‡9:6 *word of God.* His clearly stated purpose, which has not failed, because "they are not all Israel which are of Israel." Paul is not denying the election of all Israel (as a nation) but stating that within Israel there is a separation, that of unbelieving Israel and believing Israel. Physical descent is no guarantee of a place in God's family.

9:7 *seed.* Physical descendants (e.g., Ishmael and his offspring).

9:8 *children of the flesh.* Those merely biologically descended from Abraham. *children of God.* See v. 4. Not all Israelites were God's children. The reference is to the Israel of faith.

9:11 *neither having done any good or evil.* God's choice of Jacob was based on sovereign freedom, not on the fulfillment of any prior conditions. *purpose of God according to election.* God's purpose embodied in His election (see note on Eph 1:4). *not of works, but of him that calleth.* Before Rebekah's children were even born, God made a choice—a choice obviously not based on works. *calleth.* See 8:28 and note.

‡9:13 *Jacob I have loved, but Esau I have hated.* Equivalent to "Jacob I chose, but Esau I rejected." In vv. 6–13 Paul is dealing with national election—he is portraying the nation Israel (Jacob) over the nation Edom (Esau). See Mal 1:2–3. Paul's intention is evident in light of the problem he is addressing: How can God's promise stand when so many who comprise Israel (in the OT collective sense) are unbelieving and therefore cut off?

9:14 *Is there unrighteousness with God? God forbid.* Is He unjust to elect on the basis of His sovereign freedom, as with Jacob and Esau?

9:15 Paul denies injustice in God's dealing with Isaac and Ishmael, and Jacob and Esau, by appealing to God's sovereign right to dispense mercy as He chooses.

9:16 *it.* God's choice, which is not controlled in any way by man. However, Paul makes it clear that the basis for Israel's rejection was her unbelief (see vv. 30–32).

9:17 *Pharaoh.* Pharaoh of the exodus. *raised thee up.* Made you ruler of Egypt. *my name.* The character of God, particularly as revealed in the exodus (see Ex 15:13–18; Josh 2:10–11; 9:9; 1 Sam 4:8).

18 Therefore hath he mercy on whom he will *have mercy*, and whom he will he hardeneth.

19 Thou wilt say then unto me, Why doth he yet find fault? For [a]who hath resisted his will?

20 Nay but, O man, who art thou that [1]repliest against God? [a]Shall the thing formed say to him that formed *it*, Why hast thou made me thus?

21 Hath not the [a]potter power over the clay, of the same lump to make [b]one vessel unto honour, and another unto dishonour?

22 What if God, willing to shew *his* wrath, and to make his power known, endured with much longsuffering [a]*the* vessels of wrath [b][1]fitted to destruction:

23 And that he might make known [a]the riches of his glory on the vessels of mercy, which he had [b]afore prepared unto glory,

24 Even us, whom he hath called, [a]not of the Jews only, but also of the Gentiles?

25 As he saith also in Osee, [a]I will call *them* my people, which were not my people; and her beloved, which was not beloved.

26 [a]And it shall come to pass, *that* in the place where it was said unto them, Ye *are* not my people; there shall they be called the children of the living God.

27 Esaias also crieth concerning Israel, [a]Though the number of the children of Israel be as the sand of the sea, [b]a remnant shall be saved:

28 For he will finish [1]the work, and cut *it* short in righteousness: [a]because a short work will the Lord make upon the earth.

29 And as Esaias said before, [a]Except the Lord of sabaoth had left us a seed, [b]we had been as Sodoma, and been made like unto Gomorrha.

The gospel offered to the Jews

30 What shall we say then? [a]That the Gentiles, which followed not *after* righteousness, have attained to righteousness, [b]even the righteousness which is of faith.

31 But Israel, [a]which followed *after* the law of righteousness, [b]hath not attained to the law of righteousness.

32 Wherefore? Because *they sought it* not by faith, but as *it were* by the works of the law. For [a]they stumbled at *that* stumblingstone;

33 As it is written, [a]Behold, I lay in Sion a stumblingstone and rock of offence: and [b]whosoever believeth on him shall not be [1]ashamed.

10 Brethren, my heart's desire and prayer to God for Israel is, that *they* might be saved.

2 For I bear them record [a]that they have a zeal of God, but not according to knowledge.

3 For they being ignorant of [a]God's righteousness, and going about to establish their own [b]righteousness, have not submitted themselves unto the righteousness of God.

9:19 [a]2 Chr. 20:6; Dan. 4:35
9:20 [1]Or, *answerest again,* or, *disputest with God?* [a]Is. 29:16
9:21 [a]Prov. 16:4 [b]2 Tim. 2:20
9:22 [1]Or, *made up* [a]1 Thes. 5:9 [b]1 Pet. 2:8
9:23 [a]Col. 1:27 [b]ch. 8:28-30
9:24 [a]ch. 3:29
9:25 [a]Hos. 2:23
9:26 [a]Hos. 1:10
9:27 [a]Is. 10:22 [b]ch. 11:5
9:28 [1]Or, *the account* [a]Is. 28:22
9:29 [a]Is. 1:9; Lam. 3:22 [b]Is. 13:19; Jer. 50:40
9:30 [a]ch. 4:11 [b]ch. 1:17
9:31 [a]ch. 10:2 [b]Gal. 5:4
9:32 [a]Luke 2:34; 1 Cor. 1:23
9:33 [1]Or, *confounded* [a]Ps. 118:22; Is. 8:14; 28:16; Mat. 21:42; 1 Pet. 2:6-8 [b]ch. 10:11
10:2 [a]Acts 21:20; 22:3; ch. 9:31; Gal. 1:14
10:3 [a]ch. 1:17 [b]Phil. 3:9

‡9:18 The first part of this verse again echoes Ex 33:19 (see v. 15) and the last part such texts as Ex 7:3; 9:12; 14:4,17, in which God is said to harden the hearts of Pharaoh and the Egyptians. *whom he will.* Cannot mean that God is arbitrary in His mercy, because Paul ultimately bases God's rejection of Israel on her unbelief (see vv. 30–32).

9:19 Someone may object: "If God determines whose heart is hardened and whose is not, how can God blame anyone for hardening his heart?"

9:20 *who art thou that repliest against God?* Paul is not silencing all questioning of God by man, but he is speaking to those with an impenitent, God-defying attitude who want to make God answerable to man for what He does and who, by their questions, defame the character of God.

9:21 The analogy between God and the potter and between man and the pot should not be pressed to the extreme. The main point is the sovereign freedom of God in dealing with man.

9:22–23 An illustration of the principle stated in v. 21. The emphasis is on God's mercy, not His wrath.

9:22 No one can call God to account for what He does. But He does not exercise His freedom of choice arbitrarily, and He shows great patience even toward the objects of His wrath. In light of 2:4, the purpose of such patience is to bring about repentance.

9:23 *glory.* See note on 3:23.

9:25–26 In the original context these passages from Hosea refer to the spiritual restoration of Israel. But Paul finds in them the principle that God is a saving, forgiving, restoring God, who delights to take those who are "not my people" and make them "my people." Paul then applies this principle to Gentiles, whom God makes His people by sovereignly grafting them into covenant relationship (see ch. 11).

9:27–29 The two passages from Isaiah indicate that only a small remnant will survive from the great multitude of Israelites. God's calling includes both Jews and Gentiles (see v. 24), but the vast majority are Gentiles, as v. 30 suggests.

9:30–32 A new step in Paul's argument: The reason for Israel's rejection lay in the nature of her disobedience—she failed to obey her own God-given law, which in reality was pointing to Christ. She pursued the law—yet not by faith but by works. Thus the real cause of Israel's rejection was that she failed to believe.

9:31 *law of righteousness.* The law that prescribed the way to righteousness. Paul does not reject obedience to the law but righteousness by works, the attempt to use the law to put God in one's debt.

9:32 *not by faith.* The failure of Israel was not that she pursued the wrong thing (i.e., righteous standing before God), but that she pursued it by works in a futile effort to merit God's favor rather than pursuing it by faith. *that stumblingstone.* Jesus, the Messiah. God's rejection of Israel was not arbitrary but was based on Israel's rejection of God's way of gaining righteousness (faith).

9:33 The two passages from Isaiah, which are here combined, apparently were commonly used by early Christians in defense of Jesus' Messiahship (see 1 Pet 2:4,6–8; see also Ps 118:22; Luke 20:17–18).

10:1 *prayer to God for Israel.* Paul often prayed for the churches (see Eph 1:15–23; Col 1:3; 1 Thes 1:2–3; 2 Thes 1:3). Here he prays for the salvation of his fellow countrymen.

10:2 *zeal of God.* The Jews' zeal for God (see Acts 21:20; 22:3; Gal 1:14) was commendable in that God was its object, but it was flawed because it was not based on right knowledge about God's way of salvation. Paul, before his conversion, was an example of such zeal (see Gal 1:14).

10:3 *their own.* Righteous standing based on mere human effort. *righteousness of God.* Righteous standing based on faith

4 For [a]Christ *is* the end of the law for righteousness to every one that believeth.

5 For Moses describeth the righteousness which is of the law, [a]That the man which doeth those *things* shall live by them.

6 But the righteousness which is of faith speaketh on this wise, [a]Say not in thine heart, Who shall ascend into heaven? (that is, to bring Christ down *from above:*)

7 Or, Who shall descend into the deep? (that is, to bring up Christ again from the dead.)

8 But what saith it? [a]The word is nigh thee, *even* in thy mouth, and in thy heart: that is, the word of faith, which we preach;

9 That [a]if thou shalt confess with thy mouth the Lord Jesus, and shalt believe in thine heart that God hath raised him from the dead, thou shalt be saved.

10 For with the heart *man* believeth unto righteousness; and with the mouth confession is made unto salvation.

11 For the scripture saith, [a]Whosoever believeth on him shall not be ashamed.

12 For [a]there is no difference between the Jew and the Greek: for [b]the same Lord over all [c]*is* rich unto all that call upon him.

13 [a]For whosoever shall call [b]upon the name of the Lord shall be saved.

14 How then shall they call on *him* in whom they have not believed? and how shall they believe *in him* of whom they have not heard? and how shall they hear [a]without a preacher?

15 And how shall they preach, except they be sent? as it is written, [a]How beautiful *are* the feet of them that preach the gospel of peace, and bring glad tidings of good *things!*

16 But they have not all obeyed the gospel. For Esaias saith, [a]Lord, who hath believed [1]our [2]report?

17 So then faith *cometh* by hearing, and hearing by the word of God.

18 But I say, Have they not heard? Yes verily, [a]their sound went into all the earth, [b]and their words unto the ends of the world.

19 But I say, Did not Israel know? First Moses saith, [a]I will provoke you to jealousy by *them that are* no people, *and* by a [b]foolish nation I will anger you.

10:4 [a]Mat. 5:17; Gal. 3:24
10:5 [a]Lev. 18:5; Neh. 9:29; Ezek. 20:11; Gal. 3:12
10:6 [a]Deut. 30:12
10:8 [a]Deut. 30:14
10:9 [a]Mat. 10:32; Luke 12:8; Acts 8:37
10:11 [a]Is. 28:16; 49:23; Jer. 17:7
10:12 [a]Acts 15:9; ch. 3:22 [b]Acts 10:36; 1 Tim. 2:5 [c]Eph. 1:7; 2:4,7
10:13 [a]Joel 2:32; Acts 2:21 [b]Acts 9:14
10:14 [a]Tit. 1:3
10:15 [a]Is. 52:7; Nah. 1:15
10:16 [1]Gr. *the hearing of us?* [2]Or, *preaching?* [a]Is. 53:1; John 12:38
10:18 [a]Ps. 19:4; Mat. 24:14; Mark 16:15; Col. 1:6,23 [b]1 Ki. 18:10; Mat. 4:8
10:19 [a]ch. 11:11 [b]Tit. 3:3

(see 1:17), which comes from God as a gift and cannot be earned by man's works.

‡10:4 *Christ is the end of the law.* Although the Greek word for "end" (*telos*) can mean either (1) "termination," "cessation," or (2) "goal," "culmination," "fulfillment," it seems best here to understand it in the latter sense. Christ is the fulfillment of the law (see Mat 5:17) in the sense that He brought it to completion by obeying perfectly its demands and by fulfilling its types and prophecies. The Christian is no longer "under the law" (6:15), since Christ has freed him from its condemnation, but the law still plays a role in his life. He is liberated by the Holy Spirit to fulfill its moral demands (see 8:4). *righteousness.* The righteous standing before God that Christ makes available to everyone who believes (see notes on 1:17; 3:24).

10:5 *the man which doeth those things shall live by them.* Lev 18:5 (see note there; see also Deut 6:25) speaks of the righteousness to which Israel was called under the Sinai covenant. Some understand Paul's purpose in quoting it here as describing the way of obtaining righteousness ("shall live") by keeping the law (see 2:6–10). Others think that the reference is to Christ, who perfectly fulfilled the law's demands and thus makes salvation available to all who believe (see Heb 5:9).

10:6–7 The purpose of the OT quotation is to explain the nature of the righteousness that is by faith. It does not require heroic feats such as bringing Christ down from heaven or up from the grave. Deut 30:12–13 in its original context refers to the law, and Paul here applies the basic principle to Christ.

10:8 *The word is nigh thee.* In the OT passage the "word" is God's word as found in the law. Paul takes the passage and applies it to the gospel, "the word of faith"—the main point being the accessibility of the gospel. Righteousness is gained by faith, not by deeds, and is readily available to anyone who will receive it freely from God through Christ.

10:9 *confess with thy mouth the Lord Jesus.* The earliest Christian confession of faith (cf. 1 Cor 12:3), probably used at baptisms. In view of the fact that "Lord" (Greek *kyrios*) is used over 6,000 times in the Septuagint (the Greek translation of the OT) to translate the name of Israel's God (Yahweh), it is clear that Paul, when using this word of Jesus, is ascribing deity to him. *in thine heart.* In Biblical terms the heart is not merely the seat of the emotions and affections, but also of the intellect and will. *God hath raised him from the dead.* A bedrock truth of Christian doctrine (see 1 Cor 15:4,14,17) and the central thrust of apostolic preaching (see, e.g., Acts 2:31–32; 3:15; 4:10; 10:40). Christians believe not only that Jesus lived but also that He still lives. *shalt be saved.* In the future tense. Paul is thinking of final salvation—salvation at the last day.

10:10 Salvation involves inward belief ("with the heart") as well as outward confession ("with the mouth").

10:12 *no difference between the Jew and the Greek.* In the sense that both are on the same footing as far as salvation is concerned (see v. 13).

10:13 Peter cited this same passage (Joel 2:32) on the day of Pentecost (Acts 2:21).

10:14–15 Since it might be argued that Jews had never had a fair opportunity to hear and respond to the gospel, Paul, by means of a series of rhetorical questions, states (in reverse order) the conditions necessary to call on Christ and be saved: (1) a preacher sent from God, (2) proclamation of the message, (3) hearing the message, (4) believing the message.

10:15 *How beautiful are the feet of them that preach the gospel of peace.* The quotation is from Is 52:7, which refers to those who bring the exiles the good news of their imminent release from captivity in Babylon. Here it is applied to gospel preachers, who bring the good news of release from captivity to sin.

10:17 *word of God.* Either (1) the gospel concerning Christ, or (2) Christ speaking His message through His messengers.

‡10:18 *their sound.* The quotation is from Ps 19:4, which refers to the testimony of the heavens to the glory of God. Here "their sound" is applied to gospel preachers and is used to show that Israel cannot offer the excuse that she did not have opportunity to hear, since preachers went everywhere. These words (originally used to describe God's revelation in nature) aptly describe the widespread preaching of the gospel, and Paul uses them to show that Jews had ample opportunity to hear the message of redemption.

10:19 *Did not Israel know?* The quotation that follows (from Deut 32:21) answers this question by suggesting that the Gentiles, whom the Jews considered to be spiritually unenlightened, understood. Surely if they understood the message, the Jews could have. *them that are no people.* The Gentiles, those who are not a nation of God's forming in the sense that Israel was.

20 But Esaias is very bold, and saith, [a]I was
found of them that sought me not; I was made
manifest unto them that asked not after me.
21 But to Israel he saith, [a]All day long have
I stretched forth my hands unto a disobedient
and gainsaying people.

The remnant of Israel

11 I say then, [a]Hath God cast away his
people? God forbid. For [b]I also am an
Israelite, of the seed of Abraham, *of* the tribe
of Benjamin.
2 God hath not cast away his people which
[a]he foreknew. Wot ye not what the scripture
saith [1]of Elias? how he maketh intercession to
God against Israel, saying,
3 [a]Lord, they have killed thy prophets, and
digged down thine altars; and I am left alone,
and they seek my life.
4 But what saith the answer of God unto
him? [a]I have reserved to myself seven thousand men, who have not bowed the knee to
the image of Baal.
5 [a]*Even* so then at *this* present time also
there is a remnant according to the election of
grace.
6 And [a]if by grace, *then is it* no more of
works: otherwise grace is no more grace. But
if *it be* of works, *then* is it no more grace: otherwise work is no more work.
7 What then? [a]Israel hath not obtained that

10:20 [a]Is. 65:1
10:21 [a]Is. 65:2
11:1 [a]1 Sam. 12:22; Jer. 31:37 [b]2 Cor. 11:22; Phil. 3:5
11:2 [1][Gr. *in Elias?*] [a]ch. 8:29
11:3 [a]1 Ki. 19:10
11:4 [a]1 Ki. 19:18
11:5 [a]ch. 9:27
11:6 [a]ch. 4:4,5; Deut. 9:4,5; Gal. 5:4
11:7 [a]ch. 9:31
11:7 [1]Or, *hardened*
11:8 [1]Or, *remorse* [a]Is. 29:10 [b]Deut. 29:4; Is. 6:9; Jer. 5:21; Ezek. 12:2; Mat. 13:14; John 12:40; Acts 28:26
11:9 [a]Ps. 69:22
11:10 [a]Ps. 69:23
11:11 [a]Acts 13:46; 18:6; ch. 10:19
11:12 [1]Or, *decay,* or, *loss*
11:13 [a]Acts 9:15; Gal. 1:16; Eph. 3:8; 1 Tim. 2:7
11:14 [a]1 Cor. 9:22; 1 Tim. 4:16; Jas. 5:20
11:16 [a]Lev. 23:10; Jas. 1:18

which he seeketh for; but the election hath obtained *it,* and the rest were [1]blinded,
8 (According as it is written, [a]God hath giv-
en them the spirit of [1]slumber, [b]eyes that *they*
should not see, and ears that *they* should not
hear;) unto this day.
9 And David saith, [a]Let their table be made
a snare, and a trap, and a stumblingblock, and
a recompence unto them:
10 [a]Let their eyes be darkened, that *they*
may not see, and bow down their back alway.

Israel's future salvation

11 ¶ I say then, Have they stumbled that
they should fall? God forbid: but *rather*
[a]through their fall salvation *is come* unto the
Gentiles, for to provoke them to jealousy.
12 Now if the fall of them *be* the riches of
the world, and the [1]diminishing of them the
riches of the Gentiles; how much more their
fulness?
13 For I speak to you Gentiles, inasmuch as
[a]I am the apostle of the Gentiles, I magnify
mine office:
14 If by any means I may provoke to emu-
lation *them which are* my flesh, and [a]might
save some of them.
15 For if the casting away of them *be* the
reconciling of the world, what *shall* the receiving *of them be,* but life from the dead?
16 For if [a]the firstfruit *be* holy, the lump *is*

10:21 The responsibility for Israel's rejection as a nation rested with Israel herself. She had failed to meet God's requirement, namely, faith.
11:1 *cast away.* Totally rejected. There has always been a faithful remnant among the Jewish people.
11:2 *which he foreknew.* See note on 8:29.
11:5 *remnant.* As it was in Elijah's day, so it was in Paul's day. Despite widespread apostasy, a faithful remnant of Jews remained. *according to the election of grace.* The grounds for the existence of the remnant was not their good works but God's grace.
11:7 *Israel . . . seeketh.* A righteous standing before God, which eluded the greater part of Israel. *the election hath obtained it.* The faithful remnant among the Jews. *the rest were blinded.* Because they refused the way of faith (see 9:31–32), God made them impervious to spiritual truth (see notes on Is 6:8–10)—a judicial hardening of Israel.
11:8 *unto this day.* The spiritual dullness of the Jews had continued from Isaiah's day to Paul's day.
11:9–10 The passage from Ps 69:22–23 was probably originally spoken by David concerning his enemies; Paul uses it to describe the results of the divine hardening.
11:11 *their fall.* The Jews' rejection of the gospel. *to provoke them to jealousy.* See v. 14; 10:19.
11:12 *riches of the world.* Equivalent to "riches of the Gentiles," a reference to the abundant benefits of salvation already enjoyed by believing Gentiles, which had come about because of the rejection of the gospel by the Jews. That rejection caused the apostles to turn to the Gentiles (see Acts 13:46–48; 18:6). *the diminishing of them.* Equivalent to "their transgression" (see note on v. 11), but focusing on the loss that this transgression entailed. *how much more.* See note on v. 15. *their fulness.* The salvation of Israel (see vv. 26–27; see also the "fulness of the Gentiles," v. 25).
11:13 *apostle of the Gentiles.* See 1:5; Acts 9:15; Gal 1:16; 2:7,9.
11:15 *casting away.* God's temporary and partial exclusion of the Jews. *reconciling of the world.* Somewhat equivalent to "riches of the world" (see note on v. 12). *life from the dead.* Equivalent to "how much more" in v. 12. The sequence of redemptive events is: The "fall" and "diminishing" (v. 12) of Israel leads to the salvation of the Gentiles, which leads to the jealousy or envy of Israel, which leads to the "fulness" (v. 12) of Israel when the hardening is removed, which leads to even more riches for the Gentiles. But to what does the "how much more" (v. 12) for the Gentiles refer, which Paul describes here as "life from the dead"? Three views may be suggested: (1) an unprecedented spiritual awakening in the world; (2) the consummation of redemption at the resurrection of the dead; (3) a figurative expression describing the conversion of the Jews as a joyful and glorious event (like resurrection)—which will result in even greater blessing for the world. Of these three views the first seems least likely, since, before Israel's spiritual rebirth, the fullness of the Gentiles will already have come in (see v. 25). Since the Gentile mission will then be complete, there seems to be no place for a period of unprecedented spiritual awakening. The second view also seems unlikely, since the context suggests nothing of bodily resurrection.
‡11:16 The first half of this verse is a reference to Num 15:17–21. Part of the dough made from the first of the harvested grain (firstfruit) was offered to the Lord. This consecrated the whole batch. *firstfruit.* The patriarchs. *lump.* The Jewish people. *holy.* Not that all Jews are righteous (i.e., saved) but that God will be true to His promises concerning them (see 3:3–4). Paul foresaw a future for Israel, even though she was for a time set aside. *root.* The patriarchs. *branches.* The Jewish people.

also *holy:* and if the root *be* holy, so *are* the
branches.
17 And if [a]some of the branches be broken
off, [b]and thou, being a wild olive tree, wert
graffed in [1]amongst them, and with *them* par-
takest of the root and fatness of the olive tree;
18 [a]Boast not against the branches: but if
thou boast, thou bearest not the root, but the
root thee.
19 Thou wilt say then, The branches were
broken off, that I might be graffed in.
20 Well; because of unbelief they were broken off, and thou standest by faith. [a]Be not
high-minded, but [b]fear:
21 For if God spared not the natural
branches, *take heed* lest he also spare not thee.
22 Behold therefore the goodness and severity of God: on them which fell, severity; but toward thee, goodness, [a]if thou continue in *his*
goodness: otherwise [b]thou also shalt be cut off.
23 And they also, [a]if they bide not still in
unbelief, shall be graffed in: for God is able to
graff them in again.
24 For if thou wert cut out of the olive tree
which is wild by nature, and wert graffed contrary to nature into a good olive tree: how
much more shall these, which be the natural
branches, be graffed into their own olive tree?
25 ¶ For I would not, brethren, that ye
should be ignorant of this mystery, lest ye
should be [a]wise in your own conceits; that
[b][1]blindness in part is happened to Israel, [c]un-
til the fulness of the Gentiles be come in.
26 And so all Israel shall be saved: as it is
written, [a]There shall come out of Sion the Deliverer, and shall turn away ungodliness from
Jacob:
27 [a]For this *is* my covenant unto them,
when I shall take away their sins.
28 As concerning the gospel, *they are* enemies for your sakes: but as touching the election, *they are* [a]beloved for the fathers' sakes.
29 For the gifts and calling of God *are*
[a]without repentance.
30 For as ye [a]in times past have not [1]be-
lieved God, yet have now obtained mercy
through their unbelief:
31 *Even* so have these also now not [1]be-
lieved, that through your mercy they also may
obtain mercy.
32 For [a]God hath [1]concluded *them* all in
unbelief, that he might have mercy upon all.

11:17 [1]Or, *for them* [a]Jer. 11:16 [b]Acts 2:39; Eph. 2:12
11:18 [a]1 Cor. 10:12
11:20 [a]ch. 12:16 [b]Prov. 28:14; Is. 66:2
11:22 [a]1 Cor. 15:2; Heb. 3:6 [b]John 15:2
11:23 [a]2 Cor. 3:16
11:25 [1]Or, *hardness* [a]ch. 12:16 [b]2 Cor. 3:14 [c]Luke 21:24; Rev. 7:9
11:26 [a]Ps. 14:7; Is. 59:20
11:27 [a]Is. 27:9; Jer. 31:31; Heb. 8:8
11:28 [a]Deut. 7:8
11:29 [a]Num. 23:19
11:30 [1]Or, *obeyed* [a]Eph. 2:2; Col. 3:7
11:31 [1]Or, *obeyed*
11:32 [1]Or, *shut them all up together* [a]ch. 3:9

11:17 *branches.* Individual Jews. *wild olive tree.* Gentile Christians. *graffed in.* The usual procedure was to insert a shoot or slip of a cultivated tree into a common or wild one. In vv. 17–24, however, the metaphor is used, "contrary to nature" (v. 24), of grafting a wild olive branch (the Gentiles) into the cultivated olive tree. Such a procedure is unnatural, which is precisely the point. Normally, such a graft would be unfruitful. *root and fatness.* The patriarchs. The whole olive tree represents the people of God.

11:18 *thou bearest not the root, but the root thee.* The salvation of Gentile Christians is dependent on the Jews, especially the patriarchs (e.g., the Abrahamic covenant). See John 4:22.

11:19 *branches.* Unbelieving Jews.

11:20 *fear.* On the fear of God see note on Gen 20:11; see also Prov 3:7; Phil 2:12–13; Heb 4:1; 1 Pet 1:17.

‡11:22 *goodness and severity of God.* Any adequate doctrine of God must include these two elements. When we ignore His goodness, God seems a ruthless tyrant; when we ignore His sternness, He seems a doting Father.

11:23 *God is able to graff them in again.* Paul holds out hope for the Jews—God is able (see Mat 19:26; Mark 10:27; Luke 18:27).

‡11:24 *contrary to nature.* Paul recognized that such grafting was not commonly practiced (see note on v. 17). The inclusion of Gentiles in the family of God is "contrary to nature" (cf. Eph 2:12). Obviously, the reasoning in this verse is more theological than horticultural. It would be difficult horticulturally to graft broken branches back into the parent tree, but the Jews really "belong" (historically and theologically) to the parent tree. Thus they will "much more . . . be graffed into their own olive tree."

11:25 *mystery.* The so-called mystery religions of Paul's day used the Greek word (*mysterion*) in the sense of something that was to be revealed only to the initiated. Paul himself, however, used it to refer to something formerly hidden or obscure but now revealed by God for all to know and understand (see 16:25; 1 Cor 2:7; 4:1; 13:2; 14:2; 15:51; Eph 1:9; 3:3–4,9; 5:32; 6:19; Col 1:26–27; 2:2; 4:3; 2 Thes 2:7; 1 Tim 3:9,16). The word is used of (1) the incarnation (1 Tim 3:16; see note there), (2) the death of Christ (1 Cor 2:7, "the wisdom of God in a mystery"), (3) God's purpose to sum up all things in Christ (Eph 1:9) and especially to include both Jews and Gentiles in the NT church (Eph 3:3–6), (4) the change that will take place at the resurrection (1 Cor 15:51), and (5) the plan of God by which both Jew and Gentile, after a period of disobedience by both, will by His mercy be included in His kingdom (v. 25). *lest ye should be wise in your own conceits.* God's merciful plan to include the Gentiles in His great salvation plan should humble them, not fill them with arrogance. *in part.* Israel's hardening is partial, not total. *until.* Israel's hardening is temporary, not permanent. *fulness of the Gentiles.* The total number of the elect Gentiles.

11:26 *And so.* An emphatic statement that this is the way all Israel will be saved. *all Israel.* Three main interpretations of this phrase are: (1) the total number of elect Jews of every generation (equivalent to the "fulness" of Israel [v. 12], which is analogous to the "fulness ['full number'] of the Gentiles" [v. 25]); (2) the total number of the elect, both Jews and Gentiles, of every generation; (3) the great majority of Jews of the final generation. *shall be saved.* The salvation of the Jews will, of course, be on the same basis as anyone's salvation: personal faith in Jesus Christ, crucified and risen from the dead. *there shall come out of Sion the Deliverer.* The quotation is from Is 59:20, where the deliverer ("Redeemer") seems to refer to God. The Talmud understood the text to be a reference to the Messiah, and Paul appears to use it in this way. *Sion.* See note on Gal 4:26.

11:27 *covenant.* The new covenant of Jer 31:31–34. *when I shall take away their sins.* See Jer 31:34; Zech 13:1. Just as salvation for Gentiles involves forgiveness of sins, so the Jews, when they are saved, are forgiven by the mercy of God—His forgiveness based only on their repentance and faith (see v. 23; Zech 12:10–13:1).

11:28 *they are enemies.* Only temporarily. *for your sakes.* Explained in v.11. *beloved for the fathers' sakes.* Not because any merit was passed on from the patriarchs to the Jewish people as a whole, but because God in love chose Israel and that choice was irrevocable.

‡11:29 *the gifts and calling of God are without repentance.* God does not change His mind with reference to His call. Even though Israel is presently in a state of unbelief, God's purpose will be fulfilled in her.

11:32 *all.* Both groups under discussion (Jews and Gentiles).

33 ¶ O the depth of the riches both of the
wisdom and knowledge of God! [a]how unsearchable *are* his judgments, and [b]his ways
past finding out!
34 [a]For who hath known the mind of the
Lord? or [b]who hath been his counseller?
35 Or [a]who hath first given to him, and it
shall be recompensed unto him *again?*
36 For [a]of him, and through him, and to
him, *are* all *things:* [b]to [1]whom *be* glory for
ever. Amen.

Christian conduct

12 [a]I beseech you therefore, brethren,
by the mercies of God, [b]that *ye*
[c]present your bodies [d]a living sacrifice, holy,
acceptable unto God, *which is* your reasonable
service.
2 And [a]be not conformed to this world: but
[b]be ye transformed by the renewing of your
mind, that ye may [c]prove what *is that* good,
and acceptable, and perfect, will of God.
3 For I say, [a]through the grace given unto
me, to every *man* that is among you, [b]not to
think *of himself* more highly than he ought to
think; but to think [1]soberly, according as God
hath dealt [c]to every man the measure of faith.

11:33 [a]Ps. 36:6 [b]Job 11:7; Ps. 92:5
11:34 [a]Job 15:8; Is. 40:13; Jer. 23:18 [b]Job 36:22
11:35 [a]Job 35:7
11:36 [1][Gr. *him*] [a]Col. 1:16 [b]Heb. 13:21; Rev. 1:6
12:1 [a]2 Cor. 10:1 [b]1 Pet. 2:5 [c]ch. 6 [d]Heb. 10:20
12:2 [a]1 John 2:15 [b]Eph. 4:23; Col. 3:10 [c]1 Thes. 4:3
12:3 [1]Gr. *to sobriety* [a]Gal. 2:9 [b]Prov. 25:27 [c]Eph. 4:7
12:4 [a]1 Cor. 12:12; Eph. 4:16
12:5 [a]1 Cor. 10:17; Eph. 1:23
12:6 [a]1 Cor. 12:4 [b]ver. 3 [c]Acts 11:27
12:7 [a]Eph. 4:11
12:8 [1]Or, *imparteth* [2]Or, *liberally* [a]Acts 15:32 [b]Mat. 6:1-3 [c]Acts 20:28 [d]2 Cor. 9:7
12:9 [a]1 Tim. 1:5 [b]Ps. 34:14

4 For [a]as we have many members in one
body, and all members have not the same office:
5 So [a]we, being many, are one body in
Christ, and every one members one of another.
6 [a]Having then gifts differing [b]according to
the grace that is given to us, whether [c]proph-
ecy, *let us prophesy* according to the proportion of faith;
7 Or ministry, *let us wait* on *our* ministering: or [a]he that teacheth, on teaching;
8 Or [a]he that exhorteth, on exhortation:
[b]he that [1]giveth, *let him do it* [2]with simplicity; [c]he that ruleth, with diligence; he that
sheweth mercy, [d]with cheerfulness.
9 ¶ [a]*Let* love *be* without dissimulation.
[b]Abhor *that which is* evil; cleave to *that which*
is good.
10 [a]*Be* kindly affectioned one to another
[1]with brotherly love; [b]in honour preferring
one another;
11 Not slothful in business; fervent in spirit; serving the Lord;
12 [a]Rejoicing in hope; [b]patient in tribulation; [c]continuing instant in prayer;

12:10 [1]Or, *in the love of the brethren* [a]Heb. 13:1 [b]Phil. 2:3
12:12 [a]Luke 10:20 [b]Luke 21:19 [c]Luke 18:1

There has been a period of disobedience for each in order that God may have mercy on them all. Paul is in no way teaching universal salvation.

11:33–36 The doxology that ends this section of Romans is the natural outpouring of Paul's praise to God, whose wisdom and knowledge brought about His great plan for the salvation of both Jews and Gentiles.

12:1–16:27 Paul now turns to the practical application of all he has said previously in the letter. This does not mean that he has not said anything about Christian living up to this point. Chs. 6–8 have touched on this already, but now Paul goes into detail to show that Jesus Christ is to be Lord of every area of life. These chapters are not a postscript to the great theological discussions in chs. 1–11. In a real sense the entire letter has been directed toward the goal of showing that God demands our action as well as our believing and thinking. Faith expresses itself in obedience.

‡12:1 *I beseech you therefore.* Paul draws an important inference from the truth set forth in chs. 1–11. *mercies of God.* Much of the letter has been concerned with demonstrating this. *your bodies.* See 6:13 and note. *living sacrifice.* In contrast to dead animal sacrifices, or perhaps "living" in the sense of having the new life of the Holy Spirit (see 6:4). *reasonable service.* Not merely ritual activity but the involvement of heart, mind and will.

‡12:2 *this world.* With all its evil and corruption (see Gal 1:4). *be ye transformed.* Here a process, not a single event. The same word is used in the transfiguration narratives (Mat 17:2–8; Mark 9:2–8) and in 2 Cor 3:18. *mind.* Thought and will as they relate to morality (see 1:28). *that.* After the spiritual transformation just described has taken place. *good.* That which leads to the spiritual and moral growth of the Christian. *acceptable.* To God, not necessarily to us. *perfect.* No improvement can be made on the will of God. *will of God.* What God wants from the believer here and now.

12:3 *God hath dealt.* Since the power comes from God, there can be no basis for a superior attitude or self-righteousness. *measure of faith.* The power given by God to each believer to fulfill various ministries in the church (see vv. 4–8).

12:4–8 Paul likens Christians to members of a human body. There are many members and each has a different function, but all are needed for the health of the body. The emphasis is on unity within diversity (see 1 Cor 12:12–31).

12:5 *in Christ.* The key to Paul's concept of Christian unity. It is only in Jesus Christ that any unity in the church is possible. True unity is spiritually based. See notes on 6:11; Eph 1:1.

‡12:6 *gifts.* Greek *charismata,* referring to special gifts of grace—freely given by God to His people to meet the needs of the body (see notes on 1 Cor 1:7; 12:4). *prophecy.* See note on 1 Cor 12:10. *according to.* There is to be no false modesty that denies the existence of gifts or refuses to use them. *to the proportion of faith.* Probably means about the same thing as "measure of faith" in v. 3 (see note there).

12:7 *ministry.* Any kind of service needed by the body of Christ or by any of its members. *teacheth.* See notes on 1 Cor 12:28; Eph 4:11.

12:8 *exhorteth.* Exhorting others with an uplifting, cheerful call to worthwhile accomplishment. The teacher often carried out this function. In teaching, the believer is shown what he must do; in encouraging, he is helped to do it. *giveth.* Giving what is one's own, or possibly distributing what has been given by others. *ruleth.* Possibly a reference to an elder. The Ephesian church had elders by about this time (see Acts 20:17; 1 Thes 5:12; 1 Tim 5:17). *sheweth mercy.* Caring for the sick, the poor and the aged. *with cheerfulness.* Serving the needy should be a delight, not a chore.

12:9 *love.* The Christian's love for fellow Christians and perhaps also for his fellowman. *without dissimulation.* True love, not pretense. In view of the preceding paragraph, with its emphasis on social concern, the love Paul speaks of here is not mere emotion but is active love.

12:10 *brotherly love.* Love within the family of God. *in honour preferring one another.* Only a mind renewed by the Holy Spirit (see v. 2) could possibly do this (see Phil 2:3).

12:11 *fervent in spirit.* If "spirit" means "Holy Spirit" here, the reference would be to the fervor the Holy Spirit provides.

12:12 *Rejoicing in hope.* The certainty of the Christian's hope is a cause for joy (see 5:5; see also 8:16–25; 1 Pet 1:3–9).

13 [a]Distributing to the necessity of saints;
[b]given to hospitality.
14 [a]Bless them which persecute you: bless,
and curse not.
15 [a]Rejoice with them that do rejoice, and
weep with them that weep.
16 [a]*Be* of the same mind one towards another. [b]Mind not high *things,* but [1]conde-
scend to *men* of low estate. [c]Be not wise in
your own conceits.
17 [a]Recompense to no *man* evil for evil.
[b]Provide *things* honest in the sight of all men.
18 If *it be* possible, as much as lieth in you,
[a]live peaceably with all men.
19 Dearly beloved, [a]avenge not yourselves,
but *rather* give place unto wrath: for it is written, [b]Vengeance *is* mine; I will repay, saith the
Lord.
20 [a]Therefore if thine enemy hunger, feed
him; if he thirst, give him drink: for in so doing thou shalt heap coals of fire on his head.
21 Be not overcome of evil, but overcome
evil with good.

13 Let every soul [a]be subject unto the
higher powers. For [b]there is no power but of God: the powers that be are [1]or-
dained of God.
2 Whosoever therefore resisteth [a]the power, resisteth the ordinance of God: and they
that resist shall receive to themselves damnation.
3 For rulers are not a terror to good works,

12:13 [a]1 Cor. 16:1 [b]1 Tim. 3:2
12:14 [a]Mat. 5:44
12:15 [a]1 Cor. 12:26
12:16 [1]Or, *be contented with mean* things [a]Phil. 2:2 [b]Jer. 45:5 [c]Prov. 3:7
12:17 [a]Mat. 5:39 [b]2 Cor. 8:21
12:18 [a]Heb. 12:14
12:19 [a]Lev. 19:18 [b]Deut. 32:35
12:20 [a]Mat. 5:44
13:1 [1]Or, *ordered* [a]1 Pet. 2:13 [b]Dan. 2:21
13:2 [a]Tit. 3:1
13:3 [a]1 Pet. 2:14
13:5 [a]Eccl. 8:2 [b]1 Pet. 2:19
13:7 [a]Mat. 22:21; Luke 20:25
13:8 [a]Gal. 5:14; 1 Tim. 1:5
13:9 [a]Ex. 20:13; Mat. 19:18 [b]Lev. 19:18; Mark 12:31; Jas. 2:8
13:10 [a]Mat. 22:40
13:11 [a]1 Cor. 15:34; Eph. 5:14

but to the evil. Wilt thou then not be afraid of
the power? [a]do *that which is* good, and thou
shalt have praise of the same:
4 For he is the minister of God to thee for
good. But if thou do *that which is* evil, be
afraid; for he beareth not the sword in vain:
for he is the minister of God, a revenger to *execute* wrath upon him that doeth evil.
5 Wherefore [a]*ye* must needs be subject,
not only for wrath, [b]but also for conscience
sake.
6 For for this cause pay you tribute also: for
they are God's ministers, attending continually
upon this very *thing.*
7 [a]Render therefore to all *their* dues: tribute to whom tribute *is due;* custom to whom
custom; fear to whom fear; honour to whom
honour.
8 Owe no *man* any *thing,* but to love one
another: for [a]he that loveth another hath fulfilled the law.
9 For *this,* [a]Thou shalt not commit adultery, Thou shalt not kill, Thou shalt not steal,
Thou shalt not bear false witness, Thou shalt
not covet; and if *there be* any other commandment, it is briefly comprehended in this saying, namely, [b]Thou shalt love thy neighbour as
thyself.
10 Love worketh no ill to *his* neighbour:
therefore [a]love *is* the fulfilling of the law.
11 ¶ And that, knowing the time, that now
it is high time [a]to awake out of sleep: for now

---

patient. Enduring triumphantly—necessary for a Christian, because affliction is his inevitable experience (see John 16:33). *continuing instant in prayer.* One must not only pray in hard times, but also maintain communion with God through prayer at all times (see Luke 18:1; 1 Thes 5:17).

12:13 *Distributing to the . . . saints.* The Christian has social responsibility to all people, but especially to other believers (see Gal 6:10).

12:14 *Bless them which persecute you.* Paul is echoing Jesus' teaching in Mat 5:44; Luke 6:28.

12:15 Identification with others in their joys and in their sorrows is a Christian's privilege and responsibility.

12:17 *Recompence to no man evil for evil.* See Mat 5:39–42, 44–45; 1 Thes 5:15; 1 Pet 3:9. *Provide things honest in the sight of all men.* A possible reflection of Prov 3:4 in the Septuagint (the Greek translation of the OT). Christian conduct should never betray the high moral standards of the gospel, or it will provoke the disdain of unbelievers and bring the gospel into disrepute (see 2 Cor 8:21; 1 Tim 3:7).

12:18 *If it be possible . . . live peaceably.* Jesus pronounced a blessing on peacemakers (Mat 5:9), and believers are to cultivate peace with everyone to the extent that it depends on them.

12:20 *heap coals of fire on his head.* Doing good to one's enemy (v. 21), instead of trying to take revenge, may bring about his repentance (see note on Prov 25:22).

13:1 *be subject.* A significant word in vv. 1–7. *higher powers.* The civil rulers, all of whom were probably pagans at the time Paul was writing. Christians may have been tempted not to submit to them and to claim allegiance only to Christ. *ordained of God.* Even the possibility of a persecuting state did not shake Paul's conviction that civil government is ordained by God.

13:2 *damnation.* Either divine judgment or, more likely, punishment by the governing authorities, since v. 3 ("For") explains this verse; see also v. 4.

13:3 *do that which is good, and thou shalt have praise.* Paul is not stating that this will always be true but is describing the proper, ideal function of rulers. When civil rulers overstep their proper function, the Christian is to obey God rather than man (see Acts 4:19; 5:29).

13:4 *he is the minister of God.* In the order of divine providence the ruler is God's servant (see Is 45:1). *good.* Rulers exist for the benefit of society—to protect the general public by maintaining good order. *the sword.* The symbol of Roman authority on both the national and the international levels. Here we find the Biblical principle of using force for the maintenance of good order.

13:5 *for conscience sake.* Civil authorities are ordained by God, and in order to maintain a good conscience Christians must duly honor them.

13:6 *pay you tribute also.* Because rulers are God's agents, who function for the benefit of society in general.

13:8 *but to love.* To love is the one debt that is never paid off. No matter how much one has loved, he is under obligation to keep on loving. *one another.* Includes not only fellow Christians but all people. *the law.* The Mosaic law, which lays down both moral and social responsibilities.

13:9 Further explains the last statement of v. 8, namely, that love of neighbor encompasses all our social responsibilities. *thy neighbor.* Jesus taught that our neighbor is anyone in need (see Luke 10:25–37), which is probably the idea Paul has in mind here. *as thyself.* Not a command to love ourselves but a recognition of the fact that we naturally do so.

13:11–14 In this section, as in other NT passages, the certain coming of the end of the present age is used to provide moti-

is our salvation nearer than when we believed.
12 The night is far spent, the day is at
hand: [a]let us therefore cast off the works of
darkness, and [b]let us put on the armour of
light.
13 [a]Let us walk [1]honestly, as in the day;
[b]not in rioting and drunkenness, [c]not in
chambering and wantonness, [d]not in strife
and envying.
14 But [a]put ye on the Lord Jesus Christ,
and [b]make not provision for the flesh, to *fulfil*
the lusts *thereof.*

The weak and the strong

14 Him that [a]is weak in the faith receive
you, *but* [1]not to doubtful disputations.
2 For one believeth that *he* [a]may eat all
things: another, who is weak, eateth herbs.
3 Let not him that eateth despise him that
eateth not; and [a]let not him which eateth not
judge him that eateth: for God hath received
him.
4 [a]Who art thou that judgest another *man's*
servant? to his own master he standeth or falleth. Yea, he shall be holden up: for God is able
to make him stand.
5 [a]One man esteemeth one day above another: another esteemeth every day *alike.* Let
every man be [1]fully persuaded in his own
mind.
6 He that [a][1]regardeth the day, regardeth *it*
unto the Lord; and he that regardeth not the
day, to the Lord he doth not regard *it.* He that
eateth, eateth to the Lord, for [b]he giveth God
thanks; and he that eateth not, to the Lord he
eateth not, and giveth God thanks.
7 For [a]none of us liveth to himself, and no
man dieth to himself.
8 For whether we live, we live unto the
Lord; and whether we die, we die unto the
Lord: whether we live therefore, or die, we
are the Lord's.
9 For [a]to this end Christ both died, and
rose, and revived, that he might be [b]Lord both
of the dead and living.
10 ¶ But why dost thou judge thy brother?
or why dost thou set at nought thy brother? for
[a]we shall all stand before the judgment seat of
Christ.
11 For it is written, [a]*As* I live, saith the
Lord, every knee shall bow to me, and every
tongue shall confess to God.
12 So then [a]every one of us shall give account of himself to God.
13 Let us not therefore judge one another
any more: but judge this rather, that [a]no *man*

13:12 [a]Eph. 5:11 [b]Eph. 6:13
13:13 [1]Or, *decently* [a]Phil. 4:8 [b]Prov. 23:20 [c]1 Cor. 6:9 [d]Jas. 3:14
13:14 [a]Gal. 3:27; Eph. 4:24 [b]Gal. 5:16
14:1 [1]Or, *not to judge* his *doubtful thoughts* [a]1 Cor. 8:9
14:2 [a]1 Cor. 10:25; Tit. 1:15
14:3 [a]Col. 2:16
14:4 [a]Jas. 4:12
14:5 [a]Gal. 4:10
14:5 [1]Or, *fully assured*
14:6 [1]Or, *observeth* [a]Gal. 4:10 [b]1 Cor. 10:31; 1 Tim. 4:3
14:7 [a]1 Cor. 6:19; Gal. 2:20; 1 Thes. 5:10; 1 Pet. 4:2
14:9 [a]2 Cor. 5:15 [b]Acts 10:36
14:10 [a]Mat. 25:31; 2 Cor. 5:10
14:11 [a]Is. 45:23
14:12 [a]Mat. 12:36; Gal. 6:5; 1 Pet. 4:5
14:13 [a]1 Cor. 8:9

vation for godly living (see, e.g., Mat 25:31–46; Mark 13:33–37; Jas 5:7–11; 2 Pet 3:11–14).

‡13:11 *the time.* The time of salvation, the closing period of the present age, before the consummation of the kingdom. *high time.* The time for action. *salvation.* The full realization of salvation at the second coming of Jesus Christ (see 8:23; Heb 9:28; 1 Pet 1:5). *nearer.* Every day brings us closer to the second advent of Christ.

13:12 *The night.* The present evil age. *is far spent, the day is at hand.* A clear example of the NT teaching of the "nearness" of the end times (see Mat 24:33; 1 Cor 7:29; Phil 4:5; Jas 5:8–9; 1 Pet 4:7; 1 John 2:18). These texts do not mean that the early Christians believed that Jesus would return within a few years (and thus were mistaken). Rather, they regarded the death and resurrection of Christ as the crucial events of history that began the last days. Since the next great event in God's redemptive plan is the second coming of Jesus Christ, "the night," no matter how long chronologically it may last, is "almost gone." *the day.* The appearing of Jesus Christ, which ushers in the consummation of the kingdom.

13:14 *put ye on the Lord Jesus Christ.* See Gal 3:27. Paul exhorts believers to display outwardly what has already taken place inwardly—including practicing all the virtues associated with Christ.

14:1 *that is weak in the faith.* Probably Jewish Christians at Rome who were unwilling to give up the observance of certain requirements of the law, such as dietary restrictions and the keeping of the sabbath and other special days. Their concern was not quite the same as that of the Judaizers of Galatia. The Judaizers thought they could put God in their debt by works of righteousness and were trying to force this heretical teaching on the Galatian churches, but the "weak" Roman Christians did neither. They were not yet clear as to the status of OT regulations under the new covenant inaugurated by the coming of Christ. *not to doubtful disputations.* Fellowship among Christians is not to be based on everyone's agreement on disputable questions. Christians do not agree on all matters pertaining to the Christian life, nor do they need to.

14:2 *one believeth.* In contrast, Paul now describes the "strong" Christian. Here faith is used in the sense of assurance or confidence. The strong Christian's understanding of the gospel allows him to recognize that one's diet has no spiritual significance.

14:4 *another man's servant.* God's. A Christian must not reject a fellow Christian, who is also a servant of God. *to his own master he standeth or falleth.* The "weak" Christian is not the master of his "strong" brother, nor is the "strong" the master of the "weak." God is Master, and to Him alone all believers are responsible.

14:5 *one day above another.* Some feel that this refers primarily to the sabbath, but it is probably a reference to all the special days of the OT ceremonial law. *esteemeth every day alike.* All days are to be dedicated to God through holy living and godly service. *fully persuaded in his own mind.* The importance of personal conviction in disputable matters of conduct runs through this passage (see vv. 14,16,22–23).

14:6 The motivation behind the actions of both the strong and the weak is to be the same: Both should want to serve the Lord and give thanks for His provision.

14:7 *none of us liveth to himself.* The reference is to "us" Christians. We do not live to please ourselves but the Lord. *no man dieth to himself.* Even in death the important thing is one's relationship to the Lord. Paul repeats the truths of this verse in v. 8.

14:9 *Lord.* See note on 10:9. Christ's Lordship over both the dead and the living arises out of His death and resurrection.

‡14:10 *why dost thou judge thy brother?* Addressed to weak Christians. *why dost thou set at nought thy brother?* Addressed to strong Christians. *we shall all.* Refers to every Christian. *judgment seat of Christ.* All Christians will be judged, and the judgment will be based on works (see 2 Cor 5:10; cf. 1 Cor 3:10–15).

14:13 *but judge this rather.* The words that immediately follow are addressed to strong Christians. *stumblingblock.* Something that causes one to fall into sin.

put a stumblingblock or an occasion to fall in
his brother's way.
14 I know, and am persuaded by the Lord
Jesus, [a]that *there is* nothing [1]unclean of itself:
but [b]to him that esteemeth any *thing* to be
[1]unclean, to him *it is* unclean.
15 But if thy brother be grieved with *thy*
meat, now walkest thou not [1]charitably. [a]De-
stroy not him with thy meat, for whom Christ
died.
16 [a]Let not then your good be evil spoken of:
17 [a]For the kingdom of God is not meat
and drink; but righteousness, and peace, and
joy in the Holy Ghost.
18 For he that in these *things* serveth Christ
[a]*is* acceptable to God, and approved of men.
19 [a]Let us therefore follow *after* the *things*
which make for peace, and *things* wherewith
[b]one may edify another.
20 [a]For meat destroy not the work of God.
[b]All *things* indeed *are* pure; [c]but *it is* evil for
that man who eateth with offence.
21 *It is* good neither to eat [a]flesh, nor to
drink wine, nor *any thing* whereby thy brother stumbleth, or is offended, or is *made* weak.
22 Hast thou faith? have *it* to thyself before
God. [a]Happy *is* he that condemneth not himself in *that thing* which he alloweth.
23 And he that [1]doubteth is damned if he
eat, because *he eateth* not of faith: for [a]what-
soever *is* not of faith is sin.

15 We [a]then that are strong ought to
bear the [b]infirmities of the weak,
and not to please ourselves.
2 [a]Let every one of us please *his* neighbour
for *his* good [b]to edification.
3 [a]For even Christ pleased not himself;
but, as it is written, The [b]reproaches of them
that reproached thee fell on me.
4 For [a]whatsoever *things* were written
aforetime were written for our learning, that
we through patience and comfort of the scriptures might have hope.
5 [a]Now the God of patience and consolation grant you to be likeminded one towards
another [1]according to Christ Jesus:
6 That ye may [a]with one mind *and* one
mouth glorify God, even the Father of our Lord
Jesus Christ.
7 Wherefore [a]receive ye one another, [b]as
Christ also received us, to the glory of God.
8 Now I say that [a]Jesus Christ was a minister of the circumcision for the truth of God, [b]to
confirm the promises made unto the fathers:

14:14 [1]Gr. *common* [a]1 Cor. 10:25 [b]1 Cor. 8:7
14:15 [1]Gr. *according to charity* [a]1 Cor. 8:11
14:16 [a]ch. 12:17
14:17 [a]1 Cor. 8:8
14:18 [a]2 Cor. 8:21
14:19 [a]ch. 12:18 [b]1 Cor. 14:12; 1 Thes. 5:11
14:20 [a]ver. 15 [b]Mat. 15:11 [c]1 Cor. 8:9
14:21 [a]1 Cor. 8:13
14:22 [a]1 John 3:21
14:23 [1]Or, *discerneth and putteth a difference between meats* [a]Tit. 1:15
15:1 [a]Gal. 6:1 [b]ch. 14:1
15:2 [a]1 Cor. 10:33 [b]ch. 14:19
15:3 [a]Mat. 26:39 [b]Ps. 69:9
15:4 [a]1 Cor. 10:11
15:5 [1]Or, *after the example of* [a]1 Cor. 1:10
15:6 [a]Acts 4:24 15:7 [a]ch. 14:1,3 [b]ch. 5:2 15:8 [a]Mat. 15:24; John 1:11; Acts 3:25 [b]2 Cor. 1:20

‡14:14 *I know, and am persuaded by the Lord Jesus.* Now that Paul was a Christian, the old food taboos no longer applied (see Mat 15:10–11,16–20; Mark 7:14–23). *nothing unclean of itself.* For Paul's teaching elsewhere on this subject see 1 Tim 4:4; Tit 1:15. *to him that esteemeth any thing to be unclean, to him it is unclean.* Not to be generalized to mean that sin is only a matter of subjective opinion or conscience. Paul is not discussing conduct that in the light of Scripture is clearly sinful, but conduct concerning which Christians may legitimately differ (in this case, food regulations). With regard to such matters, decisions should be guided by conscience.
‡14:15 *charitably.* Love is the key to proper settlement of disputes. *for whom Christ died.* Christ so valued the weak brother as to die for him. Surely the strong Christian ought to be willing to make adjustments in his own behavior for the sake of such brothers.
14:16 *your good.* From your own understanding of Christian liberty. *be evil spoken of.* To exercise freedom without responsibility can lead to evil results.
14:17 *kingdom of God.* See notes on Mat 3:2; Luke 4:43. *is not meat and drink.* To be concerned with such trivial matters is to miss completely the essence of Christian living. *righteousness.* Righteous living. Paul's concern for the moral and ethical dimension of the Christian life stands out in all his letters. *peace.* See 5:1 and note. *joy in the Holy Ghost.* Joy given by the Holy Spirit.
14:19 *edify another.* The spiritual building up of individual Christians and of the church (see 1:11–12).
14:20 *work of God.* The weak Christian brother who as a redeemed person is God's work and in whom God continues to work (cf. Eph 2:10). *with offence.* Paul recognizes a strong Christian's right to certain freedoms, but qualifies it with the principle of regard for a weak brother's scruples.
14:22 *have it to thyself before God.* The strong Christian is not required to go against his convictions or change his standards. Yet he is not to flaunt his Christian freedom but keep it a private matter. *which he alloweth.* Probably a reference to the eating of certain foods.
14:23 *whatsoever.* The matters discussed above, namely, conduct about which there can be legitimate differences of opinion between Christians.
15:1 *We then that are strong.* Paul identifies himself with the strong Christians, those whose personal convictions allow them more freedom than the weak. *to bear.* Not merely to tolerate or put up with but to uphold lovingly. *infirmities.* Not sins, since in the matters under discussion there is no clear guidance in Scripture. *not to please ourselves.* Not that a Christian should never please himself, but that he should not insist on doing what he wants without regard to the scruples of other Christians.
15:3 *Christ pleased not himself.* He came to do the will of the Father, not His own will. This involved suffering and even death (see Mat 20:28; Mark 10:45; 1 Cor 10:33–11:1; 2 Cor 8:9; Phil 2:5–8). *The reproaches of them that reproached thee fell on me.* In the psalm quoted (69:9) "thee" refers to God and "me" refers to the righteous sufferer, whom Paul identifies with Christ. The quotation serves to show how Christ did not please himself, but voluntarily bore man's hostility toward God.
15:4 Here Paul defends his application of Ps 69:9 to Christ. In so doing, he states a great truth concerning the purpose of Scripture: It was written for our instruction, so that as we patiently endure we might be encouraged to hold fast our hope in Christ (see 1 Cor 10:6,11).
15:5 *to be likeminded.* Not that believers should all come to the same conclusions on the matters of conscience discussed above, but that they might agree to disagree in love.
‡15:7 *as Christ also received us.* See 14:3,4,15.
15:8 *Christ was a minister of the circumcision.* Clearly revealed in His earthly ministry. He was sent to the Jewish people and largely limited His ministry to them (see Mat 15:24). God gave a special priority, so far as the gospel is concerned, to the Jews (see 3:1–8). *promises made unto the fathers.* The covenant promises made to Abraham (Gen 12:1–3; 17:7; 18:19; 22:18), Isaac (Gen 26:3–4) and Jacob (Gen 28:13–15; 46:2–4).

9 And [a]that the Gentiles might glorify God for *his* mercy; as it is written, [b]For this cause I will confess to thee among the Gentiles, and sing unto thy name.

10 And again *he* saith, [a]Rejoice, *ye* Gentiles, with his people.

11 And again, [a]Praise the Lord, all ye Gentiles; and laud him, all ye people.

12 And again Esaias saith, [a]There shall be a root of Jesse, and he that *shall* rise to reign over the Gentiles; in him shall the Gentiles trust.

13 Now the God of hope fill you with all [a]joy and peace in believing, that ye may abound in hope, through the power of the Holy Ghost.

Paul's reason for writing

14 ¶ And [a]I myself also am persuaded of you, my brethren, that ye also are full of goodness, [b]filled with all knowledge, able also to admonish one another.

15 Nevertheless, brethren, I have written the more boldly unto you in some sort, as putting you in mind, [a]because of the grace that is given to me of God,

16 That [a]I should be the minister of Jesus Christ to the Gentiles, ministering the gospel of God, that the [b1]offering up of the Gentiles might be acceptable, being sanctified by the Holy Ghost.

17 I have therefore whereof *I* may glory through Jesus Christ [a]*in those things* which pertain to God.

18 For I will not dare to speak of any of *those things* [a]which Christ hath not wrought by me, [b]to make the Gentiles obedient, by word and deed,

19 [a]Through mighty signs and wonders, by the power of the Spirit of God; so that from Jerusalem, and round about unto Illyricum, I have fully preached the gospel of Christ.

20 Yea, so have I strived to preach the gospel, not where Christ was named, [a]lest I should build upon another *man's* foundation:

21 But as it is written, [a]To whom he was not spoken of, they shall see: and they that have not heard shall understand.

Paul's future plans

22 For which cause also [a]I have been [1]much hindered from coming to you.

23 But now having no more place in these parts, and [a]having a great desire these many years to come unto you;

24 Whensoever I take my journey into Spain, I will come to you: for I trust to see you in my journey, [a]and to be brought on my way thitherward by you, if first I be somewhat filled [b1]with your *company*.

25 But now [a]I go unto Jerusalem to minister unto the saints.

26 For [a]it hath pleased *them of* Macedonia and Achaia to make a certain contribution for the poor saints which are at Jerusalem.

15:9 [a]John 10:16 [b]Ps. 18:49
15:10 [a]Deut. 32:43
15:11 [a]Ps. 117:1
15:12 [a]Is. 11:1; Rev. 5:5
15:13 [a]ch. 12:12
15:14 [a]2 Pet. 1:12; 1 John 2:21 [b]1 Cor. 8:1
15:15 [a]ch. 1:5; 12:3; Gal. 1:15; Eph. 3:7,8
15:16 [1]Or, *sacrificing* [a]ch. 11:13; Gal. 2:7-9; 1 Tim. 2:7; 2 Tim. 1:11 [b]Is. 66:20; Phil. 2:17
15:17 [a]Heb. 5:1
15:18 [a]Acts 21:19; Gal. 2:8 [b]ch. 1:5; 16:26
15:19 [a]Acts 19:11; 2 Cor. 12:12
15:20 [a]2 Cor. 10:13,15,16
15:21 [a]Is. 52:15
15:22 [1]Or, *many ways*, or, *oftentimes* [a]ch. 1:13; 1 Thes. 2:17
15:23 [a]Acts 19:21; ch. 1:11
15:24 [1]Gr. *with you* [a]Acts 15:3 [b]ver. 32
15:25 [a]Acts 19:21; 24:17
15:26 [a]1 Cor. 16:1; 2 Cor. 8:1

15:9 *that the Gentiles might glorify God.* From the beginning, God's redemptive work in and for Israel had in view the redemption of the Gentiles (see Gen 12:3). They would both see God's mighty and gracious acts for His people and hear the praises of God's people as they celebrated what God had done for them (a common theme in the Psalms; see Paul's quotations in vv. 9b–12 and note on Ps 9:1). Thus they would come to know the true God and glorify Him for His mercy (see notes on Ps 46:10; 47:9). God's greatest and climactic act for Israel's salvation was the sending of the Messiah to fulfill the promises made to the patriarchs and so to gather in the great harvest of the Gentiles.

15:12 *root of Jesse.* Jesse was the father of David (see 1 Sam 16:5–13; Mat 1:6), and the Messiah was the "Son of David" (Mat 21:9). See Is 11:1; Rev 5:5. *in him shall the Gentiles trust.* The Gentile mission of the early church was a fulfillment of this prophecy, as is the continuing evangelization of the nations.

15:13 *God of hope.* Any hope the Christian has comes from God. See note on 5:5. *through the power of the Holy Ghost.* Hope cannot be conjured up by man's effort; it is God's gift by His Spirit (see 8:24–25).

‡15:15 *as putting you in mind.* Since Paul had never preached or taught in Rome, he may be referring to Christian doctrine generally known in the church of which they needed to be reminded.

‡15:16 *minister of Jesus Christ to the Gentiles.* See note on 11:13. *ministering the gospel.* The Greek word Paul used (only here in N.T.) refers to ministering as a priest. Paul's priestly function was different from that of the Levitical priests. They were involved with the rituals of the temple, whereas he preached the gospel. *the offering . . . might be acceptable, being sanctified by the Holy Ghost.* The offering Paul brought to God was the Gentile church.

15:17 *I have therefore whereof I may glory.* Paul was not boasting of his own achievements but of what Christ had accomplished through him.

15:19 *signs and wonders.* See Acts 14:8–10; 16:16–18,25–26; 20:9–12; 28:8–9; 2 Cor 12:12; Heb 2:3–4. *from Jerusalem.* The home of the mother church, where the gospel originated and its dissemination began (see Acts 1:8). *Illyricum.* A Roman province north of Macedonia (present-day Albania and Yugoslavia). Acts mentions nothing of his ministry there, and perhaps all he means is that he reached the border. *I have fully preached the gospel.* Not everyone had heard the gospel in the eastern Mediterranean, but Paul believed that his work there had been completed and it was time to move on to other places.

15:22 *much hindered from coming to you.* Paul's great desire to complete the missionary task in the eastern Mediterranean had prevented him from making a trip to Rome.

15:23 *having no more place.* Because of the principle stated in v. 20. *having a great desire these many years to come unto you.* See 1:11–15.

15:24 *to be brought on my way thitherward by you.* Paul wanted to use the Roman church as a base of operations for a mission to Spain. *be somewhat filled with your company.* More than a quick stop at Rome was contemplated (see 1:11–12).

15:25 *minister unto the saints.* Paul wanted to present the gift (see v. 26) personally to the Jerusalem church. The gift needed interpretation. It was not merely money; it represented the love and concern of the Gentile churches for their Jewish brothers and sisters. *saints.* Refers generally to believers in Jesus Christ (see note on 1:7).

15:26 *contribution.* See 1 Cor 16:1–4; 2 Cor 8–9.

27 It hath pleased them verily; and their debtors they are. For [a]if the Gentiles have been made partakers of their spiritual *things,* [b]their duty is also to minister unto them in carnal *things.*

28 When therefore I have performed this, and have sealed to them [a]this fruit, I will come by you into Spain.

29 [a]And I am sure that, when I come unto you, I shall come in the fulness of the blessing of the gospel of Christ.

30 Now I beseech you, brethren, for the Lord Jesus Christ's sake, and [a]for the love of the Spirit, [b]that *ye* strive together with me in *your* prayers to God for me;

31 [a]That I may be delivered from them that [1]do not believe in Judea; and that [b]my service which I have for Jerusalem may be accepted of the saints;

32 [a]That I may come unto you with joy [b]by the will of God, and may with you [c]be refreshed.

33 Now [a]the God of peace *be* with you all. Amen.

Commendations and greetings

16 I commend unto you Phebe our sister, which is a servant of the church which is at [a]Cenchrea:

2 [a]That ye receive her in the Lord, as becometh saints, and *that* ye assist her in whatsoever business she hath need of you: for she hath been a succourer of many, and of myself *also.*

3 Greet [a]Priscilla and Aquila my helpers in Christ Jesus:

4 Who have for my life laid down their own necks: unto whom not only I give thanks, but also all the churches of the Gentiles.

5 Likewise *greet* [a]the church that is in their house. Salute my wellbeloved Epenetus, who is [b]the firstfruits of Achaia unto Christ.

6 Greet Mary, who bestowed much labour on us.

7 Salute Andronicus and Junia, my kinsmen, and my fellowprisoners, who are of note among the apostles, who also [a]were in Christ before me.

8 Greet Amplias my beloved in the Lord.

9 Salute Urban our helper in Christ, and Stachys my beloved.

10 Salute Apelles approved in Christ. Salute them which are of Aristobulus' [1]*household.*

11 Salute Herodion my kinsman. Greet them that be of the [1]*household* of Narcissus, which are in the Lord.

12 Salute Tryphena and Tryphosa, who labour in the Lord. Salute the beloved Persis, which laboured much in the Lord.

13 Salute Rufus [a]chosen in the Lord, and his mother and mine.

14 Salute Asyncritus, Phlegon, Hermas, Patrobas, Hermes, and the brethren which are with them.

15 Salute Philologus, and Julia, Nereus, and his sister, and Olympas, and all the saints which are with them.

16 [a]Salute one another with a holy kiss. The churches of Christ salute you.

17 ¶ Now I beseech you, brethren, mark them [a]which cause divisions and offences contrary to the doctrine which ye have learned; and [b]avoid them.

18 For *they that are* such serve not our Lord Jesus Christ, but [a]their own belly; and [b]by good words and fair speeches deceive the hearts of the simple.

19 For [a]your obedience is come abroad unto all *men.* I am glad therefore on your behalf: but *yet* I would have you [b]wise unto *that which is* good, and [1]simple concerning evil.

20 And [a]the God of peace [b]shall [1]bruise

15:27 [a]ch. 11:17 [b]1 Cor. 9:11; Gal. 6:6
15:28 [a]Phil. 4:17
15:29 [a]ch. 1:11
15:30 [a]Phil. 2:1 [b]2 Cor. 1:11; Col. 4:12
15:31 [1]Or, *are disobedient* [a]2 Thes. 3:2 [b]2 Cor. 8:4
15:32 [a]ch. 1:10 [b]Acts 18:21; 1 Cor. 4:19; Jas. 4:15 [c]1 Cor. 16:18; 2 Cor. 7:13; 2 Tim. 1:16; Philem. 7,20
15:33 [a]ch. 16:20; 1 Cor. 14:33; 2 Cor. 13:11; Phil. 4:9; 1 Thes. 5:23; 2 Thes. 3:16; Heb. 13:20
16:1 [a]Acts 18:18
16:2 [a]Phil. 2:29; 3 John 5,6
16:3 [a]Acts 18:2,18,26
16:5 [a]1 Cor. 16:19; Col. 4:15; Philem. 2 [b]1 Cor. 16:15
16:7 [a]Gal. 1:22
16:10 [1]Or, friends
16:11 [1]Or, friends
16:13 [a]2 John 1
16:16 [a]1 Cor. 16:20; 2 Cor. 13:12
16:17 [a]Acts 15:1 [b]1 Cor. 5:9; 2 Tim. 3:5
16:18 [a]Phil. 3:19; 1 Tim. 6:5 [b]Col. 2:4; 2 Tim. 3:6
16:19 [1]Or, *harmless* [a]ch. 1:8 [b]Mat. 10:16
16:20 [1]Or, *tread* [a]ch. 15:33 [b]Gen. 3:15

15:27 *their spiritual things.* Especially Christ and the gospel.
15:28 *this fruit.* The collection from the Gentile churches.
15:31 *That I may be delivered from them that do not believe in Judea.* Paul wanted to go to Jerusalem. The delivery of the collection was important to him, but he had received warnings about what might happen to him there (see Acts 20:22–23). *may be accepted.* Perhaps a reference to the way in which the money was to be distributed—often a delicate and difficult task.
15:32 *be refreshed.* See 1:11–12.
15:33 *God of peace.* See notes on 5:1; 1 Thes 5:23.
‡16:1 *Phebe.* Possibly one of the carriers of the letter to Rome. *our sister.* In the sense of being a fellow believer. *servant.* One who serves or ministers in any way. Regarding women serving in the early church see notes at 1 Tim 3:8,11. *Cenchrea.* A port located about six miles east of Corinth on the Saronic Gulf.
16:3 *Priscilla and Aquila.* Close friends of Paul who worked in the same trade of tentmaking (see Acts 18:2–3).
16:4 *for my life laid down their own necks.* There is no other record of this in the NT or elsewhere, but it must have been widely known, as the last part of the verse indicates.
16:6 *Mary.* Six persons are known by this name in the NT. This one is unknown apart from this reference.
16:8–10 *Amplias . . . Urban . . . Stachys . . . Apelles.* All common slave names found in the imperial household.
16:10 *Aristobulus.* Perhaps refers to the grandson of Herod the Great and brother of Herod Agrippa I.
16:11 *my kinsman.* Perhaps a reference to his being a Jew. *Narcissus.* Sometimes identified with Tiberius Claudius Narcissus, a wealthy freedman of the Roman emperor Tiberius.
16:12 *Tryphena and Tryphosa.* Perhaps sisters, even twins, because it was common for such persons to be given names from the same root. *Persis.* Means "Persian woman."
16:14–15 None of these persons can be further identified, except that they were slaves or freedmen in the Roman church.
16:16 *holy kiss.* See 1 Cor 16:20; 2 Cor 13:12; 1 Thes 5:26; 1 Pet 5:14. Justin Martyr (A.D. 150) tells us that the holy kiss was a regular part of the worship service in his day. It is still a practice in some churches.
16:17–20 A theological application of the story of man's fall (Gen 3).
16:17 *them which cause divisions and offences.* Who these people were we cannot tell, but some of their characteristics are mentioned in v. 18.
16:19 *wise unto that which is good.* Christians are to be experts in doing good.
‡16:20 *God of peace.* See 15:33. *shall bruise Satan.* A reference to Satan's final doom (cf. Gen 3:15). For "shortly" see note on 13:12.

Satan under your feet shortly. [c]The grace of
our Lord Jesus Christ *be* with you. Amen.
21 ¶ [a]Timotheus my workfellow, and [b]Luci-
us, and [c]Jason, and [d]Sosipater, my kinsmen,
salute you.
22 I Tertius, who wrote *this* epistle, salute
you in the Lord.
23 [a]Gaius mine host, and of the whole
church, saluteth you. [b]Erastus the chamberlain of the city saluteth you, and Quartus a
brother.
24 [a]The grace of our Lord Jesus Christ *be*
with you all. Amen.
25 ¶ Now [a]to him that is of power to stablish you [b]according to my gospel, and the
preaching of Jesus Christ, [c]according to the
revelation of the mystery, [d]which was kept secret since the world began,
26 But [a]now is made manifest, and by the
scriptures of the prophets, according to the
commandment of the everlasting God, made
known to all nations for [b]the obedience of faith:
27 To [a]God only wise, *be* glory through
Jesus Christ for ever. Amen.

¶ Written to the Romans from Corinthus, *and sent* by Phebe servant of the church at Cenchrea.

16:20 [c]1 Cor. 16:23
16:21 [a]Acts 16:1; Heb. 13:23 [b]Acts 13:1 [c]Acts 17:5 [d]Acts 20:4
16:23 [a]1 Cor. 1:14 [b]Acts 19:22
16:24 [a]1 Thes. 5:28
16:25 [a]Eph. 3:20
16:25 [b]ch. 2:16 [c]Eph. 1:9 [d]Col. 1:26
16:26 [a]Eph. 1:9 [b]Acts 6:7
16:27 [a]Jude 25

16:21 *Jason.* Possibly the Jason mentioned in Acts 17:5–9. *Sosipater.* Probably Sopater son of Pyrrhus from Berea (see Acts 20:4).
16:22 *I, Tertius, who wrote this epistle.* Not mentioned elsewhere in the NT. He had functioned as Paul's secretary.
16:23 *Gaius.* Usually identified with Titius Justus, a God-fearer, in whose house Paul stayed while in Corinth (see Acts 18:7; 1 Cor 1:14). His full name would be Gaius Titius Justus. *whole church.* In Corinth. *Erastus.* At Corinth archaeologists have discovered a reused block of stone in a paved square, with the Latin inscription: "Erastus, commissioner of public works, bore the expense of this pavement." This may refer to the Erastus mentioned here. If it does, it is the earliest reference to a Christian by name outside the NT. He may also be the same person referred to in Acts 19:22 and 2 Tim 4:20, though it is difficult to be certain because the name was fairly common. *Quartus.* Means "fourth (son)."

16:25 *my gospel.* Not a gospel different from that preached by others, but a gospel Paul received by direct revelation (see Gal 1:12). *preaching of Jesus Christ.* A description of the gospel; it is about Jesus Christ, who is its content. *mystery.* See note on 11:25. *since the world began.* From eternity past (see 1 Cor 2:6–10).

‡16:26 *made manifest, and by the scriptures of the prophets.* See 1:2. *all nations.* The universality of the gospel (see Mat 28:19).

‡16:27 *To God . . . be glory.* The ultimate purpose of all things.

The First Epistle of Paul the Apostle to the
Corinthians

INTRODUCTION

Author and Date

Paul is acknowledged as the author both by the letter itself (1:1–2; 16:21) and by the early church fathers. His authorship was attested by Clement of Rome as early as A.D. 96, and today practically all NT scholars concur. The letter was written c. 55 toward the close of Paul's three-year residency in Ephesus (see 16:5–9; Acts 20:31). It is clear from his reference to staying at Ephesus until Pentecost (16:8) that he intended to remain there somewhat less than a year when he wrote 1 Corinthians.

The City of Corinth

It has been estimated that in Paul's day Corinth had a population of about 250,000 free persons, plus as many as 400,000 slaves. In a number of ways it was the chief city of Greece.

1. *Its commerce.* Located just off the Corinthian isthmus, it was a crossroads for travelers and traders. It had two harbors: (1) Cenchrea, six miles to the east on the Saronic Gulf, and (2) Lechaion, a mile and a half to the west on the Corinthian Gulf. Goods flowed across the isthmus on the Diolkos, a road by which smaller ships could be hauled fully loaded across the isthmus, and by which cargoes of larger ships could be transported by wagons from one side to the other. Goods flowed through the city from Italy and Spain to the west and from Asia Minor, Phoenicia and Egypt to the east.

2. *Its culture.* Although Corinth was not a university town like Athens, it was characterized nevertheless by typical Greek culture. Its people were interested in Greek philosophy and placed a high premium on wisdom.

3. *Its religion.* Corinth contained at least 12 temples. Whether they were all in use during Paul's time is not known for certain. One of the most infamous was the temple dedicated to Aphrodite, the goddess of love, whose worshipers practiced religious prostitution. About a fourth of a mile north of the theater stood the temple of Asclepius, the god of healing, and in the middle of the city the sixth-century B.C. temple of Apollo was located. In addition, the Jews had established a synagogue; the inscribed lintel of it has been found and placed in the museum at old Corinth.

4. *Its immorality.* Like any large commercial city, Corinth was a center for open and unbridled immorality. The worship of Aphrodite fostered prostitution in the name of religion. At one time 1,000 sacred prostitutes served her temple. So widely known did the immorality of Corinth become that the Greek verb "to Corinthianize" came to mean "to practice sexual immorality." In a setting like this it is no wonder that the Corinthian church was plagued with numerous problems.

Occasion and Purpose

Paul had received information from several sources concerning the conditions existing in the church at Corinth. Some members of the household of Chloe had informed him of the factions that had developed in the church (1:11). There were three individuals—Stephanas, Fortunatus and Achaicus—who had come to Paul in Ephesus to make some contribution to his ministry (16:17), but whether these were the ones from Chloe's household we do not know.

Some of those who had come had brought disturbing information concerning moral irregularities in the church (chs. 5—6). Immorality had plagued the Corinthian assembly almost from the beginning. From 5:9–10 it is apparent that Paul had written previously concerning moral laxness. He had urged believers "not to company with fornicators" (5:9). Because of misunderstanding he now finds it necessary to clarify his instruction (5:10–11) and to urge immediate and drastic action (5:3–5,13).

Other Corinthian visitors had brought a letter from the church that requested counsel on several subjects (see 7:1; cf. 8:1; 12:1; 16:1).

It is clear that, although the church was gifted (see 1:4–7), it was immature and unspiritual (3:1–4). Paul's purposes for writing were: (1) to instruct and restore the church in its areas of weakness, correcting erroneous practices such as divisions (1:10—4:21), immorality (ch. 5; 6:12–20), lit-

igation in pagan courts (6:1–8) and abuse of the Lord's supper (11:17–34); (2) to correct false teaching concerning the resurrection (ch. 15); and (3) to give instruction concerning the offering for poverty-stricken believers in Jerusalem (16:1–4).

Theme

The letter revolves around the theme of problems in Christian conduct in the church. It thus has to do with progressive sanctification, the continuing development of holiness of character. Obviously Paul was personally concerned with the Corinthians' problems, revealing a true pastor's (shepherd's) heart.

Relevance

This letter is timely for the church today, both to instruct and to inspire. Most of the questions and problems that confronted the church at Corinth are still very much with us—problems like immaturity, instability, divisions, jealousy and envy, lawsuits, marital difficulties, sexual immorality and misuse of spiritual gifts. Yet in spite of this concentration on problems, the book contains some of the most familiar and beloved chapters in the entire Bible—e.g., ch. 13 (on love) and ch. 15 (on resurrection).

Outline

I. Introduction (1:1–9)
II. Divisions in the Church (1:10—4:21)
  A. The Fact of the Divisions (1:10–17)
  B. The Causes of the Divisions (1:18—4:13)
    1. A wrong conception of the Christian message (1:18–3:4)

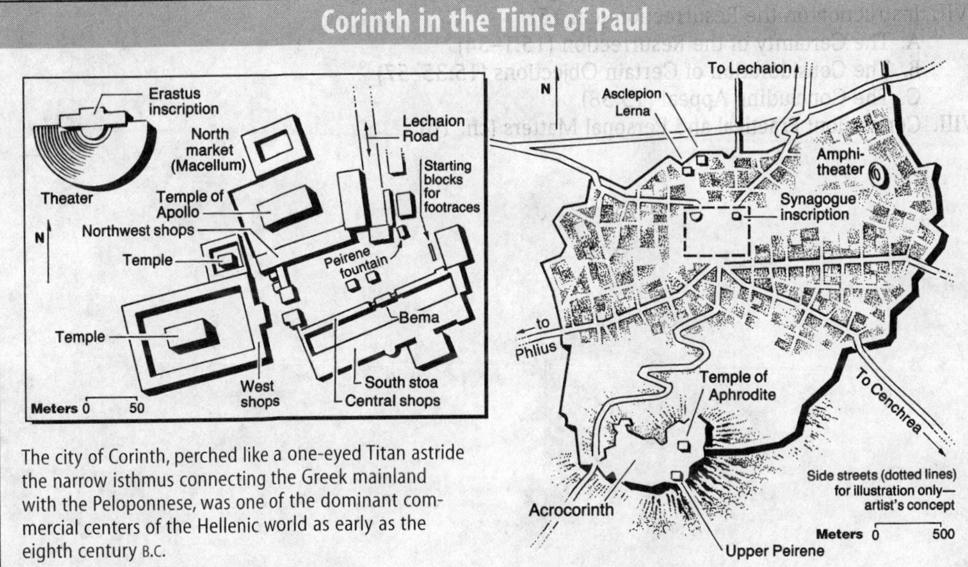

The city of Corinth, perched like a one-eyed Titan astride the narrow isthmus connecting the Greek mainland with the Peloponnese, was one of the dominant commercial centers of the Hellenic world as early as the eighth century B.C.

No city in Greece was more favorably situated for land and sea trade. With a high, strong citadel at its back, it lay between the Saronic Gulf and the Ionian Sea and ports at Lechaion and Cenchrea. A *diolkos*, or stone tramway for the overland transport of ships, linked the two seas. Crowning the Acrocorinth was the temple of Aphrodite, served, according to Strabo, by more than 1,000 pagan priestess-prostitutes.

By the time the gospel reached Corinth in the spring of A.D. 52, the city had a proud history of leadership in the Achaian League, and a spirit of revived Hellenism under Roman domination following the destruction of the city by Mummius in 146 B.C.

Paul's lengthy stay in Corinth brought him directly in contact with the major monuments of the *agora*, many of which still survive. The fountain-house of the spring *Peirene*, the temple of Apollo, the *macellum* or meat market (1 Cor 10:25) and the theater, the *bema* (Acts 18:12), and the unimpressive synagogue all played a part in the experience of the apostle. An inscription from the theater names the city official Erastus, probably the friend of Paul mentioned in Rom 16:23.

2. A wrong conception of Christian ministry and ministers (3:5—4:5)
3. A wrong conception of the Christian (4:6–13)

C. The Exhortation to End the Divisions (4:14–21)

III. Moral and Ethical Disorders in the Life of the Church (chs. 5—6)

A. Laxity in Church Discipline (ch. 5)
B. Lawsuits before Non-Christian Judges (6:1–11)
C. Licentiousness or Sexual Immorality (6:12–20)

IV. Instruction on Marriage (ch. 7)

A. The Prologue: General Principles (7:1–7)
B. The Problems of the Married (7:8–24)
C. The Problems of the Unmarried (7:25–40)

V. Instruction on Questionable Practices (8:1—11:1)

A. The Principles Involved (ch. 8)
B. The Principles Illustrated (ch. 9)
C. A Warning from the History of Israel (10:1–22)
D. The Principles Applied (10:23—11:1)

VI. Instruction on Public Worship (11:2—14:40)

A. Propriety in Worship (11:2–16)
B. The Lord's Supper (11:17–34)
C. Spiritual Gifts (chs. 12—14)

1. The test of the gifts (12:1–3)
2. The unity of the gifts (12:4–11)
3. The diversity of the gifts (12:12–31a)
4. The necessity of exercising the gifts in love (12:31b—13:13)
5. The superiority of prophecy over tongues (14:1–25)
6. Rules governing public worship (14:26–40)

VII. Instruction on the Resurrection (ch. 15)

A. The Certainty of the Resurrection (15:1–34)
B. The Consideration of Certain Objections (15:35–57)
C. The Concluding Appeal (15:58)

VIII. Conclusion: Practical and Personal Matters (ch. 16)

Paul's thanksgiving

1 Paul, [a]called *to be* an apostle of Jesus Christ [b]through the will of God, and Sosthenes *our* brother,

2 Unto the church of God which is at Corinth, to them that [a]are sanctified in Christ Jesus, [b]called *to be* saints, with all that in every place call upon the name of Jesus Christ [c]our Lord, [d]both theirs and ours:

3 [a]Grace *be* unto you, and peace, from God our Father, and *from* the Lord Jesus Christ.

4 ¶ [a]I thank my God always on your behalf, for the grace of God which is given you by Jesus Christ;

5 That in every *thing* ye are enriched by him, [a]in all utterance, and *in* all knowledge;

6 Even as [a]the testimony of Christ was confirmed in you:

7 So that ye come behind in no gift; [a]waiting for the [1]coming of our Lord Jesus Christ:

8 [a]Who shall also confirm you unto the end, [b]*that ye may be* blameless in the day of our Lord Jesus Christ.

9 [a]God *is* faithful, by whom ye were called unto [b]the fellowship of his Son Jesus Christ our Lord.

An appeal for unity

10 ¶ Now I beseech you, brethren, by the name of our Lord Jesus Christ, [a]that ye all speak the same *thing,* and *that* there be no [1]divisions among you; but *that* ye be perfectly joined together in the same mind and in the same judgment.

11 For it hath been declared unto me of you, my brethren, by them which are of the *house* of Chloe, that there are contentions among you.

12 Now this I say, [a]that every one of you saith, I am of Paul; and I of [b]Apollos; and I of [c]Cephas; and I of Christ.

13 [a]Is Christ divided? was Paul crucified for you? or were ye baptized in the name of Paul?

14 I thank God that I baptized none of you, but [a]Crispus and [b]Gaius;

15 Lest any should say that I had baptized in mine own name.

16 And I baptized also the household of [a]Stephanas: besides, I know not whether I baptized any other.

Christ, God's power and wisdom

17 ¶ For Christ sent me not to baptize, but to preach the gospel: [a]not with wisdom of [1]words, lest the cross of Christ should be made of none effect.

18 For the preaching of the cross is to [a]them that perish [b]foolishness; but unto us [c]which are saved it is the [d]power of God.

19 For it is written, [a]I will destroy the wis-

1:1 [a]Rom. 1:1 [b]2 Cor. 1:1
1:2 [a]Acts 15:9 [b]Rom. 1:7 [c]ch. 8:6 [d]Rom. 3:22
1:3 [a]Rom. 1:7; 2 Cor. 1:2
1:4 [a]Rom. 1:8
1:5 [a]ch. 12:8
1:6 [a]2 Tim. 1:8; Rev. 1:2
1:7 [1]Gr. *revelation* [a]Phil. 3:20; Tit. 2:13; 2 Pet. 3:12
1:8 [a]1 Thes. 3:13 [b]Col. 1:22
1:9 [a]Is. 49:7; 1 Thes. 5:24 [b]John 15:4
1:10 [a]2 Cor. 13:11; 1 Pet. 3:8
1:10 [1]Gr. *schisms*
1:12 [a]ch. 3:4 [b]Acts 18:24 [c]John 1:42
1:13 [a]2 Cor. 11:4
1:14 [a]Acts 18:8 [b]Rom. 16:23
1:16 [a]ch. 16:15
1:17 [1]Or, *speech* [a]ch. 2:4
1:18 [a]2 Cor. 2:15 [b]Acts 17:18 [c]ch. 15:2 [d]Rom. 1:16
1:19 [a]Is. 29:14

‡1:1 *Paul.* The Greek custom was to begin a letter with the writer's name. For more information on Paul see notes on Acts 9:1; Phil 3:4–14. *apostle of Jesus Christ.* See notes on Mark 6:30; Heb 3:1. Paul uses this title in all his letters (except Philippians, 1,2 Thessalonians and Philemon) to establish his authority as Christ's messenger—an authority that had been challenged (see ch. 9; 2 Cor 11). He reinforces his authority by adding "through the will of God," i.e., by divine initiative. *Sosthenes.* Perhaps the synagogue ruler at Corinth who was assaulted by the Greeks (Acts 18:17). If so, he obviously became a Christian—possibly while Paul was preaching at Corinth (Acts 18:18) or during Apollos's ministry there (Acts 19:1).

1:2 *church of God.* Used only by Paul and only in Acts 20:28, here and 2 Cor 1:1. Its OT counterpart is the expression "congregation (or community) of the Lord" (see Deut 23:1; see also Num 16:3; 20:4; 1 Chr 28:8). *sanctified.* Set apart for the Lord. It can also mean "made holy," which is done by (1) being declared holy through faith in Christ's atoning death on the cross (sometimes called positional sanctification), and (2) being made holy by the work of the Holy Spirit in the lives of Christians (sometimes called progressive sanctification). In spite of the fact that Paul found much in the Corinthian Christians to criticize, he still called them "sanctified"—not because of their conduct, but because of their relationship to Christ (positional sanctification).

1:3 *Grace . . . and peace.* See notes on Jonah 4:2; John 14:27; 20:19; Gal 1:3; Eph 1:2.

1:4 *thank.* See Rom 1:8.

1:5 *utterance, and in all knowledge.* Gifts of the Spirit (see 12:8; also 2 Cor 8:7).

1:6 *confirmed.* Paul's preaching about Christ had been accepted by the Corinthians, and they had proved it to be true.

‡1:7 *gift.* Probably refers to the spiritual gifts of chs. 12–14. According to those chapters, a spiritual gift is a manifestation of the Holy Spirit enabling one to minister to the needs of Christ's body, the church (see 12:7–11; 14:3,12,17). The Greek word used here stresses that it is a gift of grace.

1:8 *Who.* God the Father. *the end.* Of the age, when Christ comes again. *in the day of our Lord Jesus Christ.* When He returns (v. 7; Phil 1:6).

1:9 *God is faithful.* He may be trusted to do what He has promised (1 Thes 5:24), namely, to "confirm you unto the end" (v. 8).

1:10 *brethren.* In Christ believers have a unity similar to that of blood brothers and sisters. Paul is referring to both men and women (see 16:20; Rom 16:3,6–7,12–13,15).

1:11 *contentions.* See Gal 5:20; Jas 4:1–2.

1:12 *Apollos.* He had carried on a fruitful ministry in Corinth (Acts 18:24–28; 19:1). *Cephas.* Peter. It has been suggested that those who followed Peter in Corinth were Jewish Christians.

1:13 *Is Christ divided?* See 12:12–13. *in the name of Paul.* Implies becoming a follower or intimate associate.

1:16 *household.* Other examples of households being baptized are those of Cornelius (Acts 10:24, 48), Lydia (Acts 16:15) and the Philippian jailer (Acts 16:33–34). The term may include family members, servants or anyone who lived in the house. *Stephanas.* See 16:15,17.

1:17 *not to baptize.* Paul is not minimizing baptism; rather, he is asserting that his God-given task was primarily to preach. Jesus (John 4:2) and Peter (Acts 10:48) also had others baptize for them. *wisdom of words.* Lit. "wisdom of speech." Paul's mission was not to couch the gospel in the language of the trained orator, who had studied the techniques of influencing people by persuasive arguments.

1:19 The quotation is from Is 29:14, where God denounced the policy of the "wise" in Judah in seeking an alliance with Egypt when threatened by King Sennacherib of Assyria. *the wise.* Aristides said that on every street in Corinth one met a so-called wise man, who had his own solutions to the world's problems.

dom of the wise, and will bring to nothing the understanding of the prudent.

20 [a]Where *is* the wise? where *is* the scribe? where *is* the disputer of this world? [b]hath not God made foolish the wisdom of this world?

21 [a]For after that in the wisdom of God the world by wisdom knew not God, it pleased God by the foolishness of preaching to save them that believe.

22 For the [a]Jews require a sign, and the Greeks seek after wisdom:

23 But we preach Christ crucified, [a]unto the Jews a stumblingblock, and unto the Greeks [b]foolishness;

24 But unto them which are called, both Jews and Greeks, Christ [a]the power of God, and [b]the wisdom of God.

25 Because the foolishness of God is wiser than men; and the weakness of God is stronger than men.

26 For ye see your calling, brethren, how that [a]not many wise *men* after the flesh, not many mighty, not many noble, *are called:*

27 But [a]God hath chosen the foolish *things* of the world to confound the wise; and God hath chosen the weak *things* of the world to confound the *things which are* mighty;

28 And base *things* of the world, and *things* which are despised, hath God chosen, *yea,* and [a]*things* which are not, [b]to bring to nought *things* that are:

29 [a]That no flesh should glory in his presence.

30 But of him are ye in Christ Jesus, who of God is made unto us [a]wisdom, and [b]righteousness, and [c]sanctification, and [d]redemption:

31 That, according as it is written, [a]He that glorieth, let him glory in the Lord.

2 And I, brethren, when I came to you, [a]came not with excellency of speech or of wisdom, declaring unto you [b]the testimony of God.

2 For I determined not to know any *thing* among you, [a]save Jesus Christ, and him crucified.

3 And [a]I was with you [b]in weakness, and in fear, and in much trembling.

4 And my speech and my preaching [a]*was* not with [1]enticing words of man's wisdom, [b]but in demonstration of the Spirit and of power:

5 That your faith should not [1]stand in the wisdom of men, but [a]in the power of God.

True wisdom the gift of God

6 ¶ Howbeit we speak wisdom among *them* [a]*that are* perfect: yet not [b]the wisdom of this world, nor of the princes of this world, [c]that come to nought:

7 But we speak the wisdom of God in a mystery, *even* the hidden *wisdom,* [a]which God ordained before the world unto our glory:

8 [a]Which none of the princes of this world knew: for [b]had they known *it,* they would not have crucified the Lord of glory.

9 But as it is written, [a]Eye hath not seen,

1:20 [a]Is. 33:18 [b]Job 12:17; Is. 44:25; Rom. 1:22
1:21 [a]Mat. 11:25; Luke 10:21; Rom. 1:20
1:22 [a]Mat. 12:38; Mark 8:11; John 4:48
1:23 [a]Is. 8:14; Luke 2:34; John 6:60; Gal. 5:11 [b]ch. 2:14
1:24 [a]Rom. 1:4 [b]Col. 2:3
1:26 [a]John 7:48
1:27 [a]Mat. 11:25
1:28 [a]Rom. 4:17 [b]ch. 2:6
1:29 [a]Rom. 3:27; Eph. 2:9
1:30 [a]ver. 24 [b]Jer. 23:5; Rom. 4:25; 2 Cor. 5:21 [c]John 17:19 [d]Eph. 1:7
1:31 [a]Jer. 9:23
2:1 [a]ch. 1:17 [b]ch. 1:6
2:2 [a]Gal. 6:14; Phil. 3:8
2:3 [a]Acts 18:1 [b]2 Cor. 4:7
2:4 [1]Or, *persuasible* [a]2 Pet. 1:16 [b]Rom. 15:19
2:5 [1]Gr. *be* [a]2 Cor. 4:7
2:6 [a]ch. 14:20; Heb. 5:14 [b]2 Cor. 1:12 [c]ch. 1:28
2:7 [a]Eph. 3:5; Col. 1:26
2:8 [a]Mat. 11:25 [b]Luke 23:34
2:9 [a]Is. 64:4

1:20 *the wise.* Probably a reference to Gentile philosophers in general. *scribe.* Probably the Jewish teacher of the law (see note on Mat 2:4). *disputer of this world.* Probably refers to the Greek sophists, who engaged in long and subtle disputes. *God made foolish the wisdom of this world.* All humanly devised philosophical systems end in meaninglessness because they have a wrong concept of God and His revelation.
1:21 *wisdom . . . foolishness.* Jesus expresses a similar thought in Luke 10:21. It is God's intention that worldly wisdom should not be the means of knowing Him. *foolishness of preaching.* Not that preaching is foolish, but that the message being preached (Christ crucified) is viewed by the world as foolish.
1:22 *Greeks seek after wisdom.* True of Greeks in general, but especially of the Greek philosophers.
1:23 *Christ crucified.* See 2:2. *unto the Jews a stumblingblock.* They expected a triumphant, political Messiah (Acts 1:6), not a crucified one. *unto the Greeks foolishness.* Greeks and Romans were sure that no reputable person would be crucified, so it was unthinkable that a crucified criminal could be the Savior.
1:24 *power.* See Rom 1:4,16; Mark 12:24. *wisdom.* See v. 30. The crucified Christ is the power that saves and the wisdom that transforms seeming folly into ultimate and highest discernment.
1:26–31 The Corinthian Christians themselves were living proof that salvation does not depend on anything in man, so that when someone is saved, he must glory in the Lord (v. 31).
1:30 *of him are ye in Christ Jesus.* It is God who has called you to union and communion with Christ. *righteousness.* It is by faith in Christ that we are justified (declared righteous); see Rom 5:19. *sanctification.* See note on v. 2. *redemption.* See note on Rom 3:24.
2:1 *when I came to you.* On his initial trip to Corinth c. a.d. 51 (Acts 18). *with excellency of speech or of wisdom.* See note on 1:17. Perhaps Apollos (Acts 18:24–28) had influenced the Corinthians in such a way that they were placing undue emphasis on eloquence and intellectual ability.
2:2 *not to know any thing . . . save Jesus Christ.* Paul resolved to make Christ the sole subject of his teaching and preaching while he was with them. *Jesus Christ.* See 1:30. *him crucified.* See 1:17–18,23.
2:4 *not with enticing words of man's wisdom.* This does not give preachers a license to neglect study and preparation. Paul's letters reveal a great deal of knowledge in many areas of learning, and his eloquence is apparent in his address before the Areopagus (see Acts 17:22–31 and notes). Paul's point is that unless the Holy Spirit works in a listener's heart, the wisdom and eloquence of a preacher are ineffective. Paul's confidence as a preacher did not rest on intellectual and oratorical ability, as did that of the Greek orators (see note on 1:17). *demonstration.* The Greek word is used of producing proofs in an argument in court. Paul's preaching was marked by the convincing demonstration of the power of the Holy Spirit.
2:6 *perfect.* Wise, developed Christians; contrast the "babes" mentioned in 3:1 (see Heb 5:13–6:3).
2:7 *mystery.* Cf. Rom 16:25–26; Eph 3:4–5; 1 Tim 3:16. The mystery, or secret, was once hidden but is now known because God has revealed it to His people (v. 10). To unbelievers it is still hidden. *unto our glory.* God's wisdom will cause every believer to share eventually in Christ's glory (Rom 8:17).
2:8 *princes of this world.* Rulers of this age, such as the chief priests (Luke 24:20), Pilate and Herod Antipas (cf. Acts 4:27). *crucified the Lord of glory.* The cross is here contrasted with the majesty of the victim.
2:9 *things which God hath prepared.* Probably not to be limit-

nor ear heard, neither have entered into the heart of man, *the things* which God hath prepared for them that love him.

10 But [a]God hath revealed *them* unto us by his Spirit: for the Spirit searcheth all *things,* yea, the deep things of God.

11 For what man knoweth the *things* of a man, [a]save the spirit of man which is in him? [b]even so the *things* of God knoweth no *man,* but the Spirit of God.

12 Now we have received, not the spirit of the world, but [a]the Spirit which is of God; that we might know the *things* that are freely given to us of God.

13 Which *things* also we speak, not in the words which man's wisdom teacheth, but which the Holy Ghost teacheth; comparing spiritual *things* with spiritual.

14 [a]But the natural man receiveth not the *things* of the Spirit of God: [b]for they are foolishness unto him: [c]neither can he know *them,* because they are spiritually discerned.

15 [a]But he that is spiritual [1]judgeth all *things,* yet he himself is [1]judged of no *man.*

16 [a]For who hath known the mind of the Lord, that he [1]may instruct him? [b]But we have the mind of Christ.

Fellow labourers for God

3 And I, brethren, could not speak unto you as unto [a]spiritual, but as unto [b]carnal, *even* as unto [c]babes in Christ.

2 I have fed you with [a]milk, and not with meat: [b]for hitherto ye were not able *to bear it,* neither yet now are ye able.

3 For ye are yet carnal: for [a]whereas *there is* among you envying, and strife, and [1]divisions, are ye not carnal, and walk [2]as men?

4 For while one saith, I am of Paul; and another, I *am* of Apollos; are ye not carnal?

5 ¶ Who then is Paul, and who *is* Apollos, but [a]ministers by whom ye believed, [b]even as the Lord gave to every man?

6 [a]I have planted, [b]Apollos watered; [c]but God gave the increase.

7 So then [a]neither is he that planteth any *thing,* neither he that watereth; but God that giveth the increase.

8 Now he that planteth and he that watereth are one: [a]and every man shall receive his own reward according to his own labour.

9 For [a]we are labourers together with God: ye are God's [1]husbandry, *ye are* [b]God's building.

10 [a]According to the grace of God which is given unto me, as a wise masterbuilder, I have laid [b]the foundation, and another buildeth thereon. But let every man take heed how he buildeth thereupon.

11 For other foundation can no *man* lay than [a]that is laid, [b]which is Jesus Christ.

12 Now if any *man* build upon this foundation gold, silver, precious stones, wood, hay, stubble;

13 Every man's work shall be made manifest: for the day [a]shall declare *it,* because [b]it [1]shall be revealed by fire; and the fire shall try every man's work of what sort it is.

14 If any *man's* work abide which he hath built thereupon, he shall receive a reward.

15 If any *man's* work shall be burnt, he shall suffer loss: but he himself shall be saved; yet so as by fire.

2:10 [a]Mat. 13:11
2:11 [a]Prov. 20:27; Jer. 17:9 [b]Rom. 11:33
2:12 [a]Rom. 8:15
2:14 [a]Mat. 16:23 [b]ch. 1:18,23 [c]Jude 19
2:15 [1]Or, *discerneth* [a]1 John 4:1
2:16 [1]Gr. *shall* [a]Job 15:8 [b]John 15:15
3:1 [a]ch. 2:15 [b]ch. 2:14 [c]Heb. 5:13
3:2 [a]Heb. 5:12; 1 Pet. 2:2 [b]John 16:12
3:3 [a]Gal. 5:20; Jas. 3:16
3:3 [1]Or, *factions* [2]Gr. *according to man?*
3:5 [a]2 Cor. 3:3 [b]Rom. 12:3; 1 Pet. 4:11
3:6 [a]Acts 18:4; 2 Cor. 10:14 [b]Acts 18:24; 19:1 [c]2 Cor. 3:5
3:7 [a]2 Cor. 12:11; Gal. 6:3
3:8 [a]Ps. 62:12; Rom. 2:6; Gal. 6:4,5
3:9 [1]Or, *tillage* [a]Acts 15:4; 2 Cor. 6:1 [b]Eph. 2:20; Col. 2:7; Heb. 3:3,4
3:10 [a]Rom. 1:5; 12:3 [b]ch. 4:15
3:11 [a]Is. 28:16; Mat. 16:18; 2 Cor. 11:4 [b]Eph. 2:20
3:13 [1]Gr. *is revealed* [a]1 Pet. 1:7 [b]Luke 2:35

ed to either present or future blessing; both are involved (cf. vv. 7,12).

2:10 *Spirit searcheth all things.* Not in order to know them, for He knows all things. Instead He comprehends the depth of God's nature and His plans of grace; so He is fully competent to make the revelation claimed here.

2:12 *spirit of the world.* Cf. v. 6 ("wisdom of this world"); the spirit of human wisdom as alienated from God—the attitude of the sinful nature (Rom 8:6–7).

2:13 *which the Holy Ghost teacheth.* The message Paul proclaimed was expressed in words given by the Holy Spirit. Thus spiritual truth was aptly combined with fitting spiritual words.

2:14–3:4 This passage explains why many fail to apprehend true wisdom (2:9). It is because such wisdom is perceived by the spiritual (mature) Christian (2:14–16; cf. v. 6). The Corinthians, however, were worldly (infant) believers (3:1–4), and the proof of their immaturity was their division over human leaders (3:3–4).

2:14 *natural man.* Described in Jude 19 as one who is "sensual" (cf. Rom 8:9). The non-Christian is basically dominated by the merely physical, worldly or natural life. Because he does not possess the Holy Spirit, he is not equipped to receive appreciatively truth that comes from the Spirit. Such a person needs the new birth (John 3:1–8; Tit 3:5–6). *foolishness.* See 1:18.

2:15 *spiritual.* Mature ("perfect," v. 6). *is judged of no man.* One who does not have the Spirit is not qualified to judge the spiritual person. Thus believers are not rightfully subject to the opinions of unbelievers.

3:1 *brethren.* See note on 1:10. *spiritual.* See note on 2:15. *carnal.* See note on 2:14–3:4.

3:2 *milk . . . not with meat.* See notes on Heb 5:12–14.

3:3 *walk as men.* Like men of the world instead of men of God. They were following merely human standards.

3:4 *I am of Paul . . . Apollos.* See 1:12.

3:6 *I have planted.* See Acts 18:4–11. Paul's work was of a pioneer nature, preaching where no one had ever preached before. *Apollos watered.* See Acts 18:24–28. Apollos worked in the established church, edifying the converts Paul had won.

3:9 *God's husbandry.* The people are God's farm. *God's building.* They are also depicted as God's temple (vv. 16–17). He owns the farm and the building where both Paul and Apollos worked.

3:10 *I have laid the foundation.* By preaching Christ and Him crucified (2:2). *another.* Apollos.

3:12 *gold, silver, precious stones.* Precious, durable work that stands the test of divine judgment; symbolic of pure Christian doctrine and living. *wood, hay, stubble.* Worthless work that will not stand the test; symbolic of weak, insipid teaching and life.

3:13 Cf. 4:5; 2 Cor 5:10. *the day.* See note on 1:8. *fire.* God's judgment. The work of some believers will stand the test while that of others will disappear—emphasizing the importance of teaching the pure word of God.

3:15 *loss.* Of reward (v. 14). *yet so as by fire.* Perhaps a Greek proverbial phrase, meaning "by a narrow escape," with one's work burned up by the fire of God's pure justice and judgment.

16 [a]Know ye not that ye are the temple of God, and *that* the Spirit of God dwelleth in you?

17 If any *man* [1]defile the temple of God, him shall God destroy; for the temple of God is holy, which *temple* ye are.

18 [a]Let no *man* deceive himself. If any *man* among you seemeth to be wise in this world, let him become a fool, that he may be wise.

19 For the wisdom of this world is foolishness with God. For it is written, [a]He taketh the wise in their own craftiness.

20 And again, [a]The Lord knoweth the thoughts of the wise, that they are vain.

21 Therefore let no *man* glory in men. For [a]all *things* are yours;

22 Whether Paul, or Apollos, or Cephas, or the world, or life, or death, or *things* present, or *things* to come; all are yours;

23 And [a]ye *are* Christ's; and Christ *is* God's.

Apostles of Christ

4 Let a man so account of us, as of [a]the ministers of Christ, [b]and stewards of the mysteries of God.

2 Moreover it is required in stewards, that a man be found faithful.

3 But with me it is a very small *thing* that I should be judged of you, or of man's [1]judgment: yea, I judge not mine own self.

4 For I know nothing by myself; yet am I not hereby justified: but he that judgeth me is the Lord.

5 [a]Therefore judge nothing before the time, until the Lord come, who both will bring to light the hidden *things* of darkness, and will make manifest the counsels of the hearts: and [b]then shall every man have praise of God.

6 ¶ And these *things*, brethren, [a]I have in a figure transferred to myself and *to* Apollos for your sakes; [b]that ye might learn in us not to think *of men* above *that* which is written, that no one of you [c]be puffed up for one against another.

7 For who [1]maketh thee to differ *from another?* and [a]what hast thou that thou didst not receive? now if thou didst receive *it,* why dost thou glory, as if thou hadst not received *it?*

8 Now ye are full, [a]now ye are rich, ye have reigned as kings without us: and I would *to God* ye did reign, that we also might reign with you.

9 For I think that God hath set forth [1]us the apostles last, [a]as *it were* appointed to death: for [b]we are made a [2]spectacle unto the world, and to angels, and to men.

10 [a]We *are* [b]fools for Christ's sake, but ye *are* wise in Christ; [c]we *are* weak, but ye *are* strong; ye *are* honourable, but we *are* despised.

11 [a]Even unto this present hour we both hunger, and thirst, and [b]are naked, and [c]are buffeted, and have no certain dwelling place;

12 [a]And labour, working with our own hands: [b]being reviled, we bless; being persecuted, we suffer *it:*

13 Being defamed, we intreat: [a]we are made as the filth of the world, *and are* the offscouring of all *things* unto this day.

14 I write not these *things* to shame you, but [a]as my beloved sons I warn *you.*

3:16 [a]2 Cor. 6:16
3:17 [1]Or, *destroy*
3:18 [a]Prov. 3:7
3:19 [a]Job 5:13
3:20 [a]Ps. 94:11
3:21 [a]2 Cor. 4:5
3:23 [a]Rom. 14:8; 2 Cor. 10:7; Gal. 3:29
4:1 [a]Mat. 24:45; Col. 1:25 [b]Luke 12:42; Tit. 1:7
4:3 [1]Gr. *day*
4:5 [a]Mat. 7:1; Rom. 2:1; Rev. 20:12
4:5 [b]Rom. 2:29; 2 Cor. 5:10
4:6 [a]ch. 1:12 [b]Rom. 12:3 [c]ch. 3:21
4:7 [1]Gr. *distinguisheth thee?* [a]John 3:27
4:8 [a]Rev. 3:17
4:9 [1][Or, *us the last apostles, as*] [2]Gr. *theatre* [a]Ps. 44:22 [b]Heb. 10:33
4:10 [a]ch. 2:3 [b]Acts 17:18 [c]2 Cor. 13:9
4:11 [a]Phil. 4:12 [b]Rom. 8:35 [c]Acts 23:2
4:12 [a]Acts 18:3; 20:34; 1 Thes. 2:9; 2 Thes. 3:8; 1 Tim. 4:10 [b]Mat. 5:44; Luke 6:28; 23:34; Acts 7:60; Rom. 12:14
4:13 [a]Lam. 3:45
4:14 [a]1 Thes. 2:11

3:16 *temple of God.* God's church. Paul does not mean here that each of his readers is a temple of the Holy Spirit. He says, "Ye (plural) are God's temple (singular)." In 6:19 he speaks of each Christian as a temple of the Holy Spirit.
3:17 *him shall God destroy.* Strong language, indicating that such a foolish laborer is not one of the Lord's true servants. This is in contrast to the thought of v. 15, where the faulty Christian worker is saved, but his work is destroyed (he suffers loss of reward). In the context of chs. 1–4 Paul here refers to people who tear the local church apart by factions and quarrels (1:11–12). *holy.* Sacred, set apart for God's use and glory; so do not desecrate the church by breaking it up into various factions.
3:18 *become a fool.* Turn away from human wisdom (from being "wise in this world"). Cf. 1:18. *may be wise.* Cf. 1:21, 24.
3:21 *in men.* About being some man's disciple (see 1:12; 3:4; cf. 1:31; 4:6). *all things are yours.* All these Christian leaders belong to the whole church. No group can call one leader its very own (see vv. 22–23).
3:23 *ye are Christ's.* You are united with and belong to Christ. *Christ is God's.* Christ is in union with God the Father (John 10:30) and with God the Holy Spirit (2 Cor 13:14). Similarly, Christians are in union with the church's true leaders (v. 22) and with Christ (v. 23), who in turn is in union with the other members of the Trinity.
4:1 *stewards.* The Greek underlying this phrase means "house manager." *mysteries.* Things that human wisdom cannot discover but that are now revealed by God to His people (see note on Rom 11:25).
4:3 *judge not mine own self.* His judgment was merely human, and his conscience may be mistaken (v. 4). Only God is fully qualified to judge.
4:5 *the time.* When God will judge believers (see 3:13). *make manifest the counsels of the hearts.* Cf. Ps 19:12; 139:23–24; Heb 4:12–13.
4:6 *these things.* See 3:5–4:5. *learn in us not to think of men above that which is written.* Perhaps a proverb common among the rabbis. *which is written.* In Scripture. Our view of man should be Biblical (cf. v. 7; 1:9, 31; 3:19–20; Rom 12:3). We should recognize man's weakness and ever-present limitations. *be puffed up.* One of the root causes of divisions.
‡4:8 Paul uses irony and sarcasm here to get the Corinthians to see how poor they really are because of their haughtiness and spiritual immaturity in comparison with apostles. In the Corinthian epistles, Paul repeatedly uses a subtle form of irony (the use of a positive statement when a negative idea is intended). See 4:10, 6:4, 11:19, 14:9 and 2 Cor 12:13.
4:9 *apostles.* See note on 1:1. *spectacle.* "Theater" is derived from the Greek word used here. Paul refers to the gladiatorial contests in the arena (or perhaps to the triumphal procession of a victorious Roman general). He pictures all the world and even angels looking on while the apostles are brought in last to fight to the death.
4:10 More irony. Cf. 4:8
4:11–13 A graphic description of Paul's condition in Ephesus right up to the writing of this letter.
4:12 *labour, working with our own hands.* Paul was a tent-maker by trade (Acts 18:3; cf. 20:34–35; 1 Cor 9:6,18). *we bless.* See Mat 5:44. *we suffer it.* Instead of retaliating.
4:14 *my beloved sons.* See v. 15.

15 For though you have ten thousand in-
structors in Christ, yet *have ye* not many fathers: for [a]in Christ Jesus I have begotten you
through the gospel.
16 Wherefore I beseech you, [a]be ye followers of me.
17 For this cause have I sent unto you
[a]Timotheus, [b]who is my beloved son, and
faithful in the Lord, who shall bring you [c]into
remembrance of my ways which be in Christ,
as I [d]teach every where [e]in every church.
18 [a]Now some are puffed up, as though I
would not come to you.
19 [a]But I will come to you shortly, [b]if the
Lord will, and will know, not the speech of
them which are puffed up, but the power.
20 For [a]the kingdom of God *is* not in word,
but in power.
21 What will ye? [a]shall I come unto you
with a rod, or in love, and *in* the spirit of
meekness?

Judgment of the immoral

5 It is reported commonly *that there is* fornication among you, and such fornication as is not so much as [a]named amongst the
Gentiles, [b]that one should have *his* [c]father's
wife.
2 [a]And ye are puffed up, and have not
rather [b]mourned, that he that hath done this
deed might be taken away from among you.

4:15 [a]Acts 18:11; Gal. 4:19; Jas. 1:18
4:16 [a]ch. 11:1; 1 Thes. 1:6
4:17 [a]Acts 19:22; Phil. 2:19 [b]1 Tim. 1:2; 2 Tim. 1:2 [c]ch. 11:2 [d]ch. 7:17 [e]ch. 14:33
4:18 [a]ch. 5:2
4:19 [a]Acts 19:21; 2 Cor. 1:15 [b]Acts 18:21; Heb. 6:3; Jas. 4:15
4:20 [a]1 Thes. 1:5
4:21 [a]2 Cor. 10:2
5:1 [a]Eph. 5:3 [b]Lev. 18:8 [c]2 Cor. 7:12
5:2 [a]ch. 4:18 [b]2 Cor. 7:7
5:3 [1]Or, *determined* [a]Col. 2:5
5:4 [a]Mat. 16:19; John 20:23; 2 Cor. 2:10
5:5 [a]Ps. 109:6; 1 Tim. 1:20 [b]Acts 26:18
5:6 [a]ch. 3:21 [b]Gal. 5:9; 2 Tim. 2:17
5:7 [1]Or, *is slain* [a]Is. 53:7; 1 Pet. 1:19 [b]John 19:14
5:8 [1]Or, *holyday* [a]Ex. 12:15 [b]Deut. 16:3 [c]Mat. 16:6; Mark 8:15; Luke 12:1

3 [a]For I verily, as absent in body, but present in spirit, have [1]judged already, as though I
were present, *concerning* him that hath so
done this *deed,*
4 In the name of our Lord Jesus Christ,
when ye are gathered together, and my spirit,
[a]with the power of our Lord Jesus Christ,
5 [a]To deliver such a one unto [b]Satan for
the destruction of the flesh, that the spirit may
be saved in the day of the Lord Jesus.
6 [a]Your glorying *is* not good. Know ye not
that [b]a little leaven leaveneth the whole lump?
7 Purge out therefore the old leaven, that
ye may be a new lump, as ye are unleavened.
For even [a]Christ our [b]passover [1]is sacrificed
for us:
8 Therefore [a]let us keep [1]the feast, [b]not
with old leaven, neither [c]with the leaven of
malice and wickedness; but with the unleavened bread of sincerity and truth.
9 ¶ I wrote unto you in an epistle [a]not to
company with fornicators:
10 [a]Yet not altogether with the fornicators
[b]of this world, or with the covetous, or extortioners, or with idolaters; for then must ye
needs go [c]out of the world.
11 But now I have written unto you not to
keep company, [a]if any *man that is* called a
brother be a fornicator, or covetous, or an idol-

5:9 [a]2 Cor. 6:14; Eph. 5:11 5:10 [a]ch. 10:27 [b]ch. 1:20 [c]John 17:15; 1 John 5:19 5:11 [a]Mat. 18:17; Rom. 16:17; 2 John 10

4:15 *I have begotten you.* See 3:6,10.
4:18 *some.* Some of the Corinthians who were trying to undercut Paul's authority (see 9:1–3) were teaching that he was unstable (2 Cor 1:17) and that his ministry was not important (2 Cor 10:10).
4:19 *puffed up.* See 5:2.
4:20 *kingdom of God.* God's present reign in the lives of His people—that dynamic new life in Christ (2 Cor 5:17), the power of the new birth (John 3:3–8), showing itself in a humble life, dedicated to Christ and His church. *not in word, but in power.* Idle, empty talk is contrasted with the genuine power of the Holy Spirit.
5:1 *not . . . named amongst the Gentiles.* The Roman orator Cicero states that incest was practically unheard of in Roman society. *his father's wife.* That this expression was used rather than "his mother" suggests that the woman was his stepmother. The OT prohibited such sexual relations (Lev 18:8; Deut 27:20).
5:2 *puffed up.* Evidently proud of their liberty—a distortion of grace. *taken away from among you.* Excommunicated from the church (cf. John 9:22).
5:4 *In the name of our Lord Jesus Christ, when ye are gathered together.* The Corinthians are to pass judgment on the man by the authority of the Lord Jesus. *the power of our Lord Jesus Christ.* Jesus' power is present through His word and His Holy Spirit.
5:5 *deliver such a one unto Satan.* Abandon this sinful man to the devil that he may afflict the man as he pleases. This abandonment to Satan was to be accomplished, not by some magical incantation, but by expelling the man from the church (see v. 13; also vv. 2,7,11). To expel him was to put him out in the devil's territory, severed from any connection with God's people. *for the destruction of the flesh.* Satan is allowed to bring physical affliction on the man, which would bring him to repentance. *the spirit may be saved.* Cf. 3:15. The person put out of the church may well be a Christian. *day of the Lord Jesus.* When Christ returns (see 1:7).
‡5:6 *a little leaven . . . the whole lump.* To illustrate Christian holiness and discipline, Paul alludes to the prohibition against the use of leaven (or yeast) in the bread eaten in the passover feast (see Ex 12:15). Leaven in Scripture usually symbolizes evil or sin (see note on Mark 8:15), and the church here is called on to get rid of the leaven of sin (v. 8) because they are an unleavened batch of dough—new creations in Christ (2 Cor 5:17).
‡5:7 *Purge out therefore the old leaven.* Perhaps refers to the passover custom of sweeping all the (leavened) bread crumbs out of one's house before preparing the passover meal. *as ye are unleavened.* Positionally they were a new batch, already sanctified in God's sight (see 1:2; 6:11), but Paul calls on them to become holy also in conduct (see note on 1:2). *Christ our passover.* In His death on the cross, Christ fulfilled the true meaning of the Jewish sacrifice of the passover lamb (Is 53:7; John 1:29). Christ, the Lamb of God, was crucified on passover day, a celebration that began the evening before when the passover meal was eaten (cf. Ex 12:8).
5:8 *let us keep the feast.* Keeping the feast of unleavened bread (which followed passover) symbolizes living the Christian life in holy dedication to God (cf. Rom 12:1–2; 1 Pet 2:5) and not getting involved in such sins as malice and wickedness and incestuous relations.
5:9 *I wrote unto you in an epistle.* Paul here clarifies a previous letter (one not preserved). The Corinthians mistook that letter to mean that, on separating from sin, they should disassociate themselves from all immoral persons, including non-Christian people. Instead, Paul meant that they should separate from immoral persons in the church who claimed to be Christian brothers (vv. 10–11).
5:11 *with such a one no not to eat.* Calling oneself a Christian while continuing to live an immoral life is reprehensible and degrading, and gives a false testimony to Christ. If the true Chris-

ater, or a railer, or a drunkard, or an extortioner; with such a one [b]no not to eat.

12 For what have I to do to judge [a]them also that are without? do not ye judge [b]them that are within?

13 But them that are without God judgeth. Therefore [a]put away from among yourselves *that* wicked *person.*

Lawsuits among brethren

6 Dare any of you, having a matter against another, go to law before the unjust, and not before the saints?

2 Do ye not know that [a]the saints shall judge the world? and if the world shall be judged by you, are ye unworthy to judge the smallest matters?

3 Know ye not that we shall [a]judge angels? how much more *things* that pertain to *this* life?

4 [a]If then ye have judgments *of things* pertaining to *this* life, set them to judge who are least esteemed in the church.

5 I speak to your shame. Is it so, that there is not a wise *man* amongst you? no, not one that shall be able to judge between his brethren?

6 But brother goeth to law with brother, and that before the unbelievers.

7 Now therefore there is utterly a fault among you, because ye go to law one with another. [a]Why do ye not rather take wrong? why do ye not rather *suffer yourselves to* be defrauded?

8 Nay, you do wrong, and defraud, [a]and that *your* brethren.

9 Know ye not that the unrighteous shall not inherit the kingdom of God? Be not deceived: [a]neither fornicators, nor idolaters, nor adulterers, nor effeminate, nor abusers of themselves with mankind,

10 Nor thieves, nor covetous, nor drunkards, nor revilers, nor extortioners, shall inherit the kingdom of God.

11 And such were [a]some of you: [b]but ye are washed, but ye are sanctified, but ye are justified in the name of the Lord Jesus, and by the Spirit of our God.

God to be glorified in the body

12 ¶ [a]All *things* are lawful unto me, but all *things* are not [1]expedient: all *things* are lawful for me, but I will not be brought under the power of any.

13 [a]Meats for the belly, and the belly for meats: but God shall destroy both it and them. Now the body *is* not for fornication, but [b]for the Lord; [c]and the Lord for the body.

14 And [a]God hath both raised up the Lord, and will *also* raise up us [b]by his own power.

5:11 [b]Gal. 2:12
5:12 [a]Mark 4:11; Col. 4:5; 1 Thes. 4:12 [b]ch. 6:1-4
5:13 [a]Deut. 13:5
6:2 [a]Ps. 49:14; Dan. 7:22; Mat. 19:28; Luke 22:30
6:3 [a]2 Pet. 2:4
6:4 [a]ch. 5:12
6:7 [a]Prov. 20:22; Mat. 5:39; Luke 6:29
6:8 [a]1 Thes. 4:6
6:9 [a]Gal. 5:21; Eph. 5:5; 1 Tim. 1:9
6:11 [a]ch. 12:2 [b]Heb. 10:22
6:12 [1]Or, *profitable* [a]ch. 10:23
6:13 [a]Mat. 15:17; Rom. 14:17; Col. 2:22 [b]1 Thes. 4:3 [c]Eph. 5:23
6:14 [a]Rom. 6:5,8; 2 Cor. 4:14 [b]Eph. 1:19

tian has intimate association with someone who does this, the non-Christian world may assume that the church approves such immoral, ungodly living and thus the name of Christ would be dishonored. Questions could arise concerning the true character of the Christian's own testimony (cf. Rom 16:17–18; 2 Thes 3:6, 14–15).

5:12 *judge them that are within.* The church is to exercise spiritual discipline over the professing believers in the church (cf. Mat 18:15–18), but it is not to attempt to judge the unsaved world. There are governing authorities to do that (Rom 13:1–5), and the ultimate judgment of the world is to be left to God (v. 13; cf. Rev 20:11–15).

‡5:13 To show the severity with which sin in the assembly must be treated Paul parallels this to the stonings of the OT. See Deut 13:5; 17:7,12; 22:21,24.

6:1 *a matter against another.* Paul seems to be talking about various kinds of property court cases here (cf. the phrase "rather . . . be defrauded," v. 7), not criminal cases that should be handled by the state (Rom 13:3–4). *before the saints.* The Corinthians should take their property cases before qualified Christians for settlement. In Paul's day the Romans allowed the Jews to apply their own law in property matters, and since the Romans did not yet consider Christians as a separate class from the Jews, Christians no doubt had the same rights.

6:2 *saints shall judge the world.* With Christ. Cf. Mat 19:28; 2 Tim 2:12; Rev 20:4. *are ye unworthy to judge the smallest matters?* Paul views believers as fully competent to judge cases where Christians have claims against each other, because they view matters from a godly vantage point. In comparison with their future role in the judgment of the world and of angels, judgments concerning things of this life are insignificant.

6:3 *we shall judge angels.* Cf. 2 Pet 2:4,9; Jude 6.

‡6:4 *judge who are least esteemed.* Either the verse suggests that the least in the church are capable of judging such small matters, or it asks ironically if believers should submit their cases to pagan judges, who really are not qualified to decide on cases between Christians. See 4:8.

6:7 *utterly a fault.* Most likely by greed, retaliation and hatred, instead of practicing unselfishness, forgiveness and love—even willingness to suffer loss.

6:9 *not inherit the kingdom of God.* Cf. John 3:3–5. *fornicators.* Paul here identifies three kinds of sexually immoral persons: adulterers, male prostitutes and males who practice homosexuality. In Rom 1:26 he adds the category of females who practice homosexuality. People who engage in such practices, as well as the other offenders listed in vv. 9–10, are explicitly excluded from God's kingdom (but see next note).

6:11 *such were some of you.* God, however, does save and sanctify people like those described in vv. 9–10.

6:12 *All things are lawful unto me.* Paul is probably quoting some in the Corinthian congregation who boasted that they had a right to do anything they pleased. The apostle counters by observing that such "freedom" of action may not benefit the Christian. *not be brought under the power of any.* One may become enslaved by those actions in which he "freely" indulges (see note on 10:23).

6:13 *Meats for the belly, and the belly for meats.* Paul quotes some Corinthians again who were claiming that as the physical acts of eating and digesting food have no bearing on one's inner spiritual life, so the physical act of promiscuous sexual activity does not affect one's spiritual life. *the body is not for fornication, but for the Lord.* Paul here declares the dignity of the human body: It is intended for the Lord. Although granting that food and the stomach are transitory, Paul denies that what one does with his body is unimportant. This is particularly true of the use of sex, which the Lord has ordained in wedlock for the good of mankind (cf. Heb 13:4).

6:14 *God . . . raised up the Lord . . . also raise up us.* As an illustration of God's high regard for the body, Paul cites the resurrection of Christ's body and, eventually, the believer's body (15:51–53; 1 Thes 4:16–17). A body destined for resurrection should not be used for immorality.

15 Know ye not that [a]your bodies are the members of Christ? shall I then take the members of Christ, and make *them* the members of a harlot? God forbid.

16 What? know ye not that he which is joined to a harlot is one body? for [a]two, saith *he,* shall be one flesh.

17 [a]But he that is joined unto the Lord is one spirit.

18 [a]Flee fornication. Every sin that a man doeth is without the body; but he that committeth fornication sinneth [b]against his own body.

19 What? [a]know ye not that your body is the temple of the Holy Ghost which is in you, which ye have of God, [b]and ye are not your own?

20 For [a]ye are bought with a price: therefore glorify God in your body, and in your spirit, which are God's.

Marriage

7 Now concerning *the things* whereof ye wrote unto me: [a]*It is* good for a man not to touch a woman.

2 Nevertheless, to avoid fornication, let every man have his own wife, and let every woman have her own husband.

3 [a]Let the husband render unto the wife due benevolence: and likewise also the wife unto the husband.

4 The wife hath not power of her own body, but the husband: and likewise also the husband hath not power of his own body, but the wife.

5 [a]Defraud you not one the other, except *it be* with consent for a time, that ye may give yourselves to fasting and prayer, and come together again, that [b]Satan tempt you not for your incontinency.

6 But I speak this by permission, [a]*and* not of commandment.

7 For [a]I would that all men were [b]even as I myself. But [c]every man hath his proper gift of God, one after this manner, and another after that.

8 ¶ I say therefore to the unmarried and widows, [a]It is good for them if they abide even as I.

9 But [a]if they cannot contain, let them marry: for it is better to marry than to burn.

10 And unto the married I command, *yet* not I, but the Lord, [a]Let not the wife depart from *her* husband:

11 But and if she depart, let her remain unmarried, or be reconciled to *her* husband: and let not the husband put away *his* wife.

12 But to the rest speak I, not the Lord: If any brother hath a wife that believeth not, and

6:15 [a]Rom. 12:5; Eph. 4:12; 5:30
6:16 [a]Gen. 2:24; Mat. 19:5; Eph. 5:31
6:17 [a]John 17:21; Eph. 4:4
6:18 [a]Rom. 6:12; Heb. 13:4 [b]Rom. 1:24; 1 Thes. 4:4
6:19 [a]2 Cor. 6:16 [b]Rom. 14:7
6:20 [a]Acts 20:28; Gal. 3:13; Heb. 9:12; 1 Pet. 1:18; 2 Pet. 2:1; Rev. 5:9
7:1 [a]ver. 8,26
7:3 [a]Ex. 21:10; 1 Pet. 3:7
7:5 [a]Joel 2:16; Zech. 7:3; See Ex. 19:15; 1 Sam. 21:4 [b]1 Thes. 3:5
7:6 [a]2 Cor. 8:8; 11:17
7:7 [a]Acts 26:29 [b]ch. 9:5 [c]ch. 12:11
7:8 [a]ver. 1,26
7:9 [a]1 Tim. 5:14
7:10 [a]Mal. 2:14; Mat. 5:32; 19:6,9; Mark 10:11; Luke 16:18

6:15 *members of Christ.* See 12:27. It is not merely the spirit that is a member of Christ's body; it is the whole person, consisting of spirit and body. This fact gives dignity to the human body.

‡6:16 *one body.* In a sexual relationship the two bodies become one (cf. Gen 2:24; Mat 19:5), and a new human being may emerge from the sexual union. Sexual relations outside the marriage bond are a gross perversion of the divinely established marriage union.

‡6:17 *one spirit.* There is a higher union than the marriage bond: the believer's spiritual union with Christ, which is the perfect model for the kind of unity that should mark the marriage relationship (cf. Eph 5:21–33).

‡6:18 *Every sin . . . without the body.* Perhaps means that in a unique way, sexual immorality gratifies one's physical body. Paul may be quoting a Corinthian slogan (see note on v. 12), which he refutes in the second half of the verse. *but he that committeth fornication sinneth against his own body.* The body is a temple of the Holy Ghost (v. 19); thus to use it in prostitution disgraces God's temple. Furthermore, the prostitutes of Corinth were dedicated to the service of Aphrodite, the goddess of love and sex. See note on 7:2.

6:19 *your body is the temple of the Holy Ghost.* The Christian should value his body as a sacred place where God dwells and should realize that by the Spirit's presence and power he can be helped against such sins as sexual immorality (Rom 8:9). *not your own.* Cf. 1 Pet 2:9.

6:20 *glorify God in your body.* Cf. 10:31; Rom 6:12–13; Col 3:17.

7:1 *things whereof ye wrote.* The Corinthians had written Paul, asking him a number of vexing questions (see 8:1; 12:1). *good for a man not to touch a woman.* Because of the crisis at Corinth (vv. 26,28). Elsewhere (Eph 5:22–33; Col 3:18–19; 1 Tim 3:2,12; 5:14) Paul spoke strongly in favor of the married state, and in 1 Tim 4:1–3 he taught that forbidding to marry would be a sign of the end-time apostasy. Another possible interpretation is that Paul is again (see notes on 6:12–13,18) quoting a slogan of the Corinthians suggesting it was good for a man not to have sexual relations with a woman. He refutes this idea in v. 2 by stating that sexual relations have their proper expression in marriage.

7:2 *fornication.* Example: The temple to Aphrodite on the Acrocorinth, the rocky eminence above Corinth, at one time had in service 1,000 prostitute priestesses.

7:3 *render unto the wife due benevolence.* Married couples should have normal sexual relations. Permanent abstention deprives the other partner of his or her natural right and may be conducive to temptation.

7:4 *likewise.* Both husband and wife have conjugal rights and exclusive possession of the other in this area.

7:5 *Defraud you not one the other.* Of sexual fulfillment. *Satan tempt you not for your incontinency.* The Christian deprived of normal sexual activity with his or her marriage partner may be tempted by Satan to sexual immorality. The normal God-given sexual drive in the human being is strong.

7:6 *permission, and not of commandment.* Although marriage is desirable and according to God's plan, it was not mandatory under the difficult circumstances at Corinth (see v. 26). In another situation (1 Tim 5:14) Paul urges that "the younger women marry."

7:10 *I command, yet not I, but the Lord.* Paul is citing a command from the Lord Jesus during His earthly ministry that married couples must stay together (Mat 5:32; 19:3–9; Mark 10:2–12; Luke 16:18). Paul probably heard such commands from other disciples (cf. Gal 1:18–19) or from Jesus Himself by a special revelation.

‡7:11 *But and if she depart, let her remain unmarried, or be reconciled.* Paul argues that in the light of Christ's command she (or he) is not to marry again. Rather, the separated or divorced couple are to be reconciled. Clearly the ideal is that marriage should not be permanently disrupted.

7:12 *speak I, not the Lord.* Paul is not quoting a direct command from Jesus here. *any brother hath a wife that believeth not.* The apostle is talking here (and in v. 13) about couples already married, when one of them becomes a Christian. If at all

she be pleased to dwell with him, let him not put her away.

13 And the woman which hath a husband that believeth not, and *if* he be pleased to dwell with her, let her not leave him.

14 For the unbelieving husband is sanctified by the wife, and the unbelieving wife is sanctified by the husband: else [a]were your children unclean; but now are they holy.

15 But if the unbelieving depart, let him depart. A brother or a sister is not under bondage in such *cases:* but God hath called us [a][1]to peace.

16 For what knowest thou, O wife, whether thou shalt [a]save *thy* husband? or [1]how knowest thou, O man, whether thou shalt save *thy* wife?

17 But as God hath distributed to every man, as the Lord hath called every one, so let him walk. And [a]so ordain I in all churches.

18 Is any *man* called being circumcised? let him not become uncircumcised. Is any called in uncircumcision? [a]let him not be circumcised.

19 [a]Circumcision is nothing, and uncircumcision is nothing, but [b]the keeping of the commandments of God.

20 Let every man abide in the same calling wherein he was called.

21 Art thou called *being* a servant? care not for it: but if thou mayest be made free, use *it* rather.

22 For he that is called in the Lord, *being* a servant, is [a]the Lord's [1]freeman: likewise also he that is called, *being* free, is [b]Christ's servant.

23 [a]Ye are bought with a price; be not ye the servants of men.

24 Brethren, let every man, wherein he is called, therein abide with God.

25 ¶ Now concerning virgins [a]I have no commandment of the Lord: yet I give *my* judgment, as one [b]that hath obtained mercy of the Lord [c]to be faithful.

26 I suppose therefore that this is good for the present [1]distress, *I say,* [a]that *it is* good for a man so to be.

27 Art thou bound unto a wife? seek not to be loosed. Art thou loosed from a wife? seek not a wife.

28 But and if thou marry, thou hast not sinned; and if a virgin marry, she hath not sinned. Nevertheless such shall have trouble in the flesh: but I spare you.

29 But [a]this I say, brethren, the time *is* short: it remaineth, that both they that have wives be as though they had none;

30 And they that weep, as though they wept not; and they that rejoice, as though they rejoiced not; and they that buy, as though they possessed not;

31 And they that use this world, as not [a]abusing *it:* for [b]the fashion of this world passeth away.

32 But I would have you without carefulness. [a]He *that is* unmarried careth for the

7:14 [a]Mal. 2:15
7:15 [1]Gr. *in peace* [a]Rom. 12:18; 14:19; ch. 14:33
7:16 [1][Gr. *what*] [a]1 Pet. 3:1
7:17 [a]ch. 4:17
7:18 [a]Acts 15:1; Gal. 5:2
7:19 [a]Gal. 5:6 [b]John 15:14; 1 John 2:3; 3:24
7:22 [1]Gr. *made free* [a]John 8:36; Rom. 6:18; Philem. 16 [b]ch. 9:21; Gal. 5:13; Eph. 6:6; 1 Pet. 2:16
7:23 [a]1 Pet. 1:18; See Lev. 25:42
7:25 [a]2 Cor. 8:8 [b]1 Tim. 1:16 [c]1 Tim. 1:12
7:26 [1]Or, *necessity* [a]ver. 1,8
7:29 [a]Rom. 13:11; 1 Pet. 4:7; 2 Pet. 3:8,9
7:31 [a]ch. 9:18 [b]Ps. 39:6; Jas. 1:10; 4:14; 1 Pet. 1:24; 4:7; 1 John 2:17
7:32 [a]1 Tim. 5:5

possible, they should remain together, unless the unbeliever, whether man or woman, refuses to remain (v. 15).

7:14 *the unbelieving husband is sanctified by the wife.* The unbelieving partner is influenced by the godly life of the Christian partner; so that family is under the holy influence of the believer and in that sense is sanctified. *your children . . . now are they holy.* They at least have the advantage of being under the sanctifying influence of one Christian parent (see v. 16) and so may be called holy. Some believe that such children are called holy because they are included with their parents in the new covenant in Christ, just as the children of Abraham were included in the covenant with their father (and so were circumcised).

7:15 *A brother or the sister is not under bondage in such cases.* The believer is not under obligation to try to continue living with the unbeliever. *peace.* If the unbeliever were forced to live with the believer, there would be no peace in the home.

7:17 *as the Lord hath called every one, so let him walk.* Each Christian is to live contentedly for the Lord in whatever economic, social and religious station in life God has placed him. See v. 18 for an example.

7:18 *circumcised . . . uncircumcised.* Jew . . . Gentile. In the religious sphere, Christian Jews should not try to obliterate physically the fact that they are Jews, and Christian Gentiles should not yield to Jewish pressure for circumcision (cf. Acts 15:1–5; Gal 5:1–3).

7:21 *Art thou called being a servant?* In the social and economic sphere, the Christian slave should live contentedly in his situation, realizing that he has become free in Christ (v. 22; John 8:32, 36). *if thou mayest be made free, use it rather.* If a Christian slave has an opportunity to get his freedom, he should take advantage of it. In the Roman empire slaves were sometimes freed by Roman patricians. There is nothing wrong with seeking to improve your condition, but be content at every stage.

7:22 *he that is . . . free, is Christ's servant.* A man who was not a Roman slave should realize that in a spiritual sense he belonged to Christ, and, because of his allegiance to Christ, he must not oppress the underprivileged slave. Cf. Eph 6:5,9; Col 3:22; 4:1.

7:23 *bought with a price; be not ye the servants of men.* Christians in all stations of life should realize that their ultimate allegiance is not to men but to Christ, who bought them with His blood (6:20; 1 Pet 1:18–19).

7:25 *Now concerning virgins.* Paul answers another major question the Corinthians had asked (v. 1). *I give my judgment, as one . . . faithful.* Paul is not giving a direct command from Jesus here (as in v. 10; cf. Acts 20:35). In this matter, which is not a question of right and wrong, Paul expresses his own judgment. Even though he put it this way, he is certainly not denying that he wrote under the influence of divine inspiration (see v. 40). And since he writes under inspiration, what he recommends is clearly the better course of action.

7:26 *present distress.* Probably a reference to the pressures of the Christian life in an immoral and particularly hostile environment (cf. vv. 2,28; 5:1; 2 Tim 3:12). Paul's recommendation here does not apply to all times and all situations.

7:28 *trouble.* Times of suffering and persecution for Christ, when being married would mean even greater hardship in taking care of one's mate.

7:29 *time is short.* The time for doing the Lord's work has become increasingly short. Life is fleeting, as times of persecution remind us. Do not be unduly concerned with the affairs of this world (vv. 29–31) because material things are changing and disappearing (v. 31). Some think the reference is to the Lord's second coming.

things [1]that belong to the Lord, how he may please the Lord:

33 But he that is married careth for the *things that are* of the world, how he may please *his* wife.

34 There is difference *also* between a wife and a virgin. The unmarried *woman* [a]careth for the *things* of the Lord, that she may be holy both in body and in spirit: but she that is married careth for the *things* of the world, how she may please *her* husband.

35 And this I speak for your own profit; not that I may cast a snare upon you, but for *that which is* comely, and that you may attend upon the Lord without distraction.

36 But if any *man* think that *he* behaveth himself uncomely toward his virgin, if she pass the flower of *her* age, and need so require, let him do what he will, he sinneth not: let them marry.

37 Nevertheless he that standeth stedfast in *his* heart, having no necessity, but hath power over his own will, and hath so decreed in his heart that *he* will keep his virgin, doeth well.

38 [a]So then he that giveth *her* in marriage doeth well; but he that giveth *her* not in marriage doeth better.

39 ¶ [a]The wife is bound by the law as long as her husband liveth; but if her husband be dead, she is at liberty to be married to whom she will; [b]only in the Lord.

40 But she is happier if she so abide, [a]after my judgment: and [b]I think also that *I* have the Spirit of God.

7:32 [1][Gr. *of the Lord,* as ver. 34]
7:34 [a]Luke 10:40
7:38 [a]Heb. 13:4
7:39 [a]Rom. 7:2 [b]2 Cor. 6:14
7:40 [a]ver. 25 [b]1 Thes. 4:8

8:1 [a]Acts 15:20; ch. 10:19 [b]Rom. 14:14 [c]Rom. 14:3
8:2 [a]ch. 13:8,9; Gal. 6:3; 1 Tim. 6:4
8:3 [a]Ex. 33:12; Nah. 1:7; Mat. 7:23; Gal. 4:9
8:4 [a]Is. 41:24 [b]Deut. 4:39; 6:4; Is. 44:8; Mark 12:29; Eph. 4:6; 1 Tim. 2:5
8:5 [a]John 10:34
8:6 [1]Or, *for him* [a]Mal. 2:10; Eph. 4:6 [b]Acts 17:28; Rom. 11:36 [c]John 13:13; Acts 2:36; Eph. 4:5; Phil. 2:11 [d]John 1:3; Col. 1:16; Heb. 1:2
8:7 [a]ch. 10:28 [b]Rom. 14:14
8:8 [1]Or, *have we the more* [2]Or, *have we the less* [a]Rom. 14:17
8:9 [1]Or, *power* [a]Gal. 5:13 [b]Rom. 14:13

Food offered to idols

8 Now [a]as touching things offered unto idols, we know that we all have [b]knowledge. [c]Knowledge puffeth up, but charity edifieth.

2 And [a]if any *man* think that *he* knoweth any *thing,* he knoweth nothing yet as he ought to know.

3 But if any *man* love God, [a]the same is known of him.

4 As concerning therefore the eating of those things that are offered in sacrifice unto idols, we know that [a]an idol *is* nothing in the world, [b]and that *there is* none other God but one.

5 For though there be that are [a]called gods, whether in heaven or in earth, (as there be gods many, and lords many,)

6 But [a]to us *there is but* one God, the Father, [b]of whom *are* all *things,* and we [1]in him; and [c]one Lord Jesus Christ, [d]by whom *are* all *things,* and we by him.

7 Howbeit *there is* not in every *man that* knowledge: for some [a]with conscience of the idol unto this hour, eat *it* as a thing offered unto an idol; and their conscience being weak is [b]defiled.

8 But [a]meat commendeth us not to God: for neither, if we eat, [1]are we the better; neither, if we eat not, [2]are we the worse.

9 But [a]take heed lest by any means this [1]liberty of yours become [b]a stumblingblock to them that are weak.

10 For if any *man* see thee which hast knowledge sit at meat in the idol's temple,

7:36 *he behaveth himself uncomely toward his virgin . . . pass the flower of her age . . . let them marry.* "Virgin" here means "daughter." In the light of hostility toward believers in Corinth, a man might refrain from giving his daughter in marriage. But if he then realizes that his daughter is getting beyond her prime marriageable age and the situation thus seems unfair to her, it is perfectly proper for him to give her in marriage.

7:37 *hath power over his own will . . . doeth well.* The man who determines that there is no need for him to give his daughter in marriage under the circumstances has made a good decision too (v. 38).

7:39 *bound by the law as long as her husband liveth.* Marriage is a lifelong union (yet see the exception clause in Mat 19:9). *if her husband be dead.* Death breaks the marriage bond, and a Christian is then free to marry another Christian ("only in the Lord").

‡7:40 *if she so abide.* A widow. *I think also that I have the Spirit of God.* Paul writes as one convinced that he is guided by the Holy Spirit.

8:1 *Now as touching things offered unto idols.* Another matter the Corinthians had written about (see note on 7:1). *offered unto idols.* Offered on pagan altars. Meat left over from a sacrifice might be eaten by the priests, eaten by the offerer and his friends at a feast in the temple (see note on v. 10) or sold in the public meat market. Some Christians felt that if they ate such meat, they participated in pagan worship and thus compromised their testimony for Christ. Other Christians did not feel this way. *knowledge.* Explained in vv. 2–6. *Knowledge puffeth up.* It fills one with false pride. *charity edifieth.* Explained in vv. 7–13. The Christian should love his brother who doubts.

8:2 *he knoweth nothing.* The wisest and most knowledgeable Christian realizes that his knowledge is limited. God is the only one who knows all (cf. Rom 11:33–36).

8:3 *if any man love God, the same is known of him.* A person who tempers his knowledge with love toward God shows that he is really known and thus accepted by God as one of God's own redeemed (Gal 4:8–9; 1 John 4:7–8).

8:4 *idol is nothing in the world.* It represents no real god and possesses no power (see Ps 115:4–7; 135:15–17; Is 44:12–20). But there are demons behind them (10:20).

8:5 *called gods.* The alleged gods of Greek and Roman mythology. *as there be gods many, and lords many.* Not that there actually are many gods and lords. This would contradict the consistent and emphatic teaching of Scripture that there is but one God (Deut 6:4). Paul is recognizing the obvious fact that there are many who are worshiped as gods—though they do not actually exist, to say nothing of being deities.

8:6 *of whom are all things . . . by whom are all things.* See Heb 2:10. God the Father is the ultimate source of all creation (Acts 4:24). God the Son is the dynamic one through whom, with the Father, all things came into existence (John 1:3; Col 1:16).

8:7 *not in every man that knowledge.* The knowledge that an idol has no personal reality. *their conscience being weak is defiled.* Christians who conceive of an idol as being real cannot rid themselves of this idea. Consequently, they think that in eating meat sacrificed on pagan altars they have involved themselves in pagan worship and thus have sinned against Christ.

‡8:9 *this liberty of yours.* To eat meat sacrificed to idols because you know that an idol is nothing (v. 4). *weak.* Those Christians whose consciences are weak, who think it is wrong to eat meat sacrificed to idols.

8:10 *sit at meat in the idol's temple.* At the site of ancient Cor-

shall not [a]the conscience of him which is
weak be [1]emboldened to eat those things
which are offered to idols;
11 And [a]through thy knowledge shall the
weak brother perish, for whom Christ died?
12 But [a]when ye sin so against the brethren, and wound their weak conscience, ye sin
against Christ.
13 Wherefore, [a]if meat make my brother
to offend, I will eat no flesh while the world
standeth, lest I make my brother to offend.

Christian rights

9 [a]Am I not an apostle? am I not free?
[b]have I not seen Jesus Christ our Lord?
[c]are not you my work in the Lord?
2 If I be not an apostle unto others, yet
doubtless I am to you: for [a]the seal of mine
apostleship are ye in the Lord.
3 Mine answer to them that do examine
me is this:
4 [a]Have we not power to eat and to drink?
5 Have we not power to lead about a sister,
a [1]wife, as well as other apostles, and *as* [a]the
brethren of the Lord, and [b]Cephas?
6 Or I only and Barnabas, [a]have not we
power to forbear working?
7 Who [a]goeth a warfare any time at his
own charges? who [b]planteth a vineyard, and
eateth not of the fruit thereof? or who
[c]feedeth a flock, and eateth not of the milk of
the flock?
8 Say I these *things* as a man? or saith not
the law the same also?
9 For it is written in the law of Moses,
[a]Thou shalt not muzzle the mouth of the ox
that treadeth out the corn. Doth God take care
for oxen?
10 Or saith he *it* altogether for our sakes?
For our sakes, no doubt, *this* is written: that
[a]he that ploweth should plow in hope; and
that he that thresheth in hope should be partaker of his hope.
11 [a]If we have sown unto you spiritual
things, is it a great *thing* if we shall reap your
carnal *things?*
12 If others be partakers of *this* power over
you, *are* not we rather? [a]Nevertheless we have
not used this power; but suffer all *things,* [b]lest
we should hinder the gospel of Christ.
13 [a]Do ye not know that they which minister about holy *things* [1]live of *the things of*
the temple? *and* they which wait at the altar
are partakers with the altar?
14 Even so [a]hath the Lord ordained [b]that
they which preach the gospel should live of
the gospel.
15 But [a]I have used none of these *things:*
neither have I written these *things,* that it
should be so done unto me: for [b]*it were* better
for me to die, than that any *man* should make
my glorying void.
16 For though I preach the gospel, I have
nothing to glory of: for [a]necessity is laid upon
me; yea, woe is unto me, if I preach not the
gospel!
17 For if I do this *thing* willingly, [a]I have a
reward: but if against my will, [b]a dispensation
of the gospel is committed unto me.
18 What is my reward then? *Verily* that,
[a]when I preach the gospel, I may make the

8:10 [1]Gr. *edified* [a]ch. 10:28
8:11 [a]Rom. 14:15
8:12 [a]Mat. 25:40
8:13 [a]Rom. 14:21; 2 Cor. 11:29
9:1 [a]Acts 9:15; 13:2; 26:17; 2 Cor. 12:12; Gal. 2:7,8; 1 Tim. 2:7; 2 Tim. 1:11 [b]Acts 9:3,17; 18:9; 22:14,18; ch. 15:8 [c]ch. 3:6
9:2 [a]2 Cor. 12:12
9:4 [a]1 Thes. 2:6
9:5 [1]Or, *woman* [a]Mat. 13:55; Gal. 1:19 [b]Mat. 8:14
9:6 [a]2 Thes. 3:8
9:7 [a]2 Cor. 10:4; 1 Tim. 1:18 [b]Deut. 20:6 [c]John 21:15; 1 Pet. 5:2
9:9 [a]Deut. 25:4; 1 Tim. 5:18
9:10 [a]2 Tim. 2:6
9:11 [a]Rom. 15:27; Gal. 6:6
9:12 [a]Acts 20:33; 1 Thes. 2:6 [b]2 Cor. 11:12
9:13 [1]Or, *feed* [a]Lev. 6:16
9:14 [a]Mat. 10:10; Luke 10:7 [b]Gal. 6:6
9:15 [a]Acts 18:3 [b]2 Cor. 11:10
9:16 [a]Rom. 1:14
9:17 [a]ch. 3:8,14 [b]Gal. 2:7; Col. 1:25
9:18 [a]ch. 10:33

inth, archaeologists have discovered two temples containing rooms apparently used for pagan feasts where meat offered to idols was eaten. To such feasts Christians may have been invited by pagan friends.

8:11 *through thy knowledge shall the weak brother perish.* The weak Christian is influenced by the example of the stronger Christian and, though he feels it to be wrong, eats the meat that has been offered to an idol. The spiritual destruction that follows is explained in v. 12.

8:12 *wound their weak conscience.* Eating meat offered to idols when they feel it is wrong tends to blunt their consciences, so that doing what is wrong becomes much easier. The result may be moral tragedy. *ye sin against Christ.* Because Christ died for your brother (v. 11), even as He died for you. It is also a sin against Christ because it breaks the unity of the members of His body (the church).

8:13 *I will eat no flesh while the world standeth.* Paul will forever refrain from engaging in the harmless practice of eating meat sacrificed to idols if it will cause his weak Christian brother, who feels it is wrong, also to eat that meat.

‡9:1 *Am I not an apostle?* Some at Corinth (2 Cor 12:11–12) and elsewhere (Gal 1:1; 1:15–2:10) questioned Paul's genuine apostleship. To certify his apostleship Paul gives this proof: that he has seen the Lord Jesus (Acts 9:1–9; 22:6–16; 26:12–18), as was true of the other apostles (Acts 1:21–22). Furthermore, he adds that his ministry has produced true spiritual fruit (the Corinthians) for the Lord, which should confirm to them that he is indeed an apostle. *am I not free?* Do I not have the rights that any Christian has?

9:4 *power to eat and to drink.* Paul and Barnabas, as God's workers, have a right to have their food and other physical needs supplied at the church's expense (cf. vv. 6,13–14).

9:5 *lead about a sister, a wife.* Paul asserts his right to be married, if he wishes. This does not mean that he was married, as some have imagined (see 7:7). Other apostles, including Peter (see Mark 1:30), had wives.

9:11 *reap your carnal things.* Food, lodging and pay supplied by the Corinthians (cf. Gal 6:6). Paul here sets forth the principle that Christian workers should be paid for their labors.

9:12 *have not used this power.* The point of Paul's discussion in ch. 9. He had numerous rights that he did not claim because of his love for the Corinthians. Thus ch. 9 is an extended personal illustration of the practice advocated in ch. 8. Because of love for others, believers should be ready to surrender their rights.

9:13 *they which minister about holy things.* The Corinthian believers would understand this illustration not only from their knowledge of the OT (cf. Lev 7:28–36; Num 18:8–20) but also from the practice in pagan temples in Greece and Rome.

9:15 *my glorying.* That he had preached the gospel without charge, so that they could not say that they had paid him for it.

9:16 *necessity is laid upon me.* The Lord had laid on Paul the necessity of preaching the gospel (Acts 9:1–16; 26:16–18; see also Jer 20:9 and note).

9:18 *my reward . . . when I preach the gospel.* Paul's reward in preaching is not material things but the boasting that he has preached to the Corinthians without charge and has not taken advantage of the rights he deserves: food and drink, shelter and pay (vv. 3–12).

gospel of Christ without charge, that *I* [b]abuse not my power in the gospel.

19 For though I be [a]free from all *men,* yet have [b]I made myself servant unto all, [c]that I might gain the more.

20 And [a]unto the Jews I became as a Jew, that I might gain *the* Jews; to them that are under the law, as under the law, that I might gain them that are under the law;

21 [a]To [b]them *that are* without law, as without law, ([c]being not without law to God, but under the law to Christ,) that I might gain them *that are* without law.

22 [a]To the weak became I as weak, that I might gain the weak: [b]I am made all *things* to all *men,* [c]that I might by all means save some.

23 And this I do for the gospel's sake, that I might be partaker thereof with *you.*

24 ¶ Know ye not that they which run in a race run all, but one receiveth the prize? [a]So run, that ye may obtain.

25 And every *man* that striveth for the mastery is temperate in all *things.* Now they *do it* to obtain a corruptible crown; but we [a]an incorruptible.

26 I therefore so run, [a]not as uncertainly; so fight I, not as one that beateth the air:

27 [a]But I keep under my body, and [b]bring *it* into subjection: lest that by any means, when I have preached to others, I myself should be [c]a castaway.

The idolatry in the wilderness

10 Moreover, brethren, I would not that ye should be ignorant, how that all our fathers were under [a]the cloud, and all passed through [b]the sea;

2 And were all baptized unto Moses in the cloud and in the sea;

3 And did all eat the same [a]spiritual meat;

4 And did all drink the same [a]spiritual drink: for they drank of *that* spiritual Rock that [1]followed *them:* and *that* Rock was Christ.

5 But with many of them God was not well pleased: for they [a]were overthrown in the wilderness.

6 Now these *things* were [1]our examples, to the intent we should not lust after evil *things,* as [a]they also lusted.

7 [a]Neither be ye idolaters, as *were* some of them; as it is written, [b]The people sat down to eat and drink, and rose up to play.

8 [a]Neither let us commit fornication, as some of them committed, and [b]fell in one day three and twenty thousand.

9 Neither let us tempt Christ, as [a]some of

9:18 [b]ch. 7:31
9:19 [a]ver. 1 [b]Gal. 5:13 [c]Mat. 18:15; 1 Pet. 3:1
9:20 [a]Acts 16:3; 18:18
9:21 [a]Gal. 3:2 [b]Rom. 2:12 [c]ch. 7:22
9:22 [a]Rom. 15:1; 2 Cor. 11:29 [b]ch. 10:33 [c]Rom. 11:14
9:24 [a]Gal. 2:2; 2 Tim. 4:7
9:25 [a]Jas. 1:12; Rev. 2:10
9:26 [a]2 Tim. 2:5
9:27 [a]Rom. 8:13; Col. 3:5 [b]Rom. 6:18 [c]Jer. 6:30; 2 Cor. 13:5
10:1 [a]Ex. 13:21 [b]Ex. 14:22; Ps. 78:13
10:3 [a]Ex. 16:15; Ps. 78:24
10:4 [1]Or, *went with* them [a]Ex. 17:6; Ps. 78:15
10:5 [a]Num. 14:29; Ps. 106:26
10:6 [1]Gr. *our figures* [a]Num. 11:4
10:7 [a]ver. 14 [b]Ex. 32:6
10:8 [a]Rev. 2:14 [b]Ps. 106:29
10:9 [a]Ex. 17:2,7

9:19 *have I made myself servant unto all.* Not only did Paul not use his right to material support in preaching the gospel but he also deprived himself—curtailed his personal privileges and social and religious rights—in dealing with different kinds of people. *that I might gain.* To bring to Christ.

9:20 *them that are under the law.* Those under the OT law and religious practices (the Jews). *as under the law.* For the Jews' sake Paul conformed to the Jewish law (Acts 16:3; 18:18; 21:20–26).

9:21 *them that are without law.* Those who have not been raised under the OT law (the Gentiles). *as without law.* Paul accommodated himself to Gentile culture when it did not violate his allegiance to Christ, though he still reckoned that he was under God's law and Christ's law. (By "law to Christ" Paul is probably referring to Christ's teachings, though the term is not necessarily restricted to them.)

9:22 *the weak.* Those whose consciences are weak (8:9–12). *became I as weak.* Paul did not exercise his Christian freedom in such things as eating meat sacrificed to idols (8:9,13).

9:23 *might be partaker thereof with you.* Of the blessings of realizing that he has been faithful to Christ in preaching, of hearing the Lord's "Well done" (Mat 25:21; Luke 19:17) and of seeing others come to Christ.

9:24 *race run all.* The Corinthians were familiar with the foot races in their own Isthmian games, which occurred every other year and were second only to the Olympic games in importance. *prize.* In ancient times the prize was a perishable wreath (v. 25).

9:25 *crown . . . incorruptible.* See 2 Tim 4:8; Jas 1:12; 1 Pet 5:4; Rev 2:10; 3:11; 4:10 and notes.

9:26 *run, not as uncertainly.* See Phil 3:14.

9:27 *I keep under my body, and bring it into subjection.* Here Paul uses the figure of boxing to represent the Christian life. He does not aimlessly beat the air, but he severely disciplines his own body in serving Christ. *lest . . . I myself . . . castaway.* Paul realizes that he must with rigor serve the Lord and battle against sin. If he fails in this, he may be excluded from the reward (see 3:10–15).

10:1 *under the cloud.* Under God's leadership and guidance (Ex 13:21–22; Num 9:15–23; 14:14; Deut 1:33; Ps 78:14). His guidance did not fail them—He successfully led them through the sea (Ex 14:22,29).

10:2 As a people, they were united under God's redemptive program, and they submitted to Moses, God's appointed leader (Ex 14:31). *baptized.* A figure used to depict their submission to Moses as their deliverer and leader, just as Christian baptism depicts the believer's submission to Christ as Savior and Lord.

10:3–4 *spiritual meat . . . spiritual drink.* The manna and the water from the rock are used as figures representing the spiritual sustenance that God continually provides for His people (Ex 16:2–36; 17:1–7; Num 20:2–11; 21:16).

10:4 *that Rock was Christ.* The rock, from which the water came, and the manna were symbolic of supernatural sustenance through Christ, the bread of life and the water of life (John 4:14; 6:30–35).

10:5 *with many of them God was not well pleased.* In spite of the remarkable privileges given to Israel (vv. 1–4), they failed to obey God, thus incurring His displeasure. Of the adults who came out of Egypt, only Caleb and Joshua were allowed to enter Canaan (Num 14:22–24, 28–35; Josh 1:1–2).

10:6 *as they also lusted.* What Paul has in mind is described in vv. 7–10.

10:7 *idolaters.* Referring to the incident of the golden calf (Ex 32:1–6). The people ate a ritual meal sacrificed to an idol (cf. ch. 8).

10:8 Refers to Israel's joining herself to Baal of Peor (Num 25:1–9), participating in the worship of this god of the Moabites and engaging in sexual immorality with the prostitute virgins who worshiped this god. *three and twenty thousand.* The Hebrew and Greek (Septuagint) texts of Num 25:9 have 24,000. It is clear that Paul is not striving for exactness. He is only speaking approximately. First-century writers were not as concerned about being precise as 21st-century authors often are.

them also tempted, and [b]were destroyed of serpents.

10 Neither murmur ye, as [a]some of them also murmured, and [b]were destroyed of [c]the destroyer.

11 Now all these *things* happened unto them for [1]ensamples: and [a]they are written for our admonition, [b]upon whom the ends of the world are come.

12 Wherefore [a]let him that thinketh he standeth take heed lest he fall.

13 There hath no temptation taken you but such as is [1]common to man: but [a]God *is* faithful, [b]who will not suffer you to be tempted above that you are able; but will with the temptation also make a way to escape, that ye may be able to bear *it.*

14 Wherefore, my dearly beloved, [a]flee from idolatry.

15 I speak as to [a]wise *men;* judge ye what I say.

Prohibition of idol feasts

16 ¶ [a]The cup of blessing which we bless, is it not the communion of the blood of Christ? [b]The bread which we break, is it not the communion of the body of Christ?

17 For [a]we being many are one bread, *and* one body: for we are all partakers of *that* one bread.

18 Behold [a]Israel [b]after the flesh: [c]are not they which eat *of* the sacrifices partakers of the altar?

19 What say I then? [a]that the idol is any *thing,* or that which is offered in sacrifice to idols is any *thing?*

20 But *I say,* that *the things* which the Gentiles [a]sacrifice, they sacrifice to devils, and not to God: and I would not that ye should have fellowship with devils.

21 [a]Ye cannot drink the cup of the Lord, and [b]the cup of devils: ye cannot be partakers of the Lord's table, and of the table of devils.

22 Do we [a]provoke the Lord to jealousy? [b]are we stronger than he?

Do all to the glory of God

23 ¶ [a]All *things* are lawful for me, but all *things* are not expedient: all *things* are lawful for me, but all *things* edify not.

24 [a]Let no *man* seek his own, but every man another's *wealth.*

25 [a]Whatsoever is sold in the shambles, *that* eat, asking no question for conscience sake:

26 For [a]the earth *is* the Lord's, and the fulness thereof.

27 If any of them that believe not bid you *to a feast,* and ye be disposed to go; [a]whatsoever is set before you, eat, asking no question for conscience sake.

28 But if any *man* say unto you, This is offered in sacrifice unto idols, eat not [a]for his sake that shewed *it,* and *for* conscience *sake:*

10:9 [b]Num. 21:6
10:10 [a]Ex. 16:2 [b]Num. 14:37 [c]Ex. 12:23
10:11 [1]Or, *types* [a]Rom. 15:4 [b]Phil. 4:5; Heb. 10:25
10:12 [a]Rom. 11:20
10:13 [1]Or, *moderate* [a]ch. 1:9 [b]Ps. 125:3; 2 Pet. 2:9
10:14 [a]2 Cor. 6:17
10:15 [a]ch. 8:1
10:16 [a]Mat. 26:26 [b]Acts 2:42
10:17 [a]ch. 12:27
10:18 [a]Rom. 4:12 [b]Rom. 4:1; 2 Cor. 11:18 [c]Lev. 3:3
10:19 [a]ch. 8:4
10:20 [a]Lev. 17:7; Deut. 32:17; Ps. 106:37
10:21 [a]2 Cor. 6:15 [b]Deut. 32:38
10:22 [a]Deut. 32:21 [b]Ezek. 22:14
10:23 [a]ch. 6:12
10:24 [a]Rom. 15:1,2; ch. 13:5
10:25 [a]1 Tim. 4:4
10:26 [a]Ex. 19:5; Ps. 24:1
10:27 [a]Luke 10:7
10:28 [a]ch. 8:10,12

10:10 *Neither murmur.* As in Num 16:41. *destroyer.* Paul links the angel who brought the plague of Num 16:46–50—because of the grumbling of the Israelites against Moses and Aaron (Num 16:41)—with the destroying angel of Ex 12:23.
10:11 *written for our admonition.* See note on Rom 15:4. *the ends of the world.* The period of time inaugurated by Christ's death and resurrection and continuing into the future until Christ's second coming and beyond. It is the period of fulfillment when all that God has been doing for His people throughout all previous ages comes to its fruition in the Messiah.
10:13 *temptation.* Temptation in itself is not sin. Jesus was tempted (Mat 4:1–11). Yielding to the temptation is sin. *bear it.* Through God's enablement to resist the temptation to sin.
10:14 *flee from idolatry.* Like that described in Ex 32:1–6. Corinthian Christians had come out of a background of paganism. Temples for the worship of Apollo, Asclepius, Demeter, Aphrodite and other pagan gods and goddesses were seen daily by the Corinthians as they engaged in the activities of everyday life. The worship of Aphrodite, with its many sacred prostitutes, was a particularly strong temptation.
10:16 *cup of blessing.* One of the cups drunk at the Jewish passover, at which time the Lord's supper was instituted (Mat 26:17–30; Mark 14:12–26; Luke 22:7–23). *communion of the blood of Christ.* A memorial symbol of fellowship with the crucified Christ, not a literal drinking of His blood. When the Lord's supper was instituted, Christ had not yet poured out His blood. The Lord's supper is to remind us of Him (11:25).
10:17 *one bread.* The act of many believers partaking of one loaf of bread symbolizes the unity of the body of Christ, the church, which is nourished by the one bread of life (see John 6:33–58).
10:18 *they which eat of the sacrifices partakers of the altar.* When the people of Israel ate part of the sacrifice made at the altar (Lev 7:15; 8:31; Deut 12:17–18), they participated in the worship of God, who established the sacrifices and whose altar it was. Likewise when the pagans sacrificed, they did so to demons (vv. 20–21). Paul denies that the idol is anything, i.e., that it is a real deity (v. 19). Nor is a sacrifice offered to a so-called god anything, because the idol is nothing and the god being worshiped is no god at all. In reality, demons (not gods) were the objects of idol worship. God's people are warned that if they do eat meat sacrificed to idols, they should not eat it with pagans in their temple feasts, for to do so is to "fellowship with devils" (v. 20).
10:22 *provoke the Lord to jealousy.* By sharing in pagan idolatry and worship (cf. Ex 20:5; Deut 32:21; Ps 78:58).
10:23 *all things are not expedient.* See note on 6:12. Personal freedom and desire for one's rights are not the only considerations. One must also consider the good of his neighbor (v. 24; cf. 8:1; Gal 6:2).
10:25 *Whatsoever is sold in the shambles, that eat.* Even if it has been sacrificed to an idol, because out in the public market it has lost its pagan religious significance.
10:26 A quotation from Ps 24:1 used at Jewish mealtimes as a blessing (cf. Ps 50:12; 89:11).
10:27 *whatsoever is set before you, eat.* Whether or not it might be meat sacrificed to idols, ask no questions. As long as the subject has not been brought up, you are free to eat the meat, even if it had been offered to an idol.
10:28 *for his sake that shewed it.* If the meat has been identified as meat sacrificed to idols and you eat it, the man—whether a believer or an unbeliever—might think you condone, or even are willing to participate in, the worship of the idols the meat has been offered to. *for conscience sake.* In eating meat that has publicly been declared to have been sacrificed to idols, you may offend "another man's" conscience (v. 29)

for [b]the earth *is* the Lord's, and the fulness
thereof:
29 Conscience, I say, not thine own, but of
the other's: for [a]why is my liberty judged of
another *man's* conscience?
30 For if I by [1]grace be a partaker, why am
I evil spoken of for *that* [a]*for* which I give
thanks?
31 [a]Whether therefore ye eat, or drink, or
whatsoever ye do, do all to the glory of God.
32 [a]Give none offence, neither to the Jews,
nor to the [1]Gentiles, nor to [b]the church of
God:
33 Even as [a]I please all *men* in all *things,*
[b]not seeking mine own profit, but the *profit* of
many, that they may be saved.
11 Be [a]ye followers of me, even as I also
am of Christ.

The covering of women's heads

2 ¶ Now I praise you, brethren, [a]that you
remember me in all *things,* and [b]keep the [1]or-
dinances, as I delivered *them* to you.
3 But I would have you know, that [a]the
head of every man is Christ; and [b]the head of
the woman *is* the man; and [c]the head of
Christ *is* God.
4 Every man praying or [a]prophesying, having *his* head covered, dishonoureth his head.

10:28 [b]Deut. 10:14; Ps. 24:1
10:29 [a]Rom. 14:16
10:30 [1]Or, *thanksgiving* [a]Rom. 14:6; 1 Tim. 4:3,4
10:31 [a]Col. 3:17; 1 Pet. 4:11
10:32 [1]Gr. *Greeks* [a]Rom. 14:13; ch. 8:13 [b]Acts 20:28; 1 Tim. 3:5
10:33 [a]Rom. 15:2 [b]ver. 24
11:1 [a]Eph. 5:1; Phil. 3:17
11:2 [1]Or, *traditions* [a]ch. 4:17 [b]ch. 7:17
11:3 [a]Eph. 5:23 [b]Gen. 3:16; 1 Tim. 2:11 [c]John 14:28; Phil. 2:7-9
11:4 [a]ch. 12:10
11:5 [a]Acts 21:9 [b]Deut. 21:12
11:6 [a]Num. 5:18
11:7 [a]Gen. 1:26
11:8 [a]Gen. 2:21
11:9 [a]Gen. 2:18
11:10 [1]That is, *a covering, in sign that she is under the power of her husband* [a]Gen. 24:65 [b]Eccl. 5:6
11:11 [a]Gal. 3:28

5 But [a]every woman that prayeth or prophesieth with *her* head uncovered dishonoureth
her head: for *that* is even all one as if she were
[b]shaven.
6 For if the woman be not covered, let her
also be shorn: but *if it* be [a]a shame for a woman
to be shorn or shaven, let her be covered.
7 For a man indeed ought not to cover *his*
head, forasmuch as [a]he is the image and glory
of God: but the woman is the glory of the man.
8 For [a]the man is not of the woman; but
the woman of the man.
9 [a]Neither was the man created for the
woman; but the woman for the man.
10 For this cause ought the woman [a]to
have [1]power on *her* head [b]because of the angels.
11 Nevertheless [a]neither *is* the man without the woman, neither the woman without
the man, in the Lord.
12 For as the woman *is* of the man, *even* so
is the man also by the woman; but all *things* of
God.
13 Judge in yourselves: is it comely that a
woman pray unto God uncovered?
14 Doth not even nature itself teach you,
that, if a man have long hair, it is a shame unto
him?

by causing him to think it is all right to eat meat sacrificed to idols even though he has doubts about it. Or if he is an unbeliever, he may think that the Christian worships both God and a pagan idol.

10:29 *my liberty.* Cf. Rom 14:16. The exercise of one's personal freedom is to be governed by whether it will bring glory to God, whether it will build up the church of God and whether it will encourage the unsaved to receive Christ as Savior and Lord (vv. 31–33).

10:30 *that for which I give thanks.* Paul could thank God for meat sacrificed to idols, for the idol is nothing and the meat is a part of God's created world.

10:31 *all to the glory of God.* The all-inclusive principle that governs the discussion in chs. 8–10 is that God should be glorified in everything that is done.

10:32 *Give none offence.* The particular cause of stumbling Paul had in mind was that of eating meat offered to idols (see 8:13). Living to glorify God will result in doing what is beneficial for others, whether Christians ("the church of God") or non-Christians ("Jews, Gentiles").

10:33 *please all men in all things.* Paul does not mean that he will compromise the truths of the gospel in order to please everybody, but that he will consider his fellowman and not cause anyone's conscience to be offended by his daily life, thus keeping that person from receiving the gospel. *that they may be saved.* See 9:22.

‡11:1 Notice the order: (1) Christ is the supreme example (cf. 1 Pet 2:21); (2) Christ's apostle follows His example ("even as I also am of Christ"); (3) we are to follow the apostle's example.

‡11:2–16 Paul is not correcting belligerent Christian women who are coming to the assembly with their heads uncovered, for he praises them for doing what they have been taught (v. 2). Rather, he wants them to understand why (v. 3) it is that when praying or prophesying men's heads are to be uncovered and women's covered. Due to God's creation plan for man and woman as evidenced in the creation order of Gen 1–2, the distinctions in male and female roles need to be observed at those times during which God allows women to perform seemingly male roles of leadership and teaching (see 1 Tim 2:12). So when leading in public prayer and when exercising the spiritual gift of prophesying, women are to demonstrate the authority which is over them. This passage does not teach that women when they go to church must have their heads covered. It does however, reveal role differences that are as old as humanity. Paul's arguments are not based upon culture or first century practices, but upon God's plan at creation (see verses 7,8,9,10,12.)

11:3 Some understand the term "head" to refer primarily to the concept of honor, in that one's physical head is the seat of his honor (cf. vv. 4–5). Thus as Christ honored God, man is to honor Christ, and woman is to honor her husband. Others see in the word "head" the idea of authority (which would also include the concept of honor). They point out that Paul clearly uses the term in the sense of authority in Eph 1:21–22 ("under his feet"; "head over all things"), in Eph 5:22–23 (where headship is seen in a context of submission) and in Col 1:18; 2:10. Thus as Christ is in authority over man and is therefore to be honored by man, so the husband is in a position of authority and is therefore to be honored by his wife. See note on 15:28.

‡11:4 The first use of "head" in this verse refers to man's physical head; the second refers to his spiritual head (Christ)—or perhaps is intended in a double sense. When a man prayed or prophesied with his head covered, he failed to show the proper attitude toward Christ.

‡11:10 *power on her head.* Understood by some to refer to the woman's authority as co-ruler with man in the creation (Gen 1:26–27). Others take the phrase to refer to the man's authority as properly recognized by the woman in her head covering. *angels.* Perhaps mentioned here because they are interested in all aspects of the Christian's salvation and are sensitive to decorum in worship (cf. Eph 3:10; 1 Tim 5:21) and were observers of God's creation plan (Job 38:7).

‡11:13–14 *comely . . . nature itself.* Believers must be conscious of how their actions appear, in light of what is considered to be honorable behavior.

15 But if a woman have long hair, it is a glory to her: for *her* hair is given her for a [1]covering.

16 But [a]if any *man* seem to be contentious, we have no such custom, [b]neither the churches of God.

The Lord's supper

17 ¶ Now in this that I declare *unto you* I praise *you* not, that you come together not for the better, but for the worse.

18 For first of all, when ye come together in the church, [a]I hear that there be [1]divisions among you; and I partly believe *it.*

19 For [a]there must be also [1]heresies among you, [b]that they *which are* approved may be made manifest among you.

20 When ye come together therefore into one place, [1]*this* is not to eat the Lord's supper.

21 For in eating every one taketh before *other* his own supper: and one is hungry, and [a]another is drunken.

22 What? have ye not houses to eat and to drink *in?* or despise ye [a]the church of God, and [b]shame [1]them that have not? What shall I say to you? shall I praise you in this? I praise *you* not.

23 For [a]I have received of the Lord *that* which also I delivered unto you, [b]That the Lord Jesus the *same* night in which he was betrayed took bread:

11:15 [1]Or, *vail*
11:16 [a]1 Tim. 6:4 [b]ch. 7:17
11:18 [1]Or, *schisms* [a]ch. 1:10,11
11:19 [1]Or, *sects* [a]Mat. 18:7; Luke 17:1; 1 Tim. 4:1 [b]Luke 2:35; 1 John 2:19
11:20 [1]Or, *ye cannot eat*
11:21 [a]2 Pet. 2:13; Jude 12
11:22 [1]Or, *them that are poor?* [a]ch. 10:32 [b]Jas. 2:6
11:23 [a]ch. 15:3 [b]Mat. 26:26; Luke 22:19
11:24 [1]Or, *for a remembrance*
11:26 [1]Or, *shew ye* [a]John 14:3; Acts 1:11
11:27 [a]John 6:51
11:28 [a]2 Cor. 13:5
11:29 [1]Or, *judgment*
11:31 [a]Ps. 32:5; 1 John 1:9
11:32 [a]Ps. 94:12

24 And when he had given thanks, he brake *it,* and said, Take, eat: this is my body, which is broken for you: this do [1]in remembrance of me.

25 After the same manner also *he took* the cup, when *he* had supped, saying, This cup is the new testament in my blood: this do ye, as oft as ye drink *it,* in remembrance of me.

26 For as often as ye eat this bread, and drink this cup, [1]ye do shew the Lord's death [a]till he come.

27 [a]Wherefore whosoever shall eat this bread, and drink *this* cup of the Lord unworthily, shall be guilty of the body and blood of the Lord.

28 But [a]let a man examine himself, and so let him eat of *that* bread, and drink of *that* cup.

29 For he that eateth and drinketh unworthily, eateth and drinketh [1]damnation to himself, not discerning the Lord's body.

30 For this cause many *are* weak and sickly among you, and many sleep.

31 For [a]if we would judge ourselves, we should not be judged.

32 But when we are judged, [a]we are chastened of the Lord, that we should not be condemned with the world.

33 Wherefore, my brethren, when ye come together to eat, tarry one for another.

34 And if any *man* hunger, let him eat at

---

‡11:16 In worship services, Paul and the churches in general followed the common custom of the men wearing short hair and the women long hair. Paul was basing his remarks on common custom in the churches.

11:17 *praise you not.* Contrast v. 2.

11:18 *divisions.* Paul had already dealt with one aspect of these divisions (1:10–17).

‡11:19 *must be also heresies among you, that.* Paul appears to be using sarcasm again. See note at 4:8.

11:20 *not to eat the Lord's supper.* Their intention was to eat the Lord's supper, but it was profaned by their gluttony and discrimination.

11:21 *is hungry . . . is drunken.* The early church held the *agape* ("love") feast in connection with the Lord's supper (cf. 2 Pet 2:13; Jude 12). Perhaps the meal was something like a present-day potluck dinner. In good Greek style they brought food for all to share, the rich bringing more and the poor less, but because of their cliques the rich ate much and the poor were left hungry.

11:22 *shall I praise you . . . ?* See v. 17.

11:23–26 Observe the similarity of Paul's words here with Mat 26:26–29; Mark 14:22–25; and especially Luke 22:17–20.

11:23 *I have received of the Lord.* Paul does not necessarily mean that he received the message about the Lord's supper directly from Christ. The information probably was passed on to him by others who had heard it from Jesus.

11:24 *had given thanks.* The Jewish practice at meals. This makes it a true Eucharist ("thanksgiving"). *my body.* The broken bread is a symbol of Christ's body given for sinners (Luke 22:19). *in remembrance of me.* As the feast of passover was a commemorative meal (see Ex 12:14), so also the Lord's supper is a memorial supper, recalling and portraying Christ's death for sinners.

11:25 *the cup.* A symbol of the new covenant in Jesus' blood (Luke 22:20; cf. Jer 31:31–34). (The old covenant was the Mosaic or Sinaitic covenant; see Ex 24:3–8.) By the use of this covenant sign God signifies His bestowal of salvation upon His people, sealed and paid for by the shedding of Jesus' blood. *when he had supped.* After the passover supper. The Lord's supper was first celebrated by Jesus in connection with the passover meal (cf. Mat 26:18–30 and parallels in Mark and Luke).

11:26 *as often as you eat . . . and drink.* The Lord's supper should be held periodically, but there is no explicit instruction as to how often. *till he come.* Cf. Mat 26:29.

11:27 *unworthily.* In the irreverent and self-centered manner that characterized some of the Corinthians at their unruly *agape* supper (vv. 19–22; see note on v. 21).

‡11:28 *examine himself.* A person should test the attitude of his own heart and actions and his awareness of the significance of the supper.

11:29 *damnation.* Not God's eternal judgment, which is to come on the unbeliever, but such disciplinary judgment as physical sickness and death (v. 30). *not discerning the Lord's body.* The word "body" may refer to either the Lord's physical body or the church as the body of Christ (see 12:13,27). The first view means that the person partakes of the Lord's supper without recognizing that it symbolizes Christ's crucified body. But in that case, why is the blood not mentioned? The second view means that the participant is not aware of the nature of the church as the body of Christ, resulting in the self-centered actions of vv. 20–21.

11:30 *sleep.* A common first-century figure of speech for death.

11:32 *chastened.* As God's redeemed children we are disciplined—just as a human father disciplines his child—so that we might repent of our sins (cf. 2 Cor 7:10) and grow in grace (2 Pet 3:18; Heb 12:7–11).

11:33 *come together to eat.* Another reference to the *agape* fellowship meal (see note on v. 21). Each person was to exercise restraint and wait to eat with the others. If a person was

home; that ye come not together unto [1]con-
demnation. And the rest [a]will I set in order
when [b]I come.

The diversities of gifts

12 Now [a]concerning spiritual *gifts,* brethren, I would not have you ignorant.
2 Ye know [a]that ye were Gentiles, carried
away unto *these* [b]dumb idols, *even* as ye were
led.
3 Wherefore I give you to understand,
[a]that no *man* speaking by the Spirit of God
calleth Jesus [1]accursed: and [b]*that* no *man* can
say that Jesus is the Lord, but by the Holy
Ghost.
4 Now [a]there are diversities of gifts, but
[b]the same Spirit.
5 [a]And there are differences of [1]adminis-
trations, but the same Lord.
6 And there are diversities of operations,
but it is the same God [a]which worketh all in
all.
7 [a]But the manifestation of the Spirit is giv-
en to every man to profit withal.
8 For to one is given by the Spirit [a]the
word of wisdom; to another [b]the word of
knowledge by the same Spirit;
9 [a]To another faith by the same Spirit; to
another [b]the gifts of healing by the same
Spirit;
10 [a]To another the working of miracles; to
another [b]prophecy; [c]to another discerning of
spirits; to another [d]*divers* kinds of tongues; to
another the interpretation of tongues:
11 But all these worketh *that* one and the
selfsame Spirit, [a]dividing to every man severally [b]as he will.
12 ¶ For [a]as the body is one, and hath
many members, and all the members of *that*
one body, being many, are one body: [b]so also
is Christ.
13 For [a]by one Spirit are we all baptized
into one body, [b]whether *we be* Jews or [1]Gen-
tiles, whether *we be* bond or free; and [c]have
been all made to drink into one Spirit.
14 For the body is not one member, but
many.

11:34 [1]Or, *judgment* [a]Tit. 1:5 [b]ch. 4:19
12:1 [a]ch. 14:1,37
12:2 [a]Eph. 2:11; 1 Thes. 1:9; 1 Pet. 4:3 [b]Ps. 115:5
12:3 [1]Or, *anathema* [a]Mark 9:39; 1 John 4:2 [b]Mat. 16:17; John 15:26
12:4 [a]Rom. 12:4; 1 Pet. 4:10 [b]Eph. 4:4
12:5 [1][Or, *ministeries*] [a]Rom. 12:6; Eph. 4:11
12:6 [a]Eph. 1:23
12:7 [a]Rom. 12:6; Eph. 4:7
12:8 [a]ch. 2:6,7
12:8 [b]2 Cor. 8:7
12:9 [a]Mat. 17:19; 2 Cor. 4:13 [b]Mark 16:18; Jas. 5:14
12:10 [a]Mark 16:17; Gal. 3:5 [b]Rom. 12:6 [c]1 John 4:1 [d]Acts 2:4

12:11 [a]Rom. 12:6; 2 Cor. 10:13 [b]John 3:8 12:12 [a]Rom. 12:4,5; Eph. 4:4 [b]Gal. 3:16 12:13 [1]Gr. *Greeks* [a]Rom. 6:5 [b]Gal. 3:28; Col. 3:11 [c]John 6:63

too hungry, he should satisfy his hunger at home and not bring selfish and discriminatory practices into the church.

11:34 *the rest . . . when I come.* Paul suggests that they had other problems concerning the Lord's supper that needed his attention, but he would take care of these later.

12:1 *Now concerning.* Suggests Paul is answering another question raised by the Corinthians in their letter (cf. 7:1; 8:1; 16:1). *spiritual gifts.* For a definition see note on 1:7, though a different Greek word is used there.

12:2 *carried away unto these dumb idols.* At one time the Corinthians had been led by various influences to worship mute idols (cf. 10:19–20), but now they are to be led by the Holy Spirit.

12:3 *calleth Jesus accursed . . . Jesus is the Lord.* One who is regenerated by the Holy Spirit cannot pronounce a curse on Jesus; rather, he is the only one who from the heart can confess, "Jesus is the Lord" (cf. John 20:28; also 1 John 4:2–3). The Greek word for "Lord" here is used in the Greek translation of the OT (the Septuagint) to translate the Hebrew name *Yahweh* ("the LORD").

12:4–6 *same Spirit . . . same Lord . . . same God.* These verses, reflecting the Trinity, show the diversity and unity of spiritual gifts.

12:4 *gifts.* Gifts of grace produced by the indwelling Holy Spirit. See note on v. 1.

12:5 *administrations.* The Greek word in its various forms is used to indicate service to the Christian community, such as serving tables (Acts 6:2–3); it is also the word used a little later in the first-century Christian church for the office of deacon (Phil 1:1).

12:6 *operations.* The Greek word indicates power that is in operation. Spiritual gifts produce results that are obvious.

12:7 *manifestation . . . to every man to profit withal.* Every member of the body of Christ has been given some spiritual gift that is an evidence of the Spirit's working in his life. All the gifts are intended to build up the members of the Christian community (see 1 Pet 4:10–11). They are not to be used for selfish advantage, as some in the Corinthian community apparently were doing.

12:8 *to one . . . to another.* Not everyone has the same gift or all the gifts. *word of wisdom . . . knowledge.* Gifts that meet the need of the Christian community when knowledge or wisdom is required to make decisions or to choose proper courses of action.

12:9 *faith.* Not saving faith, which all Christians have, but faith to meet a specific need within the body of Christ. *gifts of healing.* Lit. "gifts of healings." The double plural may suggest different kinds of illnesses and the various ways God heals them.

12:10 *working of miracles.* Lit. "deeds of power." In Scripture a miracle is an action that cannot be explained by natural means. It is an act of God intended as evidence of His power and purpose. *prophecy.* A communication of the mind of God imparted to a believer by the Holy Spirit. It may be a prediction (cf. Agabus, Acts 11:28; 21:10–11) or an indication of the will of God in a given situation (cf. 14:29–30; Acts 13:1–2). *discerning of spirits.* Since there can also be false prophecies that come from evil spirits, this gift is necessary in order to distinguish the true from the false (cf. 1 John 4:1–6). *divers kinds of tongues.* Since the Greek word for "tongues" means "languages" or "dialects," some understand it to refer to the ability to speak in unlearned human languages, as the apostles did on the day of Pentecost (Acts 2:4,6,11; cf. also 1 Cor 14:9–10). Others believe that in chs. 12–14 the term "tongues" refers to both earthly and heavenly languages, including ecstatic languages of praise and prayer (13:1; 14:2,10). *interpretation of tongues.* The communication of the message spoken in a tongue so that hearers can understand and be edified (cf. 14:5, 13,27–28).

12:11 *as he will.* The Holy Spirit sovereignly determines which gift or gifts each believer should have.

12:12 *one . . . many members.* This example illustrates the unity and diversity of the different spiritual gifts exercised by God's people, who are all members of the one body of Christ. *is Christ.* Is Christ's body, the church, of which He is the head (Eph 1:22–23).

12:13 *by one Spirit . . . all baptized into one body.* Spiritually baptized, regenerated by the Holy Spirit (John 3:3,5) and united with Christ as part of His body. *Jews or Gentiles.* In Christ there is no racial or cultural distinction. *bond or free.* No social distinction. *all made to drink into one Spirit.* God has given all His people the Holy Spirit to indwell them (6:19) so that their lives may overflow with the fruit of the Spirit (Gal 5:22–23; cf. John 7:37–39).

12:14–20 Addressed mainly to those who feel that their gifts

15 If the foot shall say, Because I am not the hand, I am not of the body; is it therefore not of the body?

16 And if the ear shall say, Because I am not the eye, I am not of the body; is it therefore not of the body?

17 If the whole body *were* an eye, where *were* the hearing? If the whole *were* hearing, where *were* the smelling?

18 But now hath [a]God set the members every one of them in the body, [b]as it hath pleased him.

19 And if they were all one member, where *were* the body?

20 But now *are they* many members, yet *but* one body.

21 And the eye cannot say unto the hand, I have no need of thee: nor again the head to the feet, I have no need of you.

22 Nay, much more those members of the body, which seem to be more feeble, are necessary:

23 And those *members* of the body, which we think to be less honourable, upon these we [1]bestow more abundant honour; and our uncomely *parts* have more abundant comeliness.

24 For our comely *parts* have no need: but God hath tempered the body together, having given more abundant honour to that *part* which lacked:

25 That there should be no [1]schism in the body; but *that* the members should have the same care one for another.

26 And whether one member suffer, all the members suffer with *it;* or one member be honoured, all the members rejoice with *it.*

27 Now [a]ye are the body of Christ, and [b]members in particular.

28 ¶ And [a]God hath set some in the church, first [b]apostles, secondarily [c]prophets, thirdly teachers, after that [d]miracles, then [e]gifts of healings, [f]helps, [g]governments, [1]diversities of tongues.

29 *Are* all apostles? *are* all prophets? *are* all teachers? *are* all [1]workers of miracles?

30 Have all the gifts of healing? do all speak with tongues? do all interpret?

31 But [a]covet earnestly the best gifts: and yet shew I unto you a more excellent way.

The way of love

13 Though I speak with the tongues of men and of angels, and have not

12:18 [a]ver. 28 [b]Rom. 12:3
12:23 [1]Or, *put on*
12:25 [1]Or, *division*
12:27 [a]Rom. 12:5; Eph. 1:23; 4:12; 5:23,30; Col. 1:24 [b]Eph. 5:30
12:28 [1]Or, *kinds* [a]Eph. 4:11 [b]Eph. 2:20; 3:5 [c]Acts 13:1; Rom. 12:6 [d]ver. 10 [e]ver. 9 [f]Num. 11:17 [g]Rom. 12:8; 1 Tim. 5:17; Heb. 13:17,24
12:29 [1]Or, *powers*
12:31 [a]ch. 14:1,39

are inferior and unimportant. Apparently the more spectacular gifts (such as tongues) had been glorified in the Corinthian church, making those who did not have them feel inferior.

12:14 As the human body must have diversity to work effectively as a whole, so the members of Christ's body have diverse gifts, the use of which can help bring about the accomplishment of Christ's united purpose. Each must properly exercise his gifts or effectively use his position for the good of the whole: e.g., the gift of the message of wisdom, the message of knowledge, the position of apostle, elder (1 Pet 5:1), deacon (Acts 6:1–6).

12:18 Paul stresses the sovereign purpose of God in diversifying the parts of the body; by implication he is saying that God has arranged that different Christians in the body of Christ exercise different spiritual gifts, not the same gift. And this diversity is intended to accomplish God's unified purpose. God's method employs diversity to create unity.

12:21–26 Addressed mainly to those who feel that their gifts are superior and most important. These verses provide another indication that some gifts, like tongues, had been magnified as being preeminent.

12:21 The principle here is the interdependence of the parts of the body in the one whole. Christians in the body of Christ are mutually dependent as they exercise their distinctive functions.

12:22 *more feeble, are necessary.* Christians who seem to have less important functions in the body of Christ are actually indispensable.

‡12:23 *those members of the body, which we think to be less honourable, upon these we bestow more abundant honour.* Just as we give food to the stomach, though it is a less attractive part of the body, so we should give honor and support to the Christians in the church who have ordinary gifts (in their functions). *our uncomely parts.* Christians whose functions may be very obscure in the church are to be given special respect.

12:24 Persons with more spectacular gifts do not need to be given special honor.

12:25 *no schism.* See 1:10–12.

12:26 *all the members suffer.* In the body of Christ if one Christian suffers, all the Christians are affected (cf. Acts 12:1–5—the martyrdom of James and the imprisonment of Peter).

12:27 *ye are the body of Christ.* Addressed to the local church at Corinth. Each local church is the body of Christ just as the universal church is Christ's body.

12:28 The list here differs somewhat from that in vv. 8–10 (see notes there). Paul notes three of the gifted individuals of Eph 4:11, then five of the spiritual gifts listed in vv. 8–10. The apostles and prophets were part of the foundation of the church (Eph 2:20), and teaching was associated with the pastoral office (Eph 4:11; 1 Tim 3:2). These three gifted individuals are listed as "first," "secondarily" and "thirdly," indicating their importance in the church. The rest of the list is introduced with "then," indicating the variety that follows. Paul's lists of spiritual gifts seem to be largely random samples. Apart from v. 28a he does not rank them in importance since he has already insisted that all gifts are important (vv. 21–26). *apostles.* Those chosen by Christ during His earthly ministry to be with Him and to go out and preach (Mark 3:14). They were also to be witnesses of the resurrection (Acts 1:21–22). The term may occasionally have been used in a broader sense (Rom 16:7; Gal 1:19). *miracles . . . healings . . . tongues.* See notes on vv. 9–10. *helps.* Any act of helping others may be the product of a spiritual gift (cf. Rom 12:6–8), though the primary reference here is probably to a ministry to the poor, needy, sick and distressed (cf. Acts 6:1–6). *governments.* Those with gifts of administration were enabled by the Holy Spirit to organize and project plans and spiritual programs in the church.

12:29–30 *Are all apostles?* Christians have different gifts, and no one gift should be expected by everyone.

‡12:31 *covet earnestly the best gifts.* See v. 28; 14:1,5,12,39. An alternative translation could be "you are eagerly desiring . . . ." If this is correct, the Corinthians were apparently seeking status through the exercise of the gifts that seemed to them to be more important. *a more excellent way.* Paul now shows the right way to exercise all spiritual gifts—the way of love. He does not identify love as a gift; rather, it is a fruit of the Spirit (Gal 5:22).

13:1–3 *tongues . . . prophecy . . . faith . . . give.* Paul selects four

charity, I am become *as* sounding brass, or a tinkling cymbal.

2 And though I have *the gift of* [a]prophecy, and understand all mysteries, and all knowledge; and though I have all faith, [b]so that *I* could remove mountains, and have no charity, I am nothing.

3 And [a]though I bestow all my goods to feed *the poor,* and though I give my body to be burned, and have not charity, it profiteth me nothing.

4 [a]Charity suffereth long, *and* is kind; charity envieth not; charity [1]vaunteth not itself, is not puffed up,

5 Doth not behave itself unseemly, [a]seeketh not her own, is not easily provoked, thinketh no evil;

6 [a]Rejoiceth not in iniquity, but [b]rejoiceth [1]in the truth;

7 [a]Beareth all *things,* believeth all *things,* hopeth all *things,* endureth all *things.*

8 Charity never faileth: but whether *there be* prophecies, they shall fail; whether *there be* tongues, they shall cease; whether *there be* knowledge, it shall vanish away.

9 [a]For we know in part, and we prophesy in part.

10 But when *that which is* perfect is come, then that which is in part shall be done away.

11 When I was a child, I spake as a child, I understood as a child, I [1]thought as a child: but when I became a man, I put away childish *things.*

12 For [a]now we see through a glass, [1]darkly; but then [b]face to face: now I know in part; but then shall I know even as also I am known.

13 And now abideth faith, hope, charity, these three; but the greatest of these *is* charity.

Prophecy and tongues

14 Follow after charity, and [a]desire spiritual *gifts,* [b]but rather that ye may prophesy.

2 For he that [a]speaketh in an *unknown* tongue speaketh not unto men, but unto God: for no *man* [1]understandeth *him;* howbeit in the spirit he speaketh mysteries.

3 But he that prophesieth speaketh unto men *to* edification, and exhortation, and comfort.

4 He that speaketh in an *unknown* tongue edifieth himself; but he that prophesieth edifieth *the* church.

13:2 [a]ch. 12:8-10,28; 14:1; See Mat. 7:22 [b]Mat. 17:20; Mark 11:23; Luke 17:6
13:3 [a]Mat. 6:1,2
13:4 [1]Or, *is not rash* [a]Prov. 10:12; 1 Pet. 4:8
13:5 [a]ch. 10:24; Phil. 2:4
13:6 [1]Or, *with the truth* [a]Ps. 10:3; Rom. 1:32 [b]2 John 4
13:7 [a]Rom. 15:1; Gal. 6:2; 2 Tim. 2:24
13:9 [a]ch. 8:2
13:11 [1]Or, *reasoned*
13:12 [1]Gr. *in a riddle* [a]2 Cor. 3:18; 5:7; Phil. 3:12 [b]Mat. 18:10; 1 John 3:2
14:1 [a]ch. 12:31 [b]Num. 11:25,29
14:2 [1]Gr. *heareth* [a]Acts 2:4; 10:46

gifts as examples. He declares that even their most spectacular manifestations mean nothing unless motivated by love.

13:1 *tongues of men and of angels.* Paul uses hyperbole. Even if he could speak not only the various languages that human beings speak but even the languages used by angels—if he did not speak in love, it would be nothing but noise. *charity.* The Greek for this word indicates a selfless concern for the welfare of others that is not called forth by any quality of lovableness in the person loved, but is the product of a will to love in obedience to God's command. It is like Christ's love manifested on the cross (cf. John 13:34–35; 1 John 3:16).

13:2 *all mysteries, and all knowledge.* Again Paul uses hyperbole to express the amount of understanding possessed. Even if one's gift is unlimited knowledge, if one does not possess and exercise that knowledge in love, he is nothing. *faith . . . remove mountains.* A special capacity to trust God to meet outstanding needs. Again Paul uses hyperbole.

13:3 *give my body to be burned.* A reference to suffering martyrdom through burning at the stake, as many early Christians experienced. Even the supreme sacrifice, if not motivated by love, accomplishes nothing.

13:4–7 Love is now described both positively and negatively.

13:4 *vaunteth not itself.* See 8:1.

13:5 *behave itself unseemly.* Perhaps an indirect reference to their unruly conduct in worship (11:18–22).

13:6 *Rejoiceth not in iniquity.* As they were doing in ch. 5.

13:8 *prophecies . . . shall fail; . . . tongues . . . shall cease; . . . knowledge . . . shall vanish away.* These three will cease because they are partial in nature (v. 9) and will be unnecessary when what is complete has come (v. 10).

‡13:10 *perfect.* The Greek for this word can mean "end," "fulfillment," "completeness" or "maturity." In this context the contrast is between the partial and the complete. Some refer the verse to the return of Christ, others to the death of the Christian, others to the maturity (or establishment) of the church (see the illustration in v. 11), still others to the completion of the canon of NT Scripture.

‡13:12 *see through a glass, darkly.* The imagery is of a polished metal (probably bronze) mirror in which one could receive only an imperfect reflection (cf. Jas 1:23)—in contrast to seeing an image clearly and completely, whether the revelation of God's completed Word through the apostles or that of the person of Christ at His Coming. The two spiritual gifts of prophecy and knowledge (vs. 8) which will pass along with tongues suggest that this "perfect" thing (v. 10) related to revelation rather than to glorification.

13:13 *abideth.* Now and forever. *faith, hope and charity.* See note on 1 Thes 1:3. *the greatest of these is charity.* Because God is love (1 John 4:8) and has communicated His love to us (1 John 4:10) and commands us to love one another (John 13:34–35). Love supersedes the gifts because it outlasts them all. Long after these sought-after gifts are no longer necessary, love will still be the governing principle that controls all that God and His redeemed people are and do.

14:1–5 The basic principle Paul insists on is that whatever is done in the church must contribute to the edification (building up) of the body. This is in keeping with the declaration in 12:7 that gifts are "given to every man to profit withal." It also is in agreement with the principle of love (ch. 13). What is spoken in the church, then, must be intelligible—it must be spoken in the vernacular language or at least be interpreted in the vernacular. Prophecy is therefore more desirable than tongues (unless an interpreter is present) because prophecy is spoken in the native language of the listeners.

14:1 *Follow after charity . . . spiritual gifts.* Love is the means by which spiritual gifts are made effective. *rather that ye may prophesy.* See note on 12:10.

14:2 *tongue.* Or "another language" (also in vv. 4,13,14,19, 26,27). The hearers cannot understand what the person who speaks in a tongue is saying. Therefore what he says is a mystery unless it is interpreted. Only God understands it. *in the spirit.* It is not spoken from his mind (see vv. 14–17).

14:3 In prophesying the speaker can edify and encourage others (12:7).

‡14:4 *edifieth himself.* This edification can not involve the mind since the speaker does not understand what he has said. This statement seems to be another use of irony by Paul. See note at 4:8.

5 I would that ye all spake with tongues,
but rather that ye prophesied: for greater *is* he
that prophesieth than he that speaketh with
tongues, except he interpret, that the church
may receive edifying.
6 Now, brethren, if I come unto you speaking with tongues, what shall I profit you, except I shall speak to you either by [a]revelation,
or by knowledge, or by prophesying, or by doctrine?
7 *And* even *things* without life giving
sound, whether pipe or harp, except they give
a distinction in the [1]sounds, how shall it be
known what is piped or harped?
8 For if the trumpet give an uncertain
sound, who shall prepare himself to the battle?
9 So likewise you, except ye utter by the
tongue words [1]easy to be understood, how
shall it be known what is spoken? for ye shall
speak into the air.
10 There are, it may be, so many kinds of
voices in the world, and none of them *is* without signification.
11 Therefore if I know not the meaning of
the voice, I shall be unto him that speaketh a
barbarian, and he that speaketh *shall be* a barbarian unto me.
12 Even so ye, forasmuch as ye are zealous
[1]of spiritual *gifts,* seek that ye may excel to
the edifying of the church.
13 Wherefore let him that speaketh in an
unknown tongue pray that he may interpret.
14 For if I pray in an *unknown* tongue, my
spirit prayeth, but my understanding is unfruitful.
15 What is it then? I will pray with the
spirit, and will pray with the understanding
also: [a]I will sing with the spirit, and I will sing
[b]with the understanding also.
16 Else when thou shalt bless with the
spirit, how shall he that occupieth the room of
the unlearned say Amen [a]at thy giving of
thanks, seeing he understandeth not what
thou sayest?
17 For thou verily givest thanks well, but
the other is not edified.
18 I thank my God, I speak with tongues
more than you all:
19 Yet in the church I had rather speak five
words with my understanding, that *by my
voice* I might teach others also, than ten thousand words in an *unknown* tongue.
20 Brethren, [a]be not children in understanding: howbeit in malice [b]be ye children,
but in understanding be [1]men.
21 [a]In the law it is [b]written, With *men* of
other tongues and other lips will I speak unto
this people; and yet for all that will they not
hear me, saith the Lord.
22 Wherefore tongues are for a sign, not to
them that believe, but to them that believe
not: but prophesying *serveth* not for them that
believe not, but for them which believe.
23 If therefore the whole church be come
together into one place, and all speak with
tongues, and there come in *those that are* un-

14:6 [a]ver. 26
14:7 [1]Or, *tunes*
14:9 [1]Gr. *significant*
14:12 [1]Gr. *of spirits*

14:15 [a]Eph. 5:19; Col. 3:16 [b]Ps. 47:7
14:16 [a]ch. 11:24
14:20 [1]Gr. *perfect,* or, *of a ripe age* [a]Ps. 131:2; Mat. 11:25; 18:3; 19:14; Rom. 16:19; ch. 3:1; Eph. 4:14; Heb. 5:12,13 [b]Mat. 18:3; 1 Pet. 2:2
14:21 [a]John 10:34 [b]Is. 28:11,12

14:5 *would that ye all spake with tongues.* Paul was not opposed to tongues-speaking if it was practiced properly. *greater is he that prophesieth.* Because he serves the common good more effectively since what he says can be understood and thus edifies the church. *except he interpret.* If the tongues-speaker also has an interpreter, his speaking is as beneficial as prophecy, for then it can be understood (see v. 13).

14:6 *what shall I profit you . . . ?* It would be useless for a person to speak in tongues unless, by interpretation, he brings the church something understandable and edifying.

14:7 *pipe or harp.* Instruments that were well known in Greece. *distinction in the sounds.* For a person to recognize the tune and to understand and appreciate it, there must be a variety of notes so arranged as to create a meaningful tune. One note repeated monotonously cannot accomplish this.

14:8 *the trumpet . . . prepare himself to the battle.* All Greeks would be acquainted with the use of the trumpet or bugle for battle signals (cf. Homer's *Iliad,* 18.219), and the Jews would be familiar with the use of the ram's horn (Num 10:9; Josh 6:4,9). Again, the notes sounded must convey a message.

14:10 *many kinds of voices.* Some see vv. 10–11 as an indication that the tongues of chs. 12–14 were unlearned foreign languages.

14:12 *excel to the edifying of the church.* The basic principle of ch. 14.

14:14 *understanding is unfruitful.* When a person speaks in tongues or prays in tongues, the human mind does not produce the language.

14:15–17 *pray . . . sing . . . bless . . . say Amen . . . giving of thanks.* Elements employed in OT (1 Chr 16:36; Neh 5:13; 8:6; Ps 104:33; 136:1; 148:1) and NT worship (Rom 11:36; Eph 5:18–20). "Amen," meaning "It is true" or "So be it," is the believer's confession of agreement with the words spoken (cf. Gal 1:5). Thus it is important that a message in tongues be interpreted.

14:15 *pray with the spirit . . . with the understanding . . . sing with the spirit . . . with the understanding.* May mean that Paul will sometimes pray or sing with his spirit in a tongue; at other times he will pray or sing with his mind in his own language. Others believe that Paul was declaring his intention to pray or sing with both mind and spirit at the same time.

14:20 *be not children in understanding.* Just as in the case of infants, have no evil desires or wrong motives in wanting to excel in spiritual gifts (such as speaking in tongues) as an end in itself.

‡14:21–22 The passage from Is 28 indicates that the foreign language of the Assyrians was a sign to unbelieving Israel that judgment was coming on them. Paul deduced from this fact that tongues were intended to be a sign for unbelievers (v. 22), as, e.g., in Acts 2:4–12, and the unconvinced (vv. 23–24) as, e.g. Acts 10:45; 11:2, 15–18; and 19:1–7. Similarly, prophecy was for believers (v. 22) since it communicated revealed truth to those disposed to receive it (cf. Mat 13:11–16).

‡14:21 *In the law.* Cf. Rom 3:10–19, where Paul quotes from a number of passages from the OT, including Isaiah, and then in v. 19 collectively calls them "the law."

‡14:23 *unlearned.* Perhaps those untaught or disbelievers concerning the ministry of the Holy Spirit. *unbelievers.* Those who have made no movement toward saving faith. The context is a meeting of the church in which everyone is speaking in tongues with the result that general confusion reigns. *ye are mad.* The visitors will be repulsed by the confusion, and the phenomenon meant to be an impressive sign will have a negative effect on the unsaved.

learned, or unbelievers, [a]will they not say that ye are mad?

24 But if all prophesy, and there come in one that believeth not, or *one* unlearned, he is convinced of all, he is judged of all:

25 And thus are the secrets of his heart made manifest; and so falling down on *his* face he will worship God, and report [a]that God is in you of a truth.

The use of spiritual gifts

26 ¶ How is it then, brethren? when ye come together, every one of you hath a psalm, [a]hath a doctrine, hath a tongue, hath a revelation, hath an interpretation. [b]Let all *things* be done unto edifying.

27 If any *man* speak in an *unknown* tongue, *let it be* by two, or at the most *by* three, and *that* by course; and let one interpret.

28 But if there be no interpreter, let him keep silence in the church; and let him speak to himself, and to God.

29 Let the prophets speak two or three, and [a]let the other judge.

30 If *any thing* be revealed to another that sitteth *by,* [a]let the first hold his peace.

31 For ye may all prophesy one by one, that all may learn, and all may be comforted.

32 And [a]the spirits of the prophets are subject to the prophets:

33 For God is not *the author* of [1]confusion, but of peace, [a]as in all churches of the saints.

34 ¶ [a]Let your women keep silence in the churches: for it is not permitted unto them to speak; but *they are commanded* to be under obedience, as also saith the [b]law.

35 And if they will learn any *thing,* let them ask their husbands at home: for it is a shame for women to speak in the church.

36 What? came the word of God out from you? or came it unto you only?

37 [a]If any *man* think himself to be a prophet, or spiritual, let him acknowledge that *the things* that I write unto you are the commandments of the Lord.

38 But if any *man* be ignorant, let him be ignorant.

39 Wherefore, brethren, [a]covet to prophesy, and forbid not to speak with tongues.

40 [a]Let all *things* be done decently and in order.

The resurrection

15 Moreover, brethren, I declare unto you the gospel [a]which I preached unto you, which also you have received, and [b]wherein ye stand;

2 [a]By which also ye are saved, if ye [1]keep in memory [2]what I preached unto you, unless [b]ye have believed in vain.

14:23 [a]Acts 2:13
14:25 [a]Is. 45:14; Zech. 8:23
14:26 [a]ver. 6; ch. 12:8-10 [b]ch. 12:7; 2 Cor. 12:19; Eph. 4:12
14:29 [a]ch. 12:10
14:30 [a]1 Thes. 5:19,20
14:32 [a]1 John 4:1
14:33 [1]Gr. *tumult,* or, *unquietness* [a]ch. 11:16
14:34 [a]1 Tim. 2:11,12 [b]Gen. 3:16
14:37 [a]2 Cor. 10:7; 1 John 4:6
14:39 [a]ch. 12:31; 1 Thes. 5:20
14:40 [a]ver. 33
15:1 [a]Gal. 1:11 [b]Rom. 5:2
15:2 [1]Or, *hold fast* [2]Gr. *by what speech* [a]Rom. 1:16; ch. 1:21 [b]Gal. 3:4

14:24 *all prophesy.* Prophecy, spoken in the vernacular language and intended for believers, turns out to have a positive effect on unbelievers because they hear and understand and are convicted of their sins. (Yet see restrictions on prophesying in vv. 29–32 and notes there.)

14:26–27 *every one . . . any man . . . one.* The stress here is again on the diversity and yet complementary nature of spiritual gifts. It is also apparent that every member could participate, not just certain leaders or officers.

14:26 *a psalm . . . a doctrine . . . a tongue . . . a revelation . . . an interpretation.* Elements that made up the worship service at Corinth. Some of these elements (the hymn and the word of instruction) came from OT and synagogue worship (cf. Mat 26:30; Luke 4:16–22). All parts of Christian worship should be edifying to the church.

14:27–28 Three restrictions are placed on speaking in a tongue "in the church" (v. 28): 1. Only two or three should do so in a meeting. 2. They should do so one at a time. 3. There must be interpretation.

14:28 *let him keep silence.* The implication seems to be that it was up to the one speaking in a tongue in the Corinthian church to make certain that there was in the audience someone to interpret his message.

‡14:29 *Let the prophets speak two or three.* Apparently in turn (v. 31), as with the tongues-speakers (v. 27). *judge.* The prophets and others who had the gift of discerning the spirits (12:10) were to decide whether the messages of their fellow prophets were valid (see note on v. 32).

‡14:30 *If any thing be revealed.* Not an inspired revelation intended to become a part of written Scripture. In OT times, Scriptural revelation came through prophets, and in NT times through apostles or close associates of apostles. Prophecy referred to in chs. 12–14 could come through any member of the church (vv. 26,29–31). It could be a prediction (Agabus, Acts 11:28; 21:10–11), a divine directive (Acts 13:1–2) or a message from God designed to edify, exhort or console (v. 3).

14:32 *subject to the prophets.* Prophecy (and tongues as well) was not an uncontrollable emotional ecstasy. Paul insists that these gifts should be controlled by the recipients themselves (vv. 15, 26–32). See notes on vv. 27–29.

14:33 *God . . . of peace.* See note on 1 Thes 5:23. *confusion.* Paul was concerned that disorderly and unregulated worship at Corinth would bring discredit on the name of the God who had called them in Christ to peace and unity. *in all the churches of the saints.* A unique expression in the NT that stresses the universality and commonality of the whole visible church of God on earth. All congregations are to obey the directives that follow.

‡14:34–35 It seems best to understand vv. 34–35 in the light of the immediate context—verses 29–33. God gave to women the gift of prophesying (11:5; Acts 2:17; 21:9) but not ruling authority over men (1 Tim 2:11–12).

14:36 Paul asks these rhetorical questions sarcastically, suggesting that the Corinthians were following their own practice in these matters rather than conforming to God's word.

14:37 *commandments of the Lord.* Paul's commands are the Lord's commands and are to be followed. In a situation where so much stress was being placed on gifts, Paul insists that any genuinely gifted person will recognize the apostle's God-given authority.

‡14:38 *let him be ignorant.* Or, "one who disregards or does not recognize this." Paul and the churches will ignore such a disobedient person, and so he will be regarded as an unbeliever.

14:39 *forbid not to speak with tongues.* Paul's solution to the tongues problem in the Corinthian church was not to forbid tongues, but to correct the improper use of the gift.

14:40 *decently and in order.* As spelled out in vv. 26–35.

15:2 *if ye keep in memory.* See note on Heb 3:14. *believed in vain.* If you are not persevering in the Christian faith, this is an evidence that you did not have saving faith in the first place (cf. Judas Iscariot, who eventually showed that he was not a true believer).

3 For [a]I delivered unto you first *of all* that
[b]which I also received, how that Christ died
for our sins [c]according to the scriptures;
4 And that he was buried, and that he rose
again the third day [a]according to the scriptures:
5 [a]And that he was seen of Cephas, then
[b]of the twelve:
6 After that, he was seen of above five hundred brethren at once; of whom the greater
part remain unto this present, but some are
fallen asleep.
7 After that, he was seen of James; then [a]of
all the apostles.
8 [a]And last of all he was seen of me also, as
of [1]one born out of due time.
9 For I am [a]the least of the apostles, that
am not meet to be called an apostle, because [b]I
persecuted the church of God.
10 But [a]by the grace of God I am what I
am: and his grace which was *bestowed* upon
me was not in vain; but [b]I laboured more
abundantly than they all: [c]yet not I, but the
grace of God which was with me.
11 Therefore whether *it were* I or they, so
we preach, and so ye believed.
12 ¶ Now if Christ be preached that he rose
from the dead, how say some among you that
there is no resurrection of the dead?
13 But if there be no resurrection of the
dead, [a]then is Christ not risen:
14 And if Christ be not risen, then *is* our
preaching vain, and your faith *is* also vain.
15 Yea, and we are found false witnesses of
God; because [a]we have testified of God that he
raised up Christ: whom he raised not up, if so
be that the dead rise not.
16 For if the dead rise not, then is not
Christ raised:
17 And if Christ be not raised, your faith *is*
vain; [a]ye are yet in your sins.
18 Then they also which are fallen asleep
in Christ are perished.
19 [a]If in this life only we have hope in
Christ, we are of all men most miserable.
20 But now [a]is Christ risen from the dead,
and become [b]the firstfruits of them that slept.
21 For [a]since by man *came* death, [b]by man
came also the resurrection of the dead.
22 For as in Adam all die, even so in Christ
shall all be made alive.

15:3 [a]ch. 11:2,23 [b]Gal. 1:12 [c]Ps. 22:15; Is. 53:5,6; Dan. 9:26; Zech. 13:7; Luke 24:26,46; Acts 3:18; 26:23; 1 Pet. 1:11; 2:24
15:4 [a]Ps. 16:10; Is. 53:10; Hos. 6:2; Luke 24:26; Acts 2:25; 1 Pet. 1:11
15:5 [a]Luke 24:34 [b]Mat. 28:17; Mark 16:14; Luke 24:36; John 20:19
15:7 [a]Luke 24:50; Acts 1:3,4
15:8 [1]Or, *an abortive* [a]Acts 9:4; 22:14,18
15:9 [a]Eph. 3:8 [b]Acts 8:3; Phil. 3:6
15:10 [a]Eph. 3:7,8 [b]2 Cor. 11:23; 12:11 [c]Mat. 10:20; Rom. 15:18; 2 Cor. 3:5; Gal. 2:8; Eph. 3:7; Phil. 2:13
15:13 [a]1 Thes. 4:14
15:15 [a]Acts 2:24; 4:10,33
15:17 [a]Rom. 4:25
15:19 [a]2 Tim. 3:12
15:20 [a]1 Pet. 1:3 [b]Acts 26:23; Rev. 1:5
15:21 [a]Rom. 5:12 [b]John 11:25; Rom. 6:23

15:3–5 Two lines of evidence for the death and resurrection of Christ are given here: (1) the testimony of the OT (e.g., Ps 16:8–11; Is 53:5–6,11) and (2) the testimony of eyewitnesses (Acts 1:21–22). Six resurrection appearances are listed here. The Gospels give more.

15:3 *I delivered unto you first of all that which I also received.* Here Paul links himself with early Christian tradition. He was not its originator, nor did he receive it directly from the Lord. His source was other Christians. The verbs he uses are technical terms for receiving and transmitting tradition (see note on 11:23). What follows is the heart of the gospel: that Christ died for our sins (not for His own sins; cf. Heb 7:27), that He was buried (confirmation that He had really died) and that He was raised from the dead.

‡15:4 *the third day.* Cf. Mat 12:40. The Jews counted parts of days as whole days. Thus the three days would include part of Friday afternoon, all of Saturday, and Sunday morning. A similar way of reckoning time is seen in John 20:26 ("after eight days," NASB "a week later"); two Sundays are implied, one at each end of the expression.

15:5 *Cephas . . . the twelve.* The appearance to Peter is the one mentioned in Luke 24:34, which occurred on Easter Sunday. The appearance to the twelve seems to have taken place on Sunday evening (see Luke 24:36–43; John 20:19–23). "The twelve" seems to have been used to refer to the group of original apostles, even though Judas was no longer with them (notice, however, that the 11 disciples, the 11 apostles or "the eleven" are referred to in Mat 28:16; Mark 16:14; Luke 24:9,33; Acts 1:26).

15:6 *above five hundred . . . at once.* The appearance to this large group may be mentioned to help bolster the faith of those Corinthians who evidently had some doubts about the resurrection of Christ (cf. v. 12). This appearance may be the one in Galilee recorded in Mat 28:10,16–20, where the eleven and possibly more met the risen Lord. *some are fallen asleep.* A common expression at that time for physical death (cf. Acts 7:60).

‡15:7 *James.* Since this James is listed in addition to the apostles, he is not James son of Zebedee or James son of Alphaeus (Mat 10:2–3). This is James, the half-brother of Jesus (Mat 13:55), who did not believe in Christ before the resurrection (John 7:5) but afterward joined the apostolic band (Acts 1:14) and later became prominent in the Jerusalem church (Acts 15:13). It is not clear in Scripture when and where this appearance to James occurred. *all the apostles.* For example, Acts 1:6–11.

15:8 *last of all.* See Acts 9:1–8. This appearance to Paul came several years after the resurrection (perhaps C.A.D. 33). *one born out of due time.* Paul was not part of the original group of apostles. He had not lived with Christ as the others had. His entry into the apostolic office was not at the same time ("untimely") as the others. Furthermore, at his conversion he was abruptly snatched from his former way of life (Acts 9:3–6).

15:9 *church of God.* In persecuting the church, he was actually persecuting Christ (see Acts 9:4–5).

‡15:12–19 Some at Corinth were saying that there was no resurrection of the body, and Paul draws a number of conclusions from this false contention. If the dead do not rise from the grave, then (1) "is Christ not risen" (v. 13); (2) "is our preaching vain" (v. 14); (3) "your faith is also vain" (v. 14); (4) we are "false witnesses" that God raised Christ from the dead (v. 15); (5) "your faith is vain" (v. 17); (6) "ye are yet in your sins" (v. 17) and still carry the guilt and condemnation of sin; (7) "they also which are fallen asleep [have died] in Christ are perished" (v. 18); and (8) "we are . . . most miserable" who "in this life only . . . have hope in Christ" (v. 19) and put up with persecution and hardship.

15:12 *he rose from the dead.* Christ was raised historically on the third day. Paul uses this same verb form (that expresses the certainty of Christ's bodily resurrection) a total of seven times in this passage (vv. 4,12–14,16–17,20).

15:20 *now is Christ risen.* Paul's categorical conclusion based on his evidence set forth in vv. 3–8. *firstfruits.* The first sheaf of the harvest given to the Lord (Lev 23:10–11,17,20) as a token that all the harvest belonged to the Lord and would be dedicated to Him through dedicated lives. So Christ, who has been raised, is the guarantee of the resurrection of all of God's redeemed people (cf. 1 Thes 4:13–18).

‡15:21 *by man came death.* Through Adam (Gen 3:17–19). *by man came also the resurrection of the dead.* Through Christ, the second Adam, "the last Adam" (v. 45; cf. Rom 5:12–21).

15:22 *in Adam all die.* All who are "in Adam"—i.e., his de-

23 But [a]every man in his own order: Christ the firstfruits; afterward they that are Christ's at his coming.

24 Then *cometh* the end, when he shall have delivered up [a]the kingdom to God, even the Father; when he shall have put down all rule and all authority and power.

25 For he must reign, [a]till he hath put all enemies under his feet.

26 [a]The last enemy *that* shall be destroyed *is* death.

27 For he [a]hath put all *things* under his feet. But when *he* saith, all *things* are put under *him, it is* manifest that he is excepted, which did put all *things* under him.

28 [a]And when all *things* shall be subdued unto him, then [b]shall the Son also himself be subject unto him that put all *things* under him, that God may be all in all.

29 Else what shall they do which are baptized for the dead, if the dead rise not at all? why are they then baptized for the dead?

30 And [a]why stand we in jeopardy every hour?

31 I protest by [a][1]your rejoicing which I have in Christ Jesus our Lord, [b]I die daily.

32 If [1]after the manner of men [a]I have fought with beasts at Ephesus, what advantageth it me, if the dead rise not? [b]let us eat and drink; for to morrow we die.

33 Be not deceived: [a]evil communications corrupt good manners.

34 [a]Awake to righteousness, and sin not: [b]for some have not the knowledge of God: [c]I speak *this* to your shame.

35 ¶ But some *man* will say, [a]How are the dead raised up? and with what body do they come?

36 *Thou* fool, [a]*that* which thou sowest is not quickened, except it die:

37 And *that* which thou sowest, thou sowest not that body that shall be, but bare grain, it may chance of wheat, or of some other *grain:*

38 But God giveth it a body as it hath pleased him, and to every seed his own body.

39 All flesh *is* not the same flesh: but *there is* one *kind of* flesh of men, another flesh of beasts, another of fishes, *and* another of birds.

15:23 [a]1 Thes. 4:15
15:24 [a]Dan. 7:14
15:25 [a]Ps. 110:1; Acts 2:34; Eph. 1:22
15:26 [a]2 Tim. 1:10; Rev. 20:14
15:27 [a]Ps. 8:6
15:28 [a]Phil. 3:21 [b]ch. 3:23; 11:3
15:30 [a]2 Cor. 11:26; Gal. 5:11
15:31 [1]Some read, *our* [a]1 Thes. 2:19 [b]Rom. 8:36; 2 Cor. 4:10
15:32 [1]Or, to speak *after the manner of men* [a]2 Cor. 1:8 [b]Eccl. 2:24; Is. 22:13; Luke 12:19
15:33 [a]ch. 5:6
15:34 [a]Rom. 13:11; Eph. 5:14 [b]1 Thes. 4:5 [c]ch. 6:5
15:35 [a]Ezek. 37:3
15:36 [a]John 12:24

scendants—suffer death. *in Christ shall all be made alive.* All who are "in Christ"—i.e., who are related to Him by faith—will be made alive at the resurrection (cf. John 5:25; 1 Thes 4:16–17; Rev 20:6).

15:23 *every man in his own order.* Christ, the firstfruits, was raised in His own time in history (c. A.D. 30), and those who are identified with Christ by faith will be raised at His second coming. His resurrection is the pledge that ours will follow.

15:24 *the end.* The second coming of Christ and all the events accompanying it. This includes His handing over the kingdom to the Father, following His destroying all dominion, authority and power of the persons and forces who oppose Him.

‡15:25 *For he must reign.* During this process of Christ's destroying all dominion and handing over the kingdom to the Father, Christ must reign (Rev 20:1–6). Some take this to mean that Christ will literally reign with His saints for 1,000 years on the earth (cf. Is 2:2–4; Mic 4:1–5). Others believe that this refers to Christ's reign over the course of history and in the lives of His people, who are spiritually raised, or born again. This "spiritual" reign is viewed as occurring during the present age. *under his feet.* An OT figure for complete conquest. Verse 25 is an allusion to Ps 110:1 (cf. Mat 22:44).

15:26 This destruction of death will occur at the end of the second-coming events after Christ conquers His enemies (Rev 19:11–21; 20:5–14), at the great white throne judgment (when death and Hades will be thrown into the lake of fire).

15:28 *the Son also himself be subject unto him.* The Son will be made subject to the Father in the sense that administratively, after He subjects all things to His power, He will then turn it all over to God the Father, the administrative head. This is not to suggest that the Son is in any way inferior to the Father. All three persons of the Trinity are equal in deity and in dignity. The subordination referred to is one of function (see note on 11:3). The Father is supreme in the Trinity; the Son carries out the Father's will (e.g., in creation, redemption); the Spirit is sent by the Father and the Son to vitalize life, communicate God's truth, apply His salvation to people and enable them to obey God's will (or word). *that God may be all in all.* The triune God will be shown to be supreme and sovereign in all things.

15:29 *they . . . which are baptized for the dead.* The present tense suggests that at Corinth people were currently being baptized for the dead. But because Paul does not give any more information about the practice, many attempts have been made to interpret the concept. Three of these are: 1. Living believers were being baptized for believers who died before they were baptized, so that they too, in a sense, would not miss out on baptism. 2. Christians were being baptized in anticipation of the resurrection of the dead. 3. New converts were being baptized to fill the ranks of Christians who had died. At any rate, Paul mentions this custom almost in passing, using it in his arguments substantiating the resurrection of the dead, but without necessarily approving the practice. Probably the passage will always remain obscure.

15:30 *why stand we in jeopardy every hour?* If there is no resurrection, why should we suffer persecution and privation for Christ every day (cf. 2 Cor 11:23–29)?

‡15:32 *I have fought with beasts at Ephesus.* This statement can be taken literally or figuratively. But since from Acts 19 we have no evidence of Paul suffering imprisonment and having to face the lions, it is more likely that the expression means that the enemies in Ephesus were as ferocious as wild beasts. *let us eat and drink; for to morrow we die.* See Is 22:13; a fitting philosophy of life if there is no resurrection.

15:33 A quotation from the Greek comedy *Thais* written by the Greek poet Menander, whose writings the Corinthians would know. The application of the quotation is that those who are teaching that there is no resurrection (v. 12) are the "bad company," and they are corrupting the "good morals" of those who hold to the correct doctrine. Cf. Prov 13:20.

15:34 *sin not.* The sin of denying that there is a resurrection and thus doubting even the resurrection of Christ, all of which had a negative effect on the lives they were living. *some have not the knowledge of God.* Even in the Corinthian church. This, Paul says, is a shameful situation.

15:35–49 In discussing the nature of the resurrection body, Paul compares it to plant life (vv. 36–38), to fleshly beings (v. 39) and to celestial and earthly physical bodies (vv. 40–41).

15:36–38 Plant organisms, though organized similarly in their own order, are different; the seed sown is related to the new plant that sprouts, but the new sprout has a different and genuinely new body that God has given it.

15:39 *All flesh is not the same.* Although there is much that is

40 *There are* also celestial bodies, and bodies terrestrial: but the glory of the celestial *is*
one, and the *glory* of the terrestrial *is* another.
41 *There is* one glory of the sun, and another glory of the moon, and another glory of
the stars: for *one* star differeth from *another*
star in glory.
42 [a]So also *is* the resurrection of the dead.
It is sown in corruption; it is raised in incorruption:
43 [a]It is sown in dishonour; it is raised in
glory: it is sown in weakness; it is raised in
power:
44 It is sown a natural body; it is raised a
spiritual body. There is a natural body, and
there is a spiritual body.
45 And so it is written, The first man Adam
[a]was made a living soul; [b]the last Adam *was
made* [c]a quickening spirit.
46 Howbeit *that was* not first *which is* spiritual, but *that which is* natural; *and* afterward
that which is spiritual.
47 [a]The first man *is* of the earth, [b]earthy:
the second man *is* the Lord [c]from heaven.
48 As *is* the earthy, such *are they* also *that
are* earthy: [a]and as *is* the heavenly, such *are
they* also *that are* heavenly.
49 And [a]as we have borne the image of the
earthy, [b]we shall also bear the image of the
heavenly.
50 ¶ Now this I say, brethren, that [a]flesh

15:42 [a]Dan. 12:3; Mat. 13:43
15:43 [a]Phil. 3:21
15:45 [a]Gen. 2:7 [b]Rom. 5:14 [c]John 5:21; Phil. 3:21; Col. 3:4
15:47 [a]John 3:31 [b]Gen. 3:19 [c]John 3:13
15:48 [a]Phil. 3:20
15:49 [a]Gen. 5:3 [b]Rom. 8:29; 2 Cor. 3:18; Phil. 3:21; 1 John 3:2
15:50 [a]Mat. 16:17; John 3:3,5
15:51 [a]1 Thes. 4:15 [b]Phil. 3:21
15:52 [a]Zech. 9:14; Mat. 24:31; John 5:25
15:53 [a]2 Cor. 5:4
15:54 [a]Is. 25:8; Rev. 20:14
15:55 [1]Or, *hell* [a]Hos. 13:14
15:56 [a]Rom. 4:15
15:57 [a]Rom. 7:25 [b]1 John 5:4
15:58 [a]2 Pet. 3:14 [b]ch. 3:8
16:1 [a]Acts 11:29; Gal. 2:10

and blood cannot inherit the kingdom of God;
neither doth corruption inherit incorruption.
51 Behold, I shew you a mystery; [a]We shall
not all sleep, [b]but we shall all be changed,
52 In a moment, in the twinkling of an eye,
at the last trump: [a]for the trumpet shall sound,
and the dead shall be raised incorruptible, and
we shall be changed.
53 For this corruptible must put on incorruption, and [a]this mortal *must* put on immortality.
54 So when this corruptible shall have put
on incorruption, and this mortal shall have put
on immortality, then shall be brought to pass
the saying that is written, [a]Death is swallowed
up in victory.
55 [a]O death, where *is* thy sting? O [1]grave,
where *is* thy victory?
56 The sting of death *is* sin; and [a]the
strength of sin *is* the law.
57 [a]But thanks *be* to God, which giveth us
[b]the victory through our Lord Jesus Christ.
58 [a]Therefore, my beloved brethren, be ye
stedfast, unmoveable, always abounding in the
work of the Lord, forasmuch as you know
[b]that your labour is not in vain in the Lord.

The collection for the poor

16 Now concerning [a]the collection for
the saints, as I have given order to
the churches of Galatia, even so do ye.

similar in the organizational character of fleshly beings, each species is different: man, animals, birds, fish.

15:40–41 Here the analogy involves inanimate objects of creation: the sun, moon and stars with their differing splendor, and the earthly bodies (possibly the great mountains, canyons and seas) with their splendor. In it all, God can take similar physical material and organize it differently to accomplish His purpose.

15:42–44 In applying these analogies, the apostle says that in the case of the resurrection of the dead, God will take a perishable, dishonorable, weak (and sinful) body—"a natural body" characterized by sin—and in the resurrection make it an imperishable, glorious, powerful body. "Spiritual body" does not mean a nonmaterial body but, from the analogies, a physical one similar to the present natural body organizationally, but radically different in that it will be imperishable, glorious and powerful, fit to live eternally with God. There is continuity, but there is also change.

15:44–49 The contrast here between the natural body and the spiritual body again follows from their two representatives (see notes on vv. 21–22). One is the first Adam, who had a natural body of the dust of the ground (Gen 2:7) and through whom a natural body is given to his descendants. The other is the last Adam, Christ, the life-giving spirit (cf. John 5:26) who through His death and resurrection will at the second coming give His redeemed people a spiritual body—physical, yet imperishable, without corruption, and adaptable to live with God forever (cf. Phil 3:21). It will be a body similar to Christ's resurrected, glorified physical body (cf. Luke 24:36–43).

15:46 Adam, the earthly man, and his descendants received natural, earthly bodies. Christ, the last Adam, the man from heaven who became incarnate in a human body, received a glorified, spiritual body following His resurrection. Similarly, His redeemed people will receive a spiritual body.

15:50 Paul's final argument about the resurrection of the body: God's redeemed people must have newly organized, imperishable bodies to live with him. "Flesh and blood" stands for perishable, corrupt, weak, sinful human beings.

15:51 *mystery.* Things about the resurrection body that were not understood but are now revealed (see note on Rom 11:25). *We shall not all sleep.* Some believers will not experience death and the grave. *we shall all be changed.* All believers, whether alive when Jesus comes again or in the grave, will receive changed, imperishable bodies.

‡15:52 *In a moment.* This passage parallels Paul's revelation in 1 Thes 4:13–18 of the snatching away (Rapture) of the church—living and dead—to meet the Lord in the air and remaining with Him forever.

15:56 *The sting of death is sin.* It was sin that brought us under death's power—it was Adam's sin that brought his death and ultimately ours (see Rom 5:12). *the strength of sin is the law.* The law of God gives sin its power, for it reveals our sin and condemns us because of our sin.

15:57 *victory through our Lord Jesus Christ.* Victory over the condemnation for sin that the law brought (v. 56) and over death and the grave (vv. 54–55), through the death and resurrection of Christ (cf. Rom 4:25).

15:58 *Therefore.* Because of Christ's resurrection and ours, we know that serving Him is not empty, useless activity. *your labour is not in vain in the Lord.* Our effort is invested in the Lord's winning cause. He will also reward us at His second coming (Mat 25:21; cf. Luke 19:17).

16:1 *Now concerning.* Again an answer to one of the questions of the Corinthians (cf. 7:1; 8:1; 12:1). *the saints.* God's people at Jerusalem (cf. v. 3; Rom 15:26). *churches of Galatia.* The fact that the Galatian and Macedonian churches (2 Cor 8:1; 9:1–4) are involved, along with the Corinthians, indicates that the collection of this offering was quite widespread. The Jerusalem saints may have become poverty-stricken because of the famine

2 [a]Upon the first *day* of the week let every
one of you lay by him in store, as *God* hath
prospered him, that there be no gatherings
when I come.
3 And when I come, [a]whomsoever you
shall approve by *your* letters, them will I send
to bring your [1]liberality unto Jerusalem.
4 [a]And if it be meet that I go also, they
shall go with me.

Paul's itinerary

5 Now I will come unto you, [a]when I shall
pass through Macedonia: for I do pass through
Macedonia.
6 And it may be that I will abide, yea, and
winter with you, that ye may [a]bring me on my
journey whithersoever I go.
7 For I will not see you now by the way;
but I trust to tarry a while with you, [a]if the
Lord permit.
8 But I will tarry at Ephesus until Pentecost.
9 For [a]a great door and effectual is opened
unto me, and [b]*there are* many adversaries.
10 Now [a]if Timotheus come, see that he
may be with you without fear: for [b]he worketh
the work of the Lord, as I also *do.*
11 [a]Let no *man* therefore despise him: but
conduct him forth [b]in peace, that he may come
unto me: for I look for him with the brethren.

16:2 [a]Acts 20:7
16:3 [1]Gr. *gift* [a]2 Cor. 8:19
16:4 [a]2 Cor. 8:19
16:5 [a]Acts 19:21; 2 Cor. 1:16
16:6 [a]Acts 15:3; Rom. 15:24
16:7 [a]Acts 18:21; Jas. 4:15
16:9 [a]Acts 14:27; 2 Cor. 2:12; Col. 4:3 [b]Acts 19:9
16:10 [a]Acts 19:22 [b]Phil. 2:20; 1 Thes. 3:2
16:11 [a]1 Tim. 4:12 [b]Acts 15:33

16:12 [a]ch. 1:12
16:13 [a]Mat. 24:42; 1 Thes. 5:6; 1 Pet. 5:8 [b]Phil. 1:27; 1 Thes. 3:8; 2 Thes. 2:15 [c]Eph. 6:10; Col. 1:11
16:14 [a]1 Pet. 4:8
16:15 [a]ch. 1:16 [b]Rom. 16:5 [c]2 Cor. 8:4; Heb. 6:10
16:16 [a]Heb. 13:17 [b]Heb. 6:10
16:17 [a]2 Cor. 11:9; Phil. 2:30

12 As touching *our* brother [a]Apollos, I
greatly desired him to come unto you with the
brethren: but *his* will was not at all to come at
this time; but he will come when he shall have
convenient time.

Concluding message

13 [a]Watch ye, [b]stand fast in the faith, quit
you like men, [c]be strong.
14 [a]Let all your *things* be done with charity.
15 ¶ I beseech you, brethren, (ye know
[a]the house of Stephanas, that it is [b]the firstfruits of Achaia, and *that* they have addicted
themselves to [c]the ministry of the saints,)
16 [a]That ye submit yourselves unto such,
and to every one that helpeth with *us,* and
[b]laboureth.
17 I am glad of the coming of Stephanas
and Fortunatus and Achaicus: [a]for that which
was lacking on your part they have supplied.
18 [a]For they have refreshed my spirit and
yours: therefore [b]acknowledge ye *them that
are* such.
19 The churches of Asia salute you. Aquila
and Priscilla salute you much in the Lord,
[a]with the church that is in their house.

16:18 [a]Col. 4:8 [b]Phil. 2:29 16:19 [a]Rom. 16:5

---

recorded in Acts 11:28 (c. A.D. 44 or 46), or because of the persecution of Jerusalem Christians (cf. Acts 8:1).

16:2 *Upon the first day of the week let every one of you lay by him in store.* Every Sunday each person was to bring what he had set aside for the Lord's work—an amount proportionate to his income. Since it was to be brought on Sunday, the new day for worship (cf. Acts 20:7; Rev 1:10), probably it was collected at the worship service, not at home. Justin Martyr indicates (in his *Apology,* 1.67–68) that in his time (c. A.D. 150) offerings were brought to the church on Sundays.

16:3 For proper financial accountability and responsibility these approved men would act as auditors and guardians of the funds the Corinthians gave (cf. 2 Cor 8:16–21).

16:4 *if it be meet that I go also.* Possibly to take care of important missionary business, or to be there to explain about the gift when it arrives.

16:5 *when I shall pass through Macedonia.* After leaving Ephesus (v. 8), where he was when he wrote 1 Corinthians, Paul planned to go up to Macedonia, no doubt to visit the Philippians and others in northern Greece, and then to Corinth. He had originally planned to go to Corinth first and then to Macedonia but thought it best to change his plans (see 2 Cor 1:12–2:4).

16:6 *winter with you.* Probably the three-month stay in Greece mentioned in Acts 20:3. *bring me on my journey.* With supplies and equipment, and certainly with prayers and goodwill. However, Paul had indicated earlier in the letter (9:7–12) that he did not want to be a financial burden to them.

16:8 *until Pentecost.* The 50th day (Pentecost means "50") after passover, when the Jews celebrated the feast of firstfruits (Lev 23:10–16)—late spring.

16:9 *many adversaries.* Probably a reference to the pagan craftsmen who made the silver shrines of Artemis and to the general populace whom they had stirred up (Acts 19:23–34).

16:10 *if Timotheus come.* In Acts 19:22 Paul sends Timothy (and Erastus) into Macedonia, after which Timothy was to go on to Corinth (1 Cor 4:17). *see that he may be with you without fear.* Timothy seems to have been somewhat timid (1 Tim 4:12; 2 Tim 1:7), and Paul wants the Corinthians to treat him kindly.

16:11 *brethren.* Possibly including Erastus (cf. Acts 19:22), who was a believer from Corinth and "city treasurer" (Rom 16:23; see note there).

‡16:12 *As touching . . . Apollos.* Lit. "now concerning." The Corinthians had asked Paul about Apollos and several other matters—each addressed in turn in this epistle (cf. the similar words, in 7:1; 8:1; 12:1; 16:1) and his coming to see them.

16:15 *house of Stephanas.* Evidently the Corinthians had little respect for this household that Paul had baptized (1:16). They were among the first converts in Achaia (Greece), along with the few individuals in Athens who had believed a short time earlier (Acts 17:34). *ministry.* The whole household of Stephanas was serving.

16:17 Probably the ones who had brought to the apostle the letter from the Corinthians referred to in 7:1. Their coming supplied "that which was lacking" from the Corinthians, i.e., the affection of these three brothers supplied the affection Paul desired from the whole Corinthian church.

16:18 *refreshed my spirit and yours.* Perhaps through their willingness to come to get Paul's advice and to bring it back to them. At least a new relationship between Paul and the Corinthians was in the making.

16:19 *of Asia.* The Roman province (presently in western Turkey) in which Ephesus and the surrounding cities were located (cf. Acts 19:10). During Paul's long ministry in Ephesus all in the province of Asia heard the word. The churches of Colosse, Laodicea and Hierapolis (cf. Col 4:13–16; Rev 1:11), which were located on the border of the province of Asia, may be included in the greetings, along with the other churches of Rev 2–3. *Aquila and Priscilla.* They had helped Paul found the church at Corinth (Acts 18:1–4). *much in the Lord.* Enthusiastically as fellow believers. *the church that is in their house.* Aquila and Priscilla had left Corinth with Paul and had gone to Ephesus (Acts 18:18–19). Evidently they were still there, and a church was meeting at their house; it now sends greetings.

20 All the brethren greet you. [a]Greet ye
one another with a holy kiss.
21 ¶ [a]The salutation of *me* Paul with mine
own hand.
22 If any *man* [a]love not the Lord Jesus
Christ, [b]let him be anathema, [c]Maran-atha.
23 [a]The grace of *our* Lord Jesus Christ *be*
with you.
24 My love *be* with you all in Christ Jesus.
Amen.

16:20 [a]Rom. 16:16
16:21 [a]Col. 4:18
16:22 [a]Eph. 6:24 [b]Gal. 1:8,9 [c]Jude 14,15
16:23 [a]Rom. 16:20

¶ The first *epistle* to the Corinthians was written from Philippi by Stephanas, and Fortunatus, and Achaicus, and Timotheus.

House churches were common in this early period (cf. Rom 16:3–5; Philem 2).

16:20 *holy kiss.* The kiss of mutual respect and love in the Lord was evidently the public practice of early Christians—from a practice that was customary in the ancient East. Such a practice may have been used in the first-century A.D. synagogue—men kissing men, and women kissing women—and it would have been natural for the practice to have been continued in the early Jewish-Gentile churches.

16:21 *salutation . . . with mine own hand.* Paul now signs this letter, as was his habit (see Col 4:18; Philem 19), a mark of the authenticity of the letter (2 Thes 3:17). Someone else had been penning the letter for him up to this point (cf. Rom 16:22).

16:22 *let him be anathema.* May this person experience God's displeasure and wrath, since he has declared himself an unbeliever (John 3:36). This is not a curse based on things God has created (e.g., heaven and earth), an oath that Jesus forbids. Rather, it is a curse based on God as witness to the unbeliever's essential lack of love and obedience to God (see also Gal 1:8–9). *Maran-atha.* An expression meaning "O Lord come!", used by the early church as a cry that the second coming of Christ may soon take place.

16:23 The apostle's usual benediction (see Gal 6:18; Eph 6:24; Phil 4:23); a longer Trinitarian benediction is found in 2 Cor 13:14.

16:24 Although he has been severe with the Corinthians, Paul wants them to know that he loves them as believers in Christ Jesus.

The Second Epistle of Paul the Apostle to the Corinthians

INTRODUCTION

Author

Paul is the author of this letter (see 1:1; 10:1). It is stamped with his style and it contains more autobiographical material than any of his other writings.

Date

The available evidence indicates that the year A.D. 55 is a reasonable estimate for the writing of this letter. From 1 Cor 16:5–8 we conclude that 1 Corinthians was written from Ephesus before Pentecost (in the spring) and that 2 Corinthians was written later that same year before the onset of winter. 2 Cor 2:13; 7:5 indicate that it was written from Macedonia.

Recipients

The opening salutation of the letter states that it was addressed to the church in Corinth and to the Christians throughout Achaia (the Roman province comprising all the territory of Greece south of Macedonia).

Purpose

The Corinthian church had been infiltrated by false teachers who were challenging both Paul's personal integrity and his authority as an apostle. Because he had announced a change in his itinerary, with the result that he would now pay the Corinthians one (long) visit instead of two (short) visits, these adversaries were asserting that his word was not to be trusted. They were also saying that he was not a genuine apostle and that he was putting into his own pocket the money they had collected for the poverty-stricken believers in Jerusalem. Paul asks the Corinthians to consider that his personal life in their midst was always honorable and that his life-transforming message of salvation was true. He urges them to prepare for his impending visit by completing the collection they had started a year previously and by dealing with the troublemakers in their midst. He warns them that he means what he writes.

Structure

The structure of the letter relates primarily to Paul's impending third visit to Corinth. The letter falls naturally into three sections:

1. Paul explains the reason for the change of itinerary (chs. 1—7).
2. Paul encourages the Corinthians to complete the collection in preparation for his arrival (chs. 8—9).
3. Paul stresses the certainty of his coming, his authenticity as an apostle and his readiness as an apostle to exercise discipline if necessary (chs. 10—13).

Unity

Some have questioned the unity of this letter (see note on 2:3–4), but it forms a coherent whole, as the structure (above) shows. Tradition has been unanimous in affirming its unity (the early church fathers, e.g., knew the letter only in its present form). Furthermore, none of the early Greek manuscripts breaks up the book.

Outline

- I. Primarily Apologetic: Paul's Explanation of His Conduct and Apostolic Ministry (chs. 1—7)
  - A. Salutation (1:1–2)
  - B. Thanksgiving for Divine Comfort in Affliction (1:3–11)
  - C. The Integrity of Paul's Motives and Conduct (1:12—2:4)

D. Forgiving the Offender at Corinth (2:5–11)
E. God's Direction in the Ministry (2:12–17)
F. The Corinthian Believers—a Letter from Christ (3:1–11)
G. Seeing the Glory of God with Unveiled Faces (3:12—4:6)
H. Treasure in Earthen Vessels (4:7–16a)
I. The Prospect of Death and What It Means for the Christian (4:16b—5:10)
J. The Ministry of Reconciliation (5:11—6:10)
K. A Spiritual Father's Appeal to His Children (6:11—7:4)
L. The Meeting with Titus (7:5–16)

II. Hortatory: The Collection for the Christians at Jerusalem (chs. 8—9)
A. Generosity Encouraged (8:1–15)
B. Titus and His Companions Sent to Corinth (8:16—9:5)
C. Results of Generous Giving (9:6–15)

III. Polemical: Paul's Vindication of His Apostolic Authority (chs. 10—13)
A. Paul's Defense of His Apostolic Authority and the Area of His Mission (ch. 10)
B. Paul Forced into Foolish Boasting (chs. 11—12)
C. Final Warnings (13:1–10)
D. Conclusion (13:11–14)

The God of all comfort

1 Paul, [a]an apostle of Jesus Christ by the
will of God, and Timothy *our* brother,
unto the church of God which is at Corinth,
[b]with all the saints which are in all Achaia:
2 [a]Grace *be* to you and peace from God our
Father, and *from* the Lord Jesus Christ.
3 ¶ [a]Blessed *be* God, even the Father of our
Lord Jesus Christ, the Father of mercies, and
the God of all comfort;
4 Who comforteth us in all our tribulation,
that we may be able to comfort them which
are in any trouble, by the comfort wherewith
we ourselves are comforted of God.
5 For as [a]the sufferings of Christ abound in
us, so our consolation also aboundeth by
Christ.
6 And whether we be afflicted, [a]*it is* for
your consolation and salvation, which [1]is effectual in the enduring of the same sufferings
which we also suffer: or whether we be comforted, *it is* for your consolation and salvation.
7 And our hope of you *is* stedfast, knowing,
that [a]as you are partakers of the sufferings, so
shall ye be also of the consolation.
8 For we would not, brethren, have you ignorant of [a]our trouble which came to us in
Asia, that we were pressed out of measure,
above strength, insomuch that we despaired
even of life:
9 But we had the [1]sentence of death in
ourselves, that we should [a]not trust in ourselves, but in God which raiseth the dead:
10 [a]Who delivered us from so great a
death, and doth deliver: in whom we trust that
he will yet deliver *us;*
11 You also [a]helping together by prayer for
us, that [b]for the gift *bestowed* upon us by the
means of many persons thanks may be given
by many on our behalf.

Paul's change of plans

12 ¶ For our rejoicing is this, the testimony
of our conscience, that in simplicity and [a]god-
ly sincerity, [b]not with fleshly wisdom, but by
the grace of God, we have had our conversation in the world, and more abundantly to you-
wards.
13 For we write none other *things* unto
you, than what you read or acknowledge; and
I trust you shall acknowledge even to the end;
14 As also you have acknowledged us in
part, [a]that we are your rejoicing, even as [b]ye
also *are* ours in the day of the Lord Jesus.
15 And in this confidence [a]I was minded
to come unto you before, that you might have
[b]a second [1]benefit;
16 And to pass by you into Macedonia, and
[a]to come again out of Macedonia unto you, and
of you to be brought on *my* way toward Judea.
17 When I therefore was thus minded, did
I use lightness? or *the things* that I purpose, do
I purpose [a]according to the flesh, that with me
there should be yea yea, and nay nay?
18 But *as* God *is* true, our [1]word toward
you was not yea and nay.

1:1 [a]1 Cor. 1:1; Eph. 1:1; Col. 1:1; 1 Tim. 1:1; 2 Tim. 1:1 [b]Phil. 1:1; Col. 1:2
1:2 [a]Rom. 1:7; 1 Cor. 1:3; Gal. 1:3; Phil. 1:2; Col. 1:2; 1 Thes. 1:1; 2 Thes. 1:2
1:3 [a]Eph. 1:3; 1 Pet. 1:3
1:5 [a]Acts 9:4; ch. 4:10
1:6 [1]Or, *is wrought* [a]ch. 4:15
1:7 [a]Rom. 8:17; 2 Tim. 2:12
1:8 [a]Acts 19:23; 1 Cor. 15:32; 16:9
1:9 [1]Or, *answer* [a]Jer. 17:5,7
1:10 [a]2 Pet. 2:9
1:11 [a]Rom. 15:30; Phil. 1:19; Philem. 22 [b]ch. 4:15
1:12 [a]ch. 2:17 [b]1 Cor. 2:4
1:14 [a]ch. 5:12 [b]Phil. 2:16; 1 Thes. 2:19
1:15 [1]Or, *grace* [a]1 Cor. 4:19 [b]Rom. 1:11
1:16 [a]1 Cor. 16:5,6
1:17 [a]ch. 10:2
1:18 [1]Or, *preaching*

1:1 *apostle.* One specially commissioned by Christ (see notes on Mark 6:30; 1 Cor 1:1; Heb 3:1). *Timothy.* Evidently with Paul when this letter was written, but not necessarily a co-author. *our brother.* Our fellow believer, our brother in Christ (cf. Acts 9:17; Heb 2:11). *church of God.* The community of believers, the local representatives of the universal church (see note on 1 Cor 1:2). *saints.* Another term for God's people; it means "those who have been set apart as holy to the Lord" (see note on Rom 1:7). *Achaia.* Greece, as distinct from Macedonia in the north. Though the letter deals particularly with the situation in Corinth, it was also intended for Christians elsewhere in Greece. Presumably copies of the letter would be made in Corinth and circulated to them.
1:2 *Grace be to you and peace.* See notes on Jonah 4:2; John 14:27; 20:19; Gal 1:3; Eph 1:2.
1:3 *God.* The source of our comfort. *comfort.* Consolation and encouragement. This comfort flows to believers when they suffer for Jesus' sake, and it equips them to comfort others who are in trouble (vv. 4–7).
1:8 *our trouble.* Throughout this letter Paul uses the editorial plural (we, us, our, ourselves). Except where the context plainly indicates otherwise, these plurals should be understood as referring to Paul alone. *Asia.* The Roman province of that name in western Asia Minor, now Turkish territory. The precise location where Paul's hardships occurred is not given, nor is the nature of affliction.
1:9 Paul's hardships were so life-threatening that he regarded his survival and recovery as tantamount to being raised from the dead. *trust . . . in God.* A key principle of this letter. God's grace is all-sufficient, and our weakness is precisely the opportunity for His power to be displayed (cf. 12:9–10).
1:12 In defending his trustworthiness against the slanders being spread about him, Paul appeals to the witness of his own conscience and to the Corinthians' firsthand knowledge of his character. He had spent 18 months with them when he first came to Corinth (Acts 18:11), so they could not plead ignorance of his integrity.
1:13 In keeping with their knowledge of Paul's character, they can trust what he writes from a distance: He means what he says.
1:14 *in part.* Some in Corinth had allowed their confidence in Paul and his apostolic authority to be shaken by the false apostles who had penetrated their ranks. *day of the Lord Jesus.* His return (cf. 1 Thes 2:19–20).
1:15 *that you might have a second benefit.* Here and in v. 16 Paul refers to his change of itinerary. Originally he had planned to cross over by sea from Ephesus to Corinth, visiting the Corinthians before traveling north to Macedonia, and then, returning from Macedonia, to visit them a second time, thus giving them the benefit of two short visits. This was when he was on good terms with them. What probably occurred was that he paid them a quick visit directly from Ephesus, a visit he had not contemplated and one that he made "in heaviness" (2:1). That visit then gave rise to his letter that caused them sorrow (see 7:8–9).
1:17 *did I use lightness?* Paul's opponents in Corinth had been attempting to persuade the Christians there that this change of plan was evidence that his word was not to be trusted, that he was fickle and unreliable. The two rhetorical questions are in effect his denial that he acts lightly and that he says "Yes" and "No" at the same time so that it is impossible to know what he means. In any case, his plan to visit the Corinthians had not been abandoned; it had simply been modified.
1:18 *not yea and nay.* Paul now (vv. 18–20) appeals to the

19 For [a]the Son of God, Jesus Christ, who
was preached among you by us, *even* by me
and Silvanus and Timotheus, was not yea and
nay, [b]but in him was yea.
20 [a]For all the promises of God in him *are*
yea, and in him Amen, unto the glory of God
by us.
21 Now he which stablisheth us with you
in Christ, and [a]hath anointed us, *is* God;
22 Who [a]hath also sealed us, and [b]given
the earnest of the Spirit in our hearts.
23 ¶ Moreover [a]I call God for a record upon
my soul, [b]that to spare you I came not as yet
unto Corinth.
24 Not for [a]that we have dominion over
your faith, but are helpers of your joy: for [b]by
faith ye stand.

2 But I determined this with myself,
[a]that *I* would not come again to you in
heaviness.
2 For if I make you sorry, who is he then
that maketh me glad, but *the same* which is
made sorry by me?
3 And I wrote this same unto you, lest,
when I came, [a]I should have sorrow from *them*
of whom I ought to rejoice; [b]having confidence
in you all, that my joy is *the joy* of you all.
4 For out of much affliction and anguish of
heart I wrote unto you with many tears; [a]not
that you should be grieved, but that ye might
know the love which I have more abundantly
unto you.

1:19 [a]Mark 1:1; Luke 1:35; Acts 9:20 [b]Heb. 13:8
1:20 [a]Rom. 15:8
1:21 [a]1 John 2:20
1:22 [a]Eph. 4:30; 2 Tim. 2:19; Rev. 2:17 [b]ch. 5:5; Eph. 1:14
1:23 [a]Rom. 1:9; ch. 11:31; Gal. 1:20; Phil. 1:8 [b]1 Cor. 4:21; ch. 2:3; 12:20; 13:2,10
1:24 [a]1 Cor. 3:5; 1 Pet. 5:3 [b]Rom. 11:20; 1 Cor. 15:1
2:1 [a]ch. 1:23
2:3 [a]ch. 12:21 [b]ch. 8:22; Gal. 5:10
2:4 [a]ch. 7:8,9
2:5 [a]1 Cor. 5:1 [b]Gal. 4:12
2:6 [1]Or, *censure* [a]1 Cor. 5:4,5; 1 Tim. 5:20
2:7 [a]Gal. 6:1
2:9 [a]ch. 10:6
2:10 [1]Or, *in the sight*
2:12 [a]Acts 16:8 [b]1 Cor. 16:9
2:13 [a]ch. 7:5,6

Forgiveness of an offender

5 ¶ But [a]if any have caused grief, he hath
not [b]grieved me, but in part: that I may not
overcharge you all.
6 Sufficient to such *a man is* this [1]punish-
ment, which *was inflicted* [a]of many.
7 [a]So that contrariwise ye *ought* rather to
forgive *him,* and comfort *him,* lest perhaps
such a one should be swallowed up with overmuch sorrow.
8 Wherefore I beseech you that *you* would
confirm *your* love towards him.
9 For to this end also did I write, that I
might know the proof of you, whether ye be
[a]obedient in all *things.*
10 To whom ye forgive any *thing,* I *forgive*
also: for if I forgave any *thing,* to whom I forgave *it,* for your sakes *forgave I it* [1]in the person of Christ;
11 Lest Satan should get an advantage of
us: for we are not ignorant of his devices.

Ministers of the new testament

12 ¶ Furthermore, [a]when I came to Troas
to *preach* Christ's gospel, and [b]a door was
opened unto me of the Lord,
13 [a]I had no rest in my spirit, because I
found not Titus my brother: but taking my
leave of them, I went from *thence* into Macedonia.
14 Now thanks *be* unto God, which always
causeth us to triumph in Christ, and maketh

gospel message he had preached to them: Believing it, they had found it to be altogether true and entirely free from ambiguity, and by their experience of its dynamic power they had proved it to be one great affirmative in Christ, in whom all God's promises are "Yes."

1:20 *Amen.* The "Amen" uttered by the congregation at the end of an offering of prayer or praise (cf. 1 Cor 14:16).

1:22 *sealed.* See notes on Hag 2:23; Eph 1:13; cf. Eph 4:30. *earnest.* A part given as a guarantee that the whole will be forthcoming. The part is of the same kind as the whole. The first installment of a sum of money that has been inherited, e.g., assures the recipient that the whole will be received. This justifies the expansion of a single Greek word into several English words: "a deposit, guaranteeing what is to come."

1:23 *to spare you.* Paul's change of plans for visiting the Corinthian Christians had been motivated, not by a fickle and insensitive attitude, but by love and concern for them.

‡2:1 *come again . . . in heaviness.* Paul had already made one painful visit to Corinth, and he wanted to avoid another such visit, though he was ready to exert his authority should it prove necessary (cf. 13:2). The occasion of this former painful visit is not known to us. It could not have been his original visit to Corinth at the time when the church there was founded in response to the preaching of the gospel. Therefore he must have paid a second visit, which is confirmed by 12:14; 13:1, where he states that the visit he is now about to make will be his third. The second visit probably took place between the writing of 1 and 2 Corinthians, though some hold that it occurred before 1 Corinthians was written, for Paul revisited the churches of the first journey shortly after he had started them (see Acts 14:21-23; 16:1-5) but had not had the opportunity to revisit Corinth until his three-year stay in Ephesus.

‡2:3–4 *I wrote . . . you . . . out of much affliction and anguish.* This passage refers to a previous letter that had been sent to the Corinthians. The consensus of the church from the earliest times has been that this previous letter is 1 Corinthians. In more recent times, however, the hypothesis that the reference is to an intermediate letter, written after 1 Corinthians and before 2 Corinthians, has been widely accepted.

2:5–11 Speaks of a particular person who has been the cause of serious offense in Corinth and upon whom church discipline has been imposed. Paul admonishes the Corinthians that because the offender has shown genuine sorrow and repentance for his sin the punishment should be discontinued and he should be lovingly restored to their fellowship. Church discipline, important as it is, should not be allowed to develop into a form of graceless rigor in which there is no room for pardon and restoration. The offense in question probably took place during Paul's intermediate visit to Corinth (see note on v. 1) and was the occasion for his writing the severe letter demanding the punishment of the offender (see note on vv. 3–4). Another view is that Paul refers to the incident recorded in 1 Cor 5.

‡2:12 *when I came to Troas.* Paul had traveled up from Ephesus to Troas, a city on the Aegean coast, hoping to find Titus there and to receive news from him about the Corinthian church. But Titus, who presumably Paul knew would be following the same route in reverse, did not arrive in Troas; so Paul, anxious for news from Corinth, "went . . . into Macedonia" (v. 13), perhaps to the city of Philippi.

2:13 *my brother.* Cf. 8:23. Paul held Titus in high esteem; he entrusted Titus with the organization of the collection of funds in Corinth for the relief of the poverty-stricken Christians of Jerusalem (8:6), and he chose him to bear this letter to the Corinthian Christians (8:16–17).

2:14 At this point Paul breaks off the narrative of his itinerary and in a characteristic manner allows his spontaneous spirit to

manifest [a]the savour of his knowledge by us in
every place.
15 For we are unto God a sweet savour of
Christ, [a]in them that are saved, and [b]in them
that perish:
16 [a]To the one *we are* the savour of death
unto death; and to the other the savour of life
unto life. And [b]who *is* sufficient for these
things?
17 For we are not as many, which [a] [1]corrupt
the word of God: but as [b]of sincerity, but as of
God, in the sight of God speak we [2]in Christ.

3 Do [a]we begin again to commend ourselves? or need we, as some *others,*
[b]epistles of commendation to you, or *letters* of
commendation from you?
2 [a]Ye are our epistle written in our hearts,
known and read of all men:
3 Forasmuch as ye are manifestly declared
to be the epistle of Christ [a]ministered by us,
written not with ink, but with the Spirit of the
living God; not [b]in tables of stone, but [c]in
fleshy tables of the heart.
4 And such trust have we through Christ to
God-ward:
5 [a]Not that we are sufficient of ourselves to
think any *thing* as of ourselves; but [b]our sufficiency *is* of God;
6 Who also hath made us able [a]ministers of
[b]the new testament; not [c]of the letter, but of
the spirit: for [d]the letter killeth, [e]but the spirit [1]giveth life.

A ministry of glory

7 But if [a]the ministration of death, [b]written
and engraven in stones, was glorious, [c]so that

2:14 [a]Sol. 1:3 **2:15** [a]1 Cor. 1:18 [b]ch. 4:3 **2:16** [a]Luke 2:34; John 9:39; 1 Pet. 2:7 [b]1 Cor. 15:10 **2:17** [1]Or, *deal deceitfully with* [2][Or, *of*] [a]2 Pet. 2:3 [b]ch. 1:12 **3:1** [a]ch. 5:12 [b]Acts 18:27 **3:2** [a]1 Cor. 9:2 **3:3** [a]1 Cor. 3:5 [b]Ex. 24:12 [c]Ps. 40:8; Ezek. 11:19; Heb. 8:10 **3:5** [a]John 15:5 [b]1 Cor. 15:10 **3:6** [1]Or, *quickeneth* [a]1 Cor. 3:5; Eph. 3:7; Col. 1:25 [b]Jer. 31:31; Mat. 26:28; Heb. 8:6,8 [c]Rom. 2:27 [d]Rom. 3:20; Gal. 3:10 [e]John 6:63; Rom. 8:2 **3:7** [a]Rom. 7:10 [b]Ex. 34:1; Deut. 10:1 [c]Ex. 34:29

carry him into a lengthy digression (the narrative is not resumed until 7:5). The digression, however, is quite relevant to the main tenor of this letter, for it is an immensely rich outpouring of triumphant faith in praise of the unfailing adequacy of the grace of God for every conceivable situation, no matter how threatening and destructive it may seem to be. *causeth us to triumph.* The imagery is that of a Roman triumph in which the victorious general would lead his soldiers and the captives they had taken in festive procession, while the people watched and applauded and the air was filled with the sweet smell released by the burning of spices in the streets. So the Christian, called to spiritual warfare, is triumphantly led by God in Christ, and it is through Him that God spreads everywhere the "sweet savour" of the knowledge of Christ.

‡2:16 *savour of death . . . savour of life.* As the gospel aroma is released in the world through Christian testimony, it is always sweet-smelling, even though it may be differently received. The two ultimate categories of mankind are "them that are saved and . . . them that perish" (v. 15). To the latter, testifying Christians are the smell of death, not because the gospel message has become evil-smelling or death-dealing, but because in rejecting the life-giving grace of God unbelievers choose death for themselves. To those who welcome the gospel of God's grace, Christians with their testimony are the fragrance of life. *who is sufficient for these things?* For the answer see 3:5.

2:17 *we are not as many, which corrupt the word of God.* Paul is referring to false teachers who had infiltrated the Corinthian church. Such persons—themselves insincere, self-sufficient and boastful—artfully presented themselves in a persuasive manner, and their chief interest was to take money from gullible church members. Paul, by contrast, had preached the gospel sincerely and free of charge, taking care not to be a financial burden to the Corinthian believers (see 11:7–12; 1 Cor 9:7–15).

3:1 *Do we begin again to commend ourselves?* Paul is sensitive to the fact that virtually everything he wrote or said was liable to be twisted and used in a hostile manner by the false teachers in Corinth. *letters of commendation.* The appearance of vagrant impostors, who claimed to be teachers of apostolic truth, led to the need for letters of recommendation. Paul needed no such confirmation; but others, including the Corinthian intruders, did need authentication and, being themselves false, often resorted to unscrupulous methods for obtaining or forging letters of recommendation.

3:2 *known and read of all men.* Because of the power of the gospel demonstrated by their transformed lives.

3:3 *epistle of Christ.* Paul is no more than the instrument in the hands of the Master. *written not with ink.* As a parchment or papyrus document would be. *with the Spirit of the living God.* As though the Spirit were a substitute for ink! Ink fades and may easily be deleted or blocked out since it is no more than an inanimate fluid. But the Spirit of the living God is Himself life and therefore life-giving (v. 6), and the life He gives is eternal and without defect. *not in tables of stone.* As at Sinai (see note on v. 6). *in fleshy tables of the heart.* See Jer 31:33; Ezek 11:19; 36:26. Paul explains the significance of this contrast between the old and the new covenants in vv. 7–18.

3:5 *our sufficiency is of God.* Answers the question in 2:16: "who is sufficient for these things?"

‡3:6 *ministers of.* Those who serve the cause of (see Rom 15:16; Col 1:7; 4:7; 1 Tim 4:6). Paul will return to the theme of "this ministry" in 4:1. *new testament.* Here Paul takes up the theme suggested by the mention of "fleshy tables of the heart" (v. 3). See Heb 8–10 and note on Heb 7:22. Paul's reference to ministers of a new covenant in contrast to the "ministration of death" (v. 7) may have been occasioned by his opponents in Corinth who were Judaizers, perhaps those who claimed to be associated with Peter (1 Cor 1:12) and who are referred to as Hebrews in 11:22 (see note there). *the letter.* The "tables of stone" on which the letter of the law was originally written (see Ex 24:12; 31:18; 32:15–16). *the spirit.* The writing of the law "with the Spirit of the living God . . . in fleshy tables of the heart," which was the promise of the new covenant as foretold by the prophets (see Jer 31:31–34; 32:39–40; Ezek 11:19; 36:26). *the letter killeth, but the spirit giveth life.* Does not mean that the external, literal sense of Scripture is deadly or unprofitable while the inner, spiritual (mystical or mythical) sense is vital. "The letter" is synonymous with the law as an external standard before which all people, because they are lawbreakers, stand guilty and condemned to death. Therefore it is described as the "ministration of death" and the "ministration of condemnation" (vv. 7,9). On the other hand, the Spirit who gives life is the "Spirit of the living God" who, in fulfillment of the promise of the new covenant, writes that same law inwardly "in fleshy tables of the heart" (v. 3). He thus provides the believer with love for God's law, which previously he had hated, and with power to keep it, which previously he had not possessed.

‡3:7–18 Paul is defending his "ministry" of the new covenant in Christ (cf. v. 6; 4:1) and here compares the experiences of Moses, who mediated the old covenant of Sinai, and his own as a minister of the new covenant. But he now applies the word "ministry" to the law that was "written . . . in tables of stone" and to the Spirit, who writes "in fleshly tables of the heart" (v. 3). The point of comparison is the fading glory that shone on Moses' face and the ever-increasing glory reflected in the faces

the children of Israel could not stedfastly behold the face of Moses for the glory of his countenance; which *glory* was to be done away:

8 How shall not [a]the ministration of the spirit be rather glorious?

9 For if the ministration of condemnation *be* glory, much more doth the ministration [a]of righteousness exceed in glory.

10 For even that which was made glorious had no glory in this respect, by reason of the glory that excelleth.

11 For if that which is done away *was* glorious, much more that which remaineth *is* glorious.

12 Seeing then that we have such hope, [a]we use great [1]plainness of speech:

13 And not as Moses, [a]*which* put a vail over his face, that the children of Israel could not stedfastly look to [b]the end of that which is abolished:

14 But [a]their minds were blinded: for until this day remaineth the same vail untaken away in the reading of the old testament; which *vail* is done away in Christ.

15 But *even* unto this day, when Moses is read, the vail is upon their heart.

3:8 [a]Gal. 3:5
3:9 [a]Rom. 1:17
3:12 [1]Or, *boldness* [a]ch. 7:4; Eph. 6:19
3:13 [a]Ex. 34:33 [b]Rom. 10:4; Gal. 3:23
3:14 [a]Is. 6:10; Acts 28:26
3:16 [a]Ex. 34:34; Rom. 11:23 [b]Is. 25:7
3:17 [a]1 Cor. 15:45
3:18 [1]Or, *of the Lord the Spirit* [a]1 Cor. 13:12 [b]ch. 4:4,6 [c]Rom. 8:29
4:1 [a]ch. 3:6 [b]1 Cor. 7:25
4:2 [1]Gr. *shame* [a]ch. 2:17 [b]ch. 6:4,7 [c]ch. 5:11
4:3 [a]1 Cor. 1:18
4:4 [a]Eph. 6:12 [b]John 12:40 [c]ch. 3:8,9 [d]John 1:18; Heb. 1:3

16 Nevertheless [a]when *it* shall turn to the Lord, [b]the vail shall be taken away.

17 Now [a]the Lord is *that* Spirit: and where the Spirit of the Lord *is,* there *is* liberty.

18 But we all, with open face beholding [a]as in a glass [b]the glory of the Lord, [c]are changed *into* the same image from glory to glory, even as [1]by the Spirit of the Lord.

An honest and tried ministry

4 Therefore seeing we have [a]this ministry, [b]as we have received mercy, we faint not;

2 But have renounced the hidden *things* of [1]dishonesty, not walking in craftiness, [a]nor handling the word of God deceitfully; but [b]by manifestation of the truth [c]commending ourselves to every man's conscience in the sight of God.

3 But if our gospel be hid, [a]it is hid to them that are lost:

4 In whom [a]the god of this world [b]hath blinded the minds of them which believe not, lest [c]the light of the glorious gospel of Christ, [d]who is the image of God, should shine unto them.

of those who minister the new covenant. This contrast in regard to glory serves to highlight the temporary and inadequate character of the old covenant and the permanent and effective character of the new covenant.

3:7 *was glorious.* The law of the old covenant given at Sinai was in no way bad or evil; on the contrary, Paul describes it elsewhere as holy, righteous, good and spiritual (Rom 7:12,14). The evil is in the hearts and deeds of people who, as lawbreakers, bring upon themselves the condemnation of the law and the penalty of death—and the law engraved on stone could not purge away that evil. *glory of his countenance.* The glory of God surrounded the giving of the law and was reflected on the face of Moses when he descended from the mountain (see Ex 34:29–30).

3:8–9 *ministration of the spirit . . . ministration of righteousness.* The ministry of the Spirit gives life instead of death. "Righteousness" is here both objective (justification) and personal (sanctification).

3:11 *that which is done away.* Paul here applies the fading to the old covenant of Sinai, which was not to endure forever. In due course it was superseded by the unfading and much more glorious radiance belonging to the new covenant.

3:13 *Moses, which put a vail over his face.* See Ex 34:33–35. The purpose of the veil was to prevent the Israelites from seeing the fading of the glory.

‡3:14 *until this day remaineth the same vail.* The veil that prevented them from seeing the fading of the glory on Moses' face is still with them, preventing them from recognizing the temporary and inadequate character of the old covenant—a "veil" that is removed only in Christ. Only those who have received the new covenant in Christ have the power to see how the new covenant has transcended and replaced the old covenant—because of its greater glory.

‡3:17 *the Lord is that Spirit.* This statement should be linked with what was said at the end of v. 6: "the Spirit giveth life." It is only by turning to the Lord (v. 16) that the condemnation and the sentence of death pronounced by the law on the lawbreaker are annulled and replaced by the free life-giving grace of the new covenant. There is a close relationship between the Spirit of Christ and the Holy Spirit. Both are said to dwell in the believer (Rom 8:9; Gal 2:20). In Rom 8:9–10 the Spirit, the Spirit of God, the Spirit of Christ, and Christ all seem to be used interchangeably. Perhaps this is because the Holy Spirit proceeds from the Father and the Son, and the first two persons of the Trinity accomplish their purposes through the Spirit.

‡3:18 *with open face.* In contrast to Moses. *are changed into the same image from glory to glory.* Christ Himself is the glory of God in the fullness of its radiance (Heb 1:3); His is the eternal and unfading glory, which He had with the Father before the world began (John 17:5). We who believe are made partakers of this glory by being gradually transformed into the likeness of Christ. The reference here is to the process of Christian sanctification.

4:1 *this ministry.* See 3:6 and note. *we faint not.* When God through His mercy calls and commissions His servants, He also supplies the strength necessary for them to persevere in the face of hardships and persecutions.

4:2 *have renounced the hidden things of dishonesty.* Paul is referring to the false teachers in Corinth. By contrast, he is able to appeal to the conscience of every one of them and also to his integrity in the sight of God, because his practice was always that of setting forth the truth plainly, i.e., without veiling it or resorting to deception (cf. 1:12,18–24).

4:3 *if our gospel be hid.* See 3:13–18.

4:4 *god of this world.* The devil, who is the archenemy of God and the unseen power behind all unbelief and ungodliness. Those who follow him have in effect made him their god. *this world.* Used in contrast to the future eternal age when God's creation will be forever purged of all that now mars and defiles it. In Gal 1:4 it is called "this present evil world." *blinded the minds of them which believe not.* Paul continues to use the imagery of the veil that covers the divine glory so that those who reject the gospel fail to see that glory (3:12–18). *image of God.* Christ, who is both the incarnate Son and the Second Person of the Trinity, authentically displays God to us, for He is the very radiance of divine glory (Heb 1:3). He is the image of God in which man was originally created and into which redeemed mankind is being gloriously transformed (3:18), until at last,

5 [a]For we preach not ourselves, but Christ Jesus the Lord; and [b]ourselves your servants for Jesus' sake.

6 For God, [a]who commanded the light to shine out of darkness, [1]hath [b]shined in our hearts, to give [c]the light of the knowledge of the glory of God in the face of Jesus Christ.

7 ¶ But we have this treasure in [a]earthen vessels, [b]that the excellency of the power may be of God, and not of us.

8 *We are* [a]troubled on every *side,* yet not distressed; *we are* perplexed, but [1]not in despair;

9 Persecuted, but not forsaken; [a]cast down, but not destroyed;

10 [a]Always bearing about in the body the dying of the Lord Jesus, [b]that the life also of Jesus might be made manifest in our body.

11 For we which live [a]are alway delivered unto death for Jesus' sake, that the life also of Jesus might be made manifest in our mortal flesh.

12 So then [a]death worketh in us, but life in you.

13 We having [a]the same spirit of faith, according as it is written, [b]I believed, *and* therefore have I spoken; we also believe, and therefore speak;

4:5 [a]1 Cor. 1:13; 10:33 [b]1 Cor. 9:19
4:6 [1][Gr. is he *who hath*] [a]Gen. 1:3 [b]2 Pet. 1:19 [c]1 Pet. 2:9
4:7 [a]ch. 5:1 [b]1 Cor. 2:5
4:8 [1]Or, *not altogether without help,* or, *means* [a]ch. 7:5
4:9 [a]Ps. 37:24
4:10 [a]Phil. 3:10 [b]Rom. 8:17
4:11 [a]Rom. 8:36
4:12 [a]ch. 13:9
4:13 [a]2 Pet. 1:1 [b]Ps. 116:10
4:14 [a]Rom. 8:11; 1 Cor. 6:14
4:15 [a]Col. 1:24; 2 Tim. 2:10 [b]ch. 1:11
4:16 [a]Rom. 7:22; Col. 3:10
4:17 [a]Mat. 5:12; Rom. 8:18; 1 Pet. 1:6
4:18 [a]Rom. 8:24; Heb. 11:1
5:1 [a]Job 4:19
5:2 [a]Rom. 8:23
5:3 [a]Rev. 3:18

14 Knowing that [a]he which raised up the Lord Jesus shall raise up us also by Jesus, and shall present *us* with you.

15 For [a]all *things are* for your sakes, that [b]the abundant grace might through the thanksgiving of many redound to the glory of God.

16 For which cause we faint not; but though our outward man perish, yet [a]the inward *man* is renewed day by day.

17 For [a]our light affliction, which is but for a moment, worketh for us a far more exceeding *and* eternal weight of glory;

18 [a]While we look not at the *things* which are seen, but at the *things* which are not seen: for the *things* which are seen *are* temporal; but the *things* which are not seen *are* eternal.

A confident ministry

5 For we know that if [a]our earthly house of *this* tabernacle were dissolved, we have a building of God, a house not made with hand, eternal in the heavens.

2 For in this [a]we groan, earnestly desiring to be clothed upon with our house which is from heaven:

3 If so be that [a]being clothed we shall not be found naked.

when Christ comes again at the end of this age, we who believe will be like Him (1 John 3:2).

4:5 *we preach not ourselves.* As did the false teachers, puffed up with self-importance. Paul does not lord it over their faith (1:24), for there is only one Lord, Jesus Christ, and He is the theme of Paul's preaching.

4:6 *commanded the light to shine out of darkness.* God said this at the creation (Gen 1:2–4), and God says it again in the new creation or new birth (see 5:17; John 3:3,7; 1 Pet 1:3) as the darkness of sin is dispelled by the light of the gospel. *the light of the knowledge of the glory of God.* The light that now shines in Paul's heart (qualifying him to be a proclaimer of Christ) is the knowledge of the glory of God as it was displayed in the face of Christ—who has come, not just from an earthly tabernacle, but from the glorious presence of God in heaven itself (see John 1:14).

4:7 *this treasure.* The gospel. *earthen vessels.* It was customary to conceal treasure in clay jars, which had little value or beauty and did not attract attention to themselves and their precious contents. Here they represent Paul's human frailty and unworthiness. *excellency of the power may be of God, and not of us.* The idea that the absolute insufficiency of man reveals the total sufficiency of God pervades this letter.

4:10 *Always bearing about in the body the dying of the Lord Jesus.* The frailty of the "earthen vessel" of Paul's humanity (v. 7) is plainly seen in the constant hardships and persecutions with which he is buffeted for the sake of the gospel and through which he shares in Christ's suffering (see 1:5; Rom 8:17; Phil 3:10; Col 1:24).

4:11 *that the life also of Jesus might be made manifest in our mortal flesh.* The reference is to Christ's resurrection life and power. Once again (see note on v. 7), human weakness provides the occasion for the triumph of divine power, and daily "dying" magnifies the wonder of daily resurrection life (see 1:9).

4:13 *I believed, and therefore have I spoken.* Faith leads to testimony. Paul therefore tirelessly labored and journeyed to bring the gospel message to others.

4:16 *For which cause we faint not.* Repeating the statement in v. 1. The intervening paragraphs explain why the apostle continues to have a cheerful heart, and the remaining verses of the chapter summarize the argument he has developed. *perish.* Because of the hardships to which he is subjected. *is renewed.* Because of the inextinguishable flame of the resurrection life of Jesus burning within. Moreover, the inward renewal overcomes the outward destruction, and ultimately overcomes even death itself.

‡4:17 *light affliction, which is but for a moment.* Seen in the perspective of eternity, the Christian's difficulties, whatever they may be, diminish in importance. *for a moment . . . eternal weight of glory.* By comparison, the eternal glory is far greater than all the suffering one may face in this life (cf. Rom 8:18).

4:18 *things which are seen . . . things which are not seen.* The experiences and circumstances of this present life, often painful and perplexing, are what is visible to the Christian; but these are merely phenomena in the passing parade of our fallen age and are therefore temporary and fleeting. To fix our eyes on these visible things would cause us to lose heart (vv. 1,16). By contrast the unseen realities, which are no less real for being invisible (cf. Heb 11:1,7, 26–27), are eternal and imperishable. Accordingly, we look up and away from the impermanent appearances of this present world scene (see Phil 3:20; Heb 12:2).

5:1 *earthly house of this tabernacle.* Our present body (see 2 Pet 1:13). As a tent is a temporary and flimsy abode, so our bodies are frail, vulnerable and wasting away (4:10–12,16). *a building of God, a house . . . eternal in the heavens.* A solid structure—permanent, not temporary. This is one of the eternal realities that are as yet unseen (4:18). *not made with hands.* The work of God, and therefore perfect and permanent (see Heb 9:11).

5:2 *we groan.* Because we long for the perfection that will be ours when we put on the glorious spiritual body (cf. 1 Cor 15:42–49). *clothed upon with our house which is from heaven.* The eternal dwelling provided by God is pictured as something the Christian puts on like a garment.

5:3 *naked.* Without the clothing of a body, which is the state of those whose earthly tent-dwelling has been dismantled by death (see note on v. 8).

4 For we that are in *this* tabernacle do groan, being burdened: not for that we would be unclothed, but [a]clothed upon, that mortality might be swallowed up of life.

5 Now [a]he that hath wrought us for the selfsame *thing is* God, who also [b]hath given unto us the earnest of the Spirit.

6 Therefore *we are* always confident, knowing that, whilst we are at home in the body, we are absent from the Lord:

7 (For [a]we walk by faith, not by sight:)

8 We are confident, I say, and [a]willing rather to be absent from the body, and to be present with the Lord.

A reconciling ministry

9 ¶ Wherefore we [1]labour, that, whether present or absent, we may be accepted of him.

10 [a]For we must all appear before the judgment seat of Christ; [b]that every one may receive the *things done* in *his* body, according to that he hath done, whether *it be* good or bad.

11 Knowing therefore [a]the terror of the Lord, we persuade men; but [b]we are made manifest unto God; and I trust also are made manifest in your consciences.

12 For [a]we commend not ourselves again unto you, but give you occasion [b]to glory on our behalf, that you may have *somewhat* to *answer* them which glory [1]in appearance, and not in heart.

13 For [a]whether we be besides ourselves, *it is* to God: or whether we be sober, *it is* for your cause.

14 For the love of Christ constraineth us; because we thus judge, that [a]if one died for all, then were all dead:

15 And *that* he died for all, [a]that they which live should not henceforth live unto themselves, but unto him which died for them, and rose *again.*

16 [a]Wherefore henceforth know we no *man* after the flesh: yea, though we have known Christ after the flesh, [b]yet now henceforth know we *him* no more.

17 Therefore if any *man* [a]*be* in Christ, [1]*he is* [b]a new creature: [c]old *things* are past away; behold, all *things* are become new.

18 And all *things are* of God, [a]who hath

5:4 [a]1 Cor. 15:53
5:5 [a]Is. 29:23; Eph. 2:10 [b]Rom. 8:23; Eph. 1:14
5:7 [a]Rom. 8:24; Heb. 11:1
5:8 [a]Phil. 1:23
5:9 [1]Or, *endeavour*
5:10 [a]Rom. 14:10 [b]Gal. 6:7; Eph. 6:8; Rev. 22:12
5:11 [a]Heb. 10:31; Jude 23 [b]ch. 4:2
5:12 [1]Gr. *in the face* [a]ch. 3:1 [b]ch. 1:14
5:13 [a]ch. 11:1,16
5:14 [a]Rom. 5:15
5:15 [a]Rom. 6:11; 1 Cor. 6:19; Gal. 2:20
5:16 [a]Mat. 12:50; Col. 3:11 [b]John 6:63
5:17 [1]Or, let him be [a]Rom. 8:9 [b]Gal. 5:6 [c]Is. 65:17; Eph. 2:15; Rev. 21:5
5:18 [a]Rom. 5:10; Eph. 2:16; Col. 1:20

5:4 *mortality.* Our present mortal body. *swallowed up of life.* By our participation in the resurrection life of Jesus (4:10) our mortal being is swallowed up by life, not by death. Paul reverses the age-old imagery of death and the grave being the great swallower (see Ps 69:15; Prov 1:12), as did Isaiah (see Is 25:8; see also 1 Cor 15:54).

5:5 *God, who also hath given unto us . . . the Spirit.* The Holy Spirit, poured out by the risen and exalted Savior, applies the benefits of Christ's redeeming work to the believer's heart and makes the resurrection power of Jesus a reality of his daily experience (cf. 4:14,16). This guarantees his eventual total transformation into the likeness of Christ's glorified body (Phil 3:21). *earnest.* See note on 1:22.

5:6 *at home in the body . . . absent from the Lord.* Still living here in our earthly tent-dwelling (v. 1); it does not mean that we are deprived of the Lord's spiritual presence with us in our daily pilgrimage.

‡5:8 *absent from the body . . . present with the Lord.* The situation of the Christian after death, when he is no longer living in his "earthly house" (v. 1). This speaks of an intermediate state between death and resurrection. The believer who has died is at home with his Lord, and that is preferable to our present life in the body (cf. Phil 1:23). It is not clear whether the departed is "embodied" at this time, or awaits the resurrection body at the time of Christ's coming (cf. 1 Cor 15:51–53 and notes).

5:9 *whether present or absent.* Whether we will be alive or will have already died at His coming.

5:10 *appear before the judgment seat of Christ.* This accounting has nothing to do with justification, which is credited to the Christian fully and forever through faith in Christ; instead, it refers to what we have done with our lives as Christians (cf. 1 Cor 3:11–15). *things done in his body . . . that he hath done.* Although the body is wasting away, we are responsible for our actions while in it. Non-Christians, too, are morally responsible and liable to God's judgment (see Rom 2:5,16), but Paul has believers in mind here.

5:11 *terror of the Lord.* As the one to whom we are accountable (v. 10). *we persuade men.* Paul needs to persuade some members of the Corinthian church that he, not any of the false teachers who have invaded their ranks, is their authentic apostle.

5:12 *glory in appearance.* The pretension of the false apostles is a superficial front; their concern is not with spirituality that is true and deep, but with money and popularity and self-importance.

5:13 *besides ourselves . . . sober.* Probably Paul's enemies were asserting that he was suffering from religious mania, pointing perhaps to the sensational conversion he claimed to have experienced on the road to Damascus and to what they regarded as his insane way of life. If this is to be out of his mind, Paul does not deny it, for this whole letter shows how willingly and joyfully he endured affliction for the gospel (cf. 12:10). That, however, was essentially a matter between him and God. On the other hand, there was nothing that could be called eccentric about his manner of presenting the gospel to the Corinthians, for in this he had been, and continued to be, sensible and sober-minded, avoiding flowery rhetoric and all forms of sensationalism (cf. 1 Cor 2:1–5).

5:14 *love of Christ.* As shown in His death for us, though some hold that the meaning here is "our love for Christ." *one.* The incarnate Son. *for all.* For all mankind. *then were all dead.* Because Christ died for all, He involved all in His death. For some His death would confirm their own death, but for others (those who by faith would become united with Him) His death was their death to sin and self, so that they now live in and with the resurrected Christ (v. 15). However, some hold that Paul is not speaking specifically here about the scope of Christ's atonement but about the effect of Christ's death on the Christian life. Thus "all" would refer not to mankind in general but only to the church.

5:16 *we have known Christ after the flesh.* Paul is admitting that before his conversion he held views of Christ that were "according to the flesh"—based on purely human considerations.

5:17 *in Christ.* United with Christ through faith in Him and commitment to Him. *new creature.* Redemption is the restoration and fulfillment of God's purposes in creation (see note on 4:6), and this takes place in Christ, through whom all things were made (see John 1:3; Col 1:16; Heb 1:2) and in whom all things are restored or created anew (cf. Rom 8:18–23; Eph 2:10).

‡5:18 *all things are of God.* God takes the initiative in redemption (see Rom 5:8; John 3:16), and He sustains it and brings it to completion. *ministry of reconciliation.* We who are the re-

reconciled us to himself by Jesus Christ, and
hath given to us the ministry of reconciliation;
19 To wit, that [a]God was in Christ reconciling the world unto himself, not imputing
their trespasses unto them; and hath [1]commit-
ted unto us the word of reconciliation.
20 *Now* then we are [a]ambassadors for
Christ, as [b]though God did beseech *you* by us:
we pray *you* in Christ's stead, be ye reconciled
to God.
21 For [a]he hath made him *to be* sin for us,
who knew no sin; that we might be made [b]the
righteousness of God in him.

A suffering ministry

6 We then, *as* [a]workers together *with him,*
[b]beseech *you* also [c]that ye receive not
the grace of God in vain.
2 (For he saith, [a]I have heard thee in a
time accepted, and in the day of salvation have
I succoured thee: behold, now *is* the accepted
time; behold, now *is* the day of salvation.)
3 [a]Giving no offence in any *thing,* that the
ministry be not blamed:
4 But in all *things* [1]approving ourselves [a]as
the ministers of God, in much patience, in afflictions, in necessities, in distresses,
5 [a]In stripes, in imprisonments, [1]in tumults, in labours, in watchings, in fastings;
6 By pureness, by knowledge, by longsuffering, by kindness, by the Holy Ghost, by love
unfeigned,
7 [a]By the word of truth, by [b]the power of
God, by [c]the armour of righteousness on the
right hand and on the left,
8 By honour and dishonour, by evil report
and good report: as deceivers, and *yet* true;
9 As unknown, and [a]*yet* well known; [b]as
dying, and behold, we live; as [c]chastened, and
not killed;
10 As sorrowful, yet alway rejoicing; as
poor, yet making many rich; as having nothing, and *yet* possessing all *things.*

Believers are the temple of God

11 ¶ O *ye* Corinthians, our mouth is open
unto you, [a]our heart is enlarged.
12 Ye are not straitened in us, but [a]ye are
straitened in your own bowels.
13 Now for a recompence in the same, ([a]I
speak as unto *my* children,) be ye also enlarged.
14 [a]Be ye not unequally yoked together
with unbelievers: for [b]what fellowship hath
righteousness with unrighteousness? and
what communion hath light with darkness?
15 And what concord hath Christ with Belial? or what part hath he that believeth with
an infidel?
16 And what agreement hath the temple of
God with idols? for [a]ye are the temple of the
living God; as God hath said, [b]I will dwell in
them, and walk in *them;* and I will be their
God, and they shall be my people.
17 [a]Wherefore come out from among
them, and be ye separate, saith the Lord, and
touch not the unclean *thing;* and I will receive
you,

5:19 [1]Gr. *put in us* [a]Rom. 3:24
5:20 [a]Job 33:23; Mal. 2:7; Eph. 6:20 [b]ch. 6:1
5:21 [a]Is. 53:6,9; Gal. 3:13; 1 Pet. 2:22; 1 John 3:5 [b]Rom. 1:17; 10:3
6:1 [a]1 Cor. 3:9 [b]ch. 5:20 [c]Heb. 12:15
6:2 [a]Is. 49:8
6:3 [a]Rom. 14:13; 1 Cor. 9:12; 10:32
6:4 [1]Gr. *commending* [a]1 Cor. 4:1
6:5 [1]Or, *in tossings to and fro* [a]ch. 11:23
6:7 [a]ch. 7:14 [b]1 Cor. 2:4
6:7 [c]ch. 10:4; Eph. 6:11; 2 Tim. 4:7
6:9 [a]ch. 4:2; 5:11 [b]1 Cor. 4:9; ch. 1:9; 4:10,11 [c]Ps. 118:18
6:11 [a]ch. 7:3
6:12 [a]ch. 12:15
6:13 [a]1 Cor. 4:14
6:14 [a]Deut. 7:2,3; 1 Cor. 5:9 [b]1 Sam. 5:2,3; 1 Ki. 18:21; 1 Cor. 10:21; Eph. 5:7,11
6:16 [a]1 Cor. 3:16; 6:19; Eph. 2:21; Heb. 3:6 [b]Ex. 29:45; Lev. 26:12; Jer. 31:33; 32:38; Ezek. 11:20; Zech. 13:9
6:17 [a]Is. 52:11; Rev. 18:4

---

cipients of divine reconciliation have the privilege and obligation of now being, like Paul in a sense, the heralds and instruments in God's hands to minister the message of reconciliation throughout the world (v. 19).

5:21 *be sin.* Or "be a sin offering." *sin for us, who knew no sin.* A summary of the gospel and its logic. Christ, the only entirely righteous one, at Calvary took our sin upon himself and endured the punishment we deserved, namely, death and separation from God. Thus, by a marvelous exchange, He made it possible for us to receive His righteousness and thereby be reconciled to God. Our standing and our acceptance before God are solely in Him (cf. 1 Cor 1:30). Again, all this is God's doing; all this is freely available to us because of the initiative of divine grace.

6:1 *receive not the grace of God in vain.* To live for oneself (see 5:15) is one way to do this.

6:2 *the accepted time . . . the day of salvation.* An affirmation that is true in a general sense of all God's saving acts in the history of His people, but that finds its particular fulfillment in this present age of grace between the two comings of Christ. This understanding does not exclude from grace and salvation those who lived before Christ's coming, for the believers of the OT period received the promises that in due course were fulfilled in Christ (1:20) and they saw and welcomed their fulfillment from a distance (see John 8:56; Heb 11:13).

‡6:3 *Giving no offence in any thing.* Paul is concerned that he live an exemplary life because he does not want the ministry discredited.

6:4–10 Cf. 4:8–12.

6:4 *approving ourselves as the ministers of God.* Paul commends himself again inasmuch as the gospel he preached in Corinth is at stake; but, in contrast to the false apostles who were no better than self-servers, he does so as God's servant. His life, with all its trials and afflictions, could not have been more starkly different from that of these intruders whose concern was for their own comfort and prestige.

6:10 *making many rich.* In Christ. True wealth does not consist in worldly possessions but in being "rich toward God" (Luke 12:15,21). The believer, even if he has nothing of this world's goods, nevertheless has everything in Him who is Lord of all (cf. 1 Cor 1:4–5; 3:21–23; Eph 2:7; 3:8; Phil 4:19; Col 2:3).

6:11–13 Paul has always been completely open and sincere in his relations with the Christians in Corinth (cf. 1:12–14; 4:2), but the false apostles among them have been trying to persuade them that Paul does not really love them. Now the apostle tenderly appeals to these Corinthians, who are the beneficiaries of his love for them (cf. 11:11).

6:14 *Be ye not unequally yoked together with unbelievers.* Doubtless Paul has in mind the OT prohibition of "mixtures" as in Deut 22:10. For the Corinthian believers to cooperate with false teachers, who are in reality servants of Satan, notwithstanding their charming and persuasive ways (see notes on 11:13–14), is to become unequally yoked, destroying the harmony and fellowship that unite them in Christ.

6:15 *Belial.* A term (from Hebrew) used to designate Satan (see note on Deut 13:13).

6:16 *agreement hath the temple of God with idols.* There can be no reversion to or compromise with the idolatry they have forsaken for the gospel (cf. 1 Thes 1:9). *temple of the living God.* Built of "living stones," namely, Christian believers (1 Pet 2:5); therefore it is all the more important that they form no defiling and unholy alliances (cf. 1 Cor 6:19–20).

18 [a]And will be a Father unto you, and ye
shall be my sons and daughters, saith the Lord
Almighty.

7 Having [a]therefore these promises, dearly
beloved, let us cleanse ourselves from all
filthiness of the flesh and spirit, perfecting holiness in the fear of God.

The joy of good news

2 ¶ Receive us; we have wronged no *man,*
we have corrupted no *man,* [a]we have defrauded no *man.*
3 I speak not *this* to condemn *you:* for [a]I
have said before, that you are in our hearts to
die and live with *you.*
4 [a]Great *is* my boldness of speech toward
you, [b]great *is* my glorying of you: [c]I am filled
with comfort, I am exceeding joyful in all our
tribulation.
5 For, [a]when we were come into Macedonia, our flesh had no rest, but [b]*we were* troubled on every *side;* [c]without *were* fightings,
within *were* fears.
6 Nevertheless [a]God, that comforteth
those that are cast down, comforted us by [b]the
coming of Titus;
7 And not by his coming only, but by the
consolation wherewith he was comforted in
you, when he told us your earnest desire, your
mourning, your fervent mind toward me; so
that I rejoiced the more.
8 For though I made you sorry with a letter,
I do not repent, [a]though I did repent: for I perceive that the same epistle hath made you sorry, though *it were* but for a season.
9 Now I rejoice, not that ye were made sorry, but that ye sorrowed to repentance: for ye
were made sorry [1]after a godly manner, that
ye might receive damage by us in nothing.
10 For [a]godly sorrow worketh repentance
to salvation not to be repented of: [b]but the sorrow of the world worketh death.
11 For behold this selfsame *thing,* that ye
sorrowed after a godly sort, what carefulness it
wrought in you, yea, *what* clearing of yourselves, yea, *what* indignation, yea, *what* fear,
yea, *what* vehement desire, yea, *what* zeal,
yea, *what* revenge! In all *things* ye have approved yourselves to be clear in *this* matter.
12 Wherefore, though I wrote unto you, *I*
did it not for his cause that had done the
wrong, nor for his cause that suffered wrong,
[a]but that our care for you in the sight of God
might appear unto you.
13 Therefore we were comforted in your
comfort: *yea,* and exceedingly the more joyed
we for the joy of Titus, because his spirit [a]was
refreshed by you all.
14 For if I have boasted any *thing* to him of
you, I am not ashamed; but as we spake all
things to you in truth, even so our boasting,
which *I made* before Titus, is found a truth.
15 And his [1]inward affection is more abundant toward you, whilst he remembereth [a]the
obedience of you all, how with fear and trembling you received him.
16 I rejoice therefore that [a]I have confidence in you in all *things.*

The giving of the Macedonians

8 Moreover, brethren, we do you to wit of
the grace of God bestowed on the
churches of Macedonia;
2 How that in a great trial of affliction the
abundance of their joy and [a]their deep poverty
abounded unto the riches of their [1]liberality.
3 For to *their* power, I bear record, *yea,* and
beyond *their* power *they were* willing of themselves;
4 Praying us with much intreaty that we

6:18 [a]Jer. 31:1,9; Rev. 21:7
7:1 [a]1 John 3:3
7:2 [a]Acts 20:33
7:3 [a]ch. 6:11,12
7:4 [a]ch. 3:12 [b]1 Cor. 1:4 [c]Phil. 2:17; Col. 1:24
7:5 [a]ch. 2:13 [b]ch. 4:8 [c]Deut. 32:35
7:6 [a]ch. 1:4 [b]See ch. 2:13
7:8 [a]ch. 2:4
7:9 [1]Or, *according to God*
7:10 [a]2 Sam. 12:13; Mat. 26:75 [b]Prov. 17:22
7:12 [a]ch. 2:4
7:13 [a]Rom. 15:32
7:15 [1]Gr. *bowels* [a]ch. 2:9; Phil. 2:12
7:16 [a]2 Thes. 3:4; Philem. 8,21
8:2 [1][Gr. *simplicity*] [a]Mark 12:44

7:1 *holiness.* See 1 Thes 4:7; 1 John 3:3.

7:2 *we have wronged no man.* Implies that Paul had been accused by the false teachers of being unjust, destructive and fraudulent—the very things they themselves were guilty of.

7:3 Again he declares the depth of his affection for the Corinthian believers and appeals to them to respond, contrary to the wishes of the false teachers, by displaying their love for him, their genuine apostle (cf. 6:11–13).

7:4 *Great is my boldness . . . exceeding joyful.* The long digression that started at 2:14 concludes here on this note of exhilaration. The news he had been so anxiously awaiting from Corinth has turned out to be good and reassuring, and Paul is overjoyed to receive it.

7:5–6 *when we were come into Macedonia . . . God . . . comforted us by the coming of Titus.* Here Paul resumes the account he began in 2:12–13, where he described how his hopes of meeting Titus in Troas were disappointed and how, restless for news, he had decided to press on into Macedonia. He now explains that on reaching Macedonia, he was at last comforted by the arrival of Titus, who brought the news he most wanted to hear concerning the situation in Corinth. Titus himself had been well received in that city and was able to assure Paul (see v. 7) of the "earnest desire" and "fervent mind" of the Corinthian Christians for him and of the "mourning" they had expressed because of the grief they had caused him. Consequently, he "rejoiced the more."

7:8–9 *I do not repent . . . I did repent . . . Now I rejoice.* Paul did regret the necessity of writing a letter to the Corinthians that caused sorrow to them. However, it was not the actual writing that he regretted, but the situation that required the writing. Moreover, the fact that the letter had the desired effect made him happy, for their sorrow did not leave them embittered and hostile but led them to repentance. They became sorrowful as God intended, and so were benefited, not harmed, by the letter.

7:10 *godly sorrow . . . sorrow of the world.* The former manifests itself by repentance and the experience of divine grace; the latter brings death because, instead of being God-centered sorrow over the wickedness of sin, it is self-centered sorrow over the painful consequences of sin. The letter's primary purpose was not to deal with the notorious offender in Corinth or the person he had injured, but to test their loyalty and devotion to Paul as their apostle.

8:1–9:15 Paul addresses the question of the collection of money for the distressed Christians in Jerusalem, which the Corinthians had started but not completed.

8:1 *grace.* The "gracious work" of giving on the part of believers (v. 7) is more than matched by the self-giving "grace of our Lord Jesus Christ" (v. 9).

8:2 *abundance of their joy.* In the blessings of the gospel.

would receive the gift, and *take upon us* [a]the fellowship of the ministering to the saints.

5 And *this they did,* not as we hoped, but first gave their own selves to the Lord, and unto us by the will of God.

6 Insomuch that [a]we desired Titus, that as he had begun, so he would also finish in you the same [1]grace also.

7 Therefore, as [a]ye abound in every *thing, in* faith, and utterance, and knowledge, and *in* all diligence, and *in* your love to us, *see* [b]that ye abound in this grace also.

The example of Jesus

8 [a]I speak not by commandment, but by occasion of the forwardness of others, and to prove the sincerity of your love.

9 For ye know the grace of our Lord Jesus Christ, [a]that, though he was rich, *yet* for your sakes he became poor, that ye through his poverty might be rich.

10 And herein [a]I give *my* advice: for [b]this is expedient for you, who have begun before, not only to do, but also to be [c][1]forward a year ago.

11 Now therefore perform the doing *of it;* that as *there was* a readiness to will, so *there may be* a performance also out of that which *you* have.

12 For [a]if there be first a willing mind, *it is* accepted according to that a man hath, *and* not according to that he hath not.

13 For *I mean* not that other *men* be eased, and you burdened:

14 But by an equality, *that* now at *this* time your abundance *may be a supply* for their want, that their abundance also may be *a supply* for your want: that there may be equality:

15 As it is written, [a]He that *had gathered* much had nothing over; and he that *had gathered* little had no lack.

Coming of Titus

16 ¶ But thanks *be* to God, which put the same earnest care into the heart of Titus for you.

17 For indeed he accepted [a]the exhortation; but being more forward, of his own accord he went unto you.

18 And we have sent with him [a]the brother, whose praise *is* in the gospel throughout all the churches;

19 And not *that* only, but who was also [a]chosen of the churches to travel with us with this [1]grace, which is administered by us [b]to the glory of the same Lord, and *declaration of* your ready mind:

20 Avoiding this, that no *man* should blame us in this abundance which is administered by us:

21 [a]Providing *for* honest *things,* not only in the sight of the Lord, but also in the sight of men.

22 And we have sent with them our brother, whom we have oftentimes proved diligent in many *things,* but now much more diligent, upon the great confidence which [1]*I have* in you.

23 Whether *any do inquire* of Titus, *he is* my partner and fellowhelper concerning you: or our brethren *be inquired of, they are* [a]the

8:4 [a]Acts 11:29; 24:17; Rom. 15:25,26; 1 Cor. 16:1,3,4; ch. 9:1
8:6 [1][Or, *gift,* ver. 4,19] [a]ver. 17; ch. 12:18
8:7 [a]1 Cor. 1:5; 12:13 [b]ch. 9:8
8:8 [a]1 Cor. 7:6
8:9 [a]Mat. 8:20; Luke 9:58; Phil. 2:6,7
8:10 [1]Gr. *willing* [a]1 Cor. 7:25 [b]Prov. 19:17; Mat. 10:42; 1 Tim. 6:18, 19; Heb. 13:16 [c]ch. 9:2
8:12 [a]Mark 12:43,44; Luke 21:3
8:15 [a]Ex. 16:18
8:17 [a]ver. 6
8:18 [a]ch. 12:18
8:19 [1]Or, *gift* [a]1 Cor. 16:3,4 [b]ch. 4:15
8:21 [a]Rom. 12:17; Phil. 4:8; 1 Pet. 2:12
8:22 [1]Or, he hath
8:23 [a]Phil. 2:25

‡8:5 *first gave their own selves to the Lord.* The true principle of all Christian giving. These Macedonian Christians are an amazing example to the Corinthian believers and to the church in every age of the dynamic difference that God's grace makes in the lives and attitudes of His people—a central theme of this letter (cf. 12:9–10).

‡8:6 *we desired Titus.* The collection had been started in Corinth under the direction of Titus during the previous year (see v. 10; 9:2), but, no doubt because of the troubles in the Corinthian church, had slowed down or come to a standstill. Paul is now sending Titus back to them, taking with him this present letter, for the purpose of completing this good work, which he describes as "the same grace," i.e. a work of grace (cf. the link between the grace of God and the selfless generosity of the Macedonian churches in vv. 1–5).

8:7 *you abound in every thing.* Cf. 1 Cor 1:4–7.

8:8 *I speak not by commandment.* True charity and generosity cannot be commanded. *forwardness of others.* The remarkable example of the Macedonian churches (vv. 1–5). *sincerity of your love.* They can prove this by giving selflessly and spontaneously.

8:9 *though he was rich . . . he became poor.* The eternal Son, in His incarnation and His atoning death in our place on the cross, emptied Himself of His riches (see Phil 2:7). *through his poverty might be rich.* The supreme and inescapable incentive of all genuine Christian generosity.

8:11 *Now therefore perform the doing of it.* The work they had started "a year ago" with desire (v. 10) needs to be completed (see note on v. 6).

8:12 *according to that a man hath.* What matters is the willingness, which is the motive of true generosity, no matter how small the amount that can be afforded. An outstanding example of one who put this principle into practice is the poor widow (see Mark 12:41–44). The mechanics of the collection being made in Corinth had been proposed by Paul in his earlier letter (see 1 Cor 16:1–2).

8:15 The reference is to the gathering by the Israelites of the manna in the wilderness. Though in the daily gathering the aged and weak might collect less than the prescribed amount and the young and vigorous might collect more, there was an equal distribution, so that the excess of some ministered to the deficiency of others.

8:16 *Titus.* Had established a relationship of trust and affection with the Corinthians (see 7:6–7,13–15). He had organized the collection when it was started the previous year (see note on v. 6).

8:18 *the brother.* Probably Luke, but possibly Barnabas. In any case, it was someone who was widely known for the faithfulness of his ministry.

8:19 *chosen of the churches.* Paul provides a good example of the care that church leaders should take in handling money.

8:20 It is important not only that God sees (cf. vv. 19,21) but also that people see that one is carrying on the Lord's work in a proper, ethical and honest manner.

8:21 *Providing for honest things.* Even so, Paul is the victim of disgraceful slander (implied by 12:17–18; see Introduction: Purpose); but the integrity of his representatives (see note on v. 23) reflects well on his own integrity.

8:22 *our brother.* This second brother is anonymous, like the one already mentioned (see v. 18 and note).

8:23 *partner and fellowhelper.* See note on 2:13. *messengers*

messengers of the churches, *and* the glory of Christ.

24 Wherefore shew ye to them, and before the churches, the proof of your love, and of our [a]boasting on your behalf.

God loveth a cheerful giver

9 For as touching [a]the ministering to the saints, it is superfluous for me to write to you:

2 For I know [a]the forwardness of your mind, [b]for which I boast of you to them of Macedonia, that [c]Achaia was ready a year ago; and your zeal hath provoked very many.

3 [a]Yet have I sent the brethren, lest our boasting of you should be in vain in this behalf; that, as I said, ye may be ready:

4 Lest haply if they of Macedonia come with me, and find you unprepared, we (that we say not, you) should be ashamed in this *same* confident boasting.

5 Therefore I thought it necessary to exhort the brethren, that they would go before unto you, and make up beforehand your [1]bounty, [2]whereof *ye* had notice before, that the same might be ready, as *a matter of* [1]bounty, and not as *of* covetousness.

6 [a]But this *I say,* He which soweth sparingly shall reap also sparingly; and he which soweth bountifully shall reap also bountifully.

7 Every man according as he purposeth in *his* heart, *so let him give;* [a]not grudgingly, or of necessity: for [b]God loveth a cheerful giver.

8 [a]And God *is* able to make all grace abound towards you; that ye, always having all sufficiency in all *things,* may abound to every good work:

9 (As it is written, [a]He hath dispersed abroad; he hath given to the poor: his righteousness remaineth for ever.

10 Now he that [a]ministereth seed to the sower both minister bread for *your* food, and multiply your seed sown, and increase the fruits of your [b]righteousness;)

11 Being enriched in every *thing* to all [1 2]bountifulness, [a]which causeth through us thanksgiving to God.

12 For the administration of this service not only [a]supplieth the want of the saints, but is abundant also by many thanksgivings unto God;

13 Whiles by the experiment of this ministration they [a]glorify God for your professed subjection unto the gospel of Christ, and *for your* liberal [b]distribution unto them, and unto all *men;*

14 And by their prayer for you, which long after you for the exceeding [a]grace of God in you.

15 Thanks *be* unto God [a]for his unspeakable gift.

Paul defends his ministry

10 Now [a]I Paul myself beseech you by the meekness and gentleness of Christ, [b]who [1]in presence *am* base among you, but being absent am bold toward you:

2 But I beseech *you,* [a]that I may not be bold when I am present with *that* confidence, wherewith I [1]think to be bold against some, which [2]think of us as if we walked according to the flesh.

3 For though we walk in the flesh, we do not war after the flesh:

4 ([a]For the weapons [b]of our warfare *are* not carnal, but [c]mighty [1]through God [d]to the pulling down of strong holds;)

8:24 [a]ch. 7:14; 9:2
9:1 [a]Acts 11:29; Rom. 15:26; 1 Cor. 16:1; ch. 8:4; Gal. 2:10
9:2 [a]ch. 8:19 [b]ch. 8:24 [c]ch. 8:10
9:3 [a]ch. 8:6,17
9:5 [1]Gr. *blessing* [2]Or, *which hath been* so much *spoken of before*
9:6 [a]Prov. 11:24
9:7 [a]Deut. 15:7 [b]Ex. 35:5; Prov. 11:25; Rom. 12:8; ch. 8:12
9:8 [a]Prov. 11:24; Phil. 4:19
9:9 [a]Ps. 112:9
9:10 [a]Is. 55:10 [b]Hos. 10:12; Mat. 6:1
9:11 [1][Or, *liberality*] [2][Gr. *simplicity.* See ch. 8:2] [a]ch. 1:11
9:12 [a]ch. 8:14
9:13 [a]Mat. 5:16 [b]Heb. 13:16
9:14 [a]ch. 8:1
9:15 [a]Jas. 1:17
10:1 [1]Or, *in outward appearance* [a]Rom. 12:1 [b]ch. 12:5
10:2 [1]Or, *reckon* [2]Or, *reckon* [a]1 Cor. 4:21; ch. 13:2,10
10:4 [1]Or, *to God* [a]Eph. 6:13; 1 Thes. 5:8 [b]1 Tim. 1:18; 2 Tim. 2:3 [c]Acts 7:22; 1 Cor. 2:5 [d]Jer. 1:10

---

of the churches. Duly elected delegates of the churches at large (so that they could not be dismissed as cronies chosen by Paul alone); see note on Acts 20:4. *the glory of Christ.* Christians of outstanding faithfulness.

9:6 Probably a well-known proverb—but not taken from the OT book of Proverbs.

9:7 See Luke 6:38.

9:8 *always having all sufficiency in all things.* Through His abounding grace, God can enable each Christian to abound in generous deeds (see v. 11).

9:9–10 *righteousness.* See note on Ps 1:5.

9:12 *not only supplieth the want of the saints.* The effect of generous giving on the part of the Corinthians will extend beyond Jerusalem, the destination of their gift, to the church as a whole, causing widespread prayer and praise to be offered (see vv. 13–14).

9:14 *the exceeding grace of God in you.* Displayed in this unselfish demonstration of their loving concern for fellow believers who are in desperate need.

9:15 *unspeakable gift.* His own Son (John 3:16). God is the first giver; He first selflessly gives Himself to us in the person of His Son, and all true Christian giving is our response of gratitude for this gift that is beyond description (cf. 8:9; 1 John 4:9–11).

‡10:1 *in presence am base . . . being absent am bold.* Paul had been meek and lowly among them, but if opposition to him and rejection of his apostolic message continues, he will act boldly when he comes. From the mild tone of the first nine chapters of Paul's letter, it appears that the majority of the Corinthian believers had been won over to Paul (cf. 7:6–13), after having been alienated by his Corinthian opponents. In this final section (chs. 10–13), however, Paul deals firmly with the slanders that have been spread against him in Corinth by the remaining opposition. Those who wish to discredit him have been saying that he is bold at a distance, threatening to take severe disciplinary action, especially in his letters (cf., e.g., his warning that, if necessary, he will come "with a rod" in 1 Cor 4:18–21). But they say that he will not dare to be anything but weak and indecisive if he is present with them in person—in short, that he does not have the apostolic authority he claims to have. Paul is ready to prove otherwise, should the occasion demand, when he comes to Corinth for the third time (see vv. 6,10–11). His appeal to the meekness and gentleness of Christ is an indication of his own affectionate desire to show these same qualities when present with them. In any case, though weak in himself, Paul is strong in the Lord—as this whole letter explains—and those who are rebellious can expect to feel the force of his divinely given authority.

‡10:4 *weapons of our warfare.* Paul is prepared for warfare; his weapons, however, are not the weapons prized by this fallen world and fashioned by human pride and arrogance. *strong holds.* Of "imaginations" and "every high thing" (v. 5) defiantly raised "against the knowledge of God" (cf. Rom 1:18–23), among

5 [a]Casting down [1]imaginations, and every high thing that exalteth itself against the knowledge of God, and bringing into captivity every thought to the obedience of Christ;

6 [a]And having in a readiness to revenge all disobedience, when [b]your obedience is fulfilled.

7 ¶ [a]Do ye look on *things* after the outward appearance? [b]If any *man* trust to himself that *he* is Christ's, let him of himself think this again, that, as he *is* Christ's, even so *are* [c]we Christ's.

8 For though I should boast somewhat more [a]of our authority, which the Lord hath given us for edification, and not for your destruction, [b]I should not be ashamed:

9 That I may not seem as if *I* would terrify you by letters.

10 For *his* letters, [1]say they, *are* weighty and powerful; but [a]*his* bodily presence *is* weak, and *his* [b]speech contemptible.

11 Let such a one think this, that, such as we are in word by letters when we are absent, such *will we be* also in deed when we are present.

12 ¶ [a]For we dare not make *ourselves* of the number, or compare ourselves with some that commend themselves: but they measuring themselves by themselves, and comparing themselves amongst themselves, [1]are not wise.

13 [a]But we will not boast of *things* without *our* measure, but according to the measure of the [1]rule which God hath distributed to us, a measure to reach even unto you.

14 For we stretch not ourselves beyond *our measure,* as though we reached not unto you: [a]for we are come as far as to you also in *preaching* the gospel of Christ:

15 Not boasting of *things* without *our* measure, *that is,* [a]of other *men's* labours; but having hope, when your faith is increased, that *we* shall be [1]enlarged by you according to our rule abundantly,

16 To preach the gospel in the *regions* beyond you, *and* not to boast in another *man's* [1]line of *things* made ready to our hand.

17 [a]But he that glorieth, let him glory in the Lord.

18 For [a]not he that commendeth himself is approved, but [b]whom the Lord commendeth.

Paul's fear of false teachers

11 Would *to God* you could bear with me a little in [a]*my* folly: and indeed [1]bear with me.

2 For I am [a]jealous over you with godly jealousy: for [b]I have espoused you to one husband, [c]that *I* may present *you* [d]*as* a chaste virgin to Christ.

3 But I fear, lest by any means, as [a]the serpent beguiled Eve through his subtilty, so your minds [b]should be corrupted from the simplicity that is in Christ.

4 For if he that cometh preacheth another Jesus, whom we have not preached, or *if* ye re-

10:5 [1]Or, *reasonings* [a]1 Cor. 1:19
10:6 [a]ch. 13:2,10 [b]ch. 7:15
10:7 [a]John 7:24 [b]1 Cor. 14:37; 1 John 4:6 [c]1 Cor. 3:23; ch. 11:23
10:8 [a]ch. 13:10 [b]ch. 7:14
10:10 [1][Gr. *saith* he] [a]1 Cor. 2:3,4; Gal. 4:13 [b]1 Cor. 1:17
10:12 [1]Or, *understand* it *not* [a]ch. 5:12
10:13 [a]ver. 15
10:13 [1]Or, *line*
10:14 [a]1 Cor. 3:5
10:15 [1]Or, *magnified in you* [a]Rom. 15:20
10:16 [1]Or, *rule*
10:17 [a]Is. 65:16; Jer. 9:24; 1 Cor. 1:31
10:18 [a]Prov. 27:2 [b]Rom. 2:29; 1 Cor. 4:5
11:1 [1]Or, *you do bear with me* [a]ver. 16; ch. 5:13
11:2 [a]Gal. 4:17 [b]Hos. 2:19; 1 Cor. 4:15 [c]Col. 1:28 [d]Lev. 21:13
11:3 [a]Gen. 3:4; John 8:44 [b]Eph. 6:24; Col. 2:4,8; 1 Tim. 1:3

---

which are the faulty reasonings by which the false apostles have been trying to shake the faith of the Christians in Corinth (see 1 Cor 2:13–14).

10:5 *every thought to the obedience of Christ.* The center of man's being thus becomes fully subject to the lordship of Christ.

‡10:7 *he is Christ's.* Probably echoes the claim to superior spirituality by the Christ party (1 Cor 1:12) and the false teachers in Corinth. Paul, who had dramatically encountered and been commissioned by the risen Lord (see Acts 9:3–9; 22:6–11; 26:12–18) and who received the gospel he preached "by the revelation of Jesus Christ" (Gal 1:12; cf. 2 Cor 12:2–7), asserts that he belongs to Christ just as much.

10:8 *authority . . . for edification.* The primary purpose of Paul's apostolic authority is constructive, for building up, not destructive, for pulling down (the same statement is made again in 13:10). The demands he makes in his letters are written so that they may put right what is amiss and so that things may be in order for his arrival, thus removing the need for severe action (pulling down) and preparing the way for edification (building up).

10:9 *terrify you by letters.* See 2:3–4; 7:8–9; chs. 10–13; 1 Cor 4:18–21.

10:10 *his speech contemptible.* See note on v. 1. Paul's adversaries used a professional type of oratory as their stock in trade, designed to extract money from their gullible audiences. But Paul's manner of speaking was quite different; it was plain, straightforward and free from artificiality—and it was also free of charge (see note on 11:7), which meant, if his slanderous opponents were to be believed, that what he said was worthless. But in coming to Corinth Paul had purposely disdained academic eloquence and wisdom and was determined to proclaim the message of Christ crucified, and the transformed lives of the Corinthian believers testified to the divine power with which he spoke (cf. 1 Cor 2:1–5).

10:12 *they measuring themselves by themselves.* The false teachers in Corinth behave as though there is no standard of comparison higher than themselves, but Paul boasts only in the Lord (see vv. 13–18; cf. 1 Cor 1:31).

‡10:13 *the rule which God hath distributed to us.* The Greek word translated "rule" can also mean "sphere." The context involving both vv. 13 and 15 refers to an assigned sphere of authority.

10:15 See note on verse 13.

10:16 *regions beyond.* Spain is probably in his thoughts (see Rom 15:24,28).

11:1 *folly.* In order to compare his own ministry with that of the false apostles who have invaded the Corinthian church, Paul has to speak about himself, which inevitably seems like foolish boasting.

11:2 *godly jealousy.* Paul cannot bear the thought that there might be any rival to Christ and His gospel. *I have espoused you to one husband.* As their spiritual father (cf. 6:13), Paul has promised the Corinthian believers to Christ, who is frequently depicted in the NT as the bridegroom, with the church portrayed as His bride (Mat 9:15; John 3:29; Rom 7:4; 1 Cor 6:15; Eph 5:23–32; Rev 19:7–9; 21:2). *chaste virgin.* Undefiled by the doctrines of false teachers (see vv. 3–4).

11:4 *another Jesus, whom we have not preached.* They presented a Jesus cast in the mold of Judaistic teachings (Paul's opponents were Jews; see v. 22). *another spirit.* A spirit of bondage, fear and worldliness (cf. Rom 8:15; 1 Cor 2:12; Gal 2:4; 4:24; Col 2:20–23) instead of a spirit of freedom, love, joy, peace and power (cf. 3:17; Rom 14:17; Gal 2:4; 5:1,22; Eph 3:20; Col 1:11; 2 Tim 1:7). *another gospel.* Cf. Gal 1:6–9. *ye might well*

ceive another spirit, which ye have not received, or [a]another gospel, which ye have not
accepted, ye might well bear [1]with *him.*
5 For I suppose [a]*I* was not a whit behind
the very chiefest apostles.
6 But though [a]*I be* rude in speech, yet not
[b]in knowledge; but [c]we *have been* throughly
made manifest among you in all *things.*
7 Have I committed an offence in abasing
myself that you might be exalted, because I
have preached to you the gospel of God freely?
8 I robbed other churches, taking wages *of
them,* to do you service.
9 And when I was present with you, and
wanted, [a]I was chargeable to no *man:* for that
which was lacking to me [b]the brethren which
came from Macedonia supplied: and in all
things I have kept myself [c]from being burdensome to you, and *so* will I keep *myself.*
10 [a]*As* the truth of Christ is in me, [b][1]no
man shall stop me of this boasting in the regions of Achaia.
11 Wherefore? [a]because I love you not?
God knoweth.
12 But what I do, that I will do, [a]that I may
cut off occasion from them which desire occasion; that wherein they glory, they may be
found even as we.
13 For such [a]*are* false apostles, [b]deceitful
workers, transforming themselves into the
apostles of Christ.
14 And no marvel; for Satan himself is
transformed into [a]an angel of light.
15 Therefore *it is* no great *thing* if his ministers also be transformed as the ministers of
righteousness; [a]whose end shall be according
to their works.

Paul's rightful boasting

16 ¶ I say again, Let no *man* think me a
fool; if otherwise, yet as a fool [1]receive me,
that I may boast myself a little.
17 *That* which I speak, [a]I speak *it* not after
the Lord, but as *it were* foolishly, in this confidence of boasting.
18 Seeing that many glory after the flesh, I
will glory also.
19 For ye suffer fools gladly, [a]seeing ye
yourselves are wise.
20 For ye suffer, [a]if a man bring you into
bondage, if a man devour *you,* if a man take *of
you,* if a man exalt himself, if a man smite you
on the face.
21 I speak as concerning reproach, [a]as
though we had been weak. Howbeit [b]where-
insoever any is bold, (I speak foolishly,) I am
bold also.
22 Are they Hebrews? [a]so *am* I. Are they

11:4 [1][Or, *with me*] [a]Gal. 1:7,8
11:5 [a]1 Cor. 15:10
11:6 [a]1 Cor. 1:17 [b]Eph. 3:4 [c]ch. 12:12
11:9 [a]Acts 20:33; 1 Thes. 2:9 [b]Phil. 4:10 [c]ch. 12:14
11:10 [1]Gr. *this boasting shall not be stopped in me* [a]Rom. 9:1 [b]1 Cor. 9:15
11:11 [a]ch. 6:11
11:12 [a]1 Cor. 9:12
11:13 [a]Acts 15:24; Rom. 16:18; Gal. 1:7; Phil. 1:15; 2 Pet. 2:1; Rev. 2:2 [b]Phil. 3:2; Tit. 1:10
11:14 [a]Gal. 1:8
11:15 [a]Phil. 3:19
11:16 [1]Or, *suffer*
11:17 [a]1 Cor. 7:6
11:19 [a]1 Cor. 4:10
11:20 [a]Gal. 2:4
11:21 [a]ch. 10:10 [b]Phil. 3:4
11:22 [a]Acts 22:3; Rom. 11:1; Phil. 3:5

bear with him. They have been undiscerningly tolerant of these deceivers in their midst.

11:5 *the very chiefest apostles.* Paul's sarcastic way of referring to the false apostles who had infiltrated the Corinthian church and were in reality not apostles at all, except in their own arrogantly inflated opinion of themselves (cf. 10:12).

11:6 *though I be rude in speech.* Not using the skills, references and flourishes of professional rhetoric (see note on 10:10). *yet not in knowledge.* As the Corinthian believers well knew, Paul had knowledge of Christ that was true, powerful and God-given, totally distinct from the powerless human wisdom the false teachers were attempting to deceive them with (cf. 1 Cor 2:6–10).

11:7 *freely.* Another slanderous criticism made by Paul's adversaries was that his refusal to accept payment for his instruction proved that it was worth nothing. This accusation at the same time helped to cloak their own grasping character, since their method of operation, like that of first-century traveling philosophers and religious teachers, was to demand payment for their "professional" services. Paul, his enemies said, was lowering himself and committing a sin by breaking the rule that a teacher should receive payment in proportion to the worth of his performance.

11:8 *robbed other churches.* Accepted freely given support from established congregations.

11:9 *brethren which came from Macedonia.* They brought gifts from the churches in that province (Acts 18:5), particularly from the church at Philippi (Phil 4:15). *burdensome.* A financial liability (see note on 2:17). This reinforced his teaching that the gospel of Jesus Christ is a free gift.

11:12 *I will do.* Paul will not be deterred from presenting the gospel without charge. Actually, this practice made his adversaries look bad. They were greedy for gain, and it would have suited them better if Paul had been willing to accept money for his teaching, for this would have put him on a level with their practice. *even as we.* In financial matters.

11:13 *transforming themselves into the apostles of Christ.* Now Paul exposes these would-be "chiefest apostles" (v. 5) as false apostles and servants of Satan (v. 14) who are covering up their true identity.

‡11:14 *an angel of light.* Though he is in reality the prince of darkness.

11:16 *Let no man think me a fool.* See note on v. 1.

11:18 *glory.* By speaking of the nature of his apostolic ministry.

11:19 *ye suffer fools gladly.* Resumes the implied rebuke of v. 4, and has the same ironic tone. There it was a matter of their readiness to tolerate false teaching; here it is a matter of their willingness to put up with disgraceful treatment by these false teachers, who are described as fools because of their self-centered boasting.

11:20 *bring you into bondage.* By the imposition of tyrannical man-made rules and prohibitions (cf. Gal 5:1). *devour you.* See Mark 12:40. *take of you.* Or, "take advantage of you," made possible by the Corinthians' lack of discernment and their readiness to be impressed by outward show and clever talk. *exalt himself.* For the purpose of lording it over the members of the church (cf. 1:24). *smite you on the face.* Using physical violence to cow them into submission.

11:21 *as though we had been weak.* Compared with the crude self-seeking roughness of the impostors, Paul's conduct may well be considered weak, but he is probably speaking ironically here.

11:22 *Hebrews . . . Israelites . . . seed of Abraham.* The claims implied here on the part of the false apostles indicate that they were Jews who felt superior to Gentile Christians. From this there follows the possibility that they were Judaizers, i.e., they wished to impose distinctive Jewish practices and observances as required for Gentile converts. This, of course, was not Paul's position (see Rom 2:28–29; 1 Cor 12:13; Gal 3:28–29; Eph 2:11–18; Col 3:11). For Paul's claim see Acts 22:3–5; 26:4–5; Phil 3:5–6.

Israelites? so *am* I. Are they the seed of Abraham? so *am* I.
23 Are they ministers of Christ? (I speak as
a fool) I *am* more; [a]in labours more abundant,
[b]in stripes above measure, in prisons more frequent, [c]in deaths oft.
24 Of the Jews five times received I [a]forty
stripes save one.
25 Thrice was I [a]beaten with rods, [b]once
was I stoned, thrice I [c]suffered shipwrack, a
night and a day I have been in the deep;
26 *In* journeyings often, *in* perils of waters,
in perils of robbers, [a]*in* perils by *my own* countrymen, [b]*in* perils by the heathen, *in* perils in
the city, *in* perils in the wilderness, *in* perils in
the sea, *in* perils among false brethren;
27 In weariness and painfulness, [a]in
watchings often, [b]in hunger and thirst, in fastings often, in cold and nakedness.
28 Besides those *things* that are without,
that which cometh upon me daily, [a]the care of
all the churches.
29 [a]Who is weak, and I am not weak? who
is offended, and I burn not?
30 If I must needs glory, [a]I will glory of the
things which concern mine infirmities.
31 [a]The God and Father of our Lord Jesus
Christ, [b]which is blessed for evermore,
knoweth that I lie not.
32 [a]In Damascus the governor under Aretas the king kept the city of the Damascenes
with a garrison, desirous to apprehend me:
33 And through a window in a basket was
I let down by the wall, and escaped his hands.

Paul's visions of the Lord

12 It is not expedient for me doubtless
to glory. [1]I will come to visions and
revelations of the Lord.
2 I knew a man [a]in Christ above fourteen
years ago, (whether in the body, I cannot tell;
or whether out of the body, I cannot tell: God
knoweth;) such a one [b]caught up to the third
heaven.
3 And I knew such a man, (whether in the
body, or out of the body, I cannot tell: God
knoweth;)
4 How that he was caught up into [a]para-
dise, and heard unspeakable words, which *it is*
not [1]lawful for a man to utter.
5 Of such a one will I glory: [a]yet of myself
I will not glory, but in mine infirmities.
6 For [a]though I would desire to glory, I
shall not be a fool; for I will say the truth: but
now I forbear, lest any *man* should think of me

11:23 [a]1 Cor. 15:10 [b]Acts 9:16 [c]1 Cor. 15:30
11:24 [a]Deut. 25:3
11:25 [a]Acts 16:22 [b]Acts 14:19 [c]Acts 27:41
11:26 [a]Acts 9:23 [b]Acts 14:5
11:27 [a]Acts 20:31 [b]1 Cor. 4:11
11:28 [a]Acts 20:18; Rom. 1:14
11:29 [a]1 Cor. 8:13
11:30 [a]ch. 12:5
11:31 [a]Rom. 1:9; Gal. 1:20; 1 Thes. 2:5
11:31 [b]Rom. 9:5
11:32 [a]Acts 9:24
12:1 [1][Gr. *For I will come*]
12:2 [a]Rom. 16:7; Gal. 1:22 [b]Acts 22:17
12:4 [1]Or, *possible* [a]Luke 23:43
12:5 [a]ch. 11:30
12:6 [a]ch. 11:16

11:23 *ministers of Christ.* Paul is not granting their claim to be servants of Christ. Indeed, the consideration of the nature of his ministry and its cost to him in suffering will show that he is more Christ's servant than any or all of them. *in deaths oft.* Cf. 4:8–11. He means this literally, for the sufferings he lists here and in the verses that follow were life-threatening. The catalogue that follows makes it clear that Luke's account in Acts is selective.

11:24–25 *stripes . . . rods.* Eight floggings are mentioned here, five at the hands of the Jews (cf. Deut 25:1–3) and three at the hands of the Roman authorities, who used rods on these occasions (see Acts 16:22–23). The three beatings with rods took place despite the fact that Paul, being a Roman citizen, was legally protected from such punishment (cf. Acts 16:37–39; 22:25–29).

11:25 *stoned.* A traditional manner of Jewish execution (cf. Acts 14:19–20). *shipwrack.* Only one shipwreck is recorded in Acts, but it took place after the writing of this letter (Acts 27:39–44). The three shipwrecks referred to here could have taken place during the voyages mentioned in Acts 9:30; 11:25–26; 13:4,13; 14:25–26; 16:11; 17:14; 18:18–19, 21–22. *a night and a day . . . in the deep.* Probably as a result of one of the shipwrecks.

11:26 *in perils.* Apart from the specific incidents referred to in the preceding verses, Paul constantly faced situations of danger as well as labors and hardships (see note on Acts 14:24).

11:29 So closely did Paul identify himself with them that he felt the weakness of any member who was weak. If anyone was led into sin, he not only burned with indignation against the person responsible but also experienced the shame of the offense and longed for the restoration of the one who had stumbled.

11:30 *I will glory of the things which concern mine infirmities.* His weakness opens the way for him to experience the superabundant strength of God's grace. Therefore his boasting in its entirety, unlike that of the false apostles, is not in what he has done but in what God has done.

11:32 *Aretas the king.* Aretas IV, father-in-law of Herod Antipas, ruled over the Nabatean Arabs from c. 9 B.C.–A.D. 40. The Roman emperor Caligula may have given Damascus to Aretas since it was once part of his territory.

12:1 *visions and revelations.* If his adversaries falsely claimed to have received their teaching directly from God through visions and revelations, Paul could claim that this was truly so in his case. But he mentions this here to show that the supreme height to which he was raised through these ecstatic experiences was counterbalanced by the humbling depth of a particular affliction he was given to bear (see v. 7), so that he should continue to glory not in self but only in the "God of all grace" (1 Pet 5:10).

‡12:2–4 *caught up to the third heaven . . . caught up into paradise.* Paul is sure of this remarkable experience, but he is unsure whether this rapture (being "caught up") was one that included the body or one that took place in separation from the body. The third heaven designates a place beyond the immediate heaven of the earth's atmosphere and beyond the further heaven of outer space and its constellations into the presence of God himself. Thus the risen and glorified Lord is said to have passed "into the heavens" (Heb 4:14), and now, having "ascended up far above all heavens" (Eph 4:10), to be "made higher than the heavens" (Heb 7:26). The term "paradise" is synonymous with the third heaven, where those believers who have died are even now "present with the Lord" (5:8; cf. "with Christ," Phil 1:23). The nature of the inexpressible things that Paul heard remains unknown to us because this is something Paul was not permitted to tell. It was an experience that must have given incalculable strength to his apostleship, which involved him in such constant and extreme suffering. Moreover, as this experience was not self-induced, it afforded him no room for self-glorification (vv. 5–6).

12:5 *Of such a one will I glory.* Some believe that the man "caught up to the third heaven" (v. 2) was not Paul and that Paul here insists that he will not boast about such a glorious experience but only about his weakness.

above *that* which he seeth me *to be*, or that he
heareth of me.
7 And lest I should be exalted above measure through the abundance of the revelations,
there was given to me a [a]thorn in the flesh,
[b]the messenger of Satan to buffet me, lest I
should be exalted above measure.
8 [a]For this *thing* I besought the Lord
thrice, that it might depart from me.
9 And he said unto me, My grace is sufficient for thee: for my strength is made perfect
in weakness. Most gladly therefore [a]will I
rather glory in my infirmities, [b]that the power
of Christ may rest upon me.
10 Therefore [a]I take pleasure in infirmities, in reproaches, in necessities, in persecutions, in distresses for Christ's sake: [b]for when
I am weak, then am I strong.

The signs of a true apostle

11 I am become [a]a fool in glorying; ye have
compelled me: for I ought to have been commended of you: for [b]*in* nothing am I behind the
very chiefest apostles, though [c]I be nothing.
12 [a]Truly the signs of an apostle were
wrought among you in all patience, in signs,
and wonders, and mighty deeds.
13 [a]For what is it wherein ye were inferior
to other churches, except *it be* that [b]I myself
was not burdensome to you? forgive me [c]this
wrong.
14 ¶ [a]Behold, the third *time* I am ready to
come to you; and I will not be burdensome to
you: for [b]I seek not yours, but you: [c]for the
children ought not to lay up for the parents,
but the parents for the children.
15 And I will very gladly spend and be
spent [a]for [1]you; though [b]the more abundantly
I love you, the less I be loved.
16 But be it so, [a]I did not burden you: nevertheless, being crafty, I caught you with guile.
17 [a]Did I make a gain of you by any of
them whom I sent unto you?
18 [a]I desired Titus, and with *him* I sent a
[b]brother. Did Titus make a gain of you? walked
we not in the same spirit? *walked we* not in
the same steps?

The appeal for repentance

19 ¶ [a]Again, think you that we excuse ourselves unto you? [b]we speak before God in
Christ: [c]but *we do* all *things*, dearly beloved,
for your edifying.
20 For I fear, lest, when I come, I shall not
find you such as I would, and *that* [a]I shall be
found unto you such as ye would not: lest
there be debates, envyings, wraths, strifes,
backbitings, whisperings, swellings, tumults:
21 *And* lest, when I come again, my God
[a]will humble *me* among you, and *that* I shall
bewail many [b]which have sinned already, and
have not repented of the uncleanness and [c]for-
nication and lasciviousness which they have
committed.

13 This *is* [a]the third *time* I am coming
to you. [b]In the mouth of two or three
witnesses shall every word be established.
2 [a]I told *you* before, and foretell *you*, as if I
were present the second *time;* and being absent now I write to them [b]which heretofore
have sinned, and to all other, that, if I come
again, [c]I will not spare:
3 Since ye seek a proof of Christ [a]speaking

12:7 [a]See Ezek. 28:24; Gal. 4:13 [b]Job 2:7; Luke 13:16
12:8 [a]Deut. 3:23; Mat. 26:44
12:9 [a]ch. 11:30 [b]1 Pet. 4:14
12:10 [a]Rom. 5:3; ch. 7:4 [b]ch. 13:4
12:11 [a]ch. 11:1,16 [b]ch. 11:5; Gal. 2:6-8 [c]1 Cor. 3:7; Eph. 3:8
12:12 [a]Rom. 15:18; 1 Cor. 9:2; ch. 4:2
12:13 [a]1 Cor. 1:7 [b]1 Cor. 9:12; ch. 11:9 [c]ch. 11:7
12:14 [a]ch. 13:1 [b]Acts 20:33; 1 Cor. 10:33 [c]1 Cor. 4:14
12:15 [1]Gr. *your souls* [a]John 10:11; ch. 1:6; Col. 1:24; 2 Tim. 2:10 [b]ch. 6:12,13
12:16 [a]ch. 11:9
12:17 [a]ch. 7:2
12:18 [a]ch. 8:6,16 [b]ch. 8:18
12:19 [a]ch. 5:12 [b]Rom. 9:1; ch. 11:31 [c]1 Cor. 10:33
12:20 [a]1 Cor. 4:21; ch. 13:2,10
12:21 [a]ch. 2:1,4 [b]ch. 13:2 [c]1 Cor. 5:1
13:1 [a]ch. 12:14 [b]Num. 35:30; Deut. 17:6; Mat. 18:16; John 8:17; Heb. 10:28
13:2 [a]ch. 10:2 [b]ch. 12:21 [c]ch. 1:23
13:3 [a]Mat. 10:20; 1 Cor. 5:4

12:7 *thorn in the flesh.* The precise nature of this severe affliction remains unknown. *messenger of Satan.* A further description of Paul's thorn (cf. 1 Cor 5:5; 11:30; 1 Tim 1:20; see Job 2:10).

12:9 *My grace is sufficient for thee.* A better solution than to remove Paul's thorn. Human weakness provides the ideal opportunity for the display of divine power.

12:10 Cf. Eph 3:16; Phil 4:13.

12:11 *I am become a fool.* See note on 11:1. *ye . . . compelled me.* The Corinthian Christians have put Paul under pressure to write about himself as he did because they had accepted the claims of the "chiefest apostles" who had invaded their ranks, challenging Paul's apostolic authority.

12:12 *Truly the signs of an apostle.* Extraordinary gifts and powers had been displayed in their midst. By implication, the false teachers had come to them without these apostolic signs (cf. Heb 2:3–4).

‡12:13 *I myself was not burdensome to you.* See note on 11:9. Paul's refusal to accept any payment when preaching the gospel to the Corinthians had been slanderously twisted by his adversaries (see notes on 11:7,12). They, who had grasped at all they could get, were saying that it was he who had sinned against the Corinthians. *forgive me this wrong.* Irony—resuming the line of discussion in 11:7–12.

‡12:14 *third time.* See note on 2:1. *not be burdensome.* Chiefly now, so that the falsity and greed of the "chiefest apostles" may be clearly exposed (see 11:12). *children.* Paul is their spiritual father (cf. 6:13; 1 Cor 4:14–16).

12:15 His paternal devotion to them is shown not merely in his readiness to spend whatever money he has for them but, much more deeply, in his joyful willingness to spend himself completely for their sake.

‡12:16 *I caught you with guile.* Sarcastically echoes another of the slanders being made against Paul by the false apostles: that he was exploiting them by the trick of organizing a collection for the poverty-stricken Christians in Jerusalem—contributions that would never reach the mother-city because they went into Paul's own pocket (v. 17). No wonder, then, that he could afford not to be a burden to them! The fact is, however, that it is these false apostles who are the "deceitful workers" masquerading as "ministers of righteousness" (11:13–15). Paul is unblemished both in conduct and in conscience, and the Corinthians are fully aware of this.

12:18 *Titus . . . a brother.* See notes on 8:6,16,18–23.

12:19 *speak before God in Christ.* Paul's concern in speaking of himself is not for his own personal prestige and reputation before people (cf. 1 Cor 4:3–4). It is before God that he stands, and his standing before God is in Christ. Far from being self-centered, his concern is for the Corinthians, his dear friends—for their strengthening as they too stand before God in Christ. His entire ministry, with its sufferings, is directed to this end (cf. 10:8).

‡13:2 *I will not spare.* Paul will not hesitate to take stern disciplinary action against offenders when he comes to Corinth for the third time, as he is about to do.

13:3 *ye seek a proof of Christ speaking in me.* See note on 10:10.

in me, which to you-ward is not weak, but is
mighty [b]in you.
4 [a]For though he was crucified through
weakness, yet [b]he liveth by the power of God.
For [c]we also are weak [1]in him, but we shall
live with him by the power of God toward you.
5 Examine yourselves, whether ye be in
the faith; prove your own selves. Know ye not
your own selves, [a]how that Jesus Christ is in
you, except ye be [b]reprobates?
6 But I trust that ye shall know that we are
not reprobates.
7 Now I pray to God that ye do no evil; not
that we should appear approved, but that ye
should do *that which is* honest, though [a]we be
as reprobates.
8 For we can do nothing against the truth,
but for the truth.
9 For we are glad, [a]when we are weak, and
ye are strong: and this also we wish, [b]*even*
your perfection.

13:3 [b]1 Cor. 9:2
13:4 [1]Or, *with him* [a]Phil. 2:7,8; 1 Pet. 3:18 [b]Rom. 6:4 [c]ch. 10:3,4
13:5 [a]Rom. 8:10; Gal. 4:19 [b]1 Cor. 9:27
13:7 [a]ch. 6:9
13:9 [a]1 Cor. 4:10; ch. 11:30 [b]1 Thes. 3:10
13:10 [a]1 Cor. 4:21; ch. 12:20,21
13:11 [a]Rom. 12:16,18 [b]Rom. 15:33
13:12 [a]Rom. 16:16; 1 Cor. 16:20; 1 Thes. 5:26; 1 Pet. 5:14
13:14 [a]Rom. 16:24 [b]Phil. 2:1

10 [a]Therefore I write these *things* being
absent, lest being present I should use sharp-
ness, according to the power which the Lord
hath given me to edification, and not to destruction.

Farewell and benediction

11 ¶ Finally, brethren, farewell. Be perfect,
be of good comfort, [a]be of one mind, live in
peace; and the God of love [b]and peace shall be
with you.
12 [a]Greet one another with a holy kiss.
13 All the saints salute you.
14 [a]The grace of the Lord Jesus Christ, and
the love of God, and [b]the communion of the
Holy Ghost, *be* with you all. Amen.

¶ The second *epistle* to the Corinthians was written from Philippi, *a city* of Macedonia, by Titus and Lucas.

They will be given ample proof when he comes, unless they show a change of heart. *which to you-ward is not weak.* Rebellion against Paul is rebellion against Christ, who appointed him as His apostle. The authority of the apostle is the authority of his Master. Any who imagine that Paul is weak will find that Christ, the Lord who speaks through His apostle, is not weak but powerful.

13:4 *we shall live with him by the power of God.* Paul is referring to his present apostolic authority, and to the fact that divine power will be displayed by the punishment of any who resist that authority.

13:5 *Examine yourselves . . . prove your own selves.* Instead of demanding proof that Christ was speaking through him (v. 3), as the false apostles were inciting them to do, they should look into their own hearts.

13:7 *do that which is honest.* Then there will be no need for Paul to give evidence of his authority by taking disciplinary action when he comes to them.

13:8 *we can do nothing against the truth.* Paul can exercise his apostolic authority only in a way that supports the truth. Consequently, if the truth is acknowledged when he arrives in Corinth, there will be no need for him to take disciplinary action.

13:9 *weak.* To have no need to give proof of his apostolic strength. *strong.* In the truth.

13:11–14 These concluding exhortations and salutations exhibit a note of confidence.

13:11 *God of . . . peace.* See note on 1 Thes 5:23.

13:12 *kiss.* A token of mutual trust and affection, still in common use in the Near East—corresponding to the handshake of the Western world. For Christians it must be a holy kiss, for all greetings should be purely and sincerely exchanged in Christ (see 1:2).

‡13:14 The benediction is Trinitarian in form and has ever since been a part of Christian worship tradition. It serves to remind us that the mystery of the Holy Trinity is known to be true not through rational or philosophical explanation but through Christian experience, whereby the believer knows firsthand the grace, the love, and the fellowship that freely flow from the three Persons of the one Lord God.

The Epistle of Paul the Apostle to the Galatians

INTRODUCTION

Author

The opening verse identifies the author of Galatians as the apostle Paul. Apart from a few 19th-century scholars, no one has seriously questioned his authorship.

Date and Destination

The date of Galatians depends to a great extent on the destination of the letter. There are two main views:

1. *The North Galatian theory.* This older view holds that the letter was addressed to churches located in north-central Asia Minor (Pessinus, Ancyra and Tavium), where the Gauls had settled when they invaded the area in the third century B.C. It is held that Paul visited this area on his second missionary journey, though Acts contains no reference to such a visit. Galatians, it is maintained, was written between A.D. 53 and 57 from Ephesus or Macedonia.

2. *The South Galatian theory.* According to this view, Galatians was written to churches in the southern area of the Roman province of Galatia (Antioch, Iconium, Lystra and Derbe) that Paul had founded on his first missionary journey. Some believe that Galatians was written from Syrian Antioch in 48–49 after Paul's first journey and before the Jerusalem council meeting (Acts 15). Others say that Galatians was written in Syrian Antioch or Corinth between 51 and 53.

Occasion and Purpose

Judaizers were Jewish Christians who believed, among other things, that a number of the ceremonial practices of the OT were still binding on the NT church. Following Paul's successful campaign in Galatia, they insisted that Gentile converts to Christianity abide by certain OT rites, especially circumcision. They may have been motivated by a desire to avoid the persecution of Zealot Jews who objected to their fraternizing with Gentiles (see 6:12). The Judaizers argued that Paul was not an authentic apostle and that out of a desire to make the message more appealing to Gentiles he had removed from the gospel certain legal requirements.

Paul responded by clearly establishing his apostolic authority and thereby substantiating the gospel he preached. By introducing additional requirements for justification (e.g., works of the law) his adversaries had perverted the gospel of grace and, unless prevented, would bring Paul's converts into the bondage of legalism. It is by grace through faith alone that man is justified, and it is by faith alone that he is to live out his new life in the freedom of the Spirit.

Theological Teaching

Galatians stands as an eloquent and vigorous apologetic for the essential NT truth that man is justified by faith in Jesus Christ—by nothing less and nothing more—and that he is sanctified not by legalistic works but by the obedience that comes from faith in God's work for him, in him and through him by the grace and power of Christ and the Holy Spirit. It was the rediscovery of the basic message of Galatians that brought about the Reformation. Galatians is often referred to as "Luther's book," because Martin Luther relied so strongly on this letter in his writings and arguments against the prevailing theology of his day. A key verse is 2:16 (see note there).

Outline

- I. Introduction (1:1–9)
  - A. Salutation (1:1–5)
  - B. Denunciation (1:6–9)
- II. Personal: Authentication of the Apostle of Liberty and Faith (1:10—2:21)
  - A. Paul's Gospel Was Received by Special Revelation (1:10–12)

- B. Paul's Gospel Was Independent of the Jerusalem Apostles and the Judean Churches (1:13—2:21)
  1. Evidenced by his early activities as a Christian (1:13–17)
  2. Evidenced by his first post-Christian visit to Jerusalem (1:18–24)
  3. Evidenced by his second post-Christian visit to Jerusalem (2:1–10)
  4. Evidenced by his rebuke of Peter at Antioch (2:11–21)

III. Doctrinal: Justification of the Doctrine of Liberty and Faith (chs. 3—4)
- A. The Galatians' Experience of the Gospel (3:1–5)
- B. The Experience of Abraham (3:6–9)
- C. The Curse of the Law (3:10–14)
- D. The Priority of the Promise (3:15–18)
- E. The Purpose of the Law (3:19–25)
- F. Sons, Not Slaves (3:26—4:11)
- G. Appeal to Enter into Freedom from Law (4:12–20)
- H. The Allegory of Hagar and Sarah (4:21–31)

IV. Practical: Practice of the Life of Liberty and Faith (5:1—6:10)
- A. Exhortation to Freedom (5:1–12)
- B. Life by the Spirit, Not by the Flesh (5:13–26)
- C. Call for Mutual Help (6:1–10)

V. Conclusion (6:11–18)

No other gospel

1 Paul, an apostle, (not of men, neither by
man, but [a]by Jesus Christ, and God the
Father, [b]who raised him from the dead;)
2 And all the brethren [a]which are with me,
[b]unto the churches of Galatia:
3 [a]Grace *be* to you and peace from God the
Father, and *from* our Lord Jesus Christ,
4 [a]Who gave himself for our sins, that he
might deliver us [b]from *this* present evil world,
according to the will of God and our Father:
5 To whom *be* glory for ever and ever.
Amen.
6 ¶ I marvel that you are so soon removed
[a]from him that called you into the grace of
Christ unto another gospel:
7 [a]Which is not another; but there be some
[b]that trouble you, and would pervert the
gospel of Christ.
8 But though [a]we, or an angel from heav-
en, preach any other gospel unto you than *that*
which we have preached unto you, let him be
accursed.
9 As we said before, so say I now again, If
any *man* preach any other gospel unto you [a]than
that ye have received, let him be accursed.
10 For [a]do I now [b]persuade men, or God?
or [c]do I seek to please men? for if I yet pleased
men, I should not be the servant of Christ.

1:1 [a]Acts 9:6; Tit. 1:3 [b]Acts 2:24
1:2 [a]Phil. 2:22 [b]1 Cor. 16:1
1:3 [a]1 Thes. 1:1
1:4 [a]Mat. 20:28; Rom. 4:25; Tit. 2:14 [b]Heb. 2:5; 1 John 5:19
1:6 [a]ch. 5:8
1:7 [a]2 Cor. 11:4 [b]Acts 15:1; 2 Cor. 2:17
1:8 [a]1 Cor. 16:22
1:9 [a]Deut. 4:2; Prov. 30:6; Rev. 22:18
1:10 [a]1 Thes. 2:4 [b]1 Sam. 24:7; Mat. 28:14 [c]1 Thes. 2:4; Jas. 4:4
1:11 [a]1 Cor. 15:1
1:12 [a]1 Cor. 15:1 [b]Eph. 3:3
1:13 [a]Acts 9:1; 1 Tim. 1:13 [b]Acts 8:3
1:14 [1]Gr. *equals in years* [a]Acts 26:9; Phil. 3:6 [b]Jer. 9:14; Mat. 15:2; Mark 7:5
1:15 [a]Is. 49:1,5
1:16 [a]2 Cor. 4:6 [b]Acts 9:15; Eph. 3:8 [c]Mat. 16:17; Eph. 6:12
1:18 [1]Or, *returned* [a]Acts 9:26

Paul's authority of divine origin

11 ¶ [a]But I certify you, brethren, that the
gospel which was preached of me is not after
man.
12 For [a]I neither received it of man, neither was I taught *it,* but [b]by the revelation of
Jesus Christ.
13 For ye have heard of my conversation in
time past in the Jews' religion, how that [a]be-
yond measure I persecuted the church of God,
and [b]wasted it:
14 And profited in the Jews' religion above
many *my* [1]equals in mine own nation, [a]being
more exceedingly zealous [b]of the traditions of
my fathers.
15 But when it pleased God, [a]who separated me from my mother's womb, and called *me*
by his grace,
16 [a]To reveal his Son in me, that [b]I might
preach him among the heathen; immediately I
conferred not with [c]flesh and blood:
17 Neither went I up to Jerusalem to them
which were apostles before me; but I went
into Arabia, and returned again unto Damascus.
18 Then after three years [a]I [1]went up to Jerusalem to see Peter, and abode with him fifteen days.

1:1 *Paul.* Writers of this time customarily put their names at the beginning of letters. For more information on Paul see notes on Acts 9:1; Phil 3:4–14. *apostle.* One sent on a mission with full authority of representation; an ambassador (see note on 1 Cor 1:1). *raised him from the dead.* The resurrection is the central affirmation of the Christian faith (see Acts 17:18; Rom 1:4; 1 Cor 15:20; 1 Pet 1:3), and because Paul had seen the risen Christ he was qualified to be an apostle (see Acts 1:22 and note; 2:32; 1 Cor 15:8).
1:2 *brethren.* Fellow Christians (see 3:15; 4:12; 5:11; 6:18). *churches.* This was a circular letter to several congregations. *Galatia.* The term occurs four times in the NT. In 2 Tim 4:10 the reference is uncertain. In 1 Pet 1:1 it refers to the northern area of Asia Minor occupied by the Gauls. Here (and in 1 Cor 16:1) Paul probably uses the term to refer to the Roman province of Galatia and an additional area to the south, through which he traveled on his first missionary journey (Acts 13:14–14:23). See Introduction: Date and Destination.
1:3 *Grace.* The Christian adaptation of a common Greek form of greeting (see notes on Jon 4:2; Eph 1:2). *peace.* The common Hebrew form of greeting (see notes on John 14:27; 20:19; Eph 1:2).
1:4 *for our sins.* See Mat 1:21; John 1:29; 1 Cor 15:3; 1 Pet 2:24. *present evil world.* The present period of the world's history (see note on 2 Cor 4:4). In contrast to the age to come (the climax of the Messianic age), this present age is characterized by wickedness (Eph 2:2; 6:12).
1:5 For other doxologies see Rom 9:5; 11:36; 16:27; Eph 3:21; 1 Tim 1:17.
1:6 *so soon.* So soon after your conversion. *him that called you.* God. *grace of Christ.* The test of a pure, unadulterated gospel.
1:7 *some.* The Judaizers (see Introduction: Occasion and Purpose).
1:8 *accursed.* The Greek word (*anathema*) originally referred to a pagan temple offering in payment for a vow. Later it came to represent a curse (see v. 9; 1 Cor 12:3; 16:22; Rom 9:3).
1:10 *servant of Christ.* Paul once wore the "yoke of slavery" (5:1) but, having been set free from sin by the redemption that is in Christ, he became a slave of righteousness, a slave of God (see Rom 6:18,22).
1:11 *I certify you, brethren.* A similar phrase is found in 1 Cor 15:1, where Paul sets forth the gospel he received. *the gospel . . . preached of me.* Called "my gospel" in Rom 2:16; 16:25. Salvation is for all and is received by faith in Christ.
1:12 *by the revelation of Jesus Christ.* See Eph 3:2–6.
‡1:13 *the Jews' religion.* The Jewish faith and way of life that developed during the period between the OT and the NT. The NT counterpart of the OT assembly (see Num 16:21) or community of the Lord (Num 20:4).
1:14 *zealous.* See Phil 3:6. *traditions of my fathers.* Traditions orally transmitted from previous generations and contrasted with the written law of Moses. Cf. the "tradition of the elders" (see note on Mat 15:2).
1:15 *separated me from my mother's womb.* See Is 49:1; Jer 1:5; Rom 1:1.
1:16 *heathen.* Lit. "nations" or "peoples." The term commonly designated foreigners—hence pagans, or the non-Jewish world. *flesh and blood.* In the NT always with the implication of human weakness or ignorance (see Mat 16:17; 1 Cor 15:50; Eph 6:12). Paul received his message from God.
1:17 *Jerusalem.* The religious center of Judaism and the birthplace of Christianity. *Arabia.* The Nabatean kingdom in Transjordan stretching from Damascus southwest to the Suez. *Damascus.* Ancient capital of Syria (Aram in the OT). Paul had been converted en route from Jerusalem to Damascus (Acts 9:1–9).
1:18 *after three years.* From the time of his departure into Arabia. The text does not say he spent the three years in Arabia. *I went up to Jerusalem.* Probably the visit referred to in Acts 9:26–30, though some equate it with the one in Acts 11:30. *Peter.* Peter; from the Greek word for "stone"; the Aramaic equivalent is "Cephas" (see Mat 16:18 and note). The name designates a like quality in the bearer (see note on John 1:42).

19 But [a]other of the apostles saw I none,
save [b]James the Lord's brother.
20 Now *the things* which I write unto you,
[a]behold, before God, I lie not.
21 [a]Afterwards I came into the regions of
Syria and Cilicia;
22 And was unknown by face [a]unto the
churches of Judea which [b]were in Christ:
23 But they had heard only, That he which
persecuted us in times past now preacheth the
faith which once he destroyed.
24 And they glorified God in me.

Paul accepted by the church

2 Then fourteen years after [a]I went up
again to Jerusalem with Barnabas, and
took Titus with *me* also.
2 And I went up by revelation, [a]and communicated unto them *that* gospel which I
preach among the Gentiles, but [1]privately to
them which were of reputation, lest by any
means [b]I should run, or had run, in vain.
3 But neither Titus, who was with me, being a Greek, was compelled to be circumcised:
4 And *that* because of [a]false brethren unawares brought in, who came in privily to spy
out our [b]liberty which we have in Christ
Jesus, [c]that they might bring us into bondage:
5 To whom we gave place by subjection,
no, not for an hour; that [a]the truth of the
gospel might continue with you.
6 But of these [a]who seemed to be somewhat, (whatsoever they were, it maketh no
matter to me: [b]God accepteth no man's person:) for they who seemed *to be somewhat* [c]in
conference added nothing to me:
7 But contrariwise, [a]when they saw that
the gospel of the uncircumcision [b]was committed unto me, as *the gospel* of the circumcision *was* unto Peter;
8 (For he that wrought effectually in Peter
to the apostleship of the circumcision, [a]*the
same* was [b]mighty in me towards the Gentiles:)
9 And when James, Cephas, and John, who
seemed to be [a]pillars, perceived [b]the grace
that was given unto me, they gave to me and
Barnabas the right hands of fellowship; that
we *should go* unto the heathen, and they unto
the circumcision.
10 Only *they would* that we should remember the poor; [a]the same which I also was
forward to do.

Paul's opposition to Peter

11 ¶ [a]But when Peter was come to Antioch, I withstood him to the face, because he
was *to be* blamed.
12 For before that certain came from
James, [a]he did eat with the Gentiles: but
when they were come, he withdrew and separated himself, fearing them which were of the
circumcision.
13 And the other Jews dissembled likewise
with him; insomuch that Barnabas also was
carried away with their dissimulation.
14 But when I saw that they walked not
uprightly according to [a]the truth of the gospel,
I said unto Peter [b]before *them* all, [c]If thou, being a Jew, livest after the manner of Gentiles,
and not as do the Jews, why compellest thou
the Gentiles to live as do the Jews?
15 [a]We *who are* Jews by nature, and not
[b]sinners of the Gentiles,
16 [a]Knowing that a man is not justified by
the works of the law, but [b]by the faith of Jesus
Christ, even we have believed in Jesus Christ,

1:19 [a]1 Cor. 9:5 [b]Mat. 13:55
1:20 [a]Rom. 9:1
1:21 [a]Acts 9:30
1:22 [a]1 Thes. 2:14 [b]Rom. 16:7
2:1 [a]Acts 15:2
2:2 [1]Or, *severally* [a]Acts 15:12 [b]Phil. 2:16; 1 Thes. 3:5
2:4 [a]Acts 15:1; 2 Cor. 11:26 [b]ch. 3:25 [c]ch. 4:3,9
2:5 [a]ver. 14
2:6 [a]ch. 6:3 [b]Acts 10:34; Rom. 2:11 [c]2 Cor. 12:11
2:7 [a]Acts 13:46; Rom. 11:13; 2 Tim. 1:11 [b]1 Thes. 2:4
2:8 [a]Acts 9:15; 1 Cor. 15:10 [b]ch. 3:5
2:9 [a]Mat. 16:18; Rev. 21:14 [b]Rom. 1:5; 1 Cor. 15:10; Eph. 3:8
2:10 [a]Acts 11:30; Rom. 15:25
2:11 [a]Acts 15:35
2:12 [a]Acts 10:28
2:14 [a]ver. 5 [b]1 Tim. 5:20 [c]Acts 10:28
2:15 [a]Acts 15:10 [b]Mat. 9:11; Eph. 2:3
2:16 [a]Acts 13:38 [b]Rom. 1:17; ch. 3:24

1:19 *James.* See Introduction to James: Author. In Acts 21:18 this James appears to be the leader of the elders in the Jerusalem church. *the Lord's brother.* See note on Luke 8:19.
1:21 *Syria and Cilicia.* Provinces in Asia Minor. Specifically Paul went to Tarsus (see Acts 9:30), his hometown.
2:1 *fourteen years after.* Probably from the date of Paul's conversion. *I went up again to Jerusalem.* According to some, the visit mentioned in Acts 11:30; according to others, the one in Acts 15:1–4 (see notes on Acts 12:1; 15:2). *Barnabas.* Means "one who encourages." His given name was Joseph, and he was a Levite from the island of Cyprus (see Acts 4:36 and note). He was Paul's companion on the first missionary journey (Acts 13:1–14:28). *Titus.* A Gentile Christian who served as Paul's delegate to Corinth and later was left in Crete to oversee the church there (see Tit 1:5).
2:2 *them which were of reputation.* Paul recognized their authority, and is probably referring to James, Peter and John (v. 9; cf. v. 6). *had run, in vain.* See 1 Cor 15:58; Phil 2:16.
2:4 *false brethren.* Judaizers who held that Gentile converts should be circumcised and obey the law of Moses (cf. Acts 15:5; 2 Cor 11:26). *to spy out.* Used in the Septuagint (the Greek translation of the OT) in 2 Sam 10:3 and 1 Chr 19:3 of spying out a territory. *liberty.* See 5:1,13; Rom 6:18,20,22; 8:2.
2:6 *these who seemed to be somewhat.* See note on v. 2. *accepteth no man's person.* Cf. Deut 10:17;1 Sam 16:7; Luke 20:21; Jas 2:1.
2:7 *gospel of the uncircumcision.* Paul's ministry was not exclusively to the Gentiles. In fact, he regularly went first to the synagogue when arriving in a new location (see note on Acts 13:14). He did, however, consider himself to be foremost an apostle to the Gentiles (see Rom 11:13 and note).
2:9 *James.* See note on 1:19. *pillars.* A common metaphor for those who represent and strongly support an institution. *right hands of fellowship.* A common practice among both Hebrews and Greeks, indicating a pledge of friendship.
2:11 *Antioch.* The leading city of Syria and third leading city of the Roman empire (after Rome and Alexandria). From it Paul had been sent out on his missionary journeys (see Acts 13:1–3; 14:26). *was to be blamed.* For yielding to the pressure of the circumcision party (the Judaizers), thus going against what he knew to be right.
2:12 *them which were of the circumcision.* Judaizers, who believed that circumcision was necessary for salvation (cf. Acts 10:45; 11:2; Rom 4:12).
2:13 *the other Jews.* Jewish Christians not associated with the circumcision party but whom Peter's behavior had led astray.
2:14 *livest after the manner of Gentiles.* You do not observe Jewish customs, especially dietary restrictions (see v. 12).
2:16 A key verse in Galatians (see Introduction: Theological Teaching). Three times it tells us that no one is justified by observing the law, and three times it underscores the indispensable requirement of placing one's faith in Christ. *justified by the faith of Christ.* The essence of the gospel message (see Rom 3:20,28; Phil 3:9; see also notes on Rom 3:24,28). Faith is the

that we might be justified by the faith of Christ, and not by the works of the law: for [c]by the works of the law shall no flesh be justified.

17 But if, while we seek to be justified by Christ, we ourselves also are found [a]sinners, *is* therefore Christ the minister of sin? God forbid.

18 For if I build again the *things* which I destroyed, I make myself a transgressor.

19 For I [a]through the law [b]am dead to the law, that I might [c]live unto God.

20 I am [a]crucified with Christ: nevertheless I live; yet not I, but Christ liveth in me: and *the life* which I now live in the flesh [b]I live by the faith of the Son of God, [c]who loved me, and gave himself for me.

21 I do not frustrate the grace of God: for [a]if righteousness *come* by the law, then Christ is dead in vain.

Receiving the Spirit by faith

3 O foolish Galatians, [a]who hath bewitched you, that *you* should not obey [b]the truth, before whose eyes Jesus Christ hath been evidently set forth, crucified among you?

2 This only would I learn of you, Received ye [a]the Spirit by the works of the law, [b]or by the hearing of faith?

3 Are ye so foolish? [a]having begun in the Spirit, are ye now made perfect by [b]the flesh?

4 [a]Have ye suffered [1]so many *things* in vain? if *it be* yet in vain.

5 He therefore that ministereth to you the Spirit, and worketh miracles among you, *doeth he it* by the works of the law, or by the hearing of faith?

6 Even as [a]Abraham believed God, and it was [1]accounted to him for righteousness.

7 Know ye therefore that [a]they which are of faith, the same are the children of Abraham.

8 And [a]the scripture, foreseeing that God would justify the heathen through faith, preached before the gospel unto Abraham, *saying,* [b]In thee shall all nations be blessed.

9 So then they which be of faith are blessed with faithful Abraham.

10 For as many as are of the works of the law are under the curse: for it is written, [a]Cursed *is* every one that continueth not in all *things* which are written in the book of the law to do them.

11 But [a]that no *man* is justified by the law in the sight of God, *it is* evident: for, [b]The just shall live by faith.

12 And [a]the law is not of faith: but, [b]The man that doeth them shall live in them.

13 [a]Christ hath redeemed us from the curse of the law, being made a curse for us: for it is written, [b]Cursed *is* every one that hangeth on a tree:

14 [a]That the blessing of Abraham might come on the Gentiles through Jesus Christ; that we might receive [b]the promise of the Spirit through faith.

15 Brethren, I speak after the manner of men; [a]Though *it be* but a man's [1]covenant, *yet if it be* confirmed, no *man* disannulleth, or added thereto.

16 Now [a]to Abraham and his seed were the promises made. *He* saith not, And to

2:16 [c]Ps. 143:2; Rom. 3:20
2:17 [a]1 John 3:8
2:19 [a]Rom. 8:2 [b]Rom. 6:14 [c]Rom. 6:11; 2 Cor. 5:15; Heb. 9:14
2:20 [a]Rom. 6:6 [b]2 Cor. 5:15; 1 Pet. 4:2 [c]Eph. 5:2; Tit. 2:14
2:21 [a]Heb. 7:11; Rom. 11:6
3:1 [a]ch. 5:7 [b]ch. 2:14
3:2 [a]Acts 2:38; Eph. 1:13; Heb. 6:4 [b]Rom. 10:16
3:3 [a]ch. 4:9 [b]Heb. 7:16
3:4 [1]Or, *so great* [a]Heb. 10:35; 2 John 8
3:6 [1]Or, *imputed* [a]Gen. 15:6; Rom. 4:3,9; Jas. 2:23
3:7 [a]John 8:39
3:8 [a]Rom. 9:17 [b]Gen. 12:3; Acts 3:25
3:10 [a]Deut. 27:26; Jer. 11:3
3:11 [a]ch. 2:16 [b]Hab. 2:4; Rom. 1:17; Heb. 10:38
3:12 [a]Rom. 4:4,5 [b]Lev. 18:5; Rom. 10:5
3:13 [a]Rom. 8:3; 2 Cor. 5:21 [b]Deut. 21:23
3:14 [a]Rom. 4:9 [b]Is. 32:15; Ezek. 11:19; Acts 2:33
3:15 [1]Or, *testament* [a]Heb. 9:17
3:16 [a]Gen. 12:3

means by which justification is received, not its basis. *by the works of the law.* Paul is not depreciating the law itself, for he clearly maintained that God's law is "holy, and just, and good" (Rom 7:12). He is arguing against an illegitimate use of the OT law that made the observance of that law the grounds of acceptance with God.

2:19 *dead to the law.* See v. 20; see also note on Rom 7:4.

‡2:20 *crucified with Christ.* See 5:24; 6:14; Rom 6:8–10; 7:6; see also note on Rom 6:7. *gave himself for me.* See 1:4; 1 Tim 2:6; Tit 2:14.

2:21 *Christ is dead in vain.* To mingle legalism with grace distorts grace and makes a mockery of the cross.

3:1 *foolish.* They were not mentally deficient but simply failed to use their powers of perception (see Luke 24:25; Rom 1:14; 1 Tim 6:9; Tit 3:3). *who . . . ?* Obviously legalistic Judaizers. *set forth, crucified.* See 1 Cor 1:23; 2:2. The verb means "to publicly portray or placard." Cf. the brass serpent that Moses displayed on a pole (Num 21:9).

3:2 *the Spirit.* From this point on in Galatians Paul refers to the Holy Spirit 16 times.

3:3 *begun in the Spirit . . . made perfect.* Both salvation and sanctification are the work of the Holy Spirit. *by the flesh.* A reference to human nature in its unregenerate weakness. Trying to achieve righteousness by works, including circumcision, was a part of life in the "flesh."

3:4 Paul hopes that those who have been misled will return to the true gospel.

3:7 *children of Abraham.* Abraham was the physical and spiritual father of the Jewish race (see John 8:33,39,53; Acts 7:2; Rom 4:12). Here all believers (Jews and Gentiles) are called his spiritual children (see notes on Rom 4:11–12). They are also referred to as the "seed" or "descendants" of Abraham (v. 16; Heb 2:16).

3:8 *scripture, foreseeing.* A personification of Scripture that calls attention to its divine origin (see 1 Tim 5:18).

3:9 *faithful Abraham.* Paul develops this theme at length in Rom 4; see also Heb 11:8–19.

3:10 *are of the works of the law.* The reference is to legalists—those who refuse God's offer of grace and insist on pursuing righteousness through works. *under the curse.* Because no one under the law ever perfectly kept the law. God's blessing has never been earned, but has always been freely given. *all things.* See Jas 2:10.

3:11 *shall live.* Means here (and in v. 12) almost the same thing as "will be justified."

3:13 *Christ hath redeemed us from the curse of the law.* See 4:5; Rom 8:3. *tree.* Used in classical Greek of stocks and poles on which bodies were impaled, here of the cross (see Acts 5:30; 10:39; 1 Pet 2:24).

3:14 *the blessing of Abraham.* See v. 8; Rom 4:1–5. *promise of the Spirit.* See Ezek 36:26; 37:14; 39:29; John 14:16; cf. Eph 1:13.

3:15 *Brethren.* See note on 1:2. *man's covenant.* The Greek word normally indicates a last will or testament, which is probably the legal instrument Paul is referring to here. But in the Septuagint (the Greek translation of the OT) it had been widely used of God's covenant with His people (see also Mat 26:28; Luke 1:72; Acts 3:25; 7:8; 2 Cor 3:14; Heb 8:9), so Paul's choice of analogy was apt for his purpose.

seeds, as of many; but as of one, And to thy seed, which is [b]Christ.

17 And this I say, *that* the covenant, that was confirmed before of God in Christ, the law, [a]which was four hundred and thirty years after, cannot disannul, [b]that *it* should make the promise of none effect.

18 For if [a]the inheritance *be* of the law, [b]*it is* no more of promise: but God gave *it* to Abraham by promise.

The function of the law

19 ¶ Wherefore then *serveth* the law? [a]It was added because of transgressions, till the seed should come to whom the promise was made; *and it was* [b]ordained by angels in the hand [c]of a mediator.

20 Now a mediator is not *a mediator* of one, [a]but God is one.

21 *Is* the law then against the promises of God? God forbid: for if there had been a law given which could have given life, verily righteousness should have been by the law.

22 But the scripture hath concluded [a]all under sin, [b]that the promise by faith of Jesus Christ might be given to them that believe.

23 But before faith came, we were kept under the law, shut up unto the faith which should afterwards be revealed.

24 Wherefore [a]the law was our schoolmaster *to bring us* unto Christ, [b]that we might be justified by faith.

25 But after that faith is come, we are no longer under a schoolmaster.

26 For ye [a]are all the children of God by faith in Christ Jesus.

27 For [a]as many of you as have been baptized into Christ [b]have put on Christ.

28 [a]There is neither Jew nor Greek, there is neither bond nor free, there is neither male nor female: for ye are all [b]one in Christ Jesus.

29 And [a]if ye *be* Christ's, then are ye Abraham's seed, and [b]heirs according to the promise.

Do not return to bondage

4 Now I say, *That* the heir, as long as he is a child, differeth nothing from a servant, though he be lord of all;

2 But is under tutors and governors until the time appointed of the father.

3 Even so we, when we were children, [a]were in bondage under the [1]elements of the world:

4 But [a]when the fulness of the time was come, God sent forth his Son, [b]made [c]of a woman, [d]made under the law,

5 [a]To redeem them that were under the law, [b]that we might receive the adoption of sons.

3:16 [b]1 Cor. 12:12
3:17 [a]Ex. 12:40 [b]Rom. 4:13
3:18 [a]Rom. 8:17 [b]Rom. 4:14
3:19 [a]John 15:22; Rom. 4:15 [b]Acts 7:53 [c]Ex. 20:19; John 1:17
3:20 [a]Rom. 3:29
3:22 [a]Rom. 11:32 [b]Rom. 4:11
3:24 [a]Rom. 10:4
3:24 [b]Acts 13:39
3:26 [a]John 1:12; Rom. 8:14
3:27 [a]Rom. 6:3 [b]Rom. 13:14
3:28 [a]Rom. 10:12 [b]John 10:16; Eph. 2:14
3:29 [a]Gen. 21:10; Heb. 11:18 [b]Rom. 8:17
4:3 [1]Or, *rudiments* [a]Col. 2:8; Heb. 9:10
4:4 [a]Gen. 49:10; Mark 1:15 [b]John 1:14; Heb. 2:14 [c]Gen. 3:15; Is. 7:14; Mat. 1:23 [d]Mat. 5:17; Luke 2:27
4:5 [a]Mat. 20:28; Heb. 9:12 [b]John 1:12; Eph. 1:5

3:16 *promises.* See notes on Rom 4:13; 9:4.

3:17 *four hundred and thirty years.* See Ex 12:40–41. The period in Egypt is designated in round numbers as "400 years" in Gen 15:13; Acts 7:6.

‡3:19 *was added.* From the time of Abraham, the promise covenanted to him (Gen 12:2–3,7; 15:18–20; 17:4–8) had stood at the center of God's relationship with His people. After the exodus the law contained in the Sinaitic covenant (Ex 19–24) became an additional element in that relationship—what Jeremiah by implication called the "old covenant" when he brought God's promise of a "new covenant" (Jer 31:31–34). *till the seed should come.* After God promised through Abraham's seed (Jesus Christ) to regenerate the nations, He added the Mosaic law to reveal and restrain sin until Christ should come and provide righteousness to all who believe (Rom 10:4). The purpose of the law has been fulfilled within those who have obtained righteousness and sonship in Christ (see vv. 24–25). *by angels.* See Deut 33:2; Acts 7:38,53; Heb 2:2.

3:20 The Mosaic covenant was a formal arrangement of mutual commitments between God and Israel, with Moses as the mediator. But since the promise God covenanted with Abraham involved commitment only from God's side (and God is one; see note on Deut 6:4), no mediator was involved.

3:21 The reason the law is not opposed to the promise is that, although in itself it cannot save, it serves to reveal sin, which alienates God from man, and to show the need for the salvation that the promise offers.

‡3:23 *faith.* In Christ (v. 22). *kept under the law.* To be a prisoner of sin (v. 22) and a prisoner of law amounts to much the same, because law reveals and stimulates sin (see 4:3; Rom 7:8; Col 2:20).

3:24 *was our schoolmaster.* The expression translates the Greek *paidagogos* (from which "pedagogue" is derived). It refers to the personal slave-attendant who accompanied a freeborn boy wherever he went and exercised a certain amount of discipline over him. His function was as much that of a baby-sitter as a teacher (see 1 Cor 4:15, "tutors").

‡3:25 *no longer under a schoolmaster.* See v. 19.

‡3:26 By adoption, the justified believer is a full adult and heir in God's family, with all the attendant rights and privileges (4:1–7; Rom 8:14–17).

3:27 *baptized into Christ.* See Rom 6:3–11; 1 Cor 12:13.

‡3:28 Unity in Christ transcends ethnic, social and sexual distinctions (see Rom 10:12; 1 Cor 12:13; Eph 2:15–16). These earthly distinctions and roles remain, but all who are "in Christ" are positioned as full and equal sons and heirs of God. *free.* See 5:1,13; Rom 6:18,20,22; 8:2. "Free" and "freedom" are key words in Galatians, occurring ten times (here; 4:22–23,26,30–31; 5:1,13; cf. "liberty" in 2:4).

3:29 Christians are Abraham's true, spiritual descendants.

4:1 *child.* A minor. Contrast with "men" in 1 Cor 14:20 ("perfect" in Phil 3:15).

‡4:2 *tutors.* "Guardians" may be a better translation here, since this is a broader term than the one used in 3:24. See Mat 20:8; Luke 8:3 ("steward").

‡4:3 *in bondage.* See note on 3:23. *elements.* The Greek term meant essentially "things placed side by side in a row" (as the ABCs) and then came to mean fundamental principles or basic elements of various kinds. The context here suggests that it refers to the elemental forms of religion, whether those of the Jews (under the law, v. 5) or those of the Gentiles (under their old religious bondage, v. 8).

‡4:4 *fulness of the time was come.* The time "appointed" (v. 2) by God for His children to become adult sons and heirs. *God sent forth his Son.* See John 1:14; 3:16; Rom 1:1–6; 1 John 4:14. *made of a woman.* Showing that Christ was truly human. *made under the law.* Subject to the Jewish law.

‡4:5 *the adoption of sons.* With the full rights of sons. See Rom 8:15, where the "spirit of adoption" is contrasted with the "spirit of bondage" (cf. Eph 1:5). God takes into His family as fully

6 And because ye are sons, God hath sent forth [a]the Spirit of his Son into your hearts, crying, Abba, Father.

7 Wherefore thou art no more a servant, but a son; [a]and if a son, then an heir of God through Christ.

8 Howbeit then, [a]when ye knew not God, [b]ye did service unto them which by nature are no gods.

9 But now, [a]after that ye have known God, or rather are known of God, [b]how turn ye [1]again to [c]the weak and beggarly [2]elements, whereunto ye desire again to be in bondage?

10 [a]Ye observe days, and months, and times, and years.

11 I am afraid of you, [a]lest I have bestowed upon you labour in vain.

Paul's concern for the Galatians

12 ¶ Brethren, I beseech you, be as I *am;* for I *am* as ye *are:* [a]ye have not injured me at all.

13 Ye know how [a]through infirmity of the flesh I preached the gospel unto you at the first.

14 And my temptation which was in my flesh ye despised not, nor rejected; but received me [a]as an angel of God, [b]*even* as Christ Jesus.

15 [1]Where is then the blessedness you spake of? for I bear you record, that if *it had been* possible, ye would have plucked out your own eyes, and have given *them* to me.

16 Am I therefore become your enemy, because I tell you the truth?

17 They [a]zealously affect you, *but* not well; yea, they would exclude [1]you, that you might affect them.

18 But *it is* good to be zealously affected always in a good *thing,* and not only when I am present with you.

19 [a]My little children, of whom I travail in birth again until Christ be formed in you,

20 I desire to be present with you now, and to change my voice; for [1]I stand in doubt of you.

The allegory of Abraham

21 ¶ Tell me, ye that desire to be under the law, do ye not hear the law?

22 For it is written, that Abraham had two sons, [a]the one by a bondmaid, [b]the other by a freewoman.

23 But he who was of the bondwoman [a]was born after the flesh; [b]but he of the freewoman *was* by promise.

24 Which *things* are an allegory: for these are the two [1]covenants; the one from the mount [a][2]Sinai, which gendereth to bondage, which is Agar.

25 For *this* Agar is mount Sinai in Arabia, and [1]answereth to Jerusalem which now is, and is in bondage with her children.

26 But [a]Jerusalem which is above is free, which is the mother of us all.

4:6 [a]Rom. 5:5
4:7 [a]Rom. 8:16
4:8 [a]Eph. 2:12; 1 Thes. 4:5 [b]Rom. 1:25; 1 Cor. 12:2; 1 Thes. 1:9
4:9 [1]Or, *back* [2]Or, *rudiments* [a]1 Cor. 8:3 [b]Col. 2:20 [c]Heb. 7:18
4:10 [a]Rom. 14:5
4:11 [a]1 Thes. 3:5
4:12 [a]2 Cor. 2:5
4:13 [a]1 Cor. 2:3
4:14 [a]Mal. 2:7 [b]Luke 10:16
4:15 [1]Or, *What was then*
4:17 [1]Or, *us* [a]Rom. 10:2
4:19 [a]1 Cor. 4:15
4:20 [1]Or, *I am perplexed for you*
4:22 [a]Gen. 16:15 [b]Gen. 21:2
4:23 [a]Rom. 9:7,8 [b]Heb. 11:11
4:24 [1]Or, *testaments* [2][Gr. *Sina*] [a]Deut. 33:2
4:25 [1]Or, *is in the same rank with*
4:26 [a]Is. 2:2

recognized sons and heirs both Jews (those who had been under law) and Gentiles who believe in Christ.

4:6 *Spirit of his Son.* A new "tutor" (v. 2), identified as the "Spirit of God" in Rom 8:9 (see Rom 8:2; Eph 1:13–14). *crying.* The Greek for this phrase is a vivid verb expressing deep emotion, often used of an inarticulate cry. In Mat 27:50 it is used of Jesus' final cry. *Abba, Father.* "Abba," expressive of an especially close relationship to God, is Aramaic for "Father."

4:8 *when ye knew not God.* See 1 Cor 12:2; 1 Thes 4:5. *are no gods.* When the Galatians were pagans, they thought that the beings they worshiped were gods; but when they became Christians, they learned better.

4:9 *how turn ye again.* See 3:1–3. *weak and beggarly elements.* See note on v. 3. *desire again . . . bondage.* Legalistic trust in rituals, in moral achievement, in law, in good works, or even in cold, dead orthodoxy may indicate a relapse into second childhood on the part of those who should be knowing and enjoying the freedom of full-grown sons.

4:10 *days.* Such as the sabbath and the day of atonement (tenth day of Tishri; see Lev 16:29–34), which had never been, and can never be, in themselves means of salvation or sanctification. *months, and times.* Such as new moons (see Num 28:11–15; Is 1:13–14), passover (Ex 12:18) and firstfruits (Lev 23:10). *years.* Such as the sabbath year (see Lev 25:4). The Pharisees meticulously observed all these to gain merit before God.

4:11 *in vain.* Due to their return to the old covenant law.

4:12 *Brethren.* See note on 1:2.

4:13 *infirmity of the flesh.* On the basis of v. 15; 6:11 some suggest it was eye trouble. Others have suggested malaria or epilepsy. *preached . . . at the first.* When Paul visited Galatia on his first missionary journey (Acts 13:14–14:23).

‡4:14 *received me.* He implies that under the influence of Judaizers they have changed their attitude toward him.

4:15 *Where is then the blessedness you spake of?* Because of the restraints of legalistic Judaism they had lost their blessing and joy. *plucked out your own eyes.* A hyperbole indicating their willingness, for his benefit, to part with that which was most precious to them. See Mark 2:4, where the same verb is used of digging through a roof.

4:16 *your enemy.* Telling the truth sometimes results in loss of friends.

4:17 *They.* Judaizers (see 2:4,12).

4:19 *My little children.* For Paul's affectionate relationship to his converts see Acts 20:37–38; Phil 4:1; 1 Thes 2:7–8. The expression occurs only here in Paul's writings, but is common in John's (e.g., John 13:33; 1 John 2:1; 3:7). *until Christ be formed in you.* The goal of Paul's ministry (see Rom 8:29; Eph 4:13,15; Col 1:27).

4:22 *two sons.* Ishmael was born to the slave woman, Hagar (Gen 16:1–16), and Isaac to the free woman, Sarah (Gen 21:2–5).

4:24 *allegory.* The Sarah-Hagar account is not an allegory in the sense that it was nonhistorical, but in the sense that Paul uses the events to illustrate a theological truth. *covenants.* See note on 3:15. *mount Sinai.* Where the old covenant was established, with its law governing Israel's life (see Ex 19:2; 20:1–17).

4:25 *answereth to Jerusalem which now is.* Jerusalem can be equated with mount Sinai because it represents the center of Judaism, which is still under bondage to the law issued at mount Sinai.

‡4:26 *Jerusalem which is above.* Rabbinical teaching held that the Jerusalem above was the heavenly archetype that in the Messianic period would be let down to earth (cf. Rev 21:2). Here it refers to the heavenly city of God, in which Christ reigns and of which Christians are citizens, in contrast to the "Jerusalem which now is" (v. 25). *mother of us all.* As citizens of the heavenly Jerusalem, Christians are her children.

27 For it is written, [a]Rejoice, *thou* barren that bearest not; break forth and cry, thou that travailest not: for the desolate hath many moe children than she which hath a husband.

28 Now we, brethren, as Isaac was, are [a]the children of promise.

29 But as then [a]he that was born after the flesh persecuted him that was *born* after the Spirit, [b]even so *it is* now.

30 Nevertheless what saith [a]the scripture? [b]Cast out the bondwoman and her son: for [c]the son of the bondwoman shall not be heir with the son of the freewoman.

31 So then, brethren, we are not children of *the* bondwoman, [a]but of the free.

Liberty threatened by legalism

5 Stand fast therefore in [a]the liberty wherewith Christ hath made us free, and be not entangled again [b]with the yoke of bondage.

2 Behold, I Paul say unto you, that [a]if ye be circumcised, Christ shall profit you nothing.

3 For I testify again to every man that is circumcised, [a]that he is a debtor to do the whole law.

4 [a]Christ is become of no effect unto you, whosoever of you are justified by the law; [b]ye are fallen from grace.

5 For we through the Spirit [a]wait for the hope of righteousness by faith.

6 For [a]in Jesus Christ neither circumcision availeth any *thing*, nor uncircumcision; but [b]faith which worketh by love.

7 Ye [a]did run well; [b][1]who did hinder you that *ye* should not obey the truth?

8 *This* persuasion *cometh* not of him [a]that calleth you.

9 [a]A little leaven leaveneth the whole lump.

10 [a]I have confidence in you through the Lord, that you will be none otherwise minded: but [b]he that troubleth you [c]shall bear *his* judgment, whosoever he be.

11 [a]And I, brethren, if I yet preach circumcision, [b]why do I yet suffer persecution? then is [c]the offence of the cross ceased.

12 [a]I would they were even cut off [b]which trouble you.

Liberty defined

13 ¶ For, brethren, ye have been called unto liberty; only [a]*use* not liberty for an occasion to the flesh, but [b]by love serve one another.

14 For [a]all the law is fulfilled in one word, *even* in *this;* [b]Thou shalt love thy neighbour as thyself.

15 But if ye bite and devour one another, take heed ye be not consumed one of another.

16 *This* I say then, [a]Walk in the Spirit, and [1]ye shall not fulfil the lust of the flesh.

17 For [a]the flesh lusteth against the Spirit, and the Spirit against the flesh: and these are contrary the one to the other: [b]so that ye cannot do the *things* that ye would.

4:27 [a]Is. 54:1
4:28 [a]Acts 3:25
4:29 [a]Gen. 21:9 [b]ch. 5:11
4:30 [a]ch. 3:8,22 [b]Gen. 21:10 [c]John 8:35
4:31 [a]John 8:36
5:1 [a]Rom. 6:18 [b]Acts 15:10
5:2 [a]Acts 15:1
5:3 [a]ch. 3:10
5:4 [a]Rom. 9:31 [b]Heb. 12:15
5:5 [a]Rom. 8:24
5:6 [a]Col. 3:11
5:6 [b]1 Thes. 1:3
5:7 [1]Or, *who did drive you back?* [a]1 Cor. 9:24 [b]ch. 3:1
5:8 [a]ch. 1:6
5:9 [a]1 Cor. 5:6
5:10 [a]2 Cor. 2:3 [b]ch. 1:7 [c]2 Cor. 10:6
5:11 [a]ch. 6:12 [b]1 Cor. 15:30 [c]1 Cor. 1:23
5:12 [a]Josh. 7:25 [b]Acts 15:1,2
5:13 [a]1 Cor. 8:9; 1 Pet. 2:16 [b]1 Cor. 9:19
5:14 [a]Mat. 7:12; Jas. 2:8 [b]Mat. 22:39
5:16 [1]Or, *fulfil not* [a]Rom. 6:12; 1 Pet. 2:11
5:17 [a]Rom. 7:23 [b]Rom. 7:15

4:27 Paul applies Isaiah's joyful promise to exiled Jerusalem (in her exile "barren" of children) to the ingathering of believers through the gospel, by which "Jerusalem's" children have become many.

4:28 *children of promise.* Children by virtue of God's promise (see 3:29; Rom 9:8).

4:29 *persecuted him that was born after the Spirit.* Suggested by Gen 21:9; cf. Ps 83:5–6. *so it is now.* See Acts 13:50; 14:2–5,19; 1 Thes 2:14–16.

4:30 *Cast out the bondwoman.* Sarah's words in Gen 21:10 were used by Paul as the Scriptural basis for teaching the Galatians to put the Judaizers out of the church.

4:31 *we are not children of the bondwoman.* The believer is not enslaved to the law but is a child of promise and lives by faith (cf. 3:7,29).

5:1 *made us free.* Emphasized by its position in the Greek sentence. The freedom spoken of here is freedom from the yoke of the law. *entangled.* In classical Greek the verb meant "to be caught or entangled in." *yoke of bondage.* The burden of the rigorous demands of the law as the means for gaining God's favor—an intolerable burden for sinful man (see Acts 15:10–11).

5:2 *circumcised.* As a condition for God's acceptance.

‡5:3 *debtor to do the whole law.* The OT law is a unit; submission to it cannot be selective. See Jas 2:10.

5:4 *fallen from grace.* Placed yourself outside the scope of divine favor, because gaining God's favor by observing the law and receiving it by grace are mutually exclusive (see 2 Pet 3:17).

5:5 *the hope of righteousness.* A reference to God's final verdict of "not guilty," assured presently to the believer by faith and by the sanctifying work of the Holy Spirit. This is one of the few eschatological statements in Galatians.

5:6 *neither circumcision availeth any thing, nor uncircumcision.* See v. 2; 2:21; 6:15; 1 Cor 7:19. *faith which worketh by love.* Faith is not mere intellectual assent (see Jas 2:18–19) but a living trust in God's grace that expresses itself in acts of love (see 1 Thes 1:3).

5:7 *Ye did run well.* Before the Judaizers hindered them. Paul was fond of depicting the Christian life as a race (see, e.g., 2:2; Phil 2:16).

5:8 *persuasion.* By the Judaizers.

5:9 A proverb used here to stress the pervasive effect of Judaism. When the word "leaven" in the Bible is used as a symbol, it indicates evil or false teaching (see note on Mark 8:15), except in Mat 13:33.

5:11 *brethren.* See note on 1:2. *offence of the cross.* See Rom 9:32–33; 1 Cor 1:23.

‡5:12 *were even cut off.* The Greek word means "to cut off," or "to castrate." The Galatians would be better off if these Judaizers who are preaching circumcision were themselves "cut off." In Phil 3:2 Paul uses a related word to describe the same sort of people as "the false circumcision." His sarcasm is evident.

5:13 *use not liberty for an occasion to the flesh.* See Rom 6:1; 1 Pet 2:16. Liberty is not license but freedom to serve God and each other in love.

5:14 *all the law is fulfilled.* Doing to others what you would have them do to you expresses the spirit and intention of "the law and the prophets" (Mat 7:12; cf. Mark 12:31).

5:15 *bite and devour one another.* Opposite of vv. 13–14. Seeking to attain status with God and man by mere observance of law breeds a self-righteous, critical spirit.

5:16 *Walk.* Present tense—"go on living" (used of habitual conduct). Living by the promptings and power of the Spirit is the key to conquering sinful desires (see v. 25; Rom 8:2–4).

5:17 *are contrary the one to the other.* See Rom 7:15–23; 1 Pet 2:11.

18 But [a]if ye be led of the Spirit, ye are not
under the law.
19 Now [a]the works of the flesh are manifest, which are *these;* Adultery, fornication,
uncleanness, lasciviousness,
20 Idolatry, witchcraft, hatred, variance,
emulations, wrath, strife, seditions, heresies,
21 Envyings, murders, drunkenness, revellings, and such like: of the which I tell you before, as I have also told *you* in time past, that
[a]they which do such *things* shall not inherit
the kingdom of God.
22 But [a]the fruit of the Spirit is love, joy,
peace, longsuffering, [b]gentleness, [c]goodness,
[d]faith,
23 Meekness, temperance: [a]against such
there is no law.
24 And they that are Christ's [a]have crucified the flesh with the [1]affections and lusts.
25 [a]If we live in the Spirit, let us also walk
in the Spirit.
26 [a]Let us not be desirous of vain glory,
provoking one another, envying one another.

Fulfilling the law of Christ

6 Brethren, [a][1]if a man be overtaken in a
fault, ye [b]which are spiritual, restore
such a one [c]in the spirit of meekness; considering thyself, [d]lest thou also be tempted.
2 [a]Bear ye one another's burdens, and so
fulfil [b]the law of Christ.
3 For [a]if a man think himself to be something, when [b]he is nothing, he deceiveth himself.
4 But [a]let every man prove his own work,
and then shall he have rejoicing in himself
alone, and [b]not in another.
5 For [a]every man shall bear his own burden.
6 [a]Let him that is taught in the word communicate unto him that teacheth in all good
things.
7 [a]Be not deceived; [b]God is not mocked:
for [c]whatsoever a man soweth, that shall he
also reap.
8 [a]For he that soweth to his flesh shall of
the flesh reap corruption; but he that soweth
to the Spirit shall of the Spirit reap life everlasting.
9 And [a]let us not be weary in well doing:
for in due season we shall reap, [b]if we faint
not.
10 [a]As we have therefore opportunity, [b]let
us do good unto all *men,* especially unto them
who are of [c]the household of faith.

Paul's personal benediction

11 ¶Ye see how large a letter I have written unto you with mine own hand.
12 As many as desire to make a fair shew
in the flesh, [a]they constrain you to be circumcised; [b]only lest they should [c]suffer persecution for the cross of Christ.
13 For neither they themselves who are
circumcised keep the law; but desire to have
you circumcised, that they may glory in your
flesh.
14 [a]But God forbid that I should glory, save
in the cross of our Lord Jesus Christ, [1]by

5:18 [a]Rom. 6:14
5:19 [a]Eph. 5:3
5:21 [a]1 Cor. 6:9
5:22 [a]John 15:2; Eph. 5:9 [b]Col. 3:12 [c]Rom. 15:14 [d]1 Cor. 13:7
5:23 [a]1 Tim. 1:9
5:24 [1]Or, *passions* [a]Rom. 6:6; 1 Pet. 2:11
5:25 [a]Rom. 8:4,5
5:26 [a]Phil. 2:3
6:1 [1]Or, *although* [a]Rom. 14:1 [b]1 Cor. 2:15 [c]1 Cor. 4:21 [d]1 Cor. 7:5
6:2 [a]Rom. 15:1; 1 Thes. 5:14 [b]Jas. 2:8
6:3 [a]Rom. 12:3; 1 Cor. 8:2 [b]2 Cor. 3:5
6:4 [a]1 Cor. 11:28 [b]Luke 18:11
6:5 [a]Rom. 2:6; 1 Cor. 3:8
6:6 [a]1 Cor. 9:11
6:7 [a]1 Cor. 6:9 [b]Job 13:9 [c]Rom. 2:6; 2 Cor. 9:6
6:8 [a]Job 4:8
6:9 [a]1 Cor. 15:58 [b]Mat. 24:13; Rev. 2:10
6:10 [a]John 9:4 [b]Tit. 3:8 [c]Eph. 2:19
6:12 [a]ch. 2:3,14 [b]Phil. 3:18 [c]ch. 5:11
6:14 [1]Or, *whereby* [a]Phil. 3:3,7

5:18 *led of the Spirit.* See Rom 8:14. *not under the law.* Not under the bondage of trying to please God by minute observance of the law for salvation or sanctification (see note on Rom 6:14).

5:19–21 For other lists of vices see 1 Cor 6:9–10; Eph 5:5; Rev 22:15.

5:22–23 For other lists of virtues see 2 Cor 6:6; Eph 4:2; 5:9; Col 3:12–15. Christian character is produced by the Holy Spirit, not by the mere moral discipline of trying to live by law. Paul makes it clear that justification by faith does not result in libertinism. The indwelling Holy Spirit produces Christian virtues in the believer's life.

5:22 *fruit of the Spirit.* Compare the singular "fruit" with the plural "works" (v. 19).

5:23 *no law.* See 1 Tim 1:9.

5:24 *crucified the flesh.* See 2:20; 6:14.

‡5:25 *walk in.* A military term meaning "to keep in step with," or "to walk in line with." A different Greek word for "walk" was used in verse 16, meaning to walk or live, involving one's conduct.

6:1 *Brethren.* See note on 1:2. *ye which are spiritual.* Contrast with 1 Cor 3:1–3. *restore.* The Greek for this verb is used elsewhere for setting bones, mending nets, or bringing factions together.

‡6:2 *Bear ye one another's burdens.* The translation "burden" in verses two and five represents two different Greek nouns. Verse five requires that each one is to bear his own normal load. But we are to help others when they have an overload or are overburdened. The emphasis here is on moral burdens (see v. 1; Rom 15:1–3). *law of Christ.* See note on 1 Cor 9:21.

6:4 *let every man prove his own work.* The emphasis here is on personal responsibility (see 1 Cor 11:28; 2 Cor 13:5).

6:5 *bear his own burden.* The "for" at the beginning of the verse connects it with v. 4. Each of us is responsible before God. The reference may be to the future judgment (the verb is in the future tense), when every person will give an account to God (Rom 14:12; 2 Cor 5:10).

6:6 *communicate unto him that teacheth in all good things.* See Phil 4:14–19.

6:7 *whatsoever a man soweth, that shall he also reap.* See 2 Cor 9:6. As vv. 8–9 show, the principle applies not only negatively but also positively.

‡6:8 See Rom 8:13. *corruption.* See 5:19–21. *life everlasting.* In 5:21 Paul speaks of inheriting "the kingdom of God," here of reaping "life everlasting." The first focuses on the realm (sphere, context) that will be inherited (as Israel inherited the promised land); the second focuses on the blessed life that will be enjoyed in that realm.

‡6:10 *especially unto them who are of the household of faith.* See 1 Tim 5:8.

6:11 *large a letter.* May have been for emphasis or, as some have suggested, because he had poor eyesight (see note on 4:13). *with mine own hand.* The letter up to this point had probably been dictated to a scribe, after which Paul took the pen in his own hand and finished the letter.

6:12 *constrain you to be circumcised.* Cf. 2:3. *lest they should suffer persecution.* By advocating circumcision (see 5:11) the Judaizers were less apt to experience opposition from the Jewish opponents of Christianity. They were thinking only of themselves. See Introduction: Occasion and Purpose.

6:14 *glory, save in the cross.* See 1 Cor 1:31; 2:2. *the world.* All

whom the world is [b]crucified unto me, and I
unto the world.
15 For [a]in Christ Jesus neither circumcision availeth any *thing,* nor uncircumcision,
but [b]a new creature.
16 [a]And as many as walk [b]according to this
rule, peace *be* on them, and mercy, and upon
[c]the Israel of God.

6:14 [b]Rom. 6:6
6:15 [a]1 Cor. 7:19 [b]2 Cor. 5:17
6:16 [a]Ps. 125:5 [b]Phil. 3:16 [c]Rom. 2:29
6:17 [a]2 Cor. 1:5
6:18 [a]2 Tim. 4:22

17 From henceforth let no *man* trouble
me: for [a]I bear in my body the marks of the
Lord Jesus.
18 Brethren, [a]the grace of our Lord Jesus
Christ *be* with your spirit. Amen.

¶ Unto the Galatians written from Rome.

that is against God. *crucified unto me, and I unto the world.* See 2:19–20; 5:24; see also notes on Jas 4:4; 1 John 2:15.

6:15 *new creature.* In Christ man undergoes a transformation that results in an entirely new being. Creation again takes place (see 2 Cor 5:17).

‡6:16 *this rule.* See vv. 14–15. *peace . . . and mercy.* Cf. Ps 125:5; 128:6. *Israel of God.* Christian Jews. If the conjunction is translated as "even" instead of "and," the phrase stands in contrast to "Israel according to flesh" (a literal rendering of the Greek for "national Israel" in 1 Cor 10:18). The NT church, made up of believing Jews and Gentiles, is included in the seed of Abraham and an heir according to the promise (3:29; cf. Rom 9:6; Phil 3:3).

‡6:17 *marks.* In ancient times the Greek word was used of the brand-marks that identified slaves or animals. Paul's suffering (stoning, Acts 14:19; beatings, Acts 16:22; 2 Cor 11:25; illness, 2 Cor 12:7; Gal 4:13–14) marked him as a "servant of Christ" (1:10; cf. 2 Cor 4:10).

6:18 *Amen.* A word of confirmation often used at the close of a doxology or benediction.

The Epistle of Paul the Apostle to the
Ephesians

INTRODUCTION

Author, Date and Place of Writing

The author identifies himself as Paul (1:1; 3:1; cf. 3:7,13; 4:1; 6:19–20). Some have taken the absence of the usual personal greetings and the verbal similarity of many parts to Colossians, among other reasons, as grounds for doubting authorship by the apostle Paul. However, this was probably a circular letter, intended for other churches in addition to the one in Ephesus (see notes on 1:1,15; 6:21–23). Paul may have written it about the same time as Colossians, c. A.D. 60, while he was in prison at Rome (see 3:1; 4:1; 6:20).

The City of Ephesus

Ephesus was the most important city in western Asia Minor (now Turkey). It had a harbor that at that time opened into the Cayster River, which in turn emptied into the Aegean Sea. Because it was

Ephesus in the Time of Paul

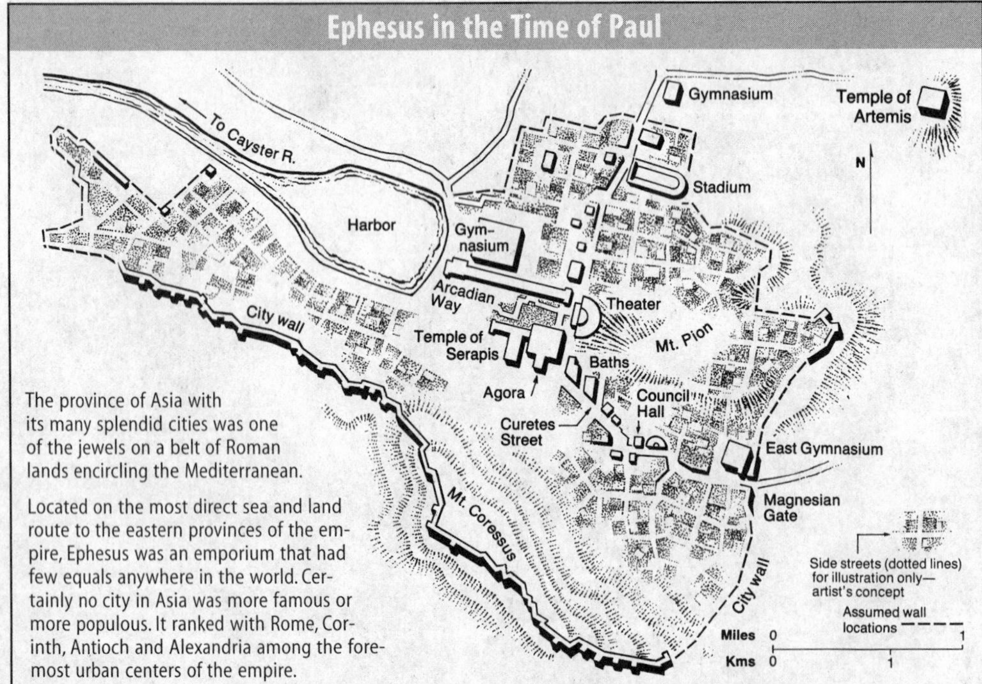

The province of Asia with its many splendid cities was one of the jewels on a belt of Roman lands encircling the Mediterranean.

Located on the most direct sea and land route to the eastern provinces of the empire, Ephesus was an emporium that had few equals anywhere in the world. Certainly no city in Asia was more famous or more populous. It ranked with Rome, Corinth, Antioch and Alexandria among the foremost urban centers of the empire.

Situated on an inland harbor (now silted up), the city was connected by a narrow channel via the Cayster River with the Aegean Sea some three miles away. Ephesus boasted impressive civic monuments, including, most prominently, the temple of Artemis (Diana), one of the seven wonders of the ancient world. Coins of the city proudly displayed the slogan Neokoros, "temple-warden."

Here in Ephesus Paul preached to large crowds of people. The silversmiths complained that he had influenced large numbers of people here in Ephesus and in practically the whole province of Asia (Acts 19:26). In one of the most dramatic events recorded in the NT, the apostle escaped a huge mob in the theater. This structure, located on the slope of Mt. Pion at the end of the Arcadian Way, could seat 25,000 people!

Other places doubtless familiar to the apostle were the Commercial Agora, the Magnesian Gate, the Town Hall or "Council House," and the Street of the Curetes. The location of the lecture hall of Tyrannus, where Paul taught, is unknown.

also at an intersection of major trade routes, Ephesus became a commercial center. It boasted a pagan temple dedicated to the Roman goddess Diana (Greek *Artemis*); cf. Acts 19:23–31. Paul made Ephesus a center for evangelism for about three years (see note on Acts 19:10), and the church there apparently flourished for some time, but later needed the warning of Rev 2:1–7.

Message

Unlike several of the other letters Paul wrote, Ephesians does not address any particular error or heresy. Paul wrote to expand the horizons of his readers, so that they might understand better the dimensions of God's eternal purpose and grace and come to appreciate the high goals God has for the church.

The letter opens with a sequence of statements about God's blessings, which are interspersed with a remarkable variety of expressions drawing attention to God's wisdom, forethought and purpose. Paul emphasizes that we have been saved, not only for our personal benefit, but also to bring praise and glory to God. The climax of God's purpose, in the "fulness of the times," is to bring all things in the universe together under Christ (1:10). It is crucially important that Christians realize this, so in 1:15–23 Paul prays for their understanding (a second prayer occurs in 3:14–21).

Having explained God's great goals for the church, Paul proceeds to show the steps toward their fulfillment. First, God has reconciled individuals to Himself as an act of grace (2:1–10). Second, God has reconciled these saved individuals to each other, Christ having broken down the barriers through His own death (2:11–22). But God has done something even beyond this: He has united these reconciled individuals in one body, the church. This is a "mystery" not fully known until it was revealed to Paul (3:1–6). Now Paul is able to state even more clearly what God has intended for the church, namely, that it be the means by which He displays His "manifold wisdom" to the "rulers and the authorities in the heavenly places" (3:7–13). It is clear through the repetition of "heavenly places" (1:3,20; 2:6; 3:10; 6:12) that Christian existence is not merely on an earthly plane. It receives its meaning and significance from heaven, where Christ is exalted at the right hand of God (1:20).

Nevertheless, that life is lived out on earth, where the practical daily life of the believer continues to work out the purposes of God. The ascended Lord gave "gifts" to the members of His church to enable them to minister to one another and so promote unity and maturity (4:1–16). The unity of the church under the headship of Christ foreshadows the uniting of "all things . . . in heaven, and . . . on earth" under Christ (1:10). The new life of purity and mutual deference stands in contrast to the old way of life without Christ (4:17—6:9). Those who are "strong in the Lord" have victory over the evil one in the great spiritual conflict, especially through the power of prayer (6:10–20).

Outline

I. Greetings (1:1–2)
II. The Divine Purpose: The Glory and Headship of Christ (1:3–14)
III. Prayer That Christians May Realize God's Purpose and Power (1:15–23)
IV. Steps Toward the Fulfillment of God's Purpose (chs. 2–3)
  A. Salvation of Individuals by Grace (2:1–10)
  B. Reconciliation of Jew and Gentile through the Cross (2:11–18)
  C. Uniting of Jew and Gentile in One Household (2:19–22)
  D. Revelation of God's Wisdom through the Church (3:1–13)
  E. Prayer for Deeper Experience of God's Fullness (3:14–21)
V. Practical Ways to Fulfill God's Purpose in the Church (4:1—6:20)
  A. Unity (4:1–6)
  B. Maturity (4:7–16)
  C. Renewal of Personal Life (4:17—5:20)
  D. Deference in Personal Relationships (5:21—6:9)
    1. Principle (5:21)
    2. Husbands and wives (5:22–33)
    3. Children and parents (6:1–4)
    4. Slaves and masters (6:5–9)
  E. Strength in the Spiritual Conflict (6:10–20)
VI. Conclusion, Final Greetings and Benediction (6:21–24)

1 Paul, an apostle of Jesus Christ [a]by the
will of God, [b]to the saints which are at
Ephesus, [c]and to the faithful in Christ Jesus:
2 [a]Grace *be* to you, and peace, from God
our Father, and *from* the Lord Jesus Christ.

Spiritual blessings in Christ

3 ¶ [a]Blessed *be* the God and Father of our
Lord Jesus Christ, who hath blessed us with all
spiritual blessings in heavenly [1]*places* in
Christ:
4 According as [a]he hath chosen us in him
[b]before the foundation of the world, that we
should [c]be holy and without blame before him
in love:
5 [a]Having predestinated us unto [b]the adoption of children by Jesus Christ to himself, [c]ac-
cording to the good pleasure of his will,
6 To the praise of the glory of his grace,
[a]wherein he hath made us accepted in [b]the
beloved:
7 [a]In whom we have redemption through
his blood, the forgiveness of sins, according to
[b]the riches of his grace;
8 Wherein he hath abounded toward us in
all wisdom and prudence;
9 [a]Having made known unto us the mystery of his will, according to his good pleasure
[b]which he had purposed in himself:
10 That in the dispensation of [a]the fulness
of times [b]*he* might gather together in one [c]all
things in Christ, both which are in [1]heaven,
and which are on earth; *even* in him:
11 [a]In whom also we have obtained an inheritance, [b]being predestinated according to
[c]the purpose of him who worketh all *things* after the counsel of his own will:
12 [a]That we should be to the praise of his
glory, [b]who first [1]trusted in Christ:
13 In whom ye also *trusted,* after that ye
heard [a]the word of truth, the gospel of your salvation: in whom also after that ye believed, [b]ye
were sealed with *that* holy Spirit of promise,
14 [a]Which is the earnest of our inheri-

1:1 [a]2 Cor. 1:1 [b]Rom. 1:7; 2 Cor. 1:1 [c]1 Cor. 4:17
1:2 [a]Gal. 1:3
1:3 [1]Or, things [a]2 Cor. 1:3
1:4 [a]Rom. 8:28 [b]1 Pet. 1:2 [c]Luke 1:75
1:5 [a]Rom. 8:29 [b]John 1:12 [c]1 Cor. 1:21
1:6 [a]Rom. 3:24 [b]Mat. 3:17
1:7 [a]Heb. 9:12
1:7 [b]Rom. 3:24
1:9 [a]Rom. 16:25 [b]2 Tim. 1:9
1:10 [1]Gr. *the heavens* [a]Gal. 4:4 [b]1 Cor. 3:22 [c]Col. 1:20
1:11 [a]Rom. 8:17 [b]ver. 5 [c]Is. 46:10
1:12 [1]Or, *hoped* [a]2 Thes. 2:13 [b]Jas. 1:18
1:13 [a]John 1:17 [b]2 Cor. 1:22
1:14 [a]2 Cor. 5:5

1:1 *apostle.* One specially commissioned by Christ (see notes on Mark 6:30; 1 Cor 1:1; Heb 3:1). *by the will of God.* Paul not only stresses his authority under God, but also anticipates the strong emphasis he will make later in this chapter and book on God's sovereign plan and purpose. *at Ephesus.* The book may have been intended as a circular letter to several churches, including the one at Ephesus (see notes on v. 15; 6:21–23; Acts 19:10). *in Christ Jesus.* This phrase (or a similar one) occurs 11 times in vv. 1–13. It refers to the spiritual union of Christ with believers, which Paul often symbolizes by the metaphor "body (of Christ)" (see, e.g., v. 23; 2:16; 4:4,12,16; 5:23,30).

1:2 *Grace be to you, and peace.* Although these words were commonly used in the greetings of secular letters, the words that follow show that Paul intended a spiritual dimension. He uses the word "grace" 12 times and "peace" 8 times in Ephesians.

1:3–14 All one sentence in Greek, this section is often called a "doxology" because it recites what God has done and is an expression of worship to honor Him. Paul speaks first of the blessings we have through the Father (v. 3), then of those that come through the Son (vv. 4–13a) and finally of those through the Holy Spirit (1:13b–14).

1:3 *Father of our Lord Jesus Christ.* Jesus' relation to God the Father is unique (see John 20:17 and note). *blessed . . . blessings.* Jewish people used the word "bless" to express both God's kindness to us and our thanks or praise to him. *heavenly places.* Occurs five times in Ephesians, emphasizing Paul's perception that in the exaltation of Christ (His resurrection and enthronement at God's right hand) and in the Christian's union with the exalted Christ ultimate issues are involved—issues that pertain to the divine realm and that in the final analysis are worked out in and from that realm. At stake are God's eternal eschatological purpose (3:11) and the titanic conflict between God and the powerful spiritual forces arrayed against Him—a purpose and a conflict that come to focus in the history of redemption. Here (v. 3) Paul asserts that, through their union with the exalted Christ, Christians have already been made beneficiaries of every spiritual blessing that belongs to and comes from the heavenly places. In vv. 20–22, he proclaims Christ's exaltation to that realm and His elevation over all other powers and titles so that He rules over all for the sake of His church. According to 2:6, those who have been made alive with Christ (2:5) share in Christ's exaltation and enthronement in heaven. Thus (3:10) by the gathering of Gentiles and Jews into one body of Christ (the church), God triumphantly displays His "manifold wisdom" to the "the principalities and powers" in the heavenly places. As a result, the spiritual struggle of the saints here and now is not so much against "flesh and blood" as against the great spiritual forces that war against God in heaven (6:12).

‡1:4 *chosen.* Divine election is a constant theme in Paul's letters (Rom 8:29–33; 9:6–26; 11:5,7,28; 16:13; Col 3:12; 1 Thes 1:4; 2 Thes 2:13; Tit 1:1). In this chapter it is emphasized in the following ways: (1) "He hath chosen us" (here); (2) "predestined us" (v. 5); (3) "also we have obtained an inheritance" (v. 11); (4) "being predestined" (v. 11). *before the foundation of the world.* See John 17:24. *holy and without blame.* See 5:27 for the same pair of words. Holiness is the result—not the basis—of God's choosing. It refers both to the holiness imparted to the believer because of Christ and to the believer's personal sanctification (see note on 1 Cor 1:2). *in love.* Cf. 3:17; 4:2,15–16; 5:2.

1:5 *adoption.* See note on Rom 8:23.

1:6 *To the praise.* See vv. 12,14. Election is for God's glory.

1:7 *redemption.* See v. 14; 4:30; Rom 3:24; Tit 2:14. The Ephesians were familiar with the Greco-Roman practice of redemption: Slaves were freed by the payment of a ransom. Similarly, the ransom necessary to free sinners from the bondage of sin and the resulting curse imposed by the law (see Gal 3:13) was the death of Christ (called here "his blood"). *through his blood.* Cf. 2:13; 1 Pet 1:18–19.

1:9 *mystery.* See notes on Rom 11:25; Col 1:26.

1:10 *the fulness of times . . . in Christ.* Paul uses a significant term here that not only has the idea of leadership but also was often used of adding up a column of figures. A contemporary way of putting it might be to say that in a world of confusion, where things do not "add up" or make sense, we look forward to the time when everything will be brought into meaningful relationship under the headship of Christ. *in him.* Christ is the center of God's plan. Whether the universe or the individual Christian is in view, it is only in relationship to Christ that there is a meaningful future destiny. Paul goes on to speak, not of the world as a whole, but of those who respond to God's call.

1:12 *who first trusted in Christ.* Probably a reference to those Jews who, like Paul, had become believers before many Gentiles had.

1:13 *ye also.* Probably refers to the majority of the Ephesians, who were Gentiles. *sealed.* In those days a seal denoted ownership.

1:14 *earnest.* See note on Rom 8:23.

tance, [b]until the redemption of [c]the purchased possession, [d]unto the praise of his glory.

Prayer for wisdom and knowledge

15 ¶ Wherefore I also, [a]after I heard of your faith in the Lord Jesus, and love unto all the saints,

16 [a]Cease not to give thanks for you, making mention of you in my prayers;

17 That [a]the God of our Lord Jesus Christ, the Father of glory, [b]may give unto you the spirit of wisdom and revelation [1]in the knowledge of him:

18 [a]The eyes of your understanding being enlightened; that ye may know what is [b]the hope of his calling, and what the riches of the glory of his inheritance in the saints,

19 And what *is* the exceeding greatness of his power to us-ward who believe, [a]according to the working [1]of his mighty power,

20 Which he wrought in Christ, when [a]he raised him from the dead, and [b]set *him* at his own right hand in the heavenly *places,*

21 [a]Far above all [b]principality, and power, and might, and dominion, and every name that is named, not only in this world, but also in that which is to come:

22 And [a]hath put all *things* under his feet, and gave him [b]*to be* the head over all *things* to the church,

1:14 [b]Rom. 8:23 [c]Acts 20:28 [d]1 Pet. 2:9
1:15 [a]Col. 1:4
1:16 [a]Rom. 1:9
1:17 [1]Or, *for the acknowledgment* [a]John 20:17 [b]Col. 1:9
1:18 [a]Acts 26:18 [b]ch. 2:12
1:19 [1]Gr. *of the might of his power* [a]Col. 2:12
1:20 [a]Acts 2:24 [b]Ps. 110:1
1:21 [a]Phil. 2:9,10 [b]Rom. 8:38
1:22 [a]Mat. 28:18 [b]Heb. 2:7
1:23 [a]Rom. 12:5 [b]Col. 2:9 [c]1 Cor. 12:6
2:1 [a]Col. 2:13 [b]ch. 4:18
2:2 [a]Col. 1:21 [b]ch. 6:12 [c]Col. 3:6
2:3 [1]Gr. *the wills* [a]1 Pet. 4:3 [b]Gal. 5:16 [c]Ps. 51:5
2:4 [a]Rom. 10:12
2:5 [1][Or, *by whose grace*] [a]Rom. 5:6,8 [b]Rom. 6:4,5
2:6 [a]ch. 1:20
2:7 [a]Tit. 3:4
2:8 [a]2 Tim. 1:9 [b]Rom. 4:16 [c]Mat. 16:17

23 [a]Which is his body, [b]the fulness of him [c]that filleth all in all.

New life with Christ

2 And [a]you *hath he quickened,* [b]who were dead in trespasses and sins;

2 [a]Wherein in time past ye walked according to the course of this world, according to [b]the prince of the power of the air, the spirit that now worketh in [c]the children of disobedience:

3 [a]Among whom also we all had our conversation in times past in [b]the lusts of our flesh, fulfilling [1]the desires of the flesh and of the mind; and [c]were by nature the children of wrath, even as others.

4 But God, [a]who is rich in mercy, for his great love wherewith he loved us,

5 [a]Even when we were dead in sins, hath [b]quickened *us* together with Christ, ([1]by grace ye are saved;)

6 And hath raised *us* up together, and made *us* sit together [a]in heavenly *places* in Christ Jesus:

7 That in the ages to come he might shew the exceeding riches of his grace in [a]*his* kindness towards us through Christ Jesus.

8 [a]For by grace are ye saved [b]through faith; and that not of yourselves: [c]*it is* the gift of God:

9 Not of works, lest any *man* should boast.

1:15 *after I heard.* This sounds strange from one who had spent several years in Ephesus. He may be referring to a greatly enlarged church there, many of whom Paul did not know, or, if Ephesians was intended as a circular letter (see note on v. 1), he may be referring to news from the whole area, only a part of which he had visited.

1:17 *God of our Lord Jesus Christ.* See note on v. 3. *him.* God the Father.

1:18 *eyes of your understanding.* Your mind or understanding or inner awareness. *hope.* Has an objective quality of certainty (see Rom 8:25). It is the assurance of eternal life guaranteed by the present possession of the Holy Spirit (see v. 14). *calling.* See Phil 3:14; 2 Tim 1:9; Heb 3:1. *the glory of his inheritance in the saints.* Either the inheritance we have from God (see v. 14; Col 1:12) or the inheritance God receives, i.e., the saints themselves. *saints.* Those whom God has called to be His own people, i.e., all Christians (see vv. 1,15). The word carried the idea of dedication to a deity.

1:19 In this verse Paul piles term upon term to emphasize that the extraordinary divine force by which Jesus Christ was raised (v. 20) is the same power at work in and through believers.

1:20 *right hand.* The symbolic place of highest honor and authority.

1:21 *all principality . . . every name that is named.* Including whatever supernatural beings his contemporaries might conceive of, for in his day many people believed not only in the existence of angels and demons, but also in that of other beings. Christ is above them all. *this world . . . that which is to come.* Like the rabbinic teachers of his day, Paul distinguishes between the present age, which is evil, and the future age when the Messiah will consummate His kingdom and there will be a completely righteous society on earth.

1:22 *under his feet.* Ps 8:5–6 emphasizes the destiny of man, and Heb 2:6–9 shows that ultimately it is the Son of man who rules over everything (cf. Heb 10:13). *head.* Christ is not only head of the church, but also head over everything (see note on v. 10).

1:23 *his body.* See 2:16; 4:4,12,16; 5:23,30. *fulness . . . filleth.* The church is the fullness of Christ probably in the sense that it is filled by Him who fills all things.

2:1–10 In ch. 1 Paul wrote of the great purposes and plan of God, culminating in the universal headship of Christ (1:10), all of which is to be for "the praise of His glory" (1:14). He now proceeds to explain the steps by which God will accomplish His purposes, beginning with the salvation of individuals.

2:1 A description of their past moral and spiritual condition, separated from the life of God.

2:2 *prince.* Satan (cf. John 14:30, "prince of this world"). *air.* Satan is no mere earthbound enemy (cf. 6:12). *spirit.* Satan is a created, but not a human, being (cf. Job 1:6; Ezek 28:15; see note on Is 14:12–15).

‡2:3 *we all.* Jews and Gentiles. *children of wrath.* See Rom 1:18–20; 2:5; 9:22.

2:5 *quickened us together with Christ.* This truth is expanded in Rom 6:1–10.

2:6 *heavenly places.* See note on 1:3. *in Christ Jesus.* Through our union with Christ.

2:7 *ages to come.* Cf. 1:21; probably refers to the future of eternal blessing with Christ. *shew.* Or "exhibit" or "prove."

2:8 A major passage for understanding God's grace, i.e., His kindness, unmerited favor and forgiving love. *are ye saved.* "Saved" has a wide range of meanings. It includes salvation from God's wrath, which we all had incurred by our sinfulness. The tense of the verb (also in v. 5) suggests a completed action with emphasis on its present effect. *through faith.* See Rom 3:21–31 (and notes on that passage), which establishes the necessity of faith in Christ as the only means of being made right with God. *not of yourselves.* No human effort can contribute to our salvation; it is the gift of God.

‡2:9 *Not of works.* One cannot earn salvation by the "deeds of

10 For we are [a]his workmanship, created in Christ Jesus unto good works, which God hath before [1]ordained that we should walk in them.

The household of God

11 ¶ Wherefore remember, that ye *being* in time passed Gentiles in the flesh, who are called Uncircumcision by that which is called [a]the Circumcision in the flesh made by hands;

12 [a]That at that time ye were without Christ, [b]being aliens from the commonwealth of Israel, and strangers from [c]the covenants of promise, [d]having no hope, [e]and without God in the world:

13 [a]But now in Christ Jesus ye who sometimes were [b]far off are made nigh by the blood of Christ.

14 For [a]he is our peace, [b]who hath made both one, and hath broken down the middle wall of partition *between us;*

15 [a]Having abolished [b]in his flesh the enmity, *even* the law of commandments *contained* in ordinances; for to make in himself of twain one [c]new man, *so* making peace;

2:10 [1]Or, *prepared* [a]Is. 19:25
2:11 [a]Col. 2:11
2:12 [a]Col. 1:21 [b]Ezek. 13:9 [c]Rom. 9:4,8 [d]1 Thes. 4:13 [e]Gal. 4:8
2:13 [a]Gal. 3:28 [b]Acts 2:39
2:14 [a]Mic. 5:5 [b]John 10:16
2:15 [a]Col. 2:14 [b]Col. 1:22 [c]Gal. 6:15
2:16 [1]Or, *in himself* [a]Col. 1:20-22 [b]Rom. 6:6
2:17 [a]Is. 57:19 [b]Ps. 148:14
2:18 [a]John 10:9 [b]1 Cor. 12:13
2:19 [a]Phil. 3:20 [b]Gal. 6:10
2:20 [a]1 Pet. 2:4 [b]Mat. 16:18 [c]1 Cor. 12:28 [d]Ps. 118:22
2:21 [a]1 Cor. 3:17
2:22 [a]1 Pet. 2:5
3:1 [a]Acts 21:33 [b]Col. 1:24
3:2 [a]Rom. 1:5 [b]Acts 9:15

16 And *that* he might [a]reconcile both unto God in one body by the cross, [b]having slain the enmity [1]thereby:

17 And came [a]and preached peace to you which were afar off, and to [b]them that were nigh;

18 For [a]through him we both have access [b]by one Spirit unto the Father.

19 Now therefore ye are no more strangers and foreigners, but [a]fellowcitizens with the saints, and of [b]the household of God;

20 And are [a]built [b]upon the foundation of the [c]apostles and prophets, Jesus Christ himself being [d]the chief corner *stone;*

21 In whom all the building fitly framed together groweth unto [a]a holy temple in the Lord:

22 [a]In whom you also are builded together for a habitation of God through the Spirit.

Paul, apostle to the Gentiles

3 For this cause I Paul, [a]the prisoner of Jesus Christ [b]for you Gentiles,

2 If ye have heard of [a]the dispensation of the grace of God [b]which is given me to you-ward:

---

the law" (Rom 3:20, 28). Such a legalistic approach to salvation (or sanctification) is consistently condemned in Scripture. *lest any man should boast.* No one can take credit for his or her salvation.

2:10 *workmanship.* The Greek for this word sometimes has the connotation of a "work of art." *before ordained.* Carries forward the theme of God's sovereign purpose and planning, seen in ch. 1.

2:11–22 From the salvation of individuals, Paul moves to another aspect of salvation in which God reconciles Jews and Gentiles, previously hostile peoples, not only to Himself but also to each other through Christ (vv. 11–16). Even more than that, God unites these now reconciled people in one body, a truth introduced in vv. 19–22 and explained in ch. 3.

‡2:11 *Wherefore.* Refers to the state of those without Christ, described in vv. 1–10. *ye . . . Gentiles.* Most of the Ephesians (cf. 1:13, "ye also"). *Uncircumcision . . . Circumcision.* The rite of circumcision was applied to all Jewish male babies; so this physical act ("in the flesh made by hands") was a clear mark of distinction between Jew and Gentile, in which Jewish people naturally took pride.

2:12 *at that time.* Before salvation, in contrast to "But now" (v. 13). *without Christ . . . without God.* All these expressions emphasize the distance of unbelieving Gentiles from Israel, as well as from Christ. *covenants.* God had promised blessings to and through the Jewish people (see note on Rom 9:4).

2:13 *But now.* Not only contrasts with "at that time" (v. 12) but also introduces the contrast between "without Christ" (v. 12) and "in Christ" (here). *blood of Christ.* Expresses the violent death of Christ as He poured out His lifeblood as a sacrifice for us (cf. 1:7).

2:14 *both.* Believing Jews and believing Gentiles. *middle wall of partition.* Vivid description of the total religious isolation Jews and Gentiles experienced from each other.

2:15 *abolished . . . the law.* Since Mat 5:17 and Rom 3:31 teach that God's moral standard expressed in the OT law is not changed by the coming of Christ, what is abolished here is probably the effect of the specific "commandments contained in ordinances" in separating Jews from Gentiles, whose nonobservance of the Jewish law renders them ritually unclean. *in himself.* Probably refers to the death of Christ. *one new man.* The united body of believers, the church.

2:16 *one body.* While this could possibly mean the body of Christ offered on the cross (cf. "in his flesh," v. 15), it probably refers to the "one new man" just mentioned, the body of believers.

2:17 *afar off . . . nigh.* Gentiles and Jews respectively.

2:19 *Now therefore.* Paul indicates that the unity described in vv. 19–22 is based on what Christ did through His death, described in vv. 14–18. *ye.* The Gentiles at Ephesus are particularly in mind here. *fellowcitizens . . . household.* Familiar imagery. The household in ancient times was what we today might call an "extended family."

2:20 *foundation.* Further metaphorical language to convey the idea of a solid, integrated structure. *apostles and prophets.* Probably refers to the founding work of the early Christian apostles and prophets as they preached and taught God's word (cf. 1 Cor 3:10–11). *corner stone.* Is 28:16, which uses the same term in its pre-Christian Greek translation (the Septuagint), refers to a foundation with a "tested" stone at the corner.

2:21 *fitly framed together.* Cf. 4:16 for the same word. Both passages speak of the close relationship between believers. *groweth.* The description of a building under construction conveys the sense of the dynamic growth of the church. *holy temple.* Paul now uses the metaphor of a temple, thereby indicating the purpose ("to become") for which God has established His church.

2:22 *habitation.* The church is to be a people or community in whom the Holy Spirit dwells.

3:1–13 Having saved people individually by His grace (2:1–10), and having reconciled them to each other as well as to Himself through the sacrificial death of Christ (2:11–22), God also now unites them on an equal basis in one body, the church. This step in God's eternal plan was not fully revealed in previous times. Paul calls it a "mystery."

3:1 *For this cause.* Because of all that God has done, explained in the preceding several verses. *prisoner.* Apparently Paul was under house arrest at this time (see Acts 28:16,30). *of Jesus Christ.* Paul's physical imprisonment was because he obeyed Christ in spite of opposition. After this verse Paul breaks his train of thought to explain the "mystery" (v. 4). He resumes his initial thought in v. 14.

3:2 *If ye have heard.* Most of the Ephesians would have heard

3 [a]How that by revelation [b]he made known unto me the mystery; (as I wrote [1]afore in few *words,*

4 Whereby, when ye read, ye may understand my knowledge in the mystery of Christ)

5 [a]Which in other ages was not made known unto the sons of men, as it is now revealed unto his holy apostles and prophets by the Spirit;

6 That the Gentiles [a]should be fellowheirs, and of the same body, and partakers of his promise in Christ by the gospel:

7 [a]Whereof I was made a minister, [b]according to the gift of the grace of God given unto me by [c]the effectual working of his power.

8 Unto me, [a]*who am* less than the least of all saints, is this grace given, that *I* should preach among the Gentiles [b]the unsearchable riches of Christ;

9 And to make all *men* see what *is* the fellowship of the mystery, [a]which from the beginning of the world hath been hid in God, [b]who created all *things* by Jesus Christ:

10 [a]To the intent that now [b]unto the principalities and powers in heavenly *places* [c]might be known by the church the manifold wisdom of God,

11 According to the eternal purpose which he purposed in Christ Jesus our Lord:

12 In whom we have boldness and access [a]with confidence by the faith of him.

13 [a]Wherefore I desire that *ye* faint not at my tribulations for you, [b]which is your glory.

Strength through the Spirit

14 For this cause I bow my knees unto the Father of our Lord Jesus Christ,

15 Of whom [a]the whole family in heaven and earth is named,

16 That he would grant you, [a]according to the riches of his glory, [b]to be strengthened with might by his Spirit in [c]the inner man;

17 [a]That Christ may dwell in your hearts by faith; that ye, [b]being rooted and grounded in love,

18 [a]May be able to comprehend with all saints [b]what *is* the breadth, and length, and depth, and height;

19 And to know the love of Christ, which passeth knowledge, that ye might be filled [a]with all the fulness of God.

20 Now [a]unto him that is able to do exceeding abundantly [b]above all that we ask or think, [c]according to the power that worketh in us,

21 [a]Unto him *be* glory in the church by

3:3 [1]Or, *a little before* [a]Acts 22:17 [b]Rom. 16:25
3:5 [a]Rom. 16:25
3:6 [a]Gal. 3:28
3:7 [a]Rom. 15:16 [b]Rom. 1:5 [c]Rom. 15:18
3:8 [a]1 Cor. 15:9 [b]Col. 1:27
3:9 [a]Rom. 16:25 [b]Ps. 33:6
3:10 [a]1 Pet. 1:12 [b]Col. 1:16 [c]1 Tim. 3:16
3:12 [a]Heb. 4:16
3:13 [a]Phil. 1:14 [b]2 Cor. 1:6
3:15 [a]ch. 1:10
3:16 [a]Phil. 4:19 [b]Col. 1:11 [c]Rom. 7:22
3:17 [a]John 14:23 [b]Col. 1:23
3:18 [a]ch. 1:18 [b]Rom. 10:3
3:19 [a]ch. 1:23
3:20 [a]Rom. 16:25 [b]1 Cor. 2:9 [c]Col. 1:29
3:21 [a]Rom. 11:36

of Paul's ministry because of his long stay there earlier. However, if this was a circular letter (see note on 1:1), the other churches may not have known much about it. *dispensation.* Paul unfolds God's administrative plan for the church and for the universe in this letter (see especially 1:3–12). He has been given a significant responsibility in the execution of this plan.

3:3 *mystery.* A truth known only by divine revelation (v. 5; see Rom 16:25; see also notes on Rom 11:25; Col 1:26). Here the word "mystery" has the special meaning of the private, wise plan of God, which in Ephesians relates primarily to the unification of believing Jews and Gentiles in the new body, the church (see v. 6). It may be thought of as a secret that is temporarily hidden, but more than that, it is a plan God is actively working out and revealing stage by stage (cf. 1:9–10; Rev 10:7). *as I wrote afore in few words.* May refer to 1:9–10.

3:5 *not made known unto the sons of men.* See note on v. 6. *holy.* Set apart for God's service. *apostles and prophets.* See note on 2:20. Although Paul was the chief recipient, others received this revelation also.

3:6 *fellowheirs . . . same body . . . partakers.* Thes words indicate the unique aspect of the mystery that was not previously known: the equality and mutuality that Gentiles had with Jews in the church, the one body. That Gentiles would turn to the God of Israel and be saved was prophesied in the OT (see Rom 15:9–12); that they would come into an organic unity with believing Jews on an equal footing was unexpected. *fellowheirs.* See note on 1:18.

‡3:8 *less than the least.* Cf. 1 Tim 1:15. Paul never ceased to be amazed that one so unworthy as he should have been chosen for so high a task. His modesty was genuine, even though we may disagree with his self-evaluation. *grace.* In this case, a special endowment that brings responsibility for service. *unsearchable.* Far beyond what we can know, but not beyond our appreciation—at least in part (cf. Rom 11:33).

‡3:10 *now.* In contrast to the previous "ages" (v. 9). *principalities and powers.* Christ had ascended over all these (1:20–21). It is a staggering thought that the church on earth is observed, so to speak, by these spiritual powers and that to the degree the church is spiritually united it portrays to them the wisdom of God. This thought may be essential in understanding the meaning of "vocation" in 4:1. *heavenly places.* See note on 1:3. *by the church.* The fact that God had done the seemingly impossible—reconciling and organically uniting Jews and Gentiles in the church—makes the church the perfect means of displaying God's wisdom. *manifold.* Variegated or multifaceted (in the way that many facets of a diamond reflect and enhance its beauty).

3:11 *eternal purpose.* The effective headship of Christ over a united church is in preparation for His ultimate assumption of headship over the universe (1:10).

3:14–21 Paul now expresses a prayer that grows out of his awareness of all that God is doing in believers. God's key gifts are "might" (vv. 16,20) and "love" (vv. 17–19).

3:14 *For this cause.* Resumes the thought of v. 1. *I bow my knees.* Expresses deep emotion and reverence, as people in Paul's day usually stood to pray.

3:15 *family.* The word in Greek is similar to the word for "father," so it can be said that the "family" derives its name (and being) from the "father." God is our Father, and we can commit our prayers to Him in confidence.

3:17 *dwell.* Be completely at home. Christ was already present in the Ephesian believers' lives (cf. Rom 8:9). *hearts.* The whole inner being.

3:19 *passeth knowledge.* Not unknowable, but so great that it cannot be completely known. *fulness.* God, who is infinite in all His attributes, allows us to draw on His resources—in this case, His love.

3:20 *exceeding abundantly above.* Has specific reference to the matters presented in this section of Ephesians but is not limited to these. *power.* See 1:19–21.

3:21 *Unto him be glory.* The ultimate goal of our existence (see 1:6 and note). *in the church by Christ Jesus.* A remarkable parallel. God has called the church to an extraordinary position and vocation (cf. v. 10; 4:1).

Christ Jesus throughout all ages, world without end. Amen.

The unity of the Spirit

4 I therefore, [a]the prisoner [1]of the Lord,
beseech you that *ye* [b]walk worthy of the
vocation wherewith ye are called,
2 [a]With all lowliness and meekness, with
longsuffering, forbearing one another in love;
3 Endeavouring to keep the unity of the
Spirit [a]in the bond of peace.
4 [a]*There is* one body, and one Spirit, even
as ye are called in one hope of your calling;
5 [a]One Lord, [b]one faith, [c]one baptism,
6 [a]One God and Father of all, who *is* above
all, and [b]through all, and in you all.
7 But [a]unto every one of us is given grace
according to the measure of the gift of Christ.
8 Wherefore *he* saith, [a]When he ascended
up on high, [b]he led [1]captivity captive, and
gave gifts unto men.

4:1 [1]Or, *in the Lord* [a]Philem. 1,9 [b]Phil. 1:27
4:2 [a]Acts 20:19
4:3 [a]Col. 3:14
4:4 [a]Rom. 12:5
4:5 [a]1 Cor. 1:13 [b]Jude 3 [c]Heb. 6:6
4:6 [a]Mal. 2:10 [b]Rom. 11:36
4:7 [a]1 Cor. 12:11
4:8 [1]Or, *a multitude of captives* [a]Ps. 68:18 [b]Judg. 5:12
4:9 [a]John 3:13
4:10 [1]Or, *fulfil* [a]Acts 1:9 [b]Acts 2:33
4:11 [a]1 Cor. 12:28 [b]Acts 21:8 [c]Acts 20:28 [d]Rom. 12:7
4:12 [a]1 Cor. 12:7 [b]1 Cor. 14:26 [c]Col. 1:24

9 ([a]Now that he ascended, what is it but
that he also descended first into the lower
parts of the earth?
10 He that descended is the same also
[a]that ascended up far above all heavens, [b]that
he might [1]fill all *things.*)
11 [a]And he gave some, apostles; and some,
prophets; and some, [b]evangelists; and some,
[c]pastors and [d]teachers;
12 [a]For the perfecting of the saints for the
work of the ministry, [b]for the edifying of [c]the
body of Christ:
13 Till we all come [1]in the unity of the
faith, and [a]of the knowledge of the Son of God,
unto [b]a perfect man, unto the measure of the
[2]stature of the fulness of Christ:
14 That we *henceforth* be no more [a]chil-
dren, [b]tossed to and fro, and carried about
with every [c]wind of doctrine, by the sleight of

4:13 [1]Or, *into the unity* [2]Or, *age* [a]Col. 2:2 [b]1 Cor. 14:20
4:14 [a]Is. 28:9 [b]Heb. 13:9 [c]Mat. 11:7

4:1–32 The chapter begins (v. 2) and ends (v. 32) with exhortations to love and forgive one another.

4:1–16 So far Paul has taught that God brought Jew and Gentile into a new relationship to each other in the church and that he called the church to display his wisdom. Paul now shows how God made provision for those in the church to live and work together in unity and to grow together into maturity.

4:1 *prisoner.* See note on 3:1. *vocation.* See 3:10,21 and notes.

4:3 *keep the unity.* Which God produced through the reconciling death of Christ (see 2:14–22). It is the heavy responsibility of Christians to keep that unity from being disturbed.

4:4 *one hope.* Has different aspects (e.g., 1:5,10; 2:7), but it is still one hope, tied to the glorious future of Christ, in which all believers share.

‡4:5 *one baptism.* Probably not the baptism of the Spirit (see 1 Cor 12:13), which was inward and therefore invisible, but water baptism (see note on Rom 6:3–4). Since Paul apparently has in mind that which identifies all believers as belonging together, he would naturally refer to that church ordinance in which every new convert participated publicly. At that time it was a more obvious common mark of identification of Christians than it is now, when it is observed differently and often only seen by those in the church.

4:7 *grace.* See 3:7–8.

4:8 Ps 68:18 (see note there) speaks of God's triumphant ascension to His throne in the temple at Jerusalem (symbol of His heavenly throne). Paul applies this to Christ's triumphal ascension into heaven. Where the psalm states further that God "received gifts among men," Paul apparently takes his cue from certain rabbinic interpretations current in his day that read the Hebrew preposition for "among" in the sense of "unto" (a meaning it often has) and the verb for "received" in the sense of "take and give" (a meaning it sometimes has—but with a different preposition; see Gen 15:9; 18:5; 27:13; Ex 25:2; 1 Ki 17:10–11). *captivity.* Probably Paul applies this to the spiritual enemies Christ defeated at the cross.

‡4:9 *ascended . . . descended.* Although Paul quoted from the psalm to introduce the idea of the "gifts unto men," he takes the opportunity to remind his readers of Christ's coming to earth (His incarnation—"descended") and His subsequent resurrection and ascension ("ascended"). This passage probably does not teach, as some think and as some translations suggest, that Christ descended into hell.

4:11 *he gave.* The quotation from Ps 68 has its ultimate meaning when applied to Christ as the ascended Lord, who Himself has given gifts. *apostles.* Mentioned here because of their role in establishing the church (see 2:20). For qualifications of the initial group of apostles see Acts 1:21–22; see also notes on Mark 6:30; Rom 1:1; 1 Cor 1:1; Heb 3:1. In a broader sense, Paul was also an apostle (see 1:1). *prophets.* People to whom God made known a message for His people that was appropriate to their particular need or situation (see 1 Cor 14:3–4; see also note on 1 Cor 12:10). *evangelists.* See Acts 21:8; 1 Cor 1:17. While the other gifted people helped the church grow through edification, the evangelists helped the church grow by augmentation. Since the objective mentioned in v. 12 is "for the perfecting of the saints for the work of ministry," we may assume that evangelists, among their various ministries, helped other Christians in their testimony. *pastors and teachers.* Because of the Greek grammatical construction (also, the word "some" introduces both words together), it is clear that these groups of gifted people are closely related. Those who have pastoral care for God's people (the image is that of shepherding) will naturally provide "food" from the Scriptures (teaching). They will be especially gifted as teachers (cf. 1 Tim 3:2).

‡4:12 *For the perfecting of the saints for the work of the ministry.* Those mentioned in v. 11 were not to do all the work for the people, but were to train the people to do the work themselves. *for the edifying of the body of Christ.* See v. 16. Spiritual gifts are for the body, the church, and are not to be exercised individualistically. (cf. 1 Pet 4:10). "Edifying" or "building up" reflects the imagery of 2:19–22. Both concepts—body and building—occurring together emphasize the key idea of growth.

‡4:13 *Till.* Expresses not merely duration but also purpose. *unity.* Carries forward the ideal of vv. 1–6. *of the faith.* Here "faith" refers to the Christians' common conviction about Christ and the doctrines concerning Him, as the following words make clear (cf. also "the apostles' doctrine" in Acts 2:42). *knowledge of the Son of God.* Unity is not just a matter of a loving attitude or religious feeling, but of truth and a common understanding about God's Son. *perfect man . . . fulness of Christ.* Not the maturity of doctrinal conviction just mentioned, nor a personal maturity that includes the ability to relate well to other people (cf. vv. 2–3), but the maturity of the perfectly balanced character of Christ.

4:14 *children.* Contrast the maturity of v. 13. *tossed.* The nautical imagery pictures the instability of those who are not strong Christians. *doctrine.* Then, as now, there were many distorted teachings and heresies that would easily throw the immature off course. *sleight . . . craftiness . . . deceive.* Sometimes those

men, and cunning craftiness, [d]whereby they
lie in wait to deceive;
15 But [a][1]speaking the truth in love, [b]may
grow *up* into him *in* all *things,* [c]which is the
head, *even* Christ:
16 [a]From whom the whole body fitly
joined together and compacted by that which
every joint supplieth, according to the effectual working in the measure of every part,
maketh increase of the body unto the edifying
of itself in love.

The old life and the new

17 ¶ This I say therefore, and testify in the
Lord, that [a]ye henceforth walk not as other
Gentiles walk, [b]in the vanity of their mind,
18 [a]Having the understanding darkened,
[b]being alienated from the life of God through
the ignorance that is in them, because of the
[c][1]blindness of their heart:
19 [a]Who being past feeling [b]have given
themselves over unto lasciviousness, to work
all uncleanness with greediness.
20 But ye have not so learned Christ;
21 If so be that ye have heard him, and have
been taught by him, as the truth is in Jesus:
22 That ye [a]put off concerning [b]the former
conversation the old man, which is corrupt according to the deceitful lusts;
23 And [a]be renewed in the spirit of your
mind;

4:14 [d]Rom. 16:18
4:15 [1]Or, *being sincere* [a]2 Cor. 4:2 [b]ch. 1:22 [c]Col. 1:18
4:16 [a]Col. 2:19
4:17 [a]Col. 3:7 [b]Rom. 1:21
4:18 [1]Or, *hardness* [a]Acts 26:18 [b]1 Thes. 4:5 [c]Rom. 1:21
4:19 [a]1 Tim. 4:2 [b]1 Pet. 4:3
4:22 [a]Col. 2:11 [b]Col. 3:7
4:23 [a]Col. 3:10
4:24 [1]Or, *holiness of truth* [a]Rom. 6:4
4:25 [a]Zech. 8:16 [b]Rom. 12:5
4:26 [a]Ps. 37:8
4:27 [a]1 Pet. 5:9
4:28 [1]Or, *to distribute* [a]Acts 20:35 [b]Luke 3:11
4:29 [1]Or, *to edify profitably* [a]Col. 3:8 [b]1 Thes. 5:11 [c]Col. 3:16
4:30 [a]Is. 7:13 [b]Luke 21:28
4:31 [a]Col. 3:8,19 [b]Jas. 4:11 [c]Tit. 3:3
4:32 [a]2 Cor. 2:10 [b]Mark 11:25
5:1 [a]Luke 6:36
5:2 [a]1 Thes. 4:9 [b]Gal. 1:4

24 And that *ye* [a]put on the new man,
which after God is created in righteousness
and [1]true holiness.
25 ¶ Wherefore putting away lying, [a]speak
every man truth with his neighbour: for [b]we
are members one of another.
26 [a]Be ye angry, and sin not: let not the
sun go down upon your wrath:
27 [a]Neither give place to the devil.
28 Let him that stole steal no more: but
rather [a]let him labour, working with *his* hands
the *thing which is* good, that he may have [1]to
give [b]to him that needeth.
29 [a]Let no corrupt communication proceed out of your mouth, but [b]that which *is*
good [1]to the use of edifying, [c]that it may minister grace unto the hearers.
30 And [a]grieve not the holy Spirit of God,
whereby ye are sealed unto the day of [b]re-
demption.
31 [a]Let all bitterness, and wrath, and
anger, and clamour, and [b]evil speaking, be put
away from you, [c]with all malice:
32 And [a]be ye kind one to another, tenderhearted, [b]forgiving one another, even as God
for Christ's sake hath forgiven you.

The works of light and darkness

5 Be [a]ye therefore followers of God, as
dear children;
2 And [a]walk in love, [b]as Christ also hath

who try to draw people away from the Christian faith are not innocently misguided but deliberately deceitful and evil (cf. 1 Tim 4:1–2).

‡4:15 *speaking the truth in love.* A truthful and loving manner of life is implied. *grow up . . . head.* A slightly different restatement of v. 13, based now on the imagery of Christ as the Head of the body, which is the church. Paul thus speaks primarily of corporate maturity. It is the "body of Christ" that needs to be edified or built up (v. 12). In v. 13 "we all" are to become "a perfect man" (mature).

4:16 Further details of the imagery of the body growing under the direction of the Head. The parts of the body help each other in the growing process, picturing the mutual ministries of God's people spoken of in vv. 11–13. *love.* Maturity and unity are impossible without it (cf. vv. 2,15).

4:17–5:20 Paul has just discussed unity and maturity as twin goals for the church, which God has brought into existence through the death of Christ. He now goes on to show that purity is also essential among those who belong to Him.

4:17 *vanity of their mind.* Life without God is intellectually frustrating, useless and meaningless (see, e.g., Eccl 1:2; Rom 1:21).

4:18 *understanding darkened.* Continues the idea of a futile thought life. *blindness of their heart.* Moral unresponsiveness.

4:19 *have given themselves over.* Just as Pharaoh's heart was hardened reciprocally by himself and by God (see Ex 7–11), so here the Gentiles have given themselves over to a sinful kind of life, while Rom 1:24,26,28 says that God gave them over to that life.

4:20 *ye.* Emphatic.

4:21 *truth is in Jesus.* The wording and the use of the name Jesus (rather than Christ) suggest that Paul is referring to the embodiment of truth in Jesus' earthly life.

‡4:22 *old man.* Refers to everything we are naturally, by birth, being part of the fallen human race. It includes our old life-style resulting from our natural deceitful desires.

4:23 *mind.* Cf. the evil thoughts of unbelievers (vv. 17–18).

‡4:24 *new man.* Refers to everything we are in Christ through rebirth. (Cf. Rom 6:6–11, 2 Cor 5:17, Gal 2:20, Col 3:9–10.)

4:25 *truth.* Cf. vv. 15,21. *neighbour.* Probably means fellow Christians in this context.

4:26 *Be ye angry.* Christians do not lose their emotions at conversion, but their emotions should be purified. Some anger is sinful, some is not. *let not the sun go down.* No anger is to outlast the day.

4:27 *the devil.* Personal sin is usually due to our evil desires (see Jas 1:14) rather than to direct tempting by the devil. However, Satan can use our sins—especially those, like anger, that are against others—to bring about greater evil, such as divisions among Christians.

4:28 *steal no more . . . labour . . . him that needeth.* It is not enough to cease from sin; one must do good. The former thief must now help those in need.

4:29 *but that. . . edifying.* An exhortation parallel to the previous one. The Christian not only stops saying unwholesome things; he also begins to say things that will help build others up.

‡4:30 *grieve.* By sin, such as "corrupt communication" (v. 29) and the sins mentioned in v. 31. The verb also demonstrates that the Holy Spirit is a person, not just an influence, for only a person can be grieved. *sealed.* See note on 1:13. *day of redemption.* See 1:14; 1 Pet 1:5 and notes.

4:31 *bitterness . . . malice.* Such things grieve the Holy Spirit. This continues the instruction concerning one's speech (v. 29).

4:32 *kind . . . tenderhearted.* The opposite of the negative qualities of v. 31. *forgiving.* This basic Christian attitude, which is a result of being forgiven in Christ, along with being kind and compassionate, brings to others what we have received from God.

‡5:1 *Be . . . followers.* One way of imitating God is to have a

loved us, and hath given himself for us an offering and a sacrifice to God [c]for a sweet-
smelling savour.
3 But [a]fornication, and all uncleanness, or
covetousness, [b]let it not be once named
amongst you, as becometh saints;
4 [a]Neither filthiness, nor foolish talking,
nor jesting, [b]which are not convenient: but
rather giving of thanks.
5 For this ye know, that [a]no whoremonger,
nor unclean *person,* nor covetous man [b]who is
an idolater, [c]hath *any* inheritance in the kingdom of Christ and of God.
6 [a]Let no *man* deceive you with vain
words: for because of these *things* [b]cometh
the wrath of God upon the children of [1]dis-
obedience.
7 Be not ye therefore partakers with them.
8 [a]For ye were sometimes darkness, but
now [b]*are ye* light in the Lord: walk as [c]chil-
dren of light:
9 (For [a]the fruit of the Spirit *is* in all goodness and righteousness and truth;)
10 [a]Proving what is acceptable unto the
Lord.

5:2 [c]2 Cor. 2:15
5:3 [a]Rom. 6:13 [b]1 Cor. 5:1
5:4 [a]Mat. 12:35 [b]Rom. 1:28
5:5 [a]1 Cor. 6:9 [b]Col. 3:5 [c]Rev. 22:15
5:6 [1]Or, *unbelief* [a]Jer. 29:8 [b]Rom. 1:18
5:8 [a]Is. 9:2 [b]2 Cor. 3:18 [c]Luke 16:8
5:9 [a]Gal. 5:22
5:10 [a]Rom. 12:2
5:11 [a]Rom. 6:21 [b]1 Tim. 5:20
5:12 [a]Rom. 1:24
5:13 [1]Or, *discovered* [a]John 3:20
5:14 [1][Or, it] [a]Is. 60:1 [b]John 5:25
5:15 [a]Col. 4:5
5:16 [a]Col. 4:5 [b]Eccl. 11:2
5:17 [a]Col. 4:5 [b]Rom. 12:2 [c]1 Thes. 4:3
5:18 [a]Prov. 20:1
5:19 [a]Acts 16:25
5:20 [a]Ps. 34:1 [b]1 Pet. 2:5

11 And have no fellowship with [a]the unfruitful works of darkness, but rather [b]reprove
them.
12 [a]For it is a shame even to speak of those
things which are done of them in secret.
13 But [a]all *things* that are [1]reproved are
made manifest by the light: for whatsoever
doth make manifest is light.
14 Wherefore [1]*he* saith, [a]Awake thou that
sleepest, and [b]arise from the dead, and Christ
shall give thee light.
15 [a]See then that ye walk circumspectly,
not as fools, but as wise,
16 [a]Redeeming the time, [b]because the
days are evil.
17 [a]Wherefore be ye not unwise, but [b]un-
derstanding [c]what the will of the Lord *is.*
18 And [a]be not drunk with wine, wherein
is excess; but be filled with the Spirit;
19 Speaking to yourselves [a]in psalms and
hymns and spiritual songs, singing and making
melody in your heart to the Lord;
20 [a]Giving thanks always for all *things*
unto God and the Father [b]in the name of our
Lord Jesus Christ;

forgiving spirit (4:32). The way we imitate our Lord is to act "even as" (4:32) He did. The sacrificial way Jesus expressed His love for us is not only the means of salvation (as seen in ch. 2) but also an example of the way we are to live for the sake of others.

5:2 *offering . . . savour.* In the OT the offering of a sacrifice pleased the Lord so much that it was described as a "sweet savour" (Gen 8:21; Ex 29:18,25,41; Lev 1:9,13,17).

5:3 *all uncleanness, or covetousness.* Paul moves from specifically sexual sins to more general sins, such as greed. These include sexual lust but refer to other kinds of excessive desire as well. *not be once named.* See v. 12. *saints.* We are also a "holy temple" (2:21; cf. 2 Cor 6:16; 1 Pet 2:5,9).

5:4 *foolish talking, nor jesting.* The context and the word "filthiness" indicate that it is not humor as such but dirty jokes and the like that are out of place. *giving of thanks.* By being grateful for all that God has given us, we can displace evil thoughts and words.

5:5 *whoremonger . . . nor covetous.* See v. 3. *idolater.* Cf. Col 3:5. The greedy person wants things more than he wants God, and puts things in place of God, thereby committing idolatry. *inheritance.* The person who persists in sexual and other kinds of greed has excluded God, who therefore excludes him from the kingdom (but see notes on 1 Cor 6:9,11).

5:7 *partakers.* Although Christians live in normal social relationships with others, as did the Lord Jesus (Luke 5:30–32; 15:1–2), they are not to participate in the sinful life-style of unbelievers.

‡5:8 *darkness . . . light.* This section emphasizes the contrast between light and darkness, showing that those who belong to Him who is "light" (1 John 1:5), i.e., pure and true, not only have their lives illumined by Him but also are the means of introducing that light into the dark areas of human conduct (cf. Mat 5:14).

‡5:9 *fruit of the Spirit.* See Gal 5:22–23.

5:11 *have no fellowship with.* See v. 7. *reprove.* Light, by nature, exposes what is in darkness, and the contrast shows sin for what it really is.

5:12 *a shame even to speak of.* Christians should not dwell on the evils that their lives are exposing in others.

5:13–14 *all things . . . made manifest . . . whatsoever doth make manifest is light.* By the repetition of these words, Paul seems to be stressing the all-pervasive nature of the light of God and its inevitable effect.

5:14 *he saith.* What follows may well be a hymn used by the early Christians (see note on Col 3:16). *sleepest . . . dead.* Two images that describe a sinner (cf. 2:1). *Christ shall give thee light.* With His life-giving light.

5:15 *fools . . . wise.* Having emphasized the contrast between light and darkness, Paul now turns to the contrast between wisdom and foolishness.

5:16 *time.* The foolish person has no strategy for life and misses opportunities to live for God in an evil environment.

5:17 *unwise . . . understanding.* The contrast continues. The foolish person not only misses opportunities to make wise use of time; he has a more fundamental problem: He does not understand what are God's purposes for mankind and for Christians. God's purposes are a basic theme in Ephesians (see ch. 1).

5:18 *be not drunk . . . be filled with the Spirit.* The Greek present tense is used to indicate that the filling of the Spirit is not a once-for-all experience. Repeatedly, as the occasion requires, the Spirit empowers for worship, service and testimony. The contrast between being filled with wine and filled with the Spirit is obvious. But there is something in common that enables Paul to make the contrast, namely, that one can be under an influence that affects him, whether of wine or of the Spirit. Since Col 3:15–4:1 is very similar to Eph 5:18–6:9, we may assume that Paul intends to convey a basically similar thought in the introductory sentences to each passage. When he speaks here of being filled with the Spirit and when he speaks in Colossians of being under the rule of the peace of Christ and indwelt by the "word" of Christ, he means to be under God's control. The effect of this control is essentially the same in both passages: a happy, mutual encouragement to praise God and a healthy, mutual relationship with people.

5:19 *psalms . . . songs.* Every kind of appropriate song—whether psalms like those of the OT, or hymns directed to God or to others that Christians were accustomed to singing—could provide a means for praising and thanking God (v. 20). Actually, however, all three terms may refer to different types of psalms (see note on Col 3:16).

21 [a]Submitting yourselves one to another in the fear of God.

Analogy of family and church

22 ¶ [a]Wives, submit yourselves unto your own husbands, [b]as unto the Lord.

23 For [a]the husband is the head of the wife, even as [b]Christ *is* the head of the church: and he is the saviour of [c]the body.

24 Therefore as the church is subject unto Christ, so *let* the wives *be* to their own husbands [a]in every *thing.*

25 [a]Husbands, love your wives, even as Christ also loved the church, and [b]gave himself for it;

26 That he might sanctify and cleanse *it* [a]with the washing of water by the word,

27 [a]That he might present it to himself a glorious church, [b]not having spot, or wrinkle, or any such *thing;* but that it should be holy and without blemish.

28 So ought men to love their wives as their own bodies. He that loveth his wife loveth himself.

29 For no *man* ever yet hated his own flesh; but nourisheth and cherisheth it, even as the Lord the church:

30 For [a]we are members of his body, of his flesh, and of his bones.

31 [a]For this cause shall a man leave his father and mother, and shall be joined unto his wife, and they [b]two shall be one flesh.

32 This is a great mystery: but I speak concerning Christ and the church.

33 Nevertheless [a]let every one of you in particular so love his wife even as himself; and the wife *see* that she [b]reverence *her* husband.

6 Children, [a]obey your parents in the Lord: for this is right.

2 [a]Honour thy father and mother; (which is the first commandment with promise;)

3 That it may be well with thee, and thou mayest live long on the earth.

4 And, [a]ye fathers, provoke not your children to wrath: but [b]bring them up in the nurture and admonition of the Lord.

5 ¶ [a]Servants, be obedient to *them that are your* masters according to the flesh, [b]with fear and trembling, [c]in singleness of your heart, as unto Christ;

6 [a]Not with eyeservice, as menpleasers; but as the servants of Christ, doing the will of God from the heart;

7 With good will doing service, as to the Lord, and not to men:

5:21 [a]Phil. 2:3
5:22 [a]Gen. 3:16 [b]ch. 6:5
5:23 [a]1 Cor. 11:3 [b]Col. 1:18 [c]ch. 1:23
5:24 [a]Tit. 2:9
5:25 [a]Col. 3:19 [b]Acts 20:28
5:26 [a]John 3:5
5:27 [a]Col. 1:22 [b]Sol. 4:7
5:30 [a]Gen. 2:23
5:31 [a]Mat. 19:5 [b]1 Cor. 6:16
5:33 [a]Col. 3:19 [b]1 Pet. 3:6
6:1 [a]Col. 3:20
6:2 [a]Ex. 20:12
6:4 [a]Col. 3:21 [b]Gen. 18:19
6:5 [a]1 Tim. 6:1 [b]2 Cor. 7:15; Phil. 2:12 [c]1 Chr. 29:17; Col. 3:22
6:6 [a]Col. 3:22

5:21–6:9 In chs. 2–4 Paul showed the way God brought believing Jews and Gentiles together into a new relationship in Christ. In 4:1–6 he stressed the importance of unity. Now he shows how believers, filled with the Spirit, can live together in a practical way in various human relationships. This list of mutual responsibilities is similar to the pattern found in Col 3:18–4:1; 1 Pet 2:13–3:12; cf. Rom 13:1–10.

‡5:21 *Submitting yourselves one to another.* Basic to the following paragraphs. Paul will show how, in each relationship, the partners can have a conciliatory attitude that will help that relationship. The grammar indicates that this submission is associated with the filling of the Spirit in v. 18. The command "be filled" (v. 18) is followed by a series of participles in the Greek: speaking, singing, making melody (v. 19), giving thanks (v. 20) and submitting (v. 21).

‡5:22 *Wives, submit yourselves.* An aspect of the submission taught in v. 21. To be subject meant to yield one's own rights. If the relationship called for it, as in the military, the term could connote obedience, but that meaning is not called for here. In fact, the word "obey" does not appear in Scripture with respect to wives, though it does with respect to children (6:1) and servants (6:5). *as unto the Lord.* Does not put a woman's husband in the place of the Lord, but shows rather that a woman ought to submit to her husband as an act of submission to the Lord. Cf. 1 Pet 3:1–6, esp. v. 6)

‡5:23-33 Throughout this crucial and very practical text, Paul instructs wives and husbands by showing that the husband is to take his cues from Christ and the wife take hers from the church. This insight is important both for the marriage partners and for the church (cf. v. 32)

5:23 *head of the wife.* See note on 1 Cor 11:3. *as Christ.* The analogy between the relationship of Christ to the church and that of the husband to the wife is basic to the entire passage. *he . . . body.* See 2:16; 4:4,12,16. *saviour.* Christ earned, so to speak, the right to His special relationship to the church.

5:25 *Husbands.* Paul now shows that this is not a one-sided submission, but a reciprocal relationship. *love.* Explained by what follows. *gave himself for it.* Not only the expression of our Lord's love, but also an example of how the husband ought to devote himself to his wife's good. To give oneself up to death for the beloved is a more extreme expression of devotion than the wife is called on to make.

5:26 *washing of water by the word.* Many attempts have been made to see marriage customs or liturgical symbolism in these words. One thing is clear: The Lord Jesus died not only to bring forgiveness, but also to effect a new life of holiness in the church, which is His "bride." A study of the concepts of washing, of water and of the word should include reference to John 3:5; 15:3; Tit 3:5; Jas 1:18; 1 Pet 1:23; 3:21.

5:27 *holy and without blemish.* See 1:4.

5:28–29 *as their own bodies . . . loveth himself . . . his own flesh.* The basis for such expressions and for the teaching of these verses is the quotation from Gen 2:24 in v. 31. If the husband and wife become "one flesh," then for the man to love his wife is to love one who has become part of himself.

5:32 *mystery.* See note on Rom 11:25. The profound truth of the union of Christ and his "bride," the church, is beyond unaided human understanding. It is not that the relationship of husband and wife provides an illustration of the union of Christ and the church, but that the basic reality is the latter, with marriage a human echo of that relationship.

5:33 *love . . . reverence.* A rephrasing and summary of the whole passage.

6:3 *on the earth.* In Deut 5:16 (see Ex 20:12), where this commandment occurs, the "promise" (v. 2) was expressed in terms of the anticipated occupation of the "land," i.e., Canaan. That specific application was, of course, not appropriate to the Ephesians, so the more general application is made here.

6:4 *provoke not.* Fathers must surrender any right they may feel they have to act unreasonably toward their children.

6:5 *Servants.* Both the OT and the NT included regulations for societal situations such as slavery and divorce (see Deut 24:1–4), which were the results of the hardness of hearts (Mat 19:8). Such regulations did not encourage or condone such situations but were divinely-given, practical ways of dealing with the realities of the day.

8 [a]Knowing that whatsoever good *thing* any man doeth, the same shall he receive of the Lord, [b]whether *he be* bond or free.

9 And, ye [a]masters, do the same *things* unto them, [1]forbearing threatening: knowing that [2]your Master also is in heaven; [b]neither is there respect of persons with him.

The whole armour of God

10 ¶ Finally, my brethren, be strong in the Lord, and in the power of his might.

11 [a]Put on the whole armour of God, that ye may be able to stand against the wiles of the devil.

12 For we wrestle not against [1]flesh and blood, but against [a]principalities, against powers, against [b]the rulers of the darkness of this world, against [2]spiritual wickedness in [3]high *places.*

13 [a]Wherefore take unto *you* the whole armour of God, that ye may be able to withstand [b]in the evil day, and [1]having done all, to stand.

14 Stand therefore, [a]having your loins girt about with truth, and [b]having on the breastplate of righteousness;

15 [a]And *your* feet shod with the preparation of the gospel of peace;

16 Above all, taking [a]the shield of faith, wherewith ye shall be able to quench all the fiery darts of the wicked.

17 And [a]take the helmet of salvation, and [b]the sword of the Spirit, which is the word of God:

18 [a]Praying always with all prayer and supplication in the Spirit, and [b]watching thereunto with all perseverance and [c]supplication for all saints;

19 [a]And for me, that utterance may be given unto me, that *I* may open my mouth [b]boldly, to make known the mystery of the gospel,

20 For which [a]I am an ambassador [1]in bonds: that [2]therein [b]I may speak boldly, as I ought to speak.

Concluding benediction

21 ¶ But that ye also may know my affairs, *and* how I do, [a]Tychicus, a beloved brother and faithful minister in the Lord, shall make known to you all *things:*

22 [a]Whom I have sent unto you for the same purpose, that ye might know our affairs, and *that* he might comfort your hearts.

23 [a]Peace *be* to the brethren, and love with faith, from God the Father and the Lord Jesus Christ.

24 Grace *be* with all them that love our Lord Jesus Christ [1]in sincerity. Amen.

¶ Written from Rome unto the Ephesians by Tychicus.

6:8 [a]Rom. 2:6; Col. 3:24 [b]Gal. 3:28
6:9 [1]Or, *moderating* [2]Some read, *both your and their Master* [a]Col. 4:1 [b]Rom. 2:11
6:11 [a]2 Cor. 6:7
6:12 [1][Gr. *blood and flesh*] [2]Or, *wicked spirits* [3]Or, *heavenly* [a]Rom. 8:38 [b]Luke 22:53
6:13 [1]Or, *having overcome all* [a]2 Cor. 10:4 [b]ch. 5:16
6:14 [a]Is. 11:5; 1 Pet. 1:13 [b]Is. 59:17
6:15 [a]Is. 52:7
6:16 [a]1 John 5:4
6:17 [a]1 Thes. 5:8 [b]Heb. 4:12
6:18 [a]Luke 18:1 [b]Mat. 26:41 [c]Phil. 1:4
6:19 [a]Acts 4:29 [b]2 Cor. 3:12
6:20 [1]Or, *in a chain* [2]Or, *thereof* [a]2 Cor. 5:20 [b]Phil. 1:20
6:21 [a]Acts 20:4
6:22 [a]Col. 4:8
6:23 [a]1 Pet. 5:14
6:24 [1]Or, *with incorruption*

6:9 *masters.* Once again Paul stresses reciprocal attitudes (cf. 5:21–6:4). See note on Tit 2:9.

6:10–20 Paul's scope in Ephesians has been cosmic. From the very beginning he has drawn attention to the unseen world (see note on 1:3; see also 1:10,20–23; 2:6; 6:10), and now he describes the spiritual battle that takes place against evil "in the high places" (v. 12).

6:10 *strong . . . might.* Implies that human effort is inadequate but God's power is invincible.

‡6:12 *not against flesh and blood.* A caution against lashing out against human opponents as though they were the real enemy and also against assuming that the battle can be fought using merely human resources. *principalities . . . spiritual wickedness.* Cf. Paul's earlier allusions to powerful beings in the unseen world (see notes on 1:21; 3:10). *high places.* The Greek phrase is the same as in 1:3 and is better translated "heavenly places." See note on 1:3.

6:13–14 *withstand . . . Stand therefore.* In this context the imagery is not that of a massive invasion of the domain of evil, but of individual soldiers withstanding assault.

‡6:14 *loins girt about with truth.* Cf. the symbolic clothing of the Messiah in Is 11:5. Character, not brute force, wins the battle, just as in the case of the Messiah. *breastplate of righteousness.* Paul is using a metaphor to show that Christians are to put on righteousness to protect their hearts as a soldier puts on a breastplate to protect himself.

6:15 *feet shod with the preparation.* Whereas the description of the messenger's feet in Is 52:7 reflects the custom of running barefooted, here the message of the gospel is picturesquely connected with the protective and supportive footgear of the Roman soldier.

6:16 *shield of faith . . . quench . . . fiery darts.* Describes the large Roman shield covered with leather, which could be soaked in water and used to put out flame-tipped arrows.

6:17–18 *sword of the Spirit . . . Praying . . . in the Spirit.* Reminders that the battle is spiritual and must be fought in God's strength, depending on the word and on God through prayer.

6:17 *helmet of salvation.* Is 59:17 has similar language, along with the breastplate imagery (see note on v. 14). The helmet both protected the soldier and provided a striking symbol of military victory.

6:21–23 Paul concludes with greetings that lack personal references such as are usually found in his letters. This is understandable if Ephesians is a circular letter (see note on 1:1).

6:21 *Tychicus.* An associate of Paul who traveled as his representative (cf. Col 4:7; 2 Tim 4:12; Tit 3:12).

The Epistle of Paul the Apostle to the Philippians

INTRODUCTION

Author, Date and Place of Writing

The early church was unanimous in its testimony that Philippians was written by the apostle Paul (see 1:1). Internally the letter reveals the stamp of genuineness. The many personal references of the author fit what we know of Paul from other NT books.

It is evident that Paul wrote the letter from prison (see 1:13–14). Some have argued that this imprisonment took place in Ephesus, perhaps c. A.D. 53–55; others put it in Caesarea c. 57–59. Best evidence, however, favors Rome as the place of origin and the date as c. 61. This fits well with the account of Paul's house arrest in Acts 28:14–31. When he wrote Philippians, he was not in the Mamertine dungeon as he was when he wrote 2 Timothy. He was in his own rented house, where for two years he was free to impart the gospel to all who came to him.

Purpose

Paul's primary purpose in writing this letter was to thank the Philippians for the gift they had sent him upon learning of his detention at Rome (1:5; 4:10–19). However, he makes use of this occasion to fulfill several other desires: (1) to report on his own circumstances (1:12–26; 4:10–19); (2) to encourage the Philippians to stand firm in the face of persecution and rejoice regardless of circumstances (1:27–30; 4:4); (3) to exhort them to humility and unity (2:1–11; 4:2–5); (4) to commend Timothy and Epaphroditus to the Philippian church (2:19–30); and (5) to warn the Philippians against the Judaizers (legalists) and antinomians (libertines) among them (ch. 3).

Philippi in the Time of Paul

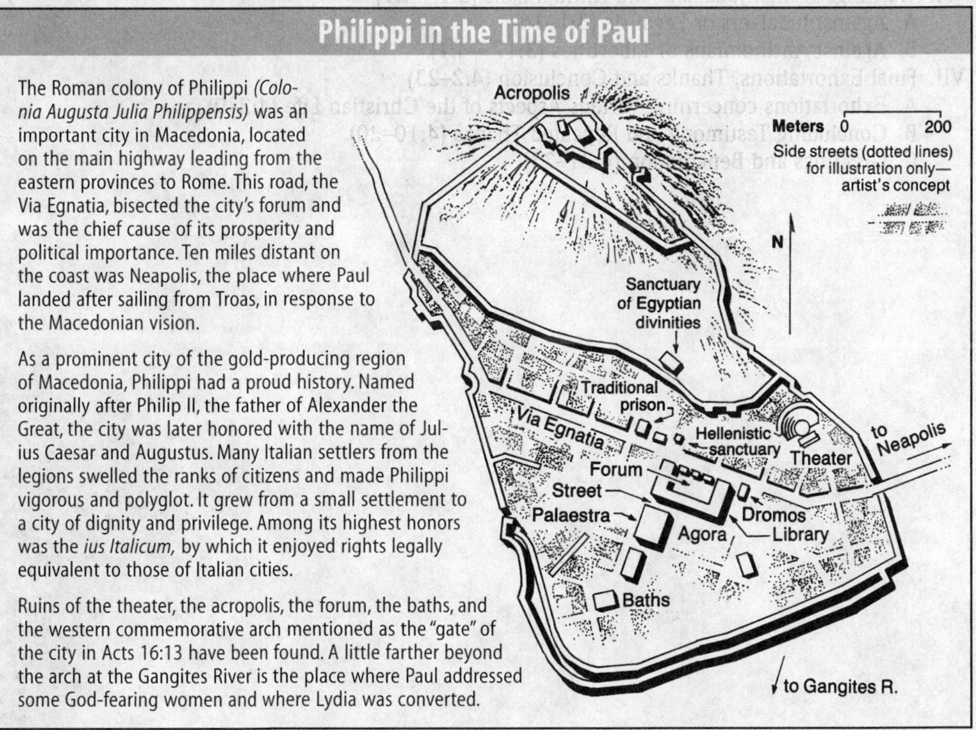

The Roman colony of Philippi *(Colonia Augusta Julia Philippensis)* was an important city in Macedonia, located on the main highway leading from the eastern provinces to Rome. This road, the Via Egnatia, bisected the city's forum and was the chief cause of its prosperity and political importance. Ten miles distant on the coast was Neapolis, the place where Paul landed after sailing from Troas, in response to the Macedonian vision.

As a prominent city of the gold-producing region of Macedonia, Philippi had a proud history. Named originally after Philip II, the father of Alexander the Great, the city was later honored with the name of Julius Caesar and Augustus. Many Italian settlers from the legions swelled the ranks of citizens and made Philippi vigorous and polyglot. It grew from a small settlement to a city of dignity and privilege. Among its highest honors was the *ius Italicum,* by which it enjoyed rights legally equivalent to those of Italian cities.

Ruins of the theater, the acropolis, the forum, the baths, and the western commemorative arch mentioned as the "gate" of the city in Acts 16:13 have been found. A little farther beyond the arch at the Gangites River is the place where Paul addressed some God-fearing women and where Lydia was converted.

Recipients

The city of Philippi was named after King Philip II of Macedon, father of Alexander the Great. It was a prosperous Roman colony, which meant that the citizens of Philippi were also citizens of the city of Rome itself. They prided themselves on being Romans (see Acts 16:21), dressed like Romans and often spoke Latin. No doubt this was the background for Paul's reference to the believer's heavenly citizenship (3:20–21). Many of the Philippians were retired military men who had been given land in the vicinity and who in turn served as a military presence in this frontier city. That Philippi was a Roman colony may explain why there were not enough Jews there to permit the establishment of a synagogue and why Paul does not quote the OT in the Philippian letter.

Characteristics

1. Philippians contains no OT quotations (but see note on Job 13:16).
2. It is a missionary thank-you letter in which the missionary reports on the progress of his work.
3. It manifests a particularly vigorous type of Christian living: (1) self-humbling (2:1–4); (2) pressing toward the goal (3:13–14); (3) lack of anxiety (4:6); (4) ability to do all things (4:13).
4. It is outstanding as the NT letter of joy; the word "joy" in its various forms occurs some 16 times.
5. It contains one of the most profound Christological passages in the NT (2:5–11). Yet, profound as it is, Paul includes it mainly for illustrative purposes.

Outline

I. Salutation (1:1–2)
II. Thanksgiving and Prayer for the Philippians (1:3–11)
III. Paul's Personal Circumstances (1:12–26)
IV. Exhortations (1:27—2:18)
  A. Living a Life Worthy of the Gospel (1:27–30)
  B. Following the Servant Attitude of Christ (2:1–18)
V. Paul's Associates in the Gospel (2:19–30)
  A. Timothy (2:19–24)
  B. Epaphroditus (2:25–30)
VI. Warnings against Judaizers and Antinomians (3:1—4:1)
  A. Against Judaizers or Legalists (3:1–16)
  B. Against Antinomians or Libertines (3:17—4:1)
VII. Final Exhortations, Thanks and Conclusion (4:2–23)
  A. Exhortations concerning Various Aspects of the Christian Life (4:2–9)
  B. Concluding Testimony and Repeated Thanks (4:10–20)
  C. Greetings and Benediction (4:21–23)

1 Paul and Timotheus, the servants of
Jesus Christ, to all the saints [a]in Christ
Jesus which are at Philippi, with the bishops
and deacons:
2 [a]Grace *be* unto you, and peace, from God
our Father, and *from* the Lord Jesus Christ.

Prayer of thankfulness

3 ¶ [a]I thank my God upon every [1]remem-
brance of you,
4 Always in every prayer of mine for you all
making request with joy,
5 [a]For your fellowship in the gospel from
the first day until now;
6 Being confident of this very *thing,* that
he which hath begun [a]a good work in you
[1]will perform *it* until the day of Jesus Christ:
7 Even as it is meet for me to think this of
you all, because [1]I have you in *my* heart; inasmuch as both in my bonds, and *in* the defence
and confirmation of the gospel, ye all are [2]par-
takers of my grace.
8 For [a]God is my record, how *greatly* I long
after you all in the bowels of Jesus Christ.

1:1 [a]1 Cor. 1:2
1:2 [a]1 Pet. 1:2
1:3 [1]Or, *mention* [a]1 Cor. 1:4
1:5 [a]Rom. 12:13
1:6 [1]Or, *will finish* it [a]John 6:29
1:7 [1]Or, *you have me in* your *heart* [2]Or, *partakers with me of grace*
1:8 [a]Rom. 1:9; Gal. 1:20
1:9 [1]Or, *sense*
1:10 [1]Or, *try* [2]Or, *differ* [a]Rom. 12:2 [b]Acts 24:16 [c]1 Cor. 1:8
1:11 [a]Eph. 2:10; Col. 1:6 [b]John 15:8
1:13 [1]Or, *for Christ* [2]Or, *Cesar's court* [3]Or, *to all others* [a]ch. 4:22
1:15 [a]ch. 2:3

9 And this I pray, that your love may
abound yet more and more in knowledge and
in all [1]judgment;
10 That [a]ye may [1]approve *things* that [2]are
excellent; [b]that ye may be sincere and without
offence [c]till the day of Christ;
11 Being filled with the fruits of righteousness, [a]which are by Jesus Christ [b]unto the glory and praise of God.

Paul's boldness in prison

12 ¶ But I would ye should understand,
brethren, that the *things which happened*
unto me have fallen out rather unto the furtherance of the gospel;
13 So that my bonds [1]in Christ are manifest
[a]in all [2]the palace, and [3]*in* all other *places;*
14 And many of the brethren in the Lord,
waxing confident by my bonds, are much
more bold to speak the word without fear.
15 Some indeed preach Christ even of
envy and [a]strife; and some also of good will:
16 The one preach Christ of contention,
not sincerely, supposing to add affliction to my
bonds:

1:1–2 As in all his letters, Paul follows the conventional letter format of his day, with its three elements: (1) identification of the sender, (2) identification of the recipients, (3) greeting.

‡1:1 *Timotheus.* See Introduction to 1 Timothy: Recipient. Timothy is identified with the contents of the letter as Paul's associate, but not as co-author. *servants.* See Rom 1:1; Tit 1:1; Philem 1. In Paul's case, this designation brings out an essential aspect of the more usual identification of himself as "apostle." *saints.* A designation, not of individual moral purity, but of spiritual union with Christ, as the following "in Christ Jesus" shows (see Rom 1:7; 1 Cor 1:2 and notes). *Philippi.* See Introduction: Recipients. *bishops and deacons.* The only place in Paul's writings where church officers as a group are singled out as recipients of a letter. *bishops.* See note on 1 Tim 3:1. *deacons.* See note on 1 Tim 3:8.

1:2 The opening greeting is not merely a matter of polite custom but is given a distinctively Christian tone and content.

1:3–4 *I thank my God . . . prayer of mine . . . with joy.* Prayers of joyful thanksgiving for his readers' response to the gospel are a hallmark of the opening sentences of Paul's letters (see Rom 1:8; 1 Cor 1:4; Col 1:3; 1 Thes 1:2; 2 Thes 1:3; 2 Tim 1:3; Philem 4).

1:5 *your fellowship in the gospel.* The basis of Paul's prayerful thanksgiving is not only their reception of the gospel but also their active support of his ministry (see 4:15). *from the first day.* When Paul first came to Philippi (see Acts 16:12). *now.* Toward the close (see 2:24) of Paul's first Roman imprisonment (see Acts 28:16–31).

1:6 *work in you.* Paul is confident, not only of what God has done "for" the readers in forgiving their sins, but also of what he has done "in" them (see v. 11). "Work" refers to God's activity in saving them. *day of Jesus Christ.* His return, when their salvation will be brought to completion (see 1:10; 2:16; 1 Cor 1:8; 5:5; 2 Cor 1:14). It is God who initiates salvation, who continues it and who will one day bring it to its consummation.

1:7 *partakers of my grace.* Not even imprisonment and persecution can change such sharing. Even in Paul's imprisonment they willingly identified themselves with Paul by sending Epaphroditus and their financial gifts. They had become one with Paul in his persecution.

1:8 *bowels of Jesus Christ.* Or, "the affection of Jesus Christ," the deep yearning and intense, compassionate love exhibited by Jesus Himself and now fostered in Paul by his union with Christ. This affection reaches out to all impartially and without exception.

‡1:9 *abound yet more and more.* Real love requires growth and maturation (see 1 Thes 3:12; 4:10; 2 Thes 1:3). *in knowledge.* The way love grows (cf. Col 1:9). *judgment.* Practical discernment and sensitivity. Christian love is not mere sentiment; it is rooted in knowledge and understanding.

‡1:10 *approve things that are excellent.* Christians are to approve (and practice) what is morally and ethically superior. *sincere and without offence.* The goal of Christians in this life is to be without any mixture of evil and not open to censure because of moral or spiritual failure. *till the day of Christ.* Then the goal will be perfectly realized (see note on v. 6), and then Christians must give an account (see 2 Cor 5:10).

1:11 *filled with the fruits of righteousness.* What is expected of all Christians (cf. Mat 5:20–48; Heb 12:11; Jas 3:18; see also Amos 6:12; Gal 5:22). *by Jesus Christ.* Produced by Christ (in union with Him) through the work of the Holy Spirit (cf. John 15:5; Eph 2:10). *unto the glory and praise of God.* The ultimate goal of all that God does in believers (see Eph 1:6,12,14).

1:12 *things which happened.* Paul's detainment in prison. *furtherance of the gospel.* Instead of hindering the gospel, Paul's imprisonment had served to make it known.

1:13 *bonds in Christ are manifest.* It has become apparent to all who know of Paul's situation that he is imprisoned, not because he is guilty of some crime, but on account of his stand for the gospel. *bonds.* Either actual chains or a broader reference to his sufferings and imprisonment (see v. 14). *all the palace.* A contingent of soldiers, numbering several thousand, would have had personal contact with Paul or would have been assigned individually to guard him during the course of his imprisonment (see Acts 28:16,30).

1:14 *are much more bold.* The unexpected result of Paul's imprisonment is that others, encouraged by his example, are forcefully proclaiming the gospel.

1:15 *even of envy and strife . . . of good will.* The gospel preaching stimulated by Paul's imprisonment stems from either one of two sharply opposed motives.

‡1:16 *The one preach Christ of contention.* Those who preach with wrong, insincere motives do so out of a sense of compe-

17 But the other of love, knowing that I am set for the defence of the gospel.

18 What then? notwithstanding, every way, whether in pretence, or in truth, Christ is preached; and I therein do rejoice, yea, and will rejoice.

19 For I know that this shall turn to my salvation [a]through your prayer, and the supply of the Spirit of Jesus Christ,

20 According to my [a]earnest expectation and *my* hope, that [b]in nothing I shall be ashamed, but *that* [c]with all boldness, as always, *so* now also Christ shall be magnified in my body, whether *it be* by life, or by death.

21 For to me to live *is* Christ, and to die *is* gain.

22 But if *I* live in the flesh, this *is* the fruit of my labour: yet what I shall choose I wot not.

23 For [a]I am in a strait betwixt two, having a desire to [b]depart, and to be with Christ; *which is* far better:

24 Nevertheless to abide in the flesh *is* more needful for you.

25 And [a]having this confidence, I know that I shall abide and continue with you all for your furtherance and joy of faith;

26 That [a]your rejoicing may be *more* abundant in Jesus Christ for me by my coming to you again.

The example of Christ

27 ¶ Only [a]let your conversation be as it becometh the gospel of Christ: that whether I come and see you, or *else* be absent, I may hear of your affairs, that ye stand fast in one spirit, [b]with one mind striving together for the faith of the gospel;

28 And in nothing terrified by *your* adversaries: [a]which is to them an evident token of perdition, [b]but to you of salvation, and that of God.

29 For unto you [a]it is given in the behalf of Christ, [b]not only to believe on him, but also to suffer for his sake;

30 [a]Having the same conflict [b]which ye saw in me, and now hear *to be* in me.

2 If *there be* therefore any consolation in Christ, if any comfort of love, [a]if any fel-

1:19 [a]2 Cor. 1:11
1:20 [a]Rom. 8:19 [b]Rom. 5:5 [c]Eph. 6:19
1:23 [a]2 Cor. 5:8 [b]2 Tim. 4:6
1:25 [a]ch. 2:24
1:26 [a]2 Cor. 1:14
1:27 [a]Eph. 4:1; 1 Thes. 2:12 [b]1 Cor. 1:10; Acts 2:36
1:28 [a]2 Thes. 1:5 [b]Rom. 8:17
1:29 [a]Rom. 5:3 [b]Eph. 2:8
1:30 [a]Col. 2:1 [b]Acts 16:19; 1 Thes. 2:2
2:1 [a]2 Cor. 13:14

tition with Paul and so think they are making his imprisonment more difficult to bear. *not sincerely.* Not all preaching of the gospel is based on proper motives

‡1:17 *the other of love.* Those who preach with a right motive recognize the true reason for Paul's imprisonment, already expressed earlier in v. 13, and are encouraged to take the same bold stand that he has taken.

1:18 *whether in pretense, or in truth, Christ is preached.* The insincere preachers are not to be viewed as being heretical. Their message is true, even though their motives are not pure. The gospel has its objectivity and validity apart from those who proclaim it; the message is more than the medium. *I . . . rejoice . . . and will rejoice.* An example of the kind of vigorous Christian experience Paul expressed. He was under arrest, and fellow Christians sought, by their preaching, to add to his difficulties; yet he kept on rejoicing.

1:19 *salvation.* Either Paul's release from prison (see v. 25; 2:24) or, in view of the immediately following verses, the deliverance brought to the believer by death (cf. Rom 8:28). Verse 25, however, seems to point to the former interpretation. *Spirit of Jesus Christ.* The Holy Spirit is not only the Spirit of God the Father (Rom 8:9,14; 1 Cor 2:10–11,14) but also the Spirit of Christ, the second person of the Trinity (Acts 16:7; Rom 8:9; Gal 4:6). He is sent by the Father (John 14:16–17,26; Gal 4:6) and by the Son (John 15:26; 16:7).

1:20 *be ashamed . . . with all boldness.* The circumstances of imprisonment, with all its attendant suffering and oppression, constitute a real temptation for Paul to abandon the gospel and his resolute service for Christ. *my body.* Where the exalted Christ dwells by His Spirit and is at work (cf. Rom 8:9–10), and so is exalted by what Paul does. *whether it be by life, or by death.* Whether his service for Christ continues or ends in death.

1:21 *to live is Christ.* Christ was the source and secret of Paul's continual joy (even in prison), for Paul's life found all its meaning in Christ. *gain.* Verse 23 specifies that the gain brought by death is "being with Christ," so that here Paul is saying that his ultimate concern and most precious possession, both now and forever, is Christ and his relationship to Him.

1:22 *fruit of my labour.* The spread of the gospel and the upbuilding of the church.

1:23–24 *depart, and to be with Christ . . . abide in the flesh.* Either alternative was a good one. While mysteries remain, this passage clearly teaches that when believers die they are with Christ, apart from the body.

1:23 *far better.* Being with Christ after death must involve some kind of conscious presence and fellowship (cf. 2 Cor 5:6,8).

1:24 *more needful for you.* Paul puts the needs of those he ministers to ahead of his personal preference.

1:25 *I shall abide.* Possibly Paul was later released from prison (see map, pp. 1738–1739). *furtherance and joy of faith.* The Christian life is to be one of joyful growth and advance (see note on v. 9 and the verses cited there).

1:27 *becometh the gospel.* Appropriate to the standards and goals given with the gospel. *in one spirit.* Having a common disposition and purpose. *with one mind striving.* Particularly where the gospel is under attack, Christians need each other and must stand together.

1:28 *token.* Persistent opposition to the church and the gospel is a sure sign of eventual destruction, since it involves rejection of the only way of salvation. By the same token, when Christians are persecuted for their faith, this is a sign of the genuineness of their salvation (see 2 Thes 1:5).

1:29 *given . . . to suffer.* Given as a gift or privilege. Christian suffering, as well as faith, is a blessing (cf. Mat 5:11–12; Acts 5:41; Jas 1:2; 1 Pet 4:14). The Christian life is to be a "not only . . . but also" proposition: not only believing but also suffering.

1:30 *same conflict.* Their common involvement with Paul in conflict with those who oppose the gospel. *ye saw.* When Paul and Silas first visited Philippi and were imprisoned (see Acts 16:19–40).

2:1 *in Christ.* In Paul's teaching, personal union with Christ is the basic reality of salvation. To be in Christ is to be saved. It is to be in intimate personal relationship with Christ the Savior. From this relationship flow all the particular benefits and fruits of salvation, like encouragement (see, e.g., 3:8–10; Rom 8:1; 2 Cor 5:17; Gal 2:20). *comfort of love.* The comforting knowledge and assurance that come from God's love in Christ, demonstrated especially in Christ's death for the forgiveness of sins and eternal life (see John 3:16; Rom 5:8; 8:38–39; 1 John 3:16; 4:9–10,16). *fellowship of the Spirit.* The fellowship among believers produced by the Spirit, who indwells each of them (see 2 Cor 13:14). *bowels and mercies.* Christians are to have intense care and deep sympathy for each other (see 1:8; Col 3:12). All

lowship of the Spirit, if any [b]bowels and mercies,
2 [a]Fulfil ye my joy, [b]that ye be likeminded,
having the same love, *being* of one accord, of
one mind.
3 [a]*Let* nothing *be done* through strife or
vainglory; but [b]in lowliness of mind *let* each
esteem other better than themselves.
4 [a]Look not every man on his own *things,*
but every man also on the *things* of others.
5 [a]Let this mind be in you, which *was* also
in Christ Jesus:
6 Who, [a]being in the form of God, thought
it not robbery to be equal with God:
7 [a]But made himself of no reputation, and
took *upon him* the form [b]of a servant, and
[c]was made in the likeness of men:
8 And being found in [1]fashion as a man, he
humbled himself, and [a]became obedient unto
death, even the death of the cross.
9 Wherefore God also [a]hath highly exalted
him, and [b]given him a name which is above
every name:
10 [a]That at the name of Jesus every knee
should bow, of *things* in heaven, and *things* in
earth, and *things* under the earth;
11 And [a]*that* every tongue should confess
that Jesus Christ *is* Lord, to the glory of God
the Father.

Obligations of Christians

12 Wherefore, my beloved, [a]as ye have always obeyed, not as in my presence only, but
now much more in my absence, work out your
own salvation with [b]fear and trembling.
13 For [a]it is God which worketh in you
both to will and to do of *his* good pleasure.
14 Do all *things* [a]without murmurings and
[b]disputings:
15 That ye may be blameless and [1]harm-

2:1 [b]Col. 3:12
2:2 [a]John 3:29 [b]Rom. 12:16; 1 Cor. 1:10
2:3 [a]Gal. 5:26; Jas. 3:14 [b]Rom. 12:10; 1 Pet. 5:5
2:4 [a]1 Cor. 13:5
2:5 [a]Mat. 11:29; 1 Pet. 2:21
2:6 [a]2 Cor. 4:4; Col. 1:15
2:7 [a]Ps. 22:6; Is. 53:3; Dan. 9:26; Mark 9:12 [b]Is. 42:1; Ezek. 34:23; Zech. 3:8; Mat. 20:28; Luke 22:27 [c]John 1:14; Rom. 1:3; Gal. 4:4
2:8 [1]Or, *habit* [a]Mat. 26:39; Heb. 5:8
2:9 [a]Acts 2:33; Heb. 2:9
2:9 [b]Heb. 1:4
2:10 [a]Is. 45:23; Mat. 28:18
2:11 [a]John 13:13; Acts 2:36
2:12 [a]ch. 1:5 [b]Eph. 6:5
2:13 [a]2 Cor. 3:5
2:14 [a]1 Pet. 4:9 [b]Rom. 14:1
2:15 [1]Or, *sincere*

these benefits—encouragement, comfort, fellowship, tenderness and compassion—are viewed by Paul as present realities for the Philippians.

2:2 *likeminded . . . same love . . . one accord . . . one mind.* Emphasizes the unity that should exist among Christians. *one mind.* Not uniformity in thought but the common disposition to work together and serve one another—the "attitude" of Christ (v. 5; see 4:2; Rom 12:16; 15:5; 2 Cor 13:11).

2:3 *strife or vainglory.* The mortal enemies of unity and harmony in the church (cf. 1:17; see Gal 5:20, where the Greek for "selfishness" is rendered "disputes" and listed among the "deeds of the flesh"). *lowliness of mind.* The source of Christian unity. This is the mind-set of the person who is not conceited but who has a right attitude toward himself. *esteem other better than themselves.* Not that everyone else is superior or more talented, but that Christian love sees others as worthy of preferential treatment (see Rom 12:10; Gal 5:13; Eph 5:21; 1 Pet 5:5).

2:4 *his own things.* These are proper, but only if there is equal concern for the interests of others (cf. Rom 15:1).

2:5 *Let this mind be in you, which was also in Christ Jesus.* In spite of all that is unique and radically different about the person and work of Christ (see vv. 6–11), Christians are to have His attitude of self-sacrificing humility and love for others (see vv. 2–4; Mat 11:29; John 13:12–17).

‡2:6–11 The poetic, even lyric, character of these verses is apparent. Many view them as an early Christian hymn (see note on Col 3:16), taken over and perhaps modified by Paul. If so, they nonetheless express his convictions. The passage treats Christ's humiliation (vv. 6–8) and exaltation (vv. 9–11). This "kenotic" pattern of suffering, followed by glory, becomes an important one for the writer, who applies it to himself (cf. 3:7–14) and his readers (cf. v. 5; 3:15–16; Rom 8:17–19).

2:6 *in the form of God.* Affirming that Jesus is fully God (see note on Rom 9:5). *form.* Essential form, the sum of those qualities that make God specifically God. *robbery.* Perhaps something to be forcibly retained—the glory Christ had with the Father before His incarnation. But He did not consider that high position to be something He could not give up. On the other hand, it may be something still to be attained, like a prize, as if He did not yet possess it. *equal with God.* The status and privileges that inevitably follow from being in very nature God.

‡2:7 *made himself of no reputation.* He did this, not by giving up deity, but by laying aside His glory (see John 17:5) and submitting to the humiliation of becoming man (see 2 Cor 8:9). Jesus is truly God and truly man. Another view is that He emptied Himself, not of deity itself, but of its prerogatives—the high position and glory of deity. *form of a servant.* Emphasizes the full reality of His servant identity (see Mat 20:28). As a servant, He was always submissive to the will of the Father.

‡2:8 *fashion as a man.* Not only was Jesus "like" a human being (v. 7), but He also took on the actual outward characteristics of a man (see John 1:14; Rom 8:3; Heb 2:17). *humbled himself.* See v. 7; 2 Cor 8:9. *obedient.* How Jesus humbled himself (cf. Heb 5:7–8). A "servant" (v. 7) obeys. *death.* Stresses both the totality and the climax of Jesus' obedience. *of the cross.* Heightens Jesus' humiliation; He died as someone cursed (see Gal 3:13; Heb 12:2). Crucifixion was the most degrading kind of execution that could be inflicted on a person.

2:9 *exalted.* See Mat 28:18; Acts 2:33; cf. Is 52:13. *a name . . . above every name.* Reference doubtless is to the office or rank conferred on Jesus—His glorious position, not His proper name (cf. Eph 1:21; Heb 1:4–5).

2:10–11 *bow . . . confess.* Cf. Is 45:23. God's design is that all people everywhere should worship and serve Jesus as Lord. Ultimately all will acknowledge Him as Lord (see Rom 14:9), whether willingly or not.

2:12 *Wherefore.* Because of Christ's incomparable example (vv. 5–11). *obeyed.* The commands of God as passed on to the Philippians by Paul (see Rom 1:5; 15:18; 2 Cor 10:5–6). *my presence.* During the course of Paul's second (see Acts 16:12–40) and third (see Acts 20:1–3,6) missionary journeys. *work out your own salvation.* Work it out to the finish; not a reference to the attempt to earn one's salvation by works, but to the expression of one's salvation in spiritual growth and development. Salvation is not merely a gift received once for all; it expresses itself in an ongoing process in which the believer is strenuously involved (cf. Mat 24:13; 1 Cor 9:24–27; Heb 3:14; 6:9–11; 2 Pet 1:5–8)—the process of perseverance, spiritual growth and maturation. *fear and trembling.* Not because of doubt or anxiety; rather, the reference is to an active reverence and a singleness of purpose in response to God's grace.

2:13 *to will and to do.* Intention, or faith, and our obedience cannot be separated (cf. Gal 5:6; Jas 2:18,20,22).

2:14–17 Some things involved in working out our salvation.

2:14 *murmurings.* Being discontented with God's will is an expression of unbelief that prevents one from doing what pleases God (v. 13; cf. 1 Cor 10:10). *disputings.* Over debatable points that do not need to be settled for the good of the church (see 2 Tim 2:23; Tit 3:9).

less, [a]the sons of God without rebuke, [b]in the
midst of [c]a crooked and perverse nation,
among whom [d2]ye shine as lights in the
world;
16 Holding forth the word of life; that [a]I
may rejoice in the day of Christ, that [b]I have
not run in vain, neither laboured in vain.
17 Yea, and if [a]I be [1]offered upon the sacrifice [b]and service of your faith, [c]I joy, and rejoice with you all.
18 *For* the same *cause* also do ye joy, and
rejoice with me.

Timotheus and Epaphroditus

19 ¶ [1]But I trust in the Lord Jesus to send
[a]Timotheus shortly unto you, that I also may
be of good comfort, when I know your state.
20 For I have no *man* [a1]likeminded, who
will naturally care for your state.
21 For all [a]seek their own, not the *things*
which are Jesus Christ's.
22 But ye know the proof of him, [a]that, as
a son *with the* father, he hath served with me
in the gospel.
23 Him therefore I hope to send presently,
so soon as I shall see how it will go with me.
24 But [a]I trust in the Lord that I also myself
shall come shortly.
25 Yet I supposed it necessary to send to
you [a]Epaphroditus, my brother, and companion in labour, and [b]fellowsoldier, [c]but your

2:15 [2]Or, *shine ye* [a]Mat. 5:45; Eph. 5:1 [b]1 Pet. 2:12 [c]Deut. 32:5 [d]Eph. 5:8
2:16 [a]2 Cor. 1:14; 1 Thes. 2:19 [b]Gal. 2:2
2:17 [1]Gr. *poured forth* [a]2 Tim. 4:6 [b]Rom. 15:16 [c]2 Cor. 7:4; Col. 1:24
2:19 [1]Or, *Moreover* [a]Rom. 16:21
2:20 [1]Or, *so dear unto me* [a]Ps. 55:13
2:21 [a]1 Cor. 10:24; 13:5; 2 Tim. 4:10
2:22 [a]1 Cor. 4:17; 1 Tim. 1:2
2:24 [a]ch. 1:25
2:25 [a]ch. 4:18 [b]Philem. 2 [c]2 Cor. 8:23 [d]2 Cor. 11:9
2:26 [a]ch. 1:8
2:29 [1]Or, *honour such* [a]1 Cor. 16:18; 1 Thes. 5:12; 1 Tim. 5:17
2:30 [a]1 Cor. 16:17
3:1 [a]2 Cor. 13:11; 1 Thes. 5:16
3:2 [a]Gal. 5:15 [b]Rom. 2:28
3:3 [a]Deut. 30:6; Jer. 4:4 [b]Rom. 7:6 [c]Gal. 6:14
3:4 [a]2 Cor. 11:18

messenger, and [d]he that ministered to my
wants.
26 [a]For he longed after you all, and *was* full
of heaviness, because that ye had heard that
he had been sick.
27 For indeed he was sick nigh unto death:
but God had mercy on him; and not on him
only, but on me also, lest I should have sorrow
upon sorrow.
28 I sent him therefore the more carefully,
that, when ye see him again, ye may rejoice,
and *that* I may be the less sorrowful.
29 Receive him therefore in the Lord with
all gladness; and [a1]hold such in reputation:
30 Because for the work of Christ he was
nigh unto death, not regarding *his* life, [a]to supply your lack of service toward me.

The example of Paul

3 Finally, my brethren, [a]rejoice in the
Lord. To write the same *things* to you, to
me indeed *is* not grievous, but for you *it is*
safe.
2 [a]Beware of dogs, beware of evil workers,
[b]beware of the concision.
3 For we are [a]the circumcision, [b]which
worship God in the spirit, and [c]rejoice in
Christ Jesus, and have no confidence in the
flesh.
4 Though [a]I *might* also have confidence in
the flesh. If any other *man* thinketh that *he*

2:15 *blameless and harmless . . . without rebuke.* Not absolute, sinless perfection, but wholehearted, unmixed devotion to doing God's will. *crooked and perverse nation.* A description of the unbelieving world (see Acts 2:40; Eph 2:1–3; cf. Mat 17:17). *shine as lights.* The contrast, like light in darkness, that Christians are to be to the world around them (cf. Mat 5:15–16).

‡2:16 *rejoice.* Because of what God has done through Paul (see 1 Thes 2:19). *day of Christ.* See note on 1:6. *in vain.* Cf. 1 Cor 9:24–27.

2:17–18 *I . . . rejoice . . . also do ye . . . rejoice.* Christian joy ought always to be mutual.

2:17 *I be offered.* The reference may be to his entire ministry as one large thanksgiving sacrifice. However, it is more probable that Paul refers to his present imprisonment, which may end in a martyr's death. His life would then be poured out as a drink offering accompanying the sacrificial service of the Philippians. *upon the sacrifice.* The OT background is the daily sacrifices in Ex 29:38–41. *of your faith.* Genuine faith is active and working (see note on v. 13).

2:19–23 Paul plans to send Timothy, who is with him in Rome (see 1:1), to discover and report on conditions in the Philippian church.

2:20 *no man likeminded.* Timothy was a good example of the kind of person envisioned in the exhortation of v. 4.

2:21 A sharp contrast between Timothy and Paul's other associates—an outstanding commendation for one so young.

2:22 *as a son with the father.* This relationship between Timothy and Paul is developed at length in 1,2 Timothy. *served with me.* Like Jesus and Paul, Timothy had a servant attitude.

2:24 Paul anticipates his release in the near future (see 1:25).

2:25–30 Epaphroditus, too, after a close brush with death (vv. 27,30), is being sent home to Philippi.

2:25 *messenger.* A broader use of the Greek word often translated "apostle," applied here to Epaphroditus as a representative of the Philippian church (cf. 2 Cor 8:23).

2:27 Cf. 1:21–26.

2:28 *sorrowful.* The legitimate cares and concerns that come with the Christian life and the gospel ministry (see note on 4:6; cf. 2 Cor 4:8; 11:28).

‡3:1 *Finally.* Marks a transition to a new section as Paul moves toward his conclusion; this does not mark the close of the letter, however (cf. 4:8). *rejoice in the Lord.* See 4:4. *same things.* Matters taken up in the verses that follow, which Paul had previously dealt with either orally when he was in Philippi or perhaps in an earlier letter. *safe.* Where serious error is present, there is safety in repetition.

3:2 *dogs.* A harsh word for Paul's opponents, showing their aggressive opposition to the gospel and the seriousness of their error and its destructive, "devouring" results (cf. Gal 5:15). Their teaching was probably similar to what Paul had to oppose in the Galatian churches (see Introduction to Galatians: Occasion and Purpose). *concision.* Or "mutilation." Again, this is a strong, painfully vivid term; the false teachers have so distorted the meaning of circumcision (cf. v. 3) that it has become nothing more than a useless cutting of the body.

3:3 *circumcision.* Its true, inner meaning is realized only in believers, who worship God with genuine spiritual worship and who glory in Christ as their Savior rather than trusting in their own human effort (cf. Rom 2:28–29; Col 2:12–13; see also Deut 30:6; Ezek 36:26). *rejoice . . . no confidence.* Everyone is a "boaster," either in Christ or in himself. *flesh.* Weak human nature. Although the term "flesh" in Paul's letters often refers to sinful human nature, it speaks here of the frailty of human nature: It is not worthy of our confidence; it cannot save.

3:4–14 Paul's personal testimony, a model for every believer; one of the most significant autobiographical sections in his letters (see Gal 1:13–24; 1 Tim 1:12–16; cf. Acts 22:1–21; 26:1–23).

hath whereof he might trust in the flesh, I more:

5 Circumcised the eighth day, of the stock of Israel, [a]of the tribe of Benjamin, [b]a Hebrew of the Hebrews; as touching the law, [c]a Pharisee;

6 [a]Concerning zeal, persecuting the church; [b]touching the righteousness which is in the law, [c]blameless.

7 But [a]what *things* were gain to me, those I counted loss for Christ.

8 Yea doubtless, and I count all *things but* loss [a]for the excellency of the knowledge of Christ Jesus my Lord: for whom I have suffered the loss of all *things,* and do count *them but* dung, that I may win Christ,

9 And be found in him, not having [a]mine own righteousness, which is of the law, but [b]that which is through the faith of Christ, the righteousness which is of God by faith:

10 That *I* may know him, and the power of his resurrection, and [a]the fellowship of his sufferings, being made conformable unto his death;

11 If by any means I might [a]attain unto the resurrection of the dead.

3:5 [a]Rom. 11:1 [b]2 Cor. 11:22 [c]Acts 23:6
3:6 [a]Acts 22:3 [b]Rom. 10:5 [c]Luke 1:6
3:7 [a]Mat. 13:44
3:8 [a]Is. 53:11
3:9 [a]Rom. 10:3 [b]Rom. 1:17
3:10 [a]Rom. 6:3-5; 8:17
3:11 [a]Acts 26:7
3:12 [a]1 Tim. 6:12 [b]Heb. 12:23
3:13 [a]Luke 9:62 [b]Heb. 6:1
3:14 [a]2 Tim. 4:7 [b]Heb. 3:1
3:15 [a]1 Cor. 2:6 [b]Gal. 5:10
3:16 [a]Rom. 12:16; 15:6 [b]Gal. 6:16
3:17 [a]1 Cor. 11:1; 1 Thes. 1:6 [b]1 Pet. 5:3
3:18 [a]Gal. 1:7; 2:21
3:19 [a]2 Cor. 11:15 [b]1 Tim. 6:5; Tit. 1:11

The high calling of God

12 Not as though I had already [a]attained, either were already [b]perfect: but I follow *after,* if that I may apprehend *that* for which also I am apprehended of Christ Jesus.

13 Brethren, I count not myself to have apprehended: but *this* one *thing I do,* [a]forgetting those *things which are* behind, and [b]reaching forth unto those *things which are* before,

14 [a]I press toward the mark for the prize of [b]the high calling of God in Christ Jesus.

15 Let us therefore, as many as *be* [a]perfect, [b]be thus minded: and if in any *thing* ye be otherwise minded, God shall reveal even this unto you.

16 Nevertheless, whereto we have *already* attained, [a]*let us* walk [b]by the same rule, *let us* mind the same *thing.*

17 ¶ Brethren, [a]be followers together of me, and mark them which walk so as [b]ye have us for an ensample.

18 (For many walk, of whom I have told you often, and now tell *you* even weeping, *that they are* [a]the enemies of the cross of Christ:

19 [a]Whose end *is* destruction, [b]whose God

3:4–6 Paul's pre-Christian confidence, rooted in his Jewish pedigree, privileges and attainments.

3:5 *eighth day.* See Gen 17:12. *of the stock of Israel.* Paul was born a Jew and was not a proselyte. *tribe of Benjamin.* His Jewish roots are deep and unambiguous. Jerusalem, the Holy City, lay on the border of the tribal territory of Benjamin. *Hebrew of the Hebrews.* In language, attitudes and life-style (see Acts 22:2–3; Gal 1:14). *Pharisee.* See Acts 22:3; 23:6; 26:5.

3:6 *righteousness . . . in the law.* Righteousness produced by using the law as an attempt to merit God's approval and blessing (cf. v. 9)—a use of the law strongly opposed by Paul as contrary to the gospel itself (see Rom 3:27–28; 4:1–5; Gal 2:16; 3:10–12). *blameless.* In terms of legalistic standards of scrupulous external conformity to the law.

3:7–14 Paul's confidence in Christ.

3:7 *what things.* The things mentioned in vv. 5–6. *gain . . . loss.* The great reversal in Paul—begun on the road to Damascus (see Acts 9:3–16)—from being self-centered to being centered in Christ.

3:8 *knowledge of Christ Jesus.* Not only a knowledge of facts but a knowledge gained through experience that, in its surpassing greatness, transforms the entire person. The following verses spell this out. *dung.* What Paul now has as a Christian is not merely preferable or a better alternative; in contrast, his former way of life was worthless and despicable.

3:9 *be found in him.* Union with Christ (see note on 2:1; cf. 1 Cor 1:30)—not simply an experience in the past, but a present, continuing relationship. *righteousness . . . of the law.* See note on v. 6. *righteousness . . . through the faith.* A principal benefit of union with Christ (see Rom 3:21–22; 1 Cor 1:30; Gal 2:16).

3:10 *know him.* As in v. 8, this knowledge is not merely factual; it includes the experience of the power of His resurrection (see Eph 1:17–20), of fellowship in His sufferings (cf. Acts 9:16) and of being like Him in His death (see 2 Cor 4:7–12; 12:9–10). Believers already share positionally in Christ's death and resurrection (cf. Rom 6:2–13; Gal 2:20; 5:24; 6:14; Eph 2:6; Col 2:12–13; 3:1). In v. 10, however, Paul speaks of the actual experience of Christ's resurrection power and of suffering with and for Him, even to the point of death.

3:11 *I might attain.* Not an indication of doubt or uncertainty, but of intense concern and involvement. *resurrection.* The great personal anticipation of every believer (see Dan 12:2; John 5:29; Acts 24:15; 1 Cor 15:23; 1 Thes 4:16).

3:12–14 The Christian life is like a race; elsewhere Paul uses athletic imagery in a similar way (1 Cor 9:24–27; 1 Tim 6:12; 2 Tim 4:7–8; cf. Mat 24:13; Heb 12:1).

3:12 *apprehend . . . I am apprehended.* Paul's goal is Christ's goal for him, and Christ supplies the resources for him to "press toward the mark" (v. 14; cf. 2:12–13).

3:13 *forgetting.* Not losing all memory of his sinful past (see vv. 4–6), but leaving it behind him as done with and settled.

3:14 *prize.* The winner of the Greek races received a wreath of leaves and sometimes a cash award; the Christian receives an award of everlasting glory. *high calling.* Paul's ultimate aspirations are found not in this life but in heaven, because Christ is there (see Col 3:1–2).

3:15 *perfect.* Those who have made reasonable progress in spiritual growth and stability (see 1 Cor 2:6; 3:1–3; Heb 5:14). *thus minded.* That expressed in vv. 12–14: There are heights yet to be scaled; do not become complacent. *otherwise minded.* If the readers accept the view set forth in vv. 12–14 and yet fail to agree in some lesser point, God will clarify the matter for them.

3:16 *let us walk by the same rule.* Put into practice the truth they have already comprehended. We are responsible for the truth we currently possess.

3:17 *be followers . . . of me.* As Paul follows the example of Christ. *mark them.* The life-styles Christians lead ought to be models worth following.

3:18 *told you often.* See v. 1. *weeping.* See Acts 20:19,31. *they are the enemies of the cross.* In glaring contrast to Paul's conduct (v. 10) and to the truth of the gospel.

3:19 *destruction.* The opposite of salvation. *God . . . belly.* A deep self-centeredness; their appetites and desires come first. *earthly things.* They have set their minds on the things of this life; they are antinomians (libertines), the opposite of the legalists of v. 2.

is their belly, and [c]*whose* glory *is* in their
shame, [d]who mind earthly *things.*)
20 For [a]our conversation is in heaven;
[b]from whence also we [c]look for the Saviour,
the Lord Jesus Christ:
21 [a]Who shall change our vile body, that it
may be fashioned like unto his glorious body,
[b]according to the working whereby he is able
[c]even to subdue all *things* unto himself.

Appeal to rejoice in the Lord

4 Therefore, my brethren dearly beloved
and [a]longed for, [b]my joy and crown, so
[c]stand fast in the Lord, *my* dearly beloved.
2 I beseech Euodias, and beseech Syntyche, [a]that *they* be of the same mind in the
Lord.
3 And I intreat thee also, true yokefellow,
help those *women* which [a]laboured with me
in the gospel, with Clement also, and *with* other my fellowlabourers, whose names *are* in
[b]the book of life.
4 ¶ [a]Rejoice in the Lord alway: *and* again I
say, Rejoice.

3:19 [c]Hos. 4:7; Gal. 6:13 [d]Rom. 8:5
3:20 [a]Eph. 2:6; Col. 3:1,3 [b]Acts 1:11 [c]1 Cor. 1:7; 1 Thes. 1:10
3:21 [a]1 Cor. 15:43; Col. 3:4 [b]Eph. 1:19 [c]1 Cor. 15:26
4:1 [a]ch. 1:8 [b]2 Cor. 1:14; ch. 2:16 [c]ch. 1:27
4:2 [a]ch. 3:16
4:3 [a]Rom. 16:3 [b]Ex. 32:32; Ps. 69:28; Dan. 12:1
4:4 [a]Rom. 12:12; 1 Thes. 5:16; 1 Pet. 4:13
4:5 [a]Heb. 10:25; 1 Pet. 4:7
4:6 [a]Ps. 55:22; Prov. 16:3; Mat. 6:25
4:7 [a]John 14:27; Rom. 5:1; Col. 3:15
4:8 [1]Or, *venerable* [a]1 Thes. 5:22
4:9 [a]ch. 3:17 [b]Rom. 15:33

5 Let your moderation be known unto all
men. [a]The Lord *is* at hand.
6 [a]Be careful for nothing; but in every *thing*
by prayer and supplication with thanksgiving
let your requests be made known unto God.
7 And [a]the peace of God, which passeth all
understanding, shall keep your hearts and
minds through Christ Jesus.
8 Finally, brethren, whatsoever *things* are
true, whatsoever *things are* [1]honest, whatsoever *things are* just, whatsoever *things are*
pure, whatsoever *things are* lovely, [a]whatsoev-
er *things are* of good report; if *there be* any
virtue, and if *there be* any praise, think on
these *things.*
9 [a]Those *things,* which ye have both
learned, and received, and heard, and seen in
me, do: and [b]the God of peace shall be with you.

The Philippian gifts

10 ¶ But I rejoiced in the Lord greatly, that
now at the last [a]your care of me [1]hath flour-

4:10 [1]Or, *is revived* [a]2 Cor. 11:9

‡3:20 *conversation.* Lit. "citizenship." In this world Christians are aliens, fully involved in it, yet not of it (cf. John 17:14–16; 1 Cor 7:29–31; 1 Pet 2:11). *in heaven.* Where Christ is and where believers are—in union with Him; contrast the "earthly things" of v. 19 (see Eph 2:6; Col 3:1–4). *from whence . . . look.* See Rom 8:19; 1 Cor 1:7; 1 Thes 1:9–10; 2 Tim 4:8.
‡3:21 *shall change.* By the Holy Spirit at the resurrection (see Rom 8:11; 1 Cor 6:14; 15:50–53). *our vile body.* More literally, "lowly," in that it is subject to weakness, decay and death, due to sin (see Rom 8:10,20–23; 1 Cor 15:42–44). *fashioned like unto his glorious body.* See Rom 8:29; 1 John 3:2. The resurrection body, received already by Christ, who is the "firstfruits," will be received by believers in the future resurrection "harvest" (see 1 Cor 15:20,49). It is "spiritual," i.e., transformed by the power of the Holy Spirit (see 1 Cor 15:44,46). *working . . . to subdue.* Christ's present power, earned by His obedience to death (see 2:8) and received in His resurrection and ascension, is universal and absolute (see Mat 28:18; 1 Cor 15:27; Eph 1:20–22).
4:1 *beloved and longed for.* See notes on 1:8; 2:1. *my joy and crown.* True not only now, but especially when Christ returns (see 1 Thes 2:19). *so.* Refers to the closing statements of ch. 3. In the face of libertine practices (3:18–19), the Philippians should follow Paul's example (3:17), having their minds set on heavenly things (3:20–21). *stand fast.* In the midst of present struggles for the sake of the gospel (cf. 1:27–30; 1 Cor 15:58).
4:2–3 The disagreement between Euodia and Syntyche is serious enough to be mentioned in a letter to be read publicly, but Paul seems confident that "those women" (v. 3) will be reconciled. His handling of the situation is a model of tact—he does not take sides but encourages others closer to the situation to promote reconciliation (see 2:2).
4:3 *laboured with me . . . fellowlabourers.* Those associated with the apostle in the cause of the gospel (women as well as men) are his equals, not subordinates (cf. 2:25; Rom 16:3,9,21; Philem 24). *Clement.* Not mentioned elsewhere in the NT. *other my fellowlabourers.* Not mentioned individually because they are known to God and their names are entered in the book of life, the heavenly register of the elect (see note on Rev 3:5).
4:4 *Rejoice in the Lord.* See 3:1. *alway.* Under all kinds of circumstances, including suffering (see Hab 3:17–18; Jas 1:2; 1 Pet 4:13).
4:5 *moderation.* Christlike consideration for others (cf. 2 Cor 10:1). It is especially essential in church leaders (see 1 Tim 3:3; Tit 3:2, "shewing all meekness"). *at hand.* See Rom 13:11; cf. Jas 5:8–9; Rev 22:7,12,20. The next great event in God's prophetic schedule is Christ's return. The whole period from Christ's first coming to the consummation of the kingdom is viewed in the NT as the last time (1 John 2:18). From God's vantage point, a thousand years are as a day. Thus there is a sense in which, for every generation, the Lord's coming is near.
4:6 *careful.* Or "anxious," with self-centered, counterproductive worry, not legitimate cares and concerns for the spread of the gospel (see 2:28 and note; 2 Cor 11:28; see also Mat 6:25–31; 1 Pet 5:7). *in every thing by prayer.* Anxiety and prayer are two great opposing forces in Christian experience. *thanksgiving.* The antidote to worry (along with prayer and petition).
4:7 *peace of God.* Not merely a psychological state of mind, but an inner tranquillity based on peace with God—the peaceful state of those whose sins are forgiven (cf. John 14:27; Rom 5:1). The opposite of anxiety, it is the tranquillity that comes when the believer commits all his cares to God in prayer and worries about them no more. *passeth all understanding.* The full dimensions of God's love and care are beyond human comprehension (see Eph 3:18–20). *keep your hearts and minds.* A military concept depicting a sentry standing guard. God's "protective custody" of those who are in Christ Jesus extends to the core of their beings and to their deepest intentions (cf. 1 Pet 1:5).
‡4:8 *Finally.* See note on 3:1. *true . . . any praise.* Paul understood the influence of one's thoughts on one's life. What a person allows to occupy his mind will sooner or later determine his speech and his action. Paul's exhortation to "think on these things" is followed by a second exhortation, "those things . . . do" (v. 9). The combination of virtues listed in vv. 8–9 is sure to produce a wholesome thought pattern, which in turn will result in a life of moral and spiritual excellence.
‡4:9 *seen in me.* See notes on 2:6–11 and 3:17. *God of peace.* See note on 1 Thes 5:23; cf. the "peace of God" (v. 7).
4:10 *at the last . . . lacked opportunity.* The delay in sending gifts to Paul was not the fault of the Philippians, nor was it because they were lacking in concern for him (cf. 2 Cor 11:9). Perhaps Paul's uncertain itinerary prior to his arrival at Rome or the lack of an available messenger had prevented the Philippians from showing their concern.

ished again; wherein ye were also careful, but ye lacked opportunity.

11 Not that I speak in respect of want: for I have learned, in whatsoever *state* I am, [a]*there-with* to be content.

12 [a]I know both *how* to be abased, and I know *how* to abound: every where and in all *things* I am instructed both to be full and to be hungry, both to abound and to suffer need.

13 I can do all *things* [a]through Christ which strengtheneth me.

14 Notwithstanding ye have well done, that [a]ye did communicate with my affliction.

15 Now ye Philippians know also, that in the beginning of the gospel, when I departed from Macedonia, [a]no church communicated with me as concerning giving and receiving, but ye only.

16 For even in Thessalonica ye sent once and again unto my necessity.

17 Not because I desire a gift: but I desire [a]fruit that *may* abound to your account.

4:11 [a] 1 Tim. 6:6
4:12 [a] 1 Cor. 4:11
4:13 [a] John 15:5
4:14 [a] ch. 1:7
4:15 [a] 2 Cor. 11:8
4:17 [a] Tit. 3:14
4:18 [1] Or, *I have received all* [a] ch. 2:25 [b] Heb. 13:16 [c] 2 Cor. 9:12
4:19 [a] Ps. 23:1 [b] Eph. 1:7
4:20 [a] Rom. 16:27
4:21 [a] Gal. 1:2
4:22 [a] ch. 1:13
4:23 [a] Rom. 16:24

18 But [1]I have all, and abound: I am full, having received [a]of Epaphroditus the *things which were sent* from you, [b]an odour of a sweet smell, [c]a sacrifice acceptable, well pleasing to God.

19 But my God [a]shall supply all your need [b]according to his riches in glory by Christ Jesus.

20 [a]Now unto God and our Father *be* glory for ever and ever. Amen.

Concluding benediction

21 ¶ Salute every saint in Christ Jesus. The brethren [a]which are with me greet you.

22 All the saints salute you, [a]chiefly they that are of Cesar's household.

23 [a]The grace of our Lord Jesus Christ *be* with you all. Amen.

¶ It was written to the Philippians from Rome by Epaphroditus.

4:11 *whatsoever state . . . to be content.* Paul genuinely appreciates the gifts from Philippi (see vv. 14,18) but he is not ultimately dependent on them (cf. 1 Tim 6:6–8).

4:12 *I know . . . abased . . . abound.* Prosperity, too, can be a source of discontent.

‡4:13 *all things.* This refers to any and all situations that Paul might face (cf. vv. 11–12). *Christ which strengtheneth me.* Christ. Union with the living, exalted Christ is the secret of being content (v. 12) and the source of Paul's abiding strength (see especially 2 Cor 12:9–10; see also John 15:5; Eph 3:16–17; Col 1:11).

4:14 *communicate.* The Philippians' gifts are a means of involving them in Paul's troubles (cf. Heb 10:33).

‡4:15 *beginning.* During Paul's second missionary journey, when he first preached in Philippi (see Acts 16:12–40). *departed.* For the south (Achaia), where Athens and Corinth were located (see Acts 17:14–16; 18:1–4). *Macedonia.* The northern part of modern-day Greece, where Berea and Thessalonica, as well as Philippi, were located. *communicated with me concerning.* Or "participated with me in an account of." Paul uses commercial language to describe "giving and receiving" (credit and debit) between the Philippians and himself (see "abound to your account," v. 17). Yet this commercial imagery is plainly transcended by the mutual concern and self-sacrifice of their relationship. *but ye only.* The generosity of the Philippian church is unique and unmatched (cf. 2 Cor 8:1–5).

4:16 *even in Thessalonica.* While he was still in Macedonia (see Acts 17:1–9). *sent once and again.* The gifts sent to Rome through Epaphroditus are the latest in a long and consistent pattern of generosity (cf. 2 Cor 8:1–5).

4:17 *abound to your account.* See note on v. 15. The "investment value" of the Philippians' gift is not primarily what Paul received, but the "spiritual dividends" they received.

4:18 *a sweet smell, a sacrifice acceptable.* The OT background is the sacrifice, not of atonement for sin, but of thanksgiving and praise (cf. Lev 7:12–15; Rom 12:1; Eph 5:2; Heb 13:15–16). *acceptable, well pleasing to God.* Because of Christ's work for us (see 1 Pet 2:5) and God's work in us (see Phil 2:13).

4:19 *my.* A personal touch (cf. "my God" in 1:3). *shall supply.* A promise given to a church that had sacrificially given to meet Paul's need. *your need.* Paul is concerned not only about his own situation but also about that of the Philippians. *his riches in glory by Christ Jesus.* The true measure of God's blessings to the church (cf. Eph 1:18; 3:16–20).

4:20 Paul cannot hold back a doxology, especially as he considers the truth of v. 19.

4:21–22 Final greetings are a typical feature of Paul's letters (see, e.g., Rom 16:3–16,21–23; 1 Cor 16:19–20; 2 Cor 13:12–13; Col 4:10–12,14–15,18).

4:21 *every saint.* See note on 1:1. *brethren which are with me.* Paul's fellow workers at Rome, especially Timothy (see 1:1,14,16).

4:22 *Cesar's household.* Not blood relatives of the emperor, but those employed (slaves or freedmen) in or around the palace area (cf. "palace," 1:13).

The Epistle of Paul the Apostle to the Colossians

INTRODUCTION

Author, Date and Place of Writing

That Colossians is a genuine letter of Paul is not usually disputed. In the early church, all who speak on the subject of authorship ascribe it to Paul. In the 19th century, however, some thought that the heresy refuted in ch. 2 was second-century Gnosticism. But a careful analysis of ch. 2 shows that the heresy referred to there is noticeably less developed than the Gnosticism of leading Gnostic teachers of the second and third centuries. Also, the seeds of what later became the full-blown Gnosticism of the second century were present in the first century and already making inroads into the churches. Consequently, it is not necessary to date Colossians in the second century at a time too late for Paul to have written the letter.

Instead, it is to be dated during Paul's first imprisonment in Rome, where he spent at least two years under house arrest (see Acts 28:16–31). Some have argued that Paul wrote Colossians from Ephesus or Caesarea, but most of the evidence favors Rome as the place where Paul penned all the Prison Letters (Ephesians, Colossians, Philippians and Philemon). Colossians should be dated c. A.D. 60, in the same year as Ephesians and Philemon.

Colosse: The Town and the Church

Several hundred years before Paul's day, Colosse had been a leading city in Asia Minor (present-day Turkey). It was located on the Lycus River and on the great east-west trade route leading from Ephesus on the Aegean Sea to the Euphrates River. By the first century A.D. Colosse was diminished to a second-rate market town, which had been surpassed long ago in power and importance by the neighboring towns of Laodicea and Hierapolis (see 4:13).

What gave Colosse NT importance, however, was the fact that, during Paul's three-year ministry in Ephesus, Epaphras had been converted and had carried the gospel to Colosse (cf. 1:7–8; Acts 19:10). The young church that resulted then became the target of heretical attack, which led to Epaphras's visit to Paul in Rome and ultimately to the penning of the Colossian letter.

Perhaps as a result of the efforts of Epaphras or other converts of Paul, Christian churches had also been established in Laodicea and Hierapolis. Some of them were house churches (see 4:15; Philem 2). Most likely all of them were primarily Gentile.

The Colossian Heresy

Paul never explicitly describes the false teaching he opposes in the Colossian letter. The nature of the heresy must be inferred from statements he made in opposition to the false teachers. An analysis of his refutation suggests that the heresy was diverse in nature. Some of the elements of its teachings were:

1. *Ceremonialism.* It held to strict rules about the kinds of permissible food and drink, religious festivals (2:16–17) and circumcision (2:11; 3:11).

2. *Asceticism.* "Touch not; taste not; handle not" (2:21; cf. 2:23).

3. *Angel worship.* See 2:18.

4. *Depreciation of Christ.* This is implied in Paul's stress on the supremacy of Christ (1:15–20; 2:2–3,9).

5. *Secret knowledge.* The Gnostics boasted of this (see 2:18 and Paul's emphasis in 2:2–3 on Christ, "in whom are hid all the treasures of wisdom").

6. *Reliance on human wisdom and tradition.* See 2:4,8.

These elements seem to fall into two categories, Jewish and Gnostic. It is likely, therefore, that the Colossian heresy was a mixture of an extreme form of Judaism and an early stage of Gnosticism (see Introduction to 1 John: Gnosticism; see also note on 2:23).

Purpose and Theme

Paul's purpose is to refute the Colossian heresy. To accomplish this goal, he exalts Christ as the very image of God (1:15), the Creator (1:16), the preexistent sustainer of all things (1:17), the head of the church (1:18), the first to be resurrected (1:18), the fullness of deity in bodily form (1:19; 2:9) and the reconciler (1:20–22). Thus Christ is completely adequate. We "are complete" in Christ (2:10). On the other hand, the Colossian heresy was altogether inadequate. It was a hollow and deceptive philosophy (2:8), lacking any ability to restrain the old sinful nature (2:23).

The theme of Colossians is the complete adequacy of Christ as contrasted with the emptiness of mere human philosophy.

Outline

- I. Introduction (1:1–14)
  - A. Greetings (1:1–2)
  - B. Thanksgiving (1:3–8)
  - C. Prayer (1:9–14)
- II. The Supremacy of Christ (1:15–23)
- III. Paul's Labor for the Church (1:24—2:7)
  - A. A Ministry for the Sake of the Church (1:24–29)
  - B. A Concern for the Spiritual Welfare of His Readers (2:1–7)
- IV. Freedom from Human Regulations through Life with Christ (2:8–23)
  - A. Warning to Guard against the False Teachers (2:8–15)
  - B. Pleas to Reject the False Teachers (2:16–19)
  - C. An Analysis of the Heresy (2:20–23)
- V. Rules for Holy Living (3:1—4:6)
  - A. The Old Self and the New Self (3:1–17)
  - B. Rules for Christian Households (3:18—4:1)
  - C. Further Instructions (4:2–6)
- VI. Final Greetings (4:7–18)

Salutation and thanksgiving

1 Paul, [a]an apostle of Jesus Christ by the
will of God, and Timotheus *our* brother,
2 To the saints [a]and faithful brethren in
Christ which are at Colosse: [b]Grace *be* unto
you, and peace, from God our Father and the
Lord Jesus Christ.
3 ¶ [a]We give thanks to God and the Father
of our Lord Jesus Christ, praying always for
you,
4 [a]Since we heard of your faith in Christ
Jesus, and of [b]the love which *ye have* to all the
saints,
5 For the hope [a]which is laid up for you in
heaven, whereof ye heard before in the word
of the truth of the gospel;
6 Which is come unto you, [a]as *it is* in all
the world; and bringeth forth fruit, as *it doth*
also in you, since the day ye heard of *it,* and
knew [b]the grace of God in truth:
7 As ye also learned of [a]Epaphras our dear
fellowservant, who is for you [b]a faithful minister of Christ;
8 Who also declared unto us your [a]love in
the Spirit.

1:1 [a]Eph. 1:1
1:2 [a]1 Cor. 4:17
[b]Gal. 1:3
1:3 [a]1 Cor. 1:4;
Eph. 1:16; Phil.
1:3
1:4 [a]Eph. 1:15
[b]Heb. 6:10
1:5 [a]1 Pet. 1:4
1:6 [a]Mat. 24:14
[b]Eph. 3:2; Tit.
2:11
1:7 [a]Philem. 23
[b]2 Cor. 11:23;
1 Tim. 4:6
1:8 [a]Rom. 15:30
1:9 [a]Eph. 1:15
[b]1 Cor. 1:5
[c]Rom. 12:2
[d]Eph. 1:8
1:10 [a]Phil. 1:27
[b]1 Thes. 4:1
[c]Heb. 13:21
1:11 [a]Eph. 3:16
[b]Eph. 4:2 [c]Acts
5:41
1:12 [a]Eph. 5:20
[b]Eph. 1:11
1:13 [1]Gr. *the
Son of his love*
[a]Eph. 6:12
[b]2 Pet. 1:11
1:14 [a]Eph. 1:7
1:15 [a]2 Cor. 4:4
[b]Rev. 3:14
1:16 [a]Heb. 1:2

Paul's prayer for the Colossians

9 ¶ [a]For this cause we also, since the day
we heard *it,* do not cease to pray for you, and
to desire [b]that ye might be filled *with* [c]the
knowledge of his will [d]in all wisdom and spiritual understanding;
10 [a]That ye might walk worthy of the Lord
[b]unto all pleasing, [c]being fruitful in every
good work, and increasing in the knowledge of
God;
11 [a]Strengthened with all might, according
to his glorious power, [b]unto all patience and
longsuffering [c]with joyfulness;
12 [a]Giving thanks unto the Father, which
hath made us meet to be partakers of [b]the inheritance of the saints in light:
13 Who hath delivered us from [a]the power
of darkness, [b]and hath translated *us* into the
kingdom of [1]his dear Son:
14 [a]In whom we have redemption through
his blood, *even* the forgiveness of sins:

Christ's preeminence

15 Who is [a]the image of the invisible God,
[b]the firstborn of every creature:
16 For [a]by him were all *things* created,

1:1 *Paul.* It was customary to put the writer's name at the beginning of a letter. For more information on Paul see notes on Acts 9:1; Phil 3:4–14. *Christ.* Paul is very Christ-centered, as seen by this short letter, in which he uses the title "Christ" 25 times and the title "Lord" (alone) 9 times. *Timotheus.* Paul also mentions Timothy in 2 Corinthians, Philippians, 1,2 Thessalonians and Philemon, but Paul is really the sole author, as seen by the constant use of "I" (see especially 4:18).

1:2 *saints.* Because of Christ's substitutionary death for the Colossian believers, they are declared holy in the sight of God, and because of the Holy Spirit's work, they are continuing to be made holy in their lives. *faithful.* See 1:7; 4:7,9. *in Christ.* Paul mentions the spiritual union with Christ 11 times in Colossians (see note on Eph 1:1). *Grace . . . and peace.* See notes on Jonah 4:2; John 14:27; 20:19; Gal 1:3; Eph 1:2.

1:3 *We.* Paul and Timothy. *give thanks to God.* Every one of Paul's letters, except Galatians, begins with thanks or praise (see note on Phil 1:3–4). In Colossians thanks is an important theme (see v. 12; 2:7; 3:15–17; 4:2). The Bible never thanks man for his faith and love, but rather God, who is the source of these virtues.

1:5 The three great Christian virtues of faith, love and hope appear also in Rom 5:2–5; 1 Cor 13:13; Gal 5:5–6; 1 Thes 1:3; 5:8; Heb 10:22–24. *hope.* Not wishful thinking but a firm assurance. For this unusual thought of faith and love coming from hope see Tit 1:2.

1:6 *in all the world.* Hyperbole, to dramatize the rapid spread of the gospel into every quarter of the Roman empire within three decades of Pentecost (see v. 23; Rom 1:8; 10:18; 16:19). In refutation of the charge of the false teachers, Paul insists that the Christian faith is not merely local or regional but worldwide.

1:7 *Epaphras.* A native (4:12) and probably founder of the Colossian church, and an evangelist in nearby Laodicea and Hierapolis (4:13). Paul loved and admired him, calling him a "fellowprisoner" (Philem 23), his dear fellow servant and a faithful minister of Christ. Epaphras was the one who told Paul at Rome about the Colossian church problem and thereby stimulated him to write this letter (vv. 4,8). His name, a shortened form of Epaphroditus (from "Aphrodite," the Greek goddess of love), suggests that he was a convert from paganism. He is not the Epaphroditus of Phil 2:25; 4:18.

1:8 *your love in the Spirit.* The Holy Spirit is the source of all Christian love.

1:9 *the knowledge of his will.* Biblical knowledge is not merely the possession of facts. Rather, knowledge and wisdom in the Bible are practical, having to do with godly living. This is borne out by vv. 10–12, where knowledge, wisdom and understanding result in a life worthy of the Lord.

‡1:12 *light.* Symbolizes holiness (Mat 5:14; 6:23; Acts 26:18; 1 John 1:5), truth (Ps 36:9; 119:105,130; 2 Cor 4:6), love (Jas 1:17; 1 John 2:9–10), glory (Is 60:1–3; 1 Tim 6:16) and life (John 1:4). Accordingly, God (1 John 1:5), Christ (John 8:12) and the Christian (Eph 5:8) are characterized by light. The "light" is the opposite of the "power of darkness" (v. 13).

1:13 *kingdom.* Does not here refer to a territory but to the authority, rule or sovereign power of a king. Here it means that the Christian is no longer under the dominion of evil (darkness) but under the benevolent rule of God's Son.

1:14 *redemption.* Deliverance and freedom from the penalty of sin by the payment of a ransom—the substitutionary death of Christ.

1:15–20 Perhaps an early Christian hymn (see note on 3:16) on the supremacy of Christ—used here by Paul to counteract the false teaching at Colosse. It is divided into two parts: (1) Christ's supremacy in creation (vv. 15–17); (2) Christ's supremacy in redemption (vv. 18–20).

‡1:15 *image.* Christ is called the "image of God" here and in 2 Cor 4:4. In Heb 1:3 He is described as the "brightness of his glory, and the express image of his person." This figure of the image suggests two truths: (1) God is invisible ("No man hath seen God at any time," John 1:18); (2) Christ, who is the eternal Son of God and who became the God-man, reflects and reveals Him (see also John 1:18; 14:9). *firstborn of every creature.* Just as the firstborn son had certain privileges and rights in the Biblical world, so also Christ has certain rights in relation to all creation—priority, preeminence and sovereignty (vv. 16–18). Also see this same idea of preeminence and sovereignty in Ps 89:27.

‡1:16 *by him were all things created.* See John 1:3. Seven times

that are in heaven, and that are in earth, visible and invisible, whether *they be* thrones, or
[b]dominions, or principalities, or powers: all
things were created [c]by him, and for him:
17 [a]And he is before all *things,* and by him
all *things* consist.
18 And [a]he is the head of the body, the
church: who is the beginning, [b]the firstborn
from the dead; that [1]in all *things* he might
have the preeminence.
19 For it pleased *the Father* that [a]in him
should all fulness dwell;
20 And, [a][1]having made peace through the
blood of his cross, [b]by him to reconcile [c]all
things unto himself; by him, *I say,* whether
they be things in earth, or *things* in heaven.

The ministry of Paul

21 ¶ And you, [a]that were sometime alienated and enemies [1]in *your* mind [b]by wicked
works, yet now hath he reconciled
22 [a]In the body of his flesh through death,
[b]to present you holy and unblameable and un-
reproveable in his sight:
23 If ye continue in the faith [a]grounded and
settled, and *be* [b]not moved away from the hope
of the gospel, which ye have heard, [c]*and* which
was preached to every creature which is under
heaven; [d]whereof I Paul am made a minister;
24 [a]Who now rejoice in my sufferings [b]for
you, and fill up [c]that which is behind of the afflictions of Christ in my flesh for [d]his body's
sake, which is the church:
25 Whereof I am made a minister, according to [a]the dispensation of God which is given
to me for you, [1]to fulfil the word of God;
26 *Even* [a]the mystery which hath been hid
from ages and from generations, [b]but now is
made manifest to his saints:
27 [a]To whom God would make known
what *is* [b]the riches of the glory of this mystery
among the Gentiles; which is Christ [1]in you,
[c]the hope of glory:
28 Whom we preach, [a]warning every man,
and teaching every man in all wisdom; [b]that we
may present every man perfect in Christ Jesus:
29 [a]Whereunto I also labour, [b]striving [c]ac-
cording to his working, which worketh in me
mightily.

2 For I would that ye knew what great
[a][1]conflict I have for you, and *for* them at
Laodicea, and *for* as many as have not seen my
face in the flesh;
2 [a]That their hearts might be comforted,
[b]being knit together in love, and unto all
riches of the full assurance of understanding,
[c]to the acknowledgement of the mystery of
God and of the Father, and of Christ;
3 [a][1]In whom are hid all the treasures of
wisdom and knowledge.

1:16 [b]Eph. 1:21 [c]Heb. 2:10 **1:17** [a]John 17:5 **1:18** [1]Or, *among all* [a]1 Cor. 11:3 [b]Rev. 1:5 **1:19** [a]John 1:16 **1:20** [1]Or, *making peace* [a]Eph. 2:14 [b]2 Cor. 5:18 [c]Eph. 1:10 **1:21** [1]Or, *by your mind in wicked works* [a]Eph. 2:1 [b]Tit. 1:15 **1:22** [a]Eph. 2:15 [b]Eph. 5:27 **1:23** [a]Eph. 3:17 [b]John 15:6 [c]Rom. 10:18 [d]Acts 1:17 **1:24** [a]2 Cor. 7:4 [b]Eph. 3:1,13 [c]2 Cor. 1:5 **1:24** [d]Eph. 1:23 **1:25** [1]Or, *fully to preach the word of God* [a]Gal. 2:7 **1:26** [a]1 Cor. 2:7 [b]2 Tim. 1:10 **1:27** [1]Or, *amongst you* [a]2 Cor. 2:14 [b]Rom. 9:23 [c]1 Tim. 1:1 **1:28** [a]Acts 20:20 [b]Eph. 5:27 **1:29** [a]1 Cor. 15:10 [b]ch. 2:1 [c]Eph. 1:19 **2:1** [1]Or, *fear,* or, *care* [a]Phil. 1:30

2:2 [a]2 Cor. 1:6 [b]ch. 3:14 [c]Phil. 3:8 **2:3** [1]Or, *Wherein* [a]1 Cor. 1:24

in vv. 15–20 Paul mentions "all creation," "all things" and "every creature," thus stressing that Christ is supreme over all. *thrones, or dominions, or principalities, or powers.* Angels. An angelic hierarchy figured prominently in the Colossian heresy (see Introduction: The Colossian Heresy).

1:17 *he is before all things.* Referring to time, as in John 1:1–2; 8:58.

1:18 *beginning.* Of the new creation. *firstborn.* Christ was the first to rise from the dead with a resurrection body. Elsewhere Paul calls Him the "firstfruits of them that slept" (1 Cor 15:20). Others who were raised from the dead (2 Ki 4:35; Luke 7:15; John 11:44; Acts 9:36–41; 20:7–11) were raised only to die again.

1:19 *fulness.* Part of the technical vocabulary of some Gnostic philosophies. In these systems it meant the sum of the supernatural forces controlling the fate of people. For Paul "fullness" meant the totality of God with all His powers and attributes (2:9).

1:20 *reconcile all things unto himself.* Does not mean that Christ by His death has saved all people. Scripture speaks of an eternal hell and makes clear that only believers are saved. When Adam and Eve sinned, not only was the harmony between God and man destroyed, but also disorder came into creation (Rom 8:19–22). So when Christ died on the cross, He made peace possible between God and man, and He restored in principle the harmony in the physical world, though the full realization of the latter will come only when Christ returns (Rom 8:21).

1:22 *death.* Christ's death.

1:23 *every creature.* See note on v. 6.

1:24 *my sufferings.* By preaching the gospel to the Gentiles, Paul experienced all kinds of affliction, but here he was probably referring especially to his imprisonment. *fill up that which is behind.* Does not mean that there was a deficiency in the atoning sacrifice of Christ. Rather, it means that Paul suffered afflictions because he was preaching the good news of Christ's atonement. Christ suffered on the cross to atone for sin, and Paul filled up Christ's afflictions by experiencing the added sufferings necessary to carry this good news to a lost world.

1:25 *fulfil the word of God.* The meaning seems to be that the word of God is brought to completion, i.e., to its intended purpose, only when it is proclaimed (cf. Is 55:11). Paul's commission to bring the word to completion, therefore, required him to make the word of God heard in Colosse as well as elsewhere. See Rom 15:19 for a similar statement.

‡1:26 *mystery.* The purpose of God, unknown to man except by revelation. This word was a popular, pagan religious term, used in the mystery religions to refer to secret information available only to an exclusive group of people. Paul changes that meaning radically by always combining it with words such as "made manifest" (here), "made known" (Eph 1:9), "make all men see" (Eph 3:9) and "revelation" (Rom 16:25). The Christian mystery is not secret knowledge for a few. It is a revelation of divine truths—once hidden but now openly proclaimed.

1:27 *Gentiles . . . Christ in you.* The mystery is the fact that Christ indwells Gentiles, for it had not been previously revealed that the Gentiles would be admitted to the church on equal terms with Israel (see note on Eph 3:6).

1:28 *perfect.* Employed by the mystery religions and the Gnostics to describe those who had become possessors of the secrets or knowledge boasted of by the particular religion (see Introduction to 1 John: Gnosticism). But in Christ every believer is one of the perfect.

2:1 *Laodicea.* This letter was to be read to the church there too (4:16). Laodicea (near modern Denizli) was only about 11 miles from Colosse.

2:2 *mystery.* See notes on 1:26; Rom 11:25.

2:3 *knowledge.* Paul stressed knowledge in this letter (v. 2; 1:9–10) because he was refuting a heresy that emphasized

4 And this I say, [a]lest any *man* should beguile you with enticing words.

5 For [a]though I be absent in the flesh, yet am I with you in the spirit, joying and beholding [b]your order, and the [c]stedfastness of your faith in Christ.

6 [a]As ye have therefore received Christ Jesus the Lord, *so* walk ye in him:

7 [a]Rooted and built up in him, and stablished in the faith, as ye have been taught, abounding therein with thanksgiving.

The sufficiency of Christ

8 ¶ Beware lest any *man* spoil you through philosophy and vain deceit, after [a]the tradition of men, after the [b][1]rudiments of the world, and not after Christ.

9 For [a]in him dwelleth all the fulness of the Godhead bodily.

10 And ye are complete in him, [a]which is the head of all [b]principality and power:

11 In whom also ye are [a]circumcised with the circumcision made without hands, in [b]putting off the body of the sins of the flesh, by the circumcision of Christ:

12 Buried with him in baptism, wherein also you are risen with *him* through [a]the faith of the operation of God, [b]who hath raised him from the dead.

13 And you, being dead in *your* sins and the uncircumcision of your flesh, hath he quickened together with him, having forgiven you all trespasses;

14 [a]Blotting out the handwriting of ordinances that was against us, which was contrary to us, and took it out of the way, nailing it to *his* cross;

15 *And* [a]having spoiled [b]principalities and powers, he made a shew of *them* openly, triumphing over them [1]in it.

16 ¶ Let no *man* therefore [a]judge you [b][1]in meat, or in drink, or [2]in respect [c]of a holyday, or of the new moon, or of the sabbath days:

17 [a]Which are a shadow of *things* to come; but the body *is* of Christ.

18 Let no *man* [1]beguile you of your reward [2]in a voluntary humility and worshipping of angels, intruding into *those things* which he hath not seen, vainly puft up by his fleshly mind,

19 And not holding [a]the head, from which all the body by joints and bands having nourishment ministered, and knit together, increaseth *with* the increase of God.

20 Wherefore if ye be [a]dead with Christ from the [1]rudiments of the world, [b]why, as though living in the world, are ye subject to ordinances,

21 ([a]Touch not; taste not; handle not;

2:4 [a]Rom. 16:18
2:5 [a]1 Thes. 2:17 [b]1 Cor. 14:40 [c]1 Pet. 5:9
2:6 [a]1 Thes. 4:1
2:7 [a]Eph. 2:21
2:8 [1]Or, *elements* [a]Gal. 1:14 [b]Gal. 4:3,9
2:9 [a]John 1:14
2:10 [a]1 Pet. 3:22 [b]ch. 1:16
2:11 [a]Deut. 10:16 [b]Rom. 6:6
2:12 [a]Eph. 1:19 [b]Acts 2:24
2:14 [a]Eph. 2:15
2:15 [1]Or, *in himself* [a]Is. 53:12 [b]Eph. 6:12
2:16 [1]Or, *for eating and drinking* [2]Or, *in part* [a]Rom. 14:3 [b]Rom. 14:2 [c]Rom. 14:5
2:17 [a]Heb. 8:5
2:18 [1]Or, *judge against you* [2]Gr. *being a voluntary in humility*
2:19 [a]Eph. 4:15
2:20 [1]Or, *elements* [a]Rom. 6:3,5 [b]Gal. 4:3,9
2:21 [a]1 Tim. 4:3

knowledge as the means of salvation (see Introduction to 1 John: Gnosticism). Paul insisted that the Christian, not the Gnostic, possessed genuine knowledge.

2:5 *absent in the flesh . . . with you in the spirit.* Similar to 1 Cor 5:3.

2:6 *walk ye in him.* The believer's intimate, spiritual, living union with Christ is mentioned repeatedly in this letter (see, e.g., vv. 7,10–13,20; 1:2,27–28; 3:1,3).

2:8 *rudiments of the world.* This term (which occurs also in v. 20 and Gal 4:3,9) means false, worldly, religious, elementary teachings. Paul was counteracting the Colossian heresy, which, in part, taught that for salvation one needed to combine faith in Christ with secret knowledge and with man-made regulations concerning such physical and external practices as circumcision, eating and drinking, and observance of religious festivals.

2:9 *fulness of the Godhead.* See note on 1:19. The declaration that the very essence of deity was present in totality in Jesus' human body was a direct refutation of Gnostic teaching.

2:10–15 Here Paul declares that the Christian is complete in Christ, rather than being deficient as the Gnostics claimed. This completeness includes the putting off of the sinful nature (v. 11), resurrection from spiritual death (vv. 12–13), forgiveness (v. 13) and deliverance from legalistic requirements (v. 14) and from evil spirit beings (v. 15).

‡2:11–12 *circumcision . . . baptism.* Both are symbolic pictures of salvation—one negative, the other positive. Circumcision pictures the cutting off of the flesh—the repudiation of the flesh. Baptism pictures the believer's death, burial and rising up to newness of life (cf. Rom 6:3–5).

2:14 *handwriting of ordinances.* A business term, meaning a certificate of indebtedness in the debtor's handwriting. Paul uses it as a designation for the Mosaic law, with all its regulations, under which everyone is a debtor to God.

2:15 *having spoiled principalities.* Not only did God cancel out the accusations of the law against the Christian, but He also conquered and disarmed the evil angels (principalities and powers, 1:16; Eph 6:12), who entice people to follow asceticism and false teachings about Christ. The picture is of conquered soldiers stripped of their clothes as well as their weapons to symbolize their total defeat. *triumphing over them.* Lit. "leading them in a triumphal procession." The metaphor recalls a Roman general leading his captives through the streets of his city for all the citizens to see as evidence of his complete victory (see 2 Cor 2:14 and note). That Christ triumphed over the devil and his cohorts is seen from Mat 12:29; Luke 10:18; Rom 16:20.

2:17 *shadow . . . body.* The ceremonial laws of the OT are here referred to as shadows (cf. Heb 8:5; 10:1) because they symbolically depicted the coming of Christ; so any insistence on the observance of such ceremonies is a failure to recognize that their fulfillment has already taken place. This element of the Colossian heresy was combined with a rigid asceticism, as vv. 20–21 reveal.

‡2:18 *beguile.* This term pictures an umpire or referee who excludes from competition any athlete who fails to follow the rules. The Colossians were not to permit any false teacher to deny the reality of their salvation because they were not delighting in mock humility and in the worship of angelic beings. *voluntary humility.* Humility in which one delights is of necessity mock humility. Paul may refer to a professed humility in view of the absolute God, who was believed to be so far above man that He could only be worshiped in the form of angels He had created. Second-century Gnosticism conceived of a list of spirit beings who had emanated from God and through whom God may be approached.

‡2:19 *not holding the head.* The central error of the Colossian heresy is a defective view of Christ, in which He is believed to be less than deity (see v. 9; 1:19).

2:20 *rudiments of the world.* See note on v. 8.

2:21 *Touch not; taste not; handle not.* The strict ascetic nature of the heresy is seen here. These prohibitions seem to carry OT ceremonial laws to the extreme.

22 Which all are to perish with the using;) [a]after the commandments and doctrines of men?

23 [a]Which *things* have indeed a shew of wisdom in will worship, and humility, and [1]neglecting of the body, not in any honour to the satisfying of the flesh.

The true center of Christian life

3 If ye then be risen with Christ, seek those *things* which are above, where [a]Christ sitteth on the right hand of God.

2 Set your [1]affection on *things* above, not on *things* on the earth.

3 [a]For ye are dead, [b]and your life is hid with Christ in God.

4 [a]When Christ, *who is* [b]our life, shall appear, then shall ye also appear with him [c]in glory.

5 ¶ [a]Mortify therefore [b]your members which are upon the earth; [c]fornication, uncleanness, inordinate affection, evil concupiscence, and covetousness, [d]which is idolatry:

6 [a]For which *things'* sake the wrath of God cometh on [b]the children of disobedience:

7 [a]In the which ye also walked sometime, when ye lived in them.

8 [a]But now you also put off all *these;* anger, wrath, malice, blasphemy, [b]filthy communication out of your mouth.

2:22 [a]Tit. 1:14
2:23 [1]Or, *punishing,* or, *not sparing* [a]1 Tim. 4:8
3:1 [a]Eph. 1:20
3:2 [1]Or, *mind*
3:3 [a]Rom. 6:2 [b]2 Cor. 5:7
3:4 [a]1 John 3:2 [b]John 14:6 [c]1 Cor. 15:43
3:5 [a]Rom. 8:13 [b]Rom. 6:13 [c]Eph. 5:3 [d]Eph. 5:5
3:6 [a]Rev. 22:15 [b]Eph. 2:2
3:7 [a]1 Cor. 6:11
3:8 [a]Eph. 4:22 [b]Eph. 4:29
3:9 [a]Eph. 4:25 [b]Eph. 4:22
3:10 [a]Rom. 12:2 [b]Eph. 4:23 [c]Eph. 2:10
3:11 [a]Gal. 3:28 [b]Eph. 1:23
3:12 [a]1 Pet. 1:2 [b]Gal. 5:22
3:13 [1]Or, *complaint* [a]Mark 11:25
3:14 [a]1 Pet. 4:8 [b]1 Cor. 13 [c]Eph. 4:3
3:15 [a]Phil. 4:7 [b]1 Cor. 7:15 [c]Eph. 4:4
3:16 [a]Eph. 5:19
3:17 [a]1 Cor. 10:31

9 [a]Lie not one to another, [b]seeing that ye have put off the old man with his deeds;

10 And have put on the new *man,* which [a]is renewed in knowledge [b]after the image of him that [c]created him:

11 Where there is neither [a]Greek nor Jew, circumcision nor uncircumcision, barbarian, Scythian, bond *nor* free: [b]but Christ *is* all, and in all.

12 Put on therefore, [a]as the elect of God, holy and beloved, [b]bowels of mercies, kindness, humbleness of mind, meekness, longsuffering;

13 [a]Forbearing one another, and forgiving one another, if any *man* have a [1]quarrel against any: even as Christ forgave you, so also *do* ye.

14 [a]And above all these *things* [b]*put on* charity, which is the [c]bond of perfectness.

15 And let [a]the peace of God rule in your hearts, [b]to the which also ye are called [c]in one body; and be ye thankful.

16 Let the word of Christ dwell in you richly in all wisdom; teaching and admonishing one another [a]in psalms and hymns and spiritual songs, singing with grace in your hearts to the Lord.

17 And [a]whatsoever ye do in word or deed, *do* all in the name of the Lord Jesus, giving thanks to God and the Father by him.

‡2:23 A rather detailed analysis of the Colossian heresy: 1. It appeared to set forth an impressive system of religious philosophy. 2. It was, however, a system created by the false teachers themselves, rather than being of divine origin. 3. The false teachers attempted to parade their humility. 4. This may have been done by a harsh asceticism that brutally misused the body. Paul's analysis is that such practices are worthless because they totally fail to control sinful desires.

‡3:1 *if ye then be risen.* Verses 1–10 set forth what has been described as the indicative and the imperative (standing and state) of the Christian. The indicative statements describe the believer's position in Christ: He is dead (v. 3); he has been raised with Christ (v. 1); he is with Christ in heaven ("hid with Christ," v. 3); he has "put off the old man" (v. 9); and he has "put on the new man" (v. 10). The imperative statements indicate what the believer is to do as a result: He is to set his heart (or mind) on things above (vv. 1–2); he is to put to death practices that belong to his earthly nature (v. 5); and he is to rid himself of practices that characterized his unregenerate self (v. 8). In summary, he is called upon to become in daily experience what he is positionally in Christ (cf. Rom 6:1–13). *then.* "Then" (or "therefore") links the doctrinal section of the letter with the practical section, just as it does in Rom 12:1; Eph 4:1; Phil 4:1.

3:4 *shall appear.* Refers to Christ's second coming.

3:6 *wrath of God.* See note on Zech 1:2. God is unalterably opposed to sin and will invariably make sure that it is justly punished.

‡3:9–10 *put off . . . put on.* cf. Gal 3:27). At salvation God changes the believer's nature, making this possible. See notes on Eph 4:22 and 24.

3:10 *renewed.* See 2 Co 5:17. *knowledge.* See 1:10; 2:2–3. *image of him that created him.* See note on Gen 1:26.

‡3:11 *barbarian.* Someone who did not speak Greek and was thought to be uncivilized. *Scythian.* Scythians were known especially for their brutality and were considered by others as little better than wild beasts. They came originally from what is today south Russia. They were the barbarian's barbarian. *Christ is all, and in all.* Christ transcends all barriers and unifies people from all cultures, races and nations. Such distinctions are no longer significant. Christ alone matters.

3:12 *elect of God.* Israel was called this (Deut 4:37), and so is the Christian community (1 Pet 2:9). Divine election is a constant theme in Paul's letters (see note on Eph 1:4), but the Bible never teaches that it dulls human responsibility. On the contrary, as this verse shows, it is precisely because the Christian has been elected to eternal salvation that he must put forth every effort to live the godly life. For Paul, divine sovereignty and human responsibility go hand in hand.

3:15 *peace of God.* The attitude of peace that Christ alone gives—in place of the attitude of bitterness and quarrelsomeness. This attitude is to "rule" (lit. "function like an umpire") in all human relationships.

3:16 *word of Christ.* Refers especially to Christ's teaching, which in the time of the Colossians was transmitted orally. But by implication it includes the OT as well as the NT. *psalms and hymns and spiritual songs.* Some of the most important doctrines were expressed in Christian hymns preserved for us now only in Paul's letters (1:15–20; Eph 5:14; Phil 2:6–11; 1 Tim 3:16). "Psalms" refers to the OT psalms (see Luke 20:42; 24:44; Acts 1:20; 13:33), some of which may have been set to music by the church. "Psalm" could also describe a song newly composed for Christian worship (cf. 1 Cor 14:26, where "hymn" is lit. "psalm" in the Greek text). A "hymn" was a song of praise, especially used in a celebration (see Mark 14:26; Heb 2:12; see also Acts 16:25), much like the OT psalms that praised God for all that He is. A "song" recounted the acts of God and praised Him for them (see Rev 5:9; 14:3; 15:3), much like the OT psalms that thanked God for all that He had done. See note on Eph 5:19.

The Christian family

18 ¶ [a]Wives, submit yourselves unto your own husbands, [b]as it is fit in the Lord.

19 [a]Husbands, love *your* wives, and be not [b]bitter against them.

20 [a]Children, obey *your* parents [b]in all *things:* for this is well pleasing unto the Lord.

21 [a]Fathers, provoke not your children *to anger,* lest they be discouraged.

22 [a]Servants, obey [b]in all *things your* masters [c]according to the flesh; not with eyeservice, as menpleasers; but in singleness of heart, fearing God:

23 [a]And whatsoever ye do, do *it* heartily, as to the Lord, and not unto men;

24 [a]Knowing that of the Lord ye shall receive the reward of the inheritance: [b]for ye serve the Lord Christ.

25 But he that doeth wrong shall receive *for* the wrong which he hath done: and [a]there is no respect of persons.

4 [a]Masters, give unto *your* servants that which is just and equal; knowing that ye also have a Master in heaven.

2 ¶ [a]Continue in prayer, and watch in the same [b]with thanksgiving;

3 [a]Withal praying also for us, that God would [b]open unto us a door of utterance, to speak [c]the mystery of Christ, [d]for which I am also in bonds:

4 That I may make it manifest, as I ought to speak.

5 [a]Walk in wisdom toward them that are without, [b]redeeming the time.

6 Let your speech *be* alway [a]with grace, [b]seasoned with salt, [c]that *you* may know how ye ought to answer every man.

3:18 [a]1 Pet. 3:1 [b]Eph. 5:3
3:19 [a]Eph. 5:25 [b]Eph. 4:31
3:20 [a]Eph. 6:1 [b]Eph. 5:24
3:21 [a]Eph. 6:4
3:22 [a]Eph. 6:5; 1 Tim. 6:1; Tit. 2:9; 1 Pet. 2:18 [b]ver. 20 [c]Philem. 16
3:23 [a]Eph. 6:6,7
3:24 [a]Eph. 6:8 [b]1 Cor. 7:22
3:25 [a]Rom. 2:11; Eph. 6:9; 1 Pet. 1:17; Deut. 10:17
4:1 [a]Eph. 6:9
4:2 [a]Luke 18:1; Rom. 12:12 [b]ch. 2:7
4:3 [a]Eph. 6:19 [b]1 Cor. 16:9; 2 Cor. 2:12 [c]Eph. 6:19 [d]Eph. 6:20; Phil. 1:7
4:5 [a]Eph. 5:15 [b]Eph. 5:16
4:6 [a]Eccl. 10:12 [b]Mark 9:50 [c]1 Pet. 3:15
4:8 [a]Eph. 6:22
4:9 [a]Philem. 10
4:10 [a]Acts 19:29 [b]Acts 15:37; 2 Tim. 4:11
4:12 [1]Or, *striving* [2]Or, *filled* [a]Philem. 23 [b]Rom. 15:30 [c]Mat. 5:48; 1 Cor. 2:6
4:14 [a]2 Tim. 4:11 [b]2 Tim. 4:10
4:15 [a]Rom. 16:5; 1 Cor. 16:19
4:16 [a]1 Thes. 5:27

Tychicus and Onesimus

7 ¶ All my state shall Tychicus declare unto you, *who is* a beloved brother, and a faithful minister and fellowservant in the Lord:

8 [a]Whom I have sent unto you for the same purpose, that he might know your estate, and comfort your hearts;

9 With [a]Onesimus, a faithful and beloved brother, who is *one* of you. They shall make known unto you all *things* which *are done* here.

Greetings and final instructions

10 [a]Aristarchus my fellowprisoner saluteth you, and [b]Marcus, sister's son to Barnabas, (touching whom ye received commandments: if he come unto you, receive him;)

11 And Jesus, which is called Justus, who are of the circumcision. These only *are my* fellowworkers unto the kingdom of God, which have been a comfort unto me.

12 [a]Epaphras, who is *one* of you, a servant of Christ, saluteth you, always [b][1]labouring fervently for you in prayers, that ye may stand [c]perfect and [2]complete in all the will of God.

13 For I bear him record, that he hath a great zeal for you, and them that are in Laodicea, and them in Hierapolis.

14 [a]Luke, the beloved physician, and [b]Demas, greet you.

15 Salute the brethren which are in Laodicea, and Nymphas, and [a]the church which is in his house.

16 And when [a]*this* epistle is read amongst you, cause that it be read also in the church of the Laodiceans; and that ye likewise read the *epistle* from Laodicea.

3:18–4:1 See notes on Eph 5:22–6:9.

3:20 *in all things.* In everything not sinful (see Acts 5:29).

‡3:22–4:1 Paul neither condones slavery nor sanctions revolt against masters. Rather, he calls on both slaves and masters to show Christian principles in their relationship and thus to attempt to change the institution from within. The reason Paul writes more about slaves and masters than about wives, husbands, children and fathers may be that the slave Onesimus (4:9) is going along with Tychicus to deliver this Colossian letter and the letter to Philemon, Onesimus's master, who also lived in Colosse. Compare the book of Philemon.

4:6 *seasoned with salt.* Salt is a preservative and is tasty. Similarly, the Christian's conversation is to be wholesome (see 3:8; Eph 4:29).

4:7 *Tychicus.* See note on Eph 6:21.

‡4:9–17 Onesimus (v. 9), Aristarchus (v. 10), Marcus (v. 10), Epaphras (v. 12), Luke (v. 14), Demas (v. 14) and Archippus (v. 17) are mentioned in Philemon. This suggests that the letters to Colosse and Philemon were written at the same time and place.

4:9 *Onesimus.* See Introduction to Philemon: Recipient, Background and Purpose.

‡4:10 *Aristarchus.* A Macedonian, who is mentioned three times in Acts: 1. He was with Paul during the Ephesian riot (Acts 19:29) and therefore was known in Colosse. 2. Both he and Tychicus (Acts 20:4) were with Paul in Greece. 3. He accompanied Paul on his trip to Rome (Acts 27:2). *Marcus.* The author of the second Gospel. Against Barnabas's advice, Paul refused to take Mark on the second missionary journey because Mark had "departed from" him at Pamphylia (Acts 15:38). But now—about 12 years later—the difficulties seem to have been ironed out, because Paul, both here and in Philem 24 (sent at the same time to Philemon, who was in Colosse), sends Mark's greetings. About five years later, Paul even writes that Mark "is profitable to me for the ministry" (2 Tim 4:11). See note on Acts 15:39.

4:13 *Hierapolis.* A town in Asia Minor (present-day Turkey), about 6 miles from Laodicea and 14 miles from Colosse. Its church may have been founded during Paul's three-year stay in Ephesus (Acts 19), but probably not by Paul himself (cf. 2:1).

4:14 *Luke.* Wrote about Paul in the book of Acts, having often accompanied him on his travels (see note on Acts 16:10). He was with Paul in Rome during his imprisonment (Acts 28), where this letter was written. *Demas.* A Christian worker who would later desert Paul (2 Tim 4:10).

4:15 *Nymphas.* Probably a Laodicean. *church which is in his house.* For the most part, the early church had no buildings, so it usually met for worship and instruction in homes. It often centered around one family, as, e.g., Priscilla and Aquila (Rom 16:5; 1 Cor 16:19), Philemon (Philem 2) and Mary the mother of John (Acts 12:12).

‡4:16 *when this epistle is read amongst you.* The practice of the early church was to read Paul's letters aloud to the assembled congregation. *epistle from Laodicea.* Does not necessarily mean a letter by the Laodiceans. Rather, it could have been a letter that the Laodiceans were to lend to the Colossians—a letter that Paul had originally written to the Laodiceans. This may have been a fourth letter that Tychicus carried to this area

17 And say to [a]Archippus, Take heed to
[b]the ministry which thou hast received in the
Lord, that thou fulfil it.
18 [a]The salutation by the hand of me Paul.
[b]Remember my bonds. [c]Grace *be* with you.
Amen.

¶ Written from Rome to the Colossians by Tychicus and Onesimus.

4:17 [a]Philem. 2 [b]1 Tim. 4:6
4:18 [a]1 Cor. 16:21; 2 Thes. 3:17 [b]Heb. 13:3 [c]Heb. 13:25

in what is present-day Turkey, in addition to Ephesians, Colossians and Philemon. Or this letter could have been Paul's letter to the Ephesians—a circular letter making the rounds from Ephesus to Laodicea to Colosse (see Introduction to Ephesians: Author, Date and Place of Writing).

4:17 *Archippus.* Philem 2 calls him Paul's "fellowsoldier."

4:18 Paul's custom was to dictate his letters (see Rom 16:22) and pen a few greetings himself (1 Cor 16:21; Gal 6:11; 2 Thes 3:17; Philem 19). His personal signature was the guarantee of the genuineness of the letter.

The First Epistle of Paul the Apostle to the Thessalonians

INTRODUCTION

Background of the Thessalonian Letters

It is helpful to trace the locations of Paul and his companions that relate to the Thessalonian correspondence. The travels were as follows:

1. Paul and Silas fled from Thessalonica to Berea (see Acts 17:10). Since Timothy is not mentioned, it is possible that he stayed in Thessalonica or went back to Philippi and then rejoined Paul and Silas in Berea (Acts 17:14).

2. Paul fled to Athens from Berean persecution, leaving Silas and Timothy in Berea (see Acts 17:14).

3. Paul sent word back, instructing Silas and Timothy to come to him in Athens (see Acts 17:15; see also note on 3:1–2).

4. Timothy rejoined Paul at Athens and was sent back to Thessalonica (see 3:1–5). Since Silas is not mentioned, it has been conjectured that he went back to Philippi when Timothy went to Thessalonica.

5. Paul moved on to Corinth (see Acts 18:1).

6. Silas and Timothy came to Paul in Corinth (see 3:6; Acts 18:5).

7. Paul wrote 1 Thessalonians and sent it to the church.

8. About six months later (A.D. 51/52) he sent 2 Thessalonians in response to further information about the church there.

Author, Date and Place of Writing

Both external and internal evidence (see 1:1; 2:18) support the view that Paul wrote 1 Thessalonians (from Corinth; see note on 3:1–2). Early church writers are agreed on the matter, with testimonies beginning as early as A.D. 140 (Marcion). Paul's known characteristics are apparent in the letter (3:1–2,8–11 compared with Acts 15:36; 2 Cor 11:28). Historical allusions in the book fit Paul's life as recounted in Acts and in his own letters (2:14–16 compared with Acts 17:5–10; 3:6 compared with Acts 17:16). In the face of such evidence, few have ever rejected authorship by Paul.

It is generally dated c. A.D. 51. Weighty support for this date was found in an inscription discovered at Delphi, Greece, that dates Gallio's proconsulship to c. 51–52 and thus places Paul at Corinth at the same time (see Acts 18:12–17). Except for the possibility of an early date for Galatians (48–49?), 1 Thessalonians is Paul's earliest canonical letter.

Thessalonica: The City and the Church

Thessalonica was a bustling seaport city at the head of the Thermaic Gulf. It was an important communication and trade center, located at the junction of the great Egnatian Way and the road leading north to the Danube. Its population numbered about 200,000, making it the largest city in Macedonia. It was also the capital of its province.

The background of the Thessalonian church is found in Acts 17:1–9. Since Paul began his ministry there in the Jewish synagogue, it is reasonable to assume that the new church included some Jews. However, 1:9–10; Acts 17:4 seem to indicate that the church was largely Gentile in membership.

Purpose

Paul had left Thessalonica abruptly (see Acts 17:5–10) after a rather brief stay. Recent converts from paganism (1:9) were thus left with little external support in the midst of persecution. Paul's purpose in writing this letter was to encourage the new converts in their trials (3:3–5), to give instruction concerning godly living (4:1–8), to urge some not to neglect daily work (4:11–12) and to give

assurance concerning the future of believers who die before Christ returns (see Theme; see also notes on 4:13,15).

Theme

Although the thrust of the letter is varied (see Purpose), the subject of eschatology (doctrine of last things) seems to be predominant in both Thessalonian letters. Every chapter of 1 Thessalonians ends with a reference to the second coming of Christ, with ch. 4 giving it major consideration (1:9–10; 2:19–20; 3:13; 4:13–18; 5:23–24). Thus, the second coming seems to permeate the letter and may be viewed in some sense as its theme. The two letters are often designated as the eschatological letters of Paul.

Outline

I. The Thanksgiving for the Thessalonians (ch. 1)
  A. The Grounds for the Thanksgiving (1:1–4)
  B. The Genuineness of the Grounds (1:5–10)
II. The Defense of the Apostolic Actions and Absence (chs. 2—3)
  A. The Defense of the Apostolic Actions (2:1–16)
  B. The Defense of the Apostolic Absence (2:17—3:10)
  C. The Prayer (3:11–13)
III. The Exhortations to the Thessalonians (4:1—5:22)
  A. Primarily concerning Personal Life (4:1–12)
  B. Concerning the Coming of Christ (4:13—5:11)
  C. Primarily concerning Church Life (5:12–22)
IV. The Concluding Prayer, Greetings and Benediction (5:23–28)

Salutation and thanksgiving

1 Paul, and [a]Silvanus, and Timotheus, unto
the church of the Thessalonians *which is*
in God the Father and *in* the Lord Jesus Christ:
[b]Grace *be* unto you, and peace, from God our
Father, and the Lord Jesus Christ.
2 ¶ [a]We give thanks to God always for you
all, making mention of you in our prayers;
3 [a]Remembering without ceasing [b]your
work of faith, [c]and labour of love, and patience of hope in our Lord Jesus Christ, in the
sight of God and our Father;
4 Knowing, brethren [1]beloved, [a]your election of God.
5 For [a]our gospel came not unto you in
word only, but also in power, and [b]in the Holy
Ghost, [c]and in much assurance; as ye know
what manner of *men* we were among you for
your sake.
6 And [a]ye became followers of us, and of
the Lord, having received the word in much
affliction, [b]with joy of the Holy Ghost:
7 So that ye were ensamples to all that believe in Macedonia and Achaia.
8 For from you [a]sounded out the word of
the Lord not only in Macedonia and Achaia,
but also [b]in every place your faith to God-ward
is spread abroad; so that we need not to speak
any *thing*.
9 For they themselves shew of us [a]what
manner of entering in we had unto you, [b]and
how ye turned to God from idols to serve the
living and true God,
10 And [a]to wait for his Son [b]from heaven,
[c]whom he raised from the dead, *even* Jesus,
which delivered us [d]from the wrath to come.

Paul's work in Thessalonica

2 For [a]yourselves, brethren, know our entrance in unto you, that it was not in
vain:
2 But even after that we had suffered before, and were shamefully entreated, as ye
know, at [a]Philippi, [b]we were bold in our God
to speak unto you the gospel of God [c]with
much contention.
3 [a]For our exhortation *was* not of deceit,
nor of uncleanness, nor in guile:
4 But as [a]we were allowed of God [b]to be
put in trust with the gospel, *even* so we speak;
[c]not as pleasing men, but God, [d]which trieth
our hearts.
5 For [a]neither at any time used we flattering words, as ye know, nor a cloke of covetousness; [b]God *is* witness:

1:1 [a]1 Pet. 5:12 [b]Eph. 1:2
1:2 [a]Rom. 1:8
1:3 [a]ch. 2:13 [b]John 6:29 [c]Rom. 16:6
1:4 [1]Or, *beloved of God, your election* [a]Col. 3:12
1:5 [a]Mark 16:20 [b]2 Cor. 6:6 [c]Heb. 2:3
1:6 [a]1 Cor. 4:16; Phil. 3:17 [b]Acts 5:41; Heb. 10:34
1:8 [a]Rom. 10:18 [b]Rom. 1:8; 2 Thes. 1:4
1:9 [a]ch. 2:1 [b]1 Cor. 12:2; Gal. 4:8
1:10 [a]Rom. 2:7; 2 Pet. 3:12 [b]Acts 1:11 [c]Acts 2:24 [d]Rom. 5:9
2:1 [a]ch. 1:5,9
2:2 [a]Acts 16:22 [b]ch. 1:5 [c]Phil. 1:30
2:3 [a]2 Cor. 7:2
2:4 [a]1 Cor. 7:25 [b]Tit. 1:3 [c]Gal. 1:10 [d]Prov. 17:3
2:5 [a]2 Cor. 2:17 [b]Rom. 1:9

1:1 *Paul.* See notes on Acts 9:1; 13:9; Phil 3:4–14. *Silvanus.* See note on Acts 15:22. He accompanied Paul on most of his second missionary journey. *Timotheus.* See Introduction to 1 Timothy: Recipient. Both he and Silas helped Paul found the Thessalonian church (see Acts 17:1–14). *in.* Indicates the vital union and living relationship that Christians have with the Father and the Son (see John 14:23; 17:21). The close connection between the Father and the Son points to the Trinitarian relationship (see 3:11; 2 Thes 1:2,8,12; 2:16; 3:5). *Grace . . . and peace.* See notes on Jonah 4:2; John 14:27; 20:19; Gal 1:3; Eph 1:2.

1:2 *thanks.* See note on Phil 1:3–4.

1:3 The triad of faith, hope and love is found often in the NT (5:8; Rom 5:2–5; 1 Cor 13:13; Gal 5:5–6; Col 1:4–5; Heb 6:10–12; 10:22–24; 1 Pet 1:3–8,21–22). *work of faith.* Faith produces action (see Rom 1:5; 16:26; Gal 5:6; 2 Thes 1:11; Jas 2:14–26). *hope.* Not unfounded wishful thinking, but firm confidence in our Lord Jesus Christ and His return (v. 10). See Heb 6:18–20 and note on Col 1:5.

1:4 *Knowing.* The reasons for Paul's conviction regarding their election are stated in vv. 5–10. *brethren.* United to each other through union with Christ. This term (including its singular form) is used 28 times in the two letters to the Thessalonians. *beloved . . . election.* Both words speak of God's electing love (see Col 3:12; 2 Thes 2:13; see also note on Eph 1:4).

‡1:5 *our gospel.* The gospel preached by Paul, Silas and Timothy and that they themselves had received by faith. It is first of all God the Father's (2:8) because He originated it, and Christ's (3:2) because it springs from His atoning death. *power.* The power that delivered them from spiritual bondage. That power is of the Holy Spirit (see Rom 15:13,18–19; 1 Cor 2:4–5), but it also resides in the gospel itself (see Rom 1:16). *much assurance.* Such assurance, on the part of both the preachers and the Thessalonians, was also of the Holy Spirit.

‡1:6 *followers.* The Greek word refers to those who follow to the point of imitation. The order in Christian imitation: (1) Believers in Macedonia and Achaia imitated the Thessalonians (v. 7), just as the Thessalonians imitated the churches in Judea (2:14); (2) the Thessalonians imitated Paul, just as the Corinthians did (1 Cor 4:6; 11:1) and just as all believers were to imitate their leaders (2 Thes 3:7,9; 1 Tim 4:12; Tit 2:7; 1 Pet 5:3); (3) Paul imitated Christ (1 Cor 11:1) as did the Thessalonians (here); (4) all were to imitate God (Eph 5:1). *much affliction.* Such as recorded in Acts 17:5–14 (see also 1 Thes 2:14).

1:7 *Macedonia and Achaia.* The two Roman provinces into which Greece was then divided (see Acts 19:21; Rom 15:26).

1:8 *in every place.* In every place they visited or knew about (see Rom 1:8; 1 Cor 1:2; 2 Cor 2:14; 1 Tim 2:8). The news spread because Thessalonica was on the important Egnatian Way; it was also a busy seaport and the capital of the Roman province of Macedonia.

1:9–10 Three marks of true conversion: (1) turning from idols, (2) serving God and (3) waiting for Christ to return. In his two short letters to the Thessalonians, Paul speaks much of the second coming of Christ (v. 10; 2:19; 3:13; 4:13–5:4; 2 Thes 1:7–10; 2:1–12).

1:10 *Jesus.* See note on Mat 1:21. *wrath.* Some see a reference here to the final judgment (see note on Rom 1:18), while others think it refers to a future period of tribulation.

2:1–12 A "manual" for a minister: 1. His message is God's good news ("gospel," v. 2). 2. His motive is not impurity (v. 3), pleasing people (v. 4), greed (v. 5) or seeking praise from people (v. 6), but pleasing God (v. 4). 3. His manner is not one of trickery (v. 3), flattery (v. 5) or a cover-up (v. 5), but of courage (v. 2), gentleness (v. 7), love (vv. 8,11), toil (v. 9) and holiness (v. 10).

‡2:1 *yourselves . . . know.* The local church could refute the accusation of insincerity that evidently had been leveled against Paul (v. 3).

2:2 *shamefully entreated.* Paul was deeply hurt by the way he had been treated in the city of Philippi (see Acts 16:19–40).

2:3 *deceit.* The Greek for this word was originally used of a lure for catching fish; it came to be used of any sort of cunning used for profit.

2:4 *our hearts.* Not simply our emotions, but also our intellects and wills.

2:5 *covetousness.* Personal profit was never Paul's aim.

6 [a]Nor of men sought we glory, neither of
you, nor *yet* of others, when [b]we might have
[1]been [c]burdensome, [d]as *the* apostles of
Christ.
7 But [a]we were gentle among you, *even* as
a nurse cherisheth her children:
8 So being affectionately desirous of you,
we were willing [a]to have imparted unto you,
not the gospel of God only, but also [b]our own
souls, because ye were dear unto us.
9 For ye remember, brethren, our labour
and travail: for [a]labouring night and day, [b]be-
cause *we* would not be chargeable unto any of
you, we preached unto you the gospel of God.
10 [a]Ye *are* witnesses, and God *also,* [b]how
holily and justly and unblameably we behaved
ourselves among you that believe:
11 As you know how we exhorted and
comforted and charged every one of you, as a
father *doth* his children,
12 [a]That ye would walk worthy of God,
[b]who hath called you unto his kingdom and
glory.

Paul's reception in Thessalonica

13 For this cause also thank we God [a]with-
out ceasing, because, when ye received the
word of God which *ye* heard of us, ye received
it [b]not as the word of men, but as it is in truth,
the word of God, which effectually worketh
also in you that believe.
14 For ye, brethren, became followers [a]of
the churches of God which in Judea are in
Christ Jesus: for [b]ye also have suffered like
things of your own countrymen, even as they
have of the Jews:
15 [a]Who both killed the Lord Jesus, and

2:6 [a]1 Tim. 5:17 [1]Or, *used authority* [b]1 Cor. 9:4 [c]2 Cor. 11:9 [d]1 Cor. 9:1
2:7 [a]1 Cor. 2:3
2:8 [a]Rom. 1:11; 15:29 [b]2 Cor. 12:15
2:9 [a]Acts 20:34; 2 Thes. 3:8 [b]2 Cor. 12:13
2:10 [a]ch. 1:5 [b]2 Cor. 7:2
2:12 [a]Col. 1:10 [b]1 Cor. 1:9; 2 Thes. 2:14
2:13 [a]ch. 1:3 [b]Gal. 4:14
2:14 [a]Gal. 1:22 [b]Acts 17:5
2:15 [a]Acts 2:23
2:15 [1]Or, *chased us out* [b]Mat. 5:12 [c]Esth. 3:8
2:16 [a]Luke 11:52; Acts 13:50 [b]Gen. 15:16; Mat. 23:32 [c]Mat. 24:6
2:17 [a]1 Cor. 5:3; Col. 2:5 [b]ch. 3:10
2:18 [a]Rom. 1:13
2:19 [1]Or, *glorying?* [a]2 Cor. 1:14 [b]Prov. 16:31 [c]1 Cor. 15:23
3:1 [a]ver. 5 [b]Acts 17:15
3:2 [a]Rom. 16:21; 1 Cor. 16:10
3:3 [a]Eph. 3:13 [b]Acts 9:16; 1 Cor. 4:9; 2 Tim. 3:12
3:4 [a]Acts 20:24
3:5 [a]ver. 1 [b]1 Cor. 7:5; 2 Cor. 11:3 [c]Gal. 2:2

[b]their own prophets, and have [1]persecuted
us; and they please not God, [c]and are contrary
to all men:
16 [a]Forbidding us to speak to the Gentiles
that they might be saved, [b]to fill up their sins
alway: [c]for the wrath is come upon them to
the uttermost.
17 ¶ But we, brethren, being taken from
you for a short time [a]in presence, not in heart,
endeavoured the more abundantly [b]to see
your face with great desire.
18 Wherefore we would have come unto
you, even I Paul, once and again; but [a]Satan
hindered us.
19 For [a]what *is* our hope, or joy, or [b]crown
of [1]rejoicing? *Are* not even ye in the presence
of our Lord Jesus Christ [c]at his coming?
20 For ye are our glory and joy.

Timotheus's visit and report

3 Wherefore [a]when we could no longer
forbear, [b]we thought it good to be left at
Athens alone;
2 And sent [a]Timotheus, our brother, and
minister of God, and our fellowlabourer in the
gospel of Christ, to establish you, and to comfort you concerning your faith:
3 [a]That no *man* should be moved by these
afflictions: for yourselves know that [b]we are
appointed thereunto.
4 [a]For verily, when we were with you, we
told you before that we should suffer tribulation; even as it came to pass, and ye know.
5 For this cause, [a]when I could no longer
forbear, I sent to know your faith, [b]lest by
some means the tempter have tempted you,
and [c]our labour be in vain.

2:6 *might have been burdensome.* Apostles were entitled to be supported by the church (see 1 Cor 9:3–14; 2 Cor 11:7–11). Paul did not always take advantage of the right, but insisted that he had it.

2:9 *labour and travail.* Greeks despised manual labor and viewed it as fit only for slaves, but Paul was not ashamed of doing any sort of work that would help further the gospel. He did not want to be unduly dependent on others.

2:12 *walk worthy of God.* See Eph 4:1. *hath called.* See note on 1:4. *kingdom.* The chief subject of Jesus' teaching. Paul did not use this term often, but used it once to sum up the message of his preaching (Acts 20:25).

‡2:13 *not as the word of men.* Not tailored to fit the popular knowledge of the day. *the word of God.* Paul knew (Gal 1:12), as did his regenerated hearers, that the message he preached was the revelation of God. The apostle Peter confirms this (1 Pet 3:15–16).

2:14 *ye also have suffered . . . of your own countrymen.* At the time of Paul's initial visit to Thessalonica, persecution instigated by the Jews apparently was carried out by Gentiles (see Acts 17:5–9). *Jews.* Although Paul had great love and deep concern for the salvation of those of his own race (see Rom 9:1–3; 10:1), he did not fail to rebuke harshly Jews who persecuted the church.

2:15 *prophets.* Throughout OT history, Israelites had persecuted their prophets (cf. Acts 7:52).

2:16 *wrath is come.* The eschatological wrath, the final outpouring of God's anger upon sinful mankind (see 1:10). It is spoken of as already present, either because it had been partially experienced by the Jews or because of its absolute certainty.

2:17 *taken from you.* Lit. "orphaned." Paul is like a mother (v. 7), a father (v. 11) and now an orphan.

2:19 *crown.* Not a royal crown, but a wreath used on festive occasions or as the prize in the Greek games. *at his coming.* The expression was used regarding the arrival of a great person, as on a royal visit.

2:20 *ye are our glory and joy.* True both now (cf. Phil 4:1) and when Christ returns.

3:1–2 Paul first went to Athens alone, then sent to Berea for Silas and Timothy (Acts 17:14–15). It is not clear whether Silas, as instructed (Acts 17:15), came to Athens with Timothy. However, when Timothy later returned from Thessalonica to Paul, who was now at Corinth, Silas came with him (Acts 18:5). See Introduction: Background of the Thessalonian Letters.

3:1 *we.* An editorial "we," referring to Paul alone.

‡3:2 *gospel of Christ.* See notes on 1:5; Mark 1:1. *establish.* Or strengthen. In Greek classical literature the word was generally used in the literal sense of putting a buttress on a building. In the NT it is mainly used figuratively, as here.

3:3 *afflictions.* The opposition and persecution suffered by the Thessalonian converts. Christians must expect troubles (see Mark 4:17; John 16:33; Acts 14:22; 2 Tim 3:12; 1 Pet 4:12), but these are not disasters, for they advance God's purposes (see Acts 11:19; Rom 5:3; 2 Cor 1:4; 4:17).

3:5 *I.* Paul uses the Greek emphatic pronoun (elsewhere used only in 2:18) to bring out his deep concern. *tempter.* Satan is

6 [a]But now when Timotheus came from you unto us, and brought us good tidings of your faith and charity, and that ye have good remembrance of us always, desiring greatly to see us, [b]as we also *to see* you:

7 Therefore, brethren, [a]we were comforted over you in all our affliction and distress, by your faith:

8 For now we live, if ye [a]stand fast in the Lord.

9 [a]For what thanks can we render to God again for you, for all the joy wherewith we joy for your sakes before our God;

10 [a]Night and day [b]praying exceedingly [c]that *we* might see your face, [d]and might perfect that which is lacking in your faith?

11 Now God himself and our Father, and our Lord Jesus Christ, [a][1]direct our way unto you.

12 And the Lord [a]make you to increase and abound in love one towards another, and towards all *men,* even as we *do* towards you:

13 To the end *he* may [a]stablish your hearts unblameable in holiness before God, even our Father, at the coming of our Lord Jesus Christ [b]with all his saints.

Living to please God

4 Furthermore then we [1]beseech you, brethren, and [2]exhort *you* by the Lord Jesus, [a]that as ye have received of us [b]how ye ought to walk [c]and to please God, *so* ye would abound more *and more.*

2 For ye know what commandments we gave you by the Lord Jesus.

3 For this is [a]the will of God, *even* [b]your sanctification, [c]that ye should abstain from fornication:

4 [a]That every one of you should know how to possess his vessel in sanctification and honour;

5 [a]Not in the lust of concupiscence, [b]even as the Gentiles [c]which know not God:

6 That no *man* go beyond and [1]defraud his brother [2]in *any* matter: because that the Lord [a]*is* the avenger of all such, as we also have forewarned you and testified.

7 For God hath not called us unto uncleanness, [a]but unto holiness.

8 [a]He therefore that [1]despiseth, despiseth not man, but God, [b]who hath also given unto us his holy Spirit.

9 ¶ But as touching brotherly love [a]ye need not that *I* write unto you: for [b]ye yourselves are taught of God [c]to love one another.

10 [a]And indeed ye do it towards all the brethren which are in all Macedonia: but we beseech you, brethren, [b]that *ye* increase more *and more;*

3:6 [a]Acts 18:1 [b]Phil. 1:8
3:7 [a]2 Cor. 1:4
3:8 [a]Phil. 4:1
3:9 [a]ch. 1:2
3:10 [a]Acts 26:7 [b]Rom. 15:32 [c]ch. 2:17 [d]Col. 4:12
3:11 [1]Or, *guide* [a]Mark 1:3
3:12 [a]ch. 4:10
3:13 [a]1 Cor. 1:8; Phil. 1:10 [b]Zech. 14:5
4:1 [1]Or, *request* [2]Or, *beseech*
4:1 [a]Phil. 1:27 [b]ch. 2:12 [c]Col. 1:10
4:3 [a]Rom. 12:2 [b]Eph. 5:27 [c]Col. 3:5
4:4 [a]Rom 6:19
4:5 [a]Col. 3:5 [b]Eph. 4:17 [c]1 Cor. 15:34
4:6 [1]Or, *oppress,* or, *overreach* [2]Or, *in the matter* [a]2 Thes. 1:8
4:7 [a]Lev. 11:44
4:8 [1]Or, *rejecteth* [a]Luke 10:16 [b]1 Cor. 2:10
4:9 [a]ch. 5:1 [b]Jer. 31:34 [c]Mat. 22:39
4:10 [a]ch. 1:7 [b]ch. 3:12

spoken of in every major division of the NT. He is supreme among evil spirits (see John 16:11; Eph 2:2). His activities can affect the physical (see 2 Cor 12:7) and the spiritual (see Mat 13:39; Mark 4:15; 2 Cor 4:4). He tempted Jesus (Mat 4:1–11), and he continues to tempt Jesus' servants (see Luke 22:3; 1 Cor 7:5). He hinders missionary work (2:18). But he has already been defeated (see Col 2:15), and Christians need not be overwhelmed by him (see Eph 6:16). His final overthrow is certain (see Rev 20:10).

‡3:6 *brought us good tidings.* The only place where the Greek for this phrase is used by Paul for anything other than the gospel. Three things caused him joy: (1) "your faith"—a right attitude toward God; (2) "charity"—a right attitude toward man; (3) "desiring greatly to see us"—a right attitude toward Paul.

3:9 *thanks . . . to God.* The preceding shows that Paul's work of evangelism had been effective. He might have congratulated himself on work well done, but instead he thanked God for the joy he had from what God had done.

3:10 *night and day.* Not prayer at two set times, but frequent prayer (see 1:2–3). *exceedingly.* Translates a strong and unusual Greek compound word (found elsewhere in the NT only in 5:13; Eph 3:20) that brings out Paul's passionate longing. *that which is lacking.* Some of the things lacking were of a practical nature, such as moral (4:1–12) and disciplinary matters (5:12–24). Others were doctrinal, such as confusion over Christ's return (4:13–5:11). *your faith.* The fifth time in the chapter that Paul speaks of their faith (see vv. 2,5–7).

3:11 In the middle of a letter Paul frequently breaks into prayer (e.g., Eph 1:15–23; 3:14–21; Phil 1:9–11; Col 1:9–12). For the link between Father and Son see note on 1:1.

3:12 *the Lord.* In Paul's writings this usually means Jesus rather than the Father.

3:13 *stablish.* See note on v. 2. *holiness.* The basic idea is "set apart [for God]." Here it refers to the completed process of sanctification (see note on 1 Cor 1:2). *saints.* Used of Christians in many NT passages. Here it may mean the departed saints who will return with Jesus, or it may mean the angels or, probably, both.

4:1 *Furthermore.* The main section of the letter is finished, though much is yet to come (see Phil 3:1 and note). *we beseech you.* Paul is not arrogant, but he does speak with authority in the Lord Jesus. He has the "mind of Christ" (1 Cor 2:16). *walk.* Paul uses this metaphor often of the Christian way (see Rom 6:4; 2 Cor 5:7; Eph 4:1; 5:15; Col 1:10; 2:6; 4:5. It points to steady progress.

4:2 *commandments.* Used of authoritative commands and has a military ring (see Acts 5:28; 16:24).

4:3 *sanctification.* See note on 3:13. *fornication.* In the first century moral standards were generally very low, and chastity was regarded as an unreasonable restriction. Paul, however, would not compromise God's clear and demanding standards. The warning was needed, for Christians were not immune to the temptation (see 1 Cor 5:1).

4:5 *as the Gentiles.* The Christian is to be different.

4:6 *defraud.* Sexual sin harms others besides those who engage in it. In adultery, e.g., the spouse is always wronged. Premarital sex wrongs the future partner by robbing him or her of the virginity that ought to be brought to marriage. *the Lord is the avenger.* A motive for chastity.

4:7 Another reason for chastity is God's call to holiness.

4:8 *God, who hath also given unto us his holy Spirit.* Still another reason for chastity is that sexual sin is against God, who gives the Holy Spirit to believers for their sanctification. To live in sexual immorality is to reject God, specifically in regard to the Holy Spirit.

4:9 *brotherly love.* Translates *philadelphia,* a Greek word that outside the NT almost without exception denoted the mutual love of children of the same father. In the NT it always means

11 And that *ye* study to be quiet, and [a]to
do your own *business,* and [b]to work with your
own hands, as we commanded you;
12 [a]That ye may walk honestly toward
them that are without, and *that* ye may have
lack [1]of no*thing.*

The sudden coming of the Lord

13 ¶ But I would not have you to be ignorant, brethren, concerning them which are
asleep, that ye sorrow not, [a]even as others
[b]which have no hope.
14 For [a]if we believe that Jesus died and
rose again, *even* so [b]them also which sleep in
Jesus will God bring with him.
15 For this we say unto you [a]by the word
of the Lord, that [b]we which are alive *and* remain unto the coming of the Lord shall not
prevent them which are asleep.
16 For [a]the Lord himself shall descend
from heaven with a shout, with the voice of
the archangel, and with [b]the trump of God:
[c]and the dead in Christ shall rise first:
17 [a]Then we which are alive *and* remain
shall be caught up together with them [b]in the
clouds, to meet the Lord in the air: and so
[c]shall we ever be with the Lord.
18 [a]Wherefore [1]comfort one another with
these words.

5 But of [a]the times and the seasons,
brethren, [b]ye have no need that *I* write
unto you.
2 For yourselves know perfectly that [a]the
day of the Lord so cometh as a thief in the
night.
3 For when they shall say, Peace and safety;
then [a]sudden destruction cometh upon them,
[b]as travail upon a *woman* with child; and they
shall not escape.
4 [a]But ye, brethren, are not in darkness,
that *that* day should overtake you as a thief.
5 Ye are all [a]the children of light, and the

4:11 [a]2 Thes. 3:11 [b]Acts 20:35; Eph. 4:28
4:12 [1]Or, *of no man* [a]Rom. 13:13
4:13 [a]Lev. 19:28; 2 Sam. 12:20 [b]Eph. 2:12
4:14 [a]1 Cor. 15:13 [b]1 Cor. 15:23
4:15 [a]1 Ki. 13:17 [b]1 Cor. 15:51
4:16 [a]Mat. 24:30; Acts 1:11 [b]1 Cor. 15:52 [c]1 Cor. 15:23
4:17 [a]1 Cor. 15:51 [b]Acts 1:9 [c]John 17:24
4:18 [1]Or, *exhort* [a]ch. 5:11
5:1 [a]Mat. 24:3 [b]ch. 4:9
5:2 [a]2 Pet. 3:10
5:3 [a]Is. 13:6-9 [b]Hos. 13:13
5:4 [a]Rom. 13:12
5:5 [a]Eph. 5:8

love of fellow believers in Christ, all of whom have the same heavenly Father. *taught of God.* Cf. Is 54:13; John 6:45; 1 Cor 2:13.

4:11 Some Thessalonians, probably because of idleness, were taking undue interest in other people's affairs. *work with your own hands.* The Greeks in general thought manual labor degrading and fit only for slaves. Christians took seriously the need for earning their own living, but some of the Thessalonians, perhaps as a result of their belief in the imminent return of Christ (see 2 Thes 3:11), were neglecting work and relying on others to support them.

4:12 *have lack of nothing.* Or "not be dependent on anyone." Both meanings are true and significant. Christians in need because of their idleness are not obedient Christians.

4:13 *them which are asleep.* For the Christian, sleep is a particularly apt metaphor for death, since death's finality and horror are removed by the assurance of resurrection. Some of the Thessalonians seem to have misunderstood Paul and thought all believers would live until Christ returns. When some died, the question arose, "Will those who have died have part in that great day?" See note on v. 15. *which have no hope.* Inscriptions on tombs and references in literature show that first-century pagans viewed death with horror, as the end of everything. The Christian attitude was in strong contrast (see 1 Cor 15:55–57; Phil 1:21–23).

4:14 *died.* Paul does not say that Christ "slept," perhaps to underscore the fact that He bore the full horror of death so that those who believe in Him would not have to. *rose again.* For the importance of the resurrection see 1 Cor 15, especially vv. 14,17–22. *them also which sleep in Jesus.* Believers who have died, trusting in Jesus.

4:15 *by the word of the Lord.* The doctrine mentioned here is not recorded in the Gospels and was either a direct revelation to Paul or something Jesus said that Christians passed on orally. *we which are alive.* Those believers who will be alive when Christ returns. "We" does not necessarily mean that Paul thought that he would be alive then. He often identified himself with those he wrote to or about. Elsewhere he says that God will raise "us" at that time (1 Cor 6:14; 2 Cor 4:14). *shall not prevent.* The Thessalonians had evidently been concerned that those among them who died would miss their place in the great events when the Lord comes, and Paul assures them this will not be the case.

4:16 *the Lord himself.* See Acts 1:11. *archangel.* The only named archangel in the Bible is Michael (Jude 9; see Dan 10:13). In Scripture, Gabriel is simply called an angel (Luke 1:19,26). *shall rise first.* Before the ascension of believers mentioned in the next verse.

‡4:17 *we which are alive.* See note on v. 15. *caught up.* Greek *harpazo,* "to snatch away." Both the dead and the living "in "Christ" (believers) are caught up into the air. A "rapture" (from the Latin Vulgate rendering) is clearly referred to. But 1 Cor 15:51–52 also refers to the same event. See note on 1 Cor 15:52. *with the Lord.* The chief hope of the believer (see 5:10; John 14:3; 2 Cor 5:8; Phil 1:23; Col 3:4).

‡4:18 *comfort one another.* The primary purpose of vv. 13–18 is to urge mutual encouragement, as shown here and in v. 13. The promise of the rapture of believers is the basis of that hope.

5:1 *times and the seasons.* See Acts 1:6–7. There have always been some Christians who try to fix the date of our Lord's return, but apparently the Thessalonians were not among them.

‡5:2 *day of the Lord.* See 1 Cor 5:5. The expression goes back to Amos 5:18. In the OT it is a time when God will come and intervene with judgment (cf. Zeph 1:14–15) and then blessing (cf. Joel 3:14–21) In the NT the thought of judgment continues (see Rom 2:5; 2 Pet 2:9), but it is also the "day of redemption" (Eph 4:30); the "day of God" (2 Pet 3:12), or of Christ (1 Cor 1:8; Phil 1:6); and the "last day" (John 6:39), the "great day" (Jude 6) or simply "that day" (2 Thes 1:10). It is first tribulation and then Christ's kingdom (Mat 24:21–31; 25:31–34). There will be some preliminary signs (e.g., 2 Thes 2:3), but the coming will be as unexpected as that of a thief in the night (cf. Mat 24:43–44; Luke 12:39–40; 2 Pet 3:10; Rev 3:3; 16:15).

5:3 *sudden.* Paul stresses the surprise of unbelievers. He uses a word found elsewhere in the NT only in Luke 21:34. *destruction.* Not annihilation, but exclusion from the Lord's presence (2 Thes 1:9); thus the ruin of life and all its proud accomplishments. *travail.* Here the idea is not the pain of childbirth so much as the suddenness and inevitability of such pains. *not.* An emphatic double negative in the Greek, a construction Paul uses only four times in all his writings.

5:4 *darkness.* Believers no longer live in darkness, nor are they of the darkness (v. 5). See John 1:5; Acts 26:18. *thief.* See note on v. 2.

5:5 In Semitic languages (such as Hebrew) to be the "son of" a quality meant to be characterized by that quality. Christians do not simply live in the light; they are characterized by light.

children of the day: we are not of the night, nor of darkness.

6 [a]Therefore let us not sleep, as *do* others; but [b]let us watch and be sober.

7 For [a]they that sleep sleep in the night; and they that be drunken [b]are drunken in the night.

8 But let us, who are of the day, be sober, [a]putting on the breastplate of faith and love; and for a helmet, the hope of salvation.

9 For [a]God hath not appointed us to wrath, [b]but to obtain salvation by our Lord Jesus Christ,

10 [a]Who died for us, that, whether we wake or sleep, we should live together with him.

11 [a]Wherefore [1]comfort yourselves together, and edify one another, even as also ye do.

12 ¶ And we beseech you, brethren, [a]to know them which labour among you, and are over you in the Lord, and admonish you;

13 And to esteem them very highly in love for their work's sake. [a]*And* be at peace among yourselves.

14 Now we [1]exhort you, brethren, [a]warn *them that are* [2]unruly, [b]comfort the feebleminded, [c]support the weak, [d]be patient toward all *men.*

15 [a]See that none render evil for evil unto any *man;* but ever [b]follow *that which is* good, both among yourselves, and to all *men.*

16 [a]Rejoice evermore.

17 [a]Pray without ceasing.

18 In every *thing* give thanks: for this *is* the will of God in Christ Jesus concerning you.

19 [a]Quench not the Spirit.

20 [a]Despise not prophesyings.

21 [a]Prove all *things;* [b]hold fast *that which is* good.

22 [a]Abstain from all appearance of evil.

23 And [a]the very God of peace [b]sanctify you wholly; and *I pray God* your whole spirit and soul and body [c]be preserved blameless unto the coming of our Lord Jesus Christ.

24 [a]Faithful *is* he that calleth you, who also will do *it.*

Conclusion

25 ¶ Brethren, [a]pray for us.

26 [a]Greet all the brethren with a holy kiss.

27 I [1]charge you by the Lord that [a]*this* epistle be read unto all the holy brethren.

5:6 [a]Mat. 25:5 [b]1 Pet. 5:8
5:7 [a]Luke 21:34 [b]Acts 2:15
5:8 [a]Eph. 6:14
5:9 [a]Rom. 9:22 [b]2 Thes. 2:13
5:10 [a]2 Cor. 5:15
5:11 [1]Or, *exhort* [a]ch. 4:18
5:12 [a]1 Cor. 16:18
5:13 [a]Mark 9:50
5:14 [1]Or, *beseech* [2]Or, *disorderly* [a]2 Thes. 3:11 [b]Heb. 12:12
5:14 [c]Rom. 14:1 [d]Gal. 5:22
5:15 [a]Lev. 19:18 [b]Gal. 6:10
5:16 [a]2 Cor. 6:10
5:17 [a]Eph. 6:18
5:19 [a]Eph. 4:30
5:20 [a]1 Cor. 14:1
5:21 [a]1 John 4:1 [b]Phil. 4:8
5:22 [a]ch. 4:12
5:23 [a]Phil. 4:9 [b]ch. 3:13 [c]1 Cor. 1:8
5:24 [a]1 Cor. 1:9
5:25 [a]Col. 4:3
5:26 [a]Rom. 16:16
5:27 [1]Or, *adjure* [a]Col. 4:16

‡5:6 *sleep.* Unbelievers are spiritually insensitive, but this kind of sleep is not for "sons of the light." *watch.* This is in keeping with the emphasis Paul is placing on Christ's coming (cf. Mat 24:42–43; 25:13; Mark 13:34–37). *sober.* A contrast with the conduct mentioned in v. 7.

5:8 *the day.* A reference to the light that characterizes Christians; perhaps it refers also to the coming of Christ (see v. 2 and note). *breastplate . . . helmet.* Paul also uses the metaphor of armor in Rom 13:12; 2 Cor 6:7; 10:4; Eph 6:13–17. He does not consistently attach a particular virtue to each piece of armor; it is the general idea of equipment for battle that is pictured. For the triad of faith, hope and love see note on 1:3.

5:9 *appointed.* God's appointment, not man's choice, is the significant thing. *wrath.* See note on 1:10. *salvation.* Our final, completed salvation.

5:10 *whether we wake or sleep.* That is, "live or die"; or, if the sense is moral, "are alert or carnal" (see v. 6). *with him.* To be Christ's is to have entered a relationship that nothing can destroy.

5:11 *edify.* The verb basically applies to building houses, but Paul frequently used it for Christians being edified.

‡5:12 *them which labour among you.* Not much is known about the organization and leadership of the church at this period, but the reference is probably to elders (cf. 1 Tim 3:1–5; 5:17; Heb 13:7,17).

5:13 *for their work's sake.* Not merely because of personal attachment or respect for their high position, but in appreciation for their work. *be at peace.* The words apply to Christian relationships in general, but here they probably refer especially to right relations between leaders and those under them.

‡5:14 *them that are unruly.* Or "those who are idle"; they were loafers. It seems that some Thessalonians were so sure that the second coming was close that they had given up their jobs in order to prepare for it, but Paul says they should work (see 2 Thes 3:10–11 and notes). *the feebleminded.* Meaning those who are fainthearted or discouraged. *the weak.* These are to be helped, not rejected, by the strong (cf. Rom 14:1–15; 1 Cor 8:13).

5:15 *render.* Retaliation is never a Christian option (cf. Rom 12:17; 1 Pet 3:9). Christians are called to forgive (see Mat 5:38–42; 18:21–35).

5:16 People are naturally happy on some occasions, but the Christian's joy is not dependent on circumstances. It comes from what Christ has done, and it is constant.

5:17 For the practice of continual (or regular) prayer see 1:3; 2:13; Rom 1:9–10; Eph 6:18; Col 1:3; 2 Tim 1:3.

5:18 As in v. 16, Christians are differentiated from the natural man. Because of what God has done, they are continually thankful whatever the circumstances (cf. Eph 5:20).

5:19 *Quench not the Spirit.* There is a warmth, a glow, about the Spirit's presence that makes this language appropriate. The kind of conduct Paul is opposing may include loafing, immorality and the other sins he has denounced. On the other hand, he may be warning against a mechanical attitude toward worship that discourages the expression of the gifts of the Spirit in the local assembly (see v. 20).

5:20 *prophesyings.* For the gift of prophecy see Rom 12:6; 1 Cor 12:10,28; 13:2; 14:29-33; Eph 4:11. For the function of prophecies see 1 Cor 14:3.

5:21 *Prove all things.* The approval of prophecy (v. 20) does not mean that anyone who claims to speak in the name of the Lord is to be accepted without question. Paul does not say what specific tests are to be applied, but he is clear that every teaching must be tested—surely they must be in agreement with his gospel.

5:23 A typical prayer. *God of peace.* A fitting reference to God in view of vv. 12–15. But Paul often refers to God in this way near the end of his letters (see Rom 15:33; 16:20; 1 Cor 14:33; 2 Cor 13:11; Phil 4:9; cf. 2 Thes 3:16). *your whole spirit and soul and body.* Paul is emphasizing the whole person, not attempting to differentiate the parts.

5:24 Paul's confidence rests in the nature of God (cf. Gen 18:25), who can be relied on to complete what He begins (see Num 23:19; Phil 1:6).

5:26 *all.* Paul sent a warm greeting to everyone, even those he had corrected. *holy kiss.* A kiss was a normal greeting of that day, similar to our modern handshake (cf. Rom 16:16; 1 Cor 16:20; 2 Cor 13:12; and a "kiss of charity," 1 Pet 5:14).

5:27 *I charge you.* Surprisingly strong language, meaning "I put

28 [a]The grace of our Lord Jesus Christ *be*
with you. Amen.

5:28 [a]Rom. 16:20

¶ The first *epistle* unto the Thessalonians was written from Athens.

you on oath." Paul clearly wanted every member of the church to read or hear his letter and to know of his concern and advice for them.

5:28 Paul always ended his letters with a benediction of grace for his readers, sometimes adding other blessings, as in 2 Cor 13:14.

The Second Epistle of Paul the Apostle to the Thessalonians

INTRODUCTION

See Introduction to 1 Thessalonians.

Author, Date and Place of Writing

Paul's authorship of 2 Thessalonians has been questioned more often than that of 1 Thessalonians, in spite of the fact that it has more support from early Christian writers. Objections are based on internal factors rather than on the adequacy of the statements of the church fathers. It is thought that there are differences in the vocabulary (ten words not used elsewhere), in the style (it is said to be unexpectedly formal) and in the eschatology (the doctrine of the "man of sin" is not taught elsewhere). However, such arguments have not convinced current scholars Most still hold to Paul's authorship of 2 Thessalonians.

Because of its similarity to 1 Thessalonians, it must have been written not long after the first letter—perhaps about six months. The situation in the church seems to have been much the same. Paul probably penned it (see 1:1; 3:17) c. A.D. 51 or 52 in Corinth, after Silas and Timothy had returned from delivering 1 Thessalonians.

Purpose

Inasmuch as the situation in the Thessalonian church has not changed substantially, Paul's purpose in writing is very much the same as in his first letter to them. He writes (1) to encourage persecuted believers (1:4–10), (2) to exhort the Thessalonians to be steadfast and to work for a living (2:13—3:15) and (3) to correct a misunderstanding concerning the Lord's return (2:1–12).

Theme

Like 1 Thessalonians, this letter deals extensively with eschatology (see Introduction to 1 Thessalonians: Theme). In fact, in 2 Thessalonians 18 out of 47 verses (38 percent) deal with this subject.

Outline

I. Introduction (ch. 1)
   A. Salutation (1:1–2)
   B. Thanksgiving for Their Faith, Love and Perseverance (1:3–10)
   C. Intercession for Their Spiritual Progress (1:11–12)
II. Instruction (ch. 2)
   A. Prophecy regarding the Day of the Lord (2:1–12)
   B. Thanksgiving for Their Election and Calling (Their Position) (2:13–15)
   C. Prayer for Their Service and Testimony (Their Practice) (2:16–17)
III. Injunctions (ch. 3)
   A. Call to Prayer (3:1–3)
   B. Charge to Discipline for the Disorderly and Lazy (3:4–15)
   C. Conclusion, Greeting and Benediction (3:16–18)

Thanksgiving and prayer

1 Paul, [a]and Silvanus, and Timotheus, unto
the church of the Thessalonians [b]in God
our Father and the Lord Jesus Christ:
2 [a]Grace unto you, and peace, from God
our Father and the Lord Jesus Christ.
3 ¶ [a]We are bound to thank God always for
you, brethren, as it is meet, because that your
faith groweth exceedingly, and the charity of
every one of you all towards each other
aboundeth;
4 So that [a]we ourselves glory in you in the
churches of God [b]for your patience and faith
[c]in all your persecutions and tribulations that
ye endure:
5 *Which is* [a]a manifest token of the righteous judgment of God, that ye may be counted worthy of the kingdom of God, [b]for which
ye also suffer:
6 [a]Seeing *it is* a righteous *thing* with God
to recompense tribulation to them that trouble
you;
7 And to you who are troubled [a]rest with
us, when [b]the Lord Jesus shall be revealed
from heaven with [1]his mighty angels,
8 [a]In flaming fire, [1]taking vengeance on
them [b]that know not God, and [c]that obey not
the gospel of our Lord Jesus Christ:
9 [a]Who shall be punished *with* everlasting
destruction from the presence of the Lord, and
[b]from the glory of his power;
10 [a]When he shall come to be glorified in
his saints, [b]and to be admired in all them that
believe (because our testimony among you
was believed) in that day.
11 Wherefore also we pray always for you,
that our God would [a][1]count you worthy of *this*
calling, and fulfil all the good pleasure of *his*
goodness, and [b]the work of faith with power:
12 [a]That the name of our Lord Jesus Christ
may be glorified in you, and ye in him, according to the grace of our God and the Lord Jesus
Christ.

The man of sin

2 Now we beseech you, brethren, [a]by the
coming of our Lord Jesus Christ, [b]and *by*
our gathering together unto him,
2 [a]That ye be not soon shaken in mind, or
be troubled, neither by spirit, nor by word,
nor by letter as from us, as that the day of
Christ is at hand.
3 [a]Let no *man* deceive you by any means:
for *that day shall not come*, [b]except there

1:1 [a]2 Cor. 1:19 [b]1 Thes. 1:1
1:2 [a]1 Cor. 1:3
1:3 [a]1 Thes. 1:2; ch. 2:13
1:4 [a]2 Cor. 7:14; 1 Thes. 2:19 [b]1 Thes. 1:3 [c]1 Thes. 2:14
1:5 [a]Phil. 1:28 [b]1 Thes. 2:14
1:6 [a]Rev. 6:10
1:7 [1]Gr. *the angels of his power* [a]Rev. 14:13 [b]1 Thes. 4:16; Jude 14
1:8 [1]Or, *yielding* [a]Heb. 12:29; 2 Pet. 3:7; Rev. 21:8 [b]Ps. 79:6 [c]Rom. 2:8
1:9 [a]Phil. 3:19; 2 Pet. 3:7 [b]Deut. 33:2; Is. 2:19
1:10 [a]Ps. 89:7 [b]Ps. 68:35
1:11 [1]Or, *vouchsafe* [a]ver. 5 [b]1 Thes. 1:3
1:12 [a]1 Pet. 1:7
2:1 [a]1 Thes. 4:16 [b]Mat. 24:31; Mark 13:27
2:2 [a]Mat. 24:4; Eph. 5:6
2:3 [a]Mat. 24:4; Eph. 5:6 [b]1 Tim. 4:1

1:1–2 See note on 1 Thes 1:1.
1:3 *bound.* Paul is obliged to give thanks where it is due (cf. 1 Thes 1:7–8; see note on Phil 1:3–4). *brethren.* See note on 1 Thes 1:4. *faith . . . charity.* Two virtues that Paul had been pleased to acknowledge in the Thessalonian church (see 1 Thes 3:6–7), but that were also somewhat lacking (1 Thes 3:10,12). *growth exceedingly.* The same verb Paul had used in his prayer that their love might grow (1 Thes 3:12). He is recording an exact answer to prayer.
1:4 *we.* Emphatic,"we ourselves." Paul seems to imply that it was unusual for the founders of a church to boast about it, though others might do so (cf. 1 Thes 1:9). But the Thessalonians were so outstanding that Paul departed from normal practice. *persecutions and tribulations.* See 1 Thes 1:6; 2:14; 3:3.
1:5 *manifest token of the righteous judgment of God.* The evidence was in the way the Thessalonians endured trials. The judgment on them was right because God did not leave them to their own resources. He provided strength to endure, and this in turn produced spiritual and moral character. It also proved that God was on their side and gave a warning to their persecutors (cf. Phil 1:28). *kingdom of God.* See notes on 1 Thes 2:12; Mat 3:2. *for which.* That is,"in the interest of which" or "in behalf of which."
1:6 *righteous thing with God.* The justice of God brings punishment on unrepentant sinners (cf. Mark 9:47–48; Luke 13:3–5), and it may be in the here and now (see Rom 1:24,26,28) as well as on judgment day.
‡1:7 *rest.* Retribution not only involves punishment of the evil but also relief for the righteous. *with us.* Paul was not merely an academic theologian writing in comfort from a distance; rather, he was suffering just as they were. *revealed.* Christ is now hidden, and many people even deny His existence. But at His second coming He will be seen by everyone for who He is. *his mighty angels.* Perhaps a class of angels (such a group is mentioned in apocalyptic writings) given special power to do God's will.
1:8 *flaming fire.* He comes to punish wickedness (cf. Is 66:15; Rev 1:14) *know not God.* Does not refer to those who have never heard of the true God but to those who refuse to recognize Him (cf. 2:10,12; Rom 1:28). *obey not.* The gospel invites acceptance, and rejection is disobedience to a royal invitation.
1:9 *destruction.* Not annihilation (see note on 1 Thes 5:3). Paul uses the word in 1 Cor 5:5, possibly of the destruction of the "flesh" for the purpose of salvation. Since, however, salvation implies resurrection of the body, annihilation cannot be in mind. The word means something like "complete ruin." Here it means being shut out from Christ's presence. This eternal separation is the penalty of sin and the essence of hell.
1:10 *glorified in his saints.* Not simply "among" but "in" them. His glory is seen in what they are. *saints.* See note on 1 Thes 3:13. *our testimony.* The preaching of the gospel is essentially bearing testimony to what God has done in Christ. *that day.* See note on 1 Thes 5:2.
1:11 *pray always for you.* See note on 1 Thes 5:17. *good pleasure of his goodness.* Lit. "resolve of goodness." God initiates every good purpose and every act prompted by faith; Paul prays accordingly that He will bring them to fulfillment.
1:12 *name.* In ancient times one's name was often more than a personal label; it summed up what a person was. Paul looks for glory to be ascribed to Christ for all He will do in the lives of the Thessalonian Christians.
‡2:1 *gathering together.* Greek *episunagogue,* "assemble together." This verse refers to the rapture of the church spoken of in 1 Thes 4:13–18. Also see 1 Cor 15:51–52.
‡2:2 *shaken.* The Greek for this verb was often used of a ship adrift from its mooring, and suggests lack of stability. *troubled.* Jesus issued a similar instruction, using the same verb (Mark 13:7). *spirit.* Paul seems to be uncertain about what was disturbing them, so he uses a general expression denoting any inspired revelation. *word.* Perhaps referring to a sermon or other oral communication. *letter as from us.* A forgery. *day of Christ.* See note on 1 Thes 5:2. *is at hand.* Obviously Christ's climactic return had not occurred, but Paul was combating the idea that the final days had begun and their completion would be imminent.

come a falling away first, and [c]*that* man of sin
be revealed, [d]the son of perdition;
4 Who opposeth and [a]exalteth himself
[b]above all that is called God, or that is worshipped; so that he as God sitteth in the temple of God, shewing himself that he is God.
5 Remember ye not, that, when I was yet
with you, I told you these *things?*
6 And now ye know what [1]withholdeth
that he might be revealed in his time.
7 For [a]the mystery of iniquity doth already
work: only he who now letteth *will let,* until
he be taken out of the way.
8 And then shall *that* Wicked be revealed,
[a]whom the Lord shall consume [b]with the spirit of his mouth, and shall destroy [c]with the
brightness of his coming:
9 *Even him,* whose coming is [a]after the
working of Satan with all power and [b]signs
and lying wonders,
10 And with all deceivableness of unrighteousness in [a]them that perish; because they
received not the love of the truth, that they
might be saved.

2:3 [c]Dan. 7:25; Rev. 13:11 [d]John 17:12
2:4 [a]Is. 14:13; Rev. 13:6 [b]1 Cor. 8:5
2:6 [1]Or, *holdeth*
2:7 [a]1 John 2:18
2:8 [a]Dan. 7:10 [b]Is. 11:4 [c]Heb. 10:27
2:9 [a]John 8:41; Rev. 18:23 [b]Deut. 13:1; Rev. 19:20
2:10 [a]2 Cor. 2:15
2:11 [a]Rom. 1:24 [b]1 Tim. 4:1
2:12 [a]Rom. 1:32
2:13 [a]ch. 1:3 [b]1 Thes. 1:4 [c]Eph. 1:4 [d]1 Pet. 1:2
2:14 [a]1 Pet. 5:10
2:15 [a]1 Cor. 16:13 [b]1 Cor. 11:2
2:16 [a]ch. 1:1,2 [b]Rev. 1:5 [c]1 Pet. 1:3

11 And [a]for this cause God shall send them
strong delusion, [b]that they should believe a
lie:
12 That they all might be damned who believed not the truth, but [a]had pleasure in unrighteousness.

Thanksgiving and appeal

13 ¶ But [a]we are bound to give thanks alway to God for you, brethren beloved of the
Lord, because God [b]hath [c]from the beginning
chosen you to salvation [d]through sanctification of the Spirit and belief of the truth:
14 Whereunto he called you by our gospel,
to [a]the obtaining of the glory of our Lord Jesus
Christ.
15 Therefore, brethren, [a]stand fast, and
hold [b]the traditions which ye have been
taught, whether by word, or by our epistle.
16 [a]Now our Lord Jesus Christ himself,
and God, even our Father, [b]which hath loved
us, and hath given *us* everlasting consolation
and [c]good hope through grace,

2:3 *a falling away.* At the last time there will be a falling away from the faith (see Mat 24:10–12; 1 Tim 4:1). But here Paul is speaking of active rebellion, the supreme opposition of evil to the things of God. *that man of sin.* The leader of the forces of evil at the last time. Only here is he called by this name. John tells us of many "antichrists" (1 John 2:18), and this may be the worst of them—the beast of Rev 13—though Paul's description of the man of sin has some distinctive features. He is not Satan, because he is clearly distinguished from him in v. 9. *revealed.* Since the Greek for this word is from the same root as that used of Jesus Christ in 1:7, it may indicate something supernatural. *son of perdition.* For all his proud claims, his final overthrow is certain. The same Greek expression is used of Judas Iscariot in John 17:12, where it is also translated "son of perdition."

‡2:4 *all that is called God, or that is worshipped.* He is not merely a political or military man, but claims a place above every god and everything associated with worship. He even claims to be God. *temple of God.* Apparently refers to a physical temple (cf. Mat 24:25; Mark 13:14) from which he makes his blasphemous pronouncements (cf. Dan 11:36–45; Rev 13:1–15).

‡2:7 *mystery.* In the NT a mystery usually denotes something people could not know by themselves but that God has revealed (see note on Rom 11:25). The expression here indicates that we know some things about evil only as God reveals them. This evil is already at work, but will in the day of the Lord (the Great Tribulation) intensify dramatically (cf. Mat 24:21–22). *he who now letteth will let.* The English word "let" in earlier centuries meant to "hinder" or "restrain" (as does the Greek word here) rather than to "allow." So the meaning is that he who now restrains will restrain until he is removed. There have been many suggestions as to the identity of this restrainer: The Roman state with its emperor, Paul's missionary work, the Jewish state, the principle of law and government embodied in the state, the Holy Spirit or the restraining ministry of the Holy Spirit through the church. Since only God is able to restrain Satan and his antichrist, it seems best to regard the Holy Spirit's presence in and work through the church as the Restrainer who will be removed at the ushering in of the tribulation period. So the day of the Lord (of Christ) with its Great Tribulation will not begin until after the Restrainer is removed and the Wicked One, the man of sin, is revealed. Paul wants the Thessalonians to understand, therefore, that the day of the Lord (the final days) has not yet come, and that they have not missed the rapture of the church. The order of events in this verse is: (1) removal of the restrainer; (2) falling away; (3) rise of the wicked one.

2:8 *that Wicked be revealed.* Evidently refers to some supernatural aspects of his appearing (see v. 9). *consume with the spirit of his mouth.* Despite his impressiveness (v. 4), the man of sin will easily be destroyed by Christ (cf. Dan 11:45; Rev 19:20). *brightness.* In 2 Tim 1:10 ("appearing") the Greek for this word refers to Jesus' first coming, but everywhere else in the NT to His second coming.

2:9 *coming.* The same word used of Christ's coming in v. 8. Satan empowers him with miracles, signs and wonders (cf. Mat 24:24). *lying.* "Producing false impressions."

2:10 *deceivableness.* The aim of the miracles of v. 9. *received not.* Their unbelief was willing and intentional. *truth.* Often closely connected with Jesus (see John 14:6; Eph 4:21) and with the gospel (see Gal 2:5; Eph 1:13).

2:11 *for this cause.* Because of their deliberate rejection of the truth (v. 10). *God shall send them strong delusion.* God uses sin to punish the sinful (cf. Rom 1:24–28). *believe a lie.* Not just any lie, but the great lie that the man of sin is God (v. 4).

2:13 *beloved of the Lord, because God hath . . . chosen.* For the connection between God's love and election see Col 3:12; 1 Thes 1:4; see also note on Eph 1:4. *from the beginning.* Election is from eternity (see Eph 1:4). *sanctification.* A necessary aspect of salvation, not something reserved for special Christians (see 1 Thes 3:13; 4:3 and notes). *truth.* See note on v. 10. All three persons of the Trinity are mentioned in this verse (see note on 1 Thes 1:1).

2:14 *called . . . by our gospel.* The past tense refers to the time when the Thessalonians were converted; but the divine call is a present reality in 1 Thes 2:12; 5:24. *our gospel.* See note on 1 Thes 1:5. *glory of our Lord Jesus Christ.* Cf. 1 Thes 2:12. Ultimately there is no glory other than God's.

2:15 *traditions.* Until the NT was written, essential Christian teaching was passed on in the "traditions," just as rabbinic law was (see note on Mat 15:2); it could be either oral or written. In 1 Cor 15:3 Paul uses the technical words for receiving and handing on traditions.

2:16–17 There is a similar prayer in about the same place in the first letter (1 Thes 3:11–13).

17 Comfort your hearts, [a]and stablish you in every good word and work.

Appeals for prayer and labour

3 Finally, brethren, [a]pray for us, that the word of the Lord [1]may have *free* course, and be glorified, even as *it is* with you:

2 And [a]that we may be delivered from [1]unreasonable and wicked men: [b]for all *men* have not faith.

3 But [a]the Lord is faithful, who shall stablish you, and [b]keep *you* from evil.

4 And [a]we have confidence in the Lord touching you, that ye both do and will do *the things* which we command you.

5 And [a]the Lord direct your hearts into the love of God, and into [1]the patient waiting for Christ.

6 ¶ Now we command you, brethren, in the name of our Lord Jesus Christ, [a]that ye withdraw yourselves [b]from every brother that walketh [c]disorderly, and not after [d]the tradition which he received of us.

7 For yourselves know [a]how *ye* ought to follow us: for [b]we behaved not ourselves disorderly among you;

8 Neither did we eat any *man's* bread for nought; but [a]wrought with labour and travail night and day, that *we* might not be chargeable to any of you:

9 [a]Not because we have not power, but to make [b]ourselves an ensample unto you to follow us.

10 For even when we were with you, this we commanded you, [a]that if any would not work, neither should he eat.

11 For we hear that *there are* some [a]which walk among you disorderly, [b]working not at all, but are busybodies.

12 [a]Now *them that are* such we command and exhort by our Lord Jesus Christ, [b]that with quietness they work, and eat their own bread.

13 But ye, brethren, [a][1]be not weary in well doing.

14 And if any *man* obey not our word [1]by *this* epistle, note that *man,* and [a]have no company with him, that he may be ashamed.

15 [a]Yet count *him* not as an enemy, [b]but admonish *him* as a brother.

Benediction

16 Now [a]the Lord of peace himself give you peace always by all means. The Lord *be* with you all.

17 ¶ [a]The salutation of Paul with mine own hand, which is the token in every epistle: so I write.

18 [a]The grace of our Lord Jesus Christ *be* with you all. Amen.

¶ The second *epistle* to the Thessalonians was written from Athens.

2:17 [a]1 Cor. 1:8
3:1 [1]Gr. *may run* [a]Eph. 6:19
3:2 [1]Gr. *absurd* [a]Rom. 15:31 [b]Acts 28:24; Rom. 10:16
3:3 [a]1 Cor. 1:9 [b]John 17:15; 2 Pet. 2:9
3:4 [a]2 Cor. 7:16
3:5 [1]Or, *the patience of Christ* [a]1 Chr. 29:18
3:6 [a]Rom. 16:17 [b]1 Cor. 5:11 [c]1 Thes. 4:11 [d]ch. 2:15
3:7 [a]1 Cor. 4:16 [b]1 Thes. 2:10
3:8 [a]Acts 18:3; 2 Cor. 11:9
3:9 [a]1 Cor. 9:6
3:9 [b]ver. 7
3:10 [a]1 Thes. 4:11
3:11 [a]ver. 6 [b]1 Tim. 5:13
3:12 [a]1 Thes. 4:11 [b]Eph. 4:28
3:13 [1]Or, *faint not* [a]Gal. 6:9
3:14 [1]Or, *signify that* man *by an epistle* [a]Mat. 18:17
3:15 [a]Lev. 19:17 [b]Tit. 3:10
3:16 [a]Rom. 15:33
3:17 [a]1 Cor. 16:21
3:18 [a]Rom. 16:24

---

‡2:17 *Comfort . . . stablish.* The prayer is for inner strength that will produce results in both action and speech.
3:1 *Finally.* See note on 1 Thes 4:1. In 1 Thes 5:25 Paul simply asked for prayer; here he mentions specifics. *even as it is with you.* Lit. "just as also with you." The expression is general enough to cover the present as well as the past (cf. 1 Thes 2:13).
3:2 *unreasonable.* The Greek for this word means "out of place," and elsewhere in the NT it is used only of things (see Luke 23:41; Acts 25:5). Perverseness is always out of place. For Paul's difficulties at Corinth (where he wrote this letter) see Acts 18:12–13.
3:3 *faithful.* In the Greek text, "faithful" immediately follows "faith" (v. 2), putting the faithfulness of God in sharp contrast with the lack of faith in people (cf. 1 Cor 1:9; 10:13; 2 Cor 1:18).
3:5 *hearts.* See note on 1 Thes 2:4. *love of God.* Paul is about to rebuke the idle, and is here reminding them of God's love. There should be no hard feelings among those who owe everything to the love of God.
3:6 *command.* An authoritative word with a military ring. *the name.* See note on 1:12. *withdraw.* Not withdrawal of all contact but withholding of close fellowship. Idleness is sinful and disruptive, but those guilty of it are still brothers (v. 15). *walketh disorderly.* The problem was mentioned in the first letter (4:11–12; 5:14; see notes there), and evidently had worsened. Paul takes it seriously and gives more attention to it in this letter than to anything else but the second coming. *tradition.* See note on 2:15.
3:7 *ye ought to follow us.* See note on 1 Thes 1:6.
3:8 *eat any man's bread.* A Hebraism for "make a living" (see, e.g., Gen 3:19; Amos 7:12). Paul is not saying that he never accepted hospitality but that he had not depended on other people for his living (see 1 Thes 2:9 and note).
3:9 *have not power.* See note on 1 Thes 2:6.
‡3:10 Pagan parallels are in the form, "He who does not work does not eat." But Paul gives an imperative: lit. "let him not eat." The Christian must not be a loafer.
3:11 *busybodies.* Worse than idle, they were interfering with other people's affairs, a problem to which an unruly or idle life often leads.
3:14 Paul realizes that some may not heed his letter. *no company with.* The Greek for this phrase is an unusual double compound, meaning "mix up together with" (used elsewhere in the NT only in 1 Cor 5:9,11—of a similar withdrawal of close fellowship). It indicates a disassociation that will bring the person back to a right attitude. *be ashamed.* And repent. The aim is not punishment but restoration to fellowship.
3:15 Discipline in the church should be brotherly, never harsh. *admonish.* See 1 Thes 5:12.
3:16 *Lord of peace.* The more usual phrase is "God of peace" (see note on 1 Thes 5:23). *you all.* Even the disorderly.
3:17 Paul normally dictated his letters (cf. Rom 16:22), but toward the end he added something in his own handwriting (see 1 Cor 16:21; Gal 6:11; Col 4:18). Here he tells us that this practice was his distinguishing mark.
3:18 See note on 1 Thes 5:28. Paul has criticized his offenders, but his last prayer is for everyone.

The Pastoral Epistles

1,2 Timothy and Titus are known as the Pastoral Epistles because they give instruction to Timothy and Titus concerning the pastoral care of churches. All three letters probably were written not long after the events of Acts 28.

After his imprisonment in Rome (c. A.D. 60–62), Paul most likely began his fourth missionary journey (see map, pp. 1738–1739). During this trip he commissioned Titus to remain as his representative in Crete, and he left Timothy in charge of the church at Ephesus. Paul then moved on to Philippi in northern Greece (Macedonia), where he wrote his first letter to Timothy and his letter to Titus (c. 63–65). Later he traveled to Rome, where he was imprisoned for the second time and where he wrote 2 Timothy shortly before he was executed (67 or 68).

Certain themes and phrases recur throughout the Pastoral Epistles: (1) God the Savior (see note on Tit 1:3); (2) sound doctrine, faith and teaching (see note on Tit 1:9); (3) godliness (see note on 1 Tim 2:2); (4) controversies (1 Tim 1:4; 6:4; 2 Tim 2:23; Tit 3:9); (5) trustworthy sayings (see note on 1 Tim 1:15).

The First Epistle of Paul the Apostle to Timothy

INTRODUCTION

Author

Both early tradition and the salutations of the Pastoral Epsitles themselves confirm Paul as their author. Some objections have been raised in recent years on the basis of an alleged uncharacteristic vocabulary and style (e.g., see notes on 1:15; 2:2), but evidence is still convincingly supportive of Paul's authorship.

Background and Purpose

During his fourth missionary journey, Paul had instructed Timothy to care for the church at Ephesus (1:3) while he went on to Macedonia (see "The Pastoral Epistles," p. 1734). When he realized that he might not return to Ephesus in the near future (3:14–15), he wrote this first letter to Timothy to develop the charge he had given his young assistant (1:3,18), to refute false teachings (1:3–7; 4:1–8; 6:3–5,20–21) and to supervise the affairs of the growing Ephesian church (church worship, 2:1–15; the appointment of qualified church leaders, 3:1–13; 5:17–25).

A major problem in the Ephesian church was a heresy that combined Gnosticism (see Introduction to 1 John: Gnosticism), decadent Judaism (1:3–7) and false asceticism (4:1–5).

Date

1 Timothy was written sometime after the events of Acts 28 (c. 63–65), at least eight years after Paul's three-year stay in Ephesus (Acts 19:8,10; 20:31).

Recipient

As the salutation indicates (1:2), Paul is writing to Timothy, a native of Lystra (in modern Turkey). Timothy's father was Greek, while his mother was a Jewish Christian (Acts 16:1). From childhood he had been taught the OT (2 Tim 1:5; 3:15). Paul called him "my own son in the faith" (1:2), perhaps having led him to Christ during his first visit to Lystra. At the time of his second visit Paul invited Timothy to join him on his missionary travels, and circumcised him so that his Greek ancestry would not be a liability in working with the Jews (Acts 16:3). Timothy shared in the evangelization of Macedonia and Achaia (Acts 17:14–15; 18:5) and was with Paul during much of his long preaching ministry at Ephesus (Acts 19:22). He traveled with Paul from Ephesus to Macedonia, to Corinth, back to Macedonia, and to Asia Minor (Acts 20:1–6). He seems even to have accompanied him all the way to Jerusalem. He was with Paul during the apostle's first imprisonment (Phil 1:1; Col 1:1; Philem 1).

Following Paul's release (after Acts 28), Timothy again traveled with him but eventually stayed at Ephesus to deal with the problems there, while Paul went on to Macedonia. Paul's closeness to and admiration of Timothy are seen in Paul's naming him as the co-sender of six of his letters (2 Corinthians, Philippians, Colossians, 1,2 Thessalonians and Philemon) and in his speaking highly of him to the Philippians (Phil 2:19–22). At the end of Paul's life he requested Timothy to join him at Rome (2 Tim 4:9,21). According to Heb 13:23, Timothy himself was imprisoned and subsequently released—whether at Rome or elsewhere, we do not know.

Timothy was not an apostle, and he was probably not an overseer since he was given instructions about overseers (3:1–7; 5:17–22). It may be best to regard him as an apostolic representative, delegated to carry out special work (see Tit 1:5).

Outline

I. Salutation (1:1–2)
II. Warning against False Teachers (1:3–11)
   A. The Nature of the Heresy (1:3–7)
   B. The Purpose of the Law (1:8–11)

III. The Lord's Grace to Paul (1:12–17)
IV. The Purpose of Paul's Instructions to Timothy (1:18–20)
V. Instructions concerning the Administration of the Church (chs. 2—3)
   A. Public Worship (ch. 2)
      1. Prayer in public worship (2:1–8)
      2. Women in public worship (2:9–15)
   B. Qualifications for Church Officers (3:1–13)
      1. Bishops (3:1–7)
      2. Deacons (3:8–13)
   C. Purpose of These Instructions (3:14–16)
VI. Methods of Dealing with False Teaching (ch. 4)
   A. False Teaching Described (4:1–5)
   B. Methods of Dealing with It Explained (4:6–16)
VII. Methods of Dealing with Different Groups in the Church (5:1—6:2)
   A. The Elderly and Younger People (5:1–2)
   B. Widows (5:3–16)
   C. Elders (5:17–25)
   D. Servants (6:1–2)
VIII. Miscellaneous Matters (6:3–19)
   A. False Teachers (6:3–5)
   B. Love of Money (6:6–10)
   C. Charge to Timothy (6:11–16)
   D. The Rich (6:17–19)
IX. Concluding Appeal (6:20–21)

1 Paul, an apostle of Jesus Christ [a]by the commandment [b]of God our Saviour, and Lord Jesus Christ, [c]*which is* our hope;

2 Unto [a]Timothy, [b]*my* own son in the faith: [c]Grace, mercy, *and* peace, from God our Father and Jesus Christ our Lord.

The problem of unsound doctrine

3 ¶ As I besought thee to abide *still* at Ephesus, [a]when I went into Macedonia, that thou mightest charge some [b]that *they* teach no other doctrine,

4 [a]Neither give heed to fables and endless genealogies, [b]which minister questions, rather than godly edifying which is in faith: *so do.*

5 Now [a]the end of the commandment is charity [b]out of a pure heart, and *of* a good conscience, and *of* faith unfeigned:

6 From which some [1]having swerved have turned aside unto [a]vain jangling;

7 Desiring to be teachers of the law; [a]understanding neither what they say, nor whereof they affirm.

8 But we know that [a]the law *is* good, if a man use it lawfully;

9 [a]Knowing this, that the law is not made for a righteous *man,* but for the lawless and disobedient, for the ungodly and for sinners, for unholy and profane, for murderers of fathers and murderers of mothers, for manslayers,

10 For whoremongers, for them that defile themselves with mankind, for menstealers, for liars, for perjured *persons,* and if *there be* any other *thing that* is contrary [a]to sound doctrine;

1:1 [a]Acts 9:15 [b]Tit. 1:3 [c]Col. 1:27
1:2 [a]Acts 16:1 [b]Tit. 1:4 [c]Gal. 1:3
1:3 [a]Acts 20:1 [b]Gal. 1:6,7
1:4 [a]Tit. 1:14 [b]ch. 6:4
1:5 [a]Rom. 13:8; Gal. 5:14 [b]2 Tim. 2:22
1:6 [1]Or, *not aiming at* [a]ch. 6:4,20
1:7 [a]ch. 6:4
1:8 [a]Rom. 7:12
1:9 [a]Gal. 3:19
1:10 [a]2 Tim. 4:3; Tit. 1:9
1:11 [a]1 Cor. 9:17; Gal. 2:7; Col. 1:25
1:12 [a]2 Cor. 12:9 [b]1 Cor. 7:25 [c]2 Cor. 3:5
1:13 [a]Acts 8:3 [b]John 4:21
1:14 [a]Rom. 5:20 [b]2 Tim. 1:13 [c]Luke 7:47
1:15 [a]2 Tim. 2:11 [b]Mat. 9:13
1:16 [a]2 Cor. 4:1 [b]Acts 13:39
1:17 [a]Ps. 10:16 [b]Rom. 1:23 [c]Heb. 11:27 [d]Rom. 16:27 [e]1 Chr. 29:11
1:18 [a]2 Tim. 2:2 [b]ch. 4:14 [c]2 Tim. 2:3
1:20 [a]2 Tim. 2:17 [b]2 Tim. 4:14 [c]1 Cor. 5:5 [d]Acts 13:45

11 According to the glorious gospel of the blessed God, [a]which was committed to my trust.

The testimony of Paul

12 And I thank Christ Jesus our Lord, [a]who hath enabled me, [b]for that he counted me faithful, [c]putting *me* into the ministry;

13 [a]Who was before a blasphemer, and a persecutor, and injurious: but I obtained mercy, because [b]I did *it* ignorantly in unbelief.

14 [a]And the grace of our Lord was exceeding abundant [b]with faith [c]and love which is in Christ Jesus.

15 [a]*This is* a faithful saying, and worthy of all acceptation, that [b]Christ Jesus came into the world to save sinners; of whom I am chief.

16 Howbeit for this cause [a]I obtained mercy, that in me first Jesus Christ might shew forth all longsuffering, [b]for a pattern to them which should hereafter believe on him to life everlasting.

17 Now unto [a]the King eternal, [b]immortal, [c]invisible, [d]the only wise God, [e]*be* honour and glory for ever and ever. Amen.

18 This charge [a]I commit unto thee, son Timothy, [b]according to the prophecies which went before on thee, that thou by them mightest [c]war a good warfare;

19 Holding faith, and a good conscience; which some having put away, concerning faith have made shipwrack:

20 Of whom is [a]Hymeneus and [b]Alexander; whom I have [c]delivered unto Satan, that they may learn not to [d]blaspheme.

1:1 *apostle.* One specially commissioned by Christ (see notes on Mark 6:30; 1 Cor 1:1; Heb 3:1). *Jesus Christ . . . our hope.* See Tit 2:13. *hope.* Expresses absolute certainty, not a mere wish.

1:2 *my own son in the faith.* My spiritual son (see 1:18; 1 Cor 4:17; 2 Tim 1:2; 2:1; Philem 10). *Grace.* See notes on Jonah 4:2; Gal 1:3; Eph 1:2. *mercy.* See Rom 9:23. *peace.* See notes on John 14:27; 20:19; Gal 1:3; Eph 1:2.

1:3–11 In this section, along with 4:1–8; 6:3–5,20–21, Paul warns against heretical teachers in the Ephesian church. They are characterized by (1) teaching false doctrines (1:3; 6:3); (2) teaching Jewish myths (Tit 1:14); (3) wanting to be teachers of the OT law (1:7); (4) building up endless, far-fetched, fictitious stories based on obscure genealogical points (1:4; 4:7; Tit 3:9); (5) being conceited (1:7; 6:4); (6) being argumentative (1:4; 6:4; 2 Tim 2:23; Tit 3:9); (7) using talk that was meaningless (1:6) and foolish (2 Tim 2:23; Tit 3:9); (8) not knowing what they were talking about (1:7; 6:4); (9) teaching ascetic practices (4:3); and (10) using their positions of religious leadership for personal financial gain (6:5). These heretics probably were forerunners of the Gnostics (6:20–21; see Introduction to 1 John: Gnosticism).

1:3 *abide still at Ephesus.* The Ephesian church was well established by this time. Paul had had an extensive ministry there on his third missionary journey about eight years earlier (Acts 19:1–20:1). After his release from prison in Rome (after Acts 28), he revisited the church, leaving Timothy in charge while he journeyed on to Macedonia. *when I went into Macedonia.* Since this incident is not recorded in Acts, it probably occurred after Acts 28, between Paul's first and second Roman imprisonments (see Introduction: Recipient).

1:4 *fables and endless genealogies.* Probably mythical stories built on OT history (genealogies) that later developed into intricate Gnostic philosophical systems (see Introduction to 1 John: Gnosticism).

1:8 *the law is good.* See Rom 7:7–12.

1:10 *sound doctrine.* See note on Tit 1:9.

1:11 *gospel.* See note on Mark 1:1. *committed.* See 6:20; 1 Cor 9:17; Gal 2:7; 1 Thes 2:4; 2 Tim 1:12,14; 2:2.

1:13 *a blasphemer, and a persecutor, and injurious.* See Acts 9:1; 22:4–5,19; 26:10–11.

1:15 *This is a faithful saying.* A clause found nowhere else in the NT but used five times in the Pastorals (here; 3:1; 4:9; 2 Tim 2:11; Tit 3:8) to identify a key saying.

‡1:18 *prophecies.* In the early church God revealed His will in various matters through prophets (see Acts 13:1–3, where prophets had an active role in the sending of Paul and Barnabas on their mission to the Gentiles). In Timothy's case this prophecy may have occurred at the time of or before his ordination (4:14), perhaps about 12 years earlier on Paul's second missionary journey (see Acts 16:3). Prophecies about Timothy seem to have pointed to the significant leadership role he was to have in the church.

‡1:20 *Hymeneus.* See 2 Tim 2:17–18. *Alexander.* Perhaps the Alexander of 2 Tim 4:14 (but see note there). *delivered unto Satan.* The reference is to church discipline (see note on Mat 18:17). Paul had excluded these two men from the church, which was considered a sanctuary from Satan's power. Out in the world, away from the fellowship and care of the church, they would "learn" (the word means basically "to discipline") not to blaspheme. The purpose of such drastic action was more re-

Prayer and sobriety

2 I [1]exhort therefore that, first of all, supplications, prayers, intercessions, *and*
giving of thanks, be made for all men;
2 [a]For kings, and [b]*for* all that are in [1]au-
thority; that we may lead a quiet and peaceable life in all godliness and honesty.
3 For this *is* [a]good and acceptable in the
sight [b]of God our Saviour;
4 [a]Who will have all men to be saved, [b]and
to come unto the knowledge of the truth.
5 [a]For *there is* one God, and [b]one mediator
between God and men, *the* man Christ Jesus;
6 [a]Who gave himself a ransom for all, [b][1]to
be testified [c]in due time.
7 [a]Whereunto I am ordained a preacher,
and an apostle, ([b]I speak the truth in Christ,
and lie not;) [c]a teacher of the Gentiles in faith
and verity.
8 I will therefore that men pray [a]every

2:1 [1]Or, *desire* 2:2 [1]Or, *eminent place* [a]Ezra 6:10 [b]Rom. 13:1 2:3 [a]Rom. 12:2 [b]2 Tim. 1:9 2:4 [a]Ezek. 18:23; Tit. 2:11 [b]John 17:3; 2 Tim. 2:25 2:5 [a]Gal. 3:20 [b]Heb. 9:15 2:6 [1]Or, a *testimony* [a]Mark 10:45 [b]1 Cor. 1:6; 2 Tim. 1:8 [c]Rom. 5:6; Eph. 1:9 2:7 [a]Eph. 3:7,8 [b]Rom. 9:1 [c]Gal. 1:16 2:8 [a]Luke 23:34

medial than punitive. For a similar situation see 1 Cor 5:5,13; see also note on 1 Cor 5:5.

2:2 *kings, and for all that are in authority.* See Jer 29:7. The notorious Roman emperor Nero (A.D. 54–68) was in power when Paul wrote these words. *godliness.* A key word (along with "godly") in the Pastorals, the Greek term occurs eight times in 1 Timothy (here; 3:16; 4:7–8; 6:3,5–6,11), once in 2 Timothy (3:5) and once in Titus (1:1), but nowhere else in the writings of Paul. It implies a good and holy life, with special emphasis on its source, a deep reverence for God.

2:4 *Who will have all men to be saved.* God desires the salvation of all people. On the other hand, the Bible indicates that God chooses some (not all) people to be saved (e.g., 1 Pet 1:2). Some interpreters understand such passages to teach that God has chosen those He, in His foreknowledge, knew would believe when confronted with the gospel and enabled to believe. Other interpreters hold that, though human reasoning cannot resolve the seeming inconsistency, the Bible teaches both truths and thus there can be no actual contradiction. Certainly there is none in the mind of God. See note on Rom 8:29.

2:5 *there is one God.* The basic belief of Judaism (Deut 6:4), which every Jew confessed daily in the Shema (see note on Mark 12:29).

2:6 *ransom.* See note on Mat 20:28. *to be testified.* The apostolic testimony that Christ gave Himself as the ransom. *due time.* See note on Gal 4:4.

2:7 *Whereunto.* To testify that, through His death, Christ has bridged the gap between God and man and made salvation available to all. *preacher.* One who with authority makes a public proclamation. *apostle.* See notes on Mark 6:30; 1 Cor 1:1.

Paul's Fourth Missionary Journey

C. A.D. 62–68

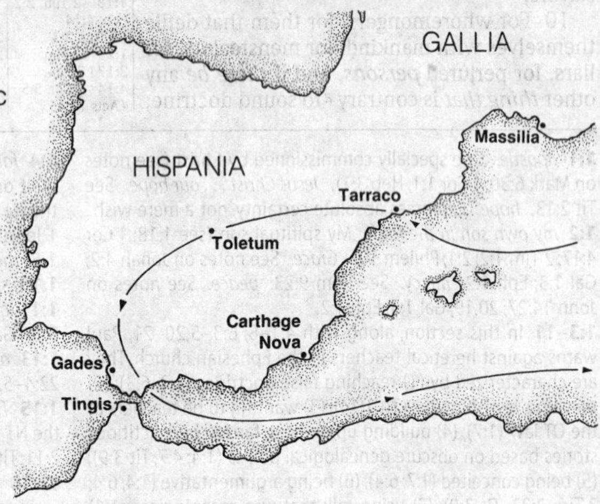

It is clear from Acts 13:1–21:17 that Paul went on three missionary journeys. There is also reason to believe that he made a fourth journey after his release from the Roman imprisonment recorded in Acts 28. The conclusion that such a journey did indeed take place is based on: (1) Paul's declared intention to go to Spain (Rom 15:24,28), (2) Eusebius's implication that Paul was released following his first Roman imprisonment (*Ecclesiastical History*, 2.22.2-3) and (3) statements in early Christian literature that he took the gospel as far as Spain (Clement of Rome, *Epistle to the Corinthians*, ch. 5; *Actus Petri Vercellenses*, chs. 1-3; Muratorian Canon, lines 34-39).

The places Paul may have visited after his release from prison are indicated by statements of intention in his earlier writings and by subsequent mention in the Pastoral Epistles. The order of his travel cannot be determined with certainty, but the itinerary at the right seems likely.

1. **Rome**—released from prison in A.D. 62
2. **Spain**—62-64 (Rom 15:24,28)
3. **Crete**—64-65 (Tit 1:5)
4. **Miletus**—65 (2 Tim 4:20)
5. **Colosse**—66 (Philem 22)
6. **Ephesus**—66 (1 Tim 1:3)
7. **Philippi**—66 (Phil 2:23-24; 1 Tim 1:3)
8. **Nicopolis**—66-67 (Tit 3:12)
9. **Rome**—67
10. Martyrdom—67/68

where, [b]lifting up holy hands, without wrath
and doubting.
9 In like manner also, that [a]women adorn
themselves in modest apparel, with shamefast-
ness and sobriety; not with [1]broided hair, or
gold, or pearls, or costly array;
10 [a]But (which becometh women professing godliness) with good works.
11 Let the woman learn in silence with all
subjection.
12 But [a]I suffer not a woman to teach, nor
to usurp authority over the man, but to be in
silence.
13 For [a]Adam was first formed, then Eve.
14 And [a]Adam was not deceived, but the
woman being deceived was in the transgression.
15 Notwithstanding she shall be saved in
childbearing, if they continue in faith and
charity and holiness with sobriety.

2:8 [b]Ps. 134:2
2:9 [1]Or, *plaited* [a]1 Pet. 3:3
2:10 [a]1 Pet. 3:4
2:12 [a]1 Cor. 14:34
2:13 [a]Gen. 1:27; 1 Cor. 11:8
2:14 [a]Gen. 3:6; 2 Cor. 11:3

‡2:8–14 Some maintain that Paul's teaching about women here is historically conditioned, not universal and timeless. Others view these verses as unaffected by the historical situation and therefore applicable to every age. See note on 1 Cor 11:2–16.
2:8 *men.* The Greek for this word does not refer to mankind (as in vv. 5–6) but to male as distinct from female. That women sometimes prayed in public, however, seems evident from 1 Cor 11:5.
2:9 Not a total ban on the wearing of jewelry or braided hair. Rather, Paul was expressing caution in a society where such things were signs of extravagant luxury and proud personal display.
2:10 See 1 Pet 3:3–4.
‡2:12 *I suffer not a woman to teach.* Paul did not allow a woman to be an official teacher in the assembled church. This is indicated by the added restriction concerning exercising "authority over a man" (see 1 Cor 11:3), i.e., functioning as a bishop (see note on 3:1).
‡2:13–14 Paul based the restrictions on Gen 2–3. The appeal to the creation account makes the restrictions universal and permanent: 1. *Adam was first formed.* Paul appeals to the priority of Adam in creation, which predates the fall. Thus he views the man-woman relationship set forth in this passage as grounded in creation. 2. *the woman being deceived.* Paul appears to argue that since the woman was deceived (and then led Adam astray), she is not to be entrusted with the teaching function of a bishop (or elder) in the public worship services of the assembled church.
‡2:15 Three possible meanings of this verse are: (1) It speaks of the godly woman finding fulfillment in her role as wife and mother in the home when her children are disciplined in godliness; (2) it refers to women being saved spiritually through the most significant birth of all, the incarnation of Christ; or (3) it refers to women being kept physically safe in childbirth.

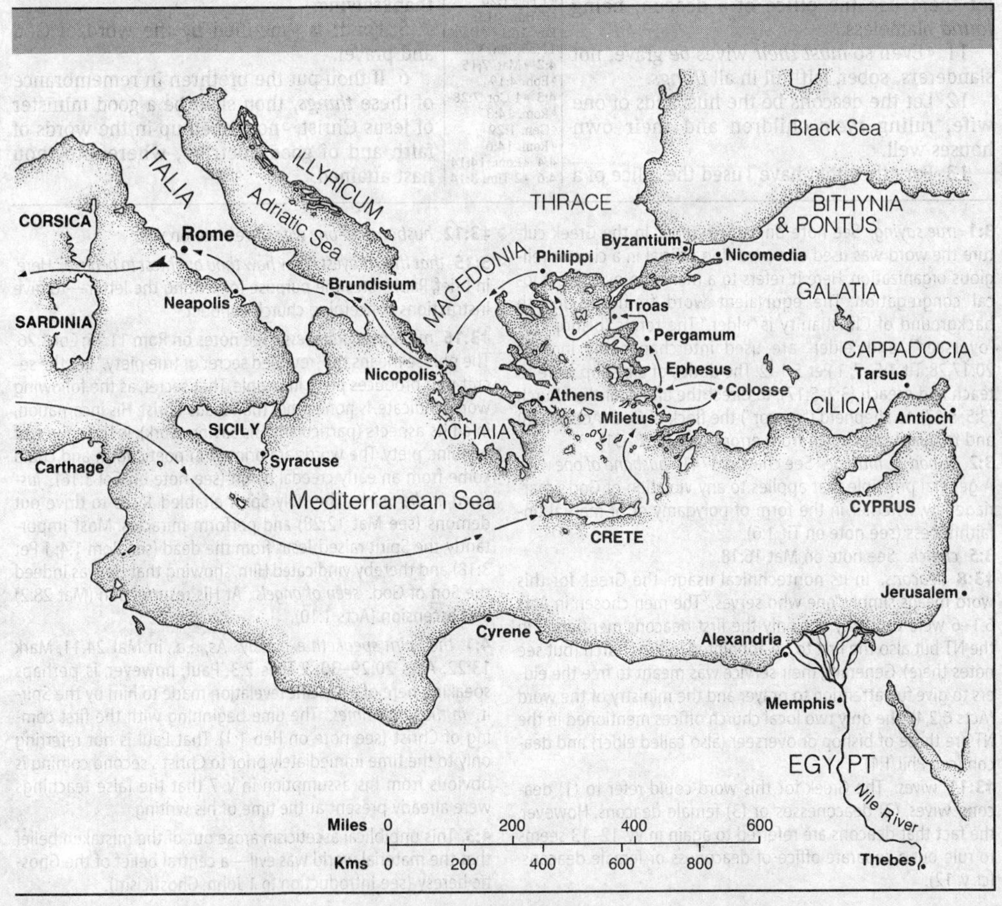

Bishops and deacons

3 *This is* a true saying, If a man desire the office of a bishop, he desireth a good work.

2 [a]A bishop then must be blameless, the husband of one wife, vigilant, sober, [1]of good behaviour, given to hospitality, [b]apt to teach;

3 [1]Not given to wine, [a]no striker, [b]not greedy of filthy lucre; but patient, not a brawler, not covetous;

4 One that ruleth well his own house, [a]having *his* children in subjection with all gravity;

5 (For if a man know not how to rule his own house, how shall he take care of the church of God?)

6 Not [1]a novice, lest being lifted up with pride he fall into the condemnation of the devil.

7 Moreover he must have a good report [a]of them which are without; lest he fall into reproach [b]and the snare of the devil.

8 Likewise *must* [a]the deacons *be* grave, not doubletongued, [b]not given to much wine, not greedy of filthy lucre;

9 [a]Holding the mystery of the faith in a pure conscience.

10 And let these also first be proved; then let them use the office of a deacon, being *found* blameless.

11 [a]Even so *must their* wives *be* grave, not slanderers, sober, faithful in all *things.*

12 Let the deacons be the husbands of one wife, ruling *their* children and their own houses well.

13 For [a]they that have [1]used the office of a deacon well purchase to themselves a good degree, and great boldness in the faith which is in Christ Jesus.

14 ¶ These *things* write I unto thee, hoping to come unto thee shortly:

15 But if I tarry long, that thou mayest know how *thou* oughtest to behave thyself [a]in the house of God, which is the church of the living God, the pillar and [1]ground of the truth.

16 And without controversy great is the mystery of godliness: [a]God was [1]manifest in the flesh, [b]justified in the Spirit, [c]seen of angels, [d]preached unto the Gentiles, [e]believed on in the world, [f]received up into glory.

Instructions for godly living

4 Now the Spirit [a]speaketh expressly, that [b]in the latter times some shall depart from the faith, giving heed [c]to seducing spirits, [d]and doctrines of devils;

2 [a]Speaking lies in hypocrisy, [b]having their conscience seared with a hot iron;

3 [a]Forbidding to marry, [b]*and commanding* to abstain from meats, which God hath created [c]to be received [d]with thanksgiving of them which believe and know the truth.

4 For [a]every creature of God *is* good, and nothing to be refused, if it be received with thanksgiving:

5 For it is sanctified by the word of God and prayer.

6 If thou put the brethren in remembrance of these *things,* thou shalt be a good minister of Jesus Christ, [a]nourished up in the words of faith and of good doctrine, whereunto thou hast attained.

3:2 [1] Or, *modest* [a] Tit. 1:6 [b] 2 Tim. 2:24
3:3 [1] Or, *Not ready to quarrel, and offer wrong, as one in wine* [a] 2 Tim. 2:24 [b] 1 Pet. 5:2
3:4 [a] Tit. 1:6
3:6 [1] Or, *one newly come to the faith*
3:7 [a] Acts 22:12; 1 Cor. 5:12 [b] 2 Tim. 2:26
3:8 [a] Acts 6:3 [b] Ezek. 44:21
3:9 [a] ch. 1:19
3:11 [a] Tit. 2:3
3:13 [1] Or, *ministered* [a] Mat. 25:21
3:15 [1] Or, *stay* [a] Eph. 2:21; 2 Tim. 2:20
3:16 [1] [Gr. *manifested*] [a] John 1:14; 1 John 1:2 [b] Mat. 3:16; Rom. 1:4 [c] Mat. 28:2; Mark 16:5 [d] Acts 10:34; Rom. 10:18 [e] Col. 1:6,23 [f] Luke 24:51
4:1 [a] John 16:13; 2 Thes. 2:3; 2 Tim. 3:1 [b] 1 Pet. 1:20 [c] 2 Tim. 3:13; Rev. 16:14 [d] Dan. 11:35; Rev. 9:20
4:2 [a] Mat. 7:15 [b] Eph. 4:19
4:3 [a] 1 Cor. 7:28 [b] Rom. 14:3 [c] Gen. 1:29 [d] Rom. 14:6
4:4 [a] Rom. 14:14
4:6 [a] 2 Tim. 3:14

3:1 *true saying.* See note on 1:15. *bishop.* In the Greek culture the word was used of a presiding official in a civic or religious organization. Here it refers to a man who oversees a local congregation. The equivalent word from the Jewish background of Christianity is "elder." The terms "bishop" (or "overseer") and "elder" are used interchangeably in Acts 20:17,28; Tit 1:5–7; 1 Pet 5:1–2. The duties of a bishop were to teach and preach (3:2; 5:17), to direct the affairs of the church (3:5; 5:17), to shepherd ("pastor") the flock of God (Acts 20:28) and to guard the church from error (Acts 20:28–31).

3:2 *bishop . . . must be.* See chart, p. 1741. *husband of one wife.* A general principle that applies to any violation of God's marriage law, whether in the form of polygamy or of marital unfaithfulness (see note on Tit 1:6).

3:5 *church.* See note on Mat 16:18.

‡3:8 *deacons.* In its nontechnical usage, the Greek for this word means simply "one who serves." The men chosen in Acts 6:1–6 were probably not only the first deacons mentioned in the NT but also the first to be appointed in the church (but see notes there). Generally, their service was meant to free the elders to give full attention to prayer and the ministry of the word (Acts 6:2,4). The only two local church offices mentioned in the NT are those of bishop or overseer (also called elder) and deacon (see Phil 1:1).

‡3:11 *wives.* The Greek for this word could refer to (1) deacons' wives, (2) deaconesses or (3) female deacons. However, the fact that deacons are referred to again in vv. 12–13 seems to rule out a separate office of deaconess or female deacons. (cf. v. 12).

‡3:12 *husbands of one wife.* See note on v. 2.

3:15 *that thou mayest know how thou oughtest to behave.* Here, in brief, Paul states the purpose for writing the letter—to give instructions concerning church conduct.

‡3:16 *mystery of godliness.* See notes on Rom 11:25; Col 1:26. The phrase means the "revealed secret of true piety," i.e., the secret that produces piety in people. That secret, as the following words indicate, is none other than Jesus Christ. His incarnation, in all its aspects (particularly His saving work), is the source of genuine piety. The words are printed in poetic form and could come from an early creedal hymn (see note on Col 3:16). *justified in the Spirit.* The Holy Spirit enabled Jesus to drive out demons (see Mat 12:28) and perform miracles. Most importantly, the Spirit raised Jesus from the dead (see Rom 1:4; 1 Pet 3:18) and thereby vindicated Him, showing that He was indeed the Son of God. *seen of angels.* At His resurrection (Mat 28:2) and ascension (Acts 1:10).

4:1 *the Spirit speaketh expressly.* As, e.g., in Mat 24:11; Mark 13:22; Acts 20:29–30; 2 Thes 2:3. Paul, however, is perhaps speaking here of a specific revelation made to him by the Spirit. *in the latter times.* The time beginning with the first coming of Christ (see note on Heb 1:1). That Paul is not referring only to the time immediately prior to Christ's second coming is obvious from his assumption in v. 7 that the false teachings were already present at the time of his writing.

4:3 This unbiblical asceticism arose out of the mistaken belief that the material world was evil—a central belief of the Gnostic heresy (see Introduction to 1 John: Gnosticism).

7 But [a]refuse profane and old wives' fables,
and [b]exercise thyself *rather* unto godliness.
8 For [a]bodily exercise profiteth [1]little: [b]but
godliness is profitable unto all *things,* [c]having
promise of the life that now is, and of that
which is to come.
9 *This is* a faithful saying and worthy of all
acceptation.
10 For therefore [a]we both labour and suffer reproach, because we trust in the living
God, [b]who is the Saviour of all men, specially
of those that believe.
11 These *things* command and teach.
12 ¶ Let no *man* despise thy youth; but [a]be
thou an example of the believers, in word, in
conversation, in charity, in spirit, in faith, in
purity.
13 Till I come, give attendance to reading,
to exhortation, to doctrine.
14 [a]Neglect not the gift that is in thee,
which was given thee [b]by prophecy, [c]with the
laying on of the hands of the presbytery.
15 Meditate upon these *things;* give thyself
wholly to them; that thy profiting may appear
[1]to all.
16 [a]Take heed unto thyself, and unto the
doctrine; continue in them: for in doing this
thou shalt both [b]save thyself, and them that
hear thee.

Pastoral duties

5 Rebuke [a]not an elder, but intreat *him* as a
father; *and* the younger *men* as brethren;
2 The elder *women* as mothers; the
younger as sisters, with all purity.
3 Honour widows that are widows indeed.
4 But if any widow have children or
nephews, let them learn first to shew [1]piety at
home, and [a]to requite *their* parents: for that is
good and acceptable before God.

4:7 [a]2 Tim. 2:16; Tit. 1:14 [b]Heb. 5:14
4:8 [1]Or, *for a little time* [a]1 Cor. 8:8 [b]ch. 6:6 [c]Ps. 37:4
4:10 [a]1 Cor. 4:11 [b]Ps. 36:6
4:12 [a]Tit. 2:7
4:14 [a]2 Tim. 1:6
4:14 [b]ch. 1:18 [c]Acts 6:6
4:15 [1]Or, *in all things*
4:16 [a]Acts 20:28 [b]Ezek. 33:9
5:1 [a]Lev. 19:32
5:4 [1]Or, *kindness* [a]Gen. 45:10; Mat. 15:4; Eph. 6:1,2

4:7 *fables.* See note on 1:4. *excercise thyself rather unto godliness.* See note on 2:2. Godliness requires self-discipline.

‡4:8 *bodily exercise.* Paul is not speaking here of keeping in good physical condition. He is speaking of religious exercises, such as asceticism—not marrying, and not eating meat (see v. 3).

‡4:9 *faithful saying.* See note on 1:15. It is possible that the expression in this instance refers back to the seemingly proverbial statement in v. 8. The words "labour and suffer reproach" in v. 10 may refer to the excercising mentioned in vv. 7b–8.

4:10 *trust.* See note on 1:1. *Saviour of all.* Obviously this does not mean that God saves every person from eternal punishment, for such universalism would contradict the clear testimony of Scripture. God is, however, the Savior of all in that He offers salvation to all and saves all who come to him.

4:12 *thy youth.* Timothy was probably in his mid–30s or younger, and in that day, such an influential position was not usually held by a man so young. For this reason, perhaps his leadership had been called into question.

4:13 *Till I come.* Paul's journey had taken him from Ephesus to Macedonia (see map, pp. 1738–1739), but he hoped to rejoin Timothy soon at Ephesus (3:14).

4:14 *prophecy.* See note on 1:18.

‡4:16 *thou shalt both save thyself, and them that hear thee.* God alone saves, but Christians can be God's instruments to bring about the salvation of others. *save thyself.* Salvation is both an event and a process. We are saved at the time of conversion but are still being saved in the sense of being made more conformed to Christ's image (1 Cor 1:18) and ultimately glorified.

‡5:3 *Honour widows that are widows indeed.* That is, widows who are truly left alone and destitute (see vv. 4 and 5). This probably means taking care of them, including the giving of material support. Widows were particularly vulnerable in ancient so-

Qualifications for Elders/Bishops and Deacons

Qualification	Office	Reference
Self-controlled	ELDER	1 Tim 3:2; Tit 1:8
Hospitable	ELDER	1 Tim 3:2; Tit 1:8
Able to teach	ELDER	1 Tim 3:2; 5:17; Tit 1:9
Not violent but gentle	ELDER	1 Tim 3:3; Tit 1:7
Not quarrelsome	ELDER	1 Tim 3:3
Not a lover of money	ELDER	1 Tim 3:3
Not a recent convert	ELDER	1 Tim 3:6
Has a good reputation with outsiders	ELDER	1 Tim 3:7
Not overbearing	ELDER	Tit 1:7
Not quick-tempered	ELDER	Tit 1:7
Loves what is good	ELDER	Tit 1:8
Upright, holy	ELDER	Tit 1:8
Disciplined	ELDER	Tit 1:8
Above reproach (blameless)	ELDER DEACON	1 Tim 3:2; Tit 1:6 1 Tim 3:9
Husband of one wife	ELDER DEACON	1 Tim 3:2; Tit 1:6 1 Tim 3:12
Temperate	ELDER DEACON	1 Tim 3:2; Tit 1:7 1 Tim 3:8
Respectable	ELDER DEACON	1 Tim 3:2 1 Tim 3:8
Not given to drunkenness	ELDER DEACON	1 Tim 3:3; Tit 1:7 1 Tim 3:8
Manages his own family well	ELDER DEACON	1 Tim 3:4 1 Tim 3:12
Sees that his children obey him	ELDER DEACON	1 Tim 3:4-5; Tit 1:6 1 Tim 3:12
Does not pursue dishonest gain	ELDER DEACON	Tit 1:7 1Ti 3:8
Holds to the truth	ELDER DEACON	Tit 1:9 1 Tim 3:9
Sincere	DEACON	1 Tim 3:8
Tested	DEACON	1 Tim 3:10

5 [a]Now she that is a widow indeed, and
desolate, trusteth in God, and [b]continueth in
supplications and prayers [c]night and day.
6 [a]But she that liveth [1]in pleasure is dead
while she liveth.
7 And these *things* give in charge, that
they may be blameless.
8 But if any provide not for his own, [a]and
specially for those of his own [1]house, [b]he hath
denied the faith, [c]and is worse than an infidel.
9 Let not a widow be [1]taken into the number under threescore years old, having been
the wife of one man,
10 Well reported of for good works; if she
have brought up children, if she have [a]lodged
strangers, if she have [b]washed the saints' feet,
if she have relieved the afflicted, if she have
diligently followed every good work.
11 But the younger widows refuse: for
when they have *begun to* wax wanton against
Christ, they will marry;
12 Having damnation, because they have
cast off *their* first faith.
13 [a]And withal they learn *to be* idle, wandering about from house to house; and not
only idle, but tattlers also and busybodies,
speaking *things* which they ought not.
14 [a]I will therefore that the younger
women marry, bear children, guide the house,
[b]give none occasion to the adversary [1]to speak
reproachfully.
15 For some are already turned aside after
Satan.
16 If any man or woman that believeth
have widows, let them relieve them, and let
not the church be charged; that it may relieve
[a]them that are widows indeed.
17 ¶ [a]Let the elders that rule well [b]be
counted worthy of double honour, especially
they who labour in the word and doctrine.

5:5 [a]1 Cor. 7:32 [b]Luke 2:37 [c]Acts 26:7
5:6 [1]Or, *delicately* [a]Jas. 5:5
5:8 [1]Or, *kindred* [a]Is. 58:7; Gal. 6:10 [b]2 Tim. 3:5; Tit. 1:16 [c]Mat. 18:17
5:9 [1]Or, *chosen*
5:10 [a]Acts 16:15; Heb. 13:2; 1 Pet. 4:9 [b]Gen. 19:2
5:13 [a]2 Thes. 3:11
5:14 [1]Gr. *for their railing* [a]1 Cor. 7:9 [b]Tit. 2:8
5:16 [a]ver. 3,5
5:17 [a]Phil. 2:29 [b]Acts 28:10
5:18 [a]Deut. 25:4; 1 Cor. 9:9 [b]Lev. 19:13; Deut. 24:14; Mat. 10:10
5:19 [1]Or, *under* [a]Deut. 19:15
5:20 [a]Tit. 1:13 [b]Deut. 13:11
5:21 [1]Or, *without prejudice* [a]ch. 6:13; 2 Tim. 2:14
5:22 [a]Acts 6:6; 2 Tim. 1:6 [b]2 John 11
5:23 [a]Ps. 104:15
5:24 [a]Gal. 5:19
6:1 [a]Eph. 6:5; Col. 3:22; Tit. 2:9; 1 Pet. 2:18 [b]Is. 52:5; Rom. 2:24; Tit. 2:5,8
6:2 [1]Or, *believing* [a]Col. 4:1
6:3 [a]2 Tim. 1:13; Tit. 1:9 [b]Tit. 1:1
6:4 [1]Or, *a fool* [2]Or, *sick* [a]1 Cor. 8:2

18 For the scripture saith, [a]Thou shalt not
muzzle the ox that treadeth out the corn. And,
[b]The labourer *is* worthy of his reward.
19 Against an elder receive not an accusation, but [a][1]before two or three witnesses.
20 [a]Them that sin rebuke before all, [b]that
others also may fear.
21 [a]I charge *thee* before God, and the Lord
Jesus Christ, and the elect angels, that thou
observe these *things* [1]without preferring *one
before another,* doing nothing by partiality.
22 [a]Lay hands suddenly on no *man,* [b]neither be partaker of other *men's* sins: keep thyself pure.
23 Drink no longer water, but use a little
wine [a]for thy stomach's sake and thine often
infirmities.
24 [a]Some men's sins are open beforehand,
going before to judgment; and some *men* they
follow after.
25 Likewise also the good works *of some*
are manifest beforehand; and they that are
otherwise cannot be hid.

6 Let as many [a]servants as are under the
yoke count their own masters worthy of
all honour, [b]that the name of God and *his* doctrine be not blasphemed.
2 And they that have believing masters, let
them not despise *them,* [a]because they are
brethren; but rather do *them* service, because
they are [1]faithful and beloved, partakers of the
benefit. These *things* teach and exhort.

The use of wealth

3 If any *man* teach otherwise, and consent
[a]not to wholesome words, *even* the *words* of
our Lord Jesus Christ, [b]and to the doctrine
which is according to godliness;
4 He is [1]proud, [a]knowing nothing, but
[2]doting about questions and strifes of words,

cieties because no pensions, government assistance, life insurance, or the like were available to them.

5:6 *dead while she liveth.* Dead spiritually while living physically.

5:9 *taken into the number.* The church in Ephesus seems to have maintained a list of widows supported by the church. While there is no evidence of an order of widows comparable to that of the bishops, it appears that those on the list were expected to devote themselves to prayer (v. 5) and good deeds (v. 10).

5:10 *washed the saints' feet.* A menial task, but necessary because of dusty roads and the wearing of sandals (see John 13:14).

5:12 *cast off their first faith.* Perhaps when a widow was added to the list she pledged special devotion to Christ, which would be diminished by remarriage. Or Paul may be referring to the believer's basic trust in Christ, which a widow would compromise by marrying outside the faith.

5:15 *Satan.* See notes on Zech 3:1; Mat 16:23; Rev 12:10.

‡5:17 All elders were to exercise leadership (3:4–5) and to teach and preach (3:2), and all were to receive honor. But those who excelled in leadership were to be counted worthy of double honor. This was especially true of those who labored at teaching and preaching. That such honor should include financial support is indicated by the two illustrations in v. 18.

5:18 *scripture.* The use of this term for both an OT (Deut 25:4) and a NT (Luke 10:7) passage shows that by this time portions of the NT (or what ultimately became a part of the NT) were considered to be equal in authority to the OT Scriptures.

5:20 *Them that sin.* The context indicates that Paul is speaking of the discipline of elders.

5:21 *elect angels.* Elect angels, in contrast to Satan and the other fallen angels.

5:22 *Lay hands suddenly on no man.* Paul is speaking of the ordination of an elder, which should not be performed until the candidate has had time to prove himself. *neither be partaker of other men's sins.* Do not ordain a person unworthy of the office of elder. *keep thyself pure.* Probably refers to refusal to become involved in the ordination of an unworthy man.

5:23 *Drink no longer water.* A parenthetical comment in Paul's discussion of elders. In view of Timothy's physical ailments, and perhaps because safe drinking water was often difficult to find, Paul advised him to drink a little wine.

5:24–25 *Some men's sins . . . good works.* Paul advises being alert to hidden sins as well as to good deeds in the lives of candidates for ordination.

6:1 *servants.* See notes on Eph 6:5; Col 3:22–4:1.

6:2 *These things teach and exhort.* Refers to the instructions to slaves.

6:3–5 Paul returns to the subject of 1:3. See note on 1:3–11.

whereof cometh envy, strife, railings, evil surmisings,

5 [a][1]Perverse disputings of men of corrupt minds, and destitute of the truth, [b]supposing that gain is godliness: [c]from such withdraw thyself.

6 But [a]godliness with contentment is great gain.

7 For [a]we brought nothing into *this* world, *and it is* certain we can carry nothing out.

8 And [a]having food and raiment let us be therewith content.

9 But [a]they that will be rich fall into temptation and a snare, and *into* many foolish and hurtful lusts, [b]which drown men in destruction and perdition.

10 [a]For the love of money is the root of all evil: which while some coveted after, they have [1]erred from the faith, and pierced themselves through with many sorrows.

The good fight of faith

11 [a]But thou, [b]O man of God, flee these *things;* and follow *after* righteousness, godliness, faith, love, patience, meekness.

12 [a]Fight the good fight of faith, [b]lay hold on eternal life, whereunto thou art also called, [c]and hast professed a good profession before many witnesses.

13 [a]I give thee charge in the sight of God, [b]who quickeneth all *things,* and *before* Christ Jesus, [c]who before Pontius Pilate witnessed a good [1]confession;

6:5 [1]Or, *Gallings one of another* [a]1 Cor. 11:16 [b]2 Pet. 2:3 [c]Rom. 16:17
6:6 [a]Ps. 37:16; Heb. 13:5
6:7 [a]Job 1:21
6:8 [a]Gen. 28:20; Heb. 13:5
6:9 [a]Prov. 15:27 [b]ch. 1:19
6:10 [1]Or, *been seduced* [a]Deut. 16:19
6:11 [a]2 Tim. 2:22 [b]Deut. 33:1
6:12 [a]ch. 1:18 [b]Phil. 3:12 [c]Heb. 13:23
6:13 [1]Or, *profession* [a]ch. 5:21 [b]1 Sam. 2:6 [c]John 18:37
6:14 [a]Phil. 1:6
6:15 [a]ch. 1:11,17
6:16 [a]John 6:46 [b]Eph. 3:21
6:17 [1]Gr. *uncertainty of riches* [a]Luke 12:21 [b]Prov. 23:5 [c]1 Thes. 1:9 [d]Acts 14:17
6:18 [1]Or, *sociable* [a]Jas. 2:5 [b]Rom. 12:13 [c]Gal. 6:6
6:19 [a]Mat. 6:20
6:20 [a]2 Tim. 1:14 [b]Tit. 1:14
6:21 [a]2 Tim. 2:18

14 That thou keep *this* commandment without spot, unrebukeable, [a]until the appearing of our Lord Jesus Christ:

15 Which in his times he shall shew, *who is* [a]the blessed and only Potentate, the King of kings, and Lord of lords;

16 Who only hath immortality, dwelling in the light which no *man* can approach unto; [a]whom no man hath seen, nor can see: [b]to whom *be* honour and power everlasting. Amen.

Final charge and benediction

17 ¶ Charge *them that are* rich in this world, that *they* be not highminded, [a]nor trust in [b][1]uncertain riches, but in [c]the living God, [d]who giveth us richly all *things* to enjoy;

18 That *they* do good, that [a]*they* be rich in good works, [b]ready to distribute, [c][1]willing to communicate;

19 [a]Laying up in store for themselves a good foundation against the time to come, that they may lay hold on eternal life.

20 O Timothy, [a]keep that which is committed to *thy* trust, [b]avoiding profane *and* vain babblings, and oppositions of science falsely so called:

21 Which some professing [a]have erred concerning the faith. Grace *be* with thee. Amen.

¶ The first to Timothy was written from Laodicea, which is the chiefest city of Phrygia Pacatiana.

6:5 *destitute of the truth.* They had once known the truth but had been led into error. *supposing that gain is godliness.* See note on 2 Cor 11:7.
6:11 *godliness.* See note on 2:2.
6:12 *lay hold on eternal life.* Timothy had possessed eternal life since he had first been saved, but Paul urges him to claim its benefits in greater fullness (see vv. 17–19 and note on 4:16). *professed a good profession.* Probably a reference to Timothy's confession of faith at his baptism during Paul's first missionary journey.
6:13 *before Pontius Pilate witnessed a good confession.* Probably a reference to Jesus' statements recorded in John 18:33–37; 19:10–11.
6:14 *this commandment.* Perhaps the whole charge given to Timothy to preach the gospel and care for the church (see v. 20)—though the preceding context may indicate that Paul used the singular "commandment" to sum up the various commands listed in vv. 11–12.
6:15 *in his times.* Just as Jesus' first coming occurred at the precise time God wanted (Gal 4:4), so also His second coming will be at God's appointed time. *King of kings, and Lord of lords.* See Rev 19:16.
6:16 *whom no man hath seen, nor can see.* See note on John 1:18.
6:19 *lay hold on eternal life.* See note on v. 12.
‡6:20 *that which is committed to thy trust.* The gospel. The same command is found in 2 Tim 1:14. *science falsely so called.* The Greek word translated "science" is normally translated "knowledge." This is a reference to an early form of the heresy of Gnosticism, which taught that one may be saved by knowledge. (The term "Gnosticism" comes from this Greek word for knowledge; see Introduction to 1 John: Gnosticism.)

The Second Epistle of Paul the Apostle to Timothy

INTRODUCTION

See "The Pastoral Epistles," p. 1734.

Author, Date and Setting

After Paul's release from prison in Rome in A.D. 62/63 (Acts 28) and after his fourth missionary journey (see map, pp. 1738–1739), during which he wrote 1 Timothy and Titus, Paul was again imprisoned under Emperor Nero c. 66–67. It was during this time that he wrote 2 Timothy. In contrast to his first imprisonment, when he lived in a rented house (Acts 28:30), he now languished in a cold dungeon (4:13), chained like a common criminal (1:16; 2:9). His friends even had a hard time finding out where he was being kept (1:17). Paul knew that his work was done and his life was nearly at an end (4:6–8).

Reasons for Writing

Paul had three reasons for writing to Timothy at this time:

1. He was lonely. Phygellus and Hermogenes, "all they which are in Asia" (1:15), and Demas (4:10) had deserted him. Crescens, Titus and Tychicus were away (4:10–12), and only Luke was with him (4:11). Paul wanted very much for Timothy to join him also. Timothy was his fellow worker (Rom 16:21), who "as a son with the father" had served closely with Paul (Phil 2:22; see 1 Cor 4:17). Of him Paul could say, "I have no man likeminded" (Phil 2:20). Paul longed for Timothy (1:4) and twice asked him to come soon (4:9,21). For more information on Timothy see Introduction to 1 Timothy: Recipient.

2. Paul was concerned about the welfare of the churches during this time of persecution under Nero, and he admonishes Timothy to guard the gospel (1:14), to persevere in it (3:14), to keep on preaching it (4:2) and, if necessary, to suffer for it (1:8; 2:3).

3. He wanted to write to the Ephesian church through Timothy (see note on 4:22).

Outline

- I. Introduction (1:1–4)
- II. Paul's Concern for Timothy (1:5–14)
- III. Paul's Situation (1:15–18)
- IV. Special Instructions to Timothy (ch. 2)
  - A. Call for Endurance (2:1–13)
  - B. Warning about Foolish Controversies (2:14–26)
- V. Warning about the Last Days (ch. 3)
  - A. Terrible Times (3:1–9)
  - B. Means of Combating Them (3:10–17)
- VI. Paul's Departing Remarks (4:1–8)
  - A. Charge to Preach the Word (4:1–5)
  - B. Paul's Victorious Prospect (4:6–8)
- VII. Final Requests and Greetings (4:9–22)

1 Paul, [a]an apostle of Jesus Christ by the
will of God, according to [b]the promise of
life which is in Christ Jesus,
2 [a]To Timothy, *my* dearly beloved son:
Grace, mercy, *and* peace, from God the Father
and Christ Jesus our Lord.

Appeal for faithfulness

3 ¶ [a]I thank God, [b]whom I serve from *my*
forefathers with pure conscience, that [c]with-
out ceasing I have remembrance of thee in my
prayers night and day;
4 [a]Greatly desiring to see thee, being
mindful of thy tears, that I may be filled with
joy;
5 When I call to remembrance [a]the unfeigned faith that is in thee, which dwelt first
in thy grandmother Lois, and [b]thy mother Eunice; and I am persuaded that in thee also.
6 Wherefore I put thee in remembrance
[a]that *thou* stir up the gift of God, which is in
thee by the putting on of my hands.
7 For [a]God hath not given us the spirit of
fear; [b]but of power, and of love, and of a sound
mind.
8 [a]Be not thou therefore ashamed of [b]the
testimony of our Lord, nor of me [c]his prisoner:
[d]but be thou partaker of the afflictions of the
gospel according to the power of God;
9 [a]Who hath saved us, and [b]called *us* with
a holy calling, [c]not according to our works, but
[d]according to his own purpose and grace,
which was given us in Christ Jesus [e]before the
world began,
10 But [a]is now made manifest by the appearing of our Saviour Jesus Christ, [b]who hath
abolished death, and hath brought life and immortality to light through the gospel:
11 [a]Whereunto I am appointed a preacher,
and an apostle, and a teacher of the Gentiles.
12 [a]For the which cause I also suffer these
things: nevertheless I am not ashamed: [b]for I
know whom I have [1]believed, and I am persuaded that he is able to [c]keep that which I
have committed unto *him* against that day.
13 [a]Hold fast [b]the form of [c]sound words,
which thou hast heard of me, [d]in faith and
love which is in Christ Jesus.
14 *That* good thing which was committed
unto *thee* keep by the Holy Ghost [a]which
dwelleth in us.
15 This thou knowest, that [a]all they which
are in Asia be turned away from me; of whom
are Phygellus and Hermogenes.
16 The Lord [a]give mercy unto the house of
Onesiphorus; [b]for he oft refreshed me, and
was not ashamed of [c]my chain:
17 But, when he was in Rome, he sought
me out very diligently, and found *me.*
18 The Lord grant unto him that *he* may
find mercy of the Lord [a]in that day: and in
how many *things* he [b]ministered *unto me* at
Ephesus, thou knowest very well.

2 Thou therefore, [a]my son, [b]be strong in
the grace that is in Christ Jesus.
2 And *the things* that thou hast heard of
me [1]among many witnesses, the same commit
thou to faithful men, who shall be able to
teach others also.
3 Thou therefore endure hardness, [a]as a
good soldier of Jesus Christ.
4 [a]No *man* that warreth entangleth himself

1:1 [a]2 Cor. 1:1 [b]Eph. 3:6; Heb. 9:15
1:2 [a]1 Tim. 1:2
1:3 [a]Rom. 1:8; Eph. 1:16 [b]Acts 22:3; Rom. 1:9 [c]1 Thes. 1:2
1:4 [a]ch. 4:9,21
1:5 [a]1 Tim. 1:5 [b]Acts 16:1
1:6 [a]1 Tim. 4:14
1:7 [a]Rom. 8:15 [b]Acts 1:8
1:8 [a]Rom. 1:16 [b]1 Tim. 2:6 [c]Eph. 3:1 [d]Col. 1:24
1:9 [a]1 Tim. 1:1 [b]Heb. 3:1 [c]Rom. 3:20 [d]Rom. 8:28 [e]Rom. 16:25
1:10 [a]Eph. 1:9 [b]1 Cor. 15:54
1:11 [a]Acts 9:15; 1 Tim. 2:7
1:12 [1]Or, *trusted* [a]Eph. 3:1 [b]1 Pet. 4:19 [c]1 Tim. 6:20
1:13 [a]Tit. 1:9; Heb. 10:23 [b]Rom. 2:20 [c]1 Tim. 6:3 [d]1 Tim. 1:14
1:14 [a]Rom. 8:11
1:15 [a]Acts 19:10
1:16 [a]Mat. 5:7 [b]Philem. 7 [c]Acts 28:20
1:18 [a]2 Thes. 1:10 [b]Heb. 6:10
2:1 [a]1 Tim. 1:2 [b]Eph. 6:10
2:2 [1]Or, *by*
2:3 [a]1 Tim. 1:18
2:4 [a]1 Cor. 9:25

1:1 *apostle.* One specially commissioned by Christ (see notes on Mark 6:30; 1 Cor 1:1; Heb 3:1). *according to the promise of life.* Paul's being chosen to be an apostle was in keeping with that promise because apostles were appointed to preach and explain the good news that eternal life is available to all who will receive it through faith in Christ.
1:2 *Timothy, my dearly beloved son.* See note on 1 Tim 1:2. *Grace . . . peace.* See notes on Jonah 4:2; John 14:27; 20:19; Gal 1:3; Eph 1:2.
1:3 *thank God . . . in my prayers.* See note on Phil 1:3–4.
1:4 *Greatly desiring to see thee.* See 4:9,21. *mindful of thy tears.* Probably refers to Timothy's tears when Paul left for Macedonia (1 Tim 1:3).
‡1:5 *thy grandmother Lois, and thy mother Eunice.* According to Acts 16:1, Timothy's mother was a Jewish Christian. Here we learn that his grandmother too was a Christian. Timothy's father, however, was a Greek and possibly an unbeliever (Acts 16:1). It was probably because of him that Timothy had not been circumcised as a child.
1:6 *stir up the gift of God.* Gifts are not given in full bloom; they need to be developed through use. *by the putting on of my hands.* Paul was God's instrument, through whom the gift came from the Holy Spirit to Timothy (see note on 1 Tim 1:18).
1:7 *God hath not given us the spirit of fear.* Apparently lack of confidence was a serious problem for Timothy (see 1 Cor 16:10–11; 1 Tim 4:12).
1:9 *not according to our works, but according to his own purpose and grace.* Salvation is by grace alone and is based not on human effort but on God's saving plan and the gracious gift of His Son (see Rom 3:28; Eph 2:8–9; Tit 3:5). *before the world began.* God's plan to save lost sinners was made in eternity past (see Eph 1:4; 1 Pet 1:20; Rev 13:8).
1:11 *preacher, and an apostle.* See note on 1 Tim 2:7.
1:12 *that day.* The day of judgment.
1:13 *sound words.* See note on Tit 1:9. *faith and love . . . in Christ.* Faith and love through union with Christ—another way of saying "Christian faith and love" (see 1 Tim 1:14).
1:14 *That good thing . . . committed unto thee.* The gospel. Paul gives the same command in 1 Tim 6:20.
1:15 *all.* Probably hyperbole, a deliberate exaggeration to express widespread desertion. *Asia.* Timothy was in Ephesus, the capital of the province of Asia, which is in western Turkey today. *Phygellus and Hermogenes.* Nothing more is known about these two people.
1:16 *Onesiphorus.* Probably he and his family lived in Ephesus (v. 18; 4:19).
1:17 *Rome.* See Introduction: Author, Date and Setting; see also v. 8; 2:9.
‡1:18 *that day.* The day of judgment. *ministered unto me at Ephesus.* Either on Paul's third missionary journey (Acts 19) or on his fourth (see map, pp. 1738–1739).
2:1 *my son.* See note on 1 Tim 1:2.
2:2 *among many witnesses.* Refers to Paul's preaching and teaching, which Timothy had heard repeatedly on all three missionary journeys and could be confirmed by many.
2:3–6 Paul gives three examples for Timothy to follow: (1) a soldier who wants to please his commander; (2) an athlete who follows the rules of the game; and (3) a farmer who works hard.

with the affairs of *this* life; that he may please him who hath chosen *him* to be a soldier.

5 And [a]if a man also strive for masteries, *yet* is he not crowned, except he strive lawfully.

6 [1]The husbandman that laboureth must be first partaker of the fruits.

7 Consider what I say; and the Lord give thee understanding in all *things.*

8 Remember that Jesus Christ [a]of the seed of David [b]*was* raised from the dead [c]according to my gospel:

9 [a]Wherein I suffer trouble, as an evil doer, [b]*even* unto bonds; [c]but the word of God is not bound.

10 Therefore [a]I endure all *things* for the elects' sakes, [b]that they may also obtain the salvation which is in Christ Jesus with eternal glory.

11 *It is* a faithful saying: For [a]if we be dead with *him,* we shall also live with *him:*

12 [a]If we suffer, we shall also reign with *him:* [b]if we deny *him,* he also will deny us:

13 [a]If we believe not, *yet* he abideth faithful: [b]he cannot deny himself.

A workman approved unto God

14 ¶ Of these *things* put *them* in remembrance, [a]charging *them* before the Lord that *they* strive not about words to no profit, *but* to the subverting of the hearers.

15 Study to shew thyself approved unto God, a workman that needeth not to be ashamed, rightly dividing the word of truth.

16 But [a]shun profane *and* vain babblings: for they will increase unto more ungodliness.

17 And their word will eat as *doth* a [1]canker: of whom is Hymeneus and Philetus;

18 Who concerning the truth have erred, [a]saying that the resurrection is past already; and overthrow the faith of some.

19 Nevertheless [a]the foundation of God standeth [1]sure, having this seal, The Lord [b]knoweth them that are his. And, Let every one that nameth the name of Christ depart from iniquity.

20 But in a great house there are not only vessels of gold and of silver, but also of wood and of earth; [a]and some to honour, and some to dishonour.

21 [a]If a man therefore purge himself from these, he shall be a vessel unto honour, sanctified, and meet for the master's use, *and* [b]prepared unto every good work.

22 Flee also youthful lusts: but follow righteousness, faith, charity, peace, with them that [a]call on the Lord [b]out of a pure heart.

23 But [a]foolish and unlearned questions avoid, knowing that they do gender strifes.

24 And [a]the servant of the Lord must not strive; but be gentle unto all *men,* [b]apt to teach, [1]patient,

25 [a]In meekness instructing those that oppose themselves; [b]if God peradventure will give them repentance [c]to the acknowledging of the truth;

26 And *that* they may [1]recover themselves [a]out of the snare of the devil, *who are* [2]taken captive by him at his will.

The coming apostasy

3 This know also, that [a]in the last days perilous times shall come.

2 For men shall be [a]lovers of their own selves, [b]covetous, [c]boasters, [d]proud, [e]blasphemers, [f]disobedient to parents, unthankful, unholy,

2:5 [a]1 Cor. 9:25
2:6 [1]Or, *The husbandman, labouring first, must be partaker of the fruits*
2:8 [a]Rom. 1:3,4 [b]1 Cor. 15:1 [c]Rom. 2:16
2:9 [a]Acts 9:16 [b]Eph. 3:1 [c]Acts 28:31; Eph. 6:19
2:10 [a]Eph. 3:13 [b]2 Cor. 1:6
2:11 [a]Rom. 6:5,8
2:12 [a]Rom. 8:17; 1 Pet. 4:13 [b]Mat. 10:33; Mark 8:38
2:13 [a]Rom. 3:3 [b]Num. 23:19
2:14 [a]1 Tim. 5:21
2:16 [a]1 Tim. 4:7
2:17 [1]Or, *gangrene*
2:18 [a]1 Cor. 15:12
2:19 [1]Or, *steady* [a]Mat. 24:24 [b]Nah. 1:7; John 10:14
2:20 [a]Rom. 9:21
2:21 [a]Is. 52:11 [b]ch. 3:17
2:22 [a]Acts 9:14; 1 Cor. 1:2 [b]1 Tim. 1:5
2:23 [a]1 Tim. 1:4
2:24 [1]Or, *forbearing* [a]Tit. 3:2 [b]Tit. 1:9
2:25 [a]Gal. 6:1; 1 Tim. 6:11 [b]Acts 8:22 [c]1 Tim. 2:4
2:26 [1]Gr. *awake* [2]Gr. *taken alive* [a]1 Tim. 3:7
3:1 [a]1 Tim. 4:1
3:2 [a]Phil. 2:21 [b]2 Pet. 2:3 [c]Jude 16 [d]1 Tim. 6:4 [e]1 Tim. 1:20 [f]Rom. 1:30

2:6 *partaker of the fruits.* In this illustration, as in the previous two (soldier, vv. 3–4; athlete, v. 5), the main lesson is that dedicated effort will be rewarded—not necessarily monetarily, but in enjoyment of seeing the gospel produce changed lives.
2:8 *seed of David was raised from the dead.* Christ's resurrection proclaims His deity, and His descent from David shows His humanity; both truths are basic to the gospel. Since Christ is God, His death has infinite value; since He is man, He could rightfully become our substitute.
2:9 *trouble, as an evil doer.* Apparently Paul was awaiting execution (see 4:6).
2:10 *I endure all things for the elects' sakes.* No suffering is too great if it brings about the salvation of God's chosen ones who will yet believe. *in Christ Jesus.* See note on 1:13. *eternal glory.* The final state of salvation.
2:11–13 Probably an early Christian hymn. The point to which Paul appeals is that suffering for Christ will be followed by glory.
2:11 *faithful saying.* See note on 1 Tim 1:15. *if we be dead with him, we shall also live with him.* The Greek grammatical construction here assumes that we died with Christ in the past, when He died for us on the cross. We are therefore assured that we will also live with Him eternally.
2:12 *If we suffer, we shall also reign.* Faithfully bearing up under suffering and trial will result in reward when Christ returns. *if we deny him.* See Mat 10:33.
2:14–18 The wording of vv. 14–16 indicates that the heresy mentioned here is an early form of Gnosticism—the same as that dealt with in 1 Timothy and Titus (see note on 1 Tim 1:3–11 and Introduction to 1 John: Gnosticism). Two leaders of this heresy, Hymenaeus (see 1 Tim 1:20) and Philetus, denied the bodily resurrection and probably asserted that there is only a spiritual resurrection (similar to the error mentioned in 1 Cor 15:12–19). Gnosticism interpreted the resurrection allegorically, not literally.
2:15 *Study.* See 4:9,21. *word of truth.* The gospel.
‡2:19 *foundation of God.* The church, which upholds the truth (1 Tim 3:15). In spite of the heresy of Hymenaeus and Philetus, Timothy should be heartened to know that the church is God's solid foundation. There are two seals on it: One stresses the security of the church ("The Lord knoweth them that are His"; here "know," as often in the Bible, means to be intimately acquainted with), while the other emphasizes human responsibility ("every one that nameth the name of Christ depart from iniquity"). *seal.* The church is owned and securely protected by God (see note on Eph 1:13).
2:22 *youthful.* See note on 1 Tim 4:12.
3:1 *last days.* The Messianic era, the time beginning with Christ's first coming (see notes on Acts 2:17; 1 Tim 4:1; Heb 1:1; 1 Pet 1:20; 1 John 2:18). That "the last days" in this passage does not refer only to the time just prior to Christ's return is apparent from Paul's command to Timothy to have nothing to do with the unbelieving and unfaithful people who characterize this time (v. 5).

3 [a]Without natural affection, [b]trucebreakers, [1]false accusers, [c]incontinent, fierce, despisers of *those that are* good,

4 [a]Traitors, heady, highminded, [b]lovers of pleasures more than lovers of God;

5 Having a form of godliness, but [a]denying the power thereof: [b]from such turn away.

6 For [a]of this sort are they which creep into houses, and lead captive silly women laden with sins, led away with divers lusts,

7 Ever learning, and never able [a]to come to the knowledge of the truth.

8 [a]Now as Jannes and Jambres withstood Moses, so do these also resist the truth: [b]men of corrupt minds, [c][1]reprobate concerning the faith.

9 But they shall proceed no further: for their folly shall be manifest unto all *men,* [a]as theirs also was.

The defence of the faith

10 [a]But [1]thou hast fully known my doctrine, manner of life, purpose, faith, longsuffering, charity, patience,

11 Persecutions, afflictions, which came unto me [a]at Antioch, [b]at Iconium, [c]at Lystra; what persecutions I endured: but [d]out of *them* all the Lord delivered me.

12 Yea, and [a]all that will live godly in Christ Jesus shall suffer persecution.

13 [a]But evil men and seducers shall wax worse and worse, deceiving, and being deceived.

14 But [a]continue thou in *the things* which thou hast learned and hast been assured of, knowing of whom thou hast learned *them;*

15 And that from a child thou hast known [a]the holy scriptures, which are able to make thee wise unto salvation through faith which is in Christ Jesus.

16 [a]All scripture *is* given by inspiration of God, [b]and *is* profitable for doctrine, for reproof, for correction, for instruction in righteousness:

17 [a]That the man of God may be perfect, [b][1]throughly furnished unto all good works.

4 [a]I charge *thee* therefore before God, and the Lord Jesus Christ, [b]who shall judge the quick and the dead at his appearing and his kingdom;

2 Preach the word; be instant in season, out of season; reprove, [a]rebuke, [b]exhort with all longsuffering and doctrine.

3 [a]For the time will come when they will not endure [b]sound doctrine; [c]but after their own lusts shall they heap to themselves teachers, having itching ears;

4 And they shall turn away *their* ears from the truth, and [a]shall be turned unto fables.

5 But watch thou in all *things,* [a]endure afflictions, do the work of [b]an evangelist, [c][1]make full proof of thy ministry.

6 For [a]I am now ready to be offered, and the time of [b]my departure is at hand.

7 [a]I have fought a good fight, I have finished *my* course, I have kept the faith:

8 Henceforth there is laid up for me [a]a crown of righteousness, which the Lord, the righteous judge, shall give me [b]at that day: and not to me only, but unto all them also that love his appearing.

3:3 [1]Or, *makebates* [a]Rom. 1:31 [b]Rom. 1:31 [c]2 Pet. 3:3
3:4 [a]2 Pet. 2:10 [b]Phil. 3:19
3:5 [a]1 Tim. 5:8 [b]1 Tim. 6:5
3:6 [a]Mat. 23:14; Tit. 1:11
3:7 [a]1 Tim. 2:4
3:8 [1]Or, *of no judgment* [a]Ex. 7:11 [b]1 Tim. 6:5 [c]Rom. 1:28
3:9 [a]Ex. 7:12
3:10 [1]Or, *thou hast been a diligent follower of* [a]1 Tim. 4:6
3:11 [a]Acts 13:45 [b]Acts 14:2 [c]Acts 14:19 [d]Ps. 34:19
3:12 [a]Ps. 34:19
3:13 [a]2 Thes. 2:11
3:14 [a]ch. 1:13
3:15 [a]John 5:39
3:16 [a]2 Pet. 1:20 [b]Rom. 15:4
3:17 [1]Or, *perfected* [a]1 Tim. 6:11 [b]ch. 2:21
4:1 [a]1 Tim. 5:21 [b]Acts 10:42
4:2 [a]1 Tim. 5:20; Tit. 1:13 [b]1 Tim. 4:13
4:3 [a]ch. 3:1 [b]1 Tim. 1:10 [c]ch. 3:6
4:4 [a]1 Tim. 1:4
4:5 [1]Or, *fulfil* [a]ch. 1:8 [b]Acts 21:8 [c]Rom. 15:19
4:6 [a]Phil. 2:17 [b]Phil. 1:23; 2 Pet. 1:14
4:7 [a]Phil. 3:14; Heb. 12:1
4:8 [a]Jas. 1:12 [b]ch. 1:12

3:6 *silly women.* Unstable women who are guilt-ridden because of their sins, torn by lust, and victims of various false teachers ("ever learning," v. 7, but never coming to a saving knowledge of Christ).

3:8 *Jannes and Jambres.* Neither of these men is mentioned in the OT, but according to Jewish tradition they were the Egyptian court magicians who opposed Moses (see Ex 7:11 and note).

3:11 *Antioch, at Iconium, at Lystra.* Three cities in the Roman province of Galatia, which Paul visited on his first and second missionary journeys (Acts 13:14–14:23; 16:1–6). Since Timothy was from Lystra, he would have known firsthand of Paul's sufferings in that region. *out of them all the Lord delivered me.* Even from execution by stoning (Acts 14:19–20).

3:12 A principle repeated elsewhere in the NT (see Mat 10:22; Acts 14:22; Phil 1:29; 1 Pet 4:12). *in Christ.* See note on 1:13.

3:14 *of whom thou hast learned them.* Perhaps a reference to Paul as well as to Timothy's mother and grandmother (1:5).

3:15 *from a child thou hast known the holy scriptures.* A Jewish boy formally began to study the OT when he was five years old. Timothy was taught at home by his mother and grandmother even before he reached this age.

3:16 *All scripture.* The primary reference is to the OT, since some of the NT books had not even been written at this time. (See 1 Tim 5:18; 2 Pet 3:15–16 for indications that some NT books—or material ultimately included in the NT—were already considered equal in authority to the OT Scriptures.) *inspiration of God.* Paul affirms God's active involvement in the writing of Scripture, an involvement so powerful and pervasive that what is written is the infallible and authoritative word of God (see 2 Pet 1:20–21 and notes).

4:1 *I charge thee.* Paul states his charge to Timothy, aware that he does so in the presence of God the Father and of Christ, who will judge all men. He is also keenly aware of the twin facts of Christ's return and the coming establishment of God's kingdom in its fullest expression. Timothy was to view a charge so given as of utmost importance.

4:2 *be instant.* Be ready in any situation to speak the needed word, whether of correction, of rebuke or of encouragement.

‡4:3 *sound doctrine.* See note on Tit 1:9. *having itching ears.* These hearers will have ears that want to be satisfied by words in keeping with their evil desires.

4:4 *fables.* See note on 1 Tim 1:4.

4:6 *be offered.* The offering of wine poured around the base of the altar (see Num 15:1–12; 28:7,24). Paul views his approaching death as the pouring out of his life as an offering to Christ (see Phil 2:17). *my departure.* His impending death (cf. Phil 1:23).

4:7 In this verse Paul looks back over 30 years of labor as an apostle (c. A.D. 36–66). Like an athlete who had engaged successfully in a contest ("fought a good fight"), he had "finished my course" and had "kept the faith," i.e., had carefully observed the rules (the teachings) of the Christian faith (see 2:5). Or, in view of the Pastorals' emphasis on sound doctrine, perhaps "the faith" refers to the deposit of Christian truth. Paul has kept (guarded) it.

4:8 *crown of righteousness.* Continuing with the same figure of speech, Paul uses the metaphor of the wreath given to the

Greetings and benediction

9 ¶ Do thy diligence to come shortly unto
me:
10 For [a]Demas hath forsaken me, [b]having
loved *this* present world, and is departed unto
Thessalonica; Crescens to Galatia, Titus unto
Dalmatia.
11 [a]Only [b]Luke is with me. Take [c]Mark,
and bring *him* with thee: for he is profitable to
me for the ministry.
12 And [a]Tychicus have I sent to Ephesus.
13 The cloke that I left at Troas with Carpus, when thou comest, bring *with thee,* and
the books, *but* especially the parchments.
14 [a]Alexander the coppersmith did me
much evil: [b]the Lord reward him according to
his works:
15 Of whom be thou ware also; for he hath
greatly withstood [1]our words.
16 At my first answer no *man* stood with
me, but all *men* forsook me: [a]*I pray God* that it
may not be laid to their charge.
17 [a]Notwithstanding the Lord stood with
me, and strengthened me; [b]that by me the
preaching might be fully known, and *that* all
the Gentiles might hear: and I was delivered
[c]out of the mouth of the lion.
18 [a]And the Lord shall deliver me from
every evil work, and will preserve *me* unto his
heavenly kingdom: [b]to whom *be* glory for ever
and ever. Amen.
19 ¶ Salute [a]Prisca and Aquila, and the
household of Onesiphorus.
20 [a]Erastus abode at Corinth: but [b]Trophi-
mus have I left at Miletum sick.
21 [a]Do thy diligence to come before winter. Eubulus greeteth thee, and Pudens, and
Linus, and Claudia, and all the brethren.
22 [a]The Lord Jesus Christ *be* with thy spirit. Grace *be* with you. Amen.

¶ The second *epistle* unto Timotheus, ordained the first bishop of the church of the Ephesians, was written from Rome, when Paul was brought before [1]Nero the second time.

4:10 [a]Col. 4:14 [b]1 John 2:15
4:11 [a]ch. 1:15 [b]Col. 4:14 [c]Acts 12:25
4:12 [a]Acts 20:4; Eph. 6:21
4:14 [a]Acts 19:33 [b]2 Sam. 3:39; Ps. 28:4
4:15 [1]Or, *our preachings*
4:16 [a]Acts 7:60
4:17 [a]Acts 23:11
4:17 [b]Acts 9:15 [c]Ps. 22:21
4:18 [a]Ps. 121:7 [b]Rom. 11:36; Gal. 1:5; Heb. 13:21
4:19 [a]Acts 18:2; Rom. 16:3
4:20 [a]Acts 19:22; Rom. 16:23 [b]Acts 20:4
4:21 [a]ver. 9
4:22 [1][Gr. *Cesar Nero,* or, *the emperor Nero*] [a]Gal. 6:18; Philem. 25

winner of a race (1 Cor 9:25). He could be referring to (1) a crown given as a reward for a righteous life, (2) a crown consisting of righteousness or (3) a crown given righteously (justly) by the righteous Judge. *that day.* The day of Christ's second coming ("appearing").

4:10 *Crescens.* Mentioned only here in the NT. *Galatia.* Either the northern area of Asia Minor (Gaul) or a Roman province in what is now central Turkey (see note on Gal 1:2). *Titus to Dalmatia.* See Introduction to Titus: Recipient. *Dalmatia.* Present-day Albania and a portion of Yugoslavia, also known in Scripture as Illyricum (Rom 15:19).

4:11 *Mark.* John Mark had deserted Paul and Barnabas on their first missionary journey (Acts 13:13). After Paul refused to take Mark on the second journey, Barnabas separated from Paul, taking Mark with him on a mission to Cyprus (Acts 15:36–41). Ultimately Mark proved himself to Paul, indicated by his presence with Paul during Paul's first Roman imprisonment (Col 4:10; Philem 24) and by Paul's request here for Timothy to bring Mark with him to Rome.

4:13 *cloke.* For protection against the cold dampness (see Introduction: Author, Date and Setting). It was probably a heavy, sleeveless, outer garment, circular in shape and with a hole in the middle for one's head. *Carpus.* Not mentioned elsewhere. *the books, but especially the parchments.* The books or scrolls (see note on Ex 17:14) were made of papyrus, and the parchments were made of the skins of animals. The latter may have been copies of parts of the OT.

4:14 *Alexander the coppersmith.* Possibly the Alexander mentioned in 1 Tim 1:20.

4:16 *my first answer.* The first court hearing of Paul's present case, not his defense on the occasion of his first imprisonment (Acts 28).

4:17 *that by me the preaching might be fully known.* Even in these dire circumstances Paul used the occasion to testify about Jesus Christ in the imperial court. *I was delivered out of the mouth of the lion.* Since, as a Roman citizen, Paul could not be thrown to the lions in the amphitheater, this must be a figurative way of saying that his first hearing did not result in an immediate guilty verdict.

4:18 *the Lord shall deliver me from every evil work.* Since Paul fully expected to die soon (v. 6), the rescue he speaks of here is spiritual, not physical. *heavenly kingdom.* Heaven itself.

4:19 *Onesiphorus.* See note on 1:16.

4:20 *Erastus.* See note on Rom 16:23. *Miletum.* A seaport on the coast of Asia Minor about 50 miles south of Ephesus.

4:21 *Linus.* Early tradition says he was bishop of Rome after the deaths of Peter and Paul.

‡4:22 *Grace.* See notes on Jonah 4:2; Gal 1:3; Eph 1:2. *you.* The word "thy" in the first part of the verse is singular, indicating that it was addressed to Timothy alone. In view of Paul's impending death and the solemn charge he gave to his timid young friend, Timothy needed such encouragement.

The Epistle of Paul to Titus

INTRODUCTION

See "The Pastoral Epistles," p. 1734.

Author

The author is Paul (see Introduction to 1 Timothy: Author).

Recipient

The letter is addressed to Titus, one of Paul's converts (1:4) and a considerable help to Paul in his ministry. When Paul left Antioch to discuss "his" gospel (2 Tim 2:8) with the Jerusalem leaders, he took Titus with him (Gal 2:1–3); acceptance of Titus (a Gentile) as a Christian without circumcision vindicated Paul's stand there (Gal 2:3–5). Presumably Titus, who is not referred to in Acts (but is mentioned 13 times in the rest of the NT), worked with Paul at Ephesus during the third missionary journey. From there the apostle sent him to Corinth to help that church with its work (see notes on 2 Cor 2:12–13; 7:5–6; 8:6).

Following Paul's release from his first Roman imprisonment (Acts 28), he and Titus worked briefly in Crete (1:5), after which he commissioned Titus to remain there as his representative and complete some needed work (1:5; 2:15; 3:12–13). Paul asked Titus to meet him at Nicopolis (on the west coast of Greece) when a replacement arrived (3:12). Later, Titus went on a mission to Dalmatia (modern Yugoslavia; see note on 2 Tim 4:10), the last word we hear about him in the NT. Considering the assignments given him, he obviously was a capable and resourceful leader.

Crete

The fourth largest island of the Mediterranean, Crete lies directly south of the Aegean Sea (see note on 1 Sam 30:14; cf. Paul's experiences there in Acts 27:7–13). In NT times life in Crete had sunk to a deplorable moral level. The dishonesty, gluttony and laziness of its inhabitants were proverbial (1:12).

Occasion and Purpose

Apparently Paul introduced Christianity in Crete when he and Titus visited the island, after which he left Titus there to organize the converts. Paul sent the letter with Zenas and Apollos, who were on a journey that took them through Crete (3:13), to give Titus personal authorization and guidance in meeting opposition (1:5; 2:1,7–8,15; 3:9), instructions about faith and conduct, and warnings about false teachers. Paul also informed Titus of his future plans for him (3:12).

Place and Date of Writing

Paul possibly wrote from Macedonia, for he had not yet reached Nicopolis (see 3:12). The letter was written after his release from the first Roman imprisonment (Acts 28), probably between A.D. 63 and 65—or possibly at a later date if he wrote after his assumed trip to Spain (see Rom 15:24).

Distinctive Characteristics

Especially significant, considering the nature of the Cretan heresy, are the repeated emphases on "good deeds" (1:16; 2:7,14; 3:1,8,14) and the classic summaries of Christian doctrine (2:11–14; 3:4–7).

Outline

I. Salutation (1:1–4)
II. Concerning Elders (1:5–9)
   A. Reasons for Leaving Titus in Crete (1:5)

- B. Qualifications of Elders (1:6–9)

III. Concerning False Teachers (1:10–16)

IV. Concerning Various Groups in the Congregations (ch. 2)
- A. The Instructions to Different Groups (2:1–10)
- B. The Foundation for Christian Living (2:11–14)
- C. The Duty of Titus (2:15)

V. Concerning Believers in General (3:1–8)
- A. Obligations as Citizens (3:1–2)
- B. Motives for Godly Conduct (3:3–8)

VI. Concerning Response to Spiritual Error (3:9–11)

VII. Conclusion (3:12–15)

1 Paul, a servant of God, and an apostle of
Jesus Christ, according to the faith of
God's elect, and [a]the acknowledging of the
truth [b]which is after godliness,
2 [a][1]In hope of eternal life, which God, [b]that
cannot lie, promised [c]before the world began;
3 [a]But hath in due times manifested his
word through preaching, [b]which is committed
unto me according to the commandment of
God our Saviour;
4 To [a]Titus, *mine* own son after the common faith: [b]Grace, mercy, *and* peace, from
God the Father and the Lord Jesus Christ our
Saviour.

Qualifications for elders

5 ¶ For this cause left I thee in Crete, that
thou shouldest [a]set in order the *things* that are
[1]wanting, and ordain elders in every city, as I
had appointed thee:
6 [a]If any be blameless, the husband of one
wife, [b]having faithful children not accused of
riot or unruly.
7 For a bishop must be blameless, as [a]the
steward of God; not selfwilled, not soon angry,
[b]not given to wine, no striker, not given to
filthy lucre;
8 [a]But a lover of hospitality, a lover of
[1]good *men*, sober, just, holy, temperate;
9 Holding fast the faithful word [1]as *he* hath
been taught, that he may be able [a]by sound
doctrine both to exhort and to convince the
gainsayers.

Dealing with false teachers

10 For [a]there are many unruly and vain
talkers and deceivers, [b]specially they of the
circumcision:
11 Whose mouths must be stopped, [a]who
subvert whole houses, teaching *things* which
they ought not, [b]for filthy lucre's sake.
12 [a]One of themselves, *even* a prophet of
their own, said, The Cretians *are* alway liars,
evil beasts, slow bellies.
13 This witness is true. [a]Wherefore rebuke
them sharply, that they may be [b]sound in the
faith;
14 [a]Not giving heed to Jewish fables, and
[b]commandments of men, that turn from the
truth.
15 [a]Unto the pure all *things are* pure: but

1:1 [a]2 Tim. 2:25 [b]1 Tim. 3:16
1:2 [1]Or, *For* [a]2 Tim. 1:1 [b]2 Tim. 2:13 [c]Rom. 16:25
1:3 [a]2 Tim. 1:10 [b]1 Thes. 2:4
1:4 [a]2 Cor. 2:13 [b]Eph. 1:2
1:5 [1]Or, *left undone* [a]1 Cor. 11:34
1:6 [a]1 Tim. 3:2 [b]1 Tim. 3:4
1:7 [a]Mat. 24:45
1:7 [b]Lev. 10:9
1:8 [1]Or, *good things* [a]1 Tim. 3:2
1:9 [1]Or, *in teaching* [a]1 Tim. 1:10
1:10 [a]1 Tim. 1:6 [b]Acts 15:1
1:11 [a]2 Tim. 3:6 [b]1 Tim. 6:5
1:12 [a]Acts 17:28
1:13 [a]2 Cor. 13:10 [b]ch. 2:2
1:14 [a]1 Tim. 1:4 [b]Is. 29:13
1:15 [a]1 Cor. 6:12

‡1:1 *servant of God.* Only here does Paul call himself a servant of God; elsewhere he says "servant of Christ" (Rom 1:1; Gal 1:10; Phil 1:1). James uses both terms of himself (Jas 1:1). *servant.* See note on Rom 1:1. *apostle.* One specially commissioned by Christ (see notes on Mark 6:30; 1 Cor 1:1; Heb 3:1). *according to the faith . . . and the acknowledging.* Paul's appointed mission as God's servant and Christ's apostle—further explained in v. 2 (see Acts 9:15; 22:15; 26:16–18).

1:2 *hope.* See note on Col 1:5. *cannot lie.* In contrast to the Cretans (v. 12)—and the devil (John 8:44).

1:3 *due times.* Crucial events in God's program occur at His designated times in history (1 Tim 2:6; 6:15). *his word.* The authoritative message that centers in Christ. *God our Saviour.* Three times in the letter God the Father is called Savior (here; 2:10; 3:4; see also 1 Tim 1:1; 2:3; 4:10), and three times Jesus is called Savior (v. 4; 2:13; 3:6; see also 2 Tim 1:10).

‡1:4 *mine own son.* Titus, like Timothy (1 Tim 1:2), was a spiritual son, having been converted through Paul's ministry. Onesimus was also called a son by Paul (Philem 10). *the common faith.* The faith shared by all true believers. *Saviour.* In all of Paul's other salutations Jesus is called "Lord." Paul uses "Savior" 12 times in all his letters, half of the references being in Titus.

1:5 *left I thee in Crete.* Implies that Paul and Titus had been together in Crete, a ministry not mentioned in Acts. On his voyage to Rome, Paul visited Crete briefly as a prisoner (Acts 27:7–8), but now that he had been released from his first Roman imprisonment he was free to travel wherever he wished (see 3:12). *ordain elders.* Though Paul and Titus perhaps had already preached in Crete, they had not had time to organize churches. The appointing of elders is consistent with Paul's usual practice (Acts 14:23).

‡1:6–9 1 Tim 3:1–7 gives a parallel list of qualifications for elders, but the two lists reflect the different situations in which Timothy and Titus ministered. See chart, p. 1741.

1:6 *husband of one wife.* Since elders, by definition, were chosen from among the older men of the congregation, Paul assumed they already would be married and have children. A qualified unmarried man was not necessarily barred. It is also improbable that the standard forbids an elder to remarry if his wife dies (cf. Rom 7:2–3; 1 Cor 7:39; 1 Tim 5:14). The most likely meaning is simply that a faithful monogamous married life must be maintained. See note on 1 Tim 3:2.

‡1:7 *bishop.* The use of "elder" in v. 5 and "bishop" (or "overseer") in v. 7 indicates that the terms were used interchangeably (cf. Acts 20:17,28; 1 Pet 5:1–2). "Elder" indicates qualification (maturity and experience), while "bishop" indicates responsibility (watching over God's flock).

1:8 *sober.* A virtue much needed in Crete (see vv. 10–14); Paul refers to it five times in two chapters (here; 2:2,4–6,12). *temperate.* Possessing the inner strength to control one's desires and actions.

1:9 *sound doctrine.* Correct teaching, in keeping with that of the apostles (see 1 Tim 1:10; 6:3; 2 Tim 1:13; 4:3). The teaching is called "sound" not only because it builds up in the faith, but because it protects against the corrupting influence of false teachers. Soundness of doctrine, faith and speech is a basic concern in all the Pastoral Epistles (1,2 Timothy; Titus). In them the word "sound" occurs ten times (see also "sound" in Rom 12:3; 2 Cor 5:13).

‡1:10 *unruly.* Against the word of God and against Paul and Titus as the Lord's authoritative ministers. These troublemakers had three main characteristics: 1. They belonged to the "circumcision," like the people of Gal 2:12, believing that, for salvation or sanctification or both, it was necessary to be circumcised and to keep the Jewish ceremonial law (see Introduction to Galatians: Occasion and Purpose). 2. They held to unscriptural Jewish myths (v. 14) and genealogies (3:9; see 1 Tim 1:4 and note there). 3. They were ascetics (vv. 14–15), having scruples against things that God declared to be good. *vain talkers.* Paul used similar language in writing to Timothy about this kind of person (1 Tim 1:6).

‡1:12 *slow bellies.* More clearly stated as "lazy gluttons." The quotation is from the poet Epimenides (a sixth-century B.C. native of Knossos, Crete), who was held in high esteem by the Cretans. Several fulfilled predictions were ascribed to him. For other uses of pagan sayings by Paul see Acts 17:28; 1 Cor 15:33 and notes. In Greek literature "to Cretanize" meant to lie.

1:14 *Jewish fables.* See note on v. 10.

‡1:15 *Unto the pure all things are pure.* To Christians, who have been purified by the atoning death of Christ, "every creature of

unto them that are defiled and unbelieving *is*
nothing pure; but even their mind and conscience is defiled.

16 They profess that *they* know God; but
[a]in works they deny *him,* being abominable,
and disobedient, [b]and unto every good work
[1]reprobate.

Christian doctrine and conduct

2 But speak thou *the things* which become
[a]sound doctrine:

2 That the aged men be [1]sober, grave, temperate, sound in faith, in charity, in patience.

3 The aged women likewise, *that they be*
in behaviour as becometh [1]holiness, not [2]false
accusers, not given to much wine, teachers of
good things;

4 That they may teach the young *women* to
be [1]sober, to love their husbands, to love their
children,

5 *To be* discreet, chaste, keepers at home,
good, [a]obedient to their own husbands, [b]that
the word of God be not blasphemed.

6 Young *men* likewise exhort to be [1]sober
minded.

7 [a]In all *things* shewing thyself a pattern of
good works: in doctrine *shewing* uncorruptness, gravity, [b]sincerity,

8 [a]Sound speech that cannot be condemned; [b]that he that is of the contrary *part*
may be ashamed, having no evil *thing* to say of
you.

9 *Exhort* [a]servants to be obedient unto
their own masters, *and* to please *them* well [b]in
all *things;* not [1]answering again;

10 Not purloining, but shewing all good fidelity; [a]that they may adorn the doctrine of
God our Saviour in all *things.*

11 For [a]the grace of God [1]that bringeth salvation [b]hath appeared to all men,

12 Teaching us [a]that denying ungodliness
[b]and worldly lusts we should live soberly, righteously, and godly, in *this* present world;

13 [a]Looking for *that* blessed [b]hope, and
the glorious [c]appearing of the great God and
our Saviour Jesus Christ;

14 [a]Who gave himself for us, that he might
redeem us from all iniquity, [b]and purify unto
himself [c]a peculiar people, [d]zealous of good
works.

1:16 [1]Or, *void of judgment* [a]2 Tim. 3:5 [b]Rom. 1:28
2:1 [a]1 Tim. 1:10
2:2 [1]Or, *vigilant*
2:3 [1]Or, *holy women* [2]Or, *makebates*
2:4 [1]Or, *wise*
2:5 [a]1 Cor. 14:34 [b]Rom. 2:24
2:6 [1]Or, *discreet*
2:7 [a]1 Tim. 4:12
2:7 [b]Eph. 6:24
2:8 [a]1 Tim. 6:3 [b]Neh. 5:9
2:9 [1]Or, *gainsaying* [a]Eph. 6:5 [b]Eph. 5:24
2:10 [a]Mat. 5:16
2:11 [1]Or, *that bringeth salvation to all men, hath appeared* [a]Rom. 5:15 [b]Luke 3:6
2:12 [a]Luke 1:75 [b]1 Pet. 4:2
2:13 [a]1 Cor. 1:7 [b]Acts 24:15 [c]Col. 3:4
2:14 [a]Gal. 1:4 [b]Heb. 9:14 [c]Ex. 15:16 [d]Eph. 2:10

God is good, and nothing to be refused if it be received with thanksgiving" (1 Tim 4:4). To understand better Paul's statements here, see Rom 14:14 with 14:20. *unto them that are defiled and unbelieving is nothing pure.* Unbelievers, especially ascetics with unbiblical scruples against certain foods, marriage and the like (cf. 1 Tim 4:3; Col 2:21), do not enjoy the freedom of true Christians, who receive all God's creation with thanksgiving. Instead, they set up arbitrary, man-made prohibitions against what they consider to be impure (see Mat 15:10–11,16–20; Mark 7:14–19; Acts 10:9–16; Rom 14:20). The principle of this verse does not conflict with the many NT teachings against practices that are morally and spiritually wrong. *conscience.* See 1 Tim 4:2–3.

1:16 *in works they deny him.* The false teachers stood condemned by the test of personal conduct. *good.* See Introduction: Distinctive Characteristics. Right knowledge is extremely important because it leads to godliness (v. 1). Paul maintained a remarkable balance between doctrine and practice.

2:1 *thou.* Emphatic, contrasting the work of Titus with that of the false teachers just denounced (1:10–16).

2:2–10 Sound doctrine demands right conduct of all believers, regardless of age, sex or position.

‡2:2 Older men, as leaders, were to be moral and spiritual examples. *temperate.* Instead of being "slow bellies" (lazy gluttons), as were Cretans in general (1:12), these older believers were to be responsible and sensible.

2:3 *likewise.* The same moral standards applied to women as to men. *not false accusers.* Slanderous talk apparently was a common vice among Cretan women.

2:4 *love their husbands.* Just as husbands are exhorted (Eph 5:25) to love their wives (though different Greek words for "love" are used in the two passages).

2:5 *that the word of God be not blasphemed.* Indicating Paul's deep spiritual concern behind these ethical instructions. See also vv. 8,10, dealing with his concern that Christian living should help rather than hinder the spread of the gospel.

2:7–8 Perhaps Titus was still a young man and was not yet well respected by the Cretan churches. The demands on a leader are all-inclusive, involving not only his word but also his life-style (Jas 3:1).

2:7 *good.* See Introduction: Distinctive Characteristics.

2:9–10 Instructions for a distinct group in the churches. Slavery was a basic element of Roman society, and the impact of Christianity upon slaves was a vital concern. Guidance for the conduct of Christian slaves was essential (see note on Eph 6:5).

2:9 *masters.* The Greek for this word, from which our English term "despot" is derived, indicates the owner's absolute authority over his slave. Roman slaves had no legal rights, their fates being entirely in their masters' hands.

2:10 *adorn the doctrine.* Christian slaves could give a unique and powerful testimony to the gospel by their willing faithfulness and obedience to their masters.

2:11–14 Briefly describes the effect grace should have on believers. It encourages rejection of ungodliness and leads to holier living—in keeping with Paul's repeated insistence that profession of Christ be accompanied by godly living (vv. 1–2,4–5, 10; 3:8).

2:11 *For.* Introduces the doctrinal basis for the ethical demands just stressed. Right conduct must be founded on right doctrine. *grace of God.* The undeserved love God showed us in Christ while we were still sinners and His enemies (Rom 5:6–10) and by which we are saved apart from any moral achievements or religious acts on our part (see 3:5; Eph 2:8–9). But this same grace instructs us that our salvation should produce good works (see note on v. 14; see also Eph 2:10).

‡2:12 *Teaching us.* The word translated "teaching" refers to more than instruction; it includes the whole process of training a child—instruction, encouragement, correction and discipline. *this present world.* See note on 2 Cor 4:4.

‡2:13 *that blessed hope, and the glorious appearing.* The second coming (see 1 Tim 6:14; 2 Tim 4:1; see also note on 2 Tim 4:8). *the great God and our Saviour Jesus Christ.* This translation is possible, but both the context (Christ's second coming) and the Greek construction favor the translation: "The great God, even our Saviour Jesus Christ." It is an explicit testimony to the deity of Christ (see note on Rom 9:5).

2:14 Salvation involves the double work of redeeming us from guilt and judgment and of producing moral purity and helpful service to others (see Introduction: Distinctive Characteristics).

15 These *things* speak, and [a]exhort, and rebuke with all authority. Let no *man* despise thee.

Faith and works

3 Put them in mind [a]to be subject to principalities and powers, to obey magistrates, [b]to be ready to every good work,

2 [a]To speak evil of no *man,* [b]to be no brawlers, *but* [c]gentle, shewing all [d]meekness unto all men.

3 For [a]we ourselves also were sometimes foolish, disobedient, deceived, serving divers lusts and pleasures, living in malice and envy, hateful, *and* hating one another.

4 But after that [a]the kindness and [1]love of [b]God our Saviour toward man appeared,

5 [a]Not by works of righteousness which we have done, but according to his mercy he saved us, by [b]the washing of regeneration, and renewing of the Holy Ghost;

6 [a]Which he shed on us [1]abundantly through Jesus Christ our Saviour;

7 [a]That being justified by his grace, [b]we should be made heirs [c]according to the hope of eternal life.

8 [a]*This is* a faithful saying, and these *things* I will that thou affirm constantly, that they which have believed in God might be careful [b]to maintain good works. These *things* are good and profitable unto men.

9 But [a]avoid foolish questions, and genealogies, and contentions, and strivings about the law; [b]for they are unprofitable and vain.

10 A man *that is* a heretick [a]after the first and second admonition, [b]reject;

11 Knowing that *he that is* such is subverted, and sinneth, [a]being condemned of himself.

Closing instruction, benediction

12 ¶ When I shall send Artemas unto thee, or [a]Tychicus, be diligent to come unto me to Nicopolis: for I have determined there to winter.

13 Bring Zenas the lawyer and [a]Apollos on their journey diligently, that nothing be wanting unto them.

14 And let ours also learn [a]to [1]maintain good works for necessary uses, that they be [b]not unfruitful.

15 All that are with me salute thee. Greet them that love us in the faith. Grace *be* with you all. Amen.

¶ It was written to Titus, ordained the first bishop of the church of the Cretians, from Nicopolis of Macedonia.

2:15 [a]2 Tim. 4:2
3:1 [a]1 Pet. 2:13 [b]Col. 1:10; Heb. 13:21
3:2 [a]Eph. 4:31 [b]2 Tim. 2:24 [c]Phil. 4:5 [d]Eph. 4:2; Col. 3:12
3:3 [a]1 Cor. 6:11; 1 Pet. 4:3
3:4 [1]Or, *pity* [a]ch. 2:11 [b]1 Tim. 2:3
3:5 [a]Rom. 3:20; 2 Tim. 1:9 [b]John 3:3; 1 Pet. 3:21
3:6 [1]Gr. *richly* [a]Ezek. 36:25; Joel 2:28
3:7 [a]Rom. 3:24 [b]Rom. 8:23 [c]ch. 1:2
3:8 [a]1 Tim. 1:15
3:8 [b]ch. 2:14
3:9 [a]1 Tim. 1:4 [b]2 Tim. 2:14
3:10 [a]2 Cor. 13:2 [b]Mat. 18:17
3:11 [a]Acts 13:46
3:12 [a]Acts 20:4
3:13 [a]Acts 18:24
3:14 [1]Or, *profess honest trades* [a]ver. 8 [b]Rom. 15:28; Phil. 1:11

2:15 A summary of Titus's responsibility and authority. *things.* The content of the whole chapter.

3:1–2 NT teaching is not confined to the area of personal salvation but includes much instruction about practical living. Although believers are citizens of heaven (Phil 3:20), they must also submit themselves to earthly government (see Rom 13:1–7; 1 Pet 2:13–17) and help promote the well-being of the community.

3:1 *to principalities and powers.* The terms refer to all forms and levels of human government (cf. Eph 3:10; 6:12 for application to angels). *good.* See Introduction: Distinctive Characteristics.

3:4 *kindness and love.* The reasons why God did not simply banish fallen man but acted to save him (cf. 2:11).

‡3:5 *according to his mercy he saved us.* Salvation is not achieved by human effort or merit but comes through God's mercy alone. *washing of regeneration.* The Greek construction suggests that as we are renewed by the work of the Holy Spirit so we are washed by the work of regeneration. *renewing of the Holy Ghost.* Also a reference to new birth.

3:8 *faithful saying.* A reference to the doctrinal summary in vv. 4–7. This phrase, which occurs only here in Titus, appears four other times in the Pastoral Epistles (1 Tim 1:15; 3:1; 4:9; 2 Tim 2:11) and nowhere else in the NT. *good.* See Introduction: Distinctive Characteristics.

3:9 *about the law.* A reference to the situation described in 1:10–16. A similar problem existed in Ephesus (see 1 Tim 1:3–7).

‡3:10 *heretick.* The Greek for this phrase became a technical term in the early church for a type of heretic who promoted dissension by propagating extreme views of legitimate Christian truths.

3:11 Stubborn refusal to listen to correction reveals inner perversion.

3:12 *Tychicus.* Paul's trusted co-worker, who on various occasions traveled with or for Paul (Acts 20:4; Eph 6:21–22; Col 4:7–8; 2 Tim 4:12). *Nicopolis.* Means "city of victory." Several cities had this name, but the reference here apparently is to the city in Epirus on the western shore of Greece. *determined there to winter.* Indicates that Paul had not arrived there when he wrote and that he was still free to travel at will, not yet having been imprisoned in Rome for the second time.

3:13 *Zenas the lawyer.* Mentioned only here in the NT. If he was a Jewish convert, "lawyer" means that he was an expert in the Mosaic law; if he was a Gentile convert, that he was a Roman jurist. *Apollos.* A native of Alexandria and one of Paul's well-known co-workers (Acts 18:24–28; 19:1; 1 Cor 1:12; 3:4–6,22; 16:12). The two travelers apparently brought the letter from Paul.

3:14 *good.* See Introduction: Distinctive Characteristics.

The Epistle of Paul to Philemon

INTRODUCTION

Author, Date and Place of Writing

Paul wrote this short letter (see vv. 1, 9, 19) probably at the same time as Colossians (c. A.D. 60; see Introduction to Colossians: Author, Date and Place of Writing) and sent it to Colosse with the same travelers, Onesimus and Tychicus. He apparently wrote both letters from prison in Rome, though possibly from Ephesus (see Introduction to Philippians: Author, Date and Place of Writing).

Recipient, Background and Purpose

Paul wrote this letter to Philemon, a believer in Colosse who, along with others, was a slave owner (cf. Col 4:1; for slavery in the NT see note on Eph 6:5). One of his slaves, Onesimus, had apparently stolen from him (cf. v. 18) and then run away, which under Roman law was punishable by death. But Onesimus met Paul and through his ministry became a Christian (see v. 10). Now he was willing to return to his master, and Paul writes this personal appeal to ask that he be accepted as a Christian brother (see v. 16).

Approach and Structure

To win Philemon's willing acceptance of Onesimus, Paul writes very tactfully and in a lighthearted tone, which he creates with a wordplay (see note on v. 11). The appeal (vv. 4–21) is organized in a way prescribed by ancient Greek and Roman teachers: to build rapport (vv. 4–10), to persuade the mind (vv. 11–19) and to move the emotions (vv. 20–21). The name Onesimus is not mentioned until the rapport has been built (v. 10), and the appeal itself is stated only near the end of the section to persuade the mind (v. 17).

Outline

I. Greetings (1–3)
II. Thanksgiving and Prayer (4–7)
III. Paul's Plea for Onesimus (8–21)
IV. Final Request, Greetings and Benediction (22–25)

1 ¶ Paul, [a]a prisoner of Jesus Christ, and Timothy *our* brother, unto Philemon *our* dearly beloved, [b]and fellowlabourer,

2 And to *our* beloved Apphia, and [a]Archippus [b]our fellowsoldier, and to [c]the church in thy house:

3 [a]Grace to you, and peace, from God our Father and the Lord Jesus Christ.

Thanksgiving and prayer

4 ¶ [a]I thank my God, making mention of thee always in my prayers,

5 [a]Hearing of thy love and faith, which thou hast toward the Lord Jesus, and toward all saints;

6 That the communication of thy faith may become effectual [a]by the acknowledging of every good *thing* which is in you in Christ Jesus.

7 For we have great joy and consolation in thy love, because the bowels of the saints [a]are refreshed by thee, brother.

Appeal for Onesimus

8 Wherefore, [a]though I might be much bold in Christ to enjoin thee that which is convenient,

9 *Yet* for love's sake I rather beseech *thee,* being such a one as Paul the aged, [a]and now also a prisoner of Jesus Christ.

10 I beseech thee for my son [a]Onesimus, [b]whom I have begotten in my bonds:

11 Which in time past was to thee unprofitable, but now profitable to thee and to me:

12 Whom I have sent again: thou therefore receive him, that is, mine own bowels:

13 Whom I would have retained with me, [a]that in thy stead he might have ministered unto me in the bonds of the gospel:

14 But without thy mind would I do nothing; [a]that thy benefit should not be as *it were* of necessity, but willingly.

15 [a]For perhaps he therefore departed for a season, that thou shouldest receive him for ever;

16 Not now as a servant, but above a servant, [a]a brother beloved, specially to me, but how much more unto thee, [b]both in the flesh, and in the Lord?

17 If thou count me therefore [a]a partner, receive him as myself.

18 If he hath wronged thee, or oweth *thee* ought, put that on mine account;

19 I Paul have written *it* with mine own hand, I will repay *it:* albeit I do not say to thee how thou owest unto me even thine own self besides.

20 Yea, brother, let me have joy of thee in the Lord: [a]refresh my bowels in the Lord.

21 [a]Having confidence in thy obedience I wrote unto thee, knowing that thou wilt also do more than I say.

22 But withal prepare me also a lodging: for [a]I trust that [b]through your prayers I shall be given unto you.

23 There salute thee [a]Epaphras, my fellowprisoner in Christ Jesus;

24 [a]Marcus, [b]Aristarchus, [c]Demas, [d]Lucas, my fellowlabourers.

25 [a]The grace of our Lord Jesus Christ *be* with your spirit. Amen.

¶ Written from Rome to Philemon, by Onesimus a servant.

1 [a]ver. 9; Eph. 3:1; 4:1; 2 Tim. 1:8 [b]Phil. 2:25
2 [a]Col. 4:17 [b]Phil. 2:25 [c]Rom. 16:5; 1 Cor. 16:19
3 [a]Eph. 1:2
4 [a]Eph. 1:16; 1 Thes. 1:2; 2 Thes. 1:3
5 [a]Eph. 1:15; Col. 1:4
6 [a]Phil. 1:9
7 [a]ver. 20; 2 Cor. 7:13; 2 Tim. 1:16
8 [a]1 Thes. 2:6
9 [a]ver. 1
10 [a]Col. 4:9 [b]1 Cor. 4:15; Gal. 4:19
13 [a]1 Cor. 16:17; Phil. 2:30
14 [a]2 Cor. 9:7
15 [a]Gen. 45:5,8
16 [a]Mat. 23:8; 1 Tim. 6:2 [b]Col. 3:22
17 [a]2 Cor. 8:23
20 [a]ver. 7
21 [a]2 Cor. 7:16
22 [a]Phil. 1:25; 2:24 [b]2 Cor. 1:11
23 [a]Col. 1:7; 4:12
24 [a]Acts 12:12,25 [b]Acts 19:29; 27:2; Col. 4:10 [c]Col. 4:14 [d]2 Tim. 4:11
25 [a]2 Tim. 4:22

‡1–2 Although Paul writes together with Timothy and although he addresses the entire church in Colosse, in this very personal letter to Philemon he uses "I" rather than "we," and "thee" (singular except in vv. 22,25).

1 *prisoner.* See notes on Eph 3:1; Phil 1:13. *Timothy.* See note on Col 1:1; see also Introduction to 1 Timothy: Recipient. *Philemon.* A Christian living in Colosse or nearby and the owner of the slave Onesimus.

2 *Apphia.* Probably Philemon's wife. *Archippus.* See Col 4:17.

4 *thank . . . making mention of thee always in my prayers.* See note on Phil 1:3–4.

‡5 *love and faith . . . toward the Lord Jesus, and toward all saints.* See Col 1:4.

‡7 *bowels.* As the heart today is regarded as the seat of emotions, in the same way were the intestines or "bowels" for the ancient Greeks (see vv. 12, 20).

10 *my son.* See note on 1 Tim 1:2. *Onesimus.* See Introduction: Recipient, Background and Purpose.

11 *unprofitable . . . profitable.* A play on the meaning of Onesimus's name ("useful").

‡12 *receive him.* The main emphasis of this brief letter is that Philemon accept and receive back his unfaithful slave not only as a servant but as a brother in the Lord (v. 16). To understand more clearly Paul's message concerning servants and masters one must read the book of Philemon in conjunction with Col 3:22—4:1.

‡17–19 Luther said, "Even as Christ did for us with God the Father, thus Paul also does for Onesimus with Philemon." But verse 19 weakens this correspondence.

‡20 *me . . . my.* Both pronouns are emphatic, making an obvious allusion to v. 7. *joy.* The Greek for this word has the sense of "benefit" and is another play on the name Onesimus.

22 *But withal.* It was not unusual for an ancient letter, though occasioned by one matter, to also include another matter. Often, as here, the second matter had to do with how and when the author planned to meet the recipient again.

23 *Epaphras.* See Col 4:12.

24 *Marcus, Aristarchus.* See note on Col 4:10. *Demas, Lucas.* See note on Col 4:14.

The Epistle of Paul the Apostle to the
Hebrews

INTRODUCTION

Author

The writer of this epistle does not identify himself, but he was obviously well known to the original recipients. For some 1,200 years (from c. A.D. 400 to 1600) the book was commonly called "The Epistle of Paul the Apostle to the Hebrews" (hence the title above), but there was no agreement in the earliest centuries regarding its authorship. Since the Reformation it has been widely agreed that Paul was not the writer. There is no disharmony between the teaching of Hebrews and that of Paul's letters, but the specific emphases and writing styles are markedly different. Contrary to Paul's usual practice, the author of Hebrews nowhere identifies himself in the letter—except to indicate that he was a man (see note on 11:32). Moreover, the statement that the message of salvation "at the first began to be spoken by the Lord, and was confirmed unto us by them that heard him" (2:3), indicates that the author had neither been with Jesus during his earthly ministry nor received special revelation directly from the risen Lord, as had Paul (Gal 1:11–12).

The earliest alternative suggestion of authorship is found in Tertullian's *De Pudicitia,* 20 (c. 200), in which he quotes from "an epistle to the Hebrews under the name of Barnabas." From the letter itself it is clear that the writer must have had authority in the apostolic church and was an intellectual Hebrew Christian well versed in the OT. Barnabas meets these requirements. He was a Jew of the priestly tribe of Levi (Acts 4:36) who became a close friend of Paul after the latter's conversion. Under the guidance of the Holy Spirit, the church at Antioch commissioned Barnabas and Paul for the work of evangelism and sent them off on the first missionary journey (Acts 13:1–4).

The other leading candidate for authorship is Apollos, whose name was first suggested by Martin Luther and who is favored by many scholars today. Apollos, an Alexandrian by birth, was also a Jewish Christian with notable intellectual and oratorical abilities. Luke tells us that Apollos was "an eloquent man, and mighty in the scriptures" (Acts 18:24). We also know that Apollos was associated with Paul in the early years of the church in Corinth (1 Cor 1:12; 3:4–6,22).

Date

Hebrews must have been written before the destruction of Jerusalem and the temple in A.D. 70 because: (1) if it had been written after this date, the author surely would have mentioned the temple's destruction and the end of the Jewish sacrificial system; and (2) the author consistently uses the Greek present tense when speaking of the temple and the priestly activities connected with it (see 5:1–3; 7:23,27; 8:3–5; 9:6–9,13,25; 10:1,3–4,8,11; 13:10–11).

Recipients

The letter was addressed primarily to Jewish converts who were familiar with the OT and who were being tempted to revert to Judaism or to Judaize the gospel (cf. Gal 2:14). Some have suggested that these professing Jewish Christians were thinking of merging with a Jewish sect, such as the one at Qumran near the Dead Sea. It has also been suggested that the recipients were from the large number of priests who "were obedient to the faith" (Acts 6:7).

Theme

The theme of Hebrews is the absolute supremacy and sufficiency of Jesus Christ as revealer and as mediator of God's grace. The prologue (1:1–4) presents Christ as God's full and final revelation, far surpassing the limited preliminary revelation given in the OT. The prophecies and promises of the OT are fulfilled in the "new covenant" (or "new testament"), of which Christ is the mediator. From the OT itself, Christ is shown to be superior to the ancient prophets, to angels, to Moses (the mediator of the former covenant) and to Aaron and the priestly succession descended from Him. Hebrews

could be called "the book of better things" since the two Greek words for "better" and "superior" occur 15 times in the letter.

Practical applications of this theme are given throughout the book. The readers are told that there can be no turning back to or continuation in the old Jewish system, which has been superseded by the unique priesthood of Christ. God's people now must look only to Him, whose atoning death, resurrection and ascension have opened the way into the true, heavenly sanctuary of God's presence. Resisting temptations to give up the struggle, believers must persevere in the spiritual contest to which they have committed themselves. Otherwise they may meet with judgment as did the rebellious generation of Israelites in the wilderness.

Outline

I. Prologue: The Superiority of God's New Revelation (1:1–4)
II. The Superiority of Christ to Leaders of the Old Covenant (1:5—7:28)
 A. Christ Is Superior to the Angels (1:5—2:18)
  1. Scriptural proof of superiority (1:5–14)
  2. Exhortation not to ignore the revelation of God in His Son (2:1–4)
  3. Further Scriptural proof of superiority over the angels (2:5–18)
 B. Christ Is Superior to Moses (3:1—4:13)
  1. Demonstration of Christ's superiority (3:1–6)
  2. Exhortation to enter His rest (3:7—4:13)
 C. Christ Is Superior to the Aaronic Priests (4:14—7:28)
  1. Exhortation to hold fast (4:14–16)
  2. Qualifications of a priest (5:1–10)
  3. Exhortation to abandon spiritual lethargy (5:11—6:12)
  4. Certainty of God's promise (6:13–20)
  5. Christ's superior priestly order (ch. 7)
III. The Superior Sacrificial Work of Our High Priest (chs. 8—10)
 A. A Better Covenant (ch. 8)
 B. A Better Sanctuary (9:1–12)
 C. A Better Sacrifice (9:13—10:18)
 D. Exhortations (10:19–39)
IV. Final Plea for Persevering Faith (chs. 11—12)
 A. Examples of Past Heroes of the Faith (ch. 11)
 B. Encouragement for Persevering Faith (12:1–11)
 C. Exhortations for Persevering Faith (12:12–17)
 D. Motivation for Persevering Faith (12:18–29)
V. Conclusion (ch. 13)
 A. Practical Rules for Christian Living (13:1–17)
 B. Request for Prayer (13:18–19)
 C. Benediction (13:20–21)
 D. Personal Remarks (13:22–23)
 E. Greetings and Final Benediction (13:24–25)

The Son is God's revelation

1 God, who at sundry times and [a]in divers
manners spake in time past unto the fathers by the prophets,
2 Hath [a]in these last days [b]spoken unto us
by *his* Son, [c]whom he hath appointed heir of
all *things,* [d]by whom also he made the worlds;
3 [a]Who being the brightness of *his* glory,
and the express image of his person, and [b]up-
holding all *things* by the word of his power,
[c]when he had by himself purged our sins, [d]sat
down on the right hand of the Majesty on
high;
4 Being made so much better than the angels, as [a]he hath by inheritance obtained a
more excellent name than they.
5 For unto which of the angels said he at
any time, [a]Thou art my Son, this day have I begotten thee? And again, [b]I will be to him a Father, and he shall be to me a Son?
6 And [1]again, when he bringeth in [a]the
firstbegotten into the world, he saith, [b]And let
all the angels of God worship him.
7 And [1]of the angels he saith, [a]Who

1:1 [a]Num. 12:6
1:2 [a]Eph. 1:10 [b]John 1:17 [c]Ps. 2:8 [d]John 1:3
1:3 [a]John 1:14 [b]John 1:4; Rev. 4:11 [c]ch. 7:27 [d]Ps. 110:1
1:4 [a]Phil. 2:9,10
1:5 [a]Ps. 2:7; Acts 13:33 [b]2 Sam. 7:14
1:6 [1][Or, *when he bringeth again*] [a]Rom. 8:29 [b]Deut. 32:43; LXX
1:7 [1][Gr. *unto*] [a]Ps. 104:4
1:8 [1]Gr. *rightness,* or, *straightness* [a]Ps. 45:6,7
1:9 [a]Is. 61:1
1:10 [a]Ps. 102:25
1:11 [a]Is. 34:4
1:13 [a]Ps. 110:1; Luke 20:42
1:14 [a]Ps. 103:20; Mat. 18:10 [b]Rom. 8:17

maketh his angels spirits, and his ministers a
flame of fire.
8 But unto the Son *he saith,* [a]Thy throne,
O God, *is* for ever and ever: a sceptre of [1]righ-
teousness *is* the sceptre of thy kingdom.
9 Thou hast loved righteousness, and hated
iniquity; therefore God, *even* thy God, [a]hath
anointed thee *with* the oil of gladness above
thy fellows.
10 And, [a]Thou, Lord, in the beginning hast
laid the foundation of the earth; and the heavens are the works of thine hands:
11 [a]They shall perish; but thou remainest;
and they all shall wax old as *doth* a garment;
12 And as a vesture shalt thou fold them
up, and they shall be changed: but thou art the
same, and thy years shall not fail.
13 But to which of the angels said he at any
time, [a]Sit on my right hand, until I make thine
enemies thy footstool?
14 [a]Are they not all ministering spirits,
sent forth to minister for them who shall be
[b]heirs of salvation?

---

‡1:1 *God. . . spake.* God is the ultimate author of both the OT and the NT. *at sundry times and in divers manners.* The OT revelation was fragmentary and occasional, lacking fullness and finality. *in time past.* Prior to Christ's coming, in contrast to "in these last days" (v. 2), the Messianic era inaugurated by the incarnation (see notes on Acts 2:17; 1 Tim 4:1; 1 John 2:18). *unto the fathers.* In contrast to "unto us" (v. 2). *by the prophets.* All OT writers are here viewed as prophets in that their testimony was preparation for the coming of Christ; cf. "by his Son" (v. 2), a new and unique category of revelation in contrast to that of the prophets.

‡1:2–3 The superiority of the Son's revelation is demonstrated by seven great descriptive statements about Him: 1. *appointed heir of all things.* The incarnate Son, having performed the work of redemption, was gloriously exalted to the position of the firstborn heir of God, i.e., He received the inheritance of God's estate ("all things"). See Rom 8:17. 2. *by whom also he made the worlds.* See John 1:3; Col 1:16. 3. *brightness of His glory.* As the brilliance of the sun is inseparable from the sun itself, so the Son's radiance is inseparable from deity, for He Himself is God, the second person of the Trinity (John 1:14,18). 4. *express image of his person.* Jesus is not merely an image or reflection of God. Because the Son Himself is God, He is the absolutely authentic representation of God's being (cf. John 14:9; Col 1:15). 5. *upholding all things.* Christ is not like Atlas, the mythical Greek god who held the world on his shoulders. The Son dynamically holds together and carries forward all that has been created through Him (Col 1:17). 6. *purged our sins.* Through His redeeming death on the cross. 7. *sat down on the right hand of the Majesty on high.* Being seated at God's right hand indicates that the work of redemption is complete and that Christ is actively ruling with God as Lord over all (see v. 13; 8:1; 10:12; 12:2; Eph 1:20; Col 3:1; 1 Pet 3:22; see also note on Mark 16:19).

1:4 *much better than the angels.* To most Jews angels were exalted beings, especially revered because they were involved in giving the law at Sinai (see note on 2:2) and to the Jews the law was God's supreme revelation. The Dead Sea Scrolls reflect the expectation that the archangel Michael would be the supreme figure in the Messianic kingdom. Whether the recipients of Hebrews were tempted to assign angels a place above Christ (Messiah) is not known. *name.* To Jews a name stood for the full character of a person in all he was and did (see note on Gen 17:5). The section that follows indicates that this name was "Son"—a name to which no angel could lay claim.

1:5–14 Christ's superiority to angels is documented by seven OT quotations, showing that He is God's Son, that He is worshiped by angels and that, though He is God, He is distinguished from the Father.

‡1:5 *Thou art My Son, this day have I begotten thee.* This passage (Ps 2:7) is quoted in Acts 13:33 as fulfilled in Christ's resurrection (cf. Rom 1:4). *I will be to him a Father and he shall be to me a Son.* Jews acknowledged 2 Sam 7:14 (of which this passage is a quotation) and Ps 2 to be Messianic in their ultimate application (see Luke 1:32–33). This royal personage is neither an angel nor an archangel; He is God's Son.

1:6 *firstbegotten.* See note on Col 1:15. *let all the angels of God worship Him.* Possibly quoted from Ps 97:7. This statement, which in the OT refers to the Lord God (Yahweh), is here applied to Christ, giving clear indication of His full deity. The very beings with whom Christ is being compared are commanded to proclaim His superiority by worshiping Him.

1:7 *Who maketh his angels spirits, and his ministers a flame of fire.* Ps 104:4 speaks of the storm wind and the lightning as agents of God's purposes. The Septuagint (the Greek translation of the OT), which the author of Hebrews quotes as the version familiar to his readers, reflects the developing doctrine of angels during the period between the OT and the NT.

1:8 *But unto the Son he saith, Thy throne, O God, is for ever.* The author selects a passage that intimates the deity of the Messianic (and Davidic) King, further demonstrating the Son's superiority over angels.

1:10 *Thou, Lord, in the beginning hast laid the foundation of the earth.* As in v. 8, a passage addressed to Yahweh ("You, Lord") is applied to the Son.

1:13 *Sit on my right hand.* See note on vv. 2–3. Ps 110 is applied repeatedly to Jesus in Hebrews (vv. 3,13; 5:6,10; 6:20; 7:3,11, 17,21; 8:1; 10:12–13; 12:2).

1:14 *ministering spirits.* Christ reigns; angels minister as those sent to serve.

The role of Christ in salvation

2 Therefore we ought to give the more
earnest heed to the *things* which we
have heard, lest at any time we should [1]let
them slip.
2 For if the word [a]spoken by angels was
stedfast, and [b]every transgression and disobedience received a just recompence of reward;
3 [a]How shall we escape, if we neglect so
great salvation; [b]which at the first began to be
spoken by the Lord, and was [c]confirmed unto
us by them that heard *him;*
4 [a]God also bearing *them* witness, [b]both
with signs and wonders, and with divers miracles, and [c][1]gifts of the Holy Ghost, [d]according
to his own will?

Christ the high priest

5 ¶ For unto *the* angels hath he not put in

2:1 [1]Gr. *run out as leaking vessels*
2:2 [a]Deut. 33:2; Acts 7:53 [b]Num. 15:30
2:3 [a]ch. 10:28
2:3 [b]Mat. 4:17 [c]Luke 1:2
2:4 [1]Or, *distributions* [a]Mark 16:20 [b]Acts 2:22 [c]1 Cor. 12:4,7, 11 [d]Eph. 1:5,9

2:1–4 The first of five warnings strategically positioned throughout the letter (see 3:7–4:13; 5:11–6:12; 10:19–39; 12:14–29).
2:1 *things which we have heard.* The message of the gospel, including that of Christ's person as the God-man and His redemptive work on the cross. *let them slip.* From the greater revelation given through the Son.
2:2 *the word spoken by angels.* The law given to Moses at Sinai. That angels were active in giving the law is indicated by Deut 33:2 ("ten thousands of saints"); Ps 68:17; Acts 7:38,53; Gal 3:19.
‡2:3 *so great salvation.* The argument here is from the lesser to the greater, and assumes that the gospel is greater than the law. Thus, if disregard for the law brought certain punishment, disregard for the gospel will bring even greater punishment. *confirmed unto us by them that heard.* The eyewitnesses, chiefly the apostles (see 2 Pet 1:16; 1 John 1:1), had vouched for the message first announced by Christ. The author himself apparently was neither an apostle nor an eyewitness (see Introduction: Author).
2:4 *signs and wonders, and with divers miracles.* God added His confirmation to the gospel message through supernatural acts such as healing the sick (see Acts 3:7–9,11–12,16). *gifts of the Holy Ghost.* Such as the gift of tongues (see Acts 2:4–12). *according to his own will.* See 1 Cor 12:4–11.
2:5–18 An exposition of Ps 8:4–6, which continues to show

Titles of Jesus in Hebrews

Jesus, the Messiah, is greater than all the people, practices and procedures of the OT, and the author of Hebrews explains how true that is. Jesus is the Son of God, the "brightness of God's glory," and he represents the Father exactly (Heb 1:3). Because of that, Jesus is greater than the angels (1:5–14) and greater than Moses (3:3). In fact, Jesus is God's ultimate "apostle" (3:1). He is our great high priest (4:14) and an "anchor of the soul" (6:19). While the animal sacrifices of the OT were temporary, Jesus' death set up a permanent way whereby we could have a relationship with God (7:24). Jesus himself makes a new covenant between us and God (9:15). Jesus is the "author and finisher of our faith" (12:2), meaning that our faith has its starting point and its ending point in him as we "may grow up into him in all things, which is the head" (Eph 4:15). He is also the one who never changes (13:8). There are at least 25 word pictures used of Jesus in the book of Hebrews.

TITLE OF JESUS	HEBREWS	TITLE OF JESUS	HEBREWS
1. Son of God	1:2–8; 6:6; 10:29	**14.** Anchor of the Soul	6:19
2. Heir of All Things	1:2	**15.** Surety of a Better Testament	7:22
3. Brightness of God's Glory	1:3	**16.** Permanent Priest	7:24
4. Express Image of God's Person	1:3	**17.** Holy, Blameless, Pure	7:26
5. Superior to the Angels	1:4–14	**18.** One Seated in Heaven	8:1; 10:12
6. "O God"	1:8	**19.** Mediator of the New Covenant	8:6; 9:15; 12:24
7. Crowned with Glory and Honor	2:9	**20.** Mediator of a New Testament	9:15
8. Captain of Salvation	2:10	**21.** Great High Priest Over the House of God	10:21
9. Merciful and Faithful High Priest	2:17	**22.** He That Shall Come	10:37
10. Apostle and High Priest	3:1	**23.** Author and Finisher of our Faith	12:2
11. Faithful Son Over God's House	3:6	**24.** Same Yesterday, Today and For Ever	13:8
12. Great High Priest	4:14	**25.** Great Shepherd of the Sheep	13:20
13. Priest For Ever after the Order of Melchisedec	5:6; 6:20; 7:1–17		

subjection [a]the world to come, whereof we speak:

6 But one in a certain place testified, saying, [a]What is man, that thou art mindful of him? or the son of man, that thou visitest him?

7 Thou madest him [1]a little lower than the angels; thou crownedst him with glory and honour, and didst set him over the works of thy hands:

8 [a]Thou hast put all *things* in subjection under his feet. For in that *he* put all in subjection under him, he left nothing *that is* not put under him. But now [b]we see not yet all *things* put under him.

9 But we see Jesus, [a]who was made a little lower than the angels, [1]for the suffering of death, [b]crowned with glory and honour; that he by the grace of God should taste death [c]for every *man*.

10 [a]For it became him, [b]for whom *are* all *things*, and by whom *are* all *things*, in bringing many sons unto glory, to make [c]the captain of their salvation [d]perfect through sufferings.

11 For [a]both he that sanctifieth and they who are sanctified [b]*are* all of one: for which cause [c]he is not ashamed to call them brethren,

12 Saying, [a]I will declare thy name unto my brethren, in the midst of the church will I sing praise unto thee.

13 And again, [a]I will put my trust in him. And again, [b]Behold, I, and the children [c]which God hath given me.

14 Forasmuch then as the children are partakers of flesh and blood, he [a]also himself likewise took part of the same; [b]that through death he might destroy him that had the power of death, that is, the devil;

15 And deliver them who [a]through fear of death were all their lifetime subject to bondage.

16 For verily [1]he took not on *him the nature of* angels; but he took on *him* the seed of Abraham.

17 Wherefore in all *things* it behoved him [a]to be made like unto *his* brethren, that he might be [b]a merciful and faithful high priest *in things* pertaining to God, to make reconciliation for the sins of the people.

18 [a]For in that he himself hath suffered being tempted, he is able to succour them that are tempted.

Christ superior to Moses

3 Wherefore, holy brethren, partakers of [a]the heavenly calling, consider [b]the

2:5 [a]2 Pet. 3:13
2:6 [a]Job 7:17
2:7 [1]Or, *a little while inferior to*
2:8 [a]Mat. 28:18; Eph. 1:22 [b]1 Cor. 15:25
2:9 [1]Or, *by* [a]Phil. 2:7-9 [b]Acts 2:33 [c]John 3:16; 2 Cor. 5:15; 1 John 2:2; Rev. 5:9
2:10 [a]Luke 24:46 [b]Rom. 11:36 [c]Acts 5:31 [d]Luke 13:32
2:11 [a]ch. 10:10 [b]Acts 17:26 [c]Mat. 28:10; John 20:17
2:12 [a]Ps. 22:22
2:13 [a]Ps. 18:2; Is. 12:2 [b]Is. 8:18 [c]John 10:29
2:14 [a]John 1:14; Phil. 2:7 [b]1 Cor. 15:54; Col. 2:15
2:15 [a]Luke 1:74; 2 Tim. 1:7
2:16 [1]Gr. *he taketh not hold of angels, but of the seed of Abraham he taketh hold*
2:17 [a]Phil. 2:7 [b]ch. 4:15
2:18 [a]ch. 4:15,16
3:1 [a]Rom. 1:7; 1 Cor. 1:2; Phil. 3:14; 2 Pet. 1:10 [b]Rom. 15:8

Christ's superiority over the angels—in fulfilling man's role as sovereign over the earth and in redeeming fallen man, not fallen angels. To accomplish all this, Christ assumed human nature (see vv. 11,14).

2:5 *unto the angels hath he not put in subjection the world to come.* Some think the readers were being enticed to believe that the future kingdom would be under the rule of angelic beings (see note on 1:4). Others see the author trying to dissuade his readers from turning back to Judaism. He shows that Christ, as bearer of the new revelation, is superior to angels who had participated in bringing the revelation at Sinai.

2:6a *one in a certain place testified.* Such a well-known passage as Ps 8:4–6 did not need precise identification.

2:6b–8 Awed by the marvelous order and immensity of God's handiwork in the celestial universe, the psalmist marveled at the high dignity God had bestowed on puny man by entrusting him with dominion over the other creatures (see Gen 1:26–28 and notes).

2:7 *angels.* See note on Ps 8:5.

2:8 *all things.* God's purpose from the beginning was that man should be sovereign in the creaturely realm, subject only to God. Due to sin, that purpose of God has not yet been fully realized. Indeed, men are themselves "subject to bondage" (v. 15).

2:9 *Jesus . . . crowned with glory and honour.* See 10:13. Ps 8 is here applied to Jesus in particular. As forerunner of man's restored dominion over the earth, He was made lower than the angels for a while but is now crowned with glory and honor at God's right hand. By His perfect life, His death on the cross and His exaltation, He has made possible for redeemed man the ultimate fulfillment of Ps 8 in the future kingdom, when man will regain sovereignty over creation.

‡2:10 *many sons unto glory.* Those who believe in Christ are made God's children through His only Son (cf. John 1:12–13). *perfect through sufferings.* Christ had not been morally or spiritually imperfect, but His incarnation was completed (perfected) when He experienced suffering. He identified with us on the deepest level of anguish, and so became qualified to pay the price for our sinful imperfection and to become our sympathetic high priest.

2:11 *both he that sanctifieth and they who are sanctified.* Christ became man to identify Himself with man and, by His substitutionary sacrifice on the cross, to restore the holiness man had lost. *to call them brethren.* Our brotherhood with Jesus is the brotherhood of the Redeemer with the redeemed, who are truly one with Him.

2:12 *I will declare thy name unto my brethren.* A quotation from Ps 22:22, a psalm describing the sufferings and triumph of God's righteous servant (see introduction to Ps 22). The key phrase is "my brethren," seen here as coming from the lips of the triumphant Messiah.

2:13 *I will put my trust in him.* An expression of true dependence on God perfectly exemplified in Christ. In Him humanity is seen as it was intended to be. *Behold, I, and the children which God hath given me.* Also seen ultimately as an utterance of the incarnate Son. The Father's children are given to the Son to be His brothers (see v. 11).

2:14 *him that had the power of death.* Satan wields the power of death only insofar as he induces people to sin and to come under sin's penalty, which is death (see Ezek 18:4; Rom 5:12; 6:23).

2:15 *deliver.* See 1 Cor 15:54–57; Rev 1:18.

2:16 *seed of Abraham.* Christ assumed not angelic nature but human nature, characterized by the descendants of Abraham.

‡2:17 *a merciful and faithful high priest.* Christ could represent mankind before God only if He became one with them. *make reconciliation.* To make atonement or satisfaction and so to turn away God's wrath. See notes on Rom 3:25; 1 John 2:2. In order for Christ to turn aside the wrath of God against guilty sinners, He had to become one with them and die as a substitute for them.

2:18 *he himself . . . tempted.* See note on 4:15.

3:1–4:13 An exposition of Ps 95:7–11, stressing Christ's superiority over Moses and warning against disobedience and unbelief.

3:1 *partakers.* See note on v. 14. *the heavenly calling.* The in-

Apostle and High Priest of our profession, Christ Jesus;

2 Who was faithful to him that [1]appointed him, as also [a]Moses *was faithful* in all his house.

3 For this *man* was counted worthy of more glory than Moses, inasmuch as [a]he who hath builded the house hath more honour than the house.

4 For every house is builded by some *man;* but [a]he that built all *things is* God.

5 [a]And Moses verily *was* faithful in all his house, as [b]a servant, [c]for a testimony of those *things* which were to be spoken after;

6 But Christ as [a]a Son over his own house; [b]whose house are we, [c]if we hold fast the confidence and the rejoicing of the hope firm unto the end.

7 Wherefore, as [a]the Holy Ghost saith, [b]To day if ye will hear his voice,

8 Harden not your hearts, as in the provocation, in the day of temptation in the wilderness:

9 When your fathers tempted me, proved me, and saw my works forty years.

10 Wherefore I was grieved with that generation, and said, They do alway err in *their* heart; and they have not known my ways.

11 So I sware in my wrath, [1]They shall not enter into my rest.

The disobedient generation

12 ¶ Take heed, brethren, lest there be in any of you an evil heart of unbelief, in departing from the living God.

13 But exhort one another daily, while it is called To day; lest any of you be hardened through the deceitfulness of sin.

14 For we are made partakers of Christ, [a]if we hold the beginning of *our* confidence stedfast unto the end;

15 Whilst it is said, [a]To day if ye will hear his voice, harden not your hearts, as in the provocation.

16 [a]For some, when they had heard, did provoke: howbeit not all that came out of Egypt by Moses.

17 But with whom was he grieved forty years? *was it* not with them that had sinned, [a]whose carcases fell in the wilderness?

18 And [a]to whom sware he that *they* should not enter into his rest, but to them that believed not?

19 So we see that they could not enter in because of unbelief.

The promise of rest

4 Let [a]us therefore fear, lest, a promise being left *us* of entering into his rest, any of you should seem to come short *of it.*

2 For unto us was the gospel preached, as well as unto them: but [1]the word preached did not profit them, [2]not being mixed with faith in them that heard *it.*

3 [a]For we which have believed do enter into rest, as *he* said, [b]As I have sworn in my

3:2 [1]Gr. *made* [a]Num. 12:7
3:3 [a]Zech. 6:12; Mat. 16:18
3:4 [a]Eph. 2:10; ch. 1:2
3:5 [a]ver. 2 [b]Ex. 14:31; Deut. 3:24 [c]Deut. 18:19
3:6 [a]ch. 1:2 [b]1 Cor. 3:16 [c]Mat. 10:22; Rom. 5:2; Col. 1:23
3:7 [a]Acts 1:16 [b]Ps. 95:7
3:11 [1]Gr. *If they shall enter*
3:14 [a]ver. 6
3:15 [a]ver. 7
3:16 [a]Num. 14:2
3:17 [a]Num. 14:22; Ps. 106:26
3:18 [a]Num. 14:30
4:1 [a]ch. 12:15
4:2 [1]Gr. *the word of hearing* [2]Or, *because they were not united by faith to*
4:3 [a]ch. 3:14 [b]Ps. 95:11

vitation that comes from heaven and leads to heaven. *Apostle.* Means "one who is sent" (see notes on Mark 6:30; 1 Cor 1:1). Jesus repeatedly spoke of Himself as having been sent into the world by the Father (e.g., Mat 10:40; 15:24; Mark 9:37; Luke 9:48; John 4:34; 5:24,30,36–38; 6:38). He is the supreme apostle, the one from whom all other apostleship flows.

3:2 A comparison of Christ and Moses, both of whom were sent by the Father to lead His people—the one to lead them from bondage under Pharaoh to the promised land, the other to lead them from bondage under the devil (2:14–15) to the rest promised to those who believe (4:3,9). The rest may be heaven, though many hold that it refers primarily to the salvation-rest of Christ's redemption. The analogy focuses on faithful stewardship.

3:3 *he who hath builded . . . hath more honour than the house.* Jesus is the actual builder of the house (or household), whereas Moses was simply a part of it.

3:4 *he that built all things is God.* Jesus is here equated with God, making it beyond question that Christ is greater than Moses.

3:5–6 *in all his house, as a servant . . . a Son over his own house.* The superiority of Christ over Moses is shown in two comparisons: (1) Moses was a servant, whereas Christ is a son, and (2) Moses was in God's house, i.e., a part of it, whereas Christ is over God's house.

3:6 *whose house are we.* The house is made up of God's people, His household (see Eph 2:19; 1 Pet 2:5). *if we hold fast the confidence and the . . . hope.* Failure to persevere reveals that a person is actually not a child of God, whereas perseverance is the hallmark of His children.

3:7–11 This quotation from Ps 95:7–11 summarizes the inglorious history of Israel under Moses' leadership in the wilderness. Three time periods are alluded to: that of the exodus, that of the psalmist and that of the writing of Hebrews. The example of Israel under Moses was used by the psalmist to warn the Israelites of his day against unbelief and disobedience. In a similar way the author of Hebrews applied the psalmist's warning to the recipients of this letter. The warning also applies today.

3:12 *departing from the living God.* To turn away rebelliously (lit. "to become apostate") from God is to turn away from life and to choose death, just as did some of the Israelites who came out of Egypt.

3:13 *while it is called To day.* See 4:7. This is still the day of divine grace and opportunity to trust God, but it will not last indefinitely.

‡3:14 *partakers of Christ.* To belong to Him and participate in the blessings (cf. v. 1). *hold the beginning of our confidence stedfast unto the end.* Salvation is evidenced by continuing in faith to the end. Such perseverance reveals those who share in Christ (see note on v. 6).

3:16–19 The argument is pursued with a series of rhetorical questions. The important truths are that the people who failed to enter Canaan were the ones who had heard God's promise concerning the land and that they refused to believe what God had promised (v. 19)—an action described as rebellion (v. 16), sin (v. 17) and disobedience (v. 18). Consequently, God in His anger closed the doors of Canaan in the face of that whole generation of Israelites (Num 14:21–35). First-century readers of Hebrews faced a similar danger spiritually.

4:1 *a promise being left us of entering into his rest.* Salvation is still available. "His rest" cannot refer ultimately to the rest in Canaan offered to the Israelites. That temporary, earthly rest gained under Joshua (see v. 8; see also note on Josh 1:13) pointed to a rest that is spiritual and eternal.

wrath, if they shall enter into my rest: although the works were finished from the foundation of the world.
4 For *he* spake in a certain place of the seventh *day* on this wise, [a]And God did rest the
seventh day from all his works.
5 And in this *place* again, If they shall enter into my rest.
6 Seeing therefore it remaineth that some
must enter therein, [a]and they to whom [1]it
was first preached entered not in because of
unbelief,
7 Again he limiteth a certain day, saying in
David, To day, after so long a time; as it is said,
[a]To day if ye will hear his voice, harden not
your hearts.
8 For if [1]Jesus had given them rest, *then*
would he not afterward have spoken of another day.
9 There remaineth therefore a [1]rest to the
people of God.
10 For he that is entered into his rest, he
also hath ceased from his own works, as God
did from his.
11 Let us labour therefore to enter into
that rest, lest any *man* fall after the same example of [1]unbelief.

4:4 [a]Ex. 20:11
4:6 [1]Or, *the gospel was first preached* [a]ch. 3:19
4:7 [a]Ps. 95:7
4:8 [1]That is, *Joshua*
4:9 [1]Or, *keeping of a sabbath*
4:11 [1]Or, *disobedience*
4:12 [a]Ps. 147:15; Jer. 23:29 [b]Is. 49:2 [c]Eph. 6:17; Rev. 1:16 [d]1 Cor. 14:25
4:13 [a]Ps. 90:8 [b]Job 26:6
4:14 [a]ch. 7:26 [b]ch. 10:23
4:15 [a]Is. 53:3 [b]Luke 22:28 [c]2 Cor. 5:21; 1 Pet. 2:22
4:16 [a]Eph. 2:18
5:1 [a]ch. 8:3

12 For the word of God *is* [a]quick, and powerful, and [b]sharper than any [c]twoedged
sword, piercing even to the dividing asunder
of soul and spirit, and of the joints and marrow, and *is* [d]a discerner of the thoughts and
intents of the heart.
13 [a]Neither is there any creature *that is*
not manifest in his sight: but all *things are*
naked [b]and opened unto the eyes of him with
whom we have to do.

Christ the way to God

14 ¶ Seeing then that we have a great high
priest, [a]that is passed into the heavens, Jesus
the Son of God, [b]let us hold fast *our* profession.
15 For [a]we have not a high priest which
cannot be touched with the feeling of our infirmities; but [b]was in all *points* tempted like as
we are, [c]*yet* without sin.
16 [a]Let us therefore come boldly unto the
throne of grace, that we may obtain mercy,
and find grace to help in time of need.
5 For every high priest taken from among
men [a]is ordained for men *in things* pertaining to God, that he may offer both gifts and
sacrifices for sins:

4:3 *we which have believed do enter into rest.* Just as entering physical rest in Canaan demanded faith in God's promise, so salvation-rest is entered only by faith in the person and work of Jesus Christ. *if they shall enter into my rest.* This literal translation of a Hebrew idiom would better be translated: "they shall not enter my rest" (also in v. 5). *the works were finished from the foundation of the world.* God rested from His work on the seventh day of creation (see v. 4; Gen 2:2), and thus His rest is already a reality. The rest God calls us to enter (vv. 10–11) is not our rest but His rest, which He invites us to share.

4:6–8 Israel's going into Canaan under Joshua was a partial and temporary entering of God's rest. That, however, was not the end of entering, as shown in the continuing invitation of Ps 95:7–8.

4:7 *To day.* See note on 3:13.

‡4:8 *Jesus.* See KJV marg. The Greek name "Jesus" and the Hebrew name "Joshua" are the same name, meaning "Savior." The context of this verse is speaking of the rest that Joshua could not give to the nation of Israel when they entered the promised land of Canaan. Ps 95 bears witness to this unfulfilled rest in Moses' and Joshua's time.

4:9 *There remaineth therefore a rest.* God's rest may still be entered by faith in His Son.

4:10 *ceased from his own works.* Whereas God rested from the work of creation, the believer ceases his efforts to gain salvation by his own works and rests in the finished work of Christ on the cross. According to some, however, the believer's final rest is in view here (see Rev 14:13).

4:11 *Let us labour.* Not a call to earn one's salvation by works, but an exhortation to enter salvation-rest by faith and not follow Israel's sad example in the wilderness.

4:12–13 The reasons for giving serious attention to the exhortation of v. 11.

4:12 *word of God.* God's truth was revealed by Jesus (the incarnate Word; see John 1:1,14), but it has also been given verbally, the word referred to here. This dynamic word of God, active in accomplishing God's purposes, appears in both the OT and the NT (see Ps 107:20; 147:18; Is 40:8; 55:11; Gal 3:8; Eph 5:26; Jas 1:18; 1 Pet 1:23). The author of Hebrews describes it as a living power that judges as with an all-seeing eye, penetrating a person's innermost being. *soul and spirit . . . joints and marrow.* The totality and depth of one's being.

4:13 *Neither . . . any creature. . . not manifest.* The author associates the activity of the word with the activity of God as though they are one and the same—which in a sense they are.

4:14–7:28 An exposition of Ps 110:4, stressing Christ's superiority over Aaron because of a better priesthood.

4:14 *great high priest.* See 2:17; 3:1. The author here begins an extended discussion of the superior priesthood of Christ. *into the heavens.* As the Aaronic high priest on the day of atonement passed from the sight of the people into the most holy place (see Lev 16:15,17), so Jesus passed from the sight of His watching disciples, ascending through the heavens into the heavenly sanctuary, His work of atonement accomplished (Acts 1:9–11). *hold fast our profession.* Suggests that the readers were in danger of letting their faith slip (see similar admonitions in 2:1; 3:6,14).

4:15 *tempted like as we are.* See 2:18. The author stresses the parallel between Christ's temptations and ours. He did not have each temptation we have but experienced every kind of temptation a person can have. *yet without sin.* The way in which Christ's temptations were completely different from ours was in the results—His temptations never led to sin (see Mat 4:1–11).

‡4:16 *Let us therefore come boldly.* Because Christ our high priest has experienced human temptation, He stands ready to give immediate and sympathetic help when we are tempted. *throne of grace.* The place where we meet God when we pray is described as: (1) a throne—a place of authority and abundant resources, and (2) of grace—a condition of favor and liberal help.

5:1–4 The high-priestly office had two specific qualifications: (1) A candidate had to be "taken from among men" (v. 1) and thus be able to represent them before God; and (2) he had to be "called of God" (v. 4).

5:1 *gifts and sacrifices.* See 8:3; 9:9; see also notes on Lev 1:2; 2:1.

2 Who [1]can have compassion on the ignorant, and on them that are out of the way; for
that he himself also is compassed with infirmity.
3 And [a]by reason hereof he ought, as for
the people, so also for himself, to offer for sins.
4 [a]And no *man* taketh *this* honour unto
himself, but he that is called of God, as [b]*was*
Aaron.
5 [a]So also Christ glorified not himself to be
made a high priest; but he that said unto him,
[b]Thou art my Son, to day have I begotten thee.
6 As he saith also in another *place,* [a]Thou
art a priest for ever after the order of Melchisedec.
7 Who in the days of his flesh, when he
had [a]offered up prayers and supplications
[b]with strong crying and tears unto him [c]that
was able to save him from death, and was
heard [d][1]in that *he* feared;
8 [a]Though he were a Son, *yet* learned he
[b]obedience by *the things* which he suffered;
9 And being made perfect, he became the
author of eternal salvation unto all them that
obey him;
10 Called of God a high priest after the order of Melchisedec.

Warning against apostasy

11 ¶ Of whom [a]we have many things to
say, and hard to be uttered, seeing ye are [b]dull
of hearing.
12 For when for the time ye ought to be
teachers, ye have need that *one* teach you
again which *be* the first principles of the oracles of God; and are become such as have need
of [a]milk, and not of strong meat.
13 For every one that useth milk [1]*is* unskilful in the word of righteousness: for he is
[a]a babe.
14 But strong meat belongeth to *them that
are* [1]of full age, *even* those who by reason [2]of
use have their senses exercised [a]to discern
both good and evil.

6 Therefore [a]leaving [1]the principles of the
doctrine of Christ, let us go on unto perfection; not laying again the foundation of repentance [b]from dead works, and of faith towards God,
2 [a]Of the doctrine of baptisms, [b]and of laying on of hands, [c]and of resurrection of the
dead, [d]and of eternal judgment.
3 And this will we do, [a]if God permit.
4 For [a]*it is* impossible for those [b]who were
once enlightened, and have tasted of [c]the

5:2 [1]Or, *can reasonably bear with*
5:3 [a]Lev. 4:3
5:4 [a]2 Chr. 26:18; John 3:27 [b]Ex. 28:1
5:5 [a]John 8:54 [b]Ps. 2:7
5:6 [a]Ps. 110:4
5:7 [1]Or, *for* his *piety* [a]Mat. 26:39; Mark 14:36; John 17:1 [b]Ps. 22:1; Mat. 27:46 [c]Mat. 26:53; Mark 14:36 [d]Mat. 26:37; Mark 14:33; Luke 22:43; John 12:27
5:8 [a]ch. 3:6 [b]Phil. 2:8
5:11 [a]John 16:12; 2 Pet. 3:16
5:11 [b]Mat. 13:15
5:12 [a]1 Cor. 3:1
5:13 [1]Gr. *hath no experience* [a]1 Cor. 13:11; Eph. 4:14; 1 Pet. 2:2
5:14 [1]Or, *perfect* [2]Or, *of a habit,* or, *perfection* [a]Is. 7:15; 1 Cor. 2:14

6:1 [1]Or, *the word of the beginning of Christ* [a]Phil. 3:12-14; ch. 5:12 [b]ch. 9:14 6:2 [a]Acts 19:4,5 [b]Acts 8:14; 19:6 [c]Acts 17:31 [d]Acts 24:25; Rom. 2:16 6:3 [a]Acts 18:21 6:4 [a]Mat. 12:31; ch. 10:26; 2 Pet. 2:20; 1 John 5:16 [b]ch. 10:32 [c]John 4:10; 6:32; Eph. 2:8

‡5:2 *the ignorant, and on them that are out of the way.* I.e."the ignorant and misguided." See Is 53:6. Contrast the unintentional sin (as in Lev 4; Num 15:27–29) with defiant rebellion against God (see Num 15:30–31; cf. Heb 6:4–6; 10:26–31).

5:4 *no man taketh this honour unto himself.* In Christ's day the high-priestly office was in the hands of a family that had bought control of it.

5:5 *Christ glorified not himself to be made a high priest.* The Son was appointed by the Father, as the two prophetic statements cited here show (Ps 2:7; 110:4). His high priesthood, however, was "according to the order of Melchisedec" (v. 6), not in the order of Aaron. *to day have I begotten thee.* See notes on 1:5; Ps 2:7–9; cf. Rom 1:4.

25:7 *days of his flesh.* The principal reference here is to Christ's agony in the Garden of Gethsemane. *unto him that was able to save Him from death.* To the Father. Jesus did not shrink from physical suffering and death but from the indescribable agony of taking mankind's sin on Himself (see Mat 27:46). Although He asked that the cup of suffering might be taken from Him, He did not waver in His determination to fulfill the Father's will (see Mat 26:36–46). *was heard.* His prayer was granted by the Father, who saved Him from death—through resurrection.

‡5:8 *learned he obedience by the things which he suffered.* He was made "perfect" (v. 9) through suffering (see note on 2:10), namely, His temptation in the wilderness and His ordeal on the cross. Though He was the eternal Son of God, it was necessary for Him as the incarnate Son to learn obedience—not that He was ever disobedient, but that He was called on to obey to an extent He had never before experienced. The temptations He faced were real and the battle for victory was difficult, but where Adam failed and fell, Jesus resisted and prevailed. His humanity was thereby completed, "made perfect" (v. 9), and on the basis of this perfection He could become "the author of eternal salvation" (v. 9; see also 9:12).

‡5:11 *Of whom we have many things to say.* The author wishes to discuss the priesthood of Melchisedec but will not until ch. 7 due to the spiritual condition described as follows. *dull of hearing.* Instead of progressing in the Christian life, the readers had become spiritually sluggish and mentally lazy (6:12).

5:12 *for the time.* They were not recent converts. *first principles of the oracles of God.* These are listed in 6:1–2 (see note there). Having taken the first steps toward becoming (mature) Christians, they had slipped back to where they started. *strong meat.* Advanced teaching such as that given in ch. 7.

5:14 *of full age.* Those who had progressed in spiritual life and had become Christians of sound judgment and discernment. *discern both good and evil.* Something neither physical nor spiritual infants can do.

6:1–2 *not laying again the foundation.* Six fundamental doctrines are mentioned: 1. *repentance.* The change of mind that causes one to turn away from sin and/or useless rituals. 2. *faith towards God.* The counterpart of repentance. As repentance is turning away from the darkness of sin, faith is turning to the light of God. 3. *doctrine of baptisms.* Probably refers to different baptisms with which the readers were familiar, such as Jewish baptism of proselytes, John the Baptist's baptism, and the baptism commanded by Jesus (Mat 28:19). 4. *laying on of hands.* Sometimes followed baptism (Acts 8:16–17; 19:5–6). Otherwise laying on of hands was practiced in connection with ordaining or commissioning (see Acts 6:6; 13:3; 1 Tim 5:22; 2 Tim 1:6), healing the sick (see Mark 6:5; 16:18; Luke 4:40; Acts 28:8) and bestowal of blessing (see Mat 19:13–15). 5. *resurrection of the dead.* The resurrection of all people in the last days (see John 5:25–29; 11:25; 2 Cor 4:14). 6. *eternal judgment.* The destiny of those who reject God's saving grace and persist in their sinful ways.

6:1 *principles of the doctrine of Christ.* See note on 5:12.

6:3 A common expression of dependence on the will of God (cf. 1 Cor 16:7). Only the Lord can open minds and hearts and bring spiritual maturity.

‡6:4–6 The most common interpretations of this difficult passage are: 1. It refers to Christians who actually lose their salvation. But the author seems to be teaching the opposite of that

heavenly gift, and [d]were made partakers of the
Holy Ghost,
5 And have tasted the good word of God,
and the powers of [a]the world to come,
6 If they shall fall away, to renew *them*
again unto repentance; [a]seeing they crucify to
themselves the Son of God afresh, and put *him*
to an open shame.
7 For the earth which drinketh *in* the rain
that cometh oft upon it, and bringeth forth
herbs meet for them [1]by whom it is dressed,
[a]receiveth blessing from God:
8 [a]But that which beareth thorns and
briers *is* rejected, and *is* nigh unto cursing;
whose end *is* to be burned.

God's oath unchanging

9 ¶ But, beloved, we are persuaded better
things of you, and *things* that accompany salvation, though we thus speak.
10 [a]For [b]God *is* not unrighteous to forget
[c]your work and labour of love, which ye have
shewed toward his name, in that ye have
[d]ministered to the saints, and do minister.
11 And we desire that [a]every one of you do
shew the same diligence [b]to the full assurance
of hope unto the end:
12 That ye be not slothful, but followers of
them who through faith and patience [a]inherit
the promises.
13 For when God made promise to Abraham, because he could swear by no greater,
[a]he sware by himself,

6:4 [d]Gal. 3:2,5; ch. 2:4
6:5 [a]ch. 2:5
6:6 [a]ch. 10:29
6:7 [1]Or, *for* [a]Ps. 65:10
6:8 [a]Is. 5:6
6:10 [a]Prov. 14:31; Mat. 10:42; 25:40; John 13:20 [b]Rom. 3:4; 2 Thes. 1:6,7 [c]1 Thes. 1:3 [d]Rom. 15:25; 2 Cor. 8:4; 2 Tim. 1:18
6:11 [a]ch. 3:6,14 [b]Col. 2:2
6:12 [a]ch. 10:36
6:13 [a]Gen. 22:16,17; Ps. 105:9; Luke 1:73

6:16 [a]Ex. 22:11
6:17 [1]Gr. *interposed himself by an oath* [a]ch. 11:9 [b]Rom. 11:29
6:18 [a]ch. 12:1
6:19 [a]Lev. 16:15; ch. 9:7
6:20 [a]ch. 4:14; 8:1; 9:24 [b]ch. 3:1; 5:6,10; 7:17
7:1 [a]Gen. 14:18
7:3 [1]Gr. *without pedigree*

14 Saying, Surely blessing I will bless thee,
and multiplying I will multiply thee.
15 And so, after he had patiently endured,
he obtained the promise.
16 For men verily swear by the greater:
and [a]an oath for confirmation *is* to them an
end of all strife.
17 Wherein God, willing more abundantly
to shew unto [a]the heirs of promise [b]the immutability of his counsel, [1]confirmed *it* by an
oath:
18 That by two immutable things, in which
it was impossible for God to lie, we might
have a strong consolation, who have fled for
refuge to lay hold upon the hope [a]set before
us:
19 Which *hope* we have as an anchor of
the soul, both sure and stedfast, [a]and which
entereth into that within the vail;
20 [a]Whither the forerunner is for us entered, *even* Jesus, [b]made a high priest for ever
after the order of Melchisedec.

The priesthood of Melchisedec

7 For this [a]Melchisedec, king of Salem,
priest of the most high God, who met
Abraham returning from the slaughter of the
kings, and blessed him;
2 To whom also Abraham gave a tenth *part*
of all; first being by interpretation King of righteousness, and after that also King of Salem,
which is, King of peace;
3 Without father, without mother, [1]with-

in 6:13–20. 2. It is a hypothetical argument to warn immature Hebrew Christians (5:11–14) that they must progress to maturity (see v. 1) or else experience divine discipline or judgment (see vv. 7–8). This view is supported by the fact that each of the five warnings expresses a condition and its consequences (2:3; 3:14; 6:6; 10:26 and 12:25); the author places himself among his hearers (10:26) and is convinced that these conditions are not really true of them (6:9). 3. It refers to professing Christians whose apostasy proves that their faith was not genuine (cf. 1 John 2:19). This view sees chs. 3–4 as a warning based on the rebellion of the Israelites in the wilderness. As Israel could not enter the promised land after spying out the region and tasting its fruit, so the professing Hebrew Christians would not be able to repent if they adamantly turned against "the light" they had received. According to this interpretation, such expressions as "enlightened," "tasted of the heavenly gift" and "partakers of the Holy Ghost" indicate that such persons had come under the influence of God's covenant blessings and had professed to turn from darkness to light but were in danger of a public and final rejection of Christ, proving they had never been regenerated.

6:5 *the world to come.* See Mark 10:30 and note; 1 Tim 6:19.

6:7–8 A short parable graphically illustrating the warning just given (see John 15:5–6; 2 Pet 2:20–22; 1 John 5:16).

6:9 *persuaded better things . . . that accompany salvation.* Although the author has suggested the possibility that some of his readers may still be unsaved, he is confident that God has been at work among them. Changed lives and works of love (v. 10) suggest that many of these persons were indeed regenerated.

6:11 *the full assurance of hope.* See 11:1; 2 Pet 1:10. *unto the end.* A call for perseverance in faith as an evidence of salvation.

6:12 *them who through faith and patience inherit the promises.* For examples see ch. 11.

‡6:13 *God made promise to Abraham.* The promise of many descendants was made with an oath to emphasize its unchanging character (see Gen 22:16–18). Ordinarily the swearing of an oath belongs to our fallen human situation, in which a man's word is not always trustworthy. God's swearing of an oath was a condescension to human frailty, thus making His word, which in itself is absolutely trustworthy, doubly dependable (see v. 18).

6:15 *after he had patiently endured.* For 25 years (see Gen 12:3–4; 21:5). *obtained the promise.* The birth of his son Isaac (Gen 17:2; 18:10; 21:5).

6:18 *two immutable things.* God's promise, which in itself is absolutely trustworthy, and God's oath confirming that promise. *might have a strong consolation.* Since we look back on the fulfillment of the promise that Abraham saw only in anticipation (11:13; John 8:56).

6:19 *as an anchor of the soul, both sure and stedfast.* Like an anchor holding a ship safely in position, our hope in Christ guarantees our safety. *within the vail.* Whereas the ship's anchor goes down to the ocean bed, the Christian's anchor goes up into the true, heavenly sanctuary, where he is moored to God himself.

6:20 *a high priest for ever after the order of Melchisedec.* The grand theme that the author is about to develop (ch. 7).

‡7:1 *Melchisedec.* See Gen 14:18–20 and notes. *king . . . priest.* Of particular significance is Melchisedec's holding both offices, one of the ways in which he prefigured Christ. *Salem.* Jerusalem (see note on Gen 14:18).

7:2 *King of righteousness . . . King of peace.* Messianic titles (see Is 9:6–7; Jer 23:5–6; 33:15–16).

out descent, having neither beginning of days, nor end of life; but made like unto the Son of God; abideth a priest continually.

4 Now consider how great this *man was,* [a]unto whom even the patriarch Abraham gave the tenth of the spoils.

5 And verily [a]they that are of the sons of Levi who receive the office of the priesthood have a commandment to take tithes of the people according to the law, that is, of their brethren, though they come out of the loins of Abraham:

6 But he whose [1]descent is not counted from them received tithes of Abraham, [a]and blessed [b]him that had the promises.

7 And without all contradiction the less is blessed of the better.

8 And here men that die receive tithes; but there he *receiveth them,* [a]of whom it is witnessed that he liveth.

9 And as *I* may so say, Levi also, who receiveth tithes, payed tithes in Abraham.

7:4 [a]Gen. 14:20
7:5 [a]Num. 18:21,26
7:6 [1]Or, *pedigree* [a]Gen. 14:19 [b]Rom. 4:13
7:8 [a]ch. 5:6; 6:20

7:11 [a]ver. 18,19; Gal. 2:21; ch. 8:7
7:14 [a]Is. 11:1; Mat. 1:3; Luke 3:33; Rom. 1:3; Rev. 5:5

10 For he was yet in the loins of his father, when Melchisedec met him.

11 [a]If therefore perfection were by the Levitical priesthood, (for under it the people received the law,) what further need *was there* that another priest should rise after the order of Melchisedec, and not be called after the order of Aaron?

12 For the priesthood being changed, there is made of necessity a change also of the law.

13 For he of whom these *things* are spoken pertaineth to another tribe, of which no *man* gave attendance at the altar.

14 For *it is* evident that [a]our Lord sprang out of Juda; of which tribe Moses spake nothing concerning priesthood.

15 And it is yet far more evident: for that after the similitude of Melchisedec there ariseth another priest,

16 Who is made, not after the law of a carnal commandment, but after the power of an endless life.

‡7:3 *Without father . . . nor end of life.* Gen 14:18–20, contrary to the practice elsewhere in the early chapters of Genesis, does not mention Melchisedec's parentage and children, or his birth and death. That he was a real, historical figure is clear, but the author of Hebrews (in accordance with Jewish interpretation) uses the silence of Scripture about Melchisedec's genealogy to portray him as a prefiguration of Christ. Melchisedec's priesthood anticipates Christ's eternal existence and His unending priesthood. Some believe the appearance of Melchisedec to Abraham was a manifestation of Christ before His incarnation, but the comparison "like unto the Son of God" argues against such an interpretation.

‡7:4 *consider how great this man was.* The one who collects a tithe is greater than the one who pays it, and "the less is blessed of the better" (v. 7). In both ways Melchisedec was greater than Abraham.

‡7:11–14 The point of these verses is that the Levitical priesthood brought with it all the regulations of the Mosaic law. So if one turns to Christ and His priesthood, he must reject the Levitical priesthood and its law, for the law disqualifies Jesus from becoming its priest, since He is from the invalid tribe of Judah.

7:11 *under it.* The Levitical priesthood. *the people received the law.* The law of Moses and the priesthood went together. All the people without exception were sinners, subject to the law's condemnation, and thus were in need of a priestly system to mediate between them and God. *after the order of Melchisedec and not . . . after the order of Aaron.* Implies that the Aaronic (or Levitical) priesthood was imperfect but that Melchisedec's was perfect. The announcement of the coming one who would be a priest forever (Ps 110:4) was written midway in the history of the Levitical priesthood, which could only mean that the existing system was to give way to something better.

‡7:16 *not after the law of a carnal commandment.* A law involving physical requirements—the tribe of Levi. In the law of Moses the priestly function was restricted to the tribe of Levi (Deut 18:1), but Jesus came from the nonpriestly tribe of Judah (vv. 14–15). *the power of an endless life.* According to Ps 110:4 the priest in the order of Melchisedec is "a priest for ever."

Old Testament Sacrifices Compared to Jesus' Sacrifice

OT SACRIFICE	HEBREWS	JESUS' SACRIFICE
Aaronic priesthood	6:19–7:25	Melchisedec's priesthood
Impermanent priesthood	7:16–17,23–24	For ever priesthood
Old covenant (temporary)	7:22; 8:6,13; 10:20	New covenant (permanent)
One year atonement	7:25; 9:12,15; 10:1–4,12	Eternal atoning sacrifice
Sinful priests	7:26–27; 9:7	Sinless priest
Daily sacrifices	7:27; 9:12,25–26; 10:9–10,12	Once-for-all sacrifice
A shadow	8:5; 9:23–24; 10:1	The reality
Obsolete promises	8:6–13	Better promises
Animal sacrifices	9:11–15,26; 10:4–10,19	Sacrifice of God's Son
Ongoing sacrifices	10:11–14,18	Sacrifices no longer needed

17 For *he* testifieth, [a]Thou *art* a priest for ever after the order of Melchisedec.

18 For there is verily a disannulling of the commandment going before for [a]the weakness and unprofitableness thereof.

19 For [a]the law made nothing perfect, [1]but the bringing in of [b]a better hope *did;* by the which [c]we draw nigh unto God.

20 And inasmuch as not without an oath *he was made priest:*

21 (For those priests were made [1]without an oath; but this with an oath by him that said unto him, [a]The Lord sware and will not repent, Thou *art* a priest for ever after the order of Melchisedec:)

22 By so much [a]was Jesus made a surety of a better testament.

23 And they truly were many priests, because *they* were not suffered to continue by reason of death:

24 But this *man,* because he continueth ever, hath [1]an unchangeable priesthood.

25 Wherefore he is able also to save them [1]to the uttermost that come unto God by him, seeing he ever liveth [a]to make intercession for them.

Christ's priesthood superior

26 ¶ For such a high priest became us, [a]*who is* holy, harmless, undefiled, separate from sinners, [b]and made higher than the heavens;

27 Who needeth not daily, as *those* high priests, to offer up sacrifice, [a]first for his own sins, [b]*and* then for the people's: for [c]this he did once, when he offered up himself.

28 For the law maketh [a]men high priests which have infirmity; but the word of the oath, which was since the law, *maketh* the Son, [b]who is [1]consecrated for evermore.

Superiority of the new covenant

8 Now of the *things* which we have spoken *this is* the sum: We have such a high priest, [a]who is set on the right hand of the throne of the Majesty in the heavens;

2 A minister [1]of [a]the sanctuary, and of [b]the true tabernacle, which the Lord pitched, and not man.

3 For [a]every high priest is ordained to offer gifts and sacrifices: wherefore [b]*it is* of necessity that this *man* have somewhat also to offer.

4 For if he were on earth, he should not be a priest, seeing that [1]there are priests that offer gifts according to the law:

5 Who serve unto the example and [a]shadow of heavenly *things,* as Moses was admonished of God when he was about to make the tabernacle: [b]for, See, saith *he, that* thou make

7:17 [a]Ps. 110:4; ch. 6:20
7:18 [a]Rom. 8:3; Gal. 4:9
7:19 [1]Or, *but it was the bringing in* [a]Acts 13:39; Rom. 3:20,21,28 [b]ch. 6:18 [c]Rom. 5:2; Eph. 2:18; ch. 4:16
7:21 [1]Or, *without swearing of an oath* [a]Ps. 110:4
7:22 [a]ch. 8:6
7:24 [1]Or, *which passeth not from one to another*
7:25 [1]Or, *evermore* [a]Rom. 8:34; 1 Tim. 2:5; 1 John 2:1
7:26 [a]ch. 4:15
7:26 [b]Eph. 1:20; 4:10
7:27 [a]Lev. 9:7 [b]Lev. 16:15 [c]Rom. 6:10
7:28 [1]Gr. *perfected* [a]ch. 5:1,2 [b]ch. 2:10; 5:9
8:1 [a]Eph. 1:20; Col. 3:1; ch. 10:12
8:2 [1]Or, *of holy things* [a]ch. 9:8,12 [b]ch. 9:11
8:3 [a]ch. 5:1 [b]Eph. 5:2; ch. 9:14
8:4 [1]Or, *they are priests*
8:5 [a]Col. 2:17; ch. 9:23 [b]Ex. 25:40; Num. 8:4; Acts 7:44

7:18 *disannulling of the commandment . . . weakness and unprofitableness.* The law is holy and good (Rom 7:12), but it is not able to make right those who sin by breaking it, nor can it give the power necessary to fulfill its demands (v. 19a).

7:19 The law was only preparatory (see Gal 3:23–25) and brought nothing to fulfillment (see Mat 5:17). *better hope.* The new covenant is better because it assures us of complete redemption and brings us into the very presence of God. See note on Col 1:5.

7:20 No divine oath was associated with the establishment of the Levitical priesthood. The priesthood pledged in Ps 110 is superior because it was divinely affirmed with an oath.

‡7:22 *better testament.* The new covenant. See chs. 8–10.

7:23 *not suffered to continue by reason of death.* Impermanence was further evidence of the imperfection of the Levitical order.

7:25 *to the uttermost.* May include the ideas of completeness and permanence. Jesus is a perfect high priest forever; so He is able to save completely and for all time. *ever liveth to make intercession.* His people will never be without a priestly representative (see John 17; 1 John 2:1).

7:26 *such a high priest.* One who meets our need for salvation from sin and its consequences.

7:27 *daily.* A reference to the endless repetition of sacrifices throughout the year (see Ex 29:36–42), evidence that these sacrifices never effectively and finally dealt with sin. *first for his own sins.* Christ's priesthood is superior because He has no personal sins for which sacrifice must be made. *this he did once.* A key concept in Hebrews (see 9:12,26; 10:2,10). The Levitical priests had to bring daily offerings to the Lord, whereas Jesus sacrificed Himself once for all. *offered up himself.* Levitical priests offered up only animals; our high priest offered Himself, the perfect substitute—Man for man.

7:28 *men . . . which have infirmity.* Because (1) they are mortal and therefore impermanent, v. 23; (2) they are sinful, v. 27; and (3) they could only offer animals, which could never provide a genuine substitute for man, who is made in the image of God (see Gen 1:26–28 and notes). *consecrated for evermore.* Christ was made perfect in that He faced temptation without succumbing to sin (see notes on 2:10; 5:8). Instead He perfectly obeyed the Father, thereby establishing a perfection that is eternal.

‡8:1–10:39 The argument of this section grows out of an exposition of Jer 31:31–34 and demonstrates that Christ is the mediator of a "better testament" (7:22).

8:1 See note on 1:2–3. *the Majesty in the heavens.* A Jewish expression for God (see 1:3).

8:2 *true tabernacle.* In contrast to the tabernacle erected by Moses, which was an imperfect and impermanent copy of the heavenly one. *which the Lord pitched, and not man.* The heavenly sanctuary built by God corresponds to the most holy place, the innermost sanctuary in Moses' tabernacle, into which the high priest briefly entered with the blood of atonement once a year (see Lev 16:13–15,34). In the heavenly sanctuary, however, our great high priest dwells eternally as our intercessor (7:25).

8:3 *gifts and sacrifices.* See note on 5:1.

‡8:4 *he should not be a priest.* By His human birth Jesus belonged to the tribe of Judah, which was not the priestly tribe (see 7:12–14). *there are priests that offer gifts.* Members of the tribe of Levi. The present tense of the verb "offer," here and elsewhere in the letter, indicates that the temple in Jerusalem was still standing. This letter, therefore, must have been written prior to the temple's destruction in A.D. 70 (see Introduction: Date).

‡8:5 *the example and shadow of heavenly things.* The heavenly reality is the sanctuary of God's presence, into which Christ our high priest entered with His own blood (see 9:11–12). *make all things according to the pattern.* Because both the tabernacle and its ministry were intended to illustrate symbolically the only way sinners may approach a holy God and find forgiveness.

all *things* according to the pattern shewed to thee in the mount.

6 But now [a]hath he obtained a more excellent ministry, by how much also he is the mediator of a better [1]covenant, which was established upon better promises.

7 ¶ [a]For if that first *covenant* had been faultless, *then* should no place have been sought for the second.

8 For finding fault with them, *he* saith, [a]Behold, the days come, saith the Lord, when I will make a new covenant with the house of Israel and with the house of Juda:

9 Not according to the covenant that I made with their fathers in the day when I took them by the hand to lead them out of the land of Egypt; because they continued not in my covenant, and I regarded them not, saith the Lord.

10 For [a]this *is* the covenant that I will make with the house of Israel after those days, saith the Lord; I will [1]put my laws into their mind, and write them [2]in their hearts: and [b]I will be to them a God, and they shall be to me a people:

11 And [a]they shall not teach every man his neighbour, and every man his brother, saying, Know the Lord: for all shall know me, from the least to the greatest.

12 For I will be merciful to their unrighteousness, [a]and their sins and their iniquities will I remember no more.

13 [a]In that *he* saith, A new *covenant,* he hath made the first old. Now that which decayeth and waxeth old *is* ready to vanish away.

Temporary sacrifices by Levites

9 Then verily the first *covenant* had also [1]ordinances of divine service, and [a]a worldly sanctuary.

2 [a]For there was a tabernacle made; the first, [b]wherein *was* [c]the candlestick, and [d]the table, and the shewbread; which is called [1]the sanctuary.

3 [a]And after the second vail, the tabernacle which is called the holiest of all;

4 Which had the golden censer, and [a]the ark of the covenant overlaid round about with gold, wherein *was* [b]the golden pot that had manna, and [c]Aaron's rod that budded, and [d]the tables of the covenant;

5 And [a]over it the cherubims of glory shadowing the mercy seat; of which *we* cannot now speak particularly.

6 Now when these *things* were thus ordained, [a]the priests went always into the first tabernacle, accomplishing the service *of God.*

7 But into the second *went* the high priest alone [a]once every year, not without blood, [b]which he offered for himself, and *for* the errors of the people:

8 [a]The Holy Ghost this signifying, that [b]the way into the holiest *of all* was not yet made manifest, while as the first tabernacle was yet standing:

9 Which *was* a figure for the time *then*

8:6 [1]Or, *testament* [a]2 Cor. 3:6,8; ch. 7:22
8:7 [a]ch. 7:11,18
8:8 [a]Jer. 31:31
8:10 [1]Gr. *give* [2]Or, *upon* [a]ch. 10:16 [b]Zech. 8:8
8:11 [a]Is. 54:13; John 6:45; 1 John 2:27
8:12 [a]Rom. 11:27
8:13 [a]2 Cor. 5:17
9:1 [1]Or, *ceremonies* [a]Ex. 25:8
9:2 [1]Or, *holy* [a]Ex. 26:1 [b]Ex. 26:35 [c]Ex. 25:31 [d]Ex. 25:23
9:3 [a]Ex. 26:31
9:4 [a]Ex. 25:10 [b]Ex. 16:33 [c]Num. 17:10 [d]Ex. 25:16; Deut. 10:2
9:5 [a]Lev. 16:2
9:6 [a]Num. 28:3
9:7 [a]Ex. 30:10 [b]ch. 7:27
9:8 [a]ch. 10:19 [b]John 14:6

8:6 *he is the mediator of a better covenant.* See 9:15; 12:24; 1 Tim 2:5. The new covenant (see vv. 8–12; Jer 31:31–34) that Jesus mediates is superior to the covenant God made through Moses at Sinai (see Ex 24:7–8). *established upon better promises.* See vv. 10–12.

8:7 *if that first covenant had been faultless.* The line of argument here is similar to that in 7:11, where the Levitical priestly order is shown to be inferior because it was replaced by the order of Melchisedec. Similarly, if the Mosaic covenant were without defect, there would have been no need to replace it with a new covenant. Concerning the fact that there was nothing essentially "wrong" with the Mosaic covenant see note on 7:18.

8:8–12 A quotation from Jer 31:31–34 containing a prophetic announcement and definition of the new covenant, which was to be different from the Mosaic covenant (v. 9). Its superior benefits are: (1) God's laws will become inner principles (v. 10a) that enable His people to delight in doing His will (cf. Ezek 36:26–27; Rom 8:2–4); (2) God and His people will have intimate fellowship (v. 10b); (3) sinful ignorance of God will be removed forever (v. 11); and (4) forgiveness of sins will be an everlasting reality (v. 12).

8:13 *decayeth and waxeth old.* The announcement of the new covenant clearly proved the impermanence of the one already in existence. To return to the old system would be to return to what is no longer valid or effective.

9:2 *there was a tabernacle made.* The tabernacle built under Moses. *candlestick.* Made of hammered gold and placed at the south side of the holy place (Ex 40:24), it had seven lamps that were kept burning every night (Ex 25:31–40). *the table, and the shewbread.* Made of acacia wood overlaid with gold, it stood on the north side of the holy place (Ex 40:22). On it were twelve loaves, arranged in two rows of six (Lev 24:5–6).

‡9:4 *Which had the golden censer.* The Greek word translated "censer" here refers to a vessel used for burning incense. So it can describe either the shovel (censer) used for carrying the coals or the altar on which the coals were placed. Since the golden altar of incense is otherwise not referred to in this enumeration of the tabernacle furniture, it seems best to understand this verse as referring to that altar. Although the altar of incense stood in the holy place, the author describes it as belonging to the most holy place. His purpose was to show its close relationship to the inner sanctuary and the ark of the covenant (cf. Ex 40:5; 1 Ki 6:22). On the day of atonement the high priest took incense from this altar, along with the blood of the sin offering, into the most holy place (Lev 16:12–14). *ark of the covenant.* A chest made of acacia wood, overlaid inside and out with gold (Ex 25:10–16). *manna . . . rod . . . tables.* See notes on Ex 16:33–34; see also Num 17:8–10.

9:5 *cherubims of glory.* Two winged figures made of pure gold, of one piece with the atonement cover, or mercy seat, and standing at either end of it. It was between them that the glory of God's presence appeared (Ex 25:17–22; Lev 16:2; Num 7:89). *mercy seat.* Fitting exactly over the top of the ark of the covenant, it was a slab of pure gold on which the blood of the sin offering was sprinkled by the high priest on the day of atonement (Lev 16:14–15).

9:7 *once every year.* On the day of atonement (*Yom Kippur*), the tenth day of the seventh month (Lev 16:29,34). For a description of its ritual see Lev 16 and notes.

9:8 *while as the first tabernacle was yet standing.* As long as the Mosaic system with its imperfect priesthood and sacrifice remained in effect (8:7–8,13).

9:9 *a figure for the time then present.* The Mosaic tabernacle,

present, in which were offered both gifts and sacrifices, [a]that could not make him that did the service perfect, as pertaining to the conscience;

10 *Which stood* only in [a]meats and drinks, and [b]divers washings, [c]and carnal [1]ordinances, imposed *on them* until the time of reformation.

11 But Christ being come [a]a high priest [b]of good *things* to come, [c]by a greater and more perfect tabernacle, not made with hands, that is to say, not of this building,

12 Neither [a]by the blood of goats and calves, but [b]by his own blood he entered in [c]once into the holy *place,* [d]having obtained eternal redemption *for us.*

13 For if [a]the blood of bulls and of goats, and [b]the ashes of a heifer sprinkling the unclean, sanctifieth to the purifying of the flesh:

14 How much more [a]shall the blood of Christ, [b]who through the eternal Spirit offered himself without [1]spot to God, [c]purge your conscience from [d]dead works [e]to serve the living God?

Christ's once-for-all sacrifice

15 ¶ [a]And for this cause [b]he is the mediator of the new testament, [c]that by means of death, for the redemption of the transgressions that were under the first testament, [d]they which are called might receive the promise of eternal inheritance.

16 For where a testament *is,* there must also of necessity [1]be the death of the testator.

17 For [a]a testament *is* of force after *men* are dead: otherwise it is of no strength at all whilst the testator liveth.

18 [a]Whereupon neither the first *testament* was [1]dedicated without blood.

19 For when Moses had spoken every precept to all the people according to the law, [a]he took the blood of calves and of goats, [b]with water, and [1]scarlet wool, and hyssop, and sprinkled both the book, and all the people,

20 Saying, [a]This *is* the blood of the testament which God hath enjoined unto you.

21 Moreover [a]he sprinkled with blood both the tabernacle, and all the vessels of the ministry.

22 And almost all *things* are by the law purged with blood; and [a]without shedding of blood is no remission.

23 *It was* therefore necessary that [a]the patterns of *things* in the heavens should be purified with these; but the heavenly *things* themselves with better sacrifices than these.

24 For [a]Christ is not entered into the holy *places* made with hands, *which are* the figures of [b]the true; but into heaven itself, now [c]to appear in the presence of God for us:

25 Nor yet that he should offer himself often, as [a]the high priest entereth into the holy *place* every year with blood of others;

26 For then must he often have suffered since the foundation of the world: but now [a]once [b]in the end of the world hath he appeared to put away sin by the sacrifice of himself.

27 [a]And as it is appointed unto men once to die, [b]but after this the judgment:

28 So [a]Christ was once [b]offered to bear the sins [c]of many; and unto them that [d]look for

9:9 [a]Gal. 3:21
9:10 [1]Or, *rites,* or, *ceremonies* [a]Col. 2:16 [b]Num. 19:7 [c]Eph. 2:15
9:11 [a]ch. 3:1 [b]ch. 10:1 [c]ch. 8:2
9:12 [a]ch. 10:4 [b]Eph. 1:7; Col. 1:14 [c]Zech. 3:9 [d]Dan. 9:24
9:13 [a]Lev. 16:14 [b]Num. 19:2
9:14 [1]Or, *fault* [a]1 John 1:7 [b]Rom. 1:4 [c]ch. 10:22 [d]ch. 6:1 [e]Luke 1:74
9:15 [a]1 Tim. 2:5 [b]ch. 7:22 [c]Rom. 3:25 [d]ch. 3:1
9:16 [1]Or, *be brought in*
9:17 [a]Gal. 3:15
9:18 [1]Or, *purified* [a]Ex. 24:6
9:19 [1]Or, *purple* [a]Ex. 24:5,6 [b]Lev. 14:4
9:20 [a]Ex. 24:8; Mat. 26:28
9:21 [a]Ex. 29:12; Lev. 8:15
9:22 [a]Lev. 17:11
9:23 [a]ch. 8:5
9:24 [a]ch. 6:20 [b]ch. 8:2 [c]Rom. 8:34; 1 John 2:1
9:25 [a]ver. 7
9:26 [a]ch. 7:27 [b]1 Cor. 10:11
9:27 [a]Gen. 3:19; Eccl. 3:20 [b]2 Cor. 5:10
9:28 [a]Rom. 6:10; 1 Pet. 3:18 [b]1 Pet. 2:24; 1 John 3:5 [c]Mat. 26:28; Rom. 5:15 [d]Tit. 2:13

though superseded, still provided instruction through its typical (symbolic) significance and was a reminder that returning to the old order was useless, since it could not deal effectively with sin. *gifts and sacrifices.* See note on 5:1.

9:10 *the time of reformation.* The new covenant, with its new priesthood, new sanctuary and new sacrifice, all introduced by Christ.

9:11 *not of this building.* It was not an earthly tabernacle, but the heavenly sanctuary of God's presence (v. 24; 8:2).

‡9:12 *he entered in once.* Not repeatedly year after year as did the Levitical high priests. Christ's sacrifice was perfect, because it was completely effective and did not need to be repeated. After He had obtained eternal redemption, Christ ascended into the true heavenly sanctuary.

9:13 *blood of bulls and of goats.* As on the day of atonement. *ashes of a heifer.* As prescribed in Num 19 for those who became ceremonially unclean as a result of contact with a corpse. *purifying of the flesh.* Such sprinkling, since it was only external, could not cleanse a person from sin.

9:14 *offered himself.* He was the one who offered the sacrifice, and He was the sacrifice itself. *without spot.* In the entirety of Christ's being, not just superficially. *purge your conscience.* Remove sin's defilement from the very core of our beings.

‡9:15 *mediator.* See 8:6 and note; 12:24; 1 Tim 2:5. *new testament.* See 7:22; 8:6,13. *for the redemption of the transgressions.* Cf. Mark 10:45 and note. By shedding His blood, He paid the necessary price to set them free from the sins committed under the first covenant, i.e., violations of Mosaic law. *the promise of eternal inheritance.* Defined in the passage from Jeremiah (31:31–34) quoted in 8:8–12. On the basis of Christ's atoning death, this inheritance has become real for those who are called by God (cf. Rom 8:28).

‡9:16 *testament.* Here and in v. 17 "testament" is used in the sense of a last will and testament. (Verse 18 returns to the concept of covenant as opposed to the idea of a will) Beneficiaries have no claim on the benefits assigned to them in a will until the testator dies (v. 17). Since Christ's death has been duly attested, "the promise of eternal inheritance" (v. 15) is available to His beneficiaries.

9:18 *without blood.* Without death—the death of the calves from which Moses took blood to seal the old covenant.

9:19–20 For the ceremony referred to here see Ex 24:4–8.

9:21 See, e.g., Lev 8:10,19,30.

9:23 *patterns of things in the heavens.* See 8:5. Whereas it was necessary for the earthly sanctuary to be purified with animal sacrifices, it was necessary for the heavenly sanctuary to be purified with the better sacrifice of Christ Himself.

9:24 *now to appear in the presence of God for us.* See 7:25; 1 John 2:1.

9:26 *end of the world.* His coming has ushered in the great Messianic era, toward which all history has moved (see note on 1:2; cf. 1 Pet 1:20).

9:27 *appointed . . . once to die, but after this the judgment.* As in the natural order man dies once (v. 27; as a consequence of sin, Rom 5:12), so Christ died once as the perfect sacrifice for sin (v. 28). And as, after death, man faces judgment, so Christ, after His death, will appear again, bringing salvation (see next note) from sin and its judgment.

him shall he appear the second time without sin unto salvation.

10 For the law having [a]a shadow [b]of good *things* to come, *and* not the very image of the things, [c]can never with those sacrifices which they offered year by year continually make the comers *thereunto* [d]perfect.

2 For then [1]would they not have ceased to be offered? because that the worshippers once purged should have had no more conscience of sins.

3 [a]But in those *sacrifices there is* a remembrance *again made* of sins every year.

4 For [a]*it is* not possible that the blood of bulls and of goats should take away sins.

5 Wherefore when he cometh into the world, he saith, [a]Sacrifice and offering thou wouldest not, but a body [1]hast thou prepared me:

6 In burnt offerings and *sacrifices* for sin thou hast had no pleasure.

7 Then said I, Lo, I come (in the volume of the book it is written of me,) to do thy will, O God.

8 Above when he said, Sacrifice and offering and burnt offerings and *offering* for sin thou wouldest not, neither hadst pleasure *therein:* which are offered by the law;

9 Then said he, Lo, I come to do thy will, O God. He taketh away the first, that he may establish the second.

10 [a]By the which will we are sanctified [b]through the offering of the body of Jesus Christ once for all.

11 And every priest standeth [a]daily ministering and offering oftentimes the same sacrifices, [b]which can never take away sins:

12 [a]But this *man,* after he had offered one sacrifice for sins for ever, sat down on the right hand of God;

13 From henceforth expecting [a]till his enemies be made his footstool.

14 For by one offering [a]he hath perfected for ever them that are sanctified.

15 *Whereof* the Holy Ghost also is a witness to us: for after that *he* had said before,

16 [a]This *is* the covenant that I will make with them after those days, saith the Lord, I will put my laws into their hearts, and in their minds will I write them;

17 [1]And their sins and iniquities will I remember no more.

18 Now where remission of these *is, there is* no more offering for sin.

The appeal to hold fast

19 ¶ Having therefore, brethren, [a][1]boldness to enter [b]into the holiest by the blood of Jesus,

20 *By* [a]a new and living way, which he hath [1]consecrated for us, [b]through the vail, that is to say, his flesh;

21 And *having* [a]a high priest over [b]the house of God;

22 [a]Let us draw near with a true heart [b]in

10:1 [a]Col. 2:17 [b]ch. 9:11 [c]ch. 9:9 [d]ver. 14
10:2 [1][Or, *they would have ceased to be offered, because, etc.*]
10:3 [a]ch. 9:7
10:4 [a]Mic. 6:6,7
10:5 [1]Or, *thou hast fitted me* [a]Ps. 40:6
10:10 [a]John 17:19
10:10 [b]ch. 9:12
10:11 [a]Num. 28:3 [b]ver. 4
10:12 [a]Col. 3:1
10:13 [a]Ps. 110:1; Acts 2:35
10:14 [a]ver. 1
10:16 [a]ch. 8:10,12
10:17 [1][Some copies have, *Then he said, And their*]
10:19 [1]Or, *liberty* [a]Eph. 2:18 [b]ch. 9:8,12
10:20 [1]Or, *new made* [a]John 10:9 [b]ch. 9:3
10:21 [a]ch. 4:14 [b]1 Tim. 3:15
10:22 [a]ch. 4:16 [b]Eph. 3:12

9:28 *look for him.* As the Israelites waited for the high priest while he was in the most holy place on the day of atonement (see 2 Tim 4:8; Tit 2:13). *unto salvation.* The consummation, in all its glorious fullness, of the salvation purchased for us on the cross (see Rom 8:29–30; Phil 3:20–21; 1 John 3:2–3).

10:1 *the law.* Together with the Levitical priesthood to which it was closely linked under the Mosaic system (see note on 7:11). *having a shadow.* The sacrifices prescribed by the law prefigured Christ's ultimate sacrifice. Thus they were repeated year after year, the very repetition bearing testimony that the perfect, sin-removing sacrifice had not yet been offered.

10:4 *not possible that the blood of bulls and of goats should take away sins.* An animal cannot possibly be a completely adequate substitute for a human being, who is made in God's image.

10:5–6 The different terms used for Levitical sacrifices represent four of the five types of offerings prescribed by the Mosaic law (Lev 1–7), namely, peace, grain ("meat"), burnt and sin.

10:5 *when he cometh into the world, he saith.* The words of this psalm of David (40:6–8) express Christ's obedient submission to the Father in coming to earth. The Mosaic sacrifices are replaced by submissive obedience to the will of God (v. 7).

10:6 *thou hast had no pleasure.* These offerings were only preparatory and temporary, looking forward to the one perfect and final offering—that of the incarnate Son of God.

10:7 *to do thy will.* The will of the Father was the Son's consuming concern (see Luke 22:42; John 4:34).

10:9 *He taketh away the first, that he may establish the second.* His perfect sacrifice, offered in complete submission, supersedes and therefore replaces all previous sacrifices.

10:10 *sanctified.* Justified, set apart in consecration to God, and now experiencing the process of continuing sanctification (see "are sanctified," v. 14; see also note on 1 Cor 1:2).

‡10:11–14 A contrast between "standeth" and "sat down." The Levitical priest always stood, because his work was never finished.

10:11 *offering . . . the same sacrifices.* Because these sacrifices were unable to accomplish what they signified. They could not remove sin, and thus had to be offered over and over again.

10:12 *he . . . sat down on the right hand of God.* In contrast to the work of the Levitical priests, which was never done (v. 11; see notes on 1:3,13), Christ's work was completed. His one sacrifice atoned for the sins of all time, making any further sacrifice unnecessary (v. 14).

10:15–18 The two quotations included in these verses are from Jer 31:31–34 (already cited in 8:8–12). The new covenant guarantees that sins will be effectively and completely forgiven (v. 17), with the result that no additional sacrifice for sins is needed (v. 18).

‡10:19 Another section of practical application and exhortation begins here (see note on 2:1–4). *boldness to enter into the holiest.* The way into the sanctuary of God's presence was closed to the people under the former covenant because the blood of animal sacrifices could never completely atone for their sins. Now, however, believers can come to the throne of grace since the perfect priest has offered the perfect sacrifice, atoning for sin once for all.

‡10:20 *the vail, that is to say, his flesh.* When Jesus died, the veil separating the holy place from the most holy place was "rent in twain from the top to the bottom" (Mark 15:38). The curtain symbolizes the body of Christ in terms of suffering: Like the curtain, His body was torn to open the way into the divine presence.

‡10:22–25 Five exhortations spring from Jesus' provision for our reconciliation to His Father: 1. "Let us draw near." 2. "Let us

full assurance of faith, having *our* hearts sprinkled [c]from an evil conscience, and [d]*our* bodies washed with pure water.

23 [a]Let us hold fast the profession of *our* hope without wavering; (for [b]he *is* faithful that promised;)

24 And let us consider one another to provoke unto love and to good works:

25 [a]Not forsaking the assembling of ourselves together, as the manner of some *is;* but exhorting *one another:* and [b]so much the more, as ye see [c]the day approaching.

26 ¶ For [a]if we sin wilfully [b]after that *we* have received the knowledge of the truth, there remaineth no more sacrifice for sins,

27 But a certain fearful looking for of judgment and [a]fiery indignation, which shall devour the adversaries.

28 [a]He that despised Moses' law died without mercy [b]under two or three witnesses:

29 [a]Of how much sorer punishment, suppose ye, shall he be thought worthy, who hath trodden under foot the Son of God, and [b]hath counted the blood of the covenant, wherewith he was sanctified, an unholy *thing,* [c]and hath done despite unto the Spirit of grace?

30 For we know him that hath said, [a]Vengeance *belongeth* unto me, I will recompense, saith the Lord. And again, [b]The Lord shall judge his people.

31 [a]*It is* a fearful *thing* to fall into the hands of the living God.

32 But [a]call to remembrance the former days, in which, [b]after ye were illuminated, ye endured [c]a great fight of afflictions;

33 Partly, whilst ye were made [a]a gazingstock both by reproaches and afflictions; and partly, whilst [b]ye became companions of them that were so used.

34 For ye had compassion *of me* [a]in my bonds, and [b]took joyfully the spoiling of your goods, knowing [1]in yourselves that [c]*ye* have in heaven a better and an enduring substance.

35 Cast not away therefore your confidence, [a]which hath great recompence of reward.

36 [a]For ye have need of patience, that, after ye have done the will of God, [b]ye might receive the promise.

37 For [a]yet a little while, *and* [b]he that shall come will come, and will not tarry.

38 Now [a]the just shall live by faith: but if *any man* draw back, my soul shall have no pleasure in him.

39 But we are not of *them* [a]who draw back unto perdition; but of *them* that [b]believe to the saving of the soul.

Faith defined and exemplified

11 Now faith is the [1]substance of *things* hoped for, the evidence [a]of things not seen.

2 For [a]by it the elders obtained a good report.

3 Through faith we understand that [a]the worlds were framed by the word of God, so that *things* which are seen were not made of *things* which do appear.

4 By faith [a]Abel offered unto God a more excellent sacrifice than Cain, by which he obtained witness that he was righteous, God testifying of his gifts: and by it he being dead [1]yet speaketh.

10:22 [c]ch. 9:14 [d]Ezek. 36:25
10:23 [a]ch. 4:14 [b]1 Cor. 1:9; 2 Thes. 3:3
10:25 [a]Acts 2:42 [b]Rom. 13:11 [c]Phil. 4:5; 2 Pet. 3:9
10:26 [a]Num. 15:30 [b]2 Pet. 2:20
10:27 [a]Zeph. 1:18; 2 Thes. 1:8
10:28 [a]ch. 2:2 [b]Mat. 18:16
10:29 [a]ch. 2:3 [b]1 Cor. 11:29 [c]Mat. 12:31; Eph. 4:30
10:30 [a]Deut. 32:35 [b]Deut. 32:36
10:31 [a]Luke 12:5
10:32 [a]Gal. 3:4 [b]ch. 6:4 [c]Phil. 1:29; Col. 2:1
10:33 [a]1 Cor. 4:9
10:33 [b]Phil. 1:7
10:34 [1][Or, *that ye have in yourselves,* or, *for yourselves*] [a]2 Tim. 1:16 [b]Mat. 5:12 [c]Mat. 6:20
10:35 [a]Mat. 5:12
10:36 [a]Luke 21:19 [b]Col. 3:24
10:37 [a]Luke 18:8 [b]Hab. 2:3,4
10:38 [a]Rom. 1:17; Gal. 3:11
10:39 [a]2 Pet. 2:20 [b]Acts 16:31; 1 Thes. 5:9; 2 Thes. 2:14
11:1 [1]Or, *ground,* or, *confidence* [a]Rom. 8:24; 2 Cor. 4:18

11:2 [a]ver. 39 11:3 [a]Gen. 1:1; Ps. 33:6; John 1:3; 2 Pet. 3:5
11:4 [1]Or, *is yet spoken of* [a]Gen. 4:4; 1 John 3:12

hold fast the profession of our hope without wavering." 3. "Let us consider one another to provoke unto love and to good works." 4. "Not forsaking the assembling of ourselves together." 5. "Exhorting one another."

‡10:22 Four conditions are given for drawing "near" to God: 1. *a true heart.* Undivided allegiance in the inner being. 2. *full assurance of faith.* Faith that knows no hesitation in trusting in and following Christ. 3. *hearts sprinkled from an evil conscience.* Total freedom from a sense of guilt, a freedom based on the once-for-all sacrifice of Christ. 4. *bodies washed with pure water.* Not an external ceremony such as baptism but a figure for inner cleansing, of which the washing of the priests under the old covenant was a symbol (see Ex 30:19–21; Lev 8:6; see also Ezek 36:25, where a similar expression is used figuratively for the cleansing resulting from the new covenant).

10:23 *profession of our hope.* See 6:18–20. *without wavering.* Without doubt or hesitation. Some of the readers were tempted to give up the struggle and turn back to a form of Judaism. *he is faithful that promised.* Cf. 2 Tim 2:13.

10:25 *Not forsaking the assembling of ourselves together.* The Greek word translated "forsaking" speaks of desertion and abandonment (see Mat 27:46; 2 Cor 4:9; 2 Tim 4:10,16). *the day.* Of the Lord's return (see 1 Thes 5:2,4; 2 Thes 1:10; 2:2; 2 Pet 3:10).

10:26–31 That these verses are a warning to persons ("some," v. 25) deserting the Christian assembly is apparent from the Greek word *gar* ("for") at the beginning of v. 26. See notes on 6:4–8, where the same spiritual condition is discussed.

10:26 *if we sin wilfully.* Committing the sin of apostasy (see v. 29; see also note on 5:2). The OT background is Num 15:27–31. *there remaineth no more sacrifice for sins.* To reject Christ's sacrifice for sins is to reject the only sacrifice; there is no other.

10:27 *judgment and fiery indignation.* See 2 Thes 1:6–9.

10:28 See Deut 17:2–7.

10:29 *blood of the covenant.* See 9:20; 13:20; Ex 24:8; Mat 26:28; Mark 14:24.

10:31 See 12:29.

10:32 *the former days.* Presumably following their first enthusiastic response to the gospel, when they had unflinchingly suffered loss and persecution and were deeply concerned for each other.

10:34 *better and an enduring substance.* Such as salvation in Christ and future reward (11:10,13–16,26,35; 13:14; Mat 5:11–12; 6:19–21; Rom 8:18).

10:38 *the just shall live by faith.* See note on Hab 2:4.

‡10:39 *draw back unto perdition.* The opposite of "believe to the saving of the soul." The author is confident that those to whom he is writing are, for the most part, among the saved (see note on 6:9).

11:1–12:29 Exhortations based on the preceding expositions of OT passages.

11:2 *elders.* Heroes of faith in the pre-Christian era, such as those listed in this chapter.

‡11:4 See Gen 4:2–5. *obtained witness that he was righteous.* Both brothers brought offerings to the Lord: Cain from the fruits of the soil, and Abel from the firstborn of his flock. The chief reason for the acceptance of Abel's sacrifice was that he offered

5 By faith [a]Enoch was translated that *he*
should not see death; and was not found, because God had translated him: for before his
translation he had this testimony, that *he*
pleased God.
6 But without faith *it is* impossible to
please *him:* for he that cometh to God must
believe that he is, and *that* he is a rewarder of
them that diligently seek him.
7 By faith [a]Noah, being warned of God of
things not seen as yet, [1]moved with fear, [b]pre-
pared an ark to the saving of his house; by the
which he condemned the world, and became
heir of [c]the righteousness which is by faith.
8 By faith [a]Abraham, when he was called
to go out into a place which he should after receive for an inheritance, obeyed; and he went
out, not knowing whither he went.
9 By faith he sojourned in the land of promise, as *in* a strange *country,* [a]dwelling in tabernacles with Isaac and Jacob, [b]the heirs with
him of the same promise:
10 For he looked for [a]a city which hath
foundations, [b]whose builder and maker *is* God.
11 Through faith also [a]Sara herself received strength to conceive seed, and [b]was delivered of a child when *she* was past age, because she judged him [c]faithful who had
promised.
12 Therefore sprang there even of one, and
[a]him as good as dead, [b]*so many* as the stars of
the sky in multitude, and as the sand which is
by the sea shore innumerable.
13 These all died [1]in faith, [a]not having received the promises, but [b]having seen them
afar off, and were persuaded of *them,* and embraced *them,* and [c]confessed that they were
strangers and pilgrims on the earth.
14 For they that say such *things* [a]declare
plainly that they seek a country.
15 And truly, if they had been mindful of
that *country* from whence they came out, they
might have had opportunity to have returned.
16 But now they desire a better *country,*
that is, a heavenly: wherefore God is not
ashamed [a]to be called their God: for [b]he hath
prepared for them a city.
17 By faith [a]Abraham, when he was tried,
offered up Isaac: and he that had received the
promises [b]offered up *his* only begotten *son,*
18 [1]Of whom it was said, [a]That in Isaac
shall thy seed be called:
19 Accounting that God [a]*was* able to raise
him up, even from the dead; from whence also
he received him in a figure.
20 By faith [a]Isaac blessed Jacob and Esau
concerning *things* to come.
21 By faith Jacob, when he was a dying,
[a]blessed both the sons of Joseph; and [b]wor-
shipped, *leaning* upon the top of his staff.
22 By faith [a]Joseph, when he died, [1]made
mention of the departing of the children of Israel; and gave commandment concerning his
bones.
23 By faith [a]Moses, when he was born,
was hid three months of his parents, because
they saw *he was* a proper child; and they were
not afraid of the king's [b]commandment.

11:5 [a]Gen. 5:22
11:7 [1]Or, *being wary* [a]Gen. 6:13 [b]1 Pet. 3:20 [c]Rom. 3:22; Phil. 3:9
11:8 [a]Gen. 12:1; Acts 7:2-4
11:9 [a]Gen. 12:8 [b]ch. 6:17
11:10 [a]ch. 12:22 [b]Rev. 21:10
11:11 [a]Gen. 17:19; 18:11,14 [b]Luke 1:36 [c]Rom. 4:21
11:12 [a]Rom. 4:19 [b]Rom. 4:18
11:13 [1]Gr. *according to faith* [a]ver. 39
11:13 [b]John 8:56 [c]Gen. 23:4; 1 Chr. 29:15; Ps. 39:12; 1 Pet. 1:17
11:14 [a]ch. 13:14
11:16 [a]Ex. 3:6,15; Mat. 22:32; Acts 7:32 [b]ch. 13:14
11:17 [a]Gen. 22:1 [b]Jas. 2:21
11:18 [1]Or, *To* [a]Gen. 21:12; Rom. 9:7
11:19 [a]Rom. 4:17
11:20 [a]Gen. 27:27
11:21 [a]Gen. 48:5 [b]Gen. 47:31
11:22 [1]Or, *remembered* [a]Gen. 50:24
11:23 [a]Ex. 2:2 [b]Ex. 1:16

it "by faith." It is implied that Cain's sacrifice was rejected because he offered it without faith, i.e., as a self-originated act of worship (see note on Gen 4:3–4; see also 1 John 3:12).

‡11:5 *Enoch.* See Gen 5:18–24. *was translated.* Taken up to God's presence (see note on Gen 5:24; cf. Ps 49:15; 73:24).

11:6 *without faith it is impossible to please him.* That Enoch pleased God is proof of his faith. *believe that he is.* Faith must have an object, and the proper object of genuine faith is God. *them that diligently seek him.* See Jer 29:13.

11:7 *Noah.* See Gen 5:28–9:29. *by the which he condemned.* When the flood came, God's word was proved to be true, Noah's faith was vindicated, and the world's unbelief was judged. *righteousness which is by faith.* Noah expressed complete trust in God and His word, even when it related to "things not seen" (v. 1), namely, the coming flood. Thus Noah also fitted the description of God's righteous ones who live by faith (10:38). His faith in God's word moved him to build the ark in a dry, landlocked region where it was inconceivable that there would ever be enough water to float the vessel.

‡11:8 *Abraham.* Presented in the NT as the outstanding example of those who live "by faith" and as the "father of all them that believe" (Rom 4:11–12,16; Gal 3:7,9,29). *called.* See Gen 12:1–3. His faith expressed itself in obedience (see note on Gen 12:4). *a place which he should after receive.* Canaan. *not knowing whither he went.* He did not go in blind faith, but in complete confidence in God's trustworthiness.

11:10 *city which hath foundations.* Speaks of permanence in contrast to the tents in which the patriarch lived (v. 9). This city is "the heavenly Jerusalem" (12:22), "the city which is to come" (13:14) and the "new Jerusalem" (Rev 21:2–4, 9–27). *builder.* Cf. Ps 147:2.

11:11 *Sara . . . received strength to conceive.* Probably referring to the fact that she was far past childbearing (Gen 18:11–12; see note on Gen 11:30).

11:12 *as good as dead.* Because he was 100 years old (see Gen 21:5; Rom 4:19). *stars of the sky . . . sand . . . by the sea shore.* See Gen 13:16 and note; 15:5; 22:17; 26:4; 1 Ki 4:20.

11:13 *having seen them afar off.* By faith they saw—dimly—these heavenly realities and were sure that what they hoped for would ultimately be theirs (see v. 1). *strangers and pilgrims on the earth.* Their true home was in heaven.

11:14 *seek a country.* That better, heavenly country (v. 16).

11:16 *prepared for them a city.* City (v. 10) and country are interchangeable in the concluding chapters of this letter (vv. 9–10,14–16; 13:14). The ultimate reality is represented by the new Jerusalem in John's vision of the believer's eternal state (see Rev 21:2).

11:17 See Gen 22. *his only begotten son.* See Gen 22:2,12,16; cf. John 3:16; Rom 8:32.

11:19 *God was able to raise . . . the dead.* So strong was Abraham's faith that he actually believed that God would raise Isaac from the dead if necessary, an event that did occur figuratively when the substitute ram was provided (Gen 22:13).

11:20 See Gen 27:27–40.

11:21 See Gen 47:29–31; 48:8–20.

11:22 See Gen 50:24–25. Jacob (v. 21) and Joseph are additional examples of those whose faith is no less strong at death than in life (v. 13).

11:23–29 See Acts 7:20–44.

11:23 *his parents.* See Ex 6:20; Num 26:58–59. *a proper child.* See note on Ex 2:2. *the king's commandment.* To kill all Israelite males at birth (Ex 1:16,22).

24 By faith [a]Moses, when he was come to years, refused to be called the son of Pharaoh's daughter;

25 [a]Choosing rather to suffer affliction with the people of God, than to enjoy the pleasures of sin for a season;

26 Esteeming [a]the reproach [1]of Christ greater riches than the treasures in Egypt: for he had respect unto [b]the recompence of the reward.

27 By faith [a]he forsook Egypt, not fearing the wrath of the king: for he endured, as [b]seeing *him who is* invisible.

28 Through faith [a]he kept the passover, and the sprinkling of blood, lest he that destroyed the firstborn should touch them.

29 By faith [a]they passed through the Red sea as by dry *land:* which the Egyptians assaying to do were drowned.

30 By faith [a]the walls of Jericho fell down, after they were compassed about seven days.

31 By faith [a]the harlot Rahab perished not with them [1]that believed not, when [b]she had received the spies with peace.

32 ¶ And what shall I more say? for the time would fail me to tell of [a]Gedeon, and *of* Barak, and *of* [b]Samson, and *of* [c]Jephthae; *of* [d]David also, and [e]Samuel, and *of* the prophets:

33 Who through faith subdued kingdoms, wrought righteousness, [a]obtained promises, [b]stopped the mouths of lions,

34 [a]Quenched the violence of fire, [b]escaped the edge of the sword, [c]out of weakness were made strong, waxed valiant in fight, [d]turned to flight the armies of the aliens.

35 [a]Women received their dead raised to life again: and others were [b]tortured, not accepting deliverance; that they might obtain a better resurrection:

36 And others had trial of *cruel* mockings and scourgings, yea, moreover [a]of bonds and imprisonment:

37 [a]They were stoned, they were sawn asunder, were tempted, were slain with the sword: [b]they wandered about [c]in sheepskins and goatskins; being destitute, afflicted, tormented;

38 (Of whom the world was not worthy:) they wandered in deserts, and *in* mountains, and [a]*in* dens and caves of the earth.

39 And these all, [a]having obtained a good report through faith, received not the promise:

40 God having [1]provided some better

11:24 [a]Ex. 2:10
11:25 [a]Ps. 84:10
11:26 [1]Or, *for Christ* [a]ch. 13:13 [b]ch. 10:35
11:27 [a]Ex. 10:28 [b]ver. 13
11:28 [a]Ex. 12:21
11:29 [a]Ex. 14:22
11:30 [a]Josh. 6:20
11:31 [1]Or, *that were disobedient* [a]Josh. 6:23 [b]Josh. 2:1
11:32 [a]Judg. 6:11 [b]Judg. 13:24 [c]Judg. 12:7 [d]1 Sam. 16:1 [e]1 Sam. 1:20
11:33 [a]2 Sam. 7:11 [b]Judg. 14:5; 1 Sam. 17:34
11:34 [a]Dan. 3:25 [b]1 Sam. 20:1 [c]2 Ki. 20:7 [d]Judg. 15:8
11:35 [a]1 Ki. 17:22 [b]Acts 22:25
11:36 [a]Gen. 39:20; Jer. 20:2
11:37 [a]1 Ki. 21:13; Acts 7:58 [b]2 Ki. 1:8; Mat. 3:4 [c]Zech. 13:4
11:38 [a]1 Ki. 18:4
11:39 [a]ver. 2,13
11:40 [1]Or, *foreseen*

11:25 *pleasures of sin.* The luxury and prestige in Egypt's royal palace.

11:26 *of Christ.* Although Moses' understanding of the details of the Messianic hope was extremely limited, he chose to be associated with the people through whom that hope was to be realized. *treasures of Egypt.* The priceless treasures of King Tutankhamun's tomb alone included several thousand pounds of pure gold.

11:27 *By faith he forsook Egypt.* Probably referring to his flight to Midian in the Sinai peninsula when he was 40 years old (Ex 2:11–15; Acts 7:23–29). *not fearing the wrath of the king.* Exodus indicates that Moses was afraid (Ex 2:14) but does not expressly say of whom. And it tells us that he fled from Pharaoh when Pharaoh tried to kill him (Ex 2:15) but does not expressly say that he fled out of fear. The author of Hebrews capitalizes on these features of the account to highlight the fact that, in his fleeing from Pharaoh, Moses was sustained by his trust in God that the liberation of Israel would come and that he would have some part in it. *he endured.* For 40 years in Midian (Acts 7:30). *seeing him who is invisible.* See vv. 1,6.

11:28 See Ex 12.

11:29 See Ex 14–15. The third and final 40-year period of Moses' life was spent leading the Israelites through the wilderness. At the age of 120 years he died in Moab (Deut 34:1–7).

11:30 Moses' place as leader was taken by Joshua, who brought the people of Israel into the land of promise. *Jericho.* The first great obstacle to their conquest of the land was captured by faith without a battle (Josh 6).

11:31 *the harlot Rahab.* A designation describing her way of life prior to her newly found faith (Josh 2:8–11; 6:22–25); also a testimony to God's boundless grace that can reach down and redeem and raise any sinner to eternal dignity. *received the spies with peace.* See Jas 2:25.

‡11:32–38 There were many more heroes of faith before the coming of Christ, and much more could be written of them. Only a small sampling is given, representing all types of men and women of faith. The great quality they had in common was that of overcoming "through faith" (v. 33).

11:32 *what shall I more say.* Translates the masculine form of a Greek verb, indicating that the author of Hebrews was a man (see Introduction: Author). *Gedeon, Barak, Samson, Jephthae.* See Judg 4:6–5:15; 6:11–8:35; 11:1–12:7; 13:24–16:31; 1 Sam 12:11, where Gideon is called Jerubbaal (see Judg 6:32 and note). *Samuel, and of the prophets.* See Ps 99:6; Jer 15:1; Acts 3:24; 13:20.

11:33 *mouths of lions.* Cf. Daniel in the lions' den (Dan 6).

11:34 *Quenched the violence of fire.* Cf. Daniel's friends, Shadrach, Meshach and Abednego, in the fiery furnace (Dan 3). *weakness were made strong.* Through God's help (see Rom 8:26; 2 Cor 12:9).

‡11:35 *Women received their dead raised to life again.* Cf. the widow of Zarephath (1 Ki 17:17–24) and the Shunammite woman (2 Ki 4:8–36). *were tortured, not accepting deliverance; that they might obtain a better resurrection.* Strongly reminiscent of the heroic Maccabean Jewish patriots of the second century B.C. (see 2 Maccabees 7). But the description applies also to countless believers, known and unknown, who demonstrated their faith in God by persevering in the face of harsh trials and afflictions.

11:37 *They were stoned.* Men like Zechariah, the son of Jehoiada the priest, who were put to death for declaring the truth (2 Chr 24:20–22; Luke 11:51). See also Introduction to Jeremiah: Author and Date. *sawn assunder.* Perhaps refers to Isaiah, who, according to tradition, met this kind of death under wicked King Manasseh (see Introduction to Isaiah: Author).

11:39 *all, having obtained a good report through faith.* Not all the heroes of faith experienced immediate triumph over their circumstances, but all were blessed by God.

11:40 *God having provided some better thing.* The fulfillment for them, as for us, is in Christ who is "the resurrection and the life" (John 11:25–26). *that they without us should not be made perfect.* All persons of faith who had gone before focused their faith on God and His promises. The fulfillment of God's promises to them has now come in Jesus Christ, and their redemption too is now complete in Him.

thing for us, that they without us should not be [a]made perfect.

Christ our example

12 Wherefore seeing we also are compassed about with so great a cloud of witnesses, [a]let us lay aside every weight, and the sin which doth so easily beset *us,* and [b]let us run [c]with patience the race that is set before us,

2 Looking unto Jesus the [1]author and finisher of *our* faith; [a]who for the joy that was set before him endured the cross, despising the shame, and [b]is set down at the right hand of the throne of God.

3 [a]For consider him that endured such contradiction of sinners against himself, [b]lest ye be wearied and faint in your minds.

An appeal for endurance

4 ¶ [a]Ye have not yet resisted unto blood, striving against sin.

5 And ye have forgotten the exhortation which speaketh unto you as unto children, [a]My son, despise not thou the chastening of the Lord, nor faint when thou art rebuked of him:

6 For [a]whom the Lord loveth he chasteneth, and scourgeth every son whom he receiveth.

7 [a]If ye endure chastening, God dealeth with you as with sons; for what son is *he* whom the father chasteneth not?

8 But if ye be without chastisement, [a]whereof all are partakers, then are ye bastards, and not sons.

9 Furthermore we have had fathers of our flesh which corrected *us,* and we gave *them* reverence: shall we not much rather be in subjection unto [a]the Father of spirits, and live?

10 For they verily for a few days chastened *us* [1]after their own pleasure; but he for *our* profit, [a]that *we* might be partakers of his holiness.

11 Now no chastening for the present seemeth to be joyous, but grievous: nevertheless afterward it yieldeth [a]the peaceable fruit of righteousness unto them which are exercised thereby.

12 Wherefore [a]lift up the hands which hang down, and the feeble knees;

13 [a]And make [1]straight paths for your feet, lest *that which is* lame be turned out of the way; [b]but let it rather be healed.

14 [a]Follow peace with all *men,* and holiness, [b]without which no *man* shall see the Lord:

15 Looking diligently [a]lest any *man* [1]fail of the grace of God; [b]lest any root of bitterness springing up trouble *you,* and thereby many be defiled;

16 [a]Lest there *be* any fornicator, or profane *person,* as Esau, [b]who for one morsel of meat sold his birthright.

17 For ye know how that afterward, [a]when he would have inherited the blessing, he was rejected: for he found no [1]place of repentance, though he sought it carefully with tears.

11:40 [a]ch. 5:9
12:1 [a]Col. 3:8 [b]1 Cor. 9:24 [c]Rom. 12:12
12:2 [1]Or, *beginner* [a]Luke 24:26; Phil. 2:8 [b]Ps. 110:1; 1 Pet. 3:22
12:3 [a]Mat. 10:24; John 15:20 [b]Gal. 6:9
12:4 [a]1 Cor. 10:13
12:5 [a]Job 5:17
12:6 [a]Ps. 94:12; Jas. 1:12
12:7 [a]Deut. 8:5
12:8 [a]1 Pet. 5:9
12:9 [a]Job 12:10
12:10 [1][Or, *as seemed good,* or, *meet to them*] [a]Lev. 11:44
12:11 [a]Jas. 3:18
12:12 [a]Job 4:3,4
12:13 [1]Or, *even* [a]Prov. 4:26 [b]Gal. 6:1
12:14 [a]Ps. 34:14; 2 Tim. 2:22 [b]Mat. 5:8; 2 Cor. 7:1
12:15 [1]Or, *fall from* [a]Gal. 5:4 [b]ch. 3:12
12:16 [a]Eph. 5:3 [b]Gen. 25:33
12:17 [1]Or, *way to change his mind* [a]Gen. 27:34

‡12:1 *compassed about with so great a cloud of witnesses.* The imagery suggests an athletic contest in a great amphitheater. The witnesses are the heroes of the past who have just been mentioned (ch. 11). They are not spectators but inspiring examples. The Greek word translated "witnesses" is the origin of the English word "martyr" and means "testifiers, witnesses." They bear testimony to the power of faith and to God's faithfulness. *run with patience.* See Acts 20:24; 1 Cor 9:24–26; Gal 2:2; 5:7; Phil 2:16; 2 Tim 4:7. The Christian life is pictured as a long-distance race rather than a short sprint. Some Hebrew Christians were tempted to drop out of the contest because of persecution.

‡12:2 *Looking unto Jesus.* Just as a runner concentrates on the finish line, we should concentrate on Jesus, the goal and objective of our faith (Phil 3:13–14). *finisher of our faith.* Our faith, which has its beginning in Him, is also completed in Him; He is both the start and the end of the race. He is also the supreme witness who has already run the race and overcome. *joy that was set before him.* His accomplishing our eternal redemption and His glorification at the Father's "right hand" (see note on 1:3; cf. Is 53:10–12). *endured the cross.* See Phil 2:5–8. *despising the shame.* As with Christ, the humiliation of our present suffering for the gospel's sake is far outweighed by the prospect of future glory (see 11:26; Mat 5:10–12; Rom 8:18; 2 Cor 4:17; 1 Pet 4:13; 5:1,10).

12:3 *consider him.* He suffered infinitely more than any of His disciples is asked to suffer—a great encouragement for us when we are weary and tempted to become discouraged. *lest ye be wearied.* See Is 40:28–31.

12:4 *not yet resisted unto blood.* Though they had suffered persecution and loss of possessions (10:32–34), they had not had to die for the faith.

12:5 *the chastening of the Lord.* Suffering and persecution should be seen as corrective and instructive training for our spiritual development as His children.

12:6 *scourgeth.* The Greek for this verb means "to whip." God chastens us in order to correct our faults.

12:7 *dealeth with you as with sons.* God's discipline is evidence that we are His children. Far from being a reason for despair, discipline is a basis for encouragement and perseverance (v. 10).

12:11 *it yieldeth the peaceable fruit of righteousness.* When received submissively (see v. 9), discipline is wholesome and beneficial.

12:13 *make straight paths.* A call for upright conduct that will help, rather than hinder, the spiritual and moral welfare of others, especially the "lame" who waver in the Christian faith.

12:14 *holiness, without which no man shall see the Lord.* Cf. 1 Pet 1:15–16; 1 John 3:2–3.

12:15 *fail of the grace of God.* "Falls short of" or "fails to lay hold of" God's grace. Such an experience is described in 2:1–4; 6:4–8. *root of bitterness.* Pride, animosity, rivalry or anything else harmful to others.

12:16 *profane person, as Esau.* See Gen 25:29–34. He had no appreciation for true values and was profane in his outlook on life (cf. Phil 3:18–19). He "despised his birthright" (Gen 25:34) by valuing food for his stomach more highly than his birthright.

‡12:17 *the blessing.* Of the firstborn. The readers were thinking of compromising their faith in order to gain relief from persecution. But to trade their spiritual birthright for temporary ease in this world would deprive them of Christ's blessing. *he was rejected.* Because he only regretted his loss, and did not repent of his sin (Gen 27, especially v. 41). His sorrow was not "godly sorrow" that "worketh repentance to salvation," but "the sorrow of the world" that "worketh death" (2 Cor 7:10). *with tears.* See Gen 27:34–38.

18 ¶ For ye are not come unto [a]the mount that might be touched, and that burned with fire, nor unto blackness, and darkness, and tempest,

19 And the sound of a trumpet, and the voice of words; which *voice* they that heard [a]intreated that the word should not be spoken to them any more:

20 (For they could not endure that which was commanded, [a]And if *so much as* a beast touch the mountain, it shall be stoned, or thrust through with a dart:

21 [a]And so terrible was the sight, *that* Moses said, I exceedingly fear and quake;)

22 But ye are come [a]unto mount Sion, [b]and unto the city of the living God, the heavenly Jerusalem, [c]and to an innumerable company of angels,

23 To the general assembly, and church of [a]the firstborn, [b]which are [1]written in heaven, and to God [c]the Judge of all, and to the spirits of just *men* [d]made perfect,

24 And to Jesus [a]the mediator of the new [1]covenant, and to [b]the blood of sprinkling, that speaketh better *things* [c]than *that of* Abel.

25 See *that* ye refuse not him that speaketh: for [a]if they escaped not who refused him that spake on earth, much more *shall not* we *escape,* if we turn away from him that *speaketh* from heaven:

26 [a]Whose voice then shook the earth: but now he hath promised, saying, [b]Yet once *more* I shake not the earth only, but also heaven.

27 And this *word,* Yet once *more,* signifieth [a]the removing of those *things* that [1]are shaken, as of *things* that are made, that those *things* which cannot be shaken may remain.

28 Wherefore we receiving a kingdom which cannot be moved, [1]let us have grace, whereby we may serve God acceptably with reverence and godly fear:

29 For [a]our God *is* a consuming fire.

Warnings and requests

13 Let [a]brotherly love continue.

2 [a]Be not forgetful to entertain strangers: for thereby [b]some have entertained angels unawares.

3 [a]Remember *them that are* in bonds, as bound with *them; and* them which suffer adversity, as being yourselves also in the body.

4 Marriage *is* honourable in all, and the bed undefiled: [a]but whoremongers and adulterers God will judge.

5 *Let your* conversation *be* without covetousness; *and* [a]*be* content with such *things* as ye have: for he hath said, [b]I will never leave thee, nor forsake thee.

6 So that we may boldly say, [a]The Lord *is* my helper, and I will not fear what man shall do unto me.

7 [a]Remember them which [1]have the rule over you, who have spoken unto you the word of God: [b]whose faith follow, considering the end of *their* conversation.

8 Jesus Christ [a]the same yesterday, and to day, and for ever.

9 [a]Be not carried about with divers and

12:18 [a]Deut. 4:11
12:19 [a]Ex. 20:19; Deut. 5:5
12:20 [a]Ex. 19:13
12:21 [a]Ex. 19:16
12:22 [a]Gal. 4:26; Rev. 3:12 [b]Phil. 3:20 [c]Deut. 33:2; Ps. 68:17
12:23 [1]Or, *enrolled* [a]Jas. 1:18 [b]Luke 10:20 [c]Ps. 94:2 [d]Phil. 3:12
12:24 [1]Or, *testament* [a]ch. 9:15 [b]Ex. 24:8 [c]Gen. 4:10
12:25 [a]ch. 2:2,3
12:26 [a]Ex. 19:18 [b]Hag. 2:6
12:27 [1]Or, *may be shaken* [a]2 Pet. 3:10
12:28 [1]Or, *let us hold fast*
12:29 [a]Ex. 24:17; Deut. 4:24
13:1 [a]Rom. 12:10; 1 Pet. 1:22
13:2 [a]Mat. 25:35; 1 Tim. 3:2 [b]Gen. 18:3
13:3 [a]Mat. 25:26
13:4 [a]1 Cor. 6:9
13:5 [a]Phil. 4:11 [b]Gen. 28:15
13:6 [a]Ps. 27:1
13:7 [1]Or, *are the guides* [a]ver. 17 [b]ch. 6:12
13:8 [a]John 8:58
13:9 [a]Eph. 4:14; Col. 2:4,8

12:18–21 These verses describe the awesome occasion when the law was given at mount Sinai (see Ex 19:10–25; Deut 4:11–12; 5:22–26), a description focusing on the old covenant's tangible mountain, ordinances, terrifying warnings and severe penalties. Believers in Jesus Christ do not have such a threatening covenant, and should not consider returning to it.

12:22 *mount Sion.* Not the literal mount Zion (Jerusalem, or its southeast portion), but the heavenly city of God and those who dwell there with Him (see 11:10,13–16; 13:14; Phil 3:20). The circumstances under which the old covenant was given (vv. 18–21) and the features of the new covenant (vv. 22–24) point up the utter contrast between the two covenants, and lay the foundation for one more warning and exhortation to those still thinking of going back to Judaism. *innumerable company of angels.* See Rev 5:11–12.

‡12:23 *church of the firstborn.* Believers in general who make up the church: (1) They cannot be angels since these have just been mentioned (v. 22); (2) "firstborn" cannot refer to Christ (though He is called firstborn, 1:6; Rom 8:29; Col 1:15–18; Rev 1:5), since here the Greek word is plural; (3) that their names are recorded in heaven reminds us of the redeemed (see Rev 3:5; 13:8; 17:8; 20:12; 21:27). The designation "firstborn" suggests their privileged position as heirs together with Christ, the supreme firstborn and "heir of all things" (Heb 1:2). *God the Judge of all.* See 4:13; Rom 14:10–12; 1 Cor 3:10–15; 2 Cor 5:10; Rev 20:11–15. *spirits of just men made perfect.* For the most part, these were pre-Christian believers such as Abel (11:4) and Noah (11:7). They are referred to as "spirits" because they are waiting for the resurrection and as "just" because God credited their faith to them as righteousness, as He did to Abraham (see Rom 4:3). Actual justification was not accomplished, however, until Christ made it complete by His death on the cross (see 11:40; Rom 3:24–26; 4:23–25).

12:24 *mediator of the new covenant.* See 7:22; 8:6 and note; 8:13; 9:15; 1 Tim 2:5. *blood . . . speaketh better than . . . Abel.* Abel's blood cried out for justice and retribution (see note on Gen 4:10), whereas the blood of Jesus shed on the cross speaks of forgiveness and reconciliation (9:12; 10:19; Col 1:20; 1 John 1:7).

12:25 *him that speaketh.* God. *spake on earth.* At Sinai. *speaketh from heaven.* Christ, who is both from and in heaven (1:1–3; 4:14; 6:20; 7:26; 9:24). Since we have greater revelation, we have greater responsibility and therefore greater danger (2:2–4).

12:26 *shook the earth.* See Ex 19:18; Judg 5:5; Ps 68:7–8.

12:27 *once more.* During the great end-time upheavals associated with the second advent of Christ. *which cannot be shaken.* The kingdom (v. 28).

12:28 *serve God acceptably.* See John 4:19–24; Rom 12:1.

12:29 Cf. Ex 24:17; Deut 9:3.

13:2 *entertained angels unawares.* As did Abraham (Gen 18), Gideon (Judg 6) and Manoah (Judg 13).

13:3 *Remember them that are in bonds . . . and them which suffer adversity.* See 10:32–34; 1 Cor 12:26.

13:5 *covetousness.* See Luke 12:15,21; Phil 4:10–13; 1 Tim 6:6–10,17–19. *be content.* See Phil 4:11–12; 1 Tim 6:8.

13:7 *which have the rule over you, who have spoken unto you the word of God.* See 2:3; 5:12. *whose faith follow.* See 6:12; 1 Cor 4:16; Eph 5:1; 1 Thes 1:6–7; 2:14; 3 John 11. *considering the end of their conversation.* Probably indicates that these exemplary leaders were now dead.

‡13:8 *Jesus Christ the same.* A confession of the changeless-

strange doctrines. For *it is* a good *thing* that
the heart be established with grace; [b]not with
meats, which have not profited them that have
been occupied therein.
10 [a]We have an altar, whereof they have
no right to eat which serve the tabernacle.
11 For [a]the bodies of those beasts, whose
blood is brought into the sanctuary by the high
priest for sin, are burnt without the camp.
12 Wherefore Jesus also, that he might
sanctify the people with his own blood, [a]suf-
fered without the gate.
13 Let us go forth therefore unto him without the camp, bearing [a]his reproach.
14 [a]For here have we no continuing city,
but we seek one to come.
15 [a]By him therefore let us offer [b]the sacrifice of praise to God continually, that is, [c]the
fruit of *our* lips [1]giving thanks to his name.
16 [a]But to do good and to communicate
forget not: for [b]with such sacrifices God is well
pleased.
17 [a]Obey them that [1]have the rule over
you, and submit yourselves: for [b]they watch
for your souls, as they that must give account,
that they may do it with joy, and not with
grief: for that *is* unprofitable for you.

13:9 [b]Rom. 14:17; 1 Tim. 4:3
13:10 [a]1 Cor. 9:13
13:11 [a]Ex. 29:14
13:12 [a]Acts 7:58
13:13 [a]1 Pet. 4:14
13:14 [a]Mic. 2:10; Phil. 3:20
13:15 [1]Gr. *confessing to* [a]Eph. 5:20 [b]Lev. 7:12 [c]Hos. 14:2
13:16 [a]Rom. 12:13 [b]2 Cor. 9:12; Phil. 4:18
13:17 [1]Or, *guide* [a]Phil. 2:29; 1 Tim. 5:17 [b]Ezek. 3:17
13:18 [a]Eph. 6:19 [b]Acts 23:1
13:20 [1]Or, *testament* [a]Rom. 15:33 [b]Rom. 4:24; Gal. 1:1 [c]1 Pet. 2:25 [d]Zech. 9:11
13:21 [1]Or, *doing* [a]1 Pet. 5:10 [b]Phil. 2:13 [c]Gal. 1:5
13:22 [a]1 Pet. 5:12
13:23 [a]1 Thes. 3:2 [b]1 Tim. 6:12

18 [a]Pray for us: for we trust we have [b]a
good conscience, in all *things* willing to live
honestly.
19 But I beseech *you* the rather to do this,
that I may be restored to you the sooner.
20 ¶ Now [a]the God of peace, [b]that brought
again from the dead our Lord Jesus, [c]*that* great
shepherd of the sheep, [d]through the blood of
the everlasting [1]covenant,
21 [a]Make you perfect in every good work
to do his will, [b1]working in you *that which is*
well pleasing in his sight, through Jesus
Christ; [c]to whom *be* glory for ever and ever.
Amen.
22 And I beseech you, brethren, suffer the
word of exhortation: for [a]I have written a letter unto you in few *words*.
23 Know ye that [a]*our* brother Timothy [b]is
set at liberty; with whom, if he come shortly, I
will see you.
24 Salute all them [a]that have the rule over
you, and all the saints. They of Italy salute you.
25 [a]Grace *be* with you all. Amen.

¶ Written to the Hebrews from Italy by Timothy.

13:24 [a]ver. 7,17 13:25 [a]Tit. 3:15

ness of Christ, no doubt related to the preceding verse. The substance of their former leaders' faith was the unchanging Christ. *yesterday.* Probably the days of Christ's life on earth, when the eyewitnesses observed Him (2:3). *today.* The Christ whom the eyewitnesses saw was still the same, and what they had said about Him was still true. *for ever.* And it will always be true. To compromise His absolute supremacy by returning to the inferior Aaronic priesthood and sacrifices (see chs. 5–10) is to undermine the gospel.

13:9 *not with meats.* I.e. "ceremonial foods." This is what the legalistic Judaizers were teaching. The old Mosaic order was done away with at the cross and must not be revived.

‡13:10 *We have an altar.* Probably refers to the cross, which marked the end of the whole Aaronic priesthood and its replacement by the order of Melchisedec, of which Christ is the unique and only priest. *no right to eat.* The priests could not eat of the sacrifice on the day of atonement, but we can partake of our sacrifice, so to speak—through spiritual reception of Christ by faith (see John 6:48–58). We have a higher privilege than the priests under the old covenant had.

13:11 *burnt without the camp.* See Lev 4:12 and note; 16:27.

13:12 *Jesus also . . . suffered without the gate.* Christ's death outside Jerusalem represented the removal of sin, as had the removal of the bodies of sacrificial animals outside the camp of Israel.

13:13 *go forth . . . unto him without the camp.* Calls for separation from Judaism to Christ. As He died in disgrace outside the city, so the readers should be willing to be disgraced by turning unequivocally from Judaism to Christ.

13:14 *no continuing city.* See notes on 11:10,14,16.

13:15 *sacrifice of praise.* "Sacrifice" is used metaphorically here to represent an offering to God (see Rom 12:1; Phil 4:18). Animal offerings are now obsolete.

13:17 *them that have the rule over you.* Their present leaders, as distinct from their first ones, now dead, mentioned in v. 7. *submit yourselves.* Dictatorial leadership is not condoned by this command (see 3 John 9–10), but respect for authority, orderliness and discipline in the church are taught throughout the NT.

13:19 *restored to you.* The identity and whereabouts of the writer are not known to us, but "restored" suggests that somehow he had been delayed in visiting those to whom he was writing, perhaps by his current ministry. That he was not under arrest is clear from v. 23.

13:20–21 This benediction provides a fitting conclusion to the letter. *God of peace.* A title for God used frequently in benedictions (see Rom 15:33; 16:20; Phil 4:9; 1 Thes 5:23).

13:20 *great shepherd.* See, e.g., Ps 23; Is 40:11; Ezek 34:11–16, 23; 37:24; John 10:2–3,11,14,27; 1 Pet 2:25; 5:4. *everlasting covenant.* The new covenant (see note on 8:8–12). What Jeremiah designates as the new covenant in 31:31 he describes as everlasting in 32:40 (see also Is 55:3 and note; 61:8). On the blood of the covenant see note on 10:29.

13:21 *every good work.* Such as faith, faithfulness, obedience and perseverance.

13:22–25 A postscript.

13:22 *word of exhortation.* The main thrust of the letter is to go on in Christian maturity and not fall away from Christ. *few words.* Compared to the lengthy treatise that would be necessary to explain adequately the superiority of Christ.

13:23 *Timothy is set at liberty.* Timothy, who was well known to the recipients of the letter, had recently been released from prison.

‡13:24 *them that have the rule over you.* Mentioned in v. 17. *They of Italy.* This phrase likely suggests that this letter was written either to or from Italy (cf. Acts 10:23). The author could, however, simply be passing on greetings from some Italian believers.

The General Epistles

The seven letters following Hebrews—James, 1,2 Peter, 1,2,3 John and Jude—have often been designated as the General Epistles. This term goes back to the early church historian Eusebius (c. A.D. 265–340), who in his *Ecclesiastical History* (2.23–25) first referred to these seven letters as Catholic Epistles, using the word "catholic" to mean "universal."

The epistles so designated may be said to be, for the most part, addressed to general audiences rather than to specific persons or localized groups. 2 and 3 John, the two epistles that seem most obviously addressed to individuals, have long been viewed as appendages of 1 John, which is clearly general in its address. However, when compared with Paul's epistles, all these letters except 3 John are clearly general in nature. By contrast, Paul addresses his letters to such recipients as the saints at Philippi, or the churches of Galatia, or Timothy or Titus.

As Eusebius noted long ago, one interesting fact connected with the General Epistles is that most of them were at one time among the disputed books of the NT. James, 2 Peter, 2 John, 3 John and Jude were all questioned extensively before being admitted to the canon of Scripture.

The General Epistle of James

INTRODUCTION

Author

The author identifies himself as James (1:1), and he was probably the brother of Jesus and leader of the Jerusalem council (Acts 15). Four men in the NT have this name. The author of this letter could not have been the apostle James, who died too early (A.D. 44) to have written it. The other two men named James had neither the stature nor the influence that the writer of this letter had.

James was one of several brothers of Christ and was probably the oldest since he heads the list in Mat 13:55. At first he did not believe in Jesus and even challenged Him and misunderstood His mission (John 7:2–5). Later he became very prominent in the church:

1. He was one of the select individuals Christ appeared to after His resurrection (1 Cor 15:7).
2. Paul called him a "pillar" of the church (Gal 2:9).
3. Paul, on his first post-conversion visit to Jerusalem, saw James (Gal 1:19).
4. Paul did the same on his last visit (Acts 21:18).
5. When Peter was rescued from prison, he told his friends to tell James (Acts 12:17).
6. James was a leader in the important council of Jerusalem (Acts 15:13).
7. Jude could identify himself simply as a "brother of James" (Jude 1:1), so well known was James.

He was martyred c. A.D. 62.

Date

Some date the letter in the early 60s. There are indications, however, that it was written before A.D. 50:

1. Its distinctively Jewish nature suggests that it was composed when the church was still predominantly Jewish.
2. It reflects a simple church order—officers of the church are called "elders" (5:14) and "masters," meaning "teachers" (3:1).
3. No reference is made to the controversy over Gentile circumcision.
4. The Greek term *synagoge* ("synagogue," "meeting," or "assembly") is used to designate the meeting or meeting place of the church (2:2).

If this early dating is correct, this letter is the earliest of all the NT writings—with the possible exception of Galatians.

Recipients

The recipients are identified explicitly only in 1:1: "the twelve tribes which are scattered abroad." Some hold that this expression refers to Christians in general, but the term "twelve tribes" would more naturally apply to Jewish Christians. Furthermore, a Jewish audience would be more in keeping with the obviously Jewish nature of the letter (e.g., the use of the Hebrew title for God, *kyrios sabaoth,* "Lord of sabaoth," 5:4). That the recipients were Christians is clear from 2:1; 5:7–8. It has been plausibly suggested that these were believers from the early Jerusalem church who, after Stephen's death, were scattered as far as Phoenicia, Cyprus and Syrian Antioch (Acts 8:1; 11:19). This would account for James's references to trials and oppression, his intimate knowledge of the readers and the authoritative nature of the letter. As leader of the Jerusalem church, James wrote as pastor to instruct and encourage his dispersed people in the face of their difficulties.

Distinctive Characteristics

Characteristics that make the letter distinctive are: (1) its unmistakably Jewish nature; (2) its emphasis on vital Christianity, characterized by good deeds and a faith that works (genuine faith must and will be accompanied by a consistent life-style); (3) its simple organization; (4) its familiarity with Jesus' teachings preserved in the Sermon on the Mount (compare 2:5 with Mat 5:3; 3:10–12 with

Mat 7:15–20; 3:18 with Mat 5:9; 5:2–3 with Mat 6:19–20; 5:12 with Mat 5:33–37); (5) its similarity to OT wisdom writings such as Proverbs; (6) its excellent Greek.

Outline

I. Greetings (1:1)
II. Trials and Temptations (1:2–18)
    A. The Testing of Faith (1:2–12)
    B. The Source of Temptation (1:13–18)
III. Listening and Doing (1:19–27)
IV. Favoritism Forbidden (2:1–13)
V. Faith and Deeds (2:14–26)
VI. Taming the Tongue (3:1–12)
VII. Two Kinds of Wisdom (3:13–18)
VIII. Warning against Worldliness (ch. 4)
    A. Quarrelsomeness (4:1–3)
    B. Spiritual Unfaithfulness (4:4)
    C. Pride (4:5–10)
    D. Slander (4:11–12)
    E. Boasting (4:13–17)
IX. Warning to Rich Oppressors (5:1–6)
X. Miscellaneous Exhortations (5:7–20)
    A. Concerning Patience in Suffering (5:7–11)
    B. Concerning Oaths (5:12)
    C. Concerning the Prayer of Faith (5:13–18)
    D. Concerning Those Who Wander from the Truth (5:19–20)

1 [a]James, [b]a servant of God and of the
Lord Jesus Christ, [c]to the twelve tribes
[d]which are scattered abroad, greeting.

Patience in temptation

2 ¶ My brethren, [a]count *it* all joy [b]when ye
fall into divers temptations;
3 [a]Knowing *this,* that the trying of your
faith worketh patience.
4 But let patience have *her* perfect work,
that ye may be perfect and entire, wanting
nothing.
5 [a]If any of you lack wisdom, [b]let him ask
of God, that giveth to all *men* liberally, and upbraideth not; and [c]it shall be given him.
6 [a]But let him ask in faith, nothing wavering: for he that wavereth is like a wave of the
sea driven with the wind and tossed.
7 For let not that man think that he shall
receive any *thing* of the Lord.
8 [a]A double minded man *is* unstable in all
his ways.
9 Let the brother of low degree [1]rejoice in
that he is exalted:
10 But the rich, in that he is made low: because [a]as the flower of the grass he shall pass
away.
11 For the sun is no sooner risen with a
burning heat, but it withereth the grass, and
the flower thereof falleth, and the grace of the
fashion of it perisheth: so also shall the rich
man fade away in his ways.
12 [a]Blessed *is* the man that endureth
temptation: for when he is tried, he shall receive [b]the crown of life, [c]which the Lord hath
promised to them that love him.
13 Let no *man* say when he is tempted, I
am tempted of God: for God cannot be tempted with [1]evil, neither tempteth he any *man:*
14 But every man is tempted, when he is
drawn away of his own lust, and enticed.
15 Then [a]when lust hath conceived, it
bringeth forth sin: and sin, when it is finished,
[b]bringeth forth death.
16 Do not err, my beloved brethren.
17 [a]Every good gift and every perfect gift is
from above, and cometh down from the Father
of lights, [b]with whom is no variableness, neither shadow of turning.
18 [a]Of his own will begat he us with the
word of truth, [b]that we should be a kind of
[c]firstfruits of his creatures.

The conduct of true religion

19 ¶ Wherefore, my beloved brethren, [a]let
every man be swift to hear, [b]slow to speak,
[c]slow to wrath:
20 For the wrath of man worketh not the
righteousness of God.
21 Wherefore [a]lay apart all filthiness and
superfluity of naughtiness, and receive with
meekness the engrafted word, [b]which is able
to save your souls.
22 But [a]be ye doers of the word, and not
hearers only, deceiving your own selves.
23 For [a]if any be a hearer of the word, and
not a doer, he is like unto a man beholding his
natural face in a glass:
24 For he beholdeth himself, and goeth his
way, and straightway forgetteth what manner
of *man* he was.
25 But [a]whoso looketh into the perfect
[b]law of liberty, and continueth *therein,* he being not a forgetful hearer, but a doer of the
work, [c]this *man* shall be blessed in his [1]deed.

1:1 [a]Acts 12:17 [b]Tit. 1:1 [c]Acts 26:7 [d]Deut. 32:26; John 7:35; Acts 2:5; 1 Pet. 1:1
1:2 [a]Acts 5:41 [b]1 Pet. 1:6
1:3 [a]Rom. 5:3
1:5 [a]1 Ki. 3:9; Prov. 2:3 [b]Mat. 7:7; Luke 11:9; John 14:13 [c]Jer. 29:12; 1 John 5:14
1:6 [a]Mark 11:24; 1 Tim. 2:8
1:8 [a]ch. 4:8
1:9 [1]Or, *glory*
1:10 [a]Job 14:2; Ps. 37:2; 1 Cor. 7:31
1:12 [a]Job 5:17; Prov. 3:11 [b]1 Cor. 9:25; 2 Tim. 4:8 [c]Mat. 10:22
1:13 [1]Or, *evils*
1:15 [a]Job 15:35; Ps. 7:14 [b]Rom. 6:21
1:17 [a]John 3:27 [b]Num. 23:19
1:18 [a]John 1:13; 1 Cor. 4:15 [b]Eph. 1:12 [c]Rev. 14:4
1:19 [a]Eccl. 5:1 [b]Prov. 10:19; Eccl. 5:2 [c]Prov. 14:17
1:21 [a]Col. 3:8; 1 Pet. 2:1 [b]Acts 13:26; Rom. 1:16; Eph. 1:13; Tit. 2:11
1:22 [a]Mat. 7:21; Rom. 2:13; 1 John 3:7
1:23 [a]Luke 6:47
1:25 [1]Or, *doing* [a]2 Cor. 3:18 [b]ch. 2:12 [c]John 13:17

1:1 *James.* See Introduction: Author. *servant.* See note on Rom 1:1. *twelve tribes.* See Introduction: Recipients.

‡1:2 *brethren.* James addresses the readers as brothers 15 times in this short letter. He has many rebukes for them, but he chides them in brotherly love. *joy.* See Mat 5:11–12; Rom 5:3; 1 Pet 1:6. *temptations.* The same Greek root lies behind the word "trials" here and the word "tempted" in v. 13. In vv. 2–3 the emphasis is on difficulties that come from outside; in vv. 13–15 it is on inner moral trials such as temptation to sin.

1:5 *wisdom.* Enables one to face trials with "joy" (v. 2). Wisdom is not just acquired information but practical insight with spiritual implications (see Prov 1:2–4; 2:10–15; 4:5–9; 9:10–12).

1:6 *wave of the sea.* See Eph 4:14.

‡1:9–10 *brother of low degree . . . the rich.* Since James's discussions of wisdom (vv. 5–8) and of the poor man and the rich man (vv. 9–11) appear between the two sections on trials (vv. 2–4 and v. 12), vv. 5–11 may also have to do with trials. The Christian who suffers the trial of poverty is to rejoice in his high position (v. 9) as a believer (see 2:5), and the wealthy Christian is to rejoice (v. 10) in trials that bring him low, perhaps including the loss of his wealth.

‡1:12 *Blessed.* See Jer 17:7–8; Mat 5:3–12; see also notes on Ps 1:1; Mat 5:3; Rev 1:3. *crown of life.* This crown of life could either refer to eternal life itself or to God's eternal reward or glory for those who overcome the severe trials of life, such as a physical handicap, a degrading status or role in life, or any number of agonies of life (see 2 Tim 4:8; 1 Pet 5:4; Rev 2:10 and note).

1:13 *tempted.* In vv. 13–14 the verb refers to temptations that test one's moral strength to resist sin (see note on Mat 4:1). *God cannot be tempted.* Because God in His very nature is holy, there is nothing in Him for sin to appeal to. *neither tempteth he any man.* See note on Gen 22:1.

‡1:15 The three stages—lust, sin, death—are seen in the temptations of Eve (Gen 3:6–22) and David (2 Sam 11:2–17).

‡1:17 *Every good gift and every perfect gift is from above.* See v. 5; 3:17. *Father of lights.* God is the Creator of the heavenly bodies, which give light to the earth, but, unlike them, He does not change.

1:18 *begat he us.* Not a reference to creation but to regeneration (see John 3:3–8). *word of truth.* The proclamation of the gospel (see 1 Pet 1:23–25). *firstfruits.* See Lev 23:9–14. Just as the first sheaf of the harvest was an indication that the whole harvest would eventually follow, so the early Christians were an indication that a great number of people would eventually be born again.

1:19 *let every man be . . . slow to speak.* See v. 26.

1:21 *word.* Of God.

1:25 *perfect law.* The moral and ethical teaching of Christianity, which is based on the OT moral law, as embodied in the ten commandments (see Ps 19:7), but brought to completion (perfection) by Jesus Christ. *liberty.* In contrast to the sinner, who is a slave to sin (John 8:34), obeying the moral law gives the Christian the joyous freedom to be what he was created for (see 2:12).

26 If any *man* among you seem to be religious, and [a]bridleth not his tongue, but deceiveth his own heart, this *man's* religion *is* vain.
27 Pure religion and undefiled before God and the Father is this, [a]To visit the fatherless and widows in their affliction, [b]*and* to keep himself unspotted from the world.

True faith impartial

2 My brethren, have not the faith of our Lord Jesus Christ, [a]*the Lord* of glory, with [b]respect of persons.
2 For if there come unto your [1]assembly a man with a gold ring, in goodly apparel, and there come in also a poor *man* in vile raiment;
3 And ye have respect to him that weareth the gay clothing, and say unto him, Sit thou here [1]in a good place; and say to the poor, Stand thou there, or sit here under my footstool:
4 Are ye not then partial in yourselves, and are become judges of evil thoughts?
5 Hearken, my beloved brethren, [a]Hath not God chosen the poor of this world [b]rich in faith, and heirs of [1]the kingdom [c]which he hath promised to them that love him?
6 But [a]ye have despised the poor. Do not rich *men* oppress you, [b]and draw you before the judgment seats?
7 Do not they blaspheme *that* worthy name by the which ye are called?
8 If ye fulfil the royal law according to the scripture, [a]Thou shalt love thy neighbour as thyself, ye do well:
9 But [a]if ye have respect to persons, ye commit sin, and are convinced of the law as transgressors.
10 For whosoever shall keep the whole law, and *yet* offend in one *point,* [a]he is guilty of all.
11 For [1]he that said, [a]Do not commit adultery, said also, Do not kill. Now if thou commit no adultery, yet *if* thou kill, thou art become a transgressor of the law.
12 So speak ye, and so do, as they that shall be judged by [a]the law of liberty.
13 For [a]he shall have judgment without mercy, that hath shewed no mercy; and [b]mercy [1]rejoiceth against judgment.

True faith evidenced by works

14 ¶ [a]What *doth it* profit, my brethren, though a man say *he* hath faith, and have not works? can faith save him?
15 [a]If a brother or sister be naked, and destitute of daily food,
16 And [a]one of you say unto them, Depart in peace, be you warmed and filled; notwithstanding ye give them not those *things which are* needful to the body; what *doth it* profit?
17 Even so faith, if it hath not works, is dead, *being* [1]alone.
18 Yea, a man may say, Thou hast faith, and I have works: shew me thy faith [1]without thy works, [a]and I will shew thee my faith by my works.
19 Thou believest that there is one God; thou doest well: the devils also believe, and tremble.
20 But wilt thou know, O vain man, that faith without works is dead?
21 Was not Abraham our father justified by works, [a]when he had offered Isaac his son upon the altar?

1:26 [a]Ps. 34:13; 1 Pet. 3:10
1:27 [a]Is. 1:16; Mat. 25:36 [b]Rom. 12:2; 1 John 5:18
2:1 [a]1 Cor. 2:8 [b]Lev. 19:15; Deut. 1:17; Mat. 22:16; Jude 16
2:2 [1]Gr. *synagogue*
2:3 [1]Or, *well,* or, *seemly*
2:5 [1]Or, that [a]John 7:48 [b]Luke 12:21 [c]Ex. 20:6; Prov. 8:17
2:6 [a]1 Cor. 11:22 [b]Acts 13:50
2:8 [a]Lev. 19:18; Mat. 22:39
2:9 [a]ver. 1
2:10 [a]Deut. 27:26; Mat. 5:19; Gal. 3:10
2:11 [1]Or, *that law which said* [a]Ex. 20:13
2:12 [a]ch. 1:25
2:13 [1]Or, *glorieth* [a]Job 22:6 [b]1 John 4:17
2:14 [a]Mat. 7:26; Mat. 15:11
2:15 [a]Luke 3:11
2:16 [a]1 John 3:18
2:17 [1]Gr. *by itself*
2:18 [1]Some copies read, *by thy works* [a]ch. 3:13
2:21 [a]Gen. 22:9

1:26 *religious.* Refers to the outward acts of religion: e.g., giving to the needy, fasting and public acts of praying and worshiping.

‡1:27 *Pure religion.* James identifies true religion as involving two actions (service and separation) which relate to two basic attributes of God (love and holiness).

‡2:1 *faith . . . with respect of persons.* God does not show favoritism—nor should believers. See Deut 1:17, Rom 2:11, Eph 6:9, and Col 3:25.

2:2 *assembly.* The Greek for this term is the origin of the English word "synagogue."

2:5–13 James gives three arguments against showing favoritism to the rich: 1. The rich persecute the poor—the believers (vv. 5–7). 2. Favoritism violates the royal law of love and thus is sin (vv. 8–11). 3. Favoritism will be judged (vv. 12–13).

2:5 *Hath not God chosen the poor.* See Luke 6:20; 1 Cor 1:26–31. *the kingdom.* The kingdom that is entered by the new birth (John 3:3,5) and that will be consummated in the future (Mat 25:34,46).

2:8 *royal law.* The law of love (Lev 19:18) is called "royal" because it is the supreme law that is the source of all other laws governing human relationships. It is the summation of all such laws (Mat 22:36–40; Rom 13:8–10).

2:10 *guilty of all.* The law is the expression of the character and will of God; therefore to violate one part of the law is to violate God's will and thus His whole law (cf. Mat 5:18–19; 23:23).

2:12 *judged.* This judgment is not for determining eternal destiny, for James is speaking to believers (v. 1), whose destiny is already determined (John 5:24). Rather, it is for giving rewards to believers (1 Cor 3:12–15; 2 Cor 5:10; Rev 22:12).

2:13 *mercy rejoiceth against judgment.* If man is merciful, God will be merciful on the day of judgment (see Prov 21:13; Mat 5:7; 6:14–15; 18:21–35).

2:14–26 In vv. 14–20,24,26 "faith" is not used in the sense of genuine, saving faith. Rather, it is demonic (v. 19), useless (v. 20) and dead (v. 26). It is a mere intellectual acceptance of certain truths without trust in Christ as Savior. James is also not saying that a person is saved by works and not by genuine faith. Rather, he is saying, to use Martin Luther's words, that a man is justified (declared righteous before God) by faith alone, but not by a faith that is alone. Genuine faith will produce good deeds, but only faith in Christ saves. (For more information on justification see note on Rom 3:24.)

2:15–16 This illustration of false faith is parallel to the illustration of false love found in 1 John 3:17. The latter passage calls for love in action; this one calls for faith in action.

2:18 *Thou hast faith, and I have works.* The false claim is that there are "faith" Christians and "works" Christians, i.e., that faith and deeds can exist independently of each other. *shew me thy faith without thy works.* Irony; James denies the possibility of this.

2:19 *there is one God.* A declaration of monotheism that reflects the well-known Jewish creed called in Hebrew the *Shema,* meaning "Hear" (Deut 6:4; Mark 12:29).

2:21 Apart from its context, this verse might seem to contradict the Biblical teaching that people are saved by faith and

22 [1]Seest thou [a]how faith wrought with his works, and by works was faith made perfect?

23 And the scripture was fulfilled which saith, [a]Abraham believed God, and it was imputed unto him for righteousness: and he was called [b]the Friend of God.

24 Ye see then how that by works a man is justified, and not by faith only.

25 Likewise also [a]was not Rahab the harlot justified by works, when she had received the messengers, and had sent *them* out another way?

26 For as the body without the [1]spirit is dead, so faith without works is dead also.

True faith evidenced by words

3 My brethren, [a]be not many masters, [b]knowing that we shall receive the greater [1]condemnation.

2 For [a]*in* many *things* we offend all. [b]If any *man* offend not in word, [c]the same *is* a perfect man, *and* able also to bridle the whole body.

3 Behold, [a]we put bits in the horses' mouths, that they may obey us; and we turn about their whole body.

4 Behold also the ships, which though they be so great, and are driven of fierce winds, *yet* are they turned about with a very small helm, whithersoever the governor listeth.

5 Even so [a]the tongue is a little member, and [b]boasteth great things. Behold, how great [1]a matter a little fire kindleth.

6 And [a]the tongue *is* a fire, a world of iniquity: so is the tongue amongst our members, that [b]it defileth the whole body, and setteth on fire the [1]course of nature; and it is set on fire of hell.

7 For every [1]kind of beasts, and of birds, and of serpents, and of *things* in the sea, is tamed, and hath been tamed of [2]mankind:

2:22 [1]Or, *Thou seest* [a]Heb. 11:17
2:23 [a]Gen. 15:6; Rom. 4:3; Gal. 3:6 [b]2 Chr. 20:7; Is. 41:8
2:25 [a]Heb. 11:31
2:26 [1]Or, *breath*
3:1 [1]Or, *judgment* [a]Mat. 23:8 [b]Luke 6:37
3:2 [a]1 Ki. 8:46; 2 Chr. 6:36; Prov. 20:9 [b]Ps. 34:13; 1 Pet. 3:10 [c]Mat. 12:37
3:3 [a]Ps. 32:9
3:5 [1]Or, *wood* [a]Prov. 12:18 [b]Ps. 12:3
3:6 [1][Gr. *wheel*] [a]Prov. 16:27 [b]Mat. 15:11
3:7 [1]Gr. *nature* [2]Gr. *nature of man*
3:8 [a]Ps. 140:3
3:9 [a]Gen. 1:26
3:11 [1]Or, *hole*
3:13 [a]Gal. 6:4 [b]ch. 2:18 [c]ch. 1:21
3:14 [a]Rom. 13:13 [b]Rom. 2:17
3:15 [1]Or, *natural* [a]Phil. 3:19
3:16 [1]Gr. *tumult,* or, *unquietness* [a]1 Cor. 3:3; Gal. 5:20
3:17 [1]Or, *without wrangling* [a]1 Cor. 2:6 [b]Rom. 12:9; 1 Pet. 1:22
3:18 [a]Prov. 11:18
4:1 [1]Or, *brawlings* [2]Or, *pleasures* [a]Rom. 7:23; Gal. 5:17
4:2 [1][Or, *envy*]
4:3 [1]Or, *pleasures* [a]Job 27:9; Ps. 18:41 [b]Ps. 66:18

8 But the tongue can no man tame; *it is* an unruly evil, [a]full of deadly poison.

9 Therewith bless we God, even the Father; and therewith curse we men, [a]which are made after the similitude of God.

10 Out of the same mouth proceedeth blessing and cursing. My brethren, these *things* ought not so to be.

11 Doth a fountain send forth at the same [1]place sweet *water* and bitter?

12 Can the fig tree, my brethren, bear olive berries? either a vine, figs? so *can* no fountain *both* yield salt water and fresh.

True and false wisdom

13 ¶ [a]Who *is* a wise *man* and endued with knowledge amongst you? let him shew out of a good conversation [b]his works [c]with meekness of wisdom.

14 But if ye have [a]bitter envying and strife in your hearts, [b]glory not, and lie *not* against the truth.

15 [a]This wisdom descendeth not from above, but *is* earthly, [1]sensual, devilish.

16 For [a]where envying and strife *is,* there *is* [1]confusion and every evil work.

17 But [a]the wisdom that is from above is first pure, then peaceable, gentle, *and* easy to be intreated, full of mercy and good fruits, [1]without partiality, [b]and without hypocrisy.

18 [a]And the fruit of righteousness is sown in peace of them that make peace.

Friendship and humility

4 From whence *come* wars and [1]fightings among you? *come they* not hence, *even* of your [2]lusts [a]that war in your members?

2 Ye lust, and have not: ye [1]kill, and desire *to have,* and cannot obtain: ye fight and war, yet ye have not, because ye ask not.

3 [a]Ye ask, and receive not, [b]because ye ask amiss, that ye may consume *it* upon your [1]lusts.

---

not by good deeds (Rom 3:28; Gal 2:15–16). But James means only that righteous action is evidence of genuine faith—not that it saves, for the verse (Gen 15:6) that he cites (v. 23) to substantiate his point says, "And he believed in the LORD; and he counted it [i.e., faith, not works] to him for righteousness." Furthermore, Abraham's act of faith recorded in Gen 15:6 occurred before he offered up Isaac, which was only a proof of the genuineness of his faith. As Paul wrote, the only thing that matters is "faith which worketh by love" (Gal 5:6). Faith that saves produces deeds.

2:23 *the Friend of God.* This designation (see 2 Chr 20:7) further describes Abraham's relationship to God as one of complete acceptance.

2:24 *not by faith only.* Not by an intellectual assent to certain truths (see note on 2:14–26).

2:25 *Rahab the harlot.* James does not approve Rahab's occupation. He merely commends her for her faith (see also Heb 11:31), which she demonstrated by helping the spies (Josh 2).

‡3:1 *masters.* "Master" has its old English meaning of a "teacher" here, as the Greek word used and the subject matter of chapter 3 show. *greater condemnation.* Because a teacher has great influence, he will be held more accountable (see Luke 20:47; cf. Mat 23:1–33).

‡3:2 *perfect man.* Since the tongue is so difficult to control, anyone who could control it perfectly could control himself in all other areas of life as well.

3:6 *world of iniquity.* Like the world in its fallenness. *set on fire of hell.* A figurative way of saying that the source of the tongue's evil is the devil (see John 8:44). See notes on Mat 5:22; Luke 16:23.

3:9 *similitude of God.* Since man has been made like God (Gen 1:26–27), to curse man is like cursing God (see Gen 9:6). See note on Gen 1:26.

‡3:13 Three elements of a true teacher are expressed by three words in this verse: "knowledge," "meekness," and "shew." *shew out of a good conversation.* Show by his good conduct in life. We cannot teach well what we cannot practice in our own life.

3:15 *from above.* From God (see 1:5,17; 1 Cor 2:6–16).

3:16 *confusion.* "God is not the author of confusion but of peace" (1 Cor 14:33).

3:17 *without partiality.* See 2:1–13.

3:18 *them that make peace.* Contrast v. 16. Discord cannot produce righteousness.

4:1 *lusts.* The Greek for this term is the source of our word "hedonism."

4:2 *kill.* Figurative (hyperbole) for "hate."

4 [a]Ye adulterers and adulteresses, know ye not that [b]the friendship of the world is enmity with God? [c]whosoever therefore will be a friend of the world is the enemy of God.

5 Do ye think that the scripture saith in vain, [a]the spirit that dwelleth in us lusteth [1]to envy?

6 But he giveth more grace. Wherefore *he* saith, [a]God resisteth the proud, but giveth grace unto the humble.

7 Submit yourselves therefore to God. [a]Resist the devil, and he will flee from you.

8 [a]Draw nigh to God, and he will draw nigh to you. [b]Cleanse *your* hands, *ye* sinners; and [c]purify *your* hearts, *ye* [d]double minded.

9 [a]Be afflicted, and mourn, and weep: let your laughter be turned to mourning, and *your* joy to heaviness.

10 [a]Humble yourselves in the sight of the Lord, and he shall lift you up.

Slander and false confidence

11 ¶ [a]Speak not evil one of another, brethren. He that speaketh evil of *his* brother, [b]and judgeth his brother, speaketh evil of the law, and judgeth the law: but if thou judge the law, thou art not a doer of the law, but a judge.

12 There is one lawgiver, [a]who is able to save and to destroy: [b]who art thou that judgest another?

13 ¶ [a]Go to now, ye that say, To day or to morrow we will go into such a city, and continue there a year, and buy and sell, and get gain:

14 Whereas ye know not what *shall be* on the morrow: for what *is* your life? [a][1]It is even a vapour, that appeareth for a little *time,* and then vanisheth away.

15 For that ye *ought* to say, [a]If the Lord will, we shall live, and do this, or that.

16 But now ye rejoice in your boastings: [a]all such rejoicing is evil.

17 Therefore [a]to him that knoweth to do good, and doeth *it* not, to him it is sin.

The miseries of the rich

5 Go [a]to now, ye rich *men,* weep and howl for your miseries that shall come upon *you.*

2 Your riches are corrupted, and [a]your garments are motheaten.

3 Your gold and silver is cankered; and the rust of them shall be a witness against you, and shall eat your flesh as *it were* fire: [a]ye have heaped treasure together for the last days.

4 Behold, [a]the hire of the labourers which have reaped *down* your fields, which is of you kept back by fraud, crieth: and [b]the cries of them which have reaped are entered into the ears of the Lord of sabaoth.

5 [a]Ye have lived in pleasure on the earth, and been wanton; ye have nourished your hearts, as in a day of slaughter.

6 [a]Ye have condemned *and* killed the just; *and* he doth not resist you.

The patience of the saints

7 ¶ [1]Be patient therefore, brethren, unto the coming of the Lord. Behold, the husbandman waiteth for the precious fruit of the earth, and hath long patience for it, until he receive [a]the early and latter rain.

8 Be ye also patient; stablish your hearts: [a]for the coming of the Lord draweth nigh.

9 [a][1]Grudge not one against another, brethren, lest ye be condemned: behold, the judge [b]standeth before the door.

4:4 [a]Ps. 73:27 [b]1 John 2:15 [c]John 15:19; Gal. 1:10
4:5 [1]Or, *enviously?* [a]Gen. 6:5; Num. 11:29
4:6 [a]Job 22:29; Ps. 138:6; Prov. 3:34; Mat. 23:12
4:7 [a]Eph. 4:27; 1 Pet. 5:9
4:8 [a]2 Chr. 15:2 [b]Is. 1:16 [c]1 Pet. 1:22; 1 John 3:3 [d]ch. 1:8
4:9 [a]Mat. 5:4
4:10 [a]Job 22:29
4:11 [a]1 Pet. 2:1 [b]Mat. 7:1
4:12 [a]Mat. 10:28 [b]Rom. 14:4
4:13 [a]Prov. 27:1
4:14 [1]Or, *For it is* [a]Job 7:7
4:15 [a]Acts 18:21
4:16 [a]1 Cor. 5:6
4:17 [a]Luke 12:47; John 9:41
5:1 [a]Prov. 11:28; Luke 6:24
5:2 [a]Job 13:28; Mat. 6:20
5:3 [a]Rom. 2:5
5:4 [a]Lev. 19:13 [b]Deut. 24:15
5:5 [a]Job 21:13; Amos 6:1
5:6 [a]ch. 2:6
5:7 [1]Or, *Be long patient,* or, *Suffer with long patience* [a]Deut. 11:14; Hos. 6:3
5:8 [a]Phil. 4:5; 1 Pet. 4:7
5:9 [1]Or, *Groan,* or, *Grieve, not* [a]ch. 4:11 [b]Mat. 24:33

4:4 *adulterers and adulteresses.* Those who are spiritually unfaithful, who love the world rather than God. For spiritual adultery see, e.g., Jer 31:32. *world.* See note on 1:27.
‡4:5 *scripture.* The passage James had in mind is not known.
4:6 See 1 Pet 5:5, which also quotes Prov 3:34.
4:7–10 These verses contain ten commands, each of which is so stated in Greek that it calls for immediate action in rooting out the sinful attitude of pride.
4:7 *Resist the devil.* See Eph 6:11–18; 1 Pet 5:8–9.
4:8 *Cleanse your hands.* Before the OT priests approached God at the tabernacle, they had to wash their hands and feet at the brass laver as a symbol of spiritual cleansing (Ex 30:17–21). See Ps 24:4 for the imagery of "clean hands and a pure heart."
4:9 *Be afflicted, and mourn, and weep.* Repent.
4:10 See Mat 23:12.
4:11 *speaketh evil of his brother . . . speaketh evil of the law.* See note on 2:8; see also Ex 20:16; Ps 15:3; 50:19–20; Prov 6:16,19. To speak against a brother is to scorn the law of love.
5:1 *rich.* These (as also in 2:2,6) are not Christians, for James warns them to repent and weep because of the coming misery. Verses 1–6 are similar to OT declarations of judgment against pagan nations, interspersed in books otherwise addressed to God's people (Is 13–23; Jer 46–51; Ezek 25–32; Amos 1:3–2:16; Zeph 2:4–15).
5:2 *garments.* One of the main forms of wealth in the ancient world (see Acts 20:33).
5:3 *rust.* The result of hoarding. It will both testify against and judge the selfish rich. *last days.* See notes on Acts 2:17; 1 Tim 4:1; 2 Tim 3:1; Heb 1:1; 1 John 2:18.
5:4 *the Lord of sabaoth.* See notes on Gen 17:1; 1 Sam 1:3.
5:5 *lived in pleasure . . . and been wanton.* See Luke 16:19–31. *a day of slaughter.* The day of judgment. The wicked rich are like cattle that continue to fatten themselves on the very day they are to be slaughtered, totally unaware of coming destruction.
5:7 *therefore.* Refers back to vv. 1–6. Since the believers are suffering at the hands of the wicked rich, they are to look forward patiently to the Lord's return. *early and latter rain.* In Israel the early rain comes in October and November soon after the grain is sown, and the late rain comes in March and April just prior to harvest (Deut 11:14; Jer 5:24; Hos 6:3; Joel 2:24).
5:9 *Grudge not.* James calls for patience toward believers as well as unbelievers (vv. 7–8). *the judge standeth before the door.* A reference to Christ's second coming (see vv. 7–8) and the judgment associated with it. The NT insistence on imminence (e.g., in Rom 13:12; Heb 10:25; 1 Pet 4:7; Rev 22:20) arises from the teaching that the "last days" began with the incarnation. We have been living in the "last days" (v. 3) ever since (see note on Heb 1:1). The next great event in redemptive history is Christ's second coming. The NT does not say when it will take place, but its certainty is never questioned and believers are consistently admonished to watch for it. It was in this light that James expected the imminent return of Christ.

10 [a]Take, my brethren, the prophets, who have spoken in the name of the Lord, for an example of suffering affliction, and of patience.
11 Behold, [a]we count them happy which endure. Ye have heard of [b]the patience of Job, and have seen [c]the end of the Lord; that [d]the Lord is very pitiful, and of tender mercy.
12 But above all *things,* my brethren, [a]swear not, neither by heaven, neither by the earth, neither by any other oath: but let your yea be yea; and *your* nay, nay; lest ye fall into condemnation.

Prayer and confession

13 Is any among you afflicted? let him pray. Is any merry? [a]let him sing psalms.
14 Is any sick among you? let him call for the elders of the church; and let them pray over him, [a]anointing him with oil in the name of the Lord:

5:10 [a]Mat. 5:12
5:11 [a]Ps. 94:12 [b]Job 2:10 [c]Job 42:10 [d]Num. 14:18
5:12 [a]Mat. 5:34
5:13 [a]Eph. 5:19
5:14 [a]Mark 6:13
5:15 [a]Is. 33:24
5:16 [a]Num. 11:2; John 9:31
5:17 [1]Or, *in his prayer* [a]Acts 14:15 [b]1 Ki. 17:1 [c]Luke 4:25
5:18 [a]1 Ki. 18:42,45
5:19 [a]Mat. 18:15
5:20 [a]Rom. 11:14 [b]Prov. 10:12; 1 Pet. 4:8

15 And the prayer of faith shall save the sick, and the Lord shall raise him up; [a]and if he have committed sins, they shall be forgiven him.
16 Confess *your* faults one to another, and pray one for another, that ye may be healed. [a]The effectual fervent prayer of a righteous *man* availeth much.
17 Elias was a man [a]subject to like passions as we are, and [b]he prayed [1]earnestly that it might not rain: [c]and it rained not on the earth *by the space of* three years and six months.
18 And [a]he prayed again, and the heaven gave rain, and the earth brought forth her fruit.
19 ¶ Brethren, [a]if any of you do err from the truth, and one convert him;
20 Let him know, that he which converteth the sinner from the error of his way [a]shall save a soul from death, and [b]shall hide a multitude of sins.

‡5:11 *patience of Job.* This refers to the endurance or perseverance of Job in the face of adversity (Job 1:20–22; 2:9–10,13–15). This is the only place in the NT where Job is mentioned, though Job 5:13 is quoted in 1 Cor 3:19.
‡5:12 *swear not.* James's words are very close to Christ's (Mat 5:33–37). James is not condemning the taking of solemn oaths, such as God's before Abraham (Heb 6:13) or Jesus' before Caiaphas (Mat 26:63–64) or Paul's (Rom 1:9; 9:1) or a man's before the Lord (Ex 22:11). Rather, he is condemning the use of "non-binding oaths" to give the impression of truthfulness. He is applying the teaching of Jesus (cf. Mt 23:16–22). James is teaching total honesty even in the most adverse circumstances.
‡5:14 *elders.* See notes on 1 Tim 3:1; 5:17. *church.* See note on Mat 16:18. *oil.* One of the best-known ancient medicines (referred to by Philo, Pliny and the physician Galen; see also Is 1:6; Luke 10:34). Some believe that James may be using the term medicinally in this passage. Others, however, regard its use here as an aid to faith, an outward sign of the healing to be brought about by God in response to prayer made in faith (v. 15; see especially Mark 6:13).
‡5:15 *prayer of faith.* Since Elijah is provided (vv. 17–18) by James as the example of the prayer of faith, this prayer must be prayer that is in harmony with the revealed and discerned will of God. Elijah prayed and acted upon the promise God had already revealed to him. He knew God's will and so was praying God's will when he fervently prayed for God to send fire from heaven to consume his sacrifice (1 Ki 18:36) and when he fervently prayed for God to send rain after a three-year drought (1 Ki 18:41–44 with 18:1). Also see note at 1 Ki 18:1.
‡5:19 *err from the truth.* The one who errs is either a professing Christian, whose faith is not genuine (cf. Heb 6:4–8; 2 Pet 2:20–21), or a sinning Christian, who needs to be restored. For the former, the death spoken of in v. 20 is the "second death" (Rev 21:8); for the latter, it is physical death (cf. 1 Cor 11:30). See note on 1 John 5:16.
5:20 *hide a multitude of sins.* The sins of the one who errs will be forgiven by God.

The First Epistle General of Peter

INTRODUCTION

Author and Date

The author identifies himself as the apostle Peter (1:1), and the contents and character of the letter support his authorship (see notes on 1:12; 4:13; 5:1–2,5,13). Moreover, the letter reflects the history and terminology of the Gospels and Acts (notably Peter's speeches); its themes and concepts reflect Peter's experiences and his associations in the period of our Lord's earthly ministry and in the apostolic age. That he was acquainted, e.g., with Paul and his letters is made clear in 2 Pet 3:15–16; Gal 1:18; 2:1–21 and elsewhere; coincidences in thought and expression with Paul's writings are therefore not surprising.

From the beginning, 1 Peter was recognized as authoritative and as the work of the apostle Peter. The earliest extant reference to it is 2 Pet 3:1, where Peter himself refers to a former letter he had written. 1 Clement (A.D. 95) seems to indicate acquaintance with 1 Peter. Polycarp, a disciple of the apostle John, makes use of 1 Peter in his letter to the Philippians. The author of the Gospel of Truth (140–150) was acquainted with 1 Peter. Eusebius (fourth century) indicated that it was universally received.

The letter was explicitly ascribed to Peter by that group of church fathers whose testimonies appear in the attestation of so many of the genuine NT writings, namely, Irenaeus (A.D. 140–203), Tertullian (150–222), Clement of Alexandria (155–215) and Origen (185–253). It is thus clear that Peter's authorship of the book has early and strong support.

Nevertheless some claim that the idiomatic Greek of this letter is beyond Peter's competence. But in his time Aramaic, Hebrew and Greek were used in Palestine, and he may well have been acquainted with more than one language. That he was not a professionally trained scribe (Acts 4:13) does not mean that he was unacquainted with Greek; in fact, as a Galilean fisherman he in all likelihood did use it. Even if he had not known it in the earliest days of the church, he may have acquired it as an important aid to his apostolic ministry in the decades that intervened between then and the writing of 1 Peter.

It is true, however, that the Greek of 1 Peter is good literary Greek, and even though Peter could no doubt speak Greek, as so many in the Mediterranean world could, it is unlikely that he would write such polished Greek. But it is at this point that Peter's remark in 5:12 concerning Silvanus may be significant. Here the apostle claims that he wrote "by" (or more lit. "by means of") Silvanus. This phrase cannot refer merely to Silvanus as a letter carrier. Thus Silvanus was the intermediate agent in writing. Some have claimed that Silvanus's qualifications for recording Peter's letter in literary Greek are found in Acts 15:22–29. It is known that a secretary in those days often composed documents in good Greek for those who did not have the language facility to do so. Thus in 1 Peter Silvanus's Greek may be seen, while in 2 Peter it may be Peter's rough Greek that appears.

Some also maintain that the book reflects a situation that did not exist until after Peter's death, suggesting that the persecution referred to in 4:14–16; 5:8–9 is descriptive of Domitian's reign (A.D. 81–96). However, the situation that was developing in Nero's time (54–68) is just as adequately described by those verses. The book can be satisfactorily dated in the early 60s. It cannot be placed earlier than 60 since it shows familiarity with Paul's Prison Epistles (e.g., Colossians and Ephesians, which are to be dated no earlier than 60): Compare 1:1–3 with Eph 1:1–3; 2:18 with Col 3:22; 3:1–6 with Eph 5:22–24. Furthermore, it cannot be dated later than 67/68, since Peter was martyred during Nero's reign.

Place of Writing

In 5:13 Peter indicates that he was in Babylon when he wrote 1 Peter. Among the interpretations that have been suggested are that he was writing from (1) Egyptian Babylon, which was a military post, (2) Mesopotamian Babylon, (3) Jerusalem and (4) Rome. Peter may well be using the name

"Babylon" symbolically, as it seems to be used in the book of Revelation (see, e.g., notes on Rev 17:9–10). Tradition connects him in the latter part of his life with Rome, and certain early writers held that 1 Peter was written there. On the other hand, it is known that Babylon existed in the first century as a small town on the Euphrates. Furthermore, it is pointed out that (1) there is no evidence that the term Babylon was used figuratively to refer to Rome until Revelation was written (c. A.D. 95), and (2) the context of 5:13 is not at all figurative or cryptic.

Recipients

See note on 1:1.

Themes

Although 1 Peter is a short letter, it touches on various doctrines and has much to say about Christian life and duties. It is not surprising that different readers have found it to have different principal themes. For example, it has been characterized as a letter of separation, of suffering and persecution, of suffering and glory, of hope, of pilgrimage, of courage, and as a letter dealing with the true grace of God. Peter says that he has written "exhorting, and testifying that this is the true grace of God" (5:12). This is a definitive general description of the letter, but it does not exclude the recognition of numerous subordinate and contributory themes. The letter is composed also of a series of exhortations (imperatives) that run from 1:13 to 5:11.

Outline

- I. Salutation (1:1–2)
- II. Praise to God for His Grace and Salvation (1:3–12)
- III. Exhortations to Holiness of Life (1:13—5:11)
  - A. The Requirement of Holiness (1:13—2:3)
  - B. The Position of Believers (2:4–12)
    1. A spiritual house (2:4–8)
    2. A chosen people (2:9–10)
    3. Aliens and strangers (2:11–12)
  - C. Submission to Authority (2:13—3:7)
    1. Submission to rulers (2:13–17)
    2. Submission to masters (2:18–20)
    3. Christ's example of submission (2:21–25)
    4. Submission of wives to husbands (3:1–6)
    5. The corresponding duty of husbands (3:7)
  - D. Duties of All (3:8–17)
  - E. Christ's Example (3:18—4:6)
  - F. Conduct in View of the End of All Things (4:7–11)
  - G. Conduct of Those Who Suffer for Christ (4:12–19)
  - H. Conduct of Elders (5:1–4)
  - I. Conduct of Young Men (5:5–11)
- IV. The Purpose of the Letter (5:12)
- V. Closing Greetings (5:13–14)

1 Peter, an apostle of Jesus Christ, to the
strangers [a]scattered throughout Pontus,
Galatia, Cappadocia, Asia, and Bithynia,
2 [a]Elect [b]according to the foreknowledge
of God the Father, [c]through sanctification of
the Spirit, unto obedience and [d]sprinkling of
the blood of Jesus Christ: [e]Grace unto you,
and peace, be multiplied.

The risen Christ

3 ¶ [a]Blessed *be* the God and Father of our
Lord Jesus Christ, which [b]according to his
[1]abundant mercy [c]hath begotten us again
unto a lively hope [d]by the resurrection of Jesus
Christ from the dead,
4 To an inheritance incorruptible, and undefiled, and that fadeth not away, [a]reserved in
heaven [1]for you,
5 [a]Who are kept by the power of God
through faith unto salvation ready to be revealed in the last time.
6 [a]Wherein ye greatly rejoice, though now
[b]for a season, if need be, [c]ye are in heaviness
through manifold temptations:
7 That [a]the trial of your faith, *being* much
more precious than of gold that perisheth,
though [b]it be tried with fire, [c]might be found
unto praise and honour and glory at the appearing of Jesus Christ:
8 [a]Whom having not seen, ye love; [b]in
whom, though now ye see *him* not, yet believing, ye rejoice with joy unspeakable and full of
glory:
9 Receiving [a]the end of your faith, *even* the
salvation of *your* souls.
10 [a]Of which salvation the prophets have
inquired and searched diligently, who prophesied of the grace *that should come* unto you:
11 Searching what, or what manner of time
[a]the Spirit of Christ which was in them did
signify, when it testified beforehand the sufferings of Christ, and the glory that should follow.
12 [a]Unto whom it was revealed, that [b]not
unto themselves, but unto us they did minister
the things, which are now reported unto you
by them that have preached the gospel unto
you with [c]the Holy Ghost sent *down* from
heaven; [d]which *things the* angels desire to
look into.

An appeal for a holy life

13 ¶ Wherefore [a]gird up the loins of your
mind, [b]be sober, and hope [1]to the end for the

1:1 [a]John 7:35; Acts 2:5,9; Jas. 1:1
1:2 [a]Eph. 1:4 [b]Rom. 8:29 [c]2 Thes. 2:13 [d]Heb. 12:24 [e]Rom. 1:7
1:3 [1]Gr. *much* [a]Eph. 1:3 [b]Tit. 3:5 [c]John 3:3,5; Jas. 1:18 [d]1 Cor. 15:20
1:4 [1]Or, *for us* [a]Col. 1:5
1:5 [a]John 10:28
1:6 [a]Mat. 5:12 [b]2 Cor. 4:17 [c]Jas. 1:2
1:7 [a]Jas. 1:3
1:7 [b]Job 23:10; Prov. 17:3 [c]Rom. 2:7
1:8 [a]1 John 4:20 [b]John 20:29
1:9 [a]Rom. 6:22
1:10 [a]Gen. 49:10
1:11 [a]2 Pet. 1:21
1:12 [a]Dan. 9:24 [b]Heb. 11:13 [c]Acts 2:4 [d]Dan. 8:13
1:13 [1]Gr. *perfectly* [a]Eph. 6:14 [b]Luke 21:34; Rom. 13:13

1:1 *Peter.* See notes on Mat 16:18; John 1:42. *apostle.* See notes on Mark 6:30; 1 Cor 1:1; Heb 3:1. *strangers.* People temporarily residing on earth but whose home is in heaven (cf. 1 Chr 29:15; Ps 39:12; Heb 13:14). *scattered throughout Pontus . . . Bithynia.* Jewish and Gentile Christians scattered throughout much of Asia Minor. People from this area were in Jerusalem on the day of Pentecost (see Acts 2:9–11). Paul preached and taught in some of these provinces (see, e.g., Acts 16:6; 18:23; 19:10,26).

1:2 *Elect.* See note on Eph 1:4. *foreknowledge.* See note on Rom 8:29. *Father . . . Spirit . . . Jesus Christ.* All three persons of the Trinity are involved in the redemption of the elect. *sanctification.* See note on 2 Thes 2:13. The order of the terms employed suggests that the sanctifying work of the Spirit referred to here is the influence of the Spirit that draws one from sin toward holiness. Peter says it is "to" (or "for") obedience and sprinkling of Christ's blood, i.e., the Spirit's sanctifying leads to obedient saving faith and cleansing from sin (see note on 1 Cor 7:14). *unto obedience.* God's choice or election is designed to bring this about. *sprinkling of the blood.* The benefits of Christ's redemption are applied to His people (cf. Ex 24:4–8; Is 52:15; Heb 9:11–14,18–28). *Grace unto you, and peace.* See notes on Jonah 4:2; John 14:27; 20:19; Gal 1:3; Eph 1:2.

1:3 *lively hope.* In spite of the frequent suffering and persecution mentioned in this letter (v. 6; 2:12,18–25; 3:13–18; 4:1,4,12–19; 5:1,7–10), hope is such a key thought in it (the word itself is used here and in vv. 13,21; 3:5,15) that it may be called a letter of hope in the midst of suffering (see Introduction: Themes). In the Bible, hope is not wishful thinking but a firm conviction, much like faith that is directed toward the future. *resurrection of Jesus Christ.* Secures for His people their new birth and the hope that they will be resurrected just as He was.

1:4 *To an inheritance.* Believers are born again not only to a hope but also to the inheritance that is the substance of the hope. The inheritance is eternal—in its essence (it is not subject to decay) and in its preservation (it is divinely kept for us).

1:5 *by the power of God through faith.* There are two sides to the perseverance of the Christian. He is shielded (1) by God's power and (2) by his own faith. Thus he is never kept contrary to his will nor apart from God's activity. *salvation.* See note on 2 Tim 1:9. The Bible speaks of salvation as (1) past—when a person first believes (see, e.g., Tit 3:5), (2) present—the continuing process of salvation, or sanctification (see v. 9; 1 Cor 1:18), and (3) future—when Christ returns and salvation, or sanctification, is completed through glorification (here; see also Rom 8:23,30; 13:11).

1:7 *That the trial of your faith . . . might be found.* See Rom 5:3; Jas 1:2–4. Not only is the faith itself precious, but Peter's words indicate that the trial of faith is also valuable. *glory.* A key word in 1,2 Peter.

1:8 *though now ye see him not, yet believing.* Similar to Jesus' saying in John 20:29, on an occasion when Peter was present.

1:9 *souls.* Implies the whole person. Peter is not excluding the body from heaven.

1:10 *prophets . . . searched diligently.* Inspiration (see 2 Pet 1:21) did not bestow omniscience. The prophets probably did not always understand the full significance of all the words they spoke.

‡1:11 *Spirit of Christ.* The Holy Spirit is called this because Christ sent Him (see John 16:7) and ministered through Him (see Luke 4:14,18, and also note on 1 Pet 3:19,20a). *the sufferings of Christ, and the glory.* A theme running through the Bible (see, e.g., Ps 22; Is 52:13–53:12; Zech 9:9–10; 13:7; Mat 16:21–23; 17:22; 20:19; Luke 24:26,46; John 2:19; Acts 3:17–21), and a basic concept in this letter (vv. 18–21; 3:17–22; 4:12–16; 5:1,4,9–10). Those who are united to Christ will also, after suffering, enter into glory. And they will benefit in the midst of their present sufferings from His having already entered into glory (vv. 3,8,21; 3:21–22).

1:12 *Holy Ghost sent down from heaven.* By Christ, on the day of Pentecost (see Acts 2:33), at which Peter was present. God the Father also sent the Spirit (see John 14:16,26). *which things the angels desire to look into.* Their intense desire is highlighted by the Greek word rendered "to look into." It means "to stoop and look intently" (see John 20:5,11).

1:13 *gird up the loins of your mind.* The first of a long series of exhortations (actually imperatives) that end at 5:11. This one is

grace that is *to be* brought unto you [c]at the
revelation of Jesus Christ;
14 As obedient children, [a]not fashioning
yourselves according to the former lusts [b]in
your ignorance:
15 [a]But as he which hath called you is
holy, so be ye holy in all *manner of* conversation;
16 Because it is written, [a]Be ye holy; for I
am holy.
17 And if ye call on the Father, [a]who without respect of persons judgeth according to
every man's work, [b]pass the time of your [c]so-
journing *here* in fear:
18 Forasmuch as ye know [a]that ye were
not redeemed with corruptible *things, as* silver and gold, from your vain conversation [b]re-
ceived by tradition from your fathers;
19 But [a]with the precious blood of Christ,
[b]as of a lamb without blemish and without
spot:
20 [a]Who verily was foreordained before
the foundation of the world, but was manifest
[b]in *these* last times for you,
21 Who by him do believe in God, [a]that
raised him up from the dead, and [b]gave him
glory; that your faith and hope might be in
God.
22 Seeing ye [a]have purified your souls in
obeying the truth through the Spirit unto unfeigned [b]love of the brethren, *see that ye* love
one another with a pure heart fervently:
23 [a]Being born again, not of corruptible
seed, but *of* incorruptible, [b]by the word of
God, which liveth and abideth for ever.
24 [1]For [a]all flesh *is* as grass, and all the glory of man as the flower of grass. The grass
withereth, and the flower thereof falleth away:
25 [a]But the word of the Lord endureth for
ever. [b]And this is the word which by the
gospel is preached unto you.

Christ our corner stone

2 Wherefore [a]laying aside all malice, and
all guile, and hypocrisies, and envies,
and all evil speakings,
2 [a]As newborn babes, desire the sincere
[b]milk of the word, that ye may grow thereby:
3 If so be ye have [a]tasted that the Lord *is*
gracious.
4 To whom coming, *as unto* a living stone,

1:13 [c]1 Cor. 1:7
1:14 [a]Rom. 12:2 [b]Acts 17:30
1:15 [a]2 Cor. 7:1
1:16 [a]Lev. 11:44
1:17 [a]Deut. 10:17 [b]Heb. 12:28 [c]Heb. 11:13
1:18 [a]1 Cor. 6:20 [b]Ezek. 20:18
1:19 [a]Acts 20:28 [b]Ex. 12:5
1:20 [a]Rom. 3:25 [b]Gal. 4:4
1:21 [a]Acts 2:24 [b]Acts 2:33
1:22 [a]Acts 15:9 [b]Heb. 13:1
1:23 [a]John 1:13 [b]Jas. 1:18
1:24 [1]Or, *For that* [a]Is. 40:6
1:25 [a]Is. 40:8 [b]John 1:1
2:1 [a]Heb. 12:1
2:2 [a]Mat. 18:3 [b]1 Cor. 3:2
2:3 [a]Heb. 6:5

a graphic call for action. In the language of the first century it meant that the reader should literally gather up his long, flowing garments and be ready for physical action. *grace that is to be brought unto you.* The final state of complete blessedness and deliverance from sin. Peter later indicates that a major purpose of this letter is to encourage and testify regarding the true grace of God (5:12).

1:14 *children.* Christians, born into the family of God (see v. 23), are children of their heavenly Father (v. 17) and can pray, "Our Father which art in heaven" (Mat 6:9). Believers are also described as being adopted into God's family (see Rom 8:15 and note).

1:16 *Be ye holy; for I am holy.* To be holy is to be set apart—set apart from sin and impurity, and set apart to God. The complete moral perfection of God, whose eyes are too pure to look on evil with favor (Hab 1:13), should move His people to strive for moral purity. 1 Peter is a letter of practical earnestness, filled with exhortations and encouragements.

1:17 *without respect of persons.* See Rom 2:11; Jas 2:1. *the time of your sojourning here.* See note on v. 1. *fear.* Not terror, but wholesome reverence and respect for God, which is the basis for all godly living (cf. Prov 1:7; 8:13; 16:6).

1:18 *redeemed.* In the Bible, to redeem means to free someone from something bad by paying a penalty, or a ransom (see e.g., Ex 21:30 and note; see also Ex 13:13). Likewise, in the Greek world slaves could be redeemed by the payment of a price, either by someone else or by the slave himself. Similarly, Jesus redeems believers from the "curse of the law" (Gal 3:13) and "all iniquity" (Tit 2:14). The ransom price is not silver or gold, but Christ's blood (Eph 1:7; 1 Pet 1:19; Rev 5:9), i.e., His death (Mat 20:28; Mark 10:45; Heb 9:15) or Christ Himself (Gal 3:13). The result is the "forgiveness of sins" (Col 1:14) and "being justified" (Rom 3:24; see note there). *vain conversation received by tradition from your fathers.* Or, "empty way of life . . . from your forefathers." Some maintain that the recipients must have been pagans because the NT stresses the emptiness of pagan life (Rom 1:21; Eph 4:17). Others think they were Jews since Jews were traditionalists who stressed the influence of the father as teacher in the home. In the light of the context of the whole letter, probably both Jews and Gentiles are addressed.

1:19 *lamb.* The OT sacrifices were types (foreshadowings) of Christ, depicting the ultimate and only effective sacrifice. Thus Christ is the passover lamb (1 Cor 5:7), who takes away the sin of the world (John 1:29). *without blemish and without spot.* See Heb 9:14 and note; see also Introduction to Leviticus: Themes.

‡1:20 *foreordained.* God knew before creation that it would be necessary for Christ to redeem man (cf. Rev 13:8), but He has revealed Christ in these last times. Or the Greek for "foreordained" may also be rendered "chosen," or foreknown. Then the meaning would be that in eternity past God "chose" Christ as Redeemer. *these last times.* See notes on Acts 2:17; 1 Tim 4:1; 2 Tim 3:1; Heb 1:1; 1 John 2:18.

1:22 *unfeigned love.* See Rom 12:9. *love one another.* A command no doubt based on John 13:34–35. See also 1 Thes 4:9–10, where, like Peter, Paul commends his readers for their love of fellow believers and then urges them to love still more.

1:23 *born again . . . but of . . . by the word of God.* The new birth comes about through the direct action of the Holy Spirit (Tit 3:5), but the word of God also plays an important role (see Jas 1:18), for it presents the gospel to the sinner and calls on him to repent and believe in Christ (see v. 25). *corruptible seed . . . incorruptible.* In this context the seed is doubtless the word of God, which is imperishable, living and enduring.

1:25 *the word of the Lord endureth for ever.* The main point of the quotation here.

2:1 *Wherefore.* Connects the exhortations that follow with 1:23–25; compare "born again" (1:23) with "newborn babes" (2:2).

2:2 *desire.* The unrestrained hunger of a healthy baby provides an example of the kind of eager desire for spiritual food that ought to mark the believer. *sincere milk of the word.* See 1:23,25. The author is speaking figuratively. Milk is not to be understood here as in 1 Cor 3:2; Heb 5:12–14—in unfavorable contrast to solid food—but as an appropriate nourishment for babies. *grow.* The Greek for this phrase is the standard term for the desirable growth of children.

2:3 *have tasted.* The tense of the Greek verb used here suggests that an initial act of tasting is referred to. Since this taste has proved satisfactory, the believers are urged to long for additional spiritual food.

2:4 *living stone.* Christ (see vv. 6–8; cf. Mat 21:42; Mark

[a]disallowed indeed of men, but chosen of God,
and precious,
5 [a]Ye also, as lively stones, [1]are built *up* [b]a
spiritual house, [c]a holy priesthood, to offer up
[d]spiritual sacrifices, [e]acceptable to God by
Jesus Christ.
6 Wherefore also it is contained in the
scripture, [a]Behold, I lay in Sion a chief corner
stone, elect, precious: and he that believeth on
him shall not be confounded.
7 Unto you therefore which believe [1]*he is*
precious: but unto them which be disobedient, [a]the stone which the builders disallowed,
the same is made the head of the corner,
8 [a]And a stone of stumbling, and a rock of
offence, [b]*even to them* which stumble at the
word, being disobedient: [c]whereunto also
they were appointed.
9 But ye *are* [a]a chosen generation, [b]a royal
priesthood, [c]a holy nation, [d][1]a peculiar people; that ye should shew forth the [2]praises of
him who hath called you out of [e]darkness into
his marvellous light:
10 [a]Which in time past *were* not a people,
but *are* now the people of God: which had not
obtained mercy, but now have obtained mercy.

Christian submission

11 ¶ Dearly beloved, I beseech *you* [a]as
strangers and pilgrims, [b]abstain from fleshly
lusts, [c]which war against the soul;
12 [a]Having your conversation honest
among the Gentiles: that, [1]whereas they speak
against you as evildoers, [b]they may by *your*
good works, *which* they shall behold, glorify
God in the day of visitation.
13 [a]Submit yourselves to every ordinance
of man for the Lord's sake: whether *it be* to the
king, as supreme;
14 Or unto governors, as unto them that
are sent by him [a]for the punishment of evildoers, and [b]*for* the praise of them that do well.
15 For so is the will of God, that [a]with well

2:4 [a]Ps. 118:22; Acts 4:11
2:5 [1]Or, *be ye built* [a]Eph. 2:21 [b]Heb. 3:6 [c]Is. 61:6 [d]Hos. 14:2; Mal. 1:11 [e]Phil. 4:18
2:6 [a]Is. 28:16
2:7 [1]Or, he is *an honour* [a]Ps. 118:22
2:8 [a]Is. 8:14 [b]1 Cor. 1:23 [c]Rom. 9:22
2:9 [1]Or, *a purchased people* [2]Or, *virtues* [a]Deut. 10:15 [b]Rev. 5:10 [c]Is. 62:12 [d]Deut. 4:20 [e]Acts 26:18
2:10 [a]Hos. 1:9
2:11 [a]Ps. 39:12 [b]Gal. 5:16 [c]Jas. 4:1
2:12 [1]Or, *wherein* [a]Phil. 2:15 [b]Mat. 5:16
2:13 [a]Rom. 13:1
2:14 [a]Rom. 13:4 [b]Rom. 13:3
2:15 [a]Tit. 2:8

12:10–11; Luke 20:17; Acts 4:11; Rom 9:33). The stone is living in that it is personal. Furthermore He is a life-giving stone. Christ as the Son of God has life in Himself (John 1:4; 5:26). See also "living water" (John 4:10–14; 7:38), "living bread" (John 6:51) and "living way" (Heb 10:20). *disallowed indeed of men, but chosen of God.* Peter repeatedly makes a contrast in Acts between the hostility of unbelieving men toward Jesus and God's exaltation of Him (Acts 2:22–36; 3:13–15; 4:10–11; 10:39–42).

2:5 *lively stones.* Believers are not literal pieces of rock, but are persons. In addition, they derive their life from Christ, who is the original living Stone to whom they have come (v. 4), the "life-giving spirit" (1 Cor 15:45). These references to stones may well reflect Jesus' words to Peter in Mat 16:18. *spiritual house.* The house is spiritual in a metaphorical sense, but also in that it is formed and indwelt by the Spirit of God. Every stone in the house has been made alive by the Holy Spirit, sent by the exalted living Stone, Jesus Christ (cf. Acts 2:33). The OT temple provides the background of this passage (cf. John 2:19; 1 Cor 3:16; Eph 2:19–22). *holy priesthood.* The whole body of believers. As priests, believers are to (1) reflect the holiness of God and that of their high priest (see 1:15; Heb 7:26; 10:10), (2) offer spiritual sacrifices (here), (3) intercede for man before God and (4) represent God before man. *spiritual sacrifices.* The NT refers to a variety of offerings: bodies offered to God (Rom 12:1), offerings of money or material goods (Phil 4:18; Heb 13:16), sacrifices of praise to God (Heb 13:15) and sacrifices of doing good (Heb 13:16). *acceptable to God.* Through the work of our Mediator, Jesus Christ (cf. John 14:6). Believers are living stones that make up a spiritual temple in which, as a holy priesthood, they offer up spiritual sacrifices.

2:6 *chief corner stone.* See Ps 118:22; Mat 21:42; Mark 12:10; Luke 20:17; Acts 4:11. This is an obvious reference to Christ, as vv. 6b–8 make clear. The corner stone, which determined the design and orientation of the building, was the most significant stone in the structure. The picture that Peter creates is of a structure made up of believers (living stones, v. 5), the design and orientation of which are all in keeping with Christ, the corner stone. *he that believeth on him.* Two attitudes toward the corner stone are evident: (1) Some trust in Him; (2) others reject Him (v. 7) and, as a result, stumble and fall (v. 8).

2:8 *whereunto also they were appointed.* Some see here an indication that some people are destined to fall and be lost. Others say that unbelievers are destined to be lost because God in His foreknowledge (cf. 1:2) saw them as unbelievers. Still others hold that Peter means that unbelief is destined to result in eternal destruction.

2:9 *chosen generation.* See Eph 1:4 and note; Is 43:10,20; 44:1–2. As Israel was called God's chosen people in the OT, so in the NT believers are designated as chosen, or elect. *royal priesthood.* See note on v. 5; see also Is 61:6. *holy nation.* See Deut 28:9. *a peculiar people.* See Deut 4:20; 7:6; 14:2; Is 43:21; Mal 3:17. Though once not the people of God, they are now the recipients of God's mercy (see Hos 1:6–10; Rom 9:25–26; 10:19). *shew forth the praises of him.* See Is 43:21; Acts 2:11.

2:10 See notes on Hos 1:6,9; 2:1,22; Rom 9:25–26. In Hosea it is Israel who is not God's people; in Romans it is the Gentiles to whom Paul applies Hosea's words; in 1 Peter the words are applied to both.

2:11 *strangers and pilgrims.* See note on 1:1. As aliens and strangers on earth, whose citizenship is in heaven, they are to be separated from the corruption of the world, not yielding to its destructive sinful desires.

2:12 *good works, which they shall behold.* Deeds that can be seen to be good (cf. Mat 5:16). The Greek word translated "behold" refers to a careful watching, over a period of time. The pagans' evaluation is not a "snap judgment." *the day of visitation.* Perhaps the day of judgment and ensuing punishment, or possibly the day when God visits a person with salvation. The believer's good life may then influence the unbeliever to repent and believe.

2:13–3:6 Peter urges that Christians submit to all legitimate authorities, whether or not the persons exercising authority are believers. The recognition of properly constituted authority is necessary for the greatest good of the largest number of people, and it is necessary to best fulfill the will of God in the world.

2:13 *every ordinance of man.* Authority established among men depends on God for its existence (Rom 13:1–2). Indirectly, when one disobeys a human ruler he disobeys God, who ordained the system of human government (cf. Rom 13:2). *to the king.* When Peter wrote, the emperor was the godless, brutal Nero, who ruled from A.D. 54 to 68 (see Introduction: Author and Date). Of course, obedience to the emperor must never be in violation of the law of God (to see this basic principle in action cf. Acts 4:19; 5:29).

2:15 *silence the ignorance.* Good citizenship counters false charges made against Christians and thus commends the gospel to unbelievers.

doing *ye* may put to silence the ignorance of
foolish men:
16 [a]As free, and not [1]using *your* liberty for
a cloke of maliciousness, but as [b]the servants
of God.
17 [a][1]Honour all *men.* [b]Love the brotherhood. [c]Fear God. Honour the king.
18 [a]Servants, *be* subject to *your* masters
with all fear; not only to the good and gentle,
but also to the froward.
19 For this *is* [a][1]thankworthy, if a man for
conscience toward God endure grief, suffering
wrongfully.
20 For what glory *is it,* if, when ye be buffeted for your faults, ye shall take it patiently?
but if, when ye do well, and suffer *for it,* ye
take it patiently, this *is* [1]acceptable with God.

Christ our great example

21 For [a]*even* hereunto were ye called: because Christ also suffered [1]for us, [b]leaving us
an example, that ye should follow his steps:
22 [a]Who did no sin, neither was guile
found in his mouth:
23 [a]Who, when he was reviled, reviled not
again; when he suffered, he threatened not;
but [b][1]committed *himself* to him that judgeth
righteously:
24 [a]Who his own self bare our sins in his
own body [1]on the tree, [b]that we, being dead
to sins, should live unto righteousness: [c]by
whose stripes ye were healed.
25 For [a]ye were as sheep going astray; but
are now returned [b]unto the Shepherd and
Bishop of your souls.

The husband and the wife

3 Likewise, [a]ye wives, *be* in subjection to
your own husbands; that, if any obey not
the word, [b]they also may without the word
[c]be won by the conversation of the wives;
2 [a]While they behold your chaste conversation *coupled* with fear.
3 [a]Whose adorning let it not be that outward *adorning* of plaiting the hair, and of
wearing of gold, or of putting on of apparel;
4 But *let it be* [a]the hidden man of the
heart, in *that which is* not corruptible, *even*
the ornament of a meek and quiet spirit,
which is in the sight of God of great price.
5 For after this manner in the old time the
holy women also, who trusted in God,

2:16 [1]Gr. *having* [a]Gal. 5:1 [b]1 Cor. 7:22
2:17 [1]Or, *Esteem* [a]Rom. 12:10 [b]Heb. 13:1 [c]Rom. 13:7
2:18 [a]Eph. 6:5
2:19 [1]Or, *thank* [a]Mat. 5:10
2:20 [1]Or, *thank*
2:21 [1]Some read, *for you* [a]Mat. 16:24 [b]1 John 2:6
2:22 [a]Is. 53:9
2:23 [a]Is. 53:7
2:23 [1]Or, *committed* his cause [b]Luke 23:46
2:24 [1]Or, *to* [a]Heb. 9:28 [b]Rom. 7:6 [c]Is. 53:5
2:25 [a]Is. 53:6 [b]Ezek. 34:23; Heb. 13:20
3:1 [a]1 Cor. 14:34 [b]1 Cor. 7:16 [c]Mat. 18:15
3:2 [a]ch. 2:12
3:3 [a]1 Tim. 2:9
3:4 [a]Rom. 2:29

2:16 *As free.* Does not authorize rebellion against constituted authority, but urges believers freely to submit to God and to earthly authorities (as long as such submission does not conflict with the law of God). *for a cloke of maliciousness.* Genuine freedom is the freedom to serve God, a freedom exercised under law. Liberty is not license to do as we please.
2:17 *Honour all men.* Because every human being bears the image of God. *Fear God.* See note on 1:17.
2:18 *Servants.* Household servants, whatever their particular training and functions. The context indicates that Peter is addressing Christian slaves. NT writers do not attack slavery as an institution (see note on Eph 6:5), but the NT contains the principles that ultimately uprooted slavery. Peter's basic teachings on the subject may apply to employer-employee relations today (see Eph 6:5–8; Col 3:22–25; 1 Tim 6:1–2; Tit 2:9–10).
2:19 *conscience toward God.* As submission to duly constituted authority is "for the Lord's sake" (v. 13; cf. Eph 6:7–8), so one will submit to the point of suffering unjustly if it is God's will.
2:21 *hereunto were ye called.* The patient endurance of injustice is part of God's plan for the Christian. It was an important feature of the true grace of God experienced by the readers (5:12). *Christ also suffered for us.* Cf. Is 52:13–53:12. Christ is the supreme example of suffering evil for doing good. His experience as the suffering Servant-Savior transforms the sufferings of His followers from misery into privilege.
2:22 Scripture declares the sinlessness of Christ in the clearest of terms, allowing for no exception (see 1:19; Acts 3:14; 2 Cor 5:21; Heb 4:15; 7:26; 1 John 3:5). *neither was guile.* Cf. v. 1; 3:10.
2:23 Prominent examples of our Lord's silent submission are found in Mat 27:12–14,34–44 and parallels. *committed himself.* Cf. 4:19.
2:24 *bare our sins.* See Is 53:12. Although dealing with the example set by Christ, Peter touches also on the redemptive work of Christ, which has significance far beyond that of setting an example. Peter here points to the substitutionary character of the atonement. Christ, like the sacrificial lamb of the OT, died for our sins, the innocent for the guilty. *tree.* A figurative reference to the cross (see Acts 5:30 and note; see also Acts 10:39; 13:29; Gal 3:13 and note). *that we, being dead to sins, should live unto righteousness.* Cf. Rom 6:3–14. Peter stresses the bearing of the cross on our sanctification. As a result of Christ's death on the cross, believers are positionally dead to sin so that they may live new lives and present themselves to God as instruments of righteousness (see note on Rom 6:11–13). *ye were healed.* See Is 53:5; not generally viewed as a reference to physical healing, though some believe that such healing was included in the atonement (cf. Mat 8:16–17). Others see spiritual healing in this passage. It is another way of asserting that Christ's death brings salvation to those who trust in Him.
2:25 *Shepherd.* A concept raised here in connection with the allusion to the wandering sheep of Is 53. The sheep had wandered from their shepherd, and to their Shepherd (Christ) they have now returned. See note on Ps 23:1; see also John 10:11,14 and note on Heb 13:20. *Bishop.* Christ (cf. 5:2,4; Acts 20:28). Elders are to be both shepherds and guardians, i.e., they are to look out for the welfare of the flock. These are not two separate offices or functions; the second term is a further explanation of the first.
3:1–6 Instructions to wives (cf. Gen 3:16; 1 Cor 11:3; Eph 5:22–24; Col 3:18; 1 Tim 2:9–10; Tit 2:5).
3:1 *Likewise.* As believers are to submit to government authorities (2:13–17), and as slaves are to submit to masters (2:18–25). *be in subjection.* The same Greek verb as is used in 2:13,18, a term that calls for submission to a recognized authority. Inferiority is not implied by this passage. The submission is one of role or function necessary for the orderly operation of the home. *the word.* The gospel message. *without the word.* Believing wives are not to rely on argumentation to win their unbelieving husbands, but on the quality of their lives. "Actions speak louder than words."
3:2 *chaste conversation coupled with fear.* Their lives are to be marked by a moral purity that springs from reverence toward God.
3:3 *hair . . . gold.* Extreme coiffures and gaudy exhibits of jewelry. Christian women should not rely on such extremes of adornment for beauty. *apparel.* The Greek for this word simply means "garment," but in this context expensive garments are meant.
3:5 *in the old time . . . women also.* The standards stated by Peter are not limited to any particular time or culture.

adorned themselves, being in subjection unto their own husbands:

6 *Even* as Sara obeyed Abraham, [a]calling him lord: whose [1]daughters ye are, as long as ye do well, and are not afraid *with* any amazement.

7 [a]Likewise, ye husbands, dwell with *them* according to knowledge, giving honour unto the wife, [b]as unto the weaker vessel, and as *being* heirs together of the grace of life; [c]that your prayers be not hindered.

Christian conduct

8 ¶ Finally, [a]*be ye* all of one mind, having compassion one of another, [b][1]love as brethren, [c]*be* pitiful, *be* courteous:

9 [a]Not rendering evil for evil, or railing for railing: but contrariwise blessing; knowing that ye are thereunto called, [b]that ye should inherit a blessing.

10 For [a]he that will love life, and see good days, [b]let him refrain his tongue from evil, and his lips that *they* speak no guile:

11 Let him [a]eschew evil, and do good; [b]let him seek peace, and ensue it.

12 For the eyes of the Lord *are* over the righteous, [a]and his ears *are open* unto their prayers: but the face of the Lord *is* [1]against them that do evil.

13 [a]And who *is* he that will harm you, if ye be followers of *that which is* good?

14 [a]But and if ye suffer for righteousness' sake, happy *are ye:* and [b]be not afraid of their terror, neither be troubled;

15 But sanctify the Lord God in your hearts: and [a]*be* ready always to *give* an answer to every *man* that asketh you a reason of the hope that is in you with meekness and [1]fear:

16 [a]Having a good conscience; [b]that, whereas they speak evil of you, as of evildoers, they may be ashamed that falsely accuse your good conversation in Christ.

17 For *it is* better, if the will of God be so, that *ye* suffer for well doing, than for evil doing.

18 For Christ also hath [a]once suffered for sins, the just for the unjust, that he might bring us to God, [b]being put to death [c]in the flesh, but [d]quickened by the Spirit:

3:6 [1]Gr. *children* [a]Gen. 18:12
3:7 [a]1 Cor. 7:3 [b]1 Cor. 12:23 [c]Job 42:8; Mat. 18:19
3:8 [1]Or, *loving to the brethren* [a]Rom. 12:16 [b]Rom. 12:10; Heb. 13:1 [c]Eph. 4:32
3:9 [a]Prov. 17:13 [b]Mat. 25:34
3:10 [a]Ps. 34:12 [b]Jas. 1:26; Rev. 14:5
3:11 [a]Ps. 37:27; 3 John 11 [b]Rom. 12:18; Heb. 12:14
3:12 [1]Gr. *upon* [a]John 9:31; Jas. 5:16
3:13 [a]Prov. 16:7
3:14 [a]Jas. 1:12; ch. 2:19 [b]Is. 8:12,13
3:15 [1]Or, *reverence* [a]Ps. 119:46; Col. 4:6; 2 Tim. 2:25
3:16 [a]Heb. 13:18 [b]Tit. 2:8
3:18 [a]Rom. 5:6 [b]2 Cor. 13:4 [c]Col. 1:21 [d]Rom. 1:4

3:6 *lord.* An expression of the submission called for in v. 1. *whose daughters . . . not afraid.* Christian women become daughters of Sarah as they become like her in doing good and in not fearing any potential disaster, but trusting in God (cf. Prov 3:25–27).

3:7 *weaker vessel.* Not a reference to moral stamina, strength of character or mental capacity, but most likely to sheer physical strength. *heirs togther of the grace of life.* Women experience the saving grace of God on equal terms with men (see Gal 3:28). *prayers be not hindered.* Spiritual fellowship, with God and with one another, may be hindered by disregarding God's instruction concerning husband-wife relationships.

3:8–12 In 2:11–17 Peter addressed all his readers, and in 2:18–25 he spoke directly to slaves; in 3:1–6 he addressed wives, and in 3:7 husbands. Now he encourages all his readers to develop virtues appropriate in their relations with others (see "ye all," v. 8).

3:8 *be ye all of one mind.* See Rom 12:16; Phil 2:2. *having compassion.* See Rom 12:15; 1 Cor 12:26. *love as brethren.* See 1 Thes 4:9–10; Heb 13:1. *pitiful.* Or "compassionate." See Col 3:12. *courteous.* See Phil 2:6–8.

3:9 See Rom 12:17–21.

3:10–12 Peter introduces this quotation from Ps 34 with the explanatory conjunction "For," showing that he views the quotation as giving reasons for obeying the exhortation of v. 9. According to the psalmist, (1) the one who does such things will find life to be most gratifying (v. 10), (2) his days will be good (v. 10), (3) God's eyes will ever be on him to bless him (v. 12), and (4) God's ears will be ready to hear his prayer (v. 12).

3:13 *who . . . harm you . . . ?* As a general rule, people are not harmed for acts of kindness. This is especially true if one is an enthusiast for doing good.

3:14 *if ye suffer.* In the Greek, this conditional clause is the furthest removed from stating a reality. Suffering for righteousness is a remote possibility, but even if it does occur, it brings special blessing to the sufferer (see Mat 5:10–12). *their terror.* In Isaiah's context God's people are not to view things as unbelievers do. They are not to make worldly judgments or be afraid of the enemies of God. Instead, they are to fear God (see Is 8:13).

3:15 *sanctify the Lord God.* An exhortation to the readers to make an inner commitment to Christ. Then they need not be speechless when called on to defend their faith. Instead, there will be a readiness to answer. *with meekness and fear.* The Christian is always to be a gentleman or gentle woman, even when opposed by unbelievers. Our apologetic ("defense") is always to be given with love, never in degrading terms.

3:16 *they may be ashamed.* Because it is shown to be obviously untrue and because the believer's loving attitude puts the opponent's bitterness in a bad light.

‡3:18 *once.* See Heb 9:28. *the just for the unjust.* Peter, like Paul in Phil 2:5–11, refers to Jesus as an example of the type of conduct that should characterize the Christian. We are to be ready to suffer for doing good (vv. 13–14,17). The thought of Christ's suffering and death, however, leads Peter to comment on what occurred after Christ's death—which leads to tangential remarks about preaching to the spirits in prison and about baptism (see vv. 19–21). *quickened by the Spirit.* "Spirit" is capitalized here to indicate that Christ was raised up by the Holy Spirit, through which at an earlier time, He "went and preached unto the spirits" which are now in prison (v. 19).

‡3:19–20a Three main interpretations of this passage have been suggested: 1. Some hold that in His preincarnate state Christ went and preached through Noah to the wicked generation of that time. This seems to be in line with the context of 1 Pet 1:10–11, where the Spirit is said to speak through the prophets. Peter refers to Noah as a "preacher of righteousness" (2 Pet 2:5). 2. Others argue that between His death and resurrection Christ went to some prison where fallen angels are supposedly incarcerated and there preached to the angels who are said to have left their proper state and married human women during Noah's time (cf. Gen 6:1–4; 2 Pet 2:4; Jude 6). The "sons of God" in Gen 6:2,4, and in Job 1:6; 2:1 are supposed to have been angels. The message He preached to these evil angels was probably a declaration of victory. 3. Still others say that between death and resurrection Christ went to the place of the dead and preached to the spirits of Noah's wicked contemporaries, again proclaiming a declaration of victory for Christ and doom for His hearers.

The strength of the first view is that it least taxes the imagination and fits with Peter's context of 1:10–11. Some feel it is weak in that it does not relate the event to the time of Christ's death and resurrection. The main problem with the second view

19 By which also he went and [a]preached
unto the spirits [b]in prison;
20 Which sometime were disobedient,
[a]when once the longsuffering of God waited in
the days of Noah, while [b]the ark was a preparing, [c]wherein few, that is, eight souls were
saved by water.
21 [a]The like figure whereunto *even* baptism doth also now save us (not the putting
away of [b]the filth of the flesh, [c]but the answer
of a good conscience toward God,) [d]by the resurrection of Jesus Christ:
22 Who is gone into heaven, and [a]is on the
right hand of God; [b]angels and authorities and
powers being made subject unto him.

4 Forasmuch then [a]as Christ hath suffered
for us in the flesh, arm yourselves likewise with the same mind: for [b]he that hath
suffered in the flesh hath ceased from sin;

3:19 [a]ch. 1:12 [b]Is. 42:7
3:20 [a]Gen. 6:3,5 [b]Heb. 11:7 [c]Gen. 7:7
3:21 [a]Eph. 5:26 [b]Tit. 3:5 [c]Rom. 10:10 [d]ch. 1:3
3:22 [a]Ps. 110:1; Rom. 8:34 [b]Rom. 8:38; 1 Cor. 15:24
4:1 [a]ch. 3:18 [b]Gal. 5:24
4:2 [a]Rom. 14:7 [b]Gal. 2:20 [c]John 1:13
4:3 [a]Ezek. 44:6 [b]Eph. 2:2; 1 Thes. 4:5; Tit. 3:3
4:4 [a]Acts 13:45
4:5 [a]Acts 10:42; Rom. 14:10; 2 Tim. 4:1
4:6 [a]ch. 3:19
4:7 [a]Rom. 13:12 [b]Mat. 26:41; Luke 21:34
4:8 [a]Col. 3:14; Heb. 13:1

2 [a]That *he* no longer [b]should live the rest
of *his* time in the flesh to the lusts of men,
[c]but to the will of God.
3 [a]For the time past of *our* life may suffice
us [b]to have wrought the will of the Gentiles,
when we walked in lasciviousness, lusts, excess of wine, revellings, banquetings, and
abominable idolatries:
4 Wherein they think it strange that you
run not with *them* to the same excess of riot,
[a]speaking evil *of you:*
5 Who shall give account to him that is
ready [a]to judge the quick and the dead.
6 For for this cause [a]was the gospel
preached also to *them that are* dead, that they
might be judged according to men in the flesh,
but live according to God in the spirit.
7 ¶ But [a]the end of all *things* is at hand: [b]be
ye therefore sober, and watch unto prayer.
8 [a]And above all *things* have fervent chari-

is that it assumes sexual relations between angels and women, and such physical relations may not be possible for angels since they are spirits. A major difficulty with the third view is that the term "spirits" is only used of human beings when qualifying terms are added. Otherwise the term seems restricted to supernatural beings. Preaching the gospel, and/or giving a "second chance," is also Biblically out of the question.

3:21 *The like figure whereunto even baptism.* There is a double figure here. The flood symbolizes baptism, and baptism symbolizes salvation. The flood was a figure of baptism in that in both instances the water that spoke of judgment (in the flood the death of the wicked, in baptism the death of Christ and the believer) is the water that saves. Baptism is a symbol of salvation in that it depicts Christ's death, burial and resurrection and our identification with Him in these experiences (see Rom 6:4). *doth also now save us.* In reality, believers are saved by what baptism symbolizes—Christ's death and resurrection. The symbol and the reality are so closely related that the symbol is sometimes used to refer to the reality (see note on Rom 6:3–4). *save us . . . by the resurrection of Jesus Christ.* In the final analysis people are saved not by any ritual, but by the supernatural power of the resurrection. *the answer of a good conscience toward God.* The act of baptism is a commitment on the part of the believer in all good conscience to make sure that what baptism symbolizes will become a reality in his life.

3:22 *gone into heaven.* See Acts 1:9–11. *on the right hand of God.* See Heb 1:3; 12:2. *angels and authorities and powers.* See Eph 1:21; 6:12.

4:1 *Forasmuch then.* Since 3:19–22 is parenthetical, 4:1 ties directly back to 3:18. The aspect of Christ's suffering that these passages stress is suffering unjustly because one has done good. Furthermore, it is physical suffering—"in the flesh." *arm yourselves likewise with the same mind.* Believers are to be prepared also to suffer unjustly, and to face such abuse with Christ's attitude—with His willingness to suffer for doing good. (For a similar principle in Paul's writings see Phil 2:5–11.) *for he that hath suffered . . . hath ceased from sin.* Such suffering enables one to straighten out his priorities. Sinful desires and practices that once seemed important now seem insignificant when one's life is in jeopardy. Serious suffering for Christ advances the progress of sanctification. (Some see a parallel between this passage and Rom 6:1–14, but Peter is not referring to being dead to sin in Paul's sense.)

4:2 *to the lusts of men, but to the will of God.* Now that Christ's attitude prevails, God's will is the determining factor in life.

4:3 *the time past.* The time before conversion. *the Gentiles.* This, along with the term "idolatries," suggests that at least some of the readers were non-Jews (see note on 1:1), converted from pagan backgrounds.

4:4 *they think it strange . . . speaking evil of you.* One of the reasons for the suffering the readers were undergoing.

4:5 *shall give account.* See Acts 17:31; Rom 2:5,16. *him that is ready to judge.* In the NT both the Father and the Son are said to be judge on the great, final judgment day. The Father is the ultimate source of judgment, but He will delegate judgment to the Son (cf. John 5:27; Acts 17:31). *the quick and the dead.* Those alive and those dead when the final judgment day dawns.

‡4:6 *for this cause.* The reason referred to is expressed in the latter part of the verse (in the "that" clause), not in the preceding verse. *was . . . preached also to them that are dead.* That is, to those who are now dead. This preaching was a past event. The preaching was done not after these people had died, but while they were still alive. (There will be no opportunity for people to be saved after death; see Heb 9:27.) *be judged according to men in the flesh.* The first reason that the gospel was preached to those now dead. Some say that this judgment is that to which all people must submit, either in this life (see John 5:24) or in the life to come (see v. 5). The gospel is preached to people in this life so that in Christ's death they may receive judgment now and avoid judgment to come. Others hold that these people are judged according to human standards by the pagan world, which does not understand why God's people no longer follow its sinful way of life (see vv. 2–4). So also the world misunderstood Christ (see Acts 2:22–24,36; 3:13–15; 5:30–32; 7:51–53). *but live according to God in the spirit.* The second reason that the gospel was preached to those now dead. Some believe this means that all gospel preaching has as its goal that the hearers may live as God lives—eternally—and that this life is given by the Holy Spirit. Others maintain that it means that the ultimate reason for the preaching of the gospel is that God's people, even though the wicked world may abuse them and put them to death, will have eternal life, which the Holy Spirit imparts.

‡4:7 *the end . . . is at hand.* See note on Jas 5:9. *therefore.* Anticipating the end times, particularly Christ's return, should influence believers' attitudes, actions and relationships (see 2 Pet 3:11–14). *sober.* I.e."of a sober spirit." Christians are to be characterized by reason; are to make wise, mature decisions; and are to have a clearly defined, decisive purpose in life. See Gal 5:23. *prayer.* Cf. 3:7; Luke 18:1; 1 Cor 7:5; Eph 6:18; 1 Thes 5:17; 1 John 5:14–15.

4:8 *have fervent charity.* See 1 Thes 4:9–10; 2 Pet 1:7; 1 John

ty among yourselves: for [b]charity [1]shall cover
the multitude of sins.
9 [a]Use hospitality one to another [b]without
grudging.
10 [a]As every man hath received *the* gift,
even so minister the same one to another, [b]as
good stewards of [c]the manifold grace of God.
11 [a]If any *man* speak, *let him speak* as the
oracles of God; [b]if any *man* minister, *let him*
do it as of the ability which God giveth: that
[c]God in all *things* may be glorified through
Jesus Christ, [d]to whom be praise and dominion for ever and ever. Amen.

The Christian and suffering

12 ¶ Beloved, think it not strange concerning [a]the fiery trial which is to try you, as
though *some* strange *thing* happened unto
you:
13 [a]But rejoice, inasmuch as [b]ye are partakers of Christ's sufferings; that, when his
glory shall be revealed, ye may be glad also
with exceeding joy.
14 [a]If ye be reproached for the name of
Christ, happy *are ye;* for the spirit of glory and
of God resteth upon you: on their part he is
evil spoken of, but on your part he is glorified.
15 But [a]let none of you suffer as a murder-
er, or *as* a thief, or *as* an evildoer, [b]or as a busybody in other men's matters.
16 Yet if *any man suffer* as a Christian, let
him not be ashamed; [a]but let him glorify God
on this behalf.
17 For the time *is come* [a]that judgment
must begin at the house of God: and [b]if *it* first
begin at us, [c]what *shall* the end *be* of them
that obey not the gospel of God?
18 [a]And if the righteous scarcely be saved,
where shall the ungodly and the sinner appear?
19 Wherefore let them that suffer according to the will of God [a]commit the keeping of
their souls *to him* in well doing, as unto a
faithful Creator.

Christian life in God's care

5 The elders which are among you I exhort, who am also [a]an elder, and [b]a witness of the sufferings of Christ, and also [c]a
partaker of the glory that shall be revealed:
2 [a]Feed the flock of God [1]which is among
you, taking the oversight *thereof,* [b]not by constraint, but willingly; [c]not for filthy lucre, but
of a ready mind;
3 Neither as [a][1]being lords over [b]*God's* heritage, but [c]being ensamples to the flock.
4 And when [a]the chief Shepherd shall appear, ye shall receive [b]a crown of glory that
fadeth not away.
5 Likewise, *ye* younger, submit yourselves
unto the elder. Yea, [a]all *of you* be subject one
to another, and be clothed with humility: for

4:8 [1]Or, *will* [b]Prov. 10:12; 1 Cor. 13:7
4:9 [a]Heb. 13:2 [b]2 Cor. 9:7
4:10 [a]Rom. 12:6 [b]Mat. 24:45; Tit. 1:7 [c]1 Cor. 12:4; Eph. 4:11
4:11 [a]Jer. 23:22 [b]1 Cor. 3:10 [c]Eph. 5:20 [d]1 Tim. 6:16
4:12 [a]1 Cor. 3:13
4:13 [a]Acts 5:41 [b]Rom. 8:17
4:14 [a]2 Cor. 12:10; Jas. 1:12
4:15 [a]ch. 2:20 [b]1 Thes. 4:11
4:16 [a]Acts 5:41
4:17 [a]Is. 10:12 [b]Luke 23:31 [c]Luke 10:12
4:18 [a]Luke 23:31
4:19 [a]2 Tim. 1:12
5:1 [a]Philem. 9 [b]Luke 24:48; Acts 1:8 [c]Rev. 1:9
5:2 [1]Or, *as much as in you* is [a]Acts 20:28 [b]1 Cor. 9:17 [c]1 Tim. 3:3
5:3 [1]Or, *overruling* [a]Ezek. 34:4 [b]Ps. 33:12 [c]Phil. 3:17
5:4 [a]Heb. 13:20 [b]2 Tim. 4:8
5:5 [a]Rom. 12:10

4:7–11. *charity shall cover the multitude of sins.* Love forgives again and again (see Mat 18:21–22; 1 Cor 13:5; Eph 4:32).

4:9 *Use hospitality.* See Rom 12:13; 1 Tim 3:2; 5:10; Tit 1:8; 3 John 5–8.

4:10 *As every man hath received the gift, even so minister.* See Rom 12:4–8; 1 Cor 12:7–11.

4:11 *oracles.* The Greek for this phrase is used to refer to the Scriptures or to words God has spoken (see Acts 7:38; Rom 3:2). *that God in all things may be glorified.* See 1 Cor 1:26–31; Jude 24–25.

4:12 *Beloved.* See 2:11. *think it not strange concerning the fiery trial.* See 1:6–7; 2:20–21.

4:13 *partakers of Christ's sufferings.* See note on Col 1:24. Peter once rebelled against the idea that Christ would suffer (see Mat 16:21–23).

4:14 *reproached for the name of Christ.* See Mat 5:11–12; John 15:18–20; Acts 5:41; 14:22; Rom 8:17; 2 Cor 1:5; Phil 3:10; 2 Tim 3:12.

4:17 *judgment must begin at the house of God.* The persecutions that believers were undergoing were divinely sent judgment intended to purify God's people. *the end be of them that obey not the gospel.* If God brings judgment on His own people, how much more serious will the judgment be that He will bring on unbelievers!

5:1 *also an elder.* See notes on Acts 20:17; 1 Tim 3:1; 5:17. Peter, who identified himself as an apostle at the beginning of his letter (1:1), chooses now to identify himself with the elders of the churches (cf. 2 John 1; 3 John 1). This would be heartening to them in light of their great responsibilities and the difficult situation faced by the churches. The churches for which these elders were responsible were scattered across much of Asia Minor (see 1:1), so if Peter was a local church officer, he must have been officially related to one of them. *witness of the sufferings of Christ.* Peter had been with Jesus from the early days of His ministry and was a witness of all its phases and aspects, including the climactic events of His suffering (cf. Mat 26:58; Mark 14:54; Luke 22:60–62; John 18:10–11,15–16). In this letter he bears notable witness to Christ's sufferings (see 2:21–24) and obeys His command in Acts 1:8. *partaker of the glory . . . be revealed.* Peter witnessed Christ's glory in His ministry in general (see John 1:14; 2:11), and, as one present at the transfiguration (see Mat 16:27; 17:8), he had already seen the glory of Christ's coming kingdom. In God's appointed time, just as Christ suffered and entered into glory, so all His people, after their sufferings, will participate in His future glory.

‡5:2 *Feed the flock of God.* A metaphor that our Lord Himself had employed (John 10:1–18; Luke 15:3–7) and that must have been etched on Peter's mind (see John 21:15–17; cf. 1 Pet 2:25). Peter is fulfilling Christ's command to feed His sheep as he writes this letter. What he writes to the elders is reminiscent of Paul's farewell address to the Ephesian elders (especially Acts 20:28). The term "shepherd" is an OT metaphor as well (see Ezek 34:1–10, where the Lord holds the leaders of Israel responsible for failing to care for the flock). *taking the oversight.* The same term is used in Acts 20:28; Phil 1:1; 1 Tim 3:2; Tit 1:7. See note on 1 Tim 3:1. It is clear from this passage, as well as from Acts 20:17,28, that the three terms "elder," "overseer" (or bishop) and "shepherd" all apply to one office. That one office has, however, several different functions (see note on Tit 1:7).

5:3 *Neither . . . lords over God's heritage.* Cf. Mat 16:24–27; Mark 10:42–45; Phil 2:6–11; 2 Thes 3:9. Although Peter has full apostolic authority (see v. 1), he does not lord it over his readers in this letter, but exemplifies the virtues he recommends.

5:4 *chief Shepherd.* Christ. When He returns, He will reward those who have served as shepherds under Him. *fadeth not away.* See 1:4.

5:5 *be subject.* The theme that runs throughout 2:13–3:6. Here it applies to church leaders. *be clothed with humility.* Peter may

[b]God resisteth the proud, and [c]giveth grace to
the humble.
6 [a]Humble yourselves therefore under the
mighty hand of God, that he may exalt you in
due time:
7 [a]Casting all your care upon him; for he
careth for you.
8 [a]Be sober, be vigilant; because [b]your adversary the devil, as a roaring lion, walketh
about, seeking whom he may devour:
9 [a]Whom resist stedfast in the faith,
[b]knowing that the same afflictions are accomplished in your brethren that are in the world.
10 But the God of all grace, [a]who hath
called us into his eternal glory by Christ
Jesus, after that ye have suffered [b]a while,
[c]make you perfect, [d]stablish, strengthen, settle *you.*
11 [a]To him *be* glory and dominion for ever
and ever. Amen.

Conclusion and benediction

12 ¶ [a]By Silvanus, a faithful brother unto
you, as I suppose, I have [b]written briefly, exhorting, and testifying [c]that this is the true
grace of God wherein ye stand.
13 The *church that is* at Babylon, elected
together with *you,* saluteth you; and *so doth*
[a]Marcus my son.
14 [a]Greet ye one another with a kiss of
charity. [b]Peace *be* with you all that are in
Christ Jesus. Amen.

5:5 [b]Jas. 4:6 [c]Is. 57:15
5:6 [a]Jas. 4:10
5:7 [a]Ps. 37:5; Heb. 13:5
5:8 [a]Luke 21:34 [b]Job 1:7
5:9 [a]Eph. 6:11 [b]Acts 14:22
5:10 [a]1 Cor. 1:9 [b]2 Cor. 4:17
5:10 [c]Heb. 13:21 [d]2 Thes. 2:17
5:11 [a]Rev. 1:6
5:12 [a]2 Cor. 1:19 [b]Heb. 13:22 [c]Acts 20:24
5:13 [a]Acts 12:12
5:14 [a]Rom. 16:16 [b]Eph. 6:23

have had in mind the footwashing scene of John 13, in which he figured prominently. Although he was at first rebellious, he writes now with understanding (see John 13:7).

5:6 See Luke 14:11. *exalt you in due time.* His help will come at just the right time.

5:7 Cf. Phil 4:6–7.

5:8 *Be sober.* See 1 Thes 5:6,8. *vigilant.* Perhaps Peter remembered his own difficulty in keeping awake during our Lord's agony in Gethsemane (see Mat 26:36–46).

5:9 *your brethren.* They are not isolated; they belong to a fellowship of suffering.

5:10 *grace.* See notes on Gal 1:3; Eph 1:2.

5:12 *By Silvanus.* Silvanus (Silas) may have been the bearer of the letter to its destination. He may also have been a scribe who recorded what Peter dictated or who aided, as an informed and intelligent secretary, in the phrasing of Peter's thoughts (see Introduction: Author and Date). *exhorting . . . grace of God.* See Introduction: Themes.

5:13 *Babylon.* See Introduction: Place of Writing. *elected.* See note on Eph 1:4. *Marcus my son.* Peter regards Mark with such warmth and affection that he calls him his son. It is possible that Peter had led Mark to Christ (see 1 Tim 1:2 and note). Early Christian tradition closely associates Mark and Peter (see Introduction to Mark: Author).

5:14 *kiss.* See note on 1 Cor 16:20. *Peace be with you all . . . in Christ.* Spiritual well-being and blessedness to all who are united to Christ. Peter thus ends with a reference to the union of believers with Christ, a concept fundamental to the understanding of the whole letter.

The Second Epistle General of Peter

INTRODUCTION

Author

The author identifies himself as Simon Peter (1:1). He uses the first person singular pronoun in a highly personal passage (1:12–15) and claims to be an eyewitness of the transfiguration (1:16–18; cf. Mat 17:1–5). He asserts that this is his second letter to the readers (3:1) and refers to Paul as "our beloved brother" (3:15; see note there). In short, the letter claims to be Peter's, and its character is compatible with that claim.

Although 2 Peter was not as widely known and recognized in the early church as 1 Peter, some may have used and accepted it as authoritative as early as the second century and perhaps even in the latter part of the first century (1 Clement [A.D. 95] may allude to it). It was not ascribed to Peter until Origen's time (185–253), and he seems to reflect some doubt concerning it. Eusebius (265–340) placed it among the questioned books, though he admits that most accept it as from Peter. After Eusebius's time, it seems to have been quite generally accepted as canonical.

In recent centuries, however, its genuineness has been challenged by a considerable number of scholars. One of the objections that has been raised is the difference in style from that of 1 Peter. But the difference is not absolute; there are noteworthy similarities in vocabulary and in other matters. In fact, no other known writing is as much like 1 Peter as 2 Peter. The differences that do exist may be accounted for by variations in subject matter, in the form and purpose of the letters, in the time and circumstances of writing, in sources or models, and in scribes who may have been employed. Perhaps most significant is the statement in 1 Pet 5:12 that Silvanus assisted in the writing of 1 Peter. No such statement is made concerning 2 Peter, which may explain its noticeable difference in style (see Introduction to 1 Peter: Author and Date).

Other objections arise from a naturalistic reconstruction of early Christian history or misunderstandings or misconstructions of the available data. For example, some argue that the reference to Paul's letters in 3:15–16 indicates an advanced date for this book—beyond Peter's lifetime. But it is quite possible that Paul's letters were gathered at an early date, since some of them had been in existence and perhaps in circulation for more than ten years (Thessalonians by as much as 15 years) prior to Peter's death. Besides, what Peter says may only indicate that he was acquainted with some of Paul's letters (communication in the Roman world and in the early church was good), not that there was a formal, ecclesiastical collection of them.

Date

2 Peter was written toward the end of Peter's life (cf. 1:12–15), after he had written a prior letter (3:1) to the same readers (probably 1 Peter). Since Peter was martyred during the reign of Nero, his death must have occurred prior to A.D. 68; so it is very likely that he wrote 2 Peter between 65 and 68.

Some have argued that this date is too early for the writing of 2 Peter, but nothing in the book requires a later date. The error combated is comparable to the kind of heresy present in the first century. To insist that the second chapter was directed against second-century Gnosticism is to assume more than the contents of the chapter warrant. While the heretics referred to in 2 Peter may well have been among the forerunners of second-century Gnostics, nothing is said of them that would not fit into the later years of Peter's life.

Some have suggested a later date because they interpret the reference to the fathers in 3:4 to mean an earlier Christian generation. However, the word is most naturally interpreted as the OT patriarchs (cf. John 6:31, "fathers"; Acts 3:13; Heb 1:1). Similarly, reference to Paul and his letters (3:15–16; see Author) does not require a date beyond Peter's lifetime.

2 Peter and Jude

There are conspicuous similarities between 2 Peter and Jude (compare 2 Pet 2 with Jude 4–18), but there are also conspicuous differences. It has been suggested that one borrowed from the other or that they both drew on a common source. If there is borrowing, it is not a slavish borrowing but one that adapts to suit the writer's purpose. While many have insisted that Jude used Peter, it is more reasonable to assume that the longer letter (Peter) incorporated much of the shorter (Jude). Such borrowing is fairly common in ancient writings. For example, many believe that Paul used parts of early hymns in Phil 2:6–11 and 1 Tim 3:16.

Purpose

In his first letter Peter feeds Christ's sheep by instructing them how to deal with persecution from outside the church (see, e.g., 1 Pet 4:12); in this second letter he teaches them how to deal with false teachers and evildoers who have come into the church (see 2:1; 3:3–4). While the particular situations naturally call for variations in content and emphasis, in both letters Peter as a pastor ("shepherd") of Christ's sheep (John 21:15–17) seeks to commend to his readers a wholesome combination of Christian faith and practice. More specifically, his purpose is threefold: (1) to stimulate Christian growth (ch. 1), (2) to combat false teaching (ch. 2) and (3) to encourage watchfulness in view of the Lord's certain return (ch. 3).

Outline

- I. Introduction (1:1–2)
- II. Exhortation to Growth in Christian Virtues (1:3–11)
  - A. The Divine Enablement (1:3–4)
  - B. The Call for Growth (1:5–7)
  - C. The Value of Such Growth (1:8–11)
- III. The Purpose and Authentication of Peter's Message (1:12–21)
  - A. His Aim in Writing (1:12–15)
  - B. The Basis of His Authority (1:16–21)
- IV. Warning against False Teachers (ch. 2)
  - A. Their Coming Predicted (2:1–3a)
  - B. Their Judgment Assured (2:3b-9)
  - C. Their Characteristics Set Forth (2:10–22)
- V. The Fact of Christ's Return (3:1–16)
  - A. Peter's Purpose in Writing Restated (3:1–2)
  - B. The Coming of Scoffers (3:3–7)
  - C. The Certainty of Christ's Return (3:8–10)
  - D. Exhortations Based on the Fact of Christ's Return (3:11–16)
- VI. Concluding Remarks (3:17–18)

1 [1]Simon Peter, a servant and an apostle of
Jesus Christ, to them that have obtained
[a]like precious faith with us through the righteousness [2]of God and our Saviour Jesus
Christ:
2 [a]Grace and peace be multiplied unto you
through the knowledge of God, and of Jesus
our Lord.

The growth of true knowledge

3 ¶ According as his divine power hath giv-
en unto us all *things* that *pertain* unto life and
godliness, through the knowledge of him [a]that
hath called us [1]to glory and virtue:
4 [a]Whereby are given unto us exceeding
great and precious promises: that by these you
might be [b]partakers of the divine nature, having escaped the corruption that is in the world
through lust:
5 And beside this, [a]giving all diligence, add
to your faith virtue; and to virtue [b]knowledge;
6 And to knowledge temperance; and to
temperance patience; and to patience godliness;
7 And to godliness brotherly kindness; and
[a]to brotherly kindness charity.
8 For if these *things* be in you, and abound,
they make *you that ye shall* neither *be* [1]barren
[a]nor unfruitful in the knowledge of our Lord
Jesus Christ.
9 But he that lacketh these *things* [a]is blind,
and cannot see far off, and hath forgotten that
he was [b]purged from his old sins.
10 Wherefore the rather, brethren, give
diligence [a]to make your calling and election
sure: for if ye do these *things,* ye shall never
fall:
11 For so an entrance shall be ministered
unto you abundantly into the everlasting kingdom of our Lord and Saviour Jesus Christ.

The basis of true knowledge

12 ¶ Wherefore [a]I will not be negligent to
put you always in remembrance of these
things, [b]though ye know *them,* and be stablished in the present truth.
13 Yea, I think it meet, [a]as long as I am in
this tabernacle, to stir you up by putting *you* in
remembrance;
14 [a]Knowing that shortly *I* must put off
this my tabernacle, even as [b]our Lord Jesus
Christ hath shewed me.
15 Moreover I will endeavour that you may
be able after my decease to have these *things*
always in remembrance.

1:1 [1][Or, *Symeon*] [2][Gr. *of our God and Saviour*] [a]Eph. 4:5
1:2 [a]Dan. 4:1
1:3 [1]Or, *by* [a]1 Thes. 2:12
1:4 [a]2 Cor. 7:1 [b]2 Cor. 3:18; Heb. 12:10
1:5 [a]ch. 3:18 [b]1 Pet. 3:7
1:7 [a]Gal. 6:10; 1 Thes. 3:12
1:8 [1][Gr. *idle*] [a]John 15:2; Tit. 3:14
1:9 [a]1 John 2:9 [b]Eph. 5:26; Heb. 9:14
1:10 [a]1 John 3:19
1:12 [a]Phil. 3:1; 1 John 2:21 [b]1 Pet. 5:12
1:13 [a]2 Cor. 5:1
1:14 [a]2 Tim. 4:6 [b]John 21:18,19

1:1 *Simon Peter.* See notes on Mat 16:18; John 1:42. *servant.* See note on Rom 1:1. *apostle.* See notes on Mark 6:30; 1 Cor 1:1; Heb 3:1. *to them.* Probably the same people as those in 1 Pet 1:1. *have obtained.* God in His justice ("righteousness") imparts to people the ability to believe. *faith.* Not here a body of truth to be believed—the faith—but the act of believing, or the God-given capacity to trust in Christ for salvation. *God and our Saviour Jesus Christ.* Assumes that Jesus is both God and Savior. For other passages that ascribe deity to Christ see note on Rom 9:5.
1:2 *Grace and peace.* See notes on Jonah 4:2; John 14:27; 20:19; Gal 1:3; Eph 1:2. *knowledge of God, and of Jesus our Lord.* The concept of Christian knowledge is prominent in 2 Peter (see 1:3,5,8; 3:18). Peter was combating heretical teaching, and one of the best antidotes for heresy is the statement of true knowledge.
1:3 *all things that pertain unto life and godliness.* God has made available all that we need spiritually through our knowledge of Him. If indeed 2 Peter was written to combat an incipient Gnosticism, the apostle may be insisting that the knowledge possessed by those in apostolic circles was entirely adequate to meet their spiritual needs. No secret, esoteric knowledge is necessary for salvation (see Introduction to 1 John: Gnosticism). *glory and virtue.* The excellence of God: "Glory" expresses the excellence of His being—His attributes and essence; "excellence" depicts excellence expressed in deeds—virtue in action.
1:4 *by these.* Through God's excellence—internal and external—He has given us great promises. Their nature is suggested in the words that follow: participation in the divine nature and escape from worldly corruption. *partakers of the divine nature.* Does not indicate that Christians become divine in any sense, but only that we are indwelt by God through His Holy Spirit (see John 14:16–17). Our humanity and His deity, as well as the human personality and the divine, remain distinct and separate.
1:5–9 The virtues that will produce a well-rounded, fruitful Christian life.
1:5 *faith.* The root of the Christian life (see v. 1 and note). *virtue.* Cf. v. 3. *knowledge.* See notes on vv. 2–3.
1:6 *temperance.* According to many of the false teachers, knowledge made self-control unnecessary; according to Peter, Christian knowledge leads to self-control. *godliness.* A genuine reverence toward God that governs one's attitude toward every aspect of life.
1:7 *brotherly kindness.* Warmhearted affection toward all in the family of faith. *charity.* The kind of outgoing, selfless attitude that leads one to sacrifice for the good of others (see note on 1 Pet 4:8).
1:8 *if these things be in you.* Peter does not mean to imply that the believer is to cultivate each listed quality in turn, one after the other until all have been perfected. Instead, they are all to be cultivated simultaneously. *abound.* Peter has continuing spiritual growth in mind. *neither be barren nor unfruitful in the knowledge.* The Christian's knowledge should affect the way he lives. It does not set him free from moral restraints, as the heretics taught (see Introduction to 1 John: Gnosticism). Rather, it produces holiness and all such virtues (cf. Col 1:9–12).
1:9 *blind.* Peter may have in mind a possible alternative meaning for "blind," namely, "to shut the eyes." Such a person is blind because he has closed his eyes to the truth.
1:10 *make your calling and election sure.* By cultivating the qualities listed in vv. 5–7, they and others can be assured that God has chosen them and called them (cf. Mat 7:20). The genuineness of their profession will be demonstrated as they express these virtues (cf. Gal 5:6; Jas 2:18). When God elects and calls, it is to obedience and holiness (1 Pet 1:2; Eph 1:3–6), and these fruits confirm their divine source. *never fall.* Those who in this way give evidence of their faith will never cease to persevere.
1:11 *entrance . . . ministered unto you abundantly.* By producing the fruits Peter is commending to them (see vv. 5–10). *everlasting kingdom.* Eternal life (cf. Mat 25:46).
‡1:13 *tabernacle.* Peter is speaking of his body, his earthly dwelling place. See John 1:14; 2 Cor 5:1 and notes.
1:14 *Christ hath shewed me.* Either the revelation recorded in John 21:18–19 or a subsequent one.
1:15 *to have these things always in remembrance.* An aim that

16 For we have not followed [a]cunningly devised fables, when we made known unto you the power and coming of our Lord Jesus Christ, but [b]were eyewitnesses of his majesty.
17 For he received from God the Father honour and glory, when there came such a voice to him from the excellent glory, [a]This is my beloved Son, in whom I am well pleased.
18 And this voice which came from heaven we heard, when we were with him in [a]the holy mount.
19 We have also a more sure word of prophecy; whereunto ye do well that ye take heed, as unto [a]a light that shineth in a dark place, until the day dawn, and [b]the day star arise in your hearts:
20 Knowing this first, that [a]no prophecy of the scripture is of *any* private interpretation.
21 For [a]the prophecy came not [1]in old time by the will of man: [b]but holy men of God spake *as they were* moved by the Holy Ghost.

False prophets and teachers

2 But [a]there were false prophets also among the people, even as [b]there shall be false teachers among you, who privily shall bring in damnable heresies, even [c]denying the Lord [d]that bought them, [e]and bring upon themselves swift destruction.
2 And many shall follow their [1]pernicious ways; by reason of whom the way of truth shall be evil spoken of.
3 And [a]through covetousness shall they with feigned words [b]make merchandise of you: [c]whose judgment now of a long time lingereth not, and their damnation slumbereth not.
4 For if God spared not [a]the angels [b]that

1:16 [a]1 Cor. 1:17 [b]Mark 9:2; 1 John 1:1
1:17 [a]Mat. 3:17; Luke 9:35
1:18 [a]Mat. 17:6
1:19 [a]Ps. 119:105; John 5:35 [b]Rev. 22:16
1:20 [a]Rom. 12:6
1:21 [1]Or, *at any time* [a]2 Tim. 3:16; 1 Pet. 1:11
1:21 [b]2 Sam. 23:2; Acts 1:16
2:1 [a]Deut. 13:1 [b]Mat. 24:11; 1 John 4:1 [c]Jude 4 [d]1 Cor. 6:20; Heb. 10:29; Rev. 5:9 [e]Phil. 3:19
2:2 [1]Or, *lascivious ways,* as some copies read
2:3 [a]Rom. 16:18; Tit. 1:11 [b]2 Cor. 2:17 [c]Deut. 32:35; Jude 4,15
2:4 [a]Job 4:18; Jude 6 [b]John 8:44

was realized, whether intentionally or unintentionally, through the Gospel of Mark, which early tradition connected with Peter.

1:16 *cunningly devised fables.* Peter's message was based on his eyewitness account of the supernatural events that marked the life of Jesus. It was not made up of myths and imaginative stories as was the message of the heretics of 2:3. *coming of our Lord Jesus Christ.* In Christ's transfiguration the disciples received a foretaste of what His coming will be like when He returns to establish His eternal kingdom (Mat 16:28). *eyewitnesses of his majesty.* A reference to Christ's transfiguration (see vv. 17–18; Mat 16:28–17:8).

1:19–21 Peter's message rests on two solid foundations: (1) the voice from God at the transfiguration (vv. 16–18) and (2) the still more significant testimony of Scripture (vv. 19–21). An alternative, but less probable, view is that the apostles' testimony to the transfiguration fulfills and thus confirms the Scriptures that predicted such things.

1:19 *more sure.* Or "very certain."

1:20 Two major views of this verse are: 1. No prophecy is to be privately or independently interpreted (cf. the false teachers in 3:16). The Holy Spirit, Scripture itself and the church should be included in the interpretative process. 2. No prophecy originated through the prophet's own interpretation. The preceding and following contexts indicate that this view is probably to be preferred. In vv. 16–19 the subject discussed is the origin of the apostolic message. Did it come from human imaginings, or was it from God? In v. 21 again the subject is origin. No prophecy of Scripture arose from a merely human interpretation of things. This understanding of v. 20 is further supported by the explanatory "for" with which v. 21 begins. Verse 21 explains v. 20 by restating its content and then affirming God as the origin of prophecy.

‡1:21 *moved by the Holy Ghost.* See note on 2 Tim 3:16. In the production of Scripture both God and man were active participants. God was the source of the content of Scripture, so that what it says is what God has said. But the human author also actively spoke; he was more than a recorder. Yet what he said came from God. Although actively speaking, he was carried along by the Holy Spirit. This verse gives the process of inspiration, whereas 2 Tim 3:16 speaks of the product of inspiration—the writings themselves.

2:1 *false prophets.* See 2 Ki 18:19; Is 9:13–17; Jer 5:31; 14:14; 23:30–32. *there shall be false teachers among you.* Numerous NT passages warn of false teachers who are already present or yet to come (see Mat 24:4–5,11; Acts 20:29–30; Gal 1:6–9; Phil 3:2; Col 2:4,8,18,20–23; 2 Thes 2:1–3; 1 Tim 1:3–7; 4:1–3; 2 Tim 3:1–8; 1 John 2:18–19,22–23; 2 John 7–11; Jude 3–4). *damnable heresies.* Divisive opinions or teachings that result in the moral and spiritual destruction of those who accept them. *the Lord that bought them.* Does not necessarily mean that the false teachers were believers. Christ's death paid the penalty for their sin, but it would not become effective for their salvation unless they trusted in Christ as Savior. (However, see vv. 20–22, where it is obvious that the heretics had at least professed knowing the Lord.) *swift destruction.* Not immediate physical calamity, but sudden doom, whether at death or at the Lord's second coming (cf. Mat 24:50–51; 2 Thes 1:9).

2:2 *pernicious ways.* Open, extreme immorality not held in check by any sense of shame. *way of truth.* See Ps 119:30. The Christian faith is not only correct doctrine but also correct living.

2:3 *through coveteousness.* They will be motivated by a desire for money and will commercialize the Christian faith to their own selfish advantage. *feigned words.* See note on 1:16. *of a long time lingereth not.* Long ago, in OT times, their condemnation was declared (see vv. 4–9 for OT examples of the fact that judgment is coming on the wicked). *damnation slumbereth not.* Although delay makes it seem that they have escaped God's judgment, destruction is a reality that is sure to come upon them.

2:4–8 Three examples showing that God will rescue the godly and destroy the wicked.

‡2:4 *angels that sinned.* Some believe this sin was the one referred to in Gen 6:2, where the sons of God are said to have intermarried with the daughters of men, meaning (according to this view) that angels married human women. The offspring of those marriages are said to have been the Nephilim (Gen 6:4; see notes on Gen 6:2,4). But since it appears impossible for angels, who are spirits, to have sexual relations with women, the sin referred to in this verse probably occurred before the fall of Adam and Eve. The angels who fell became the devil and the evil angels (probably the demons and evil spirits referred to in the NT). *cast them down to hell.* The Greek for "hell" is *Tartarus,* the term used by the Greeks to designate the place where the most wicked spirits were sent to be punished. Peter uses this term to indicate a sphere of habitation and activity that is infinitely below their former estate, and from which they cannot escape or return to the former position. Why some evil angels are imprisoned and others are free to serve Satan as demons is not explained in Scripture. *chains of darkness.* This highly figurative phrase indicates that Satan and his fallen angels can-

sinned, but [c]cast *them* down to hell, and delivered *them* into chains of darkness, *to be* reserved unto judgment;
5 And spared not the old world, but saved
[a]Noah the eighth *person,* [b]a preacher of righteousness, [c]bringing in the flood upon the
world of the ungodly;
6 And [a]turning the cities of Sodom and Gomorrha into ashes condemned *them* with an
overthrow, [b]making *them* an ensample unto
those that after should live ungodly;
7 And [a]delivered just Lot, vexed with the
filthy conversation of the wicked:
8 (For *that* righteous *man* dwelling among
them, [a]in seeing and hearing, vexed *his* righteous soul from day to day with *their* unlawful
deeds;)
9 [a]The Lord knoweth *how* to deliver the
godly out of temptations, and to reserve the
unjust unto the day of judgment *to be* punished:
10 But chiefly [a]them that walk after the
flesh in the lust of uncleanness, and despise
[1]government. [b]Presumptuous *are they,* selfwilled, they are not afraid to speak evil of dignities.
11 Whereas [a]angels, which are greater in
power and might, bring not railing accusation
[1]against them before the Lord.
12 But these, [a]as natural brute beasts,
made to be taken and destroyed, speak evil of
the things that they understand not; and shall
utterly perish in their own corruption;
13 [a]And shall receive the reward of unrighteousness, *as* they that count it pleasure
[b]to riot in the day time. [c]Spots *they are* and
blemishes, sporting themselves with their
own deceivings while [d]they feast with you;
14 Having eyes full of [1]adultery and that
cannot cease from sin; beguiling unstable
souls: [a]a heart they have exercised with covetous practices; cursed children:
15 Which have forsaken the right way, and
are gone astray, following the way of [a]Balaam
the son of Bosor, who loved the wages of unrighteousness;
16 But was rebuked for his iniquity: the
dumb ass speaking with man's voice forbad
the madness of the prophet.
17 [a]These are wells without water, clouds
that are carried with a tempest; to whom the
mist of darkness is reserved for ever.
18 For when [a]they speak great swelling

2:4 [c]Luke 8:31; Rev. 20:2
2:5 [a]Gen. 7:1; Heb. 11:7; 1 Pet. 3:20 [b]1 Pet. 3:19 [c]ch. 3:6
2:6 [a]Gen. 19:24; Deut. 29:23 [b]Num. 26:10
2:7 [a]Gen. 19:16
2:8 [a]Ps. 119:139; Ezek. 9:4
2:9 [a]Ps. 34:17; 1 Cor. 10:13
2:10 [1]Or, *dominion* [a]Jude 4,7,8 [b]Jude 8
2:11 [a]Jude 9
2:11 [1]Some read, *against themselves*
2:12 [a]Jude 10
2:13 [a]Phil. 3:19 [b]Rom. 13:13 [c]Jude 12 [d]1 Cor. 11:20
2:14 [1]Gr. *an adulteress* [a]Jude 11
2:15 [a]Num. 22:5; Jude 11
2:17 [a]Jude 12,13
2:18 [a]Jude 16

not escape. *judgment.* The final judgment, probably associated with the great white throne judgment of Rev 20:11–15.

2:5 *Noah the eighth person.* Noah's wife, three sons and three daughters-in-law (Noah was the eighth; see 1 Pet 3:20). *preacher of righteousness.* A description of Noah found nowhere else in Scripture. However, similar descriptions are used of him in Josephus (*Antiquities,* 1.3.1), *1 Clement* (7.6; 9.4) and the *Sibylline Oracles* (1.128–29). *the ungodly.* See Gen 6:5,11–12.

‡2:6 *the cities of Sodom and Gomorrha.* See Gen 19. These cities were destroyed by God for their gross wickedness, including homosexuality—not for simply being inhospitable to Lot's visitors.

2:7 *vexed with the filthy conversation of the wicked.* See Gen 19:4–9. How Lot could be so distressed, how he could be called a "righteous man," and yet offer to turn his two daughters over to the wicked townsmen to be sexually abused is difficult to understand apart from a knowledge of the code of honor characteristic of that day (see note on Gen 19:8).

2:9 States the point made in vv. 4–8—the wicked whose coming Peter predicts will surely be punished.

‡2:10 *chiefly them.* The heretics of Peter's day are certain to come under judgment for two main reasons: 1. They follow the corrupt desire of the sinful nature, perhaps referring to homosexuality, the sin of the Sodomites (see Gen 19:5). At least the author has in mind a similar inordinate sexual practice. 2. They despise authority. *despise government.* A specific example of despising authority. This could refer to the slander of earthly dignitaries such as church leaders, which might well be expected from such shameless peddlers of error. On the other hand, it could refer to the blaspheming of angels. This view seems more likely since the parallel passage in Jude 8–10 is speaking of angels.

2:11 *angels . . . bring not railing accusation.* Even good angels, who might have more right to do so because of their greater power, do not bring such accusations against inferior evil angels.

2:12 *as natural brute beasts.* A scathing denunciation. They are like irrational animals, whose lives are guided by mere instinct and who are born merely to be slaughtered. Destruction is their final lot. *things that they understand not.* The heresy to which Peter refers may have been an early form of second-century Gnosticism (see Introduction to 1 John: Gnosticism) that claimed to possess special, esoteric knowledge. If so, it is ironic that those who professed special knowledge acted out of abysmal ignorance, and the result was arrogant blasphemy.

‡2:13 *riot in the day time.* See 1 Thes 5:7. Even the pagan world carried on their corrupt practices under cover of darkness, but these heretics were utterly shameless. *their own deceivings while they feast with you.* These false teachers seem to have been involved in the sacred feasts of brotherly love that, in the early church, accompanied the Lord's supper. In fact, it appears that they injected their carousing into these holy observances and delighted in their shameless acts.

2:14 *eyes full of adultery.* Lit. "eyes full of an adulteress," which means that they desired every woman they saw, viewing her as a potential sex partner. *cannot cease from sin.* Their eyes serve as constant instruments of lust. *beguiling unstable souls.* For a parallel use of the Greek word for "enticing" see Jas 1:14. It depicts the fisherman who attempts to lure and catch fish with bait. *exercised with covetous practices.* The Greek text implies that they had exercised themselves like an athlete, not in physical activity but in greed.

2:15 *way of Balaam the son of Bosor.* See Num 22–24. Balaam was bent on cursing Israel, though God had forbidden it. He wanted the money Balak offered him. Similarly these false teachers apparently were guilty of attempting to extract money from naive listeners. For a donkey to rebuke the prophet's madness reflects not only on the foolishness of Balaam but also on that of the false teachers of Peter's day.

2:17 *wells without water.* A picture of cruel deception. The thirsty traveler comes to the spring expecting cool, refreshing water but finds it dry. So the false teachers promise satisfying truth but in reality have nothing to offer. *clouds that are carried with a tempest.* Gone before a drop of moisture falls. *mist of darkness.* Their destiny is hell.

2:18 *speak great swelling words of vanity.* Words that sound impressive to the new convert but in reality have nothing to offer. *allure.* See note on v. 14 ("beguiling"). *those that were*

words of vanity, they allure through the lusts
of the flesh, through much wantonness, those
that [b]were [1]clean escaped from them who live
in error.
19 While they promise them [a]liberty, they
themselves are [b]the servants of corruption: for
of whom a man is overcome, of the same is he
brought in bondage.
20 For [a]if after they [b]have escaped the pollutions of the world [c]through the knowledge
of the Lord and Saviour Jesus Christ, they are
again entangled therein, and overcome, the
latter *end* is worse with them than the beginning.
21 For [a]it had been better for them not to
have known the way of righteousness, than,
after they have known *it,* to turn from the holy
commandment delivered unto them.
22 But it is happened unto them according
to the true proverb, [a]The dog *is* turned to his
own vomit again; and, The sow that was
washed to *her* wallowing in the mire.

2:18 [1]Or, *for a little,* or, *a while,* as some read [b]Acts 2:40
2:19 [a]Gal. 5:13 [b]John 8:34; Rom. 6:16
2:20 [a]Mat. 12:45; Luke 11:26; Heb. 6:4 [b]ver. 18 [c]ch. 1:2
2:21 [a]Luke 12:47
2:22 [a]Prov. 26:11

3:1 [a]ch. 1:13
3:2 [a]Jude 17
3:3 [a]ch. 2:10
3:4 [a]Is. 5:19; Jer. 17:15; Ezek. 12:22; Mat. 24:48; Luke 12:45
3:5 [1]Gr. *consisting* [a]Gen. 1:6,9; Ps. 33:6; Heb. 11:3 [b]Ps. 24:2; Col. 1:17
3:6 [a]Gen. 7:11
3:7 [a]ver. 10

Christ's coming

3 This second epistle, beloved, I now write
unto you; in both which [a]I stir up your
pure minds by way of remembrance:
2 That *ye* may be mindful of the words
which were spoken before by the holy prophets, [a]and of the commandment of us the apostles of the Lord and Saviour:
3 Knowing this first, that there shall come
in the last days scoffers, [a]walking after their
own lusts,
4 And saying, [a]Where is the promise of his
coming? for since the fathers fell asleep, all
things continue as *they were* from the beginning of the creation.
5 For this they willingly are ignorant of,
that [a]by the word of God the heavens were of
old, and the earth [b][1]standing out of the water
and in the water:
6 [a]Whereby the world that then was, being
overflowed with water, perished:
7 But [a]the heavens and the earth, which

clean escaped. New converts who have just broken away from pagan friends. Thus the depraved false teachers prey on new converts, who have not yet had a chance to develop spiritual resistance.

2:19 *promise them liberty.* Probably freedom from moral restraint (cf. 1 Cor 6:12–13; Gal 5:13). The very ones who promise freedom from bondage to rules and regulations are themselves slaves of depravity. Freedom from law resulted in bondage to sin, and liberty was turned into license.

2:20–22 Some point to this passage as clear proof that a genuinely saved person may lose his salvation. He knows the Lord; he escapes the world's corruption; he knows the way of righteousness. Then he turns away from the message and goes back to his old way of life. His knowledge is said to have been genuine; his change of life was real; and his return to his old way of life was not superficial. Others insist that the knowledge of the Lord and of the way of righteousness could not have been genuine. If the person had been truly regenerated, he would have persevered in his faith. It is argued that the teaching of John 10:27–30 (especially v. 28) and Rom 8:28–39 makes it clear that no genuinely saved person can be lost. Thus, according to this view, the persons described here could not have been genuinely saved.

2:20 *if after they have escaped the pollutions of the world.* A reference to false teachers who had once apparently been believers in Christ. Their professed knowledge of Christ had at least produced a change in life-style. *again entangled therein, and overcome.* A complete return to the old sinful pattern of life.

2:21 *better . . . not to have known the way of righteousness.* Knowledge of the way increases one's responsibility and his hardness of heart if he then rejects it. In its early days, Christianity was known as "the way" (Acts 9:2; 18:25; 19:9,23; 22:4; 24:14,22). *holy commandment.* The whole Christian message that people are commanded to receive.

2:22 *The dog . . . The sow . . . in the mire.* In both cases the nature of the animal is not changed. The sow returns to the mud because by nature it is still a sow. The change was merely cosmetic.

3:1 *second epistle.* The first letter may have been 1 Peter, though there is some reason to doubt this identification. For example, 1 Peter cannot be very accurately described as a reminder. *beloved.* See vv. 8,14,17; 1 Pet 2:11; 4:12. *remembrance.* See 1:12–13,15.

3:2 *holy prophets.* OT personages. *commandment.* See note on 2:21. *us the apostles.* Peter places the OT prophets and the NT apostles on an equal plane. Both are vehicles of God's sacred truth. Peter, being one of the apostles, can speak with knowledge and authority as a representative of the apostolic group.

3:3 *first.* This expression is used in 1:20 to call attention to a matter of great importance. *last days.* An expression that refers to the whole period introduced by Christ's first coming. These days are last in comparison to OT days, which were preliminary and preparatory. Also, the Christian era is the time of the beginnings of prophetic fulfillment. *scoffers.* Perhaps the same false teachers described in ch. 2 (e.g., they follow their own evil desires; cf. 2:10,18–19). In ch. 3, however, the emphasis is on Christ's return. These people may have been early Gnostics who resisted the idea of a time of judgment and moral accountability.

3:4 *his coming.* Christ's. *since the fathers fell asleep.* Either the first Christians to die after Christ's death and resurrection (e.g., Stephen, James the brother of John, and other early Christian leaders who had died; cf. Heb 13:7) or the OT patriarchs (see Introduction: Date). *all things continue as they were.* Their argument against Christ's return was: Since it has not occurred up to this time, it will never occur. That nature is not subject to divine intervention, they say, has been proved by observation (1) of the period since the fathers died—perhaps 30 years—and (2) of the period since creation.

3:5 *For this they willingly are ignorant of.* Ignoring the flood as a divine intervention was not an oversight; it was deliberate. They did not want to face up to the fallacy in their argument. *the word of God.* Of command, such as "Let there be light" (Gen 1:3). *earth standing out of the water and in the water.* See Gen 1:6–10, where the waters on earth were separated from the atmospheric waters of the heavens, and the mountains then appeared, causing the earthly waters to be gathered into oceans.

‡3:6 Peter points out the fallacy of the scoffers' argument. There has been a divine intervention since the time of creation, namely, the flood. The term "world" may refer to the earth or, more probably, to the world of people (cf. John 3:16). All the people except Noah and his family were overcome by the flood and perished. This does not necessarily mean that the flood was universal. It may simply have extended to all the inhabited areas of earth (see note on Gen 6:17).

are now, by the same word are kept in store, reserved unto [b]fire against the day of judgment and perdition of ungodly men.

8 But, beloved, be not ignorant of this one *thing,* that one day *is* with the Lord as a thousand years, and [a]a thousand years as one day.

The concluding appeal

9 [a]The Lord is not slack concerning *his* promise, as some *men* count slackness; but [b]is longsuffering to us-ward, [c]not willing that any should perish, but [d]that all should come to repentance.

10 But [a]the day of the Lord will come as a thief in the night; in the which [b]the heavens shall pass away with a great noise, and the elements shall melt with fervent heat, the earth also and the works that are therein shall be burnt up.

11 Seeing then that all these *things shall* be dissolved, what manner *of persons* ought ye to be [a]in all holy conversation and godliness,

12 [a]Looking for and [1]hasting *unto* the coming of the day of God, wherein the heavens being on fire shall [b]be dissolved, and the elements shall [c]melt with fervent heat?

13 Nevertheless we, according to his promise, look for [a]new heavens and a new earth, wherein dwelleth righteousness.

14 Wherefore, beloved, seeing that ye look for such *things,* be diligent [a]that ye may be found of him in peace, without spot, and blameless.

15 And account *that* [a]the longsuffering of our Lord *is* salvation; even as our beloved brother Paul also according to the wisdom given unto him hath written unto you;

16 As also in all *his* epistles, [a]speaking in them of these *things;* in which are some *things* hard to be understood, which *they that are* unlearned and unstable wrest, as *they do* also the other scriptures, unto their own destruction.

17 Ye therefore, beloved, [a]seeing ye know *these things* before, [b]beware lest ye also, being led away with the error of the wicked, fall from your own stedfastness.

18 [a]But grow in grace, and *in* the knowledge of our Lord and Saviour Jesus Christ. [b]To him *be* glory both now and for ever. Amen.

3:7 [b]Mat. 25:41; 2 Thes. 1:8
3:8 [a]Ps. 90:4
3:9 [a]Hab. 2:3; Heb. 10:37 [b]Is. 30:18; 1 Pet. 3:20 [c]Ezek. 33:11 [d]Rom. 2:4; 1 Tim. 2:4
3:10 [a]Mat. 24:43; Luke 12:39; 1 Thes. 5:2 [b]Ps. 102:26; Is. 51:6; Mat. 24:35; Rom. 8:12
3:11 [a]1 Pet. 1:15
3:12 [1]Or, *hasting the coming* [a]1 Cor. 1:7; Tit. 2:13 [b]Ps. 50:3; Is. 34:4 [c]Mic. 1:4
3:13 [a]Is. 65:17; 66:22; Rev. 21:1
3:14 [a]1 Cor. 1:8; 15:58; Phil. 1:10; 1 Thes. 3:13
3:15 [a]Rom. 2:4; 1 Pet. 3:20
3:16 [a]Rom. 8:19; 1 Cor. 15:24; 1 Thes. 4:15
3:17 [a]Mark 13:23 [b]Eph. 4:14
3:18 [a]Eph. 4:15; 1 Pet. 2:2 [b]2 Tim. 4:18; Rev. 1:6

3:7 *by the same word.* The word of God that brought the world into existence (v. 5) and that brought watery destruction on the wicked of Noah's day will bring fiery destruction on the world that exists today and on its wicked people.

3:8 *a thousand years as one day.* Cf. Ps 90:4. God does not view time as humans do. He stands above time, with the result that when time is seen in the light of eternity, an age appears no longer than one short day, and a day seems no shorter than a long age. Since time is purely relative with God, He waits patiently while human beings stew with impatience.

3:9 God's seeming delay in bringing about the consummation of all things is a result not of indifference but of patience in waiting for all who will come to repentance. Thus the scoffers are wrong on two points: 1. They fail to recognize that all things have not continued without divine intervention since creation (the flood was an intervention, vv. 4–6). 2. They misunderstand the reason for apparent divine delay (God is a long-suffering God).

3:10 *day of the Lord.* See notes on Is 2:11,17,20; Amos 5:18; 1 Thes 5:2. *as a thief.* Suddenly and unexpectedly. *the heavens shall pass away with a great noise.* Apocalyptic language, common to books like Daniel and Revelation. Due to the figurative nature of such writings, we must not expect complete literalism but recognize it as an attempt to describe the indescribable, a task as impossible as it would have been for a first-century writer to describe the phenomena of our atomic age. What may be referred to is the destruction of the atmospheric heavens with a great rushing sound (see v. 12). *elements.* Refers either to the heavenly bodies or to the physical elements—in the first century, such things as earth, air, fire and water; in today's more precise scientific terminology, hydrogen, oxygen, carbon, etc. *fervent heat.* See vv. 7,12. *earth . . . burnt up.* Either the earth and its contents will disappear and not be seen anymore, or the earth and all man's works will appear before God's judgment seat.

3:11 *Seeing then that all these things shall be dissolved.* The transitory nature of the material universe ought to make a difference in one's system of values and one's priorities. The result should be lives of holiness (separated from sin and to God) and godliness (devoted to the worship and service of God). Cf. Mat 25:13; 1 Thes 5:6,8,11; 2 Pet 1:13–16.

3:12 *hasting unto the coming.* That day may be hastened by God's people as they speed up the accomplishment of His purposes. Since He is waiting for all who will come to repentance (v. 9), the sooner believers bring others to the Savior the sooner that day will dawn (cf. Acts 3:19–20). Prayer also serves to hasten the day (Mat 6:10), as does holy living (v. 11). *the day of God.* Apparently synonymous with "the day of the Lord" (v. 10) since it is characterized by the same kind of events. Cf. Rev 16:14. *heavens . . . shall be dissolved..* See v. 10. *elements shall melt with fervent heat.* See v. 10; Is 34:4.

3:13 *his promise.* New heavens and a new earth are promised by Isaiah (65:17; 66:22). This promise is confirmed by Rev 21:1. *wherein dwelleth righteousness.* Righteousness will dwell there as a permanent resident. Cf. Is 11:4–5; 45:8; Dan 9:24.

3:14 *without spot, and blameless.* Cf. 1 Pet 1:19, where the same two Greek words are applied to Christ.

3:15 *the longsuffering of our Lord is salvation.* See v. 9. *our beloved brother Paul.* Peter expresses warmth in his reference to Paul. The unity of teaching and purpose that governed their relationship, abundantly attested in Paul's letters and the book of Acts, is confirmed here by Peter. It has been suggested that what Paul wrote to the recipients of 2 Peter may have been a copy of Romans, which was sent to the churches as a circular letter (cf. Rom 16:4; see Introduction to Romans: Recipients; see also note on 1 Pet 1:1).

3:16 *As also in all his epistles.* Peter may be referring in general to the exhortations to holy living in vv. 11–14, which parallel many passages in Paul's writings. *unlearned and unstable.* The unlearned are simply those who have not been taught basic apostolic teaching and thus may be easily led astray (cf. 2:14). *the other scriptures.* Peter placed Paul's writings on the same level of authority as the God-breathed writings of the OT (see 1:21; 2 Tim 3:16).

3:17 *seeing ye know these things before.* That false teachers are coming (cf. ch. 2).

3:18 *grow in . . . knowledge.* Peter concludes by again stressing knowledge (see 1:2–3 and notes; see also 1:5), probably as an antidote to the false teachers who boasted in their esoteric knowledge.

The First Epistle General of John

INTRODUCTION

Author

The author is John son of Zebedee (see Mark 1:19–20)—the apostle and the author of the Gospel of John and Revelation (see Introductions to both books: Author). He was a fisherman whom Jesus called early in His ministry (Mat 4:18–22) and was the disciple "whom Jesus loved" (John 13:23). He with Peter and James was one of Jesus' inner circle. Thus, he was (1) on the mount of transfiguration (Mat 17:1), (2) in Gethsemane (Mat 26:37), (3) the only apostle at the crucifixion (John 19:2–27), (4) the first apostle to the empty tomb (John 20:4–5), and (5) with Peter when Jesus recommissioned him at the Sea of Galilee (John 21:15–23). He continued as a close companion and church leader with Peter after Pentecost (Acts 3:1; 4:19; 8:14; and Gal 2:9). Also see the Introduction to the Gospel of John: Author.

Unlike most NT letters, 1 John does not tell us who its author is. The earliest identification of him comes from the church fathers: Irenaeus (c. A.D. 140–203), Clement of Alexandria (c. 150–215), Tertullian (c. 155–222) and Origen (c. 185–253) all designated the writer as the apostle John. As far as we know, no one else was suggested by the early church.

This traditional identification is confirmed by evidence in the letter itself:

1. The style of the Gospel of John is markedly similar to that of this letter. Both are written in simple Greek and use contrasting figures, such as light and darkness, life and death, truth and lies, love and hate.

2. Similar phrases and expressions, such as those found in the following passages, are striking:

1 John	Gospel of John
1:1	1:1,14
1:4	16:24
1:6–7	3:19–21
2:7	13:34–35
3:8	8:44
3:14	5:24
4:6	8:47
4:9	1:14,18; 3:16
5:9	5:32,37
5:12	3:36

3. The mention of eyewitness testimony (1:1–4) harmonizes with the fact that John was a follower of Christ from the earliest days of His ministry.

4. The authoritative manner that pervades the letter (seen in its commands, 2:15,24,28; 4:1; 5:21; its firm assertions, 2:6; 3:14; 4:12; and its pointed identification of error, 1:6,8; 2:4,22) is what would be expected from an apostle.

5. The suggestions of advanced age (addressing his readers as "children," 2:1,28; 3:7) agree with early church tradition concerning John's age when he wrote the books known to be his.

6. The description of the heretics as antichrists (2:18), liars (2:22) and children of the devil (3:10) is consistent with Jesus' characterization of John as a son of thunder (Mark 3:17).

7. The indications of a close relationship with the Lord (1:1; 2:5–6,24,27–28) fit the descriptions of the disciple "whom Jesus loved" and the one who "was leaning on Jesus' bosom" (John 13:23).

Date

The letter is difficult to date with precision, but factors such as (1) evidence from early Christian writers (Irenaeus and Clement of Alexandria), (2) the early form of Gnosticism reflected in the denunciations of the letter and (3) indications of the advanced age of John suggest the end of the first century. Since the author of 1 John seems to build on concepts and themes found in the fourth Gospel

(see 1 John 2:7–11), it is reasonable to date the letter somewhere between A.D. 85 and 95, after the writing of the Gospel, which may have been written c. 85 (see Introduction to John: Date).

Recipients

1 John 2:12–14,19; 3:1; 5:13 make it clear that this letter was addressed to believers. But the letter itself does not indicate who they were or where they lived. The fact that it mentions no one by name suggests it was a circular letter sent to Christians in a number of places. Evidence from early Christian writers places the apostle John in Ephesus during most of his later years (c. A.D. 70–100). The earliest confirmed use of 1 John was in the province of Asia (in modern Turkey), where Ephesus was located. Clement of Alexandria indicates that John ministered in the various churches scattered throughout that province. It may be assumed, therefore, that 1 John was sent to the churches of the Roman province of Asia (see map No. 12 at the end of the Study Bible).

Gnosticism

One of the most dangerous heresies of the first two centuries of the church was Gnosticism. Its central teaching was that spirit is entirely good and matter is entirely evil. From this unbiblical dualism flowed five important errors:

1. Man's body, which is matter, is therefore evil. It is to be contrasted with God, who is wholly spirit and therefore good.
2. Salvation is the escape from the body, achieved not by faith in Christ but by special knowledge (the Greek word for "knowledge" is *gnosis,* hence Gnosticism).
3. Christ's true humanity was denied in two ways: (1) Some said that Christ only seemed to have a body, a view called Docetism, from the Greek *dokeo* ("to seem"), and (2) others said that the divine Christ joined the man Jesus at baptism and left him before he died, a view called Cerinthianism, after its most prominent spokesman, Cerinthus. This view is the background of much of 1 John (see 1:1; 2:22; 4:2–3).
4. Since the body was considered evil, it was to be treated harshly. This ascetic form of Gnosticism is the background of part of the letter to the Colossians (2:21–23).
5. Paradoxically, this dualism also led to licentiousness. The reasoning was that, since matter—and not the breaking of God's law (1 John 3:4)—was considered evil, breaking his law was of no moral consequence.

The Gnosticism addressed in the NT was an early form of the heresy, not the intricately developed system of the second and third centuries. In addition to that seen in Colossians and in John's letters, acquaintance with early Gnosticism is reflected in 1,2 Timothy, Titus, and 2 Peter and perhaps 1 Corinthians.

Occasion and Purpose

John's readers were confronted with an early form of Gnostic teaching of the Cerinthian variety (see Gnosticism). This heresy was also libertine, throwing off all moral restraints.

Consequently, John wrote this letter with two basic purposes in mind: (1) to expose false teachers (2:26) and (2) to give believers assurance of salvation (5:13). In keeping with his intention to combat Gnostic teachers, John specifically struck at their total lack of morality (3:8–10); and by giving eyewitness testimony to the incarnation, he sought to confirm his readers' belief in the incarnate Christ (1:3). Success in this would give the writer joy (1:4).

Outline*

I. Introduction: The Reality of the Incarnation (1:1–4)

II. The Christian Life as Fellowship with the Father and the Son (1:5–2:28)
- A. Ethical Tests of Fellowship (1:5—2:11)
  1. Moral likeness (1:5–7)
  2. Confession of sin (1:8—2:2)
  3. Obedience (2:3–6)
  4. Love for fellow believers (2:7–11)
- B. Two Digressions (2:12–17)
- C. Christological Test of Fellowship (2:18–28)
  1. Contrast: apostates versus believers (2:18–21)
  2. Person of Christ: the crux of the test (2:22–23)

3. Persistent belief: key to continuing fellowship (2:24–28)

III. The Christian Life as Divine Sonship (2:29—4:6)
   A. Ethical Tests of Sonship (2:29—3:24)
      1. Righteousness (2:29—3:10a)
      2. Love (3:10b-24)
   B. Christological Tests of Sonship (4:1–6)

IV. The Christian Life as an Integration of the Ethical and the Christological (4:7—5:12)
   A. The Ethical Test: Love (4:7—5:5)
      1. The source of love (4:7–16)
      2. The fruit of love (4:17–19)
      3. The relationship of love for God and love for one's spiritual brother (4:20—5:1)
      4. Obedience: the evidence of love for God's children (5:2–5)
   B. The Christological Test (5:6–12)

V. Conclusion: Great Christian Certainties (5:13–21)

The Word of life

1 *That* [a]which was from the beginning,
which we have heard, which we have
seen with our eyes, [b]which we have looked
upon, and [c]our hands have handled, of the
Word of life;
2 (For [a]the life [b]was manifested, and we
have seen *it,* [c]and bear witness, [d]and shew
unto you *that* eternal life, [e]which was with the
Father, and was manifested unto us;)
3 *That* which we have seen and heard declare we unto you, that ye also may have fellowship with us: and truly [a]our fellowship *is*
with the Father, and with his Son Jesus
Christ.
4 And these *things* write we unto you,
[a]that your joy may be full.

The test of righteousness

5 [a]This then is the message which we have
heard of him, and declare unto you, that [b]God
is light, and in him is no darkness at all.
6 [a]If we say that we have fellowship with
him, and walk in darkness, we lie, and do not
the truth:
7 But if we walk in the light, as he is in the
light, we have fellowship one with another,
and [a]the blood of Jesus Christ his Son
cleanseth us from all sin.
8 [a]If we say that we have no sin, we deceive ourselves, [b]and the truth is not in us.
9 [a]If we confess our sins, he is faithful and
just to forgive us *our* sins, and to [b]cleanse us
from all unrighteousness.
10 If we say that we have not sinned, we
make him a liar, and his word is not in us.

2 My little children, these *things* write I
unto you, that ye sin not. And if any *man*
sin, [a]we have an advocate with the Father,
Jesus Christ *the* righteous:
2 And [a]he is the propitiation for our sins:
and not for ours only, but [b]also for *the sins of*
the whole world.
3 And hereby we do know that we know
him, if we keep his commandments.
4 [a]He that saith, I know him, and keepeth
not his commandments, [b]is a liar, and the
truth is not in him.
5 But [a]whoso keepeth his word, [b]in him
verily is the love of God perfected: [c]hereby
know we that we are in him.
6 [a]He that saith *he* abideth in him [b]ought
himself also so to walk, even as he walked.
7 Brethren, [a]I write no new command-

1:1 [a]John 1:1 [b]John 1:14; 2 Pet. 1:16 [c]Luke 24:39; John 20:27
1:2 [a]John 1:4; 14:6 [b]Rom. 16:26; 1 Tim. 3:16 [c]John 21:24 [d]ch. 5:20 [e]John 1:1
1:3 [a]John 17:21; 1 Cor. 1:9
1:4 [a]John 16:24
1:5 [a]ch. 3:11 [b]John 1:9
1:6 [a]2 Cor. 6:14
1:7 [a]1 Cor. 6:11; Eph. 1:7; Heb. 9:14; 1 Pet. 1:19; Rev. 1:5
1:8 [a]Job 9:2; Eccl. 7:20; Jas. 3:2 [b]ch. 2:4
1:9 [a]Ps. 32:5 [b]Ps. 51:2
2:1 [a]Heb. 7:25
2:2 [a]Rom. 3:25; 2 Cor. 5:18 [b]John 1:29
2:4 [a]ch. 1:6 [b]ch. 1:8
2:5 [a]John 14:21,23 [b]ch. 4:12 [c]ch. 4:13
2:6 [a]John 15:4 [b]Mat. 11:29; 1 Pet. 2:21
2:7 [a]2 John 5

1:1–4 The introduction to this letter deals with the same subject and uses several of the same words as the introduction to John's Gospel (1:1–4)—"beginning,""Word,""life,""with."

1:1 *was from the beginning.* Has always existed. *we.* John and the other apostles. *heard . . . seen . . . looked upon . . . handled.* The apostle had made a careful examination of the Word of Life. He testifies that the one who has existed from eternity "was made flesh" (John 1:14)—i.e., a flesh-and-blood man. He was true God and true man. At the outset, John contradicts the heresy of the Gnostics (see Introduction: Gnosticism). *Word of life.* The one who is life and reveals life (see v. 2 and note). "Word" here speaks of revelation (see note on John 1:1).

1:2 *the life . . . that eternal life.* Christ. He is called "the life" because He is the living one who has life in Himself (see John 11:25; 14:6). He is also the source of life and sovereign over life (5:11). The letter begins and ends (5:20) with the theme of eternal life.

1:3 *fellowship with us.* Participation with us (vicariously) in our experience of hearing, seeing and touching the incarnate Christ (v. 1). Fellowship (Greek *koinonia*) is the spiritual union of the believer with Christ—as described in the figures of the vine and branches (John 15:1–5) and the body and the head (1 Cor 12:12; Col 1:18)—as well as communion with the Father and with fellow believers.

1:5 *heard of him.* From Christ. *light . . . darkness.* Light represents what is good, true and holy, while darkness represents what is evil and false (see John 3:19–21).

‡1:6–7 *walk in darkness . . . in the light.* Two life-styles—one characterized by wickedness and error, the other by holiness and truth.

1:6 *we.* John and his readers. *we have fellowship with him.* We are in living, spiritual union with God. *walk.* A metaphor for living. *truth.* See note on John 1:14.

1:7 *sin.* A key word in 1 John, occurring 27 times in the Greek.

1:9 *faithful and just.* Here the phrase is virtually a single concept (faithful-and-just). It indicates that God's response toward those who confess their sins will be in accordance with His nature and His gracious commitment to His people (see Ps 143:1; Zech 8:8). *faithful.* To His promise to forgive (see Jer 31:34; Mic 7:18–20; Heb 10:22–23). *to forgive us.* To provide the forgiveness that restores the communion with God that had been interrupted by sin (as requested in the Lord's prayer, Mat 6:12).

1:10 *we have not sinned.* Gnostics denied that their immoral actions were sinful.

2:1 *little children.* John, the aged apostle, often used this expression of endearment (vv. 12–13,28; 3:7,18; 4:4; 5:21; the term in 2:18 translates a different Greek word). *an advocate.* The Greek word refers to someone who speaks in court in behalf of a defendant (see note on John 14:16). *the righteous.* In God's court the defender must be, and is, sinless.

2:2 *propitiation for our sins.* Propitiation refers to turning away God's wrath (see also 4:10). God's holiness demands punishment for man's sin. God, therefore, out of love (4:10; John 3:16), sent His Son to make substitutionary atonement for the believer's sin. In this way the Father's wrath is propitiated (satisfied, appeased); His wrath against the Christian's sin has been turned away and directed toward Christ. See note on Rom 3:25. *for the sins of the whole world.* Forgiveness through Christ's atoning sacrifice is not limited to one particular group only; it has worldwide application (see John 1:29). It must, however, be received by faith (see John 3:16). Thus this verse does not teach universalism (that all people ultimately will be saved), but that God is an impartial God.

2:3 Forty-two times 1 John uses two Greek verbs normally translated "know." One of these verbs is related to the name of the Gnostics, the heretical sect that claimed to have a special knowledge (Greek *gnosis*) of God (see Introduction: Gnosticism). *keep his commandments.* Does not mean that only those who never disobey (1:8–9) know God, but simply refers to those whose lives are generally characterized by obedience.

‡2:5 *in him verily is the love of God perfected.* Means either that God's love for the believer is made complete when it moves the believer to acts of obedience (see 4:12), or that our love for God becomes complete when it expresses itself in acts of obedience (see 3:16–18). *in him.* Spiritual union with God (see John 17:21).

2:7–8 *new commandment.* See John 13:34–35. The Biblical

ment unto you, but an old commandment [b]which ye had from the beginning. The old commandment is the word which ye have heard from the beginning.

8 Again, [a]a new commandment I write unto you, which *thing* is true in him and in you: [b]because the darkness is past, and [c]the true light now shineth.

9 [a]He that saith *he* is in the light, and hateth his brother, is in darkness *even* until now.

10 [a]He that loveth his brother abideth in the light, and [b]there is none [1]occasion of stumbling in him.

11 But he that hateth his brother is in darkness, and walketh in darkness, and knoweth not whither he goeth, because that darkness hath blinded his eyes.

12 ¶ I write unto you, little children, because [a]*your* sins are forgiven you for his name's sake.

13 I write unto you, fathers, because ye have known him [a]that is from the beginning. I write unto you, young men, because you have overcome the wicked one. I write unto you, little children, because ye have known the Father.

14 I have written unto you, fathers, because ye have known him that is from the beginning. I have written unto you, young men, because [a]ye are strong, and the word of God abideth in you, and ye have overcome the wicked one.

15 [a]Love not the world, neither the *things* that are in the world. [b]If any *man* love the world, the love of the Father is not in him.

16 For all that is in the world, the lust of the flesh, [a]and the lust of the eyes, and the pride of life, is not of the Father, but is of the world.

17 And [a]the world passeth away, and the lust thereof: but he that doeth the will of God abideth for ever.

18 [a]Little children, [b]it is the last time: and as ye have heard that [c]antichrist shall come, [d]even now are there many antichrists; whereby we know [e]that it is the last time.

19 [a]They went out from us, but they were not of us; for [b]if they had been of us, they would *no doubt* have continued with us: but *they went out,* [c]that they might be made manifest that they were not all of us.

20 But [a]ye have an unction [b]from the Holy One, and [c]ye know all *things.*

21 I have not written unto you because ye know not the truth, but because ye know it, and that no lie is of the truth.

22 [a]Who is a liar but he that denieth that Jesus is the Christ? He is antichrist, that denieth the Father and the Son.

23 [a]Whosoever denieth the Son, the same hath not the Father: [*but*] [b]*he that acknowledgeth the Son hath the Father also.*

2:7 [b]2 John 5
2:8 [a]John 13:34 [b]Rom. 13:12 [c]John 1:9
2:9 [a]1 Cor. 13:2; 2 Pet. 1:9
2:10 [1]Gr. *scandal* [a]ch. 3:14 [b]2 Pet. 1:10
2:12 [a]Luke 24:47
2:13 [a]ch. 1:1
2:14 [a]Eph. 6:10
2:15 [a]Rom. 12:2 [b]Mat. 6:24
2:16 [a]Eccl. 5:11
2:17 [a]1 Cor. 7:31; 1 Pet. 1:24
2:18 [a]John 21:5 [b]Heb. 1:2 [c]2 Thes. 2:3 [d]Mat. 24:5; 2 John 7 [e]1 Tim. 4:1; 2 Tim. 3:1
2:19 [a]Deut. 13:13 [b]Mat. 24:24; John 6:37 [c]1 Cor. 11:19
2:20 [a]2 Cor. 1:21; Heb. 1:9 [b]Acts 3:14 [c]John 16:13
2:22 [a]2 John 7
2:23 [a]John 15:23; 2 John 9 [b]ch. 4:15

command to love was old (see Lev 19:18; also Mat 22:39–40). But its newness is seen in: (1) the new and dramatic illustration of divine love on the cross; (2) Christ's exposition of the OT law (see Mat 5), which seemed new to Christ's hearers; and (3) the standard given. The old standard, "thou shalt love thy neighbor as thyself" (Lev 19:18), has changed to "love one another as I have loved you" (John 13:34; 15:12).

‡2:7 *from the beginning.* The beginning of their Christian experience, when they first heard the gospel.

2:8 *true light.* Used in the NT only here and in John 1:9, this phrase refers to the gospel of Jesus Christ, who is the light of the world (John 8:12), and to its saving effects in the lives of believers.

2:9–10 *hateth . . . loveth.* In the Bible hatred and love as moral qualities are not primarily emotions, but attitudes expressed in actions (see 3:15–16).

2:9 *light . . . darkness.* See note on 1:5. *brother.* Fellow believer.

2:10 *stumbling.* Into sin.

2:12–14 *I write unto you . . . because.* By extended repetition in these verses, John assures his readers that, in spite of the rigorous tests contained in the letter, he is confident of their salvation. *little children . . . fathers . . . young men.* As elsewhere in this letter, "little children" probably refers to all John's readers (see note on v. 1), including fathers and young men. The terms "fathers" and "young men" may, however, describe two different levels of spiritual maturity. Some hold that all three terms refer to levels of spiritual maturity.

2:12 *his name's sake.* The name of Jesus (see 3:23; 5:13; see also note on Acts 4:12).

2:13–14 *him that is from the beginning.* Christ (see note on 1:1).

2:15 *the world.* Not the world of people (John 3:16) or the created world (John 17:24), but the world, or realm, of sin (v. 16; Jas 4:4), which is controlled by Satan and organized against God and righteousness (see note on John 1:9). *love of the Father.* Love for the Father.

2:18 *last time.* With other NT writers, John viewed the whole period beginning with Christ's first coming as the last days (see notes on Acts 2:17; 2 Tim 3:1; Heb 1:1; 1 Pet 1:20). They understood this to be the "last" of the days because neither former prophecy nor new revelation concerning the history of salvation indicated the coming of another era before the return of Christ. The word "last" in "last days," "last times" and "last hour" also expresses a sense of urgency and imminence. The Christian is to be alert, waiting for the return of Christ (Mat 25:1–13). *antichrist . . . many antichrists.* John assumed his readers knew that a great enemy of God and His people would arise before Christ's return. That person is called "antichrist" here, "that man of sin" (2 Thes 2:3; but see note there) and "the beast" (Rev 13:1–10). But prior to him, there will be many antichrists. These are characterized by the following: (1) They deny the incarnation (4:2; 2 John 7) and that Jesus is the divine Christ (v. 22); (2) they deny the Father (v. 22); (3) they do not have the Father (v. 23); (4) they are liars (v. 22) and deceivers (2 John 7); (5) they are many (v. 18); (6) in John's day they left the church because they had nothing in common with believers (v. 19). The antichrists referred to in John's letter were the early Gnostics. The "anti" in antichrist means "against" (cf. 2 Thes 2:4; Rev 13:6–7).

2:20 *unction.* Or "anointing," i.e. the Holy Spirit (see v. 27 and note; Acts 10:38). *Holy One.* Either Jesus Christ (Mark 1:24; John 6:69; Acts 2:27; 3:14; 22:14) or the Father (2 Ki 19:22; Job 6:10).

2:22 *Jesus is the Christ.* The man Jesus is the divine Christ (see the parallel confession in 5:5; see also Introduction: Gnosticism and note on 5:6).

2:23 See 2 John 9 for the same thought.

24 Let *that* therefore abide in you, [a]which ye have heard from the beginning. If *that* which ye have heard from the beginning shall remain in you, [b]ye also shall continue in the Son, and in the Father.

25 [a]And this is the promise that he hath promised us, *even* eternal life.

26 These *things* have I written unto you [a]concerning them that seduce you.

27 But [a]the anointing which ye have received of him abideth in you, and [b]ye need not that any *man* teach you: but as the same anointing [c]teacheth you of all *things,* and is truth, and is no lie, and even as it hath taught you, ye shall abide in [1]him.

28 And now, little children, abide in him; that, [a]when he shall appear, we may have confidence, [b]and not be ashamed before him at his coming.

29 [a]If ye know that he is righteous, [1]ye know that [b]every one which doeth righteousness is born of him.

Obedience and love

3 Behold, what manner of love the Father hath bestowed upon us, that [a]we should be called the sons of God: therefore the world knoweth us not, [b]because it knew him not.

2 Beloved, [a]now are we the sons of God, and [b]it doth not yet appear what we shall be: but we know that, when he shall appear, [c]we shall be like him; for [d]we shall see him as he is.

3 [a]And every *man* that hath this hope in him purifieth himself, even as he is pure.

4 Whosoever committeth sin transgresseth also the law: for [a]sin is the transgression of the law.

5 And ye know [a]that he was manifested [b]to take away our sins; and [c]in him is no sin.

6 Whosoever abideth in him sinneth not: [a]whosoever sinneth hath not seen him, neither known him.

7 Little children, [a]let no *man* deceive you: [b]he that doeth righteousness is righteous, even as he is righteous.

8 [a]He that committeth sin is of the devil; for the devil sinneth from the beginning. For this purpose the Son of God was manifested, [b]that he might destroy the works of the devil.

9 [a]Whosoever is born of God doth not commit sin; for [b]his seed remaineth in him: and he cannot sin, because he is born of God.

10 In this the children of God are manifest, and the children of the devil: [a]whosoever doeth not righteousness is not of God, [b]neither he that loveth not his brother.

Love in action

11 For [a]this is the [1]message that ye heard from the beginning, [b]that we should love one another.

12 Not as [a]Cain, *who* was of *that* wicked one, and slew his brother. And wherefore slew he him? Because his own works were evil, and his brother's righteous.

13 Marvel not, my brethren, if [a]the world hate you.

14 [a]We know that we have passed from death unto life, because we love the brethren. [b]He that loveth not *his* brother abideth in death.

15 [a]Whosoever hateth his brother is a murderer: and ye know that [b]no murderer hath eternal life abiding in him.

16 [a]Hereby perceive we the love *of God,* because he laid down his life for us: and we ought to lay down *our* lives for the brethren.

17 But [a]whoso hath *this* world's good, and

2:24 [a]2 John 6 [b]John 14:23
2:25 [a]John 17:3
2:26 [a]2 John 7
2:27 [1]Or, *it* [a]ver. 20 [b]ver. 21 [c]John 14:26
2:28 [a]ch. 3:2 [b]ch. 4:17
2:29 [1]Or, *know ye* [a]Acts 22:14 [b]ch. 3:7,10
3:1 [a]John 1:12 [b]John 16:3
3:2 [a]Is. 56:5; Rom. 8:15 [b]Rom 8:18; 2 Cor. 4:17 [c]Rom. 8:29; 2 Pet. 1:4 [d]Ps. 16:11; Mat. 5:8
3:3 [a]ch. 4:17
3:4 [a]Rom. 4:15
3:5 [a]ch. 1:2 [b]Is. 53:5,6 [c]2 Cor. 5:21; Heb. 4:15; 1 Pet. 2:22
3:6 [a]ch. 2:4
3:7 [a]ch. 2:26 [b]Rom. 2:13
3:8 [a]Mat. 13:38; John 8:44 [b]Luke 10:18; John 16:11
3:9 [a]ch. 5:18 [b]1 Pet. 1:23
3:10 [a]ch. 2:29 [b]ch. 4:8
3:11 [1]Or, *commandment* [a]ch. 1:5 [b]John 13:34; 2 John 5
3:12 [a]Gen. 4:4,8; Heb. 11:4
3:13 [a]John 17:14
3:14 [a]ch. 2:10 [b]ch. 2:9,11
3:15 [a]Mat. 5:21 [b]Gal. 5:21
3:16 [a]John 3:16
3:17 [a]Deut. 15:7; Luke 3:11

2:26 One of the statements of purpose for the letter (see Introduction: Occasion and Purpose).

‡2:27 *ye need not that any man teach you.* Since the Bible constantly advocates teaching (Mat 28:20; 1 Cor 12:28; Eph 4:11; Col 3:16; 1 Tim 4:11; 2 Tim 2:2,24), John is not ruling out human teachers. At the time when he wrote, however, Gnostic teachers were insisting that the teaching of the apostles was to be supplemented with the "higher knowledge" that they (the Gnostics) claimed to possess. John's response in vv. 20-27 is that true believers are indwelt by the Holy Spirit and that they have an anointing by the Holy Spirit, who shows them that Jesus Christ is God come in the flesh (cf. 4:2,15; 5:1,10). The person of Jesus Christ is the topic discussed between vv. 20 and 27. As general (natural) revelation reveals to every human that a God exists who is all powerful (Rom 1:18-20) and good (Acts 14:17), so the Holy Spirit reveals to all saints the nature of Jesus Christ (cf. 4:13-15; 5:9-10).

2:28 *abide in him.* See vv. 24,27. *confidence.* See 3:21; 4:17; 5:14.

2:29 *he . . . him.* God the Father. *doeth righteousness.* Members of God's family are marked by holy living.

3:1 *sons of God.* See note on John 1:12.

3:2 *he . . . him.* Christ.

3:3 *hope.* Not a mere wish, but unshakable confidence concerning the future (see note on Rom 5:2). *him.* Christ. *purifieth himself.* By turning from sin.

3:6 *sinneth not.* John is not asserting sinless perfection (see 1:8–10; 2:1), but explaining that the believer's life is characterized not by sin but by doing what is right.

3:8 *devil.* In this short letter John says much about the devil: 1. He is called "the devil" (here) and "that wicked one" (v. 12; 2:13–14; 5:18–19). 2. He "sinneth from the beginning" (here), i.e., from the time he first rebelled against God, before the fall of Adam and Eve (John 8:44). 3. He is the instigator of human sin, and those who continue to sin belong to him (vv. 8,12) and are his children (v. 10). 4. He is in the world (4:3) and has "the whole world" of unbelievers under his control (5:19). 5. But he cannot lay hold of the believer to harm him (5:18). 6. On the contrary, the Christian will overcome him (2:13–14; 4:4), and Christ will destroy his work.

3:9 *his seed.* The picture is of human reproduction, in which the sperm (the Greek for "seed" is *sperma*) bears the life principle and transfers the paternal characteristics. *cannot sin.* Not a complete cessation of sin, but a life that is not characterized by sin.

3:11 *from the beginning.* See note on 2:7.

3:12 *Cain.* See Heb 11:4.

3:14 *brethren.* Fellow believers.

3:15 *hateth.* See note on 2:9–10.

3:17–18 See Jas 2:14–17.

3:17 *love of God.* God's kind of love, which He pours out in the believer's heart (Rom 5:5) and which in turn enables the Chris-

seeth his brother hath need, and shutteth up
his bowels *of compassion* from him, [b]how
dwelleth the love of God in him?

The test of belief

18 My little children, [a]let us not love in
word, neither in tongue; but in deed and in
truth.
19 And hereby we know [a]that we are of the
truth, and shall [1]assure our hearts before him.
20 [a]For if *our* heart condemn us, God is
greater than our heart, and knoweth all *things.*
21 [a]Beloved, if our heart condemn us not,
[b]*then* have we confidence towards God.
22 And [a]whatsoever we ask, we receive of
him, because we keep his commandments,
[b]and do those *things* that are pleasing in his
sight.
23 [a]And this is his commandment, That
we should believe on the name of his Son
Jesus Christ, [b]and love one another, [c]as he
gave us commandment.
24 And [a]he that keepeth his commandments [b]dwelleth in him, and he in him. And
[c]hereby we know that he abideth in us, by the
Spirit which he hath given us.

4 Beloved, [a]believe not every spirit, but
[b]try the spirits whether they are of God:
because [c]many false prophets are gone out
into the world.
2 Hereby know ye the Spirit of God: [a]Every
spirit that confesseth that Jesus Christ is come
in the flesh is of God:
3 And [a]every spirit that confesseth not that
Jesus Christ is come in the flesh is not of God:
and this is *that spirit* of antichrist, whereof you
have heard that it should come; and [b]*even*
now already is it in the world.
4 [a]Ye are of God, little children, and have

3:17 [b]ch. 4:20
3:18 [a]Ezek. 33:31; Rom. 12:9; Eph. 4:15
3:19 [1]Gr. *persuade* [a]John 18:37
3:20 [a]1 Cor. 4:4
3:21 [a]Job 22:26 [b]Heb. 10:22
3:22 [a]Ps. 34:15; Prov. 15:29; Jer. 29:12; Mat. 7:8 [b]John 8:29
3:23 [a]John 6:29 [b]Mat. 22:39; John 13:34; Eph. 5:2 [c]ch. 2:8,10
3:24 [a]John 14:23 [b]John 17:21 [c]Rom. 8:9
4:1 [a]Jer. 29:8; Mat. 24:4 [b]1 Cor. 14:29; 1 Thes. 5:21; Rev. 2:2 [c]Mat. 24:5; Acts 20:30; 1 Tim. 4:1; 2 Pet. 2:1
4:2 [a]1 Cor. 12:3
4:3 [a]2 John 7 [b]2 Thes. 2:7
4:4 [a]ch. 5:4 [b]John 12:31; Eph. 2:2
4:5 [a]John 3:31 [b]John 15:19
4:6 [a]John 8:47 [b]Is. 8:20
4:7 [a]ch. 3:10,11
4:8 [a]ch. 2:4 [b]ver. 16
4:9 [a]John 3:16 [b]ch. 5:11
4:10 [a]John 15:16; Rom. 5:8; Tit. 3:4 [b]ch. 2:2
4:11 [a]Mat. 18:33; ch. 3:16
4:12 [a]John 1:18; 1 Tim. 6:16 [b]ch. 2:5
4:13 [a]John 14:20
4:14 [a]John 1:14 [b]John 3:17
4:15 [a]Rom. 10:9
4:16 [a]ver. 8 [b]ch. 3:24

overcome them: because greater is he that is
in you, than [b]he that is in the world.
5 [a]They are of the world, therefore speak
they of the world, and [b]the world heareth them.
6 We are of God: [a]he that knoweth God
heareth us; *he* that is not of God heareth not
us. Hereby know we [b]the spirit of truth, and
the spirit of error.

The source of love

7 [a]Beloved, let us love one another: for
love is of God; and every one that loveth is
born of God, and knoweth God.
8 He that loveth not, [a]knoweth not God;
for [b]God is love.
9 [a]In this was manifested the love of God
towards us, because that God sent his only begotten Son into the world, [b]that we might live
through him.
10 Herein is love, [a]not that we loved God,
but that he loved us, and sent his Son [b]*to be*
the propitiation for our sins.
11 Beloved, [a]if God so loved us, we ought
also to love one another.
12 [a]No *man* hath seen God at any time. If
we love one another, God dwelleth in us, and
[b]his love is perfected in us.
13 [a]Hereby know we that we dwell in him,
and he in us, because he hath given us of his
Spirit.
14 ¶ And [a]we have seen and do testify that
[b]the Father sent the Son *to be* the Saviour of
the world.
15 [a]Whosoever shall confess that Jesus is
the Son of God, God dwelleth in him, and he
in God.
16 And we have known and believed the
love that God hath to us. [a]God is love; and [b]he
that dwelleth in love dwelleth in God, and
God in him.

tian to love fellow believers. Or it may speak of the believer's love for God.

3:20 *God is greater than our heart.* An oversensitive conscience can be quieted by the knowledge that God Himself has declared active love to be an evidence of salvation. He knows the hearts of all—whether, in spite of shortcomings, they have been born of Him.

3:23 This command has two parts: (1) Believe in Christ (see John 6:29), and (2) love each other (see John 13:34–35). The first part is developed in 4:1–6 and the second part in 4:7–12.

‡4:1 *spirit.* A person moved by a spirit, whether by the Holy Spirit or an evil one. *try the spirits.* Cf. 1 Thes 5:21. *false prophets.* A true prophet speaks from God, being "moved by the Holy Ghost" (2 Pet 1:21). False prophets, such as the Gnostics of John's day, speak under the influence of spirits alienated from God. Christ warned against false prophets (Mat 7:15; 24:11), as did Paul (1 Tim 4:1) and Peter (2 Pet 2:1).

4:2 *confesseth.* Not only knows intellectually—for demons know, and shudder (Jas 2:19; cf. Mark 1:24)—but also confesses publicly. *Jesus Christ is come in the flesh.* See note on 1:1. Thus John excludes the Gnostics, especially the Cerinthians, who taught that the divine Christ came upon the human Jesus at his baptism and then left him at the cross, so that it was only the man Jesus who died (see Introduction: Gnosticism).

4:3 *confesseth not . . . Jesus Christ.* The incarnate Jesus Christ of 1:2 (see note on 2:18).

4:4 *of God.* An abbreviated form of the expression "born of God" (2:29; 3:9–10). *them.* The false prophets (v. 1), who were inspired by the spirit of the antichrist (v. 3). *he that is in the world.* The devil (John 12:31; 16:11). In v. 3 "world" means the inhabited earth; in vv. 4–5 it means the community, or system, of those not born of God—including the antichrists (see note on John 1:9).

4:6 *spirit of truth.* Cf. 5:6; see note on John 14:17.

4:7–5:3 The word "love" in its various forms is used 43 times in the letter, 32 times in this short section.

4:8 *knoweth not God.* Only those who are to some degree like Him truly know Him. *God is love.* In His essential nature and in all His actions, God is loving. John similarly affirms that God is spirit (John 4:24) and light (1:5), as well as holy, powerful, faithful, true and just.

4:9 *only begotten Son.* See note on John 1:18.

4:10 *propitiation for our sins.* See note on 2:2.

4:12 *No man hath seen God at any time.* See note on John 1:18. Since our love has its source in God's love, His love reaches full expression (is made complete) when we love fellow Christians. Thus the God whom "no one has seen" is seen in those who love, because God lives in them.

4:16 *God is love.* See note on v. 8.

17 Herein is [1]our love made perfect, that [a]we may have boldness in the day of judgment: [b]because as he is, so are we in this world.

18 There is no fear in love; but perfect love casteth out fear: because fear hath torment. He that feareth [a]is not made perfect in love.

19 We love him, because he first loved us.

20 [a]If a man say, I love God, and hateth his brother, he is a liar: for he that loveth not his brother whom he hath seen, how can he love God [b]whom he hath not seen?

21 And [a]this commandment have we from him, That he who loveth God love his brother also.

Faith through the Son

5 Whosoever [a]believeth that [b]Jesus is the Christ is [c]born of God: [d]and every one that loveth him that begat loveth him also that is begotten of him.

2 By this we know that we love the children of God, when we love God, and keep his commandments.

3 [a]For this is the love of God, that we keep his commandments: and [b]his commandments are not grievous.

4 For [a]whatsoever is born of God overcometh the world: and this is the victory that overcometh the world, *even* our faith.

5 Who is he that overcometh the world, but [a]he that believeth that Jesus is the Son of God?

6 This is he that came [a]by water and blood, *even* Jesus Christ; not by water only, but by water and blood. [b]And it is the Spirit that beareth witness, because the Spirit is truth.

7 For there are three that bear record in heaven, the Father, [a]the Word, and the Holy Ghost: [b]and these three are one.

8 And there are three that bear witness in earth, the Spirit, and the water, and the blood: and *these* three agree in one.

9 If we receive [a]the witness of men, the witness of God is greater: [b]for this is the witness of God which he hath testified of his Son.

10 He that believeth on the Son of God [a]hath the witness in himself: he that believeth not God [b]hath made him a liar; because he believeth not the record that God gave of his Son.

11 [a]And this is the record, that God hath given to us eternal life, and [b]this life is in his Son.

12 [a]He that hath the Son hath life; *and* he that hath not the Son of God hath not life.

The certainties of faith

13 ¶ [a]These *things* have I written unto you that believe on the name of the Son of God; [b]that ye may know that ye have eternal life, and that ye may believe on the name of the Son of God.

14 And this is the confidence that we have [1]in him, that, [a]if we ask any *thing* according to his will, he heareth us:

15 And if we know that he hear us, whatsoever we ask, we know that we have the petitions that we desired of him.

16 If any *man* see his brother sin a sin

4:17 [1] Gr. *love with us* [a] Jas. 2:13 [b] ch. 3:3
4:18 [a] ver. 12
4:20 [a] ch. 2:4 [b] ver. 12
4:21 [a] Mat. 22:37; John 13:34
5:1 [a] John 1:12 [b] ch. 2:22,23 [c] John 1:13 [d] John 15:23
5:3 [a] John 14:15; 2 John 6 [b] Mic. 6:8
5:4 [a] John 16:33
5:5 [a] 1 Cor. 15:57
5:6 [a] John 19:34 [b] John 14:17; 1 Tim. 3:16
5:7 [a] John 1:1; Rev. 19:13 [b] John 10:30
5:9 [a] John 8:17 [b] Mat. 3:16
5:10 [a] Rom. 8:16 [b] John 3:33
5:11 [a] ch. 2:25 [b] ch. 4:9
5:12 [a] John 3:36
5:13 [a] John 20:31 [b] ch. 1:1,2
5:14 [1] Or, *concerning him* [a] ch. 3:22

‡4:17 *so are we.* Like Christ. The fact that we are like Christ in love is a sign that God, who is love, lives in us; therefore we may have confidence on the day of judgment that we are saved.

4:18 *no fear in love.* There is no fear of God's judgment because genuine love confirms salvation.

4:19 All love comes ultimately from God; genuine love is never self-generated by His creatures.

4:21 *this commandment.* See John 13:34.

5:1 *Whosoever believeth that Jesus is the Christ is born of God.* Faith in Jesus as the Christ is a sign of being born again, just as love is (4:7). *the Christ.* See note on 2:22. *loveth him that begat . . . him also . . . begotten.* John wrote at a time when members of a family were closely associated as a unit under the headship of the father. He could therefore use the family as an illustration to show that anyone who loves God the Father will naturally love God's children.

5:3 *his commandments are not grievous.* Not because the commands themselves are light or easy to obey but, as John explains in v. 4, because of the new birth. The one born of God by faith is enabled by the Holy Spirit to obey.

‡5:4 *overcometh.* To overcome the world is to gain victory over its sinful pattern of life, which is another way of describing obedience to God (v. 3). Such obedience is not impossible for the believer because he has been born again and the Holy Spirit dwells within him and gives him strength. John speaks of two aspects of victory: (1) the initial victory of turning in faith from the world to God (first "overcometh"); (2) the continuing day-by-day victory of Christian living (second "overcometh"). *world.* See note on 2:15.

5:5 *Son of God.* For parallel confessions see 2:22; 4:2; 5:1.

5:6 Water symbolizes Jesus' baptism, and blood symbolizes His death. These are mentioned because Jesus' ministry began at His baptism and ended at His death. John is reacting to the heretics of his day (see Introduction: Gnosticism) who said that Jesus was born only a man and remained so until His baptism. At that time, they maintained, the Christ (the Son of God) descended on the human Jesus, but left him before his suffering on the cross—so that it was only the man Jesus who died. Throughout this letter John has been insisting that Jesus Christ is God as well as man (1:1–4; 4:2; 5:5). He now asserts that it was this God-man Jesus Christ who came into our world, was baptized and died. Jesus was the Son of God not only at His baptism but also at His death (v. 6b). This truth is extremely important, because, if Jesus died only as a man, His sacrificial atonement (2:2; 4:10) would not have been sufficient to take away the guilt of man's sin. *the Spirit that beareth witness.* The Holy Spirit testifies that Jesus is the Son of God in two ways: (1) The Spirit descended on Jesus at His baptism (John 1:32–34), and (2) He continues to confirm in the hearts of believers the apostolic testimony that Jesus' baptism and death verify that He is the Christ, the Son of God (2:27; 1 Cor 12:3).

5:7-8 *three.* The OT law required "two . . . three witnesses" (Deut 17:6; 19:15; see 1 Tim 5:19).

5:11 *hath given to us eternal life.* As a present possession (see notes on John 3:15,36).

5:13 Another statement of the letter's purpose (see 2:26). See Introduction: Occasion and Purpose.

5:14 *if we ask any thing according to His will.* For another condition for prayer see 3:21–22.

‡5:16 Verses 16–17 illustrate the kind of petition we can be

which is not unto death, he shall ask, and [a]he
shall give him life for them that sin not unto
death. [b]There is a sin unto death: [c]I do not say
that he shall pray for it.

17 [a]All unrighteousness is sin: and there is
a sin not unto death.

18 We know that [a]whosoever is born of
God sinneth not; but he that is begotten of
God [b]keepeth himself, and *that* wicked one
toucheth him not.

19 *And* we know that we are of God, and
[a]the whole world lieth in wickedness.

20 And we know that the Son of God is
come, and [a]hath given us an understanding,
[b]that we may know him *that is* true, and we
are in him *that is* true, *even* in his Son Jesus
Christ. [c]This is the true God, [d]and eternal life.

21 Little children, [a]keep yourselves from
idols. Amen.

5:16 [a]Job 42:8; Jas. 5:14 [b]Mat. 12:31; Mark 3:29; Heb. 6:4,6 [c]Jer. 7:16; John 17:9
5:17 [a]ch. 3:4
5:18 [a]1 Pet. 1:23 [b]Jas. 1:27
5:19 [a]Gal. 1:4
5:20 [a]Luke 24:45 [b]John 17:3 [c]Is. 9:6; Acts 20:28; Tit. 2:13 [d]ver. 11,12
5:21 [a]1 Cor. 10:14

sure God will answer (see vv. 14–15). *sin unto death.* In the context of this letter directed against Gnostic teaching, which denied the incarnation and threw off all moral restraints, it is probable that the "sin unto death" refers to the Gnostics' adamant and persistent denial of the truth and to their shameless immorality. This kind of unrepentant sin leads to spiritual death. Another view is that this is sin that results in physical death. It is held that, because a believer continues to sin, God in judgment takes his life (cf. 1 Cor 11:30). In either case, "sin which is not unto death" is of a less serious nature.

5:18–20 *We know.* The letter ends with three striking statements, affirming the truths that "we know" and summarizing some of the letter's major themes.

5:20 *him that is true.* God the Father. *This is the true God.* Could refer to either God the Father or God the Son. *eternal life.* The letter began with this theme (1:1–2) and now ends with it.

‡5:21 *idols.* Keep yourself from false teachings and hence from false gods, i.e., idols.

The Second Epistle of John

INTRODUCTION

Author

The author is John the apostle. Obvious similarities to 1 John and the Gospel of John suggest that the same person wrote all three books. Compare the following:

2 John 5	1 John 2:7	John 13:34–35
2 John 6	1 John 5:3	John 14:23
2 John 7	1 John 4:2–3	
2 John 12	1 John 1:4	John 15:11; 16:24

See Introductions to 1 John and the Gospel of John: Author.

Date

The letter was probably written about the same time as 1 John (A.D. 85–95), as the above comparisons suggest (see Introduction to 1 John: Date).

Occasion and Purpose

During the first two centuries the gospel was taken from place to place by traveling evangelists and teachers. Believers customarily took these missionaries into their homes and gave them provisions for their journey when they left. Since Gnostic teachers also relied on this practice (see note on 3 John 5), 2 John was written to urge discernment in supporting traveling teachers; otherwise, someone might unintentionally contribute to the propagation of heresy rather than truth.

Outline

I. Salutation (1–3)
II. Commendation (4)
III. Exhortation and Warning (5–11)
IV. Conclusion (12–13)

1 ¶ The elder unto the elect lady and her
children, [a]whom I love in the truth; and not I
only, but also all they that have known [b]the
truth;
2 For the truth's sake, which dwelleth in
us, and shall be with us for ever.
3 [a]Grace [1]be with you, mercy, *and* peace,
from God the Father, and from the Lord Jesus
Christ, the Son of the Father, in truth and love.

Counsel and warnings

4 ¶ I rejoiced greatly that I found of thy children
[a]walking in truth, as we have received a
commandment from the Father.
5 And now I beseech thee, lady, [a]not as
though I wrote a new commandment unto
thee, but *that* which we had from the beginning,
[b]that we love one another.
6 And [a]this is love, that we walk after his
commandments. This is the commandment,
That, as [b]ye have heard from the beginning, ye
should walk in it.

1 [a]3 John 1 [b]Col. 1:5
3 [1][Gr. *shall be*] [a]1 Tim. 1:2
4 [a]3 John 3
5 [a]1 John 3:11 [b]John 13:34
6 [a]1 John 2:5 [b]1 John 2:24
7 [a]1 John 4:1 [b]1 John 4:2 [c]1 John 2:22
8 [1]Or, *gained.* Some copies read, *which ye have gained, but* that *ye receive, etc.* [a]Mark 13:9 [b]Gal. 3:4
9 [a]1 John 2:23
10 [a]Rom. 16:17
12 [1]Gr. *mouth to mouth* [2][Or, *your*] [a]3 John 13 [b]John 17:13
13 [a]1 Pet. 5:13

7 For [a]many deceivers are entered into the
world, [b]who confess not that Jesus Christ is
come in the flesh. [c]This is a deceiver and an
antichrist.
8 [a]Look to yourselves, [b]that we lose not
those things which we have [1]wrought, but
that we receive a full reward.
9 [a]Whosoever transgresseth, and abideth
not in the doctrine of Christ, hath not God. He
that abideth in the doctrine of Christ, he hath
both the Father and the Son.
10 If there come any unto you, and bring
not this doctrine, receive him not into *your*
house, [a]neither bid him God speed:
11 For he that biddeth him God speed is
partaker of his evil deeds.
12 ¶ [a]Having many *things* to write unto
you, I would not *write* with paper and ink: but
I trust to come unto you, and speak [1]face to
face, [b]that [2]our joy may be full.
13 [a]The children of thy elect sister greet
thee. Amen.

---

1 *elder.* See note on 1 Tim 3:1. In his later years, John functioned as an elder, perhaps of the Ephesian church. The apostle Peter held a similar position (1 Pet 5:1). *elect lady.* Either an unknown Christian woman in the province of Asia or a figurative designation of a local church there. *her children.* Children of that Christian lady or members of that local church. *truth.* See note on John 1:14.

3 *Grace . . . peace.* See notes on Gal 1:3; Eph 1:2. *mercy.* See note on Rom 9:23.

‡5 *new commandment.* See note on 1 John 2:7–8.

6 *from the beginning.* See note on 1 John 2:7.

7–11 This section deals with the basic Gnostic heresy attacked in 1 John, namely, that the Son of God did not become flesh (John 1:14), but that He temporarily came upon the man Jesus between his baptism and crucifixion (see Introduction to 1 John: Gnosticism).

7 *Jesus Christ is come in the flesh.* See 1 John 4:2–3 and note. *antichrist.* See note on 1 John 2:18.

8 *have wrought . . . full reward.* Work faithfully accomplished on earth brings future reward (see Mark 9:41; 10:29–30; Luke 19:16–19; Heb 11:26).

‡9 *transgresseth.* In the sense of going too far. This is a reference to the Gnostics, who believed that they had advanced beyond the teaching of the apostles. *doctrine of Christ.* The similarity of this letter to 1 John, the nature of the heresy combated, and the immediate context suggest that John is not referring to teaching given by Christ, but to true teaching about Christ as the incarnate God-man.

10 *receive him not into your house.* A reference to the housing and feeding of traveling teachers (see Introduction: Occasion and Purpose). The instruction does not prohibit greeting or even inviting a person into one's home for conversation. John was warning against providing food and shelter, since this would be an investment in the "evil deeds" of false teachers and would give public approval (see v. 11).

‡12 *paper and ink.* Paper was made from papyrus reeds, which were readily available and cheap. The ink (the Greek for this word comes from a word that means "black") was made by mixing carbon, water and gum or oil. *that our joy may be full.* See 1 John 1:4.

13 *elect sister.* May be taken literally to designate another Christian woman or figuratively to refer to another local church (see note on v. 1).

The Third Epistle of John

INTRODUCTION

Author

The author is John the apostle. In the first verses of both 2 John and 3 John the author identifies himself as "the elder." Note other similarities: "love in the truth" (v. 1 of both letters), "walk in truth" (v. 4 of both letters) and the similar conclusions. See Introductions to 1 John and the Gospel of John: Author.

Date

The letter was probably written about the same time as 1 and 2 John (A.D. 85–95). See Introduction to 1 John: Date.

Occasion and Purpose

See Introduction to 2 John: Occasion and Purpose. Itinerant teachers sent out by John were rejected in one of the churches in the province of Asia by a dictatorial leader, Diotrephes, who even excommunicated members who showed hospitality to John's messengers. John wrote this letter to commend Gaius for supporting the teachers and, indirectly, to warn Diotrephes.

Outline

I. Salutation (1–2)
II. Commendation of Gaius (3–8)
III. Condemnation of Diotrephes (9–10)
IV. Exhortation to Gaius (11)
V. Example of Demetrius (12)
VI. Conclusion (13–14)

Encouragement and reproof

1 ¶ The elder unto the wellbeloved Gaius,
[a]whom I love [1]in the truth.

2 Beloved, I [1]wish above all *things* that
thou mayest prosper and be in health, even as
thy soul prospereth.

3 For I rejoiced greatly, when *the* brethren
came and testified of the truth *that is* in thee,
even as [a]thou walkest in the truth.

4 I have no greater joy than to hear that
[a]my children walk in truth.

5 Beloved, thou doest faithfully whatsoever
thou doest to the brethren, and to strangers;

6 Which have borne witness of thy charity
before the church: whom if thou bring forward on their journey [1]after a godly sort, thou
shalt do well:

7 Because that for his name's sake they
went forth, [a]taking nothing of the Gentiles.

8 We therefore ought to receive such, that
we might be fellowhelpers to the truth.

9 ¶ I wrote unto the church: but Diotrephes, who loveth to have the preeminence
among them, receiveth us not.

10 Wherefore, if I come, I will remember
his deeds which he doeth, prating against us
with malicious words: and not content therewith, neither doth he himself receive the
brethren, and forbiddeth them that would,
and casteth *them* out of the church.

11 Beloved, [a]follow not *that which is* evil,
but *that which is* good. [b]He that doeth good is
of God: but he that doeth evil hath not seen
God.

12 Demetrius [a]hath good report of all *men*,
and of the truth itself: yea, and we also bear
record; [b]and ye know that our record is true.

13 ¶ [a]I had many *things* to write, but I will
not with ink and pen write unto thee:

14 But I trust *I* shall shortly see thee, and
we shall speak [1]face to face. Peace *be* to thee.
Our friends salute thee. Greet the friends by
name.

1 [1]Or, *truly* [a]2 John 1
2 [1]Or, *pray*
3 [a]2 John 4
4 [a]1 Cor. 4:15; Philem. 10
6 [1][Gr. *worthy of God*]
7 [a]1 Cor. 9:12,15
11 [a]Ps. 37:27; Is. 1:16,17; 1 Pet. 3:11 [b]1 John 2:29; 3:6,9
12 [a]1 Tim. 3:7 [b]John 21:24
13 [a]2 John 12
14 [1]Gr. *mouth to mouth*

‡1 *The elder.* See note on 2 John 1. *wellbeloved.* Same Greek word as for "beloved." A favorite term of John (used nine times in two letters: 1 John 3:2,21; 4:1,7,11; 3 John 1,2,5,11). *Gaius.* A Christian in one of the churches of the province of Asia. Gaius was a common Roman name. *truth.* See note on John 1:14.

4 *my children.* Perhaps John's converts, or believers currently under his spiritual guidance.

5 *doest to the brethren.* The early church provided hospitality and support for missionaries. See Introduction to 2 John: Occasion and Purpose; see also note on 2 John 10.

7 *name.* See note on Acts 4:12. Today Orthodox Jews often address God by the title *Ha-Shem* ("The Name").

9 *I wrote.* There may have been a previous letter of the apostle that is now lost. *church.* Some identify this church with the chosen lady of 2 John 1. *Diotrephes.* A church leader who was exercising dictatorial power in the church. He must have had considerable influence since he was able to exclude people from the church fellowship (v. 10).

11 *doeth good.* The continual practice of good, not merely doing occasional good deeds.

13–14 See 2 John 12–13 for a similar conclusion.

14 *Peace be to thee.* Not a prayer or wish but a benedictory pronouncement (see notes on John 14:27; 20:19; Gal 1:3; Eph 1:2).

The General Epistle of Jude

INTRODUCTION

Author

The author identifies himself as Jude (v. 1), which is another form of the Hebrew name Judah (Greek "Judas"), a common name among the Jews. Of those so named in the NT, the ones most likely to be author of this letter are: (1) Judas the apostle (Luke 6:16; Acts 1:13)—not Judas Iscariot—and (2) Judas the brother of the Lord (Mat 13:55; Mark 6:3). The latter is more likely. For example, the author does not claim to be an apostle and even seems to separate himself from the apostles (see v. 17). Furthermore, he describes himself as a "brother of James" (v. 1). Ordinarily a person in Jude's day would describe himself as someone's son rather than as someone's brother. The reason for the exception here may have been James's prominence in the church at Jerusalem (see Introduction to James: Author).

Although neither Jude nor James describes himself as a brother of the Lord, others did not hesitate to speak of them in this way (see Mat 13:55; John 7:3–10; Acts 1:14; 1 Cor 9:5; Gal 1:19). Apparently they themselves did not ask to be heard because of the special privilege they had as members of the household of Joseph and Mary.

Possible references to the letter of Jude or quotations from it are found at a very early date: e.g., in Clement of Rome (c. A.D. 96). Clement of Alexandria (155–215), Tertullian (150–222) and Origen (185–253) accepted it; it was included in the Muratorian Canon (c. 170) and was accepted by Athanasius (298–373) and by the Council of Carthage (397). Eusebius (265–340) listed the letter among the questioned books, though he recognized that many considered it as from Jude.

According to Jerome and Didymus, some did not accept the letter as canonical because of its use of uninspired literature (see notes on vv. 9,14). But sound judgment has recognized that an author, writing under inspiration, may legitimately make use of uninspired literature—whether for illustrative purposes or for appropriation of historically reliable or otherwise acceptable material—and such use does not necessarily endorse that literature as inspired (cf. Acts 17:28 and note). Under the influence of the Spirit, the church came to the conviction that the authority of God stands behind the letter of Jude. The fact that the letter was questioned and tested but nonetheless was finally accepted by the churches indicates the strength of its claims to authenticity.

Date

There is nothing in the letter that requires a date beyond the lifetime of Jude the brother of the Lord. The error the author is combating, like that in 2 Peter, is not the heretical teaching of the second century, but that which could and did develop at an early date (cf. Acts 20:29–30; Rom 6:1; 1 Cor 5:1–11; 2 Cor 12:21; Gal 5:13; Eph 5:3–17; 1 Thes 4:6). (See also Introduction to 2 Peter: Date.) There is, moreover, nothing in the letter that requires a date after the time of the apostles, as some have argued. It may even be that Jude's readers had heard some of the apostles speak (see vv. 17–18). Likewise, the use of the word "faith" in the objective sense of the body of truth believed (v. 3) does not require a late dating of the letter. It was used in such a sense as early as Gal 1:23.

The question of the relationship between Jude and 2 Peter has a bearing on the date of Jude. If 2 Peter makes use of Jude—a commonly accepted view (see Introduction to 2 Peter: 2 Peter and Jude)—then Jude is to be dated prior to 2 Peter, probably c. A.D. 65. Otherwise, a date as late as c. 80 would be possible.

Recipients

The description of those to whom Jude addressed his letter is very general (see v. 1). It could apply to Jewish Christians, Gentile Christians, or both. Their location is not indicated. It should not be assumed that, since 2 Pet 2 and Jude 4–18 appear to describe similar situations, they were both written to the same people. The kind of heresy depicted in these two passages was widespread (see Date).

Occasion and Purpose

Although Jude was very eager to write to his readers about salvation, he felt that he must instead warn them about certain immoral men circulating among them who were perverting the grace of God (v. 4). Apparently these false teachers were trying to convince believers that being saved by grace gave them license to sin since their sins would no longer be held against them. Jude thought it imperative that his readers be on guard against such men and be prepared to oppose their perverted teaching with the truth about God's saving grace.

It has generally been assumed that these false teachers were Gnostics. Although this identification is no doubt correct, they must have been forerunners of fully developed, second-century Gnosticism (see Introduction to 2 Peter: Date).

Outline

- I. Salutation (1–2)
- II. Occasion for the Letter (3–4)
  - A. The Change of Subject (3)
  - B. The Reason for the Change: The Presence of Godless Apostates (4)
- III. Warning against the False Teachers (5–16)
  - A. Historical Examples of the Judgment of Apostates (5–7)
    1. Unbelieving Israel (5)
    2. Angels who fell (6)
    3. Sodom and Gomorrha (7)
  - B. Description of the Apostates of Jude's Day (8–16)
    1. Their slanderous speech deplored (8–10)
    2. Their character graphically portrayed (11–13)
    3. Their destruction prophesied (14–16)
- IV. Exhortation to Believers (17–23)
- V. Concluding Doxology (24–25)

1 ¶ Jude, the servant of Jesus Christ, and
[a]brother of James, to them that are sanctified
by God the Father, and [b]preserved *in* Jesus
Christ, *and* [c]called:
2 Mercy unto you, and [a]peace, and love, be
multiplied.

The doom of false teachers

3 ¶ Beloved, when I gave all diligence to
write unto you [a]of the common salvation, it was
needful for me to write unto you, and exhort
you that [b]*ye* should earnestly contend for the
faith which was once delivered unto the saints.
4 [a]For there are certain men crept in unawares, [b]who were before of old ordained to
this condemnation, ungodly *men,* [c]turning
[d]the grace of our God into lasciviousness, and
[e]denying the only Lord God, and our Lord
Jesus Christ.
5 I will therefore put you in remembrance,
though ye once knew this, how that [a]the Lord,
having saved the people out of the land of
Egypt, afterward [b]destroyed them that believed not.
6 And [a]the angels which kept not their
[1]first estate, but left their own habitation, [b]he
hath reserved in everlasting chains under
darkness [c]unto the judgment of the great day.
7 *Even* as [a]Sodom and Gomorrha, and the
cities about them, in like manner giving themselves over to fornication, and going after
[1]strange flesh, are set forth for an example,
suffering the vengeance of eternal fire.
8 [a]Likewise also these *filthy* dreamers defile the flesh, despise dominion, and [b]speak
evil of dignities.
9 Yet [a]Michael the archangel, when contending with the devil he disputed about the
body of Moses, [b]durst not bring against *him* a
railing accusation, but said, [c]The Lord rebuke
thee.
10 [a]But these speak evil of those *things*
which they know not: but what they know
naturally, as brute beasts, in those *things* they
corrupt themselves.
11 Woe unto them! for they have gone in
the way [a]of Cain, and [b]ran greedily after the
error of Balaam for reward, and perished [c]in
the gainsaying of Core.
12 ¶ [a]These are spots in your [b]feasts of

1 [a]Acts 1:13 [b]John 17:11; 1 Pet. 1:5 [c]Rom. 1:7
2 [a]1 Pet. 1:2; 2 Pet. 1:2
3 [a]Tit. 1:4 [b]Phil. 1:27; 2 Tim. 1:13
4 [a]Gal. 2:4; 2 Pet. 2:1 [b]Rom. 9:22 [c]2 Pet. 2:10 [d]Tit. 2:11 [e]Tit. 1:16
5 [a]1 Cor. 10:9 [b]Num. 14:29; Ps. 106:26
6 [a]John 8:44
6 [1]Or, *principality* [b]2 Pet. 2:4 [c]Rev. 20:10
7 [1]Gr. *other* [a]Gen. 19:24; 2 Pet. 2:6
8 [a]2 Pet. 2:10 [b]Ex. 22:28
9 [a]Dan. 10:13 [b]2 Pet. 2:11 [c]Zech. 3:2
10 [a]2 Pet. 2:12
11 [a]1 John 3:12 [b]2 Pet. 2:15 [c]Num. 16:1
12 [a]2 Pet. 2:13 [b]1 Cor. 11:21

‡1 *servant.* See note on Rom 1:1. *brother of James.* See Introduction: Author. *sanctified.* See notes at 1 Cor 1:2 and Rom 6:22. *preserved in Jesus Christ.* He who holds the whole universe together (see Col 1:17; Heb 1:3) will see that God's children are kept in the faith and that they reach their eternal inheritance (see John 6:37–40; 17:11–12; 1 Pet 1:3–5). *called.* See note on Rom 8:28.

2 *peace.* The profound well-being of soul that flows from the experience of God's grace (see notes on John 14:27; 20:19; Gal 1:3; Eph 1:2).

3 *Beloved.* See vv. 17,20; see also note on 2 Pet 3:1. *the common salvation.* Jude's original intention was to write a general treatment of the doctrine of salvation, probably dealing with such subjects as man's sin and guilt, God's love and grace, the forgiveness of sins and the changed life-style that follows new birth. *the faith.* Here used of the body of truth held by believers everywhere—the gospel and all its implications (see Introduction: Date; see also 1 Tim 4:6). This truth was under attack and had to be defended. *once delivered.* The truth has finality and is not subject to change.

‡4 *For.* Introduces the reason Jude felt impelled to change the subject of his letter (see Introduction: Occasion and Purpose). *before of old ordained to this condemnation.* The reference may be to OT denunciations of ungodly men or to Enoch's prophecy (vv. 14–15). Or Jude may mean that judgment has long been about to fall on them because of their sin (see 2 Pet 2:3, which may be a clarification of this clause). *ungodly men.* See vv. 15,18. *turning the grace of our God into lasciviousness.* They assume that salvation by grace gives them the right to sin without restraint, either because God in His grace will freely forgive all their sins, or because sin, by contrast, magnifies the grace of God (cf. Rom 5:20; 6:1).

5–7 Three examples of divine judgment.

5 *destroyed them that believed not.* They did not believe that God would give them the land of Canaan; consequently all unbelieving adults died in the desert without entering the promised land.

6 *angels.* See note on 2 Pet 2:4. *estate.* See note on 2 Pet 2:4. God had assigned differing areas of responsibility and authority to each of the angels (see Dan 10:20–21, where the various princes may be angels assigned to various nations). Some of these angels refused to maintain their assignments and thus became the devil and his angels (cf. Mat 25:41). *their own habitation.* Angels apparently were assigned specific locations as well as responsibilities. Some assume that they left the heavenly realm and came to earth (see note on 2 Pet 2:4). *reserved . . . chains . . . judgment.* See note on 2 Pet 2:4. *the great day.* The final judgment.

7 *Even as.* Does not mean that the sin of Sodom and Gomorrha was the same as that of the angels or vice versa. This phrase is used to introduce the third illustration of the fact that God will see to it that the unrighteous will be consigned to eternal punishment on judgment day. *fornication, and . . . strange flesh.* More specifically, homosexuality (see Gen 19:5 and note; see also note on 2 Pet 2:10). *set forth for an example, suffering . . . eternal fire.* God destroyed Sodom and Gomorrha by pouring out "brimstone and fire" (Gen 19:24)—a foretaste of the eternal fire that is to come.

8 *these filthy dreamers.* The reference to "dreaming" is either (1) because they claimed to receive revelations or, more likely, (2) because in their passion they were out of touch with truth and reality. *defile the flesh.* Probably a reference to the homosexuality in Sodom and Gomorrha (see vv. 4,7; 1 Cor 6:18). *despise dominion.* See note on 2 Pet 2:10. *speak evil of dignities.* See note on 2 Pet 2:10.

9 According to several church fathers, this verse is based on a work called The Assumption of Moses. Other NT quotations from, or allusions to, non-Biblical works include Paul's quotations of Aratus (Acts 17:28), Menander (1 Cor 15:33) and Epimenides (Tit 1:12). Such usage in no way suggests that the quotations, or the books from which they were taken, are divinely inspired. It only means that the Biblical author found the quotations to be a helpful confirmation, clarification or illustration.

10 *those things which they know not.* See note on 2 Pet 2:12; cf. 1 Cor 2:14. *as brute beasts.* See note on 2 Pet 2:12.

11 Three OT examples of the kind of persons Jude warns his readers about. *Woe unto them!* A warning that judgment is coming (see Mat 23:13,15–16,23,25,27,29). *way of Cain.* The way of selfishness and greed (see note on Gen 4:3–4) and the way of hatred and murder (see 1 John 3:12). *error of Balaam.* The error of consuming greed (see note on 2 Pet 2:15). *gainsaying of Core.* Korah ("Core") rose up against God's appointed leadership (see Num 16). Jude may be suggesting that the false

charity when they feast with *you,* feeding
themselves without fear: [c]clouds *they are*
without water, [d]carried about of winds; trees
whose fruit withereth, without fruit, twice
dead, [e]plucked up by the roots;
13 [a]Raging waves of the sea, [b]foaming out
their own shame; wandering stars, [c]to whom
is reserved the blackness of darkness for ever.
14 And Enoch also, [a]the seventh from
Adam, prophesied of these, saying, Behold, [b]the
Lord cometh with ten thousands of his saints,
15 To execute judgment upon all, and to
convince all *that are* ungodly among them of all
their ungodly deeds which they have ungodly
committed, and of all *their* [a]hard *speeches*
which ungodly sinners have spoken against him.

Hold to the true faith

16 ¶ These are murmurers, complainers,
walking after their own lusts; and [a]their mouth
speaketh great swelling *words,* [b]having *men's*
persons in admiration because of advantage.
17 [a]But, beloved, remember ye the words
which were spoken before of the apostles of
our Lord Jesus Christ;

12 [c]Prov. 25:14; 2 Pet. 2:17 [d]Eph. 4:14 [e]Mat. 15:13
13 [a]Is. 57:20 [b]Phil. 3:19 [c]2 Pet. 2:17
14 [a]Gen. 5:18 [b]Deut. 33:2
15 [a]1 Sam. 2:3; Ps. 31:18
16 [a]2 Pet. 2:18 [b]Prov. 28:21
17 [a]2 Pet. 3:2
18 [a]1 Tim. 4:1; 2 Pet. 2:1
19 [a]Prov. 18:1 [b]Jas. 3:15
20 [a]Col. 2:7 [b]Rom. 8:26
21 [a]Tit. 2:13; 2 Pet. 3:12
23 [a]Rom. 11:14 [b]Amos 4:11; Zech. 3:2 [c]Zech. 3:4,5
24 [a]Eph. 3:20 [b]Col. 1:22
25 [a]Rom. 16:27

18 How that they told you [a]there should be
mockers in the last time, who should walk after their own ungodly lusts.
19 These be they [a]who separate themselves, [b]sensual, having not the Spirit.
20 But ye, beloved, [a]building up yourselves on your most holy faith, [b]praying in the
Holy Ghost,
21 Keep yourselves in the love of God,
[a]looking for the mercy of our Lord Jesus Christ
unto eternal life.
22 And of some have compassion, making
a difference:
23 And others [a]save with fear, [b]pulling
them out of the fire; hating even [c]the garment
spotted by the flesh.

Benediction

24 ¶ [a]Now unto him that is able to keep
you from falling, and [b]to present *you* faultless
before the presence of his glory with exceeding joy,
25 [a]To the only wise God our Saviour, *be*
glory and majesty, dominion and power, both
now and ever. Amen.

---

teachers of his day were rebelling against church leadership (cf. 3 John 9–10).

‡12–13 These verses contain six graphic metaphors: 1. *spots in your feast of charity.* See 1 Cor 11:21; 2 Pet 2:13. 2. *feeding themselves.* Instead of feeding the sheep for whom they are responsible (see Ezek 34:8–10). 3. *clouds . . . without water.* Like clouds promising moisture for the parched land, the false teachers promise soul-satisfying truth, but in reality they have nothing to offer. 4. *trees whose fruit withereth, without fruit, twice dead, plucked up by the roots.* Though the trees ought to be heavy with fruit. 5. *Raging waves of the sea.* As wind-tossed waves constantly churn up rubbish, so these apostates continually stir up moral filth (see Is 57:20). 6. *wandering stars.* As shooting stars appear in the sky only to fly off into eternal oblivion, so these false teachers are destined for the darkness of eternal hell.

‡14 *Enoch also, the seventh from Adam.* Not the Enoch in the line of Cain (Gen 4:17) but the one in the line of Seth (Gen 5:18–24; 1 Chr 1:1–3). He was seventh if Adam is counted as the first. The quotation is from the book of Enoch, which purports to have been written by the Enoch of Gen 5, but actually did not appear until the first century B.C. The book of Enoch was a well-respected writing in NT times. That it was not canonical does not mean that it contained no truth; nor does Jude's quotation of the book mean that he considered it inspired (see Introduction: Author; see also note on v. 9). *prophesied.* Not in the sense of supernaturally revealing new truth, but merely in the sense of speaking things about the future that were already known (see Dan 7:9–14; Zech 14:1–5). *the Lord cometh.* Jude uses the quotation to refer to Christ's second coming and to His judgment of the wicked (see 2 Thes 1:6–10). *saints.* Or "holy ones." This could refer to: (1) angels (see Dan 4:13–17; 2 Thes 1:7); (2) raptured saints who return with the Lord (see 1 Cor 15:52; 1 Thes 3:13; 4:17); (3) or both (see Rev 19:11–14).

15 *ungodly . . . ungodly . . . ungodly . . . ungodly.* This thunderous repetition and the awesome judgment scene that is depicted emphasize the condemnation of the false teachers in v. 4.

16 *These.* The ungodly men first mentioned in v. 4 and subsequently referred to repeatedly as "these" (vv. 10,12,14,19; cf. v. 8). They are the libertine false teachers who pervert the grace of God.

17 *remember ye the words . . . spoken before of the apostles.* The coming of these godless men should not take believers by surprise, for it had been predicted by the apostles (Acts 20:29; 1 Tim 4:1; 2 Tim 3:1–5).

‡18 *they told you.* The Greek for this phrase indicates that the apostles continually or repeatedly warned that such godless apostates would come (for example, Mat 24:4–5,10–12; Acts 20:28–30; 2 Pet 2:1–3). *mockers.* In both 2 Pet 3:3 and Jude the mockers are said to be characterized by selfish lusts. *last time.* See note on 2 Pet 3:3.

19 *who separate themselves.* At the very least this phrase means that they were divisive, creating factions in the church—the usual practice of heretics. Or Jude may refer to the later Gnostics' division of men into the spiritual (the Gnostics) and the sensual (those for whom there is no hope). *sensual.* An ironic description of the false teachers, who labeled others as "sensual." *having not the Spirit.* Rather than being the spiritual ones—the privileged elite class the Gnostics claimed to be—Jude denies that they even possess the Spirit. A person who does not have the Spirit is clearly not saved (see Rom 8:9).

20 *But ye, beloved.* In contrast to the ungodly false teachers, about whom this letter speaks at length. *most holy faith.* See note on v. 3. *in the Holy Ghost.* According to the Spirit's promptings and with the power of the Spirit (see Rom 8:26–27; Gal 4:6; Eph 6:18).

21 *keep yourselves in the love of God.* God keeps believers in His love (see Rom 8:35–39), and enables them to keep themselves in His love.

‡22–23 *have compassion . . . pulling them out of the fire.* Seek to help all who have come under the influence of the apostates—whether they are wavering in the faith or on the verge of destruction.

23 *save with fear.* Even in showing mercy one may be trapped by the allurement of sin. *pulling them out of the fire.* Rescuing them from the verge of destruction. *garment spotted by the flesh.* The wicked are pictured as so corrupt that even their garments are polluted by their sinful nature.

24–25 After all the attention necessarily given in this letter to the ungodly and their works of darkness, Jude concludes his letter by focusing attention on God, who is fully able to keep those who put their trust in Him.

The Revelation
of S. John the Divine

INTRODUCTION

Author

Four times the author identifies himself as John (1:1,4,9; 22:8). From as early as Justin Martyr in the second century A.D. it has been held that this John was the apostle, the son of Zebedee (see Mat 10:2). The book itself reveals that the author was a Jew, well versed in Scripture, a church leader who was well known to the seven churches of Asia (western Turkey), and a deeply religious person fully convinced that the Christian faith would triumph over the demonic forces at work in the world.

In the third century, however, an African bishop named Dionysius compared the language, style and thought of the Apocalypse (Revelation) with that of the other writings of John and decided that the book could not have been written by the apostle John. He suggested that the author was a certain John the Presbyter, whose name appears elsewhere in ancient writings. Although many today follow Dionysius in his view of authorship, the external evidence seems overwhelmingly supportive of the traditional view.

Date

Revelation was written when Christians were entering a time of persecution. The two periods most often mentioned are the latter part of Nero's reign (A.D. 54–68) and the latter part of Domitian's reign (81–96). Most scholars date the book c. 95. There are many substantial arguments favoring the later date: (1) Domitian was the first emperor to insist upon being worshiped as god throughout the empire; (2) the lukewarm condition of the churches of Asia Minor implies they had been in existence for many years; (3) the testimony of the earliest church fathers supports a date at the end of the first century.

Occasion

Since Roman authorities at this time were beginning to enforce the cult of emperor worship, Christians—who held that Christ, not Caesar, was Lord—were facing increasing hostility. The believers at Smyrna are warned against coming opposition (2:10), and the church at Philadelphia is told of an hour of trial coming on the world (3:10). Antipas has already given his life (2:13) along with others (6:9). John has been exiled to the island of Patmos (probably the site of a Roman penal colony) for his activities as a Christian missionary (1:9). Some within the church are advocating a policy of compromise (2:14–15,20), which has to be corrected before its subtle influence can undermine the determination of believers to stand fast in the perilous days that lie ahead.

Purpose

John writes to encourage the faithful to resist staunchly the demands of emperor worship. He informs his readers that the final showdown between God and Satan is imminent. Satan will increase his persecution of believers, but they must stand fast, even to death. They are sealed against any spiritual harm and will soon be vindicated when Christ returns, when the wicked are forever destroyed, and when God's people enter an eternity of glory and blessedness.

Literary Form

For an adequate understanding of Revelation, the reader must recognize that it is a distinct kind of literature. Revelation is apocalyptic, a kind of writing that is highly symbolic. Although its visions often seem bizarre to the Western reader, fortunately the book provides a number of clues for its own interpretation (e.g., stars are angels, candlesticks (or candlesticks) are churches, 1:20; "the great harlot," 17:1, is "Babylon" [Rome?], 17:5,18; and the heavenly Jerusalem is the wife of the Lamb, 21:9–10). There is frequently a dualism between the earthly and the heavenly, good and evil, this

world and the world to come. Beasts and other animals are used figuratively to represent certain realities, and colors are used symbolically, as are some numbers—especially 3, 7, and multiples of 12.

Distinctive Features

A distinctive feature is the frequent use of the number seven (52 times). There are seven beatitudes (see note on 1:3), seven churches (1:4,11), seven spirits (1:4), seven golden candlesticks (1:12), seven stars (1:16), seven seals (5:1), seven horns and seven eyes (5:6), seven trumpets (8:2), seven thunders (10:3), seven signs (12:1,3; 13:13–14; 15:1; 16:14; 19:20), seven heads with seven crowns (12:3), seven plagues (15:6), seven golden vials (15:7), seven mountains (17:9) and seven kings (17:10), as well as other sevens. Symbolically, the number seven stands for completeness. The Revelation also uses "and" (Greek *kai*) over 1,200 times. The constant use of this conjunction creates a sense of fast-paced movement in the book from one event to the next.

Interpretation

Interpreters of Revelation normally fall into four groups:

1. *Preterists* understand the book exclusively in terms of its first-century setting, claiming that most of its events have already taken place.
2. *Historicists* take it as describing the long chain of events from Patmos to the end of history.
3. *Futurists* place the book primarily in the end times.
4. *Idealists* view it as symbolic pictures of such timeless truths as the victory of good over evil.

Fortunately, the fundamental truths of Revelation do not depend on adopting a particular point of view. They are available to anyone who will read the book for its overall message and resist the temptation to become overly enamored with the details.

Outline

I. Introduction (1:1–8)
  A. Prologue (1:1–3)
  B. Greetings and Doxology (1:4–8)
II. Jesus among the Seven Churches (1:9–20)
III. The Letters to the Seven Churches (chs. 2—3)
  A. Ephesus (2:1–7)
  B. Smyrna (2:8–11)
  C. Pergamos (2:12–17)
  D. Thyatira (2:18–29)
  E. Sardis (3:1–6)
  F. Philadelphia (3:7–13)
  G. Laodicea (3:14–22)
IV. The Throne, the Book and the Lamb (chs. 4—5)
  A. The Throne in Heaven (ch. 4)
  B. The Seven-Sealed Book (5:1–5)
  C. The Lamb Slain (5:6–14)
V. The Seal Judgments (6:1—8:1)
  A. First Seal: The White Horse (6:1–2)
  B. Second Seal: The Red Horse (6:3–4)
  C. Third Seal: The Black Horse (6:5–6)
  D. Fourth Seal: The Pale Horse (6:7–8)
  E. Fifth Seal: The Souls under the Altar (6:9–11)
  F. Sixth Seal: The Great Earthquake (6:12–17)
VI. The First Interlude (7:1—8:1)
  A. The Sealing of the 144,000 (7:1–8)
  B. The Great Multitude (7:9–17)
  C. Seventh Seal: Silence in Heaven (8:1)
VII. The Seven Trumpets (8:2—11:19)
  A. Introduction (8:2–5)
  B. First Trumpet: Hail and Fire Mixed with Blood (8:6–7)
  C. Second Trumpet: A Mountain Thrown into the Sea (8:8–9)
  D. Third Trumpet: The Star Wormwood (8:10–11)

E. Fourth Trumpet: A Third of the Sun, Moon and Stars Struck (8:12–13)
F. Fifth Trumpet: The Plague of Locusts (9:1–12)
G. Sixth Trumpet: Release of the Four Angels (9:13–21)

VIII. The Second Interlude (10:1—11:14)
A. The Angel and the Little Scroll (ch. 10)
B. The Two Witnesses (11:1–14)
C. Seventh Trumpet: Judgments and Rewards (11:15–19)

IX. Various Personages and Events (chs. 12—14)
A. The Woman and the Dragon (ch. 12)
B. The Two Beasts (ch. 13)
C. The Lamb and the 144,000 (14:1–5)
D. The Harvest of the Earth (14:6–20)

X. The Seven Vials (chs. 15—16)
A. Introduction: The Song of Moses and the Seven Angels with the Seven Plagues (ch. 15)
B. First Vial: Ugly and Painful Sores (16:1–2)
C. Second Vial: Sea Turns to Blood (16:3)
D. Third Vial: Rivers and Springs of Water Become Blood (16:4–7)
E. Fourth Vial: Sun Scorches People with Fire (16:8–9)
F. Fifth Vial: Darkness (16:10–11)
G. Sixth Vial: Euphrates River Dries Up (16:12–16)
H. Seventh Vial: Tremendous Earthquake (16:17–21)

XI. Babylon: The Great Prostitute (17:1—19:5)
A. Babylon Described (ch. 17)
B. The Fall of Babylon (ch. 18)
C. Praise for Babylon's Fall (19:1–5)

XII. Praise for the Marriage Supper of the Lamb (19:6–10)
XIII. The Return of Christ (19:11–21)
XIV. The Thousand Years (20:1–6)
XV. Satan's Doom (20:7–10)
XVI. Great White Throne Judgment (20:11–15)
XVII. New Heaven, New Earth, New Jerusalem (21:1—22:5)
XVIII. Conclusion (22:6–21)

The source of the revelation

1 The Revelation of Jesus Christ, [a]which
God gave unto him, to shew unto his servants *things* which must shortly come to pass;
and [b]he sent and signified *it* by his angel unto
his servant John:
2 [a]Who bare record of the word of God,
and of the testimony of Jesus Christ, and of all
things [b]that he saw.
3 [a]Blessed *is* he that readeth, and they that
hear the words of *this* prophecy, and keep
those *things* which are written therein: for
[b]the time *is* at hand.

The salutation

4 ¶ John to the seven churches which are
in Asia: Grace *be* unto you, and peace, from
him [a]which is, and [b]which was, and which is
to come; [c]and from the seven spirits which are
before his throne;
5 And from Jesus Christ, [a]*who is* the faithful witness, *and* the [b]first begotten of the
dead, and [c]the prince of the kings of the earth.
Unto him [d]that loved us, [e]and washed us from
our sins in his own blood,
6 And hath [a]made us kings and priests
unto God and his Father; [b]to him *be* glory and
dominion for ever and ever. Amen.
7 ¶ [a]Behold, he cometh with clouds; and
every eye shall see him, and [b]they *also* which
pierced him: and all kindreds of the earth shall
wail because of him. Even so, Amen.
8 [a]I am Alpha and Omega, the beginning
and the ending, saith the Lord, [b]which is, and
which was, and which is to come, the Almighty.

The voice and the vision

9 ¶ I John, who also am your brother, and
[a]companion in tribulation, and [b]in the kingdom and patience of Jesus Christ, was in the
isle that is called Patmos, [c]for the word of
God, and for the testimony of Jesus Christ.
10 [a]I was in the spirit on [b]the Lord's day,
and heard behind me [c]a great voice, as of a
trumpet,
11 Saying, [a]I am Alpha and Omega, [b]the
first and the last: and, What thou seest, write
in a book, and send *it* unto the seven churches
which are in Asia; unto Ephesus, and unto
Smyrna, and unto Pergamos, and unto Thyatira, and unto Sardis, and unto Philadelphia, and
unto Laodicea.
12 And I turned to see the voice that spake
with me. And being turned, [a]I saw seven gold-
en candlesticks;
13 [a]And in the midst of the seven candlesticks [b]one like unto the Son of man, [c]clothed
with a garment down to the foot, and [d]girt
about the paps with a golden girdle.
14 His head and [a]*his* hairs *were* white like

1:1 [a]John 3:32 [b]ch. 22:16
1:2 [a]1 Cor. 1:6 [b]1 John 1:1
1:3 [a]Luke 11:28 [b]Jas. 5:8
1:4 [a]Ex. 3:14 [b]John 1:1 [c]Zech. 3:9
1:5 [a]John 8:14; 1 Tim. 6:13 [b]Col. 1:18 [c]ch. 17:14 [d]John 13:34; Gal. 2:20 [e]Heb. 9:14; 1 John 1:7
1:6 [a]1 Pet. 2:5 [b]1 Tim. 6:16
1:7 [a]Dan. 7:13 [b]Zech. 12:10
1:8 [a]Is. 41:4 [b]ch. 4:8
1:9 [a]Phil. 1:7 [b]Rom. 8:17; 2 Tim. 2:12 [c]ch. 6:9
1:10 [a]Acts 10:10; 2 Cor. 12:2 [b]John 20:26 [c]ch. 4:1
1:11 [a]ver. 8 [b]ver. 17
1:12 [a]Ex. 25:37; Zech. 4:2
1:13 [a]ch. 2:1 [b]Ezek. 1:26; Dan. 7:13; 10:16 [c]Dan. 10:5 [d]ch. 15:6
1:14 [a]Dan. 7:9

1:1 *Revelation.* Apocalypse ("unveiling" or "disclosure"). *of Jesus Christ.* Can mean (1) by or from Jesus Christ, (2) about Jesus Christ or (3) both. *servants.* All believers. *shortly come to pass.* See v. 3; 22:6–7,10,20. *his angel.* A mediating angel. The word "angel" (including its plural form) occurs over 70 times in Revelation. *John.* See Introduction: Author.

1:3 *Blessed.* The first of seven beatitudes in the book (see 14:13; 16:15; 19:9; 20:6; 22:7,14). "Blessed" means much more than "happy." It describes the favorable circumstance God has put a person in (see notes on Ps 1:1; Mat 5:3). *prophecy.* Includes not only foretelling the future but also proclaiming any word from God—whether command, instruction, history or prediction. *time is at hand.* See note on Jas 5:9.

1:4 *seven churches.* Located about 50 miles apart, forming a circle in the Roman province of Asia moving clockwise north from Ephesus and coming around full circle from Laodicea (east of Ephesus). They were perhaps postal centers serving seven geographic regions. Apparently the entire book of Revelation (including the seven letters) was sent to each church (see v. 11). *Asia.* A Roman province lying in modern western Turkey. *Grace . . . and peace.* See notes on Jonah 4:2; John 14:27; 20:19; Gal 1:3; Eph 1:2. "Grace" is used only twice in Revelation (here and in 22:21) but over 100 times by Paul. *which is . . . was . . . is to come.* A paraphrase of the divine name from Ex 3:14–15. Cf. Heb 13:8. *seven spirits.* The sevenfold Spirit (see Zech 4:2 and note; cf. Zech 4:10).

‡1:6 *kings and priests unto God.* This OT designation of Israel (see notes on Ex 19:6; Zech 3) is applied in the NT to the church (1 Pet 2:5,9). This does not suggest, however, that the writer is equating the church with Israel.

1:7 *pierced.* See Ps 22:16; Is 53:5; Zech 12:10; John 19:34,37. *Even so, Amen.* A double affirmation.

1:8 *Alpha and Omega.* The first and last letters of the Greek alphabet. God is the beginning and the end (see 21:6). He sovereignly rules over all human history. In 22:13 Jesus applies the same title to Himself. *Almighty.* Nine of the ten occurrences of this term in the NT are in Revelation (here; 4:8; 11:17; 15:3; 16:7,14; 19:6,15; 21:22). The tenth occurrence is in 2 Cor 6:18.

‡1:9 *tribulation . . . kingdom . . . patience.* Three pivotal themes in Revelation: (1) "tribulation" (2:9–10,22; 7:14), (2) "kingdom" (11:15; 12:10; 16:10; 17:12,17–18), (3) "patience" (2:2–3,19; 3:10; 13:10; 14:12). *Patmos.* A small (four by eight miles), rocky island in the Aegean Sea some 50 miles southwest of Ephesus, off the coast of modern Turkey. It probably served as a Roman penal settlement. Eusebius, the "father of church history" (A.D. 265–340), reports that John was released from Patmos under the emperor Nerva (96–98).

‡1:10 *in the spirit.* In a state of spiritual exaltation—not a dream, but a vision like Peter's in Acts 10:10. *the Lord's day.* This phrase has become a technical term for the first day of the week—so named because Jesus rose from the dead on that day. It was also the day on which the Christians met (see Acts 20:7) and took up collections (see 1 Cor 16:2). It is not certain whether it meant Sunday, in this case, or whether it referred to John's being transported in spirit into "the Day of the Lord," the eschatological day of judgment.

1:11 *book.* Actually it was a scroll. Pieces of papyrus or parchment were sewn together and rolled on a spindle (see note on Ex 17:14). The book form was not invented until about the second century A.D. *seven churches.* See note on v. 4.

‡1:12 *seven.* See Introduction: Distinctive Feature. *golden candlesticks.* The seven churches (see v. 20). The word here actually refers to a candlestick. Each candlestick has a wick that draws oil from the common base, which would be symbolic of Christ.

1:13 *Son of man.* See notes on Dan 7:13; Mark 8:31. *garment . . . to the foot.* The high priest wore a full-length robe (Ex 28:4; 29:5). Reference to Christ as high priest is supported by the reference to the golden sash around His chest.

wool, *as* white as snow; and [b]his eyes *were* as
a flame of fire;
15 [a]And his feet like unto fine brass, as if
they burned in a furnace; and [b]his voice as the
sound of many waters.
16 [a]And he had in his right hand seven
stars: and [b]out of his mouth went a sharp
twoedged sword: [c]and his countenance *was* as
the sun shineth in his strength.
17 And [a]when I saw him, I fell at his feet
as dead. And [b]he laid his right hand upon me,
saying unto me, Fear not; [c]I am the first and
the last:
18 [a]I am he that liveth, and was dead; and
behold, [b]I am alive for evermore, Amen; and
[c]have the keys of hell and of death.
19 Write *the things* which thou hast seen,
[a]and *the things* which are, [b]and *the things*
which shall be hereafter;
20 The mystery of the seven stars which
thou sawest in my right hand, and the seven
golden candlesticks. The seven stars are [a]the
angels of the seven churches: and [b]the seven
candlesticks which thou sawest are the seven
churches.

1:14 [b]Dan. 10:6
1:15 [a]Ezek. 1:7; Dan. 10:6 [b]Ezek. 43:2; Dan. 10:6; ch. 14:2
1:16 [a]ch. 2:1 [b]Is. 49:2; Eph. 6:17; Heb. 4:12 [c]Acts 26:13
1:17 [a]Ezek. 1:28 [b]Dan. 8:18; 10:10 [c]Is. 41:4; 44:6; 48:12; ch. 22:13
1:18 [a]Rom. 6:9 [b]ch. 4:9 [c]Ps. 68:20; ch. 20:1
1:19 [a]ch. 2:1 [b]ch. 4:1
1:20 [a]Mal. 2:7; ch. 2:1 [b]Zech. 4:2; Mat. 5:15; Phil. 2:15
2:1 [a]ch. 1:16

The message to Ephesus

2 Unto the angel of the church of Ephesus
write; These *things* saith [a]he that hold-

1:14 *white like wool.* Cf. Dan 7:9; Is 1:18. The hoary head suggests wisdom and dignity (Lev 19:32; Prov 16:31). *eyes . . . as a flame of fire.* Penetrating insight (see 4:6).
1:16 *sharp twoedged sword.* Like a long Thracian sword (also in 2:12,16; 6:8; 19:15,21). The sword in 6:4; 13:10,14 was a small sword or dagger. The sword symbolizes divine judgment (see Is 49:2; Heb 4:12).
1:17 *fell at his feet.* A sign of great respect and awe (4:10; 5:8; 7:11; 19:10; 22:8). *I am.* See note on John 6:35. *the first and the last.* Essentially the same as the "Alpha and the Omega" (v. 8; cf. Is 44:6; 48:12).
1:18 *he that liveth.* Based on OT references to the "living God" (e.g., Josh 3:10; Ps 42:2; 84:2). In contrast to the dead gods of paganism, Christ possesses life in His essential nature. *keys of hell and of death.* Absolute control over their domain (see Mat 16:18 and note).
‡1:19 Many take the threefold division of this verse as a clue to the entire structure of the book. "The things which thou hast seen" would be the inaugural vision of ch. 1; "the things which are" would be the letters to the seven churches (chs. 2–3); "the things which shall be hereafter" would be everything from ch. 4 on. An alternative interpretation sees the initial clause as the essential unit (it parallels v. 11), followed by two explanatory clauses. The sense would be: "Write, therefore, what you are about to see, i.e., both what is now and what will take place later." Some who hold the latter view make no attempt to outline the book on this basis, maintaining that there is a mixture of "now" and "later" throughout. A "futurist" or "historicist" interpretation would support the first interpretation. The "preterist" or the "idealist" would likely favor the second view.
‡1:20 The first of several places where the symbols are interpreted (see also 17:15,18). *stars.* Either (1) heavenly messengers, (2) earthly messengers/ministers or (3) personifications of the prevailing spirit of each church. In favor of the first view is the fact that there are two other times when a star is seen to be an angel in this book (9:1–11; 12:4,7). It is also known that nations have angels assigned to them (as in Dan 10:13), so it would not be extraordinary for an angel also to have been assigned to a particular church.
2:1–3:22 Some take the seven letters as a preview of church history in its downward course toward Laodicean lukewarmness. Others interpret them as characteristic of various kinds of Christian congregations that have existed from John's day until the present time. In either case, they were historical churches in Asia Minor (see map No. 11 at the end of the Study Bible). The general pattern in the letters is commendation, complaint and correction.
2:1 *angel.* See note on 1:20. *Ephesus.* See Introduction to Ephesians: The City of Ephesus. *holdeth the seven stars.* See 1:16,20. *seven golden candlesticks.* See 1:12,20.

The Sevens in the Revelation

The frequent use of the number seven in the Revelation is a unique feature in the Apocalypse.

THE SEVENS	REVELATION	THE SEVENS	REVELATION
1. Seven churches	1:4-20; 2–3	**12.** Seven thousand	11:13
2. Seven spirits	1:4; 3:1; 4:5; 5:6	**13.** Seven heads	12:3; 13:1; 17:3-9
3. Seven candlesticks	1:12-20; 2:1	**14.** Seven crowns	12:3
4. Seven stars	1:16-20; 2:1; 3:1	**15.** Seven angels	15:1-8; 21:9
5. Seven lamps	4:5	**16.** Seven plagues	15:1-8; 21:9
6. Seven seals	5:1-5	**17.** Seven vials	15:7; 17:1; 21:9
7. Seven horns	5:6	**18.** Seven mountains	17:9
8. Seven eyes	5:6	**19.** Seven kings	17:10-11
9. Seven angels	8:2-6	**20.** (Seven) beatitudes	1:3; 14:13; 16:15; 19:9; 20:6; 22:7,14
10. Seven trumpets	8:2-6	**21.** (Seven) "I ams" of Christ	1:8,11,17,18; 21:6; 22:13,16
11. Seven thunders	10:3-4		

eth the seven stars in his right hand, [b]who
walketh in the midst of the seven golden candlesticks;
2 [a]I know thy works, and thy labour, and
thy patience, and how thou canst not bear
them which are evil: and [b]thou hast tried
them [c]which say *they* are apostles, and are
not, and hast found them liars:
3 And hast borne, and hast patience, and
for my name's sake hast laboured, and hast
[a]not fainted.
4 Nevertheless I have *somewhat* against
thee, because thou hast left thy first love.
5 Remember therefore from whence thou
art fallen, and repent, and do the first works;
[a]or else I *will* come unto thee quickly, and will
remove thy candlestick out of his place, except
thou repent.
6 But this thou hast, that thou hatest the
deeds of the Nicolaitans, which I also hate.

2:1 [b]ch. 1:13
2:2 [a]Ps. 1:6; ch. 3:1,8 [b]1 John 4:1 [c]2 Cor. 11:13; 2 Pet. 2:1
2:3 [a]Gal. 6:9; Heb. 12:3,5
2:5 [a]Mat. 21:41
2:7 [a]Mat. 11:15; 13:9,43; ch. 3:6,13 [b]ch. 22:2,14 [c]Gen. 2:9
2:8 [a]ch. 1:8,17
2:9 [a]Luke 12:21; 1 Tim. 6:18; Jas. 2:5 [b]Rom. 2:17 [c]ch. 3:9
2:10 [a]Mat. 10:22 [b]Mat. 24:13 [c]Jas. 1:12; ch. 3:11

7 [a]He that hath an ear, let him hear what
the Spirit saith unto the churches; To him that
overcometh will I give [b]to eat of [c]the tree of
life, which is in the midst of the paradise of
God.

The message to Smyrna

8 ¶ And unto the angel of the church in
Smyrna write; These *things* saith [a]the first and
the last, which was dead, and is alive;
9 I know thy works, and tribulation, and
poverty, (but thou art [a]rich) and *I know* the
blasphemy of [b]them which say they are Jews,
and are not, [c]but *are* the synagogue of Satan.
10 [a]Fear none *of those things* which thou
shalt suffer: behold, the devil shall cast *some*
of you into prison, that ye may be tried; and ye
shall have tribulation ten days: [b]be thou faithful unto death, and I will give thee [c]a crown of
life.

2:2 *hast tried them.* The necessity of testing for correct doctrine and dependable advice was widely recognized in the early church (see 1 Cor 14:29; 1 Thes 5:21; 1 John 4:1).
‡2:4 *left.* They did not lose it; they left it. *first love.* The love they had at first for one another and/or for Christ.
2:5 *remove thy candlestick.* Immediate judgment.
2:6 *Nicolaitans.* A heretical sect within the church that had worked out a compromise with the pagan society. They apparently taught that spiritual liberty gave them sufficient leeway to practice idolatry and immorality. Tradition identifies them with Nicolas, the proselyte of Antioch who was one of the first seven deacons in the Jerusalem church (Acts 6:5), though the evidence is merely circumstantial. A similar group at Pergamum held the teaching of Balaam (vv. 14–15), and some at Thyatira were followers of the woman Jezebel (v. 20). From their heretical tendencies it would appear that all three groups were Nicolaitans.
‡2:7 *overcometh.* The challenge to overcome occurs in each letter (here; vv. 11,17,26; 3:5,12,21). *paradise.* Originally a Persian word for a pleasure garden (see note on Luke 23:43). In Revelation it symbolizes the eschatological state in heaven in which God and man are restored to the perfect fellowship that existed before sin entered the world. (see 22:2; 2 Cor 12:4).
2:8 *Smyrna.* A proud and beautiful Asian city (modern Izmir) closely aligned with Rome and eager to meet its demands for emperor worship. This plus a large and actively hostile Jewish population made it extremely difficult to live there as a Christian. Polycarp, the most famous of the early martyrs, was bishop of Smyrna. *the first and the last.* See note on 1:17.
2:9 *which say they are Jews.* See Rom 2:28–29. *Satan.* Hebrew for "accuser" (see Zech 3:1; cf. Job 1:6–12; 2:1–7).
2:10 *devil.* Greek *diabolos,* meaning "accuser." *tribulation.* See the warnings by Jesus (John 15:20) and Paul (2 Tim 3:12). *crown of life.* The crown that is eternal life. "Crown" does not refer to a royal crown (12:3; 13:1; 19:12) but to the garland or wreath awarded to the winner in athletic contests (3:11; 4:4,10; 6:2; 9:7; 12:1; 14:14).

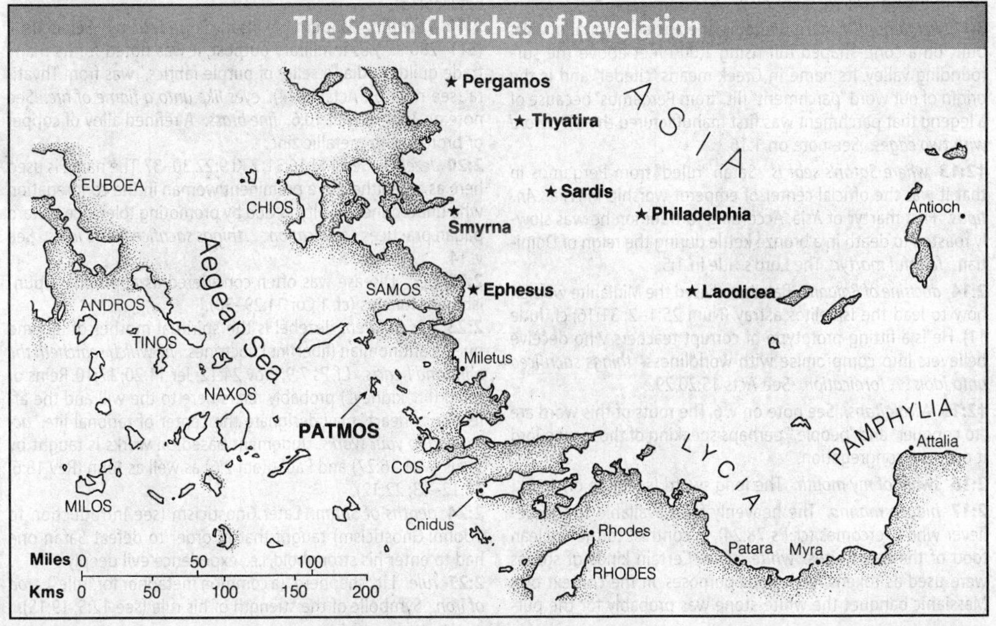

11 [a]He that hath an ear, let him hear what the Spirit saith unto the churches; He that overcometh shall not be hurt of [b]the second death.

The message to Pergamos

12 ¶ And to the angel of the church in Pergamos write; These *things* saith [a]he which hath the sharp sword with two edges;

13 I know thy works, and where thou dwellest, *even* where Satan's seat *is:* and thou holdest fast my name, and hast not denied my faith, even in *those* days wherein Antipas *was* my faithful martyr, who was slain among you, where Satan dwelleth.

14 But I have a few *things* against thee, because thou hast there them that hold the doctrine of [a]Balaam, who taught Balac to cast a stumblingblock before the children of Israel, [b]to eat things sacrificed unto idols, [c]and to commit fornication.

15 So hast thou also them that hold the doctrine of the Nicolaitans, which *thing* I hate.

16 Repent; or else I *will* come unto thee quickly, and [a]will fight against them with the sword of my mouth.

17 He that hath an ear, let him hear what the Spirit saith unto the churches; To him that overcometh will I give to eat of the hidden manna, and will give him a white stone, and in the stone [a]a new name written, which no *man* knoweth saving he that receiveth *it.*

The message to Thyatira

18 ¶ And unto the angel of the church in Thyatira write; These *things* saith the Son of God, [a]who hath his eyes like unto a flame of fire, and his feet *are* like fine brass;

19 [a]I know thy works, and charity, and service, and faith, and thy patience, and thy works; and the last *to be* more than the first.

20 Notwithstanding I have a few *things* against thee, because thou sufferest *that* woman [a]Jezebel, which calleth herself a prophetess, to teach and to seduce my servants [b]to commit fornication, and to eat things sacrificed unto idols.

21 And I gave her space [a]to repent of her fornication; and she repented not.

22 Behold, I *will* cast her into a bed, and them that commit adultery with her into great tribulation, except they repent of their deeds.

23 And I will kill her children with death; and all the churches shall know that [a]I am he which searcheth the reins and hearts: and [b]I will give unto every one of you according to your works.

24 But unto you I say, and unto the rest in Thyatira, as many as have not this doctrine, and which have not known the depths of Satan, as they speak; [a]I will put upon you none other burden.

25 But [a]*that* which ye have *already* hold fast till I come.

26 And he that overcometh, and keepeth [a]my works unto the end, [b]to him will I give power over the nations:

27 [a]And he shall rule them with a rod of iron; as the vessels of a potter *shall* they be broken to shivers: even as I received of my Father.

28 And I will give him [a]the morning star.

29 [a]He that hath an ear, let him hear what the Spirit saith unto the churches.

2:11 [a]ch. 13:9 [b]ch. 20:1; 21:8
2:12 [a]ch. 1:16
2:14 [a]Num. 24:14; 25:1; 31:16; 2 Pet. 2:15; Jude 11 [b]Acts 15:29; 1 Cor. 8:9; 10:19,20 [c]1 Cor. 6:13
2:16 [a]Is. 11:4; 2 Thes. 2:8; ch. 1:16
2:17 [a]ch. 3:12; 19:12
2:18 [a]ch. 1:14,15
2:19 [a]ver. 2
2:20 [a]1 Ki. 16:31; 21:25; 2 Ki. 9:7 [b]Ex. 34:15; Acts 15:20
2:21 [a]ch. 9:20
2:23 [a]1 Sam. 16:7; Jer. 11:20; John 2:24; Acts 1:24; Rom. 8:27 [b]Ps. 62:12; 2 Cor. 5:10
2:24 [a]Acts 15:28
2:25 [a]ch. 3:11
2:26 [a]John 6:29; 1 John 3:23 [b]Mat. 19:28; Luke 22:29; 1 Cor. 6:3
2:27 [a]Ps. 2:8,9; Dan. 7:22
2:28 [a]2 Pet. 1:19
2:29 [a]ver. 7

2:11 *He that overcometh.* See note on v. 7. *second death.* The lake of fire (20:14; see 20:6; 21:8).

2:12 *Pergamos.* Modern Bergama; the ancient capital of Asia, built on a cone-shaped hill rising 1,000 feet above the surrounding valley. Its name in Greek means "citadel" and is the origin of our word "parchment" (lit. "from Pergamos" because of a legend that parchment was first manufactured there). *sword with two edges.* See note on 1:16.

‡2:13 *where Satan's seat is.* Satan "ruled" from Pergamos in that it was the official center of emperor worship in Asia. *Antipas.* First martyr of Asia. According to tradition he was slowly roasted to death in a bronze kettle during the reign of Domitian. *faithful martyr.* The Lord's title in 1:5.

2:14 *doctrine of Balaam.* Balaam advised the Midianite women how to lead the Israelites astray (Num 25:1–2; 31:16; cf. Jude 11). He is a fitting prototype of corrupt teachers who deceive believers into compromise with worldliness. *things sacrificed unto idols . . . fornication.* See Acts 15:20,29.

‡2:15 *Nicolaitans.* See note on v. 6. The roots of this word are "to conquer" and "people," perhaps speaking of those who lord it over the congregation.

2:16 *sword of my mouth.* The long sword (see note on 1:16).

2:17 *hidden manna.* The heavenly food available to the believer who overcomes (cf. Ps 78:24), in contrast to the unclean food of the Balaamites. *white stone.* Certain kinds of stones were used as tokens for various purposes. In the context of a Messianic banquet the white stone was probably for the purpose of admission. *new name.* The name of the victor (see Is 62:2; 65:15).

2:18 *Thyatira.* Modern Akhisar. Founded by Seleucus I (311–280 B.C.) as a military outpost, it was noted for its many trade guilds. Lydia, "a seller of purple fabrics," was from Thyatira (see note on Acts 16:14). *eyes like unto a flame of fire.* See note on 1:14; cf. Dan 10:6. *fine brass.* A refined alloy of copper or bronze with metallic zinc.

2:20 *Jezebel.* See 1 Ki 16:31; 2 Ki 9:22,30–37. The name is used here as an epithet for a prominent woman in the congregation who undermined loyalty to God by promoting tolerance toward pagan practices. *fornication . . . things sacrificed unto idols.* See v. 14.

2:22 *bed.* Disease was often considered as appropriate punishment for sins (cf. 1 Cor 11:29–30).

2:23 *her children.* Jezebel is the spiritual mother of all who pursue antinomian (libertine) doctrines. *he which searcheth the reins and hearts.* Cf. Ps 7:9; Prov 24:12; Jer 11:20; 17:10. Reins or mind (lit. "kidney") probably refers here to the will and the affections; "heart" may designate the center of rational life. *according to your works.* Judgment based on works is taught by Jesus (Mat 16:27) and Paul (Rom 2:6) as well as John (Rev 18:6; 20:12–13; 22:12).

2:24 *depths of Satan.* Later Gnosticism (see Introduction to 1 John: Gnosticism) taught that in order to defeat Satan one had to enter his stronghold, i.e., experience evil deeply.

2:27 *rule.* Lit. "shepherd" (a common metaphor for "rule"). *rod of iron.* Symbolic of the strength of his rule (see 12:5; 19:15).

The message to Sardis

3 And unto the angel of the church in Sardis write; These *things* saith he [a]that
hath the seven spirits of God, and the seven
stars; [b]I know thy works, that thou hast a
name that thou livest, [c]and art dead.
2 Be watchful, and strengthen the *things*
which remain, that are ready to die: for I have
not found thy works perfect before God.
3 [a]Remember therefore how thou hast received and heard, and hold fast, and [b]repent.
[c]If therefore thou shalt not watch, I will come
on thee as a thief, and thou shalt not know
what hour I will come upon thee.
4 Thou hast [a]a few names even in Sardis,
which have not [b]defiled their garments; and
they shall walk with me [c]in white: for they are
worthy.
5 He that overcometh, [a]the same shall be
clothed in white raiment; and I will not [b]blot
out his name out of the [c]book of life, but [d]I
will confess his name before my Father, and
before his angels.
6 [a]He that hath an ear, let him hear what
the Spirit saith unto the churches.

The message to Philadelphia

7 ¶ And to the angel of the church in Philadelphia write; These *things* saith [a]he *that is*
holy, [b]he *that is* true, he that hath [c]the key of
David, [d]he that openeth, and no *man* shutteth;
and [e]shutteth, and no *man* openeth;
8 [a]I know thy works: behold, I have set before thee [b]an open door, and no *man* can shut
it: for thou hast a little strength, and hast kept
my word, and hast not denied my name.

3:1 [a]ch. 1:4,16 [b]ch. 2:2 [c]Eph. 2:1,5
3:3 [a]1 Tim. 6:20; 2 Tim. 1:13 [b]ver. 19 [c]Mat. 24:42; Mark 13:33; Luke 12:39; 1 Thes. 5:2,6; 2 Pet. 3:10
3:4 [a]Acts 1:15 [b]Jude 23 [c]ch. 4:4; 6:11
3:5 [a]ch. 19:8 [b]Ex. 32:32 [c]Phil. 4:3 [d]Luke 12:8
3:6 [a]ch. 2:7
3:7 [a]Acts 3:14 [b]1 John 5:20 [c]Is. 22:22; Luke 1:32 [d]Mat. 16:19 [e]Job 12:14
3:8 [a]ver. 1 [b]1 Cor. 16:9

3:1 *Sardis.* Modern Sart. Capital of the ancient kingdom of Lydia, it was a city of great wealth and fame. The acropolis was a natural citadel on the northern spur of mount Tmolus. It rose 1,500 feet above the lower valley.
3:3 *come on thee as a thief.* Not a reference to the second coming of Christ, because here His coming depends on the church's refusal to repent. Elsewhere in the NT the clause refers to the second advent (16:15; Mat 24:42–44; 1 Thes 5:2; 2 Pet 3:10).
3:4 *in white.* Description of the redeemed (3:18; 6:11; 7:9,13; cf. 4:4; 19:14).
‡3:5 *He that overcometh.* The overcomer is every Christian, every believer. See 1 John 5:4–5. *I will not blot out his name.* This is a positive promise of complete and total security. *book of life.* A divine ledger is first mentioned in Ex 32:32–33 (see note on Ps 69:28; cf. Dan 12:1). It was a register of all citizens in the kingdom community. To have one's name erased from this book would indicate loss of citizenship (see 13:8; 17:8; 20:12,15; 21:27; Phil 4:3).
3:7 *Philadelphia.* Modern Alashehir; a city of commercial importance conveniently located as the gateway to the high central plateau of the province of Asia in Asia Minor. The name means "brotherly love" and commemorates the loyalty and devotion of Attalus II (220–130 B.C.) to his brother Eumenes II. *holy . . . true.* See 6:10. For God as the Holy One see Is 40:25; Hab 3:2–3; Mark 1:24. *key of David.* Christ is the Davidic Messiah with authority to control entrance to the kingdom (see Is 22:22; Mat 16:19).
3:8 *open door.* Either the door of opportunity or the door to the kingdom. The context favors the latter.

Names and Titles of Jesus in Revelation

NAME / TITLE	REVELATION	NAME / TITLE	REVELATION
1. Jesus Christ	1:1	**16.** He that is holy and true	3:7
2. Faithful witness	1:5	**17.** He that hath the key of David	3:7
3. First begotten from the dead	1:5	**18.** The Amen	3:14
4. Prince of the kings of the earth	1:5	**19.** Faithful and true witness	3:14
5. Alpha and Omega	1:8	**20.** Beginning of God's creation	3:14
6. He which is, was and is to come	1:8	**21.** Lion of the tribe of Judah	5:5
7. The Almighty	1:8	**22.** Root of David	5:5
8. Son of man	1:13; 14:14	**23.** The Lamb (28 times)	
9. He that Liveth	1:18	**24.** Sovereign Lord, holy and true	6:10
10. He that holdeth the seven stars	2:1	**25.** Lord	11:8
11. He who walks among the candlesticks	2:1	**26.** Man child	12:5
12. He who has the double-edged sword	2:12	**27.** King of the saints	15:3
13. Son of God	2:18	**28.** Word of God	19:13
14. He who has eyes like a flame of fire	2:18	**29.** King of kings and Lord of lords	19:16
15. He that hath the seven spirits of God	3:1	**30.** Bright morning star	22:16

9 Behold, I *will* make [a]*them* of the synagogue of Satan, which say they are Jews, and are not, but do lie; behold, [b]I will make them to come and worship before thy feet, and to know that I have loved thee.

10 Because thou hast kept the word of my patience, [a]I also will keep thee from the hour of temptation, which shall come upon [b]all the world, to try them that dwell [c]upon the earth.

11 Behold, [a]I come quickly: [b]hold *that* fast which thou hast, that no *man* take [c]thy crown.

12 Him that overcometh will I make [a]a pillar in the temple of my God, and he shall go no more out: and [b]I will write upon him the name of my God, and the name of the city of my God, *which is* [c]new Jerusalem, which cometh down out of heaven from my God: [d]and *I will write upon him* my new name.

13 [a]He that hath an ear, let him hear what the Spirit saith unto the churches.

The message to Laodicea

14 ¶ And unto the angel of the church [1]of the Laodiceans write; [a]These *things* saith the Amen, [b]the faithful and true witness, [c]the beginning of the creation of God;

15 [a]I know thy works, that thou art neither cold nor hot: I would thou wert cold or hot.

16 So *then* because thou art lukewarm, and neither cold nor hot, I will spue thee out of my mouth.

17 Because thou sayest, [a]I am rich, and increased with goods, and have need of nothing; and knowest not that thou art wretched, and miserable, and poor, and blind, and naked:

18 I counsel thee [a]to buy of me gold tried in the fire, that thou mayest be rich; and [b]white raiment, that thou mayest be clothed, and *that* the shame of thy nakedness do not appear; and anoint thine eyes *with* eyesalve, that thou mayest see.

19 [a]As many as I love, I rebuke and chasten: be zealous therefore, and repent.

20 Behold, [a]I stand at the door, and knock: [b]if any *man* hear my voice, and open the door, [c]I will come in to him, and will sup with him, and he with me.

21 To him that overcometh [a]will I grant to sit with me in my throne, *even* as I also overcame, and am set down with my Father in his throne.

22 [a]He that hath an ear, let him hear what the Spirit saith unto the churches.

The heavenly worship

4 After this I looked, and behold, a door *was* opened in heaven: and [a]the first voice which I heard *was* as *it were* of a trumpet talking with me; which said, [b]Come up hither, [c]and I will shew thee *things* which must be hereafter.

2 And immediately [a]I was in the spirit: and behold, [b]a throne was set in heaven, and one sat on the throne.

3:9 [a]ch. 2:9 [b]Is. 49:23
3:10 [a]2 Pet. 2:9 [b]Luke 2:1 [c]Is. 24:17
3:11 [a]Phil. 4:5 [b]ch. 2:25 [c]ch. 2:10
3:12 [a]1 Ki. 7:21; Gal. 2:9 [b]ch. 14:1 [c]Heb. 12:22 [d]ch. 22:4
3:13 [a]ch. 2:7
3:14 [1]Or, *in Laodicea* [a]Is. 65:16 [b]ch. 19:11 [c]Col. 1:15
3:15 [a]ver. 1
3:17 [a]Hos. 12:8; 1 Cor. 4:8
3:18 [a]Is. 55:1; Mat. 13:44 [b]2 Cor. 5:3; ch. 7:13
3:19 [a]Job 5:17; Prov. 3:11; Heb. 12:5,6
3:20 [a]Sol. 5:2 [b]Luke 12:37 [c]John 14:23
3:21 [a]Mat. 19:28; Luke 22:30; 2 Tim. 2:12
3:22 [a]ch. 2:7
4:1 [a]ch. 1:10 [b]ch. 11:12 [c]ch. 1:19
4:2 [a]ch. 1:10 [b]Is. 6:1; Ezek. 1:26; Dan. 7:9

3:9 *synagogue of Satan.* A bold metaphor directed against unbelieving and hostile Jews. Cf. Jesus' scathing rebuke in John 8:44; see also 2 Cor 11:14–15. The Jewish synagogue was a gathering place for worship, study and communal activities. *say they are Jews.* See Rom 2:28–29. *worship before thy feet.* An appropriate act of worship in the Near East (see Is 45:14; 60:14; cf. Acts 10:25; Phil 2:10; see also note on Rev 1:17).

‡3:10 *keep thee from.* The Greek for this phrase can mean either "keep you from undergoing" or "keep you through." *hour of temptation.* This period of testing that precedes the consummation of the kingdom is the Great Tribulation period (see 13:5–10; Mat 24:4–28; cf. Dan 12:1; Mark 13:19; 2 Thes 2:1–12). Notice that the purpose of this tribulation is "to try them that dwell on the earth." See note on 6:10.

3:11 *I come quickly.* Cf. 1:1; 22:7,12,20 (see note on Jas 5:9).

3:12 *Him that overcometh.* See note on 2:7. *temple.* See note on 7:15. *name of my God.* See 14:1; 22:4. *new Jerusalem.* See 21:2,10. *write upon him my new name.* Names revealed character. Christ's new name symbolizes all that He is by virtue of His redemptive work for mankind. This awaits the second advent.

‡3:14 *Laodiceans.* Laodicea was near modern Denizli. The wealthiest city in Phrygia during Roman times, it was widely known for its banking establishments, medical school and textile industry. Its major weakness was lack of an adequate water supply. Each of these characteristics is reflected in the letter. *the Amen.* Is 65:16 speaks of "the God of truth," i.e., "the God of the Amen." As a personal designation it describes one who is perfectly trustworthy or faithful. *faithful and true witness.* See 1:5; 19:11. *beginning.* The Greek word can mean first in point of time ("beginning") or first in rank ("ruler"). Christ, the Creator of all things, is the Ruler, the One in first rank over all His creation.

‡3:16 *lukewarm, and neither cold nor hot.* Something cold is always refreshing, and "hot" may refer to the hot, medicinal waters of nearby Hierapolis. The church in Laodicea supplied neither healing for the spiritually sick nor refreshment for the spiritually weary. *spue.* Lit. "vomit."

3:18 Refers to three items in which Laodicea took great pride: financial wealth, an extensive textile industry and a famous eye salve.

3:19 *As many as I love, I . . . chasten.* See Job 5:17; Ps 94:12; Prov 3:11–12; 1 Cor 11:32; Heb 12:5–11.

‡3:20 *I stand at the door, and knock.* Usually taken as a picture of Christ's knocking on the door of the individual unbeliever's heart. In context, however, the self-deluded members of the congregation are being addressed. In this passage, the Lord of the church is pictured as knocking on the door of the church. The Laodiceans were in danger of closing Christ out of their church, just as unbelievers can close Him out of their lives.

3:21 *overcometh.* See notes on 2:7 and 3:5. *set down with my Father in his throne.* See 20:4,6; Mat 19:28; 2 Tim 2:12.

4:1–5:14 These two chapters constitute an introduction to chs. 6–20. In the throne room of heaven, the Lamb assumes the responsibility of initiating the great final conflict with the forces of evil, the end of which will see the Lamb triumphant and the devil consigned to the lake of fire.

‡4:1 *Come up hither.* Similarly, Moses was called up on mount Sinai to receive divine direction (Ex 19:20,24). Cf. also the heavenly ascent of the two witnesses (11:12). Some interpreters find the rapture of the church in this verse. *things which must be hereafter.* Indicates events that are yet to come. See 1:1,19; Dan 2:28–29,45.

4:2 *in the spirit.* In a state of heightened spiritual awareness (see note on 1:10; see also 17:3; 21:10). *throne . . . in heaven.* The depiction of God ruling from His throne in heaven is a regular feature of the OT (e.g., Ps 47:8).

3 And he that sat was to look upon like a
jasper and a sardine stone: [a]and *there was* a
rainbow round about the throne, in sight like
unto an emerald.
4 [a]And round about the throne *were* four
and twenty seats: and upon the seats I saw
four and twenty elders sitting, [b]clothed in
white raiment; and they had on their heads
crowns of gold.
5 And out of the throne proceeded [a]light-
nings and thunderings and voices: [b]and *there*
were seven lamps of fire burning before the
throne, which are [c]the seven spirits of God.
6 And before the throne *there was* [a]a sea of
glass like unto crystal: [b]and in the midst of the
throne, and round about the throne, *were* four
beasts full of eyes before and behind.
7 [a]And the first beast *was* like a lion, and
the second beast like a calf, and the third beast
had a face as a man, and the fourth beast *was*
like a flying eagle.
8 And the four beasts had each of them
[a]six wings about *him;* and *they were* full of
eyes within: and [1]they rest not day and night,
saying, [b]Holy, holy, holy, [c]Lord God Almighty,
[d]which was, and is, and is to come.
9 And when *those* beasts give glory and
honour and thanks to him that sat on the
throne, [a]who liveth for ever and ever,

4:3 [a]Ezek. 1:28
4:4 [a]ch. 11:16 [b]ch. 3:4,5
4:5 [a]ch. 8:5 [b]Ex. 37:23; 2 Chr. 4:20; Ezek. 1:13; Zech. 4:2 [c]ch. 1:4
4:6 [a]Ex. 38:8; ch. 15:2 [b]Ezek. 1:5
4:7 [a]Num. 2:2; Ezek. 1:10
4:8 [1]Gr. *they have no rest* [a]Is. 6:2 [b]Is. 6:3 [c]ch. 1:8 [d]ch. 1:4
4:9 [a]ch. 1:18
4:10 [a]ch. 5:8,14
4:11 [a]ch. 5:12 [b]Gen. 1:1; Acts 17:24; Eph. 3:9
5:1 [a]Ezek. 2:9 [b]Is. 29:11; Dan. 12:4
5:5 [a]Gen. 49:9; Heb. 7:14 [b]Is. 11:1,10; ch. 22:16 [c]ch. 6:1
5:6 [a]Is. 53:7; John 1:29; 1 Pet. 1:19

10 [a]The four and twenty elders fall down
before him that sat on the throne, and worship
him that liveth for ever and ever, and cast
their crowns before the throne, saying,
11 [a]Thou art worthy, O Lord, to receive
glory and honour and power: [b]for thou hast
created all *things,* and for thy pleasure they
are and were created.

The book and the Lamb

5 And I saw in the right hand of him that
sat on the throne [a]a book written within
and on the backside, [b]sealed with seven seals.
2 And I saw a strong angel proclaiming
with a loud voice, Who is worthy to open the
book, and to loose the seals thereof?
3 And no *man* in heaven, nor in earth, neither under the earth, was able to open the
book, neither to look thereon.
4 And I wept much, because no *man* was
found worthy to open and to read the book,
neither to look thereon.
5 And one of the elders saith unto me,
Weep not: behold, [a]the Lion of the tribe of
Juda, [b]the root of David, hath prevailed to
open the book, [c]and to loose the seven seals
thereof.
6 And I beheld, and lo, in the midst of the
throne and of the four beasts, and in the midst
of the elders, stood [a]a Lamb as *it had been*

‡4:3 *jasper . . . sardine . . . emerald.* Since God dwells in "the light which no man can approach" and is one "whom no man hath seen, nor can see" (1 Tim 6:16), He is described in terms of the reflected brilliance of precious stones—an emerald rainbow around the throne (cf. Ezek 1:26–28). In the OT the rainbow was a symbol of divine hope and a promise for the future (Gen 9:13–15).
4:4 *four and twenty elders.* Representative of either the whole company of believers in heaven or an exalted angelic order worshiping and serving God there (see vv. 9–11; 5:5–14; 7:11–17; 11:16–18; 14:3; 19:4). The number 24 is often understood to reflect the 12 Israelite tribes of the OT and the 12 apostles of the NT.
4:5 *lightnings . . . thunderings . . . burning.* Symbolic of the awesome majesty and power of God (cf. the manifestation of God at Sinai, Ex 19:16–19; cf. also the conventional OT depiction of God's coming in mighty power to deliver His people, Ps 18:12–15; 77:18). In Revelation, thunder and lightning always mark an important event connected with the heavenly temple (8:5; 11:19; 16:18). *seven spirits.* See note on 1:4; "seven" symbolizes fullness, completeness or perfection.
4:6 *sea of glass.* See 15:2. The source of the imagery may be Ezek 1:22 (cf. Ex 24:10), but it is also possible that it is the basin in the heavenly temple (cf. 11:19; 14:15,17; 15:5–6,8; 16:1,17), whose counterpart in the earthly temple was referred to as the "sea" (1 Ki 7:23–25; 2 Ki 16:17; 2 Chr 4:2,4,10,15; Jer 27:19). Other features of the temple in heaven are: the lamps (v. 5), the altar (6:9), the altar of incense (8:3) and the ark of his testament (11:19). *four beasts.* An exalted order of angelic beings whose task is to guard the heavenly throne and lead in worship and adoration of God. *full of eyes.* Nothing escapes their attention.
4:7 Ezekiel in a vision also saw four living creatures, each of which had four faces—human in front, lion on the right, ox on the left, and eagle behind (Ezek 1:6,10). In John's vision the creatures were in the form of a lion, an ox, and a flying eagle, and one had a face like that of a man.
4:8 *Holy, holy, holy.* See note on Is 6:3. *was . . . is . . . is to come.* An expansion of the divine name in Ex 3:14–15 (see note on Rev 1:4). God's power and holiness extend from eternity past to eternity yet to come (cf. Is 41:4).
4:10 *cast their crowns.* Acknowledgment that God alone is worthy of ultimate praise and worship.
4:11 *thou hast created all things.* See Gen 1.
5:1 *book.* See note on 1:11; cf. the little book of 10:2,8–10. *written within and on the backside.* Like the stone tablets of the OT covenant law (Ex 32:15; see Ezek 2:9–10). The fibers of a papyrus scroll run horizontally on the inside, which makes writing easier than on the reverse side (where the fibers are vertical). *sealed with seven seals.* Indicating absolute inviolability (cf. Is 29:11; Dan 12:4).
5:2 *strong angel.* See 18:21.
5:3 *heaven . . . earth . . . under the earth.* A conventional phrase used to express the universality of the proclamation—no creature was worthy. It is not intended to teach a threefold division of the universe (cf. Ex 20:4; Phil 2:10).
5:5 *Lion of the tribe of Juda.* A Messianic title taken from Gen 49:8–10, where Judah is named a "lion's whelp" and promised the right to rule "until Shiloh comes" (see also Ezek 21:27). *root of David.* See Is 11:1,10, which looks forward to the ideal king in the line of David. The title is interpreted Messianically in Rom 15:12.
5:6 *Lamb.* Pictured as the sacrifice for sin ("slain"; cf. Is 53:7; John 1:29) and as the mighty conqueror (17:14). Revelation uses a special word for "lamb" (29 times in Revelation and only once elsewhere in the NT—John 21:15). The idea of the lamb as a victorious military leader seems to come from the apocalyptic tradition (1 Enoch 90:9; Testament of Joseph 19:8). *as it had been slain.* Bearing the marks of its slaughter—He has come to power through His death. *seven horns.* The horn is an ancient Jewish symbol for power or strength (cf. Deut 33:17). The fourth beast of Dan 7:7,20 had ten horns (cf. Dan 8:3,5). Seven horns would symbolize full strength. *seven spirits.* See note on 4:5.

slain, having seven horns and [b]seven eyes, which are [c]the seven spirits of God sent forth into all the earth.

7 And he came and took the book out of the right hand [a]of him that sat upon the throne.

8 And when he had taken the book, [a]the four beasts and four *and* twenty elders fell down before the Lamb, having every one *of them* [b]harps, and golden vials full of [1]odours, [c]which are the prayers of saints.

9 And [a]they sung a new song, saying, [b]Thou art worthy to take the book, and to open the seals thereof: for thou wast slain, and [c]hast redeemed us to God by thy blood [d]out of every kindred, and tongue, and people, and nation;

10 [a]And hast made us unto our God kings and priests: and we shall reign on the earth.

11 ¶ And I beheld, and I heard the voice of many angels round about the throne and the beasts and the elders: and the number of them was [a]ten thousand times ten thousand, and thousands of thousands;

12 Saying with a loud voice, [a]Worthy is the Lamb that was slain to receive power, and riches, and wisdom, and strength, and honour, and glory, and blessing.

13 And [a]every creature which is in heaven, and on the earth, and under the earth, and such as are in the sea, and all that are in them, heard I saying, [b]Blessing, and honour, and glory, and power, *be* unto him [c]that sitteth upon the throne, and unto the Lamb for ever and ever.

14 [a]And the four beasts said, Amen. And the four *and* twenty elders fell down and worshipped him [b]that liveth for ever and ever.

5:6 [b]Zech. 3:9 [c]ch. 4:5
5:7 [a]ch. 4:2
5:8 [1]Or, *incense* [a]ch. 4:8,10 [b]ch. 14:2 [c]Ps. 141:2
5:9 [a]Ps. 40:3 [b]ch. 4:11 [c]Acts 20:28; Rom. 3:24; 1 Cor. 6:20; Eph. 1:7; Col. 1:14; Heb. 9:12; 1 Pet. 1:18; 2 Pet. 2:1; 1 John 1:7 [d]Dan. 4:1
5:10 [a]Ex. 19:6; 1 Pet. 2:5
5:11 [a]Ps. 68:17; Dan. 7:10; Heb. 12:22
5:12 [a]ch. 4:11
5:13 [a]Phil. 2:10 [b]1 Chr. 29:11; Rom. 9:5; 16:27; 1 Tim. 6:16; 1 Pet. 4:11; 5:11 [c]ch. 6:16
5:14 [a]ch. 19:4 [b]ch. 4:9,10
6:1 [a]ch. 5:5-7 [b]ch. 4:7
6:2 [a]Zech. 6:3; ch. 19:11 [b]Ps. 45:4,5 LXX [c]Zech. 6:11; ch. 14:14
6:3 [a]ch. 4:7
6:4 [a]Zech. 6:2
6:5 [a]ch. 4:7 [b]Zech. 6:2
6:6 [1]The word *chenix* signifieth a measure containing one wine quart, and the twelfth part of a quart [a]ch. 9:4
6:7 [a]ch. 4:7
6:8 [1]Or, *to him* [a]Zech. 6:3 [b]Ezek. 14:21 [c]Lev. 26:22
6:9 [a]ch. 8:3; 14:18 [b]ch. 20:4

Six of the seals opened

6 And [a]I saw when the Lamb opened one of the seals, and I heard, as *it were* the noise of thunder, [b]one of the four beasts saying, Come and see.

2 And I saw, and behold [a]a white horse: [b]and he that sat on him had a bow; [c]and a crown was given unto him: and he went forth conquering, and to conquer.

3 ¶ And when he had opened the second seal, [a]I heard the second beast say, Come and see.

4 [a]And there went out another horse *that was* red: and *power* was given to him that sat thereon to take peace from the earth, and that they should kill one another: and there was given unto him a great sword.

5 ¶ And when he had opened the third seal, [a]I heard the third beast say, Come and see. And I beheld, and lo [b]a black horse; and he that sat on him had a pair of balances in his hand.

6 And I heard a voice in the midst of the four beasts say, [1]A measure of wheat for a penny, and three measures of barley for a penny; and [a]*see* thou hurt not the oil and the wine.

7 ¶ And when he had opened the fourth seal, [a]I heard the voice of the fourth beast say, Come and see.

8 [a]And I looked, and behold a pale horse: and his name that sat on him *was* Death, and Hell followed with him. And power was given [1]unto them over the fourth *part* of the earth, [b]to kill with sword, and with hunger, and with death, [c]and with the beasts of the earth.

9 ¶ And when he had opened the fifth seal, I saw under [a]the altar [b]the souls of them that

---

5:8 *harps.* An ancient stringed instrument (not the large modern harp) used especially to accompany songs (Ps 33:2). *vials full of odours.* The vial was a flat, shallow cup. Incense (see KJV marg.) was a normal feature of Hebrew ritual (see Deut 33:10; cf. Ps 141:2; Rev 8:3–4). *prayers of saints.* In later Jewish thought, angels often present the prayers of saints to God (Tobit 12:15; 3 Baruch 11).

5:9 *new song.* Cf. 14:3; Ps 33:3; 96:1; 144:9; Is 42:10. In the OT a new song celebrated a new act of divine deliverance or blessing. That is also its sense here; notice the theme of the song. *redeemed us . . . by thy blood . . . kindred.* The sacrificial death of Christ is central to NT teaching (see Mark 10:45; 1 Cor 6:20).

5:10 *kings and priests.* See note on 1:6. *reign on the earth.* See 2:26–27; 20:4,6; 22:5.

5:11 *thousands of thousands.* A rhetorical phrase for an indefinitely large number (see Dan 7:10; cf. Heb 12:22).

5:12 *power . . . blessing.* See David's farewell prayer in 1 Chr 29:10–19. The attributes increase from three in 4:11 to four in 5:13 to seven in 5:12; 7:12.

5:13 *heaven . . . earth . . . under the earth.* See note on v. 3.

6:1 *seals.* The first of three sevenfold numbered series of judgments (cf. the seven trumpets in chs. 8–9 and the seven vials in ch. 16).

6:2 *white horse.* The imagery of the four horsemen comes from Zech 1:8–17; 6:1–8 (see note on Zech 6:2–3). The colors in Revelation correspond to the character of the rider; white symbolizes conquest. Major interpretations of the rider on the white horse are: (1) Christ (cf. 19:11), (2) the antichrist and (3) the spirit of conquest. The latter establishes a more natural sequence with the other three riders (which symbolize bloodshed, famine and death). *bow.* A battle weapon. *crown.* See note on 2:10.

6:4 *horse that was red.* Symbolizing bloodshed and war (cf. Zech 1:8; 6:2). *they should kill one another.* If the white horse is conquest from without, the red horse may be internal revolution. *sword.* See note on 1:16.

6:5 *black horse.* Symbolizing famine (cf. Zech 6:2,6). The sequence is thus conquest, bloodshed, famine. *pair of balances.* A balance beam with scales hung from either end. Weights were originally stones.

‡6:6 *wheat . . . barley.* One quart of wheat would be enough for only one person. Three quarts of the less nutritious barley would be barely enough for a small family. Famine had inflated prices to at least ten times their normal level—an entire day's wages just for some food. *oil and the wine.* There was even less of these precious commodities.

6:8 *pale horse.* Describes the ashen appearance of the dead; it symbolizes death. *Hell.* Equivalent to Hebrew *Sheol* (see 1:18; 20:13–14; see also note on Mat 16:18).

‡6:9 *under the altar.* In OT ritual the blood of the slaughtered animal was poured out at the base of the altar (Ex 29:12; Lev 4:7). *slain for the word of God.* These are the souls of many tribulation saints.

were slain [c]for the word of God, and for [d]the
testimony which they held:
10 And they cried with a loud voice, saying, [a]How long, O Lord, [b]holy and true, [c]dost
thou not judge and avenge our blood on them
that dwell on the earth?
11 And [a]white robes were given unto
every one of them; and it was said unto them,
[b]that they should rest yet for a little season,
until their fellowservants also and their brethren, that should be killed as they *were,* should
be fulfilled.
12 ¶ And I beheld when he had opened the
sixth seal, [a]and lo, there was a great earthquake; and [b]the sun became black as sackcloth
of hair, and the moon became as blood;
13 [a]And the stars of heaven fell unto the
earth, *even* as a fig tree casteth her [1]untimely
figs, when she is shaken of a mighty wind.
14 [a]And the heaven departed as a scrole
when it is rolled together; and [b]every mountain and island were moved out of their places.
15 And the kings of the earth, and the
great men, and the rich *men,* and the chief
captains, and the mighty *men,* and every bondman, and every free *man,* [a]hid themselves in
the dens and in the rocks of the mountains;
16 [a]And said to the mountains and rocks,
Fall on us, and hide us from the face of him
that sitteth on the throne, and from the wrath
of the Lamb:
17 [a]For the great day of his wrath is come;
[b]and who shall be able to stand?

6:9 [c]ch. 1:9 [d]2 Tim. 1:8; ch. 19:10
6:10 [a]See Zech. 1:12 [b]ch. 3:7 [c]ch. 11:18
6:11 [a]ch. 3:4,5 [b]Heb. 11:40
6:12 [a]ch. 16:18 [b]Joel 2:10; 3:15; Mat. 24:29; Acts 2:20
6:13 [1]Or, *green figs* [a]ch. 8:10; 9:1
6:14 [a]Ps. 102:26; Is. 34:4; Heb. 1:12 [b]Jer. 3:23; 4:24; ch. 16:20
6:15 [a]Is. 2:19
6:16 [a]Hos. 10:8; Luke 23:30
6:17 [a]Is. 13:6; Zeph. 1:14; ch. 16:14 [b]Ps. 76:7

7:1 [a]Dan. 7:2 [b]ch. 9:4
7:3 [a]ch. 6:6 [b]ch. 22:4
7:4 [a]ch. 9:16 [b]ch. 14:1

The sealing of God's servants

7 And after these *things* I saw four angels
standing on the four corners of the earth,
[a]holding the four winds of the earth, [b]that the
wind should not blow on the earth, nor on the
sea, nor on any tree.
2 And I saw another angel ascending from
the east, having the seal of the living God: and
he cried with a loud voice to the four angels,
to whom it was given to hurt the earth and the
sea,
3 Saying, [a]Hurt not the earth, neither the
sea, nor the trees, till we have sealed the servants of our God [b]in their foreheads.
4 [a]And I heard the number of them which
were sealed: *and there were* sealed [b]an hundred *and* forty *and* four thousand of all the
tribes of the children of Israel.
5 Of the tribe of Juda *were* sealed twelve
thousand.
Of the tribe of Reuben *were* sealed
twelve thousand.
Of the tribe of Gad *were* sealed twelve
thousand.
6 Of the tribe of Aser *were* sealed twelve
thousand.
Of the tribe of Nephthalim *were* sealed
twelve thousand.
Of the tribe of Manasses *were* sealed
twelve thousand.
7 Of the tribe of Simeon *were* sealed
twelve thousand.
Of the tribe of Levi *were* sealed twelve
thousand.

‡6:10 *them that dwell on the earth.* A regular designation in Revelation for mankind in its hostility to God (see 3:10; 8:13; 11:10; 13:8,12; 17:2,8). These are those that oppose God, receive the mark of the beast, and on whom the tribulation is focused. (See note on 3:10.)

6:11 *white robes.* Symbol of blessedness and purity (see 3:5,18; 4:4; 7:9,13; 19:14). *until their fellowservants . . . should be fulfilled.* Jewish thought held that God rules the world according to a predetermined time schedule (see 2 Esdras 4:35–37) and that the end awaits the death of a certain number of the righteous (1 Enoch 47:4). God will avenge, but only in due time.

‡6:12 *a great earthquake.* A regular feature of divine visitation (see Ex 19:18; Is 2:19; Hag 2:6), but this is more like a universe quake. *moon became as blood.* See Joel 2:31, quoted by Peter in his Pentecost sermon (Acts 2:20).

6:13 *stars . . . fell.* One of the signs immediately preceding the coming of the Son of man (Mark 13:25–26). *untimely figs.* Green figs appearing in the winter and easily blown from the tree, which at that season has no leaves.

6:14 *heaven departed as a scrole.* See Is 34:4. *every mountain and island were moved.* Perhaps suggested by Jer 4:24 or Nah 1:5; see 16:20; 20:11.

‡6:15 *chief captains.* A chief captain was a Roman officer who commanded a cohort, i.e., about 1,000 men. *hid . . . in the dens.* See Jer 4:29.

‡6:16 *wrath of the Lamb.* God's wrath is a theme that permeates NT theology. It is both present (see Rom 1:18 and note) and future (see 19:15). It is prophesied in the OT (Zeph 1:14–18; Nah 1:6; Mal 3:2). According to the pretribulation rapture, the church is removed before the tribulation begins, and thus does not experience God's wrath (1 Thes 5:9). *Lamb.* See note on 5:6.

7:1–17 A parenthesis separating the final seal from the preceding six (the same feature is found in the trumpet sequence; see 10:1–11:13). It contains two visions: (1) the sealing of the 144,000 (vv. 1–8) and (2) the innumerable multitude (vv. 9–17).

7:1 *four winds.* Destructive agents of God (see Jer 49:36).

‡7:2 *seal of the living God.* Ancient documents were folded and tied, and a lump of clay was pressed over the knot. The sender would then stamp the hardening clay with his signet ring or roll it with a cylinder seal, which authenticated and protected the contents. The sealing in ch. 7 results in the name of the Lord being stamped on the forehead of His followers (see 9:4; 14:1; cf. 22:4). Its primary purpose is to protect the 144,000 Jews in the coming judgments. For the background see Ezek 9:4, where the mark was the Hebrew letter *Taw,* made like an *X* or +.

‡7:4 *an hundred and forty and four thousand.* Some find here a reference to members of actual Jewish tribes, the faithful Jewish remnant of the "great tribulation" (v. 14). Others take the passage as symbolic of all the faithful believers who live during the period of tribulation. This must be a reference to actual Jews, because they are listed by tribes and then distinguished from the great multitude of Gentiles (v. 9–17), who are from every tongue, tribe, nation and people.

7:5 *Juda.* Perhaps listed before Reuben, his older brother, because the Messiah belonged to the tribe of Judah (but see note on Gen 37:21).

7:6 *Manasses.* One of the two Joseph tribes (Ephraim and Manasseh), yet mentioned separately, probably to make up 12 tribes since Dan is omitted. This omission is due perhaps to Dan's early connection with idolatry (Judg 18:30), or to a tradition that the antichrist was to come from that tribe.

Of the tribe of Isachar *were* sealed
twelve thousand.
8 Of the tribe of Zabulon *were* sealed
twelve thousand.
Of the tribe of Joseph *were* sealed
twelve thousand.
Of the tribe of Benjamin *were* sealed
twelve thousand.

The saints in white robes

9 ¶ After this I beheld, and lo, [a]a great multitude, which no *man* could number, [b]of all nations, and kindreds, and people, and tongues,
stood before the throne, and before the Lamb,
[c]clothed with white robes, and palms in their
hands;
10 And cried with a loud voice, saying,
[a]Salvation to our God [b]which sitteth upon the
throne, and unto the Lamb.
11 [a]And all the angels stood round about
the throne, and *about* the elders and the four
beasts, and fell before the throne on their
faces, and worshipped God,
12 [a]Saying, Amen: Blessing, and glory, and
wisdom, and thanksgiving, and honour, and
power, and might, *be* unto our God for ever
and ever. Amen.
13 And one of the elders answered, saying
unto me, What are these which are arrayed in
[a]white robes? and whence came they?
14 And I said unto him, Sir, thou knowest.
And he said to me, [a]These are they which
came out of great tribulation, and have
[b]washed their robes, and made them white in
the blood of the Lamb.
15 Therefore are they before the throne of
God, and serve him day and night in his tem-

7:9 [a]Rom. 11:25 [b]ch. 5:9 [c]ver. 14; ch. 3:5,18; 4:4; 6:11
7:10 [a]Ps. 3:8; Is. 43:11; Jer. 3:23; Hos. 13:4; ch. 19:1 [b]ch. 5:13
7:11 [a]ch. 4:6
7:12 [a]ch. 5:13,14
7:13 [a]ver. 9
7:14 [a]ch. 6:9; 17:6 [b]Is. 1:18; See Zech. 3:3-5
7:15 [a]Is. 4:5,6; ch. 21:3
7:16 [a]Is. 49:10 [b]Ps. 121:6; ch. 21:4
7:17 [a]Ps. 23:1; 36:8; John 10:11,14 [b]Is. 25:8; ch. 21:4
8:1 [a]ch. 6:1
8:2 [a]Mat. 18:10; Luke 1:19 [b]2 Chr. 29:25-28
8:3 [1]Or, *add it to the prayers* [a]ch. 5:8 [b]Ex. 30:1; ch. 6:9
8:4 [a]Ps. 141:2; Luke 1:10
8:5 [1][Or, *upon*] [a]ch. 16:18 [b]2 Sam. 22:8; 1 Ki. 19:11; Acts 4:31
8:7 [a]Ezek. 38:22 [b]ch. 16:2 [c]Is. 2:13; ch. 9:4
8:8 [a]Jer. 51:25; Amos 7:4

ple: and he that sitteth on the throne shall
[a]dwell among them.
16 [a]They shall hunger no more, neither
thirst any more; [b]neither shall the sun light on
them, nor any heat.
17 For the Lamb which is in the midst of
the throne [a]shall feed them, and shall lead
them unto living fountains of waters: [b]and
God shall wipe away all tears from their eyes.

The seventh seal

8 And [a]when he had opened the seventh
seal, there was silence in heaven about
the space of half an hour.
2 ¶ [a]And I saw the seven angels which
stood before God; [b]and to them were given
seven trumpets.
3 And another angel came and stood at the
altar, having a golden censer; and there was
given unto him much incense, that he should
[1]offer *it* with [a]the prayers of all saints upon
[b]the golden altar which was before the throne.
4 And [a]the smoke of the incense, *which*
came with the prayers of the saints, ascended
up before God out of the angel's hand.
5 And the angel took the censer, and filled
it with fire of the altar, and cast *it* [1]into the
earth: and [a]there were voices, and thunderings, and lightnings, [b]and an earthquake.
6 And the seven angels which had the sev-
en trumpets prepared themselves to sound.
7 ¶ The first angel sounded, [a]and there followed hail and fire mingled with blood, and
they were cast [b]upon the earth: and the third
part [c]of trees was burnt up, and all green grass
was burnt up.
8 ¶ And the second angel sounded, [a]and as

‡7:9 *great multitude.* Identified in v. 14 as those who have come out of the great tribulation. *of all nations, and kindreds,and people, and tongues.* All four are mentioned together also in 5:9; 11:9; 13:7; 14:6. Cf. 10:11; 17:15, in which one of the four is changed. *palms.* Palm branches were used for festive occasions (see Lev 23:40; John 12:13).

‡7:10 *Salvation to our God.* See Gen 49:18; John 2:9. These individuals were saved, but not protected as the 144,000 during the tribulation, and therefore they lost their lives.

7:11 *elders.* See note on 4:4. *four beasts.* See note on 4:6.

7:12 *Blessing . . . might.* The sevenfold list of attributes expresses complete or perfect praise (see note on 5:12).

7:13 *white robes.* See note on 6:11.

7:14 *great tribulation.* The period of final hostility prior to Christ's return. Some hold that the beginning of this hostility was already being experienced by the church of John's day.

7:15 *temple.* All 16 references to the temple in Revelation use the word that designates the inner shrine rather than the larger precincts. It is the place where God's presence dwells. *dwell among them.* The imagery would evoke memories of the tabernacle in the wilderness (Lev 26:11–13).

7:17 *shall feed them.* Ancient kings often referred to themselves as the shepherds of their people.

‡8:1 *opened the seventh seal.* There is no separate judgment associated with this seal. Instead, seven angels appear with seven trumpets to signal a seven-fold judgment as the expression of this seventh and final seal. *silence in heaven.* A dramatic pause before the next series of plagues—the final act of the drama is left undisclosed here, reserved to be presented later.

8:2 *seven trumpets.* In OT times the trumpet served to announce important events and give signals in time of war. The seven trumpets of Rev 8–9; 11:15–19 announce a series of plagues more severe than the seals but not as completely devastating as the vials (ch. 16).

8:3 *censer.* A firepan used to hold live charcoal for the burning of incense (cf. Ex 27:3; 1 Ki 7:50). *with the prayers.* Most translations consider the incense to be mingled "with" prayers. The Greek for this phrase also allows a translation that takes the incense "to be" the prayers ("incense . . . consisting of the prayers").

8:4 Although the angel is involved in presenting the prayers of the saints to God, he does not make them acceptable. The Jewish apocalyptic concept of angels as mediators finds no place in the NT.

8:5 *thunderings . . . earthquake.* See note on 4:5.

8:7 *hail and fire mingled with blood.* Cf. the imagery of the seventh plague on Egypt (Ex 9:13–25; cf. Ezek 38:22). *the third part of trees was burnt up.* This fraction indicates that the punishment announced by the trumpets is not yet complete and final (the same fraction appears in each of the next three plagues: vv. 8–9, 10–11, 12). A smaller fraction (a fourth) of devastation accompanied the opening of the fourth seal (6:8).

‡8:8 *sea became blood.* Reminiscent of the first plague on Egypt (Ex 7:20–21). This is an eschatological judgment rather

it were a great mountain burning with fire was
cast into the sea: [b]and the third *part* of the sea
[c]became blood;
9 [a]And the third *part* of the creatures
which were in the sea, and had life, died; and
the third *part* of the ships were destroyed.
10 ¶ And the third angel sounded, [a]and
there fell a great star from heaven, burning as
it were a lamp, [b]and it fell upon the third *part*
of the rivers, and upon the fountains of waters;
11 [a]And the name of the star is called
Wormwood: [b]and the third *part* of the waters
became wormwood; and many men died of
the waters, because they were made bitter.
12 ¶ [a]And the fourth angel sounded, and
the third *part* of the sun was smitten, and the
third *part* of the moon, and the third *part* of
the stars; so as the third *part* of them was darkened and the day shone not for a third *part* of
it, and the night likewise.
13 And I beheld, [a]and heard an angel flying through the midst of heaven, saying with a
loud voice, [b]Woe, woe, woe, to the inhabiters
of the earth by reason of the other voices of
the trumpet of the three angels, which are yet
to sound.

The plague of locusts

9 And the fifth angel sounded, [a]and I saw
a star fall from heaven unto the earth:
and to him was given the key of [b]the bottomless pit.
2 And he opened the bottomless pit; and
there arose a smoke out of the pit, as the smoke
of a great furnace; and the sun and the air were
darkened by reason of the smoke of the pit.
3 And there came out of the smoke [a]locusts
upon the earth: and unto them was given power, [b]as the scorpions of the earth have power.
4 And it was commanded them [a]that they
should not hurt [b]the grass of the earth, neither
any green *thing,* neither any tree; but only
those men which have not [c]the seal of God in
their foreheads.
5 And to them it was given that they should
not kill them, [a]but that they should be tormented five months: and their torment *was* as the
torment of a scorpion, when he striketh a man.
6 And in those days [a]shall men seek death,
and shall not find it; and shall desire to die,
and death shall flee from them.
7 And [a]the shapes of the locusts *were* like
unto horses prepared unto battle; [b]and on
their heads *were* as *it were* crowns like gold,
[c]and their faces *were* as the faces of men.
8 And they had hair as the hair of women,
and [a]their teeth were as *the teeth* of lions.
9 And they had breastplates, as *it were*
breastplates of iron; and the sound of their
wings *was* [a]as the sound of chariots of many
horses running to battle.
10 And they had tails like unto scorpions,
and there were stings in their tails: [a]and their
power *was* to hurt men five months.
11 [a]And they had a king over them, *which*
is [b]the angel of the bottomless *pit,* whose
name in the Hebrew tongue *is* Abaddon, but
in the Greek *tongue* hath *his* name [1]Apollyon.

8:8 [b]ch. 16:3 [c]Ezek. 14:19 8:9 [a]ch. 16:3 8:10 [a]Is. 14:12; ch. 9:1 [b]ch. 16:4 8:11 [a]Ruth 1:20 [b]Ex. 15:23 8:12 [a]Is. 13:10; Amos 8:9 8:13 [a]ch. 14:6; 19:17 [b]ch. 9:12; 11:14 9:1 [a]Luke 10:18; ch. 8:10 [b]ver. 2,11; Luke 8:31; ch. 17:8; 20:1

9:3 [a]Ex. 10:4; Judg. 7:12 [b]ver. 10 9:4 [a]ch. 6:6; 7:3 [b]ch. 8:7 [c]See Ex. 12:23; Ezek. 9:4; ch. 7:3 9:5 [a]ver. 10; ch. 11:7 9:6 [a]Job 3:21; Is. 2:19; Jer. 8:3; ch. 6:16 9:7 [a]Joel 2:4 [b]Nah. 3:17 [c]Dan. 7:8 9:8 [a]Joel 1:6 9:9 [a]Joel 2:5-7 9:10 [a]ver. 5 9:11 [1] That is to say, *A destroyer* [a]Eph. 2:2 [b]ver. 1

than natural pollution resulting from widespread volcanic upheavals. Notice that the text does not say the sea became like blood, but that it actually turned into blood.

8:10 *there fell a great star.* See notes on 6:13; 9:1.

8:11 *Wormwood.* A plant with a strong, bitter taste. It is used here as a metaphor for calamity and sorrow (see Prov 5:3–4; Jer 9:15; Lam 3:19). It is not poisonous, but its bitterness suggests death. *waters became wormwood.* The reverse of the miracle at Marah, where bitter waters were made sweet (Ex 15:25).

‡8:12 *the third part of the sun . . . smitten.* In the ninth plague on Egypt, thick darkness covered the land for three days (Ex 10:21–23). References to the Egyptian plagues suggest that in Revelation we have the final exodus of God's people from the bondage of a world controlled by hostile powers. This plague is far worse and seems to have no end.

‡8:13 *Woe, woe, woe . . . yet to sound.* These three woes correspond to the three final trumpet plagues (see 9:12; 11:14 [10:1–11:13 is a parenthesis]; the seven vial judgments of chs. 15–16 apparently constitute the third woe). The woes fall on the unbelieving world (the phrase "the inhabitants of the earth" refers to the wicked; see notes on 3:10 and 6:10), not on the righteous (see 9:4).

‡9:1 *star fall from heaven.* The star in 8:10 was part of a cosmic disturbance; here the star is a divine agent, probably an angel (cf. 1:20; 12:4; 20:1). *bottomless pit.* Conceived of as the subterranean abode of demonic hordes (see 20:1; Luke 8:31). The Greek word *abyss* means "very deep" or "bottomless," and is used in the Septuagint (the Greek translation of the OT) to translate the Hebrew word for the primeval deep (see Gen 1:2; 7:11; Prov 8:28). Seven of the nine NT occurrences of the Greek word for "bottomless pit" are in Revelation.

‡9:3 *locusts.* For background see the plague of locusts in Ex 10:1–20. Joel 1:2–2:11 interprets the locust plague as a foreshadowing of the devastations that accompany the day of the Lord. Locusts traveled in enormous swarms and could strip a land of all vegetation. *scorpions.* Small creatures that injure or kill by means of a poisonous barb in the tail. The description of these creatures indicates intelligence. Many believe they are symbolic of demons.

9:4 *men which have not the seal of God.* The first woe does not affect the "servants of our God" (see 7:3). Cf. the Israelites, who were protected from the Egyptian plagues (Ex 8:22; 9:4,26; 10:23; 11:7).

9:5 *five months.* A limited period of time suggested by the life cycle of the locust or the dry season (spring through late summer, about five months), in which the danger of a locust invasion is always present.

9:6 *seek death, and shall not find it.* Cf. Hos 10:8 (quoted in Luke 23:30). Cornelius Gallus, a Roman poet living in the first century B.C., wrote: "Worse than any wound is the wish to die and yet not be able to do so." Cf. Paul's attitude toward death in Phil 1:23–24.

9:7 *faces of men.* The locusts appear to have the cunning of intelligent beings. They do not simply use brute force.

9:8 *hair of women.* Perhaps a reference to long antennae. *teeth of lions.* Cruel, inhumane.

‡9:9 *breastplates.* The breastplate was a coat of mail that protected the front. *as it were breastplates of iron.* In Roman soldiers, thin iron pieces riveted to a leather base.

9:10 *five months.* See note on v. 5.

9:11 *Abaddon.* A personification of destruction (cf. Prov 15:11).

12 [a]One woe is past; *and* behold, there
come two woes more hereafter.
13 ¶ And the sixth angel sounded, and I
heard a voice from the four horns of the gold-
en altar which is before God,
14 Saying to the sixth angel which had the
trumpet, Loose the four angels which are
bound [a]in the great river Euphrates.
15 And the four angels were loosed, which
were prepared [1]for an hour, and a day, and a
month, and a year, for to slay the third *part* of
men.
16 And [a]the number of the army [b]of the
horsemen *were* two hundred thousand thousand: [c]and I heard the number of them.
17 And thus I saw the horses in the vision,
and them that sat on them, having breastplates
of fire, and of jacinth, and brimstone: [a]and the
heads of the horses *were* as the heads of lions;
and out of their mouths issued fire and smoke
and brimstone.
18 By these three was the third *part* of
men killed, by the fire, and by the smoke, and
by the brimstone, which issued out of their
mouths.
19 For their power is in their mouth, and
in their tails: [a]for their tails *were* like unto serpents, and had heads, and with them they do
hurt.
20 And the rest of the men which were not
killed by these plagues [a]*yet* repented not of
the works of their hands, that they should not
worship [b]devils, [c]and idols of gold, and silver,
and brass, and stone, and of wood: which neither can see, nor hear, nor walk:
21 Neither repented they of their murders,
[a]nor of their sorceries, nor of their fornication,
nor of their thefts.

9:12 [a]ch. 8:13
9:14 [a]ch. 16:12
9:15 [1]Or, *at*
9:16 [a]Ps. 68:17; Dan. 7:10 [b]Ezek. 38:4 [c]ch. 7:4
9:17 [a]1 Chr. 12:8; Is. 5:28,29
9:19 [a]Is. 9:15
9:20 [a]Deut. 31:29 [b]Lev. 17:7; Deut. 32:17; Ps. 106:37; 1 Cor. 10:20 [c]Ps. 115:4; 135:15; Dan. 5:23
9:21 [a]ch. 22:15
10:1 [a]Ezek. 1:28 [b]Mat. 17:2; ch. 1:16 [c]ch. 1:15
10:2 [a]Mat. 28:18
10:3 [a]ch. 8:5
10:4 [a]Dan. 8:26; 12:4,9
10:5 [a]Ex. 6:8; Dan. 12:7
10:6 [a]Neh. 9:6; ch. 4:11; 14:7 [b]Dan. 12:7; ch. 16:17
10:7 [a]ch. 11:15

John eats the book

10 And I saw another mighty angel
come down from heaven, clothed
with a cloud: [a]and a rainbow *was* upon *his*
head, and [b]his face *was* as *it were* the sun, and
[c]his feet as pillars of fire:
2 And he had in his hand a little book
open: [a]and he set his right foot upon the sea,
and *his* left *foot* on the earth,
3 And cried with a loud voice, as *when* a
lion roareth: and when he had cried, [a]seven
thunders uttered their voices.
4 And when the seven thunders had uttered their voices, I was about to write: and I
heard a voice from heaven saying unto me,
[a]Seal *up those things* which the seven thunders uttered, and write them not.
5 And the angel which I saw stand upon
the sea and upon the earth [a]lifted up his hand
to heaven,
6 And sware by him that liveth for ever and
ever, [a]who created heaven, and the *things* that
therein are, and the earth, and the *things* that
therein are, and the sea, and the *things* which
are therein, [b]that there should be time no
longer:
7 But [a]in the days of the voice of the sev-

9:12 *One woe.* See note on 8:13.
9:13 *horns of the golden altar.* See 8:3–5. The horns were projections at the four corners of the altar (Ex 27:2). Those fleeing judgment could seek mercy by taking hold of the horns (1 Ki 1:50–51; 2:28; see note on Amos 3:14).
9:14 *four angels.* Apparently in charge of the demonic horsemen (vv. 15–19). *Euphrates.* The longest river in western Asia (about 1,700 miles). It marked the boundary between Israel and her historic enemies (Assyria and Babylon) to the east (cf. Is 8:5–8).
9:15 *hour . . . day . . . month . . . year.* Apocalyptic thought views God as acting according to an exact timetable.
‡9:16 *two hundred thousand thousand.* The reference could be general, intending an incalculable host rather than a specific number (cf. Ps 68:17; Dan 7:10; Rev 5:11). However, this number, 200 million, is not out of question in today's world. An army from the east (China, India and Asia) could easily number this many soldiers.
9:17 *breastplates.* See note on v. 9. *out of their mouths issued fire.* Cf. the two witnesses in 11:5.
‡9:19 *tails were like unto serpents, and had heads.* Emphasizes the demonic origin of these strange creatures (cf. 12:9).
9:20 *devils.* Spiritual beings in league with Satan and exerting an evil influence on human affairs (cf. Deut 4:28; Ps 115:5–7; 1 Cor 10:20).
9:21 *Neither repented they.* See 16:9,11. Even physical pain will not change the rebellious heart. *sorceries.* Involved the mixing of various ingredients (the Greek for this phrase is *pharmakon,* from which comes the English "pharmacy") for magical purposes. Believers at Ephesus publicly burned their books of magic, valued at 50,000 drachmas (Acts 19:19). (A drachma was a silver coin worth about a day's wages.)
10:1 *mighty angel.* Perhaps the angel of 5:2. *rainbow.* Cf. Ezek 1:26–28. The rainbow became a sign of God's pledge never to destroy the earth again by a flood (Gen 9:8–17). *feet as pillars of fire.* Since the exodus supplies background for this central part of Revelation (see note on 8:12), this feature may recall the pillars of fire and cloud that guided (Ex 13:21–22) and protected (Ex 14:19,24) the Israelites during their wilderness journey.
10:2 *little book.* Not the same as the book of destiny in ch. 5, since that book was intended to reveal its contents and this book was to be eaten. Furthermore, the term "little book" sets this particular book off from all others. *right foot upon the sea . . . left foot on the earth.* Indicates his tremendous size and symbolizes that his coming has to do with the destiny of all creation (cf. v. 6).
10:3 *seven thunders.* In 8:5; 11:19; 16:18 thunder is connected with divine punishment. Here, too, it anticipates the judgment to fall on those who refuse God's love and grace.
10:4 *Seal up.* In Dan 8:26; 12:4,9 the prophecies are sealed until the last times, when they will be opened. What the seven thunders said will not be revealed until their proper time. Cf. the angel's instructions in 22:10 not to seal the prophecies of Revelation.
10:5 *lifted up his hand.* A part of oath taking (see Gen 14:22–23; Deut 32:40).
‡10:6 *him that liveth for ever and ever.* Of special encouragement in a context of impending martyrdom (cf. 1:18; 4:9–10; 15:7). *time no longer.* This does not mean that time will no longer exist, but that there should be no more delay in the judgment. The martyrs in 6:9–11 were told to rest for a while, but now the end has come (cf. Dan 12:1; Mark 13:19).
10:7 *mystery of God.* In apocalyptic thought mysteries were secrets preserved in heaven and revealed to the apocalyptist.

enth angel, when he shall begin to sound, the mystery of God should be finished, as he hath declared to his servants the prophets.

8 ¶ And [a]the voice which I heard from heaven spake unto me again, and said, Go *and* take the little book which is open in the hand of the angel which standeth upon the sea and upon the earth.

9 And I went unto the angel, and said unto him, Give me the little book. And he said unto me, [a]Take *it,* and eat it up; and it shall make thy belly bitter, but it shall be in thy mouth sweet as honey.

10 And I took the little book out of the angel's hand, and ate it up; [a]and it was in my mouth sweet as honey: and as soon as I had eaten it, [b]my belly was bitter.

11 And he said unto me, Thou must prophesy again before many peoples, and nations, and tongues, and kings.

The two witnesses

11 And there was given me [a]a reed like unto a rod: and the angel stood, saying, [b]Rise, and measure the temple of God, and the altar, and them that worship therein.

2 But [a]the court which is without the temple [1]leave out, and measure it not; [b]for it is given unto the Gentiles: and the holy city shall they [c]tread under foot [d]forty *and* two months.

3 And [1]I will give *power* unto my two [a]witnesses, [b]and they shall prophesy [c]a thousand two hundred *and* threescore days, clothed in sackcloth.

4 These are the [a]two olive trees, and the two candlesticks standing before the God of the earth.

5 And if any *man* will hurt them, [a]fire proceedeth out of their mouth, and devoureth their enemies: [b]and if any *man* will hurt them, he must in this manner be killed.

6 These [a]have power to shut heaven, that it rain not in the days of their prophecy: and have power over waters to turn them to blood, and to smite the earth with all plagues, as often as they will.

7 And when they [a]shall have finished their testimony, [b]the beast that ascendeth [c]out of the bottomless *pit* [d]shall make war against them, and shall overcome them, and kill them.

8 And their dead bodies *shall lie* in the street of [a]the great city, which spiritually is called Sodom and Egypt, [b]where also our Lord was crucified.

9 [a]And *they* of the people and kindreds and tongues and nations shall see their dead bod-

10:8 [a]ver. 4
10:9 [a]Jer. 15:16; Ezek. 2:8
10:10 [a]Ezek. 3:3 [b]Ezek. 2:10
11:1 [a]Ezek. 40:3; ch. 21:15 [b]Num. 23:18
11:2 [1]Gr. *cast out* [a]Ezek. 40:17 [b]Ps. 79:1; Luke 21:24
11:2 [c]Dan. 8:10 [d]ch. 13:5
11:3 [1]Or, *I will give unto my two witnesses that they may prophesy* [a]ch. 20:4 [b]ch. 19:10 [c]ch. 12:6
11:4 [a]Ps. 52:8; Jer. 11:16; Zech. 4:3
11:5 [a]2 Ki. 1:10; Jer. 1:10; Ezek. 43:3; Hos. 6:5 [b]Num. 16:29
11:6 [a]1 Ki. 17:1; Jas. 5:16
11:7 [a]Luke 13:32 [b]ch. 13:1,11 [c]ch. 9:2 [d]Dan. 7:21; Zech. 14:2
11:8 [a]ch. 14:8 [b]Heb. 13:12
11:9 [a]ch. 17:15

Here the mystery is that God has won the victory over the forces of evil and will reign for ever and ever (cf. 11:15).

10:9 *Take it, and eat it up.* Grasp and digest fully the contents of the book (cf. Ps 119:103).

10:10 *in my mouth sweet as honey.* God's eternal purposes will experience no further delay—the "good news." *my belly was bitter.* The message of the little book (11:1–13) will involve suffering—the "bad news."

10:11 *prophesy again.* The prophecies following the sounding of the seventh trumpet in 11:15. *peoples . . . kings.* See note on 7:9.

‡11:1 *a reed like unto a rod.* A bamboo-like cane that often reached a height of 20 feet and grew in abundance in the waters along the banks of the Jordan. Straight and light, the reed was a convenient measuring rod (see Ezek 40:3; Zech 2:1–2). *temple.* See note on 7:15. This seems to be a Jewish temple reconstructed during the tribulation period and desecrated by the antichrist (see Dan 9:27; Mat 24:15). *altar.* The context of worship suggests that this is the great altar.

‡11:2 *court which is without.* The court of the Gentiles, approximately 26 acres. *the holy city shall they tread under foot.* Cf. Ps 79:1; Is 63:18; Luke 21:24. *forty and two months.* Three and a half years. Some find the background for this period in the time of Jewish suffering under the Syrian tyrant, Antiochus Epiphanes (168–165 B.C.). Others point out that, whereas the temple was desolated for three years under Antiochus, the figure used in Revelation is three and a half years, which no doubt looks back to the dividing of the 70th "week" (Dan 9:27) into two equal parts. The same time period is also designated as 1,260 days (v. 3; 12:6) and as "a time, and times, and half a time" (12:14; cf. Dan 7:25; 12:7). Some believe that this period of time evidently became a conventional symbol for a limited period of unrestrained wickedness. However, these time periods, though each equal to one another, should be seen as literal.

‡11:3 *two witnesses.* Modeled after Moses and Elijah (see notes on vv. 5–6). Some feel they may symbolize testifying believers (the church), in the final period before Christ returns. However, they are probably two actual individuals who will be martyred for the proclamation of the truth. In fact, Mal 4:5–6 says that Elijah will return before the day of the Lord. That is why John the Baptist was asked if he were Elijah (John 1:21) after he denied being the Christ (John 1:20). Moses and Elijah appear together in Mal 4:4–5, and in the transfiguration (Mat 9, Mark 9, Luke 17). Together, they represent the law (Moses) and the prophets (Elijah)—a reference to the entire OT. *a thousand two hundred and threescore days.* See note on v. 2. These are months of 30 days (42 months x 30 days = 1,260 days). *sackcloth.* A coarse, dark cloth woven from the hair of goats or camels. It was worn as a sign of mourning and penitence (Joel 1:13; Jonah 3:5–6; Mat 11:21).

11:4 The imagery emphasizes that the power for effective testimony is supplied by the Spirit of God (see notes on Zech 4).

11:5 *fire proceedeth . . . and devoureth.* Cf. Elijah's encounters with the messengers of Ahaziah (2 Ki 1:10,12).

11:6 *power to shut heaven, that it rain not.* Cf. the drought in the days of Elijah (1 Ki 17:1; see also Luke 4:25; Jas 5:17). *waters . . . to blood.* God used Moses to bring the same plague on the Egyptians (Ex 7:17–21).

11:7 *the beast.* First mention of the major opponent of God's people in the final days (see chs. 13; 17). That he comes up from the bottomless pit (see note on 9:1) indicates his demonic character. *kill them.* They will suffer the same fate as their Lord (see v. 8).

‡11:8 *their dead bodies shall lie in the street.* In the Near East the denial of burial was a flagrant violation of decency. *great city.* Possibly Jerusalem, though some say Rome, Babylon or some other city. It may be symbolic of the world opposed to God (see 16:19; 17:18; 18:10,16,18–19,21). Sodom (see similarly Is 1:10) refers to its low level of morality (cf. Gen 19:4–11), and Egypt emphasizes oppression and slavery. *where also our Lord was crucified.* Some say that Jesus could have been crucified in Rome in the sense that her power extended throughout the known world and was immediately responsible for Christ's execution, but that seems to stretch the meaning of the clearly written text.

ies three days and a half, [b]and shall not suffer their dead bodies to be put in graves.

10 [a]And they that dwell upon the earth shall rejoice over them, and make merry, [b]and shall send gifts one to another; [c]because these two prophets tormented them that dwelt on the earth.

11 [a]And after three days and a half [b]the spirit of life from God entered into them, and they stood upon their feet; and great fear fell upon them which saw them.

12 And they heard a great voice from heaven saying unto them, Come up hither. [a]And they ascended up to heaven [b]in a cloud; [c]and their enemies beheld them.

13 And the same hour [a]was there a great earthquake, [b]and the tenth *part* of the city fell, and in the earthquake were slain [1]of men seven thousand: and the remnant were affrighted, [c]and gave glory to the God of heaven.

14 [a]The second woe is past; *and* behold, the third woe cometh quickly.

The seventh trumpet

15 ¶ And [a]the seventh angel sounded; [b]and there were great voices in heaven, saying, [c]The kingdoms of *this* world are become *the kingdoms* of our Lord, and of his Christ; [d]and he shall reign for ever and ever.

16 And [a]the four and twenty elders, which sat before God on their seats, fell upon their faces, and worshipped God,

17 Saying, We give thee thanks, O Lord God Almighty, [a]which art, and wast, and art to come; because thou hast taken *to thee* thy great power, [b]and hast reigned.

18 [a]And the nations were angry, and thy wrath is come, [b]and the time of the dead, that *they* should be judged, and that *thou* shouldest give reward unto thy servants the prophets, and to the saints, and them that fear thy name, [c]small and great; [d]and shouldest destroy them which [1]destroy the earth.

The woman and the dragon

19 ¶ And [a]the temple of God was opened in heaven, and there was seen in his temple the ark of his testament: and [b]there were lightnings, and voices, and thunderings, and an earthquake, [c]and great hail.

12 And there appeared a great [1]wonder in heaven; a woman clothed with the sun, and the moon under her feet, and upon her head a crown of twelve stars:

2 And she being with child cried, [a]travailing in birth, and pained to be delivered.

3 And there appeared another [1]wonder in heaven; and behold [a]a great red dragon, [b]having seven heads and ten horns, [c]and seven crowns upon his heads.

4 And [a]his tail drew the third *part* [b]of the stars of heaven, [c]and did cast them to the earth: and the dragon stood [d]before the woman which was ready to be delivered, [e]for to devour her child as soon as it was born.

5 And she brought forth a man child, [a]who was to rule all nations with a rod of iron: and her child was caught up unto God, and *to* his throne.

6 And [a]the woman fled into the wilderness, where she hath a place prepared of God,

11:9 [b]Ps. 79:2,3
11:10 [a]ch. 12:12 [b]Esth. 9:19 [c]ch. 16:10
11:11 [a]ver. 9 [b]Ezek. 37:5
11:12 [a]Is. 14:13 [b]Is. 60:8; Acts 1:9 [c]2 Ki. 2:1
11:13 [1]Gr. *names of men* [a]ch. 6:12 [b]ch. 16:19 [c]Josh. 7:19
11:14 [a]ch. 8:13
11:15 [a]ch. 10:7 [b]Is. 27:13 [c]ch. 12:10 [d]Dan. 2:44
11:16 [a]ch. 4:4
11:17 [a]ch. 16:5 [b]ch. 19:6
11:18 [1]Or, *corrupt* [a]ver. 2,9 [b]Dan. 7:9 [c]ch. 19:5 [d]ch. 13:10
11:19 [a]ch. 15:5,8 [b]ch. 8:5 [c]ch. 16:21
12:1 [1]Or, *sign*
12:2 [a]Is. 66:7; Gal. 4:19
12:3 [1]Or, *sign* [a]ch. 17:3 [b]ch. 17:9,10 [c]ch. 13:1
12:4 [a]ch. 9:10,19 [b]ch. 17:18 [c]Dan. 8:10 [d]ver. 2 [e]Ex. 1:16
12:5 [a]Ps. 2:9; ch. 19:15
12:6 [a]ver. 4

11:9 *three days and a half.* A short time when compared with the three and a half years of their ministry. *not suffer . . . graves.* See note on v. 8.

‡11:11 *the spirit of life from God entered into them.* A dramatic validation of the true faith (cf. Ezek 37:5,10). These two individuals are raised from the dead by God.

11:12 *ascended up to heaven in a cloud.* Cf. 1 Thes 4:17. *enemies beheld them.* Cf. 1:7.

11:13 *earthquake.* See notes on 6:12; Ezek 38:19. *gave glory to the God of heaven.* Not an act of repentance but the terrified realization that Christ, not the antichrist, is the true Lord of all.

11:14 *second woe.* Cf. 9:12.

‡11:15 *seventh angel sounded.* The series of trumpet blasts is now continued (see 9:13) and completed. As with the breaking of the seventh seal, no immediate judgment occurs. Apparently, the seven vial judgments (ch. 16) compose the seventh trumpet. There is thus a heightening of the seventh and last seal as well as the last trumpet. *kingdoms of our Lord.* Cf. Ex 15:18; Ps 10:16; Zech 14:9. *of our Lord, and of his Christ.* Cf. Ps 2:2.

11:16 *four and twenty elders.* See note on 4:4.

‡11:17 *which art, and wast, and art to come.* See 1:4,8; 4:8.

11:18 *nations were angry.* See Ps 48:4. *thy wrath.* See note on 6:16. God's wrath triumphs in 14:10–11; 16:15–21; 20:8–9. *the dead, that they should be judged.* Anticipated in 6:10, carried out in 20:11–15. *thy servants the prophets.* See Dan 9:6,10; Amos 3:7; Zech 1:6.

11:19 *ark of his testament.* The OT ark was a chest of acacia wood (Deut 10:1–2). It symbolized the throne or presence of God among His people. It was probably destroyed when Nebuzaradan destroyed the temple in Jerusalem (2 Ki 25:8–10). In the NT it symbolizes God's faithfulness in keeping covenant with His people. *lightnings . . . great hail.* See note on 4:5.

‡12:1 *a great wonder.* An extraordinary spectacle or event that points beyond itself; a sign (cf. Luke 21:11,25; Acts 2:19). *a woman clothed with the sun.* The sun was the backdrop. *the moon under her feet.* Standing on the moon. *upon her head a crown of twelve stars.* The only Biblical background for this vision is Gen 37:9–10. There Joseph sees the sun, moon, and 11 stars bowing down to him. Jacob suggests the obvious meaning as being that Joseph saw his father (Jacob, the sun), mother (Leah, the moon), and 11 brothers (11 stars) bowing down to him. It seems that John is here taking an OT picture of Israel and projecting it into the future. This woman represents Israel in the tribulation.

‡12:2 *cried . . . pained to be delivered.* Cf. the similar language describing the rebirth of Jerusalem in Is 66:7 (see Mic 4:10). This woman, Israel, gives birth to Jesus Christ the Messiah. It is unlikely that the woman represents the church because the church is pictured in Scripture as the "bride," not the "mother," of Christ.

12:3 *red dragon.* Identified in v. 9 (cf. 20:2). Dragons abound in the mythology of ancient peoples (Leviathan in Canaanite lore and Set-Typhon, the red crocodile, in Egypt). In the OT they are normally used metaphorically to depict the enemies of God and of Israel (see Ps 74:14; Is 27:1; Ezek 29:3). *seven heads.* Symbolizing universal wisdom (cf. 13:1). *ten horns.* Symbolizing great power.

12:5 *a man child.* The Messiah. *rod of iron.* See note on 2:27. *caught up unto God.* The ascension of Christ.

that they should feed her there [b]a thousand
two hundred *and* threescore days.
7 ¶ And there was war in heaven: [a]Michael
and his angels fought [b]against the dragon; and
the dragon fought and his angels,
8 And prevailed not; neither was their
place found any more in heaven.
9 And [a]the great dragon was cast *out,* [b]*that*
old serpent, called the devil, and Satan,
[c]which deceiveth the whole world: [d]he was
cast *out* into the earth, and his angels were
cast *out* with him.
10 And I heard a loud voice saying in heav-
en, [a]Now is come salvation, and strength, and
the kingdom of our God, and the power of his
Christ: for the accuser of our brethren is cast
down, [b]which accused them before our God
day and night.
11 And [a]they overcame him by the blood
of the Lamb, and by the word of their testimony; [b]and they loved not their lives unto the
death.
12 Therefore [a]rejoice, ye heavens, and ye
that dwell in them. [b]Woe to the inhabiters of
the earth and of the sea! for the devil is come
down unto you, having great wrath, [c]because
he knoweth that he hath *but* a short time.
13 ¶ And when the dragon saw that he was
cast unto the earth, he persecuted [a]the
woman which brought forth the man *child.*
14 [a]And to the woman were given two
wings of a great eagle, [b]that she might fly [c]into
the wilderness, into her place, where she is
nourished [d]for a time, and times, and half a
time, from the face of the serpent.
15 And the serpent [a]cast out of his mouth
water as a flood after the woman, that he
might cause her to be carried away of the
flood.
16 And the earth helped the woman, and
the earth opened her mouth, and swallowed
up the flood which the dragon cast out of his
mouth.
17 And the dragon was wroth with the
woman, [a]and went to make war with the remnant of her seed, [b]which keep the commandments of God, and have [c]the testimony of
Jesus Christ.

The beast from the sea

13 And I stood upon the sand of the sea,
and saw [a]a beast rise up out of the
sea, [b]having seven heads and ten horns, and
upon his horns ten crowns, and upon his
heads the [1]name of blasphemy.
2 [a]And the beast which I saw was like unto
a leopard, [b]and his feet *were* as *the feet* of a
bear, [c]and his mouth as the mouth of a lion:
and [d]the dragon gave him his power, and his
seat, [e]and great authority.
3 And I saw one of his heads [a]as *it were*
[1]wounded to death; and his deadly wound was
healed: and [b]all the world wondered after the
beast.
4 And they worshipped the dragon which
gave power unto the beast: and they worshipped the beast, saying, [a]Who *is* like unto
the beast? who is able to make war with him?
5 And there was given unto him [a]a mouth
speaking great *things* and blasphemies; and

12:6 [b]ch. 11:3
12:7 [a]Dan. 10:13 [b]ch. 20:2
12:9 [a]Luke 10:18; John 12:31 [b]Gen. 3:1,4; ch. 20:2 [c]ch. 20:3 [d]ch. 9:1
12:10 [a]ch. 11:15 [b]Job 1:9; Zech. 3:1
12:11 [a]Rom. 16:20 [b]Luke 14:26
12:12 [a]Ps. 96:11; Is. 49:13; ch. 18:20 [b]ch. 8:13 [c]ch. 10:6
12:13 [a]ver. 5
12:14 [a]Ex. 19:4 [b]ver. 6 [c]ch. 17:3 [d]Dan. 7:25
12:15 [a]Is. 59:19
12:17 [a]Gen. 3:15; ch. 11:7 [b]ch. 14:12 [c]1 Cor. 2:1; 1 John 5:10
13:1 [1]Or, *names* [a]Dan. 7:2,7 [b]ch. 12:3
13:2 [a]Dan. 7:6 [b]Dan. 7:5 [c]Dan. 7:4 [d]ch. 12:9 [e]ch. 12:4
13:3 [1]Gr. *slain* [a]ver. 12,14 [b]ch. 17:8
13:4 [a]ch. 18:18
13:5 [a]Dan. 7:8

‡12:6 *wilderness.* This is where Jesus told Israel to flee when the antichrist appeared (Mat 24:15). After three-and-one-half years of the seven year tribulation, the antichrist will break his compact with Israel by desecrating the temple (see 2 Thes 2:3–4). *a thousand two hundred and threescore days.* The time of protection corresponds to the time of persecution (see note on 11:2; cf. 13:5).

12:7 *Michael.* An archangel who defeats Satan in heavenly warfare. In Dan 12:1 he is the protector of Israel who will deliver her from tribulation in the last days.

‡12:9 *dragon was cast out . . . into the earth.* Not the original casting of Satan out of heaven, but apparently a change from being the prince of the power of the air to being confined to the earth, a further demotion—an explanation of his intense hostility against God's people in the last days (vv. 12–17). *devil, and Satan.* See notes on 2:9–10. *deceiveth.* Cf. 2 Cor 11:3; see also Luke 22:31; John 13:2.

12:10 *accuser.* See Job 1:9–11 and notes on Job 1:6; Zech 3:1. Satan (v. 9) in Hebrew means "accuser."

12:11 *blood of the Lamb.* See note on 5:9; see also 1:5; 7:14.

12:12 *he hath but a short time.* The period of final, intense hostility of Satan toward the people of God.

12:13–16 Cf. the similarity to the exodus.

‡12:14 *wilderness.* See note on v. 6. *a time, and times, and half a time.* One year plus two years plus half a year (see note on 11:2). This is the last half of the tribulation period when Satan and the antichrist seek to destroy Israel, and in so doing attempt to nullify the fulfillment of God's promises to them.

12:16 *earth opened her mouth.* In Num 16:30–33 the earth opened and swallowed Korah's men.

‡12:17 *remnant of her seed.* These are saved Jews, but those who apparently were not able to flee into the wilderness. *testimony of Jesus.* The testimony that Jesus bore (cf. 1:2,9; 19:10).

‡13:1 *beast rise up out of the sea.* First mentioned in 11:7. According to some, the beast symbolizes the Roman empire, the deification of secular authority. However, he seems to be the final, personal antichrist. The background seems to be Daniel's vision of the four great beasts (Dan 7:2–7). See 17:8–11 for the interpreting angel's explanation of the beast. *seven heads.* Seven is the total number of combined heads four in the beasts in Dan 7:1–8. See 17:12. *ten horns.* The ten horns correspond to the ten toes of the image in Dan 2:44, as well as the ten horns of Daniel's fourth beast (Dan 7:7–8,24). This is a confederation of ten kingdoms headed by one powerful man—the antichrist. *the name of blasphemy.* Roman emperors tended to assume titles of deity. Domitian, e.g., was addressed as *Dominus et Deus noster* ("Our Lord and God").

13:2 *leopard . . . bear . . . lion.* John's beast combined characteristics of Daniel's four beasts (Dan 7:4–6). *dragon.* See note on 12:3.

13:3 *wounded to death . . . healed.* Emphasizes the tremendous recuperative power of the beast. *all the world wondered.* See 17:8 for the same reaction.

‡13:5 *was given.* Four times in the Greek text of vv. 5–7 the passive "was given" occurs, emphasizing the subordinate role of the beast (see vv. 2,4). *forty and two months.* For the first half (three-and-one-half years) of the tribulation period, the antichrist is the friend of Israel, making a covenant with Israel and possibly allowing them to rebuild their temple (Dan 9:26) However, from the time the antichrist desecrates the temple (Dan

power was given unto him [1] to continue [b] forty
and two months.
6 And he opened his mouth in blasphemy
against God, to blaspheme his name, [a] and his
tabernacle, and them that dwell in heaven.
7 And it was given unto him [a] to make war
with the saints, and to overcome them: [b] and
power was given him over all kindreds, and
tongues, and nations.
8 And all that dwell upon the earth shall
worship him, [a] whose names are not written in
the book of life of the Lamb slain [b] from the
foundation of the world.
9 [a] If any *man* have an ear, let him hear.
10 [a] He that leadeth into captivity *shall* go
into captivity: [b] he that killeth with the sword
must be killed with the sword. [c] Here is the patience and the faith of the saints.

The beast from the earth

11 ¶ And I beheld another beast [a] coming
up out of the earth; and he had two horns like
a lamb, and he spake as a dragon.
12 And he exerciseth all the power of the
first beast before him, and causeth the earth
and them which dwell therein to worship the
first beast, [a] whose deadly wound was healed.
13 And [a] he doeth great wonders, [b] so that
he maketh fire come down from heaven on
the earth in the sight of men,
14 [a] And deceiveth them that dwell on the
earth [b] by the means of *those* miracles which
he had power to do in the sight of the beast;
saying to them that dwell on the earth, that
they should make an image to the beast, which
had the wound by a sword, [c] and did live.
15 And he had power to give [1] life unto the
image of the beast, that the image of the beast
should both speak, [a] and cause that as many as
would not worship the image of the beast
should be killed.
16 And he causeth all, *both* small and
great, rich and poor, free and bond, [a] [1] to receive a mark in their right hand, or in their
foreheads:
17 And that no *man* might buy or sell, save
he that had the mark, or [a] the name of the
beast, [b] or the number of his name.
18 [a] Here is wisdom. Let him that hath understanding count [b] the number of the beast:
[c] for it is the number of a man; and his number
is Six hundred threescore *and* six.

The Lamb on mount Zion

14 And I looked, and lo, [a] a Lamb stood
on the mount Sion, and with him [b] an
hundred forty *and* four thousand, [c] having his
Father's name written in their foreheads.
2 And I heard a voice from heaven, [a] as the
voice of many waters, and as the voice of a
great thunder: and I heard the voice of
[b] harpers harping with their harps:
3 And [a] they sung as *it were* a new song before the throne, and before the four beasts,
and the elders: and no *man* could learn *that*
song [b] but the hundred *and* forty *and* four
thousand, which were redeemed from the
earth.
4 These are they which were not defiled
with women; [a] for they are virgins. These are
they [b] which follow the Lamb whithersoever
he goeth. These [c] [1] were redeemed from
among men, [d] *being* the firstfruits unto God
and to the Lamb.

13:5 [1] Or, *to make war* [b] ch. 11:2
13:6 [a] John 1:14; Col. 2:9
13:7 [a] Dan. 7:21; ch. 11:7 [b] ch. 11:18
13:8 [a] Ex. 32:32; Dan. 12:1; Phil. 4:3; ch. 3:5 [b] ch. 17:8
13:9 [a] ch. 2:7
13:10 [a] Is. 33:1 [b] Gen. 9:6; Mat. 26:52 [c] ch. 14:12
13:11 [a] ch. 11:7
13:12 [a] ver. 3
13:13 [a] Deut. 13:1; Mat. 24:24; 2 Thes. 2:9; ch. 16:14 [b] 1 Ki. 18:38; 2 Ki. 1:10
13:14 [a] ch. 12:9 [b] 2 Thes. 2:9 [c] 2 Ki. 20:7
13:15 [1] Gr. *breath*
13:15 [a] ch. 16:2
13:16 [1] Gr. *to give [them]* [a] ch. 14:9
13:17 [a] ch. 14:11 [b] ch. 15:2
13:18 [a] ch. 17:9 [b] ch. 15:2 [c] ch. 21:17
14:1 [a] ch. 5:6 [b] ch. 7:4 [c] ch. 13:16
14:2 [a] ch. 1:15 [b] ch. 5:8
14:3 [a] ch. 5:9 [b] ver. 1
14:4 [1] Gr. *were bought* [a] 2 Cor. 11:2 [b] ch. 3:4 [c] ch. 5:9 [d] Jas. 1:18

9:29), he becomes Israel's adversary for these 42 months, the last half of the tribulation. See note on 11:2.

13:7 *make war.* See 12:17; see also Dan 7:7.

13:8 *book of life of the Lamb.* See note on 3:5. *Lamb slain.* Cf. Is 53:7; John 1:29,36.

‡13:11 *another beast coming up out of the earth.* According to some, he symbolizes religious power in the service of secular authorities. However, in accordance with the personal aspects of the antichrist, he is the personal false prophet (see 16:13; 19:20; 20:10). *two horns like a lamb.* He attempts to appear gentle and harmless. *spake as a dragon.* See Jesus' warning in Mat 7:15 about ravening wolves who come in sheep's clothing.

13:12 *exerciseth all the power of the first beast.* The trinity of evil is now complete. The beast from the earth is under the authority of the beast from the sea. The latter is subject to the dragon. Satan, secular power and religious compromise (or Satan, the antichrist and the false prophet) join against the cause of God: Father, Son and Holy Spirit.

13:13 *great wonders.* See the warning in Deut 13:1–3; see also Mat 24:24; 2 Thes 2:9; cf. Rev 19:20. *fire . . . from heaven.* See 1 Ki 18:24–39.

13:14 *make an image.* Cf. Dan 3:1–11; 2 Thes 2:4.

13:15 *should both speak.* Belief in statues that could speak is widely attested in ancient literature. Ventriloquism and other forms of deception were common.

13:16 *mark.* Whatever its origin—possibly the branding of slaves or enemy soldiers, the sealing and stamping of official documents, or the sign of the cross on the forehead of a new Christian—the mark of the beast apparently symbolized allegiance to the demands of the imperial cult. In the final days of the antichrist it will be the ultimate test of loyalty (cf. v. 17; 14:9,11; 15:2; 16:2; 19:20; 20:4). It imitates the sealing of the servants of God in ch. 7.

13:17 *buy or sell.* Economic boycott against all faithful believers. *number of his name.* In ancient times the letters of the alphabet served for numbers. Riddles using numerical equivalents for names were popular.

13:18 *Six hundred threescore and six.* Various schemes for decoding these numbers result in such names as Euanthas, Lateinos, and Nero Caesar. Others take 666 as a symbol for the trinity of evil and imperfection—each digit falls just short of the perfect number 7.

14:1 *Lamb.* See note on 5:6. *mount Sion.* In the OT it was first the fortress of the pre-Israelite city of Jerusalem (2 Sam 5:7), captured by David and established as his capital. Later it became a virtual synonym for Jerusalem. In Revelation, as in Heb 12:22–24, it is the heavenly Jerusalem, the eternal dwelling place of God and His people (cf. Gal 4:26). It comes down to the new earth in 21:2–3. *an hundred forty and four thousand.* See note on 7:4. *name.* Contrast 13:16–18.

14:2 *harps.* See note on 5:8.

14:3 *new song.* See note on 5:9. The theme is deliverance.

‡14:4 *not defiled with women.* This could be a symbolic description of believers who kept themselves from defiling relationships with the pagan world system, or it could signify that the 144,000 are only males. *they are virgins.* This phrase could

5 And [a]in their mouth was found no guile:
for [b]they are without fault before the throne of
God.

The angelic messages

6 ¶ And I saw another angel [a]fly in the
midst of heaven, [b]having the everlasting
gospel to preach unto them that dwell on the
earth, [c]and to every nation, and kindred, and
tongue, and people,
7 Saying with a loud voice, [a]Fear God, and
give glory to him; for the hour of his judgment
is come: [b]and worship him that made heaven,
and earth, and the sea, and the fountains of
waters.
8 And there followed another angel, say-
ing, [a]Babylon is fallen, is fallen, [b]*that* great
city, because she made all nations drink of the
wine of the wrath of her fornication.
9 And *the* third angel followed them, saying with a loud voice, [a]If any *man* worship the
beast and his image, and receive *his* mark in
his forehead, or in his hand,
10 The same [a]shall drink of the wine of the
wrath of God, which is [b]poured out without
mixture into [c]the cup of his indignation; and
[d]he shall be tormented with [e]fire and brimstone in the presence of the holy angels, and
in the presence of the Lamb:
11 And [a]the smoke of their torment ascendeth up for ever and ever: and they have no
rest day nor night, who worship the beast and
his image, and whosoever receiveth the mark
of his name.
12 [a]Here is the patience of the saints:
[b]here *are* they that keep the commandments
of God, and the faith of Jesus.
13 And I heard a voice from heaven saying
unto me, Write, [a]Blessed *are* the dead [b]which
die in the Lord [1]from henceforth: Yea, saith
the Spirit, [c]that they may rest from their
labours; and their works do follow them.
14 ¶ And I looked, and behold a white
cloud, and upon the cloud one sat [a]like unto
the Son of man, [b]having on his head a golden
crown, and in his hand a sharp sickle.
15 And another angel [a]came out of the
temple, crying with a loud voice to him that
sat on the cloud, [b]Thrust in thy sickle, and
reap: for the time is come for thee to reap; for
the harvest [c]of the earth is [1]ripe.
16 And he that sat on the cloud thrust in
his sickle on the earth; and the earth was
reaped.
17 ¶ And another angel came out of the
temple which is in heaven, he also having a
sharp sickle.
18 And another angel came out from the
altar, [a]which had power over fire; and cried
with a loud cry to him that had the sharp sickle, saying, [b]Thrust in thy sharp sickle, and
gather the clusters of the vine of the earth; for
her grapes are fully ripe.
19 And the angel thrust in his sickle into
the earth, and gathered the vine of the earth,
and cast *it* into [a]the great winepress of the
wrath of God.
20 And [a]the winepress was trodden [b]with-
out the city, and blood came out of the wine-

14:5 [a]Ps. 32:2; Zeph. 3:13 [b]Eph. 5:27; Jude 24
14:6 [a]ch. 8:13 [b]Eph. 3:9; Tit. 1:2 [c]ch. 13:7
14:7 [a]ch. 11:18 [b]Neh. 9:6; Ps. 33:6; 124:8; 146:5,6; Acts 14:15; 17:24
14:8 [a]Is. 21:9; ch. 18:2 [b]Jer. 51:7; ch. 16:19; 17:2,5; 18:3,10
14:9 [a]ch. 13:14
14:10 [a]Ps. 75:8; Is. 51:17; Jer. 25:15 [b]ch. 18:6 [c]ch. 16:19 [d]ch. 20:10 [e]ch. 19:20
14:11 [a]Is. 34:10
14:12 [a]ch. 13:10 [b]ch. 12:17
14:13 [1]Or, *from henceforth saith the Spirit, Yea* [a]Eccl. 4:1,2 [b]1 Cor. 15:18; 1 Thes. 4:16 [c]2 Thes. 1:7; Heb. 4:9,10
14:14 [a]Ezek. 1:26; Dan. 7:13 [b]ch. 6:2
14:15 [1]Or, *dried* [a]ch. 16:17 [b]Joel 3:13; Mat. 13:39 [c]Jer. 51:33; ch. 13:12
14:18 [a]ch. 16:8 [b]Joel 3:13
14:19 [a]ch. 19:15
14:20 [a]Is. 63:3; Lam. 1:15 [b]Heb. 13:12

confirm the literal interpretation. *follow the Lamb.* As His disciples (see Mat 19:21; Mark 8:34). *firstfruits.* See Lev 23:9–14. The word is used figuratively in the NT for the first converts in an area (Rom 16:5) and the first to rise from the dead (1 Cor 15:20). In Revelation believers are considered as a choice offering to God and the Lamb.

14:5 *no guile.* Contrast Rom 1:25; see Is 53:9.

‡14:6 *everlasting gospel.* The content of this "good news" is perhaps found in v. 7. Angels are given the task of preaching at this point.

14:7 *him that made heaven.* See Ex 20:11; Ps 146:6.

‡14:8 *Babylon.* Ancient Babylon in Mesopotamia was the political, commercial and religious center of a world empire. It was noted for its luxury and moral decadence. The title "that great city" is taken from Dan 4:30. According to some, it is used in Revelation (e.g., here and in 16:19; 17:5; 18:2,10,21) for Rome as the center of opposition to God and His people. According to others, it represents the whole political and religious system of the world in general. According to still others, it is to be understood as literal Babylon—rebuilt and restored. Babylon's fall is proclaimed in Is 21:9; Jer 51:8. *wine of the wrath of her fornication.* Here Babylon (Rome?) is pictured as a prostitute whose illicit relations are achieved by intoxication.

14:10 *cup of his indignation.* In the OT God's wrath is commonly pictured as a cup of wine to be drunk (Ps 75:8; Is 51:17; Jer 25:15). It is not the outworking of impersonal laws of retribution, but the response of a righteous God to those who refuse His love and grace. *fire and brimstone.* Sodom and Gomorrah were destroyed by a rain of fire and brimstone (Gen 19:24). Ps 11:6 speaks of a similar fate for the wicked. The figure occurs elsewhere in the OT and the Apocrypha. It is used several times in the final chapters of Revelation (19:20; 20:10; 21:8).

14:11 *torment . . . for ever and ever.* Revelation offers no support for the doctrine of the annihilation of the wicked (also compare 19:20 with 20:10).

14:13 *Blessed.* The second beatitude (see note on 1:3).

14:14 *Son of man.* See 1:13 and notes on Dan 7:13; Mark 8:31. *golden crown.* A victory wreath of gold. See note on 2:10 for the comparison between the victory crown and the royal crown. *sickle.* The Israelite sickle used for cutting grain was normally a flint or iron blade attached to a curved shaft of wood or bone.

14:15 *harvest of the earth.* Symbolizes in a general way the coming judgment (see Mat 13:30,40–42). Some interpreters think it refers to the ingathering of the righteous at the return of Christ.

14:18 *another angel . . . which had power over fire.* The angel of 8:3–5. Fire is commonly associated with judgment (see Mat 18:8; Luke 9:54; 2 Thes 1:7). *sharp sickle.* The context suggests (in contrast to the sickle of v. 14) the smaller grape-knife with which the farmer cut the clusters of grapes from the vine.

14:19 *great winepress.* A rock-hewn trough about eight feet square with a channel leading to a lower and smaller trough. Grapes were thrown into the upper vat and tramped with bare feet. The juice was collected in the lower vat. At times mechanical pressure was added. The treading of grapes was a common OT figure for the execution of divine wrath (see Is 63:3; Lam 1:15; Joel 3:13).

14:20 *without the city.* Bloodshed would defile the city (see Joel 3:12–14; Zech 14:1–4; cf. Heb 13:12). *a thousand and six*

press, [c]*even* unto the horse bridles, by the
space of a thousand *and* six hundred furlongs.

The seven plagues

15 And [a]I saw another sign in heaven,
great and marvellous, [b]seven angels
having the seven last plagues; [c]for in them is
filled up the wrath of God.
2 And I saw as *it were* [a]a sea of glass [b]min-
gled with fire: and them that had gotten the
victory over the beast, [c]and over his image,
and over his mark, *and* over the number of his
name, stand on the sea of glass, [d]having *the*
harps of God.
3 And they sing [a]the song of Moses the
servant of God, and the song of the Lamb, saying, [b]Great and marvellous *are* thy works,
Lord God Almighty; [c]just and true *are* thy
ways, thou King of [1]saints.
4 [a]Who shall not fear thee, O Lord, and
glorify thy name? for *thou* only *art* holy: for
[b]all nations shall come and worship before
thee; for thy judgments are made manifest.
5 ¶ And after that I looked, and, behold,
[a]the temple of the tabernacle of the testimony
in heaven was opened:
6 [a]And the seven angels came out of the
temple, having the seven plagues, [b]clothed in
pure and white linen, and having their breasts
girded with golden girdles.
7 [a]And one of the four beasts gave unto the
seven angels seven golden vials full of the
wrath of God, [b]who liveth for ever and ever.
8 And [a]the temple was filled with smoke
[b]from the glory of God, and from his power;
and no *man* was able to enter into the temple,
till the seven plagues of the seven angels were
fulfilled.

14:20 [c]ch. 19:14
15:1 [a]ch. 12:1,3 [b]ch. 21:9 [c]ch. 14:10
15:2 [a]ch. 4:6 [b]Mat. 3:11 [c]ch. 13:15 [d]ch. 5:8
15:3 [1][Or, *nations*, or, *ages*] [a]Ex. 15:1 [b]Deut. 32:4; Ps. 111:2 [c]Ps. 145:17; Hos. 14:9
15:4 [a]Ex. 15:14; Jer. 10:7 [b]Is. 66:23
15:5 [a]Num. 1:50
15:6 [a]ver. 1 [b]Ex. 28:6; Ezek. 44:17
15:7 [a]ch. 4:6 [b]1 Thes. 1:9
15:8 [a]Ex. 40:34; 2 Chr. 5:14 [b]2 Thes. 1:9
16:1 [a]ch. 15:1 [b]ch. 14:10
16:2 [a]ch. 8:7 [b]Ex. 9:9-11 [c]ch. 13:16 [d]ch. 13:14
16:3 [a]ch. 8:8 [b]Ex. 7:17 [c]ch. 8:9
16:4 [a]ch. 8:10 [b]Ex. 7:20
16:5 [a]ch. 15:3 [b]ch. 1:4,8
16:6 [a]Mat. 23:34; ch. 13:15 [b]ch. 11:18 [c]Is. 49:26
16:7 [a]ch. 15:3 [b]ch. 13:10
16:8 [a]ch. 8:12 [b]ch. 9:17,18
16:9 [1]Or, *burned* [a]ver. 11,21 [b]Dan. 5:22 [c]ch. 11:13
16:10 [a]ch. 13:2 [b]ch. 9:2 [c]ch. 11:10
16:11 [a]ver. 9,21

The vials of God's wrath

16 And I heard a great voice out of the
temple saying [a]to the seven angels,
Go your ways, and pour out the vials [b]of the
wrath of God upon the earth.
2 And the first went, and poured out his
vial [a]upon the earth; and [b]there fell a noisome
and grievous sore upon the men [c]which had
the mark of the beast, and *upon* them [d]which
worshipped his image.
3 ¶ And the second angel poured out his
vial [a]upon the sea; and [b]it became as the blood
of a dead *man:* [c]and every living soul died in
the sea.
4 ¶ And the third angel poured out his vial
[a]upon the rivers and fountains of waters; [b]and
they became blood.
5 And I heard the angel of the waters say,
[a]Thou art righteous, O Lord, [b]which art, and
wast, and shalt be, because thou hast judged
thus.
6 For [a]they have shed the blood [b]of saints
and prophets, [c]and thou hast given them
blood to drink; for they are worthy.
7 And I heard another out of the altar say,
Even so, [a]Lord God Almighty, [b]true and righteous *are* thy judgments.
8 ¶ And the fourth angel poured out his vial
[a]upon the sun; [b]and *power* was given unto
him to scorch men with fire.
9 And men were [1]scorched *with* great
heat, and [a]blasphemed the name of God,
which hath power over these plagues: [b]and
they repented not [c]to give him glory.
10 ¶ And the fifth angel poured out his vial
[a]upon the seat of the beast; [b]and his kingdom
was full of darkness; [c]and they gnawed their
tongues for pain,
11 And [a]blasphemed the God of heaven

---

hundred furlongs. The approximate length of the Holy Land from north to south.

15:1–8 Introduces the last of the three sevenfold series of judgments—the plagues, or vials of wrath (see note on 8:2).

15:1 *wrath of God.* See note on 6:16.

15:2 *sea of glass.* See note on 4:6. *victory over the beast.* Cf. the saints' victory over the devil in 12:11. *number of his name.* See notes on 13:16–18. *harps.* See note on 5:8.

15:3 *song of Moses.* See Ex 15; Deut 32. Ex 15:1–18 was sung on sabbath evenings in the synagogue to celebrate Israel's great deliverance from Egypt. *song of the Lamb.* The risen Lord triumphed over His enemies in securing spiritual deliverance for His followers (cf. Ps 22). *Great and marvellous are thy works.* See Ex 15:11; Ps 92:5; 111:2. *Almighty.* See note on 1:8. *King of saints.* See Jer 10:10; cf. 1 Tim 1:17.

15:4 Universal recognition of God is taught in both the OT (Ps 86:9; Is 45:22–23; Mal 1:11) and the NT (Phil 2:9–11).

15:5 *tabernacle of the testimony.* The dwelling place of God during the wilderness wandering of the Israelites (see Ex 40:34–35). It was so named because the ancient tent contained the two tables of the Testimony brought down from mount Sinai (Ex 32:15; 38:21; Deut 10:5).

15:6 *seven plagues.* The last series of plagues (see v. 1). *golden girdles.* Symbolic of royal and priestly functions.

15:7 *wrath of God.* Cf. 2 Thes 1:7–9.

15:8 *filled with smoke.* Cf. Ex 40:34; 1 Ki 8:10–11; Ezek 44:4. Smoke symbolizes the power and glory of God.

‡16:2 *vial.* A vial is similar to a chemistry beaker, a cereal bowl or a goblet. Each angel dips his goblet into the vial of God's wrath and casts it forth on the earth. Compare the first four vials (vv. 2–9) with the first four trumpets (8:7–12). *noisome and grievous sore.* Cf. the boils and abscesses of the sixth Egyptian plague (Ex 9:9–11; see also Job 2:7–8,13). *mark of the beast.* See 13:16 and note.

16:4 *rivers and fountains of waters.* Cf. 8:10–11; see also Ps 78:44.

16:5 *which art, and wast, and shalt be.* See note on 11:17; cf. Ex 3:14.

16:6 *given them blood to drink.* Punishment is tailored to fit the crime (see Is 49:26).

16:7 *altar.* Personified.

16:8 *fire.* Often connected with judgment in Scripture (see Deut 28:22; 1 Cor 3:13; 2 Pet 3:7).

16:9 *they repented not.* In 11:13 the nations were dazzled into homage by the great earthquake. Here they curse the name of God.

16:10 *seat of the beast.* Cf. Satan's throne in 2:13. "Throne" occurs 42 times in Revelation. The other 40 references are to the throne of God. *gnawed their tongues.* Cf. the scene in 6:15–17.

16:11 *God of heaven.* Used in Dan 2:44 of the sovereign God, who destroys the kingdoms of the world and establishes His universal and eternal reign.

because of their pains and [b]their sores, [c]and
repented not of their deeds.
12 ¶ And the sixth angel poured out his vial
[a]upon the great river Euphrates; [b]and the water thereof was dried up, [c]that the way of the
kings of the east might be prepared.
13 And I saw three unclean [a]spirits like
frogs *come* out of the mouth of [b]the dragon,
and out of the mouth of the beast, and out of
the mouth of [c]the false prophet.
14 [a]For they are the spirits of devils,
[b]working miracles, which go forth unto the
kings of the earth [c]and of the whole world, to
gather them to [d]the battle of that great day of
God Almighty.
15 [a]Behold, I come as a thief. Blessed *is* he
that watcheth, and keepeth his garments, [b]lest
he walk naked, and they see his shame.
16 [a]And he gathered them together into a
place called in the Hebrew tongue Armageddon.
17 ¶ And the seventh angel poured out his
vial into the air; and there came a great voice
out of the temple of heaven, from the throne,
saying, [a]It is done.
18 And [a]there were voices, and thunders,
and lightnings; [b]and there was a great earthquake, [c]such as was not since men were upon
the earth, so mighty an earthquake, *and* so
great.
19 And [a]the great city was *divided* into
three parts, and the cities of the nations fell:
and great Babylon [b]came in remembrance before God, [c]to give unto her the cup of the wine
of the fierceness of his wrath.
20 And [a]every island fled *away,* and the
mountains were not found.
21 [a]And there fell upon men a great hail
out of heaven, *every stone* about the weight of
a talent: and [b]men blasphemed God because
of [c]the plague of the hail; for the plague thereof was exceeding great.

16:11 [b]ver. 2 [c]ver. 9
16:12 [a]ch. 9:14 [b]Jer. 50:38 [c]Is. 41:2,25
16:13 [a]1 John 4:1 [b]ch. 12:3,9 [c]ch. 19:20
16:14 [a]1 Tim. 4:1; Jas. 3:15 [b]2 Thes. 2:9 [c]Luke 2:1 [d]ch. 17:14
16:15 [a]Mat. 24:43 [b]2 Cor. 5:3
16:16 [a]ch. 19:19
16:17 [a]ch. 21:6
16:18 [a]ch. 4:5 [b]ch. 11:13 [c]Dan. 12:1
16:19 [a]ch. 14:8; 17:18 [b]ch. 18:5 [c]Is. 51:17; ch. 14:10
16:20 [a]ch. 6:14
16:21 [a]ch. 11:19 [b]ver. 9,11 [c]Ex. 9:23

17:1 [a]ch. 21:9 [b]ch. 16:19 [c]Nah. 3:4; ch. 19:2 [d]Jer. 51:13
17:2 [a]ch. 18:3 [b]Jer. 51:7; ch. 18:3
17:3 [a]ch. 12:6,14 [b]ch. 12:3 [c]ch. 13:1 [d]ver. 9 [e]ver. 12
17:4 [1]Gr. *gilded* [a]ch. 18:12 [b]Dan. 11:38 [c]Jer. 51:7; ch. 18:6 [d]ch. 14:8
17:5 [1]Or, *fornications* [a]2 Thes. 2:7
17:6 [a]ch. 18:24 [b]ch. 13:15 [c]ch. 6:9,10
17:8 [a]ch. 11:7 [b]ch. 13:10 [c]ch. 13:3 [d]ch. 13:8
17:9 [a]ch. 13:18 [b]ch. 13:1

The woman on the beast

17 And there came [a]one of the seven angels which had the seven vials, and
talked with me, saying unto me, *Come* hither;
[b]I will shew unto thee the judgment of [c]the
great whore [d]that sitteth upon many waters:
2 [a]With whom the kings of the earth have
committed fornication, and [b]the inhabiters of
the earth have been made drunk with the
wine of her fornication.
3 So he carried me away in the spirit [a]into
the wilderness: and I saw a woman sit [b]upon a
scarlet coloured beast, full of [c]names of blasphemy, [d]having seven heads and [e]ten horns.
4 And the woman [a]was arrayed in purple
and scarlet colour, [b]and [1]decked with gold and
precious stone and pearls, [c]having a golden
cup in her hand [d]full of abominations and
filthiness of her fornication:
5 And upon her forehead *was* a name written, [a]MYSTERY, BABYLON THE GREAT, THE
MOTHER OF [1]HARLOTS AND ABOMINA-
TIONS OF THE EARTH.
6 And I saw [a]the woman drunken [b]with
the blood of the saints, and with the blood of
[c]the martyrs of Jesus: and when I saw her, I
wondered *with* great admiration.
7 And the angel said unto me, Wherefore
didst thou marvel? I will tell thee the mystery
of the woman, and of the beast that carrieth
her, which hath the seven heads and ten
horns.
8 The beast that thou sawest was, and is
not; and [a]shall ascend out of the bottomless
pit, and [b]go into perdition: and they that dwell
on the earth [c]shall wonder, [d]whose names
were not written in the book of life from the
foundation of the world, when they behold the
beast that was, and is not, and yet is.
9 *And* [a]here *is* the mind which hath wisdom. [b]The seven heads are seven mountains,
on which the woman sitteth.

‡16:12 *Euphrates.* See note on 9:14. *kings of the east.* Evidently Parthian rulers (17:15–18:24), to be distinguished from the "kings of the earth" (v. 14), who wage the final war against Christ and the armies of heaven (19:11–21).

16:13 *frogs.* Lev 11:10 classifies the frog as an unclean animal. The imagery suggests the deceptive propaganda that will, in the last days, lead people to accept and support the cause of evil.

16:14 *miracles.* Cf. 13:13. *kings of the earth.* See 6:15. *great day of God.* See 19:11–21 for this battle.

16:15 *Blessed.* The third beatitude (see note on 1:3).

‡16:16 *Armageddon.* This probably stands for Har Mageddon, "the mountain of Megiddo" (see note on Judg 5:19). Many see no specific geographical reference in the designation and take it to be a symbol of the final overthrow of evil by God. However, the city of Megiddo strategically overlooks the Jezreel Valley where this final battle will be fought. It takes its name from this city and the mound upon which it is built, thus providing the reader with a specific location for this conflict.

17:1 *seven angels.* Cf. 15:1; 16. *great whore.* See v. 18 for the angel's own identification of this symbol. In 17:5 the harlot is named "BABYLON THE GREAT." *sitteth upon many waters.* See Ps 137:1; Jer 51:13.

17:2 *wine of her fornication.* See note on 14:8; cf. 18:3; Is 23:17; Jer 51:7.

17:3 *in the spirit.* In a state of spiritual ecstasy (see notes on 1:10; 4:2; see also 21:10). *scarlet coloured beast.* The beast that rose out of the sea in ch. 13. *names of blasphemy.* See note on 13:1.

17:5 *BABYLON THE GREAT.* See note on 14:8.

17:6 *saints . . . the martyrs.* See 6:9.

17:7 *mystery.* See note on 10:7.

17:8 *was, and is not; and shall ascend.* An obvious imitation of the description of the Lamb (1:18; 2:8). Cf. the description of God in 1:4,8; 4:8. Here the phrase seems to mean that the beast appeared once, is not presently evident, but will in the future again make his presence known. Evil is persistent. *bottomless pit.* See note on 9:1. *go into perdition.* Although evil is real and persistent, there is no uncertainty about its ultimate fate. *book of life.* See note on 3:5.

17:9 *seven mountains.* It is perhaps significant that Rome began as a network of seven hill settlements on the left bank of the Tiber. Her designation as the city on seven hills is commonplace among Roman writers (e.g., Virgil, Martial, Cicero).

10 And there are seven kings: five are fallen, and one is, *and* the other is not yet come; and when he cometh, he must continue a short *space*.

11 And the beast that was, and is not, even he is the eighth, and is of the seven, [a]and goeth into perdition.

12 And [a]the ten horns which thou sawest are ten kings, which have received no kingdom as yet; but receive power as kings one hour with the beast.

13 These have one mind, and shall give their power and strength unto the beast.

14 [a]These shall make war with the Lamb, and the Lamb shall overcome them: [b]for he is Lord of lords, and King of kings: [c]and they that are with him *are* called, and chosen, and faithful.

15 And he saith unto me, [a]The waters which thou sawest, where the whore sitteth, [b]are peoples, and multitudes, and nations, and tongues.

16 And the ten horns which thou sawest upon the beast, [a]these shall hate the whore, and shall make her desolate [b]and naked, and shall eat her flesh, and [c]burn her with fire.

17 [a]For God hath put in their hearts to fulfil his will, and to agree, and give their kingdom unto the beast, [b]until the words of God shall be fulfilled.

18 And the woman which thou sawest [a]is *that* great city, [b]which reigneth over the kings of the earth.

The desolation of Babylon

18 And [a]after these *things* I saw another angel come down from heaven, having great power; [b]and the earth was lightened with his glory.

2 And he cried mightily with a strong voice, saying,

[a]Babylon the great is fallen, is fallen,
And [b]is become the habitation of devils,
And the hold of every foul spirit,
And [c]a cage of every unclean and hateful bird.

3 For all nations [a]have drunk of the wine of the wrath of her fornication,
And the kings of the earth have committed fornication with her,
[b]And the merchants of the earth are waxed rich through the [1]abundance of her delicacies.

4 ¶ And I heard another voice from heaven, saying,

[a]Come out of her, my people,
That ye be not partakers of her sins,
And that ye receive not of her plagues.
5 [a]For her sins have reached unto heaven,
And [b]God hath remembered her iniquities.
6 [a]Reward her even as she rewarded you,
And double unto her double according to her works:
[b]In the cup which she hath filled [c]fill to her double.
7 [a]How much she hath glorified herself, and lived deliciously,
So much torment and sorrow give her:
For she saith in her heart, I sit a [b]queen,
And am no widow, and shall see no sorrow.
8 Therefore shall her plagues come [a]in one day,
Death, and mourning, and famine;
And [b]she shall be utterly burnt with fire:
[c]For strong *is* the Lord God who judgeth her.
9 And [a]the kings of the earth, who have committed fornication and lived deliciously with her,
[b]Shall bewail her, and lament for her,
[c]When they shall see the smoke of her burning,
10 Standing afar off for the fear of her torment,
Saying, [a]Alas, alas, *that* great city Babylon, *that* mighty city!
[b]For in one hour is thy judgment come.
11 And [a]the merchants of the earth *shall* weep and mourn over her;
For no *man* buyeth their merchandise any more:

17:11 [a]ver. 8
17:12 [a]Dan. 7:20; Zech. 1:18
17:14 [a]ch. 16:14 [b]Deut. 10:17; 1 Tim. 6:15; ch. 19:16 [c]Jer. 50:44; ch. 14:4
17:15 [a]Is. 8:7 [b]ch. 13:7
17:16 [a]Jer. 50:41; ch. 16:12 [b]Ezek. 16:37; ch. 18:16 [c]ch. 18:8
17:17 [a]2 Thes. 2:11 [b]ch. 10:7
17:18 [a]ch. 16:19 [b]ch. 12:4
18:1 [a]ch. 17:1 [b]Ezek. 43:2
18:2 [a]Is. 13:19; Jer. 51:8 [b]Is. 13:21; Jer. 50:39 [c]Is. 14:23; Mark 5:2
18:3 [a]ch. 14:8

18:3 [1]Or, *power* [b]Is. 47:15
18:4 [a]Is. 48:20; Jer. 50:8; 2 Cor. 6:17
18:5 [a]Gen. 18:20; Jer. 51:9; Jonah 1:2 [b]ch. 16:19
18:6 [a]Ps. 137:8; Jer. 50:15 [b]ch. 14:10 [c]ch. 16:19
18:7 [a]Ezek. 28:2 [b]Is. 47:7,8; Zeph. 2:15
18:8 [a]ver. 10; Is. 47:9 [b]ch. 17:16 [c]Jer. 50:34; ch. 11:17
18:9 [a]Ezek. 26:16 [b]Jer. 50:46 [c]ch. 19:3
18:10 [a]Is. 21:9; ch. 14:8 [b]ver. 17,19
18:11 [a]Ezek. 27:27

17:10 *seven kings.* That seven heads symbolize both seven hills and seven kings illustrates the fluidity of apocalyptic symbolism, unless the hills are figurative for royal (or political) power. *five . . . one . . . the other.* Taken (1) as seven actual Roman emperors, (2) as seven secular empires or (3) symbolically as the power of the Roman empire as a whole.

17:11 *and is not.* Cf. 13:3. *the eighth.* The antichrist, who plays the role of a king ("is one of the seven") but is in reality part of the cosmic struggle between God and Satan.

17:12 *one hour.* A short time.

17:14 *Lord of lords, and King of kings.* Emphasizes the supreme sovereignty of the Lamb (cf. Deut 10:17; Ps 136:2–3; Dan 2:47; 1 Tim 6:15).

17:18 *great city.* Cf. 17:1; see notes on 11:8; 14:8.

18:1 *earth was lightened with his glory.* Cf. Ex 34:29–35; Ps 104:2; Ezek 43:1–5; 1 Tim 6:16.

‡18:2 *Babylon the great is fallen, is fallen.* The double phrase is for emphasis and certainty. Cf. Is 21:9; Jer 51:8; see notes on 11:8; 14:8.

18:3 *wine of the wrath of her fornication.* See note on 14:8.

18:4 *Come out of her.* A common prophetic warning (cf. Is 52:11; Jer 51:45; 2 Cor 6:17).

18:6 *double.* In full, sufficiently (see note on Is 40:2). *cup which she hath filled.* See 17:4.

‡18:7 *I sit a queen, And am no widow.* The ungodly system refuses to see itself as it really is.

18:9–20 Three groups lament: (1) kings (v. 9), (2) merchants (v. 11) and (3) sailers (v. 17). The passage is modeled after Ezekiel's lament over Tyre (Ezek 27). Fifteen of the 29 commodities in vv. 12–13 are also listed in Ezek 27:12–22.

18:9 *kings . . . bewail her, and lament.* Probably because of their own great financial loss (see v. 11).

12 [a]The merchandise of gold, and silver,
And precious stones, and of pearls,
And fine linen, and purple, and silk,
and scarlet,
And all [1]thyine wood, and all *manner*
vessels of ivory,
And all *manner* vessels of most
precious wood,
And of brass, and iron, and marble,
13 And cinnamon, and odours,
And ointments, and frankincense,
And wine, and oil,
And fine flour, and wheat,
And beasts, and sheep, and horses, and
chariots,
And [1]slaves, and [a]souls of men.
14 And the fruits that thy soul lusted after
are departed from thee,
And all *things which were* dainty and
goodly are departed from thee,
And thou shalt find them no more at
all.
15 [a]The merchants of these *things,* which
were made rich by her,
Shall stand afar off for the fear of her
torment,
Weeping and wailing,
16 And saying,
Alas, alas, *that* great city,
[a]That was clothed in fine linen, and
purple, and scarlet,
And decked with gold, and precious
stones, and pearls:
17 [a]For in one hour so great riches is
come to nought.

And [b]every shipmaster, and all the
company in ships,
And sailers, and as many as trade by
sea,
Stood afar off,
18 [a]And cried
When they saw the smoke of her
burning, saying,
[b]What *city is* like unto *this* great city?
19 And [a]they cast dust on their heads,
And cried, weeping and wailing,
saying,
Alas, alas, *that* great city,
Wherein were made rich all that had
ships in the sea by reason of her
costliness:
[b]For in one hour is she made desolate.
20 [a]Rejoice over her, *thou* heaven,
And ye holy apostles and prophets;
For [b]God hath avenged you on her.
21 ¶ And a mighty angel took up a stone
like a great millstone, and cast *it* into the sea,
saying,
[a]Thus with violence shall *that* great
city Babylon be thrown down, and
[b]shall be found no more at all.
22 [a]And the voice of harpers, and
musicians, and of pipers, and
trumpeters, shall be heard no more
at all in thee;
And no craftsman, of whatsoever craft
he be, shall be found any more in
thee;
And the sound of a millstone shall be
heard no more at all in thee;
23 [a]And the light of a candle shall shine
no more at all in thee;
[b]And the voice of the bridegroom and
of the bride shall be heard no more
at all in thee:
For [c]thy merchants were the great
men of the earth;
[d]For by thy sorceries were all nations
deceived.
24 And [a]in her was found the blood of
prophets, and of saints,
And of all that [b]were slain upon the
earth.

The marriage supper of the Lamb

19 And after these *things* [a]I heard a
great voice of much people in heav-
en, saying, Alleluia; [b]Salvation, and glory, and
honour, and power, unto the Lord our God:
2 For [a]true and righteous *are* his judgments: for he hath judged the great whore,
which did corrupt the earth with her fornication, and [b]hath avenged the blood of his servants at her hand.
3 And again they said, Alleluia. And [a]her
smoke rose up for ever and ever.
4 And [a]the four and twenty elders and the
four beasts fell down and worshipped God that
sat on the throne, saying, [b]Amen; Alleluia.
5 And a voice came out of the throne, saying, [a]Praise our God, all ye his servants, and
ye that fear him, [b]both small and great.
6 [a]And I heard as *it were* the voice of a
great multitude, and as the voice of many waters, and as the voice of mighty thunderings,
saying, Alleluia: for [b]the Lord God Omnipotent reigneth.

18:12 [1]Or, *sweet* [a]ch. 17:4
18:13 [1]Or, *bodies* [a]Ezek. 27:13
18:15 [a]ver. 3,11
18:16 [a]ch. 17:4
18:17 [a]ver. 10 [b]Is. 23:14; Ezek. 27:29
18:18 [a]Ezek. 27:30 [b]ch. 13:4
18:19 [a]Josh. 7:6; 1 Sam. 4:12; Job 2:12; Ezek. 27:30 [b]ver. 8
18:20 [a]Is. 44:23; 49:13; Jer. 51:48 [b]Luke 11:49; ch. 19:2
18:21 [a]Jer. 51:64 [b]ch. 12:8; 16:20
18:22 [a]Jer. 7:34; 16:9; 25:10; Ezek. 26:13
18:23 [a]Jer. 25:10 [b]Jer. 7:34; 16:9; 25:10; 33:11 [c]Is. 23:8 [d]2 Ki. 9:22; ch. 17:2,5
18:24 [a]ch. 17:6 [b]Jer. 51:49
19:1 [a]ch. 11:15 [b]ch. 4:11; 7:10,12
19:2 [a]ch. 15:3 [b]Deut. 32:43
19:3 [a]Is. 34:10; ch. 14:11
19:4 [a]ch. 4:4,6 [b]1 Chr. 16:36; Neh. 5:13; 8:6; ch. 5:14
19:5 [a]Ps. 134:1 [b]ch. 11:18; 20:12
19:6 [a]Ezek. 1:24; ch. 14:2 [b]ch. 11:15

18:12 *purple.* An expensive dye since it must be extracted a drop at a time from the murex shellfish. *thyine wood.* An expensive dark wood from north Africa—used for inlay work in costly furniture. *marble.* Used to decorate public buildings and the homes of the very rich.

18:13 *ointments,and frankincense.* Brought by the wise men as gifts for the infant Jesus (Mat 2:11). *slaves, and souls of men.* Slave trade.

18:17 *shipmaster.* The pilot of the ship rather than the owner. Both are mentioned in Acts 27:11.

18:19 *cast dust on their heads.* An act of sorrow and dismay (see Ezek 27:30). *in one hour.* See vv. 10,17.

18:21 *great millstone.* Similar to the large millstone of Mark 9:42, which was actually a "donkey millstone" (one large enough to require a donkey to turn it).

18:24 *blood of prophets.* See 6:10; 17:6; 19:2; cf. Ezek 24:7.

19:1 *much people.* See note on 7:9. *Alleluia.* Occurs four times in vv. 1–6 but nowhere else in the NT. It is derived from two Hebrew words meaning "Praise the LORD."

19:4 *four and twenty elders and the four beasts.* See notes on 4:4,6.

7 Let us be glad and rejoice, and give honour to him: for [a]the marriage of the Lamb is come, and his wife hath made herself ready.

8 And [a]to her was granted that she should be arrayed in fine linen, clean and [1]white: [b]for the fine linen is the righteousness of saints.

9 And he saith unto me, Write, [a]Blessed *are* they which are called unto the marriage supper of the Lamb. And he saith unto me, [b]These are the true sayings of God.

10 And [a]I fell at his feet to worship him. And he said unto me, [b]See *thou do it* not: I am thy fellowservant, and of thy brethren [c]that have the testimony of Jesus: worship God: for the testimony of Jesus is the spirit of prophecy.

The beast and false prophet

11 ¶ [a]And I saw heaven opened, and behold [b]a white horse; and he that sat upon him *was* called [c]Faithful and True, and [d]in righteousness he doth judge and make war.

12 [a]His eyes *were* as a flame of fire, [b]and on his head *were* many crowns; [c]and he had a name written, that no *man* knew, but he himself.

13 [a]And he *was* clothed with a vesture dipt in blood: and his name is called [b]The Word of God.

14 [a]And the armies which were in heaven followed him upon white horses, [b]clothed in fine linen, white and clean.

15 And [a]out of his mouth goeth a sharp sword, that with it he should smite the nations: and [b]he shall rule them with a rod of iron: and [c]he treadeth the winepress of the fierceness and wrath of Almighty God.

16 And [a]he hath on *his* vesture and on his thigh a name written, [b]KING OF KINGS, AND LORD OF LORDS.

17 ¶ And I saw an angel standing in the sun; and he cried with a loud voice, saying [a]to all the fowls that fly in the midst of heaven, [b]Come and gather yourselves together unto the supper of the great God;

18 [a]That ye may eat the flesh of kings, and the flesh of captains, and the flesh of mighty *men,* and the flesh of horses, and of them that sit on them, and the flesh of all *men,* both free and bond, both small and great.

19 [a]And I saw the beast, and the kings of the earth, and their armies, gathered together to make war against him that sat on the horse, and against his army.

20 [a]And the beast was taken, and with him the false prophet that wrought miracles before him, with which he deceived them that had received the mark of the beast, and [b]them that worshipped his image. [c]*These* both were cast alive into a lake of fire [d]burning with brimstone.

21 And the remnant [a]were slain with the sword of him that sat upon the horse, which *sword* proceeded out of his mouth: [b]and all the fowls [c]were filled with their flesh.

The millennial reign

20 And I saw an angel come down from heaven, [a]having the key of the bottomless *pit* and a great chain in his hand.

2 And he laid hold on [a]the dragon, *that* old serpent, which is the devil, and Satan, and bound him a thousand years,

3 And cast him into the bottomless *pit,* and shut him up, and [a]set a seal upon him, [b]that

19:7 [a]Mat. 22:2; 25:10; 2 Cor. 11:2; Eph. 5:32; ch. 21:2,9
19:8 [1][Or, *bright*] [a]Ps. 45:13; Ezek. 16:10; ch. 3:18 [b]Ps. 132:9
19:9 [a]Mat. 22:2; Luke 14:15 [b]ch. 22:6
19:10 [a]ch. 22:8 [b]Acts 10:26; ch. 22:9 [c]1 John 5:10; ch. 12:17
19:11 [a]ch. 15:5 [b]ch. 6:2 [c]ch. 3:14 [d]Is. 11:4
19:12 [a]ch. 1:14 [b]ch. 6:2 [c]ch. 2:17
19:13 [a]Is. 63:2,3 [b]John 1:1; 1 John 5:7
19:14 [a]ch. 14:20 [b]Mat. 28:3; ch. 4:4
19:15 [a]Is. 11:4; 2 Thes. 2:8; ch. 1:16 [b]Ps. 2:9; ch. 2:27 [c]Is. 63:3; ch. 14:19
19:16 [a]ver. 12
19:16 [b]Dan. 2:47; 1 Tim. 6:15; ch. 17:14
19:17 [a]ver. 21 [b]Ezek. 39:17
19:18 [a]Ezek. 39:18
19:19 [a]ch. 16:16
19:20 [a]ch. 16:13 [b]ch. 13:12 [c]Dan. 7:11; ch. 20:10 [d]ch. 14:10
19:21 [a]ver. 15 [b]ver. 17,18 [c]ch. 17:16
20:1 [a]ch. 1:18
20:2 [a]2 Pet. 2:4; Jude 6; ch. 12:9
20:3 [a]Dan. 6:17 [b]ch. 12:9

‡19:7 *marriage of the Lamb.* The imagery of a wedding to express the intimate relationship between God and His people has its roots in the prophetic literature of the OT (e.g., Is 54:5–7; Hos 2:19). Cf. the NT usage (Mat 22:2–14; Eph 5:32). The fact that this marriage takes place in heaven implies that the church has been raptured previously.

19:9 *Blessed.* The fourth beatitude (see note on 1:3).

19:10 *fell at his feet.* See note on 1:17; cf. Acts 10:25. *spirit.* Essence.

19:11 *white horse.* Probably not the white horse of 6:2. The context here indicates that the rider is Christ returning as Warrior-Messiah-King.

19:12 *name written.* A secret name whose meaning is veiled from all created beings.

19:13 *vesture dipt in blood.* Either the blood of the enemy shed in conflict (cf. 14:14–20; Is 63:1–3), or the blood of Christ shed to atone for sin.

‡19:14 *armies . . . in heaven.* Their robes of white indicate this to be the redeemed church—the bride of Christ—returning in triumph with her heavenly Bridegroom (cf. 19:8; 17:14).

19:15 *sharp sword.* See note on 1:16. *rod of iron.* See note on 2:27. *winepress.* See note on 14:19.

19:16 *KING OF KINGS.* See note on 17:14.

19:17 *supper of the great God.* A grim contrast to the "marriage supper of the Lamb" (v. 9; cf. Ezek 39:17–20).

19:20 *beast . . . false prophet.* See notes on 13:1,11. *lake of fire burning with brimstone.* See 20:10,14–15; 21:8. Punishment by fire is prominent in both Biblical and non-Biblical Jewish writings (e.g., 1 Enoch 54:1). Although the designation *gehenna* is not used here, this is what John refers to (see note on Mat 5:22). Originally the site of a cultic shrine where human sacrifices were offered (2 Ki 16:3; 23:10; Jer 7:31), it came to be equated with the "hell" of final judgment in apocalyptic literature.

19:21 *fowls were filled with their flesh.* The "supper of the great God" of vv. 17–18.

20:1–22:21 These last three chapters reflect many of the subjects and themes of the first three chapters of Genesis.

‡20:1 *bottomless pit.* Greek *abyss.* See note on 9:1.

‡20:2 *dragon.* See note on 12:3. *old serpent.* See 12:15; Gen 3:1–5. *thousand years.* The millennium (from the Latin *mille,* "thousand," and *annus,* "year"). It is taken literally by some as 1,000 actual years, while others interpret it metaphorically as a long but undetermined period of time. There are three basic approaches to the subject of the millennium: 1. Amillennialism: The millennium describes the present reign of the souls of deceased believers with Christ in heaven. 2. Premillennialism: The present form of God's kingdom is moving toward a grand climax when Christ will return to establish His kingdom in a literal, visible reign of peace and righteousness on the earth. 3. Postmillennialism: The world will eventually be Christianized, resulting in a long period of peace and prosperity called the millennium. This future period will close with Christ's second coming, the resurrection of the dead, the final judgment and the eternal state. The context favors the second view. The 1,000 years are mentioned six times, and there is every reason to take them literally, not allegorically.

he should deceive the nations no more, till the
thousand years should be fulfilled: and after
that he must be loosed a little season.
4 ¶ And I saw [a]thrones, and they sat upon
them, and [b]judgment was given unto them:
and *I saw* [c]the souls of them that were beheaded for the witness of Jesus, and for the
word of God, and [d]which had not worshipped
the beast, [e]neither his image, neither had received *his* mark upon their foreheads, or in
their hands; and they lived and [f]reigned with
Christ a thousand years.
5 But the rest of the dead lived not again
until the thousand years were finished. This *is*
the first resurrection.
6 Blessed and holy *is* he that hath part in
the first resurrection: on such [a]the second
death hath no power, but they shall be [b]priests
of God and of Christ, [c]and shall reign with
him a thousand years.

The loosing of Satan

7 ¶ And when the thousand years are expired, [a]Satan shall be loosed out of his prison,
8 And shall go out [a]to deceive the nations
which are in the four quarters of the earth,
[b]Gog and Magog, [c]to gather them together to
battle: the number of whom *is* as the sand of
the sea.
9 [a]And they went up on the breadth of the
earth, and compassed the camp of the saints
about, and the beloved city: and fire came
down from God out of heaven, and devoured
them.
10 [a]And the devil that deceived them was
cast into the lake of fire and brimstone,
[b]where the beast and the false prophet *are,*
and [c]shall be tormented day and night for ever
and ever.

The great white throne judgment

11 ¶ And I saw a great white throne, and
him that sat on it, from whose face [a]the earth
and the heaven fled *away;* [b]and there was
found no place for them.
12 And I saw the dead, [a]small and great,
stand before God; [b]and the books were
opened: and another [c]book was opened,
which is *the book* of life: and the dead were
judged out of those *things* which were written
in the books, [d]according to their works.
13 And the sea gave up the dead which
were in it; [a]and death and [1]hell delivered up
the dead which were in them: [b]and they were
judged every man according to their works.
14 And [a]death and hell were cast into the
lake of fire. [b]This is the second death.
15 And whosoever was not found written
in the book of life [a]was cast into the lake of
fire.

The new Jerusalem

21 And [a]I saw a new heaven and a new
earth: [b]for the first heaven and the
first earth were passed away; and there was no
more sea.
2 And I John saw [a]the holy city, new Jerusalem, coming down from God out of heaven,
prepared [b]as a bride adorned for her husband.
3 And I heard a great voice out of heaven
saying, Behold, [a]the tabernacle of God *is* with
men, and he will dwell with them, and they
shall be his people, and God himself shall be
with them, *and be* their God.
4 [a]And God shall wipe away all tears from
their eyes; and [b]there shall be no more death,
[c]neither sorrow, nor crying, neither shall
there be any more pain: for the former *things*
are passed away.
5 And [a]he that sat upon the throne said,
[b]Behold, I make all *things* new. And he said
unto me, Write: for [c]these words are true and
faithful.
6 And he said unto me, [a]It is done. [b]I am
Alpha and Omega, the beginning and the end.
[c]I will give unto him that is athirst of the fountain of the water of life freely.
7 He that overcometh shall inherit [1]all
things; and [a]I will be his God, and he shall be
my son.
8 [a]But the fearful, and unbelieving, and the
abominable, and murderers, and whoremongers, and sorcerers, and idolaters, and all liars,
shall have their part in [b]the lake which burneth with fire and brimstone: which is the second death.

20:4 [a]Dan. 7:9; Mat. 19:28; Luke 22:30 [b]1 Cor. 6:2,3 [c]ch. 6:9 [d]ch. 13:12 [e]ch. 13:15 [f]Rom. 8:17; 2 Tim. 2:12; ch. 5:10
20:6 [a]ch. 2:11 [b]Is. 61:6; 1 Pet. 2:9; ch. 1:6 [c]ver. 4
20:7 [a]ver. 2
20:8 [a]ver. 3,10 [b]Ezek. 38:2; 39:1 [c]ch. 16:14
20:9 [a]Is. 8:8; Ezek. 38:9
20:10 [a]ver. 8 [b]ch. 19:20 [c]ch. 14:10
20:11 [a]2 Pet. 3:7; ch. 21:1 [b]Dan. 2:35
20:12 [a]ch. 19:5 [b]Dan. 7:10 [c]Ps. 69:28; Dan. 12:1; Phil. 4:3; ch. 3:5
20:12 [d]Jer. 17:10; 32:19; Mat. 16:27; Rom. 2:6; ch. 2:23
20:13 [1]Or, *the grave* [a]ch. 6:8 [b]ver. 12
20:14 [a]1 Cor. 15:26 [b]ch. 21:8
20:15 [a]ch. 19:20
21:1 [a]Is. 65:17; 2 Pet. 3:13 [b]ch. 20:11
21:2 [a]Is. 52:1; Gal. 4:26; Heb. 11:10; 12:22; ch. 3:12 [b]Is. 54:5; 2 Cor. 11:2
21:3 [a]Lev. 26:11; Ezek. 43:7; 2 Cor. 6:16
21:4 [a]Is. 25:8 [b]1 Cor. 15:26; ch. 20:14 [c]Is. 35:10; 61:3; 65:19
21:5 [a]ch. 4:2,9; 20:11 [b]Is. 43:19; 2 Cor. 5:17 [c]ch. 19:9
21:6 [a]ch. 16:17 [b]ch. 1:8 [c]Is. 12:3; John 4:10; 7:37
21:7 [1][Or, *these things*] [a]Zech. 8:8; Heb. 8:10
21:8 [a]1 Cor. 6:9; Gal. 5:19; Eph. 5:5; 1 Tim. 1:9; Heb. 12:14 [b]ch. 20:14

20:3 *loosed a little season.* See vv. 7–10.
‡20:4 *souls of them that were beheaded.* See 6:9–11. This seems to be the souls of all those believers who died in the tribulation. *his mark.* See note on 13:16. *they lived.* The "first resurrection" (v. 5).
‡20:5 *rest of the dead.* Either the wicked, meaning all unsaved dead from Cain onward. They will not be raised until after the millennial reign of Christ.
20:6 *Blessed.* The fifth beatitude (see note on 1:3). *second death.* Defined in v. 14 as the "lake of fire" (cf. 21:8).
20:7 *thousand years.* See note on v. 2.
20:8 *Gog and Magog.* Symbolize the nations of the world as they band together for a final assault on God. The OT background is Ezek 38–39.
20:10 *tormented day and night.* See note on 14:11; cf. 14:10.
20:12 *book of life.* See note on 3:5. *judged . . . according to their works.* The principle of judgment on the basis of works is taught in Ps 62:12; Jer 17:10; Rom 2:6; 1 Pet 1:17 and elsewhere.
20:14 *death and hell.* See 6:8 and note.
20:14–15 *lake of fire.* See note on 19:20.
21:2–22:5 The "holy city" combines elements of Jerusalem, the temple and the Garden of Eden.
21:2 *bride.* See note on 19:7.
21:3 *tabernacle of God.* See Lev 26:11–12; Ezek 37:27; 2 Cor 6:16.
21:4 *wipe away all tears.* See 7:17; Is 25:8.
21:6 *Alpha and Omega.* See note on 1:8. *water of life.* Cf. Ps 36:9.
21:7 *He that overcometh.* Cf. the emphasis on overcoming in the seven letters (2:7,11,17,26; 3:5,12,21).
21:8 *sorcerers.* Cf. Acts 19:19. The magical tradition in ancient times called for the mixing of various herbs to ward off evil. *lake which burneth with fire and brimstone.* See note on 19:20.

9 ¶ And there came unto me one of [a]the seven angels which had the seven vials full of the seven last plagues, and talked with me, saying, *Come* hither, I will shew thee [b]the bride, the Lamb's wife.

10 And he carried me away [a]in the spirit to a great and high mountain, and shewed me [b]*that* great city, the holy Jerusalem, descending out of heaven from God,

11 [a]Having the glory of God: and her light *was* like unto a stone most precious, *even* like a jasper stone, clear as crystal;

12 And had a wall great and high, and had [a]twelve gates, and at the gates twelve angels, and names written *there*on, which are *the names* of the twelve tribes of the children of Israel:

13 [a]On the east three gates; on the north three gates; on the south three gates; and on the west three gates.

14 And the wall of the city had twelve foundations, and [a]in them the names of the twelve apostles of the Lamb.

15 And he that talked with me [a]had a golden reed to measure the city, and the gates thereof, and the wall thereof.

16 And the city lieth foursquare, and the length is as large as the breadth: and he measured the city with the reed, twelve thousand furlongs. The length and the breadth and the height of it are equal.

17 And he measured the wall thereof, an hundred *and* forty *and* four cubits, *according to* the measure of a man, that is, of *the* angel.

18 And the building of the wall of it was *of* jasper: and the city *was* pure gold, like unto clear glass.

19 [a]And the foundations of the wall of the city *were* garnished with all *manner of* precious stones. The first foundation *was* jasper; the second, sapphire; the third, a chalcedony; the fourth, an emerald;

20 The fifth, sardonyx; the sixth, sardius; the seventh, chrysolite; the eighth, beryl; the ninth, a topaz; the tenth, a chrysoprasus; the eleventh, a jacinth; the twelfth, an amethyst.

21 And the twelve gates *were* twelve pearls; every several gate was of one pearl: [a]and the street of the city *was* pure gold, as *it were* transparent glass.

22 [a]And I saw no temple therein: for the Lord God Almighty and the Lamb are the temple of it.

23 [a]And the city had no need of the sun, neither of the moon, to shine in it: for the glory of God did lighten it, and the Lamb *is* the light thereof.

24 [a]And the nations of them which are saved shall walk in the light of it: and the kings of the earth do bring their glory and honour into it.

25 [a]And the gates of it shall not be shut at all by day: for [b]there shall be no night there.

26 [a]And they shall bring the glory and honour of the nations into it.

27 And [a]there shall in no wise enter into it any *thing* that defileth, neither *whatsoever* worketh abomination, or *maketh* a lie: but they which are written in the Lamb's [b]book of life.

The water and tree of life

22 And he shewed me [a]a pure river of water of life, clear as crystal, proceeding out of the throne of God and of the Lamb.

2 [a]In the midst of the street of it, and of either side of the river, *was there* [b]the tree of life, which bare twelve *manner of* fruits, *and* yielded her fruit every month: and the leaves of the tree *were* [c]for the healing of the nations.

3 And [a]there shall be no more curse: [b]but the throne of God and of the Lamb shall be in it; and his servants shall serve him:

4 And [a]they shall see his face; and [b]his name *shall be* in their foreheads.

5 [a]And there shall be no night there; and they need no candle, neither light of the sun; for [b]the Lord God giveth them light: [c]and they shall reign for ever and ever.

Epilogue

6 ¶ And he said unto me, [a]These sayings *are* faithful and true: and the Lord God of the holy prophets [b]sent his angel to shew unto his servants *the things* which must shortly be done.

7 [a]Behold, I come quickly: [b]blessed *is* he that keepeth the sayings of the prophecy of this book.

21:9 [a]ch. 15:1 [b]ch. 19:7
21:10 [a]ch. 1:10 [b]Ezek. 48
21:11 [a]ch. 22:5
21:12 [a]Ezek. 48:31-34
21:13 [a]Ezek. 48:31-34
21:14 [a]Mat. 16:18; Gal. 2:9; Eph. 2:20
21:15 [a]Ezek. 40:3; Zech. 2:1
21:19 [a]Is. 54:11
21:21 [a]ch. 22:2
21:22 [a]John 4:23
21:23 [a]Is. 24:23; 60:19,20
21:24 [a]Is. 60:3; 66:12
21:25 [a]Is. 60:11 [b]Is. 60:20; Zech. 14:7; ch. 22:5
21:26 [a]ver. 24
21:27 [a]Is. 35:8; 52:1; 60:21; Joel 3:17; ch. 22:14 [b]Phil. 4:3
22:1 [a]Ezek. 47:1; Zech. 14:8
22:2 [a]Ezek. 47:12; ch. 21:21 [b]Gen. 2:9; ch. 2:7 [c]ch. 21:24
22:3 [a]Zech. 14:11 [b]Ezek. 48:35
22:4 [a]Mat. 5:8; 1 Cor. 13:12; 1 John 3:2 [b]ch. 14:1
22:5 [a]ch. 21:23 [b]Ps. 36:9 [c]Dan. 7:27; Rom. 5:17; 2 Tim. 2:12
22:6 [a]ch. 19:9 [b]ch. 1:1
22:7 [a]ch. 3:11 [b]ch. 1:3

21:9 *seven last plagues.* See 15:1.
21:10 *in the spirit.* See notes on 1:10; 4:2; 17:3.
‡21:12 *twelve gates.* See Ezek 48:30–35. The number 12 comes from the 12 tribes of Israel, the OT people of God. See v. 14, where the 12 foundations bear the names of the 12 apostles. Twelve apostles were chosen to rule over the 12 tribes of Israel (Mat 19:28).
21:15 *measure the city.* Cf. Ezek 40–41. In Rev 11 the measuring was to ensure protection; here it serves to show the size and symmetry of the eternal dwelling place of the faithful.
‡21:16 *twelve thousand furlongs.* This is a cube of about 1,500 miles square. This city may sit on the earth, in the earth, or be suspended in space near the earth. *length and the breadth and the height.* Thus a perfect cube, as was the most holy place of the tabernacle and the temple.
21:20 The precise identification of some of these precious stones is uncertain.
21:27 *Lamb's book of life.* See note on 3:5.
22:2 *tree of life.* See Gen 2:9; 3:22; Ezek 47:12.
‡22:4 *they shall see his face.* An idiom for "have an audience" with the king. In ancient times criminals were banished from the presence of the king (Esth 7:8; cf. 2 Sam 14:24). One blessing of eternity will be to see the Lord face to face (cf. 1 Cor 13:12). *his name.* See note on 3:12.
22:5 *they shall reign.* See 5:10; 20:6; Dan 7:18,27.
22:6 *his servants.* See v. 3. *things which must shortly be done.* See 1:1,19.
22:7 *I come quickly.* See vv. 12,20; 2:16; 3:11. *blessed.* The sixth beatitude (see note on 1:3).
22:8 *fell down to worship.* See note on 1:17.

8 ¶ And I John saw these *things,* and heard
them. And when I had heard and seen, [a]I fell
down to worship before the feet of the angel
which shewed me these *things.*
9 Then saith he unto me, [a]See *thou do it*
not: for I am thy fellowservant, and of thy
brethren the prophets, and of them which
keep the sayings of this book: worship God.
10 [a]And he saith unto me, Seal not the sayings of the prophecy of this book: [b]for the time
is at hand.
11 [a]He that is unjust, let him be unjust
still: and he which is filthy, let him be filthy
still: and *he that is* righteous, let him be righteous still: and *he that is* holy, let him be holy
still.
12 [a]And behold, I come quickly; and [b]my
reward *is* with me, [c]to give every man according as his work shall be.
13 [a]I am Alpha and Omega, the beginning
and the end, the first and the last.
14 [a]Blessed *are* they that do his commandments, that they may have right [b]to the tree of
life, [c]and may enter in through the gates into
the city.
15 For [a]without *are* [b]dogs, and sorcerers,
and whoremongers, and murderers, and idolaters, and whosoever loveth and maketh a lie.
16 ¶ [a]I Jesus have sent mine angel to testify unto you these *things* in the churches. [b]I
am the root and the offspring of David, *and*
[c]the bright and morning star.
17 And the Spirit and [a]the bride say,
Come. And let him that heareth say, Come.
[b]And let him that is athirst come. And whosoever will, let him take the water of life freely.
18 For I testify unto every *man* that
heareth the words of the prophecy of this
book, [a]If any *man* shall add unto these *things,*
God shall add unto him the plagues that are
written in this book:
19 And if any *man* shall take away from the
words of the book of this prophecy, [a]God shall
take away his part [1] out of the book of life, and
out of [b]the holy city, and *from* the *things*
which are written in this book.
20 He which testifieth these *things* saith,
[a]Surely I come quickly. [b]Amen. [c]Even so,
come, Lord Jesus.
21 [a]The grace of our Lord Jesus Christ *be*
with you all. Amen.

22:8 [a]ch. 19:10 **22:9** [a]ch. 19:10 **22:10** [a]Dan. 8:26 [b]ch. 1:3 **22:11** [a]Ezek. 3:27; Dan. 12:10; 2 Tim. 3:13 **22:12** [a]ver. 7 [b]Is. 40:10 [c]ch. 20:12 **22:13** [a]Is. 41:4 **22:14** [a]Dan. 12:12; 1 John 3:24 [b]ch. 2:7 [c]ch. 21:27 **22:15** [a]1 Cor. 6:9; Gal. 5:19; Col. 3:6 [b]Phil. 3:2

22:16 [a]ch. 1:1 [b]ch. 5:5 [c]Num. 24:17; Zech. 6:12; 2 Pet. 1:19 **22:17** [a]ch. 21:2,9 [b]Is. 55:1; John 7:37 **22:18** [a]Deut. 4:2; Prov. 30:6 **22:19** [1][Or, *from the tree of life*] [a]Ex. 32:33; Ps. 69:28 [b]ch. 21:2 **22:20** [a]ver. 12 [b]John 21:25 [c]2 Tim. 4:8

22:21 [a]Rom. 16:20

22:10 *Seal not the sayings.* Contrast Dan 12:4.
‡22:11 *unjust, let him be unjust still.* This verse speaks of the stability of the eternal state—both for the wicked and for the righteous.
22:12 *I come quickly.* See vv. 7,20; 2:16; 3:11. *according as his work shall be.* See notes on 2:23; 20:12.
22:13 *Alpha and Omega.* See note on 1:8.
22:14 *Blessed.* The last of the seven beatitudes (see note on 1:3).
22:15 *dogs.* A term applied to all types of ceremonially impure persons. In Deut 23:18 it designates a male prostitute.
‡22:16 *mine angel.* Cf. 1:1. *the root and the offspring of David.* See note on 5:5; cf. Is 11:1,10; Rom 1:3. *bright and morning star.* These are Messianic titles applied to Jesus Christ. See Num 24:17.
22:18–19 Cf. the commands in Deut 4:2; 12:32. The warning here relates specifically to the book of Revelation.
‡22:20 *I come quickly.* See vv. 7,12; 2:16; 3:11. *come, Lord Jesus.* See note on 1 Cor 16:22. *grace.* The NT begins with Jesus Christ (Mat 1:1) and ends with an expression of His grace. Throughout, He is the subject. The NT begins with the fact of His first coming and ends with the promise of His second.

STUDY HELPS

INDEX TO SUBJECTS

The Index to Subjects will lead you to key texts on a variety of subjects covered in the *Zondervan KJV Study Bible*.

D

H

12:23; Ps 6:5; 17:15; 30:9; 49:15; Prov 2:18; Eccl 9:10; 12:7

Principles Prov 3:1-4

Source Gen 2:7; Job 27:3; Ps 104:30; Eccl 12:7

Unfair Gen 18:25; 2 Sam 21:6,9,14; Job 1:13-19; 34:19; Ps 73:3-5; Eccl 2:26; 4:13-16

Value of 2 Ki 11:1-2; Job 3:10-16; Eccl 12:6

Without God Eccl 1:2; 6:12

Light Gen 1:14-16; Ps 13:3; 112:4; 119:105; Is 42:6; 58:8,10; 60:3; 1 John 1:5

Loneliness Ps 42:3-4; 102:6-7; 102:16-18

Lord's Supper Mat 6:29; 26:26,28; Luke 22:17-20; John 6:51-56; 21:13; Acts 1:4; 2:42,46-47; 20:7,11; 1 Cor 10:16-17; 11:20-26 24:30,35,41-43

Love

For God Num 30:2; Ps 37:4; 69:9; 112:2-8; 130:5-6; Luke 14:26; John 21:15-17; Rom 13:10; Heb 10:6,8; Rev 2:4

For others Mat 5:48; John 13:34-35; 15:12-14,17; Rom 12:18; 12:20; 13:10; 1 Cor 1:7; 3:2; 13:1-3; 1 John 4:16

Loyalty 1 Ki 11:17-19; 2 Chr 11:13-14; 11:16; Ps 16:4; 84:11; Prov 17:17

Lying Ex 1:19-20; 1 Sam 21:2; 27:8-10; 2 Ki 8:10; 10:19; 2 Chr 18:22; Ps 62:4; Jer 38:27; Acts 5:5,10

M

Magic, witchcraft, and sorcery Ex 22:18; Lev 19:26,31; 20:6,27; Deut 18:10-12,20-21; Is 2:6; 47:10-14; Jer 27:9; Mic 5:12; Mal 3:5; Acts 8:9-24; 13:6-12; 16:16-18; 19:13-19; Gal 5:20

Marriage

Choosing a spouse Ruth 3:10; 2 Chr 21:6; Prov 21:9

Customs Gen 24:50-51; 24:67; 29:18; 29:23-25; 29:27; 31:15; 34:4; Ruth 3:7-8,13-14; 1 Chr 2:21; 2:34-35

Interfaith Gen 38:2; Deut 7:3-4; Judg 12:9; 1 Ki 7:8; 11:1-4; 16:31; 2 Chr 8:11; 21:6; Neh 13:26; 13:28; 1 Cor 7:14

Interracial Lev 24:10; Ruth 1:4; Jer 31:8

Political Gen 20:2; 41:45; 1 Ki 3:1; 2 Chr 18:1

Relationship Gen 2:24; 3:16; Prov 31:23; Jer 16:2; Mark 10:8

Remarriage Deut 24:4; Mat 19:9

Martyrs 1 Ki 18:4,13; 2 Ki 21:16; Ps 37:3-25; Is 57:1-2; Dan 6:22-23; Luke 21:18; Phil 3:10; 1 Pet 1:6; Rev 6:9; 11:7; 20:4-5

Materialism Mat 5:3-12; Luke 6:20-22 1 Cor 3:3; Eph 4:13

Meaning of life Ps 73:13; 90:17; 102:9-10; Prov 1:7; Eccl 1:2; 2:3-11; 2:13-16; 8:16-17; 11:8; 2 Cor 5:10

Mercy Ps 7:11; 25:11; 39:13; 51:1; 78:39; 139:19; 143:1-2; Is 30:18; Jer 3:1; 22:2-5; 24:7; Ezek 3:7; 39:25; Hos 11:8; Nah 2:13; Jas 2:13

Messiah Ps 110:4; Is 16:5; 32:3; Jer 33:16; Nah 1:15; Zech 11:7; Mat 16:20; 17:2; 20:30; Mark 8:30; 10:47; 11:8; Luke 2:32; 18:34; 20:41-44; John 1:46

Other names for Ps 2:2; 110:1; Zech 3:8; 10:4; Luke 2:25; John 10:1-15; Rev 5:5-6

Prophecy about Is 7:14-16; 9:4-6; 32:1; 53:2; Ezek 34:11; Dan 9:24-27; Zech 6:13; 12:10; Luke 3:4-6

Son of David Ps 72:5; 132:12; Is 11:1; Ezek 17:22-24; 34:23-24; Hag 2:23; Mark 12:35-37; Luke 18:38

Miracles Ex 4:1-9; 14:21; 16:31; Josh 3:16; 10:13-14; 2 Ki 20:11; Jonah 1:17; Mark 8:12; Luke 11:29

Moderation Prov 25:16; Eccl 10:16-17

Money Deut 8; Ps 24; 62:10; Mat 6:19-34; 1 Tim 6:3-19 Jas 5:1-5

Moses Ex 2–40; Num 1–36; Deut 1–34; Mat 17:1-13; Heb 11:24-28

Murder Gen 9:6; Ex 2:12; Num 35:24-25; Deut 19:13; 21:1-9; 2 Sam 20:10; 2 Ki 11:1-2; 2 Chr 22:10

Mystery 1 Cor 15:50-58; Eph 3; Col 1:24–2:5; 1 Tim 3:16

N

Natural disasters Gen 7:11; 19:24; Is 24:1-6; Jer 27:8-15; 36:3; Amos 4:6-11

God's control Gen 9:13; Deut 3:22; 4:26; Josh 10:11; 2 Ki 3:20; 20:11; Ps 148:1-10; Is 38:7-8; Jonah 1:10; Zech 10:1; Luke 4:39; 24:31

Lessons from Ps 29:10; Prov 30:24-28

Needs (spiritual) Ps 40:17; 63:1; 70:5; 86:1; Mat 5:20

Neighbour Lev 19:18; Mat 22:37-40; Luke 10:25-37; Rom 13:8-10

Obedience

To God Ex 4:13; Num 15:3; Deut 6:3; Judg 2:22; 1 Sam 15:22; 1 Ki 17:3; Prov 1:7; 10:27; Jer 36:8-9; Mic 6:8; Hag 1–2; John 13:34-35; Heb 5:8

To the law Deut 30:11; Mark 2:27; Acts 16:21; Tit 3:1-2

To leaders 2 Ki 4:2-7; Jer 38:2-3; Dan 3:13-14; Acts 4:19; Tit 3:1-2; 1 Pet 2:13-17

To parents Gen 22:9; Jer 35:8-16; Eph 6:1

Rewards of Gen 22:2; Ex 33:12; Lev 26:3-39; Josh 6:3; 1 Ki 11:4-8; 2 Ki 24:4; 2 Chr 25:2; Mat 6:10

Occult 1 Sam 28:12; Job 31:24-28; Dan 5:11; Mic 5:12; Mat 2:2; Acts 16:17-18; 19:18-19

Astrology 2 Ki 17:16; Is 47:9,12-13; Jer 10:1-2; Mat 2:1

Black magic Gen 41:8; Ex 7:11-12,22; 8:7; Ezek 13:18; Rev 9:21

Fortune telling (divination) Gen 30:27; 44:5,15; Num 22:7; Deut 18:14-15; 2 Ki 16:15; Ezek 13:17; 21:21

Sorcery Ex 22:18; 2 Ki 9:22; Job 3:8; Is 8:19; Acts 8:9-11; 19:13

Offerings Ex 23:15; 35:21; Lev 1:14; 3:3-5; 3:16; Deut 26:2; 1 Chr 21:26; Ezra 1:4-6; Ps 96:8; Prov 3:9-10; Ezek 45:13-25; Mal 1:10; Mat 26:10; 2 Cor 8:1,7

Oil Lev 8:10; Deut 33:24; 1 Ki 1:39; Ps 45:7; 133:2; Is 21:5; Mark 6:13; Jas 5:14

Ordination Lev 8:22; 1 Ki 19:19; 2 Tim 1:6

Pain Job 16:6; 33:19; Jer 15:15-21; Hab 1–3; Rom 5:1-5; 8:28-39; Rev 21:1-4

Parables 2 Sam 14:2-3; 1 Ki 22:19-20; 2 Chr 18:18-21; 25:18-19; Mat 13:11-13; Mark 4:10-12,21-25; Luke 8:4-10

About Christ's birth Is 9:2; 40:3-5,9; Mic 5:2

About Christ's death Ps 22:16; 50:4-6; Is 52:14; 53:1-12

Examples of 1 Chr 12:18; 25:1,6-7; 2 Chr 18:9; Is 12:1-6; Jer 13:1-11; 28:10; 29:26; Hos 1:2; Mic 1:8

Fulfilled Is 49:22; Jer 31:8; 31:15; Ezek 17:22-24; Dan 2:31-45; 11:2-45; Obad v. 18-20; Mat 1:1; Luke 3:4-6; 19:41-44

Future 2 Chr 7:14; Is 41:18; Jer 7:30-34; Ezek 3:25; 4:3-6; 38:2-6; Dan 7:24

Purpose today Is 15:1-9; 21:1; Dan 12:9-10; Hos 1:11; Amos 9:11; Zech 1:8; Acts 11:27-30; 1 Cor 14:1

Understanding Jer 23:5-8; Dan 7:1; 8:27; Zeph 1:2; Zech 6:6; Mat 24:15; Mark 13:5-25; Luke 18:34; 24:45; Rev 1:19-20; 17:9-14

Warning Jer 25:15-17; Jonah 3:4; Acts 21:4,11-12

Prophets 1 Sam 10:5; 1 Cor 12:28

Mistreated Jer 11:21; 20:1-2; 26:20-23; 32:3; 36:5; 37:16; Hos 9:7

Reliable Deut 18:21; 2 Chr 18:5-6

Role 2 Sam 12:1; 1 Ki 1:9-10; 12:24; 2 Ki 4:13; Jer 1:10; John 1:6

Test 1 Ki 12:24; 22:6-7; Jer 23:18; 26:8-9; 28:8-9; 28:15-16; Dan 1:17; Mat 7:15-16; 1 Thes 5:20-21

Prostitutes Gen 19:4-5; 38:15; 38:21; 1 Ki 14:24; 2 Ki 23:7; Prov 7:4-5; 23:28; Jas 2:25

Providence of God Ps 104; Mat 10:29-30; Acts 14:14-17

Punishment Gen 20:16; Ex 34:6-7; Num 14:20-35; Mat 12:31-32; Acts 13:46; Rom 11:8; 2 Thes 1:8

Delayed Num 33:52-53; 2 Ki 23:24-26; 2 Chr 34:27-28; Ps 140:12

Limits Deut 25:3; Zech 1:15; 9:1-6

Physical Prov 26:3

Substitute Is 53:5; 53:10; Rom 9:3; Gal 3:13

Purity Lev 6:10; Josh 5:15; Mal 3:2; 1 John 3:3

Quiet time Ps 1:2; 16:7; 77:12; 119:11; 119:15; Mat 6:23

R

Racism Ex 1:9-10; Esth 2:10; Amos 1:13

Rape Gen 19:8; 34:26; Deut 22:19,29; Judg 19:24; 2 Sam 13:13

Rebellion (against God) Num 15:30; Ps 85:4; 107:11; Is 1:24; 57:17; Hos 4:4; Nah 3:1-4; Acts 26:14; Rev 16:6; 17:3

Reconciliation Mat 5:23-26; Phil 4:2-3; 2 Cor 5:11–6:2; Eph 2:11-22; Col 1:15-23

Redemption Ex 12:29; Num 35:19; Ruth 2:20; 3:12; 4:3-6; Job 19:25; Ps 54:7; 90:11-14; 130:7-8; Is 35:10; Jer 17:9; Hos 13:14; Col 1:17

Rejection Ps 88:14; John 9:22

Relationship (to God) Ps 5:5; 50:16; Eccl 12:13-14; Ezek 43:10; Acts 17:30; Rom 5:1

National Is 43:3; 59:18; Jer 18:7-10

Personal Ps 32:9; 107:33-43; Is 37:14; 64:8; Jer 22:16; Hag 1:8; Luke 18:22-30; Mat 19:21

Repentance Lev 26:41; 1 Ki 21:27; 2 Ki 6:30; 2 Chr 33:1-2; Ps 79:8; Joel 2:12-14

National Judg 3:15; 1 Sam 7:6; Neh 8:9-11; Lam 5:21; Dan 9:3; Hos 6:1-3

Personal Ps 38:4; 39:13; 143:1-2; Ezek 11:19; Zech 1:3; Mat 3:11; Luke 7:29-30; John 1:6; Philem v. 12; Rev 22:11

Respect

Elderly Job 33:2-7

God Ex 3:5; 30:20-21; Lev 16:2; 1 Chr 13:9-10; 15:29; 2 Chr 27:2; Job 9:9; 28:28; Ps 103:11; Eccl 5:1; Is 6:1-8; 54:5; Zech 2:13; Mal 2:17; John 12:3; 2 Cor 7:1

Leaders 1 Sam 26:9; 2 Sam 1:6-10; 2 Chr 24:15-16; Eccl 10:20; Rom 13:4; 1 Thes 5:12

Parents Ex 21:17; Prov 13:1; Jer 9:13-16; Mat 8:22; 12:46-50; Mark 3:31-35; John 2:4; Eph 6:1

Responsibility 2 Ki 21:9; 1 Tim 4:14

Accepting 2 Ki 6:5; Ps 104:14-15; 139:16; Is 4:4; 2 Thes 3:6-13

Resurrection Ezek 37:10; Dan 12:2,13; Mat 28:17; Luke 24:5-6; 24:31,37-39; Acts 10:41; 23:9; Rom 1:4; 1 Cor 15:2

Last days Is 26:19; John 20:17; 1 Cor 15:35-57; Heb 11:35; Rev 20:4-5

Revelation Ps 19:1-6; John 1:1-18; Acts 14:14-1; Rom 1:18-23; Heb 1; 2 Tim 3:14-17; 2 Pet 1:19-21

Revenge Ex 21:23-25; Lev 24:20; 2 Sam 19:22; 1 Ki 2:6; Ps 58:6-8; 94:1-3; 149:6-9; Jer 46:10; Ezek 25:3-7; Mat 5:39; 2 Tim 4:14

Revival 2 Ki 23:24-26; 2 Chr 15:12; 19:4-5; Neh 1:6; Ps 19:7; 80:18; Is 19:19-25; Ezek 37:10

The rich and the poor Ex 35:4-9; Deut 8:18; 1 Chr 29:3,12; Ps 62:10; 82:3-4; Hos 2:8; Mal 3:8-10; Mat 6:19-25; 19:16-21; Eph 4:28; 5:3; Col 3:5; 1 Tim 6:17-18; 1 Pet 5:2

Righteousness Ps 7; Jer 23:1-6; Mat 6:25-34; Rom 4:6-8; Gal 2:15-21; Phil 3:7-11; 1 Tim 6:11-16; 1 Pet 2:24-25

Role models Esth 4:16; Job 15:4; 2 Cor 8:8; Eph 5:1; Phil 4:9; Heb 12:1

Sacrifices Ex 20:24; 29:11-21; Lev 1:1; 17:11; Num 7:41-80; Ps 40:6; 50:5; 50:8-15; 50:23; 51:19; 1 Pet 2:5

Sadducees Mat 16:1-12; Mark 12:18-23; Acts 4:1-22; 5:17-42; 23:1-11

Salvation

Belief in Christ John 3:16-18; 6:29; 8:37,40; 8:51; 13:8; 17:2,6,9; Acts 13:48; 2 Cor 13:5; 2 Tim 2:19

By faith Gen 15:6; Ps 106:31; 127:1-2; Is 26:2; Ezek 33:13; Mat 5:20; 25:35-36; Luke 19:9; Acts 15:20; Rom 10:3-7; Heb 4:11; Jas 2:14-24

For all people Gen 35:11; Deut 4:33; Ruth 4:22; 2 Chr 6:33; Esth 13:1-3; Ps 22:27; 86:9; Is 42:6; Jer 31:31; 48:47; Amos 9:12; Jonah 2:7-9; Zeph 2:11; Zech 9:7; Mat 2:2; 15:23-26; Luke 2:32; John 10:16; Acts 10:45; 1 Tim 2:4

God's promise to Abraham Gen 12:3; Deut 26:18; 1 Ki 8:43; Ps 47:9; Is 19:19-25; Eph 3:3-4,6,9

Losing Rom 11:21-22; 1 Cor 9:27; Heb 6:6; 2 Pet 2:20-22

Understanding Ps 67:2; 87:4; 98:2-3; Prov 10:16; Is 52:15; Jer 22:16; Mat 10:5; 19:17; Acts 4:12; Rom 1:16; Phil 2:12-13

Sanctify John 17:17,19; 1 Cor 1:2; Phil 1:6; 1 Thes 4:3-12

Satan

Limited by God Job 1:12; 19:8-12; Luke 10:18; Rom 16:20; Col 2:15; 1 John 5:18

Names for 2 Sam 24:1; 2 Ki 1:2; Job 31:35; Zech 3:1; Mat 4:1; 4:1; 4:3-4; 10:25; Mark 1:12-13; 8:33; Luke 4:3; John 12:31; Col 1:13; Jas 4:7; Rev 12:11

Power of Job 1:13-19; Mat 4:8-9; 7:22-23; Luke 4:6; 22:3; John 13:27; Acts 19:19; 2 Cor 2:11; Eph 2:2; 6:12; 1 Thes 2:18; 1 Pet 5:8; 1 John 1:8; Rev 6:1-17

Scapegoat Lev 16:20-22; 2 Ki 6:32-33; 1 Pet 1:6

Second chances Lam 5:22

Second coming Mat 24–25; John 14:1-4; Acts 1:6-8; 1 Cor 15:12-28; 1 Thes 4:13–5:11; 2 Thes 2; 2 Pet 3; Rev 19–20

Self

Confidence 1 Sam 10:22; Ps 22:6-7; Prov 12:9; Rom 12:3; 1 Cor 2:3; Gal 6:4

Control Prov 6:6-11; 25:28; Tit 2:2

Defense Ex 22:3; 2 Sam 20:10

Denial Mat 7:13-14

Esteem Ex 30:15; 1 Chr 4:9-10; Ezra 2:2-61; Job 25:6; Ps 8:5; 103:14; 139:13-16; Prov 22:2; Is 41:14; 1 Pet 2:18-21

Reliance 2 Chr 12:14; Is 2:7-8; 26:18; 50:10-11

Will Judg 16:17

Service (to God and others) Num 35:2; 1 Chr 23:7-23; Mat 25:26-27; John 13:14-15; 1 Tim 3:13

Servant Is 49:1-6; 50:4-9; 52:13–53:12; Mark 10:35-45; John 13:1-17; 1 Cor 9:19-23; Gal 5:13-26; Phil 2:6-11; 1 Pet 2:18-25

Sex

Homosexuality Gen 13:13; 19:4-5; Lev 18:22; Judg 19:24; 2 Ki 23:7; Rom 1:26-27

In marriage 1 Cor 6:20

Pleasure Prov 5:18-19

Religious rituals Num 25:1; Josh 22:17; 1 Ki 14:24; 16:32; Hos 4:12; 4:14

Rules about Ex 19:15; 2 Sam 11:11

Temptation 2 Sam 11:2-3; Prov 5:3-10; 9:17; 23:28; 1 Cor 6:18

Shame Ezra 9:6-15; Ps 25; 34:1-7; Rom 1:16-17; 2 Tim 1:8-14

Sin

Acceptance Lev 26:41; Ps 38:4; John 9:41

Communal Josh 7:11; 2 Sam 24:15; Ezra 9:6; Is 59:12; Ezek 21:4; Dan 9:3; 9:5; Mal 4:6

Defeating Rom 6:2-14; 7:14-25

Development 2 Ki 18:4

Hated by God Ps 5:5

Individual Lev 20:9; Num 14:18; Deut 5:9; 23:2; Ezek 18:2

Punished 1 Chr 21:14; 1 Thes 4:6

Secret 2 Ki 17:9; Ps 90:8

Unforgivable Mat 12:31-32; Mark 3:29

Unintentional Ps 19:12; Acts 3:14-15,17; Jas 4:17

Sin's effects Gen 12:17; 1 Sam 2:31-33; 2 Sam 12:9-10; 21:6,9,14; 1 Chr 21:14; Job 5:7; 15:20; Ps 7:13,16; 51:4; 103:10; Jer 17:9; Ezek 7:27; 18:24; Mat 5:29-30; Rom 1:24,26,28; 5:13-14; 6:1; 2 Cor 7:9

Church 1 Cor 5:7; 8:12

Creation Gen 9:2; Ps 107:33-34; Jer 7:20; John 9:2; 9:3; Rom 8:20-21; Rev 8:7-11

Families Ps 79:8; Jer 2:9; 31:29; 32:18; Lam 2:11-12; Ezek 18:19-20; 18:19-20; Hos 2:4-5

God Job 35:6; Jer 12:7-8; Ezek 33:11; John 11:35

Health Gen 3:16; John 5:14

Nations Neh 1:6; Ps 51:18; Jer 9:3-8; 18:7-10; 29:21-23; Lam 2:11-12; Ezek 21:4; 22:30; Dan 9:5

Removed Rev 22:2

Slander Ps 12:5; Prov 10:18-21; Jas 4:11

Slavery Ex 10:27-28; Lev 22:6,11; 25:44-46; Josh 16:10; Judg 1:28; 1 Ki 12:18; 1 Chr 5:21; Mat 20:26-28; Mark 10:43-45; 1 Cor 7:21-24; 1 Pet 2:18-21

Son of God Mat 16:18; Luke 22:70-71; John 1:18; Heb 7:11

Son of man Ps 80:17; Ezek 2:1; Dan 7:13; 8:17; Mark 2:10; Heb 2:6-8; Rev 1:13; 14:14

Sorrow Ex 3:1-9; Mat 26:36-46

Soul Deut 6:1-5; 30:6; Ps 25:1; 42; 103; 130; Eccl 12:7; 1 Thes 5:23; Heb 4:12; Rev 6:9-10

Spirit of God Gen 6:3; Ex 24:2; 31:3; Judg 13:25; 1 Sam 11:6; 16:14; 2 Sam 23:2; 1 Chr 12:18; 28:12,19; 2 Chr 20:14; Ps 104:30; Prov 20:27; Joel 2:28; Zech 4:6; Mark 1:10

Stealing Ex 20:15; 22:1-15; Lev 19:11-13; Mal 3:8-10; Eph 4:28

Stewardship Mat 25:14-30; Luke 12:35-48; 16:10-12; Eph 5:15-16

Stubbornness Prov 29:1

Submission

In marriage Eph 5:24-33; 1 Pet 3:5-6

To God Is 18:7; 19:18; Jer 27:8-15; 29:7

To authority Col 3:18-4:1; 1 Pet 2:13-17

To others Eph 5:21

Success Deut 28:2-6; 2 Chr 26:5; Job 22:21-25; Ps 1:3-4; 90:17; Prov 6:6-11

Suffering Job 5:7; 6:24; 11:16; 34:37; Ps 88:3; Mark 8:34; 15:23; Acts 5:41; Rev 13:10

Alone Job 19:13-20; Ps 10:1; 12:1; 22:1; 88:6; 102:3-5; Lam 3:3; Mat 26:41; 27:46; Mark 14:38; 14:51-52; 15:34; Luke 22:40; 2 Tim 1:15

God's role 2 Sam 12:14-15; 2 Ki 5:1; Ps 34:17; 71:20; 97:10; Rev 13:8

Purpose of Job 32:14; 33:19; Ps 22:30-31; 102:9-10; Prov 22:4; Is 45:7; 48:10; Lam 3:38; Ezek 24:16-18; John 9:3; 1 Thes 3:3

Results Job 3:10-16; 23:10; Ps 119:67-75; Prov 17:3; Eccl 11:8; Lam 3:38; John 11:4; Rom 5:3; 2 Cor 4:12; Rev 9:20-21

Understanding Job 5:27; 9:22-24; 17:7-8; 23:10; 42:8; Is 13:16; 53:9; Rom 8:17; 2 Cor 1:5; 1 Pet 4:1

Suicide 1 Sam 31:5; 2 Sam 17:23; Is 57:1-2; Acts 1:18-19; 16:22-36

Talents 1 Chr 22:8; Mat 25:26-27; 1 Tim 4:14

Talking (with God) Gen 12:1; 18:10; Num 1:1; 7:89; Josh 1:1; 1 Sam 3:21; 30:6; Job 38:1; Ps 95:7; Hab 2:1; Mal 2:17

Temple 2 Chr 3:1; 3:3-17; Mat 24:2-3

U

V

W

INDEX TO NOTES

All entries are words or concepts in the study notes, *not* in the KJV text. For references to key words in the text, consult either the Index to Subjects or the Concordance. For location of geographical names, check both the Index to Maps and the Index to Color Maps.

A

BETHESDA, POOL OF
John 5:2

BETHLEHEM, BETH-LEHEM
Judg 12:8; 17:7; Ruth 1:1; 1 Sam 16:1; Mic 5:2; Mat 2:1,16; Luke 2:4,8,22

BETHPHAGE
Mat 21:1

BETHSAIDA
Mat 11:21; Mark 6:32,44; John 6:5

BEZALEL
Ex 31:2; 37:1; 1 Chr 2:18-24; 2 Chr 1:5; 27:1-9; Introduction to 2 Chronicles: The Building of the Temple in Chronicles—p. 588

BEZEK
Judg 1:4; 1 Sam 11:8

BEZER
Deut 4:43

BIBLE. ***See*** SCRIPTURE

BICRI
2 Sam 20:1

BIGTHANA
Esth 2:23

BIGVAI
Neh 2:10; 13:7

BILDAD
Job 2:11; 8:5-6,20; 18:1-4,17; 19:6; 26:5-14; 32:15-16

BILHAH
Ex 1:2-4; 1 Chr 7:13

BIRTHRIGHT
Gen 25:31; 27:36

BISHOP
Titus 1:7

BISITUN INSCRIPTION. ***See*** BEHISTUN INSCRIPTION

BIT ADINI
Is 37:12

BITHYNIA
Acts 16:7; 1 Pet 1:1

BLACK OBELISK
2 Ki 10:34; "Ancient Texts Relating to the Old Testament"—p. xix

BLASPHEMY
Mark 2:7; 14:64; Luke 5:21; John 8:59; 10:31,33; 19:7; Acts 6:11; 14:5; 26:11; 1 Tim 1:20

BLASTUS
Acts 12:20

BLESSED
Ps 1:1; Prov 31:28; Mat 5:3; Rev 1:3

BLESSING
Gen 12:2-3; 27:33,36; 33:11; 35:11-12; 49:2-27; Lev 26:3; Ezek 34:26; Eph 1:3

BLESSINGS AND CURSES
Deut 4:25; 28:1-14

BLOOD
Gen 9:4; Lev 4:5; 17:11; Mark 14:24; Heb 9:18; 12:24

BLOOD REVENGE
Gen 27:45; Num 35:6-15; Josh 20:1-9; 2 Sam 14:7; "Cities of Refuge"—p. 226

BOASTING. ***See also*** PRIDE
Rom 15:17; 2 Cor 11:30

BOAZ
Ruth 2:1; 3:1; 4:1

BOOK
of the Covenant
Ex 20:22-26; 21:1-36; 22:1-31; 23:1-19; 24:7; 2 Ki 23:2
of the Dead
Ezek 29:5
of Jashar
Josh 10:13; Introduction to 1 Samuel: Literary Features, Authorship and Date—p. 353
of the Law
Josh 1:8; 23:6; 2 Ki 22:8; 2 Chr 34:3-7; Neh 8:1
of Life
Ps 69:28; Rev 3:5
of Moses
Ezra 6:18
of Truth
Dan 10:21
of the Twelve
"The Book of the Twelve, or the Minor Prophets"—p. 1234
of the Wars of the Lord
Num 21:14; Ps 60:6-8

BOOTHS, FEAST OF. ***See also*** FEAST: OF INGATHERING; OF TABERNACLES
Ex 23:16; Lev 23:42

BOUNDARY STONE
Deut 19:14

BOZKATH
2 Ki 22:1

BOZRAH
Is 34:6; Jer 49:13; Amos 1:12

BRANCH
Is 4:2; Jer 23:5; Zech 3:8

BREAD OF LIFE
Jesus as
John 6:35

BREAD OF THE PRESENCE
Ex 25:30; Lev 24:8; 1 Sam 21:4

BREASTPLATE
Rev 9:9

BRIDEGROOM. ***See*** CHRIST: AS BRIDEGROOM

BROAD WALL
Neh 3:8; 11:9

BRONZE PILLARS
1 Ki 7:15

BRONZE SEA
1 Ki 7:23,24

BROOM TREE
1 Ki 19:4; Ps 120:4

BUBASTIS
Ezek 30:17

BUBONIC PLAGUE
1 Sam 6:4

BUCKTHORN
Judg 9:14

BURIAL CUSTOMS, JEWISH
Mark 14:8; Luke 23:56

BURNT OFFERING
Lev 1:3; 3:5; Neh 8:10; Ezek 40:39; "Tabernacle Furnishings"—p. 115; "Old Testament Sacrifices"—p. 141

BUSYBODIES
2 Thes 3:11

BUZITE
Job 32:2

BYBLOS
Josh 13:5; Ezek 27:9

CAESAR (Augustus)
Mat 11:21; Luke 2:1; 20:22; John 19:12; Acts 10:1; 17:7

CAESAR (Claudius)
Acts 12:21

CAESAREA
Mark 15:1; Acts 8:40; 10:1; 12:19; 19:6; 21:8; 23:33

CAESAREA PHILIPPI
Mat 16:13; Luke 23:1

CAIAPHAS
Mat 26:3; Mark 14:53-72; 15:1-15; Luke 3:2; John 11:50,51; Acts 4:6; 5:17; James 5:12

CAIN
Gen 4:3-4,5,11,13,17; 1 Sam 20:11; Heb 11:4

CALAH
Jonah 1:2; 3:3

CALAMUS
Sol 4:14; Is 43:24; Jer 6:20; Ezek 27:19

CALCOL
1 Chr 2:6

CALEB
Num 14:24; Judg 1:12; 1 Sam 25:3

CALENDAR, HEBREW
Ex 12:2; Lev 23:5,24; "Hebrew Calendar and Selected Events"—p. 92

CALF WORSHIP
Ex 32:4,5,6; 1 Ki 12:28

D

G

K

L

N

O

S

INDEX TO MAPS

All entries are place-names found on the maps within the study Bible. References are to the page on which the map is located. For additional information on place-names, see Index to Notes.

K

N

T

CONCORDANCE

TO THE OLD AND NEW TESTAMENTS

For each verse quoted in this concordance, an italicized single letter followed by a period is used to designate the word entry. The texts chosen for each word are in Bible book order under the entry. Occasionally the verses under a word entry contain different forms of that entry (for example, under the word ABASE, entries may contain "abased" or "abasing"). Those alternate forms of the word have been placed in parentheses after the key word. The context of each verse will help the reader understand which form of the word fits the italicized letter.

A

ABASE (ABASED, ABASING)
Job 40:11 every one that is proud, and *a.*
Is 31: 4 nor *a.* himself for the noise of them
Ezek 21:26 *a.* him that is high
Dan 4:37 walk in pride he is able to *a.*
Mat 23:12 exalt himself shall be *a.*
2 Cor 11: 7 offence in *a.* myself

ABATED
Gen 8: 3 fifty days the waters were *a.*
Lev 27:18 shall be *a.* from thy estimation
Deut 34: 7 nor his natural force *a.*
Judg 8: 3 their anger was *a.* towards

ABHOR (ABHORRED, ABHORREST, ABHORRETH, ABHORRING)
Ex 5:21 made our savour to be *a.*
Lev 26:11 my soul shall not *a.* you
26:15 if your soul *a.* my judgments
26:30 my soul shall *a.* you
26:43 their soul *a.* my statutes
26:44 neither will I *a.* them
Deut 23: 7 shalt not *a.* an Edomite
32:19 when the Lord saw it he *a.* them
1 Sam 2:17 for men *a.* the offering
27:12 made his people to *a.* him
Job 19:19 my inward friends *a.* me
30:10 they *a.* me, they flee
33:20 so that his life *a.* bread
42: 6 I *a.* myself, and repent
Ps 5: 6 Lord will *a.* the bloody
10: 3 covetous, whom the Lord *a.*
22:24 nor *a.* the affliction of the afflicted
36: 4 he *a.* not evil
89:38 cast off and *a.* . . . thine anointed
106:40 he *a.* his own inheritance
107:18 their soul *a.* all manner of meat
119:163 I hate and *a.* lying
Prov 22:14 *a.* of the Lord shall fall
Is 49: 7 him whom the nation *a.*
66:24 be an *a.* unto all flesh
Jer 14:21 do not *a.* us for thy name's sake
Lam 2: 7 Lord hath *a.* his sanctuary
Amos 5:10 they *a.* him that speaketh
6: 8 I *a.* the excellency of Jacob
Mic 3: 9 house of Israel that *a.* judgment
Zech 11: 8 their soul also *a.* me
Rom 2:22 thou that *a.* idols

ABIDE
Ex 16:29 *a.* ye every man in his place
Num 35:25 *a.* in it unto the death of the high
2 Sam 11:11 Israel, and Judah, *a.* in tents
Ps 15: 1 who shall *a.* in thy tabernacle
61: 4 I will *a.* in thy tabernacle
61: 7 he shall *a.* before God for ever
91: 1 *a.* under the shadow of the Almighty
Prov 7:11 her feet *a.* not in her house
19:23 that hath it shall *a.* satisfied
Hos 3: 3 shall *a.* for me many days
3: 4 Israel shall *a.* without a king
Joel 2:11 terrible; who can *a.* it
Mal 3: 2 who may *a.* the day of his
Mat 10:11 there *a.* till ye go thence
Luke 19: 5 I must *a.* at thy house
24:29 *a.* with us; for it is toward
John 14:16 Comforter, that he may *a.* with you
15: 4 *a.* in me and I in you
15:10 ye shall *a.* in my love, *a.* in his
Acts 20:23 bonds and afflictions *a.* me
1 Cor 3:14 if any man's work *a.*
7: 8 good for them if they *a.* even as I
7:20 every man *a.* in the same
7:24 is called therein *a.* with God
Phil 1:24 to *a.* in the flesh is needful
1:25 know that I shall *a.* with you
1 John 2:24 let that therefore *a.* in you
2:27 ye shall *a.* in him
2:28 little children *a.* in him

ABIDETH (ABIDING)
Ps 49:12 man being in honour *a.* not
55:19 even he that *a.* of old
Eccl 1: 4 the earth *a.* for ever
John 3:36 wrath of God *a.* on him
5:38 not his word *a.* in you
8:35 but the Son *a.* for ever
12:24 except it die it *a.* alone
12:34 Christ *a.* for ever
15: 5 he that *a.* in me bringeth forth
2 Tim 2:13 yet he *a.* faithful
1 Pet 1:23 word of God *a.* for ever
1 John 3: 6 whoso *a.* in him sinneth not
3:15 no murderer hath eternal life *a.*
3:24 hereby we know he *a.* in us

ABODE
John 14:23 make our *a.* with him

ABILITY
Mat 25:15 every man according to his several *a.*
1 Pet 4:11 as of the *a.* God giveth

ABLE
Ex 18:21 *a.* men, such as fear God,
Lev 14:22 such as he is *a.* to get
Deut 16:17 every man give as he is *a.*
2 Chr 20: 6 none is *a.* to withstand
Dan 3:17 God is *a.* to deliver
4:37 walk in pride he is *a.* to abase
Mat 3: 9 God is *a.* of these stones to raise
9:28 believe ye I am *a.* to do this?
10:28 are not *a.* to kill the soul
19:12 he that is *a.* to receive it, let
Mark 4:33 as they were *a.* to hear
John 10:29 no man is *a.* to pluck them
Rom 4:21 he was *a.* to perform
14: 4 God is *a.* to make him stand
1 Cor 3: 2 neither yet now are ye *a.*
10:13 tempted above that ye are *a.*
2 Cor 9: 8 *a.* to make all grace abound
Phil 3:21 *a.* to subdue all to himself
2 Tim 1:12 *a.* to keep that which
3:15 which are *a.* to make thee wise
Heb 2:18 *a.* to succour the tempted
5: 7 *a.* to save him from death
7:25 *a.* to save to the uttermost
11:19 *a.* to raise him from dead
Jas 1:21 *a.* to save your souls
4:12 *a.* to save and to destroy
Jude 1:24 *a.* to keep you from falling

ABOLISH (ABOLISHED)
Is 2:18 idols he shall utterly *a.*
51: 6 righteousness shall not be *a.*
Ezek 6: 6 your works may be *a.*
2 Cor 3:13 to the end of that which is *a.*
Eph 2:15 having *a.* in his flesh
2 Tim 1:10 Jesus Christ hath *a.* death

ABOMINABLE
Lev 7:21 or any *a.* unclean thing
18:30 commit not any one of these *a.* customs
1 Chr 21: 6 king's word was *a.* to Joab
Job 15:16 how much more *a.* is man
Ps 14: 1 have done *a.* works
Is 14:19 thy grave like an *a.* branch
Jer 16:18 carcases of their detestable and *a.* things
44: 4 do not this *a.* thing that I hate
Nah 3: 6 I will cast *a.* filth on thee
Tit 1:16 in works deny him being *a.*
1 Pet 4: 3 walked in *a.* idolatries
Rev 21: 8 unbelieving and *a.* shall

ABOMINATION (ABOMINATIONS)
2 Ki 21: 2 the *a.* of the heathen
Ezra 9:14 join people of these *a.*
Prov 6:16 seven things are an *a.* to Lord
11: 1 a false balance is *a.* to the Lord
11:20 they of a froward heart are *a.*
12:22 lying lips are *a.* to the Lord
15: 8 sacrifice of wicked is an *a.*
15:26 thoughts of wicked are an *a.*
16: 5 proud in heart is an *a.* to Lord
20:23 divers weights are an *a.* to the Lord
26:25 seven *a.* in his heart
28: 9 even his prayer shall be *a.*
Is 1:13 incense is an *a.* unto me
Jer 7:10 delivered to do all these *a.*
Ezek 16: 2 cause Jerusalem to know her *a.*
18:13 hath done all these *a.* shall die
Dan 9:27 for the overspreading of *a.*
11:31 place the *a.* that maketh desolate
12:11 *a.* that maketh desolate set up
Mat 24:15 see the *a.* of desolation
Luke 16:15 is *a.* in the sight of God
Rev 17: 5 mother of harlots and *a.*

ABOUND (ABOUNDED, ABOUNDING)
Prov 28:20 faithful shall *a.* with blessings
Mat 24:12 because iniquity shall *a.*
Rom 3: 7 truth of God hath more *a.*
5:20 that the offence might *a.*
6: 1 in sin that grace may *a.*
1 Cor 15:58 always *a.* in the work
Eph 1: 8 wherein he hath *a.* toward us
Phil 1: 9 that your love may *a.* yet more
4:12 both to *a.* and to suffer need
4:17 fruit that may *a.* to your account
4:18 I have all and *a.*
Col 2: 7 *a.* therein with thanksgiving
1 Thes 3:12 the Lord make you *a.* in love
2 Pet 1: 8 these things be in you and *a.*

ABOVE
Ex 20: 4 that is in the heaven *a.*
John 3:31 cometh from *a.* is *a.* all
8:23 I am from *a.*; ye are of this world
19:11 power given thee from *a.*
Gal 4:26 Jerusalem which is *a.* is free
Eph 4: 6 one God who is *a.* all
Col 3: 1 seek those things which are *a.*
3: 2 set your affection on things *a.*
Jas 1:17 every perfect gift is from *a.*
3:15 wisdom from *a.* is pure

ABSENT
2 Cor 5: 6 in body we are *a.* from the Lord
5: 8 willing rather to be *a.* from the body
5: 9 that whether present or *a.*
Col 2: 5 though I be *a.* in the flesh

ABSTAIN
Acts 15:20 that they *a.* from pollutions of idols
1 Thes 4: 3 ye should *a.* from fornication
5:22 *a.* from all appearance of evil
1 Tim 4: 3 commanding to *a.* from meats
1 Pet 2:11 *a.* from fleshly lusts

ABUNDANCE
Deut 28:47 for the *a.* of all things
Eccl 5:10 he that loveth *a.* with increase
5:12 *a.* of the rich not suffer him to
Mat 12:34 out of the *a.* of the heart the mouth
13:12 and he shall have more *a.*
Mark 12:44 cast in of their *a.*
Luke 12:15 life consisteth not in *a.*
2 Cor 8: 2 *a.* of their joy abounded
12: 7 through *a.* of revelations

ABUNDANT (ABUNDANTLY)
Ex 34: 6 *a.* in goodness and truth
Job 12: 6 whose hand God bringeth *a.*
Ps 36: 8 shall be *a.* satisfied
Sol 5: 1 yea, drink *a.* O beloved
Is 55: 7 he will *a.* pardon
John 10:10 might have life more *a.*
1 Cor 15:10 laboured more *a.* than all
2 Cor 4:15 for your sakes, that the *a.* grace
9:12 is *a.* also by many thanksgivings
11:23 in labours more *a.*
1 Tim 1:14 grace of our Lord exceeding *a.*
Tit 3: 6 shed on us *a.* through Jesus
1 Pet 1: 3 his *a.* mercy hath begotten
2 Pet 1:11 shall be ministered unto you *a.*

ABUSE (ABUSING)
1 Cor 7:31 use this world as not *a.* it
9:18 that I *a.* not my power

ACCEPT (ACCEPTED, ACCEPTEST, ACCEPTETH, ACCEPTING)
Gen 4: 7 shalt thou not be *a.*
19:21 *a.* thee concerning this thing
32:20 peradventure he will *a.* of me
Lev 26:41 *a.* of the punishment of their
Deut 33:11 *a.* the work of his hands
2 Sam 24:23 Lord thy God *a.* thee
Job 13: 8 will ye *a.* his person
32:21 not *a.* any man's person
34:19 *a.* not the persons of princes
42: 8 servant Job, him will I *a.*
Ps 119:108 *a.* freewill offerings
Prov 18: 5 not good to *a.* the person
Eccl 9: 7 God now *a.* thy works
Ezek 43:27 I will *a.* you, saith the Lord
Hos 8:13 but the Lord *a.* them not
Mal 1:13 should I *a.* this of your
Luke 4:24 no prophet is *a.* in his own
20:21 neither *a.* thou the person
Acts 10:35 worketh righteousness is *a.*
24: 3 we *a.* it always
2 Cor 5: 9 we may be *a.* of him
6: 2 behold, now is the *a.* time
Gal 2: 6 God *a.* no man's person
Eph 1: 6 made us *a.* in the beloved
Heb 11:35 were tortured not *a.* deliverance

ACCEPTABLE (ACCEPTABLY)
Ps 19:14 meditation of my heart, be *a.*
Eccl 12:10 sought out to find *a.* words
Is 49: 8 in an *a.* time I heard thee
58: 5 and an *a.* day to the Lord
61: 2 proclaim the *a.* year of the Lord
Dan 4:27 let my counsel be *a.*
Rom 12: 1 sacrifice holy *a.* to God
Eph 5:10 proving what is *a.* to Lord
Phil 4:18 a sacrifice *a.* wellpleasing
Heb 12:28 serve God *a.* with reverence
1 Pet 2: 5 *a.* to God by Jesus Christ

ACCEPTATION
1 Tim 1:15 worthy of all *a.*

ACCESS
Rom 5: 2 we have *a.* by faith
Eph 2:18 we both have *a.* by one Spirit
3:12 boldness and *a.* with confidence

ACCOMPLISH (ACCOMPLISHED, ACCOMPLISHING)
Ps 64: 6 they *a.* a diligent search
Prov 13:19 desire *a.* is sweet
Is 40: 2 her warfare is *a.* that her
55:11 it shall *a.* that which I please
Ezek 6:12 thus will I *a.* my fury
Dan 9: 2 he would *a.* seventy years
Luke 9:31 he should *a.* at Jerusalem
John 19:28 all things were now *a.*
Heb 9: 6 *a.* the service of God
1 Pet 5: 9 same afflictions are *a.*

ACCORD
Acts 1:14 continued with one *a.* in prayer
2: 1 with one *a.* in one place
2:46 continuing daily with one *a.*
4:24 voice to God with one *a.*
15:25 being assembled with one *a.*

ACCOUNT (ACCOUNTED)
Job 33:13 not *a.* of any of his matters
Ps 22:30 it shall be *a.* to the Lord
144: 3 that thou makest *a.* of him
Eccl 7:27 one by one to find out the *a.*
Is 2:22 wherein is he to be *a.* of
Mat 12:36 give *a.* thereof in the day of judgment
18:23 would take *a.* of his servants
Luke 16: 2 give an *a.* of thy stewardship
20:35 they which shall be *a.* worthy to obtain that world
21:36 you may be *a.* worthy to escape
22:24 which should be *a.* the greatest
Rom 14:12 give *a.* of himself to God
Gal 3: 6 *a.* to him for righteousness
Phil 4:17 fruit that may abound to your *a.*
Heb 13:17 as they that must give *a.*
1 Pet 4: 5 shall give *a.* to him that

ACCURSED
Deut 21:23 hanged is *a.* of God.
Josh 6:18 keep from the *a.* thing
Is 65:20 one hundred years old shall be *a.*
Rom 9: 3 wish myself *a.* from Christ
1 Cor 12: 3 the Spirit of God calleth Jesus *a.*
Gal 1: 8 unto him, let him be *a.*

ACCUSATION
Ezra 4: 6 wrote they unto him an *a.*
Mat 27:37 over his head his *a.*
Luke 6: 7 might find an *a.* against him
19: 8 from any man by false *a.*
John 18:29 What *a.* bring ye against this man
Acts 25:18 they brought none *a.* of such things
2 Pet 2:11 bring not a railing *a.*

ACCUSE (ACCUSETH, ACCUSING)
Prov 30:10 *a.* not a servant unto his master
Luke 3:14 neither *a.* any falsely
John 5:45 that I will *a.* you to the Father
Rom 2:15 their thoughts the meanwhile *a.*
Tit 1: 6 not *a.* of riot or unruly
1 Pet 3:16 falsely *a.* your good conversation
Rev 12:10 which *a.* them before our God

ACCUSERS
Acts 25:16 have the *a.* face to face
2 Tim 3: 3 trucebreakers, false *a.*
Tit 2: 3 becometh holiness not false *a.*

ACKNOWLEDGE (ACKNOWLEDGING)
Deut 33: 9 neither did he *a.* his brethren
Ps 32: 5 I *a.* my sin unto thee, and mine
51: 3 For I *a.* my transgression
Prov 3: 6 in all thy ways *a.* him
Is 33:13 ye that are near *a.* my might
63:16 though Israel *a.* us not
Jer 3:13 only *a.* thine iniquity
14:20 we *a.* our wickedness
Hos 5:15 till they *a.* their offence
1 Cor 16:18 *a.* them that are such
2 Tim 2:25 to the *a.* of the truth
Tit 1: 1 and the *a.* of the truth

ACKNOWLEDGMENT
Col 2: 2 to the *a.* of the mystery of God and of the Father

ACQUAINT (ACQUAINTED)
Job 22:21 *a.* now thyself with him
Ps 139: 3 art *a.* with all my ways
Is 53: 3 man of sorrows, and *a.* with grief

ACQUAINTANCE
Job 19:13 mine *a.* are verily estranged from me
Ps 31:11 a fear to my *a.*
55:13 my guide, and mine *a.*
88: 8 put away mine *a.* far from me
88:18 mine *a.* into the darkness

ACQUIT
Job 10:14 wilt not *a.* me from mine iniquity
Nah 1: 3 will not at all *a.* the wicked

ACT (ACTS)
Deut 11: 3 his miracles, and his *a.*
11: 7 great *a.* of the Lord
Judg 5:11 rehearse the righteous *a.*
1 Sam 12: 7 reason of all righteous *a.*
Ps 106: 2 who can utter the mighty *a.*
145: 4 declare thy mighty *a.*
Is 28:21 to pass his *a.* his strange *a.*
John 8: 4 taken in adultery in the very *a.*

ADD (ADDED, ADDETH)
Lev 5:16 shall *a.* the fifth part thereto
6: 5 shall *a.* the fifth part more thereto
Deut 4: 2 shall not *a.* unto the word
5:22 and he *a.* no more
29:19 *a.* drunkenness to thirst
1 Sam 12:19 *a.* to all our sins this evil
Ps 69:27 *a.* iniquity to their iniquity
Prov 10:22 he *a.* no sorrow with it
30: 6 *a.* not unto his words
Is 30: 1 that they may *a.* sin to sin
Jer 36:32 were *a.* many like words
45: 3 Lord *a.* grief to my sorrow
Mat 6:27 can *a.* one cubit unto his stature
Acts 2:41 there were *a.* unto them about
2:47 Lord *a.* to the church daily
5:14 believers were the more *a.*

Acts 11:24 much people was *a.* to the Lord
Phil 1:16 *a.* affliction to bonds
2 Pet 1: 5 *a.* to your faith virtue
Rev 22:18 if any man *a.* unto these things

ADDER
Gen 49:17 an *a.* in the path
Ps 91:13 tread upon the lion and *a.*

ADJURE
1 Ki 22:16 how many times shall I *a.* thee
2 Chr 18:15 How many times shall I *a.* thee
Mat 26:63 I *a.* thee by the living God
Mark 5: 7 I *a.* thee by God
Acts 19:13 We *a.* you by Jesus

ADMINISTRATION
1 Cor 12: 5 there are differences of *a.*
2 Cor 9:12 the *a.* of this service not only

ADMINISTERED
2 Cor 8:19 this grace, which is *a.* to us
8:20 this abundance which is *a.* by us

ADMONISH (ADMONISHED, ADMONISHING)
Eccl 4:13 foolish king will no more be *a.*
12:12 by these, my son be *a.*
Jer 42:19 know that I have *a.* you
Rom 15:14 able to *a.* one another
Col 3:16 *a.* one another in psalms
1 Thes 5:12 over you and *a.* you
2 Thes 3:15 *a.* him as a brother
Heb 8: 5 as Moses was *a.* of God

ADMONITION
1 Cor 10:11 they were written for our *a.*
Eph 6: 4 up in the nurture and *a.* of the Lord
Tit 3:10 after first and second *a.* reject

ADOPTION
Rom 8:15 ye have received the Spirit of *a.*
8:23 *a.*, to wit, the redemption of our body
Gal 4: 5 we might receive the *a.* of sons
Eph 1: 5 us unto the *a.* of children

ADORN (ADORNED, ADORNETH)
Is 61:10 as a bride *a.* herself
Jer 31: 4 again be *a.* with thy tabrets
Luke 21: 5 it was *a.* with goodly stones
1 Tim 2: 9 women *a.* themselves in modest
Tit 2:10 *a.* the doctrine of God our
1 Pet 3: 5 holy women *a.* themselves
Rev 21: 2 as a bride *a.* for her husband

ADULTERER (ADULTERERS)
Lev 20:10 the *a.* and adulteress shall surely
Job 24:15 eye also of the *a.* waits for twilight
Is 57: 3 seed of the *a.* and the whore
Jer 23:10 For the land is full of *a.*
9: 2 for they be all *a.*
Hos 7: 4 they are all *a.*
Mal 3: 5 the sorcerers and against *a.*
Heb 13: 4 whoremongers and *a.* God will judge
Jas 4: 4 ye *a.* and adulteresses know ye

ADULTERESS (ADULTERESSES)
Prov 6:26 *a.* hunt for the precious life
Jas 4: 4 ye adulterers and *a.* know ye

ADULTERY (ADULTERIES)
Prov 6:32 committeth *a.* with a woman lacks
Mat 5:28 committed *a.* in his heart
15:19 out of the heart proceed *a.*
2 Pet 2:14 having eyes full of *a.*

ADULTEROUS
Prov 30:20 such is the way of an *a.* woman
Mat 12:39 *a.* generation seeketh after a sign
16: 4 A wicked and *a.* generation seeketh
Mark 8:38 this *a.* and sinful generation

ADVANTAGE (ADVANTAGED)
Luke 9:25 what is a man *a.*
Rom 3: 1 What *a.* then hath the Jew
2 Cor 2:11 lest Satan get an *a.*

ADVERSARY (ADVERSARIES)
Ex 23:22 I will be an *a.* to thy *a.*
1 Sam 2:10 *a.* of the Lord shall be broken
1 Ki 5: 4 is neither *a.* nor evil
Job 31:35 my *a.* had written a book
Lam 1: 5 her *a.* are the chief, her
Mat 5:25 agree with thine *a.*
Luke 21:15 all your *a.* shall not be able
1 Cor 16: 9 and there are many *a.*
Phil 1:28 in nothing terrified by your *a.*
1 Tim 5:14 give no occasion to *a.*
Heb 10:27 shall devour the *a.*
1 Pet 5: 8 your *a.* the devil as a

ADVERSITY
1 Sam 10:19 saved you out of all *a.*
2 Sam 4: 9 redeemed my soul from all *a.*
2 Chr 15: 6 God did vex with all *a.*
Ps 10: 6 I shall never be in *a.*
31: 7 thou hast known my soul in *a.*
94:13 give rest from days of *a.*
Prov 17:17 brother is born for *a.*
Eccl 7:14 in the day of *a.* consider
Is 30:20 give you the bread of *a.*

ADVOCATE
1 John 2: 1 we have an *a.* with the Father

AFAR
Gen 22: 4 saw the place *a.* off
37:18 when they saw him *a.* off
Ps 65: 5 of them that are *a.* off
138: 6 proud he knoweth *a.*
139: 2 understandest thoughts *a.* off
Jer 23:23 Lord, and not a God *a.* off
Eph 2:17 preached peace to you *a.*
Heb 11:13 having seen promises *a.*
2 Pet 1: 9 blind and cannot see *a.*

AFFECT (AFFECTED, AFFECTETH)
Lam 3:51 mine eye *a.* my heart
Gal 4:17 they zealously *a.* you
4:18 good to be zealously *a.*

AFFECTION (AFFECTIONED)
Rom 12:10 be kindly *a.* one to another
Col 3: 5 mortify therefore your members . . . inordinate *a.*

AFFECTIONS
Rom 1:26 gave them up to vile *a.*
Gal 5:24 have crucified flesh with the *a.*

AFFLICT (AFFLICTED)
Gen 15:13 they shall *a.* them four hundred years
Ex 1:11 taskmasters to *a.* them
22:22 You shall not *a.* any widow
Num 30:13 every binding oath to *a.* the soul
2 Sam 22:28 *a.* people thou wilt save
Ezra 8:21 that we might *a.* ourselves
Job 6:14 to him that is *a.* pity should be showed
34:28 heareth the cry of the *a.*
Ps 22:24 nor abhorred the affliction of the *a.*
119:67 before I was *a.* I went astray
119:71 it is good that I have been *a.*
119:75 thou in faithfulness hast *a.* me
119:107 I am *a.* very much; quicken
140:12 wilt maintain the cause of the *a.*
Prov 15:15 all days of the *a.* are evil
Is 49:13 and will have mercy upon his *a.*
53: 4 smitten of God and *a.*
53: 7 he was oppressed and he was *a.*
58: 5 day for man to *a.* his soul
58:10 satisfy the *a.* soul
Lam 3:33 doth not *a.* willingly
Mic 4: 6 driven out, and her that I have *a.*

AFFLICTION (AFFLICTIONS)
Ex 3: 7 seen the *a.* of my people
2 Ki 14:26 For the Lord saw the *a.* of Israel
Job 5: 6 *a.* cometh not forth of dust
36: 8 and be holden in cords of *a.*
36:15 He delivereth the poor in his *a.*
36:21 this hast thou chosen rather than *a.*
Ps 25:18 look upon my *a.* and pain
34:19 many are the *a.* of the righteous
107:10 being bound in *a.* and iron
107:39 brought low through oppression, *a.*
119:92 should have perished in *a.*
132: 1 remember David and all his *a.*
Is 48:10 chosen thee in the furnace of *a.*
63: 9 in all their *a.* he was afflicted
Hos 5:15 in their *a.* they will seek
Amos 6: 6 not grieved for the *a.* of Joseph
Obad 1:13 not have looked on their *a.*
Nah 1: 9 *a.* shall not rise up the second time
Zech 1:15 and they helped forward the *a.*
Acts 7:10 delivered him out of all his *a.*
20:23 bonds and *a.* abide me
2 Cor 4:17 our light *a.* which is
Phil 4:14 communicate with my *a.*
1 Thes 1: 6 received word in much *a.*
3: 3 should be moved by these *a.*
2 Tim 1: 8 partaker of the *a.* of the gospel
Heb 10:32 endured a great fight of *a.*
11:25 choosing rather to suffer *a.*
Jas 1:27 to visit the fatherless and widows in *a.*
1 Pet 5: 9 the same *a.* accomplished

AFRAID
Lev 26: 6 and none shall make you *a.*
Num 12: 8 were ye not *a.* to speak against
Job 13:21 let not thy dread make me *a.*
Ps 56: 3 What time I am *a.*
56:11 Not be *a.* what man can do
119:120 I am *a.* of thy judgments
Is 12: 2 I will trust, and not be *a.*
Mat 14:27 it is I; be not *a.*
Mark 5:36 Be not *a.*, only believe
Luke 12: 4 Be not *a.* of them that kill
Heb 11:23 they were not *a.* of the king's commandment
1 Pet 3: 6 ye do well, and are not *a.*
3:14 be not *a.* of their terror

AGE
Job 5:26 come to thy grave in a full *a.*
Ps 39: 5 mine *a.* is as nothing before thee
John 9:21 he is of *a.* ask him
Heb 5:14 meat to those of full *a.*

AGED
Tit 2: 2 that the *a.* men be sober, grave

AGES
Eph 2: 7 that in the *a.* to come he might
3: 5 which in other *a.* was not made known
3:21 Christ Jesus throughout all *a.*
Col 1:26 mystery which hath been hid from *a.*

AGREE (AGREED)
Amos 3: 3 walk together, except they be *a.*?
Mat 5:25 *a.* with thine adversary quickly
18:19 if two shall *a.* on earth
Acts 5: 9 that ye have *a.* together
1 John 5: 8 these three *a.* in one

AGREEMENT
Is 28:15 and with hell are we at *a.*
2 Cor 6:16 *a.* hath the temple of God with idols

ALIEN, (ALIENS)
Ex 18: 3 been an *a.* in a strange land
Deut 14:21 thou mayest sell it unto an *a.*
Ps 69: 8 an *a.* unto my mother's children
Is 61: 5 sons of the *a.* shall be
Lam 5: 2 to strangers our houses to *a.*
Eph 2:12 being *a.* from the commonwealth
Heb 11:34 turned to fight the armies of the *a.*

Mat 6:17 when thou fastest, *a.* thy head
Jas 5:14 *a.* him with oil
1 John 2:27 same *a.* teacheth you of all things
Rev 3:18 *a.* thine eyes with eyesalve

ANOINTED

1 Sam 2:10 exalt the horn of his *a.*
24: 6 seeing he is the *a.* of the Lord
1 Chr 16:22 touch not my *a.*
2 Chr 6:42 turn not away the face of thine *a.*
Ps 2: 2 against the Lord and his *a.*
18:50 mercy to his *a.*, to David
20: 6 the Lord saveth his *a.*
28: 8 Lord is the saving strength of his *a.*
45: 7 *a.* thee with the oil of gladness
84: 9 look upon face of thine *a.*
89:38 hast been wroth with thine *a.*
132:17 ordained a lamp for mine *a.*
Hab 3:13 salvation with thine *a.*
Zech 4:14 two *a.* ones, that stand by the Lord
Acts 4:27 Jesus, whom thou hast *a.*
10:38 how God *a.* Jesus of Nazareth
2 Cor 1:21 who hath *a.* us is God

ANSWER

Gen 41:16 God shall give Pharaoh an *a.* of peace
Deut 20:11 if it make thee *a.* of peace
Job 9: 3 he cannot *a.* him one of a thousand
14:15 thou shalt call and I will *a.*
19:16 he gave me no *a.*; I entreated
40: 4 I am vile, what shall I *a.* thee
40: 5 once have I spoken, but I will not *a.*
Ps 91:15 call upon me and I will *a.* him
102: 2 when I call, *a.* me speedily
143: 1 in thy faithfulness *a.* me
Prov 15: 1 soft *a.* turneth away wrath
16: 1 *a.* of the tongue is from the Lord
26: 4 *a.* a fool according to his folly
Is 14:32 what shall one then *a.* the messengers
58: 9 shalt thou call, and the Lord shall *a.*
65:24 before they call, I will *a.*
66: 4 when I called none did *a.*
Jer 33: 3 Call unto me, and I will *a.* thee
Ezek 14: 7 I the Lord will *a.* him by myself
Mic 3: 7 there is no *a.* of God
Mat 25:37 then shall the righteous *a.*
Luke 12:11 what thing ye shall *a.*
13:25 he shall *a.*, I know you not
21:14 meditate not what to *a.*
Rom 11: 4 what saith the *a.* of God
2 Cor 5:12 somewhat to *a.* them
Col 4: 6 know how to *a.* every man
2 Tim 4:16 at my first *a.* no man stood
1 Pet 3:15 ready to give an *a.* to
3:21 the *a.* of a good conscience

ANSWERED (ANSWERETH, ANSWERING)

Ps 18:41 to the Lord, but he *a.* not
81: 7 I *a.* thee in the secret place
99: 6 called on the Lord and he *a.*
Prov 18:23 but the rich *a.* roughly
18:13 he that *a.* a matter before he
27:19 As in water face *a.* to face
Eccl 10:19 money *a.* all things
Tit 2: 9 in all things, not *a.* again

ANT (ANTS)

Prov 6: 6 Go to the *a.*, thou sluggard
30:25 the *a.* are a people not strong

ANTICHRIST (ANTICHRISTS)

1 John 2:18 even now are there many *a.*
2:22 he is *a.*, that denieth the Father
4: 3 this is that spirit of *a.*
2 John 1: 7 this is a deceiver and an *a.*

APOSTLE (APOSTLES)

Mat 10: 2 names of the twelve *a.*
Luke 11:49 I will send prophets and *a.*
Acts 1:26 numbered with the eleven *a.*
Rom 11:13 I am an *a.* of Gentiles
1 Cor 4: 9 God hath set forth us the *a.*
1 Cor 9: 1 am I not an *a.*? Am I not free
15: 9 I am the least of the *a.*
2 Cor 11:13 such are false *a.*; deceitful workers
12:12 signs of an *a.* were wrought
Eph 2:20 built upon the foundation of the *a.*
4:11 gave some *a.*, some prophets
Heb 3: 1 consider the *a.* and high priest
Rev 2: 2 say they are *a.* and are not
18:20 and ye holy *a.* and prophets
21:14 names of the twelve *a.* of the Lamb

APOSTLESHIP

Acts 1:25 part of this ministry and *a.*
Rom 1: 5 we have received grace and *a.*
1 Cor 9: 2 seal of mine *a.* are ye
Gal 2: 8 to the *a.* of the circumcision

APPAREL

Is 63: 1 that is glorious in his *a.*
Zeph 1: 8 such as are clothed with strange *a.*
1 Tim 2: 9 adorn themselves in modest *a.*

ADORNING

1 Pet 3: 3 let it not be that outward *a.*

APPEAR (APPEARED)

Ex 23:15 none shall *a.* before me empty
Deut 16:16 all thy males *a.* before the Lord
1 Sam 2:27 plainly *a.* unto the house of thy father
2 Chr 1: 7 did God *a.* to Solomon
Ps 42: 2 when shall I *a.* before God
Is 1:12 when ye come to *a.* before me
66: 5 shall *a.* to your joy, but they
Mat 6:16 they may *a.* to men to fast
23:27 which indeed *a.* beautiful outward
Rom 7:13 sin that it might *a.* sin
2 Cor 5:10 we must all *a.* before the judgment
Col 3: 4 shall *a.*, then shall ye also *a.*
1 Tim 4:15 that thy profiting may *a.* to all
Tit 2:11 bringeth salvation hath *a.* to all men
Heb 9:24 to *a.* in the presence of God
9:26 he *a.* to put away sin
9:28 *a.* the second time without sin to
11: 3 were not made of things which do *a.*
1 Pet 5: 4 when the chief shepherd shall *a.*
1 John 3: 2 not yet *a.* what we shall be

APPEARANCE

1 Sam 16: 7 man looketh on the outward *a.* but the Lord
John 7:24 judge not according to *a.*
1 Thes 5:22 abstain from all *a.* of evil

APPEARING

2 Tim 1:10 manifest by the *a.* of Jesus
4: 1 judge the quick and the dead at his *a.*
4: 8 all them that love his *a.*
Tit 2:13 the glorious *a.* of the great God
1 Pet 1: 7 unto praise at the *a.* of Jesus

APPLE

Deut 32:10 kept him as the *a.* of his eye
Ps 17: 8 keep me as the *a.* of the eye
Prov 7: 2 my law as the *a.* of thine eye
Zech 2: 8 toucheth the *a.* of his eye

APPOINT (APPOINTED)

Gen 30:28 *a.* me thy wages, and I will give
Job 7: 1 an *a.* time to man upon earth
14:14 all the days of my *a.* time
30:23 to the house *a.* for all living
Ps 79:11 preserve those *a.* to die
Is 26: 1 salvation will God *a.* for walls
61: 3 *a.* to them that mourn in Zion
Jer 5:24 the *a.* weeks of the harvest
Hab 2: 3 vision is yet for an *a.* time
Mat 24:51 *a.* him his portion with the hypocrites
Luke 22:29 I *a.* unto you a kingdom
1 Thes 5: 9 God hath not *a.* us to wrath
Heb 9:27 *a.* unto men once to die

APPREHEND (APPREHENDED)

Acts 12: 4 when he had *a.* him, he put him in
2 Cor 11:32 a garrison, desirous to *a.* me
Phil 3:12 which also I am *a.* of Christ Jesus
3:13 I count myself not to have *a.*

APPROACH (APPROACHING)

Lev 18: 6 none of you shall *a.* to any
Ps 65: 4 the man whom thou . . . causest to *a.*
Is 58: 2 take delight in *a.* to God
Jer 30:21 engaged his heart to *a.* unto me
1 Tim 6:16 light which none can *a.* unto
Heb 10:25 as ye see the day *a.*

APPROVE (APPROVED, APPROVEST, APPROVETH, APPROVING)

Ps 49:13 posterity *a.* their sayings
Lam 3:36 man in his cause, the Lord *a.* not
Acts 2:22 a man *a.* of God among you
Rom 2:18 *a.* the things that are more excellent
14:18 acceptable to God, and *a.* of men
16:10 Salute Apelles *a.* in Christ
1 Cor 11:19 *a.* may be made manifest among
2 Cor 6: 4 in all things *a.* ourselves
Phil 1:10 may *a.* things that are excellent

ARE

Gen 41:27 came up after them *a.* seven years
1 Cor 1:28 things which *a.* not
1:30 of him *a.* ye in Christ Jesus
8: 6 of whom *a.* all things
Heb 2:10 and by whom *a.* all things
Rev 1:19 write the things . . . which *a.*

ARIGHT

Ps 50:23 ordereth his conversation *a.*
78: 8 that set not their heart *a.*
Jer 8: 6 but they spake not *a.*

ARISE (ARISETH)

1 Chr 22:16 *a.* therefore and be doing
Ps 44:26 *A.* for our help, and redeem
68: 1 let God *a.*, let his enemies be
112: 4 Unto the upright there *a.* light
Amos 7: 2 by whom shall Jacob *a.*
Mic 7: 8 when I fall, I shall *a.*
Mal 4: 2 shall the Sun of righteousness *a.*
Mat 13:21 persecution *a.* because

ARM (ARMS)

Gen 49:24 *a.* of his hands were made strong
Ex 15:16 by the greatness of thine *a.*
Deut 33:27 underneath are the everlasting *a.*
2 Chr 32: 8 with him is an *a.* of flesh
Job 40: 9 hast thou an *a.* like God
Ps 44: 3 never did their own *a.* save them
89:13 Thou hast a mighty *a.*: strong
98: 1 his holy *a.*, hath gotten him victory
Is 33: 2 be thou their *a.* every morning
40:10 his *a.* shall rule for him
40:11 gather the lambs with his *a.*
51: 5 on my *a.* shall they trust
51: 9 put on strength, O *a.* of the Lord
53: 1 is the *a.* of the Lord revealed
62: 8 Lord hath sworn . . . by the *a.*
63:12 led them by his glorious *a.*
Jer 17: 5 maketh flesh his *a.*
Luke 1:51 he hath shown strength with his *a.*
Acts 13:17 with a high *a.* brought he them
1 Pet 4: 1 *a.* yourselves likewise with with same

ARMED

Luke 11:21 when a strong man *a.* keepeth

ARMIES

1 Sam 17:26 defy the *a.* of the living God
Job 25: 3 Is there any number of his *a.*
Ps 44: 9 goest not forth with our *a.*
Sol 6:13 it were the company of two *a.*
Rev 19:14 *a.* which were in heaven followed

ARMOUR

Rom 13:12 put on the *a.* of light

2 Cor 6: 7 by the *a.* of righteousness
Eph 6:11 put on the whole *a.* of God

ARROGANCY
1 Sam 2: 3 let not *a.* come out of your mouth
Prov 8:13 pride and *a.*, and the evil way
Is 13:11 cause the *a.* of the proud to cease

ARROW (ARROWS)
Deut 32:23 I will spend mine *a.* upon
2 Ki 13:17 the *a.* of Lord's deliverance
Job 6: 4 the *a.* of the Almighty
Ps 38: 2 thine *a.* stick fast in me
45: 5 thine *a.* are sharp in the heart
91: 5 nor for the *a.* that flieth by day
Lam 3:12 set me as a mark for the *a.*

ASCEND (ASCENDED, ASCENDING)
Gen 28:12 angels *a.* and descending
Ps 24: 3 shall *a.* into the hill of the Lord
139: 8 if I *a.* up into heaven
Prov 30: 4 who hath *a.* into heaven
John 1:51 *a.* and descending upon the Son of man
3:13 no man hath *a.* to heaven
20:17 I *a.* unto my Father and your
Eph 4: 8 when he *a.* up on high
Rev 8: 4 the smoke of the incense . . . *a.*
11:12 *a.* up to heaven in a cloud

ASCRIBE
Deut 32: 3 *a.* ye greatness unto our God
Job 36: 3 *a.* righteousness to my Maker

ASHAMED
Gen 2:25 man and his wife, and were not *a.*
Ezra 9: 6 I am *a.* and blush to lift
Ps 25: 2 let me not be *a.*
Is 49:23 not be *a.* that wait for me
Ezek 16:61 shalt remember thy ways and be *a.*
Mark 8:38 be *a.* of me and my word
Rom 1:16 I am not *a.* of the gospel
6:21 whereof ye are now *a.*
9:33 believeth on him shall not be *a.*
2 Tim 2:15 workman that needeth not to be *a.*

ASHES
Gen 18:27 which am but dust and *a.*
Job 2: 8 sat down among the *a.*
13:12 remembrances are like unto *a.*
42: 6 repent in dust and *a.*
Ps 102: 9 I have eaten *a.* like bread
Is 61: 3 give unto them beauty for *a.*
Ezek 28:18 I will bring thee to *a.*
Mal 4: 3 *a.* under the soles of your feet

ASK (ASKETH)
Jer 50: 5 They shall *a.* the way to Zion
6:16 *a.* for the old paths, where is
Mat 7: 7 *a.* and it shall be given
7: 8 For everyone that *a.* receiveth
7:11 give good things to them that *a.* him
20:22 ye know not what ye *a.*
Luke 12:48 of him they will *a.* more
John 14:14 whatsoever ye *a.* in my name
16:24 *a.* and ye shall receive
Eph 3:20 above all that we *a.* or think
Jas 1: 5 wisdom let him *a.* of God
1: 6 let him *a.* in faith, not wavering
4: 2 ye have not, because ye *a.* not
1 John 3:22 whatsoever we *a.* we receive
5:14 *a.* anything according to his will

ASLEEP
1 Cor 15: 6 but some are fallen *a.*
15:18 are fallen *a.* in Christ
1 Thes 4:13 concerning them which are *a.*

ASP (ASPS)
Deut 32:33 dragons, and cruel venom of *a.*
Job 20:14 it is the gall of *a.* within him
20:16 suck the poison of *a.*
Is 11: 8 play on the hole of the *a.*
Rom 3:13 poison of *a.* is under their lips

ASS
Is 1: 3 the *a.* his master's crib: but Israel
Zech 9: 9 lowly, and riding upon an *a.*
Mat 21: 5 meek, and sitting upon an *a.*

ASSEMBLY (ASSEMBLIES)
Ps 22:16 the *a.* of the wicked have inclosed me
89: 7 to be feared in the *a.* of the saints
Is 4: 5 and upon her *a.*, a cloud
Heb 12:23 general *a.* of the firstborn

ASSEMBLING
Heb 10:25 forsake not the *a.* of ourselves

ASSURANCE
Is 32:17 effect of righteousness quietness and *a.*
Col 2: 2 riches of the full *a.* of understanding
1 Thes 1: 5 gospel came in much *a.*
Heb 6:11 the full *a.* of hope unto the end

ASSURE
1 John 3:19 and shall *a.* our hearts before him

ASTRAY
Ps 119:176 gone *a.* like a lost sheep
Is 53: 6 all we like sheep have gone *a.*
Mat 18:12 one of them be gone *a.*
1 Pet 2:25 ye were as sheep going *a.*

ATHIRST
Judg 15:18 he was sore *a.*, and called on
Rev 21: 6 give to him that is *a.*

ATONEMENT
Ex 30:16 take the *a.* money
Lev 16:11 make an *a.* for himself
23:27 brought in to make *a.*
Num 8:19 make an *a.* for the children

ATTAIN (ATTAINED)
Ps 139: 6 high, I cannot *a.* unto it
Prov 1: 5 man of understanding shall *a.*
Ezek 46: 7 according as his hand shall *a.*
Phil 3:11 *a.* unto the resurrection of dead
3:12 as though I had already *a.*

ATTEND (ATTENDED)
Ps 55: 2 *a.* unto me, and hear me
86: 6 *a.* to the voice of my supplication
142: 6 *a.* unto my cry; for I am
Prov 4: 1 *a.* to know understanding
4:20 my son, *a.* to my words
Acts 16:14 she *a.* to things spoken

ATTENT (ATTENTIVE)
2 Chr 6:40 ears be *a.* unto the prayer
Neh 1: 6 let thine ear now be *a.*
Ps 130: 2 thine ears be *a.* to the voice
Luke 19:48 were very *a.* to hear him

AUTHOR
1 Cor 14:33 God is not the *a.* of confusion
Heb 5: 9 *a.* of eternal salvation
12: 2 Jesus the *a.* and finisher of our faith

AUTHORITY (AUTHORITIES)
Mat 7:29 taught as one having *a.*
John 5:27 *a.* to execute judgment
1 Cor 15:24 put down all rule and all *a.*
Tit 2:15 exhort, and rebuke with all *a.*
1 Pet 3:22 *a.* and powers being made . . .
Rev 13: 2 dragon gave him . . . great *a.*

AVAILETH
Esth 5:13 yet all this *a.* me nothing
Gal 5: 6 neither circumcision *a.* any thing
Jas 5:16 prayer of a righteous man *a.* much

AVENGE (AVENGED, AVENGETH, AVENGING)
Lev 19:18 thou shalt not *a.*, nor bear
26:25 *a.* the quarrel of my covenant
Deut 32:43 he will *a.* the blood of his
Judg 5: 2 praise the Lord for the *a.* of Israel
2 Sam 22:48 It is God that *a.* me
Is 1:24 I will *a.* me of my enemies
Jer 5: 9 not my soul be *a.* on such a nation
9: 9 shall not my soul be *a.* on such a
Luke 18: 7 shall not God *a.* his elect
Rom 12:19 *a.* not yourselves, but rather
Rev 6:10 dost thou not *a.* our blood
18:20 God hath *a.* you on her

AVENGER
Num 35:12 cities for refuge from the *a.*
Ps 8: 2 still the enemy and the *a.*
44:16 by reason of the enemy and *a.*
1 Thes 4: 6 the Lord is the *a.* of all

AVOID
Prov 4:15 *a.* it, pass not by it
Rom 16:17 which ye have learned and *a.* them

AWAKE (AWAKED, AWAKEST)
Job 8: 6 surely now he would *a.* for thee
Ps 35:23 *a.* to my judgment, even unto my
73:20 when thou *a.* thou shalt despise
78:65 Lord *a.* as one out of sleep
139:18 when I *a.* I am still with
1 Cor 15:34 *a.* to righteousness; and sin not
Eph 5:14 *a.* thou that sleepest; and arise

AWE
Ps 4: 4 stand in *a.*, and sin not
33: 8 of the world stand in *a.* of him

AXE (AXES)
Deut 19: 5 a stroke with the *a.* to cut down
2 Sam 12:31 under *a.* of iron, and made them
1 Ki 6: 7 neither hammer nor *a.* nor any tool
2 Ki 6: 5 the *a.* head fell into the water
Ps 74: 5 according as he had lifted up *a.*
Is 10:15 the *a.* boast itself against him
Jer 46:22 come against her with *a.*
51:20 thou art my battle *a.*
Mat 3:10 *a.* laid to root of trees

B

BABE (BABES)
Ps 8: 2 out of the mouth of *b.*
17:14 rest of their substance to their *b.*
Is 3: 4 princes and *b.* shall rule over them
Luke 1:41 the *b.* leaped in her womb
1 Cor 3: 1 as unto *b.* in Christ
1 Pet 2: 2 as newborn *b.*, desire the sincere

BACK (BACKS)
Ex 33:23 shalt see my *b.* parts
1 Sam 10: 9 turned his *b.* to go from Samuel
1 Ki 14: 9 cast me behind thy *b.*
Neh 9:26 cast thy law behind their *b.*
Ps 19:13 keep *b.* thy servant from
53: 6 when God bringeth *b.* captivity
129: 3 plowers plowed on my *b.*
Prov 26: 3 rod for the fool's *b.*
Is 38:17 cast my sins behind thy *b.*
50: 6 gave my *b.* to smiters
Jer 2:27 they have turned their *b.* unto me
18:17 show them the *b.* and not the face
Acts 20:20 kept *b.* nothing profitable

BACKBITERS (BACKBITETH, BACKBITINGS)
Ps 15: 3 He that *b.* not with his tongue
Rom 1:30 *b.*, haters of God, despiteful
2 Cor 12:20 strifes, *b.*, whisperings, swellings

BACKSLIDER
Prov 14:14 *b.* in heart shall be filled

BACKSLIDING (BACKSLIDINGS)
Jer 2:19 thy *b.* shall reprove thee
3:12 return thou *b.* Israel
5: 6 and their *b.* are increased

Jer 8: 5 slidden back by perpetual *b.*
Hos 11: 7 my people are bent to *b.*
14: 4 I will heal their *b.*

BACKWARD
Gen 9:23 went *b.* and covered the nakedness
Is 1: 4 into anger they are gone away *b.*
59:14 judgment is turned away *b.*
John 18: 6 went *b.* and fell to ground

BAG (BAGS)
Deut 25:13 have in thy *b.* divers measures
Prov 16:11 weights of his *b.* are his work
Mic 6:11 *b.* of deceitful weights
Hag 1: 6 earneth wages to put it into a *b.*
Luke 12:33 provide yourselves *b.* which wax not old
John 13:29 because Judas had the *b.*

BALANCE
Job 31: 6 be weighed in an even *b.*
Ps 62: 9 to be laid in the *b.*
Prov 11: 1 false *b.* is abomination to
Is 40:12 and the hills in a *b.*
40:15 as the small dust of the *b.*
46: 6 weigh silver in the *b.*
Dan 5:27 art weighed in the *b.*
Hos 12: 7 *b.* of deceit are in hand
Mic 6:11 count pure with wicked *b.*

BALD
2 Ki 2:23 go up, thou *b.* head
Jer 16: 6 nor make themselves *b.* for them

BALDNESS
Lev 21: 5 not make *b.* upon their head
Deut 14: 1 nor make any *b.* between your eyes
Is 3:24 instead of well set hair *b.*
22:12 to mourning, and to *b.*
Ezek 7:18 *b.* upon all their heads

BALM
Gen 37:25 bearing spicery and *b.* and myrhh
43:11 a little *b.* and a little honey
Jer 8:22 is there no *b.* in Gilead
51: 8 take *b.* for her pain if so be
Ezek 27:17 and honey, and oil, and *b.*

BANNER (BANNERS)
Ps 20: 5 we will set up our *b.*
60: 4 *b.* to them that fear thee
Sol 2: 4 his *b.* over me was love
6: 4 terrible as an army with *b.*
Is 13: 2. Lift ye up a *b.* upon the high

BANQUET
Esth 5: 4. come this day unto the *b.*
Dan 5:10 came into the *b.* house: and the queen

BAPTISM (BAPTISMS)
Mat 20:22 be baptized with the *b.* that I am
21:25 the *b.* of John, whence was it
Mark 1: 4 preach the *b.* of repentance
10:38 be baptized with the *b.* that I am
11:30 the *b.* of John, was it from heaven
Luke 7:29 being baptized with the *b.* of John
20: 4 The *b.* of John, was it from heaven
Acts 1:22 Beginning from the *b.* of John
10:37 after the *b.* which John preached
13:24 before his coming the *b.* of repentance
18:25 knowing only the *b.* of John
19: 3 they said unto John's *b.*
19: 4 verily baptized with the *b.* of repentance
Rom 6: 4 buried with him by *b.*
Eph 4: 5 One Lord, one faith, one *b.*
Heb 6: 2 doctrine of *b.* and of laying
1 Pet 3:21 even *b.* doth also now save us by

BAPTIZE
Mat 3:11 I indeed *b.* you with water
Mark 1: 4 John did *b.* in wilderness
1: 8 he shall *b.* you with the Holy Ghost
Luke 3:16 he shall *b.* you with the Holy Ghost
12:50 I have a *b.* to be baptized with
John 1:26 I *b.* with water: but there
1:33 he that sent me to *b.* with

BAPTIZED (BAPTIZING)
Mat 28:19 all nations *b.* them in the name
Mark 1: 5 were all *b.* of him in the river
1: 8 I indeed have *b.* you with water
1: 9 Jesus was *b.* of John
16:16 he that believeth and is *b.*
Luke 3: 7 came forth to be *b.* of him
3:21 when all the people were *b.*
7:29 publicans, justified God, being *b.*
John 4: 1 Jesus *b.* more disciples
Acts 1: 5 ye shall be *b.* with the Holy Ghost
2:38 repent and be *b.* every one
2:41 received his word were *b.*
8:13 Simon believed and was *b.*
8:48 Peter commanded them to be *b.*
16:15 she was *b.* and her household
16:33 was *b.* he and all his straight way
18: 8 Corinthians believed and were *b.*
22:16 arise and be *b.* wash away
Rom 6: 3 Jesus Christ were *b.* into his death
1 Cor 1:13 were ye *b.* in the name of Paul
10: 2 were all *b.* unto Moses in the cloud
12:13 are all *b.* into one body
15:29 do which are *b.* for the dead
Gal 3:27 as have been *b.* into Christ

BARE
Ex 19: 4 how I *b.* you on eagles' wings
Is 53:12 he *b.* the sin of many
1 Pet 2:24 *b.* our sins in his own body

BARN (BARNS)
Prov 3:10 shall thy *b.* be filled with plenty
Mat 6:26 neither do they reap, nor gather into *b.*
13:30 gather the wheat into my *b.*
Luke 12:24 which neither have storehouse nor *b.*
12:18 I will pull down my *b.*

BARREN
Gen 11:30 But Sarai was *b.*; she had no child
25:21 for his wife because she was *b.*
29:31 opened her womb; but Rachel was *b.*
Ex 23:26 cast their young nor be *b.*
Judg 13: 2 his wife was *b.* and bare not
1 Sam 2: 5 so that the *b.* hath borne seven
Ps 113: 9 maketh the *b.* woman to keep house
Sol 4: 2 none is *b.* among them
Is 54: 1 sing, O *b.*, thou that didst not bear
Luke 1: 7 because that Elisabeth was *b.*
2 Pet 1: 8 neither *b.* nor unfruitful

BASE (BASEST)
2 Sam 6:22 and will be *b.* in mine own sight
Ezek 29:15 It shall be the *b.* of kingdoms
Dan 4:17 setteth up over it the *b.* of men
1 Cor 1:28 *b.* things of this world
2 Cor 10: 1 who in presence am *b.* among you

BASTARD (BASTARDS)
Deut 23: 2 A *b.* shall not enter into the congregation
Zech 9: 6 And a *b.* shall dwell in Ashdod
Heb 12: 8 Then are ye *b.* and not sons

BATTLE
Gen 14: 8 *b.* of four kings against five
Josh 8:14 men of Ai against Israel to *b.*
Judg 8:13 Gideon returned from *b.*
20:14 to *b.* against the children of Israel
2 Sam 2:17 there was a very sore *b.* that day
10: 8 Ammon put the *b.* in array
2 Chr 13: 3 Abijah set the *b.* in array
14:10 Asa set the *b.* in array
25: 8 be strong for the *b.*: God shall
Ps 140: 7 covered my head in the day of *b.*
Eccl 9:11 not the *b.* to the strong neither
Jer 8: 6 as the horse rusheth into the *b.*
Rev 16:14 *b.* of the great day of God

BEAM (BEAMS)
Sol 1:17 *b.* of our house are cedar
Hab 2:11 *b.* out of the timber shall answer it
Mat 7: 3 the *b.* that is in thine own eye

BEAR
Gen 4:13 punishment greater than I can *b.*
49:15 bowed his shoulder to *b.*
Num 11:14 not able to *b.* all this people
Deut 1: 9 not able to *b.* you myself alone
Ps 75: 3 I *b.* up the pillars of it
91:12 *b.* thee up in their hands
Prov 18:14 wounded spirit who can *b.*
30:21 for four which it cannot *b.*
Lam 3:27 he *b.* the yoke in his youth
Ezek 17: 8 that it might *b.* fruit
Hos 9:16 they shall *b.* no fruit
Amos 7:10 land not able to *b.* words
Mic 7: 9 I will *b.* the indignation of Lord
Luke 13: 9 and if it *b.* fruit, well
14:27 whosoever doth not *b.* his cross
John 15: 8 that ye *b.* much fruit
16:12 ye cannot *b.* them now
Rom 15: 1 strong *b.* the infirmities of the weak
1 Cor 3: 2 hitherto ye were not able to *b.*
10:13 that ye may be able to *b.* it
Gal 6: 2 *b.* ye one another's burdens
6: 5 every man *b.* his own burden
6:17 I *b.* in my body the marks
Heb 9:28 offered to *b.* the sins of many

BEAREST (BEARETH, BEARING)
Ps 106: 4 favour that thou *b.* unto thy people
126: 6 *b.* precious seed, shall doubtless
Joel 2:22 for the tree *b.* her fruit
Mat 13:23 which also *b.* fruit, and bringeth
John 15: 2 every branch that *b.* fruit
Rom 2:15 conscience also *b.* witness
11:18 Thou *b.* not the root but the root
13: 4 *b.* the not sword in vain
1 Cor 13: 7 *b.* all things, believeth all things
Heb 13:13 without the camp, *b.* his reproach

BEARD (BEARDS)
2 Sam 10: 4 shaved off one half of their *b.*
2 Sam 19:24 nor trimmed his *b.*, nor washed his
20: 9 Joab took Amasa by the *b.*
Ezra 9: 3. off the hair of my head and of my *b.*
Ps 133: 2 that ran down upon the *b.*
Is 15: 2 be baldness and every *b.* cut off
Jer 41: 5 having their *b.* shaven
48:37 shall be bald and every *b.* clipped

BEAR (BEARS)
2 Ki 2:24 there came forth two she *b.*
Prov 17:12. Let a *b.* be robbed of her whelps
Is 59:11 We roar all like *b.*, and mourn
Dan 7: 5 beast a second, like to a *b.*
Hos 13: 8 *b.* that is bereaved of her whelps
Amos 5:19 from a lion and a *b.* met him
Rev 13: 2 were as the feet of a *b.*

BEAST (BEASTS)
Gen 1:24 and *b.* of the earth after his kind
Ps 49:12 like the *b.* that perish
73:22 I was as a *b.* before thee
Prov 9: 2 she hath killed her *b.*; she hath
Dan 7: 3 four great *b.* came up from the sea
7:11 I beheld even till the *b.* was slain
1 Cor 15:32 I fought with the *b.* at Ephesus
Rev 4: 6 were four *b.* full of eyes before and
11: 7 the *b.* that ascendeth out
13: 1 saw a *b.* rise up out of the sea
14: 3 and before the four *b.*
16:13 out of the mouth of the *b.*
17: 8 the *b.* that thou sawest was
19: 4 four *b.* fell down and worshipped God
20:10 where the *b.* and the false prophet are

BEAT (BEATEN, BEATETH)
Prov 23:14 Thou shalt *b.* him with the rod
Is 3:15 that ye *b.* my people to pieces
Luke 12:47 shall be *b.* with many stripes
1 Cor 9:26 not as one who *b.* the air

BEAUTY
Ex 28: 2 thy brother for glory and for *b.*
2 Chr 20:21 praise the *b.* of holiness
Ps 29: 2 the Lord in the *b.* of holiness
27: 4 to behold the *b.* of the Lord
39:11 makest his *b.* to consume
96: 9 the Lord in the *b.* of holiness
Prov 20:29 *b.* of old men is the gray head
31:30 favour is deceitful and *b.* is vain
Is 3:24 sackcloth; and burning instead of *b.*
33:17 eyes shall see the king in his *b.*
61: 3 to give unto them *b.* for ashes
Zech 11: 7 two staves: the one I called *B.*

BEAUTIFY
Ps 149: 4 he will *b.* the meek with salvation
Is 60:13 to *b.* the place of my sanctuary

BEAUTIFUL
Eccl 3:11 every thing *b.* in his time
Sol 6: 4 Thou art *b.*, O my love
Is 52: 1 put on thy *b.* garments, O Jerusalem
64:11 Our holy and our *b.* house
Jer 13:20 that was given thee, thy *b.* flock
Ezek 16:13 thou was exceeding *b.*
Mat 23:27 which indeed appear *b.* outside
Acts 3: 2 temple which is called *b.*
Rom 10:15 How *b.* are the feet of them

BED (BEDS)
2 Ki 4:10 let us set for him there a *b.*
Ps 41: 3 make his *b.* in sickness
Sol 3: 1 on my *b.* I sought him
Is 28:20 *b.* is shorter than that a man
Amos 6: 4 lie on *b.* of ivory
Heb 13: 4 and the *b.* undefiled but whoremongers
Rev 2:22 I will cast her into a *b.*

BEFORE
Gen 31: 2 behold, it was not toward him as *b.*
43:15 to Egypt and stood *b.* Joseph
Josh 8:10 of Israel *b.* the people to Ai
2 Sam 6:21 unto Michal, it was *b.* the Lord
1 Ki 17: 1 God of Israel liveth *b.* whom I stand
2 Ki 3:14 Lord of hosts liveth, *b.* whom I stand
Luke 22:47 one of the twelve went *b.* them
John 1:15 cometh after me is preferred *b.* me
Phil 3:13 those things which are *b.*
Col 1:17 he is *b.* all things, and by him

BEG (BEGGED, BEGGING)
Ps 37:25 forsaken, nor his seed *b.* bread
109:10 children be continually vagabonds and *b.*
Prov 20: 4 therefore shall he *b.* in harvest
Luke 16: 3 I cannot dig; to *b.* I am ashamed
John 9: 8 Is not this he that sat and *b.*

BEGGAR
1 Sam 2: 8 and lifteth up the *b.* from the
Luke 16:20 a certain *b.* named Lazarus

BEGIN
Ezek 9: 6 and *b.* at my sanctuary

BEGINNING
Gen 49: 3 my might and the *b.* of strength
Ex 12: 2 the *b.* of months
Deut 21:17 for he is the *b.* of his strength
Ps 111:10 fear of the Lord is the *b.* of wisdom
Eccl 7: 8 better the end than the *b.*
Mat 24: 8 all these are the *b.* of sorrows
Col 1:18 who is the *b.*, the firstborn
2 Pet 2:20 end is worse than the *b.*
Rev 1: 8 Alpha and the Omega, the *b.* and the
3:14 saith the *b.* of the creation of God

BEGOTTEN
Job 38:28 who hath *b.* the drops of dew
Ps 2: 7 this day have I *b.* thee
John 1:14 as of the only *b.* of the Father
3:16 that he gave his only *b.* Son
1 Pet 1: 3 *b.* us again unto a lively hope
1 John 4: 9 sent his only *b.* Son into the world
5: 1 loveth him that is *b.* of him
Rev 1: 5 Christ the first *b.* of the dead

BEGUILE (BEGUILED, BEGUILING)
Gen 3:13 The serpent *b.* me, and I did eat
2 Cor 11: 3 as the serpent *b.* Eve
Col 2: 4 lest any man should *b.* you
2 Pet 2:14 cannot cease from sin: *b.* unstable souls

BEHELD
Num 23:21 He hath not *b.* iniquity in Jacob
Luke 10:18 I *b.* Satan as lightning fall
John 1:14 we *b.* his glory, the glory as of
Rev 11:12 in a cloud and their enemies *b.* them

BEHIND
Ex 10:26 shall not an hoof left *b.*
Neh 9:26 cast thy law *b.* their backs
Ps 139: 5 thou hast beset me *b.* and before
Is 38:17 cast my sins *b.* thy back
Phil 3:13 forgetting those things which are *b.*
Col 1:24 fill up that which is *b.* of the afflictions

BEHOLD
Deut 3:27 *b.* it with thine eyes: for thou shalt
Job 19:27 mine eyes shall *b.* and not another
40: 4 *b.* I am vile; what shall I
Ps 11: 4 his eyes *b.* his eyelids try
11: 7 his countenance doth *b.* the upright
17:15 I will *b.* thy face in righteousness
27: 4 desired to *b.* the beauty of Lord
37:37 the perfect man and *b.* the upright
113: 6 he who humbleth himself to *b.*
133: 1 *b.* how good and how pleasant it is
Eccl 11: 7 it is pleasant to *b.* the sun
Is 24: 1 *b.* the Lord maketh the earth empty
32: 1 *b.* a king shall reign in righteousness
37: 7 *b.* I will send a blast upon him
40:10 *b.* the Lord will come with strong hand
42: 1 *b.* my servant, whom I uphold; mine
48:10 *b.* I have refined thee but not with
49: 1 *b.* Lord's hand is not shortened
Hab 1:13 of purer eyes than to *b.*
Mat 18:10 their angels do always *b.* the face of
John 17:24 they may *b.* my glory
19: 5 Pilate saith unto them, *b.* the man
19:26 unto his mother, Woman *b.* thy son
1 Pet 3: 2 while they *b.* your chaste conversation
Rev 1: 7 *b.* he cometh with clouds
1:18 *b.* I am alive for evermore
3: 8 *b.* I set before thee an open door
3:11 *b.* I come quickly hold that fast
3:20 *b.* I stand at the door, and knock
4: 2 *b.* a throne was set in heaven
9:12 *b.* there come two woes more
11:14 *b.* a third woe cometh quickly
21: 5 *b.* I make all things new

BEHOLDETH (BEHOLDING)
Ps 33:13 from heaven; he *b.* all the sons of men
119:37 turn away mine eyes from *b.* vanity
Prov 15: 3 *b.* the evil and the good
2 Cor 3:18 open face *b.* as in a glass
Col 2: 5 joying and *b.* your order
Jas 1:23 like unto a man *b.* his natural face
1:24 he *b.* himself and goeth his way

BEING
Ps 104:33 to my God while I have my *b.*
146: 2 unto my God while I have any *b.*
Acts 17:28 and move, and have our *b.*

BELIAL
Deut 13:13 the children of *B.* are gone out
Judg 19:22 men of the city, certain sons of *B.*
20:13 children of *B.* which are in Gibeah
1 Sam 2:12 sons of Eli were sons of *B.*
10:27 but the children of *B.* said
25:17 for he is such a son of *B.*
2 Sam 16: 7 bloody man, and thou man of *B.*
23: 6 the sons of *B.* shall be all
1 Ki 21:10 set two men, sons of *B.*, before him
2 Chr 13: 7 vain men, the children of *B.*
2 Cor 6:15 what concord hath Christ with *B.*

BELIEVE
Ex 4: 1 behold, they will not *b.* me
Num 14:11 how long will it be ere they *b.*
Deut 1:32 ye did not *b.* the Lord
2 Chr 20:20 *b.* in the Lord your God
Is 7: 9 if ye will not *b.*, surely ye shall
Mat 9:28 *b.* ye that I am able to do this
Mark 1:15 repent and *b.* the gospel
9:24 Lord, I *b.* help thou mine unbelief
11:24 *b.* that ye receive them
Luke 8:13 which for a while *b.* and in time
24:25 slow of heart to *b.* all
John 4:48 signs and wonders, ye will not *b.*
6:69 we *b.* and are sure thou art that Christ
7:39 that *b.* on him should receive
8:24 if ye *b.* not I am he, ye die
10:26 ye *b.* not, because ye are not
11:27 I *b.* that thou art the Christ
11:40 if thou wouldst *b.* thou shouldst see
11:42 they may *b.* that thou hast sent me
12:36 *b.* in the light while ye have
12:39 they could not *b.* because that Esaias
14: 1 ye *b.* in God, *b.* also in me
17:20 pray for them who shall *b.*
20:25 hand into his side, I will not *b.*
20:31 written that ye might *b.*
Acts 8:37 I *b.* Jesus Christ is the Son
13:39 all that *b.* are justified
16:31 *b.* on the Lord Jesus Christ
Rom 3: 3 for what if some did not *b.*
3:22 Jesus Christ unto all them that *b.*
10: 9 shalt *b.* in thine heart
10:14 how shall they *b.* on him
2 Cor 4: 4 blinded the mind of them that *b.* not
4:13 we *b.* and therefore speak
Phil 1:29 not only to *b.* but suffer
2 Thes 2:11 they should *b.* a lie
2:13 worketh also in you that *b.*
1 Tim 4:10 especially those that *b.*
2 Tim 2:13 we *b.* not, yet he abideth faithful
Heb 10:39 *b.* to the saving of the soul
11: 6 cometh to God must *b.* that he is
Jas 2:19 devils also *b.* and tremble
1 John 3:23 *b.* on the name of his Son Jesus Christ
4: 1 beloved, *b.* not every spirit

BELIEVED
Gen 15: 6 *b.* in Lord, and he counted
Num 20:12 because ye *b.* me not to sanctify
Ps 27:13 I had fainted unless I had *b.*
78:32 and *b.* not for his wondrous works
106:24 they *b.* not his word
116:10 I *b.* therefore have I spoken
119:66 for I *b.* thy commandments
Is 53: 1 who hath *b.* our report
Jonah 3: 5 people of Nineveh *b.* God
Mat 8:13 as thou hast *b.* so be it
21:32 publicans and harlots *b.* him
John 4:53 himself *b.* and his house
7:48 have any of the Pharisees *b.* on
17: 8 have *b.* that thou didst send me
Acts 4:32 that *b.* were of one heart
8:13 Simon *b.* and was baptized
11:21 great number *b.* and turned
13:48 were ordained to eternal life *b.*
Rom 4:18 against hope *b.* in hope
10:14 in whom they have not *b.*
13:11 salvation nearer than when we *b.*
Eph 1:13 after that ye *b.* ye were sealed

2 Thes 2:12 who *b.* not the truth
1 Tim 3:16 *b.* on in the world, recieved up
2 Tim 1:12 for I know whom I have *b.*
Heb 3:18 but to them that *b.* not

BELIEVERS
Acts 5:14 and *b.* were the more added
1 Tim 4:12 be thou an example of the *b.*

BELIEVEST (BELIEVING)
Luke 1:20 because thou *b.* not my words
John 1:50 I saw thee under the fig tree, *b.* thou
11:26 shall never die. *b.* thou this
14:10 *b.* thou not that I am in the Father
20:27 be not faithless, but *b.*
20:31 that *b.* ye might have life
Acts 8:37 if thou *b.* with all thine heart
16:34 *b.* in God with all his house
26:27 I know that thou *b.*
Rom 15:13 all joy and peace in *b.*
1 Tim 6: 2 And they that have *b.* masters
Jas 2:19 Thou *b.* that there is one God
1 Pet 1: 8 yet *b.* ye rejoice with joy

BELIEVETH
Prov 14:15 the simple *b.* every word
Is 28:16 he that *b.* shall not make haste
Mark 9:23 things possible to him that *b.*
16:16 he that *b.* shall be saved
Luke 24:41 while they yet *b.* not for joy
John 3:15 *b.* in him should not perish
3:18 that *b.* not is condemned already
3:36 *b.* on the Son hath everlasting life
5:24 *b.* on him that sent me
6:35 *b.* on me shall never thirst
6:40 and *b.* on him, may have everlasting life
7:38 that *b.* on me out of his belly shall flow
11:25 *b.* in me though he were dead
11:26 he that *b.* in me shall never die
12:44 *b.* in me, *b.* not on me, but
12:46 *b.* on me should not abide in darkness
14:12 *b.* on me the works that I do
Rom 1:16 unto salvation to every one that *b.*
3:26 justifier of him that *b.* in Jesus
4: 5 worketh not, but *b.* on him
9:33 *b.* on him shall not be ashamed
10: 4 for righteousness to every one that *b.*
14: 2 one *b.* that he may eat all things
1 Cor 7:12 brother hath a wife that *b.* not
13: 7 *b.* all things, hopeth all things
14:24 come in one that *b.* not, or one
2 Cor 6:15 he that *b.* with an infidel
1 Tim 5:16 that *b.* have widows, let them relieve
1 Pet 2: 6 *b.* on him shall not be confounded
1 John 5: 1 whosoever *b.* that Jesus is the Christ
5: 5 overcometh the world, but he that *b.*

BELLY (BELLIES)
Gen 3:14 upon thy *b.* shalt thou go
Num 5:21 thy thigh to rot, and thy *b.* to swell
25: 8 thrust them through the *b.*
Job 3:11 when I came out of the *b.*
15: 2 fill his *b.* with the east wind
15:35 their *b.* prepareth deceit
20:15 God cast them out of his *b.*
Ps 17:14 whose *b.* thou fillest with
22:10 art my God from my mother's *b.*
44:25 our *b.* cleaveth to the earth
Is 46: 3 borne by me from the *b.*
Jonah 1:17 was in the *b.* of fish
2: 1 prayed to God out of the fish's *b.*
2: 2 out of the *b.* of hell cried I
Hab 3:16 when I heard my *b.* trembled
Luke 15:16 fill his *b.* with husks
John 7:38 out of his *b.* shall flow
1 Cor 6:13 meats for the *b.* and the *b.* for
Phil 3:19 whose god is their *b.*, and whose glory
Tit 1:12 Cretians are always liars . . . slow *b.*
Rev 10: 9 it shall make thy *b.* bitter

BELONG (BELONGETH)
Gen 40: 8 interpretations *b.* to God
Deut 29:29 secret things *b.* to the Lord
Ezra 10: 4 for this matter *b.* unto thee
Ps 3: 8 salvation *b.* to the Lord
47: 9 shields of the earth *b.* to God
62:11 heard this; that power *b.* unto God
68:20 to God *b.* the issues from death
Dan 9: 8 to us *b.* confusion of face
9: 9 to the Lord *b.* mercies and forgivenesses
Mark 9:41 because ye *b.* to Christ
Luke 19:42 things that *b.* to thy peace
1 Cor 7:32 for the things that *b.* to the Lord
Heb 5:14 strong meat *b.* to them

BELOVED
Deut 21:15 two wives, one *b.* and another hated
Neh 13:26 who was *b.* of his God
Ps 60: 5 thy *b.* may be delivered
127: 2 Lord giveth his *b.* sleep
Sol 1:14 my *b.* is unto me as a cluster
4:16 let my *b.* come into his garden
5: 2 it is the voice of my *b.*
5: 9 thy *b.* more than another *b.*
6: 2 my *b.* is gone down into his garden
Is 5: 1 of my *b.* touching his vineyard
Dan 10:11 O Daniel, a man, greatly *b.*
Mat 3:17 this is my *b.* Son, in whom
17: 5 this is my *b.* Son, in whom
Rom 9:25 and her *b.* which was not *b.*
11:28 they are *b.* for the fathers' sake
16: 8 Amplias my *b.* in the Lord
Eph 1: 6 made us accepted in the *b.*
Col 3:12 as the elect of God holy and *b.*
4:14 Luke the *b.* physician
2 Pet 3:15 even as our *b.* brother Paul
Rev 20: 9 and the *b.* city: and fire came

BEND (BENDETH, BENDING, BENT)
Ps 11: 2 the wicked *b.* their bow
37:14 and have *b.* their bow, to cast
58: 7 when he *b.* his bow to shoot
Is 5:28 and all their bows *b.*
60:14 afflicted thee come *b.*
Jer 9: 3 *b.* their tongues like a bow
Lam 3:12 he hath *b.* his bow, and set
Zech 9:13 I have *b.* Judah for me

BENEFACTORS
Luke 22:25 authority upon them are called *b.*

BENEFITS
Ps 68:19 who daily loadeth us with *b.*
103: 2 forget not all his *b.*
116:12 render to Lord for all his *b.*

BEREAVED
Gen 43:14 If I be *b.* of my children
Eccl 4: 8 do I labor and *b.* my soul
Jer 15: 7 I will *b.* them of children
18:21 let their wives be *b.* of their children
Ezek 5:17 evil beasts, and they shall *b.* thee
36:12 henceforth *b.* them of men
Hos 13: 8 a bear that is *b.* of her whelps

BEREAVETH
Lam 1:20 abroad the sword *b.*, at home

BESEECH (BESOUGHT)
Deut 3:23 I *b.* the Lord at that time
2 Sam 12:16 David therefore *b.* God for the child
1 Ki 13: 6 the man of God *b.* the Lord
2 Ki 13: 4 Jehoahaz *b.* the Lord
2 Chr 33:12 he *b.* the Lord his God
Ezra 8:23 we fasted and *b.* our God for this
Mal 1: 9 *b.* God that he will be gracious
2 Cor 5:20 as though God did *b.* you by us
12: 8 I *b.* the Lord thrice

BESET
Ps 139: 5 Thou hast *b.* me behind and before
Hos 7: 2 own doings have *b.* them about
Heb 12: 1 sin which doth so easily *b.* us

BESIDE
Ps 23: 2 leadeth me *b.* the still waters
Is 32:20 ye that sow *b.* all waters
Sol 1: 8 feed thy kids *b.* the shepherds' tents
Is 56: 8 *b.* those that are gathered

BESOM
Is 14:23 sweep it with the *b.* of destruction

BEST
Ps 39: 5 man at his *b.* state is altogether vanity
Luke 15:22 bring forth the *b.* robe
1 Cor 12:31 covet earnestly the *b.* gifts

BESTOW (BESTOWED)
Ex 32:29 that he may *b.* upon you a blessing
Luke 12:17 room to *b.* my fruits
John 4:38 whereon ye *b.* no labour
1 Cor 12:23 *b.* more abundant honour
13: 3 *b.* all my goods to feed the poor
15:10 his grace which was *b.* on me
2 Cor 1:11 gift *b.* upon us by the means
8: 1 grace of God *b.* on the churches
Gal 4:11 have *b.* upon you labour in vain
1 John 3: 1 love the Father hath *b.* on us

BETRAY (BETRAYETH)
Mat 24:10 be offended, and shall *b.* one another
26:21 one of you shall *b.* me
Mark 13:12 brother shall *b.* the brother to death
14:18 which eateth with me shall *b.* me
Luke 22:21 the hand of him that *b.* me is with me
John 13:21 one of you shall *b.* me

BETROTH
Deut 28:30 Thou shalt *b.* a wife
Hos 2:19 I will *b.* thee unto me for ever
2:20 even *b.* thee unto me in faithfulness

BETTER
Judg 8: 2 grapes of Ephraim *b.* than the vintage
1 Sam 1: 8 am I not *b.* to thee than ten sons
Prov 15:16 *b.* is little with fear of the Lord
15:17 *b.* is a dinner of herbs where love
16: 8 *b.* is a little with righteousness
16:16 much *b.* to get wisdom than gold
17: 1 *b.* is a dry morsel, and quietness
27:10 *b.* is a neighbour near than
Eccl 4: 9 two are *b.* than one
4:13 *b.* is a poor and wise child than
7: 1 *b.* is a good name than precious
7: 2 *b.* to go to the house of mourning
7: 3 *b.* is sorrow than laughter
7: 5 *b.* to hear the rebuke of the wise than
7: 8 the patient in spirit is *b.* than
9:16 wisdom is *b.* than strength
9:18 wisdom is *b.* than weapons of
Sol 1: 2 for thy love is *b.* than wine
Rom 3: 9 are we *b.* than they? No, in no
1 Cor 9:15 for it were *b.* for me to die
11:17 come not for the *b.* but worse
Phil 1:23 with Christ; which is far *b.*
2: 3 esteem others *b.* than themselves
Heb 1: 4 made so much *b.* than the angels
6: 9 we are persuaded *b.* things of you
7:19 bringing in of a *b.* hope did
7:22 Jesus made a surety of a *b.* testament
8: 6 mediator of a *b.* covenant
10:34 a *b.* and an enduring substance
11:16 now they desire a *b.* country
11:35 might obtain a *b.* resurrection
11:40 God having provided some *b.* thing
12:24 blood speaketh *b.* than Abel
2 Pet 2:21 *b.* for them not to have known

BETWEEN
Gen 3:15 put enmity *b.* thee and the woman
1 Ki 3: 9 discern *b.* good and bad
18:21 how long halt ye *b.* two opinions
1 Tim 2: 5 one mediator *b.* God and men

BETWIXT
Phil 1:23 for I am in a strait *b.* two

BEWARE
Mat 7:15 *b.* of false prophets, which come
10:17 But *b.* of men: for they will
16: 6 *b.* of the leaven of Pharisees
Luke 12:15 *b.* of covetousness: for a man's life
Phil 3: 2 *b.* of dogs, *b.* of evil workers
Col 2: 8 *b.* lest any man spoil you
2 Pet 3:17 *b.* lest ye also being led away

BID (BIDDEN)
Mat 22: 9 as ye shall find, *b.* to the marriage
23: 3 whatsoever they *b.* you observe
Luke 14:10 but when thou art *b.* of any man

BILL
Deut 24: 1 let him write her a *b.* of divorcement
Is 50: 1 the *b.* of your mother's divorcement
Jer 3: 8 and given her a *b.* of divorcement
Mark 10: 4 write a *b.* of divorcement
Luke 16: 6 take thy *b.*, and sit down
16: 7 take thy *b.* and write fourscore

BILLOWS
Ps 42: 7 thy *b.* are gone over me
Jonah 2: 3 all thy *b.* and thy waves

BIND
Job 38:31 canst thou *b.* the sweet influences
31:36 I would *b.* it as a crown
Ps 105:22 *b.* his princes at pleasure
149: 8 to *b.* their kings with chains
Prov 3: 3 *b.* them about thy neck
Is 8:16 *b.* up the testimony, seal the law
Hos 6: 1 smitten, and will *b.* us up
Mat 12:29 first *b.* the strong man and
13:30 *b.* them in bundles to burn
16:19 thou shalt *b.* on earth
22:13 *b.* him hand and foot, and cast

BIRD (BIRDS)
Gen 15:10 but the *b.* divided he not
2 Sam 21:10 neither the *b.* of the air to rest
Ps 104:17 where the *b.* make their nests
124: 7 soul is escaped as a *b.*
Prov 7:23 as a *b.* hasteth to the snare
Eccl 9:12 as the *b.* that are caught
10:20 *b.* of the air shall carry the voice
Sol 2:12 the time of the singing of the *b.*
Is 31: 5 as *b.* flying so will the Lord
46:11 ravenous *b.* from the east
Jer 5:27 as a cage is full of *b.*
12: 9 the *b.* round about are against her
Mat 8:20 the *b.* of the air have nests

BIRTH
2 Ki 19: 3 for the children are come to the *b.*
Eccl 7: 1 of death than the day of one's *b.*
Is 66: 9 shall I bring to the *b.*, and not
Ezek 16: 3 thy *b.* and thy nativity
Gal 4:19 whom I travail in *b.* again

BIRTHDAY
Gen 40:20 the third day, which was Pharaoh's *b.*
Mat 14: 6 when Herod's *b.* was kept

BIRTHRIGHT
Gen 25:31 sell me this day thy *b.*
27:36 he took away my *b.*; and behold
43:33 the firstborn according to his *b.*
1 Chr 5: 1 the *b.* was given unto the sons
Heb 12:16 for one morsel of meat sold his *b.*

BISHOP (BISHOPS)
Phil 1: 1 at Philippi, with *b.* and deacons
1 Tim 3: 1 desire the office of *b.*
Tit 1: 7 for a *b.* must be blameless
1 Pet 2:25 returned unto the shepherd and *b.* of souls

BITE (BITETH, BITTEN)
Num 21: 9 if a serpent had *b.* any man
Prov 23:32 at last it *b.* like a serpent
Eccl 10:11 the serpent will *b.* without enchantment
Jer 8:17 not be charmed and they shall *b.* you
Amos 9: 3 command the serpent, and he shall *b.* thee
Mic 3: 5 prophets *b.* with their teeth
Hab 2: 7 rise up suddenly that shall *b.* thee
Gal 5:15 if ye *b.* and devour one another

BITTER
Ex 1:14 made their lives *b.* with hard bondage
12: 8 with *b.* herbs they shall eat it
Deut 32:24 devoured with *b.* destruction
32:32 grapes of gall, their clusters are *b.*
2 Ki 14:26 of Israel, that it was very *b.*
Job 3:20 life given to the *b.* in soul
13:26 write *b.* things against me
Ps 64: 3 to shoot their arrows even *b.* words
Prov 27: 7 every *b.* thing is sweet
Is 5:20 woe to them that put *b.* for sweet
Jer 2:19 it is an evil thing and *b.* that
Col 3:19 wives and be not *b.* against them
Jas 3:14 if ye have *b.* envying and strife
Rev 8:11 because they were made *b.*
10: 9 and it shall make thy belly *b.*

BITTERLY
Judg 5:23 curse ye *b.* inhabitants thereof
Is 22: 4 I will weep *b.*, labour not to comfort
Ezek 27:30 heard against thee, and shall cry *b.*
Hos 12:14 provoked him most *b.*
Mat 26:75 went out and wept *b.*

BITTERNESS
1 Sam 1:10 she was in *b.* of soul, and prayed
15:32 surely the *b.* of death is past
2 Sam 2:26 it will be *b.* in the end
Prov 14:10 heart knows its own *b.*
Acts 8:23 in gall of *b.* and bond of
Rom 3:14 whose mouth full of cursing and *b.*
Eph 4:31 let all *b.* . . . be put away from you
Heb 12:15 root of *b.* springing up trouble you

BLACK
1 Ki 18:45 the heaven was *b.* with clouds
Sol 1: 5 look not upon me because I am *b.*
Mat 5:36 canst not make one hair white or *b.*

BLACKNESS
Heb 12:18 burned with fire nor unto *b.* and darkness
Jude 1:13 reserved the *b.* of darkness for ever

BLAME (BLAMED)
Gen 43: 9 let me bear the *b.* forever
2 Cor 6: 3 that the ministry be not *b.*
8:20 no man should *b.* us in this abundance
Gal 2:11 because he was to be *b.*
Eph 1: 4 we should be holy and without *b.*

BLAMELESS
Gen 44:10 and ye shall be found *b.*
Josh 2:17 we will be *b.* of this thine oath
Judg 15: 3 now shall I be more *b.*
Mat 12: 5 profane the sabbath, and are *b.*
Luke 1: 6 in ordinances of the Lord *b.*
1 Cor 1: 8 be *b.* in the day of our Lord
Phil 3: 6 righteous which is in the law *b.*
1 Thes 5:23 soul and body be preserved *b.* unto the
1 Tim 3: 2 bishop then must be *b.*, the husband
3:10 office of a deacon being found *b.*
5: 7 give in charge, that they may be *b.*
Tit 1: 7 for a bishop must be *b.*
2 Pet 3:14 of him in peace, without spot and *b.*

BLASPHEME (BLASPHEMED, BLASPHEMETH)
Lev 24:16 *b.* the name of the Lord
2 Ki 19: 6 of Assyria have *b.* me
Ps 44:16 voice of him that reproacheth and *b.*
74:10 shall the enemy *b.* thy name forever
74:18 foolish people have *b.* thy name
Is 52: 5 my name continually every day is *b.*
Mat 9: 3 scribes said this man *b.*
Mark 3:29 *b.* against Holy Ghost hath never
Luke 12:10 unto him that *b.* against the Holy
Acts 26:11 compelled them to *b.*
Rom 2:24 is *b.* among the Gentiles through you
1 Tim 1:20 that they may learn not to *b.*
6: 1 name of God and his doctrine be not *b.*
Jas 2: 7 do they not *b.* that name
Rev 16:11 and *b.* the God of heaven because

BLASPHEMER (BLASPHEMERS)
1 Tim 1:13 who was before a *b.*, and a persecutor
2 Tim 3: 2 covetous, boasters, proud, *b.*

BLASPHEMY
2 Ki 19: 3 day of trouble, and of rebuke, and *b.*
Is 37: 3 day of trouble, and of rebuke, and of *b.*
Mat 12:31 and *b.* shall be forgiven unto men
Mark 7:22 an evil eye, *b.*, pride, foolishness
Col 3: 8 off all these; anger, wrath, malice, *b.*
Rev 2: 9 I know the *b.* of them which say

BLEMISH
Ex 12: 5 Your lamb shall be without *b.*
29: 1 and two rams without *b.*
Lev 1: 3 let him offer a male without *b.*
4:23 of the goats a male without *b.*
Dan 1: 4 children in whom was no *b.*
Eph 5:27 that it should be holy and without *b.*
1 Pet 1:19 as of a lamb without *b.* and without

BLESS
Gen 12: 2 and I will *b.* thee
12: 3 I will *b.* them that *b.* thee
22:17 in blessing I will *b.* thee
Ex 23:25 God, and he shall *b.* thy bread and water
24: 1 pleased the Lord to *b.* Israel
Num 6:24 Lord *b.* thee and keep thee
Deut 8:10 thou shalt *b.* the Lord thy God
Judg 5: 9 among the people *b.* ye the Lord
Ps 5:12 Thou, Lord wilt *b.* the righteous
16: 7 I will *b.* the Lord
28: 9 *b.* thine inheritance and feed
29:11 will *b.* his people with peace
63: 4 Thus will I *b.* thee while I live
67: 1 be merciful to us and *b.* us
103: 1 *b.* the Lord, O my soul
104:35 *b.* the Lord, O my soul
115:13 he will *b.* them that fear
132:15 I will abundantly *b.* her
134: 3 the Lord *b.* thee out of Zion
145: 2 Every day will I *b.* thee
Hag 2:19 from this day will I *b.*
Rom 12:14 *b.* them that persecute
Acts 3:26 sent him to *b.* you
1 Cor 4:12 being reviled we *b.*

BLESSED
Gen 1:22 God *b.* them, saying, Be fruitful
2: 3 God *b.* the seventh day
Ex 20:11 the Lord *b.* the sabbath day
Num 24: 9 *b.* is he that blesseth
Ps 1: 1 *b.* is the man that walketh not in the counsel
32: 1 *b.* is he whose transgression is
32: 2 *b.* is the man unto whom the Lord imputeth
33:12 *b.* is the nation whose God is
34: 8 *b.* is the man that trusteth in him
41: 1 *b.* is he that considereth the poor
65: 4 *b.* is the man whom thou choosest
84: 5 *b.* is the man whose strength is in thee
94:12 *b.* is the man whom thou chastenest
112: 1 *b.* is the man *that* feareth the Lord
Prov 8:32 *b.* are they that keep my ways
8:34 *b.* is the man that heareth me

Prov 10: 7 memory of the just is *b.*
Is 30:18 *b.* are all they that wait for him
56: 2 *b.* is the man that doeth this,
Jer 17: 7 *b.* is the man that trusteth in the Lord
Dan 12:12 *b.* is he that waiteth and cometh
Mat 5: 3 *b.* are the poor in spirit
5: 4 *b.* are they that mourn
5: 5 *b.* are the meek: for they shall
5: 6 *b.* are they which do hunger and thirst
5: 7 *b.* are the merciful: for they
5: 8 *b.* are the pure in heart
5: 9 *b.* are the peacemakers
5:10 *b.* are they which are persecuted
5:11 *b.* are ye, when men shall revile you
11: 6 *b.* is he whosoever not offended in me
13:16 *b.* are your eyes for they see
21: 9 *b.* is he that cometh in the name of the Lord
24:46 *b.* is that servant whom his lord
Mark 10:16 in his arms and *b.* them
11: 9 *b.* is he that cometh in the name of the Lord
Luke 1:28 *b.* art thou among women
1:48 all generations shall call me *b.*
11:28 *b.* are they that hear the word
John 12:13 *b.* is he that cometh in
20:29 *b.* are they that have not seen, and
Acts 20:35 it is more *b.* to give
Rom 1:25 the Creator who is *b.* for ever
4: 7 *b.* are they whose iniquities are . . .
1 Tim 1:11 glorious gospel of the *b.* God
6:15 *b.* and only Potentate
Jas 1:12 *b.* is the man that endureth temptation
Rev 1: 3 *b.* is he that readeth this prophecy
14:13 *b.* are the dead which die in the Lord
19: 9 *b.* are they which are called unto the marriage supper
20: 6 *b.* and holy is he that hath part
22: 7 *b.* is he that keepeth the sayings of this book
22:14 *b.* are they that do his commandments

BLESSEDNESS
Rom 4: 6 describeth the *b.* of the man, unto whom God
Gal 4:15 where is then the *b.* ye spake of

BLESSING (BLESSINGS)
Gen 12: 2 name great; and thou shalt be a *b.*
27:36 now he hath taken away my *b.*
28: 4 give thee *b.* of Abraham
49:25 who shall bless thee with *b.* of heaven above
Deut 11:26 set before you a *b.* and a curse
23: 5 turned curse into a *b.* unto thee
Josh 8:34 words of the law, the *b.* and the cursings
Neh 9: 5 name, which is exalted above all *b.*
Job 29:13 *b.* of him that was ready to perish
Ps 3: 8 thy *b.* is upon thy people
21: 3 preventest him with *b.* of goodness
109:17 as he delighted not in *b.*
129: 8 the *b.* of the Lord be upon you
Prov 28:20 faithful man shall abound with *b.*
Is 65: 8 destroy it not, for a *b.* is in it
Joel 2:14 repent and leave a *b.* behind him
Mal 2: 2 I will curse your *b.*: yea I have
1 Cor 10:16 cup of *b.* which we bless
Gal 3:14 *b.* of Abraham come on Gentiles
Eph 1: 3 hath blessed us with all spiritual *b.*
Jas 3:10 out of the same mouth proceedeth *b.* and cursing

BLIND
Lev 21:18 not approach, a *b.* man, or a lame
Job 29:15 I was eyes to the *b.*, and feet
Ps 146: 8 openeth the eyes of the *b.*
Is 42: 7 to open the *b.* eyes, to bring out
42:19 who is *b.* but my servant
43: 8 bring the *b.* people that have eyes
Mat 11: 5 the *b.* receive their sight
23:16 woe unto you ye *b.* guides
Luke 4:18 recovery of sight to the *b.*
2 Pet 1: 9 lacketh these things is *b.*
Rev 3:17 not that thou art . . . *b.* and naked

BLINDED
John 12:40 he hath *b.* their eyes and hardened
Rom 11: 7 obtained it, and the rest were *b.*
2 Cor 4: 4 god of this world *b.* the minds
1 John 2:11 that darkness hath *b.* his eyes

BLOOD
Gen 4:11 receive thy brother's *b.* from thy hand
49:11 his clothes in the *b.* of grapes
Job 16:18 cover thou not my *b.*, and let
Ps 9:12 when he maketh inquisition for *b.*
72:14 precious is their *b.* in his sight
Is 26:21 earth shall disclose her *b.*
Ezek 3:18 his *b.* will I require at thine hand
9: 9 land is full of *b.* and the city full
16: 6 polluted in thine own *b.*
Mic 3:10 they build up Zion with *b.*
Mat 26:28 This is my *b.* of the new testament
27: 8 that field was called the field of *b.*
27:25 his *b.* be on us and on our children
Luke 13: 1 whose *b.* Pilate had mingled with
22:44 as it were great drops of *b.*
John 1:13 born not of *b.* nor of flesh
6:54 drinketh my *b.* hath eternal life
6:55 my *b.* is drink indeed
6:56 drinketh my *b.* dwelleth in me
Acts 17:26 made of one *b.* all nations
18: 6 your *b.* be on your own heads
20:26 pure from the *b.* of all men
20:28 hath purchased with his own *b.*
Rom 3:25 through faith in his *b.*
1 Cor 11:27 guilty of the body and *b.* of the Lord
Eph 1: 7 redemption through his *b.* even forgiveness
Col 1:20 peace through the *b.* of the cross
Heb 9:20 This is the *b.* of the testament
10:19 into the holiest by the *b.* of Jesus
12: 4 ye have not yet resisted unto *b.*
12:24 *b.* of sprinkling that speaketh
1 Pet 1: 2 sprinkling of the *b.* of Jesus
1:19 with the precious *b.* of Christ
1 John 1: 7 *b.* of Jesus Christ cleanseth us
5: 6 he that came by water and *b.*
Rev 1: 5 washed us in his own *b.*
6:10 dost thou not avenge our *b.*
8: 7 hail and fire mingled with *b.*
16: 6 thou hast given them *b.* to drink
17: 6 drunken with the *b.* of saints

BLOODGUILTINESS
Ps 51:14 deliver me from *b.*, O God

BLOSSOM (BLOSSOMED)
Num 17: 5 man's rod, whom I shall choose, shall *b.*
Is 5:24 their *b.* shall go up as dust
27: 6 Israel shall *b.* and bud
35: 1 the desert shall *b.* as the rose
35: 2 it shall *b.* abundantly and rejoice
Ezek 7:10 rod hath *b.*, pride hath budded
Hab 3:17 the fig tree shall not *b.*

BLOT (BLOTTED, BLOTTETH, BLOTTING)
Ex 32:32 *b.* me out of thy book
Deut 9:14 and *b.* out their name from under heaven
2 Ki 14:27 he would *b.* out the name of Israel
Neh 4: 5 let not their sin be *b.* out
Job 31: 7 if any *b.* hath cleaved to mine hands
Ps 51: 1 *b.* out my transgressions
109:13 let their name be *b.* out
Prov 9: 7 rebuketh a wicked man getteth himself a *b.*
Is 43:25 I am he that *b.* out thy transgressions
Jer 18:23 neither *b.* out their sin from thy sight
Acts 3:19 that your sins may be *b.* out
Col 2:14 *b.* out handwriting of ordinances

BLUSH
Ezra 9: 6 and *b.* to lift up my face
Jer 6:15 ashamed neither could they *b.*

BOAST (BOASTETH)
Ps 34: 2 my soul shall make her *b.* in the Lord
52: 1 why *b.* thou thyself in mischief
Prov 20:14 he is gone his way, then he *b.*
27: 1 *b.* not thyself of tomorrow
Rom 1:30 despiteful, proud, *b.*, inventors of
11:18 *b.* not against the branches, but if thou *b.*
Eph 2: 9 not of works lest any man should *b.*
Jas 3: 5 *b.* as he that putteth it off

BOASTERS
2 Tim 3: 2 covetous, *b.* proud, blasphemers

BOASTING (BOASTINGS)
Acts 5:36 rose up Theudas, *b.* himself to be
Rom 3:27 where is *b.* then? It is excluded
Jas 4:16 now ye rejoice in your *b.*

BODY
Ex 24:10 as it were the *b.* of heaven
Deut 28:11 in the fruit of thy *b.*, and in
Job 19:26 after my skin worms destroy this *b.*
Mic 6: 7 fruit of my *b.* for the sin of
Mat 6:22 light of the body is the eye
10:28 fear not them which kill the *b.*
26:26 take, eat: this is my *b.*
John 2:21 spake of the temple of his *b.*
Rom 6: 6 *b.* of sin might be destroyed
7: 4 dead to the law by the *b.* of Christ
7:24 me from the *b.* of this death
8:10 *b.* is dead because of sin
8:13 do mortify the deeds of the *b.*
8:23 the redemption of our *b.*
1 Cor 5: 3 absent in *b.*, but present in spirit
6:18 sin that a man doeth is without the *b.*
6:19 *b.* is the temple of Holy Ghost
7: 4 wife hath not power of her own *b.*
9:27 I keep under my *b.* and bring
10:16 communion of the *b.* of Christ
11:29 not discerning the Lord's *b.*
12:14 the *b.* is not one member, but many
12:27 ye are the *b.* of Christ
15:44 it is raised a spiritual *b.*
2 Cor 5: 6 home in *b.* absent from the Lord
5: 8 to be absent from the *b.*
5:10 receive things done in his *b.*
12: 2 whether in *b.* or out I cannot
Eph 3: 6 fellowheirs of the same *b.*
4:12 for edifying the *b.* of Christ
5:23 he is the saviour of the *b.*
Phil 1:20 Christ magnified in my *b.*
3:21 shall change our vile *b.*
Col 1:18 head of the *b.* the church
2:11 putting off the *b.* of sins of flesh
2:23 humility, and neglecting of the *b.*
Heb 10: 5 but a *b.* hast thou prepared
13: 3 being yourselves also in the *b.*
Jas 3: 6 tongue defileth the whole *b.*
1 Pet 2:24 bare our sins in his own *b.*
Jude 1: 9 disputed about the *b.* of Moses

BODIES
Rom 8:11 quicken your mortal *b.* by your spirit
12: 1 present your *b.* a living sacrifice
1 Cor 6:15 your *b.* are the members of Christ
Eph 5:28 love wives as their own *b.*
Heb 10:22 our *b.* washed with pure water

BODILY
Luke 3:22 Holy Ghost in a *b.* shape
2 Cor 10:10 his *b.* presence is weak
Col 2: 9 the fulness of Godhead *b.*
1 Tim 4: 8 *b.* exercise profiteth little

BOLD (BOLDLY)
Prov 28: 1 righteous are *b.* as a lion
Mark 15:43 went in *b.* unto Pilate and craved
2 Cor 10: 1 being absent am *b.* toward you
11:21 if any is *b.* I am *b.* also
Phil 1:14 are much more *b.* to speak
Heb 4:16 come *b.* to throne of grace

BOLDNESS
2 Cor 7: 4 Great is my *b.* of speech toward
Eph 3:12 in whom we have *b.* and
Heb 10:19 *b.* to enter into the holiest
1 John 4:17 may have *b.* in the day of judgment

BOND (BONDS)
Job 12:18 He looseth looseth the *b.* of kings
Ps 116:16 handmaid: thou hast loosed my *b.*
Ezek 20:37 bring you into the *b.* of the covenant
Acts 20:23 *b.* and afflictions abide me
23:29 worthy of death or of *b.*
1 Cor 12:13 whether we be *b.* or free
Gal 3:28 there is neither *b.* nor free
Eph 4: 3 unity of Spirit in the *b.* of peace
6: 8 whether he be *b.* or free
6:20 I am an ambassador in *b.*
Phil 1:16 to add affliction to my *b.*
Col 3:11 *b.* nor free but Christ is all
3:14 charity which is the *b.* of perfectness

BONDMAN (BONDWOMAN)
Gen 21:10 cash out this *b.* and her son
Gal 4:23 but he who was of the *b.* was born
Rev 6:15 and every *b.*, and every free man

BONDAGE
Ex 13: 3 out of the of *b.*
1:14 their lives bitter with hard *b.*
2:23 sighed by reason of the *b.*
Rom 8:15 spirit of *b.* again to fear
1 Cor 7:15 brother or a sister is not under *b.*
Gal 4:24 Sinai which gendereth to *b.*
5: 1 entangled with the yoke of *b.*

BONE (BONES)
Gen 2:23 this is now *b.* of my bones
Ex 12:46 neither shall ye break a *b.* thereof
Judg 9: 2 remember also that I am your *b.*
2 Sam 19:13 art thou not of my *b.*
1 Chr 11: 1 behold we are thy *b.* and thy flesh
Ps 6: 2 heal me, my *b.* are vexed
22:14 all my *b.* are out of joint
32: 3 my *b.* waxed old through my roaring
34:20 he keepeth all his *b.*: not one of
35:10 All my *b.* shall say, Lord, who is like
38: 3 neither is there any rest in my *b.*
51: 8 *b.* which thou hast broken may
102: 3 my *b.* are burned as an hearth
102: 5 my *b.* cleave to my skin
Eccl 11: 5 how the *b.* do grow in the womb
Ezek 37: 1 valley which was full of dry *b.*
37: 3 Son of man, can these *b.* live
Mat 23:27 are within full of dead men's *b.*
John 19:36 *b.* of him shall not be broken
Eph 5:30 of his flesh, and of his *b.*

BOOK (BOOKS)
Gen 5: 1 This is the *b.* of the generations
Ex 32:32 blot me out of thy *b.*
Esth 6: 1 to bring the *b.* of the records
Job 19:23 O that they were printed in a *b.*
Ps 40: 7 in the volume of the *b.*
56: 8 tears, are they not in thy *b.*
139:16 in thy *b.* all my members were written
Eccl 12:12 of making many *b.* there is no end
Dan 7:10 judgment was set, and the *b.* were opened
John 21:25 could not contain the *b.* that should be
Phil 4: 3 whose names are in the *b.* of life
2 Tim 4:13 bring with thee, and the *b.*
Heb 10: 7 the volume of the *b.* it is written
Rev 3: 5 name out of the *b.* of life
13: 8 names are not written in the *b.*
20:12 and the *b.* were opened
20:15 not found written in the *b.* of life
22:19 words of the *b.* of this prophecy

BORN
Job 5: 7 Yet man is *b.* unto trouble
14: 1 man that is *b.* of a woman
Ps 58: 3 go astray as soon as they be *b.*
87: 4 with Ethiopia this man was *b.* there
Prov 17:17 brother is *b.* for adversity
Eccl 3: 2 a time to be *b.* and a time to die
Is 9: 6 unto us a child is *b.* unto us
66: 8 shall a nation be *b.* at once
Mat 11:11 among them that are *b.* of women
26:24 better if he had not been *b.*
Luke 7:28 among those that are *b.* of women
John 3: 3 except a man be *b.* again
3: 4 can man be *b.* when he is old
3: 5 *b.* of water and of the Spirit
3: 6 which is *b.* of the flesh is flesh
3: 7 said unto thee ye must be *b.* again
Rom 9:11 children being not yet *b.*
1 Cor 15: 8 as of one *b.* out of due time
Gal 4:23 bond woman was *b.* after the flesh
1 Pet 2: 2 as new *b.* babes desire milk of
1 John 3: 9 is *b.* of God doth not commit
4: 7 everyone that loveth if *b.* of God

BORNE
Jer 15:10 that thou hast *b.* me a man of strife

BORROW (BORROWED)
Ex 3:22 every woman shall *b.* of her neighbor
12:35 they *b.* of the Egyptians
22:14 if a man *b.* aught of his neighbour
Deut 15: 6 but thou shalt not *b.*: and thou
28:12 many nations, and thou shalt not *b.*
Mat 5:42 would *b.* of thee turn thou not away

BORROWER
Prov 22: 7 the *b.* is servant to the lender
Is 24: 2 as with the lender so with the *b.*

BOSOM
Gen 16: 5 I have given my maid into thy *b.*
Ex 4: 6 he put his hand into his *b.*
Num 11:12 carry them in thy *b.* as a
Deut 13: 6 wife of thy *b.*; or thy friend
Ps 35:13 my prayer returned into my own *b.*
74:11 pluck thy hand out of thy *b.*
79:12 sevenfold into their *b.* their reproach
89:50 how I do bear in my *b.*
Prov 5:20 and embrace the *b.* of a stranger
17:23 taketh a gift out of the *b.* to pervert
19:24 hideth his hands in his *b.*
Eccl 7: 9 anger resteth in the *b.* of fools
Is 40:11 his arm, and carry them in his *b.*
65: 6 recompense even recompense into their *b.*
Jer 32:18 fathers into the *b.* of their children
Mic 7: 5 her that lieth in thy *b.*
Luke 6:38 running over, shall men give into your *b.*
16:22 carried by the angels into Abraham's *b.*
John 13:23 leaning on Jesus' *b.* one of his disciples

BOTTLE (BOTTLES)
Gen 21:14 took bread, and a *b.* of water
Job 38:37 who can stay the *b.* of heaven
Ps 56: 8 put thou my tears into thy *b.*
119:83 I am become like a *b.* in the smoke
Jer 13:12 every *b.* filled with wine
Mat 9:17 do men put new wine into old *b.*
Mark 2:22 no man putteth new wine into new *b.*

BOUGHT
Gen 17:13 he that is *b.* with thy money
33:19 he *b.* a parcel of a field
Deut 32: 6 is not he thy father that hath *b.* thee?
Mat 13:46 sold all that he had and *b.* it
1 Cor 6:20 For ye are *b.* with a price
1 Cor 7:23 Ye are *b.* with a price
2 Pet 2: 1 denying the Lord that *b.* them

BOUND
Gen 22: 9 *b.* Isaac his son, and laid him
Job 36: 8 if they be *b.* in fetters
Ps 107:10 shadow of death being *b.* in affliction
Prov 22:15 foolishness is *b.* in the heart
Is 1: 6 have not been closed neither *b.* up
61: 1 prison to them that are *b.*
Ezek 30:21 it shall not be *b.* up to be healed
34: 4 neither have ye *b.* up that which
Hos 13:12 iniquity of Ephraim is *b.* up
Mat 16:19 bind on earth shall be *b.* in heaven
Acts 20:22 I go *b.* in the spirit
21:13 ready not to be *b.* only, but
Rom 7: 2 wife is *b.* to her husband
1 Cor 7:39 the wife is *b.* by law so long
2 Tim 2: 9 the word of God is not *b.*
Heb 13: 3 remember them in bonds as *b.* with them

BOW (BOWS)
Gen 9:13 I do set my *b.* in the clouds
49:24 his *b.* abode in strength, and the arms
Josh 24:12 not with thy sword nor with thy *b.*
1 Sam 2: 4 the *b.* of the mighty men are broken
2 Sam 1:18 children of Judah the use of the *b.*
Ps 7:12 hath bent his *b.* and made
11: 2 lo, the wicked bend their *b.*
37:15 their *b.* shall be broken
44: 6 I will not trust in my *b.*
78:57 turned aside like a deceitful *b.*
Jer 9: 3 bend their tongue like their *b.* for lies
Lam 2: 4 bent his *b.* like an enemy
3:12 bent his *b.* and set me as a mark
Hos 1: 5 break the *b.* of Israel
1: 7 I will not save them by *b.*
7:16 turned like a deceitful *b.*

BOW (BOWED, BOWETH)
Gen 23:12 Abraham *b.* down himself before the
Judg 7: 5 every one that *b.* down upon his knees
2 Ki 19:16 Lord, *b.* down thine ear
Job 31:10 let others *b.* down upon her
Ps 31: 2 *b.* down thine ear to me
38: 6 I am *b.* down greatly; I go mourning
95: 6 let us worship and *b.* down
145:14 raiseth up all that be *b.* down
Prov 22:17 *b.* down thine ear, and hear
Is 2:11 haughtiness of men shall be *b.* down

BOWELS
Gen 43:30 for his *b.* did yearn upon his brother
1 Ki 3:26 for her *b.* yearned upon her son
2 Chr 21:18 the Lord smote him in his *b.*
Ps 71: 6 took me out of my mother's *b.*
Is 63:15 the sounding of thy *b.* and of thy
Jer 4:19 my *b.* my *b.* I am pained
31:20 my *b.* are troubled for him
Acts 1:18 in the midst and, all his *b.* gushed out
2 Cor 6:12 you are straitened in your own *b.*
Phil 1: 8 I long after you in the *b.* of Christ
Col 3:12 put on the *b.* of mercies
Philem 1: 7 *b.* of the saints are refreshed
1:20 refresh my *b.* in the Lord
1 John 3:17 shutteth up his *b.* of compassion

BRAKE
Ex 32:19 and *b.* them beneath the mount
1 Sam 4:18 Eli *b.* his neck and died
1 Ki 19:11 and *b.* into pieces the rocks
2 Ki 10:27 they *b.* down the images of Baal
11:18 and *b.* it down, his altars
23:14 *b.* into pieces the images
25:10 *b.* down the walls of Jerusalem
2 Chr 14: 3 and *b.* down the images, and cut down
25:23 and *b.* down the wall of Jerusalem
Job 29:17 *b.* the jaws of the wicked

Ps 76: 3 *b.* the arrows of the bow
105:16 *b.* the whole staff of bread
107:14 *b.* their bands in sunder
Jer 31:32 my covenant they *b.* although I was
39: 8 and *b.* down the walls of Jerusalem
52:14 *b.* down all the walls of Jerusalem
Ezek 17:16 and whose covenant he *b.*, even with him
Dan 2: 1 troubled, and his sleep *b.* from him
6:24 *b.* all their bones to pieces
Mat 14:19 he blessed and *b.*, and gave the loaves
15:36 and gave thanks, and *b.* them
26:26 blessed it, and *b.* it and gave it
Mark 6:41 and blessed, and *b.* the loaves
14: 3 she *b.* the box and poured it on his
14:22 took bread, and blessed and *b.* it
Luke 22:19 took bread, and gave thanks, and *b.* it
24:30 took bread, and blessed it, and *b.*
1 Cor 11:24 he *b.* it and said, Take, eat

BRAMBLE
Judg 9:14 said all the trees unto the *b.*, Come
Luke 6:44 nor of a *b.* bush gather they grapes

BRANCH
Num 13:23 a *b.* with one cluster of grapes
Job 14: 7 the tender *b.* thereof will not cease
18:16 and above shall his *b.* be cut off
Prov 11:28 righteous shall flourish as a *b.*
Is 4: 2 shall the *b.* of the Lord be beautiful
9:14 cut off from head to tail, *b.*
11: 1 a *B.* shall grow out of
14:19 cast out like an abominable *b.*
25: 5 *b.* of the terrible ones shall be
60:21 *b.* of my planting, the work of my
Jer 23: 5 I will raise unto David a righteous *B.*
Ezek 8:17 they put the *b.* to their nose
Zech 3: 8 bring forth my servant the *B.*
6:12 behold the man whose name is the *B.*
Mal 4: 1 leave neither root nor *b.*
Mat 24:32 fig tree; when his *b.* is yet tender
John 15: 4 As the *b.* cannot bear fruit of itself
15: 6 cast forth as a *b.* and is withered

BRANCHES
Lev 23:40 *b.* of palm trees, and the boughs
Neh 8:15 fetch olive *b.*, and pine *b.*,
Job 15:30 flame shall dry up his *b.*
Ps 80:11 sent her *b.* unto the river
104:12 habitation, which sing among the *b.*
Is 16: 8 her *b.* are stretched out, they are gone
17: 6 four or five in the outmost fruitful *b.*
18: 5 take away and cut down the *b.*
Jer 11:16 the *b.* of it are broken
Ezek 17: 6 whose *b.* turned toward him
19:11 exalted among the thick *b.*
Dan 4:14 hew down the tree, and cut off his *b.*
Hos 14: 6 his *b.* shall spread and his beauty
Zech 4:12 what be these two olive *b.*
John 15: 5 I am the vine, ye are the *b.*
Rom 11:16 root be holy, so are the *b.*
11:17 if some of the *b.* be broken off
11:21 God spared not the natural *b.*

BRASEN
Num 16:39 Eleazar the priest took the *b.* censers
2 Ki 18: 4 brake in pieces the *b.* serpent
2 Chr 6:13 Solomon had made a *b.* scaffold
Jer 1:18 and *b.* walls against the whole land
Mark 7: 4 washing of cups, and pots, *b.* vessels

BRASS
Gen 4:22 instructor of every artificer in *b.* and iron
Num 21: 9 And Moses made a serpent of *b.*
Deut 8: 9 out of whose hills thou mayest dig *b.*
28:23 that is over thy head shall be *b.*
Job 6:12 strength of stones or is my flesh *b.*
41:27 he esteemeth *b.* as rotten wood
Ps 107:16 broken the gates of *b.*, and cut
Is 48: 4 thy neck iron, and thy brow *b.*

Dan 2:32 his belly and his thighs of *b.*
5: 4 of silver, of *b.*, of iron, of wood
Zech 6: 1 the mountains were mountains of *b.*
1 Cor 13: 1 I am become as sounding *b.* and
Rev 1:15 his feet like unto fine *b.*
2:18 his feet are like fine *b.*

BREACH (BREACHES)
Gen 38:29 this *b.* be upon thee: therefore his
Num 14:34 ye shall know my *b.* of promise
Judg 21:15 Lord had made a *b.* in the tribes
2 Sam 6: 8 Lord had made a *b.* upon Uzzah
Job 16:14 He breaketh me with *b.* upon *b.*
Ps 60: 2 heal the *b.* thereof; for it shaketh
106:23 his chosen stood before him in the *b.*
Is 30:13 this iniquity shall be to you as *b.*
58:12 shalt be called the repairer of the *b.*
Lam 2:13 thy *b.* is great like the sea

BREAD
Gen 3:19 sweat of thy face shalt thou eat *b.*
19: 3 and did bake unleavened *b.*
28:20 will give me *b.* to eat
49:20 Out of Asher his *b.* shall be fat
Ex 12:15 shall ye eat unleavened *b.*
16: 4 I will rain *b.* from heaven
23:25 he will bless thy *b.* and water
Lev 21: 6 *b.* of their God they do offer
26:26 I have broken the staff of your *b.*
Num 14: 9 they are *b.* for us: their defense
21: 5 soul loatheth this light *b.*
Deut 8: 3 man doth not live by *b.* only
16: 3 *b.* therewith even the *b.* of affliction
Ruth 1: 6 visited his people giving *b.*
1 Sam 2: 5 hired themselves for *b.*
25:11 take my *b.* and my water
1 Ki 18: 4 fed them with *b.* and water
Neh 5:14 not eaten *b.* of the governor
9:15 gavest them *b.* from heaven
Ps 37:25 nor his seed begging *b.*
78:20 can he give *b.* also
80: 5 feedest them with *b.* of tears
102: 9 I have eaten ashes like *b.*
105:16 he brake the whole staff of *b.*
127: 2 to eat the *b.* of sorrows
132:15 satisfy her poor with *b.*
Prov 9:17 *b.* eaten in secret is pleasant
20:17 *b.* of deceit is sweet to a man
22: 9 giveth of his *b.* to the poor
25:21 be hungry, give him *b.* to eat
31:27 she eateth not *b.* of idleness
Eccl 9:11 neither yet *b.* to the wise
11: 1 cast thy *b.* upon the waters
Is 3: 1 the staff whole stay of *b.*
30:20 Lord give you *b.* of adversity
55: 2 money for that which is not *b.*
55:10 seed to the sower, *b.* to the eater
58: 7 deal thy *b.* to the hungry
Lam 4: 4 the young children ask *b.*
Ezek 4:16 I will break the staff of *b.*
18: 7 hath given his *b.* to the hungry
Hos 2: 5 give me my *b.* and water
Amos 4: 6 want of *b.* in all your places
Mal 1: 7 ye offer polluted *b.* on mine
Mat 4: 3 these stones be made *b.*
4: 4 not live by *b.* alone
6:11 Give us this day our daily *b.*
7: 9 son ask *b.* will he give a stone
15:26 meet to take the children's *b.*
26:26 took *b.* and blessed it
Mark 7: 5 but eat *b.* with unwashen hands
8: 4 satisfy these men with *b.*
14:12 the first day of unleavened *b.*
Luke 7:33 neither eating *b.* nor drinking wine
15:17 servants of my father's have *b.* enough
22: 7 then came the day of unleavened *b.*
24:35 known to them in breaking of *b.*
John 6:32 Moses gave you not that *b.*
6:33 the *b.* of God is he that cometh
6:34 evermore give us this *b.*
6:35 I am the *b.* of life
6:50 this is the *b.* that cometh down
13:18 he that eateth *b.* with me

Acts 2:42 breaking *b.* and in prayer
2:46 breaking *b.* from house to house
20: 6 after the days of unleavened *b.*
20: 7 came together to break *b.*
27:35 he took *b.* and gave thanks
1 Cor 10:16 *b.* we break is it not the communion
5: 8 with the unleavened *b.* of sincerity and truth
10:17 we many are one *b.* and one body
11:26 for as often as ye eat this *b.*
2 Cor 9:10 both minister *b.* for your food
2 Thes 3:12 they work, and eat their own *b.*

BREAK
Ex 19:21 lest they *b.* through to come up
19:22 lest the Lord *b.* forth upon them
23:24 and quite *b.* down their images
34:13 destroy their altars, *b.* their images,
Deut 7: 5 and *b.* down their images, and cut down
Ezra 9:14 should we again *b.* thy commandments
Job 19: 2 and *b.* me in pieces with words
Ps 2: 3 let us *b.* their bands asunder
2: 9 shalt *b.* them with a rod of iron
10:15 *b.* thou the arm of the wicked
58: 6 *b.* their teeth in their mouth
72: 4 and shall *b.* into pieces the oppressor
89:31 if they *b.* my statutes
89:34 my covenant will I not *b.* nor
94: 5 they *b.* into pieces thy people
Eccl 3: 3 a time to *b.* down, and a time to
Sol 2:17 till the day *b.* and the shadow
Is 14: 7 they *b.* forth into singing
38:13 as a lion so will he *b.* all
42: 3 bruised reed shall be not *b.*
45: 2 I will *b.* into pieces the gates
55:12 the hills shall *b.* forth before you
Jer 1:14 an evil shall *b.* forth upon all
14:21 *b.* not thy covenant with us
15:12 shall iron *b.* northern iron
33:20 if ye can *b.* my covenant of the day
51:22 I will *b.* into pieces the horse
Ezek 17:15 *b.* the covenant and be delivered
Dan 2:44 but it shall *b.* into pieces
7:23 tread it down, and *b.* it into pieces
Hos 1: 5 that I will *b.* the bow of Israel
10: 2 he shall *b.* down their altars
Zech 11:10 that I might *b.* my covenant which I
Mat 5:19 *b.* one of these least commandments
6:19 thieves *b.*through and steal
Acts 21:13 mean ye to weep and to *b.* mine heart?
1 Cor 10:16 bread which we *b.*, is not the
Gal 4:27 *b.* forth and cry, that travailest

BREAKETH (BREAKING)
Gen 32:26 let me go, for the day *b.*
Job 9:17 he *b.* me with a tempest
Ps 29: 5 voice of the Lord *b.* the cedars
46: 9 *b.* the bow and cutteth the spear
119:20 my soul *b.* for the longing
Prov 25:15 a soft tongue *b.* the bone
Eccl 10: 8 *b.* an hedge, a serpent shall bite
Jer 19:11 as one *b.* a potter's vessel
23:29 like a hammer that *b.* rocks
Luke 24:35 known of them in *b.* of bread
Acts 2:42 and in *b.* of bread, and in prayer
Rom 2:23 through *b.* the law dishonourest thou God?

BREAST (BREASTS)
Gen 49:25 blessings of the *b.*, and of the womb
Job 3:12 why *b.* that I should suck
21:24 his *b.* are full of milk
Ps 22: 9 I was upon my mother's *b.*
Prov 5:19 let her *b.* satisfy thee at
Sol 1:13 all night between my *b.*
4: 5 thy *b.* are like two roes
7: 7 thy *b.* to clusters of grapes
8: 1 sucked the *b.* of my mother
8: 8 a little sister, and she hath no *b.*
8:10 I am a wall, and my *b.* like towers
Is 28: 9 from the milk and drawn from the *b.*

Is 60:16 and shalt suck the *b.* of kings
66:11 satisfied with the *b.* of her consolation
Lam 4: 3 sea monsters draw out the *b.*
Ezek 16: 7 thy *b.* are fashioned, and thine hair
23: 3 there were their *b.* pressed
23: 8 they bruised the *b.* of her virginity
Hos 2: 2 adulteries from between her *b.*
9:14 given them a miscarrying womb and dry *b.*
Joel 2:16 the children, and those that suck *b.*
Luke 23:48 smote their *b.* and returned
John 13:25 He then lying on Jesus' *b.*
21:20 which also leaned on his *b.* at supper
Rev 15: 6 their *b.* girded with golden girdles

BREASTPLATE (BREASTPLATE)

Ex 28: 4 garments which they shall make; a *b.*
Eph 6:14 having on the *b.* of righteousness
1 Thes 5: 8 putting on the *b.* of faith and love
Rev 9:17 having *b.* of fire and of jacinth

BREATH

Gen 2: 7 into his nostrils the *b.* of life
Job 12:10 the *b.* of all mankind
15:30 by the *b.* of his mouth
17: 1 my *b.* is corrupt, my days are extinct
33: 4 *b.* of the Almighty hath given me life
34:14 if he gather his spirit and *b.*
37:10 by the *b.* of God frost is given
41:21 his *b.* kindleth coals
Ps 33: 6 host of them, by the *b.* of his mouth
104:29 thou takest away their *b.*
135:17 neither any *b.* in their mouths
146: 4 *b.* goeth forth, he returneth
Eccl 3:19 the other; yea they have all one *b.*
Is 2:22 whose *b.* is in his nostrils
11: 4 the *b.* of his lips shall he slay
30:28 his *b.*, as an overflowing stream
30:33 the *b.* of the Lord doth kindle it
33:11 your *b.* as fire shall devour you
42: 5 giveth *b.* unto the people
Jer 10:14 and there is no *b.* in them
Lam 4:20 the *b.* of our nostrils
Dan 5:23 in whose hand thy *b.* is
Hab 2:19 no *b.* at all in the midst
Acts 17:25 giveth to all life and *b.*

BREATHE (BREATHED, BREATHING)

Ps 27:12 such as *b.* out cruelty
Ezek 37: 9 come *b.* upon these slain
John 20:22 he *b.* on them, and saith unto
Acts 9: 1 *b.* out threatenings and slaughter

BREED (BRED, BREEDING)

Gen 8:17 that they may *b.* abundantly
Ex 16:20 *b.* worms and stank; and Moses was wroth
Deut 32:14 lambs and rams of the *b.* of Bashan
Zeph 2: 9 even the *b.* of nettles, and salt pits

BRETHREN

Gen 13: 8 and thy headmen for we be *b.*
19: 7 I pray you *b.* do not so wickedly
24:27 me to the house of my master's *b.*
42: 3 Joseph's ten *b.* went to buy corn
42: 6 *b.* bowed down themselves before him
45:16 Joseph's *b.* are come: and it pleased
49: 5 Simeon and Levi are *b.*
49:26 of him that was separate from his *b.*
50:15 Joseph's *b.* saw their father was dead
Num 27: 4 give therefore a possession among the *b.*
27:10 if he have no *b.*, they ye shall give
Deut 17:20 be not lifted up above his *b.*
25: 5 if *b.* dwell together, and one of them die
33: 9 neither did he acknowledge his *b.*
33:24 let him be acceptable to his *b.*
Josh 6:23 brought out Rahab . . . and her *b.*
Judg 9: 1 went to Shechem unto his mother's *b.*
2 Ki 10:13 we are *b.* of Ahaziah
1 Chr 4: 9 more honourable than his *b.*
5: 2 prevailed above his *b.*
12: 2 Saul's *b.* of Benjamin
26: 7 whose *b.* were strong men, Elihu and
27:18 Elihu one of the *b.* of David
2 Chr 21: 2 he had *b.* the sons of Jehoshaphat
22: 8 the sons of the *b.* of Ahaziah
Job 6:15 my *b.* dealt deceitfully
19:13 put my *b.* far from me
Ps 22:22 declare thy name unto my *b.*
69: 8 become a stranger to my *b.*
122: 8 for my *b.* and companions' sakes
133: 1 for *b.* to dwell in unity
Prov 6:19 soweth discord among *b.*
17: 2 part of the inheritance of *b.*
Hos 13:15 though he be fruitful among his *b.*
Mat 4:18 Jesus . . . saw two *b.*, Simon called
12:48 my mother, who are my *b.*
19:29 forsaken houses, or *b.* or sisters
20:24 moved against the two *b.*
22:25 now there were with us seven *b.*
23: 8 even Christ and all ye are *b.*
25:40 the least of these my *b.* ye have
28:10 go tell my *b.* that they go
Mark 10:29 man that hath left house or *b.*
Luke 14:26 hate not . . . *b.*, sisters, yea,
16:28 for I have five *b.*; that he may
21:16 betrayed by both by parents and *b.*
John 7: 5 neither did his *b.* believe
20:17 go to my *b.* and say, I ascend
Acts 6: 3 *b.* look ye out among you seven men
7:26 sirs, ye are *b.* why do ye
9:30 when the *b.* knew, they brought him
10:23 certain *b.* from Joppa accompanied
11:12 these six *b.* accompanied me
11:29 determined send relief to the *b.*
12:17 show these things to James and to the *b.*
14: 2 evil affected against the *b.*
15: 3 caused great joy to all the *b.*
15:22 chief men among the *b.*
15:32 exhorted the *b.* with many words
15:40 by the *b.* unto the grace of God
17: 6 drew Jason and certain *b.*
17:10 *b.* sent away Paul and Silas
18:18 Paul took leave of the *b.*
18:27 *b.* wrote exhorting the disciples
20:32 now *b.* I commend you to God
23: 6 men and *b.* I am a Pharisee
Rom 8:29 the firstborn among many *b.*
9: 3 accursed from Christ for my *b.*
1 Cor 6: 5 to judge between his *b.*
8:12 when ye sin so against the *b.*
15: 6 seen of above five hundred *b.* at once
Gal 2: 4 false *b.* unawares brought in
1 Tim 4: 6 If thou put the *b.* in remembrance
5: 1 a father and the younger men as *b.*
Heb 2:11 is not ashamed to call them *b.*
1 Pet 1:22 the Spirit unto unfeigned love of the *b.*
3: 8 love as *b.* be pitiful, courteous
1 John 3:14 unto life because we love the *b.*
3:16 to lay down our lives for the *b.*
3 John 1:10 neither doth receive the *b.*

BRIBE (BRIBES)

1 Sam 8: 3 turned aside after lucre, and took *b.*
12: 3 have I received any *b.* to blind
Ps 26:10 and their right hand is full of *b.*
Is 33:15 that shaketh his hands from holding *b.*
Amos 5:12 they take a *b.*, and they turn aside

BRIBERY

Job 15:34 fire shall consume the tabernacles of *b.*

BRICK (BRICKS)

Gen 11: 3 and they had *b.* for stone
Ex 1:14 hard bondage, in mortar and in *b.*
5: 7 give the people straw to make *b.*
Is 9:10 the *b.* are fallen down
65: 3 burneth incense upon altars of *b.*

BRIDE

Is 49:18 bind them on thee, as a *b.* doeth
61:10 as a *b.* adorneth herself
Jer 2:32 can a *b.* forget her attire
Joel 2:16 of his chamber, and the *b.* out of her closet
John 3:29 hath *b.* is the bridegroom
Rev 21: 2 as a *b.* adorned for her husband
21: 9 I will show thee the *b.* the Lamb's wife

BRIDEGROOM

Ps 19: 5 as *b.* coming out of the chamber
Is 61:10 as a *b.* decketh himself
62: 5 as a *b.* rejoiceth over the bride
Jer 7:34 I cause to cease the voice of the *b.*
33:11 the voice of the *b.*, and the voice of
Joel 2:16 let the *b.* go forth of his chamber
Mat 9:15 as long as the *b.* is with them
25: 1 went forth to meet the *b.*
John 2: 9 the governor of the feast called the *b.*
3:29 friend of *b.* rejoiceth
Rev 18:23 and the voice of the *b.* and of the

BRIDLE

Job 30:11 let loose the *b.* before me
Ps 32: 9 must be held in with bit and *b.*
39: 1 I will keep my mouth as with a *b.*
Prov 26: 3 a *b.* for the ass, and a rod for
Is 37:29 put my *b.* in thy lips
Jas 3: 2 able to *b.* the whole body

BRIDLES

Rev 14:20 even unto the horse *b.*, by thy space

BRIDLETH

Jas 1:26 *b.* not his tongue, but deceiveth

BRIER (BRIERS)

Judg 8:16 and thorns of the wilderness and *b.*
Is 5: 6 come up *b.* and thorns
7:23 it shall even be for *b.* and thorns
9:18 it shall devour the *b.* and thorns
27: 4 set *b.* against me in battle
55:13 instead of *b.* shall come up myrtle
Ezek 2: 6 though *b.* and thorns be with thee
28:24 no more a pricking *b.* unto
Mic 7: 4 the best of them is as a *b.*
Heb 6: 8 that which beareth thorns and *b.* is rejected

BRIGHT

Lev 13: 2 a scab, or *b.* spot and it be in
Job 37:11 he scattereth his *b.* cloud
Sol 5:14 his belly is as *b.* ivory
Jer 51:11 make *b.* the arrows; gather the shields
Ezek 1:13 the fire was *b.* and out of
21:15 it is made *b.*, it is wrapped
Nah 3: 3 up both the *b.* sword and the glittering
Zech 10: 1 the Lord shall make *b.* clouds
Mat 17: 5 a *b.* cloud overshadowed them
Luke 11:36 *b.* shining of a candle doth give thee
Acts 10:30 a man stood in *b.* clothing
Rev 22:16 of David, and the *b.* and morning star

BRIGHTNESS

2 Sam 22:13 through the *b.* before him were
Job 31:26 beheld the moon walking in *b.*
Is 59: 9 for *b.* but we walk in darkness
Ezek 1:28 the appearance of the *b.* round about
8: 2 as the appearance of *b.*
10: 4 full of the *b.* of the Lord's glory
28: 7 they shall defile thy *b.*
28:17 corrupted thy wisdom by reason of thy *b.*
Dan 4:36 mine honour and *b.* returned unto me
12: 3 shine as the *b.* of the firmament
Amos 5:20 even very dark and no *b.* in it?
Hab 3: 4 and his *b.* was as the light
Acts 26:13 a light above the *b.* of the sun
2 Thes 2: 8 Lord with the *b.* of his coming

Heb 1: 3 being the *b.* of his glory

BRIMSTONE

Gen 19:24 Lord rained upon Sodom and upon Gomorrah *b.*
Deut 29:23 the whole land thereof is *b.*
Ps 11: 6 rain snares, fire, and *b.*
Is 30:33 of the Lord like a stream of *b.*
34: 9 dust thereof into *b.*, land burning
Ezek 38:22 great hailstones, fire, and *b.*
Luke 17:29 it rained fire and *b.* from heaven
Rev 9:17 issued fire and smoke and *b.*
19:20 cast into a lake of fire and *b.*

BRING

Gen 1:11 let the earth *b.* forth grass
1:24 the earth *b.* forth the living creature
6:17 even I, do *b.* a flood of waters
Josh 23:15 *b.* upon you all the evil
1 Ki 8:32 to *b.* his way on his head
2 Ki 19: 3 there is not strength to *b.* forth
Job 14: 4 who can *b.* a clean thing
15:35 and *b.* forth vanity
33:30 to *b.* back his soul from the pit
Ps 37: 6 he shall *b.* forth thy righteousness
60: 9 who will *b.* me into the strong city
92:14 they shall still bring forth fruit in old age
Prov 27: 1 knowest not what a day may *b.* forth
Eccl 11: 9 God will *b.* thee into judgment
Sol 8: 2 *b.* thee to my mother's house
Is 1:13 *b.* no more vain oblations
41:21 *b.* forth your strong reasons
42: 1 *b.* forth judgment to the Gentiles
43: 5 I will *b.* thy seed from the east
43: 6 *b.* my sons from afar, and
46:13 I *b.* near my righteousness
66: 8 shall earth be made to *b.* forth in one day?
66: 9 *b.* to the birth and not cause
Hos 2:14 *b.* her into wilderness and speak
Zeph 2: 2 before the decree *b.* forth
3: 5 every morning doth he *b.* his judgment
Mat 1:21 she shall *b.* forth a son
Mark 4:20 *b.* forth fruit some thirtyfold
Luke 2:10 I *b.* you good tidings of great joy
3: 8 *b.* forth fruits worthy of repentance
8:14 this life, and *b.* no fruit to perfection
John 12:24 if it die it *b.* much fruit
14:26 and *b.* all to your remembrance
15: 2 that it may *b.* forth more fruit
Acts 5:28 intend to *b.* this man's blood on us
1 Cor 1:28 *b.* to nought things that are
4: 5 *b.* to light the hidden things
1 Thes 4:14 will God *b.* with him
1 Pet 3:18 that he might *b.* us to God

BRINGETH

Ps 1: 3 *b.* forth fruit in his season
Hos 10: 1 He *b.* forth fruit unto himself
Mat 3:10 every tree which *b.* not forth good fruit
7:19 every tree that *b.* not forth good fruit
Luke 6:43 a good tree *b.* not forth corrupt fruit
Jas 1:15 when lust hath conceived, it *b.* forth sin

BROAD

Num 16:39 they were made *b.* plates for a covering
Job 36:16 out of the strait into a *b.* place
Ps 119:96 but thy commandment is exceeding *b.*
Is 33:21 be unto us a place of *b.* rivers
Nah 2: 4 one against another in the *b.* ways
Mat 7:13 *b.* is the way that leadeth to destruction
23: 5 they make *b.* their phylacteries

BROKEN

Gen 17:14 he hath *b.* my covenant
Ps 34:18 nigh unto them that are of a *b.* heart
44:19 sore *b.* us in the place of dragons
51: 8 bones which thou hast *b.* rejoice
51:17 a *b.* spirit, a *b.* and a contrite heart
55:20 he hath *b.* his covenant
147: 3 He healeth the *b.* in heart, and bindeth
Prov 17:22 but a *b.* spirit drieth the bones
Eccl 4:12 a threefold cord is not quickly *b.*
Is 24: 5 the ordinance *b.* the everlasting covenant
61: 1 sent me to bind up the *b.* hearted
Jer 2:13 hewed them out cisterns, *b.* cisterns
5: 5 these have altogether *b.* the yoke
33:21 then may also my covenant be *b.*
Ezek 44: 7 they have *b.* my covenant
Dan 2:42 partly strong and partly *b.*
Hos 5:11 Ephraim is oppressed and *b.* in judgment
Mat 21:44 fall on this stone shall be *b.*

BROOK (BROOKS)

Job 20:17 the floods, the *b.* of honey and butter
Ps 110: 7 drink of the *b.* in the way
Is 19: 6 the *b.* of defence shall be emptied

BROTHER

Prov 17:17 a *b.* is born for adversity
18:19 a *b.* offended is harder to be won
18:24 a friend that sticketh closer than a *b.*
27:10 neighbour that is near, than a *b.* far off
Jer 9: 4 trust ye not in any *b.* for every *b.*
Mat 10:21 *b.* shall deliver up *b.* to death
Mark 13:12 *b.* shall betray the *b.* to death
Acts 9:17 on him said, *b.* Saul, the Lord, even Jesus
1 Cor 5:11 *b.* be a fornicator or
7:15 A *b.* or sister is not under bondage
8:11 though thy knowledge shall the weak *b.* perish
1 Thes 4: 6 no man go beyond and defraud his *b.*
2 Thes 3:15 as an enemy, but admonish him as a *b.*
Jas 1: 9 let the *b.* of low degree rejoice

BROTHERHOOD

Zech 11:14 I might break the *b.* between Judah and
1 Pet 2:17 Love the *b.*. Fear God.

BROTHERLY

Amos 1: 9 and remembered not the *b.* covenant
Rom 12:10 affectioned one to another with *b.* love
1 Thes 4: 9 as touching *b.* love, ye need not that
Heb 13: 1 let *b.* love continue
2 Pet 1: 7 to godliness *b.* kindness; and to *b.*

BROUGHT

Deut 33:14 precious fruits *b.* forth by the sun
2 Sam 7:18 that thou hast *b.* me hitherto
Neh 4:15 God had *b.* their counsel to nought
9:33 thou art just in all that is *b.* on
Ps 45:14 be *b.* unto the king in raiment
79: 8 mercies prevent us: we are *b.* low
90: 2 before the mountains were *b.* forth
106:43 *b.* low for their iniquities
107:39 *b.* low through oppression
Is 1: 2 nourished and *b.* up children
66: 7 before she travailed, she *b.* forth
Mat 10:18 ye shall *b.* before governors and kings
Luke 12:16 ground of a certain rich man *b.* forth
1 Cor 6:12 I will not be *b.* under the power of any
Gal 2: 4 because of false brethren unawares *b.* in
1 Tim 6: 7 we *b.* nothing into this world, and it
Jas 5:18 the earth *b.* forth her fruit

BRUISE (BRUISED)

Gen 3:15 it shall *b.* thy head, and thou shalt
2 Ki 18:21 trustest upon the staff of this *b.* reed
Is 42: 3 a *b.* reed shall he not break
53: 5 He was *b.* for our iniquities
53:10 it pleased the Lord to *b.* him.
Ezek 23: 3 there they *b.* the teats of their virginity
Luke 4:18 to set at liberty them that are *b.*
Rom 16:20 God of peace shall *b.* Satan

BRUTISH

Ps 92: 6 a *b.* man knoweth not; neither doth a
94: 8 understand ye *b.* among the people
Prov 12: 1 but he that hateth reproof is *b.*
Jer 10:14 every man is *b.* in his knowledge

BUCKET (BUCKETS)

Num 24: 7 He shall pour the water out of his *b.*
Is 40:15 the nations are as a drop of a *b.*

BUCKLER

1 Chr 5:18 men able to bear *b.* and sword
Job 15:26 upon the thick bosses of his *b.*
Ps 91: 4 his truth shall be thy shield and *b.*
Sol 4: 4 where on there hang a thousand *b.*

BUILD (BUILDETH)

Josh 6:26 cursed be the man that . . . *b.* this city
Ps 51:18 *b.* thou the walls of Jerusalem
102:16 when the Lord shall *b.* up Zion, he shall
127: 1 except the Lord *b.* the house they labour
Prov 14: 1 Every wise woman *b.* her house: but
Eccl 3: 3 break down and a time to *b.* up
Jer 22:13 woe to him that *b.* the house
Amos 9: 6 that *b.* his stories in heaven
Mic 3:10 they *b.* up Zion with blood
Hab 2:12 him that *b.* a town with blood
Acts 20:32 his grace, which is able to *b.* you up
1 Cor 3:10 the foundations and another *b.* thereon

BUILDER

Ps 118:22 stone which the *b.* refused is become head
Mat 21:42 stone which the *b.* rejected
Mark 12:10 stone which the *b.* rejected
Acts 4:11 stone which was set at nought of you *b.*
Heb 11:10 foundations whose *b.* and maker is God
1 Pet 2: 7 the stone which the *b.* disallowed

BUILDING

1 Cor 3: 9 God's husbandry, ye are God's *b.*
2 Cor 5: 1 we have a *b.* of God, an house
Eph 2:21 all the *b.* fitly framed together

BUILT

Job 22:23 to the Almighty, thou shalt be *b.* up
Ps 89: 2 mercy shall be *b.* up for ever
Mat 7:24 wise man which *b.* his house upon a rock
Eph 2:20 ye are *b.* on the foundation of
Heb 3: 4 he that *b.* all things is God
1 Pet 2: 5 *b.* up a spiritual house, an holy

BULLS

Ps 22:12 many *b.* have compassed me: strong *b.*
50:13 will I eat the flesh of *b.*, or drink
68:30 rebuke the multitude of *b.*
Heb 9:13 if the blood of *b.* and goats

BULLOCK (BULLOCKS)

Ps 51:19 they offer *b.* on thine altar
69:31 better than an ox or *b.* that hath horns
Is 1:11 delight not in the blood of *b.*
Jer 31:18 as a *b.* unaccustomed to the yoke: turn

BULRUSH (BULRUSHES)

Ex 2: 3 took for him an ark of *b.*
Is 18: 2 even in vessels of *b.*
58: 5 Is it to bow down his head as a *b.*

BULWARKS
Ps 48:13 mark ye well her *b.*
Is 26: 1 salvation will God appoint for walls and *b.*

BURDEN
Ex 18:22 shall bear the *b.* with thee
23: 5 ass lying under his *b.*
Deut 1:12 how can I bear your *b.*
2 Sam 15:33 thou shalt be a *b.* unto
19:35 servant be yet a *b.* unto my lord
2 Ki 5:17 two mules' *b.* of earth
9:25 the Lord laid this *b.* upon him
2 Chr 35: 3 not be a *b.* on your shoulders
Neh 13:19 no *b.* brought in on the sabbath day
Job 7:20 so that I am a *b.* to myself
Ps 38: 4 a *b.* they are too heavy for me
55:22 cast thy *b.* upon the Lord
81: 6 I removed his shoulder from the *b.*
Eccl 12: 5 grasshopper shall be a *b.*
Is 9: 4 thou hast broken the yoke of his *b.*
13: 1 the *b.* of Babylon, which Isaiah
30:27 the *b.* thereof is heavy: his lips full
Ezek 12:10 this *b.* concerneth the prince in Jerusalem
Nah 1: 1 the *b.* of Nineveh. The book of
Hab 1: 1 the *b.* which Habakkuk the prophet
Zeph 3:18 reproach of it was a *b.*
Zech 9: 1 the *b.* of the word of the Lord
12: 3 all that *b.* themselves with it shall
Mal 1: 1 *b.* of the word of the Lord
Mat 11:30 my yoke is easy, my *b.* is light
Acts 15:28 no greater *b.* than necessary
2 Cor 12:16 But be it so, I did not *b.* you
Gal 6: 5 every man bear his own *b.*
Rev 2:24 put on you no other *b.*

BURDENED
2 Cor 5: 4 in this tabernacle do groan being *b.*
8:13 not that other men be eased and ye *b.*

BURDENS
Gen 49:14 couching down between two *b.*
Ex 1:11 taskmasters to afflict them with their *b.*
Is 58: 6 to undo the heavy *b.* and let the
Lam 2:14 seen for thee false *b.* and causes of
Mat 23: 4 bind heavy *b.* and grievous to be born
Gal 6: 2 bear one another's *b.* and fulfil

BURN (BURNED, BURNETH)
Gen 44:18 let not thine anger *b.*
Ex 3: 2 the bush *b.* with fire
29:13 and *b.* them upon the altar
Lev 1: 9 the priest shall *b.* all on the altar
6:15 *b.* it upon the altar for a sweet
Deut 9:15 the mount *b.* with fire
32:22 shall *b.* unto the lowest hell
Ps 46: 9 *b.* the chariot in the fire
74: 8 they have *b.* up all the synagogues of God
Is 9:18 wickedness *b.* as the fire
27: 4 go through them, I would *b.* them
Mal 4: 1 day cometh shall *b.* as an oven
Luke 3:17 chaff he will *b.* with fire
24:32 did not our heart *b.* within us?
1 Cor 3:15 if man's work shall be *b.*, he shall
7: 9 it is better to marry than to *b.*
13: 3 though I give my body to be *b.* and
2 Cor 11:29 who is offended and I *b.* not?
Heb 6: 8 whose end is to be *b.*
12:18 not come to the mount that *b.*
Rev 21: 8 lake which *b.* with fire

BURNING (BURNINGS)
Gen 15:17 a *b.* lamp that passed between
Ex 21:25 *b.* for *b.*, wound for wound
Deut 28:22 smite thee with extreme *b.*
Is 3:24 of sackcloth and *b.* instead of beauty
4: 4 judgment and by the spirit of *b.*
33:14 shall dwell with everlasting *b.*
Jer 20: 9 word was in mine heart as a *b.* fire
Ezek 1:13 their appearance was like *b.* coals of fire
Amos 4:11 as a firebrand plucked out of the *b.*
Luke 12:35 loins be girded about, and your lights *b.*
John 5:35 He was a *b.* and a shining light
Rev 4: 5 there were seven lamps of fire *b.*

BURNT
Gen 8:20 and offered *b.* offerings on the altar
Deut 12: 6 hither shall ye bring your *b.* offerings
1 Sam 15:22 great delight in *b.* offerings and sacrifices
Ps 51:16 thou delightest not in *b.* offering
Is 1:11 I am full of the *b.* offerings
64:11 is *b.* up with fire
Jer 7:21 put your *b.* offerings unto your sacrifices
Hos 6: 6 knowledge of God more than *b.* offerings
Mic 6: 6 shall I come before him with *b.* offerings
Mat 22: 7 and *b.* up their city
Mark 12:33 is more than all *b.* offerings
Heb 10: 6 In *b.* offerings and sacrifices
2 Pet 3:10 works that are therein shall be *b.*

BURST
Jer 2:20 broken thy yoke, and *b.* thy bands
5: 5 broken the yoke and *b.* the bonds
Mark 2:22 new wine doth *b.* the bottles
Acts 1:18 he *b.* asunder in the midst

BURY (BURIED, BURYING)
Gen 23: 4 *b.* my dead out of my sight
47:30 bury me in their *b.* place
49:29 *b.* me with my fathers in the cave
Ps 79: 3 there was none to *b.* them
Mat 8:21 first to go and *b.* my father
8:22 let the dead *b.* their dead
Rom 6: 4 we are *b.* with him by baptism into death
1 Cor 15: 4 he was *b.* and rose again
Col 2:12 *b.* with him in baptism, wherein

BUSHEL
Mat 5:15 and put it under a *b.*; but on a
Luke 11:33 neither under a *b.*, but on a

BUSINESS
Gen 39:11 went into the house to do his *b.*
Deut 24: 5 neither shall he be charged with any *b.*
Ps 107:23 in ships, that do *b.* in great waters
Dan 8:27 rose up and did the king's *b.*
Luke 2:49 must be about my Father's *b.*
Rom 12:11 not slothful in *b.*; fervent
1 Thes 4:11 study to be quiet, and to do your own *b.*

BUTTER
Gen 18: 8 and he took *b.*, and milk, and the calf
2 Sam 17:29 and honey, and *b..* and sheep
Job 20:17 the brooks of honey and *b.*
Ps 55:21 words were smoother than *b.*
Is 7:15 *b.* and honey shall he eat

BUY (BUYETH)
Prov 23:23 *b.* the truth, and sell it not
Is 55: 1 *b.* and eat, yea, *b.* wine
Mat 13:44 selleth all and *b.* that field
Jas 4:13 *b.* and sell, and get gain
Rev 3:18 I counsel thee to *b.* gold
13:17 no man might *b.* or sell
18:11 no man *b.* their merchandise

BUYER
Prov 20:14 it is naught, saith the *b.*
Is 24: 2 as with *b.* so with seller
Ezek 7:12 let not the *b.* rejoice, nor

BYWORD
Deut 28:37 and a *b.* among all nations
1 Ki 9: 7 Israel shall be a . . . *b.* among
Job 17: 6 he hath made me also a *b.* of the prophet
Ps 44:14 makest us a *b.* among the heathen

C

CAKE (CAKES)
Gen 18: 6 make *c.* upon the hearth
Lev 24: 5 flour and bake twelve *c.* thereof
Judg 7:13 *c.* of barley tumbled into the host
1 Ki 17:12 I have not a *c.* but meal
Jer 7:18 make *c.* to the queen of heaven
Hos 7: 8 Ephraim is a *c.* not turned

CALAMITY (CALAMITIES)
Deut 32:35 the day of their *c.* is at hand
Job 6: 2 my *c.* laid in the balances
Ps 18:18 prevented me in the day of my *c.*
57: 1 until these *c.* be overpast
141: 5 my prayer shall be in their *c.*
Prov 1:26 I will laugh at your *c.*
17: 5 glad at *c.* shall not be unpunished
19:13 a foolish son is the *c.* of his
27:10 brother's house in the day of thy *c.*
Jer 18:17 not the face in the day of their *c.*
46:21 day of their *c.* is come
Ezek 35: 5 the sword in the day of their *c.*
Obad 1:13 my people in the day of their *c.*

CALF (CALVES)
Gen 18: 7 fetched a *c.* tender and good
Ex 32: 4 made a molten *c.*
Lev 9: 2 thee a young *c.* for a sin offering
Deut 9:16 had made a molten *c.*
1 Ki 12:28 made two *c.* of gold for you
Neh 9:18 they had made them a molten *c.*
Job 21:10 calveth and casteth not her *c.*
Ps 29: 6 them also to skip like a *c.*
106:19 They made a *c.* in Horeb
Is 11: 6 *c.* and the young lion
27:10 there shall the *c.* feed
Jer 34:18 they cut the *c.* in twain
Hos 8: 5 thy *c.*, O Samaria, hath cast thee
14: 2 we will render the *c.* of our lips
Mic 6: 6 come with *c.* of a year old
Mal 4: 2 grow up as *c.* of the stall
Luke 15:23 bring hither the fatted *c.*
Heb 9:12 blood of goats and *c.*, but by his
Rev 4: 7 the second beast like a *c.*

CALL
Gen 2:19 to see what he would *c.* them
4:26 began men to *c.* upon the name of the Lord
12: 8 and *c.* upon the name of the Lord
24:57 we will *c.* the damsel and inquire
30:13 daughters will *c.* me blessed
Deut 4: 7 God is in all things that we *c.* upon
4:26 I *c.* heaven and earth to witness
1 Sam 3: 6 for thou didst *c.* me
1 Ki 8:52 in all that they *c.* for
18:24 and I will *c.* on the name of the Lord
2 Ki 5:11 and *c.* on the name of the Lord
Job 5: 1 *C.* now if there be any to answer
13:22 *c.* thou, and I will answer
27:10 will he always *c.* upon God
Ps 4: 1 hear me when I *c.*, O God
14: 4 they *c.* not upon the Lord
49:11 *c.* their lands after their own names
50:15 And *c.* upon me in the day of trouble
91:15 He shall *c.* upon me
77: 6 I *c.* to remembrance my song
80:18 quicken us and we will *c.* on thy name
86: 5 plenteous in mercy to all that *c.*
116: 4 then I *c.* upon the name of the Lord
145:18 nigh to all that *c.* upon him
Prov 1:28 then shall they *c.* upon me
Is 5:20 woe unto them that *c.* evil good
22:12 Lord God of hosts *c.* to weeping
58: 9 thou shalt *c.* and Lord will answer
65:24 before they *c.* I will answer
Jer 25:29 I will *c.* for a sword upon all

Jer 29:12 then shall ye *c.* upon me
Joel 2:32 whosoever shall *c.* on the name
Jonah 1: 6 arise, *c.* upon thy God
Zeph 3: 9 that all may *c.* upon the name of the Lord
Zech 13: 9 shall *c.* upon thy name
Mal 3:12 all nations shall *c.* you blessed
3:15 and now we *c.* the proud happy
Mat 9:13 I am not come to *c.* the righteous
22: 3 *c.* them that were bidden
23: 9 *c.* no man your father on earth
Luke 1:48 all generations will *c.* me blessed
6:46 why *c.* ye me Lord, Lord and
14:12 a supper *c.* not thy friends
14:13 a feast *c.* the poor, the maimed
John 4:16 *c.* thy husband and come hither
13:13 ye *c.* me Master and Lord
15:15 I *c.* you not servants, but friends
Acts 2:21 shall *c.* on the name of the Lord
2:39 as many as the Lord shall *c.*
24:14 after the way which they *c.* heresy
Rom 9:25 I will *c.* them my people
10:12 rich in mercy to all that *c.* on him
10:13 shall *c.* upon the name of the Lord
1 Cor 1: 2 *c.* upon the name of Jesus Christ
2 Cor 1:23 I *c.* God for a record upon my soul
Heb 2:11 not ashamed to *c.* them brethren
Jas 5:14 *c.* for the elders of the church
1 Pet 1:17 if ye *c.* on the Father

CALLED

Gen 21:17 angel of God *c.* to Hagar
22:11 angel of Lord *c.* to Abraham
Ex 3: 4 God *c.* him out of the bush
Judg 15:18 sore athirst and *c.* on the Lord
2 Ki 8: 1 Lord hath *c.* for a famine
1 Chr 4:10 Jabez *c.* on the God of Israel
21:26 David *c.* upon the Lord and he
2 Chr 6:33 have built is *c.* by my name
7:14 which are *c.* by my name
Ps 17: 6 I have *c.* upon thee
18: 6 in my distress I *c.* upon the Lord
79: 6 that have not *c.* on thy name
88: 9 I have *c.* daily upon thee
118: 5 I *c.* on the Lord in my distress
Prov 1:24 I have *c.* and ye refused
Sol 5: 6 I *c.* him, he gave no answer
Is 41: 2 who *c.* him to his foot
42: 6 I the Lord *c.* thee in righteousness
43: 1 I have *c.* thee by thy name
43: 7 that is *c.* by my name
48: 1 *c.* by the name of Israel
49: 1 the Lord *c.* me from the womb
50: 2 when I *c.*, was there none to answer
51: 2 I *c.* him alone, and blessed him
61: 3 might be *c.* trees of righteousness
62: 4 thou shalt be *c.* Hephzibah
65:12 when I *c.* ye did not answer
Jer 7:11 which is *c.* by my name
15:16 I am *c.* by thy name
25:29 city which is *c.* by my name
34:15 House which is *c.* by my name
Lam 1:19 I *c.* for my lovers
3:55 I *c.* upon thy name, O Lord
Dan 9:19 people are *c.* by thy name
Hos 11: 1 I *c.* my son out of Egypt
Amos 7: 4 the Lord *c.* to contend by fire
9:12 heathen which are *c.* by my name
Hag 1:11 I *c.* for a drought on the land
Mark 14:72 Peter *c.* to mind the word
Luke 15:19 not worthy to be *c.* thy son
John 1:48 before that Philip *c.* thee
10:35 if he *c.* them gods to whom
15:15 but I have *c.* you friends
Acts 9:21 destroy them which *c.* on this name
9:41 when he had *c.* the saints
10:24 *c.* together his kinsmen and near friends
11:26 disciples were *c.* Christians first
13: 2 for the work whereto I *c.* them
15:17 Gentiles upon whom my name is *c.*
19:40 we are in danger to be *c.* in question
24:21 of the dead I am *c.* in question
Rom 1: 1 *c.* to be an apostle
Rom 1: 6 ye also the *c.* of Jesus Christ
Rom 1: 7 beloved of God *c.* to be saints
Rom 2:17 art *c.* a Jew, and restest in the law
8:28 the *c.* according to his purpose
8:30 predestinate, them he also *c.*
9:24 whom he *c.*, not of Jews only
1 Cor 1: 9 ye were *c.* unto the fellowship
1:26 not many wise, not many noble are *c.*
5:11 if any man that is *c.* a brother
7:17 as the Lord hath *c.* every one,
7:18 any man *c.* being circumcised?
7:24 wherein he is *c.* therein abide
15: 9 not meet to be *c.* an apostle
Gal 1: 6 *c.* you into the grace of Christ
1:15 God who *c.* me by his grace
5:13 ye have been *c.* to liberty
Eph 2:11 who are *c.* uncircumcision
4: 4 are *c.* in one hope of your calling
Col 3:15 peace of God to which ye are *c.*
1 Thes 2:12 who hath *c.* you unto his Kingdom
4: 7 God hath not *c.* us to uncleanness
2 Thes 2: 4 above all that is *c.* God
2:14 he *c.* you by our gospel
1 Tim 6:12 life, whereunto thou art *c.*
2 Tim 1: 9 *c.* us with holy calling
Heb 3:13 while it is *c.* today
5: 4 *c.* of God, as was Aaron
11:16 not ashamed to be *c.* their God
11:24 be *c.* the son of Pharaoh's daughter
Jas 2: 7 name by the which ye are *c.*
1 Pet 1:15 as he that *c.* you is holy
2: 9 who *c.* you out of darkness
2:21 For even hereunto were ye *c.*
5:10 God *c.* us to his eternal glory
2 Pet 1: 3 *c.* us to glory and virtue
1 John 3: 1 we should be *c.* sons of God
Jude 1: 1 preserved in Christ Jesus and *c.*
Rev 17:14 that are with him are *c.* and chosen
19: 9 are *c.* unto the marriage supper

CALLETH

1 Ki 8:43 that the stranger *c.* to thee
Ps 42: 7 deep *c.* unto deep at the noise
147: 4 stars, he *c.* them by all their
Is 59: 4 none *c.* for justice nor for truth
64: 7 none that *c.* upon thy name
Hos 7: 7 none among them that *c.* unto me
Amos 5: 8 that *c.* for waters of the sea
Luke 15: 6 home, he *c.* together his friends
John 10: 3 he *c.* his own sheep by name
Rom 4:17 *c.* those things which be not
9:11 not of works but of him that *c.*
Gal 5: 8 cometh not of him that *c.* you
1 Thes 5:24 faithful is he that *c.* you

CALLING

Is 41: 4 *c.* the generations from the beginning
Mat 11:16 children sitting in the markets, and *c.*
Mark 11:21 Peter *c.* to remembrance saith unto
Acts 7:59 they stoned Stephen, *c.* upon God
22:16 *c.* on the name of the Lord
Rom 11:29 the gifts and *c.* of God
1 Cor 1:26 ye see your *c.*, brethren
7:20 let every man abide in the same *c.*
Eph 1:18 know what is the hope of his *c.*
4: 4 called in one hope of your *c.*
Phil 3:14 prize of the high *c.* of God
2 Thes 1:11 count worthy of this *c.*
2 Tim 1: 9 and called us with a holy *c.*
Heb 3: 1 partakers of the heavenly *c.*
1 Pet 3: 6 obeyed Abraham, *c.* him lord
2 Pet 1:10 make your *c.* and election sure

CALM

Ps 107:29 he maketh the storm a *c.*, so that
Jonah 1:11 sea may be *c.* unto us
Mat 8:26 there was a great *c.*
Mark 4:39 and there was a great *c.*
Luke 8:24 and there was a great *c.*

CAME

2 Chr 7: 3 how the fire *c.* down
Mat 20:28 Son of man *c.* not to be ministered
John 1:11 He *c.* unto his own and his own
1:17 grace and truth *c.* by Jesus Christ
3:13 he that *c.* down from heaven
6:38 I *c.* down from heaven not to do
6:51 bread which *c.* down from heaven
16:28 I *c.* forth from the Father
18:37 for this cause *c.* I into the world
Rom 9: 5 concerning the flesh Christ *c.*
1 Tim 1:15 Christ Jesus *c.* into the world
1 John 5: 6 he that *c.* by water and blood
Rev 20: 9 fire *c.* down from God out of heaven

CAMEL

Mat 3: 4 John had his raiment of *c.*'s hair
19:24 it is easier for a *c.* to go through
23:24 strain at a gnat, and swallow a *c.*

CAMP

Ex 14:19 angel of God which went before the *c.*
16:13 quails came up and covered the *c.*
32:17 noise of war in the *c.*
36: 6 proclaimed throughout the *c.*
Num 11:26 and they prophesied in the *c.*
11:31 let the quails fall by the *c.*
Deut 23:14 therefore shall thy *c.* be holy
Judg 13:25 began to move him at times in the *c.*
Heb 13:13 go unto him without the *c.*
Rev 20: 9 compassed the *c.* of the saints

CAN

Gen 41:38 *c.* we find such a one as this is
Deut 1:12 how *c.* I myself alone bear your
32:39 neither is there any that *c.* deliver
2 Sam 7:20 what *c.* David say more unto thee
2 Chr 1:10 for who *c.* judge this thy people
Esth 8: 6 how *c.* I endure to see the evil
Job 8:11 *c.* the rush grow up without mire
25: 4 how *c.* man be justified with God?
34:29 who then *c.* make trouble?
Eccl 4:11 but how *c.* one be warm alone
Is 49:15 *c.* a woman forget her sucking child
Jer 2:32 *c.* the maid forget her ornaments
Ezek 22:14 *c.* thine heart endure or can thine
37: 3 Son of man, *c.* these bones live?
Amos 3: 3 *c.* two walk together except
Mat 12:34 how *c.* ye speak good things?
19:25 amazed, saying who then *c.* be saved?
Mark 2: 7 who *c.* forgive sins but God?
2:19 *c.* the children of the bridechamber
3:27 no man *c.* enter into a strong man's
10:38 *c.* ye drink of the cup that I
John 3: 4 how *c.* man be born when old?
3: 9 said unto him how *c.* these things be
5:19 the Son *c.* do nothing of himself
6:44 no man *c.* come to me except
6:60 an hard saying who *c.* hear it?
9: 4 night cometh, when no man *c.* work
14: 5 how *c.* we know the way?
15: 4 no more *c.* ye, except ye abide
1 Cor 12: 3 no man *c.* say that Jesus is Lord
2 Cor 13: 8 *c.* do nothing against the truth
1 Tim 6: 7 is certain we *c.* carry nothing out
Heb 10:11 sacrifices which *c.* never take away sins
Jas 2:14 have not works, *c.* faith save him?

CANNOT

Gen 32:12 which *c.* be numbered for multitude
Num 23:20 blessed, I *c.* reverse it
Josh 24:19 ye *c.* serve the Lord; for he
1 Sam 12:21 after vain things which *c.* profit
1 Ki 8:27 heaven of heavens *c.* contain thee
2 Chr 6:18 heaven of heavens *c.* contain thee
Ezra 9:15 we *c.* stand before thee
Job 9: 3 contend with him he *c.* answer him
12:14 he breaketh down and it *c.* be
14: 5 appointed his bounds that he *c.* pass
28:15 it *c.* be gotten for gold
36:18 a great ransom *c.* deliver thee

Acts 16:23 they *c.* them into prison
Rom 11: 1 hath God *c.* away his people
13:12 let us *c.* off the works of darkness
2 Cor 4: 9 *c.* down but not destroyed
7: 6 comforteth those that are *c.* down
Gal 4:30 *c.* out this bondwoman and her son
Heb 10:35 *c.* not away your confidence
1 Tim 5:12 they *c.* off their first faith
Rev 2:10 *c.* some of you into prison
2:22 I will *c.* her into a bed, and them
12: 9 and the great dragon was *c.* out
20: 3 *c.* him into the bottomless pit

CASTETH

Job 21:10 cow *c.* not her calf
Ps 147: 6 *c.* the wicked to the ground
Jer 6: 7 so she *c.* out wickedness
Mat 9:34 he *c.* out devils through Beelzebub
Mark 3:22 of the devils *c.* he out devils
Luke 11:15 *c.* out devils through Beelzebub
1 John 4:18 perfect love *c.* out fear
3 John 1:10 *c.* them out of the church

CASTING

Job 6:21 ye see my *c.* down and are afraid
Rom 11:15 if the *c.* away of them be
2 Cor 10: 5 *c.* down imaginations and every high
1 Pet 5: 7 *c.* all your care upon him

CATTLE

Ps 50:10 the *c.* upon a thousand hills
104:14 grass to grow for the *c.*
Ezek 34:17 I judge between *c.* and *c.*
John 4:12 drank thereof and his *c.*

CATCH (CAUGHT)

Judg 21:21 and *c.* you every man his wife
Ps 10: 9 he lieth in wait to *c.* the poor
35: 8 his net that he hid *c.* himself
109:11 let the extortioner *c.* all he hath
Prov 7:13 so she *c.* him and kissed him
Jer 5:26 they set a trap, they *c.* men
Mark 12:13 they *c.* him in his words
Luke 5:10 henceforth thou shalt *c.* men
John 21: 3 that night they *c.* nothing
Acts 8:39 Spirit of the Lord *c.* away Philip
2 Cor 12: 4 he was *c.* up into paradise
1 Thes 4:17 remain shall be *c.* up together with
Rev 12: 5 her child was *c.* up unto God

CAUSE

Ex 9:16 for this *c.* have I raised thee up
22: 9 *c.* of both parties shall come before
23: 2 shalt thou speak in a *c.* to decline
23: 3 countenance a poor man in his *c.*
23: 6 wrest judgment of thy poor in his *c.*
Deut 1:17 the *c.* that is too hard for you
Job 5: 8 to God would I commit my *c.*
6:24 *c.* me to understand wherein I
Ps 9: 4 maintained my right and my *c.*
10:17 wilt *c.* thine ear to hear
35:23 judgment even unto my *c.*, my God
85: 4 *c.* thine anger towards us to cease
143: 8 *c.* me to know the way
Prov 3:30 with a man without *c.*
18:17 that is first in his own *c.*
25: 9 debate thy *c.* with thy neighbour
Eccl 7:10 the *c.* that is former days
Is 3:12 which lead thee, *c.* thee to err
51:22 pleadeth the *c.* of his people
58:14 I will *c.* thee to ride
66: 9 and not *c.* to bring forth
Jer 3:12 not *c.* my anger to fall
5:28 the *c.* of the fatherless
7: 3 *c.* you to dwell in this place
15: 4 *c.* them to be removed
15:11 *c.* the enemy to treat thee well
18: 2 I will *c.* thee to hear my words
32:37 I will *c.* them to dwell safely
Lam 3:32 though he *c.* grief
3:36 to subvert a man in his *c.*
Ezek 36:27 *c.* you to walk in statutes
37: 5 *c.* breath to enter into you
Dan 9:17 *c.* thy face to shine upon thy
Mat 5:22 without *c.* shall be in danger
19: 3 put away his wife for every *c.*
19: 5 For this *c.* shall a man
John 15:25 hated me without *c.*
1 Cor 11:30 this *c.* many are weak and sickly
2 Cor 4:16 for which *c.* we faint not
5:13 if we be sober it is for your *c.*
Eph 5:31 For this *c.* shall a man
1 Tim 9: 1 for this *c.* I obtained mercy

CAUSED (CAUSETH)

Prov 7:21 fair speech *c.* him to yield
10: 5 in harvest is a son *c.* shame
18:18 the lot *c.* contentions to cease
19:27 cease instruction that *c.* to err
Mat 5:32 *c.* her to commit adultery
2 Cor 2:14 always *c.* us to triumph

CAVE (CAVES)

Gen 19:30 he dwelt in a *c.*, he and his
23:19 buried Sarah his wife in the *c.*
25: 9 buried Abraham in the *c.*
49:29 bury me with my fathers in the *c.*
Josh 10:16 hid themselves in a *c.*
Is 2:19 go to *c.* for fear of the Lord
Ezek 33:27 be in the *c.* shall die of pestilence
John 11:38 to the grave. It was a *c.*
Heb 11:38 wandered in the *c.* of the earth

CEASE (CEASETH)

Gen 8:22 day and night shall not *c.*
Neh 6: 3 why should the work *c.*
Job 3:17 wicked *c.* from troubling
Ps 12: 1 Help, Lord; for the godly man *c.*
37: 8 *c.* from anger and wrath
46: 9 he maketh wars to *c.* unto the end
Prov 19:27 *c.* to hear instruction
23: 4 *c.* from thine own wisdom
26:20 where there is no talebearer, the strife *c.*
Acts 13:10 wilt thou not *c.* to pervert
1 Cor 13: 8 tongues, they shall *c.*
Eph 1:16 *c.* not to give thanks for
Col 1: 9 *c.* not to pray for you
2 Pet 2:14 that cannot *c.* from sin

CEASING

Rom 1: 9 without *c.* I make mention
1 Thes 5:17 pray without *c.*
2:13 thank we God without *c.*.
2 Tim 1: 3 without *c.* I have remembrance

CEDAR (CEDARS)

Lev 14: 4 and *c.* wood and scarlet
2 Ki 14: 9 sent to *c.* that was in Lebanon
Ps 29: 5 voice of the Lord breaketh *c.*
92:12 grow like a *c.* in Lebanon
Sol 1:17 beams of our house are *c.*
5:15 countenance excellent as *c.*
Is 9:10 we will change them into *c.*
Ezek 17: 3 took the highest branch of the *c.*
31: 3 the Assyrian was a *c.* in Lebanon

CHAFF

Job 21:18 as *c.* that the storm carrieth away
Ps 1: 4 the *c.* which the wind driveth away
35: 5 be as *c.* before the wind
Is 5:24 the flame consumeth the *c.*
17:13 chased as the *c.* of mountains
33:11 ye shall conceive *c.*
41:15 make the hills as *c.*
Jer 23:28 what is the *c.* to the wheat
Dan 2:35 became like *c.* of the summer
Hos 13: 3 as the *c.* that is driven
Zeph 2: 2 before the day pass as the *c.*
Mat 3:12 burn up the *c.* in unquenchable
Luke 3:17 the *c.* he will burn with fire

CHAIN (CHAINS)

Gen 41:42 gold *c.* about his neck
Ps 73: 6 compasseth them as a *c.*
149: 8 to bind their kings with *c.*
Prov 1: 9 thy head and *c.* about thy neck
Is 3:19 Lord will take away thy *c.*
Ezek 7:23 Make a *c.* for the land is full
16:11 I put a *c.* on thy neck
Dan 5: 7 have a gold *c.* about his neck
Acts 12: 7 Peter's *c.* fell from his hands
28:20 I am bound with this *c.*
2 Tim 1:16 was not ashamed of my *c.*
2 Pet 2: 4 delivered into the *c.* of darkness
Jude 1: 6 reserved in everlasting *c.*
Rev 20: 1. a great *c.* in his hand

CHAMBER (CHAMBERS)

Gen 43:30 Joseph entered into his *c.* and wept
Job 9: 9 Pleiades, and the *c.* of the south
Ps 19: 5 bridegroom coming out of his *c.*
104: 3 beams of his *c.* in the waters
Prov 7:27 going down to the *c.* of death
Sol 1: 4 the king brought me to his *c.*
Is 26:20 enter thou into thy *c.* and shut
Joel 2:16 bridegroom go forth of his *c.*
Dan 6:10 windows being open in his *c.* toward Jerusalem
Mat 24:26 he is in the secret *c.*

CHANCE

1 Sam 6: 9 it was a *c.* that happened
2 Sam 1: 6 I happened by *c.* upon Mount Gilboa
Eccl 9:11 time and *c.* happeneth to them all
Luke 10:31 by *c.* there came down a certain priest

CHANGE (CHANGED, CHANGETH)

Job 14:14 time will I wait till my *c.* come
17:12 *c.* the night into day
Ps 102:26 as a vesture shalt thou *c.* them
Prov 24:21 with them that are given to *c.*
Jer 13:23 can the Ethiopian *c.* his skin
Dan 2:21 he *c.* times and seasons
3:27 neither were their coats *c.*
7:25 think to *c.* times and laws
Mal 3: 6 I am the Lord, I *c.* not
Rom 1:23 *c.* the glory of the uncorruptible God
1:25 *c.* the truth of God into a lie
1:26 women did *c.* the natural use
2 Cor 3:18 *c.* into the same image into glory
Phil 3:21 Christ shall *c.* our vile bodies
Heb 1:12 they shall be *c.*: but thou art
7:12 necessity a *c.* also of the law

CHANGES

Job 10:17 *c.* and war are against me
Ps 55:19 they have no *c.*, therefore they fear

CHARGE (CHARGED)

Gen 26: 5 obeyed my voice and kept my *c.*
28: 6 as he blessed him he gave him a *c.*
Ex 6:13 gave them a *c.* unto the children
Job 1:22 nor *c.* God foolishly
4:18 *c.* his angels with folly
Ps 35:11 to my *c.* things that I knew not
91:11 give his angels *c.* over thee
Sol 2: 7 I *c.* you, O daughters of Jerusalem
8: 4 I *c.* you, O daughters of Jerusalem
Mat 4: 6 He shall give his angels *c.*
Luke 4:10 He shall give his angels *c.*
9:21 and he straightly *c.* them
Acts 7:60 lay not to their *c.*
16:24 such a *c.* thrust into the inner prison
23:29 nothing laid to his *c.* worthy of
Rom 8:33 lay to the *c.* of God's elect
1 Cor 9:18 make the gospel without *c.*
1 Thes 2:11 *c.* every one as a father
1 Tim 1:18 this *c.* I commit to thee
6:13 I give thee *c.* in the sight of God
6:17 *c.* them that are rich
2 Tim 4:16 be laid to their *c.*

CHARIOT (CHARIOTS)

Gen 41:43 the second *c.* which he had
Ex 14: 6 made ready his *c.*
14:25 and took off their *c.* wheels
Josh 17:16 of the valley have *c.* of iron
1 Sam 8:11 take sons for his *c.*
2 Sam 8: 4 took from him a thousands *c.*

1 Ki 10:26 Solomon gathered together *c.* and horsemen
6:17 mountain full of *c.* and horses
2 Ki 14: 2 *c.* of fire
13:14 the *c.* of Israel
Ps 20: 7 some trust in *c.*,
68:17 the *c.* of God are twenty thousand
104: 3 who maketh the clouds his *c.*
Sol 1: 9 a company of horses in Pharaoh's *c.*
6:12 like the *c.* of Amminadib
Is 21: 7 a *c.* of asses, and a *c.* of
22:18 there the *c.* of thy glory
31: 1 stay on horses and trust in *c.*
Hab 3: 8 and thy *c.* of salvation
Zech 6: 1 four *c.* between two mountains
Acts 8:28 sitting in his *c.* read Esaias
Rev 9: 9 sound of wings as of *c.*

CHARITY

1 Cor 8: 1 knowledge puffeth up but *c.* edifieth
13: 2 have not *c.* I am nothing
13:13 faith, hope, *c.* . . . but the greatest is *c.*
Col 3:14 above all these things put on *c.*
1 Thes 3: 6 tidings of your faith and *c.*
2 Thes 1: 3 *c.* of every one aboundeth
1 Tim 1: 5 end of commandment is *c.*
2:15 if they continue in faith and *c.*
4:12 be thou an example in *c.*
2 Tim 2:22 follow righteousness, faith, *c.*
3:10 known my doctrine, faith, *c.*
Tit 2: 2 aged men be sound in *c.*
1 Pet 4: 8 fervent *c.* among yourselves for *c.*
5:14 greet one another with a kiss of *c.*
2 Pet 1: 7 to brotherly kindness, *c.*
3 John 1: 6 borne witness of thy *c.*
Jude 1:12 spots in your feasts of *c.*
Rev 2:19 I know thy works and *c.*

CHARITABLY

Rom 14:15 now walkest thou not *c.*

CHASTE

2 Cor 11: 2 as a *c.* virgin to Christ
Tit 2: 5 young women discreet, *c.*
1 Pet 3: 2 they behold your *c.* conversation

CHASTEN (CHASTENED, CHASTENEST)

Deut 8: 5 as man *c.* his son so the Lord
2 Sam 7:14 I will *c.* him with the rod
Ps 6: 1 neither *c.* me in thy
69:10 *c.* my soul with fasting
94:12 blessed is the man whom thou *c.*
118:18 the Lord hath *c.* me sore
Prov 13:24 loveth him *c.* him betimes
19:18 *c.* thy son while there is hope
Dan 10:12 to *c.* thyself before God
1 Cor 11:32 we are *c.* of the Lord
2 Cor 6: 9 as *c.* and not killed
Heb 12: 6 whom the Lord loveth he *c.*
12:10 fathers for few days *c.* us
Rev 3:19 as many as I love, I *c.*

CHASTENING

Job 5:17 despise not thou *c.* of the Lord
Prov 3:11 despise not the *c.* of
Is 26:16 when thy *c.* was upon them
Heb 12: 5 despise not thou *c.* of the Lord
12: 7 if ye endure *c.*, God dealeth
12:11 no *c.* for present seemeth joyous

CHASTISE

Lev 26:28 will *c.* you seven times
Deut 22:18 the elders shall *c.* him
Hos 7:12 I will *c.* as their congregation
10:10 my desire that I should *c.* them
Luke 23:16 *c.* him and release him

CHASTISEMENT

Job 34:31 I have borne *c.*, I will not
Is 53: 5 *c.* of our peace was upon him
Jer 30:14 with the *c.* of a cruel one
Heb 12: 8 without *c.* then are ye bastards

CHEEK

1 Ki 22:24 smote Micaiah on the *c.*
Job 16:10 smitten me upon the *c.* reproachfully
Mic 5: 1 judge of Israel, with a rod upon the *c.*
Mat 5:39 smite thee on the right *c.*, turn
Luke 6:29 smiteth thee on the one *c.* offer

CHEER (CHEERETH)

Deut 24: 5 and shall *c.* up his wife
Judg 9:13 leave my wine, which *c.* God and man
Eccl 11: 9 let thy heart *c.* thee
Mat 9: 2 Son, be of good *c.*; thy sins be
14:27 Be of good *c.*; it is I; be
John 16:33 be of good *c.*, I have overcome
Acts 23:11 Be of good *c.*, Paul
27:25 be of good *c.*, for I believe

CHERISHETH

Eph 5:29 own flesh but nourisheth and *c.* it
1 Thes 2: 7 as a nurse *c.* her children

CHICKENS

Mat 23:37 gathereth her *c.* under her wings

CHIEF

Num 31:26 the *c.* fathers of the congregation
2 Ki 25:18 took Seraiah the *c.* priest
1 Chr 7: 3 all of them *c.* men
Job 40:19 he is the *c.* of the ways of God
Ps 78:51 the *c.* of their strength
Mat 16:21 the elders and *c.* priests and scribes
20:27 whoso will be *c.* among you
Luke 22:26 is *c.*, as he that serveth
Eph 2:20 himself being the *c.* corner stone
1 Tim 1:15 sinners, of whom I am *c.*
1 Pet 2: 6 in Sion a *c.* corner stone

CHILD

2 Sam 12:16 David besought God for a *c.*
1 Ki 3: 7 I am not but a little *c.*
3:25 divide the living *c.* in two
2 Ki 5:14 like unto the flesh of a little *c.*
Job 33:25 shall be fresher than a *c.*
Ps 131: 2 quieted as a *c.* that is weaned
Prov 20:11 even a *c.* is known by his doings
22: 6 train up a *c.* in the way he
22:15 bound in the heart of the *c.*
Eccl 4:13 better is as poor and wise *c.*
10:16 woe when thy king is a *c.*
Is 7:16 before the *c.* shall know to refuse
9: 6 for unto us a *c.* is born
11: 6 and a little *c.* shall lead them
11: 8 and the sucking *c.* shall play
65:20 for the *c.* shall die an hundred
Jer 31:20 is he a pleasant *c.*?
Hos 11: 1 when Israel was a *c.* I loved
Mat 18: 5 receive one such little *c.* in my name
Luke 2:34 this *c.* is set for the fall
9:48 shall receive this *c.* in my name
18:17 as a little *c.* shall in no wise
Gal 4: 1 as long as he is a *c.*
Rev 12: 5 a man *c.* who was to rule

CHILDBEARING

1 Tim 2:15 she shall be saved in *c.* if

CHILDISH

1 Cor 13:11 a man, I put away *c.* things

CHILDLESS

Gen 15: 2 seeing I go *c.*, and the steward
Jer 22:30 write ye this man *c.*

CHILDREN

Gen 3:16 thou shalt bring forth *c.*
18:19 he will command his *c.*
30: 1 give me *c.* or else I die
50:25 an oath of the *c.* of Israel
Ex 1: 7 *c.* of Israel were fruitful
13:15 firstborn of my *c.* I redeem
20: 5 iniquity of the fathers upon the *c.*
29:45 dwell among the *c.* of Israel
Ex 34: 7 upon the *c.* and the children's *c.*
Lev 25:45 *c.* of the strangers that do sojourn
Num 14:33 your *c.* shall wander forty years
Deut 6: 7 teach them diligently unto thy *c.*
24:16 to death for the *c.*, neither shall the *c.*
32: 5 their spot is not the spot of his *c.*
1 Ki 2: 4 thy *c.* take heed to their way
6:13 dwell among the *c.* of Israel
9:20 were not of the *c.* of Israel
2 Ki 17:31 Sepharvites burnt their *c.*
2 Chr 33: 6 cause his *c.* to pass through
Ps 17:14 they are full of *c.* and leave
69: 8 an alien to my mother's *c.*
72: 4 he shall save the *c.* of the needy
82: 6 all of you are *c.* of the Most High
89:30 If his *c.* forsake my law
103:17 righteousness unto children's *c.*
127: 4 mighty men so are *c.* of the youth
128: 3 thy *c.* like olive plants
128: 6 thou shalt see thy children's *c.*
147:13 hath blessed thy *c.* within thee
Prov 17: 6 glory of *c.* are their fathers
20: 7 his *c.* are blessed after him
31:28 her *c.* rise and call her blessed
Is 1: 2 I brought up *c.* and they rebelled
2: 6 in the *c.* of strangers
8:18 I and the *c.* whom the Lord hath
54:13 thy *c.* shall be taught of the Lord
57: 5 slaying the *c.* in the valleys
Jer 3:14 backsliding *c.*, wise to evil
7:18 *c.* gather wood, and the fathers
31:15 Rahel weeping for her *c.*
Lam 4: 4 the young *c.* ask for bread
Ezek 16:21 that thou hast slain my *c.*
Dan 5:13 of the *c.* of the captivity of Judah
Nah 3:10 her young *c.* also were dashed in pieces
Mal 4: 6 turn the hearts of fathers to the *c.*
Mat 2:18 Rachel weeping for her *c.*,
3: 9 raise up the *c.* unto Abraham
5: 9 be called the *c.* of God
5:45 *c.* of the Father in heaven
8:12 but the *c.* of the kingdom
11:19 wisdom is justified of her *c.*
21:15 the *c.* crying in the temple
23:31 the *c.* of them which killed
23:37 have gathered thy *c.* together
Luke 6:32 *c.* sitting in the marketplace
6:35 ye shall be *c.* of the Highest
11: 7 my *c.* are with me in bed
16: 8 for the *c.* of this world are in
20:34 the *c.* of this world marry
20:36 *c.* of God being the *c.* of the resurrection
John 11:52 together in one the *c.* of God
12:36 ye may be the *c.* of light
Acts 2:39 promise unto you and to your *c.*
3:25 ye are the *c.* of the prophets
Rom 8:16 we are the *c.* of God
8:17 if *c.* then heirs; heirs of God
8:21 liberty of the *c.* of God
9: 7 seed of Abraham, are they all *c.*
9: 8 *c.* of the promise are counted
9:26 they shall be called *c.* of the
1 Cor 14:20 in malice be ye *c.* in understanding
2 Cor 12:14 *c.* ought not to lay up for the
Gal 3: 7 same are the *c.* of Abraham
3:26 all the *c.* of God by
4: 3 we, when we were *c.*, were in bondage
4:28 are the *c.* of the promise
Eph 1: 5 unto the adoption of *c.* by Jesus
2: 3 by nature the *c.* of wrath
4:14 no more *c.* tossed to and fro
5: 6 upon the *c.* of disobedience
5: 8 walk as *c.* of light
6: 1 *c.*, obey your parents
6: 4 fathers provoke not your *c.*
Col 3: 6 on the *c.* of disobedience
3:20 *c.*, obey your parents
3:21 provoke not your *c.* to anger
1 Thes 5: 5 ye are all *c.* of light
1 Tim 5: 4 if any widow have *c.* or

Heb 2:14 as the c. are partakers of flesh
12: 5 speaketh unto you as unto c.
1 Pet 1:14 as obedient c.; not fashioning
1 John 3:10 c. of God are manifest, and the c.
5: 2 that we love the c. of God

CHOKE (CHOKED)

Mat 13: 7 thorns sprung up and c. them
Mark 4:19 things entering in c. the word
5:13 and were c. in the sea
Luke 8:14 and are c. with cares and riches

CHOOSE (CHOOSEST, CHOOSING, CHOSE)

Gen 13:11 Lot c. the plain of
Num 17: 5 the man's rod whom I shall c.
Deut 12: 5 place the Lord God shall c.
17:10 the Lord shall c. shall show
17:15 whom the Lord thy God shall c.
30:19 therefore c. life, that both thou
Josh 24:15 c. you this day whom ye will serve
2 Sam 24:12 three things, c. thee one of them
Neh 9: 7 Lord God didst c. Abraham
Ps 65: 4 blessed is the man whom thou c.
Prov 1:29 did not c. the fear of the Lord
Is 7:15 refuse evil and c. good
14: 1 the Lord will yet c. Israel
56: 4 c. the things that please me
Zech 1:17 I shall yet c. Jerusalem
Luke 6:13 he c. twelve, whom
Phil 1:22 what I shall c. I wot not
Heb 11:25 c. rather to suffer affliction with the

CHOSEN

Judg 10:14 unto the gods which you have c.
1 Sam 16: 8 neither hath the Lord c. this
1 Ki 8:48 city which thou hast c.
Job 36:21 iniquity c. rather than affliction
Ps 105:43 with joy and his c. with gladness
119:30 I have c. the way of truth
119: 73 I have c. his precepts
Prov 16:16 rather to be c. than silver
Is 41: 8 Jacob, whom I have c., the seed
41: 9 my servant, I have c. thee
43:20 give drink to my people, my c.
44: 1 Israel, whom I have c.
48:10 I have c. thee in the furnace of
58: 5 is it such a fast that I have c.
65:15 for a curse unto my c.
Jer 8: 3 death shall be c. rather than
33:24 families which the Lord hath c.
49:19 who is a c. man that I may
Mat 20:16 many be called, but few c.
Mark 13:20 elect's sake, whom he hath c.
Luke 10:42 Mary hath c. that good part
23:35 Christ the c. of God
John 13:18 I know whom I have c.
15:16 Ye have not c. me
Acts 9:15 for he is a c. vessel unto me
1 Cor 1:27 God hath c. the foolish
Eph 1: 4 c. us in him before the foundation
1 Pet 2: 4 c. of God, and precious
Rev 17:14 called, and c. and faithful

CHRIST

Mat 2: 4 where C. should be born
16:16 thou art the C. the Son
23: 8 one is your master, even C.,
Mark 9:41 because ye belong to C.
Luke 2:26 not die before seeing C.
4:41 the devils knew he was C.
24:26 ought not C. to have suffered
24:46 it behooved C. to suffer and rise
John 4:25 Messias cometh which is called C.
7:26 that this is the very C.
7:27 when C. cometh, no man knoweth
7:41 shall C. come out of Galilee?
7:42 C. cometh of the seed of David
11:27 I believe that thou art the C.
12:34 that C. abideth for ever
Acts 8: 5 Samaria, and preached C. unto them
Rom 5: 6 C. died for the ungodly
5: 8 while yet sinners, C. died for us
6: 8 if we be dead with C.
Rom 8: 1 them which are in C. Jesus
8: 2 law of the spirit of life in C. Jesus
8: 9 have not the Spirit of C., he is none of
8:10 if C. be not in you, the body is dead
8:17 heirs of God and joint heirs with C.
12: 5 many, one body in C.
15: 3 for C. pleased not himself; but
1 Cor 1:24 C. the power of God and
1:30 but of him are ye in C. Jesus
2: 2 save Jesus C., and him crucified
3:23 ye are C.'s, and C. is God's
5: 7 C. our passover is sacrificed
15:14 if C. be not risen, then is
15:16 if dead rise not, C. is not raised
15:18 fallen asleep in C. are perished
15:19 if in this life only we have hope in C.
2 Cor 5:17 if any man be in C.
5:19 God was in C. reconciling the world
6:16 though we have known C. after
12: 2 I knew a man in C. above fourteen years
13: 5 know ye not C. Jesus is in you?
Gal 1:22 churches which were in C.
2:20 I am crucified with C.
3:13 C. hath redeemed us from the curse
3:28 ye are all one in C. Jesus
4:19 travail till C. be formed in you
5: 6 in C. Jesus neither circumcision nor
Eph 1: 1 faithful in C. Jesus
2: 5 quickened us together with C.
2:10 created in C. Jesus unto good works
2:12 ye were without C., aliens
3:17 that C. dwell in your hearts
4:20 ye have not so learned C., if so
5:14 dead, and C. shall give thee light
5:23 wife, as C. is head of the church
6: 5 in singleness of heart, as unto C.
Phil 1:13 so that my bonds in C. are manifest in all
1:21 to live is C. and to die
1:23 desire to depart and be with C.
2: 1 if there be any consolation in C.
2:11 confess that C. Jesus is Lord
3: 3 rejoice in C. Jesus
3: 8 that I may win C.
3:12 for which I am apprehended of C. Jesus
4:13 I can do all things through C.
Col 1: 2 saints and faithful in C.
1:27 C. in you hope of glory
2: 6 received C. Jesus the Lord
2:20 if ye be dead with C. from the
3: 3 and your life is hid with C. in God
1 Thes 4:16 the dead in C. shall rise first
1 Tim 1:15 C. Jesus came into world to save
2 Tim 2: 3 as a good soldier of C. Jesus
3:12 will live godly in C. Jesus shall suffer
Heb 13: 8 C. Jesus the same yesterday, and
Rev 20: 4 reigned with C. a thousand years

CHRISTIAN (CHRISTIANS)

Acts 11:26 were called C. first at Antioch
26:28 persuadest me to be a C.

CHURCH

Mat 16:18 this rock I will build my c.
18:17 tell it unto the c.
Acts 2:47 the Lord added to the c. daily
5:11 great fear came on all the c.
8: 1 great persecution against the c.
11:26 assembled themselves with the c.
14:27 and had gathered the c. together
15: 3 brought on their way by the c.
15:22 pleased elders, with the whole c.
20:28 to feed the c. of God
1 Cor 1: 2 c. of God which is at Corinth
4:17 teach every where in the c.
10:32 nor to the c. of God
14: 4 he that prophesieth edifieth the c.
16:19 c. that is in their house,
2 Cor 1: 1 unto the c. of God
Eph 1:22 head over all things to the c.
3:10 heavenly places known by the c.
Eph 5:24 as the c. is subject unto Christ
5:25 as Christ loved the c. and gave
5:27 present to himself a glorious c.
5:32 I speak concerning Christ and the c.
Phil 3: 6 Concerning zeal, persecuting the c.
4:15 no c. communicated with me
Col 1:18 he is head of the body, the c.
1:24 for his body's sake, which is the c.
4:15 the c. which is in his house
1 Tim 3: 5 take care of the c. of God
5:16 let not the c. be charged
Heb 12:23 assembly and c. of the firstborn
3 John 1: 6 witness of thy charity before the c.
1: 9 I wrote unto the c.: but

CHURCHES

Acts 9:31 then had the c. rest throughout
15:41 and Cilicia, confirming the c.
16: 5 the c. established in faith
Rom 16:16 c. of Christ salute you
1 Cor 7:17 and so ordain I in all c.
14:33 as in all c. of the saints
14:34 women keep silence in the c.
1 Thes 2:14 became followers of the c. of God
2 Thes 1: 4 glory in you in the c. of God
Rev 1: 4 seven c. which are in Asia
2: 7 hear what the Spirit saith unto the c.
22:16 testify these things in the c.

CIRCUMCISE (CIRCUMCISED)

Gen 17:10 every male shall be c.
17:11 ye shall c. the flesh
21: 4 Abraham c. his son Isaac, being eight
Deut 30: 6 the Lord will c. thy heart
10:16 c. therefore the foreskin
Josh 5: 2 c. again the children of Israel
5: 4 the cause why Joshua did c.
Jer 4: 4 c. yourselves to the Lord
9:25 all which are c. with uncircumcised
Acts 15: 1 except the c. cannot be saved
15:24 ye must be c. and keep the law
16: 3 c. him because of the Jews
Gal 2: 3 Titus . . . was compelled to be c.
Phil 3: 5 c. the eighth day, of the stock
Col 2:11 in whom also ye are c.

CIRCUMCISION

John 7:22 Moses therefore gave unto you c.
Acts 7: 8 God gave the covenant of c.
Rom 2:25 c. verily profiteth if thou keep the
2:29 c. is that of the heart, in the spirit
3: 1 what profit is there of c.?
3:30 which shall justify the c. by faith
4: 9 cometh this blessedness on the c. only?
4:11 he received the sign of c.
15: 8 Christ was minister of the c.
1 Cor 7:19 c. is nothing, but the keeping
Gal 2: 7 as the gospel of c. was unto Peter
5: 6 neither c. availeth nor uncircumcision
Phil 3: 3 we are the c. which worship
Col 2:11 with the c. made without hands
Tit 1:10 deceivers, specially of the c.

CISTERN (CISTERNS)

2 Ki 18:31 every one the waters of his c.
Prov 5:15 waters out of thine own c.
Jer 2:13 hewed them out c., broken c.

CITY

Gen 4:17 he builded a c., and called the name
Josh 21:13 to be a c. of refuge
Neh 11: 1 to dwell in Jerusalem the holy c.
Ps 48: 2 the c. of the great King
107: 4 they found no c. to dwell in
127: 1 except the Lord keep the c.
Prov 16:32 than he that taketh a c.
Sol 3: 2 I will go about the c. in
Is 1:21 is the faithful c. become a harlot
22: 2 a tumultuous c. a joyous c.
26: 1 We have a strong c., salvation
33:20 look on Zion, c. of our solemnities
48: 2 call themselves of the holy c.

Is 62:12 sought out, a *c.* not forsaken
Jer 3:14 take you one of a *c.*, two of a
29: 7 seek the peace of the *c.*
Lam 1: 1 How doth the *c.* sit solitary
Dan 9:24 upon thy holy *c.* to finish
Amos 4: 7 to rain on one *c.* not on
Zeph 2:15 this is the rejoicing *c.*
Zech 8: 3 shall be called the *c.* of truth
Mat 4: 5 devil taketh him into the holy *c.*
5:14 *c.* on a hill cannot be hid
5:35 the *c.* of the great king
9: 1 and came into his own *c.*
27:53 resurrections and went into the holy *c.*
Luke 10: 8 whatsoever *c.* ye enter
10:12 tolerable for Sodom than for that *c.*
19:41 he beheld the *c.* and wept over it
Heb 11:10 he looked for a *c.* which
11:16 he hath prepared for them a *c.*
12:22 to the *c.* of the living God
13:14 have here no continuing *c.*
Rev 3:12 name of the *c.* of my God
11: 2 holy *c.* shall they tread
21: 2 John saw the holy *c.*
21:18 the *c.* was pure gold, like unto
21:23 *c.* had no need of the sun
22:19 and out of the holy *c.*

CITIES
Num 35:15 these six *c.* shall be refuge
Luke 19:17 have thou authority over ten *c.*
Rev 16:19 the *c.* of the nations fell

CITIZEN (CITIZENS)
Luke 15:15 joined himself to a *c.*
19:14 but his *c.* hated him
Acts 21:39 a *c.* of no mean city
Eph 2:19 fellow *c.* with the saints

CLAY
Job 10: 9 that thou hast made me as *c.*
4:19 them tat dwell in houses of *c.*
38:14 it is turned as *c.* to the seal
Is 41:25 as the potter treadeth *c.*
45: 9 shall the *c.* say to him
64: 8 we are the *c.*, thou our potter
Jer 18: 4 that he made of *c.* was marred
18: 6 the *c.* is in the potter's hands
43: 9 hide them in the *c.* in the kiln
Dan 2:33 feet part of iron, part of *c.*
John 9: 6 made *c.* of spittle and anointed
Rom 9:21 power over the *c.*

CLEAN
Gen 7: 2 of every *c.* beast thou shalt
8:20 took of every *c.* beast
Lev 10:10 unholy and between unclean and *c.*
Job 14: 4 bring a *c.* thing out of unclean
17: 9 he that hath *c.* hands shall be
25: 4 how can he be *c.* that is born
Ps 19: 9 the fear of the Lord is *c.*
22:15 my tongue *c.* to my jaws
24: 4 that hath *c.* hands and
44:25 our belly *c.* unto the earth
51:10 in me a *c.* heart, O God
73: 1 such as are of a *c.* heart
Prov 16: 2 ways of man are *c.* in his own
Is 1:16 wash you, make you *c.*; put
52:11 be ye *c.* that bear the vessels
Jer 13:27 wilt thou not be made *c.*
Ezek 22:26 between unclean and *c.*
36:25 *c.* water upon you, and ye shall be *c.*
44:23 discern between the unclean and the *c.*
Mat 8: 3 I will, be thou *c.*
23:25 make *c.* the outside of the cup
Luke 11:41 all things are *c.* to you
John 13:11 said he, Ye are not all *c.*
Rev 19: 8 fine linen, *c.* and white

CLEANNESS
Ps 18:24 according to the *c.* of my hands
Amos 4: 6 given you *c.* of teeth

CLEANSE (CLEANSED, CLEANSETH)
2 Chr 30:19 though he be not *c.* according
Ps 19:12 *c.* me from secret faults
51: 2 *c.* me from my sin
73:13 I have *c.* my heart in vain
119: 9 shall a young man *c.* his way
Jer 33: 8 I will *c.* them from all sin
Ezek 36:25 from idols will I *c.* you
36:33 *c.* you from all iniquities
Mat 10: 8 heal the sick, *c.* the lepers
11: 5 lame walk, the lepers are *c.*
Luke 17:17 were there not ten *c.*
Acts 10:15 what God hath *c.*, that call not
2 Cor 7: 1 let us *c.* ourselves from
Eph 5:26 *c.* with washing of water
Jas 4: 8 *c.* your hands, ye sinners
1 John 1: 7 blood of Jesus Christ *c.* us from all

CLEAR
Ex 34: 7 no means *c.* the guilty
Ps 51: 4 be *c.* when thou judgest
Sol 6:10 *c.* as the sun, and terrible as
Zech 14: 6 light shall not be *c.* nor dark

CLEAVE (CLEAVETH)
Gen 2:24 and shall *c.* unto his wife
Deut 4: 4 ye that did *c.* to the Lord
11:22 his ways, and to *c.* unto him
Josh 23: 8 but *c.* unto the Lord your God
Ps 137: 6 tongue *c.* to the roof of my mouth
Mat 19: 5 and shall *c.* to his wife
Mark 10: 7 mother and *c.* to his wife
Rom 12: 9 *c.* to that which is good

CLOAK
Is 59:17 and was clad with zeal as a *c.*
Mat 5:40 let him have thy *c.* also
John 15:22 have no *c.* for their sin
2 Tim 4:13 the *c.* that I left at Troas
1 Pet 2:16 liberty for a *c.* of maliciousness

CLOSET
Joel 2:16 and the bride out of her *c.*
Mat 6: 6 when thou prayest, enter thy *c.*

CLOTHE (CLOTHED)
Gen 3:21 God make coats of skins and *c.* them
Job 10:11 *c.* me with skin and flesh
Ps 35:26 let them be *c.* with shame
104: 1 *c.* with honour and majesty
109:18 he *c.* himself with cursing
132: 9 priests be *c.* with righteousness
132:18 his enemies will I *c.* with shame
Is 61:10 *c.* with garments of salvation
Ezek 16:10 I *c.* thee with broidered
Zeph 1: 8 *c.* with strange apparel
Zech 3: 3 Joshua was *c.* with filthy garments
Mat 6:30 God so *c.* the grass of the
11: 8 a man *c.* in soft raiment
25:36 naked, and ye *c.* me: I was
2 Cor 5: 2 desiring to be *c.* upon with
5: 4 not unclothed, but *c.* upon
1 Pet 5: 5 be *c.* with humility: for
Rev 3: 5 be *c.* with white raiment
12: 1 a woman *c.* with the sun
19:13 *c.* in vesture dipped in blood
19:14 *c.* in fine linen, clean and white

CLOTHING
Job 22: 6 stripped naked of their *c.*
Ps 45:13 her *c.* is of wrought gold
Prov 31:25 strength and honour are her *c.*
Is 59:17 garment of vengeance for *c.*
Mat 7:15 which come to you in sheep's *c.*
Mark 12:38 love to go in long *c.*
Acts 10:30 stood before me in bright *c.*
Jas 2: 3 to him that weareth the gay *c.*

CLOUD (CLOUDS)
Gen 9:13 set my bow in the *c.*
Ex 14:20 it was a *c.* and darkness to them
19: 9 I come unto thee in a thick *c.*
Judg 5: 4 the *c.* also dropped water
2 Sam 23: 4 even a morning without *c.*
Ps 36: 5 faithfulness reacheth to the *c.*
57:10 and thy truth unto the *c.*
104: 3 who maketh *c.* his chariot
Eccl 11: 4 regardeth the *c.* shall not reap
Is 44:22 blotted out as a thick *c.*
Mat 24:30 coming in the *c.* of heaven
Mark 14:62 coming in the *c.* of heaven
1 Cor 10: 1 our fathers were under the *c.*
1 Thes 4:17 with them in the *c.*, to meet
Heb 12: 1 so great a *c.* of witnesses
2 Pet 2:17 *c.* that are carried with a tempest
Jude 1:12 *c.* without water, carried about
Rev 1: 7 he cometh with the *c.*
11:12 ascended up to heaven in a *c.*

COAL (COALS)
2 Sam 14: 7 shall quench my *c.* which
Job 41:21 his breath kindleth *c.*
Ps 18: 8 *c.* were kindled by it
140:10 let burning *c.* fall upon them
Prov 6:28 can one go upon hot *c.*
25:22 heap *c.* of fire on his head
26:21 as *c.* are to burning *c.*
Sol 8: 6 thereof are *c.* of fire
Is 6: 6 a live *c.* in his hands
47:14 shall not be a *c.* to warm
Lam 4: 8 visage is blacker than *c.*
John 18:18 who had made a fire of *c.*
21: 9 they saw a fire of *c.* there
Rom 12:20 heap *c.* of fire on his head

COAT (COATS)
Gen 37: 3 made him a *c.* of many colors
Ex 28: 4 and a broidered *c.*, a mitre
Sol 5: 3 put off my *c.*; how shall I
John 19:23 the *c.* was without seam
21: 7 Peter girt his fisher's *c.*

COLD
Gen 3:21 God make *c.* of skin and clothe
8:22 and *c.* and heat, and summer and
Job 24: 7 have no covering in the *c.*
Mat 10:10 neither two *c.*, neither shoes
24:12 the love of many shall wax *c.*
Luke 3:11 he that hath two *c.* let him
Acts 9:39 *c.* and garments which Dorcas made
Rev 3:15 thou art neither *c.* nor hot

COLLECTION
1 Cor 16: 1 the *c.* for the saints

COME
Gen 49: 6 my soul, *c.* not thou into
Ex 20:24 where I record my name, I will *c.*
1 Sam 17:45 I *c.* to thee in the name of
1 Chr 29:14 all things *c.* of thee
Job 22:21 good shall *c.* unto thee
38:11 hitherto shalt thou *c.*, but no
Ps 40: 7 lo I *c.*: in the volume of the
65: 2 to thee shall all flesh *c.*
Eccl 9: 2 all things *c.* alike to all
Sol 4:16 north wind; and *c.*, thou south
Is 1:18 *c.* let us reason together
35: 4 your God will *c.* and save you
55: 1 that thirsteth *c.* ye to the waters
55: 3 incline your ear, and *c.* unto me
Jer 3:22 we *c.* to thee for thou art Lord
Hos 6: 1 *C.* let us return unto the Lord
Mic 6: 6 wherewith shall I *c.* before
Hab 2: 3 it will surely *c.* it will not tarry
Mal 3: 1 Lord shall suddenly *c.* to his temple
4: 6 lest I *c.* and smite the earth
Mat 8:11 many shall *c.* from east and west
11: 3 art thou he that should *c.* or look we
11:28 *c.* unto me all ye that labour and
16:24 if any man will *c.* after me
17:10 say scribes Elias must first *c.*
22: 4 all things ready, *c.* to marriage
Luke 7: 8 I say *c.* and he cometh
14:20 married a wife, I cannot *c.*
John 1:39 saith unto them *c.* and see
4:29 *C.* see a man, which told me all
5:40 ye will not *c.* to me
6:44 no man can *c.* to me, except

John 7:37 if any man thirst, let him *c.*
14:18 leave you comfortless, I will *c.* to
Acts 1:11 this Jesus shall so *c.* as
16: 9 *C.* over into Macedonia
1 Cor 11:26 Lord's death till he *c.*
2 Cor 6:17 *c.* out from among them
1 Tim 4: 8 promise of the life to *c.*
Heb 4:16 *c.* boldly unto the throne of
7:25 save them that *c.* to God by him
10:37 he that shall *c.* will *c.*
Rev 6: 1 four beasts, saying *c.* and see
17: 1 saying unto me *c.* hither
18: 4 *c.* out of her, my people
21: 9 *C.* hither, I will show thee
22:17 the Spirit and the bride say, *c.*

COMETH

Ps 118:26 *c.* in the name of the Lord
Is 63: 1 who is this that *c.* from Edom
Mat 3:11 he that *c.* after me is
Luke 6:47 whoso *c.*, heareth, doeth, is
John 3:31 he that *c.* from above
6:35 *c.* to me shall never hunger
6:37 *c.* to me, I will in no wise cast out
6:45 hath learned of the Father *c.* unto me
Heb 11: 6 that *c.* to God must believe
Jas 1:17 gift *c.* down from the Father

COMING

Ps 19: 5 as a bridegroom *c.* out of his
121: 8 the Lord shall preserve thy *c.* in
Mal 3: 2 who may abide the day of his *c.*
Mat 24: 3 what is the sign of thy *c.*
John 1:27 *c.* after me is preferred before
1 Cor 1: 7 waiting for the *c.* of our
15:23 that are Christ's at his *c.*
1 Thes 2:19 presence of Jesus Christ at his *c.*
3:13 at the *c.* of our Lord
5:23 unto the *c.* of our Lord Jesus
2 Thes 2: 1 by the *c.* of our Lord
Jas 5: 8 for the *c.* of the Lord
1 Pet 2: 4 to whom *c.* as unto a living stone
2 Pet 1:16 power and *c.* of the Lord
3:12 hasting unto the *c.* of the day of God

COMELY

1 Sam 16:18 and a *c.* person, and the Lord
Job 41:12 his power, nor his *c.* proportion
Ps 33: 1 praise is *c.* for the upright
Prov 30:29 yea, four are *c.* in going
Sol 1: 5 I am black but *c.*
6: 4 *c.* as Jerusalem, terrible as an
Jer 6: 2 Zion to a *c.* and delicate woman
1 Cor 12:24 our *c.* parts have no need

COMELINESS

Is 53: 2 he hath no form nor *c.*
Ezek 16:14 it was perfect through my *c.*

COMFORT (COMFORTED)

Gen 5:29 this same shall *c.* us concerning
24:67 Isaac was *c.* after his mother's
37:35 but he refused to be *c.*
Job 7:13 my bed shall *c.* me
Ps 23: 4 thy rod and thy staff they *c.* me
119:50 is my *c.* in my affliction
Is 40: 1 *c.* ye *c.* ye my people
49:13 Lord hath *c.* his people
51: 3 for the Lord shall *c.* Zion
51:12 I, even I am he that *c.*
54:11 tossed with tempest, and not *c.*
61: 2 to *c.* all that mourn
Jer 31:13 I will *c.* and make them rejoice
31:15 Rahel weeping . . . refused to be *c.*
Lam 1: 2 she hath none to *c.* her
Mat 9:22 be of good *c.*, thy faith hath
Luke 16:25 he is *c.*, thou art tormented
Acts 9:31 walking in the *c.* of the Holy Ghost
Rom 1:12 I may be *c.* together with you
1 Cor 14: 3 edification and exhortation and *c.*
14:31 all prophesy one by one all be *c.*
2 Cor 1: 4 we may be able to *c.* them
7:13 we were *c.* in your comfort
Phil 2: 1 if any *c.* of love, if any
Col 4:11 which have been a *c.* unto me
1 Thes 3: 7 *c.* over you by your faith
4:18 *c.* one another with these
5:11 *c.* selves together, and edify one
5:14 *c.* the feeble minded, support the weak
2 Thes 2:17 Lord Jesus *c.* your hearts and

COMFORTABLY

2 Sam 19: 7 speak *c.* unto thy servants
2 Chr 30:22 spake *c.* unto all the Levites
32: 6 spake *c.* to them, saying
Is 40: 2 speak ye *c.* to Jerusalem
Hos 2:14 wilderness and speak *c.* unto her

COMFORTERS

Job 16: 2 miserable *c.* are ye all
Ps 69:20 and for *c.*, but I found none

COMFORTLESS

John 14:18 I will not leave you *c.*

COMMAND (COMMANDETH, COMMANDING)

Gen 18:19 Abraham will *c.* his children
Deut 28: 8 Lord shall *c.* thy blessing upon thee
Ps 42: 8 Lord will *c.* his lovingkindness
Is 45:11 work of my hands, *c.* me
Lam 3:37 when the Lord *c.* it not
Mat 4: 3 *c.* these stones be made bread
John 15:14 if ye do whatsoever I *c.*
Acts 17:30 now *c.* all men to repent
1 Cor 7:10 unto the married I *c.*
1 Tim 4: 3 *c.* to abstain from meats, which God
4:11 these things I *c.* and teach

COMMANDED

Ps 111: 9 he hath *c.* his covenant for ever
119: 4 hast *c.* us to keep thy precepts
133: 3 Lord *c.* the blessing, even life
148: 5 Lord *c.* and they were created
Mat 28:20 whatsoever I have *c.* you
2 Cor 4: 6 God who *c.* the light to
Heb 12:20 not endure that which was *c.*

COMMANDMENT

Num 23:20 I have received *c.* to bless
Ps 119:96 thy *c.* is exceeding broad
Prov 6:23 the *c.* is a lamp; and law is light
8:29 waters should not pass his *c.*
Hos 5:11 willingly walked after the *c.*
Mat 22:38 is the first and great *c.*
Mark 7: 9 reject the *c.* of God
John 10:18 this *c.* I received of my Father
12:50 his *c.* is life everlasting
13:34 a new *c.* give I unto you
15:12 this is my *c.* that ye love one
Rom 7: 8 sin taking occasion by the *c.*
7: 9 when the *c.* came, sin revived
1 Tim 1: 5 end of the *c.* is charity
Heb 7:16 not after the law of a carnal *c.*
2 Pet 2:21 turn from the holy *c.*
1 John 2: 7 an old *c.* which ye had
3:23 this is his *c.* that we believe

COMMANDMENTS

Ex 34:28 words of the covenant the ten *c.*
Ps 111: 7 all his *c.* are sure
112: 1 delighteth greatly in his *c.*
119: 6 I have respect unto all thy *c.*
119:19 hide not thy *c.* from me
119:21 which do err from thy *c.*
119:35 make me to go in the path of thy *c.*
119:48 thy *c.* which I have loved
119:66 I have believed thy *c.*
119:73 give understanding to learn thy *c.*
119:127 I love thy *c.* above gold
119:131 I longed for thy *c.*
119:172 all thy *c.* are righteousness
Mat 15: 9 for doctrines the *c.* of men
22:40 on these two *c.* hang all the law
Mark 10:19 thou knowest the *c.*, do not commit
Luke 1: 6 walking in all the *c.* and ordinances
Col 2:22 after the *c.* and doctrines of men
1 John 3:24 he that keepeth his *c.* dwelleth
2 John 1: 6 that we walk after his *c.*

COMMEND (COMMENDED, COMMENDETH)

Gen 12:15 and *c.* her before pharaoh
Luke 23:46 to thy hands I *c.* my spirit
Acts 14:23 *c.* them to the Lord on whom
Rom 3: 5 if our unrighteousness *c.* the righteousness
5: 8 God *c.* his love toward us
16: 1 I *c.* unto you Phebe our sister
1 Cor 8: 8 meat *c.* us not to God
2 Cor 5:12 we *c.* not ourselves again unto
10:12 ourselves with some that *c.* themselves
10:18 not he that *c.* self is approved

COMMENDATION

2 Cor 3: 1 as some others epistles of *c.*

COMMIT (COMMITTED, COMMITTETH)

Ex 20:14 thou shalt not *c.* adultery
Job 5: 8 to God would I *c.* my cause
Ps 10:14 the poor *c.* himself unto thee
31: 5 to thy hand I *c.* my spirit
37: 5 *c.* thy way unto the Lord
Prov 16: 3 *c.* thy works unto the Lord
Mat 5:27 thou shalt not *c.* adultery
19:18 thou shalt not *c.* adultery
Luke 12:48 to whom men have *c.* much
16:11 who will *c.* to your trust
John 2:24 did not *c.* himself unto them
5:22 *c.* all judgment to the Son
8:34 who *c.* sin is servant of sin
Rom 1:32 *c.* such things are worthy of death
1 Cor 9:17 dispensation of the gospel is *c.* unto
Gal 2: 7 uncircumcision was *c.* unto me
1 Tim 1:11 God's which was *c.* to my trust
1:18 this charge I *c.* unto thee
2 Tim 1:12 which I have *c.* unto him against
1 Pet 2:23 *c.* himself to him that judgeth
4:19 *c.* the keeping of their souls
1 John 3: 8 who *c.* sin is of the devil
3: 9 born of God doth not *c.* sin
Jude 1:15 which they have ungodly *c.*

COMMON

Lev 4:27 one of the *c.* people sin through
Num 16:29 the *c.* death of all men
Jer 31: 5 and shall eat them as *c.* things
Ezek 23:42 men of the *c.* sort were brought
Mark 12:37 the *c.* people heard him gladly
Acts 2:44 together and had all things *c.*
10:15 God hath cleansed, that call not *c.*
1 Cor 10:13 such as is *c.* to man
Jude 1: 3 write unto you of the *c.* salvation

COMMONLY

Mat 28:15 this saying is *c.* reported

COMMONWEALTH

Eph 2:12 from the *c.* of Israel

COMMUNE (COMMUNED)

Ex 25:22 I will *c.* with thee from above
Ps 4: 4 *c.* with your own heart
Luke 6:11 they *c.* one with another

COMMUNICATE (COMMUNICATED)

Gal 2: 2 *c.* unto them that gospel which
6: 6 taught in the word *c.* unto him
Phil 4:14 ye did *c.* with my affliction
4:15 no church *c.* with me in
1 Tim 6:18 ready to distribute, willing to *c.*
Heb 13:16 do good and to *c.* forget not

COMMUNICATION (COMMUNICATIONS)

Luke 24:17 what manner of *c.* are these
1 Cor 15:33 evil *c.* corrupt good manners
Eph 4:29 let no corrupt *c.* proceed
Col 3: 8 filthy *c.* out of your mouth

COMMUNION
1 Cor 10:16 is it not the *c.* of the blood of
2 Cor 6:14 what *c.* hath light with darkness?
13:14 *c.* of the Holy Ghost be with you

COMPANY
Gen 32:21 lodged that night in the *c.*
Ps 55:14 to the house of God in *c.*
Prov 29: 3 keepeth *c.* with harlots
Sol 6:13 as it were the *c.* of two armies
Acts 6: 7 a great *c.* of the priests
Rom 15:24 first filled with your *c.*
1 Cor 5:11 not to keep *c.*, if any man
2 Thes 3:14 have no *c.* with him, that he may
Heb 12:22 an innumerable *c.* of angels

COMPANION (COMPANIONS)
Ps 119:63 I am a *c.* of all them that
45:14 the virgins, her *c.* that follow
122: 8 for my brethren and *c.* sakes
Prov 13:20 *c.* of fools shall be destroyed
Is 1:23 are rebellious and *c.* of thieves
Mal 2:14 thy *c.* and thy wife of the covenant
Phil 2:25 Epaphroditus my *c.* in labour
Rev 1: 9 your brother and *c.* in tribulation

COMPARE (COMPARED, COMPARING)
Ps 89: 6 who in heaven can be *c.*
Prov 3:15 desire are not to be *c.* unto her
Sol 1: 9 *c.* thee, O my love to a company
Is 40:18 what likeness will ye *c.* unto him
46: 5 *c.* me, that we may be like
Rom 8:18 not worthy to be *c.* with the glory
1 Cor 2:13 *c.* spiritual things with spiritual
2 Cor 10:12 *c.* ourselves with some that commend

COMPASS (COMPASSED, COMPASSEST, COMPASSETH)
Ps 5:12 with favour *c.* him as with
18: 4 the sorrows of death *c.* me
26: 6 innocency: so will I *c.* thy altar
32:10 mercy shall *c.* him about
73: 6 pride *c.* them about as a chain
116: 3 sorrows of death *c.* me
118:10 all nations *c.* me about
139: 3 thou *c.* my path and my lying
Is 50:11 *c.* yourselves with sparks
Jer 31:22 a woman shall *c.* a man
Hos 11:12 Ephraim *c.* me with lies
Jonah 2: 3 and the floods *c.* me about
Hab 1: 4 wicked doth *c.* the righteous
Mat 23:15 ye *c.* sea and land to

COMPASSION (COMPASSIONS)
Ex 2: 6 babe wept. And she had *c.*
Deut 30: 3 Lord turn captivity and have *c.*
1 Ki 8:50 give them *c.* before them who
Ps 78:38 being full of *c.* forgave their
111: 4 Lord is gracious and full of *c.*
145: 8 and full of *c.*
Jer 12:15 return and have *c.* on them
Lam 3:22 consumed because his *c.* fail not
3:32 cause grief, yet will he have *c.*
Mic 7:19 he will have *c.* on us
Zech 7: 9 and show mercy and *c.* every man
Mat 9:36 he was moved with *c.* on them
14:14 was moved with *c.* toward them
15:32 I have *c.* on the multitude
18:27 servant was moved with *c.*
20:34 So Jesus had *c.* on them
Mark 1:41 Jesus, moved with *c.* put forth
5:19 friends, tell how the Lord had *c.* on
9:22 canst do any thing have *c.* on us
Luke 7:13 Lord had *c.* and said, Weep not
15:20 off, his father saw him, and had *c.*
Rom 9:15 will have *c.* on whom I will have *c.*
Heb 5: 2 who can have *c.* on the ignorant
1 Pet 3: 8 having *c.* one of another
1 John 3:17 shutteth up his bowels of *c.*
Jude 1:22 And of some have *c.*, making a

COMPEL (COMPELLED, COMPELLEST)
2 Chr 21:11 fornication and *c.* Judah thereto
Mat 5:41 shall *c.* thee to go a mile
Mark 15:21 they *c.* one Simon a Cyrenian
Luke 14:23 and *c.* them to come in
Acts 26:11 I *c.* them to blaspheme
2 Cor 12:11 I am a fool ye *c.* me
Gal 2: 3 not *c.* to be circumcised
2:14 *c.* Gentiles to live as Jews

COMPREHEND (COMPREHENDED)
Job 37: 5 doeth he which we cannot *c.*
John 1: 5 and the darkness *c.* it not
Rom 13: 9 it is briefly *c.* in this saying
Eph 3:18 be able to *c.* with all saints

CONCEAL (CONCEALETH, CONCEALED)
Gen 37:26 slay our brother and *c.* his blood
Job 6:10 not *c.* words of the Holy One
27:11 the Almighty will I not *c.*
Ps 40:10 not *c.* thy lovingkindness and thy
Prov 12:23 a prudent man *c.* knowledge

CONCEIT (CONCEITS)
Prov 18:11 and as an high wall in his own *c.*
26: 5 lest he be wise in his own *c.*
28:11 rich man is wise in his own *c.*
Rom 11:25 should be wise in your own *c.*

CONCEIVE (CONCEIVED)
Gen 30:38 should *c.* when they came to drink
Num 11:12 have I *c.* all this people?
Job 3: 3 there is a man child *c.*
15:35 they *c.* mischief, and bring forth
Ps 7:14 hath *c.* mischief, and brought forth
51: 5 in sin did my mother *c.* me
Is 59: 4 they *c.* mischief, and bring forth
7:14 a virgin shall *c.* and bear a son
Jer 49:30 *c.* a purpose against you
Mat 1:20 *c.* in her is of the Holy Ghost
Luke 1:31 thou shalt *c.* in thy womb
1:36 Elizabeth, she hath also *c.* a son
2:21 so named before he was *c.*
Acts 5: 4 why hast thou *c.* in thy heart
Heb 11:11 Sara also received strength to *c.*
Jas 1:15 when lust hath *c.* it bringeth

CONCORD
2 Cor 6:15 what *c.* hath Christ with Belial

CONCUBINE (CONCUBINES)
Judg 19: 1 a *c.* out of Bethlehem-Judah
2 Sam 16:21 go in unto thy father's *c.*
1 Ki 11: 3 and three hundred *c.*: and his wives
1 Chr 1:32 Keturah, Abraham's *c.*: she bare
Dan 5: 2 and his *c.* might drink therein

CONCUPISCENCE
Rom 7: 8 in me all manner of *c.*
Col 3: 5 affection, evil *c.*, and covetousness
1 Thes 4: 5 not in the lust of *c.*, even

CONDEMN (CONDEMNED, CONDEMNETH)
2 Chr 36: 3 *c.* the land in a hundred talents
Job 9:20 my own mouth shall *c.* me
10: 2 I will say to God, do not *c.* me
Ps 37:33 nor *c.* him when judged
94:21 righteous and *c.* the innocent blood
Is 50: 9 Lord will help me, who shall *c.*?
Prov 17:15 he that *c.* the just, even they
Mat 12:37 by thy words thou shalt be *c.*
12:41 this generation and shall *c.* it
Luke 6:37 *c.* not and ye shall not be condemned
John 3:17 into the world to *c.* the world
8:11 neither do I *c.* thee, go and sin
Rom 8: 3 for sin, *c.* sin in the flesh
8:34 who is he that *c.*? It is Christ
14:22 Happy is he that *c.* not himself
1 Cor 11:32 we should not be *c.* with the world
Tit 2: 8 sound speech cannot be *c.*

CONDEMNATION
Luke 23:40 seeing thou art in the same *c.*
John 3:19 this is the *c.*, that light is
5:24 shall not come into *c.* but is
Rom 5:16 judgment by one to *c.*, but free
8: 1 no *c.* to them which are in
2 Cor 3: 9 the ministration of *c.* be glory
1 Tim 3: 6 fall into *c.* of the devil
Jas 3: 1 we shall receive the greater *c.*
5:12 swear not, lest ye fall into *c.*
Jude 1: 4 of old ordained to this *c.*

CONFESS (CONFESSED, CONFESSETH, CONFESSING)
Lev 5: 5 he shall *c.* that he hath
26:40 if they *c.* their iniquity
1 Ki 8:35 and *c.* thy name, and turn from
Neh 1: 6 *c.* the sins of the children
Ps 32: 5 I will *c.* my transgressions unto
Prov 28:13 whoso *c.* and forsaketh them shall
Dan 9:20 *c.* my sin and the sin of my
Mat 3: 6 baptized in the Jordan *c.* their sins
10:32 shall *c.* me before men
Luke 12: 8 him will the Son of Man also *c.*
Rom 10: 9 *c.* with thy mouth the Lord Jesus;
Heb 11:13 *c.* that they were strangers
Jas 5:16 *c.* your faults one to another
1 John 1: 9 if we *c.* our sins, he is faithful
4:15 *c.* Jesus is the Son of God
2 John 1: 7 *c.* not that Jesus Christ is come

CONFESSION
Josh 7:19 make *c.* unto him; and tell me
2 Chr 30:22 making *c.* to the Lord God
Ezra 10:11 make *c.* unto the Lord God of
Dan 9: 4 made my *c.* and said, O Lord
Rom 10:10 mouth *c.* is made unto salvation
1 Tim 6:13 Pontius Pilate witnessed a good *c.*

CONFIDENCE (CONFIDENCES)
Ps 65: 5 *c.* of all the ends of the earth
118: 8 than to put *c.* in man
Prov 3:26 the Lord shall be thy *c.*
Jer 2:37 the Lord hath rejected thy *c.*
48:13 Israel ashamed of Beth-el, their *c.*
Ezek 29:16 no more the *c.* of Israel
Mic 7: 5 put ye not *c.* in a guide,
Eph 3:12 in whom we have access with *c.*
Phil 3: 3 we have no *c.* in the flesh
Heb 3: 6 if we hold fast the *c.*
1 John 3:21 then have we *c.* toward God
2:28 we may have *c.*, and not

CONFIRM (CONFIRMED, CONFIRMING)
Is 35: 3 and *c.* the feeble knees
44:26 that *c.* the word of his servant
Dan 9:27 he shall *c.* the covenant
Mark 16:20 and *c.* the word with the signs
Rom 15: 8 to *c.* the promises made unto
1 Cor 1: 8 shall also *c.* you unto the end
2 Cor 2: 8 *c.* your love toward him
Heb 6:17 of his counsel *c.* it by an oath

CONFORMED
Rom 8:29 predestined to be *c.* to the image
12: 2 be not *c.* to this world

CONFOUND (CONFOUNDED)
Gen 11: 7 and there *c.* their language
Ps 97: 7 *c.* be all they that serve graven
Jer 1:17 lest I *c.* thee before them
17:18 but let not me be *c.*: let them
Ezek 16:52 be thou *c.* also and bear thy shame
Mic 3: 7 and the diviners *c.*: yea, they
7:16 nations shall see and be *c.*
Acts 2: 6 multitude came together and were *c.*
9:22 *c.* the Jews which dwelt at
1 Cor 1:27 foolish things of the world to *c.*
1 Pet 2: 6 believeth shall not be *c.*

CONFUSION
Ezra 9: 7 to a spoil and to *c.* of face
Ps 44:15 my *c.* is continually before

Ps 71: 1 let me never be put to *c.*
Is 24:10 the city of *c.* is broken
1 Cor 14:33 God is not the author of *c.*

CONGREGATION
Ex 16: 2 the whole *c.* of the children
16:22 the rulers of the *c.* came
27:21 tabernacle of the *c.* without the
40: 2 tabernacle of the tent of the *c.*
Lev 4:15 elders of the *c.* shall lay their hands
Num 4:34 chief of the *c.* numbered
14:27 I bear with this evil *c.*
16: 2 famous in the *c.*, men of renown
31:26 chief fathers of the *c.*
Josh 9:15 princes of the *c.* sware
22:30 princes of the *c.* and heads
Judg 21:13 whole *c.* sent some to speak
21:16 elders of the *c.* said
Neh 13: 1 into the *c.* of God forever
Ps 22:25 be of thee in the great *c.*
Is 14:13 the mount of the *c.* in the sides
Lam 1:10 heathen not enter the *c.*,
Mic 2: 5 cast a cord by lot in the *c.*

CONQUER (CONQUERING)
Rev 6: 2 he went forth *c.* and to *c.*

CONQUERORS
Rom 8:37 we are more than *c.* through him

CONSCIENCE
John 8: 9 convicted by their own *c.*
Acts 23: 1 in all good *c.* before God
24:16 a *c.* void of offence
Rom 2:15 their *c.* also bearing witness
9: 1 my *c.* also bearing me witness
13: 5 also for *c.* sake
1 Cor 8: 7 some with *c.* of the idol
10:28 and for *c.* sake
2 Cor 1:12 testimony of our *c.*
1 Tim 3: 9 of faith in a pure *c.*
4: 2 having their *c.* seared with hot
2 Tim 1: 3 my forefathers with pure *c.*
Tit 1:15 their mind and *c.* is defiled
Heb 9:14 purge *c.* from dead works
10: 2 *c.* of sins
13:18 we have a good *c.*
1 Pet 3:21 answer of a good *c.* toward God

CONSENT (CONSENTING)
Gen 34:15 we will *c.* unto you
Prov 1:10 entice thee, *c.* thou not
Hos 6: 9 murder in the way by *c.*
Luke 14:18 all with one *c.* began
Acts 8: 1 was *c.* unto his death
22:20 and *c.* unto his death
Rom 7:16 I *c.* unto the law
1 Tim 6: 3 and *c.* not to wholesome

CONSIDER (CONSIDERED, CONSIDEREST)
Deut 4:39 *c.* it in thy heart
32:29 would *c.* their latter end
1 Sam 12:24 *c.* how great things he
Job 1: 8 hast thou *c.* my servant Job
Ps 8: 3 when I *c.* thy heavens
31: 7 thou hast *c.* my trouble
41: 1 blessed is he that *c.* the poor
77: 5 have *c.* days of old, the years
Eccl 7:13 *c.* the work of God
Is 1: 3 my people doth not *c.*
5:12 neither *c.* operation of his hands
Hag 1: 5 saith the Lord, *c.* your ways
Mat 6:28 *c.* the lilies of the field
7: 3 *c.* not the beam
Mark 6:52 *c.* not the miracle of the loaves
Rom 4:19 *c.* not his own body dead
2 Tim 2: 7 *c.* what I say, and Lord give
Heb 3: 1 *c.* the Apostle and the High Priest
10:24 *c.* one another to provoke to
12: 3 *c.* him that endured such

CONSOLATION (CONSOLATIONS)
Job 15:11 are the *c.* of God small
Is 66:11 with the breasts of her *c.*
Luke 2:25 waiting for the *c.* of Israel
6:24 woe are rich, have received your *c.*
Acts 4:36 being interpreted the son of *c.*
Rom 15: 5 God of *c.* grant you to
2 Cor 1: 5 our *c.* aboundeth by Christ
Phil 2: 1 if therefore any *c.* in Christ
Heb 6:18 might have a strong *c.*

CONSTRAIN (CONSTRAINED)
Acts 16:15 abide there and she *c.* us
2 Cor 5:14 for the love of Christ *c.*
Gal 6:12 they *c.* you to be circumcised

CONSTRAINT
1 Pet 5: 2 not by *c.* but willingly

CONSUME (CONSUMED)
Ex 3: 2 bush was not *c.*
33: 3 lest I *c.* thee in the way
Deut 5:25 this great fire will *c.* us
Ps 37:20 they shall *c.*; into smoke
78:33 their days did he *c.* in vanity
90: 7 we are *c.* by thine anger
119:139 my zeal hath *c.* me, because
Prov 5:11 thy flesh and body are *c.*
Lam 3:22 of the Lord's mercies not *c.*
Ezek 4:17 *c.* for the iniquity
Gal 5:15 not *c.* one of another
2 Thes 2: 8 Lord shall *c.* with the spirit of
Jas 4: 3 *c.* it upon your lusts

CONSUMING
Deut 4:24 thy God is a *c.* fire
Heb 12:29 our God is a *c.* fire

CONTAIN (CONTAINED, CONTAINING)
1 Ki 8:27 heaven of heavens cannot *c.*
John 2: 6 *c.* two or three firkins
21:25 itself could not *c.* the books
Rom 2:14 the things *c.* in the law
1 Cor 7: 9 if they cannot *c.*, let them marry

CONTEMN
Ps 10:13 doth the wicked *c.* God
Ezek 21:13 if sword *c.* the rod

CONTEMNED
Ps 15: 4 a vile person is *c.*

CONTEMPT
Ps 123: 3 we are filled with *c.*
Dan 12: 2 shame and everlasting *c.*

CONTEMPTIBLE
Mal 1: 7 table of the Lord *c.*
2: 9 have I made you *c.* before all
2 Cor 10:10 weak, his speech *c.*

CONTEND (CONTENDETH)
Deut 2: 9 neither *c.* with them in battle
Job 40: 2 he that *c.* with the Almighty
Is 49:25 I will *c.* with them that *c.*
50: 8 who will *c.* with me
57:16 I will not *c.* for ever
Jer 12: 5 then how canst thou *c.* with horses?
Amos 7: 4 the Lord God called to *c.* by fire
Jude 1: 3 earnestly *c.* for the faith

CONTENTION (CONTENTIONS)
Prov 13:10 only by pride cometh before *c.*
17:14 water, leave off *c.* before it be
18: 6 A fool's lips enter into *c.* and
22:10 out the scorner, and *c.* shall go out
Jer 15:10 borne me a man of *c.* to
Hab 1: 3 raise up strife and *c.*
Acts 15:39 and the *c.* was so sharp between them
Phil 1:16 the one preach Christ of *c.*
1 Thes 2: 2 gospel of God with much *c.*

CONTENTIOUS
Prov 18:18 lot causeth *c.* to cease
19:13 and the *c.* of a wife are a
21:19 than with a *c.* and an angry woman
26:21 so is a *c.* man to kindle
27:15 rainy day and a *c.* woman are alike
Rom 2: 8 them that are *c.*, and do not obey
1 Cor 1:11 there are *c.* among you
11:16 but if any man seem to be *c.*
Tit 3: 9 and *c.* and strivings about the law

CONTENT
Josh 7: 7 would to God we had been *c.*
Prov 6:35 neither will he rest *c.*
Luke 3:14 be *c.* with your wages
Phil 4:11 therewith to be *c.*
1 Tim 6: 8 food and raiment let us be *c.*
Heb 13: 5 be *c.* with such things

CONTENTMENT
1 Tim 6: 6 but godliness with *c.* is great gain

CONTINUAL (CONTINUALLY)
Gen 6: 5 heart was only evil *c.*
Ex 28:30 upon his heart before the Lord *c.*
29:42 there shall be a *c.* burnt offering
Ps 34: 1 his praise *c.* in my mouth
52: 1 goodness of God endureth *c.*
71: 3 habitation whereto I may *c.* resort
71:14 I will hope *c.*, and will yet
73:23 I am *c.* with thee
Prov 6:21 bind *c.* upon thine heart
Is 58:11 the Lord shall guide thee *c.*
Hos 12: 6 turn and wait on thy God *c.*
Acts 6: 4 give ourselves *c.* to prayer
Rom 9: 2 great heaviness and *c.* sorrow in my heart
Heb 13:15 sacrifice of praise to God *c.*

CONTINUANCE
Ps 139:16 which in *c.* were fashioned
Rom 2: 7 to them who by patient *c.* in well doing

CONTINUE
1 Sam 12:14 *c.* following the Lord your God
Ps 36:10 O *c.* thy lovingkindness unto
102:28 children of thy servants shall *c.*
119:91 *c.* according to thine ordinances
Mat 15:32 because they *c.* with me
John 8:31 *c.* in my word, then are ye my disciples
15: 9 *c.* ye in my love
Acts 13:43 to *c.* in the grace of God
14:22 exhorting them to *c.* in the faith
26:22 I *c.* unto this day, witnessing
Rom 6: 1 shall we *c.* in sin that grace
Col 1:23 if ye *c.* in faith grounded
4: 2 *c.* in prayer, and watch
1 Tim 2:15 if they *c.* in faith and charity
4:16 doctrine; *c.* in them: for
2 Tim 3:14 *c.* thou in things learned
Heb 13: 1 let brotherly love *c.*
Rev 13: 5 to *c.* forty-two months

CONTINUED (CONTINUETH, CONTINUING)
Neh 5:16 I *c.* in the work of this wall
Jer 30:23 with fury, a *c.* whirlwind
Dan 1:21 Daniel *c.* even unto the first year
Luke 6:12 *c.* all night in prayer
22:28 *c.* with me in my temptations
Acts 1:14 *c.* with one accord in prayer
2:42 *c.* stedfastly in the apostles' doctrine
2:46 *c.* daily with one accord
20: 7 *c.* his speech till midnight
Rom 12:12 patient in tribulation, *c.* instant in prayer
Gal 3:10 that *c.* not in all things
1 Tim 5: 5 *c.* in supplication and prayer
Heb 7:24 this man, because he *c.* ever
8: 9 because they *c.* not in my covenant
13:14 for here have we no *c.* city
Jas 1:25 law of liberty, and *c.* therein
1 John 2:19 would have *c.* with us

CONTRARY
Lev 26:21 if ye walk *c.* unto me
Ezek 16:34 therefore thou art *c.*
Mat 14:24 for the wind was *c.*
Acts 18:13 to worship God *c.* to the law
26: 9 things *c.* to the name of Jesus
27: 4 because the winds were *c.*
Rom 11:24 and wert grafted *c.* to nature
Gal 5:17 these are *c.* the one to another
Col 2:14 against us, which was *c.* to us
1 Thes 2:15 not God, and are *c.* to all men
1 Tim 1:10 other thing that is *c.* to sound doctrine

CONVENIENT
Prov 30: 8 feed with food *c.* for me
Acts 24:25 I have a *c.* season I will call
Rom 1:28 over to do things not *c.*
Eph 5: 4 nor jesting which are not *c.*
Philem 1: 8 that which is *c.*

CONVERSATION
Ps 37:14 such as be of upright *c.*
50:23 ordereth his *c.* aright will I
2 Cor 1:12 we have had our *c.* in the world
Gal 1:13 ye have heard of my *c.* in times
Eph 2: 3 we all had our *c.* in times past
4:22 the former *c.* the old man
Phil 1:27 *c.* be as becometh the gospel
3:20 our *c.* is in heaven
1 Tim 4:12 an example of believers in *c.*
Heb 13: 5 let your *c.* be without covetousness
Jas 3:13 show out of good *c.* his works
1 Pet 1:15 holy in all manner of *c.*
2:12 *c.* honest among the Gentiles
3: 1 won by *c.* of the wives
3:16 accuse your good *c.* in Christ
2 Pet 2: 7 with the filthy *c.* of the wicked
3:11 in all holy *c.* and godliness

CONVERT (CONVERTED)
Ps 51:13 sinners be *c.* to thee
Is 6:10 understand with their heart and *c.* and be healed
60: 5 abundance of sea, *c.* to thee
Mat 13:15 be *c.* and I should heal them
18: 3 except ye be *c.* and become as
Luke 22:32 when thou art *c.* strengthen
Acts 3:19 be *c.* and your sins blotted out
Jas 5:19 err from the truth, and one *c.* him

CONVERTS
Is 1:27 her *c.* with rightousness

CORD (CORDS)
Josh 2:15 let them down by a *c.*
Job 30:11 he hath loosed my *c.*, and afflicted me

CORDS
Job 36: 8 be holden in *c.* of affliction
Ps 118:27 bind the sacrifice with *c.*
2: 3 cast away their *c.* from us
129: 4 asunder of *c.* of the wicked
Prov 5:22 holden with the *c.* of his sins
Eccl 4:12 threefold *c.* not quickly broken
Is 54: 2 spare not, lengthen thy *c.*, and strengthen
Jer 10:20 all my *c.* are broken
Hos 11: 4 *c.* of a man, bands of love
Mic 2: 5 shall cast a *c.* by lot
John 2:15 made a scourge of small *c.*

CORN
Gen 41:49 gathered *c.* as the sand of the sea
Deut 7:13 thy *c.*, and thy wine, and thine oil
25: 4 ox that treadeth out *c.*
Josh 5:11 eat of the old *c.* of the land
Neh 13: 5 the tithes of the *c.*, the new wine
Job 5:26 as a shock of *c.* cometh in
Ps 65: 9 thou preparest them *c.*
72:16 handful of *c.* in the earth
78:24 given them *c.* of heaven to eat
Is 62: 8 no more than give *c.* to enemies
Ezek 36:29 call for *c.* and increase
Hos 2: 8 did not know that I gave her *c.*
Zech 9:17 *c.* shall make the young men
Mat 12: 1 began to pluck the ears of *c.*
John 12:24 except a *c.* of wheat fall
1 Cor 9: 9 ox that treadeth out the *c.*
1 Tim 5:18 ox that treadeth out the *c.*

CORNER (CORNERS)
Lev 19: 9 shalt not reap the *c.* of thy field
19:27 mar the *c.* of thy beard
Job 38: 6 who laid the *c.* stone thereof
Ps 118:22 is become the head of the *c.*
144:12 daughters may be as *c.* stones
Prov 7: 8 through the street near her *c.*
21: 9 it is better to dwell in a *c.*
Is 28:16 a precious *c.* stone
30:20 not thy teachers be removed into a *c.*
Zech 10: 4 out of him came forth the *c.*
Mat 6: 5 synagogues and in *c.* of the streets
21:42 same has become the head of the *c.*
Acts 4:11 has become the head of the *c.*
Eph 2:20 himself being the chief *c.* stone
1 Pet 2: 6 in Sion a chief *c.* stone

CORRECT (CORRECTED, CORRECTETH)
Job 5:17 happy is the man whom God *c.*
Ps 39:11 with rebukes dost *c.* man
94:10 chastiseth the heathen, shall not he *c.*?
Prov 3:12 whom the Lord loveth he *c.*
29:17 *c.* thy son, and he shall give
Jer 2:19 thine own wickedness shall *c.* thee
10:24 *c.* me, but with judgment
Heb 12: 9 our flesh which *c.* us

CORRECTION
Job 37:13 whether for *c.*, or for his land
Prov 3:11 but be not weary of his *c.*
22:15 rod of *c.* shall drive foolishness
23:13 withhold not *c.* from the child
Hab 1:12 established them for *c.*
2 Tim 3:16 Scripture profitable for *c.*

CORRUPT
Job 17: 1 My breath is *c.*, my days
Ps 14: 1 they are *c.*, they have done
38: 5 wounds stink and are *c.*
Mat 6:19 moth and rust doth *c.*
7:17 but a *c.* tree bringeth forth
12:33 or else make the tree *c.*
1 Cor 15:33 evil communications *c.* good manners
2 Cor 2:17 not as many which *c.* word
Eph 4:22 the old man which is *c.*
1 Tim 6: 5 men of *c.* minds and destitute
2 Tim 3: 8 men of *c.* minds, reprobate
Jude 1:10 in those they *c.* themselves

CORRUPTED
Ex 32: 7 Egypt, have *c.* themselves
Hos 9: 9 have deeply *c.* themselves
Mal 2: 8 ye have *c.* the covenant of Levi
2 Cor 7: 2 we have *c.* no man, we have

CORRUPTIBLE
1 Cor 9:25 do it to obtain a *c.* crown
15:53 For this *c.* must put in
1 Pet 1:18 redeemed with *c.* things

CORRUPTION
Job 17:14 I have said to *c.*
Ps 16:10 Holy one to see *c.*
Is 38:17 from the pit of *c.*
Dan 10: 8 turned in me into *c.*
Jonah 2: 6 brought up my life from *c.*
Acts 2:31 his flesh did see *c.*
13:34 now no more to return to *c.*
Rom 8:21 from the bondage of *c.*
1 Cor 15:42 It is sown in *c.*, it is raised
Gal 6: 8 shall of the flesh reap *c.*
2 Pet 1: 4 having escaped through *c.*

COST
2 Sam 19:42 eaten all of the king's *c.*
24:24 of that which doth *c.* me nothing
1 Chr 21:24 offer burnt offering without *c.*
Luke 14:28 and counteth the *c.*, whether we

COUNCIL
Ps 68:27 princes of Judah and their *c.*
Mat 5:22 shall be in danger of the *c.*
10:17 they will deliver you up to the *c.*
26:59 and all the *c.* sought false witness
Mark 15: 1 scribes and the whole *c.*, and bound
Acts 4:15 them to go aside out of the *c.*

COUNSEL
Num 27:21 who shall ask *c.* for him
31:16 through the *c.* of Balaam
1 Ki 12: 8 forsook the *c.* of the old men
Job 5:13 *c.* of froward is carried headlong
12:13 he hath *c.* and understanding
21:16 *c.* of the wicked far from me
38: 2 who is this that darkeneth *c.*
Ps 1: 1 walketh not in the *c.* of the ungodly
14: 6 ye have shamed the *c.* of the poor
33:10 *c.* of the Lord stands for ever
55:14 we took sweet *c.* together
83: 3 taken crafty *c.* against thy people
Prov 1:25 set at nought all my *c.*
8:14 *c.* is mine and sound wisdom
11:14 where no *c.* is the people fall
20:18 purpose established by *c.*
21:30 nor *c.* against the Lord
24: 6 by wise *c.* make war, in multitude
27: 9 a man's friend by hearty *c.*
Is 11: 2 the spirit of *c.* and might
28:29 which is wonderful in *c.* and
40:14 with whom took he *c.* and who
Jer 32:19 great in thy *c.* and mighty in thy work
Zech 6:13 *c.* of peace between them
Luke 7:30 rejected the *c.* of God against
Acts 2:23 delivered by the determinate *c.*
5:38 if this *c.* be of men it will come
20:27 declare to you all the *c.* of God
Eph 1:11 after the *c.* of his own will

COUNSELLOR (COUNSELLORS)
2 Sam 15:12 Ahithophel the Gilonite, David's *c.*
1 Chr 26:14 Zechariah his son, a wise *c.*
2 Chr 22: 3 mother was his *c.* to do wickedly
Ezra 4: 5 and hired *c.* against them
Ps 119:24 thy testimonies are my *c.*
Prov 11:14 in a multitude of the *c.* safety
Is 1:26 restore the *c.* as at the beginning
9: 6 called Wonderful, *C.*, the mighty God
Dan 3:24 spake and said unto his *c.*
Mark 15:43 Joseph of Arimathaea, an honourable *c.*
Rom 11:34 who has been his *c.*

COUNT (COUNTED)
Gen 15: 6 *c.* to him for righteousness
Ex 12: 4 shall make your *c.* for the lamb
Num 23:10 who can *c.* the dust of Jacob
Job 31: 4 doth not he *c.* all my steps
Ps 106:31 and that was *c.* unto him for
139:18 if I should *c.* them, they are more
Is 40:17 *c.* to him less than nothing
Hos 8:12 law *c.* as a strange thing
10:29 *c.* the blood of the covenant unholy
Acts 20:24 neither *c.* I my life dear
Rom 4: 3 it was *c.* unto him for rightousness
Phil 3: 7 those I *c.* loss for Christ
3:13 I *c.* not to have apprehended
Jas 1: 2 *c.* it all joy when ye fall

COUNTENANCE
Gen 4: 5 Cain was very wroth and his *c.* fell
31: 2 and Jacob beheld the *c.* of Laban
Num 6:26 Lord lift up his *c.* upon thee
1 Sam 1:18 and her *c.* was no more sad
16: 7 look not on his *c.* or height
Neh 2: 2 why is thy *c.* sad, seeing thou art
Job 29:24 the light of my *c.* they cast not

Ps 4: 6 the light of thy *c.* upon us
90: 8 secret sins in the light of thy *c.*
Sol 2:14 let me see thy *c.*, let me hear
Mat 6:16 as hypocrites of a sad *c.*
Acts 2:28 full of joy with thy *c.*

COUNTRY
Prov 25:25 good news from a far *c.*
Mat 21:33 and went into a far *c.*
25:14 a man traveling into a far *c.*
Luke 15:13 his journey into a far *c.*
20: 9 into a far *c.* for a long time
Heb 11:14 declare plainly they seek a *c.*
11:16 they desire a better *c.*

COURAGE
Num 13:20 and be ye of good *c.*
Deut 31: 6 be strong and of good *c.*
Josh 1: 6 be strong and of good *c.*
2:11 any more *c.* in any man
2 Sam 10:12 be of good *c.*, and let us
1 Chr 28:20 be strong and of good *c.*
Ezra 10: 4 be of good *c.* and do it
Ps 27:14 Wait on the Lord: be of good *c.*
Is 41: 6 Be of good *c.*
Acts 28:15 he thanked God, and took *c.*

COURAGEOUS
Josh 23: 6 be ye therefore very *c.*
2 Sam 13:28 be *c.* and be valiant

COURSE (COURSES)
1 Chr 23: 6 divided them into *c.* among the sons
Ps 82: 5 foundations of the earth are out of *c.*
Acts 20:24 finish my *c.* with joy
1 Cor 14:27 at most by three, and that by *c.*
Eph 2: 2 according to the *c.* of this world
2 Thes 3: 1 word may have free *c.* and
2 Tim 4: 7 I have finished my *c.*
Jas 3: 6 setteth on fire the *c.* of nature

COURT (COURTS)
Ex 27: 9 make the *c.* of tabernacle
Ps 65: 4 that he may dwell in thy *c.*
84:10 for a day in thy *c.* is better
100: 4 enter his *c.* with praise
Is 1:12 who required, to tread my *c.*
34:13 for dragons and a *c.* for owls
62: 9 drink it in the *c.* of my holiness
Amos 7:13 and it is the king's *c.*
Rev 11: 2 *c.* without the temple leave

COVENANT
Gen 9: 9 I establish my *c.* with you
9:12 this is the token of the *c.*
9:15 and I will remember my *c.*
15:18 Lord made a *c.* with Abraham
17: 7 will establish my *c.* between me and thee
17: 9 thou shalt keep my *c.* therefore
17:11 token of the *c.* betwixt me and you
Ex 2:24 God remembered his *c.* with Abraham
6: 4 have established my *c.* with them
6: 5 I have remembered my *c.*
19: 5 obey my voice indeed, and keep my *c.*
24: 7 he took the book of the *c.*
34:27 I have made a *c.* with thee
34:28 wrote upon the tables the words of the *c.*
Num 10:33 the ark of the *c.* of the Lord
25:13 *c.* of an everlasting priesthood
Deut 5: 2 made a *c.* with us in Horeb
7: 9 which keepeth *c.* and mercy
9:15 tables of the *c.* were in my two
Josh 7:11 also transgressed my *c.*
Judg 2: 1 never brake the *c.* with you
2:20 people hath transgressed my *c.*
2 Sam 23: 5 made with me an everlasting *c.*
1 Ki 8:23 who keepest *c.* and mercy
11:11 thou hast kept my *c.* and statues
2 Ki 18:12 but transgressed his *c.*, and all
23: 3 made a *c.* before the Lord
1 Chr 16:15 be ye mindful always of his *c.*
16:17 Even of the *c.* which he made
2 Chr 6:14 the earth; which keepest my *c.*
Neh 1: 5 that keepeth *c.* and mercy for them
9:32 who keepest *c.* and mercy
Job 31: 1 I made a *c.* with mine eyes
Ps 25:10 keep his *c.* and testimonies
25:14 he will shew them his *c.*
50: 5 made a *c.* with me by sacrifice
74:20 Have respect to the *c.*: for the
89: 3 I have made a *c.* with my chosen
103:18 to such as keep his *c.*
105:10 to Israel for an everlasting *c.*
106:45 he remembered for them his *c.*
132:12 if thy children keep my *c.*
Prov 2:17 forgetteth the *c.* of her God
Is 28:15 we have made a *c.* with death
42: 6 give thee for a *c.* of the people
54:10 nor the *c.* of my peace be removed
55: 3 I will make an everlasting *c.* with
61: 8 will make an everlasting *c.* with them
Jer 14:21 break not the *c.* with us
31:31 will make a new *c.* with the house
32:40 I will make an everlasting *c.* with them
34:18 men that have transgressed my *c.*
50: 5 to the Lord in a perpetual *c.*
Ezek 16:60 I will remember my *c.*
20:37 bring into the bond of the *c.*
Dan 9: 4 keeping the *c.* and mercy to them
9:27 confirm the *c.* with many for one
Hos 8: 1 they have transgressed my *c.*
6: 7 like men, have transgressed the *c.*
10: 4 swearing falsely in making a *c.*
Amos 1: 9 remembered not thy brotherly *c.*
Mal 2: 4 that my *c.* might be with Levi
2:14 thy companion, the wife of the *c.*
Luke 1:72 to remember his holy *c.*
Acts 3:25 ye the children of the *c.*
Rom 9: 4 adoption, and glory and *c.*
Eph 2:12 strangers from the *c.* of promise
Heb 8: 6 the mediator of a better *c.*
8:13 A new *c.*, he hath made the first
12:24 the mediator of the new *c.*
13:20 through the blood of an everlasting *c.*

COVER (COVERED, COVEREST, COVERETH)
Ex 21:33 dig a pit and not *c.* it
33:22 I will *c.* thee with my hand
Deut 33:12 Lord shall *c.* him all day
1 Sam 24: 3 went in to *c.* his feet
Job 16:18 O earth *c.* not my blood
31:33 if I *c.* my transgressions
Ps 32: 1 is forgiven whose sin is *c.*
73: 6 violence *c.* them as a garment
91: 4 *c.* thee with his feathers
104: 2 *c.* thyself with light as with
Prov 10:12 but love *c.* all sins
Is 11: 9 as the waters *c.* the sea
58: 7 seest the naked that thou *c.* him
Lam 3:44 *c.* thyself with a cloud
Hos 10: 8 say to the mountains, *c.* us
Rom 4: 7 and whose sins are *c.*
1 Cor 11: 7 man ought not to *c.* his head
1 Pet 4: 8 charity shall *c.* a multitude of

COVET (COVETED)
Ex 20:17 thou shalt not *c.* thy neighbor's house
Acts 20:33 I have *c.* no man's silver, or gold
1 Cor 12:31 *c.* earnestly the best gifts
14:39 *c.* to prophesy and forbid not
1 Tim 6:10 which while some *c.* after, they

COVETOUS
Ps 10: 3 blesseth the *c.*, whom the Lord
Luke 16:14 Pharisees also who were *c.*, heard
1 Cor 5:10 of this world or with *c.*, or
6:10 nor the *c.* inherit the kingdom of God
Eph 5: 5 Person, nor *c.* man, who is an
1 Tim 3: 3 but patient, not a brawler, not *c.*
2 Tim 3: 2 lovers of their own selves, covetous
2 Pet 2:14 heart they have exercised with *c.*

COVETOUSNESS
Ex 18:21 fear God, men of truth, hating *c.*
Ps 119:36 thy testimonies and not to *c.*
Ezek 33:31 their heart goeth after their *c.*
Luke 12:15 and beware of *c.*: for man's life
Col 3: 5 and *c.* which is idolatry
Heb 13: 5 let your conversation be without *c.*

CRAFTY
Job 5:12 disappoint devices of the *c*
15: 5 choosest the tongue of the *c.*

CRAFTINESS
Job 5:13 in their own *c.*
Luke 20:23 but he perceived their *c.*, and said
1 Cor 3:19 taketh the wise in their own *c.*
2 Cor 4: 2 not walking in *c.*, nor handling
Eph 4:14 and cunning *c.*, whereby

CREATE (CREATED)
Gen 1: 1 God *c.* the heavens and the earth
Ps 51:10 *c.* in me a clean heart
102:18 people which shall be *c.* shall
104:30 forth thy spirit, they are *c.*
Is 4: 5 will *c.* upon every dwelling place
43: 7 I have *c.* him for my glory
45: 7 I form light and *c.* darkness
57:19 I *c.* the fruit of the lips, peace
65:18 rejoice for ever in that which I *c.*
Jer 31:22 *c.* a new thing in the earth
Mal 2:10 hath not one God *c.* us
Eph 2:10 *c.* in Christ Jesus to good works
3: 9 *c.* all things by Jesus Christ
Col 1:16 all things were *c.* by him
3:10 after the image of him that *c.* him
1 Tim 4: 3 which God *c.* to be received
Rev 4:11 thou hast *c.* all things
10: 6 *c.* heaven and things therein

CREATION
Mark 10: 6 from the beginning of the *c.*
13:19 from the beginning of the *c.*
Rom 1:20 of him from the *c.* of the world
8:22 the whole *c.* groaneth
Rev 3:14 beginning of the *c.* of God

CREATOR
Eccl 12: 1 remember now thy *C.* in the days
Is 40:28 the Lord is the *C.* of ends of earth
43:15 *C.* of Israel, your king
Rom 1:25 more than the blessed *C.*
1 Pet 4:19 in well doing as unto a faithful *C.*

CREATURE
Gen 1:20 moving *c.* that hath life
Lev 11:46 of every living *c.* that moveth
Mark 16:15 preach the gospel to every *c.*
Rom 8:20 *c.* was made subject to vanity
8:21 *c.* itself also shall be delivered
2 Cor 5:17 man in Christ is a new *c.*
Gal 6:15 availeth anything but a new *c.*
Col 1:15 the firstborn of every *c.*
1 Tim 4: 4 for every *c.* of God is good
Heb 4:13 neither is there any *c.* that

CRIB
Job 39: 9 to serve thee or abide by thy *c.*
Prov 14: 4 no oxen are, the *c.* is clean
Is 1: 3 and the ass his master's *c.*

CROOKED
Deut 32: 5 are a perverse and *c.* generation
Job 26:13 hand hath formed the *c.* serpent
Ps 125: 5 their *c.* ways
Eccl 1:15 *c.* cannot be made straight
Is 27: 1 leviathon that *c.* serpent
40: 4 the *c.* shall be made straight
Luke 3: 5 the *c.* shall be made straight
Phil 2:15 a *c.* and perverse generation

DARKENED
Ex 10:15 so that the land was *d.*
Ps 69:23 let eyes be *d.* that they see not
Mat 24:29 shall the sun be *d.*
Rom 1:21 their foolish heart was *d.*
11:10 Let their eyes be *d.* that they may
Eph 4:18 having the understanding *d.*

DARKLY
1 Cor 13:12 now we see through a glass *d.*

DARKNESS
Gen 1: 2 *d.* was upon the face of the deep
Deut 28:29 as the blind gropeth in *d.*
1 Sam 2: 9 wicked shall be silent in *d.*
2 Sam 22:29 Lord will lighten my *d.*
Job 34:22 no *d.* nor shadow of death
Ps 104:20 makest *d.,* and it is night
107:10 such as sit in *d.* and in the
Is 5:20 *d.* for light, and light for *d.*
9: 2 that walked in *d.* have seen
29:18 out of obscurity and out of *d.*
45: 7 I form light and create *d.*
Mat 4:16 sat in *d.* saw a great light
6:23 whole body full of *d.*
8:12 cast out into outer *d.*
John 1: 5 light shineth in the *d.*
3:19 men loved *d.* rather than light
12:35 light lest *d.* come upon you
Acts 26:18 turn them from *d.* to light
Rom 13:12 cast off the works of *d.*
1 Cor 4: 5 the hidden things of *d.*
2 Cor 4: 6 light to shine out of *d.*
Eph 5: 8 ye were sometimes *d.* but
5:11 the unfruitful works of *d.*
6:12 the rulers of the *d.* of this world
1 Thes 5: 4 but ye brethren are not in *d.*
1 Pet 2: 9 called you out of the *d.*
2 Pet 2: 4 delivered into chains of *d.*
1 John 1: 5 in him is no *d.* at all
2: 8 *d.* is past, and the true light shineth
2:11 because *d.* hath blinded his eyes
Jude 1:13 blackness of *d.* for ever

DARTS
Eph 6:16 quench all the fiery *d.* of the wicked

DASH (DASHED, DASHETH)
Ex 15: 6 hath *d.* in pieces the enemy
2 Ki 8:12 wilt *d.* their children, and rip up
Ps 2: 9 *d.* in pieces like a potter's vessel
91:12 lest thou *d.* thy foot against a stone
137: 9 *d.* thy little ones against the stones
Is 13:18 bows shall *d.* the young men
Jer 13:14 will *d.* them one against another
Hos 10:14 the mother was *d.* in pieces

DAY
Gen 1: 5 and God called the light *d.*
Ps 19: 2 *d.* unto *d.* uttereth speech
20: 1 Lord hear in the *d.* of trouble
50:15 call on me in the *d.* of trouble
59:16 my defence and refuge in the *d.* of trouble
77: 2 in the *d.* of trouble I sought the
84:10 a *d.* in thy courts is better than
118:24 this is the *d.* which the Lord
Prov 27: 1 what a *d.* may bring forth
Is 2:12 *d.* of the Lord of Hosts
13: 9 the *d.* of the Lord cometh
34: 8 the *d.* of the Lord's vengeance
37: 3 This *d.* is a *d.* of trouble and
Jer 46:10 the *d.* of the Lord of Hosts
Lam 2:22 a solemn *d.* my terrors round
Ezek 7: 7 time is come, the *d.* of trouble is near
30: 3 For the *d.* is near, even the day
Joel 1:15 the *d.* of the Lord is at hand
3:14 the *d.* of the Lord is near
Amos 5:18 that desire the *d.* of the Lord
6: 3 put far away the evil *d.*
Obad 1:15 the *d.* of the Lord is near
Nah 1: 7 a strong hold in the *d.* of trouble
Hab 3:16 I might rest in the *d.* of trouble
Zeph 1:15 a *d.* of trouble and distress
2: 3 be hid in the *d.* of the Lord's anger
Zech 4:10 despised the *d.* of small things
14: 1 the *d.* of the Lord cometh
Mal 4: 5 the great and dreadful *d.*
Mat 6:34 sufficient to the *d.* is the evil
10:15 in the *d.* of judgment than for
12:36 thereof in the *d.* of judgment
Mark 6:11 in the *d.* of judgment than for
John 8:56 Abraham rejoiced to see my *d.*
1 Cor 1: 8 blameless in the *d.* of our Lord
3:13 the *d.* shall declare it
5: 5 the *d.* of the Lord Jesus
2 Cor 1:14 in the *d.* of the Lord Jesus
Phil 1: 6 the *d.* of Jesus Christ
1 Thes 5: 5 children of the *d.*
5: 2 the *d.* of the Lord so cometh
2 Thes 2: 2 as that the *d.* of Christ
2 Pet 1:19 *d.* star arise in your hearts
2: 9 unto the *d.* of judgment
3: 7 the *d.* of judgment and perdition
3:10 *d.* of the Lord will come
Rev 1:10 the Spirit on the Lord's *d.*

DAYS
Gen 49: 1 which shall befall you in the last *d.*
Num 24:14 to thy people in the latter *d.*
Deut 31:29 befall you in the latter *d.*
Job 7: 6 my *d.* are swifter than a
7:16 let me alone, my *d.* are vanity
8: 9 *d.* on earth as a shadow
14: 1 of few *d.* and full of trouble
32: 7 *d.* should speak, and multitude
Ps 39: 4 to know the end, and measure of my *d.*
90:12 teach us to number our *d.*
102: 3 my *d.* are consumed like smoke
102:23 in the way; he shortened my *d.*
Prov 3:16 length of *d.* is in her right
Eccl 7:10 former *d.* better than these
11: 8 remember the *d.* of darkness; many
12: 1 while the evil *d.* come not
Is 2: 2 it shall come to pass in the last *d.*
39: 8 peace and truth in my *d.*
Jer 2:32 forgotten me *d.* without number
20:18 my *d.* are consumed with shame
23:20 in the latter *d.* ye shall
30:24 in the latter *d.* ye shall consider
Dan 10:14 befall thy people in the latter *d.*
Hos 3: 5 his goodness in the latter *d.*
Mic 4: 1 in the last *d.* it shall
Acts 2:17 come to pass in the last *d.*
Gal 4:10 observe the *d.,* months, and years
Eph 5:16 time because the *d.* are evil
2 Tim 3: 1 that in the last *d.* perilous
Heb 1: 2 in these last *d.* spoken unto us
Jas 5: 3 treasure together in the last *d.*
1 Pet 3:10 love life and see good *d.*
2 Pet 3: 3 come in the last *d.* scoffers

DAILY
Ps 61: 8 I may *d.* perform my vows
Prov 8:34 watching *d.* at my gates
Is 58: 2 seek me *d.* and delight in
Acts 2:47 the Lord added to the church *d.*
Heb 3:13 but exhort one another *d.,* while

DEACONS
Phil 1: 1 at Philippi with the bishops and *d.*
1 Tim 3: 8 likewise must the *d.* be grave

DEAD
Gen 20: 3 behold thou art but a *d.* man
23: 3 up from before his *d.*
Num 16:48 stood between *d.* and living
1 Sam 24:14 after a *d.* dog, after a flea
Ps 88:10 shall the *d.* arise and praise
115:17 the *d.* praise not the Lord
Eccl 9: 5 the *d.* know not any thing
10: 1 *d.* flies cause the ointment to
Mat 8:22 let the *d.* bury their own *d.*
22:32 not the God of the *d.* but of the
Luke 8:52 she is not *d.* but sleepeth
John 5:25 *d.* hear the voice of the Son of God
John 11:25 though *d.* yet shall he live
Rom 6: 8 now if we be *d.* with Christ
6:11 *d.* indeed unto sin, but alive
Gal 2:19 I through the law am *d.* to the law
Eph 2: 1 who were *d.* in trespasses and sins
Col 2:13 being *d.* in your sins and the
1 Thes 4:16 *d.* in Christ rise first
2 Tim 2:11 *d.* with him, we shall live
Heb 11: 4 by it he being *d.* yet speaketh
Rev 14:13 blessed are the *d.* which die

DEAF
Ex 4:11 who maketh the dumb or *d.*
Lev 19:14 thou shalt not curse the *d.*
Ps 38:13 I, as a *d.* man, heard not
Is 35: 5 ears of the *d.* shall be unstopped
42:18 hear, ye *d.* and look, ye blind
42:19 or *d.* as my messenger that I sent?
43: 8 and the *d.* people that have ears
Mic 7:16 their mouth, their ears shall be *d.*
Mat 11: 5 the *d.* hear, the dead are raised up
Mark 7:32 unto him the one that was *d.*

DEATH
Gen 21:16 not see the *d.* of the child
Num 23:10 let me die the *d.* of the righteous
Deut 30:15 set before you life and *d.*
Ps 6: 5 in *d.* no remembrance of thee
68:20 to the Lord belong issues from *d.*
73: 4 have no bands in their *d.*: but
89:48 liveth and shall not see *d.*
116:15 Lord is the *d.* of his saints
118:18 he hath not given me over unto *d.*
Prov 2:18 her house inclineth to *d.*
8:36 all they that hate me love *d.*
18:21 *d.* and life in the power of the tongue
Eccl 7:26 more bitter than *d.* the woman
8: 8 hath power in the day of *d.*
Is 25: 8 he will swallow up *d.* in victory
28:15 we have made a covenant with *d.*
38:18 *d.* cannot celebrate thee
Jer 8: 3 *d.* chosen rather than life
21: 8 you a way of life, a way of *d.*
Hos 13:14 O *d.,* I will be thy plagues
Mat 16:28 which shall not taste of *d.*
26:38 exceeding sorrowful even unto *d.*
John 5:24 is passed from *d.* unto life
8:51 he shall never see *d.,*
12:33 what *d.* he should die
Acts 2:24 having loosed the pains of *d.*
Rom 5:12 sin entered, and *d.* by sin
6: 5 planted in the likeness of his *d.*
6: 9 *d.* hath no more dominion over
6:21 for the end of those things is *d.*
7: 5 to bring forth fruit unto *d.*
8: 2 free from the law of sin and *d.*
8: 6 for to be carnally minded is *d.*
8:38 *d.* nor life shall separate us from
1 Cor 3:22 or life, or *d.* or things
11:26 ye show the Lord's *d.* till he come
15:21 by man came *d.* by man also
15:54 *d.* is swallowed up in victory
15:55 O *d.,* where is thy sting
15:56 sting of *d.* is sin, and strength
2 Cor 1: 9 sentence of *d.* in ourselves
1:10 deliver from so great a *d.* and doth
2:16 we are the savour of *d.* unto *d.*
4:11 delivered to *d.* for Jesus' sake
4:12 *d.* worketh in us, but life in you
Phil 2: 8 *d.* even the *d.* of the cross
Heb 2: 9 should taste *d.* for every man
2:15 through fear of *d.* are subject to
11: 5 should not see *d.,*
Jas 1:15 sin finished bringeth *d.*
1 Pet 3:18 put to *d.* in the flesh
1 John 3:14 but is passed from *d.* unto life
5:16 there is a sin unto *d.*: I do not
Rev 1:18 I have the keys of hell and *d.*
2:10 be faithful unto *d.* and I will
20: 6 on such second *d.* hath no power
21: 4 there shall be no more *d.* nor

DEBATE
Prov 25: 9 *d.* thy cause with thy neighbour

Is 27: 8 thou wilt *d.* with it he stayeth
58: 4 fast for strife and *d.*
Rom 1:29 full of envy, murder, *d.*
2 Cor 12:20 lest there be *d.* envyings

DEBT (DEBTS)
Mat 6:12 forgive us our *d.*
18:27 and forgave him the *d.*
Rom 4: 4 reckoned of grace, but of *d.*

DEBTOR (DEBTORS)
Ezek 18: 7 restored the *d.* his pledge
Luke 7:41 creditor which had two *d.*
Rom 1:14 I am *d.* both to the Greeks
8:12 brethren, we are *d.*; not to the
15:27 verily; and their *d.* they are
Gal 5: 3 he is a *d.* to do the whole law

DECEIT
Ps 72:14 redeem thy soul from *d.*
101: 7 worketh *d.* shall not dwell
Prov 20:17 bread of *d.* is sweet to man
Is 53: 9 neither was any *d.* in his mouth
Jer 5:27 their houses full of *d.*
8: 5 they hold fast *d.* they refuse
9: 8 an arrow shot out; it speaketh *d.*
Col 2: 8 spoil through philosophy and vain *d.*

DECEITFUL (DECEITFULLY)
Job 13: 7 and talk *d.* for him
Ps 5: 6 abhor the bloody and *d.* man
24: 4 unto vanity, nor sworn *d.*
35:20 they devise *d.* matters against
55:23 *d.* men shall not live half their days
78:57 turned aside like a *d.* bow
109: 2 mouth of the *d.* are opened
Prov 11:18 wicked worketh a *d.* work
14:25 but a *d.* witness speaketh lies
27: 6 kisses of an enemy are *d.*
Jer 17: 9 heart *d.* above all things
48:10 the work of the lord *d.*
Hos 7:16 they are like a *d.* bow
2 Cor 4: 2 handling the word of God *d.*
Eph 4:22 corrupt according to the *d.* lusts

DECEITFULNESS
Mat 13:22 *d.* of riches, choke the word

DECEIVE (DECEIVED, DECEIVING, DECEIVETH)
Deut 11:16 that your heart be not *d.*
2 Ki 4:28 did I not say Do not *d.* me
18:29 Let not Hezekiah *d.* you
Job 12:16 *d.* and the deceiver are
Prov 24:28 and *d.* not with thy lips
26:19 the man that *d.* his neighbor
Is 44:20 a *d.* heart hath turned
Jer 20: 7 O Lord, thou hast *d.* me
Ezek 14: 9 I, Lord, have *d.* that prophet
Obad 1: 3 pride of thine heart hath *d.* thee
Mat 24: 4 take heed no man *d.* you
24:24 if possible *d.* the very elect
Rom 7:11 sin *d.* me, and by it slew me
1 Cor 3:18 let no man *d.* himself
Gal 6: 3 when he is nothing, he *d.* himself
1 Tim 2:14 and Adam was not *d.* but the woman
2 Tim 3:13 and worse, *d.* and being *d.*
Jas 1:26 but *d.* his own heart, this man's
1 John 1: 8 no sin, we *d.* ourselves
Rev 12: 9 which *d.* the whole world

DECEIVER (DECEIVERS)
Gen 27:12 shall seem to him as a *d.*
Mal 1:14 but cursed be the *d.*, which hath
Mat 27:63 remember that the *d.* said
2 Cor 6: 8 as *d.* and yet true
Tit 1:10 and vain talkers and *d.*, specially
2 John 1: 7 many *d.* are entered into the world

DECLARE (DECLARED, DECLARETH)
Gen 41:24 there was none that could *d.* it
Ps 22:22 I will *d.* thy name unto brethren
38:18 I will *d.* my iniquity and
50:16 to do to *d.* my statutes
78: 6 may *d.* them to their children
145: 4 shall *d.* thy mighty acts
Is 3: 9 they *d.* their sin as Sodom
42: 9 and new things do I *d.*
53: 8 who shall *d.* his generation
Amos 4:13 *d.* to man his thought
Acts 17:23 worship him *d.* I unto you
20:27 not shunned to *d.* all counsel
Rom 1: 4 *d.* to be the Son of God
3:25 to *d.* his righteousness for the
Heb 11:14 say such things *d.* plainly
1 John 1: 3 seen and heard *d.* we unto you

DECREE (DECREED, DECREES)
Job 28:26 he made a *d.* for rain
Ps 2: 7 I will declare the *d.*
Prov 8:15 reign, and princes *d.* justice
8:29 gave to the sea his *d.*
Is 10: 1 unto them that *d.* unrighteous *d.*
10:22 the consumption *d.* shall overflow
Jer 5:22 bound of the sea by a perpetual *d.*
Dan 4:17 by the *d.* of the watchers
Zeph 2: 2 before the *d.* bring forth
Luke 2: 1 went out a *d.* from Caesar
Acts 17: 7 contrary to the *d.* of Caesar
1 Cor 7:37 and hath *d.* in his heart

DEDICATE (DEDICATED)
Deut 20: 5 and another man *d.* it
2 Sam 8:11 King David did *d.* unto the Lord
1 Chr 26:20 the treasures of the *d.* things
26:27 battles did they *d.* to maintain
Ezek 44:29 and every *d.* thing in Israel

DEDICATION
Num 7:84 this was the *d.* of the altar
2 Chr 7: 9 they kept the *d.* of the altar
Ezra 6:17 at the *d.* of this house
Neh 12:27 the *d.* of the wall of Jerusalem
John 10:22 the feast of the *d.*, and it was

DEED (DEEDS)
Judg 19:30 no such *d.* done nor seen
2 Sam 12:14 by this *d.* thou hast
Neh 13:14 wipe not out my good *d.*
Ps 28: 4 give them according to their *d.*
Jer 25:14 them according to their *d.*
John 3:19 because their *d.* were evil
Rom 2: 6 every man according to his *d.*
3:20 by *d.* of law no flesh justified
8:13 do mortify the *d.* of the body
15:18 obedient by word and *d.*
Col 3: 9 the old man with his *d.*
3:17 whatsoever ye do in word or *d.*
1 John 3:18 in tongue but in *d.* and in truth
2 John 1:11 partaker of his evil *d.*

DEEP
Gen 1: 2 was upon the face of the *d.*
7:11 fountains of the great *d.*
Job 38:30 the face of the *d.* is frozen
Ps 36: 6 thy judgments are a great *d.*
42: 7 *d.* calleth unto *d.* at the noise
1 Cor 2:10 yea, the *d.* things of God
2 Cor 11:25 I have been in the *d.*

DEEPLY
Is 31: 6 children of Israel have *d.* revolted
Hos 9: 9 they have *d.* corrupted themselves
Mark 8:12 sighed *d.* in spirit, and saith

DEFENCE
2 Chr 11: 5 built cities for *d.* in Judah
Num 14: 9 their *d.* is departed from them
Job 22:25 the Almighty shall be thy *d.*
Ps 59: 9 upon thee; for God is my *d.*
62: 2 he is my *d.*, I shall not
89:18 for the Lord is our *d.*
94:22 but the Lord is my *d.*
Eccl 7:12 for wisdom is a *d.*, and money
Is 4: 5 on all the glory shall be the *d.*
19: 6 brooks of *d.* shall be emptied
33:16 place of *d.* shall be the munitions

DEFER (DEFERRED, DEFERRETH)
Prov 13:12 hope *d.* maketh the heart sick
19:11 discretion of a man *d.* his anger
Eccl 5: 4 *D.* not to pay it, for he
Is 48: 9 name's sake will I defer my anger
Dan 9:19 *d.* not for thine own sake

DEFILE (DEFILED, DEFILETH)
Lev 18:25 and the land is *d.*, therefore
Is 24: 5 the earth also is *d.*
Dan 1: 8 he would not *d.* himself
Mat 15:18 and they *d.* the man
Mark 7: 2 his disciples eat bread with *d.*
1 Cor 3:17 if any *d.* the temple of God
Tit 1:15 mind and conscience is *d.*
Heb 12:15 and thereby many be *d.*
Rev 3: 4 have not *d.* their garments
21:27 not enter any thing that *d.*

DEFRAUD (DEFRAUDED)
Lev 19:13 thou shalt not *d.* thy neighbor
1 Sam 12: 3 or whom have I *d.*? whom have I
1 Cor 6: 7 why not rather be *d.*
2 Cor 7: 2 we have *d.* no man

DELAY (DELAYED, DELAYETH)
Ex 22:29 not *d.* to offer the first
32: 1 Moses *d.* to come down
Ps 119:60 I *d.* not to keep thy commandments
Mat 24:48 my lord *d.* his coming
Acts 9:38 he would not *d.* to come

DELICATE (DELICATES)
Deut 28:56 tender and *d.* woman among you
Is 47: 1 no more be called tender and *d.*
Jer 6: 2 a comely and *d.* woman
51:34 filled his belly with my *d.*
Mic 1:16 poll thee for thy *d.* children

DELICATELY
1 Sam 15:32 Agag came unto him *d.*
Prov 29:21 he that *d.* bringeth up his servant
Lam 4: 5 that did feed *d.* are desolate
Luke 7:25 gorgeously apparelled, and live *d.*

DELIGHT (DELIGHTED, DELIGHTETH)
Gen 34:19 he had *d.* in Jacob's daughter
Num 14: 8 If the Lord *d.* in us
Deut 10:15 Lord had a *d.* in thy fathers
1 Sam 15:22 as great *d.* in burnt offerings
2 Sam 22:20 because he *d.* in me
24: 3 Why doth the king *d.* in this thing?
Esth 2:14 except the king *d.* in her
6: 6 whom the king *d.* to honour
Job 22:26 thy *d.* in the Almighty
27:10 will he *d.* himself in
Ps 1: 2 his *d.* is in the law
16: 3 saints in whom is all my *d.*
22: 8 deliver him, seeing he *d.* in him
40: 8 I *d.* to do thy will, O my God
94:19 thy comforts *d.* my soul
109:17 he *d.* not in blessing, so let
147:10 he *d.* not in the strength of the horse
Prov 3:12 the son in whom he *d.*
11: 1 just weight is his *d.*
11:20 in their way is his *d.*
15: 8 prayer of the upright is his *d.*
Sol 2: 3 under his shadow with *d.*
Is 1:11 I *d.* not in the blood of bullocks
42: 1 elect in whom my soul *d.*
55: 2 let your soul *d.* itself in
58: 2 take *d.* in approaching to God
62: 4 Beulah: for the Lord *d.* in thee
Jer 9:24 in these things I *d.* saith Lord
Mic 7:18 for ever, because he *d.* in mercy
Rom 7:22 I *d.* in the law of God

DELIGHTS
Ps 119:92 thy law had been my *d.*
Prov 8:31 my *d.* were with sons of men
Sol 7: 6 how pleasant, O love, for *d.*

DELIGHTSOME
Mal 3:12 ye shall be a *d.* land

DELIVER
Ex 3: 8 come down to *d.* them
5:18 ye shall *d.* the tale
Job 5:19 *d.* thee in six troubles
10: 7 none can *d.* out of thy hand
Ps 33:19 to *d.* their soul from death
50:15 I will *d.* thee, and thou
91:15 I will *d.* him and honour him
56:13 wilt thou not *d.* my feet
74:19 *d.* not the soul of thy turtledove
Eccl 8: 8 shall wickedness *d.* those that are
Ezek 14:14 should *d.* but their own souls
34:10 I will *d.* my flock from their mouth
Dan 3:17 our God is able to *d.* us
Hos 11: 8 how shall I *d.* thee, Israel
Rom 7:24 shall *d.* me from the body
1 Cor 5: 5 to *d.* such a one to Satan
2 Tim 4:18 Lord shall *d.* me from every evil
Heb 2:15 *d.* them who through fear
2 Pet 2: 9 Lord knoweth how to *d.* the godly

DELIVERED
Prov 28:26 walketh wisely shall and be *d.*
Is 38:17 *d.* it from the pit of corruption
49:24 or the lawful captive *d.*?
Jer 7:10 *d.* to do all abominations
Ezek 3:19 but thou hast *d.* thy soul
33: 9 but thou hast *d.* thy soul
Dan 12: 1 at that time thy people shall be *d.*
Joel 2:32 name of the Lord shall be *d.*
Mic 4:10 Babylon, there shalt thou be *d.*
Mat 11:27 all *d.* to me of my Father
Acts 2:23 *d.* by the determinate counsel
Rom 4:25 who was *d.* for our offences
7: 6 now we are *d.* from the law, that
8:32 *d.* him up for us all
2 Cor 1:10 who *d.* us from so great a death
4:11 *d.* to death for Jesus' sake
1 Thes 1:10 *d.* us from the wrath to come
1 Tim 1:20 whom I have *d.* to Satan
Jude 1: 3 faith once *d.* to the saints

DELIVERANCE
Gen 45: 7 save your lives by a great *d.*
Judg 15:18 this great *d.* into the hand
2 Ki 5: 1 had given *d.* to Syria
13:17 the arrow of the Lord's *d.*
1 Chr 11:14 saved them by a great *d.*
Ezra 9:13 given us such *d.* as this
Esth 4:14 *d.* arise to the Jews from another
Ps 18:50 great *d.* giveth he to
32: 7 about with songs of *d.*
Joel 2:32 and in Jerusalem shall be *d.*
Obad 1:17 upon mount Zion shall be *d.*
Luke 4:18 to preach *d.* to the captives
Heb 11:35 tortured, not accepting *d.*

DELUSION (DELUSIONS)
Is 66: 4 I also will choose their *d.*
2 Thes 2:11 God shall send them a strong *d.*

DEN (DENS)
Judg 6: 2 the *d.* which are in the mountains
Job 37:17 beasts go into *d.*, and remain
Ps 10: 9 as a lion in his *d.*
104:22 lay them down in their *d.*
Sol 4: 8 from the lion's *d.*, from the
Jer 7:11 become a *d.* of robbers in your eyes
9:11 and a *d.* of dragons, and I
10:22 desolate and a *d.* of dragons
Dan 6:24 cast them into the *d.* of lions
Amos 3: 4 young lion cry out of his *d.*
Nah 2:12 and his *d.* with ravin
Mat 21:13 have made it a *d.* of thieves
Heb 11:38 in *d.* and caves of the earth
Rev 6:15 hid themselves in the *d.* and in the

DENY (DENIED, DENYING)
1 Ki 2:16 one petition of thee, *d.* me not
Job 8:18 then it shall *d.* him
Prov 30: 9 lest I be full, and *d.* thee
Mat 10:33 shall *d.* me before men
16:24 let him *d.* himself and take up
26:34 cock crow thou shalt *d.* me
26:35 yet will I not *d.* thee
Mark 14:30 thou shalt *d.* me thrice
1 Tim 5: 8 he hath *d.* the faith
2 Tim 2:12 if we *d.* him, he will *d.* us
Tit 1:16 but in works they *d.* him
2:12 *d.* ungodliness and the worldly
2 Pet 2: 1 *d.* the Lord that bought them
Rev 2:13 and hast not *d.* my faith

DEPART (DEPARTED, DEPARTETH, DEPARTING, DEPARTS)
2 Sam 22:22 have not wickedly *d.* from my God
Job 21:14 they say unto God, *d.* from us
28:28 *d.* from evil is understanding
Ps 18:21 not wickedly *d.* from my God
34:14 *d.* from evil and do good
37:27 *d.* from evil and do good
119:102 have *d.* from thy judgments
Prov 14:16 feareth and *d.* from evil
3: 7 fear the Lord and *d.* from evil
16:17 the upright is to *d.* from evil
Is 59:15 that *d.* from evil makes himself prey
Hos 9:12 woe also to them when I *d.*
Mat 7:23 *d.* from me, ye that work
25:41 *d.* from me, ye cursed, into
Luke 2:29 lettest thy servant *d.* in peace
5: 8 saying, *d.* from me, for I am a
Acts 20:29 after my *d.* shall grievous wolves
Phil 1:23 having a desire to *d.* and
Heb 3:12 unbelief, in *d.* from the living God
1 Tim 4: 1 some shall *d.* from faith

DEPARTURE
Ezek 26:18 shall be trouble at thy *d.*
2 Tim 4: 6 time of my *d.* is at hand

DEPTH (DEPTHS)
Ex 15: 5 the *d.* have covered them
Job 38:16 walked in search of the *d.*
Ps 68:22 from the *d.* of the sea
130: 1 out of the *d.* have I cried
Prov 8:27 upon the face of the *d.*
9:18 are in the *d.* of hell
Mic 7:19 cast all their sins into the *d.*
Mat 18: 6 drowned in the *d.* of the sea
Mark 4: 5 because it had no *d.* of earth
Rom 8:39 neither height nor *d.* nor any other
Eph 3:18 breadth, length, *d.* and height
Rev 2:24 have not known the *d.* of Satan

DERISION
Job 30: 1 younger than I have me in *d.*
Ps 2: 4 Lord shall have them in *d.*
44:13 a scorn and *d.* to them
119:51 have had me greatly in *d.*
Jer 20: 8 reproach unto me, and a *d.* daily

DESCEND (DESCENDED, DESCENDING)
Gen 28:12 angels of God ascending and *d.*
Ex 19:18 Lord *d.* upon it in fire
33: 9 the cloudy pillar *d.*, and stood
Ps 49:17 glory not *d.* after him
Is 5:14 rejoiceth shall *d.* into it
Mat 3:16 the Spirit of God *d.* like a dove
Mark 1:10 like a dove *d.* upon him
John 1:32 saw the spirit *d.* from heaven
1:51 angels of God ascending and *d.*
1 Thes 4:16 Lord shall *d.* from heaven

DESERT (DESERTS)
Ex 3: 1 to the backside or the *d.*
5: 3 three days journey into the *d.*
2 Chr 26:10 also he built towers in the *d.*
Job 24: 5 as wild asses in the *d.*
Ps 78:40 and grieve him in the *d.*
102: 6 like an owl of the *d.*
Is 13:21 wild beasts of the *d.* shall lie
21: 1 the burden of the *d.* of the sea
35: 1 and the *d.* shall rejoice
35: 6 break out and streams in the *d.*
40: 3 in the *d.* a highway for our God
41:19 set in the *d.* the fir tree
43:19 and rivers in the *d.*
Is 51: 3 her *d.* like the garden
Jer 2: 6 through a land of *d.* and of pits
Ezek 13: 4 like the foxes in the *d.*
Mark 1:45 but was without in *d.* places
Luke 1:80 in *d.* till the day of showing
John 6:31 fathers did eat manna in the *d.*
Heb 11:38 wandered in *d.* and mountains

DESIRE
Gen 3:16 *d.* shall be to thy husband
Ex 34:24 nor any man *d.* thy land
Deut 18: 6 come with all the *d.* of his mind
2 Chr 15:15 and sought him with their whole *d.*
Neh 1:11 who *d.* to fear thy name
Job 14:15 wilt have a *d.* to the work of
21:14 we *d.* not knowledge of thy ways
Ps 38: 9 all my *d.* is before thee
145:16 satisfieth the *d.* of every living
Prov 10:24 *d.* of righteous shall be granted
11:23 *d.* of the righteous is only good
13:19 *d.* accomplished is sweet
Eccl 12: 5 *d.* shall fail because man goeth
Is 26: 8 *d.* of our soul is to thy name
Hag 2: 7 the *d.* of all nations shall
Luke 22:15 with *d.* I have desired to eat
Jas 4: 2 *d.* to have and cannot obtain
Rev 9: 6 *d.* to die, and death shall flee

DESIRED (DESIRES, DESIREST, DESIRETH)
Job 7: 2 servant earnestly *d.* the shadow
Ps 19:10 more to be *d.* are they than gold
27: 4 one thing have I *d.* of the Lord
34:12 what man *d.* life and loveth
37: 4 give thee the *d.* of thine heart
51: 6 thou *d.* truth in the inward parts
51:16 thou *d.* not sacrifice, else would
68:16 hill which God *d.* to dwell in
Prov 12:12 wicked *d.* the net of evil men
13: 4 soul of the sluggard *d.* and hath
21:10 soul of wicked *d.* evil
Is 26: 9 with my soul have I *d.* thee
Jer 17:16 neither have I *d.* the woeful day
Hos 6: 6 I *d.* mercy, not sacrifice
Eph 2: 3 fulfilling *d.* of the flesh

DESOLATE
2 Sam 13:20 Tamar remained *d.* in her brother
Job 15:28 he dwelleth in *d.* cities and in
16: 7 thou hast made *d.* all my company
Ps 25:16 I am *d.* and afflicted
Is 49:21 I have lost my children, and am *d.*
54: 1 for more are the children of the *d.*
Mat 23:38 behold your house is left unto you *d.*
Rev 17:16. and shall make her *d.* and naked

DESOLATIONS
Jer 25:12 and will make it perpetual *d.*
Ezek 35: 9 I will make thee perpetual *d.*
Dan 9: 2 seventy years in the *d.* of Jerusalem

DESPAIR
Eccl 2:20 to cause my heart to *d.*
2 Cor 4: 8 we are perplexed, but not in *d.*

DESPERATE (DESPERATELY)
Job 6:26 speeches of one that is *d.*
Is 17:11 in the day of grief and of *d.* sorrow
Jer 17: 9 deceitful above all things and *d.* wicked

DESPISE (DESPISED, DESPISEST, DESPISETH, DESPISING)
Gen 16: 4 her mistress was *d.* in her eyes
Lev 26:15 if ye shall *d.* my statutes
1 Sam 2:30 they that *d.* me be lightly
2 Sam 6:16 she *d.* him in her heart
Job 5:17 *d.* not the chastening of the Almighty
36: 5 God is mighty and *d.* not any
Ps 102:17 destitute and will not *d.* their
Prov 11:12 void of wisdom *d.* his neighbour
12: 9 he that is *d.* and hath a servant
13:13 whoso *d.* the word shall be destroyed
15:32 refuseth instruction *d.* his soul

Prov 19:16 he that *d.* his ways shall die
23:22 *d.* not thy mother when she is old
30:17 and *d.* to obey his mother
Is 33:15 he that *d.* the gain of oppression
53: 3 he is *d.* and rejected
Amos 5:21 I *d.* your feast days
Zech 4:10 who *d.* the day of small things
Mat 6:24 hold to one, and *d.* the other
Luke 10:16 he that *d.* you, *d.* me, and he that
18: 9 they were righteous and *d.* others
Rom 2: 4 *d.* thou the riches of goodness
14: 3 that eateth *d.* him that eateth not
1 Thes 4: 8 *d.* not man but God who hath also
1 Tim 4:12 no man *d.* thy youth
Heb 10:28 he that *d.* Moses' law died without
12: 2 *d.* the shame, and is set down

DESPISERS
Acts 13:41 behold, ye *d.*, and wonder, and perish
2 Tim 3: 3 *d.* of those that are good

DESPITE
Heb 10:29 done *d.* unto the Spirit of grace

DESTROY (DESTROYED)
Gen 19:13 for we will *d.* this place
Esth 4:14 thy father's house shall be *d.*
Ps 37:38 transgressors shall be *d.* together
101: 8 I will *d.* the wicked of the land
Prov 1:32 prosperity of fools shall *d.* them
13:20 a companion of fools shall be *d.*
Eccl 7:16 why shouldest thou *d.* thyself
Dan 2:44 kingdom which shall never be *d.*
Hos 4: 6 are *d.* for lack of knowledge
13: 9 Israel, thou hast *d.* thyself
10: 8 the sin of Israel, shall be *d.*
Mat 5:17 not come to *d.* but to fulfil
21:41 miserably *d.* those wicked men
John 2:19 *d.* this temple, and in three days
Rom 14:15 *d.* not him with thy meat
14:20 for meat *d.* not the work of God
1 Cor 3:17 defile the temple of God shall God *d.*
6:13 God shall *d.* both it and them
15:26 that shall be *d.* is death
2 Cor 4: 9 cast down, but not *d.*
Jas 4:12 who is able to save and to *d.*
1 John 3: 8 might *d.* the works of the devil

DESTROYER
Job 15:21 in prosperity the *d.* shall come upon
Ps 17: 4 kept me from the paths of the *d.*
Prov 28:24 same is the companion of a *d.*
Jer 4: 7 *d.* of the Gentiles is on his way
1 Cor 10:10 and were destroyed of the *d.*

DESTRUCTION
Deut 7:23 shall destroy them with a mighty *d.*
Job 5:22 at *d.* and famine shall laugh
21:30 wicked is reserved to the day of *d.*
26: 6 *d.* before him hath no covering
31:23 *d.* from God was a terror to me
Ps 90: 3 thou turnest man to *d.*
91: 6 *d.* that wasteth at noonday
Prov 10:29 *d.* shall be to workers of iniquity
15:11 Hell and *d.* are before the Lord
16:18 pride goeth before *d.*, and an
18:12 before *d.* the heart of man is haughty
27:20 hell and *d.* are never full
Jer 4:20 *d.* upon *d.* is cried, for
Hos 13:14 O grave, I will be thy *d.*
Mat 7:13 the way, that leadeth to *d.*
Rom 3:16 *d.* and misery are in their ways
1 Cor 5: 5 for the *d.* of the flesh
2 Cor 10: 8 and not for your *d.*, I should
1 Thes 5: 3 sudden *d.* cometh on them
2 Pet 2: 1 bring upon themselves swift *d.*
3:16 scriptures unto their own *d.*

DETERMINED
2 Chr 25:16 God hath *d.* to destroy thee
Is 10:23 even *d.*, in the midst of all the land
Dan 9:24 seventy weeks are *d.* upon thy people

Acts 4:28 thy counsel *d.* before to be done
17:26 hath *d.* the times before appointed
1 Cor 2: 2 I *d.* not to know any thing among you

DEVICE (DEVICES)
Job 5:12 he disappointeth the *d.* of the crafty
Ps 33:10 he maketh the *d.* of the people
Prov 1:31 and be filled with their own *d.*
14:17 a man of wicked *d.* is hated
Eccl 9:10 for there is no work nor *d.*
Jer 18:12 we will walk after our own *d.*
2 Cor 2:11 we are not ignorant of his *d.*

DEVIL
Mat 4: 1 wilderness to be tempted of the *d.*
13:39 the enemy that sowed is the *d.*
John 6:70 twelve, and one of you is a *d.*
7:20 thou hast a *d.*: who goeth about
8:44 ye are of your father the *d.*
13: 2 *d.* having now put into the heart
Eph 4:27 neither give place to the *d.*
1 Tim 3: 6 fall into condemnation of the *d.*
2 Tim 2:26 recover out of the snare of the *d.*
Jas 4: 7 resist the *d.* and he will flee
1 Pet 5: 8 because your adversary the *d.*
1 John 3: 8 to destroy the works of the *d.*
3:10 children of God and children of the *d.*
Rev 2:10 the *d.* shall cast some of you

DEVILS
Lev 17: 7 offer their sacrifices unto *d.*
2 Chr 11:15 the high places and for the *d.*
Ps 106:37 sacrificed their sons to *d.*
Mat 4:24 which were possessed with *d.*
10: 8 raise the dead, cast out *d.*
Mark 16: 9 out of whom he had cast seven *d.*
Luke 8:36 he that was possessed of the *d.*
10:17 even *d.* are subject to us
1 Tim 4: 1 to seducing spirits and doctrines of *d.*
Jas 2:19 the *d.* also believe and tremble

DEVISE (DEVISETH)
Prov 3:29 *d.* not evil against thy neighbour
14:22 do they not err that *d.* evil
16: 9 a man's heart *d.* his ways
Jer 18:18 *d.* devices against Jeremiah
Mic 2: 1 woe to them that *d.* iniquity

DEVOUR (DEVOURED)
Gen 49:27 he shall *d.* the prey
Is 9:12 they shall *d.* Israel with open mouth
Prov 30:14 to *d.* the poor off the earth
Is 24: 6 hath curse *d.* the earth
Jer 3:24 shame hath *d.* the labour
50:17 Israel the king of Assyria hath *d.*
Hos 7: 7 and have *d.* their judges
Mat 23:14 for ye *d.* widows' houses, and
2 Cor 11:20 if a man *d.* you, if a man take
Gal 5:15 if ye bite and *d.* one another
Heb 10:27 which shall *d.* the adversaries
1 Pet 5: 8 seeking whom he may *d.*

DEVOURING
Ex 24:17 like *d.* fire on top of the mount
Ps 52: 4 thou lovest all *d.* words
Is 29: 6 and the flame of *d.* fire
33:14 shall dwell with the *d.* fire

DEVOUT
Luke 2:25 the same man was just and *d.*
Acts 2: 5 dwelling at Jerusalem Jews, *d.* men
8: 2 and *d.* men carried Stephen
10: 2 a *d.* man, and one that feared God
13:50 Jews stirred up the *d.* and honourable women
17: 4 and of the *d.* Greeks a great multitude
22:12 Ananias, a *d.* man according to the law

DEW
Gen 27:28 God give thee of the *d.* of heaven

Deut 32: 2 my speech shall distill as the *d.*
Ps 110: 3 thou hast the *d.* of thy youth
Is 26:19 thy *d.* is as the *d.* of herbs
Hos 6: 4 goodness is as the early *d.*
14: 5 I will be as *d.* to Israel
Mic 5: 7 many people as a *d.* from the Lord

DIE
Gen 2:17 thereof thou shalt surely *d.*
3: 4 ye shall not surely *d.*
6:17 everything that is in the earth shall *d.*
Ex 20:19 let not God speak with us, lest we *d.*
1 Sam 14:44 for thou shalt surely *d.*, Jonathan
1 Ki 2:42 that thou shalt surely *d.*
Job 14:14 if a man *d.* shall he live again?
Ps 82: 7 but ye shall *d.* like men
Prov 23:13 with the rod, he shall not *d.*
Eccl 3: 2 born and a time to *d.*
7:17 why shouldst thou *d.* before thy time
Is 22:13 for tomorrow we shall *d.*
Jer 26: 8. him, saying Thou shalt surely *d.*
31:30 *d.* for his own iniquity
Ezek 3:18 wicked man shall *d.* in his iniquity
3:19 he shall *d.* in his iniquity
18:31 why will ye *d.* O house of Israel
Jonah 4: 3 better for me to *d.* than to live
Mat 26:35 though I should *d.* with thee
Luke 20:36 neither can they *d.* any more
John 8:21 ye shall *d.* in your sins
11:50 that one man should *d.* for the people
Rom 14: 8 we *d.* we *d.* unto the Lord
1 Cor 9:15 better for me to *d.* than
Phil 1:21 to live is Christ, to *d.* is gain
Heb 9:27 appointed unto men once to *d.*
Rev 3: 2 which remain that are ready to *d.*

DIED (DIETH)
Rom 5: 6 Christ *d.* for the ungodly
5: 8 while we were yet sinners, Christ *d.*
6: 9 being raised from the dead *d.* no more
6:10 for in that he *d.* he *d.* unto sin
7: 9 sin revived and I *d.*
14: 7 no man *d.* to himself
14: 9 to this end Christ *d.* and rose
1 Cor 15: 3 Christ *d.* for our sins
2 Cor 5:15 he *d.* for all, that they
1 Thes 5:10 who *d.* for us that whether
Heb 11:13 these all *d.* in faith, not

DYING
2 Cor 4:10 the *d.* of the Lord Jesus
6: 9 yet well known as *d.* and, behold
Heb 11:21 By faith, Jacob, when he was *d.*

DILIGENCE
Prov 4:23 keep thy heart with all *d.*
Luke 12:58 give *d.* that thou mayest be delivered
Rom 12: 8 he that ruleth, with *d.*
2 Cor 8: 7 in all *d.* and in your love to us
2 Tim 4: 9 Do thy *d.* to come shortly unto me
4:21 do thy *d.* to come before winter
2 Pet 1: 5 giving all *d.*, add to your faith
1:10 give *d.* to make your calling
Jude 1: 3 when I gave all *d.* to write

DILIGENT (DILIGENTLY)
Ex 15:26 if thou wilt *d.* hearken to
Deut 4: 9 keep thy soul *d.*, lest thou forget
6:17 *d.* keep the commandments of the Lord
19:18 judges shall make *d.* inquisition
28: 1 thou shalt hearken *d.* unto the voice
Ps 37:10 thou shalt *d.* consider his place
64: 6 they accomplish a *d.* search
Prov 10: 4 hand of the *d.* maketh rich
12:24 hand of the *d.* shall bear rule
13: 4 soul of the *d.* shall be made fat
21: 5 thoughts of the *d.* tend to plenty
22:29 man *d.* in his business
Jer 17:24 if ye *d.* hearken unto me
Zech 6:15 if ye will *d.* obey the voice

Luke 15: 8 seek *d.* till she find it
1 Pet 1:10 prophets have inquired and searched *d.*
2 Pet 3:14 be *d.* to be found of him

DINNER
Prov 15:17 better is a *d.* of herbs
Luke 14:12 when thou makest a *d.* or a supper

DIP (DIPPED)
Ruth 2:14 and *d.* thy morsel in the vinegar
Ps 68:23 thy foot may be *d.* in the blood
John 13:26 when he had *d.* the sop

DIRECT (DIRECTED)
Ps 5: 3 will I *d.* my prayer to thee
119: 5 my ways were *d.* to keep
Prov 3: 6 he shall *d.* thy paths
16: 9 the Lord *d.* his steps
Eccl 10:10 but wisdom is profitable to *d.*
Is 40:13 who hath *d.* the spirit of the Lord
45:13 and I will *d.* all his ways
61: 8 I will *d.* their work in truth
Jer 10:23 walketh to *d.* his steps

DISCERN (DISCERNED, DISCERNETH, DISCERNING)
2 Sam 14:17 the king to *d.* good and bad
Eccl 8: 5 a wise man's heart *d.* both time
Mal 3:18 *d.* between the righteous and the
1 Cor 2:14 because they are spiritually *d.*
11:29 not *d.* the Lord's body
12:10 to another *d.* of spirits
Heb 5:14 to *d.* both good and evil

DISCIPLE (DISCIPLES)
Mat 10:24 *d.* is not above his master
10:42 cup of water in the name of a *d.*
Luke 14:26 life also he cannot be my *d.*
John 8:31 then are ye my *d.* indeed
9:28 thou art his *d.*; but we are
19:38 Joseph of Arimathaea, being a *d.*
Acts 21:16 an old *d.* with whom

DISEASED
John 6: 2 he did on them that were *d.*

DISEASES
Ex 15:26 I will put none of these *d.*
2 Chr 16:12 in his *d.* he sought not the Lord
Ps 38: 7 are filled with a loathsome *d.*
103: 3 who healeth all thy *d.*
Eccl 6: 2 and it is an evil *d.*
Mat 4:23 and all manner of *d.* among the people

DISHONOUR (DISHONOURETH)
Ezra 4:14 not meet for us to see the king's *d.*
Ps 35:26 clothed with shame and *d.*
Prov 6:33 a wound and *d.* shall he get
Mic 7: 6 for the son *d.* his father
Rom 1:24 to *d.* their own bodies
1 Cor 15:43 it is sown in *d.* it is raised
2 Cor 6: 8 by honour and *d.*, by evil report

DISOBEDIENCE
Rom 5:19 by one man's *d.* many were made
2 Cor 10: 6 readiness to revenge all *d.*
Eph 2: 2 worketh in the children of *d.*
5: 6 wrath of God upon the children of *d.*
Col 3: 6 cometh upon the children of *d.*
Heb 2: 2 if every *d.* received just

DISOBEDIENT
1 Ki 13:26 who was *d.* unto the word of God
Neh 9:26 nevertheless they were against *d.*
Luke 1:17 *d.* to the wisdom of the just
Rom 1:30 of evil things *d.* to parents
1 Tim 1: 9 law made for lawless and *d.*
2 Tim 3: 2 *d.* to parents, unthankful, unholy
Tit 1:16 deny him being abominable, and *d.*
1 Pet 3:20 which sometime were *d.* which once

DISPENSATION
1 Cor 9:17 a *d.* of the gospel is committed
Eph 1:10 in the *d.* of the fulness of time
3: 2 the *d.* of the grace of God
Col 1:25 according to the *d.* of God

DISPLEASED
Gen 38:10 the thing which he did *d.* the Lord
2 Sam 11:27 that David had done *d.* the Lord
1 Chr 21: 7 God was *d.* with this thing
Zech 1:15 I am very sore *d.* with the heathen
Mark 10:14 he was much *d.*, and said

DISPLEASURE
Deut 9:19 afraid of the anger and hot *d.*
Ps 2: 5 and vex them in his sore *d.*

DISPUTE (DISPUTED, DISPUTING)
Job 23: 7 there the righteous might *d.* with him
Mark 9:33 what was it that ye *d.* among yourselves
Acts 6: 9 Cilicia and of Asia, *d.* with Stephen
9:29 and *d.* against the Grecians
17:17 therefore *d.* he in the synagogue
19: 9 disciples, *d.* daily in the school

DISPUTATIONS
Rom 14: 1 but not to doubtful *d.*

DISSENSION
Acts 15: 2 Paul and Barnabas had no small *d.*
23:10 when there arose a great *d.*

DISSOLVED (DISSOLVEST)
Job 30:22 upon it and *d.* my substance
Ps 75: 3 all the inhabitants thereof are *d.*
Is 24:19 the earth is clean *d.*
2 Cor 5: 1 house of this tabernacle were *d.*
2 Pet 3:11 all these things shall be *d.*

DISTRESS
Gen 35: 3 answered me in the day of my *d.*
42:21 therefore is this *d.* come upon us
2 Sam 22: 7 in my *d.* I called upon the Lord
1 Ki 1:29 redeemed thy soul out of *d.*
Neh 9:37 and we are in great *d.*
Ps 4: 1 enlarged me when I was in *d.*
18: 6 in my *d.* I called upon the Lord
120: 1 In my *d.* I cried unto the Lord
Prov 1:27 when *d.* and anguish cometh
Is 25: 4 strength to the needy in his *d.*
Zeph 1:15 day of trouble and *d.*, a day of
Luke 21:25 upon the earth *d.* of nations
Rom 8:35 shall tribulation, or *d.*, or persecution

DISTRESSED
Gen 32: 7 Then Jacob was greatly afraid and *d.*
2 Sam 1:26 I am *d.* for thee, my brother Jonathan
2 Chr 28:20 and *d.* him, but strengthened him not

DISTRIBUTE (DISTRIBUTING, DISTRIBUTETH)
Job 21:17 God *d.* sorrows in anger
Luke 18:22 and *d.* unto the poor, and thou
Rom 12:13 *d.* to the necessity of saints
1 Tim 6:18 ready to *d.*, willing to communicate

DISTRIBUTION
Acts 4:35 *d.* was made to every man
2 Cor 9:13 for your liberal *d.* unto them

DITCH (DITCHES)
2 Ki 3:16 make this valley full of *d.*
Job 9:31 shalt thou plunge me in the *d.*
Ps 7:15 and is fallen into the *d.*
Prov 23:27 for a whore is a deep *d.*
Is 22:11 made also a *d.* between the two walls
Mat 15:14 both shall fall into the *d.*

DIVIDE (DIVIDED, DIVIDING)
Gen 1: 6 *d.* the waters from the waters
1:14 to *d.* the day from the night
10:25 isles of the Gentiles *d.* in their
Ex 14:16 thine hand over the sea, and *d.* it
Josh 19:51 *d.* for an inheritance land by lot
Ps 55: 9 destroy O Lord and *d.* their tongues
Is 53:12 will I *d.* him a portion
Dan 2:41 the kingdom shall be *d.*
Mat 12:25 city or house *d.* against itself
Luke 12:13 to *d.* the inheritance with me
1 Cor 1:13 is Christ *d.*? was Paul
12:11 *d.* to every man severally as he will
2 Tim 2:15 rightly *d.* the word of truth
Heb 4:12 to the *d.* asunder of soul and spirit

DIVISION (DIVISIONS)
Judg 5:16 for the *d.* of Reuben there were
Luke 12:51 I tell you Nay, but rather *d.*

DIVINE
1 Sam 28: 8 *d.* unto me by the familiar spirit
Prov 16:10 a *d.* sentence is in the lips
Mic 3:11 prophets thereof *d.* for money
Heb 9: 1 had also ordinances of *d.* service
2 Pet 1: 3 his *d.* power hath given

DIVINATION
Num 22: 7 the rewards of *d.* in their hand
Deut 18:10 or that useth *d.* or an observer
Ezek 21:21 of the two ways, to use *d.*
Acts 16:16 possessed with a spirit of *d.*

DIVINERS
1 Sam 6: 2 called for the priests and the *d.*
Is 44:25 and maketh *d.* mad, that turneth
Mic 3: 7 and the *d.* confounded: yea, they
Zech 10: 2 and the *d.* have seen a lie

DIVORCE (DIVORCED)
Lev 22:13 Priest's daughter be a widow, or *d.*
Num 30: 9 and of her that is *d.*
Jer 3: 8 and given her a bill of *d.*

DIVORCEMENT
Deut 24: 1 let him write her a bill of *d.*
Is 50: 1 where is the bill of your mother's *d.*
Mat 5:31 let him give her a writing of *d.*

DO
Gen 18:25 not the Judge of all the earth *d.* right
Mat 7:12 men *d.* to you, *d.* ye even so
John 15: 5 without me ye can *d.* nothing
Rom 7:15 what I would that *d.* I not
Phil 4:13 I can *d.* all things all through Christ
Heb 4:13 with whom we have to *d.*
Rev 19:10 see thou *d.* it not

DOERS
Rom 2:13 *d.* of it shall be justified
Jas 1:22 be ye *d.* of word and not

DOING (DOINGS)
Lev 18: 3 after the *d.* of the land of Canaan
Ps 64: 9 they shall wisely consider of his *d.*
118:23 this is the Lord's *d.*
Prov 20:11 even a child is known by his *d.*
Jer 7: 3 amend your ways and your *d.*
Acts 10:38 who went about *d.* good
Rom 2: 7 by patient continuance in well *d.*
Gal 6: 9 let us not be weary in well *d.*
Eph 6: 6 *d.* the will of God from the heart
2 Thes 3:13 brethren, be not weary in well *d.*
1 Pet 2:15 that with well *d.* ye may put
3:17 that ye suffer for well *d.*
4:19 of their souls to him in well *d.*

DOCTOR (DOCTORS)
Luke 2:46 sitting in the midst of the *d.*
5:17 there were Pharisees and *d.* of the law
Acts 5:34 Gamaliel, a *d.* of the law

DOCTRINE
Deut 32: 2 my *d.* shall drop as the rain
Is 28: 9 whom shall he make to understand *d.*?

Luke 21:34 be overcharged with surfeiting, and *d.*
Rom 13:13 not in rioting and *d.*
Gal 5:21 murders, *d.*, revelling, and such like

DROP (DROPPED)
Ps 65:11 goodness; and thy paths *d.* fatness
Prov 5: 3 *d.* as an honeycomb, and her mouth
Sol 4:11 O my spouse, *d.* as the honeycomb
5: 5 my hands *d.* with myrrh
Is 40:15 nations as a *d.* of a bucket

DROPS
Job 36:27 he maketh small the *d.* of water
38:28 who hath begotten the *d.* of dew
Sol 5: 2 my locks with the *d.* of the night
Luke 22:44 as it were great *d.* of blood

DROSS
Ps 119:119 all the wicked of the earth like *d.*
Is 1:25 purely purge away thy *d.*
Ezek 22:18 the house of Israel is to me become *d.*

DRY
Judg 6:37 if it be *d.* upon all the earth
Prov 17: 1 better is a *d.* morsel
Is 44: 3 and floods upon the *d.* ground
56: 3 behold, I am a *d.* tree
Jer 4:11 a *d.* wind of the high places
Ezek 17:24 have made the *d.* tree to flourish
Hos 9:14 a miscarrying womb and *d.* breasts

DUE
Deut 32:35 foot shall slide in *d.* time
1 Chr 15:13 sought him not after *d.* order
Ps 104:27 meat in *d.* season
Prov 3:27 good from them to whom it is *d.*
15:23 a word spoken in *d.* season
Eccl 10:17 thy princes eat in *d.* season
Mat 18:34 pay all that was *d.* unto him
24:45 to give them their meat in *d.* season
Luke 12:42 their portion of meat in *d.* season
23:41 we receive the *d.* reward of our deeds
Rom 13: 7 tribute to whom tribute is *d.*
Gal 6: 9 in *d.* season we shall reap
1 Cor 15: 8 as one born out of *d.* time
1 Tim 2: 6 to be testified in *d.* time

DUMB
Ps 38:13 I was as a *d.* man
Prov 31: 8 open thy mouth for the *d.*
Is 35: 6 tongue of the *d.* to sing
53: 7 as a sheep before her shearers is *d.*
56:10 watchmen are all *d.* dogs
Ezek 3:26 that thou shalt be *d.*, and shalt
Hab 2:18 therein to make *d.* idols
Mat 9:33 devil was cast out, the *d.* spake
Mark 9:25 thou *d.* and deaf spirit
Luke 1:20 behold, thou shalt be *d.*
1 Cor 12: 2 carried away unto these *d.* idols
2 Pet 2:16 the *d.* ass speaking with man's voice

DUNG
Mal 2: 3 even the *d.* of your solemn feasts
Phil 3: 8 I count them but *d.*

DUST
Gen 3:19 unto *d.* thou shalt return
13:16 thy seed as the *d.* of the earth
18:27 which am but *d.* and ashes
28:14 seed shall be as the *d.* of the earth
Ex 8:17 smote the *d.* of the land
Num 23:10 who can count the *d.* of Jacob
Deut 28:24 make the rain of thy land powder and *d.*
2 Chr 1: 9 like the *d.* of the earth in multitude
Job 10: 9 wilt thou bring me into *d.* again
30:19 I am become like *d.* and ashes
42: 6 repent in *d.* and ashes
Ps 7: 5 lay mine honour in the *d.*
18:42 beat them small as the *d.* before
22:15 brought me into the *d.* of death
Ps 30: 9 shall the *d.* praise thee
102:14 stones and favour the *d.* thereof
103:14 remembereth that we are *d.*
104:29 they die, and return to their *d.*
Eccl 12: 7 shall the *d.* return to the earth
Is 26:19 awake and sing, ye that dwell in *d.*
41: 2 he gave them as the *d.* to his sword
Lam 3:29 he putteth his mouth in the *d.*
Dan 12: 2 sleep in the *d.* of the earth
Amos 2: 7 that pant after the *d.* of the earth
Mat 10:14 shake off the *d.* of your feet
Acts 13:51 they shook off the *d.* of their feet
Rev 18:19 they cast *d.* on their heads

DUTY
Ex 21:10 and her *d.* of marriage shall he not
2 Chr 8:14 as the *d.* of every day required
Eccl 12:13 this is the whole *d.* of man
Luke 17:10 which was our *d.* to do

DWELL (DWELLETH, DWELT)
Ps 15: 1 who shall *d.* in thy holy hill
23: 6 *d.* in house of Lord for ever
84:10 than to *d.* in the tents of wickedness
120: 5 that I *d.* in the tents of Kedar
132:14 here will I *d.* for I desired
Is 33:14 who *d.* with devouring fire
33:16 he shall *d.* on high
Ezek 43: 7 I will *d.* in the midst of the children
John 1:14 Word made flesh and *d.*
6:56 *d.* in me, and I in him
14:10 Father that *d.* in me, he doeth
14:17 ye know him for he *d.* with you
Acts 7:48 *d.* not in temples made with hands
13:17 they *d.* as strangers in the land of
Rom 7:17 sin that *d.* in me
7:18 in my flesh *d.* no good thing
8: 9 Spirit of God *d.* in you
2 Cor 6:16 I will *d.* in them, and walk in
Eph 3:17 that Christ may *d.* in your hearts
Col 1:19 that in him should all fulness *d.*
2: 9 in Christ *d.* all the fulness of
3:16 let the word of Christ *d.* in you richly
2 Tim 1: 5 which *d.* first in thy grandmother
1:14 Holy Ghost which *d.* in us
Jas 4: 5 spirit which *d.* in us lusteth
2 Pet 3:13 wherein *d.* righteousness
1 John 3:17 how *d.* the love of God in him
4:12 God *d.* in us, and his love is
4:13 know that we *d.* in him
4:15 God *d.* in him, and he in God
2 John 1: 2 truth's sake which *d.* in us
Rev 21: 3 he will *d.* with them, and

DWELLING (DWELLINGS)
Ps 87: 2 more than all the *d.* of Jacob
1 Tim 6:16 *d.* in the light which no man
Heb 11: 9 *d.* in tabernacles with Isaac
2 Pet 2: 8 righteous man *d.* among them

E

EAGLE (EAGLES)
Ex 19: 4 I bare you on *e.* wings
Deut 28:49 as swift as the *e.* flieth
2 Sam 1:23 they were swifter than *e.*, stronger
Job 9:26 *e.* that hasteth to the prey
39:27 doth the *e.* mount up
Ps 103: 5 thy youth is renewed like the *e.*
Prov 30:17 the young *e.* shall eat it
30:19 way of an *e.* in the air
Is 40:31 they shall mount up with wings as *e.*
Jer 49:16 thy nest as high as the *e.*
Lam 4:19 persecutors swifter than *e.*
Ezek 10:14 the fourth the face of an *e.*
17: 3 a great *e.* with great wings
Dan 7: 4 like a lion and had *e.* wings
Hos 8: 1 he shall come as an *e.* against the house
Obad 1: 4 thou exalt thyself as the *e.*
Mic 1:16 enlarge thy baldness as the *e.*
Hab 1: 8 they shall fly as the *e.* that
Rev 4: 7 beast was like a flying *e.*
Rev 12:14 given two wings of a great *e.*

EAR
Ex 21: 6 shall bore his *e.* through with an awl
29:20 blood upon the tip of the right *e.*
Deut 32: 1 Give *e.* O ye heavens
Judg 5: 3 give *e.*, o ye princes
2 Ki 19:16 bow down thine *e.*, and hear
Neh 1: 6 let thine *e.* now be attentive
Job 4:12 mine *e.* received a little thereof
36:10 God openeth man's *e.*
42: 5 heard of thee by hearing of the *e.*
Ps 5: 1 give *e.* to my words, O Lord
10:17 cause thine *e.* to hear
17: 6 incline thine *e.* unto me
49: 1 give *e.*, all ye inhabitants
54: 2 give *e.* to the words of my mouth
78: 1 give *e.*, O my people, to my law
86: 6 give *e.*, O Lord, unto my prayer
94: 9 He that planted the *e.* shall
130: 2 let thine *e.* be attentive
Prov 15:31 *e.* that heareth reproof
20:12 The hearing *e.* and seeing eye
25:12 wise reprover on an obedient *e.*
Is 1: 2 hear, O heavens, and give *e.*
8: 9 give *e.*, all ye of far countries
37:17 incline thine *e.*, O Lord
48: 8 time thine *e.* was not opened
50: 5 Lord God hath opened mine *e.* and
Jer 6:10 *e.* is uncircumcised and they cannot
Joel 1: 2 hear this, ye old men, and give *e.*
Amos 3:12 two legs or a piece of an *e.*
Luke 12: 3 which ye have spoken in the *e.*
1 Cor 2: 9 eye hath not seen nor *e.* heard

EARS
Deut 29: 4 eyes to see and *e.* to hear
2 Sam 7:22 all that we have heard with our *e.*
22: 7 my cry did enter into his *e.*
2 Chr 6:40 let thine *e.* be attent
Job 15:21 a dreadful sound in his *e.*
33:16 He openeth the *e.* of men
Ps 34:15 his *e.* are open unto their cry
40: 6 my *e.* hast thou opened
44: 1 we have heard with our *e.*
49: 4 I will incline mine *e.* to a parable
78: 1 incline your *e.* to the words
115: 6 they have *e.* but they hear not
Prov 23:12 apply thine *e.* to words of knowledge
Is 30:21 thine *e.* shall hear a word behind
32: 3 *e.* of hearers shall hearken
35: 5 the *e.* of the deaf shall be unstopped
43: 8 and the deaf that have *e.*
55: 3 incline your *e.* and come unto me
Jer 5:21 which have *e.*, and hear not
Ezek 3:10 and hear with thine *e.*
23:25 shall take away thy nose and thine *e.*
Zech 7:11 and stopped their *e.* that they
Mat 11:15 *e.* to hear, let him hear
13: 9 who hath *e.* to hear, let him hear
Mark 7:33 Jesus put his fingers into his *e.*
8:18 having *e.* hear ye not?
Luke 9:44 let sayings sink into your *e.*
Rev 2: 7 he that hath an *e.*, let him hear

EARLY
Gen 19:27 Abraham gat up *e.* in the morning
Ps 46: 5 God shall help her and that right *e.*
57: 8 I myself will awake *e.*
90:14 satisfy us *e.* with thy mercy
Prov 1:28 seek me *e.* and not find
8:17 that seek me *e.* shall find me
Is 26: 9 within me will I seek thee *e.*
Jer 26: 5 both rising up *e.*, and sending them
Hos 5:15 in affliction will seek me *e.*
John 18:28 hall of judgment and it was *e.*
20: 1 cometh Mary Magdalene *e.*
Jas 5: 7 receive *e.* and latter rain

EARNEST (EARNESTLY)
Job 7: 2 servant *e.* desireth shadow
Jer 11: 7 I *e.* protested unto your fathers
Mic 7: 3 do evil with both hands *e.*
Luke 22:44 in agony, he prayed more *e.*

Rom 8:19 for the *e.* expectation of
1 Cor 12:31 covet *e.* the best gifts
2 Cor 1:22 given the *e.* of the Spirit in our hearts
5: 2 in this we groan, *e.* desiring
5: 5 given unto us the *e.* of the Spirit
7: 7 told us of your *e.* desire
Eph 1:14 which is the *e.* of our inheritance
Phil 1:20 according to my *e.* expectation
Heb 2: 1 we ought to give the more *e.* heed
Jas 5:17 prayed *e.* that it might not rain
Jude 1: 3 ye should *e.* contend for the faith

EARRINGS

Gen 35: 4 and all their *e.* which were in
Ex 32: 2 break off the golden *e.*
Num 31:50 bracelets, rings, *e.*, and tablets
Judg 8:24 every man the *e.* of his prey
Ezek 16:12 and *e.* in thine ears
Hos 2:13 decked herself with her *e.*

EARTH

Gen 6:11 the *e.* also was corrupt
11: 1 whole *e.* of one language
41:47 *e.* brought forth by handfuls
Ex 9:29 that the *e.* is the Lord's
Num 16:32 *e.* opened her mouth
Deut 10:14 the *e.* also, with all that therein is
28:23 *e.* under thee be iron
32: 1 hear O *e.* the words of my mouth
Judg 5: 4 the *e.* trembled and the heavens
1 Sam 2: 8 pillars of the *e.* are the Lord's
1 Chr 16:31 and let the *e.* rejoice: and let
Job 9: 6 shaketh the *e.* out of her place
11: 9 longer than the *e.*, broader than the sea
16:18 O *e.* cover not thou my blood
26: 7 and hangeth the *e.* upon nothing
30: 8 base men, viler than the *e.*
38: 4 I laid the foundations of the *e.*
Ps 24: 1 the *e.* is the Lord's
33: 5 *e.* is full of the goodness of the Lord
65: 9 visitest the *e.* and waterest it
67: 2 way be known upon the *e.*, thy saving
67: 6 shall the*e.* yield her increase
72:19 let the whole *e.* be filled
73:25 none upon the *e.* that I desire
78:69 like the *e.* established for ever
89:11 are thine, the *e.* also is thine
97: 4 the world: the *e.* saw and trembled
104:24 the *e.* is full of thy riches
106:17 the *e.* opened and swallowed up Dathan
115:16 *e.* hath he given to the children
139:15 in lowest parts of the *e.*
Prov 25: 3 heaven for height and *e.* for depth
Eccl 1: 4 but the *e.* abideth for ever
5: 2 God is in heaven and thou upon *e.*
7:20 not a just man upon *e.* that doeth good
10: 7 princes walking as servants upon the *e.*
Is 6: 3 the whole *e.* is full of his glory
11: 4 smite the *e.* with the rod
11: 9 *e.* shall be full of the knowledge
13:13 *e.* shall remove out of her place
24: 1 Lord maketh the *e.* empty
24: 4 the *e.* mourneth and fadeth away
24: 5 the *e.* also is defiled under the
24:19 the *e.* is utterly broken down
24:20 *e.* shall reel to and fro like a
26:19 *e.* shall cast out the dead
66: 1 *e.* is my footstool, where is
Jer 22:29 O *e.* *e.* *e.* hear the word
Ezek 34:27 *e.* shall yield her increase
43: 2 the *e.* shined with his glory
Hos 2:22 *e.* shall hear the corn, and
Hab 2:14 for the *e.* shall be filled
3: 3 and *e.* was full of his praise
Mat 13: 5 where they had not much *e.*
Luke 5:24 Son of man power upon *e.* to forgive
John 3:31 he that is of *e.* is earthly
1 Cor 10:28 the *e.* is the Lord's

Col 3: 5 mortify your members which are upon the *e.*
Heb 6: 7 *e.* which drinketh in the rain that
Rev 12:16 and the *e.* helped the woman

EARTHEN

Jer 19: 1 get a potter's *e.* bottle
Lam 4: 2 how they are esteemed as *e.* pitchers

EARTHLY

John 3:31 he that is of the earth is *e.*
2 Cor 4: 7 we have this treasure in *e.* vessels
5: 1 if our *e.* house of this tabernacle
Phil 3:19 their shame who mind *e.* things

EARTHQUAKE (EARTHQUAKES)

1 Ki 19:12 and after the *e.* a fire
Is 29: 6 with thunder, and with *e.*
Amos 1: 1 two years before the *e.*
Zech 14: 5 as ye fled from before the *e.*
Mat 24: 7 and *e.* in divers places
27:54 with him, watching Jesus, saw the *e.*
28: 2 behold, there was a great *e.*
Acts 16:26 suddenly there was a great *e.*
Rev 11:19 and an *e.*, and great hail
16: 8 and there was a great *e.*

EASE

Job 12: 5 the thought of him that is at *e.*
Ps 25:13 his soul shall dwell at *e.*
Is 1:24 I will *e.* me of adversaries
32:11 tremble, ye women that are at *e.*
Jer 46:27 and be in rest and at *e.*
Ezek 23:42 and a voice of a multitude being at *e.*
Amos 6: 1 woe to them that are at *e.*
Zech 1:15 with the heathen that are at *e.*
Luke 12:19 take thine *e.* and be merry

EASY (EASIER, EASILY)

Prov 14: 6 knowledge is *e.* to him
Mat 9: 5 for whether is *e.*, to say
11:30 my yoke is *e.*, and my burden
Luke 16:17 *e.* for heaven and earth to pass
1 Cor 14: 9 words *e.* to be understood
Heb 12: 1 sin which doth so *e.* beset
Jas 3:17 gentle, *e.* to be entreated

EAST

Gen 28:14 abroad to the west and to the *e.*
41: 6 blasted with the *e.* wind
Ex 14:21 go back by a strong *e.* wind
Ps 48: 7 ships of Tarshish with an *e.* wind
103:12 as far as the *e.* is from the west
Is 27: 8 in the day of the *e.* wind
43: 5 bring thy seed from the *e.*
Hos 13:15 an *e.* wind shall come
Hab 1: 9 faces shall sup up as the *e.* wind
Mat 2: 1 there came wise men from the *e.*
8:11 many shall come from the *e.*

EAT

Gen 2:16 tree of the garden thou mayest freely *e.*
2:17 good and evil thou shalt not *e.*
3:14 dust shalt thou *e.* all the days
3:19 thy face shalt thou *e.* bread
9: 4 the blood thereof, shall ye not *e.*
18: 8 by them under the tree and they did *e.*
27: 4 bring it to me that I may *e.*
Ex 10: 5 shall *e.* the residue of that
12:48 no uncircumcised person shall *e.* thereof
16:35 Israel did *e.* manna forty years, until
32: 6 people sat down to *e.* and to drink
Lev 7:21 and *e.* of the flesh of the sacrifice
11: 2 are the beasts which ye shall *e.*
11:22 of them ye may *e.*, the locusts
17:14 *e.* the blood of no manner of flesh
19:25 shall ye *e.* of the fruit thereof
26:38 land of your enemies shall *e.* you up
Num 6: 3 nor *e.* moist grapes, or dried
11: 5 fish we *e.* in Egypt, melons, leeks
Deut 4:28 gods which neither *e.* nor

Deut 14:21 shall not *e.* anything that dieth
14:23 *e.* before Lord God tithe, firstlings
28:55 flesh of his children whom he shall *e.*
1 Sam 14:32 the people did *e.* them with the blood
1 Ki 13: 9 *e.* no bread, drink no water
19: 5 and said unto him Arise and *e.*
21:23 dogs shall *e.* Jezebel
2 Ki 4:43 give the people that they may *e.*
6:29 boiled my son, and did *e.* him
Neh 8:10 *e.* the fat, drink the sweet
Ps 22:26 meek shall *e.* and be satisfied
53: 4 *e.* up my people as bread
78:25 man did *e.* angels' food
128: 2 *e.* the labour of thine hands
Prov 1:31 *e.* the fruit of their own way
13: 2 *e.* good by the fruit of his mouth
25:16 *e.* so much as is sufficient
Eccl 3:13 every man should *e.* and drink
9: 7 *e.* thy bread with joy
Sol 5: 1 *e.* O friends; drink, yea
Is 1:19 if obedient ye shall *e.*
3:10 shall *e.* the fruit of their doings
4: 1 we will *e.* our own bread, only let
7:15 butter and honey shall he *e.*
9:20 *e.* every man the flesh of his own
11: 7 and the lion shall *e.* straw
30:24 young asses that ear the ground shall *e.*
37:30 *e.* this year such as groweth of itself
51: 8 worm shall *e.* them as wool
55: 1 buy and *e.*, yea, come buy
55: 2 *e.* that is good, let your soul delight
61: 6 ye shall *e.* the riches of the Gentiles
62: 9 they that have gathered it shall *e.* it
65: 4 which *e.* swine's flesh, and broth of
Jer 15:16 words were found and I did *e.*
Ezek 3: 1 *e.* this roll, and go speak
4:13 Israel *e.* their defiled bread among the Gentiles
4:16 *e.* bread by weight, and with care
5:10 fathers shall *e.* the sons
22: 9 they *e.* upon the mountains
Dan 1:12 let them give us pulse to *e.*
4:33 and did *e.* grass as oxen
Hos 4:10 *e.* and not have enough
Amos 7:12 there *e.* bread, and prophesy
9:14 gardens, and *e.* the fruit of them
Mic 3: 3 *e.* the flesh of my people
Zech 7: 6 did not ye *e.* for yourselves?
Mat 6:25 no thought what ye shall *e.*
26:26 Jesus said, Take *e.* this is my body
Mark 1: 6 *e.* locusts and wild honey
7: 5 *e.* bread with unwashen hands
7:28 dogs *e.* of the children's crumbs
14:22 as they did *e.*, Jesus took bread
Luke 10: 8 *e.* such things as are set before you
15:23 let us *e.*, and be merry
22:30 ye may *e.* and drink at my table
John 4:31 I have meat to *e.* that ye
6:26 because ye did *e.* of the loaves
6:53 except ye *e.* the flesh of the Son
Acts 2:46 did *e.* their meat with gladness
1 Cor 5:11 with such an one, no not to *e.*
8: 7 *e.* it as a thing offered unto an idol
10: 7 the people sat down to *e.* and drink
10:31 whether therefore ye *e.* or drink
11:24 take, *e.*: this is my body
2 Thes 3:10 not work, neither should he *e.*
Jas 5: 3 *e.* your flesh as it were fire
Rev 2: 7 will I give to *e.* of the tree
10: 9 take it and *e.* it up
17:16 shall *e.* her flesh, and burn

EATEN (EATETH, EATING)

Num 13:32 is a land that *e.* up the inhabitants
Deut 26:14 not *e.* thereof in my mourning
1 Sam 30:16 *e.* and drinking, and dancing,
Ps 69: 9 zeal of thine house hath *e.* me up
Prov 9:17 bread *e.* in secret is pleasant
Eccl 4: 5 together and *e.* his own flesh
Hos 10:13 having *e.* the fruit of lies
Joel 1: 4 hath the locust *e.*, and that

Amos 7: 2 end of e. the grass of the land
Mat 9:11 why e. your master with publicans and
11:18 John came neither e. nor drinking.
14:21 e. were about five thousand
24:38 were e. and drinking, marrying and
26:26 as they were e. Jesus took
Luke 13:26 e. and drunk in thy presence
John 2:17 the zeal of thine house hath e. me up
6:54 whoso e. my flesh and drinketh
6:58 he that e. this bread shall live
Acts 12:23 he was e. of worms
Rom 14: 6 he that e. e. to the Lord
14:20 for that man who e. with offence
1 Cor 11:29 e. and drinketh unworthily, e. and

EATER
Judg 14:14 out of the e. came forth meat
Is 55:10 seed to the sower, bread to the e.
Nah 3:12 fall into the mouth of the e.

EDIFY (EDIFIED, EDIFIETH)
Acts 9:31 and were e., and walking in the fear
Rom 14:19 wherewith one may e. another
1 Cor 8: 1 knowledge puffeth up, but charity e.
10:23 but all things e. not
14:17 but the other is not e.
1 Thes 5:11 yourselves together, and e. one

EDIFICATION
Rom 15: 2 please his neighbour for his good to e.
1 Cor 14: 3 speaketh unto men to e.
2 Cor 10: 8 which the Lord hath given us for e.

EDIFYING
1 Cor 14:12 may excel to the e. of the church
2 Cor 12:19 we do all for your e.
Eph 4:12 for the e. of the body of Christ
4:16 body unto the e. of itself in love
4:29 but that which is good to the use of e.
1 Tim 1: 4 questions rather than godly e.

EFFECT
Is 32:17 e. of righteousness quietness
Mat 15: 6 commandment of God of none e.
Mark 7:13 making the word of God of none e.
Rom 3: 3 make the faith of God without e.
9: 6 word of God had taken none e.
1 Cor 1:17 cross of Christ be made of none e.
Gal 5: 4 Christ is become of no e. to you

EFFECTUAL
1 Cor 16: 9 great door and e. is opened unto
2 Cor 1: 6 which is e. in the enduring
Eph 3: 7 by the e. working of his power
Philem 1: 6 thy faith may become e. by the
Jas 5:16 e. fervent prayer of a righteous

EFFEMINATE
1 Cor 6: 9 nor adulterers, nor e., nor abusers

EGG (EGGS)
Deut 22: 6 whether they be young ones, or e.
Job 6: 6 any taste in the white of an e.
Is 10:14 as one gathereth e. that are left
Jer 17:11 as the partridge sitteth on e.
Luke 11:12 or if he shall ask an e.

ELDER (ELDERS)
Gen 10:21 the brother of Japheth the e.
25:23 the e. shall serve the younger
Deut 32: 7 thy e. and they will tell thee
Ezra 10: 8 according to the counsel of the e.
Joel 2:16 assemble the e., gather the
Acts 14:23 ordained them e. in every church
15:23 e. and brethren send greeting
20:17 Ephesus, and called the e. of the church
Rom 9:12 the e. shall serve the younger
1 Tim 5: 1 rebuke not an e. but entreat
5: 2 the e. women as mothers
5:17 e. that rule well be counted
Tit 1: 5 ordain e. in every city
Heb 11: 2 e. obtained a good report
Jas 5:14 let him call for the e. of the church
1 Pet 5: 1 e. which are among you I exhort
5: 5 younger, submit yourselves unto the e.
2 John 1: 1 the e. unto the elect lady
3 John 1: 1 the e. unto the well-beloved Gaius
Rev 4: 4 four and twenty e. sitting
11:16 and the four and twenty e., which sat

ELECT
Is 42: 1 e. in whom my soul delighteth
65: 9 mine e. shall inherit it
Mat 24:22 for the e.'s sake those days shall shortened
24:24 if possible deceive the very e.
24:31 gather his e. from the four winds
Luke 18: 7 God avenge his own e.
Rom 8:33 to the charge of God's e.
Col 3:12 put on as the e. of God
1 Tim 5:21 the e. angels, that thou observe
2 Tim 2:10 I endure all things for the e.'s sake
Tit 1: 1 according to the faith of God's e.
1 Pet 1: 2 e. according to the foreknowledge of God
2: 6 corner stone, e., precious
2 John 1: 1 the elder unto the e. lady

ELECTED
1 Pet 5:13 e. together with you, saluteth you

ELECTION
Rom 9:11 according to e. might stand
11: 5 remnant according to the e. of grace
11: 7 but the e. hath obtained it
1 Thes 1: 4 brethren beloved, your e. of God
2 Pet 1:10 make your calling and e. sure

ELEMENTS
Gal 4: 9 again to the weak and beggarly e.

EMPTY
Gen 37:24 into a pit: and the pit was e.
41:27 the seven e. ears blasted with
Ex 23:15 and none shall appear before me e.
Deut 15:13 shalt not let him go away e.
16:16 they shall not appear before the Lord e.
Judg 7:16 in every man's hand, with e. pitchers
2 Sam 1:22 sword of Saul returned not e.
2 Ki 4: 3 even e. vessels; borrow not a few
Hos 10: 1 Israel is an e. vine, he bringeth
Luke 1:53 the rich he hath sent e. away

EMPTINESS
Is 34:11 confusion and the stones of e.

END
Gen 6:13 the e. of all flesh is come
Num 23:10 let my last e. be like his
Deut 8:16 to do thee good at thy latter e.
32:20 see what their e. shall be
Job 42:12 Lord blessed the latter e. of Job more
Ps 37:37 the e. of that man is peace
39: 4 make me to know mine e.
73:17 then understood I their e.
102:27 and thy years shall have no e.
119:33 I shall keep it unto the e.
119:96 seen an e. of all perfection
Prov 5: 4 her e. is bitter as wormwood
19:20 thou mayest be wise in thy latter e.
Eccl 4: 8 there is no e. of his labour
7: 2 for that is the e. of all men
7: 8 better is the e. of a thing
Is 9: 7 of his government there shall be no e.
Jer 4:27 yet will I not make a full e.
5:31 what will ye do in the e.
12: 4 he shall not see our last e.
17:11 days, and at his e. shall be a fool
31:17 and there is hope in thine e.
Lam 4:18 our e. is come, our e. is near
Ezek 11:13 wilt thou make a full e. of the remnant
21:25 when iniquity shall have an e.
Dan 6:26 dominion shall be even unto the e.
8:19 at the time appointed the e. shall
Amos 8: 2 e. is come upon my people of Israel
Hab 2: 3 at the e. it shall speak
Mat 13:39 harvest is the e. of the world
24: 3 and of the e. of the world
24: 6 but the e. is not yet
24:13 he that shall endure unto the e.
28:20 even unto the e. of the world
Luke 21: 9 but the e. is not by and by
John 13: 1 he loved them unto the e.
Rom 6:21 the e. of those things is death
6:22 and the e. everlasting life
14: 9 to this e. Christ both died and rose
1 Cor 1: 8 who shall also confirm you unto the e.
1 Tim 1: 5 e. of the commandment is charity
Heb 3:14 beginning of our confidence stedfast unto the e.
6: 8 whose e. is to be burned
6:11 assurance of hope unto the e.
6:16 is to them an e. of all strife
7: 3 beginning of days, nor e. of life
Jas 5:11 seen the e. of the Lord
1 Pet 1: 9 receiving the e. of your faith
4: 7 the e. of all things is at hand
4:17 e. of those that obey not the gospel
2 Pet 2:20 the latter e. is worse with them
Rev 1: 8 Alpha and Omega, the beginning and the e.
2:26 overcometh, and keepeth my works unto the e.
21: 6 Omega, the beginning and the e.
22:13 Alpha and Omega, the beginning and the e.

ENDS
Ps 22:27 the e. of the world shall remember
67: 7 all the e. of the earth shall fear him
Is 45:22 be ye saved, all the e. of the earth
52:10 all the e. of the earth shall see
Zech 9:10 even to the e. of the earth
Acts 13:47 salvation unto the e. of the earth
1 Cor 10:11 upon whom the e. of the world are come

ENDURE (ENDURED)
Gen 33:14 as children are able to e.
Ps 9: 7 the Lord shall e. forever
30: 5 weeping may e. for a night
72:17 His name shall e. forever
81:15 time should have e. for ever
89:36 his seed shall e. forever,
102:26 they shall perish, but thou shalt e.
Prov 27:24 crown e. to every generation
Ezek 22:14 can thine heart e. or can thine
Mat 24:13 he that shall e. to the end
Mark 4:17 no root, and e. but for a time
13:13 that shall e. unto the end shall
Rom 9:22 e. with much longsuffering
2 Tim 2: 3 e. hardness as a good soldier
2:10 e. all things for the elect's sake
3:11 what persecutions I e., but out of
4: 5 watch thou, e. afflictions, do the
Heb 6:15 he had patiently e., he obtained
11:27 e. as seeing him who is invisible
12: 2 that was set before him e. the cross
12: 7 if ye e. chastening, God dealeth
Jas 5:11 we count them happy which e.

ENDURETH
1 Chr 16:34 for his mercy e. for ever
2 Chr 5:13 for his mercy e. forever
Ezra 3:11 for his mercy e. forever toward Israel
Ps 30: 5 his anger e. but a moment
100: 5 his truth e. to all generations
106: 1 for his mercy e. forever
111:10 his praise e. for ever
112: 3 his righteousness e. for ever
117: 2 the truth of the Lord e. for ever
119:160 thy righteous judgments e. for ever

Ps	135:13	thy name, O Lord, *e.* for ever
	136: 1	for his mercy *e.* forever
	138: 8	thy mercy, O Lord, *e.* forever
	145:13	and thy dominion *e.* throughout all
Mat	10:22	that *e.* to end shall be saved
John	6:27	meat which *e.* unto life
1 Cor	13: 7	hopeth all things, *e.* all things
Jas	1:12	blessed is the man that *e.* temptation
1 Pet	1:25	the word of the Lord *e.* for ever

ENEMY

Ex	23:22	I will be an *e.* unto thine enemies
Deut	32:27	not that I feared the wrath of the *e.*
1 Sam	24:19	find his *e.* will he let him go
1 Ki	21:20	hast thou found me, O mine *e.*
Job	33:10	he counteth me for his *e.*
Ps	7: 5	let the *e.* persecute my soul
	8: 2	mightest still the *e.* and avenger
Prov	27: 6	kisses of an *e.* are deceitful
Mic	7: 8	rejoice not against me, O mine *e.*
1 Cor	15:26	the last *e.* destroyed is death
Gal	4:16	am I therefore become your *e.*
2 Thes	3:15	count him not as an *e.*, but
Jas	4: 4	friend of the world is the *e.* of God

ENEMIES

Gen	22:17	seed shall possess the gate of his *e.*
Ex	23:22	I will be an enemy unto thine *e.*
Deut	28:48	therefore shalt thou serve thine *e.*
Judg	5:31	let all thine *e.* perish, O Lord
Ps	68: 1	let his *e.* be scattered
	92: 9	for lo, thine *e.* shall perish
	132:18	his *e.* will I clothe with shame
Prov	16: 7	he maketh even his *e.* to be at peace
Is	66: 6	that rendereth recompence to his *e.*
Mic	7: 6	man's *e.* are the men of his own house
Mat	22:44	till I make thine *e.* thy footstool
Rom	5:10	if when we were *e.* we were reconciled
1 Cor	15:25	put all *e.* under his feet
Col	1:21	*e.* in your mind by wicked works
Heb	1:13	until I make thine *e.* thy footstool
	10:13	till his *e.* be made his footstool

ENMITY

Gen	3:15	I will put *e.* between thee and
Rom	8: 7	carnal mind is *e.* against God
Eph	2:15	abolished in his flesh the *e.*

ENJOY

Lev	26:34	shall the land *e.* her sabbaths
Num	36: 8	children of Israel may *e.* every man
Deut	28:41	thou shalt not *e.* them; for they
Acts	24: 2	we *e.* great quietness
Heb	11:25	*e.* the pleasures of sin for a season

ENLARGE (ENLARGED, ENLARGETH)

Gen	9:27	God shall *e.* Japheth and he
Deut	33:20	blessed be he that *e.* Gad
2 Sam	22:37	thou hast *e.* my steps under me
Ps	4: 1	thou hast *e.* me when in distress
	25:17	troubles of my heart are *e.*
Is	5:14	hell hath *e.* herself, and opened
	54: 2	*e.* the place of thy tent, and let
Hab	2: 5	*e.* his desire as hell and is as
2 Cor	6:11	unto you our heart is *e.*

ENLIGHTEN (ENLIGHTENED)

Ps	18:28	the Lord my God will *e.* my darkness
Eph	1:18	eyes of your understanding being *e.*
Heb	6: 4	impossible for those who were once *e.*

ENOUGH

Gen	33:11	with me and because I have *e.*
	45:28	is *e.* Joseph my son is yet alive
Ex	36: 5	people bring more than *e.* for the
2 Sam	24:16	Lord said to the angel, It is *e.*
1 Ki	19: 4	it is *e.* now, O Lord
Prov	30:15	say not, it is *e.*
Mat	10:25	it is *e.* for the disciple that
Mark	14:41	it is *e.* the hour is come
Luke	15:17	bread *e.* and to spare

ENSIGN (ENSIGNS)

Ps	74: 4	set up their *e.* for signs
Is	5:26	he will lift up an *e.* to the nations
	11:10	stand for an *e.* to the people
Zech	9:16	lifted up as an *e.* upon his land

ENTER

Num	20:24	for he shall not *e.* into the land
Job	22: 4	will he *e.* with thee into judgment
Ps	100: 4	*e.* his gates with thanksgiving
	118:20	gate into which the righteous shall *e.*
Prov	4:14	*e.* not into the path of the wicked
	23:10	*e.* not into the fields of the fatherless
Is	2:10	*e.* into the rock and hide
	26:20	*e.* into thy chambers, and shut
	57: 2	he shall *e.* into peace
Dan	11:17	set his face to *e.* with the strength
Mat	5:20	no case *e.* into the kingdom
	6: 6	when thou prayest, *e.* into thy closet
	7:21	shall *e.* into the kingdom of heaven
	18: 8	it is better to *e.* into life halt
	19:24	than for rich men to *e.* into the kingdom
	25:21	*e.* thou into the joy of thy Lord
	26:41	that ye *e.* not into temptation
Mark	14:38	watch and pray, lest ye *e.* into temptation
Luke	13:24	seek to *e.* but not able
	24:26	things and to *e.* into his glory
John	3: 4	can he *e.* the second time into his
	3: 5	he cannot *e.* into the kingdom of God
	10: 9	I am the door; by me if any man *e.*
Acts	14:22	tribulation *e.* into the kingdom of God
Heb	4: 3	believed do *e.* into rest
	10:19	*e.* into the holiest by the blood of Jesus
Rev	15: 8	no man was able to *e.* the temple
	22:14	*e.* through the gates into the city

ENTERED (ENTERETH)

Gen	19:23	the earth when Lot *e.* into Zoar
Ex	33: 9	as Moses *e.* into the tabernacle
Luke	11:52	ye *e.* not in yourselves, and them
John	4:38	ye are *e.* into their labours
	10: 1	*e.* not by the door, but climbeth up
Rom	5:12	by one man sin *e.* into the world
	5:20	law *e.* that offence might abound
Heb	4: 6	*e.* not because of unbelief

ENTERTAIN

Heb	13: 2	be not forgetful to *e.* strangers

ENTREAT (ENTREATED)

Gen	12:16	and he *e.* Abram well for her sake
Ex	9:28	*e.* the Lord (for it is enough)
1 Sam	2:25	if a man sin who shall *e.*
Jer	15:11	I will cause the enemy to *e.* thee well
1 Cor	4:13	being defamed, we *e.*: we are made
1 Tim	5: 1	not an elder but *e.* him as a father
Jas	3:17	easy to be *e.*, full of mercy

ENTREATY (ENTREATIES)

Prov	18:23	the poor useth *e.*, but the rich
2 Cor	8: 4	praying us with much *e.* that we

ENVY (ENVIES)

Job	5: 2	and *e.* slayeth the silly one
Prov	3:31	*e.* thou not the oppressor, and
	14:30	*e.* is the rottenness of bones
	23:17	let not thy heart *e.* sinners
	27: 4	who is able to stand before *e.*
Is	11:13	*e.* also of Ephraim shall depart
Ezek	35:11	and according to thine *e.* which thou
Mat	27:18	for *e.* they delivered him
Acts	7: 9	moved with *e.* sold Joseph into
	17: 5	which believed not, moved with *e.*
Phil	1:15	some indeed preach Christ even of *e.*
1 Tim	6: 4	whereof cometh *e.*, strife, railings
Tit	3: 3	living in malice, *e.*, hateful and
Jas	4: 5	spirit in us lusteth to *e.*
1 Pet	2: 1	hypocrisies and *e.* and all evil

ENVIED (ENVIEST, ENVYING)

Gen	26:14	the Philistines *e.* him
Num	11:29	*e.* thou for my sake? would God
Ps	106:16	they *e.* Moses also in the camp
Eccl	4: 4	work, that for this a man is *e.*
Rom	13:13	wantonness, not in strife and *e.*
1 Cor	3: 3	*e.* and strife, and divisions, are ye
Gal	5:26	provoking one another, *e.* one another

ENVIOUS

Ps	37: 1	neither be thou *e.*
Prov	24: 1	be not thou *e.* against the workers

EPHOD

Ex	39: 2	made the *e.* of gold, blue, and purple
Judg	8:27	and Gideon made an *e.* thereof
	17: 5	and made an *e.*, and teraphim
1 Sam	2:18	girded with a linen *e.*
	21: 9	wrapped in a cloth behind the *e.*
	23: 9	the priest, bring hither the *e.*
	30: 7	pray thee, bring me hither the *e.*
2 Sam	6:14	David was girded with a linen *e.*
Hos	3: 4	without an image, and without an *e.*

EPISTLE

Acts	15:30	together they delivered the *e.*
Rom	16:22	I Tertius, who wrote this *e.*
1 Cor	5: 9	I wrote unto you in an *e.*
2 Cor	3: 2	*e.* written in our hearts
	7: 8	the same *e.* hath made you sorry
Col	4:16	ye likewise read the *e.* from Laodicea
1 Thes	5:27	this *e.* be read unto all
2 Thes	2:15	whether by word, or our *e.*
2 Pet	3: 1	this second *e.*, beloved, I now write

EQUAL (EQUALS)

Is	40:25	Or shall I be *e.*? saith the Holy
Ezek	18:25	ye say, the way of the Lord is not *e.*
Mat	20:12	thou hast made them *e.* unto us
Luke	20:36	for they are *e.* unto the angels
John	5:18	making himself *e.* with God
Gal	1:14	my *e.* in mine own nation
Phil	2: 6	it not robbery to be *e.* with God
Col	4: 1	servants that which is just and *e.*
Rev	21:16	breadth, and the height of it are *e.*

EQUALITY

2 Cor	8:14	but by an *e.*, that now

EQUITY

Ps	98: 9	and the people with *e.*
	99: 4	thou dost establish *e.*, thou
Prov	1: 3	wisdom, justice, judgment, *e.*
	17:26	nor to strike princes for *e.*
Eccl	2:21	labour is in wisdom, knowledge, *e.*
Is	11: 4	reprove with *e.* for the meek
	59:14	truth fallen, *e.* cannot enter
Mic	3: 9	princes that pervert all *e.*
Mal	2: 6	Levi walked with me in *e.*

ERR (ERRED)

Num	15:22	and if ye have *e.*, and not
1 Sam	26:21	the fool, and have *e.* exceedingly
Job	6:24	understand wherein I have *e.*
Ps	95:10	do *e.* in their heart
	119:21	which do *e.* from thy commandments
	119:110	I *e.* not from thy precepts
Prov	14:22	do they not *e.* that devise evil
Is	9:16	leaders of this people cause them to *e.*
	30:28	jaws of the people, causing them to *e.*
	28: 7	and prophet have *e.* through strong drink
	35: 8	wayfaring men, though fools, shall not *e.*
	63:17	why hast thou made us to *e.* from thy
Jer	23:13	and caused my people Israel to *e.*
Mic	3: 5	prophets that make my people *e.*
Mat	22:29	ye do *e.* not knowing the scripture
1 Tim	6:10	have *e.* from the faith, and pierced
	6:21	professing have *e.* concerning the faith

2 Tim 2:18 who concerning the truth have *e.*
Jas 5:19 if any of you *e.* from the truth

ERROR (ERRORS)
2 Sam 6: 7 God smote him there for his *e.*
Job 19: 4 mine *e.* remaineth with myself
Ps 19:12 who can understand his *e.*
Eccl 10: 5 as an *e.* which proceedeth from the ruler
Is 32: 6 utter *e.* against the Lord
Jer 10:15 are vanity and the work of *e.*
Dan 6: 4 neither was any *e.* or fault
Rom 1:27 recompence of their *e.* which was
Heb 9: 7 and for the *e.* of the people
Jas 5:20 sinner from the *e.* of his way
2 Pet 2:18 from them who live in *e.*
1 John 4: 6 spirit of truth and the spirit of *e.*
Jude 1:11 after the *e.* of Balaam for reward

ESCAPE (ESCAPED)
Gen 19:22 haste thee, *e.* thither, for I cannot
32: 8 the other company which is left shall *e.*
Ezra 9: 8 to leave us a remnant to *e.*
9:15 for we remain yet *e.*, as it
Esth 4:13 think not that thou shalt *e.*
Job 1:15 I only alone am *e.* to tell
11:20 fail, and they shall not *e.*
Ps 56: 7 shall they *e.* by iniquity
71: 2 deliver me and cause me to *e.*
124: 7 our soul is *e.* as a bird
141:10 own nets, whilst I withal *e.*
Prov 19: 5 that speaketh lies shall not *e.*
Eccl 7:26 pleaseth God shall *e.* from her
Is 20: 6 Assyria: and how shall we *e.*
45:20 that are *e.* of the nations
Jer 11:11 which they shall not be able to *e.*
Ezek 17:15 shall he *e.* that doeth such things
Mat 23:33 can ye *e.* the damnation of hell
Luke 21:36 accounted worthy to *e.* all these
John 10:39 he *e.* out of their hand
Rom 2: 3 thou shalt *e.* the judgment of God
1 Cor 10:13 temptation also make a way to *e.*
1 Thes 5: 3 child; and they shall not *e.*
Heb 2: 3 how shall we *e.* if we neglect
12:25 *e.* not who refused him that spake
2 Pet 1: 4 *e.* the corruption that is in the
2:18 allure those that were clean *e.*

ESTABLISH
Gen 9: 9 I *e.* my covenant with you, and
17: 7 I will *e.* my covenant between me and
Lev 26: 9 and *e.* my covenant with you
Deut 8:18 that he may *e.* his covenant which he sware
1 Sam 1:23 only the Lord *e.* his word
2 Sam 7:12 and I will *e.* his kingdom
2 Chr 9: 8 God loved Israel to *e.* them
Ps 7: 9 but *e.* the just: for the righteous
48: 8 our God: God will *e.* it for ever
89: 2 faithfulness shalt thou *e.* in heaven
89: 4 thy seed will I *e.* for ever
90:17 *e.* the work of our hands
99: 4 thou dost *e.* equity, thou
Prov 15:25 will *e.* the border of the widow
Is 9: 7 order it, and to *e.* it with judgment
49: 8 to *e.* the earth, to cause to
62: 7 no rest till he *e.* Jerusalem
Ezek 16:60 I will *e.* unto thee an everlasting covenant
Rom 3:31 God forbid: yea, we *e.* the law
3:10 to *e.* their own righteousness
1 Thes 3:13 *e.* your hearts

ESTABLISHED
Gen 41:32 the thing is *e.* by God
Ex 6: 4 I have also *e.* my covenant with them
15:17 which thy hands have *e.*
Ps 40: 2 upon a rock, he *e.* my goings
78: 5 he *e.* a testimony in Jacob
93: 2 thy throne is *e.* of old
119:90 hast *e.* the earth, and it abideth

Prov 3:19 by understanding hath he *e.* the heavens
4:26 let all thy ways be *e.*
12: 3 man not be *e.* by wickedness
16:12 throne is *e.* by righteousness
20:18 every purpose is *e.* by counsel
Is 7: 9 surely, ye shall not be *e.*
16: 5 in mercy shall the throne be *e.*
Jer 10:12 hath *e.* the world by his wisdom
Hab 1:12 thou hast *e.* them for correction
Mat 18:16 or three witnesses every word may be *e.*
Acts 16: 5 so were the churches *e.* in the faith
Rom 1:11 gift to the end ye may be *e.*
Heb 8: 6 *e.* upon better promises
13: 9 that the heart be *e.* with grace
2 Pet 1:12 and be *e.* in the present truth

ESTATE
Ps 136:23 who remembered us in our low *e.*
Prov 27:23 know the *e.* of thy flocks
Luke 1:48 the low *e.* of his handmaiden
Jude 1: 6 angels that kept not their first *e.*

ESTEEM (ESTEEMED, ESTEEMETH, ESTEEMING)
Deut 32:15 and lightly *e.* the rock of his salvation
1 Sam 2:30 they that despise me shall be lightly *e.*
Job 23:12 *e.* the words of his mouth more than
Ps 119:128 I *e.* all thy precepts concerning
Is 53: 4 we did *e.* him stricken of God
Luke 16:15 which is highly *e.* among men is
Rom 14: 5 one man *e.* one day above another
14:14 to him that *e.* it, it is unclean
Phil 2: 3 *e.* each other better than themselves
1 Thes 5:13 *e.* them very highly in love for
Heb 11:26 *e.* the reproach of Christ

ESTRANGED
Ps 58: 3 wicked are *e.* from the womb
78:30 not *e.* from their lusts
Ezek 78:14 they are all *e.* from me

ETERNAL
Deut 33:27 the *e.* God is thy refuge
Is 60:15 make thee an *e.* excellency
Mat 19:16 that I may have *e.* life
25:46 the righteous into life *e.*
Mark 3:29 is in danger of *e.* damnation
10:17 that I may inherit *e.* life
10:30 and in the world to come *e.* life
Luke 10:25 what shall I do to inherit *e.* life
John 3:15 should not perish but have *e.* life
4:36 wages, gathereth fruit unto *e.* life
6:54 hath *e.* life and I will raise him up
6:68 we go? thou hast the words of *e.* life
10:28 and I give unto them *e.* life
12:25 shall keep it unto *e.* life
17: 3 this is life *e.*, that they might
Acts 13:48 ordained to *e.* life believed
Rom 1:20 even his *e.* power and Godhead
2: 7 honour, immortality, and *e.* life
6:23 the gift of God is *e.* through Jesus
2 Cor 4:17 exceeding and *e.* weight of glory
4:18 the things which are not seen are *e.*
5: 1 hands, *e.* in the heavens
Eph 3:11 according to the *e.* purpose
1 Tim 1:17 unto the King *e.* immortal, invisible
6:12 lay hold on *e.* life
2 Tim 2:10 which is in Christ Jesus with *e.* glory
Tit 1: 2 in hope of *e.* life which God
3: 7 heirs according to the hope of *e.* life
Heb 5: 9 author of *e.* salvation unto all
9:12 obtained *e.* redemption for us
9:14 through the *e.* Spirit offered himself
1 Pet 5:10 called us unto his *e.* glory
1 John 1: 2 *e.* life which was with the Father
3:15 ye know that no murderer hath *e.* life
5:11 God has given to us *e.* life
Jude 1:21 our Lord Jesus Christ unto *e.* life

EUNUCH (EUNUCHS)
2 Ki 9:32 looked out to him two or three *e.*
20:18 they shall be *e.* in the palace
Is 56: 3 neither *e.* say, I am a dry tree
Mat 19:12 themselves *e.* for the kingdom of heaven's sake
Acts 8:27 *e.* of great authority under Candace

EVEN *or* EVENING
Gen 1: 5 the *e.* and the morning were the first
19: 1 there came two angels to Sodom at *e.*
1 Ki 18:29 offering of the *e.* sacrifice
Ezra 9: 5 at the *e.* sacrifice I arose
Ps 141: 2 my hands as the *e.* sacrifice
Dan 9:21 about the time of the *e.* oblation
Hab 1: 8 horses more fierce than *e.* wolves
Zeph 3: 3 her judges are *e.* wolves
Zech 14: 7 at *e.* time it shall be light

EVER
Gen 3:22 and eat and live for *e.*
Ex 15:18 Lord reigneth for *e.* and *e.*
Deut 19: 9 to walk *e.* in his way
32:40 to heaven and say, I live for *e.*
Josh 4:24 fear the Lord your God for *e.*
1 Ki 10: 9 because the Lord loved Israel for *e.*
11:39 afflict seed of David, but not for *e.*
Ps 5:11 let them *e.* shout for joy
9: 7 for the Lord shall endure for *e.*
10:16 the Lord is king for *e.*
12: 7 them from this generation for *e.*
22:26 your heart shall live for *e.*
23: 6 dwell in the house of the Lord for *e.*
25:15 my eyes are *e.* towards the Lord
25:37 he is *e.* merciful and lendeth
30:12 I will give thanks unto thee for *e.*
33:11 counsel of the Lord standeth for *e.*
37:18 their inheritance shall be for *e.*
45: 6 thy throne, O God, is for *e.*
48:14 this God is our God for *e.*
49: 9 he should still live for *e.*
51: 3 and my sin is *e.* before me
73:26 my heart and my portion for *e.*
74:19 the congregation of thy poor for *e.*
81:15 their time should have endured for *e.*
92: 7 that they shall be destroyed for *e.*
103: 9 neither will he keep his anger for *e.*
105: 8 hath remembered his covenant for *e.*
111: 8 commandments stand fast for *e.*
119:44 I will keep thy law for *e.*
119:111 have I taken as an heritage for *e.*
119:145 I will bless thy name for *e.*
146: 6 which keepeth truth for *e.*
Prov 27:24 riches are not for *e.*
Eccl 1: 4 the earth abideth for *e.*
Is 26: 4 trust in the Lord for *e.*
32:17 quietness and assurance for *e.*
40: 8 the word of our God shall stand for *e.*
57:16 I will not contend for *e.*
Jer 3: 5 will he reserve anger for *e.*
32:39 that they may fear me for *e.*
Lam 3:31 the Lord will not cast off for *e.*
Mic 4: 5 the Lord our God for *e.* and *e.*
7:18 retaineth not his anger for *e.*
Zech 1: 5 prophets, do they live for *e.*
Luke 15:31 son, thou art *e.* with me
John 6:51 of this bread, he shall live for *e.*
8:35 but the son abideth *e.*
Rom 1:25 the Creator who is blessed for *e.*
9: 5 who is over all, God blessed for *e.*
2 Cor 9: 9 his righteousness remaineth for *e.*
Gal 1: 5 to whom be glory for *e.* and *e.*
Phil 4:20 our Father be glory for *e.* and *e.*
1 Thes 4: 5 *e.* follow that which is good
4:17 shall we *e.* be with the Lord
1 Tim 1:17 be honour and glory and *e.* and *e.*
2 Tim 3: 7 *e.* learning, and never able to
Heb 7:24 this man, because he continueth *e.*
7:25 he *e.* liveth to make intercession
13: 8 the same, yesterday today and for *e.*
13:21 to whom be glory for *e.* and *e.*
1 Pet 1:23 the word of God abideth for *e.*
1:25 word of the Lord endureth for *e.*
4:11 be praise and dominion for *e.* and *e.*

1 John 2:17 doeth the will of God abideth for *e.*
Jude 1:25 to God be glory now and *e.*
Rev 1: 6 to him be glory and dominion for *e.* and *e.*
4: 9 who liveth for *e.* and *e.*

EVERLASTING

Gen 17: 8 land of Canaan, an *e.* possession
21:33 on the name of the Lord, the *e.* God
49:26 unto the utmost bound of the *e.* hills
Ex 40:15 *e.* priesthood throughout their generations
Deut 33:27 and underneath are the *e.* arms
Ps 24: 7 be ye lift up ye *e.* doors
41:13 blessed be God from *e.* to *e.*
90: 2 even from *e.* to *e.* thou art
103:17 mercy of Lord from *e.* to *e.*
112: 6 the righteous shall be in *e.* remembrance
139:24 lead me in the way *e.*
145:13 thy kingdom is an *e.* kingdom
Prov 10:25 righteous is an *e.* foundation
Is 9: 6 The mighty God, the *e.* Father
26: 4 in the Lord Jehovah is *e.* strength
33:14 who dwell with *e.* burnings
35:10 songs and *e.* joy upon their heads
40:28 the *e.* God, the Lord, the Creator
45:17 Israel saved with *e.* salvation
55:13 to the Lord for a name, an *e.* sign
56: 5 I will give them an *e.* name
60:19 the Lord shall be an *e.* light
Jer 10:10 he is the living God, and an *e.* King
20:11 *e.* confusion shall never be forgotten
23:40 I will bring an *e.* reproach
31: 3 I have loved thee with an *e.* love
Dan 4:34 whose dominion is an *e.* dominion
12: 2 awake some to *e.* life, and some
Mic 5: 2 goings forth of old, from *e.*
Hab 1:12 art thou not from *e.*, O Lord my God
3: 6 the *e.* mountains were scattered
Mat 18: 8 to be cast into *e.* fire
19:29 and shall inherit *e.* life
25:46 shall go into *e.* punishment
Luke 16: 9 may receive you into *e.* habitations
18:30 in the world to come *e.* life
John 3:16 not perish but have *e.* life
3:36 believeth on the Son hath *e.* life
4:14 well of water springing up into *e.* life
5:24 that heareth my word hath *e.* life
6:27 meat which endureth to *e.* life
6:40 whoso believeth may have *e.* life
12:50 his commandment is *e.* life
Acts 13:46 yourselves unworthy of *e.* life
Rom 6:22 holiness and the end *e.* life
Gal 6: 8 shall of the Spirit reap *e.* life
2 Thes 1: 9 shall be punished with *e.* destruction
1 Tim 1:16 believe on him to life *e.*
6:16 to whom be honour and power *e.*
2 Pet 1:11 *e.* kingdom of our Lord Jesus Christ
Jude 1: 6 hath reserved in *e.* chains under
Rev 14: 6 having the *e.* gospel to preach unto

EVIL

Gen 6: 5 thoughts of his heart only *e.*
Deut 29:21 I will separate him to *e.*
30:15 life and good, death and *e.*
Josh 24:15 if it seem *e.* unto you to serve the
Job 2:10 shall we not receive *e.*
5:19 there shall no *e.* touch thee
30:26 looked for good then *e.* came
Ps 23: 4 I will fear no *e.* for thou
34:21 *e.* shall slay the wicked, and they
51: 4 have done this *e.* in thy sight
52: 3 thou lovest *e.* more than good
91:10 shall no *e.* befall thee, neither
97:10 ye that love the Lord, hate *e.*
Prov 5:14 I was almost in all *e.* in the midst
12:21 there shall no *e.* happen to the just
14:19 the *e.* bow before the good
15: 3 beholding the *e.* and the good
15:15 all the days of the afflicted are *e.*
31:12 will do him good and not *e.*
Eccl 5:13 sore *e.* which I have seen
9: 3 heart of the sons of men is full of *e.*
Is 1: 4 a seed of *e.* doers, children that
5:20 them that call *e.* good, and good *e.*
7:15 know to refuse the *e.*, and choose
45: 7 I make peace and create *e.*
57: 1 taken away from the *e.* to come
59: 7 feet run to *e.* and make haste
Jer 17:17 art my hope in the day of *e.*
18:11 I frame *e.* against you, and devise
29:11 thoughts of peace and not of *e.*
44:27 I will watch over them for *e.*
Lam 3:38 most High proceedeth not *e.* and good
Ezek 7: 5 an *e.*, an only *e.*, behold is come
Dan 9:12 bringing upon us a great *e.*
Amos 3: 6 shall there be *e.* in a city
5:14 seek good and not *e.*, that ye may
9: 4 set eyes on them for *e.*, and not for
Hab 1:13 purer eyes than to behold *e.*, and
Mat 5:11 all manner of *e.* against you falsely
5:45 his sun to rise on the *e.* and the
6:34 sufficient to the day is the *e.* thereof
7:11 if ye, being *e.*, know how to give
Luke 6:35 kind to the unthankful and to the *e.*
John 3:19 light because their deeds were *e.*
Rom 2: 9 on every soul that doeth *e.*
7:19 *e.* which I would not that I do
7:21 I would do good *e.* is present with me
12:17 recompense to no man *e.* for *e.*
12:21 be not overcome of *e.* but overcome *e.*
1 Cor 13: 5 not easily provoked, thinketh no *e.*
Eph 5:16 time because the days are *e.*
1 Thes 5:15 none render *e.* for *e.* unto any man
5:22 abstain from all appearance of *e.*
1 Tim 6:10 love of money is the root of all *e.*
Tit 3: 2 to speak *e.* of no man, to be no
Heb 5:14 exercised discern both good and *e.*
3 John 1:11 follow not that which is *e.*
Jude 1:10 speak *e.* of those things which they

EXALT (EXALTED, EXALTETH)

Ex 15: 2 my father's God, I will *e.*
Num 24: 7 and his kingdom shall be *e.*
1 Sam 2:10 *e.* the horn of his anointed
2 Sam 22:47 *e.* be the God of my salvation
Neh 9: 5 *e.* above all blessing and praise
Job 5:11 which mourn may be *e.* to safety
Ps 34: 3 let us *e.* his name together
89:16 in righteousness shall be *e.*
99: 5 *e.* ye the Lord our God
118:28 my God, I will *e.* thee
Prov 11:11 blessing of the upright, the city is *e.*
14:34 righteousness *e.* a nation, but sin
Is 2: 2 and shall be *e.* above the hills
2:11 Lord alone shall be *e.* in that day
40: 4 every valley shall be *e.*
Ezek 21:26 *e.* him that is low, and abase
Hos 13: 1 Ephraim was *e.* in Israel
Mat 11:23 Capernaum, which art *e.* to heaven
23:12 humbleth himself shall be *e.*
Luke 1:52 their seats and *e.* them of low degree
14:11 *e.* himself shall be abased
18:14 for every one that *e.* himself shall be
Acts 2:33 by right hand of God *e.*
5:31 Him hath God *e.* with his right hand
2 Cor 12: 7 I should be *e.* above measure through
Phil 2: 9 God hath highly *e.* him
2 Thes 2: 4 *e.* himself above all that is called
1 Pet 5: 6 that he may *e.* you in due time

EXAMINE (EXAMINED)

Ps 26: 2 *e.* me, O Lord, and prove me
Luke 23:14 having *e.* him before you, have found
Acts 4: 9 this day be *e.* of the good deed
1 Cor 11:28 and so let a man *e.* himself
2 Cor 13: 5 *e.* yourselves, whether ye be in the faith

EXAMPLE (EXAMPLES)

Mat 1:19 not make her a public *e.*
John 13:15 I have given you an *e.*
1 Cor 10: 6 these things were our *e.*
1 Cor 10:11 happened unto them for *e.*
Phil 3:17 as ye have us for an *e.*
1 Thes 1: 7 ye were *e.* to all that believe
2 Thes 3: 9 to make ourselves an *e.*
1 Tim 4:12 an *e.* of the believers in word
Heb 4:11 after the same *e.* of unbelief
8: 5 serve unto the *e.* and shadow
Jas 5:10 for an *e.* of suffering affliction
1 Pet 2:21 suffered for us leaving us an *e.*
5: 3 but being *e.* to the flock
2 Pet 2: 6 making them an *e.* unto those
Jude 1: 7 for an *e.* suffering the vengeance

EXCEED

Mat 5:20 your righteousness shall *e.* the
2 Cor 3: 9 ministration of righteousness *e.*

EXCEEDING (EXCEEDINGLY)

Gen 13:13 wicked and sinners before the Lord *e.*
17: 6 I will make thee *e.* fruitful
27:34 Esau cried with a great and *e.* bitter
Num 14: 7 search it, it is an *e.* good land
1 Sam 2: 3 talk no more so *e.* proudly
1 Ki 4:29 gave Solomon wisdom *e.* much
1 Chr 22: 5 builded for the Lord must be *e.* magnifical
Ps 43: 4 I will go to God my *e.* joy
68: 3 yea, let them *e.* rejoice
119:167 thy testimonies I love *e.*
Mat 5:12 rejoice and be *e.* glad
Rom 7:13 commandment might become *e.* sinful
2 Cor 4:17 a far more *e.* and eternal weight
7: 4 I am *e.* joyful in all tribulation
Eph 1:19 *e.* greatness of his power to us-ward
2: 7 might show *e.* riches of his grace
3:20 him that is able to do *e.* abundantly
1 Thes 3:10 praying *e.* that we might see your face
2 Thes 1: 3 that your faith groweth *e.*
1 Tim 1:14 grace was *e.* abundant with faith
2 Pet 1: 4 *e.* great and precious promises
Jude 1:24 presence of his glory with *e.* joy

EXCEL (EXCELLEST, EXCELLETH)

Ps 103:20 angels that *e.* in strength
Prov 31:29 virtuously but thou *e.* them all
Eccl 2:13 wisdom *e.* folly, as far as light
1 Cor 14:12 seek that ye may *e.* to the edifying
2 Cor 3:10 respect by reason of glory that *e.*

EXCELLENCY

Gen 49: 3 the *e.* of dignity and the *e.* of
Ex 15: 7 in the greatness of thine *e.*
Deut 33:26 rideth in his *e.* on sky
Job 13:11 shall not his *e.* make you afraid
37: 4 thunders with the voice of his *e.*
40:10 deck thyself now with *e.*
Ps 47: 4 *e.* of Jacob, whom he loved
68:34 his *e.* is over Israel, and his
Is 35: 2 see glory and *e.* of our God
Amos 6: 8 I abhor the *e.* of Jacob, and hate
1 Cor 2: 1 not with *e.* of speech or of wisdom
2 Cor 4: 7 *e.* of the power may be of God, and
Phil 3: 8 loss for the *e.* of the knowledge of Christ

EXCELLENT

Esth 1: 4 the honour of his *e.* majesty
Ps 8: 1 how *e.* is thy name in all the earth
16: 3 saints, *e.* in whom my delight
36: 7 how *e.* is thy lovingkindness
148:13 the Lord, for his name alone is *e.*
Prov 12:26 the righteous is more *e.* than his
17:27 man of understanding is of *e.* spirit
Is 12: 5 Lord hath done *e.* things
Ezek 16: 7 and thou art come to *e.* ornaments
Dan 5:12 an *e.* spirit and knowledge and
Rom 2:18 the things that are more *e.*
1 Cor 12:31 I show unto you a more *e.* way
Phil 1:10 approve things that are *e.*
Heb 1: 4 obtained a more *e.* name than they
11: 4 offered a more *e.* sacrifice

2 Pet 1:17 such a voice from the *e.* glory

EXCUSE (EXCUSING)

Luke 14:18 with one consent began to make *e.*
Rom 1:20 so that they are without *e.*
2:15 while accusing or else *e.* one another

EXECUTE

Ex 12:12 I will *e.* judgment; I am the Lord
Num 5:30 priest shall *e.* upon her all this law
8:11 they may *e.* the service of the Lord
Deut 10:18 he doth *e.* the judgment of the
Ps 119:84 when wilt thou *e.* judgment on them
149: 7 *e.* vengeance upon the heathen
Is 16: 3 take counsel, *e.* judgment; make thy
Jer 7: 5 if ye thoroughly *e.* judgment
Hos 11: 9 not *e.* the fierceness of mine anger
Mic 7: 9 plead my cause, and *e.* judgment for me
Zech 8:16 *e.* the judgment of truth and peace
John 5:27 hath given him authority to *e.* judgment
Rom 13: 4 a revenger to *e.* wrath upon him that
Jude 1:15 to *e.* judgment upon all

EXHORT (EXHORTED, EXHORTING)

Acts 2:40 did he testify and *e.*, saying
11:23 was glad, and *e.* them all
2 Cor 9: 5 thought it necessary to *e.* the brethren
1 Thes 2:11 how we *e.* and comforted and charged
5:14 now we *e.* you, brethren
2 Thes 3:12 *e.* by our Lord Jesus Christ
1 Tim 2: 1 I *e.* therefore, that, first of all
2 Tim 4: 2 *e.* with all longsuffering and doctrine
Tit 1: 9 both to *e.* and to convince the gainsayers
Heb 3:13 *e.* one another daily while it
10:25 but *e.* one another, and so much the
1 Pet 5: 1 I *e.*, who am also an elder
Jude 1: 3 and *e.* you that ye should earnestly contend

EXHORTATION

Luke 3:18 in his *e.* preached he unto the people
Acts 13:15 if ye have any word of *e.* for the
20: 2 and had given them much *e.*
Rom 12: 8 or he that exhorteth, on *e.*
1 Cor 14: 3 to edification, and *e.*, and comfort
2 Cor 8:17 for indeed he accepted the *e.*
1 Thes 2: 3 for our *e.* was not of deceit
1 Tim 4:13 give attendance to reading, to *e.*, to doctrine
Heb 12: 5 ye have forgotten the *e.* which
13:22 suffer the word of *e.*: for I have

EXPECTATION

Ps 9:18 *e.* of the poor shall not perish for
62: 5 on God; for my *e.* is from him
Prov 10:28 but the *e.* of the wicked shall perish
11:23 but the *e.* of the wicked is wrath
23:18 thine *e.* shall not be cut off
Is 20: 5 and ashamed of Ethiopia, their *e.*
Luke 3:15 as the people were in *e.*
Acts 12:11 from all the *e.* of the people
Rom 8:19 *e.* of the creature waiteth for the
Phil 1:20 according to my earnest *e.* and my

EXPEDIENT

John 11:50 nor consider that it is *e.* for us
16: 7 *e.* for you that I go away
1 Cor 6:12 but all things are not *e.*
12: 1 it is not *e.* for me to glory

EXTEND (EXTENDED, EXTENDETH)

Ezra 9: 9 but hath *e.* mercy unto us
Ps 16: 2 my goodness *e.* not to thee
109:12 none to *e.* mercy unto him
Is 66:12 *e.* peace to her like a river

EXTOL (EXTOLLED)

Ps 30: 1 I will *e.* thee, O Lord
68: 4 *e.* him that rideth upon the heavens
145: 1 I will *e.* thee, my God, O king
Is 52:13 he shall be exalted and *e.*
Dan 4:37 I Nebuchadnezzar praise and *e.* and honour

EXTORTION

Ezek 22:12 gained of thy neighbors by *e.*
Mat 23:25 within they are full of *e.*

EXTORTIONER

Ps 109:11 Let the *e.* catch all that he hath
Is 16: 4 for the *e.* is at an end, the spoiler
1 Cor 5:11 or a drunkard, or an *e.*; with such a

EXTORTIONERS

Luke 18:11 not as other men are, *e.*, unjust
1 Cor 6:10 nor revilers, nor *e.*, shall inherit

EYE

Ex 21:24 *e.* for *e.*, tooth for tooth
Deut 32:10 kept him as the apple of his *e.*
Job 24:15 no *e.* shall see me, and disguiseth
Ps 17: 8 keep me as the apple of thine *e.*
33:18 the *e.* of the Lord is upon them
Prov 20:12 the seeing *e.*, the Lord hath
23: 6 bread of him that hath an evil *e.*
Eccl 1: 8 the *e.* is not satisfied with seeing
Is 64: 4 neither hath the *e.* seen, O God
Jer 13:17 mine *e.* shall weep sore, because
Mat 5:38 an *e.* for an *e.*, and a tooth
6:22 light of the body is the *e.*
18: 9 if thine *e.* offend thee, pluck it out
Mark 7:22 an evil *e.*, blasphemy, pride
Luke 11:34 the light of the body is the *e.*
1 Cor 2: 9 *e.* hath not seen nor ear heard
Rev 1: 7 and every *e.* shall see him, and they

EYELIDS

Job 16:16 on my *e.* is the shadow of death
Ps 11: 4 his eyes behold, his *e.* try
Prov 4:25 let thine *e.* look straight before thee
30:13 and their *e.* are lifted up
Jer 9:18 our *e.* gush out with waters

EYEWITNESSES

Luke 1: 2 from the beginning were *e.*
2 Pet 1:16 but were *e.* of his majesty

EYES

Gen 3: 5 then your *e.* shall be opened and ye
6: 8 Noah found grace in the *e.* of the Lord
Deut 12: 8 whatsoever is right in his own *e.*
13:18 right in the *e.* of the Lord
Judg 17: 6 which was right in his own *e.*
21:25 that which was right in his own *e.*
1 Sam 26:24 be much set by in the *e.* of the Lord
2 Sam 15:25 find favour in the *e.* of the Lord
1 Ki 15:11 was right in the *e.* of the Lord
1 Ki 22:43 which was right in the *e.* of the Lord
2 Chr 16: 9 *e.* of the Lord run to and fro
Job 10: 4 hast thou *e.* of flesh or seest thou
32: 1 he was righteous in his own *e.*
Ps 15: 4 whose *e.* a vile person is condemned
25:15 mine *e.* are ever towards the Lord
34:15 *e.* of the Lord are upon the righteous
101: 6 mine *e.* shall be upon the faithful
119:148 mine *e.* prevent the night watches
123: 2 our *e.* wait on the Lord
139:16 thine *e.* did see my substance
141: 8 mine *e.* are unto thee, O God
145:15 the *e.* of all wait upon thee and thou
Prov 5:21 ways of man before the *e.* of the Lord
15: 3 the *e.* of the Lord are in every place
22:12 the *e.* of the Lord preserve knowledge
23: 5 set thine *e.* on that which is not
Eccl 2:14 wise man's *e.* are in his head
11: 7 for the *e.* to behold the sun
Is 1:15 I will hide mine *e.* from you
3:16 stretched forth necks and wanton *e.*
29:18 *e.* of the blind see out of obscurity
29:32 *e.* of them that see shall not dim
30:20 thine *e.* shall see thy teachers
Is 35: 5 *e.* of the blind shall be opened
43: 8 Blind people that have *e.*
49: 5 be glorious in the *e.* of the Lord
65:12 did evil before mine *e.*
Jer 5: 3 are not thine *e.* upon the truth
5:21 have *e.* and see not; which have
9: 1 that mine *e.* were a fountain of tears
14:17 let mine *e.* run down with tears
24: 6 set mine *e.* upon them for good
Ezek 24:16 take away the desire of thine *e.*
Amos 9: 4 set mine *e.* upon them for evil
9: 8 the *e.* of the Lord God are upon
Hab 1:13 art of purer *e.* than to behold evil
Zech 3: 9 on one stone shall be seven *e.*
Mat 13:16 blessed are your *e.* for they see
18: 9 having two *e.* to be cast into hell fire
20:33 that our *e.* may be opened
Mark 8:18 having *e.* see ye not
Luke 2:30 mine *e.* have seen thy salvation
4:20 *e.* of all were fastened on him
10:23 blessed are the *e.* which see
John 9: 6 anointed the *e.* of blind man
Rom 11: 8 *e.* that they should not see, and ears
Eph 1:18 *e.* of your understanding being
Heb 4:13 all open unto the *e.* of him
2 Pet 2:14 *e.* full of adultery, and that cannot
1 John 1: 1 which we have seen with our *e.*
2:16 lust of the *e.* and pride
Rev 1:14 his *e.* were as a flame of fire
2:18 who hath his *e.* like unto a flame
3:18 and anoint thine *e.* with eyesalve
4: 6 four beasts full of *e.* before and behind
19:12 His *e.* were as a flame of fire

F

FABLES

1 Tim 4: 7 refuse profane and old wives' *f.*
2 Tim 4: 4 and shall be turned unto *f.*
Tit 1:14 not giving heed to Jewish *f.*
2 Pet 1:16 not followed cunningly devised *f.*

FACE

Lev 19:32 honour the *f.* of the old man
Num 6:25 the Lord make his *f.* shine upon thee
2 Chr 6:42 turn not the *f.* of thine anointed
Ps 17:15 behold thy *f.* in righteousness
31:16 make thy *f.* to shine upon
84: 9 behold the *f.* of the anointed
119:135 make thy *f.* to shine upon thy
Ezek 1:10 *f.* of a man, and the *f.* of a lion
Dan 9:17 cause thy *f.* to shine upon
Hos 5: 5 Israel doth testify to his *f.*
Mat 11:10 my messenger before thy *f.*
Luke 9:52 sent messengers before his *f.*
Acts 2:25 foresaw the Lord always before my *f.*
1 Cor 13:12 glass darkly but then *f.* to *f.*
2 Cor 3:18 with open *f.* beholding as in a glass
Jas 1:23 his natural *f.* in a glass
Rev 4: 7 third beast had a *f.* like a man

FADE (FADETH)

Is 64: 6 we all do *f.* as a leaf
Jas 1:11 rich man *f.* away in his ways
1 Pet 1: 4 inheritance that *f.* not away
5: 4 crown of glory that *f.* not away

FAIL (FAILED, FAILETH)

Deut 31: 6 Lord will not *f.* nor forsake
Josh 1: 5 not *f.* thee, nor forsake thee
1 Chr 28:20 he will not *f.* thee, nor forsake
Ps 12: 1 faithful *f.* from among the children of men
31:10 strength *f.* because of mine iniquity
40:12 therefore my heart *f.* me
71: 9 forsake me not when my strength *f.*
77: 8 doth his promise *f.* for evermore
143: 7 my spirit *f.*; hide not thy face
Sol 5: 6 soul *f.* when he spake, I sought
Lam 3:22 because his compassions *f.* not
Luke 12:33 treasure in heaven that *f.* not
16: 9 when ye *f.* they may receive you

Luke 16:17 than one tittle of the law to *f.*
22:32 prayed that thy faith *f.* not
1 Cor 13: 8 charity never *f.*, but whether there
Heb 12:15 lest any *f.* of the grace

FAINT (FAINTED, FAINTETH)

Ps 27:13 *f.* unless I believed to see the
84: 2 even *f.* for the courts of the Lord
119:81 my soul *f.* for thy salvation
Is 1: 5 head is sick, and the whole heart *f.*
40:28 of the ends of the earth *f.* not
40:29 he giveth power to the *f.*
40:30 youths shall *f.* and be weary
40:31 wait on the Lord shall walk and not *f.*
2 Cor 4: 1 we have received mercy we *f.* not
Gal 6: 9 we shall reap if we *f.* not
Heb 12: 5 nor *f.* when thou art rebuked of him
Rev 2: 3 hast laboured and hast not *f.*

FAIR (FAIRER)

Ps 45: 2 *f.* than the children of men
Prov 7:21 with her much *f.* speech, she caused
Sol 1:15 behold thou art *f.*; thou hast
Jer 12: 6 they speak *f.* words unto thee
Dan 1:15 their countenances appeared *f.* and fatter
Acts 7:20 Moses was born and was exceeding *f.*
Gal 6:12 desire to make a *f.* show in

FAITH

Deut 32:20 children in whom is no *f.*
Hab 2: 4 just shall live by *f.*
Mat 6:30 clothe you, O ye of little *f.*
8:10 not found so great *f.*
8:26 are ye fearful, O ye of little *f.*
9: 2 Jesus seeing their *f.* said unto
9:22 thy *f.* hath made thee whole
14:31 O thou of little *f.*, wherefore didst
15:28 O woman, great is thy *f.* be it unto
17:20 *f.* as a grain of mustard seed
21:21 have *f.* and doubt not, ye shall not
23:23 omitted judgment, mercy, and *f.*
Mark 4:40 how is it ye have no *f.*
Luke 7: 9 I have not found so great *f.*
7:50 thy *f.* hath saved thee
8:25 where is your *f.*
17: 5 unto the Lord, increase our *f.*
17: 6 if ye had *f.* ye might say to this
18: 8 shall he find *f.* on the earth
22:32 I have prayed that thy *f.* fail not
Acts 3:16 the *f.* which is by him hath given him
6: 5 Stephen, a man full of *f.*
6: 7 company of priests obedient to the *f.*
11:24 man, full of the Holy Ghost and of *f.*
14: 9 that he had *f.* to be healed
15: 9 purifying their hearts by *f.*
16: 5 churches established in the *f.*
20:21 *f.* toward our Lord Jesus Christ
Rom 1: 5 for obedience to the *f.* among all
1: 8 your *f.* is spoken of through
1:12 by the mutual *f.* both of you and me
1:17 righteousness of God revealed from *f.* to *f.*
2:19 I know thy works and *f.*
3: 3 make the *f.* of God without effect
3:25 propitiation through *f.* in his blood
3:27 Nay, but by the law of *f.*
3:28 conclude a man is justified by *f.*
3:30 which shall justify circumcision by *f.*
4: 5 his *f.* is counted for righteousness
4:11 circumcision, a seal of righteousness
4:13 through the righteousness of *f.*
4:14 law be heirs, *f.* is made void
4:19 not weak in *f.*, he considered not
4:20 strong in *f.* giving glory to God
5: 1 being justified by *f.* we have peace
9:32 not by *f.* but by the works of the law
10: 8 the word of *f.* which we preach
10:17 *f.* cometh by hearing, and hearing
11:20 broken off, and thou standest by *f.*
12: 3 to every man the measure of *f.*
12: 6 according to the proportion of *f.*
Rom 14:22 hast thou *f.*? have it to thyself before God
16:26 nations for the obedience of *f.*
1 Cor 2: 5 that your *f.* not stand in wisdom
12: 9 to another *f.* by the same spirit
13: 2 though I have all *f.* to remove
13:13 now abideth *f.*, hope, charity
15:14 your *f.* is also vain
16:13 stand fast in the *f.*, quit you like men
2 Cor 1:24 of your joy; for by *f.* ye stand
4:13 having the same Spirit of *f.*
5: 7 we walk by *f.* and not by sight
8: 7 ye abound in *f.* and utterance
10:15 when your *f.* is increased, we
13: 5 examine whether ye be in *f.*
Gal 1:23 preacheth the *f.* which once he
2:16 by the works of the law, but by *f.*
2:20 I live by the *f.* of the Son of God
3: 2 Spirit by the hearing of *f.*
3: 8 God would justify the heathen through *f.*
3:11 The just shall live by *f.*
3:12 the law is not of *f.* but the man
3:14 receive the promise of the Spirit through *f.*
3:22 the promise by *f.* of Jesus Christ be given
3:23 before *f.* came, we were under the law
3:25 after that *f.* is come, we are no
3:26 children of God by *f.* in Jesus Christ
5: 5 for hope of righteousness by *f.*
5: 6 but *f.* which worketh by love
5:22 but the fruit of the Spirit is . . . *f.*
Eph 1:15 heard of your *f.* in the Lord Jesus
2: 8 by grace ye are saved through *f.*
3:12 with confidence by the *f.* of him
3:17 Christ dwell in your hearts by *f.*
4: 5 one Lord, one *f.*, one baptism
6:16 above all taking the shield of *f.*
6:23 love with *f.* from God the Father
Phil 1:25 for your furtherance and joy of the *f.*
1:27 striving together for *f.* of the gospel
2:17 sacrifice and service of your *f.*
3: 9 which is through the *f.* of Christ
Col 1: 4 since we heard of your *f.* in Christ Jesus
1:23 if ye continue in *f.* grounded
2: 5 the stedfastness of your *f.*
2:12 through the *f.* of the operation of God
1 Thes 1: 3 remember your work of *f.*
1: 8 your *f.* to God-ward is spread
3: 2 comfort you concerning your *f.*
3: 5 I sent to know your *f.*, lest
3: 6 brought us good tidings of your *f.*
3: 7 comforted in affliction by your *f.*
3:10 perfect that which is lacking in your *f.*
5: 8 putting on the breastplate of *f.*
2 Thes 1: 3 your *f.* groweth exceedingly
1: 4 for your patience and *f.* in all
3: 2 for all men have not *f.*
1 Tim 1: 2 Timothy, my own son in the *f.*
1: 4 godly edifying which is in *f.*
1: 5 charity out of *f.* unfeigned
1:14 exceeding abundant with *f.* and love
2: 7 teacher of the Gentiles in *f.*
2:15 if they continue in *f.* and charity
3: 9 holding the mystery of the *f.*
3:13 great boldness in the *f.* which is in
4: 1 some shall depart from the *f.*
4: 6 nourished up in the words of *f.*
5: 8 he hath denied the *f.* and is worse
5:12 because they have cast off their first *f.*
6:12 fight the good fight of *f.*
2 Tim 1: 5 unfeigned *f.* that is in thee
1:13 in *f.* and love which is in Christ Jesus
2:18 and overthrow the *f.* of some
2:22 follow righteousness, *f.*, charity
3: 8 reprobate concerning the *f.*
3:10 fully known my doctrine, manner of life, *f.*
2 Tim 3:15 salvation through *f.* in Jesus
4: 7 I have kept the *f.*
Tit 1: 1 according to the *f.* of God's elect
1:13 that they may be sound in *f.*
3:15 greet them that love us in *f.*
Philem 1: 6 that the communication of thy *f.*
Heb 4: 2 not being mixed with *f.* in them
6: 1 dead works and of *f.* toward God
6:12 through *f.* and patience inherit promises
10:22 draw near in assurance of *f.*
10:23 hold fast the profession of our *f.*
11: 1 *f.* is the substance of things hoped
11: 3 through *f.* we understand the worlds
11: 4 by *f.* Abel offered unto God
11: 6 without *f.* it is impossible to please him
11:13 these died in *f.* not having
11:28 through *f.* Moses kept the passover
11:33 through *f.* subdued kingdoms
11:39 obtained a good report through *f.*
12: 2 Jesus the finisher of our *f.*
13: 7 whose *f.* follow, considering the end
Jas 1: 1 like precious *f.* with us through
1: 3 trying of your *f.* worketh patience
1: 6 ask in *f.*, nothing wavering
2: 1 have not the *f.* of our Lord Jesus
2: 5 poor of this world rich in *f.*
2:17 *f.* if it hath not works, is dead
2:18 show me thy *f.* without thy works
2:22 how *f.* wrought with his works
2:24 justified by works, not by *f.*
5:15 prayer of *f.* shall save the sick
1 Pet 1: 5 kept by the power of God through *f.*
1: 7 trial of your *f.* being precious
1: 9 receiving the end of your *f.*
1:21 that your *f.* and hope might be in God
5: 9 whom resist, stedfast in the *f.*
2 Pet 1: 5 add to your *f.* virtue, and to virtue
1 John 5: 4 overcometh the world, even our *f.*
Jude 1: 3 contend earnestly for the *f.*
1:20 building up yourselves on holy *f.*
Rev 2:13 hast not denied my *f.*
13:10 here is the *f.* of the saints
14:12 which keep the *f.* of Jesus

FAITHLESS

Mat 17:17 O *f.* and perverse generation
John 20:27 be not *f.* but believing

FAITHFUL

Num 12: 7 who is *f.* in all my house
Deut 7: 9 God, the *f.* God which keepeth covenant
1 Sam 2:35 I will raise me up a *f.* priest
2 Sam 20:19 that are peaceable and *f.* in Israel
Neh 7: 2 a *f.* man, and feared God
9: 8 foundest his heart *f.* before thee
13:13 for they were counted *f.*
Ps 12: 1 *f.* fail from among the children of
31:23 Lord preserveth the *f.*, and
89:37 and as a *f.* witness in heaven
101: 6 mine eyes be upon the *f.* of the land
119:86 all thy commandments are *f.*: they
Prov 11:13 He that is of a *f.* spirit
13:17 a *f.* ambassador is health
14: 5 a *f.* witness will not lie
20: 6 a *f.* man who can find?
27: 6 *f.* are the wounds of a friend
28:20 *f.* man shall abound with blessings
Is 1:21 the *f.* city become an harlot
1:26 city of righteousness, *f.* city
8: 2 I took *f.* witnesses to record
49: 7 Lord is *f.* and the Holy One of Israel
Jer 42: 5 the Lord be a *f.* witness
Hos 11:12 and is *f.* with the saints
Dan 6: 4 forasmuch as he was *f.*
Mat 25:21 well done thou good and *f.* servant
25:23 *f.* over a few things, I will
Luke 12:42 who is that *f.* steward
16:10 *f.* in least is *f.* also in much
16:12 not *f.* in what is another man's
Acts 16:15 judged me *f.* to the Lord

1 Cor 1: 9 God is *f.* by whom ye were called
4: 2 required in stewards, a man *f.*
4:17 Timothy who is *f.* in the Lord
10:13 God is *f.* who will not suffer
Eph 1: 1 *f.* in Christ Jesus
6:21 *f.* minister in the Lord, shall make
1 Thes 5:24 *f.* is he that calleth you who
2 Thes 3: 3 but the Lord is *f.* who will
1 Tim 1:12 for he counted me *f.*, putting me
1:15 a *f.* saying and worthy of all acceptation
3:11 slanderers, sober, *f.* in all things
6: 2 because they are *f.* and beloved
2 Tim 2: 2 same commit thou to *f.* men, who shall
2:11 it is a *f.* saying: for if we be
2:13 abideth *f.* he cannot deny himself
Tit 1: 6 one wife, having *f.* children
1: 9 holding fast the *f.* word as taught
3: 8 this is a *f.* saying, and these things
Heb 2:17 might be a merciful and *f.* high priest
3: 2 Moses was *f.* in all his house
10:23 *f.* is he that promised
1 Pet 4:19 well doing as unto a *f.* Creator
5:12 by Silvanus, a *f.* brother
1 John 1: 9 he is *f.* and just to forgive
Rev 1: 5 *f.* witness and the first begotten
17:14 are called, they are chosen and *f.*
21: 5 for these words are true and *f.*

FAITHFULNESS
1 Sam 26:23 his righteousness and his *f.*
Ps 5: 9 no *f.* in their mouth
36: 5 thy *f.* reacheth to the clouds
40:10 I have declared thy *f.* and thy
88:11 or thy *f.* in destruction?
89: 1 make known thy *f.* to all generations
89: 5 praise thy *f.* in the congregation
89: 8 who is like to thy *f.* round about thee
89:24 my *f.* shall be with him
89:33 nor suffer my *f.* to fail
92: 2 to show forth thy *f.* every night
119:75 thou in *f.* hast afflicted me
119:90 thy *f.* is unto all generations
143: 1 in thy *f.* answer me, and in thy
Is 11: 5 *f.* the girdle of his reins
Lam 3:23 new every morning, great is thy *f.*
Hos 2:20 I will betroth thee to me in *f.*

FALL
Gen 45:24 *f.* not out by the way
2 Sam 24:14 *f.* into the hand of Lord
Ps 37:24 though he *f.* he shall not
45: 5 whereby people *f.* under thee
141:10 let the wicked *f.* into their own nets
145:14 the Lord upholdeth all that *f.*
Prov 11: 5 wicked shall *f.* by his own wickedness
24:16 wicked shall *f.* into mischief
26:27 whoso diggeth a pit shall *f.* therein
28:14 hardeneth his heart shall *f.*
Eccl 4:10 if they *f.* one will lift up
Is 8:15 many shall stumble and *f.*
Dan 11:35 them of understanding shall *f.*
Hos 10: 8 and to the hills *f.* on us
Mic 7: 8 rejoice not when I *f.*
Mat 7:27 great was the *f.* of it
10:29 sparrow not *f.* on the ground
15:14 blind lead the blind, both shall *f.* into
Luke 2:34 set for the *f.* and rising of many
23:30 say to the mountains, *f.* on us
Rom 11:11 stumbled that they should *f.*
11:11 through their *f.* salvation is come
1 Cor 10:12 take heed lest he *f.*
1 Tim 3: 6 *f.* into the condemnation of the devil
6: 9 will be rich *f.* into temptation
Heb 4:11 *f.* after the same example of unbelief
6: 6 if they shall *f.* away, to renew them
10:31 *f.* into the hands of the living God
Jas 1: 2 when ye *f.* into divers temptations
2 Pet 1:10 ye do these things, ye shall never *f.*
3:17 lest ye *f.* from stedfastness
Rev 6:16 *f.* on us and hide us from the face

FALLEN (FALLING)
Ps 16: 6 *f.* unto me in pleasant places
56:13 wilt not thou deliver my feet from *f.*
116: 8 from tears and my feet from *f.*
Hos 14: 1 thou hast *f.* by thine iniquity
Gal 5: 4 by the law, ye are *f.* from grace
2 Thes 2: 3 there come a *f.* away first
Jude 1:24 able to keep you from *f.*
Rev 2: 5 remember whence thou art *f.*

FALSE
Ex 20:16 not bear *f.* witness against thy neighbour
23: 1 thou shalt not raise a *f.* report
23: 7 keep thee far from a *f.* matter
Deut 5:20 shalt thou bear *f.* witness
Ps 119:104 therefore I hate every *f.* way
Prov 6:19 a *f.* witness that speaketh lies
11: 1 a *f.* balance is abomination to the
21:28 a *f.* witness shall perish
25:18 a man that beareth *f.* witness against
Jer 14:14 prophesy unto you a *f.* vision and
23:32 against them that prophesy *f.* dreams
Zech 8:17 love no *f.* oath: for all these
Mal 3: 5 against *f.* swearers, and against
Mat 7:15 beware of *f.* prophets which come to
15:19 fornications, thefts, *f.* witnesses, blasphemies
19:18 thou shalt not bear *f.* witness
24:24 arise *f.* Christs and *f.* prophets
Luke 6:26 so did their fathers to the *f.* prophets
Rom 13: 9 thou shalt not bear *f.* witness
1 Cor 15:15 and we are found *f.* witnesses of God
2 Cor 11:13 for such are *f.* apostles, deceitful
Gal 2: 4 because of *f.* brethren unawares brought in
2 Tim 3: 3 affection, trucebreakers, *f.* accusers
2 Pet 2: 1 there were *f.* prophets also among the people
1 John 4: 1 many *f.* prophets are gone out

FALSEHOOD
Ps 119:118 their deceit is *f.*
144: 8 hand is a right hand of *f.*
Is 57: 4 children of transgression, a seed of *f.*
59:13 from the heart words of *f.*
Jer 10:14 for his molten image is *f.*

FALSELY
Lev 6: 3 and lieth concerning it, and sweareth *f.*
19:12 ye shall not swear by my name *f.*
Ps 44:17 neither have we dealt *f.* in thy covenant
Jer 6:13 unto the priest, every one dealeth *f.*
Zech 5: 4 house of him that sweareth *f.*
Mat 5:11 evil against you *f.* for my sake
Luke 3:14 neither accuse any *f.*, and be content
1 Pet 3:16 be ashamed that *f.* accuse

FAMILY (FAMILIES)
Gen 10: 5 after their *f.*, in their nations
Lev 20: 5 against that man, and against his *f.*
Ps 68: 6 God setteth the solitary in *f.*
Amos 3: 2 known of all the *f.* of the earth
Zech 12:12 mourn, every *f.* apart
Eph 3:15 whole *f.* in heaven and earth is named

FAMINE
Gen 12:10 and there was a *f.* in the land
41:27 shall be seven years of *f.*
Job 5:20 in *f.* he shall redeem thee
Ps 33:19 keep them alive in *f.*
37:19 the days of *f.* they shall be satisfied
Ezek 5:16 evil arrows of *f.*, which shall be
Amos 8:11 not a *f.* of bread, nor a thirst for

FAR
Ex 23: 7 keep thee *f.* from a false matter
Ps 73:27 that are *f.* from thee shall perish
Mark 12:34 not *f.* from the kingdom of God
Eph 2:13 were *f.* off are made nigh by the
Phil 1:23 to be with Christ; which is *f.* better

FASHION (FASHIONED, FASHIONETH, FASHIONING)
Job 10: 8 made me and *f.* me together
Ps 33:15 he *f.* their hearts alike, he
119:73 thy hands have made me and *f.* me
139:16 which in continuance were *f.*
Ezek 16: 7 thy breasts are *f.*, and thine hair
1 Cor 7:31 for the *f.* of this world passeth away
Phil 2: 8 being found in *f.* as a man
3:21 be *f.* like his glorious body
1 Pet 1:14 as obedient children, not *f.* yourselves

FAST
2 Sam 12:21 thou didst *f.* and weep for the child
1 Ki 21: 9 saying, proclaim a *f.*, and set Naboth
2 Chr 20: 3 proclaimed a *f.* throughout all Judah
Ezra 8:21 then I proclaimed a *f.* there
Esth 4:16 and *f.* ye for me and neither eat
Is 58: 4 ye *f.* for strife and debate
58: 5 is it such a *f.* that I have chosen
Jer 14:12 when they *f.* I will not hear
36: 9 they proclaimed a *f.* before the Lord
Joel 1:14 sanctify ye a *f.*, call a solemn
Jonah 3: 5 Nineveh believed God, and proclaimed a *f.*
Zech 7: 5 did ye at all *f.* unto me
8:19 the *f.* of the fourth month
Mat 6:16 ye *f.* be not as the hypocrites
9:14 why do we *f.* but thy disciples *f.* not
9:15 taken from them and then shall they *f.*
Luke 18:12 I *f.* twice in the week
Acts 27: 9 because the *f.* was now already past

FASTED
Judg 20:26 and *f* that day until even
2 Sam 1:12 wept and *f.* till even for Saul and
12:16 David *f.* and lay all night on
Ezra 8:23 we *f.* and besought the Lord
Is 58: 3 why have we *f.* and thou
Mat 4: 2 when he had *f.* forty days
Acts 13: 2 ministered to the Lord, and *f.* and

FASTING (FASTINGS)
Neh 9: 1 of Israel were assembled with *f.*
Esth 4: 3 great mourning among the Jews and *f.*
Ps 109:24 my knees are weak through *f.*
Jer 36: 6 in the Lord's house upon the *f.* day
Dan 6:18 palace and passed the night *f.*
9: 3 to seek by prayer and supplication with *f.*
Joel 2:12 with all your hearts and *f.*
Mat 15:32 not send them away *f.*
Luke 2:37 with *f.* and prayers night and day
Acts 10:30 days ago I was *f.* till this hour
14:23 and had prayed with *f.*, they commended
1 Cor 7: 5 give yourselves to *f.* and prayer
2 Cor 6: 5 in tumults, in labours, in watchings, in *f.*
11:27 in hunger and thirst, in *f.* often

FAT
Lev 3:16 all the *f.* is the Lord's
4: 8 *f.* of the bullock for the sin offering
Prov 11:25 liberal soul shall be made *f.*
13: 4 soul of the diligent shall be made *f.*
15:30 good report maketh the bones *f.*
28:25 trust in the Lord shall be made *f.*
Is 25: 6 *f.* things full of marrow

FATNESS
Job 36:16 on thy table should be full of *f.*
Ps 36: 8 satisfied with the *f.* of thy house
63: 5 satisfied as with marrow and *f.*
65:11 goodness, and thy paths drop *f.*
Is 55: 2 let your soul delight in *f.*
Jer 31:14 satiate the soul of the priests with *f.*
Rom 11:17 root and *f.* of the olive tree

FATHER
Gen 2:24 a man shall leave his *f.*

Gen 4:21 he was the *f.* of all such
17: 4 be a *f.* of many nations
Ex 15: 2 my *f.*'s God, and I will exalt
Num 11:12 as a nursing *f.* beareth the sucking child
2 Sam 7:14 I will be his *f.*, and he shall be
Job 29:16 I was a *f.* to the poor, and the cause
31:18 brought up with me as with a *f.*
38:28 hath the rain a *f.* or who
Ps 68: 5 a *f.* of the fatherless and a judge
103:13 as a *f.* pitieth his children
Is 9: 6 the everlasting *F.*, prince of
Jer 31: 9 I am a *f.* to Israel and
Mal 1: 6 if I be a *f.* where is my honour
2:10 Have we not all one *f.*?
Mat 5:16 glorify your *F.* in heaven
23: 9 call no man your *f.* on earth
John 5:17 my *F.* worketh hitherto and I work
5:19 what he seeth the *F.* do
5:20 the *F.* loveth the Son
5:21 as the *F.* raiseth up the dead and
5:22 the *F.* judgeth no man
5:26 as the *F.* hath life in himself
8:18 *F.* that sent me beareth witness of me
8:29 *F.* hath not left me alone
8:41 ye do the deeds of your *f.*
10:30 I and my *f.* are one
14:20 that I am in my *F.* and ye in me
14:28 I go unto the *F.*, for my *F.* is
16:32 I am not alone, because the *F.* is
20:17 I ascend to my *F.* and your *f.*
Acts 1: 4 wait for the promise of the *F.*
1: 7 the *F.* hath put in his own power
Rom 4:11 the *f.* of all that believe
4:12 and the *f.* of circumcision
1 Cor 8: 6 *F.* of whom are all things, and we
2 Cor 1: 3 be God even the *F.* of our Lord
6:18 I will be a *F.* to you and ye
Eph 1: 3 Blessed be the God and *f.*
1 Tim 5: 1 intreat him as a *f.*
Heb 1: 5 I will be to him a *f.*
12: 9 subjection to the *F.* of spirits
Jas 1:17 and cometh down from the *F.* of lights
1 Pet 1: 3 the God and *F.* of our Lord Jesus

FATHERS
Neh 9:16 our *f.* dealt proudly, and hardened
Ps 22: 4 our *f.* trusted in thee, they trusted
39:12 sojourner, as all my *f.* were
Lam 5: 7 our *f.* have sinned, and are not
Acts 15:10 our *f.* nor we were able to bear

FATHERLESS
Ex 22:22 not afflict any widow, or *f.* child
Deut 10:18 execute judgment of the *f.*
Ps 10:14 thou art the helper of the *f.*
68: 5 a father of the *f.*, and a judge
146: 9 he relieveth the *f.* and widow
Is 1:17 judge the *f.*, plead for the widow
Hos 14: 3 in thee the *f.* findeth mercy
Jas 1:27 visit the *f.* in affliction

FAULT (FAULTS)
Ps 19:12 cleanse thou me from secret *f.*
Mat 18:15 tell him his *f.* between thee and him
Luke 23: 4 I find no *f.* in this man
John 18:38 I find in him no *f.* at all
19: 6 for I find no *f.* in him
1 Cor 6: 7 there is utterly a *f.* among you
Gal 6: 1 if a man be overtaken in a *f.*
1 Pet 2:20 if when ye be buffeted for your *f.*

FAVOUR
1 Sam 2:26 and was in *f.* both with the Lord
Job 10:12 thou hast granted me life and *f.*
Ps 5:12 with *f.* wilt thou compass him as
30: 5 in his *f.* is life; weeping may endure
Prov 31:30 *f.* is deceitful, and beauty is vain
Luke 2:52 in *f.* with God and man

FEAR
Gen 9: 2 and the *f.* of you and the dread
15: 1 *f.* not I am thy shield
20:11 *f.* of God is not in this place
42:18 this do and live, for I *f.* God
Ex 15:16 *f.* and dread shall fall upon them
18:21 such as *f.* God, men of truth
Num 14: 9 Lord is with us, *f.* not them
Deut 1:21 *f.* not, neither be discouraged
4:10 learn to *f.* me all the days that
5:29 such a heart that would *f.* me
6: 2 mightest *f.* the Lord, thy God, to
6:13 thou shalt *f.* the Lord thy God
6:24 to *f.* the Lord our God for our good
10:12 but to *f.* the Lord thy God, to walk
14:23 learn to *f.* the Lord thy God
28:58 mayest *f.* this glorious name
Josh 4:24 ye might *f.* the Lord your God
8: 1 *f.* not, neither be thou dismayed
24:14 therefore *f.* the Lord and serve him
1 Sam 12:14 if ye will *f.* the Lord and serve
12:24 *f.* the Lord and serve him in truth
2 Sam 23: 3 must be just ruling in the *f.* of God
1 Ki 18:12 thy servant did *f.* the Lord
2 Ki 17:28 how they should *f.* the Lord
1 Chr 16:30 *f.* before him, all the earth
2 Chr 6:31 that they may *f.* thee, to walk in
Neh 1:11 servants, desire to *f.* thy name
5:15 not I because of the *f.* of God
Job 28:28 the *f.* of the Lord, that is wisdom
37:24 therefore men do *f.* him
Ps 2:11 serve the Lord with *f.*, and rejoice
15: 4 he honoureth them that *f.* the Lord
19: 9 the *f.* of the Lord is clean, enduring
22:23 ye that *f.* the Lord trust in him
23: 4 I will *f.* no evil, for thou
25:14 of the Lord is with them that *f.* him
31:19 goodness laid up for those that *f.*
33: 8 let all the earth *f.* the Lord
33:18 the Lord is upon them that *f.* him
34:11 children, I will teach you the *f.* of the Lord
36: 1 there is no *f.* of God before his eyes
53: 5 in great *f.* where no *f.* was
56: 4 I will not *f.* what flesh can do
61: 5 heritage of them that *f.* thy name
66:16 come and hear, all that *f.* God
85: 9 salvation is nigh them that *f.* him
86:11 unite my heart to *f.* thy name
90:11 according to thy *f.* so is wrath
103:13 Lord pitieth them that *f.* him
115:13 he will bless them that *f.* the Lord
118: 4 let them that *f.* the Lord say
119:38 servant who is devoted to thy *f.*
119:120 flesh trembleth for *f.* of thee
135:20 ye that *f.* the Lord, bless the Lord
147:11 Lord taketh pleasure in them that *f.*
Prov 1:26 I will mock when *f.* cometh
1:29 they did not choose the *f.* of the Lord
3: 7 *f.* the Lord and depart from evil
8:13 the *f.* of the Lord is to hate evil
10:27 the *f.* of the Lord prolongeth days
14:26 the *f.* of the Lord is strong confidence
15:33 the *f.* of the Lord is instruction of wisdom
16: 6 by the *f.* of the Lord men depart
19:23 the *f.* of the Lord tendeth to life
22: 4 by the *f.* of the Lord are riches
23:17 be thou in the *f.* of the Lord all
24:21 my son, *f.* the Lord and meddle not
29:25 the *f.* of man bringeth a snare
Eccl 5: 7 vanities, *f.* thou God
8:12 shall be well with them that *f.* God
12:13 *f.* God and keep his commandments
Is 8:12 neither *f.* ye their *f.* nor be afraid
29:13 their *f.* toward me is taught
33: 6 the *f.* of the Lord is his treasure
41:10 *f.* thou not for I am with thee
43: 5 *f.* not; for I am with thee
63:17 hardened our heart from thy *f.*
Jer 5:22 *f.* ye not me, saith the Lord
5:24 let us *f.* the Lord that giveth rain
10: 7 who would not *f.* thee, O king of
26:19 did not he *f.* the Lord
30:10 *f.* thou not, O my servant Jacob
32:39 heart that may *f.* me for ever
32:40 but I put my *f.* in their hearts
Hos 3: 5 and shall *f.* the Lord and his goodness
Jonah 1: 9 I *f.* the Lord the God of heaven
Mal 1: 6 if I be a master where is my *f.*
Mat 10:28 *f.* thou not them that kill the body
Luke 1:50 his mercy on them that *f.* him from
12: 5 *f.* him, which after he hath killed
12:32 *f.* not little flock, for it is your
Acts 9:31 walking in the *f.* of the Lord and comfort
Rom 8:15 the spirit of bondage again to *f.*
11:20 be not highminded, but *f.*
13: 7 render *f.* to whom *f.*, honour to
2 Cor 7: 1 perfecting holiness in the *f.* of God
Phil 2:12 work out your own salvation with *f.*
2 Tim 1: 7 spirit of *f.* but of power and of
Heb 2:15 who through *f.* of death were all
4: 1 *f.* lest a promise being left us
12:21 Moses said, I exceedingly *f.* and quake
12:28 with reverence and godly *f.*
13: 6 I will not *f.* what man shall do
1 Pet 1:17 time of sojourning here in *f.*
1 John 4:18 there is no *f.* in love, but perfect
Rev 2:10 *f.* none of those things which thou
11:18 saints and them that *f.* thy name

FEARED (FEAREST, FEARETH)
Gen 22:12 I know that thou *f.* God
Ex 1:17 midwives *f.* God and did not
14:31 people *f.* the Lord and believed
1 Sam 12:18 all the people greatly *f.* the Lord
Neh 7: 2 faithful man and *f.* God above many
Job 1: 1 that *f.* God and eschewed evil
1: 8 one that *f.* God and escheweth
Ps 25:12 what man is he that *f.* the Lord
76: 7 thou, even thou art to be *f.*
89: 7 God is greatly to be *f.* in the
96: 4 Lord is to be *f.* above all gods
112: 1 blessed is the man that *f.* the Lord
Prov 28:14 happy man that *f.* always
Is 50:10 who is among you that *f.* the Lord
Mal 3:16 they that *f.* the Lord spake often
Acts 10: 2 one that *f.* God with all his house
10:22 one that *f.* God and of good report
10:35 that *f.* God and worketh righteousness
13:26 whosoever among you *f.* God to you is
Heb 5: 7 and was heard in that he *f.*

FEARFUL (FEARFULLY)
Ex 15:11 glorious in holiness, *f.* in praises
Ps 139:14 I am *f.* and wonderfully made
Mat 8:26 why are ye *f.*, O ye of little faith
Heb 10:27 certain *f.* looking for of judgment
10:31 *f.* thing to fall into the hands
Rev 21: 8 *f.* and unbelieving shall have their part

FEARFULNESS
Ps 55: 5 *f.* and trembling are come upon me
Is 33:14 *f.* hath surprised the hypocrites

FEAST
Prov 15:15 merry heart hath a continual *f.*
Eccl 10:19 a *f.* is made for laughter, and wine
Is 25: 6 unto all people a *f.* of fat things
1 Cor 5: 8 let us keep the *f.*, not with

FEEBLE
Ps 105:37 not one *f.* person among
Is 35: 3 weak hands and confirm the *f.* knees
Zech 12: 8 he that is *f.* shall be as David
1 Thes 5:14 comfort the *f.* minded, support the
Heb 12:12 hang down and lift up the *f.* knees

FEED (FEEDETH, FED)
Ps 28: 9 *f.* them also and lift them up for
37: 3 verily thou shalt be *f.*
49:14 death shall *f.* on them; and the
Prov 10:21 lips of the righteous *f.* many
30: 8 *f.* me with food convenient for me

Sol 1: 8 *f.* thy kids beside the shepherds' tents
2:16 I am his; he *f.* among the lilies
Is 44:20 he *f.* on ashes: a deceived heart
58:14 *f.* thee with the heritage of Jacob
Jer 3:15 pastors *f.* you with knowledge
Hos 12: 1 Ephraim *f.* on the wind and followeth
Mic 7:14 *f.* thy people with thy rod
John 21:15 he saith unto him *f.* my lambs
Rom 12:20 if thine enemy hunger, *f.* him
Acts 20:28 to *f.* the church of God, which he
1 Cor 3: 2 I have *f.* you with milk, and
9: 7 who *f.* a flock and eateth not
13: 3 give my goods to *f.* the poor
1 Pet 5: 2 *f.* the flock of God among

FEET
1 Sam 2: 9 keep the *f.* of his saints
Neh 9:21 and their *f.* swelled not
Job 12: 5 is ready to slip with his *f.*
29:15 and *f.* was I to the lame
Ps 73: 2 as for me, my *f.* were almost gone
116: 8 delivered my *f.* from falling
119:101 refrained my *f.* from every evil
119:105 thy word is a lamp to my *f.*
Prov 4:26 ponder the path of thy *f.*
Is 59: 7 their *f.* run to evil, and
Luke 1:79 guide our *f.* into the way of
Eph 6:15 *f.* shod with the preparation of
Heb 12:13 and make straight paths for your *f.*
Rev 11:11 they stood upon their *f.*

FELLOW
Eccl 4:10 if they fall, one will lift up his *f.*
Acts 24: 5 found this man a pestilent *f.*
Rom 16: 7 my kinsmen and *f.* prisoners
2 Cor 8:23 he is my partner and *f.* helper
Eph 2:19 *f.* citizens with the saints, and of
Phil 2:25 companion in labour, and *f.* soldier
4: 3 I entreat thee also, true yoke *f.*
Col 1: 7 of Epaphras our dear *f.* servant
4:10 Aristarchus my *f.* prisoner
1 Thes 3: 2 our *f.* labourer in the gospel
3 John 1: 8 that we might be *f.* helpers
Rev 6:11 until their *f.* servants also and their
22: 9 for I am thy *f.* servant

FELLOWSHIP
Ps 94:20 throne of iniquity have *f.* with thee
Acts 2:42 stedfastly in the apostles' doctrine and *f.*
1 Cor 1: 9 called unto the *f.* of his Son
10:20 should have *f.* with devils
2 Cor 6:14 what *f.* hath righteousness with unrighteousness
8: 4 *f.* of the ministering to the saints
Gal 2: 9 gave us right hands of *f.* that we
Eph 5:11 and have no *f.* with works of
Phil 1: 5 for your *f.* in the gospel
2: 1 if there be any *f.* of the spirit
3:10 know him and the *f.* of his sufferings
1 John 1: 3 ye also may have *f.* with us: and
1: 6 if we say we have *f.* with him

FERVENT (FERVENTLY)
Acts 18:25 and being *f.* in the spirit
Rom 12:11 *f.* in spirit, serving the Lord
2 Cor 7: 7 your *f.* mind toward me; so that I
Col 4:12 Epaphras always labouring *f.* for you
Jas 5:16 *f.* prayer of a righteous man availeth
1 Pet 1:22 love one another with a pure heart *f.*
4: 8 have *f.* charity among yourselves
2 Pet 3:10 the elements shall melt with *f.* heat

FEW
Gen 29:20 seemed unto him but a *f.* days
Ps 105:12 when they were but a *f.* men
Mat 7:14 *f.* there be that find it
20:16 many be called, but *f.* chosen
1 Pet 3:20 *f.* that is, eight souls were saved
Rev 2:14 I have a *f.* things against you
3: 4 thou hast a *f.* names in Sardis

FIERY
Deut 33: 2 from his right hand went a *f.* law
Num 21: 6 Lord sent *f.* serpents among the people
Ps 21: 9 thou shalt make them as a *f.* oven
Eph 6:16 quench all the *f.* darts of the wicked
Heb 10:27 *f.* indignation which shall devour
1 Pet 4:12 not strange concerning the *f.* trial

FIGHT
Ex 14:14 the Lord shall *f.* for you
1 Sam 17:20 as the host was going forth to the *f.*
Acts 5:39 found to *f.* against God
23: 9 let us not *f.* against God
1 Tim 6:12 *f.* the good *f.* of faith
2 Tim 4: 7 I have fought a good *f.*
Heb 10:32 a great *f.* of afflictions

FIG (FIGS)
Gen 3: 7 they sewed *f.* leaves together
Judg 9:10 to the *f.* tree, come thou and
1 Ki 4:25 under his vine and under his *f.* tree
Is 34: 4 as a falling *f.* from the *f.* tree
36:16 and every one of his *f.* tree

FIGS
Jer 24: 2 one basket had very good *f.*
Nah 3:12 strong holds shall be like *f.* trees
Zech 3:10 the vine and under the *f.* tree
Mat 7:16 grapes of thorns or *f.* of thistles?
21:19 presently the *f.* tree withered away
Luke 13: 7 I come seeking fruit on this *f.* tree
John 1:50 I saw thee under the *f.* tree
Jas 3:12 can the *f.* tree, my brethren, bear
Rev 6:13 even as a *f.* tree casteth her

FILL (FILLED)
Job 8:21 till he *f.* thy mouth with laughing
Ps 72:19 earth be *f.* with his glory
81:10 open thy mouth wide, and I will *f.* it
Jer 23:24 do I not *f.* heaven and earth
Luke 1:15 and he shall be *f.* with the Holy Ghost
1:53 hath *f.* the hungry with good things
Acts 9:17 and be *f.* with the Holy Ghost
2: 4 they were all *f.* with the Holy Ghost
4:31 they were all *f.* with the Holy Ghost
13: 9 *f.* with the Holy Ghost, set his eyes
Rom 15:13 God *f.* you with all joy
15:14 *f.* with all knowledge, able also to
2 Cor 7: 4 I am *f.* with comfort; I am exceeding
Eph 3:19 be *f.* with all fulness of God
4:10 that he might *f.* all things
Phil 1:11 *f.* with the fruits of righteousness
Col 1: 9 *f.* with the knowledge of his will
2 Tim 1: 4 that I may be *f.* with joy

FILTHINESS
Ezek 36:25 from all *f.* will I cleanse you
2 Cor 7: 1 cleanse ourselves from all *f.* of
Jas 1:21 lay apart all *f.* and superfluity of

FILTHY
Job 15:16 more abominable and *f.* is man
Ps 14: 3 they are altogether become *f.*
Is 64: 6 our righteousness as *f.* rags
Col 3: 8 *f.* communication out of your mouth
1 Tim 3: 3 not greedy of *f.* lucre
Tit 1:11 they ought not, for *f.* lucre's sake
1 Pet 5: 2 but willingly, not for *f.* lucre
2 Pet 2: 7 vexed with the *f.* conversation of the
Rev 22:11 that is *f.* let him be *f.*

FINALLY
2 Cor 13:11 *f.*, brethren, farewell. Be perfect
Eph 6:10 *f.*, my brethren, be strong in the Lord
Phil 3: 1 *f.*, my brethren, rejoice in the Lord
2 Thes 3: 1 *f.*, brethren, pray for us
1 Pet 3: 8 *f.*, be ye all of one mind

FIND (FINDETH)
Num 32:23 your sin will *f.* you out
Prov 1:28 me early but they shall not *f.* me
8:35 whoso *f.* me *f.* life
18:22 whoso *f.* a wife *f.* a good thing
Eccl 9:10 whatsoever thy hand *f.* to do
Sol 5: 6 I sought but could not *f.*
Jer 6:16 ye shall *f.* rest for your souls
29:13 shall seek me and *f.* me, when ye
Mat 7: 7 seek and ye shall *f.*, knock and it
7: 8 and he that seeketh *f.*; and to him
7:14 way to life, few there be that *f.* it
10:39 that *f.* his life shall lose it: and
11:29 ye shall *f.* rest unto your souls
Luke 11:10 receiveth and he that seeketh *f.*
11:25 when he cometh, he *f.* it swept
John 7:34 shall seek me, and shall not *f.* me
2 Tim 1:18 he may *f.* mercy of the Lord in that
Heb 4:16 *f.* grace to help in time of need
Rev 9: 6 seek death and shall not *f.* it

FINGER (FINGERS)
Ex 8:19 this is the *f.* of God
31:18 written with the *f.* of God
Deut 9:10 written with the *f.* of God
1 Ki 12:10 my little *f.* shall be thicker
Ps 8: 3 the work of thy *fingers*
Prov 6:13 he teacheth with his *f.*
Luke 11:20 with the *f.* of God cast out
11:46 the burdens with one of your *f.*
John 20:27 reach hither thy *f.*

FINISH (FINISHED)
Dan 9:24 to *f.* the transgression, and to make
John 17: 4 I have *f.* the work which thou
19:30 he said, It is *f.*
Acts 20:24 I might *f.* my course with joy
2 Cor 8: 6 he would *f.* in you the same grace
2 Tim 4: 7 I have *f.* my course
Jas 1:15 sin when it is *f.* bringeth death

FINISHER
Heb 12: 2 author and *f.* of faith

FIRE
Gen 19:24 Lord rained brimstone and *f.*
Ex 3: 2 unto him in a flame of *f.*
9:24 and *f.* mingles with hail
40:38 *f.* was on it by night
Lev 10: 1 offered a strange *f.* before the Lord
Ps 11: 6 rain *f.* and brimstone on the wicked
39: 3 while I was musing the *f.* burned
Prov 6:27 can man take *f.* in his bosom
25:22 heap coals of *f.* on head
Sol 8: 6 coals thereof are coals of *f.*
Is 9:18 wickedness burneth as a *f.*
10:17 light of Israel for a *f.*
31: 9 Lord whose *f.* is in Zion
43: 2 walkest through the *f.* thou shalt
Jer 23:29 is not my word like *f.*
Amos 5: 6 lest the Lord break out like *f.*
7: 4 Lord God called to contend by *f.*
Hab 2:13 people shall labour in the very *f.*
Zech 2: 5 I will be a wall of *f.*
Mal 3: 2 he is like a refiner's *f.*
Mat 3:10 hewn down, and cast into the *f.*
Mark 9:43 into the *f.* that never shall be quenched
Luke 3:17 he will burn with *f.* unquenchable
9:54 command *f.* to come down
12:49 am come to send *f.* on earth
Rom 12:20 thou shalt heap coals of *f.* on his head
1 Cor 3:13 revealed by *f.* and *f.* shall try
Heb 12:29 our God is a consuming *f.*
Jude 1:23 pulling them out of the *f.*

FIRST
Is 41: 4 the Lord is the *f.* and the last
44: 6 I am the *f.* and I am the last
Mat 6:33 seek ye *f.* the kingdom of God
7: 5 hypocrite *f.* cast out the beam
19:30 many that are *f.* shall be last
Acts 26:23 Christ should be the *f.* to rise
Rom 11:35 who hath *f.* given to him
1 Cor 15:45 *f.* Adam was made a living soul
2 Cor 8: 5 *f.* gave their own selves to the Lord
8:12 if there be *f.* a willing mind

1 Pet 4:17 if it *f.* begin at us, what shall
1 John 4:19 because he *f.* loved us
Rev 2: 4 because thou hast left thy love *f.*
20: 5 this is the *f.* resurrection

FIRSTBORN
Mat 1:25 brought forth her *f.* son
Luke 2: 7 brought forth her *f.* son
Rom 8:29 might be the *f.* among many brethren
Col 1:15 God, the *f.* of every creature
1:18 beginning the *f.* from the dead
Heb 12:23 assembly and church of the *f.*

FIRSTFRUIT (FIRSTFRUITS)
Prov 3: 9 with the *f.* of all thine increase
Rom 8:23 which have the *f.* of the Spirit
11:16 if the *f.* be holy the lump also
1 Cor 15:20 Christ is the *f.* of them that slept
Jas 1:18 we should be a kind of *f.*
Rev 14: 4 being the *f.* unto God

FISH
Ezek 29: 5 all the *f.* of thy rivers
47:10 their *f.* shall be according to

FISHERS
Jer 16:16 I will send for many *f.*
Ezek 47:10 the *f.* shall stand upon it
Mat 4:19 I will make you *f.* of men
John 21: 7 he girt his *f.* coat

FLAME
Ex 3: 2 appeared unto him in a *f.*
Judg 13:20 ascended in the *f.* of the altar
Is 10:17 his Holy One for a *f.*
Heb 1: 7 his ministers a *f.* of fire

FLAMING
2 Thes 1: 8 in *f.* fire taking on them that

FLATTER (FLATTERETH, FLATTERING)
Job 32:22 I know not to give *f.* titles
Ps 78:36 they did *f.* him with
Prov 2:16 the stranger which *f.*
20:19 not with him that *f.* with his lips
1 Thes 2: 5 at any time used we *f.* words

FLEE (FLED)
Prov 28: 1 wicked *f.* when no man
Is 10: 3 will ye *f.* for help
Mat 3: 7 who warned you to *f.* from the wrath
1 Cor 6:18 my dearly beloved *f.* from fornication
10:14 dearly beloved *f.* from idolatry
2 Tim 2:22 *f.* also youthful lusts
Heb 6:18 who have *f.* for refuge
Jas 4: 7 resist the devil, he will *f.*

FLESH
Gen 2:23 and *f.* of my *f.*: she shall
2:24 they shall be one *f.*
Job 10:11 clothed with skin and *f.*
19:26 in my *f.* shall I see God
Ps 56: 4 not fear what *f.* can do to me
65: 2 to thee shall all *f.* come
63: 1 my *f.* longeth for thee in a day
78:39 remember they are but *f.*
Is 40: 6 all *f.* is grass, and all the
49:26 all *f.* know I am thy Redeemer
Jer 17: 5 in man and maketh *f.* his arm
32:27 I am the Lord, God of all *f.*
Joel 2:28 I will pour my Spirit on all *f.*
Mat 16:17 *f.* and blood hath not revealed
19: 5 they twain shall be one *f.*
26:41 is willing, but the *f.* is weak
Luke 3: 6 all *f.* shall see the salvation of God
John 1:13 born not of will but of the *f.*
1:14 the Word was made *f.*
3: 6 which is born of the *f.* is *f.*
6:53 eat the *f.* of the Son of man
6:63 *f.* profiteth nothing, words are
8:15 ye judge after the *f.*
17: 2 given him power over all *f.*
Rom 7: 5 when we were in the *f.*
7:18 that is, in my *f.*
7:25 with the *f.* the law of sin
8: 1 walk not after the *f.*
8: 5 the *f.* mind things of the *f.*
8: 8 are in the *f.* cannot please God
8:13 if ye live after the *f.* ye shall die
9: 5 of whom concerning the *f.* Christ
9: 8 which are the children of the *f.*
13:14 make not provision for the *f.*
1 Cor 1:26 not many wise men after the *f.*
1:29 that no *f.* should glory
6:16 saith he, shall be one *f.*
10:18 Israel after the *f.*, are not they
15:50 *f.* and blood cannot inherit the
2 Cor 1:17 purpose according to the *f.*
5:16 we have known Christ after the *f.*
10: 2 walked according to the *f.*
Gal 5:19 works of the *f.* are manifest
5:24 crucified the *f.* with affections
6: 8 shall of the *f.* reap corruption
6:13 they may glory in your *f.*
Eph 2: 3 *f.* fulfilling the desires of the *f.*
5:30 members of his body, of his *f.*
5:31 they two shall be one *f.*
6: 5 masters according to the *f.*
6:12 we wrestle not against *f.* and blood
Heb 2:14 partakers of *f.* and blood
12: 9 we had fathers of our *f.*
1 Pet 1:24 for all *f.* is as grass, and all
3:18 he was put to death in the *f.*
3:21 not putting away filth of the *f.*
2 Pet 2:10 after the *f.* in lust of uncleanness
1 John 2:16 lust of the *f.* lust of the eyes
Jude 1: 7 going after strange *f.*
1:23 hating the garment spotted by *f.*

FLESHLY
2 Cor 1:12 not with *f.* wisdom but by
Col 2:18 puffed up by his *f.* mind
1 Pet 2:11 abstain from *f.* lusts

FLOCK (FLOCKS)
Gen 32: 5 I have oxen, and asses, *f.*
Ps 77:20 leddest thy people like a *f.*
Is 40:11 he shall feed his *f.* like
63:11 with the shepherd of his *f.*
Jer 13:20 given thee, thy beautiful *f.*
Zech 11: 4 feed the *f.* of slaughter
Acts 20:28 to yourselves and to all the *f.*
1 Pet 5: 2 feed the *f.* of God among you

FOLLOW (FOLLOWED)
Ex 23: 2 thou shalt not *f.* a multitude
Num 14:24 hath *f.* me fully, him I will bring
32:12 for they have wholly *f.* the Lord
Deut 16:20 is altogether just shalt thou *f.*
Josh 14: 8 I wholly *f.* the Lord
Ps 23: 6 goodness and mercy shall *f.* me
Is 51: 1 that *f.* after righteousness
Hos 6: 3 if we *f.* on to know the Lord
Mat 4:19 *f.* me and I will make you
9: 9 saith unto him, *f.* me
16:24 take up his cross and *f.* me
Luke 18:22 sell all thou hast, and *f.* me
John 1:43 saith unto him, *f.* me
12:26 if any serve me let him *f.* me
21:19 saith unto him, *f.* me
Rom 9:30 *f.* not after, have attained to righteousness
14:19 *f.* things that make for peace
1 Cor 14: 1 *F.* after charity, and desire spiritual
Phil 3:12 but I *f.* that I may apprehend
1 Thes 5:15 *f.* that which is good
1 Tim 6:11 *f.* after righteousness, godliness, faith
2 Tim 2:22 *f.* righteousness, faith, charity, peace
Heb 12:14 *f.* peace with all men, and holiness
13: 7 whose faith *f.* considering the end
1 Pet 2:21 example that ye *f.* his steps
Rev 14:13 their works do *f.* them

FOLLY
Gen 34: 7 had wrought *f.* in Israel
Josh 7:15 hath wrought *f.* in Israel
Job 4:18 angels he charged with *f.*
Ps 49:13 their way is their *f.*
Prov 26: 5 answer a fool according to his *f.*
2 Tim 3: 9 their *f.* shall be manifest

FOOD
Gen 3: 6 saw that the tree was good for *f.*
Deut 10:18 in giving him *f.* and raiment
Job 23:12 his mouth more than my necessary *f.*
Ps 78:25 men did eat the angels' *f.*
146: 7 which giveth *f.* to the hungry
Prov 30: 8 feed me will *f.* convenient for me
Acts 14:17 filling our hearts with *f.*
2 Cor 9:10 ministered bread for your *f.*, and
1 Tim 6: 8 having *f.* and raiment let us be

FOOL (FOOLS)
Ps 14: 1 the *f.* hath said in his heart
75: 4 *f.* deal not foolishly: and to the
94: 8 and ye *f.* when will ye be wise
Prov 13:20 companion of *f.* shall be destroyed
14: 8 folly of the *f.* is deceitful
14: 9 *f.* make a mock at sin: but among
Eccl 5: 4 he hath no pleasure in *f.*
Jer 17:11 at his end shall be a *f.*
Mat 5:22 say to brother, Thou *f.*
23:17 ye *f.* and blind, for whether is greater
Luke 12:20 thou *f.* this night thy soul
Rom 1:22 professing to be wise became *f.*
1 Cor 3:18 let him become a *f.* that
4:10 we are *f.* for Christ's sake
2 Cor 11:16 let no man think me a *f.*
Eph 5:15 circumspectly, not as *f.*, but as wise

FOOLISH (FOOLISHLY)
Gen 31:28 thou hast done *f.* in so doing
Num 12:11 wherein we have done *f.*
Deut 32: 6 Lord, requite *f.* people and unwise
1 Sam 13:13 to Saul, thou hast done *f.*
2 Sam 24:10 I have done very *f.*
Job 1:22 not nor charged God *f.*
Ps 5: 5 *f.* shall not stand in thy sight
73:22 so *f.* was I and ignorant
Prov 14:17 He that is soon angry dealeth *f.*
Mat 7:26 likened unto a *f.* man which built
25: 2 them were wise and five were *f.*
Rom 1:21 and their *f.* heart darkened
2 Cor 11:21 (I speak *f.*,) I am bold also
Gal 3: 1 O *f.* Galatians, who hath
Eph 5: 4 neither filthiness, nor *f.* talking
Tit 3: 3 we ourselves also were sometimes *f.*

FOOLISHNESS
2 Sam 15:31 counsel of Ahithophel into *f.*
Prov 12:23 heart of fools proclaimeth *f.*
14:24 *f.* of fools is their folly
15:14 mouth of fools feedeth on *f.*
22:15 *f.* is bound in the heart of a child
24: 9 the thought of *f.* is sin; and the
27:22 yet will not his *f.* depart
1 Cor 1:18 cross to them that perish *f.*
1:21 God by the *f.* of preaching to save
2:14 they are *f.* to him; neither can he
3:19 wisdom of this world is *f.* with God

FOOT
Prov 3:23 thy *f.* shall not stumble
Eccl 5: 1 keep thy *f.* when thou goest to
Is 58:13 turn away thy *f.* from the sabbath
Mat 18: 8 if thy *f.* offend thee, cut
1 Cor 12:15 if *f.* shall say, because I am not
Heb 10:29 trodden under *f.* the Son of God

FORBID (FORBIDDING)
Mark 10:14 and *f.* them not: for of such is
Luke 18:16 and *f.* them not: for of such is
Acts 24:23 that he should *f.* none
28:31 all confidence no man *f.* him
1 Thes 2:16 *f.* us to speak to the Gentiles
1 Tim 4: 3 *f.* to marry, and commanding to abstain

FOREHEAD (FOREHEADS)
Ex 28:38 it shall be on Aaron's *f.*

Jer 3: 3 thou hast a whore's *f.*
Ezek 3: 8 thy *f.* strong against their foreheads
Rev 7: 3 sealed in their *f.*
9: 4 the seal of God on their *f.*
22: 4 his name shall be in their *f.*

FOREIGNER (FOREIGNERS)

Ex 12:45 a *f.* and a hired servant
Deut 15: 3 of a *f.* thou mayest exact it
Obad 1:11 the *f.* entered into his gates
Eph 2:19 ye are no more strangers and *f.*

FOREKNOW (FOREKNEW)

Rom 8:29 whom he did *f.*, he also did
11: 2 cast away his people which he *f.*

FOREKNOWLEDGE

Acts 2:23 determinate counsel, and *f.* of God
1 Pet 1: 2 according to the *f.* of God

FOREORDAINED

1 Pet 1:20 who was verily *f.* before the foundation

FORGET (FORGETTETH, FORGETTING, FORGOTTEN)

Deut 9: 7 *f.* not, how thou provokedst the
32:18 thou hast *f.* God that formed
Job 8:13 paths of all that *f.* God
Ps 9:12 he *f.* not the cry of the humble
10:11 God hath *f.*: he hideth his face
42: 9 why hast thou *f.* me
45:10 *f.* also thine own people, and thy
50:22 consider this, ye that *f.* God
77: 9 hath God *f.* to be gracious
103: 2 and *f.* not all his benefits
119:16 I will not *f.* thy words
119:61 I have not *f.* thy law
Prov 2:17 *f.* the covenant of her God
3: 1 my son *f.* not my law
Is 17:10 *f.* the God of thy salvation
49:14 Zion said, my Lord hath *f.* me
49:15 can a woman *f.* her sucking child
Jer 2:32 can a maid *f.* her ornaments or a
3:21 have *f.* the Lord their God
50: 5 covenant that shall not be *f.*
Phil 3:13 *f.* those things which are behind
Heb 6:10 unrighteous to *f.* your labour of love
12: 5 ye have *f.* the exhortation which
13:16 to do good and to communicate *f.* not
Jas 1:24 straightway *f.* what manner of man

FORGIVE (FORGAVE, FORGAVEST, FORGIVEN, FORGIVETH, FORGIVING)

Ex 32:32 if thou wilt *f.* their sin
34: 7 *f.* iniquity and transgression and sin, and
Ps 32: 1 transgression is *f.*, whose sin is
32: 5 thou *f.* the iniquity of my sin
78:38 *f.* their iniquity, and destroyed
85: 2 *f.* the iniquity of thy people
86: 5 art good and ready to *f.*
99: 8 thou wast a God that *f.* them
103: 3 *f.* thine iniquities; who healeth
Is 2: 9 humbleth himself therefore *f.* them not
33:24 people shall be *f.* their iniquity
Jer 31:34 for I will *f.* their iniquity
Mat 6:12 *f.* us our debts, as we *f.*
6:14 if ye *f.* men their trespasses
9: 6 Son of man hath power on earth to *f.*
18:27 and loosed him, *f.* him the debt
Luke 6:37 *f.* and ye shall be forgiven
7:42 frankly *f.* them both tell me therefore
7:43 that he, to whom the *f.* most
7:47 to whom little is *f.* the same loveth
17: 3 if he repent, *f.* him
23:34 Father, *f.* them, they know not
Rom 4: 7 are those whose iniquities are *f.*
2 Cor 2:10 to whom ye *f.* any thing
Eph 4:32 as God for Christ's sake hath *f.* you
Col 3:13 as Christ *f.* you, so also do ye
Jas 5:15 sins, they shall be *f.* him
1 John 1: 9 faithful to *f.* us our sins
1 John 2:12 because your sins are *f.* you

FORGIVENESS (FORGIVENESSES)

Dan 9: 9 to the Lord our God belong mercies and *f.*
Acts 5:31 repentance to Israel and *f.* of sins
26:18 may receive *f.* of sins by faith
Col 1:14 redemption, even the *f.* of sins

FORM

Gen 1: 2 the earth was without *f.*
1 Sam 28:14 said unto her what *f.* is he of
Is 45: 7 I *f.* the light and create darkness
53: 2 hath no *f.* nor comeliness
Rom 2:20 which hast the *f.* of knowledge
6:17 from the heart that *f.* of doctrine
Phil 2: 6 who being in the *f.* of God
2: 7 took upon him the *f.* of a servant
2 Tim 1:13 hold the *f.* of sound words
3: 5 having the *f.* of godliness

FORMED

Ps 94: 9 that *f.* the eye shall he not see?
Prov 26:10 great God that *f.* all things both
Is 27:11 *f.* them will show them no favour
43:21 this people I *f.* for myself
44: 2 thee and *f.* thee from the womb
54:17 no weapon *f.* against thee shall prosper
Rom 9:20 thing *f.* say to him that *f.*
Gal 4:19 till Christ be *f.* in you

FORNICATION (FORNICATIONS)

2 Chr 21:11 inhabitants of Jerusalem to commit *f.*
Is 23:17 shall commit *f.* with all the kingdoms
Ezek 16:15 pouredst out thy *f.* on everyone
16:26 committed *f.* with the Egyptians
Mat 15:19 adulteries, *f.*, thefts
John 8:41 we be not born of *f.*
Acts 15:20 from *f.*, and from things strangled
Rom 1:29 filled with *f.*, wickedness
1 Cor 5: 1 there is *f.* among you, and such *f.* as
6:13 Now the body not for *f.*, but
6:18 *f.*. Every sin that a man doeth
7: 2 to avoid *f.* have thy own wife
10: 8 neither let us commit *f.*
2 Cor 12:21 not repented of their *f.*
Gal 5:19 works of flesh, adultery, *f.*
Eph 5: 3 But *f.* and all uncleanness, or covetousness
Col 3: 5 *f.*, uncleanliness, inordinate affection
1 Thes 4: 3 should abstain from *f.*
Jude 1: 7 giving themselves to *f.*
Rev 2:14 sacrificed unto idols and to commit *f.*
2:21 I gave her space to repent her *f.*
9:21 neither repented of their *f.*
14: 8 the wine of the wrath of her *f.*
17: 4 abominations and filthiness of her *f.*
18: 3 the earth have committed *f.* with her
19: 2 did corrupt the earth with her *f.*

FORNICATORS

1 Cor 5: 9 an epistle not to company with *f.*
6: 9 be not deceived: neither *f.*, nor
Heb 12:16 Lest there be any *f.* or profane

FORSAKE (FORSAKEN, FORSAKETH, FORSOOK)

Deut 4:31 will not *f.* thee neither destroy thee
12:19 thou *f.* not the Levite as long
31:16 will *f.* me, and break my covenant
32:15 then he *f.* God which made him
Josh 1: 5 I will not fail thee nor *f.* thee
1 Sam 8:57 let him not leave nor *f.* us
12:22 Lord will not *f.* his people
1 Chr 28:20 will not fail thee, nor *f.* thee
Ps 22: 1 my God, why hast thou *f.* me
27:10 when my father and my mother *f.* me
71:11 God hath *f.* him: persecute and take
94:14 neither will he *f.* the inheritance
119:87 I *f.* not thy precepts
Prov 2:17 which *f.* the guide of her youth
28:13 and *f.* them shall have mercy
Is 41:17 God of Israel will not *f.* them
49:14 But Zion said, the Lord hath *f.* me
54: 7 for a small moment have I *f.* thee
55: 7 let the wicked *f.* his way
Jer 2:13 *f.* me the fountain of living waters
17:13 that *f.* thee shall be ashamed
Jonah 2: 8 lying vanities *f.* their own mercy
Mat 19:27 we have *f.* all, and followed thee
27:46 my God, why hast thou *f.* me
2 Cor 4: 9 Persecuted but not *f.*; cast down
2 Tim 4:16 stood with me, but all men *f.* me
Heb 13: 5 never leave thee, nor *f.* thee

FORTRESS

2 Sam 22: 2 my rock, and my *f.*
Ps 18: 2 The Lord is my rock and my *f.*
31: 3 for thou art my rock and my *f.*
71: 3 for thou art my rock and my *f.*
91: 2 He is my refuge and my *f.*: my God
144: 2 my goodness, and my *f.*; my high tower
Jer 16:19 my strength, and my *f.*, and my refuge

FOUND

Gen 26:19 and *f.* there a well of springing
31:37 thou *f.* of all thy household
Eccl 7:27 this have I *f.* that
Sol 3: 1 I sought him, but I *f.* him not
3: 4 I *f.* him whom my soul
Is 55: 6 seek the Lord while he may be *f.*
65: 1 *f.* of them that sought me not
Ezek 22:30 I sought a man and *f.* none
Dan 5:27 in the balance and *f.* wanting
2 Pet 3:14 be *f.* of him in peace

FOUNDED

Ps 24: 2 hath *f.* it upon the seas
Is 14:32 the Lord hath *f.* Zion
Mat 7:25 For it was *f.* on a rock

FOUNDATION (FOUNDATIONS)

Job 4:19 whose *f.* is in the dust
Ps 11: 3 if the *f.* be destroyed
104: 5 Who laid the *f.* of the earth
Prov 8:29 appointed the *f.* of the earth
10:25 righteous is an everlasting *f.*
Is 28:16 I lay in Zion a sure *f.*
51:16 and lay the *f.* of the earth
John 17:24 before the *f.* of the world
Rom 15:20 build on another man's *f.*
1 Cor 3:10 I have laid the *f.*
Eph 1: 4 before the *f.* of the world
2:20 built on the *f.* of prophets
1 Tim 6:19 a good *f.* against the time to come
2 Tim 2:19 the *f.* of God standeth sure
Heb 11:10 looked for a city which hath *f.*
1 Pet 1:20 before the *f.* of the world
Rev 13: 8 from the *f.* of the world
21:14 the city hath twelve *f.*

FOUNTAIN (FOUNTAINS)

Gen 7:11 the *f.* of the great deep broken up
Deut 8: 7 of *f.* and depths that spring
33:28 *f.* of Jacob shall be upon a land
Ps 36: 9 with thee is the *f.* of life
68:26 bless the Lord from the *f.* of Israel
Prov 5:18 let thy *f.* be blessed
13:14 law of the wise is a *f.* of life
14:27 fear of the Lord is a *f.* of life
Eccl 12: 6 a pitcher broken at the *f.*
Sol 4:12 a spring shut up, a *f.* sealed
Jer 2:13 forsaken me, the *f.* of living waters
9: 1 that my eyes were a *f.* of tears
Joel 3:18 a *f.* out of the house of the Lord
Zech 13: 1 a *f.* opened to the house of David
Jas 3:12 can a *f.* both yield salt
Rev 21: 6 the *f.* of the water of life

FOX (FOXES)

Judg 15: 4 caught three hundred *f.*
Ps 63:10 they shall be a portion for *f.*
Sol 2:15 take us the *f.*, the little foxes
Lam 5:18 the *f.* walk upon it

Ezek 13: 4 prophets are like *f.* in the deserts
Mat 8:20 The *f.* have holes, and the birds of
Luke 13:32 Go ye, and tell that *f.*

FRAME (FRAMED)
Ps 103:14 For he knoweth our *f.*
Is 29:16 thing *f.* say of him that *f.*
Jer 18:11 I *f.* evil against you, and devise
Eph 2:21 the building fitly *f.* together
Heb 11: 3 the worlds were *f.* by the word

FREE
Ex 21: 2 he shall go out *f.* for nothing
Lev 19:20 because she was not *f.*
2 Chr 29:31 as many as were of a *f.* heart
Ps 51:12 uphold with thy *f.* spirit
88: 5 *f.* among the dead, like the slain
John 8:32 truth shall make you *f.*
8:36 Son make you *f.* you shall be *f.* indeed
Rom 5:15 so also is a *f.* gift
5:18 the *f.* gift came on all men
1 Cor 7:22 he that is called, being *f.*
Gal 3:28 There is neither bond nor *f.*
Col 3:11 bond nor *f.*, but Christ is all
2 Thes 3: 1 word of Lord may have *f.* course
1 Pet 2:16 *f.* and not using liberty

FREELY
Hos 14: 4 I will love them *f.*
Mat 10: 8 *f.* ye have received, *f.* give
Rom 3:24 justified *f.* by his grace
8:32 with him *f.* give us all things
1 Cor 2:12 things *f.* given us of God
Rev 21: 6 fountain of the water of life *f.*

FRIEND (FRIENDS)
Ex 33:11 as a man speaketh to his *f.*
Deut 13: 6 *f.* which is as his own soul
2 Sam 16:17 is this kindness to thy *f.*
2 Chr 20: 7 the seed of Abraham thy *f.* forever
Prov 17:17 *f.* loveth at all times
18:24 a *f.* closer than a brother
27:10 own *f.* and thy father's *f.*
Sol 5:16 and this is my *f.*, O daughters
Jer 6:21 neighbor and his *f.* shall perish
Hos 3: 1 beloved of her *f.*, yet an adulteress
Mic 7: 5 trust ye not in a *f.*
John 15:13 lay down his life for his *f.*
Jas 2:23 he was called the *f.* of God

FRIENDSHIP
Prov 22:24 make no *f.* with an angry man
Jas 4: 4 *f.* of the world is enmity with God

FROWARD (FROWARDLY)
Deut 32:20 for they are a very *f.* generation
Job 5:13 counsel of the *f.* is carried
Ps 18:26 *f.* wilt show thyself *f.*
101: 4 *f.* heart shall depart from
Prov 4:24 put away from thee a *f.* mouth
10:31 the *f.* tongue shall be cut
11:20 are of a *f.* heart are abomination
17:20 hath a *f.* heart findeth no good
Is 57:17 he went on *f.* in the way
1 Pet 2:18 good and gentle, but also to the *f.*

FRUIT
Gen 4: 3 brought of the *f.* of the ground
30: 2 withheld from thee the *f.* of the womb
Ex 21:22 hurt so that the *f.* depart
Lev 19:24 all the *f.* thereof shall be holy
2 Ki 19:30 downward, and bear the *f.* upward
Ps 92:14 shall bring forth *f.* in old age
127: 3 the *f.* of the womb is his reward
Prov 11:30 *f.* of the righteous tree of life
Sol 2: 3 his *f.* was sweet to taste
Is 3:10 eat the *f.* of their doings
27: 9 all the *f.* to take away sin
57:19 I create the *f.* of the lips
Hos 10: 1 he bringeth *f.* unto himself
Mic 6: 7 *f.* of my body for the sin of my soul
Mat 7:17 good tree bringeth forth good *f.*
12:33 make his tree corrupt and his *f.* corrupt
26:29 drink henceforth of this *f.* of the vine
Luke 1:42 blessed is the *f.* of thy womb
John 4:36 gathereth *f.* to life eternal
15: 2 branch beareth not *f.* he taketh away
Rom 6:21 what *f.* had ye then
7: 4 should bring forth *f.* unto God
15:28 have sealed to them this *f.*
Gal 5:22 *f.* of the Spirit is love, joy
Eph 5: 9 *f.* of Spirit is in all goodness
Phil 4:17 I desire *f.* that may abound
Heb 12:11 peaceable *f.* of righteousness
Jas 3:18 *f.* of righteousness sown
Rev 22: 2 and yielded her *f.* every month

FRUITS
Sol 4:13 with pleasant *f.*; camphire
7:13 all manner of pleasant *f.*
Mat 3: 8 therefore *f.* meet for repentance
2 Cor 9:10 increase the *f.* of your righteousness
Phil 1:11 filled with the *f.* of righteousness
Jas 3:17 full of mercy and good *f.*

FULL
Deut 34: 9 Nun was *f.* of the spirit of wisdom
Ruth 1:21 I went out *f.*, and the Lord hath
1 Sam 2: 5 that were *f.* have hired
Job 5:26 come to the grave in *f.* age
Ps 17:14 they are *f.* of children, and leave
Prov 27: 7 the *f.* soul loatheth an honeycomb
30: 9 lest I be *f.* and deny thee
Luke 4: 1 Jesus *f.* of the Holy Ghost
6:25 woe to you that are *f.*
John 1:14 was made flesh, *f.* of grace and truth
Phil 4:12 know both to be *f.* and
Col 2: 2 and unto all riches of the *f.* assurance
2 Tim 4: 5 make *f.* proof of thy ministry
Heb 6:11 to the *f.* assurance of hope
10:22 near in *f.* assurance of faith

FULFILL (FULFILLED, FULFILLING)
Gen 29:27 He will *f.* her week, and we will
Ps 145:19 *f.* the desire of them
Mat 3:15 us to *f.* all righteousness
Luke 21:24 until the times of the Gentiles be *f.*
Acts 13:22 which shall *f.* all my will
Gal 5:14 all the law is *f.* in one word
5:16 shall not *f.* the lust of the flesh
6: 2 bear the burden and so *f.* the law of
Eph 2: 3 *f.* the desires of the flesh, mind
Phil 2: 2 *f.* ye my joy, that ye be
Col 4:17 in the Lord that thou *f.* it
Jas 2: 8 if ye *f.* the royal law
Rev 17:17 put in their hearts to *f.* his will

FULNESS
Job 20:22 in the *f.* of his sufficiency
John 1:16 of his *f.* have we received
Rom 11:25 till the *f.* of the Gentiles become
15:29 *f.* of the blessing of the Gospel
Gal 4: 4 when the *f.* of the time was come
Eph 1:10 dispensation of the *f.* of times
1:23 *f.* of him that filleth all in all
3:19 filled with the *f.* of God
4:13 to the stature of the *f.* of Christ
Col 1:19 in him should all *f.* dwell
2: 9 all the *f.* of the Godhead

FURNACE
Deut 4:20 you forth out of the iron *f.*
Ps 12: 6 tried in a *f.* of the earth
Is 31: 9 fire is in Zion, his *f.* in Jerusalem
48:10 chosen thee in a *f.* of affliction
Dan 3:11 into the midst of a burning fiery *f.*
Mat 13:50 cast them into the *f.*
Rev 1:15 if they burned in a *f.*

G

GAIN (GAINED)
Job 27: 8 hope of the hypocrite though he hath *g.*
Is 33:15 despiseth the *g.* of oppressions
Mat 16:26 if he shall *g.* the whole world
18:15 thou hast *g.* thy brother
Luke 19:16 Lord, thy pound hath *g.* ten pounds
1 Cor 9:19 servant to all, that I might *g.*
Phil 1:21 to live is Christ, to die is *g.*
1 Tim 6: 5 supposing that *g.* godliness

GALL
Deut 29:18 root beareth *g.* and wormwood
Job 16:13 poureth out my *g.* upon the earth
20:25 sword cometh out of his *g.*
Ps 69:21 gave me *g.* for meat
Jer 8:14 given us water of *g.*
Lam 3:19 my misery, wormwood and the *g.*
Mat 27:34 vinegar drink mixed with *g.*
Acts 8:23 in the *g.* of bitterness

GARDEN
Gen 2:15 took the man, and put him in the *g.*
3:23 sent him forth from the *g.*
13:10 as the *g.* of the Lord
Sol 4:12 a *g.* enclosed is my sister
Is 58:11 thou shalt be like a watered *g.*
Jer 31:12 their soul shall be as a watered *g.*

GARMENT (GARMENTS)
Josh 7:21 a goodly Babylonish *g.*
Ezra 9: 3 rent my *g.*, and my mantle
Job 37:17 How thy *g.* are warm, when he
Ps 22:18 part my *g.* among them
Is 9: 5 and *g.* rolled in blood
59:17 put on *g.* of vengeance
Joel 2:13 rend your hearts not *g.*
Mat 21: 8 spread their *g.* in the way
Acts 9:39 coats and *g.* Dorcas made
Rev 3: 4 have not defiled their *g.*
16:15 watcheth and keepeth his *g.*

GATE (GATES)
Gen 19: 1 sat at the *g.* of Sodom
22:17 shall possess the *g.* of his enemies
28:17 and this is the *g.* of heaven
34:24 went out of the *g.* of his city
Job 29: 7 I went out to the *g.* through
Ps 9:13 lifteth me up from the *g.* of death
24: 7 lift up your heads, O ye *g.*
100: 4 enter his *g.* with thanksgiving
118:19 open to me the *g.* of righteousness
118:20 this *g.* of the Lord, into which the
Is 38:10 go to the *g.* of the grave
Mat 7:13 enter ye at the strait *g.*
16:18 the *g.* of hell shall not prevail
Heb 13:12 suffered without the *g.*

GATHER (GATHERED, GATHERETH)
Deut 30: 3 *g.* thee from all the nations
Neh 1: 9 yet will I *g.* them from thence
Ps 26: 9 *g.* not my soul with sinners
Jer 29:14 I will *g.* you from all the nations
Zeph 3:18 *g.* them that are sorrowful
Mat 3:12 *g.* his wheat into garner
7:16 do men *g.* grapes of thorns
23:37 would I have *g.* thy children together
John 4:36 *g.* fruit unto life eternal
Eph 1:10 *g.* in one all things in Christ

GAVE (GAVEST)
Gen 14:20 and *g.* him tithes of all
Ex 11: 3 the Lord *g.* the people favour
Ps 21: 4 asked life of thee, thou *g.* it
81:12 *g.* them up unto their own hearts' lust
Is 42:24 who *g.* Jacob for a spoil and Israel
John 1:12 *g.* he power to become the sons
3:16 God *g.* his only begotten Son
17: 4 The work which thou *g.* me to do
17:22 And the glory which thou *g.* me
18: 9 of them which thou *g.* me
1 Cor 3: 6 Apollos watered; but God *g.* the increase
2 Cor 8: 5 first *g.* their own selves to the
Gal 1: 4 who *g.* himself for our sins
2:20 who loved me *g.* himself for me

Eph 4: 8 captive, and *g.* gifts unto men
4:11 *g.* some apostles; and some, prophets
1 Tim 2: 6 *g.* himself a ransom for all
Tit 2:14 who *g.* himself for us

GENEALOGIES
1 Tim 1: 4 heed to fables and endless *g.*
Tit 3: 9 avoid foolish questions and *g.*

GENERATION (GENERATIONS)
Gen 2: 4 these are the *g.* of the heavens
6: 9 These are the *g.* of Noah
Deut 32: 5 perverse and crooked *g.*
32:20 a very froward *g.* in whom
Ps 14: 5 God is in the *g.* of righteous
22:30 the accounted to the Lord for a *g.*
24: 6 this is the *g.* of them that seek
33:11 the thoughts of his heart to all *g.*
45:17 name to be remembered in all *g.*
72: 5 sun and moon endure, throughout all *g.*
79:13 show forth thy praise to all *g.*
89: 4 build thy throne to all *g.*
90: 1 our dwelling place in all *g.*
100: 5 his truth endureth to all *g.*
102:18 written for the *g.* to come
102:24 thy years are throughout all *g.*
112: 2 *g.* of upright shall be blessed
119:90 thy faithfulness is to all *g.*
145: 4 one *g.* shall praise thy works
145:13 dominion endureth to all *g.*
Mat 3: 7 O *g.* of vipers, who hath warned
Acts 13:36 had served his own *g.* by the will
Col 1:26 mystery hid from ages and *g.*
1 Pet 2: 9 ye are a chosen *g.* a royal

GENTILES
Gen 10: 5 the isles of the *G.* divided
Is 11:10 to it shall the *G.* seek
42: 6 the people, for a light of the *G.*
49: 6 give a light to the *G.*
60: 3 *g.* shall come to thy light
60:62 *g.* shall see thy righteousness
Mat 6:32 after these things do the *g.* seek
Luke 2:32 A light to lighten the *G.*
21:24 till the times of the *g.* be
John 7:35 dispersed among the *g.*, teach the *g.*
Acts 13:46 everlasting life, lo, we turn to the *g.*
13:47 set thee to be a light to the *G.*
14:27 opened the door of faith unto the *g.*
Rom 2:14 *g.* which have not the law
3:29 is he not also of the *g.*?
11:25 until the fulness of the *g.* become
15:10 rejoice, ye *g.*, with his people
15:12 reign over the *g.*; in him shall *g.* trust
Eph 3: 6 that the *g.* should be fellowheirs
1 Tim 2: 7 teacher of the *g.* in faith
3:16 God in flesh, preached to the *g.*

GENTLE (GENTLY)
Is 40:11 *g.* lead those with young
1 Thes 2: 7 we were *g.* among you even as a
2 Tim 2:24 servant of the Lord must be *g.*
Tit 3: 2 be *g.* showing all meekness
Jas 3:17 wisdom from above is *g.*
1 Pet 2:18 not only to the *g.* but to

GENTLENESS
Ps 18:35 thy *g.* made me great
2 Cor 10: 1 by the meekness and *g.* of Christ
Gal 5:22 longsuffering, *g.*, goodness

GIFT (GIFTS)
Ex 23: 8 take no *g.* for a *g.* blindeth the wise
Ps 68:18 thou hast received *g.* for men
Prov 17: 8 A *g.* is as a precious stone
18:16 a man's *g.* maketh room for
21:14 a *g.* in secret pacifieth anger
Eccl 7: 7 a *g.* destroyeth the heart
Mat 7:11 to give good *g.* unto your children
John 4:10 if thou knewest the *g.* of God
Rom 6:23 *g.* of God is eternal life
11:29 for the *g.* and calling of God are
1 Cor 1: 7 ye come behind in no *g.*
1 Cor 7: 7 every man hath his proper *g.*
Eph 2: 8 it is the *g.* of God
4: 8 captivity captive gave *g.* to men
Phil 4:17 not because I desire a *g.*
1 Tim 4:14 neglect not the *g.* that
Heb 6: 4 have tasted of the heavenly *g.*

GIRD (GIRDED, GIRDETH, GIRT)
Ps 18:32 God that *g.* me with strength
30:11 sackcloth, and *g.* me with gladness
Luke 12:35 let your loins be *g.*
Eph 6:14 have your loins *g.* about with truth
1 Pet 1:13 *g.* up the loins of the mind

GIRDLE (GIRDLES)
Is 11: 5 shall be the *g.* of his loins
Mat 3: 4 leathern *g.* about his loins
Rev 1:13 the paps with a golden *g.*
15: 6 their breasts girded with golden *g.*

GIVE (GIVEN, GIVETH)
Gen 12: 7 unto thy seed will I *g.* this land
30:31 thou shalt not *g.* me anything
1 Ki 3: 5 ask what I shall *g.* thee
Ps 2: 8 I shall *g.* thee the heathen
29:11 Lord will *g.* strength to his
37:21 righteous showeth mercy and *g.*
84:11 Lord will *g.* grace and glory
104:27 mayest *g.* them their meat
109: 4 I *g.* myself unto prayer
Prov 28:27 he that *g.* to the poor shall
Is 40:29 He *g.* power to the faint
42: 5 he that *g.* breath unto the people on earth
Jer 17:10 to *g.* every man according to his works
32:19 to *g.* everyone according to his ways
Hos 11: 8 how shall I *g.* thee up
Mat 13:12 whosoever hath, to him shall be *g.*
13:11 it is *g.* to you to know mysteries
Luke 6:38 *g.* and it shall be given
12:48 to whomsoever much is *g.*
John 10:28 I *g.* to them eternal life
Acts 3: 6 such as I have *g.* I thee
20:35 more blessed to *g.* than to receive
Rom 8:32 not with him also freely *g.* us all
11:35 Or who hath first *g.* to him
1 Cor 2:12 know things freely *g.* of God
Eph 4:28 have to *g.* to him that needeth
1 Tim 4:15 *g.* thyself wholly to them
6:17 *g.* us richly all things to enjoy
Jas 1: 5 that *g.* to all men liberally
Rev 22:12 to *g.* every man according to his work

GIVER
2 Cor 9: 7 God loveth the cheerful *g.*

GLAD (GLADLY)
Ps 16: 9 therefore, my heart is *g.*
31: 7 I will be *g.* and rejoice in
64:10 righteous shall be *g.* in the Lord
104:34 I will be *g.* in the Lord
122: 1 I was *g.* when they said unto me
Mark 6:20 many things; and heard him *g.*
Luke 8:40 was returned, the people *g.* received him
Acts 2:41 that *g.* received his word
2 Cor 12:15 I will very *g.* spend and be spent

GLADNESS
Ps 4: 7 thou hast put *g.* in my heart
30:11 sackcloth and girded me with *g.*
45: 7 anointed thee with the oil of *g.*
51: 8 make me to hear joy and *g.* come before
100: 2 serve the Lord with *g.*, and sorrow
106: 5 rejoice in the *g.* of thy nation
Is 35:10 obtain joy and *g.*
Acts 2:46 eat their meat with *g.*
14:17 filling our hearts with food and *g.*

GLASS
1 Cor 13:12 now we see through a *g.*, darkly
2 Cor 3:18 beholding as in a *g.* the glory
Jas 1:23 beholding a natural face in *g.*
Rev 4: 6 a sea of *g.* like unto crystal
21:18 the city of pure gold like clear *g.*

GLORY
Ex 16: 7 ye shall see the *g.* of the Lord
1 Sam 4:21 saying the *g.* departed from Israel
1 Chr 16:10 *G.* ye in his holy name: let the heart
29:11 and the power and the *g.*
Job 29:20 my *g.* was fresh in me
Ps 8: 5 crowned him with *g.* and honour
19: 1 declare the *g.* of God
29: 9 every one speak of his *g.*
57: 8 Awake up my *g.*; awake, psaltery
64:10 upright in heart shall *g.*
72:19 filled with his *g.*; Amen, and Amen
73:24 afterward receive me to *g.*
89:17 art the *g.* of their strength
104:31 *g.* of the Lord shall endure forever
145:11 speak of the *g.* of thy kingdom
Prov 3:35 the wise shall inherit *g.*
16:31 hoary head is a crown of *g.*
25:27 to search their own *g.* is not *g.*
Is 4: 5 upon all the *g.* shall be a defence
6: 3 the whole earth is full of his *g.*
23: 9 to stain the pride of all *g.*
24:16 heard songs, even *g.* to the righteous
28: 5 Lord shall be for a crown of *g.*
40: 5 *g.* of the Lord shall be revealed
41:16 shalt *g.* in the Holy One of
42: 8 my *g.* will I not give
45:25 seed of Israel be justified, and *g.*
48:11 not give my *g.* unto another
60: 1 the *g.* of the Lord is risen
60: 7 I will glorify the house of my *g.*
Jer 2:11 my people have changed their *g.*
Ezek 1:28 likeness of the *g.* of the Lord
20: 6 which is the *g.* of all lands
43: 5 the *g.* of the Lord filled the house
Hos 4: 7 will I change their *g.* into shame
Hab 3: 3 his *g.* covered the heavens
Hag 2: 7 I will fill this house with *g.*
Zech 2: 5 will be the *g.* in the midst
6:13 build the temple and bear the *g.*
Mat 6: 2 that they may have *g.* of men
6:13 thine is the kingdom, the power the *g.*
25:31 son of man shall come in his *g.*
Luke 2: 9 the *g.* of the Lord shone round
2:14 *g.* to God in the highest
2:32 light of Gentiles, *g.* of thy people
John 1:14 his *g.*, *g.* as of the only begotten Son
2:11 manifested forth his *g.*; and his disciples
17:22 *g.* which thou gavest me I have
17:24 I am; that they may behold my *g.*
Rom 2: 7 seek for *g.* and honour and immortality
4: 2 hath whereof to *g.* but not
5: 2 rejoice in the hope and *g.* of God
5: 3 we *g.* in tribulations also
11:36 to whom be *g.* for ever, Amen
16:27 wise be the *g.* through Christ
1 Cor 10:31 do all to the *g.* of God
11: 7 is the image and *g.* of God
15:43 sown in dishonour, raised in *g.*
2 Cor 3:18 as in a glass, the *g.* of the Lord
4:17 exceeding and eternal weight of *g.*
5:12 occasion to *g.* on our behalf
11:18 many *g.* after the flesh, I *g.* also
12: 1 it is not expedient for me to *g.*
12: 9 will I rather *g.* in my infirmities
Gal 6:14 God forbid I should *g.*
Eph 1: 6 praise of the *g.* of his grace
1:12 to the praise of his *g.*
3:21 to him be *g.* in the church
3:13 my tribulation for you is your *g.*
Phil 3:19 whose *g.* is in their shame
Col 1:27 Christ in you, the hope of *g.*
3: 4 ye also appear with him in *g.*
1 Thes 2:12 called you to his kingdom and *g.*
2:20 ye are our *g.* and joy
1 Tim 3:16 The world received up into *g.*

Heb 1: 3 who, being the brightness of his *g.*
13:21 to whom be *g.* for ever and ever
1 Pet 1: 8 joy unspeakable, full of *g.*
1:11 the sufferings of Christ, and the *g.* that
4:13 when his *g.* shall be revealed
5: 1 partaker of the *g.* to be revealed
5: 4 ye shall receive a crown of *g.*
5:10 called us to eternal *g.* by Christ
2 Pet 1: 3 called us to *g.* and virtue
1:17 came a voice from excellent *g.*
Rev 4:11 and worthy, O lord, to receive *g.*
5:12 and honour, and *g.*, and blessing
21:11 having the *g.* of God

GLORIFY (GLORIFIED)

Lev 10: 3 before all I will be *g.*
Is 25: 3 shall the strong people *g.* thee
60: 7 I will *g.* the house of my glory
Mat 5:16 *g.* your Father in heaven
John 7:39 Jesus was not yet *g.*
12:23 Son of man should be *g.*
12:28 Father, *g.* thy name
15: 8 herein is my Father *g.*
17: 1 *g.* thy Son that the Son *g.* thee
17:10 all mine are thine, I am *g.*
21:19 by what death he should *g.* God
Acts 3:13 God of our fathers hath *g.* his Son
4:21 all men *g.* God for that which was
Rom 1:21 they *g.* him not as God
1 Cor 6:20 *g.* God in your body and
Gal 1:24 they *g.* God in me
2 Thes 1:10 come to be *g.* in his saints
3: 1 word have free course and be *g.*
Heb 5: 5 even Christ *g.* not himself
1 Pet 2:12 *g.* God in the day of visitation
Rev 15: 4 who shall not fear thee, and *g.*
18: 7 how she hath *g.* herself

GLORIOUS

Ex 15: 6 Lord, is become *g.* in power
15:11 who is like thee, *g.* in holiness
Deut 28:58 fear this *g.* and fearful name
1 Chr 29:13 thank thee, and praise thy *g.* name
Ps 45:13 king's daughter is all *g.* within
66: 2 make his praise be *g.*
72:19 blessed be his *g.* name
87: 3 *g.* things spoken of thee
111: 3 his work is honourable and *g.*
145: 5 speak of the *g.* honour of thy
145:12 the *g.* majesty of his kingdom
Is 4: 2 branch of Lord shall be *g.*
11:10 his rest shall be *g.*
22:23 be for a *g.* throne to his father's house
30:30 cause his *g.* voice to be heard
49: 5 I be *g.* in eyes of the Lord
60:13 make the place of my feet *g.*
63:12 hand of Moses with his *g.* arm
Jer 17:12 a *g.* high throne from the beginning
Rom 8:21 *g.* liberty of the children of God
2 Cor 3: 7 written and engraves in stone, was *g.*
4: 4 light of the *g.* gospel should shine
Eph 5:27 present it to himself a *g.* church
Phil 3:21 fashioned like unto his *g.* body
Col 1:11 according to his *g.* power
1 Tim 1:11 according to the *g.* gospel of
Tit 2:13 and the *g.* appearing of the great

GLUTTON

Deut 21:20 he is a *g.* and a drunkard
Prov 23:21 the drunkard and the *g.*

GLUTTONOUS

Mat 11:19 and they say behold a man *g.*
Luke 7:34 and ye say behold a *g.* man

GOINGS

Job 34:21 and he seeth all his *g.*
Ps 17: 5 hold up my *g.* in thy paths
40: 2 rock, and established my *g.*
68:24 they have seen thy *g.*, O God
Prov 5:21 he pondereth all his *g.*
20:24 man's *g.* are of the Lord

Mic 5: 2 whose *g.* are of old, from

GOAT (GOATS)

Lev 3:12 if his offering be a *g.*, then
16:21 hands upon the head of the live *g.*
Is 1:11 of bullocks or of lambs, or of he *g.*
Ezek 34:17 judge between rams and *g.*
Zech 10: 3 I punished the *g.*: for the Lord
Mat 25:32 set *g.* on his left hand
Heb 9:12 Neither by the blood of *g.*
10: 4 blood of bulls and of *g.*

GOD

Job 33:12 *G.* is greater than man
Ps 18:31 who is *G.* save the Lord
86:10 wondrous things, thou art *G.* alone
Dan 11:36 marvelous things against the *G.* of gods
Mic 7:18 who a *G.* like thee
Mat 6:24 cannot serve *G.* and mammon
19:17 none good but one, that is *G.*
Mark 12:32 one *G.* and none other
John 1: 1 with *G.*, and the Word was *G.*
1:18 hath seen *G.* at anytime
17: 3 know thee the only true *G.*
Acts 7: 2 *G.* of glory appeared to Abraham
Rom 3: 4 *G.* forbid: yea, let *G.* be true
8:31 if *G.* be for us, who can be against
9: 5 over all, *G.* blessed for ever
15: 5 *G.* of patience and consolation
15:13 *G.* of hope fill you with all joy
1 Cor 15:28 that *G.* may be all in all
2 Cor 1: 3 mercies, and the *G.* of all comfort
2 Thes 2: 4 above all that is called *G.*
1 Tim 3:16 *G.* was manifest in the flesh
1 Pet 5:10 *G.* of all grace, who hath called
1 John 4:12 no man hath seen *G.* at any time
5:20 This is the true *G.*

GODHEAD

Acts 17:29 *G.* is like unto gold
Rom 1:20 his eternal power and *G.*
Col 2: 9 the fulness of the *G.* bodily

GODLY

Ps 4: 3 that is *g.* for himself
32: 6 every one that is *g.* pray
Mal 2:15 he might seek a *g.* seed
2 Cor 1:12 in simplicity and *g.* sincerity
7: 9 sorrow after a *g.* manner
Tit 2:12 live soberly, righteously and *g.*
Heb 12:28 with reverence and *g.* fear
2 Pet 2: 9 deliver the *g.* out of
3 John 1: 6 journey after a *g.* sort

GODLINESS

1 Tim 2: 2 quiet and peaceable life in all *g.*
3:16 great is the mystery of *g.*
4: 7 exercise thyself rather unto *g.*
4: 8 *g.* is profitable to all things
6: 3 doctrine which is according to *g.*
6: 6 *g.* with contentment is great gain
6:11 follow after righteousness, *g.*
2 Tim 3: 5 having a form of *g.* but
Tit 1: 1 truth which is after *g.*
2 Pet 1: 3 all that pertain to life and *g.*
1: 6 Patience; and to patience and *g.*
3:11 in all holy conversation and *g.*

GOLD

Gen 2:11 land of Havilah where there is *g.*
13: 2 in silver, and in *g.*
Job 23:10 I shall come forth as *g.*
31:24 if I have made *g.* my hope, or
Ps 19:10 more desired than *g.*, yea
119:127 love thy commandments above *g.*
Prov 8:19 my fruit is better than *g.*
Is 2: 7 full of silver and *g.*
13:12 man more precious than fine *g.*
Zech 13: 9 and will try them as *g.* is tried
1 Cor 3:12 build on this foundation, *g.*
1 Tim 2: 9 not with braided hair, or *g.*
1 Pet 1: 7 trial of faith more precious than *g.*
3: 3 the hair and of wearing of *g.*

Rev 3:18 buy of me *g.* tried in the fire

GOOD

Gen 1:31 every thing was very *g.*
2:18 not *g.* for man to be alone
32:12 thou saidst, I will do thee *g.*
50:20 God meant it unto *g.*
2 Ki 20:19 *g.* is the word of the Lord
Neh 2:18 their hands for this *g.* work
Ps 34: 8 taste and see that the Lord is *g.*
73: 1 truly God is *g.* to Israel
86: 5 Lord, art *g.*, ready to forgive
106: 5 may see the *g.* of thy chosen
145: 9 Lord is *g.* to all; and his tender
Lam 3:25 Lord *g.* to them that wait
Mic 6: 8 shown thee what is *g.*
Mat 19:17 Why callest thou me *g.*?
26:10 she has wrought a *g.* work upon me
John 10:32 many *g.* works have I shown you
10:33 for a *g.* work we stone thee not
Acts 9:36 Dorcas was full of *g.* works
Rom 3: 8 do evil that *g.* may come
7:18 that which is *g.* I find not
13: 3 not a terror to *g.* works
2 Cor 9: 8 abound to every *g.* work
Eph 2:10 in Jesus Christ unto *g.* works
Phil 1: 6 begun a *g.* work will finish it
Col 1:10 being fruitful in every *g.* work
1 Thes 5:15 follow that which is *g.*
2 Thes 2:17 establish you in every *g.* work
1 Tim 2:10 (women professing godliness) with *g.* works
5:10 have diligently followed every *g.* work
5:25 the *g.* works of some are manifest
Tit 1:16 and unto every *g.* work reprobate
3: 1 to be ready to every *g.* work
3: 8 careful to maintain *g.* works
Heb 10:24 provoke unto love and to *g.* works
13:21 perfect in every *g.* work
1 Pet 2:12 may by your *g.* works which

GOODNESS

Ex 33:19 I will make my *g.* pass
34: 6 God abundant in *g.* and truth
2 Chr 6:41 let saints rejoice in *g.*
Neh 9:25 delight themselves in *g.*
9:35 not served thee in thy great *g.*
Ps 16: 2 my *g.* extendeth not to
23: 6 *g.* and mercy shall follow me
27:13 believed to see the *g.* of the Lord
31:19 how great is thy *g.*, which thou
33: 5 earth full of the *g.* of the Lord
52: 1 the *g.* of God endureth continually
52:11 crownest the year with thy *g.*
52:65 satisfied with the *g.* of thy house
Is 63: 7 great *g.* bestowed on Israel
Hos 3: 5 fear the Lord and his *g.*
Rom 2: 4 *g.* of God leadeth to repentance
11:22 behold the *g.* and severity of God
Gal 5:22 longsuffering, gentleness, *g.*
Eph 5: 9 fruit of Spirit in all *g.*

GOSPEL

Mat 4:23 preaching the *g.* of the kingdom
Mark 1: 1 the beginning of the *g.*
8:35 for my sake, and the *g.*
16:15 preach the *g.* to every creature
Acts 20:24 testify the *g.* of the grace of God
Rom 1: 1 separated unto *g.* of God
1 Cor 1:17 but to preach the *g.*
4:15 begotten you through the *g.*
2 Cor 4: 3 if our *g.* hid, it is hid
11: 4 another *g.* which ye have not accepted
Eph 1:13 truth, the *g.* of your salvation
6:15 preparation of the *g.* of peace
Phil 1: 5 For your fellowship in the *g.*
1:27 as it becometh the *g.* of Christ
Col 1: 5 the word of truth of the *g.*
1 Thes 1: 5 our *g.* came to you not only
1 Tim 1:11 according to the glorious *g.*
Heb 4: 2 unto us was the *g.* preached
1 Pet 4: 6 *g.* was preached to the dead

Rev 14: 6 having the everlasting *g.* to preach

GOVERNMENT (GOVERNMENTS)

Is 9: 6 *g.* shall be upon his shoulder
22:21 commit thy *g.* into his hand
1 Cor 12:28 gifts of healing, helps *g.*
2 Pet 2:10 uncleanliness, and despise *g.*

GRACE

Ezra 9: 8 for a little space *g.* hath been
Esth 2:17 she obtained *g.* and favor
Ps 84:11 Lord will give *g.* and glory
Prov 3:34 but he giveth *g.* to the lowly
Zech 4: 7 with shoutings, crying, *g. g.* unto it
12:10 spirit of *g.* and supplications
Luke 2:40 *g.* of God was upon him
Acts 15:11 *g.* of our Lord Jesus Christ
18:27 which we had believed through *g.*
Rom 1: 7 *g.* and peace to you
3:24 justified freely by his *g.*
5:20 *g.* did much more abound
6:14 not under law, but *g.*
11: 5 according to the election of *g.*
11: 6 if by *g.* then not of works
16:20 *g.* of our Lord Jesus Christ
1 Cor 16:23 *g.* of our Lord Jesus Christ
2 Cor 1:12 by the *g.* of God our conversation
6: 1 receive not the *g.* of God in vain
8: 1 *g.* of God bestowed on the churches
9:14 for the exceeding *g.* of God in you
12: 9 my *g.* sufficient for thee
13:14 *g.* of the Lord Jesus Christ
Gal 2:21 I do not frustrate the *g.* of God
6:18 *g.* of our Lord Jesus Christ
Eph 2: 5 by *g.* ye are saved
2: 7 show exceeding riches of his *g.*
2: 8 by *g.* are ye saved
4:29 minister *g.* to the hearers
Phil 4:23 *g.* of our Lord Jesus Christ
Col 1: 6 knew the *g.* of God in truth
1 Thes 5:28 *g.* of our Lord Jesus Christ
2 Thes 3:18 *g.* of our Lord Jesus Christ
Tit 3: 7 justified by his *g.*
Heb 4:16 come boldly to the throne of *g.*
13: 9 heart be established with *g.*
Jas 4: 6 he giveth more *g.* unto the humble
1 Pet 3: 7 heirs of the *g.* of life
4:10 stewards of the manifold *g.* of God
5: 5 and giveth *g.* to the humble
5:12 this the true *g.* of God wherein ye stand
2 Pet 3:18 grow in *g.* and knowledge
Jude 1: 4 turning the *g.* of God into lasciviousness
Rev 22:21 *g.* of our Lord Jesus Christ

GRACIOUS (GRACIOUSLY)

Gen 33: 5 which God hath *g.* given thy servant
43:29 God be *g.* unto thee my son
Ex 22:27 I will hear, for I am *g.*
22:19 I will be *g.* to whom I will be *g.*
34: 6 Lord God merciful and *g.*
Num 6:25 and be *g.* unto thee
2 Chr 30: 9 God is *g.* and merciful
Neh 9:31 thou art a *g.* and merciful God
Job 33:24 then he is *g.* to him
Ps 77: 9 hath God forgotten to be *g.*
86:15 full of compassion and *g.*
103: 8 Lord is merciful and *g.*
119:29 grant me thy law *g.*
Hos 14: 2 all iniquity, and receive us *g.*
Joel 2:13 for he is *g.* and merciful
Amos 5:15 the Lord God of hosts will be *g.*
Jonah 4: 2 knew thou art a *g.* God
Mal 1: 9 he will be *g.* unto us
1 Pet 2: 3 tasted that the Lord is *g.*

GRAPES

Deut 32:32 their *g.* are *g.* of gall
Sol 2:13 the tender *g.* give a good smell
Is 5: 4 brought it forth wild *g.*
Ezek 18: 2 fathers have eaten sour *g.*
Mic 7: 1 fruits, as the *g.* gleanings of vintage

GRASS

Ps 37: 2 soon be cut down like the *g.*
90: 5 like the *g.* which groweth up
103:15 as for man his days are like *g.*
Is 40: 6 shall I cry? All flesh is *g.*
51:12 shall be made as *g.*
Mat 6:30 if God so clothe the *g.*
Jas 1:11 but it withereth the *g.*
1 Pet 1:24 for all flesh is as *g.*
Rev 8: 7 all green *g.* was burnt up

GRAVE

1 Sam 2: 6 Lord bringeth down to the *g.*
Job 5:26 come to thy *g.* in full age
14:13 hide me in the *g.*
Ps 6: 5 in the *g.* who shall give thanks
Prov 1:12 swallow alive, as the *g.*
Eccl 9:10 nor wisdom in the *g.*
Is 38:18 the *g.* cannot praise thee
Hos 13:14 ransom them from the power of the *g.*
1 Cor 15:55 O *g.* where is thy victory

GRAVEN

Job 19:24 they were *g.* with an iron
Is 49:16 have *g.* thee on the palms
Jer 17: 1 it is sin *g.* upon table of their heart

GREAT

Gen 6: 5 wickedness of man was *g.*
12: 2 make of thee a *g.* nation
30: 8 with *g.* wrestlings have I wrestled
Ex 32:11 land of Egypt with a *g.* power
Deut 29:24 the heat of this *g.* anger
1 Sam 6: 9 he hath done us this *g.* evil
Neh 13:27 to do all this *g.* evil
Job 5: 9 *g.* things and unsearchable
Ps 47: 2 a *g.* king over all the earth
48: 2 the city of the *g.* king
147: 5 *g.* is our Lord, and of *g.* power
Eccl 2:21 vanity and a *g.* evil
Jer 45: 5 seekest thou *g.* things for thyself
Dan 9:12 bringing upon us a *g.* evil
Hos 8:12 written to him the *g.* things
Joel 3:13 for their wickedness is *g.*
Nah 1: 3 slow to anger and *g.* in power
Mal 1:14 I am a *g.* king
Luke 1:49 hath done to me *g.* things
Acts 4:33 with *g.* power gave the apostles
Rev 11:17 taken to thee thy *g.* power

GREATER

Job 33:12 God is *g.* than man
Mat 12:42 *g.* than Solomon is here
John 1:50 see *g.* things than these
4:12 art thou *g.* than our father Jacob
10:29 gave them me, is *g.* than all
14:28 my father is *g.* than I
1 Cor 14: 5 *g.* is he that prophesieth
1 John 3:20 God *g.* than our heart
4: 4 *g.* he that is in you
5: 9 witness of God is *g.*

GREATLY

1 Sam 30: 6 David was *g.* distressed
2 Sam 24:10 I have sinned *g.* in that I
1 Ki 18: 3 Obadiah feared the Lord *g.*
1 Chr 16:25 great is the Lord and *g.* to be praised
2 Chr 33:12 humbled himself *g.* before the God
Job 3:25 thing I *g.* feared is come
Ps 28: 7 therefore my heart *g.* rejoiceth
89: 7 God is *g.* to be feared in the assembly
116:10 have I spoken I was *g.* afflicted
145: 3 great is the Lord, and *g.* to be praised
Dan 9:23 O man, *g.* beloved
Mark 12:27 ye therefore do *g.* err

GREATNESS

Ex 15: 7 *g.* of thy excellency
Num 14:19 according to the *g.* of thy mercy
Deut 32: 3 ascribe ye *g.* to our God
Ps 66: 3 through the *g.* of thy power
145: 3 and his *g.* is unsearchable
Is 63: 1 travelling in *g.* of strength
Eph 1:19 the exceeding *g.* of his power

GREEDY

Prov 1:19 every one that is *g.* of gain
15:27 he that is *g.* of gain troubleth
Is 56:11 they are *g.* dogs, never
1 Tim 3: 3 not *g.* of filthy lucre

GREEDINESS

Eph 4:19 to work all uncleanness with *g.*

GRIEF

Is 53: 3 sorrows, and acquainted with *g.*
Heb 13:17 with joy, and not with *g.*

GRIEVE (GRIEVED)

Gen 6: 6 earth, and it *g.* him at his heart
Judg 10:16 his soul was *g.* for misery
Ps 95:10 forty years long was I *g.*
119:158 I beheld transgressors and was *g.*
139:21 *g.* with those that rise up
Is 54: 6 called thee as a woman forsaken and *g.*
Jer 5: 3 stricken, they have not *g.*
Lam 3:33 nor *g.* the children of men
Amos 6: 6 they are not *g.* for affliction
Mark 3: 5 *g.* for hardness of their hearts
Rom 14:15 if thy brother be *g.* with thy meat

GRIEVIOUS

Ps 10: 5 His ways are always *g.*; thy judgments
Mat 8: 6 sick of the palsy, *g.* tormented
23: 4 burdens *g.* to be borne
Acts 20:29 shall *g.* wolves enter
1 John 5: 3 his commandments are not *g.*

GROAN (GROANED, GROANETH)

John 11:33 *g.* in spirit, and was troubled
Rom 8:22 whole creation *g.* and travaileth
2 Cor 5: 4 we that are in this tabernacle do *g.*

GROANING (GROANINGS)

Ps 6: 6 I was weary with my *g.*
38: 9 my *g.* is not hid from thee
102:20 to hear the *g.* of the prisoner
Rom 8:26 *g.* which cannot be uttered

GROW (GROWETH)

Gen 48:16 let them *g.* into a multitude
2 Sam 23: 5 although he make it not to *g.*
Ps 92:12 *g.* like a cedar in Lebanon
Hos 14: 5 he shall *g.* as a lily
Eph 2:21 *g.* unto an holy temple in the Lord
4:15 *g.* up into him in all things
1 Pet 2: 2 milk of word that ye may *g.*
2 Pet 3:18 *g.* in grace, and in knowledge

GUIDE

Ps 48:14 he will be our *g.* even unto death
73:24 *g.* me with thy counsel
Prov 2:17 forsaketh the *g.* of youth
Is 58:11 Lord shall *g.* thee continually
Jer 3: 4 Father, thou art the *g.* of my youth
Luke 1:79 *g.* our feet into the way of peace
John 16:13 he will *g.* you into all truth
1 Tim 5:14 bear children, *g.* the house

GUILE

Ex 21:14 to slay him with *g.*
Ps 32: 2 in whose spirit is no *g.*
34:13 keep thy lips from speaking *g.*
55:11 deceit and *g.* depart not from her
John 1:47 Israelite indeed in whom is no *g.*
2 Cor 12:16 I caught you with *g.*
1 Thes 2: 3 nor of uncleanliness, nor in *g.*
1 Pet 2: 1 laying aside malice and *g.*

GUILTY

Ex 34: 7 will by no means clear the *g.*
Lev 4:13 not be done, and are *g.*
Num 14:18 by no means clearing the *g.*
Rom 3:19 all the world may become *g.* before

1 Cor 11:27 *g.* of the body and blood of
Jas 2:10 offend in one point, *g.* of all

GUILTLESS
Ex 20: 7 not hold him *g.* that taketh

H

HABITATION (HABITATIONS)
Deut 26:15 look down from thy holy *h.*
2 Chr 29: 6 from the *h.* of the Lord
Ps 26: 8 loved the *h.* of thy house
68: 5 God in his holy *h.*
71: 3 be thou my strong *h.* whereunto
74:20 earth full of *h.* of cruelty
89:14 are the *h.* of thy throne
91: 9 hast made the Most High thy *h.*
Prov 3:33 he blesseth the *h.* of the just
Is 33:20 see Jerusalem a quiet *h.*
63:15 behold from the *h.* of thy holiness
Jer 31:23 Lord bless thee, O *h.* of justice
Zech 2:13 out of his holy *h.*
Luke 16: 9 receive into everlasting *h.*
Jude 1: 6 angels which left their own *h.*
Rev 18: 2 Babylon is become the *h.* of

HAIR (HAIRS)
Ps 40:12 more than the *h.* of mine head
Hos 7: 9 gray *h.* are here and there
Mat 5:36 not make one *h.* white or
10:30 *h.* of your head are all numbered
1 Cor 11:14 if a man hath long *h.*
1 Tim 2: 9 not with braided *h.*, or gold
1 Pet 3: 3 plaiting the *h.*, and wearing of gold

HAND
Gen 3:22 he put forth his hand
16:12 every man's *h.* against him
Num 11:23 is the Lord's *h.* waxed short
Deut 33: 3 all his saints are in thy *h.*
2 Sam 24:14 fall now into the *h.* of the Lord
Ezra 7: 9 good *h.* of his God on him
8:22 *h.* of our God is upon all
Job 2:10 good at the *h.* of God and not evil
12: 6 into whose *h.* God bringeth
12: 9 *h.* of the Lord hath wrought this
Ps 16: 8 he is at my right *h.*
16:11 at thy right *h.* are pleasures for
18:35 thy right *h.* hath holden me up
31: 5 into thy *h.* I commend my spirit
48:10 thy right *h.* is full of righteousness
73:23 hast holden me by my right *h.*
110: 5 Lord at thy right *h.* shall strike
137: 5 let my right *h.* forget her cunning
139:10 thy *h.* lead and thy right *h.*
145:16 thou openest thy *h.* and satisfiest
Prov 3:16 length of days is in her right *h.*
10: 4 *h.* of the diligent maketh rich
11:21 though *h.* join in *h.*
30:32 lay thy *h.* upon thy mouth
Eccl 9: 1 wise and their works in the *h.* of God
9:10 whatsoever thy *h.* findeth to do
10: 2 wise man's heart at his right *h.*
Sol 2: 6 his right *h.* doth embrace me
Is 1:12 who required this at your *h.*
26:11 when thy *h.* is lifted up, they
40: 2 received of the *h.* of the Lord double
59: 1 *h.* of the Lord is not shortened
Mat 5:30 if thy right *h.* offend thee
6: 3 left *h.* know what thy right *h.*
18: 8 if thy *h.* or thy foot offend
20:21 one on the right *h.*, the other on
22:13 bind him *h.* and foot
25:33 sheep on the right *h.*, goats on left
Mark 14:62 sitting on right *h.* of power
16:19 sat on the right *h.* of God
Luke 1:74 out of the *h.* of our enemies
Acts 2:33 the right *h.* of God exalted
4:28 to do whatsoever thy *h.* and
7:55 Jesus standing on the right *h.*
Rom 8:34 even at the right *h.* of God
Col 3: 1 sitteth on the right *h.* of God
Heb 1: 3 sat down on the right *h.*
8: 1 who is set on the right *h.*
10:12 sat down on the right *h.*
1 Pet 3:22 is on the right *h.* of God
5: 6 under the mighty *h.* of God

HANDS
Gen 27:22 *h.* are the *h.* of Esau
Ex 17:12 Moses' *h.* were heavy, and they
Job 17: 9 clean *h.* shall be stronger
Ps 24: 4 clean *h.* and a pure heart
119:73 thy *h.* have made me and fashioned
Prov 31:20 reacheth thy *h.* to the needy
31:31 give her of the fruit of her *h.*
Is 1:15 when ye spread forth your *h.*
Mic 7: 3 do evil with both *h.*
Mat 9:44 delivered into the *h.* of men
18: 8 having two *h.* or feet
Luke 23:46 into thy *h.* I commend my spirit
John 13: 3 given all things into his *h.*
13: 9 but also my *h.* and head
2 Cor 5: 1 house not made with *h.*
Eph 4:28 let him labour, working with his *h.*
1 Tim 2: 8 pray every where, lifting up holy *h.*
Heb 9:11 tabernacle, not made with *h.*
10:31 fall into the *h.* of the living God
Jas 4: 8 cleanse your *h.* ye sinners
1 John 1: 1 and our *h.* have handled of the

HANG (HANGED, HANGETH)
Deut 21:23 that is *h.* is accursed of God
28:66 thy life shall *h.* in doubt
Josh 8:29 he *h.* on a tree until eventide
Job 26: 7 he *h.* the earth on nothing
Ps 137: 2 we *h.* our harps upon the willows
Mat 18: 6 millstone were *h.* about his neck
22:40 commandments *h.* all the law and the prophets
Gal 3:13 everyone that *h.* on a tree
Heb 12:12 lift up the hands which *h.* down

HAPPY
Gen 30:13 *H.* am I for the daughters
Deut 33:29 *h.* art thou, O Israel
1 Ki 10: 8 *h.* are thy men, *h.* are these
Job 5:17 *h.* the man whom God correcteth
Ps 127: 5 *h.* the man who hath his quiver
128: 2 *h.* shalt thou be, and be well
144:15 *h.* is that people, that is in such
146: 5 *h.* is he that hath the God
Prov 3:13 *h.* is the man that findeth wisdom
14:21 that hath mercy on poor, *h.* is he
16:20 who trusteth in Lord, *h.* is he
28:14 *h.* is man that feareth always
29:18 he that keepeth the law, *h.* is he
Mal 3:15 now we call the proud *h.*
John 13:17 *h.* are ye if ye do them
Rom 14:22 *h.* is he that condemneth not
1 Pet 3:14 suffer for righteousness' sake, *h.* are ye
4:14 reproached for the name of Christ, *h.* are ye

HARD
Gen 18:14 any thing too *h.* for the Lord
35:17 she was in *h.* labour
Ex 1:14 made their lives bitter with *h.* bondage
18:26 the *h.* causes they brought unto Moses
2 Sam 13: 2 thought it *h.* for him to do anything
2 Ki 2:10 thou hast asked a *h.* thing
Ps 60: 3 shown thy people *h.* things
88: 7 wrath lieth *h.* upon me
Prov 13:15 way of transgressors is *h.*
Jer 32:17 nothing too *h.* for thee
Mark 10:24 how *h.* is it for them that trust
Acts 9: 5 *h.* for thee to kick against the pricks
26:14 it is *h.* for thee to kick
2 Pet 3:16 things too *h.* to be understood
Jude 1:15 of all their *h.* speeches which ungodly

HARDEN (HARDENED)
Ex 4:21 I will *h.* his heart
Deut 15: 7 thou shalt not *h.* thy heart
Josh 11:20 was of the Lord to *h.* their hearts
Job 9: 4 hath *h.* himself against him
Ps 95: 8 *h.* not your heart, as in the provocation
Is 63:17 *h.* our heart from thy fear
Mark 6:52 loaves; for their heart was *h.*
Heb 3: 8 *h.* not your hearts, as in the
3:13 *h.* through the deceitfulness of sin

HARDNESS
Mat 19: 8 *h.* of your hearts suffered you
Mark 3: 5 grieved for the *h.* of their
Rom 2: 5 after thy *h.* and impenitent
2 Tim 2: 3 endure *h.* as a good soldier

HARLOT (HARLOTS)
Gen 34:31 sister as with a *h.*
Josh 2: 1 came into an *h.* house named Rahab
Judg 11: 1 was the son of a *h.*
Prov 7:10 woman with the attire of an *h.*
Is 1:21 the faithful city become as an *h.*
23:15 Tyre sing as a *h.*
Jer 2:20 thou wanderest, playing the *h.*
Ezek 16:15 own beauty, and playedst the *h.*
Hos 2: 5 mother hath played the *h.*
4:15 though thou Israel, play the *h.*
Mat 21:31 *h.* into the kingdom of God
1 Cor 6:16 joined to a *h.* is one body
Heb 11:31 by faith the *h.* Rahab
Jas 2:25 Rahab the *h.* justified by works
Rev 17: 5 mother of *h.* and abominations

HARM
Gen 31:52 pillar unto me, for *h.*
1 Chr 16:22 do my prophets no *h.*
Ps 105:15 do my prophets no *h.*
Prov 3:30 have done thee no *h.*
Jer 39:12 look well to him and do him no *h.*
Acts 28: 5 into the fire and felt no *h.*
1 Pet 3:13 who is he that will *h.* you

HARMLESS
Mat 10:16 as serpents and *h.* as doves
Phil 2:15 ye may be blameless and *h.*

HARVEST
Gen 8:22 remaineth, seedtime and *h.*
30:14 went in the days of wheat *h.*
Ex 34:21 in *h.* thou shalt rest
Is 9: 3 according to the joy in *h.*
Jer 5:24 unto us the appointed weeks of the *h.*
8:20 *h.* is past, summer is ended
51:33 time of her *h.* shall come
Joel 3:13 sickle for the *h.* is ripe
Mat 9: 3 pray ye the Lord of the *h.*
13:39 *h.* is the end of the world
Rev 14:15 for the *h.* of earth is ripe

HASTE
Ex 12:33 out of the land in *h.*
Ps 31:22 I said in my *h.*, I am cut off
38:22 make *h.* to help me, O Lord
40:13 O Lord, make *h.* to help me
71:12 O my God, make *h.* for my help
119:60 I made *h.* and delayed not
141: 1 make *h.* unto me; give ear unto
Sol 8:14 make *h.*, my beloved and be thou
Is 28:16 believeth shall not make *h.*
49:17 thy children shall make *h.*
52:12 ye shall not go out with *h.*

HASTEN
Ps 16: 4 multiplied that *h.* after another god
Is 5:19 let him make speed and *h.*
60:22 I the Lord will *h.* it in his time
Jer 1:12 I will *h.* my word to perform it

HASTY (HASTILY)
Prov 20:21 inheritance may be gotten *h.*
29:20 a man that is *h.* in words?

HATE
Gen 24:60 the gate of those which *h.* them
Lev 19:17 shall not *h.* thy brother
Deut 7:10 repayeth them that *h.* him
Ps 68: 1 let them that *h.* him flee
97:10 ye that love the Lord, *h.* evil
119:104 I *h.* every false way
119:113 I *h.* vain thoughts
139:21 do not I *h.* them that *h.*
Prov 8:13 fear of Lord is to *h.* evil
8:36 all they that *h.* me love death
Jer 44: 4 abominable thing that I *h.*
Amos 5:15 *h.* the evil, and love the good
Luke 14:26 and *h.* not his father
Rom 7:15 what I *h.* that do I
1 John 3:13 marvel not if the world *h.*
Rev 2: 6 *h.* deeds, which I *h.*
17:16 these shall *h.* the whore

HATED (HATEST, HATETH)
Ex 23: 5 ass of him that *h.* thee lying
Deut 21:15 one beloved, and another *h.*
Ps 5: 5 thou *h.* all workers of iniquity
50:17 seeing thou *h.* instruction
Prov 1:29 for that they *h.* knowledge
5:12 how have I *h.* instruction
13:24 spareth rod, *h.* his son
Is 66: 5 your brethren that *h.* you
Mal 1: 3 I *h.* Esau, and laid his mountains
Mat 10:22 shall be *h.* of all men
Luke 19:14 his citizens *h.* him, and sent
John 12:25 *h.* his life in this world
15:24 *h.* both seen, and me and my Father
Rom 9:13 loved, but Esau have I *h.*
Eph 5:29 no man *h.* his own flesh
1 John 2: 9 *h.* his brother is in darkness
3:15 *h.* his brother is a murderer
4:20 and *h.* his brother

HATEFUL
Tit 3: 3 living in malice and envy, *h.*
Jude 1:23 *h.* garment spotted by flesh

HATERS
Rom 1:30 backbiters, *h.* of God

HAUGHTY
Ps 131: 1 Lord, my heart is not *h.*
Prov 16:18 and an *h.* spirit before a fall
21:24 proud and *h.* scorner is his name
Zeph 3:11 thou shalt no more be *h.* because

HAUGHTINESS
Is 2:11 *h.* of men shall be bowed down
13:11 will lay low the *h.* of the
16: 6 he is very proud: even of his *h.*

HEAD
Gen 3:15 it shall bruise thy *h.* and
49:26 blessings on Joseph's *h.*
Ezra 9: 6 iniquity increased over thy *h.*
Ps 38: 4 iniquities gone over my *h.*
Prov 16:31 hoary *h.* is a crown of glory
20:29 beauty of the old men is a gray *h.*
25:22 heap coals of fire upon his *h.*
Eccl 2:14 wise man's eyes are in his *h.*
9: 8 let thy *h.* lack no ointment
Sol 5: 2 my *h.* is filled with dew
5:11 his *h.* is as most fine gold
Is 1: 5 whole *h.* is sick and the whole
1: 6 the sole of the foot even unto the *h.*
Jer 9: 1 Oh that my *h.* were waters
48:37 every *h.* shall be bald
Ezek 9:10 their way on their *h.*
16:43 thy way upon thy *h.*
Dan 2:28 visions of thy *h.* on a bed
2:38 thou art this *h.* of gold
Zech 4: 7 bring forth the *h.* stone
Mat 8:20 where to lay his *h.*
14: 8 give me the *h.* of John Baptist
Rom 12:20 coals of fire on his *h.*
Eph 1:22 gave him to be *h.* over all
4:15 which is the *h.* even Christ
5:23 husband is the *h.* of the wife
Col 1:18 he is the *h.* of the body
2:19 holding the *h.* from which all
Rev 19:12 on his *h.* were many crowns

HEADS
Gen 2:10 was parted and became into four *h.*
Ps 24: 7 lift up your *h*, O ye gates
Is 35:10 everlasting joy upon their *h.*
Luke 21:28 look up, and lift up your *h.*
Rev 13: 1 having seven *h.* and ten horns

HEAL (HEALED, HEALETH)
Ex 15:26 I the Lord that *h.* thee
Num 12:13 Lord, saying, *h.* her now, O God
Deut 32:39 I make alive; I wound, and I *h.*
2 Chr 7:14 and will *h.* their land
30:20 Hezekiah, and *h.* the people
Ps 6: 2 *h.* me, for my bones are
30: 2 unto thee and thou hast *h.* me
41: 4 *h.* my soul, for I have sinned
103: 3 who *h.* all thy diseases
147: 3 he *h.* the broken in heart
Is 6:10 with their heart, and convert and be *h.*
30:26 *h.* the stroke of their wound
53: 5 with his stripes we are *h.*
57:18 seen his ways and will *h.* him
Jer 3:22 I will *h.* your backslidings
6:14 *h.* the hurt of the daughter
15:18 which refuseth to be *h.*
17:14 *h.* me, and I shall be healed
Hos 6: 1 hath torn and he will *h.* us
7: 1 I would have *h.* Israel
Mat 4:24 had the palsy, and he *h.* them
12:15 followed him, and he *h.* them all
Luke 4:18 sent me to *h.* the brokenhearted
4:23 will say, Physician, *h.* thyself
John 12:40 converted and I should *h.*
Acts 28:27 and I should *h.* them
Heb 12:13 let it rather be *h.*
Jas 5:16 pray that ye may be *h.*
1 Pet 2:24 by whose stripes ye were *h.*
Rev 13: 3 his deadly wound was *h.*

HEALING
Jer 14:19 for the time of *h.*, and behold
30:13 thou hast no *h.* medicine
Mal 4: 2 righteousness arise with *h.* in his wings
Mat 4:23 *h.* all manner of sickness
1 Cor 12: 9 to another the gifts of *h.*
Rev 22: 2 tree were for the *h.* of the nations

HEALTH
Ps 42:11 *h.* of countenance, and my God
Prov 3: 8 shall be *h.* to thy navel, and marrow
12:18 the tongue of the wise is *h.*
Jer 8:15 looked for a time of *h.*
30:17 I will restore *h.* and heal

HEAP (HEAPED, HEAPETH)
Deut 32:23 I will *h.* mischiefs upon
Job 36:13 hypocrites in heart *h.* up wrath
Ps 39: 6 he *h.* up riches, and knoweth not
Prov 25:22 shalt *h.* coals of fire on
2 Tim 4: 3 shall they *h.* to themselves teachers
Jas 5: 3 ye have *h.* treasure together for

HEAPS
Judg 15:16 *h.* upon *h.* with the jaw of an

HEAR
Deut 30:17 if thou wilt not *h.*
1 Ki 8:30 *h.* thou in heaven thy dwellingplace
2 Ki 19:16 bow thine ear, and *h.*
2 Chr 6:21 *h.* from thy dwelling
Job 5:27 *h.* it and know it for good
Ps 4: 1 mercy upon me, and *h.* my prayer
10:17 thou wilt cause thine ear to *h.*
39:12 mercy upon me, and *h.* my prayer oh Lord
51: 8 make me to *h.* joy and gladness
59: 7 who, say they, doth *h.*
66:16 come and *h.* all ye that
84: 8 Lord God of hosts, *h.* my prayer
115: 6 they have ears, but *h.* not
143: 1 *h.* my prayer, O Lord, give ear
Prov 19:27 cease to *h.* instruction
Eccl 5: 1 be more ready to *h.* than
Sol 2:14 let me *h.* thy voice
Is 1: 2 *h.* O heavens, and give ear
6:10 lest they *h.* with ears
55: 3 *h.* and your soul shall live
Dan 9:19 O Lord, *h.*; oh Lord forgive
Zech 10: 6 the Lord their God, and will *h.* them
Mat 10:27 what ye *h.* in the ear
13:17 to *h.* those things which ye *h.*
17: 5 I am well pleased, *h.* ye him
18:17 if he neglect to *h.* them
Mark 4:24 take heed in what ye *h.*
4:33 as they were able to *h.*
Luke 8:18 take heed therefore how ye *h.*
John 5:25 they that *h.* shall live
Acts 10:33 to *h.* all things that are commanded
Jas 1:19 every man be swift to *h.*
Rev 3:20 if any *h.* my voice, and open

HEARD
Ex 2:24 God *h.* their groaning, and God remembered
Ps 6: 9 Lord hath *h.* my supplication
10:17 hast *h.* the desire of the humble
34: 4 I sought the Lord, and he *h.*
61: 5 thou O God, hast *h.* my vows
66:19 verily God hath *h.* me
118:21 I will praise thee, for thou hast *h.* me
120: 1 I cried to Lord, and he *h.*
Is 40:28 hast thou not *h.* that God
Jer 8: 6 I hearkened and *h.*, but they spake
Jonah 2: 2 I cried to Lord and he *h.*
Mal 3:16 and the Lord hearkened and *h.* it
Mat 6: 7 be *h.* for much speaking
Luke 1:13 thy prayer is *h.* and thy
John 3:32 what he hath seen and *h.*
8: 6 wrote as though he *h.* them not
Rom 10:14 of whom they have not *h.*
1 Cor 2: 9 eye hath not seen nor ear *h.*
Phil 4: 9 learned and received and *h.*
Heb 4: 2 with faith in them that *h.*
5: 7 was *h.* in that he feared
Jas 5:11 ye have *h.* of the patience of Job
Rev 3: 3 how thou hast received and *h.*

HEARER (HEARERS)
Rom 2:13 not the *h.* of the law are just
Eph 4:29 minister grace unto the *h.*
Jas 1:22 doers of the word, and not *h.* only
1:25 not a forgetful *h.* but a doer

HEAREST (HEARETH)

HEARETH
1 Sam 3: 9 speak, Lord; for thy servant *h.*
Ps 65: 2 O thou that *h.* prayer, unto thee
Prov 8:34 blessed the man that *h.* me
Mat 7:24 whoso *h.* these sayings of mine
Luke 10:16 he that *h.* you *h.* me
John 9:31 God *h.* not sinners, but
11:42 I knew thou *h.* me always
1 John 5:14 ask according to his will he *h.*
Rev 22:17 let him that *h.* say, Come

HEARING
Job 42: 5 of thee by the *h.* of the ear
Prov 20:12 the *h.* ear, and the seeing eye
28: 9 turneth away his ear from *h.*
Rom 10:17 faith cometh by *h.* and *h.* by
Heb 5:11 seeing ye are dull of *h.*
2 Pet 2: 8 in seeing and *h.* vexed his

HEARKEN
Deut 28: 1 if thou *h.* diligently
28:15 if thou wilt not *h.* unto the voice
1 Sam 15:22 to *h.* better than the fat of rams
Ps 103:20 angels *h.* to the voice of his word
Is 46:12 *h.* unto me, ye stouthearted
51: 1 *h.* unto me, ye that follow
55: 2 *h.* diligently unto me, eat

HEART
Ex 35: 5 whosoever is of a willing *h.*
Deut 6: 5 love God with all thy *h.* and soul
11:13 serve him with all your *h.* and soul
26:16 keep and do them with all thy *h.* and
Josh 22: 5 serve him with all your *h.*
1 Sam 1:13 she spake in her *h.* only
10: 9 God gave him another *h.*
16: 7 but the Lord looketh on the *h.*
24: 5 David's *h.* smote him because
2 Ki 20: 3 thee in truth and with perfect *h.*
1 Chr 16:10 let the *h.* of them rejoice
22:19 now set your *h.* and your soul
28: 9 serve him with a perfect *h.*
2 Chr 17: 6 *h.* lifted up in the Lord's ways
30:19 prepareth his *h.* to seek God
Ps 22:26 your *h.* shall live for ever
24: 4 clean hands and a pure *h.*
37:31 law of his God is in his *h.*
45: 1 my *h.* is inditing a good
51:17 a broken and contrite *h.*, O God
57: 7 my *h.* is fixed, O God
64: 6 every one of them, and the *h.*, is deep
73:26 my flesh and my *h.* faileth, but
78:37 their *h.* was not right with
84: 2 my *h.* and my flesh crieth for the
Prov 3: 5 trust in Lord with all thy *h.*
4:23 keep thy *h.* with diligence
10:20 *h.* of the wicked is little worth
14:10 *h.* knoweth its own bitterness
16: 9 a man's *h.* deviseth his way
27:19 so the *h.* of man to man
Eccl 7: 4 *h.* of the wise is in the house
10: 2 wise man's *h.* at his right hand
Sol 3:11 day of the gladness of his *h.*
5: 2 I sleep, but my *h.* waketh
Is 6:10 make the *h.* of this people fat
57:15 to revive the *h.* of the contrite ones
Jer 3:15 give pastors according to my *h.*
11:20 triest reins and the *h.* let me see
12:11 no man layeth it to *h.*
17: 9 *h.* is deceitful above all things
24: 7 I will give them an *h.* to know
29:13 search for me with all your *h.*
32:39 And I will give them one *h.*
Lam 3:41 lift up our *h.* with hands
Ezek 11:19 I will give them an *h.* of flesh
18:31 make you a new *h.*, and a new spirit
36:26 I will take away the stony *h.*
Joel 2:13 rend your *h.* not garments
Mal 4: 6 turn the *h.* of the fathers
Mat 5: 8 blessed are the pure in *h.*
6:21 there will your *h.* be also
12:35 of good treasure of the *h.*
15:19 out of the *h.* proceed evil thoughts
22:37 Lord thy God with all thy *h.*
Luke 2:19 pondered them in her *h.*
2:51 mother kept all these sayings in her *h.*
10:27 love the Lord thy God, with all thy *h.*
24:25 O fools, slow of *h.* to believe
24:32 did not our *h.* burn within us
John 14: 1 let not your *h.* be troubled
Acts 5:33 that they were cut to the *h.*
11:23 with the purpose of *h.* they would cleave
13:22 found a man after mine own *h.*
Rom 10:10 with the *h.* man believeth
1 Cor 2: 9 nor entered into the *h.* of man
2 Cor 3: 3 in fleshy tables of the *h.*
1 Tim 1: 5 charity out of a pure *h.*
2 Tim 2:22 call on the Lord out of a pure *h.*
1 Pet 1:22 love one another with pure *h.*
3: 4 the hidden man of the *h.*
1 John 3:20 if the *h.* condemn us, God

HEATHEN
Lev 25:44 shall be of the *h.* that are round
26:45 in the sight of the *h.*
Ps 2: 1 why do the *h.* rage
2: 8 give thee the *h.* for thine
Acts 4:25 why did the *h.* rage
Gal 3: 8 justify the *h.* through faith

HEAVEN
1 Ki 8:27 the *h.* and the *h.* of heavens
2 Chr 6:18 behold, *h.*, and the *h.* of heavens
Ps 73:25 whom have I in *h.* but thee
103:11 as *h.* is high above the
115:16 *h.* even the heavens are the Lord's
Prov 25: 3 *h.* for height, and earth
Eccl 5: 2 God is in *h.* thou upon earth
Is 66: 1 *h.* is my throne, and the earth
Jer 31:37 if *h.* can be measured
Hag 1:10 *h.* is stayed from dew
Luke 15:18 sinned against *h.*, and before thee
John 1:51 you shall see *h.* open and angels
Acts 3:21 the *h.* must receive until the times
7:49 *h.* is my throne, and the earth
Heb 10:34 have in *h.* a better substance
1 Pet 1: 4 inheritance reserved in *h.*
Rev 21: 1 saw a new *h.* and a new earth

HEAVENS
Ps 8: 3 when I consider thy *h.*
19: 1 the *h.* declare the glory of God
89:11 the *h.* are thine, and earth also
Is 65:17 I create new *h.* and a new earth
66:22 for as the new *h.* and the new earth
2 Cor 5: 1 a house eternal in the *h.*
Eph 4:10 ascended far above all *h.*
2 Pet 3:12 *h.* being on fire shall be dissolved

HEAVENLY
Mat 6:14 your *h.* Father will also
18:35 likewise shall my *h.* Father do
Luke 11:13 your *h.* father give the
John 3:12 if I tell you of *h.* things
1 Cor 15:48 and as is the *h.* such are they
Eph 1: 3 all spiritual blessings in *h.* places
2: 6 in *h.* places in Christ Jesus
2 Tim 4:18 will preserve me unto his *h.* kingdom
Heb 3: 1 partakers of the *h.* calling

HEAVY
Prov 31: 6 wine to those of *h.* hearts
Is 6:10 make their ears *h.* lest
58: 6 to undo the *h.* burdens, and to let
Mat 11:28 that labour and are *h.* laden
23: 4 bind *h.* burdens and grievous

HEAVINESS
Ps 69:20 I am full of *h.*: and I looked
119:28 my soul melteth for *h.*
Prov 12:25 *h.* in the heart maketh it stoop
14:13 end of that mirth is *h.*
Rom 9: 2 I have great *h.* and sorrow
1 Pet 1: 6 in *h.* through manifold temptations

HEED
Deut 2: 4 take good *h.* to yourselves
Josh 22: 5 take diligent *h.* to do the
2 Sam 20:10 But Amasa took no *h.* to the sword
2 Ki 10:31 took no *g.* to walk in the law
Ps 119: 9 by taking *h.* thereto according to
Jer 18:18 not give *h.* to any of his

HEEL (HEELS)
Gen 3:15 thou shalt bruise his *h.*
Ps 41: 9 lifted his *h.* against me
49: 5 iniquity of *h.* shall compass
Hos 12: 3 he took his brother by the *h.*
John 13:18 lifted up his *h.* against me

HEIFER
Num 19: 2 that they bring thee a red *h.*
Jer 46:20 Egypt is like a fair *h.*
Hos 4:16 slideth back as a backsliding *h.*
Heb 9:13 the ashes of an *h.* sprinkling

HEIR (HEIRS)
Gen 15: 4 own bowels shall be thine *h.*
21:10 bondwoman shall not be *h.*
Jer 49: 1 Israel no sons? Hath he no *h.*
Rom 4:13 should be *h.* of the world
8:17 *h.* of God, joint *h.* with Christ
Gal 3:29 Abraham's seed and *h.* according to
4: 7 if a son, then an *h.* of God
Eph 3: 6 Gentiles should be fellow *h.*
Heb 1: 2 whom he hath appointed *h.* of all
6:17 willing to show *h.* of promise
11: 7 became *h.* of the righteousness
1 Pet 3: 7 *h.* together of the grace of life

HELL
Deut 32:22 shall burn to the lowest *h.*
2 Sam 22: 6 the sorrows of *h.* compassed me
Job 11: 8 it is deeper than *h.*; what
26: 6 *h.* is naked before him and
Ps 9:17 wicked shall be turned into *h.*
16:10 not leave my soul in *h.*
55:15 let them go down quick into *h.*
86:13 delivered my soul from lowest *h.*
139: 8 make my bed in *h.* thou art
Prov 5: 5 her steps take hold on *h.*
7:27 her house is the way to *h.*
9:18 her guests are in the depths of *h.*
15:11 *h.* and destruction before the Lord
15:24 that he may depart from *h.*
23:14 shalt deliver his soul from *h.*
27:20 *h.* and destruction are never full
Is 5:14 *h.* hath enlarged herself, and opened
14: 9 *h.* from beneath is moved for thee
14:15 thou shalt be brought down to *h.*
57: 9 debase thyself even to *h.*
Amos 9: 2 though they dig into *h.*
Jonah 2: 2 out of the belly of *h.* cried I
Hab 2: 5 enlargeth his desire as *h.*
Mat 5:22 be in danger of *h.* fire
5:29 body should be cast into *h.*
10:28 destroy soul and body in *h.*
11:23 heaven shalt be brought down to *h.*
16:18 gates of *h.* shall not prevail
18: 9 to be cast into *h.* fire
23:15 twofold more than the child of *h.*
Mark 9:45 to be cast into *h.*
Luke 12: 5 power to cast into *h.*
16:23 in *h.* he lift up his eyes
Acts 2:27 wilt not leave my soul in *h.*
2:31 his soul not left in *h.*
Jas 3: 6 tongue set on the fire of *h.*
2 Pet 2: 4 cast them down to *h.*
Rev 1:18 have the keys of *h.* and
6: 8 Death, and *H.* followed with
20:13 death and *h.* delivered up the dead
20:14 death and *h.* were cast into

HELMET
1 Sam 17: 5 he had an *h.* of brass
2 Chr 26:14 and spears, and *h.*, and habergeons
Eph 6:17 take the *h.* of salvation
1 Thes 5: 8 an *h.*, hope of salvation

HELP
Gen 2:18 make him an *h.* meet for him
Deut 33:29 Lord, the shield of thy *h.*
Judg 5:23 came not to the *h.* of the Lord
2 Chr 14:11 nothing with thee to *h.*
Ps 27: 9 thou hast been my *h.*
33:20 he is our *h.* and shield
40:13 make haste to *h.* me
40:17 thou art my *h.* and my deliverer
46: 1 God a very present *h.* in trouble
60:11 vain is the *h.* of man
71:12 my God, make haste for my *h.*
89:19 laid *h.* on one that is mighty
115: 9 Lord is our *h.* and shield
124: 8 our *h.* is in the name of Lord
Is 41:10 I will *h.* thee
63: 5 I looked and there was none to *h.*
Hos 13: 9 but in me is thy *h.*
Acts 16: 9 come to Macedonia, and *h.* us
26:22 having obtained the *h.* of God
Heb 4:16 find grace to *h.* in time

HELPED (HELPETH)
1 Sam 7:12 hitherto hath the Lord *h.* us
Is 49: 8 in the day of salvation I *h.*
Zech 1:15 and they *h.* forward the affliction
Acts 18:27 *h.* them much which believed
Rom 8:26 the Spirit also *h.* our infirmities
Rev 12:16 the earth *h.* the woman

Ps 29: 2 worship the Lord in the beauty of *h.*
30: 4 thanks at the remembrance of his *h.*
47: 8 God sitteth upon the throne of his *h.*
60: 6 God hath spoken in his *h.*
89:35 I have sworn by my *h.*
93: 5 *h.* becometh thine house, O Lord
110: 3 in the beauties of *h.*; from the
Is 23:18 shall be *h.* to the Lord
35: 8 shall be called the way of *h.*
62: 9 drink it in the courts of my *h.*
63:18 the people of thy *h.* have possessed
Jer 2: 3 Israel was *h.* unto the Lord
23: 9 because of the Lord and words of his *h.*
Amos 4: 2 Lord hath sworn by his *h.*
Obad 1:17 deliverance and there shall be *h.*
Zech 14:20 on horse bells, *h.* to Lord
Mal 2:11 Judah profaned the *h.* of the Lord
Luke 1:75 in *h.* and righteousness
Acts 3:12 by your own power or *h.*
Rom 1: 4 according to the Spirit of *h.*
6:22 ye have your fruit unto *h.*
2 Cor 7: 1 perfecting *h.* in the fear of God
Eph 4:24 in righteousness and true *h.*
1 Thes 3:13 unblameable in *h.* before God
1 Tim 2:15 charity, *h.* with sobriety
Tit 2: 3 behaviour as becometh *h.*
Heb 12:10 we might be partakers of his *h.*
12:14 follow peace with all men, and *h.*

HOLY GHOST

Mat 1:18 was found with child of the *H.*
3:11 ye shall be baptize you with the *H.*
3:12 blasphemy against the *H.*
Mark 12:36 for David himself said by the *H.*
13:11 not ye that speak, but the *H.*
Luke 1:15 *H.* shall come upon thee
1:26 revealed unto him by the *H.*
3:22 *H.* descended in bodily shape
12:12 *H.* shall teach you what to say
John 7:39 for the *H.* was not yet given
14:26 Comforter, which is the *H.*
20:22 unto them receive ye the *H.*
Acts 1: 2 through the *H.* had given commandment
1: 5 baptized with the *H.*
1: 8 after that the *H.* is come upon you
2:38 receive the gift of the *H.*
5: 3 filled thine heart to lie to the *H.*
5:32 and so is also the *H.*
7:51 ye do always resist the *H.*
8:15 they might receive the *H.*
9:31 walking in the comfort of the *H.*
10:38 with the *H.*, and with power
10:44 the *H.* fell on all them which
11:16 be baptized with the *H.*
13: 2 and fasted, the *H.* said; Separate me
13: 4 they being sent forth by the *H.*
15:28 it seemed good to the *H.* and us
16: 6 forbidden of the *H.* to preach in
20:23 save that the *H.* witnesseth
20:28 flock over which the *H.* made you overseers
21:11 thus saith the *H.* so shall the Jews
Rom 5: 5 by the *H.* which is given
9: 1 conscience bearing witness in the *H.*
14:17 righteousness, peace, joy in the *H.*
15:16 being sanctified by the *H.*
1 Cor 2:13 in words the *H.* teacheth
6:19 your body is the temple of the *H.*
2 Cor 6: 6 by the *H.* by love unfeigned
13:14 communion of the *H.* be with you
1 Thes 1: 5 in power and in the *H.*
2 Tim 1:14 keep by the *H.* which
Tit 3: 5 by the renewing of the *H.*
Heb 2: 4 with gifts of the *H.*
3: 7 as the *H.* saith, today if
9: 8 *H.* this signifying, that the way
1 Pet 1:12 preached gospel with the *H.*
2 Pet 1:21 they were moved by the *H.*
1 John 5: 7 Father, Word, and the *H.*
Jude 1:20 holy faith praying in the *H.*

HOLY SPIRIT

Ps 51:11 take not thy *H.* from me
Is 63:10 rebelled and vexed his *H.*
63:11 where is he that put his *H.* within
Luke 11:13 give the *H.* to them that ask
Eph 1:13 sealed with the *H.*
4:30 grieve not the *H.* of God
1 Thes 4: 8 God, who hath given his *H.*

HOME

Ruth 1:21 Lord hath brought me *h.* again empty
Job 39:12 he will bring *h.* thy seed
Ps 68:12 tarried at *h.* divided the spoil
Eccl 12: 5 man goeth to his long *h.*
2 Cor 5: 6 whilst at *h.* in body, absent
Tit 2: 5 chaste, keepers at *h.*, good

HONEST (HONESTLY)

Luke 8:15 which in an *h.* and good heart
Acts 6: 3 seven men of *h.* report, full
Rom 12:17 provide things *h.* in the sight
13:13 let us walk *h.* as in the day
2 Cor 8:21 Providing for *h.* things not only
13: 7 should do that which is *h.*
Phil 4: 8 are true whatsoever things are *h.*
1 Thes 4:12 ye may walk *h.* toward them
Heb 13:18 in all things willing to live *h.*
1 Pet 2:12 having your conversation *h.* among

HONEY

Gen 43:11 and a little *h.*, spices myrrh
Ex 16:31 taste was like wafers made with *h.*
Judg 14:18 what is sweeter than *h.*
1 Ki 14: 3 and a cruse of *h.*, and go to him
Ps 19:10 fine gold sweeter also than *h.*
81:16 with *h.* out of the rock should I
Sol 4:11 *h.* and milk under thy tongue
Is 7:15 butter and *h.* shall he eat
Ezek 27:17 Pannag, and *h.*, and oil, and balm
Mat 3: 4 his meat locusts and wild *h.*
Rev 10: 9 shall be in thy mouth sweet as *h.*

HONEYCOMB

1 Sam 14:27 and dipped it in an *h.*

HONOUR

Gen 49: 6 to their assembly, mine *h.*
Ex 14:17 I will get me *h.* upon Pharaoh
Judg 4: 9 shall not be for thine *h.*
1 Sam 2:30 that *h.* me I will *h.*
15:30 *h.* me before the elders
1 Chr 29:12 both riches and *h.* come of thee
2 Chr 26:18 shall it be for thine *h.*
Ps 7: 5 lay mine *h.* in the dust
8: 5 crowned him with glory and *h.*
26: 8 place where thine *h.* dwelleth
49:20 man in *h.* understandeth not
149: 9 this *h.* have all his saints
Prov 3: 9 *h.* the Lord with substance
3:16 her left hand riches and *h.*
14:28 the people is the king's *h.*
15:33 wisdom: and before *h.* is humility
20: 3 it is an *h.* to cease from strife
21:21 findeth life, righteousness, and *h.*
25: 2 *h.* of kings to search a matter
26: 1 *h.* is not seemly for a fool
29:23 *h.* shall uphold the humble
Is 29:13 with their lips do *h.* me
Mat 13:57 prophet is not without *h.*
John 5:41 I receive not *h.* from men
5:23 *h.* the Son as they *h.* the Father
12:26 serve me, him will my Father *h.*
Rom 2: 7 in well doing seek glory, *h.*
9:21 make one vessel to *h.*, and another
12:10 in *h.* preferring one another
2 Cor 6: 8 by *h.* and dishonour, by evil report
1 Tim 5: 3 *h.* widows that are widows indeed
Heb 5: 4 taketh this *h.* to himself
1 Pet 1: 7 found unto praise and *h.*
2:17 *h.* all men. Love thy brotherhood
3: 7 giving *h.* unto the wife

HOPE

Ezra 10: 2 now there is *h.* in Israel
Job 11:20 *h.* shall be as giving up
17:15 where is now my *h.*? as for my *h.*
31:24 if I have made gold my *h.*
Ps 16: 9 my flesh shall rest in *h.*
22: 9 didst make me *h* on my mother's
33:18 them that *h.* in his mercy
39: 7 wait I for my *h.* is in thee
42: 5 *h.* thou in God, for I shall
78: 7 might set their *h.* in God
119:49 thou hast caused me to *h.*
119:81 I *h.* in thy word
Prov 10:28 *h.* of the righteous shall be gladness
11: 7 *h.* of unjust men perisheth
14:32 righteous hath *h.* in his death
19:18 chasten thy son while there is *h.*
26:12 more *h.* of a fool than of him
Is 57:10 saidst thou not, There is no *h.*
Jer 14: 8 the *h.* of Israel, the Saviour
17: 7 blessed whose *h.* the Lord is
18:12 they said, there is no *h.*
50: 7 the *h.* of their fathers
Lam 3:26 good that a man should *h.*
3:29 if so be there be *h.*
Ezek 37:11 bones are dried and our *h.* is lost
Hos 2:15 valley of Achor for the door of *h.*
Joel 3:16 Lord will be the *h.* of his people
Zech 9:12 to the strong hold, ye prisoners of *h.*
Acts 24:15 have *h.* towards God, which they
28:20 for the *h.* of Israel I am bound
Rom 5: 4 patience experience; experience, *h.*
5: 5 *h.* maketh not ashamed; because
8:24 we are saved by *h.*: but *h.*
8:25 if we *h.* for that we see not
15: 4 comfort of scriptures, have *h.*
1 Cor 13:13 now abideth faith, *h.*, charity
15:19 in this life only we have *h.*
Gal 5: 5 wait for the *h.* of righteousness
Eph 2:12 having no *h.* and without God
Col 1:23 away from the *h.* of the gospel
1 Thes 4:13 as others which have no *h.*
5: 8 for the helmet, the *h.* of salvation
1 Tim 1: 1 Jesus Christ who is our *h.*
Tit 2:13 looking for that blessed *h.*
Heb 6:11 to the full assurance of *h.*
6:19 which *h.* we have as an anchor
1 Pet 1: 3 begotten again to lively *h.*
1:13 be sober and *h.* to the end
3:15 asketh a reason of *h.* in you
1 John 3: 3 every man that hath this *h.*

HORN (HORNS)

1 Sam 2: 1 my *h.* is exalted in the Lord
Ps 18: 2 and the *h.* of my salvation
92:10 my *h.* is as the *h.* of a unicorn
148:14 he exalteth the *h.* of his
Mic 4:13 I will make thy *h.* iron
Rev 5: 6 as it had been slain having seven *h.*
13: 1 having seven heads and ten *h.*

HORSE (HORSES)

Ex 15:21 the *h.* and his rider hath he thrown
Ps 32: 9 be ye not as the *h.* or mule
33:17 *h.* is a vain thing for safety
147:10 delighteth not in the strength of the *h.*
Eccl 10: 7 have seen servants on *h.*
Jer 8: 6 as the *h.* rusheth into battle
12: 5 canst thou contend with *h.*
Hos 14: 3 we will not ride upon *h.*
Zech 1: 8 there red *h.* speckled and white
6: 6 black *h.* which are there
Rev 6: 8 and behold a pale *h.*

HOSPITALITY

Rom 12:13 necessity of saints; given to *h.*
1 Tim 3: 2 of good behavior, given to *h.*
Tit 1: 8 but a lover of *h.*, a lover of
1 Pet 4: 9 use *h.* one to another

HOST (HOSTS)

Ps 27: 3 an *h.* should encamp against me
33:16 by the multitude of an *h.*
148: 2 praise ye him, all his *h.*
103:21 Bless ye the Lord, all ye his *h.*

Is 40:26 bringeth out their *h.* by number
Jer 3:19 a goodly heritage of the *h.*
Luke 2:13 multitude of the heavenly *h.*
10:35 and gave them to the *h.*
Rom 16:23 Gaius, mine *h.*, and of the whole

HOT
Ps 38: 1 chasten me in thy *h.* displeasure
39: 3 my heart was *h.* within me
Prov 6:28 can one go upon *h.* coals
Hos 7: 7 they are all *h.* as an oven
1 Tim 4: 2 seared with a *h.* iron
Rev 3:15 thou art neither cold nor *h.*

HOUR
Dan 3:15 shall be cast the same *h.*
4:33 the same *h.* was the thing
Mat 10:19 given you in that same *h.*
24:36 day and *h.* knoweth no man
25:13 know neither day nor *h.*
Luke 12:12 Holy Ghost shall teach you that same *h.*
22:53 this is your *h.* and power
John 2: 4 mine *h.* is not yet come
4:23 *h.* cometh, and now is when
7:30 his *h.* was not yet come
Rev 3: 3 not know what *h.* I come
3:10 keep from the *h.* of temptation
17:12 power as kings one *h.* with the beast
18:10 in one *h.* is thy judgment

HOUSE
Gen 28:17 is none other but the *h.* of God
Ex 12:30 not a *h.* where there was not one
Deut 6: 7 when thou sittest in thine *h.*
Josh 24:15 as for me and my *h.*
2 Sam 23: 5 although my *h.* be not so with God
Job 21:28 where is the *h.* of the prince
30:23 *h.* appointed for all living
Ps 23: 6 in the *h.* of the Lord
26: 8 I loved the habitation of thine *h.*
36: 8 satisfied with the fatness of thine *h.*
55:14 unto the *h.* of God in company
101: 2 I will walk within my *h.* with
105:21 him lord of all his *h.*
112: 3 wealth and riches shall be in his *h.*
Prov 3:33 curse of the Lord is in the *h.* of
7:27 her *h.* is the way to hell
12: 7 *h.* of the righteous shall stand
Eccl 5: 1 goest to the *h.* of God
7: 2 go to the *h.* of mourning
12: 3 when keepers of the *h.* tremble
Sol 2: 4 brought me to the banqueting *h.*
Is 2: 3 to the *h.* of the God of Jacob
5: 8 woe to them that join *h.* to *h.*
38: 1 set thine *h.* in order, for thou
60: 7 I will glorify the *h.* of my
64:11 our holy and beautiful *h.*
Mic 4: 2 to the *h.* of the God of Jacob
Mat 10:13 if the *h.* be worthy, let your peace
12:25 a *h.* divided against itself shall not
12:44 I will return into my *h.* from
23:38 *h.* is left unto you desolate
Luke 11:17 and a *h.* divided against a *h.*
11:24 I will return unto my *h.*
12: 3 proclaimed upon the *h.* tops
John 4:53 believed and his whole *h.*
14: 2 in my Father's *h.* are many
Acts 10: 2 feared God with all his *h.*
11:14 thou and all thine *h.* saved
16:31 thou shalt be saved, and thy *h.*
16:34 believing in God with all his *h.*
Rom 16: 5 greet the church that is in their *h.*
1 Cor 16:19 church that is in their *h.*
Col 4:15 the church which is in his *h.*
1 Tim 3:15 behave thyself in the *h.* of God
5: 8 specially for those of his own *h.*
2 Tim 1:16 mercy to the *h.* of Onesiphorus
Philem 1: 2 to the church in thy *h.*
Heb 3: 2 faithful in all his *h.*
3: 3 *h.* more honour than the *h.*
1 Pet 4:17 must begin at the *h.* of God
2 John 1:10 receive him not to your *h.*

HOUSES
Job 4:19 dwell in *h.* of clay
Ps 49:11 *h.* shall continue for ever
Prov 19:14 *h.* and riches are the inheritance
Mat 11: 8 wear soft clothing are in king's *h.*
19:29 everyone that hath forsaken *h.*
23:14 hypocrites! for ye devour widows' *h.*
Mark 10:29 no man that hath left the *h.*
Luke 16: 4 may receive me into their *h.*
20:47 which devour widows *h.*, and for a show
1 Cor 11:22 have ye not *h.* to eat and drink in
1 Tim 3:12 their children and their own *h.* well
2 Tim 3: 6 they which creep into *h.* and lead
Tit 1:11 subvert whole *h.* teaching things

HOUSEHOLD
Acts 16:15 baptized and her whole *h.*
Gal 6:10 who are of the *h.* of faith
Eph 2:19 saints of the *h.* of God

HUMBLE (HUMBLED)
Ex 10: 3 thou refuse to *h.* thyself
Lev 26:41 if uncircumcised hearts be *h.*
Deut 8: 2 to *h.* thee, and prove
2 Ki 22:19 hast *h.* thyself before the Lord
2 Chr 7:14 shall *h.* themselves
12: 6 Israel and the kings *h.* themselves
12:12 And when he *h.* himself the wrath
33:23 *h.* not himself before the Lord
34:27 didst *h.* thyself before God
Ps 9:12 forgetteth not the cry of the *h.*
10:12 up thine hand: forget not the *h.*
34: 2 *h.* shall hear thereof, and be glad
35:13 I *h.* my soul with fasting
Prov 6: 3 *h.* thyself, make sure thy friend
16:19 to be of an *h.* spirit
Is 2:11 lofty looks of man shall be *h.*
5:15 *h.* and eyes of the lofty shall be *h.*
10:33 haughty shall be *h.*
57:15 *h.* spirit, to revive the spirit of
Jer 13:18 to the queen, *h.* yourselves
44:10 they are not *h.* unto this day
Lam 3:20 my soul is *h.* in me
Dan 5:22 hast not *h.* thy heart
Mat 18: 4 whosoever therefore shall *h.* himself
23:12 he that shall *h.* himself
2 Cor 12:21 my God will *h.* me
Phil 2: 8 *h.* himself and became obedient
Jas 4: 6 But giveth grace unto the *h.*
4:10 *h.* yourselves in the sight of Lord
1 Pet 5: 5 giveth grace to the *h.*
5: 6 *h.* yourselves under the mighty hand

HUMILITY
Prov 15:33 wisdom: and before honour is *h.*
18:12 man is haughty, and before honour is *h.*
22: 4 by *h.* are riches and honour
Acts 20:19 serving the Lord with all *h.*
Col 2:18 of your reward in a voluntary *h.*
1 Pet 5: 5 be clothed with *h.*: For God resisteth

HUNGER
Deut 8: 3 suffered thee to *h.*, and fed thee
Ps 34:10 do lack, and suffer *h.*
Prov 19:15 idle soul shall suffer *h.*
Is 49:10 shall not *h.* nor thirst
Lam 4: 9 sword better than slain with *h.*
Mat 5: 6 blessed are they which do *h.*
Luke 6:21 blessed are ye that *h.* now
6:25 unto you that are full! Ye shall *h.*
John 6:35 cometh to me shall never *h.*
Rom 12:20 Therefore if thine enemy *h.* feed
1 Cor 4:11 we both *h.* and thirst, and are naked
11:34 if any man *h.* let him eat at

HUNGRY
Ps 107: 9 filleth the *h.* soul with goodness
146: 7 God giveth food to the *h.*
Prov 25:21 if thine enemy be *h.* give him
27: 7 to the *h.* soul every bitter thing is sweet
Is 58: 7 to deal thy bread to the *h.*
58:10 if thou draw out thy soul to the *h.*
65:13 shall eat; but ye shall be *h.*
Ezek 18: 7 hath given his bread to the *h.*
Luke 1:53 filled the *h.* with good things
Phil 4:12 how to be full and to be *h.*

HURT
Gen 4:23 and a young man to my *h.*
26:29 thou wilt do us no *h.*
Josh 24:20 will turn and do you *h.*
Ps 15: 4 sweareth to his own *h.*
Eccl 5:13 owners thereof to their *h.*
Jer 6:14 healed the *h.* of the daughter
8:11 they have healed the *h.*
Rev 2:11 shall not be *h.* of second death

HUSBAND (HUSBANDS)
Gen 3:16 to thy *h.*, and he shall rule over
29:32 therefore my *h.* will love me
Ex 4:25 surely a bloody *h.* art thou to me
Is 54: 5 for thy Maker is thine *h.*
Mark 10:12 if a woman put away her *h.*
John 4:17 I have no *h.*. Jesus said unto
4:18 thou hast had five *h.*
1 Cor 7:14 unbelieving *h.* is sanctified by
7:34 careth how she may please her *h.*
14:35 let them ask the *h.* at home
2 Cor 11: 2 I have espoused you to one *h.*
Eph 5:22 wives, submit to your *h.*
5:23 the *h.* is the head of wife
5:33 wife see that she reverence her *h.*
5:25 *h.*, love your wives, as Christ
Col 3:19 *h.* love your wives, and be not bitter
3:18 wives, submit to your *h.*
1 Pet 3: 1 ye wives be in subjection to your own *h.*
3: 7 likewise ye *h.*, dwell with them

HUSBANDMAN
John 15: 1 my father is the *h.*
Jas 5: 7 *h.* waiteth for the precious fruit

HUSBANDRY
1 Cor 3: 9 together with God: ye are God's *h.*

HYMN (HYMNS)
Mat 26:30 when they had sung a *h.*
Eph 5:19 in psalms and *h.*, and spiritual psalms
Col 3:16 admonishing one another in psalms and *h.*

HYPOCRISY
Is 32: 6 to practice *h.* and to utter
Mat 23:28 within ye are full of *h.*
Mark 12:15 knowing their *h.*, said unto them
Luke 12: 1 the pharisees, which is *h.*
1 Tim 4: 2 speaking lies in *h.* having their conscience
Jas 3:17 without partiality and without *h.*
1 Pet 2: 1 and all guile and *h.*

HYPOCRITE (HYPOCRITES)
Job 8:13 the *h's.* hope shall perish
15:34 congregation of *h.* shall be desolate
20: 5 joy of the *h.* for a moment
27: 8 what is the hope of the *h.*
Is 9:17 every one is a *h.* and evil
33:14 fearfulness hath surprised the *h.*
Mat 6: 2 as the *h.* do in the synagogues
7: 5 thou *h.*, first cast out the beam
15: 7 ye *h.*, well did Esaias
16: 3 oh ye *h.*, ye can discern
23:13 scribes and pharisees, *h.*!
24:51 appoint him portion with *h.*
Luke 6:42 thou *h.* cast out first the beam out
13:15 thou *h.*. doth not each one

I

IDLE
Prov 19:15 an *i.* soul shall suffer
Mat 12:36 every *i.* word that men shall speak
20: 6 ye stand here all the day *i.*

Luke 24:11 words seemed as *i.* tales

IDLENESS
Prov 31:27 eateth not the bread of *i.*
Eccl 10:18 and through *i.* of hands
Ezek 16:49 abundance of *i.* was in her

IDOL (IDOLS)
Ps 96: 5 gods of nations are *i.*
Is 2: 8 land is full of *i.*; they worship
66: 3 as if he blessed an *i.*
Jer 50:38 they are mad upon *i.*
Hos 4:17 Ephraim is joined to *i.*
Zech 11:17 woe to the *i.* shepherd
Acts 15:20 abstain from the pollutions of *i.*
Rom 2:22 thou that abhorrest *i.* dost thou commit
1 Cor 8: 1 touching things offered to *i.*
8: 4 an *i.* is nothing in the world
1 John 5:21 keep yourselves from *i.*
Rev 2:14 eat things sacrificed to *i.*
9:20 not worship devils and *i.* of gold

IDOLATER (IDOLATERS)
1 Cor 5:11 or an *i.*, or a railer
6: 9 nor *i.*, nor adulterers
10: 7 neither be ye *i.*, as were some
Eph 5: 5 covetous man, who is an *i.*
Rev 21: 8 and sorcerers, and *i.*, and all liars
22:15 and *i.*, and whosoever loveth

IDOLATRY
Acts 17:16 city wholly given to *i.*
1 Cor 10:14 dearly beloved, flee from *i.*
Gal 5:20 *i.*, witchcraft, hatred, variance
Col 3: 5 concupiscence, and covetousness, which is *i.*

IGNORANCE
Lev 4:13 congregation of Israel sin through *i.*
Num 15:25 be forgiven them for it is *i.*
Acts 3:17 I wot that through *i.* ye did it
17:30 the times of this *i.* God winked at
Eph 4:18 alienated from God through *i.*

IGNORANT (IGNORANTLY)
Is 63:16 our father, though Abraham be *i.* of
Rom 10: 3 for being *i.* of God's righteousness
Acts 17:23 when therefore ye *i.* worship
1 Cor 14:38 if man be *i.* let him be *i.*
1 Tim 1:13 I did it *i.* in unbelief
Heb 5: 2 can have compassion on the *i.*

IMAGE
Gen 1:26 let us make man in our *i.*
5: 3 in his own likeness after his *i.*
9: 6 for in the *i.* of God
Lev 26: 1 set up any *i.* of stone
Ps 73:20 thou shalt despise their *i.*
Dan 2:31 this great *i.* whose brightness
Mat 22:20 whose is this *i.* and superscription
Rom 8:29 conformed to the *i.* of the Son
1 Cor 15:49 *i.* of earthy shall also bear *i.*
2 Cor 4: 4 Christ who is the *i.* of God
Col 1:15 the *i.* of the invisible God
3:10 after the *i.* of him that
Heb 1: 3 express the *i.* of his person
Rev 13:14 make an *i.* to the beast

IMMORTAL
1 Tim 1:17 the King *i.*, invisible

IMMORTALITY
Rom 2: 7 seek for glory, honour, *i.*
1 Cor 15:53 this mortal must put on *i.*
2 Tim 1:10 brought life and *i.* to light

IMPOSSIBLE
Mat 17:20 nothing shall be *i.* unto you
19:26 with men this is *i.* but with God
Luke 1:37 with God nothing shall be *i.*
17: 1 it is *i.* but offences will come
Heb 6: 4 *i.* for those once enlightened
6:18 in two things it was *i.* for God to

Heb 11: 6 without faith it is *i.* to please

IMPUTED (IMPUTETH, IMPUTING)
Lev 7:18 shall it be *i.* unto him that offereth
17: 4 blood shall be *i.* unto that man
Ps 32: 2 whom the Lord *i.* not iniquity
Rom 4: 6 God *i.* righteousness without work
4:11 righteousness might be *i.*
4:22 *i.* to him for righteousness
5:13 sin is not *i.* when there is no law
2 Cor 5:19 not *i.* their trespasses unto them
Jas 2:23 *i.* unto him for righteousness

INCLINE (INCLINED)
Josh 24:23 *i.* your heart unto the God
Judg 9: 3 their hearts *i.* to follow Abimelech
1 Ki 8:58 that he may *i.* our hearts unto him
Ps 40: 1 he *i.* unto me and heard
78: 1 *i.* your ears to the words
116: 2 he hath *i.* his ear unto me
119:36 *i.* my heart unto thy testimonies
Prov 2: 2 *i.* thine ear unto wisdom
5:13 nor *i.* mine ear to them
Is 55: 3 *i.* your ear and come unto me
Jer 7:26 nor *i.* their ear, but hardened
17:23 obeyed not, neither *i.* their ear
34:14 not unto me neither *i.* their ear
44: 5 nor *i.* their ear to turn

INCORRUPTIBLE (UN-)
Rom 1:23 the glory of the *i.* God
1 Cor 9:25 corruptible crown; but we an *i.*
15:52 dead shall be raised *i.*, and we shall
1 Pet 1: 4 to an inheritance *i.* and undefiled
1:23 not of corruptible seed, but of *i.*

INCORRUPTION
1 Cor 15:50 neither doth corruption inherit *i.*

INCREASE (INCREASED)
Lev 19:25 yield unto you the *i.* thereof
25:36 take no usury of him nor *i.*
Num 32:14 your father's stead an *i.* of sinful men
Deut 16:15 bless thee in all thine *i.*
Ezra 9: 6 iniquities are *i.* over our head
Ps 62:10 if riches *i.* set not your heart
67: 6 shall the earth yield her *i.*
Prov 1: 5 will hear, and will *i.* learning
Eccl 5:11 when goods *i.* they are
Is 9: 3 and not *i.* the joy: they joy before
9: 7 of the *i.* of his government
29:19 the meek shall also *i.* their joy
Ezek 18: 8 neither taken any *i.* that hath
Luke 2:52 Jesus *i.* in wisdom and
17: 5 said unto the Lord, *i.* our faith
John 3:30 he must *i.* but I decrease
Acts 6: 7 the word of God *i.* and the
1 Cor 3: 6 Apollos watered; but God gave the *i.*
Col 2:19 increaseth with the *i.* of God
1 Thes 3:12 Lord make you to *i.* and abound
2 Tim 2:16 for they will *i.* to more ungodliness
Rev 3:17 I am rich and *i.* with goods

INDIGNATION
Neh 4: 1 took great *i.* and mocked the Jews
Esth 5: 9 full of *i.* against Mordecai
Ps 78:49 his anger, wrath, and *i.*, and trouble
102:10 thine *i.*, and thy wrath
Is 10: 5 staff in their hand is mine *i.*
Mic 7: 9 I will bear the *i.* of the Lord
Nah 1: 6 who can stand before his *i.*
Mat 20:24 moved with *i.* against the two
26: 8 when disciples saw it, they had *i.*
Rom 2: 8 *i.* and wrath, tribulation
2 Cor 7:11 yea, what *i.*, yea, what fear
Heb 10:27 fiery *i.* which shall devour
Rev 14:10 poured into the cup of his *i.*

INFINITE
Job 22: 5 and thine iniquities, *i.*
Ps 147: 5 of great power: his understanding is *i.*
Nah 3: 9 her strength, and it was *i.*

INFIRMITY (INFIRMITIES)
Ps 77:10 this is my *i.*: but
Prov 18:14 spirit of man will sustain *i.*
Mat 8:17 himself took our *i.*, and bare our
Rom 8:26 the Spirit helpeth our *i.*
2 Cor 12: 9 will I rather glory in my *i.*
12:10 pleasure in *i.*, in reproaches
1 Tim 5:23 stomach's sake and thine often *i.*
Heb 4:15 with the feeling of our *i.*
5: 2 himself is compassed with *i.*
7:28 maketh men high priests which have *i.*

INHERIT
Gen 15: 8 shall I know that I shall *i.* it
1 Sam 2: 8 make them *i.* the throne of glory
Ps 25:13 his seed shall *i.* the earth
37:11 the meek shall *i.* the earth
37:29 the righteous shall *i.* the land
82: 8 O God, thou shalt *i.* all nations
Prov 3:35 wise shall *i.* glory; but
8:21 that love me to *i.* substance
Mat 5: 5 they shall *i.* the earth
25:34 *i.* the kingdom prepared for you
Mark 10:17 what shall I do that I may *i.* eternal
1 Cor 6: 9 unrighteous shall not *i.* the kingdom
15:50 flesh and blood cannot *i.* the kingdom
Gal 5:21 shall not *i.* the kingdom of God
Heb 6:12 faith and patience *i.* the promises
1 Pet 3: 9 that ye should *i.* a blessing
Rev 21: 7 overcometh shall *i.* all things

INHERITANCE
Num 18:20 I am thy part and thine *i.*
Deut 4:20 a people of *i.*, as ye are this day
10: 9 no part nor *i.* with his brethren
18: 2 the Lord is their *i.*
1 Ki 8:36 hast given to thy people for an *i.*
Ps 16: 5 Lord is a portion of mine *i.*
28: 9 save thy people and bless thine *i.*
78:62 and was wroth with his *i.*
94:14 neither will he forsake his *i.*
106:40 that he abhorred his own *i.*
Prov 19:14 riches are the *i.* of fathers
Eccl 7:11 wisdom is good with an *i.*
Is 19:25 and Israel mine *i.*
Jer 51:19 Israel is the rod of his *i.*
Ezek 44:28 *i.*: I am their *i.*: and ye shall
Acts 20:32 and to give you an *i.*
Eph 1:11 in whom we obtained an *i.*
1:14 earnest of our *i.* until the
5: 5 any *i.* in the kingdom of Christ
Col 1:12 partakers of the *i.* of saints
3:24 shall receive the reward of *i.*
Heb 9:15 the promise of eternal *i.*
1 Pet 1: 4 to an *i.* incorruptible and undefiled

INIQUITY
Gen 15:16 for the *i.* of the Amorites
Ex 20: 5 visiting the *i.* of the fathers upon
34: 7 forgiving *i.*, and transgression
Lev 26:41 accept the punishment of their *i.*
Num 23:21 hath not beheld *i.* in Jacob
Job 4: 8 they that plow *i.* and sow wickedness
5:16 and *i.* stoppeth her mouth
15:16 man which drinketh *i.* like water
22:23 put away *i.* far from thy tabernacles
34:22 workers of *i.* may hide
34:32 if I have done *i.* I will do no
Ps 5: 5 thou hatest all workers of *i.*
18:23 kept myself from mine *i.*
32: 5 mine *i.* have I not hid
39:11 dost correct man for his *i.*
51: 5 behold, I was shapen in *i.*
66:18 if I regard *i.* in my heart
69:27 add *i.* unto their *i.*: and let them
92: 7 workers of *i.* do flourish
119: 3 they also do no *i.*: they walk
119:133 let not any *i.* have dominion
Prov 21:15 shall be to the workers of *i.*
Eccl 3:16 place of righteousness there *i.* was
Is 1: 4 people laden with *i.*, a seed
5:18 woe to them that draw *i.* with

Is 62: 1 *J.* sake I will not rest
Jer 3:17 the name of the Lord to *J.*
Joel 2:32 in mount Zion, and in *J.*
Zech 12:10 upon the inhabitants of *J.*
Gal 4:26 *J.* which is above is free
Heb 12:22 living God, the heavenly *J.*
Rev 3:12 which is new *J.*, which cometh down
21: 2 the holy city, new *J.*

JESUS
Mat 1:21 thou shalt call his name *J.*
2: 1 *J.* was born in Bethlehem
8:29 do with thee *J.* thou Son of God
14: 1 tetrarch heard of the fame of *J.*
27:37 This is *J.* the King of the Jews
1 Cor 12: 3 Spirit of God calleth *J.* accursed
2 Cor 4: 5 but Christ *J.* the Lord, and ourselves
Eph 4:21 taught by him as the truth is in *J.*
Heb 2: 9 But we see *J.*, who was made a little
12: 2 looking unto *J.* the author and
Rev 22:16 I *J.* have sent my angel

JEW (JEWS)
Rom 1:16 the *J.* first, and also to the Greek
2:10 *J.* first, and also to the Gentile
2:28 *J.* which is one outwardly, but a *J.*
10:12 no difference between *J.* and Greek
1 Cor 9:20 to Jews I became as a *J.*
Gal 3:28 there is neither *J.* nor Greek, there
Col 3:11 there is neither Greek nor *J.*
Rev 2: 9 say they are *J* and are not
3: 9 say they are *J.*, and are not

JOIN (JOINED)
Ex 1:10 they *j.* also unto our enemies
Num 25: 3 Israel *j.* himself to Baal-Peor
Ezra 9:14 and *j.* in affinity with the people
Prov 11:21 hand *j.* in hand, the wicked shall
Eccl 9: 4 for him that is *j.* to the living
Is 5: 8 woe to them that *j.* house to house
Jer 50: 5 let us *j.* ourselves to the Lord
Hos 4:17 Ephraim is *j.* to idols
Zech 2:11 nations shall be *j.* to the Lord
Mat 19: 6 what God hath *j.* together let not
Acts 5:13 durst no man *j.* himself
1 Cor 1:10 that ye be perfectly *j.* together
Eph 5:31 shall be *j.* to his wife

JOINTS
Col 2:19 which all the body by *j.* and bands
Heb 4:12 and of the *j.* and marrow

JOY
1 Chr 12:40 there was *j.* in Israel
2 Chr 20:27 go again to Jerusalem with *j.*
Neh 8:10 *j.* of the Lord is your strength
Esth 8:17 Jews had *j.* and gladness
Job 20: 5 *j.* of the hypocrite but for
Ps 16:11 thy presence is fulness of *j.*
43: 4 unto God my exceeding *j.*
51: 8 make me hear *j.* and gladness
51:12 restore to me the *j.* of thy salvation
126: 5 that sow in tears shall reap in *j.*
Eccl 9: 7 eat thy bread with *j.*
Is 9: 3 according to the *j.* in harvest
12: 3 with *j.* shall ye draw water out
35:10 with songs and everlasting *j.*
61: 3 give them the oil of *j.* for mourning
61: 7 everlasting *j.* shall be to them
66: 5 he shall appear to your *j.*
Zeph 3:17 will *j.* over thee with singing
Mat 2:10 rejoiced with great *j.*
13:20 hear the word, and with *j.*
Luke 1:44 babe leaped in the womb for *j.*
15: 7 *j.* shall be in heaven over one
John 15:11 and that your *j.* might be full
16:20 your sorrow be turned into *j.*
16:22 your *j.* no man taketh from you
16:24 that your *j.* may be full
17:13 my *j.* fulfilled in themselves
Acts 20:24 finish my course with *j.*
Rom 15:13 fill you with all *j.* and peace
2 Cor 1:24 but are helpers of your *j.*
2: 3 my *j.* is the *j.* of you all
Gal 5:22 fruit of the Spirit is love, *j.*
Phil 4: 1 my *j.* and crown, so stand fast in
1 Thes 1: 6 receive the word with *j.* of
Heb 12: 2 who for the *j.* set before
Jas 1: 2 count it all *j.* when ye
1 Pet 1: 8 rejoice with *j.* unspeakable
4:13 be glad with exceeding *j.*
1 John 1: 4 write that your *j.* may be full

JOYFUL (JOYFULLY)
Ezra 6:22 the Lord hath made them *j.*
Ps 35: 9 my soul shall be *j.* in the Lord
63: 5 I will praise thee with *j.* lips
89:15 people that know the *j.* sound
Eccl 7:14 in the day of prosperity be *j.*
9: 9 live *j.* with the wife whom thou
Is 56: 7 make them *j.* in my house
61:10 my soul shall be *j.* in God
2 Cor 7: 4 exceeding *j.* in all our tribulation
Heb 10:34 took *j.* the spoiling of goods

JOYFULNESS
Deut 28:47 servedst not the Lord thy God with *j.*
Col 1:11 all patience longsuffering with *j.*

JOYING
Col 2: 5 *j.* and beholding your order, and the

JOYOUS
Heb 12:11 for the present seemeth to be *j.*

JUDGE
Gen 16: 5 Lord *j.* between me and thee
18:25 shall not the *J.* of the earth
Ex 2:14 thee a prince and a *j.* over us
Deut 32:36 the Lord shall *j.* his people
1 Sam 2:25 the *j.* shall *j.* him; but
24:12 Lord *j.* between me and thee
Ps 7: 8 Lord shall *j.* the people
9: 8 Lord shall *j.* the world in righteousness
68: 5 father of the fatherless and *j.* of widows
75: 7 God is the *j.*: he putteth down
98: 9 with righteousness shall he *j.*
Is 33:22 The Lord is our *j.*, the Lord is our
Mic 3:11 heads thereof *j.* for reward
Mat 7: 1 *j.* not, that ye be not judged
Luke 12:14 who made me a *j.* or a divider
John 5:30 as I hear I *j.* and my judgment
12:47 I came not to *j.* the world
Acts 7:27 made thee ruler and a *j.*
10:42 to be the *J.* of the quick and dead
17:31 in which he will *j.* the world in
23: 3 sittest thou to *j.* me after the law
Rom 2:16 when God shall *j.* the secrets of men
3: 6 then how shall God *j.* the world
14:10 why dost thou *j.* thy brother
1 Cor 4: 3 I *j.* not mine own self
4: 5 *j.* nothing before the time
6: 3 know ye not that we shall *j.* angels
11:31 if we would *j.* ourselves, we
14:29 two or three and let the other *j.*
Col 2:16 let no man *j.* you in meat
2 Tim 4: 1 who shall *j.* the quick and the dead
4: 8 Lord the righteous *j.*, shall give me
Heb 10:30 Lord shall *j.* his people
12:23 are come to God the *J.*
Jas 4:11 if thou *j.* the law thou art not a
5: 9 the *J.* standeth before the door

JUDGETH (JUDGING)
Deut 1:17 ye shall not respect persons in *j.*
Ps 7:11 God *j.* the righteous and God is
58:11 he is a God that *j.* in earth
Mat 19:28 *j.* the twelve tribes of Israel
Luke 22:30 sit on thrones, *j.* the twelve
1 Cor 2:15 but he that is spiritual *j.* all things
4: 4 he that *j.* me is the Lord

JUDGMENT
Deut 1:17 for the *j.* is God's: and the cause
Ps 1: 5 ungodly not stand in the *j.*
9:16 Lord is known by the *j.* he executeth
101: 1 I will sing of mercy and *j.*
143: 2 enter not into *j.* with thy servant
149: 9 to execute upon them the *j.*
Prov 21:15 it is joy to the just to do *j.*
29:26 every man's *j.* cometh from the Lord
Eccl 11: 9 God will bring thee into *j.*
Is 1:27 Zion shall be redeemed with *j.*
28:17 *j.* also will I lay to the line
30:18 for the Lord is a God of *j.*
42: 1 he shall bring *j.* to the Gentiles
53: 8 he was taken from prison and *j.*
61: 8 I the Lord love *j.*, I hate
Jer 5: 1 if there be any that executeth *j.*
8: 7 people know not the *j.* of the Lord
10:24 correct me, but with *j.*; not in
Dan 4:37 whose works are truth and his ways *j.*
7:22 and *j.* was given to the saints
Hos 12: 6 keep mercy and *j.*, wait on
Amos 5: 7 who turn *j.* to wormwood
5:24 let *j.* run down as waters, and
Mat 5:21 kill shall be in danger of the *j.*
12:20 till he send *j.* unto victory
John 5:27 and given him authority to execute *j.*
9:39 for *j.* I am come into the world
16: 8 and of righteousness, and of *j.*
Acts 24:25 temperance, and *j.* to come
Rom 5:18 *j.* came upon all men to condemnation
14:10 must all stand before the *j.* seat
1 Pet 4:17 *j.* begin at the house of God
Jude 1:15 execute *j.* upon all, and to convince
Rev 17: 1 show thee *j.* of a great whore

JUDGMENTS
Ps 19: 9 *j.* of the Lord are true and righteous
36: 6 thy *j.* are a great deep
119:75 I know, O Lord, that thy *j.* are right
119:108 O Lord, teach me thy *j.*
119:120 and I am afraid of thy *j.*
Is 26: 8 in the way of thy *j.*, O Lord, have
26: 9 when thy *j.* are in the earth
Jer 12: 1 let me talk with thee of thy *j.*
Rom 11:33 how unsearchable are his *j.*, and his

JUST
Gen 6: 9 Noah was a *j.* man and perfect
Lev 19:36 *j.* balance, *j.* weights, a *j.* ephah
Deut 16:20 that which is *j.* shalt thou follow
25:15 shalt have a perfect and *j.* weight
32: 4 without iniquity *j.* and right is he
2 Sam 23: 3 he that ruleth men must be *j.*
Neh 9:33 art *j.* in all that is brought upon us
Prov 4:18 path of the *j.* is as a shining
10: 6 blessings are on the head of the *j.*
11: 1 but a *j.* weight is his delight
12:21 no evil shall happen to the *j.*
17:26 to punish the *j.* is not good
18:17 in his own cause seemeth *j.*
20: 7 the *j.* man walketh in his integrity
24:16 *j.* man falleth seven times
Eccl 7:15 there is a *j.* man that perisheth
7:20 there is not a *j.* man on earth
8:14 be *j.* men, to whom it happeneth
Is 26: 7 way of the *j.* is uprightness
45:21 no God beside me; a *j.* God
Ezek 18: 9 he is *j.*, he shall live
Hab 2: 4 *j.* shall live by his faith
Zeph 3: 5 the *j.* Lord is in the midst
Luke 15: 7 more than over ninety-nine *j.* persons
20:20 who should feign themselves *j.*
John 5:30 I judge and my judgment is *j.*
Acts 7:52 the coming of the *J.* One
24:15 both of the *j.* and the unjust
Rom 1:17 *j.* shall live by faith
2:13 not hearers of the law are *j.*
3:26 he might be *j.* and the justifier
7:12 commandment holy, *j.* and
Gal 3:11 *j.* shall live by faith
Phil 4: 8 whatsoever things are *j.*
Col 4: 1 that which is *j.* and
Heb 2: 2 received a *j.* recompence
10:38 *j.* shall live by faith

Is 43:15 Creator of Israel, your *K.*
Hos 3: 5 Lord their God and David their *k.*
7: 5 in the day of our *k.* the princes
13:11 I gave thee a *k.* in mine anger
Zech 9: 9 behold, thy *K.* cometh
Luke 23: 2 he himself is Christ, a *K.*
John 6:15 by force to make him *k.*
1 Tim 1:17 now unto the *K.* eternal
6:15 *K.* of kings, and Lord of lords
1 Pet 2:17 fear God, honour thy *k.*
Rev 15: 3 thy ways, thou *k.* of saints
17:14 Lord of Lords, and *k.* of kings
19:16 *k.* of kings, and Lord of Lords

KINGS (KINGS')
Ps 72:11 *k.* shall fall before him
76:12 terrible to the *k.* of earth
102:15 *k.* of the earth be thy glory
144:10 that giveth salvation to *k.*
149: 8 to bind their *k.* with chains
Prov 8:15 by me *k.* reign, and princes
Is 62: 2 and all *k.* thy glory: and thou
Hos 8: 4 they set up *k.* but not by
Mat 11: 8 soft clothing in *k.* houses
Luke 22:25 *k.* of Gentiles exercise authority
1 Cor 4: 8 reigned as *k.* without us
1 Tim 2: 2 *k.* and for all that are in authority
Rev 1: 6 made us *k.* and priests to God
5:10 unto our God, *k.* and priests

KINGDOM
Ex 19: 6 be a *k.* of priests, and an
1 Sam 10:25 people the manner of the *k.*
1 Chr 29:11 thine is the *k.*, O Lord
Ps 22:28 for the *k.* is the Lord's
Dan 2:44 God of heaven set up a *k.*
4:17 High ruleth in the *k.* of men
7:27 whose *k.* is an everlasting *k.*
Mat 3: 2 for the *k.* of heaven is at hand
4:17 for the *k.* of heaven is at hand
5: 3 theirs is the *k.* of heaven
6:13 for thine is the *k.* and the
6:33 seek ye first the *k.* of God
11:12 *k.* of heaven suffereth violence
12:25 every *k.* divided against itself
12:28 the *k.* of God is come unto you
13:19 heareth the word of the *k.*
13:38 good seed are the children of the *k.*
16:19 the keys of the *k.* of heaven
23:13 shut up the *k.* of heaven against men
25: 1 *k.* of heaven be likened unto ten
25:34 inherit the *k.* prepared for you
Mark 1:15 the *k.* of God is at hand
11:10 blessed be the *k.* of our father David
Luke 10:11 *k.* of God is come nigh unto you
12:32 good pleasure to give you the *k.*
17:21 *k.* of God is within you
19:12 to receive for himself a *k.*
21:31 *k.* of God is nigh at hand
22:29 I appoint unto you a *k.* as my
John 3: 3 he cannot see the *k.* of God
18:36 my *k.* is not of this world
Rom 14:17 *k.* of God is not meat and drink
1 Cor 4:20 *k.* of God is not in word
6: 9 shall not inherit the *k.* of God
15:24 delivered up the *k.* to God
Eph 5: 5 hath any inheritance in the *k.* of God
Col 1:13 translated us into the *k.* of
2 Thes 1: 5 be counted worthy of the *k.* of God
2 Tim 4:18 preserve me to the heavenly *k.*
Jas 2: 5 rich in faith, heirs of the *k.*
2 Pet 1:11 into the everlasting *k.* of our Lord
Rev 1: 9 in the *k.* and patience of Jesus
12:10 strength and the *k.* of our God
17:17 to give their *k.* to the beast

KINGDOMS
Rev 11:15 *k.* of this world are become the *k.*

KISS (KISSED)
Ps 2:12 *k.* the son lest he be angry
85:10 peace have *k.* each other
Sol 1: 2 let him *k.* me with the kisses
Luke 7:38 *k.* his feet and anointed

Rom 16:16 salute one another with an holy *k.*
1 Pet 5:14 with the *k.* of charity

KISSES
Prov 27: 6 *k.* of an enemy are deceitful

KNEE (KNEES)
Gen 30: 3 she shall bear upon my *k.*
41:43 bow the *k.*: and he made him
Is 35: 3 confirm the feeble *k.*
45:23 to God every *k.* shall bow
Dan 5: 6 *k.* smote one against another
Nah 2:10 the *k.* smite together and much pain
Mat 27:29 they bowed the *k.* before him
Rom 14:11 every *k.* shall bow to me
Eph 3:14 I bow my *k.* unto the Lord
Phil 2:10 of Jesus every *k.* should bow
Heb 12:12 which hang down and the feeble *k.*

KNOCK
Mat 7: 7 *k.* and it shall be opened
Rev 3:20 I stand at the door and *k.*

KNEW (KNEWEST)
Gen 3: 7 they *k.* they were naked
4: 1 Adam *k.* Eve his wife, and she
28:16 Lord in this place, I *k.* it not
Deut 34:10 whom the Lord *k.* face to face
Jer 1: 5 in the belly I *k.* thee
Mat 7:23 I never *k.* you: depart ye
John 4:10 if thou *k.* the gift of God
Rom 1:21 *k.* God they glorified him not
1 John 3: 1 us not, because it *k.* him not

KNOW
Gen 18:19 *k.* him that he will command
22:12 now I *k.* that thou fearest God
Ex 4:14 I *k.* that he can speak
Deut 8: 2 to *k.* what was in thy
Josh 22:22 Israel he shall *k.*; if it be in
1 Sam 3: 7 Samuel did not yet *k.* Lord
1 Ki 8:38 shall *k.* every man the plague of
2 Ki 19:27 I *k.* thy abode and thy going
1 Chr 28: 9 *k.* thou the God of thy father
Job 5:27 *k.* thou it for thy good
8: 9 are but of yesterday, and *k.* nothing
13:23 make me to *k.* my transgression
19:25 I *k.* that my Redeemer liveth
22:13 how doth God *k.*? can he judge
Ps 4: 3 *k.* that Lord doth set apart the godly
9:10 that *k.* thy name will trust in
41:11 by this I *k.* thou favourest
46:10 be still, and *k.* that I am God
51: 6 thou shalt make me to *k.* wisdom
73:16 when I thought to *k.* this
139:23 search me O God and *k.* my heart
Eccl 11: 9 *k.* thou that for all these
Is 58: 2 seek me daily and delight to *k.*
Jer 10:23 I *k.* that the way of man is not
17: 9 desperately wicked, who can *k.* it
22:16 was not this to *k.* me, saith Lord
24: 7 I will give them a heart to *k.*
29:11 I *k.* the thoughts that I think
31:34 *k.* the Lord, for they shall all *k.*
44:28 shall *k.* whose words shall
Ezek 2: 5 shall *k.* that there hath been a
Hos 2:20 faithfulness, and thou shalt *k.* the
Mic 3: 1 is it not for you to *k.* judgment
Mat 6: 3 let not the left hand *k.* what
7:11 *k.* how to give good gifts
25:12 say unto ye, I *k.* you not
John 4:42 we *k.* this is the Christ
7:17 he shall *k.* of the doctrine
10: 4 sheep follow him, for they *k.*
10:14 and *k.* my sheep and am known
13: 7 knowest not now, but thou shalt *k.*
13:17 if ye *k.* these things, happy are
13:18 I *k.* whom I have chosen
13:35 by this shall all men *k.*
Acts 1: 7 it is not for you to *k.* the times
26:27 I *k.* that thou believest
Rom 7:18 I *k.* that in me, that is in my
1 Cor 2:14 neither can he *k.* them
4: 4 for I *k.* nothing by myself

1 Cor 4:19 and will *k.* not the speech
8: 2 knoweth nothing as he ought to *k.*
13:12 now I *k.* in part; but then
Eph 3:19 to *k.* the love of Christ
Phil 4:12 I *k.* both how to be abased
2 Tim 1:12 I *k.* whom I have believed
Tit 1:16 profess they *k.* God, but
1 John 2: 4 he that saith I *k.* him, and keepeth
Rev 2: 2 I *k.* thy works and thy labor
3: 1 I *k.* thy works, that thou hast

KNOWETH (KNOWN)
Ps 1: 6 Lord *k.* the way of the righteous
9:16 Lord is *k.* by judgment which he
31: 7 hast *k.* my soul in adversities
67: 2 that thy way may be *k.* on earth
94:11 Lord *k.* the thoughts of man that
103:14 he *k.* our frame, that we
138: 6 the proud he *k.* afar off
139:14 my soul *k.* right well
Eccl 9: 1 no man *k.* either love or
Is 1: 3 ox *k.* his owner, and ass his
45: 4 thou hast not *k.* me
Jer 8: 7 stork *k.* her appointed times
Zeph 3: 5 the unjust *k.* no shame
Mat 6: 8 Father *k.* things ye have need of
10:26 hid that shall not be *k.*
24:36 of that day and hour *k.* no man
Luke 19:42 if thou hadst *k.*, even thou, at
Acts 15:18 *k.* to God are all his works
Rom 1:19 that which may be *k.* of God
7: 7 I had not *k.* sin but by the law
1 Cor 8: 3 love God, the same is *k.* of him
13:12 even as I am also *k.*
Gal 4: 9 *k.* God, or rather are *k.* of God
2 Tim 2:19 Lord *k.* them that are his
3:15 from a child thou hast *k.*
2 Pet 2: 9 Lord *k.* how to deliver
1 John 3: 1 the world *k.* us not
Rev 2:17 a name which no man *k.*
2:24 have not *k.* the depths of Satan

KNOWLEDGE
Gen 2:17 of the tree of *k.* of good and evil
1 Sam 2: 3 the Lord is a God of *k.*
Ps 19: 2 night unto night showeth *k.*
73:11 is there *k.* in the Most High
139: 6 such *k.* is too wonderful
Prov 8:12 I find out *k.* of witty inventions
9:10 *k.* of the holy is understanding
14: 6 *k.* is easy to him that understandeth
19: 2 soul be without *k.* is not good
30: 3 nor have the *k.* of the holy
Eccl 9:10 nor device nor *k.* nor wisdom
Is 28: 9 whom shall he teach *k.*
53:11 by his *k.* shall my righteous
Jer 3:15 feed you with *k.* and understanding
Dan 12: 4 and *k.* shall be increased
Hos 4: 6 are destroyed for lack of *k.*
Hab 2:14 earth shall be filled with the *k.* of
Mal 2: 7 priest's lips should keep *k.*
Rom 2:20 hast the form of *k.* and of the
3:20 for by the law is the *k.* of sin
10: 2 a zeal of God, but not according to *k.*
1 Cor 8: 1 all have *k.* *K.* puffeth up
Eph 3:19 love of Christ which passeth *k.*
Phil 3: 8 loss for excellency of the *k.* of
Col 2: 3 treasures of wisdom and *k.*
3:10 renewed in *k.* after the image
1 Pet 3: 7 dwell with them according to their *k.*
2 Pet 1: 5 faith virtue and to virtue *k.*
3:18 grow in grace and in the *k.* of the

L

LABOUR
Gen 31:42 and the *l.* of my hands
35:16 and she had hard *l.*
Ps 90:10 yet is their strength *l.*
104:23 work to his *l.* until
128: 2 thou shalt eat the *l.* of thine
Prov 14:23 in all *l.* there is profit
23: 4 *l.* not to be rich; cease

Eccl 1: 8 all things are full of *l.*
4: 8 yet is there no end of all his *l.*
Is 55: 2 ye spend your *l.* for that which
Mat 11:28 ye that *l.* and are heavy laden
John 4:38 reap that whereon ye bestowed no *l.*
6:27 *l.* not for the meat that
1 Cor 15:58 your *l.* is not in vain in
1 Thes 1: 3 work of faith, *l.* of love
5:12 know them which *l.* among you, and
Heb 4:11 let us *l.* to enter into

LABOURED
Is 49: 4 I have *l.* in vain
John 4:38 other men *l.* and ye are entered
1 Cor 15:10 I *l.* more abundantly than they
Phil 2:16 not run in vain, neither *l.* in vain

LABOURER (LABOURERS)
Mat 9:37 plenteous but the *l.* are few
Luke 10: 2 send forth *l.* into his harvest
10: 7 the *l.* is worthy of his hire
1 Cor 3: 9 for we are *l.* together with God
1 Tim 5:18 the *l.* is worthy of his reward

LABOURS
Rev 14:13 that they may rest from their *l.*

LACK (LACKING)
Hos 4: 6 for *l.* of knowledge: because thou
Mat 19:20 my youth up: what I *l.* yet
2 Cor 11: 9 that which was *l.* to me
1 Thes 3:10 which is *l.* in your faith
Jas 1: 5 If any of you *l.* wisdom

LADY (LADIES)
Judg 5:29 her wise *l.* answered her
Esth 1:18 *l.* of Persia and Media say this
Is 47: 5 no more be called the *l.* of kingdoms
47: 7 I shall be a *l.* for ever
2 John 1: 1 unto the elect *l.* and her children

LAMB (LAMBS)
Gen 22: 7 where is the *l.* for a burnt offering
22: 8 God will provide himself a *l.*
Ex 12: 3 to them every man a *l.*
2 Sam 12: 3 had nothing save one little ewe *l.*
Is 11: 6 wolf shall dwell with the *l.*
53: 7 brought as a *l.* to slaughter
John 1:29 behold the *L.* of God
21:15 Jesus said to Peter, Feed my *l.*
1 Pet 1:19 as a *l.* without blemish
Rev 5:12 worthy is the *L.* that was slain
7:14 white in the blood of the *L.*
7:17 *L.* in the midst of the throne
13: 8 *L.* slain from the foundation

LAME
Lev 21:18 a blind man, or a *l.*, or he
Job 29:15 eyes to the blind, feet to the *l.*
Prov 26: 7 legs of the *l.* are not equal
Is 35: 6 shall the *l.* man leap as an hart
Mal 1:13 that which was torn, and the *l.*
Heb 12:13 *l.* be turned out of the way

LAMP
Ex 25:37 make the seven *l.* thereof
27:20 to cause the *l.* to burn
Num 8: 2 the *l.*, the seven *l.* shall
2 Sam 22:29 thou art my *l.* O Lord
1 Ki 15: 4 give him a *l.* in Jerusalem
Job 12: 5 is as a *l.* despised in the thought
Ps 119:105 thy word a *l.* to my feet
132:17 I have ordained a *l.* for mine
Prov 6:23 the commandment is a *l.* and the law
13: 9 *l.* of wicked shall be put out
Is 62: 1 salvation as the *l.* that burneth
Zech 4: 2 and his seven *l.* thereon, and seven
Mat 25: 1 which took their *l.* went forth
Rev 4: 5 were seven *l.* of fire

LANGUAGE
Gen 11: 1 earth was of one *l.*
Neh 13:24 could not speak in the Jew's *l.*
Ps 81: 5 I heard a *l.* that I understood not
Is 19:18 speak the *l.* of Canaan
Zeph 3: 9 I turn to the people a pure *l.*

LASCIVIOUSNESS
Mark 7:22 deceit, *l.*, an evil eye
2 Cor 12:21 fornication and *l.*, which they have
Gal 5:19 fornication, uncleanness, *l.*
Eph 4:19 given themselves over to *l.*
1 Pet 4: 3 when we walked in *l.*
Jude 1: 4 turning the grace of God into *l.*

LATTER
Job 19:25 stand at the *l.* upon earth
Prov 19:20 be wise in the *l.* end
Hag 2: 9 glory of this *l.* house
1 Tim 4: 1 that in the *l.* times

LAUGH (LAUGHING)
Gen 17:17 upon his face and *l.*
18:15 he said, Nay, but thou didst *l.*
Job 5:22 thou shalt *l.* neither shalt thou be
8:21 till he fill thy mouth with *l.*
Ps 2: 4 he that sitteth in heavens shall *l.*
37:13 Lord shall *l.* at him for he seeth
52: 6 righteous shall see and fear and *l.*
Prov 1:26 I will *l.* at your calamity
Luke 6:21 weep now for ye shall *l.*
6:25 woe to you that *l.*

LAUGHTER
Ps 126: 2 was our mouth filled with *l.*
Prov 14:13 in *l.* the heart is sorrowful
Eccl 2: 2 I said of *l.*, It is mad
7: 3 sorrow is better than *l.*
Jas 4: 9 let *l.* be turned to mourning

LAW
Gen 47:26 made it a *l.* over the land
Deut 33: 2 from his right hand went a fiery *l.*
Neh 8: 7 caused people to understand the *l.*
9:26 cast thy *l.* behind their backs
10:28 of the lands unto the *l.* of God
Job 22:22 *l.* from his mouth and lay up his
Ps 19: 7 *l.* of the Lord is perfect
37:31 *l.* of his God is in his heart
40: 8 thy *l.* is within my heart
78: 5 appointed a *l.* in Israel
94:12 teachest him out of thy *l.*
119:18 wondrous things out of thy *l.*
119:70 I delight in thy *l.*
119:72 *l.* of thy mouth is better
119:97 how I love thy *l.*
Prov 6:23 the *l.* is the light: and reproofs
7: 2 keep my *l.* as the apple of thine eye
13:14 the *l.* of the wise is a fountain
28: 9 away his ear from hearing the *l.*
29:18 keepeth the *l.* happy is he
Is 2: 3 out of Zion shall go forth the *l.*
8:16 seal the *l.* among my disciples
8:20 to the *l.* and the testimony
42:21 magnify the *l.* and make it
51: 7 people in whose heart is my *l.*
Jer 18:18 *l.* shall not perish from the priest
31:33 I will put the *l.* in inward parts
Hos 8:12 great things of my *l.*, but they were
Mal 2: 7 they should seek the *l.* at his mouth
Luke 16:16 *l.* and prophets were until John
John 1:17 *l.* was given by Moses
19: 7 we have a *l.* and by our *l.* he
Acts 13:39 not justified by the *l.* of Moses
Rom 2:12 without the *l.* perish without the *l.*
2:13 not hearers of the *l.*
2:14 having not the *l.* are a *l.*
3:20 *l.* shall no flesh be justified
3:31 do we make void the *l.*?
4:15 *l.* worketh wrath; where no *l.*
5:13 sin is not imputed where no *l.*
7: 7 known sin but by the *l.*
7: 8 for without the *l.* sin was dead
7: 9 I was alive without the *l.*
7:12 the *l.* is holy, just, and good
7:14 *l.* is spiritual, but I am carnal
7:22 I delight in the *l.* of God
7:23 warring against the *l.* of my mind
Rom 8: 2 made me free from the *l.* of sin
10: 5 righteousness which is of the *l.*
1 Cor 6: 1 go to *l.* before the unjust
6: 7 brother goeth to the *l.* with brother
Gal 2:16 man not justified by works of the *l.*
2:19 I through the *l.* am dead to the *l.*
3:10 of works of the *l.* are under a curse
3:12 the *l.* is not of faith, but the
3:13 us from the curse of the *l.*
5:23 love, faith, against such is no *l.*
Phil 3: 9 righteousness which is of the *l.*
1 Tim 1: 8 the *l.* is good, if a man use
1: 9 that *l.* is not made for the righteous
Heb 7:19 for the *l.* made nothing perfect
Jas 1:25 whoso looketh into the perfect *l.*
1 John 3: 4 sin transgresseth the *l.*

LAWFUL
Ezek 18: 5 do that which is *l.* and right
33:19 do that which is *l.* and right
1 Cor 6:12 all things are *l.* unto me
10:23 All things are *l.* for me

LAY
Gen 19:35 perceived when she *l.* down
Eccl 7: 2 the living will *l.* it to heart
Is 28:16 I *l.* in Zion for a foundation
Mal 2: 2 ye do not *l.* it to heart
Mat 6:20 *l.* up for yourselves treasure
8:20 hath not where to *l.* his head
John 10:15 I *l.* down my life for the sheep
Acts 7:60 *l.* not this sin to their charge
15:28 *l.* on you no greater burden
1 Tim 5:22 *l.* hands suddenly on no man
6:12 *l.* hold on eternal life
Heb 6:18 *l.* hold upon the hope set before
12: 1 *l.* aside every weight
Jas 1:21 *l.* apart all filthiness and superfluity
1 John 3:16 we ought to *l.* down our lives

LAID (LAYETH, LAYING)
1 Sam 21:12 David *l.* up these words in his
Job 21:19 God *l.* up his iniquity
Ps 31:19 *l.* up for them that fear
62: 9 to be *l.* in the balance
89:19 I *l.* help on one that is
Prov 2: 7 *l.* up sound wisdom for the righteous
26:24 and *l.* up deceit within him
Sol 7:13 *l.* up for thee O my beloved
Is 53: 6 Lord hath *l.* on him the iniquity
56: 2 that *l.* hold on it
57: 1 no man *l.* it to heart
Jer 12:11 because no man *l.* it to heart
Luke 1:66 *l.* up in their hearts
12:19 much goods *l.* up for many years
1 Cor 3:10 I have *l.* the foundation
Col 1: 5 hope which is *l.* up for you
2 Tim 4: 8 *l.* up for me a crown of
Heb 6: 1 not *l.* again the foundation
6: 2 *l.* on of hands, and of resurrection
1 Pet 2: 1 *l.* aside all malice and all guile
1 Tim 6:19 *l.* up in store for themselves

LEAD (LEADETH, LED)
Ex 15:10 sank as *l.* in the mighty waters
Ps 5: 8 *l.* me O Lord in thy righteousness
23: 2 *l.* me beside still waters
25: 5 *l.* me in thy truth and teach
61: 2 *l.* me to the rock that is higher
139:24 *l.* me in the way everlasting
Sol 8: 2 I would *l.* thee and bring thee
Is 11: 6 a little child shall *l.* them
40:11 gently *l.* those with young
Zech 5: 8 weight of *l.* upon the mouth
Mat 7:13 broad is the way that *l.* to
7:14 narrow is the way that *l.* to life
15:14 blind *l.* the blind, both shall fall
John 10: 3 calleth sheep and *l.* them out
Rom 8:14 as are *l.* by the spirit
Gal 5:18 ye be *l.* of the spirit
1 Tim 2: 2 may *l.* a quiet and peaceable life
Rev 7:17 and shall *l.* them unto living

LEAN (LEANING, LEANED)
Job 8:15 he shall *l.* upon his house
Prov 3: 5 *l.* not unto thine own understanding
Sol 8: 5 wilderness *l.* on her beloved
Mic 3:11 yet will they *l.* on the Lord
John 13:23 *l.* on Jesus' bosom one of his
21:20 which also *l.* on his breast

LEAP (LEAPED, LEAPING)
Sol 2: 8 cometh *l.* upon the mountains
Is 35: 6 shall the lame man *l.*
Zeph 1: 9 I punish all those that *l.*
Luke 1:41 the babe *l.* in her womb
6:23 rejoice in that day and *l.* for joy

LEARN (LEARNED)
Deut 4:10 that they may *l.* to fear
31:13 and *l.* to fear the Lord
Ps 106:35 among the heathen *l.* their works
119:71 that I might *l.* thy statutes
Prov 22:25 lest thou *l.* his ways
Is 1:17 *l.* to do well, seek
26:10 yet will he not *l.* righteousness
50: 4 given me the tongue of the *l.*
Jer 10: 2 *l.* not the way of the heathen
Mat 9:13 *l.* what that meaneth, I will have
11:29 *l.* of me, for I am meek
John 6:45 hath *l.* of Father cometh unto me
Acts 7:22 Moses was *l.* in all wisdom
Eph 4:20 ye have not so *l.* Christ
Tit 3:14 also *l.* to maintain good
Heb 5: 8 he were a Son, yet *l.* he obedience
Rev 14: 3 no man could *l.* that song

LEARNING
Acts 26:24 much *l.* doth make thee mad
Rom 15: 4 were written for our *l.*
2 Tim 3: 7 ever *l.* and never able to

LEAST
Gen 32:10 not worthy of the *l.* of all the
Jer 31:34 shall know me from the *l.* of them
Luke 16:10 in that which is *l.* is faithful
1 Cor 6: 4 them to judge who are *l.* esteemed
15: 9 I am the *l.* of the apostles
Eph 3: 8 less than the *l.* of all saints

LEAVE
Gen 2:24 man shall *l.* his father and mother
1 Ki 8:57 let him not *l.* us, nor
Ps 16:10 not *l.* my soul in hell
27: 9 *l.* me not, neither forsake me
Mat 5:24 *l.* there thy gift before the altar
19: 5 shall a man *l.* father and mother
23:23 and not to *l.* the other undone
Mark 10: 7 man *l.* his father and mother
John 14:18 will not *l.* you comfortless
14:27 peace I *l.* with you, my peace
Acts 2:27 not *l.* my soul in hell
Eph 5:31 man *l.* his father and mother
Heb 13: 5 I will never *l.* thee, nor forsake

LEAVEN
Ex 12:15 put away *l.* our of your houses
Lev 2:11 ye shall burn no *l.*, nor any honey
Mat 13:33 heaven is like unto *l.* which a woman
16: 6 beware of the *l.* of the Pharisees
Luke 12: 1 beware ye of the *l.* of the Pharisees
1 Cor 5: 6 a little *l.* leaveneth a whole lump
5: 8 not with old *l.*, neither with the

LEND (LENDETH, LENT)
Ex 22:25 *l.* money to any of my people
Deut 23:20 stranger thou mayest *l.* upon usury
1 Sam 1:28 I have *l.* him to the Lord
Ps 37:26 merciful and *l.*, and his seed is
112: 5 showeth favour and *l.*, he will guide
Prov 19:17 hath pity upon the poor *l.* to Lord
Jer 15:10 I have neither *l.* on usury, nor

LENDER
Prov 22: 7 borrower is servant to the *l.*

LEOPARD (LEOPARDS)
Sol 4: 8 the mountains of the *l.*
Is 11: 6 *l.* shall lie down with the kid
Jer 5: 6 a *l.* shall watch over their cities
13:23 or the *l.* his spots; then may ye
Hos 13: 7 as a *l.* by the way will I
Hab 1: 8 also are swifter than the *l.*

LEVIATHAN
Job 41: 1 draw out *l.* with an hook
Ps 74:14 breakest the heads of *l.*

LIAR (LIARS)
Ps 116:11 All men are *l.*
Is 44:25 frustrateth the tokens of *l.*
John 8:44 he is a *l.* and the father
Rom 3: 4 let God be true, every man a *l.*
Tit 1:12 the Cretians are always *l.*
1 John 1:10 we make him a *l.*, and his word
5:10 hath made him a *l.* because he
2: 4 keepeth not his commandments is a *l.*
Rev 2: 2 not and hast found them *l.*

LIBERAL (LIBERALLY)
Prov 11:25 *l.* soul shall be made fat
Is 32: 8 the *l.* deviseth *l.* things
2 Cor 9:13 your *l.* distribution unto them
Jas 1: 5 giveth to all men *l.*, and upbraideth

LIBERALITY
1 Cor 16: 3 bring your *l.* into Jerusalem
2 Cor 8: 2 unto the riches of their *l.*

LIBERTY
Lev 25:10 and proclaim *l.* throughout all the land
Ps 119:45 I will walk at *l.* for I seek
Is 61: 1 proclaim *l.* to the captives
Jer 34: 8 to proclaim *l.* unto them
Luke 4:18 to set at *l.* the bruised
Rom 8:21 glorious *l.* of the children of God
Gal 5: 1 stand fast in the *l.* wherewith Christ
5:13 use not *l.* for an occasion to
Jas 1:25 looketh into the perfect law of *l.*
2:12 be judged by the law of *l.*

LIE
Ps 62: 9 men of high degree are a *l.*
Num 23:19 God is not a man, that he should *l.*
Is 63: 8 children that will not *l.*
Hab 2: 3 it shall speak and not *l.*
Col 3: 9 *l.* not one to another, seeing
2 Thes 2:11 they should believe a *l.*
Tit 1: 2 God that cannot *l.* hath promised
Heb 6:18 it was impossible for God to *l.*

LIES
Job 11: 3 should thy *l.* make men hold
Ps 58: 3 as they are born, speaking *l.*
101: 7 that telleth *l.* shall not tarry
Hos 11:12 compasseth me about with *l.*
1 Tim 4: 2 speaking *l.* in hypocrisy

LYING
Ps 119:29 remove from me the way of *l.*
119:163 I hate and abhor *l.* but love thy law
Prov 12:19 a *l.* tongue is but for a moment
Jer 7: 4 trust ye not in *l.* words, saying
Hos 4: 2 by swearing and *l.* and killing and
Jonah 2: 8 observe *l.* vanities forsake their own
Eph 4:25 wherefore putting away *l.*

LIFE
Gen 2: 9 tree of *l.* also in the midst
44:30 is bound up in the lad's *l.*
Deut 30:15 before thee this day, *l.* and good
32:47 because it is your *l.*: and
1 Sam 25:29 bound in the bundle of *l.*
1 Ki 19: 4 O Lord, take away my *l.*
Job 2: 4 hath will he give for his *l.*
10:12 granted me *l.* and favour
Ps 16:11 show me the path of *l.*
21: 4 asked *l.* of thee and thou gavest
36: 9 with thee is the fountain of *l.*
63: 3 lovingkindness better than *l.*
66: 9 God holdeth our soul in *l.*
91:16 with long *l.* will I satisfy
Prov 8:35 whoso findeth me findeth *l.*
15:24 way of *l.* is above to the wise
18:21 death and *l.* are in the power of the
Is 57:10 thou hast found the *l.* of thine hand
Mat 6:25 take no thought for your *l.*
10:39 findeth his *l.* shall loose it
20:28 to give his *l.* a ransom for many
John 1: 4 in him was *l.* and the *l.* was
3:36 believeth on the Son hath everlasting *l.*
5:40 come to me, that ye might have *l.*
6:35 I am the bread of *l.*
6:51 flesh which I will give for the *l.*
6:63 are spirit, and they are *l.*
8:12 but shall have the light of *l.*
10:10 I am come that they might have *l.*
11:25 I am the resurrection and the *l.*
14: 6 I am the way, the truth, and the *l.*
Rom 5:10 reconciled shall be saved by his *l.*
5:17 reign in *l.* by one, Jesus Christ
8: 2 law of the Spirit of *l.* in Christ
8: 6 to be spiritually minded is *l.* and
2 Cor 2:16 to the other, the savour of *l.* unto *l.*
3: 6 letter killeth, the spirit giveth *l.*
4:11 *l.* of Jesus might be manifest
5: 4 mortality swallowed up of *l.*
Gal 2:20 the *l.* which I now live in the flesh
Eph 4:18 alienated from a *l.* of God
Col 3: 3 your *l.* is hid with Christ
3: 4 when Christ our *l.* shall appear
1 Tim 2: 2 a peaceable *l.* in all godliness
4: 8 having the promise of the *l.* that
2 Tim 1:10 brought *l.* and immortality to light
2 Pet 1: 3 that pertain unto *l.* and godliness
1 John 5:12 he that hath the Son hath *l.*

LIFT UP (LIFTED, LIFTING)
Num 6:26 *l.* his countenance upon thee
2 Chr 17: 6 heart *l.* in ways of the Lord
Ps 4: 6 Lord *l.* the light of countenance
7: 6 Lord *l.* thyself because of rage
24: 7 *l.* up your heads, O ye gates
25: 1 to thee I *l.* my soul
75: 4 wicked *l.* not the horn
83: 2 they that hate thee *l.* the head
102:10 thou hast *l.* and cast me down
121: 1 *l.* mine eyes unto the hills
141: 2 *l.* of my hands as the evening
Eccl 4:10 one will *l.* his fellow
Is 33:10 now will I *l.* myself
26:11 Lord, when thy hand is *l.*
42: 2 he shall not cry, nor *l.*
Jer 7:16 neither *l.* cry nor prayer for them
Lam 3:41 let us *l.* our hearts with
Hab 2: 4 his soul which is *l.* is not upright
John 3:14 so must the Son of man be *l.*
8:28 when ye have *l.* the Son of man
12:32 if I be *l.* will draw all men
1 Tim 2: 8 *l.* holy hands, without wrath
Heb 12:12 *l.* the hands which hang
Jas 4:10 Lord and he shall *l.* you up

LIGHT
Gen 1: 3 let there be *l.*
Num 21: 5 our soul loatheth this *l.* bread
Judg 9: 4 vain and *l.* persons which followed
1 Ki 16:31 it had been a *l.* thing
Job 18: 5 *l.* of the wicked put out
25: 3 on whom doth not his *l.* arise
33:30 enlightened with the *l.* of the living
Ps 4: 6 lift up the *l.* of thy countenance
36: 9 in thy *l.* shall we see *l.*
43: 3 O send out thy *l.* and thy truth
90: 8 sins in the *l.* of thy countenance
97:11 *l.* is sown for the righteous
104: 2 coverest thyself with *l.* as a
112: 4 to the upright ariseth *l.* in
119:105 and a *l.* unto my path
Prov 4:18 path of the just is as shining *l.*
6:23 and the law is *l.*, and reproofs

Prov 15:30 *l.* of the eyes rejoiceth the
Eccl 11: 7 *l.* is sweet and a pleasant
Is 5:20 darkness for *l.* and *l.* for
5:30 the *l.* is darkened in the heavens
8:20 because there is no *l.* in them
9: 2 in darkness have seen a great *l.*
30:26 *l.* of the moon shall be as the *l.*
42: 6 a *l.* of the Gentiles
45: 7 I form *l.* and create darkness
49: 6 it is a *l.* thing
50:10 walketh in darkness and hath no *l.*
58: 8 thy *l.* break forth as morning
58:60 shine; for thy *l.* is come
Ezek 8:17 Is it a *l.* thing
Zeph 3: 4 her prophets are *l.* and
Zech 14: 6 *l.* shall not be clear nor
14: 7 evening time it shall be *l.*
Mat 5:14 ye are the *l.* of the world
5:16 let your *l.* so shine before men
11:30 my yoke easy, my burden *l.*
Luke 2:32 a *l.* to lighten the Gentiles
16: 8 wiser than the children of *l.*
John 1: 4 the life was the *l.* of men
1: 7 came to bear witness of the *l.*
1: 9 true *l.* that lighteth every man
3:19 loved darkness rather than *l.*
3:20 neither cometh to the *l.*, lest
5:35 a burning and a shining *l.*
8:12 I am the *l.* of the world
8:12 shall have the *l.* of life
12:35 walk while ye have the *l.*
Acts 13:47 I have set thee for a *l.*
26:18 turn them from darkness to *l.*
Rom 13:12 put on the armour of *l.*
2 Cor 4: 4 the *l.* of the glorious gospel
4:17 our *l.* affliction which is
6:14 what communion hath *l.* with darkness
Eph 5: 8 walk as children of *l.*
5:14 Christ shall give thee *l.*
1 Thes 5: 5 ye are the children of *l.*
1 Pet 2: 9 to his marvellous *l.*
1 John 1: 5 God is *l.* and in him is
Rev 21:23 the Lamb is the *l.* thereof

LIGHTS
Ps 136: 7 to him that made great *l.*; for his
Ezek 32: 8 all the bright *l.* of heaven
Luke 12:35 girded about and your *l.* burning
Phil 2:15 ye shine as *l.* in the world
Jas 1:17 down from the father of *l.*

LIGHTEN (LIGHTENED)
2 Sam 22:29 Lord will *l.* my darkness
Ezra 9: 8 God may *l.* our eyes
Ps 13: 3 God: *l.* mine eyes lest I sleep
34: 5 looked unto him, and were *l.*
Rev 21:23 glory of God did *l.* it

LIGHTNING (LIGHTNINGS)
Ex 19:16 there were thunders and *l.*
Ps 18:14 and he shot out *l.*
Mat 24:27 as the *l.* cometh out of the
28: 3 his countenance was like *l.*
Luke 10:18 Satan as *l.* fall from heaven

LIKE
1 Cor 16:13 quit you *l.* men, be strong
Heb 2:17 be made *l.* his brethren
1 John 3: 2 we shall be *l.* him

LIKENESS
Gen 1:26 in our image, after our *l.*
5: 3 begat a son in his own *l.*
Ps 17:15 when I awake with thy *l.*
Rom 6: 5 together in the *l.* of his death
8: 3 in the *l.* of sinful flesh
Phil 2: 7 made in the *l.* of men

LINE (LINES)
Ps 16: 6 *l.* are fallen unto me in pleasant
Is 28:13 *l.* upon *l.*, *l.* upon *l.*
28:17 judgment will I lay to the *l.*
34:11 stretch out on it a *l.* of confusion

2 Cor 10:16 boast in another man's *l.* of things

LION (LIONS)
Gen 49: 9 Judah is a *l.* whelp
Judg 14:18 what is stronger than a *l.*
Job 4:11 *l.* should perish for lack of prey
28: 8 the *l.* whelps have not trodden
Ps 7: 2 tear my soul like a *l.*
22:13 ravening and a roaring *l.*
Prov 22:13 there is a *l.* without
28: 1 righteous are bold as a *l.*
Is 11: 6 calf and young *l.* and the fatling
35: 9 no *l.* shall be there, nor
38:13 as a *l.* so will he break all my
65:25 *l.* shall eat straw like the bullock
Ezek 1:10 face of a *l.*, on the right side
Hos 5:14 and as a young *l.* to the house
2 Tim 4:17 delivered out of the mouth of the *l.*
1 Pet 5: 8 the devil as a roaring *l.* walketh
Rev 4: 7 beast was like a *l.*
5: 5 *L.* of the tribe of Judah

LIPS
Ex 6:30 I am of uncircumcised *l.*
Ps 12: 3 cut off all flattering *l.*
17: 1 goeth not out of feigned *l.*
17: 4 by the word or thy *l.* I have kept me
31:18 lying *l.* be put to silence
45: 2 grace is poured into thy *l.*
51:15 open thou my *l.*
63: 3 my *l.* shall praise thee
63: 5 praise thee with joyful *l.*
141: 3 keep the door of my *l.*
Prov 10:18 hideth hatred with lying *l.*
10:21 *l.* of the righteous feed many
16:10 in the *l.* of the king
17: 4 giveth heed to false *l.*
26:23 burning *l.* and a wicked heart
Sol 7: 9 *l.* of those that are asleep to speak
Is 6: 5 I am a man of unclean *l.*
57:19 I create the fruit of the *l.*
59: 3 your *l.* have spoken lies
Mal 2: 7 priest's *l.* should keep knowledge

LITTLE
Ezra 9: 8 now for a *l.* space grace hath
Neh 9:32 trouble seem *l.* before thee
Ps 2:12 his wrath is kindled but a *l.*
8: 5 a *l.* lower than the angels
37:16 a *l.* that a righteous man hath
Prov 6:10 a *l.* sleep, a *l.* slumber, a *l.*
15:16 better is a *l.* with fear
16: 8 better is a *l.* with righteousness
Is 28:10 here a *l.* and there a *l.*
54: 8 in a *l.* wrath I hid my face
Ezek 11:16 will I be to them as a *l.* sanctuary
Mat 6:30 O ye of *l.* faith
14:31 O thou of *l.* faith
Luke 12:32 fear not, *l.* flock, it is
19:17 been faithful in a very *l.*
1 Tim 4: 8 bodily exercise profiteth *l.*
Heb 2: 7 a *l.* lower then the angels
Rev 3: 8 hast a *l.* strength, and hast kept

LIVE
Gen 3:22 of life and eat and *l.* forever
17:18 Ishmael might *l.* before thee
Lev 18: 5 if a man do, he shall *l.*
Job 14:14 if a man die, shall he *l.* again
Ps 55:23 men shall not *l.* out half their days
63: 4 will I bless thee while I *l.*
118:17 I shall not die, but *l.* and
146: 2 while I *l.* will I praise
Is 38:16 recover me and make me to *l.*
55: 3 hear, and your soul shall *l.*
Ezek 3:21 he shall surely *l.*, because he is
16: 6 wast in thy blood, *L.*; yea, I said
18:32 turn yourselves and *l.*
33:16 lawful and right, he shall surely *l.*
Hab 2: 4 the just shall *l.* by faith
Mat 4: 4 man shall not *l.* by bread alone
Acts 17:28 in him we *l.* and move and have
Rom 8:13 if ye *l.* after the flesh, ye
10: 5 those things shall *l.* by them

Rom 14: 8 whether we *l.*, we *l.* unto the Lord
1 Cor 9:14 they which preach the gospel *l.* of
2 Cor 5:15 which *l.* should not *l.* to themselves
6: 9 as dying, and behold we *l.*
13:11 be of one mind, *l.* in peace
Gal 2:20 *l.* in the flesh, I *l.* by the faith
3:12 shall *l.* in them
5:25 if we *l.* in Spirit, walk in
Phil 1:21 to *l.* is Christ, and to die is
2 Tim 3:12 all that will *l.* godly in Christ
Tit 2:12 we should *l.* soberly
Heb 13:18 willing to *l.* honestly
1 Pet 2:24 should *l.* unto righteousness, by
1 John 4: 9 would that we might *l.* through him

LIVED (LIVETH)
Job 19:25 for I know that my Redeemer *l.*
Acts 23: 1 *l.* in all good conscience before God
Rom 6:10 in that he *l.*, he *l.* unto God
1 Tim 5: 6 *l.* in pleasure is dead while she *l.*
Heb 7:25 he ever *l.* to make intercession
Jas 5: 5 ye have *l.* in pleasure on the earth
Rev 1:18 he that *l.* and was dead
18: 9 *l.* deliciously with her, shall bewail

LIVELY
Acts 7:38 received the *l.* oracles to give unto
1 Pet 1: 3 begotten again to a *l.* hope
2: 5 ye, as *l.* stones, are built up a

LIVING
Eccl 7: 2 *l.* will lay it to heart
Is 38:19 the *l.*, the *l.* shall praise
Jer 2:13 fountain of *l.* waters, and hewed them
Mat 22:32 God of the dead, but of the *l.*
John 7:38 shall flow rivers of *l.* water
Rom 12: 1 present your bodies a *l.* sacrifice
14: 9 Lord both of the dead and *l.*
1 Cor 15:45 first man Adam made a *l.* soul
Heb 10:20 by a new and *l.* way, which he hath
1 Pet 2: 4 coming as to a *l.* stone, disallowed
Rev 7:17 lead them to *l.* fountains

LOFTY
Ps 131: 1 not haughty nor mine eyes *l.*
Prov 30:13 how *l.* are their eyes
Is 2:11 *l.* looks of man shall be humbled
57:15 *l.* One that inhabiteth eternity

LOINS
Prov 31:17 she girdeth her *l.* with strength
Is 11: 5 shall be the girdle of his *l.*
Luke 12:35 let your *l.* be girded
Eph 6:14 *l.* girt about with truth
1 Pet 1:13 gird up the *l.* of your mind

LONG (LONGED, LONGETH, LONGING)
Job 6: 8 the thing that I *l.* for
Ps 63: 1 my flesh *l.* for thee
84: 2 my soul *l.*, yea, even fainteth
107: 9 he satisfieth the *l.* soul
119:20 my soul breaketh for the *l.*
119:40 I have *l.* after thy precepts
119:131 I have *l.* for thy commandments
119:174 I have *l.* for thy salvation
Rom 1:11 for I *l.* to see you

LONGSUFFERING
Ex 34: 6 gracious, *l.*, and abundant
Num 14:18 the Lord is *l.* and of great mercy
Ps 86:15 compassion, and gracious, *l.*
Jer 15:15 take me not away in thy *l.*
Rom 2: 4 goodness, and forbearance, and *l.*
9:22 endured with much *l.* the vessels
Gal 5:22 joy peace, *l.*, gentleness
Eph 4: 2 meekness, with *l.*, forbearing one
Col 1:11 unto all patience, and *l.*
3:12 humbleness of mind, meekness, and *l.*
1 Tim 1:16 Christ might show forth all *l.*
2 Tim 3:10 purpose, faith, *l.*, charity, patience
4: 2 exhort with all *l.* and doctrine

1 Pet 3:20 when once the *l.* of God waited in
2 Pet 3: 9 but is *l.* to us-ward

LOOK (LOOKED)
Gen 13:14 and *l.* from the place where
29:32 the Lord *l.* on my affliction
Ex 2:25 God *l.* upon the children
4:31 he had *l.* upon their affliction
10:10 *l.* to it; for evil is before you
Ps 34: 5 they *l.* to him and were lightened
Sol 1: 6 *l.* not upon me, because I am black
Is 5: 7 he *l.* for judgment, but behold
8:17 of Jacob, and I will *l.* for him
22:11 ye have not *l.* to the maker of
45:22 *l.* unto me and be saved
64: 3 didst terrible things we *l.* not for
66: 2 to this man will I *l.*
Jer 8:15 we *l.* for peace, but no good came
Mic 7: 7 I will *l.* unto the Lord
Hag 1: 9 ye *l.* for much and lo, it came to
Luke 2:38 that *l.* for redemption in Jerusalem
7:19 or *l.* we for another
22:61 the Lord turned and *l.* upon Peter
2 Cor 4:18 we *l.* not at things seen
Phil 2: 4 *l.* not every man on his own
3:20 heaven, from whence also we *l.* for
Heb 9:28 unto them that *l.* for him he shall
11:10 for he *l.* for a city which hath
1 Pet 1:12 things the angels desire to *l.* into
1 John 1: 1 that which we have *l.* on

LOOKETH (LOOKING)
1 Sam 16: 7 *l.* on outward appearance, but the
Ps 33:13 the Lord *l.* from heaven
Prov 14:15 prudent man *l.* well to his
Sol 2: 9 he *l.* forth at the windows, showing
Is 38:14 mine eyes fail with *l.* upward
Mat 5:28 whosoever *l.* on a woman to lust after
24:50 come in a day he *l.* not for
Luke 9:62 *l.* back is fit for the kingdom of God
Tit 2:13 *l.* for that blessed hope
Heb 10:27 a certain fearful *l.* for
12: 2 *l.* to Jesus, the author and
Jas 1:25 *l.* into the perfect law of
2 Pet 3:12 *l.* for and hasting unto the coming
Jude 1:21 *l.* for the mercy of our Lord

LOOKS
Ps 18:27 wilt bring down high *l.*

LOOSE (LOOSED, LOOSETH)
Deut 25: 9 and *l.* his shoe from his foot
Josh 5:15 *l.* thy shoe from thy foot
Ps 102:20 to *l.* those appointed to death
146: 7 Lord *l.* the prisoners
Eccl 12: 6 or ever the silver cord be *l.*
Acts 2:24 *l.* the pains of death
1 Cor 7:27 seek not to be *l.* Art thou *l.*

LORD
Gen 15: 6 he believed in the *L.*
Ex 34: 6 *L.*, the *L.* God, merciful
Deut 4:35 *L.* he is God; there is none else
6: 4 O Israel, the *L.* our God is one *L.*
10:17 the *L.* your God is God of gods
1 Sam 2: 1 heart rejoiced in the *L.*
1 Ki 18:39 the *L.*, he is the God
2 Ki 18: 5 he trusted in the *L.* God
Neh 9: 6 art thou, even thou *L.* alone; thou
Ps 4: 5 put your trust in the *L.*
31:24 hope in the *L.*
34: 2 soul make her boast in the *L.*
37: 3 Trust in the *L.*
37: 4 delight thyself in the *L.*
97:12 rejoice in the *L.*, ye righteous
100: 3 the *L.*, he is God, it is he that
104:34 will be glad in the *L.*
118:27 God is the *L.*, which hath shown
Prov 3: 5 trust in the *L.* with
Is 26: 4 trust ye in the *L.*
37:20 therefore, oh *L.* our God
45:17 Israel shall be saved in the *L.*
45:24 in the *L.* have I righteousness
45:25 in the *L.* all the seed of Israel
61:10 greatly rejoice in the *L.*
Dan 2:47 and a *L.* of kings, and a revealer
Joel 2:23 rejoice in the *L.* your God
Zeph 3: 2 she trusted not in the *L.*
Zech 10: 7 heart shall rejoice in the *L.*
Mark 2:28 Son of man is *L.* of the sabbath
Acts 2:36 crucified, both *L.* and Christ
Rom 10:12 same *L.* over all is rich
14: 9 *L.* of the dead and of the living
16:12 labour in the *L.*
1 Cor 2: 8 have crucified the *L.* of glory
8: 6 one God, one *L.* Jesus Christ
15:47 second man is the *L.* from heaven
15:58 abounding in the work of the *L.*
Eph 4: 5 one *L.*, one faith, one baptism
Phil 3: 1 rejoice in the *L.*
Col 4: 7 fellow servant in the *L.*
1 Thes 5:12 over you in the *L.*
1 Tim 6:15 king of kings and *L.* of lords
Rev 14:13 dead which die in the *L.*
17:14 he is the *L.* of lords, and king
19:16 and *L.* of lords

LOSE (LOST)
Ps 119:176 astray like *l.* sheep
Prov 23: 8 and *l.* thy sweet words
Eccl 3: 6 and a time to *l.*; a time to
Ezek 37:11 our hope is *l.*, we are cut
Mat 5:13 if salt have *l.* his savour
10: 6 to the *l.* sheep of the house of
10:42 in no wise *l.* his reward
16:26 and *l.* his own soul
18:11 save that which was *l.*
Luke 15: 4 hundred sheep, if he *l.* one
19:10 save that which is *l.*
15:32 thy brother was *l.* and is found
John 6:39 I should *l.* nothing
2 Cor 4: 3 gospel be hid, hid to them that are *l.*
2 John 1: 8 that we *l.* not those things

LOSS
1 Cor 3:15 he shall suffer *l.*
Phil 3: 8 I have suffered the *l.*

LOT (LOTS)
Lev 16:10 on which the *l.* fell
Josh 15: 1 the *l.* of the tribe
1 Sam 14:41 Give a perfect *l.*
Ps 16: 5 thou maintainest my *l.*
22:18 cast *l.* upon my vesture
125: 3 not rest upon the *l.* of the righteous
Prov 16:33 the *l.* is cast into the lap
18:18 *l.* causeth contentions to cease
Mat 27:35 parted his garments, casting *l.*
Mark 15:24 casting *l.* upon them
Acts 1:26 the *l.* fell on Matthias

LOVE
Gen 27: 4 meat, such as I *l.*
Lev 19:18 thou shalt *l.* thy neighbour as thyself
Deut 6: 5 shalt *l.* the Lord thy God with all
7: 7 Lord did not set his *l.* upon you
10:12 to *l.* him and to serve
2 Sam 1:26 passing the *l.* of women
Ps 18: 1 I will *l.* thee, oh Lord
31:23 *l.* the Lord, all ye his saints
116: 1 I *l.* the Lord because
119:97 O, how *l.* I thy law. It is
145:20 Lord preserveth them that *l.* him
Eccl 9: 1 no man knoweth either *l.*
Sol 1: 4 the upright *l.* thee
2: 5 I am sick of *l.*
8: 6 *l.* is strong as death
Jer 2: 2 the *l.* of thine espousals
31: 3 loved thee with everlasting *l.*
Ezek 16: 8 thy time was the time of *l.*
33:31 their mouth they show much *l.*
Zech 8:19 *l.* the truth and peace
Mat 5:44 *l.* your enemies, bless
19:19 *l.* thy neighbor as thyself
22:37 *l.* the Lord thy God
22:39 *l.* thy neighbor as thyself
24:12 *l.* of many shall wax cold
Luke 11:42 over judgment, and the *l.* of God
John 5:42 have not the *l.* of God
13:34 that ye also *l.* one another
14:23 if a man *l.* me, he will keep
15: 9 continue ye in my *l.*
15:13 greater *l.* hath no man than this
15:17 that ye *l.* one another
Rom 5: 5 *l.* of God is shed abroad in our
8:35 separate us from the *l.* of Christ
12: 9 let *l.* be without dissimulation
13: 8 but to *l.* one another
13:10 *l.* is the fulfilling of the law
15:30 Christ's sake, and the *l.* of Spirit
1 Cor 16:22 if any man *l.* not the Lord
2 Cor 5:14 *l.* of Christ constraineth
13:14 and the *l.* of God, and the communion
Gal 5: 6 faith which worketh by *l.*
5:13 by *l.* serve one another
5:14 *l.* thy neighbor as thyself
5:22 fruit of the Spirit is *l.*, joy, peace
Eph 1: 4 without blame before him in *l.*
3:17 rooted and grounded in *l.*
4: 2 forbearing one another in *l.*
4:15 speaking truth in *l.*
5: 2 walk in *l.* as Christ hath loved
5:25 *l.* your wives, even as Christ
Col 2: 2 knit together in *l.* and
3:19 Husbands, *l.* your wives
1 Thes 1: 3 your labour of *l.*, and patience of
3:12 abound in *l.* toward one another
5: 8 breastplate of faith and *l.*
5:13 esteem very highly in *l.*
2 Thes 2:10 received not the *l.* of truth
3: 5 hearts into the *l.* of God
2 Tim 4: 8 unto them also that *l.* his appearing
Heb 13: 1 let brotherly *l.* continue
Jas 2: 8 *l.* thy neighbor as thyself
1 Pet 1: 8 having not seen, ye *l.*
1:22 see that ye *l.* one another
2:17 *l.* the brotherhood
1 John 2: 5 in him is the *l.* of God perfected
2:15 *l.* not the world, neither the things
3: 1 what manner of *l.* the Father hath
3:16 perceive we the *l.* of God
3:23 and *l.* one another
4: 7 for *l.* is of God
4: 8 knoweth not God, for God is *l.*
4: 9 in this was manifested the *l.* of God
4:12 If we *l.* one another
4:18 there is no fear in *l.*
4:19 we *l.* him because he first
4:21 who loveth God *l.* his brother
5: 3 the *l.* of God that we keep his commandments
2 John 1: 1 whom I *l.* in the truth, and
Rev 2: 4 thou hast left thy first *l.*
3:19 as many as I *l.* I rebuke

LOVED
Deut 7: 8 because the Lord *l.* you
33: 3 he *l.* the people, all his saints
1 Sam 18: 1 *l.* him as his own soul
2 Sam 12:24 and the Lord *l.* him.
1 Ki 3: 3 Solomon *l.* the Lord
10: 9 the Lord *l.* Israel for ever
Hos 11: 1 Israel was a child, then I *l.* him
Mal 1: 2 yet I have *l.* Jacob
Mark 10:21 Jesus beholding him, *l.* him
Luke 7:47 are forgiven, for she *l.* much
John 3:16 God so *l.* the world that
3:19 men *l.* darkness rather than
12:43 *l.* the praise of men more
13: 1 having *l.* his own, which were in
13:23 one of his disciples whom Jesus *l.*
14:28 if ye *l.* me, ye would rejoice
15: 9 as my Father *l.* me, so have I *l.*
16:27 Father loveth you because ye *l.* me
17:23 hast *l.* them as thou hast *l.* me
17:26 wherewith thou hast *l.* me
21: 7 whom Jesus *l.* saith unto Peter
Rom 8:37 conquerors through him that *l.* us
9:13 Jacob I *l.*, Esau I hated
Gal 2:20 Son of God, who *l.* me

Eph 2: 4 great love wherewith he *l.* us
5: 2 walk in love, as Christ *l.* us
5:25 wives as Christ *l.* the church
2 Thes 2:16 Father, which hath *l.* us
2 Tim 4:10 *l.* this present world, and is
Heb 1: 9 hast *l.* righteousness and hated
2 Pet 2:15 who *l.* the wages of unrighteousness
1 John 4:10 that we *l.* God, but that he *l.* us
Rev 1: 5 that *l.* us and washed us
12:11 *l.* not their lives unto death

LOVETH
Ps 146: 8 the Lord *l.* the righteous
Prov 3:12 whom the Lord *l.* he correcteth
17:17 a friend *l.* at all times
21:17 he that *l.* pleasure shall be poor
Sol 1: 7 whom my soul *l.*, where thou
Mat 10:37 *l.* father or mother more than me
John 3:35 Father *l.* the Son and hath
2 Cor 9: 7 God *l.* a cheerful giver
Heb 12: 6 whom the Lord *l.*, he chasteneth
3 John 1: 9 Diotrephes, who *l.* to have the
Rev 22:15 whosoever *l.* and maketh a lie

LOVINGKINDNESS
Ps 36: 7 how excellent is thy *l.*
36:10 O continue thy *l.* unto them
63: 3 thy *l.* is better than life
103: 4 who crowneth thee with *l.*
Is 63: 7 I will mention the *l.* of the Lord
Jer 9:24 the Lord which exercise *l.*
31: 3 with *l.* have I drawn thee
32:18 thou showest *l.* to thousands
Hos 2:19 in *l.* and in mercies

LOW
Deut 28:43 shalt come down very *l.*
Job 40:12 that is proud and bring him *l.*
Ps 49: 2 both *l.* and high, rich and
136:23 remembered us in our *l.* estate
Prov 29:23 man's pride shall bring him *l.*
Is 26: 5 the lofty city, he layeth it *l.*
32:19 city shall be *l.* in a *l.* place
Luke 1:48 he hath regarded the *l.* estate
3: 5 every mountain and hill shall be brought *l.*

LOWLINESS
Eph 4: 2 with all *l.* and meekness
Phil 2: 3 but in *l.* of mind let each

LOWLY
Ps 138: 6 yet hath he respect to the *l.*
Prov 3:34 he giveth grace unto the *l.*
11: 2 with the *l.* is wisdom
Mat 11:29 learn of me, I am meek and *l.*

LUCRE
1 Tim 3: 3 not greed of filthy *l.*
3: 8 not greedy of filthy *l.*
Tit 1: 7 not given to filthy *l.*
1 Pet 5: 2 not for filthy *l.*, but of a ready

LUKEWARM
Rev 3:16 then because thou art *l.*

LUST (LUSTETH)
Ex 15: 9 my *l.* shall be satisfied
Ps 78:18 asking meat for their *l.*
81:12 up to their own hearts' *l.*
Mat 5:28 looketh on a woman to *l.* after her
Rom 7: 7 I had not known *l.* except the law
1 Cor 10: 6 not *l.* after evil things
Gal 5:16 shall not fulfil the *l.* of the flesh
5:17 flesh *l.* against the Spirit
1 Thes 4: 5 not in the *l.* of concupiscence
Jas 4: 2 Ye *l.* and have not: ye kill
1 John 2:16 *l.* of the flesh, and *l.* of

LUSTS
Mark 4:19 *l.* of other things entering in
John 8:44 *l.* of your father ye will do
Rom 6:12 ye should obey it in the *l.* thereof
13:14 for the flesh, to fulfil the *l.*
Rom 13:24 crucified flesh with affections and *l.*
1 Tim 6: 9 foolish and hurtful *l.*
2 Tim 2:22 flee also youthful *l.*: but follow
3: 6 laden with sins, led away with *l.*
Tit 2:12 denying ungodliness and worldly *l.*
3: 3 serving divers *l.* and pleasures
Jas 4: 3 ye may consume it upon your *l.*
1 Pet 2:11 abstain from fleshly *l.*
4: 2 no longer live to the *l.* of men
2 Pet 3: 3 walking after their own *l.*
Jude 1:18 walk after their own ungodly *l.*

M

MAD
Deut 28:34 thou shalt be *m.* for the sight
1 Sam 21:13 feigned himself *m.* in their hands
Jer 50:38 they are *m.* upon idols
Hos 9: 7 prophet is a fool, spiritual man is *m.*
John 10:20 he hath a devil and is *m.*
Acts 26:11 being exceedingly *m.* against them, I
26:24 much learning doth make thee *m.*

MADNESS
Deut 28:28 Lord shall smite thee with *m.*
Eccl 1:17 and to know *m.* and folly
2:12 myself to behold wisdom and *m.*
Zech 12: 4 astonishment, and his horse with *m.*
Luke 6:11 they were filled with *m.*
2 Pet 2:16 forbad the *m.* of the prophet

MAGNIFY (MAGNIFIED)
Gen 19:19 thou hast *m.* thy mercy
Josh 3: 7 I begin to *m.* thee
2 Sam 7:26 let thy name be *m.* for
1 Chr 29:25 the Lord *m.* Solomon exceedingly
Job 7:17 man, that thou shouldest *m.* him
Ps 34: 3 *m.* the Lord with me
35:27 let the Lord be *m.*
69:30 *m.* him with thanksgiving
138: 2 hast *m.* thy word above
Is 42:21 *m.* the law, and make it
Luke 1:46 my soul doth *m.* the Lord
Acts 10:46 spake with tongues, *m.* God
19:17 name of Lord Jesus was *m.*
Phil 1:20 Christ be *m.* in my body

MAJESTY
1 Chr 29:11 victory and the *m.*: for all that is
Job 40:10 deck thyself now with *m.*
Ps 21: 5 honour and *m.* hast thou laid
29: 4 voice of the Lord is full of *m.*
45: 4 in thy *m.* ride prosperously
93: 1 he is clothed with *m.*; the Lord
145: 5 of the glorious honour of thy *m.*
145:12 and the glorious *m.* of his kingdom
Is 2:10 for glory of his *m.*
Dan 4:36 excellent *m.* was added unto
Heb 1: 3 right hand of the *M.* on high
8: 1 throne of the *M.* in the heavens
2 Pet 1:16 but were eyewitnesses of his *m.*
Jude 1:25 be glory and *m.*, dominion and power

MAINTAIN (MAINTAINED)
1 Ki 8:45 their supplication and *m.* their cause
Job 13:15 I will *m.* mine own ways
Ps 9: 4 of my cup thou hast *m.* my right
140:12 the Lord will *m.* the cause
Tit 3: 8 might be careful to *m.* good works

MAINTAINEST
Ps 16: 5 thou *m.* my lot

MAKE (MADE)
Gen 1:26 Let us *m.* man in our
3: 6 desired to *m.* one wise
Ex 2:14 who *m.* thee a prince
Deut 32:35 come upon them *m.* haste
1 Sam 20:38 *m.* speed, haste, stay not
2 Sam 13: 6 and *m.* himself sick
Ps 104:24 in wisdom hast thou *m.* them all
139:14 fearfully and wonderfully *m.*
Prov 16: 4 Lord hath *m.* all things for himself
John 1: 3 all things were *m.* by him
Rom 1: 3 Christ, *m.* of the seed of David
1:20 being understood by things that are *m.*
1 Cor 1:30 who of God is *m.* unto us
4: 5 will *m.* manifest the counsels
9:22 *m.* all things to all men
Gal 4: 4 *m.* of a woman, *m.* under the law
Phil 2: 7 *m.* in the likeness of men

MAKER
Job 4:17 more pure than his *m.*?
32:22 my *m.* would soon take me
35:10 where is God my *m.*
36: 3 ascribe righteousness to my *m.*
Prov 14:31 the poor, reproacheth his *m.*
22: 2 Lord is the *m.* of them all
Is 17: 7 day shall man look to his *m.*
22:11 looked to the *m.* thereof
45: 9 unto him that striveth with his *m.*
51:13 forgettest the Lord thy *m.*
54: 5 thy *m.* is thy husband; the
Heb 11:10 whose builder and *m.* is God

MALE
Gen 1:27 *m.* and female created he them
Num 5: 3 both *m.* and female shall ye put out
Mal 1:14 hath in his flock a *m.*
Mat 19: 4 made them *m.* and female
Gal 3:28 there is neither *m.* nor female

MALICE
1 Cor 5: 8 with the leaven of *m.*
14:20 in *m.* be children, but in
Eph 4:31 away from you, with all *m.*
Col 3: 8 anger, wrath, *m.*, blasphemy
Tit 3: 3 living in *m.* and envy
1 Pet 2: 1 laying aside all *m.*

MAMMON
Mat 6:24 you cannot serve God and *m.*
Luke 16: 9 friends of the *m.* of righteousness

MAN (MAN'S)
Gen 1:27 God created *m.* in his own image
Ex 15: 3 the Lord is a *m.* of war
Num 23:19 God is not a *m.* that he
Deut 33: 1 Moses the *m.* of God blessed the
Judg 13: 8 let the *m.* of God which thou didst
2 Ki 1:13 said unto him, O *m.* of God
9:11 know the *m.*, and his communication
Job 4:17 *m.* be more just than God?
7:17 what is *m.* that thou shouldest be
11:12 for vain *m.* would be wise
14: 1 *m.* born of woman is of few days
15:14 What is *m.*, that he should be clean?
25: 4 How can *m.* be justified with God?
25: 6 much less *m.* that is a worm
Ps 8: 4 what is *m.* that thou art mindful
10:18 *m.* of the earth may no more oppress
25:12 what *m.* is he that feareth the Lord
49:12 *m.* being in honour abideth not
90: 3 thou turnest *m.* to destruction
104:23 *m.* goeth forth to his work
118: 6 not fear; what can *m.* do
Prov 1: 5 a wise *m.* will hear, and will
9: 8 rebuke a wise *m.* and he will love thee
14:16 a wise *m.* feareth and departeth
20:24 *m.* goings are of the Lord
Eccl 2:14 a wise *m.* eyes are in his head
6:10 it is known that it is *m.*
7:29 God made *m.* upright, but
10: 2 a wise *m.* heart is at his right hand
12: 5 *m.* goeth to his long home
Is 2:22 cease ye from *m.* whose breath
47: 3 I will not meet thee as a *m.*
53: 3 a *m.* of sorrows and acquainted
Jer 9:23 let not the wise *m.* glory in wisdom
15:10 borne me a *m.* of strife and
31:22 a woman shall compass a *m.*
Zech 13: 7 awake against the *m.* that
Mat 4: 4 *m.* shall not live by bread

Mat 8: 9 I am a *m.* under the authority
16:26 what shall a *m.* give in exchange
26:72 I know not the *m.*
John 3: 3 except a *m.* be born again
7:46 never *m.* spake like this *m.*
Acts 10:26 I myself also am a *m.*
Rom 6: 6 old *m.* crucified with him
7:22 in the law of God after the inward *m.*
1 Cor 2:11 *m.* knoweth the things of a *m.*
2:14 natural *m.* receiveth not things
11: 8 *m.* is not of the woman, but the
15:47 first *m.* is of the earth earthy; the
2 Cor 4:16 though outward *m.* perish, yet inward *m.* is renewed
12: 2 I knew a *m.* in Christ
Eph 4:22 the old *m.* which is corrupt
4:24 put on the new *m.*
Phil 2: 8 in fashion as a *m.* he humbled
Col 3:10 put on the new *m.*
1 Tim 6:11 O *m.* of God, flee these things
2 Tim 3:17 the *m.* of God may be perfect
Jas 3:13 who is a wise *m.* and endued with
1 Pet 3: 4 be the hidden *m.* of the heart

MANIFEST (MANIFESTED)
Eccl 3:18 that God might *m.* them
Mark 4:22 which shall not be *m.*
John 2:11 *m.* forth his glory, and his
14:21 love him and will *m.* myself to him
17: 6 I have *m.* thy name unto men
1 Cor 4: 5 make *m.* the counsels of the hearts
15:27 it is *m.* that he is excepted
Gal 5:19 works of the flesh are *m.*
1 Tim 3:16 God was *m.* in the flesh
1 John 3: 5 was *m.* to take away sin
3:10 in this children of God are *m.*
4: 9 in this was *m.* the love of God

MANIFESTATION
Rom 8:19 *m.* of the sons of God
1 Cor 12: 7 *m.* of the Spirit is given

MANIFOLD
Neh 9:27 according to thy *m.* mercies
Ps 104:24 how *m.* are thy works
Amos 5:12 I know your *m.* transgressions
Luke 18:30 receive *m.* more in this present time
Eph 3:10 known by the church the *m.* wisdom of God
1 Pet 1: 6 in heaviness through *m.* temptations
4:10 good stewards of the *m.* grace of God

MANNA
Ex 16:15 It is *m.*; for they wist not
Num 11: 6 this *m.* before our eyes
Deut 8: 3 and fed thee with *m.* which thou
8:16 fed thee in the wilderness with *m.*
Josh 5:12 the *m.* ceased on the morrow
Neh 9:20 withheldest not thy *m.* from their
Ps 78:24 rained down *m.* upon them
John 6:31 fathers did eat *m.* in
Rev 2:17 will I give to eat of the hidden *m.*

MARK (MARKED, MARKS)
Job 7:20 set me as a *m.* against thee
Ps 37:37 *m.* the perfect man and behold
130: 3 if thou shouldest *m.* iniquity
Jer 2:22 thine iniquity is *m.* before me
Ezek 9: 4 set thy *m.* on the foreheads
Rom 16:17 *m.* them which cause divisions
Gal 6:17 I bear in my body the *m.* of
Phil 3:14 I press toward the *m.*
Rev 13:17 save he that had the *m.*

MARRIAGE
Mat 22: 2 king made a *m.* for his son
25:10 that were ready went into the *m.*
John 2: 1 there was a *m.* in Cana
Heb 13: 4 *m.* is honourable in all
Rev 19: 7 *m.* of Lamb is come

MARROW
Job 21:24 bones moistened with *m.*
Ps 63: 5 soul is satisfied as with *m.*

Prov 3: 8 health to thy naval and *m.*
Is 25: 6 feast of fat things full of *m.*
Heb 4:12 joints and *m.*, and is a discerner

MARRY (MARRIED, MARRIETH)
Gen 38: 8 thy brother's wife, and *m.* her
Deut 25: 5 the wife of the dead shall not *m.*
Is 62: 5 as a young man *m.* a virgin
Jer 3:14 I am *m.* to you, saith Lord
Luke 14:20 I have *m.* a wife, and
1 Cor 7: 9 better to *m.* than to burn
1 Tim 4: 3 forbidding to *m.* and commanding
5:14 that younger women *m.* and

MARTYR (MARTYRS)
Acts 22:20 the blood of thy *m.* Stephen
Rev 2:13 Antipas was my faithful *m.*
17: 6 the blood of the *m.* of Jesus

MARVEL (MARVELLED)
Ps 48: 5 they saw it and so they *m.*
Eccl 5: 8 *m.* not at the matter
Mat 8:10 when Jesus heard it, he *m.*
8:27 but the men *m.*, saying, What
21:20 disciples saw it they *m.*
Mark 6: 6 he *m.* because of their unbelief
Luke 1:63 name is John And they *m.* all
John 3: 7 *M.* not that I said unto thee
5:28 *M.* not at this: for the hour
Acts 3:12 why *m.* ye at this
2: 7 were all amazed and *m.*
4:13 unlearned and ignorant men, they *m.*
1 John 3:13 *M.* not my brethren, if

MARVELLOUS
1 Chr 16:12 remember his *m.* works
Job 5: 9 unsearchable *m.* things without number
10:16 showed thyself *m.* upon me
Ps 17: 7 show thy *m.* kindness
98: 1 for he hath done *m.* things
105: 5 remember his *m.* works
139:14 *m.* are thy works; and that my soul
Mic 7:15 show unto him *m.* things
1 Pet 2: 9 out of darkness into his *m.* light
Rev 15: 3 Great and *m.* are thy works

MASTER (MASTERS)
Eccl 12:11 by the *m.* of assemblies
Is 24: 2 the servant so with his *m.*
Mal 1: 6 and a servant his *m.*
Mat 6:24 no man can serve two *m.*
23:10 neither be ye called *m.*
John 3:10 art thou a *m.* of Israel
13:13 ye call me *M.* and Lord
13:14 your Lord and *M.* have washed your
Rom 14: 4 to his own *m.* he standeth
Eph 6: 9 ye *m.* do the same thing unto them
Col 4: 1 *m.* give unto your servants that
Jas 3: 1 be not many *m.*, knowing we shall

MATTER (MATTERS)
Ex 18:22 that every great *m.* they bring
1 Sam 10:16 of the *m.* of the kingdom
Job 32:18 for I am full of *m.*
33:13 account of any of his *m.*
Ps 45: 1 my heart is inditing a good *m.*
131: 1 exercise myself in great *m.*
Dan 7:28 I kept the *m.* in my heart
Acts 8:21 part nor lot in this *m.*
2 Cor 9: 5 be ready as a *m.* of bounty
1 Pet 4:15 busybody in other men's *m.*

MEAN (MEANT)
Gen 50:20 but God *m.* it unto good
Ex 12:26 what *m.* you by this service
Deut 6:20 what *m.* the testimonies
Josh 4:21 What *m.* these stones
Ezek 17:12 Know ye not what these things *m.*
Acts 17:20 know therefore what these things *m.*
21:13 what *m.* ye to weep and to break

MEANEST
Ezek 37:18 what thou *m.* by these

Jonah 1: 6 what *m.* thou O sleeper

MEANS
Ps 49: 7 by any *m.* redeem his brother
Jer 5:31 priests bear rule by their *m.*
1 Cor 9:22 might by all *m.* save some
Phil 3:11 If by any *m.* I might attain
1 Thes 3: 5 lest by some *m.* the tempter

MEASURE
Lev 19:35 in weight or in *m.*
Deut 25:15 perfect and just *m.* shalt
Job 11: 9 the *m.* is longer than the earth
Ps 39: 4 the *m.* of my days, what it is
Is 27: 8 in *m.* when it shooteth forth
Jer 30:11 I will correct thee in *m.*
Mat 7: 2 with what *m.* ye mete
23:32 fill up the *m.* of your fathers
John 3:34 giveth not the Spirit by *m.*
2 Cor 1: 8 that we were pressed out of *m.*
12: 7 lest I be exalted above *m.*
Eph 4: 7 according to the *m.* of the gift of
4:13 unto the *m.* of the stature of
Rev 11: 1 Rise, and *m.* the temple of God

MEAT (MEATS)
Job 6: 7 are as my sorrowful *m.*
Ps 42: 3 my tears have been my *m.*
104:27 give them their *m.* in due season
111: 5 given *m.* to them that fear him
Prov 6: 8 provideth her *m.* in the summer
Hos 11: 4 I laid *m.* unto them
Hab 1:16 is fat and their *m.* plenteous
3:17 the fields shall yield no *m.*
Hag 2:12 or wine, or oil, of any *m.*
Mal 1:12 even his *m.* is contemptible
Mat 6:25 is not life more than *m.*
John 4:32 I have *m.* to eat ye know
4:34 my *m.* is to do the will of him
6:27 labour not for *m.* which perisheth
6:55 my flesh is *m.* indeed
Rom 14:15 destroy not him with thy *m.*
14:17 kingdom of God is not *m.* and drink
1 Cor 6:13 *m.* for the belly, and the belly
8: 8 *m.* commendeth us not to God
10: 3 did all eat the same spiritual *m.*

MEDIATOR
Gal 3:19 by angels in the hand of a *m.*
3:20 a *m.* is not a *m.* of one
1 Tim 2: 5 one *m.* between God and men
Heb 8: 6 he is the *m.* of a better covenant
9:15 he is the *m.* of a new testament
12:24 to Jesus the *m.* of a new covenant

MEDICINE (MEDICINES)
Prov 17:22 merry heart doeth good like a *m.*
Jer 30:13 thou hast no healing *m.*
46:11 in vain shalt thou use many *m.*
Ezek 47:12 the leaf thereof, for *m.*

MEDITATE
Gen 24:63 Issac went out to *m.* in
Josh 1: 8 shalt *m.* therein, day and
Ps 1: 2 in his law doth he *m.* day and night
63: 6 *m.* on thee in the night watches
77:12 I will *m.* also of all thy work
119:15 I will *m.* in thy precepts
Is 33:18 thine heart shall *m.* terror
Luke 21:14 not *m.* before what ye shall answer
1 Tim 4:15 *m.* upon these things

MEDITATION
Ps 5: 1 words, O Lord, consider my *m.*
49: 3 *m.* of my heart shall be of understanding
104:34 my *m.* of him shall be sweet
119:97 thy law! It is my *m.* all the day
119:99 thy testimonies are my *m.*

MEEK
Num 12: 3 Moses was very *m.* above all
Ps 22:26 *m.* shall eat and be satisfied
25: 9 *m.* will he guide in judgment

Ps 37:11 *m.* shall inherit the earth
147: 6 the Lord lifteth up the *m.*
149: 4 beautify the *m.* with salvation
Is 11: 4 reprove with equity for the *m.*
29:19 *m.* shall increase their joy
61: 1 preach good tidings to the *m.*
Amos 2: 7 turn aside the way of the *m.*
Mat 5: 5 blessed are the *m.*: for they shall
11:29 I am *m.* and lowly in heart
1 Pet 3: 4 ornament of the *m.* and quiet spirit

MEEKNESS
Ps 45: 4 because of truth and *m.*
Zeph 2: 3 seek righteousness, seek *m.*
1 Cor 4:21 love, and in the spirit of *m.*
2 Cor 10: 1 beseech you by the *m.* and gentleness
Gal 5:23 *m.*, temperance, against such
6: 1 one in the spirit of *m.*
Eph 4: 2 walk with lowliness, *m.*
1 Tim 6:11 follow after love, patience, *m.*
2 Tim 2:25 in *m.* instructing those that oppose
Tit 3: 2 showing all *m.* unto all men
Jas 1:21 receive with *m.* the engrafted word
3:13 works with *m.* of wisdom
1 Pet 3:15 hope that is in you with *m.* and fear

MEET (MEETEST)
Gen 2:18 make him an help *m.* for him
Job 34:31 it is *m.* to be said to God
Is 47: 3 I will not *m.* thee as a man
64: 5 thou *m.* him that rejoiceth
Hos 13: 8 I will *m.* them as a bear
Amos 4:12 prepare to *m.* thy God
Mat 3: 8 therefore fruits *m.* for repentance
Acts 26:20 do works *m.* for repentance
1 Cor 15: 9 not *m.* to be called an apostle
Col 1:12 *m.* to be partakers of the inheritance
1 Thes 4:17 caught up to *m.* the Lord
2 Tim 2:21 *m.* for the master's use, and prepared
Heb 6: 7 herbs *m.* for them by whom it is dressed

MEMBER (MEMBERS)
Ps 139:16 book all my *m.* were written
Mat 5:29 that one of thy *m.* should perish
Rom 6:13 neither yield ye your *m.* as
7:23 I see another law in my *m.*
12: 5 every one *m.* one of another
1 Cor 6:15 your bodies *m.* of Christ
12:12 body is one, and hath many *m.*
12:14 the body is not one *m.*, but many
Jas 3: 5 tongue is a little *m.* and
Eph 4:25 we are *m.* one of another
5:30 *m.* of his body, his flesh and
Col 3: 5 mortify your *m.* on earth

MEMORY
Ps 109:15 he may cut off the *m.* of them
145: 7 utter the *m.* of thy great goodness
Prov 10: 7 *m.* of the just is blessed
Eccl 9: 5 for the *m.* of them is forgotten
Is 26:14 made all their *m.* to perish
1 Cor 15: 2 if ye keep in *m.* what I

MEMORIAL
Ex 3:15 this is my *m.* to all generations
13: 9 for a *m.* between thine eyes
17:14 write this for a *m.* in the book
Hos 12: 5 God of hosts; the Lord is his *m.*
Mat 26:13 hath done, be told for a *m.* of her
Acts 10: 4 alms are come up for a *m.* before God

MEN
Gen 32:28 with *m.*, and hast prevailed
42:11 we are true *m.*, thy servants
Ps 9:20 know themselves to be but *m.*
17:14 *m.* which are thy hand, O Lord
82: 7 ye shall die like *m.* and fall
Eccl 12: 3 strong *m.* shall bow
Is 31: 3 Egyptians are *m.*, not God
Hos 6: 7 they like *m.* have transgressed
Mat 7:12 ye would that *m.* should do to you
Eph 6: 6 with eyeservice, as *m.* pleasers
Col 3:22 not with eyeservice as with *m.* pleasers
1 Thes 2: 4 not as pleasing *m.*, but God

MENTION
Ex 23:13 make no *m.* of the name
Job 28:18 no *m.* shall be made of coral
Ps 71:16 make *m.* of thy righteousness
Is 26:13 by thee only will we make *m.* of
62: 6 ye that make *m.* of the Lord
Rom 1: 9 make *m.* of you in my prayers
Eph 1:16 making *m.* of you in my prayers
1 Thes 1: 2 making *m.* of you in my prayers
Philem 1: 4 *m.* of thee always in my prayers

MERCY
Gen 19:19 thou hast magnified thy *m.*
Ex 34: 7 keeping *m.* for thousands, forgiving
Num 14:18 and of great *m.*, forgiving iniquity
Deut 7: 9 which keepeth covenant and *m.*
1 Ki 8:23 who keepest covenant and *m.*
Neh 9:32 who keepest covenant and *m.*
Ps 23: 6 goodness and *m.* shall follow me
25:10 all paths of the Lord are *m.* and
33:18 them that hope in his *m.*
52: 8 I trust in the *m.* of God
57: 3 God shall send forth his *m.*
66:20 prayer nor his *m.* from me
69:13 in the multitude of thy *m.*, hear me
86: 5 plenteous in *m.* to all
101: 1 I will sing of his *m.* and
103: 8 slow to anger and plenteous in *m.*
103:17 *m.* of the Lord is from everlasting
106: 1 his *m.* endureth for ever
107: 1 his *m.* endureth forever
Prov 16: 6 by *m.* and truth iniquity is purged
20:28 *m.* and truth preserve the king and
Dan 9: 4 keeping the covenant and *m.* to them
Hos 6: 6 I desired *m.* and not sacrifice
14: 3 in thee the fatherless findeth *m.*
Jonah 2: 8 vanities forsake their own *m.*
Mic 6: 8 to do justly, and love *m.*
7:18 because he delighteth in *m.*
7:20 and the *m.* to Abraham which thou
Luke 1:50 his *m.* is on them that fear him
1:78 through the tender *m.* of our God
Rom 9:15 *m.* on whom I will have *m.*
9:23 on vessels of *m.* prepared
11:31 through your *m.* they obtain *m.*
15: 9 might glorify God for his *m.*
2 Cor 4: 1 as we have received *m.*
1 Tim 1: 2 Grace *m.* and peace from God
1:13 I obtained *m.* because I did it
2 Tim 1:18 that he may find *m.* in
Heb 4:16 we may obtain *m.* and
Jas 2:13 shall have judgment without *m.*
3:17 full of *m.* and good fruits
5:11 Lord is very pitiful and of tender *m.*
2 John 1: 3 Grace be with you, *m.*
Jude 1: 2 *m.* unto you, and peace

MERCIES
Gen 32:10 not worthy of the least of all the *m.*
1 Chr 21:13 for very great are his *m.*
Ps 25: 6 thy tender *m.* and thy lovingkindness
40:11 not thou thy tender *m.* from me
51: 1 the multitude of thy tender *m.*
145: 9 his tender *m.* are over all his
Is 55: 3 even the sure *m.* of David
Dan 9: 9 to the Lord our God belong *m.* and
Acts 13:34 will give you the sure *m.*
Rom 12: 1 I beseech you by the *m.* of God
2 Cor 1: 3 Father of *m.* and God of
Col 3:12 put on bowels of *m.*

MERCIFUL
Ex 34: 6 Lord God *m.* and gracious
2 Chr 30: 9 God is *m.* and gracious
Neh 9:31 art a *m.* and gracious God
Ps 18:25 thou wilt show thyself *m.*
37:26 he is ever *m.* and lendeth
103: 8 The Lord is *m.* and gracious
117: 2 his *m.* kindness is great toward us
Is 57: 1 *m.* men are taken away
Jer 3:12 I am *m.*, saith the Lord
Joel 2:13 for he is gracious and *m.*
Jonah 4: 2 thou art a gracious God, and *m.*
Mat 5: 7 blessed are the *m.*, for they shall
Luke 6:36 *m.*, as your Father also is *m.*
Heb 2:17 a *m.* and faithful high priest
8:12 I will be *m.* to their unrighteousness

MESSAGE
Judg 3:20 I have a *m.* from God
Hag 1:13 Lord's *m.* unto the people
1 John 1: 5 the *m.* which ye have heard

MESSENGER (MESSENGERS)
Job 33:23 if there be a *m.* with him, an
Is 14:32 answer the *m.* of a nation
42:19 who is blind or deaf, as my *m.*
44:26 that performeth counsel of his *m.*
Mal 2: 7 he is the *m.* of the Lord

MIDST
Ps 22:14 in the *m.* of my bowels
46: 5 God is in the *m.* of her, she
110: 2 in the *m.* of thine enemies
Prov 4:21 in the *m.* of thine heart
Is 41:18 in the *m.* of the valleys
Ezek 43: 9 dwell in the *m.* of them
Joel 2:27 I am in the *m.* of Israel
Zeph 3: 5 Lord is in the *m.* thereof
Phil 2:15 in the *m.* of a crooked and
Rev 1:13 in the *m.* of seven candlesticks
5: 6 in the *m.* of the elders
7:17 Lamb in the *m.* of the throne

MIGHT
Gen 49: 3 firstborn, my *m.*, and the beginning
Num 14:13 this people in thy *m.* from among them
Deut 6: 5 all thy soul, and with all thy *m.*
2 Ki 23:25 turned to the Lord with *m.*
2 Chr 20:12 no *m.* against this great company
Ps 76: 5 none of the men of *m.* found
145: 6 speak of the *m.* of thy terrible acts
Eccl 9:10 do it with thy *m.*
Is 40:29 to them that have no *m.*
Zech 4: 6 not by *m.*, nor by power, but
Eph 3:16 strengthened with *m.* by his Spirit
6:10 and in the power of his *m.*
Col 1:11 strengthened with all *m.*, according

MIGHTY (MIGHTILY)
Deut 7:23 with a *m.* destruction, until they
10:17 a great God, a *m.* and a
Judg 5:23 help of the Lord against the *m.*
Ps 24: 8 Lord strong and *m.*, the Lord *m.*
Is 5:22 *m.* to drink wine, men of strength
Jer 32:19 great in counsel, *m.* in work
Acts 18:28 he *m.* convinced the Jews
19:20 so *m.* grew the word of God
1 Cor 1:26 many *m.*, not many noble are called
2 Cor 10: 4 but *m.* through God to the pulling
Col 1:29 which worketh in me *m.*

MILK
Gen 18: 8 and he took butter and *m.*
49:12 and his teeth white with *m.*
Job 10:10 hast poured me out as *m.*
Sol 4:11 and *m.* under thy tongue
5: 1 I drunk my wine with my *m.*
Is 55: 1 buy wine and *m.* without
Joel 3:18 the hills shall flow with *m.*
Heb 5:12 such as have need of *m.*
1 Pet 2: 2 desire the sincere *m.* of the word

MIND
Gen 26:35 a grief of *m.* unto Isaac and to
Lev 24:12 the *m.* of the Lord might be shown
1 Chr 28: 9 heart and with a willing *m.*
Neh 4: 6 people had a *m.* to work
Is 26: 3 whose *m.* is stayed on thee
Luke 12:29 neither be ye of doubtful *m.*
Acts 17:11 with readiness of *m.*, and searched
20:19 serving Lord with all humility of *m.*

Luke 21:15 will give you a *m.* and
Rom 10:10 with the *m.* confession is made

MULTIPLY
Gen 16:10 I will *m.* thy seed

MULTITUDE
Ex 12:38 a mixed *m.* went up
Num 11: 4 mixed *m.* that was among them
Job 32: 7 *m.* of years should teach wisdom
Ps 5: 7 in the *m.* of thy mercy
5:10 cast them out in the *m.* of their
33:16 no king saved by the *m.* of
51: 1 unto the *m.* of thy tender mercies
94:19 in the *m.* of my thoughts
106:45 to the *m.* of his mercies
Prov 10:19 in *m.* of words wanteth not sin
11:14 in *m.* of counsellors safety
15:22 in the *m.* of counsellors
24: 6 in *m.* of counsellors there is
Eccl 5: 3 voice is known by *m.* of words
Jas 5:20 and shall hide a *m.* of sins
1 Pet 4: 8 shall cover the *m.* of sins

MURDER (MURDERS)
Mat 15:19 proceed evil thoughts, *m.*
Rom 1:29 full of envy, *m.*, debate
Gal 5:21 envyings, *m.*, drunkenness
Rev 9:21 repented they of their *m.*

MURDERER
Job 24:14 *m.* rising with the light killeth
Hos 9:13 forth his children to the *m.*
John 8:44 was a *m.* from the beginning
1 Pet 4:15 none suffer as a *m.*, or as an

MURMURED
Deut 1:27 ye *m.* in your tents
Ps 106:25 but *m.* in their tents an hearkened

MURMURERS
Jude 1:16 these are *m.*, complainers

MURMURINGS
Ex 16: 7 he heareth your *m.* against the
Phil 2:14 without *m.* and disputings

MYSTERY (MYSTERIES)
Mark 4:11 know the *m.* of the kingdom
Rom 11:25 ye should be ignorant of this *m.*
16:25 according to revelation of the *m.*
1 Cor 2: 7 wisdom of God in a *m.*, even the
4: 1 stewards of the *m.* of God
13: 2 prophecy and understand all *m.*
14: 2 in the spirit he speaketh *m.*
Eph 1: 9 made known the *m.* of
3: 4 my knowledge in the *m.* of Christ
3: 9 what is the fellowship of the *m.*
6:19 make known the *m.* of the gospel
Col 1:26 *m.* which hath been hid
1:27 glory of this *m.* among Gentiles
2: 2 acknowledgement of the *m.* of God
4: 3 to speak the *m.* of Christ
2 Thes 2: 7 *m.* of iniquity doth already work
1 Tim 3: 9 holding the *m.* of the faith
3:16 great is the *m.* of godliness
Rev 1:20 write the *m.* of seven stars
10: 7 *m.* of God should be finished

N

NAIL (NAILS)
Judg 5:26 put her hand to the *n.*
Eccl 12:11 *n.* fastened by the masters
Is 22:23 fasten him as a *n.* in a
Zech 10: 4 out of him the *n.*, out of him

NAKED
Gen 2:25 they were both *n.*, the man and
3: 7 knew that they were *n.*
3:11 told thee that thou wast *n.*
Ex 32:25 when Moses saw the people were *n.*
2 Chr 28:19 he made Judah *n.*, and transgressed
Job 1:21 *n.* came I out of my mother's womb
Mat 25:36 *n.* and ye clothed me: I was
1 Cor 4:11 hunger and thirst and are *n.*
2 Cor 5: 3 clothed we shall not be found *n.*
Heb 4:13 all things are *n.* and open
Rev 16:15 keepeth his garments, lest he walk *n.*

NAME (NAME'S)
Ex 23:13 no mention of the *n.* of other gods
23:21 for my *n.* is in him
28:12 Aaron bear their *n.* before the Lord
34:14 whose *n.* is jealous, is a jealous
Lev 18:21 profane the *n.* of thy God
2 Chr 14:11 in thy *n.* we go against this
Ps 8: 1 how excellent is thy *n.* in all
20: 1 the *n.* of the God of Jacob
48:10 according to thy *n.* so is thy
72:17 his *n.* shall endure for ever
75: 1 thy *n.* is near, thy wondrous works declare
76: 1 his *n.* is great in Israel
106: 8 he saved them for his *n.* sake
109:13 let their *n.* be blotted
138: 2 praise thy *n.* for thy lovingkindness
Prov 10: 7 the *n.* of the wicked shall rot
22: 1 a good *n.* is rather to be chosen
30: 3 what is his *n.* and what is his
Eccl 7: 1 good *n.* better than precious ointment
Sol 1: 3 thy *n.* is as ointment poured
Is 9: 6 his *n.* shall be called Wonderful
26: 8 desire of our soul is to thy *n.*
48: 9 for my *n.* sake I defer anger
55:13 shall be to the Lord for a *n.*
56: 5 a *n.* better than of sons and
62: 2 thou shalt be called by a new *n.*
64: 7 none that calleth on thy *n.*
Jer 13:11 for a people, and for a *n.*
32:20 made thee a *n.* as at this day
33: 9 shall be to me a *n.* of joy
Ezek 20: 9 wrought for my *n.* sake
Mic 4: 5 walk in the *n.* of the Lord
6: 9 man of wisdom shall see thy *n.*
Zech 14: 9 shall be one Lord and his *n.*
Mal 1:14 my *n.* is dreadful among the
2: 2 lay it to heart, to give glory to my *n.*
Mat 10:22 hated of all for my *n.* sake
10:41 receive prophet in the *n.* of
Luke 6:22 cast out your *n.* as evil
John 14:13 ask in my *n.*, that will I do
15:16 ask of the father in my *n.*
16:24 asked nothing in my *n.*
16:26 ye shall ask in my *n.*
17:12 I kept them in thy *n.*
20:31 ye might have life through his *n.*
Acts 9:15 a chosen vessel to bear my *n.*
Rom 2:24 *n.* of God is blasphemed
Eph 1:21 every *n.* that is named
Phil 2: 9 a *n.* above every *n.*
Col 3:17 do all in the *n.* of the Lord
2 Tim 2:19 that nameth the *n.* of Christ
Heb 1: 4 obtained a more excellent *n.*
1 Pet 4:14 reproached for the *n.* of Christ
1 John 3:23 believe on the *n.* of the Son
Rev 2: 3 for my *n.* sake hast laboured, and
2:13 holdest fast my *n.*, and hast not
2:17 new *n.* written, which no man
3: 1 thou hast a *n.* that thou livest
3: 5 confess his *n.* before my father
3: 8 and hast not denied my *n.*
3:12 write on him the *n.* of my God
14: 1 his Father's *n.* written in their

NAMES
Deut 12: 3 destroy the *n.* of them
Ps 16: 4 nor take up their *n.* into my
49:11 call lands after their *n.*
Luke 10:20 your *n.* are written in heaven
Rev 3: 4 hast a few *n.* in Sardis which have

NARROW (NARROWER)
1 Ki 6: 4 made windows of *n.* slits
Prov 23:27 strange woman is a *n.* pit
Is 28:20 covering *n.* then that he can wrap
49:19 now be too *n.* by reason of the
Mat 7:14 and *n.* is the way which leadeth

NATION (NATIONS)
Gen 10:32 after their generations in their *n.*
15:14 and also that *n.*, whom they
17: 6 I will make *n.* of thee and kings
20: 4 wilt slay a righteous *n.*
21:13 the bondwoman will I make a *n.*
Ex 19: 6 priests, and an holy *n.*
Num 14:12 make of thee a greater *n.*
2 Sam 7:23 what one *n.* in the earth
Ps 9:20 *n.* may know themselves to be but
33:12 *n.* whose God is the Lord
113: 4 Lord high above all *n.*, and his
147:20 not dealt so with any *n.*
Is 1: 4 Ah sinful *n.*, a people laden
2: 2 all *n.* shall flow unto it
2: 4 *n.* shall not lift the sword against *n.*
40:17 *n.* before him are as nothing
49: 7 him whom the *n.* abhorreth
55: 5 *n.* that knew thee not shall
66: 8 shall a *n.* be born at once
Jer 4: 2 *n.* shall bless themselves in
Zech 2:11 many *n.* be joined to the Lord
Mat 25:32 before him be gathered all *n.*
24: 7 *n.* shall rise against *n.*
Luke 7: 5 he loveth our *n.* and he hath built
Acts 10:35 in every *n.* he that feareth
14:16 suffered all *n.* to walk in
Rom 10:19 by a foolish *n.* I will
Phil 2:15 midst of a crooked and perverse *n.*
1 Pet 2: 9 ye are an holy *n.*, a peculiar people
Rev 5: 9 kindred and tongue, and people and *n.*
21:24 *n.* of them that are saved

NATURAL (NATURALLY)
Deut 34: 7 nor his *n.* force abated
Rom 1:27 the *n.* use of the women
11:24 would be the *n.* branches
1 Cor 2:14 the *n.* man receiveth not
15:46 but that which is *n.*
Phil 2:20 who will *n.* care for your state
2 Tim 3: 3 without *n.* affection, trucebreakers
Jas 1:23 beholding his *n.* face in a glass
2 Pet 2:12 as *n.* brute beasts, made to be
Jude 1:10 they know *n.* as brute beasts

NATURE
Rom 1:26 that which is against *n.*
2:14 do by *n.* things contained in
2:27 uncircumcision, which is by *n.*
1 Cor 11:14 doth not even *n.* itself teach
Gal 4: 8 them which by *n.* are no gods
Eph 2: 3 by *n.* the children of wrath
Heb 2:16 on him the *n.* of angels
Jas 3: 6 setteth on fire the course of *n.*
2 Pet 1: 4 might be partakers of the divine *n.*

NECK (NECKS)
2 Ki 17:14 but hardened their *n.*; like to the
Neh 9:29 and hardened their *n.*, and would
Sol 1:10 thy *n.* with chains of gold
Is 48: 4 thy *n.* is an iron sinew
Jer 7:26 but hardened their *n.*, they did worse
Acts 15:10 upon the *n.* of the disciples
Rom 16: 4 laid down their own *n.*

NEED (NEEDETH)
Mat 6:32 ye have *n.* of all these things
9:12 they that are whole *n.* not
Luke 15: 7 just persons which *n.* no repentance
Eph 4:28 give to him that *n.*
Heb 4:16 grace to help in time of *n.*
1 Pet 1: 6 if *n.* be, ye are in heaviness
1 John 2:27 *n.* not that any man teach you
Rev 3:17 and have *n.* of nothing
21:23 the city had no *n.* of sun
22: 5 and they *n.* no candle

NEEDFUL
Luke 10:42 one thing is *n.*, and Mary hath

NEEDY
Ps 9:18 *n.* shall not always be forgotten
72:12 he shall deliver the *n.*
113: 7 lifteth the *n.* out of the dunghill
Is 14:30 *n.* shall lie down in safety

NEGLECT
Mat 18:17 he shall *n.* to hear them
1 Tim 4:14 *n.* not the gift that is in thee
Heb 2: 3 if we *n.* so great a salvation

NEIGHBOUR
Ex 3:22 every woman shall borrow of her *n.*
11: 2 every woman of her *n.* jewels of
20:16 not bear false witness against thy *n.*
Lev 19:13 thou shalt not defraud thy *n.*
19:17 thou shalt in any wise rebuke thy *n.*
19:18 shalt love thy *n.* as thyself
Ps 15: 3 nor doeth evil to his *n.*
Prov 27:10 better is a *n.* that is near
Jer 31:34 teach no more every man his *n.*
Mat 19:19 love thy *n.* as thyself
22:39 love thy *n.* as thyself
Luke 10:29 Jesus, and who is my *n.*
Rom 13: 9 love thy *n.* as thyself
13:10 love worketh no ill to his *n.*
15: 2 let every one of us please his *n.*
Gal 5:14 love thy *n.* as thyself
Jas 2: 8 love thy *n.* as thyself

NEST (NESTS)
Job 29:18 I shall die in my *n.*
Ps 84: 3 the swallow a *n.* for herself
Prov 27: 8 bird that wandereth from her *n.*
Is 10:14 my hand has found as a *n.* the riches
Hab 2: 9 set his *n.* on high, that he may
Mat 8:20 birds of the air have *n.*

NET (NETS)
Job 19: 6 hath compassed me with his *n.*
Ps 9:15 in the *n.* which they hid
31: 4 Pull me out of the *n.*
35: 8 his *n.* that he hath hid
66:11 broughtest us into the *n.*
Eccl 7:26 woman whose heart is snares and *n.*
Is 51:20 as a wild bull in a *n.*
Hab 1:16 they sacrifice unto their *n.*
Mat 13:47 heaven in like unto a *n.*

NEW
Num 16:30 Lord make a *n.* thing, and the
Deut 32:17 to *n.* gods that came newly up
Judg 5: 8 chose *n.* gods: then there was
Ps 33: 3 sing unto him a *n.* song
Eccl 1: 9 there is no *n.* thing under the sun
Is 42:10 sing unto the Lord a *n.* song
62: 2 be called by a *n.* name
65:17 *n.* heavens and a *n.* earth
66:22 *n.* heavens and the *n.* earth
Jer 31:22 created a *n.* thing in the earth
Ezek 11:19 put a *n.* spirit within you
36:26 a *n.* heart also will I give
Mat 9:16 putteth *n.* cloth unto an old garment
9:17 neither put *n.* wine in old bottles
13:52 his treasure things *n.* and old
Mark 1:27 what *n.* doctrine is this
John 13:34 a *n.* commandment I give unto you
Acts 17:19 we know what this *n.* doctrine
17:21 to tell or to hear some *n.* thing
1 Cor 5: 7 that ye may be a *n.* lump
2 Cor 5:17 *n.* creature; behold, all things are become *n.*
Gal 6:15 nor uncircumcision, but a *n.* creature
Eph 4:24 put on the *n.* man
Col 3:10 put on the *n.* man
2 Pet 3:13 *n.* heavens and a *n.* earth
1 John 2: 8 a *n.* commandment I write unto you
Rev 2:17 a *n.* name written, which
5: 9 they sung a *n.* song, saying
21: 1 a *n.* heaven and a *n.* earth

NEWNESS
Rom 6: 4 should walk in the *n.* of life
7: 6 should serve in the *n.* of spirit

NIGH
Deut 4: 7 who hath God so *n.* unto
30:14 word is very *n.* to thee
Ps 34:18 Lord is *n.* unto them that are
145:18 Lord is *n.* them that call on
Mat 15: 8 draweth *n.* unto me with their mouth
Rom 10: 8 the word is *n.* thee
Eph 2:13 made *n.* by the blood of Christ
2:17 and to them that were *n.*

NIGHT
Gen 1: 5 and the darkness he called *n.*
26:24 appeared unto him the same *n.*
Ex 12:42 this is that *n.* of the Lord
Job 35:10 giveth songs in the *n.*
Ps 16: 7 instruct me in the *n.* seasons
19: 2 *n.* unto *n.* showeth knowledge
30: 5 weeping may endure for a *n.*
42: 8 in the *n.* his song shall be
77: 6 I call to remembrance my song in the *n.*
119:55 in the *n.*, and have kept thy law
134: 1 which by *n.* stand in the house
139:11 *n.* shall be light about me
Is 21:11 Watchman, what of *n.*?
30:29 ye shall have a song as in the *n.*
59:10 stumble at noonday as in the *n.*
Jer 14: 8 turneth aside to tarry for a *n.*
Luke 6:12 continued all *n.* in prayer
12:20 this *n.* thy soul shall be required
John 3: 2 the same came to Jesus by *n.*
9: 4 *n.* cometh when no man can work
11:10 if a man walk in the *n.* he stumbleth
19:39 first came to Jesus by *n.*
Rom 13:12 *n.* is far spent; the day is at hand
1 Thes 5: 7 sleep in the *n.* and they that
Rev 21:25 shall be no *n.* there

NOBLE (NOBLES)
Ex 24:11 upon the *n.* of the children
Ezra 4:10 whom the great *n.* Asnapper brought
Neh 13:17 contended with the *n.* of Judah
Esth 6: 9 the king's most *n.* princes
Ps 149: 8 their *n.* with fetters of iron
Prov 8:16 by me princes rule, and *n.*
Eccl 10:17 when thy king is a son of *n.*
Jer 2:21 planted thee a *n.* vine
Acts 17:11 these were more *n.* than those
1 Cor 1:26 not many *n.* are called

NOBLEMAN
Luke 19:12 *n.* went into a far country
John 4:49 the *n.* saith unto him, Sir, come

NOSE
Prov 30:33 the wringing of the *n.*
Is 65: 5 these are a smoke in my *n.*

NOSTRILS
Is 2:22 man, whose breath is in his *n.*
Lam 4:20 the breath of our *n.*, the anointed

NOTHING
Gen 11: 6 now *n.* will be restrained
Ex 12:10 let *n.* of it remain
Num 6: 4 eat *n.* that is made of
Josh 11:15 he left *n.* undone, of all
2 Sam 24:24 which doth cost me *n.*
1 Ki 8: 9 *n.* in the ark save the two tables
Neh 8:10 send to them for whom *n.* is prepared
Job 6:21 for now ye are *n.*; ye see my
8: 9 of yesterday, and know *n.*
26: 7 and hangeth the earth upon *n.*
34: 9 it profiteth a man *n.*
Ps 17: 3 tried me, and shalt find *n.*
49:17 when he dieth, shall carry *n.* away
119:165 *n.* shall offend them
Prov 13: 4 sluggard desireth and hath *n.*
13: 7 maketh himself rich, yet hath *n.*
Is 40:17 all nations before him are as *n.*
Jer 10:24 lest thou bring me to *n.*
Lam 1:12 is it *n.* to you, all ye that
Luke 1:37 with God *n.* shall be impossible
John 14:30 cometh and hath *n.* in me
15: 5 without me ye can do *n.*
1 Cor 1:19 bring to *n.* the understanding
13: 2 and have not charity, I am *n.*
2 Cor 6:10 having *n.* yet possessing all
1 Tim 6: 7 we brought *n.* into world

NUMBER (NUMBERED, NUMBEREST, NUMBERS)
Job 14:16 for now thou *n.* my steps
Ps 71:15 I know not the *n.* thereof
90:12 teach us to *n.* our days
Is 53:12 *n.* with the transgressors, and he
65:12 I will *n.* you to the sword
Jer 33:22 host of heaven cannot be *n.*
Hos 1:10 which cannot be measured nor *n.*
Rev 7: 9 multitude no man could *n.*
13:17 beast, or the *n.* of his name

NURSE (NURSING)
Is 49:23 *n.* fathers and their queens *n.* mothers
1 Thes 2: 7 a *n.* cherisheth her children

O

OATH
Gen 24: 8 thou shalt be clear from this my *o.*
1 Sam 14:26 people feared the *o.*
2 Sam 21: 7 Lord's *o.* that was between
2 Chr 15:15 all Judah rejoiced at the *o.*
Eccl 8: 2 in regard of the *o.* of God
Ezek 16:59 which hast despised the *o.*
Luke 1:73 *o.* which he sware to our
Heb 6:16 and an *o.* for confirmation is
Jas 5:12 neither by any other *o.*

OBEY (OBEYED)
Gen 27: 8 therefore, my son, *o.* my voice
Ex 5: 2 the Lord, that I should *o.* his voice
Deut 11:27 blessing if ye *o.*
13: 4 keep his commandments and *o.* his voice
Josh 24:24 his voice will we *o.*
1 Sam 12:14 serve him and *o.* his voice
15:22 to *o.* is better than sacrifice
Jer 7:23 *o.* my voice and I will be your God
Acts 5:29 ought to *o.* God rather than men
Rom 2: 8 contentious, and do not *o.* truth
6:16 servants ye are to whom ye *o.*
6:17 but ye have *o.* from the heart
Eph 6: 1 children, *o.* your parents in the Lord
Col 3:20 Children, *o.* your parents in all things
3:22 servants, *o.* in all things
2 Thes 1: 8 that *o.* not the gospel
3:14 if any man *o.* not our word
Tit 3: 1 to *o.* magistrates, to be ready to
Heb 5: 9 salvation to all them that *o.*
13:17 *o.* them that have rule over
1 Pet 3: 1 if any *o.* not the word
3: 6 even as Sarah *o.* Abraham

OBEDIENCE
Rom 1: 5 for *o.* to the faith among all nations
5:19 by the *o.* of one shall many be
16:19 your *o.* is come abroad
16:26 to all nations for the *o.* of faith
1 Cor 14:34 they are commanded to be under *o.*
2 Cor 7:15 he remembereth the *o.* of you
10: 5 every thought to the *o.* of Christ
10: 6 when your *o.* is fulfilled
Heb 5: 8 learned *o.* by things suffered
1 Pet 1: 2 sanctification of the Spirit to *o.*

OBEDIENT
Ex 24: 7 will we do, and be *o.*
Num 27:20 children of Israel may be *o.*
Deut 4:30 turn and be *o.* to his voice
8:20 perish; because ye would not be *o.*
2 Sam 22:45 they shall be *o.* unto me
Prov 25:12 the wise reprover upon an *o.* ear

Is 1:19 if ye be willing and *o.*
42:24 neither were they *o.* to his law
Acts 6: 7 priests were *o.* to the faith
Rom 15:18 to make Gentiles *o.* by word
2 Cor 2: 9 whether ye be *o.* in all
Eph 6: 5 servants, be *o.* to them
Phil 2: 8 he became *o.* unto death
Tit 2: 9 exhort servants to be *o.*
1 Pet 1:14 as *o.* children, not fashioning

OBSERVE (OBSERVED)

Ex 12:17 *o.* the feast of unleavened bread
12:42 it is a night to be much *o.*
34:11 *o.* thou that which I command thee
Ps 107:43 who is wise and will *o.*
119:34 *o.* it with my whole heart
Prov 23:26 let thine eyes *o.* my ways
Jonah 2: 8 they that *o.* lying vanities
Mat 28:20 teaching them to *o.* all things
Mark 6:20 man and an holy, and *o.* him
10:20 all these I *o.* from my youth
Gal 4:10 ye *o.* days and months and times

OBSERVATION

Luke 17:20 kingdom of God cometh not with *o.*

OBTAIN (OBTAINED)

Prov 8:35 and shall *o.* favour of the Lord
Is 35:10 they shall *o.* joy and gladness, and
Hos 2:23 her that had not *o.* mercy
Luke 20:35 worthy to *o.* that world
Acts 26:22 having therefore *o.* help of God
Rom 11: 7 the election hath *o.* it
1 Cor 9:24 so run, that ye may *o.*
Eph 1:11 whom also we have *o.* an inheritance
1 Tim 1:13 but I *o.* mercy, because I did
Heb 1: 4 inheritance *o.* a more excellent name
4:16 we may *o.* mercy and find grace
6:15 patiently endured, he *o.* the promise
8: 6 hath he *o.* a more excellent ministry
9:12 *o.* eternal redemption for us
11:35 they might *o.* a better resurrection
Jas 4: 2 ye desire to have, and cannot *o.*

OCCASION (OCCASIONS)

2 Sam 12:14 given great *o.* to the enemies
Job 33:10 he findeth *o.* against me
Jer 2:24 in her *o.* who can turn
Rom 7: 8 sin, taking *o.* by the commandment
14:13 *o.* to fall in his brother's way
2 Cor 11:12 I may cut off *o.* from them
Gal 5:13 use not liberty for *o.* to the flesh
1 Tim 5:14 give none *o.* to the adversary
1 John 2:10 there is none *o.* of stumbling in him

OFFENCE (OFFENCES)

1 Sam 25:31 nor *o.* of heart unto my lord
Eccl 10: 4 yielding pacifieth great *o.*
Is 8:14 rock of *o.* to both the houses of Israel
Mat 16:23 thou art an *o.* unto me
Acts 24:16 conscience void of *o.*
Rom 4:25 who was delivered for our *o.* and
5:15 the *o.* so also is the free gift
5:17 by one man's *o.* death reigned
9:33 a stumblingstone and rock of *o.*
14:20 for him that eateth with *o.*
16:17 cause divisions and *o.* contrary to
2 Cor 6: 3 giving no *o.* in any thing
11: 7 have I committed an *o.* in abasing
Gal 5:11 then is the *o.* of the cross ceased
Phil 1:10 without *o.* till the day of Christ
1 Pet 2: 8 and a rock of *o.*, even to them

OFFEND (OFFENDED)

Job 34:31 I will not *o.* any more
Ps 73:15 I should *o.* against the generation
119:165 law: and nothing shall *o.* them
Prov 18:19 a brother *o.* is harder to be won
Jer 2: 3 all that devour him shall *o.*
50: 7 we *o.* not because they have
Hos 4:15 harlot, yet let not Judah *o.*
Mat 5:29 if thy right eye *o.* thee
11: 6 whosoever shall not be *o.* in me
13:41 of his kingdom all things that *o.*
17:27 yet lest we should *o.* them, go
18: 6 shall *o.* one of these little ones
26:33 yet will I never be *o.*
Mark 4:17 immediately they are *o.*
9:43 if thy hand *o.* thee, cut it off
Rom 14:21 thy brother stumbleth or is *o.*
2 Cor 11:29 who is *o.* and I burn not
Jas 2:10 yet *o.* in one point he is guilty
3: 2 in many things we *o.* all

OFFER (OFFERED)

Gen 31:54 then Jacob *o.* sacrifice upon the mount
Lev 1: 3 he shall *o.* it of his own voluntary
Mat 5:24 then come and *o.* thy gift
Phil 2:17 *o.* upon the sacrifice and service
2 Tim 4: 6 I am now ready to be *o.*, and the time
Heb 9:14 Spirit *o.* himself without spot to God
9:28 Christ was once *o.* to bear sins
11: 4 by faith Abel *o.* unto God a more
11:17 Abraham, when he was tried, *o.* up Isaac
13:15 let us *o.* the sacrifice of praise
Rev 8: 3 *o.* it with the prayers of all saints

OFFERING

Eph 5: 2 an *o.* and a sacrifice to God
Heb 10: 5 sacrifice and *o.* thou wouldest not
10:14 by one *o.* he hath perfected for ever

OFFSCOURING

Lam 3:45 thou hast made us as the *o.*
1 Cor 4:13 we are the *o.* of all things

OFTEN

Prov 29: 1 he, that being *o.* reproved
Mal 3:16 the Lord spake *o.* one to another
Mat 23:37 how *o.* would I have gathered
1 Cor 11:26 as *o.* as ye eat this bread
Phil 3:18 many walk, of whom I have told you *o.*
Heb 9:25 yet that he should offer himself *o.*

OIL

Gen 28:18 and poured *o.* upon the top of it
Ex 25: 6 *o.* for the light, spices for anointing
Ps 45: 7 anointed thee with the *o.* of gladness
89:20 with my holy *o.* have I anointed
92:10 I shall be anointed with fresh *o.*
104:15 *o.* to make his face to shine
141: 5 it shall be an excellent *o.*
Is 61: 3 *o.* of joy for mourning, the garment
Mic 6: 7 with ten thousands of rivers of *o.*
Mat 25: 3 and took no *o.* with them
25: 4 wise took *o.* in their vessels
25: 8 give us of your *o.* for our lamps
Luke 7:46 head with *o.* didst not anoint
10:34 pouring in *o.* and wine, and set him
Heb 1: 9 anointed thee with the *o.* of gladness

OINTMENT (OINTMENTS)

Ps 133: 2 it is like precious *o.* upon the head
Prov 27:16 and the *o.* of his right hand
Eccl 7: 1 good name is better than precious *o.*
Sol 1: 3 the savour of thy good *o.*
Is 1: 6 bound up neither mollified with *o.*
Amos 6: 6 anoint themselves with chief *o.*
Mat 26:12 she hath poured this *o.* on my body
Luke 7:37 brought an alabaster box of *o.*
John 12: 5 why was not this *o.* sold

OLD

Gen 5:32 and Noah was five hundred years *o.*
18:13 of a surety bear a child, which am *o.*
25: 8 and died in a good *o.* age
Ps 37:25 I have been young, and now am *o.*
71: 9 me not off in the time of *o.* age
92:14 still bring forth fruit in *o.* age
Prov 22: 6 when he is *o.* he will not depart from
Jer 6:16 ask for the *o.* paths, where is the
Rom 6: 6 our *o.* man is crucified with him
1 Cor 5: 7 purge out the *o.* leaven
2 Cor 5:17 *o.* things are passed away
Eph 4:22 concerning the former conversation the *o.* man
Col 3: 9 ye have put off the *o.* man
2 Pet 1: 9 purged from his *o.* sins

OMEGA

Rev 1: 8 I am the Alpha and the *O.*
1:11 Alpha and *O.*, the first and the last
21: 6 Alpha and *O.*, the beginning and the end
22:13 Alpha and *O.*, the beginning and the end

ONE

Gen 2:24 and they shall be *o.* flesh
Ps 89:19 laid help upon *o.* that is mighty
Eccl 4: 9 two are better than *o.*
Jer 3:14 *o.* of a city, and two of a
Mat 19: 5 and they twain shall be *o.* flesh
19:17 none good but *o.*, that is God
Luke 10:42 but *o.* thing is needful: and Mary
John 10:30 I and my Father are *o.*
1 Cor 8: 4 there is none other God but *o.*
10:17 we being many are *o.* bread and *o.* body
Gal 3:20 not mediator of *o.*, but God is *o.*
Phil 3:13 this *o.* thing I do, forgetting
1 John 5: 7 Ghost: and these three are *o.*

OPEN (OPENED, OPENEST)

Gen 3: 7 eyes of them both were *o.*
Ps 51:15 O Lord, *o.* thou my lips: and my
81:10 *o.* thy mouth wide, and I will fill
104:28 thou *o.* thine hand, they are
119:18 *o.* thou mine eyes, that I may
145:16 thou *o.* thine hand, and satisfiest
Prov 31: 8 *o.* thy mouth for the dumb in the
Sol 5: 2 *o.* to me, my sister, my love
Is 22:22 shall *o.* and none shall shut
35: 5 eyes of the blind shall be *o.*
42: 7 to *o.* the blind eyes, to bring out
53: 7 yet he *o.* not his mouth
Ezek 16:63 never *o.* thy mouth any more because
Mat 7: 7 knock, and it shall be *o.*
25:11 saying, Lord, Lord, *o.* to us
Acts 14:27 *o.* the door of faith to the Gentiles
16:14 whose heart the Lord *o.*
26:18 to *o.* their eyes, and to turn them
1 Cor 16: 9 great door and effectual is *o.*
2 Cor 2:12 door *o.* unto me of the Lord
Col 4: 3 *o.* to us a door of utterance
Heb 4:13 naked and *o.* unto the eyes of
Rev 5: 2 who is worthy to *o.* the book

OPPORTUNITY

Mat 26:16 he sought *o.* to betray him
Gal 6:10 as we have therefore *o.*, let us do good
Phil 4:10 were also careful, but ye lacked *o.*
Heb 11:15 they might have had *o.* to have returned

OPPRESS (OPPRESSED)

Ex 3: 9 wherewith the Egyptians *o.* them
22:21 neither vex a stranger nor *o.* him
Lev 25:14 ye shall not *o.* one another
Judg 10:12 and the Maonites did *o.* you
Job 10: 3 good unto thee that thou shouldest *o.*
Ps 9: 9 Lord also will be a refuge for the *o.*
10:18 that man of the earth may no more *o.*
Prov 22:22 neither *o.* the afflicted in the gate
Eccl 4: 1 tears of such as were *o.*
Is 1:17 relieve the *o.*, judge the fatherless
58: 6 and to let the *o.* go free
Zech 7:10 *o.* not the widow, nor the fatherless
Mal 3: 5 witness against those that *o.*
Acts 10:38 healing all that were *o.* of the devil
Jas 2: 6 do not rich men *o.* you?

OPPRESSION (OPPRESSIONS)

Deut 26: 7 looked on our labour and our *o.*
2 Ki 13: 4 for he saw the *o.* of Israel

Ps 12: 5 for the *o.* of the poor, for the
62:10 trust not in *o.* and become
Eccl 4: 1. considered all the *o.* that are done
7: 7 *o.* maketh a wise man mad
Is 5: 7 judgment, but behold *o.*; for
33:15 he that despiseth gain of *o.*

OPPRESSOR (OPPRESSORS)
Ps 54: 3 and *o.* seek after my soul
72: 4 shall break in pieces the *o.*
Prov 3:31 envy thou not the *o.*
28:16 is also a great *o.*; but he
Is 3:12 children are their *o.*, and women
51:13 because of the fury of the *o.*

ORACLES
Acts 7:38 who received the lively *o.* to give
Rom 3: 2 unto them were committed the *o.* of God
Heb 5:12 first principles of the *o.* of God
1 Pet 4:11 let him speak as the *o.* of God

ORDAIN (ORDAINED)
Ps 8: 2 hast thou *o.* strength because of
132:17 *o.* a lamp for mine anointed
Is 26:12 Lord, thou wilt *o.* peace for us
30:33 Tophet is *o.* of old, for
Jer 1: 5 *o.* thee a prophet to the nations
Hab 1:12 Lord, thou hast *o.* them for judgment
Acts 13:48 as many as were *o.* to eternal life
14:23 *o.* them elders in every church
17:31 judge by that man whom he *o.*
Rom 7:10 the commandment which was *o.* to life
13: 1 powers that be are *o.* of God
Gal 3:19 *o.* by angels in the hand of
Eph 2:10 God hath before *o.* that we should
1 Tim 2: 7 *o.* a preacher and an apostle
Tit 1: 5 and *o.* elders in every city
Heb 5: 1 *o.* for men in things pertaining to
Jude 1: 4 before of old *o.* to this condemnation

ORDER
Gen 22: 9 laid the wood in *o.*, and bound Isaac
Job 23: 4 I would *o.* my cause before him
33: 5 set thy words in *o.* before me
Ps 40: 5 be reckoned up in *o.* unto thee
50:21 set them in *o.* before thine eyes
1 Cor 14:40 things be done decently and in *o.*
Col 2: 5 joying and beholding your *o.*
Tit 1: 5 set in *o.* things wanting

ORDINANCE (ORDINANCES)
Lev 22: 9 they shall therefore keep mine *o.*
Neh 10:32 also we made *o.* for us
Is 58: 2 ask of me the *o.* of justice
Jer 31:35 *o.* of the moon and of the stars
Ezek 11:20 keep mine *o.* and do them
Luke 1: 6 in all commandments and *o.* of the Lord
Rom 13: 2 resisteth the *o.* of God
1 Cor 11: 2 remember me in all things, and keep the *o.*
Eph 2:15 law of commandments contained in *o.*
Col 2:14 out the handwriting of *o.* that was
Heb 9: 1 had also *o.* of divine service, and a
1 Pet 2:13 submit to every *o.* of man

OUTSIDE
Ezek 40: 5. a wall on the *o.* of the house
Mat 23:25 make clean the *o.* of the cup

OUTSTRETCHED
Deut 26: 8 and with an *o.* arm and with
Jer 21: 5 fight against you with an *o.* hand
27: 5 my great power and by my *o.* arm

OUTWARD (OUTWARDLY)
1 Sam 16: 7 man looketh on the *o.* appearance
Mat 23:28 even so ye also *o.* appear righteous
Rom 2:28 not a Jew, which is one *o.*
2 Cor 4:16 though our *o.* man perish
1 Pet 3: 3. let it not be that *o.* adorning

OVERCOME (OVERCOMETH)
Gen 49:19 he shall *o.* at the last
Num 13:30 for we are well able to *o.* it
Sol 6: 5 for they have *o.* me: thy hair
John 16:33 good cheer, I have *o.* the world
1 John 2:13 ye have *o.* the wicked one
2:14 ye have *o.* the wicked one
4: 4 are of God, little children, and have *o.*
5: 4 born of God *o.* the world
Rev 2: 7 to him that *o.* I will give
2:11 he that *o.* shall not be hurt of
3: 5 he that *o.* shall be clothed
3:12 him that *o.* will I make a pillar
3:21 him that *o.* will I grant to sit
17:14 the Lamb shall *o.* them: for he is

OVERSEER (OVERSEERS)
Prov 6: 7 which having no guide, *o.*, or ruler
Acts 20:28 the Holy Ghost hath made you *o.*

OVERSIGHT
Gen 43:12 peradventure it was an *o.*
1 Pet 5: 2 taking the *o.* thereof, not by constraint

OVERTHROW (OVERTHROWETH, OVERTHROWN)
Deut 12: 3 ye shall *o.* their altars
Job 12:19 princes away spoiled, and *o.* the mighty
Ps 140:11 hunt the violent man to *o.* him
Prov 13: 6 but wickedness *o.* the sinner
21:12 God *o.* the wicked for their wickedness
Amos 4:11 I have *o.* some of you, as God
Acts 5:39 be of God, ye cannot *o.* it
2 Tim 2:18 and *o.* the faith of some

OWE (OWED)
Mat 18:24 which *o.* him ten thousand talents
Rom 13: 8 *o.* no man anything, but to love

OWN
Deut 24:16 be put to death for his *o.* sin
Judg 7: 2 mine *o.* hand hath saved me
John 1:11 his *o.* and his *o.* received him not
1 Cor 6:19 and ye are not your *o.*
10:24 let no man seek his *o.*, but
Phil 2: 4 look not every man on his *o.* things

OX (OXEN)
Ps 144:14 that our *o.* may be strong to labour
Prov 7:22 as an *o.* goeth to the slaughter
15:17 than a stalled *o.* and hatred therewith
Is 1: 3 the *o.* knoweth his owner
22:13 behold joy and gladness, slaying *o.*
Mat 22: 4 my *o.* and my fatlings are killed
Luke 14:19 I have bought five yoke of *o.*
John 2:14 in the temple those that sold *o.*
1 Cor 9: 9 doth God take care for *o.*

P

PAIN (PAINS)
Ps 116: 3 *p.* of hell gat hold on me
Is 21: 3 are my loins filled with *p.*
66: 7 before her *p.* came, she was delivered
Jer 6:24 and *p.*, as of a woman in travail
Mic 4:10 be in *p.* and labour to bring forth
Acts 2:24 loosed the *p.* of death
Rev 21: 4 neither shall there be any more *p.*

PAINED
Ps 55: 4 my heart is sore *p.*
Is 23: 5 they be sorely *p.* at the report of Tyre
Jer 4:19 I am *p.* at my very heart
Joel 2: 6 the people shall be much *p.*
Rev 12: 2 travailing in birth and *p.*

PALACE
1 Chr 29:19 and to build the *p.*, for which
Ps 45:15 they shall enter into the king's *p.*
Sol 8: 9 will build upon her a *p.* of silver
Is 25: 2 a *p.* of strangers to be no city
Phil 1:13 in Christ are manifest in all the *p.*

PARABLE (PARABLES)
Ps 49: 4 incline mine ear to a *p.*
78: 2 I will open my mouth in a *p.*
Prov 26: 9 is a *p.* in the mouth of fools
Ezek 20:49 doth he not speak *p.*
Mic 2: 4 shall one take up a *p.* against you
Mat 13: 3 spake many things unto them in *p.*
Luke 5:36 spake also a *p.* unto them; no man
13: 6 he spake also this *p.*; a certain man
21:29 and he spake to them a *p.*

PARADISE
Luke 23:43 today shalt thou be with me in *p.*
2 Cor 12: 4 he was caught up into *p.*
Rev 2: 7 in the midst of the *p.* of God

PARDON (PARDONED, PARDONETH)
Ex 34: 9 *p.* our iniquity, and our sin
23:21 he will not *p.* your transgressions
Num 14:19 *p.* the iniquity of the people
1 Sam 15:25 *p.* my sin and turn again with me
2 Ki 24: 4 which the Lord would not *p.*
2 Chr 30:18 the good Lord *p.* every one
Neh 9:17 thou art a God ready to *p.*
Job 7:21 why dost thou not *p.* my transgression
Ps 25:11 thy name's sake O Lord *p.* my iniquity
Is 40: 2 that her iniquity is *p.*
55: 7 to our God, for he will abundantly *p.*
Jer 5: 7 how shall I *p.* thee for this
33: 8 I will *p.* all their iniquities
50:20 I will *p.* them whom I reserve
Mic 7:18 who is God like unto thee that *p.*

PARENTS
Mat 10:21 children rise up against their *p.*
Luke 2:27 when the *p.* brought in the child Jesus
8:56 and her *p.* were astonished
18:29 no man hath left house, or *p.*
21:16 ye shall be betrayed both by *p.*
Rom 1:30 of evil things, disobedient to *p.*
2 Cor 12:14 the *p.* but the *p.* for the children
1 Tim 5: 4 to requite their *p.*: for that
2 Tim 3: 2 disobedient to *p.*, unthankful, unholy

PART
Ex 29:26 the Lord: and it shall be thy *p.*
Num 18:20 thy *p.* and thine inheritance among
Ps 5: 9 their inward *p.* is very wickedness
118: 7 Lord taketh my *p.* with them
Luke 10:42 Mary hath chosen that good *p.*
Acts 8:21 neither *p.* nor lot in this matter
1 Cor 13: 9 know in *p.* and we prophesy in *p.*

PARTAKER (PARTAKERS)
Ps 50:18 thou hast been *p.* with adulterers
Rom 15:27 made *p.* of their spiritual things
1 Cor 9:10 in hope should be *p.* of his hope
9:13 wait at the altar are *p.* with the altar
10:17 we are all *p.* of that one bread
10:21 cannot be *p.* of the Lord's table
10:30 if I by grace be a *p.* why am I
Eph 5: 7 be ye not therefore *p.* with them
1 Tim 5:22 be not *p.* of other men's sins
Heb 3:14 for we are made *p.* of Christ
6: 4 and were made *p.* of the Holy Ghost
12:10 might be *p.* of his holiness
1 Pet 5: 1 a *p.* of the glory that shall be revealed
2 John 1:11 God speed is *p.* of his evil deeds

PARTIAL
Mal 2: 9 but have been *p.* in the law
Jas 2: 4 are ye not then *p.* in yourselves

PARTIALITY
1 Tim 5:21 before another, doing nothing by *p.*
Jas 3:17 without *p.*, and without hypocrisy

PASS (PASSED, PASSEST, PASSETH)
Is 43: 2 when thou *p.* through the waters
Mic 7:18 *p.* by the transgression of the remnant
Mark 14:35 the hour might *p.* from him
Luke 16:17 easier for heaven and earth to *p.*
John 5:24 but is *p.* from death unto life
1 Cor 7:31 fashion of this world *p.* away
Phil 4: 7 peace of God *p.* all understanding
1 John 2:17 world *p.* away and the lust thereof

PASSOVER
Ex 12:11 it is the Lord's *p.*
Deut 16: 2. therefore sacrifice the *p.* unto the Lord
Josh 5:11 on the morrow after the *p.*
2 Chr 30:15 killed the *p.* on the fourteenth day
35:11 they killed the *p.*, and the priests
1 Cor 5: 7 Christ our *p.* is sacrificed
Heb 11:28 through faith he kept the *p.*

PASTOR (PASTORS)
Jer 3:15 I will give you *p.* according
17:16 have not hastened from being a *p.*
Eph 4:11 and some, *p.* and teachers

PASTURE (PASTURES)
Ps 23: 2 maketh me to lie down in green *p.*
74: 1 against the sheep of thy *p.*
95: 7 we are the people of his *p.*
100: 3 his people and the sheep of his *p.*
Is 49: 9 their *p.* shall be in all high places
Ezek 34:18 to have eaten up the good *p.*
John 10: 9 shall go in and out, and find *p.*

PATH (PATHS)
Num 22:24 angel of the Lord stood in a *p.*
Job 28: 7 there is a *p.* which no fowl knoweth
Ps 16:11 wilt show me the *p.* of life
17: 4 kept me from the *p.* of the destroyer
17: 5 hold up my goings in thy *p.*
25:10 all *p.* of the Lord are mercy
27:11 lead me in a plain *p.*
65:11 and thy *p.* drop fatness
119:35 go in the *p.* of thy commandments
139: 3 thou compassest my *p.*, and my lying
Prov 3:17 all her *p.* are peace
4:18 *p.* of just is as a shining light
4:26 ponder the *p.* of thy feet
5: 6 lest thou ponder the *p.* of life
Is 26: 7 thou dost weigh the *p.* of the just
59: 7 destruction are in their *p.*
59: 8 they have made them crooked *p.*
Hos 2: 6 she shall not find her *p.*
Mat 3: 3 way of the Lord make his *p.* straight
Heb 12:13 make straight *p.* for your feet

PATIENCE
Mat 18:29 have *p.* with me, and I will pray
Luke 8:15 bring forth fruit with *p.*
21:19 in your *p.* possess ye your souls
Rom 5: 3 knowing that tribulation worketh *p.*
15: 4 that we through *p.* and comfort of
15: 5 now the God of *p.* and consolation
2 Cor 12:12 wrought among you in all *p.*
Col 1:11 unto all *p.* and longsuffering
1 Thes 1: 3 *p.* of hope in our Lord Jesus
2 Thes 1: 4 for your *p.* and faith in all your
1 Tim 6:11 godliness, faith, love *p.* meekness
2 Tim 3:10 purpose, faith, longsuffering, charity, *p.*
Tit 2: 2 sound in faith, in charity, in *p.*
Heb 6:12 through faith and *p.* inherit the promises
10:36 have need of *p.*, that after ye have
12: 1 run with *p.* the race that is set before us
Jas 1: 3 trying of your faith worketh *p.*
1: 4 let *p.* have her perfect work
5:10 for an example of suffering affliction and of *p.*
5:11 ye have heard of the *p.* of Job
2 Pet 1: 6 and to temperance *p.*, and to *p.*
Rev 1: 9 in the kingdom and *p.* of Jesus
2: 2 I know thy works and thy labour, and thy *p.*
13:10 here is the *p.* of saints

PATIENT
Eccl 7: 8 the *p.* in spirit better than the proud
Rom 2: 7 by *p.* continuance in well doing
12:12 *p.* in tribulation, instant in
2 Thes 3: 5 into the *p.* waiting for Christ
1 Tim 3: 3 not greedy of filthy lucre, but *p.*
2 Tim 2:24 gentle unto all men, apt to teach, *p.*
Jas 5: 7 *p.* therefore, brethren, unto the coming of the Lord

PATIENTLY
Ps 37: 7 in the Lord, and wait *p.* for him
40: 1 I waited *p.* for the Lord
Heb 6:15 after he had *p.* endured, he obtained
1 Pet 2:20 for your faults, ye shall take it *p.*

PATTERN (PATTERNS)
Ezek 43:10 and let them measure the *p.*
1 Tim 1:16 show forth all longsuffering, for a *p.*
Tit 2: 7 showing thyself a *p.* of good works
Heb 8: 5 make all things according to the *p.*
9:23 that the *p.* of things in the heavens

PEACE
Num 6:26 countenance upon thee, and give thee *p.*
Job 22:21 acquaint now thyself with him and be at *p.*
Ps 34:14 do good; seek *p.* and pursue it
37:37 the end of that man is *p.*
85: 8 he will speak *p.* unto his people
119:165 great *p.* have they which love
120: 7 I am for *p.*: but when I speak
122: 6 pray for the *p.* of Jerusalem
125: 5 but *p.* shall be upon Israel
Prov 16: 7 his enemies to be at *p.* with him
Is 9: 6 everlasting Father, Prince of *P.*
26: 3 thou wilt keep him in perfect *p.*
27: 5 that he may make *p.* with me
45: 7 I make *p.* and create evil
48:18 had thy *p.* been as a river
48:22 there is no *p.*, saith the Lord
57:19 *p.*, *p.* to him that is far off
59: 8 way of *p.* they know not
60:17 I will also make thy officers *p.*
66:12 extend *p.* to her like a river
Jer 6:14 saying *p.*, *p.* when there is no *p.*
8:15 looked for *p.* but no good came
29: 7 seek the *p.* of the city
29:11 thoughts of *p.* and not of evil
Ezek 13:10 saying *p.*, and there was no *p.*
Mic 5: 5 this man shall be the *p.*
Zech 8:19 therefore love the truth and *p.*
Mat 10:34 I came not to send *p.* but a sword
Mark 9:50 have *p.* one with another
Luke 2:14 on earth *p.*, good will towards
2:29 lettest thou thy servant depart in *p.*
19:42 things that belong to thy *p.*
John 14:27 *p.* I leave with you; my *p.* I give
16:33 that in me ye might have *p.*
Rom 5: 1 we have *p.* with God through Jesus Christ
8: 6 spiritually minded is life and *p.*
14:17 righteousness, and *p.* and joy in the
1 Cor 7:15 God hath called us to *p.*
2 Cor 13:11 live in *p.*, and the God of
Gal 5:22 fruit of the Spirit is love, joy, *p.*
Eph 2:14 he is our *p.*, who hath made both
Phil 4: 7 the *p.* of God, which passeth all
1 Thes 5:13 and be at *p.* among yourselves
Heb 12:14 follow *p.* with all men and holiness
Jas 3:18 fruit of righteousness is sown in *p.*
1 Pet 3:11 let him seek *p.* and ensue
2 Pet 3:14 ye may be found of him in *p.*

PEACEABLE (PEACEABLY)
Rom 12:18 lieth in you live *p.* with all men
1 Tim 2: 2 that we may lead a quiet and *p.* life
Jas 3:17 from above is first pure, then *p.*

PEACEMAKERS
Mat 5: 9 blessed are the *p.*: for they

PEARL (PEARLS)
Mat 7: 6 cast not *p.* before swine
13:46 found one *p.* of great price
Rev 21:21 the twelve gates were twelve *p.*

PECULIAR
Ex 19: 5 ye shall be a *p.* treasure unto me
Deut 14: 2 chosen thee to be a *p.* people
26:18 thee this day to be his *p.* people
Ps 135: 4 Israel for his *p.* treasure
Eccl 2: 8 *p.* treasure of kings, and of the
Tit 2:14 purify unto himself a *p.* people
1 Pet 2: 9 an holy nation, a *p.* people

PEOPLE
Gen 27:29 let *p.* serve thee, and nations bow
Ex 6: 7 I will take you to me for a *p.*
Ps 50: 7 hear, O my *p.* and I will speak
100: 3 we are his *p.* and the sheep of his
144:15 happy is that *p.* whose God
148:14 the children of Israel a *p.* near unto
Is 1: 4 a *p.* laden with iniquity, a seed of
10: 6 against the *p.* of my wrath
27:11 a *p.* of no understanding
34: 5 upon the *p.* of my curse
63: 8 they are my *p.* that will not lie
Jer 30:22 ye shall be my *p.*, and I will be
31:33 their God, and they shall be my *p.*
Ezek 36:28 and ye shall be my *p.*, and I will
Hos 1: 9 Lo-ammi: for ye are not my *p.*
4: 9 there shall be like *p.* like priest
Zech 8: 8 they shall be my *p.*, and I will
Mat 1:21 Jesus shall save his *p.* from their sins
Rom 11: 2 God hath not cast away his *p.*
2 Cor 6:16 their God and they shall be my *p.*
Heb 4: 9 remaineth a rest to the *p.* of God
11:25 suffer affliction with the *p.* of God
1 Pet 2:10 but are now the *p.* of God

PERDITION
John 17:12 is lost but the son of *p.*
Phil 1:28 to them an evident token of *p.*
2 Thes 2: 3 be revealed, the son of *p.*
1 Tim 6: 9 drown men in destruction and *p.*
Heb 10:39 of them who draw back unto *p.*
2 Pet 3: 7 judgment and *p.* of ungodly men
Rev 17:11 of the seven, and goeth into *p.*

PERFECT
Gen 6: 9 Noah was a just man and *p.*
17: 1 walk before me, and be *p.*
Deut 18:13 shalt be *p.* with the Lord thy God
2 Sam 22:31 As for God, his way is *p.*
Job 1: 1 and that man was *p.* and upright
Ps 19: 7 law of the Lord is *p.*
37:37 mark the *p.* man, and behold
Mat 5:48 *p.* even as your Father which is in
19:21 if thou wilt be *p.* go and sell
1 Cor 2: 6 among them that are *p.*
2 Cor 12: 9 my strength is made *p.* in weakness
13:11 farewell be *p.*, be of good comfort
Eph 4:13 a *p.* man, unto the measure of
Phil 3:12 either were already *p.*: but I follow
Col 1:28 present every man *p.* in Christ
4:12 may stand *p.* and complete
2 Tim 3:17 man of God may be *p.*
Heb 2:10 make the captain of their salvation *p.*
7:19 the law made nothing *p.*
12:23 spirits of just men made *p.*
13:21 make you *p.* in every good work
Jas 1: 4 let patience have her *p.* work
1:17 good gift and every *p.* gift is from above
1 John 4:18 *p.* love casteth out fear
Rev 3: 2 I have not found thy works *p.*

PERFECTING
2 Cor 7: 1 *p.* holiness in the fear of God
Eph 4:12 for the *p.* of the saints

PERFECTION
Job 11: 7 thou find out the Almighty unto *p.*
Ps 119:96 have seen an end of all *p.*
Luke 8:14 bring no fruit to *p.*
2 Cor 13: 9 this also we wish, even your *p.*
Heb 6: 1 let us go on unto *p.*

PERFORM (PERFORMED, PERFORMETH)
Ruth 3:13 that if he will *p.* unto thee
Neh 9: 8 hast *p.* thy words; for thou art
Job 5:12 hands cannot *p.* their enterprise
Ps 57: 2 God that *p.* all things
119:106 have sworn and will *p.* it
119:112 inclined mine heart to *p.* thy statutes
Is 9: 7 zeal of the Lord of hosts will *p.*
10:12 Lord *p.* his whole work
44:26 and *p.* the counsel of his messengers
44:28 shall *p.* all my pleasure
Jer 51:29 purpose of the Lord shall be *p.*
Mic 7:20 thou wilt *p.* truth to Jacob
Rom 4:21 promised, was able to *p.*
7:18 how to *p.* that which is good
Phil 1: 6 *p.* it until day of Jesus Christ

PERISH (PERISHED)
Gen 41:36 land *p.* not through the famine
Lev 26:38 ye shall *p.* among the heathen
Num 17:12 we die, we *p.*, we all *p.*
Esth 4:16 if I *p.*, I *p.*
Ps 2:12 ye *p.* from the way, when his wrath
119:92 should then have *p.* in my affliction
Prov 29:18 there is no vision, the people *p.*
Mat 8:25 him, saying Lord, save us, we *p.*
John 3:15 believeth in him should not *p.*
3:16 should not *p.* but have everlasting life
10:28 they shall never *p.*; neither shall
1 Cor 8:11 the weak *p.* for whom Christ died
2 Pet 3: 9 not willing that any *p.*

PERSECUTES (PERSECUTED, PERSECUTEST)
Job 19:22 why *p.* me as God
Ps 10: 2 wicked in his pride doth *p.* the poor
35: 6 let the angel of the Lord *p.* them
83:15 *p.* them with thy tempest
109:16 *p.* the poor and needy man
119:161 princes *p.* me without cause
143: 3 the enemy hath *p.* my soul
Mat 5:11 when men shall revile you and *p.* you
5:44 despitefully use you and *p.* you
10:23 when they *p.* you in this city
John 15:20 they *p.* me they will persecute you
Acts 9: 4 Saul, Saul, why *p.* thou me?
22: 4 I *p.* this way unto the death
26:11 I *p.* them to strange cities
Rom 12:14 bless them which *p.* you: bless and
1 Cor 4:12 we bless; being *p.* we suffer it
15: 9 because I *p.* the church of God
2 Cor 4: 9 *p.* but not forsaken, cast
Gal 1:13 I *p.* the church of God
4:29 *p.* him born after the Spirit

PERSECUTION
2 Tim 3:12 godly in Christ Jesus shall suffer *p.*

PERSECUTOR
1 Tim 1:13 who was before a blasphemer and a *p.*

PERSEVERANCE
Eph 6:18 watching thereunto with all *p.*

PERSON (PERSONS)
Lev 19:15 nor honour the *p.* of the mighty
Deut 10:17 which regardeth not *p.*, nor taketh
Mal 1: 8 will he accept thy *p.*
Mat 22:16 thou regardest not the *p.* of men
Acts 10:34 God is no respecter of *p.*
Gal 2: 6 God accepteth no man's *p.*
Eph 6: 9 neither is there respect of *p.* with him
Col 3:25 and there is no respect of *p.*
Heb 1: 3 and the express image of his *p.*
1 Pet 1:17 who without respect of *p.* judgeth
2 Pet 3:11 what manner of *p.* ought ye to be
Jude 1:16 men's *p.* in admiration because of

PERSUADE (PERSUADED)
Acts 13:43 *p.* them to continue in the grace
21:14 when he would not be *p.*
Rom 8:38 I am *p.* that neither death
2 Cor 5:11 we *p.* men, but we are made manifest
Gal 1:10 do I *p.* men, or God
Heb 6: 9 are *p.* better things of you
11:13 were *p.* of them, and embraced them

PERSUASION
Gal 5: 8 this *p.* cometh not of him that calleth

PERVERSE
Num 22:32 because thy way is *p.* before me
Deut 32: 5 they are a *p.* and crooked generation
Job 6:30 cannot my taste discern *p.* things
Prov 4:24 and *p.* lips put far from thee
17:20 he that hath a *p.* tongue falleth
Is 19:14 the Lord hath mingled a *p.* spirit
Mat 17:17 O faithless and *p.* generation
Acts 20:30 shall men arise, speaking *p.* things
Phil 2:15 in the midst of a crooked and *p.* nation
1 Tim 6: 5 *p.* disputings of men or corrupt minds

PERVERT (PERVERTED, PERVERTING)
Deut 24:17 thou shalt not *p.* the judgment
1 Sam 8: 3 and took bribes, and *p.* judgment
Job 33:27 sinned and *p.* that which was right
34:12 neither will the Almighty *p.* judgment
Prov 17:23 to *p.* the ways of judgment
Jer 3:21 they have *p.* their way
Mic 3: 9 that abhor judgment, and *p.* all equity
Luke 23: 2 this fellow *p.* the nation
Acts 13:10 not cease to *p.* the right

PESTILENCE (PESTILENCES)
2 Sam 24:15 so the Lord sent a *p.* upon Israel
1 Ki 8:37 if there be *p.*, blasting, mildew
Ps 78:50 but gave their life over to the *p.*
Jer 14:12 by the famine, and by the *p.*
Ezek 5:12 part of thee shall die with the *p.*
Amos 4:10 I have sent among you the *p.*
Hab 3: 5 before him went the *p.*
Mat 24: 7 there shall be famines, and *p.*

PETITION (PETITIONS)
1 Sam 1:17 grant thee thy *p.*, that thou hast
Esth 5: 6 what is thy *p.*? and it shall
Ps 20: 5 the Lord fulfil all thy *p.*
1 John 5:15 we have the *p.* that we desired

PHYSICIAN
Job 13: 4 ye are all *p.* of no value
Jer 8:22 is there no *p.* there
Mat 9:12 that be whole need not a *p.*
Luke 4:23 say unto me, *P.* heal thyself
Col 4:14 Luke the beloved *p.* and Demas

PIECE
Prov 6:26 is brought to a *p.* of bread
28:21 for a *p.* of bread that man will
Mat 9:16 no man putteth a *p.* of new cloth
Luke 14:18 I have bought a *p.* of ground

PIERCE (PIERCED, PIERCING)
Num 24: 8. and *p.* them through with his arrows
2 Ki 18:21 go into his hand and *p.* it
Ps 22:16 they *p.* my hands and my feet
Luke 2:35 sword shall *p.* through thy
1 Tim 6:10 *p.* themselves through with many sorrows
Heb 4:12 *p.* even to the dividing asunder of
Rev 1: 7 they also which *p.* him

PILGRIMS
Heb 11:13 were strangers and *p.* on the earth
1 Pet 2:11 I beseech you as strangers and *p.*

PILGRIMAGE
Gen 47: 9 the years of my *p.* are an hundred
Ex 6: 4 the land of their *p.*, wherein they
Ps 119:54 my songs in the house of my *p.*

PILLAR (PILLARS)
Gen 19:26 she became a *p.* of salt
Ex 13:21 by day in a *p.* of cloud
Num 14:14 and in a *p.* of fire by night
Deut 31:15 tabernacle in a *p.* of a cloud
Neh 9:12 in the night by a *p.* of fire
Job 9: 6 the *p.* thereof tremble
26:11 the *p.* of heaven tremble
Ps 75: 3 I bear up the *p.* of it
99: 7 spake unto them in the cloudy *p.*
Prov 9: 1 hath hewn out her seven *p.*
Sol 3: 6 *p.* of smoke perfumed with myrrh
3:10 made the *p.* thereof of silver
5:15 his legs are as *p.* of marble
Is 19:19 *p.* at the border thereof to the Lord
Jer 1:18 I made thee an iron *p.*
1 Tim 3:15 God the *p.* and ground of the truth
Rev 3:12 make a *p.* in the temple

PILLOW
Gen 28:11 put them for his *p.*, and lay down
Ezek 13:18 the women that sew *p.* to all armholes

PIT
Gen 37:20 cast him into some *p.*, and we will
Ex 21:33 if a man shall dig a *p.*, and not
Job 33:24 deliver him from going down to the *p.*
Ps 9:15 sunk down in the *p.* they had made
28: 1 like them that go down to the *p.*
40: 2 out of an horrible *p.*
55:23 bring them down into the *p.* of destruction
88: 4 them that go down into the *p.*
143: 7 unto them that go down into the *p.*
Prov 1:12 as those that go down into the *p.*
22:14 mouth of strange women is a deep *p.*
23:27 and a strange woman is a narrow *p.*
Is 38:17 it from the *p.* of corruption
38:18 they that go down into the *p.*
51: 1 hole of the *p.* whence ye are digged
Zech 9:11 sent prisoners out of the *p.*
Rev 20: 1 having the key of the bottomless *p.*

PITS
Ps 119:85 proud digged *p.* for me, which are
Jer 14: 3 came to the *p.* and found no water

PITY
Deut 7:16 thine eye shall have no *p.* upon them
Job 6:14 *p.* should be shown from his friend
19:21 have *p.* on me, have *p.*
Is 63: 9 in his *p.* he redeemed them
Ezek 36:21 had *p.* for my holy name
Mat 18:33 even as I had *p.* on thee

PITIETH
Ps 103:13 *p.* his children, so the Lord *p.*

PITIFUL
Jas 5:11 that the Lord is very *p.*
1 Pet 3: 8 as brethren be *p.*, be courteous

PLACE (PLACES)
Ex 3: 5 the *p.* whereon thou standest is holy
Deut 12:14 in the *p.* which the Lord shall choose
Job 7:10 neither shall his *p.* know him any more
Ps 16: 6 lines fallen unto me in pleasant *p.*

Ps 26: 8 the *p.* where thine honour dwelleth
32: 7 thou art my hiding *p.*; thou shalt
90: 1 Lord, thou hast been our dwelling *p.*
Prov 8: 2 she standeth in the top of high *p.*
15: 3 eyes of the Lord are in every *p.*
Is 40: 4 and the rough *p.* plain
66: 1 where is the *p.* of my rest
Hos 5:15 will go and return to my *p.*
10: 8 the high *p.* also of Aven
Amos 4:13 treadeth upon the high *p.* of the earth
Hab 3:19 make me to walk upon mine high *p.*
John 8:37 my word hath no *p.* in you
11:48 take away both our *p.* and nation
Rom 12:19 avenge not, but rather give *p.*
1 Cor 4:11 and have no certain dwelling *p.*
11:20 ye come together into one *p.*
Eph 1: 3 all spiritual blessings in heavenly *p.*
2: 6 in heavenly *p.* in Christ Jesus
3:10 principalities and powers in heavenly *p.*
4:27 neither give *p.* to the devil
6:12 against spiritual wickedness in high *p.*
Rev 12: 6 she hath a *p.* prepared of God

PLAGUE (PLAGUES)

1 Ki 8:38 every man the *p.* of his own heart
Ps 89:23 and *p.* them that hate him
Hos 13:14 O death, I will be thy *p.*
Rev 16: 9 which hath power over these *p.*
18: 8 therefore shall her *p.* come in one day
22:18 God shall add unto him the *p.*

PLAIN (PLAINLY)

Gen 25:27 Jacob was a *p.* man
Ps 27:11 lead me in a *p.* path
Prov 8: 9 they are all *p.* to him
Zech 4: 7 thou shalt become a *p.*
John 16:29 unto him, Lo now speakest thou *p.*

PLAINNESS

2 Cor 3:12 we use great *p.* of speech

PLANT (PLANTED, PLANTETH, PLANTS)

Gen 2: 5 and every *p.* of the field
Job 14: 9 bring forth boughs like a *p.*
Ps 1: 3 a tree *p.* by the rivers
92:13 *p.* in the house of the Lord
128: 3 thy children like olive *p.* around
Is 40:24 yea, they shall not be *p.*
Jer 2:21 I *p.* thee a noble vine
18: 9 kingdom, to build it and to *p.* it
24: 6 *p.* them and not pluck
17: 8 as a tree *p.* by the waters
Ezek 34:29 raise up for them a *p.* of renown
Mat 15:13 my heavenly Father hath not *p.*
21:33 *p.* a vineyard and hedged it
Rom 6: 5 we have been *p.* together
1 Cor 3: 6 I have *p.*, Apollos watered
9: 7 who *p.* a vineyard and eateth not

PLANTING

Is 60:21 the branch of my *p.*, the work of
61: 3 trees of righteousness, the *p.* of the Lord

PLAY

Ex 32: 6 and to drink, and rose up to *p.*
2 Sam 2:14 now arise and *p.* before us
Ezek 33:32 can *p.* well on an instrument
1 Cor 10: 7 eat and drink, and rose up to *p.*

PLEAD

Judg 6:31 he that will *p.* for him
Job 13:19 who will *p.* with me
16:21 might *p.* for man with God
23: 6 will he *p.* against me with great power
Is 1:17 the fatherless; *p.* for the widow
43:26 let us *p.* together: declare thou
66:16 by fire and sword will the Lord *p.*
Jer 2:29 wherefore will ye *p.* with me
12: 1 righteous art thou, Lord, when I *p.*
25:31 he will *p.* with all flesh
Hos 2: 2 *p.* with your mother, *p.*
Joel 3: 2 I will *p.* for them there

PLEASE

2 Sam 7:29 now let it *p.* thee to bless
Ps 69:31 this also shall *p.* the Lord
Prov 16: 7 when man's ways *p.* the Lord
Is 55:11 accomplish that which I *p.*
56: 4 choose the things that *p.* me
Rom 8: 8 that are in flesh cannot *p.* God
15: 1 and not to *p.* ourselves
15: 2 let every one of us *p.* his neighbour
1 Cor 7:32 how he may *p.* the Lord
10:33 I *p.* men in all things
Gal 1:10 do I seek to *p.* men
1 Thes 4: 1 how ye ought to walk, and to *p.* him
Heb 11: 6 without faith it is impossible to *p.*

PLEASED (PLEASETH, PLEASING)

Ps 115: 3 God hath done whatsoever he *p.*
Eccl 7:26 whoso *p.* God shall escape
8: 3 he doeth whatsoever *p.* him
Is 42:21 Lord is well *p.* for his
53:10 it *p.* the Lord to bruise him
Mic 6: 7 will the Lord be *p.* with thousands
Mat 3:17 Son, in whom I am well *p.*
17: 5 in whom I am well *p.*, hear ye him
Rom 15: 3 for even Christ *p.* not himself
Col 1:10 worthy of the Lord unto all *p.*
1:19 it *p.* the Father that in him should
1 Thes 2: 4 not as *p.* men, but God
Heb 11: 5 he had this testimony, that he *p.* God
13:16 with such sacrifices God is well *p.*
13:21 working in you that which is well *p.*
1 John 3:22 do things *p.* in his sight

PLEASANT

Gen 2: 9 every tree that is *p.* to the sight
3: 6 that it was *p.* to the eyes
2 Sam 1:23 Saul and Jonathan were lovely and *p.*
Ps 16: 6 lines fallen to me in *p.* places
133: 1 how *p.* for brethren to dwell
Prov 2:10 knowledge is *p.* to the soul
5:19 as a loving hind and *p.* roe
9:17 bread eaten in secret is *p.*
Eccl 11: 7 *p.* for the eyes to behold the sun
Sol 1:16 thou art fair, my beloved, yea, *p.*
7: 6 how *p.* art thou, O love, for delights
Jer 31:20 dear son? is he a *p.* child
Mic 2: 9 have ye cast out from their *p.* houses

PLEASANTNESS

Prov 3:17 her ways are ways of *p.*

PLEASURE

Gen 18:12 shall I have *p.*, my lord being old
1 Chr 29:17 and hast *p.* in uprightness. As for
Ps 5: 4 not a God that hath *p.* in
35:27 hath *p.* in the prosperity of his
51:18 do good in thy good *p.* unto Zion
102:14 servants take *p.* in her stones
103:21 ministers of his that do his *p.*
147:11 Lord taketh *p.* in them
Prov 21:17 he that loveth *p.* shall be poor
Eccl 5: 4 for he hath no *p.* in fools
12: 1 say, I have no *p.* in them
Is 44:28 shall perform all my *p.*
53:10 the *p.* of the Lord shall prosper in
Jer 22:28 is he a vessel wherein is no *p.*
Ezek 18:32 no *p.* in the death of him that dieth
Mal 1:10 I have no *p.* in you, saith the Lord
Luke 12:32 it is your Father's good *p.*
2 Cor 12:10 I take *p.* in infirmities
Eph 1: 5 according to the good *p.* of
Phil 2:13 and to do of his good *p.*
2 Thes 1:11 fulfil all good *p.* of his
Heb 10:38 my soul shall have no *p.*
12:10 chastened us after their own *p.*
Rev 4:11 for thy *p.* they are and were created

PLEASURES

Ps 16:11 at thy right hand *p.* for evermore
36: 8 drink of the river of thy *p.*
2 Tim 3: 4 lovers of *p.* more than lovers of God
Tit 3: 3 serving divers lusts and *p.*
Heb 11:25 than to enjoy the *p.* of sin

PLENTY

Job 37:23 in judgment, and in *p.* of justice

PLENTEOUS

Ps 86: 5 *p.* in mercy unto all them that call
103: 8 slow to anger, and *p.* in mercy
130: 7 with him is *p.* redemption
Mat 9:37 harvest is *p.*, but the labourers

PLOUGH (PLOW, PLOWED, PLOWETH)

Deut 22:10 thou shalt not *p.* with an ox and an
Judg 14:18 if ye had not *p.* with my heifer
Job 4: 8 they that *p.* iniquity, and
Ps 129: 3 the plowers *p.* on my back: they made
Prov 20: 4 sluggard will not *p.* by reason of
Is 28:24 doth plowman *p.* all day
Jer 26:18 Zion shall be *p.* like a field
Hos 10:13 ye have *p.* wickedness, ye have
Luke 9:62 having put his hand to the *p.*
1 Cor 9:10 he that *p.* should plow in hope; and

PLOWMAN

Is 61: 5 shall be your *p.* and your vinedressers
Amos 9:13 the *p.* shall overtake the reaper

PLOWSHARES

Is 2: 4 they shall beat their swords into *p.*
Joel 3:10 beat your *p.* into swords
Mic 4: 3 shall beat their swords into *p.*

POLLUTE (POLLUTED)

Num 18:32 neither shall ye *p.* the holy things
Ezek 7:21 for a spoil; and they shall *p.* it
Mic 2:10 because it is *p.*, it shall destroy you
Zeph 3: 1 woe to her that is filthy and *p.*
Mal 1:12 the table of the Lord is *p.*

POLLUTIONS

Acts 15:20 they abstain from *p.* of idols
2 Pet 2:20 they have escaped the *p.* of the world

PONDER (PONDERED, PONDERETH)

Prov 4:26 *p.* the way of thy feet and let
21: 2 but the Lord *p.* the hearts
24:12 he that *p.* the heart consider it
Luke 2:19 *p.* them in her heart

POOR

Ex 23:11 that the *p.* of thy people may eat
30:15 the *p.* shall not give less
Lev 19:15 not respect the person of the *p.*
Deut 15:11 for the *p.* shall never cease out
1 Sam 2: 7 Lord maketh *p.* and maketh rich
2: 8 raiseth the *p.* out of dust
Job 5:16 so the *p.* hath hope, and iniquity
36:15 deliver the *p.* in affliction
Ps 10:14 *p.* committeth himself to thee
69:33 the Lord heareth the *p.* and
72: 4 he shall judge the *p.* of the
132:15 satisfy her *p.* with bread
140:12 and the right of the *p.*
Prov 13: 7 there is that maketh himself *p.*
14:20 *p.* is hated of his neighbour
14:31 oppresseth the *p.* reproacheth his Maker
19: 4 *p.* is separated from his neighbour
19: 7 all brethren of the *p.* do hate him
22:22 rob not the *p.* because he is *p.*
30: 9 lest I be *p.* and steal
Is 14:32 *p.* of his people shall trust
29:19 *p.* among men shall rejoice
41:17 when the *p.* and needy seek water
58: 7 bring the *p.* that are cast out to thy

Is 66: 2 that is *p.* and of a contrite
Jer 5: 4 surely these are *p.*; they are foolish
Amos 2: 6 and the *p.* for a pair of shoes
Zeph 3:12 an afflicted and *p.* people
Zech 11:11 *p.* of the flock waited on me
Mat 5: 3 blessed are the *p.* in spirit
11: 5 *p.* have the gospel preached to
26:11 ye have the *p.* always with you
Luke 6:20 blessed be ye *p.*: for yours is the
2 Cor 6:10 as *p.*, yet making many rich
8: 9 for your sakes he became *p.*
9: 9 he hath given to the *p.*
Gal 2:10 we should remember the *p.*
Jas 2: 5 God chosen the *p.* of this world
Rev 3:17 thou art wretched, and miserable and *p.*

PORTION
Deut 21:17 by giving him a double *p.* of all
33:21 in a *p.* of the lawgiver, was he
32: 9 Lord's *p.* is his people
2 Ki 2: 9 double *p.* of thy spirit
Job 24:18 their *p.* is cursed in earth
26:14 how little a *p.* is heard
31: 2 what *p.* of God is from above
Ps 16: 5 Lord is the *p.* of mine inheritance
17:14 have their *p.* in this life
63:10 they shall be a *p.* for foxes
73:26 of my heart and my *p.* for ever
142: 5 art my *p.* in him a *p.* with the
Is 61: 7 they shall rejoice in their *p.*
Jer 10:16 the *p.* of Jacob not like them
Hab 1:16 because by them their *p.* is fat
Zech 2:12 Lord shall inherit Judah his *p.*

POSSESS (POSSESSED, POSSESSING)
Gen 22:17 thy seed shall *p.* the gate of his
Judg 11:24 wilt thou not *p.* that which Chemosh
Job 7: 3 made to *p.* months of vanity
13:26 *p.* the iniquities of my youth
Ps 139:13 for thou hast *p.* my reins: thou
Prov 8:22 Lord *p.* me in the beginning
Is 63:18 people of thy holiness *p.* it a little
Luke 21:19 in your patience *p.* ye your souls
1 Cor 7:30 they that buy as though they *p.* not
2 Cor 6:10 as having nothing yet *p.* all
1 Thes 4: 4 you should know how to *p.* his vessel

POSSESSION
Eph 1:14 until the redemption of the purchased *p.*

POSSIBLE
Mat 19:26 with God all things are *p.*
24:24 if *p.* shall deceive the very elect
Mark 9:23 all things are *p.* to him that
14:36 Father, all things are *p.* to thee
Luke 18:27 impossible with men are *p.* with God
Rom 12:18 if it be *p.*, as much as lieth in you
Heb 10: 4 not *p.* that the blood of bulls

POT (POTS)
Ex 16:33 take a *p.* and put an omer full
Ps 68:13 though you have lain among the *p.*
Jer 1:13 I said, I see a seething *p.*
Zech 14:21 every *p.* in Jerusalem and in Judah

POTTER (POTTER'S)
Is 29:16 shall be esteemed as the *p.* clay
64: 8 and thou our *p.*, ad we all are
Jer 18: 6 cannot I do with you as this *p.*
Lam 4: 2 the work of the hands of the *p.*
Rom 9:21 hath not the *p.* power over the clay
Rev 2:27 as the vessels of the *p.* shall they

POUR (POURED, POURETH)
Job 10:10 hast thou not *p.* me out as milk
12:21 he *p.* contempt upon princes
16:20 mine eye *p.* out tears unto God
30:16 my soul is *p.* out upon me
Ps 45: 2 grace is *p.* into thy lips
62: 8 *p.* out your heart before him
79: 6 *p.* out thy wrath on the heathen
107:40 he *p.* contempt upon princes
Prov 1:23 I will *p.* out my Spirit
Sol 1: 3 name is as ointment *p.* forth
Is 32:15 the Spirit be *p.* upon us from on high
42:25 he hath *p.* upon him the fury
44: 3 *p.* water on him that is thirsty
53:12 *p.* out his soul unto death
Jer 7:20 my fury shall be *p.* out
10:25 *p.* out thy fury upon the heathen
Lam 2:19 *p.* thine heart like water before
Ezek 20: 8 I will *p.* out my fury upon them
30:15 I will *p.* my fury upon Sin
Zeph 3: 8 to *p.* upon them my indignation
Rev 16: 1 *p.* vials of the wrath of God

POVERTY
Gen 45:11 all that thou hast, come to *p.*
Prov 6:11 so shall thy *p.* come as one
10:15 destruction of the poor is their *p.*
11:24 but it tendeth to *p.*
20:13 love not sleep lest thou come to *p.*
30: 8 give me neither *p.* nor riches
2 Cor 8: 2 their deep *p.* abounded unto the
8: 9 ye through his *p.* might be rich
Rev 2: 9 I know thy works, and tribulation, and *p.*

POWER
Gen 32:28 for as a prince hast thou *p.* with God
49: 3 dignity and excellency of *p.*
Deut 8:18 giveth thee *p.* to get wealth
32:36 when he seeth that their *p.* is gone
2 Sam 22:33 God is my strength and *p.*
1 Chr 29:11 is the greatness, and the *p.* and
Ezra 8:22 *p.* and his wrath is against all them
Job 26: 2 thou helped him that is without *p.*
26:14 thunder of his *p.* who can
Ps 62:11 that the *p.* belongeth unto God
Prov 3:27 when it is in the *p.* of thine hand
18:21 and life are in the *p.* of the tongue
Eccl 8: 4 the word of the king is, there is *p.*
8: 8 no man that hath *p.* over the spirit to
Is 40:29 he giveth *p.* to the faint
Jer 10:12 he hath made the earth by his *p.*
Hos 12: 3 by strength he had *p.* with God
Mic 3: 8 I am full of *p.* by the Spirit
Hab 1:11 imputing *p.* to his God
3: 4 there was the hiding of his *p.*
Zech 4: 6 not by might, nor by *p.* but by
Mat 9: 6 hath *p.* on earth to forgive sins
9: 8 glorified God which had given such *p.*
22:29 the scriptures nor the *p.* of God
28:18 all *p.* is given unto me in heaven
Mark 9: 1 kingdom of God come with *p.*
Luke 1:35 *p.* of the Highest shall overshadow
5:17 *p.* of the Lord to heal them
22:53 this is your hour and *p.* of
24:49 till ye be endued with *p.*
John 1:12 gave he *p.* to become the sons of God
10:18 *p.* to lay it down and *p.* to
17: 2 given him *p.* over all flesh
19:10 that I have *p.* to crucify thee
Acts 26:18 them from the *p.* of Satan to God
Rom 1:16 gospel is the *p.* of God unto salvation
1:20 even his eternal *p.* and Godhead
9:22 to make his *p.* known, endured with
13: 1 there is no *p.* but of God
1 Cor 1:24 Christ the *p.* of God, and the wisdom
2: 4 demonstration of the Spirit and *p.*
4:19 which are puffed up, but the *p.*
5: 4 together with the *p.* of our Lord
6:12 not be brought under the *p.* of
9: 4 have we not *p.* to eat and
2 Cor 4: 7 excellency of the *p.* may be of God
13:10 according to the *p.* which the Lord hath given
Eph 1:19 exceeding greatness of his *p.*
2: 2 to the prince of the *p.* of the air
Phil 3:10 know the *p.* of his resurrection
Col 1:11 according to his glorious *p.*
1:13 delivered from the *p.* of darkness
2:10 head of all principality and *p.*
2 Thes 1: 9 and from the glory of his *p.*
1 Tim 6:16 to whom be honour and *p.* everlasting
2 Tim 1: 7 Spirit of *p.* and of love
3: 5 form of godliness, denying *p.*
Heb 1: 3 all things by the word of his *p.*
2:14 destroy him that had the *p.* of death
6: 5 the good word of God and the *p.*
1 Pet 1: 5 kept by the *p.* of God through faith
2 Pet 1: 3 his divine *p.* hath given
Jude 1:25 be glory and majesty, dominion and *p.*
Rev 2:26 him will I give *p.* over nations
4:11 to receive glory and honour and *p.*
5:13 blessing and honour and glory and *p.*
7:12 and *p.* and might be unto our God
11: 3 I give *p.* unto my two witnesses
11:17 hast taken to thee thy great *p.*
12:10 of our God and the *p.* of his Christ
16: 9 hath *p.* over these plagues
19: 1 honour and *p.*, unto the Lord our God

POWERS
Eph 6:12 against principalities, against *p.*
Col 1:16 or dominions or principalities, or *p.*
1 Pet 3:22 authorities and *p.* being made subject unto him

PRAISE (PRAISED)
Deut 10:21 he is thy *p.* and thy God
Judg 5: 3 I will sing *p.* to the Lord God
2 Sam 22: 4 who is worthy to be *p.*: so shall
1 Chr 16:25 greatly to be *p.*: he also is to
Neh 9: 5 above all blessing and *p.*
Ps 7:17 I will *p.* the Lord according to his
9: 1 I will *p.* thee, O Lord, with my
22:25 my *p.* shall be of thee
30: 9 shall the dust *p.* thee? shall it
33: 1 *p.* is comely for the upright
42: 5 shall *p.* him for the help of his
48: 1 greatly to be *p.* in the city of
63: 3 my lips shall *p.* thee
65: 1 *p.* waiteth for thee, O God
88:10 shall the dead arise and *p.*
96: 4 great and greatly to be *p.*
109: 1 hold not peace, God of my *p.*
119:164 seven times a day do I *p.* thee
145: 3 Lord, and greatly to be *p.*
145:10 all thy works shall *p.* thee
Prov 27: 2 let another man *p.* thee, and not
27:21 so is a man to his *p.*
31:31 her own works *p.* her in the gates
Is 38:18 the grave cannot *p.* thee
38:19 the living shall *p.* thee as I do
60:18 walls Salvation and thy gates *P.*
62: 7 make Jerusalem a *p.* in the earth
Jer 13:11 for a *p.* and for a glory
17:14 be saved: for thou art my *p.*
Joel 2:26 eat in plenty and be satisfied and *p.*
Hab 3: 3 earth was full of his *p.*
John 12:43 *p.* of men more than the *p.* of God
Rom 2:29 whose *p.* is not of men
Eph 1: 6 *p.* of the glory of his grace
Phil 4: 8 if there be any *p.*, think on
Heb 13:15 offer the sacrifice of *p.* to God
1 Pet 2:14 for the *p.* of them that do well

PRAISES (PRAISING)
Ex 15:11 glorious in holiness, fearful in *p.*
2 Chr 5:13 to be heard in *p.*, and thanking thee
Ezra 3:11 sang together by course in *p.*
Ps 22: 3 that inhabitest the *p.* of Israel
78: 4 generation to come the *p.* of the
84: 4 they will still be *p.* thee
149: 6 high *p.* of God be in their mouth
Is 60: 6 shall show forth the *p.* of the Lord
63: 7 and the *p.* of the Lord, according
Luke 2:13 multitude of the heavenly host *p.* God
Acts 2:47 *p.* God, and having favour with all
1 Pet 2: 9 ye should show forth the *p.* of him

PRAY
Gen 20: 7 *p.* for thee and thou shalt live

1 Sam 7: 5 I will *p.* for you to the Lord
2 Sam 7:27 found in his heart to *p.* this
Job 21:15 profit shall we have, if we *p.*
42: 8 my servant Job shall *p.* for
Ps 5: 2 my God: to thee will I *p.*
55:17 morning and noon will I *p.*
122: 6 *p.* for the peace of Jerusalem
Jer 7:16 therefore *p.* not for this people
Mat 5:44 *p.* for them which despitefully
26:41 watch and *p.* that ye enter not
Mark 11:24 things ye desire when ye *p.*
Luke 11: 1 teach us to *p.* as John also
16:27 I *p.* thee therefore, father
18: 1 end, that men ought always to *p.*
21:36 watch ye and *p.* always
John 16:26 I will *p.* the Father for
17: 9 I *p.* for them: I *p.* not
17:20 neither *p.* I for these alone
Acts 8:22 *p.* God, if perhaps the thought of
10: 9 Peter went on the housetop to *p.*
Rom 8:26 know not what we should *p.* for
1 Cor 14:15 I will *p.* with the spirit
2 Cor 5:20 we *p.* you in Christ's stead
Col 1: 9 do not cease to *p.* for you
1 Thes 5:17 *p.* without ceasing
5:25 brethren, *p.* for us
2 Thes 3: 1 finally, brethren, *p.* for us
1 Tim 2: 8 that men *p.* every where lifting up
Heb 13:18 *p.* for us, for we trust we have
Jas 5:13 any afflicted? let him *p.*
5:16 *p.* one for another, that ye may

PRAYING (PRAYED)

Luke 22:32 I have *p.* for thee that thy faith
22:44 in an agony he *p.* more earnestly
Acts 10: 2 gave much alms to people and *p.* to God
20:36 he kneeled down and *p.* with them all
Eph 6:18 *p.* always with all prayer and supplication
Jas 5:17 he *p.* earnestly that it might not rain

PRAYER

2 Sam 7:27 to pray this *p.* to thee
1 Ki 8:28 respect unto the *p.* of thy servant
8:38 what *p.* and supplication soever be
8:45 hear thou in heaven their *p.*
Neh 1: 6 mayest hear the *p.* of thy servant
4: 9 we made our *p.* to our God
Job 15: 4 off fear, and restrainest *p.* before God
Ps 65: 2 thou that hearest *p.* unto thee
102:17 he will regard the *p.* of the destitute
109: 4 but I give myself unto *p.*
Prov 15: 8 *p.* of the upright is his delight
15:29 Lord heareth the *p.* of the righteous
28: 9 even his *p.* shall be abomination
Is 26:16 they poured out a *p.* when thy
56: 7 an house of *p.* for all people
Lam 3:44 our *p.* should not pass through
Dan 9: 3 to seek by *p.* and supplications
Mat 17:21 this kind goeth not out but by *p.*
23:14 for a pretence, make long *p.*
Luke 6:12 continued all night in *p.* to God
Acts 1:14 continued with one accord in *p.* and
3: 1 to the temple at the hour of *p.*
6: 4 give ourselves continually to *p.*
12: 5 *p.* was made without ceasing
16:13 where *p.* was wont to be made
Rom 12:12 continuing instant in *p.*
1 Cor 7: 5 may give yourselves to *p.*
2 Cor 1:11 ye also helping together by *p.* for us
Phil 4: 6 in every thing by *p.* and supplication
Col 4: 2 continue in *p.*, and watch
1 Tim 4: 5 sanctified by the word of God and *p.*
Jas 5:15 *p.* of faith shall save the sick
5:16 effectual fervent *p.* of a righteous
1 Pet 4: 7 be ye therefore sober and watch unto *p.*

PRAYERS

Ps 72:20 *p.* of David the son of Jesse are
Acts 10: 4 thy *p.* and thine alms are
1 Tim 2: 1 first of all that supplications, *p.*
1 Pet 3: 7 that your *p.* be not hindered
3:12 his ears are open to their *p.*
Rev 5: 8 which are the *p.* of saints

PREACH

Neh 6: 7 appointed prophets to *p.* of thee
Jonah 3: 2 *p.* unto it the preaching that I bid
Mat 4:17 Jesus began to *p.* and to say
10:27 what ye hear in thine ear, that *p.* ye
Mark 1: 4 and *p.* the baptism of repentance for
Luke 4:18 to *p.* deliverance to the captives
9:60 go and *p.* the kingdom of God
Acts 10:42 commanded us to *p.* unto the people
15:21 in every city them that *p.* him
Rom 10: 8 word of faith which we *p.*
10:15 how shall they *p.* except they
1 Cor 1:23 we *p.* Christ crucified, unto the
15:11 so we *p.* and so ye believed
2 Cor 4: 5 we *p.* not ourselves but Christ
Phil 1:15 some indeed *p.* Christ even of envy
2 Tim 4: 2 *p.* the word; be instant in season

PREACHED (PREACHETH, PREACHING)

Ps 40: 9 I have *p.* righteousness in the great
Mark 2: 2 he *p.* the word unto them
6:12 he *p.* that men should repent
16:20 *p.* everywhere, the Lord working with
Luke 4:44 he *p.* in the synagogues of Galilee
24:47 remission of sins should be *p.* in his
Acts 8: 5 Samaria, and *p.* Christ unto them
9:20 he *p.* Christ in the synagogues
10:36 *p.* peace by Jesus Christ: (he is Lord)
11:19 *p.* the word to none but Jews
13:38 through this man is *p.* unto you
1 Cor 1:18 *p.* of the cross is to them
1:21 by foolishness of *p.* to save them
2: 4 my *p.* was not with enticing words
9:27 when I have *p.* to others, I myself
15: 1 gospel which I *p.* unto you
15: 2 keep in memory what I *p.*
15:12 if Christ be *p.* that he rose
15:14 then is our *p.* vain, and faith
Gal 1:23 *p.* the faith he once destroyed
Col 1:23 which was *p.* to every creature
1 Tim 3:16 *p.* unto the Gentiles believed on
Heb 4: 2 the word *p.* did not profit them
1 Pet 3:19 went and *p.* unto the spirits in prison

PREACHER

Eccl 1: 1 the words of the *p.*, the son of
12: 9 because the *p.* was wise, he still
1 Tim 2: 7 ordained a *p.*, and an apostle
2 Tim 1:11 whereunto I am appointed a *p.*

PRECEPTS

Neh 9:14 commandedst them *p.*, statutes, and laws
Ps 119: 4 commanded us to keep thy *p.*
119:15 I will meditate in thy *p.*
119:27 to understand the way of thy *p.*
119:45 at liberty: for I seek thy *p.*
119:56 had, because I kept thy *p.*
119:110 I erred not from thy *p.*
119:128 I esteem all thy *p.* to be right
119:141 I do not forget thy *p.*
119:159 consider I love thy *p.*: quicken
Is 28:10 *p.* upon *p.* upon *p.*
29:13 fear is taught by *p.* of men

PRECIOUS

1 Sam 3: 1 word of the Lord was *p.*
26:21 my soul was *p.* in thine eyes
Ps 49: 8 redemption of the soul is *p.*
116:15 *p.* in the sight of the Lord
126: 6 goeth forth and weepeth, bearing *p.* seed
139:17 how *p.* are thy thoughts
Eccl 7: 1 good name is better than *p.* ointment
Is 13:12 I will make a man more *p.* than gold
28:16 a tried stone, a *p.* corner stone
43: 4 since thou wast *p.* in my sight
Jer 15:19 if thou take *p.* from vile
Lam 4: 2 *p.* sons of Zion are comparable to
Jas 5: 7 husbandman waiteth for the *p.* fruit
1 Pet 1: 7 the trial of your faith is more *p.*
1:19 redeemed with the *p.* blood of Christ
2: 4 stone chosen of God and *p.*
2 Pet 1: 1 obtained like *p.* faith with us
1: 4 exceeding great and *p.* promises

PREDESTINATE (PREDESTINATED)

Rom 8:30 whom he did *p.* them he also called
Eph 1: 5 having *p.* us unto the adoption

PREFER (PREFERRED, PREFERRING)

Ps 137: 6 if I *p.* not Jerusalem above my chief
John 1:15 cometh after me is *p.* before me
Rom 12:10 in honour *p.* one another
1 Tim 5:21 without *p.* one before another

PREPARATION (PREPARATIONS)

Prov 16: 1 the *p.* of the heart in man
Mark 15:42 it was the *p.*, that is, the day

PREPARE

Ex 15: 2 I will *p.* him an habitation
1 Sam 7: 3 *p.* your hearts to the Lord
1 Chr 29:18 *p.* their heart unto thee
2 Chr 35: 6 sanctify yourselves, and *p.* your brethren
Job 11:13 if thou *p.* thy heart and
Ps 10:17 thou wilt *p.* their heart
61: 7 O *p.* mercy and truth, which may
Prov 24:27 *p.* thy work without, and make it
Is 40: 3 *p.* ye the way of the Lord
Amos 4:12 *p.* to meet thy God, O Israel
Mic 3: 5 they even *p.* war against him
Mat 11:10 shall *p.* thy way before thee
John 14: 2 I go to *p.* a place for you

PREPARED (PREPAREST, PREPARETH)

2 Chr 19: 3 hast *p.* thine heart to seek God
27: 6 he *p.* his ways before the Lord
29:36 God had *p.* the people: for the thing
30:19 that *p.* his heart to seek God
Neh 8:10 unto them for whom nothing is *p.*
Ps 23: 5 thou *p.* a table before me in the
65: 9 thou *p.* them corn, when thou hast
68:10 *p.* of thy goodness for the poor
147: 8 who *p.* rain for the earth
Is 64: 4 what he hath *p.* for him
Hos 6: 3 his going forth is *p.* as the
Mat 20:23 to them for whom it is *p.*
22: 4 I have *p.* my dinner; my oxen
25:34 inherit the kingdom *p.* for you
Luke 1:17 ready a people *p.* for the Lord
12:47 knew his lord's will, and *p.* not
Rom 9:23 of mercy which he had afore *p.* to
2 Tim 2:21 *p.* and unto every good work
Heb 10: 5 but a body hast thou *p.* me
11:16 for he hath *p.* for them a city
Rev 12: 6 where she hath a place *p.* of God
21: 2 *p.* as a bride adorned for her husband

PRESENT

Ps 46: 1 a very *p.* help in trouble
Acts 10:33 all here *p.* before God
Rom 7:18 for to will is *p.* with me
8:38 nor things *p.* nor things to come
12: 1 *p.* your bodies a living sacrifice
1 Cor 3:22 or thing *p.*, or things to come
5: 3 absent in body, but *p.* in spirit
2 Cor 5: 8 to be *p.* with the Lord
11: 2 *p.* you as a chaste virgin
Gal 1: 4 deliver us from this *p.* evil world
Col 1:22 to *p.* you holy and unblameable and
1:28 *p.* every man perfect in Christ
2 Tim 4:10 having loved this *p.* world
2 Pet 1:12 and be established in the *p.* truth
Jude 1:24 *p.* you faultless before the presence

PRESENCE

Gen 3: 8 themselves from the *p.* of the Lord
4:16 Cain went from the *p.* of the Lord
Job 1:12 Satan went forth from the *p.* of the
23:15 I am troubled at his *p.*: when I

Ps 16:11 in thy *p.* is fulness of joy
31:20 hide them in the secret of thy *p.*
51:11 cast me not away from thy *p.*
100: 2 come before his *p.* with singing
114: 7 thou earth, at the *p.* of the Lord
139: 7 whither shall I flee from thy *p.*
140:13 upright shall dwell in thy *p.*
Is 63: 9 angel of his *p.* saved them
Jer 4:26 broken down at the *p.* of the Lord
5:22 will ye not tremble at my *p.*
Jonah 1:10 fled from the *p.* of the Lord
1 Cor 1:29 no flesh glory in his *p.*
2 Cor 10: 1 who in *p.* am base among you
Jude 1:24 present you faultless before the *p.*
Rev 14:10 *p.* of the holy angels and in *p.* of

PRESERVE (PRESERVED, PRESERVETH)

Gen 45: 7 sent me before you to *p.* you a posterity
2 Sam 8: 6 the Lord *p.* David whithersoever he
Job 10:12 and thy visitation hath *p.* my spirit
Ps 12: 7 thou shalt *p.* them from this generation
16: 1 *p.* me, O God, for in thee
25:21 let integrity and uprightness *p.* me
32: 7 thou shalt *p.* me from trouble
41: 2 Lord will *p.* and keep him alive
61: 7 mercy and truth may *p.* him
64: 1 *p.* my life from fear of the enemy
86: 2 *p.* my soul, for I am holy
97:10 he *p.* the souls of his saints
116: 6 the Lord *p.* the simple: I was brought
121: 7 Lord shall *p.* thee from all evil
140: 1 *p.* me from the violent man
145:20 Lord *p.* all them that love him
146: 9 Lord *p.* the stranger; he relieveth
Prov 2: 8 he *p.* the way of his saints
2:11 discretion shall *p.* thee
Luke 17:33 shall lose his life shall *p.* it
1 Thes 5:23 soul and body be *p.* blameless unto
2 Tim 4:18 *p.* me to his heavenly kingdom
Jude 1: 1 and *p.* in Jesus Christ, and called

PRESERVER

Job 7:20 O thou *p.* of men? why hast thou

PRESS (PRESSED, PRESSETH)

Gen 40:11 and *p.* them into Pharaoh's cup
Judg 16:16 she *p.* him daily with her words
Ps 38: 2 me, and thy hand *p.* me sore
Amos 2:13 *p.* under you as a cart is *p.*
Luke 6:38 good measure, *p.* down, and shaken
Acts 18: 5 Paul was *p.* in the spirit and
2 Cor 1: 8 were *p.* out of measure, above strength
Phil 3:14 I *p.* towards the mark for

PRETENCE

Mat 23:14 and for a *p.* make long prayer
Phil 1:18 whether in *p.*, or in truth, Christ is

PREVAIL (PREVAILED, PREVAILEST)

Gen 7:20 fifteen cubits upward did the waters *p.*
32:28 power with God and men, and hast *p.*
Ex 17:11 held up his hand, Israel *p.*
Judg 16: 5 by what means we may *p.* against him
1 Sam 2: 9 by strength shall no man *p.*
Job 14:20 thou *p.* for ever against him
Ps 9:19 arise, O Lord, let not man *p.*
65: 3 iniquities *p.* against me
Eccl 4:12 if one *p.* against him, two shall
Hos 12: 4 power over the angel, and *p.*: he wept
Mat 16:18 gates of hell shall not *p.*
Acts 19:20 mightily grew the word of God and *p.*

PREY

Gen 49:27 the morning he shall devour the *p.*
Esth 9:16 they laid not their hands on the *p.*

Ps 124: 6 not given us a *p.* to their teeth
Is 49:24 *p.* be taken from the mighty
59:15 departeth from evil maketh himself a *p.*
Jer 21: 9 life shall be unto him for a *p.*

PRICE

Lev 25:16 thou shalt increase the *p.* thereof
Deut 23:18 or the *p.* of a dog, into the house
Job 28:13 man knoweth not the *p.* thereof
Prov 17:16 a *p.* in the hand of a fool
Is 55: 1 and milk without money and without *p.*
Mat 13:46 pearl of great *p.*, went and sold
Acts 5: 2 kept back part of the *p.*, his wife
1 Cor 6:20 for ye are bought with a *p.*
1 Pet 3: 4 in the sight of God of great *p.*

PRICKS (PRICKED)

Ps 73:21 I was *p.* in my reins
Acts 2:37 they were *p.* in their heart
9: 5 for thee to kick against the *p.*
26:14 for thee to kick against the *p.*

PRIDE

2 Chr 32:26 humbled himself for the *p.* of his
Job 33:17 hide purpose, and *p.* from man
Ps 10: 2 wicked in his *p.* doth persecute
31:20 hide them from the *p.* of man
73: 6 *p.* compasseth them about as a chain
Prov 8:13 hate evil, *p.* and arrogancy
11: 2 when *p.* cometh, then cometh shame
13:10 by *p.* cometh contention: but with the
16:18 *p.* goeth before destruction
29:23 man's *p.* shall bring him low
Jer 13:17 weep in secret for your *p.*
Ezek 7:10 rod hath blossomed, *p.* hath budded
16:49 iniquity of Sodom, *p.*, fulness of bread
Dan 4:37 those that walk in *p.*
Hos 5: 5 *p.* of Israel doth testify to his
Obad 1: 3 *p.* of thine heart hath deceived thee
1 Tim 3: 6 lest being lifted up with *p.* he fall
1 John 2:16 lust of the eyes, and the *p.* of life

PRIEST

Gen 14:18 he was the *p.* of the most high God
Ex 2:16 the *p.* of Midian had seven daughters
Lev 5: 6 the *p.* shall make an atonement
21:10 is the high *p.* among his brethren
Is 24: 2 as with people, so with the *p.*
28: 7 *p.* and prophet have erred through
Jer 23:11 prophet and *p.* are profane; yea
Ezek 7:26 law shall perish from the *p.*
Hos 4: 4 they that strive with the *p.*
4: 9 and there shall be like people, like *p.*
Heb 2:17 a merciful and faithful high *p.*
3: 1 consider the Apostle and High *p.* of
5: 1 every high *p.* taken from among men
5: 6 thou art a *p.* for ever after the
6:20 Jesus, made an high *p.* for ever
7:26 for such an high *p.* became us
8: 3 every high *p.* is ordained to offer
9:11 Christ being come an high *p.* of good
10:21 having an high *p.* over the house of God

PRIESTS

Ps 132: 9 thy *p.* be clothed with righteousness
Is 61: 6 ye be named *P.* of the Lord
Jer 5:31 *p.* bear rule by their means
31:14 satiate the soul of the *p.* with fatness
Ezek 22:26 her *p.* have violated my law
Joel 1: 9 the *p.*, the Lord's ministers, mourn
Mat 12: 5 *p.* in the temple profane the sabbath
Acts 6: 7 company of the *p.* were obedient to
Rev 1: 6 kings and *p.* unto God and his Father
5:10 made us unto our God kings and *p.*

PRIESTHOOD

Ex 40:15 everlasting *p.* throughout their generations
Heb 7:24 ever hath an unchangeable *p.*

1 Pet 2: 5 an holy *p.*, to offer up spiritual
2: 9 ye are a chosen generation, a royal *p.*

PRINCE

Gen 23: 6 thou art a mighty *p.* among us
32:28 as a *p.* hast thou power with
34: 2 *p.* of the country saw her, he took
Ex 2:14 who made thee a *p.* and judge over
2 Sam 3:38 *p.* and great man fallen this day
Job 31:37 as a *p.* would I go near
Is 9: 6 everlasting Father, *P.* of Peace
Ezek 34:24 my servant David, a *p.* among them
Dan 10:21 in these things but Michael your *p.*
12: 1 Michael stand up, the great *p.*
Hos 3: 4 asking, and without a *p.*
John 12:31 now shall the *p.* of this world
14:30 *p.* of this world cometh and hath
16:11 the *p.* of this world is judged
Acts 3:15 And killed the *P.* of life, whom God
5:31 to be a *P.* and a Saviour
Eph 2: 2 *p.* of the power of the air
Rev 1: 5 the *p.* of the kings of the earth

PRINCES

Job 12:19 he leadeth *p.* away spoiled
12:21 he poureth contempt upon *p.*
34:19 that accepteth not persons of *p.*
Ps 45:16 thou mayest make *p.* in earth
76:12 he shall cut off the spirit of *p.*
82: 7 shall fall like one of the *p.*
118: 9 than to put confidence in *p.*
119:23 *p.* did sit and speak against me
119:161 *p.* persecuted me without cause
Prov 8:15 kings reign, and *p.* decree justice
17:26 not good, nor to strike *p.* for equity
28: 2 of a land many are the *p.* thereof
31: 4 drank wine; nor for *p.* strong drink
Is 3: 4 give children to be their *p.*
Hos 7: 5 *p.* have made him sick with bottles
8: 4 made *p.* and I knew it not
Mat 20:25 *p.* of Gentiles exercise dominion over
1 Cor 2: 6 nor of the *p.* of this world

PRINCIPALITY (PRINCIPALITIES)

Jer 13:18 for your *p.* shall come down
Rom 8:38 nor angels, nor *p.*, nor powers
Eph 1:21 far above all *p.*, and power and might
6:12 but against *p.*, against powers
Col 2:10 which is the head of all *p.* and power
Tit 3: 1 be subject to *p.* and powers

PRISON

Gen 39:20 put him into the *p.*, a place where
Is 42: 7 bring out the prisoners from the *p.*
53: 8 he was taken from *p.* and from
61: 1 opening of *p.* to them that are bound
Mat 5:25 and thou be cast into *p.*
18:30 cast into *p.* till he should pay
25:36 I was in *p.* and ye came
1 Pet 3:19 preached unto the spirits in *p.*
Rev 2:10 devil cast some of you into *p.*

PRISONER (PRISONERS)

Ps 69:33 hungry. The Lord despiseth not his *p.*
79:11 let the sighing of the *p.* come before
102:20 to hear the groaning of the *p.*
146: 7 the Lord looseth the *p.*
Zech 9:11 sent forth thy *p.* out of the pit
9:12 turn to the stronghold, ye *p.* of hope
Eph 4: 1 I a *p.* of the Lord beseech you

PRIVATE (PRIVATELY)

Gal 2: 2. but *p.* to them which were of reputation
2 Pet 1:20 scripture is of any *p.* interpretation

PRIZE

1 Cor 9:24 run all, but one receiveth the *p.*
Phil 3:14 for the *p.* of the high calling

PROCEED (PROCEEDED, PROCEEDETH)

Gen 24:50 thing *p.* from the Lord: we cannot

Deut 8: 3 by every word that *p.* out of the mouth
1 Sam 24:13 wickedness *p.* from the wicked
Is 29:14 I will *p.* to do a marvellous work
51: 4 a law shall *p.* from me
Jer 9: 3 they *p.* from evil to evil
Lam 3:38 mouth of the most High *p.* not evil
Mat 4: 4 word that *p.* out of the mouth of God
15:19 out of the heart *p.* evil thoughts
Luke 4:22 gracious words which *p.* out of his mouth
John 8:42 I *p.* forth and came from God
15:26 Spirit of truth, which *p.* from the
Eph 4:29 no corrupt communication *p.* out of
2 Tim 3: 9 they shall *p.* no further
Jas 3:10 out of the same mouth *p.* blessing
Rev 11: 5 fire *p.* out of their mouth

PROCLAIM (PROCLAIMED)

Ex 33:19 I will *p.* the name of the Lord
34: 6 Lord passed before him and *p.*
Lev 23: 2 which ye shall *p.* to be holy
Deut 20:10 then *p.* peace unto it
Prov 20: 6 men *p.* every one his own goodness
Is 61: 2 to *p.* the acceptable year of the Lord

PROFANE (PROFANED, PROFANING)

Lev 18:21 shalt thou *p.* the name of thy God
19:12 shalt thou *p.* the name of thy God
21: 6 and not *p.* the name of their God
Neh 13:17 that ye do and *p.* the sabbath day
Ezek 22: 8 things, and hast *p.* my sabbaths
22:26 no difference between the holy and *p.*
Mal 1:12 have *p.* it, in that ye say
2:10 *p.* the covenant of our fathers
2:11 Judah *p.* the holiness of the Lord
Mat 12: 5 priests in the temple *p.* the sabbath
1 Tim 1: 9 law is for the unholy and *p.*
4: 7 refuse *p.* and old wives' fables
6:20 avoiding *p.* and vain babblings
Heb 12:16 there be any fornicator or *p.* person

PROFESS

Deut 26: 3 I *p.* this day unto the Lord thy God
Tit 1:16 they *p.* that they know God

PROFESSION

1 Tim 6:12 and hast professed a good *p.*
Heb 3: 1 High Priest of our *p.*, Christ Jesus
4:14 Son of God, let us hold fast our *p.*
10:23 let us hold fast the *p.* of our faith

PROFIT (PROFITETH)

1 Sam 12:21 which cannot *p.* nor deliver
Job 34: 9 it *p.* a man nothing that he should
Prov 10: 2 treasures of wickedness *p.* nothing
11: 4 riches *p.* not in the day of wrath
14:23 in all labour there is *p.*
Eccl 7:11 by it there is *p.* to them that
Is 30: 5 not *p.* then nor be an help nor *p.*
57:12 for they shall not *p.* thee
Jer 2: 8 walked after things that do not *p.*
16:19 wherein there is no *p.*
23:32 they shall not *p.* this people at all
John 6:63 the flesh *p.* nothing: the words that
1 Cor 13: 3 have not charity, it *p.* me nothing
Gal 5: 2 Christ shall *p.* you nothing
2 Tim 2:14 they strive not about words to no *p.*
Heb 4: 2 the word preached did not *p.* them
12:10 but he for our *p.* that we might
Jas 2:14 what doth it *p.* my brethren

PROFITABLE

Job 22: 2 is wise may be *p.* unto himself
Eccl 10:10 strength: but wisdom is *p.* to direct
Acts 20:20 kept back nothing that was *p.* unto
1 Tim 4: 8 godliness is *p.* unto all things
2 Tim 3:16 inspiration of God, and is *p.* for doctrine
Tit 3: 8 these things are good and *p.* unto men
Philem 1:11 now *p.* to thee and to me

PROFITING

1 Tim 4:15 that thy *p.* may appear to all

PROMISE (PROMISES)

Num 14:34 ye shall know my breach of *p.*
Neh 5:12 that they should do according to this *p.*
Ps 77: 8 doth his *p.* fail for evermore
Luke 24:49 the *p.* of my Father upon you
Acts 1: 4 wait for the *p.* of the Father
Rom 4:16 *p.* might be sure to all the seed
9: 4 the service of God and the *p.*
9: 8 children of the *p.* are counted for
15: 8 confirm the *p.* made unto the fathers
2 Cor 1:20 all the *p.* of God in him are yea
7: 1 having therefore these *p.*
Gal 3:21 is the law against the *p.*
4:28 as Isaac was, are the children of *p.*
Eph 1:13 with that holy Spirit of *p.*
6: 2 the first commandment with *p.*
1 Tim 4: 8 *p.* of the life that now is, and
Heb 4: 1 lest a *p.* being left us of
6:12 through faith and patience inherit the *p.*
6:17 willing to show unto the heirs of *p.*
8: 6 which was established upon better *p.*
9:15 receive the *p.* of eternal inheritance
11:17 he that had received *p.*
2 Pet 1: 4 us exceeding great and precious *p.*
3: 4 where is the *p.* of his coming?
1 John 2:25 *p.* that he promised us, even eternal

PROMISED

Rom 1: 2 which he had *p.* afore by his prophets
Tit 1: 2 which God, that cannot lie, *p.* before
Heb 10:23 for he is faithful that *p.*
11:11 she judged him faithful who had *p.*
12:26 but now he hath *p.* saying

PROPHECY

1 Cor 12:10 the working of miracles; to another *p.*
1 Tim 4:14 which was given thee by *p.*
2 Pet 1:20 no *p.* of the scripture is of any
Rev 1: 3 they that hear the words of this *p.*
11: 6 it rain not in the days of their *p.*
19:10 testimony of Jesus is the spirit of *p.*
22: 7 keepeth the sayings of the *p.* of

PROPHESY (PROPHESIED)

Num 11:25 them, they *p.* and did not cease
1 Ki 22: 8 doth not *p.* good concerning me
Is 30:10 *p.* not right things *p.* deceits
Jer 23:21 I have not spoken to them, yet they *p.*
Joel 2:28 thy sons and thy daughters shall *p.*
Amos 2:12 commanded the prophets, saying *p.* not
3: 8 Lord God hath spoken, who can but *p.*
Mat 7:22 have we not *p.* in thy name
11:13 prophets and the law *p.* until John
John 11:51 *p.* that Jesus should die
1 Cor 13: 9 know in part and we *p.* in part
14: 1 but rather that ye may *p.*
14:31 for ye may all *p.* one by one
14:39 covet to *p.* and forbid not to
1 Pet 1:10 *p.* of the grace that should come
Jude 1:14 Enoch also the seventh from Adam *p.*
Rev 10:11 thou must *p.* again before many

PROPHET

Gen 20: 7 he is a *p.* and shall pray for thee
Ex 7: 1 and Aaron thy brother shall be thy *p.*
Deut 18:15 raise up unto thee a *p.*
18:18 raise them up a *p.* from among
2 Ki 5:13 if the *p.* had bid thee do some
Ezek 33:33 know that a *p.* hath been among them
Hos 9: 7 *p.* is a fool, the spiritual man
12:13 by a *p.* was he preserved
Mat 10:41 he that receiveth a *p.* in the name
13:57 a *p.* is not without honour save in
Luke 7:28 there is not a greater *p.*
13:33 a *p.* perish out of Jerusalem
24:19 *p.* mighty in deed and word
John 7:40 said, Of a truth this is the *P.*
7:52 out of Galilee ariseth no *p.*
Acts 3:22 a *p.* shall the Lord raise
3:23 will not hear the *p.* shall be destroyed
Tit 1:12 even a *p.* of their own, said
2 Pet 2:16 forbad the madness of the *p.*

PROPHETS

Num 11:29 all the Lord's people were *p.*, and
Ps 105:15 anointed, and do my *p.* no harm
Jer 5:13 the *p.* shall become wind, and the
23:26 are *p.* of the deceit of their
Lam 2:14 *p.* have seen vain and foolish things
Hos 6: 5 I hewed them by the *p.*
Mic 3:11 *p.* thereof divine for money: yet
Zeph 3: 4 her *p.* are light and treacherous
Mat 5:17 come to destroy the law, or *p.*
7:12 this is the law and the *p.*
13:17 many *p.* and righteous men have desired
22:40 on these hang all the law and the *p.*
23:34 I send you *p.* and wise men
Luke 1:70 spake by the mouth of his holy *p.*
6:23 so did their fathers unto the *p.*
16:29 they have Moses and the *p.*
16:31 if they hear not Moses and the *p.*
24:25 to believe all that the *p.* have spoken
24:44 *p.*, and in the psalms, concerning me
John 8:52 Abraham is dead, and the *p.*
Acts 3:18 by the mouth of all his *p.*
3:25 ye are children of the *p.*
10:43 to him give all the *p.* witness
13:27 knew him not nor yet voices of *p.*
26:22 things which the *p.* and Moses
26:27 believest thou the *p.*?
Rom 1: 2 which he had promised afore by his *p.*
3:21 being witnessed by the law and the *p.*
1 Cor 12:28 first apostles, secondarily *p.*
14:32 spirits of the *p.* are subject to the *p.*
Eph 2:20 the foundation of the apostles and *p.*
1 Thes 2:15 killed the Lord Jesus and their own *p.*
Heb 1: 1 spake in the past unto the fathers by the *p.*
Jas 5:10 take, my brethren, the *p.* who have spoken
Rev 18:20 rejoice, ye apostles and *p.*
22: 6 Lord God of the holy *p.* sent his
22: 9 and of thy brethren the *p.*

PROPITIATION

Rom 3:25 God hath set forth to be a *p.*
1 John 2: 2 he is the *p.* for our sins
4:10 his Son to be the *p.* for our sins

PROSPER (PROSPERED)

Gen 24:40 and *p.* thy way; and thou shalt
39: 3 Lord made all that he did to *p.*
Deut 29: 9 that ye may *p.* in that all ye do
Josh 1: 7 thou mayest *p.* whithersoever thou goest
Neh 1:11 and *p.*, I pray thee, thy servant
Job 12: 6 tabernacles of robbers *p.* and they
Ps 1: 3 whatsoever he doeth shall *p.*
122: 6 they shall *p.* that love thee
Is 53:10 the pleasure of the Lord shall *p.*
54:17 no weapon against thee shall *p.*
55:11 shall *p.* in the thing whereto
Jer 12: 1 Wherefore doth the way of the wicked *p.*
23: 5 a King shall reign and *p.*
1 Cor 16: 2 as God hath *p.* him, that there be

PROSPERITY

1 Ki 10: 7 thy wisdom and *p.* exceedeth the fame
Job 36:11 spend their days in *p.*
Ps 30: 6 in my *p.* I said I shall never

Ps 73: 3 when I saw the *p.* of the wicked
118:25 Lord, I beseech thee, send now *p.*
122: 7 walls, and *p.* be in thy palaces
Prov 1:32 *p.* of fools shall destroy them
Eccl 7:14 in the day of *p.* be joyful
Jer 22:21 I spake to thee in thy *p.*

PROUD

Job 9:13 the *p.* helpers do stoop under him
Ps 12: 3 the tongue that speaketh *p.* things
40: 4 respecteth not the *p.* nor
138: 6 the *p.* he knoweth afar off
Prov 6:17 *p.* look, a lying tongue, and hands
21: 4 high look and a *p.* heart, and the
Eccl 7: 8 patient in spirit is better than the *p.*
Mal 3:15 now we call the *p.* happy; yea
Luke 1:51 the *p.* in the imagination of their
Jas 4: 6 God resisteth the *p.*, but giveth grace
1 Pet 5: 5 for God resisteth the *p.*, and giveth

PROUDLY

Ex 18:11 wherein they dealt *p.* he was above
1 Sam 2: 3 talk no more so exceeding *p.*
Neh 9:10 knewest that they dealt *p.* against
Ps 17:10 with their mouth they speak *p.*
Is 3: 5 child behave *p.* against ancient

PROVE (PROVED)

Ex 16: 4 that I may *p.* them, whether they will
20:20 fear not, for God is come to *p.* you
Deut 8:16 and that he might *p.* thee
33: 8 whom thou didst *p.* at Massah
1 Ki 10: 1 she came to *p.* him with hard
Job 9:20 mouth shall *p.* me perverse
Ps 17: 3 thou hast *p.* mine heart
26: 2 examine me, O Lord, *p.* me
66:10 thou, O God, hast *p.* us as
95: 9 tempted me, *p.* me, and saw my work
Mal 3:10 *p.* me now herewith, saith the Lord
Rom 12: 2 that ye may *p.* what is that good and
2 Cor 8: 8 to *p.* the sincerity of your love
13: 5 *p.* your own selves, know ye not
Gal 6: 4 let every man *p.* his work
1 Thes 5:21 *p.* all things; hold fast
Heb 3: 9 your father tempted me, *p.* me

PROVERB (PROVERBS)

Deut 28:37 thou shalt become an astonishment, a *p.*
1 Ki 4:32 he spake three thousand *p.*
9: 7 and Israel shall be a *p.*
Ps 69:11 and I became a *p.* to them
Prov 1: 1 the *p.* of Solomon, the son of David
10: 1 the *p.* of Solomon. A wise son
25: 1 these are also *p.* of Solomon
Eccl 12: 9 he set in order many *p.*
Is 14: 4 thou shalt take up this *p.* against
Jer 24: 9 to be a reproach and a *p.*
Ezek 14: 8 will make him a sign and a *p.*
John 16:25 things have I spoken unto you in *p.*
2 Pet 2:22 unto them according to the true *p.*

PROVIDE (PROVIDETH)

Gen 22: 8 God will *p.* himself a lamb
Job 38:41 who *p.* for the raven his food
Ps 78:20 can he *p.* flesh for people
Prov 6: 8 *p.* her meat in the summer
Mat 10: 9 *p.* neither gold nor silver nor brass
Luke 12:33 *p.* bags which wax not old
Rom 12:17 *p.* things honest in the sight of all
1 Tim 5: 8 if any *p.* not for his own

PROVOKE (PROVOKED)

Ex 23:21 obey his voice, *p.* him not
Num 14:11 how long will this people *p.* me
14:23 neither any of them that *p.* me
16:30 these men have *p.* the Lord
Deut 9: 8 ye *p.* the Lord to wrath
31:20 and *p.* me, and break my covenant
1 Ki 14:22 *p.* him to jealousy with their sins
2 Ki 23:26 that Manasseh *p.* him withal
1 Chr 21: 1 and *p.* David to number Israel
Ezra 5:12 our fathers had *p.* God to
Ps 78:40 how oft did they *p.* him
78:56 and *p.* the most high God, and
106: 7 *p.* him at the sea, even at the Red
106:33 because they *p.* his spirit, so that
106:43 they *p.* him with their counsel
Is 3: 8 to *p.* the eyes of his glory
Jer 7:19 do they *p.* me to anger
44: 8 ye *p.* me to wrath with your
Zech 8:14 when your fathers *p.* me to wrath
Luke 11:53 to *p.* him to speak of many things
Rom 10:19 I will *p.* you to jealousy
1 Cor 10:22 do we *p.* the Lord to jealousy
2 Cor 9: 2 and your zeal hath *p.* very many
Heb 3:16 for some when they heard, did *p.*
10:24 to *p.* unto love and good works

PRUDENT

1 Sam 16:18 a man of war, and *p.* in matters
Prov 12:16 known but a *p.* man covereth shame
12:23 *p.* man concealeth knowledge: but the
13:16 *p.* man dealeth with knowledge
14: 8 wisdom of the *p.* is to understand
14:15 the *p.* man looketh well to his
14:18 the *p.* are crowned with knowledge
15: 5 he that regardeth reproof is *p.*
16:21 wise in heart shall be called *p.*
18:15 heart of the *p.* getteth knowledge
19:14 a *p.* wife is from the Lord
22: 3 a *p.* man foreseeth the evil
Is 5:21 and *p.* in their own sight
Hos 14: 9 is *p.* and he shall know them? for
Mat 11:25 hid these things from the wise and *p.*
1 Cor 1:19 to nothing the understanding of the *p.*

PRUDENCE

2 Chr 2:12 endued with *p.* and understanding
Prov 8:12 I wisdom dwell with *p.*
Eph 1: 8 abounded toward us in all wisdom and *p.*

PRUDENTLY

Is 52:13 my servant shall deal *p.*

PSALM (PSALMS)

1 Chr 16: 7 David delivered first this *p.* to thank
16: 9 sing *p.* unto him, talk ye of all
Ps 81: 2 take a *p.*, and bring hither the timbrel
95: 2 joyful noise unto him with *p.*
98: 5 and with the voice of a *p.*
Acts 13:33 it is also written in the second *p.*
1 Cor 14:26 every one of you hath a *p.*
Eph 5:19 speaking to yourselves in *p.*
Jas 5:13 merry? let him sing *p.*

PUBLICAN (PUBLICANS)

Mat 5:46 do not even the *p.* the same
11:19 a friend of *p.* and sinners
18:17 unto thee as an heathen man and a *p.*
21:31 *p.* and harlots go into the kingdom
21:32 *p.* and harlots believed him
Luke 3:12 came also *p.* to be baptized
7:29 the *p.*, justified God, being baptized
18:13 and the *p.*, standing afar off

PUBLISH (PUBLISHED)

Deut 32: 3 I will *p.* the name of the Lord
2 Sam 1:20 *p.* it not in the streets
Ps 26: 7 *p.* with a voice of thanksgiving
Is 52: 7 bringeth good tidings, that *p.* peace
Jer 4:15 and *p.* affliction from mount Ephraim
Acts 13:49 word of the Lord was *p.*

PUFFED (PUFFETH)

1 Cor 4:19 the speech of them which are *p.* up
5: 2 and ye are *p.* up, and have not
8: 1 knowledge *p.* up, but charity edifieth
13: 4 charity vaunteth not itself, is not *p.* up
Col 2:18 vainly *p.* up by his fleshly mind

PUNISH (PUNISHED)

Lev 26:18 I will *p.* you seven times more
Ezra 9:13 God hast *p.* us less than we deserve
Is 10:12 *p.* the fruit of the stout heart
13:11 I will *p.* the world for their
Jer 9:25 *p.* all them which are circumcised with
Hos 4:14 I will not *p.* your daughters
12: 2 will *p.* Jacob according to his ways
2 Thes 1: 9 be *p.* with everlasting destruction
2 Pet 2: 9 unto the day of judgment to be *p.*

PUNISHMENT

Gen 4:13 my *p.* is greater than I can
Lev 26:41 accept the *p.* of their iniquity
Lam 3:39 a man for the *p.* of his sins
Amos 1: 3 I will not turn away the *p.*
Mat 25:46 go into everlasting *p.*
2 Cor 2: 6 sufficient to such a man is this *p.*
Heb 10:29 of how much sorer *p.*, suppose
1 Pet 2:14 sent by him, for the *p.* of

PURCHASED

Ps 74: 2 thy congregation, which thou hast *p.*
Acts 8:20 the gift of God may be *p.* with money
20:28 which he hath *p.* with his own blood
Eph 1:14 until the redemption of the *p.* possession

PURE

Ex 27:20 they bring thee *p.* olive oil
30:34 these sweet spices with *p.* frankincense
2 Sam 22:27 with the *p.* thou wilt show thyself *p.*
Job 4:17 man can be more *p.* than his Maker
25: 5 stars are not *p.* in his sight
Ps 12: 6 words of the Lord are *p.* words
19: 8 commandment of the Lord is *p.*
24: 4 clean hands and a *p.* heart
Prov 15:26 words of the *p.* are pleasant
30: 5 every word of God is *p.*
30:12 generation that are *p.* in their own eyes
Zeph 3: 9 turn to the people a *p.* language
Acts 20:26 I am *p.* from the blood of all
Rom 14:20 all things indeed are *p.*; but it is
Phil 4: 8 are just, whatsoever things are *p.*
1 Tim 3: 9 faith in a *p.* conscience
5:22 other men's sins: keep thyself *p.*
Tit 1:15 to the *p.* all things are *p.*
Heb 10:22 our bodies washed with *p.* water
Jas 1:27 *p.* religion and undefiled before God
3:17 wisdom from above is first *p.*
2 Pet 3: 1 I stir up your *p.* minds

PURITY

1 Tim 4:12 in charity, in spirit, in faith, in *p.*

PURGE (PURGED)

Ps 51: 7 *p.* me with hyssop, and I shall be
65: 3 transgressions, thou shalt *p.*
79: 9 *p.* away our sins for thy name's
Is 6: 7 iniquity is taken, and sin *p.*
27: 9 shall the iniquity of Jacob be *p.*
Mal 3: 3 purify and *p.* them as gold
Mat 3:12 he will thoroughly *p.* his floor, and
1 Cor 5: 7 *p.* out therefore the old leaven
2 Tim 2:21 if a man therefore *p.* himself from
Heb 1: 3 had by himself *p.* our sins
9:14 *p.* your conscience from dead works
2 Pet 1: 9 he was *p.* from old sins

PURIFY (PURIFIED, PURIFIETH, PURIFYING)

Ps 12: 6 in a furnace of earth *p.* seven times
Dan 12:10 many shall be *p.* and made white
Mal 3: 3 and he shall *p.* the sons of Levi
Acts 15: 9 *p.* their hearts by faith
Heb 9:13 sanctifieth to the *p.* of the flesh
Tit 2:14 *p.* unto himself a peculiar
Jas 4: 8 *p.* your hearts, ye double
1 Pet 1:22 *p.* your souls in obeying the truth
1 John 3: 3 *p.* himself, even as he is pure

PURPOSE (PURPOSED)
Job 33:17 withdraw man from his *p.*
Prov 20:18 every *p.* is established by counsel
Eccl 3:17 a time there for every *p.* and for
Is 14:26 the *p.* that is purposed upon the whole
Jer 51:29 *p.* of the Lord shall be performed
Acts 11:23 with *p.* of heart they would cleave
Rom 8:28 called according to his *p.*
Eph 1: 9 which he hath *p.* in himself
1:11 according to the *p.* of him who
3:11 according to the eternal *p.* which
2 Tim 1: 9 according to his own *p.* and grace
1 John 3: 8 for this *p.* the Son of God

PUT
Gen 2: 8 there he *p.* the man whom he had formed
3:15 I will *p.* enmity between thee and
28:20 bread to eat and raiment to *p.* on
Ezra 7:27 which hath *p.* such a thing as this
Neh 2:12 what God *p.* in the heart
3: 5 nobles *p.* not their necks
Job 4:18 he *p.* no trust in his servants
29:14 I *p.* on righteousness and it
38:36 hath *p.* wisdom in inward parts
Ps 4: 7 hast *p.* gladness in my heart
8: 6 *p.* all things under his feet
9:20 *p.* them in fear, that they may
Eccl 10:10 then must he *p.* to more strength
Sol 5: 3 *p.* off my coat, how shall I *p.* it on?
Is 5:20 woe to them that *p.* darkness for light
42: 1 I have *p.* my Spirit upon him
43:26 *p.* me in remembrance: let us plead
51: 9 awake, *p.* on strength, O arm of
59:17 *p.* on righteousness as a breastplate
63:11 who *p.* his holy spirit within him
Jer 31:33 *p.* my law in their inward parts
32:40 I will *p.* my fear in their hearts
Ezek 11:19 *p.* a new spirit within you
36:27 I will *p.* my Spirit in you
Mic 7: 5 *p.* ye not confidence in a guide
Mat 5:15 *p.* it under a bushel, but on a
6:25 nor for body, what ye shall *p.* on
19: 6 let not man *p.* asunder
Luke 1:52 *p.* down the mighty from their seats
Acts 1: 7 Father hath *p.* in his own power
15: 9 *p.* no difference between us
Rom 13:12 *p.* on the armour of light
13:14 *p.* on the Lord Jesus Christ
Gal 3:27 baptized into Christ have *p.* on Christ
Eph 4:22 *p.* off concerning the former conversation
6:11 *p.* on the whole armour of God
Col 3: 9 that ye have *p.* off the old man
3:12 *p.* on therefore as the elect
3:14 above all things *p.* on charity
2 Pet 1:14 I must *p.* off this tabernacle
Rev 17:17 God hath *p.* in their hearts

PUTTETH (PUTTING)
Num 22:38 word that God *p.* in my mouth
Job 15:15 he *p.* no trust in saints
Ps 15: 5 that *p.* not out his money
75: 7 God *p.* down one, and setteth
Sol 2:13 the fig tree *p.* forth her green figs
Lam 3:29 he *p.* his mouth in the dust; if so be
Mal 2:16 saith that he hateth *p.* away
Eph 4:25 *p.* away lying, speak every man truth
Col 2:11 in *p.* off the body of sins
1 Thes 5: 8 *p.* on the breastplate of faith
1 Pet 3: 3 wearing of gold or *p.* on of
3:21 not *p.* away of the filth of the flesh

Q

QUAKE (QUAKED, QUAKING)
Ex 19:18 the whole mount *q.* greatly
Ezek 12:18 eat thy bread with *q.*
Dan 10: 7 but a great *q.* fell upon them
Mat 27:51 the bottom; and the earth did *q.*

QUEEN (QUEENS)
1 Ki 10: 1 the *q.* of Sheba heard of the fame
Ps 45: 9 did stand the *q.* in gold of Ophir
Sol 6: 8 there are threescore *q.* and fourscore
Jer 44:25 to burn incense to the *q.* of heaven
Mat 12:42 the *q.* of the south shall rise up
Rev 18: 7 I sit a *q.*, and am no widow

QUENCH (QUENCHED)
2 Sam 14: 7 so they shall *q.* my coal
21:17 that thou *q.* not the light of Israel
Sol 8: 7 many waters cannot *q.* love
Is 42: 3 smoking flax shall he not *q.*
Mark 9:43 fire that never shall be *q.*
Eph 6:16 to *q.* the fiery darts of wicked
1 Thes 5:19 *q.* not the Spirit

QUESTION (QUESTIONS)
1 Ki 10: 1 came to prove him with hard *q.*
Mark 12:34 no man after that durst ask him any *q.*
Luke 2:46 hearing them, and asking them *q.*
1 Cor 10:25 asking no *q.* for conscience sake
1 Tim 1: 4 which minister *q.*, rather than godly
2 Tim 2:23 but foolish and unlearned *q.* avoid

QUICK (QUICKLY)
Ex 32: 8 turned aside *q.* out of the way
Num 16:30 they go down *q.* into the pit
Deut 11:17 lest ye perish *q.* from off the good
Ps 55:15 let them go down *q.* into hell
Eccl 4:12 threefold cord is not *q.* broken
Is 11: 3 of *q.* understanding in fear
Mat 5:25 agree with thine adversary *q.*
Acts 10:42 to be the Judge of *q.* and dead
2 Tim 4: 1 who shall judge the *q.* and dead
Rev 3:11 behold, I come *q.*: hold that

QUICKEN (QUICKENED, QUICKENETH, QUICKENING)
Ps 71:20 *q.* me again and shalt bring me
80:18 *q.* us, and we will call on thy name
119:25 *q.* thou me according to thy word
119:37 *q.* thou me in thy way
119:40 *q.* me in thy righteousness
119:50 for thy word hath *q.* me
119:149 *q.* me according to thy judgment
John 5:21 even so the Son *q.* whom he will
6:63 it is the Spirit that *q.*
Rom 8:11 *q.* your mortal bodies by his
1 Cor 15:45 last Adam was made a *q.* spirit
Col 2:13 hath he *q.* together with him
1 Pet 3:18 in the flesh, but *q.* by the Spirit

QUIET
Eccl 9:17 words of the wise are heard in *q.*
Is 7: 4 take heed and be *q.*, fear not
1 Thes 4:11 study to be *q.* and to do your own
1 Tim 2: 2 lead a *q.* and peaceable life in all
1 Pet 3: 4 ornament of a meek and *q.* spirit

QUIETNESS
1 Chr 22: 9 shall give peace and *q.* to Israel
Job 20:20 he shall not feel *q.* in his belly
34:29 when he giveth *q.* who then can make
Eccl 4: 6 better is a handful with *q.*
Is 30:15 in *q.* and confidence shall be your
32:17 effect of righteousness shall be *q.*
2 Thes 3:12 exhort that with *q.* they work

QUIVER
Ps 127: 5 the man that hath his *q.* full of them
Is 49: 2 in his *q.* hath he hid me
Jer 5:16 *q.* is as an open sepulchre

R

RACE
Ps 19: 5 strong man to run a *r.*
Eccl 9:11 that the *r.* is not to the swift
1 Cor 9:24 they which run in a *r.* run all
Heb 12: 1 run with patience the *r.* that is set

RAGE (RAGED, RAGETH, RAGING)
2 Ki 5:12 he turned and went away in a *r.*
2 Chr 16:10 for he was in a *r.* with him
28: 9 ye have slain them in a *r.*
Ps 46: 6 the heathen *r.*, the kingdoms were
89: 9 rulest the *r.* of the sea
Prov 6:34 jealousy is the *r.* of a man
14:16 the fool *r.* and is confident
20: 1 wine is a mocker, strong drink is *r.*
29: 9 whether he *r.* or laugh is no
Jude 1:13 *r.* waves of the sea, foaming out

RAGS
Prov 23:21 drowsiness shall clothe a man with *r.*
Is 64: 6 our righteousnesses are as filthy *r.*

RAIMENT
Gen 28:20 bread to eat and *r.* to put on
Ex 21:10 *r.* and her duty of marriage, shall he
Deut 8: 4 thy *r.* waxed not old upon
24:17 not take the widow's *r.* to
Zech 3: 4 clothe thee with change of *r.*
Mat 6:25 meat, and the body more than *r.*
11: 8 man clothed in soft *r.*? Behold
17: 2 his *r.* was white as the light
1 Tim 6: 8 having food and *r.* let us be therewith
Rev 3: 5 shall be clothed in white *r.*

RAIN
Lev 26: 4 I will give you *r.* in due season
Deut 32: 2 my doctrine shall drop as the *r.*
2 Sam 23: 4 by clear shining after *r.*
1 Ki 8:35 no *r.* because they have sinned
2 Chr 7:13 that there be no *r.*, or if I command
Job 5:10 who giveth *r.* on the earth
28:26 he made a decree for the *r.*
38:26 cause it to *r.* on the earth
Ps 11: 6 upon the wicked he shall *r.* snares
68: 9 didst send a plentiful *r.*
72: 6 he shall come down like *r.*
147: 8 who prepareth *r.* for the earth
Prov 16:15 favour is as a cloud of the latter *r.*
Eccl 12: 2 nor clouds return after *r.*
Sol 2:11 winter is past; the *r.* is over
Is 4: 6 a covert from storm and from *r.*
5: 6 clouds that they *r.* no *r.* upon
55:10 as the *r.* cometh down from
Jer 5:24 Lord our God, that giveth *r.*
Hos 10:12 till he come and *r.* righteousness
Amos 4: 7 withholden the *r.* from you, when
Zech 10: 1 ask ye of the Lord *r.* in the time of
14:17 even upon them shall be no *r.*
Mat 5:45 sendeth *r.* on the just and on
Heb 6: 7 earth which drinketh in *r.*
Jas 5:18 prayed again, the heaven gave *r.*

RAISE (RAISED, RAISETH)
Ex 9:16 for this cause I have *r.* thee up
Deut 18:18 I will *r.* them up a Prophet
2 Sam 12:11 I will *r.* up evil against thee
Ps 113: 7 he *r.* up the poor out of dust
145:14 *r.* up those that are bowed down
Is 44:26 *r.* up the decayed places thereof
58:12 *r.* up the foundations of many
Hos 6: 2 third day he will *r.* us up
Amos 9:11 I will *r.* up the tabernacle of
Mat 11: 5 deaf hear, the dead are *r.* up
Luke 1:69 *r.* up an horn of salvation
John 6:40 I will *r.* him up at the last day
Rom 4:25 *r.* again for our justification
6: 4 as Christ was *r.* from the dead
1 Cor 6:14 God hath both *r.* up the Lord
2 Cor 4:14 he which *r.* up the Lord Jesus
Eph 2: 6 hath *r.* us up together and made us

RANSOM
Ex 21:30 he shall give for the *r.* of his life
30:12 give every man a *r.* for
Job 33:24 to the pit. I have found a *r.*
36:18 great *r.* cannot deliver thee
Ps 49: 7 nor give to God a *r.* for him
Prov 6:35 he will not regard any *r.*
13: 8 *r.* of man's life are his riches
21:18 the wicked shall be a *r.* for the

Is 43: 3 I gave Egypt for thy *r.*
Mat 20:28 to give his life a *r.* for
1 Tim 2: 6 gave himself a *r.* for all

READ (READEST, READETH)
Ex 24: 7 and *r.* in the audience of the people
Deut 17:19 *r.* therein all the days of his life
Neh 13: 1 they *r.* in the book of Moses
Acts 8:30 understandest thou what thou *r.*
15:21 *r.* in the synagogues every Sabbath
2 Cor 3: 2 known and *r.* of all men
Col 4:16 that ye likewise *r.* the epistle from
1 Thes 5:27 epistle be *r.* unto all
Rev 1: 3 blessed is he that *r.*

READY
Neh 9:17 thou art a God *r.* to pardon
Ps 45: 1 tongue is the pen of a *r.* writer
Eccl 5: 1 more *r.* to hear, than
Mat 24:44 be ye also *r.* for in such an
Mark 14:38 spirit is *r.* but the flesh
Acts 21:13 *r.* not to be bound only
1 Tim 6:18 do good, *r.* to distribute
2 Tim 4: 6 for I am now *r.* to be offered
Tit 3: 1 to be *r.* to every good work
Rev 3: 2 that are *r.* to die: for I have

REAP (REAPED, REAPETH)
Lev 19: 9 when ye *r.* the harvest of your land
Hos 10:12 *r.* in mercy, break up your fallow
10:13 plowed wickedness, ye have *r.* iniquity
Mat 6:26 sow not, neither do they *r.*
John 4:36 he that *r.* receiveth wages
1 Cor 9:11 a great thing if we *r.*
Gal 6: 7 man soweth, that shall he also *r.*
6: 8 shall of the Spirit *r.* life everlasting
6: 9 shall *r.* if we faint not
Rev 14:16 earth; and the earth was *r.*

REAPERS
Mat 13:39 world; and the *r.* are the angels

REASON
Prov 26:16 seven men that can render a *r.*
Dan 4:36 my *r.* returned unto me, and for the
1 Pet 3:15 asketh a *r.* of the hope

REASONABLE
Rom 12: 1 which is your *r.* service

REBEL (REBELLED)
Num 14: 9 only *r.* not ye against the Lord
Josh 22:19 but *r.* not against the Lord
Neh 9:26 and *r.* against thee, and cast thy
Job 24:13 of those that *r.* against the light
Is 63:10 *r.* and vexed his holy Spirit

REBELLION
1 Sam 15:23 *r.* is as the sin of witchcraft

REBELLIOUS
Deut 9: 7 ye have been *r.* against the Lord
Is 30: 9 this is a *r.* people, lying
50: 5 I was not *r.* neither turned away
65: 2 all the day unto a *r.* people
Jer 4:17 she hath been *r.* against me
5:23 people hath a revolting and *r.* heart
Ezek 2: 5 for they are a *r.* house
12: 3 though they be a *r.* house
44: 6 thou shalt say to the *r.*

REBELS
Num 20:10 hear now, ye *r.*; must we fetch
Ezek 20:38 purge out from you the *r.*

REBUKE
Lev 19:17 shalt in any wise *r.* thy neighbour
2 Ki 19: 3 a day of trouble, *r.* and blasphemy
Ps 6: 1 *r.* me not in thine anger, nor
Prov 9: 8 *r.* a wise man, he will love
27: 5 open *r.* is better than secret love
Zech 3: 2 Lord said to Satan, The Lord *r.* thee
Mat 16:22 Peter took him and began to *r.* him
Luke 17: 3 brother trespass against thee *r.* him
Phil 2:15 sons of God, without *r.*
1 Tim 5: 1 *r.* not an elder, entreat
5:20 them that sin *r.* before all
Tit 1:13 wherefore *r.* them sharply that

RECEIVE
Job 2:10 shall we *r.* good at the hand of God
22:22 *r.* I pray thee the law from his mouth
Ps 6: 9 the Lord will *r.* my prayer
49:15 grave: for he shall *r.* me
73:24 and afterward *r.* me to glory
75: 2 when I shall *r.* the congregation
Mat 10:41 shall *r.* a prophet's reward; and he
18: 5 *r.* one such little child in my name
19:11 all men cannot *r.* this saying
21:22 ask in prayer, believing, ye shall *r.*
Mark 4:16 heard the word, immediately *r.* it with
11:24 believe that ye *r.* them, and ye shall
Luke 16: 9 *r.* you into everlasting habitations
John 3:27 man can *r.* nothing except
5:44 which *r.* honour one of another
16:24 ask, and ye shall *r.*, that your joy
Acts 2:38 shall *r.* the gift of the Holy Ghost
7:59 Lord Jesus, *r.* my spirit
10:43 whosoever believeth shall *r.* remission
20:35 more blessed to give than to *r.*
26:18 may *r.* forgiveness of sins
Rom 14: 1 him that is weak in faith *r.* ye
1 Cor 3: 8 every man *r.* his own reward
2 Cor 5:10 may *r.* things done in the body
6: 1 *r.* not the grace of God in vain
Gal 3:14 *r.* the promise of the Spirit
Eph 6: 8 same shall he *r.* of the Lord
Col 3:24 *r.* the reward of inheritance
Jas 1:21 *r.* with meekness the engrafted word
3: 1 we shall *r.* the greater condemnation
1 Pet 5: 4 shall *r.* a crown of glory
1 John 3:22 whatsoever we ask, we *r.*
2 John 1: 8 but that we *r.* a full reward

RECEIVED (RECEIVETH, RECEIVING)
Job 4:12 mine ear *r.* a little thereof
Ps 68:18 thou hast *r.* gifts for men
Jer 7:28 nor *r.* correction, truth is perished
Mat 7: 8 every one that asketh *r.*
10: 8 freely ye have *r.*, freely give
10:40 he that *r.* you *r.* me
Luke 6:24 ye have *r.* your consolation
John 1:11 own, and his own *r.* him not
3:32 no man *r.* his testimony
12:48 rejecteth me, and *r.* not my words
Acts 8:17 them, and they *r.* the Holy Ghost
17:11 *r.* the word with all readiness
20:24 ministry which I *r.* of the Lord
Rom 5:11 by whom we have *r.* atonement
8:15 have *r.* the spirit of adoption
14: 3 him that eateth, for God hath *r.* him
15: 7 ye one another, as Christ also *r.* us
1 Cor 2:14 natural man *r.* not the things
11:23 For I have *r.* of the Lord
Phil 4:15 as concerning giving and *r.*, but ye
1 Tim 3:16 in the world *r.* up into glory
4: 3 meats which God hath created to be *r.*
Heb 11:13 in faith not having *r.* promises
12:28 wherefore we *r.* a kingdom
1 Pet 1: 9 *r.* the end of your faith

RECOMPEN(C)SE
Deut 32:35 to me belongeth vengeance and *r.*
Job 15:31 vanity shall be his *r.*
Prov 12:14 and the *r.* of a man's hands
Is 35: 4 even God with a *r.*; he will come
66: 6 render *r.* to his enemies
Jer 25:14 *r.* them according to their deeds
Hos 9: 7 the days of *r.* are come
Luke 14:12 again and a *r.* be made thee
14:14 they cannot *r.* thee: for thou shalt
Rom 12:17 *r.* to no man evil for evil
Heb 2: 2 disobedience received just *r.* of reward
10:35 confidence, which hath great *r.* of
11:26 he had respect unto *r.* of

RECOMPENSED
2 Sam 22:21 cleanness of my hands hath he *r.* me
Prov 11:31 the righteous shall be *r.*
Jer 18:20 shall evil be *r.* for good
Rom 11:35 it shall be *r.* unto him again

RECONCILE (RECONCILED, RECONCILING)
Lev 6:30 to *r.* withal in the holy place
Mat 5:24 first be *r.* to thy brother
Rom 5:10 when we were enemies we were *r.*
2 Cor 5:18 God, who hath *r.* us to himself
5:19 God was in Christ *r.* the world
5:20 in Christ's stead, be ye *r.* to God
Col 1:20 to *r.* all things to himself

RECONCILIATION
Lev 8:15 sanctified it, to make *r.* upon it
2 Chr 29:24 they made *r.* with their blood
Ezek 45:17 to make *r.* for the house of Israel
Dan 9:24 and to make *r.* for iniquity
2 Cor 5:18 given to us the ministry of *r.*
5:19 committed to us the word of *r.*
Heb 2:17 make *r.* for the sins of the people

RECORD
Ex 20:24 in all places where I *r.* my name
Deut 30:19 I call heaven and earth to *r.* this day
Job 16:19 in heaven and my *r.* is on high
John 1:32 And John bare *r.* saying, I saw
12:17 and raised him from the dead, bare *r.*
19:35 and he that saw it bare *r.*
Rom 10: 2 for I bear them *r.* that they have
Gal 4:15 for I bear ye *r.*, that if it had
2 Cor 1:23 I call God for a *r.* upon my
Phil 1: 8 for God is my *r.*, how greatly
1 John 5: 7 three bear *r.* in heaven
Rev 1: 2 bare *r.* of the word of God

RED
Ps 75: 8 and the wine is *r.*; it is full of
Is 1:18 though they be *r.* like crimson
27: 2 a vineyard of *r.* wine
63: 2 wherefore art thou *r.* in thine apparel
Zech 1: 8 a man riding upon a *r.* horse
Rev 6: 4 went out another horse that was *r.*
12: 3 behold a great *r.* dragon

REDEEM (REDEEMED, REDEEMETH)
Gen 48:16 angel which *r.* me from all evil
Ex 6: 6 I will *r.* you with a stretched out arm
2 Sam 4: 9 *r.* my soul out of adversity
7:23 Israel whom God went to *r.*
Job 5:20 in famine he shall *r.* thee
Ps 34:22 the Lord *r.* the soul of his servants
49:15 God will *r.* my soul from power
103: 4 who *r.* thy life from destruction
130: 8 *r.* Israel from all his iniquities
136:24 *r.* us from our enemies: for his
Is 1:27 Zion shall be *r.* with judgment
52: 3 shall be *r.* without money
63: 9 love and in his pity he *r.* them
Hos 13:14 I will *r.* them from death
Luke 1:68 he hath visited and *r.* his people
24:21 which should have *r.* Israel
Gal 3:13 Christ hath *r.* us from the curse of
Eph 5:16 *r.* the time because the days are evil
Col 4: 5 that are without, *r.* the time
Tit 2:14 might *r.* us from all iniquity
1 Pet 1:18 not *r.* with corruptible things as
Rev 5: 9 hast *r.* us to God by thy blood
14: 4 these were *r.* from among men

REDEEMER
Job 19:25 I know that my *r.* liveth
Ps 19:14 O Lord, my strength and my *r.*
Prov 23:11 their *r.* is mighty
Is 63:16 our father and *r.*; he shall plead
Jer 50:34 their *R.* is strong; the Lord of hosts

REDEMPTION
Lev 25:24 ye shall grant a r. for the land
Num 3:49 Moses took the r. money of them
Ps 49: 8 r. of their soul is precious
111: 9 he sent r. unto his people
Luke 2:38 looked for r. in Jerusalem
21:28 heads, for your r. draweth nigh
Rom 3:24 through r. that is in Christ Jesus
8:23 waiting for the r. of our body
1 Cor 1:30 righteousness, and sanctification, and r.
Eph 1: 7 in whom we have r. through his blood
1:14 until the r. of the purchased possession
4:30 sealed unto the day of r.
Col 1:14 in whom we have r. through his blood
Heb 9:12 obtained eternal r. for us

REFINE (REFINED)
Is 25: 6 of wines on the lees well r.
48:10 behold, I have r. thee, but not
Zech 13: 9 and will r. them as silver is refined

REFINER
Mal 3: 3 he shall sit as a r. and purifier

REFRESHING
Is 28:12 this is the r., yet they would not hear
Acts 3:19 when the times of r. shall come from

REFUGE
Num 35:13 six cities shall ye have for r.
Deut 33:27 the eternal God is thy r.
Josh 20: 3 they shall be your r. from the avenger
Ps 9: 9 the Lord also will be a r.
46: 1 God is our r. and strength; a
57: 1 thy wings will I make my r., until
59:16 hast been my defence and r. in the
62: 7 my strength and my r. is in God
Is 4: 6 and for a place of r., and for a
28:15 we have made lies our r.
Jer 16:19 Lord my strength my fortress and my r.
Heb 6:18 fled for r. to lay hold on

REFUSE (REFUSED)
Neh 9:17 r. to obey, neither were mindful
Ps 77: 2 my soul r. to be comforted
118:22 the stone which the builders r.
Jer 5: 3 have r. to receive correction
8: 5 hold fast deceit, they r. to return
31:15 r. to be comforted for her children
Lam 3:45 made us as the offscouring and r.
Amos 8: 6 and sell the r. of the wheat
1 Tim 4: 4 nothing to be r. if it be received
4: 7 r. profane and old wives' fables
Heb 12:25 r. him that spake on earth

REGARD (REGARDED, REGARDEST, REGARDETH)
Deut 10:17 which r. not persons nor taketh
Job 34:19 nor r. the rich more than the
Ps 28: 5 they r. not the works of the Lord
66:18 if I r. iniquity in my heart
102:17 will r. the prayer of the destitute
106:44 he r. their affliction and
Prov 12:10 righteous r. the life of the beast
13:18 he that r. reproof shall be
15: 5 he that r. reproof is prudent
Is 5:12 that r. not the work of the Lord
Mat 22:16 thou r. not the person of men
Luke 1:48 r. the low estate of his handmaiden
Rom 14: 6 he that r. the day r. it
Heb 8: 9 I r. them not saith the Lord

REGENERATION
Mat 19:28 in the r. when the Son of man shall sit
Tit 3: 5 saved us by the washing of r.

REIGN (REIGNED, REIGNEST, REIGNETH)
Gen 37: 8 shalt thou indeed r. over us
Ex 15:18 Lord shall r. for ever and ever
Lev 26:17 they that hate you shall r. over you
1 Chr 29:12 thou r. over all; and in thine
Ps 93: 1 the Lord r., he is clothed with majesty
99: 1 the Lord r., let the people tremble
146:10 the Lord shall r. for ever
Prov 8:15 by me kings r. and princes
Is 52: 7 saith unto Zion, Thy God r.
Jer 23: 5 a King shall r. and prosper
Luke 19:14 not have this man to r. over us
Rom 5:14 nevertheless death r. from Adam to Moses
5:17 r. in life by one, Jesus
5:21 that as sin r. unto death so
1 Cor 4: 8 I would to God ye did r.
2 Tim 2:12 if we suffer, we shall r.
Rev 5:10 we shall r. on the earth
19: 6 for the Lord God omnipotent r.
20: 4 r. with Christ a thousand years
22: 5 they shall r. for ever and ever

REINS
Ps 7: 9 God trieth the hearts and r.
16: 7 my r. also instruct me in the night
73:21 I was pricked in my r.
Prov 23:16 my r. shall rejoice, when thy lips
Jer 12: 2 mouth, and far from their r.
17:10 search the heart, I try the r.
Rev 2:23 I am he which searcheth the r. and

REJECT (REJECTED)
1 Sam 8: 7 have not r. thee, but they have
2 Ki 17:20 and the Lord r. all the seed of Israel
Is 53: 3 is despised and r. of men
Jer 6:19 nor to my law, but r. it
6:30 because the Lord hath r. them
8: 9 they r. the word of the Lord
Lam 5:22 thou hast utterly r. us
Hos 4: 6 because thou hast r. knowledge
Mark 6:26 sat with him, he would not r. her
7: 9 ye r. the commandment of God
Luke 7:30 r. the counsel of God
John 12:48 he that r. me, and receiveth not
Gal 4:14 ye despised not, nor r.
Heb 12:17 he was r. for he found no
Tit 3:10 after the first and second admonition r.

REJOICE
Deut 28:63 Lord will r. over you
1 Sam 2: 1 because I r. in thy salvation
2 Chr 6:41 let thy saints r. in goodness
20:27 the Lord made them to r.
Neh 12:43 God made them r. with
Ps 2:11 Lord with fear and r. with trembling
5:11 put their trust in thee r.
9:14 I will r. in thy salvation
33: 1 r. in the Lord, O ye righteous
51: 8 bones which thou hast broken may r.
58:10 righteous shall r. when he
65: 8 morning and evening to r.
68: 3 let them r. before God
85: 6 that thy people may r. in thee
86: 4 r. the soul of thy servant
104:31 Lord shall r. in his works
105: 3 heart of them r. that seek the
119:162 I r. at thy word as one
Prov 5:18 r. with the wife of thy youth
24:17 r. not when thine enemy falleth
Is 29:19 poor among men shall r. in the Holy One
41:16 thou shalt r. in the Lord
62: 5 shall thy God r. over thee
65:13 my servants shall r., but ye shall
Jer 32:41 I will r. over them to do
Joel 2:23 and r. in the Lord your God
Hab 3:18 Yet I will r. in the Lord
Zeph 3:17 r. over thee with joy
Zech 10: 7 their heart shall r. as through wine
Luke 6:23 r. ye in that day; leap
10:20 rather r. because your names
John 5:35 for a season to r. in his light
14:28 if ye loved me ye would r.
Rom 5: 2 r. in hope of the glory of God
12:15 r. with them that do r.
1 Cor 7:30 that r., as though they rejoiced not
Phil 3: 3 and r. in Christ Jesus, and have no
4: 4 r. in the Lord always: and again
Col 1:24 r. in my sufferings for you
1 Thes 5:16 r. evermore
Jas 1: 9 brother of low degree r. in that he
1 Pet 1: 8 r. with joy unspeakable and full of

REJOICED (REJOICETH)
Ex 18: 9 and Jethro r. for all the goodness
Ps 28: 7 my heart greatly r.: and with my
119:14 I have r. in the way of thy
Prov 13: 9 the light of the righteous r.
15:30 light of the eyes r. the heart
Is 62: 5 bridegroom r. over the bride
64: 5 thou meetest him that r.
Luke 1:47 my spirit hath r. in God my
10:21 Jesus r. in spirit and said
John 8:56 father Abraham r. to see my day
1 Cor 7:30 as though they r. not; and they that
13: 6 r. not in iniquity but r. in
Jas 2:13 mercy; and mercy r. against judgment

REJOICING
Ps 19: 8 statutes of Lord are right, r. the heart
119:111 for they are the r. of my heart
Prov 8:31 r. in the habitable part
Jer 15:16 thy word was the joy and r. of my
Acts 5:41 r. that they were counted worthy
8:39 he went on his way r.
2 Cor 1:12 our r. is this, the testimony
Gal 6: 4 shall he have r. in himself
Heb 3: 6 r. of hope firm unto the end

RELIGION
Acts 26: 5 straitest sect of our r. I lived
Gal 1:14 and profited in the Jews' r.
Jas 1:27 pure r. and undefiled before God and

RELIGIOUS
Acts 13:43 Jews and r. proselytes followed Paul
Jas 1:26 any man among you seem to be r.

REMEMBER
Gen 9:16 look upon it that I may r.
40:23 yet did not the chief butler r. Joseph
Ex 13: 3 r. this day in which ye came out of Egypt
Lev 26:42 will I r. my covenant with Jacob
Deut 5:15 r. that thou wast a servant in
7:18 shalt well r. what the Lord thy God did
8:18 thou shalt r. the Lord thy God
9: 7 r. and forget not how thou provokedst
2 Ki 20: 3 r. now how I walked before thee
Neh 1: 8 r., I beseech thee, the word that thou
13:14 r. me O my God, concerning
Ps 20: 7 we will r. the name of the Lord
25: 6 r. O Lord thy tender mercies
63: 6 when I r. thee upon my bed
74: 2 r. thy congregation, which thou hast
77:11 I will r. the works of the Lord
79: 8 O r. not against us former iniquities
89:47 r. how short my time is
119:49 r. thy word unto thy servant
132: 1 r. David and all his afflictions
Eccl 12: 1 r. now thy Creator in days of
Sol 1: 4 we will r. thy love more
Is 43:25 I will not r. thy sins
46: 8 r. this, show yourselves men
Jer 2: 2 for I r. thee, the kindness of thy youth
31:20 I do earnestly r. him still
31:34 I will r. their sin no more
Ezek 16:60 I will r. my covenant with thee
16:61 shalt r. thy ways, and be ashamed
36:31 shall ye r. your own evil ways

Mic 6: 5 *r.* now what Balak king of Moab consulted
Hab 3: 2 in wrath *r.* mercy
Luke 1:72 to *r.* his holy covenant
17:32 *r.* Lot's wife
Gal 2:10 that we should *r.* the poor
Col 4:18 *r.* my bonds. Grace be with you
Heb 8:12 iniquities will I *r.* no more
13: 3 *r.* them that are in bonds

REMEMBERED (REMEMBERETH)

Gen 8: 1 God *r.* Noah and every living thing
19:29 God *r.* Abraham and sent Lot
30:22 God *r.* Rachel, and God hearkened to her
Ex 2:24 and God *r.* his covenant with Abraham
Num 10: 9 ye shall be *r.* before the Lord
Ps 77: 3 I *r.* God and was troubled
78:39 he *r.* they were but flesh
98: 3 hath *r.* his mercy and truth
119:52 I *r.* thy judgments of old
119:55 I have *r.* thy name, O Lord, in the
136:23 who *r.* us in our low estate
137: 1 we wept when we *r.* Zion
Lam 1: 9 she *r.* not her last end
Mat 26:75 Peter *r.* the word of Jesus
Luke 24: 8 and they *r.* his words
John 2:17 disciples *r.* that it was written
Rev 18: 5 God hath *r.* her iniquities

REMEMBRANCE

1 Ki 17:18 unto me to call my sin to *r.*
Ps 6: 5 in death is no *r.* of
Is 26: 8 to thy name, and to the *r.* of thee
Lam 3:20 my soul hath them still in *r.*
Mal 3:16 a book of *r.* was written
Luke 1:54 Israel in *r.* of his mercy
22:19 for you: this do in *r.* of me
John 14:26 bring all things to your *r.*
Acts 10:31 thine alms are had in *r.*
1 Cor 11:25 ye drink it, in *r.* of me
2 Tim 1: 6 wherefore I put thee in *r.*
2 Pet 3: 1 stir up your pure minds by way of *r.*
Jude 1: 5 I will therefore put you in *r.*
Rev 16:19 Babylon came in *r.* before God

REMIT (REMITTED)

John 20:23 whosesoever sins ye *r.* they are *r.*

REMISSION

Mat 26:28 shed for many for the *r.* of sins
Mark 1: 4 baptism of repentance for the *r.* of
Luke 1:77 by the *r.* of their sins
Acts 2:38 of Jesus Christ for the *r.* of sins
10:43 shall receive *r.* of sins
Rom 3:25 his righteousness for the *r.* of sins
Heb 9:22 without shedding of blood is no *r.*
10:18 where *r.* of these is, there is no

REMNANT

Lev 2: 3 the *r.* of the meat offering
Deut 3:11 king of Bashan remained of the *r.* of giants
2 Ki 19: 4 lift up thy prayer for the *r.*
Ezra 9: 8 leave us a *r.* to escape
Is 1: 9 left unto us a very small *r.*
10:21 the *r.* shall return, even the *r.* of
Jer 23: 3 I will gather the *r.* of my flock
Ezek 6: 8 yet will I leave a *r.*
Rom 9:27 a *r.* shall be saved
11: 5 *r.* according to the election of grace

REMOVE (REMOVED)

Ps 39:10 *r.* thy stroke away from me
103:12 so far hath he *r.* our transgressions
119:22 *r.* from me reproach and
119:29 *r.* from me the way of lying
Prov 4:27 nor the left: *r.* thy foot from evil
10:30 righteous shall never be *r.*
30: 8 *r.* far from me vanity and lies
Eccl 11:10 *r.* sorrow from thy heart
Is 30:20 shall not thy teachers be *r.*
Ezek 36:17 as the uncleanness of a *r.* woman
Mat 17:20 to yonder place; and it shall *r.*
Luke 22:42 if thou be willing, *r.* this cup
Rev 2: 5 I will *r.* thy candlestick out of

REND

Is 64: 1 thou wouldest *r.* the heavens
Joel 2:13 *r.* your heart and not your garments

RENDER

Deut 32:43 will *r.* vengeance to his adversaries
2 Chr 6:30 *r.* to every man according to his ways
Job 33:26 he will *r.* to man his righteousness
34:11 work of a man shall he *r.* to
Ps 116:12 what shall I *r.* to the Lord
Prov 26:16 seven men that can *r.* a reason
Hos 14: 2 we will *r.* the calves of our lips
Mat 22:21 *r.* therefore unto Caesar the things
Rom 13: 7 *r.* therefore to all their dues
1 Thes 5:15 that none *r.* evil for evil

RENEW (RENEWED, RENEWEST, RENEWING)

Ps 51:10 *r.* a right spirit in me
103: 5 thy youth is *r.* like the eagle's
104:30 *r.* the face of the earth
Is 40:31 upon the Lord shall *r.* their strength
Rom 12: 2 transformed by the *r.* of your mind
2 Cor 4:16 inward man is *r.* day by day
Eph 4:23 be *r.* in the spirit of your mind
Tit 3: 5 the *r.* of the Holy Ghost
Heb 6: 6 *r.* them again unto repentance

REPAY (REPAID)

Deut 7:10 he will *r.* him to his face
Job 41:11 that I should *r.* him
Prov 13:21 to the righteous good shall be *r.*
Is 59:18 to their deeds accordingly he will *r.*
Rom 12:19 I will *r.*, saith the Lord

REPENT

Ex 32:12 *r.* of this evil against my
Num 23:19 neither the son of man that he should *r.*
Deut 32:36 shall judge his people and *r.* himself
1 Ki 8:47 *r.*, and make supplication unto thee
Job 42: 6 I abhor myself and *r.* in dust
Ps 90:13 let it *r.* thee concerning
135:14 will *r.* himself concerning
Jer 18: 8 I will *r.* of the evil I thought
Ezek 14: 6 *r.* and turn yourselves from your
Jonah 3: 9 if God will turn and *r.*
Mat 3: 2 *r.* ye, for the kingdom of heaven is
Mark 1:15 *r.* and believe the gospel
6:12 preached that men should *r.*
Luke 13: 3 except ye *r.* ye shall all likewise
16:30 went unto them from dead, they will *r.*
17: 3 if he *r.* forgive him
Acts 2:38 *r.* and be baptized everyone
3:19 *r.* and be converted, that
8:22 *r.* of this thy wickedness
17:30 commandeth all men everywhere to *r.*
26:20 should *r.* and turn to God
Rev 2: 5 whence thou art fallen, and *r.*
2:16 *r.*; or I will come unto thee
3:19 be zealous therefore, and *r.*

REPENTANCE

Hos 13:14 *r.* shall be hid from mine eyes
Mat 3: 8 fruits meet for *r.*
3:11 baptize you with water unto *r.*
9:13 not righteous but sinners to *r.*
Mark 1: 4 and preach the baptism of *r.*
Luke 15: 7 just persons which need no *r.*
24:47 that *r.* and remission of sins be
Acts 5:31 give *r.* to Israel and forgiveness of
11:18 God also to the Gentiles granted *r.*
13:24 preached the baptism of *r.* to all
Rom 2: 4 goodness of God leadeth to *r.*
11:29 gifts and calling of God without *r.*
2 Cor 7:10 godly sorrow worketh *r.* to salvation
Heb 6: 1 not laying again the foundation of *r.*
12:17 found no place of *r.*, though he
2 Pet 3: 9 that all should come to *r.*

REPENTED (REPENTETH)

Gen 6: 6 and it *r.* the Lord that he had
Ex 32:14 the Lord *r.* of the evil which he
Judg 2:18 it *r.* the Lord because of their groanings
2 Sam 24:16 the Lord *r.* him of the evil
Jer 8: 6 no man *r.* him of his wickedness
Mat 21:29 but afterward he *r.* and went
27: 3 *r.* himself, and brought again the
Luke 15: 7 one sinner that *r.*, more than over

REPORT

Gen 37: 2 brought unto his father their evil *r.*
Ex 23: 1 shalt not raise a false *r.*
Num 13:32 brought up an evil *r.* of the land
Neh 6:13 they might have matter for an evil *r.*
Is 53: 1 who hath believed our *r.*
John 12:38 Lord, who hath believed our *r.*
Rom 10:16 Esaias saith Lord, who hath believed our *r.*
2 Cor 6: 8 by evil *r.* and good *r.*
Heb 11: 2 by it the elders obtained a good *r.*

REPROACH (REPROACHED, REPROACHES)

Josh 5: 9 have I rolled away the *r.* of Egypt
Neh 1: 3 are in great affliction and *r.*
Job 27: 6 my heart shall not *r.* me
Ps 15: 3 up a *r.* against his neighbour
69: 7 for thy sake I have borne *r.*
69: 9 *r.* of them that reproached
69:20 *r.* hath broken my heart
Prov 14:34 sin is a *r.* to any people
18: 3 also contempt, and with ignominy *r.*
Is 51: 7 fear ye not the *r.* of men
54: 4 not remember the *r.* of thy widowhood
Jer 31:19 I did bear the *r.* of my youth
Zeph 3:18 the *r.* of it was a burden
2 Cor 12:10 I take pleasure in infirmities, in *r.*
Heb 11:26 esteeming the *r.* of Christ greater riches
13:13 without the camp, bearing his *r.*
1 Pet 4:14 if ye be *r.* for the name of Christ

REPROBATE (REPROBATES)

Jer 6:30 *r.* silver shall men call them
Rom 1:28 God gave them over to a *r.* mind
2 Cor 13: 6 ye shall know we are not *r.*
2 Tim 3: 8 corrupt minds, *r.* concerning the faith
Tit 1:16 unto every good work *r.*

REPROOF

Job 26:11 are astonished at his *r.*
Prov 1:23 turn you at my *r.*: behold I will
1:25 counsel, and would none of my *r.*
10:17 he that refuseth *r.* erreth
12: 1 he that hateth *r.* is brutish
13:18 he that regardeth *r.* shall be honoured
15: 5 he that regardeth *r.* is prudent
15:31 heareth *r.* of life abideth among the wise
15:32 heareth *r.* getteth understanding
17:10 *r.* entereth more into a wise
29:15 the rod and *r.* give wisdom
2 Tim 3:16 is profitable for doctrine, for *r.*

REPROVE (REPROVED, REPROVETH)

Ps 50:21 I will *r.* thee, and set them
105:14 he *r.* kings for their sakes
141: 5 let him *r.* me, it shall be an
Prov 9: 7 that *r.* a scorner getteth
9: 8 *r.* not a scorner, lest he
15:12 a scorner loveth not one that *r.*
29: 1 he that being often *r.* hardeneth
Is 29:21 that *r.* in the gate, and turn aside
Hos 4: 4 let no man strive nor *r.*
John 16: 8 *r.* the world of sin, righteousness
3:20 lest his deeds should be *r.*
Eph 5:13 all things that are *r.* are

REPUTATION
Eccl 10: 1 that is in *r.* for wisdom and honour
Acts 5:34 had in *r.* among all the people
Gal 2: 2 privately to them which were of *r.*
Phil 2: 7 made himself of no *r.*, and took

REQUEST (REQUESTS)
Ps 106:15 he gave them their *r.*; but sent
Phil 4: 6 let your *r.* be made known unto God

REQUIRE (REQUIRED)
Gen 9: 5 hand of every beast will I *r.*
42:22 behold also his blood is *r.*
Deut 10:12 what doth the Lord *r.*
1 Ki 8:59 maintain as the matter shall *r.*
1 Chr 4: 2 it is *r.* in stewards, that
Prov 30: 7 two things have I *r.* of thee
Is 1:12 who *r.* this at your hand
Ezek 3:20 his blood will I *r.* at thine
33: 8 his blood will I *r.* at thine
Mic 6: 8 what doth the Lord *r.*
Luke 12:20 thy soul shall be *r.* of thee
12:48 of him shall much be *r.*

REQUITE (REQUITING)
Gen 50:15 will certainly *r.* us all
Deut 32: 6 do ye thus *r.* the Lord
2 Sam 16:12 Lord will *r.* me good for his
2 Chr 6:23 by *r.* the wicked, by recompensing
1 Tim 5: 4 and to *r.* their parents: for that is

RESERVE (RESERVED, RESERVETH)
Job 21:30 wicked is *r.* to the day of
Jer 3: 5 will he *r.* his anger for ever
50:20 will pardon them whom I *r.*
Nah 1: 2 and he *r.* wrath for his enemies
1 Pet 1: 4 not away, *r.* in heaven for you
2 Pet 2: 9 and to *r.* the unjust unto the day
Jude 1: 6 *r.* in everlasting chains under

RESIST (RESISTED, RESISTETH)
Zech 3: 1 at his right hand to *r.* him
Mat 5:39 I say unto you that ye *r.* not evil
Acts 7:51 ye do always *r.* the Holy Ghost
Rom 9:19 who hath *r.* his will?
13: 2 therefore *r.* the power *r.* the
2 Tim 3: 8 so do these *r.* the truth
Heb 12: 4 have not yet *r.* unto blood
Jas 4: 6 God *r.* the proud, but giveth grace
4: 7 *r.* the devil, and he will
1 Pet 5: 5 God *r.* the proud, and giveth grace
5: 9 whom *r.* stedfast in the faith

RESPECT (RESPECTETH)
Gen 4:4 Lord had *r.* unto Abel and to his
Ex 2:25 Israel, and God had *r.* unto them
Lev 19:15 thou shalt not *r.* the person
26: 9 I will have *r.* unto you
2 Ki 13:23 and had *r.* unto them, because of his
2 Chr 19: 7 nor *r.* of persons, nor taking of
Ps 40: 4 *r.* not the proud, nor such
119: 6 *r.* to all thy commandments
138: 6 yet hath he *r.* unto the lowly
Prov 24:23 not good to have *r.* of persons
Rom 2:11 there is no *r.* of persons
Eph 6: 9 neither is there *r.* of persons
Col 3:25 there is no *r.* of persons
Heb 11:26 he had *r.* unto the recompence of the
Jas 2: 1 Lord of glory, with *r.* of persons
2: 9 if ye have *r.* to persons, ye commit
1 Pet 1:17 who without *r.* of persons

RESPECTER
Acts 10:34 God is no *r.* of persons

REST
Ex 16:23 the *r.* of the holy sabbath
Deut 12: 9 as yet come to the *r.* and to the
Ps 16: 9 my flesh shall *r.* in hope
95:11 they should not enter into my *r.*
125: 3 rod of the wicked shall not *r.*
132:14 this is my *r.* for ever: here will I
Is 11:10 his *r.* shall be glorious
30:15 in returning and *r.* shall ye be saved
Ps 57: 2 he shall *r.* in their beds
57:20 the troubled sea, when it cannot *r.*
62: 7 give him no *r.* till he establish
Jer 6:16 ye shall find *r.* for your souls
Mic 2:10 this is not your *r.*: because it is
Hab 3:16 I might *r.* in the day of trouble
Acts 9:31 then had the churches *r.* throughout
2 Thes 1: 7 to you who are troubled *r.* with us
Heb 4: 9 a *r.* to the people of God
4:10 entered into his *r.*, he also hath
Rev 14:11 they have no *r.* day nor night
14:13 they may *r.* from their labours

RESTEST (RESTETH)
Prov 14:33 wisdom *r.* in the heart of him
Eccl 7: 9 anger *r.* in bosom of fools
Rom 2:17 art called a Jew, and *r.* in
1 Pet 4:14 glory and of God *r.* upon you

RESTING
Num 10:33 search out a *r.* place for them
2 Chr 6:41 into thy *r.* place, thou, and the ark
Prov 24:15 spoil not his *r.* place
Is 32:18 and in quiet *r.* places
Jer 50: 6 they have forgotten their *r.* place

RESTORE (RESTORED, RESTORETH)
Ps 23: 3 He *r.* my soul: he leadeth me
51:12 *R.* unto me the joy of thy
69: 4 I *r.* that which I took not away
Luke 19: 8 accusation, I *r.* him fourfold
Gal 6: 1 *r.* such an one in the spirit

RESTORER
Is 58:12 the *r.* of paths to dwell in

RESTITUTION
Ex 22: 3 he should make full *r.*; as if he have
Acts 3:21 until the times of *r.* of all things

RESURRECTION
Mat 22:23 Sadducees which say that there is no *r.*
Luke 20:36 being the children of the *r.*
John 5:29 done good unto the *r.* of life
11:25 I am the *r.* and the life
Acts 17:18 preached unto them Jesus and the *r.*
23: 8 Sadducees say that there is no *r.*
24:15 there shall be a *r.* of the dead
Rom 6: 5 together in the likeness of his *r.*
1 Cor 15:12 there is no *r.* of the dead
Phil 3:10 and the power of his *r.*, and the
Heb 6: 2 and of *r.* of the dead, and of
11:35 that they might obtain a better *r.*
Rev 20: 5 This is the first *r.*

RETURN
Gen 3:19 till thou *r.* unto the ground
1 Ki 8:48 *r.* to thee with all their heart
Job 1:21 naked shall I *r.* thither
Ps 73:10 his people *r.* hither; and waters
116: 7 *r.* unto thy rest, O my soul
Eccl 12: 7 dust shall *r.* to the earth
Sol 6:13 *r. r.* O Shulamite; *r. r.*
Is 10:21 remnant shall *r.*, even the remnant
35:10 the ransomed of the Lord shall *r.*
55:11 shall not *r.* unto me void
Jer 3:12 *r.*, thou backsliding Israel, saith
4: 1 if thou wilt *r.*, O Israel, saith
5: 3 they have refused to *r.*
15:19 let them *r.* unto thee, but *r.*
Hos 2: 7 I will go and *r.* to my first husband
5:15 I will go and *r.* to my place
7:16 they *r.*, but not to the Most High
11: 5 *r.* into the land of Egypt
11: 9 I will not *r.* to destroy Ephraim
Mal 3: 7 *r.* to me, and I will *r.* to
3:18 then shall ye *r.* and discern

RETURNED (RETURNING)
Ps 35:13 my prayer *r.* into my bosom
78:34 they *r.* and inquired early after God
Is 30:15 in *r.* and rest shall ye be
Amos 4: 6 yet have ye not *r.* unto me
1 Pet 2:25 but are now *r.* unto the Shepherd

REVEAL (REVEALED, REVEALETH)
Deut 29:29 things which are *r.* belong unto us
Job 20:27 heaven shall *r.* his iniquity
Prov 11:13 talebearer *r.* secrets: but he that is
Is 22:14 it was *r.* in mine ears
53: 1 whom is the arm of the Lord *r.*
Dan 2:19 then was the secret *r.* unto Daniel
Amos 3: 7 *r.* his secret to his servants
Mat 10:26 covered that shall not be *r.*
11:25 and hast *r.* them unto babes
16:17 flesh and blood hath not *r.*
Rom 1:17 righteousness of God *r.* from faith to
8:18 glory which shall be *r.* in us
1 Cor 2:10 God hath *r.* them to us
Gal 1:16 To *r.* his Son in me, that I
2 Thes 1: 7 when the Lord Jesus shall be *r.*
2: 3 and that man of sin be *r.*; the Son

REVELATION (REVELATIONS)
Rom 2: 5 wrath and *r.* of the righteous
16:25 according to the *r.* of the mystery
2 Cor 12: 1 I will come to visions and *r.*
Gal 1:12 taught it, but by the *r.* of Jesus
Eph 1:17 the spirit of wisdom and *r.* in the
3: 3 by *r.* he made known unto me the
1 Pet 1:13 unto you at the *r.* of Jesus Christ
Rev 1: 1 the *r.* of Jesus Christ, which God

REVENGE (REVENGETH)
Jer 15:15 *r.* me of my persecutors; take me not
Nah 1: 2 the Lord *r.* and is furious
2 Cor 7:11 yea, what zeal, yea, what *r.*
10: 6 readiness to *r.* all disobedience

REVENGER
Num 35:19 the *r.* of blood himself shall slay
Rom 13: 4 a *r.* to execute wrath upon him that

REVERENCE
Lev 19:30 my sabbaths, and *r.* my sanctuary
Ps 89: 7 to be had in *r.* of all them
Eph 5:33 wife see that she *r.* her
Heb 12:28 serve God acceptably with *r.*

REVEREND
Ps 111: 9 holy and *r.* is his name

REVILE (REVILED)
Ex 22:28 shalt not *r.* the gods, nor curse the
Mat 5:11 when men shall *r.* you, and persecute
1 Cor 4:12 being *r.* we bless; being persecuted
1 Pet 2:23 when he was *r. r.* not

REVILERS
1 Cor 6:10 nor drunkards, nor *r.*, nor

REVILINGS
Is 51: 7 be ye afraid of their *r.*
Zeph 2: 8 and the *r.* of the children

REVIVE (REVIVED)
Ps 85: 6 wilt thou not *r.* us again
Is 57:15 *r.* the spirit of the humble, to *r.*
Hos 6: 2 after two days will he *r.* us
14: 7 they shall *r.* as the corn, and
Rom 7: 9 commandment came, sin *r.* and I died
14: 9 Christ both died and rose, and *r.*

REVOLT (REVOLTED, REVOLTING)
Is 1: 5 ye will *r.* more and more
31: 6 children of Israel have deeply *r.*
Jer 5:23 hath a *r.* and a rebellious heart

REVOLTERS
Jer 6:28 they are all grievious *r.*
Hos 5: 2 And the *r.* are profound to make
9:15 no more: all their princes are *r.*

REWARD
Gen 15: 1 thy exceeding great *r.*
Deut 10:17 regardeth not persons, nor taketh *r.*

Ps 19:11 in keeping them is great *r.*
58:11 there is a *r.* for the righteous
127: 3 fruit of the womb is his *r.*
Prov 11:18 righteousness shall be sure *r.*
Is 3:11 *r.* of his hands shall be
Mic 7: 3 the judge asketh for a *r.*
Mat 5:12 great is your *r.* in heaven
6: 2 I say unto you, They have their *r.*
6: 4 secret himself shall *r.* thee openly
10:41 shall receive a prophet's *r.*
Rom 4: 4 is the *r.* not reckoned of
1 Cor 3: 8 every man shall receive his own *r.*
Col 2:18 no man beguile you of your *r.*
3:24 receive the *r.* of inheritance
1 Tim 5:18 labourer is worthy of his *r.*
2 Tim 4:14 Lord *r.* him according to his works
Heb 2: 2 received a just recompence of *r.*
2 John 1: 8 but that we receive a full *r.*
Rev 18: 6 *r.* her as she rewarded you
22:12 I come quickly; and my *r.* is with

REWARDED (REWARDETH)

Ps 31:23 and plentifully *r.* the proud doer
103:10 nor *r.* us according to our iniquities
Is 3: 9 have *r.* evil to themselves

REWARDER

Heb 11: 6 *r.* of them that diligently seek

RICH

Gen 13: 2 Abram was very *r.* in cattle
14:23 I have made Abram *r.*
Ex 30:15 the *r.* shall not give more
Prov 10: 4 hand of the diligent maketh *r.*
10:22 blessing of the Lord, it maketh *r.*
14:20 but the *r.* hath many friends
18:11 *r.* man's wealth is his strong city
22: 2 *r.* and poor meet together
23: 4 labour not to be *r.*: cease from
28:11 *r.* man wise in his own conceit
28:20 that maketh haste to be *r.* shall
Eccl 5:12 abundance of the *r.* will not suffer
10:20 curse not the *r.* in thy bedchamber
Jer 9:23 let not the *r.* man glory in his
Mat 19:23 *r.* man shall hardly enter into the
Luke 1:53 *r.* he hath sent empty away
6:24 woe unto you that are *r.*
16: 1 certain *r.* man which had
18:23 sorrowful: for he was very *r.*
2 Cor 6:10 as poor yet making many *r.*
8: 9 though he was *r.* yet for your sakes
Eph 2: 4 God, who is *r.* in mercy, for his
1 Tim 6: 9 they that will be *r.* fall into
6:17 charge them that are *r.* in this
6:18 that they be *r.* in good works
Jas 2: 5 poor of this world *r.* in faith
Rev 2: 9 thy poverty, (but thou art *r.*)
3:17 because thou sayest, I am *r.*

RICHES

1 Chr 29:12 both *r.* and honour come of thee
Ps 39: 6 he heapeth up *r.*, and knoweth not
49: 6 boast themselves in multitude of their *r.*
52: 7 trusted in the abundance of his *r.*
62:10 if *r.* increase, set not your heart
104:24 the earth is full of thy *r.*
112: 3 wealth and *r.* shall be in his house
Prov 3:16 in her left hand *r.* and
11: 4 *r.* profit not in the day of wrath
11:28 that trusteth in his *r.* shall fall
13: 8 ransom of man's life are his *r.*
14:24 crown of the wise is their *r.*
23: 5 *r.* certainly make themselves wings
27:24 *r.* are not for ever, nor the
30: 8 give me neither poverty nor *r.*
Jer 17:11 so he that getteth *r.* and
Mat 13:22 deceitfulness of *r.*, choke the word
Luke 16:11 to your trust the true *r.*
Rom 2: 4 despisest thou the *r.*
11:12 the fall of them be the *r.* of
2 Cor 8: 2 unto the *r.* of their liberality
Eph 1: 7 according to the *r.* of his
2: 7 show exceeding *r.* of grace
Col 1:27 the *r.* of the glory of this mystery
2: 2 unto all *r.* of the full assurance
1 Tim 6:17 not trust in uncertain *r.*
Jas 5: 2 your *r.* are corrupted, and your

RICHLY

Col 3:16 word of Christ dwell in you *r.*
1 Tim 6:17 who giveth us *r.* all things to enjoy

RIDE (RIDETH)

Deut 33:26 who *r.* upon thy heaven
Ps 45: 4 *r.* prosperously because of truth
66:12 caused men to *r.* over our heads
68: 4 extol him that *r.* upon thy
68:33 that *r.* upon the heavens of heavens
Is 19: 1 Lord *r.* upon a stiff cloud
Hab 3: 8 thou didst ride upon thin horses

RIGHT

Gen 18:25 Judge of all the earth do *r.*
Num 27: 7 Zelophehad speak *r.*: thou shalt
Deut 21:17 the *r.* of the firstborn is his
Ezra 8:21 seek of him a *r.* way for
Job 34:23 not lay upon man more than *r.*
Ps 19: 8 the statutes of the Lord are *r.*
51:10 renew a *r.* spirit within me
119:128 concerning all things to be *r.*
Prov 4:11 I have led thee in *r.* paths
8: 9 *r.* to them that find knowledge
12: 5 thoughts of the righteous are *r.*
14:12 a way which seemeth *r.* to
21: 2 way of man is *r.* in his own eyes
Is 30:10 prophesy not unto us *r.* things
Ezek 18: 5 do that which is lawful and *r.*
Hos 14: 9 ways of the Lord are *r.*
Amos 3:10 they know not to do *r.*
Mark 5:15 and in his *r.* mind: and they were
Luke 12:57 judge ye not what is *r.*
Acts 4:19 whether it be *r.* in the sight of God
8:21 heart is not *r.* in the sight of
13:10 not cease to pervert *r.* ways
Eph 6: 1 parents in the Lord: for this is *r.*
2 Pet 2:15 forsaken the *r.* way, and are gone
Rev 22:14 have a *r.* to the tree of life

RIGHTLY

2 Tim 2:15 *r.* dividing the word of truth

RIGHTEOUS

Gen 7: 1 thee have I seen *r.* before me
18:23 also destroy the *r.* with the wicked
Num 23:10 let me die the death of the *r.*
Deut 25: 1 shall justify the *r.* and condemn
Job 4: 7 where were the *r.* cut off?
17: 9 the *r.* shall hold on his way
Ps 1: 6 Lord knoweth the way of the *r.*
5:12 thou, Lord, wilt bless the *r.*
7:11 God judgeth the *r.* and God is angry
32:11 glad in the Lord and rejoice, ye *r.*
34:17 *r.* cry, and the Lord heareth
34:19 many are the afflictions of the *r.*
37:25 have I not seen the *r.* forsaken
37:29 the *r.* shall inherit the land
55:22 never suffer the *r.* to be moved
58:11 there is a reward for the *r.*
64:10 *r.* shall be glad in the Lord
68: 3 let the *r.* be glad; let them rejoice
92:12 the *r.* shall flourish like a palm tree
97:11 light is sown for the *r.*, and gladness
112: 6 the *r.* shall be in everlasting
125: 3 shall not rest on the lot of the *r.*
145:17 the Lord is *r.* in all his ways
146: 8 the Lord loveth the *r.*
Prov 3:32 his secret is with the *r.*
10: 3 the soul of the *r.* to famish
10:21 the lips of the *r.* feed many
10:24 desire of the *r.* shall be granted
10:25 *r.* is an everlasting foundation
10:28 the hope of the *r.* shall be gladness
10:30 the *r.* shall never be removed
10:32 lips of the *r.* know what is acceptable
11: 8 *r.* is delivered out of trouble
11:21 seed of the *r.* shall be delivered
11:28 the *r.* shall flourish as a branch
Prov 11:30 fruit of the *r.* is a tree of life
11:31 the *r.* shall be recompensed in
12: 3 root of the *r.* shall not be moved
12: 5 the thoughts of the *r.* are *r.*
12: 7 the house of the *r.* shall stand
12:10 *r.* man regardeth the life of his beast
12:12 root of the *r.* yieldeth fruit
12:26 *r.* is more excellent than his
13: 9 the light of the *r.* rejoiceth
13:25 *r.* eateth to the satisfying of his
14:32 *r.* hath hope in his death
15: 6 in the house of the *r.* is
15:19 the way of the *r.* is made plain
15:29 he heareth the prayer of the *r.*
28: 1 the *r.* are bold as a lion
Eccl 7:16 be not *r.* over much, nor
9: 2 one event to the *r.* and to the wicked
Is 3:10 say ye to *r.*, it shall be well
41: 2 who raised up the *r.* man from the east
57: 1 the *r.* perisheth, and no man layeth
60:21 thy people also shall be all *r.*
Ezek 3:20 when a *r.* man doth turn
Mal 3:18 discern between the *r.* and the
Mat 9:13 not come to call the *r.*, but
10:41 shall receive the *r.* man's reward
25:46 but the *r.* into life eternal
Luke 1: 6 they were both *r.* before God
18: 9 that they were *r.* and despised
Rom 3:10 there is none *r.*, no not one
5: 7 scarcely for a *r.* man will one
2 Thes 1: 5 a token of the *r.* judgment of God
1 Tim 1: 9 law is not made for a *r.*
Jas 5:16 fervent prayer of the *r.* man
1 Pet 4:18 and if the *r.* scarcely be saved
Rev 22:11 he that is *r.* let him be *r.*

RIGHTEOUSLY

Tit 2:12 live soberly, *r.*, and godly, in this

RIGHTEOUSNESS

Gen 15: 6 and he counted it to him for *r.*
Deut 6:25 it shall be our *r.* if
9: 5 nor for thy *r.*, or for the
33:19 offer sacrifices of *r.*
1 Ki 8:32 give him according to his *r.*
Job 29:14 I put on *r.* and it clothed
36: 3 and will ascribe *r.* to my Maker
Ps 11: 7 righteous Lord loveth *r.*
15: 2 walketh uprightly and worketh *r.*
40:10 I have not hid thy *r.* within my
50: 6 heavens shall declare his *r.*
51:14 tongue shall sing aloud of thy *r.*
85:10 *r.* and peace have kissed each other
97: 2 *r.* and judgment are the habitation
106: 3 he that doeth *r.* at all times
106:31 that was counted unto him for *r.*
Prov 10: 2 nothing but *r.* delivereth from death
11: 5 *r.* of the perfect shall direct his way
11: 6 *r.* of the upright shall deliver them
11:18 to him that soweth *r.* a sure
11:19 as *r.* tendeth to life; so he that
12:28 in the way of *r.* is life
13: 6 *r.* keepeth him that is upright in
14:34 *r.* exalteth a nation: but sin
15: 9 he loveth him that followeth *r.*
16:12 the throne is established by *r.*
16:31 if it be found in the way of *r.*
Is 11: 5 *r.* shall be the girdle of his loins
26: 9 inhabitants of the world will learn *r.*
28:17 to line and *r.* to the plummet
32:17 work of *r.* shall be peace
45:24 in the Lord have I *r.* and
46:12 stouthearted, that are far from *r.*
46:13 I bring near my *r.*; it shall not
54:17 their *r.* is of me, saith the Lord
57:12 I will declare thy *r.*, and the works
61: 3 might be called trees of *r.*
61:10 covered me with the robe of *r.*
62: 2 Gentiles shall see thy *r.*, and all
64: 5 that rejoiceth and worketh *r.*
64: 6 and all our *r.* are as filthy rags
Jer 23: 6 be called THE LORD OUR *R.*
Dan 4:27 break off thy sins by *r.*

Dan 9: 7 O Lord, *r.* belongeth unto thee
9:24 to bring in everlasting *r.*
12: 3 they that turn many to *r.*
Zeph 2: 3 seek *r.*, seek meekness: it may be
Mal 4: 2 Sun of *r.* arise with healing
Mat 3:15 it becometh us to fulfil all *r.*
5: 6 which do hunger and thirst after *r.*
5:20 except your *r.* exceed the *r.* of
6:33 God, and his *r.*; and all these
21:32 came unto you in the way of *r.*
Luke 1:75 in holiness and *r.* before
John 16: 8 the world of sin, and of *r.*
Acts 10:35 worketh *r.*, is accepted, wilt thou
13:10 thou enemy of all *r.*
Rom 1:17 therein is the *r.* of God revealed
3:22 even *r.* of God which is by faith of
3:25 his *r.* for the remission of sins
4: 5 his faith is counted for *r.*
4: 6 man to whom God imputeth *r.*
4:22 it was imputed to him for *r.*
5:18 by the *r.* of one the free gift came
5:21 grace reign through *r.* unto eternal
6:13 members as instruments of *r.*
6:19 members servants to *r.* unto holiness
8: 4 that the *r.* of the law might
9:30 have attained to *r.*, even *r.*, 31.
10: 3 ignorant of God's *r.*, and going about
10: 4 the end of the law for *r.* to every
10: 6 *r.* which is of faith speaketh
10:10 heart of man believeth unto *r.*
14:17 but *r.*, and peace, and joy
1 Cor 1:30 made unto us wisdom and *r.*
15:34 awake to *r.* and sin not
2 Cor 5:21 might be made the *r.* of God in him
6: 7 armour of *r.* on the right hand
9:10 increase the fruits of your *r.*
11:15 transformed as ministers of *r.*
Gal 2:21 if *r.* come by the law, then
3: 6 and it was accounted to him for *r.*
Eph 6:14 having on the breastplate of *r.*
Phil 1:11 being filled with fruits of *r.*
3: 6 *r.* which is in the law blameless
3: 9 not mine own *r.* but the *r.* which
1 Tim 6:11 follow after *r.*, godliness, faith
Heb 12:11 peaceable fruit of *r.* unto them
Jas 1:20 man worketh not the *r.* of God
3:18 fruit of *r.* is sown in peace
1 Pet 3:14 if ye suffer for *r.* sake
2 Pet 1: 1 through the *r.* of God and our
3:13 new earth, wherein dwelleth *r.*
1 John 2:29 one that doeth *r.* is born of him
Rev 19: 8 fine linen is the *r.* of saints

RIOT
Tit 1: 6 not accused or *r.* or unruly
1 Pet 4: 4 to the same excess of *r.*, speaking
2 Pet 2:13 it pleasure to *r.* in the daytime

RIOTING
Rom 13:13 not in *r.* and drunkenness, not in

RIOTOUS
Prov 23:20 winebibbers; among *r.* eaters of flesh
Luke 15:13 wasted his substance with *r.* living

RIPE
Gen 40:10 thereof brought forth *r.* grapes
Ex 22:29 to offer the first of thy *r.* fruits
Num 18:13 whatsoever is first *r.* in the land
Jer 24: 2 like the figs that are first *r.*
Hos 9:10 saw your fathers as the first *r.*
Joel 3:13 the sickle, for the harvest is *r.*
Mic 7: 1 my soul desired the first *r.* fruit
Nah 3:12 fig trees with the first *r.* figs
Rev 14:15 harvest of the earth is *r.*

RIPENING
Is 18: 5 sour grape is *r.* in the flower

RISE
Sol 3: 2 I will *r.* now, and go about
Is 14:21 that they do not *r.*, nor possess the
26:14 deceased, they shall not *r.*
43:17 together, they shall not *r.*
54:17 every tongue that shall *r.* against thee
58:10 then shall thy light *r.* in obscurity
1 Thes 4:16 dead in Christ shall *r.* first

RISING
Prov 30:31 king against whom there is no *r.*
Luke 2:34 set for the fall and *r.* again

RIVER (RIVERS)
Ex 1:22 is born ye shall cast into the *r.*
Job 20:17 he shall not see the *r.*
40:23 he drinketh up a *r.*, and hasteth not
Ps 36: 8 drink of the *r.* of thy pleasures
46: 4 There is a *r.*, the streams whereof
65: 9 enrichest it with the *r.* of God
119:136 *R.* of water run down mine eyes
Prov 21: 1 of the Lord, as the *r.* of water
Is 33:21 a place of broad *r.* and streams
48:18 then had thy peace been as a *r.*
66:12 I will extend peace to her like a *r.*
Mic 6: 7 or with ten thousands of *r.* of oil
John 7:38 belly shall flow *r.* of living water
Rev 22: 2 on either side of the *r.*

ROAR
Is 42:13 he shall cry, yea *r.*; he shall
Jer 25:30 mightily *r.* upon his habitation
Hos 11:10 *r.*, then the children shall tremble
Joel 3:16 Lord also shall *r.* out of Zion
Amos 1: 2 Lord will *r.* from Zion, and utter

ROB (ROBBED)
Lev 19:13 defraud thy neighbour neither *r.*
Prov 22:22 *R.* not the poor, because he is poor
Is 42:22 this is a people *r.* and spoiled
Mal 3: 8 Will a man *r.* God? Yet ye have
2 Cor 11: 8 I *r.* other churches, taking wages of

ROBBER
Job 5: 5 the *r.* swalloweth up their substance
John 10: 1 other way is a thief and a *r.*

ROBBERY
Ps 62:10 become not vain in *r.*: if riches
Prov 21: 7 *r.* of the wicked shall destroy
Is 61: 8 I hate *r.* for burnt offering
Amos 3:10 who store up violence and *r.*
Phil 2: 6 thought it not *r.* to be equal

ROBE (ROBES)
Is 61:10 covered me with the *r.* of righteousness
Rev 7: 9 clothed with white *r.*, and palms in
7:14 and have washed their *r.*

ROCK (ROCKS)
Ex 17: 6 thou shalt smite the *r.*
Num 20:11 with his rod he smote the *r.* twice
Deut 32: 4 He is the *R.*, his work is perfect
Ps 18: 2 the Lord is my *r.*
31: 3 thou art my *r.* and my fortress
61: 2 lead me to the *r.* that is higher than
62: 2 he only is my *r.* and my salvation
89:26 and the *r.* of my salvation
94:22 God is the *r.* of my refuge
Mat 7:24 wise man, which built his house on a *r.*
16:18 on this *r.* I will build my church
1 Cor 10: 4 them: and that *R.* was Christ
Rev 6:16 said to the mountains and *r.*

ROD
Ex 4:20 Moses took the *r.* of God
Num 17: 8 the *r.* of Aaron for the house
Ps 23: 4 thy *r.* and staff they comfort
125: 3 *r.* of the wicked shall not rest upon
Prov 13:24 spareth his *r.* hateth his son
23:14 shalt beat him with the *r.*
29:15 *r.* and reproof give wisdom
Ezek 20:37 cause to pass under the *r.*
Mic 6: 9 hear ye the *r.* and who hath
7:14 feed thy people with thy *r.*
Rev 2:27 he shall rule with a *r.* of iron
12: 5 rule all nations with a *r.*

ROOT
Deut 29:18 among you a *r.* that beareth gall
Job 19:28 seeing the *r.* of the matter
Ps 52: 5 *r.* thee out of the land of the living
Is 11:10 there shall be *r.* of Jesse
37:31 take the *r.* downward, and bear fruit
Mat 3:10 laid to the *r.* of the trees
13: 6 because they had no *r.*, they
Luke 17: 6 be thou plucked up by the *r.*
Rom 11:16 if the *r.* be holy, so are the
1 Tim 6:10 love of money is the *r.* of all

ROOTED
Mat 15:13 not planted, shall be *r.* up
Eph 3:17 being *r.* and grounded in love
Col 2: 7 *r.* and built up in him, and

ROSE
Sol 2: 1 I am the *r.* of Sharon
Is 35: 1 shall rejoice and blossom as the *r.*

ROYAL
Is 62: 3 and a *r.* diadem in the hand
Jas 2: 8 if ye fulfil the *r.* law according
1 Pet 2: 9 a *r.* priesthood, an holy nation

RUBIES
Job 28:18 Price of wisdom is above *r.*
Prov 3:15 she is more precious than *r.*
8:11 for wisdom is better than *r.*
31:10 for her price is far above *r.*

RULE (RULETH)
Esth 9: 1 Jews had *r.* over them that hated them
Ps 103:19 his kingdom *r.* over all
Prov 16:23 he that *r.* his spirit than
17: 2 wise servant shall have *r.* over a
25:28 that hath no *r.* over his own spirit
Hos 11:12 deceit: but Judah yet *r.* with God
Gal 6:16 walk according to this *r.*
Phil 3:16 let us walk by the same *r.*
Col 3:15 let the peace of God *r.* in
1 Tim 3: 5 man know not how to *r.* his own house
5:17 elders that *r.* well be counted worthy
Heb 13: 7 remember them which have *r.* over you
Rev 12: 5 man child who was to *r.* all

RULER (RULERS)
Mic 5: 2 unto me that is to be *r.* in Israel
Mat 25:21 I will make thee *r.* over many things
Rom 13: 3 *r.* are not a terror to good works
Eph 6:12 *r.* of the darkness of this world

RUN (RUNNETH)
Gen 49:22 whose branches *r.* over the wall
Lev 15: 3 whether his flesh *r.* with his issue
1 Sam 8:11 some shall *r.* before his chariots
2 Chr 16: 9 eyes of the Lord *r.* to and fro
Ps 19: 5 rejoiceth as a strong man to *r.* a race
23: 5 my head with oil; my cup *r.* over
119:32 I will *r.* the way of thy commandments
Eccl 1: 7 all the rivers *r.* into the sea
Sol 1: 4 draw me, we will *r.* after
Is 40:31 shall *r.* and not be weary
Dan 12: 4 many shall *r.* to and fro
Rom 9:16 nor of him that *r.* but of God
Gal 2: 2 *r.*, or had *r.* in vain
Heb 12: 1 *r.* with patience the race
1 Pet 4: 4 *r.* not with them to the same excess

S

SABBATH (SABBATHS)
Ex 16:29 Lord hath given your the *s.*
20: 8 Remember the *s.* day, to keep it holy
Lev 19: 3 and his father, and keep my *s.*
23: 3 seventh day is the *s.* of rest
26: 2 Ye shall keep my *s.*, and reverence
Neh 9:14 known unto them thy holy *s.*

Neh 13:18 upon Israel by profaning the *s.*
Is 56: 2 keepeth the *s.* from polluting it
56: 4 Eunuchs that keep my *s.*
56: 6 everyone that keepeth the *s.*
58:13 call the *s.* a delight, the holy
Ezek 20:13 my *s.* they greatly polluted
23:38 and have profaned my *s.*
46: 3 in the *s.* and in the new moons
Mat 12: 5 priests in the temple profane the *s.*
28: 1 end of the *s.*, as it began to dawn
Acts 13:42 preached to them the next *s.*
18: 4 reasoned in the synagogue every *s.*

SACKCLOTH
Gen 37:34 put *s.* upon his loins, and mourned
Job 16:15 I have sewed *s.* upon my skin
Ps 30:11 thou hast put off my *s.*, and
35:13 were sick, my clothing was *s.*
Is 22:12 to baldness and to girding with *s.*
Rev 11: 3 threescore days, clothed in *s.*

SACRIFICE
Gen 31:54 then Jacob offered *s.* upon the mount
Ex 8:25 *s.* to your God in the land
1 Sam 2:29 wherefore kick ye at my *s.*
3:14 Eli's house not purged with *s.*
15:22 to obey is better than *s.*
Ps 50: 5 made covenant with me by *s.*
107:22 *s.* the sacrifices of thanksgiving
141: 2 up of my hands as the evening *s.*
Prov 15: 8 *s.* of the wicked is abomination
21: 3 more acceptable to Lord than *s.*
Eccl 5: 1 than to give the *s.* of fools
Dan 8:11 by him the daily *s.* was taken away
9:27 cause *s.* and oblation to cease
11:31 take away daily *s.*
Hos 6: 6 for I desired mercy and not *s.*
Mat 9:13 I will have mercy, and not *s.*
Mark 9:49 and every *s.* be salted with salt
Rom 12: 1 present your bodies a living *s.*
Eph 5: 2 a *s.* to God for a sweetsmelling
Phil 2:17 offered on the *s.* and service of
4:18 a *s.* acceptable, wellpleasing to God
Heb 9:26 put away sin by *s.* of himself

SACRIFICED (SACRIFICES)
Ps 4: 5 offer the *s.* of righteousness
51:17 *s.* of God are a broken spirit
1 Cor 5: 7 Christ our passover is *s.* for us
Heb 13:15 offer the *s.* of praise to God
1 Pet 2: 5 priesthood, to offer up spiritual *s.*

SAD
1 Sam 1:18 and her countenance was no more *s.*
Ezek 13:22 whom I have not made *s.*; and
Mark 10:22 he was *s.* at that saying, and went

SADNESS
Eccl 7: 3 *s.* of the countenance the heart

SAINTS
Deut 33: 2 came with ten thousands of the *s.*
33: 3 all his *s.* are in thy hand
1 Sam 2: 9 he will keep the feet of his *s.*
Job 15:15 he putteth no trust in his *s.*
Ps 16: 3 to the *s.* that are in the earth
50: 5 gather my *s.* together unto me
52: 9 it is good before thy *s.*
89: 5 in the congregation of the *s.*
97:10 he preserveth the souls of his *s.*
116:15 is the death of his *s.*
Prov 2: 8 preserveth the way of his *s.*
Dan 7:18 *s.* of most High shall take
Hos 11:12 and is faithful with the *s.*
Zech 14: 5 Lord shall come, and all *s.*
Rom 1: 7 beloved of God, called to be *s.*
8:27 intercession for the *s.*, according
12:13 to the necessity of the *s.*
15:25 Jerusalem, to minister unto the *s.*
1 Cor 1: 2 called to be *s.*, with all that
6: 2 that the *s.* shall judge the world
16: 1 concerning the collection for the *s.*
2 Cor 1: 1 *s.* which are in all Achaia
8: 4 of the ministering to the *s.*
2 Cor 9:12 supplieth the want of the *s.*
Eph 1: 1 the *s.* which are at Ephesus
3: 8 less than the least of all *s.*
6:18 supplication for all *s.*
Col 1: 2 to the *s.* and faithful brethren
1 Thes 3:13 Lord Jesus Christ, with all his *s.*
2 Thes 1:10 to be glorified in his *s.*
Heb 6:10 ye have ministered to the *s.*
Jude 1:14 cometh with ten thousand of his *s.*
Rev 5: 8 which are the prayers of the *s.*
11:18 to the *s.* and them that fear
13: 7 to make war with the *s.*
14:12 here is the patience of the *s.*
15: 3 thy ways, thou King of *s.*
16: 6 shed the blood of the *s.* and prophets
19: 8 fine linen is the righteousness of *s.*
20: 9 compassed the camp of the *s.*

SALT
Gen 19:26 she became a pillar of *s.*
Lev 2:13 offerings thou shalt offer *s.*
Mat 5:13 ye are the *s.* of the earth: but if
Mark 9:50 Have *s.* in yourselves, and have peace
Col 4: 6 grace, seasoned with *s.*, that ye may

SALVATION
Ex 14:13 see the *s.* of the Lord
15: 2 he is become my *s.*: he is my
2 Sam 23: 5 this is all my *s.*, and all my
2 Chr 20:17 see the *s.* of the Lord with you
Ps 3: 8 *s.* belongeth to the Lord
14: 7 that the *s.* of Israel were come out
18: 2 the horn of my *s.*, and my high
27: 1 my light and my *s.*; whom shall I
37:39 *s.* of the righteous is of the Lord
50:23 I will show him the *s.* of God
51:14 thou God of my *s.*, and my tongue
53: 6 *s.* of Israel were come out of Zion
68:20 God is the God of *s.*
85: 9 his *s.* is nigh them that fear him
88: 1 O Lord God of my *s.*, I have cried
89:26 God, and the rock of my *s.*
118:14 and song, and is become my *s.*
119:155 *s.* is far from the wicked
132:16 I will also clothe her priests with *s.*
140: 7 Lord, the strength of my *s.*
149: 4 will beautify the meek with *s.*
Is 12: 2 Behold, God is my *s.*; I will trust
25: 9 be glad and rejoice in his *s.*
26: 1 *s.* will God appoint for walls
33: 2 be our *s.* also in the time
33: 6 thy times, and strength of *s.*
45:17 Lord with an everlasting *s.*
46:13 I will place *s.* in Zion for
52:10 shall see the *s.* of our God
59:16 his arm brought *s.* unto him
59:17 for an helmet of *s.* upon his
60:18 call thy walls *S.*, thy gates
61:10 clothed me with garments of *s.*
62: 1 *s.* thereof as a lamp that burneth
Jer 3:23 in vain is *s.* hoped for
Lam 3:26 quietly wait for the *s.* of the Lord
Jonah 2: 9 have vowed *S.* is of the Lord
Mic 7: 7 I will wait for the God of my *s.*
Hab 3: 8 thine horses and thy chariots of *s.*
3:18 I will joy in the God of my *s.*
Zech 9: 9 he is just and having *s.*
Luke 19: 9 this day is *s.* come to this house
John 4:22 worship: for *s.* is of the Jews
Acts 4:12 neither is there *s.* in any
13:26 is the word of this *s.* sent
Rom 1:16 it is the power of God to *s.*
11:11 through their fall *s.* is come
13:11 now is our *s.* nearer than
2 Cor 1: 6 it is for your consolation and *s.*
6: 2 behold, now is the day of *s.*
Eph 6:17 take the helmet of *s.*
Phil 2:12 work out your own *s.* with
1 Thes 5: 8 for an helmet, the hope of *s.*
2 Thes 2:13 from the beginning chosen you to *s.*
2 Tim 2:10 to obtain *s.* which is in Christ
3:15 able to make thee wise unto *s.*
Tit 2:11 grace of God that bringeth *s.*
Heb 1:14 who shall be heirs of *s.*
2: 3 escape, if we neglect so great *s.*
5: 9 he became the author of eternal *s.*
6: 9 things that accompany *s.*, though we
9:28 second time without sin unto *s.*
1 Pet 1: 5 through faith to *s.*, ready to be
Jude 1: 3 write unto you of common *s.*
Rev 7:10 *S.* to our God, which sitteth upon
12:10 Now is come *s.*, and strength, and
19: 1 *S.*, and glory, and honour

SANCTIFY
Ex 13: 2 *s.* unto me all the firstborn
19:10 *s.* them today and tomorrow
31:13 I am the Lord that doth *s.*
Lev 20: 7 *s.* yourselves therefore and be ye holy
Is 8:13 *s.* the Lord of hosts himself
Ezek 38:23 I magnify myself and *s.* myself
Joel 1:14 *s.* ye a fast, call a solemn assembly
2:16 *s.* the congregation, assemble the
John 17:17 *s.* them through thy truth
17:19 for their sakes I *s.* myself
1 Thes 5:23 very God of peace *s.* you wholly
Heb 13:12 that he might *s.* the people
1 Pet 3:15 *s.* the Lord God in your hearts

SANCTIFIED (SANCTIFIETH)
Gen 2: 3 blessed seventh day and *s.* it
Lev 10: 3 I will be *s.* in them that
Deut 32:51 ye *s.* me not in the midst of
Job 1: 5 Job sent and *s.* them and
Is 5:16 God that is holy shall be *s.*
Jer 1: 5 I *s.* thee, and I ordained thee
Ezek 20:41 *s.* in you before the heathen
Mat 23:17 or the temple that *s.* the gold
John 10:36 him whom the Father hath *s.*
Acts 20:32 among all them which are *s.*
Rom 15:16 being *s.* by the holy ghost
1 Cor 1: 2 to them that are *s.* in Christ Jesus
6:11 ye are washed, but ye are *s.*
7:14 unbelieving husband is *s.* by the wife
1 Tim 4: 5 *s.* by the word of God
Heb 2:11 they who are *s.* are all of one
10:14 perfected for ever them that are *s.*

SANCTIFICATION
1 Cor 1:30 righteousness, and *s.*, and redemption
1 Thes 4: 4 possess his vessel in *s.* and honour
2 Thes 2:13 chosen you to salvation through *s.*
1 Pet 1: 2 *s.* of the spirit, unto obedience

SANCTUARY
Ps 63: 2 seen thee in the *s.*
73:17 I went into the *s.* of God
Is 8:14 he shall be for a *s.*
Ezek 11:16 be to them as a little *s.*
Dan 9:17 thy face to shine upon thy *s.*
Heb 9: 2 the showbread; which is called the *s.*

SAND
Gen 22:17 *s.* which is upon the seashore
32:12 thy seed as the *s.* of the sea
Job 6: 3 heavier than the *s.* of the sea
29:18 multiply my days as the *s.*
Is 10:22 Israel be as the *s.* of the sea
Mat 7:26 built his house upon the *s.*

SATAN
1 Chr 21: 1 *S.* stood up against Israel
Job 1: 6 *S.* came also among them
Ps 109: 6 let *S.* stand at his right
Mat 4:10 get thee hence, *S.*: for it is
16:23 unto Peter, Get thee behind me *S.*
Luke 10:18 I beheld *S.* as lightning fall
22: 3 then entered *S.* into Judas
Acts 26:18 turn from the power of *S.*
Rom 16:20 God of peace shall bruise *S.*
1 Cor 5: 5 deliver such an one to *S.*
7: 5 *S.* tempt you not for your incontinency
2 Cor 2:11 lest *S.* should get an advantage
11:14 *S.* is linen formed into an angel

Is 50: 4 know how to speak a word in *s.*
Luke 4:13 he departed from him for a *s.*
John 5:35 willing for a *s.* to rejoice
Acts 1: 7 for you to know the times or *s.*
14:17 and fruitful *s.*, filling our hearts
1 Thes 5: 1 of times and *s.* brethren ye have
2 Tim 4: 2 be instant in *s.*, out of *s.*
Heb 11:25 enjoy the pleasures of sin for a *s.*
1 Pet 1: 6 greatly rejoice, though now for a *s.*

SEASONED
Col 4: 6 speech be always with grace *s.*

SECRET (SECRETS)
Gen 49: 6 come not thou into their *s.*
Job 11: 6 he would show thee the *s.* of wisdom
15: 8 hast thou heard the *s.* of God
29: 4 *s.* of God was on my tabernacle
40:13 and bind their faces in *s.*
Ps 25:14 *s.* of the Lord is with them that
27: 5 in the *s.* of his tabernacle
44:21 he knoweth the *s.* of the heart
139:15 when I was made in *s.*, and curiously
Prov 3:32 his *s.* is with the righteous
9:17 bread eaten in *s.* is pleasant
11:13 A talebearer revealeth *s.*, but he
Dan 2:28 God in heaven that revealeth *s.*
Amos 3: 7 revealeth his *s.* to his servants
Mat 6: 4 thine alms may be in *s.*: and thy
John 18:20 in *s.* have I said nothing
Rom 2:16 God shall judge the *s.* of men by

SECRETLY
John 19:38 but *s.* for fear of the Jews

SEE (SEEN, SEETH)
Ps 34: 8 O taste and *s.* that the Lord is good
Mat 5: 8 in heart: for they shall *s.* God
6: 1 before men to be *s.* of them
13:17 which ye *s.* and have not *s.* them
23: 5 their works they do to be *s.* of men
John 1:18 no man hath *s.* God at any time
12:45 he that *s.* me *s.* him that
14: 9 he that hath *s.* me hath *s.* the Father
14:17 because it *s.* him not, neither
14:19 the world *s.* me no more; but ye
16:22 I will *s.* you again, and your heart
20:29 blessed are they that have not *s.* and
2 Cor 4:18 things which are *s.* are temporal
1 Tim 6:16 whom no man hath *s.*, nor can *s.*
11: 1 the evidence of things not *s.*
1 Pet 1: 8 whom not having *s.*, ye love
1 John 1: 1 that which we have *s.* and
3: 2 we shall *s.* him as he is
4:12 no man hath *s.* God at any time
Rev 1: 7 and every eye shall *s.* him
22: 4 they shall *s.* his face: and his

SEED (SEEDS)
Gen 1:11 whose *s.* is in itself upon the earth
17: 7 between me and thee and thy *s.*
38: 9 that the *s.* should not be his
Ps 37:28 *s.* of wicked shall be cut off
69:36 *s.* of his servants shall inherit it
126: 6 bearing precious *s.* shall doubtless
Prov 11:21 *s.* of righteous shall be
Eccl 11: 6 in the morning, sow thy *s.*
Is 1: 4 laden with iniquity, *s.* of evildoers
45:25 all the *s.* of Israel be justified
53:10 see his *s.*, he shall prolong his days
55:10 that it may give *s.* to the sower
Mal 2:15 he might seek a godly *s.*
Mat 13:38 good *s.* are the children of the kingdom
Luke 8:11 the *s.* is the word of God
Rom 9: 8 children of promise are counted for *s.*
9:29 Lord of Sabaoth had left us a *s.*
Gal 3:16 And to *s.*, as of many; but as
1 John 3: 9 his *s.* remaineth in him

SEEK
Deut 4:29 thou *s.* him with all thy heart
1 Chr 28: 9 thou *s.* him, he will be found
2 Chr 15: 2 be with him: and if ye *s.* him
Ezra 8:21 to *s.* of him a right way
8:22 upon them for good that *s.* him
Job 5: 8 I would *s.* unto God, and unto God
Ps 9:10 not forsake them that *s.*
10:15 *s.* out his wickedness till thou
63: 1 my God, early will I *s.* thee
69:32 heart shall live that *s.* God
119: 2 blessed are they that *s.* him
119:176 *s.* thy servant, for I do not forget
Prov 8:17 that *s.* me early shall find
Sol 3: 2 *s.* him whom my soul loveth
Is 26: 9 within me will I *s.* thee early
45:19 *s.* ye me in vain: I the Lord
Jer 29:13 ye shall *s.* me and find
Amos 5: 4 *s.* ye me, ye shall live
Zeph 2: 3 *s.* righteousness, *s.* meekness
Mal 2: 7 should *s.* the law at his mouth
2:15 that he might *s.* the godly seed
Mat 6:33 *s.* ye first the kingdom of God
7: 7 *s.* and ye shall find; knock
Luke 13:24 many will *s.* to enter in
19:10 *s.* and to save that which was lost
John 8:21 ye shall *s.* me and shall die in your
Rom 2: 7 *s.* for glory and honour and
1 Cor 10:24 let no man *s.* his own but
Phil 2:21 all *s.* their own, not the things
Col 3: 1 *s.* those things which are above
1 Pet 3:11 let him *s.* peace, and ensue it

SEEKETH (SEEKING)
John 4:23 Father *s.* such to worship
1 Cor 13: 5 *s.* not her own, is not easily
1 Pet 5: 8 walketh about *s.* whom he may devour

SELL (SELLETH)
Gen 25:31 *S.* me this day thy birthright
Prov 23:23 buy truth and *s.* it not
Mat 13:44 *s.* all that he hath and buyeth
19:21 go, and *s.* that thou hast

SEND
Ps 20: 2 *S.* thee help from the sanctuary
43: 3 O *s.* out thy light and
57: 3 he shall *s.* from heaven and
Mat 9:38 *s.* forth labourers into his harvest
John 14:26 whom the Father will *s.* in my name
16: 7 if I depart I will *s.* him unto
2 Thes 2:11 God shall *s.* them strong delusion

SENTENCE (SENTENCES)
Deut 17: 9 show thee the *s.* of judgment
Prov 16:10 a divine *s.* is in the lips
Eccl 8:11 because the *s.* is not executed
Dan 5:12 of dreams, and showing of hard *s.*
2 Cor 1: 9 we had the *s.* of death in

SEPARATE (SEPARATED)
Gen 13: 9 *s.* thyself, I pray thee, from me
49:26 him that was *s.* from his brethren
Ex 33:16 so shall we be *s.*, I and thy
Deut 29:21 Lord shall *s.* him unto evil
Is 59: 2 iniquities have *s.* between you and
Acts 13: 2 *s.* me Barnabas and Saul for the work
19: 9 departed from them and *s.* the disciples
Rom 8:35 who shall *s.* us from love of Christ
8:39 *s.* us from the love of God
2 Cor 6:17 and be ye *s.*, saith the Lord
Gal 1:15 who *s.* me from my mother's womb
Heb 7:26 *s.* from sinners, and made higher

SERAPHIMS
Is 6: 2 above it stood the *s.*
6: 6 flew one of the *s.* unto me

SERPENT (SERPENTS)
Gen 3: 1 the *s.* was more subtle
49:17 Dan shall be a *s.* by the way
Num 21: 6 Lord sent fiery *s.* among the people
Prov 23:32 at last it biteth like a *s.*
Mat 7:10 will he give him a *s.*
10:16 be ye wise as *s.*, harmless as
John 3:14 as Moses lifted up the *s.* in the
2 Cor 11: 3 as the *s.* beguiled Eve through his
Rev 12: 9 that old *s.*, called the Devil

SERVE
Deut 10:20 him thou shalt *s.*, and to him
11:13 *s.* him with all your heart
13: 4 shall *s.* him, and cleave
Josh 22: 5 *s.* him with all your heart
24:14 fear the Lord, *s.* him
24:15 choose you this day whom ye will *s.*
1 Sam 12:20 *s.* the Lord with all your heart
1 Chr 28: 9 *s.* him with a perfect heart
Job 21:15 Almighty that we should *s.* him
Ps 2:11 *S.* Lord with fear, rejoice
Mat 6:24 ye cannot *s.* God and mammon
Luke 1:74 *s.* him without fear in
12:37 will come forth and *s.* them
John 12:26 if any man *s.* me let him
Acts 6: 2 leave the word of God and *s.* the tables
27:23 whose I am, and whom I *s.*
Rom 1: 9 whom I *s.* with my spirit
7: 6 we should *s.* in newness of spirit
7:25 I myself *s.* the law of God
16:18 they *s.* not the Lord Jesus Christ
Gal 5:13 but by love *s.* one another
Col 3:24 for ye *s.* the Lord Christ
1 Thes 1: 9 to *s.* the living and true God
Heb 9:14 from dead works to *s.* the living God
12:28 whereby we may *s.* God acceptably
Rev 7:15 *s.* him day and night in his temple

SERVANT (SERVANTS)
Ezra 5:11 are the *s.* of the God of heaven
Is 24: 2 with the *s.* so with his master
42: 1 behold my *s.* whom I uphold
49: 3 thou art my *s.*, O Israel, in
52:13 my *s.* shall deal prudently
Dan 3:26 ye *s.* of the most high God
Mat 20:27 among you, let him be your *s.*
25:21 well done, good and faithful *s.*
John 8:34 committeth sin is the *s.* of sin
13:16 *s.* not greater than the lord
Acts 16:17 *s.* of the most high God
Rom 6:16 yield yourselves *s.* to obey
6:17 ye were the *s.* of sin
6:18 ye became *s.* of righteousness
1 Cor 7:21 art thou called, being a *s.*
7:23 be not ye the *s.* of men
9:19 have I made myself a *s.* to all
Gal 1:10 should not be the *s.* of Christ
Phil 1: 1 the *s.* of Jesus Christ, to all the
2: 7 took on him the form of a *s.*
2 Tim 2:24 the *s.* of the Lord must not strive
1 Pet 2:16 but as the *s.* of God
2 Pet 2:19 themselves are the *s.* of corruption
Rev 7: 3 we have sealed the *s.* of our God
22: 3 and his *s.* shall serve him

SERVICE
Jer 22:13 useth his neighbour's *s.* without
Rom 12: 1 which is your reasonable *s.*

SERVING
Luke 10:40 Martha was cumbered about much *s.*
Acts 20:19 *s.* the Lord with all humility
26: 7 twelve tribes instantly *s.* God
Rom 12:11 fervent in spirit; *s.* the Lord
Tit 3: 3 *s.* divers lusts and pleasures

SETTLE (SETTLED)
Luke 21:14 *S.* it therefore in your hearts
Col 1:23 in faith grounded and *s.*
1 Pet 5:10 stablish, strengthen, *s.* you

SEVERITY
Rom 11:22 the goodness and *s.* of God

SHADE
Ps 121: 5 the Lord is thy *s.* upon thy

SHADOW (SHADOWS)
1 Chr 29:15 days on the earth are as a *s.*

John 1:29 taketh away the *s.* of the world
5:14 *s.* no more lest a worse thing
Rom 5:12 by one man *s.* entered into the world
6:14 *s.* shall not have dominion
7: 9 *s.* revived, and I died
7:13 but *s.*, that it might appear *s.*
7:14 I am carnal, sold under *s.*
7:17 but *s.* that dwelleth in me
7:25 with the flesh the law of *s.*
8: 2 made me free from the law of *s.*
2 Cor 5:21 him to be *s.* for us, who knew no *s.*
Eph 4:26 be ye angry and *s.* not
Jas 1:15 lust bringeth forth *s.*, and *s.*
1 Pet 2:22 who did no *s.*, neither was guile
1 John 1: 8 if we say we have no *s.*
2: 1 ye *s.* not; if any man *s.* we have
3: 9 he cannot *s.* because he is born of God
5:16 there is *s.* unto death

SINS

Josh 24:19 your transgressions, nor your *s.*
Ps 19:13 thy servant from presumptuous *s.*
90: 8 our secret *s.* in the light
103:10 dwelt with us after our *s.*
Is 43:25 and will not remember thy *s.*
59: 2 your *s.* have hid his face
59:12 our *s.* testify against us
Jer 5:25 *s.* have withholden good things
Ezek 33:16 none of his *s.* that he hath committed
Dan 9:16 for our *s.*, and for the iniquities
9:24 to make an end of *s.*
John 8:21 shall die in your *s.*: whither I go
1 Cor 15: 3 Christ died for our *s.*
15:17 ye are yet in your *s.*
Gal 1: 4 gave himself for our *s.*
1 Tim 5:22 partaker of other men's *s.*
2 Tim 3: 6 silly women laden with *s.*
Heb 1: 3 had by himself purged our *s.*
1 Pet 2:24 bare our *s.* in his own body
1 John 2: 2 he is the propitiation for our *s.*
Rev 1: 5 and washed us from our *s.*

SINNED (SINNETH)

Ex 9:27 I have *s.* this time: the Lord
32:33 whosoever hath *s.* against me, him
Num 22:34 angel of the Lord, I have *s.*
Josh 7:20 I have *s.* against the Lord God
Judg 10:10 We have *s.* against thee
2 Sam 12:13 I have *s.* against the Lord
Job 1:22 in all this Job *s.* not
33:27 I have *s.* and perverted
Ps 51: 4 thee only have I *s.*, and done this evil
106: 6 we have *s.* with our fathers
Prov 8:36 but he that *s.* against me wrongeth
Eccl 7:20 man that doeth good, and *s.* not
Is 42:24 he against whom we have *s.*
Jer 3:25 we have *s.* against the Lord
Lam 1: 8 Jerusalem hath grievously *s.*
5:16 woe unto us, that we have *s.*
Ezek 18: 4 soul that *s.* it shall die
Dan 9: 5 We have *s.*, and have committed iniquity
Mic 7: 9 because I have *s.* against him
Mat 27: 4 *s.* in that I have betrayed
Luke 15:18 Father, I have *s.* against heaven
15:21 I have *s.* against heaven
Rom 2:12 many as *s.* without the law
3:23 all have *s.* and come short
1 John 1:10 if we say we have not *s.*
5:18 whosoever is born of God *s.* not

SINNER (SINNERS)

Gen 13:13 wicked and *s.* before the Lord
Ps 1: 1 nor standeth in the way of *s.*
25: 8 therefore will he teach *s.* in the way
Eccl 7:26 the *s.* shall be taken by her
9:18 one *s.* destroyeth much good
Is 33:14 the *s.* in Zion are afraid
Mat 9:13 I am not come to call righteous, but *s.*
Luke 13: 2 were *s.* above all the Galilaeans
13: 4 think ye that they were *s.*
15: 7 joy in heaven over one *s.* that
18:13 God be merciful to me a *s.*
John 9:31 we know that God heareth not *s.*
Rom 5: 8 while we were yet *s.* Christ died
5:19 disobedience many were made *s.*
Gal 2:15 and not the *s.* of the Gentiles
1 Tim 1:15 came into world to save *s.*
Heb 7:26 separate from *s.*, and made higher
Jas 4: 8 cleanse your hands, ye *s.*
5:20 converteth the *s.* from the error
1 Pet 4:18 shall the ungodly and the *s.* appear
Jude 1:15 speeches which ungodly *s.* have spoken

SINCERE

Phil 1:10 that ye may be *s.* and without
1 Pet 2: 2 desire the *s.* milk of the word

SINCERITY

Josh 24:14 serve him in *s.* and in truth
1 Cor 5: 8 with the unleavened bread of *s.*
2 Cor 1:12 in simplicity and godly *s.* we have
8: 8 to prove the *s.* of your love
Eph 6:24 that love our Lord Jesus Christ in *s.*
Tit 2: 7 showing uncorruptness, gravity, *s.*

SINEW (SINEWS)

Job 10:11 fenced me with bones and *s.*
Is 48: 4 thy neck is an iron *s.*

SING

Ex 15: 1 I will *s.* unto the Lord
15:21 *S.* ye to the Lord for he hath
Judg 5: 3 I will *s.* praise to the Lord
1 Chr 16:23 *S.* unto the Lord all the earth
Job 29:13 I caused the widows heart to *s.*
Ps 9:11 *S.* praises to the Lord which
27: 6 I will *s.*, yea, I will *s.*
30: 4 *S.* unto the Lord O ye saints
47: 7 of all the earth: *s.* ye praises
57: 7 I will *s.* and give praise
68: 4 *s.* unto God, *s.* praises to his
92: 1 *s.* praises unto thy name, O most
95: 1 let us *s.* unto the Lord
101: 1 I will *s.* of mercy and judgment
135: 3 *s.* praises unto his name; for it is
144: 9 I will *s.* a new song unto thee
145: 7 and shall *s.* of thy righteousness
147: 1 it is good to *s.* praises
147: 7 *S.* unto the Lord with thanksgiving
Prov 29: 6 the righteous doth *s.* and rejoice
Is 5: 1 I will *s.* to my wellbeloved
12: 5 *S.* unto the Lord; for he hath
35: 6 and the tongue of the dumb *s.*
65:14 my servants shall *s.* for joy
1 Cor 14:15 I will *s.* with the spirit
Jas 5:13 is any merry? let him *s.*

SINGING

Eph 5:19 *s.* and making melody in your heart

SINGLE

Mat 6:22 therefore thine eye be *s.*
Luke 11:34 when thine eye is *s.*, thy whole

SINGLENESS

Acts 2:46 with gladness and *s.* of heart
Eph 6: 5 trembling, in *s.* of your heart
Col 3:22 in *s.* of heart, fearing God

SKIN (SKINS)

Job 2: 4 *s.* for *s.*, yea all that a man
10:11 clothed me with *s.* and flesh
19:26 after my *s.*, worms destroy this body
Jer 13:23 Can the Ethiopian change his *s.*
Heb 11:37 in sheep *s.* and goat *s.*

SKIP (SKIPPED, SKIPPING)

Ps 29: 6 them also to *s.* like a calf
114: 4 mountains *s.* like rams, and the
Sol 2: 8 upon the mountains, *s.* upon the hills

SLACK (SLACKED)

Deut 7:10 will not be *s.* to him that hateth
Prov 10: 4 poor that dealeth with a *s.* hand
Hab 1: 4 Therefore, the law is *s.*
Zeph 3:16 Let not thine hands be *s.*
2 Pet 3: 9 The Lord is not *s.* concerning

SLAY (SLAIN)

Lev 14:13 he shall *s.* the lamb in the place
Job 13:15 Though he *s.* me, yet will I
Ps 139:19 thou wilt *s.* the wicked
Eph 2:16 having *s.* in his flesh the enmity
Rev 5: 9 wast *s.* and hast redeemed
13: 8 of the Lamb *s.* from the foundation

SLEEP

Gen 2:21 caused a deep *s.* to fall upon
15:12 a deep *s.* fell upon Abraham
1 Sam 26:12 a deep *s.* from the Lord
Job 4:13 deep *s.* falleth on men
Ps 76: 6 are cast into a dead *s.*
90: 5 they are as a *s.*: in the morning
127: 2 he giveth his beloved *s.*
132: 4 will not give *s.* to mine eyes
Prov 3:24 and thy *s.* shall be sweet
6: 4 give not *s.* to thine eyes, nor
19:15 Slothfulness casteth into a deep *s.*
20:13 love not *s.* lest thou come to poverty
Eccl 5:12 *s.* of the labouring man is sweet
Sol 5: 2 I *s.* but my heart waketh
Is 29:10 upon you the spirit of deep *s.*
Jer 31:26 beheld: and my *s.* was sweet to me
51:39 *s.* a perpetual *s.*, and not wake
Luke 9:32 with him were heavy with *s.*
Rom 13:11 time to awake out of *s.*
1 Cor 11:30 sickly among you, and many *s.*
15:51 we shall not all *s.* but shall
1 Thes 4:14 them also which *s.* in Jesus died
5: 6 let us not *s.* as others; but
5: 7 they that *s. s.* in the night
5:10 whether we wake or *s.* we should

SLEEPEST (SLEPT)

Ps 3: 5 I laid me down and *s.*; I awaked
76: 5 they have *s.* their sleep: and none
1 Cor 15:20 firstfruits of them that *s.*
Eph 5:14 he saith, awake, thou that *s.*

SLING

1 Sam 25:29 them shall he *s.* out as out of
Jer 10:18 I will *s.* out the inhabitants

SLIP (SLIPPETH)

Ps 18:36 under me, that my feet did not *s.*
94:18 I said, My foot *s.*; thy mercy
Heb 2: 1 at any time we should let them *s.*

SLIPPERY

Ps 35: 6 Let their way be dark and *s.*
73:18 thou didst send them into *s.* places
Jer 23:12 unto them as *s.* ways in the darkness

SLOTHFUL (SLOTHFULNESS)

Prov 12:24 but the *s.* shall be under tribute
12:27 *s.* man roasteth not that which he
15:19 way of the *s.* man is as a hedge of
18: 9 *s.* in his work is the brother to
19:15 *s.* casteth into a deep sleep
21:25 desire of the *s.* killeth him
24:30 I went by the field of the *s.*
26:14 door turneth on hinges, so doth the *s.*
Heb 6:12 be not *s.* but followers of them

SLOW

Prov 14:29 He that is *s.* to wrath is of great
Luke 24:25 fools *s.* of heart to believe
Jas 1:19 *s.* to speak, *s.* to wrath

SLUGGARD

Prov 6: 6 Go to the ant, thou *s.*
6: 9 how long wilt thou sleep, O *s.*
13: 4 the soul of the *s.* desireth
20: 4 *s.* will not plow by reason

Prov 26:16 *s.* is wiser in his own conceit

SLUMBER (SLUMBERED, SLUMBERETH)
Ps 132: 4 mine eyes, or *s.* to mine eyelids
Mat 25: 5 tarried, they all *s.* and
Rom 11: 8 given them the spirit of *s.*
2 Pet 2: 3 not, and their damnation *s.* not

SMITE (SMITEST, SMITTEN)
Deut 28:22 The Lord shall *s.* thee with a
Ps 141: 5 let the righteous *s.* me; it shall
Is 53: 4 him stricken, *s.* of God, and
Jer 18:18 let us *s.* him with the tongue
Hos 6: 1 hath *s.* and he will bind us up
Mat 5:39 *s.* thee on thy right cheek
John 18:23 but if well, why *s.* thou me

SMOKE (SMOKING)
Gen 19:28 the *s.* of the country went up
Ex 19:18 Sinai was altogether on a *s.*
Deut 29:20 his jealousy shall *s.* against
Ps 74: 1 why doth thine anger *s.* against
Is 42: 3 *s.* flax shall he not quench
Rev 14:11 *s.* of their torment ascendeth

SNARE (SNARES)
Ex 23:33 it will surely be a *s.*
Judg 2: 3 gods shall be a *s.* unto you
Ps 11: 6 on the wicked he will rain *s.*
18: 5 the *s.* of death prevented me
69:22 let their table become a *s.*
91: 3 deliver thee from the *s.* of
119:110 wicked have laid a *s.* for me
124: 7 *s.* is broken, and we are escaped
Prov 13:14 depart from the *s.* of death
29:25 fear of man bringeth a *s.*: but whoso
2 Tim 2:26 out of the *s.* of the devil

SNOW
Ps 51: 7 shall be whiter than *s.*
68:14 it was white as *s.* in Salmon
Is 1:18 they shall be as white as *s.*
Dan 7: 9 did sit, whose garment was white as *s.*
Mat 28: 3 lightning, and his raiment white as *s.*
Rev 1:14 white like wool, as white as *s.*

SOBER
2 Cor 5:13 whether we be *s.*, it is for you
1 Thes 5: 6 let us watch and be *s.*
1 Tim 3: 2 vigilant, *s.*, of good behavior
3:11 wives be grave, not slanderers, *s.*
Tit 1: 8 *s.*, just, holy, temperate
2: 2 that the aged men be *s.*, grave
2: 4 teach young women to be *s.*
1 Pet 1:13 up the loins of your mind, be *s.*
4: 7 be ye therefore *s.* and watch unto prayer
5: 8 be *s.*, be vigilant: because your

SOBERLY
Rom 12: 3 but to think *s.*, according as God
Tit 2:12 worldly lusts, we should live *s.*

SOBERNESS
Acts 26:25 forth the words of truth and *s.*

SOFT
Job 23:16 for God maketh my heart *s.*
Prov 15: 1 *s.* answer turneth away wrath: but
25:15 and a *s.* tongue breaketh the bone
Mat 11: 8 to see? A man clothed in *s.* raiment

SOJOURN (SOJOURNING)
Gen 12:10 went down into Egypt to *s.* there
Ex 12:40 the *s.* of the children of Israel
Ps 120: 5 I *s.* in Mesech, that I dwell
1 Pet 1:17 the time of your *s.* here in fear

SOJOURNER (SOJOURNERS)
Lev 25:23 are strangers and *s.* with me
1 Chr 29:15 strangers before thee, and *s.*
Ps 39:12 stranger with thee, and a *s.*

SOLD
1 Ki 21:20 hast *s.* thyself to work evil
2 Ki 17:17 *s.* themselves to do evil
Rom 7:14 I am carnal, *s.* under sin

SOLDIER
2 Tim 2: 3 as a good *s.* of Jesus Christ
2: 4 him who hath chosen him to be a *s.*

SON
Num 23:19 neither the *s.* of man, that he
2 Sam 18:33 O Absalom, my *s.*, my *s.*
Job 25: 6 *s.* of man, which is a worm
Ps 2:12 kiss the *S.* lest he be angry
8: 4 *s.* of man, that thou visitest
80:17 upon the *s.* of man whom thou
Prov 10: 1 a wise *s.* maketh a glad father
Dan 3:25 is like the *S.* of God
7:13 one like the *S.* of man came
Mal 3:17 as a man spareth his own *s.*
Mat 4: 3 thou be the *S.* of God
11:27 no man knoweth the *S.*, but the Father
16:16 the *S.* of the living God
17: 5 this is my beloved *S.*, in whom
Luke 10: 6 if the *s.* of peace be there
John 1:18 only begotten *S.*, which is in the
3:16 gave his only begotten *s.*
5:21 *S.* quickeneth whom he will
5:23 men should honour the *S.*
8:35 but the *S.* abideth ever
8:36 if the *S.* shall make you free
Acts 3:13 hath glorified his *s.* Jesus
Rom 1: 3 concerning his *S.* Jesus
5:10 by the death of his *s.*
8: 3 sending his own *S.* in the likeness
8:32 spared not his own *s.*
1 Cor 1: 9 fellowship of his *S.* Jesus
Gal 1:16 To reveal his *S.* in me, that I
4: 4 God sent forth his *S.*, made of a
4: 7 if a *s.* then an heir of God
1 Thes 1:10 wait for his *S.* from heaven
Heb 1: 2 spoken unto us by his *S.*
5: 8 though he were a *S.* yet learned he
1 John 1: 7 blood of Jesus Christ his *S.*
2:22 that denieth the father the *S.*
3:23 believe on the name of his *S.*
5:11 and this life is in his *S.*
5:12 *S.* hath life, hath not the *S.*

SONS
Gen 6: 2 *s.* of God saw the daughters
Job 1: 6 *s.* of God came to present themselves
38: 7 all the *s.* of God shouted for joy
Ps 144:12 that our *s.* may be as plants
Sol 2: 3 so is my beloved among *s.*
Hos 1:10 Ye are the *s.* of the living God
Mal 3: 3 purify the *s.* of Levi
Mark 3:17 Boanerges, which is, The *s.* of
John 1:12 become the *s.* of God, even to them
Rom 8:14 of God, they are the *s.* of God
1 Cor 4:14 as my beloved *s.* I warn
Gal 4: 6 because ye are *s.*, God hath sent
Phil 2:15 *s.* of God without rebuke, in the midst
Heb 2:10 bringing many *s.* to glory
12: 7 God dealeth with you as with *s.*
1 John 3: 1 we should be called the *s.* of God
3: 2 Beloved, now are we the *s.* of God

SONG (SONGS)
Ex 15: 2 Lord is my strength and my *s.*
Job 30: 9 And now am I their *s.*, yea
35:10 who giveth *s.* in the night
Ps 32: 7 me about with *s.* of deliverance
33: 3 sing unto him a new *s.*
42: 8 his *s.* shall be with me and my
96: 1 sing unto the Lord a new *s.*
119:54 *s.* in house of my pilgrimage
149: 1 Sing unto the Lord a new *s.*
Is 30:29 Ye shall have a *s.*, as in the
42:10 Sing unto the Lord a new *s.*
Ezek 33:32 to them as a very lovely *s.*
Eph 5:19 in psalms and hymns and spiritual *s.*
Rev 5: 9 they sung a new *s.* saying, Thou
14: 3 no man could learn that *s.*
15: 3 sing the *s.* of Moses the servant of

SORCERER (SORCERERS)
Jer 27: 9 nor to your *s.*, which speak unto
Mal 3: 5 swift witness against the *s.*
Acts 13: 8 But Elymas the *s.* (for so is his
Rev 21: 8 whoremongers, and *s.*, and idolaters

SORCERIES
Acts 8:11 he had bewitched them with *s.*

SORRY
Ps 38:18 I will be *s.* for my sin
2 Cor 2: 2 if I make you *s.*, who is he then
7: 8 the same epistle hath made you *s.*

SORROW (SORROWS)
Ps 18: 4 *s.* of death compassed me
18: 5 the *s.* of hell compassed me
90:10 is their strength, labour and *s.*
127: 2 sit up late to eat the bread of *s.*
Prov 15:13 by *s.* of the heart the spirit
Eccl 1:18 increaseth knowledge increaseth *s.*
7: 3 *s.* is better than laughter
Is 35:10 *s.* and sighing shall flee away
50:11 ye shall lie down in *s.*
53: 3 man of *s.*, and acquainted with
53: 4 carried our *s.*: yet we did esteem
Jer 31:12 shall not *s.* any more at all
Lam 1:12 there be any *s.* like unto my *s.*
Mat 24: 8 all these are the beginning of *s.*
John 16: 6 *s.* hath filled your heart
16:20 your *s.* shall be turned into joy
2 Cor 2: 7 swallowed up with overmuch *s.*
7:10 for godly *s.* worketh repentance
Phil 2:27 lest I should have *s.* upon *s.*
1 Thes 4:13 *s.* not, as others which have no hope
1 Tim 6:10 and pierced through with many *s.*
Rev 21: 4 no more death, neither *s.*

SORROWED
2 Cor 7: 9 but that ye *s.* to repentance: for

SORROWFUL
Job 6: 7 to touch are as my *s.* meat
Prov 14:13 in laughter the heart is *s.*
Jer 31:25 replenished the *s.* soul
Zeph 3:18 gather them that are *s.*
Mat 19:22 that saying, he went away *s.*
26:22 they were exceeding *s.*, and began

SOUGHT
Ex 33: 7 every one which *s.* the Lord
1 Chr 15:13 *s.* him not after the due
2 Chr 14: 7 because we have *s.* the Lord
16:12 *s.* not to the Lord, but to the
Ps 34: 4 I *s.* the Lord, and he heard
78:34 then they *s.* him: and they returned
111: 2 *s.* out of all them that have
119:10 with my whole heart have I *s.* thee
Eccl 7:29 they have *s.* out many inventions
Sol 5: 6 I *s.* him, but I could not
Is 62:12 shall be called, *S.* out, a city not
65: 1 found of them that *s.* me not
Jer 8: 2 and whom they have *s.*, and whom they
Rom 9:32 *s.* it not by faith, but by

SOUL
Ex 30:12 every man a ransom for his *s.*
Lev 26:15 your *s.* abhor my judgments
Deut 6: 5 and with all thy *s.*, and with all
11:13 heart and with all your *s.*
13: 3 your heart and with your *s.*
Josh 22: 5 your heart and with all your *s.*
Judg 10:16 his *s.* was grieved for misery
1 Sam 18: 1 *s.* of Jonathan knit with the *s.*
1 Ki 8:48 and with all their *s.*, in the land of
2 Ki 23:25 with all his *s.*, and with all
1 Chr 22:19 *s.* to seek the Lord your God
Job 27: 8 when God taketh away his *s.*
Ps 16:10 not leave my *s.* in hell

Ps 19: 7 Lord is perfect, converting the *s.*
31: 7 hast known my *s.* in adversities
34:22 Lord redeemeth the *s.* of his servants
35: 3 say to my *s.* I am thy salvation
35: 9 my *s.* shall be joyful in the Lord
42: 5 why cast down, O my *s.*
49: 8 redemption of their *s.* is precious
62: 1 Truly my *s.* waiteth upon God
62
5My *s.*, wait thou only upon God
63: 1 my *s.* thirsteth for thee, my flesh
63: 8 my *s.* followeth hard after thee
74:19 deliver not the *s.* of thy turtledove
107: 9 filleth the hungry *s.* with goodness
Prov 10: 3 not suffer the *s.* of the righteous
19: 2 that *s.* be without knowledge
27: 7 the full *s.* loatheth an honeycomb
Is 26: 8 the desire of our *s.* is to thy
26: 9 with my *s.* have I desired thee
55: 2 let your *s.* delight in fatness
55: 3 hear and your *s.* shall live
58:10 and satisfy the afflicted *s.*
61:10 my *s.* shall be joyful in my God
Jer 31:25 I have satiated the weary *s.*
38:16 Lord liveth, that made us this *s.*
Ezek 3:19 but thou hast delivered thy *s.*
Hab 2: 4 his *s.* lifted up is not upright
Mat 10:28 not able to kill the *s.*: but rather
16:26 gain the whole world, and lose his *s.*
22:37 and with all thy *s.*, and with all
26:38 My *s.* is exceedingly sorrowful
Mark 12:33 and with all the *s.*, and with all
Luke 1:46 my *s.* doth magnify the Lord
12:20 this night thy *s.* shall be
John 12:27 Now is my *s.* troubled; and what
Rom 13: 1 let every *s.* be subject to
1 Thes 5:23 *s.* and body be preserved blameless
Heb 4:12 dividing asunder of *s.* and spirit
10:39 believe to the saving of the *s.*
3 John 1: 2 be in health even as thy *s.* prospereth

SOULS
Josh 23:14 all your hearts and in all your *s.*
Prov 11:30 and he that winneth *s.* is wise
Is 57:16 and the *s.* which I have made
Jer 6:16 ye shall find rest for your *s.*
Ezek 14:14 they should deliver but their own *s.*
Mat 11:29 ye shall find rest unto your *s.*
Luke 21:19 your patience possess ye your *s.*
Heb 13:17 they watch for your *s.*, as they that
1 Pet 1:22 ye have purified your *s.* in obeying
2:25 Shepherd and Bishop of your *s.*
4:19 commit the keeping of their *s.* to him
2 Pet 2:14 beguiling unstable *s.*: an heart they
Rev 6: 9 *s.* of them that were slain for the
20: 4 *s.* of them that were beheaded for

SOUND
Job 15:21 dreadful *s.* is in his ears
Ps 47: 5 Lord with the *s.* of a trumpet
89:15 people that know joyful *s.*
119:80 let my heart be *s.* in thy statutes
Prov 2: 7 he layeth up *s.* wisdom
Eccl 12: 4 *s.* of the grinding is low
Amos 6: 5 that chant to the *s.* of the viol
Rom 10:18 *s.* went into all the earth
1 Tim 1:10 thing that is contrary to *s.* doctrine
2 Tim 1: 7 and of love and of a *s.* mind
1:13 hold fast the form of *s.* words
Tit 2: 2 temperate, *s.* in faith, in charity

SOUNDNESS
Ps 38: 3 there is no *s.* in my flesh
Is 1: 6 there is no *s.* in it

SOW (SOWETH, SOWN)
Job 4: 8 *s.* wickedly, reap the same
Ps 97:11 light is *s.* for the righteous, and
126: 5 *s.* in tears shall reap in joy
Prov 11:18 to him that *s.* righteousness
22: 8 *s.* iniquity shall reap vanity
Eccl 11: 4 observeth the wind shall not *s.*
Jer 4: 3 fallow ground, and *s.* not among thorns
31:27 I will *s.* the house of Israel
Hos 8: 7 *s.* wind, they shall reap whirlwind
10:12 *s.* to yourselves in righteousness, reap
Mic 6:15 thou shalt *s.* but thou shalt not
Mat 13: 3 Behold, a sower went forth to *s.*
Luke 12:24 the ravens; for they neither *s.* nor
19:22 reaping that I did not *s.*
John 4:37 true, and one *s.*, another reapeth
1 Cor 9:11 have *s.* to you spiritual things
15:42 it is *s.* in corruption; it is raised
15:43 *s.* in dishonour, it is raised
2 Cor 9: 6 *s.* sparingly shall reap also
9:10 multiply your seed *s.*, and increase
Gal 6: 7 whatsoever a man *s.*, that shall
Jas 3:18 fruit of righteousness *s.* in peace

SOWER
Is 55:10 it may give seed to the *s.*

SPARE (SPARED, SPARETH)
Gen 18:26 I will *s.* all the place
Neh 13:22 *s.* me according to the greatness of
Ps 39:13 *s.* me that I may recover strength
Prov 13:24 he that *s.* the rod hateth his
Joel 2:17 *s.* thy people O Lord and give not
Mal 3:17 I will *s.* them, as a man spareth
Rom 8:32 He that *s.* not his own Son, but
11:21 if God *s.* not the natural branches
2 Pet 2: 4 God *s.* not angels that sinned

SPARKS
Job 5: 7 trouble, as the *s.* fly upward
Is 50:11 that compass yourself about with *s.*

SPARROW (SPARROWS)
Ps 102: 7 am as a *s.* along upon the house
Mat 10:29 two *s.* sold for a farthing

SPEAK
Gen 18:27 taken on me to *s.* to the Lord
Ex 4:14 I know he can *s.* well
34:35 went in to *s.* with him
1 Sam 3: 9 *S.*, Lord, for thy servant heareth
Ps 85: 8 he will *s.* peace to his people
Is 50: 4 how to *s.* a word in season
Jer 18: 7 at what instant I shall *s.*
Mat 10:19 how or what ye shall *s.*
Luke 6:26 when all men *s.* well of
John 3:11 we *s.* that we do know and testify
Acts 4:20 cannot but *s.* the things which we
1 Cor 1:10 ye all *s.* the same thing
Tit 3: 2 to *s.* evil of no man to be no
Jas 1:19 swift to hear, slow to *s.*
2 Pet 2:10 not afraid to *s.* evil of dignities
Jude 1:10 *s.* evil of things which they

SPEAKETH (SPEAKING)
Is 58:13 pleasure, nor *s.* thine own words
65:24 while they are *s.* I will hear
Dan 9:20 whiles I was *s.* and praying, and
Mat 6: 7 shall be heard for their much *s.*
12:32 *s.* a word against the Son of man
12:34 abundance of the heart the mouth *s.*
Eph 4:15 But *s.* the truth in love may
4:31 evil *s.*, be put away from you, with
5:19 *s.* to yourselves in psalms
1 Tim 4: 2 *s.* lies in hypocrisy
Heb 11: 4 he being dead yet *s.*
12:24 *s.* better things than that of Abel
12:25 refuse not him that *s.*
Rev 13: 5 a mouth *s.* great things

SPEECH (SPEECHES)
Gen 11: 1 one language and of one *s.*
Mat 26:73 them; for thy *s.* betrayeth thee
Rom 16:18 by fair *s.* deceive the hearts
1 Cor 2: 1 not with excellency of *s.*
2 Cor 3:12 use great plainness of *s.*
10:10 weak, and his *s.* contemptible
Col 4: 6 let your *s.* be always with grace
Tit 2: 8 sound *s.*, that cannot be condemned
Jude 1:15 of all their hard *s.* which ungodly

SPEECHLESS
Mat 22:12 garment? And he was *s.*

SPEND (SPENT)
Job 21:13 they *s.* their days in wealth
Ps 90: 9 *s.* our years as a tale that
Is 49: 4 have *s.* my strength for nought
55: 2 *s.* money for that which is
Rom 13:12 night is far *s.*, the day is at
2 Cor 12:15 gladly spend and be *s.* for you

SPEW (SPEWING)
Lev 18:28 the land *s.* not you out also
Jer 25:27 be drunken, and *s.* and fall
Hab 2:16 shameful *s.* shall be on thy glory
Rev 3:16 I will *s.* thee out

SPIRIT
Gen 1: 2 the *s.* of God moved upon the face
6: 3 my *s.* shall not always strive
Ex 35:21 everyone whom his *s.* made willing
Num 11:17 take of the *s.* which is on
14:24 Caleb had another *s.* with
2 Ki 2: 9 double portion of thy *s.*
2 Chr 15: 1 *s.* of God came upon Azariah
Ezra 1: 5 whose *s.* God had raised, to go up to
Neh 9:20 gavest also thy good *s.* to instruct
Job 26:13 by his *s.* he garnished the
32:18 the *s.* within constraineth me
Ps 31: 5 to thine hand I commit my *s.*
32: 2 in whose *s.* there is no guile
34:18 such as be of a contrite *s.*
51:10 renew a right *s.* within me
51:11 take not thy holy *s.* from me
51:12 uphold me with thy free *s.*
51:17 sacrifices of God are a broken *s.*
76:12 he shall cut off the *s.* of princes
78: 8 *s.* was not stedfast with God
139: 7 whither should I go from thy *s.*
142: 3 when my *s.* was overwhelmed within
143: 7 O Lord, my *s.* faileth
Prov 14:29 hasty of *s.* exalteth folly
15:13 by sorrow of heart the *s.* is broken
16:18 and an haughty *s.* before a fall
16:32 he that ruleth his *s.* than he
18:14 a wounded *s.* who can bear?
20:27 *s.* of man is the candle of the Lord
Eccl 3:21 who knoweth the *s.* of man
8: 8 power over the *s.* to retain the *s.*
12: 7 the *s.* shall return to God
Is 32:15 until the *s.* be poured upon us
34:16 his *s.* it hath gathered them
38:16 these things is the life of my *s.*
57:15 to revive the *s.* of the humble
57:16 the *s.* should fail before me
61: 3 garment of praise for the *s.* of
66: 2 that is poor and of a contrite *s.*
Ezek 11:24 Afterwards the *s.* took me up
36:27 I will put my *s.* within you
Mic 2:11 walking in *s.* and falsehood
Zech 4: 6 but by my *s.*, saith the Lord
12: 1 formeth the *s.* of man within
12:10 *s.* of grace and supplication
13: 2 the prophets of the unclean *s.*
Mat 3:16 *S.* of God descending like a dove
12:28 cast out devils by the *s.*
12:43 when the unclean *s.* is gone out of a
22:43 doth in *s.* call him Lord
26:41 *s.* is willing, but the flesh weak
Luke 1:47 my *s.* hath rejoiced in God my
1:80 child grew, and waxed strong in *s.*
2:27 he came by the *S.* into the temple
8:55 *s.* came again and she arose
9:55 know not what manner of *s.* ye are
23:46 into thy hands I commend my *s.*
24:39 *s.* hath not flesh and bones
John 3: 5 born of water and of *s.* he cannot
3: 6 that which is born of the *S.* is *s.*
4:24 God is a *S.*: and they that
6:63 it is the *s.* that quickeneth
Acts 6:10 resist the wisdom and the *s.*

Acts 7:59 Lord Jesus, receive my *s.*
16: 7 the *S.* suffered them not
17:16 *s.* was stirred in him when he saw
18: 5 Paul was pressed in *s.* and
Rom 1: 9 whom I serve with my *s.* in the
8: 1 not after flesh, but after the *S.*
8: 2 *S.* of the life in Christ Jesus made
8: 9 if any have not the *S.* of Christ, he
8:13 through the *S.* do mortify the deeds
8:14 as many as are led by the *S.* of God
8:15 ye have received the *S.* of adoption
8:16 *S.* beareth witness with our *s.*
1 Cor 2:10 *s.*: for the *S.* searcheth all things
2:14 the things of the *S.* of God
3:16 the *S.* of God dwelleth in you
5: 5 the *s.* may be saved in the day of
6:11 Jesus, and by the *S.* of our God
6:17 joined unto the Lord is one *s.*
12: 3 speaking by the *S.* of God
12:13 all made to drink into one *S.*
14:14 unknown tongue, my *s.* prayeth
2 Cor 3: 3 with the *S.* of the living God
3: 6 not of the letter but of the *s.*
3:17 *S.* of the Lord is, there is liberty
7: 1 from filthiness of flesh and *s.*
Gal 3: 3 begun in *S.* are ye now perfect
4: 6 sent forth the *S.* of his Son into your
5:17 flesh lusteth against *S.* and *S.*
5:18 led of the *S.* ye are not under the
5:22 fruit of the *S.* is love, joy, peace
5:25 live in the *S.* let us also walk in
6:18 Lord Jesus Christ be with your *s.*
Eph 1:13 sealed with that holy *S.* of promise
4: 4 there is one body, and one *S.* even
4:23 be renewed in the *s.* of your mind
4:30 grieve not the holy *S.* of God
5: 9 fruit of *S.* is in all goodness
6:18 prayer and supplication in the *s.*
Col 2: 5 yet am I with you in the *s.*
1 Thes 5:23 whole *s.* be preserved blameless unto
Heb 4:12 diving asunder of soul and *s.*
9:14 through the eternal *S.* offered himself
Jas 4: 5 *s.* that dwelleth in us lusteth
1 Pet 3: 4 the ornament of a meek and quiet *s.*
3:18 in flesh, but quickened by the *S.*
4:14 *s.* of glory and of God resteth
1 John 4: 1 believe not every *s.*, but try
4: 2 Hereby know ye the *s.* of God
Jude 1:19 themselves sensual, having not the *S.*
Rev 1:10 I was in the *S.* on the Lord's day
11:11 *S.* of life from God entered
14:13 yea, saith the *S.*, that they may

SPIRITS
Num 16:22 God of the *s.* of all flesh
Prov 16: 2 but the Lord weigheth the *s.*
Mat 10: 1 gave them power against unclean *s.*
Luke 10:20 rejoice not that the *s.* are subject to you
Acts 5:16 them which were vexed with unclean *s.*
8: 7 unclean *s.*, crying with loud voice
1 Cor 14:32 *s.* of the prophets are subject
Heb 12:23 to the *s.* of just men made
1 Pet 3:19 preached unto the *s.* in prison
1 John 4: 1 believe not every spirit but try the *s.*
Rev 16:14 they are the *s.* of devils

SPIRITUAL
Hos 9: 7 the *s.* man is mad for the multitude
Rom 1:11 impart unto you some *s.* gift
7:14 that the law is *s.*, but I am carnal
15:27 partakers of their *s.* things
1 Cor 2:13 comparing *s.* things with *s.*
2:15 he that is *s.* judgeth all things
3: 1 not speak unto you as unto the *s.*
9:11 if we have sown unto you *s.* things
10: 3 did all eat the same *s.* meat
10: 4 of that *s.* Rock that followed them
15:44 natural body, it is raised a *s.* body
Gal 6: 1 ye which are *s.* restore
Eph 1: 3 blessed us with all *s.* blessings
5:19 psalms and hymns and *s.* songs
6:12 against *s.* wickedness in high places
Col 3:16 psalms and hymns and *s.* songs
1 Pet 2: 5 are built up a *s.* house, an holy

SPIRITUALLY
Rom 8: 6 to be *s.* minded is life and peace
1 Cor 2:14 because they are *s.* discerned
Rev 11: 8 which *s.* is called Sodom and Egypt

SPOIL (SPOILED, SPOILING)
Gen 49:27 at night he shall divide the *s.*
Ex 12:36 And they *s.* the Egyptians
Ps 68:12 tarried at home divided the *s.*
Is 53:12 divide the *s.* with the strong
Mat 12:29 and then he will *s.* his house
Col 2: 8 beware lest any man *s.* you
2:15 having *s.* principalities and powers
Heb 10:34 took joyfully the *s.* of your goods

SPOT
Num 19: 2 bring thee a red heifer without *s.*
Deut 32: 5 *s.* is not the *s.* of his children
Job 11:15 shalt thou lift up thy face without *s.*
Sol 4: 7 there is no *s.* in thee
1 Tim 6:14 keep this commandment without *s.*
Heb 9:14 offered himself without *s.* to God
1 Pet 1:19 lamb without blemish and without *s.*
2 Pet 3:14 peace, without *s.*, and blameless

SPRING (SPRINGING, SPRUNG)
Ps 65:10 thou blesses the *s.* thereof
85:11 Truth shall *s.* out of the earth
Mat 13: 5 forthwith they *s.* up because they
13: 7 and the thorns *s.* up, and choked
John 4:14 *s.* up into everlasting life
Heb 12:15 root of bitterness *s.* up trouble you

SPRINKLE (SPRINKLED, SPRINKLING)
Lev 14: 7 he shall *s.* upon him that is to
Is 52:15 so shall he *s.* many nations
Ezek 36:25 then will I *s.* clean water upon you
Heb 10:22 hearts *s.* from an evil conscience
12:24 to blood of *s.*, that speaketh
1 Pet 1: 2 *s.* of the blood of Jesus Christ

SPY
Num 13:16 which Moses sent out to *s.* the land
Josh 2: 1 two men to *s.* secretly, saying, Go
Gal 2: 4 to *s.* out our liberty

STAFF
Gen 32:10 with my *s.* I passed over
Ps 23: 4 thy rod and thy *s.* they comfort me
Is 3: 1 from Judah the stay and the *s.*
9: 4 burden, and the *s.* of his shoulder
10: 5 *s.* in their hand is mine indignation
Zech 11:10 And I took my *s.*, even Beauty, and

STAND
Ex 9:11 magicians could not *s.* before Moses
14:13 *s.* still, and see the salvation of
Josh 10:12 *s.* thou still upon Gibeon
1 Sam 6:20 is able to *s.* before his holy Lord
2 Chr 20:17 set yourselves, *s.* ye still
Job 19:25 *s.* at the latter day upon the earth
Ps 76: 7 who may *s.* in thy sight
130: 3 iniquities, O Lord, who shall *s.*
Prov 19:21 the counsel of the Lord, that shall *s.*
Is 46:10 my counsel shall *s.*, and I will
Ezek 29: 7 their loins to be at a *s.*
Nah 1: 6 who can *s.* before his indignation
Mal 3: 2 who shall *s.* when he appeareth?
Mat 12:25 against itself shall not *s.*
Luke 21:36 *s.* before the Son of man
Rom 5: 2 this grace wherein we *s.*
14:10 shall all *s.* before the judgment seat
1 Cor 16:13 *s.* fast in the faith quit you
2 Cor 1:24 your joy: for by faith ye *s.*
Gal 5: 1 *s.* fast in liberty wherewith
Phil 1: 4 *s.* fast in the Lord, dearly beloved
1:27 that ye *s.* fast in one spirit
1 Thes 3: 8 we live, if ye *s.* fast in Lord
2 Thes 2:15 *s.* fast, and hold the traditions
1 Pet 5:12 grace of God wherein ye *s.*
Rev 3:20 I *s.* at the door and knock
20:12 small and great, *s.* before God

STANDETH
Ps 1: 1 nor *s.* in the way of sinners
33:11 counsel of the Lord *s.* forever
Prov 8: 2 She *s.* in the top of high
Is 3:13 The Lord *s.* up to plead, and *s.*
Rom 14: 4 to his own master he *s.* or falleth
1 Cor 10:12 *s.* take heed lest he fall
2 Tim 2:19 the foundation of God *s.* sure, having
Jas 5: 9 the Judge *s.* before the door

STAR (STARS)
Num 24:17 there shall come a *S.* out of Jacob
Judg 5:20 the *s.* in their courses fought
Job 25: 5 *s.* are not pure in his sight
38: 7 the morning *s.* sang together
Dan 12: 3 to righteousness as the *s.* for ever
Mat 2: 2 we have seen his *s.* in the east
Rev 12: 1 on her head a crown of twelve *s.*

STATURE
Mat 6:27 can add one cubit unto his *s.*
Eph 4:13 measure of the *s.* of the fulness of

STATUTES
Ex 15:26 and keep all his *s.*, I will put
Deut 6:17 his testimonies and his *s.*
2 Ki 17:15 they rejected his *s.*, and his
Neh 9:14 precepts, *s.*, and laws, by the hand
Ps 18:22 not put away his *s.* from me
19: 8 *s.* of the Lord are right
105:45 that they might observe his *s.*
Ezek 20:24 had despised my *s.* and had polluted
33:15 walk in the *s.* of life without
Mic 6:16 the *s.* of Omri are kept

STEAL (STOLE, STOLEN)
Ex 20:15 Thou shalt not *s.*
Prov 6:30 thief, if he *s.* to satisfy his soul
9:17 *s.* waters are sweet, and bread
Jer 23:30 saith the Lord, that *s.* my words
Mat 6:19 thieves break through and *s.*
27:64 come by night, and *s.* him away
Eph 4:28 let him that *s.*, steal no more

STEDFAST
Job 11:15 yea, thou shalt be *s.*, and shalt
Ps 78: 8 whose spirit was not *s.* with God
Dan 6:26 living God, and *s.* forever
1 Cor 15:58 be ye *s.* unmoveable, always abounding
Heb 3:14 of our confidence *s.* to the end
1 Pet 5: 9 whom resist *s.* in the faith, knowing

STEADFASTNESS
Col 2: 5 the *s.* of your faith in Christ
2 Pet 3:17 of the wicked fall from your own *s.*

STEPS
Ex 20:26 thou go up by *s.* unto mine altar
Ps 18:36 thou hast enlarged my *s.* under me
37:23 *s.* of a good man are ordered
37:31 none of his *s.* shall slide
119:133 order my *s.* in thy word
Prov 16: 9 but the Lord directeth his *s.*
Jer 10:23 man that walketh to direct his *s.*
Rom 4:12 who also walk in the *s.* of that faith
1 Pet 2:21 that ye should follow his *s.*

STEWARD (STEWARDS)
Luke 12:42 that faithful and wise *s.*
16: 2 for thou mayest be no longer *s.*
1 Cor 4: 1 and *s.* of the mysteries of God
Tit 1: 7 must be blameless, as the *s.* of God
1 Pet 4:10 as good *s.* of the manifold grace

STIFF (STIFFENETH)
Deut 31:27 I know thy rebellion, and thy *s.* neck
2 Chr 36:13 he *s.* his neck, and hardened his
Jer 17:23 made their neck *s.*, that they might

STIFFNECKED
Ex 32: 9 and, behold, it is a *s.* people

Ex 34: 9 it is a *s.* people; and pardon
Deut 9:13 and, behold, it is a *s.* people
10:16 heart, and be no more *s.*
Acts 7:51 *s.* and uncircumcised in heart

STILL (STILLETH)
Ex 15:16 they shall be as *s.* as a stone
Ps 4: 4 own heart upon your bed, and be *s.*
8: 2 *s.* the enemy and the avenger
46:10 be *s.* and know that I am God
65: 7 which *s.* the noise of the seas
83: 1 thy peace, be not *s.* O God
89: 9 thereof arise, thou *s.* them
139:18 I awake, I am *s.* with thee
Is 30: 7 their strength is to sit *s.*
Mark 4:39 Peace, be *s.* And the wind

STIR
Num 24: 9 great lion: who shall *s.* him up
Ps 35:23 *s.* up thyself, and awake to my
78:38 away, and did not *s.* up all his wrath
Sol 2: 7 that ye *s.* not up, nor awake
2 Tim 1: 6 *s.* up the gift of God that is

STONE (STONES)
Gen 49:24 is the shepherd, the *s.* of Israel
Ps 118:22 *s.* which the builders refused
Is 8:14 *s.* of stumbling and for a rock
28:16 a *s.*, a tried *s.*, a precious corner *s.*
Dan 2:34 *s.* cut out without hands
Hab 2:11 *s.* shall cry out of the wall
Zech 3: 9 on one *s.* shall be seven eyes
Mat 3: 9 God is able of these *s.* to raise
7: 9 ask for bread, will he give him a *s.*
Luke 19:40 the *s.* would immediately cry out
Rom 9:33 lay in Zion, a stumbling *s.*
1 Pet 2: 4 whom coming, as unto a living *s.*
2: 6 chief corner *s.*, elect, precious

STORM
Ps 55: 8 escape from the windy *s.*
83:15 make them afraid with thy *s.*
107:29 he maketh the *s.* a calm
Is 4: 6 for a covert from *s.* and from
25: 4 refuge from the *s.*, a shadow
Nah 1: 3 his way in the whirlwind, and in the *s.*
Mark 4:37 arose a great *s.* of wind

STORMY
Ps 148: 8 *s.* wind fulfilling his word

STRAIGHT
Josh 6: 5 ascend up every man *s.*
Ps 5: 8 thy way *s.* before my face
Eccl 1:15 which is crooked cannot be made *s.*
Is 40: 3 make *s.* in the desert a highway for our
45: 2 make the crooked places *s.*
Jer 31: 9 rivers of waters in a *s.* way
Luke 3: 4 way of Lord, make his paths *s.*
3: 5 crooked shall be made *s.*
Heb 12:13 make *s.* paths for your feet

STRAIT
2 Sam 24:14 I am in a great *s.*: let us fall
Job 36:16 removed thee out of the *s.*
Is 49:20 place is too *s.* for me
Mat 7:13 enter in at the *s.* gate
Phil 1:23 I am in a *s.* betwixt two

STRAITENED
Mic 2: 7 is the spirit of Lord *s.*?
Luke 12:50 how am I *s.* till it be accomplished
2 Cor 6:12 not *s.* in us, but ye are *s.* in

STRANGE
Ex 21: 8 sell her unto a *s.* nation
Lev 10: 1 and offered *s.* fire before
Judg 11: 2 for thou art the son of a *s.* woman
Ezra 10:11 the land, and from the *s.* wives
Ps 81: 9 there shall no *s.* god be in thee
Prov 2:16 deliver thee from the *s.* woman
Is 28:21 do his *s.* work; and bring to pass
Jer 2:21 plant of a *s.* vine unto me
Hos 8:12 they were counted as a *s.* thing
Zeph 1: 8 such as are clothed with *s.* apparel
Luke 5:26 we have seen *s.* things today
Heb 11: 9 of promise, as in a *s.* country
13: 9 about with divers and *s.* doctrines
1 Pet 4: 4 think it *s.* that ye run not
4:12 think it not *s.* concerning the fiery
Jude 1: 7 going after *s.* flesh are set forth

STRANGER (STRANGERS)
Gen 23: 4 *s.* and a sojourner with you
1 Chr 29:15 For we are *s.* before thee
Ps 39:12 for I am a *s.* with thee, and
105:12 yea, very few and *s.* in it
119:19 I am a *s.* in the earth
146: 9 the Lord preserveth the *s.*
Jer 14: 8 why shouldest thou be as a *s.*
Mat 25:35 I was a *s.* and ye took me in
Luke 17:18 glory to God, save this *s.*
John 10: 5 a *s.* will they not follow
Eph 2:19 are no more *s.* and foreigners
Heb 11:13 confessed that they were *s.* and
13: 2 be not forgetful to entertain *s.*
1 Pet 2:11 beseech you as *s.* and

STREAM (STREAMS)
Ps 46: 4 There is a river the *s.* whereof
126: 4 as the *s.* in the south
Sol 4:15 living waters and *s.* from Lebanon
Is 30:25 rivers and *s.* of waters in the day
30:33 like a *s.* of brimstone doth kindle
33:21 a place of broad rivers and *s.*
35: 6 break out, and *s.* in the desert
66:12 Gentiles like a flowing *s.*
Dan 7:10 fiery *s.* issued and came forth
Amos 5:24 and righteousness as a mighty *s.*
Luke 6:48 the *s.* beat vehemently upon that

STREET (STREETS)
Prov 1:20 uttereth her voice in the *s.*
Sol 3: 2 go about the city in the *s.* and in
Luke 14:21 Go out quickly into the *s.*
Rev 11: 8 bodies shall lie in the *s.*
21:21 *s.* of the city was pure gold
22: 2 In the midst of the *s.* of it

STRENGTH
Gen 49: 3 and the beginning of my *s.*, the
49:24 But his bow abode in *s.*, and
Ex 15: 2 The Lord is my *s.* and song
1 Sam 2: 9 by *s.* shall no man prevail
15:29 the *S.* of Israel will not lie
Job 6:12 Is my *s.* the *s.* of stones
9:19 if I speak of *s.* lo, he is
12:13 with him is wisdom and *s.*
Ps 18: 2 my *s.*, in whom I will trust
18:32 It is God that girdeth me with *s.*
27: 1 the Lord is the *s.* of my life
28: 7 Lord is my *s.* and my shield
29:11 Lord will give *s.* to his people
33:16 mighty not delivered by much *s.*
39:13 spare me that I recover *s.*
43: 2 For thou art the God of my *s.*
46: 1 God is our refuge and *s.*, a very
68:35 he that giveth *s.* and power unto his
73:26 God is the *s.* of my heart
84: 5 blessed is the man whose *s.* is in
84: 7 they go from *s.* to *s.*, every one
93: 1 the Lord is clothed with *s.*
96: 6 *s.* and beauty are in his sanctuary
102:23 He weakened my *s.* in the way
118:14 The Lord is my *s.* and song, and
138: 3 strengthenedst me with *s.* in my soul
140: 7 Lord, the *s.* of my salvation
Eccl 9:16 wisdom is better than *s.*
10:10 then must he put to more *s.*
Is 12: 2 Jehovah is my *s.* and my song
25: 4 a *s.* to the poor, a *s.* to the needy
26: 4 the Lord Jehovah is everlasting *s.*
40:29 that have no might he increaseth *s.*
45:24 in the Lord have I righteousness and *s.*
49: 5 my God shall be my *s.*
Jer 16:19 O Lord, my *s.*, and my fortress
Hab 3:19 the Lord God is my *s.*, and he will
Joel 3:16 and the *s.* of the children of Israel
Luke 1:51 he hath shown *s.* with his arm
Rom 5: 6 when we were without *s.*
1 Cor 15:56 is sin; and *s.* of sin is the law
2 Cor 12: 9 my *s.* is made perfect in weakness
Rev 3: 8 thou hast a little *s.* and
5:12 wisdom, and *s.*, and honour
12:10 now is come salvation and *s.*

STRENGTHEN (STRENGTHENED, STRENGTHENEDST, STRENGTHENETH)
1 Sam 23:16 wood, and *s.* his hand in God
Ps 20: 2 sanctuary, and *s.* thee out of Zion
27:14 he shall *s.* thine heart
41: 3 *s.* him on the bed of languishing
104:15 bread which *s.* man's heart
138: 3 *s.* me with strength in my soul
Ezek 34: 4 diseased have ye not *s.*
Is 35: 3 *s.* ye the weak hands, and confirm
41:10 I will *s.* thee, yea, I will
54: 2 lengthen thy cords, and *s.* thy stakes
Dan 11: 1 stood to confirm and *s.* him
Zech 10:12 I will *s.* them in the Lord
Luke 22:32 thou art converted, *s.* thy brethren
Eph 3:16 to be *s.* with might by his
Phil 4:13 through Christ which *s.* me
Col 1:11 *s.* with all might according to
2 Tim 4:17 Lord stood with me and *s.* me
1 Pet 5:10 make you perfect, stablish, *s.*
Rev 3: 2 watchful and *s.* the things which remain

STRETCH (STRETCHED, STRETCHETH)
Gen 22:10 Abraham *s.* forth his hand
1 Ki 17:21 *s.* himself upon the child three times
1 Chr 21:16 sword *s.* out over Jerusalem
Job 11:13 *s.* out thine hands towards him
15:25 he *s.* out his hand against God
Prov 31:20 she *s.* out her hand to the poor
Is 5:25 but his hand is *s.* out still
40:22 *s.* out the heavens as a curtain
45:12 hands, have *s.* out the heavens
51:13 that hath *s.* forth the heavens
Jer 10:12 hath *s.* out the heavens by his
Amos 6: 4 *s.* themselves on their couches
Zech 12: 1 which *s.* forth the heavens
Mat 12:13 *s.* forth thy hand. And he *s.*
John 21:18 thou shalt *s.* forth thy hands
Rom 10:21 all day I have *s.* forth my hands

STRIFE (STRIFES)
Gen 13: 8 there be no *s.* between me and thee
Ps 80: 6 makest us a *s.* to our neighbours
Prov 10:12 hatred stirreth up *s.*, but love
15:18 wrathful man stirreth up *s.*
16:28 A froward man soweth *s.*: and a
20: 3 honour for a man to cease from *s.*
28:25 a proud heart stirreth up *s.*
29:22 an angry man stirreth up *s.*
30:33 forcing of wrath bringeth *s.*
Is 58: 4 ye fast for *s.* and debate
Jer 15:10 hast borne me a man of *s.*
Luke 22:24 there was also a *s.* among them
1 Cor 3: 3 there is among you envying, *s.*
Gal 5:20 wrath, *s.*, seditions, heresies
Phil 1:15 preach Christ even of envy and *s.*
2: 3 let nothing be done through *s.*
1 Tim 6: 4 whereof cometh envy, *s.*, railings
2 Tim 2:23 that they do gender *s.*
Jas 3:14 if ye have bitter envying and *s.*

STRIPES
Prov 17:10 than an hundred *s.* into a fool
20:30 so do *s.* the inward parts of the
Is 53: 5 with his *s.* we are healed
Luke 12:48 commit things worthy of *s.*
1 Pet 2:24 by whose *s.* ye were healed

STRIVE (STRIVETH, STRIVING)
Gen 6: 3 Spirit shall not always *s.*

Ex 21:22 men *s.*, and hurt a woman
Job 33:13 why dost thou *s.* against him
Prov 3:30 *s.* not with a man without cause
Is 45: 9 woe to him that *s.* with his Maker
Mat 12:19 he shall not *s.* nor cry
Luke 13:24 *s.* to enter in at the strait gate
Phil 1:27 one mind *s.* together for the faith
2 Tim 2:24 the servant of Lord must not *s.*
Heb 12: 4 resisted unto blood, *s.* against sin

STRONG

Josh 14:11 I am as *s.* this day as I was in
Ps 24: 8 The Lord *s.* and mighty, the Lord
30: 7 made my mountain to stand *s.*
31: 2 be thou my *s.* rock, for an house
71: 7 but thou art my *s.* refuge
Prov 10:15 rich man's wealth is his *s.* city
14:26 fear of the Lord is *s.* confidence
18:10 name of the Lord is a *s.* tower
24: 5 a wise man is *s.*; yea, a man of
Eccl 9:11 the swift, nor the battle to the *s.*
12: 3 and the *s.* men shall bow themselves
Sol 8: 6 love is *s.* as death; jealousy
Is 1:31 the *s.* shall be as tow, and the maker
26: 1 we have a *s.* city
35: 4 Be *s.*, fear not: behold, your God
53:12 shall divide the spoil with the *s.*
Jer 50:34 their Redeemer is *s.*, the Lord of
Joel 3:10 let the weak say, I am *s.*
Hag 2: 4 now, be *s.*, o Zerubbabel
Luke 11:21 *s.* man armed keepeth his palace
Rom 4:20 but was *s.* in faith, giving
15: 1 we that are *s.* ought to bear the infirmities
1 Cor 16:13 quit you like men, be *s.*
2 Cor 12:10 when I am weak, then am I *s.*
Eph 6:10 be *s.* in the Lord, and in the
2 Tim 2: 1 be *s.* in the grace that is in
Heb 11:34 out of weakness were made *s.*

STRONGER

Job 17: 9 clean hands shall be *s.* and *s.*
Jer 20: 7 thou art *s.* than I and hast
1 Cor 1:25 weakness of God is *s.* than men

STUBBORN (STUBBORNNESS)

Deut 9:27 look not unto the *s.* of this people
21:18 a man have a *s.* and rebellious son
1 Sam 15:23 and *s.* is as iniquity and idolatry
Ps 78: 8 a *s.* and rebellious generation

STUDY (STUDIETH)

Prov 15:28 heart of the righteous *s.*
24: 2 their heart *s.* destruction and their
Eccl 12:12 much *s.* is a weariness of the flesh
1 Thes 4:11 that ye *s.* to be quiet and to do
2 Tim 2:15 *S.* to show thyself approved

STUMBLE (STUMBLED, STUMBLETH)

Prov 3:23 thy foot shall not *s.*
4:12 runnest, thou shalt not *s.*
4:19 they know not at what they *s.*
Is 5:27 none shall be weary nor *s.*
8:15 many among them shall *s.* and fall
28: 7 err in vision, *s.* in judgment
John 11: 9 if a man walk in the day he *s.* not
Rom 9:32 they *s.* at that stumblingstone
14:21 whereby thy brother *s.* or is offended
1 Pet 2: 8 even to them which *s.* at the word

STUMBLING

Is 8:14 but for a stone of *s.* and for a
Rom 9:32 stumbled at the *s.* stone
1 Pet 2: 8 stone of *s.*, and a rock of offense
1 John 2:10 there is none occasion of *s.* in him

STUMBLINGBLOCK (STUMBLINGBLOCKS)

Lev 19:14 put a *s.* before the blind
Is 57:14 take up the *s.* out of the way
Jer 6:21 I will lay *s.* before this people
Ezek 3:20 I lay a *s.* before him
Rom 11: 9 a trap, snare, and a *s.*, and a
14:13 put a *s.* or an occasion to fall in

1 Cor 1:23 unto the Jews a *s.*, and unto the
Rev 2:14 taught Balac to cast a *s.*

SUBDUE (SUBDUED)

Mic 7:19 upon us; he will *s.* our iniquities
Phil 3:21 able to *s.* all things unto himself
Heb 11:33 who through faith *s.* kingdoms

SUBJECT

Luke 10:20 spirits are *s.* unto you; but rather
Rom 8: 7 it is not *s.* to the law of God
8:20 creature was made *s.* to vanity
13: 1 every soul be *s.* unto the higher powers
1 Cor 14:32 spirits of the prophets are *s.* to
15:28 shall be *s.* unto him that put all
Eph 5:24 as the church is *s.* to Christ
Heb 2:15 all their lifetime *s.* to bondage
Jas 5:17 Elias was a man *s.* to like passions
1 Pet 2:18 servants be *s.* to your masters
5: 5 all of you be *s.* one to another

SUBJECTION

1 Cor 9:27 under my body, and bring it into *s.*
1 Tim 2:11 woman learn in silence with all *s.*
3: 4 having his children in *s.*
Heb 2: 8 put all in *s.* under him
12: 9 be in *s.* unto the father
1 Pet 3: 5 in *s.* unto their own husbands

SUBMIT (SUBMITTED, SUBMITTING)

Gen 16: 9 and *s.* thyself under her hands
Ps 18:44 strangers shall *s.* themselves unto
68:30 till everyone *s.* himself
Rom 10: 3 have not *s.* unto the righteousness of
1 Cor 16:16 that ye *s.* yourselves unto such
Eph 5:21 *s.* yourselves one to another
Col 3:18 *s.* yourselves unto your own
Heb 13:17 rule over you, and *s.* yourselves
Jas 4: 7 *S.* yourselves therefore to God
1 Pet 2:13 *S.* yourselves to every ordinance
5: 5 *s.* yourselves unto the elder

SUBSTANCE

Gen 7: 4 every living *s.* that I have made
15:14 they come out with great *s.*
Deut 33:11 bless, Lord, his *s.* and accept
Job 30:22 upon it and dissolvest my *s.*
Ps 139:15 my *s.* was not hid from thee
Prov 3: 9 honour the Lord with thy *s.*
Hos 12: 8 I have found me out *s.*: in all my
Luke 8: 3 ministered to him of their *s.*
Heb 10:34 a better and an enduring *s.*
11: 1 faith is the *s.* of things hoped for

SUBTLE

Gen 3: 1 serpent was more *s.* than any beast
Prov 7:10 attire of an harlot, and *s.* of heart

SUBTLETY

Prov 1: 4 to give *s.* to the simple
Acts 13:10 full of all *s.* and mischief
2 Cor 11: 3 beguiled Eve through his *s.*

SUCK (SUCKED, SUCKING)

Gen 21: 7 should have given children *s.*
Deut 32:13 made him to *s.* honey out of
33:19 they shall *s.* of the abundance
Job 20:16 he shall *s.* the poison of asps
Is 11: 8 the *s.* child shall play on the hole
49:15 can a woman forget her *s.* child
60:16 *s.* the milk of the Gentiles
Lam 4: 4 the tongue of the *s.* child cleaveth
Mat 24:19 to them that give *s.* in those
Luke 11:27 blessed are paps which thou hast *s.*
23:29 paps which never gave *s.*

SUFFER

Ex 12:23 will not *s.* the destroyer
Lev 19:17 neighbour, and not *s.* sin upon him
Ps 55:22 never *s.* the righteous to be moved
89:33 nor *s.* my faithfulness to fail
121: 3 not *s.* thy foot to be moved
Prov 10: 3 not *s.* the soul of righteous to famish

Mat 16:21 *s.* many things of the elders and
17:17 how long shall I *s.* you?
19:14 *s.* little children, and forbid them
1 Cor 4:12 being persecuted, we *s.* it
10:13 God will not *s.* you to be tempted
Phil 1:29 but also to *s.* for his sake
2 Tim 2:12 if we *s.* we shall also reign
Heb 11:25 choosing rather to *s.* affliction
13:22 *s.* the word of exhortation
1 Pet 4:15 none of you *s.* as a murderer
4:19 that *s.* according to the will of God

SUFFERED (SUFFERETH)

Ps 105:14 he *s.* no man to do them wrong
Mat 11:12 kingdom of heaven *s.* violence
Acts 14:16 *s.* all nations to walk in their own
16: 7 the Spirit *s.* them not
1 Cor 13: 4 Charity *s.* long, and is kind
Phil 3: 8 for whom I *s.* loss of all
Heb 5: 8 obedience by the things which he *s.*
1 Pet 2:21 Christ also *s.* for us, leaving us
5:10 after that ye have *s.* a while

SUFFERINGS

Rom 8:18 the *s.* of this present times
2 Cor 1: 6 enduring of the same *s.*
Phil 3:10 the fellowship of his *s.*
Col 1:24 now rejoice in my *s.* for you
Heb 2:10 of their salvation perfect through *s.*
1 Pet 1:11 testified beforehand the *s.* of Christ
4:13 ye are partakers of Christ's *s.*

SUFFICIENT

Mat 6:34 *s.* unto the day is the evil
2 Cor 2:16 who is *s.* for these things?
3: 5 not that we are *s.* of ourselves
12: 8 my grace is *s.* for thee

SUMMER

Gen 8:22 heat, and *s.* and winter, and day
Ps 74:17 thou hast made *s.* and winter
Prov 6: 8 provideth her meat in the *s.*
10: 5 that gathereth in the *s.* is a wise son
Is 18: 6 fowls shall *s.* upon them
Zech 14: 8 in *s.* and in winter shall it be

SUN

Josh 10:12 *s.*, stand thou still upon Gibeon
Ps 19: 4 he set a tabernacle for the *s.*
74:16 prepared the light and the *s.*
104:19 *s.* knoweth his going down
121: 6 *s.* shall not smite thee by day
136: 8 *s.* to rule the day: for his mercy
Sol 1: 6 because the *s.* looked on me
6:10 fair as the moon, clear as the *s.*
Is 30:26 light of the *s.* shall be sevenfold
60:19 *s.* shall be no more thy light by day
60:20 thy *s.* shall no more go down
Jer 31:35 giveth *s.* for a light by day
Mal 4: 2 *S.* of righteousness arise
Mat 5:45 his *s.* to rise on evil and
13:43 shine forth as the *s.* in the kingdom
1 Cor 15:41 there is one glory of the *s.*
Eph 4:26 let not the *s.* go down upon
Rev 7:16 neither shall the *s.* light on them
10: 1 his face was as it the *s.*
21:23 city had no need of the *s.*

SUP

Hab 1: 9 their faces shall *s.* up as the east
Luke 17: 8 make ready wherewith I may *s.*, and
Rev 3:20 and will *s.* with him, and he with

SUPPER

Luke 14:16 A certain man made a great *s.*
22:20 also the cup after *s.*, saying
1 Cor 11:20 is not to eat the Lord's *s.*
Rev 19: 9 the marriage *s.* of the Lamb

SUPERSTITION (SUPERSTITIOUS)

Acts 17:22 in all things ye are too *s.*
25:19 against him of their own *s.*

SUPPLICATION (SUPPLICATIONS)
1 Ki 8:28 thy servant and to his *s.*, O Lord
Job 8: 5 and make thy *s.* to the almighty
Ps 6: 9 Lord hath heard my *s.*; the Lord
55: 1 hide not thyself from my *s.*
119:170 Let my *s.* come before thee
Dan 6:11 making *s.* before his God
Hos 12: 4 wept, and made *s.* unto him
Zech 12:10 the spirit of grace and of *s.*
Eph 6:18 prayer and *s.* in the spirit
Phil 4: 6 prayer and *s.* with thanksgiving
1 Tim 5: 5 continueth in *s.* and prayers
2: 1 first of all *s.*, prayers, intercessions
Heb 5: 7 offered up prayers and *s.*

SUPPLY (SUPPLIETH)
2 Cor 9:12 only *s.* the want of the saints
Eph 4:16 by that which every joint *s.*
Phil 1:19 the *s.* of the Spirit of Jesus
4:19 my God shall *s.* all your need

SURE
Gen 23:17 borders round about, were made *s.*
2 Sam 23: 5 ordered in all things, and *s.*
Ps 19: 7 testimony of the Lord is *s.*
93: 5 thy testimonies are very *s.*
111: 7 all his commandments are *s.*
Prov 11:15 he that hateth suretyship is *s.*
11:18 righteousness shall be a *s.* reward
Is 22:25 nail that is fastened in a *s.* place
28:16 a *s.* foundation: he that believeth
33:16 given him; his waters shall be *s.*
55: 3 even the *s.* mercies of David
John 6:69 are *s.* that thou art that Christ
Acts 13:34 give you the *s.* mercies of David
Rom 4:16 promise might be *s.* to all
2 Tim 2:19 foundation of God standeth *s.*
2 Pet 1:10 to make your calling and election *s.*
1:19 a more *s.* word of prophecy

SWALLOW (SWALLOWED)
Ex 15:12 thy right hand, the earth *s.* them
Num 16:32 opened her mouth, and *s.* them up
Ps 84: 3 the *s.* a nest for herself
Jer 8: 7 the *s.* observe the time of their
Is 25: 8 will *s.* up death in victory
Mat 23:24 strain at a gnat, *s.* a camel
2 Cor 2: 7 should be *s.* up with overmuch sorrow
5: 4 mortality be *s.* up of life

SWEAR (SWEARETH, SWEARING)
Num 30: 2 *s.* an oath to bind his soul
Deut 6:13 and shalt *s.* by his name
Ps 15: 4 he that *s.* to his own hurt
Eccl 9: 2 that *s.* as he that feareth
Is 45:23 shall bow, every tongue shall *s.*
65:16 shall *s.* by the God of truth
Jer 4: 2 shalt *s.*, The Lord liveth
23:10 because of *s.* the land mourneth
Hos 4: 2 by *s.*, and lying, and killing
10: 4 *s.* falsely in making a covenant
Zeph 1: 5 Lord, and that *s.* by Malcham
Zech 5: 3 every one that *s.* shall be cut off
Mat 5:34 *s.* not at all; neither by
Jas 5:12 *s.* not, neither by heaven, neither

SWEARERS
Mal 3: 5 and against false *s.*, and against

SWEAT
Gen 3:19 In the *s.* of thy face shalt thou
Luke 22:44 *s.* was as it were great drops

SWEET
Job 20:12 wickedness be *s.* in his mouth
Ps 55:14 We took *s.* counsel together
104:34 meditation of him shall be *s.*
119:103 how *s.* are thy words unto my taste
Prov 3:24 thy sleep shall be *s.*
9:17 stolen waters are *s.*, and bread
27: 7 hungry soul every bitter thing is *s.*
Eccl 5:12 sleep of the labouring man is *s.*
Sol 2: 3 his fruit was *s.* to my taste
Sol 2:14 *s.* is thy voice and thy countenance
5:16 his mouth is most *s.*; yea, he is
Is 5:20 put bitter for *s.* and *s.* for bitter
Phil 4:18 an odour of a *s.* smell a sacrifice
Rev 10: 9 in thy mouth *s.* as honey

SWEETER
Ps 19:10 much fine gold *s.* also than honey

SWIFT
Deut 28:49 as *s.* as the eagle flieth
Job 9:26 passed away as the *s.* ships
Eccl 9:11 the race is not to the *s.*
Rom 3:15 their feet are *s.* to shed blood
Jas 1:19 *s.* to hear, slow to speak
2 Pet 2: 1 bring on themselves *s.* destruction

SWIFTER
Job 7: 6 days *s.* than a weaver's shuttle
9:25 my days are *s.* than a post

SWIFTLY
Ps 147:15 his word runneth very *s.*
Joel 3: 4 if ye recompense me, *s.* and speedily

SWIM
2 Ki 6: 6 in thither, and the iron did *s.*
Ps 6: 6 make I my bed to *s.*; I water my
Ezek 47: 5 waters to *s.* in, a river

SWORD (SWORDS)
Gen 3:24 cherubims and a flaming *s.*
Ex 32:27 put man his *s.* by his side
Lev 26: 6 shall the *s.* go through your land
26:25 I will bring a *s.* upon you
Judg 7:20 the *s.* of the Lord and of Gideon
2 Sam 12:10 *s.* shall never depart from thine
Ps 17:13 from the wicked, which is thy *s.*
55:21 yet were they drawn *s.*
59: 7 *s.* are in their lips: for who
Prov 30:14 whose teeth are as *s.*
Sol 3: 8 every man hath his *s.* on
Is 2: 4 beat their *s.* into plowshares
Jer 9:16 I will send a *s.* after them
15: 2 such as are for the *s.* to the *s.*
Ezek 21:13 what if the *s.* contemn even the rod
32:27 they have laid their *s.* under their
Joel 3:10 Beat your plowshares into *s.*
Zech 11:17 *s.* shall be upon his arm
Mat 10:34 not to send peace, but the *s.*
Luke 2:35 a *s.* shall pierce through
Rom 13: 4 he beareth not the *s.* in vain
Eph 6:17 *s.* of the Spirit which is the word
Heb 4:12 sharper than any twoedged *s.*
Rev 1:16 mouth went a sharp twoedged *s.*
19:15 out of his mouth goeth a sharp *s.*

SYNAGOGUE (SYNAGOGUES)
Ps 74: 8 they have burned up all the *s.*
Mat 6: 5 love to pray standing in the *s.*
23: 6 and the chief seats in the *s.*
Luke 7: 5 he hath built us a *s.*
John 9:22 should be put out of the *s.*
18:20 I ever taught in the *s.* and in
Acts 15:21 read in the *s.* every sabbath day
Rev 2: 9 are not but are the *s.* of Satan
3: 9 will make them of the *s.* of Satan

T

TABERNACLE (TABERNACLES)
Ex 26: 1 make the *t.* with ten curtains
29:43 the *t.* shall be sanctified
Job 5:24 thy *t.* shall be in peace
12: 6 the *t.* of robbers prosper
Ps 15: 1 who shall abide in thy *t.*
84: 1 how amiable are thy *t.*
118:15 salvation is in the *t.* of the
Prov 14:11 *t.* of the upright shall flourish
Is 33:20 a *t.* that shall not be taken down
Amos 9:11 will I raise up the *t.* of David
Acts 15:16 will build again the *t.* of David
2 Cor 5: 1 if our earthly house of this *t.*
2 Cor 5: 4 we that are in this *t.* do groan
Heb 8: 2 sanctuary and the true *t.*, which the
11: 9 dwelling in *t.* with Isaac and
2 Pet 1:13 as long as I am in this *t.*
1:14 knowing I must put off this my *t.*
Rev 21: 3 the *t.* of God is with men

TABLE (TABLES)
Ex 25:23 make a *t.* of shittim wood
Deut 10: 4 he wrote on the *t.* according to
2 Chr 4:19 *t.* whereon the showbread was set
Job 36:16 on thy *t.* should be full of fatness
Ps 23: 5 Thou preparest a *t.* before me
69:22 let their *t.* become a snare
128: 3 like olive plants round about thy *t.*
Prov 3: 3 write them on the *t.* of thy heart
Sol 1:12 while the king sitteth at his *t.*
Is 28: 8 for all *t.* are full of vomit, and
Jer 17: 1 is graven on the *t.* of their heart
Ezek 40:41 Four *t.* were on this side
Hab 2: 2 make it plain upon the *t.*
Mal 1: 7 *t.* of Lord is contemptible
Mat 15:27 which fall from the masters' *t.*
Acts 6: 2 hear the word of God and serve *t.*
1 Cor 10:21 partakers of the Lord's *t.*
2 Cor 3: 3 not in *t.* of stone, but fleshy *t.*
Heb 9: 4 budded, and the *t.* of the covenant

TAKE
Ex 6: 7 I will *t.* you to me for a people
20: 7 not *t.* the name of the Lord in vain
34: 9 *t.* us for thine inheritance
Ps 27:10 the Lord will *t.* me up
51:11 *t.* not thy holy spirit from me
116:13 I will *t.* the cup of salvation
119:43 *t.* not the word of truth out
Hos 14: 2 *t.* with you words, and turn to
Mat 16:24 *t.* up his cross and follow
18:16 *t.* with thee one or two more
18:23 would *t.* account of his servants
20:14 *T.*, that thine is, and go
26:26 said *T.*, eat; this is my body
Luke 12:19 *t.* thine ease, eat, drink
John 10:17 my life, that I might *t.* it again
1 Cor 11:24 *T.* eat, this is my body
Eph 6:13 *t.* unto you the whole armour
6:17 *t.* the helmet of salvation
Rev 3:11 that no man *t.* thy crown

TAKEN (TAKING)
Ps 40:12 my iniquities have *t.* hold
83: 3 *t.* crafty counsel against thy people
119: 9 by *t.* heed thereto according to
119:111 thy testimonies have I *t.*
119:143 trouble and anguish have *t.* hold of
Is 6: 7 thine iniquity is *t.* away and thy sin
16:10 gladness is *t.* away and joy out of
53: 8 he was *t.* from prison and
57: 1 and merciful men are *t.* away
Lam 4:20 was *t.* in their pits of whom we
Mat 6:27 which of you by *t.* thought can
21:43 kingdom of God shall be *t.* from
24:40 one shall be *t.*, the other left
Mark 4:25 shall be *t.* even that which he hath
Luke 10:42 good part not be *t.* away from
Acts 1: 9 he was *t.* up; and a cloud
Rom 7: 8 sin, *t.* occasion by the commandment
2 Cor 3:16 Lord, the veil shall be *t.* away
Eph 6:16 above all *t.* the shield of faith
2 Tim 2:26 *t.* captive by him at his will

TALE (TALES)
Ps 90: 9 our years as a *t.* that is told
Ezek 22: 9 that carry *t.* to shed blood
Luke 24:11 seemed to them as idle *t.*

TALEBEARER
Lev 19:16 go up and down as a *t.*
Prov 11:13 A *t.* revealeth secrets: but he that
18: 8 The words of a *t.* are as wounds
20:19 goeth about as a *t.* revealeth secrets
26:22 words of a *t.* are as wounds

TALENT (TALENTS)
Mat 18:24 which owed him ten thousand *t.*
25:25 hid thy *t.* in the earth

TALK (TALKETH, TALKING)
Deut 6: 7 *t.* of them when thou sittest
1 Sam 2: 3 *t.* no more so exceeding proudly
Job 13: 7 for God? and *t.* deceitfully for him
Ps 37:30 his tongue *t.* of judgment
71:24 my tongue shall *t.* righteousness
105: 2 *t.* ye of all his wondrous works
145:11 glory of thy kingdom and *t.* of thy
Jer 12: 1 *t.* with thee of thy judgments
John 14:30 I will not *t.* much with
Eph 5: 4 nor foolish *t.*, nor jesting

TALKERS
Tit 1:10 are many unruly and vain *t.*

TARRY (TARRIED)
2 Ki 14:10 glory of this and *t.* at home
1 Chr 19: 5 *T.* at Jericho until your beards
Ps 68:12 she that *t.* at home divided the spoil
101: 7 telleth lies shall not *t.* in my sight
Prov 23:30 that *t.* long at wine; they that
Jer 14: 8 turneth aside to *t.* for a night
Hab 2: 3 though it *t.* wait for it
Mat 25: 5 bridegroom *t.*, they all slumbered
26:38 *t.* ye here and watch with me
Luke 2:43 child Jesus *t.* behind in Jerusalem
John 21:22 that he *t.* till I come what is that
1 Cor 11:33 together to eat, *t.* one for another

TASTE (TASTED)
Ex 16:31 the *t.* was like wafers
1 Sam 14:43 I did but *t.* a little honey
Job 6: 6 *t.* in the white of an egg?
Ps 34: 8 O *t.* and see that the Lord is good
Sol 2: 3 his fruit was sweet to my *t.*
Jer 48:11 therefore his *t.* remained in him
Mat 16:28 shall not *t.* of death till they see
Luke 14:24 were bidden shall *t.* of my supper
John 8:52 keep my saying shall never *t.* death
Col 2:21 touch not, *t.* not, handle not
Heb 2: 9 of God should *t.* death for every man
6: 4 have *t.* of the heavenly gift
1 Pet 2: 3 if ye have *t.* that the Lord is gracious

TAUGHT
2 Chr 30:22 *t.* the good knowledge of the Lord
Ps 71:17 hast *t.* me from my youth
Eccl 12: 9 wise, he still *t.* the people knowledge
Is 54:13 children shall be *t.* of the Lord
John 6:45 they shall be all *t.* of God
Acts 20:20 *t.* you publicly, and from house to
Gal 6: 6 let him that is *t.* in the word
1 Thes 4: 9 yourselves are *t.* of God to love

TEACH
Ex 4:12 *t.* thee what thou shalt say
Lev 10:11 ye may *t.* the children of Israel
Deut 4: 9 *t.* them thy sons, and thy sons' sons
33:10 They shall *t.* Jacob thy judgments
1 Sam 12:23 I will *t.* you the good and the
2 Chr 17: 7 to *t.* in the cities of Judah
Job 21:22 shall any *t.* God knowledge
34:32 that which I see not *teach* thou me
Ps 25: 5 lead me in thy truth, and *t.* me
25: 8 will he *t.* sinners in the way
27:11 *T.* me thy way, O Lord
34:11 I will *t.* you the fear of the Lord
51:13 will I *t.* transgressors thy ways
90:12 so *t.* us to number our days
119:12 thou O Lord: *t.* my thy statutes
119:66 *T.* me good judgment and knowledge
119:108 O Lord, *t.* me thy judgments
143:10 *T.* me to do thy will; for thou
Is 2: 3 and he will *t.* us of his ways
Jer 31:34 *t.* no more every man his neighbour
Mat 28:19 go ye therefore and *t.* all nations
John 9:34 and dost thou *t.* us?
14:26 he shall *t.* you all things
1 Cor 4:17 as I *t.* every where in every church
1 Tim 2:12 I suffer not a woman to *t.*
1 Tim 3: 2 given to hospitality, apt to *t.*
2 Tim 2: 2 be able to *t.* others also
Heb 5:12 have need that one *t.* you
1 John 2:27 need not that any man *t.* you

TEACHER (TEACHERS)
Ps 119:99 more understanding than all my *t.*
Is 30:20 shall not thy *t.* be removed
Hab 2:18 and a *t.* of lies, that the maker
John 3: 2 thou art a *t.* come from God
Rom 2:20 a *t.* of babes which hast the
1 Tim 2: 7 a *t.* of the Gentiles in faith
2 Tim 1:11 and a *t.* of the Gentiles
4: 3 heap to themselves *t.*, having itching
Tit 2: 3 to much wine *t.* of good things
Heb 5:12 ye ought to be *t.* ye have need

TEACHEST (TEACHETH, TEACHING)
2 Chr 15: 3 and without a *t.* priest
Job 35:11 who *t.* us more than beasts
36:22 his power: who *t.* like him
Ps 18:34 *t.* my hands to war so that a
94:12 O Lord, and *t.* him out of thy law
Is 48:17 Lord thy God which *t.* thee to profit
Mat 15: 9 *t.* for doctrines the commandments
22:16 *t.* the way of God in truth
28:20 *t.* them to observe all things
Rom 2:21 *t.* another, *t.* thou not thyself
1 Cor 2:13 wisdom *t.* but which the Holy Ghost *t.*
Col 1:28 *t.* every man in all wisdom
Tit 2:12 *t.* us that denying ungodliness
1 John 2:27 same anointing *t.* you of all things

TEARS
Job 16:20 mine eye poureth out *t.*
Ps 6: 6 water my couch with my *t.*
56: 8 put thou my *t.* in thy bottle
80: 5 feedest them with the bread of *t.*
126: 5 they that sow in *t.* shall reap in joy
Is 25: 8 wipe away all *t.* from off all faces
Jer 9: 1 mine eyes were a fountain of *t.*
Luke 7:38 to wash his feet with *t.*
Acts 20:19 with many *t.* and temptations
20:31 warn everyone night and day with *t.*
2 Cor 2: 4 I wrote unto you with many *t.*
2 Tim 1: 4 being mindful of thy *t.*, that I may
Heb 5: 7 with strong crying and *t.* unto him
Rev 7:17 wipe all *t.* from their eyes

TEETH
Gen 49:12 his *t.* white with milk
Job 4:10 the *t.* of the young lions
Ps 3: 7 broken the *t.* of the ungodly
112:10 he shall gnash with his *t.*
Sol 4: 2 *t.* like a flock of sheep
Jer 31:29 his *t.* shall be set on edge
Ezek 18: 2 children's *t.* are set on edge
Amos 4: 6 cleanness of the *t.* in all cities
Mat 8:12 shall be weeping and gnashing of *t.*
24:51 shall be weeping and gnashing of *t.*
25:30 shall be weeping and gnashing of *t.*

TELL
2 Sam 1:20 *T.* it not in Gath, publish it
Ps 48:13 *t.* it to the generation following
Prov 30: 4 name, if thou canst *t.*
Mat 8: 4 see thou *t.* no man; but go
18:15 go and *t.* him his fault
John 3: 8 not *t.* whence it cometh, and whither
4:25 when he is come he will *t.* us all
8:14 ye cannot *t.* whence I come
2 Cor 12: 2 out of the body, I cannot *t.*
Gal 4:16 because I *t.* you the truth
Phil 3:18 now *t.* you even weeping that they

TEMPERANCE
Acts 24:25 as he reasoned of righteousness, *t.*
Gal 5:23 *t.*: against such there is no law
2 Pet 1: 6 And to knowledge *t.*, and to *t.*

TEMPERATE
1 Cor 9:25 mastery is to *t.* in all things
Tit 1: 8 sober, just, holy, *t.*
2: 2 men be sober, grave, *t.*

TEMPLE (TEMPLES)
1 Sam 1: 9 by a post of the *t.* of the Lord
1 Ki 6: 5 of the *t.* and the oracle
Ps 29: 9 in his *t.* doth every one speak of
Sol 4: 3 thy *t.* are like a piece of a
Jer 7: 4 The *t.* of the Lord are these
Mal 3: 1 suddenly come to his *t.*, even the
Mat 12: 6 place is one greater than the *t.* is
John 2:19 destroy this *t.* and in three days
2:21 he spake of the *t.* of his body
Acts 7:48 most High dwelleth not in *t.*
1 Cor 3:16 ye are the *t.* of God
6:19 body is the *t.* of the Holy Ghost
9:13 live of the things of the *t.*
2 Cor 6:16 hath the *t.* of God with idols
Rev 7:15 serve him day and night in the *t.*
11:19 *t.* of God was opened in heaven
21:22 God and the Lamb are the *t.*

TEMPT (TEMPTED, TEMPTING)
Gen 22: God did *t.* Abraham, and said unto
Ex 17: 7 because they *t.* the Lord
Num 14:22 *t.* me now these ten times
Deut 6:16 ye shall not *t.* the Lord
Ps 78:18 they *t.* God in their heart by asking
78:56 *t.* and provoked the most high God
95: 9 when your fathers *t.* me
Is 7:12 not ask, neither will I *t.* the Lord
Mal 3:15 they that *t.* God are even delivered
Mat 4: 1 to be *t.* of the devil
4: 7 thou shalt not *t.* the Lord
16: 1 *t.* desired him that he would
22:18 why *t.* ye me, ye hypocrites
22:35 asked him a question, *t.* him
Luke 10:25 stood up, and *t.* him, saying
11:16 others, *t.* him, sought of him
John 8: 6 This they said, *t.* him
Acts 5: 9 have agreed together to *t.* the Spirit
15:10 why *t.* ye God to put a yoke
1 Cor 7: 5 that Satan *t.* you not for
10:13 not suffer you to be *t.*
Gal 6: 1 lest thou also be *t.*
1 Thes 3: 5 the tempter have *t.* you
Heb 2:18 being *t.* he is able to succour
4:15 in all points *t.* as we are
Jas 1:13 is *t.*, I am *t.* of God
1:14 say when is he *t.* when he is drawn

TEMPTATION (TEMPTATIONS)
Deut 4:34 by *t.*, by signs, and by wonders
Ps 95: 8 as in the day of *t.* in the wilderness
Mat 6:13 lead us not into *t.*, but deliver us
Luke 4:13 the devil had ended all *t.*
8:13 in time of *t.* fall away
22:28 have continued with me in my *t.*
Acts 20:19 with many tears and *t.*
1 Cor 10:13 no *t.* taken you but such
Gal 4:14 *t.* which was in my flesh
Heb 3: 8 day of *t.* in the wilderness
Jas 1: 2 when ye fall into diver's *t.*
1:12 blessed is man that endureth *t.*
1 Pet 1: 6 heaviness through manifold *t.*
2 Pet 2: 9 deliver the godly out of *t.*
Rev 3:10 keep thee from the hour of *t.*

TEMPTER
Mat 4: 3 when the *t.* came to him, he said
1 Thes 3: 5 the *t.* have tempted you, and our labour

TENDER
2 Ki 22:19 Because thine heart was *t.*
Luke 1:78 Through the *t.* mercy of our God
Jas 5:11 pitiful, and of *t.* mercy

TENDERHEARTED
Eph 4:32 be ye kind to one another, *t.*

TENTS
Gen 9:27 he shall dwell in the *t.*
Num 24: 5 how goodly are thy *t.*, O Jacob

1 Ki 12:16 to your *t.*, O Israel: now see to
Ps 84:10 dwell in the *t.* of wickedness
120: 5 I dwell in the *t.* of Kedar
Sol 1: 8 feed thy kids beside shepherds' *t.*

TERRIBLE
Ex 34:10 it is a *t.* thing that I will
Deut 1:19 that great and *t.* wilderness
7:21 is among you, a mighty God and *t.*
10:21 for thee these great and *t.* things
Neh 1: 5 the great and *t.* God
9:32 the great and mighty and *t.* God
Job 37:22 with God is *t.* majesty
Ps 45: 4 hand shall teach thee *t.* things
47: 2 for the Lord most high is *t.*
66: 3 how *t.* art thou in thy works
66: 5 God is *t.* in his doing
76:12 he is *t.* to the kings of the earth
99: 3 praise thy great and *t.* name
Sol 6: 4 *t.* as an army with banners
Jer 20:11 is with me as a mighty *t.* one
Joel 2:11 Lord is great and very *t.*
Zeph 2:11 The Lord will be *t.* unto them: for
Heb 12:21 so *t.* was the sight that Moses

TERROR
Gen 35: 5 *t.* of God was upon the cities
Deut 32:25 sword without, and *t.* within
Job 31:23 destruction from God was a *t.*
Jer 17:17 be not a *t.* unto me: thou art my
20: 4 make thee a *t.* to thyself, and to
Ezek 26:21 I will make thee a *t.*, and thou
Rom 13: 3 rulers are not a *t.* to good
2 Cor 5: 1 knowing therefore the *t.* of the Lord

TESTAMENT
Mat 26:28 my blood of the new *t.*
Luke 22:20 This cup is the new *t.*
1 Cor 11:25 This cup is the new *t.*
2 Cor 3:14 the reading of the old *t.*
Heb 7:22 Jesus made a surety of a better *t.*
9:16 where a *t.* is, there must also
Rev 11:19 in his temple the ark of his *t.*

TESTATOR
Heb 9:16 necessity be death of the *t.*
9:17 no strength at all while the *t* liveth

TESTIFY (TESTIFIED. TESTIFYING)
Num 35:30 one witness shall not *t.*
Deut 8:19 I *t.* against you this day
2 Chr 24:19 they *t.* against them: but they
Neh 9:34 thou didst *t.* against them
13:15 and I *t.* against them in the day
Ps 50: 7 I will *t.* against thee
81: 8 I will *t.* unto thee: O Israel
Is 59:12 our sins *t.* against us: for our
Jer 14: 7 our iniquities *t.* against us
Hos 5: 5 pride of Israel *t.* to his face
John 3:11 do know and *t.* that we have seen
Acts 20:24 *t.* the gospel of the grace of God
23:11 thou hast *t.* of me in Jerusalem
1 Tim 2: 6 for all, to be *t.* in due time
Heb 11: 4 God *t.* of his gifts
1 Pet 5:12 *t.* that it is the true grace
1 John 4:14 *t.* that the Father sent
5: 9 he hath *t.* of his son

TESTIMONY (TESTIMONIES)
2 Ki 11:12 upon him, and gave him the *t.*
Ps 25:10 keep his covenant and his *t.*
78: 5 for he established a *t.* in Jacob
93: 5 Thy *t.* are very sure: holiness
119: 2 Blessed are they that keep his *t.*
119:14 rejoiced in the way of thy *t.*
Is 8:16 bind up the *t.*, seal the law
Mat 10:18 for a *t.* against them and the
John 3:32 testifieth, and no man receiveth his *t.*
Acts 14: 3 *t.* to the word of his grace
2 Cor 1:12 the *t.* of our conscience
Heb 11: 5 before his translation he had this *t.*
Rev 1: 9 God, and for the *t.* of Jesus Christ
11: 7 shall have finished their *t.*
19:10 the *t.* of Jesus is the spirit

THANK
1 Chr 16: 4 to *t.* and praise the Lord
Mat 11:25 I *t.* thee, O Father, Lord of heaven
Luke 6:33 good to you, what *t.* have ye
17: 9 Doth he *t.* that servant because he
18:11 God, I *t.* thee, that I am not
John 11:41 I *t.* thee that thou hast heard
Rom 1: 8 I *t.* my God through Jesus Christ
7:25 I *t.* God through Jesus Christ
1 Cor 1: 4 I *t.* my God always on your behalf
1 Tim 1:12 I *t.* Jesus Christ our Lord

THANKFUL
Ps 100: 4 be *t.* unto him, and bless his
Rom 1:21 as God, neither were *t.*
Col 3:15 in one body, and be ye *t.*

THANKS
Dan 6:10 gave *t.* before his God, as he did
Mat 26:27 took the cup and gave *t.*
Mark 8: 6 seven loaves, and gave *t.*
Luke 22:17 took the cup and gave *t.*
1 Cor 15:57 But *t.* be to God which giveth
2 Cor 8:16 But *t.* be to God which put
9:15 *t.* be to God for his unspeakable
Eph 1:16 Cease not to give *t.* for you
5: 4 but rather giving of *t.*
1 Thes 3: 9 what *t.* can we render to God
5:18 In every thing, give *t.*
2 Thes 2:13 we are bound to give *t.*
1 Tim 2: 1 giving of *t.*, be made for all men
Heb 13:15 our lips giving *t.* to his name

THANKSGIVING
Lev 7:12 If he offer it for a *t.*
Neh 11:17 the principal to begin the *t.*
Ps 26: 7 publish with the voice of *t.*
100: 4 Enter his gates with *t.*
116:17 offer to thee the sacrifice of *t.*
Is 51: 3 *t.*, and the voice of melody
Phil 4: 6 by prayer and supplication with *t.*
1 Tim 4: 3 created to be received with *t.*
Rev 7:12 wisdom, and *t.*, and honour

THINK
Neh 5:19 *T.* upon me, my God, for good
Jer 29:11 thoughts that I *t.* toward you
Rom 12: 3 *t.* of himself more highly
1 Cor 8: 2 if any man *t.* that he knoweth
Gal 6: 3 if a man *t.* himself to be something
Eph 3:20 above all that we ask or *t.*
Phil 4: 8 be any praise, *t.* on these things

THOUGHT
Gen 50:20 As for you, ye *t.* evil against me
Ps 48: 9 we have *t.* of thy lovingkindness
119:59 I *t.* on my ways and turned
139: 2 understandest my *t.* afar
Prov 24: 9 the *t.* of foolishness is sin
Eccl 10:20 curse not the king, no not in thy *t.*
Mal 3:16 and that *t.* on his name
Mat 6:25 take no *t.* for your life
6:34 take therefore no *t.* for the morrow
Mark 13:11 take no *t.* beforehand what ye
14:72 when he *t.* thereon he wept
Luke 12:22 take no *t.* for your life
1 Cor 13:11 I *t.* as a child, but when
2 Cor 10: 5 bringeth into captivity every *t.*
Phil 2: 6 *t.* it not robbery to be equal

THOUGHTS
Gen 6: 5 imagination of the *t.* of his heart
Judg 5:15 were great *t.* of the heart
1 Chr 28: 9 the imaginations of the *t.*
29:18 keep for ever in imagination of *t.*
Ps 10: 4 God is not in all his *t.*
33:11 the *t.* of his heart to all
40: 5 thy *t.* which are to us-ward
94:11 Lord knoweth the *t.* of man
94:19 in the multitude of my *t.* within me
139:17 how precious are thy *t.* to me
139:23 know my heart, try me, and know my *t.*
Prov 12: 5 The *t.* of the righteous are right
15:26 *t.* of the wicked are the abomination
16: 3 thy *t.* shall be established
Is 55: 7 way, and the unrighteous man his *t.*
55: 8 my *t.* are not your *t.*
59: 7 their *t.* are *t.* of iniquity
66:18 I know their works and their *t.*
Jer 4:14 how long shall thy vain *t.*
Mic 4:12 know not the *t.* of the Lord
Mat 15:19 out of heart proceed evil *t.*
Luke 2:35 the *t.* of many hearts may be revealed
Rom 2:15 witness and their *t.* the mean while
1 Cor 3:20 the Lord knoweth the *t.* of the wise
Heb 4:12 a discerner of the *t.* and intents
Jas 2: 4 and are become judges of evil *t.*

THIRST (THIRSTETH)
Deut 28:48 hunger, and in *t.*, and in nakedness
Ps 42: 2 my soul *t.* for God, for the living
Is 49:10 they shall not hunger nor *t.*
55: 1 Ho, every one that *t.*, come ye
Mat 5: 6 do hunger and *t.* after righteousness
John 4:14 shall never *t.*, but the water that
6:35 believeth on me shall never *t.*
7:37 if any man *t.*, let him come unto me
Rom 12:20 feed him; if he *t.* give him drink
Rev 7:16 neither *t.* any more; neither shall

THORNS
Gen 3:18 *T.* also thistles shall it bring
Num 33:55 and *t.* in your sides, and shall vex
Josh 23:13 and *t.* in your eyes, until ye perish
Judg 2: 3 be as *t.* in your sides
2 Sam 23: 6 as *t.* thrust away, because they
Jer 4: 3 ground, and sow not among *t.*
12:13 sown wheat, but shall reap *t.*
Mat 7:16 do men gather grapes of *t.*?
13: 7 some fell among *t.*; and the *t.*

THREE
2 Sam 24:12 I offer thee *t.* things; choose thee
Prov 30:15 *t.* things that are never satisfied
30:21 *t.* things the earth is disquieted
30:29 *t.* things which go well, yea, four
Amos 1: 3 For *t.* transgressions of Damascus
2: 1 For *t.* transgressions of Moab
1 Cor 14:27 or at the most by *t.*, and that
1 John 5: 7 For there are *t.* that bear record in
Rev 16:13 *t.* unclean spirits like frogs

THRESH (THRESHETH, THRESHING)
Lev 26: 5 and your *t.* shall reach
Is 21:10 my *t.*, and the corn
41:15 thou shalt *t.* the mountains
Mic 4:13 Arise and *t.*, O daughter of Zion
Hab 3:12 thou didst *t.* the heathen in anger
1 Cor 9:10 that he that *t.* in hope

THRESHINGFLOOR
2 Sam 24:18 the *t.* of Araunah, the Jebusite
24:21 To buy the *t.* of thee to build
24:24 So David bought the *t.*
Jer 51:33 Babylon is like a *t.*, it is time

THROAT
Ps 5: 9 their *t.* is an open sepulchre; they
69: 3 weary of my crying, my *t.* is dried
Prov 23: 2 put a knife to thy *t.*

THRONE
Ps 11: 4 the Lord's *t.* is heaven: his eyes
45: 6 Thy *t.*, O God, is for ever
89:14 are the habitation of thy *t.*
94:20 *t.* of iniquity have fellowship
Prov 25: 5 *t.* shall be established in righteousness
Is 22:23 a glorious *t.* to his father's house
Jer 14:21 do not disgrace the *t.* of thy glory
17:12 A glorious high *t.* from
Lam 5:19 thy *t.* from generation to
Dan 7: 9 his *t.* was like a fiery flame

Mat 19:28 shall sit in the *t.* of his glory
25:31 shall sit on the *t.* of his glory
Heb 1: 8 Thy *t.*, O God, is for ever
4:16 boldly to the *t.* of grace
Rev 3:21 with my Father in his *t.*
20:11 And I saw a great white *t.*
22: 3 *t.* of God and the Lamb shall be in

THUNDER (THUNDERETH)
Job 26:14 but the *t.* of his power who can
40: 9 canst thou *t.* with a voice
Ps 29: 3 the God of glory *t.*: the Lord is
81: 7 in the secret place of *t.*
Mark 3:17 Boanerges, which is, The sons of *t.*

THUNDERINGS
Rev 4: 5 lightnings and *t.*, and voices
8: 5 voices, and *t.*, and lightnings
11:19 voices, and *t.*, and an earthquake
19: 6 as the voice of mighty *t.*

TIDINGS
Ex 33: 4 people heard these evil *t.*
Ps 112: 7 not be afraid of evil *t.*
Luke 1:19 and to show thee these glad *t.*
2:10 I bring you good *t.* of great joy
8: 1 preaching and showing the glad *t.*
Acts 13:32 we declare unto you glad *t.*
Rom 10:15 bring glad *t.* of good things

TIME
Ps 32: 6 in a *t.* when thou mayest be found
37:19 be ashamed in the evil *t.*
41: 1 deliver him in *t.* of trouble
69:13 in an acceptable *t.*
89:47 remember how short my *t.* is
Eccl 3: 1 and a *t.* to every purpose
3: 8 a *t.* of war and a *t.* of peace
9:11 *t.* and chance happeneth to them all
Ezek 16: 8 thy *t.* was the *t.* of love
Dan 7:25 till a *t.* and times
12: 7 that it shall be for a *t.*
Amos 5:13 keep silent in that *t.*
Luke 19:44 knewest not the *t.* of thy visitation
John 7: 6 my *t.* is not yet come: your *t.*
Acts 17:21 spent their *t.* in nothing else
Rom 13:11 it is high *t.* to awake out of sleep
2 Cor 6: 2 Behold, now is the accepted *t.*
Eph 5:16 redeeming the *t.*, because the days
Col 4: 5 are without, redeeming the *t.*
1 Pet 1:17 pass the *t.* of your sojourning
Rev 10: 6 there should be *t.* no longer
12:14 times, and a half *t.*

TIMES
Ps 31:15 my *t.* are in thy hand
34: 1 bless the Lord at all *t.*
62: 8 trust in him at all *t.*; ye people
106: 3 that doeth righteousness at all *t.*
119:20 unto thy judgments at all *t.*
Prov 5:19 let her breasts satisfy thee at all *t.*
17:17 a friend loveth at all *t.*
Luke 21:24 till the *t.* of the Gentiles
Acts 1: 7 not for you to know the *t.*
3:19 *t.* of refreshing shall come
17:26 determined the *t.* before appointed
1 Tim 4: 1 that in the latter *t.* some shall
2 Tim 3: 1 in the last days perilous *t.*

TITHE (TITHES)
Gen 14:20 he gave him *t.* of all
Amos 4: 4 and your *t.* after three years
Mal 3: 8 we robbed thee? In *t.* and offerings
Mat 23:23 ye pay *t.* of mint and anise and cummin
Luke 18:12 I give *t.* of all that I

TOGETHER
Ps 2: 2 rulers take counsel *t.* against
Prov 22: 2 rich and poor meet *t.*: the Lord is
Rom 8:28 all things work *t.* for good
1 Cor 3: 9 we are labourers *t.* with God
2 Cor 6: 1 as workers *t.* with him, beseech
Eph 2: 5 quickened us *t.* with Christ
Eph 2: 6 raised us up *t.* and made us sit *t.*

TOKEN (TOKENS)
Gen 9:13 shall be for a *t.* of a covenant
17:11 it shall be a *t.* of the covenant
Ps 65: 8 uttermost parts are afraid at thy *t.*
86:17 show me a *t.* for good; that they
135: 9 who sent *t.* and wonders into the midst
Phil 1:28 to them an evident *t.* of perdition
2 Thes 1: 5 a manifest *t.* of righteous judgment

TONGUE
Ex 11: 7 shall not a dog move his *t.* against
Josh 10:21 none moved his *t.* against any
Job 5:21 be hid from the scourge of the *t.*
20:12 though he hide it under his *t.*
Ps 34:13 keep thy *t.* from evil, and thy lips
35:28 *t.* shall speak of thy righteousness
45: 1 my *t.* is the pen of a ready
137: 6 let my *t.* cleave to the roof
Prov 10:20 *t.* of the just is as choice silver
12:18 but the *t.* of the wise is health
15: 4 wholesome *t.* is a tree of life
18:21 death and life are in power of the *t.*
21: 6 getting of treasures by a lying *t.*
21:23 keepeth his *t.* keepeth his soul
25:15 a soft *t.* breaketh the bone
Is 30:27 his *t.* as a devouring fire
50: 4 Lord hath given me the *t.* of the learned
Jer 9: 5 taught their *t.* to speak lies
Acts 2:26 heart rejoice and my *t.* was glad
Jas 1:26 and bridleth not his *t.*
3: 5 *t.* is a little member and boasteth
3: 8 the *t.* can no man tame; it is an
1 Pet 3:10 refrain his *t.* from evil

TONGUES
Ps 31:20 pavilion from the strife of *t.*
55: 9 O Lord, and divide their *t.*
Mark 16:17 they shall speak with new *t.*
Acts 19: 6 spake with *t.* and prophesied
1 Cor 12:10 to another divers kinds of *t.*
14:23 and all speak with *t.*, another come

TOOK
Ps 22: 9 he that *t.* me out of the womb
Phil 2: 7 *t.* on him the form of a servant
Heb 10:34 *t.* joyfully the spoiling of your

TORMENT (TORMENTED)
Mat 8:29 art thou come hither to *t.* us
Luke 16:24 for I am *t.* in this flame
16:28 come to this place of *t.*
Heb 11:37 being destitute, afflicted, *t.*
Rev 14:11 smoke of their *t.* ascendeth up for
18: 7 so much *t.* and sorrow give her: for

TOSS (TOSSED)
Ps 109:23 I am *t.* up and down like a locust
Is 22:18 violently turn and *t.* thee like a
Jer 5:22 though the waves thereof *t.* themselves
Jas 1: 6 driven with the wind and *t.*
Eph 4:14 be no more children *t.* to and fro

TOUCH (TOUCHED, TOUCHETH)
1 Sam 10:26 men whose hearts God had *t.*
Job 5:19 in seven there shall no evil *t.*
19:21 hand of God hath *t.* me
Ps 105:15 *T.* not mine anointed and do my
Is 52:11 *t.* no unclean thing; go ye out of
Zech 2: 8 he that *t.* you *t.* the apple
Mat 9:21 If I may but *t.* his garment
14:36 only *t.* the hem of his garment
Mark 10:13 that he should *t.* them: and his
Luke 11:46 *t.* not the burdens with one of your
John 20:17 *t.* me not, for I am not yet
1 Cor 7: 1 good for a man not to *t.* a woman
2 Cor 6:17 *t.* not the unclean thing; and I
Col 2:21 *t.* not, taste not, handle not
1 John 5:18 that wicked one *t.* him not

TOWER
Ps 61: 3 a strong *t.* from the enemy
144: 2 my high *t.*, and my deliverer
Sol 4: 4 thy neck like the *t.* of David
7: 4 thy neck is as a *t.* of ivory
Is 5: 2 built a *t.* in the midst of
Mat 21:33 winepress in it, and built a *t.*

TRADITION (TRADITIONS)
Mat 15: 3 commandment of God by your *t.*
Gal 1:14 exceedingly jealous of the *t.*
Col 2: 8 after the *t.* of men after the
2 Thes 2:15 hold the *t.* which ye have been taught
3: 6 disorderly, and not after the *t.*
1 Pet 1:18 received by *t.* from your fathers

TRAIN
Prov 22: 6 *T.* up a child in the way
Is 6: 1 up, and his *t.* filled the temple

TRANCE
Num 24: 4 falling into a *t.*, but having
Acts 10:10 they made ready, he fell into a *t.*
11: 5 in a *t.*, I saw a vision
22:17 prayed in the temple, I was in a *t.*

TRANSFIGURED
Mat 17: 2 And was *t.* before them: and his
Mark 9: 2 themselves: and he was *t.* before them

TRANSFORMED
Rom 12: 2 be ye *t.* by the renewing of your
2 Cor 11:15 *t.* as the ministers of rightousness

TRANSGRESS (TRANSGRESSED, TRANSGRESSETH)
Num 14:41 now do ye *t.* the commandments
Deut 26:13 I have not *t.* thy commandments
Josh 7:11 they have also *t.* my covenant
1 Sam 2:24 make the Lord's people to *t.*
2 Chr 24:20 why *t.* ye the commandments of the Lord?
Neh 1: 8 if ye *t.* I will scatter you
Ps 17: 3 my mouth shall not *t.*
25: 3 be ashamed which *t.* without cause
Prov 28:21 piece of bread that man will *t.*
Is 43:27 teachers have *t.* against
Jer 2: 8 pastors also *t.* against me
Lam 3:42 we have *t.* and have rebelled
Ezek 2: 3 they and their fathers have *t.*
Dan 9:11 all Israel have *t.* thy law, even
Hos 6: 7 they like men have *t.* the covenant
Amos 4: 4 come to Bethel and *t.*; at Gilgal
Hab 2: 5 Yea, also, because he *t.* by wine
Mat 15: 2 do thy disciples *t.* the traditions
Rom 2:27 and circumcision dost *t.* the law
1 John 3: 4 whosoever committeth sin *t.*

TRANSGRESSION
Ex 34: 7 forgiving iniquity, *t.*, and sin
Num 14:18 great mercy, forgiving iniquity and *t.*
1 Chr 10:13 Saul died for his *t.*
Job 13:23 make me to know my *t.*
Ps 19:13 innocent from the great *t.*
32: 1 blessed he whose *t.* is forgiven
89:32 I will visit their *t.* with the rod
107:17 Fools because of their *t.* are afflicted
Prov 17: 9 that covereth *t.* seeketh love
Is 53: 8 the *t.* of my people was he stricken
58: 1 show my people their *t.*, and the house
59:20 them that turn from *t.* in Jacob
Dan 9:24 to finish the *t.* and make an end
Amos 4: 4 at Gilgal multiply *t.*; and bring your
Mic 3: 8 to declare to Jacob his *t.*
6: 7 shall I give my firstborn for my *t.*
Rom 4:15 where no law is, there is no *t.*
1 John 3: 4 sin is the *t.* of the law

TRANSGRESSIONS
Ex 23:21 for he will not pardon your *t.*
Lev 16:21 all their *t.* in all their sins

Josh 24:19 will not forgive your *t.* nor your
Job 31:33 If I covered my *t.* as Adam, by
Ps 25: 7 sins of my youth, nor my *t.*
32: 5 I said, I will confess my *t.*
39: 8 deliver me from all my *t.*
51: 1 tender mercies blot out my *t.*
51: 3 I acknowledge my *t.* and my sin is
103:12 so far hath he removed our *t.*
Is 43:25 I am he that blotteth out thy *t.*
44:22 blotted out as a thick cloud thy *t.*
53: 5 he was wounded for our *t.*, he was
59:12 our *t.* are multiplied before thee
Ezek 18:31 cast away from you all *t.*
Heb 9:15 for the redemption of the *t.*

TRANSGRESSOR (TRANSGRESSORS)

Ps 51:13 Then will I teach *t.* thy ways
59: 5 be not merciful to any wicked *t.*
119:158 I beheld the *t.* and was grieved
Prov 13:15 the way of the *t.* is hard
Is 48: 8 called a *t.* from the womb
53:12 made intercession for the *t.*
Hos 14: 9 the *t.* shall fall therein
Jas 2: 9 convinced of the law as *t.*
2:11 if thou kill, thou art become a *t.*

TRAVAIL (TRAVAILED, TRAVAILETH, TRAVAILING)

Job 15:20 wicked man *t.* with pain all his
Eccl 1:13 this sore *t.* hath God given
4: 4 I considered all *t.*, and every
5:14 those riches perish by evil *t.*
Is 13: 8 be in pain as a woman that *t.*
53:11 He shall see of the *t.*
66: 7 before she *t.*, she brought forth
66: 8 as soon as Zion *t.*, she brought
Jer 31: 8 her that *t.* with child together
Hos 13:13 The sorrows of a *t.* woman
Gal 4:19 children, of whom I *t.*
2 Thes 3: 8 labour and *t.* night and day
Rev 12: 2 being with child, *t.* in birth

TREACHEROUS (TREACHEROUSLY)

Is 21: 2 treacherous dealer dealeth *t.*
24:16 *t.* dealers have dealt *t.*
Jer 9: 2 an assembly of *t.* men
3:20 wife *t.* departeth from her husband
Hos 5: 7 they have dealt *t.* against Lord
Mal 2:15 none deal *t.* against the wife

TREAD (TREADETH)

Deut 25: 4 not muzzle the ox when he *t.* out
Job 40:12 and *t.* down the wicked
Ps 7: 5 let him *t.* down my life
44: 5 through thy name will we *t.* them under
Is 1:12 of your hand, to *t.* my courts?
63: 3 I will *t.* them in mine anger
1 Cor 9: 9 the ox that *t.* out the corn
1 Tim 5:18 ox that *t.* out the corn
Rev 11: 2 holy city shall they *t.*

TREASURE (TREASURES)

Ex 19: 5 shall ye be a peculiar *t.* unto me
Deut 28:12 Lord shall open to thee his good *t.*
32:34 sealed up among my *t.*
Ps 135: 4 and Israel for his peculiar *t.*
Prov 2: 4 searchest for her as for hid *t.*
10: 2 *t.* of wickedness profit nothing
21: 6 getting *t.* by a lying tongue
15: 6 house of the righteous is much *t.*
21:20 there is *t.* to be desired and oil
Is 33: 6 fear of the Lord is his *t.*
Mat 6:19 not up for yourselves *t.* on earth
6:20 lay up for yourselves *t.* in heaven
6:21 where your *t.* is, there will
12:35 a good man out of the good *t.* of
13:52 bringeth forth out of his *t.*
19:21 thou shalt have *t.* in heaven
Luke 12:21 layeth up *t.* for himself, and is not
2 Cor 4: 7 we have this *t.* in earthen vessels
Col 2: 3 hid all the *t.* of wisdom
Heb 11:26 greater riches than *t.* in

TREE (TREES)

Gen 2:16 Of every *t.* of the garden
3:22 take also the *t.* of life
Ps 1: 3 like a *t.* planted by rivers
37:35 spreading himself like a bay *t.*
52: 8 I am like a green olive *t.*
104:16 *t.* of the Lord are full of sap
Prov 3:18 she is a *t.* of life to them
11:30 fruit of the righteous is the *t.* of
Is 6:13 shall be eaten: as a teil *t.*
61: 3 might be called *t.* of righteousness
Jer 17: 8 a *t.* planted by the waters
Ezek 47:12 grow all *t.* for meat whose leaf
Mat 3:10 every *t.* which bringeth not forth
7:17 good *t.* bringeth forth good fruit
12:33 the *t.* is known by his fruit
Mark 8:24 I see men as *t.* walking
1 Pet 2:24 in his own body on the *t.*
Jude 1:12 *t.* whose fruit withereth without
Rev 2: 7 will I give to eat of the *t.* of life
22: 2 in midst of street was the *t.* of life
22:14 may have right to the *t.* of life

TREMBLE (TREMBLED, TREMBLING)

Deut 28:65 give thee there a *t.* heart
1 Sam 4:13 for his heart *t.* for the ark of God
13: 7 all the people followed him *t.*
Ezra 9: 4 every one that *t.* at the words of God
10: 9 of God *t.* because of this matter
10: 3 those that *t.* at the commandment
Ps 2:11 Lord with fear, and rejoice with *t.*
Eccl 12: 3 keepers of the house shall *t.*
Is 66: 5 ye that *t.* at his word
Jer 5:22 will ye not *t.* at my presence?
10:10 at his wrath the earth shall *t.*
Ezek 12:18 drink thy water with *t.*, and with
26:16 clothe themselves with *t.*
Dan 6:26 men *t.* and fear before the God
Hos 13: 1 when Ephraim spake *t.*, he exalted
Zech 12: 2 make Jerusalem a cup of *t.*
Acts 24:25 as he reasoned Felix *t.*
1 Cor 2: 3 in fear, in weakness, and in much *t.*
Phil 2:12 your own salvation with fear and *t.*
Jas 2:19 devils also believe and *t.*

TRESPASS (TRESPASSES)

Lev 26:40 with their *t.* which the trespassed
1 Ki 8:31 any man *t.* against his neighbor
Ezra 9: 6 our *t.* is grown up unto the heavens
9:15 we are before thee in our *t.*
Ezek 39:26 and all their *t.* whereby they have
Mat 6:14 if ye forgive men their *t.*
6:15 if ye forgive not men their *t.*
18:15 thy brother shall *t.* against thee
18:35 every one his brother their *t.*
Luke 17: 3 If thy brother *t.* against thee, rebuke
2 Cor 5:19 not imputing their *t.* to
Eph 2: 1 who were dead in *t.* and sins
Col 2:13 having forgiven you all *t.*

TRIAL

Job 9:23 laugh at the *t.* of the innocent
Ezek 21:13 Because it is a *t.*, and what if the
2 Cor 8: 2 in a great *t.* of affliction
Heb 11:36 others had a *t.* of cruel mockings
1 Pet 1: 7 That the *t.* of your faith, being much
4:12 strange concerning the fiery *t.*

TRIBES

Num 24: 2 in his tents according to their *t.*
Ps 105:37 not one feeble person among their *t.*
122: 4 whither the *t.* go up, the *t.* of
Mat 24:30 shall all the *t.* of the earth
Acts 26: 7 promise our twelve *t.* instantly

TRIBULATION

Deut 4:30 When thou art in *t.*, and all these
Judg 10:14 in the time of your *t.*
1 Sam 26:24 deliver me out of all *t.*
Mat 13:21 when *t.* or persecution ariseth, because
24:29 immediately after the *t.* of those days
John 16:33 in the world ye shall have *t.*
Acts 14:22 we must through much *t.* enter into
Rom 2: 9 *t.* and anguish upon every soul
5: 3 knowing that *t.* worketh patience
8:35 from the love of Christ? shall *t.*
12:12 rejoicing in hope, patient in *t.*
2 Cor 1: 4 comforteth us in all our *t.*
7: 4 exceeding joyful in all our *t.*
2 Thes 1: 6 to recompense *t.* to them that trouble
Rev 1: 9 brother and companion in *t.*
2: 9 I know thy works and *t.*
2:10 ye shall have *t.* ten days
2:22 into great *t.* except they repent
7:14 which came out of great *t.*

TRIBULATIONS

1 Sam 10:19 of all your adversities and your *t.*
Rom 5: 3 glory in *t.* also: knowing that *t.*
Eph 3:13 faint not at my *t.* for you
2 Thes 1: 4 persecutions and *t.* that ye endure

TRIBUTE

Gen 49:15 bear, and became a servant unto *t.*
Num 31:28 levy a *t.* unto the Lord of the men
Prov 12:24 slothful shall be under *t.*
Mat 17:24 doth not the master pay *t.*
22:17 is it lawful to give *t.* to Caesar
Rom 13: 7 *t.* to whom *t.* is due; custom

TRIUMPH (TRIUMPHED, TRIUMPHING)

Ex 15: 1 he hath *t.* gloriously: the horse
15:21 for he hath *t.* gloriously: the horse
2 Sam 1:20 daughters of the uncircumcised *t.*
Job 20: 5 the *t.* of the wicked is short
Ps 25: 2 let not mine enemies *t.* over me
92: 4 *t.* in the works of thy hands
2 Cor 2:14 God, which always causeth us to *t.*
Col 2:15 of them openly, *t.* over them in it

TRODDEN

Judg 5:21 thou hast *t.* down strength
Ps 119:118 *t.* down all them that err
Is 63: 3 I have *t.* the winepress alone
Luke 21:24 Jerusalem shall be *t.* down of the
Heb 10:29 who hath *t.* under foot the Son of God

TROUBLE (TROUBLES)

Job 5: 6 neither doth *t.* spring out of the
5: 7 man is born to *t.* as sparks fly
14: 1 is of few days and full of *t.*
Ps 9: 9 the oppressed a refuge in times of *t.*
25:17 *t.* of my heart are enlarged
27: 5 in time of *t.* he shall hide me
34:17 deliver them out of all their *t.*
37:39 their strength in the time of *t.*
46: 1 a very present help in *t.*
60:11 give us help from *t.*: for vain
71:20 shown me great and sore *t.*
88: 3 my soul is full of *t.*
91:15 I will be with him in *t.*
119:143 *t.* and anguish have taken hold
143:11 bring my soul out of *t.*
Prov 11: 8 righteous delivered out of *t.*
Is 26:16 Lord, in *t.* have they visited
33: 2 our salvation also in time of *t.*
Jer 8:15 time of health, and behold *t.*
14: 8 saviour thereof in time of *t.*
14:19 for a time of healing, and behold *t.*
Dan 12: 1 there shall be a time of *t.*
1 Cor 7:28 shall have *t.* in the flesh

TROUBLED (TROUBLETH)

Ex 14:24 Lord *t.* the host of Egypt
1 Ki 18:17 Art thou he that *t.* Israel
Job 23:16 soft, and the Almighty *t.* me
Ps 30: 7 hide thy face, and I was *t.*
77: 3 I remembered God, and was *t.*
Prov 11:17 he that is cruel *t.* his own flesh
11:29 he that *t.* his own house shall
Is 57:20 wicked are like the *t.* sea
Luke 18: 5 because this widow *t.* me, I will
John 5: 4 *t.* the water: whosoever then first
12:27 now is my soul *t.*; and what shall
14: 1 let not your heart be *t.*

U

UNAWARES
Deut 4:42 which should kill his neighbor *u.*
Ps 35: 8 destruction come upon him at *u.*
Luke 21:34 that day come upon you *u.*
Heb 13: 2 some have entertained angels *u.*
Jude 1: 4 certain men crept in *u.*

UNBELIEF
Mat 13:58 works there because of their *u.*
Mark 6: 6 marvelled because of their *u.*
9:24 I believe; help thou mine *u.*
16:14 upbraided them with their *u.*
Rom 4:20 promise of God through *u.*
11:20 because of *u.* they were broken off
11:32 hath concluded them all in *u.*
1 Tim 1:13 I did it ignorantly in *u.*
Heb 3:12 you an evil heart of *u.*, in departing

UNBELIEVERS
Luke 12:46 his portion with the *u.*
1 Cor 6: 6 and that before the *u.*
14:23 are unlearned or *u.*, will they not
2 Cor 6:14 unequally yoked together with *u.*

UNBELIEVING
Acts 14: 2 *u.* Jews stirred up the Gentiles
1 Cor 7:14 the *u.* husband is sanctified by the
7:15 But if the *u.* depart, let him depart
Tit 1:15 defiled and *u.* is nothing pure
Rev 21: 8 fearful, and *u.*, and the abominable

UNCIRCUMCISED
Ex 6:30 I am of *u.* lips, and how shall
Jer 6:10 behold, their ear is *u.*
9:26 all these nations are *u.*
Acts 7:51 Ye stiffnecked and *u.* in heart

UNCIRCUMCISION
Rom 2:26 if the *u.* keep the righteous
3:30 by faith, and *u.* through faith
4:10 he was in circumcision, or in *u.*
1 Cor 7:19 and *u.* is nothing, but the keeping
Gal 2: 7 gospel of *u.* was committed
5: 6 availeth any thing, nor *u.*
6:15 availeth any thing, nor *u.*
Col 2:13 dead in your sins and the *u.*
3:11 Jew, circumcision nor *u.*, Barbarian

UNCLEAN
Lev 5: 2 a soul touch any *u.* thing
10:10 difference between *u.* and clean
11: 4 not the hoof; he is *u.* unto you
13:15 the raw flesh is *u.*: it is a
Num 19:19 person shall sprinkle on the *u.*
Is 6: 5 I am a man of *u.* lips
Lam 4:15 depart ye; it is *u.*; depart
Ezek 44:23 discern between *u.* and clean
Hag 2:13 *u.* by a dead body touch any of
Rom 14:14 there is nothing *u.* of itself
1 Cor 7:14 else were your children *u.*
Eph 5: 5 nor *u.* person, nor covetous man

UNCLEANNESS
Num 5:19 hast not gone aside to *u.*
Ezra 9:11 to another with their *u.*
Mat 23:27 dead men's bones, and of all *u.*
Rom 6:19 members servants to *u.*, and to
Eph 4:19 to work all *u.* with greediness
5: 3 all *u.* let it not once be named
1 Thes 4: 7 hath not called us to *u.*

UNCTION
1 John 2:20 but ye have an *u.* from the Holy One

UNDEFILED
Ps 119: 1 Blessed are the *u.*, in the way
Sol 5: 2 my dove, my *u.*: for my head is
Heb 7:26 holy, harmless, *u.*, separate from
13: 4 honourable in all, and the bed *u.*
Jas 1:27 pure religion and *u.* before God and
1 Pet 1: 4 to an inheritance incorruptible, *u.*

UNDERSTAND (UNDERSTANDEST, UNDERSTANDETH, UNDERSTOOD)
Gen 11: 7 they may not *u.* one another's speech
Deut 32:29 they were wise that they *u.* this
1 Chr 28: 9 *u.* all the imaginations of the thoughts
Neh 8: 7 caused people to *u.* the law
Ps 19:12 who can *u.* his errors?
73:17 then *u.* I their end
107:43 shalt *u.* the lovingkindness of the Lord
119:100 I *u.* more than the ancients
139: 2 thou *u.* my thought afar off
Prov 2: 5 shalt thou *u.* the fear of the Lord
8: 5 O ye simple, *u.* wisdom: and, ye
8: 9 are all plain to him that *u.*
19:25 understanding and he will *u.* knowledge
28: 5 that seek the Lord *u.* all things
Is 32: 4 heart also of the rash shall *u.*
Jer 9:24 glory in this, that he *u.*
Mat 13:19 and *u.* it not, then cometh the
13:51 have ye *u.* all these things
John 12:16 *u.* not his disciples at the first
Acts 8:30 *u.* thou what thou readest?
Rom 3:11 none that *u.*, none that seeketh
1 Cor 13: 2 prophecy, and to *u.* all mysteries
13:11 I *u.* as a child, I thought as a
2 Pet 3:16 are some things hard to be *u.*

UNDERSTANDING
Ex 31: 3 wisdom and in *u.*, and in knowledge
Deut 4: 6 is your wisdom and your *u.*
1 Ki 3:11 hast asked for thyself *u.* to discern
4:29 gave Solomon wisdom and *u.*
7:14 filled with wisdom and *u.*
1 Chr 12:32 were men that had *u.* of the time
2 Chr 26: 5 who had *u.* in the visions of God
Job 12:13 and strength, he hath counsel and *u.*
12:20 he taketh away the *u.* of the aged
17: 4 hast hid their heart from *u.*
28:28 to depart from evil is *u.*
32: 8 the Almighty giveth them *u.*
38:36 who hath given *u.* to the heart
39:17 neither imparted to her *u.*
Ps 47: 7 sing ye praises with *u.*
49: 3 meditation of my heart be of *u.*
119:34 give me *u.* and I shall keep
119:99 have more *u.* than all my teachers
119:104 through thy precepts I get *u.*
119:130 it giveth *u.* unto the simple
147: 5 great power; his *u.* is infinite
Prov 2: 2 apply thine heart to *u.*
2:11 preserve thee, *u.* shall keep thee
3: 5 lean not unto thine own *u.*
3:13 happy is the man that getteth *u.*
4: 5 get wisdom, get *u.*,: forget it
8: 1 *u.* put forth her voice
8: 5 ye fools, be ye of an *u.* heart
8:14 I am *u.*; I have strength
9: 6 and go in the way of *u.*
9:10 knowledge of the holy is *u.*
14:29 slow to wrath is of great *u.*
16:22 *u.* is a wellspring of life
19: 8 keepeth *u.* shall find good
21:30 *u.* nor counsel against the Lord
23:23 all wisdom, and instruction, and *u.*
30: 2 I have not the *u.* of a man
Eccl 9:11 nor yet riches to men of *u.*
Is 11: 2 spirit of wisdom and *u.*, the spirit
11: 3 make him of quick *u.* in the fear
27:11 it is a people of no *u.*
40:28 is no searching of his *u.*
Jer 51:15 stretched out heaven by his *u.*
Mark 12:33 with all the heart and with all the *u.*
Luke 2:47 were astonished at his *u.* and answers
24:45 then opened he their *u.*
1 Cor 1:19 bring to nothing the *u.* of the prudent
14:14 spirit prayeth, but *u.* is unfruitful
14:15 I will sing with the *u.* also
14:20 Brethren, be not children in *u.*
Eph 1:18 eyes of your *u.* being enlightened
4:18 the *u.* darkened, being alienated
Phil 4: 7 peace of God which passeth all *u.*
Col 1: 9 in all wisdom and spiritual *u.*
2: 2 riches of the full assurance of *u.*
2 Tim 2: 7 give thee *u.* in all things

UNDONE
Is 6: 5 Woe is me! for I am *u.*
Mat 23:23 not to leave the other *u.*

UNFEIGNED
2 Cor 6: 6 by the Holy Ghost, by love *u.*
1 Tim 1: 5 conscience, and of faith *u.*
2 Tim 1: 5 the *u.* faith that is in thee
1 Pet 1:22 through the Spirit unto *u.* love

UNFRUITFUL
Mat 13:22 choke the word, and he becometh *u.*
1 Cor 14:14 my understanding is *u.*
Eph 5:11 fellowship with the *u.* works
Tit 3:14 that they be not *u.*
2 Pet 1: 8 barren nor *u.* in the knowledge

UNGODLY
2 Sam 22: 5 *u.* men made me afraid
2 Chr 19: 2 shouldest thou help the *u.*, and love
Job 16:11 God hath delivered me to the *u.*
Ps 1: 1 walketh not in the counsel of the *u.*
1: 4 the *u.* are not so, but are like
1: 5 *u.* shall not stand in the judgment
1: 6 way of the *u.* shall perish
3: 7 hast broken the teeth of the *u.*
43: 1 plead my cause against an *u.* nation
Prov 16:27 An *u.* man diggeth up evil
19:28 an *u.* witness scorneth judgment
Rom 4: 5 him that justifieth the *u.*
5: 6 in due time Christ died for the *u.*
1 Tim 1: 9 disobedient for the *u.* and for sinners
1 Pet 4:18 where shall the *u* and the sinner
2 Pet 2: 5 the flood upon the world of the *u.*
2: 6 those that after should live *u.*
3: 7 day of judgment and perdition of *u.* men
Jude 1: 4 *u.* men, turning the grace of God
1:15 all their *u.* deeds, which they have
1:18 walk after their own *u.* lusts

UNGODLINESS
Rom 1:18 against all *u.* and unrighteousness
11:26 turn away the *u.* from Jacob
Tit 2:12 denying *u.* and worldly lusts

UNITE (UNITED)
Gen 49: 6 honour, be not thou *u.*: for in their
Ps 86:11 *u.* my heart to fear thy name

UNITY
Ps 133: 1 brethren to dwell together in *u.*
Eph 4: 3 Endeavouring to keep *u.* of the Spirit
4:13 till we all come in *u.* of faith

UNJUST
Ps 43: 1 from the deceitful and *u.* man
Prov 11: 7 hope of *u.* men perisheth
28: 8 by usury and *u.* gain increaseth his
29:27 *u.* man is an abomination to
Zeph 3: 5 the *u.* knoweth no shame
Mat 5:45 rain on the just and the *u.*
Luke 16: 8 lord commended the *u.* steward
18: 6 hear what the *u.* judge saith
18:11 other men are, extortioners, *u.*, adulterers
Acts 24:15 both of the just and *u.*
1 Pet 3:18 suffered for sins, the just the for *u.*
2 Pet 2: 9 reserve the *u.* to the day of
Rev 22:11 that is *u.* let him be *u.*

UNJUSTLY
Ps 82: 2 how long will ye judge *u.*, and
Is 26:10 in land of uprightness will he deal *u.*

UNKNOWN
Acts 17:23 this inscription, To the *u.* god

Gal 1:22 And was *u.* by face unto the churches
1 Cor 14: 2 he that speaketh in an *u.* tongue
14: 4 he that speaketh in an *u.* tongue
14:27 If any man speak in an *u.* tongue
2 Cor 6: 9 as *u.* and yet well known

UNLEARNED

Acts 4:13 perceived that they were *u.*
1 Cor 14:16 he that occupieth the room of the *u.*
14:23 those that are *u.*, of unbelievers
14:24 believeth not, or one *u.*
2 Tim 2:23 But foolish and *u.* questions
2 Pet 3:16 they that are *u.* and unstable wrest

UNLEAVENED

Ex 12:39 and they baked *u.* cakes
1 Cor 5: 7 be a new lump, as ye are *u.*

UNPROFITABLE

Job 15: 3 should he reason with *u.* talk
Mat 25:30 cast ye the *u.* servant to the outer
Luke 17:10 you say, we are *u.* servants
Rom 3:12 they are together become *u.*
Tit 3: 9 for they are *u.* and vain
Heb 13:17 for that is *u.* for you

UNRIGHTEOUS

Is 10: 1 unto them that decree *u.* decrees
Luke 16:11 not been faithful in *u.* mammon
Rom 3: 5 is God *u.* who taketh vengeance?
1 Cor 6: 9 *u.* shall not inherit the kingdom
Heb 6:10 God is not *u.* to forget

UNRIGHTEOUSNESS

Lev 19:15 Ye shall do no *u.* in
Jer 22:13 woe to him that buildeth his house by *u.*
Luke 16: 9 friends of the mammon of *u.*
John 7:18 is true, and no *u.* in him
Rom 1:18 who hold the truth in *u.*
6:13 members as instruments of *u.*
9:14 is there *u.* with God? God forbid
2 Cor 6:14 what fellowship hath righteousness with *u.*
2 Thes 2:10 all deceivableness of *u.*
2:12 believed not the truth, but had pleasure in *u.*
Heb 8:12 will be merciful to their *u.*
2 Pet 2:15 loved the wages of *u.*
1 John 1: 9 to cleanse us from all *u.*
5:17 all *u.* is sin

UNSEARCHABLE

Job 5: 9 doeth great things and *u.*
Ps 145: 3 praised; and his greatness is *u.*
Prov 25: 3 and the heart of kings is *u.*
Eph 3: 8 Gentiles the *u.* riches of Christ

UNSPEAKABLE

2 Cor 9:15 unto God for his *u.* gift
12: 4 and heard *u.* words, which it is
1 Pet 1: 8 rejoice with joy *u.* and full of

UNSPOTTED

Jas 1:27 keep himself *u.* from the world

UNSTABLE

Gen 49: 4 *U.* as water, thou shalt not excel
Jas 1: 8 man is *u.* in all his ways
2 Pet 2:14 beguiling *u.* souls: an heart
3:16 they that are unlearned and *u.* wrest

UNWISE

Deut 32: 6 O foolish people and *u.*
Hos 13:13 he is an *u.* son; for he should
Rom 1:14 to the wise and to the *u.*
Eph 5:17 Wherefore be ye not *u.*

UNWORTHY (UNWORTHILY)

Acts 13:46 judge yourselves *u.* of everlasting
1 Cor 6: 2 are ye *u.* to judge the smallest
11:27 drink this cup of the Lord *u.*

UPBRAID (UPBRAIDED, UPBRAIDETH)

Judg 8:15 with whom ye did *u.* me
Mat 11:20 Then began he to *u.* the cities
Mark 16:14 and *u.* them with their unbelief
Jas 1: 5 to all men liberally, and *u.* not

UPHOLD (UPHOLDEST, UPHOLDETH, UPHOLDING)

Ps 37:17 but the Lord *u.* the righteous
41:12 thou *u.* me in my integrity
51:12 *u.* me with thy free spirit
63: 8 thy right hand *u.* me
119:116 *u.* me according unto thy word
145:14 The Lord *u.* all that fall
Prov 29:23 honour shall *u.* the humble
Is 41:10 I will *u.* thee with the right hand
Heb 1: 3 *u.* all things by word of

UPRIGHT

Ps 7:10 saveth the *u.* in heart
11: 7 his countenance doth behold the *u.*
18:23 I was also *u.* before him
18:25 *u.* man thou wilt show thyself *u.*
25: 8 good and *u.* is the Lord
37:37 perfect man, and behold the *u.*
64:10 all the *u.* in heart shall glory
112: 2 generation of the *u.* shall be blessed
112: 4 to the *u.* there ariseth light
140:13 *u.* shall dwell in thy presence
Prov 2:21 *u.* shall dwell in the land
10:29 way of Lord is strength to the *u.*
11: 3 integrity of the *u.* shall guide
11: 6 righteousness of the *u.* shall deliver
12: 6 mouth of the *u.* shall deliver
13: 6 righteousness keepeth him that is *u.*
14:11 tabernacle of the *u.* shall flourish
28:10 *u.* shall have good things
Eccl 7:29 found, that God hath made man *u.*
Sol 1: 4 more than wine: the *u.* love thee
Hab 2: 4 is lifted up is not *u.* in him

UPRIGHTLY

Ps 15: 2 He that walketh *u.*, and worketh
58: 1 do ye judge *u.*, O ye sons of
84:11 from them that walk *u.*
Prov 2: 7 buckler to them that walk *u.*
15:21 man of understanding walketh *u.*
Is 33:15 righteously, and speaketh *u.*,
Mic 2: 7 to him that walketh *u.*
Gal 2:14 I saw they walked not *u.*

UPRIGHTNESS

Deut 9: 5 or for the *u.* of thine heart
1 Chr 29:17 heart, and hast pleasure in *u.*
Job 33:23 to show unto man his *u.*
Ps 25:21 let integrity and *u.* preserve me
143:10 lead me into the land of *u.*
Is 26: 7 the way of the just is *u.*

URIM

Ex 28:30 breastplate of judgment the *U.*
Lev 8: 8 in the breastplate the *U.*
Num 27:21 for him after the judgment of *U.*
Deut 33: 8 Thummim and thy *U.* be with
1 Sam 28: 6 neither by dreams nor by *U.*
Ezra 2:63 a priest with *U.* and Thummim
Neh 7:65 there stood up a priest with *U.*

USE (USES)

Rom 1:26 natural *u.* into that which is
1 Cor 7:31 *u.* this world, as not abusing
Gal 5:13 *u.* not liberty for the occasion
Eph 4:29 good to the *u.* of edifying
1 Tim 1: 8 if a man *u.* it lawfully
Tit 3:14 good works for necessary *u.*
Heb 5:14 by reason of *u.* have their senses

USURY

Ex 22:25 neither shalt thou lay upon him *u.*
Lev 25:37 give him thy money upon *u.*
Deut 23:20 thou mayest lend upon *u.*
Neh 5:10 let us leave off this *u.*
Ps 15: 5 putteth not out his money to *u.*
Prov 28: 8 by *u.* and unjust gain increaseth
Is 24: 2 as with the taker of *u.*, so with
Jer 15:10 men have lent to me on *u.*
Ezek 18:13 Hath given forth upon *u.*
22:12 thou hast taken *u.* and increase
Mat 25:27 should have received mine own with *u.*
Luke 19:23 required mine own with *u.*

UTTER (UTTERED, UTTERETH)

Ps 19: 2 day to day *u.* speech, and
78: 2 I will *u.* dark sayings
94: 4 they *u.* and speak hard things
Rom 8:26 groanings which cannot be *u.*
2 Cor 12: 4 words not lawful for man to *u.*
Heb 5:11 things to say and hard to be *u.*

UTTERANCE

Acts 2: 4 as Spirit gave them *u.*
Eph 6:19 that *u.* may be given me
Col 4: 3 God would open unto us the door of *u.*

UTTERMOST

1 Thes 2:16 wrath is come upon them to the *u.*
Heb 7:25 save them to the *u.* that come

VAIN

Ex 5: 9 let them not regard *v.* words
20: 7 the name of the Lord thy God in *v.*
Deut 32:47 it is not a *v.* thing for
1 Sam 12:21 should ye go after *v.* things
Job 11:12 for a *v.* man would be wise
Ps 39: 6 they are disquieted in *v.*
60:11 for *v.* is the help of man
73:13 cleansed my heart in *v.*
89:47 why hast thou made all men in *v.*
119:113 I hate *v.* thoughts, but thy law
127: 1 the watchman waketh but in *v.*
127: 2 it is *v.* for you to rise up early
Is 45:19 seek ye me in *v.*: I the Lord
Jer 3:23 in *v.* is salvation hoped for from
4:14 how long shall thy *v.* thoughts
Mat 6: 7 use not *v.* repetitions
15: 9 in *v.* do they worship me
Rom 1:21 but became *v.* in their imaginations
13: 4 beareth not the sword in *v.*
1 Cor 3:20 thoughts of the wise are *v.*
15:58 your labour is not in *v.*
2 Cor 6: 1 receive not the grace of God in *v.*
Eph 5: 6 deceive you with *v.* words
Phil 2:16 run in *v.* neither laboured in *v.*
Jas 1:26 this man's religion is *v.*
1 Pet 1:18 from your *v.* conversation received

VANITY (VANITIES)

2 Ki 17:15 they followed *v.*, and became vain
Job 7: 3 made to possess months of *v.*
7:16 let me along; for my days are *v.*
Ps 12: 2 speak *v.* every one with his neighbour
24: 4 hath not lifted up his soul to *v.*
31: 6 hated them that regard lying *v.*
39: 5 his best state is altogether *v.*
39:11 surely every man is *v.*
62: 9 men of low degree are *v.*
94:11 thoughts of man that they are *v.*
119:37 turn away mine eyes from beholding *v.*
144: 4 man is like to *v.*: his days as a
144: 8 whose mouth speaketh *v.*
Prov 22: 8 soweth iniquity shall reap *v.*
Eccl 1: 2 *v.* of *v.*, all is *v.*
3:19 above a beast: for all is *v.*
12: 8 saith the preacher; all is *v.*
11:10 childhood and youth are *v.*
Is 5:18 draw iniquity with cords of *v.*
40:17 less than nothing and *v.*
Jer 10: 8 the stock is a doctrine of *v.*
Jonah 2: 8 that observe lying *v.*
Hab 2:13 weary themselves for very *v.*
Acts 14:15 turn from these *v.* unto the

Rom 8:20 creature was made subject to *v.*
Eph 4:17 walk in the *v.* of their mind
2 Pet 2:18 great swelling worlds of *v.*

VALIANT (VALIANTLY)

Num 24:18 and Israel shall do *v.*
Ps 60:12 Through God we shall do *v.*
108:13 Through God we shall do *v.*
118:16 hand of the Lord doeth *v.*
Sol 3: 7 threescore *v.* men are about it
Is 10:13 put down the inhabitants like a *v.* man
Jer 9: 3 they are not *v.* for the truth
Heb 11:34 waxed *v.* in fight, turned to

VALUE

Job 13: 4 are all physicians of no *v.*
Mat 10:31 Ye are of more *v.* than many sparrows

VEIL

Gen 24:65 therefore she took a *v.*
Sol 5: 7 took away my *v.* from me
Is 25: 7 the *v.* that is spread over all
Mat 27:51 *v.* of the temple was rent
2 Cor 3:13 Moses put a *v.* over his
Heb 6:19 entereth into that within the *v.*
10:20 the *v.*, that is to say, his flesh

VENGEANCE

Gen 4:15 *v.* shall be taken on him
Deut 32:35 to me belongeth *v.* and recompence
Ps 58:10 rejoice when he seeth *v.*
94: 1 God, to whom *v.* belongeth
Is 34: 8 the day of the Lord's *v.*
Jer 11:20 let me see thy *v.*
51: 6 time of the Lord's *v.*
Luke 21:22 these be days of *v.*, that all
Rom 12:19 *V.* is mine; I will repay, saith
2 Thes 1: 8 in flaming fire taking *v.*
Heb 10:30 *V.* belongeth unto me, I will recompense
Jude 1: 7 suffering the *v.* of eternal fire

VESSEL (VESSELS)

Ps 2: 9 pieces like a potter's *v.*
31:12 I am like a broken *v.*
Jer 18: 4 *v.* that he made of clay
22:28 a *v.* wherein is no pleasure
48:11 not been emptied from *v.* to *v.*
Acts 9:15 he is a chosen *v.* unto me
Rom 9:21 make one *v.* unto honour and another
9:22 *v.* of wrath fitted to destruction
2 Cor 4: 7 we have this treasure in earthen *v.*
1 Thes 4: 4 possess his *v.* in sanctification
2 Tim 2:21 be a *v.* unto honour, sanctified
1 Pet 3: 7 honour to the wife as to the weaker *v.*

VEXED

Job 27: 2 The Almighty who hath *v.* my soul
Ps 6: 2 heal me; for my bones are *v.*
6: 3 soul is also sore *v.*
6:10 enemies be ashamed and sore *v.*
Is 63:10 they rebelled and *v.* his holy spirit
2 Pet 2: 7 Lot, *v.* with filthy conversation

VICTORY

1 Chr 29:11 glory, and the *v.*, and the majesty
Ps 98: 1 his holy arm hath gotten him *v.*
Is 25: 8 He will swallow up death in *v.*
1 Cor 15:15 death is swallowed up in *v.*
15:55 O grave, where is thy *v.*?
15:57 thanks to God, who giveth us *v.*
1 John 5: 4 the *v.* that overcometh the world, even

VIGILANT

1 Tim 3: 2 husband of one wife, *v.*, sober
1 Pet 5: 8 Be sober, be *v.*, because your

VILE

Deut 25: 3 brother should seem *v.* unto thee
1 Sam 3:13 sons made themselves *v.*
2 Sam 6:22 I will yet be more *v.*
Ps 15: 4 whose eyes a *v.* person is contemned
Is 32: 6 *v.* person will speak villany
Jer 15:19 take forth the precious from the *v.*
Rom 1:26 gave them up to *v.* affections
Phil 3:21 shall change our *v.* body

VINE

Deut 32:32 for their *v.* is the *v.* of Sodom
1 Ki 4:25 every man under his *v.* and under
Ps 128: 3 wife shall be as a fruitful *v.*
Jer 2:21 I planted thee a noble *v.*
Hos 10: 1 Israel is an empty *v.*
Mic 4: 4 sit every man under his *v.*
Mat 26:29 not drink of this fruit of the *v.*
John 15: 1 I am the true *v.* and my Father
15: 5 I am the *v.*, ye are the branches

VINEYARD

Ps 80:15 *v.* which thy right hand hath planted
Prov 24:30 and by the *v.* of the man
Sol 1: 6 mine own *v.* have I not kept
8:12 My *v.* which is mine
Is 5: 1 My wellbeloved hath a *v.*
Mat 20: 1 hire labourers into his *v.*
21:33 householder which planted a *v.*
Luke 13: 6 planted in his *v.*; and he came
1 Cor 9: 7 who planteth a *v.*, and eateth not

VIOLENCE

Gen 6:11 earth was filled with *v.*
Lev 6: 2 a thing taken away by *v.*
2 Sam 22: 3 thou savest me from *v.*
Ps 72:14 redeem their soul from deceit and *v.*
73: 6 *v.* covereth them as a garment
Hab 1: 2 cry out unto thee of *v.*
Mat 11:12 kingdom of heaven suffereth *v.*
Luke 3:14 do *v.* to no man, and be
Heb 11:34 quenched the *v.* of fire

VIRGIN (VIRGINS)

Sol 1: 3 therefore do the *v.* love thee
Is 7:14 Behold a *v.* shall conceive
Mat 1:23 Behold, a *v.* shall be with child
2 Cor 11: 2 present you as a chaste *v.*
Rev 14: 4 for they are *v.*. These are they

VIRTUE

Mark 5:30 *v.* had gone out of him
Luke 6:19 there went *v.* out of him
Phil 4: 8 if there be any *v.*, think
2 Pet 1: 3 called us to glory and *v.*

VIRTUOUS

Prov 12: 4 A *v.* woman is a crown
31:10 Who can find a *v.* woman

VISION

1 Sam 3: 1 in those days there was no open *v.*
Ps 89:19 Then thou spakest in *v.* to thy holy
Prov 29:18 where there is no *v.* the people perish
Ezek 13:16 see *v.* of peace for her, and
Hos 12:10 I have multiplied *v.*, and used
Joel 2:28 young men shall see *v.*
Hab 2: 2 write the *v.*, and make it plain
2: 3 the *v.* is yet for an appointed time
Mat 17: 9 Tell the *v.* to no man
Acts 2:17 your young men shall see *v.*
10:19 Peter thought on the *v.*
16: 9 a *v.* appeared to Paul in the night

VISIT (VISITED, VISITING)

Gen 50:25 God will surely *v.* you
Ex 13:19 God will surely *v.* you
20: 5 *v.* the iniquity of the fathers
34: 7 *v.* the iniquity of the fathers
Num 14:18 *v.* the iniquity of the fathers
Deut 5: 9 *v.* the iniquity of the fathers
Job 7:18 thou shouldest *v.* him every
Ps 17: 3 thou hast *v.* me in the night
106: 4 *v.* me with thy salvation
Jer 5: 9 shall I not *v.* for these things?
Lam 4:22 he will *v.* thine iniquity
Hos 2:13 I will *v.* upon her the days of
8:13 and *v.* their sins: they shall return
Mat 25:36 I was sick and ye *v.*
Luke 1:68 he hath *v.* and redeemed his people
1:78 dayspring from on high hath *v.* us
Acts 7:23 *v.* his brethren the children of
15:36 *v.* our brethren in every city
15:14 did *v.* the Gentiles, to take out of
Jas 1:27 to *v.* the fatherless and

VOICE

Gen 4:10 *v.* of thy brother's blood
27:22 The *v.* is Jacob's *v.*, but the hands
Ex 5: 2 the Lord that I should obey his *v.*?
Ps 5: 3 my *v.* shalt thou hear in the morning
18:13 the Highest gave his *v.*
42: 4 to the house of God, with the *v.* of
95: 7 today, if ye will hear his *v.*
103:20 hearkening to the *v.* of his word
Sol 2:14 let me hear thy *v.*; for sweet is
Is 30:19 unto thee at the *v.* of thy cry
50:10 obeyeth the *v.* of his servant
Ezek 33:32 that hath a pleasant *v.*
John 5:25 dead shall hear the *v.* of
10: 3 sheep hear his *v.*: and he calleth
Gal 4:20 to change my *v.*; for I stand in
1 Thes 4:16 with the *v.* of the archangel
Rev 3:20 if any man hear my *v.*

VOID

Deut 32:28 a nation *v.* of counsel
Ps 89:39 made *v.* the covenant of thy servant
119:126 for they have made *v.* thy law
Is 55:11 it shall not return to me *v.*
Acts 24:16 conscience *v.* of offence toward
1 Cor 9:15 man should make my glorying *v.*

VOMIT

Job 20:15 he shall *v.* them up again
Prov 23: 8 thou hast eaten shalt thou *v.* up
26:11 dog returneth to his *v.*
Is 19:14 drunken man staggereth in his *v.*
2 Pet 2:22 dog is turned to his own *v.*

VOW (VOWED, VOWS, VOWEDST)

Gen 28:20 Jacob *v.* a *v.*, saying, if God
31:13 thou *v.* a *v.* unto me
Deut 23:21 when thou shalt *v.* a *v.*,
Num 6: 2 to *v.* a *v.* of a Nazarite
30: 2 man *v.* a *v.* unto the Lord
1 Sam 1:11 And she *v.* a *v.*, and said, O
2 Sam 15: 8 thy servant *v.* a *v.*
Job 22:27 thou shalt pay thy *v.*
Ps 50:14 pay thy *v.* to the most High
56:12 thy *v.* are upon me, O God
61: 5 for thou, O God, hast heard my *v.*
61: 8 I may daily perform my *v.*
65: 1 unto thee shall the *v.* be performed
76:11 *v.*, and pay unto the Lord
Prov 20:25 after *v.* to make inquiry
31: 2 and what, the son of my *v.*
Eccl 5: 4 a *v.* to God, defer not to pay
Is 19:21 they shall *v.* a *v.* unto the Lord
Jonah 1:16 to the Lord, and made *v.*
2: 9 I will pay that that I have *v.*

W

WAGES

Lev 19:13 the *w.* of him that is hired
Ezek 29:18 yet had he no *w.*, nor his army
Hag 1: 6 earneth *w.* to put into the bag
Mal 3: 5 oppress the hireling in his *w.*
Luke 3:14 be content with your *w.*
Rom 6:23 the *w.* of sin is death

WAIT

Job 14:14 my appointed time will I *w.*
Ps 25: 5 on thee do I *w.* all the day
27:14 *w.* on the Lord: be of good
37:34 *w.* on the Lord and keep his way
62: 5 *w.* thou only upon God
104:27 these *w.* all upon thee; that thou

Ps 130: 5 I *w.* for the Lord, my soul doth *w.*
145:15 eyes of all *w.* upon thee
Prov 20:22 *w.* on the Lord and he will save
Is 8:17 I will *w.* upon the Lord
30:18 blessed are all they that *w.* for him
40:31 that *w.* on Lord shall renew
Lam 3:25 good to them that *w.* for
3:26 quietly *w.* for the salvation of the
Hos 12: 6 *w.* on thy God continually
Mic 7: 7 *w.* for the God of my salvation
Hab 2: 3 *w.* for it, because it will surely
Zeph 3: 8 *w.* ye on me
Luke 12:36 men that *w.* for their lord
1 Thes 1:10 to *w.* for his Son from heaven

WAITED (WAITETH, WAITING)

Gen 49:18 I have *w.* for thy salvation
Ps 33:20 our soul *w.* for the Lord
40: 1 I *w.* patiently for the Lord
130: 6 my soul *w.* for the Lord more
Prov 8:34 *w.* at the posts of my doors
Is 25: 9 our God, we have *w.* for him
26: 8 O Lord, have we *w.* for thee
33: 2 O Lord, we have *w.* for thee
64: 4 prepared for him that *w.* for him
Zech 11:11 poor of the flock that *w.* upon me
Mark 15:43 which also *w.* for the kingdom of God
Luke 2:25 *w.* for the consolation of Israel
Rom 8:23 within ourselves *w.* for the adoption
1 Cor 1: 7 *w.* for the coming of our Lord
2 Thes 3: 5 into the patient *w.* for Christ
1 Pet 3:20 longsuffering of God *w.* in the days

WAKETH (WAKENETH, WAKENED)

Ps 127: 1 watchman *w.* but in vain
Sol 5: 2 but my heart *w.*: it is the voice
Is 50: 4 he *w.* morning by morning, he *w.* my
Joel 3:12 let the heathen be *w.*

WALK

Gen 17: 1 *w.* before me and be thou perfect
24:40 Lord before whom I *w.* will send
Ex 16: 4 they will *w.* in my law or no
Lev 26:12 I will *w.* among you and will be
26:21 if ye *w.* contrary unto me
26:23 but will *w.* contrary unto me
26:24 will I also *w.* contrary unto you
Deut 5:33 *w.* in all the ways which the Lord
13: 4 ye shall *w.* after the Lord
Ps 23: 4 though I *w.* through the valley
84:11 withhold from them that *w.* uprightly
116: 9 I will *w.* before the Lord
119: 3 do no iniquity, they *w.* in his ways
Eccl 11: 9 *w.* in the ways of thine heart
Is 2: 3 and we will *w.* in his paths
2: 5 let us *w.* in the light of the Lord
30:21 this is the way, *w.* ye in it
40:31 they shall *w.* and not faint
Jer 23:14 they commit adultery and *w.* in lies
Dan 4:37 those that *w.* in pride he is able
Hos 14: 9 just shall *w.* in them
Amos 3: 3 can two *w.* together except they
Mic 6: 8 *w.* humbly with thy God
Zech 10:12 *w.* up and down in his name
John 8:12 not *w.* in darkness, but shall have
11: 9 *w.* in day he stumbleth not
12:35 *w.* while ye have light
Rom 4:12 *w.* in the steps of that faith
6: 4 should *w.* in newness of life
8: 1 *w.* not after the flesh but after
13:13 let us *w.* honestly as in the day
2 Cor 5: 7 we *w.* by faith, not by sight
10: 3 though we *w.* in the flesh, we do not war
Gal 5:16 *w.* in the Spirit, and not fulfil the
5:25 if we live in the Spirit, let us *w.* in
6:16 as many as *w.* according to this rule
Eph 2:10 ordained that we should *w.* in
4: 1 that ye *w.* worthy of the vocation
5: 2 *w.* in love, as Christ also hath loved
5: 8 *w.* as children of light
5:15 *w.* circumspectly, not as fools
Phil 3:16 let us *w.* by the same rule
Col 1:10 that ye might *w.* worthy
Col 2: 6 Jesus the Lord, so *w.* ye in him
4: 5 *w.* in wisdom toward them that
1 Thes 2:12 ye would *w.* worthy of God, who
4: 1 how ye ought to *w.* and to please
1 John 1: 7 if we *w.* in the light, as he is
2: 6 so to *w.* as he walked
3 John 1: 4 my children *w.* in truth
Rev 3: 4 shall *w.* with me in white
16:15 lest he *w.* naked and they see his
21:24 shall *w.* in the light of

WALKED (WALKEST, WALKETH, WALKING)

Gen 3: 8 voice of Lord God *w.* in the garden
Ps 15: 2 he that *w.* uprightly and worketh
39: 6 every man *w.* in a vain show
55:14 we *w.* unto the house of God
81:12 *w.* in their own counsels
81:13 and Israel had *w.* in my ways
Is 9: 2 people that *w.* in darkness
57: 2 each one *w.* in his uprightness
Jer 6:28 revolters *w.* with slanders
Mic 2:11 a man *w.* in the spirit and falsehood
2: 7 do good to him that *w.* uprightly
Luke 1: 6 God, *w.* in all the commandments and
Acts 9:31 *w.* in the fear of the Lord
Rom 14:15 thy meat, now *w.* thou not charitably
2 Cor 4: 2 not *w.* in craftiness, nor handling the
10: 2 as if we *w.* according to the flesh
12:18 *w.* we not in the same spirit
Gal 2:14 saw they *w.* not uprightly
Eph 2: 2 in time past ye *w.* according to the
Col 3: 7 ye also *w.* some time, when ye lived
2 Thes 3: 6 from every brother that *w.* disorderly
1 Pet 4: 3 when we *w.* in lasciviousness
5: 8 *w.* about, seeking whom he may
2 Pet 3: 3 *w.* after their own lusts
Rev 2: 1 *w.* in the midst of seven golden

WANT

Deut 28:48 and in *w.* of all things
Job 31:19 any perish for *w.* of clothing
Ps 23: 1 is my shepherd; I shall not *w.*
34: 9 no *w.* to them that fear him
2 Cor 8:14 a supply for your *w.*: that there may
Phil 4:11 not that I speak in respect of *w.*

WAR

Ex 13:17 people repent when they see *w.*
17:16 Lord will have *w.* with Amalek
Job 10:17 changes and *w.* are against me
Ps 18:34 He teacheth my hands to *w.*
27: 3 though *w.* should rise against me
120: 7 when I speak, they are for *w.*
Prov 20:18 with good advice make *w.*
Eccl 8: 8 is no discharge in that *w.*
Is 2: 4 neither shall they learn *w.* any more
Mic 3: 5 they even prepare *w.* against him
2 Cor 10: 3 we do not *w.* after the flesh
1 Tim 1:18 them mightest *w.* a good warfare
1 Pet 2:11 fleshly lusts which *w.* against the
Rev 11: 7 pit shall make *w.* against them, and
12: 7 there was *w.* in heaven: Michael
17:14 these shall make *w.* with the Lamb
19:11 he doth judge and make *w.*

WARS (WARRETH)

Num 21:14 in the book of the *w.* of the Lord
Ps 46: 9 he maketh *w.* to cease unto the end
Mat 24: 6 hear of *w.* and rumours of *w.*
2 Tim 2: 4 no man that *w.* entangleth himself
Jas 4: 1 from whence come *w.* and fightings

WARFARE

Is 40: 2 that her *w.* is accomplished
1 Cor 9: 7 Who goeth a *w.* any time at his
2 Cor 10: 4 weapons of *w.* are not carnal
1 Tim 1:18 by them mightest war a good *w.*

WARN (WARNED, WARNING)

2 Chr 19:10 ye shall even *w.* them
Ps 19:11 by them is thy servant *w.*
Jer 6:10 to whom shall I speak, and give *w.*
Ezek 3:19 if thou *w.* the wicked
33: 3 blow trumpet, *w.* the people
Mat 3: 7 who hath *w.* you to flee
Acts 10:22 *w.* from God by an holy angel
20:31 I ceased not to *w.* every one night
1 Cor 4:14 my beloved sons I *w.* you
Col 1:28 whom we preach, *w.* every man, and
1 Thes 5:14 *w.* them that are unruly comfort
Heb 11: 7 Noah being *w.* of God

WASH (WASHED, WASHING)

Lev 6:27 thou shalt *w.* that whereon
15:16 he shall *w.* all his flesh in water
Job 9:30 if I *w.* myself with snow water
29: 6 when I *w.* my steps with butter
Ps 26: 6 *w.* my hands in innocency
51: 2 *w.* me thoroughly from mine iniquity
51: 7 *w.* me and I shall be whiter than
58:10 he shall *w.* his feet in blood
Sol 5: 3 I have *w.* my feet; how shall I
Is 1:16 *w.* you, make you clean
4: 4 *w.* away the filth of thy daughters
Jer 2:22 thou *w.* thee with nitre
4:14 *w.* thy heart from wickedness
Ezek 16: 4 neither wast thou *w.* in water
Luke 7:38 to *w.* his feet with tears
John 13: 5 began to *w.* the disciples' feet
13: 8 I *w.* thee not, thou hast no part
13:14 ought to *w.* one another's feet
Acts 22:16 be baptized and *w.* away
Eph 5:26 *w.* of water by the word
Tit 3: 5 saved us, by the *w.* of regeneration
Heb 10:22 our bodies *w.* with pure water
Rev 1: 5 *w.* us from our sins in his own blood
7:14 *w.* their robes, and made them white

WATCH

Neh 4: 9 and set a *w.* against them
Job 7:12 thou settest a *w.* over me
14:16 dost thou not *w.* over my sin?
Ps 102: 7 I *w.* and am as a sparrow
130: 6 they that *w.* for morning
141: 3 set a *w.*, O Lord, before my mouth
Jer 44:27 I will *w.* over them for evil
Mat 24:42 *w.* therefore, for ye know not
Mark 13:33 take ye heed, *w.* and pray
1 Cor 16:13 *w.* ye, stand fast in the
Col 4: 2 *w.* in the same with thanksgiving
1 Thes 5: 6 let us *w.* and be sober
2 Tim 4: 5 *w.* thou in all things endure
Heb 13:17 for they *w.* for your souls
1 Pet 4: 7 be sober, *w.* unto prayer
Rev 3: 3 if therefore thou shalt not *w.* I will

WATCHED (WATCHES, WATCHETH, WATCHING)

Ps 37:32 the wicked *w.* the righteous, and
63: 6 meditate on thee in the night *w.*
Prov 8:34 *w.* daily at my gates, waiting
Lam 2:19 in the beginning of the *w.*
Ezek 7: 6 the end is come; it *w.* for thee
Jer 20:10 familiars *w.* for my halting
31:28 like as I have *w.* over them
Mat 24:43 he would have *w.*, and would not
Eph 6:18 *w.* thereunto with all perseverance
Rev 16:15 blessed is he that *w.* and

WATCHFUL

Rev 3: 2 be *w.*, and strengthen the things which

WATCHINGS

2 Cor 6: 5 tumults in labours, in *w.*, in fastings
11:27 painfulness, in *w.* often in hunger

WATCHMAN (WATCHMEN)

Sol 3: 3 The *w.* that go about the city
Is 21:11 *W.*, what of the night
52: 8 Thy *w.* shall lift up thy voice
62: 6 I have set *w.* upon thy walls
Jer 31: 6 that the *w.* upon the mount
Ezek 3:17 I have made thee a *w.*
33: 7 I have set thee a *w.*

WATER
Gen 49: 4 Unstable as *w.*, thou shalt not excel
Ex 12: 9 nor sodden at all with *w.*
17: 6 come *w.* out of it, that the people
2 Sam 14:14 we are as *w.* spilt on the ground
Job 15:16 drinketh iniquity like *w.*
Ps 22:14 I am poured out like *w.*
Is 12: 3 draw *w.* out of wells of salvation
27: 3 I will *w.* it every moment
30:20 *w.* of affliction, yet shall not thy
41:17 when the poor and needy seek *w.* and
44: 3 pour *w.* on him that is thirsty
58:11 a spring of *w.*, whose waters fail
Lam 1:16 eye runneth down with *w.*
Ezek 36:25 will I sprinkle clean *w.* upon you
Amos 8:11 nor a thirst for *w.*, but of hearing
Mat 3:11 I indeed baptize you with *w.*
10:42 cup of cold *w.* only in the name of a
Luke 16:24 dip the tip of his finger in *w.*
John 3: 5 except a man be born of *w.*
3:23 baptized because there was much *w.*
4:14 shall be in him a well of *w.*
7:38 flow rivers of living *w.*
19:34 came there out blood and *w.*
Acts 8:38 went down both into the *w.*
10:47 can any man forbid *w.*, that these
Eph 5:26 cleanse it with the washing of *w.*
1 John 5: 6 he that came by *w.* and blood, even
5: 8 witness in earth, spirit, *w.* and
Jude 1:12 clouds they are without *w.*
Rev 21: 6 fountain of the *w.* of life
22:17 take the *w.* of life freely

WATERED
Is 58:11 thou shalt be like a *w.* garden
1 Cor 3: 6 I have planted, Apollos *w.*

WATERS
Ps 23: 2 leadeth me beside still *w.*
124: 4 *w.* had overwhelmed us
Prov 5:15 drink *w.* out of thine own cistern
9:17 stolen *w.* are sweet, and bread
Eccl 11: 1 cast thy bread upon the *w.*
Sol 4:15 a well of living *w.*, and streams
Is 32:20 are ye that sow beside all *w.*
33:16 given him; his *w.* shall be sure
35: 6 in the wilderness shall *w.* break forth
43:20 I give *w.* in the wilderness
54: 9 this is as the *w.* of Noah unto me
58:11 a spring of water, whose *w.* fail not
Jer 2:13 fountain of living *w.*
9: 1 O that my head were *w.*
Ezek 47: 1 *w.* issued out from under
Hab 2:14 Lord, as the *w.* cover the sea
Zech 14: 8 *w.* shall go out from Jerusalem
Rev 1:15 sound of many *w.*
19: 6 his voice as the sound of many *w.*
7:17 lead them unto living fountains of *w.*

WAY
Ex 13:21 to lead them the *w.*; and by night
32: 8 turned aside quickly out of the *w.*
1 Sam 12:23 teach you the good and right *w.*
1 Ki 2: 2 I go the *w.* of all the earth
8:32 bring his *w.* on his head
Ezra 8:21 seek of him a right *w.*
Job 17: 9 righteous shall hold on his *w.*
Ps 1: 6 *w.* of the ungodly shall perish
2:12 and ye perish from the *w.*
18:30 as for God, his *w.* is perfect
25: 8 teach sinners in the *w.*
37:23 delighteth in his *w.*
49:13 their *w.* is their folly
67: 2 that thy *w.* may be known
78:50 He made a *w.* to his anger
119: 9 shall a young man cleanse his *w.*
119:14 I rejoiced in the *w.* of thy testimonies
119:30 I have chosen the *w.* of truth
119:32 run the *w.* of thy commandments
139:24 lead me in the *w.* everlasting
Prov 2: 8 Lord preserveth the *w.* of his saints
10:29 *w.* of the Lord is strength
14: 8 prudent is to understand his *w.*
14:12 a *w.* which seemeth right
15: 9 *w.* of the wicked is abomination
15:24 *w.* of life is above to the wise
16: 9 man's heart deviseth his *w.*
Eccl 11: 5 knowest not what is the *w.* of the
Is 26: 7 *w.* of the just is uprightness
26: 8 in the *w.* of thy judgments
30:21 this is the *w.*, walk ye in it
35: 8 shall be called The *w.* of holiness
43:19 make a *w.* in the wilderness
55: 7 let the wicked forsake his *w.*
59: 8 *w.* of peace they know not
Jer 6:16 where is the good *w.* and
10:23 *w.* of man is not in himself
21: 8 the *w.* of life and the *w.* of death
32:39 give them one heart and one *w.*
50: 5 shall ask the *w.* to Zion
Mat 5:25 whiles thou art in the *w.* with him
7:13 broad is the *w.*, that leadeth
21:32 John came in the *w.* of righteousness
Luke 1:79 guide our feet in the *w.* of peace
John 1:23 straight is the *w.* of the Lord
14: 4 ye know, and the *w.* ye know
14: 6 I am the *w.*, the truth, and
Acts 16:17 show unto us the *w.* of salvation
18:25 instructed in the *w.* of the Lord
1 Cor 10:13 make a *w.* to escape, that ye may
12:31 show I unto you a more excellent *w.*
2 Pet 2: 2 the *w.* of truth shall be evil spoken

WAYS
Deut 32: 4 all his *w.* are judgment
Job 21:14 desire not the knowledge of thy *w.*
40:19 he is chief of the *w.* of God
Ps 84: 5 in whose heart are the *w.* of
91:11 keep thee in all thy *w.*
145:17 Lord is righteous in all his *w.*
Prov 3:17 Her *w.* are *w.* of pleasantness
4:26 let all thy *w.* be established
5:21 *w.* of man are before the eyes of the
16: 2 *w.* of a man are clean in his own
16: 7 when a man's *w.* please the Lord
Is 2: 3 he will teach us of his *w.*
63:17 made us err from thy *w.*
Jer 7: 3 amend your *w.* and your doings
Lam 1: 4 the *w.* of Zion do mourn
3:40 let us search and try our *w.*
Ezek 16:61 thou shalt remember thy *w.*
Dan 5:23 whose are all thy *w.* hast thou
Mic 4: 2 he will teach us of his *w.*
Rom 11:33 and his *w.* past finding out
Rev 15: 3 just and true are thy *w.*

WEAK
2 Chr 15: 7 let not your hands be *w.*
Job 4: 3 thou hast strengthened the *w.* hands
Ps 6: 2 O Lord; for I am *w.*: O Lord heal
Is 35: 3 strengthen ye the *w.* hands
Ezek 16:30 how *w.* is thine heart, saith the
Mat 26:41 willing, but the flesh is *w.*
Rom 4:19 and being not *w.* in faith
14: 1 him that is *w.* in the faith receive
1 Cor 4:10 we are *w.* but ye are strong
9:22 to the *w.* became I as *w.*
11:30 for this cause many are *w.* and sickly
12:10 I am *w.* then am I strong
1 Thes 5:14 support the *w.*, be patient toward

WEAKEN (WEAKENED, WEAKENETH)
Job 12:21 and *w.* the strength of the mighty
Ps 102:23 He *w.* my strength in the way
Is 14:12 thou didst *w.* the nations

WEAKER
2 Sam 3: 1 house of Saul waxed *w.* and *w.*
1 Pet 3: 7 the wife, as unto the *w.* vessel

WEAKNESS
1 Cor 1:25 the *w.* of God is stronger
2: 3 I was in you with *w.*
15:43 it is sown in *w.*; it is raised
2 Cor 12: 9 my strength is made perfect in *w.*
13: 4 he was crucified through *w.*
Heb 11:34 out of *w.* were made strong

WEALTH
Gen 34:29 And all their *w.*, and all their
Deut 8:17 mine hand hath gotten me this *w.*
8:18 giveth thee power to get *w.*
Job 21:13 They spend their days in *w.*
Ps 49: 6 They that trust in their *w.*
49:10 and leave their *w.* to others
112: 3 *w.* and riches shall be in his
Prov 10:15 rich man's *w.* is his strong city
13:11 *w.* gotten by vanity shall be
13:22 *w.* of the sinner is laid up for
19: 4 *w.* maketh many friends
1 Cor 10:24 but every man another's *w.*

WEAPON (WEAPONS)
Deut 23:13 have a paddle upon thy *w.*
Neh 4:17 the other hand held a *w.*
Job 20:24 He shall flee from the iron *w.*
Is 13: 5 the *w.* of his indignation
54:17 No *w.* that is formed against thee
2 Cor 10: 4 *w.* of warfare are not carnal

WEARY
Gen 27:46 I am *w.* of my life because
Job 3:17 there the *w.* be at rest
10: 1 my soul is *w.* of my life; I will
Prov 3:11 nor be *w.* of his correction
Is 7:13 *w.* men, will ye *w.* my God
40:28 fainteth not, neither is *w.*
40:31 shall run and not be *w.*
50: 4 word in season to him that is *w.*
Jer 6:11 I am *w.* with holding in: I will
9: 5 *w.* themselves to commit iniquity
20: 9 I was *w.* with forbearing
31:25 I have satiated the *w.* soul
Gal 6: 9 let us not be *w.* in well doing
2 Thes 3:13 brethren, be not *w.* in well doing

WEDDING
Mat 22: 3 them that were bidden to the *w.*
Luke 14: 8 any man to a *w.*, sit not down in

WEEK (WEEKS)
Dan 9:24 Seventy *w.* are determined
9:27 covenant with many for one *w.*
10: 2 Daniel was mourning three full *w.*
Mat 28: 1 toward the first day of the *w.*
Luke 18:12 I fast twice in the *w.*
Acts 20: 7 upon the first day of the *w.*
1 Cor 16: 2 Upon the first day of the *w.*
Jer 5:24 reserveth unto us the appointed *w.*

WEEP (WEEPEST, WEEPETH)
1 Sam 1: 8 why *w.* thou? and why eatest thou
Job 30:25 Did not I *w.* for him
Ps 126: 6 he that goeth forth and *w.*
Is 30:19 thou shalt *w.* no more
Jer 9: 1 I might *w.* day and night
13:17 my soul shall *w.* in secret
Lam 1: 2 she *w.* sore in the night
Joel 2:17 *w.* between the porch and the altar
Luke 6:21 blessed are ye that *w.* now: for ye
23:28 *w.* not for me, but *w.* for yourselves
John 20:13 say unto her Woman, why *w.* thou
Rom 12:15 *w.* with them that *w.*
1 Cor 7:30 that *w.* as though they wept not
Jas 5: 1 rich men, *w.* and howl

WEEPING
Ps 30: 5 *w.* may endure for a night
Is 22:12 Lord God of hosts call to *w.* and
Joel 2:12 with fasting and with *w.*
Mal 2:13 covering the altar of the Lord with *w.*
Mat 8:12 *w.* and gnashing of teeth
22:13 be *w.* and gnashing of teeth
25:30 be *w.* and gnashing of teeth

WEIGH (WEIGHED, WEIGHETH)
Job 31: 6 let me be *w.* in an even balance
Prov 16: 2 but the Lord *w.* the spirits
Is 26: 7 doth *w.* the path of the just
Dan 5:27 art *w.* in the balances

WEIGHT (WEIGHTS)
Lev 19:36 balances, just *w.*, a just ephah
Deut 25:13 not have in thy bag divers *w.*
Prov 11: 1 just *w.* is his delight
16:11 just *w.* and balance are the Lord's
20:23 Divers *w.* are an abomination
2 Cor 4:17 exceeding and eternal *w.* of glory
Heb 12: 1 let us lay aside every *w.*

WELL
Gen 4: 7 if thou doest *w.* shalt
Ex 1:20 God dealt *w.* with the midwives
Ps 119:65 hast dealt *w.* with thy servant
128: 2 it shall be *w.* with thee
Eccl 8:12 it shall be *w.* with them
Is 3:10 shall be *w.* with him
Rom 2: 7 patient continuance in *w.* doing
Gal 6: 9 not be weary in *w.* doing
2 Thes 3:13 be not weary in *w.* doing
1 Pet 2:15 with *w.* doing ye may put to silence
3:17 ye suffer for *w.* doing
4:19 their souls to him in *w.* doing

WELLS (WELLS)
Ps 84: 6 valley of Baca make it a *w.*
Prov 5:15 running waters out of thine own *w.*
10:11 righteous man is a *w.* of life
Sol 4:15 a *w.* of living waters and streams
Is 12: 3 ye draw water out of *w.*
John 4:14 a *w.* of water springing up
2 Pet 2:17 These are *w.* without water

WEPT
Neh 1: 4 I sat down and *w.*, and mourned
Ps 69:10 When I *w.*, and chastened
Hos 12: 4 he *w.*, and made supplication
Mat 26:75 went out and *w.* bitterly
Luke 19:41 beheld the city, and *w.* over it
John 11:35 Jesus *w.*

WHEAT
Ps 81:16 with the finest of the *w.*
Prov 27:22 among *w.* with a pestle yet will
Sol 7: 2 heap of *w.* set about with lilies
Jer 12:13 they have sown *w.*, but shall reap
Amos 8: 5 we may set forth *w.*, making
Mat 3:12 gather his *w.* into the garner
Luke 22:31 that he may sift you as *w.*
John 12:24 except a corn of *w.* fall

WHEEL (WHEELS)
Ex 14:25 took off their chariot *w.*
Judg 5:28 why tarry the *w.* of his chariot
Ps 83:13 my God, make them like a *w.*
Prov 20:26 bringeth the *w.* over them
Ezek 1:16 appearance of the *w.* and their work
10:13 it was cried unto them, O *w.*
Dan 7: 9 and his *w.* as burning fire
Nah 3: 2 the rattling of the *w.*

WHIRLWIND (WHIRLWINDS)
2 Ki 2:11 went up by a *w.* into heaven
Prov 1:27 destruction cometh as a *w.*
10:25 As the *w.* passeth, so is the wicked
Is 66:15 his chariots like a *w.*
Hos 8: 7 they shall reap the *w.*
13: 3 the *w.* out of the floor
Nah 1: 3 Lord hath his way in the *w.*
Hab 3:14 came out as a *w.* to scatter me
Zech 7:14 I scatter them with a *w.*
9:14 shall go with *w.* of the south

WHITE (WHITER)
Lev 13: 4 spot be *w.* in the skin
Num 12:10 Miriam became leprous, *w.* as snow
Job 6: 6 any taste in the *w.* of an egg
Ps 51: 7 and I shall be *w.* than snow
68:14 it was *w.* as snow in Salmon
Eccl 9: 8 thy garments be always *w.*
Sol 5:10 my beloved is *w.* and ruddy
Is 1:18 they shall be as *w.* as snow; though
Lam 4: 7 they were *w.* than milk
Dan 11:35 to purge and to make them *w.*
12:10 many shall be purified and be made *w.*
Mat 17: 2 his raiment was *w.* as the light
Rev 2:17 and will give him a *w.* stone
3: 4 they shall walk with me in *w.*
4: 4 elders sitting clothed in *w.* raiment
15: 6 clothed in pure and *w.* linen
19:14 clothed in fine linen, *w.* and clean

WHOLE
Job 5:18 he woundeth and his hands make *w.*
Ps 9: 1 with my *w.* heart; I will show
119:10 with my *w.* heart have I sought thee
Is 54: 5 The God of the *w.* earth
Mic 4:13 the Lord of the *w.* earth
Zech 4:14 Lord of the *w.* earth
Mat 9:21 touch his garment, I shall be *w.*
Mark 5:34 thy faith hath made thee *w.*
John 5: 4 *w.* of whatsoever disease
5: 6 unto him wilt thou be made *w.*
Acts 9:34 Jesus Christ maketh thee *w.*: arise
1 John 2: 2 for the sins of the *w.* world
5:19 the *w.* world lieth in wickedness

WHOLESOME
Prov 15: 4 A *w.* tongue is a tree
1 Tim 6: 3 consent not to *w.* words

WHOLLY
Num 32:11 they have not *w.* followed me
Deut 1:36 he hath *w.* followed the Lord
Jer 46:28 not leave thee *w.* unpunished
1 Thes 5:23 God of peace sanctify you *w.*
1 Tim 4:15 give thyself *w.* to them

WHORE
Lev 19:29 cause her to be a *w.*
21: 9 profane herself by playing the *w.*
Deut 22:21 the *w.* in her father's house
23:18 not bring the hire of a *w.*
Prov 23:27 a *w.* is a deep ditch; and a strange
Ezek 16:28 thou hast played the *w.* also with
Rev 17: 1 judgment of the great *w.* that sitteth
17:16 these shall hate the *w.*

WHOREDOM (WHOREDOMS)
Jer 3: 9 through the lightness of her *w.*
Ezek 16:26 hast increased thy *w.* to provoke
Hos 2: 2 put away her *w.* out of her
2: 4 they be the children of *w.*
4:12 spirit of *w.* hath caused them to
5: 4 spirit of *w.* is in the midst

WHOREMONGER (WHOREMONGERS)
Eph 5: 5 no *w.*, nor unclean person
1 Tim 1:10 *w.*, for them that defile themselves
Heb 13: 4 *w.* and adulterers God will judge
Rev 21: 8 murderers, and *w.*, and sorcerers
22:15 sorcerers, and *w.*, and murderers

WICKED
Gen 18:25 slay the righteous with the *w.*
Ex 23: 7 I will not justify the *w.*
Deut 15: 9 a thought in thy *w.* heart
25: 1 righteous, and condemn the *w.*
1 Sam 2: 9 the *w.* shall be silent in
Job 21:30 that the *w.* is reserved to the day
Ps 7:11 God is angry with the *w.*
9:17 *w.* shall be turned into hell
11: 6 on the *w.* he shall rain snares
58: 3 *w.* are estranged from the womb
119:155 salvation is far from the *w.*
145:20 but all the *w.* will he destroy
Prov 11: 5 *w.* shall fall by his own wickedness
21:12 God overthroweth the *w.* for their
28: 1 *w.* flee when no man pursueth
Eccl 7:17 be not overmuch *w.*, neither be
Is 55: 7 let the *w.* forsake his way
Jer 17: 9 heart is deceitful and desperately *w.*
25:31 them that are *w.* to the sword
Ezek 3:18 warn the *w.* from his *w.* way
33: 9 if thou warn the *w.* of his way to
Dan 12:10 *w.* shall do wickedly: and none of

WICKEDLY
Gen 19: 7 pray you, brethren, do not so *w.*
1 Sam 12:25 if ye shall still do *w.*
Job 13: 7 will ye speak *w.* for God?
Ps 18:21 have not *w.* departed

WICKEDNESS
Gen 6: 5 God saw that the *w.*
39: 9 how can I do this great *w.*
1 Sam 24:13 *w.* proceedeth from the wicked
Job 4: 8 and sow *w.* shall reap same
Ps 7: 9 *w.* of the wicked come to an end
45: 7 righteousness, and hatest *w.*
Prov 8: 7 *w.* is an abomination to my lips
10: 2 treasures of *w.* profit nothing
Eccl 8: 8 neither shall *w.* deliver those
Is 9:18 *w.* burneth as the fire: it shall
Jer 2:19 thine own *w.* shall correct thee
4:14 O Jerusalem, wash thy heart from *w.*
14:20 we acknowledge, O Lord, our *w.*
Hos 10:13 ye have plowed *w.*, ye have reaped
Acts 8:22 repent therefore of this thy *w.*
1 John 4:19 whole world lieth in *w.*

WIDOW (WIDOWS)
Deut 10:18 judgment of the fatherless and *w.*, and
Ps 68: 5 a judge of the *w.*, is God in his
146: 9 he relieveth the fatherless and *w.*
Jer 49:11 and let the *w.* trust in me
Mat 23:14 for ye devour *w.* houses
Mark 12:42 there came a certain poor *w.*
Luke 18: 3 there was a *w.* in that city
18: 5 yet because this *w.* troubleth me
1 Tim 5: 3 honour *w.* that are *w.* indeed
5: 5 now she that is a *w.* indeed
Jas 1:27 fatherless and *w.* in their affliction

WIFE (WIVES)
Ex 20:17 not covet thy neighbor's *w.*
Lev 21:13 take a *w.* in her virginity
Prov 5:18 rejoice with the *w.* of thy youth
18:22 findeth a *w.* findeth a good thing
19:14 a prudent *w.* is from the Lord
Eccl 9: 9 live joyfully with the *w.*
Mal 2:15 against the *w.* of his youth
Luke 17:32 remember Lot's *w.*
1 Cor 7:29 *w.* be as though they have none
Eph 5:28 love their *w.* their own bodies
5:33 love his *w.* even as
Col 3:19 Husbands, love your *w.*
1 Tim 3:11 even so must their *w.* be grave
1 Pet 3: 1 ye *w.*, be in subjection to your
Rev 19: 7 his *w.* hath made herself ready
21: 9 show thee the bride, the Lamb's *w.*

WILDERNESS
Deut 32:10 land, and in the waste howling *w.*
Prov 21:19 better to dwell in the *w.*
Is 35: 6 in the *w.* shall waters break out
41:19 I will plant in the *w.*
42:11 Let the *w.* and the cities
Rev 12: 6 woman fled into the *w.*

WILES
Num 25:18 vex you with their *w.*
Eph 6:11 against the *w.* of the devil

WILL
Lev 1: 3 of his own voluntary *w.*
22:19 ye shall offer at your own *w.*
Deut 33:16 the good *w.* of him that
Ezra 7:18 do after the *w.* of your God
Ps 40: 8 I delight to do thy *w.*, O my God
Mat 7:21 doeth the *w.* of my Father
6:10 Thy *w.* be done in earth
26:42 I drink it, thy *w.* be done
Mark 3:35 shall do the *w.* of God
Luke 22:42 not my *w.*, but thine, be done
John 1:13 *w.* of flesh, nor of the *w.* of man
4:34 my meat is to do the *w.* of him that
6:40 this is the *w.* of him that sent
7:17 any man *w.* do his *w.*
15: 7 ask what ye *w.* and it

John 17:24 I *w.* that they also, whom thou hast
Acts 13:22 which shall fulfil all my *w.*
21:14 the *w.* of the Lord be done
22:14 thou shouldest know his *w.*
Rom 1:10 journey by the *w.* of God
2:18 And knowest his *w.*, and approvest
7:18 to *w.* is present with me
8:27 according to the *w.* of God
9:18 on whom he *w.* have mercy
12: 2 and perfect, *w.* of God
1 Cor 1: 1 through the *w.* of God
2 Cor 8: 5 unto us by the *w.* of God
Gal 1: 4 according to the *w.* of God
Eph 1: 9 known unto us, the mystery of his *w.*
6: 6 doing the *w.* of God
Phil 2:13 worketh both to *w.* and to do
Col 1: 9 knowledge of his *w.* in all wisdom
4:12 complete in all the *w.* of God
1 Thes 4: 3 this is the *w.* of God
2 Tim 2:26 captive by him at his *w.*
Heb 10: 9 I come to do thy *w.*, O God
10:36 ye have done the *w.* of God
13:21 in every good work to do his *w.*
1 Pet 4:19 according to the *w.* of God
1 John 2:17 doeth the *w.* of God abideth for ever
5:14 any thing according to his *w.*
Rev 17:17 in their hearts to fulfil his *w.*
22:17 whosoever *w.*, let him take the water of

WILLING (WILLINGLY)

Ex 35: 5 whosoever is of a *w.* heart
35:22 as many as were *w.* hearted.
Judg 5: 2 people *w.* offered themselves
1 Chr 28: 9 with a perfect heart and with a *w.* mind
Ps 110: 3 thy people shall be *w.* in the day
Lam 3:33 he doth not afflict *w.* nor grieve thee
Hos 5:11 he *w.* walked after the commandment
Mat 26:41 spirit is indeed *w.* but the flesh
Luke 22:42 if thou be *w.*, remove this cup
John 5:35 *w.* for a season to rejoice in his
2 Cor 5: 8 *w.* rather to be absent from the body
1 Tim 6:18 ready to distribute, *w.* to communicate
Heb 13:18 in all things *w.* to live
1 Pet 5: 2 not by constraint, but *w.*
2 Pet 3: 9 not *w.* that any should perish

WILL-WORSHIP

Col 2:23 of wisdom in *w.*, and humility, and

WIN (WINNETH)

Prov 11:30 and he that *w.* souls is wise
Phil 3: 8 them but dung, that I may *w.* Christ

WIND (WINDS)

Job 7: 7 O remember that my life is *w.*
30:15 pursue my soul as the *w.*
Ps 103:16 *w.* passeth over it, and it is gone
135: 7 he bringeth the *w.* out of
Prov 11:29 house shall inherit the *w.*
Eccl 11: 4 he that observeth the *w.*
Is 26:18 we have as it were brought forth *w.*
27: 8 he stayeth his rough *w.* in
Jer 5:13 prophets shall become *w.*, and the
10:13 forth the *w.* out of his treasures
Ezek 37: 9 come from the four *w.*. O breath
Hos 8: 7 sown the *w.*, and they shall reap
12: 1 feedeth on *w.*, and followeth after the
Mat 8:26 rebuked the *w.* and the sea
Luke 8:25 commandeth even the *w.* and the water
John 3: 8 *w.* bloweth where it listeth
Eph 4:14 about with every *w.* of doctrine, by

WINDOWS

Gen 7:11 *w.* of heaven were opened
Eccl 12: 3 that look out of the *w.* be darkened
Sol 2: 9 he looketh forth at the *w.*, showing
Is 60: 8 and as the doves to their *w.*
Jer 9:21 death is come up into your *w.*

WINE

Ps 104:15 *w.* maketh glad the heart
Prov 20: 1 *w.* is a mocker, strong drink is
21:17 loveth *w.* and oil shall not be rich
23:31 look not thou upon the *w.* when it is red
31: 6 and *w.* to those that be of heavy heart
Sol 1: 2 love is better than *w.*
Is 5:11 until night, till *w.* inflame them
5:12 pipe and *w.* are in their feasts
28: 7 they have erred through *w.*
55: 1 buy *w.* and milk without money and
Hos 2: 9 and my *w.* in the season thereof, and
3: 1 look to other gods, love flagons of *w.*
Hab 2: 5 he transgresseth by *w.*, he is a proud
Eph 5:18 be not drunk with *w.* wherein is
1 Tim 3: 3 not given to *w.*, no striker, not
3: 8 Not given to much *w.*, not greedy of
5:23 use a little *w.* for thy stomach's sake
Tit 1: 7 not given to *w.*, no striker

WINEBIBBER (WINEBIBBERS)

Prov 23:20 Be not among *w.*
Mat 11:19 a man gluttonous, and a *w.*

WINGS

Ruth 2:12 under whose *w.* thou art come to trust
2 Sam 22:11 seen upon the *w.* of wind
Ps 17: 8 hide me under the shadow of thy *w.*
18:10 fly upon the *w.* of the wind
36: 7 trust under the shadow of thy *w.*
91: 4 under his *w.* shalt thou trust
Prov 23: 5 riches certainly make themselves *w.*
Is 6: 2 seraphims, each one had six *w.*
Mal 4: 2 with healing in his *w.*

WINTER

Sol 2:11 For, lo, the *w.* is past, the rain
Zech 14: 8 summer and in *w.* it shall be

WISE

Gen 41:39 discreet and *w.* as thou art
Ex 23: 8 gift blindeth the *w.* and perverteth
Deut 16:19 doth blind the eyes of the *w.*
Job 11:12 vain man would be *w.*, though man be
32: 9 great men are not always *w.*
Ps 2:10 Be *w.*, now therefore, O ye kings
19: 7 Lord is sure, making *w.* the simple
107:43 whoso is *w.* and will observe
Prov 3: 7 be not *w.* in thine own eyes
3:35 the *w.* shall inherit glory
13:20 walketh with *w.* men shall be *w.*
26:12 a man *w.* in his own conceit
Eccl 7: 4 heart of the *w.* is in the house of
9: 1 the *w.* and their work are
Is 5:21 are *w.* in their own eyes, and prudent
Jer 4:22 they are *w.* to do evil, but to do
Dan 12: 3 *w.* shall shine as brightness
Hos 14: 9 who is *w.* and he shall understand
Mat 10:16 be ye therefore *w.* as serpents
10:42 in no *w.* lose his reward
11:25 hid these things from the *w.*
Luke 18:17 shall in no *w.* enter therein
John 6:37 cometh to me I will in no *w.* cast
Rom 1:22 professing themselves to be *w.*
16:19 be *w.* to that which is good
1 Cor 3:18 seemeth to be *w.* in this world
4:10 but ye are *w.* in Christ
Eph 5:15 circumspectly not as fools but as *w.*
Rev 21:27 shall in no *w.* enter into it

WISDOM

Deut 4: 6 is your *w.*, and your understanding
1 Ki 4:29 God gave Solomon *w.*, and understanding
Job 28:28 the fear of the Lord, that is *w.*
Ps 111:10 Lord is the beginning of *w.*
Prov 4: 5 get *w.*, get understanding: forget
4: 7 *w.* is the principal thing
9:10 Lord is the begining of *w.*
16:16 better is it to get *w.* than gold
19: 8 he that getteth *w.* loveth his own soul
23: 4 cease from thine own *w.*
23:23 sell it not; also *w.*, and instruction
Eccl 1:18 in much *w.* is much grief
8: 1 a man's *w.* maketh his face
Mat 11:19 But *w.* is justified of her children
1 Cor 1:17 not with *w.* of words, lest the
1:24 power of God, and the *w.* of God
1:30 who of God is made unto us *w.*
2: 6 we speak *w.* among them that are perfect
3:19 *w.* of this world is foolishness
2 Cor 1:12 not with fleshly *w.*, but by the grace
Col 1: 9 in all *w.* and spiritual understanding
Jas 1: 5 you lack *w.* let him ask of God
3:17 *w.* from above is first pure
Rev 5:12 worthy is the Lamb to receive *w.*
13:18 here is *w.*: Let him that hath
17: 9 is the mind which hath *w.*

WITCH

Ex 22:18 not suffer a *w.* to live
Deut 18:10 of times, or an enchanter or a *w.*

WITCHCRAFT

1 Sam 15:23 rebellion is as the sin of *w.*
Gal 5:20 Idolatry, *w.*, hatred, variance

WITHHOLD (WITHHOLDETH, WITHHELD)

Gen 20: 6 I also *w.* thee from sinning
22:12 thou hast not *w.* thy son
Job 31:16 If I have *w.* the poor from their
Ps 40:11 *W.* not thou thy tender mercies
84:11 no good thing will he *w.*
Prov 3:27 *w.* no good from them to whom it is
11:24 *w.* more than is meet but it tendeth
23:13 *w.* not correction from child
2 Thes 2: 6 now ye know what *w.* that he might

WITHSTAND (WITHSTOOD)

Eccl 4:12 two shall *w.* him, and a threefold
Acts 11:17 who was I, that I could *w.* God
Gal 2:11 I *w.* him to the face, because he was
Eph 6:13 able to *w.* in the evil day
2 Tim 4:15 for he hath greatly *w.* our words

WITNESS

Gen 31:48 This heap is a *w.* between me and thee
Lev 5: 1 swearing, and is a *w.*, whether he hath
Num 35:30 one *w.* shall not testify
Deut 17: 6 at the mouth of one *w.*
Judg 11:10 Lord be *w.*, between us
1 Sam 12: 5 The Lord is *w.* against you
Job 16:19 my *w.* is in heaven, and my record is
Ps 89:37 as a faithful *w.* in heaven
Is 55: 4 him for a *w.* to the people
Jer 42: 5 true and faithful *w.* between us
Mic 1: 2 the Lord God be *w.* against you
Mal 2:14 Lord hath been *w.* between thee
3: 4 I will be a swift *w.* against
John 3:11 seen; and ye receive not our *w.*
5:37 sent me hath borne *w.* of me
Acts 14:17 left not himself without *w.*
1 John 5:10 believeth on the Son of God hath *w.*
Rev 1: 5 Christ, who is the faithful *w.*
20: 4 beheaded for the *w.* of Jesus

WITNESSES

Num 35:30 put to death by the mouth of *w.*
Deut 17: 6 At the mouth of two *w.*
Josh 24:22 *w.* against yourselves that ye have
Is 43:10 ye are my *w.*, saith the Lord
Mat 18:16 mouth of two or three *w.*
2 Cor 13: 1 two or three *w.* shall every word be
1 Thes 2:10 ye are *w.* and God also
1 Tim 5:19 but before two or three *w.*
6:12 a good profession before many *w.*
Heb 10:28 without mercy, under two or three *w.*

Heb 12: 1 so great a cloud of *w.*
Rev 11: 3 power unto my two *w.*, and they share

WOMAN

Gen 2:23 she shall be called *W.*
3:15 enmity between thee and the *w.*
Lev 18:23 any *w.* stand before a beast
20:13 as he lieth with a *w.* both of
Num 30: 3 If a *w.* also vow a vow also
Prov 11:16 gracious *w.* retaineth honour
12: 4 a virtuous *w.* is a crown to her
14: 1 every wise *w.* buildeth her house
31:10 who can find a virtuous *w.*
31:30 a *w.* that feareth the Lord, she shall
Eccl 7:26 *w.* whose heart is snares and nets
7:28 *w.* among all those have I not found
Is 49:15 can a *w.* forget her sucking child
54: 6 called thee as a *w.* forsaken
Jer 31:22 the earth. A *w.* shall compass a man
Mat 5:28 looketh on a *w.* to lust
John 2: 4 *w.*, what have I to do with thee
8: 3 brought unto him a *w.* taken in adultery
19:26 his mother, *w.*, behold thy son
Rom 1:27 the natural use of *w.*
1 Cor 11: 7 the *w.* is the glory of the man
Gal 4: 4 sent forth his Son, made of a *w.*
1 Tim 2:11 let *w.* learn in silence with
2:12 I suffer not a *w.* to teach
Rev 12: 1 *w.* clothed with the sun, and the moon
17:18 *w.* which thou sawest is that great city

WOMEN

Judg 5:24 blessed above *w.* shall Jael the wife
Prov 31: 3 give not thy strength to *w.*
Sol 1: 8 O thou fairest among *w.*, go thy
Is 3:12 their oppressors, and *w.* rule over
32:11 tremble, ye *w.* that are at ease
Jer 9:17 call for the mourning *w.*, that they
Lam 4:10 *w.* have sodden their own children
Mat 11:11 born of *w.*, there hath not risen
Luke 1:28 blessed art thou among *w.*
Rom 1:26 *w.* did change the natural use
1 Cor 14:34 let your *w.* keep silence in the
1 Tim 2: 9 *w.* adorn themselves in modest apparel
5:14 therefore that the younger *w.* marry
2 Tim 3: 6 lead captive silly *w.* laden with sins
1 Pet 3: 5 in the old time holy *w.* also, who
Rev 14: 4 were not defiled with *w.*

WOMB (WOMBS)

Gen 25:23 Two nations are in thy *w.*
29:31 he opened her *w.*: but Rachel was
49:25 of the breasts, and of the *w.*
Ps 22: 9 he that took me out of the *w.*
22:10 I was cast upon thee from the *w.*
127: 3 fruit of the *w.* is his reward
139:13 covered me in my mother's *w.*
Eccl 11: 5 how the bones do grow in the *w.*
Is 44: 2 formed thee from the *w.*, which will
66: 9 to bring forth, and shut the *w.*
Hos 9:14 give them a miscarrying *w.*
Luke 1:42 blessed is fruit of thy *w.*
11:27 blessed is *w.* that bare thee
23:29 barren, and the *w.* that never bare

WONDER (WONDERED)

Deut 13: 1 giveth thee a sign of *w.*
Ps 71: 7 I am as a *w.* unto many; but thou
Is 29:14 marvelous work and a *w.*
59:16 *w.* that there was no intercessor
Zech 3: 8 they are men *w.* at: for, behold, I
Luke 4:22 *w.* at the gracious words
Acts 13:41 ye despisers, and *w.* and perish
Rev 12: 1 And there appeared a great *w.*

WONDERFUL

Deut 28:59 the Lord will make thy plagues *w.*
Job 42: 3 things too *w.* for me, which I knew
Ps 119:129 thy testimonies are *w.*: therefore doth
139: 6 such knowledge is too *w.* for me
Prov 30:18 three things which are too *w.* for
Is 9: 6 his name shall be called *W.*
25: 1 thou hast done *w.* things
Jer 5:30 a *w.* and horrible thing is committed

WONDERS

Ex 3:20 smite Egypt with all thy *w.*
7: 3 multiply my signs and my *w.*
15:11 holiness, fearful in praises, doing *w.*
Job 9:10 out yea, and *w.* without numbers
Ps 77:14 thou art the God that doest *w.*
78:11 his *w.* that he had shown them
88:10 wilt thou show *w.* to the dead?
136: 4 who alone doeth great *w.*
Dan 12: 6 shall it be to the end of these *w.*?
Joel 2:30 And I will show *w.* in the heavens
John 4:48 except ye see signs and *w.*
Acts 2:43 many *w.* and signs were done
Rom 15:19 mighty signs and *w.* by the power of
Rev 13:13 he doeth great *w.*, so that he

WORD

Num 23: 5 put a *w.* in Balaam's mouth
Deut 4: 2 Ye shall not add unto the *w.*
8: 3 every *w.* that proceedeth out
30:14 But the *w.* is very nigh unto thee
2 Ki 20:19 *w.* of the Lord which thou hast spoken
Ps 18:30 *w.* of the Lord is tried: he is a
68:11 the Lord gave the *w.*: great was
119:11 thy *w.* have I hid in mine heart
119:49 remember the *w.* to thy servant
119:105 thy *w.* is a lamp unto my feet
119:160 thy *w.* is true from the beginning
130: 5 in his *w.* do I hope
147:19 showeth his *w.* unto Jacob
Prov 15:23 *w.* spoken in due season, how good it
25:11 a *w.* fitly spoken is like apples
30: 5 Every *w.* of God is pure
Is 29:21 make a man an offender for a *w.*
30:21 shall hear a *w.* behind thee
40: 8 the *w.* of our God shall stand
44:26 confirmeth the *w.* of his servant
50: 4 how to speak a *w.* in season
Jer 5:13 the *w.* is not in them
15:16 thy *w.* was unto me joy and
20: 9 his *w.* was in mine heart as fire
Mat 8: 8 speak the *w.* only and my
12:36 every idle *w.* that men shall speak
Mark 7:13 Making the *w.* of God of none effect
Luke 4:36 what a *w.* is this? for with authority
John 1: 1 in the beginning was the *W.*
1:14 the *W.* was made flesh, and dwelt
5:38 have not his *w.* abiding in you
8:31 If ye continue in my *w.*, then
15: 3 ye are clean through the *w.*
17: 6 they have kept thy *w.*
17:17 through thy truth: thy *w.* is truth
Acts 2:41 that gladly received his *w.*
13:15 any *w.* of exhortation for the people
13:26 to you is the *w.* of this salvation sent
17:11 received the *w.* with all readiness
20:32 and to the *w.* of his grace
Rom 10:17 hearing by the *w.* of God
1 Cor 4:20 kingdom of God is not in *w.*, but
Gal 6: 6 taught in the *w.* communicate unto
Eph 5:26 washing of water by the *w.*
Col 3:16 let the *w.* of Christ dwell in
3:17 whatsoever ye do in *w.* or deed
1 Thes 2:13 truth, the *w.* of God, which effectually
2 Thes 2:17 stablish you in every good *w.*
3: 1 *w.* of the Lord may have free course
3:14 if any obey not our *w.*
1 Tim 5:17 labour in *w.* and doctrine
Tit 1: 9 holding fast the faithful *w.*
Heb 4: 2 the *w.* preached did not profit
4:12 For the *w.* of God is quick
5:13 is unskilful in the *w.* of righteousness
13:22 suffer the *w.* of exhortation
Jas 1:21 receive with meekness the engrafted *w.*
3: 2 if any man offend not in *w.*
1 Pet 1:23 incorruptible, by the *w.* of God
1:25 *w.* of the Lord endureth forever
3: 1 if any obey not the *w.* they also
2 Pet 1:19 also a more sure *w.* of prophecy
1 John 1: 1 hands have handled of the *W.*
Rev 3: 8 and hast kept my *w.*, and hast not
3:10 kept the *w.* of my patience
12:11 overcame by the *w.* of their testimony
19:13 name is called the *W.* of God

WORDS

Job 23:12 I have esteemed the *w.* of his mouth
Ps 50:17 instruction, and castest my *w.* behind
Prov 15:26 *w.* of the pure are pleasant *w.*
19: 7 he pursueth them with *w.*
22:17 bow down thine ear, hear the *w.*
Eccl 10:12 the *w.* of a wise man's mouth
12:10 to find out acceptable *w.*
12:11 *w.* of the wise are as goads
Is 59:21 *w.* which I have put in thy mouth
Jer 5:14 I will make thy *w.* in thy mouth
7: 4 trust ye not in lying *w.*
44:28 know whose *w.* shall stand
Dan 7:25 speak great *w.* against the most High
Hos 6: 5 slain them by the *w.* of my mouth
14: 2 take with you *w.*, and turn to
Mic 2: 7 do not my *w.* do good
Zech 1:13 good *w.* and comfortable *w.*
Mat 26:44 the third time, saying the same *w.*
Mark 8:38 ashamed of me and of my *w.*
13:31 my *w.* shall not pass away
Luke 4:22 the gracious *w.* which proceeded
John 5:47 how shall ye believe my *w.*
15: 7 my *w.* abide in you, ye shall ask
Acts 7:22 was mighty in *w.* and in deeds
15:24 troubled you with *w.*, subverting
20:35 remember the *w.* of the Lord
26:25 speak forth the *w.* of truth and soberness
1 Cor 2: 4 not with enticing *w.* of
2 Tim 1:13 hold fast the form of sound *w.*
2:14 strive not about *w.* to no profit
Rev 1: 3 hear the *w.* of this prophecy
22:18 the *w.* of the prophesy of this book

WORK

Gen 2: 3 rested from all his *w.* which God
Ex 20:10 in it thou shalt not do any *w.*
31:14 whosoever doeth any *w.* therein
Deut 33:11 and accept the *w.* of his hands
1 Sam 14: 6 the Lord will *w.* for us
Job 1:10 thou hast blessed the *w.* of his hands
10: 3 shouldest despise the *w.* of thine hands
14:15 a desire to the *w.* of thine hands
36: 9 he showeth them their *w.*
Ps 8: 3 heavens, the *w.* of thy fingers
9:16 wicked is snared in the *w.* of his own
101: 3 I hate the *w.* of them that turn
119:126 time for thee, O Lord, to *w.*
143: 5 muse on the *w.* of thy hands
Eccl 8:14 according to the *w.* of the wicked
8:17 I beheld all the *w.* of God
12:14 God shall bring every *w.* into judgment
Is 10:12 performed his whole *w.* upon mount Zion
28:21 do his *w.*, his strange *w.*
29:16 shall the *w.* say of him that made it
43:13 I will *w.* and who shall
45:11 concerning the *w.* of my hands
49: 4 the Lord, and my *w.* with my God
64: 8 we all are the *w.* of thy hand
Jer 10:15 vanity and the *w.* of errors
18: 3 potter wrought a *w.* on the
John 6:28 might *w.* the works of God
9: 4 I must *w.* the works of him
17: 4 finished the *w.* which thou gavest
Acts 5:38 if this *w.* be of men it will come
13: 2 for the *w.* whereto I have called

Rom 2:15 show the *w.* of the law written
11: 6 otherwise the *w.* is no more *w.*
1 Cor 3:13 every man's *w.* shall be made
9: 1 are not ye my *w.* in the Lord?
Eph 4:12 for the *w.* of the ministry
1 Thes 4:11 and to *w.* with your own hands, as we
2 Thes 1:11 goodness, and the *w.* of faith with
2: 7 iniquity doth already *w.*
2:17 stablish you in every good *w.*
3:10 if any would not *w.*, neither should he eat
2 Tim 4: 5 do the *w.* of an evangelist
Jas 1: 4 let patience have her perfect *w.*
1:25 doer of the *w.* this man shall be blessed
1 Pet 1:17 judgeth according to every man's *w.*

WORKS (WORKS)

Job 37:14 consider the wondrous *w.* of God
Ps 17: 4 concerning the *w.* of men
40: 5 are thy wonderful *w.* which thou hast
46: 8 *w.* of the Lord, what desolations he
78: 4 wonderful *w.* that he hath done
78: 7 not forget the *w.* of God but keep
92: 4 triumph in the *w.* of thy hands
107: 8 wonderful *w.* to the children
111: 7 *w.* of his hands are verity
138: 8 forsake not the *w.* of thine own hands
Prov 31:31 let her own *w.* praise
Eccl 11: 5 knowest not the *w.* of God
Is 26:12 wrought all our *w.* in us
Dan 4:37 all whose *w.* are truth
Mat 7:22 thy name done many wonderful *w.*
John 5:20 will show him greater *w.* than these
9: 3 *w.* of God should be made manifest in
10:32 of those *w.* do ye stone me?
10:38 believe the *w.*: that ye may know
14:11 believe me for the very *w.* sake
14:12 greater *w.* than these shall he do
Acts 2:11 our tongues the wonderful *w.* of God
26:20 God, and do *w.* meet for repentance
Rom 3:27 of *w.*? nay: but by the law of faith
4: 6 God imputeth righteousness without *w.*
9:11 not of *w.* but of him that calleth
9:32 but as it were by the *w.* of the law
11: 6 then is it no more of *w.*
Gal 2:16 by the *w.* of the law shall no flesh be
3:10 as many as are of the *w.* of the law
5:19 *w.* of the flesh are manifest
Eph 2: 9 not of *w.*, lest any man should
2:10 Jesus unto good *w.*, which God hath
5:11 with the unfruitful *w.* of darkness
Col 1:21 enemies in your mind by wicked *w.*
1 Thes 5:13 highly in love for their *w.* sake
2 Tim 1: 9 not according to our *w.*, but according
Tit 1:16 in *w.* they deny him, being abominable
3: 5 not by *w.* or righteousness which
Heb 6: 1 repentance from dead *w.*
9:14 conscience from dead *w.* to serve the
Jas 2:14 and have not *w.*? can faith save
2:21 Abraham our father justified by *w.*
2:22 by *w.* was faith made perfect
2:24 by *w.* a man is justified
2:25 harlot justified by *w.*, when she had
1 John 3: 8 he might destroy the *w.* of the devil
Rev 9:20 repented not of the *w.* of their
18: 6 her double according to her *w.*
20:12 in the books according to their *w.*
20:13 judged every man according to their *w.*

WORKETH

Prov 11:18 wicked *w.* a deceitful work
Is 64: 5 that rejoiceth and *w.* righteousness
John 5:17 my Father *w.* hitherto, and I *w.*
Acts 10:35 and *w.* righteousness, is accepted with
Rom 4: 4 to him that *w.* is the reward not
1 Cor 12: 6 same God which *w.* all in all
2 Cor 4:17 *w.* for us a far more exceeding
Gal 5: 6 but faith which *w.* by love
Eph 1:11 *w.* all things after the counsel of
Phil 2:13 it is God which *w.* in you
1 Thes 2:13 effectually *w.* also in you that

WORKING

Is 28:29 wonderful in counsel, excellent in *w.*
Rom 7:13 sin, *w.* death in me by that which
Eph 1:19 according to the *w.* of his mighty
3: 7 by effectual *w.* of his power
4:28 *w.* with his hands the thing
Phil 3:21 according to *w.* whereby he is able
2 Thes 3:11 *w.* not at all, but are busybodies
Heb 13:21 *w.* in you that which is well pleasing

WORKERS

2 Cor 6: 1 as *w.* together with him beseech you
11:13 are false apostles, deceitful *w.*
Phil 3: 2 beware of evil *w.*, beware of the

WORKMAN

Mat 10:10 for the *w.* is worthy of his meat
2 Tim 2:15 *w.* that needeth not to be ashamed

WORKMAMSHIP

Ex 31: 3 knowledge, and in all manner of *w.*
Eph 2:10 we are his *w.*, created in Christ

WORLD

1 Sam 2: 8 he hath set the *w.* upon them
1 Chr 16:30 *w.* also shall be stable, that it
Ps 17:14 from men of the *w.*, which have their
50:12 *w.* is mine and the fulness
93: 1 *w.* also is stablished that it
96:10 *w.* also shall be established
Eccl 3:11 hath set the *w.* in their heart
Is 26: 9 inhabitants of the *w.* will learn
Jer 10:12 established the *w.* by his wisdom
Mat 12:32 neither in the *w.* to come
16:26 gain the whole *w.* and lose his
18: 7 woe to the *w.* because of offences
24: 3 coming, and of the end of the *w.*
Mark 16:15 go ye into all the *w.* and
Luke 20:35 accounted worthy to obtain that *w.*
John 1:29 which taketh away the sin of the *w.*
3:16 God so loved the *w.* that he gave
3:17 *w.* through him might be saved
7: 7 the *w.* cannot hate you, but
8:23 ye are of this *w.*; I am not
12:47 to judge the *w.* but to save the *w.*
14:17 whom the *w.* cannot receive
14:19 *w.* seeth me no more; but ye see
14:31 *w.* may know that I love the Father
15:18 if the *w.* hate you, ye know that it
15:19 chosen you out of the *w.*
16:28 I leave the *w.* and go to the Father
17: 9 I pray not for the *w.*, but for them
17:11 I am no more in the *w.*, but these
17:16 not of the *w.*, even as I am not
17:18 thou hast sent me into the *w.*
17:23 *w.* may know that thou hast sent
Rom 3:19 all the *w.* may become guilty
12: 2 But be not conformed to this *w.*
1 Cor 1:21 *w.* by wisdom knew not God, it
Gal 6:14 *w.* is crucified unto me, and I unto
Col 1: 6 as it is in all the *w.*; and bringeth
1 Tim 6: 7 brought nothing into this *w.*
Tit 1: 2 promised before the *w.* began
Heb 2: 5 put in subjection the *w.* to come
11:38 of whom the *w.* was not worthy
1 John 2: 2 for the sins of the whole *w.*
2:17 *w.* passeth away and the lust
3: 1 the *w.* knoweth us not, because it knew
4: 5 *w.* therefore speak they of the *w.* and the
5:19 the whole *w.* lieth in wickedness
Rev 3:10 temptation shall come on all the *w.*
13: 3 all the *w.* wondered after the beast

WORLDS

Heb 1: 2 by whom also he made the *w.*
11: 3 the *w.* were framed by the word of

WORM (WORMS)

Ex 16:20 and it bred *w.*, and stank: and
Job 25: 6 How much less man, that is a *w.*
Ps 22: 6 I am a *w.* and no man
Is 41:14 fear not, thou *w.* Jacob
51: 8 *w.* shall eat them like wool
66:24 their *w.* shall not die, neither shall
Mark 9:48 their *w.* dieth not, and the fire

WORMWOOD

Deut 29:18 a root that beareth gall and *w.*
Prov 5: 4 But her end is bitter as *w.*
Lam 3:19 my misery, the *w.* and the gall
Amos 5: 7 ye who turn judgment to *w.*
Rev 8:11 the name of the star is called *W.*

WORSHIP (WORSHIPPED)

Ex 4:31 bowed their heads and *w.*
32: 8 them a molten calf, and have *w.* it
1 Chr 16:29 *w.* the Lord in the beauty of holiness
29:20 *w.* the Lord, and the king
Ps 29: 2 *w.* the Lord in the beauty of holiness
96: 9 *w.* the Lord in the beauty of holiness
99: 5 *w.* at his footstool; for he is
Jer 1:16 *w.* the works of their own hands
Mat 4:10 Thou shalt *w.* the Lord thy God, and
15: 9 in vain do they *w.* me, teaching for
John 4:24 *w.* him must *w.* him in spirit
Acts 17:23 whom therefore ye ignorantly *w.*
24:14 so *w.* I the God of my fathers
Rom 1:25 and *w.* and served the creature
2 Thes 2: 4 all that is called God, or that is *w.*
Rev 3: 9 to come and *w.* before thy feet
5:14 fell down and *w.* him that liveth for
7:11 on their faces, and *w.* God
13: 4 they *w.* the dragon which gave power
13:12 to *w.* first the beast
19:10 to *w.* God: for the testimony of
22: 9 sayings of this book: *w.* God

WORTHY

Gen 32:10 I am not *w.* of the least
Mat 8: 8 not *w.* that thou shouldest come
10:10 workman is *w.* of his meat
10:13 if the house be *w.* let your peace
22: 8 which were bidden were not *w.*
Luke 3: 8 forth therefore fruits *w.* of repentance
7: 4 *w.* for whom he should do this
10: 7 labourer is *w.* of his hire
15:19 no more *w.* to be called thy son
15:21 no more *w.* to be called thy son
20:35 accounted *w.* to obtain that world
21:36 *w.* to escape all these things
Acts 5:41 counted *w.* to suffer shame
Rom 8:18 not *w.* to be compared with the glory
Eph 4: 1 walk *w.* of the vocation wherewith
1 Thes 2:12 walk *w.* of God, who hath called you
2 Thes 1: 5 *w.* of the kingdom of God
1:11 God would count you *w.* of this calling
1 Tim 1:15 *w.* of all acceptation, that Christ
5:18 labourer is *w.* of his reward
6: 1 count their masters *w.* of all honour
Heb 3: 3 *w.* of more glory than Moses
10:29 sorer punishment shall he be thought *w.*
Rev 3: 4 in white, for they are *w.*
5:12 *w.* is the Lamb that was slain
16: 6 blood to drink; for they are *w.*

WOULD

Neh 9:30 yet *w.* they not give ear: therefore
Ps 81:11 voice, and Israel *w.* none of me
Prov 1:25 counsel, and *w.* none of my reproof
1:30 they *w.* none of my counsel
Is 30:15 your strength: and ye *w.* not
Mat 7:12 whatsoever ye *w.* that men should do
18:30 And he *w.* not: but went and
23:37 *w.* have gathered thy children
Rom 7:15 what I *w.*, that I do not
11:25 For I *w.* not, brethren

Gal 5:17 cannot do the things ye *w.*
Rev 3:15 I *w.* thou wert cold or hot

WOUND (WOUNDED, WOUNDETH, WOUNDS)

Ex 21:25 *w.* for *w.*, stripe for stripe
Deut 32:39 I *w.* and I heal: neither is there
Job 5:18 he *w.* and his hands make whole
Ps 69:26 grief of those whom thou hast *w.*
109:22 my heart is *w.* within me
Prov 6:33 A *w.* and dishonour shall he get
18:14 a *w.* spirit who can bear?
27: 6 Faithful are the *w.* of a friend
Sol 5: 7 they smote me, they *w.* me
Is 1: 6 *w.*, and bruises, and putrifying sores
53: 5 But he was *w.* for our transgressions
Jer 10:19 my *w.* is grievous: but I said
15:18 pain perpetual, and my *w.* incurable
30:14 with the *w.* of an enemy, with the
30:17 heal thee of thy *w.*, saith the
Mic 1: 9 For her *w.* is incurable
1 Cor 8:12 and *w.* their weak conscience, ye sin
Rev 13: 3 his deadly *w.* was healed: and all the

WRATH

Gen 49: 7 their *w.*, for it was cruel
Ex 32:11 Lord, why doth thy *w.* wax
Num 16:46 *w.* gone out from the Lord
25:11 hath turned my *w.* away
Deut 32:27 feared the *w.* of the enemy
Ezra 8:22 power and his *w.* is against all
Neh 13:18 bring more *w.* on Israel
Job 5: 2 *w.* killeth the foolish man
Ps 76:10 *w.* of man shall praise thee
78:38 did not stir up all his *w.*
95:11 I sware in my *w.* that they should
Is 10: 6 against the people of my *w.*
54: 8 in a little *w.* I hid my face
60:10 in my *w.* I smote thee, but in my
Jer 10:10 at his *w.*, the earth shall tremble
Ezek 7:14 my *w.* is upon all the multitude
Hos 5:10 pour out my *w.* upon them
Hab 3: 2 make known; in *w.* remember mercy
Mat 3: 7 flee from the *w.* to come
Rom 2: 5 *w.* against the day of *w.*
5: 9 saved from *w.* through him
12:19 but rather give place unto *w.*
13: 5 for *w.* but also for conscience
Eph 2: 3 by nature children of *w.*
4:26 let not the sun go down on your *w.*
1 Thes 1:10 delivered us from the *w.* to come
5: 9 For God hath not appointed us to *w.*
1 Tim 2: 8 holy hands without *w.* and doubting
Heb 11:27 not fearing the *w.* of the king
Jas 1:19 slow to speak, slow to *w.*
1:20 *w.* of man worketh not the righteousness
Rev 6:16 from the *w.* of the Lamb
6:17 great day of his *w.* is come; and
14: 8 wine of *w.* of her fornication

WRESTLE (WRESTLED)

Gen 32:25 out of joint as he *w.* with him
32:24 and there *w.* with a man
Eph 6:12 we *w.* not against flesh and blood

WRETCHED

Rom 7:24 O *w.* man that I am! who shall
Rev 3:17 thou art *w.*, and miserable, and poor

WRINKLE (WRINKLES)

Job 16: 8 thou hast filled me with *w.*
Eph 5:27 spot, or *w.*, or any such thing

WRITE (WRITTEN)

Ex 34:27 *W.* thou these words: for after the
Deut 6: 9 *w.* them upon the posts of thy house
27: 3 thou shalt *w.* upon them all the words
Ps 69:28 and not be *w.* with the righteous
102:18 shall be *w.* for the generation to come
Prov 3: 3 *w.* them on table of thine heart
22:20 have not I *w.* to thee
Eccl 12:10 and that which was *w.* was upright
Is 8: 1 *w.* in it with a man's pen concerning
Jer 30: 2 *W.* thee all the words that I have
Hab 2: 2 *w.* the vision, and make it plain
1 Cor 10:11 and they are *w.* for our admonition
2 Cor 3: 2 ye are our epistle *w.* in our hearts
3: 3 *w.* not with ink but with the Spirit
Heb 12:23 are *w.* in heaven, and to God
1 John 2: 1 these things *w.* I unto you that ye
2: 7 I *w.* no new commandment unto you
2: 8 a new commandment I *w.* unto you
2:13 I *w.* unto you, fathers
2:14 I have *w.* to you, fathers
2:21 I have not *w.* unto you because ye
2:26 these things have I *w.* unto you

WRONG (WRONGED, WRONGETH)

Ps 105:14 suffered no man to do them *w.*
Prov 8:36 *w.* his own soul: all they that
Jer 22: 3 and do no *w.*, do no violence
22:13 and his chambers by *w.*; that useth
1 Cor 6: 7 why do ye not rather take *w.*
2 Cor 7: 2 we have *w.* no man, we have corrupted
Col 3:25 he that doeth *w.* shall receive
Philem 1:18 If he hath *w.* thee or oweth thee

WROUGHT

1 Sam 6: 6 he had *w.* wonderfully among them
14:45 hath *w.* this great salvation
Ps 139:15 curiously *w.* in the lowest parts
Is 26:12 thou also hast *w.* all our works in us
Ezek 20: 9 I *w.* for my name's sake that it
John 3:21 that they are *w.* in God
Rom 7: 8 *w.* in me all manner of concupiscence
2 Cor 5: 5 that hath *w.* us for the selfsame
1 Pet 4: 3 have *w.* the will of Gentiles

YEA

Mat 5:37 communication be *y.*, *y.*; Nay, nay
2 Cor 1:18 toward you was not *y.* and nay
1:20 *y.* and in him Amen unto the glory

YEAR (YEARS)

Job 10: 5 are thy *y.* as man's days
Ps 90: 4 a thousand *y.* in thy sight are but
Is 61: 2 proclaim the acceptable *y.* of the Lord
63: 4 *y.* of my redeemed is come
Jer 11:23 even the *y.* of their visitation
Luke 4:19 preach the acceptable *y.* of the Lord
2 Pet 3: 8 a thousand *y.* as one day
Rev 20: 2 Satan, and bound him a thousand *y.*

YESTERDAY

Job 8: 9 we are but of *y.*, and know
Heb 13: 8 the same *y.*, and today, and for ever

YIELD (YIELDED, YIELDETH)

2 Chr 30: 8 but *y.* yourselves unto the Lord
Ps 67: 6 shall the earth *y.* her increase
Rom 6:13 *y.* ye your members as instruments
6:16 whom ye *y.* yourselves servants to
6:19 ye have *y.* your members servants to
Heb 12:11 *y.* the peaceable fruit of righteousness

YOKE (YOKED)

Deut 28:48 shall put a *y.* of iron upon thy neck
1 Ki 12: 4 Thy father made our *y.* grievous
Is 9: 4 broken the *y.* of his burden
10:27 the *y.* shall be destroyed
Lam 1:14 *y.* of my transgressions is bound by
Mat 11:29 take my *y.* upon you, and learn of
11:30 my *y.* is easy and my burden is light
2 Cor 6:14 be ye not unequally *y.* together with
Gal 5: 1 entangled again with the *y.* of bondage

YOUNG

Ps 37:25 I have been *y.*, and now am
Is 40:11 gently lead those that are with *y.*

YOUNGER

1 Tim 5: 1 and the *y.* men as brethren
5:14 I will therefore that *y.* women marry
1 Pet 5: 5 ye *y.* submit yourselves to the elder

YOUTH

Gen 8:21 imagination of man is evil from his *y.*
1 Ki 18:12 fear the Lord from my *y.*
Job 13:26 possess iniquities of my *y.*
Ps 25: 7 sins of my *y.*, nor my transgressions
Eccl 11: 9 Rejoice, O young man, in thy *y.*
11:10 childhood and *y.* are vanity
Jer 2: 2 the kindness of thy *y.*, the love of
1 Tim 4:12 let no man despise thy *y.*

YOUTHFUL

2 Tim 2:22 flee also *y.* lusts: but follow

Z

ZEAL

2 Ki 10:16 with me, and see my *z.* for the Lord
Ps 69: 9 the *z.* of thine house hath
119:139 my *z.* hath consumed me because
Is 9: 7 *z.* of the Lord of hosts will perform
59:17 and was clad with *z.* as a cloak
63:15 where is thy *z.* and thy strength
Rom 10: 2 record that they have a *z.* of God
Phil 3: 6 concerning *z.*, persecuting the church

ZEALOUS (ZEALOUSLY)

Num 25:13 because he was *z.* for his God
Acts 22: 3 and was *z.* toward God as ye all are
Gal 4:18 *z.* affected always in a good thing
Tit 2:14 peculiar people *z.* of good works
Rev 3:19 be *z.* therefore and repent

ZION (ZION'S)

2 Sam 5: 7 David took the stronghold of *Z.*
1 Ki 8: 1 city of David, which is *Z.*
2 Ki 19:31 they that escape out of mount *Z.*
Ps 2: 6 my king upon my holy hill of *Z.*
9:11 to the Lord, which dwelleth in *Z.*
48: 2 joy of the whole earth is mount *Z.*
146:10 even thy God, O *Z.*, unto all
147:12 O Jerusalem; praise thy God, O *Z.*
Is 1:27 *Z.* shall be redeemed with judgment
60:14 The *Z.* of the Holy One of Israel
62: 1 For *Z.* sake will I not hold my peace
Heb 12:22 But ye are come unto mount *Z.*

INDEX TO COLOR MAPS

The Index to Color Maps will lead you to place-names found on the color maps in the back of this Bible. References are to the map number and map margin markings.

K

L

M

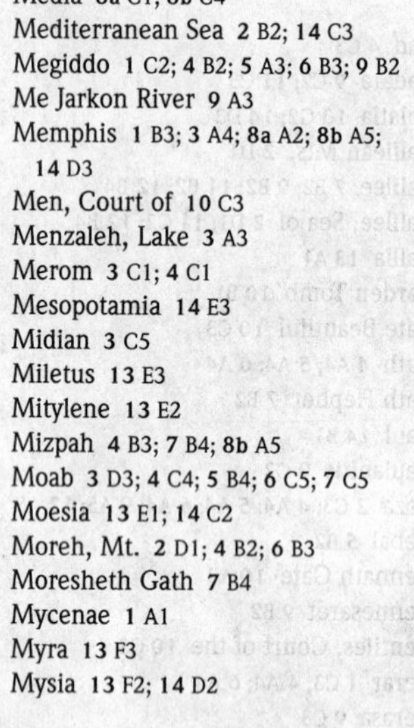

N

O

P

Q

R

S

Map 1: **WORLD OF THE PATRIARCHS**

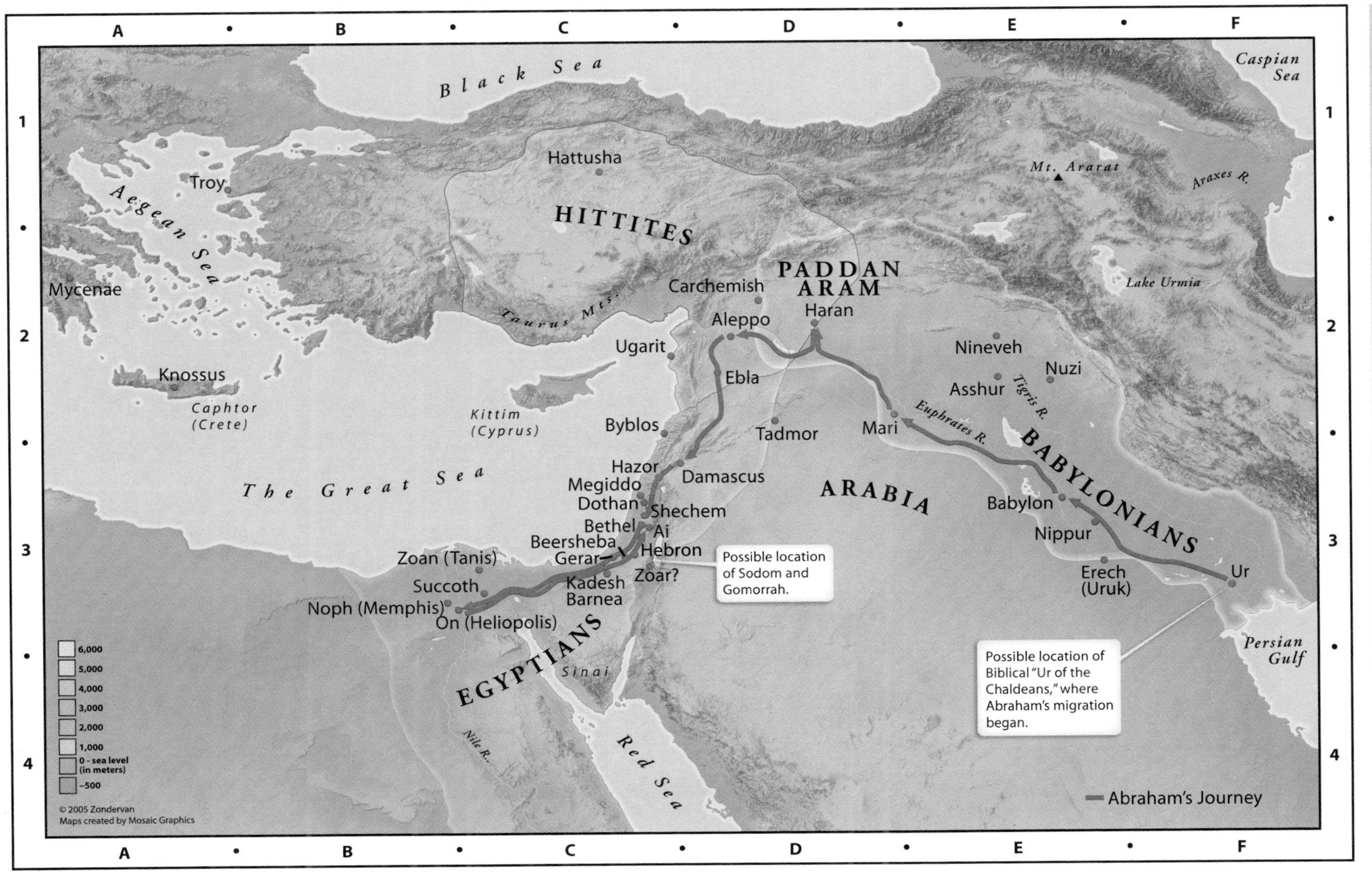

Black Sea
Caspian Sea
Aegean Sea
The Great Sea
Red Sea
Persian Gulf
Araxes R.
Lake Urmia
Mt. Ararat
Tigris R.
Euphrates R.
Nile R.
Taurus Mts.
Sinai
HITTITES
PADDAN ARAM
BABYLONIANS
ARABIA
EGYPTIANS
Kittim (Cyprus)
Caphtor (Crete)
Troy
Mycenae
Knossus
Hattusha
Carchemish
Aleppo
Ebla
Haran
Mari
Tadmor
Ugarit
Byblos
Damascus
Hazor
Megiddo
Dothan
Shechem
Bethel
Ai
Hebron
Zoar?
Beersheba
Gerar
Kadesh Barnea
Zoan (Tanis)
Succoth
On (Heliopolis)
Noph (Memphis)
Nineveh
Asshur
Nuzi
Babylon
Nippur
Erech (Uruk)
Ur
Possible location of Sodom and Gomorrah.
Possible location of Biblical "Ur of the Chaldeans," where Abraham's migration began.
Abraham's Journey
6,000
5,000
4,000
3,000
2,000
1,000
0 - sea level (in meters)
-500
© 2005 Zondervan
Maps created by Mosaic Graphics

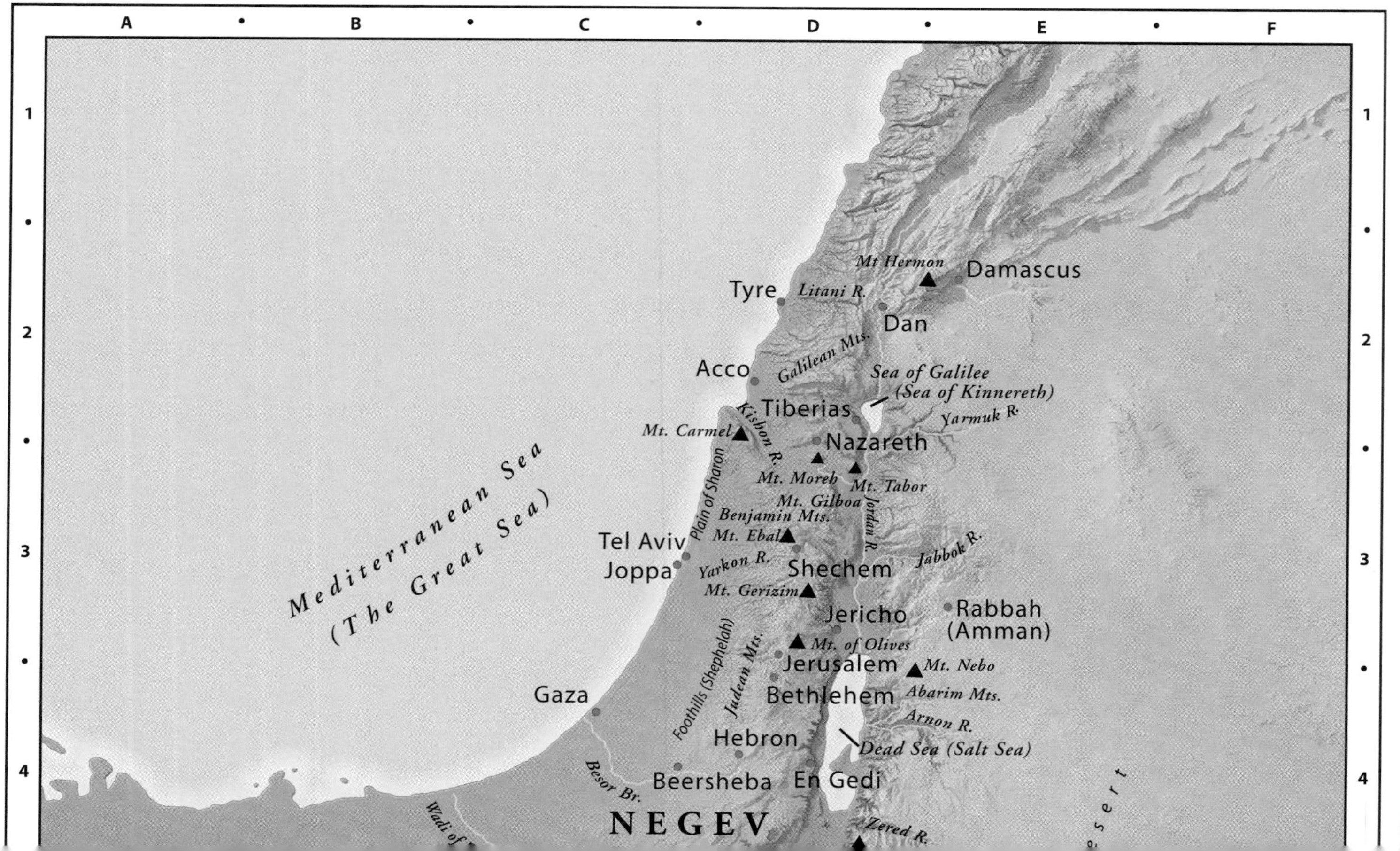

A
B
C
D
E
F
1
2
3
4
Mt Hermon
Damascus
Tyre
Litani R.
Dan
Acco
Galilean Mts.
Sea of Galilee
(Sea of Kinnereth)
Tiberias
Yarmuk R.
Mt. Carmel
Kishon R.
Nazareth
Mediterranean Sea
(The Great Sea)
Plain of Sharon
Mt. Moreh
Mt. Tabor
Mt. Gilboa
Jordan R.
Benjamin Mts.
Mt. Ebal
Tel Aviv
Joppa
Yarkon R.
Shechem
Jabbok R.
Mt. Gerizim
Jericho
Rabbah
(Amman)
Foothills (Shephelah)
Judean Mts.
Mt. of Olives
Jerusalem
Mt. Nebo
Gaza
Bethlehem
Abarim Mts.
Arnon R.
Hebron
Dead Sea (Salt Sea)
Besor Br.
Beersheba
En Gedi
NEGEV
Zered R.

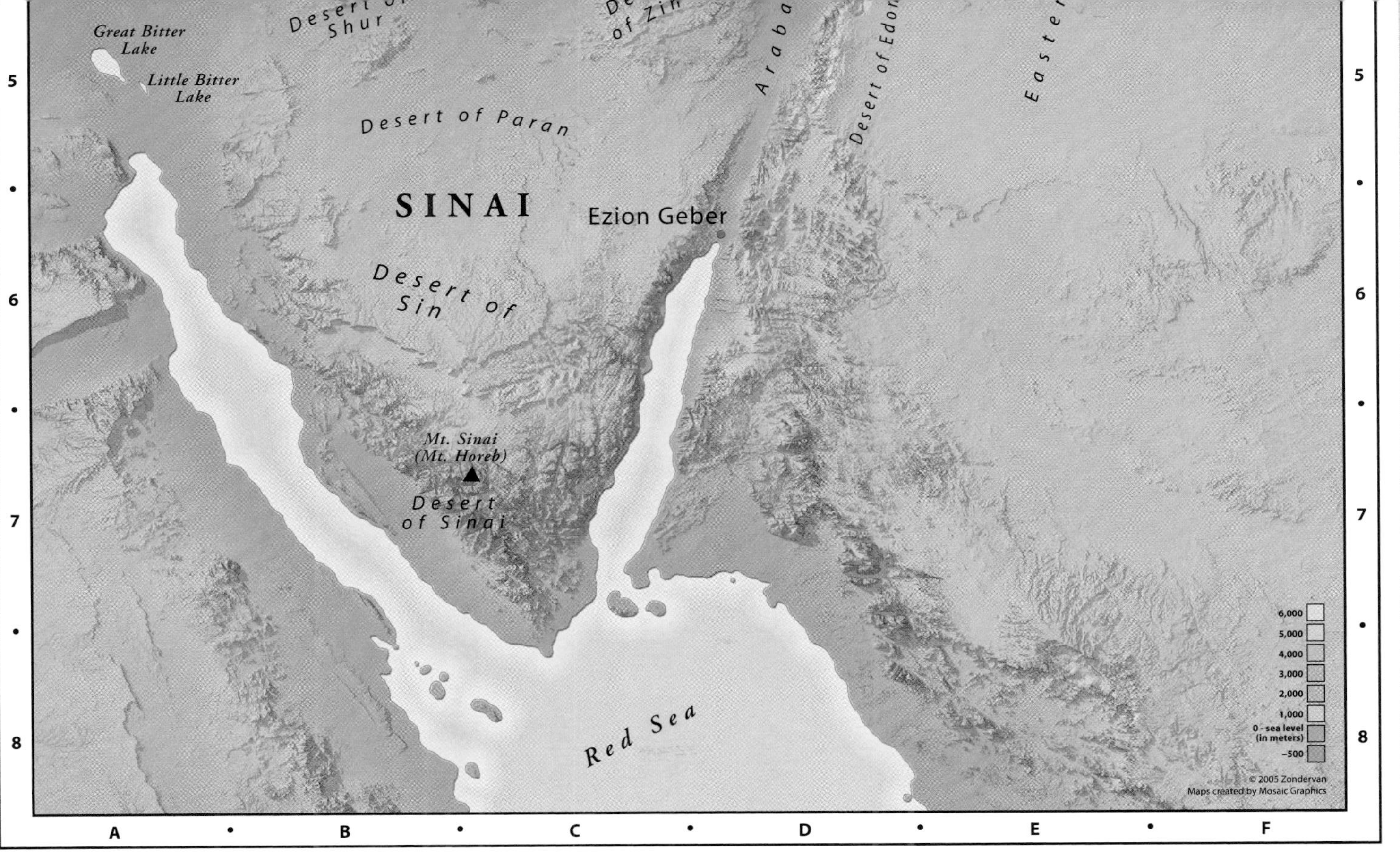
Great Bitter Lake
Little Bitter Lake
Shur
Desert of Paran
SINAI
Ezion Geber
Desert of Sin
Mt. Sinai (Mt. Horeb)
Desert of Sinai
Red Sea
6,000
5,000
4,000
3,000
2,000
1,000
0 - sea level (in meters)
-500
© 2005 Zondervan
Maps created by Mosaic Graphics
A
B
C
D
E
F
5
6
7
8

Map 3: **EXODUS AND CONQUEST OF CANAAN**

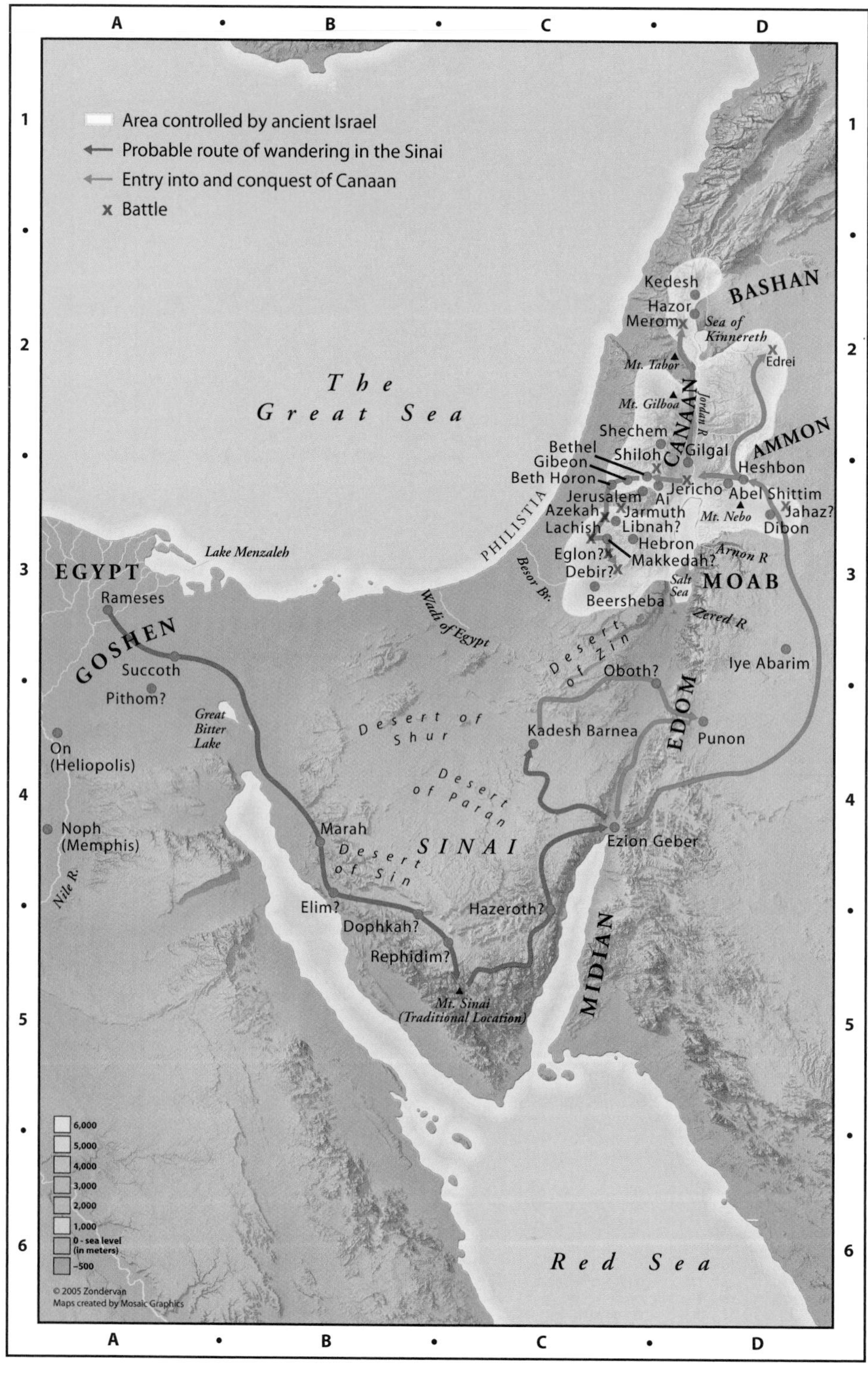
A
B
C
D
1
2
3
4
5
6
Area controlled by ancient Israel
Probable route of wandering in the Sinai
Entry into and conquest of Canaan
x Battle
The Great Sea
Kedesh
BASHAN
Hazor
Merom
Sea of Kinnereth
Mt. Tabor
Edrei
Mt. Gilboa
Jordan R.
CANAAN
Shechem
Bethel
Shiloh
Gilgal
AMMON
Gibeon
Heshbon
Beth Horon
Jericho
Abel Shittim
Jerusalem
Ai
Azekah
Jarmuth
Mt. Nebo
Jahaz?
Dibon
Lachish
Libnah?
Hebron
PHILISTIA
Eglon?
Makkedah?
Arnon R.
Debir?
Besor Br.
Salt Sea
MOAB
Beersheba
Zered R.
Lake Menzaleh
EGYPT
Rameses
GOSHEN
Succoth
Pithom?
Wadi of Egypt
Desert of Zin
Oboth?
Iye Abarim
EDOM
Great Bitter Lake
Desert of Shur
Kadesh Barnea
Punon
On (Heliopolis)
Desert of Paran
Noph (Memphis)
Marah
SINAI
Ezion Geber
Desert of Sin
Nile R.
Elim?
Hazeroth?
Dophkah?
MIDIAN
Rephidim?
Mt. Sinai (Traditional Location)
6,000
5,000
4,000
3,000
2,000
1,000
0 - sea level (in meters)
–500
Red Sea

Map 4: **LAND OF THE TWELVE TRIBES**

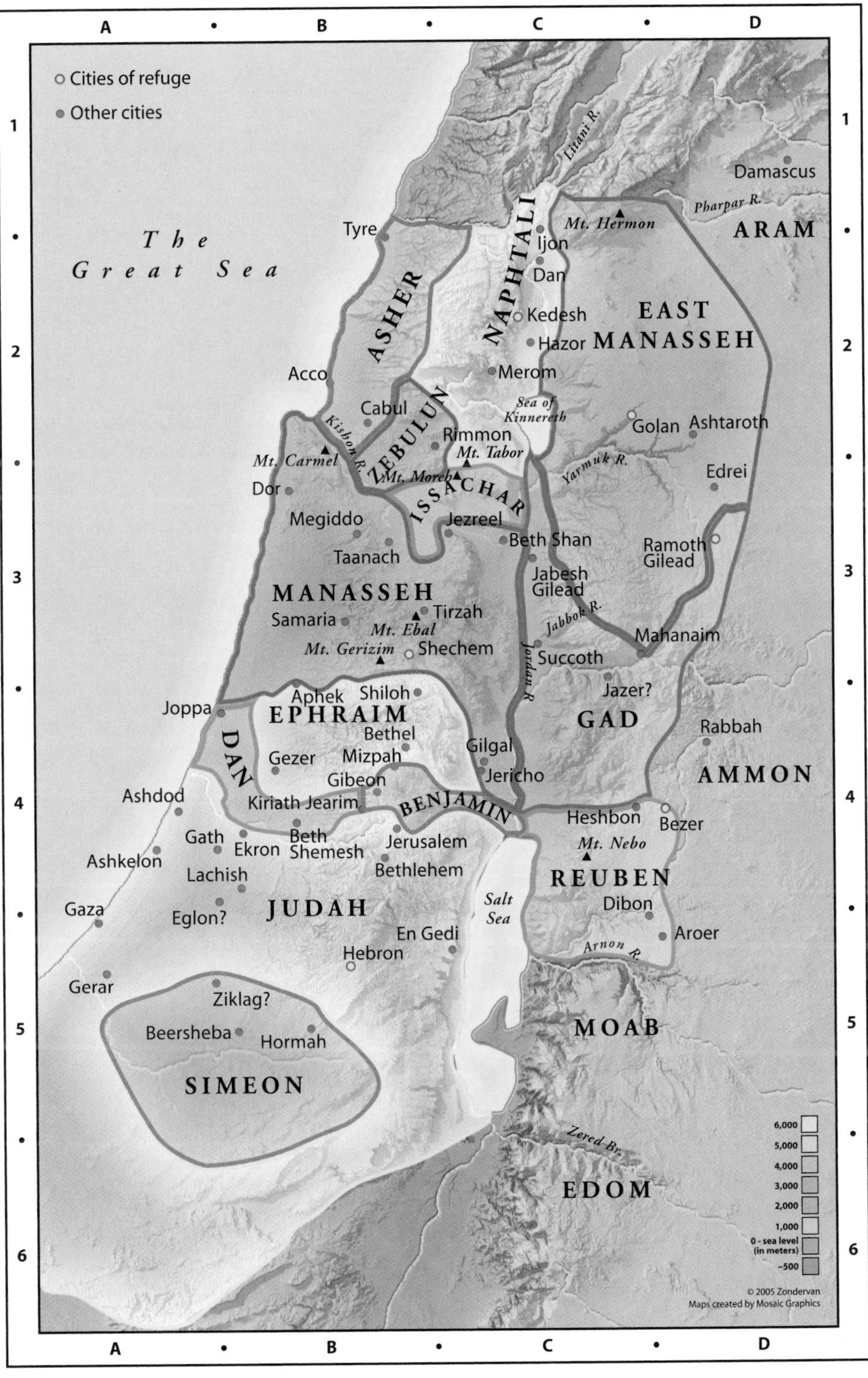

Map 5: **KINGDOM OF DAVID AND SOLOMON**

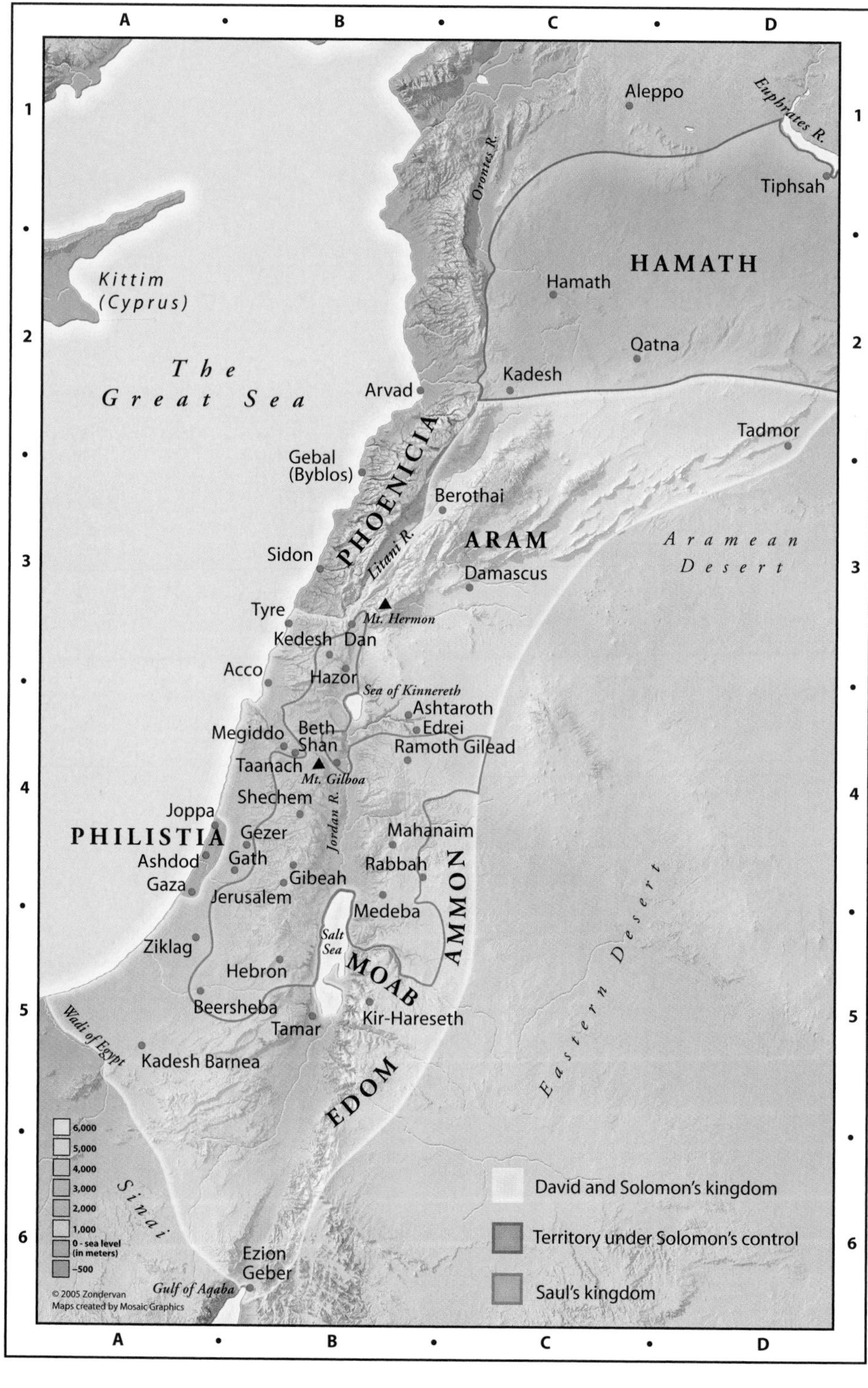

A
B
C
D
1
2
3
4
5
6
Aleppo
Euphrates R.
Tiphsah
Orontes R.
HAMATH
Hamath
Qatna
Kadesh
Kittim
(Cyprus)
The
Great Sea
Arvad
PHOENICIA
Tadmor
Gebal
(Byblos)
Berothai
ARAM
Aramean
Desert
Sidon
Litani R.
Damascus
Tyre
Mt. Hermon
Kedesh
Dan
Acco
Hazor
Sea of Kinnereth
Ashtaroth
Edrei
Megiddo
Beth
Shan
Ramoth Gilead
Taanach
Mt. Gilboa
Shechem
Jordan R.
Joppa
PHILISTIA
Gezer
Mahanaim
Ashdod
Gath
Rabbah
Gaza
Gibeah
Jerusalem
AMMON
Medeba
Salt
Sea
Ziklag
MOAB
Hebron
Eastern Desert
Beersheba
Tamar
Kir-Hareseth
Wadi of Egypt
Kadesh Barnea
EDOM
6,000
5,000
4,000
3,000
2,000
1,000
0 - sea level
(in meters)
-500
Sinai
David and Solomon's kingdom
Territory under Solomon's control
Saul's kingdom
Ezion
Geber
Gulf of Aqaba
© 2005 Zondervan
Maps created by Mosaic Graphics

Map 6: **KINGDOMS OF ISRAEL AND JUDAH**

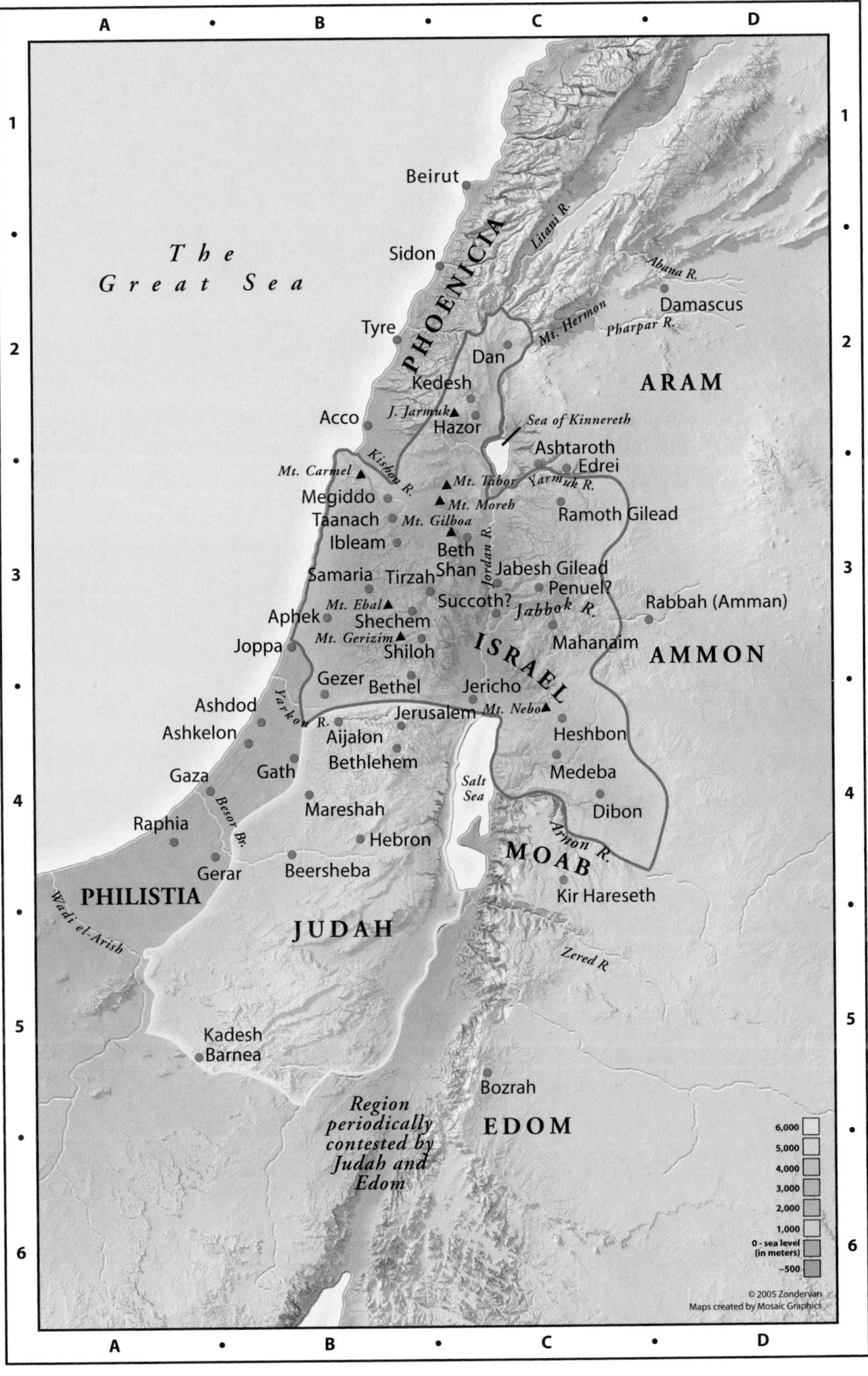

A
B
C
D
1
2
3
4
5
6
The Great Sea
Beirut
Sidon
Tyre
PHOENICIA
Litani R.
Abana R.
Damascus
Mt. Hermon
Pharpar R.
Dan
ARAM
Kedesh
J. Jarmuk
Hazor
Acco
Sea of Kinnereth
Ashtaroth
Edrei
Kishon R.
Mt. Carmel
Mt. Tabor
Yarmuk R.
Megiddo
Mt. Moreh
Taanach
Mt. Gilboa
Ramoth Gilead
Ibleam
Beth Shan
Jordan R.
Samaria
Tirzah
Jabesh Gilead
Penuel?
Mt. Ebal
Succoth?
Jabbok R.
Rabbah (Amman)
Aphek
Shechem
Mt. Gerizim
Mahanaim
Joppa
Shiloh
ISRAEL
AMMON
Gezer
Bethel
Jericho
Ashdod
Yarkon R.
Jerusalem
Mt. Nebo
Ashkelon
Aijalon
Heshbon
Bethlehem
Gaza
Gath
Salt Sea
Medeba
Mareshah
Dibon
Besor Br.
Raphia
Hebron
Arnon R.
Gerar
Beersheba
MOAB
PHILISTIA
Kir Hareseth
Wadi el-Arish
JUDAH
Zered R
Kadesh Barnea
Bozrah
Region periodically contested by Judah and Edom
EDOM
6,000
5,000
4,000
3,000
2,000
1,000
0 - sea level (in meters)
–500

Map 7: **PROPHETS IN ISRAEL AND JUDAH**

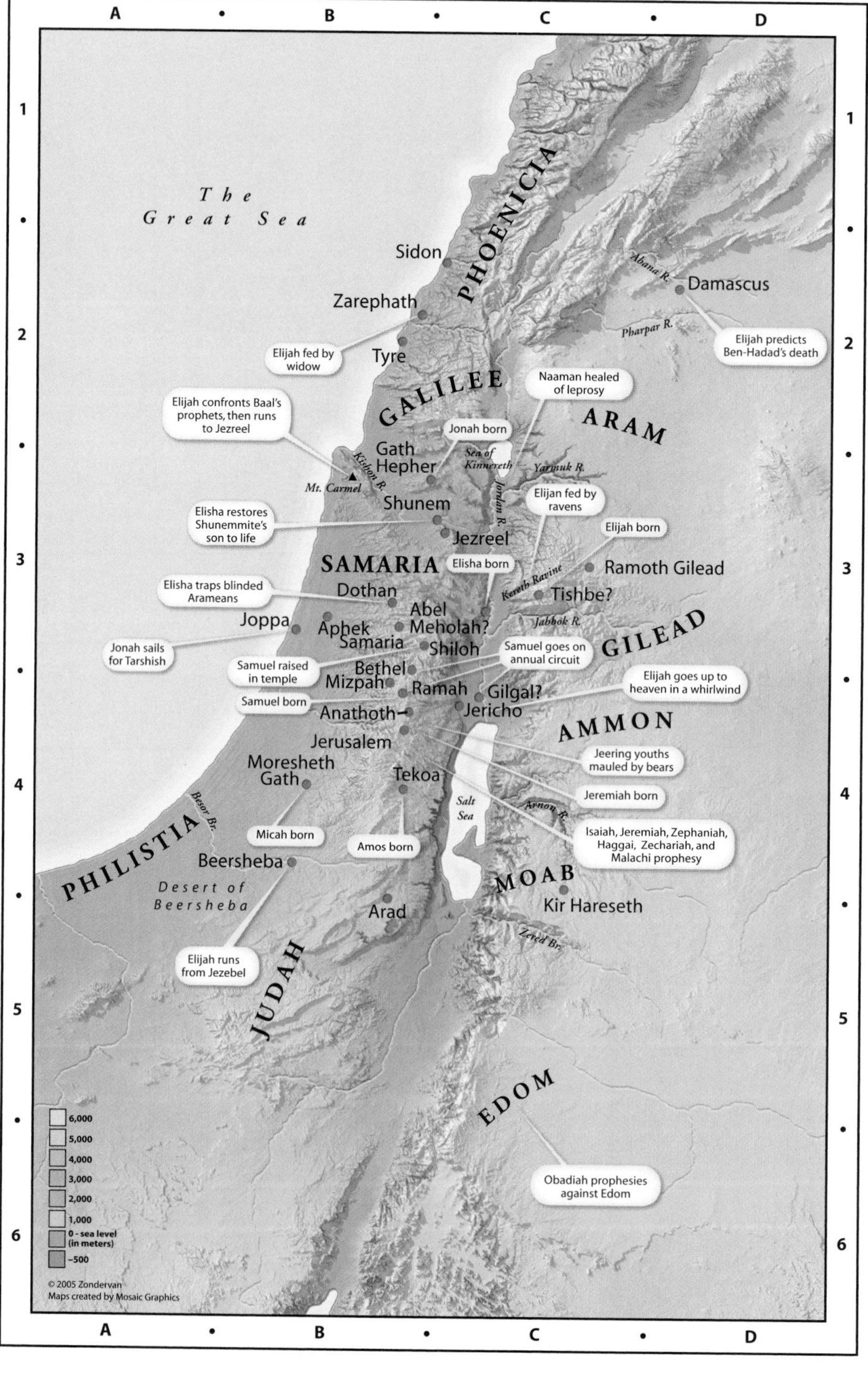

A
B
C
D
1
2
3
4
5
6
The Great Sea
PHOENICIA
Sidon
Zarephath
Tyre
Elijah fed by widow
Abana R.
Damascus
Pharpar R.
Elijah predicts Ben-Hadad's death
GALILEE
Naaman healed of leprosy
ARAM
Elijah confronts Baal's prophets, then runs to Jezreel
Jonah born
Gath Hepher
Sea of Kinnereth
Yarmuk R.
Kishon R.
Mt. Carmel
Jordan R.
Shunem
Elijan fed by ravens
Elisha restores Shunemmite's son to life
Jezreel
Elijah born
SAMARIA
Elisha born
Ramoth Gilead
Kereth Ravine
Elisha traps blinded Arameans
Dothan
Tishbe?
Abel Meholah?
Jabbok R.
Joppa
Aphek
Samaria
GILEAD
Jonah sails for Tarshish
Shiloh
Samuel goes on annual circuit
Samuel raised in temple
Bethel
Mizpah
Ramah
Gilgal?
Elijah goes up to heaven in a whirlwind
Samuel born
Anathoth
Jericho
AMMON
Jerusalem
Jeering youths mauled by bears
Moresheth Gath
Tekoa
Jeremiah born
Besor Br.
Salt Sea
Arnon R.
Isaiah, Jeremiah, Zephaniah, Haggai, Zechariah, and Malachi prophesy
PHILISTIA
Micah born
Amos born
Beersheba
MOAB
Desert of Beersheba
Arad
Kir Hareseth
Zered Br.
Elijah runs from Jezebel
JUDAH
EDOM
Obadiah prophesies against Edom
6,000
5,000
4,000
3,000
2,000
1,000
0 - sea level (in meters)
–500

Map 8: **ASSYRIAN AND BABYLONIAN EMPIRES**

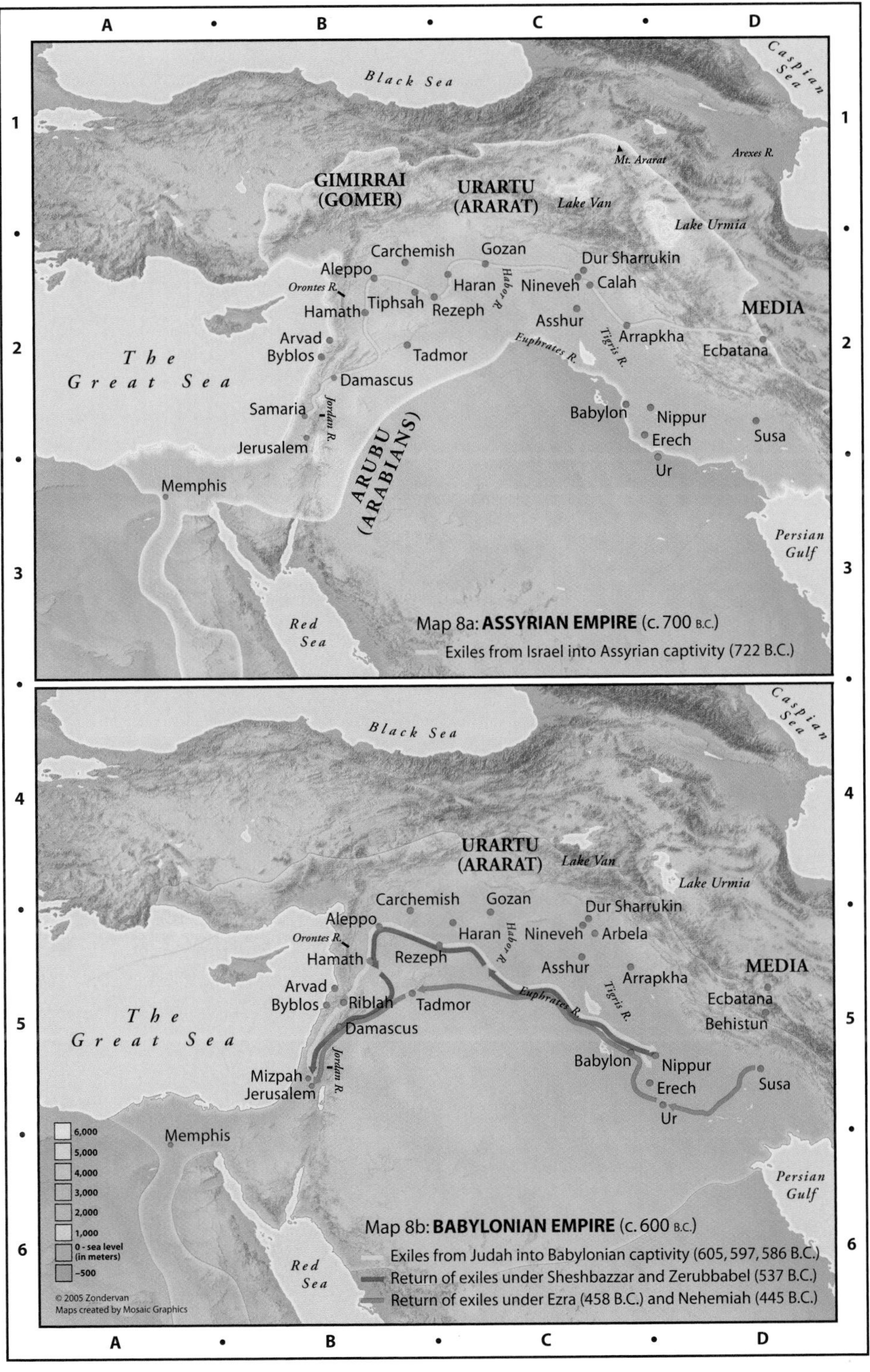

Map 9: **HOLY LAND IN THE TIME OF JESUS**

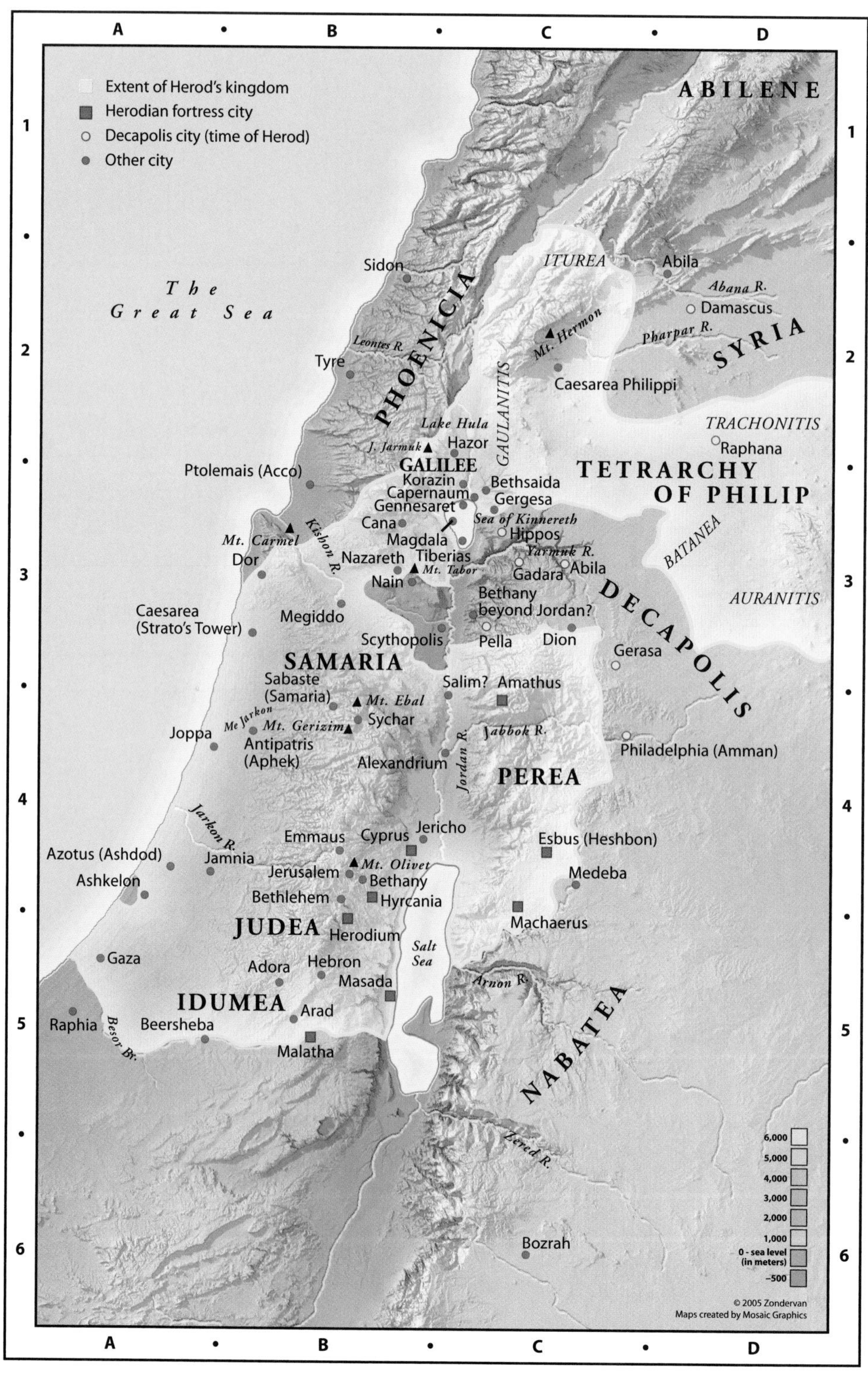
A
B
C
D
1
2
3
4
5
6
Extent of Herod's kingdom
Herodian fortress city
Decapolis city (time of Herod)
Other city
ABILENE
The Great Sea
Sidon
PHOENICIA
ITUREA
Abila
Abana R.
Damascus
Mt. Hermon
Pharpar R.
SYRIA
Leontes R.
Tyre
GAULANITIS
Caesarea Philippi
Lake Hula
TRACHONITIS
J. Jarmuk
Hazor
Raphana
GALILEE
TETRARCHY OF PHILIP
Ptolemais (Acco)
Korazin
Bethsaida
Capernaum
Gergesa
Gennesaret
Cana
Sea of Kinnereth
Hippos
Mt. Carmel
Kishon R.
Magdala
BATANEA
Yarmuk R.
Dor
Nazareth
Tiberias
Mt. Tabor
Gadara
Abila
Nain
DECAPOLIS
Bethany beyond Jordan?
AURANITIS
Caesarea (Strato's Tower)
Megiddo
Scythopolis
Pella
Dion
Gerasa
SAMARIA
Sabaste (Samaria)
Mt. Ebal
Salim?
Amathus
Me Jarkon
Mt. Gerizim
Sychar
Jabbok R.
Joppa
Antipatris (Aphek)
Jordan R.
Philadelphia (Amman)
Alexandrium
PEREA
Jarkon R.
Emmaus
Cyprus
Jericho
Esbus (Heshbon)
Azotus (Ashdod)
Jamnia
Mt. Olivet
Jerusalem
Bethany
Medeba
Ashkelon
Bethlehem
Hyrcania
JUDEA
Machaerus
Herodium
Salt Sea
Gaza
Adora
Hebron
Masada
Arnon R.
IDUMEA
Arad
NABATEA
Raphia
Besor Br.
Beersheba
Malatha
Zered R.
Bozrah
6,000
5,000
4,000
3,000
2,000
1,000
0 - sea level (in meters)
−500
© 2005 Zondervan
Maps created by Mosaic Graphics

Map 10: **JERUSALEM IN THE TIME OF JESUS**

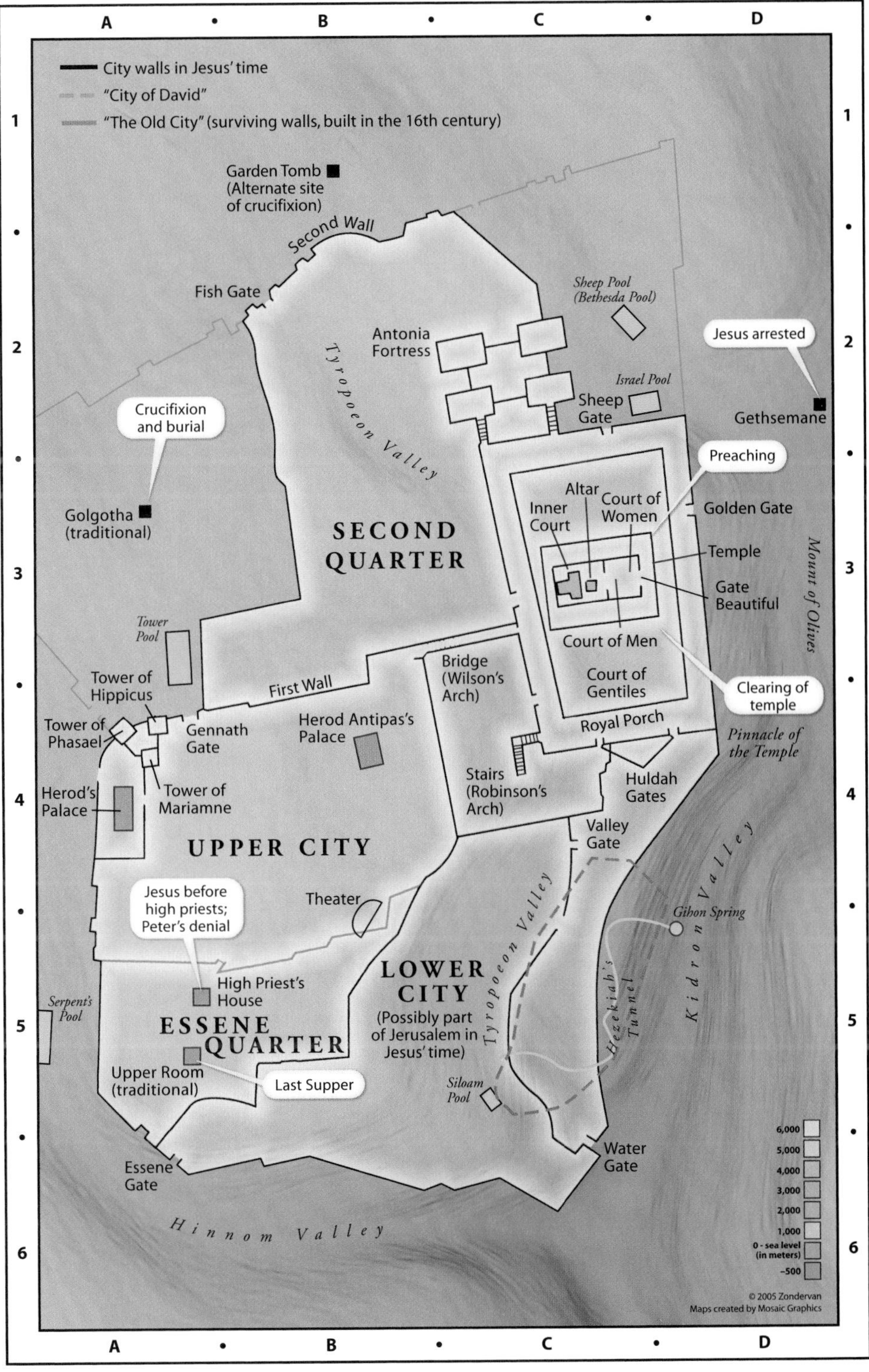

City walls in Jesus' time
"City of David"
"The Old City" (surviving walls, built in the 16th century)
Garden Tomb (Alternate site of crucifixion)
Second Wall
Fish Gate
Antonia Fortress
Tyropoeon Valley
Sheep Pool (Bethesda Pool)
Israel Pool
Sheep Gate
Jesus arrested
Gethsemane
Crucifixion and burial
Golgotha (traditional)
Preaching
Altar
Inner Court
Court of Women
Golden Gate
SECOND QUARTER
Temple
Gate Beautiful
Mount of Olives
Tower Pool
Court of Men
Court of Gentiles
Bridge (Wilson's Arch)
Tower of Hippicus
First Wall
Clearing of temple
Tower of Phasael
Gennath Gate
Herod Antipas's Palace
Royal Porch
Pinnacle of the Temple
Stairs (Robinson's Arch)
Huldah Gates
Herod's Palace
Tower of Mariamne
Valley Gate
UPPER CITY
Kidron Valley
Jesus before high priests; Peter's denial
Theater
Gihon Spring
LOWER CITY
High Priest's House
Hezekiah's Tunnel
Serpent's Pool
ESSENE QUARTER
(Possibly part of Jerusalem in Jesus' time)
Upper Room (traditional)
Last Supper
Siloam Pool
Water Gate
Essene Gate
Hinnom Valley
6,000
5,000
4,000
3,000
2,000
1,000
0 - sea level (in meters)
-500
© 2005 Zondervan
Maps created by Mosaic Graphics
A B C D
1 2 3 4 5 6

Map 11: **JESUS' MINISTRY**

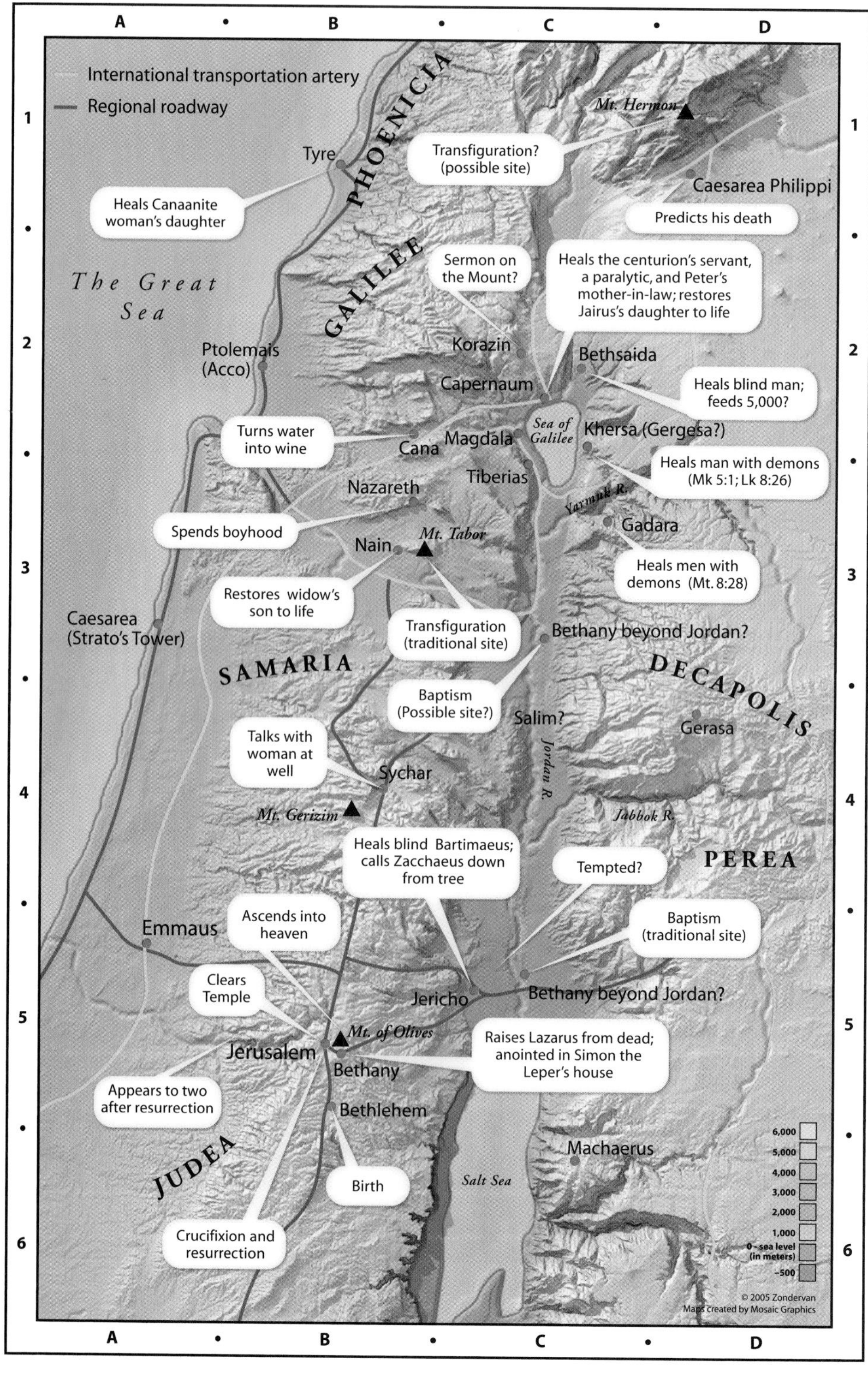
A
B
C
D
1
2
3
4
5
6
International transportation artery
Regional roadway
PHOENICIA
Mt. Hermon
Tyre
Transfiguration? (possible site)
Heals Canaanite woman's daughter
Caesarea Philippi
Predicts his death
GALILEE
Sermon on the Mount?
Heals the centurion's servant, a paralytic, and Peter's mother-in-law; restores Jairus's daughter to life
The Great Sea
Ptolemais (Acco)
Korazin
Bethsaida
Capernaum
Heals blind man; feeds 5,000?
Sea of Galilee
Turns water into wine
Cana
Magdala
Khersa (Gergesa?)
Tiberias
Heals man with demons (Mk 5:1; Lk 8:26)
Nazareth
Yarmuk R.
Spends boyhood
Gadara
Nain
Mt. Tabor
Heals men with demons (Mt. 8:28)
Restores widow's son to life
Caesarea (Strato's Tower)
Transfiguration (traditional site)
Bethany beyond Jordan?
SAMARIA
DECAPOLIS
Baptism (Possible site?)
Salim?
Gerasa
Talks with woman at well
Sychar
Jordan R.
Mt. Gerizim
Jabbok R.
Heals blind Bartimaeus; calls Zacchaeus down from tree
Tempted?
PEREA
Ascends into heaven
Baptism (traditional site)
Emmaus
Clears Temple
Jericho
Bethany beyond Jordan?
Mt. of Olives
Raises Lazarus from dead; anointed in Simon the Leper's house
Jerusalem
Bethany
Appears to two after resurrection
Bethlehem
Machaerus
JUDEA
Birth
Salt Sea
Crucifixion and resurrection
6,000
5,000
4,000
3,000
2,000
1,000
0 - sea level (in meters)
-500
© 2005 Zondervan
Maps created by Mosaic Graphics

Map 12: **APOSTLES' EARLY TRAVELS**

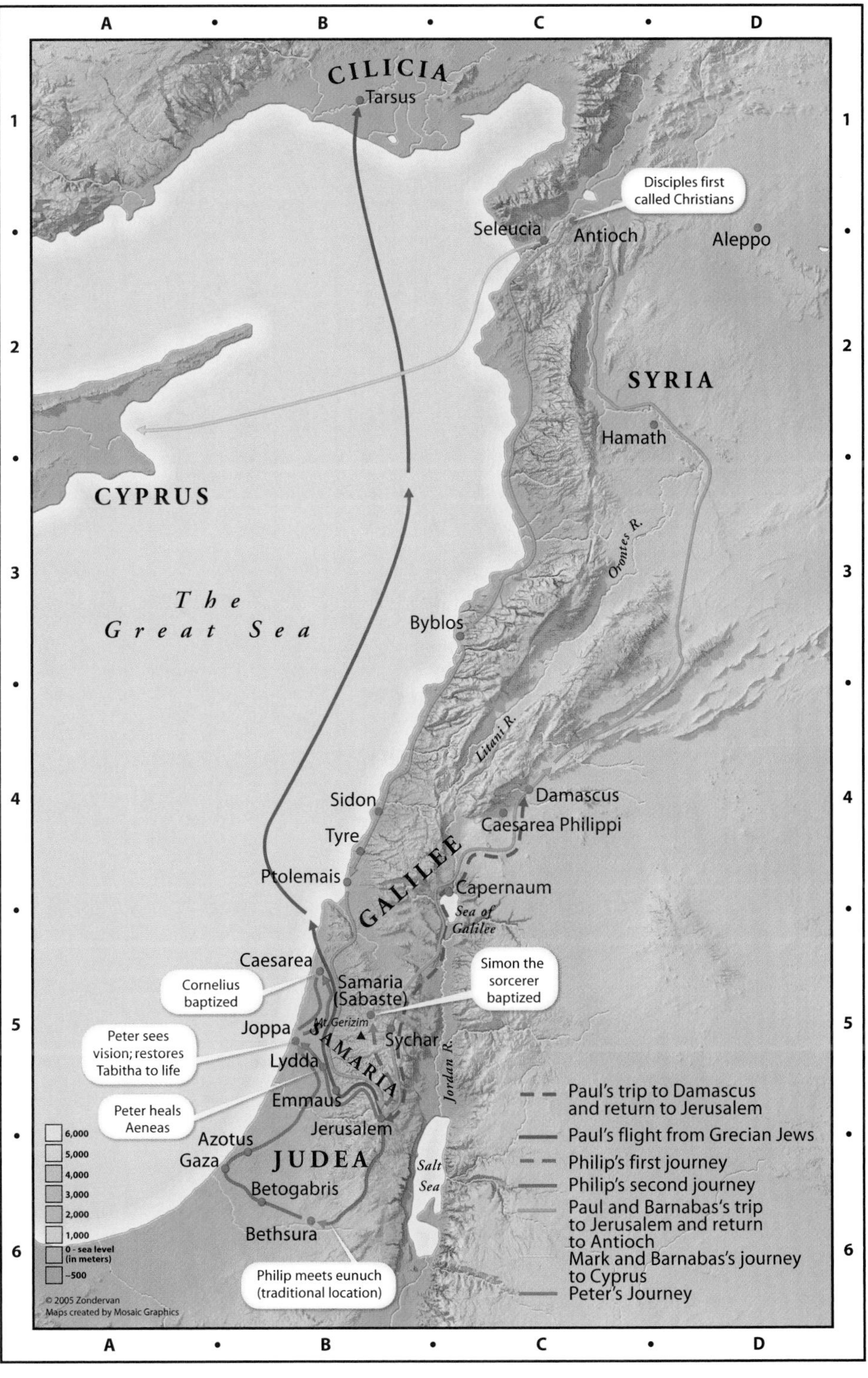

A
B
C
D
1
2
3
4
5
6
CILICIA
Tarsus
Disciples first called Christians
Seleucia
Antioch
Aleppo
SYRIA
Hamath
CYPRUS
Orontes R.
The Great Sea
Byblos
Litani R.
Damascus
Sidon
Caesarea Philippi
Tyre
GALILEE
Ptolemais
Capernaum
Sea of Galilee
Caesarea
Simon the sorcerer baptized
Cornelius baptized
Samaria (Sabaste)
Mt. Gerizim
Joppa
SAMARIA
Sychar
Peter sees vision; restores Tabitha to life
Lydda
Jordan R.
Emmaus
Peter heals Aeneas
Jerusalem
Azotus
Gaza
JUDEA
Salt Sea
Betogabris
Bethsura
Philip meets eunuch (traditional location)
6,000
5,000
4,000
3,000
2,000
1,000
0 - sea level (in meters)
-500
Paul's trip to Damascus and return to Jerusalem
Paul's flight from Grecian Jews
Philip's first journey
Philip's second journey
Paul and Barnabas's trip to Jerusalem and return to Antioch
Mark and Barnabas's journey to Cyprus
Peter's Journey
© 2005 Zondervan
Maps created by Mosaic Graphics

Map 13: **PAUL'S MISSIONARY JOURNEYS**

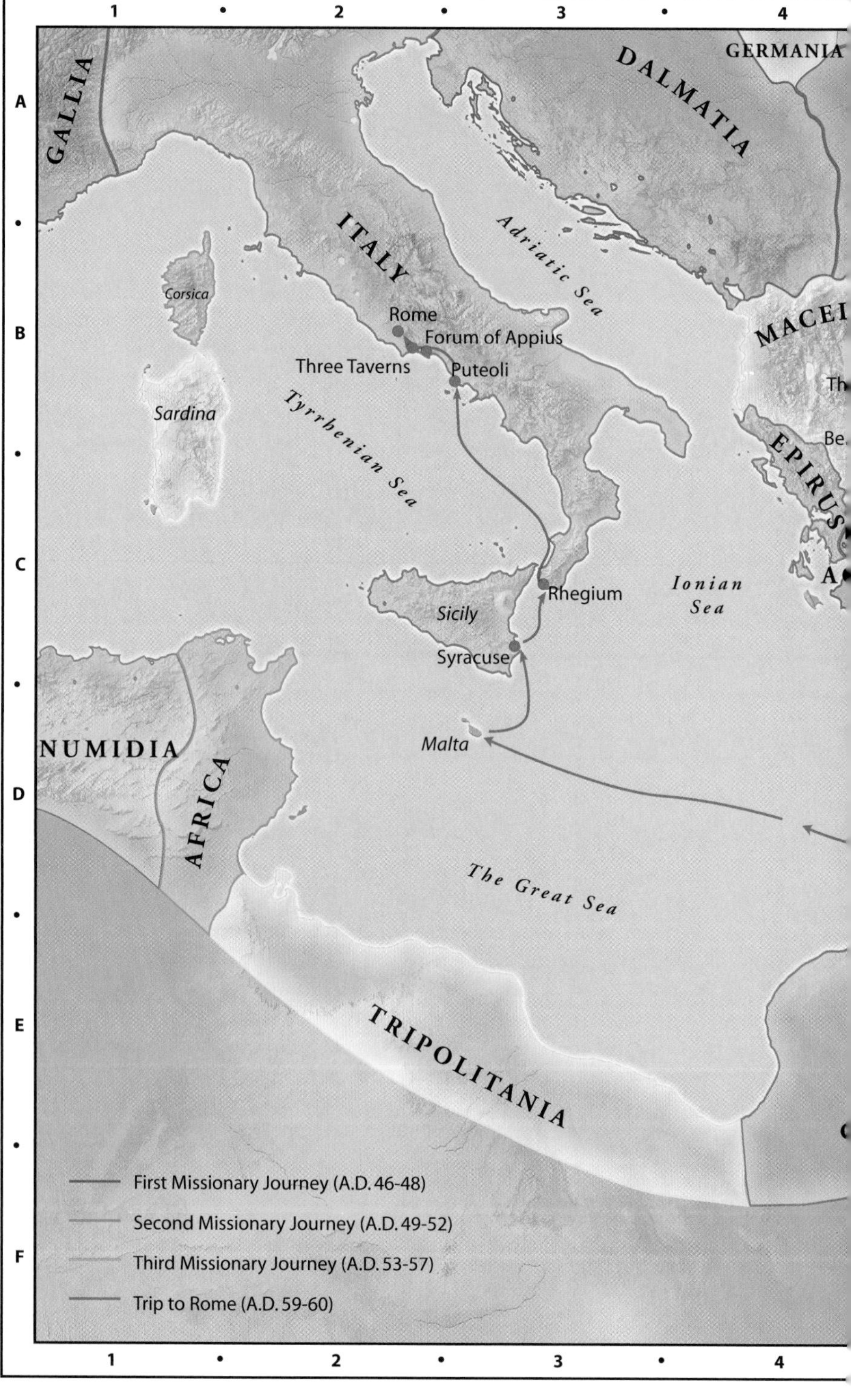

1
2
3
4
A
B
C
D
E
F
GALLIA
GERMANIA
DALMATIA
ITALY
Adriatic Sea
Corsica
Rome
Forum of Appius
Three Taverns
Puteoli
MACE
Sardina
Tyrrhenian Sea
EPIRUS
Rhegium
Ionian Sea
Sicily
Syracuse
NUMIDIA
AFRICA
Malta
The Great Sea
TRIPOLITANIA
First Missionary Journey (A.D. 46-48)
Second Missionary Journey (A.D. 49-52)
Third Missionary Journey (A.D. 53-57)
Trip to Rome (A.D. 59-60)

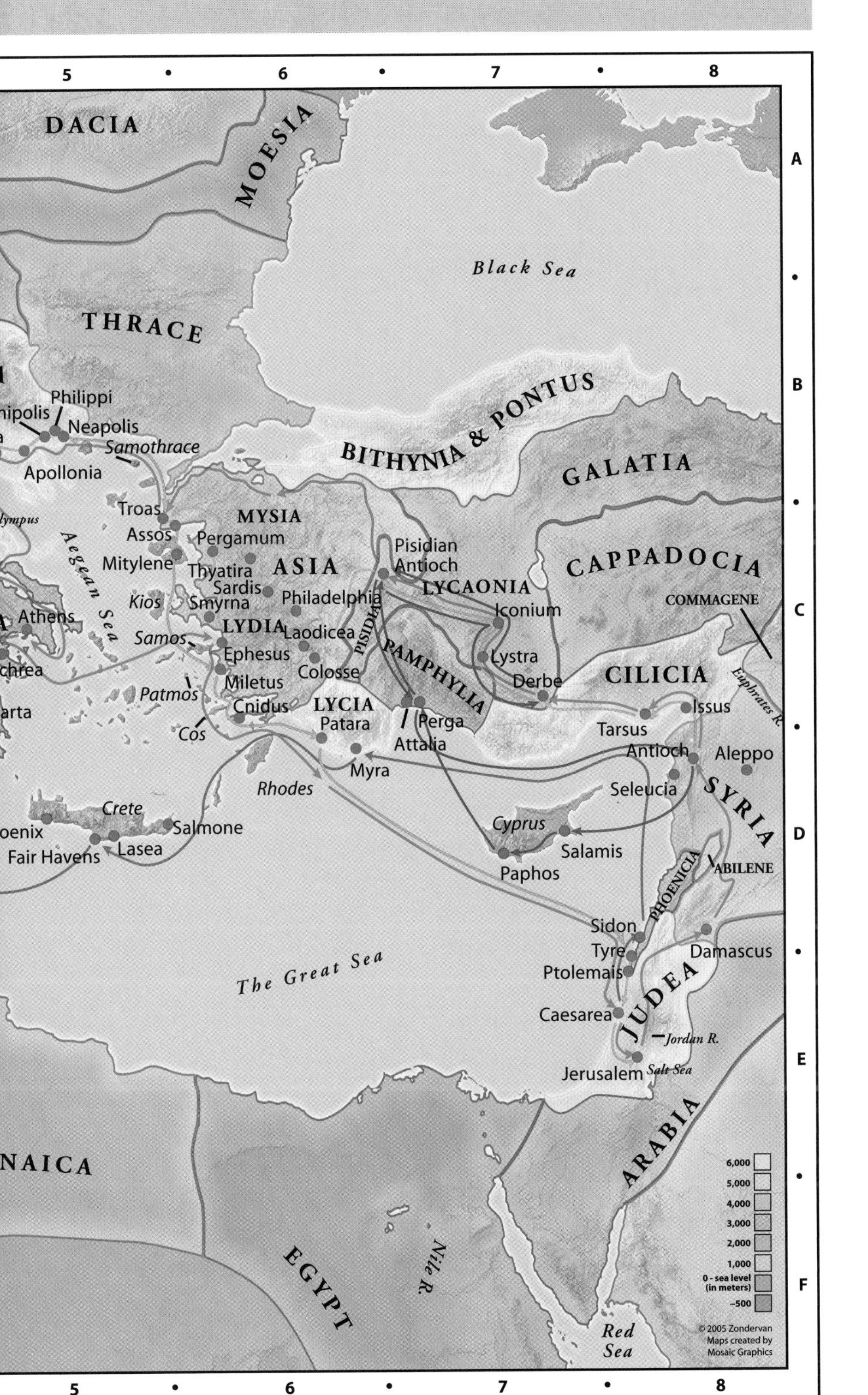
5
6
7
8
A
B
C
D
E
F
DACIA
MOESIA
Black Sea
THRACE
Philippi
Neapolis
Samothrace
Apollonia
BITHYNIA & PONTUS
GALATIA
Troas
MYSIA
Assos
Pergamum
Aegean Sea
Mitylene
Thyatira
ASIA
Pisidian Antioch
CAPPADOCIA
Sardis
LYCAONIA
Kios
Smyrna
Philadelphia
Iconium
COMMAGENE
Athens
LYDIA
Samos
Laodicea
PISIDIA
Ephesus
PAMPHYLIA
Lystra
Colosse
Miletus
Derbe
CILICIA
Euphrates R.
Patmos
LYCIA
Cnidus
Issus
Perga
Patara
Tarsus
Cos
Attalia
Antioch
Aleppo
Myra
Rhodes
Seleucia
SYRIA
Crete
Cyprus
Salmone
Lasea
Fair Havens
Salamis
Paphos
ABILENE
PHOENICIA
Sidon
Tyre
Damascus
Ptolemais
JUDEA
The Great Sea
Caesarea
Jordan R.
Jerusalem
Salt Sea
ARABIA
EGYPT
Nile R.
Red Sea
6,000
5,000
4,000
3,000
2,000
1,000
0 - sea level (in meters)
–500
© 2005 Zondervan
Maps created by Mosaic Graphics

Map 14: **ROMAN EMPIRE**

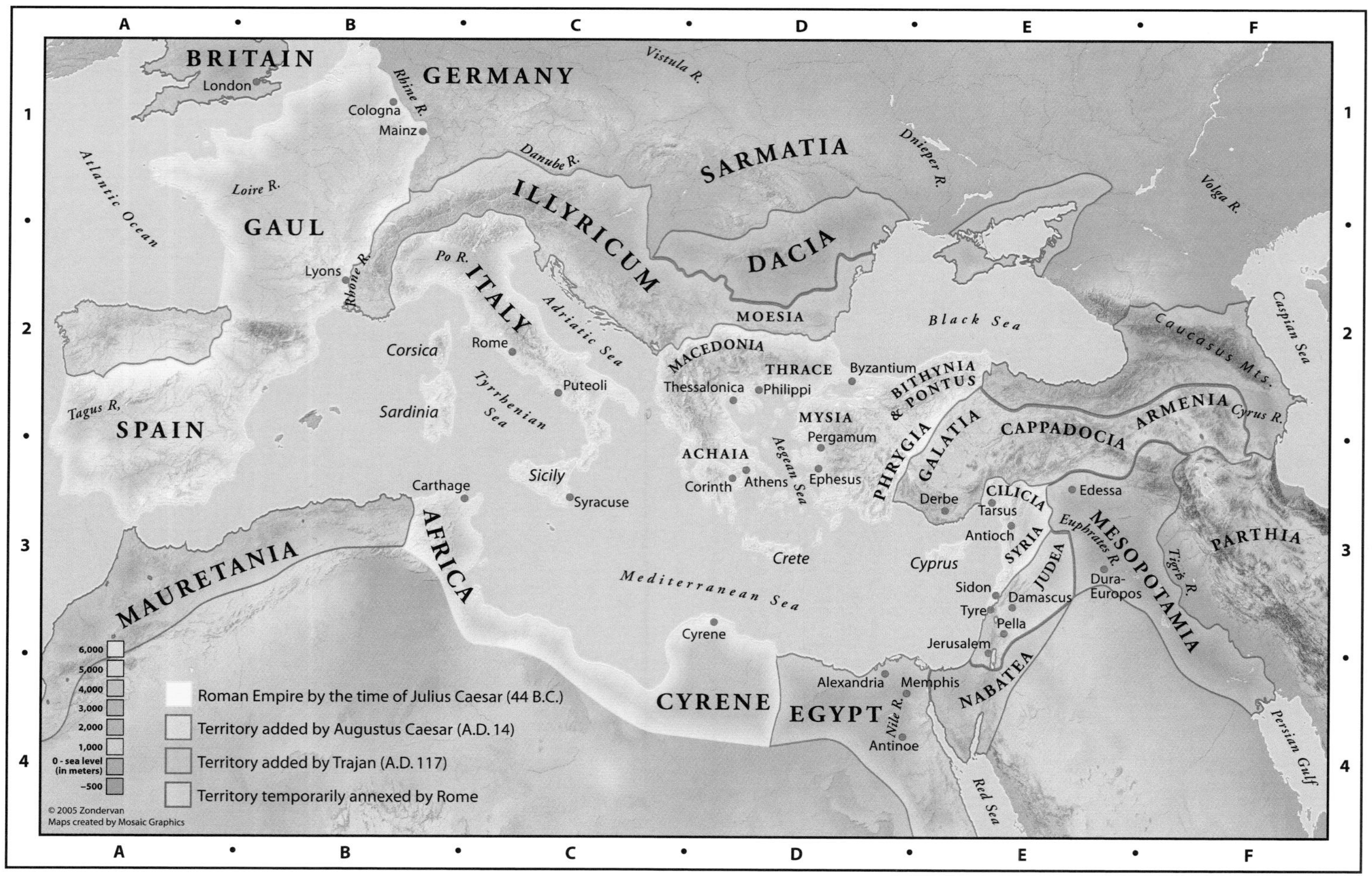